REFERENCE

ISSN: 1053-1874

A GALE CAREER INFORMATION GUIDE

JOB HUNTER'S SOURCEBOOK

Where to find employment leads and other job search resources

EIGHTH EDITION

Bohdan Romaniuk, Project Editor

GALE
CENGAGE Learning™

Detroit • New York • San Francisco • New Haven, Conn • Waterville, Maine • London

MT/BW

GALE
CENGAGE Learning™

Job Hunter's Sourcebook, 8th Edition

Project Editor: Bohdan Romaniuk

Editorial Support Services: Thomas Potts

Composition: Evi Abou-El-Seoud

Manufacturing: Rita Wimberley

Product Management: David Forman

For product information and technology assistance, contact us at
Gale Customer Support, 1-800-877-4253.
For permission to use material from this text or product, submit all requests online at **www.cengage.com/permissions.**
Further permissions questions can be emailed to
permissionrequest@cengage.com

While every effort has been made to ensure the reliability of the information presented in this publication, Gale, a part of Cengage Learning, does not guarantee the accuracy of the data contained herein. Gale accepts no payment for listing; and inclusion in the publication of any organization, agency, institution, publication, service, or individual does not imply endorsement of the editors or publisher. Errors brought to the attention of the publisher, and verified to the satisfaction of the publisher, will be corrected in future editions.

EDITORIAL DATA PRIVACY POLICY: Does this product contain information about you as an individual? If so, for more information about our editorial data privacy policies, please see our Privacy Statement at www.gale.cengage.com.

Gale, Cengage Learning
27500 Drake Rd.
Farmington Hills, MI 48331-3535

ISBN-13: 978-1-4144-0784-5
ISBN-10: 1-4144-0784-X

ISSN 1053-1874

Printed in the United States of America
1 2 3 4 5 6 7 12 11 10 09 08

10/02/08

Contents

  Provides sources of help-wanted ads, placement and job
  referral services, employer directories and networking lists,
  handbooks and manuals, employment agencies and search
  firms, online job sources and services, tradeshows, and other
  leads for various careers.

Part Two: Sources of Essential Job-Hunting Information
  Includes reference works; newspapers, magazines, and
  journals; audio/visual resources; online and database services;
  software; and other sources about the following topics:

"The person who gets hired is not necessarily the one who can do that job best; but, the one who knows the most about how to get hired."

Richard Bolles

What Color Is Your Parachute?

Job hunting is often described as a campaign, a system, a strategic process. According to Joan Moore, principal of The Arbor Consulting Group, Inc. in Plymouth, Michigan, "Launching a thorough job search can be a full-time job in itself. It requires as much energy as you would put into any other major project—and it requires a creative mix of approaches to ensure its success."

Job Hunting Is Increasingly Complex

Today's competitive job market has become increasingly complex, requiring new and resourceful approaches to landing a position. The help-wanted ads are no longer the surest route to employment. In fact, most estimates indicate that only a small percentage of all jobs are found through the classified sections of local newspapers.

Although approaches vary among individual job seekers and the levels of jobs sought, a thorough job search today should involve the use of a wide variety of resources. Professional associations, library research, executive search firms, college placement offices, direct application to employers, professional journals, and networking with colleagues and friends are all approaches commonly in use. Job hotlines and resume referral services may be elements of the search as well. High-tech components might include the use of resume databases, and electronic bulletin boards that list job openings.

More than 7 Million Job Seekers

Just as the methods of job seeking have changed, so have the job hunters themselves. By choice or by chance, the U.S. Department of Labor, Bureau of Labor Statistics, Current Population Survey estimates that at any given time more than 7.5 million Americans are seeking employment. This number includes the ranks of students pursuing their first—but probably not only—jobs. As Joyce Slayton Mitchell notes in College to Career, "Today, the average young person can look for-ward to six or seven different jobs, six or seven minicareers, that will make up his or her lifetime of work." Lifelong commitment to one employer is no longer the norm; professionals seeking to change companies, workers re-entering the job market after a period of absence, and people exploring new career options are also represented in significant numbers in the job seeking pool. And in a time of significant corporate change, restructuring, divestiture, and downsizing, many job seekers are in the market unexpectedly. These include a growing number of white-collar workers who find themselves competing against other professionals in a shrinking market.

Help for Job Hunters

As the job market has become more competitive and complex, job seekers have increasingly looked for job search assistance. The rapid growth in the number of outplacement firms and employment agencies during the last 30 years reflects the perceived need for comprehensive help. Similarly, the library has become an increasingly important and valuable resource in the job hunt. In fact, some librarians report that their most frequently asked reference questions pertain to job seeking. In response to this need, many libraries have developed extensive collections of career and job-hunting publications, periodicals that list job openings, and directories of employers. Some libraries have developed centralized collections of career information, complemented by such offerings as resume preparation software, career planning databases, and interviewing skills videotapes.

Valuable Guide for Job Seekers

Job Hunter's Sourcebook (JHS) was designed to assist those planning job search strategies. Any job hunter—the student looking for an internship, the recent graduate, the executive hoping to relocate—will find *JHS* an important first step in the job search process because it identifies and organizes employment leads quickly and comprehensively. Best of all, *JHS* provides all the information a job hunter needs to turn a local public library into a customized employment agency, available free-of-charge. *Library Journal* and the New York Public Library concurred, and gave the first edition of this work their annual outstanding reference awards.

Job Hunter's Sourcebook (*JHS*) is a comprehensive guide to sources of information on employment leads and other job search resources. It streamlines the job-seeking process by identifying and organizing the wide array of publications, organizations, audio-visual and electronic resources, and other job hunting tools.

JHS completes much of the research needed to begin a job search, with in-depth coverage of information sources for more than 200 specific professional and vocational occupations. Listings of resources on more than 30 essential topics of interest to job hunters complement the profiles on specific occupations, providing the job seeker with leads to all the information needed to design a complete job search strategy.

Job Hunter's Sourcebook can be used to:

Find a job. *JHS* is designed for use by job seekers at all levels—from those seeking a first job, to executives on the move, to those in transition. Each individual may select from the wide range of resources presented to develop a customized job campaign.

Use career resources more effectively. As library research becomes an increasingly important component in the job hunting process, librarians are providing more information and support to job seekers. *JHS* helps users go directly to the most appropriate library material by providing comprehensive lists of job hunting resources on high-interest professional and vocational occupations.

Build a better career resources collection. Librarians, career counselors, outplacement firms, spouse relocation services, job referral agencies, and others who advise job seekers can use *JHS* to start or expand their collections of career and job hunting materials.

Comprehensive Coverage and Convenient Arrangement

The job search resources in *JHS* are conveniently arranged into two parts, which are followed by a master index:

Part One: Sources of Job-Hunting Information by Professions and Occupations—identifies information sources on employment opportunities for 228 specific types of jobs. A "List of Profiled Professions and Occupations" lists hundreds of alternate, popular, synonymous, and related job titles and links them to the jobs profiled in *JHS*, providing quick access to information sources on specific occupations or fields of interest by all their variant names—from accountant to aircraft mechanic and sports official to stockbroker. Each profile contains complete contact information and lists a variety of sources of job-opportunity information organized into eight easy-to-use categories:

1. Sources of Help-Wanted Ads
2. Placement and Job Referral Services
3. Employer Directories and Networking Lists
4. Handbooks and Manuals
5. Employment Agencies and Search Firms
6. Online Job Sources and Services
7. Tradeshows
8. Other Sources, including internships and resources such as job hotlines

Part Two: Sources of Essential Job-Hunting Information—features such employment topics as:

- Interviewing Skills
- Employment Issues for Disabled Workers
- Electronic Job Search Information
- Working at Home
- Opportunities for Freelance Workers and Independent Contractors
- Opportunities for Temporary Workers

Each category includes:

- Reference Works
- Newspapers, Magazines, and Journals
- Audio/Visual Resources
- Online and Database Services
- Software
- Other Sources, such as special associations, job-hunting kits, and organizers

The information sources listed under each topic are arranged by type of resource and include complete contact information.

Index to Information Sources—comprehensively lists all of the publications, organizations, electronic resources, and other sources of job hunting information contained in *JHS*.

Please consult the User's Guide for more information about the arrangement, content, and indexing of the information sources cited in *JHS*.

JHS Profiles High-Interest Professions and Occupations

JHS catalogs job hunting resources for more than 200 professional, technical, and trade occupations, carefully selected to provide a broad cross-section of occupations of interest to today's job seekers. The majority are profiled in the Department of Labor's *Occupational Outlook Handbook (OOH)*, a leading career resource containing detailed descriptions of professional and vocational occupations. Most of the professions cited in *OOH* are also included in *JHS*, as are representative vocational occupations selected from those listed in *OOH*. To round out this list, additional occupations were included on the basis of Bureau of Labor Statistics data projecting them as high-growth positions.

Coverage of Employment Alternatives and Trends

In addition to focusing on such "how-to" topics as resume-writing and interviewing, the "Sources of Essential Job-Hunting Information" offers resources for non-traditional work options and diverse segments of the work force. Working part-time, at home, and in your own business are featured chapters, as are opportunities for minorities, older workers, women, disabled workers, and gay and lesbian job seekers. A chapter covering sources of electronic job search information is included, as well as a category titled, "Online Job Sources and Services." This category lists Internet websites related to specific job profiles.

New to this Edition

The eighth edition is a complete revision of the previous *JHS*, incorporating thousands of updates to organization and publication data. This edition also features 6 new career profiles, such as counterterrorism and intelligence analyst, video game designer, and vintner.

Method of Compilation

JHS contains citations compiled from direct contact with a wide range of associations and organizations, from dozens of publisher catalogs and other secondary sources, and from selected information from other Gale databases. While many resources cited in *JHS* contain career planning information, their usefulness in the job hunting process was the primary factor in their selection. Their annotations are tailored to support that function.

Comments and Suggestions Are Welcome

Libraries, associations, employment agencies, executive search firms, referral services, publishers, database producers, and other organizations involved in helping job seekers find opportunities or companies find candidates are encouraged to submit information about their activities and products for use in future editions of *JHS*. Comments and suggestions for improving this guide are also welcome. Please contact:

Project Editor
Job Hunter's Sourcebook
Gale, Cengage Learning
27500 Drake Rd.
Farmington Hills, MI 48331-3535
Phone: (248) 699-4253
Fax: (248) 699-8075
URL: gale.cengage.com

Job Hunter's Sourcebook (*JHS*) is divided into two parts:

- Part One: Sources of Job-Hunting Information by Professions and Occupations
- Part Two: Sources of Essential Job-Hunting Information

Access to entries is facilitated by a "List of Profiled Professions and Occupations" and an "Index to Information Sources." Users should consult each section to benefit fully from the information in *JHS*.

Master List of Profiled Professions and Occupations

A "List of Profiled Professions and Occupations" alphabetically lists the job titles used to identify the professions and occupations appearing in Part One of *JHS*, as well as alternate, popular, synonymous, and related job titles and names, and occupational specialties contained within job titles. Citations include "See" references to the appropriate occupational profiles and their beginning page numbers.

JHS is designed to meet the needs of job seekers at all levels of experience in a wide range of fields. Managers as well as entry-level job hunters will find information sources that will facilitate their career-specific searches. In addition, information on professions and occupations related to those profiled will be found.

All Career Levels. The title assigned to each profile identifies its occupational field or subject area; these titles are not meant to indicate the level of positions for which information is provided. Information systems managers, for example, will find highly useful information in the "Computer Programmers" and "Computer Systems Analysts" profiles, while financial analysts will benefit from information in the "Financial Managers" profile. The "General Managers and Top Executives" profile, on the other hand, is broad in nature and useful to any management-level search; it does not focus upon a specific profession or occupation.

Other Occupations. Job seekers not finding their specific career fields listed in this guide will discover that related profiles yield valuable sources of information. For example,

legal secretaries will find relevant information about employment agencies serving the legal profession and about prospective employers in the "Legal Assistants" and "Lawyers" profiles. An individual interested in finding a position in radio advertising sales might look to the entries in the broadcasting- and sales-related profiles to find appropriate resources. Career changers, too, can use *JHS* profiles to identify new professions to which their previously acquired skills would be transferable.

Part One: Sources of Job-Hunting Information by Professions and Occupations

This section features profiles of job-hunting information for 228 specific careers. Profiles are listed alphabetically by profession or occupation. Each profile contains up to eight categories of information sources, as described below. Within each category, entries are arranged in alphabetical order by name or title. Entries are numbered sequentially, beginning with the first entry in the first profile. All resources listed are included in each relevant profile (and in Part Two chapters, as appropriate) providing a complete selection of information sources in each occupational profile.

Sources of Help-Wanted Ads. Includes professional journals, industry periodicals, association newsletters, placement bulletins, and online services. In most cases, periodicals that focus on a specific field are cited here; general periodical sources such as the *National Business Employment Weekly* are listed in Part Two under "Help-Wanted Ads." Publications specific to an industry will be found in all profiles related to that industry. Candidates in some occupational areas, such as word processing, are usually recruited from the local marketplace and therefore are not as likely to find openings through a professional publication. Profiles for these occupations may contain fewer ad sources as job hunters are better served by local newspapers and periodicals. Entries include: the source's title and the name, address, and phone number of its publisher or producer; publication frequency; subscription rate; description of contents; toll-free or additional phone numbers; and fax numbers, when applicable. Source titles appear in italics.

Placement and Job Referral Services. Various services designed to match job seekers with opportunities are included in this category. Primarily offered by professional associations, these services range from job banks to placement services to employment clearinghouses, operating on the national and local levels. Entries include: the association's or organization's name, address, and phone number; its membership, activities, and services; toll-free or additional phone numbers; and fax numbers. E-mail and website addresses are provided, when available.

Employer Directories and Networking Lists. Covers directories and rankings of companies, membership rosters from professional associations, and other lists of organizations or groups that can be used to target prospective employers and identify potential contacts for networking purposes. In some cases, Who's Who titles are included where these can provide a source of contact information in a specialized field. General directories of companies such as Standard and Poor's Register of Corporations, Directors, and Executives are cited in Part Two in the "Identifying Prospective Employers" profile. Entries include: the title and name, address, and phone number of the publisher or distributor; publication date or frequency; price; description of contents; arrangement; indexes; toll-free or additional phone numbers; and fax numbers, when available. Directory titles appear in italics.

Handbooks and Manuals. This category notes books, pamphlets, brochures, and other published materials that provide guidance and insight to the job-hunting process in a particular occupational field. Entries include: the title and name, address, and phone number of its publisher or distributor; editor's or author's name; publication date or frequency; price; number of pages; description of contents; toll-free or additional phone numbers; and fax numbers, when known. Publication titles appear in italics.

Employment Agencies and Search Firms. Features firms used by companies to recruit candidates for positions and, at times, by individuals to pursue openings. The following firms are covered:

1. Employment agencies, which are generally geared toward filling openings at entry- to mid-levels in the local job market. Candidates sometimes pay a fee for using their services. When possible, *JHS* lists agencies where the employer pays the fee.

2. Executive search firms, which are paid by the hiring organization to recruit professional and managerial candidates, usually for higher-level openings and from a regional or national market. Executive search firms are of two types: contingency, where the firm is paid only if it fills the position, and retainer, where the firm is compensated to undertake a recruiting assignment, regardless of whether or not that firm actually fills the opening. The majority of the search firms cited in *JHS* are contingency firms. Although executive search firms work for the hiring organization and contact candidates only when recruiting for a specific position, most will accept unsolicited resumes, and some may accept phone calls.

3. Temporary employment agencies, which also are included in some profiles because they can be a way to identify and obtain regular employment.

For the most part, each profile lists firms that typically service that career. Firms specializing in a particular industry are included in all profiles relevant to that industry. *JHS* covers a mix of large and small firms. Major national search firms, which are quite broad in scope, are listed only under the "General Managers and Top Executives" profile. Some occupations are not served by employment agencies or search firms (fire fighter, for example); therefore, there are no entries for this category in such profiles. Entries include: the firm's name, address, and phone number; whether it's an employment agency, executive search firm, or temporary agency; descriptive information, as appropriate; toll-free and additional phone numbers; and fax numbers, when applicable.

Online Job Sources and Services. Publicly available electronic databases, including websites that facilitate matching job hunters with openings are cited. Many are tailored to specific occupations. Entries include: the name of the product or service; the name, address, and phone number of the distributor or producer; price; special formats or arrangements; descriptive information; toll-free or additional phone numbers; and fax numbers, when applicable. For websites, URL is included along with descriptive information.

Tradeshows. Covers exhibitions and tradeshows held in the United States. Entries include: the name of the tradeshow; the name of the sponsoring organization; contact information for the sponsoring organization, including address, phone number, toll-free or additional phone numbers, fax number, email address, and URL; types of exhibits; and dates and locations, when available.

Other Sources. This category comprises a variety of resources available to the job seeker in a specific field: job hotlines providing 24-hour recordings of openings; lists of internships, fellowships, and apprenticeships; bibliographies of job-hunting materials; video and audio cassettes; and salary surveys to be used as a guide when discussing compensation. Professional associations of significance or those that provide job hunting assistance (but not full placement services) are also included here. Because of the trend toward entrepreneurship, this section offers information sources on being one's own boss in a given field as well. Resources on job and career alternatives are provided for certain professions (such as educators), as is information on working abroad.

Entries for associations and organizations include: name, address, and phone number; the membership, activities, and services of associations; toll-free or additional phone numbers; and fax numbers. E-mail and website addresses are provided, when available. Entries for other resources include: title of the publication or name of the product or service; the name, address, and phone number of its publisher, distributor, or producer; editor's or author's name; publication date or frequency; price; special formats or arrangements; descriptive information; hotline, toll-free, or additional phone numbers; and fax numbers, when available. Publication, videocassette, and audiocassette titles appear in italics.

Part Two: Sources of Essential Job-Hunting Information

This section presents 32 profiles on topics of interest to any job hunter, such as resume writing or interviewing, as well as those of specialized interest, such as working at home (see "List of Profiled Professions and Occupations" for the complete list). Profiles are arranged alphabetically by topic and contain up to six categories of information, as listed below. Within each category, citations are organized alphabetically by name or title. Entries are also numbered sequentially, continuing the number sequence from Part One. The publications, periodicals, and other sources listed are fully cited in all relevant chapters (and in Part One profiles, as appropriate), providing the reader with a complete selection of resources in a single, convenient location.

Reference Works. Includes handbooks and manuals, directories, pamphlets, and other published sources of information. Entries include: the title and name, address, and phone number of its publisher or distributor; editor's or author's name; publication date or frequency; price; number of pages; description of contents; toll-free or additional phone numbers; and fax numbers, when known. Publication titles appear in italics.

Newspapers, Magazines, and Journals. Lists items published on a serial basis. Entries include: the title and name, address, and phone number of its publisher or distributor; frequency; price; description of contents; toll-free or additional phone numbers; and fax numbers, when known. Publication titles appear in italics.

Audio/Visual Resources. Features audiocassettes, videocassettes, and filmstrips. Entries include: the title and name, address, and phone number of its distributor or producer; date; price; special formats; descriptive information;

toll-free or additional phone numbers; and fax numbers, when applicable. Videocassette and audiocassette titles appear in italics.

Online and Database Services. Publicly available electronic databases, including websites that facilitate matching job hunters with openings are cited. Entries include: the name of the product or service; the name, address, and phone number of the distributor or producer; price; special formats or arrangements; descriptive information; toll-free or additional phone numbers; and fax numbers, when applicable. For websites: the online address (URL) is included along with descriptive information.

Software. This category notes software programs designed to help with various aspects of job hunting, such as resume preparation. Entries include: the name of the product or service; the name, address, and phone number of the distributor or producer; price; special formats or arrangements; hardware compatibility, if relevant; descriptive information; toll-free or additional phone numbers; and fax numbers, when applicable.

Other Sources. Varied resources such as special associations and organizations and job-hunting bibliographies, kits, and organizers are covered in this section. Citations for journal and newspaper articles are provided if a topic is relatively new. Entries include: the title of the publication or name of the organization, product, or service; the name, address, and phone number of the organization, publisher, distributor, or producer; editor's or author's name; publication date or frequency; price; special formats or arrangements; descriptive information; toll-free or additional phone numbers; and fax numbers, when applicable. Publication titles appear in italics. For article citations: the article title, publication date, and journal or newspaper title, as well as a description of the article.

Index to Information Sources

JHS provides a comprehensive Index to Information Sources that lists all publications, periodicals, associations, organizations, firms, online and database services, and other resources cited in Parts One and Two. Entries are arranged alphabetically and are referenced by their entry numbers. Titles of publications, audiocassettes, and videocassettes appear in italics.

List of Profiled Professions and Occupations

This list outlines references to occupations and professions by job titles, alternate names contained within job titles, popular names, and synonymous and related names. Beginning page numbers for each occupation's profile are provided. Titles of profiles appear in boldface.

Accountants and Auditors

SOURCES OF HELP-WANTED ADS

★1★ Accounting for Banks

LexisNexis Group
1275 Broadway
Albany, NY 12204
Fr: 800-227-9597
URL: http://www.lexisnexis.com

Description: Provides analysis and advice to accounting and banking professionals on day to day operations, internal accounting, investments, finances, assets, and more.

★2★ Accounting and Finance

Wiley-Blackwell
350 Main St. Commerce Pl.
Malden, MA 02148
Ph: (781)388-8200   Fax: (781)388-8210
Fr: 800-759-6120
URL: http://www.blackwellpublishing.com/journal.asp?ref=0810-5391

Quarterly. $163.00/year for institutions, print plus premium online, Australia/New Zealand; $148.00/year for institutions, print plus standard online, Australia/New Zealand; $141.00/year for institutions, premium online only, Australia/New Zealand; $432.00/year for institutions, print plus premium online; $393.00/year for institutions, print plus standard online; $373.00/year for institutions, premium online only; $300.00/year for institutions, other countries, print plus premium online; $273.00/year for institutions, other countries, print plus standard online; $259.00/year for institutions, other countries, premium online only. Journal focusing on accounting and finance.

★3★ Accounting Horizons

American Accounting Association
5717 Bessie Dr.
Sarasota, FL 34233-2399
Ph: (941)921-7747   Fax: (941)923-4093
URL: http://aaahq.org/index.cfm

Quarterly. $265.00/year for individuals, print only; $265.00/year for individuals, online, vol.13 through current issue; $290.00/year for individuals, online and print. Publication covering the banking, finance, and accounting industries.

★4★ The Accounting Review

American Accounting Association
5717 Bessie Dr.
Sarasota, FL 34233-2399
Ph: (941)921-7747   Fax: (941)923-4093
URL: http://aaahq.org/index.cfm

$315.00/year for individuals, print; $315.00/year for individuals, online from volume 74 through current issue; $350.00/year for individuals, online and print. Accounting education, research, financial reporting, and book reviews.

★5★ Auditwire

Institute of Internal Auditors Inc.
247 Maitland Ave.
Altamonte Springs, FL 32701-4201
Ph: (407)937-1100   Fax: (407)937-1101
Fr: 877-867-4957
URL: http://www.theiia.org

Description: Six issues/year. Covers internal auditing's role in a global business environment; communicates the IIA's perspectives on current and emerging issues; and delivers news about the people, places, and events that shape the profession. Columns include: Feedback; Business & Industry; Close-Up; IS Saavy; Newsmakers; Classifieds; Affiliates; Tribute; and Calendar.

★6★ Bank Auditing and Accounting Report

Thomson RIA
395 Hudson St.
New York, NY 10014
Ph: (212)367-6300   Fr: 800-950-1216
URL: http://ria.thomson.com/

Description: Monthly. Provides practical guidance for resolving issues that confront bank professionals every day.

★7★ The CPA Journal

New York State Society of CPAs
3 Park Ave., 18th Fl.
New York, NY 10016-5991
Ph: (212)719-8300   Fax: (212)719-3364
Fr: 800-633-6320
URL: http://www.cpajournal.com/

Monthly. $42.00/year for individuals; $135.00/year for individuals, U.S. 3 years; $99.00/year for individuals, foreign 3 years; $54.00/year for other countries; $74.00 for two years; $98.00/year for other countries, 2 years. Refereed accounting journal.

★8★ CPA Magazine

CPA Magazine
1705 West Northwest Hwy., Ste. 175
Grapevine, TX 76051
Ph: (817)442-1177   Fax: (817)442-1177
Fr: 888-610-1144
E-mail: cpa@cpamagazine.com
URL: http://www.cpamag.com/

Bimonthly. Magazine for certified professional accountants.

★9★ The Edge

American Society of Women Accountants
8405 Greensboro Dr., Ste. 800
McLean, VA 22102
Ph: (703)506-3265   Fax: (703)506-3266
Fr: 800-326-2163
URL: http://www.aswachicago.org

Monthly. free with membership. Magazine containing information on the accounting and financial service professions and its leaders. Provides guidance in maintaining work/life balance.

★10★ Foundations and Trends in Accounting

Now Publishers
PO Box 1024
Hanover, MA 02339
Ph: (781)871-0245
URL: http://www.nowpublishers.com/product.aspx?product=ACC

$315.00/year online only; $355.00/year print and online; $315.00/year online only; $355.00/year print and online. Academic journal publishing new research in all branches of accounting.

★11★ **Government Financial Management Topics**

Association of Government Accountants
2208 Mt. Vernon Ave.
Alexandria, VA 22301
Ph: (703)684-6931   Fax: (703)548-9367
Fr: 800-242-7211
E-mail: mforce@agacgfm.com
URL: http://www.agacgfm.org/publications/cgfm/

Description: Biweekly, Monday. Updates the latest developments relating to government financial management, educational registration forms, and general association news. Recurring features include news of research, a calendar of events, reports of meetings, news of educational opportunities, job listings, notices of publications available, and a column titled Presidential Perspective, interviews with leading government financial managers.

★12★ **Internal Auditor**

Institute of Internal Auditors Inc.
247 Maitland Ave.
Altamonte Springs, FL 32701-4201
Ph: (407)937-1100   Fax: (407)937-1101
Fr: 877-867-4957
E-mail: editor@theiia.org
URL: http://www.theiia.org

Bimonthly. $60.00/year for individuals; $10.00 for single issue; $84.00/year for other countries. Internal auditing.

★13★ **International Journal of Accounting Information Systems**

Elsevier Science Inc.
360 Park Ave. S
New York, NY 10010
Ph: (212)989-5800   Fax: (212)633-3990
URL: http://www.elsevier.com/wps/find/journaldescription.cws_home/620400/description#description

Quarterly. $110.00/year for individuals, for all countries except Europe, Japan and Iran; Journal examining the rapidly evolving relationship between accounting and information technology.

★14★ **International Journal of Auditing**

Wiley-Blackwell
350 Main St. Commerce Pl.
Malden, MA 02148
Ph: (781)388-8200   Fax: (781)388-8210
Fr: 800-759-6120
URL: http://www.blackwellpublishing.com/journal.asp?ref=1090-6738

$72.00/year for individuals, print and online; $52.00/year for students, print and online; $729.00/year for institutions, print and premium online; $672.00/year for institutions, print and standard online; $638.00/year for institutions, premium online only; Journal focusing on global auditing perspectives.

★15★ **Journal of Accountancy**

The American Institute of Certified Public Accountants
1211 Ave. of the Americas
New York, NY 10036-8775
Ph: (212)596-6200   Fax: (212)596-6213
URL: http://www.aicpa.org/

Monthly. $75.00/year for individuals; $60.00/year for members. Accounting journal.

★16★ **Journal of Accounting Research**

Wiley-Blackwell
350 Main St. Commerce Pl.
Malden, MA 02148
Ph: (781)388-8200   Fax: (781)388-8210
Fr: 800-759-6120
URL: http://www.blackwellpublishing.com/journal.asp?ref=0021-8456

$114.00/year for individuals, print and online; $44.00/year for students, print and online; $694.00/year for institutions, print and premium online; $631.00/year for institutions, print and standard online; $599.00/year for institutions, premium online only. Journal focusing on accounting.

★17★ **Journal of Bank Cost & Management Accounting**

Association for Management Information in Financial Services
3895 Fairfax Ct.
Atlanta, GA 30339
Ph: (770)444-3557   Fax: (770)444-9084
URL: http://www.amifs.org/

Subscription included in membership. Journal covering various areas of management accounting and outstanding presentations from association conferences and workshops.

★18★ **Journal of Business Finance and Accounting**

Wiley-Blackwell
350 Main St. Commerce Pl.
Malden, MA 02148
Ph: (781)388-8200   Fax: (781)388-8210
Fr: 800-759-6120
URL: http://www.blackwellpublishing.com/journal.asp?ref=0306-686X

$210.00/year for individuals, U.S. print + online; $1,618.00/year for institutions, U.S. print + premium online; $1,471.00/year for institutions, U.S. print + standard online; $1,397.00/year for institutions, U.S. premium online only. Journal focusing on finance and economic aspects of accounting.

★19★ **The Journal of the Society of Depreciation Professionals**

Society of Depreciation Professionals
8100-M4 Wyoming Blvd. NE, No. 228
Albuquerque, NM 87113
Ph: (505)867-9513   Fax: (505)867-0917
URL: http://www.depr.org/journal.htm

Annual. Professional journal covering depreciation issues for accountants.

★20★ **The Journal of Taxation**

RIA Group
395 Hudson St., 4th Fl.
New York, NY 10014
Ph: (212)367-6300   Fax: (212)367-6314
Fr: 800-431-9025
URL: http://ria.thomson.com/estore/detail.aspx?ID=JTAX

Monthly. $300.00/year for individuals, print; $450.00/year for individuals, online/print bundle; $345.00/year for individuals, online. Journal for sophisticated tax practitioners.

★21★ **Management Accounting Quarterly**

Institute of Management Accountants
10 Paragon Dr.
Montvale, NJ 07645-1718
Ph: (201)573-9000   Fax: (201)474-1603
Fr: 800-638-4427
URL: http://www.imanet.org

Quarterly. $60.00/year for individuals, online. Trade publication covering accounting theory and practices for accountants.

★22★ **National Association of Black Accountants-News Plus**

National Association of Black Accountants Inc.
7249-A Hanover Pkwy.
Greenbelt, MD 20770
Ph: (301)474-6222   Fax: (301)474-3114
Fr: 888-571-2939
E-mail: customerservice@nabainc.org
URL: http://www.nabainc.org/

Description: Quarterly. Addresses concerns of black business professionals, especially in the accounting profession. Reports on accounting education issues, developments affecting the profession, and the Association's activities on the behalf of minorities in the accounting profession. Recurring features include member profiles, job listings, reports of meetings, news of research, and a calendar of events.

★23★ **NewsAccount**

Colorado Society of Certified Public Accountants
7979 E Tufts Ave., Ste. 1000
Denver, CO 80237-2847
Ph: (303)773-2877   Fax: (303)773-6344
Fr: 800-523-9082
URL: http://www.cocpa.org/members/news_account_advert.asp

Description: Six issues/year. Relays information on issues and trends affecting the Society, its members, and the accounting profession. Recurring features include letters to the editor, job listings, a calendar of events and columns titled Committees in Action, Student Corner, SEC Corner, and Technical Update.

★24★ NPA Magazine

National Society of Accountants
1010 N Fairfax St.
Alexandria, VA 22314-1504
Ph: (703)549-6400   Fax: (703)549-2984
Fr: 800-966-6679
URL: http://www.nsacct.org/npa_is-
sues.asp?id=532

Bimonthly. Public accounting magazine.

★25★ Strategic Finance

Institute of Management Accountants
10 Paragon Dr.
Montvale, NJ 07645-1718
Ph: (201)573-9000   Fax: (201)474-1603
Fr: 800-638-4427
E-mail: sfmag@imanet.org
URL: http://www.imanet.org

Monthly. $195.00/year for individuals;
$195.00/year for other countries; $195.00/
year for individuals, corporate libraries;
$195.00/year for individuals, international
libraries; $98.00/year for individuals, non-
profit U.S. libraries only. Magazine reporting
on corporate finance, accounting, cash management, and budgeting.

PLACEMENT AND JOB REFERRAL SERVICES

**★26★ Association for Accounting
Administration (AAA)**

136 S Keowee St.
Dayton, OH 45402
Ph: (937)222-0030   Fax: (937)222-5794
E-mail: aaainfo@cpaadmin.org
URL: http://www.cpaadmin.org

Description: Promotes the profession of
accounting administration and office management in accounting firms and corporate
accounting departments. Sponsors activities,
including consulting and placement services,
seminars, salary and trends surveys, and
speakers' bureau. Provides a forum for
representation and exchange. Offers group
purchasing opportunities.

**★27★ Association of Chartered
Accountants in the United States
(ACAUS)**

341 Lafayette St., Ste. 4246
New York, NY 10012-2417
Ph: (212)334-2078   Fax: (212)431-5786
E-mail: admin@acaus.org
URL: http://www.acaus.org

Members: Chartered accountants from England, Wales, Scotland, Ireland, Canada,
Australia, New Zealand, and South Africa in
commerce and public practice. **Purpose:**
Represents the interests of chartered accountants; promotes career development
and international mobility of professionals.
Activities: Offers educational and research
programs. Maintains speakers' bureau and
placement service.

**★28★ Association of Latino
Professionals in Finance and
Accounting (ALPFA)**

801 S Grand Ave., Ste. 400
Los Angeles, CA 90017
Ph: (213)243-0004   Fax: (213)243-0006
E-mail: acepero@bdo.com
URL: http://www.alpfa.org

Members: Hispanic certified public accountants from the private and public sectors,
accounting firms, universities, and banks.
Purpose: Maintains and promotes professional and moral standards of Hispanics in
the accounting field. Assists members in
practice development and develops business opportunities for members. **Activities:**
Sponsors continuing professional education
seminars; provides employment services.

**★29★ Hospitality Financial and
Technology Professionals (HFTP)**

11709 Boulder Ln., Ste. 110
Austin, TX 78726-1832
Ph: (512)249-5333   Fax: (512)249-1533
Fr: 800-646-4387
E-mail: frank.wolfe@hftp.org
URL: http://www.hftp.org

Members: Accountants, financial officers
and MIS managers in 50 countries working
in hotels, resorts, casinos, restaurants, and
clubs. **Purpose:** Develops uniform system of
accounts. **Activities:** Conducts education,
training, and certification programs; offers
placement service; maintains hall of fame.

**★30★ International Newspaper
Financial Executives (INFE)**

21525 Ridgetop Cir., Ste. 200
Sterling, VA 20166
Ph: (703)421-4060   Fax: (703)421-4068
E-mail: infehq@infe.org
URL: http://www.infe.org

Members: Controllers, chief accountants,
auditors, business managers, treasurers,
secretaries and related newspaper executives, educators, and public accountants.
Activities: Conducts research projects on
accounting methods and procedures for
newspapers. Offers placement service;
maintains Speaker's Bureau. Produces conferences and seminars.

EMPLOYER DIRECTORIES AND NETWORKING LISTS

**★31★ American Society of Women
Accountants-Membership Directory**

American Society of Women Accountants
8405 Greensboro Dr., Ste. 800
McLean, VA 22102
Ph: (703)506-3265   Fax: (703)506-3266
Fr: 800-326-2163
URL: http://www.aswa.org/

Annual. Covers approximately 5,000 members in accounting and accounting-related
fields. Entries include: Name, address,

phone, fax, e-mail. Arrangement: Classified
by chapter, then alphabetical.

**★32★ American Woman's Society of
Certified Public Accountants-Roster**

American Woman's Society of Certified
Public Accountants
136 S Keowee St.
Dayton, OH 45402
Ph: (937)222-1872   Fax: (937)222-5794
Fr: 800-297-2721
URL: http://www.awscpa.org

Annual, October. Number of listings: 1,400.
Entries include: Name, title; company name,
address, phone; home address and phone;
membership classification. Arrangement:
Classified by type of membership, then
geographical. Indexes: Alphabetical.

**★33★ Emerson's Directory of Leading
U.S. Accounting Firms**

Emerson Co.
12342 Northup Way
Bellevue, WA 98005
Ph: (425)869-0655   Fax: (425)869-0746
URL: http://www.emersoncompany.com

Biennial, March of even years. Covers 500
CPA firms in the U.S. Entries include: Company name, address, phone, fax, names and
titles of key personnel, number of employees, geographical area served, description
of services provided and industries served.
Arrangement: Geographical. Indexes: Alphabetical, by state, by size of firm, by specialty
practice.

**★34★ National Society of Public
Accountants-Yearbook**

National Society of Accountants
1010 N Fairfax St.
Alexandria, VA 22314-1504
Ph: (703)549-6400   Fax: (703)549-2984
Fr: 800-966-6679

$35.00 for individuals. Covers association
members and committees; also includes lists
of affiliated state organizations and members
of governing board. Entries include: Member
listings include name, address, phone, and
code indicating type of membership. Other
listings include name, address, and phone.
Arrangement: Geographical.

**★35★ Peterson's Job Opportunities for
Business Majors**

Peterson's
Princeton Pke. Corporate Ctr., 2000
Lenox Dr.
PO Box 67005
Lawrenceville, NJ 08648
Ph: (609)896-1800   Fax: (609)896-4531
Fr: 800-338-3282
URL: http://www.petersons.com/

Irregular; latest edition 16th, 2000. Covers
the 2,000 largest U.S. employers hiring in
several fields, including financial services,
management consulting, consumer products, and media/entertainment. Entries include: Organization name, address, phone,
name and title of contact, number of employ-

ees, type of organization. Arrangement: Alphabetical. Indexes: Type of organization.

★36★ Who Audits America

Data Financial Press
PO Box 668
Menlo Park, CA 94026
Ph: (650)321-4553   Fax: (707)598-3560
URL: http://goliath.ecnext.com/coms2/product-compint-0000710741-p

Reported as semiannual, June and December; latest edition June 2001. Covers 12,000 publicly held corporations that report to the Securities and Exchange Commission, and their accounting firms. Entries include: For companies–Name, location, SIC classification, number of employees, financial data, and abbreviation indicating accounting firm used. For accounting firms–Name, address, list of clients with their annual sales, and stock trading symbols. Arrangement: Companies are alphabetical; accounting firms are geographical. There is a separate alphabetical section of "Big Eight" accounting firms, with list of their clients having more than 1 billion dollars annual sales.

HANDBOOKS AND MANUALS

★37★ Accountants' Handbook, Set

John Wiley & Sons, Inc.
111 River St.
Hoboken, NJ 07030
Ph: (201)748-6000   Fax: (201)748-6088
E-mail: info@wiley.com
URL: http://www.wiley.com/WileyCDA/

D.R. Carmichael and Paul H. Rosenfield. 2007. $95.00. Series covering accounting and financial reporting of interest to accountants, auditors, financial analysts, and users of accounting information.

★38★ Accounting Ethics: Critical Perspectives on Business and Management

Routledge
270 Madison Ave., No. 3
New York, NY 10016-0601
Fr: 800-634-7064

J. Edward Ketz. $1,370.00. 2006. This research collection includes important papers from key journals and books that reassess theories, research studies, and professional practices in the field of accounting ethics.

★39★ Accounting Trends & Techniques

American Institute of Certified Public Accountants
Harborside Financial Ctr.
201 Plaza Three
Jersey City, NJ 07311-3881
Ph: (201)938-3000   Fax: (201)938-3329
Fr: 888-777-7077

URL: http://www.aicpa.org
Rick Rikert. 1999. $99.00 (paper).

★40★ Best Resumes for Accountants and Financial Professionals

John Wiley & Sons, Inc.
111 River St.
Hoboken, NJ 07030
Ph: (201)748-6000   Fax: (201)748-6088
E-mail: info@wiley.com
URL: http://www.wiley.com/WileyCDA/

Kim Marino. 1994. $19.95 (paper). 208 pages. Contains examples of accounting and financial resumes. Also includes details on job search techniques.

★41★ Best Websites for Financial Professionals, Business Appraisers, & Accountants

John Wiley & Sons Inc.
111 River St.
Hoboken, NJ 07030-5774
Ph: (201)748-6000   Fax: (201)748-5774
E-mail: custserv@wiley.com
URL: http://www.wiley.com/WileyCDA/

Eva M. Lang and Jan Davis Tudor. Second edition, 2003. $49.95 (paper). 256 pages.

★42★ Careers in Accounting

The McGraw-Hill Companies
PO Box 182604
Columbus, OH 43272
Fax: (614)759-3749   Fr: 877-883-5524
E-mail: customer.service@mcgraw-hill.com
URL: http://www.mcgraw-hill.com

Gloria L. Gaylord and Glenda E. Ried. Third edition; Revised. 1997. $17.95; $13.95 (paper). 167 pages. Details opportunities in public, corporate, government, and not-for-profit accounting. Topics range from choosing a specialty to finding a mentor and networking on the job.

★43★ Careers for Financial Mavens and Other Money Movers

The McGraw-Hill Companies
PO Box 182604
Columbus, OH 43272
Fax: (614)759-3749   Fr: 877-883-5524
E-mail: customer.service@mcgraw-hill.com
URL: http://www.mcgraw-hill.com

Marjorie Eberts and Margaret Gisler. Second edition, 2004. $13.95; $9.95 (paper). 153 pages.

★44★ Careers for Number Crunchers and Other Quantitative Types

The McGraw-Hill Companies
PO Box 182604
Columbus, OH 43272
Fax: (614)759-3749   Fr: 877-883-5524
E-mail: customer.service@mcgraw-hill.com
URL: http://www.mcgraw-hill.com

Rebecca Burnett. Second edition, 2002. $22.95 (paper). 192 pages. Provides information to math-oriented job hunters on how

to become statisticians, field researchers, computer programmers, stock analysts, investment managers, bankers, engineers, accountants, underwriters, economists, market analysts, mathematicians, systems analysts, and more.

★45★ CIMA Study Systems 2006: Financial Accounting Fundamentals

CIMA Publishing
525 B St., Ste. 1900
San Diego, CA 92101
Ph: (619)231-6616   Fax: (619)699-6422
Fr: 800-545-2522
E-mail: usbkinfo@elsevier.com
URL: http://www.elsevier.com

Henry Lunt and Margaret Weaver. 2005. $52.95. Provides comprehensive study material for the exams; incorporates legislative and syllabus changes.

★46★ The CPA Profession: Opportunities, Responsibilities & Services

Prentice Hall PTR
1 Lake St.
Upper Saddle River, NJ 07458
Ph: (201)236-7000   Fax: 800-445-6991
Fr: 800-428-5331
URL: http://www.phptr.com/index.asp?rl=1

Harry T. Magill, Gary J. Previts and Thomas R. Robinson. 1997. $54.00 (paper). 252 pages.

★47★ The I Hate Selling Book: Business-Building Advice for Consultants, Attorneys, Accountants, Engineers, Architects, and Other Professionals

AMACOM
1601 Broadway, 12th Fl.
New York, NY 10019-7420
Ph: (212)586-8100   Fax: (212)903-8168
Fr: 800-262-9699
URL: http://www.amanet.org

Allan S. Boress. 2001. $29.95. 240 pages.

★48★ Opportunities in Accounting Careers

The McGraw-Hill Companies
PO Box 182604
Columbus, OH 43272
Fax: (614)759-3749   Fr: 877-883-5524
E-mail: customer.service@mcgraw-hill.com
URL: http://www.mcgraw-hill.com

Martin Rosenberg. 1996. $14.95; $11.95 (paper). 160 pages. Covers job opportunities in a variety of fields and specialties and how to pursue them. Illustrated.

★49★ Opportunities in Financial Careers

The McGraw-Hill Companies
PO Box 182604
Columbus, OH 43272
Fax: (614)759-3749   Fr: 877-883-5524
E-mail: customer.service@mcgraw-hill.com

URL: http://www.mcgraw-hill.com

Michael Sumichrast. 2004. $13.95; $11.95 (paper). 160 pages. A guide to planning for and seeking opportunities in this challenging field.

★50★ **Opportunities in Insurance Careers**

The McGraw-Hill Companies
PO Box 182604
Columbus, OH 43272
Fax: (614)759-3749   Fr: 877-883-5524
E-mail: customer.service@mcgraw-hill.com
URL: http://www.mcgraw-hill.com

Robert M. Schrayer. Revised, 2007. $14.95 (paper). 160 pages. A guide to planning for and seeking opportunities in the field. Contains bibliography and illustrations.

★51★ **Opportunities in International Business Careers**

The McGraw-Hill Companies
PO Box 182604
Columbus, OH 43272
Fax: (614)759-3749   Fr: 877-883-5524
E-mail: customer.service@mcgraw-hill.com
URL: http://www.mcgraw-hill.com

Jeffrey Arpan. 1994. $11.95 (paper). 147 pages. Describes what types of jobs exist in international business, where they are located, what challenges and rewards they bring, and how to prepare for and obtain jobs in international business.

★52★ **Opportunities in Office Occupations**

The McGraw-Hill Companies
PO Box 182604
Columbus, OH 43272
Fax: (614)759-3749   Fr: 877-883-5524
E-mail: customer.service@mcgraw-hill.com
URL: http://www.mcgraw-hill.com

Blanche Ettinger. 1995. $14.95; $11.95 (paper). 146 pages. Covers a variety of office positions and discusses trends for the next decade. Describes the job market, opportunities, job duties, educational preparation, the work environment, and earnings.

★53★ **Opportunities in State and Local Government Careers**

The McGraw-Hill Companies
PO Box 182604
Columbus, OH 43272
Fax: (614)759-3749   Fr: 877-883-5524
E-mail: customer.service@mcgraw-hill.com
URL: http://www.mcgraw-hill.com

Neale J. Baxter. Revised edition, 1992. $14.95; $10.95 (paper). 148 pages. Points out the incentives and drawbacks of a government career. Describes hiring procedures and provides tips on filling out applications, taking physical and aptitude tests, handling interviews, and finding jobs. Describes the jobs in which 75% of all state and local government workers are employed. For each occupation, covers the nature of the work and the training required.

★54★ **Power Publicity for Accountants**

Clifford Publishing
PO Box 43596
Upper Montclair, NJ 07043-0596
Ph: (973)857-4142

2006. $79.00. Ideas for press releases for accounting businesses seeking publicity. A full year calendar with ideas for every month is included.

★55★ **Research on Professional Responsibility and Ethics in Accounting**

Elsevier
525 B St., Ste. 1900
San Diego, CA 92101
Ph: (619)231-6616   Fax: (619)699-6422
Fr: 800-545-2522
E-mail: usbkinfo@elsevier.com
URL: http://www.elsevier.com

Cynthia Jeffrey. 2006. $99.95. Presents research and cases focusing on the professional responsibilities of accountants and addresses ways in which to deal with ethical issues.

★56★ **Resumes for Banking and Financial Careers**

The McGraw-Hill Companies
PO Box 182604
Columbus, OH 43272
Fax: (614)759-3749   Fr: 877-883-5524
E-mail: customer.service@mcgraw-hill.com
URL: http://www.mcgraw-hill.com

Second edition, 2001. $11.95 (paper). 160 pages.

★57★ **Top 10 Technology Opportunities: Tips & Tools**

American Institute of Certified Public Accountants
Harborside Financial Ctr.
201 Plaza Three
Jersey City, NJ 07311-3881
Ph: (201)938-3000   Fax: (201)938-3329
Fr: 888-777-7077
URL: http://www.aicpa.org

Sandi Smith. 1998. $24.95 (paper). 248 pages. Part of the American Institute of CPAs Audit Guides Series.

EMPLOYMENT AGENCIES AND SEARCH FIRMS

★58★ **Abel Fuller & Zedler LLC**

440 Benmar, Ste. 1085
Houston, TX 77060
Ph: (281)447-3334   Fax: (281)447-3334
E-mail: agarcia@execufirm.com
URL: http://www.execufirm.com

Executive search firm.

★59★ **AD Check Associates Inc.**

116 Doran Dr.
Wilkes Barre, PA 18708
Ph: (570)829-5066   Fax: (570)820-8293
E-mail: check204@aol.com

Executive search firm.

★60★ **Adams Executive Search**

3416 Fairfield Trail
Clearwater, FL 33761
Ph: (727)772-1536   Fax: (815)328-3792
E-mail: info@axsearch.com
URL: http://www.axsearch.com

Executive search firm.

★61★ **Allen Personnel Agency Inc.**

160 Broadway Lbby, Ste. 200
New York, NY 10038-4201
Ph: (212)571-1150   Fax: (212)766-1015
Fr: 800-486-1150

Personnel consultants specializing in business and finance recruitment, specifically insurance, banking, stock brokerage, law and accounting. Industries served: all.

★62★ **Aureus Group**

13609 California St.
Omaha, NE 68154
Ph: (402)891-6900   Fax: (402)891-1290
Fr: 888-239-5993
E-mail: info@aureusgroup.com
URL: http://www.aureusgroup.com

Provides human capital management services in a wide variety of industries. Executive search and recruiting consultants specializing in six areas: accounting and finance, data processing, aerospace, engineering, manufacturing and medical professionals. Industries served: hospitals, all mainframe computer shops and all areas of accounting.

★63★ **Bishop Partners**

708 3rd Ave., Ste. 2200
New York, NY 10017
Ph: (212)986-3419   Fr: (212)986-3350
E-mail: info@bishoppartners.com
URL: http://www.bishoppartners.com

Executive search firm focuses on legal and accounting fields.

★64★ **Boyce Cunnane Inc.**

PO Box 19064
Baltimore, MD 21284-9064
Ph: (410)583-5511   Fax: (410)583-5518
E-mail: bc@cunnane.com
URL: http://www.cunnane.com

Executive search firm.

★65★ **Buxbaum/Rink Consulting L.L.C.**

1 Bradley Rd., Ste. 901
Woodbridge, CT 06525-2296
Ph: (203)389-5949   Fax: (203)397-0615
E-mail: gen@buxbaumrink.com

URL: http://www.buxbaumrink.com

Personnel consulting firms offer contingency search, recruitment and placement of accounting and finance, as well as other business management positions. In addition to serving these two major career areas, also provides similar services to operations, marketing and human resources executives. Industries served: manufacturing, financial services, and service.

★66★ Capstone Consulting Inc.
723 S. Dearborn St.
Chicago, IL 60605
Ph: (312)922-9556   Fax: (312)922-9558
E-mail: Lori@CapstoneConsulting.com
URL: http://www.capstoneconsulting.com

Executive search firm.

★67★ Chanko-Ward Ltd.
2 W 45th St., Ste. 1201
New York, NY 10036
Ph: (212)869-4040   Fax: (212)869-0281
E-mail: info@chankoward.com
URL: http://www.chankoward.com

Primarily engaged in executive recruiting for individuals and corporations, where disciplines of accounting, planning, mergers and acquisitions, finance, or MIS are required. In addition will function as the internal personnel department of a corporation, either to augment present staff or in a situation where there is no formal personnel department. Serves private industries as well as government agencies.

★68★ Consultants to Executive Management Company Ltd.
20 S Clark St., Ste. 610
Chicago, IL 60603
Ph: (312)855-1500   Fax: (312)855-1510
Fr: 800-800-2362
E-mail: cemco@cemcoltd.com
URL: http://www.cemcoltd.com

National personnel consultancy specializes in executive search with focus on accounting and finance, management information systems, professional medical, and real estate fields. Industries served: all.

★69★ Cornell Global
PO Box 7113
Wilton, CT 06897
Ph: (203)762-0730   Fax: (203)761-9507
E-mail: infor@cornellglobal.com
URL: http://www.cornellglobal.com

Executive search firm.

★70★ DBL Associates
1334 Park View Ave., Ste. 100
Manhattan Beach, CA 90266
Ph: (310)546-8121   Fax: (310)546-8122
E-mail: dlong@dblsearch.com
URL: http://www.dblsearch.com

Executive search firm focused on the financial industry.

★71★ Dellosso and Greenberg
525 E. 82nd St., Ste. 2B
New York, NY 10028
Ph: (212)570-5350   Fax: (212)327-0613
E-mail: esearch@dellossoandgreenberg.com
URL: http://www.dellossoandgreenberg.com

Executive search firm.

★72★ DGL Consultants
189 S. Main St.
PO Box 450
Richford, VT 05476
Ph: (802)848-7764   Fax: (802)848-3117
E-mail: info@dglconsultants.com
URL: http://www.dglconsultants.com

Executive search firm.

★73★ Elinvar
1804 Hillsborough St.
Raleigh, NC 27605
Ph: (919)878-4454
E-mail: info@elinvar.com
URL: http://www.elinvar.com

Executive search firm.

★74★ Houser Martin Morris
110th Ave. NE, 110 Atrium Pl., Ste. 580
110 Atrium Pl.
Bellevue, WA 98004
Ph: (425)453-2700   Fax: (425)453-8726
E-mail: info@houser.com
URL: http://www.houser.com

Focus is in the areas of retained executive search, professional and technical recruiting. Areas of specialization include software engineering, sales and marketing, information technology, legal, human resources, accounting and finance, manufacturing, factory automation, and engineering.

★75★ International Search
9717 E 42nd St.
PO Box 470898
Tulsa, OK 74147-0898
Ph: (918)627-9070   Fax: (918)524-8604

Personnel consulting group provides placement expertise in engineering, accounting, and data processing. Industries served: energy, manufacturing, oil and gas, and services.

★76★ KForce
Fr: 888-663-3626
URL: http://www.kforce.com

Executive search firm. More than 30 locations throughout the United States.

★77★ O'Shea System of Employment Inc.
PO Box 2134
Aston, PA 19014
Ph: (610)364-3964   Fax: (610)364-3962
Fr: 800-220-5203

E-mail: fcomeau@osheasystem.com
URL: http://www.osheasystem.com

Offers personnel staff recruiting nationally in the following fields: Insurance, Health Care, Financial, Information Technology, Administration, Human resource, Manufacturing and Sales.

★78★ Pate Resources Group Inc.
595 Orleans, Ste. 707
Beaumont, TX 77701
Ph: (409)833-4514   Fax: (409)833-4646
Fr: 800-669-4514
E-mail: opportunities@pateresourcesgroup.com
URL: http://www.pateresourcesgroup.com

Offers executive search and recruiting services to professionals who include physicians, healthcare administrators, engineers, accounting and financial disciplines, legal, outplacement, sales and marketing. Industries served: healthcare, petrochemicals, accounting, utility, legal, and municipalities.

★79★ Penn Search Inc.
1045 1st Ave., Ste. 110
PO Box 688
Wayne, PA 19087
Ph: (610)964-8820   Fax: (610)964-8916
E-mail: charlied@pennsearch.com
URL: http://www.pennsearch.com

Assists in recruiting and hiring accounting and financial professionals from staff accountant to chief financial officer. Industries served: all.

★80★ Phillips Personnel/Search; Phillips Temps
1675 Broadway, Ste. 2410
Denver, CO 80202
Ph: (303)893-1850   Fax: (303)893-0639
E-mail: info@phillipspersonnel.com
URL: http://www.phillipspersonnel.com

Personnel recruiting and staffing consultants in: accounting/finance, MIS, sales/marketing, engineering, administration and general/executive management. Industries served: telecommunications, distribution, financial services, and general business.

★81★ Raymond Alexander Associates
97 Lackawanna Ave., Ste. 102
Totowa, NJ 07512
Ph: (973)256-1000   Fax: (973)256-5871
E-mail: raa@raymondalexander.com
URL: http://www.raymondalexander.com

Personnel consulting firm conducts executive search services in the specific areas of accounting, tax and finance. Industries served: manufacturing, financial services, and public accounting.

★82★ Roberson & Co.
10751 Parfet St.
Broomfield, CO 80021
Ph: (303)410-6510
E-mail: roberson@recruiterpro.com

URL: http://www.recruiterpro.com

A contingency professional and executive recruiting firm working the national and international marketplace. Specialize in accounting, finance, data processing and information services, healthcare, environmental and mining, engineering, manufacturing, human resources, and sales and marketing.

★83★ Rocky Mountain Recruiters, Inc.

1776 S. Jackson St., Ste. 412
Denver, CO 80210
Ph: (303)296-2000   Fax: (303)296-2223
E-mail: resumes@rmrecruiters.com
URL: http://www.rmrecruiters.com

Accounting, financial, and executive search firm.

★84★ SHS of Cherry Hill

496 N Kings Hwy., Ste. 125
Cherry Hill, NJ 08034
Ph: (856)779-9030   Fax: (856)779-0898
E-mail: shs@shsofcherryhill.com
URL: http://www.shsofcherryhill.com

Personnel recruiters operating in the disciplines of accounting, sales, insurance, engineering, and administration. Industries served: insurance, distribution, manufacturing, and service.

★85★ Spherion Pacific Enterprises L.L.C.

2050 Spectrum Blvd.
Fort Lauderdale, FL 33309
Ph: (954)938-7600   Fax: (954)938-7666
Fr: 800-900-4686
E-mail: info@spherion.com
URL: http://www.spherion.com

Firm specializes in recruiting, assessing and deploying talent. It provides the widest range of services available including consulting, managed staffing, outsourcing, search/recruitment and flexible staffing. The company has expertise in industries such as information technology, outsourcing, accounting and finance, law, manufacturing and human resources; as well as clerical, administrative and light industrial.

★86★ Wendell L. Johnson Associates Inc.

12 Grandview Dr., Ste. 1117
Danbury, CT 06811-4321
Ph: (203)743-4112   Fax: (203)778-5377

Executive search firm specializing in areas of workforce diversity, accounting/finance, human resources, marketing/sales, strategic planning, and MIS.

★87★ Whitney & Associates Inc.

920 2nd Ave. S, Ste. 625
Minneapolis, MN 55422-4103
Ph: (612)338-5600   Fax: (612)349-6129
E-mail: dwhitney@whitneyinc.com

Accounting and financial personnel recruiting consultants providing full-time placement and temporary staffing service with specialized expertise and emphasis in the accounting discipline.

ONLINE JOB SOURCES AND SERVICES

★88★ Accounting.com

E-mail: info@accounting.com
URL: http://www.accounting.com

Description: Job board for those seeking accounting jobs. Employers may also post positions available. Contains directory of CPA firms, discussion forum for job seekers, CPE resources, news bulletins and accounting links.

★89★ American Accounting Association Placement Advertising

5717 Bessie Dr.
Sarasota, FL 34233-2399
Ph: (941)921-7747   Fax: (941)923-4093
E-mail: office@aahq.org
URL: http://aaahq.org/placements/default.cfm

Description: Visitors may apply for membership to the Association at this site. **Main files include:** Placement Postings, Placement Submission Information, Faculty Development, Marketplace, more.

★90★ American Association of Finance and Accounting

E-mail: feedback@aafa.com
URL: http://www.aafa.com

Description: AAFA is the largest and oldest alliance of executive search firms specializing in the recruitment and placement of finance and accounting professionals. Contains career opportunities site with job board for both job seekers and hiring employers. One does not have to be a member to search for jobs.

★91★ Association of Certified Fraud Examiners

716 W. Ave.
Austin, TX 78701-2727
Ph: (512)478-9000   Fax: (512)478-9297
Fr: 800-245-3321
E-mail: memberservices@acfe.com
URL: http://www.cfenet.com

Description: Website for membership organization contains Career Center with job databank, ability to post jobs and career resources and links. Must be a member of organization in order to access databank.

★92★ California Society of Certified Public Accountants Classifieds

1235 Radio Rd.
Redwood City, CA 94065-1217
Fr: 800-922-5272
E-mail: info@calcpa.org

URL: http://www.calcpa.org

Description: An accounting job search tool for CPAs in California. Details steps to become a CPA, provides job search posting opportunities for seekers and candidates' pages for employers looking to fill positions.

★93★ Financial Job Network

15030 Ventura Blvd., No. 378
Sherman Oaks, CA 91403
E-mail: info@fjn.com
URL: http://www.fjn.com

Description: Contains information on international and national employment opportunities for those in the financial job market. Job listings may be submitted, as well as resumes. **Main files include:** Testimonials, Calendar, Corporate Listings, FJN Clients, more. **Fee:** Free to candidates.

★94★ Illinois Certified Public Accountant Society Career Services

550 W. Jackson, Ste. 900
Chicago, IL 60661-5716
Ph: (312)993-0407   Fax: (312)993-9954
URL: http://www.icpas.org/icpas/career-services/job-seekers.asp

Description: Offers job hunting aid to members of the Illinois CPA Society only. Opportunity for non-members to join online. **Main files include:** Overview of Services, Resume Match, Career Seminars, Career Resources, Free Job Listings, Per Diem Pool, and Career Bibliographies.

★95★ Society of Financial Examiners

174 Grace Blvd.
Altamonte Springs, FL 32714
Ph: (407)682-4930   Fax: (407)682-3175
E-mail: pkeyes@sofe.org
URL: http://www.sofe.org

Description: Website for membership organization contains classified advertisements for financial examiner positions as well as links to resources about the profession and an opportunity to enroll in an annual career development seminar. Visitors do not have to be members of the association to view job postings.

★96★ Spherion

2050 Spectrum Blvd.
Fort Lauderdale, FL 33309
Ph: (954)308-7600
E-mail: help@spherion.com
URL: http://www.spherion.com

Description: Recruitment firm specializing in accounting and finance, sales and marketing, interim executives, technology, engineering, retail and human resources.

TRADESHOWS

★97★ American Accounting Association Annual Meeting

American Accounting Association
5717 Bessie Dr.
Sarasota, FL 34233-2399
Ph: (941)921-7747   Fax: (941)923-4093
E-mail: office@aaahq.org
URL: http://aaahq.org/index.cfm

Annual. **Primary Exhibits:** Accounting equipment, supplies, and services.

★98★ American Association of Attorney-Certified Public Accountants Annual Conference

American Association of Attorney-Certified Public Accountants
24196 Alicia Pky., Ste. K
Mission Viejo, CA 92691
Ph: (949)768-0336
URL: http://www.attorney-cpa.com

Annual. **Primary Exhibits:** Exhibits for persons licensed both as attorneys and CPAs.

★99★ American Association of Hispanic CPAs

American Association of Hispanic CPAs
64 Hunter Rd.
Fairfield, CT 06824
Ph: (203)255-7003   Fax: (203)259-2872

Annual. **Primary Exhibits:** Practice development and employment, educational opportunities.

★100★ Annual Accounting Show

Florida Institute of Certified Public Accountants
PO Box 5437
Tallahassee, FL 32314
Ph: (850)224-2727

Primary Exhibits: Accounting information and services.

★101★ Association of Insolvency and Restructuring Advisors

Association of Insolvency Accountants
132 W. Main, Ste. 200
Medford, OR 97501
Ph: (541)858-1665   Fax: (541)858-9187

Annual. **Primary Exhibits:** Exhibits for CPAs and licensed public accountants, attorneys, examiners, trustees and receivers involved in insolvency accounting.

★102★ Business & Technology Solutions Show

Illinois Certified Public Accounting Society
550 W. Jackson
Ste 900
Chicago, IL 60661
Ph: (312)933-0407   Fax: (312)993-9954
Fr: 800-993-0407
URL: http://www.icpas.org

Annual. **Primary Exhibits:** Computers, office equipment, software publishing and educational supplies, and financial services.

★103★ Florida Accounting and Business Expo

Florida Institute of Certified Public Accountants
PO Box 5437
Tallahassee, FL 32314
Ph: (850)224-2727

Primary Exhibits: Accounting equipment, supplies, and services.

★104★ IASA Annual

Corcoran Expositions, Inc.
100 W. Monroe St., Ste. 1001
Chicago, IL 60603
Ph: (312)541-0567   Fax: (312)541-0573
E-mail: info@corcexpo.com
URL: http://www.corcexpo.com

Annual. **Primary Exhibits:** equipment, supplies, and services for finance, accounting, administration, and data management.

★105★ Institute of Internal Auditors - USA International Conference

Institute of Internal Auditors - USA
247 Maitland Ave.
Altamonte Springs, FL 32701-4201
Ph: (407)937-1100   Fax: (407)937-1101
E-mail: iia@theiia.org
URL: http://www.theiia.org

Annual. **Primary Exhibits:** Internal auditing equipment, supplies, and services, software, computer related equipment.

★106★ Institute of Management Accountants Conference

Institute of Management Accountants, Inc.
10 Paragon Dr.
Montvale, NJ 07645-1718
Ph: (201)573-9000   Fax: (201)573-9000
Fr: 800-638-4427
E-mail: info@imanet.org
URL: http://www.imanet.org

Annual. **Primary Exhibits:** Management accounting equipment, supplies, and services. Review courses, shipping companies, software companies, and risk management consultants.

★107★ Insurance Accounting and Systems Association Conference

Insurance Accounting and Systems Association
PO Box 51340
4705 University Dr., Ste. 280
Durham, NC 27717-3409
Ph: (919)489-0991   Fax: (919)489-1994
E-mail: info@iasa.org
URL: http://www.iasa.org

Annual. **Primary Exhibits:** Insurance equipment, supplies, and services.

★108★ National Association of Tax Professionals Conference

National Association of Tax Professionals
720 Association Dr.
PO Box 8002
Appleton, WI 54912-8002
Ph: (920)749-1040   Fax: 800-747-0001
Fr: 800-558-3402
E-mail: natp@natptax.com
URL: http://www.natptax.com

Annual. **Primary Exhibits:** Computer hardware, tax accounting and planning software, tax research information, tax forms, one-write accounting, financial planning information, office products, business equipment, and tax business solutions.

★109★ National Society of Accountants Convention

National Society of Accountants
1010 N Fairfax St.
Alexandria, VA 22314-1574
Ph: (703)549-6400   Fax: (703)549-2984
Fr: 800-966-6679
E-mail: arichman@nsacct.org
URL: http://www.nsacct.org

Annual. **Primary Exhibits:** Professional organization and its affiliates represent 30,000 members who provide auditing, accounting, tax preparation, financial and estate planning and management services to approximately 19 million individuals and business clients.

★110★ National Society of Public Accountants Annual Convention

National Society of Public Accountants
1010 N. Fairfax St.
Alexandria, VA 22314-1574
Ph: (703)549-6400   Fax: (703)549-2984
Fr: 800-966-6679
E-mail: NSA@wizard.net
URL: http://www.nsa.org

Annual. **Primary Exhibits:** Exhibits related to public accounting.

★111★ New Jersey Accounting, Business & Technology Show & Conference

Flagg Management, Inc.
353 Lexington Ave.
New York, NY 10016
Ph: (212)286-0333   Fax: (212)286-0086
E-mail: flaggmgmt@msn.com
URL: http://www.flaggmgmt.com

Annual. **Primary Exhibits:** Information and technology, financial and business services, computer accounting systems, software, tax preparation, accounting, audit, practice management software - windows, and computer and business systems. Banking, insurance, financial and business software. Internet, online systems and middle market software and investment services.

OTHER SOURCES

★112★ Accountants Global Network (AGN)

2851 S Parker Rd., Ste. 850
Aurora, CO 80014
Ph: (303)743-7880   Fax: (303)743-7660
E-mail: rhood@agn.org
URL: http://www.agn.org

Description: Represents and promotes the fields of separate and independent accounting and consulting firms serving business organizations.

★113★ Accreditation Council for Accountancy and Taxation (ACAT)

1010 N Fairfax St.
Alexandria, VA 22314-1574
Fax: (703)549-2512   Fr: 888-289-7763
E-mail: info@acatcredentials.org
URL: http://www.acatcredentials.org

Description: Strives to raise professional standards and improve the practices of accountancy and taxation. Identifies persons with demonstrated knowledge of the principles and practices of accountancy and taxation. Ensures the continued professional growth of accredited individuals by setting stringent continuing education requirements. Fosters increased recognition for the profession in the public, private, and educational sectors.

★114★ Affiliated Conference of Practicing Accountants International (ACPA)

30 Massachusetts Ave.
North Andover, MA 01845-3413
Ph: (978)689-9420   Fax: (978)689-9404
E-mail: acpaintl@acpaintl.org
URL: http://acpa.careerbank.com

Description: Certified public and chartered accounting firms. Encourages the interchange of professional and legislative information among members with the aim of: enhancing service and technical and professional competency; maintaining effective management administration and practice development; increasing public awareness of members' capabilities. Facilitates availability and use of specialists and industry expertise among members in areas such as manufacturing, real estate, legal and medical services, finance, wholesaling, retailing, and municipal government. Makes client referrals; compiles revenue, operating expense, and cost ratio comparisons among firms.

★115★ Alliance of Practicing Certified Public Accountants (APCPA)

12149 Fremont St.
Yucaipa, CA 92399
Ph: (909)705-7505   Fax: (909)790-7646
E-mail: bmvalek@earthlink.net

Description: Represents and promotes practicing certified public accountants.

★116★ American Accounting Association (AAA)

5717 Bessie Dr.
Sarasota, FL 34233-2330
Ph: (941)921-7747   Fax: (941)923-4093
E-mail: office@aaahq.org
URL: http://aaahq.org

Description: Professors and practitioners of accounting. Promotes worldwide excellence in accounting education, research and practice.

★117★ American Institute of Certified Public Accountants (AICPA)

1211 Ave. of the Americas
New York, NY 10036-8775
Ph: (212)596-6001   Fax: (212)596-6030
Fr: 888-777-7077
E-mail: bmelancon@aicpa.org
URL: http://www.aicpa.org

Members: Professional society of accountants certified by the states and territories. **Purpose:** Responsibilities include establishing auditing and reporting standards; influencing the development of financial accounting standards underlying the presentation of U.S. corporate financial statements; preparing and grading the national Uniform CPA Examination for the state licensing bodies. **Activities:** Conducts research and continuing education programs and oversight of practice. Maintains over 100 committees including Accounting Standards, Accounting and Review Services, AICPA Effective Legislation Political Action, Auditing Standards, Taxation, Consulting Services, Professional Ethics, Quality Review, Women and Family Issues, and Information Technology.

★118★ American Society of Tax Professionals (ASTP)

PO Box 1213
Lynnwood, WA 98046-1213
Ph: (425)774-1996   Fax: (425)672-0461
Fr: 877-674-1996
E-mail: carol.kraemer1@verizon.net

Members: Tax preparers, accountants, attorneys, bookkeepers, accounting services, and public accounting firms seeking to uphold high service standards in professional tax preparation. **Purpose:** Works to enhance the image of tax professionals and make tax practice more profitable; keep members abreast of tax law and service and delivery changes; promote networking among members for mutual assistance. **Activities:** Offers continuing education and training courses and public relations and marketing planning and preparation services. Supports Certified Tax Preparer Program.

★119★ American Society of Women Accountants (ASWA)

8405 Greensboro Dr., Ste. 800
McLean, VA 22102-5120
Ph: (703)506-3265   Fax: (703)506-3266
Fr: 800-326-2163
E-mail: aswa@aswa.org
URL: http://www.aswa.org

Description: Professional society of women accountants, educators, and others in the field of accounting dedicated to the achievement of personal, professional, and economic potential. Assists women accountants in their careers and promotes development in the profession. Conducts educational and research programs.

★120★ American Woman's Society of Certified Public Accountants (AWSCPA)

136 S Keowee St.
Dayton, OH 45402
Ph: (937)222-1872   Fax: (937)222-5794
Fr: 800-297-2721
E-mail: info@awscpa.org
URL: http://www.awscpa.org

Description: Citizens who hold Certified Public Accountant certificates as well as those who have passed the CPA examination but do not have certificates. Works to improve the status of professional women and to make the business community aware of the professional capabilities of the woman CPA. Conducts semiannual statistical survey of members; offers specialized education and research programs.

★121★ Association of Government Accountants (AGA)

2208 Mt. Vernon Ave.
Alexandria, VA 22301-1314
Ph: (703)684-6931   Fax: (703)548-9367
Fr: 800-AGA-7211
E-mail: rvandaniker@agacgfm.org
URL: http://www.agacgfm.org

Description: Professional society of financial managers employed by federal, state, county, and city governments in financial management and administrative positions. Conducts research; offers education and professional development programs.

★122★ Association of Healthcare Internal Auditors (AHIA)

10200 W 44th Ave., Ste. 304
Wheat Ridge, CO 80033
Ph: (303)327-7546   Fax: (303)422-8894
Fr: 888-ASK-AHIA
E-mail: ahia@ahia.org
URL: http://www.ahia.org

Members: Health care internal auditors and other interested individuals. **Purpose:** Promotes cost containment and increased productivity in health care institutions through internal auditing. Serves as a forum for the exchange of experience, ideas, and information among members; provides continuing professional education courses and informs members of developments in health care internal auditing. **Activities:** Offers employment clearinghouse services.

★123★ Association of Insolvency and Restructuring Advisors (AIRA)

221 Stewart Ave., Ste. 207
Medford, OR 97501
Ph: (541)858-1665   Fax: (541)858-9187
E-mail: aira@airacira.org

URL: http://www.airacira.org

Members: Certified and licensed public accountants, attorneys, examiners, trustees, and receivers. **Purpose:** Seeks to define and develop the accountant's role provided by the Bankruptcy Reform Act of 1978 and to improve accounting skills used in insolvency cases. Promotes the primary role of creditors in insolvency situations and the enforcement of ethical standards of practice. Seeks to develop judicial reporting standards for insolvency and provide technical, analytical, and accounting skills necessary in insolvent situations. Works to educate others in the field of the role of the accountant in order to foster better working relationships. **Activities:** Provides information about legislative issues that affect members and testifies before legislative bodies. Offers technical referral service. Administers the Certified Insolvency and Restructuring Advisor (CIRA) program.

★124★ Association of Practicing Certified Public Accountants (AP-CPA)

932 Hungerford Dr., No. 17
Rockville, MD 20850
Ph: (301)340-3340   Fax: (301)340-3343
E-mail: paul-cpa@erols.com

Activities: Provides seminars and courses that are approved by local CPAs.

★125★ BKR International (BKR)

19 Fulton St., Ste. 306
New York, NY 10038
Ph: (212)964-2115   Fax: (212)964-2133
Fr: 800-BKR-INTL
E-mail: bkr@bkr.com
URL: http://www.bkr.com

Members: Accounting firms in the U.S. and abroad. **Purpose:** Seeks to create an international group of competent professional firms, which will provide full services in major markets of the world and enable member firms to send and receive referrals. **Activities:** Helps reduce operating costs of member firms by: developing consolidated purchasing arrangements for services and supplies at the lowest possible cost; developing recruiting programs, marketing materials, and advertising to reduce the collective recruiting effort of group members; expanding the group to reduce the burden on individual member firms and increase their potential scope of services. Compiles statistics to provide member firms with data helpful to sound management decisions. Organizes clinical and administrative peer reviews to insure quality and provide management with professional counsel. Develops forms, procedures, and manuals to provide guidance and accommodate the needs of partners. Conducts 12 continuing education programs per year in all areas of expertise.

★126★ CPA Associates International (CPAAI)

Meadows Office Complex
301 Rte. 17 N
Rutherford, NJ 07070
Ph: (201)804-8686   Fax: (201)804-9222

E-mail: homeoffice@cpaai.com
URL: http://www.cpaai.com

Members: Independent firms of Certified Public Accountants (CPAs) offering professional accounting, auditing, tax, and management advisory services. **Purpose:** Fosters exchange of ideas and information among members; works to improve the profitability and practice of the accounting profession.

★127★ Financial Occupations

Delphi Productions
3159 6th St.
Boulder, CO 80304
Ph: (303)443-2100   Fax: (303)443-4022
Fr: 888-443-2400
E-mail: support@delphivideo.com
URL: http://www.delphivideo.com

$95.00. 50 minutes. Part of the Careers for the 21st Century Video Library.

★128★ Foundation for Accounting Education (FAE)

3 Park Ave., 18th Fl.
New York, NY 10016-5991
Ph: (212)719-8300   Fax: (212)719-3364
Fr: 800-633-6320
E-mail: aschmelkin@nysscpa.org
URL: http://www.nysscpa.org

Purpose: Conducts educational and technical programs, seminars, workshops, and conferences for CPAs in private practice and industry.

★129★ Information Systems Audit and Control Association and Foundation (ISACA)

3701 Algonquin Rd., Ste. 1010
Rolling Meadows, IL 60008
Ph: (847)253-1545   Fax: (847)253-1443
E-mail: membership@isaca.org
URL: http://www.isaca.org

Description: Acts as a harmonizing source for IT control practices and standards all over the world. Serves its members and other constituencies by providing education, research (through its affiliated Foundation), a professional certification, conferences and publications.

★130★ Institute of Internal Auditors (IIA)

247 Maitland Ave.
Altamonte Springs, FL 32701-4201
Ph: (407)937-1100   Fax: (407)937-1101
E-mail: iia@theiia.org
URL: http://www.theiia.org

Members: Members in internal auditing, governance, internal control, IT audit, education, and security. Provides comprehensive professional, educational and development opportunities; standards and other professional practice guidance; and certification programs.

★131★ Institute of Management Accountants (IMA)

10 Paragon Dr.
Montvale, NJ 07645
Ph: (201)573-9000   Fax: (201)474-1600
Fr: 800-638-4427
E-mail: ima@imanet.org
URL: http://www.imanet.org

Members: Management accountants in industry, public accounting, government, and academia; other persons interested in internal and management uses of accounting. **Purpose:** Conducts research on accounting methods and procedures and the management purposes served. **Activities:** Established Institute of Certified Management Accountants to implement and administer examinations for the Certified Management Accountant (CMA) program and the Certified in Financial Management (CFM) program. Annually presents chapter medals for competition, manuscripts and for the highest scores on the CMA Examination. Offers continuing education programs comprising courses, conferences, and a self-study program in management accounting areas. Offers ethics counseling services for members by telephone. Sponsors the Foundation for Applied Research.

★132★ Interamerican Accounting Association (IAA)

275 Fountainebleau Blvd., Ste. 245
Miami, FL 33172
Ph: (305)225-1991   Fax: (305)225-2011
E-mail: oficina@contadoresaic.org
URL: http://www.contadoresaic.org

Description: National associations representing 1,100,000 accountants in the Americas. Objectives are to maintain high technical and ethical standards for the accounting profession; further accounting as a scientific discipline by fostering contacts between members and institutions of higher learning; provide members with information on current accounting practices and concepts; encourage members to establish ties with accounting groups worldwide; assure that professional services rendered by members contribute to the social and economic development of their community. Operates speakers' bureau.

★133★ International Federation of Accountants (IFAC)

545 5th Ave., 14th Fl.
New York, NY 10017
Ph: (212)286-9344   Fax: (212)286-9570
E-mail: julissaguevara@ifac.org
URL: http://www.ifac.org

Members: Accounting bodies recognized by law or general consensus representing over 1,000,000 individuals in 78 countries. **Purpose:** Seeks to achieve international technical, ethical, and educational guidelines and standards for the accountancy profession. **Activities:** Fosters cooperation among members and encourages development of regional groups with similar goals.

★134★ Leading Edge Alliance (LEA)
621 Cedar St.
St. Charles, IL 60174
Ph: (630)513-9814   Fax: (630)524-9014
URL: http://www.leadingedgealliance.com

Description: Represents independently owned accounting and consulting firms. Provides business development, professional training and education, and peer-to-peer networking opportunities. Offers business advisory expertise and experience and conducts accounting, tax and consulting services.

★135★ Moore Stephens North America (MSNA)
One Penn Plz.
250 W 34th St., 36th Fl.
New York, NY 10119
Ph: (212)896-3946   Fax: (212)849-6901
E-mail: theteam@msnainc.org
URL: http://www.msnainc.com

Members: North American public accounting and consulting firms. **Purpose:** Aids certified public accounting firms in increasing, expanding, and diversifying their practices. Capitalizes on diversity of resources resident throughout the network to build a stronger revenue base for all members. **Activities:** Sponsors training programs in areas such as industry niche development, service niche development tax, staff, and computer auditing; conducts tax and management seminars. Compiles statistics. Offers networking forums, marketing assistance, and technology consulting to member firms.

★136★ National Asian American Society of Accountants (NAASA)
PO Box 8689
New York, NY 10116
E-mail: dylan.jeng@naasa.org
URL: http://www.naasa.org

Description: Enhances the influence and presence of Asian Americans in the accounting profession. Cultivates growth of accounting knowledge. Advances business development opportunities.

★137★ National Association of Black Accountants (NABA)
7249-A Hanover Pkwy.
Greenbelt, MD 20770
Ph: (301)474-6222   Fax: (301)474-3114
Fr: 888-571-2939

E-mail: customerservice@nabainc.org
URL: http://www.nabainc.org

Description: Minority students and professionals currently working, or interested in the fields of accounting, finance, technology, consulting or general business. Seeks, promotes, develops, and represents the interests of current and future minority business professionals.

★138★ National Association of Tax Professionals (NATP)
PO Box 8002
Appleton, WI 54914-8002
Fax: 800-747-0001   Fr: 800-558-3402
E-mail: natp@natptax.com
URL: http://www.natptax.com

Description: Serves professionals who work in all areas of tax practice, including individual practitioners, enrolled agents, certified public accountants, accountants, attorneys and certified financial planners.

★139★ National Society of Accountants (NSA)
1010 N Fairfax St.
Alexandria, VA 22314
Ph: (703)549-6400   Fax: (703)549-2984
Fr: 800-966-6679
E-mail: members@nsacct.org
URL: http://www.nsacct.org

Description: Professional organization and its affiliates represent 30,000 members who provide auditing, accounting, tax preparation, financial and estate planning, and management services to approximately 19 million individuals and business clients. Most members are sole practitioners or partners in small to mid-size accounting firms.

★140★ National Society of Accountants for Cooperatives (NSAC)
136 S Keowee St.
Dayton, OH 45402
Ph: (937)222-6707   Fax: (937)222-5794
E-mail: info@nsacoop.org
URL: http://www.nsacoop.org

Members: Employees of cooperatives, certified public accountants, auditors, chief financial officers, attorneys, and bankers. **Purpose:** Unites persons performing accounting, auditing, financial, and legal services for cooperative and non-profit associations. **Activities:** Holds technical sessions annually. Compiles statistics.

★141★ Polaris International North American Network (PINAN)
3700 Crestwood Pkwy., Ste. 350
Duluth, GA 30096
Ph: (770)279-4560   Fax: (770)279-4566
E-mail: rbeilfuss@pkfnan.org
URL: http://www.pkfnan.org

Members: Independent certified public accounting firms practicing on a regional or local basis. **Purpose:** Objectives are to: strengthen accounting practices; increase competency and quality of service; provide a practice management program; maintain technical competence in accounting principles and auditing standards; make available a reservoir of specialists who are immediately accessible to members; provide for the sharing of skills, knowledge and experience. **Activities:** Offers technical, marketing, and public relations support; promotes continuing professional education; facilitates networking. Conducts 4 staff development, 2 tax training, and 3 manager/partner training courses per year; operates committees and task forces.

★142★ Professional Accounting Society of America (PASA)
PO Box 251451
Los Angeles, CA 90025
E-mail: info@thepasa.org
URL: http://www.thepasa.org

Description: Represents entry-level and mid-level associates working at accounting firms across America. Addresses the issues that affect entry-level and mid-level accounting professionals. Serves as a voice for everyone in the public accounting industry.

★143★ Professional Specialty Occupations
Delphi Productions
3159 6th St.
Boulder, CO 80304
Ph: (303)443-2100   Fax: (303)443-4022
Fr: 888-443-2400
E-mail: support@delphivideo.com
URL: http://www.delphivideo.com

$95.00. 53 minutes. Part of the Careers for the 21st Century Video Library.

Actors, Directors, and Producers

SOURCES OF HELP-WANTED ADS

★144★ Act Preview Magazine
American Conservatory Theater
  Foundation
30 Grant Ave., 6th Fl.
San Francisco, CA 94108-5800
Ph: (415)834-3200   Fax: (415)749-2291
URL: http://act-sf.org

Magazine covering theater.

★145★ ArtSEARCH
Theatre Communications Group
520 8th Ave., 24th Fl.
New York, NY 10018-4156
Ph: (212)609-5900   Fax: (212)609-5901
E-mail: tcg@tcg.org
URL: http://www.tcg.org

Description: Biweekly. Publishes classified listings for job opportunities in the arts, especially theatre, dance, music, and educational institutions. Listings include opportunities in administration, artistic, education, production, and career development.

**★146★ AV Video & Multimedia
  Producer**
Access Intelligence L.L.C.
4 Choke Cherry Rd., 2nd Fl.
Rockville, MD 20850
Ph: (301)354-2000   Fax: (301)309-3847
Fr: 800-777-5006

Monthly. Magazine covering audio-visual, video and multimedia production, presentation, people, technology and techniques.

★147★ Back Stage West
VNU Business Media USA
770 Broadway
New York, NY 10003
Ph: (646)654-4500
URL: http://www.vnubusinessmedia.com/
box/bp/div_fpa_pa_backs.html

Weekly. $3.00/year for individuals, NY, CT, NJ; $3.00/year for elsewhere; $95.00/year

for individuals, 1 year; $3.00/year for individuals; $3.00/year for elsewhere; $89.00/year for individuals, 1 year. Trade publication covering the entertainment industry.

★148★ Broadcasting & Cable
Reed Business Information
360 Park Ave. S
New York, NY 10010
Ph: (646)746-6400   Fax: (646)746-7431
URL: http://www.reedbusiness.com

Weekly. $199.99/year for individuals. News magazine covering The Fifth Estate (radio, TV, cable, and satellite), and the regulatory commissions involved.

★149★ Contemporary Theatre Review
Taylor & Francis Group Journals
325 Chestnut St., Ste. 800
Philadelphia, PA 19106
Ph: (215)625-8900   Fax: (215)625-8914
Fr: 800-354-1420
URL: http://www.tandf.co.uk/journals/titles/
10486801.asp

Quarterly. $652.00/year for institutions, print and online; $619.00/year for institutions, online only; $90.00/year for individuals. Journal focusing on wide variety of playwrights to theatres.

★150★ Daily Variety
Reed Business Information
5700 Wilshire Blvd., Ste. 120
Los Angeles, CA 90036
Ph: (323)857-6600   Fax: (323)857-0494
URL: http://www.reedbusiness.com/in-
dex.asp?layout=theListProfile&

Daily. Global entertainment newspaper (tabloid).

★151★ Dance Chronicle
Taylor & Francis Group Journals
325 Chestnut St., Ste. 800
Philadelphia, PA 19106
Ph: (215)625-8900   Fax: (215)625-8914
Fr: 800-354-1420
URL: http://www.tandf.co.uk/journals/titles/
01472526.asp

$951.00/year for institutions, print and on-line; $903.00/year for institutions, online only; $115.00/year for individuals, print only. Journal covering a wide variety of topics, including dance and music, theater, film, literature, painting, and aesthetics.

**★152★ Entertainment Employment
  Journal**
Studiolot Publishing
5632 Van Nuys Blvd., Ste. 320
Van Nuys, CA 91401-4600
Ph: (818)776-2800   Fr: 800-335-4335
E-mail: support@eejonline.com
URL: http://www.eej.com

Semimonthly. Subscription included in membership. Trade magazine covering business and technical careers in broadcast, electronic media, and motion pictures.

★153★ FMedia!
FM Atlas Publishing
PO Box 336
Esko, MN 55733-0336
Ph: (218)879-7676   Fr: 800-605-2219
URL: http://members.aol.com/fmatlas/
home.html

Description: Monthly. Lists information on the facilities and formats of FM radio, including new station grants and applications. Also provides official and unofficial news and comments, as well as FM Dxing and FM reception concerns. Recurring features include letters to the editor, news of research, job listings, and notices of publications available.

★154★ The Hollywood Reporter
The Nielsen Co.
770 Broadway
New York, NY 10003
Ph: (646)654-5000   Fax: (646)654-5002
URL: http://www.hollywoodreporter.com/thr/
index.jsp

Daily (morn.). $3.00 for single issue; $6.00/year for U.S., weekly; $299.00/year for individuals, print; $175.00/year for U.S., weekly print; $299.00/year for U.S., print/online combination; $265.00/year for U.S., weekly print/online combination. Film, TV, and entertainment trade newspaper.

★155★ *HOW*

F & W Publications Inc.
4700 E Galbraith Rd.
Cincinnati, OH 45236
Ph: (513)531-2690   Fax: (513)531-0798
Fr: 800-289-0963
URL: http://www.howdesign.com

Bimonthly. $29.96/year for U.S. $45.00/year for Canada; $52.00/year for other countries. Instructional trade magazine.

★156★ *Live Design*

Penton Media Inc.
9800 Metcalf Ave.
Overland Park, KS 66212
Ph: (913)341-1300   Fax: (913)967-1898
URL: http://www.etecnyc.net

Monthly. $36.00/year for individuals; $72.00 for two years; $75.00/year for Canada; $150.00 for two years; $102.00/year for other countries; $204.00 for two years. The business of entertainment technology and design.

★157★ *Millimeter*

Penton Media Inc.
9800 Metcalf Ave.
Overland Park, KS 66212
Ph: (913)341-1300   Fax: (913)967-1898
URL: http://digitalcontentproducer.com

Monthly. Magazine focusing on the process of motion picture and television production.

★158★ *Music and Media*

VNU Business Media USA
770 Broadway
New York, NY 10003
Ph: (646)654-4500
URL: http://www.vnubusinessmedia.com

Weekly. Publication covering the music and entertainment industries.

★159★ *Post*

Post Pro Publishing Inc.
One Park Ave.
New York, NY 10016
Ph: (212)951-6600   Fax: (212)951-6793
URL: http://www.postmagazine.com/post

Monthly. Magazine serving the field of television, film, video production and post-production.

★160★ *Producers Masterguide*

Producers Masterguide
60 E 8th St., 34th Fl.
New York, NY 10003-6514
Ph: (212)777-4002   Fax: (212)777-4101
URL: http://
www.producers.masterguide.com

Annual. $155.00/year for U.S. $165.00/year for Canada; $195.00/year for other countries. An international film and TV production

directory and guide for the professional motion picture, broadcast television, feature film, TV commercial, cable/satellite, digital and videotape industries in the U.S., Canada, the UK, the Caribbean Islands, Mexico, Australia, New Zealand, Europe, Israel, Morocco, the Far East, and South America.

★161★ *Ross Reports Television and Film*

VNU Business Media USA
770 Broadway
New York, NY 10003
Ph: (646)654-4500
URL: http://www.vnubusinessmedia.com/
box/bp/div_fpa_pa_rossr.html

Bimonthly. $65.00/year for individuals; $10.00/year for individuals. Trade publication covering talent agents and casting directors in New York and Los Angeles, as well as television and film production. Special national issue of agents and casting directors is published annually. Sister publication to Back Stage, Back Stage West.

★162★ *SMPTE Journal*

Society of Motion Picture and Television Engineers
3 Barker Ave.
White Plains, NY 10601
Ph: (914)761-1100
URL: http://www.smpte.org

Monthly. $130.00/year for individuals. Journal containing articles pertaining to new developments in motion picture and television technology; standards and recommended practices; general news of the industry.

★163★ *TelevisionWeek*

Crain Communications Inc.
1155 Gratiot Ave.
PO Box 07924
Detroit, MI 48207-2997
Ph: (313)446-6000   Fax: (313)446-0347
Fr: 888-909-9111
URL: http://www.tvweek.com/

Weekly. $119.00/year for individuals; $171.00/year for Canada, including GST; $309.00/year for other countries, airmail. Newspaper covering management, programming, cable and trends in the television and the media industry.

★164★ *Variety*

Reed Business Information
5700 Wilshire Blvd., Ste. 120
Los Angeles, CA 90036
Ph: (323)857-6600   Fax: (323)857-0494
URL: http://www.variety.com

Weekly. $259.00/year for individuals, year; $25.00/year for individuals, monthly. Newspaper reporting on theatre, television, radio, music, records, and movies.

PLACEMENT AND JOB REFERRAL SERVICES

★165★ **American Conservatory Theater Foundation (ACT)**

30 Grant Ave., 6th Fl.
San Francisco, CA 94109-5800
Ph: (415)834-3200   Fax: (415)749-2291
E-mail: tickets@act-sf.org
URL: http://www.act-sf.org

Description: Provides resources for the American Conservatory Theater which functions as a repertory theatre and accredited acting school, offering a Master of Fine Arts degree. Holds national auditions for the MFA program in Chicago, IL, New York City, and Los Angeles, CA, usually in February. Holds student matinees, school outreach programs, and in-theatre discussions between artist and audiences. Conducts professional actor-training programs, a summer training congress, and a young conservatory evening academy program for children aged 8-18. Offers children's services. Operates speakers' bureau and placement service.

★166★ **Health Science Communications Association (HeSCA)**

39 Wedgewood Dr., Ste. A
Jewett City, CT 06351-2420
Ph: (860)376-5915   Fax: (860)376-6621
E-mail: hesca@hesca.org
URL: http://www.hesca.org

Description: Represents media managers, graphic artists, biomedical librarians, producers, faculty members of health science and veterinary medicine schools, health professional organizations, and industry representatives. Acts as a clearinghouse for information used by professionals engaged in health science communications. Coordinates Media Festivals Program that recognizes outstanding media productions in the health sciences. Offers placement service.

★167★ **National Association of Broadcasters (NAB)**

1771 N St. NW
Washington, DC 20036
Ph: (202)429-5300   Fax: (202)429-4199
E-mail: nab@nab.org
URL: http://www.nab.org

Description: Representatives of radio and television stations and networks; associate members include producers of equipment and programs. Seeks to ensure the viability, strength, and success of free, over-the-air broadcasters; serves as an information resource to the industry. Monitors and reports on events regarding radio and television broadcasting. Maintains Broadcasting Hall of Fame. Offers minority placement service and employment clearinghouse.

★168★ **Texas International Theatrical Arts Society (TITAS)**

3625 N Hall St., Ste. 740
Dallas, TX 75219
Ph: (214)528-6112   Fax: (214)528-2617

E-mail: csantos@titas.org
URL: http://www.titas.org

Description: Theatrical agencies working to book entertainers and international acts into all live music venues. Provides placement service; conducts educational seminars.

★169★ **University Film and Video Association (UFVA)**

University of Illinois Press
1325 S Oak St.
Champaign, IL 61820-6903
Ph: (217)244-0626   Fax: (217)244-9910
Fr: (866)244-0626
E-mail: journals@uiuc.edu
URL: http://www.ufva.org

Description: Professors and video/filmmakers concerned with the production and study of film and video in colleges and universities. Conducts research programs; operates placement service; presents annual grants; bestows scholarships and awards.

EMPLOYER DIRECTORIES AND NETWORKING LISTS

★170★ **Academy Players Directory**

Academy of Motion Picture Arts & Sciences
8949 Wilshire Blvd.
Beverly Hills, CA 90211
Ph: (310)247-3000   Fax: (310)859-9619
URL: http://www.playersdirectory.com

Semiannual, January and July. $95.33 for individuals. Covers over 18,000 members of Screen Actors Guild (SAG), American Federation of Television and Radio Artists (AFTRA), and Actors Equity Association (AEA). All listings are paid. Entries include: Name of actor, name of agency and/or personal manager with phone; photograph, contact number. Arrangement: Classified by role type in 4 sections: Part I, Academy Award Nominee and Winners, Leading women/Ingenues; Part II, Academy Award Nominees and Winners, Leading men/Younger male leads; Part III, Characters/Comedy actors and actresses; Part IV, Children/Master index. Indexes: General, ethnic/disabled.

★171★ **Billboard's International Talent and Touring Guide**

Billboard Books
770 Broadway
New York, NY 10003
Ph: (646)654-5000   Fax: (646)654-5487
Fr: 800-278-8477
URL: http://www.orderbillboard.com

Annual, published 2007. $139.00 for individuals. Covers over 12,900 artists, managers and agents from 76 countries worldwide, including the U.S. and Canada; tour facilities and services; venues; entertainers, booking agents, hotels, and others in the entertainment industry. Entries include: Company name, address, phone, fax, names and titles

of key personnel. Arrangement: Classified by line of business; venues are then geographical. Indexes: Product/service.

★172★ **Broadcasting & Cable Yearbook**

R.R. Bowker L.L.C.
630 Central Ave.
New Providence, NJ 07974
Ph: (908)286-1090   Fr: 888-269-5372
URL: http://www.bowker.com

Annual; latest edition 2007, published October 2006. $235.00 for individuals. Covers over 17,000 television and radio stations in the United States, its territories, and Canada; cable MSOs and their individual systems; television and radio networks, broadcast and cable group owners, station representatives, satellite networks and services, film companies, advertising agencies, government agencies, trade associations, schools, and suppliers of professional and technical services, including books, serials, and videos; communications lawyers. Entries include: Company name, address, phone, fax, names of executives. Station listings include broadcast power, other operating details. Arrangement: Stations and systems are geographical, others are alphabetical. Indexes: Alphabetical.

★173★ **Career Opportunities in the Film Industry**

Facts On File Inc.
132 W 31st St., 17th Fl.
New York, NY 10001
Ph: (212)967-8800   Fax: 800-678-3633
Fr: 800-322-8755
URL: http://www.factsonfile.com

Published 2003. $49.50 for individuals; $44.55 for libraries. Covers more than 75 jobs in the field, from the high-profile positions of director, producer, screenwriter, and actor to the all-important behind-the-scenes positions such as casting director, gaffer, and production designer.

★174★ **Career Opportunities in Theater and the Performing Arts**

Facts On File Inc.
132 W 31st St., 17th Fl.
New York, NY 10001
Ph: (212)967-8800   Fax: 800-678-3633
Fr: 800-322-8755
URL: http://www.factsonfile.com

April 2006. $49.50 for individuals; $44.55 for libraries. Covers 70 careers, from acting to designing to dance therapy.

★175★ **Careers in Focus: Performing Arts**

Facts On File Inc.
132 W 31st St., 17th Fl.
New York, NY 10001
Ph: (212)967-8800   Fax: 800-678-3633
Fr: 800-322-8755
URL: http://www.factsonfile.com

Latest edition 2nd, 2006. $29.95 for individuals; $26.95 for libraries. Covers an overview

of performing arts, followed by a selection of jobs profiled in detail, including the nature of the job, earnings, prospects for employment, what kind of training and skills it requires, and sources for further information.

★176★ **Contemporary Theatre, Film, and Television**

Gale, Cengage Learning
27500 Drake Rd.
Farmington Hills, MI 48331-3535
Ph: (248)699-4253   Fax: (248)699-8065
Fr: 800-877-4253
URL: http://www.gale.com

Bimonthly, volume 72; published December, 2006. $215.00 for individuals. Covers more than 15,000 leading and up-and-coming performers, directors, writers, producers, designers, managers, choreographers, technicians, composers, executives, and dancers in the United States, Canada, Great Britain and the rest of the world. Each volume includes updated biographies for people listed in previous volumes and in "Who's Who in the Theatre," which this series has superseded. Entries include: Name, agent and/or office addresses, personal and career data; stage, film, and television credits; writings, awards, other information. Arrangement: Alphabetical. Indexes: Cumulative name index also covers entries in "Who's Who in the Theatre" editions 1-17 and in "Who Was Who in the Theatre.".

★177★ **Directors Guild of America-Directory of Members**

Directors Guild of America Inc.
7920 Sunset Blvd.
Los Angeles, CA 90046
Ph: (310)289-2000   Fax: (310)289-2029
Fr: 800-421-4173
E-mail: directory@dga.wise.net
URL: http://www.dga.org

Annual, February. $22.00. Covers over 11,000 motion picture and television directors and their assistants providing films and tapes for entertainment, commercial, industrial, and other non-entertainment fields; international coverage. Entries include: DGA member name; contact or representative address, phone; specialty; brief description of experience and credits. Arrangement: Alphabetical. Indexes: Geographical, women and minority members, agents.

★178★ **Discovering Careers for Your Future: Film**

Facts On File Inc.
132 W 31st St., 17th Fl.
New York, NY 10001
Ph: (212)967-8800   Fax: 800-678-3633
Fr: 800-322-8755
URL: http://www.factsonfile.com

Published 2004. $21.95 for individuals; $19.75 for libraries. Covers actors, cartoonists and animators, film directors, lighting technicians, music directors and conductors, stunt performers, and talent agents and scouts; links career education to curriculum, helping children investigate the subjects they are interested in, and the careers those subjects might lead to.

★179★ Discovering Careers for Your Future: Performing Arts

Facts On File Inc.
132 W 31st St., 17th Fl.
New York, NY 10001
Ph: (212)967-8800   Fax: 800-678-3633
Fr: 800-322-8755
URL: http://www.factsonfile.com

Latest edition 2nd, 2005. $21.95 for individuals; $19.75 for libraries. Covers actors, comedians, disc jockeys, film and television directors, orchestra conductors, songwriters, stage production technicians, and more; links career education to curriculum, helping children investigate the subjects they are interested in, and the careers those subjects might lead to.

★180★ Dramatics Magazine-Summer Theatre Directory Issue

International Thespian Society
2343 Auburn Ave.
Cincinnati, OH 45219
Ph: (513)421-3900   Fax: (513)421-7077
URL: http://www.edta.org/

Annual, February; latest edition 2007. $9.00 for individuals. Publication includes: List of more than 200 study and performance opportunities in summer theater education programs and summer stock. Entries include: Organization, school or group name, address, phone, name of contact; description of program, dates, requirements, cost, financial aid availability, etc. Arrangement: Geographical.

★181★ The Dramatists Guild Resource Directory

The Dramatists Guild of America Inc.
1501 Broadway, Ste. 701
New York, NY 10036-5505
Ph: (212)398-9366   Fax: (212)944-0420
URL: http://www.dramatistsguild.com

Annual, September. Publication includes: Lists of Broadway and off-Broadway producers; theater and producing organizations; agents; regional theaters; sources of grants, fellowships, residencies; conferences and festivals; playwriting contests; and sources of financial assistance. Entries include: For producers–Name, address, credits, types of plays accepted for consideration. For groups–Name, address, contact name, type of material accepted for consideration, future commitment, hiring criteria, response time. For agents–Name, address. For theaters–Theater name, address, contact name, submission procedure, types of plays accepted for consideration, maximum cast, limitations, equity contract, opportunities, response time. For grants, fellowships, residencies, financial assistance, conferences, and festivals–Name, address, contact name, description, eligibility and application requirements, deadline. For play contests–Name, address, prize, deadline, description. Arrangement: Contests are by deadline; others are classified.

★182★ Fashion & Print Directory

Peter Glenn Publications
235 SE 5th Ave., Ste. R
Delray Beach, FL 33483
Ph: (561)404-4275   Fax: (561)279-4672
Fr: 888-332-6700
URL: http://www.pgdirect.com

Annual, November; latest edition 47th. $39.95 for individuals. Covers advertising agencies, PR firms, marketing companies, 1,000 client brand companies and related services in the U.S. and Canada. Includes photographers, marketing agencies, suppliers, sources of props and rentals, fashion houses, and beauty services. Entries include: Company name, address, phone; paid listings numbering 5,000 include description of products or services, key personnel. Arrangement: Classified by line of business.

★183★ Film Directors

Hollywood Creative Directory
5055 Wilshire Blvd.
Los Angeles, CA 90036-4396
Ph: (323)525-2369   Fax: (323)525-2398
Fr: 800-815-0503
URL: http://www.hcdonline.com

Annual, latest edition 16. Covers over 5,000 living and primarily active theatrical and television film directors who have made films with running times of one hour or more; over 350 deceased directors; directors of video-taped television dramas are not included. Entries include: Name, date and place of birth, address and phone (or that of agent), and chronological list of films that meet stated criteria. Over 42,000 film credits. Arrangement: Alphabetical. Indexes: Director, agent/manager, film title, foreign director name, academy awards and nominations by year, guilds.

★184★ HOLA Pages

The Hispanic Organization of Latin Actors
107 Suffolk St., Ste. 302
New York, NY 10002-3305
Ph: (212)253-1015   Fax: (212)253-9651
URL: http://www.hellohola.org/HP5/

Biennial, January of odd years. Covers about 500 Hispanic performing artists from New York, New Jersey, and California; all listings are paid. Entries include: Name, photograph, profession(s), phone number(s). Persons listed are contacted through the publisher. Arrangement: Alphabetical.

★185★ Hollywood Agents & Managers Directory

Hollywood Creative Directory
5055 Wilshire Blvd.
Los Angeles, CA 90036-4396
Ph: (323)525-2369   Fax: (323)525-2398
Fr: 800-815-0503
URL: http://www.hcdonline.com

$28.26. Covers 1,300 agencies and management companies, 4,500 agents and managers. Entries include: companies in Los Angeles, New York and across the nation.

★186★ Hollywood Representation Directory

The Nielsen Co.
770 Broadway
New York, NY 10003
Ph: (646)654-5000   Fax: (646)654-5002
URL: http://www.hcdonline.com/

Twice yearly (March and September); latest edition 33rd. $64.95 for individuals. Covers over 1,300 agencies and management companies, and over 4,600 agents and personal managers within those companies. Majority of listings are located in Los Angeles and New York. Entries include: Company name, staff names and titles, address, phone, fax, e-mail address, web site address, company type, types of clients, and guild and organization affiliations. Arrangement: Alphabetical by company. Indexes: Client category, affiliation, individual names.

★187★ International Dictionary of Films and Filmmakers

St. James Press
PO Box 9187
Farmington Hills, MI 48331-9187
Ph: (248)699-4253   Fax: (248)699-8035
Fr: 800-877-4253
URL: http://www.gale.com/

Every five years, latest edition 4th; December 2000. $200.00 for individuals. Covers, in an illustrated multi-volume set, approximately 500 directors and filmmakers, 650 actors and actresses, and 520 writers and production artists (in volumes 2, 3, and 4 respectively). Both historical and contemporary artists are listed, chosen on the basis of international importance in film history. Entries include: Name; personal, education and career data; address, when available; filmography; bibliography of monographs and articles on and by the subject, critical essay, illustrations. Volume 1 contains entries describing approximately 680 significant films. Arrangement: Alphabetical in each volume. Indexes: Film title and nationality indexes in volumes 2, 3, and 4; geographic and personal name indexes in volume 1.

★188★ International Motion Picture Almanac

Quigley Publishing Company Inc.
64 Wintergreen Ln.
Groton, MA 01450
Ph: (978)448-0272   Fax: (978)448-9325
Fr: 800-231-8239
URL: http://hometown.aol.com/quigleypub/mp.html

Annual, January; Latest edition 2007. $195.00 for individuals. Covers motion picture producing companies, firms serving the industry, equipment manufacturers, casting agencies, literary agencies, advertising and publicity representatives, motion picture theater circuits, buying and booking organizations, independent theaters, international film festivals, associations, theatre equipment supply companies. Entries include: Generally, company name, address, phone. For manufacturers–Products or service provided, name of contact. For producing companies–Additional details. For theaters–Name of owner, screen size. Companion volume is the "International Television and Video Almanac". Arrangement: Classified by service or activity.

★189★ **International Television and Video Almanac**

Quigley Publishing Company Inc.
64 Wintergreen Ln.
Groton, MA 01450-4129
Ph: (860)228-0247   Fax: (860)228-0157
Fr: 800-231-8239
URL: http://hometown.aol.com/quigleypub/mp.html

Annual, January; latest edition 2007. $175.00 for individuals. Covers "Who's Who in Motion Pictures and Television and Home Video," television networks, major program producers, major group station owners, cable television companies, distributors, firms serving the television and home video industry, equipment manufacturers, casting agencies, literary agencies, advertising and publicity representatives, television stations, associations, list of feature films produced for television, statistics, industry's year in review, award winners, satellite and wireless cable providers, primetime programming, video producers, distributors, wholesalers. Entries include: Generally, company name, address, phone; manufacturer and service listings may include description of products and services and name of contact; producing, distributing, and station listings include additional details and contacts for cable and broadcast networks. Arrangement: Classified by service or activity. Indexes: Full.

★190★ **National Directory of Arts Internships**

National Network for Artist Placement
935 W Ave. 37
Los Angeles, CA 90065
Ph: (323)222-4035   Fax: (323)225-5711
Fr: 800-354-5348
URL: http://www.artistplacement.com

Biennial, odd years; latest edition 10th. $95.00 for individuals. Covers over 5,000 internship opportunities in dance, music, theater, art, design, film, and video & over 1,250 host organizations. Entries include: Name of sponsoring organization, address, name of contact; description of positions available, eligibility requirements, stipend or salary (if any), application procedures. Arrangement: Classified by discipline, then geographical.

★191★ **New England Theatre Conference-Resource Directory**

New England Theatre Conference Inc.
215 Knob Hill Dr.
Hamden, CT 06518
Ph: (617)851-8535   Fax: (203)288-5938
URL: http://www.netconline.org

Annual, January. Covers 800 individuals and 100 groups. Entries include: For individuals–Name, address, telephone, e-mail and fax; indicate type or level of theater activity, theater and school affiliation. For groups–Name, address; telephone, box of-

fice, fax, e-mail, names and addresses of delegates. Arrangement: Alphabetical. Indexes: Members by division.

★192★ **Regional Theater Directory**

American Theatre Works Inc.
2349 W. Rd.
PO Box 159
Dorset, VT 05251
Ph: (802)867-9333   Fax: (802)867-2297
URL: http://www.theatredirectories.com

Annual, May. $29.50 for individuals. Covers regional theater companies and dinner theatres with employment opportunities in acting, design, production, and management. Entries include: Company name, address, phone, name and title of contact; type of company, activities, and size of house; whether union affiliated, whether nonprofit or commercial; year established; hiring procedure and number of positions hired annually/seasonally; description of stage; internships; description of artistic policy and audience. Arrangement: Geographical. Indexes: Company name, type of plays produced.

★193★ **Stage Managers Directory**

Stage Managers' Association
PO Box 275, Times Square Sta.
New York, NY 10108-2020
Ph: (212)330-7019   Fax: (212)543-9567
URL: http://www.stagemanagers.org/smdir.htm

Every few years. Free. Covers about 500 stage managers experienced in theater, ballet, opera, music, and other productions, nationally. Entries include: Name, address, phone, union affiliations, name of production or theater company, position held, contract or type of production (stock, opera, dance, etc.), related skills, etc. Arrangement: Alphabetical. Indexes: Name, type of experience (Broadway, Off-Broadway, opera, dance, etc.), foreign language skill, geographical.

★194★ **Summer Theater Directory**

American Theatre Works Inc.
2349 W. Rd.
PO Box 159
Dorset, VT 05251
Ph: (802)867-9333   Fax: (802)867-2297
URL: http://www.theatredirectories.com

Annual, December. $29.50 for individuals. Covers summer theater companies, theme parks and cruise lines that offer employment opportunities in acting, design, production, and management; summer theater training programs. Entries include: Company name, address, phone, name and title of contact; type of company, activities and size of house; whether union affiliated, whether nonprofit or commercial; year established; hiring procedure and number of positions hired annually/seasonally; description of stage; internships; description of company's artistic goals and audience. Arrangement: Geographical. Indexes: Company name.

★195★ **Theatrical Index**

Theatrical Index Ltd.
888 8th Ave., 16th Fl.
New York, NY 10019
Ph: (212)586-6343   Fax: (212)307-6162

Weekly. Covers theatrical presentations in pre-production stage that are seeking investors; also covers producers, agents, and theaters. Entries include: For productions–Production name, brief details, contact. For agents and producers–Name, address, phone. For theaters–Name, address, box office and backstage phone numbers.

HANDBOOKS AND MANUALS

★196★ **100 Best Careers in Entertainment**

Arco Pub.
200 Old Tappan Rd.
Old Tappan, NJ 07675
Fr: 800-428-5331

Shelly Field. 1995. $15.00 (paper). 340 pages.

★197★ **Acting A to Z: The Young Person's Guide to a Stage or Screen Career**

Watson-Guptill Publications
770 Broadway
New York, NY 10003
Ph: (646)654-5400   Fax: (646)654-5487
Fr: 800-278-8477
E-mail: info@watsonguptill.com
URL: http://www.watsonguptill.com

Katherine Mayfield. 2nd Revised edition, 2007. $16.95 (paper). Author explains exactly what it's like to be an actor, including what kind of training the young person will need, comparisons of the different types of acting, how to find work, how to prepare for an audition, and what to expect during rehearsal. 192 pages.

★198★ **Acting in Commercials: A Guide to Auditioning & Performing on Camera**

Watson-Guptill Publications
770 Broadway
New York, NY 10003
Ph: (646)654-5400   Fax: (646)654-5487
Fr: 800-278-8477
E-mail: info@watsonguptill.com
URL: http://www.watsonguptill.com

Joan See. Second edition, 1998. $17.95 (paper). 192 pages.

★199★ **Acting in Film: An Actor's Take on Movie Making**

Applause Theatre Book Publishers
151 W 46th St., 8th Fl.
New York, NY 10036
Ph: (212)575-9265   Fax: (646)562-5852

Michael Caine and Maria Aitken. 2000. $29.95.

★200★ Acting Professionally: Raw Facts about Careers in Acting

McGraw-Hill Companies
PO Box 182604
Columbus, OH 43272
Fax: (614)759-3749   Fr: 877-883-5524
E-mail: customer.service@mcgraw-hill.com
URL: http://www.mcgraw-hill.com

Robert Cohen. 6th edition, 2007. $31.25 (paper). 224 pages. Includes bibliography.

★201★ The Actor's Guide to the Internet

Heinemann
PO Box 6926
Portsmouth, NH 03802
Fax: 877-231-6980   Fr: 800-225-5800
E-mail: ustserv@heinemann.com
URL: http://www.heinemann.com/

Rob Kozlowski. 1999. $18.95 (paper). 136 pages.

★202★ Actor's Guide to Promoting Your Own Career

Smith & Kraus, Inc.
400 Bedford St., Ste. 322
Manchester, NH 03101
Ph: (603)699-7032   Fax: (603)699-7945
Fr: 888-282-2881
URL: http://www.smithkraus.com/

Glenn Alterman, editor. 1996. $11.95 (paper). Part of the Career Development and Actor's Guides Series.

★203★ The Actor's Guide Southeast: An Introductory Guide to the Southeast Regional Film & Television Market

Illustrata, Inc.
931 Monroe Dr., Ste. 102-301
Atlanta, GA 30308-1778
Ph: (404)622-6786   Fax: (404)786-4784
Fr: 800-594-3457
E-mail: info@illustrata.net
URL: http://illustrata.net/illustrata/Illustrata.html

Nan McElroy and Melissa Ohlman-Roberge. Second edition, 2001. 207 pages. Concise, comprehensive and realistic guide to what's involved in pursuing an on-camera career in the southeast region.

★204★ The Actor's Other Career Book: Using Your Chops to Survive and Thrive

Allworth Press
10 E 23rd St., Ste. 510
New York, NY 10010
Ph: (212)777-8395   Fax: (212)777-8261
Fr: 800-491-2808
URL: http://www.allworth.com/

Lisa Mulcahy. 2006. $19.95. Fifty various positions for actors that are available in cruise ships, trade shows, retail stores, advertising agencies, corporate settings, education, social outreach, tourist attractions, physical fitness, and other areas are outlined.

★205★ Actors-Take Action: A Career Guide for the Competitive Actor

Heinemann Drama
PO Box 6926
Portsmouth, NH 03802
Fax: 877-231-6980   Fr: 800-225-5800
E-mail: custserv@heinemann.com
URL: http://www.heinemanndrama.com/

Brian O'Neil. 1996. $13.95 (paper). Collects the most frequently asked follow-up questions to the basics of Acting As a Business and answers them in-depth. 112 pages.

★206★ Actors Turned Directors: On Eliciting the Best Performance from an Actor and Other Secrets of Successful Directing

Silman-James Press
3624 Shannon Rd.
Los Angeles, CA 90027
Ph: (323)661-9922   Fax: (323)661-9933
URL: http://www.silmanjamespress.com/

Jon Stevens. 1997. $19.95. 383 pages. Guidelines for directors.

★207★ Agents on Actors: Sixty Professionals Share Their Secrets to Finding Work on the Stage and Screen

Back Stage Books
545 Eighth St. SE
Washington, DC 20003
Ph: (202)544-5744
E-mail: backstagebooks@aol.com
URL: http://www.backstagebooks.com

Hettie Lynne Hurtes. 2000. $18.95 (paper). 192 pages.

★208★ Breaking into Commercials

Guildamerica Books
401 Franklin Ave.
Garden City, NY 11530
Ph: (516)873-4561   Fax: (516)873-4714

Terry Berland and Deborah Ouellette. 1997. $15.95 (paper). 272 pages.

★209★ Breaking into Film

Peterson's Guides
2000 Lenox Dr.
Box 67005
Lawrenceville, NJ 08648
Ph: (609)896-1800   Fax: (609)896-4531
Fr: 800-338-3282
E-mail: custsvc@petersons.com
URL: http://www.petersons.com

Kenna Mchugh. 1998. $14.95 (paper). 240 pages. Provides insight into jobs dealing with film and video and explains how to get a job in the film industry, with a list of key employers. Also offers advice from industry insiders and internship information.

★210★ Breaking into Television

Peterson's Guides
2000 Lenox Dr.
Box 67005
Lawrenceville, NJ 08648
Ph: (609)896-1800   Fax: (609)896-4531
Fr: 800-338-3282
E-mail: custsvc@petersons.com
URL: http://www.petersons.com

Dan Weaver. 1998. $14.95 (paper). 244 pages. Explains how to get a job in the television industry, with a list of internship opportunities.

★211★ Career Opportunities in Theater and the Performing Arts

Checkmark Books
132 W. 31st St., 17th Fl.
New York, NY 10001-2006
Ph: (212)967-8800   Fax: (212)967-9196
Fr: 800-322-8755

Shelly Field. Third edition, 2006. $18.95 (paper). 320 pages. Offers a complete range of information about job opportunities in the performing arts. Part of Career Opportunities Series.

★212★ Careers for Film Buffs and Other Hollywood Types

The McGraw-Hill Companies
PO Box 182604
Columbus, OH 43272
Fax: (614)759-3749   Fr: 877-883-5524
E-mail: customer.service@mcgraw-hill.com
URL: http://www.mcgraw-hill.com

Jaq Greenspon. Second edition, 2003. $13.95; $9.95 (paper). 208 pages. Describes job descriptions in production, camera, sound, special effects, grips, electrical, makeup, costumes, etc.

★213★ Careers for Night Owls and Other Insomniacs

The McGraw-Hill Companies
PO Box 182604
Columbus, OH 43272
Fax: (614)759-3749   Fr: 877-883-5524
E-mail: customer.service@mcgraw-hill.com
URL: http://www.mcgraw-hill.com

Louise Miller. Second edition, 2002. $12.95 (paper). 160 pages.

★214★ Careers for the Stagestruck and Other Dramatic Types

The McGraw-Hill Companies
PO Box 182604
Columbus, OH 43272
Fax: (614)759-3749   Fr: 877-883-5524
E-mail: customer.service@mcgraw-hill.com
URL: http://www.mcgraw-hill.com

Lucia Mauro. Second edition, 2004. $12.95 (paper). 160 pages. Includes bibliographical references.

★215★ Commercialmania: The Successful TV Commercial Actor's Manual

Dog Gone Books
29 Yawl St., No. A
Marina del Rey, CA 90292-7159
Ph: (310)823-2704

Karl Preston. 1998. $24.95 (paper). 171 pages.

★216★ Enter the Playmakers: Directors and Choreographers on the New York Stage

Scarecrow Press, Inc.
4501 Forbes Blvd., Ste. 200
Lanham, MD 20706-4310
Ph: (301)459-3366   Fax: (301)429-5748
Fr: 800-462-6420
E-mail: custserv@rowman.com
URL: http://www.scarecrowpress.com/

Thomas S. Hischak. 2006. $45.00. Features famous artists such as Elia Kazan and Jerome Robbins as well as lesser known artists of the American theatre. A biography of each director or choreographer is included.

★217★ Getting into Films & Television: How to Find the Best Way In

Trans-Atlantic Publications, Inc.
311 Bainbridge St.
Philadelphia, PA 19147
Ph: (215)925-5083   Fax: (215)925-1912
E-mail: jeffgolds@comcast.net
URL: http://www.transatlanticpub.com

Robert Angell. 8th Rev Ed edition, 2005. $22.00 (paper). Part of the Jobs and Careers Series. 203 pages.

★218★ Great Jobs for Theater Majors

The McGraw-Hill Companies
PO Box 182604
Columbus, OH 43272
Fax: (614)759-3749   Fr: 877-883-5524
E-mail: customer.service@mcgraw-hill.com
URL: http://www.mcgraw-hill.com

Jan Goldberg and Julie DeGalan. 2005. $15.95 (paper). 192 pages.

★219★ Hollywood, Here I Come!: An Insider's Guide to a Successful Acting & Modeling Career in Los Angeles

Yellow Deer Press
PO Box 7309A
Santa Monica, CA 90406-7309
Ph: (213)871-8755   Fr: 800-437-3267

Cynthia Hunter. 2001. $19.95. 275 pages.

★220★ How to Become a Working Actor

Citadel Press
120 Enterprise Ave.
Secaucus, NJ 07094
Ph: (201)866-0490   Fax: (201)866-8159
Fr: 800-447-2665

URL: http://kensingtonbooks.com/

Susan Wright. 1997. $10.95 (paper). 154 pages.

★221★ International Directory of Film, Photography, Video and Television

Penrose Press
PO Box 470925
San Francisco, CA 94147
Ph: (415)567-4157   Fax: (415)567-4165

Raymond Lavzzana and Denise Penrose, editors. Fifth edition, 1996. $70.00 (paper). 200 pages. Part of the International Directory of Design Series. Includes references for educational programs, professional organizations and periodical publications. The subjects covered span the range of subjects of interest to photographers, cinematographers and videographers practicing in entertainment and documentation industries, including photography, cinematography, filmaking, videography and electronic imaging. Contact information includes street addresses, telephone and fax numbers, e-mail addresses and URL links to home pages. This directory is one of ten supplemental directories that are domain-specific guides to educational programs, professional societies, trade organizations, scholarly journals, and trade magazines throughout the world.

★222★ It's Showtime: How to Perform on Television & Radio

Book Marketing Works
50 Lovely St.
Avon, CT 06001
Fax: (203)729-5335   Fr: 800-562-4357
E-mail: brianjud@bookmarketing.com
URL: http://www.bookmarketingworks.com

Brian Jud, Charles Lipka, Roberta Buland, and Storm Robinson 1997. $14.95 (paper). 100 pages.

★223★ A Killer Life: How an Independent Film Producer Survives Deals and Disasters in Hollywood and Beyond

Hal Leonard Corporation
PO Box 13819
Milwaukee, WI 53213
URL: http://www.halleonard.com/

Christine Vachon, as told to Austin Bunn. 2007. $16.95. Christine Vachon chronicles twenty years of working in the film industry.

★224★ Lights, Camera, Action!: Careers in Film, Television, & Video

BFI
601 N. Morton St.
Bloomington, IN 47404-3797
Ph: (812)855-4203   Fax: (812)855-7931
Fr: 800-842-6796

Josephine Langham. Second edition, 1997. $22.50 (paper). 287 pages.

★225★ The Los Angeles Agent Book

Sweden Press
Box 1612
Studio City, CA 91614
Ph: (818)995-4250   Fax: (818)995-4399
URL: http://www.swedenpress.com/

K. Callan. Eighth edition, 2003. $19.95 (paper). 300 pages. Describes the actor-agent relationship, provides guidance for selecting the right agent, and gives a list of agents in Los Angeles with background information on each.

★226★ The Lost Soul Companion: Comfort & Constructive Advice for Struggling Actors, Musicians, Artists, Writers & Other Free Spirits

Dell
1745 Broadway
New York, NY 10019
Ph: (212)782-9000   Fax: (212)572-6066
Fr: 800-733-3000
URL: http://www.randomhouse.com/bantamdell

Susan M. Brackney. 2001. $10.00. 176 pages.

★227★ The Media Jungle: A Survival Guide

Media Masters
872 Franklin Trace
Zionsville, IN 46077-1169
Ph: (317)733-9440   Fax: (317)873-4493

Carrie Van Dyke. 1996. $15.00. 87 pages.

★228★ The National Casting Guide

Peter Glenn Publications
42 Riverside Ave.
Westport, CT 06880
Ph: (203)227-4949   Fax: (203)227-6170
Fr: 888-332-6700

Jean Walkinshaw, Gregory James, and Tricia Blount. 2002. $24.95. Volume 2. 200 pages.

★229★ Opportunities in Acting Careers

The McGraw-Hill Companies
PO Box 182604
Columbus, OH 43272
Fax: (614)759-3749   Fr: 877-883-5524
E-mail: customer.service@mcgraw-hill.com
URL: http://www.mcgraw-hill.com

Dick Moore. 2005. $13.95 (paper). 160 pages. A guide to planning for and seeking opportunities in acting.

★230★ Opportunities in Entertainment Careers

The McGraw-Hill Companies
PO Box 182604
Columbus, OH 43272
Fax: (614)759-3749   Fr: 877-883-5524
E-mail: customer.service@mcgraw-hill.com
URL: http://www.mcgraw-hill.com

Jan Goldberg. 1999. $11.95 (paper). 148 pages.

★231★ Opportunities in Film Careers

The McGraw-Hill Companies
PO Box 182604
Columbus, OH 43272
Fax: (614)759-3749   Fr: 877-883-5524
E-mail: customer.service@mcgraw-hill.com
URL: http://www.mcgraw-hill.com

Jan Bone and Ana Fernandez. 2004. $12.95 (paper). 160 pages. Provides advice on obtaining a job in film and in corporate non-broadcast film/video production. Illustrated.

★232★ Promoting Your Acting Career: Step-by-Step Guide to Opening the Right Doors

Allworth Press
10 E. 23rd St., Ste. 510
New York, NY 10010
Ph: (212)777-8395   Fax: (212)777-8261
Fr: 800-491-2808
URL: http://www.allworth.com/

Glenn Alterman. 2004. $19.95 (paper). 240 pages.

★233★ Resumes for Performing Arts Careers

The McGraw-Hill Companies
PO Box 182604
Columbus, OH 43272
Fax: (614)759-3749   Fr: 877-883-5524
E-mail: customer.service@mcgraw-hill.com
URL: http://www.mcgraw-hill.com

2004. $10.95 (paper). 160 pages.

★234★ Role of a Lifetime: Four Professional Actors & How They Built Their Careers

Watson-Guptill Publications
770 Broadway
New York, NY 10003
Ph: (646)654-5400   Fax: (646)654-5487
Fr: 800-278-8477
E-mail: info@watsonguptill.com
URL: http://www.watsonguptill.com

Robert Simonson. 1999. $16.95 (paper). 176 pages.

★235★ The Seven Steps to Stardom: How to Become a Working Actor in Movies, TV, and Commercials

Applause Theatre & Cinema Books
19 W 21st St., Ste. 201
New York, NY 10010
Ph: (212)575-9265   Fax: (212)575-9270

Christina Ferra-Gilmor and Wink Martindale. 2006. $19.95. The founder of a leading acting school offers seven steps for becoming an actor.

★236★ Smart Actors, Foolish Choices: A Self-Help Guide to Coping with the Emotional Stresses

Back Stage Books
545 Eighth St. SE
Washington, DC 20003
Ph: (202)544-5744

E-mail: backstagebooks@aol.com
URL: http://www.backstagebooks.com

Katherine Mayfield. 1996. $16.95 (paper). 176 pages.

★237★ So You Want to be an Actor?

Nick Hern Books
1045 Westgate Dr., Ste. 90
St. Paul, MN 55114-1065
Ph: (651)221-9035   Fax: (651)917-6406
Fr: 800-283-3572

Timothy West and Prunella Scales. 2006. $20.95. Advice is given to any individual interested in the field of acting.

★238★ Theater Artist's Resource: The Watson-Guptill Guide to Workshops, Conferences & Artists' Colonies

Watson-Guptill Publications
770 Broadway
New York, NY 10003
Ph: (646)654-5400   Fax: (646)654-5487
Fr: 800-278-8477
E-mail: info@watsonguptill.com
URL: http://www.watsonguptill.com

Ruth Mayleas. 1999. $19.95 (paper). Part of the Getting Your Act Together Series. 172 pages.

★239★ Working in Show Business: Behind-the-Scenes Careers in Theater, Film and Television

Back Stage Books
545 Eighth St. SE
Washington, DC 20003
Ph: (202)544-5744
E-mail: backstagebooks@aol.com
URL: http://www.backstagebooks.com

Lynne Rogers. 1998. $18.95 (paper). 242 pages.

EMPLOYMENT AGENCIES AND SEARCH FIRMS

★240★ Filcro Media Staffing

521 5th Ave., Fl. 18
New York, NY 10175
Ph: (212)599-0909   Fax: (212)599-1023
E-mail: mail@executivesearch.tv
URL: http://www.executivesearch.tv

Executive search firm for the entertainment industry.

★241★ Howard Fischer Associates International Inc.

1800 JFK Blvd., Ste. 700
Philadelphia, PA 19103
Ph: (215)568-8363   Fax: (215)568-4815
E-mail: search@hfischer.com
URL: http://www.hfischer.com

Executive search firm. Branches in Campbell, CA and Boston, MA.

ONLINE JOB SOURCES AND SERVICES

★242★ Mandy's International Film and TV Production Directory

E-mail: Directory@mandy.com
URL: http://www.mandy.com/1/filmtvjobs.cfm

Description: Employment site intended for film and tv professionals. Employers may post free Jobs Offered listings. Job seekers may post free Jobs Wanted ads.

TRADESHOWS

★243★ International Society for the Performing Arts Foundation Annual Conference

International Society for the Performing Arts Foundation
17 Purdy Ave.
PO Box 909
Rye, NY 10580
Ph: (914)921-1550   Fax: (914)921-1593
E-mail: info@ispa.org
URL: http://www.ispa.org

Annual, and December. **Primary Exhibits:** Information of performing artists, agents and managers. **Dates and Locations:** 2008 Jan 08-10; New York, NY.

OTHER SOURCES

★244★ Academy of Motion Picture Arts and Sciences (AMPAS)

8949 Wilshire Blvd.
Beverly Hills, CA 90211-1907
Ph: (310)247-3000
E-mail: ampas@oscars.org
URL: http://www.oscars.org

Description: Represents motion picture producers, directors, writers, cinematographer, editors, actors, and craftsmen.

★245★ Academy of Television Arts and Sciences (ATAS)

5220 Lankershim Blvd.
North Hollywood, CA 91601-3109
Ph: (818)754-2800   Fax: (818)761-2827
E-mail: membership@emmys.org
URL: http://www.emmys.org

Members: Professionals in the television and film industry. **Purpose:** Aims to advance the arts and sciences of television through services to the industry in education, preservation of television programs, and information and community relations; to foster creative leadership in the television industry. **Activities:** Sponsors Television Academy Hall of Fame. Maintains library on television credits and historical material, the Television Academy Archives, and archives at UCLA of over 35,000 television programs. Offers internships to students. Holds luncheon and speakers series and meetings on problems of the various crafts.

★246★ Actors' Fund of America

729 Seventh Ave., 10th Fl.
New York, NY 10019
Ph: (212)221-7300   Fax: (212)764-0238
Fr: 800-221-7303
E-mail: info@actorsfund.org
URL: http://www.actorsfund.org

Description: Helps all professionals - both performers and those behind the scenes - in performing arts and entertainment. Serves those in film, theatre, television, music, opera, and dance with a broad spectrum of programs including comprehensive social services, health services, supportive and affordable housing, emergency financial assistance, employment and training services, and skilled nursing and assisted living care. Administered from offices in New York, Los Angeles, and Chicago, it serves as a safety net, providing programs and services for those who are in need, crisis, or transition.

★247★ Alliance for Inclusion in the Arts

1560 Broadway, Ste. 1600
New York, NY 10036
Ph: (212)730-4750   Fax: (212)730-4820
E-mail: info@ntcp.org
URL: http://www.inclusioninthearts.org

Description: Advocates the elimination of discrimination in theatre, film, and television. Works to increase the employment of artists of color and artists with disabilities by encouraging cultural diversity throughout the artistic process and all levels of production and administration, and offering consultative services. Maintains the Artist Files containing pictures and resumes of 3,000 actors, directors, writers, designers, and stage managers of color as well as those with disabilities. Sponsors forums.

★248★ Alliance of Resident Theatres/ New York (ART/NY)

575 8th Ave., Ste. 1720
New York, NY 10018-3054
Ph: (212)244-6667   Fax: (212)714-1918
E-mail: lstevenson@art-newyork.com
URL: http://www.offbroadwayonline.com

Description: Nonprofit professional theatres in New York City and interested theatre-related associations. Promotes recognition of the nonprofit theatre community. Provides members with administrative services and resources pertinent to their field. Facilitates discussion among the theatres; helps to solve real estate problems; serves as a public information source. Acts as advocate on behalf of members with government, corporate, and foundation funders to encourage greater support for New York's not-for-profit theatres. Sponsors seminars, roundtables, and individual consultations for members in areas such as financial management,

board development and marketing. Organizes Passports to Off Broadway, an industry-wide marketing campaign.

★249★ American Association of Community Theatre (AACT)

8402 Briar Wood Cir.
Lago Vista, TX 78645
Ph: (512)267-0711   Fax: (512)267-0712
Fr: (866)687-2228
E-mail: info@aact.org
URL: http://www.aact.org

Description: Community theatre organizations and individuals involved in community theatre. Promotes excellence in community theatre through networking, workshops, publications, and festivals of community theatre productions.

★250★ Association of Independent Video and Filmmakers (AIVF)

304 Hudson St., 6th Fl.
New York, NY 10013
Ph: (212)807-1400   Fax: (212)463-8519
E-mail: info@aivf.org
URL: http://www.aivf.org

Description: Represents independent media artists working at all levels across all genres. Mission is to increase the creative and professional opportunities for independent video and filmmakers and to enhance the growth of independent media by providing services, advocacy, and information. Goals are to create new opportunities for the field; to engender a strong sense of community among the very diverse constituencies of independent media artists; and to promote media arts to a broader public.

★251★ Association for Theatre in Higher Education (ATHE)

PO Box 1290
Boulder, CO 80306-1290
Ph: (303)530-2167   Fax: (303)530-2168
Fr: 888-284-3737
E-mail: info@athe.org
URL: http://www.athe.org

Members: Universities, colleges, and professional education programs; artists, scholars, teachers, and other individuals; students. **Purpose:** Promotes the exchange of information among individuals engaged in theatre study and research, performance, and crafts. Provides advocacy and support services. Encourages excellence in postsecondary theatre training, production, and scholarship.

★252★ Black Filmmaker Foundation (BFF)

11 W 42nd St., 9th Fl.
New York, NY 10036
Ph: (212)253-1690
E-mail: info@dvrepublic.org
URL: http://www.dvrepublic.org

Description: Assists emerging filmmakers and builds audiences for their work. Administers the DV Republic online community which hosts public discussion and social

critiques of film and television. Administers a laboratory that develops digital films and interactive online filmmaking that is entertainment driven and socially concerned.

★253★ Coalition of Asian Pacifics in Entertainment (CAPE)

PO Box 251855
Los Angeles, CA 90025
Ph: (310)278-2313
E-mail: info@capeusa.org
URL: http://www.capeusa.org

Description: Supports Asian Pacifics in the arts and entertainment. Increases the social, educational and professional opportunities for Asian Pacifics in the entertainment industry. Serves as a forum for Asian Pacifics in feature film, television, video, publishing, music and other entertainment fields to share common interests and concerns through such programs as screenings, panels, workshops, and hosted conversations with notable executives and artists.

★254★ Directors Guild of America (DGA)

7920 Sunset Blvd.
Los Angeles, CA 90046
Ph: (310)289-2000   Fax: (310)289-2029
Fr: 800-420-4173
E-mail: darrellh@dga.org
URL: http://www.dga.org

Purpose: Independent. Negotiates agreements for members.

★255★ Independent Film and Television Alliance (IFTA)

10850 Wilshire Blvd., 9th Fl.
Los Angeles, CA 90024-4321
Ph: (310)446-1000   Fax: (310)446-1600
E-mail: info@ifta-online.org
URL: http://www.ifta-online.org

Description: Trade association for the worldwide independent film and television industry. Contributes to negotiations with foreign producer associations; develops standardized theatrical, TV and video contracts for international distribution. Established and maintains the IFTA International Arbitration Tribunal, a system through which prominent entertainment attorneys throughout the world assist members and consenting clients in reaching equitable and binding agreements. Facilitates the formulation of policies, standardized private practices and language contracts, and the exchange of information and experience among members. Produces the American Film Market (AFM), the largest international motion picture trade event in the world.

★256★ Media and the Arts Occupations

Delphi Productions
3159 6th St.
Boulder, CO 80304
Ph: (303)443-2100   Fax: (303)443-4022
Fr: 888-443-2400
E-mail: support@delphivideo.com

URL: http://www.delphivideo.com

$95.00. 50 minutes. Part of the Careers for the 21st Century Video Library.

★257★ Media Communications Association International (MCA-I)

2810 Crossroads Dr., Ste. 3800
Madison, WI 53718
Ph: (608)443-2464   Fax: (608)443-2474
E-mail: info@mca-i.org
URL: http://www.mca-i.org

Description: Individuals engaged in multimedia communications needs analysis, scriptwriting, producing, directing, consulting, and operations management in the video, multimedia, and film fields. Seeks to advance the benefits and image of media communications professionals.

★258★ New England Theatre Conference (NETC)

215 Knob Hill Dr.
Hamden, CT 06518
Ph: (617)851-8535   Fax: (203)288-5938
E-mail: mail@netconline.org
URL: http://netconline.org

Members: Individuals and theatre-producing groups in New England who are actively engaged in or have a particular interest in theatre activity either professionally or as an avocation. **Purpose:** Aims to develop, expand, and assist theatre activity on community, educational, and professional levels in New England. **Activities:** Activities include: auditions for jobs in New England summer theatres; workshops on performance, administrative, and technical aspects of production.

★259★ Southeastern Theatre Conference (SETC)

PO Box 9868
Greensboro, NC 27429
Ph: (336)272-3645   Fax: (336)272-8810
E-mail: setc@setc.org
URL: http://www.setc.org

Description: Serves the needs of individuals and theatre organizations involved in professional, university/college, community, children/youth, and secondary school theatres. Brings together people interested in theatre and theatre artists and craftsmen from 10 southeastern states of the U.S., across the nation and internationally in order to promote high standards and to stimulate creativity in all phases of theatrical endeavor. Services include: job contact service for technical hiring and job listings, resume service, etc.; playwriting projects for new plays; scholarships for a variety of theatre interests; and annual auditions (spring and fall) for professional, dinner, repertory, summer indoor and outdoor theatres, cruise lines and entertainment venues.

★260★ Women in Film (WIF)

8857 W Olympic Blvd., Ste. 201
Beverly Hills, CA 90211
Ph: (310)657-5144   Fax: (310)657-5154
E-mail: info@wif.org
URL: http://www.wif.org

Purpose: Supports women in the film and television industry and serves as a network for information on qualified women in the entertainment field. **Activities:** Sponsors screenings and discussions of pertinent issues. Provides speakers' bureau. Maintains Women in Film Foundation, which offers financial assistance to women for education, research, and/or completion of film projects.

Actuaries

SOURCES OF HELP-WANTED ADS

★261★ Actuarial Digest

Actuarial Digest
PO Box 1127
Ponte Vedra Beach, FL 32004
Ph: (904)273-1245

Description: Quarterly. Covers issues of concern to working actuaries. Recurring features include letters to the editor, news of research, news of educational opportunities, job listings, book reviews, notices of publications available, and a column titled What's New.

★262★ ASCnet Quarterly

Applied Systems Client Network
801 Douglas Ave., Ste. 205
Altamonte Springs, FL 32714
Ph: (407)869-0404   Fax: (407)869-0418
Fr: 800-605-1045
URL: http://www.ascnetquarterly.org/

Quarterly. Subscription included in membership. Professional magazine covering technical information, association news, and industry information for insurance professionals.

★263★ Best's Review

A.M. Best Company, Inc.
Ambest Rd.
Oldwick, NJ 08858
Ph: (908)439-2200
E-mail: editor_br@ambest.com
URL: http://www.ambest.com/sales/news-overview.asp#br

Monthly. Magazine covering issues and trends for the management personnel of life/health insurers, the agents, and brokers who market their products.

★264★ Business Insurance

Crain Communications Inc.
1155 Gratiot Ave.
Detroit, MI 48207-2997
Ph: (313)446-6000

URL: http://www.businessinsurance.com

Weekly. $97.00/year for individuals; $173.00 for two years; $200.00/year for individuals, daily online only; $130.00/year for Canada and Mexico; $234.00 for Canada and Mexico, two years; $230.00/year for individuals, includes expedited airmail other countries; $436.00 for two years, includes expedited airmail other countries. International newsweekly reporting on corporate risk and employee benefit management news.

★265★ Contingencies

American Academy of Actuaries
1100 Seventeenth St. NW, Seventh Fl.
Washington, DC 20036
Ph: (202)223-8196   Fax: (202)872-1948
E-mail: contingencies@actuary.org

Bimonthly. $24.00/year for individuals. Magazine on actuarial science and its relevance to current business problems and social issues.

★266★ The Future Actuary

Society of Actuaries
475 N Martingale, Ste. 800
Schaumburg, IL 60173-2226
Ph: (847)706-3500   Fax: (847)706-3599
URL: http://www.beanactuary.org/

Description: Four issues/year. Provides actuarial students with the latest information on jobs, internships, study techniques, career development, professional conduct, and ethics. Recurring features include a calendar of events, news of educational opportunities, and job listings.

★267★ Insurance & Technology

CMP Media L.L.C.
600 Community Dr.
Manhasset, NY 11030
Ph: (516)562-5000   Fax: (516)562-7830
URL: http://www.insurancetech.com

Monthly. Publication for insurance professionals covering the role of the Internet in financial services organizations.

★268★ National Underwriter Property and Casualty/Risk and Benefits Management

National Underwriter Co.
5081 Olympic Blvd.
Erlanger, KY 41018
Ph: (859)692-2100   Fr: 800-543-0874
E-mail: nup&c@nuco.com
URL: http://www.nunews.com/pandc/subscribe/

Weekly. $94.00/year for individuals, 2nd class; $133.00/year for Canada, air mail; $178.00/year for U.S. and Canada, air mail; $211.00/year for other countries, air mail. Newsweekly for agents, brokers, executives, and managers in risk and benefit insurance.

★269★ Pensions & Investments

Crain Communications Inc.
1155 Gratiot Ave.
Detroit, MI 48207-2997
Ph: (313)446-6000
URL: http://www.pionline.com

Biweekly. $239.00/year for individuals; $595.00/year for individuals, daily email; $695.00/year for individuals. Magazine containing news and features on investment management, pension management, corporate finance, and cash management.

EMPLOYER DIRECTORIES AND NETWORKING LISTS

★270★ Best's Insurance Reports

A.M. Best Co.
Ambest Rd.
Oldwick, NJ 08858
Ph: (908)439-2200   Fax: (908)439-2688
URL: http://www.ambest.com

Annual, latest edition 2007. $1,295.00 for individuals. Published in three editions–Life-health insurance, covering about 1,750 companies; property-casualty insurance, covering over 3,200 companies; and international, covering more than 1,200 insurers. Each edition lists state insurance commissioners and related companies and agencies (mutual funds, worker compensation funds, underwriting agencies, etc.). Entries include: For each company–Company name, address, phone; history; states in which licensed; names of officers and directors; financial data; financial analysis and Best's rating. Arrangement: Alphabetical.

★271★ **Insurance Phone Book and Directory**

Douglas Publications L.L.C.
2807 N Parham Rd., Ste. 200
Richmond, VA 23294
Ph: (804)762-9600   Fax: (804)217-8999
Fr: 800-794-6086
URL: http://www.douglaspublications.com/

Annual; latest edition 2006-2007. $195.00 for print product; $249.00 for print product/CD, combined. Covers about 3,500 life, accident and health, worker's compensation, auto, fire and casualty, marine, surety, and other insurance companies; 2,100 executive contacts, from presidents and CEOs to claims and customer service managers. Entries include: Company name, address, phone, fax, toll-free number, type of insurance provided. Arrangement: Alphabetical.

★272★ **Who's Who in Insurance**

Underwriter Printing and Publishing Co.
50 E Palisade Ave.
Englewood, NJ 07631
Ph: (201)569-8808   Fr: 800-526-4700

Annual, February. Covers over 5,000 insurance officials, brokers, agents, and buyers. Entries include: Name, title, company name, address, home address, educational background, professional club and association memberships, personal and career data. Arrangement: Alphabetical.

HANDBOOKS AND MANUALS

★273★ **Actuaries' Survival Guide: How to Succeed in One of the Most Desirable Professions**

Elsevier
11830 Westline Industrial Dr.
St. Louis, MO 63146
Ph: (314)453-7010   Fax: (314)453-7095
Fr: 800-545-2522
E-mail: usbkinfo@elsevier.com
URL: http://www.elsevier.com

Fred E. Szabo. 2004. $43.95. 268 pages. Explores the function of actuaries.

★274★ **Careers for Number Crunchers and Other Quantitative Types**

The McGraw-Hill Companies
PO Box 182604
Columbus, OH 43272
Fax: (614)759-3749   Fr: 877-883-5524
E-mail: customer.service@mcgraw-hill.com
URL: http://www.mcgraw-hill.com

Rebecca Burnett. Second edition, 2002. $22.95 (paper). 192 pages. Provides information to math-oriented job hunters on how to become statisticians, field researchers, computer programmers, stock analysts, investment managers, bankers, engineers, accountants, underwriters, economists, market analysts, mathematicians, systems analysts, and more.

★275★ **Introductory Stochastic Analysis for Finance and Insurance**

John Wiley & Sons, Inc.
111 River St.
Hoboken, NJ 07030
Ph: (201)748-6000   Fax: (201)748-6088
E-mail: info@wiley.com
URL: http://www.wiley.com/WileyCDA/

X. Sheldon Lin. 2006. $89.95. Introductory stochastic analysis for finance, written specifically for actuaries.

★276★ **Opportunities in Insurance Careers**

The McGraw-Hill Companies
PO Box 182604
Columbus, OH 43272
Fax: (614)759-3749   Fr: 877-883-5524
E-mail: customer.service@mcgraw-hill.com
URL: http://www.mcgraw-hill.com

Robert M. Schrayer. Revised, 2007. $14.95 (paper). 160 pages. A guide to planning for and seeking opportunities in the field. Contains bibliography and illustrations.

★277★ **Probability: An Introductory Guide for Actuaries and Other Business Professionals**

BPP Professional Education
PO Box 2100
Torrington, CT 06790
Ph: (860)489-6001   Fax: (866)365-7657
Fr: 888-277-6001
E-mail: info@bpptraining.com
URL: http://www.bpptraining.com/

David J. Carr and Michael A. Gauger. 2004.

EMPLOYMENT AGENCIES AND SEARCH FIRMS

★278★ **The Alexander Group**

2700 Post Oak Blvd., Ste. 2400
Houston, TX 77056
Ph: (713)993-7900   Fax: (713)993-7979
E-mail: info@thealexandergroup.com
URL: http://www.thealexandergroup.com

Executive search firm. Second location in San Francisco.

★279★ **Godfrey Personnel Inc.**

300 W. Adams, Ste. 612
Chicago, IL 60606-5194
Ph: (312)236-4455   Fax: (312)580-6292
E-mail: jim@godfreypersonnel.com
URL: http://www.godfreypersonnel.com

Search firm specializing in insurance industry.

★280★ **International Insurance Personnel, Inc.**

300 W. Wieuca Rd., Bldg. 2, Ste. 101
Atlanta, GA 30342
Ph: (404)255-9710   Fax: (404)255-9864
E-mail: info@intlinspersonnel.com
URL: http://yp.bellsouth.com/sites/intlinspersonnel/index.html

Employment agency specializing in the area of insurance.

★281★ **O'Shea System of Employment Inc.**

PO Box 2134
Aston, PA 19014
Ph: (610)364-3964   Fax: (610)364-3962
Fr: 800-220-5203
E-mail: fcomeau@osheasystem.com
URL: http://www.osheasystem.com

Offers personnel staff recruiting nationally in the following fields: Insurance, Health Care, Financial, Information Technology, Administration, Human resource, Manufacturing and Sales.

★282★ **Questor Consultants, Inc.**

2515 N. Broad St.
Colmar, PA 18915
Ph: (215)997-9262   Fax: (215)997-9226
E-mail: sbevivino@questorconsultants.com
URL: http://www.questorconsultants.com

Executive search firm specializing in the insurance and legal fields.

ONLINE JOB SOURCES AND SERVICES

★283★ **Financial Job Network**

15030 Ventura Blvd., No. 378
Sherman Oaks, CA 91403
E-mail: info@fjn.com
URL: http://www.fjn.com

Description: Contains information on international and national employment opportunities for those in the financial job market. Job listings may be submitted, as well as resumes. **Main files include:** Testimonials, Calendar, Corporate Listings, FJN Clients, more. **Fee:** Free to candidates.

★284★ **Great Insurance Jobs**

Fr: 800-818-4898
URL: http://www.greatinsurancejobs.com

Description: Contains varied insurance positions. Job seekers may browse employee profiles, post resumes, and read descriptions of hundreds of recently-posted insurance jobs.

★285★ National Insurance Recruiters Association

URL: http://www.insurancerecruiters.com

Description: Contains lists of recruiters (listed by department and line of business) and available insurance positions.

TRADESHOWS

★286★ Public Agency Risk Managers Association Convention

Public Agency Risk Managers Association
PO Box 6810
San Jose, CA 95150
Ph: 888-907-2762   Fax: 888-412-5913
Fr: 888-90-PARMA
E-mail: brenda.reisinger@parma.com
URL: http://www.parma.com

Annual. **Primary Exhibits:** Risk management equipment, supplies, and services.

OTHER SOURCES

★287★ American Academy of Actuaries

1100 17th St. NW, 7th Fl.
Washington, DC 20036
Ph: (202)223-8196   Fax: (202)872-1948
E-mail: cronin@actuary.org
URL: http://www.actuary.org

Description: Ensures that the American public recognizes and benefits from the independent expertise of the actuarial profession in the formulation of public policy and the adherence of actuaries to high professional standards in discharging their responsibilities. Represents the entire profession: Casualty Actuarial Society; Conference of Consulting Actuaries; Society of Actuaries; Fraternal Actuarial Association (now defunct). Maintains speakers' bureau.

★288★ American Council of Life Insurers (ACLI)

101 Constitution Ave. NW
Washington, DC 20001-2133
Ph: (202)624-2000   Fax: (202)624-2319
Fr: 877-674-4659

E-mail: media@acli.com
URL: http://www.acli.com

Description: Represents the interests of legal reserve life insurance companies in legislative, regulatory and judicial matters at the federal, state and municipal levels of government and at the NAIC. Member companies hold majority of the life insurance in force in the United States.

★289★ American Society of Pension Professionals and Actuaries (ASPPA)

4245 N Fairfax Dr., Ste. 750
Arlington, VA 22203
Ph: (703)516-9300   Fax: (703)516-9308
E-mail: asppa@asppa.org
URL: http://www.aspa.org

Description: Aims to educate pension actuaries, consultants, administrators, and other benefits professionals. Seeks to preserve and enhance the private pension system as part of the development of a cohesive and coherent national retirement income policy.

★290★ Casualty Actuarial Society (CAS)

4350 N Fairfax Dr., Ste. 250
Arlington, VA 22203
Ph: (703)276-3100   Fax: (703)276-3108
E-mail: office@casact.org
URL: http://www.casact.org

Description: Professional society of property/casualty actuaries. Seeks to advance the body of knowledge of actuarial science applied to property, casualty and similar risk exposures, to maintain qualification standards, promote high standards of conduct and competence, and increase awareness of actuarial science. Examinations required for membership.

★291★ Conference of Consulting Actuaries (CCA)

3880 Salem Lake Dr., Ste. H
Long Grove, IL 60047-6400
Ph: (847)719-6500   Fax: (847)719-6506
E-mail: conference@ccactuaries.org
URL: http://www.ccactuaries.org

Description: Full-time consulting actuaries or governmental actuaries. Develops and maintains structure and programs to reinforce, enhance, or add to members' knowledge and skills; this includes continuing education, through diverse delivery methods, for all practice areas and for consulting and business skills.

★292★ Insurance Information Institute (III)

110 William St.
New York, NY 10038
Ph: (212)346-5500   Fr: 800-331-9146

E-mail: johns@iii.org
URL: http://www.iii.org

Description: Property and casualty insurance companies. Provides information and educational services to mass media, educational institutions, trade associations, businesses, government agencies, and the public.

★293★ LOMA

2300 Windy Ridge Pkwy., Ste. 600
Atlanta, GA 30339-8443
Ph: (770)951-1770   Fax: (770)984-0441
Fr: 800-275-5662
E-mail: askloma@loma.org
URL: http://www.loma.org

Description: Life and health insurance companies and financial services in the U.S. and Canada; and overseas in 45 countries; affiliate members are firms that provide professional support to member companies. Provides research, information, training, and educational activities in areas of operations and systems, human resources, financial planning and employee development. Administers FLMI Insurance Education Program, which awards FLMI (Fellow, Life Management Institute) designation to those who complete the ten-examination program.

★294★ National Association of Insurance Women International (NAIW)

6528 E 101st St., Ste. D-1
PMB No. 750
Tulsa, OK 74133
Fax: (918)743-1968   Fr: 800-766-6249
E-mail: joinnaiw@naiw.org
URL: http://www.naiw.org

Members: Insurance industry professionals. **Purpose:** Promotes continuing education and networking for the professional advancement of its members. **Activities:** Offers education programs, meetings, services, and leadership opportunities. Provides a forum to learn about other disciplines in the insurance industry.

★295★ Society of Actuaries (SOA)

475 N Martingale Rd., No. 600
Schaumburg, IL 60173
Ph: (847)706-3500   Fax: (847)706-3599
E-mail: membership@soa.org
URL: http://www.soa.org

Description: Serves as a professional organization of individuals trained in the application of mathematical probabilities to the design of insurance, pension, and employee benefit programs. Sponsors series of examinations leading to designation of fellow or associate in the society. Maintains speakers' bureau; conducts educational and research programs.

Acupuncturists

SOURCES OF HELP-WANTED ADS

★296★ *Acupressure News*
Jin Shin Do Foundation
PO Box 416
Idyllwild, CA 92549
Ph: (951)659-5707   Fax: (951)659-5707
E-mail: jinshindo@earthlink.net
URL: http://www.jinshindo.com

Description: Annual. Provides information on bodymind acupressure, news, and main contacts in the U.S., Canada, and Europe. Features a product catalog, a class catalog and articles.

EMPLOYER DIRECTORIES AND NETWORKING LISTS

★297★ *Careers in Focus: Alternative Healthcare*
Facts On File Inc.
132 W 31st St., 17th Fl.
New York, NY 10001
Ph: (212)967-8800   Fax: 800-678-3633
Fr: 800-322-8755
URL: http://www.factsonfile.com

Latest edition 2nd, 2003. $29.95 for individuals; $26.95 for libraries. Covers an overview of alternative healthcare, followed by a selection of jobs profiled in detail, including the nature of the job, earnings, prospects for employment, what kind of training and skills it requires, and sources for further information.

★298★ *The Gale Encyclopedia of Alternative Medicine*
Gale, Cengage Learning
27500 Drake Rd.
Farmington Hills, MI 48331-3535
Ph: (248)699-4253   Fax: (248)699-8065
Fr: 800-877-4253
URL: http://www.gale.com

latest edition 2nd, November, 2004. $470.00 for individuals. Publication includes: Listing of organizations relevant to the alternative medicine industry. Principal content of publication is a discussion of 150 different types of modern-day therapies being practiced including reflexology, acupressure, acupuncture, biofeedback and yoga along with 275 conditions and diseases, 300 herbs and plants used, and 39 biographies of pioneers in the field. Arrangement: Alphabetical.

★299★ *Health & Wellness Resource Center-Alternative Health Module*
Gale, Cengage Learning
27500 Drake Rd.
Farmington Hills, MI 48331-3535
Ph: (248)699-4253   Fax: (248)699-8065
Fr: 800-877-4253
URL: http://www.galegroup.com

Database includes: Focus upon alternative medicine topics. This information is located in the Health Organization Directory component-listings of agencies, schools and organizations; journals, newsletters, and publishers websites; hospitals, health care facilities, programs and special care. Data is derived from the Medical and Health Information Directory. Entries include: Contact information. Principal content of database consists of a medical encyclopedia, drug and herb locator, health assessment tools, medical dictionary, links to other sites, and health news and includes references to homeopathic treatments, yoga, massage therapy, etc.

HANDBOOKS AND MANUALS

★300★ *Careers in Alternative Medicine*
Rosen Publishing Group, Inc.
29 E. 21st St.
New York, NY 10010
Ph: (212)777-3017   Fax: 888-436-4643
Fr: 800-237-9932
URL: http://www.rosenpublishing.com/

Alan Steinfeld. Revised edition, 2003.

$31.95. 192 pages. Presents different ways to become involved in alternative medicine.

★301★ *A Manual of Acupuncture*
Eastland Press
1240 Activity Dr., Ste. D
Vista, CA 92081
Ph: (760)598-9695   Fax: (760)598-6083
Fr: 800-453-3278
E-mail: info@eastlandpress.com
URL: http://www.eastlandpress.com/

Peter Deadman, Kevin Baker, and Mazin Al-Khafaji. 1998. $140.00. 670 pages. Describes and illustrates the channels and collaterals, the various categories of points, and methods of selection, location, and needling.

★302★ *Opportunities in Health and Medical Careers*
The McGraw-Hill Companies
PO Box 182604
Columbus, OH 43272
Fax: (614)759-3749   Fr: 877-883-5524
E-mail: customer.service@mcgraw-hill.com
URL: http://www.mcgraw-hill.com

I. Donald Snook, Jr. and Leo D'Orazio. 2004. $13.95 (paper). 157 pages. Covers the full range of medical and health occupations. Illustrated.

★303★ *Opportunities in Holistic Health Care Careers*
The McGraw-Hill Companies
PO Box 182604
Columbus, OH 43272
Fax: (614)759-3749   Fr: 877-883-5524
E-mail: customer.service@mcgraw-hill.com
URL: http://www.mcgraw-hill.com

Gillian Tierney. 2006. $13.95; $11.95 (paper). 160 pages.

★304★ Planning Your Career in Alternative Medicine

Penguin
375 Hudson St.
New York, NY 10014
Ph: (212)366-2000   Fax: (212)366-2666
Fr: 800-847-5515
URL: http://us.penguingroup.com/

Dianne J. Boulerice Lyons. Second edition, 2000. $22.95. $16.95 (paper). 522 pages. Provides information on getting started in a wide range of alternative medicine careers.

ONLINE JOB SOURCES AND SERVICES

★305★ Acupuncture Today

PO Box 4139
Huntington Beach, CA 92605-4139
Ph: (714)230-3150   Fax: (714)899-4273
E-mail: advertising@acupuncturetoday.com
URL: http://www.acupuncturetoday.com

Description: Provides the latest news, articles and featured items that are of interest to, and can be implemented by, the acupuncture and Oriental medicine profession.

★306★ Medhunters.com

Fr: 800-664-0278
E-mail: info@medhunters.com
URL: http://www.medhunters.com

Description: Career search site for jobs in all health care specialties; educational resources; visa and licensing information for relocation; interesting articles; relocation tools; links to professional organizations and general resources.

★307★ Medzilla

URL: http://www.medzilla.com

Description: General medical website which matches employers and job hunters to their ideal employees and jobs through search capabilities. **Main files include:** Post Jobs, Search Resumes, Post Resumes, Search Jobs, Head Hunters, Articles, Salary Survey.

★308★ ProHealthJobs

Fr: 800-796-1738
E-mail: Info@prohealthedujobs.com
URL: http://www.prohealthjobs.com

Description: Career resources site for the medical and health care field. Lists professional opportunities, product information, continuing education and open positions.

OTHER SOURCES

★309★ Accreditation Commission for Acupuncture and Oriental Medicine (ACAOM)

7501 Greenway Center Dr., Ste. 820
Greenbelt, MD 20770
Ph: (301)313-0855   Fax: (301)313-0912
E-mail: dort.bigg@acaom.org
URL: http://www.acaom.org

Description: Acts as an independent body to evaluate first professional master's degree and first professional master's level certificate and diploma programs in acupuncture and in Oriental medicine with concentrations in both acupuncture and herbal therapy for a level of performance, integrity and quality that entitles them to the confidence of the educational community and the public they serve. Evaluates doctoral programs in oriental medicine. Establishes accreditation criteria, arranges site visits, evaluates those programs that desire accredited status and publicly designates those programs that meet the criteria.

★310★ Acupuncture and Oriental Medicine Alliance

PO Box 738
Gig Harbor, WA 98335
Ph: (253)238-8134   Fax: (866)698-8994
Fr: (866)698-8994
E-mail: info@aomalliance.com
URL: http://www.aomalliance.org

Description: Works to the advancement of acupuncture and Oriental medicine.

★311★ American Academy of Acupuncture and Oriental Medicine (AAAOM)

1925 W County Rd., B2
Roseville, MN 55113
Ph: (651)631-0204
E-mail: webmaster@aaaom.org
URL: http://www.aaaom.org

Description: Seeks to advance acupuncture and oriental medicine.

★312★ American Academy of Medical Acupuncture (AAMA)

4929 Wilshire Blvd., Ste. 428
Los Angeles, CA 90010
Ph: (323)937-5514   Fax: (323)937-0959
E-mail: jdowden@prodigy.net
URL: http://www.medicalacupuncture.org

Members: Professional society of physicians and osteopaths who utilize acupuncture in their practices. **Purpose:** Provides ongoing training and information related to the Chinese practice of puncturing the body at specific points to cure disease or relieve pain. **Activities:** Offers educational and research programs.

★313★ American Association of Oriental Medicine (AAOM)

PO Box 162340
Sacramento, CA 95816
Ph: (916)443-4770   Fax: (916)443-4766
Fr: (866)455-7999
E-mail: info@aaom.org
URL: http://www.aaom.org

Members: Professional acupuncturists and Oriental Medicine Practitioners. **Purpose:** Seeks to: elevate the standards of education and practice of acupuncture and oriental medicine; establish laws governing acupuncture; provide a forum to share information on acupuncture techniques; increase public awareness of acupuncture; support research in the field. **Activities:** Conducts educational programs; compiles statistics. Operates speakers' bureau.

★314★ American Manual Medicine Association (AMMA)

1845 Lakeshore Dr., Ste. 7
Muskegon, MI 49441
Fax: (231)755-2963   Fr: 888-375-7245
E-mail:
info@americanmanualmedicine.com
URL: http://
www.americanmanualmedicine.com

Description: Promotes manual therapy as an allied health care profession. Seeks to advance the practice of manual therapy and manual acupuncture through professional standards, education and testing. Offers training to clinicians in order for them to provide quality medical care to patients. Provides National Board Certification Diplomate status to qualified members.

★315★ California State Oriental Medical Association

703 Market St., Ste. 250
San Francisco, CA 94103-2100
Fax: (415)357-1940   Fr: 800-477-4564
E-mail: info@csomaonline.org
URL: http://www.csomaonline.org

Description: Offers free referrals to over 800 California-based member health professionals who practice Acupuncture and Oriental Medicine.

★316★ Council of Colleges of Acupuncture and Oriental Medicine (CCAOM)

3909 National Dr., Ste. 125
Burtonsville, MD 20866
Ph: (301)476-7790   Fax: (301)476-7792
E-mail: ccaomcnt@verizon.net
URL: http://www.ccaom.org

Description: Represents acupuncture and oriental medicine colleges. Aims to advance the status of acupuncture and oriental medicine through educational programs. Works to provide high-quality classroom and clinical instruction. Promotes the improvement of research and teaching methods.

★317★ **Health Assessment & Treating Occupations**

Delphi Productions
3159 6th St.
Boulder, CO 80304
Ph: (303)443-2100   Fax: (303)443-4022
Fr: 888-443-2400
E-mail: support@delphivideo.com
URL: http://www.delphivideo.com

$95.00. 50 minutes. Part of the Careers for the 21st Century Video Library.

★318★ **Health Service Occupations**

Delphi Productions
3159 6th St.
Boulder, CO 80304
Ph: (303)443-2100   Fax: (303)443-4022
Fr: 888-443-2400
E-mail: support@delphivideo.com
URL: http://www.delphivideo.com

$95.00. 50 minutes. Part of the Careers for the 21st Century Video Library.

★319★ **International Veterinary Acupuncture Society**

PO Box 271395
Fort Collins, CO 80527-1395
Ph: (970)266-0666   Fax: (970)266-0777
E-mail: office@ivas.org
URL: http://www.ivas.org

Description: Veterinarians and veterinary students. Encourages knowledge and research of the philosophy, technique, and practice of veterinary acupuncture. Fosters high standards in the field; promotes scientific investigation. Accumulates resources for scientific research and education; collects data concerning clinical and research cases where animals have been treated with acupuncture; disseminates information to veterinary students, practitioners, other scientific groups, and the public. Offers 120-contact hour basic veterinary acupuncture course; administers certification examination; also offers advanced traditional Chinese herbal veterinary medicine.

★320★ **Medicine & Related Occupations**

Delphi Productions
3159 6th St.
Boulder, CO 80304
Ph: (303)443-2100   Fax: (303)443-4022
Fr: 888-443-2400
E-mail: support@delphivideo.com
URL: http://www.delphivideo.com

$95.00. 45 minutes. Part of the Careers for the 21st Century Video Library.

★321★ **National Certification Commission for Acupuncture and Oriental Medicine (NCCAOM)**

76 S Laura St., Ste. 1290
Jacksonville, FL 32202
Ph: (904)598-1005   Fax: (904)598-5001
E-mail: info@nccaom.org
URL: http://www.nccaom.org

Description: Serves as national certification agency for practitioners of acupuncture, Chinese herbology, and Asian bodywork therapy in the United States. **Purpose:** Establishes and maintains standards of competence for the safe and effective practice of Oriental medicine; to evaluate an applicant's qualifications in relation to these established standards through the administration of national board examinations; to certify practitioners who meet these standards. Acts as a consultant to state agencies in regulation, certification, and licensing of the practice of acupuncture and Oriental medicine.

★322★ **Society for Acupuncture Research (SAR)**

PO Box 385
Ann Arbor, MI 48106
E-mail: info@acupunctureresearch.org
URL: http://www.acupunctureresearch.org

Description: Seeks to elevate the standards of education and practice of acupuncture and Oriental medicine. Promotes, advances and disseminates scientific inquiry into Oriental medicine systems, which include acupuncture, herbal therapy and other modalities. Stimulates scholarship in acupuncture and Oriental medicine.

Administrative Assistants

SOURCES OF HELP-WANTED ADS

★323★ Business Performance Management

Penton Media Inc.
249 W 17th St.
New York, NY 10011
Ph: (212)204-4200
URL: http://www.bpmmag.net/

Free to qualified subscribers. Magazine for business managers. Covers organizing, automating, and analyzing of business methodologies and processes.

★324★ CXO

IDG Communications Inc.
5 Speen St., 3rd. Fl
Framingham, MA 01701
Ph: (508)875-5000   Fax: (508)988-7888
URL: http://www.idg.com

Monthly. Magazine providing technology information for chief officers and managers.

★325★ D & O Advisor

American Lawyer Media L.P.
345 Pk. Ave. S
New York, NY 10010
Ph: (212)779-9200   Fax: (212)481-8110
Fr: 800-888-8300
URL: http://www.alm.com

Quarterly. Magazine that offers advice and perspective on corporate oversight responsibilities for directors and officers.

★326★ E Journal of Organizational Learning and Leadership

WeLEAD Inc.
PO Box 202
Litchfield, OH 44253
Fr: 877-778-5494
URL: http://www.weleadinlearning.org/ejournal.htm

Continuous. Free. Online academic journal about organizational leadership.

★327★ Event Management

Cognizant Communications Corp.
3 Hartsdale Rd.
Elmsford, NY 10523-3701
Ph: (914)592-7720   Fax: (914)592-8981
URL: http://www.cognizantcommunication.com/filecabinet/EventManag

Quarterly. $325.00/year for institutions, library; $360.00/year for institutions, rest of the world, library; $585.00/year for institutions, library, 2 years; $648.00/year for institutions, rest if the world, library, 2 years; $45.00/year professional; $52.00/year for other countries, professional. Journal covering research and analytic needs of a rapidly growing profession focused on events.

★328★ Executive Legal Adviser

American Lawyer Media L.P.
345 Pk. Ave. S
New York, NY 10010
Ph: (212)779-9200   Fax: (212)481-8110
Fr: 800-888-8300
URL: http://www.executivelegaladviser.com

Bimonthly. Free to qualified subscribers. Magazine that offers legal advice for corporate executives.

★329★ Fleet Maintenance

Cygnus Business Media Inc.
3 Huntington Quadrangle, Ste. 301 N
Melville, NY 11747
Ph: (631)845-2700   Fax: (631)845-7109
Fr: 800-308-6397
URL: http://www.fleetmag.com

Bimonthly. Business tabloid magazine offering a chapterized curriculum of technical, regulatory and managerial information designed to help maintenance managers, directors and supervisors better perform their jobs and reduce their overall cost-per-mile.

★330★ Forrester

Forrester Research Inc.
400 Technology Sq.
Cambridge, MA 02139
Ph: (617)613-6000   Fax: (617)613-5000
URL: http://www.forrester.com/mag

Free. Journal that aims to provide ideas and advice that are relevant to today's CEOs.

★331★ International Journal of Business Research

Academy of International Business and Economics
PO Box 2536
Ceres, CA 95307
URL: http://www.aibe.org

Peer-reviewed journal publishing theoretical, conceptual, and applied research on topics related to research, practice and teaching in all areas of business, management, and marketing.

★332★ Journal of Academic Leadership

Academic Leadership
600 Park St.
Rarick Hall 219
Hays, KS 67601-4099
Ph: (785)628-4547
URL: http://www.academicleadership.org/

Journal focusing on the leadership issues in the academic world.

★333★ Journal of Business and Psychology

Springer-Verlag New York Inc.
233 Spring St.
New York, NY 10013
Ph: (212)460-1500   Fax: (212)460-1575
URL: http://www.springer.com/journal/10869/

Journal covering all aspects of psychology that apply to the business segment. Includes topics such as personnel selection and training, organizational assessment and development, risk management and loss control, marketing and consumer behavior research.

★334★ Journal of International Business Strategy

Academy of International Business and Economics
PO Box 2536
Ceres, CA 95307
URL: http://www.AIBE.org

Peer-reviewed journal publishing theoretical, conceptual, and applied research on topics related to strategy in international business.

★335★ OfficePRO

Stratton Publishing and Marketing Inc.
5285 Shawnee Rd., Ste. 510
Alexandria, VA 22312-2334
Ph: (703)914-9200   Fax: (703)914-6777

Magazine for administrative assistants, office managers, and secretaries featuring information on trends in business, technology, career development, and management.

★336★ Organization Management Journal

Eastern Academy of Management
c/o Craig Tunwall, VP
Empire State College
2805 State Hwy. 67
Johnstown, NY 12095
Ph: (518)762-4651   Fax: (518)736-1716
URL: http://www1.wnec.edu/omj

Free to qualified subscribers. Refereed, online journal focusing on organization management issues.

★337★ Personal Report for the Administrative Professional

National Institute of Business Management
PO Box 906
Williamsport, PA 17703-9933
Ph: (570)567-0166   Fax: (570)567-0166
Fr: 800-433-0622
E-mail: customer@nibm.net
URL: http://www.nibm.net/newsletter.asp?pub=PRPS

Description: Monthly. Advises secretaries and administrative assistants concerning career, workload, supervisors, coworkers, and personal life. Recurring features include letters to the editor, interviews, and Skills Check.

★338★ Public Performance and Management Review

M.E. Sharpe Inc.
80 Business Pk. Dr.
Armonk, NY 10504
Ph: (914)273-1800   Fax: (914)273-2106
Fr: 800-541-6563
URL: http://www.mesharpe.com/mall/results1.asp?ACR=pmr

Quarterly. $85.00/year for individuals; $399.00/year for institutions; $101.00/year for other countries, individual; $431.00/year for institutions, other countries. Journal addressing a broad range of factors influencing the performance of public and nonprofit organizations and agencies. Aims to facili-

tate the development of innovative techniques and encourage a wider application of those already established; stimulate research and critical thinking about the relationship between public and private management theories; present integrated analyses of theories, concepts, strategies and techniques dealing with productivity, measurement and related questions of performance improvement; and provide a forum for practitioner-academic exchange. Continuing themes include managing for productivity, measuring and evaluating performance, improving budget strategies, managing human resources, building partnerships, and applying new technologies.

★339★ Supply Chain Management Review

Reed Business Information
225 Wyman St.
Waltham, MA 02451-1216
URL: http://www.scmr.com

$199.00/year for U.S. and Canada; $241.00/year for other countries. Publication covering business and management.

EMPLOYER DIRECTORIES AND NETWORKING LISTS

★340★ Careers in Focus: Clerks & Administrative Workers

Facts On File Inc.
132 W 31st St., 17th Fl.
New York, NY 10001
Ph: (212)967-8800   Fax: 800-678-3633
Fr: 800-322-8755
URL: http://www.factsonfile.com

Published 2003. $29.95 for individuals; $26.95 for libraries. Covers an overview of clerks and administrative workers, followed by a selection of jobs profiled in detail, including the nature of the job, earnings, prospects for employment, what kind of training and skills it requires, and sources for further information.

★341★ Peterson's Job Opportunities for Business Majors

Peterson's
Princeton Pke. Corporate Ctr., 2000 Lenox Dr.
PO Box 67005
Lawrenceville, NJ 08648
Ph: (609)896-1800   Fax: (609)896-4531
Fr: 800-338-3282
URL: http://www.petersons.com/

Irregular; latest edition 16th, 2000. Covers the 2,000 largest U.S. employers hiring in several fields, including financial services, management consulting, consumer products, and media/entertainment. Entries include: Organization name, address, phone, name and title of contact, number of employees, type of organization. Arrangement: Alphabetical. Indexes: Type of organization.

HANDBOOKS AND MANUALS

★342★ Basic Administrative Law for Paralegals

Aspen Publishers Inc.
76 Ninth Ave., 7th Fl.
New York, NY 10011
Ph: (212)771-0600   Fax: (212)771-0885
Fr: 800-234-1660
URL: http://www.aspenpublishers.com/

Anne Adams. Third edition, 2006. $88.95. 360 Pages. Explore the basics of Administrative Law.

★343★ Careers Inside the World of Offices

Pearson Learning Group
135 S. Mt. Zion Rd.
PO Box 2500
Lebanon, IN 46052
Fax: 800-393-3156   Fr: 800-526-9907
URL: http://www.pearsonatschool.com

Carolyn Simpson. Revised edition, 1998. $21.30. 64 pages. Describes skills needed to work in office settings for reluctant readers.

★344★ The Complete Job-Finding Guide for Secretaries and Administrative Support Staff

AMACOM
1601 Broadway, 12th Fl.
New York, NY 10019-7420
Ph: (212)586-8100   Fax: (212)903-8168
Fr: 800-262-9699
URL: http://www.amanet.org

Paul Falcone. 1995. $16.95 (paper). 256 pages. Covers several secretarial and administrative staff support positions and includes tips on resume writing, interview preparation, and other aspects of the job search.

★345★ From Secretary Track to Fast Track

AMACOM
1601 Broadway, 12th Fl.
New York, NY 10019-7420
Ph: (212)586-8100   Fax: (212)903-8168
Fr: 800-262-9699
URL: http://www.amanet.org

Ken Lizotte and Barbara A. Litwak. 1996. $15.95. 191 pages. Subtitled: The Get Ahead Guide for Administrative Assistants, Secretaries, Office Managers, Receptionists, and Everyone Who Wants More.

★346★ Great Jobs for History Majors

The McGraw-Hill Companies
PO Box 182604
Columbus, OH 43272
Fax: (614)759-3749   Fr: 877-883-5524
E-mail: customer.service@mcgraw-hill.com
URL: http://www.mcgraw-hill.com

Julie DeGalan and Stephen Lambert. 2001. $15.95 (paper). 256 pages.

★347★ Opportunities in Federal Government Careers

The McGraw-Hill Companies
PO Box 182604
Columbus, OH 43272
Fax: (614)759-3749   Fr: 877-883-5524
E-mail: customer.service@mcgraw-hill.com
URL: http://www.mcgraw-hill.com

Neale Baxter. Second edition, 1994. $14.95; $10.95 (paper). 150 pages. Describes the spectrum of government employment, including professional, administrative, scientific, blue-collar, clerical, and technical opportunities, and how to land a job. Illustrated. Part of the "Opportunities in ..." Series.

★348★ Opportunities in Office Occupations

The McGraw-Hill Companies
PO Box 182604
Columbus, OH 43272
Fax: (614)759-3749   Fr: 877-883-5524
E-mail: customer.service@mcgraw-hill.com
URL: http://www.mcgraw-hill.com

Blanche Ettinger. 1995. $14.95; $11.95 (paper). 146 pages. Covers a variety of office positions and discusses trends for the next decade. Describes the job market, opportunities, job duties, educational preparation, the work environment, and earnings.

★349★ Opportunities in Secretarial Careers

The McGraw-Hill Companies
PO Box 182604
Columbus, OH 43272
Fax: (614)759-3749   Fr: 877-883-5524
E-mail: customer.service@mcgraw-hill.com
URL: http://www.mcgraw-hill.com

Blanche Ettinger. 1999. 160 pages. $14.95; $11.95 (paper). Includes a chapter on finding a secretarial job with sample resumes and interview questions.

★350★ Opportunities in State and Local Government Careers

The McGraw-Hill Companies
PO Box 182604
Columbus, OH 43272
Fax: (614)759-3749   Fr: 877-883-5524
E-mail: customer.service@mcgraw-hill.com
URL: http://www.mcgraw-hill.com

Neale J. Baxter. Revised edition, 1992. $14.95; $10.95 (paper). 148 pages. Points out the incentives and drawbacks of a government career. Describes hiring procedures and provides tips on filling out applications, taking physical and aptitude tests, handling interviews, and finding jobs. Describes the jobs in which 75% of all state and local government workers are employed. For each occupation, covers the nature of the work and the training required.

★351★ Style and Sense For the Legal Profession: A Handbook for Court Reporters, Transcribers, Paralegals and Secretaries

ETC Publications
1456 Rodeo Rd.
Palm Springs, CA 92262
Ph: (760)316-9695   Fax: (760)316-9681
Fr: (866)514-9969
URL: http://www.etcpublications.com/

Audrey Fatooh and Barbara R. Mauk. Revised, 1996. $22.95. 228 pages

---

EMPLOYMENT AGENCIES AND SEARCH FIRMS

★352★ Apple One Employment Services

990 Knox St.
Torrance, CA 90504
Ph: (310)516-1572   Fr: 800-564-5644
E-mail: cduque@appleonee.com
URL: http://www.appleone.com

Employment agency. Additional offices in Anaheim, Oakland, Cerritos, San Francisco, Manhattan Beach, and Glendale.

★353★ Career Center, Inc.

194 Passaic St.
Hackensack, NJ 07601
Ph: (201)342-1777   Fax: (201)342-1776
Fr: 800-227-3379
E-mail: career@careercenterinc.com
URL: http://www.careercenterinc.com

Employment agency.

★354★ Express Professional Staffing

8516 NW Expressway
Oklahoma City, OK 73162
Ph: (405)840-5000   Fr: 800-222-4057
URL: http://www.expresspersonnel.com

Temporary help service. Also provides some permanent placements. Several locations across the United States as well as international offices.

★355★ The Linde Group, Inc.

12158 Natural Bridge Rd., Ste 102
Bridgeton, MO 63044
Ph: (314)738-0101   Fax: (314)209-7968
E-mail: info@thelindegroup.com
URL: http://www.thelindegroup.com

Permanent placement and temporary help service.

★356★ Snelling Personnel Services

24301 Southland Dr., Ste. 621
Hayward, CA 94545
Ph: (510)887-2423   Fax: (510)887-2399
E-mail: Hayward@snelling.com

Permanent employment agency and temporary help service.

★357★ Sullivan and Cogliano

230 2nd Ave
Waltham, MA 02451
Ph: (781)890-7890   Fr: 888-785-2641
E-mail: contract@sullivansogliano.com
URL: http://www.sullivancogliano.com

Technical staffing firm.

★358★ Winters and Ross

442 Main St.
Fort Lee, NJ 07024
Ph: (201)947-8400   Fax: (201)947-1035
E-mail: wintersandross@aol.com
URL: http://www.wintersandross.com

Permanent employment agency serving a variety of industries.

ONLINE JOB SOURCES AND SERVICES

★359★ Admin Exchange

E-mail: info@adminexchange.com
URL: http://www.adminexchange.com

Description: Contains links to job search and career-related websites.

★360★ Office Team

Fr: 800-804-8367
URL: http://www.officeteam.com

Description: Job search site for administrative support staff. Contains resume submission and job databank, plus resources and e-mail notification of available jobs.

OTHER SOURCES

★361★ Business and Administration Support Occupations

Delphi Productions
3159 6th St.
Boulder, CO 80304
Ph: (303)443-2100   Fax: (303)443-4022
Fr: 888-443-2400
E-mail: support@delphivideo.com
URL: http://www.delphivideo.com

$95.00. 42 minutes. Part of the Careers for the 21st Century Video Library.

Adoption Agents

SOURCES OF HELP-WANTED ADS

★362★ Adoptalk

North American Council on Adoptable
 Children
970 Raymond Ave., Ste. 106
St. Paul, MN 55114
Ph: (651)644-3036   Fax: (651)644-9848
E-mail: info@nacac.org
URL: http://www.nacac.org/

Description: Quarterly. Provides legal and activity updates concerning adoption.

★363★ Adoption

National Adoption Center
1500 Walnut St., Ste. 701
Philadelphia, PA 19102
Ph: (215)735-9988   Fax: (215)735-9410
Fr: 800-TO-ADOPT
URL: http://www.adopt.org

Description: Semiannual. Informs on activities of the center. Recurring features include interviews, news of research, and a calendar of events.

★364★ Adoption Today Newsletter

Concerned Persons for Adoption
PO Box 179
Whippany, NJ 07981
Ph: (973)684-1130
E-mail: cybermommy@compuserve.com
URL: http://www.cpfanj.org/

Description: Monthly, September-June. Reflects the organization's aim to offer support and information to the adoption community. Features updates on legislative actions and other developments affecting adoption in the U.S. and abroad. Provides information on the organization's educational, financial, and social services for children and families. Recurring features include news of research and a calendar of events.

★365★ National Adoption Reports

National Council for Adoption
225 N Washington St.
Alexandria, VA 22314-2561
Ph: (703)299-6633   Fax: (703)299-6004
E-mail: ncfa@adoptioncouncil.org
URL: http://www.adoptioncouncil.org/

Description: Quarterly. Provides information on current issues, legislation, events, practices, and policies for adoption. Recurring features include news of research, a calendar of events, reports of meetings, book reviews, and notices of publications available.

**★366★ National Council For Adoption-
Memo**

National Council for Adoption
225 N Washington St.
Alexandria, VA 22314-2561
Ph: (703)299-6633   Fax: (703)299-6004
E-mail: ncfa@adoptioncouncil.org
URL: http://www.ncfa-usa.org/

Description: Monthly. Reviews news and developments concerning adoption programs and services. Provides legislative updates, research reports, and Council news.

PLACEMENT AND JOB REFERRAL SERVICES

**★367★ Association of Administrators
of the Interstate Compact on the
Placement of Children (AAICPC)**

810 1st St. NE, Ste. 500
Washington, DC 20002
Ph: (202)682-0100   Fax: (202)289-6555
E-mail: icpcinbox@aphsa.org
URL: http://icpc.aphsa.org

Description: State public social service agency personnel who have been appointed compact administrators and who are responsible for the operation of the Interstate Compact on the Placement of Children. (ICPC is a uniform law that has been enacted in 50 states, the District of Columbia, and the Virgin Islands. Governs the placement of children across state lines for foster care and pre-adoptive placement by legally establishing the extension of responsibility and jurisdiction of the sending party, and the concomitant responsibility of the receiving state.) Enhances arrangements for the delivery of protective and supportive services in situations having interjurisdictional considerations. Provides forum for cooperation, consultation, and exchange of information among the states in relation to the placement of children from one state to another. Compiles statistics.

**★368★ World Partners Adoption
(WPAdopt)**

2205 Summit Oaks Ct.
Lawrenceville, GA 30043
Ph: (770)962-7860   Fax: (770)513-7767
Fr: 800-350-7338
E-mail: wpajim@aol.com
URL: http://www.worldpartnersadoption.org

Description: International child placement agency specializing in international adoptions from the Republic of Kazakhstan, China, Ukraine, and Russia. Children waiting for immediate adoption are age 6 months to 10 years old. Provides families with comprehensive and compassionate assistance during the entire adoption process.

EMPLOYER DIRECTORIES AND NETWORKING LISTS

★369★ National Adoption Directory

National Adoption Information
 Clearinghouse
330 C St. SW., 8th FL.
Washington, DC 20024
Ph: (703)352-3488   Fax: (703)385-3206
Fr: 888-251-0075

Semiannual. Covers the National Adoption Information Clearinghouse, containing information about agencies and support groups, as well as national adoption organizations.

★370★ National Adoption Training and Educational Directory

National Adoption Information
  Clearinghouse
330 C St. SW., 8th FL.
Washington, DC 20024
Ph: (703)352-3488   Fax: (703)385-3206
Fr: 888-251-0075

Annual. Covers adoption training opportunities, conferences, curricula, and accredited schools of social work.

★371★ NCFA Directory of Member Agencies

National Council for Adoption
225 N Washington St.
Alexandria, VA 22314-2561
Ph: (703)299-6633   Fax: (703)299-6004
URL: http://www.adoptioncouncil.org/agency/mem_benefits.html

Periodic. Covers National Council for Adoption member agency information.

★372★ Supervised Visitation Network Standards and Guidelines

Supervised Visitation Network
2804 Paran Pointe Dr.
Cookeville, TN 38506
Ph: (931)537-3414   Fax: (931)537-6348
URL: http://www.svnetwork.net/

Covers forums for networking and sharing of information between supervised child access providers and other professionals involved in providing support to children and parents who are not living together.

ONLINE JOB SOURCES AND SERVICES

★373★ Adoption Forums
URL: http://forums.adoption.com
Description: Includes job postings for adoption professionals.

TRADESHOWS

★374★ Adoption Conference

Adoptive Families Today
PO Box 1726
Barrington, IL 60011-1726
Ph: (847)382-0858   Fax: (847)382-0831
E-mail: adopadvo@aol.com
URL: http://www.adoptivefamiliestoday.org

Annual. **Primary Exhibits:** Pre and post adoptive families and adoption professionals; pre and post adoption and parenting issues.

★375★ American Adoption Congress Conference

American Adoption Congress
PO Box 42730
Washington, DC 20015
Ph: (202)483-3399
E-mail: ameradoptioncong@aol.com
URL: http://
www.americanadoptioncongress.org/

Annual. **Primary Exhibits:** Adopted persons, birthparents, and adoptive parents; members of related organizations devoted to leadership in adoption reform.

★376★ National Council for Adoption Conference

National Council for Adoption
225 N Washington St.
Alexandria, VA 22314-2561
Ph: (703)299-6633   Fax: (703)299-6004
E-mail: ncfa@ncfa-usa.org
URL: http://www.adoptioncouncil.org

Annual. **Primary Exhibits:** Represents voluntary agencies, adoptive parents, adoptees, and birthparents.

★377★ North American Council on Adoptable Children Conference

North American Council on Adoptable
  Children
970 Raymond Ave., Ste. 106
St. Paul, MN 55114
Ph: (651)644-3036   Fax: (651)644-9848
E-mail: info@nacac.org
URL: http://www.nacac.org

Annual. **Primary Exhibits:** Exhibits related to adoption and post-adoption.

OTHER SOURCES

★378★ Adoptee-Birthparent Support Network (ABSN)

6439 Woodridge Rd.
Alexandria, VA 22312-1336
Ph: (301)442-9106
E-mail: absnmail@verizon.net
URL: http://www.metroreunionregistry.org/ABSN.html

Members: Adoptees, adoptive parents, birthparents (biological parents), and siblings; social workers, and adoption professionals. **Purpose:** Seeks to provide support, information, and education to members and help them come to terms with the effects of adoption. **Activities:** Provides search assistance to adoptees and birthparents who wish to locate their biological relatives. Administers public outreach and education programs; conducts legislative efforts.

★379★ Adoption Information Services (AIS)

558 Dovie Pl.
Lawrenceville, GA 30045
Ph: (770)339-7236   Fax: (770)277-6912

E-mail: aismarcia@comcast.net
URL: http://www.adoptioninfosvcs.com

Members: Adoptive parents, adoptees, birth parents. **Purpose:** Dedicated to providing information regarding adoption, long term foster care opportunities and search information. **Activities:** Sponsors adoption information events.

★380★ American Adoption Congress (AAC)

PO Box 42730
Washington, DC 20015
Ph: (202)483-3399
E-mail: ameradoptioncong@aol.com
URL: http://
www.americanadoptioncongress.org

Description: Adopted persons, birthparents, and adoptive parents; members of related organizations devoted to leadership in adoption reform. Purposes are to: further information on adoptions and related social-psychological issues in the U.S. by study, research, teaching, and conferences; collect, publish, and disseminate information; act as a national clearinghouse and public information center. Develops alternative model plans for adoption; conducts regional educational conferences; provides research referrals to adoption-related services.

★381★ Families Adopting Children Everywhere (FACE)

PO Box 28058
Baltimore, MD 21239
Ph: (410)488-2656
E-mail: info@faceadoptioninfo.org

Description: Offers comprehensive course that covers practical topics on adoption, such as picking an adoption agency, current information on trends in domestic and intercountry adoptions, various choices in adoption, the terminology, the emotions, the monetary costs, etc.

★382★ Human Services Occupations

Delphi Productions
3159 6th St.
Boulder, CO 80304
Ph: (303)443-2100   Fax: (303)443-4022
Fr: 888-443-2400
E-mail: support@delphivideo.com
URL: http://www.delphivideo.com

$95.00. 50 minutes. Part of the Careers for the 21st Century Video Library.

★383★ Independent Search Consultants (ISC)

PO Box 10192
Costa Mesa, CA 92627
E-mail: referrals@iscsearch.com
URL: http://www.iscsearch.com

Description: Individuals assisting in searches for birth-families separated by adoption. Seeks to: provide a means of certification for active search consultants; promote ethical standards of conduct and quality assistance; encourage public understanding of the rights of the adoptee, the adoptive parent, and the birthparent; serve as a professional association for search consultants. Offers search consultant certification on national, state, and specialized levels. Individuals qualify for certification by taking an exam, documenting 500 hours of search assistance or volunteer service, and securing personal recommendations. Sponsors panels, seminars, and workshops on adoption search. Offers speakers on all aspects of adoption education and referrals to search agencies, support groups, and certifiedconsultants

★384★ Institute for Adoption Information

PO Box 4405
Bennington, VT 05201
Ph: (802)442-2845
E-mail:
info@adoptioninformationinstitute.org
URL: http://
www.adoptioninformationinstitute.org

Description: Represents adoptees, birth parents, adoptive parents, and adoption professionals. Promotes adoption. Provides positive support to members of adoption triad, and enhances the understanding of adoption.

★385★ Liberal Education for Adoptive Families (LEAF)

1295 Omaha Ave. N
Stillwater, MN 55082
Ph: (651)436-2215

Description: A post-adoption service organization providing legislative and agency policy reform, client counseling (including search assistance and referrals), training and technical assistance for public and private agencies, public education seminars, and media presentations. Cosponsors Minnesota Reunion Registry, which is fed into the system of the International Soundex Reunion Registry, which contains input from adoptees and birthparents throughout the U.S., Mexico, Canada, and abroad.

★386★ National Adoption Center (NAC)

1500 Walnut St., Ste. 701
Philadelphia, PA 19102
Fr: 800-TO-ADOPT
E-mail: kmullner@nacenter.adopt.org
URL: http://www.adopt.org

Description: Expands adoption opportunities for children throughout the United States, particularly the adoption of children with special needs and children from minority cultures, through public awareness and information and referral with families nationwide. Pictures and descriptions of waiting children are highlighted on Website.

★387★ National Council for Adoption (NCFA)

225 N Washington St.
Alexandria, VA 22314
Ph: (703)299-6633   Fax: (703)299-6004
E-mail: ncfa@adoptioncouncil.org
URL: http://www.adoptioncouncil.org

Description: Represents voluntary agencies, adoptive parents, adoptees, and birthparents. Works to protect the institution of adoption and ensure the confidentiality of all involved in the adoption process. Promotes appropriate adoption practice with legislators, policymakers, human service agencies and staff, and the public. Strives for the regulation of all adoptions to ensure the protection of birthparents, children, and adoptive parents. Serves as an information clearinghouse; provides technical assistance. Conducts research programs; monitors state and national legislation affecting adoption and maternity services. Maintains hall of fame. Compiles statistics. Operates speakers' bureau; compiles statistics.

★388★ North American Council on Adoptable Children (NACAC)

970 Raymond Ave., Ste. 106
St. Paul, MN 55114
Ph: (651)644-3036   Fax: (651)644-9848
E-mail: info@nacac.org
URL: http://www.nacac.org

Members: Members of citizen adoption groups (composed primarily of adoptive parents of "special needs" children) and other individuals from judicial, child welfare, and legislative areas. **Purpose:** Advocates the right of every child to a permanent, loving home. **Activities:** Provides direct assistance to local and state advocacy efforts; acts as a clearinghouse for adoption information; liaises with other adoption organizations. Sponsors an annual national training conference. Also sponsors Adoption Awareness Month. Conducts extensive education and outreach through the media and pre- and post-adoptive support programs. Provides resources for local advocacy programs.

★389★ Organized Adoption Search Information Services (OASIS)

PO Box 53-0761
Miami Shores, FL 33153
Ph: (305)947-8788
E-mail: rayrivers@netzero.com

Description: Offers individual assistance to adult adoptees, birth and/or adoptive parents and others who are searching for or wish to be reunited with members of birth families. Maintains confidential search files for each searching member and a cross-match birth index registry.

★390★ Orphan Foundation of America (OFA)

21351 Gentry Dr., Ste. 130
Sterling, VA 20166
Ph: (571)203-0270   Fax: (571)203-0273
E-mail: aja@orphan.org
URL: http://www.orphan.org

Description: Orphaned and abandoned youth; volunteers and contributors. Assists orphaned, abandoned, and foster-care youth by providing guidance, support, friendship, and emergency help that is seldom available to children raised outside of the traditional family setting. Advocates orphaned and abandoned youth rights nationwide; administers project that develops public policy initiatives. Offers independent living support services and volunteer referral services. Sponsors Project Bridge Program, a community-based volunteer support network that assists youth in their transition from the child welfare system to independent young adulthood. Adult volunteers guide and assist orphans in goal planning, independent living and life skills, career development, job search, maintaining employment, and recreation. Provides research services. Maintains speakers' bureau, resource center, and orphan hall of fame.

★391★ Orphan Voyage (OV)

13906 Pepperrell Dr.
Tampa, FL 33624
Ph: (813)961-1393   Fax: (904)396-8523
E-mail: asyman@aug.com
URL: http://www.geocities.com/orphanvoyage1953

Description: Adult adopted people, adoptive parents, and professionals engaged in adoption practice or related to people in adoption; natural parents of children who were adopted. Assists in building relationships between adult adopted people and their birth families; informs adoptive parents and professionals of the needs of adopted children; offers guidance and hope to birth parents whose children were adopted. Maintains liaison with groups and individuals working along similar lines through correspondence and distribution of materials. Develops museum.

★392★ Stars of David International (SDI)

3175 Commercial Ave., Ste. 100
Northbrook, IL 60062-1915
Ph: (847)509-9929   Fax: (847)509-9545
Fr: 800-STAR-349
E-mail: info@starsofdavid.org
URL: http://www.starsofdavid.org

Description: Works as a Jewish adoption information and support network. Provides a network of support, adoption information and education to prospective parents, adoptive families, adult adoptees, birth families, and the Jewish community.

Adult and Vocational Education Teachers

SOURCES OF HELP-WANTED ADS

★393★ Community Colleges Journal
American Association of Community Colleges
1 Dupont Cir. NW, Ste. 410
Washington, DC 20036
Ph: (202)728-0200   Fax: (202)833-2467
URL: http://www.aacc.nche.edu

Bimonthly. $28.00/year for nonmembers; $5.50 for single issue. Educational magazine.

★394★ Tech Directions
Prakken Publications Inc.
832 Phoenix Dr.
PO Box 8623
Ann Arbor, MI 48108
Ph: (734)975-2800   Fax: (734)975-2787
Fr: 800-530-9673
E-mail: tdedit@techdirections.com
URL: http://www.techdirections.com

Monthly. $30.00/year for individuals, U.S.; $20.00/year for students; $40.00/year for elsewhere; $55.00 for two years, U.S.; $75.00 for two years, elsewhere. Free to qualified subscribers. Magazine covering issues, programs, and projects in industrial education, technology education, trade and industry, and vocational-technical career education. Articles are geared toward teacher and administrator use and reference from elementary school through postsecondary levels.

PLACEMENT AND JOB REFERRAL SERVICES

★395★ International Educator's Institute (TIE)
PO Box 513
Cummaquid, MA 02637
Ph: (508)790-1990   Fax: (508)790-1922
Fr: 877-375-6668

E-mail: tie@tieonline.com
URL: http://www.tieonline.com

Description: Facilitates the placement of teachers and administrators in American, British, and international schools. Seeks to create a network that provides for professional development opportunities and improved financial security of members. Offers advice and information on international school news, recent educational developments, job placement, and investment, consumer, and professional development opportunities. Makes available insurance and travel benefits. Operates International Schools Internship Program.

★396★ National Association for Industry-Education Cooperation (NAIEC)
235 Hendricks Blvd.
Buffalo, NY 14226-3304
Ph: (716)834-7047   Fax: (716)834-7047
E-mail: naiec@pcom.net
URL: http://www2.pcom.net/naiec

Description: Representatives of business, industry, education, government, labor, and the professions. Fosters industry-education collaboration in continuous school improvement and workforce preparation in order to develop responsive academic and vocational programs which will more effectively serve the needs of both the students and employers as well as further human resources and economic development. Provides technical assistance to schools implementing industry-education councils, high-performance sustainable education systems and business- or industry-sponsored programs. Promotes improved career and entrepreneurship education and supports school-based job placement. Provides staff development programs to improve instruction and curricula and the efficiency and effectiveness of educational management through use of corporate and volunteer services. Acts as national clearinghouse for information on industry involvement in education; serves as liaison between organizations involved in industry-education cooperation, including American Association for Career Education, National Research Center for Career and Technical, and American Society for Training and Development. Conducts research and policy studies.

EMPLOYER DIRECTORIES AND NETWORKING LISTS

★397★ Chronicle Two-Year College Databook
Chronicle Guidance Publications Inc.
66 Aurora St.
Moravia, NY 13118-3569
Ph: (315)497-0330   Fax: (315)497-0339
Fr: 800-899-0454
URL: http://tnt.spidergraphics.com

Annual, latest edition 2006-2007 edition. $25.47 for individuals. Covers over 815 associate, certificate, occupational, and transfer programs offered by more than 2,555 technical institutes, two-year colleges, and universities in the United States. Entries include: College charts section giving college name, address, phone; accreditation, enrollment, admissions, costs, financial aid; accrediting associations' names, addresses, and phone numbers. Arrangement: Part I is classified by college major; part II is geographical. Indexes: College name.

★398★ Chronicle Vocational School Manual
Chronicle Guidance Publications Inc.
66 Aurora St.
Moravia, NY 13118-3569
Ph: (315)497-0330   Fax: (315)497-0339
Fr: 800-899-0454
URL: http://tnt.spidergraphics.com

Annual, latest edition 2006-2007. $25.46 for individuals. Covers over 945 programs of study offered by more than 2,700 vocational schools. Entries include: School name, city and ZIP code, phone, programs offered, admissions requirements, costs, enrollment information, financial aid programs, year established, student services. Arrangement: Geographical. Indexes: Vocation/course.

★399★ Distance Learning for Higher Education

Libraries Unlimited Inc.
88 Post Rd. W
Westport, CT 06881
Ph: (203)226-3571   Fax: (203)222-1502
Fr: 800-225-5800
URL: http://lu.com/

Published July 16, 2002. $38.00 for individuals. Publication includes: List of Web sites that deal with accreditation, as well as related associations, organizations, discussion groups, print and online journals, and newsletters. Indexes: Alphabetical.

★400★ Guide to Technical, Trade, & Business Schools (TTB)

Riverside Publishing/Wintergreen Orchard House
425 Springlake Dr.
Itasca, IL 60143-2079
Ph: (630)467-7000   Fax: (630)467-7192
Fr: 800-323-9540

Biennial, even years. $175.53 for individuals. Covers over 3,800 accredited public and proprietary post-secondary schools offering programs in auto mechanics, aviation, business, electronics, and other technical, trade, or business fields. Available in a four-volume national edition or as four regional editions. Entries include: School name, address, phone, accrediting body, admissions contact, course offerings, placement services, and profile. Arrangement: Geographical. Indexes: Subject, special programs, sports, professional accreditations.

★401★ National Faculty Directory

Gale, Cengage Learning
27500 Drake Rd.
Farmington Hills, MI 48331-3535
Ph: (248)699-4253   Fax: (248)699-8065
Fr: 800-877-4253
E-mail: businessproducts@gale.com
URL: http://www.galegroup.com

Annual; latest edition 39th, October 2007. $985.00 for individuals. Covers more than 740,000 (90,000 more in supplement) teaching faculty members at over 3,600 junior colleges, colleges, and universities in the United States and those in Canada that give instruction in English. Entries include: Name, department name, institution, address, and phone and fax numbers. Directory combines main edition and supplement. Arrangement: Alphabetical.

★402★ Online Directory of ESL Resources

National Clearinghouse for English Language Acquisition and Language Instruction Educational Programs
2121 K St. NW, Ste. 260
Washington, DC 20037
Ph: (202)467-0867   Fax: (202)467-4283
Fr: 800-321-6223

Free. Covers English as a second language resources on the Internet, especially geared to teachers. Includes government resources, clearinghouses, and professional associations.

★403★ Opportunities Abroad for Educators

Fulbright Teacher and Administrator Exchange Program
600 Maryland Ave. SW, Ste. 320
Washington, DC 20024-2520
Ph: (202)314-3527   Fax: (202)479-6806
Fr: 800-726-0479
URL: http://www.fulbrightexchanges.org

Annual. Covers opportunities available for elementary and secondary teachers, two-year college instructors, and school administrators to attend seminars or to teach abroad under the Mutual Educational and Cultural Exchange Act of 1961. Entries include: Countries of placement, dates, eligibility requirements, teaching assignments. Arrangement: Geographical.

★404★ Peterson's Vocational and Technical Schools and Programs

Peterson's
Princeton Pke. Corporate Ctr., 2000 Lenox Dr.
PO Box 67005
Lawrenceville, NJ 08648
Ph: (609)896-1800   Fax: (609)896-4531
Fr: 800-338-3282
URL: http://www.petersons.com/

Latest edition 6th. Covers approximately 5,800 accredited vocational and technical schools that offer training programs in over 370 career fields. Available in separate eastern and western U.S. regional editions. Entries include: Institution name, address, phone, name and title of contact, type of institution, year founded, accreditation, enrollment, faculty-to-student ratio, registration fee, student body profile, programs offered, student services, financial aid. Arrangement: Classified by program type.

★405★ School Guide

School Guide Publications
210 N Ave.
New Rochelle, NY 10801
Ph: (914)632-7771   Fax: (914)632-3412
Fr: 800-433-7771
URL: http://distance.schoolguides.com/

Annual, September. Covers over 3,000 colleges, vocational schools, and nursing schools in the United States. Entries include: Institution name, address, phone, courses offered, degrees awarded. Arrangement: Classified by type of institution, then geographical. Indexes: Subject.

HANDBOOKS AND MANUALS

★406★ Building Professional Pride in Literacy: A Dialogical Guide to Professional Development for Practitioners of Adult Literacy and Basic Education

Krieger Publishing Company
PO Box 9542
Melbourne, FL 32902-9542
Ph: (321)724-9542   Fax: (321)951-3671
Fr: 800-724-0025
E-mail: info@krieger-publishing.com
URL: http://www.krieger-publishing.com/

B. Allan Quigley. $34.25. 2006. Professional development for adult literacy practitioners.

★407★ Careers in Education

The McGraw-Hill Companies
PO Box 182604
Columbus, OH 43272
Fax: (614)759-3749   Fr: 877-883-5524
E-mail: customer.service@mcgraw-hill.com
URL: http://www.mcgraw-hill.com

Roy A. Edelfelt, Alan Reiman. Fourth edition, 2003. $15.95. 192 pages E-book, netLibrary.

★408★ Collaborative Professional Development for Teachers of Adults

Krieger Publishing Company
PO Box 9542
Melbourne, FL 32902-9542
Ph: (321)724-9542   Fax: (321)951-3671
Fr: 800-724-0025
E-mail: info@krieger-publishing.com
URL: http://www.krieger-publishing.com/

Joseph J. Moran. 2001. $28.00. Principles of self-directed learning, cooperative learning, and critical reflection are integrated into this guide for teachers of adults.

★409★ How to Get the Teaching Position You Want: Teacher Candidate Guide

Educational Enterprises
PO Box 1836
Spring Valley, CA 91979
Ph: (619)660-7720

Phyllis Murton. Second edition, revised, 1996. $19.95 (paper). 110 pages. This book provides a comprehensive guide for the teacher candidate's job search, as the format offers information that includes: interview questions most often asked in the teaching interview (grade-level and subject-matter specific); sample forms for applications, cover letters, and resumes that will impact principals and district personnel; strategies on preparing for the teaching interview; interview follow-up techniques; inside tips from a superintendent, a principal and a counselor.

★410★ Non-Profits and Education Job Finder

Planning Communications
7215 Oak Ave.
River Forest, IL 60305-1935
Ph: (708)366-5200   Fax: (708)366-5280
Fr: 888-366-5200
E-mail: info@planningcommunications.com
URL: http://jobfindersonline.com

Daniel Lauber. 1997. $32.95; $16.95 (paper). 340 pages. Covers 1600 sources. Discusses how to use sources of non-profit sector job vacancies in a number of specialties and state-by-state, including job-matching services, job hotlines, specialty periodicals with job ads, salary surveys, and directories. Covers a variety of fields from education to religion. Includes chapters on resume and cover letter preparation and interviewing.

★411★ Opportunities in Marketing Careers

The McGraw-Hill Companies
PO Box 182604
Columbus, OH 43272
Fax: (614)759-3749   Fr: 877-883-5524
E-mail: customer.service@mcgraw-hill.com
URL: http://www.mcgraw-hill.com

Margery Steinberg. 2005. $13.95; $11.95 (paper). 176. Gives guidance on identifying and pursuing job opportunities. Illustrated.

★412★ Vocational Entry-Skills for Secondary and Adult Students with Learning Disabilities

High Noon Books
20 Commercial Blvd.
Novato, CA 94949-6191
Ph: (415)883-3314   Fax: 888-287-9975
Fr: 800-422-7249
E-mail: sales@academictherapy.com
URL: http://www.academictherapy.com/

Winifred Washburn. 1999. $18.00. 192 pages. Explores vocational skills for adults with learning disabilities.

EMPLOYMENT AGENCIES AND SEARCH FIRMS

★413★ Educational Placement Service

6510-A S. Academy Blvd.
Colorado Springs, CO 80906
Ph: (719)579-9911   Fax: (719)579-5050
E-mail: accounting@educatorjobs.com
URL: http://www.educatorjobs.com

Employment agency. Focuses on teaching, administrative, and education-related openings.

OTHER SOURCES

★414★ American Association for Adult and Continuing Education (AAACE)

10111 Martin Luther King, Jr. Hwy., Ste. 200C
Bowie, MD 20720
Ph: (301)459-6261   Fax: (301)459-6241
E-mail: aaace10@aol.com
URL: http://www.aaace.org

Purpose: Provides leadership in advancing adult education as a lifelong learning process. Serves as a central forum for a wide variety of adult and continuing education special interest groups. Works to stimulate local, state, and regional adult continuing education efforts; encourages mutual cooperation and support; monitors proposed legislation and offers testimony to congress.

★415★ American Association of Community Colleges (AACC)

1 Dupont Cir. NW, Ste. 410
Washington, DC 20036-1176
Ph: (202)728-0200   Fax: (202)833-2467
E-mail: gboggs@aacc.nche.edu
URL: http://www.aacc.nche.edu

Members: Community colleges; individual associates interested in community college development; corporate, educational, foundation, and international associate members. **Purpose:** Office of Federal Relations monitors federal educational programming and legislation. **Activities:** Compiles statistics through data collection and policy analysis. Conducts seminars and professional training programs.

★416★ American Association for Women in Community Colleges (AAWCC)

PO Box 336603
Greeley, CO 80633-0611
Ph: (970)352-2079   Fax: (970)352-2080
E-mail: aawcc@comcast.net
URL: http://www.aawccnatl.org

Description: Women faculty members, administrators, staff members, students, and trustees of community colleges. Objectives are to: develop communication and disseminate information among women in community, junior, and technical colleges; encourage educational program development; obtain grants for educational projects for community college women. Disseminates information on women's issues and programs. Conducts regional and state professional development workshops and forums. Recognizes model programs that assist women in community colleges. An affiliate council of the American Association of Community Colleges.

★417★ American Federation of Teachers (AFT)

555 New Jersey Ave. NW
Washington, DC 20001
Ph: (202)879-4400   Fax: (202)879-4545
Fr: 800-238-1133

E-mail: online@aft.org
URL: http://www.aft.org

Description: Affiliated with the AFL-CIO. Works with teachers and other educational employees at the state and local level in organizing, collective bargaining, research, educational issues, and public relations. Conducts research in areas such as educational reform, teacher certification, and national assessments and standards. Represents members' concerns through legislative action; offers technical assistance. Serves professionals with concerns similar to those of teachers, including state employees, healthcare workers, and paraprofessionals.

★418★ Association for Career and Technical Education (ACTE)

1410 King St.
Alexandria, VA 22314
Ph: (703)683-3111   Fax: (703)683-7424
Fr: 800-826-9972
E-mail: acte@acteonline.org
URL: http://www.acteonline.org

Description: Represents teachers, supervisors, administrators, and others interested in the development and improvement of vocational, Technical, and practical arts education. Areas of interest include: secondary, postsecondary, and adult vocational education; education for special population groups; cooperative education. Works with such government agencies as: Bureau of Apprenticeship in Department of Labor; Office of Vocational Rehabilitation in Department of Health and Human Services; Veterans Administration; Office of Vocational and Adult Education of the Department of Education. Maintains hall of fame.

★419★ College Reading and Learning Association (CRLA)

PO Box 382
El Dorado, KS 67042
Ph: (307)382-1725   Fax: (316)322-7369
E-mail: staylor@wwcc.wy.edu
URL: http://www.crla.net

Description: Professionals involved in college/adult reading, learning assistance, developmental education, and tutorial services. Promotes communication for the purpose of professional growth.

★420★ Education and Training

Cambridge Educational
PO Box 2053
Princeton, NJ 08543-2053
Ph: 800-257-5126   Fax: (609)671-0266
Fr: 800-468-4227
E-mail: custserv@films.com
URL: http://www.cambridgeeducational.com

VHS and DVD. $89.95. 2002. 18 minutes. Presents four distinct occupations in the field: elementary teachers, teacher's aides, administrators, and librarians. People working in these jobs discuss their responsibilities.

★421★ International Reading Association (IRA)

PO Box 8139
Newark, DE 19714-8139
Ph: (302)731-1600   Fax: (302)731-1057
Fr: 800-336-7323
E-mail: pubinfo@reading.org
URL: http://www.reading.org

Description: Represents teachers, reading specialists, consultants, administrators, supervisors, researchers, psychologists, librarians, and parents interested in promoting literacy. Seeks to improve the quality of reading instruction and promote literacy worldwide. Disseminates information pertaining to research on reading, including information on adult literacy, early childhood and literacy development, international education, literature for children and adolescents, and teacher education and professional development. Maintains over 40 special interest groups and over 70 committees.

★422★ International Technology Education Association - Council for Supervisors (ITEA-CS)

PO Box 144200
Salt Lake City, UT 84114-4200
Ph: (801)538-7598   Fax: (801)538-7868
E-mail: mrobinson@schools.utah.gov
URL: http://www.iteawww.net/CS

Description: Technology education supervisors from the U.S. Office of Education; local school department chairpersons; state departments of education, local school districts, territories, provinces, and foreign countries. Improves instruction and supervision of programs in technology education. Conducts research; compiles statistics. Sponsors competitions. Maintains speakers' bureau.

★423★ National Association of Blind Teachers (NABT)

1155 15th St. NW, Ste. 1004
Washington, DC 20005
Ph: (202)467-5081   Fax: (202)467-5085
Fr: 800-424-8666
E-mail: info@acb.org
URL: http://www.acb.org

Description: Public school teachers, college and university professors, and teachers in residential schools for the blind. Promotes employment and professional goals of blind persons entering the teaching profession or those established in their respective teaching fields. Serves as a vehicle for the dissemination of information and the exchange of ideas addressing special problems of members. Compiles statistics.

★424★ National Community Education Association (NCEA)

3929 Old Lee Hwy., No. 91-A
Fairfax, VA 22030-2421
Ph: (703)359-8973   Fax: (703)359-0972
E-mail: ncea@ncea.com
URL: http://www.ncea.com

Description: Community school directors, principals, superintendents, professors, teachers, students, and laypeople. **Purpose:** Promotes and establishes community schools as an integral part of the educational plan of every community. Emphasizes community and parent involvement in the schools, lifelong learning, and enrichment of K-12 and adult education. Serves as a clearinghouse for the exchange of ideas and information, and the sharing of efforts. **Activities:** Offers leadership training.

★425★ National Council of Teachers of Mathematics (NCTM)

1906 Association Dr.
Reston, VA 20191-1502
Ph: (703)620-9840   Fax: (703)476-2970
Fr: 800-235-7566
E-mail: inquiries@nctm.org
URL: http://www.nctm.org

Description: Aims to improve teaching and learning of mathematics.

★426★ North American Council of Automotive Teachers (NACAT)

PO Box 80010
Charleston, SC 29416
Ph: (843)556-7068   Fax: (843)556-7068
E-mail: office@nacat.com
URL: http://www.nacat.com

Description: Provides support for automotive educators, secondary, post-secondary, and industry. Enhances technical training opportunities, peer interaction and resources sharing. Represents automotive teachers on councils and committees where automotive teachers' interests are involved.

★427★ Overseas Employment Opportunities for Educators: Department of Defense Dependents Schools

DIANE Publishing Co.
PO Box 617
Darby, PA 19023-0617
Ph: (610)461-6200   Fax: (610)461-6130
Fr: 800-782-3833
URL: http://www.dianepublishingcentral.com

Barry Leonard, editor. 2000. $15.00. 54 pages. An introduction to teachings positions in the Dept. of Defense Dependents Schools (DoDDS), a worldwide school system, operated by the DoD in 14 countries.

★428★ Teaching & Related Occupations

Delphi Productions
3159 6th St.
Boulder, CO 80304
Ph: (303)443-2100   Fax: (303)443-4022
Fr: 888-443-2400
E-mail: support@delphivideo.com
URL: http://www.delphivideo.com

$95.00. 50 minutes. Part of the Careers for the 21st Century Video Library.

★429★ Vocational Careers Sourcebook

Gale, Cengage Learning
27500 Drake Rd.
Farmington Hills, MI 48331-3535
Ph: (248)699-GALE   Fax: (248)699-8069
Fr: 800-877-GALE
E-mail: galeord@gale.com
URL: http://www.gale.com

Sixth edition, 2006. $160.00. 700 pages. Directs users to career information sources related to specific occupations, such as insurance and real estate sales, corrections and police work, mechanics, armed forces options, agriculture and forestry, production work, and the trades. Contains information on general career guides, career information and services provided by trade associations, standards and certification agencies, directories of educational programs and institutions, basic reference guides and handbooks related to the occupation, trade periodicals, and more. Indexes: Alphabetical.

Aerospace Engineers

★430★ Aerospace Engineering

Society of Automotive Engineers Inc.
400 Commonwealth Dr.
Warrendale, PA 15096-0001
Ph: (724)776-4841   Fax: (724)776-5760
Fr: 877-606-7323
E-mail: magazines@sae.org
URL: http://www.sae.org/aeromag

Monthly. $85.00/year for U.S., Canada, and Mexico; $145.00/year for other countries; $120.00/year for U.S., Canada, and Mexico, 2 years; $245.00 for two years, other countries. Magazine for aerospace manufacturing engineers providing technical and design information.

★431★ AeroSpaceNews.com

AeroSpaceNews.com
PO Box 1748
Ojai, CA 93024-1748
Ph: (805)985-2320
URL: http://www.aerospacenews.com/content/view/41/33/

Monthly. $19.95/year for individuals, private; $53.95/year for two years, individual, private; $79.95/year for individuals, trade; $143.95 for two years, individual. Journal reporting on the insights, impressions and images of tomorrow's technological wonders in the field of aerospace.

★432★ AIE Perspectives Newsmagazine

American Institute of Engineers
4630 Appian Way, Ste. 206
El Sobrante, CA 94803-1875
Ph: (510)758-6240   Fax: (510)758-6240

Monthly. Professional magazine covering engineering.

★433★ Air Jobs Digest

World Air Data
PO Box 42724
Washington, DC 20015
Ph: (301)990-6800   Fr: 800-247-5627
URL: http://www.airjobsdaily.com

Monthly. $96.00/year for individuals. Newspaper covering job listings in aviation and aerospace worldwide.

★434★ Aviation Maintenance

Access Intelligence L.L.C.
4 Choke Cherry Rd., 2nd Fl.
Rockville, MD 20850
Ph: (301)354-2000   Fax: (301)309-3847
Fr: 800-777-5006
URL: http://www.aviationtoday.com

Monthly. $207.00/year for individuals. Magazine covering aviation maintenance.

★435★ Aviation Week & Space Technology

McGraw-Hill Inc.
1221 Ave. of the Americas
New York, NY 10020-1095
Ph: (212)512-2000   Fax: (212)512-3840
Fr: 877-833-5524
URL: http://www.aviationweek.com/aw/generic/channel_.jsp?channel=

Weekly. $109.00/year for Canada and Mexico; $103.00/year U.S.; $160.00/year Europe. Magazine serving the aviation and aerospace market worldwide.

★436★ Engineering Conferences International Symposium Series

Berkeley Electronic Press
2809 Telegraph Ave., Ste. 202
Berkeley, CA 94705
Ph: (510)665-1200   Fax: (510)665-1201
URL: http://services.bepress.com/eci/

Journal focusing on advance engineering science.

★437★ Engineering Times

National Society of Professional Engineers
1420 King St.
Alexandria, VA 22314
Ph: (703)684-2800
URL: http://www.nspe.org

Monthly. Magazine (tabloid) covering professional, legislative, and techology issues for an engineering audience.

★438★ ENR: Engineering News-Record

McGraw-Hill Inc.
1221 Ave. of the Americas
New York, NY 10020-1095
Ph: (212)512-2000   Fax: (212)512-3840
Fr: 877-833-5524
E-mail: enr_web_editors@mcgraw-hill.com
URL: http://www.mymags.com/moreinfo.php?itemID=20012

Weekly. $94.00/year for individuals, print. Magazine focusing on engineering and construction.

★439★ Graduating Engineer & Computer Careers

Career Recruitment Media
211 W Wacker Dr., Ste. 900
Chicago, IL 60606
Ph: (312)525-3100
URL: http://www.graduatingengineer.com

Quarterly. $15.00/year for individuals. Magazine focusing on employment, education, and career development for entry-level engineers and computer scientists.

★440★ High Technology Careers Magazine

HTC
4701 Patrick Henry Dr., No. 1901
Santa Clara, CA 95054-1847
Fax: (408)567-0242
URL: http://www.hightechcareers.com

Bimonthly. $29.00/year; $35.00/year for Canada; $85.00/year for out of country. Magazine (tabloid) containing employment opportunity information for the engineering and technical community.

★441★ *InterJournal*

New England Complex Systems Institute
24 Mt. Auburn St.
Cambridge, MA 02138
Ph: (617)547-4100　　Fax: (617)661-7711
URL: http://www.interjournal.org/

Journal covering the fields of science and engineering.

★442★ *International Archives of Bioscience*

International Archives of Bioscience
PO Box 737254
Elmhurst, NY 11373-9997
URL: http://www.iabs.us/jdoc/aboutiabs.htm

Free, online only. Journal reporting multidisciplinary coverage and interaction between scientists in biology, informatics, mathematics, physics, engineering and other sciences.

★443★ *Journal of Engineering Education*

American Society for Engineering Education
1818 North St., NW, Ste. 600
Washington, DC 20036-2479
Ph: (202)331-3500
URL: http://www.asee.org/publications/jee/index.cfm

Quarterly. Journal covering scholarly research in engineering education.

★444★ *NASA Tech Briefs*

Associated Business Publications Company Ltd.
1466 Broadway, Ste. 910
New York, NY 10036
Ph: (212)490-3999　　Fax: (212)986-7864
URL: http://www.nasatech.com/

Monthly. Free. Publication covering technology for American industry and government in the fields of electronics, computers, physical sciences, materials, mechanics, machinery, fabrication technology, math and information sciences, and the life sciences.

★445★ *NSBE Magazine*

NSBE Publications
205 Daingerfield Rd.
Alexandria, VA 22314
Ph: (703)549-2207　　Fax: (703)683-5312
URL: http://www.nsbe.org/publications/premieradvertisers.php

Journal providing information on engineering careers, self-development, and cultural issues for recent graduates with technical majors.

★446★ *SWE, Magazine of the Society of Women Engineers*

Society of Women Engineers
230 East Ohio St., Ste. 400
Chicago, IL 60611-3265
Ph: (312)596-5223
E-mail: hq@swe.org
URL: http://www.swe.org

Quarterly. $30.00/year for nonmembers. Magazine for engineering students and for women and men working in the engineering and technology fields. Covers career guidance, continuing development and topical issues.

★447★ *The Technology Interface*

New Mexico State University
College of Engineering
PO Box 30001
Las Cruces, NM 88003-8001
Ph: (505)646-0111
URL: http://engr.nmsu.edu/etti/

Journal for the engineering technology profession serving education and industry.

★448★ *TEST Engineering & Management*

The Mattingley Publishing Company Inc.
3756 Grand Ave., Ste. 205
Oakland, CA 94610-1545
Ph: (510)839-0909　　Fax: (510)839-2950
URL: http://www.testmagazine.biz/

Bimonthly. $40.00/year for individuals; $55.00/year for other countries; $5.00 for single issue. Trade publication that covers physical and mechanical testing and environmental simulation; edited for test engineering professionals.

★449★ *Uratie*

IDG Communications Inc.
5 Speen St., 3rd. Fl
Framingham, MA 01701
Ph: (508)875-5000　　Fax: (508)988-7888
URL: http://www.idg.com

Magazine providing job offers for graduates, engineers and information technology professionals.

★450★ *WEPANEWS*

Women in Engineering Programs & Advocates Network
1901 E. Asbury Ave., Ste. 220
Denver, CO 80208
Ph: (303)871-4643　　Fax: (303)871-6833
E-mail: dmatt@wepan.org
URL: http://www.wepan.org

Description: 2/year. Seeks to provide greater access for women to careers in engineering. Includes news of graduate, undergraduate, freshmen, pre-college, and re-entry engineering programs for women. Recurring features include job listings, faculty, grant, and conference news, international engineering program news, action group news, notices of publications available, and a column titled Kudos.

PLACEMENT AND JOB REFERRAL SERVICES

★451★ American Indian Science and Engineering Society (AISES)

PO Box 9828
Albuquerque, NM 87119-9828
Ph: (505)765-1052　　Fax: (505)765-5608
E-mail: info@aises.org
URL: http://www.aises.org

Description: Represents American Indian and non-Indian students and professionals in science, technology, and engineering fields; corporations representing energy, mining, aerospace, electronic, and computer fields. Seeks to motivate and encourage students to pursue undergraduate and graduate studies in science, engineering, and technology. Sponsors science fairs in grade schools, teacher training workshops, summer math/science sessions for 8th-12th graders, professional chapters, and student chapters in colleges. Offers scholarships. Adult members serve as role models, advisers, and mentors for students. Operates placement service.

★452★ American Institute of Aeronautics and Astronautics (AIAA)

1801 Alexander Bell Dr., Ste. 500
Reston, VA 20191-4344
Ph: (703)264-7500　　Fax: (703)264-7551
Fr: 800-NEW-AIAA
E-mail: custserv@aiaa.org
URL: http://www.aiaa.org

Description: Represents scientists and engineers in the field of aeronautics and astronautics. Facilitates interchange of technological information through publications and technical meetings in order to foster overall technical progress in the field and increase the professional competence of members. Operates Public Policy program to provide federal decision-makers with the technical information and policy guidance needed to make effective policy on aerospace issues. Public Policy program activities include congressional testimony, position papers, section public policy activities, and workshops. Offers placement assistance; compiles statistics; offers educational programs. Provides abstracting services through its AIAA Access.

★453★ Engineering Society of Detroit (ESD)

2000 Town Ctr., Ste. 2610
Southfield, MI 48075
Ph: (248)353-0735　　Fax: (248)353-0736
E-mail: esd@esd.org
URL: http://esd.org

Description: Engineers from all disciplines; scientists and technologists. Conducts technical programs and engineering refresher courses; sponsors conferences and expositions. Maintains speakers' bureau; offers placement services; although based in Detroit, MI, society membership is international.

★454★ Korean-American Scientists and Engineers Association (KSEA)

1952 Gallows Rd., Ste. 300
Vienna, VA 22182
Ph: (703)748-1221   Fax: (703)748-1331
E-mail: admin@ksea.org
URL: http://www.ksea.org

Description: Represents scientists and engineers holding single or advanced degrees. Promotes friendship and mutuality among Korean and American scientists and engineers; contributes to Korea's scientific, technological, industrial, and economic developments; strengthens the scientific, technological, and cultural bonds between Korea and the U.S. Sponsors symposium. Maintains speakers' bureau, placement service, and biographical archives. Compiles statistics.

★455★ Society of Hispanic Professional Engineers (SHPE)

5400 E Olympic Blvd., Ste. 210
Los Angeles, CA 90022
Ph: (323)725-3970   Fax: (323)725-0316
E-mail: shpenational@shpe.org
URL: http://oneshpe.shpe.org/wps/portal/national

Description: Represents engineers, student engineers, and scientists. Aims to increase the number of Hispanic engineers by providing motivation and support to students. Sponsors competitions and educational programs. Maintains placement service and speakers' bureau; compiles statistics.

EMPLOYER DIRECTORIES AND NETWORKING LISTS

★456★ American Men and Women of Science

Gale, Cengage Learning
27500 Drake Rd.
Farmington Hills, MI 48331-3535
Ph: (248)699-4253   Fax: (248)699-8065
Fr: 800-877-4253
URL: http://www.gale.com

Biennial, latest edition 23rd, October 2006; new edition expected 24th, January 2008. $1,075.00 for individuals. Covers over 129,700 U.S. and Canadian scientists active in the physical, biological, mathematical, computer science, and engineering fields; includes references to previous edition for deceased scientists and nonrespondents. Entries include: Name, address, education, personal and career data, memberships, honors and awards, research interest. Arrangement: Alphabetical. Indexes: Discipline (in separate volume).

★457★ Career Opportunities in Aviation and the Aerospace Industry

Facts On File Inc.
132 W 31st St., 17th Fl.
New York, NY 10001
Ph: (212)967-8800   Fax: 800-678-3633
Fr: 800-322-8755

URL: http://www.factsonfile.com

Published 2005. $49.50 for individuals; $44.55 for libraries. Covers eighty up-to-date job profiles, providing detailed information about the duties, salaries, and prospects of aviation mechanics, designers, technicians, scientists, and administrators.

★458★ Careers in Focus: Engineering

Facts On File Inc.
132 W 31st St., 17th Fl.
New York, NY 10001
Ph: (212)967-8800   Fax: 800-678-3633
Fr: 800-322-8755
URL: http://www.factsonfile.com

3rd edition, 2007. $29.95 for individuals; $26.95 for libraries. Publication includes: List of resources to consult for more information. Principal content of publication consists of job descriptions, advancement opportunities, educational requirements, employment outlook, salary information, and working conditions for careers in the field of engineering. Indexes: Alphabetical.

★459★ Directory of Contract Staffing Firms

C.E. Publications Inc.
PO Box 3006
Bothell, WA 98041-3006
Ph: (425)806-5200   Fax: (425)806-5585
URL: http://www.cjhunter.com/dcsf/overview.html

Covers nearly 1,300 contract firms actively engaged in the employment of engineering, IT/IS, and technical personnel for 'temporary' contract assignments throughout the world. Entries include: Company name, address, phone, name of contact, email, web address. Arrangement: Alphabetical. Indexes: Geographical.

★460★ Indiana Society of Professional Engineers-Directory

Indiana Society of Professional Engineers
PO Box 20806
Indianapolis, IN 46220
Ph: (317)255-2267   Fax: (317)255-2530
URL: http://www.indspe.org

Annual, fall. Covers member registered engineers, land surveyors, engineering students, and engineers in training. Entries include: Member name, address, phone, type of membership, business information, specialty. Arrangement: Alphabetical by chapter area.

★461★ Peterson's Job Opportunities in Engineering and Technology

Peterson's Guides
2000 Lenox Dr.
Box 67005
Lawrenceville, NJ 08648
Ph: (609)896-1800   Fax: (609)896-4531
Fr: 800-338-3282
E-mail: custsvc@petersons.com
URL: http://www.petersons.com

Compiled by the Peterson's staff. Fourth

edition, 1996. $21.95 (paper). 379 pages. Profiles 2,000 high-tech companies looking primarily for technical personnel in such fields as biotechnology, telecommunications, software, computers and peripherals, defense, and aerospace. Contains job-search strategies and career options to help match education and expertise to the job market. Indexed geographically, by industry, and by hiring needs.

HANDBOOKS AND MANUALS

★462★ The Best Resumes for Scientists and Engineers

John Wiley & Sons Inc.
1 Wiley Dr.
Somerset, NJ 08873
Ph: (732)469-4400   Fax: (732)302-2300
Fr: 800-225-5945
E-mail: custserv@wiley.com
URL: http://www.wiley.com/WileyCDA/

Adele Lewis and David J. Moore. Second edition, 1993. $37.50; $19.95 (paper). 224 pages. Presents an extensive collection of scientific and engineering resumes, highlighting the important differences between these and resumes written for other occupations.

★463★ Careers in High Tech

The McGraw-Hill Companies
PO Box 182604
Columbus, OH 43272
Fax: (614)759-3749   Fr: 877-883-5524
E-mail: customer.service@mcgraw-hill.com
URL: http://www.mcgraw-hill.com

Nick Basta. Second edition, 1998. $17.95 (paper). 98 pages. Examines new career opportunities in such fields as biotechnology, computers, aerospace, telecommunications, and others.

★464★ Great Jobs for Engineering Majors

The McGraw-Hill Companies
PO Box 182604
Columbus, OH 43272
Fax: (614)759-3749   Fr: 877-883-5524
E-mail: customer.service@mcgraw-hill.com
URL: http://www.mcgraw-hill.com

Geraldine O. Garner. Second edition, 2002. $14.95. 256 pages. Covers all the career options open to students majoring in engineering.

★465★ How to Succeed as an Engineer: A Practical Guide to Enhance Your Career

Institute of Electrical & Electronics Engineers
445 Hoes Lane
Piscataway, NJ 08854
Ph: (732)981-0060   Fax: (732)981-9667
Fr: 800-678-4333

URL: http://www.ieee.org

Todd Yuzuriha. 1999. $29.95 (paper). 367 pages.

★466★ **The I Hate Selling Book: Business-Building Advice for Consultants, Attorneys, Accountants, Engineers, Architects, and Other Professionals**

AMACOM
1601 Broadway, 12th Fl.
New York, NY 10019-7420
Ph: (212)586-8100   Fax: (212)903-8168
Fr: 800-262-9699
URL: http://www.amanet.org

Allan S. Boress. 2001. $29.95. 240 pages.

★467★ **Keys to Engineering Success**

Prentice Hall PTR
One Lake St.
Upper Saddle River, NJ 07458
Ph: (201)236-7000   Fr: 800-428-5331
URL: http://www.phptr.com/index.asp?rl=1

Jill S. Tietjen, Kristy A. Schloss, Carol Carter, Joyce Bishop, and Sarah Lyman. 2000. $46.00 (paper). 288 pages.

★468★ **The New Engineer's Guide to Career Growth & Professional Awareness**

Institute of Electrical & Electronics Engineers
445 Hoes Lane
Piscataway, NJ 08854
Ph: (732)981-0060   Fax: (732)981-9667
Fr: 800-678-4333
URL: http://www.ieee.org

Irving J. Gabelman, editor. 1996. $39.95 (paper). 275 pages.

★469★ **Opportunities in Aerospace Careers**

The McGraw-Hill Companies
PO Box 182604
Columbus, OH 43272
Fax: (614)759-3749   Fr: 877-883-5524
E-mail: customer.service@mcgraw-hill.com
URL: http://www.mcgraw-hill.com

Wallace R. Maples. Third edition, 2002 $13.95 (paper). 160 pages. Surveys jobs with the airlines, airports, the government, the military, in manufacturing, and in research and development. Includes information on job opportunities with NASA in the U.S. space program.

★470★ **Opportunities in Engineering Careers**

The McGraw-Hill Companies
PO Box 182604
Columbus, OH 43272
Fax: (614)759-3749   Fr: 877-883-5524
E-mail: customer.service@mcgraw-hill.com
URL: http://www.mcgraw-hill.com

Nicholas Basta. Revised second edition, 2002. $13.95; $11.95 (paper). 160 pages.

Outlines typical job titles, salaries, career paths, and employment prospects.

★471★ **Opportunities in High Tech Careers**

The McGraw-Hill Companies
PO Box 182604
Columbus, OH 43272
Fax: (614)759-3749   Fr: 877-883-5524
E-mail: customer.service@mcgraw-hill.com
URL: http://www.mcgraw-hill.com

Gary Colter and Deborah Yanuck. 1999. $14.95; $11.95 (paper). 160 pages. Explores high technology careers. Describes job opportunities, how to make a career decision, how to prepare for high technology jobs, job hunting techniques, and future trends.

★472★ **Opportunities in Research and Development Careers**

The McGraw-Hill Companies
PO Box 182604
Columbus, OH 43272
Fax: (614)759-3749   Fr: 877-883-5524
E-mail: customer.service@mcgraw-hill.com
URL: http://www.mcgraw-hill.com

Jan Goldberg. 1996. $11.95 (paper). 146 pages.

★473★ **Real People Working in Engineering**

The McGraw-Hill Companies
PO Box 182604
Columbus, OH 43272
Fax: (614)759-3749   Fr: 877-883-5524
E-mail: customer.service@mcgraw-hill.com
URL: http://www.mcgraw-hill.com

Blythe Camenson, Jan Goldberg. 1997. $17.95 (paper). 160 pages. Interviews and profiles of working professionals capture a range of opportunities in this field.

★474★ **Resumes for Engineering Careers**

The McGraw-Hill Companies
PO Box 182604
Columbus, OH 43272
Fax: (614)759-3749   Fr: 877-883-5524
E-mail: customer.service@mcgraw-hill.com
URL: http://www.mcgraw-hill.com

Third edition, 2005. $11.95 (paper). 144 pages. Contains sample resumes and cover letters applicable to any engineering field.

★475★ **Resumes for Scientific and Technical Careers**

The McGraw-Hill Companies
PO Box 182604
Columbus, OH 43272
Fax: (614)759-3749   Fr: 877-883-5524
E-mail: customer.service@mcgraw-hill.com
URL: http://www.mcgraw-hill.com

Third edition, 2007. $12.95 (paper). 144 pages. Provides resume advice for individuals interested in working in scientific and technical careers. Includes sample resumes and cover letters.

★476★ **The Standard Handbook for Aeronautical and Astronautical Engineers**

The McGraw-Hill Companies
PO Box 182604
Columbus, OH 43272
Fax: (614)759-3749   Fr: 877-883-5524
E-mail: customer.service@mcgraw-hill.com
URL: http://www.mcgraw-hill.com

Mark Davies. 2002. $175.00. 1360 pages. Educational manual for aeronautical and astronautical engineers.

★477★ **Taking Flight: Education & Training for Aviation Careers**

National Academies Press
500 5th St. NW
Lockbox 285
Washington, DC 20055
Ph: (202)334-3313   Fax: (202)334-2793
Fr: 888-624-8373
URL: http://www.nap.edu/

Janet S. Hansen and Clinton V. Oster, editors. 1997. $40.25 (paper). 192 pages.

EMPLOYMENT AGENCIES AND SEARCH FIRMS

★478★ **Adams & Associates International**

520 Shorely Dr. 201
PO Box 129
Barrington, IL 60011-0129
Ph: (847)304-5300   Fax: (847)400-0798
URL: http://www.leanthinking.net

Global executive search firm.

★479★ **Amtec Engineering Corp.**

2749 Saturn St.
Brea, CA 92821
Ph: (714)993-1900   Fax: (714)993-2419
E-mail: info@amtechc.com
URL: http://www.amtec-eng.com

Employment agency.

★480★ **The Arcus Group Inc.**

5001 LBJ Freeway, Ste. 875
Dallas, TX 75244
Ph: (214)294-0516   Fax: (214)871-1338
URL: http://www.arcusgroup.com

Executive search firm. Branch in Chicago.

★481★ **The Aspire Group**

52 Second Ave, 1st Fl
Waltham, MA 02451-1129
Fax: (718)890-1810   Fr: 800-487-2967
URL: http://www.bmanet.com

Employment agency.

★482★ Aureus Group

13609 California St.
Omaha, NE 68154
Ph: (402)891-6900   Fax: (402)891-1290
Fr: 888-239-5993
E-mail: info@aureusgroup.com
URL: http://www.aureusgroup.com

Provides human capital management services in a wide variety of industries. Executive search and recruiting consultants specializing in six areas: accounting and finance, data processing, aerospace, engineering, manufacturing and medical professionals. Industries served: hospitals, all mainframe computer shops and all areas of accounting.

★483★ Brentwood International

9841 Airport Blvd., Ste. 420
Los Angeles, CA 90045
Ph: (310)338-5470   Fax: (310)338-5484
E-mail: postmaster@brentwoodintl.com
URL: http://www.brentwoodintl.com

Executive search firm with focus on information technology. Branch in Fairfield, CA.

★484★ Claddagh Resources America

3169 Holcomb Bridge Rd., Ste. 700
Norcross, GA 30071
Ph: (678)405-4400   Fax: (770)840-6071
E-mail: awood@claddaghresources.net
URL: http://www.claddaghresources.net

Executive search firm. Additional office in Ireland.

★485★ Colli Associates

414 Caboose Ln.
Valrico, FL 33594
Ph: (813)681-2145   Fax: (813)661-5217
E-mail: colli@gte.net

Employment agency. Executive search firm.

★486★ DMR Global Inc.

10230 W. Sample Rd.
Coral Springs, FL 33065
Ph: (954)796-5043   Fax: (954)796-5044
E-mail: rdaratany@dmrglobal.com
URL: http://www.dmrglobal.com

Executive search firm.

★487★ Eastbourne Associates Inc.

104 Sandy Hollow Rd.
Northport, NY 11768
Ph: (631)757-1217   Fax: (631)757-1417
E-mail: search@eastbourneassociates.com
URL: http://www.eastbourneassociates.com

Executive search firm.

★488★ Engineer One, Inc.

PO Box 23037
Knoxville, TN 37933
Fax: (865)691-0110
E-mail: engineerone@engineerone.com
URL: http://www.engineerone.com

Engineering employment service specializes in engineering and management in the chemical process, power utilities, manufacturing, mechanical, electrical, and electronic industries. Established an Information Technology Division in 1998 that works nationwide across all industries. Also provides systems analysis consulting services specializing in VAX based systems.

★489★ ESA Professional Consultants

141 Durham Rd., Ste. 16
Madison, CT 06443
Ph: (203)245-1983   Fax: (203)245-8428

Executive search firm.

★490★ Fisher Personnel Management Services

2351 N. Filbert Rd.
Exeter, CA 93221
Ph: (559)594-5774   Fax: (559)594-5777
E-mail: hookme@fisheads.net
URL: http://www.fisheads.net

Executive search firm.

★491★ Focus Learning Corp.

173 Cross St., Ste. 200
San Luis Obispo, CA 93401
Ph: (805)543-4895   Fax: (805)543-4897
Fr: 800-458-5116
E-mail: info@focuslearning.com
URL: http://www.focuslearning.com

Provides professional services to corporations for the development and implementation of training programs. Assists clients with needs assessment related to training and professional development, goals definition, and development of training materials. Industries served include: government, utility, aerospace, business, and computer.

★492★ Global Employment Solutions

10375 Park Meadows Dr., Ste. 375
Littleton, CO 80124
Ph: (303)216-9500   Fax: (303)216-9533
E-mail: careers@global
URL: http://www.gesnetwork.com

Employment agency.

★493★ International Staffing Consultants

17310 Redhill Ave., No. 140
Irvine, CA 92614
Ph: (949)255-5857   Fax: (949)767-5959
E-mail: iscinc@iscworld.com
URL: http://www.iscworld.com

Employment agency. Provides placement on regular or temporary basis. Affiliate office in London.

★494★ Johnson Personnel Co.

1639 N Alpine Rd.
Rockford, IL 61107
Ph: (815)964-0840   Fax: (815)964-0855
E-mail: darrell@nsonpersonnel.com

URL: http://www.johnsonpersonnel.com

Provide technical and managerial placement in industry. Industries served: aerospace, automotive, machine tool and consumer products.

★495★ J.R. Bechtle & Company

67 S. Bedford St., Ste. 400W
Burlington, MA 01803-5177
Ph: (781)229-5804   Fax: (781)359-1829
E-mail: jrb.boston@jrbechtle.com
URL: http://www.jrbechtle.com

Executive search firm.

★496★ Louis Rudzinsky Associates Inc.

394 Lowell St., Ste. 17
PO Box 640
Lexington, MA 02420
Ph: (781)862-6727   Fax: (781)862-6868
E-mail: lra@lra.com
URL: http://www.lra.com

Provides recruitment, placement, and executive search to industry (software, electronics, optics) covering positions in general management, manufacturing, engineering, and marketing. Personnel consulting activities include counsel to small and startup companies. Industries served: electronics, aerospace, optical, laser, computer, software, imaging, electro-optics, biotechnology, advanced materials, and solid-state/semiconductor.

★497★ R.J. Evans Associates Inc.

26949 Chagrin Blvd., Ste. 300
Beachwood, OH 44122
Ph: (216)464-5100   Fax: (866)404-6266
E-mail: resume@rjevans.com
URL: http://www.rjevens.com

Executive search firm.

★498★ Robert Drexler Associates Inc.

PO Box 151
Saddle River, NJ 07458
Ph: (201)760-2300   Fax: (201)760-2301
E-mail: drexler@engineeringemployment.com
URL: http://www.engineeringemployment.com

Executive search firm.

★499★ Search and Recruit International

4455 South Blvd. Ste. 110
Virginia Beach, VA 23452
Ph: (757)625-2121   Fr: 800-800-5627

Employment agency. Headquartered in Virginia Beach. Other offices in Bremerton, WA; Charleston, SC; Jacksonville, FL; Memphis, TN; Pensacola, FL; Sacramento, CA; San Bernardino, CA; San Diego, CA.

★500★ Techtronix Technical Search

4805 N 24th Pl.
PO Box 17713
Milwaukee, WI 53217-0173
Ph: (414)466-3100   Fax: (414)466-3598

Firm specializes in recruiting executives for the engineering, information systems, manufacturing, marketing, finance, and human resources industries.

★501★ Timothy D. Crowe Jr.

26 Higate Rd.
Chelmsford, MA 01824
Ph: (978)256-2008

Executive search firm.

★502★ Tri-Serv Inc.

22 W. Padonia Rd., Ste. C-353
Timonium, MD 21093
Ph: (410)561-1740   Fax: (410)252-7417
E-mail: info@tri-serv.coom
URL: http://www.tri-serv.com

Employment agency for technical personnel.

★503★ Winters Technical Staffing Services

6 Lansing Sq., Ste. 101
Toronto, ON, Canada M2J 1T5
Ph: (416)495-7422   Fax: (416)495-8479
E-mail: brian@winterstaffing.com
URL: http://www.winterstaffing.com

Technical staffing service for permanent and contract positions in all facets of engineering. Serves government agencies, consulting engineers, and all areas of manufacturing in Canada and northeast United States.

ONLINE JOB SOURCES AND SERVICES

★504★ American Institute of Aeronautics and Astronautics Career Planning and Placement Services

1801 Alexander Bell Dr., Ste. 500
Reston, VA 20191-4344
Ph: (703)264-7500   Fax: (703)264-7551
Fr: 800-639-2422
E-mail: custserv@aiaa.org
URL: http://www.aiaa.org

Description: Site for AIAA members to place recruitment advertisements, browse career opportunities listings, post resumes, and seek additional employment assistance. Non-members may become members though this site.

★505★ Spherion

2050 Spectrum Blvd.
Fort Lauderdale, FL 33309
Ph: (954)308-7600
E-mail: help@spherion.com
URL: http://www.spherion.com

Description: Recruitment firm specializing in accounting and finance, sales and marketing, interim executives, technology, engineering, retail and human resources.

TRADESHOWS

★506★ AeroMat Conference and Exposition

ASM International
9639 Kinsman Rd.
Materials Park, OH 44073-0002
Ph: (440)338-5151   Fax: (440)338-4634
Fr: 800-336-5152
E-mail: CustomerService@asminternational.org
URL: http://www.asminternational.org

Annual. **Primary Exhibits:** Providing information covering materials, material applications and processes for designing the next generation of aviation and space vehicles and systems.

★507★ Aerospace Congress and Exhibition

SAE - Society of Automotive Engineers, International
400 Commonwealth Dr.
Warrendale, PA 15096-0001
Ph: (724)772-4841   Fax: (724)776-0790
E-mail: exhibitions@sae.org
URL: http://www.sae.org

Biennial. **Primary Exhibits:** Equipment for the aerospace industry.

★508★ Aerospace Manufacturing and Automated Fastening Conference & Exhibition

SAE - Society of Automotive Engineers, International
400 Commonwealth Dr.
Warrendale, PA 15096-0001
Ph: (724)772-4841   Fax: (724)776-0790
E-mail: exhibitions@sae.org
URL: http://www.sae.org

Annual. **Primary Exhibits:** Aerospace parts, materials, components, systems, and techniques.

★509★ Aerospace Medical Association Annual Scientific Meeting

Aerospace Medical Association
320 S. Henry St.
Alexandria, VA 22314-3579
Ph: (703)739-2240   Fax: (703)739-9652
E-mail: jcarter@asma.org
URL: http://www.asma.org

Annual. **Primary Exhibits:** Products related to aerospace medicine; safety products; diagnostic and research instrumentation for the field of human factors. **Dates and Locations:** 2008 May 11-15; Boston, MA; 2009 May 03-07; Los Angeles, CA ; 2010 May 08-13; Phoenix, AZ.

★510★ AIAA Aerospace Sciences Meeting and Exhibition

American Institute of Aeronautics and Astronautics (AIAA)
1801 Alexander Bell Dr., Ste. 500
Reston, VA 20191-4344
Ph: (703)264-7500   Fax: (703)264-7551
Fr: 800-639-AIAA
URL: http://www.aiaa.org

Annual. **Primary Exhibits:** Computer and software technologies for the aerospace industry.

★511★ AIAA Applied Aerodynamics Conference and Exhibit

American Institute of Aeronautics and Astronautics (AIAA)
1801 Alexander Bell Dr., Ste. 500
Reston, VA 20191-4344
Ph: (703)264-7500   Fax: (703)264-7551
Fr: 800-639-AIAA
URL: http://www.aiaa.org

Annual. **Primary Exhibits:** Technologies related to aerospace guidance, navigation, and control; atmospheric flight; modeling and simulation; and astrodynamics.

★512★ AIAA/ASME/SAE/ASEE Joint Propulsion Conference and Exhibit

American Institute of Aeronautics and Astronautics (AIAA)
1801 Alexander Bell Dr., Ste. 500
Reston, VA 20191-4344
Ph: (703)264-7500   Fax: (703)264-7551
Fr: 800-639-AIAA
URL: http://www.aiaa.org

Annual. **Primary Exhibits:** Aerospace propulsion related exhibits.

★513★ AIAA Space Conference & Exposition

American Institute of Aeronautics and Astronautics (AIAA)
1801 Alexander Bell Dr., Ste. 500
Reston, VA 20191-4344
Ph: (703)264-7500   Fax: (703)264-7551
Fr: 800-639-AIAA
URL: http://www.aiaa.org

Annual. **Primary Exhibits:** Aerospace technologies.

★514★ Air Force Association Aerospace Technology Exposition

J. Spargo & Associates, Inc.
11212 Waples Mill Rd., Ste. 104
Fairfax, VA 22030
Ph: (703)631-6200   Fax: (703)818-9177
Fr: 800-564-4220
E-mail: info@jspargo.com
URL: http://www.jspargo.com

Annual. **Primary Exhibits:** Aerospace technology, airplanes, rockets, helicopters, radar, computers, software, and communications systems.

★515★ World Space Congress

American Institute of Aeronautics and
Astronautics (AIAA)
1801 Alexander Bell Dr., Ste. 500
Reston, VA 20191-4344
Ph: (703)264-7500   Fax: (703)264-7551
Fr: 800-639-AIAA
URL: http://www.aiaa.org

Primary Exhibits: Aerospace technologies.

OTHER SOURCES

★516★ American Association of Engineering Societies (AAES)

1620 I St. NW, Ste. 210
Washington, DC 20006
Ph: (202)296-2237   Fax: (202)296-1151
Fr: 888-400-2237
E-mail: dbateson@aaes.org
URL: http://www.aaes.org

Description: Coordinates the efforts of the member societies in the provision of reliable and objective information to the general public concerning issues which affect the engineering profession and the field of engineering as a whole; collects, analyzes, documents, and disseminates data which will inform the general public of the relationship between engineering and the national welfare; provides a forum for the engineering societies to exchange and discuss their views on matters of common interest; and represents the U.S. engineering community abroad through representation in WFEO and UPADI.

★517★ American Engineering Association (AEA)

4116 S Carrier Pkwy., Ste. 280-809
Grand Prairie, TX 75052
Ph: (201)664-6954
E-mail: info@aea.org
URL: http://www.aea.org

Description: Members consist of Engineers and engineering professionals. Purpose to advance the engineering profession and U.S. engineering capabilities. Issues of concern include age discrimination, immigration laws, displacement of U.S. Engineers by foreign workers, trade agreements, off shoring of U.S. Engineering and manufacturing jobs, loss of U.S. manufacturing and engineering capability, and recruitment of foreign students. Testifies before Congress. Holds local Chapter meetings.

★518★ Association for International Practical Training (AIPT)

10400 Little Patuxent Pkwy., Ste. 250
Columbia, MD 21044-3519
Ph: (410)997-2200   Fax: (410)992-3924
E-mail: aipt@aipt.org
URL: http://www.aipt.org

Description: Providers worldwide of on-the-job training programs for students and professionals seeking international career development and life-changing experiences. Arranges workplace exchanges in hundreds of professional fields, bringing employers and trainees together from around the world. Client list ranges from small farming communities to Fortune 500 companies.

★519★ Engineering Occupations

Delphi Productions
3159 6th St.
Boulder, CO 80304
Ph: (303)443-2100   Fax: (303)443-4022
Fr: 888-443-2400
E-mail: support@delphivideo.com
URL: http://www.delphivideo.com

$95.00. 50 minutes. Part of the Careers for the 21st Century Video Library.

★520★ High Frontier (HF)

500 N Washington St.
Alexandria, VA 22314-2314
Ph: (703)535-8774   Fax: (703)535-8776
E-mail: high.frontier@verizon.net
URL: http://www.highfrontier.org

Description: Represents scientists, space engineers, strategists and economists. Advocates the use of outer space for non nuclear commercial and military purposes. Seeks to open space for both economic and defensive military uses by the U.S. and its allies. Aims to provide protection for Americans and their property. The group advocates use of equipment currently in development. Maintains Speaker's Bureau; sponsors educational programs. Has produced High Frontier: A New National Strategy (television documentary show).

★521★ International Experimental Aerospace Society (IEAS)

14870 Granada Ave., No. 316
Apple Valley, MN 55124
Ph: (952)432-3918
E-mail: cab@ieas.org
URL: http://www.ieas.org

Description: Represents education and research societies of rocketry and space technology experimenters from around the world. Promotes experimental aerospace. Provides opportunities for exchange of information and coordination of services that will enable private individuals to safely engage in experimental aerospace activities. Assists and encourages regulatory authorities to permit safe experimental activities.

★522★ ISA - Instrumentation, Systems, and Automation Society

67 Alexander Dr.
PO Box 12277
Research Triangle Park, NC 27709
Ph: (919)549-8411   Fax: (919)549-8288
E-mail: info@isa.org
URL: http://www.isa.org

Description: Sets the standard for automation by helping over 30,000 worldwide members and other professionals solve difficult technical problems, while enhancing their leadership and personal career capabilities. Develops standards; certifies industry professionals; provides education and training; publishes books and technical articles; and hosts the largest conference and exhibition for automation professionals in the Western Hemisphere. Is the founding sponsor of The Automation Federation.

★523★ National Action Council for Minorities in Engineering (NACME)

440 Hamilton Ave., Ste. 302
White Plains, NY 10601-1813
Ph: (914)539-4010   Fax: (914)539-4032
E-mail: webmaster@nacme.org
URL: http://www.nacme.org

Description: Leads the national effort to increase access to careers in engineering and other science-based disciplines. Conducts research and public policy analysis, develops and operates national demonstration programs at precollege and university levels, and disseminates information through publications, conferences and electronic media. Serves as a privately funded source of scholarships for minority students in engineering.

★524★ National Society of Professional Engineers (NSPE)

1420 King St.
Alexandria, VA 22314-2794
Ph: (703)684-2800   Fax: (703)836-4875
Fr: 888-285-6773
E-mail: memserv@nspe.org
URL: http://www.nspe.org

Description: Represents professional engineers and engineers-in-training in all fields registered in accordance with the laws of states or territories of the U.S. or provinces of Canada; qualified graduate engineers, student members, and registered land surveyors. Is concerned with social, professional, ethical, and economic considerations of engineering as a profession; encompasses programs in public relations, employment practices, ethical considerations, education, and career guidance. Monitors legislative and regulatory actions of interest to the engineering profession.

★525★ Scientific, Engineering, and Technical Services

Cambridge Educational
PO Box 2053
Princeton, NJ 08543-2053
Ph: 800-257-5126   Fax: (609)671-0266
Fr: 800-468-4227
E-mail: custserv@films.com
URL: http://www.cambridgeeducational.com

VHS and DVD. $89.95. 2002. 18 minutes. 2002. Part of the Career Cluster Series.

★526★ Society of Women Engineers (SWE)

230 E Ohio St., Ste. 400
Chicago, IL 60611-3265
Ph: (312)596-5223   Fax: (312)596-5252
Fr: 877-SWE-INFO
E-mail: hq@swe.org

URL: http://www.swe.org

Description: Educational and service organization representing both students and professional women in engineering and technical fields.

★527★ **Women in Engineering**
Her Own Words
PO Box 5264
Madison, WI 53705-0264
Ph: (608)271-7083   Fax: (608)271-0209

E-mail: herownword@aol.com
URL: http://www.herownwords.com/

Video. Jocelyn Riley. $95.00. 15 minutes. Resource guide also available for $45.00.

Agricultural Engineers

★528★ AIE Perspectives Newsmagazine

American Institute of Engineers
4630 Appian Way, Ste. 206
El Sobrante, CA 94803-1875
Ph: (510)758-6240   Fax: (510)758-6240

Monthly. Professional magazine covering engineering.

★529★ Engineering Conferences International Symposium Series

Berkeley Electronic Press
2809 Telegraph Ave., Ste. 202
Berkeley, CA 94705
Ph: (510)665-1200   Fax: (510)665-1201
URL: http://services.bepress.com/eci/

Journal focusing on advance engineering science.

★530★ Engineering Times

National Society of Professional
  Engineers
1420 King St.
Alexandria, VA 22314
Ph: (703)684-2800
URL: http://www.nspe.org

Monthly. Magazine (tabloid) covering professional, legislative, and techology issues for an engineering audience.

★531★ Farmland News

Farmland News
104 Depot St.
PO Box 240
Archbold, OH 43502-0240
Ph: (419)445-9456   Fax: (419)445-4444

Weekly (Tues.). $27.00/year for individuals; $48.00 for two years. Rural human-interest newspaper (tabloid).

★532★ InterJournal

New England Complex Systems Institute
24 Mt. Auburn St.
Cambridge, MA 02138
Ph: (617)547-4100   Fax: (617)661-7711
URL: http://www.interjournal.org/

Journal covering the fields of science and engineering.

★533★ International Archives of Bioscience

International Archives of Bioscience
PO Box 737254
Elmhurst, NY 11373-9997
URL: http://www.iabs.us/jdoc/aboutiabs.htm

Free, online only. Journal reporting multidisciplinary coverage and interaction between scientists in biology, informatics, mathematics, physics, engineering and other sciences.

★534★ Journal of Agricultural Safety and Health

American Society of Agricultural
  Engineers
2950 Niles Rd.
St. Joseph, MI 49085
Ph: (269)429-0300   Fax: (269)429-3852

Quarterly. $63.00/year for members, print; $3.00/year for members, postage fees outside the U.S., print; $125.00/year for non-members, list price, print; $10.00/year for nonmembers, postage fees outside the U.S., print. Journal covering issues related to farm safety and health.

★535★ Journal of Crop Improvement

The Haworth Press Inc.
10 Alice St.
Binghamton, NY 13904
Ph: (607)722-5857   Fr: 800-429-6784
URL: http://www.haworthpress.com/store/product.asp?sid=PC3BHEAN6

Biennial. $80.00/year for individuals; $116.00/year for individuals, Canada; $124.00/year for individuals, elsewhere; $300.00/year for institutions, agency, library; $435.00/year for institutions, Canada, agency, library; $465.00/year for institutions, other countries, agency, library. Journal focus-ing on improvements in crop production productivity, quality, and safety to meet the food, feed, and fiber needs of an ever-growing world population.

★536★ Journal of Engineering Education

American Society for Engineering
  Education
1818 North St., NW, Ste. 600
Washington, DC 20036-2479
Ph: (202)331-3500
URL: http://www.asee.org/publications/jee/index.cfm

Quarterly. Journal covering scholarly research in engineering education.

★537★ The Journal of Southern Agricultural Education Research

American Association for Agricultural
  Education
c/o Robert A. Martin
Dept. of Agricultural Education & Studies
Iowa State University
201 Curtiss Hall
Ames, IA 50011
Ph: (515)294-0896   Fax: (515)294-0530
URL: http://aaae.okstate.edu/

Journal covering agricultural education.

★538★ NSBE Magazine

NSBE Publications
205 Daingerfield Rd.
Alexandria, VA 22314
Ph: (703)549-2207   Fax: (703)683-5312
URL: http://www.nsbe.org/publications/premieradvertisers.php

Journal providing information on engineering careers, self-development, and cultural issues for recent graduates with technical majors.

★539★ Resource

American Society of Agricultural
  Engineers
2950 Niles Rd.
St. Joseph, MI 49085
Ph: (269)429-0300   Fax: (269)429-3852

URL: http://www.asabe.org

$86.00/year for nonmembers, plus foreign postage; $7.50/year for nonmembers, single issue; $5.50/year for members, single issue; $20.00/year for students and preprofessionals; $32.00/year for students, graduates; $32.00/year for students, 2 years after graduation; $32.00/year for students, post-undergraduate; $90.00/year for members, aged 34 and under; $118.00/year for members, aged 35 to 64; $50.00/year for members, aged 65 to 74. Magazine covering technology for food and agriculture.

★540★ Scaffolds Fruit Journal

Cornell University New York State
 Agricultural Experiment Station
630 W North St.
Geneva, NY 14456
Ph: (315)787-2011
URL: http://www.nysaes.cornell.edu/ent/
scaffolds/2005/050912.html

Weekly. Magazine focusing on pest management and crop development.

**★541★ SWE, Magazine of the Society
of Women Engineers**

Society of Women Engineers
230 East Ohio St., Ste. 400
Chicago, IL 60611-3265
Ph: (312)596-5223
E-mail: hq@swe.org
URL: http://www.swe.org

Quarterly. $30.00/year for nonmembers. Magazine for engineering students and for women and men working in the engineering and technology fields. Covers career guidance, continuing development and topical issues.

★542★ The Technology Interface

New Mexico State University
College of Engineering
PO Box 30001
Las Cruces, NM 88003-8001
Ph: (505)646-0111
URL: http://engr.nmsu.edu/etti/

Journal for the engineering technology profession serving education and industry.

★543★ Uratie

IDG Communications Inc.
5 Speen St., 3rd. Fl
Framingham, MA 01701
Ph: (508)875-5000   Fax: (508)988-7888
URL: http://www.idg.com

Magazine providing job offers for graduates, engineers and information technology professionals.

PLACEMENT AND JOB REFERRAL SERVICES

**★544★ American Society of
Agricultural and Biological Engineers
(ASABE)**

2950 Niles Rd.
St. Joseph, MI 49085-8607
Ph: (269)429-0300   Fax: (269)429-3852
Fr: 800-371-2723
E-mail: hq@asabe.org
URL: http://www.asabe.org

Description: International professional and technical organization of individuals interested in engineering and technology for agriculture, food and biological systems. Publishes textbooks and journals. Develops engineering standards used in agriculture, food and biological systems. Sponsors technical meetings and continuing education programs. Maintains biographical archives and placement services. Sponsors competitions and special in-depth conferences. Maintains over 200 committees.

EMPLOYER DIRECTORIES AND NETWORKING LISTS

**★545★ Agricultural & Industrial
Manufacturers Representatives
Association-Membership Directory**

Agricultural & Industrial Manufacturers
 Representatives Association
7500 Flying Cloud Dr., Ste. 900
Eden Prairie, MN 55344-3756
Ph: (952)253-6230   Fax: (952)835-4774
Fr: (866)759-2467
URL: http://www.aimrareps.org

Annual, October. Covers 120 members; coverage includes Canada. Entries include: Company name, address, phone, name of principal executive, territory covered. Arrangement: Alphabetical.

★546★ Careers in Focus: Engineering

Facts On File Inc.
132 W 31st St., 17th Fl.
New York, NY 10001
Ph: (212)967-8800   Fax: 800-678-3633
Fr: 800-322-8755
URL: http://www.factsonfile.com

3rd edition, 2007. $29.95 for individuals; $26.95 for libraries. Publication includes: List of resources to consult for more information. Principal content of publication consists of job descriptions, advancement opportunities, educational requirements, employment outlook, salary information, and working conditions for careers in the field of engineering. Indexes: Alphabetical.

**★547★ Indiana Society of Professional
Engineers-Directory**

Indiana Society of Professional Engineers
PO Box 20806
Indianapolis, IN 46220
Ph: (317)255-2267   Fax: (317)255-2530
URL: http://www.indspe.org

Annual, fall. Covers member registered engineers, land surveyors, engineering students, and engineers in training. Entries include: Member name, address, phone, type of membership, business information, specialty. Arrangement: Alphabetical by chapter area.

HANDBOOKS AND MANUALS

**★548★ Choosing a Career in
Agriculture**

Rosen Publishing Group, Inc.
29 E. 21st St.
New York, NY 10010
Ph: (212)777-3017   Fax: (212)777-0277
Fr: 800-237-9932
URL: http://www.rosenpublishing.com/

Olesky, Walter. 2001. $29.25. 64 pages.

**★549★ Great Jobs for Engineering
Majors**

The McGraw-Hill Companies
PO Box 182604
Columbus, OH 43272
Fax: (614)759-3749   Fr: 877-883-5524
E-mail: customer.service@mcgraw-hill.com
URL: http://www.mcgraw-hill.com

Geraldine O. Garner. Second edition, 2002. $14.95. 256 pages. Covers all the career options open to students majoring in engineering.

★550★ Keys to Engineering Success

Prentice Hall PTR
One Lake St.
Upper Saddle River, NJ 07458
Ph: (201)236-7000   Fr: 800-428-5331
URL: http://www.phptr.com/index.asp?rl=1

Jill S. Tietjen, Kristy A. Schloss, Carol Carter, Joyce Bishop, and Sarah Lyman. 2000. $46.00 (paper). 288 pages.

**★551★ Opportunities in Agriculture
Careers**

The McGraw-Hill Companies
PO Box 182604
Columbus, OH 43272
Fax: (614)759-3749   Fr: 877-883-5524
E-mail: customer.service@mcgraw-hill.com
URL: http://www.mcgraw-hill.com

William C. White and Donald N. Collins. 1987. $13.95. 150 pages.

★552★ Workforce Management for Farms and Horticultural Businesses: Finding, Training and Keeping Good Employees

Natural Resource, Agricultural & Engineering Service
Cornell University
152 Riley Robb Hall
Ithaca, NY 14853-5170
Ph: (607)255-7654   Fax: (607)254-8770
1999. $15.00 (paper). 140 pages.

EMPLOYMENT AGENCIES AND SEARCH FIRMS

★553★ AGRI-Associates
116 W. 47th St
Kansas City, MO 64112
Ph: (816)531-7980   Fax: (816)531-7982
Fr: 800-550-7980
E-mail: gip@agriassociates.com
URL: http://www.agriassociates.com
Agribusiness executive search firm.

★554★ Agri-Personnel
5120 Old Bill Cook Rd.
Atlanta, GA 30349-0319
Ph: (404)768-5701   Fax: (404)768-5705
Agribusiness consultants active in executive/professional/technical recruitment and placement, and in mergers, acquisitions, and divestitures in various industries including dairy, feed, food, fertilizer, farm chemicals, poultry and egg, animal health, and pulp and paper.

★555★ Boyle & Associates Retained Search Group
PO Box 16658
St. Paul, MN 55116
Ph: (651)223-5050   Fax: (651)699-5378
E-mail: paul@talenthunt.com
URL: http://www.talenthunt.com
Executive search firm.

★556★ The Chase Group Inc.
10955 Lowell Ave., Ste. 500
Overland Park, KS 66210
Ph: (913)663-3100   Fax: (913)663-3131
E-mail: chase@chasegroup.com
URL: http://www.chasegroup.com
Executive search firm in the life sciences industries.

★557★ Emplex Associates
10051 E. Highland Rd. Ste. 29-353
Howell, MI 48843
Ph: (517)548-2800   Fr: 888-203-1010
E-mail: emplex@emplexcorp.com
URL: http://www.emplexcorp.com
Executive search firm.

★558★ First Search America Inc.
26746 Main St.
Ardmore, AL 35739
Ph: (256)423-8800   Fax: (256)423-8801
Fr: 800-468-9214
E-mail: firstsearch@ardmore.net
URL: http://www.firstsearchamerica.com
Executive search firm.

★559★ Florasearch, Inc.
1740 Lake Markham Rd.
Sanford, FL 32771
Ph: (407)320-8177   Fax: (407)320-8083
E-mail: search@florasearch.com
URL: http://www.florasearch.com
Employment agency for the horticulture industry.

★560★ The Jack De Jong Group
3763 W. Hardydale
Tucson, AZ 85742
Ph: (520)579-2848   Fax: (520)579-5293
URL: http://www.jackdejonggroup.com/
Agribusiness executive search firm.

★561★ Management Recruiters of Spencer
589 Hwy. 71 S
PO Box 840
Arnolds Park, IA 51331
Ph: (712)332-2011   Fax: (712)332-2051
Executive search firm.

★562★ Miller & Associates Inc.
9036 NW 37th St.
Polk City, IA 50226
Ph: (515)965-5727   Fax: (515)965-5794
Fr: 888-965-2727
E-mail: rmiller@ag-careers.com
URL: http://www.ag-careers.com
Agricultural personnel agency.

★563★ The Montgomery Group Inc.
PO Box 30791
Knoxville, TN 37930-0791
Ph: (865)693-0325   Fax: (865)691-1900
E-mail: tmg@tmgincknox.com
URL: http://www.tmgincknox.com
Executive search firm for the food and agribusiness industries.

★564★ MRI of Williamsburg
600 Court St.
PO Box 1136
Williamsburg, IA 52361-1136
Ph: (319)668-2881   Fax: (319)668-1404
E-mail: info@wburgcareers.com
URL: http://www.wburgcareers.com
Executive search firm.

★565★ PERC Ltd.
4140 E. Vernon Ave.
Phoenix, AZ 85008
Ph: (602)553-9896   Fax: (602)553-9897
Fr: 800-874-7246
E-mail: gordonstoa@qwest.net
Executive search firm.

★566★ Robert Connelly & Associates Inc.
520 Wilson Rd
Minneapolis, MN 55424
Ph: (952)925-3039   Fax: (952)922-3762
E-mail: INFO@robertconnelly.com
URL: http://www.robertconnelly.com
Executive search firm.

★567★ Robert Drexler Associates Inc.
PO Box 151
Saddle River, NJ 07458
Ph: (201)760-2300   Fax: (201)760-2301
E-mail: drexler@engineeringemployment.com
URL: http://www.engineeringemployment.com
Executive search firm.

★568★ Search North America Inc.
PO Box 3577
Sunriver, OR 97707-0577
Ph: (503)222-6461   Fax: (503)227-2804
E-mail: mylinda@searchna.com
URL: http://www.searchna.com
An executive search and recruiting firm whose focus is placing engineers, operations and maintenance managers, sales and marketing management, financial and general management executives (both domestic and international). Industries served: forest products, pulp and paper, waste to energy, environmental services, consulting and equipment suppliers for above related industries.

★569★ Sherwood Lehman Massucco Inc.
3455 W Shaw Ave., Ste. 110
Fresno, CA 93711-3201
Ph: (559)276-8572   Fax: (559)276-2351
E-mail: slinc@employmentexpert.com
URL: http://www.employmentexpert.com
Executive search firm.

★570★ Smith, Brown & Jones
7304 W. 130th St., Ste. 300
Overland Park, KS 66213
Ph: (913)814-7770   Fax: (913)814-8440
E-mail: dlsmith@smithbrownjones.com
URL: http://www.smithbrownjones.com
Executive search firm.

★571★ **Smith & Laue Search**

1 Centerpointe Dr.
Lake Oswego, OR 97035
Ph: (503)460-9181   Fax: (503)460-9182
E-mail: chuck@smithlaue.com

Executive search firm.

★572★ **Spencer Stuart**

401 N Michigan Ave., Ste. 3400
Chicago, IL 60611
Ph: (312)822-0080   Fax: (312)822-0116
URL: http://www.spencerstuart.com

Executive search firm.

★573★ **Steven Douglas Associates Retainer Division**

3040 Universal Blvd., Ste. 190
Weston, FL 33331
Ph: (954)385-8595   Fax: (954)385-1414
E-mail: Sabrina@stevendouglas.com
URL: http://www.stevendouglas.com

Executive search firm.

★574★ **Tom Allison Associates**

625 Stagecoach Rd. SE
Rio Rancho, NM 87124
Ph: (505)275-7771   Fax: (505)275-7771
E-mail: tallison@spinn.net

Executive search firm.

★575★ **Trambley the Recruiter**

5325 Wyoming Blvd. NE
Albuquerque, NM 87109-3132
Ph: (505)821-5440   Fax: (505)821-8509

Personnel consultancy firm recruits and places engineering professionals in specific areas of off-road equipment design and manufacturing. Industries served: construction, agricultural, lawn and garden, oil exploration and mining equipment manufacturing.

OTHER SOURCES

★576★ **American Engineering Association (AEA)**

4116 S Carrier Pkwy., Ste. 280-809
Grand Prairie, TX 75052
Ph: (201)664-6954
E-mail: info@aea.org
URL: http://www.aea.org

Description: Members consist of Engineers and engineering professionals. Purpose to advance the engineering profession and U.S. engineering capabilities. Issues of concern include age discrimination, immigration laws, displacement of U.S. Engineers by foreign workers, trade agreements, off shoring of U.S. Engineering and manufacturing jobs, loss of U.S. manufacturing and engineering capability, and recruitment of foreign students. Testifies before Congress. Holds local Chapter meetings.

★577★ **Council for Agricultural Science and Technology (CAST)**

4420 W Lincoln Way
Ames, IA 50014-3447
Ph: (515)292-2125   Fax: (515)292-4512
E-mail: info@cast-science.org
URL: http://www.cast-science.org

Members: Scientific societies, associate societies, individuals, corporations, foundations, and trade associations. **Purpose:** Promotes science-based information on food, fiber, agricultural, natural resource, and related societal and environmental issues.

★578★ **Engineering Occupations**

Delphi Productions
3159 6th St.
Boulder, CO 80304
Ph: (303)443-2100   Fax: (303)443-4022
Fr: 888-443-2400

E-mail: support@delphivideo.com
URL: http://www.delphivideo.com

$95.00. 50 minutes. Part of the Careers for the 21st Century Video Library.

★579★ **Growing Opportunities: Careers in Agriculture**

JIST Publishing
875 Montreal Way
St. Paul, MN 55102
Fax: 800-547-8329   Fr: 800-648-5478
E-mail: info@jist.com
URL: http://www.jist.com

2004. $99. 23 minutes. Video includes thumbnail descriptions of 23 careers that exist in the agricultural industry.

★580★ **Scientific, Engineering, and Technical Services**

Cambridge Educational
PO Box 2053
Princeton, NJ 08543-2053
Ph: 800-257-5126   Fax: (609)671-0266
Fr: 800-468-4227
E-mail: custserv@films.com
URL: http://www.cambridgeeducational.com

VHS and DVD. $89.95. 2002. 18 minutes. 2002. Part of the Career Cluster Series.

★581★ **Women in Engineering**

Her Own Words
PO Box 5264
Madison, WI 53705-0264
Ph: (608)271-7083   Fax: (608)271-0209
E-mail: herownword@aol.com
URL: http://www.herownwords.com/

Video. Jocelyn Riley. $95.00. 15 minutes. Resource guide also available for $45.00.

Agricultural Scientists

SOURCES OF HELP-WANTED ADS

★582★ AgBiotech Reporter
Agra Informa Inc.
2302 W 1st St.
Cedar Falls, IA 50613-1879
Ph: (319)277-3599   Fax: (319)277-3783
Fr: 800-959-3276
E-mail: marketing@agra-net.com
URL: http://www.agra-net.com

Description: Monthly. Concerned with the business and technical aspects of agricultural biotechnology internationally. Offers news items, reviews of producteports of meetings, and news of educational opportunities.

★583★ Agricultural Research Magazine
U.S. Department of Agriculture
Economic Research Service
1800 M St. NW, Rm. N4165
Washington, DC 20036-5831
Ph: (202)694-5110
URL: http://www.ars.usda.gov/

Monthly. $50.00/year for individuals; $70.00/year international. Magazine on agricultural research.

★584★ Agriculture & Food
National Technical Information Service
5285 Port Royal Rd.
Springfield, VA 22161
Ph: (703)605-6585   Fax: (703)605-6900
Fr: 888-584-8332
E-mail: info@ntis.gov
URL: http://www.ntis.gov/new/alerts_print-ed.asp

Description: Biweekly. Publishes abstracts of reports on agricultural chemistry, agricultural equipment, facilities, and operations. Also covers agronomy, horticulture, and plant pathology; fisheries and aquaculture; animal husbandry and veterinary medicine; and food technology. Also available via e-mail.

★585★ American Journal of Alternative Agriculture
Henry A. Wallace Institute for Alternative Agriculture
9200 Edmonston Rd., Ste. 117
Greenbelt, MD 20770-4575
Ph: (301)441-8777   Fax: (301)220-0164
URL: http://eap.mcgill.ca/MagRack/AJAA/ajaa_ind.htm

Quarterly. $24.00/year for individuals, U.S.; $26.00/year for individuals, Canada & Mexico; $28.00/year for individuals, other countries; $44.00/year for institutions, U.S.; $46.00/year for institutions, Canada & Mexico; $48.00/year for institutions, other countries; $12.00/year for students, U.S.; $14.00/year for students, Canada & Mexico; $16.00/year for students, other countries. Journal covering agricultural science.

★586★ Cell
Cell Press
600 Technology Sq.
Cambridge, MA 02139
Ph: (617)661-7057   Fax: (617)661-7061
Fr: (866)314-2355
E-mail: advertising@cell.com
URL: http://www.cell.com

$179.00/year for U.S. and Canada, individual, print and online; $269.00/year for other countries, individual, print and online; $179.00/year for U.S. and Canada, online only, individual; $179.00/year for other countries, online only, individual; $997.00/year for U.S. and Canada, institutions; $1122.00/year for institutions, other countries, print. Journal on molecular and cell biology.

★587★ CSANews
American Society of Agronomy
677 S Segoe Rd.
Madison, WI 53711
Ph: (608)273-8080   Fax: (608)273-2021
E-mail: news@agronomy.org
URL: http://www.asa-cssa-sssa.org

Description: Monthly. Publishes information on agronomy, crop science, soil science, and related topics. Provides news of the societies and members; reports of annual meetings; listings of publications; announcements of awards, retirements, and deaths; job listings; and a calendar of events.

★588★ Culture and Agriculture
American Anthropological Association
2200 Wilson Blvd., Ste. 600
Arlington, VA 22201
Ph: (703)528-1902   Fax: (703)528-3546
URL: http://www.aaanet.org/

Description: Quarterly. Provides information on agriculture and related policies and practices and the consequences they have on the environment and human life.

★589★ Farmland News
Farmland News
104 Depot St.
PO Box 240
Archbold, OH 43502-0240
Ph: (419)445-9456   Fax: (419)445-4444

Weekly (Tues.). $27.00/year for individuals; $48.00 for two years. Rural human-interest newspaper (tabloid).

★590★ Feedstuffs
Miller Publishing Co.
12400 Whitewater Dr., Ste. 160
Minnetonka, MN 55343
Ph: (952)931-0211   Fax: (952)938-1832
URL: http://www.feedstuffs.com/ME2/Default.asp

Weekly. $144.00/year for individuals; $230.00 for two years; $150.00/year for Canada; $235.00/year Europe and Middle East, airmail; $280.00/year for other countries, Japan, Far East/Australia airmail; $210.00/year Mexico/Central/South America; $196.00/year print and internet version; $334.00 for two years, print and internet version; $202.00/year for Canada, print and internet version; $287.00/year Europe/Middle East by air/print and internet version. Magazine serving the grain and feed industries and animal agriculture.

★591★ ICASA News

International Consortium for Agricultural Systems Applications
2440 Campus Rd.
PO Box 527
Honolulu, HI 96822
Ph: (808)956-2713   Fax: (808)956-2711
E-mail: icasa@icasa.net
URL: http://www.icasa.net

Description: 2/year. Reports on the development and application of system simulation products and tools for agricultural production. Recurring features include news of research and a calendar of events.

★592★ Journal of Agricultural & Food Industrial Organization

Berkeley Electronic Press
2809 Telegraph Ave., Ste. 202
Berkeley, CA 94705
Ph: (510)665-1200   Fax: (510)665-1201
E-mail: info@bepress.com
URL: http://www.bepress.com/jafio/

$250.00/year academic; $750.00/year corporate. Journal dealing with the research in industrial organization mainly focusing on the agricultural and food industry worldwide.

★593★ Journal of Crop Improvement

The Haworth Press Inc.
10 Alice St.
Binghamton, NY 13904
Ph: (607)722-5857   Fr: 800-429-6784
URL: http://www.haworthpress.com/store/product.asp?sid=PC3BHEAN6

Biennial. $80.00/year for individuals; $116.00/year for individuals, Canada; $124.00/year for individuals, elsewhere; $300.00/year for institutions, agency, library; $435.00/year for institutions, Canada, agency, library; $465.00/year for institutions, other countries, agency, library. Journal focusing on improvements in crop production productivity, quality, and safety to meet the food, feed, and fiber needs of an ever-growing world population.

★594★ The Journal of Southern Agricultural Education Research

American Association for Agricultural Education
c/o Robert A. Martin
Dept. of Agricultural Education & Studies
Iowa State University
201 Curtiss Hall
Ames, IA 50011
Ph: (515)294-0896   Fax: (515)294-0530
URL: http://aaae.okstate.edu/

Journal covering agricultural education.

★595★ Journal of Vegetable Science

The Haworth Press Inc.
10 Alice St.
Binghamton, NY 13904
Ph: (607)722-5857   Fr: 800-429-6784
URL: http://www.haworthpress.com/store/product.asp?sid=3CXTKNPDX

Quarterly. $48.00/year for individuals; $260.00/year for institutions, agency, library; $70.00/year for Canada, individual; $377.00/year for institutions, Canada, agency, library; $74.00/year for other countries, individual; $403.00/year for institutions, other countries, agency, library. Journal focusing on all aspects of vegetable science from land preparation to consumption.

★596★ Nature International Weekly Journal of Science

Nature Publishing Group
75 Varick St., 9th Fl.
New York, NY 10013-1917
Ph: (212)726-9200   Fax: (212)696-9006
Fr: 888-331-6288
E-mail: nature@natureny.com
URL: http://www.nature.com

Weekly. $145.00/year for individuals; $49.00/year for institutions. Magazine covering science and technology, including the fields of biology, biochemistry, genetics, medicine, earth sciences, physics, pharmacology, and behavioral sciences.

★597★ NewsCAST

Council for Agricultural Science & Technology
4420 W Lincoln Way
Ames, IA 50014-3447
Ph: (515)292-2125   Fax: (515)292-4512
E-mail: info@cast-science.org
URL: http://www.cast-science.org/cast/src/cast_newscast.php

Description: Semiannual. Serves a consortium of food and agricultural science societies, which promotes understanding by providing a background in agricultural science and technology. Carries features of interest to food and agricultural scientists and news of the organization's activities and programs. Recurring features include announcements of available publications and honors awarded; and a progress report on the work of authorized task forces.

★598★ Resource

American Society of Agricultural Engineers
2950 Niles Rd.
St. Joseph, MI 49085
Ph: (269)429-0300   Fax: (269)429-3852
URL: http://www.asabe.org

$86.00/year for nonmembers, plus foreign postage; $7.50/year for nonmembers, single issue; $5.50/year for members, single issue; $20.00/year for students and preprofessionals; $32.00/year for students, graduates; $32.00/year for students, 2 years after graduation; $32.00/year for students, post-undergraduate; $90.00/year for members, aged 34 and under; $118.00/year for members, aged 35 to 64; $50.00/year for members, aged 65 to 74. Magazine covering technology for food and agriculture.

★599★ Scaffolds Fruit Journal

Cornell University New York State Agricultural Experiment Station
630 W North St.
Geneva, NY 14456
Ph: (315)787-2011
URL: http://www.nysaes.cornell.edu/ent/scaffolds/2005/050912.html

Weekly. Magazine focusing on pest management and crop development.

★600★ The Scientist

The Scientist Inc.
400 Market St., No. 1250
Philadelphia, PA 19106
Ph: (215)351-1660   Fax: (215)351-1146
URL: http://www.the-scientist.com

Bimonthly. $49.95/year for individuals, online; $74.95/year for individuals, online plus print edition; $124.95/year for out of country, online plus print edition (air freight); $29.95/year for individuals; $19.95 for individuals, 6 months; $14.95 for individuals, 1 month; $9.95 for individuals, 1 week; $4.95 for individuals, 1 week. News journal (tabloid) for life scientists featuring news, opinions, research, and professional section.

PLACEMENT AND JOB REFERRAL SERVICES

★601★ American Society of Agronomy (ASA)

677 S Segoe Rd.
Madison, WI 53711
Ph: (608)273-8080   Fax: (608)273-2021
E-mail: headquarters@agronomy.org
URL: http://www.agronomy.org

Description: Professional society of agronomists, plant breeders, physiologists, soil scientists, chemists, educators, technicians, and others concerned with crop production and soil management, and conditions affecting them. Sponsors fellowship program and student essay and speech contests. Provides placement service.

★602★ Association of Applied IPM Ecologists (AAIE)

PO Box 12181
Fresno, CA 93776
Ph: (559)907-4897
E-mail: director@aaie.net

Description: Professional agricultural pest management consultants, entomologists, and field personnel. Promotes the implementation of integrated pest management in agricultural and urban environments. Provides a forum for the exchange of technical information on pest control. Offers placement service.

★603★ Federation of American Societies for Experimental Biology (FASEB)

9650 Rockville Pike
Bethesda, MD 20814
Ph: (301)634-7000   Fax: (301)634-7001
E-mail: membershipdirectoryinfo@faseb.org
URL: http://www.faseb.org

Description: Federation of scientific societies with a total of 40,000 members: the American Physiological Society; American Society for Biochemistry and Molecular Biology; American Society for Pharmacology and Experimental Therapeutics; American Society for Investigative Pathology; American Society for Nutritional Sciences; the American Association of Immunologists; the American Society for Bone and Mineral Research; American Society for Clinical Investigation; the Indocrine Society; the American Society of Human Genetics; Society for Developmental Biology; Biophysical Society; American Association of Anatomists; and the Protein Society. **Activities:** Maintains placement service.

★604★ Korean-American Scientists and Engineers Association (KSEA)

1952 Gallows Rd., Ste. 300
Vienna, VA 22182
Ph: (703)748-1221   Fax: (703)748-1331
E-mail: admin@ksea.org
URL: http://www.ksea.org

Description: Represents scientists and engineers holding single or advanced degrees. Promotes friendship and mutuality among Korean and American scientists and engineers; contributes to Korea's scientific, technological, industrial, and economic developments; strengthens the scientific, technological, and cultural bonds between Korea and the U.S. Sponsors symposium. Maintains speakers' bureau, placement service, and biographical archives. Compiles statistics.

EMPLOYER DIRECTORIES AND NETWORKING LISTS

★605★ Agricultural & Industrial Manufacturers Representatives Association-Membership Directory

Agricultural & Industrial Manufacturers Representatives Association
7500 Flying Cloud Dr., Ste. 900
Eden Prairie, MN 55344-3756
Ph: (952)253-6230   Fax: (952)835-4774
Fr: (866)759-2467
URL: http://www.aimrareps.org

Annual, October. Covers 120 members; coverage includes Canada. Entries include: Company name, address, phone, name of principal executive, territory covered. Arrangement: Alphabetical.

★606★ American Men and Women of Science

Gale, Cengage Learning
27500 Drake Rd.
Farmington Hills, MI 48331-3535
Ph: (248)699-4253   Fax: (248)699-8065
Fr: 800-877-4253
URL: http://www.gale.com

Biennial, latest edition 23rd, October 2006; new edition expected 24th, January 2008. $1,075.00 for individuals. Covers over 129,700 U.S. and Canadian scientists active in the physical, biological, mathematical, computer science, and engineering fields; includes references to previous edition for deceased scientists and nonrespondents. Entries include: Name, address, education, personal and career data, memberships, honors and awards, research interest. Arrangement: Alphabetical. Indexes: Discipline (in separate volume).

★607★ Career Opportunities in Science

Facts On File Inc.
132 W 31st St., 17th Fl.
New York, NY 10001
Ph: (212)967-8800   Fax: 800-678-3633
Fr: 800-322-8755
URL: http://www.factsonfile.com

Published 2003. $49.50 for individuals; $44.55 for libraries. Covers more than 80 jobs, such as biochemist, molecular biologist, bioinformatic specialist, pharmacologist, computer engineer, geographic information systems specialist, science teacher, forensic scientist, patent agent, as well as physicist, astronomer, chemist, zoologist, oceanographer, and geologist.

★608★ Colorado Agricultural Outlook Forum Directory

Colorado Department of Agriculture
700 Kipling St., Ste. 4000
Lakewood, CO 80215-8000
Ph: (303)239-4114   Fax: (303)239-4125
URL: http://www.state.co.us/

Latest edition 2004. Covers groups involved with agriculture in Colorado including agricultural associations in Colorado and nationally, Colorado land trusts, state government agencies, federal government agencies, congressional offices of Colorado senators and representatives, farm/ranch management assistance groups, Colorado State University (CSU) research centers and cooperative extension offices by county, and Future Farmers of America (FFA) high school chapters. Entries include: Name, address, phone, fax, and URL. For CSU and FFA information–Name, phone number. Arrangement: By category, then alphabetical.

★609★ Directory of State Departments of Agriculture

U.S. Department of Agriculture
1400 Independence Ave. SW, Rm. 3077-S
PO Box 0201
Washington, DC 20250-0201
Ph: (202)720-4276   Fax: (202)720-8477

URL: http://www.ams.usda.gov

Biennial, late summer of odd years. Free. Covers state departments of agriculture and their officials. Entries include: Department name, address, phone, names and titles of key personnel, department branches. Arrangement: Geographical.

★610★ Peterson's Job Opportunities in Engineering and Technology

Peterson's Guides
2000 Lenox Dr.
Box 67005
Lawrenceville, NJ 08648
Ph: (609)896-1800   Fax: (609)896-4531
Fr: 800-338-3282
E-mail: custsvc@petersons.com
URL: http://www.petersons.com

Compiled by the Peterson's staff. Fourth edition, 1996. $21.95 (paper). 379 pages. Profiles 2,000 high-tech companies looking primarily for technical personnel in such fields as biotechnology, telecommunications, software, computers and peripherals, defense, and aerospace. Contains job-search strategies and career options to help match education and expertise to the job market. Indexed geographically, by industry, and by hiring needs.

HANDBOOKS AND MANUALS

★611★ The Best Resumes for Scientists and Engineers

John Wiley & Sons Inc.
1 Wiley Dr.
Somerset, NJ 08873
Ph: (732)469-4400   Fax: (732)302-2300
Fr: 800-225-5945
E-mail: custserv@wiley.com
URL: http://www.wiley.com/WileyCDA/

Adele Lewis and David J. Moore. Second edition, 1993. $37.50; $19.95 (paper). 224 pages. Presents an extensive collection of scientific and engineering resumes, highlighting the important differences between these and resumes written for other occupations.

★612★ Careers in Health Care

The McGraw-Hill Companies
PO Box 182604
Columbus, OH 43272
Fax: (614)759-3749   Fr: 877-883-5524
E-mail: customer.service@mcgraw-hill.com
URL: http://www.mcgraw-hill.com

Barbara M. Swanson. Fifth edition, 2005. $15.95 (paper). 192 pages. Describes job duties, work settings, salaries, licensing and certification requirements, educational preparation, and future outlook. Gives ideas on how to secure a job.

★613★ Guide to Nontraditional Careers in Science

Taylor & Francis
325 Chestnut St., 8th Fl.
Philadelphia, PA 19106
Ph: (215)625-8900   Fax: (215)269-0363
Fr: 800-821-8312
URL: http://www.taylorandfrancis.com

Karen Young Kreeger. 1998. $45.95 (paper). Guidebook aids the reader in evaluating and finding career opportunities in non-academic research fields. 263 pages.

★614★ Math for Soil Scientists

Cengage Learning
PO Box 6904
Florence, KY 41022
Fax: 800-487-8488   Fr: 800-354-9706
URL: http://www.cengage.com/

Mark S. Coyne and James A. Thompson. 2005. $31.95. Soil science students and practitioners are offered a review of basic mathematical operations in the field.

★615★ Opportunities in Agriculture Careers

The McGraw-Hill Companies
PO Box 182604
Columbus, OH 43272
Fax: (614)759-3749   Fr: 877-883-5524
E-mail: customer.service@mcgraw-hill.com
URL: http://www.mcgraw-hill.com

William C. White and Donald N. Collins. 1987. $13.95. 150 pages.

★616★ Opportunities in Environmental Careers

The McGraw-Hill Companies
PO Box 182604
Columbus, OH 43272
Fax: (614)759-3749   Fr: 877-883-5524
E-mail: customer.service@mcgraw-hill.com
URL: http://www.mcgraw-hill.com

Odom Fanning. Revised, 2002. $12.95 (paper). 174 pages. Describes a broad range of opportunities in fields such as environmental health, recreation, physics, and hygiene, and provides job search advice. Part of the "Opportunities in ..." Series.

★617★ Opportunities in Research and Development Careers

The McGraw-Hill Companies
PO Box 182604
Columbus, OH 43272
Fax: (614)759-3749   Fr: 877-883-5524
E-mail: customer.service@mcgraw-hill.com
URL: http://www.mcgraw-hill.com

Jan Goldberg. 1996. $11.95 (paper). 146 pages.

★618★ Resumes for Scientific and Technical Careers

The McGraw-Hill Companies
PO Box 182604
Columbus, OH 43272
Fax: (614)759-3749   Fr: 877-883-5524

E-mail: customer.service@mcgraw-hill.com
URL: http://www.mcgraw-hill.com

Third edition, 2007. $12.95 (paper). 144 pages. Provides resume advice for individuals interested in working in scientific and technical careers. Includes sample resumes and cover letters.

★619★ To Boldly Go: A Practical Career Guide for Scientists

Amer Global Pub
2000 Florida Ave., NW
Washington, DC 20009
Ph: (202)462-6900   Fax: (202)328-0566
Fr: 800-966-2481

Peter S. Fiske. 1996. $19.00 (paper). 188 pages.

EMPLOYMENT AGENCIES AND SEARCH FIRMS

★620★ Agra Placements, Ltd.

8435 University Ave., Ste. 6
Des Moines, IA 50325
Ph: (515)225-6563   Fax: (515)225-7733
Fr: 888-696-5624
E-mail: careers@agrapl.com
URL: http://www.agraplacements.com

Executive search firm. Branch offices in Peru, IN, Lincoln, IL, Andover, KS and Madison, SD.

★621★ Management Search, Inc.

3013 NW 59th St.
Oklahoma City, OK 73112
Ph: (405)842-3173   Fax: (405)842-8360
E-mail: dorwig@mgmtsearch.com
URL: http://www.mgmtsearch.com

Executive search firm specializing in the field of agri-business.

TRADESHOWS

★622★ Agri News Farm Show

Agri News Farm Show
PO Box 6118
18 1st Ave. SE
Rochester, MN 55903-6118
Ph: (507)285-7600   Fax: (507)281-7436
Fr: 800-533-1727
URL: http://www.agrinews.com

Annual. **Primary Exhibits:** Agricultural equipment, supplies, and services.

★623★ American Feed Industry Association Feed Industries Show

American Feed Industry Association
1501 Wilson Blvd., Ste. 1100
Arlington, VA 22209
Ph: (703)524-0810   Fax: (703)524-1921
E-mail: afia@afia.org
URL: http://www.afia.org/

Biennial. **Primary Exhibits:** Feed equipment, services, and ingredients.

★624★ Empire Farm Days

Empire State Potato Growers, Inc.
PO Box 566
Stanley, NY 14561
Ph: (585)526-5326   Fax: (716)526-6576
Fr: 877-697-7837
E-mail: mwickham@empirepotatogrowers.com
URL: http://www.empirepotatogrowers.com

Annual. **Primary Exhibits:** Agricultural equipment, supplies, and services.

★625★ Farm Progress Show

Farm Progress Companies, Inc.
191 S. Gary Ave.
Carol Stream, IL 60188-2095
Ph: (319)622-6090   Fax: (630)588-2081
Fr: (866)264-7469
E-mail: dtourte@farmprogress.com
URL: http://www.farmprogressshow.com

Annual. **Primary Exhibits:** Farm machinery and equipment, trucks, livestock equipment, buildings, seed, chemicals, computers, and other agricultural products and services.

★626★ Mid-America Farm Show

Salina Area Chamber of Commerce
120 W Ash
PO Box 586
Salina, KS 67402-0586
Ph: (785)827-9301
URL: http://www.salinakansas.org

Annual. **Primary Exhibits:** Agricultural equipment, supplies, and services, including irrigation equipment, fertilizer, farm implements, hybrid seed, agricultural chemicals, tractors, feed, farrowing crates and equipment, silos and bins, storage equipment, and farm buildings.

★627★ Mid-South Farm and Gin Supply Exhibit

Southern Cotton Ginners Association
874 Cotton Gin Pl.
Memphis, TN 38106
Ph: (901)947-3104   Fax: (901)947-3103
E-mail: carmen.griffin@southerncottonginners.org
URL: http://www.southerncottonginners.org

Annual. **Primary Exhibits:** Agricultural equipment, supplies and services.

★628★ Midwest Farm Show

North Country Enterprises LLC
PO Box 832
Chippewa Falls, WI 54729
Ph: (715)723-2775   Fax: (715)723-2775

Annual. **Primary Exhibits:** Farm materials handling equipment, supplies, and services.

★629★ National Western Stock Show and Rodeo

The Western Stock Show Association
4655 Humboldt St.
Denver, CO 80216
Ph: (303)297-1166   Fax: (303)292-1708
Fr: 800-336-6977
URL: http://www.nationalwestern.com

Annual. **Primary Exhibits:** Jewelry, apparel, household goods, agricultural products, and service groups. A great blend of agriculture, western and urban products including agriculture equipment, supplies and services, horse items, household products, apparel, jewelry, buildings, children's' items, art, food and tools.

★630★ North American Farm and Power Show

Tradexpos, Inc.
811 Oakland Ave. W
PO Box 1067
Austin, MN 55912
Ph: (507)437-4697   Fax: (507)437-8917
Fr: 800-347-5225
E-mail: tradexpo@smig.net
URL: http://www.tradexpos.com

Annual. **Primary Exhibits:** Farm equipment, supplies, and services; lawn and garden equipment; industrial equipment.

★631★ Northwest Agricultural Show

Northwest Horticultural Congress
4672 Drift Creek Rd. SE
Sublimity, OR 97385
Ph: (503)769-7120   Fax: (503)769-3549

Annual. **Primary Exhibits:** Agricultural equipment and services.

★632★ Triumph of Agriculture Exposition - Farm and Ranch Machinery Show

Mid-America Expositions, Inc.
7015 Spring St.
Omaha, NE 68106-3518
Ph: (402)346-8003   Fax: (402)346-5412
Fr: 800-475-SHOW
E-mail: showoffice@aol.com
URL: http://www.showofficeonline.com

Annual. **Primary Exhibits:** Farm equipment and supplies.

★633★ Western Farm Show

Western Retail Implement and Hardware Association
PO Box 419264
Kansas City, MO 64141-6264
Ph: (816)561-5323   Fax: (816)561-1249

URL: http://www.southwesternassn.com

Annual. **Primary Exhibits:** equipment, supplies, and services relating to the agricultural industry. **Dates and Locations:** 2008 Feb 23-25; Kansas City, MO.

OTHER SOURCES

★634★ American Institute of Biological Sciences (AIBS)

1444 I St. NW, Ste. 200
Washington, DC 20005
Ph: (202)628-1500   Fax: (202)628-1509
Fr: 800-992-2427
E-mail: rogrady@aibs.org
URL: http://www.aibs.org

Members: Professional member organization and federation of biological associations, laboratories, and museums whose members have an interest in the life sciences. **Purpose:** Promotes unity and effectiveness of effort among persons engaged in biological research, education, and application of biological sciences, including agriculture, environment, and medicine. Seeks to further the relationships of biological sciences to other sciences and industries. Conducts roundtable series; provides names of prominent biologists who are willing to serve as speakers and curriculum consultants; provides advisory committees and other services to the Department of Energy, Environmental Protection Agency, National Science Foundation, Department of Defense, and National Aeronautics and Space Administration. Maintains educational consultant panel.

★635★ American Society for Horticultural Science (ASHS)

113 SW St., Ste. 200
Alexandria, VA 22314-2851
Ph: (703)836-4606   Fax: (703)836-2024
E-mail: ashs@ashs.org
URL: http://www.ashs.org

Description: Promotes and encourages scientific research and education in horticulture throughout the world. Members represent all areas of horticulture science.

★636★ Association for International Practical Training (AIPT)

10400 Little Patuxent Pkwy., Ste. 250
Columbia, MD 21044-3519
Ph: (410)997-2200   Fax: (410)992-3924
E-mail: aipt@aipt.org
URL: http://www.aipt.org

Description: Providers worldwide of on-the-job training programs for students and professionals seeking international career development and life-changing experiences. Arranges workplace exchanges in hundreds of professional fields, bringing employers and trainees together from around the world. Client list ranges from small farming communities to Fortune 500 companies.

★637★ Council for Agricultural Science and Technology (CAST)

4420 W Lincoln Way
Ames, IA 50014-3447
Ph: (515)292-2125   Fax: (515)292-4512
E-mail: info@cast-science.org
URL: http://www.cast-science.org

Members: Scientific societies, associate societies, individuals, corporations, foundations, and trade associations. **Purpose:** Promotes science-based information on food, fiber, agricultural, natural resource, and related societal and environmental issues.

★638★ Growing Opportunities: Careers in Agriculture

JIST Publishing
875 Montreal Way
St. Paul, MN 55102
Fax: 800-547-8329   Fr: 800-648-5478
E-mail: info@jist.com
URL: http://www.jist.com

2004. $99. 23 minutes. Video includes thumbnail descriptions of 23 careers that exist in the agricultural industry.

★639★ Minorities in Agriculture, Natural Resources and Related Sciences (MANRRS)

PO Box 381017
Germantown, TN 38183-1017
Ph: (901)757-9700   Fax: (901)757-9706
E-mail: exec.office@manrrs.org
URL: http://www.manrrs.org

Description: Promotes natural and agricultural sciences and other related fields among ethnic minorities in all phases of career preparation and participation. Provides a network to support the professional development of minorities.

★640★ Minority Women In Science (MWIS)

Directorate for Education and Human Resources Programs
1200 New York Ave. NW
Washington, DC 20005
Ph: (202)326-7019   Fax: (202)371-9849
E-mail: ygeorge@aaas.org

Description: A national network group of the American association for the Advancement of Science (AAAS), Education and Human Resources Directorate. The objectives of this group are: to identify and share information on resources and programs that could help in mentoring young women and minorities interested in science and engineering careers, and to strengthen communication among women and minorities in science and education.

★641★ National Postsecondary Agricultural Student Organization (PAS)

PO Box 68960
Indianapolis, IN 46278-1370
Ph: (317)802-4214   Fax: (317)802-5214
E-mail: eschilling@nationalpas.org

URL: http://www.nationalpas.org

Description: Agriculturally-related student organization; provides opportunity for individual growth, leadership and career preparation. Promotes development of leadership abilities through employment programs, course work, and organization activities.

★642★ **Scientific, Engineering, and Technical Services**
Cambridge Educational
PO Box 2053
Princeton, NJ 08543-2053
Ph: 800-257-5126   Fax: (609)671-0266
Fr: 800-468-4227

E-mail: custserv@films.com
URL: http://www.cambridgeeducational.com
VHS and DVD. $89.95. 2002. 18 minutes. 2002. Part of the Career Cluster Series.

★643★ **Scientific Occupations**
Delphi Productions
3159 6th St.
Boulder, CO 80304
Ph: (303)443-2100   Fax: (303)443-4022
Fr: 888-443-2400
E-mail: support@delphivideo.com
URL: http://www.delphivideo.com

$95.00. 60 minutes. Part of the Careers for the 21st Century Video Library.

★644★ **Soil Science Society of America (SSSA)**
677 S Segoe Rd.
Madison, WI 53711
Ph: (608)273-8080   Fax: (608)273-2021
E-mail: headquarters@agronomy.org
URL: http://www.soils.org

Description: Professional soil scientists, including soil physicists, soil classifiers, land use and management specialists, chemists, microbiologists, soil fertility specialists, soil cartographers, conservationists, mineralogists, engineers, and others interested in fundamental and applied soil science.

AI Programmers

SOURCES OF HELP-WANTED ADS

★645★ AI Magazine

American Association for Artificial
Intelligence
445 Burgess Dr., Ste. 100
Menlo Park, CA 94025-3442
Ph: (650)328-3123   Fax: (650)321-4457
URL: http://www.aaai.org/Magazine/maga-
zine.php

Quarterly. Magazine about artificial intelligence.

★646★ Biomedical Technology & Human Factors Engineering

National Technical Information Service
5285 Port Royal Rd.
Springfield, VA 22161
Ph: (703)605-6585   Fax: (703)605-6900
Fr: 800-553-6847
E-mail: info@ntis.gov.
URL: http://www.ntis.gov/new/alerts_print-
ed.asp

Description: Biweekly. Carries abstracts of
reports on biomedical facilities, instrumentation, and supplies. Also covers human factors engineering and man-machine relations;
bionics and artificial intelligence; prosthetics
and mechanical organs; life-support systems; space biology; and tissue preservation
and storage. Recurring features include a
form for ordering reports from NTIS. Also
available via e-mail.

★647★ Cybernetics and Systems

Taylor & Francis Group Journals
325 Chestnut St., Ste. 800
Philadelphia, PA 19106
Ph: (215)625-8900   Fax: (215)625-8914
Fr: 800-354-1420
URL: http://www.tandf.co.uk/journals/titles/
01969722.asp

$487.00/year for individuals, print only;
$1,860.00/year for individuals, online only;
$1,958.00/year for individuals, print and on-
line. International forum for developments in

cybernetics with applications spanning artificial intelligence to economics.

★648★ Dr. Dobb's Journal

CMP Media L.L.C.
2800 Campus Dr.
San Mateo, CA 94403
Ph: (650)513-4300   Fax: (650)513-4618
Fr: 800-842-0798
E-mail: webmaster@ercb.com
URL: http://www.ddj.com

Monthly. $25.00/year for individuals; $99.95/
year for individuals, CD-ROM library. Magazine covering computer programming.

★649★ eIntelligence

Edward Rosenfeld
PO Box 20008
New York, NY 10025-1510
Ph: (212)222-1123   Fax: (212)222-1123
Fr: 800-638-7257
E-mail: subs@eintelligence.com
URL: http://eintelligence.com

Description: Monthly. Covers technologies
that affect the future of computing and offers
viewpoints. Concentrates on business, research and government activities in neural
networks, parallel processing, pattern recognition, natural language interfaces, voice and
speech technologies, and art and graphics.
Recurring features include editorials and
news of research, and columns on the Net,
Nanotechnologies, and Quantum computing.

★650★ International Journal on Artificial Intelligence Tools

World Scientific Publishing
27 Warren St., Ste. 401-402
Hackensack, NJ 07601
Ph: (201)487-9655   Fax: (201)487-9656
Fr: 800-227-7562
URL: http://www.wspc.com

Bimonthly. $670.00/year for institutions,
electronic + print; $637.00/year for institu-
tions, electronic only; $243.00/year for indi-
viduals, print only; $40.00/year for individu-
als, postage; $592.00/year for institutions,
electronic + print; $562.00/year for institu-
tions, electronic only; $215.00/year for indi-

viduals, print only; $31.00/year for individu-
als, postage. Journal covering design, development, and testing of AI tools.

★651★ Journal of Artificial Intelligence Research (JAIR)

American Association for Artificial
Intelligence Press
445 Burgess Dr.
Menlo Park, CA 94025
Ph: (650)328-3123   Fax: (650)321-4457
URL: http://www.jair.org

Covers all areas of artificial intelligence.

★652★ PC AI Online

Knowledge Technology Inc.
PO Box 30130
Phoenix, AZ 85046-0130
Ph: (602)971-1869   Fax: (602)971-2321
E-mail: info@pcai.com

Bimonthly. Geared toward practical application of intelligent technology, covers developments in robotics, expert systems, neural
networks, fuzzy logic, object-oriented development, languages and all other areas of
artificial intelligence.

★653★ Presence

MIT Press
55 Hayward St.
Cambridge, MA 02142-1493
Ph: (617)253-5646   Fax: (617)258-6779
Fr: 800-405-1619
E-mail: presence@mit.edu
URL: http://www-mitpress.mit.edu

Bimonthly. $90.00/year for individuals, for
print plus electronic access; $80.00/year for
individuals, for electronic access; $570.00/
year for institutions, for print plus electronic
access; $514.00/year for institutions, for
electronic access; $48.00/year for students,
for print plus electronic access; $43.00/year
for students, for electronic access. Scholarly
journal on teleoperators and virtual environments.

★654★ Robotica

Cambridge University Press
32 Ave. of the Americas
New York, NY 10013-2473
Ph: (212)924-3900   Fax: (212)691-3239
Fr: 800-221-4512
E-mail: journals_advertising@cup.org
URL: http://uk.cambridge.org

Bimonthly. $485.00/year for institutions, online & print; $415.00/year for institutions, online; $132.00/year for individuals, online & print; $825.00/year for institutions, online & print; $700.00/year for institutions, online; $210.00/year for individuals, online & print; $198.00/year for individuals, print only. Journal robotics studies.

★655★ Robotics World

Douglas Publications L.L.C.
2807 N Parham Rd., Ste. 200
Richmond, VA 23294
Ph: (804)762-9600   Fax: (804)217-8999
Fr: 800-794-6086
URL: http://www.roboticsworld.com

Bimonthly. $72.00/year. Free, in U.S. $99.00/year for Canada and Mexico; $112.00/year for other countries; $162.00/year for Canada and Mexico, 2 years; $162.00/year for other countries, 2 years. Professional magazine covering flexible automation and intelligent machines.

★656★ Software Development

CMP Media L.L.C.
600 Community Dr.
Manhasset, NY 11030
Ph: (516)562-5000   Fax: (516)562-7830
E-mail: aweber@cmp.com
URL: http://www.cmp.com/pubinfo?pubid=68

Monthly. $19.95/year for individuals. Magazine for the computer programming industry.

EMPLOYER DIRECTORIES AND NETWORKING LISTS

★657★ Advanced Manufacturing Technology

Wiley-Blackwell
111 River St.
Hoboken, NJ 07030-5773
Ph: (201)748-6000   Fax: (201)748-6088
Fr: 800-225-5945
E-mail: amtinfo@insights.com
URL: http://www.apnf.org/frostbody.htm

Monthly. Publication includes: List of companies involved in developing advanced manufacturing technologies such as robotics, artificial intelligence in computers, ultrasonics, lasers, and waterjet cutters; also lists sources of information and education on high-technology. Entries include: Company or organization name, address, phone, name of contact; description of process, product, or service. Principal content is articles and analysis of advanced manufacturing technology. Arrangement: Classified by subject.

★658★ Robot Builder's Sourcebook

Electronic Privacy Information Center
1718 Connecticut Ave. NW, Ste. 200
Washington, DC 20009
Ph: (202)483-1140   Fax: (202)483-1248

$18.74 for individuals. Covers over 2,500 mail-order suppliers and other sources for amateur robotics materials. Entries include: Name, address, phone, e-mail address, URL, and information about the resource. Arrangement: By category, then alphabetical.

HANDBOOKS AND MANUALS

★659★ AI Application Programming

Charles River Media
25 Thomson Pl.
Boston, MA 02210
Ph: (617)757-7900   Fax: (617)757-7969
Fr: 800-382-8505
E-mail: info@charlesriver.com
URL: http://www.charlesriver.com

M. Tim Jones. 2005. Second Edition. $54.95. 473 pages. Software engineer Jones demystifies techniques associated with artificial intelligence and shows how they can be useful in everyday applications.

★660★ Artificial Intelligence: A Modern Approach

Prentice Hall/Pearson Education
1 Lake St.
Upper Saddle River, NJ 07458
Ph: (201)236-7000   Fax: (201)236-7696
E-mail: communications@pearsoned.com
URL: http://www.pearsoned.com

Stuart J. Russell and Peter Norvig. Second edition. 2002. $115.00. 1132 pages. Provides an introduction to the theory and practice of artificial intelligence.

★661★ Career Opportunities in Computers and Cyberspace

Facts On File Inc.
132 W. 31st St., 17th Fl.
New York, NY 10001-2006
Ph: (212)967-8800   Fax: 800-678-3633
Fr: 800-322-8755
E-mail: custserv@factsonfile.com
URL: http://www.factsonfile.com

Harry Henderson. Second edition, 2004. $18.95 (paper). Part of the Career Opportunities Series. 256 pages.

★662★ Choosing a Career in Computers

Rosen Publishing Group, Inc.
29 E. 21st St.
New York, NY 10010
Ph: (212)777-3017   Fax: (212)777-0277
Fr: 800-237-9932
URL: http://www.rosenpublishing.com/

Weigant, Chris. 2000. $29.25. Presents many of the options available to people interested in the technical side of the computer world-from designing and building computers to writing manuals explaining how to use them.

★663★ Computer Job Survival Guide

Technion Books
PO Box 402
Turners Falls, MA 01376
E-mail: admin@realrates.com
URL: http://www.phlaunt.com/technion/

Janet Ruhl. 2002. 211 pages. Learn from seasoned professionals the secrets of how to break into the computer field and create a long-term, high-earning computer career.

★664★ Expert Resumes for Computer and Web Jobs

Jist Publishing
875 Montreal Way
St. Paul, MN 55102
Fr: 800-648-5478
E-mail: info@jist.com
URL: http://www.jist.com

Wendy Enelow and Louis Kursmark. Second edition, 2005. $16.95 (paper). 286 pages.

★665★ Mathematical Methods in Artificial Intelligence

John Wiley & Sons Inc.
111 River St.
Hoboken, NJ 07030-5774
Ph: (201)748-6000   Fax: (201)748-6088
Fr: 800-225-5945
URL: http://www.wiley.com

Edward A. Bender. 1996. $63.95. Hardcover. 656 pages. Introduces the important mathematical foundations and tools in AI and describes their applications to the design of AI algorithms.

★666★ Preparing for an Outstanding Career in Computers: Questions and Answers for Professionals and Students

Rafi Systems, Incorporated
750 N. Diamond Bar Blvd., Ste. 224
Diamond Bar, CA 91765
Ph: (909)593-8124   Fax: (909)629-1034
Fr: 800-584-6706
E-mail: rafisystems@rafisystems.com
URL: http://www.rafisystems.com/

Mohamed Rafiquzzaman. 2001. $19.95. 204 pages. Book contains over 300 questions and answers on various important aspects of computers. Topics include basic and state-of-the-art concepts from digital logic to the design of a complete microcomputer.

★667★ Unlocking the Clubhouse: Women in Computing

MIT Press
55 Hayward St.
Cambridge, MA 02142-1493
Ph: (617)253-5646   Fax: (617)258-6779
Fr: 800-405-1619
URL: http://mitpress.mit.edu/main/home/default.asp

Jane Margolis and Allan Fisher. 2003. $15.00. 182 pages.

ONLINE JOB SOURCES AND SERVICES

★668★ ComputerJobs.com

280 Interstate N. Cir. SE, Ste. 300
Atlanta, GA 30339-2411
Fr: 800-850-0045
URL: http://www.computerjobs.com

Description: Provides listings of computer-related job opportunities.

★669★ Guru.com

5001 Baum Blvd., Ste. 760
Pittsburgh, PA 15213
Ph: (412)687-1316   Fax: (412)687-4466
URL: http://www.guru.com

Description: Job board specializing in contract jobs for creative and information technology professionals. Also provides online incorporation and educational opportunities for independent contractors along with articles and advice.

★670★ ZDNet Tech Jobs

URL: http://www.zdnet.com/

Description: Site houses a listing of national employment opportunities for professionals in high tech fields. Also contains resume building tips and relocation resources.

TRADESHOWS

★671★ IJCAI - International Joint Conference on Artificial Intelligence

International Joint Conferences on Artificial Intelligence
PO Box 5490
Somerset, NJ 08875
Ph: (313)667-4669   Fax: (313)667-4616
E-mail: info@ijcai.org
URL: http://www.ijcai.org

Biennial. **Primary Exhibits:** Artificial intelligence systems, projects, and services.

OTHER SOURCES

★672★ American Association for Artificial Intelligence (AAAI)

445 Burgess Dr., Ste. 100
Menlo Park, CA 94025
Ph: (650)328-3123   Fax: (650)321-4457
E-mail: info7contact@aaai.org
URL: http://www.aaai.org

Members: Artificial Intelligence researchers; students, libraries, corporations, and others interested in the subject. (Artificial Intelligence is a discipline in which an attempt is made to approximate the human thinking process through computers.) **Purpose:** Seeks to unite researchers and developers of Artificial Intelligence in order to provide an element of cohesion in the field. Serves as focal point and organizer for conferences; areas of interest include interpretation of visual data, robotics, expert systems, natural language processing, knowledge representation, and Artificial Intelligence programming technologies. **Activities:** Holds tutorials.

★673★ Cognitive Science Society (CSS)

University of Texas
Department of Psychology
1 University Sta. A8000
Austin, TX 78712-0187
Ph: (512)471-2030   Fax: (512)471-3053
E-mail: cogsci@psy.utexas.edu
URL: http://www.cognitivesciencesociety.org

Description: Represents published PhD's (500); students and PhD's not actively publishing (300) in the fields of psychology, artificial intelligence, and cognitive science. Promotes the dissemination of research in cognitive science and allied sciences. (Cognitive science is a branch of artificial intelligence that seeks to simulate human reasoning and associative powers on a computer, using specialized software).

★674★ Computer Occupations

Delphi Productions
3159 6th St.
Boulder, CO 80304
Ph: (303)443-2100   Fax: (303)443-4022
Fr: 888-443-2400
E-mail: support@delphivideo.com
URL: http://www.delphivideo.com

$95.00. 50 minutes. Part of the Careers for the 21st Century Video Library.

★675★ Computing Research Association (CRA)

1100 Seventeenth St. NW, Ste. 507
Washington, DC 20036-4632
Ph: (202)234-2111   Fax: (202)667-1066
E-mail: info@cra.org
URL: http://www.cra.org/

Description: An association of more than 200 North American academic departments of computer science, computer engineering, and related fields; laboratories and centers in industry government, and academia engaging in basic computing research; and affiliated professional societies.

★676★ IEEE Computer Society (CS)

1730 Massachusetts Ave. NW
Washington, DC 20036-1992
Ph: (202)371-0101   Fax: (202)728-9614
E-mail: help@computer.org
URL: http://www.computer.org

Description: Computer professionals. Promotes the development of computer and information sciences and fosters communication within the information processing community. Sponsors conferences, symposia, workshops, tutorials, technical meetings, and seminars. Operates Computer Society Press. Presents scholarships; bestows technical achievement and service awards and certificates.

★677★ IEEE Systems, Man, and Cybernetics Society (SMCS)

3 Park Ave., 17th Fl.
New York, NY 10016-5997
Ph: (212)419-7900   Fax: (212)752-4929
Fr: 800-678-4333
E-mail: lohall@ieee.org
URL: http://www.ieeesmc.org

Description: A society of the Institute of Electrical and Electronics Engineers. Serves as a forum on the theoretical and practical considerations of systems engineering, human machine systems, and cybernetics–with a particular focus on synthetic and natural systems involving humans and machines.

★678★ IMAGE Society

PO Box 6221
Chandler, AZ 85246-6221
E-mail: image@asu.edu
URL: http://www.public.asu.edu/~image

Description: Individuals and organizations interested in the technological advancement and application of real-time visual simulation (medical, virtual reality, telepresence, aeronautical, and automotive) and other related virtual reality technologies.

★679★ Information Technology Services

Cambridge Educational
PO Box 2053
Princeton, NJ 08543-2053
Ph: 800-257-5126   Fax: (609)671-0266
Fr: 800-468-4227
E-mail: custserv@films.com
URL: http://www.cambridgeeducational.com

VHS and DVD. $89.95. 2002. 19 minutes. Part of the Career Cluster Series.

★680★ **International Association for Artificial Intelligence and Law (IAAIL)**

College of Computer and Information Science
Northeastern University
202 WVH
Boston, MA 02115
Ph: (617)373-5116   Fax: (617)373-5121
E-mail: secretary@iaail.org
URL: http://www.iaail.org

Members: Computer science and law academics and professionals. **Purpose:** Promotes research and development in the field of artificial intelligence and law.

★681★ **International Society of Applied Intelligence (ISAI)**

Texas State University, San Marcos
Department of Computer Science
601 University Dr.
San Marcos, TX 78666-4616
Ph: (512)245-3409   Fax: (512)245-8750
E-mail: ma04@txstate.edu
URL: http://isai.cs.txstate.edu

Members: Researchers, academicians, computer scientists, industry professionals, and others with an interest in Intelligent systems' Technology. **Purpose:** Promotes dissemination of Research in the area of intelligent systems' technology and improves scientific literacy. **Activities:** Sponsors an International conference on Industrial, Engineering, and other Applications of Applied Intelligent Systems.

★682★ **MIT Computer Science and Artificial Intelligence Laboratory**

32 Vassar St.
Cambridge, MA 02139
Ph: (617)253-5851   Fax: (617)258-8682
E-mail: webmaster@csail.mit.udu
URL: http://www.csail.mit.edu

Description: Active since 1959. Interdisciplinary laboratory of over 200 people that spans several academic departments and has active projects ongoing with members of every academic school at MIT. Offers research, current job listings, and educational outreach.

★683★ **Society for Modeling and Simulation International (SCS)**

PO Box 17900
San Diego, CA 92177-7900
Ph: (858)277-3888   Fax: (858)277-3930
E-mail: info@scs.org
URL: http://www.scs.org

Members: Persons professionally engaged in simulation, particularly through the use of computers and similar devices that employ mathematical or physical analogies. **Activities:** Maintains speakers' bureau.

★684★ **Special Interest Group on Artificial Intelligence (SIGART)**

Association for Computing Machinery
2 Penn Plz., Ste. 701
New York, NY 10121-0701
Ph: (212)869-7440   Fax: (212)302-5826
Fr: 800-342-6626
E-mail: frawley@acm.org
URL: http://www.sigart.org

Description: A special interest group of the Association for Computing Machinery. Individuals interested in the application of computers to tasks normally requiring human intelligence. Enhances the capabilities of computers in this area.

★685★ **Special Interest Group on Simulation (SIGSIM)**

2 Penn Plz., Ste. 701
New York, NY 10036-5701
Ph: (212)626-0500   Fax: (212)944-1318
Fr: 800-342-6626
E-mail: sigsim@acm.org
URL: http://www.sigsim.org

Description: A special interest group of Association for Computing Machinery. Researchers and practitioners in computer simulation including professionals in business and industry. Holds technical meetings at annual conference of ACM. Promotes research and conducts surveys on topics such as the type of computer simulation courses being offered at colleges and universities. Researches the application of simulation principles and theory to sub disciplines of computer science.

★686★ **SRI International Artificial Intelligence Center**

333 Ravenswood Ave.
Menlo Park, CA 94025-3493
Ph: (650)859-2641   Fax: (650)859-3735
E-mail: aic@ai.sri.com
URL: http://www.ai.sri.com

Description: SRI International's Artificial Intelligence Center (AIC) is one of the world's major centers of research in artificial intelligence.

Air Traffic Controllers

$29.00 for two years, add 8 per year for Canada & other countries; $22.00/year for individuals; $12.00 for two years. General aviation magazine.

★698★ **General Aviation News**
Flyer Media Inc.
5611 76th St. W
PO Box 39099
Lakewood, WA 98439-0099
Ph: (253)471-9888   Fax: (253)471-9911
Fr: 800-426-8538
E-mail: comments@generalaviationnews.com
URL: http://www.flyer-online.com

Semimonthly. $35.00/year; $55.00 for two years; $70.00/year three years. General aviation newspaper (tabloid) for aircraft pilots and owners.

★699★ **In Flight USA**
In Flight USA
PO Box 5402
San Mateo, CA 94402
Ph: (650)358-9908   Fax: (650)358-9254
URL: http://www.inflightusa.com/index.html

Monthly. $24.95/year for individuals; $44.95 for two years. Magazine on Aviation.

★700★ **Regional Aviation News**
Access Intelligence L.L.C.
4 Choke Cherry Rd.
Rockville, MD 20850
Ph: (301)354-2000   Fax: (301)309-3847
Fr: 800-777-5006
E-mail: info@accessintel.com
URL: http://www.accessintel.com

Description: Weekly. Covers the commuter/regional airline industry, including airline management, marketing, labor, personnel changes, aircraft acquisitions, new products, and the financial and operational environment. Recurring features include interviews, news of research, a calendar of events, reports of meetings, job listings, and notices of publications available.

EMPLOYER DIRECTORIES AND NETWORKING LISTS

★701★ **AOPA's Airport Directory**
Aircraft Owners and Pilots Association
421 Aviation Way
Frederick, MD 21701
Ph: (301)695-2000   Fax: (301)695-2375
Fr: 800-872-2672
E-mail: airportdirectory@aopa.org
URL: http://www.aopa.org

Biennial, January. Covers 5,300 U.S. public-use landing facilities, including airports, heliports, seaplane bases, and approximately 1,800 private-use landing facilities; 5,000 aviation service companies. Entries include: For landing facilities–Airport type and name,

city, phone, runway dimensions, types of instrument approaches, hours operated, communications frequencies, runway light system, local attractions, ground transportation, restaurants, hotels. For aviation service companies–Company name, phone, airport affiliation, operating hours, fuel type, unicom frequency. Arrangement: Geographical. Indexes: Cross-Reference index of U.S. landing facilities.

★702★ **Discovering Careers for Your Future: Transportation**
Facts On File Inc.
132 W 31st St., 17th Fl.
New York, NY 10001
Ph: (212)967-8800   Fax: 800-678-3633
Fr: 800-322-8755
URL: http://www.factsonfile.com

Published 2002. $21.95 for individuals; $19.75 for libraries. Covers air traffic controllers, auto mechanics, locomotive engineers, pilots, public transportation operators, railroad conductors, and truck drivers; links career education to curriculum, helping children investigate the subjects they are interested in, and the careers those subjects might lead to.

★703★ **National Air Transportation Association-Aviation Business Resource Book and Official Membership Directory**
National Air Transportation Association
4226 King St.
Alexandria, VA 22302
Ph: (703)845-9000   Fax: (703)845-8176
Fr: 800-808-6282
URL: http://www.nata.aero/login.jsp?uri=%2Fdirectory%2Fmember%2F

Annual, October. $50.00 for nonmembers; $25.00 for members. Covers more than 1,000 regular, associate, and affiliate members; regular members include airport service organizations, air taxi operators, and commuter airlines. Entries include: Company name, address, phone, fax number, name and title of contact. Arrangement: Regular members are classified by service; associate and affiliate members are alphabetical in separate sections. Indexes: Geographical.

★704★ **World Aviation Directory & Aerospace Database (WAD&AD)**
Aviation Week
1200 G St. NW, Ste. 200
Washington, DC 20005
Ph: (202)383-2484   Fax: (202)383-2478
Fr: 800-551-2015
E-mail: wad@mcgraw-hill.com
URL: http://a1.ecom01.com/aw_marketdatacenter?s_id=7

Semiannual, March and September. $269.00 for U.S. Database covers: 19,000 airlines, manufacturers, MRO stations, airports military/government and distributors/suppliers; 6,000 product/service categories and 150,000 listings; 60,000 aviation/aerospace professionals; 500,000 users across all 3 platforms/formats; and commercial, military & business aviation fleet data. Ar-

rangement: Classified by major activity (manufacturers, airlines, etc.). Indexes: Company and organization, personnel, product, trade name.

HANDBOOKS AND MANUALS

★705★ **Careers for Night Owls and Other Insomniacs**
The McGraw-Hill Companies
PO Box 182604
Columbus, OH 43272
Fax: (614)759-3749   Fr: 877-883-5524
E-mail: customer.service@mcgraw-hill.com
URL: http://www.mcgraw-hill.com

Louise Miller. Second edition, 2002. $12.95 (paper). 160 pages.

★706★ **Opportunities in Aerospace Careers**
The McGraw-Hill Companies
PO Box 182604
Columbus, OH 43272
Fax: (614)759-3749   Fr: 877-883-5524
E-mail: customer.service@mcgraw-hill.com
URL: http://www.mcgraw-hill.com

Wallace R. Maples. Third edition, 2002 $13.95 (paper). 160 pages. Surveys jobs with the airlines, airports, the government, the military, in manufacturing, and in research and development. Includes information on job opportunities with NASA in the U.S. space program.

★707★ **Staffing the ATM System: The Selection of Air Traffic Controllers**
Ashgate Publishing Co.
101 Cherry St.
Ste. 420
Burlington, VT 05401-4405
Ph: (802)865-7641   Fax: (802)865-7847
URL: http://www.ashgate.com

Hinnerk Eissfeldt, Dana Broach, and Michael C. Heil. 2002. $99.95. Illustrated. 200 pages.

★708★ **Taking Flight: Education & Training for Aviation Careers**
National Academies Press
500 5th St. NW
Lockbox 285
Washington, DC 20055
Ph: (202)334-3313   Fax: (202)334-2793
Fr: 888-624-8373
URL: http://www.nap.edu/

Janet S. Hansen and Clinton V. Oster, editors. 1997. $40.25 (paper). 192 pages.

TRADESHOWS

★709★ Air Traffic Control Association Convention ATCA Annual Conference and Exposition

Air Traffic Control Association
1101 King St., Ste. 300
Alexandria, VA 22314-2944
Ph: (703)299-2430   Fax: (703)299-2437
E-mail: info@atca.org
URL: http://www.atca.org

Annual. **Primary Exhibits:** ATC/aviation equipment, supplies, and services. **Dates and Locations:** 2008 Nov 02-05; Washington, DC; Marriott Wardman Park Hotel.

★710★ Airports Council International - North America Convention

Airports Council International - North America
1775 K St. NW, Ste. 500
Washington, DC 20006
Ph: (202)293-8500   Fax: (202)331-1362
E-mail: MemberServices@aci-na.org
URL: http://www.aci-na.org

Annual. **Primary Exhibits:** Air Aviation industry equipment, products and services.

OTHER SOURCES

★711★ Air Traffic Control Association (ATCA)

1101 King St., Ste. 300
Alexandria, VA 22314
Ph: (703)299-2430   Fax: (703)299-2437
E-mail: info@atca.org
URL: http://www.atca.org

Members: Air traffic controllers; private, commercial, and military pilots; private and business aircraft owners and operators; aircraft and electronics engineers; airlines, aircraft manufacturers, and electronic and human engineering firms. **Purpose:** Promotes the establishment and maintenance of a safe and efficient air traffic control system. **Activities:** Conducts special surveys and studies on air traffic control problems. Participates in aviation community conferences.

★712★ Math at Work: Women in Nontraditional Careers

Her Own Words
PO Box 5264
Madison, WI 53705-0264
Ph: (608)271-7083   Fax: (608)271-0209
E-mail: herownword@aol.com
URL: http://www.herownwords.com/

Video. Jocelyn Riley. $95.00. 15 minutes. Resource guide also available for $45.00.

★713★ National Black Coalition of Federal Aviation Employees (NBCFAE)

77 Southgate Rd.
Valley Stream, NY 11581
Ph: (516)245-3104
E-mail: hilary.king@nbcfae.org
URL: http://www.nbcfae.org

Description: Federal Aviation Administration employees. Purposes are to: promote professionalism and equal opportunity in the workplace; locate and train qualified minorities for FAA positions; help the FAA meet its affirmative action goals; monitor black, female, and minority trainees; educate members and the public about their rights and FAA personnel and promotion qualifications; develop a voice for black, female, and minority FAA employees. Recruits minorities from community and schools who qualify for employment; sponsors seminars for members and for those who wish to be employed by the FAA. Maintains speaker's bureau; sponsors competitions.

★714★ Technical & Related Occupations

Delphi Productions
3159 6th St.
Boulder, CO 80304
Ph: (303)443-2100   Fax: (303)443-4022
Fr: 888-443-2400
E-mail: support@delphivideo.com
URL: http://www.delphivideo.com

$95.00. 49 minutes. Part of the Careers for the 21st Century Video Library.

Aircraft Mechanics and Engine Specialists

SOURCES OF HELP-WANTED ADS

★715★ AeroSpaceNews.com

AeroSpaceNews.com
PO Box 1748
Ojai, CA 93024-1748
Ph: (805)985-2320
URL: http://www.aerospacenews.com/content/view/41/33/

Monthly. $19.95/year for individuals, private; $53.95/year for two years, individual, private; $79.95/year for individuals, trade; $143.95 for two years, individual. Journal reporting on the insights, impressions and images of tomorrow's technological wonders in the field of aerospace.

★716★ Air Jobs Digest

World Air Data
PO Box 42724
Washington, DC 20015
Ph: (301)990-6800   Fr: 800-247-5627
URL: http://www.airjobsdaily.com

Monthly. $96.00/year for individuals. Newspaper covering job listings in aviation and aerospace worldwide.

★717★ Aviation Maintenance

Access Intelligence L.L.C.
4 Choke Cherry Rd., 2nd Fl.
Rockville, MD 20850
Ph: (301)354-2000   Fax: (301)309-3847
Fr: 800-777-5006
URL: http://www.aviationtoday.com

Monthly. $207.00/year for individuals. Magazine covering aviation maintenance.

★718★ Aviation Week & Space Technology

McGraw-Hill Inc.
1221 Ave. of the Americas
New York, NY 10020-1095
Ph: (212)512-2000   Fax: (212)512-3840
Fr: 877-833-5524
URL: http://www.aviationweek.com/aw/gen-eric/channel_.jsp?channel=

Weekly. $109.00/year for Canada and Mexico; $103.00/year U.S.; $160.00/year Europe. Magazine serving the aviation and aerospace market worldwide.

★719★ Avion Magazine

World Airline Entertainment Association
8201 Greensboro Dr., Ste. 300
Mc Lean, VA 22102
Ph: (703)610-9021   Fax: (703)610-9005
Fr: (866)890-7356
URL: http://www.waea.org

Quarterly. Magazine covering aviation.

★720★ Business & Commercial Aviation

Aviation Week
1200 G St. NW, Ste. 200
Washington, DC 20005
Ph: (202)383-2484   Fax: (202)383-2478
Fr: 800-551-2015

Monthly. $54.00/year in U.S.; $58.00/year for Canada and Mexico; $79.00/year for elsewhere. Magazine covering business issues relevant to professionals in commercial aviation.

★721★ Executive Flyer Magazine

McCormick Communications LLC
1801 South Federal Hwy., Ste. 224
Delray Beach, FL 33483
Ph: (561)279-0605   Fax: (561)279-0433
URL: http://www.executiveflyer.com

Quarterly. Free to qualified subscribers. Magazine for small aircraft manufacturers, fractional ownership companies and charter/aircraft management companies.

★722★ Flying

Hachette Filipacchi Media U.S. Inc.
1633 Broadway
New York, NY 10019
Ph: (212)767-6000   Fax: (212)767-5631
URL: http://www.hfmus.com/

Monthly. $17.00/year for individuals, add 8 per year for Canada & other countries; $29.00 for two years, add 8 per year for Canada & other countries; $22.00/year for individuals; $12.00 for two years. General aviation magazine.

★723★ General Aviation News

Flyer Media Inc.
5611 76th St. W
PO Box 39099
Lakewood, WA 98439-0099
Ph: (253)471-9888   Fax: (253)471-9911
Fr: 800-426-8538
E-mail: comments@generalaviationnews.com
URL: http://www.flyer-online.com

Semimonthly. $35.00/year; $55.00 for two years; $70.00/year three years. General aviation newspaper (tabloid) for aircraft pilots and owners.

★724★ In Flight USA

In Flight USA
PO Box 5402
San Mateo, CA 94402
Ph: (650)358-9908   Fax: (650)358-9254
URL: http://www.inflightusa.com/index.html

Monthly. $24.95/year for individuals; $44.95 for two years. Magazine on Aviation.

★725★ Rotor & Wing

Access Intelligence L.L.C.
4 Choke Cherry Rd., 2nd Fl.
Rockville, MD 20850
Ph: (301)354-2000   Fax: (301)309-3847
Fr: 800-777-5006
URL: http://www.pbimedia.com

Monthly. Free. Magazine covering helicopters.

EMPLOYER DIRECTORIES AND NETWORKING LISTS

★726★ AOPA's Airport Directory

Aircraft Owners and Pilots Association
421 Aviation Way
Frederick, MD 21701
Ph: (301)695-2000   Fax: (301)695-2375
Fr: 800-872-2672
E-mail: airportdirectory@aopa.org
URL: http://www.aopa.org

Biennial, January. Covers 5,300 U.S. public-use landing facilities, including airports, heliports, seaplane bases, and approximately 1,800 private-use landing facilities; 5,000 aviation service companies. Entries include: For landing facilities–Airport type and name, city, phone, runway dimensions, types of instrument approaches, hours operated, communications frequencies, runway light system, local attractions, ground transportation, restaurants, hotels. For aviation service companies–Company name, phone, airport affiliation, operating hours, fuel type, unicom frequency. Arrangement: Geographical. Indexes: Cross-Reference index of U.S. landing facilities.

★727★ National Air Transportation Association-Aviation Business Resource Book and Official Membership Directory

National Air Transportation Association
4226 King St.
Alexandria, VA 22302
Ph: (703)845-9000   Fax: (703)845-8176
Fr: 800-808-6282
URL: http://www.nata.aero/login.jsp?uri=%2Fdirectory%2Fmember%2F

Annual, October. $50.00 for nonmembers; $25.00 for members. Covers more than 1,000 regular, associate, and affiliate members; regular members include airport service organizations, air taxi operators, and commuter airlines. Entries include: Company name, address, phone, fax number, name and title of contact. Arrangement: Regular members are classified by service; associate and affiliate members are alphabetical in separate sections. Indexes: Geographical.

★728★ World Aviation Directory & Aerospace Database (WAD&AD)

Aviation Week
1200 G St. NW, Ste. 200
Washington, DC 20005
Ph: (202)383-2484   Fax: (202)383-2478
Fr: 800-551-2015
E-mail: wad@mcgraw-hill.com
URL: http://a1.ecom01.com/aw_marketdatacenter?s_id=7

Semiannual, March and September. $269.00 for U.S. Database covers: 19,000 airlines, manufacturers, MRO stations, airports military/government and distributors/suppliers; 6,000 product/service categories and 150,000 listings; 60,000 aviation/aerospace professionals; 500,000 users across all 3 platforms/formats; and commercial, military & business aviation fleet data. Arrangement: Classified by major activity (manufacturers, airlines, etc.). Indexes: Company and organization, personnel, product, trade name.

HANDBOOKS AND MANUALS

★729★ The Air Crafters: Airplane Mechanics

Xlibris Corporation
International Plaza II, Ste. 340
Philadelphia, PA 19113
Ph: (610)915-5214   Fax: (610)915-0294
Fr: 888-795-4274
E-mail: info@xlibris.com
URL: http://www2.xlibris.com

Reginaldo L. Ortiz. 2002. $30.99. 156 pages.

★730★ Careers in Travel, Tourism, and Hospitality

The McGraw-Hill Companies
PO Box 182604
Columbus, OH 43272
Fax: (614)759-3749   Fr: 877-883-5524
E-mail: customer.service@mcgraw-hill.com
URL: http://www.mcgraw-hill.com

Marjorie Eberts, Linda Brothers, and Ann Gisler. Second edition, 2005. $15.95 (paper). 224 pages.

★731★ Introduction to Aircraft Flight Mechanics

American Institute of Aeronautics & Astronautics
1801 Alexander Bell Dr., Ste. 500
Reston, VA 20191-4344
Ph: (703)264-7500   Fax: (703)264-7551
Fr: 800-639-2422
URL: http://www.aiaa.org/

Thomas R. Yechout, Steven L. Morris, David E. Bossert, and Wayne F. Hallgren. 2003. $109.95. Illustrated. 634 pages. Beginner's education on flight mechanics.

★732★ Opportunities in Aerospace Careers

The McGraw-Hill Companies
PO Box 182604
Columbus, OH 43272
Fax: (614)759-3749   Fr: 877-883-5524
E-mail: customer.service@mcgraw-hill.com
URL: http://www.mcgraw-hill.com

Wallace R. Maples. Third edition, 2002 $13.95 (paper). 160 pages. Surveys jobs with the airlines, airports, the government, the military, in manufacturing, and in research and development. Includes information on job opportunities with NASA in the U.S. space program.

★733★ Opportunities in Airline Careers

The McGraw-Hill Companies
PO Box 182604
Columbus, OH 43272
Fax: (614)759-3749   Fr: 877-883-5524
E-mail: customer.service@mcgraw-hill.com
URL: http://www.mcgraw-hill.com

Adrian A. Paradis. 1997. $14.95; $11.95 (paper). 148 pages.

★734★ Opportunities in Travel Careers

The McGraw-Hill Companies
PO Box 182604
Columbus, OH 43272
Fax: (614)759-3749   Fr: 877-883-5524
E-mail: customer.service@mcgraw-hill.com
URL: http://www.mcgraw-hill.com

Robert Scott Milne. Second edition, 2003. $14.95 (paper). 141 pages. Discusses what the jobs are and where to find them in airlines, shipping lines, and railroads. Discusses related opportunities in hotels, motels, resorts, travel agencies, public relation firms, and recreation departments. Illustrated.

★735★ Taking Flight: Education & Training for Aviation Careers

National Academies Press
500 5th St. NW
Lockbox 285
Washington, DC 20055
Ph: (202)334-3313   Fax: (202)334-2793
Fr: 888-624-8373
URL: http://www.nap.edu/

Janet S. Hansen and Clinton V. Oster, editors. 1997. $40.25 (paper). 192 pages.

EMPLOYMENT AGENCIES AND SEARCH FIRMS

★736★ Amtec Engineering Corp.

2749 Saturn St.
Brea, CA 92821
Ph: (714)993-1900   Fax: (714)993-2419
E-mail: info@amtechc.com
URL: http://www.amtec-eng.com

Employment agency.

OTHER SOURCES

★737★ Aircraft Electronics Association (AEA)

4217 S Hocker
Independence, MO 64055-0963
Ph: (816)373-6565   Fax: (816)478-3100
E-mail: info@aea.net
URL: http://www.aea.net

Members: Companies engaged in the sales, engineering, installation, and service of electronic aviation equipment and systems. **Purpose:** Seeks to: advance the science of aircraft electronics; promote uniform and stable regulations and uniform standards of performance; establish and maintain a code of ethics; gather and disseminate technical data; advance the education of members and the public in the science of aircraft electronics. **Activities:** Offers supplement type certificates, test equipment licensing, temporary FCC licensing for new installations, spare parts availability and pricing, audiovisual technician training, equipment and spare parts loan, profitable installation, and service facility operation. Provides employment information, equipment exchange information and service assistance on member installations anywhere in the world.

★738★ **Math at Work: Women in Nontraditional Careers**

Her Own Words
PO Box 5264
Madison, WI 53705-0264
Ph: (608)271-7083   Fax: (608)271-0209
E-mail: herownword@aol.com
URL: http://www.herownwords.com/

Video. Jocelyn Riley. $95.00. 15 minutes. Resource guide also available for $45.00.

★739★ **Mechanics & Repairers**

Delphi Productions
3159 6th St.
Boulder, CO 80304
Ph: (303)443-2100   Fax: (303)443-4022
Fr: 888-443-2400
E-mail: support@delphivideo.com
URL: http://www.delphivideo.com

$95.00. 50 minutes. Part of the Careers for the 21st Century Video Library.

★740★ **Professional Aviation Maintenance Association (PAMA)**

400 Commonwealth Dr.
Warrendale, PA 15096
Ph: (724)772-4092   Fax: (724)772-4064
Fr: (866)865-7262
E-mail: hq@pama.org
URL: http://www.pama.org

Members: Airframe and powerplant (A&P) technicians and aviation industry-related companies. **Purpose:** Strives to increase the professionalism of the individual aviation technician through greater technical knowledge and better understanding of safety requirements. Establishes communication among technicians throughout the country. Fosters and improves methods, skills, learning, and achievement in the aviation maintenance field.

Aircraft Pilots and Flight Engineers

Monthly. $24.95/year for individuals; $44.95 for two years. Magazine on Aviation.

★752★ *International Women Pilots*

The Ninety-Nines Inc.
4300 Amelia Earhart Rd.
Oklahoma City, OK 73159
Ph: (405)685-7969   Fax: (405)685-7985
Fr: 800-994-1929
E-mail: 99s@ninety-nines.org
URL: http://www.ninety-nines.org/

Description: Bimonthly. Includes material of interest to the members of The Ninety-Nines, Inc., an international organization of women pilots. Recurring features include interviews, news of research, letters to the editor, news of educational opportunities, a calendar of events, and columns titled President's and Careers.

★753★ *NAFI Mentor*

National Association of Flight Instructors
PO Box 3086
Oshkosh, WI 54903-3086
Ph: (920)426-6801   Fax: (920)426-6865
E-mail: nafi@eaa.org
URL: http://www.nafinet.org/

Description: Monthly. Supports NAFI in its efforts to serve as a central point for dissemination of knowledge, methodology, and new information relative to flight instruction. Recurring features include letters to the editor, news of research, reports of meetings, and notices of publications available. Also includes news of relevant legislative and regulatory activity.

★754★ *Professional Pilot*

Queensmith Communications Corp.
30 S Quaker LN Ste. 300
Alexandria, VA 22314
Ph: (703)370-0606   Fax: (703)370-7082
URL: http://www.propilotmag.com

Monthly. $36.00/year for individuals; $5.00 for single issue; $8.00/year directory issues. Magazine serving pilots of corporate, charter, and commuter airlines.

★755★ *Regional Aviation News*

Access Intelligence L.L.C.
4 Choke Cherry Rd.
Rockville, MD 20850
Ph: (301)354-2000   Fax: (301)309-3847
Fr: 800-777-5006
E-mail: info@accessintel.com
URL: http://www.accessintel.com

Description: Weekly. Covers the commuter/regional airline industry, including airline management, marketing, labor, personnel changes, aircraft acquisitions, new products, and the financial and operational environment. Recurring features include interviews, news of research, a calendar of events, reports of meetings, job listings, and notices of publications available.

★756★ *Rotor & Wing*

Access Intelligence L.L.C.
4 Choke Cherry Rd., 2nd Fl.
Rockville, MD 20850
Ph: (301)354-2000   Fax: (301)309-3847
Fr: 800-777-5006
URL: http://www.pbimedia.com

Monthly. Free. Magazine covering helicopters.

PLACEMENT AND JOB REFERRAL SERVICES

★757★ **Organization of Black Airline Pilots (OBAP)**

8630 Fenton St., Ste. 126
Silver Spring, MD 20910
Ph: (703)753-2047   Fr: 800-JET-OBAP
E-mail: nationaloffice@obap.org
URL: http://www.obap.org

Description: Cockpit crew members of commercial air carriers, corporate pilots, and other interested individuals. Seeks to enhance minority participation in the aerospace industry. Maintains liaison with airline presidents and minority and pilot associations. Conducts lobbying efforts, including congressional examinations into airline recruitment practices. Provides scholarships; co-sponsors Summer Flight Academy for Youth. Offers job placement service and charitable program; operates speakers' bureau; compiles statistics on airline hiring practices.

EMPLOYER DIRECTORIES AND NETWORKING LISTS

★758★ *AOPA's Airport Directory*

Aircraft Owners and Pilots Association
421 Aviation Way
Frederick, MD 21701
Ph: (301)695-2000   Fax: (301)695-2375
Fr: 800-872-2672
E-mail: airportdirectory@aopa.org
URL: http://www.aopa.org

Biennial, January. Covers 5,300 U.S. public-use landing facilities, including airports, heliports, seaplane bases, and approximately 1,800 private-use landing facilities; 5,000 aviation service companies. Entries include: For landing facilities–Airport type and name, city, phone, runway dimensions, types of instrument approaches, hours operated, communications frequencies, runway light system, local attractions, ground transportation, restaurants, hotels. For aviation service companies–Company name, phone, airport affiliation, operating hours, fuel type, unicom frequency. Arrangement: Geographical. Indexes: Cross-Reference index of U.S. landing facilities.

★759★ *Career Opportunities in Aviation and the Aerospace Industry*

Facts On File Inc.
132 W 31st St., 17th Fl.
New York, NY 10001
Ph: (212)967-8800   Fax: 800-678-3633
Fr: 800-322-8755
URL: http://www.factsonfile.com

Published 2005. $49.50 for individuals; $44.55 for libraries. Covers eighty up-to-date job profiles, providing detailed information about the duties, salaries, and prospects of aviation mechanics, designers, technicians, scientists, and administrators.

★760★ *Careers in Focus: Aviation*

Facts On File Inc.
132 W 31st St., 17th Fl.
New York, NY 10001
Ph: (212)967-8800   Fax: 800-678-3633
Fr: 800-322-8755
URL: http://www.factsonfile.com

Published 2005. $29.95 for individuals; $26.95 for libraries. Covers an overview of aviation, followed by a selection of jobs profiled in detail, including the nature of the job, earnings, prospects for employment, what kind of training and skills it requires, and sources for further information.

★761★ *National Air Transportation Association-Aviation Business Resource Book and Official Membership Directory*

National Air Transportation Association
4226 King St.
Alexandria, VA 22302
Ph: (703)845-9000   Fax: (703)845-8176
Fr: 800-808-6282
URL: http://www.nata.aero/login.jsp?uri=%2Fdirectory%2Fmember%2F

Annual, October. $50.00 for nonmembers; $25.00 for members. Covers more than 1,000 regular, associate, and affiliate members; regular members include airport service organizations, air taxi operators, and commuter airlines. Entries include: Company name, address, phone, fax number, name and title of contact. Arrangement: Regular members are classified by service; associate and affiliate members are alphabetical in separate sections. Indexes: Geographical.

★762★ *World Aviation Directory & Aerospace Database (WAD&AD)*

Aviation Week
1200 G St. NW, Ste. 200
Washington, DC 20005
Ph: (202)383-2484   Fax: (202)383-2478
Fr: 800-551-2015
E-mail: wad@mcgraw-hill.com
URL: http://a1.ecom01.com/aw_marketdatacenter?s_id=7

Semiannual, March and September. $269.00 for U.S. Database covers: 19,000 airlines, manufacturers, MRO stations, airports military/government and distributors/suppliers; 6,000 product/service categories and 150,000 listings; 60,000 aviation/aerospace professionals; 500,000 users across all 3 platforms/formats; and commercial, military & business aviation fleet data. Arrangement: Classified by major activity (manufacturers, airlines, etc.). Indexes: Company and organization, personnel, product, trade name.

HANDBOOKS AND MANUALS

★763★ Ace the Technical Pilot Interview

The McGraw-Hill Companies
PO Box 182604
Columbus, OH 43272
Fax: (614)759-3749   Fr: 877-883-5524
E-mail: customer.service@mcgraw-hill.com
URL: http://www.mcgraw-hill.com

Gary Bristow. 2002. $29.95 (paper). 346 pages.

★764★ Boeing 747 Classics: An Introduction for Pilots

Spirit Publications
6049 N 4th Pl.
Phoenix, AZ 85012
Ph: (602)909-1835

Philip Terpstra. 2005. $38.00. 160 pages.

★765★ Careers for Night Owls and Other Insomniacs

The McGraw-Hill Companies
PO Box 182604
Columbus, OH 43272
Fax: (614)759-3749   Fr: 877-883-5524
E-mail: customer.service@mcgraw-hill.com
URL: http://www.mcgraw-hill.com

Louise Miller. Second edition, 2002. $12.95 (paper). 160 pages.

★766★ Careers in Travel, Tourism, and Hospitality

The McGraw-Hill Companies
PO Box 182604
Columbus, OH 43272
Fax: (614)759-3749   Fr: 877-883-5524
E-mail: customer.service@mcgraw-hill.com
URL: http://www.mcgraw-hill.com

Marjorie Eberts, Linda Brothers, and Ann Gisler. Second edition, 2005. $15.95 (paper). 224 pages.

★767★ Flight Engineer FAA Written Exam

Gleim Publications
PO Box 12848, University Sta.
Gainesville, FL 32604
Ph: (352)375-0772   Fax: (352)375-6940
Fr: 800-874-5346
E-mail: ask@gleim.com
URL: http://www.gleim.com/

Irvin N. Gleim. 2000. $26.95. 378 pages.

★768★ Flight Plan to the Flight Deck: Strategies for a Pilot Career

Cage Consulting, Inc.
3333 Quebec, Ste. 1022
Denver, CO 80207
Ph: (520)579-4318   Fr: 888-899-2243
E-mail: angie@cageconsulting.com
URL: http://www.cageconsulting.com/

Judy A. Tarver. 1997. $16.95 (paper). 120 pages.

★769★ Opportunities in Aerospace Careers

The McGraw-Hill Companies
PO Box 182604
Columbus, OH 43272
Fax: (614)759-3749   Fr: 877-883-5524
E-mail: customer.service@mcgraw-hill.com
URL: http://www.mcgraw-hill.com

Wallace R. Maples. Third edition, 2002. $13.95 (paper). 160 pages. Surveys jobs with the airlines, airports, the government, the military, in manufacturing, and in research and development. Includes information on job opportunities with NASA in the U.S. space program.

★770★ Opportunities in Airline Careers

The McGraw-Hill Companies
PO Box 182604
Columbus, OH 43272
Fax: (614)759-3749   Fr: 877-883-5524
E-mail: customer.service@mcgraw-hill.com
URL: http://www.mcgraw-hill.com

Adrian A. Paradis. 1997. $14.95; $11.95 (paper). 148 pages.

★771★ Opportunities in Travel Careers

The McGraw-Hill Companies
PO Box 182604
Columbus, OH 43272
Fax: (614)759-3749   Fr: 877-883-5524
E-mail: customer.service@mcgraw-hill.com
URL: http://www.mcgraw-hill.com

Robert Scott Milne. Second edition, 2003. $14.95 (paper). 141 pages. Discusses what the jobs are and where to find them in airlines, shipping lines, and railroads. Discusses related opportunities in hotels, motels, resorts, travel agencies, public relation firms, and recreation departments. Illustrated.

★772★ The Proficient Pilot Series

Aviation Supplies & Academics, Incorporated
7005 132nd Pl., SE
Newcastle, WA 98059-3153
Ph: (425)235-1500   Fax: (425)235-0128
Fr: 800-272-2359
URL: http://www.asa2fly.com/

Barry Schiff. 2002. $54.95. 1019 pages.

★773★ Taking Flight: Education & Training for Aviation Careers

National Academies Press
500 5th St. NW
Lockbox 285
Washington, DC 20055
Ph: (202)334-3313   Fax: (202)334-2793
Fr: 888-624-8373
URL: http://www.nap.edu/

Janet S. Hansen and Clinton V. Oster, editors. 1997. $40.25 (paper). 192 pages.

TRADESHOWS

★774★ AOPA Expo - Aircraft Owners and Pilots Association

Aircraft Owners and Pilots Association
421 Aviation Way
Frederick, MD 21701
Ph: (301)695-2000   Fax: (301)695-2375
Fr: 800-USA-AOPA
URL: http://www.aopa.org

Annual. **Primary Exhibits:** Single-engine and multi-engine aircraft, avionics, airframes, power plant and equipment, financing information, and related equipment, supplies, and services. **Dates and Locations:** 2008 Nov 05-07; Tampa, FL; 2008 Nov 06-08; San Jose, CA.

★775★ National Business Aviation Association Annual Meeting & Convention

National Business Aviation Association
1200 18th St. NW, Ste. 400
Washington, DC 20036-2527
Ph: (202)783-9000   Fax: (202)331-8364
Fr: 800-FLY-NBAA
E-mail: info@nbaa.org
URL: http://www.nbaa.org

Annual. **Primary Exhibits:** Products and services limited to the design, operation, or servicing of business aircraft.

OTHER SOURCES

★776★ American Almanac of Jobs and Salaries

HarperCollins
10 E. 53rd St.
New York, NY 10022
Ph: (212)207-7000   Fr: 800-242-7737
URL: http://www.harpercollins.com/

John W. Wright. Revised edition, 2000. $20.00 (paper). 672 pages. This is a comprehensive guide to the wages of hundreds of occupations in a wide variety of industries and organizations.

★777★ **Math at Work: Women in Nontraditional Careers**

Her Own Words
PO Box 5264
Madison, WI 53705-0264
Ph: (608)271-7083   Fax: (608)271-0209
E-mail: herownword@aol.com
URL: http://www.herownwords.com/

Video. Jocelyn Riley. $95.00. 15 minutes. Resource guide also available for $45.00.

★778★ **National Black Coalition of Federal Aviation Employees (NBCFAE)**

77 Southgate Rd.
Valley Stream, NY 11581
Ph: (516)245-3104
E-mail: hilary.king@nbcfae.org
URL: http://www.nbcfae.org

Description: Federal Aviation Administration employees. Purposes are to: promote professionalism and equal opportunity in the workplace; locate and train qualified minorities for FAA positions; help the FAA meet its affirmative action goals; monitor black, female, and minority trainees; educate members and the public about their rights and FAA personnel and promotion qualifications; develop a voice for black, female, and minority FAA employees. Recruits minorities from community and schools who qualify for employment; sponsors seminars for members and for those who wish to be employed by the FAA. Maintains speaker's bureau; sponsors competitions.

★779★ **Ninety-Nines, International Organization of Women Pilots**

4300 Amelia Earhart Rd.
Oklahoma City, OK 73159
Ph: (405)685-7969   Fax: (405)685-7985
Fr: 800-994-1929
E-mail: 99s@ninety-nines.org
URL: http://www.ninety-nines.org

Members: Represents women pilots. **Purpose:** Fosters a better understanding of aviation. **Activities:** Encourages cross-country flying; provides consulting service and gives indoctrination flights; flies missions for charitable assistance programs; endorses air races. Develops programs and courses for schools and youth organizations and teaches ground school subjects. Participates in flying competitions. Maintains resource center and women's aviation museum. Conducts lecture on personal aviation experience, and charitable event. Compiles statistics.

★780★ **Professional Specialty Occupations**

Delphi Productions
3159 6th St.
Boulder, CO 80304
Ph: (303)443-2100   Fax: (303)443-4022
Fr: 888-443-2400
E-mail: support@delphivideo.com
URL: http://www.delphivideo.com

$95.00. 53 minutes. Part of the Careers for the 21st Century Video Library.

★781★ **Women in Engineering**

Her Own Words
PO Box 5264
Madison, WI 53705-0264
Ph: (608)271-7083   Fax: (608)271-0209
E-mail: herownword@aol.com
URL: http://www.herownwords.com/

Video. Jocelyn Riley. $95.00. 15 minutes. Resource guide also available for $45.00.

★782★ **Women in Nontraditional Careers: An Introduction**

Her Own Words
PO Box 5264
Madison, WI 53705
Ph: (608)271-7083   Fax: (608)271-0209
E-mail: herownword@aol.com
URL: http://www.herownwords.com/

Video. Jocelyn Riley. $95.00. 15 minutes. Resource guide also available for $45.00.

Alcohol and Drug Abuse Counselors

SOURCES OF HELP-WANTED ADS

★783★ *AAAP News*

American Academy of Addiction
  Psychiatry
345 Blackstone Blvd., 2nd Fl. RCH
Providence, RI 02906
Ph: (401)524-3076   Fax: (401)272-0922
URL: http://www.aaap.org/pulications.htm

$45.00/year for individuals; $15.00 for individuals, per issue; $50.00/year for individuals, international; $20.00 for individuals, per issue, international. Professional journal covering addiction psychiatry.

★784★ *Alcoholism*

Wiley-Blackwell
350 Main St. Commerce Pl.
Malden, MA 02148
Ph: (781)388-8200   Fax: (781)388-8210
Fr: 800-759-6120
E-mail: mnewcomb-acer@earthlink.net
URL: http://www.blackwellpublishing.com/
journal.asp?ref=0145-6008

Monthly. Publishing original clinical and research studies on alcoholism and alcohol-induced organ damage.

★785★ *The American Journal of Drug and Alcohol Abuse*

Marcel Dekker Inc.
270 Madison Ave.
New York, NY 10016
Ph: (212)696-9000   Fax: (212)685-4540
Fr: 800-228-1160
E-mail: custserv@dekker.com
URL: http://www.tandf.co.uk/journals/journal.asp?issn=0095-2990&l

$325.00/year for individuals, print only; $1,230.00/year for institutions, online only; $1,295.00/year for institutions, print & online; $785.00/year for institutions, print & online; $746.00/year for institutions, online only; $197.00/year for individuals, print only. Medical Journal focusing on the preclinical, clinical, pharmacological, administrative, and social aspects of substance misuse.

★786★ *AMHCA Advocate*

American Mental Health Counselors
  Association
801 N Fairfax St., Ste. 304
Alexandria, VA 22314
Ph: (703)548-6002   Fax: (703)548-4775
Fr: 800-326-2642
E-mail: Lmorano@amhca.org
URL: http://www.amhca.org

Description: Monthly. Publishes news of the programs, members, and activities of AMHCA. Provides updates regarding credentialing of counselors, mental health-related legislation, and insurance coverage of the expenses of mental health counseling. Recurring features include news of meetings and conferences and articles on topics of interest to clinical mental health counselors.

★787★ *Counseling Today*

American Counseling Association
5999 Stevenson Ave.
Alexandria, VA 22304
Ph: (703)823-6862   Fax: (703)823-0252
Fr: 800-347-6647
E-mail: ct@counseling.org
URL: http://www.counseling.org/ctonline

Description: Monthly. Covers news and issues relevant to the counseling profession.

★788★ *Counselor Education and Supervision*

American Counseling Association
5999 Stevenson Ave.
Alexandria, VA 22304
Ph: (703)823-6862   Fax: 800-473-2329
Fr: 800-347-6647
URL: http://www.counseling.org/

Quarterly. $50.00/year for individuals, nonmember; $80.00/year for institutions, nonmember. Journal covering research in counselor teaching, training, and trends.

★789★ *Journal of Addictions Nursing*

Taylor & Francis Group Journals
325 Chestnut St., Ste. 800
Philadelphia, PA 19106
Ph: (215)625-8900   Fax: (215)625-8914
Fr: 800-354-1420

URL: http://www.tandf.co.uk/journals/titles/
10884602.asp

$443.00/year for institutions, print and online; $421.00/year for institutions, online only; $135.00/year for individuals. Journal for nursing addiction professionals.

★790★ *Journal of Child and Adolescent Substance Abuse*

The Haworth Press Inc.
10 Alice St.
Binghamton, NY 13904
Ph: (607)722-5857   Fr: 800-429-6784
URL: http://www.haworthpress.com/store/
product.asp?sid=RGDXP14RA

Quarterly. $99.00/year for individuals; $145.00/year for individuals, Canada; $152.00/year for individuals, other countries; $430.00/year for institutions, agency, library; $616.00/year for institutions, Canada, agency, library; $655.00/year for institutions, other countries, agency, library. Journal covering strategies for chemically dependent adolescents and their families.

★791★ *Journal of Counseling Psychology*

American Psychological Association
750 1st St. NE
Washington, DC 20002-4242
Ph: (202)336-5540   Fax: (202)336-5549
Fr: 800-374-2721
E-mail: journals@apa.org
URL: http://www.apa.org/journals/cou.html

Quarterly. $50.00/year for members, domestic; $66.00/year for members, foreign, surface freight; $78.00/year for members, foreign, air mail; $29.00/year for students, domestic; $45.00/year for students, foreign, surface freight; $57.00/year for students, foreign, air mail; $98.00/year for nonmembers, domestic; $119.00/year for nonmembers, foreign, surface freight; $129.00/year for nonmembers, foreign, air mail; $267.00/year for institutions, domestic. Journal presenting empirical studies about counseling processes and interventions, theoretical articles about counseling, and studies dealing with evaluation of counseling applications and programs.

★792★ Journal of Studies on Alcohol and Drugs

Rutgers University
607 Allison Rd.
Piscataway, NJ 08854-8001
Ph: (732)445-3510   Fax: (732)445-3500
URL: http://www.jsad.com/

Bimonthly. $140.00/year for individuals; $29.00 for single issue. Journal containing original research reports about alcohol and other drugs, their use and misuse, and their biomedical, behavioral, and sociocultural effects.

★793★ Monitor on Psychology

American Psychological Association
750 1st St. NE
Washington, DC 20002-4242
Ph: (202)336-5540   Fax: (202)336-5549
Fr: 800-374-2721
E-mail: journals@apa.org
URL: http://www.apa.org/monitor/

Monthly. $46.00/year for nonmembers; $86.00/year for individuals, foreign, surface freight; $113.00/year for individuals, foreign, air freight; $87.00/year for institutions, non-member, foreign, surface freight; $168.00/year for institutions, foreign, air freight; $195.00/year for institutions, air freight; $3.00/year for single issue. Magazine of the APA. Reports on the science, profession, and social responsibility of psychology, including latest legislative developments affecting mental health, education, and research support.

★794★ Spectrum

Association for Counselor Education and Supervision (ACES)
1678 Asylum Ave
West Hartford, CT 06117
Ph: (860)231-6778   Fax: (860)231-5774
Fr: 800-347-6647
E-mail: jdurham@sjc.edu
URL: http://www.acesonline.net/

Description: Quarterly. Focuses on "the need for quality education and supervision of counselors in all work settings," the accreditation process, and professional development activities for counselors. Recurring features include news of the activities, programs, and members of ACES and related organizations.

★795★ Substance Use & Misuse

Marcel Dekker Inc.
270 Madison Ave.
New York, NY 10016
Ph: (212)696-9000   Fax: (212)685-4540
Fr: 800-228-1160
URL: http://www.tandf.co.uk/journals/journal.asp?issn=1082-6084&s

Monthly. $450.00/year for individuals, print only; $3,095.00/year for institutions, print & online; $2,940.00/year for institutions, online only. Medical Journal reporting individual and community problems brought on by drug, alcohol, and tobacco use, abuse, and dependency. Also considers legal and social aspects of addiction.

PLACEMENT AND JOB REFERRAL SERVICES

★796★ National Association on Drug Abuse Problems (NADAP)

355 Lexington Ave.
New York, NY 10017
Ph: (212)986-1170   Fax: (212)697-2939
E-mail: volunteer@nadap.com
URL: http://www.nadap.org

Description: Serves as an information clearinghouse and referral bureau for corporations and local communities interested in prevention of substance abuse and treatment of substance abusers. Provides: resources to local communities seeking to combat drug and alcohol abuse; corporate services for employers interested in creating a drug-free workplace. Makes available vocational education services including training in job hunting, job interview workshops, training programs for substance abuse treatment professionals, and individual consultations for recovering substance abusers seeking to return to the job market. Provides placement services; has conducted surveys on the employability of rehabilitated drug users and found that former addicts perform comparably with others hired for similar jobs. Operates Neighborhood Prevention Network, through which local communities develop parent support groups and youth peer leadership groups dedicated to combating drug and alcohol abuse. Maintains speakers' bureau.

EMPLOYER DIRECTORIES AND NETWORKING LISTS

★797★ Directory of Alcoholism Resources and Services

Alcoholism Council of New York
2-26 Washington St. 7th Fl.
New York, NY 10004
Ph: (212)252-7001   Fax: (212)252-7021
Fr: 800-56S-OBER

Biennial. $40.00 for individuals. Covers over 100 detoxification facilities, sobering-up stations, inpatient rehabilitation agencies, residences, halfway houses, outpatient alcohol abuse services, and related agencies and organizations in New York City. Entries include: Organization or facility name, address, phone, services offered, and other data. Arrangement: Classified by type of treatment or service offered.

★798★ Directory of Drug and Alcohol Residential Rehabilitation Facilities

Grey House Publishing
185 Millerton Rd.
PO Box 860
Millerton, NY 12546
Ph: (518)789-8700   Fax: (518)789-0556
Fr: 800-562-2139

URL: http://www.greyhouse.com

Published 2003. $165.00 for individuals. Covers more than 6,000 facilities for drug and alcohol residential rehabilitation in the United States, including drug rehab centers, addiction counseling services, support groups, drug and alcohol addiction resources, recovery homes, residential treatment centers, and alcohol treatment centers. Entries include: Name, contact information for each one, including mailing address, phone and faxes, email and websites, mission statement, type of treatment programs, cost, average length of stay, numbers of residents and counselors, accreditation, insurance plans accepted, type of environment, religious affiliation, education components. Arrangement: Alphabetical by state.

★799★ Drug Information for Teens

Omnigraphics Inc.
615 Griswold St.
PO Box 31-1640
Detroit, MI 48226
Ph: (313)961-1340   Fax: (313)961-1383
Fr: 800-234-1340
URL: http://www.omnigraphics.com

Latest edition 2nd; Published 2006. $58.00 for individuals. Publication includes: List of state and national organizations with additional information and assistance regarding substance abuse. Principal content of publication is information about various aspects of drug and alcohol abuse. Indexes: Alphabetical.

★800★ Drugs, Alcohol, and Tobacco

Macmillan Reference USA
300 Park Ave. S, 9th Fl.
New York, NY 10010-5354
Fr: 800-877-4253
URL: http://www.gale.com

November 2002. $360.00. Publication includes: List of organizations of interest regarding addictions. Entries include: Name, address, phone, and URL. Principal content of publication is information focusing on drugs, alcohol, and tobacco addictions and their relation to society. Indexes: Alphabetical.

★801★ Drugs and Controlled Substances

Gale, Cengage Learning
27500 Drake Rd.
Farmington Hills, MI 48331-3535
Ph: (248)699-4253   Fax: (248)699-8065
Fr: 800-877-4253
URL: http://www.galegroup.com

Published November 2002. $177.00 for individuals. Publication includes: List of Web sites for each entry. Principal content of publication is information about legal addictive drugs, illegal drugs, other controlled substances, and often-abused prescription and over-the-counter drugs. Indexes: Alphabetical.

★802★ Iowa Substance Abuse & Gambling Service Directory

Iowa Substance Abuse Information Center
500 1st St. SE
Cedar Rapids, IA 52401
Ph: (319)398-5133   Fax: (319)398-0476
Fr: (866)242-4111
URL: http://www.drugfreeinfo.org

Annual, fall. Free. Covers about 190 alcohol and drug abuse treatment and prevention programs. Entries include: For treatment and prevention programs–Name, organization name, address, phone, services; names, addresses, and phone numbers of branch offices and counties covered; code indicating whether a recipient of state or federal substance abuse funds. For others–Name, name and title of contact, address, phone. Arrangement: Classified by activity; treatment programs, gambling treatment programs and prevention programs are geographical. Indexes: Program name, program county.

★803★ National Directory of Drug and Alcohol Abuse Treatment Programs

Substance Abuse and Mental Health
  Services Administration
1 Choke Cherry Rd.
Rockville, MD 20857
Ph: (240)276-1250   Fax: (240)276-1260
URL: http://www.findtreatment.samhsa.gov

Annual. Covers about 11,000 federal, state, local, and privately funded facilities providing drug abuse and alcoholism treatment services. Entries include: Facility name, address, phone, and selected services provided; based on the National Survey of Substance Abuse Treatment Services. Arrangement: State, city, alphabetical by facility.

HANDBOOKS AND MANUALS

★804★ Careers in Counseling & Human Services

Accelerated Development
7625 Empire Dr.
Florence, KY 41042
Fr: 800-821-8312
URL: http://www.tandf.co.uk/homepages/a-dhome.html

Brooke B. Collison and Nancy J. Garfield, editors. Second edition, 1996. $32.95 (paper). 153 pages.

★805★ Careers in Social and Rehabilitation Services

The McGraw-Hill Companies
PO Box 182604
Columbus, OH 43272
Fax: (614)759-3749   Fr: 877-883-5524
E-mail: customer.service@mcgraw-hill.com
URL: http://www.mcgraw-hill.com

Geraldine O. Garner. 2001. $19.95; 14.95 (paper). 128 pages.

★806★ Clinical Supervision in Alcohol and Drug Abuse Counseling: Principles, Models, Methods

Jossey-Bass
989 Market St.
San Francisco, CA 94103
Ph: (415)433-1740   Fax: (415)433-0499
Fr: 800-255-5945
E-mail: custserv@wiley.com
URL: http://www.josseybass.com/WileyCDA/

David J. Powell, Archie Brodsky. 2004. $45.00. 448 pages.

★807★ Essentials of Chemical Dependency Counseling

Aspen Publishers
1 Lake St.
Upper Saddle River, NJ 07458
Ph: (201)236-7000   Fax: 800-445-6991
Fr: 800-638-8437
URL: http://www.aspenpublishers.com/

Dan Ellis, Gary W. Lawson, and P. Clayton Rivers. Third edition, 2003. $57.00. 227 pages.

★808★ Global Criteria: The 12 Core Functions of the Substance Abuse Counselor

Learning Publications, Inc.
PO Box 1338
Holmes Beach, FL 34218-1338
Fr: 800-222-1525

John W. Herdman. Third edition, 2000. $23.95 (paper). 128 pages.

★809★ Great Jobs for Liberal Arts Majors

The McGraw-Hill Companies
PO Box 182604
Columbus, OH 43272
Fax: (614)759-3749   Fr: 877-883-5524
E-mail: customer.service@mcgraw-hill.com
URL: http://www.mcgraw-hill.com

Blythe Camenson. Second edition, 2001. $14.95 (paper). 256 pages.

★810★ Introduction to Alcoholism Counseling: A Bio-Psycho-Social Approach

Routledge
270 Madison Ave.
New York, NY 10016
Ph: (212)216-7800   Fax: (212)563-2269
URL: http://www.routledge.com/

Jerome D. Levin. Second edition, 1995. $104.95; $38.95 (paper). 225 pages. Book examines the medical and then the social, anthropological and psychological underpinnings of alcoholism.

★811★ Opportunities in Counseling and Development Careers

The McGraw-Hill Companies
PO Box 182604
Columbus, OH 43272
Fax: (614)759-3749   Fr: 877-883-5524

E-mail: customer.service@mcgraw-hill.com
URL: http://www.mcgraw-hill.com

Neale J.Baxter, Mark U. Toch, and Philip A. Perry. 1997. $14.95; $11.95 (paper). 160 pages. A guide to planning for and seeking opportunities in this challenging field. Illustrated.

★812★ Opportunities in Mental Health Careers

The McGraw-Hill Companies
PO Box 182604
Columbus, OH 43272
Fax: (614)759-3749   Fr: 877-883-5524
E-mail: customer.service@mcgraw-hill.com
URL: http://www.mcgraw-hill.com

Philip A. Perry. 1996. $14.95; $11.95 (paper) 160 pages. Part of the "Opportunities in ..." Series.

★813★ Professional Alcohol and Drug Counselor Supervisor's Handbook

Learning Publications, Inc.
PO Box 1338
Holmes Beach, FL 34218-1338
Fr: 800-222-1525

Lawrence Clayton and Randy Van Nostrand. 2002. $18.95 (paper). 112 pages.

★814★ The Treatment of Drinking Problems: A Guide for Helping Professions

Cambridge University Press
32 Ave. of the Americas
New York, NY 10013
Ph: (212)924-3900   Fax: (212)691-3239
E-mail: newyork@cambridge.org
URL: http://www.cambridge.org

Griffith Edwards, Christopher C. H. Cook and Jane Marshall. Fourth edition, 2003. $80.00. Covers modern trends relating to psychological and pharmacological interventions and reappraises the role of self-help groups. 428 pages.

TRADESHOWS

★815★ American Counseling Association World Conference

American Counseling Association
5999 Stevenson Ave.
Alexandria, VA 22304-3300
Ph: (703)823-9800   Fax: (703)823-6862
Fr: 800-347-6647
E-mail: meetings@counseling.org
URL: http://www.counseling.org

Annual. **Primary Exhibits:** Books, career development information, college selection, student financial aid, testing and measurement techniques, practice management companies, software, rehabilitation aids, and community agencies and private clinics specializing in substance abuse and mental health.

★816★ Association for Counselor Education and Supervision National Conference

Association for Counselor Education and Supervision
c/o American Counseling Association
PO Box 791006
Baltimore, MD 21279-1006
Ph: (703)823-9800   Fax: (703)823-0252
Fr: 800-347-6647
E-mail: feitstep@isu.edu
URL: http://www.acesonline.net

Annual. **Primary Exhibits:** Exhibits relating to the professional preparation of counselors.

OTHER SOURCES

★817★ Alcoholics Anonymous World Services (AA)

PO Box 459
New York, NY 10163
Ph: (212)870-3400
URL: http://www.aa.org

Description: Individuals recovering from alcoholism. Maintains that members can solve their common problem and help others achieve sobriety through a twelve step program that includes sharing their experience, strength, and hope with each other. Self-supported through members' contributions, not an allied with any sect, denomination, political organization, or institution and does not endorse nor oppose any cause.

★818★ American Academy of Addiction Psychiatry (AAAP)

345 Blackstone Blvd., 2nd Fl. - RCH
Providence, RI 02906
Ph: (401)524-3076   Fax: (401)272-0922
E-mail: cj@aaap.org
URL: http://www.aaap.org

Members: Psychiatrists and other health care and mental health professionals treating people with addictive behaviors. **Purpose:** Promotes accessibility to highest quality treatment for all who need it; promotes excellence in clinical practice in addiction psychiatry; educates the public to influence public policy regarding addictive illness; provides continuing education for addiction professionals; disseminates new information in the field of addiction psychiatry; and encourages research on the etiology, prevention, identification, and treatment of the addictions.

★819★ American Council on Alcoholism (ACA)

1000 E Indian School Rd.
Phoenix, AZ 85014
Fax: (602)264-7403   Fr: 800-527-5344
E-mail: info@aca-usa.org
URL: http://www.aca-usa.org

Description: Works to educate the public about the effects of alcohol, alcoholism, alcohol abuse, and the need for prompt, effective, affordable, and available treatment.

★820★ American Society of Addiction Medicine (ASAM)

4601 N Park Ave., Upper Arcade No. 101
Chevy Chase, MD 20815
Ph: (301)656-3920   Fax: (301)656-3815
E-mail: email@asam.org
URL: http://www.asam.org

Description: Physicians with special interest and experience in the field of alcoholism and other drug dependencies and who wish to share this experience with other professionals in order to extend their knowledge of addictive diseases; promote dissemination of that knowledge; enlighten the public regarding these problems; advance education and research in the field of addiction. Holds annual Ruth Fox Course for Physicians, annual Medical-Scientific Conference and five other conferences/courses.

★821★ Christian Addiction Rehabilitation Association (CARA)

Whosoever Gospel Mission
101 E Chelten Ave.
Philadelphia, PA 19144
Ph: (215)438-3094   Fr: 800-624-5156
E-mail: agrm@agrm.org
URL: http://www.iugm.org/cara.html

Description: Provides support and serves as a clearinghouse of information for individuals involved in ministry to addicts. Conducts two conferences per year.

★822★ Do It Now Foundation (DINF)

PO Box 27568
Tempe, AZ 85285-7568
Ph: (480)736-0599   Fax: (480)736-0771
E-mail: info@doitnow.org
URL: http://www.doitnow.org

Description: Works to provide factual information to students and adults about prescription drugs, over-the-counter drugs, street drugs, alcohol, eating disorders, AIDS, and related health issues. Assists organizations engaged in alcohol and drug abuse education.

★823★ Hazelden Foundation (HF)

PO Box 11-C03
Center City, MN 55012-0011
Ph: (651)213-4200   Fax: (651)213-4411
Fr: 800-257-7810
E-mail: info@hazelden.org
URL: http://www.hazelden.org

Description: Provides treatment, recovery, education, and professional services for chemical dependency and other addictive behaviors. Operates: Hazelden Foundation Center, a treatment center; Fellowship Club in New York, St. Paul and West Palm Beach, Florida, an intermediate care facility; Hazelden Center for Youth and Families for adolescents and young adults; Hazelden Renewal Center for individuals recovering from addictive behaviors and their families; Hanley-Hazelden Center in West Palm Beach, Florida, for inpatient and outpatient treatment; Provides: aftercare therapy; counselor training; 5-7 day, live-in family program that acquaints relatives and other associates of chemically-dependent individuals with problems of chemical dependency; continuing education programs for professionals; and communities.

★824★ Health Assessment & Treating Occupations

Delphi Productions
3159 6th St.
Boulder, CO 80304
Ph: (303)443-2100   Fax: (303)443-4022
Fr: 888-443-2400
E-mail: support@delphivideo.com
URL: http://www.delphivideo.com

$95.00. 50 minutes. Part of the Careers for the 21st Century Video Library.

★825★ Institute for Integral Development (IID)

PO Box 2172
Colorado Springs, CO 80901
Ph: (719)634-7943   Fax: (719)630-7025
Fr: 800-544-9562
E-mail: iidevo@aol.com
URL: http://www.institutefortraining.com

Description: Provides a forum for discussion of issues pertaining to alcoholism and other addictions; seeks to train educators, medical professionals, and mental health practitioners in understanding and assisting addicted individuals. Sponsors seminars and workshops; provides educational audiotapes; offers consulting services. Maintains speakers' bureau; operates small library.

★826★ International Commission for the Prevention of Alcoholism and Drug Dependency (ICPA)

12501 Old Columbia Pike
Silver Spring, MD 20904
Ph: (301)680-6719
E-mail: the_icpa@hotmail.com

Members: Representatives of national public health committees and other individuals interested in the physical and social effects of alcoholism and drug dependency. **Purpose:** Fosters the scientific study of alcohol and drugs, their effects on the physical, mental, and moral powers of the individual, and their effects on social, economic, political, and religious life. **Activities:** Encourages preventive education; disseminates information on drug and alcohol abuse. Serves as a liaison with similar groups around the world. Sponsors exchange and research programs. Conducts film shows, forums, and radio and television events.

★827★ NAADAC The Association for Addiction Professionals (NAADAC)

1001 N Fairfax St., Ste. 201
Alexandria, VA 22314
Ph: (703)741-7686   Fax: (703)741-7698
Fr: 800-548-0497

E-mail: naadac@naadac.org
URL: http://www.naadac.org

Description: Promotes excellence in care by promoting the highest quality and most up-to-date, science-based services to clients, families and communities. Provides education, clinical training and certification. Among the organization's national certification programs are the National Certified Addiction Counselor, Tobacco Addiction Credential and the Masters Addiction Counselor designations.

★828★ Narcotic Educational Foundation of America (NEFA)

28245 Ave. Crocker, Ste. 230
Santa Clarita, CA 91355-1201
Ph: (661)775-6960   Fax: (661)775-1648
Fr: 877-775-6272

E-mail: info@cnoa.org
URL: http://www.cnoa.org/NEFA.htm

Description: Conducts an education program revealing the dangers that result from the illicit and abusive use of narcotics and dangerous drugs, so that youth and adults will be protected from both mental and physical drug dependency and harm.

★829★ National Association of Substance Abuse Trainers and Educators (NASATE)

6400 Press Dr.
Southern University at New Orleans
New Orleans, LA 70126
Ph: (504)286-5234
E-mail: eharrell@suno.edu

Members: Accredited colleges and universities offering 12 or more course credit hours in the field of substance abuse. **Purpose:** Goal is to provide a network for exchange on courses, student population, degreed and nondegreed programs, and graduate study in chemical dependency training. Acts as a clearinghouse for students interested in substance abuse training programs; assists universities with the development of such programs. Provides for the exchange of information among universities concerning certificates, continuing education units, degrees, and opportunities for transfer and enrollment in undergraduate, graduate, and professional schools. Examines the educational and training needs of students and their career mobility as substance abuse practitioners.

Animal Caretakers, Technicians, and Trainers

SOURCES OF HELP-WANTED ADS

★830★ American Bee Journal
Dadant & Sons Inc.
51 S 2nd St.
Hamilton, IL 62341
Ph: (217)847-3324   Fax: (217)847-3660
Fr: 888-922-1293
E-mail: abj@dadant.com
URL: http://www.dadant.com/journal/index.html

Monthly. $80.00/year for individuals, air-Asia, Africa, Mideast; $41.95/year for individuals, foreign, surface mail; $23.95/year for U.S., U.S. standard mail; $47.00/year for Canada, airmail; $83.00/year for individuals, airmail; $54.00/year for individuals, airmail Mexico; $89.00/year for individuals, airmail, Australia, New Zealand. Magazine for hobbyist and professional beekeepers. Covers hive management, honey handling, disease control, honey markets, foreign beekeeping, beekeeping history, bee laws, honey plants, marketing, and government beekeeping research.

★831★ American Journal of Veterinary Research
American Veterinary Medical Association
1931 N Meacham Rd., Ste. 100
Schaumburg, IL 60173
Ph: (847)925-8070   Fax: (847)925-1329
Fr: 800-248-2862
URL: http://www.avma.org/journals/ajvr/ajvr_about.asp

Monthly. $205.00/year for individuals; $215.00/year for other countries; $25.00 for single issue; $30.00 for single issue, other countries. Veterinary research on nutrition and diseases of domestic, wild, and furbearing animals.

★832★ American Mustang and Burro Association Journal
American Mustang and Burro Association
PO Box 1013
Grass Valley, CA 95945-1013
URL: http://www.ambainc.net/

Quarterly. Journal covering horses and burros.

★833★ Animal Guardian
Doris Day Animal League
227 Massachusetts Ave. NE, Ste. 100
Washington, DC 20002
Ph: (202)546-1761   Fax: (202)546-2193
URL: http://www.ddal.org/animalguardian/

Quarterly. Subscription included in membership. Membership magazine covering animal welfare.

★834★ Animal Keepers' Forum
American Association of Zoo Keepers Inc.
3601 SW 29th St., Ste. 133
Topeka, KS 66614-2054
E-mail: akfeditor@zk.kscoxmail.com
URL: http://aazk.org

Monthly. $10.00/year for members; $20.00/year for Canada, members. Professional journal of the American Association of Zoo Keepers, Inc.

★835★ ASA Bulletin
Avicultural Society of America
c/o Helen Hanson
PO Box 5516
Riverside, CA 92517-5516
Ph: (951)780-4102   Fax: (951)789-9366
URL: http://www.asabirds.org

Monthly. Covers the care, feeding, and breeding of birds in captivity. Contains membership roster and listings of bird specialty organizations and new members.

★836★ California Thoroughbred
California Thoroughbred Breeders Association
PO Box 60018
Arcadia, CA 91066-6018
Ph: (626)445-7800   Fax: (626)574-0852
Fr: 800-573-2822
URL: http://www.ctba.com/

Monthly. $125.00/year for members. Magazine about horse breeding and racing.

★837★ Cats & Kittens
Pet Publishing
7-L Dundas Cir.
Greensboro, NC 27407
Ph: (336)292-4047   Fax: (336)292-4272
URL: http://www.petpublishing.com/catkit/

$14.97/year for individuals. Magazine dedicated to cats. Covering feline stories, reports on feline medicine, breed profiles, and training advice.

★838★ The Chronicle of the Horse
The Chronicle of the Horse Inc.
PO Box 46
108 De Plains
Middleburg, VA 20118
Ph: (540)687-6341   Fax: (540)687-3937
E-mail: staff@chronofhorse.com
URL: http://www.chronofhorse.com

Weekly. $59.00/year; $79.00/year, Canada and all other countries; $108.00 for two years; $148.00 for two years, Canada and all other countries. $2.95 for single issue. Magazine covering English riding and horse sports.

★839★ CME Supplement to Veterinary Clinics of North America
Elsevier Science Inc.
360 Park Ave. S
New York, NY 10010
Ph: (212)989-5800   Fax: (212)633-3990
URL: http://www.elsevier.com

$55.00/year for individuals. Journal covering veterinary medicine, surgical treatment of animals.

★840★ Dog World
Fancy Publications - A Division of Bowtie, Inc.
PO Box 6050
Mission Viejo, CA 92690
Ph: (949)855-8822   Fax: (949)855-3045
E-mail: letters@dogworld.com
URL: http://www.dogworldmag.com/DogWorldMag

Monthly. $56.00/year for individuals, foreign surface delivery; $56.00/year for other countries, foreign air delivery. Magazine serving breeders, exhibitors, hobbyists and professionals in kennel operations, groomers, veterinarians, animal hospitals/clinics and pet suppliers.

★841★ DVM Newsmagazine

Advanstar Communications
641 Lexington Ave.
8th Fl.
New York, NY 10022
Ph: (212)951-6600   Fax: (212)951-6793
Fr: 800-225-4569
E-mail: dvmnewsmagazine@advanstar.com
URL: http://www.advanstar.com

Monthly. Magazine for veterinarians in private practices in the U.S.

★842★ Equus

Primedia Equine Network
656 Quince Orchard Rd., Ste. 600
Gaithersburg, MD 20878
Ph: (301)977-3900   Fax: (301)990-9015
E-mail: eqletters@primedia.com
URL: http://www.equisearch.com/equus

Monthly. $30.00 for two years; $20.00/year for individuals. Magazine featuring health, care, and understanding of horses.

★843★ Journal of Animal Science

American Society of Animal Science
1111 N Dunlap Ave.
Savoy, IL 61874
Ph: (217)356-9050   Fax: (217)398-4119
URL: http://jas.fass.org/

Monthly. Professional journal covering animal science.

★844★ The Morgan Horse

American Morgan Horse Association
122 Bostwick Rd.
PO Box 960
Shelburne, VT 05482-0960
Ph: (802)985-4944   Fax: (802)985-8897

Monthly. $31.50/year for individuals, 2nd class; $70.00/year for individuals, 1st class; $53.50/year for Canada and Mexico; $61.50/year for other countries. Magazine for Morgan horse enthusiasts.

★845★ Mushing

Mushing Magazine
PO Box 246
3875 Geist Rd., Ste. E, No. 246
Fairbanks, AK 99709-3549
Ph: (917)929-6118   Fax: (973)300-0455
URL: http://www.mushing.com/

Bimonthly. $26.00/year for U.S. $48.00 for two years; $35.00/year for Canada; $63.00 for Canada, two years; $47.00/year for other countries; $84.00 for other countries, two years. Magazine dealing with all aspects of dog-powered sports.

★846★ New Methods

Ronald S. Lippert, A.H.T.
713 S Main St., C-1
Willits, CA 95490
Ph: (707)456-1262

Description: Monthly. Examines common problems and concerns in the field of animal health technology. Provides professionals with items on animal care and protection and medical breakthroughs. Recurring features include letters to the editor, interviews, notices of publications available, job listings, news of educational opportunities, and news of research.

★847★ Newsletter-Animal Behavior Society

Animal Behavior Society
Animal Behavior Office
Indiana University
2611 E. 10th St., No. 170
Bloomington, IN 47408-2603
Ph: (812)856-5541   Fax: (812)856-5542
URL: http://www.animalbehavior.org/ABS/Newsletters/Directory/

Description: Quarterly. Informs members of the Society of activities, events, meetings, announcements and opportunities in the field of animal behavior. Recurring features include a news of educational opportunities, job listings, and notices of publications available.

★848★ The Pointing Dog Journal

Village Press Publications
2779 Aero Park Dr.
PO Box 968
Traverse City, MI 49685
Fax: (231)946-3289   Fr: 800-327-7377
URL: http://www.pointingdogjournal.com/

$26.95/year for individuals; $49.95 for two years. Magazine covering tips on nutrition, healthcare, and first-aid for sporting dogs.

★849★ Saddle Horse Report

Saddle Horse Report
730 Madison St.
Shelbyville, TN 37162-1007
Ph: (931)684-8123   Fax: (931)684-8196
E-mail: info@saddlehorsereport.com
URL: http://www.saddlehorsereport.com

Weekly. $60.00/year for individuals; $95.00 for two years; $135.00/year for individuals, 3 years. Newspaper containing national coverage of horse shows and sales.

★850★ TRENDS Magazine

American Animal Hospital Association
12575 West Bayaud Ave.
Lakewood, CO 80228
Ph: (303)986-2800   Fax: (303)986-1700
Fr: 800-883-6301
URL: http://www.aahanet.org

Bimonthly. $60.00/year for U.S. and Canada; $70.00/year for other countries; $20.00 for single issue. Professional magazine covering the management of small animal veterinary practices.

★851★ Veterinary Practice News

Bowtie Inc.
1500 Broadway, Ste. 2302
New York, NY 10036
Ph: (212)302-8080   Fax: (212)302-8289
URL: http://www.veterinarypracticenews.com/

Monthly. Magazine covering veterinary practice in the United States featuring developments and trends affecting companion animals and livestock.

★852★ Western Horseman

Western Horseman
3850 N Nevada Ave.
PO Box 7980
Colorado Springs, CO 80933-7980
Ph: (719)633-5524   Fax: (719)473-0997
URL: http://www.westernhorseman.com/

Monthly. $22.00/year for individuals; $42.00/year for individuals, for international orders; $32.00/year for individuals, for U.S. orders. Magazine covering forms of horsemanship and all breeds of horses; emphasizing western stock horses and western lifestyle.

PLACEMENT AND JOB REFERRAL SERVICES

★853★ American Veterinary Medical Association (AVMA)

1931 N Meacham Rd., Ste. 100
Schaumburg, IL 60173
Ph: (847)925-8070   Fax: (847)925-1329
Fr: 800-248-2862
E-mail: avmainfo@avma.org
URL: http://www.avma.org

Description: Professional society of veterinarians. Conducts educational and research programs. Provides placement service. Sponsors American Veterinary Medical Association Foundation (also known as AVMF Foundation) and Educational Commission for Foreign Veterinary Graduates. Compiles statistics. Accredits veterinary medical education programs and veterinary technician education programs.

★854★ National Animal Control Association (NACA)

PO Box 480851
Kansas City, MO 64148-0851
Ph: (913)768-1319   Fax: (913)768-1378
E-mail: naca@interserv.com
URL: http://www.nacanet.org

Description: Animal control agencies, humane societies, public health and safety agencies, corporations, and individuals. Works to educate and train personnel in the animal care and control professions. Seeks to teach the public responsible pet ownership; operates the NACA Network to provide animal control information; evaluates animal control programs. Provides training guides for animal control officers; makes available audiovisual materials. Conducts research.

Operates placement service and speakers' bureau.

EMPLOYER DIRECTORIES AND NETWORKING LISTS

★855★ Directory of Animal Care and Control Agencies

American Humane Association
63 Inverness Dr. E
Englewood, CO 80112-5117
Ph: (303)792-9900   Fax: (303)792-5333
Fr: 800-227-4645

Updated continuously; printed on request. Covers over 6,000 animal protection agencies; Canadian and some other foreign agencies are available; national and individual state editions are available. Entries include: Agency name, address, phone, contact. Arrangement: Geographical.

HANDBOOKS AND MANUALS

★856★ Careers with Animals

Barron's Educational Series, Incorporated
250 Wireless Blvd.
Hauppauge, NY 11788-3917
Ph: (631)434-3311   Fax: (631)434-3723
Fr: 800-645-3476
E-mail: fbrown@barronseduc.com
URL: http://barronseduc.com

Audrey Pavia. 2001. $10.95. 176 pages. Explores careers within the animal industry.

★857★ Careers with Dogs

Barron's Educational Series, Inc.
250 Wireless Blvd.
Hauppauge, NY 11788-3917
Ph: (631)434-3311   Fax: (631)434-3723
Fr: 800-645-3476
E-mail: fbrown@barronseduc.com
URL: http://barronseduc.com

Audrey Pavia. 1998. $8.95 (paper). 137 pages. Covers various types of work available for animal lovers. Includes information on salaries, qualifications, and job-hunting.

★858★ Careers in Veterinary Medicine

Rosen Publishing Group, Inc.
29 E. 21st St.
New York, NY 10010
Ph: (212)777-3017   Fax: 888-436-4643
Fr: 800-237-9932
URL: http://www.rosenpublishing.com/

Jane Caryl Duncan. Revised edition, 1994. $16.95; $9.95 (paper). Contains advice from a real veterinarian and a description of her work.

★859★ Kicked, Bitten, and Scratched: Life and Lessons at the World's Premier School for Exotic Animal Trainers

Penguin Group (USA)
375 Hudson St.
New York, NY 10014
Ph: (212)366-2000   Fax: (212)366-2666
URL: http://us.penguingroup.com/

Amy Sutherland. 2006. $25.95.

★860★ Large Animal Clinical Procedures for Veterinary Technicians

Elsevier
1600 John F. Kennedy Blvd., Ste. 1800
Philadelphia, PA 19103
Ph: (215)239-3900   Fax: (215)239-3990
Fr: 800-523-4069
URL: http://us.elsevierhealth.com

Elizabeth A. Hanie. 2005. $48.95. Large animal medical and surgical techniques are described. The book is divided into four parts: equine, bovine, small ruminant (sheep and goats), and swine.

★861★ Opportunities in Animal and Pet Care Careers

The McGraw-Hill Companies
PO Box 182604
Columbus, OH 43272
Fax: (614)759-3749   Fr: 877-883-5524
E-mail: customer.service@mcgraw-hill.com
URL: http://www.mcgraw-hill.com

Mary Price Lee and Richard S. Lee. 2001. $13.95. 160 pages. Covers the field from small animal medicine to large animal medicine, and provides job-hunting advice. Illustrated.

TRADESHOWS

★862★ American Humane Association Annual Conference

American Humane Association
63 Inverness Dr., E.
Englewood, CO 80112-5117
Ph: (303)792-9900   Fax: (303)792-5333
URL: http://www.americanhumane.org

Annual. **Primary Exhibits:** Animal welfare equipment, including pet food, cages, trucks, ID programs, and health and veterinary products.

OTHER SOURCES

★863★ American Association for Laboratory Animal Science (AALAS)

9190 Crestwyn Hills Dr.
Memphis, TN 38125-8538
Ph: (901)754-8620   Fax: (901)753-0046
E-mail: info@aalas.org

URL: http://www.aalas.org

Members: Persons and institutions professionally concerned with the production, use, care, and study of laboratory animals. **Purpose:** Serves as clearinghouse for collection and exchange of information on all phases of laboratory animal care and management and on the care, use, and procurement of laboratory animals used in biomedical research. **Activities:** Conducts examinations and certification through its Animal Technician Certification Program.

★864★ American Boarding Kennels Association (ABKA)

1702 E Pikes Peak Ave.
Colorado Springs, CO 80909-5717
Ph: (719)667-1600   Fax: (719)667-0116
Fr: 877-570-7788
E-mail: info@abka.com
URL: http://www.abka.com

Members: Persons or firms that board pets; kennel suppliers; others interested in the facility boarding kennel industry. **Purpose:** Seeks to upgrade the industry through accreditation educational programs, seminars and conventions. **Activities:** Provides insurance resources for members and supplies pet care information to the public. Promotes code of ethics and accreditation program for recognition and training of superior kennel operators. Compiles boarding facility statistics.

★865★ American Border Leicester Association (ABLA)

494 Evans Rd.
Chepachet, RI 02814
Ph: (401)949-4619
E-mail: khop4811@aol.com
URL: http://www.ablasheep.org

Members: Owners and admirers of Border Leicester sheep. **Purpose:** Promotes Border Leicesters as a source of wool and meat. **Activities:** Sets breed standards and confers certification; maintains breed registry. Sponsors competitions; conducts educational programs.

★866★ American Water Spaniel Club (AWSC)

37499 Farris Rd.
Scio, OR 97374
Ph: (503)394-3047
E-mail: jeannie@awspaniels.com
URL: http://
www.americanwaterspanielclub.org

Members: Owners, breeders, and admirers of water spaniels. **Purpose:** Promotes quality breeding and acceptance of breed standards as approved by the American Kennel Club. **Activities:** Represents the interests of breeders; provides shelter and care to abandoned and abused water spaniels; conducts educational programs; sponsors competitions; compiles statistics.

★867★ International Police Work Dog Association (IPWDA)

PO Box 7455
Greenwood, IN 46143
E-mail: k9cop496@aol.com
URL: http://www.ipwda.org
Description: Aims to unite and assist all law enforcement agencies in the training and continued progress of all police work dogs. Seeks to establish a working standard for all police work dogs, handlers, and trainers through an accreditation program. Promotes the image of the police work dog.

★868★ National Dog Groomers Association of America (NDGAA)

PO Box 101
Clark, PA 16113-0101
Ph: (724)962-2711   Fax: (724)962-1919
E-mail: ndga@nationaldoggroomers.com
URL: http://www.nationaldoggroomers.com
Description: Dog groomers and supply distributors organized to upgrade the profession. Conducts state and local workshops; sponsors competitions and certification testing. Makes groomer referrals.

Anthropologists

SOURCES OF HELP-WANTED ADS

★869★ Anthropology in Action

Berghahn Journals
150 Broadway, Ste. 812
New York, NY 10038
Ph: (212)233-6004   Fax: (212)233-6007
Fr: 800-540-8663
URL: http://journals.berghahnbooks.com/aia/

$117.00/year for institutions, print and on-line; $113.00/year for institutions, online only; $45.00/year for individuals; $18.00/year for students. Journal featuring the use of anthropology in all areas of policy and practice.

★870★ Anthropology of Consciousness

American Anthropological Association
2200 Wilson Blvd., Ste. 600
Arlington, VA 22201
Ph: (703)528-1902   Fax: (703)528-3546
URL: http://www.aaanet.org/

Description: 2/year. Serves as an information exchange for researchers investigating the effect of culture on man's psychological and supernatural behavior patterns. Examines the topics of dreaming, altered states of consciousness, spirit possession, healing, divination, extrasensory perception, mysticism, myth, shamanism, and psychic archeology. Recurring features include book reviews, queries, notices of publications and symposia, news of members, and obituaries.

★871★ Anthropology News

American Anthropological Association
2200 Wilson Blvd., Ste. 600
Arlington, VA 22201
Ph: (703)528-1902   Fax: (703)528-3546
URL: http://www.aaanet.org/press/an/index.htm

Monthly. Free to qualified subscribers, members of AAA. Periodical covering anthropology, including archaeological, biological, ethnological, and linguistic research.

★872★ Anthropology of Work Review

American Anthropological Association
2200 Wilson Blvd., Ste. 600
Arlington, VA 22201
Ph: (703)528-1902   Fax: (703)528-3546
URL: http://www.aaanet.org/

Description: Quarterly. Promotes the development of ideas, data, and methods concerning all aspects of the study of anthropology of work.

★873★ The Asia Pacific Journal of Anthropology

Taylor & Francis Group Journals
325 Chestnut St., Ste. 800
Philadelphia, PA 19106
Ph: (215)625-8900   Fax: (215)625-8914
Fr: 800-354-1420
URL: http://www.tandf.co.uk/journals/titles/14442213.asp

$373.00/year for institutions, print and on-line; $354.00/year for institutions, online only; $94.00/year for online only; $100.00/year for individuals. Journal focusing on anthropological study.

★874★ AWIS Magazine

Association for Women in Science
1200 New York Ave. NW, Ste. 650
Washington, DC 20005
Ph: (202)326-8940   Fax: (202)326-8960
Fr: (866)657-2947
E-mail: awis@awis.org
URL: http://www.awis.org/

Description: Bimonthly. Covers issues, legislation, and trends related to science education for girls, women, and minorities. Includes information on grants and fellowships, job openings, educational programs, events, and notices of publications available.

★875★ Classical Antiquity

University of California Press/Journals
2120 Berkeley Way
Berkeley, CA 94704-1012
Ph: (510)642-4247   Fax: (510)643-7127
URL: http://www.ucpress.edu/journals/ca

Biennial. $45.00/year   for   individuals; $158.00/year for institutions, print & electronic; $25.00/year for students; $135.00/year for institutions, electronic only; $22.00 for single issue, individuals/students; $87.00 for single issue, institutions. Scholarly journal covering interdisciplinary research and issues in Classics-Greek and Roman literature, history, art, philosophy, archaeology, and philology.

★876★ Field Methods

Sage Publications Inc.
2455 Teller Rd.
Thousand Oaks, CA 91320
Ph: (805)499-0721   Fax: (805)499-8096
URL: http://qualquant.net/FM

Quarterly. $690.00/year for institutions, combined (print & e-access); $725.00/year for institutions, print & all online; $621.00/year for institutions, e-access; $656.00/year for institutions, all online content; $676.00/year for institutions, print only; $131.00/year for individuals, print only; $186.00 for institutions, single print; $43.00 for individuals, single print; $621.00 for institutions, e-access thru 1999. Journal covering issues concerning scholars, students, and professionals who do fieldwork in cultural anthropology.

★877★ Human Nature

Transaction Publishers
Rutgers - The State University of New Jersey
35 Berrue Cir.
Piscataway, NJ 08854-8042
Ph: (732)445-2280   Fax: (732)445-3138
URL: http://www.transactionpub.com

Quarterly. $85.00/year for individuals, online only; $85.00/year for individuals, print only; $95.00/year for individuals, print & online only; $320.00/year for institutions, online only; $320.00/year for institutions, print only; $338.00/year for institutions, print & online only. Interdisciplinary journal covering the biological, social and environmental factors behind human behavior.

★878★ ISEM Newsletter

Institute for the Study of Earth and Man
N.L. Heroy Hall
PO Box 0274
Dallas, TX 75275-0274
Ph: (214)768-2425   Fax: (214)768-4289
E-mail: isem@mail.smu.edu
URL: http://www.smu.edu/isem/

Description: Semiannual. Reports on research in the anthropological, geological, and statistical sciences. Includes notices of research funds, grants, and contracts awarded. Provides biographical sketches of new faculty members in the anthropological, geological, and statistical sciences departments at Southern Methodist University. Recurring features include news of research and news of members.

★879★ Journal of Folklore Research

Indiana University Press
601 N Morton St.
Bloomington, IN 47404-3797
Ph: (812)855-6657   Fax: (812)855-8817
Fr: 800-842-6796
URL: http://inscribe.iupress.org/loi/jfr

$29.50/year for U.S. $39.50/year for individuals, through surface mail; $50.50/year for individuals, through air mail; $76.00/year; $65.00/year; $55.00/year; $76.00/year for institutions, foreign air mail; $65.00/year for institutions, foreign surface; $55.00/year for institutions, U.S. Journal covering anthropology and folklore.

★880★ Journal of the Society for the Anthropology of Europe

University of California Press/Journals
2120 Berkeley Way
Berkeley, CA 94704-1012
Ph: (510)642-4247   Fax: (510)643-7127
URL: http://www.h-net.org/%7Esae/sae/JSAE.htm

Semiannual. $46.00/year for individuals, non-members; $46.00/year for institutions. Journal containing articles and book reviews related to European anthropology.

★881★ Kansas Anthropological Association Newsletter

Kansas Anthropological Association
PO Box 750962
Topeka, KS 66675-0962
Ph: (785)272-8681   Fax: (785)272-8682
URL: http://www.kshs.org/resource/kaa.htm

Description: Four issues/year. Covers Association field projects, conferences, and fundraising activities. Contains reports from local chapters. Recurring features include news of research, a calendar of events, and news of educational opportunities.

★882★ NAPA Bulletin

University of California Press/Journals
2120 Berkeley Way
Berkeley, CA 94704-1012
Ph: (510)642-4247   Fax: (510)643-7127
URL: http://

www.practicinganthropology.org/napabulletin/

Annual. $12.50/year for individuals, AAA members; $25.00/year for individuals, non-members; $25.00/year for institutions. Journal focusing on information relevant to the advancement of professionals in the field from the National Association for the Practice of Anthropology (NAPA).

★883★ North American Dialogue

American Anthropological Association
2200 Wilson Blvd., Ste. 600
Arlington, VA 22201
Ph: (703)528-1902   Fax: (703)528-3546
URL: http://sananet.org/journal.html

Semiannual. Journal of the Society for the Anthropology of North America.

★884★ Oral History Review

University of California Press/Journals
2120 Berkeley Way
Berkeley, CA 94704-1012
Ph: (510)642-4247   Fax: (510)643-7127
URL: http://www.ucpress.edu/journals/ohr

Biennial. $65.00/year for individuals; $35.00/year for students; $80.00/year for individuals, contributing individuals; $140.00/year for institutions, member print & electronic; $116.00/year for individuals, electronic; $34.00 for single issue, individuals/students/retired; $69.00 for single issue, institutions. Scholarly journal of the Oral History Association covering oral history of people who have participated in important political, cultural, and economic social developments in modern times.

★885★ Society for Historical Archaeology Newsletter

Society for Historical Archaeology
15245 Shady Grove Rd.,Ste. 130
Department of Anthropology
Rockville, MD 20850
Ph: (301)990-2454   Fax: (301)990-9771
E-mail: hq@sha.org
URL: http://www.sha.org/Publications/publications.htm

Description: Quarterly. Supports the aims of the Society, which "promotes scholarly research and the dissemination of knowledge concerning historical archeology." Presents information on current research, legislative developments, and Society meetings and activities. Recurring features include editorials, letters to the editor, news of members, and a calendar of events.

★886★ Voices

American Anthropological Association
2200 Wilson Blvd., Ste. 600
Arlington, VA 22201
Ph: (703)528-1902   Fax: (703)528-3546
URL: http://sscl.berkeley.edu/%7Eafaweb/voices.html

Annual. Periodical covering activities in feminist anthropology.

★887★ WAS Newsletter

World Archaeological Society
120 Lakewood Dr.
Hollister, MO 65672
Ph: (417)334-2377
E-mail: ronwriterartist@aol.com
URL: http://www.worldarchaeologicalsociety.com

Description: Periodic. Promotes the scientific and constructive study of antiquity within the international fields of archaeology, anthropology, and art history. Recurring features include announcements of recommended books; items on people, museums, and societies; news of research; letters to the editor; obituaries; verses; and columns titled Career Notes and Democracy Club.

PLACEMENT AND JOB REFERRAL SERVICES

★888★ African Studies Association (ASA)

Douglass Campus
132 George St.
New Brunswick, NJ 08901-1400
Ph: (732)932-8173   Fax: (732)932-3394
E-mail: asaed@rci.rutgers.edu
URL: http://www.africanstudies.org

Members: Persons specializing in teaching, writing, or research on Africa including political scientists, historians, geographers, anthropologists, economists, librarians, linguists, and government officials; persons who are studying African subjects; institutional members are universities, libraries, government agencies, and others interested in receiving information about Africa. **Purpose:** Seeks to foster communication and to stimulate research among scholars on Africa. **Activities:** Sponsors placement service; conducts panels and discussion groups; presents exhibits and films.

★889★ Program on the Analysis and Resolution of Conflicts (PARC)

Syracuse University
400 Eggers Hall
Syracuse, NY 13244-1090
Ph: (315)443-2367   Fax: (315)443-3818
E-mail: rar@syr.edu
URL: http://www.maxwell.syr.edu/parc

Members: Anthropologists. **Purpose:** Fosters research on the social and cultural dynamics of peace and war. **Activities:** Provides curricular services; operates speakers' bureau and placement service; compiles statistics. Sponsors seminars and professional workshops.

EMPLOYER DIRECTORIES AND NETWORKING LISTS

★890★ American Journal of Physical Anthropology-American Association of Physical Anthropologists Membership Directory Issue

American Association of Physical
Anthropologists
244 Lord Hall, 124 W 17th Ave.
380 MFAC
Columbus, OH 43210
URL: http://www.physanth.org/pubs/

Annual, December. Publication includes: 1,500 physical anthropologists and scientists in closely related fields interested in the advancement of the science of physical anthropology through research and teaching of human variation, primate paleoanthropology, and primate evolution. Entries include: Name, affiliation, address. Arrangement: Alphabetical.

★891★ Diplomates, American Board of Forensic Anthropology Directory

American Board of Forensic Anthropology
c/o Leslie Eisenberg, Sec.
Burial Sites Preservation Program
State Historical Society of Wisconsin
Madison, WI 53706
Ph: (608)264-6503   Fax: (608)264-6542

Annual. Covers current diplomates in forensic anthropology.

★892★ Newsletter-Society for Historical Archaeology Membership Directory Issue

Society for Historical Archaeology
15245 Shady Grove Rd., Ste. 130
Rockville, MD 20850
Ph: (301)990-2454   Fax: (301)990-9771
URL: http://www.sha.org

Annual, June. Publication includes: List of about 2,100 member archaeologists, historians, anthropologists, and ethnohistorians, and other individuals and institutions having an interest in historical archaeology or allied fields. Entries include: Name, address. Arrangement: Alphabetical.

HANDBOOKS AND MANUALS

★893★ Careers in Anthropology

Mayfield Publishing Co.
1280 Villa St.
Mountain View, CA 94041-1176
Ph: (650)960-3222   Fax: (650)960-0328
Fr: 800-433-1279
URL: http://www.mhhe.com/

John T. Omohundro. Second edition, 1997. $23.75. 119 pages.

★894★ Doing Fieldwork in Japan

University of Hawaii Press
2840 Kolowalu St.
Honolulu, HI 96822-1888
Ph: (808)956-8255   Fax: (808)988-6052
E-mail: uhpbooks@hawaii.edu
URL: http://www.uhpress.hawaii.edu

Theodore C. Bestor, Patricia G. Steinhoff, and Victoria Lyon Bestor. 2003. $28.00. Illustrated. 428 pages. Exploring social sciences in Japan.

★895★ A Guide to Careers in Physical Anthropology

Greenwood Publishing Group Inc.
80 Post Rd. W
Westport, CT 06881
Ph: (203)266-3571   Fax: (203)222-1502
Fr: 800-225-5800
URL: http://www.greenwood.com/

Alan S. Ryan. 2001. $109.95. 328 pages.

★896★ Opportunities in Social Science Careers

The McGraw-Hill Companies
PO Box 182604
Columbus, OH 43272
Fax: (614)759-3749   Fr: 877-883-5524
E-mail: customer.service@mcgraw-hill.com
URL: http://www.mcgraw-hill.com

Rosanne J. Marek. 2004. $13.95. 160 Pages. VGM Opportunities Series.

★897★ Visions of Culture: An Introduction to Anthropological Theories and Theorists

AltaMira Press
4501 Forbes Blvd., Ste. 200
Lanham, MD 20706
Ph: (301)459-3366   Fax: (301)429-5748
URL: http://www.altamirapress.com/

Jerry D. Moore. Second edition, 2004. $29.95. 400 pages. Focused on college students interested in Anthropology.

TRADESHOWS

★898★ American Association of Physical Anthropologists Scientific/Professional Meeting

American Association of Physical
Anthropologists
PO Box 1897
Lawrence, KS 66044-8897
URL: http://www.physanth.org

Annual. **Primary Exhibits:** Exhibits for the advancement of the science of physical anthropology through research and teaching of human variation, primate paleoanthropology, and primate evolution. **Dates and Locations:** 2008 Apr 07-13; Columbus, OH.

★899★ American Society for Ethnohistory Conference

American Society for Ethnohistory
c/o R. David Edmunds, Pres.
University of Texas at Dallas
2601 N Floyd Rd.
Richardson, TX 75080
URL: http://ethnohistory.org

Annual. **Primary Exhibits:** Exhibits relating to the cultural history of ethnic groups worldwide.

★900★ Congress of the International Society for Human Ethology

International Society for Human Ethology
PO Box 418
Nyack, NY 10960
Ph: (207)581-2044   Fax: (207)581-6128
E-mail: karl.grammer@univie.ac.at

Biennial. **Primary Exhibits:** Books, journals, and equipment for observational research.

★901★ Organization of American Historians Annual Meeting

Organization of American Historians
112 N Bryan Ave.
PO Box 5457
Bloomington, IN 47408-5457
Ph: (812)855-7311   Fax: (812)855-0696
E-mail: oah@oah.org
URL: http://www.oah.org

Annual. **Primary Exhibits:** Equipment, supplies, and services of interest to historians, including textbooks and computer software.

OTHER SOURCES

★902★ American Academy of Forensic Sciences (AAFS)

410 N 21st St.
Colorado Springs, CO 80904-2712
Ph: (719)636-1100   Fax: (719)636-1993
E-mail: awarren@aafs.org
URL: http://www.aafs.org

Description: Represents criminalists, scientists, members of the bench and bar, pathologists, biologists, psychiatrists, examiners of questioned documents, toxicologists, odontologists, anthropologists, and engineers. Works to: encourage the study, improve the practice, elevate the standards, and advance the cause of the forensic sciences; improve the quality of scientific techniques, tests, and criteria; plan, organize, and administer meetings, reports, and other projects for the stimulation and advancement of these and related purposes. Maintains Forensic Sciences Job Listing; conducts selected research for the government; offers forensic expert referral service.

★903★ American Anthropological Association

2200 Wilson Blvd., Ste. 600
Arlington, VA 22201-3357
Ph: (703)528-1902   Fax: (703)528-3546
E-mail: members@aaanet.org
URL: http://www.aaanet.org

Description: Aims to further the professional interests of anthropologists; to disseminate anthropological knowledge and its use to address human problems; to promote the entire field of anthropology in all its diversity; to represent the discipline nationally and internationally, in the public and private sectors; to bring together anthropologists from all subfields and specializations, providing networking opportunities across the broad range of the discipline.

★904★ American Association of Physical Anthropologists (AAPA)

PO Box 7050
Lawrence, KS 66044
Fax: (785)843-1234   Fr: 800-627-0326
E-mail: aapamember@allenpress.com
URL: http://www.physanth.org

Description: Professional society of physical anthropologists and scientists in closely related fields interested in the advancement of the science of physical anthropology through research and teaching of human variation, paleoanthropology and primatology.

★905★ American Society for Eighteenth-Century Studies (ASECS)

Wake Forest University
PO Box 7867
Winston-Salem, NC 27109
Ph: (336)727-4694   Fax: (336)727-4697
E-mail: asecs@wfu.edu
URL: http://asecs.press.jhu.edu

Description: Scholars and others interested in the cultural history of the 18th century. Encourages and advances study and research in this area; promotes the interchange of information and ideas among scholars from different disciplines (such as librarianship and bibliography) who are interested in the 18th century. Co-sponsors seven fellowship programs; sponsors Graduate Student Caucus.

★906★ American Society of Primatologists (ASP)

University of California
Department of Psychology
1 Shields Ave.
Davis, CA 95616
Ph: (530)754-5890   Fax: (530)752-2087
E-mail: klbales@ucdavis.edu
URL: http://www.asp.org

Description: Promotes the discovery and exchange of information regarding nonhuman primates, including all aspects of their anatomy, behavior, development, ecology, evolution, genetics, nutrition, physiology, reproduction, systematics, conservation, husbandry and use in biomedical research.

★907★ American Studies Association (ASA)

1120 19th St. NW, Ste. 301
Washington, DC 20036
Ph: (202)467-4783   Fax: (202)467-4786
E-mail: asastaff@theasa.net
URL: http://www.georgetown.edu/cross-roads/asainfo.html

Description: Serves as professional society of persons interested in American literature, American history, sociology, anthropology, political science, philosophy, fine arts, and other disciplines; librarians, museum directors, and government officials. Concerned with any field of study relating to American life and culture, past and present. Members are interested in research and teaching that crosses traditional departmental lines.

★908★ Amerind Foundation (AF)

PO Box 400
2100 N Amerind Rd.
Dragoon, AZ 85609
Ph: (520)586-3666   Fax: (520)586-4679
E-mail: amerind@amerind.org
URL: http://www.amerind.org

Purpose: Conducts research in anthropology and archaeology of the greater American southwest and northern Mexico and ethnology in the Western Hemisphere. **Activities:** Offers artist shows; volunteer opportunities; public programs, and visiting scholar program. Operates museum.

★909★ Anthropology Film Center

HC70 Box 3209
Glorieta, NM 87535
Ph: (505)757-2219
E-mail: info@anthrofilm.org

Description: General anthropologists, visual anthropologists, culture and communication specialists, applied anthropologists, musicologists, linguists, and educators. Seeks to further scholarship, research, and practice in visual anthropology by using consultation and research services, seminars, publications, teaching, equipment outfitting, and specialized facilities. Has Anthropology Film Center that develops, reviews, and administers research projects in the following areas: generation and analysis of anthropology film (design, collection, and investigation of naturally occurring human behavior in context through visual technologies and methodologies); film as visual communication; sociovidistics (investigation of the social organization surrounding the production, use, and display of photographs and film materials in their cultural contexts); culture and human perception; visual/aural arts and media. Conducts other activities including: generation and publication of research films and reports; consultation with universities and institutions; resident fellow program. Offers Ethnographic and Documentary Film Program which provides introductory basics in photography, film making and ethnology, and hands on training with story boarding, camera, sound, editing and lighting exercises.

★910★ Association of Black Anthropologists (ABA)

Social Sciences Division
735 Anderson Hill Rd.
Purchase, NY 10577-1402
Ph: (914)251-6624
E-mail: dana-ain.davis@purchase.edu
URL: http://www.aaanet.org/assembly.htm

Description: A section of the American Anthropological Association. Anthropologists and others interested in the study of blacks and other people subjected to exploitation and oppression. Works to: formulate conceptual and methodological frameworks to advance understanding of all forms of human diversity and commonality; advance theoretical efforts to explain the conditions that produce social inequalities based on race, ethnicity, class, or gender; develop research methods that involve the people studied and local scholars in all stages of investigation and dissemination of findings.

★911★ Biological Anthropology Section (BAS)

Univ. of Alabama
Dept. of Anthropology
PO Box 870210
Tuscaloosa, AL 35487
Ph: (205)348-1958
E-mail: jbindon@tenhoor.as.ua.edu
URL: http://www.as.ua.edu/bas

Description: A unit of American Anthropological Association. International group of anthropologists concerned with the biological aspects of anthropology. Aims to maintain communication among biological anthropologists. Promotes scientific and public understanding of human origins and the interaction between biological and cultural dimensions that underlie the evolution of humans.

★912★ Institute for the Study of Man (ISM)

1133 13th St. NW, Ste. C-2
Washington, DC 20005
Ph: (202)371-2700   Fax: (202)371-1523
E-mail: iejournal@aol.com
URL: http://www.jies.org

Description: Aims to publish books and journals in areas related to anthropology, historical linguistics, and the human sciences.

★913★ International Studies Association (ISA)

University of Arizona
324 Social Sciences Bldg.
Tucson, AZ 85721
Ph: (520)621-7715   Fax: (520)621-5780
E-mail: isa@u.arizona.edu
URL: http://www.isanet.org

Members: Social scientists and other scholars from a wide variety of disciplines who are specialists in international affairs and cross-cultural studies; academicians; government officials; officials in international organizations; business executives; students. **Purpose:** Promotes research, improved teaching, and the orderly growth of knowledge in the field of international studies; emphasizes a multidisciplinary approach to problems. **Activities:** Conducts conventions, workshops and discussion groups.

★914★ **International Women's Anthropology Conference (IWAC)**

Anthropology Department
25 Waverly Pl.
New York University
New York, NY 10003
Ph: (212)998-8550   Fax: (212)995-4014
E-mail: constance.sutton@nyu.edu
URL: http://homepages.nyu.edu/~crs2/index.html

Members: Women anthropologists and sociologists who are researching and teaching topics such as women's role in development, feminism, and the international women's movement. **Purpose:** Encourages the exchange of information on research, projects, and funding; addresses policies concerning women from an anthropological perspective. Conducts periodic educational meetings with panel discussions.

★915★ **Kroeber Anthropological Society (KAS)**

Department of Anthropology
232 Kroeber Hall
Berkeley, CA 94720-3710
Ph: (510)642-3391   Fax: (510)643-8557
E-mail: kas@sscl.berkeley.edu
URL: http://anthropology.berkeley.edu/kas.html

Description: Represents anthropologists, students, interested laypersons and institutional members (300 major universities and anthropological institutions).

★916★ **National Association for the Practice of Anthropology (NAPA)**

2200 Wilson Blvd., Ste. 600
Arlington, VA 22201
Ph: (703)528-1902   Fax: (703)528-3546
E-mail: wiedmand@fiu.edu
URL: http://www.practicinganthropology.org

Description: A section of the American Anthropological Association. Professional anthropologists serving social service organizations, government agencies, and business and industrial firms. Works to help anthropologists develop and market their expertise in areas such as social and political analysis, and program design, evaluation, and management. Compiles statistics.

★917★ **National Association of Student Anthropologists (NASA)**

2200 Wilson Blvd., Ste. 600
Arlington, VA 22201
Ph: (703)528-1902   Fax: (703)528-3546
E-mail: kapu0004@umn.edu
URL: http://www.aaanet.org/nasa

Description: Anthropology graduate and undergraduate students. Promotes the interests and involvement of students as anthropologists-in-training; provides a network of students for finding jobs, attending graduate school or field programs, networking, and more.

★918★ **Professional Specialty Occupations**

Delphi Productions
3159 6th St.
Boulder, CO 80304
Ph: (303)443-2100   Fax: (303)443-4022
Fr: 888-443-2400
E-mail: support@delphivideo.com
URL: http://www.delphivideo.com

$95.00. 53 minutes. Part of the Careers for the 21st Century Video Library.

★919★ **Scientific, Engineering, and Technical Services**

Cambridge Educational
PO Box 2053
Princeton, NJ 08543-2053
Ph: 800-257-5126   Fax: (609)671-0266
Fr: 800-468-4227
E-mail: custserv@films.com
URL: http://www.cambridgeeducational.com

VHS and DVD. $89.95. 2002. 18 minutes. 2002. Part of the Career Cluster Series.

★920★ **Scientific Occupations**

Delphi Productions
3159 6th St.
Boulder, CO 80304
Ph: (303)443-2100   Fax: (303)443-4022
Fr: 888-443-2400
E-mail: support@delphivideo.com
URL: http://www.delphivideo.com

$95.00. 60 minutes. Part of the Careers for the 21st Century Video Library.

★921★ **Society for Applied Anthropology (SfAA)**

PO Box 2436
Oklahoma City, OK 73101-2436
Ph: (405)843-5113   Fax: (405)843-8553
E-mail: info@sfaa.net
URL: http://www.sfaa.net

Description: Professional society of **Members:** anthropologists, sociologists, psychologists, health professionals, industrial researchers, and educators. **Purpose:** Promotes scientific investigation of the principles controlling relations between human beings, and encourages wide application of these principles to practical problems.

★922★ **Society for Cultural Anthropology (SCA)**

University of Chicago
Department of Anthropology
1126 E 59th St.
Chicago, IL 60637
E-mail: farquhar@uchicago.edu
URL: http://www.aaanet.org/sca

Description: A section of the American Anthropological Association, dedicated to the study of culture. Compiles statistics.

★923★ **Society for Linguistic Anthropology (SLA)**

George Washington University
Department of Anthropology
2112 G St. NW, Rm. 201
Washington, DC 20052
Ph: (202)994-6545
E-mail: kuipers@gwu.edu
URL: http://www.aaanet.org/sla

Description: Serves as section of the American Anthropological Association. Represents University faculty; students. Promotes the anthropological study of language.

★924★ **Society for Urban, National and Transnational/Global Anthropology (SUNTA)**

Syracuse University
The Maxwell School
209 Maxwell Hall
Syracuse, NY 13244
E-mail: dpellow@maxwell.syr.edu
URL: http://www.sunta.org

Description: Seeks to advance the science and profession of urban, national and transnational/global anthropology. Promotes the advancement of research and the professional interests of urban national and transnational/global anthropologists. Encourages the distribution and application of knowledge acquired in the study of urban, national and transnational/global anthropology.

★925★ **World Archaeological Society (WAS)**

120 Lakewood Dr.
Hollister, MO 65672
Ph: (417)334-2377
E-mail: ronwriterartist@aol.com
URL: http://www.worldarchaeologicalsociety.com

Members: Professional and amateur archaeologists, anthropologists, and art historians in 32 countries. **Purpose:** Promotes the scientific and constructive study of antiquity within the fields of archaeology, anthropology, and art history. **Activities:** Conducts research on biblical archaeology, democracy, and the anthropology of drug addiction. Projects include the "Living" Museum of Democracy and the restoration of old Bibles. Conducts special research projects upon request. Supplies tape lectures for special programs. Provides ink and color illustrations for researchers.

Archaeologists

SOURCES OF HELP-WANTED ADS

★926★ American Archaeology
Archaeological Conservancy
5301 Central Ave. NE, Ste. 902
Albuquerque, NM 87108-1517
Ph: (505)266-1540
URL: http://www.americanarchaeology.com/aamagazine.html

Quarterly. $25.00/year for individuals. Magazine covering archaeology in the Americas.

★927★ American Indian Rock Art
American Rock Art Research Association
Arizona State Museum
University of Arizona
PO Box 210026
Tucson, AZ 85721-0026
Fax: 888-668-0052   Fr: 888-668-0052

Annual. Journal covering issues related to archaeology.

★928★ American Journal of Archaeology
Archaeological Institute of America
656 Beacon St., 6th Fl.
Boston, MA 02215-2006
Ph: (617)353-9361   Fax: (617)353-6550
URL: http://www.archaeological.org/webinfo.php?page=10041

Quarterly. $75.00/year for individuals, domestic; $95.00/year for individuals, international; $47.00/year for students, domestic; $67.00/year for students, other countries, international; $250.00/year for institutions, domestic; $290.00/year for institutions, other countries, international. Professional journal covering archaeological subjects.

★929★ Artifax
Institute for Biblical Archeology
5606 Medical Cir.
Madison, WI 53719
Ph: (608)271-1025   Fax: (608)271-1150
Fr: 800-373-9692

E-mail: scribe@broadcast.net
URL: http://www.bibleartifax.com

Description: Quarterly. Contains the latest information on developments in the field of Biblical Archeology, as well as thoughtful background articles for the layman interested in Biblical Archeology. Recurring features include letters to the editor, interviews, news of research, reports of meetings, news of educational opportunities, job listings, and book reviews. Also contains a column titled Archeology News Digest.

★930★ ASOR Newsletter
American Schools of Oriental Research
656 Beacon St., 5th Fl.
Boston, MA 02215
Ph: (617)353-6570   Fax: (617)353-6575
E-mail: asorpubs@asor.org
URL: http://www.asor.org/pubs/news/news.html

Description: Quarterly. Carries news and reports from archaeological institutes in Amman, Jerusalem, and Cyprus. Recurring features include news of research, a calendar of events, reports of meetings, news of educational opportunities, job listings, and notices of publications available.

★931★ AWIS Magazine
Association for Women in Science
1200 New York Ave. NW, Ste. 650
Washington, DC 20005
Ph: (202)326-8940   Fax: (202)326-8960
Fr: (866)657-2947
E-mail: awis@awis.org
URL: http://www.awis.org/

Description: Bimonthly. Covers issues, legislation, and trends related to science education for girls, women, and minorities. Includes information on grants and fellowships, job openings, educational programs, events, and notices of publications available.

★932★ Classical Antiquity
University of California Press/Journals
2120 Berkeley Way
Berkeley, CA 94704-1012
Ph: (510)642-4247   Fax: (510)643-7127

URL: http://www.ucpress.edu/journals/ca

Biennial. $45.00/year for individuals; $158.00/year for institutions, print & electronic; $25.00/year for students; $135.00/year for institutions, electronic only; $22.00 for single issue, individuals/students; $87.00 for single issue, institutions. Scholarly journal covering interdisciplinary research and issues in Classics-Greek and Roman literature, history, art, philosophy, archaeology, and philology.

★933★ East Asian Art & Archaeology Newsletter
Department of the History of Art
3405 Woodland Walk
Philadelphia, PA 19104
Ph: (215)898-8327   Fax: (215)573-2210
URL: http://www.arthistory.upenn.edu

Description: Three issues/year. Functions as an information guide to Asian exhibitions, museums, symposia, cultural research, and lectures. Recurring features include news of research, a calendar of events, reports of meetings, news of educational opportunities, job listings, book reviews, and notices of publications available.

★934★ PE & RS Photogrammetric Engineering & Remote Sensing
The Imaging and Geospatial Information Society
5410 Grosvenor Ln., Ste. 210
Bethesda, MD 20814-2160
Ph: (301)493-0290   Fax: (301)493-0208
E-mail: asprs@asprs.org
URL: http://www.asprs.org/

Monthly. $250.00/year for individuals, U.S.D 15 discount per subscp. off the base rate; $120.00/year for individuals, active; $80.00/year for individuals, associate; $45.00/year for students, domestic. Journal covering photogrammetry, remote sensing, geographic information systems, cartography, and surveying, global positioning systems, digital photogrammetry.

★935★ SAA Bulletin

Society for American Archaeology
900 2nd St. NE, No. 12
Washington, DC 20002-3560
Ph: (202)789-8200   Fax: (202)789-0284
E-mail: headquarters@saa.org
URL: http://www.saa.org

Description: 5/yr. Publishes informative articles about archaeology. Recurring features include letters to the editor, job listings, a calendar of events, notices of publications available, and columns titled Obituaries and News and Notes.

★936★ Sea History Gazette

National Maritime Historical Society
5 John Walsh Blvd.
PO Box 68
Peekskill, NY 10566
Ph: (914)737-7878   Fax: (914)737-7816
Fr: 800-221-6647
E-mail: editorial@seahistory.org
URL: http://www.seahistory.org/public_html/pblctn.htm

Description: Quarterly. Carries news from the fields of maritime history and preservation, including items on ship preservation, marine archaeology, sail training, and museum and exhibit openings. Designed for the layman and professional involved with the maritime heritage community. Recurring features include a calendar of events, reports of meetings, job listings, and book reviews.

★937★ Stanford Journal of Archaeology

Stanford University
Bldg. 120, Rm. 160
Stanford, CA 94305-2047
Ph: (650)725-6793   Fax: (650)725-6471
URL: http://archaeology.stanford.edu/journal/newdraft/

Irregular. Free, online. Online scholarly journal that publishes research in archaeology.

PLACEMENT AND JOB REFERRAL SERVICES

★938★ American Philological Association (APA)

292 Logan Hall
249 S 36th St.
Philadelphia, PA 19104-6304
Ph: (215)898-4975   Fax: (215)573-7874
Fr: 800-548-1784
E-mail: apaclassics@sas.upenn.edu
URL: http://www.apaclassics.org

Members: Teachers of Latin and Greek, classical archaeologists with literary interests, and comparative linguists. **Purpose:** Works for the advancement and diffusion of philological information. **Activities:** Sponsors placement service and campus advisory service to provide advice on instructional programs in classical studies.

★939★ Archaeological Institute of America (AIA)

656 Beacon St., 6th Fl.
Boston, MA 02215-2006
Ph: (617)353-9361   Fax: (617)353-6550
Fr: 877-524-5300
E-mail: aia@aia.bu.edu
URL: http://www.archaeological.org

Purpose: Educational and scientific society of archaeologists and others interested in archaeological study and research. Founded five schools of archaeology: American School of Classical Studies (Athens, 1881); School of Classical Studies of the American Academy (Rome, 1895); American Schools of Oriental Research (Jerusalem, 1900 and Baghdad, 1921); School of American Research (1907, with headquarters at Santa Fe, NM). Is allied with three research institutes: American Research Institute in Turkey; American Institute of Iranian Studies; American Research Center in Egypt. **Activities:** Maintains annual lecture programs for all branch societies. Operates placement service for archeology educators. Sponsors educational programs for middle school children.

★940★ Society for American Archaeology (SAA)

900 2nd St. NE, No. 12
Washington, DC 20002-3560
Ph: (202)789-8200   Fax: (202)789-0284
E-mail: headquarters@saa.org
URL: http://www.saa.org

Members: Professionals, vocationals, students, and others interested in American archaeology. **Purpose:** Stimulates scientific research in the archaeology of the New World by: creating closer professional relations among archaeologists, and between them and others interested in American archaeology; advocating the conservation of archaeological data and furthering the control or elimination of commercialization of archaeological objects; promoting a more rational public appreciation of the aims and limitations of archaeological research. **Activities:** Maintains placement service and educational programs.

EMPLOYER DIRECTORIES AND NETWORKING LISTS

★941★ Newsletter-Society for Historical Archaeology Membership Directory Issue

Society for Historical Archaeology
15245 Shady Grove Rd., Ste. 130
Rockville, MD 20850
Ph: (301)990-2454   Fax: (301)990-9771
URL: http://www.sha.org

Annual, June. Publication includes: List of about 2,100 member archaeologists, historians, anthropologists, and ethnohistorians, and other individuals and institutions having an interest in historical archaeology or allied

fields. Entries include: Name, address. Arrangement: Alphabetical.

HANDBOOKS AND MANUALS

★942★ Careers for Mystery Buffs and Other Snoops and Sleuths

The McGraw-Hill Companies
PO Box 182604
Columbus, OH 43272
Fax: (614)759-3749   Fr: 877-883-5524
E-mail: customer.service@mcgraw-hill.com
URL: http://www.mcgraw-hill.com

Blythe Camenson. Second edition, 2004. $12.95 (paper); $14.95 (cloth). 160 pages.

★943★ Opportunities in Social Science Careers

The McGraw-Hill Companies
PO Box 182604
Columbus, OH 43272
Fax: (614)759-3749   Fr: 877-883-5524
E-mail: customer.service@mcgraw-hill.com
URL: http://www.mcgraw-hill.com

Rosanne J. Marek. 2004. $13.95. 160 Pages. VGM Opportunities Series.

TRADESHOWS

★944★ American Society for Ethnohistory Conference

American Society for Ethnohistory
c/o R. David Edmunds, Pres.
University of Texas at Dallas
2601 N Floyd Rd.
Richardson, TX 75080
URL: http://ethnohistory.org

Annual. **Primary Exhibits:** Exhibits relating to the cultural history of ethnic groups worldwide.

★945★ Conference on Historical and Underwater Archaeology

Society for Historical Archaeology
15245 Shady Grove Rd.
Rockville, MD 20850
Ph: (301)990-2454   Fax: (301)990-9771
E-mail: hq@sha.org
URL: http://www.sha.org

Annual. **Primary Exhibits:** Archaeologists, historians, anthropologists, and ethnohistorians; other individuals and institutions with an interest in historical archaeology or allied fields.

★946★ Society for American Archaeology Conference

Society for American Archaeology
900 2nd St. NE, No. 12
Washington, DC 20002-3557
Ph: (202)789-8200   Fax: (202)789-0284
E-mail: headquarters@saa.org
URL: http://www.saa.org

Annual. **Primary Exhibits:** Archaeological equipment, supplies, and services academic books, GPS, GIS, software. **Dates and Locations:** 2008 Mar 26-30; Vancouver, BC, Canada ; 2009 Apr 22-26; Atlanta, GA.

OTHER SOURCES

★947★ Amerind Foundation (AF)

PO Box 400
2100 N Amerind Rd.
Dragoon, AZ 85609
Ph: (520)586-3666   Fax: (520)586-4679
E-mail: amerind@amerind.org
URL: http://www.amerind.org

Purpose: Conducts research in anthropology and archaeology of the greater American southwest and northern Mexico and ethnology in the Western Hemisphere. **Activities:** Offers artist shows; volunteer opportunities, public programs, and visiting scholar program. Operates museum.

★948★ Archaeological Conservancy (AC)

5301 Central Ave. NE, Ste. 902
Albuquerque, NM 87108-1517
Ph: (505)266-1540   Fax: (505)266-0311
E-mail: tacinfo@nm.net
URL: http://www.americanarchaeology.com

Members: People interested in preserving prehistoric and historic sites for interpretive or research purposes (most members are not professional archaeologists). **Purpose:** Seeks to acquire for permanent preservation, through donation or purchase, the ruins of past American cultures, primarily those of American Indians. Works throughout the U.S. to preserve cultural resources presently on private lands and protect them from the destruction of looters, modern agricultural practices, and urban sprawl. **Activities:** Operates with government agencies, universities, and museums to permanently preserve acquired sites.

★949★ ASPRS - The Imaging and Geospatial Information Society

5410 Grosvenor Ln., Ste. 210
Bethesda, MD 20814-2160
Ph: (301)493-0290   Fax: (301)493-0208
E-mail: asprs@asprs.org
URL: http://www.asprs.org

Members: Firms, individuals, government employees and academicians engaged in photogrammetry, photointerpretation, remote sensing, and geographic information systems and their application to such fields as archaeology, geographic information systems, military reconnaissance, urban planning, engineering, traffic surveys, meteorological observations, medicine, geology, forestry, agriculture, construction and topographic mapping. Mission is to advance knowledge and improve understanding of these sciences and to promote responsible applications. **Activities:** Offers voluntary certification program open to persons associated with one or more functional area of photogrammetry, remote sensing and GIS. Surveys the profession of private firms in photogrammetry and remote sensing in the areas of products and services.

★950★ Center for American Archeology (CAA)

PO Box 366
Kampsville, IL 62053
Ph: (618)653-4316   Fax: (618)653-4232
E-mail: caa@caa-archeology.org
URL: http://www.caa-archeology.org

Description: Philanthropic organizations, foundations, corporations, professional and amateur archaeologists, students, and others interested in archaeology in the U.S. Conducts archaeological research and disseminates the results. Excavates, analyzes, and conserves archaeological sites and artifacts. Sponsors tours, lectures, and educational and outreach programs, including university, middle school and junior high, and high school field schools; offers professional training at levels of detail ranging from secondary to postgraduate. Maintains speakers' bureau. Operates Visitors Center.

★951★ Epigraphic Society (ES)

97 Village Post Rd.
Danvers, MA 01923
Ph: (978)774-1275
E-mail: donalbb@epigraphy.org
URL: http://www.epigraphy.org

Description: Launches expeditions to North America and overseas. Reports discoveries and decipherments and assesses their historical implications. Participates in group lecture and teaching programs with other archaeological societies and university departments of archaeology and history.

★952★ Register of Professional Archaeologists (RPA)

5024-R Campbell Blvd.
Baltimore, MD 21236
Ph: (410)933-3486   Fax: (410)931-8111
E-mail: info@rpanet.org
URL: http://www.rpanet.org

Description: Represents archaeologists satisfying basic requirements in training and experience, including private consultants, individuals working with large firms, and academic personnel. Seeks to define professionalism in archaeology; provide a measure against which to evaluate archaeological actions and research; establish certification standards; provide for grievance procedures; demonstrate to other archaeologists and the public the nature of professional archaeology. Monitors related legislative activities; maintains register archives. Is developing educational programs and drafting standards and guidelines for field schools.

★953★ Scientific, Engineering, and Technical Services

Cambridge Educational
PO Box 2053
Princeton, NJ 08543-2053
Ph: 800-257-5126   Fax: (609)671-0266
Fr: 800-468-4227
E-mail: custserv@films.com
URL: http://www.cambridgeeducational.com

VHS and DVD. $89.95. 2002. 18 minutes. 2002. Part of the Career Cluster Series.

★954★ Society for Historical Archaeology (SHA)

15245 Shady Grove Rd., Ste. 130
Rockville, MD 20850
Ph: (301)990-2454   Fax: (301)990-9771
E-mail: hq@sha.org
URL: http://www.sha.org

Description: Represents archaeologists, historians, anthropologists, and ethnohistorians; other individuals and institutions with an interest in historical archaeology or allied fields. Aims to bring together persons interested in studying specific historic sites, manuscripts, and published sources, and to develop generalizations concerning historical periods and cultural dynamics as these emerge through the techniques of archaeological excavation and analysis. Main focus is the era beginning with the exploration of the non-European world by Europeans, and geographical areas in the Western Hemisphere, but also considers Oceanian, African, and Asian archaeology during the relatively late periods.

Architects

SOURCES OF HELP-WANTED ADS

★955★ American Institute of Architects-AIArchitect

American Institute of Architects Press
1735 New York Ave., NW
Washington, DC 20006-5292
Ph: (202)626-7300   Fax: (202)626-7547
Fr: 800-242-3837
E-mail: infocentral@aia.org
URL: http://www.aia.org/

Description: Monthly. Concerned with the architectural profession. Discusses business and legislative trends, practice and design information, and AIA activities. Recurring features include news of members and a calendar of events.

★956★ Architectural Products

Construction Business Media LLC
579 First Bank Dr., Ste. 220
Palatine, IL 60067
Ph: (847)359-6493   Fax: (847)359-6754
URL: http://www.arch-products.com/

Bimonthly. Free. Magazine provides product and product application information to architects, designers and product specifiers.

★957★ Architectural Record

McGraw-Hill Inc.
1221 Ave. of the Americas
New York, NY 10020-1095
Ph: (212)512-2000   Fax: (212)512-3840
Fr: 877-833-5524
URL: http://archrecord.construction.com

Monthly. $49.00/year for individuals. Magazine focusing on architecture.

★958★ Axis Journal

American Institute of Architects, Golden
  Empire Chapter
4450 California Ave., Ste. 88
Bakersfield, CA 93309-1152
Ph: (661)633-7755
E-mail: info@aiage.org

URL: http://www.aiage.org

Description: Monthly. Covers activities of American Institute of Architects, Golden Empire Chapter. Provides information to clients and public leaders on architects' concerns and activities.

★959★ Builder

Hanley-Wood L.L.C.
1 Thomas Cir., NW, Ste. 600
Washington, DC 20005
Ph: (202)452-0800   Fax: (202)785-1974
URL: http://www.hanleywood.com/default.aspx?page=b2bbd

$29.95/year for individuals, 13 issues; $54.95/year for Canada, 26 issues; $192.00/year for out of country, 13 issues. Magazine covering housing and construction industry.

★960★ Builder and Developer

Peninsula Publishing
1602 Monrovia Ave.
Newport Beach, CA 92663
Ph: (949)631-0308   Fax: (949)631-2475
URL: http://www.bdmag.com/new_site/

Magazine for homebuilders.

★961★ Building Industry Technology

National Technical Information Service
5285 Port Royal Rd.
Springfield, VA 22161
Ph: (703)605-6585   Fax: (703)605-6900
Fr: 800-553-6847
E-mail: info@ntis.gov
URL: http://www.ntis.gov/new/alerts_print-ed.asp

Description: Biweekly. Consists of abstracts of reports on architectural and environmental design, building standards, construction materials and equipment, and structural analyses. Recurring features include a form for ordering reports from NTIS. Also available via e-mail.

★962★ Civil Engineering-ASCE

American Society of Civil Engineers
1801 Alexander Bell Dr.
Reston, VA 20191-4400
Ph: (703)295-6300   Fax: (703)295-6222
Fr: 800-548-2723
URL: http://www.asce.org/cemagazine/1006/

Monthly. Professional magazine.

★963★ Custom Home

Hanley-Wood L.L.C.
1 Thomas Cir., NW, Ste. 600
Washington, DC 20005
Ph: (202)452-0800   Fax: (202)785-1974
URL: http://www.hanleywood.com/default.aspx?page=b2bch

$192.00/year for individuals; $36.00/year for Canada. Trade publication.

★964★ Design Cost Data

DC & D Technologies Inc.
8602 North 40th St.
Tampa, FL 33604-2434
Ph: (813)989-9300   Fax: (813)980-3982
Fr: 800-533-5680
E-mail: webmaster@dcd.com
URL: http://www.dcd.com

Bimonthly. $89.40/year for individuals; $149.28 for two years. Publication providing real cost data case studies of various types completed around the country for design and building professionals.

★965★ Design Line

American Institute of Building Design
7059 Blair Rd. NW, Ste. 201
Washington, DC 20012
Fax: (202)249-2473   Fr: 800-366-2423
E-mail: Info@AIBD.org
URL: http://www.aibd.org/

Description: Quarterly. Focuses on all aspects of building design. Recurring features include letters to the editor, interviews, a collection, reports of meetings, news of educational opportunities, and notices of publications available.

★966★ Energy Design Update

Cutter Information Corp.
37 Broadway, Ste. 1
Arlington, MA 02474
Ph: (781)648-8700   Fax: (781)648-1950
Fr: 800-964-5118
E-mail: service@cutter.com
URL: http://www.cutter.com

Description: Monthly. Reports developments in energy-efficient design and construction. Provides information on matters such as insulation, passive solar heating, pressurization testing, and indoor air quality. Contains news of regulatory trends, standards, and legal decisions. Recurring features include profiles of energy-conserving homes in North America, a calendar of national and international events, an annual special report on superinsulation, news of research, reviews of computer software, reviews of new products and materials, and construction tips.

★967★ Environmental & Architectural Phenomenology Newsletter

David Seamon
211 Seaton Hall
Architecture Dept.
Kansas State University
Manhattan, KS 66506-2901
Ph: (785)532-5953   Fax: (785)532-6722
URL: http://www.arch.ksu.edu/seamon/EAP.html

Description: Three/year. Focuses on the nature of environmental and architectural experience.

★968★ Fabric Architecture

Industrial Fabrics Association International
1801 County Rd. B W
Roseville, MN 55113
Ph: (651)222-2508   Fax: (651)631-9334
Fr: 800-225-4324
URL: http://www.ifai.com/awning/fabricarchitecturemagazine.cfm

Bimonthly. Magazine specializing in interior and exterior design ideas and technical information for architectural fabric applications in architecture and the landscape.

★969★ Green Home Builder

Peninsula Publishing
1602 Monrovia Ave.
Newport Beach, CA 92663
Ph: (949)631-0308   Fax: (949)631-2475
URL: http://www.greenhomebuildermag.com/

Quarterly. Magazine for home builders and home building industry.

★970★ Grey Room

MIT Press
55 Hayward St.
Cambridge, MA 02142-1493
Ph: (617)253-5646   Fax: (617)258-6779
Fr: 800-405-1619
E-mail: editors@greyroom.org
URL: http://mitpress.mit.edu/catalog/item/default.asp?ttype=4&tid

Quarterly. $61.00/year for individuals, for online; $68.00/year for individuals, for print and online; $36.00/year for individuals, retired, online; $40.00/year for individuals, retired, print and online; $207.00/year for institutions, online; $230.00/year for institutions, print and online; $36.00/year for students, online; $40.00/year for students, print and online. Scholarly journal devoted to the theorization of modern and contemporary architecture, art, media, and politics. Dedicated to the task of promoting and sustaining critical investigation into each of these fields separately and into their mutual interactions. Develops a rigorous, cross-disciplinary dialogue among the fields of architecture, art, and media to forge and promote a politically-informed, critical discourse uniquely relevant to the current historical situation.

★971★ Journal of Architectural Education

Wiley-Blackwell
350 Main St. Commerce Pl.
Malden, MA 02148
Ph: (781)388-8200   Fax: (781)388-8210
Fr: 800-759-6120
URL: http://www.blackwellpublishing.com/journal.asp?ref=1046-4883

Quarterly. $61.00/year for individuals, U.S. print and online; $292.00/year for institutions, U.S. print and premium online; $265.00/year for institutions, U.S. print and standard online; $252.00/year for institutions, U.S. premium online only; $58.00/year for individuals, print and premium online; $187.00/year for institutions, other countries, print and premium online; $170.00/year for institutions, other countries, print and standard online; $162.00/year for institutions, other countries, premium online only; $39.00/year for individuals, print and online. Journal focusing on architecture.

★972★ Journal of Architectural Education (JAE)

MIT Press
55 Hayward St.
Cambridge, MA 02142-1493
Ph: (617)253-5646   Fax: (617)258-6779
Fr: 800-405-1619

Quarterly. Peer-reviewed journal acting as a resource for original scholarship, criticism, and theory in architecture. Features regular sections on design, which offer extensive illustrations, often in full color. Themes include Globalization and the Profession, Construction Practices, and Recycling and Reuse.

★973★ Kitchen and Bath Design News

Cygnus Business Media Inc.
3 Huntington Quadrangle, Ste. 301 N
Melville, NY 11747
Ph: (631)845-2700   Fax: (631)845-7109
Fr: 800-308-6397
URL: http://www.cygnusb2b.com

Monthly. Trade journal.

★974★ Metal Architecture

Modern Trade Communications Inc.
7450 Skokie Blvd.
Skokie, IL 60077
Ph: (847)674-2200   Fax: (847)674-3676
URL: http://www.moderntrade.com/UI/wfHome.aspx?mag=ma&

Monthly. $60.00/year for Canada and Mexico; $140.00/year for other countries. Trade journal serving architectural, engineering, and construction firms.

★975★ The Military Engineer

The Society of American Military Engineers
607 Prince St.
Alexandria, VA 22314-3117
Ph: (703)549-3800   Fax: (703)684-0231
URL: http://www.same.org/i4a/pages/index.cfm?pageid=4273

Bimonthly. $78.00/year for U.S. and Canada, individual, second class mail; $148.00/year for U.S. and Canada, two years; $196.00/year for U.S. and Canada, 3 years; $148.00/year for other countries, air mail, individual; $286.00/year for other countries, two years, air mail; $419.00/year for other countries, 3 years, air mail; $16.00/year for students, U.S., Canada, and foreign (regular mail). Journal on military and civil engineering.

★976★ Municipal Art Society Newsletter

Municipal Art Society
457 Madison Ave.
New York, NY 10022
Ph: (212)935-3960   Fax: (212)753-1816
E-mail: info@mas.org
URL: http://www.mas.org/GetInvolved/Urbanists.cfm#membership

Description: Six issues/year. Provides updates on advocacy efforts, exhibitions, and programming on urban issues. Recurring features include a calendar of events and tour schedule.

★977★ PM Network

Project Management Institute
4 Campus Blvd.
Newtown Square, PA 19073
Ph: (610)356-4600   Fax: (610)356-4647
URL: http://www.pmi.org

Monthly. $42.00/year for members, (included in annual dues). Professional journal covering industry applications and practical issues in managing projects.

★978★ Professional Builder

Reed Business Information
360 Park Ave. S
New York, NY 10010
Ph: (646)746-6400   Fax: (646)746-7431
E-mail: ncrum@reedbusiness.com
URL: http://www.housingzone.com/toc-archive-pbx

Monthly. Free. The integrated engineering

magazine of the building construction industry.

★979★ *Residential Architect*

Hanley-Wood L.L.C.
1 Thomas Cir., NW, Ste. 600
Washington, DC 20005
Ph: (202)452-0800   Fax: (202)785-1974
URL: http://www.hanleywood.com/default.aspx?page=b2bra

Magazine for architects, designers, and building professionals.

★980★ *Residential Contractor*

Peninsula Publishing
1602 Monrovia Ave.
Newport Beach, CA 92663
Ph: (949)631-0308   Fax: (949)631-2475
URL: http://
www.residentialcontractormag.com/

Quarterly. Magazine for small volume residential builders, contractors, and specialty trades.

★981★ *SARAScope*

Society of American Registered Architects
14 E. 38th Fl., 11th Fl.
New York, NY 10016
Ph: (218)728-4293   Fax: (218)728-5361
Fr: 888-985-7272
URL: http://www.sara-national.org/main/sarascope.htm

Description: Bimonthly. Tracks Society activities at national and local levels.

★982★ *Texas Architect*

Texas Society of Architects
816 Congress Ave., Ste. 970
Austin, TX 78701-2443
Ph: (512)478-7386   Fax: (512)478-0528
E-mail: coti@texasarchitect.org
URL: http://texasarchitect.org/

Bimonthly. $25.00/year for individuals; $46.00 for two years; $19.00/year for students. Magazine for design professionals and their clients.

★983★ *The Times*

Council on Tall Buildings & Urban Habitat
Illinois Institute of Technology
S.R. Crown Hall
3360 S State St.
Chicago, IL 60616-3796
Ph: (312)567-3307   Fax: (610)694-0238
E-mail: awood@ctbuh.org
URL: http://www.ctbuh.org

Description: 3-4 issues/year. Concerned with all aspects of the planning, design, construction, and operation of tall buildings. Examines the role of tall buildings in the urban environment and acts as a forum for exchange of information among engineering, architectural, and planning professionals. Recurring features include news of research, book reviews, notices of publications available, reports on the committees of the

Council, a calendar of events, and a column titled On My Mind.

PLACEMENT AND JOB REFERRAL SERVICES

★984★ CoreNet Global

260 Peachtree St., Ste. 1500
Atlanta, GA 30303-1237
Ph: (404)589-3200   Fax: (404)589-3201
Fr: 800-726-8111
E-mail: jclarke@corenetglobal.org
URL: http://www.corenetglobal.org

Description: Executives, attorneys, real estate department heads, architects, engineers, analysts, researchers, and anyone responsible for the management, administration, and operation of national and regional real estate departments of national and international corporations. Encourages professionalism within corporate real estate through education and communication; protects the interests of corporate realty in dealing with adversaries, public or private; maintains contact with other real estate organizations; publicizes the availability of fully qualified members to the job market. Conducts seminars, including concentrated workshops on the corporate real estate field. Compiles statistics; sponsors competitions; maintains biographical archives and placement service.

★985★ Council of Educational Facility Planners, International (CEFPI)

9180 E Desert Cove Dr., Ste. 104
Scottsdale, AZ 85260-6231
Ph: (480)391-0840   Fax: (480)391-0940
E-mail: contact@cefpi.org
URL: http://www.cefpi.org

Members: Individuals and firms who are responsible for planning, designing, creating, maintaining, and equipping the physical environment of education. **Purpose:** Sponsors an exchange of information, professional experiences, best practices research results, and other investigative techniques concerning educational facility planning. **Activities:** Activities include publication and review of current and emerging practices in educational facility planning; identification and execution of needed research; development of professional training programs; strengthening of planning services on various levels of government and in institutions of higher learning; leadership in the development of higher standards for facility design and the physical environment of education. Operates speakers' bureau; sponsors placement service; compiles statistics.

★986★ Professional Women in Construction (PWC)

315 E 56th St.
New York, NY 10022-3730
Ph: (212)486-7745   Fax: (212)486-0228
E-mail: pwcusa1@aol.com

URL: http://www.pwcusa.org

Description: Management-level women and men in construction and allied industries; owners, suppliers, architects, engineers, field personnel, office personnel, and bonding/surety personnel. Provides a forum for exchange of ideas and promotion of political and legislative action, education, and job opportunities for women in construction and related fields; forms liaisons with other trade and professional groups; develops research programs. Strives to reform abuses and to assure justice and equity within the construction industry. Sponsors mini-workshops. Maintains Action Line, which provides members with current information on pertinent legislation and on the association's activities and job referrals.

★987★ Society of American Registered Architects (SARA)

14 E 38th St., 11th Fl.
New York, NY 10016
Ph: (218)724-5568   Fax: (218)724-5589
Fr: 888-385-7272
E-mail: president@sara-national.org
URL: http://www.sara-national.org

Description: Architects registered or licensed under the laws of states and territories of the U.S. Sponsors seminars and professional and student design competitions. Offers placement service.

EMPLOYER DIRECTORIES AND NETWORKING LISTS

★988★ *Almanac of Architecture and Design*

Greenway Consulting
25 Technology Pkwy. S, Ste. 101
Norcross, GA 30092
Ph: (678)879-0929   Fax: (678)879-0930
URL: http://www.greenway.us

Annual, latest edition 8, 2007. $49.50 for individuals. Publication includes: Lists of professional organizations, degree programs, and leading firms in architecture and design. Principal content of publication is a collection of information regarding architecture and design.

★989★ *Athletic Business-Professional Directory Section*

Athletic Business Publications Inc.
4130 Lien Rd.
Madison, WI 53704
Ph: (608)249-0186   Fax: (608)249-1153
Fr: 800-722-8764

Monthly. $8.00. Publication includes: List of architects, engineers, contractors, and consultants in athletic facility planning and construction; all listings are paid. Entries include: Company name, address, phone, fax and short description of company. Arrangement: Alphabetical.

★990★ Career Ideas for Teens in Architecture and Construction

Facts On File Inc.
132 W 31st St., 17th Fl.
New York, NY 10001
Ph: (212)967-8800   Fax: 800-678-3633
Fr: 800-322-8755
URL: http://www.factsonfile.com

Published 2005. $40.00 for individuals; $36.00 for libraries. Covers a multitude of career possibilities based on a teenager's specific interests and skills and links his/her talents to a wide variety of actual professions.

★991★ ENR-Top 500 Design Firms Issue

McGraw-Hill Inc.
1221 Ave. of the Americas
New York, NY 10020-1095
Ph: (212)512-2000   Fax: (212)512-3840
Fr: 877-833-5524
URL: http://enr.construction.com/people/sourcebooks/top500Design/

Annual, latest edition 2007. $50.00 for individuals. Publication includes: List of 500 leading architectural, engineering, and specialty design firms selected on basis of annual billings. Entries include: Company name, headquarters location, type of firm, current and prior year rank in billings, types of services, countries in which operated in preceding year. Arrangement: Ranked by billings.

★992★ International Architecture Centres

John Wiley & Sons Inc.
111 River St.
Hoboken, NJ 07030-5774
Ph: (201)748-6000   Fax: (201)748-6088
Fr: 800-825-7550
URL: http://as.wiley.com/WileyCDA/Wiley-Title/productCd-0470853271

Published June, 2003. $85.00 for individuals. Publication includes: A directory of international architecture centers. Principal content of publication consists of articles regarding issues that mold the work of architecture centers in the United Kingdom, Europe and North America, such as regeneration, sustainability, government policy, culture, housing and others.

★993★ The Military Engineer-Directory

The Society of American Military Engineers
607 Prince St.
Alexandria, VA 22314-3117
Ph: (703)549-3800   Fax: (703)684-0231
URL: http://www.same.org

Updated daily. Database covers: About 2,800 member architect, engineer, engineering-related firms and government agencies and equipment manufacturers, suppliers and contractors who provide products and services to government and private sector entities; also lists firms with experience and equipment useable in event of disasters/emergencies. Database includes: Firm name, address, phone, e-mail, home page, names of principals, business class, type of ownership, number of employees, and the engineering specialties of the firm. Arrangement: Alphabetical. Indexes: Alphabetical by state and country; alphabetical by business class.

★994★ ProFile

Reed Construction Data
30 Technology Pkwy. S, Ste. 100
Norcross, GA 30092
Fr: 800-424-3996
E-mail: profile@reedbusiness.com
URL: http://www.reedfirstsource.com

Annual. Covers more than 27,000 architectural firms. Entries include: For firms–Firm name, address, phone, fax, year established, key staff and their primary responsibilities (for design, specification, etc.), number of staff personnel by discipline, types of work, geographical area served, projects. "ProFile" is an expanded version of, and replaces, the "Firm Directory." Arrangement: Firms are geographical. Indexes: Firm name; key individuals; specialization by category; consultants.

★995★ Society of American Registered Architects-National Directory

Society of American Registered Architects
14 E 38th St., 11th Fl.
New York, NY 10016
Ph: (218)724-5568   Fax: (218)724-5589
URL: http://www.sara-national.org/

Annual, January. Covers 1,000 architects registered or licensed under the laws of states and territories of the United States. Entries include: Name, affiliation, address, phone, office size, specialties, and dollar volume of work. Arrangement: Alphabetical. Indexes: Cross-referenced by state registration.

HANDBOOKS AND MANUALS

★996★ Architect?: A Candid Guide to the Profession

MIT Press
55 Hayward St.
Cambridge, MA 02142-1493
Ph: (617)253-5646   Fax: (617)258-6779
Fr: 800-405-1619
URL: http://mitpress.mit.edu/main/home/default.asp

Roger K. Lewis. 1998. $25.00 (paper). 304 pages.

★997★ Architect's Handbook of Professional Practice, Student Edition

John Wiley & Sons Inc.
1 Wiley Dr.
Somerset, NJ 08873
Ph: (732)469-4400   Fax: (732)302-2300
Fr: 800-225-5945
E-mail: custserv@wiley.com
URL: http://www.wiley.com/WileyCDA/

The American Institute of Architects. Thirteenth edition, 2001. $99.00. 624 pages.

★998★ Architectural Knowledge: The Idea of a Profession

Routledge
270 Madison Ave.
New York, NY 10016
Ph: (212)216-7800   Fax: (212)563-2269
URL: http://www.routledge.com/

Francis Duffy and Les Hutton. 1998. $71.95 (paper). 217 pages.

★999★ How to Start and Operate Your Own Design Firm

The McGraw-Hill Companies
PO Box 182604
Columbus, OH 43272
Fax: (614)759-3749   Fr: 877-883-5524
E-mail: customer.service@mcgraw-hill.com
URL: http://www.mcgraw-hill.com

Albert W. Rubeling, Jr. 2007. $24.95. 256 pages.

★1000★ The I Hate Selling Book: Business-Building Advice for Consultants, Attorneys, Accountants, Engineers, Architects, and Other Professionals

AMACOM
1601 Broadway, 12th Fl.
New York, NY 10019-7420
Ph: (212)586-8100   Fax: (212)903-8168
Fr: 800-262-9699
URL: http://www.amanet.org

Allan S. Boress. 2001. $29.95. 240 pages.

★1001★ Information Technologies for Construction Managers, Architects, and Engineers

Cengage Learning
PO Box 6904
Florence, KY 41022
Fax: 800-487-8488   Fr: 800-354-9706
URL: http://www.cengage.com/

Trefor Williams. 2006. $77.50. Profiles information technology applications in construction trades, from traditional computer applications to emerging Web-based and mobile technologies.

★1002★ Opportunities in Architecture Careers

The McGraw-Hill Companies
PO Box 182604
Columbus, OH 43272
Fax: (614)759-3749   Fr: 877-883-5524
E-mail: customer.service@mcgraw-hill.com
URL: http://www.mcgraw-hill.com

Robert J. Piper and Richard D. Rush. 2006. $13.95 (paper). 160 pages. Guide to planning for and seeking opportunities in the field. Illustrated. Includes training and education requirements, salary statistics, and professional and Internet resources.

★1003★ Opportunities in Environmental Careers

The McGraw-Hill Companies
PO Box 182604
Columbus, OH 43272
Fax: (614)759-3749   Fr: 877-883-5524
E-mail: customer.service@mcgraw-hill.com
URL: http://www.mcgraw-hill.com

Odom Fanning. Revised, 2002. $12.95 (paper). 174 pages. Describes a broad range of opportunities in fields such as environmental health, recreation, physics, and hygiene, and provides job search advice. Part of the "Opportunities in ..." Series.

★1004★ Opportunities in Real Estate Careers

The McGraw-Hill Companies
PO Box 182604
Columbus, OH 43272
Fax: (614)759-3749   Fr: 877-883-5524
E-mail: customer.service@mcgraw-hill.com
URL: http://www.mcgraw-hill.com

Mariwyn Evansand and Richard Mendenhal. Second edition, 2002. $12.95 (paper). 160 pages.

★1005★ Resumes for Architecture and Related Careers

The McGraw-Hill Companies
PO Box 182604
Columbus, OH 43272
Fax: (614)759-3749   Fr: 877-883-5524
E-mail: customer.service@mcgraw-hill.com
URL: http://www.mcgraw-hill.com

VGM Career Horizons Editors. First edition. 2004. $10.95 (paper). 160 pages.

EMPLOYMENT AGENCIES AND SEARCH FIRMS

★1006★ Agra Placements, Ltd.

8435 University Ave., Ste. 6
Des Moines, IA 50325
Ph: (515)225-6563   Fax: (515)225-7733
Fr: 888-696-5624
E-mail: careers@agrapl.com
URL: http://www.agraplacements.com

Executive search firm. Branch offices in Peru, IN, Lincoln, IL, Andover, KS and Madison, SD.

★1007★ Claremont-Branan, Inc.

1298 Rockbridge Rd., Ste. B
Stone Mountain, GA 30087
Ph: (770)925-2915   Fax: (770)925-2601
Fr: 800-875-1292
E-mail: ohil@cbisearch.com
URL: http://cbisearch.com

Employment agency. Executive search firm.

★1008★ The Coxe Group Inc.

1904 Third Ave., Ste. 229
Seattle, WA 98101-1194
Ph: (206)467-4040   Fax: (206)467-4038
E-mail: consultants@coxegroup.com
URL: http://www.coxegroup.com

Executive search firm.

★1009★ RitaSue Siegel Resources, Inc.

162 Fifth Ave., 11th Fl.
New York, NY 10010-5969
Ph: (212)682-2100   Fax: (212)682-2946
E-mail: ritasues@ritasue.com
URL: http://www.ritasuesiegelresources.com

Executive search firm specializing in industrial and product design.

★1010★ Specialized Search Associates

7780 Dundee Ln.
Delray Beach, FL 33446
Ph: (561)499-3711   Fax: (561)499-3770
Fr: 888-405-2650

Executive search firm that specializes in construction, engineering, and sales.

TRADESHOWS

★1011★ American Institute of Architects National Convention

American Institute of Architects
1735 New York Ave. NW
Washington, DC 20006-5292
Ph: (202)626-7300   Fax: (202)626-7547
Fr: 800-AIA-3837
E-mail: infocentral@aia.org
URL: http://www.aia.org

Annual. **Primary Exhibits:** Architects equipment, supplies, and services. **Dates and Locations:** 2008 May 15-17; Boston, MA.

★1012★ Annual American Institute of Architects, Minnesota Convention and Exhibition

American Institute of Architects, Minnesota Chapter
275 Market St., Ste. 54
Minneapolis, MN 55405
Ph: (612)338-6763   Fax: (612)338-7981
E-mail: wald@aia-mn.org
URL: http://www.aia-mn.org

Annual. **Primary Exhibits:** Windows, concrete, roofing, millwork, tile, construction management companies, and other construction products.

★1013★ Texas Society of Architects Design Products & Ideas Expo

Texas Society of Architects
816 Congress Ave., Ste. 970
Austin, TX 78701-2443
Ph: (512)478-7386   Fax: (512)478-0528
Fr: 800-478-7386
E-mail: info@texasarchitect.org
URL: http://www.texasarchitect.org

Annual. **Primary Exhibits:** Designing and building materials and systems for both interior/exterior residential and commercial projects.

OTHER SOURCES

★1014★ American Institute of Architects (AIA)

1735 New York Ave. NW
Washington, DC 20006-5292
Ph: (202)626-7300   Fax: (202)626-7547
Fr: 800-AIA-3837
E-mail: infocentral@aia.org
URL: http://www.aia.org

Description: Represents architects, licensed architects, graduate architects, not yet licensed and retired architects. Fosters professionalism and accountability among members through continuing education and training. Promotes design excellence by influencing change in the industry. Sponsors educational programs with schools of architecture, graduate students, and elementary and secondary schools. Advises on professional competitions. Supplies construction documents. Established the American Architectural Foundation. Sponsors Octagon Museum; operates bookstore; stages exhibitions; compiles statistics. Provides monthly news service on design and construction. Conducts professional development programs, research programs, charitable activities, and children's services.

★1015★ Asian American Architects and Engineers (AAAE)

The Albert Group
114 Sansome St., Ste. 710
San Francisco, CA 94104
Ph: (415)957-8788
E-mail: leschau@kennedyjenks.com
URL: http://www.aaaenc.org

Members: Minorities. **Purpose:** Provides contracts and job opportunities for minorities in the architectural and engineering fields. **Activities:** Serves as a network for the promotion in professional fields.

★1016★ Association for International Practical Training (AIPT)

10400 Little Patuxent Pkwy., Ste. 250
Columbia, MD 21044-3519
Ph: (410)997-2200   Fax: (410)992-3924
E-mail: aipt@aipt.org
URL: http://www.aipt.org

Description: Providers worldwide of on-the-job training programs for students and professionals seeking international career development and life-changing experiences. Arranges workplace exchanges in hundreds of professional fields, bringing employers and trainees together from around the world. Client list ranges from small farming communities to Fortune 500 companies.

★1017★ **Math at Work: Women in Nontraditional Careers**

Her Own Words
PO Box 5264
Madison, WI 53705-0264
Ph: (608)271-7083   Fax: (608)271-0209
E-mail: herownword@aol.com
URL: http://www.herownwords.com/

Video. Jocelyn Riley. $95.00. 15 minutes. Resource guide also available for $45.00.

★1018★ **National Center for Construction Education and Research (NCCER)**

3600 NW 43rd St., Bldg. G
Gainesville, FL 32606
Ph: (352)334-0911   Fax: (352)334-0932
Fr: 888-622-3720
URL: http://www.nccer.org

Description: Education foundation committed to the development and publication of Contren(TM) Learning Series, the source of craft training, management education and safety resources for the construction industry.

★1019★ **National Council of Architectural Registration Boards (NCARB)**

1801 K St. NW, Ste. 1100-K
Washington, DC 20006-1310
Ph: (202)783-6500   Fax: (202)783-0290
E-mail: customerservice@ncarb.org
URL: http://www.ncarb.org

Members: Federation of state boards for the registration of architects in the United States, District of Columbia, Puerto Rico, Virgin Islands, Guam, and the Northern Mariana Islands.

★1020★ **Professional Specialty Occupations**

Delphi Productions
3159 6th St.
Boulder, CO 80304
Ph: (303)443-2100   Fax: (303)443-4022
Fr: 888-443-2400
E-mail: support@delphivideo.com
URL: http://www.delphivideo.com

$95.00. 53 minutes. Part of the Careers for the 21st Century Video Library.

★1021★ **Women in Building Construction**

Her Own Words
PO Box 5264
Madison, WI 53705-0264
Ph: (608)271-7083   Fax: (608)271-0209
E-mail: herownword@aol.com
URL: http://www.herownwords.com/

Video. Jocelyn Riley. $95.00. 15 minutes. Resource guide also available for $45.00.

Archivists and Curators

★1022★ The Abbey Newsletter

Abbey Publications Inc.
7105 Geneva Dr.
Austin, TX 78723
Ph: (512)929-3992   Fax: (512)929-3995
E-mail: abbeypub@grandecom.net
URL: http://palimpsest.stanford.edu/byorg/abbey/

Description: Six issues/year. Encourages the development of library and archival conservation, particularly technical advances and cross-disciplinary research in the field. Covers book repair and the conservation of books, papers, photographs, and non-paper materials. Recurring features include book reviews, news of research, job listings, convention reports, a calendar of events, and an occasional column about equipment and supplies.

★1023★ ACDA Bulletin

Association of Catholic Diocesan
  Archivists
711 W Monroe St.
Chicago, IL 60661-3515
Ph: (773)736-5150
E-mail: kwhite@diopitt.org

Description: Three issues/year. Recurring features include reports of meetings, news of educational opportunities, job listings, book reviews, and notices of publications available.

★1024★ Alabama Archivist

University of South Alabama Archives
307 N. University Blvd.
Mobile, AL 36688
Ph: (215)434-3800
E-mail: cellis@jaguar1.usouthal.edu
URL: http://www.alarchivists.org

Description: Semiannual. Provides news of archival activities in Alabama, covering archival repositories and significant historical collections, special work by archivists, legislative matters relating to historical records,

and general information concerning the archival profession and standards. Recurring features include Society reports, news of research, and a calendar of events.

★1025★ AMIA Newsletter

Association of Moving Image Archivists
1313 N.Vine St.
Hollywood, CA 90028
Ph: (323)463-1500   Fax: (323)463-1506
E-mail: AMIA@amianet.org
URL: http://www.amianet.org

Description: Quarterly. Presents information on the preservation of film and video materials, and the moving image archival profession. REC news of research, a calendar of events, reports of meetings, job listings, book reviews, and notices of publications available.

★1026★ Annotation

National Historical Publications and
  Records Commission
700 Pennsylvania Ave. NW, Rm. 106
Washington, DC 20408-0001
Ph: (202)357-5010   Fax: (202)357-5914
E-mail: nhprc@nara.gov
URL: http://www.archives.gov/nhprc/annotation/

Description: Quarterly. Contains information of interest to National Historical Publications and Records Commission members. Recurring features include columns titled From the Editor, and The Executive Director's Column.

★1027★ Archival Outlook

Society of American Archivists
17 N. State St., Ste. 1425
Chicago, IL 60602
Ph: (312)606-0722   Fax: (312)606-0728
Fr: (866)SAA-7858
E-mail: info@archivists.org
URL: http://www.archivists.org/periodicals/

Description: Bimonthly. Publishes news of relevance to the professional archival community. Recurring features include a calendar of events, news from constituent groups,

news of educational opportunities, professional resources available, and job listings.

★1028★ Children and Libraries

American Library Association
50 E Huron St.
Chicago, IL 60611
Fr: 800-545-2433
URL: http://www.ala.org

$50.00/year for elsewhere; $40.00/year for nonmembers. Journal that focuses on the continuing education of librarians working with children.

★1029★ Choice

Association of College and Research
  Libraries
50 E Huron St.
Chicago, IL 60611-2795
Ph: (312)280-2523   Fax: (312)280-2520
Fr: 800-545-2433
URL: http://www.ala.org/ala/acrl/acrlpubs/choice/about.htm

Online journal providing reviews of academic books, electronic media, and internet resources.

★1030★ Collections (Walnut Creek)

AltaMira Press
4501 Forbes Blvd., Ste. 200
Lanham, MD 20706
Ph: (301)459-3366   Fax: (301)429-5748
Fr: 800-462-6420
URL: http://www.altamirapress.com/rla/journals/collections/

Quarterly. $40.00/year for individuals; $89.00/year for institutions, museum; $149.00/year for institutions, non-museum. Journal that offers information on handling, preserving, researching, and organizing museum and archive collections.

**★1031★ Conference of Intermountain
  Archivists (CIMA) Newsletter**

Conference of Intermountain Archivists
300 S. Rio Grande
Salt Lake City, UT 84101-1182
Ph: (801)533-3543

E-mail: swhetsto@utah.gov
URL: http://www.lib.utah.edu/cima/news.html

Description: Quarterly. Concerned with the preservation and use of archival and manuscript materials in the Intermountain West and adjacent areas. Disseminates information on research materials and archival methodology; provides a forum for the discussion of common concerns; and cooperates with similar cultural and educational organizations. Recurring features include news of research, preservation, members, and job openings.

★1032★ ConservatioNews

Arizona State University Libraries
Box 871006
Tempe, AZ 85287
Ph: (480)965-6164   Fax: (480)965-9169
E-mail: asulib@asu.edu
URL: http://www.asu.edu/lib

Description: Quarterly. Concerned with the preservation of paper documents, magnetic media, published materials, photographs, and film. Carries articles on the theory and practice of conservation, questions and answers to specific problems, and product news. Recurring features include news of members, book reviews, and a calendar of events.

★1033★ Dirty Goat

Host Publications, Inc.
451 Greenwich St., Ste. 7J
New York, NY 10013
Ph: (212)905-2365   Fax: (212)905-2369
URL: http://www.thedirtygoat.com/index.html

Semiannual. Journal covering poetry, prose, drama, literature and visual art.

★1034★ Dusty Shelf

Kansas City Area Archivists
University of Missouri-Kansas City, 320 Newcomb Hall
5100 Rockhill Rd.
Kansas City, MO 64110-2499
Ph: (816)235-1539   Fax: (816)235-5500
URL: http://www.umkc.edu/kcaa/dustyshelf/dusty.htm

Description: Three issues/year. Contains essays and editorials on local and national archives. Recurring features include a calendar of events, reports of meetings, news of educational opportunities, job listings, notices of publications available, and a column titled Conservation Notes.

★1035★ Film History

Indiana University Press
601 N Morton St.
Bloomington, IN 47404-3797
Ph: (812)855-6657   Fax: (812)855-8817
Fr: 800-842-6796
E-mail: filmhist@aol.com
URL: http://inscribe.iupress.org/loi/fil

Quarterly. $77.00/year for individuals, print

and online, for U.S. $63.00/year for individuals, electronic only, for U.S. Journal tracing the history of the motion picture with reference to social, technological, and economic aspects, covering various aspects of motion pictures such as production, distribution, exhibition, and reception.

★1036★ History News

American Association for State & Local History
1717 Church St.
Nashville, TN 37203-2991
Ph: (615)320-3203   Fax: (615)327-9013
URL: http://www.aaslh.org/historynews.htm

Quarterly. Magazine for employees of historic sites, museums, and public history agencies. Coverage includes museum education programs and techniques for working with volunteers.

★1037★ IFLA Journal

Sage Publications Inc.
2455 Teller Rd.
Thousand Oaks, CA 91320
Ph: (805)499-0721   Fax: (805)499-8096
URL: http://www.ifla.org

Quarterly. $315.00/year for institutions, print & e-access; $331.00/year for institutions, print & all online; $284.00/year for institutions, e-access; $300.00/year for institutions, backfile lease, e-access plus backfile all online; $579.00/year for institutions, backfile purchase, e-access (content through 1999); $309.00/year for institutions, print only; $84.00/year for individuals, print only; $85.00 for single issue, institutional; $27.00 for single issue, individual. Journal of the International Federation of Library Associations and Institutions (IFLA).

★1038★ Infinity

Society of American Archivists, Preservation Section
17 N. State St., Ste. 1425
Chicago, IL 60602
Ph: (312)606-0722   Fax: (312)606-0728
Fr: (866)SAA-7858
E-mail: info@archivists.org
URL: http://www.archivists.org

Description: Quarterly. Informs members of the Society of archives news and events. Recurring features include news of research, a calendar of events, reports of meetings, news of educational opportunities, book reviews, notices of publications available, and a column titled From the Chair.

★1039★ Journal of Access Services

The Haworth Press Inc.
10 Alice St.
Binghamton, NY 13904
Ph: (607)722-5857   Fr: 800-429-6784
URL: http://www.haworthpress.com/store/product.asp?sid=9EQS2STUT

Quarterly. $69.00/year for individuals; $101.00/year for individuals, Canada; $106.00/year for other countries, individual; $190.00/year for institutions, agency, library;

$283.00/year for institutions, other countries, agency, library; $268.00/year for institutions, Canada, agency, library. Journal focusing on the basic business of providing library users with access to information and helping librarians stay up to date on continuing education and professional development in the field of access services.

★1040★ Journal of Classification

Classification Society of North America
c/o Stanley Sclove
IDS Dept., University of Illinois M/C 294
CSNA Business Office
601 South Morgan St.
Chicago, IL 60607-7124
Ph: (312)996-2676   Fax: (312)413-0385
URL: http://www.cs-na.org

Semiannual. Journal of the Classification Society of North America.

★1041★ Journal of Interlibrary Loan, Document Delivery & Electronic Reserve

The Haworth Press Inc.
10 Alice St.
Binghamton, NY 13904
Ph: (607)722-5857   Fr: 800-429-6784
URL: http://www.haworthpress.com/store/product.asp?sid=PC3BHEAN6

Quarterly. $40.00/year for individuals; $58.00/year for individuals, Canada; $62.00/year for individuals, elsewhere; $275.00/year for institutions, agency, library; $399.00/year for institutions, Canada, agency, library; $426.00/year for institutions, other countries, agency, library. Journal focusing on a broad spectrum of library and information center functions that rely heavily on interlibrary loans, document delivery, and electronic reserve.

★1042★ Journal of Librarianship and Information Science

Sage Publications Inc.
2455 Teller Rd.
Thousand Oaks, CA 91320
Ph: (805)499-0721   Fax: (805)499-8096
URL: http://www.sagepub.com/journalsProdDesc.nav?prodId=Journal20

Quarterly. $539.00/year for institutions, print & e-access; $566.00/year for institutions, print & all online; $485.00/year for institutions, e-access; $512.00/year for institutions, e-access & all online; $1,237.00/year for institutions, e-access; $528.00/year for institutions, print only; $84.00/year for individuals, print only; $146.00 for institutions, single print; $27.00 for individuals, single print. Journal for librarians, information scientists, specialists, managers, and educators.

★1043★ MAC Newsletter

Midwest Archives Conference
4300 S. U.S. Highway One, Ste. 203-293
Jupiter, FL 33477
E-mail: Membership@midwestarchives.org
URL: http://www.midwestarchives.org/

Description: Quarterly. Covers activities of Midwest Archives Conference. Includes employment opportunities, conference reports, financial statements, meeting minutes, news of members, and listing of publications available.

★1044★ **MAHD Bulletin**

Museums, Arts, and Humanities Div., Special Libraries Assn.
331 S. Patrick St.
Alexandria, VA 22314-3501
Ph: (703)647-4900   Fax: (703)647-4901
E-mail: sla@sla.org
URL: http://www.sla.org/

Description: Four issues/year. Discusses pertinent events, issues, and publications concerning special libraries. Recurring features include interviews, news of research, a calendar of events, reports of meetings, news of educational opportunities, book reviews, notices of publications available, and a column titled On My Mind.

★1045★ **Mid-Atlantic Archivist**

Mid-Atlantic Regional Archives Conference
PO Box 710215
Oak Hill, VA 20171
Ph: (703)476-1807   Fax: (703)476-1806
E-mail: marac@lamoureux.us
URL: http://www.lib.umd.edu/MARAC/

Description: Quarterly. Contains news and information for and about members of the Conference. Seeks exchange of information between colleagues, improvement of competence among archivists, and encourages professional involvement of persons actively engaged in the preservation and use of historical research materials. Recurring features include letters to the editor, news of members, book reviews, a calendar of events, and columns titled Preservation News, Reference Shelf, Session Abstracts, Software News, and Employment Opportunities.

★1046★ **Museum Archivist**

Society of American Archivists, Museum Archives Section
17 N. State St., Ste. 1425
Chicago, IL 60602
Ph: (312)606-0722   Fax: (312)606-0728
Fr: (866)SAA-7858
E-mail: info@archivists.org
URL: http://www.archivists.org/

Description: 2/year. Provides news of Society and Section activities, meetings, symposia, educational programs, project research, repository reports, notes, and announcements. Recurring features include letters to the editor, news of research, reports of meetings, and news of educational opportunities.

★1047★ **New England Archivists Newsletter**

New England Archivists
Gordon Library
100 Institute Road
Worcester, MA 01609
Ph: (617)727-2816
URL: http://www.newenglandarchivists.org/newsletter/index.html

Description: Quarterly. Contains regional archival news and announcements. Recurring features include a calendar of events, reports of meetings, job listings, book reviews, workshops, reports on repositories, and feature articles on archival subjects.

★1048★ **Preservation**

National Trust for Historic Preservation
1785 Massachusetts Ave. NW
Washington, DC 20036
Ph: (202)588-6000   Fax: (202)588-6038
Fr: 800-944-6847
URL: http://www.nationaltrust.org

Bimonthly. $20.00/year for individuals; $30.00/year for family membership. Magazine featuring historic preservation.

★1049★ **The Primary Source**

Society of Mississippi Archivists
The University of Southern Mississippi
PO Box 1151
Jackson, MS 39215-1151
Ph: (601)359-6889   Fax: (601)359-6964
E-mail: info@msarchivists.org
URL: http://www.msarchivists.org/

Description: Quarterly. Focuses on activities and trends in the archival and library community both regionally and nationally. Includes information on conservation and articles on state repositories and their holdings. Recurring features include news of research, book reviews, and a calendar of events.

★1050★ **Research Strategies**

Elsevier Science Inc.
360 Park Ave. S
New York, NY 10010
Ph: (212)989-5800   Fax: (212)633-3990
URL: http://www.elsevier.com

Journal covering library literature and the educational mission of the library.

★1051★ **The Rocky Mountain Archivist**

Society of Rocky Mountain Archivists
c/o Morgan Library
Colorado State Univ.
Fort Collins, CO 80523
Ph: (970)491-1939
E-mail: Patricia.Rettig@ColoState.edu
URL: http://www.srmarchivists.org/

Description: Quarterly. Covers activities of Society of Rocky Mountain Archivists. Includes local and national news on archives and special collections.

★1052★ **The Southwestern Archivist**

Society of Southwest Archivists
PO Box 225
Gaithersburg, MD 20884
URL: http://southwestarchivists.org

Description: Quarterly. Supports the aims of the Society, which include: "to provide a means for effective cooperation among people concerned with the documentation of human experience," and "to promote the adoption of sound principles and standards for the preservation and administration of records." Recurring features include news of research, news of members, and a calendar of events.

★1053★ **Tennessee Archivist**

Society of Tennessee Archivists
c/o Tennessee State Library & Archives
403 Seventh Ave. N.
Nashville, TN 37243-0312
Ph: (615)253-6450   Fax: (615)532-9293
E-mail: amber.barfield@state.tn.us
URL: http://www.geocities.com/tennarchivists/

Description: Quarterly. Provides information on state and national archival activities. Announces professional meetings and workshops, archival job openings, and new collections. Features articles on archives and records repositories in Tennessee. Recurring features include a calendar of events, reports of meetings, news of educational opportunities, job listings, notices of publications available, and columns titled Editorial, Message from the President, and Committee Reports.

PLACEMENT AND JOB REFERRAL SERVICES

★1054★ **American Society for Information Science and Technology (ASIS&T)**

1320 Fenwick Ln., Ste. 510
Silver Spring, MD 20910
Ph: (301)495-0900   Fax: (301)495-0810
E-mail: asis@asis.org
URL: http://www.asis.org

Members: Information specialists, scientists, librarians, administrators, social scientists, and others interested in the use, organization, storage, retrieval, evaluation, and dissemination of recorded specialized information. **Purpose:** Seeks to improve the information transfer process through research, development, application, and education. **Activities:** Provides a forum for the discussion, publication, and critical analysis of work dealing with the theory, practice, research, and development of elements involved in communication of information. Members are engaged in a variety of activities and specialties including classification and coding systems, automatic and associative indexing, machine translation of languages, special librarianship and library systems analysis, and copyright issues. Sponsors National Auxiliary Publications Service, which provides reproduction services and a central depository for all types of information. Maintains placement service. Sponsors numerous special interest groups. Conducts continuing education programs and professional development workshops.

★1055★ Print Council of America (PCA)

Department of Drawings and Prints
The Metropolitan Museum of Art
1000 Fifth Ave.
New York, NY 10025
E-mail: nadine.orenstein@metmuseum.org
URL: http://www.printcouncil.org

Description: Museum professionals. Fosters the study and appreciation of new and old prints, drawings, and photographs; stimulates discussion. Sponsors educational programs and research publications; offers placement services.

★1056★ Special Libraries Association (SLA)

331 S Patrick St.
Alexandria, VA 22314-3501
Ph: (703)647-4900   Fax: (703)647-4901
E-mail: sla@sla.org
URL: http://www.sla.org

Description: International association of information professionals who work in special libraries serving business, research, government, universities, newspapers, museums, and institutions that use or produce specialized information. Seeks to advance the leadership role of special librarians. Offers consulting services to organizations that wish to establish or expand a library or information services. Conducts strategic learning and development courses, public relations, and government relations programs. Provides employment services. Operates knowledge exchange on topics pertaining to the development and management of special libraries. Maintains Hall of Fame.

EMPLOYER DIRECTORIES AND NETWORKING LISTS

★1057★ Directory of Special Libraries and Information Centers

Gale, Cengage Learning
27500 Drake Rd.
Farmington Hills, MI 48331-3535
Ph: (248)699-4253   Fax: (248)699-8065
Fr: 800-877-4253
E-mail: businessproducts@gale.com
URL: http://www.gale.com

Annual; latest edition 33rd, April 2007. $1210.00 for individuals. Covers over 34,800 special libraries, information centers, documentation centers, etc.; about 500 networks and consortia; major special libraries abroad also included. Volume 1 part 3 contains 6 other appendices (beside networks and con-

sortia): Regional and Subregional Libraries for the Blind and Physically Handicapped, Patent and Trademark Depository Libraries, Regional Government Depository Libraries, United Nations Depository Libraries, World Bank Depository Libraries, and European Community Depository Libraries. Entries include: Library name, address, phone, fax, e-mail address; contact; year founded; sponsoring organization; special collections; subject interests; names and titles of staff; services (copying, online searches); size of collection; subscriptions; computerized services and automated operations; Internet home page address; publications; special catalogs; special indexes. For consortia and networks–Name, address, phone, contact. Other appendices have varying amounts of directory information. Contents of Volume 1 are available in "Subject Directory of Special Libraries and Information Centers." Arrangement: Libraries are alphabetical by name of sponsoring organization or institution; consortia and networks are geographical. Indexes: Subject. Geographic and personnel indexes constitute volume 2.

★1058★ Guide to Employment Sources in the Library & Information Professions

Office for Human Resource Development and Recruitment
50 E Huron St.
Chicago, IL 60611
Ph: (312)280-4282   Fax: (312)280-3256
Fr: 800-545-2433
URL: http://www.ala.org/hrdr/employment_guide.html

Annual, spring. Covers library job sources, such as specialized and state and regional library associations, state library agencies, federal library agencies, and overseas exchange programs. Entries include: Library, company, or organization name, address, phone; contact name, description of services, publications, etc. This is a reprint of a segment of the "Bowker Annual of Library and Book Trade Information." Arrangement: Classified by type of source.

★1059★ Midwest Archives Conference-Membership Directory

Midwest Archives Conference
c/o Menzi Behrnd-Klodt
7422 Longmeadow Rd.
Madison, WI 53717
Ph: (608)827-5727
URL: http://www.midwestarchives.org

Annual. Covers more than 1,000 individual and institutional members, largely librarians, archivists, records managers, manuscripts curators, historians, and museum and historical society personnel, as well as about 25 archival associations in the Midwest. Entries include: For institutions–Name of archives, parent organization, address, phone. For individuals–Name, title, business address, phone. Arrangement: Separate alphabetical sections for individuals and institutions.

★1060★ Official Museum Directory

LexisNexis Group
PO Box 933
Dayton, OH 45401-0933
Ph: (937)865-6800   Fax: (518)487-3584
Fr: 800-543-6862

Annual, December. Covers approximately 7,850 institutions of art, history, and science in the United States, including general museums, college and university museums, children's and junior museums, company museums, national park and nature center displays, and highly specialized museums. Also includes a separate volume of 2,000 suppliers of services and products to museums. Entries include: For museums–Name, address, phone, date established, personnel, governing authority, brief description of museum and type of collections, facilities, activities, publications, hours of operation, admission prices, membership fees, attendance figures. For suppliers–Company name, address, phone, name and title of contact. Arrangement: Museums are geographical; suppliers are by specialty. Indexes: Museum personnel (with name, title, affiliation, city, and state); type of museum (with name, city, and state); alphabetical; special collection.

HANDBOOKS AND MANUALS

★1061★ Advocating Archives: An Introduction to Public Relations for Archivists

Scarecrow Press, Inc.
4501 Forbes Blvd., Ste. 200
Lanham, MD 20706-4310
Ph: (301)459-3366   Fax: (301)429-5748
URL: http://www.scarecrowpress.com/

Elsie Freeman Finch. March 2003. $42.95. Illustrated. 186 pages. Study on archiving public relations.

★1062★ Ethics and the Archival Profession: Introduction and Case Studies

Society of American Archivists
527 S. Wells St., 5th Fl.
Chicago, IL 60607-3992
Ph: (312)922-0140   Fax: (312)347-1452
URL: http://www.archivists.org/

Karen M. Benedict. November 2003. $34.95. 91 pages.

★1063★ Great Jobs for History Majors

The McGraw-Hill Companies
PO Box 182604
Columbus, OH 43272
Fax: (614)759-3749   Fr: 877-883-5524
E-mail: customer.service@mcgraw-hill.com
URL: http://www.mcgraw-hill.com

Julie DeGalan and Stephen Lambert. 2001. $15.95 (paper). 256 pages.

★1064★ Great Jobs for Liberal Arts Majors

The McGraw-Hill Companies
PO Box 182604
Columbus, OH 43272
Fax: (614)759-3749   Fr: 877-883-5524
E-mail: customer.service@mcgraw-hill.com
URL: http://www.mcgraw-hill.com

Blythe Camenson. Second edition, 2001. $14.95 (paper). 256 pages.

★1065★ Museum Archives: An Introduction

Society of American Archivists
527 S. Wells St., 5th Fl.
Chicago, IL 60607-3992
Ph: (312)922-0140   Fax: (312)347-1452
URL: http://www.archivists.org/

Deborah Wythe. Second edition, 2004. $62.00. 256 pages.

★1066★ Museum Careers & Training: A Professional Guide

Greenwood Press
88 Post Rd., W.
Westport, CT 06881-5007
Ph: (203)226-3571   Fax: (203)222-1502
Fr: 800-225-5800
URL: http://www.greenwood.com/

Victor J. Danilov. 1994. $126.95 560 pages. Describes various museum positions and training programs available.

★1067★ Museum Jobs from A-Z: What They Are, How to Prepare, and Where to Find Them

Batax Museum Publishing
2051 Wheeler Ln.
Switzerland, FL 32259
Ph: (904)287-2464

G.W. Bates. 1994. $9.95 (paper). 137 pages. Provides information, including descriptions and training needs, for 62 museum occupations.

★1068★ Opportunities in Museum Careers

The McGraw-Hill Companies
PO Box 182604
Columbus, OH 43272
Fax: (614)759-3749   Fr: 877-883-5524
E-mail: customer.service@mcgraw-hill.com
URL: http://www.mcgraw-hill.com

Blythe Camenson. 2006. $13.95; $11.95 (paper). 160 pages.

EMPLOYMENT AGENCIES AND SEARCH FIRMS

★1069★ Gossage Sager Associates LLC

351 Town Pl. Cir., Ste. 508
Buffalo Grove, IL 60089
Ph: (312)961-5536   Fax: (847)419-7743
E-mail: dsager@gossagesager.com
URL: http://www.gossagesager.com

Executive search firm. Concentrates in placement of library and information professionals on permanent basis nationwide.

OTHER SOURCES

★1070★ American Association of Museums (AAM)

1575 Eye St. NW, Ste. 400
Washington, DC 20005
Ph: (202)289-1818   Fax: (202)289-6578
E-mail: membership@aam-us.org
URL: http://www.aam-us.org

Description: Represents directors, curators, registrars, educators, exhibit designers, public relations officers, development officers, security managers, trustees, and volunteers in museums as well as all museums, including art, history, science, military and maritime, and youth, as well as aquariums, zoos, botanical gardens, arboretums, historic sites, and science and technology centers. Dedicated to promoting excellence within the museum community. Assists museum staff, boards, and volunteers through advocacy, professional education, information exchange, accreditation, and guidance.

★1071★ American Institute for Conservation of Historic and Artistic Works (AIC)

1717 K St. NW, Ste. 200
Washington, DC 20036
Ph: (202)452-9545   Fax: (202)452-9328
E-mail: info@aic-faic.org
URL: http://www.aic-faic.org

Members: Professionals, scientists, administrators, and educators in the field of art conservation; interested individuals. **Purpose:** Advances the practice and promotes the importance of the preservation of cultural property. **Activities:** Coordinates the exchange of knowledge, research, and publications. Establishes and upholds professional standards. Publishes conservation literature. Compiles statistics. Represents membership to allied professional associations and advocates on conservation-related issues. Solicits and dispenses money exclusively for charitable, scientific, and educational objectives.

★1072★ College Art Association (CAA)

275 7th Ave., 18th Fl.
New York, NY 10001
Ph: (212)691-1051   Fax: (212)627-2381
E-mail: nyoffice@collegeart.org
URL: http://www.collegeart.org

Description: Professional organization of artists, art historians and fine art educators, museum directors, and curators. Seeks to raise the standards of scholarship and of the teaching of art and art history throughout the country.

★1073★ Society of American Archivists (SAA)

527 S Wells St., 5th Fl.
Chicago, IL 60607
Ph: (312)922-0140   Fax: (312)347-1452
E-mail: info@archivists.org
URL: http://www.archivists.org

Description: Individuals and institutions concerned with the identification, preservation, and use of records of historical value.

★1074★ Women's Caucus for Art (WCA)

Canal St. Sta.
PO Box 1498
New York, NY 10013
Ph: (212)634-0007
E-mail: info@nationalwca.com
URL: http://www.nationalwca.org

Members: Professional women in visual art fields: artists, critics, art historians, museum and gallery professionals, arts administrators, educators and students, and collectors of art. **Purpose:** Aims to increase recognition for contemporary and historical achievements of women in art. Ensures equal opportunity for employment, art commissions, and research grants. Encourages professionalism and shared information among women in art. Stimulates and publicizes research and publications on women in the visual arts. **Activities:** Conducts workshops, periodic affirmative action research, and statistical surveys.

Art Therapists

SOURCES OF HELP-WANTED ADS

★1075★ American Art Therapy Association Newsletter

American Art Therapy Association Inc.
5999 Stevenson Ave.
Alexandria, VA 22304
Ph: (703)212-2238   Fr: 888-290-0878
E-mail: info@arttherapy.org
URL: http://www.arttherapy.org

Description: Quarterly. Publishes news of developments and events in art therapy. Provides information on Association activities, related organizations, and available resources. Recurring features include legislative updates, letters to the editor, news of members, a calendar of events, board and committee reports, conference and symposia information.

★1076★ Art Therapy

American Art Therapy Association, Inc.
5999 Stevenson Ave.
Alexandria, VA 22304
Fax: (703)212-2238   Fr: 888-290-0878
E-mail: info@arttherapy.org

Quarterly. $125.00/year for individuals, U.S. $200.00/year for institutions, U.S. $200.00/year for individuals, out of the country; $225.00/year for institutions, out of the country. Journal for art therapists.

★1077★ ArtSEARCH

Theatre Communications Group
520 8th Ave., 24th Fl.
New York, NY 10018-4156
Ph: (212)609-5900   Fax: (212)609-5901
E-mail: tcg@tcg.org
URL: http://www.tcg.org

Description: Biweekly. Publishes classified listings for job opportunities in the arts, especially theatre, dance, music, and educational institutions. Listings include opportunities in administration, artistic, education, production, and career development.

★1078★ Dirty Goat

Host Publications, Inc.
451 Greenwich St., Ste. 7J
New York, NY 10013
Ph: (212)905-2365   Fax: (212)905-2369
URL: http://www.thedirtygoat.com/index.html

Semiannual. Journal covering poetry, prose, drama, literature and visual art.

★1079★ Film History

Indiana University Press
601 N Morton St.
Bloomington, IN 47404-3797
Ph: (812)855-6657   Fax: (812)855-8817
Fr: 800-842-6796
E-mail: filmhist@aol.com
URL: http://inscribe.iupress.org/loi/fil

Quarterly. $77.00/year for individuals, print and online, for U.S. $63.00/year for individuals, electronic only, for U.S. Journal tracing the history of the motion picture with reference to social, technological, and economic aspects, covering various aspects of motion pictures such as production, distribution, exhibition, and reception.

HANDBOOKS AND MANUALS

★1080★ Approaches to Art Therapy: Theory and Technique

Brunner-Routledge
270 Madison Ave.
New York, NY 10016
Ph: (212)216-7800   Fax: (212)563-2269
Fr: 800-634-7064
URL: http://www.routledgementalhealth.com/

Judith Aron Rubin. 2001. $46.95. 360 pages. Brings together the foundations and the practice of art therapy. Illustrates how various approaches to psychotherapy are applied in art therapy and presents therapeutic possibilities and an understanding of theoretical constructs.

★1081★ Art Therapy Activities: A Practical Guide for Teachers, Therapists and Parents

Charles C Thomas Publisher, Ltd.
2600 S 1st St.
Springfield, IL 62704
Ph: (217)789-8980   Fax: (217)789-9130
Fr: 800-258-8980
E-mail: books@ccthomas.com
URL: http://www.ccthomas.com/

Pamela J. Stack. 2006. $31.95. Profiles activities used for art therapy.

★1082★ Art Therapy: An Introduction

Routledge
270 Madison Ave.
New York, NY 10016
Ph: (212)216-7800   Fax: (212)563-2269
URL: http://www.routledge.com/

Judith A. Rubin. 2008. $52.95. 325 pages. Part of the Basic Principles Into Practice Series.

★1083★ Careers in Social and Rehabilitation Services

The McGraw-Hill Companies
PO Box 182604
Columbus, OH 43272
Fax: (614)759-3749   Fr: 877-883-5524
E-mail: customer.service@mcgraw-hill.com
URL: http://www.mcgraw-hill.com

Geraldine O. Garner. 2001. $19.95; 14.95 (paper). 128 pages.

★1084★ A Consumer's Guide to Art Therapy: For Prospective Employers, Clients and Students

Charles C Thomas Publisher, Ltd.
2600 S 1st St.
PO Box 19265
Springfield, IL 62794-9265
Ph: (217)789-8980   Fax: (217)789-9130
Fr: 800-258-8980
E-mail: books@ccthomas.com
URL: http://www.ccthomas.com

Susan R. Makin. 1996. $19.95 (paper). 112 pages.

★1085★ Counseling As an Art: The Creative Arts in Counseling

American Counseling Association
5999 Stevenson Ave.
Alexandria, VA 22304-3300
Ph: (703)823-9800   Fax: 800-473-2329
Fr: 800-347-6647
URL: http://www.counseling.org/

Samuel T. Gladding. Third edition, 2004. $42.95 (paper). 237 pages.

★1086★ Handbook of Art Therapy

Guildford Press
72 Spring St.
New York, NY 10012
Fr: 800-365-7006
E-mail: info@guilford.com
URL: http://www.guilford.com/

Cathy A. Malchiodi. 2002. $55.00. 461 pages. Provides complete and practical overview of art therapy.

★1087★ A Therapist's Guide to Art Therapy Assessments: Tools of the Trade

Charles C Thomas Publisher, Ltd.
2600 S. 1st.
PO Box 19265
Springfield, IL 62794-9265
Ph: (217)789-8980   Fax: (217)789-9130
Fr: 800-258-8980
E-mail: books@ccthomas.com
URL: http://www.ccthomas.com

Stephanie L. Brooke. Second edition, 2004. $53.95. 240 pages.

★1088★ Working with Images: The Art of Art Therapist

Charles C Thomas Publisher, Ltd.
2600 S 1st St.
PO Box 19265
Springfield, IL 62794-9265
Ph: (217)789-8980   Fax: (217)789-9130
Fr: 800-258-8980
E-mail: books@ccthomas.com
URL: http://www.ccthomas.com

Bruce L. Moon. January 2002. $48.95 (paper) $74.95 (hardcover). 241 pages. Explores art therapy.

TRADESHOWS

★1089★ American Art Therapy Association Conference

Stygar Associates, Inc.
1202 Allanson Rd.
Mundelein, IL 60060-3808
Ph: (847)566-4566   Fax: (847)566-4580
Fr: 888-290-0878
E-mail: estygarIII@aol.com
URL: http://www.stygarassociates.com

Annual. **Primary Exhibits:** Art supplies, books, therapeutic materials, and schools. **Dates and Locations:** 2008 Nov; Clevland, OH.

★1090★ The Silver Symposium of the Buckeye Art Therapy Association

The Buckeye Art Therapy Association
c/o Carrie Burick, Treas.
3562 W 120th St.
Cleveland, OH 44111
E-mail: cburick@core.com
URL: http://www.buckeyearttherapy.org

Annual. **Primary Exhibits:** Art therapy equipment, supplies, and services.

OTHER SOURCES

★1091★ American Art Therapy Association (AATA)

5999 Stevenson Ave.
Alexandria, VA 22304
Ph: (703)212-2238   Fr: 888-290-0878
E-mail: info@arttherapy.org
URL: http://www.arttherapy.org

Description: Art therapists, students, and individuals in related fields. Supports the progressive development of therapeutic uses of art, the advancement of research, and improvements in the standards of practice. Has established specific professional criteria for training art therapists. Facilitates the exchange of information and experience. Compiles statistics.

★1092★ American Society of Psychopathology of Expression (ASPE)

74 Lawton St.
Brookline, MA 02446
Ph: (617)738-9821   Fax: (617)975-0411

Description: Psychiatrists, psychologists, art therapists, sociologists, art critics, artists, social workers, linguists, educators, criminologists, writers, and historians. At least two-thirds of the members must be physicians. Fosters collaboration among specialists in the United States who are interested in the problems of expression and in the artistic activities connected with psychiatric, sociological, and psychological research. Disseminates information about research and clinical applications in the field of psychopathology of expression. Sponsors consultations, seminars, and lectures on art therapy.

★1093★ International Expressive Arts Therapy Association (IEATA)

PO Box 320399
San Francisco, CA 94132
Ph: (415)522-8959
URL: http://www.ieata.org/

Description: Provides resources about the expressive arts and how they may relate to other discipline, such as psychology, education and business.

★1094★ National Art Education Association (NAEA)

1916 Association Dr.
Reston, VA 20191-1502
Ph: (703)860-8000   Fax: (703)860-2960
E-mail: info@naea-reston.org
URL: http://www.naea-reston.org

Members: Teachers of art at elementary, middle, secondary, and college levels; colleges, libraries, museums, and other educational institutions. **Purpose:** Studies problems of teaching art; encourages research and experimentation. **Activities:** Serves as a clearinghouse for information on art education programs, materials, and methods of instruction. Sponsors special institutes. Cooperates with other national organizations for the furtherance of creative art experiences for youth.

★1095★ National Coalition of Creative Arts Therapies Associations (NCCATA)

8455 Colesville Rd., Ste. 1000
Silver Spring, MD 20910
Ph: (703)250-3414   Fax: (703)250-3414
E-mail: dianne.dulicai@cox.net
URL: http://www.nccata.org

Description: Creative arts therapists. Promotes therapeutic and rehabilitative uses of the arts in medicine, mental health, special education, and forensic and social services; coordinates member associations' activities and efforts in meeting common objectives while supporting and advancing each group's discipline. Works to: represent members' interests in legislative activities; define joint positions on public policy issues; facilitate communication among members; initiate educational and research programs. Compiles statistics.

Auctioneers

★1096★ **The Auctioneer**

National Auctioneers Association
8880 Ballentine
Overland Park, KS 66214
Ph: (913)541-8084   Fax: (913)894-5281
URL: http://www.auctioneers.org

Monthly. Trade magazine for auctioneers.

PLACEMENT AND JOB REFERRAL SERVICES

★1097★ **Florida Auctioneer Academy**

10376 E. Colonial Dr.
Orlando, FL 32817
Ph: (407)382-6699   Fr: 800-422-9155
E-mail: info@f-a-a.com
URL: http://www.f-a-a.com

Purpose: School for the training of auctioneers. **Activities:** Provides students information on career opportunities and licensing, as well as acting as a job placement service upon graduation.

EMPLOYER DIRECTORIES AND NETWORKING LISTS

★1098★ **Antique Week**

Mayhill Publications
27 N Jefferson St.
PO Box 90
Knightstown, IN 46148
Ph: (765)345-5133   Fax: (765)345-3398
Fr: 800-876-5133
URL: http://www.antiqueweek.com

Weekly. $41.00 for individuals. Covers in each issue, 100-150 antiques auctions and antique shows, occurring during the week or two after publication. Each issue also contains separate calendar of about 200-300 antique shows, flea markets, and auctions occurring during the months after publication; separate Central edition (Illinois, Indiana, Iowa, Kentucky, Michigan, Minnesota, Missouri, Ohio, western Pennsylvania, Tennessee, and Wisconsin), and Eastern edition (Connecticut, Delaware, District of Columbia, Maryland, New Jersey, New York, North Carolina, Pennsylvania, Rhode Island, South Carolina, Virginia, and West Virginia). Entries include: Name of event, location, type of event, dates, name of show manager or auctioneer. Arrangement: Geographical.

★1099★ **Arizona State Auctioneers Association**

Echo Lake Press
3660 E. University Dr., Ste. 8
Mesa, AZ 85205
Ph: (480)422-6010
E-mail: mgeyer@jpking.com
URL: http://www.azauctioneers.org/

Ted W. Parod. 1996. $9.95 (paper). Includes members of the Auctioneer Association of Arizona and their contact information.

★1100★ **Auctioneer-Directory Issue**

National Auctioneers Association
8880 Ballentine
Overland Park, KS 66214
Ph: (913)541-8084   Fax: (913)894-5281
URL: http://www.auctioneers.org

Annual, February. Publication includes: List of about 6,000 auctioneers. Entries include: Name, address, phone, fax, e-mail, website, specialization. Arrangement: Geographical and alphabetical.

★1101★ **Clark's Flea Market U.S.A.**

Clark's Publications
712 Cricket Cir.
Cantonment, FL 32533
Ph: (850)968-9595   Fax: (850)968-9596
Fr: 888-942-5275
URL: http://www.clarksfleamarketdirectory.com/index.htm

Quarterly; latest edition 2007. $10.00 for individuals. Covers over 3,000 flea markets and regular swap meets as well as auctions. Listings require payment of $ 75 fee. Entries include: For flea markets and swap meets–Name, location, dates or days held. For auctions–Name, location, date held, phone. Arrangement: Geographical.

★1102★ **Directory of Licensed Auctioneers, Apprentice Auctioneers, and Auction Firms Engaged in the Auction Profession**

South Carolina Department of LLR-Auctioneers Commission
Synergy Business Pk., Kingstree Bldg.,
  110 Centerview Dr.
PO Box 11329
Columbia, SC 29210
Ph: (803)896-4300   Fax: (803)896-4484
URL: http://www.llr.state.sc.us

Annual, December. Free. Covers approximately 1,500 auctioneers, apprentices, and firms licensed in South Carolina, including resident and non-resident licensees. Entries include: Company or personal name, address, phone, and license number. Arrangement: Geographical. Indexes: Alphabetical.

★1103★ **List of Licensed Auctioneers**

Florida Department of Business and
  Professional Regulation
1940 N Monroe St.
Tallahassee, FL 32399-1027
Ph: (850)487-1395   Fax: (850)921-0038
Fr: (866)532-1440
URL: http://www.myflorida.com/

Annual. Covers approximately 2,200 licensed auctioneers in Florida, 1,500 auction businesses. Entries include: Individual name, address. Arrangement: Alphabetical.

★1104★ **National Auto Auction Association-Membership Directory**

National Auto Auction Association
5320 Spectrum Dr., Ste. D
Frederick, MD 21703-7337
Ph: (301)696-0400   Fax: (301)631-1359
URL: http://www.naaa.com

Annual, February. Covers 25,446 automobile auction firms. Entries include: Company name, address, names and phone numbers of auction personnel; pick up, delivery, and reconditioning services available. Arrangement: Geographical.

HANDBOOKS AND MANUALS

★1105★ *Practical Treatise on the Law of Auctions: With Forms, Tables, Statutes and Cases and Directions to Auctioneers*

William S. Hein & Co.
1285 Main St.
Buffalo, NY 14209
Ph: (716)882-2600   Fax: (716)883-8100
Fr: 800-828-7571
E-mail: mail@wshein.com
URL: http://www.wshein.com/

Joseph Bateman. 1994. $47.50. 360 pages.

ONLINE JOB SOURCES AND SERVICES

★1106★ Auctioneer Talk
URL: http://www.auctioneertalk.com

Description: Serves as a discussion board for auctioneers that includes help-wanted ads, classifieds, and a list of upcoming auctions.

★1107★ National Auction List
URL: http://www.nationalauctionlist.com

Description: Provides a list of professional auctioneers, a list of upcoming auctions, and current auction news.

OTHER SOURCES

★1108★ American Academy of Auctioneers
1222 Kenwood Dr.
Broken Arrow, OK 74012-1931
Ph: (918)251-0058
URL: http://www.webspawner.com/users/auctioneerschool/index.html

Activities: Provides an at home training course in all phases of auctioneering, including how to begin a career as a professional auctioneer.

★1109★ AuctionServices.com
PO Box 20038
Roanoke, VA 24018
Ph: (540)206-3311   Fax: 877-644-4571
E-mail: inquiries@auctionservices.com
URL: http://www.auctionservices.com

Purpose: Develops and creates websites for professional auctioneers. Provides secure hosting for individual websites. **Activities:** Offers the auction industry websites to promote professionalism and connect with other auctioneers worldwide.

★1110★ California State Auctioneers Association
8880 Ballentine
Overland Park, KS 66214
Fr: 888-541-8084
E-mail: aherman@auctioneers.org
URL: http://www.caauctioneers.org

Members: Professional auctioneers. **Purpose:** Promotes professionalism, growth, and competency in the auction profession. **Activities:** Develops ethical standards in the industry, provides members with learning opportunities, reviews and develops information on technology changes in the industry, and provides opportunities to network and exchange ideas with professionals in the industry.

★1111★ Kentucky Auctioneers Association
PO Box 65
Smiths Grove, KY 42171-0065
Ph: (270)782-0065
E-mail: kaa@charleswhitley.com
URL: http://www.kentuckyauctioneers.org

Members: Professional auctioneers. **Purpose:** Promotes and advances the profession and fosters and encourages cooperation and mutual aid among those engaged in the auction profession. **Activities:** Acts as a networking forum for its members, provides information for writing contracts, and publishes a membership directory and quarterly magazine.

★1112★ Michigan State Auctioneers Association
4529 Gibbs NW
Grand Rapids, MI 49544
Ph: (616)785-8288   Fax: (616)785-8506
E-mail: info@msaa.org

URL: http://www.msaa.org

Members: Professional auctioneers. **Purpose:** Represents the interests of auctioneers and provides a forum for networking and sharing ideas and experiences. **Activities:** Sponsors educational courses and seminars, publishes an annual directory, and provides networking opportunities with other auctioneers.

★1113★ National Association of Public Auto Auctions
PO Box 41368
Raleigh, NC 27629
Ph: (919)876-0687
E-mail: execman@worldnet.att.net
URL: http://www.publicautoauctionassoc.org

Members: Professional auctioneers specializing in automobile auctions.

★1114★ National Auctioneers Association (NAA)
8880 Ballentine
Overland Park, KS 66214
Ph: (913)541-8084   Fax: (913)894-5281
E-mail: bob@auctioneers.org
URL: http://www.auctioneers.org

Description: Professional auctioneers. Provides continuing education classes for auctioneers, promotes use of the auction method of marketing in both the private and public sectors. Encourages the highest ethical standards for the profession.

★1115★ Virginia Auctioneers Association
PO Box 41368
Raleigh, NC 27629
Ph: (919)878-0601   Fax: (919)878-7413
Fr: 888-878-0601
E-mail: execman@worldnet.att.net
URL: http://www.vaa.org

Members: Professional auctioneers. **Activities:** Provides a membership directory and networking opportunities with other auctioneers.

★1116★ World Wide College of Auctioneering
PO Box 949
Mason City, IA 50402-0949
Fax: (641)423-3067   Fr: 800-423-5242
URL: http://worldwidecollegeofauctioneering.com

Purpose: Provides instruction and training in professional auctioneering. **Activities:** Offers advice on setting up an auctioneering business upon completion of the course.

Auto and Diesel Mechanics

SOURCES OF HELP-WANTED ADS

★1117★ Automotive Body Repair News
Reed Business Information
360 Park Ave. S
New York, NY 10010
Ph: (646)746-6400   Fax: (646)746-7431
URL: http://www.abrn.com/abrn/static/staticHtml.jsp?id=7442#about

Monthly. Magazine reporting automotive repair industry news.

★1118★ Automotive Cooling Journal
NARSA
15000 Commerce Pkwy., Ste. C
Mount Laurel, NJ 08054
Ph: (856)439-1575   Fax: (856)439-9596
Fr: 800-551-3232
E-mail: acj@narsa.org
URL: http://www.narsa.org

Monthly. $30.00/year for individuals; $55.00 for two years; $48.50/year for Canada; $92.00 for Canada, two years. Automotive trade magazine.

★1119★ Automotive Fleet
Bobit Business Media
3520 Challenger St.
Torrance, CA 90503
Ph: (310)533-2400   Fax: (310)533-2500
URL: http://www.bobit.com

Monthly. Free. Automotive magazine covering the car and light truck fleet market.

★1120★ Automotive News
Crain Communications Inc.
1155 Gratiot Ave.
PO Box 07924
Detroit, MI 48207-2997
Ph: (313)446-6000   Fax: (313)446-0347
Fr: 888-909-9111
URL: http://www.autonews.com

Weekly. $155.00/year for individuals; $239.00/year for Canada; $395.00/year for other countries; $266.00 for two years;

$418.00 for Canada, two years; $730.00 for other countries, two years. Tabloid reporting on all facets of the automotive and truck industry, as well as related businesses.

★1121★ The Blue Seal
National Institute for Automotive Service
  Excellence
101 Blue Seal Dr. SE, No. 101
Leesburg, VA 20175
Ph: (703)669-6600   Fax: (703)669-6123
Fr: 877-ASE-TECH
URL: http://www.asecert.org

Description: Quarterly. Covers news of the Institute's efforts to certify auto, medium/heavy truck, engine machinists, collision repair technicians, and parts specialists. Discusses industry trends, vehicle repair tips, and training information, and highlights activities of ASE-certified technicians.

★1122★ BodyShop Business
Babcox
3550 Embassy Pky.
Akron, OH 44333
Ph: (330)670-1234   Fax: (330)670-0874
E-mail: dlloyd@babcox.com
URL: http://www.bodyshopbusiness.com

Monthly. Free to qualified subscribers. Magazine providing management and technical information that can be applied to running an efficient and profitable collision repair shop.

★1123★ Bus Ride
Power Trade Media L.L.C.
4742 N 24th St., Ste. 340
Phoenix, AZ 85016
Ph: (602)265-7600   Fax: (602)227-7588
Fr: 800-541-2670
URL: http://www.busride.com

Monthly. $59.00/year for individuals, rush delivery; $94.00/year for two years, rush delivery; $39.00/year for individuals, regular mail; $64.00 for two years, regular mail; $64.00/year for Canada, one year, rush delivery; $106.00 for two years, rush delivery to Canada; $42.00/year for Canada, one year, regular mail; $69.00/year for two years, regular mail to Canada; $75.00/year for

elsewhere, one year; $125.00 for two years, other countries. Magazine for managers of bus, motorcoach and transit operations.

★1124★ Engine Builder
Babcox
3550 Embassy Pky.
Akron, OH 44333
Ph: (330)670-1234   Fax: (330)670-0874
URL: http://www.engine-builder.com

Monthly. Free to qualified subscribers. Magazine covering management topics, technical information, and new product news for owners and managers of leading volume rebuilding businesses.

★1125★ GEARS Magazine
Automatic Transmission Rebuilders
  Association
2400 Latigo Ave.
Oxnard, CA 93030
Ph: (805)604-2000   Fax: (805)604-2002
Fr: (866)664-2872
E-mail: atra@atra-gears.com
URL: http://www.atraonline.com

Description: Monthly. Contains news of the Association, its chapters, and Association programs. Lists service contract and insurance information, job listings, and personnel changes in the Association. Recurring features include news of research, notices of publications available, reports of meetings, news of educational opportunities, and a calendar of events.

★1126★ Import Automotive Parts &
  Accessories
Meyers Publishing
799 Camarillo Springs Rd.
Camarillo, CA 93012-8111
Ph: (805)445-8881   Fax: (805)445-8882
URL: http://www.meyerspublishing.com

Monthly. $75.00/year for Canada and Mexico; $105.00/year for other countries; $55.00/year for U.S. $10.00 for single issue; $25.00/year for individuals, import industry sourcebook; $35.00/year for individuals, import industry sourcebook outside the U.S.; $20.00 for single issue, outside the U.S.

Trade magazine for the automotive after-market.

★1127★ *Import Car*
Babcox
3550 Embassy Pky.
Akron, OH 44333
Ph: (330)670-1234   Fax: (330)670-0874
E-mail: jstankard@babcox.com
URL: http://www.import-car.com

Monthly. Free. Magazine serves import specialist repair shops that derive more than 50% of revenue from servicing import nameplates.

★1128★ *The Motion Systems Distributor*
Penton Media Inc.
1300 E 9th St.
Cleveland, OH 44114
Ph: (216)696-7000   Fax: (216)696-1752
URL: http://www.penton.com/

Bimonthly. Completely separate from PT Design, this bi-monthly publication is tailored to the informational needs of the motion systems distributor. Published six times, this sales and management magazine goes to sales and branch management personnel, owners/operators of distributor companies in the U.S. and their technical personnel, and selected suppliers.

★1129★ *Motor Age*
Adams Business Media
833 W Jackson, 7th Fl.
Chicago, IL 60607
Ph: (312)846-4600   Fax: (312)977-1042
URL: http://www.motorage.com

Monthly. $49.00/year for individuals; $75.00 for two years; $90.00/year for other countries. Magazine for auto repair shops.

★1130★ *Popular Mechanics*
Hearst Magazines
300 W 57th St.
New York, NY 10019-1497
Ph: (212)841-8480
E-mail: popularmechanics@hearst.com
URL: http://www.popularmechanics.com/

Monthly. $12.00/year for individuals, 12 issues; $18.00/year for individuals, 24 issues. Magazine focusing on autos, the home, and leisure. Prints Latin American Edition.

★1131★ *Transmission Digest*
MD Publications Inc.
3057 E Cairo
PO Box 2210
Springfield, MO 65802
Ph: (417)866-3917   Fax: (417)866-2781
Fr: 800-274-7890
URL: http://www.transmissiondigest.com/

Monthly. $39.00/year for individuals; $4.75 for single issue. Automotive transmission industry news.

★1132★ *Transport Topics*
American Trucking Associations Inc.
2200 Mill Rd.
Alexandria, VA 22314-4677
Ph: (703)838-1700   Fax: (703)683-2292
Fr: 800-517-7370
URL: http://www.ttnews.com

Weekly. $99.00/year for individuals, one year; $179.00/year for two years; $139.00/year for Canada and Mexico; $249.00/year for Canada and Mexico, 2 years. Newspaper (tabloid) covering the trucking industry, for executives and managers of large and small fleets at for-hire and private carriers.

★1133★ *Undercar Digest*
MD Publications Inc.
3057 E Cairo
PO Box 2210
Springfield, MO 65802
Ph: (417)866-3917   Fax: (417)866-2781
Fr: 800-274-7890
URL: http://www.mdpublications.com

Monthly. $49.00/year for individuals. Magazine for the undercar service and supply industry.

★1134★ *Underhood Service*
Babcox
3550 Embassy Pky.
Akron, OH 44333
Ph: (330)670-1234   Fax: (330)670-0874
E-mail: jstankard@babcox.com
URL: http://www.underhoodservice.com

Monthly. $35.00/year for individuals. Magazine covering service and repair shops doing 50% or more of service underhood.

EMPLOYER DIRECTORIES AND NETWORKING LISTS

★1135★ *Career Opportunities in the Automotive Industry*
Facts On File Inc.
132 W 31st St., 17th Fl.
New York, NY 10001
Ph: (212)967-8800   Fax: 800-678-3633
Fr: 800-322-8755
URL: http://www.factsonfile.com

Published 2005. $49.50 for individuals; $44.55 for libraries. Covers 70 jobs from pit crew mechanic to restoration expert, from mechanical engineer to parts distribution director, from RV specialist to exotic car museum director.

HANDBOOKS AND MANUALS

★1136★ *Auto Mechanic (Diesel)*
National Learning Corporation
212 Michael Dr.
Syosset, NY 11791
Ph: (516)921-8888   Fax: (516)921-8743
Fr: 800-645-6337

Jack Rudman. 2000. $29.95. Profiles diesel automotive repair.

★1137★ *Careers in Trucking*
Rosen Publishing Group, Inc.
29 E. 21st St.
New York, NY 10010
Ph: (212)777-3017   Fax: 888-436-4643
Fr: 800-237-9932
URL: http://www.rosenpublishing.com/

Donald D. Schauer. Revised edition, 2000. $31.95. 132 pages. Describes employment in the trucking industry including driving, operations, maintenance, sales, and administration. Covers qualifications, training, future outlook, and salaries. Offers career planning and job hunting advice.

TRADESHOWS

★1138★ *AERA Expo*
AERA - Engine Rebuilders Association
330 Lexington Dr.
Buffalo Grove, IL 60089-6998
Ph: (847)541-6550   Fax: 888-329-2372
Fr: 888-326-2372
URL: http://www.aera.org

Annual. **Primary Exhibits:** Automotive services equipment, parts, tools, supplies, and services.

★1139★ *International Autobody Congress and Exposition - NACE*
VNU Expositions, Inc. - Bill Communications, Inc.
1199 S. Belt Line Rd., Ste. 100
Coppell, TX 75019
Ph: (972)906-6500   Fax: (972)906-6501
E-mail: jlerner@vnuemedia.com
URL: http://www.vnuexpo.com

Annual. **Primary Exhibits:** Auto body repair equipment, supplies, and services.

★1140★ *National Automotive Radiator Service Association Annual Trade Show and Convention*
National Automotive Radiator Service Association
PO Box 97
East Greenville, PA 18041
Ph: (215)541-4500   Fax: (215)679-4977

Annual. **Primary Exhibits:** Manufacturers in the automotive cooling industry.

OTHER SOURCES

★1141★ Auto Mechanic

Cambridge Educational
PO Box 2053
Princeton, NJ 08543-2053
Fax: (609)671-0266   Fr: 800-257-5126
E-mail: custserv@films.com
URL: http://www.cambridgeeducational.com

VHS and DVD. $39.95. 15 minutes. 1989. Part of the Vocational Visions Career series.

★1142★ Automotive Service Association (ASA)

PO Box 929
Bedford, TX 76095-0929
Ph: (817)283-6205   Fax: (817)685-0225
Fr: 800-272-7467
E-mail: asainfo@asashop.org
URL: http://www.asashop.org

Members: Automotive service businesses including body, paint, and trim shops, engine rebuilders, radiator shops, brake and wheel alignment services, transmission shops, tune-up services, and air conditioning services; associate members are manufacturers and wholesalers of automotive parts, and the trade press. **Purpose:** Represents independent business owners and managers before private agencies and national and state legislative bodies. Promotes confidence between consumer and the automotive service industry, safety inspection of motor vehicles, and better highways.

★1143★ COIN Career Guidance System

COIN Educational Products
3361 Executive Pky., Ste. 302
Toledo, OH 43606
Ph: (419)536-5353   Fax: (419)536-7056
Fr: 800-274-8515
URL: http://www.coinedu.com/

CD-ROM. Provides career information through seven cross-referenced files covering postsecondary schools, college majors, vocational programs, military service, apprenticeship programs, financial aid, and scholarships. Apprenticeship file describes national apprenticeship training programs, including information on how to apply, contact agencies, and program content. Military file describes more than 200 military occupations and training opportunities related to civilian employment.

★1144★ Gasoline and Automotive Service Dealers Association (GASDA)

78 Harvard Ave., Ste. 260
Stamford, CT 06902
Ph: (203)327-4773   Fax: (203)323-6935
E-mail: info@gasda.org
URL: http://www.gasda.org

Members: Owners/operators or dealers of service stations or automotive repair facilities; interested individuals. **Purpose:** Aims to educate, inform, and help increase professionalism of members and of the industry. **Activities:** Offers periodic technical training clinics, and other educational programs including advanced automotive technical training, prepaid group legal services plan and group health insurance, and liaison with government agencies. Informs members of political and legislative action or changes affecting their industry.

★1145★ Mechanics & Repairers

Delphi Productions
3159 6th St.
Boulder, CO 80304
Ph: (303)443-2100   Fax: (303)443-4022
Fr: 888-443-2400
E-mail: support@delphivideo.com
URL: http://www.delphivideo.com

$95.00. 50 minutes. Part of the Careers for the 21st Century Video Library.

★1146★ National Institute for Automotive Service Excellence (ASE)

101 Blue Seal Dr. SE, Ste. 101
Leesburg, VA 20175
Ph: (703)669-6600   Fax: (703)669-6127
Fr: 888-ASE-TEST
E-mail: webmaster@asecert.org
URL: http://www.asecert.org

Members: Governed by a 40-member board of directors selected from all sectors of the automotive service industry and from education, government, and consumer groups. **Purpose:** Encourages and promotes the highest standards of automotive service in the public interest. **Activities:** Conducts continuing research to determine the best methods for training automotive technicians; encourages the development of effective training programs. Tests and certifies the competence of automobile, medium/heavy truck, collision repair, school bus and engine machinist technicians as well as parts specialists.

★1147★ Truck-Frame and Axle Repair Association (TARA)

3741 Enterprise Dr. SW
Rochester, MN 55902
Fax: (507)529-0380   Fr: 800-232-8272
E-mail: w.g.reich@att.net
URL: http://www.taraassociation.com

Members: Owners and operators of heavy-duty truck repair facilities and their mechanics; allied and associate members are manufacturers of heavy-duty trucks and repair equipment, engineers, trade press and insurance firms. **Purpose:** Seeks to help members share skills and technical knowledge and keep abreast of new developments and technology to better serve customers in areas of minimum downtime, cost and maximum efficiency. **Activities:** Conducts studies and surveys regarding safety, fuel conservation and heavy-duty truck maintenance and repairs. Has formed TARA's Young Executives to help make young people at members' repair facilities more proficient in normal business functions and to ensure the future of the Association.

★1148★ Women in Nontraditional Careers: An Introduction

Her Own Words
PO Box 5264
Madison, WI 53705
Ph: (608)271-7083   Fax: (608)271-0209
E-mail: herownword@aol.com
URL: http://www.herownwords.com/

Video. Jocelyn Riley. $95.00. 15 minutes. Resource guide also available for $45.00.

Bakers

SOURCES OF HELP-WANTED ADS

★1149★ Milling & Baking News

Sosland Publishing Co.
4800 Main St., Ste. 100
Kansas City, MO 64112
Ph: (816)756-1000   Fax: (816)756-0494
Fr: 800-338-6201
E-mail:
mbncirc@sosland.com?subject=mbn
URL: http://www.bakingbusiness.com

Weekly (Tues.). $128.00/year for individuals; $200.00 for individuals, 2 years; $276.00 for individuals, 3 years; $183.00/year for out of country; $310.00 for out of country, 2 years; $441.00 for out of country, 3 years. Trade magazine covering the grain-based food industries.

PLACEMENT AND JOB REFERRAL SERVICES

★1150★ Les Amis d'Escoffier Society of New York

787 Ridgewood Rd.
Millburn, NJ 07041
Ph: (212)414-5820   Fax: (973)379-3117
E-mail: kurt@escoffier-society.com
URL: http://www.escoffier-society.com

Members: An educational organization of professionals in the food and wine industries. **Activities:** Maintains museum, speakers' bureau, hall of fame, and placement service. Sponsors charitable programs.

HANDBOOKS AND MANUALS

★1151★ Career Opportunities in the Food and Beverage Industry

Facts on File, Inc.
132 W. 31st St., 17th Fl.
New York, NY 10001-2006
Ph: (212)967-8800   Fax: 800-678-3633
Fr: 800-322-8755
E-mail: custserv@factsonfile.com
URL: http://www.factsonfile.com

Barbara Sims-Bell. Second edition, 2001. $18.95 (paper). 223 pages. Provides the job seeker with information about locating and landing 80 skilled and unskilled jobs in the industry. Includes detailed job descriptions for many specific positions and lists trade associations, recruiting organizations, and major agencies. Contains index and bibliography.

★1152★ Careers for Gourmets and Others Who Relish Food

The McGraw-Hill Companies
PO Box 182604
Columbus, OH 43272
Fax: (614)759-3749   Fr: 877-883-5524
E-mail: customer.service@mcgraw-hill.com
URL: http://www.mcgraw-hill.com

Mary Donovan. Second edition, 2002. $15.95; $12.95 (paper). 192 pages. Discusses such job prospects as foods columnist, cookbook writer, test kitchen worker, pastry chef, recipe developer, food festival organizer, restaurant manager, and food stylist.

★1153★ Choosing a Career in the Restaurant Industry

Rosen Publishing Group, Inc.
29 E. 21st St.
New York, NY 10010
Ph: (212)777-3017   Fax: 888-436-4643
Fr: 800-237-9932
URL: http://www.rosenpublishing.com/

Eileen Beal. Revised edition, 2000. $25.25. 64 pages. Explores various jobs in the restaurant industry. Describes job duties, salaries, educational preparation, and job hunting. Contains information about fast food, catering, and small businesses.

★1154★ Culinary Arts Career Starter

LearningExpress, LLC
55 Broadway, 8th Fl.
New York, NY 10006
Ph: (212)995-2566   Fax: (212)995-5512
Fr: 800-295-9556
E-mail: customservice@learningexpressllc.com
URL: http://www.learningexpressllc.com

Mary Masi. 1999. $15.95 (paper). 208 pages.

★1155★ How to Open a Financially Successful Bakery

Atlantic Publishing Company
1210 SW 23rd Pl.
Ocala, FL 34474-7014
Fax: (352)622-1875   Fr: 800-814-1132
E-mail: sales@atlantic-pub.com
URL: http://www.atlantic-pub.com/

Sharon L. Fullen. 2004. $39.95 (CD-ROM, paper). Success in business for bakers. 288 pages.

★1156★ Opportunities in Culinary Careers

The McGraw-Hill Companies
PO Box 182604
Columbus, OH 43272
Fax: (614)759-3749   Fr: 877-883-5524
E-mail: customer.service@mcgraw-hill.com
URL: http://www.mcgraw-hill.com

Mary Deirdre Donovan. 2003. $13.95; $11.95 (paper). 149 pages. Describes the educational preparation and training of chefs and cooks and explores a variety of food service jobs in restaurants, institutions, and research and development. Lists major culinary professional associations and schools. Offers guidance on landing a first job in cooking and related fields.

★1157★ Opportunities in Restaurant Careers

The McGraw-Hill Companies
PO Box 182604
Columbus, OH 43272
Fax: (614)759-3749   Fr: 877-883-5524
E-mail: customer.service@mcgraw-hill.com
URL: http://www.mcgraw-hill.com

Carol Caprione Chmelynski. 2004. $13.95 (paper). 150 pages. Covers opportunities in the food service industry and details salaries, benefits, training opportunities, and professional associations. Special emphasis is put on becoming a successful restaurant manager by working up through the ranks. Illustrated.

TRADESHOWS

★1158★ American School Food Service Association Annual National Conference

American School Food Service Association
700 S. Washington St., Ste. 300
Alexandria, VA 22314-4287
Ph: (703)739-3900   Fax: (703)739-3915
Fr: 800-877-8822
E-mail: servicecenter@asfsa.org
URL: http://www.asfsa.org

Annual. **Primary Exhibits:** Food service supplies and equipment, including educational services and computers.

★1159★ Dairy-Deli-Bake

International Dairy-Deli-Bakery Association
313 Price Pl., Ste. 202
PO Box 5528
Madison, WI 53705-0528
Ph: (608)310-5000   Fax: (608)238-6330
E-mail: iddba@iddba.org
URL: http://www.iddba.org

Annual. **Primary Exhibits:** Dairy, deli, and bakery products, packaging, and equipment. **Dates and Locations:** 2008 Jun 01-03; Orlando, FL.

★1160★ Institute of Food Technologists Annual Meeting and Food Expo

Institute of Food Technologists
525 W, Van Buren St., Ste. 1000
Chicago, IL 60607-3814
Ph: (312)782-8424   Fax: (312)782-8348
E-mail: info@ift.org
URL: http://www.ift.org

Annual. **Primary Exhibits:** Food ingredients, equipment, laboratory equipment and supplies, and other services rendered to the food processing industry.

★1161★ International Baking Industry Exposition

IBIE Exhibition Management
401 N. Michigan Ave.
Chicago, IL 60611
Ph: (312)644-6610   Fax: (312)644-0575
E-mail: pdwyer@smithbucklin.com
URL: http://www.bakingexpo.com

Primary Exhibits: Baking equipment, supplies, and services.

★1162★ National Restauraunt Association Restaurant and Hotel-Motel Show

National Restaurant Association
(Convention Office)
150 N. Michigan Ave., Ste. 2000
Chicago, IL 60601
Ph: (312)853-2525   Fax: (312)853-2548

Annual. **Primary Exhibits:** Food service equipment, supplies, and services and food and beverage products for the hospitality industry. Includes International Cuisine Pavilion. **Dates and Locations:** 2008 May 17-20; Chicago, IL; McCormick Place.

★1163★ The Retailer's Bakery Association Marketplace

The Retailer's Bakery Association
8201 Greensboro Dr., Ste. 300
McLean, VA 22102
Ph: (703)610-9035   Fax: (703)610-9005
Fr: 800-638-0924
E-mail: info@rbanet.com
URL: http://www.rbanet.com

Annual. **Primary Exhibits:** Ingredients, raw materials, packaging supplies, equipment, services for the retail bakery industry.

OTHER SOURCES

★1164★ Allied Trades of the Baking Industry (ATBI)

2001 Shawnee Mission Pkwy.
Mission Woods, KS 66205
Ph: (913)890-6300
E-mail: t.miller@cerealfood.com
URL: http://www.atbi.org

Members: Salespeople from the allied trades servicing the baking industry. **Purpose:** Promotes the industry through cooperative service to national, state, and local bakery associations; encourages mutual understanding and goodwill between the baking industry and the allied trades. **Activities:** Carries out promotional and service activities.

★1165★ American Bakers Association (ABA)

1300 I St. NW, Ste. 700 W
Washington, DC 20005
Ph: (202)789-0300   Fax: (202)898-1164
E-mail: info@americanbakers.org
URL: http://www.americanbakers.org

Members: Manufacturers and wholesale distributors of bread, rolls, and pastry products; suppliers of goods and services to bakers. **Activities:** Conducts seminars and expositions.

★1166★ American Culinary Federation (ACF)

180 Center Place Way
St. Augustine, FL 32095
Ph: (904)824-4468   Fax: (904)825-4758
Fr: 800-624-9458
E-mail: hcramb@acfchefs.net
URL: http://www.acfchefs.org

Description: Aims to promote the culinary profession and provide on-going educational training and networking for members. Provides opportunities for competition, professional recognition, and access to educational forums with other culinary experts at local, regional, national, and international events. Operates the National Apprenticeship Program for Cooks and pastry cooks. Offers programs that address certification of the individual chef's skills, accreditation of culinary programs, apprenticeship of cooks and pastry cooks, professional development, and the fight against childhood hunger.

★1167★ American Institute of Baking (AIB)

1213 Bakers Way
PO Box 3999
Manhattan, KS 66505-3999
Ph: (785)537-4750   Fax: (785)537-1493
Fr: 800-633-5137
E-mail: info@aibonline.org
URL: http://www.aibonline.org

Members: Baking research and educational center. **Purpose:** Conducts basic and applied research, educational and hands-on training, and in-plant sanitation and worker safety audits. **Activities:** Maintains museum. Provides bibliographic and reference service. Serves as registrar for ISO-9000 quality certification.

★1168★ American Society of Baking

533 1st St. E
Sonoma, CA 95476
Ph: (707)935-0103   Fax: (707)935-0174
Fr: (866)920-9885
E-mail: tmatthias@asbe.org
URL: http://www.asbe.org

Description: Professional organization of persons engaged in bakery production; chemists, production supervisors, engineers, technicians, and others from allied fields. Maintains information service and library references to baking and related subjects.

★1169★ BEMA, The Baking Industry Suppliers Association (BEMA)

7101 College Blvd., Ste. 1505
Overland Park, KS 66210
Ph: (913)338-1300   Fax: (913)338-1327
E-mail: info@bema.org

URL: http://www.bema.org

Members: Baking and food industries.

★1170★ **Independent Bakers Association (IBA)**
PO Box 3731
Washington, DC 20007
Ph: (202)333-8190   Fax: (202)337-3809
E-mail: independentbaker@yahoo.com
URL: http://www.mindspring.com/~independentbaker

Members: Trade association representing small-medium wholesale bakers and allied trade members. **Purpose:** Represents independent wholesale bakers on federal legislative and regulatory issues. **Activities:** Offers annual Smith-Schaus-Smith internships.

★1171★ **International Association of Culinary Professionals (IACP)**
304 W Liberty St., Ste. 201
Louisville, KY 40202
Ph: (502)581-9786   Fax: (502)589-3602
Fr: 800-928-4227
E-mail: iacp@hqtrs.com
URL: http://www.iacp.com

Description: Represents cooking school owners, food writers, chefs, caterers, culinary specialists, directors, teachers, cookbook authors, food stylists, food photographers, student/apprentices, and individuals in related industries in 20 countries. Promotes the interests of cooking schools, teachers, and culinary professionals. Encourages the exchange of information and education. Promotes professional standards and accreditation procedures. Maintains a Foundation to award culinary scholarships and grants.

★1172★ **International Council on Hotel, Restaurant, and Institutional Education (CHRIE)**
2810 N Parham Rd., Ste. 230
Richmond, VA 23294
Ph: (804)346-4800   Fax: (804)346-5009
E-mail: kmccarty@chrie.org
URL: http://www.chrie.org

Description: Schools and colleges offering specialized education and training in hospitals, recreation, tourism and hotel, restaurant, and institutional administration; individuals, executives, and students. Provides networking opportunities and professional development.

★1173★ **Quality Bakers of America Cooperative (QBA)**
1055 Parsippany Blvd., Ste. 201
Parsippany, NJ 07054
Ph: (973)263-6970   Fax: (973)263-0937
E-mail: info@qba.com
URL: http://www.qba.com

Members: Independent national and international wholesale bakeries; composed of three major consulting divisions: marketing, manufacturing and technical research. Offers expertise in business strategy and management, product development, marketing and consumer research, process development, training and procurement.

★1174★ **Retailer's Bakery Association (RBA)**
8201 Greensboro Dr., Ste. 300
McLean, VA 22102
Ph: (703)610-9035   Fax: (703)610-9005
Fr: 800-638-0924
E-mail: info@rbanet.com
URL: http://www.rbanet.com

Members: Independent and in-store bakeries, food service, specialty bakeries (2500), suppliers of ingredients, tools and equipment (780); other (220). **Activities:** Provides information, management, production, merchandising, and small business services.

★1175★ **Wholesale Variety Bakers Association (WVBA)**
215 Eva St.
St. Paul, MN 55107
Ph: (651)224-5761   Fax: (651)224-9047

Description: Bakeries. Facilitates exchange of information among members and between members and other bakeries.

Bill and Account Collectors

SOURCES OF HELP-WANTED ADS

★1176★ Accounting and Finance
Wiley-Blackwell
350 Main St. Commerce Pl.
Malden, MA 02148
Ph: (781)388-8200   Fax: (781)388-8210
Fr: 800-759-6120
URL: http://www.blackwellpublishing.com/
journal.asp?ref=0810-5391

Quarterly. $163.00/year for institutions, print plus premium online, Australia/New Zealand; $148.00/year for institutions, print plus standard online, Australia/New Zealand; $141.00/year for institutions, premium online only, Australia/New Zealand; $432.00/year for institutions, print plus premium online; $393.00/year for institutions, print plus standard online; $373.00/year for institutions, premium online only; $300.00/year for institutions, other countries, print plus premium online; $273.00/year for institutions, other countries, print plus standard online; $259.00/year for institutions, other countries, premium online only. Journal focusing on accounting and finance.

★1177★ Accounting Horizons
American Accounting Association
5717 Bessie Dr.
Sarasota, FL 34233-2399
Ph: (941)921-7747   Fax: (941)923-4093
URL: http://aaahq.org/index.cfm

Quarterly. $265.00/year for individuals, print only; $265.00/year for individuals, online, vol.13 through current issue; $290.00/year for individuals, online and print. Publication covering the banking, finance, and accounting industries.

★1178★ Brookings Papers on Economic Activity
Brookings Institution Press
1775 Massashusetts Ave. NW
Washington, DC 20036-2188
Ph: (202)536-3600   Fax: (202)536-3623
Fr: 800-275-1447

URL: http://www.brookings.edu/press/journals.htm#bpea
Semiannual. $70.00/year for individuals; $84.00/year for institutions, other countries; $50.00/year for individuals; $64.00/year for individuals, foreign. Publication covering economics and business.

★1179★ Business Credit
National Association of Credit Management
8840 Columbia 100 Pkwy.
Columbia, MD 21045-2158
Ph: (410)740-5560   Fax: (410)740-5574
URL: http://www.nacm.org/bcmag/bcm_index.shtml

$54.00/year for individuals, business; $48.00/year for libraries; $60.00/year for Canada; $65.00/year for other countries. Magazine covering finance, business risk management, providing information for the extension of credit, maintenance of accounts receivable, and cash asset management.

★1180★ Commercial Lending Review
Aspen Publishers Inc.
76 Ninth Ave., 7th Fl.
New York, NY 10011
Ph: (212)771-0600   Fax: (212)771-0885
Fr: 800-638-8437
URL: http://
www.commerciallendingreview.com/

Bimonthly. Journal covering all aspects of lending for commercial banks, community and regional banks and other financial institutions.

★1181★ Foundations and Trends in Finance
Now Publishers
PO Box 1024
Hanover, MA 02339
Ph: (781)871-0245
URL: http://www.nowpublishers.com/product.aspx?product=FIN

Irregular. $315.00/year online only; $355.00/year print and online; $315.00/year online only; $355.00/year print and online. Academic journal that covers corporate finance, financial markets, asset pricing, and derivatives.

★1182★ Journal of Applied Finance
INFORMS
7240 Parkway Dr., Ste. 310
Hanover, MD 21076
Ph: (443)757-3500   Fax: (443)757-3515
Fr: 800-446-3676
URL: http://www.fma.org/

Journal for financial practice and education developments.

★1183★ U.S. Banker
Thomson Financial
195 Broadway
New York, NY 10007
Ph: (646)822-2000   Fax: (646)822-3230
Fr: 888-605-3385
URL: http://www.americanbanker.com/usb.html

Monthly. $109.00/year for individuals; $139.00/year for individuals, Canada; $139.00/year for individuals, outside North America; $179.00/year for two years; $239.00 for two years, Canada; $239.00/year for two years, outside North America. Magazine serving the financial services industry.

★1184★ Wilmott Magazine
John Wiley & Sons Inc.
111 River St.
Hoboken, NJ 07030-5774
Ph: (201)748-6000   Fax: (201)748-6088
Fr: 800-825-7550
URL: http://www.wilmott.com

$695/year for non-UK institutions. Journal focusing on the quantitative finance community and concentrating on practicalities.

PLACEMENT AND JOB REFERRAL SERVICES

★1185★ Commercial Finance Association (CFA)
225 W 34th St., Ste. 1815
New York, NY 10122
Ph: (212)594-3490   Fax: (212)564-6053
E-mail: info@cfa.com
URL: http://www.cfa.com

Members: Organizations engaged in asset-based financial services including commercial financing and factoring and lending money on a secured basis to small- and medium-sized business firms. **Purpose:** Acts as a forum for information and consideration about ideas, opportunities, and legislation concerning asset-based financial services. Seeks to improve the industry's legal and operational procedures. **Activities:** Offers job placement and reference services for members. Sponsors School for Field Examiners and other educational programs. Compiles statistics; conducts seminars and surveys; maintains Speaker's Bureau and 21 committees.

★1186★ Society of Certified Credit Executives (SCCE)
PO Box 390106
Minneapolis, MN 55439
Ph: (952)926-6547   Fax: (952)926-1624
E-mail: scce@collector.com
URL: http://www.acainternational.org

Description: A division of the International Credit Association. Credit executives who have been certified through SCCE's professional certification programs. Seeks to improve industry operations while expanding the knowledge of its members. Maintains placement service.

EMPLOYER DIRECTORIES AND NETWORKING LISTS

★1187★ Career Opportunities in Banking, Finance, and Insurance
Facts On File Inc.
132 W 31st St., 17th Fl.
New York, NY 10001
Ph: (212)967-8800   Fax: 800-678-3633
Fr: 800-322-8755
URL: http://www.factsonfile.com/

Latest edition 2nd, February 2007. $49.50 for individuals; $44.45 for libraries. Publication includes: Lists of colleges with programs supporting banking, finance, and industry; professional associations; professional certifications; regulatory agencies; and Internet resources for career planning. Principal content of publication consists of job descriptions for professions in the banking, finance, and insurance industries. Indexes: Alphabetical.

HANDBOOKS AND MANUALS

★1188★ Careers in Banking and Finance
Rosen Publishing Group, Inc.
29 E. 21st St.
New York, NY 10010
Ph: (212)777-3017   Fax: 888-436-4643
Fr: 800-237-9932
URL: http://www.rosenpublishing.com/

Patricia Haddock. Revised edition, 2001. $31.95. 139 pages. Offers advice on job hunting. Describes jobs at all levels in banking and finance. Contains information about the types of financial organizations where the jobs are found, educational requirements, job duties, and salaries.

EMPLOYMENT AGENCIES AND SEARCH FIRMS

★1189★ American Human Resources Associates Ltd. (AHRA)
PO Box 18269
Cleveland, OH 44118-0269
Ph: (440)995-7120   Fr: 877-342-5833
E-mail: inquiry@ahrasearch.com
URL: http://www.ahrasearch.com

Executive search firm. Focused on real estate, banking and credit & collection.

★1190★ Barkston Group LLC
113 South St.
PO Box 218
Litchfield, CT 06759-0218
Ph: (860)567-2400   Fax: (860)567-1466
E-mail: dpatenge@barkstongroup.com
URL: http://www.barkstongroup.com

Executive search firm focused on the banking industry.

★1191★ J Nicolas Arthur
77 Franklin St., Fl. 10
Boston, MA 02110
Ph: (617)204-9000   Fax: (617)303-8934
E-mail: nicholas.bogard@jnicholasarthur.com
URL: http://www.jnicholasarthur.com/

Executive search firm specializing in the finance industry.

OTHER SOURCES

★1192★ Account Management Systems
12121 Little Rd., Ste. 306
Hudson, FL 34667
Fr: 800-231-7645
URL: http://www.amscollects.com

Description: National and international commercial debt collection agency. Specializes in business-to-business debt collection.

★1193★ Allied Finance Adjusters
PO Box 60146
San Angelo, TX 76906
Fr: 800-843-1232
E-mail: fedauto@bellsouth.net
URL: http://www.alliedfinanceadjusters.com

Description: Association of professional repossessors, investigators, and recovery agents.

★1194★ American Bankers Association (ABA)
1120 Connecticut Ave. NW
Washington, DC 20036
Ph: (202)663-5000   Fax: (202)663-7543
Fr: 800-BAN-KERS
E-mail: custserv@aba.com
URL: http://www.aba.com

Members: Members are principally commercial banks and trust companies; combined assets of members represent approximately 90% of the U.S. banking industry; approximately 94% of members are community banks with less than $500 million in assets. **Purpose:** Seeks to enhance the role of commercial bankers as preeminent providers of financial services through communications, research, legal action, lobbying of federal legislative and regulatory bodies, and education and training programs. Serves as spokesperson for the banking industry; facilitates exchange of information among members. Maintains the American Institute of Banking, an industry-sponsored adult education program. **Activities:** Conducts educational and training programs for bank employees and officers through a wide range of banking schools and national conferences. Maintains liaison with federal bank regulators; lobbies Congress on issues affecting commercial banks; testifies before congressional committees; represents members in U.S. postal rate proceedings. Serves as secretariat of the International Monetary Conference and the Financial Institutions Committee for the American National Standards Institute. Files briefs and lawsuits in major court cases affecting the industry. Conducts teleconferences with state banking associations on such issues as regulatory compliance; works to build consensus and coordinate activities of leading bank and financial service trade groups. Provides services to members including: public advocacy; news media contact; insurance program providing directors and officers with liability coverage, financial institution bond, and trust errors and omissions coverage; research service operated through ABA Center for Banking Information; fingerprint set processing in conjunction with the Federal Bureau of Investigation; discounts on operational and income-producing projects through the Corporation for American Banking. Conducts conferences, forums, and workshops covering subjects such as small business, consumer credit, agricultural and community banking, trust management, bank operations, and automation. Sponsors ABA Educational Foundation and the Personal Economics Program, which educates schoolchildren and the community on banking, economics, and personal finance.

★1195★ American Financial Services Association (AFSA)

919 18th St. NW, Ste. 300
Washington, DC 20006-5517
Ph: (202)296-5544   Fax: (202)223-0321
E-mail: cstinebert@afsamail.org
URL: http://www.afsaonline.org

Description: Represents companies whose business is primarily direct credit lending to consumers and/or the purchase of sales finance paper on consumer goods. Has members that have insurance and retail subsidiaries; some are themselves subsidiaries of highly diversified parent corporations. Encourages the business of financing individuals and families for necessary and useful purposes at reasonable charges, including interest; promotes consumer understanding of basic money management principles as well as constructive uses of consumer credit. Includes educational services such as films, textbooks, and study units for the classroom and budgeting guides for individuals and families. Compiles statistical reports; offers seminars.

★1196★ Association of Credit and Collection Professionals

PO Box 390106
Minneapolis, MN 55439
Ph: (952)926-6547   Fax: (952)926-1624
E-mail: aca@acainternational.org
URL: http://www.acainternational.org

Description: Organization of credit and col-

lection professionals that provides accounts receivable management services.

★1197★ Association for Financial Professionals (AFP)

4520 E West Hwy., Ste. 750
Bethesda, MD 20814
Ph: (301)907-2862   Fax: (301)907-2864
E-mail: afp@afponline.org
URL: http://www.afponline.org

Purpose: Seeks to establish a national forum for the exchange of concepts and techniques related to improving the management of treasury and the careers of professionals through research, education, publications, and recognition of the treasury management profession through a certification program. **Activities:** Conducts educational programs. Operates career center.

★1198★ Consumer Data Industry Association (CDIA)

1090 Vermont Ave. NW, Ste. 200
Washington, DC 20005-4905
Ph: (202)371-0910   Fax: (202)371-0134
Fr: (866)696-7227
E-mail: cdia@cdiaonline.org
URL: http://www.cdiaonline.org

Description: Serves as international association of credit reporting and collection service offices. Maintains hall of fame and biographical archives; conducts specialized educational programs. Offers computerized services and compiles statistics.

★1199★ Credit Professionals International (CPI)

525 B N Laclede Station Rd.
St. Louis, MO 63119
Ph: (314)961-0031   Fax: (314)961-0040

E-mail: creditpro@creditprofessionals.org
URL: http://www.creditprofessionals.org

Description: Represents individuals employed in credit or collection departments of business firms or professional offices. Conducts educational program in credit work. Sponsors Career Club composed of members who have been involved in credit work for at least 25 years.

★1200★ National Association of Credit Management (NACM)

8840 Columbia 100 Pkwy.
Columbia, MD 21045-2158
Ph: (410)740-5560   Fax: (410)740-5574
URL: http://www.nacm.org/

Description: Provides information, products and services for effective business credit and accounts receivable management.

★1201★ National Association of Credit Union Services Organizations (NACUSO)

PMB 3419 Via Lido, No. 135
Newport Beach, CA 92663
Ph: (949)645-5296   Fax: (949)645-5297
Fr: 888-462-2870
E-mail: info@nacuso.org
URL: http://www.nacuso.org

Members: Credit union service organizations and their employees. **Purpose:** Promotes professional advancement of credit union service organization staff; seeks to insure adherence to high standards of ethics and practice among members. **Activities:** Conducts research and educational programs; formulates and enforces standards of conduct and practice; maintains speakers' bureau; compiles statistics.

Biological Scientists

★1202★ AAPG Explorer

American Association of Petroleum
  Geologists
1444 S Boulder
PO Box 979
Tulsa, OK 74101-0979
Ph: (918)584-2555   Fax: (918)560-2694
Fr: 800-364-AAPG
URL: http://www.aapg.org

Monthly. $63.00/year for nonmembers;
$60.00/year for individuals, airmail service.
Magazine containing articles about energy
issues with an emphasis on exploration for
hydrocarbons and energy minerals.

**★1203★ The American Biology
  Teacher**

National Association of Biology Teachers
12030 Sunrise Valley Dr., Ste. 110
Reston, VA 20191-3409
Fax: (703)264-7778   Fr: 800-406-0775
E-mail: publication@nabt.org
URL: http://www.nabt.org

Monthly. Journal featuring articles on biology, science, and education for elementary,
high school and college level biology teachers. Includes audio-visual, book, computer,
and research reviews.

**★1204★ American Biotechnology
  Laboratory**

International Scientific Communications
  Inc.
30 Controls Dr.
PO Box 870
Shelton, CT 06484
Ph: (203)926-9300   Fax: (203)926-9310
URL: http://
www.americanbiotechnologylaboratory.com

Bimonthly. $160.00/year for individuals. Bio-
technology magazine.

**★1205★ American Journal of
  Agricultural and Biological Science**

Science Publications
Vails Gate Heights Dr.
PO Box 879
Vails Gate, NY 12584
URL: http://www.scipub.org/scipub/
c4p.php?j_id=AJAB

Quarterly. $1,100.00/year for individuals;
$300.00 for single issue. Scholarly journal
covering sciences relevant to biology and
agriculture.

★1206★ American Laboratory News

International Scientific Communications
  Inc.
30 Controls Dr.
PO Box 870
Shelton, CT 06484
Ph: (203)926-9300   Fax: (203)926-9310
URL: http://www.americanlaboratory.com

Monthly. Trade magazine for scientists.

★1207★ Annual Review of Genetics

Annual Reviews Inc.
4139 El Camino Way
PO Box 10139
Palo Alto, CA 94303-0139
Ph: (650)493-4400   Fax: (650)424-0910
Fr: 800-523-8635
URL: http://www.annualreviews.org/

Annual. $80.00/year for individuals, print &
online; $80.00/year for out of country, print &
online; $226.00/year for institutions, print &
online; $226.00/year for institutions, other
countries, print & online; $188.00/year for
institutions, online; $188.00/year for institu-
tions, other countries, online; $188.00/year
for institutions, print; $188.00/year for institu-
tions, other countries, print. Periodical covering issues in genetics and the biological
sciences.

**★1208★ Annual Review of
  Microbiology**

Annual Reviews Inc.
4139 El Camino Way
PO Box 10139
Palo Alto, CA 94303-0139
Ph: (650)493-4400   Fax: (650)424-0910
Fr: 800-523-8635
URL: http://www.annualreviews.org/

Annual. $80.00/year for individuals, print &
online; $80.00/year for out of country, print &
online; $222.00/year for institutions, print &
online; $222.00/year for institutions, other
countries, print & online; $185.00/year for
institutions, online; $185.00/year for institu-
tions, other countries, online; $185.00/year
for institutions, print; $185.00/year for institu-
tions, other countries, print. Periodical covering microbiology and the biological sciences.

★1209★ ASPB News

American Society of Plant Biologists
15501 Monona Dr.
Rockville, MD 20855-2768
Ph: (301)251-0560   Fax: (301)279-2996
E-mail: info@aspb.org
URL: http://www.aspb.org/newsletter/

Description: Bimonthly. Offers news of interest to plant physiologists, biochemists,
horticulturists, and plant molecular and cell
biologists engaged in research and teaching.
Alerts members to public policy issues,
educational opportunities, meetings, seminars, and conventions pertinent to the field.
Recurring features include letters to the
editor, reports of meetings, job listings, a
calendar of events, news from regional sections, and teaching ideas.

★1210★ AWIS Magazine

Association for Women in Science
1200 New York Ave. NW, Ste. 650
Washington, DC 20005
Ph: (202)326-8940   Fax: (202)326-8960
Fr: (866)657-2947
E-mail: awis@awis.org
URL: http://www.awis.org/

Description: Bimonthly. Covers issues, legislation, and trends related to science education for girls, women, and minorities. Includes information on grants and fellow-

ships, job openings, educational programs, events, and notices of publications available.

★1211★ Cell

Cell Press
600 Technology Sq.
Cambridge, MA 02139
Ph: (617)661-7057   Fax: (617)661-7061
Fr: (866)314-2355
E-mail: advertising@cell.com
URL: http://www.cell.com

$179.00/year for U.S. and Canada, individual, print and online; $269.00/year for other countries, individual, print and online; $179.00/year for U.S. and Canada, online only, individual; $179.00/year for other countries, online only, individual; $997.00/year for U.S. and Canada, institutions; $1122.00/year for institutions, other countries, print. Journal on molecular and cell biology.

★1212★ Cell Biology Education

American Society for Cell Biology
8120 Woodmont Ave., Ste. 750
Bethesda, MD 20814-2762
Ph: (301)347-9300   Fax: (301)347-9310
URL: http://www.cellbioed.org

Quarterly. Journal that offers information on biology education grades k-20.

★1213★ Chemistry & Biology

Elsevier Science Inc.
360 Park Ave. S
New York, NY 10010
Ph: (212)989-5800   Fax: (212)633-3990
URL: http://www.elsevier.com/

Monthly. $1,745/year for institutions, U.S. and Canada; $369.00/year for individuals, U.S. and Canada. Journal focused on genetic, computational, or theoretical information of chemistry and biology, substantiating experimental data.

★1214★ Current Advances in Genetics & Molecular Biology

Elsevier Science Inc.
360 Park Ave. S
New York, NY 10010
Ph: (212)989-5800   Fax: (212)633-3990
URL: http://www.elsevier.com

Monthly. $4,096.00/year for institutions, all countries except Europe, Japan and Iran; $177.00/year for individuals, all countries except Europe, Japan and Iran. Journal covering current details of genetics and molecular biology.

★1215★ Earth Work

Student Conservation Association
689 River Rd.
PO Box 550
Charlestown, NH 03603
Ph: (603)543-1700   Fax: (603)543-1828
E-mail: earthwork@sca-inc.org
URL: http://www.thesca.org/

Description: Monthly. Contains listings of environmental positions, ranging from intern-

ships and administrative assistants for environmental groups to camp directors, state natural resource managers, and biologists.

★1216★ The Electrochemical Society Interface

The Electrochemical Society Inc.
65 S Main St., Bldg. D
Pennington, NJ 08534-2839
Ph: (609)737-1902   Fax: (609)737-2743
E-mail: interface@electrochem.org
URL: http://www.electrochem.org/dl/interface/

Quarterly. $15.00/year for members; $68.00/year for nonmembers; $15.00 for single issue, members; $20.00 for single issue, nonmembers. Publication featuring news and articles of interest to members of the Electrochemical Society.

★1217★ Engineering in Life Sciences

John Wiley & Sons Inc.
111 River St.
Hoboken, NJ 07030-5774
Ph: (201)748-6000   Fax: (201)748-6088
Fr: 800-825-7550
URL: http://as.wiley.com/WileyCDA/WileyTitle/productCd-2129.html

Bimonthly. $765.00/year for institutions, rest of Europe; $1,170.00/year for institutions, Switzerland and Liechtenstein; $1,005.00/year for institutions, rest of world; $842.00/year for institutions, print with online rest of Europe; $1,287.00/year for institutions, print with online Switzerland and Liechtenstein; $1,106.00/year for institutions, print with online rest of world. Journal focusing on the field of biotechnology and related topics including microbiology, genetics, biochemistry, and chemistry.

★1218★ Epigenetics

Landes Bioscience
1002 West Ave., 2nd Fl.
Austin, TX 78701
Ph: (512)637-6050   Fax: (512)637-6079
Fr: 800-736-9948
URL: http://www.landesbioscience.com/index.php

Journal devoted to practicing physicians, residents and students.

★1219★ Flora of North America Newsletter

Flora of North America Association
PO Box 299
St. Louis, MO 63166
Ph: (314)577-9563   Fax: (314)577-9596
E-mail: martha.hill@mobot.org
URL: http://hua.huh.harvard.edu/FNA/

Description: Quarterly. Communicates news of FNA projects and other topics of interest to floristic researchers. Recurring features include news of research, reports of meetings, job listings, and notices of publications available.

★1220★ International Archives of Bioscience

International Archives of Bioscience
PO Box 737254
Elmhurst, NY 11373-9997
URL: http://www.iabs.us/jdoc/aboutiabs.htm

Free, online only. Journal reporting multidisciplinary coverage and interaction between scientists in biology, informatics, mathematics, physics, engineering and other sciences.

★1221★ Invertebrate Biology

Allen Press Inc.
810 E 10th St.
Lawrence, KS 66044
Ph: (785)843-1234   Fax: (785)843-1244
Fr: 800-627-0326
URL: http://www.amicros.org/

Quarterly. $38.00/year for members; $19.00/year for students. Scientific journal covering the biology of invertebrate animals and research in the fields of cell and molecular biology, ecology, physiology, systematics, genetics, biogeography and behavior.

★1222★ Journal of Bacteriology

ASM Journals
1752 N St. NW
Washington, DC 20036-2904
Ph: (202)737-3600   Fax: (202)942-9333
URL: http://www.journals.asm.org

Semimonthly. $180.00/year for individuals; $290.00/year for individuals, print; $1,440.00/year for institutions; $1,534.00/year for institutions, Canada; $1,557.00/year for institutions, Europe; $1,597.00/year for institutions, Latin America; $1,602.00/year for institutions, other countries. Journal publishing articles about bacteria and other microorganisms, including fungi and other unicellular, eukaryotic organisms.

★1223★ Lab Animal

Nature Publishing Group
75 Varick St., 9th Fl.
New York, NY 10013-1917
Ph: (212)726-9200   Fax: (212)696-9006
Fr: 888-331-6288
E-mail: editors@labanimal.com
URL: http://www.labanimal.com/laban/index.html

Monthly. $225.00/year for individuals; $1,260.00/year for institutions; $125.00/year for individuals; $780.00/year for institutions. Life science magazine.

★1224★ Nature Biotechnology

Nature Publishing Group
75 Varick St., 9th Fl.
New York, NY 10013-1917
Ph: (212)726-9200   Fax: (212)696-9006
Fr: 888-331-6288
E-mail: biotech@natureny.com
URL: http://www.nature.com/nbt/index.html

Monthly. Scientific research journal.

★1225★ **Nature International Weekly Journal of Science**

Nature Publishing Group
75 Varick St., 9th Fl.
New York, NY 10013-1917
Ph: (212)726-9200   Fax: (212)696-9006
Fr: 888-331-6288
E-mail: nature@natureny.com
URL: http://www.nature.com

Weekly. $145.00/year for individuals; $49.00/year for institutions. Magazine covering science and technology, including the fields of biology, biochemistry, genetics, medicine, earth sciences, physics, pharmacology, and behavioral sciences.

★1226★ **OnLine Journal of Biological Sciences**

Science Publications
Vails Gate Heights Dr.
PO Box 879
Vails Gate, NY 12584
URL: http://www.scipub.us/

Quarterly. $1,800.00/year for individuals; $400.00 for single issue. Scholarly journal covering all aspects of biological science.

★1227★ **Ornithological Newsletter**

Ornithological Societies of North America
5400 Bosque Blvd., Ste. 680
Waco, TX 76710
Ph: (254)399-9636   Fax: (254)776-3767
E-mail: business@osnabirds.org
URL: http://birds.cornell.edu/OSNA/orn-newsl.htm

Description: Bimonthly. Provides information of interest to ornithologists. Recurring features include listings of available grants and awards, news of members, a calendar of events, activities of sponsoring societies, and notices of publications available. Notices of employment opportunities are also available on the Web version.

★1228★ **PALAIOS**

SEPM Publications
6128 E 38th St., Ste. 308
Tulsa, OK 74135-5814
Ph: (918)610-3361   Fax: (918)621-1685
Fr: 800-865-9765
URL: http://www.sepm.org/

Bimonthly. $200.00/year for individuals, for U.S. online version with CD-ROM; $235.00/year for individuals, for U.S. print and online version with CD-ROM; $200.00/year for other countries, online version with CD-ROM; $245.00/year for other countries, print and online version with CD-ROM. Journal providing information on the impact of life on Earth history as recorded in the paleontological and sedimentological records. Covers areas such as biogeochemistry, ichnology, sedimentology, stratigraphy, paleoecology, paleoclimatology, and paleoceanography.

★1229★ **Perspectives in Biology and Medicine**

The Johns Hopkins University Press
2715 N Charles St.
Baltimore, MD 21218-4363
Ph: (410)516-6989   Fax: (410)516-6968
URL: http://www.press.jhu.edu/journals/perspectives_in_biology_an

Quarterly. $45.00/year for individuals, electronic; $126.00/year for institutions, print; $45.00/year for individuals, print; $40.00/year for students, print; $252.00 for institutions, print, 2 years; $90.00 for individuals, print, 2 years; $80.00 for students, print, 2 years; $135.00 for individuals, print, 3 years; $378.00 for institutions, print, 3 years. Journal publishing articles of current interest in medicine and biology in a context with humanistic, social, and scientific concerns. Covers a wide range of biomedical topics such as neurobiology, biomedical ethics and history, genetics and evolution, and ecology.

★1230★ **Plant Science Bulletin**

Botanical Society of America
PO Box 299
St. Louis, MO 63166
Ph: (314)577-9566   Fax: (314)577-9515
E-mail: bsa-manager@botany.org
URL: http://www.botany.org

Description: Quarterly. Carries news of this Association of plant scientists, with some issues including brief articles of more general interest in the field. Recurring features include notices of awards, meetings, courses, and study and professional opportunities; annotated lists of botanical books; and book reviews.

★1231★ **PLoS Biology**

Public Library of Science
185 Berry St., Ste. 3100
San Francisco, CA 94107
Ph: (415)624-1200   Fax: (415)546-4090
URL: http://biology.plosjournals.org/perlserv/?request=index-html

Monthly. Free, online. Open access, peer-reviewed general biology journal.

★1232★ **Popular Science**

Time4 Media Inc.
2 Park Ave., 9th Fl.
New York, NY 10016-5614
Ph: (212)779-5000   Fax: (212)779-5588
URL: http://www.popsci.com/popsci

Monthly. $4.00/year; $20.00/year for individuals, 2 years, 24 issues; $30.00/year for individuals, 3 years, 36 issues; $28.00/year for Canada, 24 issues; $68.00/year for Canada, 36 issues. General interest science magazine.

★1233★ **Science**

American Association for the Advancement of Science
1200 New York Ave. NW
Washington, DC 20005
Ph: (202)326-6400   Fax: (202)371-9227

URL: http://www.scienceonline.org

Weekly (Fri.). $142.00/year for members, professional; $119.00/year for individuals, NPA postdoctoral; $99.00/year for individuals, postdoctoral/resident; $75.00/year for students; $142.00/year for individuals, k-12 teacher; $310.00/year for individuals, patron; $110.00/year for individuals, emeritus. Magazine devoted to science, scientific research, and public policy.

★1234★ **The Scientist**

The Scientist Inc.
400 Market St., No. 1250
Philadelphia, PA 19106
Ph: (215)351-1660   Fax: (215)351-1146
URL: http://www.the-scientist.com

Bimonthly. $49.95/year for individuals, online; $74.95/year for individuals, online plus print edition; $124.95/year for out of country, online plus print edition (air freight); $29.95/year for individuals, 6 months; $19.95 for individuals, 6 months; $14.95 for individuals, 1 month; $9.95 for individuals, 1 week; $4.95 for individuals, 1 week. News journal (tabloid) for life scientists featuring news, opinions, research, and professional section.

★1235★ **Seed Technologist News**

Association of Official Seed Analysts Inc.
601 S. Washington, Ste. 285
Stillwater, OK 74074-4539
Ph: (405)780-7372   Fax: (405)780-7372
E-mail: aosaoffice@sbcglobal.net
URL: http://www.aosaseed.com

Description: Three issues/year. Relates activities of the Society, with reports from various chapters across the U.S. and Canada. Publishes technical information about testing seeds and ensuring seed quality. Recurring features include news of research, a calendar of events, reports of meetings, news of educational opportunities, job listings, book reviews, and notices of publications available.

★1236★ **The World Wide Web Journal of Biology**

Epress, Inc.
130 Union Terrace Ln.
Plymouth, MN 55441
URL: http://www.epress.com/w3jbio/
Journal on Bio-informatics.

PLACEMENT AND JOB REFERRAL SERVICES

★1237★ **American Society for Biochemistry and Molecular Biology (ASBMB)**

9650 Rockville Pike
Bethesda, MD 20814-3996
Ph: (301)634-7145   Fax: (301)634-7126
E-mail: asmb@asbmb.org

URL: http://www.asbmb.org

Members: Biochemists and molecular biologists who have conducted and published original investigations in biological chemistry and/or molecular biology. **Activities:** Operates placement service.

★1238★ American Society for Cell Biology (ASCB)
8120 Woodmont Ave., Ste. 750
Bethesda, MD 20814-2762
Ph: (301)347-9300   Fax: (301)347-9310
E-mail: ascbinfo@ascb.org
URL: http://www.ascb.org

Description: Represents scientists with educational or research experience in cell biology or an allied field. Offers placement service.

★1239★ American Society for Histocompatibility and Immunogenetics (ASHI)
15000 Commerce Pkwy., Ste. C
Mount Laurel, NJ 08054
Ph: (856)638-0428   Fax: (856)439-0525
E-mail: info@ashi-hla.org
URL: http://www.ashi-hla.org

Members: Scientists, physicians, and technologists involved in research and clinical activities related to histocompatibility testing (a state of mutual tolerance that allows some tissues to be grafted effectively to others). **Activities:** Conducts proficiency testing and educational programs. Maintains liaison with regulatory agencies; offers placement services and laboratory accreditation. Has cosponsored development of histocompatibility specialist and laboratory certification program.

★1240★ American Society for Microbiology (ASM)
1752 N St. NW
Washington, DC 20036
Ph: (202)737-3600   Fax: (202)942-9333
E-mail: oed@asmusa.org
URL: http://www.asm.org

Description: Scientific society of microbiologists. Promotes the advancement of scientific knowledge in order to improve education in microbiology. Encourages the highest professional and ethical standards, and the adoption of sound legislative and regulatory policies affecting the discipline of microbiology at all levels. Communicates microbiological scientific achievements to the public. Maintains numerous committees and 23 divisions, and placement services; compiles statistics.

★1241★ American Society of Plant Biologists (ASPB)
15501 Monona Dr.
Rockville, MD 20855-2768
Ph: (301)251-0560   Fax: (301)279-2996
E-mail: info@aspb.org
URL: http://www.aspb.org

Members: Professional society of plant biol-

ogists, plant biochemists, and other plant scientists engaged in research and teaching. **Activities:** Offers placement service for members; conducts educational and public affairs programs.

★1242★ American Water Works Association (AWWA)
6666 W Quincy Ave.
Denver, CO 80235-3098
Ph: (303)794-7711   Fax: (303)347-0804
Fr: 800-926-7337
E-mail: rrenner@awwa.org
URL: http://www.awwa.org

Members: Water utility managers, superintendents, engineers, chemists, bacteriologists, and other individuals interested in public water supply; municipal- and investor-owned water departments; boards of health; manufacturers of waterworks equipment; government officials and consultants interested in water supply. **Purpose:** Develops standards and supports research programs in waterworks design, construction, operation, and management. **Activities:** Conducts in-service training schools and prepares manuals for waterworks personnel. Maintains hall of fame. Offers placement service via member newsletter; compiles statistics. Offers training; children's services; and information center on the water utilities industry, potable water, and water reuse.

★1243★ Association of Applied IPM Ecologists (AAIE)
PO Box 12181
Fresno, CA 93776
Ph: (559)907-4897
E-mail: director@aaie.net

Description: Professional agricultural pest management consultants, entomologists, and field personnel. Promotes the implementation of integrated pest management in agricultural and urban environments. Provides a forum for the exchange of technical information on pest control. Offers placement service.

★1244★ Biophysical Society (BPS)
9650 Rockville Pike
Bethesda, MD 20814
Ph: (301)634-7114   Fax: (301)634-7133
E-mail: society@biophysics.org
URL: http://www.biophysics.org

Description: Biophysicists, physical biochemists, and physical and biological scientists interested in the application of physical laws and techniques to the analysis of biological or living phenomena. Maintains placement service.

★1245★ Engineering Society of Detroit (ESD)
2000 Town Ctr., Ste. 2610
Southfield, MI 48075
Ph: (248)353-0735   Fax: (248)353-0736
E-mail: esd@esd.org
URL: http://esd.org

Description: Engineers from all disciplines;

scientists and technologists. Conducts technical programs and engineering refresher courses; sponsors conferences and expositions. Maintains speakers' bureau; offers placement services; although based in Detroit, MI, society membership is international.

★1246★ Environmental Mutagen Society (EMS)
1821 Michael Faraday Dr., Ste. 300
Reston, VA 20190
Ph: (703)438-8220   Fax: (703)438-3113
E-mail: emshq@ems-us.org
URL: http://www.ems-us.org

Members: Bioscientists in universities, governmental agencies, and industry. **Purpose:** Promotes basic and applied studies of mutagenesis (the area of genetics dealing with mutation and molecular biology); disseminates information relating to environmental mutagenesis. **Activities:** Offers placement service.

★1247★ Federation of American Societies for Experimental Biology (FASEB)
9650 Rockville Pike
Bethesda, MD 20814
Ph: (301)634-7000   Fax: (301)634-7001
E-mail: membershipdirectoryinfo@faseb.org
URL: http://www.faseb.org

Description: Federation of scientific societies with a total of 40,000 members: the American Physiological Society; American Society for Biochemistry and Molecular Biology; American Society for Pharmacology and Experimental Therapeutics; American Society for Investigative Pathology; American Society for Nutritional Sciences; the American Association of Immunologists; the American Society for Bone and Mineral Research; American Society for Clinical Investigation; the Indocrine Society; the American Society of Human Genetics; Society for Developmental Biology; Biophysical Society; American Association of Anatomists; and the Protein Society. **Activities:** Maintains placement service.

★1248★ Korean-American Scientists and Engineers Association (KSEA)
1952 Gallows Rd., Ste. 300
Vienna, VA 22182
Ph: (703)748-1221   Fax: (703)748-1331
E-mail: admin@ksea.org
URL: http://www.ksea.org

Description: Represents scientists and engineers holding single or advanced degrees. Promotes friendship and mutuality among Korean and American scientists and engineers; contributes to Korea's scientific, technological, industrial, and economic developments; strengthens the scientific, technological, and cultural bonds between Korea and the U.S. Sponsors symposium. Maintains speakers' bureau, placement service, and biographical archives. Compiles statistics.

★1249★ **Society for Cryobiology (SC)**

1 Millennium Way
Branchburg, NJ 08876
Ph: (908)947-1176   Fax: (908)947-1085
E-mail: wsun@lifecell.com
URL: http://www.societyforcryobiology.org

Description: Basic and applied research in the field of low temperature biology and medicine. Promotes interdisciplinary approach to freezing, freeze-drying, hypothermia, hibernation, physiological effects of low environmental temperature on animals and plants, medical applications of reduced temperatures, cryosurgery, hypothermic perfusion and cryopreservation of organs, cryoprotective agents and their pharmacological action, and pertinent methodologies. Operates charitable program and placement service.

★1250★ **Society for In Vitro Biology (SIVB)**

514 Daniels St., Ste. 411
Raleigh, NC 27605
Ph: (919)420-7940   Fax: (919)420-7939
Fr: 888-588-1923
E-mail: sivb@sivb.org
URL: http://www.sivb.org

Description: Professional society of individuals using mammalian, invertebrate, plant cell tissue, and organ cultures as research tools in chemistry, physics, radiation, medicine, physiology, nutrition, and cytogenetics. Aims are to foster collection and dissemination of information concerning the maintenance and experimental use of tissue cells in vitro and to establish evaluation and development procedures. Operates placement service.

★1251★ **Society for Industrial Microbiology (SIM)**

3929 Old Lee Hwy., Ste. 92A
Fairfax, VA 22030-2421
Ph: (703)691-3357   Fax: (703)691-7991
E-mail: simhq@simhq.org
URL: http://www.simhq.org

Description: Mycologists, bacteriologists, biologists, chemists, engineers, zoologists, and others interested in biological processes as applied to industrial materials and processes concerning microorganisms. Serves as liaison between the specialized fields of microbiology. Maintains placement service; conducts surveys and scientific workshops in industrial microbiology.

EMPLOYER DIRECTORIES AND NETWORKING LISTS

★1252★ *American Men and Women of Science*

Gale, Cengage Learning
27500 Drake Rd.
Farmington Hills, MI 48331-3535
Ph: (248)699-4253   Fax: (248)699-8065
Fr: 800-877-4253

URL: http://www.gale.com

Biennial, latest edition 23rd, October 2006; new edition expected 24th, January 2008. $1,075.00 for individuals. Covers over 129,700 U.S. and Canadian scientists active in the physical, biological, mathematical, computer science, and engineering fields; includes references to previous edition for deceased scientists and nonrespondents. Entries include: Name, address, education, personal and career data, memberships, honors and awards, research interest. Arrangement: Alphabetical. Indexes: Discipline (in separate volume).

★1253★ *Biotechnology Directory*

Nature Publishing Group
75 Varick St., 9th Fl.
New York, NY 10013-1917
Ph: (212)726-9200   Fax: (212)696-9006
Fr: 888-331-6288
URL: http://www.npg.nature.com/

Annual; latest edition February 2005. $315.00 for individuals; $195.00 for elsewhere. Covers more than 11,000 companies, universities, research centers, and government agencies, and suppliers of products and services to the field. Entries include: Organization name, address, phone, telex, fax, contact; description of products, services, or research. Arrangement: Geographical. Indexes: Product, organization.

★1254★ *Career Ideas for Teens in Health Science*

Facts On File Inc.
132 W 31st St., 17th Fl.
New York, NY 10001
Ph: (212)967-8800   Fax: 800-678-3633
Fr: 800-322-8755
URL: http://www.factsonfile.com

Published 2005. $40.00 for individuals; $36.00 for libraries. Covers a multitude of career possibilities based on a teenager's specific interests and skills and links his/her talents to a wide variety of actual professions.

★1255★ *Career Opportunities in Science*

Facts On File Inc.
132 W 31st St., 17th Fl.
New York, NY 10001
Ph: (212)967-8800   Fax: 800-678-3633
Fr: 800-322-8755
URL: http://www.factsonfile.com

Published 2003. $49.50 for individuals; $44.55 for libraries. Covers more than 80 jobs, such as biochemist, molecular biologist, bioinformatic specialist, pharmacologist, computer engineer, geographic information systems specialist, science teacher, forensic scientist, patent agent, as well as physicist, astronomer, chemist, zoologist, oceanographer, and geologist.

★1256★ *Careers in Focus: Earth Science*

Facts On File Inc.
132 W 31st St., 17th Fl.
New York, NY 10001
Ph: (212)967-8800   Fax: 800-678-3633
Fr: 800-322-8755
URL: http://www.factsonfile.com

Published 2002. $29.95 for individuals; $26.95 for libraries. Covers an overview of earth science, followed by a selection of jobs profiled in detail, including the nature of the job, earnings, prospects for employment, what kind of training and skills it requires, and sources for further information.

★1257★ *Discovering Careers for Your Future: Nature*

Facts On File Inc.
132 W 31st St., 17th Fl.
New York, NY 10001
Ph: (212)967-8800   Fax: 800-678-3633
Fr: 800-322-8755
URL: http://www.factsonfile.com

Published 2002. $21.95 for individuals; $19.75 for libraries. Covers botanists, ecologists, fish and game wardens, naturalists, oceanographers, park rangers, wildlife photographers, and zoologists; links career education to curriculum, helping children investigate the subjects they are interested in, and the careers those subjects might lead to.

★1258★ *Federation of American Societies for Experimental Biology-Directory of Members*

Federation of American Societies for Experimental Biology
9650 Rockville Pke.
Bethesda, MD 20814-3998
Ph: (301)634-7100   Fax: (301)634-7809
Fr: 800-433-2732
URL: http://www.faseb.org/directory/

Annual, fall. Covers about 63,000 members of The American Physiological Society, American Society for Biochemistry and Molecular Biology, American Society for Pharmacology and Experimental Therapeutics, American Society for Investigative Pathology, American Society for Nutritional Sciences, The American Association of Immunologists, Biophysical Society, American Association of Anatomists, The Protein Society, The American Society for Bone and Mineral Research, American Society for Clinical Investigation, The Endocrine Society, The American Society of Human Genetics, Society for Developmental Biology, American Peptide Society, Society for the Study of Reproduction and Radiation Research Society. Entries include: Name, address, title, affiliation, memberships in federation societies, highest degree, year elected to membership, phone, fax and electronic mail address. Membership directories of the Biophysical Society, The Protein Society, The American Society for Bone and Mineral Research, and American Society for Clinical Investigation are also available separately. Arrangement: Alphabetical. Indexes: Geographical.

★1259★ Peterson's Job Opportunities in Engineering and Technology

Peterson's Guides
2000 Lenox Dr.
Box 67005
Lawrenceville, NJ 08648
Ph: (609)896-1800   Fax: (609)896-4531
Fr: 800-338-3282
E-mail: custsvc@petersons.com
URL: http://www.petersons.com

Compiled by the Peterson's staff. Fourth edition, 1996. $21.95 (paper). 379 pages. Profiles 2,000 high-tech companies looking primarily for technical personnel in such fields as biotechnology, telecommunications, software, computers and peripherals, defense, and aerospace. Contains job-search strategies and career options to help match education and expertise to the job market. Indexed geographically, by industry, and by hiring needs.

HANDBOOKS AND MANUALS

★1260★ The Best Resumes for Scientists and Engineers

John Wiley & Sons Inc.
1 Wiley Dr.
Somerset, NJ 08873
Ph: (732)469-4400   Fax: (732)302-2300
Fr: 800-225-5945
E-mail: custserv@wiley.com
URL: http://www.wiley.com/WileyCDA/

Adele Lewis and David J. Moore. Second edition, 1993. $37.50; $19.95 (paper). 224 pages. Presents an extensive collection of scientific and engineering resumes, highlighting the important differences between these and resumes written for other occupations.

★1261★ Careers in Horticulture and Botany

The McGraw-Hill Companies
PO Box 182604
Columbus, OH 43272
Fax: (614)759-3749   Fr: 877-883-5524
E-mail: customer.service@mcgraw-hill.com
URL: http://www.mcgraw-hill.com

Jerry Garner. 2006. 15.95 (paper). 192 pages. Includes bibliographical references.

★1262★ Conducting Meaningful Experiments: 40 Steps to Becoming a Scientist

Sage Publications, Inc.
2455 Teller Rd.
Thousand Oaks, CA 91320-2218
Ph: (805)499-0721   Fax: (805)499-0871
E-mail: info@sagepub.com
URL: http://www.sagepub.com/

R. Barker Bausell. 1994. $48.95 (paper). 149 pages.

★1263★ Great Jobs for Biology Majors

The McGraw-Hill Companies
PO Box 182604
Columbus, OH 43272
Fax: (614)759-3749   Fr: 877-883-5524
E-mail: customer.service@mcgraw-hill.com
URL: http://www.mcgraw-hill.com

Blythe Camenson. Second edition, 2003. $15.95 (paper). 240 pages. Written for students entering the workforce. Describes jobs and career paths, as well as the process of writing resumes, networking, interviewing, and evaluating job offers.

★1264★ Guide to Nontraditional Careers in Science

Taylor & Francis
325 Chestnut St., 8th Fl.
Philadelphia, PA 19106
Ph: (215)625-8900   Fax: (215)269-0363
Fr: 800-821-8312
URL: http://www.taylorandfrancis.com

Karen Young Kreeger. 1998. $45.95 (paper). Guidebook aids the reader in evaluating and finding career opportunities in non-academic research fields. 263 pages.

★1265★ Opportunities in Biological Science Careers

The McGraw-Hill Companies
PO Box 182604
Columbus, OH 43272
Fax: (614)759-3749   Fr: 877-883-5524
E-mail: customer.service@mcgraw-hill.com
URL: http://www.mcgraw-hill.com

Charles A. Winter. 2004. $13.95; $11.95 (paper). 160 pages. Identifies employers and outlines opportunities in plant and animal biology, biological specialties, biomedical sciences, applied biology, and other areas. Illustrated.

★1266★ Opportunities in Environmental Careers

The McGraw-Hill Companies
PO Box 182604
Columbus, OH 43272
Fax: (614)759-3749   Fr: 877-883-5524
E-mail: customer.service@mcgraw-hill.com
URL: http://www.mcgraw-hill.com

Odom Fanning. Revised, 2002. $12.95 (paper). 174 pages. Describes a broad range of opportunities in fields such as environmental health, recreation, physics, and hygiene, and provides job search advice. Part of the "Opportunities in ..." Series.

★1267★ Opportunities in High Tech Careers

The McGraw-Hill Companies
PO Box 182604
Columbus, OH 43272
Fax: (614)759-3749   Fr: 877-883-5524
E-mail: customer.service@mcgraw-hill.com
URL: http://www.mcgraw-hill.com

Gary Colter and Deborah Yanuck. 1999. $14.95; $11.95 (paper). 160 pages. Explores high technology careers. Describes job opportunities, how to make a career decision, how to prepare for high technology jobs, job hunting techniques, and future trends.

★1268★ Opportunities in Research and Development Careers

The McGraw-Hill Companies
PO Box 182604
Columbus, OH 43272
Fax: (614)759-3749   Fr: 877-883-5524
E-mail: customer.service@mcgraw-hill.com
URL: http://www.mcgraw-hill.com

Jan Goldberg. 1996. $11.95 (paper). 146 pages.

★1269★ Plant Functional Genomics

Haworth Press, Inc.
10 Alice St.
Binghamton, NY 13904-1580
Ph: (607)722-5857   Fax: 800-895-0582
Fr: 800-429-6784
E-mail: getinfo@haworthpress.com
URL: http://www.haworthpressinc.com/

Dario Leister. 2005. $89.95. Profiles research in plant functional genomics of interest to scientists, researchers and advanced students in botany.

★1270★ Resumes for Environmental Careers

The McGraw-Hill Companies
PO Box 182604
Columbus, OH 43272
Fax: (614)759-3749   Fr: 877-883-5524
E-mail: customer.service@mcgraw-hill.com
URL: http://www.mcgraw-hill.com

Second edition, 2002. $10.95 (paper). 160 pages. Provides resume advice tailored to people pursuing careers focusing on the environment. Includes sample resumes and cover letters.

★1271★ Resumes for Scientific and Technical Careers

The McGraw-Hill Companies
PO Box 182604
Columbus, OH 43272
Fax: (614)759-3749   Fr: 877-883-5524
E-mail: customer.service@mcgraw-hill.com
URL: http://www.mcgraw-hill.com

Third edition, 2007. $12.95 (paper). 144 pages. Provides resume advice for individuals interested in working in scientific and technical careers. Includes sample resumes and cover letters.

★1272★ To Boldly Go: A Practical Career Guide for Scientists

Amer Global Pub
2000 Florida Ave., NW
Washington, DC 20009
Ph: (202)462-6900   Fax: (202)328-0566
Fr: 800-966-2481

Peter S. Fiske. 1996. $19.00 (paper). 188 pages.

EMPLOYMENT AGENCIES AND SEARCH FIRMS

★1273★ Ambler Associates
14881 Quorum Dr., Ste. 450
Dallas, TX 75254
Ph: (972)404-8712   Fax: (972)404-8761
Fr: 800-728-8712
Executive search firm.

★1274★ Amtec Engineering Corp.
2749 Saturn St.
Brea, CA 92821
Ph: (714)993-1900   Fax: (714)993-2419
E-mail: info@amtechc.com
URL: http://www.amtec-eng.com
Employment agency.

★1275★ Biomedical Search Consultants
275 Wyman St.
Waltham, MA 02451
Ph: (978)952-6425   Fax: (781)890-1082
E-mail: kprovost@biomedicalsearchconsultants.com
URL: http://www.biomedicalsearchconsultants.com
Employment agency.

★1276★ Caliber Associates
6336 Greenwich Dr., Ste. C
San Diego, CA 92122
Ph: (858)551-7880   Fax: (858)551-7887
E-mail: info@caliberassociates.com
URL: http://www.caliberassociates.com
Executive search firm.

★1277★ CEO Resources Inc.
PO Box 2883
Framingham, MA 01703-2883
Ph: (508)877-2775   Fax: (508)877-8433
E-mail: info@ceoresourcesinc.com
URL: http://ceoresourcesinc.com
Executive search firm.

★1278★ Clark Executive Search Inc.
135 N. Ferry Rd.
PO Box 560
Shelter Island, NY 11964
Ph: (631)749-3540   Fax: (631)749-3539
E-mail: mail@clarksearch.com
URL: http://www.clarksearch.com
Executive search firm.

★1279★ CTR Group
11843-C Canon Blvd.
Newport News, CA 23606
Ph: (757)462-5900   Fax: (757)873-6724
Fr: 800-462-5309
URL: http://www.ctrc.com/jobs/
Executive search firm.

★1280★ The Custer Group
6005 Tattersall Ct.
Brentwood, TN 37027
Ph: (615)309-0577
E-mail: general@custergroup.com
URL: http://www.custergroup.com
Executive search firm.

★1281★ Daly & Company Inc.
175 Federal St.
Boston, MA 02110-2210
Ph: (617)262-2800   Fax: (617)728-4477
E-mail: info@dalyco.com
URL: http://www.dalyco.com
Executive search firm.

★1282★ Diversified Search
2005 Market St., Ste. 3300
1 Commerce Square
Philadelphia, PA 19103
Ph: (215)732-6666   Fax: (215)568-8399
E-mail: info@diversifiedsearch.com
URL: http://www.diversifiedsearch.com
Executive search firm. Branches in Burlington, MA and New York.

★1283★ The Domann Organization Inc.
1 Market St., Fl. 35
San Francisco, CA 94105
Ph: (415)726-9704   Fr: 800-923-6626
E-mail: info@domann.net
URL: http://www.domann.net
Executive search firm.

★1284★ Dynamic Synergy Corp.
600 Entrada Dr., Fl. 2
Santa Monica, CA 90402
Ph: (650)493-2000
E-mail: info@dynamicsynergy.com
URL: http://www.dynamicsynergy.com
Executive search firm.

★1285★ Empire International
1147 Lancaster Ave.
Berwyn, PA 19312
Ph: (610)647-7976   Fax: (610)647-8488
E-mail: emhunter@empire-internl.com
URL: http://www.empire-internl.com
Executive search firm.

★1286★ Erspamer Associates
4010 W. 65th St., Ste. 100
Edina, MN 55435
Ph: (952)925-3747   Fax: (952)925-4022
E-mail: hdhuntrel@aol.com
Executive search firm specializing in technical management.

★1287★ Eton Partners
1 Baltimore Pl., Ste. 130
Atlanta, GA 30308
Ph: (404)685-9088   Fax: (404)685-9208
E-mail: ebirchfield@etonpartners.com
URL: http://etonpartners.com
Executive search firm.

★1288★ Intech Summit Group, Inc.
3450 Bonita Rd., Ste. 203
Chula Vista, CA 91910
Ph: (619)862-2720   Fax: (619)862-2699
Fr: 800-750-8100
E-mail: isg@isgsearch.com
URL: http://www.isgsearch.com
Employment agency and executive recruiter with a branch in Carlsbad, CA.

★1289★ JPM International
26034 Acero
Mission Viejo, CA 92691
Ph: (949)699-4300   Fax: (949)699-4333
Fr: 800-685-7856
E-mail: trish@jpmintl.com
URL: http://www.jpmintl.com
Executive search firm and employment agency.

★1290★ The Katonah Group Inc.
33 Flying Point Rd.
Southampton, NY 11968
Ph: (631)287-9001   Fax: (631)287-9773
E-mail: info@katonahgroup.com
URL: http://www.katonahgroup.com
Company specializes in executive recruiting for companies in the fields of life sciences (genomic and proteomic instrumentation), bio-informatics, chem-informatics, medical devices, clinical diagnostics, and scientific and analytical instrumentation.

★1291★ K.S. Frary & Associates
16 Schooner Ridge, Ste. 301
Marblehead, MA 01945
Ph: (781)631-2464   Fax: (781)631-2465
E-mail: ksfrary@comcast.net
URL: http://www.ksfrary.com
Executive search firm.

★1292★ Lybrook Associates, Inc.
266 N. Farm Dr.
Bristol, RI 02809
Ph: (401)254-5840
Executive search firm specializing in the field of chemistry.

★1293★ Professional Placement Associates, Inc.
287 Bowman Ave., Ste. 309
Purchase, NY 10577-2517
Ph: (914)251-1000   Fax: (914)251-1055
E-mail: careers@ppasearch.com
URL: http://www.ppasearch.com
Executive search firm specializing in the health and medical field.

★1294★ Team Placement Service, Inc.
1414 Prince St., Ste. 202
Alexandria, VA 22314
Ph: (703)820-8618   Fax: (703)820-3368
Fr: 800-495-6767
E-mail: 4jobs@teamplace.com
URL: http://www.teamplace.com

Full-service personnel consultants provide placement for healthcare staff, physician and dentist, private practice, and hospitals. Conduct interviews, tests, and reference checks to select the top 20% of applicants. Survey applicants' skill levels, provide backup information on each candidate, select compatible candidates for consideration, and insure the hiring process minimizes potential legal liability. Industries served: healthcare and government agencies providing medical, dental, biotech, laboratory, hospitals, and physician search.

ONLINE JOB SOURCES AND SERVICES

★1295★ American Institute of Biological Sciences Classifieds
1444 I St., Ste. 200
Washington, DC 20005
Ph: (202)628-1500   Fax: (202)628-1509
URL: http://www.aibs.org/classifieds/

Description: Section of the American Institute of Biological Sciences website used for posting available positions, research awards and fellowships, and other classified ads.

★1296★ American Society of Plant Biologists Job Bank
15501 Monona Dr.
Rockville, MD 20855-2768
Ph: (301)251-0560   Fax: (301)279-2996
E-mail: info@aspb.org
URL: http://www.aspb.org/jobbank/

Description: A service of the American Society of Plant Biologists, intended to aid its members in locating jobs and job resources. Site lists new jobs weekly in its job bank. **Fee:** A fee of $150 is charged for all academic/government/industry permanent positions and for all positions, regardless of rank, posted by private companies. Postdoctoral Positions; Research/Technical Positions (non-Ph.D.); and Assistantships, Fellowships, and Internships at universities and not-for-profit agencies are published for a fee of $25.

★1297★ Bio.com Career Center
E-mail: careers@bio.com
URL: http://www.bio.com/jobs/index.jhtml

Description: Contains a job index searchable by employer name, discipline, or location. Suitable for job hunters tracking down specific medical, biological, biochemical, or pharmaceutical companies and positions. Also references at Career Guide and Career Forum sections.

★1298★ FASEB Career Resources
9650 Rockville Pike
Bethesda, MD 20814-3998
Ph: (301)634-7000   Fax: (301)634-7001
E-mail: careers@faseb.org.
URL: http://www.faseb.org/careers/

Description: A career opportunity site combined with a development service that attempts to pair applicants at all career levels with employers who hire biomedical scientists and technicians. Biomedical career development is highlighted through career resource tools. **Main files include:** Careers Online DataNet, Career Online Classified.

★1299★ GrantsNet
E-mail: grantsnet@aaas.org
URL: http://www.grantsnet.org/search/srch_specify.cfm

Description: Grant-locating site intended for scientists in training who may become vulnerable in an era of competitive funding. Includes a directory of over 600 programs with contact information within a searchable database.

★1300★ The SciWeb Biotechnology Career Home Page
E-mail: info@biocareer.com
URL: http://www.biocareer.com

Description: Career resource center resulting from the collaboration of the Biotechnology Industry Organization (BIO) and *SciWeb*. Aims to connect job seekers with recruiters in the biotechnology industry. **Main files include:** Post Resume, Search Resume, Post Job, Search Job, Career Resources. **Fee:** 150.00 for the first two months, $75.00 per additional monthly renewal. Academic PostDoctoral Listings are posted for free.

TRADESHOWS

★1301★ American Institute of Biological Sciences Annual Meeting
American Institute of Biological Sciences
1444 I St. NW, Ste. 200
Washington, DC 20005
Ph: (202)628-1500   Fax: (202)628-1509
Fr: 800-992-2427
URL: http://www.aibs.org

Annual. **Primary Exhibits:** Publishers, scientific equipment companies.

★1302★ American Society for Biochemistry and Molecular Biology Annual Meeting
American Society for Biochemistry and Molecular Biology
9650 Rockville Pike
Bethesda, MD 20814-3996
Ph: (301)634-7145   Fax: (301)634-7126
E-mail: asbmb@asbmb.org
URL: http://www.asbmb.org

Annual. **Primary Exhibits:** Biological chem-

istry and molecular biology equipment, supplies, and services.

★1303★ American Society for Cell Biology Annual Meeting
American Society for Cell Biology (ASCB)
8120 Woodmont Ave. Ste. 750
Bethesda, MD 20814-2762
Ph: (301)347-9300   Fax: (301)347-9310
E-mail: ascbinfo@ascb.org
URL: http://www.ascb.org

Annual. **Primary Exhibits:** Equipment, supplies, and services related to doing research in cell and molecular biology.

★1304★ American Society of Cytopathology Annual Scientific Meeting
American Society of Cytopathology
400 W 9th St., Ste. 201
Wilmington, DE 19801
Ph: (302)429-8802   Fax: (302)429-8807
E-mail: asc@cytopathology.org
URL: http://www.cytopathology.org

Annual. **Primary Exhibits:** Cytopathology microscopes, analysis equipment and supplies, and publishers. **Dates and Locations:** 2008 Nov 07-12; Orlando, FL; Wyndham Palace Resort & Spa.

★1305★ Biophysical Society Annual Meeting
Biophysical Society
9650 Rockville Pike
Bethesda, MD 20814
Ph: (301)634-7114   Fax: (301)634-7133
E-mail: society@biophysics.org
URL: http://www.biophysics.org

Annual. **Primary Exhibits:** Biomedical research equipment, supplies, and services, including instruments and publications. **Dates and Locations:** 2008 Feb 02-06; Long Beach, CA; 2009 Mar 07-11; Fort Lauderdale, FL.

★1306★ Society for Developmental Biology Annual Meeting
Society for Developmental Biology
9650 Rockville Pike
Bethesda, MD 20814-3998
Ph: (301)634-7815   Fax: (301)634-7825
E-mail: ichow@faseb.org
URL: http://www.sdbonline.org

Annual. **Primary Exhibits:** Exhibits related to problems of development and growth of organisms, scienrfic journals & scientific tools & post-doc. openings.

OTHER SOURCES

★1307★ **American Academy of Clinical Toxicology (AACT)**

777 E Park Dr.
PO Box 8820
Harrisburg, PA 17105-8820
Ph: (717)558-7847   Fax: (717)558-7841
Fr: 888-633-5784
E-mail: swilson@pamedsoc.org
URL: http://www.clintox.org

Members: Physicians, veterinarians, pharmacists, nurses research scientists, and analytical chemists. **Purpose:** Objectives are to: unite medical scientists and facilitate the exchange of information; encourage the development of therapeutic methods and technology; **Activities:** Conducts professional training in poison information and emergency service personnel.

★1308★ **American Academy of Forensic Sciences (AAFS)**

410 N 21st St.
Colorado Springs, CO 80904-2712
Ph: (719)636-1100   Fax: (719)636-1993
E-mail: awarren@aafs.org
URL: http://www.aafs.org

Description: Represents criminalists, scientists, members of the bench and bar, pathologists, biologists, psychiatrists, examiners of questioned documents, toxicologists, odontologists, anthropologists, and engineers. Works to: encourage the study, improve the practice, elevate the standards, and advance the cause of the forensic sciences; improve the quality of scientific techniques, tests, and criteria; plan, organize, and administer meetings, reports, and other projects for the stimulation and advancement of these and related purposes. Maintains Forensic Sciences Job Listing; conducts selected research for the government; offers forensic expert referral service.

★1309★ **American Association of Anatomists (AAA)**

9650 Rockville Pike
Bethesda, MD 20814-3998
Ph: (301)634-7910   Fax: (301)634-7965
E-mail: exec@anatomy.org
URL: http://www.anatomy.org

Description: Represents biomedical researchers and educators focusing on anatomical form and function. Focuses on imaging, cell biology, genetics, molecular development, endocrinology, histology, neuroscience, forensics, microscopy, physical anthropology, and other areas. Promotes the three-dimensional understanding of structure as it relates to development and function, from molecule to organism through research and education.

★1310★ **American Institute of Biological Sciences (AIBS)**

1444 I St. NW, Ste. 200
Washington, DC 20005
Ph: (202)628-1500   Fax: (202)628-1509
Fr: 800-992-2427
E-mail: rogrady@aibs.org
URL: http://www.aibs.org

Members: Professional member organization and federation of biological associations, laboratories, and museums whose members have an interest in the life sciences. **Purpose:** Promotes unity and effectiveness of effort among persons engaged in biological research, education, and application of biological sciences, including agriculture, environment, and medicine. Seeks to further the relationships of biological sciences to other sciences and industries. Conducts roundtable series; provides names of prominent biologists who are willing to serve as speakers and curriculum consultants; provides advisory committees and other services to the Department of Energy, Environmental Protection Agency, National Science Foundation, Department of Defense, and National Aeronautics and Space Administration. Maintains educational consultant panel.

★1311★ **Association for International Practical Training (AIPT)**

10400 Little Patuxent Pkwy., Ste. 250
Columbia, MD 21044-3519
Ph: (410)997-2200   Fax: (410)992-3924
E-mail: aipt@aipt.org
URL: http://www.aipt.org

Description: Providers worldwide of on-the-job training programs for students and professionals seeking international career development and life-changing experiences. Arranges workplace exchanges in hundreds of professional fields, bringing employers and trainees together from around the world. Client list ranges from small farming communities to Fortune 500 companies.

★1312★ **Biotechnology Occupations**

Delphi Productions
3159 6th St.
Boulder, CO 80304
Ph: (303)443-2100   Fax: (303)443-4022
Fr: 888-443-2400
E-mail: support@delphivideo.com
URL: http://www.delphivideo.com

$95.00. 49 minutes. Part of the Emerging Careers Video Library.

★1313★ **Forensic Sciences Foundation (FSF)**

410 N 21st St.
Colorado Springs, CO 80904
Ph: (719)636-1100   Fax: (719)636-1993
E-mail: awarren@aafs.org
URL: http://www.aafs.org

Purpose: Purposes are to: conduct research in the procedures and standards utilized in the practice of forensic sciences; develop and implement useful educational and training programs and methods of benefit to forensic sciences; conduct programs of public education concerning issues of importance to the forensic sciences; engage in activities which will promote, encourage, and assist the development of the forensic sciences. **Activities:** Provides referral service for forensic scientists. Compiles statistics. Operates the Forensic Sciences Foundation Press.

★1314★ **Minority Women In Science (MWIS)**

Directorate for Education and Human Resources Programs
1200 New York Ave. NW
Washington, DC 20005
Ph: (202)326-7019   Fax: (202)371-9849
E-mail: ygeorge@aaas.org

Description: A national network group of the American association for the Advancement of Science (AAAS), Education and Human Resources Directorate. The objectives of this group are: to identify and share information on resources and programs that could help in mentoring young women and minorities interested in science and engineering careers, and to strengthen communication among women and minorities in science and education.

★1315★ **Radiation Research Society (RRS)**

PO Box 7050
Lawrence, KS 66044
Fax: (785)843-1274   Fr: 800-627-0326
E-mail: info@radres.org
URL: http://www.radres.org

Description: Professional society of biologists, physicists, chemists, and physicians contributing to knowledge of radiation and its effects. Promotes original research in the natural sciences relating to radiation; facilitates integration of different disciplines in the study of radiation effects.

★1316★ **Scientific, Engineering, and Technical Services**

Cambridge Educational
PO Box 2053
Princeton, NJ 08543-2053
Ph: 800-257-5126   Fax: (609)671-0266
Fr: 800-468-4227
E-mail: custserv@films.com
URL: http://www.cambridgeeducational.com

VHS and DVD. $89.95. 2002. 18 minutes. 2002. Part of the Career Cluster Series.

★1317★ **Scientific Occupations**

Delphi Productions
3159 6th St.
Boulder, CO 80304
Ph: (303)443-2100   Fax: (303)443-4022
Fr: 888-443-2400
E-mail: support@delphivideo.com
URL: http://www.delphivideo.com

$95.00. 60 minutes. Part of the Careers for the 21st Century Video Library.

★1318★ Society for Biological Engineering (SBE)

3 Park Ave., 19th Fl.
New York, NY 10016
E-mail: bio@aiche.org
URL: http://www.aiche.org/SBE

Description: Promotes the integration of biology with engineering and its benefits through bioprocessing, biomedical, and biomolecular applications. Raises interest, understanding, and recognition of engineers' and scientists' roles in biological engineering. Provides opportunities for the successful interaction of engineers and scientists.

★1319★ Soil Science Society of America (SSSA)

677 S Segoe Rd.
Madison, WI 53711
Ph: (608)273-8080   Fax: (608)273-2021
E-mail: headquarters@agronomy.org
URL: http://www.soils.org

Description: Professional soil scientists, including soil physicists, soil classifiers, land use and management specialists, chemists, microbiologists, soil fertility specialists, soil cartographers, conservationists, mineralogists, engineers, and others interested in fundamental and applied soil science.

★1320★ Teratology Society (TS)

1821 Michael Faraday Dr., Ste. 300
Reston, VA 20190
Ph: (703)438-3104   Fax: (703)438-3113
E-mail: tshq@teratology.org
URL: http://www.teratology.org

Description: Individuals from academia, government, private industry, and the professions. Stimulates scientific interest in, and promotes the exchange of ideas and information about, problems of abnormal biological development and malformations at the fundamental or clinical level. Sponsors annual education course, and presentations. Establishes archives of society documents and history.

Biomedical Engineers

SOURCES OF HELP-WANTED ADS

★1321★ AIE Perspectives Newsmagazine

American Institute of Engineers
4630 Appian Way, Ste. 206
El Sobrante, CA 94803-1875
Ph: (510)758-6240   Fax: (510)758-6240

Monthly. Professional magazine covering engineering.

★1322★ American Biotechnology Laboratory

International Scientific Communications Inc.
30 Controls Dr.
PO Box 870
Shelton, CT 06484
Ph: (203)926-9300   Fax: (203)926-9310
URL: http://www.americanbiotechnologylaboratory.com

Bimonthly. $160.00/year for individuals. Biotechnology magazine.

★1323★ Annual Review of Genetics

Annual Reviews Inc.
4139 El Camino Way
PO Box 10139
Palo Alto, CA 94303-0139
Ph: (650)493-4400   Fax: (650)424-0910
Fr: 800-523-8635
URL: http://www.annualreviews.org/

Annual. $80.00/year for individuals, print & online; $80.00/year for out of country, print & online; $226.00/year for institutions, print & online; $226.00/year for institutions, other countries, print & online; $188.00/year for institutions, online; $188.00/year for institutions, other countries, online; $188.00/year for institutions, print; $188.00/year for institutions, other countries, print. Periodical covering issues in genetics and the biological sciences.

★1324★ Annual Review of Microbiology

Annual Reviews Inc.
4139 El Camino Way
PO Box 10139
Palo Alto, CA 94303-0139
Ph: (650)493-4400   Fax: (650)424-0910
Fr: 800-523-8635
URL: http://www.annualreviews.org/

Annual. $80.00/year for individuals, print & online; $80.00/year for out of country, print & online; $222.00/year for institutions, print & online; $222.00/year for institutions, other countries, print & online; $185.00/year for institutions, online; $185.00/year for institutions, other countries, online; $185.00/year for institutions, print; $185.00/year for institutions, other countries, print. Periodical covering microbiology and the biological sciences.

★1325★ AWIS Magazine

Association for Women in Science
1200 New York Ave. NW, Ste. 650
Washington, DC 20005
Ph: (202)326-8940   Fax: (202)326-8960
Fr: (866)657-2947
E-mail: awis@awis.org
URL: http://www.awis.org/

Description: Bimonthly. Covers issues, legislation, and trends related to science education for girls, women, and minorities. Includes information on grants and fellowships, job openings, educational programs, events, and notices of publications available.

★1326★ The Blue Sheet - Health Policy & Biomedical Research

F-D-C Reports Inc.
5550 Friendship Blvd., Ste. 1
Chevy Chase, MD 20815
Ph: (240)221-4500   Fax: (240)221-4400
Fr: 800-332-2181
E-mail: Customer.Service@elsevier.com
URL: http://www.thebluesheet.net

Description: Weekly. Reviews health policy and biomedical research. Discusses NIH-related topics, public health, health professions education, and issues affecting the National Science Foundation and other federal research efforts and regulations. Recurring

features include news of research and a calendar of events.

★1327★ BMES Bulletin

Biomedical Engineering Society
8401 Corporate Dr., Ste. 225
Landover, MD 20785-2224
Ph: (301)459-1999   Fax: (301)459-2444
URL: http://www.bmes.org/pdf/vol28_2.pdf

Description: Quarterly. Provides news and information on the Society; presents articles on bioengineering science. Recurring features include letters to the editor, news of research, a calendar of events, reports of meetings, news of educational opportunities, job listings, and columns titled Public Affairs, Student Chapter News, and Society News.

★1328★ Cell

Cell Press
600 Technology Sq.
Cambridge, MA 02139
Ph: (617)661-7057   Fax: (617)661-7061
Fr: (866)314-2355
E-mail: advertising@cell.com
URL: http://www.cell.com

$179.00/year for U.S. and Canada, individual, print and online; $269.00/year for other countries, individual, print and online; $179.00/year for U.S. and Canada, online only, individual; $179.00/year for other countries, online only, individual; $997.00/year for U.S. and Canada, institutions; $1122.00/year for institutions, other countries, print. Journal on molecular and cell biology.

★1329★ Cell Biology Education

American Society for Cell Biology
8120 Woodmont Ave., Ste. 750
Bethesda, MD 20814-2762
Ph: (301)347-9300   Fax: (301)347-9310
URL: http://www.cellbioed.org

Quarterly. Journal that offers information on biology education grades k-20.

★1330★ Chemistry & Biology

Elsevier Science Inc.
360 Park Ave. S
New York, NY 10010
Ph: (212)989-5800   Fax: (212)633-3990
URL: http://www.elsevier.com/

Monthly. $1,745/year for institutions, U.S. and Canada; $369.00/year for individuals, U.S. and Canada. Journal focused on genetic, computational, or theoretical information of chemistry and biology, substantiating experimental data.

★1331★ Current Advances in Genetics & Molecular Biology

Elsevier Science Inc.
360 Park Ave. S
New York, NY 10010
Ph: (212)989-5800   Fax: (212)633-3990
URL: http://www.elsevier.com

Monthly. $4,096.00/year for institutions, all countries except Europe, Japan and Iran; $177.00/year for individuals, all countries except Europe, Japan and Iran. Journal covering current details of genetics and molecular biology.

★1332★ Engineering Conferences International Symposium Series

Berkeley Electronic Press
2809 Telegraph Ave., Ste. 202
Berkeley, CA 94705
Ph: (510)665-1200   Fax: (510)665-1201
URL: http://services.bepress.com/eci/

Journal focusing on advance engineering science.

★1333★ Engineering in Life Sciences

John Wiley & Sons Inc.
111 River St.
Hoboken, NJ 07030-5774
Ph: (201)748-6000   Fax: (201)748-6088
Fr: 800-825-7550
URL: http://as.wiley.com/WileyCDA/Wiley-Title/productCd-2129.html

Bimonthly. $765.00/year for institutions, rest of Europe; $1,170.00/year for institutions, Switzerland and Liechtenstein; $1,005.00/year for institutions, rest of world; $842.00/year for institutions, print with online rest of Europe; $1,287.00/year for institutions, print with online Switzerland and Liechtenstein; $1,106.00/year for institutions, print with online rest of world. Journal focusing on the field of biotechnology and related topics including microbiology, genetics, biochemistry, and chemistry.

★1334★ Epigenetics

Landes Bioscience
1002 West Ave., 2nd Fl.
Austin, TX 78701
Ph: (512)637-6050   Fax: (512)637-6079
Fr: 800-736-9948
URL: http://www.landesbioscience.com/index.php

Journal devoted to practicing physicians, residents and students.

★1335★ Graduating Engineer & Computer Careers

Career Recruitment Media
211 W Wacker Dr., Ste. 900
Chicago, IL 60606
Ph: (312)525-3100
URL: http://www.graduatingengineer.com

Quarterly. $15.00/year for individuals. Magazine focusing on employment, education, and career development for entry-level engineers and computer scientists.

★1336★ High Technology Careers Magazine

HTC
4701 Patrick Henry Dr., No. 1901
Santa Clara, CA 95054-1847
Fax: (408)567-0242
URL: http://www.hightechcareers.com

Bimonthly. $29.00/year; $35.00/year for Canada; $85.00/year for out of country. Magazine (tabloid) containing employment opportunity information for the engineering and technical community.

★1337★ InterJournal

New England Complex Systems Institute
24 Mt. Auburn St.
Cambridge, MA 02138
Ph: (617)547-4100   Fax: (617)661-7711
URL: http://www.interjournal.org/

Journal covering the fields of science and engineering.

★1338★ International Archives of Bioscience

International Archives of Bioscience
PO Box 737254
Elmhurst, NY 11373-9997
URL: http://www.iabs.us/jdoc/aboutiabs.htm

Free, online only. Journal reporting multidisciplinary coverage and interaction between scientists in biology, informatics, mathematics, physics, engineering and other sciences.

★1339★ Invertebrate Biology

Allen Press Inc.
810 E 10th St.
Lawrence, KS 66044
Ph: (785)843-1234   Fax: (785)843-1244
Fr: 800-627-0326
URL: http://www.amicros.org/

Quarterly. $38.00/year for members; $19.00/year for students. Scientific journal covering the biology of invertebrate animals and research in the fields of cell and molecular biology, ecology, physiology, systematics, genetics, biogeography and behavior.

★1340★ Journal of Engineering Education

American Society for Engineering Education
1818 North St., NW, Ste. 600
Washington, DC 20036-2479
Ph: (202)331-3500

URL: http://www.asee.org/publications/jee/index.cfm

Quarterly. Journal covering scholarly research in engineering education.

★1341★ NABR Update

National Association for Biomedical Research
818 Connecticut Ave. NW, Ste. 900
Washington, DC 20006
Ph: (202)857-0540   Fax: (202)659-1902
E-mail: info@nabr.org
URL: http://www.nabr.org

Description: Periodic. Apprises Association members of government, legal, and media-based activity regarding biomedical research and the animal rights movement. Summarized news items are provided in the Association's sister publication, NABR Alert.

★1342★ NSBE Magazine

NSBE Publications
205 Daingerfield Rd.
Alexandria, VA 22314
Ph: (703)549-2207   Fax: (703)683-5312
URL: http://www.nsbe.org/publications/premieradvertisers.php

Journal providing information on engineering careers, self-development, and cultural issues for recent graduates with technical majors.

★1343★ PALAIOS

SEPM Publications
6128 E 38th St., Ste. 308
Tulsa, OK 74135-5814
Ph: (918)610-3361   Fax: (918)621-1685
Fr: 800-865-9765
URL: http://www.sepm.org/

Bimonthly. $200.00/year for individuals, for U.S. online version with CD-ROM; $235.00/year for individuals, for U.S. print and online version with CD-ROM; $200.00/year for other countries, online version with CD-ROM; $245.00/year for other countries, print and online version with CD-ROM. Journal providing information on the impact of life on Earth history as recorded in the paleontological and sedimentological records. Covers areas such as biogeochemistry, ichnology, sedimentology, stratigraphy, paleoecology, paleoclimatology, and paleoceanography.

★1344★ Perspectives in Biology and Medicine

The Johns Hopkins University Press
2715 N Charles St.
Baltimore, MD 21218-4363
Ph: (410)516-6989   Fax: (410)516-6968
URL: http://www.press.jhu.edu/journals/perspectives_in_biology_an

Quarterly. $45.00/year for individuals, electronic; $126.00/year for institutions, print; $45.00/year for individuals, print; $40.00/year for students, print; $252.00 for institutions, print, 2 years; $90.00 for individuals, print, 2 years; $80.00 for students, print, 2 years; $135.00 for individuals, print, 3 years;

$378.00 for institutions, print, 3 years. Journal publishing articles of current interest in medicine and biology in a context with humanistic, social, and scientific concerns. Covers a wide range of biomedical topics such as neurobiology, biomedical ethics and history, genetics and evolution, and ecology.

★1345★ *PLoS Biology*

Public Library of Science
185 Berry St., Ste. 3100
San Francisco, CA 94107
Ph: (415)624-1200   Fax: (415)546-4090
URL: http://biology.plosjournals.org/perl-serv/?request=index-html

Monthly. Free, online. Open access, peer-reviewed general biology journal.

★1346★ *PLoS Genetics*

Public Library of Science
185 Berry St., Ste. 3100
San Francisco, CA 94107
Ph: (415)624-1200   Fax: (415)546-4090
E-mail: plosgenetics@plos.org
URL: http://journals.plos.org/plosgenetics/guidelines.php

Free, online. Open access, peer-reviewed journal that publishes research and case studies in the field of genetics.

★1347★ *SWE, Magazine of the Society of Women Engineers*

Society of Women Engineers
230 East Ohio St., Ste. 400
Chicago, IL 60611-3265
Ph: (312)596-5223
E-mail: hq@swe.org
URL: http://www.swe.org

Quarterly. $30.00/year for nonmembers. Magazine for engineering students and for women and men working in the engineering and technology fields. Covers career guidance, continuing development and topical issues.

★1348★ *The Technology Interface*

New Mexico State University
College of Engineering
PO Box 30001
Las Cruces, NM 88003-8001
Ph: (505)646-0111
URL: http://engr.nmsu.edu/etti/

Journal for the engineering technology profession serving education and industry.

★1349★ *Uratie*

IDG Communications Inc.
5 Speen St., 3rd. Fl
Framingham, MA 01701
Ph: (508)875-5000   Fax: (508)988-7888
URL: http://www.idg.com

Magazine providing job offers for graduates, engineers and information technology professionals.

★1350★ *WEPANEWS*

Women in Engineering Programs & Advocates Network
1901 E. Asbury Ave., Ste. 220
Denver, CO 80208
Ph: (303)871-4643   Fax: (303)871-6833
E-mail: dmatt@wepan.org
URL: http://www.wepan.org

Description: 2/year. Seeks to provide greater access for women to careers in engineering. Includes news of graduate, undergraduate, freshmen, pre-college, and re-entry engineering programs for women. Recurring features include job listings, faculty, grant, and conference news, international engineering program news, action group news, notices of publications available, and a column titled Kudos.

★1351★ *The World Wide Web Journal of Biology*

Epress, Inc.
130 Union Terrace Ln.
Plymouth, MN 55441
URL: http://www.epress.com/w3jbio/

Journal on Bio-informatics.

PLACEMENT AND JOB REFERRAL SERVICES

★1352★ **American Indian Science and Engineering Society (AISES)**

PO Box 9828
Albuquerque, NM 87119-9828
Ph: (505)765-1052   Fax: (505)765-5608
E-mail: info@aises.org
URL: http://www.aises.org

Description: Represents American Indian and non-Indian students and professionals in science, technology, and engineering fields; corporations representing energy, mining, aerospace, electronic, and computer fields. Seeks to motivate and encourage students to pursue undergraduate and graduate studies in science, engineering, and technology. Sponsors science fairs in grade schools, teacher training workshops, summer math/science sessions for 8th-12th graders, professional chapters, and student chapters in colleges. Offers scholarships. Adult members serve as role models, advisers, and mentors for students. Operates placement service.

★1353★ **Engineering Society of Detroit (ESD)**

2000 Town Ctr., Ste. 2610
Southfield, MI 48075
Ph: (248)353-0735   Fax: (248)353-0736
E-mail: esd@esd.org
URL: http://esd.org

Description: Engineers from all disciplines; scientists and technologists. Conducts technical programs and engineering refresher courses; sponsors conferences and expositions. Maintains speakers' bureau; offers

placement services; although based in Detroit, MI, society membership is international.

★1354★ **Society For Biomaterials (SFB)**

15000 Commerce Pkwy., Ste. C
Mount Laurel, NJ 08054
Ph: (856)439-0826   Fax: (856)439-0525
E-mail: info@biomaterials.org
URL: http://www.biomaterials.org

Members: Bioengineers and materials scientists; dental, orthopedic, cardiac, and other surgeons and scientists interested in developing biomaterials as tissue replacements in patients; corporations interested in the research manufacture of biomaterials. **Purpose:** Provides an interdisciplinary forum for research in biomaterials. Promotes research, development, and education in the biomaterials sciences.

★1355★ **Society of Hispanic Professional Engineers (SHPE)**

5400 E Olympic Blvd., Ste. 210
Los Angeles, CA 90022
Ph: (323)725-3970   Fax: (323)725-0316
E-mail: shpenational@shpe.org
URL: http://oneshpe.shpe.org/wps/portal/national

Description: Represents engineers, student engineers, and scientists. Aims to increase the number of Hispanic engineers by providing motivation and support to students. Sponsors competitions and educational programs. Maintains placement service and speakers' bureau; compiles statistics.

★1356★ **Society for Industrial Microbiology (SIM)**

3929 Old Lee Hwy., Ste. 92A
Fairfax, VA 22030-2421
Ph: (703)691-3357   Fax: (703)691-7991
E-mail: simhq@simhq.org
URL: http://www.simhq.org

Description: Mycologists, bacteriologists, biologists, chemists, engineers, zoologists, and others interested in biological processes as applied to industrial materials and processes concerning microorganisms. Serves as liaison between the specialized fields of microbiology. Maintains placement service; conducts surveys and scientific workshops in industrial microbiology.

EMPLOYER DIRECTORIES AND NETWORKING LISTS

★1357★ *AGT International Membership Directory*

Association of Genetic Technologists
AGT Executive Office
PO Box 15945-288
Lenexa, KS 66285-5945
Ph: (913)895-4605   Fax: (913)895-4652
URL: http://www.agt-info.org/IntMember-

shipDir.html

Monthly. Covers about 520 laboratories studying heritable and acquired chromosomal disorders using cytogenetic, genetics, and cellular biology techniques. Entries include: Laboratory name, address, phone, areas of specialization, techniques, numbers and types of laboratory tests performed, and names of director and cytogenetic technologists. Arrangement: Geographical. Indexes: Director name, ACT member name.

★1358★   American Men and Women of Science

Gale, Cengage Learning
27500 Drake Rd.
Farmington Hills, MI 48331-3535
Ph: (248)699-4253   Fax: (248)699-8065
Fr: 800-877-4253
URL: http://www.gale.com

Biennial, latest edition 23rd, October 2006; new edition expected 24th, January 2008. $1,075.00 for individuals. Covers over 129,700 U.S. and Canadian scientists active in the physical, biological, mathematical, computer science, and engineering fields; includes references to previous edition for deceased scientists and nonrespondents. Entries include: Name, address, education, personal and career data, memberships, honors and awards, research interest. Arrangement: Alphabetical. Indexes: Discipline (in separate volume).

★1359★   Biotechnology Directory

Nature Publishing Group
75 Varick St., 9th Fl.
New York, NY 10013-1917
Ph: (212)726-9200   Fax: (212)696-9006
Fr: 888-331-6288
URL: http://www.npg.nature.com/

Annual; latest edition February 2005. $315.00 for individuals; $195.00 for elsewhere. Covers more than 11,000 companies, universities, research centers, and government agencies, and suppliers of products and services to the field. Entries include: Organization name, address, phone, telex, fax, contact; description of products, services, or research. Arrangement: Geographical. Indexes: Product, organization.

Handbooks and Manuals

★1360★   The Best Resumes for Scientists and Engineers

John Wiley & Sons Inc.
1 Wiley Dr.
Somerset, NJ 08873
Ph: (732)469-4400   Fax: (732)302-2300
Fr: 800-225-5945
E-mail: custserv@wiley.com
URL: http://www.wiley.com/WileyCDA/

Adele Lewis and David J. Moore. Second edition, 1993. $37.50; $19.95 (paper). 224 pages. Presents an extensive collection of scientific and engineering resumes, highlighting the important differences between these and resumes written for other occupations.

★1361★   The Biomedical Engineering Handbook

CRC
6000 Broken Sounds Pkwy. NW, Ste. 300
Boca Raton, FL 33487
Ph: (561)994-0555   Fax: 800-374-3401
Fr: 800-272-7737
E-mail: orders@crcpress.com
URL: http://www.crcpress.com

Joseph D. Bronzino, editor. Third edition, 2006. $149.95. 1,560 pages. Beginning with an overview of physiology and physiological modeling, simulation, and control, the book explores bioelectric phenomena, biomaterials, biomechanics, rehabilitation and human performance engineering, and ethical issues.

★1362★   Careers in High Tech

The McGraw-Hill Companies
PO Box 182604
Columbus, OH 43272
Fax: (614)759-3749   Fr: 877-883-5524
E-mail: customer.service@mcgraw-hill.com
URL: http://www.mcgraw-hill.com

Nick Basta. Second edition, 1998. $17.95 (paper). 98 pages. Examines new career opportunities in such fields as biotechnology, computers, aerospace, telecommunications, and others.

★1363★   Careers in Science and Engineering

National Academies Press
500 5th St. NW
Lockbox 285
Washington, DC 20055
Ph: (202)334-3313   Fax: (202)334-2793
Fr: 888-624-8373
URL: http://www.nap.edu/

1996. $11.95. 134 pages. Covers planning for graduate school and beyond.

★1364★   Hidden Job Market

Peterson's Guides
2000 Lenox Dr.
Box 67005
Lawrenceville, NJ 08648
Ph: (609)896-1800   Fax: (609)896-4531
Fr: 800-338-3282
E-mail: custsvc@petersons.com
URL: http://www.petersons.com

Ninth edition, 1999. $18.95 (paper). 319 pages. Guide to 2,000 fast-growing companies that are hiring now. Focuses on high technology companies in such fields as environmental consulting, genetic engineering, home health care, telecommunications, alternative energy systems, and others. Part of Peterson's Hidden Job Market series.

★1365★   The I Hate Selling Book: Business-Building Advice for Consultants, Attorneys, Accountants, Engineers, Architects, and Other Professionals

AMACOM
1601 Broadway, 12th Fl.
New York, NY 10019-7420
Ph: (212)586-8100   Fax: (212)903-8168
Fr: 800-262-9699
URL: http://www.amanet.org

Allan S. Boress. 2001. $29.95. 240 pages.

★1366★   Introduction to Biomedical Engineering

Elsevier
11830 Westline Industrial Dr.
St. Louis, MO 63146
Ph: (314)453-7010   Fax: (314)453-7095
Fr: 800-545-2522
E-mail: usbkinfo@elsevier.com
URL: http://www.elsevier.com

Susan M. Blanchard, Joseph D. Bronzino and John Denis Enderle, editors. Second edition. 2005. $93.95. 1144 pages. Provides a historical perspective of the major developments in the biomedical field.

★1367★   Opportunities in Biological Science Careers

The McGraw-Hill Companies
PO Box 182604
Columbus, OH 43272
Fax: (614)759-3749   Fr: 877-883-5524
E-mail: customer.service@mcgraw-hill.com
URL: http://www.mcgraw-hill.com

Charles A. Winter. 2004. $13.95; $11.95 (paper). 160 pages. Identifies employers and outlines opportunities in plant and animal biology, biological specialties, biomedical sciences, applied biology, and other areas. Illustrated.

★1368★   Opportunities in Engineering Careers

The McGraw-Hill Companies
PO Box 182604
Columbus, OH 43272
Fax: (614)759-3749   Fr: 877-883-5524
E-mail: customer.service@mcgraw-hill.com
URL: http://www.mcgraw-hill.com

Nicholas Basta. Revised second edition, 2002. $13.95; $11.95 (paper). 160 pages. Outlines typical job titles, salaries, career paths, and employment prospects.

★1369★   Opportunities in High Tech Careers

The McGraw-Hill Companies
PO Box 182604
Columbus, OH 43272
Fax: (614)759-3749   Fr: 877-883-5524
E-mail: customer.service@mcgraw-hill.com
URL: http://www.mcgraw-hill.com

Gary Colter and Deborah Yanuck. 1999. $14.95; $11.95 (paper). 160 pages. Explores high technology careers. Describes job opportunities, how to make a career decision,

how to prepare for high technology jobs, job hunting techniques, and future trends.

★1370★ **Opportunities in Research and Development Careers**

The McGraw-Hill Companies
PO Box 182604
Columbus, OH 43272
Fax: (614)759-3749   Fr: 877-883-5524
E-mail: customer.service@mcgraw-hill.com
URL: http://www.mcgraw-hill.com

Jan Goldberg. 1996. $11.95 (paper). 146 pages.

★1371★ **Peterson's Job Opportunities in Engineering and Technology**

Peterson's Guides
2000 Lenox Dr.
Box 67005
Lawrenceville, NJ 08648
Ph: (609)896-1800   Fax: (609)896-4531
Fr: 800-338-3282
E-mail: custsvc@petersons.com
URL: http://www.petersons.com

Compiled by the Peterson's staff. Fourth edition, 1996. $21.95 (paper). 379 pages. Profiles 2,000 high-tech companies looking primarily for technical personnel in such fields as biotechnology, telecommunications, software, computers and peripherals, defense, and aerospace. Contains job-search strategies and career options to help match education and expertise to the job market. Indexed geographically, by industry, and by hiring needs.

★1372★ **Real People Working in Engineering**

The McGraw-Hill Companies
PO Box 182604
Columbus, OH 43272
Fax: (614)759-3749   Fr: 877-883-5524
E-mail: customer.service@mcgraw-hill.com
URL: http://www.mcgraw-hill.com

Blythe Camenson, Jan Goldberg. 1997. $17.95 (paper). 160 pages. Interviews and profiles of working professionals capture a range of opportunities in this field.

★1373★ **Resumes for Engineering Careers**

The McGraw-Hill Companies
PO Box 182604
Columbus, OH 43272
Fax: (614)759-3749   Fr: 877-883-5524
E-mail: customer.service@mcgraw-hill.com
URL: http://www.mcgraw-hill.com

Third edition, 2005. $11.95 (paper). 144 pages. Contains sample resumes and cover letters applicable to any engineering field.

★1374★ **Resumes for Scientific and Technical Careers**

The McGraw-Hill Companies
PO Box 182604
Columbus, OH 43272
Fax: (614)759-3749   Fr: 877-883-5524

E-mail: customer.service@mcgraw-hill.com
URL: http://www.mcgraw-hill.com

Third edition, 2007. $12.95 (paper). 144 pages. Provides resume advice for individuals interested in working in scientific and technical careers. Includes sample resumes and cover letters.

EMPLOYMENT AGENCIES AND SEARCH FIRMS

★1375★ **1 Exec Street**
201 Post St., Ste. 401
San Francisco, CA 94108
Ph: (415)982-0555   Fax: (415)982-0550
Fr: 888-554-6845
E-mail: contactus@1execstreet.com
URL: http://www.1execstreet.com

Executive search firm.

★1376★ **Amtec Engineering Corp.**
2749 Saturn St.
Brea, CA 92821
Ph: (714)993-1900   Fax: (714)993-2419
E-mail: info@amtechc.com
URL: http://www.amtec-eng.com

Employment agency.

★1377★ **Aureus Group**
13609 California St.
Omaha, NE 68154
Ph: (402)891-6900   Fax: (402)891-1290
Fr: 888-239-5993
E-mail: info@aureusgroup.com
URL: http://www.aureusgroup.com

Provides human capital management services in a wide variety of industries. Executive search and recruiting consultants specializing in six areas: accounting and finance, data processing, aerospace, engineering, manufacturing and medical professionals. Industries served: hospitals, all mainframe computer shops and all areas of accounting.

★1378★ **Battalia Winston International**
555 Madison Ave.
New York, NY 10022
Ph: (212)308-8080   Fax: (212)308-1309
E-mail: info@battaliawinston.com
URL: http://www.battaliawinston.com

Executive search firm. Branches in Los Angeles; Chicago; Wellesley Hills, MA; Edison, NJ.

★1379★ **Biomedical Search Consultants**
275 Wyman St.
Waltham, MA 02451
Ph: (978)952-6425   Fax: (781)890-1082
E-mail: kprovost@biomedicalsearchconsultants.com

URL: http://www.biomedicalsearchconsultants.com
Employment agency.

★1380★ **BioPharmMed**
550 North Reo St., Ste. 300
Tampa, FL 33609
Ph: (813)261-5117
E-mail: bpm@ix.netcom.com
URL: http://www.biopharmmed.com

Executive search firm.

★1381★ **BioQuest**
100 Spear St., Ste. 1125
San Francisco, CA 94105-1526
Ph: (415)777-4363
E-mail: info@bioquestinc.com
URL: http://www.bioquestinc.com

Executive search firm focused in healthcare and life sciences.

★1382★ **The Caplan Taylor Group**
550 Bear Canyon Ln.
Arroyo Grande, CA 93420
Ph: (805)481-3000
E-mail: jcaplan@caplantaylorgroup.com

Executive search firm.

★1383★ **The Cassie-Shipherd Group**
26 Main St.
Toms River, NJ 08753
Ph: (732)473-1779   Fax: (732)473-1023
E-mail: cassiegroup@cassie.com
URL: http://www.cassie.com

Executive search firm. Branches in San Diego; Bridgewater, NJ; New Bern, NC; and Salt Lake City.

★1384★ **The Coelyn Group**
1 Park Plaza, Ste. 600
Irvine, CA 92614
Ph: (949)553-8855   Fax: 888-436-2171
E-mail: contact@coelyngroup.com
URL: http://www.coelyngroup.com

Executive search firm.

★1385★ **D'Antoni Partners Inc.**
122 W. John Carpenter Fwy., Ste. 525
Irving, TX 75039
Ph: (972)719-4400   Fax: (972)719-4401
E-mail: richard@dantonipartners.com
URL: http://www.dantonipartners.com

Executive search firm.

★1386★ **Day & Associates**
577 Airport Blvd., Ste. 130
Burlingame, CA 94010
Ph: (650)343-2660   Fax: (650)344-8460
E-mail: info@dayassociates.net
URL: http://www.dayassociates.net

Executive search firm.

★1387★ Elwell & Associates Inc.
3100 W. Liberty Rd., Ste. E
Ann Arbor, MI 48103
Ph: (734)662-8775   Fax: (734)662-2045
E-mail: elwallas@elwellassociates.com
URL: http://www.elwellassociates.com

Executive search firm.

★1388★ Emerging Medical Technologies Inc.
7784 S. Addison Way
Aurora, CO 80016
Ph: (303)699-1990
E-mail: tcmemt@aol.com

Executive search firm focused on the medical devices industry.

★1389★ Erspamer Associates
4010 W. 65th St., Ste. 100
Edina, MN 55435
Ph: (952)925-3747   Fax: (952)925-4022
E-mail: hdhuntrel@aol.com

Executive search firm specializing in technical management.

★1390★ Evenium Inc.
520 Marquette Ave.
Minneapolis, MN 55402
Ph: (612)436-3200   Fax: (612)436-3157
URL: http://www.eveniumgroup.com/

Executive search firm.

★1391★ J. Blakslee International Inc.
336 Bon Air Shopping Ctr., Ste. 369
Greenbrae, CA 94904-3208
Ph: (415)389-7300   Fax: (415)389-7302
E-mail: resumes@jblakslee.com

Executive search firm.

★1392★ JPM International
26034 Acero
Mission Viejo, CA 92691
Ph: (949)699-4300   Fax: (949)699-4333
Fr: 800-685-7856
E-mail: trish@jpmintl.com
URL: http://www.jpmintl.com

Executive search firm and employment agency.

★1393★ Lloyd Staffing
445 Broadhollow Rd., Ste. 119
Melville, NY 11747
Ph: (631)777-7600   Fax: (631)777-7626
Fr: 888-292-6678
E-mail: info@lloydstaffing.com
URL: http://www.lloydstaffing.com

Personnel agency and search firm.

★1394★ O'Keefe and Partners
4 Corporate Dr., Ste 490
Shelton, CT 06484
Ph: (203)929-4222   Fax: (203)926-0073

E-mail: smoore@okeefepartners.com
URL: http://www.okeefepartners.com

Executive search firm.

★1395★ Rosemary Cass Ltd.
175 Post Rd. W
Westport, CT 06880
Ph: (203)454-2920   Fax: (203)454-4643
E-mail: resumes@rosemarycassltd.com
URL: http://www.rosemarycassltd.com/

Executive search firm.

★1396★ Techtronix Technical Search
4805 N 24th Pl.
PO Box 17713
Milwaukee, WI 53217-0173
Ph: (414)466-3100   Fax: (414)466-3598

Firm specializes in recruiting executives for the engineering, information systems, manufacturing, marketing, finance, and human resources industries.

★1397★ Winters Technical Staffing Services
6 Lansing Sq., Ste. 101
Toronto, ON, Canada M2J 1T5
Ph: (416)495-7422   Fax: (416)495-8479
E-mail: brian@winterstaffing.com
URL: http://www.winterstaffing.com

Technical staffing service for permanent and contract positions in all facets of engineering. Serves government agencies, consulting engineers, and all areas of manufacturing in Canada and northeast United States.

ONLINE JOB SOURCES AND SERVICES

★1398★ Bio.com Career Center
E-mail: careers@bio.com
URL: http://www.bio.com/jobs/index.jhtml

Description: Contains a job index searchable by employer name, discipline, or location. Suitable for job hunters tracking down specific medical, biological, biochemical, or pharmaceutical companies and positions. Also references at Career Guide and Career Forum sections.

★1399★ FASEB Career Resources
9650 Rockville Pike
Bethesda, MD 20814-3998
Ph: (301)634-7000   Fax: (301)634-7001
E-mail: careers@faseb.org
URL: http://www.faseb.org/careers/

Description: A career opportunity site combined with a development service that attempts to pair applicants at all career levels with employers who hire biomedical scientists and technicians. Biomedical career development is highlighted through career re-

source tools. **Main files include:** Careers Online DataNet, Career Online Classified.

★1400★ Genetics Society of America:Positions Open
E-mail: society@genetics-gsa.org
URL: http://www.genetics-gsa.org

Description: Listing of position announcements formerly published in Genetics. Members may e-mail job listings to the site to be posted.

★1401★ GrantsNet
E-mail: grantsnet@aaas.org
URL: http://www.grantsnet.org/search/srch_specify.cfm

Description: Grant-locating site intended for scientists in training who may become vulnerable in an era of competitive funding. Includes a directory of over 600 programs with contact information within a searchable database.

★1402★ The SciWeb Biotechnology Career Home Page
E-mail: info@biocareer.com
URL: http://www.biocareer.com

Description: Career resource center resulting from the collaboration of the Biotechnology Industry Organization (BIO) and *SciWeb*. Aims to connect job seekers with recruiters in the biotechnology industry. **Main files include:** Post Resume, Search Resume, Post Job, Search Job, Career Resources. **Fee:** 150.00 for the first two months, $75.00 per additional monthly renewal. Academic PostDoctoral Listings are posted for free.

★1403★ Spherion
2050 Spectrum Blvd.
Fort Lauderdale, FL 33309
Ph: (954)308-7600
E-mail: help@spherion.com
URL: http://www.spherion.com

Description: Recruitment firm specializing in accounting and finance, sales and marketing, interim executives, technology, engineering, retail and human resources.

TRADESHOWS

★1404★ American Society for Engineering Education Annual Conference and Exposition
American Society for Engineering Education
1818 N. St. NW, Ste. 600
Washington, DC 20036-2479
Ph: (202)331-3500   Fax: (202)265-8504
E-mail: conferences@asee.org
URL: http://www.asee.org

Annual. **Primary Exhibits:** Publications, engineering supplies and equipment, computers, software, and research companies all products and services related to engineering education.

OTHER SOURCES

★1405★ American Association of Engineering Societies (AAES)

1620 I St. NW, Ste. 210
Washington, DC 20006
Ph: (202)296-2237   Fax: (202)296-1151
Fr: 888-400-2237
E-mail: dbateson@aaes.org
URL: http://www.aaes.org

Description: Coordinates the efforts of the member societies in the provision of reliable and objective information to the general public concerning issues which affect the engineering profession and the field of engineering as a whole; collects, analyzes, documents, and disseminates data which will inform the general public of the relationship between engineering and the national welfare; provides a forum for the engineering societies to exchange and discuss their views on matters of common interest; and represents the U.S. engineering community abroad through representation in WFEO and UPADI.

★1406★ Biomedical Engineering Society (BMES)

8401 Corporate Dr., Ste. 140
Landover, MD 20785-2224
Ph: (301)459-1999   Fax: (301)459-2444
E-mail: info@bmes.org
URL: http://www.bmes.org

Members: Biomedical, chemical, electrical, civil, agricultural and mechanical engineers, physicians, managers, and university professors representing all fields of biomedical engineering; students and corporations. **Purpose:** Encourages the development, dissemination, integration, and utilization of knowledge in biomedical engineering.

★1407★ Biotechnology Occupations

Delphi Productions
3159 6th St.
Boulder, CO 80304
Ph: (303)443-2100   Fax: (303)443-4022
Fr: 888-443-2400
E-mail: support@delphivideo.com
URL: http://www.delphivideo.com

$95.00. 49 minutes. Part of the Emerging Careers Video Library.

★1408★ Engineering Occupations

Delphi Productions
3159 6th St.
Boulder, CO 80304
Ph: (303)443-2100   Fax: (303)443-4022
Fr: 888-443-2400
E-mail: support@delphivideo.com
URL: http://www.delphivideo.com

$95.00. 50 minutes. Part of the Careers for the 21st Century Video Library.

★1409★ International Functional Electrical Stimulation Society (IFESS)

1854 Los Encinos Ave.
Glendale, CA 91208-2240
Ph: (661)362-1755   Fax: (818)246-1389
E-mail: paul.meadows@bionics.com
URL: http://www.ifess.org

Description: Represents academic leaders in the field of biomedical engineering, physical therapists, medical doctors, members of the electrical stimulation manufacturing community, and students and users of functional electrical stimulation (FES) technology. Promotes the research, application, and understanding of electrical stimulation as it is utilized in the field of medicine. Facilitates cooperation and fellowship among members.

★1410★ National Action Council for Minorities in Engineering (NACME)

440 Hamilton Ave., Ste. 302
White Plains, NY 10601-1813
Ph: (914)539-4010   Fax: (914)539-4032
E-mail: webmaster@nacme.org
URL: http://www.nacme.org

Description: Leads the national effort to increase access to careers in engineering and other science-based disciplines. Conducts research and public policy analysis, develops and operates national demonstration programs at precollege and university levels, and disseminates information through publications, conferences and electronic media. Serves as a privately funded source of scholarships for minority students in engineering.

★1411★ National Society of Professional Engineers (NSPE)

1420 King St.
Alexandria, VA 22314-2794
Ph: (703)684-2800   Fax: (703)836-4875
Fr: 888-285-6773
E-mail: memserv@nspe.org
URL: http://www.nspe.org

Description: Represents professional engineers and engineers-in-training in all fields registered in accordance with the laws of states or territories of the U.S. or provinces of Canada; qualified graduate engineers, student members, and registered land surveyors. Is concerned with social, professional, ethical, and economic considerations of engineering as a profession; encompasses programs in public relations, employment practices, ethical considerations, education, and career guidance. Monitors legislative and regulatory actions of interest to the engineering profession.

★1412★ Resumes for High Tech Careers

The McGraw-Hill Companies
PO Box 182604
Columbus, OH 43272
Fax: (614)759-3749   Fr: 877-883-5524
E-mail: customer.service@mcgraw-hill.com
URL: http://www.mcgraw-hill.com

Third edition, 2003. $10.95 (paper). 160 pages. Demonstrates how to tailor a resume that catches a high tech employer's attention. Part of "Resumes for ..." series.

★1413★ Scientific, Engineering, and Technical Services

Cambridge Educational
PO Box 2053
Princeton, NJ 08543-2053
Ph: 800-257-5126   Fax: (609)671-0266
Fr: 800-468-4227
E-mail: custserv@films.com
URL: http://www.cambridgeeducational.com

VHS and DVD. $89.95. 2002. 18 minutes. 2002. Part of the Career Cluster Series.

★1414★ Society for Biological Engineering (SBE)

3 Park Ave., 19th Fl.
New York, NY 10016
E-mail: bio@aiche.org
URL: http://www.aiche.org/SBE

Description: Promotes the integration of biology with engineering and its benefits through bioprocessing, biomedical, and biomolecular applications. Raises interest, understanding, and recognition of engineers' and scientists' roles in biological engineering. Provides opportunities for the successful interaction of engineers and scientists.

★1415★ Society of Women Engineers (SWE)

230 E Ohio St., Ste. 400
Chicago, IL 60611-3265
Ph: (312)596-5223   Fax: (312)596-5252
Fr: 877-SWE-INFO
E-mail: hq@swe.org
URL: http://www.swe.org

Description: Educational and service organization representing both students and professional women in engineering and technical fields.

★1416★ Women in Engineering

Her Own Words
PO Box 5264
Madison, WI 53705-0264
Ph: (608)271-7083   Fax: (608)271-0209
E-mail: herownword@aol.com
URL: http://www.herownwords.com/

Video. Jocelyn Riley. $95.00. 15 minutes. Resource guide also available for $45.00.

★1417★ World Association for Chinese Biomedical Engineers (WACBE)
University of Pittsburgh
Musculoskeletal Research Ctr.
405 Center for Bioengineering
300 Technology Dr.
Pittsburgh, PA 15219

Ph: (412)427-2000   Fax: (412)427-2001
E-mail: ddecenzo@pitt.edu
URL: http://www.pitt.edu/~zmli/wacbe

Description: Networks the worldwide Chinese professionals and students in the field of biomedical engineering. Promotes basic and translational research in the field. Encourages students to become biomedical engineers. Facilitates the professional and career development of members. Promotes cooperation among and between industrialists and academics.

Border Patrol Agents

SOURCES OF HELP-WANTED ADS

★1418★ Copcareer.com
URL: http://www.copcareer.com
Online job posting site for law enforcement professionals, including border patrol agents.

★1419★ Homeland Response
Penton Media Inc.
249 W 17th St.
New York, NY 10011
Ph: (212)204-4200
URL: http://
www.respondersafetyonline.com/
Bimonthly. Magazine covering homeland security.

★1420★ HSToday
HSToday
6800 Fleetwood Rd., Ste. 114
Mc Lean, VA 22101
URL: http://www.hstoday.us
Monthly. Free to qualified subscribers. Magazine covering topics of interest to homeland security professionals.

EMPLOYER DIRECTORIES AND NETWORKING LISTS

★1421★ What Can I Do Now
Facts On File Inc.
132 W 31st St., 17th Fl.
New York, NY 10001
Ph: (212)967-8800   Fax: 800-678-3633
Fr: 800-322-8755
URL: http://www.factsonfile.com
$22.95 for individuals; $20.65 for libraries. Covers border patrol officers, corrections officers, crime analysts, emergency medical technicians, FBI agents, firefighters, and police officers.

HANDBOOKS AND MANUALS

★1422★ Border Patrol Agent: Questions and Answers
U.S. Department of Justice
950 Pennsylvania Ave. NW
Washington, DC 20530-0001
Ph: (202)514-2000
URL: http://www.cbp.gov/xp/cgov/toolbox/questions/
U.S. Dept. of Justice. 1995. Study guide for the border patrol agent examination.

★1423★ Border Patrol Exam
LearningExpress, LLC
55 Broadway, 8th Fl.
New York, NY 10006
Fax: (212)995-5512   Fr: 888-551-5627
E-mail: customerservice@learningexpressllc.com
URL: http://www.learningexpressllc.com
Shirley Tarbell and Byron Demmer. Second edition, 2001. $26.99. 192 pages. Contains instruction on all areas covered by the examination, as well as three practice tests. Includes information on the procedures and requirements for applying for a position as a border patrol agent.

ONLINE JOB SOURCES AND SERVICES

★1424★ 911hotjobs.com Employment Portal
E-mail: contact@911hotjobs.com
URL: http://www.911hotjobs.com
Description: Online site for those seeking job opportunities in public safety. Testing requirements and job postings are available to those seeking employment in law enforcement, fire careers, and EMS services.

★1425★ Honor First
PO Box 11325
Palm Desert, CA 92255-1325
URL: http://www.honorfirst.com
Description: Serves as the unofficial website of the United States Border Patrol. Includes information on how to apply, pay and benefits, hiring process, study guides for the examination, and class schedules. Provides links to other sites with information on becoming a border patrol agent.

★1426★ USAjobs Inc.
677 E. Quality Dr., S104
American Fork, UT 84003-3305
Fr: 877-789-5882
URL: http://www.usajobs.org
Description: The federal government's official one-stop source for federal jobs and employment information. Includes resume posting, current job listings, and search functions.

OTHER SOURCES

★1427★ National Border Patrol Council (NBPC)
PO Box 678
Campo, CA 91906
Ph: (619)478-5145   Fr: 888-583-7237
E-mail: nbpc-info@nbpc.net
URL: http://www.nbpc.net
Purpose: Represents employees of the U.S. Border Patrol.

★1428★ Transportation Security Administration
601 South 12th St.
Arlington, VA 22202-4220
Fr: 800-887-1895

URL: http://www.tsa.gov
Governmental agency that lists available jobs on its website, including those for border patrol agents.

★1429★ U.S. Border Patrol Supervisors' Association
539 Telegraph Canyon Rd., PMB No. 656
Chula Vista, CA 91910-6497
URL: http://www.bpsups.org
Members: Border patrol supervisors. **Purpose:** Promotes opportunities for training, liaison with other law enforcement associations, and political action efforts for career and retirement goals. **Activities:** Maintains an online chat room and message board to promote networking among its members.

★1430★ U.S. Customs and Border Protection
950 Pennsylvania Ave. NW
Washington, DC 20530-0001
Ph: (202)514-2000
URL: http://www.cbp.gov
Activities: Provides news releases and fact sheets on border patrol initiatives.

★1431★ U.S. Customs and Border Protection - Blaine Sector
2410 Nature's Path Way
Blaine, WA 98230-9114
Ph: (360)332-9200   Fax: (360)332-9263
URL: http://www.cbp.gov/xp/cgov/border_security/border_patrol/border_patrol_sectors/blaine_sector_wa/
Activities: Services the states of Alaska, Oregon, and the western half of the state of Washington. Stations are located in Blaine, Washington; Lynden, Washington; Bellingham, Washington; Port Angeles, Washington; and Roseburg, Oregon. Information about employment opportunities may be obtained by contacting the recruiter at the Sector office.

★1432★ U.S. Customs and Border Protection - Buffalo Sector
201 Lang Blvd.
Grand Island, NY 14072
Ph: (716)774-7200
URL: http://www.cbp.gov/xp/cgov/border_security/border_patrol/border_patrol_sectors/buffalo_sector_ny/
Activities: Covers 450 miles of border with Canada from the Ohio/Pennsylvania state line to Jefferson County, New York. Stations are located in Niagara Falls, New York; Buffalo, New York; Fulton, New York; and Watertown, New York. Information about employment opportunities may be obtained by contacting the recruiter at the Sector office.

★1433★ U.S. Customs and Border Protection - Del Rio Sector
2401 Dodson Ave.
Del Rio, TX 78840
Ph: (830)778-7000
URL: http://www.cbp.gov/xp/cgov/border_security/border_patrol/border_patrol_sectors/delrio_sector_tx/
Activities: Covers 41 counties in the state of Texas. Stations are located in Abilene, Brackettville, Carrizo Springs, Comstock, Del Rio, Eagle Pass, Llano, Rocksprings, San Angelo, and Uvalde. Information about employment opportunities may be obtained by contacting the recruiter at the Sector office.

★1434★ U.S. Customs and Border Protection - Detroit Sector
PO Box 450040
Selfridge ANGB, MI 48045-0040
Ph: (586)307-2160
URL: http://www.cbp.gov/xp/cgov/border_security/border_patrol/border_patrol_sectors/detroit_sector_mi/
Activities: Area of responsibility includes Illinois, Indiana, Michigan, and Ohio. Stations are located in Detroit, Michigan; Port Huron, Michigan; Sault Ste. Marie, Michigan; and Trenton, Michigan. Information about employment opportunities may be obtained by contacting the recruiter at the Sector office.

★1435★ U.S. Customs and Border Protection - El Centro Sector
1111 N. Imperial Ave.
El Centro, CA 92243
Ph: (760)352-3241
URL: http://www.cbp.gov/xp/cgov/border_security/border_patrol/border_patrol_sectors/elcentro_sector_ca/
Activities: Covers the counties of Imperial and Riverside in California. Stations are located in Calexico, California; El Centro, California; Indio, California; and Riverside, California. Information about employment opportunities may be obtained by contacting the recruiter at the Sector office.

★1436★ U.S. Customs and Border Protection - El Paso Sector
8901 Montana Ave.
El Paso, TX 79925-1212
Ph: (915)834-8350
URL: http://www.cbp.gov/xp/cgov/border_security/border_patrol/border_patrol_sectors/elpaso_sector_tx/
Activities: Covers the entire state of New Mexico and Hudspeth and El Paso counties in Texas, totaling 125,500 square miles of territory. Stations are located in El Paso, Texas; Fabens, Texas; Fort Hancock, Texas; Ysleta, Texas; Alamagordo, New Mexico; Albuquerque, New Mexico; Carlsbad, New Mexico; Deming, New Mexico; Las Cruces, New Mexico; Lordsburg, New Mexico; Truth or Consequences, New Mexico; and Santa Teresa, New Mexico. Information about employment opportunities may be

obtained by contacting the recruiter at the Sector office.

★1437★ U.S. Customs and Border Protection - Grand Forks Sector
2320 S. Washington St.
Grand Forks, ND 58201
Ph: (701)775-6259
URL: http://www.cbp.gov/xp/cgov/border_security/border_patrol/border_patrol_sectors/grandforks_sector_nd/
Activities: Covers the states of North Dakota, Minnesota, Wisconsin, South Dakota, Iowa, Nebraska, Kansas, and Missouri. Stations are located in Grand Forks, North Dakota; Bottineau, North Dakota; Duluth, Minnesota; International Falls, Minnesota; Pembina, North Dakota; Portal, North Dakota; and Warroad, Minnesota. Information about employment opportunities may be obtained by contacting the recruiter at the Sector office.

★1438★ U.S. Customs and Border Protection - Havre Sector
2605 Fifth Ave. SE
Havre, MT 59501
Ph: (406)265-6781
URL: http://www.cbp.gov/xp/cgov/border_security/border_patrol/border_patrol_sectors/havre_sector_mt/
Activities: Patrols 452 miles of border area between Montana and Canada, Wyoming, Colorado, Utah, as well as part of Idaho. Stations are located in Havre, Montana; Plentywood, Montana; Shelby, Montana; and Twin Falls, Idaho. Information about employment opportunities may be obtained by contacting the recruiter at the Sector office.

★1439★ U.S. Customs and Border Protection - Houlton Sector
96 Calais Rd.
Hodgdon, ME 04730
Ph: (207)532-6521   Fr: 800-851-8727
URL: http://www.cbp.gov/xp/cgov/border_security/border_patrol/border_patrol_sectors/houlton_sector_me/
Activities: Covers the entire state of Maine. Stations are located in Calais, Fort Fairfield, Houlton, Van Buren, Jackman, and Rangeley. Information about employment opportunities may be obtained by contacting the recruiter at the Sector office.

★1440★ U.S. Customs and Border Protection - Laredo Sector
207 W. Del Mar Blvd.
Laredo, TX 78041
Ph: (956)764-3200
URL: http://www.cbp.gov/xp/cgov/border_security/border_patrol/border_patrol_sectors/laredo_sector_tx/
Activities: Encompasses 116 counties and covers 101,439 square miles of southwest and northeast Texas. Stations are located Zapata, Hebbronville, Cotulla, Dallas, San Antonio, and Laredo. Information about em-

ployment opportunities may be obtained by contacting the recruiter at the Sector office.

★1441★ U.S. Customs and Border Protection - Marfa Sector

300 Madrid St.
Marfa, TX 79843
Ph: (432)729-5200
URL: http://www.cbp.gov/xp/cgov/border_
security/border_patrol/border_patrol_sectors/
marfa_sector_tx/

Activities: Covers over 135,000 square miles encompassing over 118 counties in Texas and Oklahoma, the largest geographical area of any sector along the southwest border. Stations are located in Sierra Blanca, Van Horn, Marfa, Presidio, Alpine, Sanderson, Pecos, Ft. Stockton, Midland, and Lubbock. Information about employment opportunities may be obtained by contacting the recruiter at the Sector office.

★1442★ U.S. Customs and Border Protection - Miami Sector

15720 Pines Blvd.
Pembroke Pines, FL 33023
Ph: (954)965-6300
URL: http://www.cbp.gov/xp/cgov/border_
security/border_patrol/border_patrol_sectors/
miami_sector_fl/

Activities: Covers the states of Florida, Georgia, North Carolina, and South Carolina. Stations are located in Pembroke Pines, Florida; West Palm Beach, Florida; Orlando, Florida; Jacksonville, Florida; and Tampa, Florida. Information about employment opportunities may be obtained by contacting the recruiter at the Sector office.

★1443★ U.S. Customs and Border Protection - New Orleans Sector

PO Box 6218
New Orleans, LA 70174-6218
Ph: (504)376-2800
URL: http://www.cbp.gov/xp/cgov/border_
security/border_patrol/border_patrol_sectors/
neworleans_sector_la/

Activities: Maintains jurisdiction over a seven-state area, which encompasses 592 counties and parishes and approximately 362,310 square miles. Stations are located in New Orleans, Louisiana; Lake Charles, Louisiana; Baton Rouge, Louisiana; Gulfport, Mississippi; Mobile, Alabama; and Little Rock, Arkansas. Information about employment opportunities may be obtained by contacting the recruiter at the Sector office.

★1444★ U.S. Customs and Border Protection - Ramey Sector

PO Box 250467
Ramey, PR 00604
Ph: (787)882-3560
URL: http://www.cbp.gov/xp/cgov/border_
security/border_patrol/border_patrol_sectors/
ramey_sector_puertorico/

Activities: Responsible for Puerto Rico and the U.S. Virgin Islands. The Sector's only station is located in Ramey. Information about employment opportunities may be obtained by contacting the recruiter at the Sector office.

★1445★ U.S. Customs and Border Protection - Rio Grande Valley Sector

4400 S. Expressway 281
Edinburg, TX 78539
Ph: (956)289-4800
URL: http://www.cbp.gov/xp/cgov/border_
security/border_patrol/border_patrol_sectors/
rio_grande_valley_sector/

Activities: Covers over 17,000 square miles in southeast Texas. Stations are located in Port Isabel, Weslaco, Harlingen, McAllen, Rio Grande City, Falfurrias, Kingsville, and Corpus Christi. Information about employment opportunities may be obtained by contacting the recruiter at the Sector office.

★1446★ U.S. Customs and Border Protection - San Diego Sector

2411 Boswell Rd.
Chula Vista, CA 91914-3519
Ph: (619)216-4000
URL: http://www.cbp.gov/xp/cgov/border_
security/border_patrol/border_patrol_sectors/
sandiego_sector_ca/

Activities: Covers San Diego County in the state of California. Stations are located in Brown Field (the nation's largest Border Patrol station), Chula Vista, El Cajon, Imperial Beach, San Clemente, and Temecula. Information about employment opportunities may be obtained by contacting the recruiter at the Sector office.

★1447★ U.S. Customs and Border Protection - Spokane Sector

10710 N. Newport Hwy.
Spokane, WA 99218
Ph: (509)353-2747
URL: http://www.cbp.gov/xp/cgov/border_
security/border_patrol/border_patrol_sectors/
spokane_sector_wa/

Activities: Patrols eastern Washington, Idaho, and western Montana up to the Continental Divide. Stations are located in Spokane, Washington; Colville, Washington; Curlew, Washington; Metaline Falls, Washington; Oroville, Washington; Pasco, Washington; Wenatchee, Washington; Eureka, Montana; Whitefish, Montana; and Bonners Ferry, Idaho. Information about employment opportunities may be obtained by contacting the recruiter at the Sector office.

★1448★ U.S. Customs and Border Protection - Swanton Sector

155 Grand Ave.
Swanton, VT 05488
Ph: (802)868-3361   Fr: 800-247-2434
URL: http://www.cbp.gov/xp/cgov/border_
security/border_patrol/border_patrol_sectors/
swanton_sector_vt/swanton_gener al.xml

Activities: Encompasses 24,000 square miles and includes the state of Vermont; Clinton, Essex, Franklin, St. Lawrence, and Herkimer counties in New York; and Coos, Grafton, and Carroll counties in New Hampshire. Stations are located in Ogdensburg, New York; Massena, New York; Burke, New York; Champlain, New York; Swanton, Vermont; Richford, Vermont; Newport, Vermont; and Beecher Falls, Vermont. Information about employment opportunities may be obtained by contacting the recruiter at the Sector office.

★1449★ U.S. Customs and Border Protection - Tucson Sector

2430 S. Swan Rd.
Tucson, AZ 85711
Ph: (520)748-3000
URL: http://www.cbp.gov/xp/cgov/border_
security/border_patrol/border_patrol_sectors/
tucson_sector_az/

Activities: Covers the state of Arizona. Stations are located in Ajo, Casa Grande, Douglas, Naco, Nogales, Sonoita, Tucson, and Wilcox. Information about employment opportunities may be obtained by contacting the recruiter at the Sector office.

★1450★ U.S. Customs and Border Protection - Yuma Sector

4035 South Ave. A
Yuma, AZ 85364
Ph: (928)341-6500
URL: http://www.cbp.gov/xp/cgov/border_
security/border_patrol/border_patrol_sectors/
yuma_sector_az/

Activities: Patrols 118 miles of border with Mexico between the Yuma-Pima County line in Arizona and the Imperial Sand Dunes in California. Stations are located in Yuma, Arizona; Wellton, Arizona; and Blythe, California. Information about employment opportunities may be obtained by contacting the recruiter at the Sector office.

★1451★ U.S. Office of Personnel Management

1900 E St. NW
Washington, DC 20415-1000
Ph: (202)606-1800
URL: http://www.opm.gov

Purpose: The federal government's human resources agency. **Activities:** Provides information on the specific requirements necessary to qualify as a border patrol agent, including education, experience, testing, language, firearms use, medical, and age.

Bricklayers and Cement Masons

SOURCES OF HELP-WANTED ADS

★1452★ BIA News
Brick Industry Association
1850 Centennial Park Dr., Ste. 301
Reston, VA 20191-1525
Ph: (703)620-0010   Fax: (703)620-3928

Monthly. $30.00/year for individuals. Trade publication covering issues for the brick industry.

★1453★ Builder
Hanley-Wood L.L.C.
1 Thomas Cir., NW, Ste. 600
Washington, DC 20005
Ph: (202)452-0800   Fax: (202)785-1974
URL: http://www.hanleywood.com/default.aspx?page=b2bbd

$29.95/year for individuals, 13 issues; $54.95/year for Canada, 26 issues; $192.00/year for out of country, 13 issues. Magazine covering housing and construction industry.

★1454★ Building Systems Magazine
Active Interest Media
300 Continental Blvd., Ste. 650
El Segundo, CA 90245
Ph: (310)356-4100   Fax: (310)356-4110
Fr: 800-423-4880
URL: http://www.buildingsystems.com/

Bimonthly. Magazine featuring innovative construction technologies for builders, developers and general contractors.

★1455★ Concrete Products
Penton Media Inc.
9800 Metcalf Ave.
Overland Park, KS 66212
Ph: (913)341-1300   Fax: (913)967-1898
E-mail: dmarsh@prismb2b.com
URL: http://www.concreteproducts.com/

Monthly. Free, online; $96.00/year for other countries, print. Magazine on concrete products and ready-mixed concrete.

★1456★ Constructor
Associated General Contractors of America
2300 Wilson Blvd., Ste. 400
Arlington, VA 22201
Ph: (703)548-3118   Fax: (703)548-3119
URL: http://www.agc.org

Monthly. Management magazine for the Construction Industry.

★1457★ Custom Home Outdoors
Hanley-Wood L.L.C.
1 Thomas Cir., NW, Ste. 600
Washington, DC 20005
Ph: (202)452-0800   Fax: (202)785-1974
URL: http://www.hanleywood.com/default.aspx?page=b2bcho

Quarterly. Magazine featuring latest trends and products for building professionals.

★1458★ Green Home Builder
Peninsula Publishing
1602 Monrovia Ave.
Newport Beach, CA 92663
Ph: (949)631-0308   Fax: (949)631-2475
URL: http://www.greenhomebuildermag.com/

Quarterly. Magazine for home builders and home building industry.

★1459★ Professional Builder
Reed Business Information
360 Park Ave. S
New York, NY 10010
Ph: (646)746-6400   Fax: (646)746-7431
E-mail: ncrum@reedbusiness.com
URL: http://www.housingzone.com/toc-archive-pbx

Monthly. Free. The integrated engineering magazine of the building construction industry.

★1460★ Residential Concrete
Hanley-Wood L.L.C.
1 Thomas Cir., NW, Ste. 600
Washington, DC 20005
Ph: (202)452-0800   Fax: (202)785-1974
URL: http://www.hanleywood.com/default.aspx?page=b2bresconcrete

Bimonthly. Magazine featuring the use of concrete in residential concrete construction.

★1461★ Tools of the Trade
Hanley-Wood L.L.C.
1 Thomas Cir., NW, Ste. 600
Washington, DC 20005
Ph: (202)452-0800   Fax: (202)785-1974
URL: http://www.hanleywood.com/default.aspx?page=b2btt

Bimonthly. Magazine featuring tools for commercial and residential construction.

★1462★ WIT
Vermont Works for Women
51 Park St.
Essex Junction, VT 05452
Ph: (802)878-0004   Fax: (802)878-0050
Fr: 800-639-1472
URL: http://www.nnetw.org/

Description: Three issues/year. Provides a network of support, information, and skill sharing for women in skilled trades professions.

PLACEMENT AND JOB REFERRAL SERVICES

★1463★ National Association of Home Builders (NAHB)
1201 15th St. NW
Washington, DC 20005
Ph: (202)266-8200   Fax: (202)266-8400
Fr: 800-368-5242
E-mail: info@nahb.com
URL: http://www.nahb.org

Description: Single and multifamily home builders, commercial builders, and others associated with the building industry. Lobbies on behalf of the housing industry and conducts public affairs activities to increase public understanding of housing and the economy. Collects and disseminates data on current developments in home building and home builders' plans through its Economics Department and nationwide Metropolitan Housing Forecast. Maintains NAHB Research Center, which functions as the research arm of the home building industry. Sponsors seminars and workshops on construction, mortgage credit, labor relations, cost reduction, land use, remodeling, and business management. Compiles statistics; offers charitable program, spokesman training, and placement service; maintains speakers' bureau, and Hall of Fame. Subsidiaries include the National Council of the Housing Industry. Maintains over 50 committees in many areas of construction; operates National Commercial Builders Council, National Council of the Multifamily Housing Industry, National Remodelers Council, and National Sales and Marketing Council.

EMPLOYER DIRECTORIES AND NETWORKING LISTS

★1464★ ABC Today-Associated Builders and Contractors National Membership Directory Issue

Associated Builders & Contractors Inc.
4250 N Fairfax Dr., 9th Fl.
Arlington, VA 22203-1607
Ph: (703)812-2000   Fax: (703)812-8203
URL: http://www.abc.org/wmspage.cfm?parm1=2033

Annual, December. $150.00. Publication includes: List of approximately 19,000 member construction contractors and suppliers. Entries include: Company name, address, phone, name of principal executive, code to volume of business, business specialty. Arrangement: Classified by chapter, then by work specialty.

★1465★ Constructor-AGC Directory of Membership and Services Issue

AGC Information Inc.
2300 Wilson Blvd., Ste. 400
Arlington, VA 22201
Ph: (703)548-3118   Fax: (703)548-3119
Fr: 800-282-1423
URL: http://www.agc.org

Annual, August; latest edition 2004 edition. Publication includes: List of over 8,500 member firms and 24,000 national associate member firms engaged in building, highway, heavy, industrial, municipal utilities, and railroad construction (SIC 1541, 1542, 1611, 1622, 1623, 1629); listing of state and local chapter officers. Entries include: For firms—Company name, address, phone, fax, names of principal executives, and code indicating type of construction undertaken. For officers—Name, title, address. Arrangement: Geographical, alphabetical. Indexes: Company name.

★1466★ ENR-Top 400 Construction Contractors Issue

McGraw-Hill Inc.
1221 Ave. of the Americas
New York, NY 10020-1095
Ph: (212)512-2000   Fax: (212)512-3840
Fr: 877-833-5524
URL: http://construction.ecnext.com/coms2/summary_0249-137077_ITM

Annual; 22nd, May 2006. $35.00 for individuals. Publication includes: List of 400 United States contractors receiving largest dollar volumes of contracts in preceding calendar year. Separate lists of 50 largest design/construction management firms; 50 largest program and construction managers; 25 building contractors; 25 heavy contractors. Entries include: Company name, headquarters location, total value of contracts received in preceding year, value of foreign contracts, countries in which operated, construction specialities. Arrangement: By total value of contracts received.

HANDBOOKS AND MANUALS

★1467★ Exploring Careers in Construction

Prentice Hall PTR
1 Lake St.
Upper Saddle River, NJ 07458
Ph: (201)236-7000   Fax: 800-445-6991
Fr: 800-428-5331
URL: http://www.phptr.com/index.asp?rl=1

National Center for Construction Educ. 1998. $18.67. 92 pages.

★1468★ Opportunities in Building Construction Trades

The McGraw-Hill Companies
PO Box 182604
Columbus, OH 43272
Fax: (614)759-3749   Fr: 877-883-5524
E-mail: customer.service@mcgraw-hill.com
URL: http://www.mcgraw-hill.com

Michael Sumichrast. Second edition, 1998. $14.95; $11.95 (paper). 104 pages. From custom builder to rehabber, the many kinds of companies that employ craftspeople and contractors are explored. Includes job descriptions, requirements, and salaries for dozens of specialties within the construction industry. Contains a complete list of Bureau of Apprenticeship and Training state and area offices. Illustrated.

★1469★ Opportunities in Masonry Careers

The McGraw-Hill Companies
PO Box 182604
Columbus, OH 43272
Fax: (614)759-3749   Fr: 877-883-5524
E-mail: customer.service@mcgraw-hill.com
URL: http://www.mcgraw-hill.com

Chris Santilli. 1994. $11.95 (paper). 147 pages.

★1470★ Your Opportunities in the Trades

Energeia Publishing, Inc.
1307 Fairmount Ave., S
Salem, OR 97302-4313
Ph: (503)362-1480   Fax: (503)362-2123
Fr: 800-639-6048

Ramel Waltman. 1994. $2.50 (paper). 8 pages. Covers the construction and building industries.

TRADESHOWS

★1471★ Brick Show

Brick Industry Association
1850 Centennial Park Dr., Ste. 301
Reston, VA 20191
Ph: (703)620-0010   Fax: (703)620-3928
E-mail: brickinfo@bia.org
URL: http://www.bia.org

Annual. **Primary Exhibits:** Displays related to the brick industry.

★1472★ ICCON - International Commercial Construction Exposition

National Association of Home Builders of the United States
1201 15th St. NW
Washington, DC 20005
Ph: (202)266-8200   Fax: (202)266-8223
Fr: 800-368-5242
E-mail: exposales@nahb.com
URL: http://www.nahb.org

Annual. **Primary Exhibits:** Equipment, supplies, and services for the construction industries.

★1473★ World of Concrete

Hanley-Wood Exhibitions
8600 Freeport Parkway
Irving, TX 75063
Ph: (972)536-6300   Fax: (972)536-6301
Fr: 800-869-8522
URL: http://www.hanley-wood.com

Annual. **Primary Exhibits:** Equipment and services for the construction industry. **Dates and Locations:** 2008 Jan 22-25; Las Vegas, NV; 2009 Feb 03-06; Las Vegas, NV.

OTHER SOURCES

★1474★ Associated Builders and Contractors (ABC)

4250 N Fairfax Dr., 9th Fl.
Arlington, VA 22203-1607
Ph: (703)812-2000   Fax: (703)812-8200
E-mail: gotquestions@abc.org
URL: http://www.abc.org

Description: Construction contractors, subcontractors, suppliers, and associates. Aims to foster and perpetuate the principles of rewarding construction workers and management on the basis of merit. Sponsors management education programs and craft training; also sponsors apprenticeship and skill training programs. Disseminates technological and labor relations information.

★1475★ **Associated General Contractors of America (AGC)**
2300 Wilson Blvd., Ste. 400
Arlington, VA 22201
Ph: (703)548-3118   Fax: (703)548-3119
Fr: 800-242-1767
E-mail: info@agc.org
URL: http://www.agc.org

Description: General construction contractors; subcontractors; industry suppliers; service firms. Provides market services through its divisions. Conducts special conferences and seminars designed specifically for construction firms. Compiles statistics on job accidents reported by member firms. Maintains 65 committees, including joint cooperative committees with other associations and liaison committees with federal agencies.

★1476★ **Associated Specialty Contractors (ASC)**
3 Bethesda Metro Ctr., Ste. 1100
Bethesda, MD 20814
Ph: (703)548-3118
E-mail: dgw@necanet.org
URL: http://www.assoc-spec-con.org

Description: Works to promote efficient management and productivity. Coordinates the work of specialized branches of the industry in management information, research, public information, government relations and construction relations. Serves as a liaison among specialty trade associations in the areas of public relations, government relations, and with other organizations. Seeks to avoid unnecessary duplication of effort and expense or conflicting programs

among affiliates. Identifies areas of interest and problems shared by members, and develops positions and approaches on such problems.

★1477★ **Building Trades**
Delphi Productions
3159 6th St.
Boulder, CO 80304
Ph: (303)443-2100   Fax: (303)443-4022
Fr: 888-443-2400
E-mail: support@delphivideo.com
URL: http://www.delphivideo.com

$95.00. 46 minutes. Part of the Careers for the 21st Century Video Library.

★1478★ **COIN Career Guidance System**
COIN Educational Products
3361 Executive Pky., Ste. 302
Toledo, OH 43606
Ph: (419)536-5353   Fax: (419)536-7056
Fr: 800-274-8515
URL: http://www.coinedu.com/

CD-ROM. Provides career information through seven cross-referenced files covering postsecondary schools, college majors, vocational programs, military service, apprenticeship programs, financial aid, and scholarships. Apprenticeship file describes national apprenticeship training programs, including information on how to apply, contact agencies, and program content. Military file describes more than 200 military occupations and training opportunities related to civilian employment.

★1479★ **Mason Contractors Association of America (MCAA)**
33 S Roselle Rd.
Schaumburg, IL 60193
Ph: (847)301-0001   Fax: (847)301-1110
Fr: 800-536-2225

URL: http://www.masoncontractors.org

Description: Masonry construction firms. Conducts specialized education and research programs. Compiles statistics.

★1480★ **The Masonry Society (TMS)**
3970 Broadway, Ste. 201-D
Boulder, CO 80304-1135
Ph: (303)939-9700   Fax: (303)541-9215
E-mail: info@masonrysociety.org
URL: http://www.masonrysociety.org

Description: Represents individuals interested in the art and science of masonry. Serves as professional, technical and educational association dedicated to the advancement and knowledge of masonry. Gathers and disseminates technical information.

★1481★ **National Association of Women in Construction (NAWIC)**
327 S Adams St.
Fort Worth, TX 76104
Ph: (817)877-5551   Fax: (817)877-0324
Fr: 800-552-3506
E-mail: nawic@nawic.org
URL: http://www.nawic.org

Description: Seeks to enhance the success of women in the construction industry.

★1482★ **Women in Nontraditional Careers: An Introduction**
Her Own Words
PO Box 5264
Madison, WI 53705
Ph: (608)271-7083   Fax: (608)271-0209
E-mail: herownword@aol.com
URL: http://www.herownwords.com/

Video. Jocelyn Riley. $95.00. 15 minutes. Resource guide also available for $45.00.

Broadcast Technicians

★1483★ Advanced Imaging

Cygnus Business Media Inc.
3 Huntington Quadrangle, Ste. 301 N
Melville, NY 11747
Ph: (631)845-2700   Fax: (631)845-7109
Fr: 800-308-6397
URL: http://www.cygnusb2b.com

Magazine covering the full range of electronic imaging technology and its uses.

★1484★ AV Video & Multimedia Producer

Access Intelligence L.L.C.
4 Choke Cherry Rd., 2nd Fl.
Rockville, MD 20850
Ph: (301)354-2000   Fax: (301)309-3847
Fr: 800-777-5006

Monthly. Magazine covering audio-visual, video and multimedia production, presentation, people, technology and techniques.

★1485★ Billboard Radio Monitor

VNU Business Media USA
770 Broadway
New York, NY 10003
Ph: (646)654-4500
URL: http://www.billboardradiomonitor.com/radiomonitor/index.jsp

Weekly. $299.00 for individuals, per year; $6.99 for single issue. Magazine covering every format of music radio, regulatory developments, news radio, talk radio, and satellite radio.

★1486★ Broadcasting & Cable

Reed Business Information
360 Park Ave. S
New York, NY 10010
Ph: (646)746-6400   Fax: (646)746-7431
URL: http://www.reedbusiness.com

Weekly. $199.99/year for individuals. News magazine covering The Fifth Estate (radio,

TV, cable, and satellite), and the regulatory commissions involved.

★1487★ CED (Communications Engineering & Design)

Communications Engineering & Design
PO Box 266007
Highlands Ranch, CO 80163-6007
Ph: (303)470-4800   Fax: (303)470-4890
URL: http://www.cedmagazine.com

Monthly. Technical/business publication serving the engineering/management community within broadband/cable TV networks, telecommunications carriers, data and interactive networks.

★1488★ Community Radio News

National Federation of Community Broadcasters
1970 Broadway, Ste. 1000
Oakland, CA 94612
Ph: (510)451-8200   Fax: (510)451-8208
E-mail: newsletter@nfcb.org
URL: http://www.nfcb.org

Description: Monthly. Serves as a medium of communication for independent, community-licensed radio stations. Contains brief articles and news items on such topics as public broadcasting and programming, legislative developments, activities of the Federal Communications Commission, and local stations. Recurring features include notices of grants and awards, job openings, and a calendar of events/conferences for noncommercial broadcasters.

★1489★ Entertainment Employment Journal

Studiolot Publishing
5632 Van Nuys Blvd., Ste. 320
Van Nuys, CA 91401-4600
Ph: (818)776-2800   Fr: 800-335-4335
E-mail: support@eejonline.com
URL: http://www.eej.com

Semimonthly. Subscription included in membership. Trade magazine covering business and technical careers in broadcast, electronic media, and motion pictures.

★1490★ Feminist Media Studies

Taylor & Francis Group Journals
325 Chestnut St., Ste. 800
Philadelphia, PA 19106
Ph: (215)625-8900   Fax: (215)625-8914
Fr: 800-354-1420
URL: http://www.tandf.co.uk/journals/titles/14680777.asp

Quarterly. $552.00/year for institutions, print and online; $106.00/year for individuals, print only; $524.00/year for institutions, online only. Journal covering media and communication studies.

★1491★ FMedia!

FM Atlas Publishing
PO Box 336
Esko, MN 55733-0336
Ph: (218)879-7676   Fr: 800-605-2219
URL: http://members.aol.com/fmatlas/home.html

Description: Monthly. Lists information on the facilities and formats of FM radio, including new station grants and applications. Also provides official and unofficial news and comments, as well as FM Dxing and FM reception concerns. Recurring features include letters to the editor, news of research, job listings, and notices of publications available.

★1492★ The Hollywood Reporter

The Nielsen Co.
770 Broadway
New York, NY 10003
Ph: (646)654-5000   Fax: (646)654-5002
URL: http://www.hollywoodreporter.com/thr/index.jsp

Daily (morn.). $3.00 for single issue; $6.00/year for U.S., weekly; $299.00/year for individuals, print; $175.00/year for U.S., weekly print; $299.00/year for U.S., print/online combination; $265.00/year for U.S., weekly print/online combination. Film, TV, and entertainment trade newspaper.

★1493★ Journal of the Audio Engineering Society

Audio Engineering Society Inc.
60 East 42nd St., Rm. 2520
New York, NY 10165-2520
Ph: (212)661-8528   Fax: (212)682-0477
URL: http://www.aes.org/journal

Monthly. $210.00/year for individuals, surface mail; $260.00/year for individuals, airmail. Newsletter reporting engineering developments and scientific progress in audio engineering for audio professionals, educators, executives, consumers, and students.

★1494★ Millimeter

Penton Media Inc.
9800 Metcalf Ave.
Overland Park, KS 66212
Ph: (913)341-1300   Fax: (913)967-1898
URL: http://digitalcontentproducer.com

Monthly. Magazine focusing on the process of motion picture and television production.

★1495★ Mix

Penton Media
249 W 17th St.
New York, NY 10011
Ph: (212)204-4200
E-mail: gpetersen@mixonline.com
URL: http://mixonline.com

Monthly. $40.00/year for individuals, 13 issues. Magazine focusing on audio and video music production in the recording industry. Covers a wide range of topics including: recording, live sound and production, broadcast production, audio for film and video, and music technology.

★1496★ Post

Post Pro Publishing Inc.
One Park Ave.
New York, NY 10016
Ph: (212)951-6600   Fax: (212)951-6793
URL: http://www.postmagazine.com/post

Monthly. Magazine serving the field of television, film, video production and post-production.

★1497★ Producers Masterguide

Producers Masterguide
60 E 8th St., 34th Fl.
New York, NY 10003-6514
Ph: (212)777-4002   Fax: (212)777-4101
URL: http://
www.producers.masterguide.com

Annual. $155.00/year for U.S. $165.00/year for Canada; $195.00/year for other countries. An international film and TV production directory and guide for the professional motion picture, broadcast television, feature film, TV commercial, cable/satellite, digital and videotape industries in the U.S., Canada, the UK, the Caribbean Islands, Mexico, Australia, New Zealand, Europe, Israel, Morocco, the Far East, and South America.

★1498★ QST

American Radio Relay League Inc.
225 Main St.
Newington, CT 06111-1494
Ph: (860)594-0200   Fax: (860)594-0259
Fr: 888-277-5289
E-mail: qst@arrl.org
URL: http://www.arrl.org/qst/

Monthly. $34.00/year for individuals. Amateur radio magazine.

★1499★ SMPTE Journal

Society of Motion Picture and Television
  Engineers
3 Barker Ave.
White Plains, NY 10601
Ph: (914)761-1100
URL: http://www.smpte.org

Monthly. $130.00/year for individuals. Journal containing articles pertaining to new developments in motion picture and television technology; standards and recommended practices; general news of the industry.

★1500★ TelevisionWeek

Crain Communications Inc.
1155 Gratiot Ave.
PO Box 07924
Detroit, MI 48207-2997
Ph: (313)446-6000   Fax: (313)446-0347
Fr: 888-909-9111
URL: http://www.tvweek.com/

Weekly. $119.00/year for individuals; $171.00/year for Canada, including GST; $309.00/year for other countries, airmail. Newspaper covering management, programming, cable and trends in the television and the media industry.

PLACEMENT AND JOB REFERRAL SERVICES

★1501★ Broadcast Foundation of College/University Students (BROADCAST)

89 Longview Rd.
Port Washington, NY 11050
Ph: (516)883-0159   Fax: (516)883-0159
E-mail: rstarleton@aol.com

Members: College students interested in broadcasting and professional broadcasters interested in encouraging practical broadcasting experience in colleges and universities. **Activities:** Conducts annual survey of all professional broadcasting stations for part-time and summer employment for college students. Sponsors job advisory and placement service.

★1502★ Health Science Communications Association (HeSCA)

39 Wedgewood Dr., Ste. A
Jewett City, CT 06351-2420
Ph: (860)376-5915   Fax: (860)376-6621

E-mail: hesca@hesca.org
URL: http://www.hesca.org

Description: Represents media managers, graphic artists, biomedical librarians, producers, faculty members of health science and veterinary medicine schools, health professional organizations, and industry representatives. Acts as a clearinghouse for information used by professionals engaged in health science communications. Coordinates Media Festivals Program that recognizes outstanding media productions in the health sciences. Offers placement service.

★1503★ National Association of Broadcasters (NAB)

1771 N St. NW
Washington, DC 20036
Ph: (202)429-5300   Fax: (202)429-4199
E-mail: nab@nab.org
URL: http://www.nab.org

Description: Representatives of radio and television stations and networks; associate members include producers of equipment and programs. Seeks to ensure the viability, strength, and success of free, over-the-air broadcasters; serves as an information resource to the industry. Monitors and reports on events regarding radio and television broadcasting. Maintains Broadcasting Hall of Fame. Offers minority placement service and employment clearinghouse.

EMPLOYER DIRECTORIES AND NETWORKING LISTS

★1504★ Bacon's Metro California Media

Cision US Inc.
332 S Michigan Ave., Ste. 900
Chicago, IL 60604
Ph: (312)922-2400   Fax: (312)922-9387
Fr: (866)639-5087
URL: http://www.bacons.com

Annual, November; latest edition 2005. $385.65 for individuals. Covers consumer media in the state of California, including newspapers, radio television and cable stations, magazines, and broadcast programs, ethnic media, news services and syndicates. Entries include: Name, address, phone, names of editors and creative staff, with titles or indication of assignments. Arrangement: Geographical, classified by type of outlet. Indexes: Alphabetical.

★1505★ Bacon's Radio/TV/Cable Directory, Volume 1

Cision US Inc.
332 S Michigan Ave., Ste. 900
Chicago, IL 60604
Ph: (312)922-2400   Fax: (312)922-9387
Fr: (866)639-5087
URL: http://www.bacons.com

Annual; latest edition 2007. $450.00 for individuals. Covers over 13,500 radio and television stations, including college radio and public television stations, and cable companies. Entries include: For radio and television stations–Call letters, address, phone, names and titles of key personnel; programs, times broadcast, name of contact, network affiliation, frequency or channel number, target audience data. For cable companies–Name, address, phone, description of activities. Arrangement: Geographical.

★1506★ **BIA's Television Yearbook**

BIA Financial Network Inc.
15120 Enterprise Ct.
Chantilly, VA 20151
Ph: (703)818-2425 Fax: (703)803-3299
Fr: 800-331-5086
E-mail: sales@bia.com
URL: http://www.bia.com

Annual, May. $150.00 for individuals. Covers U.S. Television markets and their inclusive stations, television equipment manufacturers, and related service providers and trade associations. Entries include: For stations–Call letters, address; name and phone number of general manager, owner, and other key personnel; technical attributes, rep. firm, network affiliation, last acquisition date and price and ratings for total day and prime time. For others–Company or organization name, address, phone, description. Arrangement: Classified by market. Indexes: Numerical by market rank; call letters.

★1507★ **Bowker's News Media Directory**

R.R. Bowker L.L.C.
630 Central Ave.
New Providence, NJ 07974
Ph: (908)286-1090 Fr: 888-269-5372
E-mail: wpn@bowker.com
URL: http://www.bowker.com

Annual; latest edition November 2006. $635.00 for individuals, set; $385.00 for individuals, per volume. Covers, in three separate volumes, syndicates and over 8,500 daily and weekly newspapers; 1,750 newsletters; over 16,800 radio and television stations; 5,500 magazines; 1,000 internal publications. Entries include: Name of publication or station, address, phone, fax, e-mail and URL, names of executives, editors, writers, etc., as appropriate. Broadcasting and magazine volumes include data on kinds of material accepted. Technical and mechanical requirements for publications are given. Arrangement: Magazines are classified by subject; newspapers and broadcasting stations geographical. Indexes: Newspaper department/editor by interest, metro area, feature syndicate subject; magazine subject, publication title; television director/personnel by subject, radio personnel and director by subject.

★1508★ **Broadcasting & Cable Yearbook**

R.R. Bowker L.L.C.
630 Central Ave.
New Providence, NJ 07974
Ph: (908)286-1090 Fr: 888-269-5372

URL: http://www.bowker.com

Annual; latest edition 2007, published October 2006. $235.00 for individuals. Covers over 17,000 television and radio stations in the United States, its territories, and Canada; cable MSOs and their individual systems; television and radio networks, broadcast and cable group owners, station representatives, satellite networks and services, film companies, advertising agencies, government agencies, trade associations, schools, and suppliers of professional and technical services, including books, serials, and videos; communications lawyers. Entries include: Company name, address, phone, fax, names of executives. Station listings include broadcast power, other operating details. Arrangement: Stations and systems are geographical, others are alphabetical. Indexes: Alphabetical.

★1509★ **CPB Public Broadcasting Directory**

Corporation for Public Broadcasting
401 9th St. NW
Washington, DC 20004-2129
Ph: (202)879-9600 Fax: (202)879-9700
Fr: 800-272-2190
URL: http://www.cpb.org/stations/publicdirectory/

Annual. Covers public television and radio stations, national and regional public broadcasting organizations and networks, state government agencies and commissions, and other related organizations. Entries include: For radio and television stations–Station call letters, frequency or channel, address, phone, licensee name, licensee type, date on air, antenna height, area covered, names and titles of key personnel. For organizations–Name, address, phone, name and title of key personnel. Arrangement: National and regional listings are alphabetical; state groups and the public radio and television stations are each geographical; other organizations and agencies are alphabetical. Indexes: Geographical, personnel, call letter, licensee type (all in separate indexes for radio and television).

★1510★ **FM Atlas**

FM Atlas Publishing
PO Box 336
Esko, MN 55733-0336
Ph: (218)879-7676 Fr: 800-605-2219
URL: http://members.aol.com/fmatlas/home.html

Irregular; latest edition 20th. $21.00 for individuals. Covers approximately 10,500 FM stations located in North America. Entries include: Call letters, location, musical format, transmitting radius in kilometers, whether stereo or monaural, FM subcarriers, etc. Arrangement: Geographical, then by frequency.

★1511★ **International Motion Picture Almanac**

Quigley Publishing Company Inc.
64 Wintergreen Ln.
Groton, MA 01450
Ph: (978)448-0272 Fax: (978)448-9325
Fr: 800-231-8239
URL: http://hometown.aol.com/quigleypub/mp.html

Annual, January; Latest edition 2007. $195.00 for individuals. Covers motion picture producing companies, firms serving the industry, equipment manufacturers, casting agencies, literary agencies, advertising and publicity representatives, motion picture theater circuits, buying and booking organizations, independent theaters, international film festivals, associations, theatre equipment supply companies. Entries include: Generally, company name, address, phone. For manufacturers–Products or service provided, name of contact. For producing companies–Additional details. For theaters–Name of owner, screen size. Companion volume is the "International Television and Video Almanac". Arrangement: Classified by service or activity.

★1512★ **International Television and Video Almanac**

Quigley Publishing Company Inc.
64 Wintergreen Ln.
Groton, MA 01450-4129
Ph: (860)228-0247 Fax: (860)228-0157
Fr: 800-231-8239
URL: http://hometown.aol.com/quigleypub/mp.html

Annual, January; latest edition 2007. $175.00 for individuals. Covers "Who's Who in Motion Pictures and Television and Home Video," television networks, major program producers, major group station owners, cable television companies, distributors, firms serving the television and home video industry, equipment manufacturers, casting agencies, literary agencies, advertising and publicity representatives, television stations, associations, list of feature films produced for television, statistics, industry's year in review, award winners, satellite and wireless cable providers, primetime programming, video producers, distributors, wholesalers. Entries include: Generally, company name, address, phone; manufacturer and service listings may include description of products and services and name of contact; producing, distributing, and station listings include additional details and contacts for cable and broadcast networks. Arrangement: Classified by service or activity. Indexes: Full.

★1513★ **The R & R Directory**

Radio and Records Inc.
2049 Century Pk. E, 41St. Fl.
Los Angeles, CA 90067-4004
Ph: (310)553-4330 Fax: (310)203-9763
E-mail: moreinfo@rronline.com
URL: http://www.radioandrecords.com/RRDirectory/Directory_Main.as

Semiannual, spring and fall. $75.00. Covers more than 3,000 radio group owners, equipment manufacturers, jingle producers, TV production houses and spot producers, record companies, representative firms, research companies, consulting firms, media brokers, networks, program suppliers, trade associations, and other organizations involved in the radio and record industry. Entries include: Organization name, address, phone, fax, e-mail, name and title of contacts, branch offices or subsidiary names and locations. Arrangement: Alphabetical; classified by subject. Indexes: Company.

★1514★ **Radio Advertising Source**
SRDS
1700 Higgins Rd.
Des Plaines, IL 60018-5605
Ph: (847)375-5000   Fax: (847)375-5001
Fr: 800-851-7737
URL: http://www.srds.com

Quarterly. $614.00 for individuals. Covers over 10,500 AM and FM stations, networks, syndicators, group owners, and representative firms. Entries include: Call letters, name of owning company, address, phone; names of representatives and station personnel; demonstration detail, station format, signal strength, programming opportunities, special features. Arrangement: Geographical by state, then by Arbitron metro and non-metro areas.

★1515★ **Radio Programming Profile**
BF/Communication Services Inc.
66 Chestnut Ln.
Woodbury, NY 11797
Ph: (516)364-2593
URL: http://www.prplace.com/pr_pub.html

Three times yearly. Covers about 3,000 AM and FM radio stations in top 200 markets, with hour-by-hour format information (type of music, news, etc.) for each. Entries include: Station call letters, address, phone, names of executives, hour-by-hour format information. Arrangement: Alphabetical by market and call letters. Volume 1 has top 70 ranking markets; volume 2 has markets 71-200.

★1516★ **RTNDA Communicator-
Directory Issues**
Radio-Television News Directors Association
1600 K St. NW, No. 700
Washington, DC 20006-2838
Ph: (202)659-6510   Fax: (202)223-4007
Fr: 800-80R-TNDA
URL: http://www.rtnda.org

Semiannual, January and July. Number of listings: 3,000; membership includes Canada and some foreign countries. Entries include: Member name, address, phone, and name of radio or television station, network, or other news organization with which affiliated. Arrangement: Same information given in alphabetical and geographical arrangements.

★1517★ **Television & Cable Factbook**
Warren Communications News Inc.
2115 Ward Ct. NW
Washington, DC 20037
Ph: (202)872-9202   Fax: (202)318-8350
Fr: 800-771-9202
URL: http://www.warren-news.com/factbook.htm

Annual. $925.00 for individuals, print product; $995.00 for individuals, full online database. Covers commercial and noncommercial television stations and networks, including educational, low-power and instructional TV stations, as well as translators; United States cable television systems; cable and television group owners; program and service suppliers; and brokerage and financing companies. Entries include: For stations–Call letters, licensee name and address, studio address and phone; identification of owners, sales and legal representatives and chief station personnel; rates, technical data, map of service area, and Nielsen circulation data. For cable systems–Name, address, basic and pay subscribers, programming and fees, physical plant; names of personnel and ownership. Arrangement: Geographical by state, province, city, county, or country. Indexes: Call letters; product/service; name; general subject.

★1518★ **TV and Cable Source**
SRDS
1700 Higgins Rd.
Des Plaines, IL 60018-5605
Ph: (847)375-5000   Fax: (847)375-5001
Fr: 800-851-7737
URL: http://www.srds.com

Quarterly. $602.00 for single issue. Covers all domestic and international commercial television stations and networks; public television stations, cable networks, systems, interconnects, rep. firms, and group owners. Includes separate section showing production specifications of stations and systems. Entries include: Call letters, parent company, address, phone, representative, personnel, facilities, special features, programming. Production specifications section shows call letters or system name, address, and preferred specifications for ad copy. Arrangement: Classified by DMA ranking, then by call letters.

HANDBOOKS AND MANUALS

★1519★ **Breaking into Television**
Peterson's Guides
2000 Lenox Dr.
Box 67005
Lawrenceville, NJ 08648
Ph: (609)896-1800   Fax: (609)896-4531
Fr: 800-338-3282
E-mail: custsvc@petersons.com
URL: http://www.petersons.com

Dan Weaver. 1998. $14.95 (paper). 244 pages. Explains how to get a job in the

television industry, with a list of internship opportunities.

★1520★ **Careers in Communications**
The McGraw-Hill Companies
PO Box 182604
Columbus, OH 43272
Fax: (614)759-3749   Fr: 877-883-5524
E-mail: customer.service@mcgraw-hill.com
URL: http://www.mcgraw-hill.com

Shonan Noronha. Fourth edition, 2004. $15.95 (paper). 192 pages. Examines the fields of journalism, photography, radio, television, film, public relations, and advertising. Gives concrete details on job locations and how to secure a job. Suggests many resources for job hunting.

★1521★ **Great Jobs for Music Majors**
The McGraw-Hill Companies
PO Box 182604
Columbus, OH 43272
Fax: (614)759-3749   Fr: 877-883-5524
E-mail: customer.service@mcgraw-hill.com
URL: http://www.mcgraw-hill.com

Jan Goldberg, Stephen Lambert, Julie DeGalan. Second edition, 2004. $15.95 (paper). 180 pages.

★1522★ **Inside Broadcasting**
Routledge
270 Madison Ave.
New York, NY 10016
Ph: (212)216-7800   Fax: (212)563-2269
URL: http://www.routledge.com/

1997. $24.99. 232 pages. Part of the Career Builders Guide Series.

★1523★ **Lights, Camera, Action!:
Careers in Film, Television, & Video**
BFI
601 N. Morton St.
Bloomington, IN 47404-3797
Ph: (812)855-4203   Fax: (812)855-7931
Fr: 800-842-6796

Josephine Langham. Second edition, 1997. $22.50 (paper). 287 pages.

★1524★ **On-the-Air Anywhere: A
Beginner's Guide to Broadcasting**
Dorrance Publishing Company, Inc.
701 Smithfield St., Ste. 301
Pittsburgh, PA 15222
Ph: (412)288-4543   Fax: (412)288-1786
Fr: 800-788-7654
URL: http://www.dorrancepublishing.com/

Charlie Pullen. 1996. $8.00 (paper). 80 pages.

★1525★ **Opportunities in Broadcasting
Careers**
The McGraw-Hill Companies
PO Box 182604
Columbus, OH 43272
Fax: (614)759-3749   Fr: 877-883-5524

E-mail: customer.service@mcgraw-hill.com
URL: http://www.mcgraw-hill.com

Elmo I. Ellis. 2004. $14.95; $11.95 (paper). 176 pages. Discusses opportunities and job search techniques in broadcasting, television, and radio. Illustrated.

★1526★ **Opportunities in Television and Video Careers**

The McGraw-Hill Companies
PO Box 182604
Columbus, OH 43272
Fax: (614)759-3749   Fr: 877-883-5524
E-mail: customer.service@mcgraw-hill.com
URL: http://www.mcgraw-hill.com

Shonan Noronha. Second edition, 2003. $12.95 (paper). 160 pages. Details the employment opportunities open in television, cable, corporate video, institutional and government media, including independent production, and discusses how to land a job. Illustrated.

★1527★ **Working in Show Business: Behind-the-Scenes Careers in Theater, Film and Television**

Back Stage Books
545 Eighth St. SE
Washington, DC 20003
Ph: (202)544-5744
E-mail: backstagebooks@aol.com
URL: http://www.backstagebooks.com

Lynne Rogers. 1998. $18.95 (paper). 242 pages.

EMPLOYMENT AGENCIES AND SEARCH FIRMS

★1528★ **Baker Scott & Co.**

1259 Rte. 46
Parsippany, NJ 07054
Ph: (973)263-3355   Fax: (973)263-9255
E-mail: exec.search@bakerscott.com
URL: http://www.bakerscott.com

Consulting services include executive recruiting, employment attitude surveys, and screening organization plans. Industries served: telecommunication, cable TV, broadcasting entertainment, and financial institutions. The firm is intergrated horizontally across functional discipline such as accounting, administration, call center, data processing, engineering, finance, genral operations, marketing and technical & plant operations.

★1529★ **The Cheyenne Group**

60 E. 42nd St., Ste. 2821
New York, NY 10165
Ph: (212)471-5000   Fax: (212)471-5050
E-mail: contact_us@cheyennegroup.com
URL: http://www.cheyennegroup.com

Executive search firm.

★1530★ **Jim Young & Associates Inc.**

Holland Creek
1424 Clear Lake Rd.
Weatherford, TX 76086-5806
Ph: (817)599-7623   Fax: (817)599-4483
Fr: 800-433-2160
E-mail: jyoung@staffing.net

Specializes in the placement of cable television, telecommunications, cellular telephone, RF engineering and satellite communications personnel. Industries served: cable television, telecommunications, and cellular.

★1531★ **Warren and Morris Ltd.**

2190 Carmel Valley Rd.
Del Mar, CA 92014
Ph: (858)481-3388   Fax: (858)481-6221
E-mail: info@warrenmorrisltd.com
URL: http://www.warrenmorrisltd.com

Offers the following services: executive search and recruitment, providing clients with pre-screened, qualified candidates; and EEO management and labor relations consulting. Industries served: cable TV and wireless communications, multimedia and competitive telephone.

ONLINE JOB SOURCES AND SERVICES

★1532★ **Society of Broadcast Engineers Job Line**

Ph: (317)846-9000   Fax: (317)846-9120
E-mail: kjones@sbe.org
URL: http://www.sbe.org/jobline.html

Description: Job Line is one benefit of membership in the Society of Broadcast Engineers. Includes a resume service to distribute resumes to employers, job contact information, and descriptions of job openings. Also accessible via telephone.

TRADESHOWS

★1533★ **CES - Spring**

CEMA - Consumer Electronics
  Manufacturers Association
2500 Wilson Blvd.
Arlington, VA 22201-3834
Ph: (703)907-7600   Fax: (703)907-7675
Fr: (866)233-7968
E-mail: cea@ce.org
URL: http://www.cesweb.org

Annual. **Primary Exhibits:** Audio hardware, computer and multimedia hardware, cellular and wireless communications, home office equipment, video hardware, home theater products, and digital photography equipment, accessories, audio hardware and software, blank media, bluetooth technology, broadband technology, computer hardware & software, digital car, digital hollywood, digital TV/HDTV, E-Commerce, electronic gaming, global positioning systems, hand-held information devices, high-end audio, home appliances, home/personal health-care, home security & automation, home theater & custom installation, internet applications & services, mobile electronics, MP3/internet audio, personal electronics, photography/digital imaging, retail resources, robotics, satellite systems, small office/home office, speech technology, telematics & vehicle navigation, telephony equipment, video hardware & software, WI-FI technology, wireless/mobile communications.

★1534★ **National Association of State Telecommunications Directors Conference**

National Association of State
  Telecommunications Directors
2760 Research Park Dr.
PO Box 11910
Lexington, KY 40578-1910
Ph: (859)244-8186   Fax: (859)244-8001
E-mail: pjohson@csg.org
URL: http://www.nastd.org

Annual. **Primary Exhibits:** Exhibits for state telecommunications systems.

★1535★ **SMPTE Technical Conference Exhibition**

Society of Motion Picture and Television
  Engineers
3 Barker Ave.
White Plains, NY 10601
Ph: (914)761-1100   Fax: (914)761-3115
E-mail: smpte@smpte.org
URL: http://www.smpte.org

Annual. **Primary Exhibits:** Equipment, lights, cameras, film, tape, and lenses.

★1536★ **Society of Broadcast Engineers Engineering Conference**

Society of Broadcast Engineers
9247 N Meridian St., Ste. 305
Indianapolis, IN 46260
Ph: (317)846-9000   Fax: (317)846-9120
URL: http://www.sbe.org

Annual. **Primary Exhibits:** Equipment, supplies, and services for the broadcast industry.

★1537★ **Southern States Communication Association Convention**

Southern States Communication
  Association
North Carolina University
Communication Department
201 Winston Hall Campus Box 8104
Raleigh, NC 27695
Ph: (919)515-9736   Fax: (919)515-9456
E-mail: ca.smith@ncsu.edu
URL: http://www.ssca.net

Annual. **Primary Exhibits:** Communications equipment; textbooks.

OTHER SOURCES

★1538★ Association for Educational Communications and Technology (AECT)

1800 N Stonelake Dr., Ste. 2
Bloomington, IN 47404
Ph: (812)335-7675   Fax: (812)335-7678
Fr: 877-677-AECT
E-mail: aect@aect.org
URL: http://www.aect.org

Description: Instructional technology professionals. Provides leadership in educational communications and technology by linking professionals holding a common interest in the use of educational technology and its application of the learning process.

★1539★ Corporation for Public Broadcasting (CPB)

401 9th St. NW
Washington, DC 20004-2129
Ph: (202)879-9600   Fax: (202)879-9700
Fr: 800-272-2190
E-mail: comments@cpb.org
URL: http://www.cpb.org

Description: Promotes and finances the growth and development of noncommercial radio and television. Makes grants to local public television and radio stations, program producers, and program distribution networks; studies emerging technologies; works to provide adequate long-range financing from the U.S. government and other sources for public broadcasting. Supports children's services; compiles statistics; sponsors training programs.

★1540★ Country Radio Broadcasters (CRB)

819 18th Ave. S
Nashville, TN 37203
Ph: (615)327-4487   Fax: (615)329-4492
E-mail: info@crb.org
URL: http://www.crb.org

Description: Seeks to advance and promote the study of the science of broadcasting through the mutual exchange of ideas by conducting seminars and workshops, as well as providing scholarships to broadcasting students.

★1541★ Media Alliance (MA)

1904 Franklin St., Ste. 500
Oakland, CA 94612
Ph: (510)832-9000   Fax: (510)238-8557
E-mail: information@media-alliance.org
URL: http://www.media-alliance.org

Description: Writers, photographers, editors, broadcast workers, public relations practitioners, videographers, filmmakers, commercial artists and other media workers and aspiring media workers. Supports free press and independent, alternative journalism that services progressive politics and social justice.

★1542★ Media and the Arts Occupations

Delphi Productions
3159 6th St.
Boulder, CO 80304
Ph: (303)443-2100   Fax: (303)443-4022
Fr: 888-443-2400
E-mail: support@delphivideo.com
URL: http://www.delphivideo.com

$95.00. 50 minutes. Part of the Careers for the 21st Century Video Library.

★1543★ National Association of Black Owned Broadcasters (NABOB)

1155 Connecticut Ave. NW, Ste. 600
Washington, DC 20036
Ph: (202)463-8970   Fax: (202)429-0657
E-mail: nabob@nabob.org
URL: http://www.nabob.org

Description: Black broadcast station owners; black formatted stations not owned or controlled by blacks; organizations having an interest in the black consumer market or black broadcast industry; individuals interested in becoming owners; and communications schools, departments, and professional groups and associations. Represents the interests of existing and potential black radio and television stations. Works with the Office of Federal Procurement Policy to determine which government contracting major advertisers and advertising agencies are complying with government initiatives to increase the amount of advertising dollars received by minority-owned firms. Conducts lobbying activities; provides legal representation for the protection of minority ownership policies. Sponsors annual Communications Awards Dinner each March. Conducts workshops; compiles statistics.

★1544★ National Cable and Telecommunications Association (NCTA)

25 Massachusetts Ave. NW, Ste. 100
Washington, DC 20001
Ph: (202)222-2300   Fax: (202)222-2514
E-mail: webmaster@ncta.com
URL: http://www.ncta.com

Description: Franchised cable operators, programmers, and cable networks; associate members are cable hardware suppliers and distributors; affiliate members are brokerage and law firms and financial institutions; state and regional cable television associations cooperate, but are not affiliated, with the organization. Serves as national medium for exchange of experiences and opinions through research, study, discussion, and publications. Represents the cable industry before Congress, the Federal Communications Commission and various courts on issues of primary importance. Conducts research program in conjunction with National Academy of Cable Programming. Sponsors, in conjunction with Motion Picture Association of America, the Coalition Opposing Signal Theft, an organization designed to deter cable signal theft and to develop anti-piracy materials. Provides promotional aids and information on legal, legislative and regulatory matters. Compiles statistics.

★1545★ National Religious Broadcasters (NRB)

9510 Technology Dr.
Manassas, VA 20110
Ph: (703)330-7000   Fax: (703)330-7100
E-mail: info@nrb.org
URL: http://www.nrb.org

Description: Christian communicators. Fosters electronic media access for the Gospel; promotes standards of excellence; integrity and accountability; and provides networking and fellowship opportunities for members.

★1546★ Society of Broadcast Engineers (SBE)

9102 N Meridian St., Ste. 150
Indianapolis, IN 46260
Ph: (317)846-9000   Fax: (317)846-9120
E-mail: jporay@sbe.org
URL: http://www.sbe.org

Description: Broadcast engineers, students, and broadcast professionals in closely allied fields. Promotes professional abilities of members and provides information exchange. Provides support to local chapters. Maintains certification program; represents members' interests before the Federal Communications Commission and other governmental and industrial groups. Offers educational workshops and seminars. Provides volunteer frequency coordination service for the nation's broadcasters.

★1547★ Technical & Related Occupations

Delphi Productions
3159 6th St.
Boulder, CO 80304
Ph: (303)443-2100   Fax: (303)443-4022
Fr: 888-443-2400
E-mail: support@delphivideo.com
URL: http://www.delphivideo.com

$95.00. 49 minutes. Part of the Careers for the 21st Century Video Library.

★1548★ Women in Cable Telecommunications (WICT)

PO Box 791305
Baltimore, MD 21279-1305
Ph: (703)234-9810   Fax: (703)817-1595
E-mail: bfmosley@wict.org
URL: http://www.wict.org

Description: Empowers and educates women to achieve their professional goals by providing opportunities for leadership, networking and advocacy.

Budget Analysts

SOURCES OF HELP-WANTED ADS

★1549★ Accounting and Finance

Wiley-Blackwell
350 Main St. Commerce Pl.
Malden, MA 02148
Ph: (781)388-8200   Fax: (781)388-8210
Fr: 800-759-6120
URL: http://www.blackwellpublishing.com/journal.asp?ref=0810-5391

Quarterly. $163.00/year for institutions, print plus premium online, Australia/New Zealand; $148.00/year for institutions, print plus standard online, Australia/New Zealand; $141.00/year for institutions, premium online only, Australia/New Zealand; $432.00/year for institutions, print plus premium online; $393.00/year for institutions, print plus standard online; $373.00/year for institutions, premium online only; $300.00/year for institutions, other countries, print plus premium online; $273.00/year for institutions, other countries, print plus standard online; $259.00/year for institutions, other countries, premium online only. Journal focusing on accounting and finance.

★1550★ Accounting Horizons

American Accounting Association
5717 Bessie Dr.
Sarasota, FL 34233-2399
Ph: (941)921-7747   Fax: (941)923-4093
URL: http://aaahq.org/index.cfm

Quarterly. $265.00/year for individuals, print only; $265.00/year for individuals, online, vol.13 through current issue; $290.00/year for individuals, online and print. Publication covering the banking, finance, and accounting industries.

★1551★ Boomer Market Advisor

Wiesner Publishing L.L.C.
7009 South Potomac St., Ste. 200
Centennial, CO 80112
Ph: (303)397-7600   Fax: (303)397-7619
URL: http://www.boomermarketadvisor.com

Monthly. Magazine for financial planners who work with variable products.

★1552★ Brookings Papers on Economic Activity

Brookings Institution Press
1775 Massashusetts Ave. NW
Washington, DC 20036-2188
Ph: (202)536-3600   Fax: (202)536-3623
Fr: 800-275-1447
URL: http://www.brookings.edu/press/journals.htm#bpea

Semiannual. $70.00/year for individuals; $84.00/year for institutions, other countries; $50.00/year for individuals; $64.00/year for individuals, foreign. Publication covering economics and business.

★1553★ Commercial Lending Review

Aspen Publishers Inc.
76 Ninth Ave., 7th Fl.
New York, NY 10011
Ph: (212)771-0600   Fax: (212)771-0885
Fr: 800-638-8437
URL: http://www.commerciallendingreview.com/

Bimonthly. Journal covering all aspects of lending for commercial banks, community and regional banks and other financial institutions.

★1554★ Foundations and Trends in Finance

Now Publishers
PO Box 1024
Hanover, MA 02339
Ph: (781)871-0245
URL: http://www.nowpublishers.com/product.aspx?product=FIN

Irregular. $315.00/year online only; $355.00/year print and online; $315.00/year online only; $355.00/year print and online. Academic journal that covers corporate finance, financial markets, asset pricing, and derivatives.

★1555★ Journal of Applied Finance

INFORMS
7240 Parkway Dr., Ste. 310
Hanover, MD 21076
Ph: (443)757-3500   Fax: (443)757-3515
Fr: 800-446-3676
URL: http://www.fma.org/

Journal for financial practice and education developments.

★1556★ Journal of Public Budgeting and Finance

American Association for Budget and Program Analysis
PO Box 1157
Falls Church, VA 22041
Ph: (703)941-4300   Fax: (703)941-1535

Quarterly. Journal covering public finance.

★1557★ Wilmott Magazine

John Wiley & Sons Inc.
111 River St.
Hoboken, NJ 07030-5774
Ph: (201)748-6000   Fax: (201)748-6088
Fr: 800-825-7550
URL: http://www.wilmott.com

$695/year for non-UK institutions. Journal focusing on the quantitative finance community and concentrating on practicalities.

EMPLOYER DIRECTORIES AND NETWORKING LISTS

★1558★ Barron's Finance and Investment Handbook

Barron's Educational Series Inc.
250 Wireless Blvd.
Hauppauge, NY 11788-3924
Ph: (631)434-3311   Fax: (631)434-3723
Fr: 800-645-3476
URL: http://www.barronseduc.com/0764155547.html

$39.99. Covers More than 6,000 publicly traded corporations in the U.S. and Canada.

Entries include: Name, address, phone, fax of all brokerage and mutual funds firms, banks, savings and loan companies, insurance companies, federal and state regulators, and major investment publications.

★1559★ Career Opportunities in Banking, Finance, and Insurance

Facts On File Inc.
132 W 31st St., 17th Fl.
New York, NY 10001
Ph: (212)967-8800   Fax: 800-678-3633
Fr: 800-322-8755
URL: http://www.factsonfile.com/

Latest edition 2nd, February 2007. $49.50 for individuals; $44.45 for libraries. Publication includes: Lists of colleges with programs supporting banking, finance, and industry; professional associations; professional certifications; regulatory agencies; and Internet resources for career planning. Principal content of publication consists of job descriptions for professions in the banking, finance, and insurance industries. Indexes: Alphabetical.

★1560★ City Government Finance & Taxation Directory

infoUSA Inc.
5711 S 86th Cir.
PO Box 27347
Omaha, NE 68127-0347
Ph: (402)593-4593   Fax: (402)596-7688
Fr: 800-555-6124
URL: http://www.infousa.com

Annual. Number of listings: 7,204. Entries include: Name, address, phone (including area code), size of advertisement, year first in "Yellow Pages," name of owner or manager, number of employees. Compiled from telephone company "Yellow Pages," nationwide. Arrangement: Geographical.

★1561★ Internet Guide to Personal Finance and Investment

Greenwood Publishing Group Inc.
88 Post Rd. W
Westport, CT 06881
Ph: (203)226-3571
URL: http://www.greenwood.com

Published 2001. $71.95 for single issue. Covers over 1,400 Web sites regarding personal finance and investment. Entries include: Name of Web site, URL, sponsor of site, and description of contents. Indexes: Website title; sponsor; subject.

HANDBOOKS AND MANUALS

★1562★ The Basics of Budgeting

AMACOM
1601 Broadway, 12th Fl.
New York, NY 10019
Ph: (212)586-8100   Fax: (212)903-8168
Fr: 800-262-9699
URL: http://www.amanet.org

Robert G. Finney. 1993. $19.95. 196 pages.

★1563★ Careers in Finance

The McGraw-Hill Companies
PO Box 182604
Columbus, OH 43272
Fax: (614)759-3749   Fr: 877-883-5524
E-mail: customer.service@mcgraw-hill.com
URL: http://www.mcgraw-hill.com

Trudy Ring, editor. Third edition, 2004. $15.95 and $17.95. 182 pages. Covers financial careers in such areas as higher education, corporate and public finance, and commercial and investment banking.

★1564★ Handbook of Budgeting

John Wiley & Sons Inc.
1 Wiley Dr.
Somerset, NJ 08873
Ph: (732)469-4400   Fax: (732)302-2300
Fr: 800-526-5368
E-mail: custserv@wiley.com
URL: http://www.wiley.com/WileyCDA/

Robert Rachlin, William R. Lalli, editors. Fourth edition, 2001. $170.00 (Cloth). $65.00 (Paper). 224 pages. Discusses budgeting preparation, presentation, and analysis. Contains examples of forms, techniques, and reports.

★1565★ Opportunities in Federal Government Careers

The McGraw-Hill Companies
PO Box 182604
Columbus, OH 43272
Fax: (614)759-3749   Fr: 877-883-5524
E-mail: customer.service@mcgraw-hill.com
URL: http://www.mcgraw-hill.com

Neale Baxter. Second edition, 1994. $14.95; $10.95 (paper). 150 pages. Describes the spectrum of government employment, including professional, administrative, scientific, blue-collar, clerical, and technical opportunities, and how to land a job. Illustrated. Part of the "Opportunities in ..." Series.

★1566★ The Portable MBA in Finance and Accounting

John Wiley & Sons Inc.
1 Wiley Dr.
Somerset, NJ 08873
Ph: (732)469-4400   Fax: (732)302-2300
Fr: 800-526-5368
E-mail: custserv@wiley.com

URL: http://www.wiley.com/WileyCDA/
John Leslie Livingstone. 2001. $37.95. 704 pages. Offers advice to businesses. Includes preparing budgets, implementing business plans, and evaluating acquisition targets.

EMPLOYMENT AGENCIES AND SEARCH FIRMS

★1567★ Chrisman & Company Inc.

350 S. Figueroa St., Ste. 550
Los Angeles, CA 90071
Ph: (213)620-1192   Fax: (213)620-1693
E-mail: info@chrismansearch.com
URL: http://www.chrismansearch.com

Executive search firm.

★1568★ David M. Ellner Associates

41 Barkers Point Rd.
Port Washington, NY 11050
Ph: (516)767-9480
E-mail: elldoda@aol.com

Executive search firm.

ONLINE JOB SOURCES AND SERVICES

★1569★ American Association of Finance and Accounting

E-mail: feedback@aafa.com
URL: http://www.aafa.com

Description: AAFA is the largest and oldest alliance of executive search firms specializing in the recruitment and placement of finance and accounting professionals. Contains career opportunities site with job board for both job seekers and hiring employers. One does not have to be a member to search for jobs.

OTHER SOURCES

★1570★ Financial Occupations

Delphi Productions
3159 6th St.
Boulder, CO 80304
Ph: (303)443-2100   Fax: (303)443-4022
Fr: 888-443-2400
E-mail: support@delphivideo.com
URL: http://www.delphivideo.com

$95.00. 50 minutes. Part of the Careers for the 21st Century Video Library.

Carpenters

★1571★ Archetype

Woodwork Institute
PO Box 980247
West Sacramento, CA 95798
Ph: (916)372-9943   Fax: (916)372-9950
URL: http://www.wicnet.org/publications/archetype.asp

Semiannual. Journal of the Woodwork Institute.

★1572★ Builder

Hanley-Wood L.L.C.
1 Thomas Cir., NW, Ste. 600
Washington, DC 20005
Ph: (202)452-0800   Fax: (202)785-1974
URL: http://www.hanleywood.com/default.aspx?page=b2bbd

$29.95/year for individuals, 13 issues; $54.95/year for Canada, 26 issues; $192.00/year for out of country, 13 issues. Magazine covering housing and construction industry.

★1573★ Builder and Developer

Peninsula Publishing
1602 Monrovia Ave.
Newport Beach, CA 92663
Ph: (949)631-0308   Fax: (949)631-2475
URL: http://www.bdmag.com/new_site/

Magazine for homebuilders.

★1574★ Concrete & Masonry Construction Products

Hanley-Wood LLC
One Thomas Cir. NW, Ste. 600
Washington, DC 20005
Ph: (202)452-0800   Fax: (202)785-1974
E-mail: cmcp@omeda.com
URL: http://www.hanleywood.com/default.aspx?page=cdconmas

Bimonthly. Free. Publication that covers carpenter tips, tools, and up keep.

★1575★ Constructor

Associated General Contractors of America
2300 Wilson Blvd., Ste. 400
Arlington, VA 22201
Ph: (703)548-3118   Fax: (703)548-3119
URL: http://www.agc.org

Monthly. Management magazine for the Construction Industry.

★1576★ Green Home Builder

Peninsula Publishing
1602 Monrovia Ave.
Newport Beach, CA 92663
Ph: (949)631-0308   Fax: (949)631-2475
URL: http://www.greenhomebuildermag.com/

Quarterly. Magazine for home builders and home building industry.

★1577★ Kitchen and Bath Design News

Cygnus Business Media Inc.
3 Huntington Quadrangle, Ste. 301 N
Melville, NY 11747
Ph: (631)845-2700   Fax: (631)845-7109
Fr: 800-308-6397
URL: http://www.cygnusb2b.com

Monthly. Trade journal.

★1578★ Oxymag

Elsevier Science Inc.
360 Park Ave. S
New York, NY 10010
Ph: (212)989-5800   Fax: (212)633-3990
URL: http://www.elsevier.com

Bimonthly. $190.00/year for institutions in all countries except Europe, Japan and Iran; $89.00/year for individuals in all countries except Europe, Japan and Iran; $63.00/year for students in all countries except Europe, Japan and Iran. Journal related to the construction field covering information in the manufacture of commercial, industrial, spark proof and decorative terrazzo floors, flooring for railroad boxcars, industrial fireproof coatings, fire-resistant marine interior deckings and a variety of building units.

★1579★ Panel World

Hatton-Brown Publishers Inc.
225 Hanrick St.
PO Box 2268
Montgomery, AL 36104
Ph: (334)834-1170   Fax: (334)834-4525
Fr: 800-669-5613
URL: http://www.panelworldmag.com/

Bimonthly. $50.00/year for U.S. $60.00/year for Canada; $24.95/year for individuals, full online; $9.95/year for individuals, online. Business magazine serving the worldwide veneer, plywood, and panel board industry.

★1580★ Professional Builder

Reed Business Information
360 Park Ave. S
New York, NY 10010
Ph: (646)746-6400   Fax: (646)746-7431
E-mail: ncrum@reedbusiness.com
URL: http://www.housingzone.com/toc-archive-pbx

Monthly. Free. The integrated engineering magazine of the building construction industry.

★1581★ Replacement Contractor

Hanley-Wood LLC
One Thomas Cir. NW, Ste. 600
Washington, DC 20005
Ph: (202)452-0800   Fax: (202)785-1974
URL: http://www.omeda.com/rcon/

Bimonthly. Magazine for contractors engaged in roofing, siding, decking and window replacement.

★1582★ Residential Contractor

Peninsula Publishing
1602 Monrovia Ave.
Newport Beach, CA 92663
Ph: (949)631-0308   Fax: (949)631-2475
URL: http://www.residentialcontractormag.com/

Quarterly. Magazine for small volume residential builders, contractors, and specialty trades.

★1583★ WIT

Vermont Works for Women
51 Park St.
Essex Junction, VT 05452
Ph: (802)878-0004   Fax: (802)878-0050
Fr: 800-639-1472
URL: http://www.nnetw.org/

Description: Three issues/year. Provides a network of support, information, and skill sharing for women in skilled trades professions.

★1584★ Wood Digest's Finishing Magazine

Cygnus Business Media Inc.
3 Huntington Quadrangle, Ste. 301 N
Melville, NY 11747
Ph: (631)845-2700   Fax: (631)845-7109
Fr: 800-308-6397
URL: http://www.woodworkingpro.com

Quarterly. Magazine serving commercial and industrial wood finishers of cabinets, furniture and millwork. Provides coverage on technical advances in equipment and supplies to assist its readers in overcoming productivity challenges.

★1585★ Wood & Wood Products

Vance Publishing Corp.
400 Knightsbridge Pky.
Lincolnshire, IL 60069
Ph: (847)634-2600   Fax: (847)634-4379
URL: http://www.vancepublishing.com

Monthly. Magazine for furniture, cabinet, and woodworking industry.

PLACEMENT AND JOB REFERRAL SERVICES

★1586★ National Association of Home Builders (NAHB)

1201 15th St. NW
Washington, DC 20005
Ph: (202)266-8200   Fax: (202)266-8400
Fr: 800-368-5242
E-mail: info@nahb.com
URL: http://www.nahb.org

Description: Single and multifamily home builders, commercial builders, and others associated with the building industry. Lobbies on behalf of the housing industry and conducts public affairs activities to increase public understanding of housing and the economy. Collects and disseminates data on current developments in home building and home builders' plans through its Economics Department and nationwide Metropolitan Housing Forecast. Maintains NAHB Research Center, which functions as the research arm of the home building industry. Sponsors seminars and workshops on construction, mortgage credit, labor relations, cost reduction, land use, remodeling, and business management. Compiles statistics; offers charitable program, spokesman training, and placement service; maintains

speakers' bureau, and Hall of Fame. Subsidiaries include the National Council of the Housing Industry. Maintains over 50 committees in many areas of construction; operates National Commercial Builders Council, National Council of the Multifamily Housing Industry, National Remodelers Council, and National Sales and Marketing Council.

EMPLOYER DIRECTORIES AND NETWORKING LISTS

★1587★ ABC Today-Associated Builders and Contractors National Membership Directory Issue

Associated Builders & Contractors Inc.
4250 N Fairfax Dr., 9th Fl.
Arlington, VA 22203-1607
Ph: (703)812-2000   Fax: (703)812-8203
URL: http://www.abc.org/
wmspage.cfm?parm1=2033

Annual, December. $150.00. Publication includes: List of approximately 19,000 member construction contractors and suppliers. Entries include: Company name, address, phone, name of principal executive, code to volume of business, business specialty. Arrangement: Classified by chapter, then by work specialty.

★1588★ Constructor-AGC Directory of Membership and Services Issue

AGC Information Inc.
2300 Wilson Blvd., Ste. 400
Arlington, VA 22201
Ph: (703)548-3118   Fax: (703)548-3119
Fr: 800-282-1423
URL: http://www.agc.org

Annual, August; latest edition 2004 edition. Publication includes: List of over 8,500 member firms and 24,000 national associate member firms engaged in building, highway, heavy, industrial, municipal utilities, and railroad construction (SIC 1541, 1542, 1611, 1622, 1623, 1629); listing of state and local chapter officers. Entries include: For firms–Company name, address, phone, fax, names of principal executives, and code indicating type of construction undertaken. For officers–Name, title, address. Arrangement: Geographical, alphabetical. Indexes: Company name.

★1589★ ENR-Top 400 Construction Contractors Issue

McGraw-Hill Inc.
1221 Ave. of the Americas
New York, NY 10020-1095
Ph: (212)512-2000   Fax: (212)512-3840
Fr: 877-833-5524
URL: http://construction.ecnext.com/coms2/
summary_0249-137077_ITM

Annual; 22nd, May 2006. $35.00 for individuals. Publication includes: List of 400 United States contractors receiving largest dollar volumes of contracts in preceding calendar

year. Separate lists of 50 largest design/construction management firms; 50 largest program and construction managers; 25 building contractors; 25 heavy contractors. Entries include: Company name, headquarters location, total value of contracts received in preceding year, value of foreign contracts, countries in which operated, construction specialities. Arrangement: By total value of contracts received.

HANDBOOKS AND MANUALS

★1590★ Opportunities in Building Construction Trades

The McGraw-Hill Companies
PO Box 182604
Columbus, OH 43272
Fax: (614)759-3749   Fr: 877-883-5524
E-mail: customer.service@mcgraw-hill.com
URL: http://www.mcgraw-hill.com

Michael Sumichrast. Second edition, 1998. $14.95; $11.95 (paper). 104 pages. From custom builder to rehabber, the many kinds of companies that employ craftspeople and contractors are explored. Includes job descriptions, requirements, and salaries for dozens of specialties within the construction industry. Contains a complete list of Bureau of Apprenticeship and Training state and area offices. Illustrated.

★1591★ Opportunities in Carpentry Careers

The McGraw-Hill Companies
PO Box 182604
Columbus, OH 43272
Fax: (614)759-3749   Fr: 877-883-5524
E-mail: customer.service@mcgraw-hill.com
URL: http://www.mcgraw-hill.com

Roger Sheldon. 2007. $13.95; $11.95 (paper). 221 pages. Discusses how to get started and covers the job market. Illustrated.

★1592★ Working Alone: Tips and Techniques for Solo Building

Taunton Press, Incorporated
63 S. Main St., Box 5506
Newtown, CT 06470-5506
Ph: (203)426-8171   Fax: (203)426-3434
Fr: 800-477-8727
URL: http://www.taunton.com/

John Carroll. 2000. $17.95. 152 pages.

TRADESHOWS

★1593★ Florida Industrial Woodworking Expo

Trade Shows, Inc.
PO Box 2000
Claremont, NC 28610-2000
Ph: (828)459-9894   Fax: (828)459-1312
E-mail: tsi@tsiexpos.com
URL: http://www.tsiexpos.com

Biennial. **Primary Exhibits:** Machinery, tooling, supplies, and services for the furniture, cabinet, casegoods, millwork, and industrial wood products industries.

★1594★ ICCON - International Commercial Construction Exposition

National Association of Home Builders of the United States
1201 15th St. NW
Washington, DC 20005
Ph: (202)266-8200   Fax: (202)266-8223
Fr: 800-368-5242
E-mail: exposales@nahb.com
URL: http://www.nahb.org

Annual. **Primary Exhibits:** Equipment, supplies, and services for the construction industries.

★1595★ International Woodworking Machinery and Furniture Supply Fair - USA

Marketing/Association Services Inc.
4342 Redwood Ave., No. C309
Marina del Rey, CA 90292-6480
Ph: (310)302-1077   Fax: (310)306-5288
E-mail: eschwa1511@aol.com

Biennial. **Primary Exhibits:** Woodworking machinery and supplies for furniture, woodworking, kitchen cabinets, architectural woodwork, and specialty wood products.

★1596★ Mid-Atlantic Industrial Woodworking Expo

Trade Shows, Inc.
PO Box 2000
Claremont, NC 28610-2000
Ph: (828)459-9894   Fax: (828)459-1312
E-mail: tsi@tsiexpos.com
URL: http://www.tsiexpos.com

Annual. **Primary Exhibits:** Woodworking and furniture industry equipment, supplies, and services.

★1597★ Wood Technology Clinic and Show

CMP Media LLC (San Mateo)
2800 Campus Dr.
San Mateo, CA 94403
Ph: (650)513-4300
E-mail: cmp@cmp.com
URL: http://www.cmp.com

Annual. **Primary Exhibits:** Equipment, supplies, and services related to the wood products industry, including sawmilling panel production and woodworking. **Dates and Locations:** 2008 Mar 12-14; Portland, OR; Oregon Convention Center.

OTHER SOURCES

★1598★ Associated Builders and Contractors (ABC)

4250 N Fairfax Dr., 9th Fl.
Arlington, VA 22203-1607
Ph: (703)812-2000   Fax: (703)812-8200
E-mail: gotquestions@abc.org
URL: http://www.abc.org

Description: Construction contractors, subcontractors, suppliers, and associates. Aims to foster and perpetuate the principles of rewarding construction workers and management on the basis of merit. Sponsors management education programs and craft training; also sponsors apprenticeship and skill training programs. Disseminates technological and labor relations information.

★1599★ Associated General Contractors of America (AGC)

2300 Wilson Blvd., Ste. 400
Arlington, VA 22201
Ph: (703)548-3118   Fax: (703)548-3119
Fr: 800-242-1767
E-mail: info@agc.org
URL: http://www.agc.org

Description: General construction contractors; subcontractors; industry suppliers; service firms. Provides market services through its divisions. Conducts special conferences and seminars designed specifically for construction firms. Compiles statistics on job accidents reported by member firms. Maintains 65 committees, including joint cooperative committees with other associations and liaison committees with federal agencies.

★1600★ Associated Specialty Contractors (ASC)

3 Bethesda Metro Ctr., Ste. 1100
Bethesda, MD 20814
Ph: (703)548-3118
E-mail: dgw@necanet.org
URL: http://www.assoc-spec-con.org

Description: Works to promote efficient management and productivity. Coordinates the work of specialized branches of the industry in management information, research, public information, government relations and construction relations. Serves as a liaison among specialty trade associations in the areas of public relations, government relations, and with other organizations. Seeks to avoid unnecessary duplication of effort and expense or conflicting programs among affiliates. Identifies areas of interest and problems shared by members, and develops positions and approaches on such problems.

★1601★ Building Trades

Delphi Productions
3159 6th St.
Boulder, CO 80304
Ph: (303)443-2100   Fax: (303)443-4022
Fr: 888-443-2400
E-mail: support@delphivideo.com
URL: http://www.delphivideo.com

$95.00. 46 minutes. Part of the Careers for the 21st Century Video Library.

★1602★ COIN Career Guidance System

COIN Educational Products
3361 Executive Pky., Ste. 302
Toledo, OH 43606
Ph: (419)536-5353   Fax: (419)536-7056
Fr: 800-274-8515
URL: http://www.coinedu.com/

CD-ROM. Provides career information through seven cross-referenced files covering postsecondary schools, college majors, vocational programs, military service, apprenticeship programs, financial aid, and scholarships. Apprenticeship file describes national apprenticeship training programs, including information on how to apply, contact agencies, and program content. Military file describes more than 200 military occupations and training opportunities related to civilian employment.

★1603★ National Association of Women in Construction (NAWIC)

327 S Adams St.
Fort Worth, TX 76104
Ph: (817)877-5551   Fax: (817)877-0324
Fr: 800-552-3506
E-mail: nawic@nawic.org
URL: http://www.nawic.org

Description: Seeks to enhance the success of women in the construction industry.

★1604★ Women in Building Construction

Her Own Words
PO Box 5264
Madison, WI 53705-0264
Ph: (608)271-7083   Fax: (608)271-0209
E-mail: herownword@aol.com
URL: http://www.herownwords.com/

Video. Jocelyn Riley. $95.00. 15 minutes. Resource guide also available for $45.00.

★1605★ Women in Nontraditional Careers: An Introduction

Her Own Words
PO Box 5264
Madison, WI 53705
Ph: (608)271-7083   Fax: (608)271-0209
E-mail: herownword@aol.com
URL: http://www.herownwords.com/

Video. Jocelyn Riley. $95.00. 15 minutes. Resource guide also available for $45.00.

Caterers

SOURCES OF HELP-WANTED ADS

★1606★ Chow

Instant Comma Inc.
4596 19th St.
San Francisco, CA 94114
URL: http://www.chowmag.com/

Bimonthly. $18.95/year for individuals. Magazine that covers food preparation techniques, recipes, columns on specialty food items, how-to articles and editorials.

★1607★ Cooking Smart

Coincide Publishing LLC
7944 E Beck Ln., Ste. 230
Scottsdale, AZ 85260-1664
Ph: (480)237-7100   Fax: (480)237-7103
URL: http://cookingsmartmagazine.com/a-boutus.htm

$17.95/year for individuals; $24.95/year for individuals; $29.94/year for individuals, newsstand, 6 issues; $59.88/year for individuals, newsstand. Magazine features articles about healthy cooking as well as recipes.

★1608★ EatingWell

Eating Well Inc.
823A Ferry Rd.
PO Box 1010
Charlotte, VT 05445
Ph: (802)425-5700   Fax: (802)425-3700
Fr: 800-337-0402
URL: http://www.eatingwell.com/

Bimonthly. $14.97/year for individuals. Magazine of food & health that includes nutritional recipes.

★1609★ Foodservice East

The Newbury Street Group Inc.
165 New Boston St., No. 236
Woburn, MA 01801
Ph: (781)376-9080   Fax: (781)376-0010
Fr: 800-852-5212
E-mail: fdsvceast@.aol.com

Bimonthly. $30.00/year for individuals. Compact tabloid covering trends and analysis of the foodservice industry in the Northeast. A business-to-business publication featuring news, analysis and trends for the Northeast food service professional.

★1610★ Good Things to Eat

Ogden Publications
1503 SW 42nd St.
Topeka, KS 66609-1265
Ph: (785)274-4300   Fax: (785)274-4305
Fr: 800-234-3368
URL: http://www.somegoodthingstoeat.com/

Quarterly. $9.95/year for U.S. Magazine featuring food and recipes.

★1611★ The Gourmet Connection Magazine

CAPCO Marketing
PO Box 1727
Cicero, NY 13039
Ph: (315)699-1687   Fax: (315)699-1689
URL: http://tgcmagazine.com/

Magazine on gourmet food and the finer things in life. Covers a wide range of topics from nutritional information, and diet tips, to recipes, and information on arranging parties.

★1612★ Kitchen & Cook

Kitchen & Cook
800 Connecticut Ave.
Norwalk, CT 06854

$19.97/year for individuals; $26.00/year for Canada; $39.00/year for elsewhere. Magazine offers information on how to cook according to the Culinary Institute of America.

★1613★ Midwest Food Network

Pinnacle Publishing Group
8205-F Estates Pky.
Plain City, OH 43064
Fax: (614)873-1650
URL: http://www.midwestfoodnetwork.com/

Bimonthly. $24.00/year. Free to qualified subscribers; $24.00/year for individuals, others. Food service trade magazine featuring new products and suppliers and other industry news including food news, restaurant association updates, news of chefs, restaurant concepts, earnings, and openings and closings.

★1614★ The National Culinary Review

American Culinary Federation Inc.
180 Center Place Way
St. Augustine, FL 32095
Ph: (904)824-4468   Fax: (904)825-4758
Fr: 800-624-9458
E-mail: acf@acfchefs.net
URL: http://www.acfchefs.org

Monthly. $50.00/year for individuals, U.S. Trade magazine covering food and cooking.

★1615★ Plate

Marketing & Technology Group
1415 N Dayton St.
Chicago, IL 60622
Ph: (312)266-3311   Fax: (312)266-3363
URL: http://www.plateonline.com

Bimonthly. Magazine that aims to inform food service professionals and owners food and focuses on how menu items are come up with.

★1616★ Real Food

Greenspring Media Group
600 US Trust Bldg.
730 2nd Ave. S
Minneapolis, MN 55402
Ph: (612)371-5800   Fax: (612)371-5801
Fr: 800-933-4398
URL: http://www.realfoodmag.com/

Quarterly. Magazine featuring food choices.

★1617★ Restaurant Business

VNU Business Publications
770 Broadway
New York, NY 10003
Ph: (646)654-5000
URL: http://www.foodservicetoday.com

Monthly. $119.00/year for individuals;

$212.00/year for Canada; $468.00/year for other countries, rest of the world. Trade magazine for restaurants and commercial food service.

★1618★ **Restaurant Hospitality**

Penton Media Inc.
1300 E 9th St.
Cleveland, OH 44114
Ph: (216)696-7000   Fax: (216)696-1752
URL: http://www.restaurant-hospitality.com/

Monthly. Free. Dedicated to the success of full service restaurants and edited for chefs and other commercial foodservice professionals. Includes new food and equipment products and trends, menu and recipe ideas, industry news, new technology, food safety, emerging new concepts, consumer attitudes and trends, labor and training, and profiles of successful operations.

★1619★ **Simple & Delicious**

Reiman Publications
5400 South 60th St.
Greendale, WI 53129
Ph: (414)423-0100   Fr: 800-344-6913
URL: http://recipes.bestsimplerecipes.com/

Bimonthly. $14.98/year for individuals. Magazine covering recipes and kitchen shortcuts, 10-minute dishes, 5-ingredient recipes, 30-minute meals, and mix and match meal planner.

★1620★ **Sizzle**

American Culinary Federation Inc.
180 Center Place Way
St. Augustine, FL 32095
Ph: (904)824-4468   Fax: (904)825-4758
Fr: 800-624-9458

Quarterly. $20.00 for individuals, one year (4 issues); $35.00 for two years, (8 issues); $10.00 for individuals, each for one year, bulk. Magazine for culinary students offering food trends, career information, and how-tos.

PLACEMENT AND JOB REFERRAL SERVICES

★1621★ **Les Amis d'Escoffier Society of New York**

787 Ridgewood Rd.
Millburn, NJ 07041
Ph: (212)414-5820   Fax: (973)379-3117
E-mail: kurt@escoffier-society.com
URL: http://www.escoffier-society.com

Members: An educational organization of professionals in the food and wine industries. **Activities:** Maintains museum, speakers' bureau, hall of fame, and placement service. Sponsors charitable programs.

HANDBOOKS AND MANUALS

★1622★ **Career Opportunities in the Food and Beverage Industry**

Facts on File, Inc.
132 W. 31st St., 17th Fl.
New York, NY 10001-2006
Ph: (212)967-8800   Fax: 800-678-3633
Fr: 800-322-8755
E-mail: custserv@factsonfile.com
URL: http://www.factsonfile.com

Barbara Sims-Bell. Second edition, 2001. $18.95 (paper). 223 pages. Provides the job seeker with information about locating and landing 80 skilled and unskilled jobs in the industry. Includes detailed job descriptions for many specific positions and lists trade associations, recruiting organizations, and major agencies. Contains index and bibliography.

★1623★ **Careers for Gourmets and Others Who Relish Food**

The McGraw-Hill Companies
PO Box 182604
Columbus, OH 43272
Fax: (614)759-3749   Fr: 877-883-5524
E-mail: customer.service@mcgraw-hill.com
URL: http://www.mcgraw-hill.com

Mary Donovan. Second edition, 2002. $15.95; $12.95 (paper). 192 pages. Discusses such job prospects as foods columnist, cookbook writer, test kitchen worker, pastry chef, recipe developer, food festival organizer, restaurant manager, and food stylist.

★1624★ **Catering on Campus: A Guide to Catering in Colleges and Universities**

Colman Publishers
1147 Elmwood
Stockton, CA 95204
Ph: (209)464-9503   Fax: (209)262-4257

Paul Fairbrook. 2004. $50.00. Designed to help catering managers at colleges do a better job of selling and providing quality and profitable catering services.

★1625★ **Catering Service Business Possibility Encyclopedia**

Frieda Carrol Communications
PO Box 416
Denver, CO 80201-0416
Ph: (303)575-5676   Fax: (970)292-2136

1997. $59.95 (ringbound).

★1626★ **Choosing a Career in the Restaurant Industry**

Rosen Publishing Group, Inc.
29 E. 21st St.
New York, NY 10010
Ph: (212)777-3017   Fax: 888-436-4643
Fr: 800-237-9932
URL: http://www.rosenpublishing.com/

Eileen Beal. Revised edition, 2000. $25.25.

64 pages. Explores various jobs in the restaurant industry. Describes job duties, salaries, educational preparation, and job hunting. Contains information about fast food, catering, and small businesses.

★1627★ **Culinary Arts Career Starter**

LearningExpress, LLC
55 Broadway, 8th Fl.
New York, NY 10006
Ph: (212)995-2566   Fax: (212)995-5512
Fr: 800-295-9556
E-mail: customerservice@learningexpressllc.com
URL: http://www.learningexpressllc.com

Mary Masi. 1999. $15.95 (paper). 208 pages.

★1628★ **How to Start a Catering Business: When You Don't Know What the Hell You're Doing**

1st Books Library
1663 Liberty Dr., Ste. 200
Bloomington, IN 47403
Ph: (812)339-6554   Fr: 800-839-8640

Jennifer Williams. 2003. $11.45.

★1629★ **How to Start a Home-Based Catering Business**

The Globe Pequot Press
246 Goose Ln.
Guilford, CT 06437
Ph: (203)458-4500   Fax: 800-820-2329
Fr: 888-249-7586
E-mail: info@globepequot.com
URL: http://www.globepequot.com/

Denise Vivaldo. Fifth edition, 2005. $18.95. 264 pages. Part of the Home-Based Business Series.

★1630★ **Opportunities in Culinary Careers**

The McGraw-Hill Companies
PO Box 182604
Columbus, OH 43272
Fax: (614)759-3749   Fr: 877-883-5524
E-mail: customer.service@mcgraw-hill.com
URL: http://www.mcgraw-hill.com

Mary Deirdre Donovan. 2003. $13.95; $11.95 (paper). 149 pages. Describes the educational preparation and training of chefs and cooks and explores a variety of food service jobs in restaurants, institutions, and research and development. Lists major culinary professional associations and schools. Offers guidance on landing a first job in cooking and related fields.

★1631★ **Opportunities in Restaurant Careers**

The McGraw-Hill Companies
PO Box 182604
Columbus, OH 43272
Fax: (614)759-3749   Fr: 877-883-5524
E-mail: customer.service@mcgraw-hill.com
URL: http://www.mcgraw-hill.com

Carol Caprione Chmelynski. 2004. $13.95

(paper). 150 pages. Covers opportunities in the food service industry and details salaries, benefits, training opportunities, and professional associations. Special emphasis is put on becoming a successful restaurant manager by working up through the ranks. Illustrated.

★1632★ The Professional Caterer's Handbook: How to Open and Operate a Financially Successful Catering Business

Atlantic Publishing Company
1210 SW 23rd Pl.
Ocala, FL 34474-7014
Fax: (352)622-1875   Fr: 800-814-1132
E-mail: sales@atlantic-pub.com
URL: http://www.atlantic-pub.com/

Douglas Robert Brown and Lora Arduser. 2005. $79.95. Comprehensive guide for planning, starting, and operating a catering business; includes companion CD-ROM. Covers marketing, management, budgeting, home-based catering, ways for restaurants to add catering services to existing businesses, forms, Web sites, and more.

★1633★ Successful Catering: Managing the Catering Operation for Maximum Profit

Atlantic Publishing Company
1210 SW 3rd Pl.
Ocala, FL 34474-7014
Fax: (352)622-1875   Fr: 800-814-1132
E-mail: sales@atlantic-pub.com
URL: http://www.atlantic-pub.com/

Sony Bode. January 2003. $19.95. 144 Pages. Illustrated.

★1634★ Working in Hotels and Catering

Cengage Learning
PO Box 6904
Florence, KY 41022
Fax: 800-487-8488   Fr: 800-354-9706
URL: http://www.cengage.com

Roy Woods. Second edition, 1997. $46.99 (paper). 252 pages.

★1635★ Working in Hotels and Catering: How to Find Great Employment Opportunities Worldwide

Trans-Atlantic Publications, Inc.
311 Bainbridge St.
Philadelphia, PA 19147
Ph: (215)925-5083   Fax: (215)925-1912
E-mail: jeffgolds@comcast.net
URL: http://www.transatlanticpub.com/

Mark Hempshell. 1997. $19.95 (paper). Part of the Jobs and Careers Series. 174 pages.

ONLINE JOB SOURCES AND SERVICES

★1636★ Food Industry Jobs.com

HRsmart, Inc.
2929 N. Central Expressway, Ste. 110
Richardson, TX 75080
E-mail: jobboards@hrsmart.com
URL: http://www.foodindustryjobs.com

Description: Job databank and resume submission service for food industry workers.

TRADESHOWS

★1637★ American School Food Service Association Annual National Conference

American School Food Service Association
700 S. Washington St., Ste. 300
Alexandria, VA 22314-4287
Ph: (703)739-3900   Fax: (703)739-3915
Fr: 800-877-8822
E-mail: servicecenter@asfsa.org
URL: http://www.asfsa.org

Annual. **Primary Exhibits:** Food service supplies and equipment, including educational services and computers.

★1638★ Annual Hotel, Motel, and Restaurant Supply Show of the Southeast

Leisure Time Unlimited, Inc.
708 Main St.
PO Box 332
Myrtle Beach, SC 29577
Ph: (843)448-9483   Fax: (843)626-1513
Fr: 800-261-5591
E-mail: dickensshow@sc.rr.com

Annual. **Primary Exhibits:** Carpeting, furniture, coffee makers, produce companies, wine and beer and food companies, and services to motels, hotels, and restaurants.

★1639★ Institute of Food Technologists Annual Meeting and Food Expo

Institute of Food Technologists
525 W, Van Buren St., Ste. 1000
Chicago, IL 60607-3814
Ph: (312)782-8424   Fax: (312)782-8348
E-mail: info@ift.org
URL: http://www.ift.org

Annual. **Primary Exhibits:** Food ingredients, equipment, laboratory equipment and supplies, and other services rendered to the food processing industry.

★1640★ International Baking Industry Exposition

IBIE Exhibition Management
401 N. Michigan Ave.
Chicago, IL 60611
Ph: (312)644-6610   Fax: (312)644-0575
E-mail: pdwyer@smithbucklin.com
URL: http://www.bakingexpo.com

Primary Exhibits: Baking equipment, supplies, and services.

★1641★ Louisiana Foodservice Expo

Louisiana Restaurant Association
2700 N. Arnoult Rd.
Metairie, LA 70002
Ph: (504)454-2277   Fax: (504)454-2663
Fr: 800-256-4572
E-mail: sandyr@lra.org

Annual. **Primary Exhibits:** Food service equipment, supplies, and services, food products.

★1642★ Midsouthwest Foodservice Convention and Exposition

Oklahoma Restaurant Association
3800 N. Portland
Oklahoma City, OK 73112
Ph: (405)942-8181   Fax: (405)942-0541
Fr: 800-375-8181
URL: http://www.okrestaurants.com

Annual. **Primary Exhibits:** Providers of foodservice and hospitality products, services and equipment.

★1643★ National Restauraunt Association Restaurant and Hotel-Motel Show

National Restaurant Association (Convention Office)
150 N. Michigan Ave., Ste. 2000
Chicago, IL 60601
Ph: (312)853-2525   Fax: (312)853-2548

Annual. **Primary Exhibits:** Food service equipment, supplies, and services and food and beverage products for the hospitality industry. Includes International Cuisine Pavilion. **Dates and Locations:** 2008 May 17-20; Chicago, IL; McCormick Place.

★1644★ South Carolina Foodservice Expo

South Carolina Foodservice Expo
111 Shannon Dr.
Spartanburg, SC 29301
Ph: (864)574-9323   Fax: (864)574-0784
E-mail: scsfsa@aol.com

Annual. **Primary Exhibits:** Food and foodservice equipment, supplies, and services.

★1645★ **Upper Midwest Hospitality, Restaurant, and Lodging Show - UP Show**

Hospitality Minnesota - Minnesota's Restaurant, Hotel, and Resort Associations
305 E Roselawn Ave.
St. Paul, MN 55117-2031
Ph: (651)778-2400   Fax: (651)778-2424
E-mail: info@hospitalitymn.com
URL: http://www.hospitalitymn.com

Annual. **Primary Exhibits:** Food, beverages, hospitality business services, lodging supplies, and foodservice equipment.

OTHER SOURCES

★1646★ **International Association of Culinary Professionals (IACP)**

304 W Liberty St., Ste. 201
Louisville, KY 40202
Ph: (502)581-9786   Fax: (502)589-3602
Fr: 800-928-4227
E-mail: iacp@hqtrs.com
URL: http://www.iacp.com

Description: Represents cooking school owners, food writers, chefs, caterers, culinary specialists, directors, teachers, cookbook authors, food stylists, food photographers, student/apprentices, and individuals in related industries in 20 countries. Promotes the interests of cooking schools, teachers, and culinary professionals. Encourages the exchange of information and education. Promotes professional standards and accreditation procedures. Maintains a Foundation to award culinary scholarships and grants.

★1647★ **International Council on Hotel, Restaurant, and Institutional Education (CHRIE)**

2810 N Parham Rd., Ste. 230
Richmond, VA 23294
Ph: (804)346-4800   Fax: (804)346-5009
E-mail: kmccarty@chrie.org
URL: http://www.chrie.org

Description: Schools and colleges offering specialized education and training in hospitals, recreation, tourism and hotel, restaurant, and institutional administration; individuals, executives, and students. Provides networking opportunities and professional development.

★1648★ **International Flight Service Association (IFSA)**

1100 Johnson Ferry Rd., Ste. 300
Atlanta, GA 30342
Ph: (404)252-3663   Fax: (404)252-0774
E-mail: ifsa@kellencompany.com
URL: http://www.ifsanet.com

Members: Works to serve the needs and interests of the airline and railway personnel, in-flight and railway caterers and suppliers responsible for providing passenger foodservice on regularly scheduled travel routes.

★1649★ **National Restaurant Association (NRA)**

1200 17th St. NW
Washington, DC 20036
Ph: (202)331-5900   Fax: (202)331-2429
Fr: 800-424-5156
E-mail: info@dineout.org
URL: http://www.restaurant.org

Description: Represents restaurants, cafeterias, clubs, contract foodservice management, drive-ins, caterers, institutional food services, and other members of the foodservice industry; also represents establishments belonging to non-affiliated state and local restaurant associations in governmental affairs. Supports foodservice education and research in several educational institutions. Is affiliated with the Educational Foundation of the National Restaurant Association to provide training and education for operators, food and equipment manufacturers, distributors, and educators. Has 300,000 member locations.

Chefs and Cooks

SOURCES OF HELP-WANTED ADS

★1650★ Chef

Talcott Communications Corp.
20 W Kinzie, Ste. 1200
Chicago, IL 60610
Ph: (312)849-2220   Fax: (312)849-2174
E-mail: chef@talcott.com
URL: http://www.chefmagazine.com

$32.00/year for individuals; $47.00 for two years; $64.00 for individuals, 3 years; $43.00/year for Canada; $96.00/year for other countries. Food information for chefs.

★1651★ Chow

Instant Comma Inc.
4596 19th St.
San Francisco, CA 94114
URL: http://www.chowmag.com/

Bimonthly. $18.95/year for individuals. Magazine that covers food preparation techniques, recipes, columns on specialty food items, how-to articles and editorials.

★1652★ Cooking Smart

Coincide Publishing LLC
7944 E Beck Ln., Ste. 230
Scottsdale, AZ 85260-1664
Ph: (480)237-7100   Fax: (480)237-7103
URL: http://cookingsmartmagazine.com/aboutus.htm

$17.95/year for individuals; $24.95/year for individuals; $29.94/year for individuals, newsstand, 6 issues; $59.88/year for individuals, newsstand. Magazine features articles about healthy cooking as well as recipes.

★1653★ EatingWell

Eating Well Inc.
823A Ferry Rd.
PO Box 1010
Charlotte, VT 05445
Ph: (802)425-5700   Fax: (802)425-3700
Fr: 800-337-0402
URL: http://www.eatingwell.com/

Bimonthly. $14.97/year for individuals. Magazine of food & health that includes nutritional recipes.

★1654★ Field & Feast

Field & Feast
PO Box 205
Four Lakes, WA 99014
URL: http://www.fieldandfeast.net

Quarterly. $19.00/year for individuals. Magazine that offers information on organic food cultivation and its health benefits.

★1655★ Foodservice East

The Newbury Street Group Inc.
165 New Boston St., No. 236
Woburn, MA 01801
Ph: (781)376-9080   Fax: (781)376-0010
Fr: 800-852-5212
E-mail: fdsvceast@.aol.com

Bimonthly. $30.00/year for individuals. Compact tabloid covering trends and analysis of the foodservice industry in the Northeast. A business-to-business publication featuring news, analysis and trends for the Northeast food service professional.

★1656★ Good Things to Eat

Ogden Publications
1503 SW 42nd St.
Topeka, KS 66609-1265
Ph: (785)274-4300   Fax: (785)274-4305
Fr: 800-234-3368
URL: http://
www.somegoodthingstoeat.com/

Quarterly. $9.95/year for U.S. Magazine featuring food and recipes.

★1657★ The Gourmet Connection Magazine

CAPCO Marketing
PO Box 1727
Cicero, NY 13039
Ph: (315)699-1687   Fax: (315)699-1689
URL: http://tgcmagazine.com/

Magazine on gourmet food and the finer things in life. Covers a wide range of topics from nutritional information, and diet tips, to recipes, and information on arranging parties.

★1658★ Hotel & Motel Management

Questex Media Group
275 Grove St., 2-130
Newton, MA 02466
Ph: (617)219-8300   Fax: (617)219-8310
Fr: 888-552-4346
URL: http://www.hotelmotel.com

$53.50/year for individuals; $74.00/year for individuals, Canada and Mexico; $130.00/year for individuals, all other countries; $75.00/year for individuals, all other countries. Free to qualified subscribers. Magazine covering the global lodging industry.

★1659★ Kitchen & Cook

Kitchen & Cook
800 Connecticut Ave.
Norwalk, CT 06854

$19.97/year for individuals; $26.00/year for Canada; $39.00/year for elsewhere. Magazine offers information on how to cook according to the Culinary Institute of America.

★1660★ Midwest Food Network

Pinnacle Publishing Group
8205-F Estates Pky.
Plain City, OH 43064
Fax: (614)873-1650
URL: http://www.midwestfoodnetwork.com/

Bimonthly. $24.00/year. Free to qualified subscribers; $24.00/year for individuals, others. Food service trade magazine featuring new products and suppliers and other industry news including food news, restaurant association updates, news of chefs, restaurant concepts, earnings, and openings and closings.

★1661★ **The National Culinary Review**
American Culinary Federation Inc.
180 Center Place Way
St. Augustine, FL 32095
Ph: (904)824-4468   Fax: (904)825-4758
Fr: 800-624-9458
E-mail: acf@acfchefs.net
URL: http://www.acfchefs.org

Monthly. $50.00/year for individuals, U.S. Trade magazine covering food and cooking.

★1662★ **Plate**
Marketing & Technology Group
1415 N Dayton St.
Chicago, IL 60622
Ph: (312)266-3311   Fax: (312)266-3363
URL: http://www.plateonline.com

Bimonthly. Magazine that aims to inform food service professionals and owners food and focuses on how menu items are come up with.

★1663★ **Real Food**
Greenspring Media Group
600 US Trust Bldg.
730 2nd Ave. S
Minneapolis, MN 55402
Ph: (612)371-5800   Fax: (612)371-5801
Fr: 800-933-4398
URL: http://www.realfoodmag.com/

Quarterly. Magazine featuring food choices.

★1664★ **Restaurant Business**
VNU Business Publications
770 Broadway
New York, NY 10003
Ph: (646)654-5000
URL: http://www.foodservicetoday.com

Monthly. $119.00/year for individuals; $212.00/year for Canada; $468.00/year for other countries, rest of the world. Trade magazine for restaurants and commercial food service.

★1665★ **Restaurant Hospitality**
Penton Media Inc.
1300 E 9th St.
Cleveland, OH 44114
Ph: (216)696-7000   Fax: (216)696-1752
URL: http://www.restaurant-hospitality.com/

Monthly. Free. Dedicated to the success of full service restaurants and edited for chefs and other commercial foodservice professionals. Includes new food and equipment products and trends, menu and recipe ideas, industry news, new technology, food safety, emerging new concepts, consumer attitudes and trends, labor and training, and profiles of successful operations.

★1666★ **Restaurant Startup & Growth**
Specialized Publications Company
5215 Crooked Rd.
Parkville, MO 64152
Ph: (816)741-5151   Fax: (816)741-6458
URL: http://www.restaurantowner.com/mag/

Monthly. $39.95/year for U.S. $48.95/year for Canada; $54.95/year for elsewhere; $69.95/year for U.S., 2 years; $87.95/year for Canada, 2 years; $99.95/year for elsewhere, 2 years; $89.95/year for U.S., 3 years; $116.95/year for Canada, 3 years; $134.95/year for elsewhere, 3 years. Magazine about starting and operating a restaurant business.

★1667★ **Restaurants & Institutions**
Reed Business Information
360 Park Ave. S
New York, NY 10010
Ph: (646)746-6400   Fax: (646)746-7431
URL: http://www.reedbusiness.com/

Semimonthly. Free. Magazine focusing on foodservice and lodging management.

★1668★ **Simple & Delicious**
Reiman Publications
5400 South 60th St.
Greendale, WI 53129
Ph: (414)423-0100   Fr: 800-344-6913
URL: http://recipes.bestsimplerecipes.com/

Bimonthly. $14.98/year for individuals. Magazine covering recipes and kitchen shortcuts, 10-minute dishes, 5-ingredient recipes, 30-minute meals, and mix and match meal planner.

★1669★ **Sizzle**
American Culinary Federation Inc.
180 Center Place Way
St. Augustine, FL 32095
Ph: (904)824-4468   Fax: (904)825-4758
Fr: 800-624-9458

Quarterly. $20.00 for individuals, one year (4 issues); $35.00 for two years, (8 issues); $10.00 for individuals, each for one year, bulk. Magazine for culinary students offering food trends, career information, and how-tos.

★1670★ **Western Itasca Review & Deerpath Shopper**
Lebhar-Friedman, Inc.
425 Park Ave., 6th Fl.
New York, NY 10022
Ph: (212)756-5000   Fax: (212)756-5215

Weekly (Mon.). $34.50/year for individuals. Local newspaper and shopper.

PLACEMENT AND JOB REFERRAL SERVICES

★1671★ **Chefs de Cuisine Association of America (CCAA)**
155 E 55th St., Ste. 302B
New York, NY 10022
Ph: (212)832-4939
E-mail: info@chefsdecuisineofamerica.com

Description: Professional executive chefs;

chefs who own restaurants; pastry chefs for hotels, clubs, and restaurants. Maintains 350 volume library and placement service for members.

★1672★ **Les Amis d'Escoffier Society of New York**
787 Ridgewood Rd.
Millburn, NJ 07041
Ph: (212)414-5820   Fax: (973)379-3117
E-mail: kurt@escoffier-society.com
URL: http://www.escoffier-society.com

Members: An educational organization of professionals in the food and wine industries. **Activities:** Maintains museum, speakers' bureau, hall of fame, and placement service. Sponsors charitable programs.

EMPLOYER DIRECTORIES AND NETWORKING LISTS

★1673★ **Careers in Focus: Food**
Facts On File Inc.
132 W 31st St., 17th Fl.
New York, NY 10001
Ph: (212)967-8800   Fax: 800-678-3633
Fr: 800-322-8755
URL: http://www.factsonfile.com

Latest edition 3rd, 2007. $29.95 for individuals; $26.95 for libraries. Covers an overview of the food industry, followed by a selection of jobs profiled in detail, including the nature of the job, earnings, prospects for employment, what kind of training and skills it requires, and sources for further information.

★1674★ **Discovering Careers for Your Future: Food**
Facts On File Inc.
132 W 31st St., 17th Fl.
New York, NY 10001
Ph: (212)967-8800   Fax: 800-678-3633
Fr: 800-322-8755
URL: http://www.factsonfile.com

Published 2005. $21.95 for individuals; $19.75 for libraries. Covers brewers, cookbook and recipe writers, cooks and chefs, dietitians and nutritionists, food service workers, supermarket managers, winemakers, and more; links career education to curriculum, helping children investigate the subjects they are interested in, and the careers those subjects might lead to.

HANDBOOKS AND MANUALS

★1675★ **Becoming a Chef**
John Wiley & Sons Inc.
1 Wiley Dr.
Somerset, NJ 08873
Ph: (732)469-4400   Fax: (732)302-2300
Fr: 800-225-5945

E-mail: custserv@wiley.com
URL: http://www.wiley.com/WileyCDA/

A. Dornenburg and Karen Page. Revised edition, 2003. $29.95. Part of Culinary Arts series. 400 pages.

★1676★ Career Opportunities in the Food and Beverage Industry

Facts on File, Inc.
132 W. 31st St., 17th Fl.
New York, NY 10001-2006
Ph: (212)967-8800   Fax: 800-678-3633
Fr: 800-322-8755
E-mail: custserv@factsonfile.com
URL: http://www.factsonfile.com

Barbara Sims-Bell. Second edition, 2001. $18.95 (paper). 223 pages. Provides the job seeker with information about locating and landing 80 skilled and unskilled jobs in the industry. Includes detailed job descriptions for many specific positions and lists trade associations, recruiting organizations, and major agencies. Contains index and bibliography.

★1677★ Careers for Gourmets and Others Who Relish Food

The McGraw-Hill Companies
PO Box 182604
Columbus, OH 43272
Fax: (614)759-3749   Fr: 877-883-5524
E-mail: customer.service@mcgraw-hill.com
URL: http://www.mcgraw-hill.com

Mary Donovan. Second edition, 2002. $15.95; $12.95 (paper). 192 pages. Discusses such job prospects as foods columnist, cookbook writer, test kitchen worker, pastry chef, recipe developer, food festival organizer, restaurant manager, and food stylist.

★1678★ Careers in Travel, Tourism, and Hospitality

The McGraw-Hill Companies
PO Box 182604
Columbus, OH 43272
Fax: (614)759-3749   Fr: 877-883-5524
E-mail: customer.service@mcgraw-hill.com
URL: http://www.mcgraw-hill.com

Marjorie Eberts, Linda Brothers, and Ann Gisler. Second edition, 2005. $15.95 (paper). 224 pages.

★1679★ Choosing a Career in the Restaurant Industry

Rosen Publishing Group, Inc.
29 E. 21st St.
New York, NY 10010
Ph: (212)777-3017   Fax: 888-436-4643
Fr: 800-237-9932
URL: http://www.rosenpublishing.com/

Eileen Beal. Revised edition, 2000. $25.25. 64 pages. Explores various jobs in the restaurant industry. Describes job duties, salaries, educational preparation, and job hunting. Contains information about fast food, catering, and small businesses.

★1680★ The Cook's Book: Techniques and Tips from the World's Master Chefs

Dorling Kindersley Publishing, Inc.
375 Hudson St., 2nd Fl.
New York, NY 10014
Ph: (201)256-0017   Fax: (201)256-0000
Fr: 800-788-6262
URL: http://us.dk.com/

Jill Norman. 2005. $50.00. Tips for home cooks from top chefs around the world; includes concise directions and color photography.

★1681★ Creating Chefs: A Journey Through Culinary School with Recipes and Lessons

The Lyons Press
246 Goose Ln.
Guilford, CT 06437
Ph: (203)458-4500   Fax: (203)458-4604
Fr: 888-249-7586
E-mail: info@globepequot.com
URL: http://www.lyonspress.com/

Carol W. Maybach. 2005. $16.95. Highlights the wisdom and secrets of the author's chef instructors from culinary school; recipes with instructions and photographs of American and ethnic dishes are presented to help readers master special cooking techniques.

★1682★ Culinary Arts Career Starter

LearningExpress, LLC
55 Broadway, 8th Fl.
New York, NY 10006
Ph: (212)995-2566   Fax: (212)995-5512
Fr: 800-295-9556
E-mail: customerservice@learningexpressllc.com
URL: http://www.learningexpressllc.com

Mary Masi. 1999. $15.95 (paper). 208 pages.

★1683★ How to Get a Job with a Cruise Line

Ticket to Adventure, Inc.
PO Box 41005
St. Petersburg, FL 33743-1005
Ph: (727)822-5029   Fax: (727)821-3409
Fr: 800-929-7447

Mary Fallon Miller. Fifth edition, 2001. $16.95 (paper). 352 pages. Explores jobs with cruise ships, describing duties, responsibilities, benefits, and training. Lists cruise ship lines and schools offering cruise line training. Offers job hunting advice.

★1684★ How I Learned to Cook: Culinary Educations from the World's Greatest Chefs

Bloomsbury Publishing
175 5th Ave., Ste. 300
New York, NY 10010
Fr: 888-330-8477

Kimberly Witherspoon and Peter Meehan. 2007. $14.95.

★1685★ Opportunities in Culinary Careers

The McGraw-Hill Companies
PO Box 182604
Columbus, OH 43272
Fax: (614)759-3749   Fr: 877-883-5524
E-mail: customer.service@mcgraw-hill.com
URL: http://www.mcgraw-hill.com

Mary Deirdre Donovan. 2003. $13.95; $11.95 (paper). 149 pages. Describes the educational preparation and training of chefs and cooks and explores a variety of food service jobs in restaurants, institutions, and research and development. Lists major culinary professional associations and schools. Offers guidance on landing a first job in cooking and related fields.

★1686★ Opportunities in Restaurant Careers

The McGraw-Hill Companies
PO Box 182604
Columbus, OH 43272
Fax: (614)759-3749   Fr: 877-883-5524
E-mail: customer.service@mcgraw-hill.com
URL: http://www.mcgraw-hill.com

Carol Caprione Chmelynski. 2004. $13.95 (paper). 150 pages. Covers opportunities in the food service industry and details salaries, benefits, training opportunities, and professional associations. Special emphasis is put on becoming a successful restaurant manager by working up through the ranks. Illustrated.

★1687★ Purchasing for Chefs: A Concise Guide

John Wiley & Sons, Inc.
111 River St.
Hoboken, NJ 07030
Ph: (201)748-6000   Fax: (201)748-6088
E-mail: info@wiley.com
URL: http://www.wiley.com/WileyCDA/

Andrew H. Feinstein and John M. Stefanelli. 2006. $45.00. Guide details purchasing principles to chefs and hospitality managers for obtaining goods and services for their business.

ONLINE JOB SOURCES AND SERVICES

★1688★ Food Industry Jobs.com

HRsmart, Inc.
2929 N. Central Expressway, Ste. 110
Richardson, TX 75080
E-mail: jobboards@hrsmart.com
URL: http://www.foodindustryjobs.com

Description: Job databank and resume submission service for food industry workers.

★1689★ StarChefs.com

9 E. 19th St., 9th Fl.
New York, NY 10003
Ph: (212)966-3775   Fax: (212)477-6644
E-mail: liz@starchefs.com
URL: http://www.starchefs.com

Description: Contains job board, resume writing service and career advice for job seekers in the culinary arts. Seekers can sign up for free e-mail account and receive job notifications through this service.

TRADESHOWS

★1690★ American School Food Service Association Annual National Conference

American School Food Service Association
700 S. Washington St., Ste. 300
Alexandria, VA 22314-4287
Ph: (703)739-3900   Fax: (703)739-3915
Fr: 800-877-8822
E-mail: servicecenter@asfsa.org
URL: http://www.asfsa.org

Annual. **Primary Exhibits:** Food service supplies and equipment, including educational services and computers.

★1691★ International Baking Industry Exposition

IBIE Exhibition Management
401 N. Michigan Ave.
Chicago, IL 60611
Ph: (312)644-6610   Fax: (312)644-0575
E-mail: pdwyer@smithbucklin.com
URL: http://www.bakingexpo.com

Primary Exhibits: Baking equipment, supplies, and services.

★1692★ National Restauraunt Association Restaurant and Hotel-Motel Show

National Restaurant Association (Convention Office)
150 N. Michigan Ave., Ste. 2000
Chicago, IL 60601
Ph: (312)853-2525   Fax: (312)853-2548

Annual. **Primary Exhibits:** Food service equipment, supplies, and services and food and beverage products for the hospitality industry. Includes International Cuisine Pavilion. **Dates and Locations:** 2008 May 17-20; Chicago, IL; McCormick Place.

OTHER SOURCES

★1693★ American Culinary Federation (ACF)

180 Center Place Way
St. Augustine, FL 32095
Ph: (904)824-4468   Fax: (904)825-4758
Fr: 800-624-9458
E-mail: hcramb@acfchefs.net
URL: http://www.acfchefs.org

Description: Aims to promote the culinary profession and provide on-going educational training and networking for members. Provides opportunities for competition, professional recognition, and access to educational forums with other culinary experts at local, regional, national, and international events. Operates the National Apprenticeship Program for Cooks and pastry cooks. Offers programs that address certification of the individual chef's skills, accreditation of culinary programs, apprenticeship of cooks and pastry cooks, professional development, and the fight against childhood hunger.

★1694★ Association for International Practical Training (AIPT)

10400 Little Patuxent Pkwy., Ste. 250
Columbia, MD 21044-3519
Ph: (410)997-2200   Fax: (410)992-3924
E-mail: aipt@aipt.org
URL: http://www.aipt.org

Description: Providers worldwide of on-the-job training programs for students and professionals seeking international career development and life-changing experiences. Arranges workplace exchanges in hundreds of professional fields, bringing employers and trainees together from around the world. Client list ranges from small farming communities to Fortune 500 companies.

★1695★ Chef

Cambridge Educational
PO Box 2053
Princeton, NJ 08543-2053
Ph: 800-257-5126   Fax: (609)671-0266
Fr: 800-468-4227
E-mail: custserv@films.com
URL: http://www.cambridgeeducational.com

VHS and DVD. $39.95. 14 minutes. 1990. Part of the Vocational Visions Career series.

★1696★ International Association of Culinary Professionals (IACP)

304 W Liberty St., Ste. 201
Louisville, KY 40202
Ph: (502)581-9786   Fax: (502)589-3602
Fr: 800-928-4227
E-mail: iacp@hqtrs.com
URL: http://www.iacp.com

Description: Represents cooking school owners, food writers, chefs, caterers, culinary specialists, directors, teachers, cookbook authors, food stylists, food photographers, student/apprentices, and individuals in related industries in 20 countries. Promotes the interests of cooking schools, teachers, and culinary professionals. Encourages the exchange of information and education. Promotes professional standards and accreditation procedures. Maintains a Foundation to award culinary scholarships and grants.

★1697★ International Council on Hotel, Restaurant, and Institutional Education (CHRIE)

2810 N Parham Rd., Ste. 230
Richmond, VA 23294
Ph: (804)346-4800   Fax: (804)346-5009
E-mail: kmccarty@chrie.org
URL: http://www.chrie.org

Description: Schools and colleges offering specialized education and training in hospitals, recreation, tourism and hotel, restaurant, and institutional administration; individuals, executives, and students. Provides networking opportunities and professional development.

★1698★ National Restaurant Association (NRA)

1200 17th St. NW
Washington, DC 20036
Ph: (202)331-5900   Fax: (202)331-2429
Fr: 800-424-5156
E-mail: info@dineout.org
URL: http://www.restaurant.org

Description: Represents restaurants, cafeterias, clubs, contract foodservice management, drive-ins, caterers, institutional food services, and other members of the foodservice industry; also represents establishments belonging to non-affiliated state and local restaurant associations in governmental affairs. Supports foodservice education and research in several educational institutions. Is affiliated with the Educational Foundation of the National Restaurant Association to provide training and education for operators, food and equipment manufacturers, distributors, and educators. Has 300,000 member locations.

★1699★ United States Personal Chef Association

610 Quantum Road NE
Rio Rancho, NM 87124
Ph: (505)994-6372   Fr: 800-995-2138
URL: http://www.uspca.com

Description: The largest organization dedicated to the personal service industry.

Chemical Engineers

SOURCES OF HELP-WANTED ADS

★1700★ Adhesives Age

Penton Media Inc.
9800 Metcalf Ave.
Overland Park, KS 66212
Ph: (913)341-1300   Fax: (913)967-1898
URL: http://www.chemweek.com/verticals/

Monthly. Magazine containing news and technology for those engaged in the manufacturing, application, research, and marketing of adhesives, sealants, and related products.

★1701★ American Institute of Chemical Engineers Journal

John Wiley & Sons Inc.
111 River St.
Hoboken, NJ 07030-5774
Ph: (201)748-6000   Fax: (201)748-6088
Fr: 800-825-7550
URL: http://as.wiley.com/WileyCDA/Wiley-Title/productCd-AIC.html

Monthly. $1,680.00/year for U.S., print only; $1,824.00/year for Canada and Mexico, print only; $1,908.00/year for other countries, print only; $1,848.00/year for U.S., combined; $1,992.00/year for Canada and Mexico, combined; $2,076.00/year for other countries, combined. Journal focusing on technological advances in core areas of chemical engineering as well as in other relevant engineering disciplines.

★1702★ Chemical Engineering

Chemical Week Associates
110 Williams St.
New York, NY 10038
Ph: (212)621-4900   Fax: (212)621-4800
URL: http://www.che.com

Monthly. $60.00/year for individuals, print; $80.00/year for individuals; $159.00/year for other countries. Chemical process industries magazine.

★1703★ Chemical Engineering Communications

Taylor & Francis Group Journals
325 Chestnut St., Ste. 800
Philadelphia, PA 19106
Ph: (215)625-8900   Fax: (215)625-8914
Fr: 800-354-1420
URL: http://www.informaworld.com/open-url?genre=journal&issn=0098-

Monthly. $2,053.00/year for individuals, print only; $4,712/year for online subscription; $4,960/year for online and print subscription. Journal focusing on the results of basic and applied research in chemical engineering.

★1704★ Chemical & Engineering News

American Chemical Society
1155 16th St. NW
Washington, DC 20036
Ph: (202)872-4600   Fax: (202)872-4615
Fr: 800-227-5558
URL: http://pubs.acs.org/cen/about.html

Weekly. Magazine on chemical and engineering news.

★1705★ Chemical Engineering Progress

American Institute of Chemical Engineers
3 Park Ave.
New York, NY 10016-5991
Ph: (212)591-7333   Fax: (212)591-8888
Fr: 800-242-4363
URL: http://www.aiche.org/CEP/index.aspx

Monthly. $160.00/year for nonmembers, in North America; $250.00/year for nonmembers, international; $200.00/year for nonmembers, with online; in North America; $290.00/year for nonmembers, with online; international. Chemical process industries magazine.

★1706★ Chemical Engineering and Technology

John Wiley & Sons Inc.
111 River St.
Hoboken, NJ 07030-5774
Ph: (201)748-6000   Fax: (201)748-6088
Fr: 800-825-7550
E-mail: cet@wiley-vch.de

URL: http://www3.interscience.wiley.com/cgi-bin/jhome/10008333

Monthly. $4,026.00/year for institutions; $458.00/year for individuals. Journal focusing on all aspects of chemical and process engineering.

★1707★ Chemical Equipment

Reed Business Information
360 Park Ave. S
New York, NY 10010
Ph: (646)746-6400   Fax: (646)746-7431
URL: http://www.reedbusinessinteractive.com

Free, for qualified professionals; $72.90/year for individuals, cover price. Tabloid on the chemical process industry.

★1708★ Chemical Market Reporter

Schnell Publishing Company Inc.
360 Park Ave. S
12th Fl.
New York, NY 10010
Ph: (212)791-4200   Fax: (212)791-4321

Weekly (Mon.). International tabloid newspaper for the chemical process industries. Includes analytical reports on developments in the chemical marketplace, plant expansions, new technology, corporate mergers, finance, current chemical prices, and regulatory matters.

★1709★ The Chemical Record

John Wiley & Sons Inc.
111 River St.
Hoboken, NJ 07030-5774
Ph: (201)748-6000   Fax: (201)748-6088
Fr: 800-825-7550
URL: http://www3.interscience.wiley.com/cgi-bin/jhome/72515006

Bimonthly. $100.00/year for U.S., print only rates; $100.00/year for Canada and Mexico, print only rates, add 6%GST in Canada; $130.00/year for other countries, print only rates; $435.00/year for U.S. institutions, print only rates; $507.00/year for institutions, Canada and Mexico, print only rates, in Canada, please add 6% GST; $549.00/year for institutions, other countries, print only rates;

$479.00/year for U.S. institutions, combined print with online access rates; $551.00/year for institutions, Canada and Mexico, print with online rates, in Canada, 6%GST; $593.00/year for institutions, other countries, combined print with online access rates. Journal publishing overviews of new developments at the cutting edge of chemistry of interest to a wide audience of chemists.

★1710★ **The Chemist**

American Institute of Chemists Inc.
315 Chestnut St.
Philadelphia, PA 19106-2702
Ph: (215)873-8224   Fax: (215)629-5224
E-mail: info@theaic.org
URL: http://www.theaic.org

Description: Six issues/year. Covers news items relating to the chemical profession and membership in the Institute. Reports on legislation, licensure, earnings, awards, and professional education. Recurring features include news of employment opportunities and news of members. Published alternate months as a magazine.

★1711★ **Chemistry & Biology**

Elsevier Science Inc.
360 Park Ave. S
New York, NY 10010
Ph: (212)989-5800   Fax: (212)633-3990
URL: http://www.elsevier.com/

Monthly. $1,745/year for institutions, U.S. and Canada; $369.00/year for individuals, U.S. and Canada. Journal focused on genetic, computational, or theoretical information of chemistry and biology, substantiating experimental data.

★1712★ **The Electrochemical Society Interface**

The Electrochemical Society Inc.
65 S Main St., Bldg. D
Pennington, NJ 08534-2839
Ph: (609)737-1902   Fax: (609)737-2743
E-mail: interface@electrochem.org
URL: http://www.electrochem.org/dl/interface/

Quarterly. $15.00/year for members; $68.00/year for nonmembers; $15.00 for single issue, members; $20.00 for single issue, nonmembers. Publication featuring news and articles of interest to members of the Electrochemical Society.

★1713★ **Engineering in Life Sciences**

John Wiley & Sons Inc.
111 River St.
Hoboken, NJ 07030-5774
Ph: (201)748-6000   Fax: (201)748-6088
Fr: 800-825-7550
URL: http://as.wiley.com/WileyCDA/WileyTitle/productCd-2129.html

Bimonthly. $765.00/year for institutions, rest of Europe; $1,170.00/year for institutions, Switzerland and Liechtenstein; $1,005.00/year for institutions, rest of world; $842.00/year for institutions, print with online rest of Europe; $1,287.00/year for institutions, print

with online Switzerland and Liechtenstein; $1,106.00/year for institutions, print with online rest of world. Journal focusing on the field of biotechnology and related topics including microbiology, genetics, biochemistry, and chemistry.

★1714★ **Engineering Times**

National Society of Professional Engineers
1420 King St.
Alexandria, VA 22314
Ph: (703)684-2800
URL: http://www.nspe.org

Monthly. Magazine (tabloid) covering professional, legislative, and techology issues for an engineering audience.

★1715★ **ENR: Engineering News-Record**

McGraw-Hill Inc.
1221 Ave. of the Americas
New York, NY 10020-1095
Ph: (212)512-2000   Fax: (212)512-3840
Fr: 877-833-5524
E-mail: enr_web_editors@mcgraw-hill.com
URL: http://www.mymags.com/moreinfo.php?itemID=20012

Weekly. $94.00/year for individuals, print. Magazine focusing on engineering and construction.

★1716★ **Graduating Engineer & Computer Careers**

Career Recruitment Media
211 W Wacker Dr., Ste. 900
Chicago, IL 60606
Ph: (312)525-3100
URL: http://www.graduatingengineer.com

Quarterly. $15.00/year for individuals. Magazine focusing on employment, education, and career development for entry-level engineers and computer scientists.

★1717★ **High Technology Careers Magazine**

HTC
4701 Patrick Henry Dr., No. 1901
Santa Clara, CA 95054-1847
Fax: (408)567-0242
URL: http://www.hightechcareers.com

Bimonthly. $29.00/year; $35.00/year for Canada; $85.00/year for out of country. Magazine (tabloid) containing employment opportunity information for the engineering and technical community.

★1718★ **Journal of Chemical Theory and Computation**

American Chemical Society
1155 16th St. NW
Washington, DC 20036
Ph: (202)872-4600   Fax: (202)872-4615
Fr: 800-227-5558
URL: http://pubs.acs.org/journals/jctcce

$1,106.00/year for institutions, North America; $1,159.00/year for institutions, outside

North America; $205.00/year for students, outside North America. Journal presenting new theories, methodology, and/or important applications in quantum chemistry, molecular dynamics, and statistical mechanics.

★1719★ **Modern Plastics**

Chemical Week Associates
110 Williams St.
New York, NY 10038
Ph: (212)621-4900   Fax: (212)621-4800
URL: http://www.modplas.com

Monthly. $59.00/year for individuals; $99.00 for two years, U.S. and possessions; $110.00/year for Canada; $199.00 for two years, for Canada; $150.00/year for other countries; $250.00 for two years. Magazine for the plastics industry.

★1720★ **Nanoparticle News**

BCC Research
70 New Canaan Ave.
Norwalk, CT 06850
Ph: (203)750-9783   Fax: (203)229-0087
Fr: (866)285-7215
URL: http://www.the-infoshop.com/newsletter/bc4377_fine_particle_

Monthly. $575.00/year for individuals; $661.25/year for individuals, order electronic copy; $495.00 for single issue, web access and archive; $590.00 for single issue, hard copy, web access and archive (North America). Publication covering issues in the chemical industry.

★1721★ **NSBE Magazine**

NSBE Publications
205 Daingerfield Rd.
Alexandria, VA 22314
Ph: (703)549-2207   Fax: (703)683-5312
URL: http://www.nsbe.org/publications/premieradvertisers.php

Journal providing information on engineering careers, self-development, and cultural issues for recent graduates with technical majors.

★1722★ **PALAIOS**

SEPM Publications
6128 E 38th St., Ste. 308
Tulsa, OK 74135-5814
Ph: (918)610-3361   Fax: (918)621-1685
Fr: 800-865-9765
URL: http://www.sepm.org/

Bimonthly. $200.00/year for individuals, for U.S. online version with CD-ROM; $235.00/year for individuals, for U.S. print and online version with CD-ROM; $200.00/year for other countries, online version with CD-ROM; $245.00/year for other countries, print and online version with CD-ROM. Journal providing information on the impact of life on Earth history as recorded in the paleontological and sedimentological records. Covers areas such as biogeochemistry, ichnology, sedimentology, stratigraphy, paleoecology, paleoclimatology, and paleoceanography.

★1723★ Plastics Engineering

Society of Plastics Engineers
14 Fairfield Dr.
PO Box 403
Brookfield, CT 06804-0403
Ph: (203)775-0471   Fax: (203)775-8490
E-mail: advertising@4spe.org
URL: http://www.4spe.org/pub

Monthly. $142.00/year for nonmembers; $242.00/year for nonmembers, outside North America; $180.00/year for institutions, corporate libraries; $280.00/year for institutions, corporate libraries outside North America. Plastics trade magazine.

★1724★ Plastics News

Crain Communications Inc.
1725 Merriman Rd.
Akron, OH 44313-5283
Ph: (330)836-9180   Fax: (313)446-6777
Fr: 800-678-9595
E-mail: editorial@plasticsnews.com
URL: http://www.plasticsnews.com

Weekly. $79.00/year for U.S., print + web; $129.00/year for Canada, print + web; $177.00/year for individuals, print + web, Mexico; $287.00/year for other countries, print + web; $99.00/year for other countries, web only. Magazine (tabloid) for the plastics industry providing business news.

★1725★ Powder and Bulk Engineering

CSC Publishing Inc.
1155 Northland Dr.
St. Paul, MN 55120-1288
Fax: (651)287-5600
URL: http://www.powderbulk.com/

Monthly. $100.00/year for individuals, outside North America, or digital format. Journal serving chemical, food, plastics, pulp and paper, and electronic industries.

★1726★ Power

McGraw-Hill Inc.
1221 Ave. of the Americas
New York, NY 10020-1095
Ph: (212)512-2000   Fax: (212)512-3840
Fr: 877-833-5524
E-mail: robert_peltier@platts.com
URL: http://online.platts.com/PPS/ P=m&s=1029337384756.1478827&e=1

Monthly. Magazine for engineers in electric utilities, process and manufacturing plants, commercial and service establishments, and consulting, design, and construction engineering firms working in the power technology field.

★1727★ Rubber World

Rubber World
1867 W Market St.
Akron, OH 44313-6901
Ph: (330)864-2122   Fax: (330)864-5298
E-mail: jhl@rubberworld.com
URL: http://www.rubberworld.com/

$34.00/year for individuals; $39.00/year for Canada; $89.00/year for other countries, airmail. Rubber manufacturing magazine.

★1728★ SWE, Magazine of the Society of Women Engineers

Society of Women Engineers
230 East Ohio St., Ste. 400
Chicago, IL 60611-3265
Ph: (312)596-5223
E-mail: hq@swe.org
URL: http://www.swe.org

Quarterly. $30.00/year for nonmembers. Magazine for engineering students and for women and men working in the engineering and technology fields. Covers career guidance, continuing development and topical issues.

★1729★ WEPANEWS

Women in Engineering Programs & Advocates Network
1901 E. Asbury Ave., Ste. 220
Denver, CO 80208
Ph: (303)871-4643   Fax: (303)871-6833
E-mail: dmatt@wepan.org
URL: http://www.wepan.org

Description: 2/year. Seeks to provide greater access for women to careers in engineering. Includes news of graduate, undergraduate, freshmen, pre-college, and re-entry engineering programs for women. Recurring features include job listings, faculty, grant, and conference news, international engineering program news, action group news, notices of publications available, and a column titled Kudos.

PLACEMENT AND JOB REFERRAL SERVICES

★1730★ American Indian Science and Engineering Society (AISES)

PO Box 9828
Albuquerque, NM 87119-9828
Ph: (505)765-1052   Fax: (505)765-5608
E-mail: info@aises.org
URL: http://www.aises.org

Description: Represents American Indian and non-Indian students and professionals in science, technology, and engineering fields; corporations representing energy, mining, aerospace, electronic, and computer fields. Seeks to motivate and encourage students to pursue undergraduate and graduate studies in science, engineering, and technology. Sponsors science fairs in grade schools, teacher training workshops, summer math/ science sessions for 8th-12th graders, professional chapters, and student chapters in colleges. Offers scholarships. Adult members serve as role models, advisers, and mentors for students. Operates placement service.

★1731★ American Oil Chemists' Society (AOCS)

PO Box 17190
Urbana, IL 61803-7190
Ph: (217)359-2344   Fax: (217)351-8091

E-mail: general@aocs.org
URL: http://www.aocs.org

Members: Chemists, biochemists, chemical engineers, research directors, plant personnel, and others in laboratories and chemical process industries concerned with animal, marine, and vegetable oils and fats, and their extraction, refining, safety, packaging, quality control, and use in consumer and industrial products such as foods, drugs, paints, waxes, lubricants, soaps, and cosmetics. **Activities:** Sponsors short courses; certifies referee chemists; distributes cooperative check samples; sells official reagents. Maintains 100 committees. Operates job placement service for members only.

★1732★ Engineering Society of Detroit (ESD)

2000 Town Ctr., Ste. 2610
Southfield, MI 48075
Ph: (248)353-0735   Fax: (248)353-0736
E-mail: esd@esd.org
URL: http://esd.org

Description: Engineers from all disciplines; scientists and technologists. Conducts technical programs and engineering refresher courses; sponsors conferences and expositions. Maintains speakers' bureau; offers placement services; although based in Detroit, MI, society membership is international.

★1733★ Korean-American Scientists and Engineers Association (KSEA)

1952 Gallows Rd., Ste. 300
Vienna, VA 22182
Ph: (703)748-1221   Fax: (703)748-1331
E-mail: admin@ksea.org
URL: http://www.ksea.org

Description: Represents scientists and engineers holding single or advanced degrees. Promotes friendship and mutuality among Korean and American scientists and engineers; contributes to Korea's scientific, technological, industrial, and economic developments; strengthens the scientific, technological, and cultural bonds between Korea and the U.S. Sponsors symposium. Maintains speakers' bureau, placement service, and biographical archives. Compiles statistics.

★1734★ National Organization for the Professional Advancement of Black Chemists and Chemical Engineers (NOBCChE)

PO Box 77040
Washington, DC 20013
Fax: (202)667-1705   Fr: 800-776-1419
E-mail: president@nobcche.org
URL: http://www.nobcche.org

Description: Black professionals in science and chemistry. Seeks to aid black scientists and chemists in reaching their full professional potential; encourages black students to pursue scientific studies and employment; promotes participation of blacks in scientific research. Provides volunteers to teach science courses in selected elementary schools; sponsors scientific field trips for students; maintains speakers' bureau for schools. Conducts technical seminars in Africa. Sponsors competitions; presents awards for significant achievements to individuals in the field. Maintains placement service; compiles statistics.

★1735★ **Society of Hispanic Professional Engineers (SHPE)**

5400 E Olympic Blvd., Ste. 210
Los Angeles, CA 90022
Ph: (323)725-3970　　Fax: (323)725-0316
E-mail: shpenational@shpe.org
URL: http://oneshpe.shpe.org/wps/portal/national

Description: Represents engineers, student engineers, and scientists. Aims to increase the number of Hispanic engineers by providing motivation and support to students. Sponsors competitions and educational programs. Maintains placement service and speakers' bureau; compiles statistics.

EMPLOYER DIRECTORIES AND NETWORKING LISTS

★1736★ **American Institute of Chemists-Professional Directory**

American Institute of Chemists Inc.
315 Chestnut St.
Philadelphia, PA 19106-2702
Ph: (215)873-8224　　Fax: (215)629-5224
URL: http://www.theaic.org

Annual, spring. Covers more than 3,500 member chemists. Entries include: Individual name and title, address, phone, name of employer, position title, principal job responsibility, principal field of chemistry, highest academic degree, certification, year elected to membership, membership category, local affiliation. Commercial use requires special permission. Arrangement: Alphabetical. Indexes: Geographical.

★1737★ **American Men and Women of Science**

Gale, Cengage Learning
27500 Drake Rd.
Farmington Hills, MI 48331-3535
Ph: (248)699-4253　　Fax: (248)699-8065
Fr: 800-877-4253
URL: http://www.gale.com

Biennial, latest edition 23rd, October 2006; new edition expected 24th, January 2008. $1,075.00 for individuals. Covers over 129,700 U.S. and Canadian scientists active in the physical, biological, mathematical, computer science, and engineering fields; includes references to previous edition for deceased scientists and nonrespondents. Entries include: Name, address, education, personal and career data, memberships, honors and awards, research interest. Arrangement: Alphabetical. Indexes: Discipline (in separate volume).

★1738★ **Careers in Focus: Engineering**

Facts On File Inc.
132 W 31st St., 17th Fl.
New York, NY 10001
Ph: (212)967-8800　　Fax: 800-678-3633
Fr: 800-322-8755
URL: http://www.factsonfile.com

3rd edition, 2007. $29.95 for individuals; $26.95 for libraries. Publication includes: List of resources to consult for more information. Principal content of publication consists of job descriptions, advancement opportunities, educational requirements, employment outlook, salary information, and working conditions for careers in the field of engineering. Indexes: Alphabetical.

★1739★ **Chemical Week-Buyers Guide Issue**

Chemical Week Associates
110 Williams St.
New York, NY 10038
Ph: (212)621-4900　　Fax: (212)621-4800
URL: http://www.chemweekbuyersguide.com/public/

Annual, October. $115.00. Publication includes: About 4,200 manufacturers and suppliers of chemical raw materials to the chemical process industries; 400 manufacturers of packaging materials; and suppliers of products and services to the chemical process industries, including hazardous waste/environmental services, computer services, plant design, construction, consulting, shipping, and transportation. Entries include: Over 17,000 product/service listings, company name, address, phone; local addresses and phone numbers for up to 25 sales locations. Arrangement: Separate alphabetical sections for chemical, packaging, and hazardous waste/environmental services. Indexes: Product (all sections); trade name (chemical and packaging sections only).

★1740★ **Consulting Services**

Association of Consulting Chemists and Chemical Engineers Inc.
PO Box 297
Sparta, NJ 07871
Ph: (973)729-6671　　Fax: (973)729-7088
URL: http://www.chemconsult.org

Biennial, even years. $30.00 for individuals. Covers about 160 member consultants in chemistry, chemical engineering, metallurgy, etc. Entries include: Individual name, address, certificate number, qualifications, affiliation, experience, facilities, staff. Arrangement: Classified by area of expertise. Indexes: Personal name, geographical.

★1741★ **Directory of Chemical Producers-United States**

SRI Consulting
4300 Bohannon Dr., Ste. 200
Menlo Park, CA 94025-3477
Ph: (650)384-4300
E-mail: dcp@sric.sri.com
URL: http://www.sriconsulting.com

Annual; latest edition June 2007. Covers over 1,200 United States basic chemical producers manufacturing 7,900 chemicals in commercial quantities at more than 3,500 plant locations. Entries include: For companies–Company name, division or subsidiary names, corporate address, phone, fax, telex, location of each subsidiary, division, and manufacturing plant, and the products made at each plant location. For products–Producer name and plant locations, alternate product names (if any). Subscription price includes bound volume, plus access to the directory staff for inquiries. Arrangement: Companies are alphabetical; products are alphabetical and by group (dyes, pesticides, etc.); manufacturing plants are geographical. Indexes: Geographical, product.

★1742★ **Directory of Contract Staffing Firms**

C.E. Publications Inc.
PO Box 3006
Bothell, WA 98041-3006
Ph: (425)806-5200　　Fax: (425)806-5585
URL: http://www.cjhunter.com/dcsf/overview.html

Covers nearly 1,300 contract firms actively engaged in the employment of engineering, IT/IS, and technical personnel for 'temporary' contract assignments throughout the world. Entries include: Company name, address, phone, name of contact, email, web address. Arrangement: Alphabetical. Indexes: Geographical.

★1743★ **Directory of World Chemical Producers**

Chemical Information Services Inc.
9101 LBJ Fwy., Ste. 310
PO Box 743512
Dallas, TX 75243
Ph: (214)349-6200　　Fax: (214)349-6286
URL: http://www.chemicalinfo.com/_shop/products.plx?product=all

Annual; latest edition 2007. $1,350.00 for book version; $3,365.00 for global single user version, Internet format; $3,860.00 for global single user version, CD format. Covers over 20,000 producers of all classes of chemicals worldwide, including bulk pharmaceuticals, fire chemicals, agrochemicals, dyes, pigments, cosmetics, food ingredients, intermediates, etc. Entries include: Company name, address, phone, fax, telex, E-mail address, websites, contact information. Arrangement: Product, CAS#, geographical.

★1744★ **Indiana Society of Professional Engineers-Directory**

Indiana Society of Professional Engineers
PO Box 20806
Indianapolis, IN 46220
Ph: (317)255-2267　　Fax: (317)255-2530
URL: http://www.indspe.org

Annual, fall. Covers member registered engineers, land surveyors, engineering students, and engineers in training. Entries include: Member name, address, phone, type of membership, business information, specialty. Arrangement: Alphabetical by chapter area.

★1745★ LabGuide
American Chemical Society
1155 16th St. NW
Washington, DC 20036
Ph: (202)872-4600　　Fax: (202)872-4615
Fr: 800-227-5558
E-mail: labguide@acs.org
URL: http://www.mediabrains.com

Annual; latest edition 49. Publication includes: List of about 2,200 manufacturers of scientific instruments, equipment, chemicals, and other supplies for scientific research and chemical laboratories; laboratory supply houses; analytical and research services. Entries include: Company name, address, phone, fax, e-mail, URL, products, and services. Arrangement: Alphabetical. Indexes: Product, chemical, service, instrument, company name.

★1746★ Peterson's Job Opportunities in Engineering and Technology
Peterson's Guides
2000 Lenox Dr.
Box 67005
Lawrenceville, NJ 08648
Ph: (609)896-1800　　Fax: (609)896-4531
Fr: 800-338-3282
E-mail: custsvc@petersons.com
URL: http://www.petersons.com

Compiled by the Peterson's staff. Fourth edition, 1996. $21.95 (paper). 379 pages. Profiles 2,000 high-tech companies looking primarily for technical personnel in such fields as biotechnology, telecommunications, software, computers and peripherals, defense, and aerospace. Contains job-search strategies and career options to help match education and expertise to the job market. Indexed geographically, by industry, and by hiring needs.

★1747★ U.S. National Committee for the International Union of Pure and Applied Chemistry-Directory
U.S. National Committee for the International Union of Pure and Applied Chemistry
Keck Center
WS 550
Washington, DC 20001
Ph: (202)334-2807　　Fax: (202)334-2231
URL: http://www7.nationalacademies.org/usnc-iupac/

Annual, July. Covers 29 member chemists and chemical engineers in the United States.

HANDBOOKS AND MANUALS

★1748★ The Best Resumes for Scientists and Engineers
John Wiley & Sons Inc.
1 Wiley Dr.
Somerset, NJ 08873
Ph: (732)469-4400　　Fax: (732)302-2300
Fr: 800-225-5945
E-mail: custserv@wiley.com

URL: http://www.wiley.com/WileyCDA/
Adele Lewis and David J. Moore. Second edition, 1993. $37.50; $19.95 (paper). 224 pages. Presents an extensive collection of scientific and engineering resumes, highlighting the important differences between these and resumes written for other occupations.

★1749★ Career Management for Scientists and Engineers
American Chemical Society
1155 16th St., NW
Washington, DC 20036
Ph: (202)872-4600　　Fr: 800-227-5558
URL: http://www.acs.org/

John K. Borchardt. May 2000. $24.95. Illustrated. 272 pages. College level studies.

★1750★ Careers for Chemists: A World Outside the Lab
American Chemical Society
1155 16th St., NW
Washington, DC 20036
Ph: (202)872-4600　　Fr: 800-227-5558
URL: http://portal.acs.org/portal/acs/corg/content

Fred Owens, Roger Uhler and Corrine A. Marasco. 1997. 211 pages.

★1751★ Great Jobs for Chemistry Majors
The McGraw-Hill Companies
PO Box 182604
Columbus, OH 43272
Fax: (614)759-3749　　Fr: 877-883-5524
E-mail: customer.service@mcgraw-hill.com
URL: http://www.mcgraw-hill.com

Mark Rowh. Second edition, 2005. $15.95 (paper). 208 pages.

★1752★ Great Jobs for Engineering Majors
The McGraw-Hill Companies
PO Box 182604
Columbus, OH 43272
Fax: (614)759-3749　　Fr: 877-883-5524
E-mail: customer.service@mcgraw-hill.com
URL: http://www.mcgraw-hill.com

Geraldine O. Garner. Second edition, 2002. $14.95. 256 pages. Covers all the career options open to students majoring in engineering.

★1753★ How to Succeed as an Engineer: A Practical Guide to Enhance Your Career
Institute of Electrical & Electronics Engineers
445 Hoes Lane
Piscataway, NJ 08854
Ph: (732)981-0060　　Fax: (732)981-9667
Fr: 800-678-4333
URL: http://www.ieee.org

Todd Yuzuriha. 1999. $29.95 (paper). 367 pages.

★1754★ The I Hate Selling Book: Business-Building Advice for Consultants, Attorneys, Accountants, Engineers, Architects, and Other Professionals
AMACOM
1601 Broadway, 12th Fl.
New York, NY 10019-7420
Ph: (212)586-8100　　Fax: (212)903-8168
Fr: 800-262-9699
URL: http://www.amanet.org

Allan S. Boress. 2001. $29.95. 240 pages.

★1755★ Is There a Chemical Engineer Inside You?: A Student's Guide to Exploring Chemical Engineering
Bonamy Publishing
PO Box 70362
Eugene, OR 97401
Ph: (541)988-1005　　Fax: (541)988-1008
Fr: 877-644-6337

Celeste Baine. $9.00 (paper). 35 pages. 2004. Explores Chemical Engineering as a career.

★1756★ The New Engineer's Guide to Career Growth & Professional Awareness
Institute of Electrical & Electronics Engineers
445 Hoes Lane
Piscataway, NJ 08854
Ph: (732)981-0060　　Fax: (732)981-9667
Fr: 800-678-4333
URL: http://www.ieee.org

Irving J. Gabelman, editor. 1996. $39.95 (paper). 275 pages.

★1757★ Opportunities in Chemistry Careers
The McGraw-Hill Companies
PO Box 182604
Columbus, OH 43272
Fax: (614)759-3749　　Fr: 877-883-5524
E-mail: customer.service@mcgraw-hill.com
URL: http://www.mcgraw-hill.com

John H. Woodburn and John Hazlett. Second edition, 2002. $14.95 (paper). 145 pages. Part of the VGM Opportunities Series.

★1758★ Opportunities in Engineering Careers
The McGraw-Hill Companies
PO Box 182604
Columbus, OH 43272
Fax: (614)759-3749　　Fr: 877-883-5524
E-mail: customer.service@mcgraw-hill.com
URL: http://www.mcgraw-hill.com

Nicholas Basta. Revised second edition, 2002. $13.95; $11.95 (paper). 160 pages. Outlines typical job titles, salaries, career paths, and employment prospects.

★1759★ *Opportunities in High Tech Careers*

The McGraw-Hill Companies
PO Box 182604
Columbus, OH 43272
Fax: (614)759-3749   Fr: 877-883-5524
E-mail: customer.service@mcgraw-hill.com
URL: http://www.mcgraw-hill.com

Gary Colter and Deborah Yanuck. 1999. $14.95; $11.95 (paper). 160 pages. Explores high technology careers. Describes job opportunities, how to make a career decision, how to prepare for high technology jobs, job hunting techniques, and future trends.

★1760★ *Opportunities in Research and Development Careers*

The McGraw-Hill Companies
PO Box 182604
Columbus, OH 43272
Fax: (614)759-3749   Fr: 877-883-5524
E-mail: customer.service@mcgraw-hill.com
URL: http://www.mcgraw-hill.com

Jan Goldberg. 1996. $11.95 (paper). 146 pages.

★1761★ *Real People Working in Engineering*

The McGraw-Hill Companies
PO Box 182604
Columbus, OH 43272
Fax: (614)759-3749   Fr: 877-883-5524
E-mail: customer.service@mcgraw-hill.com
URL: http://www.mcgraw-hill.com

Blythe Camenson, Jan Goldberg. 1997. $17.95 (paper). 160 pages. Interviews and profiles of working professionals capture a range of opportunities in this field.

★1762★ *Resumes for Engineering Careers*

The McGraw-Hill Companies
PO Box 182604
Columbus, OH 43272
Fax: (614)759-3749   Fr: 877-883-5524
E-mail: customer.service@mcgraw-hill.com
URL: http://www.mcgraw-hill.com

Third edition, 2005. $11.95 (paper). 144 pages. Contains sample resumes and cover letters applicable to any engineering field.

★1763★ *Resumes for Scientific and Technical Careers*

The McGraw-Hill Companies
PO Box 182604
Columbus, OH 43272
Fax: (614)759-3749   Fr: 877-883-5524
E-mail: customer.service@mcgraw-hill.com
URL: http://www.mcgraw-hill.com

Third edition, 2007. $12.95 (paper). 144 pages. Provides resume advice for individuals interested in working in scientific and technical careers. Includes sample resumes and cover letters.

EMPLOYMENT AGENCIES AND SEARCH FIRMS

★1764★ ARI International
1501 Ocean Ave.
Seal Beach, CA 90740
Ph: (562)795-5111   Fax: (562)596-9794
E-mail: ari.ron@att.net
URL: http://www.ariinternationalsearch.com

International executive search firm.

★1765★ Asset Group Inc.
PO Box 211
Verona, NJ 07044
Ph: (973)641-0967   Fax: (973)571-1387
E-mail: ralley@assetgroupsearch.com
URL: http://www.assetgroupsearch.com

International executive search firm.

★1766★ The Baer Group
53 Perimeter Center E., Ste. 100
Atlanta, GA 30346
Ph: (770)557-4900   Fax: (770)557-3499
URL: http://www.baergroup.com

Executive search firm.

★1767★ The Beam Group
1835 Market St., Ste. 502
Philadelphia, PA 19103
Ph: (215)988-2100   Fax: (215)988-1558
E-mail: info@beamgroup.com
URL: http://www.beamgroup.com

Executive search firm.

★1768★ Brooke Chase Associates Inc.
1543 2ND St., Ste. 201
Sarasota, FL 34236
Ph: (941)358-3111   Fax: (866)851-5693
Fr: 877-374-0039
E-mail: jmcelmeel@brookechase.com
URL: http://www.brookechase.com

Executive search firm. Branches in San Rafael, CA; Chicago; and Charlotte, NC.

★1769★ Capstone Inc.
971 Albany Shaker Rd.
Latham, NY 12110
Ph: (518)783-9300   Fax: (518)783-9328
E-mail: info@capstone-inc.com
URL: http://www.capstone-inc.com

Executive search firm.

★1770★ Catalyx Group
303 W. 42nd St., Ste. 607
New York, NY 10036
Ph: (212)956-3525
E-mail: lposter@catalyx.com
URL: http://www.catalyx.com

Executive search firm.

★1771★ Cochran, Cochran & Yale LLC
955 E. Henrietta Rd.
Rochester, NY 14623
Ph: (585)424-6060   Fax: (585)424-6069
E-mail: roch@ccy.com
URL: http://www.ccy.com

Executive search firm. Branches in Denver, CO and Williamsville, NY.

★1772★ Colli Associates
414 Caboose Ln.
Valrico, FL 33594
Ph: (813)681-2145   Fax: (813)661-5217
E-mail: colli@gte.net

Employment agency. Executive search firm.

★1773★ Conboy, Sur & Associates Inc.
15 E. Churchville Rd., Ste. 170
Bel Air, MD 21014-3837
Ph: (410)925-4122
E-mail: wksur@conboysur.com
URL: http://www.conboysur.com

Executive search firm.

★1774★ Crowder & Company
40950 Woodward Ave., Ste. 335
Bloomfield Hills, MI 48304
Ph: (248)645-0909   Fax: (248)645-2366
E-mail: ewc@crowdercompany.com
URL: http://www.crowdercompany.com

Executive search firm.

★1775★ ETI Search International
990 Hammond Dr., Ste. 825
Atlanta, GA 30328
Ph: (770)399-8492   Fax: (770)399-8487

Executive search firm.

★1776★ ExecuTech
500 S. Depeyster St.
PO Box 707
Kent, OH 44240
Ph: (330)677-0010   Fax: (330)677-0148
E-mail: recruiter@executech.org
URL: http://www.executech.org/

Executive search firm. Second location in Nathalie, VA.

★1777★ Executive Directions
PO Box 223
Foxboro, MA 02035
Ph: (505)698-3030   Fax: (508)543-6047
E-mail: info@execdir.com
URL: http://www.executivedirections.com

Executive search firm.

★1778★ Executive Recruiters Agency
14 Office Park Dr., Ste. 100
PO Box 21810
Little Rock, AR 72221-1810
Ph: (501)224-7000   Fax: (501)224-8534

E-mail: jobs@execrecruit.com
URL: http://www.execrecruit.com

Personnel service firm.

★1779★ **Global Employment Solutions**
10375 Park Meadows Dr., Ste. 375
Littleton, CO 80124
Ph: (303)216-9500   Fax: (303)216-9533
E-mail: careers@global
URL: http://www.gesnetwork.com

Employment agency.

★1780★ **JW Barleycorn & Associates Inc.**
1614 Lancaster Ave.
Reynoldsburg, OH 43068
Ph: (614)861-4400   Fax: (614)861-5558

Executive search firm.

★1781★ **Ken Clark International**
2000 Lenox Dr., Ste. 200
Lawrenceville, NJ 08648
Ph: (609)308-5200   Fax: (609)308-5250
E-mail: info-princeton@kenclark.com
URL: http://www.kenclark.com

Executive search firm. Branches in Newport Beach, CA; Deerfield, IL; Waltham, MA; and Wayne, PA.

★1782★ **Polly Brown Associates Inc.**
230 Park Ave., Ste. 1152
New York, NY 10169
Ph: (212)661-7575   Fax: (212)808-4126
E-mail: pbrown@pollybrownassociates.com
URL: http://www.pollybrownassociates.com

Executive search firm.

★1783★ **Quality Search Personnel Inc.**
1100 S Calumet Rd.
Chesterton, IN 46304
Ph: (219)926-8202   Fax: (219)926-3834
E-mail: info@qsjobs.com
URL: http://www.qsjobs.com

Technical recruiting specialists for placing technical and engineering personnel. The current concentration of assignments involves technical and engineering positions with a specialization in packaging and quality control. Assignments are primarily taken on a contingency basis. Industries served: consumer products, food, pharmaceutical and cosmetic, chemical, computer, heavy and light industrial.

★1784★ **Rand Personnel**
1200 Truxtun Ave., Ste. 130
Bakersfield, CA 93301
Ph: (805)325-0751   Fax: (805)325-4120

Personnel service firm serving a variety of fields.

★1785★ **Search and Recruit International**
4455 South Blvd. Ste. 110
Virginia Beach, VA 23452
Ph: (757)625-2121   Fr: 800-800-5627

Employment agency. Headquartered in Virginia Beach. Other offices in Bremerton, WA; Charleston, SC; Jacksonville, FL; Memphis, TN; Pensacola, FL; Sacramento, CA; San Bernardino, CA; San Diego, CA.

★1786★ **Tri-Serv Inc.**
22 W. Padonia Rd., Ste. C-353
Timonium, MD 21093
Ph: (410)561-1740   Fax: (410)252-7417
E-mail: info@tri-serv.coom
URL: http://www.tri-serv.com

Employment agency for technical personnel.

★1787★ **Winters Technical Staffing Services**
6 Lansing Sq., Ste. 101
Toronto, ON, Canada M2J 1T5
Ph: (416)495-7422   Fax: (416)495-8479
E-mail: brian@winterstaffing.com
URL: http://www.winterstaffing.com

Technical staffing service for permanent and contract positions in all facets of engineering. Serves government agencies, consulting engineers, and all areas of manufacturing in Canada and northeast United States.

ONLINE JOB SOURCES AND SERVICES

★1788★ **American Chemical Society**
1155 16th St. NW
Washington, DC 20036
Ph: 800-227-5558   Fr: 888-667-7988
E-mail: service@acs.org
URL: http://www.cen-chemjobs.org

Description: Offers online interviewing between employers and potential employees, postings for positions available and situations wanted, and regularly updated career advice and information for American Chemical Society members only.

★1789★ **Spherion**
2050 Spectrum Blvd.
Fort Lauderdale, FL 33309
Ph: (954)308-7600
E-mail: help@spherion.com
URL: http://www.spherion.com

Description: Recruitment firm specializing in accounting and finance, sales and marketing, interim executives, technology, engineering, retail and human resources.

TRADESHOWS

★1790★ **ACS National Meeting and Exposition**
American Chemical Society
1155 16th St. NW,
Washington, DC 20036
Ph: (202)872-4600   Fax: (202)776-8258
Fr: 800-227-5558
E-mail: help@acs.org
URL: http://www.acs.org

Primary Exhibits: Products related to all chemical disciplines.

★1791★ **American Chemical Society Southeastern Regional Conference and Exhibition**
American Chemical Society
1155 16th St. NW,
Washington, DC 20036
Ph: (202)872-4600   Fax: (202)776-8258
Fr: 800-227-5558
E-mail: help@acs.org
URL: http://www.acs.org

Annual. **Primary Exhibits:** Chemical equipment, supplies, and services.

★1792★ **American Society for Engineering Education Annual Conference and Exposition**
American Society for Engineering Education
1818 N. St. NW, Ste. 600
Washington, DC 20036-2479
Ph: (202)331-3500   Fax: (202)265-8504
E-mail: conferences@asee.org
URL: http://www.asee.org

Annual. **Primary Exhibits:** Publications, engineering supplies and equipment, computers, software, and research companies all products and services related to engineering education.

★1793★ **AOCS Annual Meeting & Expo**
American Oil Chemist Society
2710 S. Boulder
Urbana, IL 61802-6996
Ph: (217)359-2344   Fax: (217)351-8091
E-mail: general@aocs.org
URL: http://www.aocs.org

Annual. **Primary Exhibits:** Fat and oil processing plant equipment, supplies, and services; laboratory instrumentation; chemical ingredients for foods, detergents, and personal care products; and publications.

★1794★ **National Industrial Automation Show & Conference**
Reed Exhibitions (North American Headquarters)
383 Main Ave.
Norwalk, CT 06851
Ph: (203)840-5337   Fax: (203)840-9570
E-mail: export@reedexpo.com
URL: http://www.reedexpo.com

Annual. **Primary Exhibits:** Chemical engineering & processing, electronics, machinery equipment, supplies, and services.

OTHER SOURCES

★1795★ American Academy of Environmental Engineers (AAEE)

130 Holiday Ct., Ste. 100
Annapolis, MD 21401
Ph: (410)266-3311   Fax: (410)266-7653
E-mail: info@aaee.net
URL: http://www.aaee.net

Members: Environmentally oriented registered professional engineers certified by examination as Diplomates of the Academy. **Purpose:** Seeks to improve the standards of environmental engineering. Certifies those with special knowledge of environmental engineering. Furnishes lists of those certified to the public. **Activities:** Maintains speakers' bureau. Recognizes areas of specialization: Air Pollution Control; General Environmental; Hazardous Waste Management; Industrial Hygiene; Radiation Protection; Solid Waste Management; Water Supply and Wastewater. Requires written and oral examinations for certification. Works with other professional organizations on environmentally oriented activities. Identifies potential employment candidates through Talent Search Service.

★1796★ American Association of Engineering Societies (AAES)

1620 I St. NW, Ste. 210
Washington, DC 20006
Ph: (202)296-2237   Fax: (202)296-1151
Fr: 888-400-2237
E-mail: dbateson@aaes.org
URL: http://www.aaes.org

Description: Coordinates the efforts of the member societies in the provision of reliable and objective information to the general public concerning issues which affect the engineering profession and the field of engineering as a whole; collects, analyzes, documents, and disseminates data which will inform the general public of the relationship between engineering and the national welfare; provides a forum for the engineering societies to exchange and discuss their views on matters of common interest; and represents the U.S. engineering community abroad through representation in WFEO and UPADI.

★1797★ American Chemical Society (ACS)

1155 16th St. NW
Washington, DC 20036
Ph: (202)872-4600   Fax: (202)872-4615
Fr: 800-227-5558
E-mail: help@acs.org
URL: http://portal.chemistry.org/portal/acs/corg/memberapp

Members: Scientific and educational society of chemists and chemical engineers. **Activi-** ties: Conducts: studies and surveys; special programs for disadvantaged persons; legislation monitoring, analysis, and reporting; courses for graduate chemists and chemical engineers; radio and television programming. Offers career guidance counseling; administers the Petroleum Research Fund and other grants and fellowship programs. Operates Employment Clearing Houses. Compiles statistics. Maintains Speaker's Bureau and 33 divisions.

★1798★ American Institute of Chemical Engineers (AIChE)

3 Park Ave.
New York, NY 10016-5991
Ph: (212)591-8100   Fax: (212)591-8888
Fr: 800-242-4363
E-mail: xpress@aiche.org
URL: http://www.aiche.org

Description: Serves as professional society of chemical engineers. Establishes standards for chemical engineering curricula; offers employment services. Presents technical conferences, petrochemical and refining exposition, and continuing education programs. Sponsors competitions. Offers speakers' bureau; complies statistics.

★1799★ American Institute of Chemists (AIC)

315 Chestnut St.
Philadelphia, PA 19106-2702
Ph: (215)873-8224   Fax: (215)629-5224
E-mail: info@theaic.org
URL: http://www.theaic.org

Description: Represents chemists and chemical engineers. Promotes advancement of chemical professions in the U.S.; protects public welfare by establishing and enforcing high practice standards; represents professional interests of chemists and chemical engineers. Sponsors National Certification Commission in Chemistry and Chemical Engineering and AIC Foundation.

★1800★ Association for International Practical Training (AIPT)

10400 Little Patuxent Pkwy., Ste. 250
Columbia, MD 21044-3519
Ph: (410)997-2200   Fax: (410)992-3924
E-mail: aipt@aipt.org
URL: http://www.aipt.org

Description: Providers worldwide of on-the-job training programs for students and professionals seeking international career development and life-changing experiences. Arranges workplace exchanges in hundreds of professional fields, bringing employers and trainees together from around the world. Client list ranges from small farming communities to Fortune 500 companies.

★1801★ Engineering Occupations

Delphi Productions
3159 6th St.
Boulder, CO 80304
Ph: (303)443-2100   Fax: (303)443-4022
Fr: 888-443-2400

E-mail: support@delphivideo.com
URL: http://www.delphivideo.com

$95.00. 50 minutes. Part of the Careers for the 21st Century Video Library.

★1802★ International Society of India Chemists and Chemical Engineers (ISICCE)

Advanced Research Chemicals
1110 W Keystone Ave.
Catoosa, OK 74015
Ph: (918)266-6789   Fax: (918)266-6796
E-mail: sales@fluoridearc.com

Description: Chemists and chemical engineers from India. Goal is to bring together Indians in the chemical profession who live in the U.S. Aids members in securing jobs in their fields. Provides consultation to industries in India and helps individuals to start their own chemical companies in the U.S. Provides a forum for the exchange of social and technical issues. Plans to organize symposia, short courses, and exchange program. Compiles statistics.

★1803★ Iranian Chemists' Association of the American Chemical Society (ICA-ACS)

35 Meadowbrook Ln.
Woodbury, CT 06798
Ph: (203)573-3220   Fax: (203)573-3660
E-mail: banijamali@ica-acs.org
URL: http://www.ica-acs.org

Description: Encourages and enhances the interchange and sharing of scientific knowledge and friendship among chemists and chemistry-related professionals of Iranian descent. Provides opportunities for members to assist each other in pursuit of academic and professional development and growth. Promotes awareness of scientific contributions made by Iranian scientists.

★1804★ ISA - Instrumentation, Systems, and Automation Society

67 Alexander Dr.
PO Box 12277
Research Triangle Park, NC 27709
Ph: (919)549-8411   Fax: (919)549-8288
E-mail: info@isa.org
URL: http://www.isa.org

Description: Sets the standard for automation by helping over 30,000 worldwide members and other professionals solve difficult technical problems, while enhancing their leadership and personal career capabilities. Develops standards; certifies industry professionals; provides education and training; publishes books and technical articles; and hosts the largest conference and exhibition for automation professionals in the Western Hemisphere. Is the founding sponsor of The Automation Federation.

★1805★ National Action Council for Minorities in Engineering (NACME)

440 Hamilton Ave., Ste. 302
White Plains, NY 10601-1813
Ph: (914)539-4010   Fax: (914)539-4032

E-mail: webmaster@nacme.org
URL: http://www.nacme.org

Description: Leads the national effort to increase access to careers in engineering and other science-based disciplines. Conducts research and public policy analysis, develops and operates national demonstration programs at precollege and university levels, and disseminates information through publications, conferences and electronic media. Serves as a privately funded source of scholarships for minority students in engineering.

★1806★ National Society of Professional Engineers (NSPE)

1420 King St.
Alexandria, VA 22314-2794
Ph: (703)684-2800   Fax: (703)836-4875
Fr: 888-285-6773
E-mail: memserv@nspe.org
URL: http://www.nspe.org

Description: Represents professional engineers and engineers-in-training in all fields registered in accordance with the laws of states or territories of the U.S. or provinces of Canada; qualified graduate engineers, student members, and registered land surveyors. Is concerned with social, professional, ethical, and economic considerations of engineering as a profession; encompasses programs in public relations, employment practices, ethical considerations, education, and career guidance. Monitors legislative and regulatory actions of interest to the engineering profession.

★1807★ Scientific, Engineering, and Technical Services

Cambridge Educational
PO Box 2053
Princeton, NJ 08543-2053
Ph: 800-257-5126   Fax: (609)671-0266
Fr: 800-468-4227
E-mail: custserv@films.com
URL: http://www.cambridgeeducational.com

VHS and DVD. $89.95. 2002. 18 minutes. 2002. Part of the Career Cluster Series.

★1808★ Society of Women Engineers (SWE)

230 E Ohio St., Ste. 400
Chicago, IL 60611-3265
Ph: (312)596-5223   Fax: (312)596-5252
Fr: 877-SWE-INFO
E-mail: hq@swe.org
URL: http://www.swe.org

Description: Educational and service organization representing both students and professional women in engineering and technical fields.

★1809★ Women in Engineering

Her Own Words
PO Box 5264
Madison, WI 53705-0264
Ph: (608)271-7083   Fax: (608)271-0209
E-mail: herownword@aol.com
URL: http://www.herownwords.com/

Video. Jocelyn Riley. $95.00. 15 minutes. Resource guide also available for $45.00.

Chemists

SOURCES OF HELP-WANTED ADS

★1810★ AATCC Review

American Association of Textile Chemists
and Colorists
PO Box 12215
Research Triangle Park, NC 27709
Ph: (919)549-8141   Fax: (919)549-8933
URL: http://www.aatcc.org

Monthly. Magazine focusing on dyeing, finishing of fibers and fabrics.

★1811★ Adhesives Age

Penton Media Inc.
9800 Metcalf Ave.
Overland Park, KS 66212
Ph: (913)341-1300   Fax: (913)967-1898
URL: http://www.chemweek.com/verticals/

Monthly. Magazine containing news and technology for those engaged in the manufacturing, application, research, and marketing of adhesives, sealants, and related products.

★1812★ American Biotechnology Laboratory

International Scientific Communications
Inc.
30 Controls Dr.
PO Box 870
Shelton, CT 06484
Ph: (203)926-9300   Fax: (203)926-9310
URL: http://
www.americanbiotechnologylaboratory.com

Bimonthly. $160.00/year for individuals. Biotechnology magazine.

★1813★ American Institute of Chemical Engineers Journal

John Wiley & Sons Inc.
111 River St.
Hoboken, NJ 07030-5774
Ph: (201)748-6000   Fax: (201)748-6088
Fr: 800-825-7550
URL: http://as.wiley.com/WileyCDA/Wiley-

Title/productCd-AIC.html

Monthly. $1,680.00/year for U.S., print only; $1,824.00/year for Canada and Mexico, print only; $1,908.00/year for other countries, print only; $1,848.00/year for U.S., combined; $1,992.00/year for Canada and Mexico, combined; $2,076.00/year for other countries, combined. Journal focusing on technological advances in core areas of chemical engineering as well as in other relevant engineering disciplines.

★1814★ Applied Occupational & Environmental Hygiene

Applied Industrial Hygiene Inc.
1330 Kemper Meadow Dr., Ste. 600
Cincinnati, OH 45240
Ph: (513)742-2020   Fax: (513)742-3355
URL: http://www.acgih.org

Monthly. $223.00/year for individuals, individual membership; $623.00/year for institutions, institution or organization. Peer-reviewed journal presenting applied solutions for the prevention of occupational and environmental disease and injury.

★1815★ AWIS Magazine

Association for Women in Science
1200 New York Ave. NW, Ste. 650
Washington, DC 20005
Ph: (202)326-8940   Fax: (202)326-8960
Fr: (866)657-2947
E-mail: awis@awis.org
URL: http://www.awis.org/

Description: Bimonthly. Covers issues, legislation, and trends related to science education for girls, women, and minorities. Includes information on grants and fellowships, job openings, educational programs, events, and notices of publications available.

★1816★ Chemical Engineering Communications

Taylor & Francis Group Journals
325 Chestnut St., Ste. 800
Philadelphia, PA 19106
Ph: (215)625-8900   Fax: (215)625-8914
Fr: 800-354-1420
URL: http://www.informaworld.com/open-

url?genre=journal&issn=0098-

Monthly. $2,053.00/year for individuals, print only; $4,712/year for online subscription; $4,960/year for online and print subscription. Journal focusing on the results of basic and applied research in chemical engineering.

★1817★ Chemical & Engineering News

American Chemical Society
1155 16th St. NW
Washington, DC 20036
Ph: (202)872-4600   Fax: (202)872-4615
Fr: 800-227-5558
URL: http://pubs.acs.org/cen/about.html

Weekly. Magazine on chemical and engineering news.

★1818★ Chemical Engineering and Technology

John Wiley & Sons Inc.
111 River St.
Hoboken, NJ 07030-5774
Ph: (201)748-6000   Fax: (201)748-6088
Fr: 800-825-7550
E-mail: cet@wiley-vch.de
URL: http://www3.interscience.wiley.com/
cgi-bin/jhome/10008333

Monthly. $4,026.00/year for institutions; $458.00/year for individuals. Journal focusing on all aspects of chemical and process engineering.

★1819★ Chemical Equipment

Reed Business Information
360 Park Ave. S
New York, NY 10010
Ph: (646)746-6400   Fax: (646)746-7431
URL: http://
www.reedbusinessinteractive.com

Free, for qualified professionals; $72.90/year for individuals, cover price. Tabloid on the chemical process industry.

★1820★ Chemical Processing

Putman Media
555 W Pierce Rd., Ste. 301
Itasca, IL 60143-2649
Ph: (630)467-1301   Fax: (630)467-0197

URL: http://www.chemicalprocessing.com
Monthly. $68.00/year for individuals, U.S. and Canada; $115.00/year for other countries, international surface; $200.00/year for other countries, international airmail. Magazine for the chemical process industry.

★1821★ The Chemical Record
John Wiley & Sons Inc.
111 River St.
Hoboken, NJ 07030-5774
Ph: (201)748-6000   Fax: (201)748-6088
Fr: 800-825-7550
URL: http://www3.interscience.wiley.com/cgi-bin/jhome/72515006

Bimonthly. $100.00/year for U.S., print only rates; $100.00/year for Canada and Mexico, print only rates, add 6%GST in Canada; $130.00/year for other countries, print only rates; $435.00/year for U.S. institutions, print only rates; $507.00/year for institutions, Canada and Mexico, print only rates, in Canada, please add 6% GST; $549.00/year for institutions, other countries, print only rates; $479.00/year for U.S. institutions, combined print with online access rates; $551.00/year for institutions, Canada and Mexico, print with online rates, in Canada, 6%GST; $593.00/year for institutions, other countries, combined print with online access rates. Journal publishing overviews of new developments at the cutting edge of chemistry of interest to a wide audience of chemists.

★1822★ The Chemist
American Institute of Chemists Inc.
315 Chestnut St.
Philadelphia, PA 19106-2702
Ph: (215)873-8224   Fax: (215)629-5224
E-mail: info@theaic.org
URL: http://www.theaic.org

Description: Six issues/year. Covers news items relating to the chemical profession and membership in the Institute. Reports on legislation, licensure, earnings, awards, and professional education. Recurring features include news of employment opportunities and news of members. Published alternate months as a magazine.

★1823★ Chemistry & Biology
Elsevier Science Inc.
360 Park Ave. S
New York, NY 10010
Ph: (212)989-5800   Fax: (212)633-3990
URL: http://www.elsevier.com/

Monthly. $1,745/year for institutions, U.S. and Canada; $369.00/year for individuals, U.S. and Canada. Journal focused on genetic, computational, or theoretical information of chemistry and biology, substantiating experimental data.

★1824★ The Electrochemical Society Interface
The Electrochemical Society Inc.
65 S Main St., Bldg. D
Pennington, NJ 08534-2839
Ph: (609)737-1902   Fax: (609)737-2743

E-mail: interface@electrochem.org
URL: http://www.electrochem.org/dl/interface/

Quarterly. $15.00/year for members; $68.00/year for nonmembers; $15.00 for single issue, members; $20.00 for single issue, nonmembers. Publication featuring news and articles of interest to members of the Electrochemical Society.

★1825★ Engineering in Life Sciences
John Wiley & Sons Inc.
111 River St.
Hoboken, NJ 07030-5774
Ph: (201)748-6000   Fax: (201)748-6088
Fr: 800-825-7550
URL: http://as.wiley.com/WileyCDA/WileyTitle/productCd-2129.html

Bimonthly. $765.00/year for institutions, rest of Europe; $1,170.00/year for institutions, Switzerland and Liechtenstein; $1,005.00/year for institutions, rest of world; $842.00/year for institutions, print with online rest of Europe; $1,287.00/year for institutions, print with online Switzerland and Liechtenstein; $1,106.00/year for institutions, print with online rest of world. Journal focusing on the field of biotechnology and related topics including microbiology, genetics, biochemistry, and chemistry.

★1826★ Journal of Chemical Theory and Computation
American Chemical Society
1155 16th St. NW
Washington, DC 20036
Ph: (202)872-4600   Fax: (202)872-4615
Fr: 800-227-5558
URL: http://pubs.acs.org/journals/jctcce

$1,106.00/year for institutions, North America; $1,159.00/year for institutions, outside North America; $205.00/year for students, outside North America. Journal presenting new theories, methodology, and/or important applications in quantum chemistry, molecular dynamics, and statistical mechanics.

★1827★ Modern Plastics
Chemical Week Associates
110 Williams St.
New York, NY 10038
Ph: (212)621-4900   Fax: (212)621-4800
URL: http://www.modplas.com

Monthly. $59.00/year for individuals; $99.00 for two years, U.S. and possessions; $110.00/year for Canada; $199.00 for two years, for Canada; $150.00/year for other countries; $250.00 for two years. Magazine for the plastics industry.

★1828★ Nanoparticle News
BCC Research
70 New Canaan Ave.
Norwalk, CT 06850
Ph: (203)750-9783   Fax: (203)229-0087
Fr: (866)285-7215
URL: http://www.the-infoshop.com/newsletter/bc4377_fine_particle_

Monthly. $575.00/year for individuals; $661.25/year for individuals, order electronic copy; $495.00 for single issue, web access and archive; $590.00 for single issue, hard copy, web access and archive (North America). Publication covering issues in the chemical industry.

★1829★ Nature Biotechnology
Nature Publishing Group
75 Varick St., 9th Fl.
New York, NY 10013-1917
Ph: (212)726-9200   Fax: (212)696-9006
Fr: 888-331-6288
E-mail: biotech@natureny.com
URL: http://www.nature.com/nbt/index.html

Monthly. Scientific research journal.

★1830★ Nature International Weekly Journal of Science
Nature Publishing Group
75 Varick St., 9th Fl.
New York, NY 10013-1917
Ph: (212)726-9200   Fax: (212)696-9006
Fr: 888-331-6288
E-mail: nature@natureny.com
URL: http://www.nature.com

Weekly. $145.00/year for individuals; $49.00/year for institutions. Magazine covering science and technology, including the fields of biology, biochemistry, genetics, medicine, earth sciences, physics, pharmacology, and behavioral sciences.

★1831★ PALAIOS
SEPM Publications
6128 E 38th St., Ste. 308
Tulsa, OK 74135-5814
Ph: (918)610-3361   Fax: (918)621-1685
Fr: 800-865-9765
URL: http://www.sepm.org/

Bimonthly. $200.00/year for individuals, for U.S. online version with CD-ROM; $235.00/year for individuals, for U.S. print and online version with CD-ROM; $200.00/year for other countries, online version with CD-ROM; $245.00/year for other countries, print and online version with CD-ROM. Journal providing information on the impact of life on Earth history as recorded in the paleontological and sedimentological records. Covers areas such as biogeochemistry, ichnology, sedimentology, stratigraphy, paleoecology, paleoclimatology, and paleoceanography.

★1832★ Paper, Film & Foil Converter
Primedia Business
330 North Wabash Ave., Ste. 2300
Chicago, IL 60611-3698
Ph: (312)595-1080   Fax: (312)595-0295
Fr: 800-621-9907
E-mail: pffceditor@primediabusiness.com
URL: http://pffc-online.com/

Monthly. $90.00/year for Canada; $112.00/year. Free, in U.S. $310.00/year for other countries, airmail/first class. Magazine focusing on flexible packaging, paperboard, and film.

★1833★ **Plastics Engineering**

Society of Plastics Engineers
14 Fairfield Dr.
PO Box 403
Brookfield, CT 06804-0403
Ph: (203)775-0471   Fax: (203)775-8490
E-mail: advertising@4spe.org
URL: http://www.4spe.org/pub

Monthly. $142.00/year for nonmembers; $242.00/year for nonmembers, outside North America; $180.00/year for institutions, corporate libraries; $280.00/year for institutions, corporate libraries outside North America. Plastics trade magazine.

★1834★ **Powder and Bulk Engineering**

CSC Publishing Inc.
1155 Northland Dr.
St. Paul, MN 55120-1288
Fax: (651)287-5600
URL: http://www.powderbulk.com/

Monthly. $100.00/year for individuals, outside North America, or digital format. Journal serving chemical, food, plastics, pulp and paper, and electronic industries.

★1835★ **Science**

American Association for the
 Advancement of Science
1200 New York Ave. NW
Washington, DC 20005
Ph: (202)326-6400   Fax: (202)371-9227
URL: http://www.scienceonline.org

Weekly (Fri.). $142.00/year for members, professional; $119.00/year for individuals, NPA postdoctoral; $99.00/year for individuals, postdoctoral/resident; $75.00/year for students; $142.00/year for individuals, k-12 teacher; $310.00/year for individuals, patron; $110.00/year for individuals, emeritus. Magazine devoted to science, scientific research, and public policy.

★1836★ **The Scientist**

The Scientist Inc.
400 Market St., No. 1250
Philadelphia, PA 19106
Ph: (215)351-1660   Fax: (215)351-1146
URL: http://www.the-scientist.com

Bimonthly. $49.95/year for individuals, online; $74.95/year for individuals, online plus print edition; $124.95/year for out of country, online plus print edition (air freight); $29.95/year for individuals; $19.95 for individuals, 6 months; $14.95 for individuals, 1 month; $9.95 for individuals, 1 week; $4.95 for individuals, 1 week. News journal (tabloid) for life scientists featuring news, opinions, research, and professional section.

★1837★ **Soap/Cosmetics/Chemical Specialties**

Cygnus Business Media Inc.
3 Huntington Quadrangle, Ste. 301 N
Melville, NY 11747
Ph: (631)845-2700   Fax: (631)845-7109
Fr: 800-308-6397

Monthly. Trade magazine for household and personal care products.

PLACEMENT AND JOB REFERRAL SERVICES

★1838★ **American Microchemical Society (AMS)**

2 June Way
Middlesex, NJ 08846
E-mail: ella_osnovikova@permacel.com
URL: http://www.microchem.org

Purpose: Promotes interest in the practice and teaching of microchemistry. **Activities:** Participates in exhibits and symposia. Maintains placement service.

★1839★ **American Oil Chemists' Society (AOCS)**

PO Box 17190
Urbana, IL 61803-7190
Ph: (217)359-2344   Fax: (217)351-8091
E-mail: general@aocs.org
URL: http://www.aocs.org

Members: Chemists, biochemists, chemical engineers, research directors, plant personnel, and others in laboratories and chemical process industries concerned with animal, marine, and vegetable oils and fats, and their extraction, refining, safety, packaging, quality control, and use in consumer and industrial products such as foods, drugs, paints, waxes, lubricants, soaps, and cosmetics. **Activities:** Sponsors short courses; certifies referee chemists; distributes cooperative check samples; sells official reagents. Maintains 100 committees. Operates job placement service for members only.

★1840★ **American Society for Biochemistry and Molecular Biology (ASBMB)**

9650 Rockville Pike
Bethesda, MD 20814-3996
Ph: (301)634-7145   Fax: (301)634-7126
E-mail: asmb@asbmb.org
URL: http://www.asbmb.org

Members: Biochemists and molecular biologists who have conducted and published original investigations in biological chemistry and/or molecular biology. **Activities:** Operates placement service.

★1841★ **American Society for Neurochemistry (ASN)**

9037 Ron Den Ln.
Windermere, FL 34786-8328
Ph: (407)876-0750   Fax: (407)876-0750
E-mail: amazing@iag.net
URL: http://www.asneurochem.org

Description: Represents investigators in the field of neurochemistry and scientists who are qualified specialists in other disciplines and are interested in the activities of the society. Aims to advance and promote the science of neurochemistry and related neurosciences and to increase and enhance neurochemical knowledge; to facilitate the dissemination of information concerning neurochemical research; to encourage the research of individual neurochemists. Con-

ducts roundtables; distributes research communications. Maintains placement service.

★1842★ **American Society of Plant Biologists (ASPB)**

15501 Monona Dr.
Rockville, MD 20855-2768
Ph: (301)251-0560   Fax: (301)279-2996
E-mail: info@aspb.org
URL: http://www.aspb.org

Members: Professional society of plant biologists, plant biochemists, and other plant scientists engaged in research and teaching. **Activities:** Offers placement service for members; conducts educational and public affairs programs.

★1843★ **American Water Works Association (AWWA)**

6666 W Quincy Ave.
Denver, CO 80235-3098
Ph: (303)794-7711   Fax: (303)347-0804
Fr: 800-926-7337
E-mail: rrenner@awwa.org
URL: http://www.awwa.org

Members: Water utility managers, superintendents, engineers, chemists, bacteriologists, and other individuals interested in public water supply; municipal- and investor-owned water departments; boards of health; manufacturers of waterworks equipment; government officials and consultants interested in water supply. **Purpose:** Develops standards and supports research programs in waterworks design, construction, operation, and management. **Activities:** Conducts in-service training schools and prepares manuals for waterworks personnel. Maintains hall of fame. Offers placement service via member newsletter; compiles statistics. Offers training; children's services; and information center on the water utilities industry, potable water, and water reuse.

★1844★ **Engineering Society of Detroit (ESD)**

2000 Town Ctr., Ste. 2610
Southfield, MI 48075
Ph: (248)353-0735   Fax: (248)353-0736
E-mail: esd@esd.org
URL: http://esd.org

Description: Engineers from all disciplines; scientists and technologists. Conducts technical programs and engineering refresher courses; sponsors conferences and expositions. Maintains speakers' bureau; offers placement services; although based in Detroit, MI, society membership is international.

★1845★ **Federation of Analytical Chemistry and Spectroscopy Societies (FACSS)**

PO Box 24379
Santa Fe, NM 87502
Ph: (505)820-1648   Fax: (505)989-1073
E-mail: facss@facss.org
URL: http://www.facss.org

Members: Professional societies representing 9,000 analytical chemists and spectroscopists. Members are: Analysis Instrumentation Division of the Instrument Society of America; Association of Analytical Chemists; Coblentz Society; Division of Analytical Chemistry of the American Chemical Society; Division of Analytical Chemistry of the Royal Society of Chemistry; Society for Applied Spectroscopy. **Purpose:** Aims to provide a forum to address the challenges of analytical chemistry, chromatography, and spectroscopy. **Activities:** Reviews technical papers; maintains placement service.

★1846★ Korean-American Scientists and Engineers Association (KSEA)

1952 Gallows Rd., Ste. 300
Vienna, VA 22182
Ph: (703)748-1221   Fax: (703)748-1331
E-mail: admin@ksea.org
URL: http://www.ksea.org

Description: Represents scientists and engineers holding single or advanced degrees. Promotes friendship and mutuality among Korean and American scientists and engineers; contributes to Korea's scientific, technological, industrial, and economic developments; strengthens the scientific, technological, and cultural bonds between Korea and the U.S. Sponsors symposium. Maintains speakers' bureau, placement service, and biographical archives. Compiles statistics.

★1847★ National Organization for the Professional Advancement of Black Chemists and Chemical Engineers (NOBCChE)

PO Box 77040
Washington, DC 20013
Fax: (202)667-1705   Fr: 800-776-1419
E-mail: president@nobcche.org
URL: http://www.nobcche.org

Description: Black professionals in science and chemistry. Seeks to aid black scientists and chemists in reaching their full professional potential; encourages black students to pursue scientific studies and employment; promotes participation of blacks in scientific research. Provides volunteers to teach science courses in selected elementary schools; sponsors scientific field trips for students; maintains speakers' bureau for schools. Conducts technical seminars in Africa. Sponsors competitions; presents awards for significant achievements to individuals in the field. Maintains placement service; compiles statistics.

★1848★ Society of Cosmetic Chemists (SCC)

120 Wall St., Ste. 2400
New York, NY 10005-4088
Ph: (212)668-1500   Fax: (212)668-1504
E-mail: scc@scconline.org
URL: http://www.scconline.org

Description: Serves a professional society of scientists involved in the cosmetic industry. Sponsors educational institution support programs to stimulate growth of cosmetic science-related programs. Maintains placement service.

★1849★ Society for In Vitro Biology (SIVB)

514 Daniels St., Ste. 411
Raleigh, NC 27605
Ph: (919)420-7940   Fax: (919)420-7939
Fr: 888-588-1923
E-mail: sivb@sivb.org
URL: http://www.sivb.org

Description: Professional society of individuals using mammalian, invertebrate, plant cell tissue, and organ cultures as research tools in chemistry, physics, radiation, medicine, physiology, nutrition, and cytogenetics. Aims are to foster collection and dissemination of information concerning the maintenance and experimental use of tissue cells in vitro and to establish evaluation and development procedures. Operates placement service.

EMPLOYER DIRECTORIES AND NETWORKING LISTS

★1850★ American Board of Clinical Chemistry-Directory of Active Diplomates

American Board of Clinical Chemistry
1850 K St. NW, Ste. 625
Washington, DC 20006-2213
Ph: (202)835-8727   Fax: (202)833-4576
URL: http://www.aacc.org/abcc/

Annual, Winter. Covers about 800 chemists trained in clinical and toxicological chemistry and certified by the board. Entries include: Name, office address. Arrangement: Alphabetical.

★1851★ American Institute of Chemists-Professional Directory

American Institute of Chemists Inc.
315 Chestnut St.
Philadelphia, PA 19106-2702
Ph: (215)873-8224   Fax: (215)629-5224
URL: http://www.theaic.org

Annual, spring. Covers more than 3,500 member chemists. Entries include: Individual name and title, address, phone, name of employer, position title, principal job responsibility, principal field of chemistry, highest academic degree, certification, year elected to membership, membership category, local affiliation. Commercial use requires special permission. Arrangement: Alphabetical. Indexes: Geographical.

★1852★ American Men and Women of Science

Gale, Cengage Learning
27500 Drake Rd.
Farmington Hills, MI 48331-3535
Ph: (248)699-4253   Fax: (248)699-8065
Fr: 800-877-4253
URL: http://www.gale.com

Biennial, latest edition 23rd, October 2006; new edition expected 24th, January 2008. $1,075.00 for individuals. Covers over 129,700 U.S. and Canadian scientists active in the physical, biological, mathematical, computer science, and engineering fields; includes references to previous edition for deceased scientists and nonrespondents. Entries include: Name, address, education, personal and career data, memberships, honors and awards, research interest. Arrangement: Alphabetical. Indexes: Discipline (in separate volume).

★1853★ Chemical Week-Buyers Guide Issue

Chemical Week Associates
110 Williams St.
New York, NY 10038
Ph: (212)621-4900   Fax: (212)621-4800
URL: http://www.chemweekbuyersguide.com/public/

Annual, October. $115.00. Publication includes: About 4,200 manufacturers and suppliers of chemical raw materials to the chemical process industries; 400 manufacturers of packaging materials; and suppliers of products and services to the chemical process industries, including hazardous waste/environmental services, computer services, plant design, construction, consulting, shipping, and transportation. Entries include: Over 17,000 product/service listings, company name, address, phone; local addresses and phone numbers for up to 25 sales locations. Arrangement: Separate alphabetical sections for chemical, packaging, and hazardous waste/environmental services. Indexes: Product (all sections); trade name (chemical and packaging sections only).

★1854★ Consulting Services

Association of Consulting Chemists and Chemical Engineers Inc.
PO Box 297
Sparta, NJ 07871
Ph: (973)729-6671   Fax: (973)729-7088
URL: http://www.chemconsult.org

Biennial, even years. $30.00 for individuals. Covers about 160 member consultants in chemistry, chemical engineering, metallurgy, etc. Entries include: Individual name, address, certificate number, qualifications, affiliation, experience, facilities, staff. Arrangement: Classified by area of expertise. Indexes: Personal name, geographical.

★1855★ Directory of Chemical Producers-United States

SRI Consulting
4300 Bohannon Dr., Ste. 200
Menlo Park, CA 94025-3477
Ph: (650)384-4300
E-mail: dcp@sric.sri.com
URL: http://www.sriconsulting.com

Annual; latest edition June 2007. Covers over 1,200 United States basic chemical producers manufacturing 7,900 chemicals in commercial quantities at more than 3,500 plant locations. Entries include: For companies—Company name, division or subsidiary names, corporate address, phone, fax, telex, location of each subsidiary, division, and manufacturing plant, and the products made at each plant location. For pro-ducts–Producer name and plant locations, alternate product names (if any). Subscription price includes bound volume, plus access to the directory staff for inquiries. Arrangement: Companies are alphabetical; products are alphabetical and by group (dyes, pesticides, etc.); manufacturing plants are geographical. Indexes: Geographical, product.

★1856★ **LabGuide**
American Chemical Society
1155 16th St. NW
Washington, DC 20036
Ph: (202)872-4600   Fax: (202)872-4615
Fr: 800-227-5558
E-mail: labguide@acs.org
URL: http://www.mediabrains.com

Annual; latest edition 49. Publication includes: List of about 2,200 manufacturers of scientific instruments, equipment, chemicals, and other supplies for scientific research and chemical laboratories; laboratory supply houses; analytical and research services. Entries include: Company name, address, phone, fax, e-mail, URL, products, and services. Arrangement: Alphabetical. Indexes: Product, chemical, service, instrument, company name.

★1857★ **Peterson's Job Opportunities in Engineering and Technology**
Peterson's Guides
2000 Lenox Dr.
Box 67005
Lawrenceville, NJ 08648
Ph: (609)896-1800   Fax: (609)896-4531
Fr: 800-338-3282
E-mail: custsvc@petersons.com
URL: http://www.petersons.com

Compiled by the Peterson's staff. Fourth edition, 1996. $21.95 (paper). 379 pages. Profiles 2,000 high-tech companies looking primarily for technical personnel in such fields as biotechnology, telecommunications, software, computers and peripherals, defense, and aerospace. Contains job-search strategies and career options to help match education and expertise to the job market. Indexed geographically, by industry, and by hiring needs.

★1858★ **U.S. National Committee for the International Union of Pure and Applied Chemistry-Directory**
U.S. National Committee for the International Union of Pure and Applied Chemistry
Keck Center
WS 550
Washington, DC 20001
Ph: (202)334-2807   Fax: (202)334-2231
URL: http://www7.nationalacademies.org/usnc-iupac/

Annual, July. Covers 29 member chemists and chemical engineers in the United States.

HANDBOOKS AND MANUALS

★1859★ **The Best Resumes for Scientists and Engineers**
John Wiley & Sons Inc.
1 Wiley Dr.
Somerset, NJ 08873
Ph: (732)469-4400   Fax: (732)302-2300
Fr: 800-225-5945
E-mail: custserv@wiley.com
URL: http://www.wiley.com/WileyCDA/

Adele Lewis and David J. Moore. Second edition, 1993. $37.50; $19.95 (paper). 224 pages. Presents an extensive collection of scientific and engineering resumes, highlighting the important differences between these and resumes written for other occupations.

★1860★ **Career Management for Chemists**
Springer-Verlag New York, Inc.
233 Spring St.
New York, NY 10013
Ph: (212)460-1501   Fax: (212)460-1595
URL: http://www.springer.com/

John Fetzer. 2004. $39.95. Illustrated. 266 pages. Vocational guide for Chemists.

★1861★ **Careers for Chemists: A World Outside the Lab**
American Chemical Society
1155 16th St., NW
Washington, DC 20036
Ph: (202)872-4600   Fr: 800-227-5558
URL: http://portal.acs.org/portal/acs/corg/content

Fred Owens, Roger Uhler and Corrine A. Marasco. 1997. 211 pages.

★1862★ **Great Jobs for Chemistry Majors**
The McGraw-Hill Companies
PO Box 182604
Columbus, OH 43272
Fax: (614)759-3749   Fr: 877-883-5524
E-mail: customer.service@mcgraw-hill.com
URL: http://www.mcgraw-hill.com

Mark Rowh. Second edition, 2005. $15.95 (paper). 208 pages.

★1863★ **Guide to Nontraditional Careers in Science**
Taylor & Francis
325 Chestnut St., 8th Fl.
Philadelphia, PA 19106
Ph: (215)625-8900   Fax: (215)269-0363
Fr: 800-821-8312
URL: http://www.taylorandfrancis.com

Karen Young Kreeger. 1998. $45.95 (paper). Guidebook aids the reader in evaluating and finding career opportunities in non-academic research fields. 263 pages.

★1864★ **Opportunities in Chemistry Careers**
The McGraw-Hill Companies
PO Box 182604
Columbus, OH 43272
Fax: (614)759-3749   Fr: 877-883-5524
E-mail: customer.service@mcgraw-hill.com
URL: http://www.mcgraw-hill.com

John H. Woodburn and John Hazlett. Second edition, 2002. $14.95 (paper). 145 pages. Part of the VGM Opportunities Series.

★1865★ **Opportunities in Environmental Careers**
The McGraw-Hill Companies
PO Box 182604
Columbus, OH 43272
Fax: (614)759-3749   Fr: 877-883-5524
E-mail: customer.service@mcgraw-hill.com
URL: http://www.mcgraw-hill.com

Odom Fanning. Revised, 2002. $12.95 (paper). 174 pages. Describes a broad range of opportunities in fields such as environmental health, recreation, physics, and hygiene, and provides job search advice. Part of the "Opportunities in ..." Series.

★1866★ **Opportunities in High Tech Careers**
The McGraw-Hill Companies
PO Box 182604
Columbus, OH 43272
Fax: (614)759-3749   Fr: 877-883-5524
E-mail: customer.service@mcgraw-hill.com
URL: http://www.mcgraw-hill.com

Gary Colter and Deborah Yanuck. 1999. $14.95; $11.95 (paper). 160 pages. Explores high technology careers. Describes job opportunities, how to make a career decision, how to prepare for high technology jobs, job hunting techniques, and future trends.

★1867★ **Opportunities in Research and Development Careers**
The McGraw-Hill Companies
PO Box 182604
Columbus, OH 43272
Fax: (614)759-3749   Fr: 877-883-5524
E-mail: customer.service@mcgraw-hill.com
URL: http://www.mcgraw-hill.com

Jan Goldberg. 1996. $11.95 (paper). 146 pages.

★1868★ **Resumes for Scientific and Technical Careers**
The McGraw-Hill Companies
PO Box 182604
Columbus, OH 43272
Fax: (614)759-3749   Fr: 877-883-5524
E-mail: customer.service@mcgraw-hill.com
URL: http://www.mcgraw-hill.com

Third edition, 2007. $12.95 (paper). 144 pages. Provides resume advice for individuals interested in working in scientific and technical careers. Includes sample resumes and cover letters.

★1869★ Theoretical and Quantum Mechanics: Fundamentals for Chemists

Springer Publishing Co.
11 West 42nd St., 15th Fl.
New York, NY 10036
Ph: (212)460-1500   Fax: (212)473-6272
Fr: 877-687-7476
E-mail: contactus@springerpub.com
URL: http://www.springerpub.com/

Stefan Ivanov. 2005. $169.00. Offers an introduction into theoretical and quantum mechanics for chemists. The book focuses on the atom and bridges the gap between classical physics, general and inorganic chemistry, and quantum mechanics.

★1870★ To Boldly Go: A Practical Career Guide for Scientists

Amer Global Pub
2000 Florida Ave., NW
Washington, DC 20009
Ph: (202)462-6900   Fax: (202)328-0566
Fr: 800-966-2481

Peter S. Fiske. 1996. $19.00 (paper). 188 pages.

★1871★ What's Cooking in Chemistry?: How Leading Chemists Succeed in the Kitchen

John Wiley and Sons, Inc.
1 Wiley Dr.
Somerset, NJ 08875-1272
Ph: (732)469-4400   Fax: (732)302-2300
Fr: 800-225-5945
E-mail: custserv@wiley.com
URL: http://www.wiley.com/WileyCDA/

Hubertus P. Bell. 2003. $39.95. Illustrated. 243 pages.

EMPLOYMENT AGENCIES AND SEARCH FIRMS

★1872★ Amtec Engineering Corp.

2749 Saturn St.
Brea, CA 92821
Ph: (714)993-1900   Fax: (714)993-2419
E-mail: info@amtechc.com
URL: http://www.amtec-eng.com

Employment agency.

★1873★ Biomedical Search Consultants

275 Wyman St.
Waltham, MA 02451
Ph: (978)952-6425   Fax: (781)890-1082
E-mail: kprovost@biomedicalsearchconsultants.com
URL: http://
www.biomedicalsearchconsultants.com

Employment agency.

★1874★ The Brentwood Group Inc.

170 Kinnelon Rd., Ste. 7
Kinnelon, NJ 07405
Ph: (973)283-1000   Fax: (973)283-1220
E-mail: info@thebrentwoodgroup.com
URL: http://www.thebrentwoodgroup.com

Executive search firm.

★1875★ Briant Associates Inc.

18 E. Dundee Rd. Bldg 2, Ste. 202
Barrington, IL 60010
Ph: (847)382-5725   Fax: (847)382-7265
E-mail: rbingham@briantassociates.com
URL: http://www.briantassociates.com

Executive search firm.

★1876★ Colucci, Blendow & Johnson

643 Main St., Ste. 7
PO Box 10
Half Moon Bay, CA 94019-1988
Ph: (650)712-0103   Fax: (650)712-0105
E-mail: exsearch@ix.netcom.com

Executive search consultants in the medical technology area that includes pharmaceuticals, medical equipment and device manufacturers, biotechnology, therapeutic supplies, diagnostic laboratory equipment and supplies, diagnostic imaging equipment and supplies, medical services, chemicals, cosmetic and toiletries, dental, veterinarian, and agricultural genetics companies.

★1877★ Ellington & Associates

1755 Park St., Ste. 200
PO Box 2544
Naperville, IL 60563
Ph: (708)305-0088   Fax: (630)305-0088

Offers executive search services for the chemical, food, pulp and paper industries. Industries include chemical, waste management and construction. Firms include wheelabrator engineered systems and nalco chemical.

★1878★ Erspamer Associates

4010 W. 65th St., Ste. 100
Edina, MN 55435
Ph: (952)925-3747   Fax: (952)925-4022
E-mail: hdhuntrel@aol.com

Executive search firm specializing in technical management.

★1879★ Intech Summit Group, Inc.

3450 Bonita Rd., Ste. 203
Chula Vista, CA 91910
Ph: (619)862-2720   Fax: (619)862-2699
Fr: 800-750-8100
E-mail: isg@isgsearch.com
URL: http://www.isgsearch.com

Employment agency and executive recruiter with a branch in Carlsbad, CA.

★1880★ Lybrook Associates, Inc.

266 N. Farm Dr.
Bristol, RI 02809
Ph: (401)254-5840

Executive search firm specializing in the field of chemistry.

★1881★ Professional Placement Associates, Inc.

287 Bowman Ave., Ste. 309
Purchase, NY 10577-2517
Ph: (914)251-1000   Fax: (914)251-1055
E-mail: careers@ppasearch.com
URL: http://www.ppasearch.com

Executive search firm specializing in the health and medical field.

★1882★ Team Placement Service, Inc.

1414 Prince St., Ste. 202
Alexandria, VA 22314
Ph: (703)820-8618   Fax: (703)820-3368
Fr: 800-495-6767
E-mail: 4jobs@teamplace.com
URL: http://www.teamplace.com

Full-service personnel consultants provide placement for healthcare staff, physician and dentist, private practice, and hospitals. Conduct interviews, tests, and reference checks to select the top 20% of applicants. Survey applicants' skill levels, provide backup information on each candidate, select compatible candidates for consideration, and insure the hiring process minimizes potential legal liability. Industries served: healthcare and government agencies providing medical, dental, biotech, laboratory, hospitals, and physician search.

★1883★ Tri-Serv Inc.

22 W. Padonia Rd., Ste. C-353
Timonium, MD 21093
Ph: (410)561-1740   Fax: (410)252-7417
E-mail: info@tri-serv.coom
URL: http://www.tri-serv.com

Employment agency for technical personnel.

ONLINE JOB SOURCES AND SERVICES

★1884★ American Chemical Society

1155 16th St. NW
Washington, DC 20036
Ph: 800-227-5558   Fr: 888-667-7988
E-mail: service@acs.org
URL: http://www.cen-chemjobs.org

Description: Offers online interviewing between employers and potential employees, postings for positions available and situations wanted, and regularly updated career advice and information for American Chemical Society members only.

★1885★ American Oil Chemists Society Career Opportunities

2710 S. Boulder
Urbana, IL 61802-6996
Ph: (217)359-2344   Fax: (217)351-8091
E-mail: general@aocs.org
URL: http://www.aocs.org/member/jobcent/

Description: Section of the AOCS homepage intended to aid members in finding jobs in the oil chemistry field. Job areas include analytical, health and nutrition, processing, surfactants and detergents, general fats and oils/chemistry, and others. Jobs may be posted and searched.

TRADESHOWS

★1886★ AOAC International Annual Meeting and Exposition

AOAC International
481 North Frederick Ave., Ste. 500
Gaithersburg, MD 20877-2417
Ph: (301)924-7077   Fax: (301)924-7089
Fr: 800-379-2622
E-mail: aoac@aoac.org
URL: http://www.aoac.org

Annual. **Primary Exhibits:** Scientific and laboratory supplies and publications exhibits and posters.

OTHER SOURCES

★1887★ AACC International

3340 Pilot Knob Rd.
St. Paul, MN 55121
Ph: (651)454-7250   Fax: (651)454-0766
Fr: 800-328-7560
E-mail: aacc@scisoc.org
URL: http://www.aaccnet.org

Description: Serves as professional society of scientists and other individuals in the grain processing industry (milling, baking, convenience foods, and feeds). Encourages research on cereal grains, oil seeds, pulses, and related materials, and studies their processing, utilization, and products. Seeks to develop and standardize analytical methods used in cereal and seed chemistry and to disseminate scientific and technical information through workshops and publications. Offers honors for outstanding research. Maintains over 20 technical subcommittees. Conducts short courses for continuing education and annual sanitation certification program.

★1888★ American Academy of Clinical Toxicology (AACT)

777 E Park Dr.
PO Box 8820
Harrisburg, PA 17105-8820
Ph: (717)558-7847   Fax: (717)558-7841
Fr: 888-633-5784

E-mail: swilson@pamedsoc.org
URL: http://www.clintox.org

Members: Physicians, veterinarians, pharmacists, nurses research scientists, and analytical chemists. **Purpose:** Objectives are to: unite medical scientists and facilitate the exchange of information; encourage the development of therapeutic methods and technology; **Activities:** Conducts professional training in poison information and emergency service personnel.

★1889★ American Association of Textile Chemists and Colorists (AATCC)

PO Box 12215
Research Triangle Park, NC 27709-2215
Ph: (919)549-8141   Fax: (919)549-8933
E-mail: danielsj@aatcc.org
URL: http://www.aatcc.org

Description: Professional association for textile design, processing and testing. Works as an authority for industry standard test methods and evaluation procedures.

★1890★ American Chemical Society (ACS)

1155 16th St. NW
Washington, DC 20036
Ph: (202)872-4600   Fax: (202)872-4615
Fr: 800-227-5558
E-mail: help@acs.org
URL: http://portal.chemistry.org/portal/acs/corg/memberapp

Members: Scientific and educational society of chemists and chemical engineers. **Activities:** Conducts: studies and surveys; special programs for disadvantaged persons; legislation monitoring, analysis, and reporting; courses for graduate chemists and chemical engineers; radio and television programming. Offers career guidance counseling; administers the Petroleum Research Fund and other grants and fellowship programs. Operates Employment Clearing Houses. Compiles statistics. Maintains Speaker's Bureau and 33 divisions.

★1891★ American Crystallographic Association (ACA)

PO Box 96
Buffalo, NY 14207-0090
Ph: (716)898-8690   Fax: (716)898-8695
E-mail: aca@hwi.buffalo.edu
URL: http://aca.hwi.buffalo.edu

Members: Chemists, biochemists, physicists, mineralogists, and metallurgists interested in crystallography and in the application of X-ray, electron, and neutron diffraction. **Purpose:** Promotes the study of the arrangement of atoms in matter, its causes, its nature, and its consequences, and of the tools and methods used in such studies. **Activities:** Maintains employment clearinghouse for members and employers.

★1892★ American Institute of Chemists (AIC)

315 Chestnut St.
Philadelphia, PA 19106-2702
Ph: (215)873-8224   Fax: (215)629-5224
E-mail: info@theaic.org
URL: http://www.theaic.org

Description: Represents chemists and chemical engineers. Promotes advancement of chemical professions in the U.S.; protects public welfare by establishing and enforcing high practice standards; represents professional interests of chemists and chemical engineers. Sponsors National Certification Commission in Chemistry and Chemical Engineering and AIC Foundation.

★1893★ Association of Consulting Chemists and Chemical Engineers (ACC&CE)

PO Box 297
Sparta, NJ 07871-0297
Ph: (973)729-6671   Fax: (973)729-7088
E-mail: info@chemconsult.org
URL: http://www.chemconsult.org

Description: Serves the chemical and related industries through its expertise on a wide variety of technical and business knowledge. Provides experienced counseling for new members.

★1894★ Association for International Practical Training (AIPT)

10400 Little Patuxent Pkwy., Ste. 250
Columbia, MD 21044-3519
Ph: (410)997-2200   Fax: (410)992-3924
E-mail: aipt@aipt.org
URL: http://www.aipt.org

Description: Providers worldwide of on-the-job training programs for students and professionals seeking international career development and life-changing experiences. Arranges workplace exchanges in hundreds of professional fields, bringing employers and trainees together from around the world. Client list ranges from small farming communities to Fortune 500 companies.

★1895★ Biomedical Engineering Society (BMES)

8401 Corporate Dr., Ste. 140
Landover, MD 20785-2224
Ph: (301)459-1999   Fax: (301)459-2444
E-mail: info@bmes.org
URL: http://www.bmes.org

Members: Biomedical, chemical, electrical, civil, agricultural and mechanical engineers, physicians, managers, and university professors representing all fields of biomedical engineering; students and corporations. **Purpose:** Encourages the development, dissemination, integration, and utilization of knowledge in biomedical engineering.

★1896★ Council for Chemical Research (CCR)

1730 Rhode Island Ave. NW, Ste. 302
Washington, DC 20036
Ph: (202)429-3971   Fax: (202)429-3976

E-mail: danthony@ccrhq.org
URL: http://www.ccrhq.org

Description: Represents universities that grant advanced degrees in chemistry or chemical engineering; chemical companies, government laboratories, and independent research laboratories that employ chemists and chemical engineers in research and development. Aims to promote more effective interactions between university chemistry and chemical engineering departments and the research function of industry and government and to support basic research in chemistry and chemical engineering. Strives for continued vitality of chemical science, engineering, and technology in the U.S., and the greater recognition of the global nature of the chemical research enterprise. Sponsors charitable programs; produces educational materials; compiles statistics. Maintains speakers' bureau.

★1897★ Electrochemical Society (ECS)

65 S Main St., Bldg. D
Pennington, NJ 08534-2839
Ph: (609)737-1902   Fax: (609)737-2743
E-mail: ecs@electrochem.org
URL: http://www.electrochem.org

Description: Serves as technical society of electrochemists, chemists, chemical and electrochemical engineers, metallurgists and metallurgical engineers, physical chemists, physicists, electrical engineers, research engineers, teachers, technical sales representatives, and patent attorneys. Seeks to advance the science and technology of electrochemistry, electronics, electrothermics, electrometallurgy, and applied subjects.

★1898★ Geochemical Society (GS)

Washington University
E&PS Bldg., Rm. 334
One Brookings Dr., CB 1169
St. Louis, MO 63130-4899
Ph: (314)935-4131   Fax: (314)935-4121
E-mail: gsoffice@geochemsoc.org
URL: http://gs.wustl.edu

Members: Professional society of geochemists, chemists, geologists, physicists, biologists, oceanographers, mathematicians, meteorologists, and other scientists interested in the application of chemistry to the solution of geological and cosmological problems. The Organic Geochemistry Division focuses on biogeochemistry and organic processes at the Earth's surface and subsurface.

★1899★ International Society of Chemical Ecology (ISCE)

Dept. of Entomology
North Dakota State University
Fargo, ND 58105
Ph: (701)231-6444   Fax: (701)231-8557
E-mail: stephen.foster@ndsu.edu
URL: http://www.chemecol.org

Description: Chemists, ecologists, biologists, and others with an interest in chemical ecology. Promotes understanding of the origin, function, and importance of natural chemicals that mediate communication and interactions within and among organisms. Seeks to broaden the scope of chemical ecology and to stimulate cooperation and exchange of information among members of diverse scientific fields. Conducts educational programs designed to foster knowledge in the area of chemical ecology.

★1900★ International Society of India Chemists and Chemical Engineers (ISICCE)

Advanced Research Chemicals
1110 W Keystone Ave.
Catoosa, OK 74015
Ph: (918)266-6789   Fax: (918)266-6796
E-mail: sales@fluoridearc.com

Description: Chemists and chemical engineers from India. Goal is to bring together Indians in the chemical profession who live in the U.S. Aids members in securing jobs in their fields. Provides consultation to industries in India and helps individuals to start their own chemical companies in the U.S. Provides a forum for the exchange of social and technical issues. Plans to organize symposia, short courses, and exchange program. Compiles statistics.

★1901★ Iranian Chemists' Association of the American Chemical Society (ICA-ACS)

35 Meadowbrook Ln.
Woodbury, CT 06798
Ph: (203)573-3220   Fax: (203)573-3660
E-mail: banijamali@ica-acs.org
URL: http://www.ica-acs.org

Description: Encourages and enhances the interchange and sharing of scientific knowledge and friendship among chemists and chemistry-related professionals of Iranian descent. Provides opportunities for members to assist each other in pursuit of academic and professional development and growth. Promotes awareness of scientific contributions made by Iranian scientists.

★1902★ Minority Women In Science (MWIS)

Directorate for Education and Human
  Resources Programs
1200 New York Ave. NW
Washington, DC 20005
Ph: (202)326-7019   Fax: (202)371-9849
E-mail: ygeorge@aaas.org

Description: A national network group of the American association for the Advancement of Science (AAAS), Education and Human Resources Directorate. The objectives of this group are: to identify and share information on resources and programs that could help in mentoring young women and minorities interested in science and engineering careers, and to strengthen communication among women and minorities in science and education.

★1903★ National Registry of Certified Chemists (NRCC)

927 S Walter Reed Dr., No. 11
Arlington, VA 22204
Ph: (703)979-9001
E-mail: nrcc6@aol.com
URL: http://www.nrcc6.org

Description: Certifies programs for chemical hygiene officers, clinical chemists, clinical chemistry technologists, environmental analytical chemists, environmental analytical technicians, and toxicological chemists based on education, experience, and examination.

★1904★ Pan-American Association for Biochemistry and Molecular Biology (PABMB)

Michigan State Univ.
Dept. of Biochemistry and Molecular
East Lansing, MI 48824-1319
Ph: (517)353-3137   Fax: (517)353-9334
E-mail: preiss@pilot.msu.edu
URL: http://pabmb.fcien.edu.uy

Members: Societies of professional biochemists in the Americas and culturally related European countries. **Purpose:** Promotes the science of biochemistry by disseminating information and encouraging contacts between its members. Cooperates with other organizations having similar objectives. **Activities:** Conducts workshops and symposia.

★1905★ Radiation Research Society (RRS)

PO Box 7050
Lawrence, KS 66044
Fax: (785)843-1274   Fr: 800-627-0326
E-mail: info@radres.org
URL: http://www.radres.org

Description: Professional society of biologists, physicists, chemists, and physicians contributing to knowledge of radiation and its effects. Promotes original research in the natural sciences relating to radiation; facilitates integration of different disciplines in the study of radiation effects.

★1906★ Scientific, Engineering, and Technical Services

Cambridge Educational
PO Box 2053
Princeton, NJ 08543-2053
Ph: 800-257-5126   Fax: (609)671-0266
Fr: 800-468-4227
E-mail: custserv@films.com
URL: http://www.cambridgeeducational.com

VHS and DVD. $89.95. 2002. 18 minutes. 2002. Part of the Career Cluster Series.

★1907★ Scientific Occupations

Delphi Productions
3159 6th St.
Boulder, CO 80304
Ph: (303)443-2100   Fax: (303)443-4022
Fr: 888-443-2400
E-mail: support@delphivideo.com

URL: http://www.delphivideo.com

$95.00. 60 minutes. Part of the Careers for the 21st Century Video Library.

★1908★ **Society of Flavor Chemists**

3301 Rte. 66, Bldg. C, Ste. 205
Neptune, NJ 07753
Ph: (732)922-3393   Fax: (732)922-3590
E-mail: administrator@flavorchemist.org
URL: http://www.flavorchemist.org

Description: Works to advance the field of flavor technology and related sciences. Encourages the exchange of ideas and personal contacts among flavor chemists.

★1909★ **Society of Rheology (SOR)**

Rheology Research Center
University of Wisconsin
Madison, WI 53706
Ph: (608)262-7473   Fax: (608)265-2316
E-mail: giacomin@wisc.edu
URL: http://www.rheology.org/sor

Members: Professional society of chemical engineers, chemists, physicists, biologists, and others interested in the theory and precise measurement of the deformation and flow of matter and application of the physical data in fields such as biology, food, high polymers and plastics, metals, petroleum products, rubber, paint, printing ink, ceramics and glass, starch, floor preparations, and cosmetics.

★1910★ **Soil Science Society of America (SSSA)**

677 S Segoe Rd.
Madison, WI 53711
Ph: (608)273-8080   Fax: (608)273-2021
E-mail: headquarters@agronomy.org
URL: http://www.soils.org

Description: Professional soil scientists, including soil physicists, soil classifiers, land use and management specialists, chemists, microbiologists, soil fertility specialists, soil cartographers, conservationists, mineralogists, engineers, and others interested in fundamental and applied soil science.

★1911★ **Water Environment Federation (WEF)**

601 Wythe St.
Alexandria, VA 22314-1994
Ph: (703)684-2400   Fax: (703)684-2492
Fr: 800-666-0206
E-mail: csc@wef.org
URL: http://www.wef.org

Description: Technical societies representing chemists, biologists, ecologists, geologists, operators, educational and research personnel, industrial wastewater engineers, consultant engineers, municipal officials, equipment manufacturers, and university professors and students dedicated to the enhancement and preservation of water quality and resources. Seeks to advance fundamental and practical knowledge concerning the nature, collection, treatment, and disposal of domestic and industrial wastewaters, and the design, construction, operation, and management of facilities for these purposes. Disseminates technical information; and promotes good public relations and regulations that improve water quality and the status of individuals working in this field. Conducts educational and research programs.

Child Care Workers and Nannies

SOURCES OF HELP-WANTED ADS

★1912★ Education & Treatment of Children
West Virginia University Press
44 Stansbury Hall
PO Box 6295
Morgantown, WV 26506
Ph: (304)293-8400   Fax: (304)293-6585
Fr: (866)988-7737
URL: http://
www.educationandtreatmentofchildren.net

Quarterly. $85.00/year for institutions; $45.00/year for individuals; $100.00/year for institutions, elsewhere; $60.00/year for individuals, elsewhere. Periodical featuring information concerning the development of services for children and youth. Includes reports written for educators and other child care and mental health providers focused on teaching, training, and treatment effectiveness.

PLACEMENT AND JOB REFERRAL SERVICES

★1913★ International Nanny Association (INA)
3801 Kirby Dr., Ste. 540
Houston, TX 77098
Ph: (713)526-2670   Fax: (713)526-2667
Fr: 888-878-1477
E-mail: ina@nanny.org
URL: http://www.nanny.org

Description: An educational association for nannies and those who educate, place, employ, and support professional in-home child care. Membership is open to those who are directly involved with the in-home child care profession, including nannies, nanny employers, nanny placement agency owners (and staff), nanny educators, and providers of special services related to the nanny profession.

HANDBOOKS AND MANUALS

★1914★ Careers for Caring People and Other Sensitive Types
The McGraw-Hill Companies
PO Box 182604
Columbus, OH 43272
Fax: (614)759-3749   Fr: 877-883-5524
E-mail: customer.service@mcgraw-hill.com
URL: http://www.mcgraw-hill.com

Adrian Paradis. Second edition, 2003. $13.95 (paper). 208 pages.

★1915★ Careers in Child Care
The McGraw-Hill Companies
PO Box 182604
Columbus, OH 43272
Fax: (614)759-3749   Fr: 877-883-5524
E-mail: customer.service@mcgraw-hill.com
URL: http://www.mcgraw-hill.com

Marjorie Eberts and Margaret Gisler. Third edition, 2007. $16.95 (paper). $19.95 (hardcover). 192 pages. Know what to expect when you start out. Familiarize yourself with current salaries, benefits, and the best job prospects.

★1916★ Careers for Kids at Heart and Others Who Adore Children
The McGraw-Hill Companies
PO Box 182604
Columbus, OH 43272
Fax: (614)759-3749   Fr: 877-883-5524
E-mail: customer.service@mcgraw-hill.com
URL: http://www.mcgraw-hill.com

Marjorie Eberts and Margaret Gisler. Third edition, 2006. $13.95 (paper). 160 pages.

★1917★ Child and Adult Care Professionals
The McGraw-Hill Companies
PO Box 182604
Columbus, OH 43272
Fax: (614)759-3749   Fr: 877-883-5524
E-mail: customer.service@mcgraw-hill.com
URL: http://www.mcgraw-hill.com

Karen Stephens and Maxine Hammonds-Smith. Third edition, 2002. $64.64. Illustrated. 688 pages.

★1918★ Household Careers: Nannies, Butlers, Maids and More: The Complete Guide for Finding Household Employment or 'If the Dog Likes You, You're Hired!'
Five Star Publications, Inc.
PO Box 6698
Chandler, AZ 85246-6698
Ph: (480)940-8182   Fax: (480)940-8787
Fr: (866)471-0777
URL: http://www.fivestarpublications.com/

Linda F. Radke. 2001. 120 pages. $14.95.

★1919★ Opportunities in Child Care Careers
The McGraw-Hill Companies
PO Box 182604
Columbus, OH 43272
Fax: (614)759-3749   Fr: 877-883-5524
E-mail: customer.service@mcgraw-hill.com
URL: http://www.mcgraw-hill.com

Renee Wittenberg. 2006. $13.95 (paper). 160 pages. Discusses various job opportunities and how to secure a position. Illustrated.

★1920★ Opportunities in Homecare Services Careers
The McGraw-Hill Companies
PO Box 182604
Columbus, OH 43272
Fax: (614)759-3749   Fr: 877-883-5524
E-mail: customer.service@mcgraw-hill.com
URL: http://www.mcgraw-hill.com

Anna deSola Cardoza. 1994. $14.95; $11.95 (paper). 150 pages. Professional child care careers, including various types of therapy and post-intensive surgery assistance.

★1921★ Opportunities in Mental Health Careers
The McGraw-Hill Companies
PO Box 182604
Columbus, OH 43272
Fax: (614)759-3749   Fr: 877-883-5524

E-mail: customer.service@mcgraw-hill.com
URL: http://www.mcgraw-hill.com

Philip A. Perry. 1996. $14.95; $11.95 (paper) 160 pages. Part of the "Opportunities in ..." Series.

★1922★ *Starting and Operating A Child Care Center: A Guide*

Readers Press
523 Burning Embers Ln.
Jacksonville, FL 32225-5146

Lillie M. Robinson. 1997. $29.95. 171 pages. The guide focuses on making the decision to direct a center; finding a suitable location; equipping the center; attracting, hiring, using incentives, evaluating and separating the staff; enrolling and caring for the children; establishing relationships with parents, substitutes, and volunteers; managing and accounting for income, expenses and inventory. It deals with health, safety and nutritional needs of the children and ways of using objective evaluation procedures to assess the program, staff and children.

★1923★ *Working with Children: How to Find the Right Qualifications, Training and Job Opportunities*

Trans-Atlantic Publications, Inc.
311 Bainbridge St.
Philadelphia, PA 19147
Ph: (215)925-5083   Fax: (215)925-1912
E-mail: jeffgolds@comcast.net
URL: http://www.transatlanticpub.com/

Meg Jones. 1997. 142 pages. Part of the Jobs and Careers Series.

★1924★ *Working with Young Children: Teacher's Resource*

Goodheart Willcox Publisher
18604 W. Creek Dr.
Tinley Park, IL 60477-6243
Ph: (708)687-5000   Fax: 888-409-3900
Fr: 800-323-0440
E-mail: custserv@g-w.com
URL: http://www.g-w.com/

Judy Herr. 2001. $62.00 (Compact Disc). Illustrated. 471 pages. Educational format.

EMPLOYMENT AGENCIES AND SEARCH FIRMS

★1925★ Capitol Search

215 E. Ridgewood Ave., Ste. 205
Ridgewood, NJ 07450
Ph: (201)444-6666

Employment agency.

TRADESHOWS

★1926★ Association for Childhood Education International Annual International Conference & Exhibition

Association for Childhood Education International
17904 Georgia Ave., Ste. 215
Olney, MD 20832
Ph: (301)570-2111   Fax: (301)570-2212
Fr: 800-423-3563
E-mail: headquarters@acei.org
URL: http://www.acei.org

Annual. **Primary Exhibits:** Commercial and educational exhibits of interest to teachers, teacher educators, college students, day care personnel and other care givers. **Dates and Locations:** 2008 Mar 26-29; Atlanta, GA; Westin Peachtree Plaza; 2009 Mar 18-21; Chicago, IL; Westin Michigan Avenue.

★1927★ National Association for the Education of Young Children Annual Conference

National Association for the Education of Young Children
1509 16th St., NW
Washington, DC 20036
Ph: (202)232-8777   Fax: (202)328-1846
Fr: 800-424-2460
E-mail: naeyc@naeyc.org
URL: http://www.naeyc.org

Annual. **Primary Exhibits:** Educational materials and equipment designed for children ages birth through eight years old.

★1928★ Southern Early Childhood Association Annual Meeting

Southern Early Childhood Association
7107 W. 12th., No. 102
PO Box 55930
Little Rock, AR 72215-5930
Fax: (501)227-5297   Fr: 800-305-7322
E-mail: seca@aristotle.net
URL: http://www.southernearlychildhood.org

Annual. **Primary Exhibits:** Publications, school supplies, playground equipment, and toys.

OTHER SOURCES

★1929★ Center for the Child Care Workforce, A Project of the American Federation of Teachers Educational Foundation (CCW/AFTEF)

555 New Jersey Ave. NW
Washington, DC 20001
Ph: (202)662-8005   Fax: (202)662-8006
E-mail: ccw@aft.org
URL: http://ccw.cleverspin.com

Purpose: Purposes are: to develop innovative solutions to the child care crisis to improve salaries, working conditions, and status of child care workers; to increase public awareness about the importance of child care work and the training and skill it demands; to develop resources and create an information sharing network for child care workers nationwide. **Activities:** Gathers current information on salaries and benefits; offers consultation services. Sponsors research projects; compiles statistics; operates Speaker's Bureau. Maintains extensive file of materials on working conditions and research on child care workers.

★1930★ Education and Training

Cambridge Educational
PO Box 2053
Princeton, NJ 08543-2053
Ph: 800-257-5126   Fax: (609)671-0266
Fr: 800-468-4227
E-mail: custserv@films.com
URL: http://www.cambridgeeducational.com

VHS and DVD. $89.95. 2002. 18 minutes. Presents four distinct occupations in the field: elementary teachers, teacher's aides, administrators, and librarians. People working in these jobs discuss their responsibilities.

★1931★ National Association for the Education of Young Children (NAEYC)

1313 L St. NW, Ste. 500
Washington, DC 20005
Ph: (202)232-8777   Fax: (202)328-1846
Fr: 800-424-2460
E-mail: naeyc@naeyc.org
URL: http://www.naeyc.org

Description: Teachers and directors of preschool and primary schools, kindergartens, child care centers, and early other learning programs for young childhood; early childhood education and child development educators, trainers, and researchers and other professionals dedicated to young children's healthy development.

★1932★ National Association of Nannies

4604 N. Lakefront Dr.
Glen Allen, VA 23060
Ph: (843)548-0105   Fr: 800-344-6266
E-mail: apn@hargray.com
URL: http://www.nannyassociation.com

Description: Promotes the nanny as a legitimate career choice.

★1933★ Personal & Building Service Occupations

Delphi Productions
3159 6th St.
Boulder, CO 80304
Ph: (303)443-2100   Fax: (303)443-4022
Fr: 888-443-2400
E-mail: support@delphivideo.com
URL: http://www.delphivideo.com

$95.00. 48 minutes. Part of the Careers for the 21st Century Video Library.

★1934★ Working with Children
Cambridge Educational
PO Box 2053
Princeton, NJ 08543-2053
Ph: 800-257-5126　　Fax: (609)671-0266
Fr: 800-468-4227

E-mail: custserv@films.com
URL: http://www.cambridgeeducational.com

VHS and DVD. $89.95. 2000. 24 minutes. This program examines alternative positions offering the opportunity to work with children of different ages and the qualifications necessary for those jobs. A nanny, social worker, non-faculty school worker, and retail salesperson describe their job responsibilities and explain why they find their work so enjoyable.

Chiropractors

PLACEMENT AND JOB REFERRAL SERVICES

★1935★ Christian Chiropractors Association (CCA)

2550 Stover, No. B-102
Fort Collins, CO 80525
Ph: (970)482-1404   Fax: (970)482-1538
Fr: 800-999-1970
E-mail: bkaseman@gmail.com
URL: http://www.christianchiropractors.org

Description: Works to spread the Gospel of Christ throughout the U.S. and abroad. Offers Christian fellowship and works to unify Christian chiropractors around the essentials of the faith, "leaving minor points of doctrine to the conscience of the individual believer." Focuses on world missions; organizing short-term trips and aiding in the placement of Christian chiropractors as missionaries.

EMPLOYER DIRECTORIES AND NETWORKING LISTS

★1936★ Women's Auxiliary of the International Chiropractors Association-Membership Roster

Women's Auxiliary of the International Chiropractors Association
1110 N Glebe Rd., Ste. 1000
Arlington, VA 22201
Ph: (703)528-5000   Fax: (703)351-7893
Fr: 800-423-4690
URL: http://www.chiropractic.org/

Biennial. Covers about 500 women who are chiropractic assistants, chiropractors, or related to members of the ICA.

HANDBOOKS AND MANUALS

★1937★ The Business of Chiropractic: How to Prosper after Startup

Do Write Publishing
1227 Cedar Hill Rd.
Dandridge, TN 37725
Ph: (865)397-4358   Fax: (423)397-4358

Ivan Delman. Second edition, 2002. $29.95 (paper). $37.50. 182 pages.

★1938★ Careers in Medicine

The McGraw-Hill Companies
PO Box 182604
Columbus, OH 43272
Fax: (614)759-3749   Fr: 877-883-5524
E-mail: customer.service@mcgraw-hill.com
URL: http://www.mcgraw-hill.com

Terence J. Sacks. Third edition, 2006. $15.95 (paper). 192 pages. Examines the many paths open to M.D.s, D.O.s, and M.D./Ph.D.s, including clinical private or group practice, hospitals, public health organizations, the armed forces, emergency rooms, research institutions, medical schools, pharmaceutical companies and private industry, and research/advocacy groups like the World Health Organization. A special chapter on osteopathy and chiropractic explores this branch of medicine.

★1939★ Chiropractors for Wellness

Chiropractic Journal
2950 N Dobson Rd., Ste. 1
Chandler, AZ 85224
Fax: (602)732-9313   Fr: 800-374-1011

Terry A. Rondberg. 2004. $12.95.

★1940★ Opportunities in Chiropractic Careers

The McGraw-Hill Companies
PO Box 182604
Columbus, OH 43272
Fax: (614)759-3749   Fr: 877-883-5524
E-mail: customer.service@mcgraw-hill.com
URL: http://www.mcgraw-hill.com

Bart Green, Claire Johnson, and Louis Sportelli. 2004. $13.95; $10.95 (paper). 160 pages. A guide to planning for and building a career in the field. Illustrated.

★1941★ Opportunities in Sports and Athletics Careers

The McGraw-Hill Companies
PO Box 182604
Columbus, OH 43272
Fax: (614)759-3749   Fr: 877-883-5524
E-mail: customer.service@mcgraw-hill.com
URL: http://www.mcgraw-hill.com

William Ray Heitzmann. 1993. 160 pages. $11.95 (paper). A guide to planning for and seeking opportunities in this growing field. Illustrated.

★1942★ Opportunities in Sports Medicine Careers

The McGraw-Hill Companies
PO Box 182604
Columbus, OH 43272
Fax: (614)759-3749   Fr: 877-883-5524
E-mail: customer.service@mcgraw-hill.com
URL: http://www.mcgraw-hill.com

William Ray Heitzmann. 1992. $11.95 (paper). 160 pages. Discusses a variety of opportunities in this field and how to pursue them. Contains bibliography and illustrations.

★1943★ Power Publicity for Chiropractors

Clifford Publishing
PO Box 43596
Upper Montclair, NJ 07043-0596
Ph: (973)857-4142

Paul Hartunian. 2006. $79.00. Profiles marketing ideas for chiropractors using press releases as a tool for publicity; includes a full year calendar with story ideas and headlines for each month.

★1944★ Resumes for Health and Medical Careers

The McGraw-Hill Companies
PO Box 182604
Columbus, OH 43272
Fax: (614)759-3749   Fr: 877-883-5524
E-mail: customer.service@mcgraw-hill.com
URL: http://www.mcgraw-hill.com

Third edition, 2003. $11.95 (paper). 160 pages.

ONLINE JOB SOURCES AND SERVICES

★1945★ Medhunters.com

Fr: 800-664-0278
E-mail: info@medhunters.com
URL: http://www.medhunters.com

Description: Career search site for jobs in all health care specialties; educational resources; visa and licensing information for relocation; interesting articles; relocation tools; links to professional organizations and general resources.

★1946★ ProHealthJobs

Fr: 800-796-1738
E-mail: Info@prohealthedujobs.com
URL: http://www.prohealthjobs.com

Description: Career resources site for the medical and health care field. Lists professional opportunities, product information, continuing education and open positions.

TRADESHOWS

★1947★ American Chiropractic Association Annual Convention and Exhibition

American Chiropractic Association
1701 Clarendon Blvd.
Arlington, VA 22209
Ph: (703)276-8800   Fax: (703)243-2593
Fr: 800-986-4636
E-mail: memberinfo@amerchiro.org
URL: http://www.amerchiro.org/

Annual. **Primary Exhibits:** Chiropractic tables and products; nutritional supplements; computer services and equipment, mattress companies, and publishers.

★1948★ California Chiropractic Association Annual Convention

California Chiropractic Association
1600 Sacramento Inn Way, Ste. 106
Sacramento, CA 95815-3458
Ph: (916)648-2727   Fax: (916)648-2738
E-mail: cca@calchiro.org
URL: http://www.calchiro.org

Annual. **Primary Exhibits:** Publications, office equipment and supplies, computers, health foods, insurance companies, and X-ray equipment; nutritional, chiropractic equipment, physical therapy, orthopedics.

★1949★ Florida Chiropractic Association National Convention and Expo

Florida Chiropractic Association
217 N Kirkman Rd., Ste. 1
Orlando, FL 32811
Ph: (407)290-5883   Fax: (407)295-7191
URL: http://www.fcachiro.org

Annual. **Primary Exhibits:** Chiropractic examining/adjusting tables; X-ray equipment and products; diagnostic equipment and supplies; office furniture; computer systems and software; nutritional supplements; physical therapy equipment; orthopedic appliances; medical books; patient educational material, and uniforms.

★1950★ North American Spine Society Annual Meeting

North American Spine Society
22 Calendar Ct., 2nd Fl.
La Grange, IL 60525
Fr: 877-Spine-Dr
URL: http://www.spine.org

Annual. **Primary Exhibits:** Products & services directly and indirectly related to spinal diagnosis, treatment and surgery, the general practice of medicine aid peripheral products and services.

OTHER SOURCES

★1951★ American Chiropractic Association (ACA)

1701 Clarendon Blvd.
Arlington, VA 22209
Ph: (703)276-8800   Fax: (703)243-2593
Fr: 800-986-4636
E-mail: memberinfo@acatoday.org
URL: http://www.amerchiro.org

Description: Enhances the philosophy, science, and art of chiropractic, and the professional welfare of individuals in the field. Promotes legislation defining chiropractic health care and improves the public's awareness and utilization of chiropractic. Conducts chiropractic survey and statistical study; maintains library. Sponsors Correct Posture Week in May and Spinal Health Month in October. Chiropractic colleges have student groups.

★1952★ American College of Chiropractic Orthopedists (ACCO)

40 W Foster St.
Melrose, MA 02176
Ph: (781)665-1497   Fax: (781)662-7111
E-mail: dosdc@aol.com
URL: http://www.accoweb.org

Members: Certified and non-certified chiropractic orthopedists; students enrolled in a postgraduate chiropractic orthopedic program. **Purpose:** Seeks to establish and maintain optimal educational and clinical standards within the field of chiropractic orthopedics. **Activities:** Sponsors educational programs.

★1953★ Council on Chiropractic Education (CCE)

8049 N 85th Way
Scottsdale, AZ 85258-4321
Ph: (480)443-8877   Fax: (480)483-7333
E-mail: cce@cce-usa.org
URL: http://www.cce-usa.org

Description: Advocates high standards in chiropractic education; establishes criteria of institutional excellence for educating chiropractic physicians; acts as national accrediting agency for chiropractic colleges. Conducts workshops for college teams, consultants, and chiropractic college staffs.

★1954★ Council of Chiropractic Physiological Therapeutics and Rehabilitation (CCPT)

312 Courtyard Dr.
Hillsborough, NJ 08844
Ph: (908)722-9075   Fax: (908)722-1144
E-mail: rehabdc18@aol.com
URL: http://www.ccptr.org

Description: Represents chiropractors who use physiotherapy and rehabilitation in their practice and are dedicated to furthering the extended use of physiotherapy in the chiropractic field.

★1955★ Exploring Health Occupations

Cambridge Educational
PO Box 2053
Princeton, NJ 08543-2053
Ph: 800-257-5126   Fax: (609)671-0266
Fr: 800-468-4227
E-mail: custserv@films.com
URL: http://www.cambridgeeducational.com

VHS and DVD. $159.90. 1999. Two-part series provides a detailed view of the field of medical technicians and technologists, EMTs, nurses, therapists, and assistants.

★1956★ Foundation for Chiropractic Education and Research (FCER)

PO Box 400
Norwalk, IA 50211-0400
Ph: (515)981-9888   Fax: (515)981-9427
Fr: 800-622-6309
E-mail: fcer@fcer.org
URL: http://www.fcer.org

Description: Chiropractors and laymen. Provides funding for scientific research and research training that will "enhance the knowledge and practice of chiropractic as a conservative approach to health care restoration, maintenance, and disease prevention".

★1957★ **Health Service Occupations**

Delphi Productions
3159 6th St.
Boulder, CO 80304
Ph: (303)443-2100   Fax: (303)443-4022
Fr: 888-443-2400
E-mail: support@delphivideo.com
URL: http://www.delphivideo.com
$95.00. 50 minutes. Part of the Careers for the 21st Century Video Library.

★1958★ **Holistic Dental Association (HDA)**

PO Box 151444
San Diego, CA 92175
Ph: (619)923-3120   Fax: (619)615-2228
E-mail: info@holisticdental.org
URL: http://www.holisticdental.org
Description: Represents dentists, chiropractors, dental hygienists, physical therapists, and medical doctors. Aims to provide a holistic approach to better dental care for patients, and to expand techniques, medications, and philosophies that pertain to extractions, anesthetics, fillings, crowns, and orthodontics. Encourages the use of homeopathic medications, acupuncture, cranial osteopathy, nutritional techniques, and physical therapy in treating patients in addition to conventional treatments. Sponsors training and educational seminars.

★1959★ **International Chiropractors Association (ICA)**

1110 N Glebe Rd., Ste. 650
Arlington, VA 22201
Ph: (703)528-5000   Fax: (703)528-5023
Fr: 800-423-4690
E-mail: chiro@chiropractic.org
URL: http://www.chiropractic.org
Description: Serves as professional society of chiropractors, chiropractic educators, students, and laypersons. Sponsors professional development programs and practice management seminars.

★1960★ **Medicine & Related Occupations**

Delphi Productions
3159 6th St.
Boulder, CO 80304
Ph: (303)443-2100   Fax: (303)443-4022
Fr: 888-443-2400
E-mail: support@delphivideo.com
URL: http://www.delphivideo.com
$95.00. 45 minutes. Part of the Careers for the 21st Century Video Library.

Civil Engineers

★1972★ Graduating Engineer & Computer Careers

Career Recruitment Media
211 W Wacker Dr., Ste. 900
Chicago, IL 60606
Ph: (312)525-3100
URL: http://www.graduatingengineer.com

Quarterly. $15.00/year for individuals. Magazine focusing on employment, education, and career development for entry-level engineers and computer scientists.

★1973★ High Technology Careers Magazine

HTC
4701 Patrick Henry Dr., No. 1901
Santa Clara, CA 95054-1847
Fax: (408)567-0242
URL: http://www.hightechcareers.com

Bimonthly. $29.00/year; $35.00/year for Canada; $85.00/year for out of country. Magazine (tabloid) containing employment opportunity information for the engineering and technical community.

★1974★ InterJournal

New England Complex Systems Institute
24 Mt. Auburn St.
Cambridge, MA 02138
Ph: (617)547-4100   Fax: (617)661-7711
URL: http://www.interjournal.org/

Journal covering the fields of science and engineering.

★1975★ International Archives of Bioscience

International Archives of Bioscience
PO Box 737254
Elmhurst, NY 11373-9997
URL: http://www.iabs.us/jdoc/aboutiabs.htm

Free, online only. Journal reporting multidisciplinary coverage and interaction between scientists in biology, informatics, mathematics, physics, engineering and other sciences.

★1976★ ITE Journal

Institute of Transportation Engineers
1099 14th St. NW, Ste. 300 W
Washington, DC 20005-3438
Ph: (202)289-0222   Fax: (202)289-7722
URL: http://www.ite.org/itejournal/

Monthly. $65.00/year for individuals, U.S., Canada and Mexico; $85.00/year for out of country; $160.00 for three years for individuals, U.S., Canada and Mexico; $200.00 for three years for individuals, out of country. Technical magazine focusing on the plan, design, and operation of surface transportation systems.

★1977★ Journal of Engineering Education

American Society for Engineering Education
1818 North St., NW, Ste. 600
Washington, DC 20036-2479
Ph: (202)331-3500

URL: http://www.asee.org/publications/jee/index.cfm

Quarterly. Journal covering scholarly research in engineering education.

★1978★ MainStream

American Water Works Association
6666 W Quincy Ave.
Denver, CO 80235
Ph: (303)794-7711   Fax: (303)347-0804
Fr: 800-926-7337
URL: http://www.awwa.org/communications/mainstream/

Description: Biweekly, online; print issue is quarterly. Carries news of the Association and features about the drinking water industry, including regulations, legislation, conservation, treatment, quality, distribution, management, and utility operations. Recurring features include letters to the editor, a calendar of events, reports of meetings, news of educational opportunities, notices of publications available, education and job opportunities in the industry and legislative news.

★1979★ The Military Engineer

The Society of American Military Engineers
607 Prince St.
Alexandria, VA 22314-3117
Ph: (703)549-3800   Fax: (703)684-0231
URL: http://www.same.org/i4a/pages/index.cfm?pageid=4273

Bimonthly. $78.00/year for U.S. and Canada, individual, second class mail; $148.00/year for U.S. and Canada, two years; $196.00/year for U.S. and Canada, 3 years; $148.00/year for other countries, air mail, individual; $286.00/year for other countries, two years, air mail; $419.00/year for other countries, 3 years, air mail; $16.00/year for students, U.S., Canada, and foreign (regular mail). Journal on military and civil engineering.

★1980★ The Municipality

League of Wisconsin Municipalities
122 W Washington Ave., Ste. 300
Madison, WI 53703-2718
Ph: (608)267-2380   Fax: (608)267-0645
Fr: 800-991-5502
URL: http://www.lwm-info.org/index.asp?Type=B_BASIC&SEC=¢0702EE8F

Monthly. Magazine for officials of Wisconsin's local municipal governments.

★1981★ NSBE Magazine

NSBE Publications
205 Daingerfield Rd.
Alexandria, VA 22314
Ph: (703)549-2207   Fax: (703)683-5312
URL: http://www.nsbe.org/publications/premieradvertisers.php

Journal providing information on engineering careers, self-development, and cultural issues for recent graduates with technical majors.

★1982★ PM Network

Project Management Institute
4 Campus Blvd.
Newtown Square, PA 19073
Ph: (610)356-4600   Fax: (610)356-4647
URL: http://www.pmi.org

Monthly. $42.00/year for members, (included in annual dues). Professional journal covering industry applications and practical issues in managing projects.

★1983★ Public Works

Hanley-Wood LLC
One Thomas Cir. NW, Ste. 600
Washington, DC 20005
Ph: (202)452-0800   Fax: (202)785-1974
URL: http://www.pwmag.com

$60.00/year for individuals; $75.00/year for individuals, Canada; $90.00/year for individuals, international. Trade magazine covering the public works industry nationwide for city, county, and state.

★1984★ Roads & Bridges Magazine

Scranton Gillette Communications Inc.
3030 W Salt Creek Ln., Ste. 201
Arlington Heights, IL 60005-5025
Ph: (847)391-1000   Fax: (847)390-0408
URL: http://www.roadsbridges.com

Monthly. Free to qualified subscribers. Magazine containing information on highway, road, and bridge design, construction, and maintenance for government agencies, contractors, and consulting engineers.

★1985★ Structure Magazine

American Consulting Engineers Council
1015 15th St. NW, 8th Fl.
Washington, DC 20005-2605
Ph: (202)347-7474   Fax: (202)898-0068
URL: http://www.structuremag.org

Annual. $65.00/year for nonmembers; $35.00/year for students; $90.00/year for Canada; $125.00/year for other countries. Magazine focused on providing tips, tools, techniques, and innovative concepts for structural engineers.

★1986★ SWE, Magazine of the Society of Women Engineers

Society of Women Engineers
230 East Ohio St., Ste. 400
Chicago, IL 60611-3265
Ph: (312)596-5223
E-mail: hq@swe.org
URL: http://www.swe.org

Quarterly. $30.00/year for nonmembers. Magazine for engineering students and for women and men working in the engineering and technology fields. Covers career guidance, continuing development and topical issues.

★1987★ The Technology Interface

New Mexico State University
College of Engineering
PO Box 30001
Las Cruces, NM 88003-8001
Ph: (505)646-0111
URL: http://engr.nmsu.edu/etti/

Journal for the engineering technology profession serving education and industry.

★1988★ Uratie

IDG Communications Inc.
5 Speen St., 3rd. Fl
Framingham, MA 01701
Ph: (508)875-5000   Fax: (508)988-7888
URL: http://www.idg.com

Magazine providing job offers for graduates, engineers and information technology professionals.

★1989★ WEPANEWS

Women in Engineering Programs &
  Advocates Network
1901 E. Asbury Ave., Ste. 220
Denver, CO 80208
Ph: (303)871-4643   Fax: (303)871-6833
E-mail: dmatt@wepan.org
URL: http://www.wepan.org

Description: 2/year. Seeks to provide greater access for women to careers in engineering. Includes news of graduate, undergraduate, freshmen, pre-college, and re-entry engineering programs for women. Recurring features include job listings, faculty, grant, and conference news, international engineering program news, action group news, notices of publications available, and a column titled Kudos.

★1990★ Western City

League of California Cities
1400 K St., Ste. 400
Sacramento, CA 95814
Ph: (916)658-8200   Fax: (916)658-8240
Fr: 800-262-1801
URL: http://www.westerncity.com

Monthly. $39.00/year for individuals; $63.00 for two years; $52.00/year for other countries; $26.50/year for students. Municipal interest magazine.

PLACEMENT AND JOB REFERRAL SERVICES

★1991★ American Indian Science and Engineering Society (AISES)

PO Box 9828
Albuquerque, NM 87119-9828
Ph: (505)765-1052   Fax: (505)765-5608
E-mail: info@aises.org
URL: http://www.aises.org

Description: Represents American Indian and non-Indian students and professionals in science, technology, and engineering fields;

corporations representing energy, mining, aerospace, electronic, and computer fields. Seeks to motivate and encourage students to pursue undergraduate and graduate studies in science, engineering, and technology. Sponsors science fairs in grade schools, teacher training workshops, summer math/science sessions for 8th-12th graders, professional chapters, and student chapters in colleges. Offers scholarships. Adult members serve as role models, advisers, and mentors for students. Operates placement service.

★1992★ American Water Works Association (AWWA)

6666 W Quincy Ave.
Denver, CO 80235-3098
Ph: (303)794-7711   Fax: (303)347-0804
Fr: 800-926-7337
E-mail: rrenner@awwa.org
URL: http://www.awwa.org

Members: Water utility managers, superintendents, engineers, chemists, bacteriologists, and other individuals interested in public water supply; municipal- and investor-owned water departments; boards of health; manufacturers of waterworks equipment; government officials and consultants interested in water supply. **Purpose:** Develops standards and supports research programs in waterworks design, construction, operation, and management. **Activities:** Conducts in-service training schools and prepares manuals for waterworks personnel. Maintains hall of fame. Offers placement service via member newsletter; compiles statistics. Offers training; children's services; and information center on the water utilities industry, potable water, and water reuse.

★1993★ Engineering Society of Detroit (ESD)

2000 Town Ctr., Ste. 2610
Southfield, MI 48075
Ph: (248)353-0735   Fax: (248)353-0736
E-mail: esd@esd.org
URL: http://esd.org

Description: Engineers from all disciplines; scientists and technologists. Conducts technical programs and engineering refresher courses; sponsors conferences and expositions. Maintains speakers' bureau; offers placement services; although based in Detroit, MI, society membership is international.

★1994★ Korean-American Scientists and Engineers Association (KSEA)

1952 Gallows Rd., Ste. 300
Vienna, VA 22182
Ph: (703)748-1221   Fax: (703)748-1331
E-mail: admin@ksea.org
URL: http://www.ksea.org

Description: Represents scientists and engineers holding single or advanced degrees. Promotes friendship and mutuality among Korean and American scientists and engineers; contributes to Korea's scientific, technological, industrial, and economic developments; strengthens the scientific, technological, and cultural bonds between Korea and

the U.S. Sponsors symposium. Maintains speakers' bureau, placement service, and biographical archives. Compiles statistics.

★1995★ Society of Hispanic Professional Engineers (SHPE)

5400 E Olympic Blvd., Ste. 210
Los Angeles, CA 90022
Ph: (323)725-3970   Fax: (323)725-0316
E-mail: shpenational@shpe.org
URL: http://oneshpe.shpe.org/wps/portal/national

Description: Represents engineers, student engineers, and scientists. Aims to increase the number of Hispanic engineers by providing motivation and support to students. Sponsors competitions and educational programs. Maintains placement service and speakers' bureau; compiles statistics.

EMPLOYER DIRECTORIES AND NETWORKING LISTS

★1996★ American Men and Women of Science

Gale, Cengage Learning
27500 Drake Rd.
Farmington Hills, MI 48331-3535
Ph: (248)699-4253   Fax: (248)699-8065
Fr: 800-877-4253
URL: http://www.gale.com

Biennial, latest edition 23rd, October 2006; new edition expected 24th, January 2008. $1,075.00 for individuals. Covers over 129,700 U.S. and Canadian scientists active in the physical, biological, mathematical, computer science, and engineering fields; includes references to previous edition for deceased scientists and nonrespondents. Entries include: Name, address, education, personal and career data, memberships, honors and awards, research interest. Arrangement: Alphabetical. Indexes: Discipline (in separate volume).

★1997★ Careers in Focus: Engineering

Facts On File Inc.
132 W 31st St., 17th Fl.
New York, NY 10001
Ph: (212)967-8800   Fax: 800-678-3633
Fr: 800-322-8755
URL: http://www.factsonfile.com

3rd edition, 2007. $29.95 for individuals; $26.95 for libraries. Publication includes: List of resources to consult for more information. Principal content of publication consists of job descriptions, advancement opportunities, educational requirements, employment outlook, salary information, and working conditions for careers in the field of engineering. Indexes: Alphabetical.

★1998★ Directory of Contract Staffing Firms

C.E. Publications Inc.
PO Box 3006
Bothell, WA 98041-3006
Ph: (425)806-5200   Fax: (425)806-5585
URL: http://www.cjhunter.com/dcsf/overview.html

Covers nearly 1,300 contract firms actively engaged in the employment of engineering, IT/IS, and technical personnel for 'temporary' contract assignments throughout the world. Entries include: Company name, address, phone, name of contact, email, web address. Arrangement: Alphabetical. Indexes: Geographical.

★1999★ ENR-Top 500 Design Firms Issue

McGraw-Hill Inc.
1221 Ave. of the Americas
New York, NY 10020-1095
Ph: (212)512-2000   Fax: (212)512-3840
Fr: 877-833-5524
URL: http://enr.construction.com/people/sourcebooks/top500Design/

Annual, latest edition 2007. $50.00 for individuals. Publication includes: List of 500 leading architectural, engineering, and specialty design firms selected on basis of annual billings. Entries include: Company name, headquarters location, type of firm, current and prior year rank in billings, types of services, countries in which operated in preceding year. Arrangement: Ranked by billings.

★2000★ Indiana Society of Professional Engineers-Directory

Indiana Society of Professional Engineers
PO Box 20806
Indianapolis, IN 46220
Ph: (317)255-2267   Fax: (317)255-2530
URL: http://www.indspe.org

Annual, fall. Covers member registered engineers, land surveyors, engineering students, and engineers in training. Entries include: Member name, address, phone, type of membership, business information, specialty. Arrangement: Alphabetical by chapter area.

★2001★ Peterson's Job Opportunities in Engineering and Technology

Peterson's Guides
2000 Lenox Dr.
Box 67005
Lawrenceville, NJ 08648
Ph: (609)896-1800   Fax: (609)896-4531
Fr: 800-338-3282
E-mail: custsvc@petersons.com
URL: http://www.petersons.com

Compiled by the Peterson's staff. Fourth edition, 1996. $21.95 (paper). 379 pages. Profiles 2,000 high-tech companies looking primarily for technical personnel in such fields as biotechnology, telecommunications, software, computers and peripherals, defense, and aerospace. Contains job-search strategies and career options to help match

education and expertise to the job market. Indexed geographically, by industry, and by hiring needs.

HANDBOOKS AND MANUALS

★2002★ The Best Resumes for Scientists and Engineers

John Wiley & Sons Inc.
1 Wiley Dr.
Somerset, NJ 08873
Ph: (732)469-4400   Fax: (732)302-2300
Fr: 800-225-5945
E-mail: custserv@wiley.com
URL: http://www.wiley.com/WileyCDA/

Adele Lewis and David J. Moore. Second edition, 1993. $37.50; $19.95 (paper). 224 pages. Presents an extensive collection of scientific and engineering resumes, highlighting the important differences between these and resumes written for other occupations.

★2003★ Career Development: A Special Issue of the Journal of Management in Engineering

American Society of Civil Engineers
1801 Alexander Bell Dr.
Reston, VA 20191-4400
Ph: (703)295-6300   Fax: (703)295-6222
Fr: 800-548-2723
URL: http://www.asce.org/asce.cfm

Stuart G. Walesh, editor. 1998. $15.00 (paper). 68 pages.

★2004★ Changing Our World: True Stories of Women Engineers

American Society of Civil Engineers
1801 Alexander Bell Dr.
Reston, VA 20191-4400
Ph: (703)295-6300   Fax: (703)295-6222
Fr: 800-548-2723
URL: http://www.asce.org/asce.cfm

Sybil E. Hatch. $54.00. 2006.

★2005★ Great Jobs for Engineering Majors

The McGraw-Hill Companies
PO Box 182604
Columbus, OH 43272
Fax: (614)759-3749   Fr: 877-883-5524
E-mail: customer.service@mcgraw-hill.com
URL: http://www.mcgraw-hill.com

Geraldine O. Garner. Second edition, 2002. $14.95. 256 pages. Covers all the career options open to students majoring in engineering.

★2006★ How to Succeed as an Engineer: A Practical Guide to Enhance Your Career

Institute of Electrical & Electronics Engineers
445 Hoes Lane
Piscataway, NJ 08854
Ph: (732)981-0060   Fax: (732)981-9667
Fr: 800-678-4333
URL: http://www.ieee.org

Todd Yuzuriha. 1999. $29.95 (paper). 367 pages.

★2007★ The I Hate Selling Book: Business-Building Advice for Consultants, Attorneys, Accountants, Engineers, Architects, and Other Professionals

AMACOM
1601 Broadway, 12th Fl.
New York, NY 10019-7420
Ph: (212)586-8100   Fax: (212)903-8168
Fr: 800-262-9699
URL: http://www.amanet.org

Allan S. Boress. 2001. $29.95. 240 pages.

★2008★ Keys to Engineering Success

Prentice Hall PTR
One Lake St.
Upper Saddle River, NJ 07458
Ph: (201)236-7000   Fr: 800-428-5331
URL: http://www.phptr.com/index.asp?rl=1

Jill S. Tietjen, Kristy A. Schloss, Carol Carter, Joyce Bishop, and Sarah Lyman. 2000. $46.00 (paper). 288 pages.

★2009★ The New Engineer's Guide to Career Growth & Professional Awareness

Institute of Electrical & Electronics Engineers
445 Hoes Lane
Piscataway, NJ 08854
Ph: (732)981-0060   Fax: (732)981-9667
Fr: 800-678-4333
URL: http://www.ieee.org

Irving J. Gabelman, editor. 1996. $39.95 (paper). 275 pages.

★2010★ Opportunities in Civil Engineering Careers

McGraw-Hill
PO Box 182604
Columbus, OH 43272
Fax: (614)759-3749   Fr: 877-883-5524
E-mail: customer.service@mcgraw-hill.com
URL: http://www.mcgraw-hill.com

Joseph Hagerty, Louis F. Cohn, Philip Pessy, and Tom Cosgrove. 1996. $11.95 (paper). 160 pages. Describes career opportunities in the different fields of civil engineering and tells how to prepare for and launch such a career.

★2011★ Opportunities in Engineering Careers

The McGraw-Hill Companies
PO Box 182604
Columbus, OH 43272
Fax: (614)759-3749   Fr: 877-883-5524
E-mail: customer.service@mcgraw-hill.com
URL: http://www.mcgraw-hill.com

Nicholas Basta. Revised second edition, 2002. $13.95; $11.95 (paper). 160 pages. Outlines typical job titles, salaries, career paths, and employment prospects.

★2012★ Opportunities in High Tech Careers

The McGraw-Hill Companies
PO Box 182604
Columbus, OH 43272
Fax: (614)759-3749   Fr: 877-883-5524
E-mail: customer.service@mcgraw-hill.com
URL: http://www.mcgraw-hill.com

Gary Colter and Deborah Yanuck. 1999. $14.95; $11.95 (paper). 160 pages. Explores high technology careers. Describes job opportunities, how to make a career decision, how to prepare for high technology jobs, job hunting techniques, and future trends.

★2013★ Opportunities in Research and Development Careers

The McGraw-Hill Companies
PO Box 182604
Columbus, OH 43272
Fax: (614)759-3749   Fr: 877-883-5524
E-mail: customer.service@mcgraw-hill.com
URL: http://www.mcgraw-hill.com

Jan Goldberg. 1996. $11.95 (paper). 146 pages.

★2014★ Opportunities in State and Local Government Careers

The McGraw-Hill Companies
PO Box 182604
Columbus, OH 43272
Fax: (614)759-3749   Fr: 877-883-5524
E-mail: customer.service@mcgraw-hill.com
URL: http://www.mcgraw-hill.com

Neale J. Baxter. Revised edition, 1992. $14.95; $10.95 (paper). 148 pages. Points out the incentives and drawbacks of a government career. Describes hiring procedures and provides tips on filling out applications, taking physical and aptitude tests, handling interviews, and finding jobs. Describes the jobs in which 75% of all state and local government workers are employed. For each occupation, covers the nature of the work and the training required.

★2015★ Preparing for Design-Build Projects: A Primer for Owners, Engineers, and Contractors

American Society of Civil Engineers
1801 Alexander Bell Dr.
Reston, VA 20191-4400
Ph: (703)295-6300   Fax: (703)295-6222
Fr: 800-548-2723
URL: http://www.asce.org/asce.cfm

Douglas D. Gransberg, James A. Koch and Keith R. Molenaar. 2006. $64.00

★2016★ Real People Working in Engineering

The McGraw-Hill Companies
PO Box 182604
Columbus, OH 43272
Fax: (614)759-3749   Fr: 877-883-5524
E-mail: customer.service@mcgraw-hill.com
URL: http://www.mcgraw-hill.com

Blythe Camenson, Jan Goldberg. 1997. $17.95 (paper). 160 pages. Interviews and profiles of working professionals capture a range of opportunities in this field.

★2017★ Resumes for Engineering Careers

The McGraw-Hill Companies
PO Box 182604
Columbus, OH 43272
Fax: (614)759-3749   Fr: 877-883-5524
E-mail: customer.service@mcgraw-hill.com
URL: http://www.mcgraw-hill.com

Third edition, 2005. $11.95 (paper). 144 pages. Contains sample resumes and cover letters applicable to any engineering field.

★2018★ Resumes for Scientific and Technical Careers

The McGraw-Hill Companies
PO Box 182604
Columbus, OH 43272
Fax: (614)759-3749   Fr: 877-883-5524
E-mail: customer.service@mcgraw-hill.com
URL: http://www.mcgraw-hill.com

Third edition, 2007. $12.95 (paper). 144 pages. Provides resume advice for individuals interested in working in scientific and technical careers. Includes sample resumes and cover letters.

EMPLOYMENT AGENCIES AND SEARCH FIRMS

★2019★ Claremont-Branan, Inc.

1298 Rockbridge Rd., Ste. B
Stone Mountain, GA 30087
Ph: (770)925-2915   Fax: (770)925-2601
Fr: 800-875-1292
E-mail: ohil@cbisearch.com
URL: http://cbisearch.com

Employment agency. Executive search firm.

★2020★ Engineer One, Inc.

PO Box 23037
Knoxville, TN 37933
Fax: (865)691-0110
E-mail: engineerone@engineerone.com
URL: http://www.engineerone.com

Engineering employment service specializes in engineering and management in the

chemical process, power utilities, manufacturing, mechanical, electrical, and electronic industries. Established an Information Technology Division in 1998 that works nationwide across all industries. Also provides systems analysis consulting services specializing in VAX based systems.

★2021★ Global Employment Solutions

10375 Park Meadows Dr., Ste. 375
Littleton, CO 80124
Ph: (303)216-9500   Fax: (303)216-9533
E-mail: careers@global
URL: http://www.gesnetwork.com

Employment agency.

★2022★ International Staffing Consultants

17310 Redhill Ave., No. 140
Irvine, CA 92614
Ph: (949)255-5857   Fax: (949)767-5959
E-mail: iscinc@iscworld.com
URL: http://www.iscworld.com

Employment agency. Provides placement on regular or temporary basis. Affiliate office in London.

★2023★ Search and Recruit International

4455 South Blvd. Ste. 110
Virginia Beach, VA 23452
Ph: (757)625-2121   Fr: 800-800-5627

Employment agency. Headquartered in Virginia Beach. Other offices in Bremerton, WA; Charleston, SC; Jacksonville, FL; Memphis, TN; Pensacola, FL; Sacramento, CA; San Bernardino, CA; San Diego, CA.

★2024★ Tri-Serv Inc.

22 W. Padonia Rd., Ste. C-353
Timonium, MD 21093
Ph: (410)561-1740   Fax: (410)252-7417
E-mail: info@tri-serv.coom
URL: http://www.tri-serv.com

Employment agency for technical personnel.

ONLINE JOB SOURCES AND SERVICES

★2025★ Spherion

2050 Spectrum Blvd.
Fort Lauderdale, FL 33309
Ph: (954)308-7600
E-mail: help@spherion.com
URL: http://www.spherion.com

Description: Recruitment firm specializing in accounting and finance, sales and marketing, interim executives, technology, engineering, retail and human resources.

TRADESHOWS

★2026★ American Society of Civil Engineers Annual Conference and Exposition

American Society of Civil Engineers
1801 Alexander Bell Dr.
Reston, VA 20191-4400
Ph: (703)295-6024   Fax: (703)295-6222
Fr: 800-548-2723
E-mail: conferences@asce.org
URL: http://www.asce.org

Annual. **Primary Exhibits:** Industry related products and services.

★2027★ Structures Congress

American Society of Civil Engineers
1801 Alexander Bell Dr.
Reston, VA 20191-4400
Ph: (703)295-6024   Fax: (703)295-6222
Fr: 800-548-2723
E-mail: conferences@asce.org
URL: http://www.asce.org

Annual. **Primary Exhibits:** Civil engineering equipment, supplies, and services.

OTHER SOURCES

★2028★ American Academy of Environmental Engineers (AAEE)

130 Holiday Ct., Ste. 100
Annapolis, MD 21401
Ph: (410)266-3311   Fax: (410)266-7653
E-mail: info@aaee.net
URL: http://www.aaee.net

Members: Environmentally oriented registered professional engineers certified by examination as Diplomates of the Academy. **Purpose:** Seeks to improve the standards of environmental engineering. Certifies those with special knowledge of environmental engineering. Furnishes lists of those certified to the public. **Activities:** Maintains speakers' bureau. Recognizes areas of specialization: Air Pollution Control; General Environmental; Hazardous Waste Management; Industrial Hygiene; Radiation Protection; Solid Waste Management; Water Supply and Wastewater. Requires written and oral examinations for certification. Works with other professional organizations on environmentally oriented activities. Identifies potential employment candidates through Talent Search Service.

★2029★ American Association of Blacks in Energy (AABE)

927 15th St. NW, Ste. 200
Washington, DC 20005-2321
Ph: (202)371-9530   Fax: (202)371-9218
Fr: 800-466-0204
E-mail: aabe@aabe.org
URL: http://www.aabe.org

Description: Seeks to increase the knowledge, understanding, and awareness of the minority community in energy issues by serving as an energy information source for policymakers, recommending blacks and other minorities to appropriate energy officials and executives, encouraging students to pursue professional careers in the energy industry, and advocating the participation of blacks and other minorities in energy programs and policymaking activities. Updates members on key legislation and regulations being developed by the Department of Energy, the Department of Interior, the Department of Commerce, the Small Business Administration, and other federal and state agencies.

★2030★ American Association of Engineering Societies (AAES)

1620 I St. NW, Ste. 210
Washington, DC 20006
Ph: (202)296-2237   Fax: (202)296-1151
Fr: 888-400-2237
E-mail: dbateson@aaes.org
URL: http://www.aaes.org

Description: Coordinates the efforts of the member societies in the provision of reliable and objective information to the general public concerning issues which affect the engineering profession and the field of engineering as a whole; collects, analyzes, documents, and disseminates data which will inform the general public of the relationship between engineering and the national welfare; provides a forum for the engineering societies to exchange and discuss their views on matters of common interest; and represents the U.S. engineering community abroad through representation in WFEO and UPADI.

★2031★ American Engineering Association (AEA)

4116 S Carrier Pkwy., Ste. 280-809
Grand Prairie, TX 75052
Ph: (201)664-6954
E-mail: info@aea.org
URL: http://www.aea.org

Description: Members consist of Engineers and engineering professionals. Purpose to advance the engineering profession and U.S. engineering capabilities. Issues of concern include age discrimination, immigration laws, displacement of U.S. Engineers by foreign workers, trade agreements, off shoring of U.S. Engineering and manufacturing jobs, loss of U.S. manufacturing and engineering capability, and recruitment of foreign students. Testifies before Congress. Holds local Chapter meetings.

★2032★ American Society of Civil Engineers (ASCE)

1801 Alexander Bell Dr.
Reston, VA 20191-4400
Ph: (703)295-6300   Fax: (703)295-6222
Fr: 800-548-2723
E-mail: webmaster@asce.org
URL: http://www.asce.org

Description: Enhances the welfare of humanity by advancing the science and profession of engineering. Offers continuing education courses and technical specialty conferences. Develops technical codes and standards. Works closely with Congress, the White House and federal agencies to build sound national policy on engineering issues. Supports research of new civil engineering technology and material. Informs the public about various engineering-related topics.

★2033★ Asian American Architects and Engineers (AAAE)

The Albert Group
114 Sansome St., Ste. 710
San Francisco, CA 94104
Ph: (415)957-8788
E-mail: leschau@kennedyjenks.com
URL: http://www.aaaenc.org

Members: Minorities. **Purpose:** Provides contracts and job opportunities for minorities in the architectural and engineering fields. **Activities:** Serves as a network for the promotion in professional fields.

★2034★ Association for International Practical Training (AIPT)

10400 Little Patuxent Pkwy., Ste. 250
Columbia, MD 21044-3519
Ph: (410)997-2200   Fax: (410)992-3924
E-mail: aipt@aipt.org
URL: http://www.aipt.org

Description: Providers worldwide of on-the-job training programs for students and professionals seeking international career development and life-changing experiences. Arranges workplace exchanges in hundreds of professional fields, bringing employers and trainees together from around the world. Client list ranges from small farming communities to Fortune 500 companies.

★2035★ Engineering Occupations

Delphi Productions
3159 6th St.
Boulder, CO 80304
Ph: (303)443-2100   Fax: (303)443-4022
Fr: 888-443-2400
E-mail: support@delphivideo.com
URL: http://www.delphivideo.com

$95.00. 50 minutes. Part of the Careers for the 21st Century Video Library.

★2036★ National Action Council for Minorities in Engineering (NACME)

440 Hamilton Ave., Ste. 302
White Plains, NY 10601-1813
Ph: (914)539-4010   Fax: (914)539-4032
E-mail: webmaster@nacme.org
URL: http://www.nacme.org

Description: Leads the national effort to increase access to careers in engineering and other science-based disciplines. Conducts research and public policy analysis, develops and operates national demonstration programs at precollege and university levels, and disseminates information through publications, conferences and electronic media. Serves as a privately funded source of scholarships for minority students in engineering.

★2037★ National Association of Traffic Accident Reconstructionists and Investigators (NATARI)

PO Box 2588
West Chester, PA 19382
Ph: (610)696-1919
E-mail: natari@natari.org
URL: http://www.natari.org

Description: Represents engineers, attorneys, police officers, private investigators, medical examiners, and other individuals involved in the analysis of motor vehicle traffic accidents. Gathers and disseminates information on techniques and equipment of potential use to members; reviews literature in the field. Participating Organization of the Accreditation Commission for Traffic Accident Reconstruction.

★2038★ Scientific, Engineering, and Technical Services

Cambridge Educational
PO Box 2053
Princeton, NJ 08543-2053
Ph: 800-257-5126   Fax: (609)671-0266
Fr: 800-468-4227
E-mail: custserv@films.com
URL: http://www.cambridgeeducational.com

VHS and DVD. $89.95. 2002. 18 minutes. 2002. Part of the Career Cluster Series.

★2039★ Society of Women Engineers (SWE)

230 E Ohio St., Ste. 400
Chicago, IL 60611-3265
Ph: (312)596-5223   Fax: (312)596-5252
Fr: 877-SWE-INFO
E-mail: hq@swe.org
URL: http://www.swe.org

Description: Educational and service organization representing both students and professional women in engineering and technical fields.

★2040★ Water Environment Federation (WEF)

601 Wythe St.
Alexandria, VA 22314-1994
Ph: (703)684-2400   Fax: (703)684-2492
Fr: 800-666-0206
E-mail: csc@wef.org
URL: http://www.wef.org

Description: Technical societies representing chemists, biologists, ecologists, geologists, operators, educational and research personnel, industrial wastewater engineers, consultant engineers, municipal officials, equipment manufacturers, and university professors and students dedicated to the enhancement and preservation of water quality and resources. Seeks to advance fundamental and practical knowledge concerning the nature, collection, treatment, and disposal of domestic and industrial wastewaters, and the design, construction, operation, and management of facilities for these purposes. Disseminates technical information; and promotes good public relations and regulations that improve water quality and the status of individuals working in this field. Conducts educational and research programs.

★2041★ Women in Engineering

Her Own Words
PO Box 5264
Madison, WI 53705-0264
Ph: (608)271-7083   Fax: (608)271-0209
E-mail: herownword@aol.com
URL: http://www.herownwords.com/

Video. Jocelyn Riley. $95.00. 15 minutes. Resource guide also available for $45.00.

★2042★ Women in Highway Construction

Her Own Words
PO Box 5264
Madison, WI 53705-0264
Ph: (608)271-7083   Fax: (608)271-0209
E-mail: herownword@aol.com
URL: http://www.herownwords.com/

Video. Jocelyn Riley. $95.00. 15 minutes. Resource guide also available for $45.00.

Claims Examiners

SOURCES OF HELP-WANTED ADS

★2043★ Best's Review

A.M. Best Company, Inc.
Ambest Rd.
Oldwick, NJ 08858
Ph: (908)439-2200
E-mail: editor_br@ambest.com
URL: http://www.ambest.com/sales/news-overview.asp#br

Monthly. Magazine covering issues and trends for the management personnel of life/health insurers, the agents, and brokers who market their products.

★2044★ Business Insurance

Crain Communications Inc.
1155 Gratiot Ave.
Detroit, MI 48207-2997
Ph: (313)446-6000
URL: http://www.businessinsurance.com

Weekly. $97.00/year for individuals; $173.00 for two years; $200.00/year for individuals, daily online only; $130.00/year for Canada and Mexico; $234.00 for Canada and Mexico, two years; $230.00/year for individuals, includes expedited airmail other countries; $436.00 for two years, includes expedited airmail other countries. International newsweekly reporting on corporate risk and employee benefit management news.

★2045★ Claims

Claims
15112 64th Ave. W
Edmonds, WA 98026
Ph: (425)745-6394
E-mail: editor@claimsmag.com
URL: http://www.claimsmag.com

Monthly. $54.00/year for individuals; $75.00/year for Canada; $113.00/year for other countries. Magazine for the property-casualty insurance claims industry.

★2046★ National Underwriter Property and Casualty/Risk and Benefits Management

National Underwriter Co.
5081 Olympic Blvd.
Erlanger, KY 41018
Ph: (859)692-2100   Fr: 800-543-0874
E-mail: nup&c@nuco.com
URL: http://www.nunews.com/pandc/subscribe/

Weekly. $94.00/year for individuals, 2nd class; $133.00/year for Canada, air mail; $178.00/year for U.S. and Canada, air mail; $211.00/year for other countries, air mail. Newsweekly for agents, brokers, executives, and managers in risk and benefit insurance.

EMPLOYER DIRECTORIES AND NETWORKING LISTS

★2047★ Best's Insurance Reports

A.M. Best Co.
Ambest Rd.
Oldwick, NJ 08858
Ph: (908)439-2200   Fax: (908)439-2688
URL: http://www.ambest.com

Annual, latest edition 2007. $1,295.00 for individuals. Published in three editions–Life-health insurance, covering about 1,750 companies; property-casualty insurance, covering over 3,200 companies; and international, covering more than 1,200 insurers. Each edition lists state insurance commissioners and related companies and agencies (mutual funds, worker compensation funds, underwriting agencies, etc.). Entries include: For each company–Company name, address, phone; history; states in which licensed; names of officers and directors; financial data; financial analysis and Best's rating. Arrangement: Alphabetical.

★2048★ Business Insurance-Third-Party Claims Administrators Issue

Business Insurance
360 N Michigan Ave.
Chicago, IL 60601-3806
Ph: (312)649-5319   Fax: (312)280-3174
Fr: 800-678-2724
URL: http://www.businessinsurance.media.com

Annual; latest edition January 2005. Publication includes: List of approximately 150 third-party claims administration, adjusting, and auditing firms that process claims for self-insured clients, including employee benefit and property/casualty claims. Entries include: Company name, address, phone, fax, number of employees, number of claims processing staff, number of clients, method of compensation, prior year's revenues (when available), along with percent attributed to claims administration, adjusting and auditing for self-insured clients; claims volume by number of projects conducted; specialty or area of expertise. Arrangement: Alphabetical by company.

★2049★ Insurance Phone Book and Directory

Douglas Publications L.L.C.
2807 N Parham Rd., Ste. 200
Richmond, VA 23294
Ph: (804)762-9600   Fax: (804)217-8999
Fr: 800-794-6086
URL: http://www.douglaspublications.com/

Annual; latest edition 2006-2007. $195.00 for print product; $249.00 for print product/CD, combined. Covers about 3,500 life, accident and health, worker's compensation, auto, fire and casualty, marine, surety, and other insurance companies; 2,100 executive contacts, from presidents and CEOs to claims and customer service managers. Entries include: Company name, address, phone, fax, toll-free number, type of insurance provided. Arrangement: Alphabetical.

★2050★ Kirshner's Insurance Directories

National Underwriter Co.
5081 Olympic Blvd.
Erlanger, KY 41018
Ph: (859)692-2100   Fr: 800-543-0874

URL: http://www.nationalunderwriter.com/kirschners/

Annual; latest edition 2007. Covers insurance agents and agencies in all 50 states and the District of Columbia. Published in separate editions for Southern California, Northern California, Pacific Northwest (AK, ID, HI, OR, WA, MT), Michigan, Illinois, New England states (CT, ME, MA, NH, RI, VT), Ohio, Rocky Mountain states (AZ, CO, NV, NM, UT, WY), South Central states (GA, AL, MS), Indiana, Texas, Kentucky/Tennessee, East Central states (VA, WV, NC, SC), South Central West states (AR, OK, LA), Wisconsin, Central states (KS, MO, NE), North Central states (IA, MN, ND, SD), Mid-Atlantic states (DE, MD, NJ, DC), Pennsylvania, Florida. Entries include: For companies–Name, address, key personnel (with addresses and phone numbers). Arrangement: Separate alphabetical sections for insurance companies, wholesalers, field agents, and agencies. Indexes: Type of insurance.

★2051★ **Mergent Bank and Finance Manual**

Mergent Inc.
5250 77 Center Dr., Ste. 150
Charlotte, NC 28217
Ph: (704)527-2700   Fax: (704)559-6960
Fr: 800-937-1398
URL: http://www.mergent.com

Annual, July; supplements in 'Mergent Bank & Finance News Reports'. $2,095.00. Covers, in four volumes, over 12,000 national, state, and private banks, savings and loans, mutual funds, unit investment trusts, and insurance and real estate companies in the United States. Entries include: Company name, headquarters and branch offices, phone numbers, names and titles of principal executives, directors, history, Moody's rating, and extensive financial and statistical data. Arrangement: Classified by type of business. Indexes: Company name.

★2052★ **National Association of Catastrophe Adjusters-Membership Roster**

National Association of Catastrophe Adjusters Inc.
PO Box 821864
PO Box 821864
North Richland Hills, TX 76182
Ph: (817)498-3466   Fax: (817)498-0480
URL: http://www.nacatadj.org/

Annual, March; latest edition 2006-2007. Covers about 400 insurance catastrophe claims adjusters and adjusting firms; about 150 related insurance firms (associate members). Entries include: Name, address, phone, spouse's name. Arrangement: Separate geographical sections for regular associate and business associate members. Indexes: Alphabetical; geographical.

★2053★ **National Insurance Association-Member Roster**

National Insurance Association
411 Chapel Hill Dr., Ste. 633
Durham, NC 27701
Ph: (919)683-5328

Annual, June. Covers about 13 insurance companies owned or controlled by African-Americans. Entries include: Company name, address, phone, date founded, states in which licensed, officers. Arrangement: Alphabetical.

★2054★ **Who's Who in Insurance**

Underwriter Printing and Publishing Co.
50 E Palisade Ave.
Englewood, NJ 07631
Ph: (201)569-8808   Fr: 800-526-4700

Annual, February. Covers over 5,000 insurance officials, brokers, agents, and buyers. Entries include: Name, title, company name, address, home address, educational background, professional club and association memberships, personal and career data. Arrangement: Alphabetical.

★2055★ **Yearbook**

American Association of Managing General Agents
150 S Warner Rd., Ste. 156
King of Prussia, PA 19406
Ph: (610)225-1999   Fax: (610)225-1996
URL: http://www.aamga.org/

Annual, spring. Covers 250 managing general agents of insurance companies and their more than 500 branch offices; coverage includes Canada. Entries include: Name, address, names and titles of principal figures and contact, insurance companies represented. Arrangement: Geographical.

HANDBOOKS AND MANUALS

★2056★ **Best Websites for Financial Professionals, Business Appraisers, & Accountants**

John Wiley & Sons Inc.
111 River St.
Hoboken, NJ 07030-5774
Ph: (201)748-6000   Fax: (201)748-5774
E-mail: custserv@wiley.com
URL: http://www.wiley.com/WileyCDA/

Eva M. Lang and Jan Davis Tudor. Second edition, 2003. $49.95 (paper). 256 pages.

★2057★ **Opportunities in Insurance Careers**

The McGraw-Hill Companies
PO Box 182604
Columbus, OH 43272
Fax: (614)759-3749   Fr: 877-883-5524
E-mail: customer.service@mcgraw-hill.com
URL: http://www.mcgraw-hill.com

Robert M. Schrayer. Revised, 2007. $14.95

(paper). 160 pages. A guide to planning for and seeking opportunities in the field. Contains bibliography and illustrations.

EMPLOYMENT AGENCIES AND SEARCH FIRMS

★2058★ **Employment Advisors**

815 Nicollet Mall
Minneapolis, MN 55402
Ph: (612)339-0521

Employment agency. Places candidates in variety of fields.

★2059★ **Godfrey Personnel Inc.**

300 W. Adams, Ste. 612
Chicago, IL 60606-5194
Ph: (312)236-4455   Fax: (312)580-6292
E-mail: jim@godfreypersonnel.com
URL: http://www.godfreypersonnel.com

Search firm specializing in insurance industry.

★2060★ **International Insurance Personnel, Inc.**

300 W. Wieuca Rd., Bldg. 2, Ste. 101
Atlanta, GA 30342
Ph: (404)255-9710   Fax: (404)255-9864
E-mail: info@intlinspersonnel.com
URL: http://yp.bellsouth.com/sites/intlinspersonnel/index.html

Employment agency specializing in the area of insurance.

★2061★ **Questor Consultants, Inc.**

2515 N. Broad St.
Colmar, PA 18915
Ph: (215)997-9262   Fax: (215)997-9226
E-mail: sbevivino@questorconsultants.com
URL: http://www.questorconsultants.com

Executive search firm specializing in the insurance and legal fields.

OTHER SOURCES

★2062★ **Business and Administration Support Occupations**

Delphi Productions
3159 6th St.
Boulder, CO 80304
Ph: (303)443-2100   Fax: (303)443-4022
Fr: 888-443-2400
E-mail: support@delphivideo.com
URL: http://www.delphivideo.com

$95.00. 42 minutes. Part of the Careers for the 21st Century Video Library.

★2063★ Insurance Agent

Cambridge Educational
PO Box 2053
Princeton, NJ 08543-2053
Ph: 800-257-5126   Fax: (609)671-0266
Fr: 800-468-4227
E-mail: custserv@films.com
URL: http://www.cambridgeeducational.com

VHS and DVD. $39.95. 11 minutes. 1989.
Part of the Vocational Visions Career Series.

**★2064★ Insurance Information Institute
(III)**

110 William St.
New York, NY 10038
Ph: (212)346-5500   Fr: 800-331-9146
E-mail: johns@iii.org
URL: http://www.iii.org

Description: Property and casualty insurance companies. Provides information and educational services to mass media, educational institutions, trade associations, businesses, government agencies, and the public.

★2065★ LOMA

2300 Windy Ridge Pkwy., Ste. 600
Atlanta, GA 30339-8443
Ph: (770)951-1770   Fax: (770)984-0441
Fr: 800-275-5662
E-mail: askloma@loma.org
URL: http://www.loma.org

Description: Life and health insurance companies and financial services in the U.S. and Canada; and overseas in 45 countries; affiliate members are firms that provide professional support to member companies. Provides research, information, training, and educational activities in areas of operations and systems, human resources, financial planning and employee development. Administers FLMI Insurance Education Program, which awards FLMI (Fellow, Life Management Institute) designation to those who complete the ten-examination program.

**★2066★ National Association of
Insurance Women International
(NAIW)**

6528 E 101st St., Ste. D-1
PMB No. 750
Tulsa, OK 74133
Fax: (918)743-1968   Fr: 800-766-6249

E-mail: joinnaiw@naiw.org
URL: http://www.naiw.org

Members: Insurance industry professionals.
Purpose: Promotes continuing education and networking for the professional advancement of its members. **Activities:** Offers education programs, meetings, services, and leadership opportunities. Provides a forum to learn about other disciplines in the insurance industry.

**★2067★ National Association of Public
Insurance Adjusters (NAPIA)**

21165 Whitfield Pl., No. 105
Potomac Falls, VA 20165
Ph: (703)433-9217   Fax: (703)433-0369
E-mail: info@napia.com
URL: http://www.napia.com

Members: Professional society of public insurance adjusters. **Activities:** Sponsors certification and professional education programs.

Clinical Laboratory Technologists and Technicians

SOURCES OF HELP-WANTED ADS

★2068★ ACTA Cytologica

Science Printers and Publishers Inc.
8342 Olive Blvd.
St. Louis, MO 63132-2814
Ph: (314)991-4440   Fax: (314)991-4654
E-mail: editor@acta-cytol.com
URL: http://www.acta-cytol.com

Bimonthly. $295.00/year for individuals, Missouri residents add 7.075% tax; $385.00/year for other countries; $395.00/year for institutions, Missouri residents add 7.075% tax; $485.00/year for institutions, other countries. Journal publishing scientific articles offering significant contributions to the advancement of clinical cytology.

★2069★ ADVANCE for Medical Laboratory Professionals

Merion Publications Inc.
2900 Horizon Dr.
PO Box 61556
King of Prussia, PA 19406
Ph: (610)278-1400   Fr: 800-355-5627
E-mail: advance@merion.com
URL: http://www.advanceformlp.com

Biweekly. Free. Magazine reaches technologists and laboratory managers with professional news and employment opportunities.

★2070★ American Laboratory News

International Scientific Communications Inc.
30 Controls Dr.
PO Box 870
Shelton, CT 06484
Ph: (203)926-9300   Fax: (203)926-9310
URL: http://www.americanlaboratory.com

Monthly. Trade magazine for scientists.

★2071★ ASPB News

American Society of Plant Biologists
15501 Monona Dr.
Rockville, MD 20855-2768
Ph: (301)251-0560   Fax: (301)279-2996

E-mail: info@aspb.org
URL: http://www.aspb.org/newsletter/

Description: Bimonthly. Offers news of interest to plant physiologists, biochemists, horticulturists, and plant molecular and cell biologists engaged in research and teaching. Alerts members to public policy issues, educational opportunities, meetings, seminars, and conventions pertinent to the field. Recurring features include letters to the editor, reports of meetings, job listings, a calendar of events, news from regional sections, and teaching ideas.

★2072★ CAP Today

College of American Pathologists
325 Waukegan Rd.
Northfield, IL 60093-2750
Ph: (847)832-7000   Fax: (847)832-8000
Fr: 800-323-4040
URL: http://www.cap.org

Monthly. $95.00/year for individuals; $30.00/year for U.S. and Canada, single copy; $190.00/year for other countries; $120.00/year for Canada; $40.00/year for other countries, single copy. Magazine covering advances in pathology tests and equipment, clinical lab management and operations trends, and related regulatory and legislative changes.

★2073★ Cell

Cell Press
600 Technology Sq.
Cambridge, MA 02139
Ph: (617)661-7057   Fax: (617)661-7061
Fr: (866)314-2355
E-mail: advertising@cell.com
URL: http://www.cell.com

$179.00/year for U.S. and Canada, individual, print and online; $269.00/year for other countries, individual, print and online; $179.00/year for U.S. and Canada, online only, individual; $179.00/year for other countries, online only, individual; $997.00/year for U.S. and Canada, institutions; $1122.00/year for institutions, other countries, print. Journal on molecular and cell biology.

★2074★ Clinical Laboratory News

American Association for Clinical Chemistry
2101 L St. NW, Ste. 202
Washington, DC 20037-1558
Ph: (202)857-0717   Fax: (202)887-5093
Fr: 800-892-1400
URL: http://www.aacc.org/AACC/publications/cln/

Monthly. Free to qualified subscribers, living in U.S. Scholarly magazine providing current news in the field of clinical laboratory science.

★2075★ Cytometry

John Wiley & Sons Inc.
111 River St.
Hoboken, NJ 07030-5774
Ph: (201)748-6000   Fax: (201)748-6088
Fr: 800-825-7550
E-mail: csd_ord@wiley.com.sg
URL: http://www.wiley.com/WileyCDA/WileyTitle/productCd-CYTO.html

$1,360.00/year for institutions, print; $1,576.00/year for institutions, Canada and Mexico, print only; $1,702.00/year for institutions, other countries, print only; $1,496.00/year for institutions, print & online; $1,712.00/year for institutions, Canada and Mexico, print & online; $1,838.00/year for institutions, other countries, print & online. International journal covering all aspects of analytical cytology.

★2076★ Laboratory Medicine

American Society for Clinical Pathology
33 West Monroe, Ste. 1600
Chicago, IL 60603
Ph: (312)541-4999   Fax: (312)541-4998
Fr: 800-267-2727
E-mail: labmed@ascp.org
URL: http://www.labmedicine.com/

Monthly. $105.00/year for individuals, print and online; $105.00/year for other countries, print and online, individual; $140.00/year for other countries, print and online, individual expedited; $116.00/year for institutions, other countries, print and online, individual expedited; $20.00 for single issue, print and online; $15.00 for single issue, print and online, rest of world; $130.00/year for institutions, print and online; $130.00/year for institutions, other countries, print and online; $165.00/year for institutions, other countries, print and online, expedited. Professional journal covering medical technology and pathology.

★2077★ *Medical Laboratory Observer (MLO)*

Nelson Publishing Inc.
2500 Tamiami Trl. N
Nokomis, FL 34275
Ph: (941)966-9521   Fax: (941)966-2590
URL: http://www.mlo-online.com

Monthly. Free, to qualified clinical laboratory professionals. Magazine for clinical laboratory professionals.

★2078★ *MEEN Imaging Technology News*

Reilly Communications Group
16 E Schaumburg Rd.
Schaumburg, IL 60194-3536
Ph: (847)882-6336   Fax: (847)882-0631
URL: http://www.itnonline.net

Trade magazine (tabloid) serving users and buyers of medical imaging technologies and services.

★2079★ *Nature International Weekly Journal of Science*

Nature Publishing Group
75 Varick St., 9th Fl.
New York, NY 10013-1917
Ph: (212)726-9200   Fax: (212)696-9006
Fr: 888-331-6288
E-mail: nature@natureny.com
URL: http://www.nature.com

Weekly. $145.00/year for individuals; $49.00/year for institutions. Magazine covering science and technology, including the fields of biology, biochemistry, genetics, medicine, earth sciences, physics, pharmacology, and behavioral sciences.

★2080★ *Vantage Point*

Clinical Laboratory Management Association
989 Old Eagle School Rd., Ste. 815
Wayne, PA 19087
Ph: (610)995-2640   Fax: (610)995-9568
E-mail: publications@clma.org
URL: http://www.clma.org

Description: Semimonthly. Features general, health care, and laboratory management tips, trends, and legislative news. Recurring features include news of educational opportunities, job listings, and columns titled Manager's Workshop, Healthcare Management Briefs, Career Corner, Online Update and Legislative Update.

PLACEMENT AND JOB REFERRAL SERVICES

★2081★ **Clinical Ligand Assay Society (CLAS)**

3139 S Wayne Rd.
Wayne, MI 48184
Ph: (734)722-6290   Fax: (734)722-7006
E-mail: clas@clas.org
URL: http://www.clas.org

Description: Seeks to establish and promote high standards in the science and application of ligand assay technology by encouraging research, education practitioners, and fostering communication and cooperation among individuals in laboratories in medicine, academia, and industry. Sponsors job placement service.

★2082★ **Endocrine Society**

8401 Connecticut Ave., Ste. 900
Chevy Chase, MD 20815-5817
Ph: (301)941-0200   Fax: (301)941-0259
Fr: 888-363-6274
E-mail: societyservices@endo-society.org
URL: http://www.endo-society.org

Purpose: Promotes excellence in research, education, and clinical practice in endocrinology and related disciplines. **Activities:** Maintains placement service.

EMPLOYER DIRECTORIES AND NETWORKING LISTS

★2083★ *AGT International Membership Directory*

Association of Genetic Technologists
AGT Executive Office
PO Box 15945-288
Lenexa, KS 66285-5945
Ph: (913)895-4605   Fax: (913)895-4652
URL: http://www.agt-info.org/IntMembershipDir.html

Monthly. Covers about 520 laboratories studying heritable and acquired chromosomal disorders using cytogenetic, genetics, and cellular biology techniques. Entries include: Laboratory name, address, phone, areas of specialization, techniques, numbers and types of laboratory tests performed, and names of director and cytogenetic technologists. Arrangement: Geographical. Indexes: Director name, ACT member name.

★2084★ *AHA Guide to the Health Care Field*

American Hospital Association
1 N Franklin
Chicago, IL 60606
Ph: (312)422-2050   Fax: (312)422-4700
Fr: 800-424-4301

Annual, August. Covers hospitals, networks, multi-health care systems, freestanding am-

bulatory surgery centers, psychiatric facilities, long-term care facilities, substance abuse programs, and other health-related organizations. Entries include: For hospitals–Facility name, address, phone, administrator's name, number of beds, facilities and services, number of employees, expenses, other statistics. For other organizations–Name, address, phone, fax, name and title of contact. Arrangement: Geographical. Indexes: Hospital name.

★2085★ *Directory of Accredited Laboratories*

American Association for Laboratory Accreditation
5301 Buckeystown Pke., Ste. 350
Frederick, MD 21704-8307
Ph: (301)644-3248   Fax: (301)662-2974
URL: http://www.a2la.org

Weekly, on Web site. Free. Covers over 1,600 testing and calibration laboratories and inspection agencies accredited for technical competence as measured against national and international standards in the following fields of testing: metrology, acoustics and vibration, construction materials, biology, chemistry, electricity, environmental, geotechnical, mechanical, thermal, and nondestructive. Entries include: Name of laboratory, address, phone, contact, certificate number, current period of accreditation, fields of accreditation technologies and methodologies. Arrangement: Alphabetical. Indexes: Fields of accreditation.

★2086★ *Directory of Hospital Personnel*

Grey House Publishing
185 Millerton Rd.
PO Box 860
Millerton, NY 12546
Ph: (518)789-8700   Fax: (518)789-0556
Fr: 800-562-2139
URL: http://www.greyhouse.com/hospital_personnel.htm

Annual. $325.00 for print product; $545.00 for online database subscription; $650.00 for online database subscription and print product combined. Covers 200,000 executives at 7,000 U.S. hospitals. Entries include: Name of hospital, address, phone; number of beds; type and JCAHO status of hospital; names and titles of key department heads and staff; medical and nursing school affiliations; number of residents, interns, and nursing students. Arrangement: Geographical. Indexes: Hospital name, personnel, hospital size.

★2087★ *Guide to Careers in the Health Professions*

The Princeton Review
2315 Broadway
New York, NY 10024
Ph: (212)874-8282   Fax: (212)874-0775
Fr: 800-733-3000
URL: http://www.princetonreview.com/

Published January, 2001. $24.95 for individuals. Presents advice and information for those searching for satisfying careers in the health professions. Publication includes: Directory of schools and academic programs. Entries include: Name, address, phone, tuition, program details, employment profiles.

★2088★ Hospital Blue Book

Billian Publishing Inc./Transworld
  Publishing Inc.
2100 Powers Ferry Rd. SE
Atlanta, GA 30339
Ph: (770)955-5656   Fax: (770)952-0669
Fr: 800-533-8484
E-mail: blu-book@billian.com

2005. $300.00 for individuals. Covers more than 6,687 hospitals; some listings also appear in a separate southern edition of this publication. Entries include: Name of hospital, accreditation, mailing address, phone, fax, number of beds, type of facility (nonprofit, general, state, etc.); list of administrative personnel and chiefs of medical services, with specific titles. Arrangement: Geographical.

★2089★ Medical and Health Information Directory

Gale, Cengage Learning
27500 Drake Rd.
Farmington Hills, MI 48331-3535
Ph: (248)699-4253   Fax: (248)699-8065
Fr: 800-877-4253
E-mail: businessproducts@gale.com
URL: http://www.gale.com

Annual; latest edition 20th, July 2007. $375.00/volume. Covers in Volume 1, more than 26,500 medical and health oriented associations, organizations, institutions, and government agencies, including health maintenance organizations (HMOs), preferred provider organizations (PPOs), insurance companies, pharmaceutical companies, research centers, and medical and allied health schools. In Volume 2, over 12,000 medical book publishers; medical periodicals, directories, audiovisual producers and services, medical libraries and information centers, electronic resources, and health-related internet search engines. In Volume 3, more than 35,500 clinics, treatment centers, care programs, and counseling/diagnostic services for 34 subject areas. Entries include: Institution, service, or firm name, address, phone, fax, email and URL; many include names of key personnel and, when pertinent, descriptive annotations. Volume 3 was formerly listed separately as Health Services Directory. Arrangement: Classified by organization activity, service, etc. Indexes: Each volume has a complete alphabetical name and keyword index.

HANDBOOKS AND MANUALS

★2090★ Careers in Health Care

The McGraw-Hill Companies
PO Box 182604
Columbus, OH 43272
Fax: (614)759-3749   Fr: 877-883-5524

E-mail: customer.service@mcgraw-hill.com
URL: http://www.mcgraw-hill.com

Barbara M. Swanson. Fifth edition, 2005. $15.95 (paper). 192 pages. Describes job duties, work settings, salaries, licensing and certification requirements, educational preparation, and future outlook. Gives ideas on how to secure a job.

★2091★ Opportunities in Clinical Laboratory Science Careers

The McGraw-Hill Companies
PO Box 182604
Columbus, OH 43272
Fax: (614)759-3749   Fr: 877-883-5524
E-mail: customer.service@mcgraw-hill.com
URL: http://www.mcgraw-hill.com

Karen R. Karni, Luisa Gerasimo and Cheryl R. Caskey. $13.95 (netLibrary). 198 pages. Second edition, 2002. Explores clinical laboratory science careers.

★2092★ Opportunities in Health and Medical Careers

The McGraw-Hill Companies
PO Box 182604
Columbus, OH 43272
Fax: (614)759-3749   Fr: 877-883-5524
E-mail: customer.service@mcgraw-hill.com
URL: http://www.mcgraw-hill.com

I. Donald Snook, Jr. and Leo D'Orazio. 2004. $13.95 (paper). 157 pages. Covers the full range of medical and health occupations. Illustrated.

★2093★ Opportunities in Medical Imaging Careers

The McGraw-Hill Companies
PO Box 182604
Columbus, OH 43272
Fax: (614)759-3749   Fr: 877-883-5524
E-mail: customer.service@mcgraw-hill.com
URL: http://www.mcgraw-hill.com

Clifford J. Sherry. 2006. $13.95. 160 pages.

★2094★ Opportunities in Medical Technology Careers

The McGraw-Hill Companies
PO Box 182604
Columbus, OH 43272
Fax: (614)759-3749   Fr: 877-883-5524
E-mail: customer.service@mcgraw-hill.com
URL: http://www.mcgraw-hill.com

Karen R. Karni. Revised, 1996. $14.95; $11.95 (paper). 148 pages. Details opportunities for various technical medical personnel and supplies up-to-date information on salary levels and employment outlook. Appendices list associations and unions in each field. Illustrated.

★2095★ Resumes for the Health Care Professional

John Wiley & Sons Inc.
1 Wiley Dr.
Somerset, NJ 08873
Ph: (732)469-4400   Fax: (732)302-2300
Fr: 800-225-5945
E-mail: custserv@wiley.com
URL: http://www.wiley.com/WileyCDA/

Kim Marino. Second edition, 2000. $21.50 (paper). 224 pages.

★2096★ Resumes for Health and Medical Careers

The McGraw-Hill Companies
PO Box 182604
Columbus, OH 43272
Fax: (614)759-3749   Fr: 877-883-5524
E-mail: customer.service@mcgraw-hill.com
URL: http://www.mcgraw-hill.com

Third edition, 2003. $11.95 (paper). 160 pages.

★2097★ Resumes for Science Careers

The McGraw-Hill Companies
PO Box 182604
Columbus, OH 43272
Fax: (614)759-3749   Fr: 877-883-5524
E-mail: customer.service@mcgraw-hill.com
URL: http://www.mcgraw-hill.com

1997. $11.95 (paper). 144 pages.

★2098★ VGM's Handbook of Health Care Careers

The McGraw-Hill Companies
PO Box 182604
Columbus, OH 43272
Fax: (614)759-3749   Fr: 877-883-5524
E-mail: customer.service@mcgraw-hill.com
URL: http://www.mcgraw-hill.com

VGM Career Horizons Staff. Second edition, revised, 1997. $12.95 (paper). 112 pages.

EMPLOYMENT AGENCIES AND SEARCH FIRMS

★2099★ The Coelyn Group

1 Park Plaza, Ste. 600
Irvine, CA 92614
Ph: (949)553-8855   Fax: 888-436-2171
E-mail: contact@coelyngroup.com
URL: http://www.coelyngroup.com

Executive search firm.

★2100★ The Domann Organization Inc.

1 Market St., Fl. 35
San Francisco, CA 94105
Ph: (415)726-9704   Fr: 800-923-6626
E-mail: info@domann.net
URL: http://www.domann.net

Executive search firm.

★2101★ Durakis Executive Search

PO Box 1382
Brooklandville, MD 21022-1382
Ph: (410)252-2055
E-mail: resumes@durakis.com
URL: http://www.durakis.com

Executive search firm.

★2102★ Fitzgerald Associates

21 Muzzey St.
Lexington, MA 02421-5259
Ph: (781)863-1945   Fax: (781)863-8872
E-mail: info@fizsearch.com
URL: http://www.fitzsearch.com

Executive search firm specifically for the healthcare industry.

★2103★ Flannery, Sarna & Associates LLC

N14 W23953 Paul Rd., Ste. 204
Pewaukee, WI 53072
Ph: (262)523-1206   Fax: (262)523-1873
E-mail: shari@flannerysearch.com
URL: http://www.flannerysearch.com

Executive search firm.

ONLINE JOB SOURCES AND SERVICES

★2104★ Medhunters.com

Fr: 800-664-0278
E-mail: info@medhunters.com
URL: http://www.medhunters.com

Description: Career search site for jobs in all health care specialties; educational resources; visa and licensing information for relocation; interesting articles; relocation tools; links to professional organizations and general resources.

★2105★ ProHealthJobs

Fr: 800-796-1738
E-mail: Info@prohealthedujobs.com
URL: http://www.prohealthjobs.com

Description: Career resources site for the medical and health care field. Lists professional opportunities, product information, continuing education and open positions.

TRADESHOWS

★2106★ American Association of Blood Banks Annual Meeting and TXPO

American Association of Blood Banks
8101 Glenbrook Rd.
Bethesda, MD 20814-2749
Ph: (301)907-6977   Fax: (301)907-6895
E-mail: aabb@aabb.org

URL: http://www.aabb.org

Annual. **Primary Exhibits:** Products related to blood banking and transfusion medicine: gloves, donor coaches, chairs, recruitment articles.

★2107★ APIC Annual Meeting and Educational Conference

Hachero Hill Conference and Exhibition Managers, Inc.
11260 Roger Bacon Dr., Ste. 402
Reston, VA 20190
Ph: (703)964-1240   Fax: (703)964-1246
E-mail: anne-betts@conferencemanagers.com
URL: http://conferencemanagers.com/

Annual. **Primary Exhibits:** Pharmaceuticals, disinfectants, soaps, data processing software, sterilization devices, chemicals, housekeeping equipment and supplies, and related products. **Dates and Locations:** 2008 Jun 15-19; Denver, CO; Colorado Convention Center; 2009 Jun 07-11; Fort Lauderdale, FL ; 2010 Jun 11-15; New Orleans, LA.

★2108★ College of American Pathologists and American Society of Clinical Pathologists Fall Meeting

American Society of Clinical Pathologists
33 W. Monroe, Ste. 1600
Chicago, IL 60603
Ph: (312)541-4999   Fax: (312)541-4998
Fr: 800-267-2727
E-mail: info@ascp.org
URL: http://www.ascp.org

Annual. **Primary Exhibits:** Technical, scientific, and laboratory equipment.

OTHER SOURCES

★2109★ Accrediting Bureau of Health Education Schools (ABHES)

7777 Leesburg Pike, Ste. 314 N
Falls Church, VA 22043
Ph: (703)917-9503   Fax: (703)917-4109
E-mail: info@abhes.org
URL: http://www.abhes.org

Description: Serves as a nationally recognized accrediting agency of health education institutions and schools conducting medical laboratory technician and medical assistant education programs. Establishes criteria and standards for the administration and operation of health education institutions. Seeks to enhance the profession through the improvement of schools, courses, and the competence of graduates. Schools must apply voluntarily for accreditation; once accredited, they must report to the bureau annually and be reexamined at least every 6 years. Has accredited 15 programs for medical laboratory technicians, 124 medical assistants, and 80 institutions of allied health.

★2110★ American Association for Clinical Chemistry (AACC)

1850 K St. NW, Ste. 625
Washington, DC 20006
Ph: (202)857-0717   Fax: (202)887-5093
Fr: 800-892-1400
E-mail: custserv@aacc.org
URL: http://www.aacc.org

Members: Clinical laboratory scientists and others engaged in the practice of clinical laboratory science in independent laboratories, hospitals, and allied institutions. Sponsors education programs; publishes books.

★2111★ American Medical Technologists (AMT)

10700 W Higgins Rd.
Rosemont, IL 60018
Ph: (847)823-5169   Fax: (847)823-0458
Fr: 800-275-1268
URL: http://www.amt1.com

Description: Represents medical technologists, medical laboratory technicians, medical assistants, medical administrative specialists, dental assistants, office laboratory technicians, phlebotomy technicians, laboratory consultants, and allied health instructors. Provides allied health professionals with professional certification services and membership programs to enhance their professional and personal growth. Aims to issue certification credentials to medical and dental assistants, clinical laboratory personnel, laboratory consultants, and allied health instructors.

★2112★ American Society for Clinical Laboratory Science (ASCLS)

6701 Democracy Blvd., Ste. 300
Bethesda, MD 20817
Ph: (301)657-2768   Fax: (301)657-2909
E-mail: ascls@ascls.org
URL: http://www.ascls.org

Members: Primarily clinical laboratory personnel who have an associate or baccalaureate degree and clinical training and specialists who hold at least a master's degree in one of the major fields of clinical laboratory science such as bacteriology, mycology, or biochemistry; also includes technicians, specialists, and educators with limited certificates and students enrolled in approved programs of clinical laboratory studies and military medical technology schools. **Purpose:** Promotes and maintains high standards in clinical laboratory methods and research and advances standards of education and training of personnel. **Activities:** Conducts educational program of seminars and workshops. Approves programs of continuing education and maintains records on participation in continuing education programs formembers

★2113★ American Society of Cytopathology (ASC)

400 W 9th St., Ste. 201
Wilmington, DE 19801
Ph: (302)429-8802   Fax: (302)429-8807
E-mail: asc@cytopathology.org

URL: http://www.cytopathology.org

Description: Represents physicians, cyto-technologists, and scientists dedicated to the cytologic method of diagnostic pathology.

★2114★ Commission on Accreditation of Allied Health Education Programs (CAAHEP)
1361 Park St.
Clearwater, FL 33756
Ph: (727)210-2350   Fax: (727)210-2354
E-mail: megivern@caahep.org
URL: http://www.caahep.org
Description: Serves as a nationally recognized accrediting agency for allied health programs in 18 occupational areas.

★2115★ Exploring Health Occupations
Cambridge Educational
PO Box 2053
Princeton, NJ 08543-2053
Ph: 800-257-5126   Fax: (609)671-0266
Fr: 800-468-4227
E-mail: custserv@films.com
URL: http://www.cambridgeeducational.com
VHS and DVD. $159.90. 1999. Two-part series provides a detailed view of the field of medical technicians and technologists, EMTs, nurses, therapists, and assistants.

★2116★ Health Service Occupations
Delphi Productions
3159 6th St.
Boulder, CO 80304
Ph: (303)443-2100   Fax: (303)443-4022
Fr: 888-443-2400
E-mail: support@delphivideo.com
URL: http://www.delphivideo.com
$95.00. 50 minutes. Part of the Careers for the 21st Century Video Library.

★2117★ Health Technologists & Technicians
Delphi Productions
3159 6th St.
Boulder, CO 80304
Ph: (303)443-2100   Fax: (303)443-4022
Fr: 888-443-2400
E-mail: support@delphivideo.com
URL: http://www.delphivideo.com
$95.00. 50 minutes. Part of the Careers for the 21st Century Video Library.

★2118★ Medical Technicians and Technologists
Cambridge Educational
PO Box 2053
Princeton, NJ 08543-2053
Ph: 800-257-5126   Fax: (609)671-0266
Fr: 800-468-4227
E-mail: custserv@films.com
URL: http://www.cambridgeeducational.com
VHS and DVD. $79.95. 18 minutes. 2000.

Part of the Exploring Health Occupations Series.

★2119★ Medicine & Related Occupations
Delphi Productions
3159 6th St.
Boulder, CO 80304
Ph: (303)443-2100   Fax: (303)443-4022
Fr: 888-443-2400
E-mail: support@delphivideo.com
URL: http://www.delphivideo.com
$95.00. 45 minutes. Part of the Careers for the 21st Century Video Library.

★2120★ National Credentialing Agency for Laboratory Personnel (NCA)
PO Box 15945-289
Lenexa, KS 66285
Ph: (913)895-4613   Fax: (913)895-4652
E-mail: nca-info@goamp.com
URL: http://www.nca-info.org
Description: Persons who direct, educate, supervise, or practice in clinical laboratory science. Assures the public and employers of the competence of clinical laboratory personnel; provides a mechanism for individuals demonstrating competency in the field to achieve career mobility. Develops and administers competency-based examinations for certification of clinical laboratory personnel; provides for periodic recertification by examination or through documentation of continuing education. Compiles statistics.

College and University Faculty

SOURCES OF HELP-WANTED ADS

★2121★ AAEE Connections

American Association for Employment in Education
3040 Riverside Dr., Ste. 125
Columbus, OH 43221
Ph: (614)485-1111   Fax: (614)485-9609
E-mail: office@aaee.org
URL: http://www.aaee.org/

Description: Quarterly. Publishes news of the Association, whose aim is "to enhance and promote the concept of career planning and placement as an integral part of the educational process and to undertake activities designed to help schools, colleges, and universities meet their educational staffing needs." Also concerned with teacher education and the supply of/demand for teachers. Recurring features include news of members, state and regional news, and announcements of upcoming conferences and meetings.

★2122★ AATSEEL Newsletter

American Association of Teachers of Slavic and East European Languages (AATSEEL)
PO Box 569
Beloit, WI 53512-0569
Ph: (608)361-9697   Fax: (608)363-7129
E-mail: aatseel@sbcglobal.net
URL: http://www.aatseel.org

Description: 4/academic year. Carries articles of interest to teachers of Slavic languages. Reports on study programs, teaching innovations, and Association news. Recurring features include news of members, notices of employment opportunities, a calendar of events, reviews of materials, and columns titled Chapter Minutes, Computer Information, Communicative Corner, and Russian Language Features.

★2123★ About Campus

John Wiley & Sons Inc.
111 River St.
Hoboken, NJ 07030-5774
Ph: (201)748-6000   Fax: (201)748-6088
Fr: 800-825-7550
URL: http://www3.interscience.wiley.com/cgi-bin/jhome/86513696

Bimonthly. $60.00/year for individuals, for print; $60.00/year for Canada and Mexico, for print; $96.00/year for individuals, for print (rest of world); $159.00/year for institutions, for print; $219.00/year for institutions, Canada and Mexico, for print; $270.00/year for institutions, for print (rest of world); $175.00/year for institutions, for print and online; $235.00/year for institutions, Canada and Mexico, for print and online; $286.00/year for institutions, for print and online, (rest of world); $111.00/year for individuals, print only. Journal focused on the critical issues faced by both student affairs and academic affairs staff as they work on helping students learn.

★2124★ Academician Magazine

National Association of State Approved Colleges and Universities
808 17th St. NW, Ste. 410
Washington, DC 20006
Ph: (202)293-0090

Monthly. Magazine covering higher education.

★2125★ The Accounting Review

American Accounting Association
5717 Bessie Dr.
Sarasota, FL 34233-2399
Ph: (941)921-7747   Fax: (941)923-4093
URL: http://aaahq.org/index.cfm

$315.00/year for individuals, print; $315.00/year for individuals, online from volume 74 through current issue; $350.00/year for individuals, online and print. Accounting education, research, financial reporting, and book reviews.

★2126★ American Academic

American Federation of Teachers
555 New Jersey Ave. NW
Washington, DC 20001
Ph: (202)879-4400
URL: http://www.aft.org/pubs-reports/american_academic/index.htm

Higher education policy journal.

★2127★ The American Biology Teacher

National Association of Biology Teachers
12030 Sunrise Valley Dr., Ste. 110
Reston, VA 20191-3409
Fax: (703)264-7778   Fr: 800-406-0775
E-mail: publication@nabt.org
URL: http://www.nabt.org

Monthly. Journal featuring articles on biology, science, and education for elementary, high school and college level biology teachers. Includes audio-visual, book, computer, and research reviews.

★2128★ American School & University

Penton Media Inc.
9800 Metcalf Ave.
Overland Park, KS 66212
Ph: (913)341-1300   Fax: (913)967-1898
URL: http://www.primediabusiness.com

Monthly. Trade magazine.

★2129★ Annals of Medicine

Taylor & Francis Group Journals
325 Chestnut St., Ste. 800
Philadelphia, PA 19106
Ph: (215)625-8900   Fax: (215)625-8914
Fr: 800-354-1420
URL: http://www.ingentaconnect.com

$418.00/year for institutions, print and online; $397.00/year for institutions, online only; $155.00/year for individuals. Journal covering health science and medical education.

★2130★ Assessment & Evaluation in Higher Education

Taylor & Francis Group Journals
325 Chestnut St., Ste. 800
Philadelphia, PA 19106
Ph: (215)625-8900   Fax: (215)625-8914
Fr: 800-354-1420
E-mail: aehe@bath.ac.uk
URL: http://www.tandf.co.uk/journals/titles/02602938.asp

Bimonthly. $1,982.00/year for institutions, print and online; $1,882.00/year for institutions, online only; $466.00/year for individuals. Journal focusing on publishing papers and reports on all aspects of assessment and evaluation within higher education.

★2131★ Brookings Papers on Education Policy

Brookings Institution Press
1775 Massashusetts Ave. NW
Washington, DC 20036-2188
Ph: (202)536-3600   Fax: (202)536-3623
Fr: 800-275-1447
URL: http://www.brookings.edu/press/journals.htm

$46.00/year for institutions; $35.00/year for individuals. Journal dealing with all aspects of American education.

★2132★ Change

Heldref Publications
1319 18th St., NW
Washington, DC 20036-1802
Ph: (202)296-6267   Fr: 800-365-9753
E-mail: ch@heldref.org
URL: http://www.heldref.org/change.php

Bimonthly. $58.00/year for individuals, print only; $144.00/year for institutions, print only; $62.00/year for individuals, print and online; $173.00/year for institutions, print and online. Magazine dealing with contemporary issues in higher learning.

★2133★ The Chronicle of Higher Education

The Chronicle of Higher Education
1255 23rd St. NW 7th Fl.
Washington, DC 20037-1125
Ph: (202)466-1050   Fax: (202)452-1033
Fr: 800-728-2803
URL: http://chronicle.com

Weekly. $82.50/year for individuals, 49 issues; $45.00/year for individuals, 24 issues; $41.25/year for students, 49 issues; $22.50/year for students, 24 issues. Higher education magazine (tabloid).

★2134★ Columbia Journalism Review

Columbia Journalism Review
2950 Broadway, Journalism Bldg.
Columbia University
New York, NY 10027
Ph: (212)854-1881   Fax: (212)854-8580
Fr: 888-425-7782
E-mail: cjr@columbia.edu
URL: http://www.cjr.org/

Bimonthly. $19.95/year for U.S. $27.95 for single issue, Canadian & international orders. Magazine focusing on journalism.

★2135★ Communication Quarterly

MetaPress
PO Box 1943
Birmingham, AL 35201
Fr: 877-773-3833

Periodical focusing on research, criticism, communication theory, and excellence in teaching.

★2136★ Community College Journal of Research & Practice

Taylor & Francis Group Journals
325 Chestnut St., Ste. 800
Philadelphia, PA 19106
Ph: (215)625-8900   Fax: (215)625-8914
Fr: 800-354-1420
URL: http://www.tandf.co.uk/journals/titles/10668926.aspttp://www

Monthly. $778.00/year for institutions, print and online; $739.00/year for institutions, online only; $208.00/year for individuals. Journal focusing on exchange of ideas, research, and empirically tested educational innovations.

★2137★ Community Colleges Journal

American Association of Community Colleges
1 Dupont Cir. NW, Ste. 410
Washington, DC 20036
Ph: (202)728-0200   Fax: (202)833-2467
URL: http://www.aacc.nche.edu

Bimonthly. $28.00/year for nonmembers; $5.50 for single issue. Educational magazine.

★2138★ Connections

Association of Jesuit Colleges and Universities
1 Dupont Cir., Ste. 405
Washington, DC 20036
Ph: (202)862-9893   Fax: (202)862-8523
E-mail: publications@ajcunet.edu
URL: http://www.ajcunet.edu

Description: Monthly, except July and August. Furnishes information on legislative action affecting higher education and on Jesuit colleges and universities in the U.S. Recurring features include news of research, calendar of events, reports of meetings, notices of publications available, and columns titled Federal Relations, New Programs, and News from the Campuses. Only available online.

★2139★ E-Journal of Teaching and Learning in Diverse Settings

Southern University at Baton Rouge
PO Box 9942
Baton Rouge, LA 70813
Ph: (225)771-3184   Fax: (225)771-4400
URL: http://www.subr.edu/coeducation/ejournal

Online academic journal that publishes research and scholarly articles in the field of education and learning.

★2140★ Education & Treatment of Children

West Virginia University Press
44 Stansbury Hall
PO Box 6295
Morgantown, WV 26506
Ph: (304)293-8400   Fax: (304)293-6585
Fr: (866)988-7737
URL: http://www.educationandtreatmentofchildren.net

Quarterly. $85.00/year for institutions; $45.00/year for individuals; $100.00/year for institutions, elsewhere; $60.00/year for individuals, elsewhere. Periodical featuring information concerning the development of services for children and youth. Includes reports written for educators and other child care and mental health providers focused on teaching, training, and treatment effectiveness.

★2141★ Educational Policy

Sage Publications Inc.
2455 Teller Rd.
Thousand Oaks, CA 91320
Ph: (805)499-0721   Fax: (805)499-8096
URL: http://www.sagepub.com/journalsProdDesc.nav?prodId=Journal20

Annual. $749.00/year for institutions, combined (print & e-access); $824.00/year for institutions, backfile lease, combined plus backfile; $674.00/year for institutions, e-access; $749.00/year for institutions, backfile lease, e-access plus backfile; $687.48/year for institutions, backfile puchase, e-access (content through 1999); $734.00/year for institutions, print only; $159.00/year for individuals, print only; $135.00 for institutions, single print; $34.00 for individuals, single print. Journal for educators, policy makers, administrators, researchers, teachers, and graduate students.

★2142★ Educational Research and Evaluation

Taylor & Francis Group Journals
325 Chestnut St., Ste. 800
Philadelphia, PA 19106
Ph: (215)625-8900   Fax: (215)625-8914
Fr: 800-354-1420
URL: http://www.tandf.co.uk/journals/titles/13803611.asp

Bimonthly. $616.00/year for institutions, print and online; $585.00/year for institutions, online only; $239.00/year for individuals. Journal on theory and practice.

★2143★ Educational Researcher

American Educational Research Association
1230 17th St. NW
Washington, DC 20036
Ph: (202)223-9485   Fax: (202)775-1824
URL: http://www.aera.net/publications/?id=317

Monthly. $48.00/year for individuals, plus

foreign mailing charges; $150.00/year for institutions, plus foreign mailing charges. Educational research journal.

★2144★ Environmental Education Research

Taylor & Francis Group Journals
325 Chestnut St., Ste. 800
Philadelphia, PA 19106
Ph: (215)625-8900   Fax: (215)625-8914
Fr: 800-354-1420
URL: http://www.tandf.co.uk/journals/titles/13504622.asp

Journal covering all aspects of environmental education.

★2145★ Essays in Education

University of South Carolina
471 University Pky.
Aiken, SC 29801
Ph: (803)648-6851   Fax: (803)641-3461
Fr: 888-969-8722
URL: http://www.usca.edu/essays/

Monthly. Journal covering issues that impact and influence education.

★2146★ Financial Management

Financial Management Association International
4202 East Fowler Ave.
BSN 3331
Tampa, FL 33620-5500
Ph: (813)974-2084   Fax: (813)974-3318
E-mail: fma@coba.usf.edu
URL: http://www.fma.org/fm.htm

Quarterly. $95.00/year for individuals; $20.00 for single issue. Journal covering business, economics, finance and management.

★2147★ Hematology

American Society of Hematology
1900 M St. NW, Ste. 200
Washington, DC 20036
Ph: (202)776-0544   Fax: (202)776-0545
URL: http://asheducationbook.hematologylibrary.org

Semiweekly. $60.00/year for members; $90.00/year for nonmembers. Journal providing continuing medical education for physicians.

★2148★ The International Electronic Journal of Health Education

American Alliance for Health, Physical Education, Recreation & Dance
1900 Association Dr.
Reston, VA 20191-1598
Ph: (703)476-3400   Fax: (703)476-9527
Fr: 800-213-7193
URL: http://www.aahperd.org/iejhe/template.cfm?template=about.htm

Annual. Free to health education professionals and students. Journal promoting health through education and other systematic strategies.

★2149★ International Journal of Early Years Education

Taylor & Francis Group Journals
325 Chestnut St., Ste. 800
Philadelphia, PA 19106
Ph: (215)625-8900   Fax: (215)625-8914
Fr: 800-354-1420
URL: http://www.tandf.co.uk/journals/titles/09669760.asp

$512.00/year for institutions, print and online; $486.00/year for institutions, online only; $184.00/year for individuals. Journal focusing on education world-wide.

★2150★ International Journal of Inclusive Education

Taylor & Francis Group Journals
325 Chestnut St., Ste. 800
Philadelphia, PA 19106
Ph: (215)625-8900   Fax: (215)625-8914
Fr: 800-354-1420
URL: http://www.tandf.co.uk/journals/titles/13603116.asp

Bimonthly. $320.00/year for individuals, print only; $616.00/year for institutions, online only; $649.00/year for individuals, print and online; $193.00/year for individuals, print only; $376.00/year for institutions, online only; $396.00/year for institutions, print and online. Journal providing information on the nature of schools, universities and technical colleges for the educators and educational policy-makers.

★2151★ International Journal of Leadership in Education

Taylor & Francis Group Journals
325 Chestnut St., Ste. 800
Philadelphia, PA 19106
Ph: (215)625-8900   Fax: (215)625-8914
Fr: 800-354-1420
E-mail: ijle@txstate.edu
URL: http://www.tandf.co.uk/journals/tf/13603124.html

Quarterly. $196.00/year for individuals; $536.00/year for institutions, print and online; $509.00/year for institutions, online only; Journal dealing with leadership in education.

★2152★ International Journal of Progressive Education

International Journal of Progressive Education
c/o Mustafa Yunus Eryaman, Mng. Ed.
2108 S Orchard St., No. D
Urbana, IL 61801
URL: http://www.inased.org/ijpe.htm

$35.00/year for members; $45.00/year for individuals; $140.00/year for institutions, library; $35.00/year for students; $25.00 for single issue. U.S. Peer reviewed online journal that aims to create an open and continuing dialogue about current educational issues and future conceptions of educational theory.

★2153★ International Journal of Research & Method in Education

Taylor & Francis Group Journals
325 Chestnut St., Ste. 800
Philadelphia, PA 19106
Ph: (215)625-8900   Fax: (215)625-8914
Fr: 800-354-1420
URL: http://www.tandf.co.uk/journals/titles/1743727x.asp

$1809.00/year for institutions, print and online; $1718.00/year for institutions, online only; $271.00/year for individuals. Professional journal to further international discourse in education with particular focus on method.

★2154★ International Journal of Whole Schooling

Whole Schooling Press
Wayne State University
217 Education
Detroit, MI 48202
URL: http://www.wholeschooling.net/Journal_of_Whole_Schooling/IJW

Free to qualified subscribers. International, refereed academic journal dedicated to exploring ways to improve learning and schooling for all children.

★2155★ Journal of Academic Leadership

Academic Leadership
600 Park St.
Rarick Hall 219
Hays, KS 67601-4099
Ph: (785)628-4547
URL: http://www.academicleadership.org/

Journal focusing on the leadership issues in the academic world.

★2156★ Journal of Cases in Educational Leadership

Sage Publications Inc.
2455 Teller Rd.
Thousand Oaks, CA 91320
Ph: (805)499-0721   Fax: (805)499-8096
URL: http://www.sagepub.com/journalsProdDesc.nav?prodId=Journal20

Quarterly. $319.00/year for institutions, e-access; $83.00/year for individuals, e-access. Journal covering cases appropriate for use in programs that prepare educational leaders.

★2157★ Journal of College Teaching & Learning

The Clute Institute for Academic Research
PO Box 620760
Littleton, CO 80162
Ph: (303)904-4750   Fax: (303)978-0413
URL: http://www.cluteinstitute.com/JCTLMain.htm

Monthly. $100.00/year for individuals; $200.00/year for other countries, with postage; $495.00/year for institutions. Refereed academic journal covering all areas of college level teaching, learning and administration.

★2158★ The Journal of Continuing Education in Nursing

SLACK Inc.
6900 Grove Rd.
Thorofare, NJ 08086-9447
Ph: (856)848-1000   Fax: (856)853-5991
URL: http://www.slackinc.com/allied/jcen

Bimonthly. $99.00/year for individuals; $245.00/year for institutions; $168.00 for individuals, two years; $416.00 for institutions, two years; $32.00 for single issue. Journal for nurses involved in planning and implementing educational programs for the practitioner and others in patient care.

★2159★ Journal of Curriculum and Supervision

Association for Supervision and Curriculum Development
1703 N Beauregard St.
Alexandria, VA 22311-1714
Ph: (703)578-9600   Fax: (703)575-5400
Fr: 800-933-2723
URL: http://www.ascd.org/portal/site/ascd/menuitem.0545410c9839aa

Scholarly journal focusing on curriculum and supervision.

★2160★ Journal of Direct Instruction

Association for Direct Instruction
PO Box 10252
Eugene, OR 97440
Ph: (541)485-1293   Fax: (541)683-7543
Fr: 800-995-2464
URL: http://www.adihome.org/phpshop/articles/articles.php?type=JD

Quarterly. Subscription included in membership. Journal covering education.

★2161★ Journal of Engineering Education

American Society for Engineering Education
1818 North St., NW, Ste. 600
Washington, DC 20036-2479
Ph: (202)331-3500
URL: http://www.asee.org/publications/jee/index.cfm

Quarterly. Journal covering scholarly research in engineering education.

★2162★ Journal of Higher Education Outreach and Engagement (JHEOE)

Institute of Higher Education
Meigs Hall
Athens, GA 30602
Ph: (706)542-3464   Fax: (706)542-7588
E-mail: jheoe@uga.edu
URL: http://www.uga.edu/jheoe/

Semiannual. $35.00/year for individuals; $45.00/year for Canada; $60.00/year for elsewhere, surface mail; $70.00/year for elsewhere, airmail; $95.00/year for institutions; $105.00/year for institutions, Canada;

$110.00/year for institutions, other countries, surface mail; $120.00/year for institutions, other countries, airmail. Journal covering higher education outreach and engagement for scholars, practitioners, and professionals.

★2163★ Journal of Language, Identity, and Education

Lawrence Erlbaum Associates Inc.
10 Industrial Ave.
Mahwah, NJ 07430
Ph: (201)258-2200   Fax: (201)236-0072
Fr: 800-926-6579
E-mail: journals@erlbaum.com
URL: http://www.erlbaum.com

Quarterly. $50.00/year for U.S. and Canada, individual, online and print; $80.00/year for elsewhere, individual, online and print; $360.00/year for U.S. and Canada, institution, online and print; $390.00/year for elsewhere, institution, online and print; $290.00/year for U.S. and Canada, institution, online only; $290.00/year for elsewhere, institution, online only; $325.00/year for U.S. and Canada, institution, print only; $355.00/year for elsewhere, institution, print only. Scholarly, interdisciplinary journal covering issues in language, identity and education worldwide for academics, educators and policy specialists in a variety of disciplines, and others.

★2164★ Journal of Latinos and Education

Lawrence Erlbaum Associates Inc.
10 Industrial Ave.
Mahwah, NJ 07430
Ph: (201)258-2200   Fax: (201)236-0072
Fr: 800-926-6579
URL: http://www.erlbaum.com/

Quarterly. $50.00/year for individuals, online and print - U.S./Canada; $80.00/year for individuals, online and print - all other countries; $360.00/year for institutions, online and print - U.S./Canada; $390.00/year for institutions, online and print - all other countries; $290.00/year for institutions, online only - U.S./Canada; $290.00/year for institutions, online only - all other countries; $325.00/year for institutions, print only - U.S./Canada; $355.00/year for institutions, print only - all other countries. Scholarly, multidisciplinary journal covering educational issues that impact Latinos for researchers, teaching professionals, academics, scholars, institutions, and others.

★2165★ Journal of STEM Education

Auburn University
9088 Haley Ctr.
Auburn, AL 36849
Ph: (334)844-4000   Fax: (334)844-9027
URL: http://www.auburn.edu/research/litee/jstem/index.php

Semiannual. Journal for educators in Science, Technology, Engineering, and Mathematics (STEM) education.

★2166★ Leadership and Policy in Schools

Taylor & Francis Group Journals
325 Chestnut St., Ste. 800
Philadelphia, PA 19106
Ph: (215)625-8900   Fax: (215)625-8914
Fr: 800-354-1420
URL: http://www.tandf.co.uk/journals/titles/15700763.asp

Quarterly. $477.00/year for institutions, print and online; $453.00/year for institutions, online only; $227.00/year for individuals; $60.00/year for ICSEI members. Journal providing information about leadership and policy in primary and secondary education.

★2167★ NAIA News

National Association of Intercollegiate Athletics
1200 Grand Blvd
Kansas City, MO 64106
Ph: (816)595-8000   Fax: (816)595-8200
E-mail: naianews@naia.org
URL: http://www.naia.org

Description: Daily. Provides news and information on the Association, which strives to "develop intercollegiate athletic programs as an integral part of the total educational program of the college rather than as a separate commercial or promotional adjunct." Aims toward uniformity and equity in policies and practices. Recurring features include news of members and events, notices of awards, and job listings.

★2168★ NewsNet, the Newsletter of the AAASS

American Association for the Advancement of Slavic Studies (AAASS)
8 Story St.
Cambridge, MA 02138
Ph: (617)495-0677   Fax: (617)495-0680
E-mail: aaass@fas.harvard.edu
URL: http://www.fas.harvard.edu/~aaass/

Description: Bimonthly. Reports on Association activities and on Slavic study research in institutions throughout the world. Alerts readers to research grants, internships, and fellowship opportunities as well as to employment opportunities in universities across the country. Announces awards, upcoming conferences, courses, new scholarly publications, and annual research.

★2169★ Notices of the American Mathematical Society

American Mathematical Society
201 Charles St.
Providence, RI 02904-2294
Ph: (401)455-4000   Fax: (401)331-3842
Fr: 800-321-4267
URL: http://www.ams.org/notices

Monthly. $417.00/year for individuals;. Free, members. AMS journal publishing programs, meeting reports, new publications, announcements, upcoming mathematical meetings, scientific development trends, computer software reviews, and federal funding reports.

★2170★ **Nurse Educator**

Lippincott Williams & Wilkins
530 Walnut St.
Philadelphia, PA 19106-3621
Ph: (215)521-8300   Fax: (215)521-8902
Fr: 800-638-3030
E-mail: needitor@aol.com
URL: http://www.nurseeducatoronline.com/

Bimonthly. $103.91/year for individuals, U.S.; $292.96/year for institutions, U.S.; $189.94/year for individuals, international; $375.94/year for institutions, international. Journal for nursing educators.

★2171★ **OECD Observer**

Organization for Economic Cooperation and Development
2001 L St., NW, Ste. 650
Washington, DC 20036-4922
Ph: (202)785-6323   Fax: (202)785-0350
Fr: 800-456-6323
E-mail: observer@oecd.org
URL: http://www.oecdobserver.org

Bimonthly. $75.00/year for individuals; $105.00 for individuals, two years. Magazine on economic affairs, science, and technology.

★2172★ **Oxford Review of Education**

Taylor & Francis Group Journals
325 Chestnut St., Ste. 800
Philadelphia, PA 19106
Ph: (215)625-8900   Fax: (215)625-8914
Fr: 800-354-1420
URL: http://www.tandf.co.uk/journals/titles/03054985.asp

$1,031.00/year for institutions, print and online; $979.00/year for institutions, online only; $396.00/year for individuals. Journal covering advance study of education.

★2173★ **The Physics Teacher**

American Association of Physics Teachers
1 Physics Ellipse
College Park, MD 20740-3845
Ph: (301)209-3300   Fax: (301)209-0845
E-mail: tpt@appstate.edu
URL: http://www.aapt.org/Publications/

$335.00/year for nonmembers, international; $105.00/year for members, regular. Scientific education magazine.

★2174★ **Research Strategies**

Elsevier Science Inc.
360 Park Ave. S
New York, NY 10010
Ph: (212)989-5800   Fax: (212)633-3990
URL: http://www.elsevier.com

Journal covering library literature and the educational mission of the library.

★2175★ **School Effectiveness and School Improvement**

Taylor & Francis Group Journals
325 Chestnut St., Ste. 800
Philadelphia, PA 19106
Ph: (215)625-8900   Fax: (215)625-8914
Fr: 800-354-1420
URL: http://www.tandf.co.uk/journals/titles/09243453.asp

Quarterly. $305.00/year for institutions, print and online; $231.00/year for institutions, online only; $153.00/year for individuals, print only; $520.00/year for institutions, print and online; $494.00/year for institutions, online only; $255.00/year for individuals, print only. Journal focusing on educational progress of all students.

★2176★ **The Science Teacher**

National Science Teachers Association
1840 Wilson Blvd.
Arlington, VA 22201
Ph: (703)243-7100   Fax: (703)243-7177
URL: http://www.nsta.org/highschool/

Journal on science education.

★2177★ **Teaching and Learning in Nursing**

Elsevier Science Inc.
360 Park Ave. S
New York, NY 10010
Ph: (212)989-5800   Fax: (212)633-3990
URL: http://www.elsevier.com

Quarterly. $119.00/year for institutions, U.S. $167.00/year for institutions, other countries; $75.00/year for individuals, U.S. $104.00/year for individuals, other countries. Journal devoted to associate degree nursing education and practice.

★2178★ **The Technology Teacher**

International Technology Education Association
1914 Association Dr., Ste. 201
Reston, VA 20191-1539
Ph: (703)860-2100   Fax: (703)860-0353

$35.00/year for individuals, professional U.S., 2year; $70.00/year for individuals, professional U.S., 1year; $30.00/year for students, undergrad student- first time member, 1year; $35.00/year for students, full-time grad/renewing undergrad student, 1year; $55.00/year for students, bridge - one-time student to professional, 1year; $410.00/year for institutions, group membership, 2 year; $210.00/year for institutions, group membership, 1 year; $690.00/year for individuals, group membership, 2year; $350.00/year for individuals, group membership, 1year; $270.00/year for individuals, group membership, 2year. Magazine on technology education.

★2179★ **Theory and Research in Education**

Sage Publications Inc.
2455 Teller Rd.
Thousand Oaks, CA 91320
Ph: (805)499-0721   Fax: (805)499-8096

URL: http://tre.sagepub.com/

$459.00/year for institutions, print and online; $413.00/year for institutions, online only; $450.00/year for institutions, print only; $77.00/year for individuals, print only. Interdisciplinary journal covering normative and theoretical issues concerning education including multi-faceted philosophical analysis of moral, social, political and epistemological problems and issues arising from educational practice.

★2180★ **University Aviation Association Newsletter**

University Aviation Association
3410 Skyway Dr.
Auburn, AL 36830-6444
Ph: (334)844-2434   Fax: (334)844-2432
E-mail: deweech@auburn.edu
URL: http://www.uaa.aero/

Description: Bimonthly. Provides information on Association activities and projects, events of other aviation organizations that bear on higher education, and the future impact of collegiate aviation education. Recurring features include feature articles on outstanding individual and institutional members, statistics, a calendar of events, news of members, news of research, an editorial, letters to the editor, book reviews, employment information, and the president's report.

★2181★ **Uratie**

IDG Communications Inc.
5 Speen St., 3rd. Fl
Framingham, MA 01701
Ph: (508)875-5000   Fax: (508)988-7888
URL: http://www.idg.com

Magazine providing job offers for graduates, engineers and information technology professionals.

★2182★ **Weatherwise**

Heldref Publications
1319 18th St., NW
Washington, DC 20036-1802
Ph: (202)296-6267   Fr: 800-365-9753
URL: http://www.heldref.org/ww.php

Bimonthly. $40.00/year for individuals, print only; $106.00/year for institutions, print only; $44.00/year for individuals, print and online; $127.00/year for institutions, print and online. Popular weather magazine for students, teachers, and professionals.

★2183★ **Wisconsin Lawyer**

State Bar of Wisconsin
PO Box 7158
Madison, WI 53707-7158
Ph: (608)257-3838   Fax: (608)257-5502
Fr: 800-728-7788
E-mail: wislawyer@wisbar.org
URL: http://www.wisbar.org/wislawmag/

Monthly. $48.00/year for individuals. Official monthly publication of the State Bar of Wisconsin.

PLACEMENT AND JOB REFERRAL SERVICES

★2184★ Academy of Management (AOM)

PO Box 3020
Briarcliff Manor, NY 10510-8020
Ph: (914)923-2607   Fax: (914)923-2615
E-mail: aom@pace.edu
URL: http://www.aomonline.org

Description: Professors in accredited universities and colleges who teach management; selected business executives who have made significant written contributions to the literature in the field of management and organization. Offers placement service.

★2185★ American Academy of Religion (AAR)

825 Houston Mill Rd. NE, Ste. 300
Atlanta, GA 30329
Ph: (404)727-3049   Fax: (404)727-7959
E-mail: aar@aarweb.org
URL: http://www.aarweb.org

Description: Professional society of scholars and teachers in the field of religion. Encourages scholarship, research, and publications in the study of religion, and stimulates effective teaching. Hosts annual meeting, publishes academic journal, offers research grants and placement services to members; compiles statistics.

★2186★ American Association for Employment in Education (AAEE)

3040 Riverside Dr., Ste. 125
Columbus, OH 43221-2550
Ph: (614)485-1111   Fax: (614)485-9609
E-mail: aaee@osu.edu
URL: http://www.aaee.org

Description: Represents colleges, universities, and other post-secondary educational institutions, which are not-for-profit. Prepares teachers and other educational personnel for service in public and private educational institutions, organizations and agencies. Provides information or services relating to career planning, placement, and recruitment activities in education.

★2187★ American Association of Teachers of French (AATF)

Southern Illinois University
Mail Code 4510
Carbondale, IL 62901
Ph: (618)453-5731   Fax: (618)453-5733
E-mail: abrate@siu.edu
URL: http://www.frenchteachers.org

Members: Teachers of French in public and private elementary and secondary schools, colleges and universities. **Activities:** Sponsors National French Week each November to take French out of the classroom and into the schools and community. Conducts National French Contest in elementary and secondary schools and awards prizes at all levels. Maintains Materials Center with promotional and pedagogical materials; National French Honor Society (high school), Placement Bureau, summer scholarships.

★2188★ American Association of Teachers of Spanish and Portuguese (AATSP)

900 Ladd Rd.
Walled Lake, MI 48390
Ph: (248)960-2180   Fax: (248)960-9570
E-mail: corporate@aatsp.org
URL: http://www.aatsp.org

Description: Teachers of Spanish and Portuguese languages and literatures and others interested in Hispanic culture. Operates placement bureau and maintains pen pal registry. Sponsors honor society, Sociedad Honoraria Hispanica and National Spanish Examinations for secondary school students.

★2189★ American Classical League (ACL)

Miami University
422 Wells Mills Dr.
Oxford, OH 45056-1694
Ph: (513)529-7741   Fax: (513)529-7742
E-mail: info@aclclassics.org
URL: http://www.aclclassics.org

Members: Teachers of classical languages in high schools and colleges. **Purpose:** Works to promote the teaching of Latin and other classical languages. Presents scholarship. **Activities:** Maintains placement service, teaching materials, and resource center at Miami University in Oxford, OH to sell teaching aids to Latin and Greek teachers.

★2190★ American Mathematical Society (AMS)

201 Charles St.
Providence, RI 02904-2213
Ph: (401)455-4000   Fax: (401)331-3842
Fr: 800-321-4AMS
E-mail: ams@ams.org
URL: http://www.ams.org

Description: Professional society of mathematicians and educators. Promotes the interests of mathematical scholarship and research. Holds institutes, seminars, short courses, and symposia to further mathematical research; awards prizes. Offers placement services; compiles statistics.

★2191★ American Philosophical Association (APA)

University of Delaware
31 Amstel Ave.
Newark, DE 19716-4797
Ph: (302)831-1112   Fax: (302)831-8690
E-mail: apaonline@udel.edu
URL: http://www.apa.udel.edu/apa/index.html

Members: College and university teachers of philosophy and others with an interest in philosophy. **Purpose:** Facilitates exchange of ideas in philosophy, encourages creative and scholarly activity in philosophy, and fosters the professional work of teachers of philosophy. **Activities:** Participates in international congresses of philosophy and maintains affiliations with national and international philosophical organizations. Maintains placement service; sponsors competitions. Oversees selection of Romanell, Schutz and Carus lecturers and other prizes and awards.

★2192★ American Political Science Association (APSA)

1527 New Hampshire Ave. NW
Washington, DC 20036-1206
Ph: (202)483-2512   Fax: (202)483-2657
E-mail: apsa@apsanet.org
URL: http://www.apsanet.org

Description: College and university teachers of political science, public officials, research workers, and businessmen. Encourages the impartial study and promotes the development of the art and science of government. Develops research projects of public interest and educational programs for political scientists and journalists; seeks to improve the knowledge of and increase citizen participation in political and governmental affairs. Serves as clearinghouse for teaching and research positions in colleges, universities, and research bureaus in the U.S. and abroad and for positions open to political scientists in government and private business; conducts Congressional Fellowship Program. Conducts Committee on Professional Ethic, and Rights and Freedom. Offers placement service.

★2193★ Association of American Law Schools (AALS)

1201 Connecticut Ave. NW, Ste. 800
Washington, DC 20036-2717
Ph: (202)296-8851   Fax: (202)296-8869
E-mail: aals@aals.org
URL: http://www.aals.org

Description: Law schools association. Seeks to improve the legal profession through legal education. Interacts for law professors with state and federal government, other legal education and professional associations, and other national higher education and learned society organizations. Compiles statistics; sponsors teacher placement service. Presents professional development programs.

★2194★ Association for Direct Instruction (ADI)

PO Box 10252
Eugene, OR 97440
Ph: (541)485-1293   Fax: (541)868-1397
Fr: 800-995-2464
E-mail: info@adihome.org
URL: http://www.adihome.org

Members: Public school regular and special education teachers and university instructors. **Purpose:** Encourages, promotes, and engages in research aimed at improving educational methods. Promotes dissemination of developmental information and skills that facilitate the education of adults and children. **Activities:** Administers a preschool for developmentally delayed children. Offers educational training workshops for instructors. Maintains speaker's bureau and placement service.

★2195★ **Association of University Professors of Ophthalmology (AUPO)**

PO Box 420369
San Francisco, CA 94142-0369
Ph: (415)561-8548   Fax: (415)561-8531
E-mail: aupo@aao.org
URL: http://www.aupo.org

Members: Heads of departments or divisions of ophthalmology in accredited medical schools throughout the U.S. and Canada; directors of ophthalmology residency programs in institutions not connected to medical schools. **Purpose:** Promotes medical education, research, and patient care relating to ophthalmology. **Activities:** Operates Ophthalmology Matching Program and faculty placement service, which aids ophthalmologists interested in being associated with university ophthalmology programs to locate such programs.

★2196★ **College Language Association (CLA)**

Fayetteville State University
Dept. of English and Foreign Languages
1200 Murchison Rd.
Fayetteville, NC 28301
Ph: (910)672-1347   Fax: (910)672-1425
E-mail: banthony@uncfsu.edu
URL: http://www.clascholars.org

Description: Teachers of English and modern foreign languages, primarily in historically black colleges and universities. Maintains placement service.

★2197★ **College Media Advisers (CMA)**

University of Memphis
Department of Journalism
3711 Veterans Ave., Rm. 300
Memphis, TN 38152-6661
Ph: (901)678-2403   Fax: (901)678-4798
E-mail: rsplbrgr@memphis.edu
URL: http://www.collegemedia.org

Members: Professional association serving advisers, directors, and chairmen of boards of college student media (newspapers, yearbooks, magazines, handbooks, directories, and radio and television stations); heads of schools and departments of journalism; and others interested in junior college, college, and university student media. **Purpose:** Serves as a clearinghouse for student media; acts as consultant on student theses and dissertations on publications. Encourages high school journalism and examines its relationships to college and professional journalism. **Activities:** Conducts national survey of student media in rotation each year by type: newspapers, magazines, and yearbooks; radio and television stations. Compiles statistics. Maintains placement service and speakers' bureau.

★2198★ **Decision Sciences Institute (DSI)**

Georgia State University
J. Mack Robinson College of Business
University Plz.
Atlanta, GA 30303
Ph: (404)413-7710   Fax: (404)413-7714
E-mail: clatta@gsu.edu
URL: http://www.decisionsciences.org

Members: Businesspersons and members of business school faculties. **Activities:** Maintains placement service.

★2199★ **Financial Management Association International (FMA)**

University of South Florida
College of Business Administration
4202 E Fowler Ave., BSN 3331
Tampa, FL 33620-5500
Ph: (813)974-2084   Fax: (813)974-3318
E-mail: fma@coba.usf.edu
URL: http://www.fma.org

Members: Professors of financial management; corporate financial officers. **Purpose:** Facilitates exchange of ideas among persons involved in financial management or the study thereof. **Activities:** Conducts workshops for comparison of current research projects and development of cooperative ventures in writing and research. Sponsors honorary society for superior students at 300 colleges and universities. Offers placement services.

★2200★ **International Association of Baptist Colleges and Universities (IABCU)**

8120 Sawyer Brown Rd., Ste. 108
Nashville, TN 37221-1410
Ph: (615)673-1896   Fax: (615)662-1396
E-mail: tim_fields@baptistschools.org
URL: http://www.baptistschools.org

Members: Southern Baptist senior colleges, universities, junior colleges, academies, and Bible schools. **Purpose:** Promotes Christian education through literature, faculty workshops, student recruitment, teacher placement, trustee orientation, statistical information, and other assistance to members.

★2201★ **International Educator's Institute (TIE)**

PO Box 513
Cummaquid, MA 02637
Ph: (508)790-1990   Fax: (508)790-1922
Fr: 877-375-6668
E-mail: tie@tieonline.com
URL: http://www.tieonline.com

Description: Facilitates the placement of teachers and administrators in American, British, and international schools. Seeks to create a network that provides for professional development opportunities and improved financial security of members. Offers advice and information on international school news, recent educational developments, job placement, and investment, consumer, and professional development opportunities. Makes available insurance and trav-

el benefits. Operates International Schools Internship Program.

★2202★ **National Alliance of Black School Educators (NABSE)**

310 Pennsylvania Ave.
Washington, DC 20003
Ph: (202)608-6310   Fax: (202)608-6319
Fr: 800-221-2654
E-mail: lavette@nabse.org
URL: http://www.nabse.org

Description: Black educators from all levels; others indirectly involved in the education of black youth. Promotes awareness, professional expertise, and commitment among black educators. Goals are to: eliminate and rectify the results of racism in education; work with state, local, and national leaders to raise the academic achievement level of all black students; increase members' involvement in legislative activities; facilitate the introduction of a curriculum that more completely embraces black America; improve the ability of black educators to promote problem resolution; create a meaningful and effective network of strength, talent, and professional support. Sponsors workshops, commission meetings, and special projects. Encourages research, especially as it relates to blacks, and the presentation of papers during national conferences. Plans to establish a National Black Educators Data Bank and offer placement service.

★2203★ **National Association for Sport and Physical Education (NASPE)**

1900 Association Dr.
Reston, VA 20191-1598
Ph: (703)476-3400   Fax: (703)476-8316
Fr: 800-213-7193
E-mail: naspe@aahperd.org
URL: http://www.naspeinfo.org

Description: Men and women professionally involved with physical activity and sports. Seeks to improve the total sport and physical activity experience in America. Conducts research and education programs in such areas as sport psychology, curriculum development, kinesiology, history, philosophy, sport sociology, and the biological and behavioral basis of human activity. Develops and distributes public information materials which explain the value of physical education programs. Supports councils involved in organizing and supporting elementary, secondary, and college physical education and sport programs; administers the National Council of Athletic Training in conjunction with the National Association for Girls and Women in Sport; serves the professional interests of coaches, trainers, and officials. Maintains hall of fame, placement service, and media resource center for public information and professional preparation. Member benefits include group insurance and discounts.

★2204★ **National Association of Teachers' Agencies (NATA)**

797 Kings Hwy.
Fairfield, CT 06825
Ph: (203)333-0611   Fax: (203)334-7224

E-mail: info@jobsforteachers.com

Description: Private employment agencies engaged primarily in the placement of teaching and administration personnel. Works to standardize records and promote a strong ethical sense in the placement field. Maintains speakers' bureau.

★2205★ National Communication Association (NCA)

1765 N St. NW
Washington, DC 20036
Ph: (202)464-4622   Fax: (202)464-4600
E-mail: rsmitter@natcom.org
URL: http://www.natcom.org

Members: Elementary, secondary, college, and university teachers, speech clinicians, media specialists, communication consultants, students, theater directors, and other interested persons; libraries and other institutions. **Purpose:** Works to promote study, criticism, research, teaching, and application of the artistic, humanistic, and scientific principles of communication, particularly speech communication. Sponsors the publication of scholarly volumes in speech. **Activities:** Conducts international debate tours in the U.S. and abroad. Maintains placement service.

★2206★ U.S.-China Education Foundation (USCEF)

4140 Oceanside Blvd., Ste. 159 - No. 112
Oceanside, CA 92056-6005
Ph: (760)644-0977
E-mail: uscef@sage-usa.net
URL: http://www.sage-usa.net/uscef.htm

Purpose: Aims to promote the learning of the Chinese languages (including Mandarin, Cantonese, and minority languages such as Mongolian) by Americans, and the learning of English by Chinese. **Activities:** Conducts short-term travel-study program to prepare Americans and Chinese for stays of four, six, or eight months or one to four years in China or the U.S., respectively. Operates teacher placement service and speakers' bureau. A project of The Society for the Development of Global Education (S.A.G.E. Inc.).

★2207★ University Photographers Association of America (UPAA)

SUNY Brockport
350 New Campus Dr.
Brockport, NY 14420-2931
Ph: (585)395-2133
E-mail: jdusen@brockport.edu
URL: http://www.upaa.org

Description: College and university personnel engaged professionally in photography, audiovisual work, or journalism for universities. Seeks to advance applied photography and the profession through the exchange of thoughts and opinions among its members. Awards fellowship for exceptional work in the advancement of photography. Provides a medium for exchange of ideas and technical information on photography, especially university photographic work. Sponsors exhib-

its. Provides placement service for members.

EMPLOYER DIRECTORIES AND NETWORKING LISTS

★2208★ 50 State Educational Directories

Career Guidance Foundation
8090 Engineer Rd.
San Diego, CA 92111
Ph: (858)560-8051   Fax: (858)278-8960
Fr: 800-854-2670
URL: http://www.cgf.org

Annual. Microfiche. Collection consists of reproductions of the state educational directories published by the departments of education of individual 50 states. Directory contents vary, but the majority contain listings of elementary and secondary schools, colleges and universities, and state education officials. Amount of detail in each also varies. Entries include: Usually, institution name, address, and name of one executive.

★2209★ Accredited Institutions of Postsecondary Education

Oryx Press
4041 N Central Ave., Ste. 700
PO Box 33889
Phoenix, AZ 85021-3397
Ph: (602)265-2651   Fax: 800-279-4663
Fr: 800-279-6799
URL: http://isbndb.com

Annual, latest edition 2006-2007. Covers more than 7,000 accredited institutions and programs of postsecondary education in the United States and U.S.-chartered schools in 14 countries. Entries include: Institution name, address, phone, whether public or private, any religious affiliation, type of institution and student body, branch campuses or affiliated institutions, date of first accreditation and latest reaffirmation of accrediting body, accredited programs in professional fields, level of degrees offered, name of chief executive officer, size and composition of enrollment, type of academic calendar. Arrangement: Geographical. Indexes: Institution.

★2210★ Association of American University Presses-Directory

Association of American University Presses
71 W 23rd St.
New York, NY 10010-4102
Ph: (212)989-1010   Fax: (212)989-0275
URL: http://www.aaupnet.org

Annual; latest edition spring 2007. $21.00 for individuals. Covers 124 presses and affiliates worldwide. Entries include: Press name, address, phone, e-mail, URL; titles and names of complete editorial and managerial staffs; editorial program; mailing, warehouse, printing, and/or customer service

addresses; other details. Arrangement: Classified by press affiliation, alphabetical by press name. Indexes: Personal name.

★2211★ Chronicle Four-Year College Databook

Chronicle Guidance Publications Inc.
66 Aurora St.
Moravia, NY 13118-3569
Ph: (315)497-0330   Fax: (315)497-0339
Fr: 800-899-0454
URL: http://tnt.spidergraphics.com

Annual, September; latest edition 2006-2007 edition. $25.48 for individuals. Covers more than 825 baccalaureate, master's, doctoral, and first professional programs offered by more than 2,450 colleges and universities in the United States. Entries include: College charts section gives college name, address, phone; accreditation, enrollment, admissions, costs, financial aid; accreditation associations' names, addresses, and phone numbers. Appendices give details on admissions and other information special to each college. Arrangement: Part I, classified by college major; part II, geographical. Indexes: College name.

★2212★ Chronicle Two-Year College Databook

Chronicle Guidance Publications Inc.
66 Aurora St.
Moravia, NY 13118-3569
Ph: (315)497-0330   Fax: (315)497-0339
Fr: 800-899-0454
URL: http://tnt.spidergraphics.com

Annual, latest edition 2006-2007 edition. $25.47 for individuals. Covers over 815 associate, certificate, occupational, and transfer programs offered by more than 2,555 technical institutes, two-year colleges, and universities in the United States. Entries include: College charts section giving college name, address, phone; accreditation, enrollment, admissions, costs, financial aid; accrediting associations' names, addresses, and phone numbers. Arrangement: Part I is classified by college major; part II is geographical. Indexes: College name.

★2213★ Directory of Interior Design Programs Accredited by FIDER

Council for Interior Design Accreditation
146 Monroe Ctr. NW, Ste. 1318
Grand Rapids, MI 49503
Ph: (616)458-0400   Fax: (616)458-0460
URL: http://www.fider.org

Semiannual, June and November. Covers 128 interior design programs in the United States and Canada in conformance with the accreditation standards of the foundation. Entries include: Type of program, name of institution, name of department chair or program head, phone, dates of last and next accreditation review, degrees offered, e-mail and web addresses. Arrangement: Geographical, degree level offered, then alphabetical by institution name.

★2214★ Employment Information in the Mathematical Sciences

American Mathematical Society
201 Charles St.
Providence, RI 02904-2294
Ph: (401)455-4000   Fax: (401)331-3842
Fr: 800-321-4267
E-mail: eims-info@ams.org
URL: http://www.ams.org/eims/

Five times a year. Covers colleges and universities with departments in the mathematical sciences, and non-academic and foreign organizations with employment openings. Entries include: For departments–Name, address, name and title of contact; job title, job description, salary (if applicable). Arrangement: Classified as academic or nonacademic, then geographical.

★2215★ Fulbright Scholar Program Grants for U.S. Faculty and Professionals

Council for International Exchange of Scholars
3007 Tilden St. NW, Ste. 5L
Washington, DC 20008-3009
Ph: (202)686-4000   Fax: (202)362-3442
URL: http://www.cies.org/

Annual, March. Free. Covers about 800 grants available for postdoctoral university lecturing and advanced research by American citizens in more than 140 countries. Entries include: Periods in which grants are tenable; number of grants available for the country; language or other requirement; fields in which lectures and research are desired; stipends; housing; additional income for dependents; applications and reference forms. Arrangement: Geographical. Indexes: Professional, discipline.

★2216★ Grants, Fellowships, and Prizes of Interest to Historians

American Historical Association
400 A St. SE
Washington, DC 20003-3889
Ph: (202)544-2422   Fax: (202)544-8307
E-mail: grantguide@theaha.org
URL: http://www.historians.org

Annual; latest edition 2006. For American Historical Association members. Covers over 450 sources of funding (scholarships, fellowships, internships, awards, and book and essay prizes) in the United States and abroad for graduate students, postdoctoral researchers, and institutions in the humanities. Entries include: Name of source, institution name or contact, address, phone, eligibility and proposal requirements, award or stipend amount, location requirements for research, application deadlines. Arrangement: Alphabetical in three categories: support for individual research and teaching; grants for groups and organizations for research and education; and book, article, essay, and manuscript prizes.

★2217★ Higher Education Directory

Higher Education Publications Inc.
6400 Arlington Blvd., Ste. 648
Falls Church, VA 22042-2342
Ph: (703)532-2300   Fax: (703)532-2305
Fr: 888-349-7715
URL: http://www.hepinc.com/hed.htm

Annual; latest edition 2007. $75.00 for individuals. Covers over 4,364 degree granting colleges and universities accredited by approved agencies recognized by the U.S. Secretary of Education and by the Council of Higher Education Accreditation (CHEA); 103 systems offices; over 550 related associations and state government agencies; recognized accrediting agencies. Entries include: For institutions–Name, address, congressional district, phone, fax, year established; Carnegie classification; enrollment; type of student body; religious or other affiliation; undergraduate tuition and fees; type of academic calendar; highest degree offered; accreditations; IRS status; names, titles and job classification codes for academic and administrative officers. For associations and state agencies–Name, address, phone, name of chief executive officer. Same content and coverage as the base volume of the Department of Education's publication "Directory of Postsecondary Institutions". Arrangement: Geographical, alphabetical by state. Indexes: Administrator name (with phone and e-mail addresses), accreditation, FICE numbers, college or university name.

★2218★ Mathematical Sciences Professional Directory

American Mathematical Society
201 Charles St.
Providence, RI 02904-2294
Ph: (401)455-4000   Fax: (401)331-3842
Fr: 800-321-4267
URL: http://www.ams.org

Annual; latest edition 2006. $55.00. Covers 37 professional organizations concerned with mathematics, government agencies, academic institutions with department in the mathematical sciences, nonacademic organizations, and individuals. Entries include: For professional organizations and government agencies–Name, address, names and titles of key personnel. For institutions–Name, address; name, title, and address of department chair. Arrangement: Classified by type of organization; institutions are then geographical; others, alphabetical. Indexes: University or college name.

★2219★ Modern Language Association of America-Job Information List

Modern Language Association of America
26 Broadway, 3rd Fl.
New York, NY 10004-1789
Ph: (646)576-5000   Fax: (646)458-0030
URL: http://www.mla.org

Quarterly, February, April, October, and December. Covers available positions for college teachers of English and foreign languages in four-year colleges and universities; February issue includes separate section of openings in two-year institutions. Separate editions for English and American language and literature and for foreign language openings. Entries include: Department chair statement, including institution name; contact name, address, phone; definite or possible openings; related information for job seekers (change in deadline date, or job description, notice of a vacancy filled, etc.). Arrangement: First section–Statements of department chairmen. Second section (in October and February only)–List of departments reporting no vacancies.

★2220★ National Directory of College Athletics

Collegiate Directories Inc.
PO Box 450640
Cleveland, OH 44145
Ph: (440)835-1172   Fax: (440)835-8835
Fr: 800-426-2232
URL: http://www.collegiatedirectories.com/shopping/index.asp

Annual; latest edition 2007-2008. $45.95 for individuals. Covers men's athletic departments of 2,100 senior and junior colleges in the United States and Canada. Entries include: School name, address, enrollment, colors, team nicknames, stadium and/or gym capacity; names of president, men's athletic director, athletic administrative staff, physical education director and coaches for each sport; athletic department phones, faxes, etc.; association affiliations. Arrangement: Alphabetical. Indexes: Schools by program and division; alphabetical by advertisers and products.

★2221★ National Faculty Directory

Gale, Cengage Learning
27500 Drake Rd.
Farmington Hills, MI 48331-3535
Ph: (248)699-4253   Fax: (248)699-8065
Fr: 800-877-4253
E-mail: businessproducts@gale.com
URL: http://www.galegroup.com

Annual; latest edition 39th, October 2007. $985.00 for individuals. Covers more than 740,000 (90,000 more in supplement) teaching faculty members at over 3,600 junior colleges, colleges, and universities in the United States and those in Canada that give instruction in English. Entries include: Name, department name, institution, address, and phone and fax numbers. Directory combines main edition and supplement. Arrangement: Alphabetical.

★2222★ Opportunities Abroad for Educators

Fulbright Teacher and Administrator Exchange Program
600 Maryland Ave. SW, Ste. 320
Washington, DC 20024-2520
Ph: (202)314-3527   Fax: (202)479-6806
Fr: 800-726-0479
URL: http://www.fulbrightexchanges.org

Annual. Covers opportunities available for elementary and secondary teachers, two-year college instructors, and school administrators to attend seminars or to teach abroad under the Mutual Educational and Cultural Exchange Act of 1961. Entries include:

Countries of placement, dates, eligibility requirements, teaching assignments. Arrangement: Geographical.

★2223★ Patterson's Schools Classified

Educational Directories Inc.
PO Box 68097
Schaumburg, IL 60168
Ph: (847)891-1250   Fax: (847)891-0945
Fr: 800-357-6183
URL: http://www.ediusa.com

Annual; latest edition 2007, volume 57. $18.00 for individuals. Covers over 7,000 accredited colleges, universities, community colleges, junior colleges, career schools and teaching hospitals. Entries include: School name, address, phone, URL, e-mail, name of administrator or admissions officer, description, professional accreditation (where applicable). Updated from previous year's edition of 'Patterson's American Education'. Arrangement: Classified by area of study, then geographical by state. Indexes: Alphabetical by name.

★2224★ School Guide

School Guide Publications
210 N Ave.
New Rochelle, NY 10801
Ph: (914)632-7771   Fax: (914)632-3412
Fr: 800-433-7771
URL: http://distance.schoolguides.com/

Annual, September. Covers over 3,000 colleges, vocational schools, and nursing schools in the United States. Entries include: Institution name, address, phone, courses offered, degrees awarded. Arrangement: Classified by type of institution, then geographical. Indexes: Subject.

★2225★ Who's Who in American Law

Marquis Who's Who L.L.C.
890 Mountain Ave., Ste. 300
New Providence, NJ 07974-1218
Ph: (908)673-1001   Fax: (908)673-1189
Fr: 800-473-7020
E-mail: law@marquiswhoswho.com
URL: http://www.marquiswhoswho.com/

Biennial; latest edition 2007-2008. $345.00 for individuals. Covers over 15,000 lawyers, judges, law school deans and professors, and other legal professionals. Entries include: Name, home and office addresses, place and date of birth, educational background, career history, civic positions, professional memberships, publications, awards, special achievements. Arrangement: Alphabetical. Indexes: Fields of practice; professional area.

HANDBOOKS AND MANUALS

★2226★ America's Top Medical, Education, and Human Service Jobs, Fifth Edition

JIST Publishing
875 Montreal Way
St. Paul, MN 55102
Fax: 800-547-8329   Fr: 800-648-5478
E-mail: info@jist.com
URL: http://www.jist.com

Michael Farr. 2001. $9.95. 352 pages. Targeted reference organized into three sections that offer comprehensive job descriptions, job search advice, and current trends in jobs and industries.

★2227★ Career Opportunities for Writers

Facts On File Inc.
132 W. 31st St., 17th Fl.
New York, NY 10001-2006
Ph: (212)967-8800   Fax: 800-678-3633
Fr: 800-322-8755
E-mail: custserv@factsonfile.com
URL: http://www.factsonfile.com

Rosemary Ellen Guiley and Janet Frick. 2nd edition, 1991. $49.50. 230 pages. Part of the Career Opportunities Series. Describes more than 100 jobs in eight major fields, offering such details as duties, salaries, perquisites, employment and advancement opportunities, organizations to join, and opportunities for women and minorities.

★2228★ Careers in Horticulture and Botany

The McGraw-Hill Companies
PO Box 182604
Columbus, OH 43272
Fax: (614)759-3749   Fr: 877-883-5524
E-mail: customer.service@mcgraw-hill.com
URL: http://www.mcgraw-hill.com

Jerry Garner. 2006. 15.95 (paper). 192 pages. Includes bibliographical references.

★2229★ Careers in Journalism

The McGraw-Hill Companies
PO Box 182604
Columbus, OH 43272
Fax: (614)759-3749   Fr: 877-883-5524
E-mail: customer.service@mcgraw-hill.com
URL: http://www.mcgraw-hill.com

Jan Goldberg. Third edition, 2005. $15.95 (paper). 192 pages.

★2230★ Clinician to Academician: A Handbook for Those who Aspire to Become Faculty Members

American Occupational Therapy
  Association Inc.
4720 Montgomery Ln.
PO Box 31220
Bethesda, MD 20824-1220
Ph: (301)652-2682   Fax: (301)652-7711
Fr: 800-729-2682

URL: http://www.aota.org/

Caroline R. Brayley. 1996. $20.00 (paper). 158 pages.

★2231★ Educational Pathways: A Faculty Development Resource

Cengage Learning
PO Box 6904
Florence, KY 41022
Fax: 800-487-8488   Fr: 800-354-9706
URL: http://www.cengage.com/

Kathryn Kalanick. 2006. $69.95. Provides a three-track approach to address the training needs of instructors and educators by following the experiences of three educators from various backgrounds.

★2232★ Great Jobs for English Majors

The McGraw-Hill Companies
PO Box 182604
Columbus, OH 43272
Fax: (614)759-3749   Fr: 877-883-5524
E-mail: customer.service@mcgraw-hill.com
URL: http://www.mcgraw-hill.com

Julie DeGalan. Third edition, 2006. $15.95 (paper). 192 pages.

★2233★ Great Jobs for History Majors

The McGraw-Hill Companies
PO Box 182604
Columbus, OH 43272
Fax: (614)759-3749   Fr: 877-883-5524
E-mail: customer.service@mcgraw-hill.com
URL: http://www.mcgraw-hill.com

Julie DeGalan and Stephen Lambert. 2001. $15.95 (paper). 256 pages.

★2234★ Great Jobs for Liberal Arts Majors

The McGraw-Hill Companies
PO Box 182604
Columbus, OH 43272
Fax: (614)759-3749   Fr: 877-883-5524
E-mail: customer.service@mcgraw-hill.com
URL: http://www.mcgraw-hill.com

Blythe Camenson. Second edition, 2001. $14.95 (paper). 256 pages.

★2235★ Great Jobs for Music Majors

The McGraw-Hill Companies
PO Box 182604
Columbus, OH 43272
Fax: (614)759-3749   Fr: 877-883-5524
E-mail: customer.service@mcgraw-hill.com
URL: http://www.mcgraw-hill.com

Jan Goldberg, Stephen Lambert, Julie DeGalan. Second edition, 2004. $15.95 (paper). 180 pages.

★2236★ Great Jobs for Sociology Majors

The McGraw-Hill Companies
PO Box 182604
Columbus, OH 43272
Fax: (614)759-3749   Fr: 877-883-5524

E-mail: customer.service@mcgraw-hill.com
URL: http://www.mcgraw-hill.com

Stephen Lambert. Second edition, 2002. $15.95 (paper). 224 pages.

★2237★ Great Jobs for Theater Majors

The McGraw-Hill Companies
PO Box 182604
Columbus, OH 43272
Fax: (614)759-3749   Fr: 877-883-5524
E-mail: customer.service@mcgraw-hill.com
URL: http://www.mcgraw-hill.com

Jan Goldberg and Julie DeGalan. 2005. $15.95 (paper). 192 pages.

★2238★ How to Get the Teaching Position You Want: Teacher Candidate Guide

Educational Enterprises
PO Box 1836
Spring Valley, CA 91979
Ph: (619)660-7720

Phyllis Murton. Second edition, revised, 1996. $19.95 (paper). 110 pages. This book provides a comprehensive guide for the teacher candidate's job search, as the format offers information that includes: interview questions most often asked in the teaching interview (grade-level and subject-matter specific); sample forms for applications, cover letters, and resumes that will impact principals and district personnel; strategies on preparing for the teaching interview; interview follow-up techniques; inside tips from a superintendent, a principal and a counselor.

★2239★ Increasing Faculty Diversity: The Occupational Choices of High-Achieving Minority Students

Harvard University Press
79 Garden St
Cambridge, MA 02138
Ph: (401)531-2800   Fax: 800-406-9145
Fr: 800-405-1619
URL: http://www.hup.harvard.edu/

Stephen Cole, Elinor Barber. January 2003. $51.50. Illustrated. 384 pages. Education teachers about minority opportunities.

★2240★ Job Search in Academe: Strategic Rhetorics for Faculty Job Candidates

Routledge
270 Madison Ave.
New York, NY 10016
Ph: (212)216-7800   Fax: (212)563-2269
URL: http://www.routledge.com/

Dawn M. Formo and Cheryl Reed. 1999. $51.95. 230 pages. Identifies opportunities for job seekers in the humanities and social sciences, and advises on the preparation of effective CV's and portfolios.

★2241★ On the Market: Surviving the Academic Job Search

Riverhead Books
375 Hudson St.
New York, NY 10014
Ph: (212)366-2000   Fax: (212)366-2385
URL: http://us.penguingroup.com/static/html/riverhead/index.html

Christina Boufis and Victoria C. Olsen, editors. 1997. $12.95 (paper). 381 pages. A guide for Ph.D.'s seeking an academic position.

★2242★ Opportunities in Overseas Careers

The McGraw-Hill Companies
PO Box 182604
Columbus, OH 43272
Fax: (614)759-3749   Fr: 877-883-5524
E-mail: customer.service@mcgraw-hill.com
URL: http://www.mcgraw-hill.com

Blythe Camenson. 2004. $13.95 (paper). 173 pages.

★2243★ Opportunities in Teaching Careers

The McGraw-Hill Companies
PO Box 182604
Columbus, OH 43272
Fax: (614)759-3749   Fr: 877-883-5524
E-mail: customer.service@mcgraw-hill.com
URL: http://www.mcgraw-hill.com

Janet Fine. 2005. $13.95 (paper). 160 pages. Discusses licensing and accreditation programs, sources of placement information, job-seeking correspondence, selection procedures, and paths to advancement. Also covers professional associations, non-traditional teaching opportunities, and jobs abroad.

★2244★ Opportunities in Technical Education Careers

The McGraw-Hill Companies
PO Box 182604
Columbus, OH 43272
Fax: (614)759-3749   Fr: 877-883-5524
E-mail: customer.service@mcgraw-hill.com
URL: http://www.mcgraw-hill.com

Robert Connelly. 1998. 160 pages. $14.95; $11.95 (paper).

★2245★ Real People Working in Education

The McGraw-Hill Companies
PO Box 182604
Columbus, OH 43272
Fax: (614)759-3749   Fr: 877-883-5524
E-mail: customer.service@mcgraw-hill.com
URL: http://www.mcgraw-hill.com

Blythe Camenson, Jan Goldberg. 1997. $17.95; $12.95 (paper). 160 pages/ Interviews and profiles of working professionals capture a range of opportunities in this field.

★2246★ Tomorrow's Professor: Preparing for Academic Careers in Science and Engineering

John Wiley & Sons Inc.
1 Wiley Dr.
Somerset, NJ 08873
Ph: (732)469-4400   Fax: (732)302-2300
Fr: 800-225-5945
E-mail: custserv@wiley.com
URL: http://www.wiley.com/WileyCDA/

Rick Reis. 2001. $62.95 (paper). 440 pages. Contains advice for graduate students, post-doctorate fellows and workers, nontenured professors, and future PhD's.

EMPLOYMENT AGENCIES AND SEARCH FIRMS

★2247★ Berardi & Associates

1140 Ave. of the Americas, Fl. 8
New York, NY 10036
Ph: (212)403-6180   Fax: (212)764-9690
E-mail: jmiranda@spges.com
URL: http://www.spgjobs.com

Executive search firm.

★2248★ Boston Search Group Inc.

224 Clarendon St., Ste. 41
Boston, MA 02116-3729
Ph: (617)266-4333   Fax: (781)735-0562
E-mail: rprotsik@bostonsearchgroup.com
URL: http://www.bostonsearchgroup.com

Executive search firm.

★2249★ Brigham Hill Consultancy

2909 Cole Ave., Ste. 220
Dallas, TX 75204
Ph: (214)871-8700   Fax: (214)871-6004
E-mail: brigham@brighamhill.com
URL: http://www.brighamhill.com

Executive search firm.

★2250★ CHM Partners International LLC

466 Southern Blvd.
Chatham, NJ 07928
Ph: (973)966-1600   Fax: (973)966-6933
E-mail: solutions@chm-partners.com
URL: http://www.chm-partners.com

Executive search firm.

★2251★ Compass Group Ltd.

Birmingham Place Bldg.
401 S. Old Woodward, Ste. 460
Birmingham, MI 48009-6613
Ph: (248)540-9110   Fax: (248)647-8288
E-mail: executiveserach@compassgroup.com
URL: http://www.compassgroup.com

Executive search firm. Second location in Oak Brook, IL.

★2252★ The Dalley Hewitt Company

3075 Howell Mill Rd., NW Unit 11
Atlanta, GA 30327
Ph: (404)992-5065   Fax: (404)355-6136
E-mail: rives@dalleyhewitt.com
URL: http://www.dalleyhewitt.com

Executive search firm.

★2253★ Deerfield Associates

572 Washington St., Ste. 15
Wellesley, MA 02482
Ph: (781)237-2800   Fax: (781)237-5600
E-mail: jobs@deerfieldassociates.com
URL: http://www.deerfieldassociates.com

Executive search firm.

★2254★ Development Resource Group Inc (DRG)

104 E. 40th St., Ste. 304
New York, NY 10016
Ph: (212)983-1600   Fax: (212)983-1687
E-mail: search@drgnyc.com
URL: http://www.drgnyc.com

Executive search firm.

★2255★ Dunn Associates

229 Limberline Dr.
Greensburg, PA 15601
Ph: (724)832-9822   Fax: (724)832-9836
Fr: 877-586-2538
E-mail: maddunn@aol.com
URL: http://www.dunnassociatesinc.com/

Executive search firm.

★2256★ EFL Associates

7101 College Blvd., Ste. 550
Overland Park, KS 66210-2075
Ph: (913)451-8866   Fax: (913)451-7490
E-mail: eflinfo@eflassociates.com
URL: http://www.eflassociates.com

Executive search firm. Locations in Englewood, CO and Lake Forest, IL.

★2257★ Ford Webb Associates Inc.

27 Main St.
Concord, MA 01742
Ph: (978)371-4900
E-mail: info@fordwebb.com
URL: http://www.fordwebb.com

Executive search firm.

★2258★ Perez-Arton Consultants Inc.

23 Spring St., Ste. 204B
Ossining, NY 10562
Ph: (914)762-2103   Fax: (914)762-7834
E-mail: perezart@bestweb.net

Provides executive searches for major academic and administrative units. Conducts institutional evaluations and executive staff assessments. Firm works for colleges, universities and education-related non-profits only.

★2259★ P.N. French Associates Inc.

126 Noell Farm Rd.
Carlisle, MA 01741
Ph: (978)369-4569

Executive search firm.

★2260★ Sunny Bates Associates

1123 Broadway, Ste. 311
New York, NY 10010
Ph: (212)691-5252   Fax: (212)691-3133
E-mail: info@sunnybates.com
URL: http://www.sunnybates.com

Executive search firm.

★2261★ Witt/Kieffer

2015 Spring Rd., Ste. 510
Oak Brook, IL 60523
Ph: (630)990-1370   Fax: (630)990-1382
URL: http://www.wittkieffer.com

Executive search firm with five locations throughout the United States.

ONLINE JOB SOURCES AND SERVICES

★2262★ Academic360.com

Internet Employment Linkage, Inc.
E-mail: webmaster@academic360.com
URL: http://www.academic360.com/

Description: Site is a collection of internet resources gathered for the academic job hunter. Contains links to over 1,400 colleges and universities that advertise job openings online. Positions listed are not limited to teaching positions.

TRADESHOWS

★2263★ American Association of Physics Teachers Winter Meeting

American Association of Physics Teachers (AAPT)
1 Physics Ellipse
College Park, MD 20740-3845
Ph: (301)209-3300   Fax: (301)209-0845
E-mail: aapt-web@aapt.org
URL: http://www.aapt.org

Annual. **Primary Exhibits:** Physics textbooks, apparatus, and software.

★2264★ American Society for Engineering Education Annual Conference and Exposition

American Society for Engineering Education
1818 N. St. NW, Ste. 600
Washington, DC 20036-2479
Ph: (202)331-3500   Fax: (202)265-8504
E-mail: conferences@asee.org
URL: http://www.asee.org

Annual. **Primary Exhibits:** Publications, engineering supplies and equipment, computers, software, and research companies all products and services related to engineering education.

★2265★ American Technical Education Association National Conference on Technical Education

American Technical Education Association
c/o North Dakota State College of Science
800 N. 6th St.
Wahpeton, ND 58076-0002
Ph: (701)671-2301   Fax: (701)671-2260
URL: http://www.ateaonline.org

Annual. **Primary Exhibits:** Supplies and services related to post secondary technical education.

★2266★ Association for Education in Journalism and Mass Communication Annual Convention

Association for Education in Journalism and Mass Communication
234 Outlet Point Blvd.
Columbia, SC 29210-5667
Ph: (803)798-0271   Fax: (803)772-3509
E-mail: aejmcmemsub@aol.com
URL: http://www.aejmc.org

Annual. **Primary Exhibits:** Publications, information retrieval services, and special programs.

★2267★ Council of Graduate Schools Annual Meeting

Council of Graduate Schools
1 Dupont Cir. NW, Ste. 430
Washington, DC 20036-1173
Ph: (202)223-3791   Fax: (202)331-7157
E-mail: ngaffney@cgs.nche.edu
URL: http://www.cgsnet.org

Annual. **Primary Exhibits:** Exhibits related to the improvement and advancement of graduate education.

★2268★ Northwest Association of Schools and Colleges Meeting

Northwest Association of Schools and Colleges
1910 University Dr.
Boise, ID 83725-1060
Ph: (208)426-5727   Fax: (208)334-3228
E-mail: Northwest@boisestate.edu
URL: http://www2.boisestate.edu/nasc

Annual. **Primary Exhibits:** Educational equipment, supplies, and services.

★2269★ Southwestern Federation of Administrative Disciplines Convention

Southwestern Federation of Administrative Disciplines
2700 Bay Area Blvd.
Houston, TX 77058
Ph: (713)283-3122   Fax: (713)283-3951

Annual. **Primary Exhibits:** Educational materials and services.

★2270★ UCEA Annual Conference

National University Continuing Education Association
1 Dupont Cir., Ste. 615
Washington, DC 20036
Ph: (202)659-3130   Fax: (202)785-0374
URL: http://www.ucea.edu

Annual. **Primary Exhibits:** Exhibits related to continuing education and online learning at institutions of higher learning.

OTHER SOURCES

★2271★ Academy of International Business (AIB)

The Eli Broad College of Business
Michigan State University
7 Eppley Center
East Lansing, MI 48824-1121
Ph: (517)432-1452   Fax: (517)432-1009
E-mail: aib@aib.msu.edu
URL: http://aib.msu.edu

Description: Consists primarily of university professors, doctoral students, researchers, writers, consultants, executives, and policy setters in the international business/trade research and education fields. Facilitates information exchange among people in academia, business, and government and encourages research activities that advance the knowledge of international business operations and increase the available body of teaching materials. Compiles an inventory of collegiate courses in international business, a survey of research projects, and statistics.

★2272★ Academy of Legal Studies in Business (ALSB)

120 Upham Hall - Dept. of Finance
Miami University
Oxford, OH 45056
Fax: (513)523-8180
E-mail: herrondj@muohio.edu
URL: http://www.alsb.org

Description: Teachers of business law and legal environment in colleges and universities. Promotes and encourages business law scholarship and teaching outside of the law school environment.

★2273★ Academy of Marketing Science (AMS)

University of Miami
School of Business Administration
PO Box 248012
Coral Gables, FL 33124-6536
Ph: (305)284-6673   Fax: (305)284-3762
E-mail: ams.sba@miami.edu
URL: http://www.ams-web.org

Description: Marketing academicians and practitioners; individuals interested in fostering education in marketing science. Aims to promote the advancement of knowledge and the furthering of professional standards in the field of marketing. Explores the special application areas of marketing science and its responsibilities as an economic, ethical, and social force; promotes research and the widespread dissemination of findings. Facilitates exchange of information and experience among members, and the transfer of marketing knowledge and technology to developing countries; promotes marketing science on an international level. Provides a forum for discussion and refinement of concepts, methods and applications, and the opportunity to publish papers in the field. Assists member educators in the development of improved teaching methods, devices, directions, and materials. Offers guidance and direction in marketing practice and reviewer assistance on scholarly works. Contributes to the solution of marketing problems encountered by individual firms, industries, and society as a whole. Encourages members to utilize their marketing talents to the fullest through redirection, reassignment, and relocation. Sponsors competitions.

★2274★ American Almanac of Jobs and Salaries

HarperCollins
10 E. 53rd St.
New York, NY 10022
Ph: (212)207-7000   Fr: 800-242-7737
URL: http://www.harpercollins.com/

John W. Wright. Revised edition, 2000. $20.00 (paper). 672 pages. This is a comprehensive guide to the wages of hundreds of occupations in a wide variety of industries and organizations.

★2275★ American Association of Community Colleges (AACC)

1 Dupont Cir. NW, Ste. 410
Washington, DC 20036-1176
Ph: (202)728-0200   Fax: (202)833-2467
E-mail: gboggs@aacc.nche.edu
URL: http://www.aacc.nche.edu

Members: Community colleges; individual associates interested in community college development; corporate, educational, foundation, and international associate members. **Purpose:** Office of Federal Relations monitors federal educational programming and legislation. **Activities:** Compiles statistics through data collection and policy analysis. Conducts seminars and professional training programs.

★2276★ American Association for Health Education (AAHE)

1900 Association Dr.
Reston, VA 20191-1599
Ph: (703)476-3437   Fax: (703)476-6638
Fr: 800-213-7193
E-mail: aahe@aahperd.org
URL: http://www.aahperd.org/aahe

Members: Professionals who have responsibility for health education in schools, colleges, communities, hospitals and clinics, and industries. **Purpose:** Aims to advance the health education through program activities and federal legislation; encourage close working relationships between all health education and health service organizations; achieve good health and well-being for all Americans automatically, without conscious thought and endeavor. Member of the American Alliance for Health, Physical Education, Recreation and Dance.

★2277★ American Association of Teachers of German (AATG)

112 Haddontowne Ct., No. 104
Cherry Hill, NJ 08034-3668
Ph: (856)795-5553   Fax: (856)795-9398
E-mail: headquarters@aatg.org
URL: http://www.aatg.org

Description: Represents teachers of German at all levels; individuals interested in German language and culture. Offers in-service teacher-training workshops, materials, student honor society, national German examination and stipends/scholarships.

★2278★ American Association for Women in Community Colleges (AAWCC)

PO Box 336603
Greeley, CO 80633-0611
Ph: (970)352-2079   Fax: (970)352-2080
E-mail: aawcc@comcast.net
URL: http://www.aawccnatl.org

Description: Women faculty members, administrators, staff members, students, and trustees of community colleges. Objectives are to: develop communication and disseminate information among women in community, junior, and technical colleges; encourage educational program development; obtain grants for educational projects for community college women. Disseminates information on women's issues and programs. Conducts regional and state professional development workshops and forums. Recognizes model programs that assist women in community colleges. An affiliate council of the American Association of Community Colleges.

★2279★ American Catholic Philosophical Association (ACPA)

University of St. Thomas
Centre for Thomistic Studies
3800 Montrose Blvd.
Houston, TX 77006
Ph: (713)942-3483   Fax: (713)942-3464
E-mail: osborntm@stthom.edu
URL: http://www.acpaweb.org

Description: College and university teachers of philosophy; students engaged in research; writers and others interested in philosophical knowledge.

★2280★ **American Society of Psychopathology of Expression (ASPE)**

74 Lawton St.
Brookline, MA 02446
Ph: (617)738-9821   Fax: (617)975-0411

Description: Psychiatrists, psychologists, art therapists, sociologists, art critics, artists, social workers, linguists, educators, criminologists, writers, and historians. At least two-thirds of the members must be physicians. Fosters collaboration among specialists in the United States who are interested in the problems of expression and in the artistic activities connected with psychiatric, sociological, and psychological research. Disseminates information about research and clinical applications in the field of psychopathology of expression. Sponsors consultations, seminars, and lectures on art therapy.

★2281★ **Art Directors Club (ADC)**

106 W 29th St.
New York, NY 10001
Ph: (212)643-1440   Fax: (212)643-4266
E-mail: info@adcglobal.org
URL: http://www.adcglobal.org

Members: Art directors of advertising magazines and agencies, visual information specialists, and graphic designers; associate members are artists, cinematographers, photographers, copywriters, educators, journalists, and critics. **Purpose:** Promotes and stimulates interest in the practice of art direction. **Activities:** Sponsors Annual Exhibition of Advertising, Editorial and Television Art and Design; International Traveling Exhibition. Provides educational, professional, and entertainment programs; on-premise art exhibitions; portfolio review program. Conducts panels for students and faculty.

★2282★ **Association of Departments of English (ADE)**

26 Broadway, 3rd Fl.
New York, NY 10004-1789
Ph: (646)576-5130   Fax: (646)835-4056
E-mail: dlaurence@mla.org
URL: http://www.ade.org

Description: Administrators of college and university departments of English, humanities, rhetoric, and communications. Works to improve the teaching of English and the administration of English departments. Conducts studies and surveys of literature and writing courses. Sponsors sessions at major English conventions and conferences nationwide. Sponsored by Modern Language Association of America.

★2283★ **Association for Education in Journalism and Mass Communication (AEJMC)**

234 Outlet Pointe Blvd.
Columbia, SC 29210-5667
Ph: (803)798-0271   Fax: (803)772-3509

E-mail: aejmc@aejmc.org
URL: http://www.aejmc.org

Description: Professional organization of college and university journalism and communication teachers. Works to improve methods and standards of teaching and stimulate research. Compiles statistics on enrollments and current developments in journalism education. Maintains a listing of journalism and communication teaching positions available and teaching positions wanted, revised bimonthly.

★2284★ **Association for Library and Information Science Education (ALISE)**

65 E Wacker Pl., Ste. 1900
Chicago, IL 60601-7246
Ph: (312)795-0996   Fax: (312)419-8950
E-mail: contact@alise.org
URL: http://www.alise.org

Description: Graduate schools offering degree programs in library science and their faculties. Seeks to: promote excellence in education for library and information science as a means of increasing the effectiveness of library and information services; provide a forum for the active interchange of ideas and information among library educators; promote research related to teaching and to library and information science; formulate and promulgate positions on matters related to library education. Offers employment program at annual conference.

★2285★ **Association for the Study of Higher Education (ASHE)**

Michigan State University
424 Erickson Hall
East Lansing, MI 48824
Ph: (517)432-8805   Fax: (517)432-8806
E-mail: ashemsu@msu.edu
URL: http://www.ashe.ws

Description: Professors, researchers, administrators, policy analysts, graduate students, and others concerned with the study of higher education. Aims to advance the study of higher education and facilitate and encourage discussion of priority issues for research in the study of higher education.

★2286★ **College Reading and Learning Association (CRLA)**

PO Box 382
El Dorado, KS 67042
Ph: (307)382-1725   Fax: (316)322-7369
E-mail: staylor@wwcc.wy.edu
URL: http://www.crla.net

Description: Professionals involved in college/adult reading, learning assistance, developmental education, and tutorial services. Promotes communication for the purpose of professional growth.

★2287★ **Conference on College Composition and Communication (CCCC)**

1111 W Kenyon Rd.
Urbana, IL 61801-1096
Ph: (217)328-3870   Fax: (217)328-9645
Fr: 877-369-6283
E-mail: public_info@ncte.org

Description: Represents college and university educators involved in teaching composition and communication.

★2288★ **Council of American Instructors of the Deaf (CAID)**

PO Box 377
Bedford, TX 76095-0377
Ph: (817)354-8414
E-mail: caid@swbell.net
URL: http://www.caid.org

Members: Professional organization of teachers, administrators, and professionals in allied fields related to education of the deaf and hard-of-hearing. **Purpose:** Provides opportunities for a free interchange of views concerning methods and means of educating the deaf and hard-of-hearing. Promotes such education by the publication of reports, essays, and other information. Develops more effective methods of teaching deaf and hard-of-hearing children.

★2289★ **Eastern Finance Association (EFA)**

Auburn Montgomery
School of Business
PO Box 244023
Montgomery, AL 36124-4023
E-mail: membershipservices@blackwellpublishers.co.uk
URL: http://www.easternfinance.org

Description: College and university professors and financial officers; libraries. Provides a meeting place for persons interested in any aspect of finance, including financial management, investments, and banking. Sponsors research competitions.

★2290★ **Education and Training**

Cambridge Educational
PO Box 2053
Princeton, NJ 08543-2053
Ph: 800-257-5126   Fax: (609)671-0266
Fr: 800-468-4227
E-mail: custserv@films.com
URL: http://www.cambridgeeducational.com

VHS and DVD. $89.95. 2002. 18 minutes. Presents four distinct occupations in the field: elementary teachers, teacher's aides, administrators, and librarians. People working in these jobs discuss their responsibilities.

★2291★ **Friends Council on Education (FCE)**

1507 Cherry St.
Philadelphia, PA 19102
Ph: (215)241-7245   Fax: (215)241-7299
E-mail: info@friendscouncil.org
URL: http://www.friendscouncil.org

Members: Representatives appointed by Friends Yearly Meetings; heads of Quaker secondary and elementary schools and colleges; members-at-large. **Purpose:** Acts as a clearinghouse for information on Quaker schools and colleges. **Activities:** Holds meetings and conferences on education and provides in-service training for teachers, administrators and trustees in Friends schools.

★2292★ How to Prepare Your Curriculum Vitae

The McGraw-Hill Companies
PO Box 182604
Columbus, OH 43272
Fax: (614)759-3749   Fr: 877-883-5524
E-mail: customer.service@mcgraw-hill.com
URL: http://www.mcgraw-hill.com

Acy L. Jackson. Third edition, 2003. $12.95 (paper). 136 pages. Dozens of examples from academics in all disciplines and at all career levels illustrate the principles of writing an effective C.V. Worksheets guide the reader through a step-by-step process that begins with describing, in draft form, all pertinent experiences, and then helps shape, organize, and edit experiences and credentials into a professional curriculum vitae. Includes sample cover letters tailored to academic institutions.

★2293★ Modern Language Association of America (MLA)

26 Broadway, 3rd Fl.
New York, NY 10004-1789
Ph: (646)576-5000   Fax: (646)458-0300
E-mail: execdirector@mla.org
URL: http://www.mla.org

Description: Provides opportunities for the members to share their scholarly findings and teaching experiences with colleagues and to discuss trends in the academy. Works to strengthen the study and teaching of language and literature.

★2294★ NAFSA/Association of International Educators (NAFSA)

1307 New York Ave. NW, 8th Fl.
Washington, DC 20005-4701
Ph: (202)737-3699   Fax: (202)737-3657
E-mail: inbox@nafsa.org
URL: http://www.nafsa.org

Description: Individuals, organizations, and institutions dealing with international educational exchange, including foreign student advisers, overseas educational advisers, credentials and admissions officers, administrators and teachers of English as a second language, community support personnel, study-abroad administrators, and embassy cultural or educational personnel. Promotes self-regulation standards and responsibilities in international educational exchange; offers professional development opportunities primarily through publications, workshops, grants, and regional and national conferences. Advocates for increased awareness and support of international education and exchange on campuses, in government, and

in communities. Offers services including: a job registry for employers and professionals involved with international education; a consultant referral service. Sponsors joint liaison activities with a variety of other educational and government organizations to conduct a census of foreign student enrollment in the U.S.; conducts workshops about specific subjects and countries.

★2295★ National Art Education Association (NAEA)

1916 Association Dr.
Reston, VA 20191-1502
Ph: (703)860-8000   Fax: (703)860-2960
E-mail: info@naea-reston.org
URL: http://www.naea-reston.org

Members: Teachers of art at elementary, middle, secondary, and college levels; colleges, libraries, museums, and other educational institutions. **Purpose:** Studies problems of teaching art; encourages research and experimentation. **Activities:** Serves as a clearinghouse for information on art education programs, materials, and methods of instruction. Sponsors special institutes. Cooperates with other national organizations for the furtherance of creative art experiences for youth.

★2296★ National Association of Blind Teachers (NABT)

1155 15th St. NW, Ste. 1004
Washington, DC 20005
Ph: (202)467-5081   Fax: (202)467-5085
Fr: 800-424-8666
E-mail: info@acb.org
URL: http://www.acb.org

Description: Public school teachers, college and university professors, and teachers in residential schools for the blind. Promotes employment and professional goals of blind persons entering the teaching profession or those established in their respective teaching fields. Serves as a vehicle for the dissemination of information and the exchange of ideas addressing special problems of members. Compiles statistics.

★2297★ National Association of College and University Business Officers (NACUBO)

1110 Vermont Ave. NW, Ste. 800
Washington, DC 20005
Ph: (202)861-2500   Fax: (202)861-2583
Fr: 800-462-4916
E-mail: john.walda@nacubo.org
URL: http://www.nacubo.org

Members: Colleges, universities, and companies that are members of a regional association. **Purpose:** Develops and maintains national interest in improving the principles and practices of business and financial administration in higher education. **Activities:** Sponsors workshops in fields such as cash management, grant and contract maintenance, accounting, investment, student loan administration, and costing. Conducts research and information exchange programs between college and university personnel; compiles statistics.

★2298★ National Council for Geographic Education (NCGE)

206A Martin Hall
Jacksonville State University
Jacksonville, AL 36265-1602
Ph: (256)782-5293   Fax: (256)782-5336
E-mail: ncge@ncge.org
URL: http://www.ncge.org

Description: Teachers of geography and social studies in elementary and secondary schools, colleges and universities; geographers in governmental agencies and private businesses. Encourages the training of teachers in geographic concepts, practices, teaching methods and techniques; works to develop effective geographic educational programs in schools and colleges and with adult groups; stimulates the production and use of accurate and understandable geographic teaching aids and materials.

★2299★ National Council of Teachers of Mathematics (NCTM)

1906 Association Dr.
Reston, VA 20191-1502
Ph: (703)620-9840   Fax: (703)476-2970
Fr: 800-235-7566
E-mail: inquiries@nctm.org
URL: http://www.nctm.org

Description: Aims to improve teaching and learning of mathematics.

★2300★ Organization of American Historians (OAH)

PO Box 5457
Bloomington, IN 47407-5457
Ph: (812)855-9852   Fax: (812)855-0696
E-mail: oah@oah.org
URL: http://www.oah.org

Description: Professional historians, including college faculty members, secondary school teachers, graduate students, and other individuals in related fields; institutional subscribers are college, university, high school and public libraries, and historical agencies. Promotes historical research and study. Sponsors 12 prize programs for historical writing; maintains speakers' bureau. Conducts educational programs.

★2301★ Overseas Employment Opportunities for Educators: Department of Defense Dependents Schools

DIANE Publishing Co.
PO Box 617
Darby, PA 19023-0617
Ph: (610)461-6200   Fax: (610)461-6130
Fr: 800-782-3833
URL: http://www.dianepublishingcentral.com

Barry Leonard, editor. 2000. $15.00. 54 pages. An introduction to teachings positions in the Dept. of Defense Dependents Schools (DoDDS), a worldwide school system, operated by the DoD in 14 countries.

★2302★ Teaching & Related Occupations

Delphi Productions
3159 6th St.
Boulder, CO 80304

Ph: (303)443-2100   Fax: (303)443-4022
Fr: 888-443-2400
E-mail: support@delphivideo.com
URL: http://www.delphivideo.com

$95.00. 50 minutes. Part of the Careers for the 21st Century Video Library.

Computer and Information Systems Managers

★2303★ ACM Transactions on Internet Technology (ACM TOIT)
Association for Computing Machinery
2 Penn Plz., Ste. 701
New York, NY 10121-0701
Ph: (212)869-7440   Fax: (212)944-1318
Fr: 800-342-6626
URL: http://www.acm.org/pubs/periodicals/toit/

Quarterly. $35.00/year for members; $30.00/year for students; $140.00/year for nonmembers; $170.00/year for individuals, print only; $136.00 for single issue, online only; $204.00 for single issue, online & print. Publication of the Association for Computing Machinery. Brings together many computing disciplines including computer software engineering, computer programming languages, middleware, database management, security, knowledge discovery and data mining, networking and distributed systems, communications, performance and scalability, and more. Covers the results and roles of the individual disciplines and the relationships among them.

★2304★ AVIOS Journal
Applied Voice Input/Output Society
PO Box 20817
San Jose, CA 95160
Ph: (408)323-1783   Fax: (408)323-1782
E-mail: info@avios.org
URL: http://www.avios.com/

Annual. Journal covering issues in computer science.

★2305★ Communications of the ACM
Association for Computing Machinery
2 Penn Plz., Ste. 701
New York, NY 10121-0701
Ph: (212)869-7440   Fax: (212)944-1318
Fr: 800-342-6626
URL: http://www.acm.org/pubs/cacm/

Monthly. $179.00/year for nonmembers; $36.00/year for members. Computing news magazine.

★2306★ Component Development Strategies
Paul Harmon
37 Broadway, Ste. 1
Arlington, MA 02474
Ph: (781)648-8700   Fax: (781)648-8707
E-mail: service@cutter.com
URL: http://www.cutter.com

Description: Monthly. Contains product reviews, industry news and trends, and market forecasts. Recurring features include a calendar of events, reports of meetings, and notices of publications available.

★2307★ Computer Economics Networking Strategies Report
Computer Economics Inc.
2082 Business Center Dr. Ste 240
Irvine, CA 92612
Ph: (949)831-8700   Fax: (949)442-7688
Fr: 800-326-8100
URL: http://www.computereconomics.com

Description: Monthly. Provides an executive overview for Management Information Systems (MIS) and network professionals who are involved in network strategic planning and implementation. Covers such topics as comparative analyses of hardware and software systems, costs of ownership studies, analyses of emerging protocols and standards, and cost-saving opportunities.

★2308★ Computer Economics Report
Computer Economics Inc.
2082 Business Center Dr. Ste 240
Irvine, CA 92612
Ph: (949)831-8700   Fax: (949)442-7688
Fr: 800-326-8100
URL: http://www.computereconomics.com

Description: Monthly. Provides analyses of new IBM technologies and acquisition and financial management strategies from an end-user perspective. Recurring features include cost comparisons, price/performance analyses, new product forecasts, and evaluations of acquisition techniques for medium and large computer systems. Also available in international edition.

★2309★ Computers and Composition
Elsevier Science Inc.
360 Park Ave. S
New York, NY 10010
Ph: (212)989-5800   Fax: (212)633-3990
URL: http://www.elsevier.com

$353.00/year for institutions; $69.00/year for individuals. Journal covering computers in writing classes, programs, and research.

★2310★ Computers Programs/PC World
IDG Communications Inc.
5 Speen St., 3rd. Fl
Framingham, MA 01701
Ph: (508)875-5000   Fax: (508)988-7888
URL: http://www.idg.com

Magazine devoted to IT specialists, covering practical questions of computing including purchase and usage of the computer technology, software, computer components and peripherals.

★2311★ Computerworld/Correio Informatico
IDG Communications Inc.
5 Speen St., 3rd. Fl
Framingham, MA 01701
Ph: (508)875-5000   Fax: (508)988-7888
URL: http://www.idg.com

Weekly. Magazine providing news on latest developments in computer industry.

★2312★ Computerworld Top 100
IDG Communications Inc.
5 Speen St., 3rd. Fl
Framingham, MA 01701
Ph: (508)875-5000   Fax: (508)988-7888
URL: http://www.idg.com

Annual. Magazine for analyzing trends and events of information technology business.

★2313★ Computing SA

IDG Communications Inc.
5 Speen St., 3rd. Fl
Framingham, MA 01701
Ph: (508)875-5000   Fax: (508)988-7888
URL: http://www.idg.com

Monthly. Newspaper focusing computer hardware, software, networking, telecommunications, channel management and online computing.

★2314★ Consumer Electronics Lifestyles

Sandhills Publishing
120 W Harvest Dr.
Lincoln, NE 68521
Ph: (402)479-2181   Fax: (402)479-2195
Fr: 800-331-1978
E-mail: editor@ceLifestyles.com
URL: http://www.celifestyles.com/

Monthly. $12.00/year. Magazine for computer and electronic gadget enthusiasts.

★2315★ Cutter IT Journal

Cutter Information Corp.
37 Broadway, Ste. 1
Arlington, MA 02474
Ph: (781)648-8700   Fax: (781)648-1950
E-mail: itjournal@cutter.com
URL: http://www.cutter.com/itjournal

Description: Monthly. Provides IT managers with practical and objective views on the latest technology and management trends.

★2316★ CXO

IDG Communications Inc.
5 Speen St., 3rd. Fl
Framingham, MA 01701
Ph: (508)875-5000   Fax: (508)988-7888
URL: http://www.idg.com

Monthly. Magazine providing technology information for chief officers and managers.

★2317★ Eclipse Review

BZ Media LLC
7 High St., Ste. 407
Huntington, NY 11743
Ph: (631)421-4158   Fax: (631)421-4130
URL: http://www.eclipsesource.com/contact.htm

Magazine for IT professionals.

★2318★ ENA powered by Network World

IDG Communications Inc.
5 Speen St., 3rd. Fl
Framingham, MA 01701
Ph: (508)875-5000   Fax: (508)988-7888
URL: http://www.idg.com

Monthly. Journal covering information on networking.

★2319★ Foundations of Computational Mathematics

Springer-Verlag New York Inc.
233 Spring St.
New York, NY 10013
Ph: (212)460-1500   Fax: (212)460-1575

Academic journal that publishes articles related to the connections between mathematics and computation, including the interfaces between pure and applied mathematics, numerical analysis and computer science.

★2320★ Foundations and Trends in Networking

Now Publishers
PO Box 1024
Hanover, MA 02339
Ph: (781)871-0245
URL: http://www.nowpublishers.com/product.aspx?product=NET

$315.00/year online only; $355.00/year print and online; $315.00/year online only; $355.00/year print and online. Academic journal publishing new research in computer networking.

★2321★ Government Computer News

PostNewsweek Tech Media
10 G St. NE, Ste. 500
Washington, DC 20002-4228
Ph: (202)772-2500   Fax: (202)772-2511
Fr: (866)447-6864

Semimonthly. Magazine for professionals interested in government IT.

★2322★ HIMSS Insider

Healthcare Information and Management Systems Society
230 E. Ohio St., Ste. 500
Chicago, IL 60611-3270
Ph: (312)664-4467   Fax: (312)664-6143
URL: http://www.himss.org

Description: Monthly. Reports the news of the Healthcare Information and Management Systems Society (HIMSS), which provides leadership in healthcare for the management of technology, information, and change through publications, educational opportunities, and member services.

★2323★ I/S Analyzer

The 400 Group
11300 Rockville Pike, Ste. 1100
Rockville, MD 20852
Ph: (301)287-2700   Fax: (301)816-8945
Fr: 877-440-0477
E-mail: customer@iSeries400experts.com
URL: http://www.iseries400experts.com/ts4/index.jsp

Description: Monthly. Focuses on management issues of concern to information systems and data processing executives. Focuses in-depth on one topic per issue, with commentary, relevant case studies, and a concluding summary.

★2324★ IEEE Security & Privacy Magazine

IEEE Computer Society
10662 Los Vaqueros Cir.
PO Box 3014
Los Alamitos, CA 90720-1314
Ph: (714)821-8380   Fax: (714)821-4010
Fr: 800-272-6657
URL: http://www.computer.org/portal/site/security/

Bimonthly. $24.00/year for members; $29.00/year for nonmembers; $28.00/year for members; $565.00/year for libraries, institution. Journal that aims to explore role and importance of networked infrastructure and developing lasting security solutions.

★2325★ Information Executive

Association of Information Technology Professionals
401 N. Michigan Ave., Ste. 2400
Chicago, IL 60611-4267
Ph: (847)825-8124   Fax: (312)527-6636
Fr: 800-224-9371
E-mail: aitp_hq@aitp.org
URL: http://www.aitp.org/index.jsp

Description: Ten issues/year. Provides up-to-date information on the changes and developments of the information systems industry.

★2326★ Information Security

TechTarget
117 Kendrick St., Ste. 800
Needham, MA 02494
Ph: (781)657-1000   Fax: (781)657-1100
URL: http://searchsecurity.techtarget.com/

Monthly. Free to qualified subscribers. Magazine covering information security topics.

★2327★ Information Technology Adviser

Progressive Business Publications
370 Technology Dr.
Malvern, PA 19355
Ph: (610)695-8600   Fax: (610)647-8089
Fr: 800-220-5000
E-mail: Customer_Service@pbp.com.
URL: http://www.pbp.com/ita1.html

Description: Semimonthly. Presents information to keep IT/IS managers up-to-date on how technology cuts costs, boosts productivity, and makes companies more successful. Recurring features include interviews, news of research, a calendar of events, news of educational opportunities, and a column titled Sharpen Your Judgment.

★2328★ InfoWorld

InfoWorld Media Group
501 Second St.
San Francisco, CA 94107
Fr: 800-227-8365
E-mail: letters@infoworld.com
URL: http://www.infoworld.com/

Weekly. Free to qualified subscribers; $180.00/year for individuals. Weekly publication.

★2329★ IT Focus

IDG Communications Inc.
5 Speen St., 3rd. Fl
Framingham, MA 01701
Ph: (508)875-5000   Fax: (508)988-7888
URL: http://www.idg.com

Online journal focusing mainly on information technology.

★2330★ IT Solutions Guide

SYS-CON Media
135 Chestnut Ridge Rd.
Montvale, NJ 07645
Ph: (201)802-3000   Fax: (201)782-9600
Fr: 888-303-5282
URL: http://itsolutions.sys-con.com/

Quarterly. $4.00/year for individuals, single pdf issue. Magazine for IT professionals.

★2331★ Journal of Computer Science

Science Publications
Vails Gate Heights Dr.
PO Box 879
Vails Gate, NY 12584
URL: http://www.scipub.us/

Bimonthly. $3,500.00/year for individuals; $300.00/year for single issue. Scholarly journal covering many areas of computer science, including: concurrent, parallel and distributed processing; artificial intelligence; image and voice processing; quality software and metrics; computer-aided education; wireless communication; real time processing; evaluative computation; and data bases and information recovery and neural networks.

★2332★ Journal of Computer Systems, Networks, and Communications

Hindawi Publishing Corp.
410 Park Ave., 15th Fl.
287 PMB
New York, NY 10022
E-mail: jcsnc@hindawi.com
URL: http://www.hindawi.com/journals/jcsnc/

$195.00/year for individuals. Journal covering important areas of information technology.

★2333★ Kompiuterija PC World

IDG Communications Inc.
5 Speen St., 3rd. Fl
Framingham, MA 01701
Ph: (508)875-5000   Fax: (508)988-7888
URL: http://www.idg.com

Monthly. Journal providing professionals, business people and users with up-to-date information on computers and the internet.

★2334★ Mikro PC

IDG Communications Inc.
5 Speen St., 3rd. Fl
Framingham, MA 01701
Ph: (508)875-5000   Fax: (508)988-7888
URL: http://www.idg.com

Monthly. Magazine focusing on information technology and digital lifestyle.

★2335★ Monitor

Capital PC User Group
19209 Mt. Airey Rd.
Brookeville, MD 20833
Ph: (301)560-6442   Fax: (301)760-3303
URL: http://monitor.cpcug.org/index.html

Quarterly. Magazine covering computer hardware and software reviews, special interest user group news, advertisers and author/subject index, and calendar of events.

★2336★ NetWorld

IDG Communications Inc.
5 Speen St., 3rd. Fl
Framingham, MA 01701
Ph: (508)875-5000   Fax: (508)988-7888
URL: http://www.idg.com

Monthly. Magazine focusing on networks, security, infrastructure management, wireless, mobile and VOIP technologies.

★2337★ PC Magazine

Ziff-Davis Publishing Co.
28 East 28th St.
New York, NY 10016
Ph: (212)503-3500
E-mail: pcmag@ziffdavis.com
URL: http://www.ziffdavisinternet.com/websites/pcmag

Biweekly. $19.97/year for individuals, 25 issues. Tabloid featuring microcomputer products and developments.

★2338★ PC WORLD

101 Communications
9121 Oakdale Ave., Ste. 101
Chatsworth, CA 91311
Ph: (818)734-1520   Fax: (818)734-1522
URL: http://www.pcworld.com

Quarterly. $20.00/year for individuals, 12 issues; $30.00/year for individuals, 24 issues. Technology or business magazine meeting the informational needs of tech-savvy managers, both at work and at home.

★2339★ Queue

Association for Computing Machinery
2 Penn Plz., Ste. 701
New York, NY 10121-0701
Ph: (212)869-7440   Fax: (212)944-1318
Fr: 800-342-6626
URL: http://www.acmqueue.org/

Monthly. Free, U.S./Canadian residents and all members. Online magazine aimed at the computer professional. Magazine editorial does not provide solutions for the "here-and-now," but instead helps decision-makers plan future projects by examining the challenges and problems they are most likely to face.

★2340★ Report on IBM

DataTrends Publications Inc.
PO Box 4460
Leesburg, VA 20177-8541
Ph: (703)779-0574   Fax: (703)779-2267
E-mail: info-request@datatrendspublications.com
URL: http://www.datatrendspublications.com

Description: Weekly. Involved with International Business Machines Corporation (IBM) activities and lines of business, with emphasis on information systems in businesses, factories and homes. Contains news and articles on new IBM introductions, new markets and market strategies, and industry trends.

★2341★ Revenue

Montgomery Media International
300 Montgomery St., Ste. 1135
San Francisco, CA 94104
Ph: (415)397-2400   Fax: (415)397-2420
URL: http://www.revenuetoday.com/

$30.00/year for individuals. Magazine covering internet marketing strategies.

★2342★ SIGMIS Management Information Systems

Association for Computing Machinery
2 Penn Plaza, Ste.701
New York, NY 10121-0701
Ph: (212)626-0500   Fax: (212)944-1318
Fr: 800-342-6626
E-mail: acmhelp@acm.org
URL: http://www.acm.org/sigmis

Description: Quarterly. Covers information systems and technologies for management.

★2343★ SMB Data

IDG Communications Inc.
5 Speen St., 3rd. Fl
Framingham, MA 01701
Ph: (508)875-5000   Fax: (508)988-7888
URL: http://www.idg.com

Magazine focusing on information technology systems at small and medium-size businesses.

★2344★ SME World

IDG Communications Inc.
5 Speen St., 3rd. Fl
Framingham, MA 01701
Ph: (508)875-5000   Fax: (508)988-7888
URL: http://www.idg.com

Magazine covering articles on technology, technology investments, IT products and services.

★2345★ TecCHANNEL Compact

IDG Communications Inc.
5 Speen St., 3rd. Fl
Framingham, MA 01701
Ph: (508)875-5000   Fax: (508)988-7888
URL: http://www.idg.com

Quarterly. Magazine covering issues of information technology.

★2346★ Technology Trends

Enterprise Technology Corp.
9005 Copper Leaf Lane
Fairfax Station, VA 22039
Ph: (703)690-6147   Fax: (703)690-2057
E-mail: info@enterprisetechcorp.com
URL: http://www.enterprisetechcorp.com

Description: Six issues/year. Discusses news on computer software technology and its perceived value to the business community.

★2347★ Tips & Trucs

IDG Communications Inc.
5 Speen St., 3rd. Fl
Framingham, MA 01701
Ph: (508)875-5000   Fax: (508)988-7888
URL: http://www.idg.com

Monthly. Magazine covering topics on computer hardware, software and the internet.

★2348★ Top 100

IDG Communications Inc.
5 Speen St., 3rd. Fl
Framingham, MA 01701
Ph: (508)875-5000   Fax: (508)988-7888
URL: http://www.idg.com

Annual. Magazine providing analyses, assessments and statistics on information technology industry.

★2349★ Ubiquity

Association for Computing Machinery
2 Penn Plz., Ste. 701
New York, NY 10121-0701
Ph: (212)869-7440   Fax: (212)944-1318
Fr: 800-342-6626
URL: http://www.acm.org/ubiquity/

Weekly. Free to members; $163.00/year for nonmembers, 12 issues. Web-based magazine of the Association for Computing Machinery dedicated to fostering critical analysis and in-depth commentary, including book reviews, on issues relating to the nature, constitution, structure, science, engineering, cognition, technology, practices and paradigms of the IT profession.

★2350★ WebLogic Pro

Fawcette Technical Publications
2600 S El Camino Real, Ste. 300
San Mateo, CA 94403-2332
Ph: (650)378-7100   Fax: (650)570-6307
Fr: 800-848-5523
URL: http://www.weblogicpro.com

Bimonthly. Free to qualified subscribers. Magazine that aims to provides IT solutions for developers, architects, and administrators.

★2351★ WITI FastTrack

CMP Media L.L.C.
600 Community Dr.
Manhasset, NY 11030
Ph: (516)562-5000   Fax: (516)562-7830
URL: http://www.witi.com/corporate/fast-track.php

Semiannual. Semiannual publication featuring in-depth content on the issues facing today's women professionals in technology.

★2352★ The World Wide Web Journal of Biology

Epress, Inc.
130 Union Terrace Ln.
Plymouth, MN 55441
URL: http://www.epress.com/w3jbio/

Journal on Bio-informatics.

EMPLOYER DIRECTORIES AND NETWORKING LISTS

★2353★ A-Z of Computer Scientists

Facts On File Inc.
132 W 31st St., 17th Fl.
New York, NY 10001
Ph: (212)967-8800   Fax: 800-678-3633
Fr: 800-322-8755
URL: http://www.factsonfile.com

Published 2003. $45.00 for individuals; $40.50 for libraries. Covers the lives, work, and enduring influence of more than 150 computer pioneers and investigates the way individuals developed their ideas, overcame technical and institutional challenges, collaborated with colleagues, and created products or institutions of lasting importance.

★2354★ Career Opportunities in Computers and Cyberspace

Facts On File Inc.
132 W 31st St., 17th Fl.
New York, NY 10001
Ph: (212)967-8800   Fax: 800-678-3633
Fr: 800-322-8755
URL: http://www.factsonfile.com

Published 2004. $49.50 for individuals; $44.55 for libraries. Covers nearly 200 professions, clustering them by skill, objectives, and work conditions. Entries include: Education, salaries, employment prospects.

★2355★ Careers in Focus: Computers

Facts On File Inc.
132 W 31st St., 17th Fl.
New York, NY 10001
Ph: (212)967-8800   Fax: 800-678-3633
Fr: 800-322-8755
URL: http://www.factsonfile.com

Latest edition 4th, 2004. $29.95 for individuals; $26.95 for libraries. Covers an overview of computers, followed by a selection of jobs profiled in detail, including the nature of the job, earnings, prospects for employment,

what kind of training and skills it requires, and sources for further information.

HANDBOOKS AND MANUALS

★2356★ America's Top 101 Computer and Technical Jobs

Jist Publishing
875 Montreal Way
St. Paul, MN 55102
Fr: 800-648-5478
E-mail: info@jist.com
URL: http://www.jist.com

Michael J. Farr. 2004. $26.20. 359 pages. Job hunting in computer and technical industries.

★2357★ Career Opportunities in Computers and Cyberspace

Facts On File Inc.
132 W. 31st St., 17th Fl.
New York, NY 10001-2006
Ph: (212)967-8800   Fax: 800-678-3633
Fr: 800-322-8755
E-mail: custserv@factsonfile.com
URL: http://www.factsonfile.com

Harry Henderson. Second edition, 2004. $18.95 (paper). Part of the Career Opportunities Series. 256 pages.

★2358★ Careers Inside the World of Technology

Pearson Learning Group
135 S. Mt. Zion Rd.
PO Box 2500
Lebanon, IN 46052
Fax: 800-393-3156   Fr: 800-526-9907
URL: http://www.pearsonatschool.com

Jean W. Spencer. Revised edition, 2000. $13.50. 64 pages. Describes computer-related careers for reluctant readers.

★2359★ Choosing a Career in Computers

Rosen Publishing Group, Inc.
29 E. 21st St.
New York, NY 10010
Ph: (212)777-3017   Fax: (212)777-0277
Fr: 800-237-9932
URL: http://www.rosenpublishing.com/

Weigant, Chris. 2000. $29.25. Presents many of the options available to people interested in the technical side of the computer world-from designing and building computers to writing manuals explaining how to use them.

★2360★ The Digital Frontier Job & Opportunity Finder

Moon Lake Media
PO Box 251466
Los Angeles, CA 90025
Ph: (310)535-2453

Don B. Altman. 1996. $19.95 (paper). 245 pages.

★2361★ The e-learning Question and Answer Book: A Survival Guide for Trainers and Business Managers

AMACOM
1601 Broadway, 12th Fl.
New York, NY 10019-7420
Ph: (212)586-8100 Fax: (212)903-8168
Fr: 800-262-9699
URL: http://www.amanet.org

Allan J. Henderson. 2003. $19.95. Illustrated. 240 pages. Education for the internet.

★2362★ Get Your IT Career in Gear!

The McGraw-Hill Companies
PO Box 182604
Columbus, OH 43272
Fax: (614)759-3749 Fr: 877-883-5524
E-mail: customer.service@mcgraw-hill.com
URL: http://www.mcgraw-hill.com

Goff, Leslie. 2001. $24.99 (Trade paper). 401 pages.

★2363★ Hiring and Retaining Top IT Professionals: The Guide for Savvy Hiring Managers and Job Hunters Alike

The McGraw-Hill Companies
PO Box 182604
Columbus, OH 43272
Fax: (614)759-3749 Fr: 877-883-5524
E-mail: customer.service@mcgraw-hill.com
URL: http://www.mcgraw-hill.com

Adamsky, Howard. 2001. $24.99 (Trade paper). 256 pages.

★2364★ The New High-Tech Manager: Six Rules for Success in Changing Times

Artech House, Inc.
685 Canton St.
Norwood, MA 02062
Ph: (781)769-9750 Fax: (781)769-6334
Fr: 800-225-9977
E-mail: artech@artechhouse.com
URL: http://www.artechhouse.com/

Durham, Kenneth and Bruce Kennedy. 1997. $71.00 (Trade cloth). 201 pages.

★2365★ Opportunities in Computer Systems Careers

The McGraw-Hill Companies
PO Box 182604
Columbus, OH 43272
Fax: (614)759-3749 Fr: 877-883-5524
E-mail: customer.service@mcgraw-hill.com
URL: http://www.mcgraw-hill.com

Julie King Burns. 1996. $14.95; $11.95 (paper). 160 pages.

★2366★ Preparing for an Outstanding Career in Computers: Questions and Answers for Professionals and Students

Rafi Systems, Inc.
750 N. Diamond Bar Blvd., Ste. 224
Diamond Bar, CA 91765
Ph: (909)593-8124 Fax: (909)629-1034
Fr: 800-584-6706
E-mail: rafisystems@rafisystems.com
URL: http://www.rafisystems.com/

Mohamed Rafiquzzaman. 2001. $19.95. 204 pages. Book contains over 300 questions and answers on various important aspects of computers. Topics include basic and state-of-the-art concepts from digital logic to the design of a complete microcomputer.

★2367★ Winning Resumes for Computer Personnel

Barron's Educational Series, Inc.
250 Wireless Blvd.
Hauppauge, NY 11788-3917
Ph: (631)434-3311 Fax: (631)434-3723
Fr: 800-645-3476
E-mail: fbrown@barronseduc.com
URL: http://barronseduc.com

Anne Hart. Second edition, 1998. $14.95 (paper). 260 pages.

EMPLOYMENT AGENCIES AND SEARCH FIRMS

★2368★ 1 Exec Street

201 Post St., Ste. 401
San Francisco, CA 94108
Ph: (415)982-0555 Fax: (415)982-0550
Fr: 888-554-6845
E-mail: contactus@1execstreet.com
URL: http://www.1execstreet.com

Executive search firm.

★2369★ Ashton Computer Professionals Inc.

15 Chesterfield Pl., Unit C
North Vancouver, BC, Canada V6E 3V7
Ph: (604)904-0304 Fax: (604)904-0305
E-mail: acp@axionet.com
URL: http://www.acprecruit.com

Provides personnel recruitment and temporary contract services, specializing in advanced computer technology based fields, i.e., management information services, software engineering, product manufacturing, telecommunications, management personnel in all technology based disciplines. Serves private industries as well as government agencies.

★2370★ Berkana International Ltd.

20021 Ballinger Way NE, Ste. C
Seattle, WA 98155
Ph: (206)363-6970 Fax: (206)547-3843
E-mail: sonja@headhunters.com
URL: http://www.berkanainternational.com

Executive search firm.

★2371★ BioPharmMed

550 North Reo St., Ste. 300
Tampa, FL 33609
Ph: (813)261-5117
E-mail: bpm@ix.netcom.com
URL: http://www.biopharmmed.com

Executive search firm.

★2372★ The Brentwood Group Ltd.

4949 SW Meadows Rd., Ste. 140
Lake Oswego, OR 97035
Ph: (503)697-8136 Fax: (503)697-8161
E-mail: contact@brentwoodgroup.com
URL: http://www.brentwoodgroup.com

Executive search firm focused on the high technology industry.

★2373★ Busch International

1000 Fremont Ave., Ste. 195
Los Altos, CA 94024
Ph: (650)949-6500
E-mail: olga@buschint.com
URL: http://www.buschint.com

Executive search firm focused solely on high-technology electronics.

★2374★ Carol Maden Group

2019 Cunningham Dr., Ste. 218
Hampton, VA 23666-3316
Ph: (757)827-9010 Fax: (757)827-9081
E-mail: cmaden@hroads.net

Personnel consultants offering placement service in computer technology and engineering; servicing manufacturing and private industries nationwide. Temporary placement servicing clerical and light industrial.

★2375★ cFour Partners

100 Wilshire Blvd., Ste. 1840
Santa Monica, CA 90401
Ph: (310)394-2639 Fax: (310)394-2669
E-mail: info@cfour.com
URL: http://www.cfour.com

Executive search firm.

★2376★ Chaves & Associates

222 Post Road E.
Westport, CT 06880
Ph: (203)222-2222 Fax: (203)259-5200
E-mail: admin@insitesearch.com
URL: http://www.insitesearch.com

Executive search firm.

★2377★ CJA Executive Search

17852 17th St., Ste. 209
Tustin, CA 92780
Ph: (714)573-1820   Fax: (714)731-3952
Fr: 800-559-2559
E-mail: lindas@cjapower.com

Executive search firm. Second location in Los Angeles.

★2378★ CNR Search & Services

30752 Via Conquista
San Juan Capistrano, CA 92675
Ph: (949)488-0065
E-mail: cnrkenmiller@juno.com
URL: http://www.cnrsearch.com

Provides staffing services of permanent and temporary employees. Works primarily on a retained basis. Contingency on a limited basis. Services include human resources consulting, mergers and acquisitions in high-technology firms. Industries served: computer; information services; insurance, pharmaceutical and healthcare.

★2379★ Dahl-Morrow International

11260 Roger Bacon Dr., Ste. 204
Reston, VA 20190
Ph: (703)787-8117   Fax: (703)787-8114
E-mail: dmi@dahl-morrowintl.com
URL: http://www.dahl-morrowintl.com/

Executive search firm specializes in high technology.

★2380★ Dean Associates

PO Box 1079
Santa Cruz, CA 95061
Ph: (831)423-2931
E-mail: marydearn@deanassociates.com
URL: http://www.deanassociates.com

Executive search firm focused on the high technology industry.

★2381★ DillonGray

1796 Equestrian Dr., Ste. 112
Pleasanton, CA 94588
Ph: (925)743-4444   Fax: (925)743-1144
E-mail: info@dillongray.com
URL: http://www.dillongray.com

Executive search firm focused on technology related companies.

★2382★ Doleman Enterprises

11160-F S Lakes Dr., Ste. 326
Reston, VA 20191
Ph: (703)742-5454   Fax: (703)708-6992
E-mail: doleman@patriot.net

Human resources firm specializes in recruiting for the high-tech, data and computer engineering and pharmaceutical industries.

★2383★ Durakis Executive Search

PO Box 1382
Brooklandville, MD 21022-1382
Ph: (410)252-2055
E-mail: resumes@durakis.com
URL: http://www.durakis.com

Executive search firm.

★2384★ Dynamic Search Systems Inc.

220 W Campus Dr.
Arlington Heights, IL 60004
Ph: (847)259-3444   Fax: (847)259-3480
E-mail: candidate@dssjobs.com
URL: http://www.dssjobs.com

Provides executive and professional search services to the IT community. Firm specializes in the placement of developers, programmers, programmer analysts, systems analysts, project leaders, project managers, systems programmers, data processing consultants, IT directors, and other information technology related candidates. Industries served: all.

★2385★ Effective Search Inc.

301 N Main St., Ste. 1320
Wichita, KS 67203
Ph: (316)267-9180   Fax: (316)267-9187
Fr: 800-844-8456
E-mail: effsrch@aol.com

Conducts executive professional level searches only. Firm specializes in information technology (IT).

★2386★ Executive Directions Inc.

PO Box 223
Foxboro, MA 02035
Ph: (508)698-3030   Fax: (508)543-6047
URL: http://www.execdir.com

Executive search firm.

★2387★ Faircastle Technology Group LLC

27 Wells Rd., Ste. 1117
Monroe, CT 06468-1266
Ph: (203)459-0631   Fax: (203)459-0778
E-mail: resumes@faircastle.com
URL: http://www.faircastle.com

Executive search firm focused on high technology.

★2388★ Fisher & Associates

1063 Lenor Way
San Jose, CA 95128
Ph: (408)554-0156   Fax: (408)246-7807
E-mail: fisherassoc@aol.com

Executive search firm focused on the high technology industry.

★2389★ Focus Learning Corp.

173 Cross St., Ste. 200
San Luis Obispo, CA 93401
Ph: (805)543-4895   Fax: (805)543-4897
Fr: 800-458-5116
E-mail: info@focuslearning.com
URL: http://www.focuslearning.com

Provides professional services to corporations for the development and implementa-tion of training programs. Assists clients with needs assessment related to training and professional development, goals definition, and development of training materials. Industries served include: government, utility, aerospace, business, and computer.

★2390★ George Houchens Associates

11356 Tall Shadows Ct.
Pinckney, MI 48169-8471
Ph: (734)649-9250   Fax: (734)665-4961
E-mail: houchens@techie.com
URL: http://www.houchens.com

Specializes in recruiting top quality executive, technical, and sales/marketing professionals for permanent positions in the computer, electronics, biomedical, and other high technology industries. Positions handled include: computer product engineering, (software and hardware), management information systems, office automation and related systems, computer networking and communications, Wireless/RF/Mobile, computer aided engineering, expert systems, quality assurance, CIM/CAM, industrial control, robotics, image processing, motion control, automated inspection, material handling, and other related specialties. served: Primarily Midwest.

★2391★ Howard Fischer Associates International Inc.

1800 JFK Blvd., Ste. 700
Philadelphia, PA 19103
Ph: (215)568-8363   Fax: (215)568-4815
E-mail: search@hfischer.com
URL: http://www.hfischer.com

Executive search firm. Branches in Campbell, CA and Boston, MA.

★2392★ James Bangert & Associates Inc.

15500 Wayzata Blvd.
Wayzata, MN 55391
Ph: (952)475-3454   Fax: (952)473-4306
E-mail: jab@bangertassoc.com

Executive search firm.

★2393★ JES Search Firm Inc.

1021 Stovall Blvd., Ste. 600
950 E Paces Ferry Rd., Ste. 2245
Atlanta, GA 30319
Ph: (404)812-0622   Fax: (404)812-1910
E-mail: bde1@jessearch.com
URL: http://www.jessearch.com

Contract and permanent information technology search firm specializing in placing software developers as well as other information systems professionals.

★2394★ Jim Ward Associates

35 Browning Ave.
Toronto, ON, Canada M4K 1V8
Ph: (416)463-1661   Fax: (416)463-1688
Fr: 888-384-8884
E-mail: wardassociates@on.aibn.com

Placement service provides careers and

contract positions and professionals specifically related to the computing field. Providing personnel from operations to senior management within the information systems world. Industries served: various industries from government to small business; including banking, service, retail, distribution, manufacturing that use central, distributed or network computing facilities.

★**2395**★ **Louis Rudzinsky Associates Inc.**
394 Lowell St., Ste. 17
PO Box 640
Lexington, MA 02420
Ph: (781)862-6727   Fax: (781)862-6868
E-mail: lra@lra.com
URL: http://www.lra.com

Provides recruitment, placement, and executive search to industry (software, electronics, optics) covering positions in general management, manufacturing, engineering, and marketing. Personnel consulting activities include counsel to small and startup companies. Industries served: electronics, aerospace, optical, laser, computer, software, imaging, electro-optics, biotechnology, advanced materials, and solid-state/semiconductor.

★**2396**★ **LW Foote Company**
301 116th Ave. SE, Ste. 105
Bellevue, WA 98004
Ph: (425)451-1660   Fax: (425)451-1535
E-mail: email@lwfoote.com
URL: http://www.lwfoote.com

Executive search firm.

★**2397**★ **Management Architects**
6484 Washington St., Ste. B
Yountville, CA 94599
Ph: (707)945-1340   Fax: (707)945-1345
E-mail: doug@managementarchitects.net
URL: http://www.caywood.com

Executive search firm. Focuses on networking industries.

★**2398**★ **Michael Anthony Associates Inc.**
42 Washington St., Ste. 301
Wellesley, MA 02481-1802
Ph: (781)237-4950   Fax: (781)237-6811
Fr: 800-337-4950
E-mail: saymes@maainc.com
URL: http://www.maainc.com

Applications development, systems programming, communications, and database specialists servicing the IBM mainframe, midrange, and PC marketplace. Provides technical expertise of conversions, system software installation and upgrades, performance and tuning, capacity planning, and data communications. In addition to contract services also provide retained search and contingency placement of computer professionals ranging from senior staff to senior management. Also act as brokers for independent consultants and small consulting firms requiring the services of marketing

specialists. Industries served: banking, financial services, hospitals, HMO's, manufacturers, software development, universities, defense, and consulting firms.

★**2399**★ **Penn Search Inc.**
1045 1st Ave., Ste. 110
PO Box 688
Wayne, PA 19087
Ph: (610)964-8820   Fax: (610)964-8916
E-mail: charlied@pennsearch.com
URL: http://www.pennsearch.com

Assists in recruiting and hiring accounting and financial professionals from staff accountant to chief financial officer. Industries served: all.

★**2400**★ **R.J. Evans Associates Inc.**
26949 Chagrin Blvd., Ste. 300
Beachwood, OH 44122
Ph: (216)464-5100   Fax: (866)404-6266
E-mail: resume@rjevans.com
URL: http://www.rjevens.com

Executive search firm.

★**2401**★ **Robohm Management Group Inc.**
3 Goose Cove Rd.
Bath, ME 04530-4017
Ph: (207)442-7070   Fax: (207)442-8995
E-mail: baldwinsearch@aol.com

Executive search firm focused on the high-technology industry.

★**2402**★ **Timothy D. Crowe Jr.**
26 Higate Rd.
Chelmsford, MA 01824
Ph: (978)256-2008

Executive search firm.

★**2403**★ **TRC Staffing Services Inc.**
100 Ashford Ctr. N, Ste. 500
Atlanta, GA 30338
Ph: (770)392-1411   Fax: (770)393-2742
E-mail: info@trcstaff.com
URL: http://www.trcstaff.com

A full-service executive search company with permanent placements encompassing engineering, industrial sales, financial and computer science positions. Screen, interview, and verify past employment for all candidates prior to referral. Also assist personnel staffs in the attainment of their EEO/AAP goals with the placement of talented individuals in positions which are underutilized with minorities and/or women. Industries served: all.

ONLINE JOB SOURCES AND SERVICES

★**2404**★ **ComputerJobs.com**
280 Interstate North Cir., SE, Ste. 300
Atlanta, GA 30339-2411
Ph: 800-850-0045
URL: http://www.computerjobs.com

Description: The site is an employment tool for technology professionals. Information on positions is updated hourly for seekers. Jobs may be searched by skill, or by location nationally or in a specific state or city job market. Contains thousands of job postings. National jobs may be posted for free. Also career resources for IT professionals.

★**2405**★ **Computerwork.com**
Fr: 800-691-8413
E-mail: contactus@computerwork.com
URL: http://www.computerwork.com/

Description: Job search and resume submission service for professionals in information technology.

★**2406**★ **Computerworld Careers**
URL: http://www.computerworld.com/careertopics/careers

Description: Offers career opportunities for IT (information technology) professionals. Job seekers may search the jobs database, register at the site, and read about job surveys and employment trends. Employers may post jobs.

★**2407**★ **Computing Research Association Job Announcements**
1100 17th St., NW
Washington, DC 20036-4632
Ph: (202)234-2111   Fax: (202)667-1066
URL: http://www.cra.org/main/cra.jobs.html

Description: Contains dated links to national college and university computer technology positions.

★**2408**★ **Dice.com**
4101 NW Urbandale Dr.
Urbandale, IA 50322
Fax: (515)280-1452   Fr: 877-386-3323
URL: http://www.dice.com

Description: Job search database for computer consultants and high-tech professionals, listing thousands of high tech permanent contract and consulting jobs for programmers, software engineers, systems administrators, web developers, and hardware engineers. Also free career advice e-mail newsletter and job posting e-alerts.

★**2409**★ **Guru.com**
5001 Baum Blvd., Ste. 760
Pittsburgh, PA 15213
Ph: (412)687-1316   Fax: (412)687-4466
URL: http://www.guru.com

Description: Job board specializing in contract jobs for creative and information technology professionals. Also provides online incorporation and educational opportunities for independent contractors along with articles and advice.

★2410★ Ittalent.com

E-mail: ewsmith@ITtalent.com
URL: http://www.ittalent.com

Description: Job search and resume submission service for professionals in information technology.

★2411★ Spherion

2050 Spectrum Blvd.
Fort Lauderdale, FL 33309
Ph: (954)308-7600
E-mail: help@spherion.com
URL: http://www.spherion.com

Description: Recruitment firm specializing in accounting and finance, sales and marketing, interim executives, technology, engineering, retail and human resources.

★2412★ ZDNet Tech Jobs

URL: http://www.zdnet.com/

Description: Site houses a listing of national employment opportunities for professionals in high tech fields. Also contains resume building tips and relocation resources.

TRADESHOWS

★2413★ The CSI Computer Security Conference and Exhibition

CMP Media LLC (San Mateo)
2800 Campus Dr.
San Mateo, CA 94403
Ph: (650)513-4300
E-mail: cmp@cmp.com
URL: http://www.cmp.com

Annual. **Primary Exhibits:** Computer products and services and information security equipment, supplies and services.

★2414★ XPLOR Conference

XPLOR International
24238 Hawthorne Blvd.
Torrance, CA 90505-6505
Ph: (310)373-3633   Fax: (310)375-4240
Fr: 800-669-7567
E-mail: info@xplor.org
URL: http://www.xplor.org

Annual. **Primary Exhibits:** Equipment, supplies, and services for users and manufacturers of advanced electronic document systems.

OTHER SOURCES

★2415★ AFCOM

742 E Chapman Ave.
Orange, CA 92866
Ph: (714)997-7966   Fax: (714)997-9743
E-mail: afcom@afcom.com
URL: http://www.afcom.com

Members: Data center, networking and enterprise systems management professionals from medium and large scale mainframe, midrange and client/server data centers worldwide. **Purpose:** Works to meet the professional needs of the enterprise system management community. **Activities:** Provides information and support through educational events, research and assistance hotlines, and surveys.

★2416★ Association of Information Technology Professionals (AITP)

401 N Michigan Ave., Ste. 2400
Chicago, IL 60611-4267
Ph: (312)245-1070   Fax: (312)673-6659
Fr: 800-224-9371
E-mail: aitp_hq@aitp.org
URL: http://www.aitp.org

Members: Managerial personnel, staff, educators, and individuals interested in the management of information resources. Founder of the Certificate in Data Processing examination program, now administered by an intersociety organization. **Purpose:** Maintains Legislative Communications Network. Professional education programs include EDP-oriented business and management principles self-study courses and a series of videotaped management development seminars. Sponsors student organizations around the country interested in information technology and encourages members to serve as counselors for the Scout computer merit badge. Conducts research projects, including a business information systems curriculum for two- and four-year colleges.

★2417★ Association for Women in Computing (AWC)

41 Sutter St., Ste. 1006
San Francisco, CA 94104
Ph: (415)905-4663   Fax: (415)358-4667
E-mail: info@awc-hq.org
URL: http://www.awc-hq.org

Members: Individuals interested in promoting the education, professional development, and advancement of women in computing.

★2418★ Computer Occupations

Delphi Productions
3159 6th St.
Boulder, CO 80304
Ph: (303)443-2100   Fax: (303)443-4022
Fr: 888-443-2400

E-mail: support@delphivideo.com
URL: http://www.delphivideo.com

$95.00. 50 minutes. Part of the Careers for the 21st Century Video Library.

★2419★ Computing Technology Industry Association (CompTIA)

1815 S Meyers Rd., Ste. 300
Oakbrook Terrace, IL 60181-5228
Ph: (630)678-8300   Fax: (630)678-8384
E-mail: information@comptia.org
URL: http://www.comptia.org

Description: Trade association of more than 19,000 companies and professional IT members in the rapidly converging computing and communications market. Has members in more than 89 countries and provides a unified voice for the industry in the areas of e-commerce standards, vendor-neutral certification, service metrics, public policy and workforce development. Serves as information clearinghouse and resource for the industry; sponsors educational programs.

★2420★ IEEE Computer Society (CS)

1730 Massachusetts Ave. NW
Washington, DC 20036-1992
Ph: (202)371-0101   Fax: (202)728-9614
E-mail: help@computer.org
URL: http://www.computer.org

Description: Computer professionals. Promotes the development of computer and information sciences and fosters communication within the information processing community. Sponsors conferences, symposia, workshops, tutorials, technical meetings, and seminars. Operates Computer Society Press. Presents scholarships; bestows technical achievement and service awards and certificates.

★2421★ Information Technology Occupations

Delphi Productions
3159 6th St.
Boulder, CO 80304
Ph: (303)443-2100   Fax: (303)443-4022
Fr: 888-443-2400
E-mail: support@delphivideo.com
URL: http://www.delphivideo.com

$95.00. 52 minutes. Part of the Emerging Careers Video Library.

★2422★ Information Technology Services

Cambridge Educational
PO Box 2053
Princeton, NJ 08543-2053
Ph: 800-257-5126   Fax: (609)671-0266
Fr: 800-468-4227
E-mail: custserv@films.com
URL: http://www.cambridgeeducational.com

VHS and DVD. $89.95. 2002. 19 minutes. Part of the Career Cluster Series.

Computer Operators

★2423★ ACM Transactions on Internet Technology (ACM TOIT)
Association for Computing Machinery
2 Penn Plz., Ste. 701
New York, NY 10121-0701
Ph: (212)869-7440   Fax: (212)944-1318
Fr: 800-342-6626
URL: http://www.acm.org/pubs/periodicals/toit/

Quarterly. $35.00/year for members; $30.00/year for students; $140.00/year for nonmembers; $170.00/year for individuals, print only; $136.00 for single issue, online only; $204.00 for single issue, online & print. Publication of the Association for Computing Machinery. Brings together many computing disciplines including computer software engineering, computer programming languages, middleware, database management, security, knowledge discovery and data mining, networking and distributed systems, communications, performance and scalability, and more. Covers the results and roles of the individual disciplines and the relationships among them.

★2424★ AVIOS Journal
Applied Voice Input/Output Society
PO Box 20817
San Jose, CA 95160
Ph: (408)323-1783   Fax: (408)323-1782
E-mail: info@avios.org
URL: http://www.avios.com/

Annual. Journal covering issues in computer science.

★2425★ Communications of the ACM
Association for Computing Machinery
2 Penn Plz., Ste. 701
New York, NY 10121-0701
Ph: (212)869-7440   Fax: (212)944-1318
Fr: 800-342-6626
URL: http://www.acm.org/pubs/cacm/

Monthly. $179.00/year for nonmembers; $36.00/year for members. Computing news magazine.

★2426★ Computers and Composition
Elsevier Science Inc.
360 Park Ave. S
New York, NY 10010
Ph: (212)989-5800   Fax: (212)633-3990
URL: http://www.elsevier.com

$353.00/year for institutions; $69.00/year for individuals. Journal covering computers in writing classes, programs, and research.

★2427★ Computers Programs/PC World
IDG Communications Inc.
5 Speen St., 3rd. Fl
Framingham, MA 01701
Ph: (508)875-5000   Fax: (508)988-7888
URL: http://www.idg.com

Magazine devoted to IT specialists, covering practical questions of computing including purchase and usage of the computer technology, software, computer components and peripherals.

★2428★ Computerworld
101 Communications
9121 Oakdale Ave., Ste. 101
Chatsworth, CA 91311
Ph: (818)734-1520   Fax: (818)734-1522
URL: http://www.computerworld.com

Weekly. $99.00/year for individuals, new Australian subscribers; $99.00/year for individuals, renewals Australian; $250.00/year for other countries, airmail; $375.00/year for other countries, overseas (airmail). Newspaper for information systems executives.

★2429★ Computerworld/Correio Informatico
IDG Communications Inc.
5 Speen St., 3rd. Fl
Framingham, MA 01701
Ph: (508)875-5000   Fax: (508)988-7888
URL: http://www.idg.com

Weekly. Magazine providing news on latest developments in computer industry.

★2430★ Computerworld Top 100
IDG Communications Inc.
5 Speen St., 3rd. Fl
Framingham, MA 01701
Ph: (508)875-5000   Fax: (508)988-7888
URL: http://www.idg.com

Annual. Magazine for analyzing trends and events of information technology business.

★2431★ Computing SA
IDG Communications Inc.
5 Speen St., 3rd. Fl
Framingham, MA 01701
Ph: (508)875-5000   Fax: (508)988-7888
URL: http://www.idg.com

Monthly. Newspaper focusing computer hardware, software, networking, telecommunications, channel management and online computing.

★2432★ Consumer Electronics Lifestyles
Sandhills Publishing
120 W Harvest Dr.
Lincoln, NE 68521
Ph: (402)479-2181   Fax: (402)479-2195
Fr: 800-331-1978
E-mail: editor@ceLifestyles.com
URL: http://www.celifestyles.com/

Monthly. $12.00/year. Magazine for computer and electronic gadget enthusiasts.

★2433★ CXO
IDG Communications Inc.
5 Speen St., 3rd. Fl
Framingham, MA 01701
Ph: (508)875-5000   Fax: (508)988-7888
URL: http://www.idg.com

Monthly. Magazine providing technology information for chief officers and managers.

★2434★ Datamation

Reed Business Information
225 Wyman St.
Waltham, MA 02451-1216
URL: http://www.datamation.com

Semimonthly. Magazine on computers and information processing.

★2435★ Eclipse Review

BZ Media LLC
7 High St., Ste. 407
Huntington, NY 11743
Ph: (631)421-4158   Fax: (631)421-4130
URL: http://www.eclipsesource.com/contact.htm

Magazine for IT professionals.

★2436★ ENA powered by Network World

IDG Communications Inc.
5 Speen St., 3rd. Fl
Framingham, MA 01701
Ph: (508)875-5000   Fax: (508)988-7888
URL: http://www.idg.com

Monthly. Journal covering information on networking.

★2437★ Foundations of Computational Mathematics

Springer-Verlag New York Inc.
233 Spring St.
New York, NY 10013
Ph: (212)460-1500   Fax: (212)460-1575

Academic journal that publishes articles related to the connections between mathematics and computation, including the interfaces between pure and applied mathematics, numerical analysis and computer science.

★2438★ Foundations and Trends in Networking

Now Publishers
PO Box 1024
Hanover, MA 02339
Ph: (781)871-0245
URL: http://www.nowpublishers.com/product.aspx?product=NET

$315.00/year online only; $355.00/year print and online; $315.00/year online only; $355.00/year print and online. Academic journal publishing new research in computer networking.

★2439★ Government Computer News

PostNewsweek Tech Media
10 G St. NE, Ste. 500
Washington, DC 20002-4228
Ph: (202)772-2500   Fax: (202)772-2511
Fr: (866)447-6864

Semimonthly. Magazine for professionals interested in government IT.

★2440★ IEEE Security & Privacy Magazine

IEEE Computer Society
10662 Los Vaqueros Cir.
PO Box 3014
Los Alamitos, CA 90720-1314
Ph: (714)821-8380   Fax: (714)821-4010
Fr: 800-272-6657
URL: http://www.computer.org/portal/site/security/

Bimonthly. $24.00/year for members; $29.00/year for nonmembers; $28.00/year for members; $565.00/year for libraries, institution. Journal that aims to explore role and importance of networked infrastructure and developing lasting security solutions.

★2441★ IEEE Software

IEEE Computer Society
10662 Los Vaqueros Cir.
PO Box 3014
Los Alamitos, CA 90720-1314
Ph: (714)821-8380   Fax: (714)821-4010
Fr: 800-272-6657
E-mail: software@computer.org
URL: http://www.computer.org/software

Bimonthly. $77.00/year for nonmembers, individual; $46.00/year for members, plus online access to software articles; $76.00/year for members; $765.00/year for institutions, library. Magazine covering the computer software industry for the community of leading software practitioners.

★2442★ Information Security

TechTarget
117 Kendrick St., Ste. 800
Needham, MA 02494
Ph: (781)657-1000   Fax: (781)657-1100
URL: http://searchsecurity.techtarget.com/

Monthly. Free to qualified subscribers. Magazine covering information security topics.

★2443★ iSeries News Magazine

Penton Media
221 E 29th St.
Loveland, CO 80538
Ph: (970)663-4700   Fax: (970)667-2321
Fr: 800-621-1544
E-mail: service@iseriesnetwork.com
URL: http://www.systeminetwork.com/info/networkpubs/news400/about

$149.00/year for U.S. and Canada; $199.00/year for other countries. Trade magazine for programmers and data processing managers who use IBM iSeries.

★2444★ IT Focus

IDG Communications Inc.
5 Speen St., 3rd. Fl
Framingham, MA 01701
Ph: (508)875-5000   Fax: (508)988-7888
URL: http://www.idg.com

Online journal focusing mainly on information technology.

★2445★ IT Solutions Guide

SYS-CON Media
135 Chestnut Ridge Rd.
Montvale, NJ 07645
Ph: (201)802-3000   Fax: (201)782-9600
Fr: 888-303-5282
URL: http://itsolutions.sys-con.com/

Quarterly. $4.00/year for individuals, single pdf issue. Magazine for IT professionals.

★2446★ Journal of Computer Science

Science Publications
Vails Gate Heights Dr.
PO Box 879
Vails Gate, NY 12584
URL: http://www.scipub.us/

Bimonthly. $3,500.00/year for individuals; $300.00/year for single issue. Scholarly journal covering many areas of computer science, including: concurrent, parallel and distributed processing; artificial intelligence; image and voice processing; quality software and metrics; computer-aided education; wireless communication; real time processing; evaluative computation; and data bases and information recovery and neural networks.

★2447★ Journal of Computer Systems, Networks, and Communications

Hindawi Publishing Corp.
410 Park Ave., 15th Fl.
287 PMB
New York, NY 10022
E-mail: jcsnc@hindawi.com
URL: http://www.hindawi.com/journals/jcsnc/

$195.00/year for individuals. Journal covering important areas of information technology.

★2448★ Kompiuterija PC World

IDG Communications Inc.
5 Speen St., 3rd. Fl
Framingham, MA 01701
Ph: (508)875-5000   Fax: (508)988-7888
URL: http://www.idg.com

Monthly. Journal providing professionals, business people and users with up-to-date information on computers and the internet.

★2449★ Mikro PC

IDG Communications Inc.
5 Speen St., 3rd. Fl
Framingham, MA 01701
Ph: (508)875-5000   Fax: (508)988-7888
URL: http://www.idg.com

Monthly. Magazine focusing on information technology and digital lifestyle.

★2450★ Monitor

Capital PC User Group
19209 Mt. Airey Rd.
Brookeville, MD 20833
Ph: (301)560-6442   Fax: (301)760-3303
URL: http://monitor.cpcug.org/index.html

Quarterly. Magazine covering computer

hardware and software reviews, special interest user group news, advertisers and author/subject index, and calendar of events.

★2451★ *NetWorld*

IDG Communications Inc.
5 Speen St., 3rd. Fl
Framingham, MA 01701
Ph: (508)875-5000   Fax: (508)988-7888
URL: http://www.idg.com

Monthly. Magazine focusing on networks, security, infrastructure management, wireless, mobile and VOIP technologies.

★2452★ *PC Magazine*

Ziff-Davis Publishing Co.
28 East 28th St.
New York, NY 10016
Ph: (212)503-3500
E-mail: pcmag@ziffdavis.com
URL: http://www.ziffdavisinternet.com/websites/pcmag

Biweekly. $19.97/year for individuals, 25 issues. Tabloid featuring microcomputer products and developments.

★2453★ *Queue*

Association for Computing Machinery
2 Penn Plz., Ste. 701
New York, NY 10121-0701
Ph: (212)869-7440   Fax: (212)944-1318
Fr: 800-342-6626
URL: http://www.acmqueue.org/

Monthly. Free, U.S./Canadian residents and all members. Online magazine aimed at the computer professional. Magazine editorial does not provide solutions for the "here-and-now," but instead helps decision-makers plan future projects by examining the challenges and problems they are most likely to face.

★2454★ *Revenue*

Montgomery Media International
300 Montgomery St., Ste. 1135
San Francisco, CA 94104
Ph: (415)397-2400   Fax: (415)397-2420
URL: http://www.revenuetoday.com/

$30.00/year for individuals. Magazine covering internet marketing strategies.

★2455★ *SMB Data*

IDG Communications Inc.
5 Speen St., 3rd. Fl
Framingham, MA 01701
Ph: (508)875-5000   Fax: (508)988-7888
URL: http://www.idg.com

Magazine focusing on information technology systems at small and medium-size businesses.

★2456★ *SME World*

IDG Communications Inc.
5 Speen St., 3rd. Fl
Framingham, MA 01701
Ph: (508)875-5000   Fax: (508)988-7888
URL: http://www.idg.com

Magazine covering articles on technology, technology investments, IT products and services.

★2457★ *TecCHANNEL Compact*

IDG Communications Inc.
5 Speen St., 3rd. Fl
Framingham, MA 01701
Ph: (508)875-5000   Fax: (508)988-7888
URL: http://www.idg.com

Quarterly. Magazine covering issues of information technology.

★2458★ *Tips & Trucs*

IDG Communications Inc.
5 Speen St., 3rd. Fl
Framingham, MA 01701
Ph: (508)875-5000   Fax: (508)988-7888
URL: http://www.idg.com

Monthly. Magazine covering topics on computer hardware, software and the internet.

★2459★ *Top 100*

IDG Communications Inc.
5 Speen St., 3rd. Fl
Framingham, MA 01701
Ph: (508)875-5000   Fax: (508)988-7888
URL: http://www.idg.com

Annual. Magazine providing analyses, assessments and statistics on information technology industry.

★2460★ *Ubiquity*

Association for Computing Machinery
2 Penn Plz., Ste. 701
New York, NY 10121-0701
Ph: (212)869-7440   Fax: (212)944-1318
Fr: 800-342-6626
URL: http://www.acm.org/ubiquity/

Weekly. Free to members; $163.00/year for nonmembers, 12 issues. Web-based magazine of the Association for Computing Machinery dedicated to fostering critical analysis and in-depth commentary, including book reviews, on issues relating to the nature, constitution, structure, science, engineering, cognition, technology, practices and paradigms of the IT profession.

★2461★ *WebLogic Pro*

Fawcette Technical Publications
2600 S El Camino Real, Ste. 300
San Mateo, CA 94403-2332
Ph: (650)378-7100   Fax: (650)570-6307
Fr: 800-848-5523
URL: http://www.weblogicpro.com

Bimonthly. Free to qualified subscribers. Magazine that aims to provides IT solutions for developers, architects, and administrators.

★2462★ *WITI FastTrack*

CMP Media L.L.C.
600 Community Dr.
Manhasset, NY 11030
Ph: (516)562-5000   Fax: (516)562-7830
URL: http://www.witi.com/corporate/fast-track.php

Semiannual. Semiannual publication featuring in-depth content on the issues facing today's women professionals in technology.

★2463★ *The World Wide Web Journal of Biology*

Epress, Inc.
130 Union Terrace Ln.
Plymouth, MN 55441
URL: http://www.epress.com/w3jbio/

Journal on Bio-informatics.

EMPLOYER DIRECTORIES AND NETWORKING LISTS

★2464★ *Computer Directory*

Computer Directories Inc.
23815 Nichols Sawmill Rd.
Hockley, TX 77447
Ph: (281)356-7880   Fr: 800-234-4353
URL: http://www.compdirinc.com

Annual, fall. Covers approximately 130,000 computer installation companies; 19 separate volumes for Alaska/Hawaii, Connecticut/New Jersey, Dallas/Ft. Worth, Eastern Seaboard, Far Midwest, Houston, Illinois, Midatlantic, Midcentral, Mideast, Minnesota/Wisconsin, North Central, New England, New York Metro, Northwest, Ohio, Pennsylvania/West Virginia, Southeast, and Southwest Texas. Entries include: Company name, address, phone, fax, e-mail, name and title of contact, hardware used, software application, operating system, programming language, computer graphics, networking system. Arrangement: Geographical. Indexes: Alphabetical; industry; hardware.

★2465★ *Directory of Top Computer Executives*

Applied Computer Research
PO Box 41730
Phoenix, AZ 85080-1730
Ph: (602)216-9100   Fax: (602)548-4800
Fr: 800-234-2227
URL: http://www.itmarketintelligence.com

Semiannual, June and December. Covers, in three volumes, over 55,000 U.S. and Canadian executives with major information technology or communications responsibilities in over 30,000 U.S. and Canadian companies. Entries include: Company name, address, phone, subsidiary and/or division names, major systems installed, names and titles of top information system executives, number of IT employees, number of PCs, and web address. Arrangement: Geographical within separate eastern, western, and Canadian volumes. Indexes: Industry; alphabetical by company name.

★2466★ Discovering Careers for Your Future: Computers

Facts On File Inc.
132 W 31st St., 17th Fl.
New York, NY 10001
Ph: (212)967-8800   Fax: 800-678-3633
Fr: 800-322-8755
URL: http://www.factsonfile.com

Published 2001. $21.95 for individuals; $19.75 for libraries. Covers computer operators, programmers, database specialists, and software engineers; links career education to curriculum, helping children investigate the subjects they are interested in, and the careers those subjects might lead to.

HANDBOOKS AND MANUALS

★2467★ America's Top 101 Computer and Technical Jobs

Jist Publishing
875 Montreal Way
St. Paul, MN 55102
Fr: 800-648-5478
E-mail: info@jist.com
URL: http://www.jist.com

Michael J. Farr. 2004. $26.20. 359 pages. Job hunting in computer and technical industries.

★2468★ Career Opportunities in Computers and Cyberspace

Facts On File Inc.
132 W. 31st St., 17th Fl.
New York, NY 10001-2006
Ph: (212)967-8800   Fax: 800-678-3633
Fr: 800-322-8755
E-mail: custserv@factsonfile.com
URL: http://www.factsonfile.com

Harry Henderson. Second edition, 2004. $18.95 (paper). Part of the Career Opportunities Series. 256 pages.

★2469★ Careers for Computer Buffs and Other Technological Types

The McGraw-Hill Companies
PO Box 182604
Columbus, OH 43272
Fax: (614)759-3749   Fr: 877-883-5524
E-mail: customer.service@mcgraw-hill.com
URL: http://www.mcgraw-hill.com

Marjorie Eberts and Margaret Gisler. Third edition, 2006. $13.95 (paper). 160 pages. Suggested jobs in a wide range of settings, from the office to the outdoors.

★2470★ Careers in Computers

The McGraw-Hill Companies
PO Box 182604
Columbus, OH 43272
Fax: (614)759-3749   Fr: 877-883-5524

E-mail: customer.service@mcgraw-hill.com
URL: http://www.mcgraw-hill.com

Lila B. Stair and Leslie Stair. 2002. $19.95; $14.95 (paper). 192 pages. Describes trends affecting computer careers and explores a wide range of job opportunities from programming to consulting. Provides job qualifications, salary data, job market information, personal and educational requirements, career paths, and the place of the job in the organizational structure. Offers advice on education, certification, and job search.

★2471★ Careers Inside the World of Technology

Pearson Learning Group
135 S. Mt. Zion Rd.
PO Box 2500
Lebanon, IN 46052
Fax: 800-393-3156   Fr: 800-526-9907
URL: http://www.pearsonatschool.com

Jean W. Spencer. Revised edition, 2000. $13.50. 64 pages. Describes computer-related careers for reluctant readers.

★2472★ The Digital Frontier Job & Opportunity Finder

Moon Lake Media
PO Box 251466
Los Angeles, CA 90025
Ph: (310)535-2453

Don B. Altman. 1996. $19.95 (paper). 245 pages.

★2473★ Expert Resumes for Computer and Web Jobs

Jist Publishing
875 Montreal Way
St. Paul, MN 55102
Fr: 800-648-5478
E-mail: info@jist.com
URL: http://www.jist.com

Wendy Enelow and Louis Kursmark. Second edition, 2005. $16.95 (paper). 286 pages.

★2474★ Get Your IT Career in Gear!

The McGraw-Hill Companies
PO Box 182604
Columbus, OH 43272
Fax: (614)759-3749   Fr: 877-883-5524
E-mail: customer.service@mcgraw-hill.com
URL: http://www.mcgraw-hill.com

Leslie Goff. 2001. $24.99 (paper). 401 pages.

★2475★ Great Jobs for Computer Science Majors

The McGraw-Hill Companies
PO Box 182604
Columbus, OH 43272
Fax: (614)759-3749   Fr: 877-883-5524
E-mail: customer.service@mcgraw-hill.com
URL: http://www.mcgraw-hill.com

Jan Goldberg, Stephen Lambert, Julie De-Galan. Second edition, 2002. $14.95 (paper). 224 pages.

★2476★ The JobBank Guide to Computer and High-Tech Companies

Adams Media Corp.
57 Littlefield St.
Avon, MA 02322
Ph: (508)427-7100   Fax: (508)427-6790
Fr: 800-872-5627
URL: http://www.adamsmedia.com

Steven Graber, Marcie Dipietro, and Michelle Roy Kelly. Second edition, 1999. $17.95 (paper). 700 pages. Contains profiles of more than 4,500 high-tech employers.

★2477★ Opportunities in Computer Careers

The McGraw-Hill Companies
PO Box 182604
Columbus, OH 43272
Fax: (614)759-3749   Fr: 877-883-5524
E-mail: customer.service@mcgraw-hill.com
URL: http://www.mcgraw-hill.com

Julie Kling Burns. $12.95 (netLibrary). 160 pages. 2001. Computer vocational guidance and counseling.

★2478★ Opportunities in Office Occupations

The McGraw-Hill Companies
PO Box 182604
Columbus, OH 43272
Fax: (614)759-3749   Fr: 877-883-5524
E-mail: customer.service@mcgraw-hill.com
URL: http://www.mcgraw-hill.com

Blanche Ettinger. 1995. $14.95; $11.95 (paper). 146 pages. Covers a variety of office positions and discusses trends for the next decade. Describes the job market, opportunities, job duties, educational preparation, the work environment, and earnings.

★2479★ Preparing for an Outstanding Career in Computers: Questions and Answers for Professionals and Students

Rafi Systems, Incorporated
750 N. Diamond Bar Blvd., Ste. 224
Diamond Bar, CA 91765
Ph: (909)593-8124   Fax: (909)629-1034
Fr: 800-584-6706
E-mail: rafisystems@rafisystems.com
URL: http://www.rafisystems.com/

Mohamed Rafiquzzaman. 2001. $19.95. 204 pages. Book contains over 300 questions and answers on various important aspects of computers. Topics include basic and state-of-the-art concepts from digital logic to the design of a complete microcomputer.

★2480★ Unlocking the Clubhouse: Women in Computing

MIT Press
55 Hayward St.
Cambridge, MA 02142-1493
Ph: (617)253-5646   Fax: (617)258-6779
Fr: 800-405-1619
URL: http://mitpress.mit.edu/main/home/default.asp

Jane Margolis and Allan Fisher. 2003. $15.00. 182 pages.

★2481★ **The Unofficial Guide to Getting a Job at Microsoft**
The McGraw-Hill Companies
PO Box 182604
Columbus, OH 43272
Fax: (614)759-3749   Fr: 877-883-5524
E-mail: customer.service@mcgraw-hill.com
URL: http://www.mcgraw-hill.com
Rebecca Smith. 2000. $16.95 (paper). 192 pages.

★2482★ **Winning Resumes for Computer Personnel**
Barron's Educational Series, Inc.
250 Wireless Blvd.
Hauppauge, NY 11788-3917
Ph: (631)434-3311   Fax: (631)434-3723
Fr: 800-645-3476
E-mail: fbrown@barronseduc.com
URL: http://barronseduc.com
Anne Hart. Second edition, 1998. $14.95 (paper). 260 pages.

EMPLOYMENT AGENCIES AND SEARCH FIRMS

★2483★ **The Aspire Group**
52 Second Ave, 1st Fl
Waltham, MA 02451-1129
Fax: (718)890-1810   Fr: 800-487-2967
URL: http://www.bmanet.com
Employment agency.

★2484★ **Data Systems Search Consultants**
1615 Bonanza St., Ste. 405
Walnut Creek, CA 94596
Ph: (925)256-0635   Fax: (925)256-9099
E-mail: dsscinfo@dssc.com
URL: http://www.dssc.com
Employment agency. Executive search firm.

★2485★ **Dean Associates**
PO Box 1079
Santa Cruz, CA 95061
Ph: (831)423-2931
E-mail: marydearn@deanassociates.com
URL: http://www.deanassociates.com
Executive search firm focused on the high technology industry.

★2486★ **Jim Ward Associates**
35 Browning Ave.
Toronto, ON, Canada M4K 1V8
Ph: (416)463-1661   Fax: (416)463-1688
Fr: 888-384-8884
E-mail: wardassociates@on.aibn.com

Placement service provides careers and contract positions and professionals specifically related to the computing field. Providing personnel from operations to senior management within the information systems world. Industries served: various industries from government to small business; including banking, service, retail, distribution, manufacturing that use central, distributed or network computing facilities.

★2487★ **KForce**
Fr: 888-663-3626
URL: http://www.kforce.com
Executive search firm. More than 30 locations throughout the United States.

★2488★ **The Murphy Group**
245 W Roosevelt Rd., Bldg.15, Ste.101
Chicago, IL 60605
Ph: (630)639-5110   Fax: (630)639-5113
E-mail: info@murphygroup.com
URL: http://www.murphygroup.com
Employment agency. Places personnel in a variety of positions. Additional offices located in Napierville, Park Ridge, and OakBrook.

★2489★ **Tri-Serv Inc.**
22 W. Padonia Rd., Ste. C-353
Timonium, MD 21093
Ph: (410)561-1740   Fax: (410)252-7417
E-mail: info@tri-serv.coom
URL: http://www.tri-serv.com
Employment agency for technical personnel.

★2490★ **Worlco Computer Resources, Inc.**
997 Old Eagle School Rd., Ste. 219
Wayne, PA 19087
Ph: (610)293-9070   Fax: (610)293-1027
E-mail: parisi@worlco.com
URL: http://www.worlco.com
Employment agency and executive search firm. Second location in Cherry Hill, New Jersey.

ONLINE JOB SOURCES AND SERVICES

★2491★ **ComputerJobs.com**
280 Interstate North Cir., SE, Ste. 300
Atlanta, GA 30339-2411
Ph: 800-850-0045
URL: http://www.computerjobs.com
Description: The site is an employment tool for technology professionals. Information on positions is updated hourly for seekers. Jobs may be searched by skill, or by location nationally or in a specific state or city job market. Contains thousands of job postings. National jobs may be posted for free. Also career resources for IT professionals.

★2492★ **Computerwork.com**
Fr: 800-691-8413
E-mail: contactus@computerwork.com
URL: http://www.computerwork.com/
Description: Job search and resume submission service for professionals in information technology.

★2493★ **Computerworld Careers**
URL: http://www.computerworld.com/careertopics/careers
Description: Offers career opportunities for IT (information technology) professionals. Job seekers may search the jobs database, register at the site, and read about job surveys and employment trends. Employers may post jobs.

★2494★ **Computing Research Association Job Announcements**
1100 17th St., NW
Washington, DC 20036-4632
Ph: (202)234-2111   Fax: (202)667-1066
URL: http://www.cra.org/main/cra.jobs.html
Description: Contains dated links to national college and university computer technology positions.

★2495★ **Guru.com**
5001 Baum Blvd., Ste. 760
Pittsburgh, PA 15213
Ph: (412)687-1316   Fax: (412)687-4466
URL: http://www.guru.com
Description: Job board specializing in contract jobs for creative and information technology professionals. Also provides online incorporation and educational opportunities for independent contractors along with articles and advice.

★2496★ **Ittalent.com**
E-mail: ewsmith@ITtalent.com
URL: http://www.ittalent.com
Description: Job search and resume submission service for professionals in information technology.

★2497★ **ZDNet Tech Jobs**
URL: http://www.zdnet.com/
Description: Site houses a listing of national employment opportunities for professionals in high tech fields. Also contains resume building tips and relocation resources.

TRADESHOWS

★2498★ **Computer & Technology Showcase - Tulsa**
Event Management Services
519 Cleveland St., Ste. 205
Clearwater, FL 33755
Ph: (503)234-1552   Fax: (503)234-4253
Fr: 800-422-0251

E-mail: mfriedman@event-management.com
URL: http://www.event-management.com

Annual. **Primary Exhibits:** Products and services for computers, imaging, wireless communication, networking, application development, and e-commerce.

★2499★ The CSI Computer Security Conference and Exhibition

CMP Media LLC (San Mateo)
2800 Campus Dr.
San Mateo, CA 94403
Ph: (650)513-4300
E-mail: cmp@cmp.com
URL: http://www.cmp.com

Annual. **Primary Exhibits:** Computer products and services and information security equipment, supplies and services.

★2500★ XPLOR Conference

XPLOR International
24238 Hawthorne Blvd.
Torrance, CA 90505-6505
Ph: (310)373-3633   Fax: (310)375-4240
Fr: 800-669-7567
E-mail: info@xplor.org
URL: http://www.xplor.org

Annual. **Primary Exhibits:** Equipment, supplies, and services for users and manufacturers of advanced electronic document systems.

OTHER SOURCES

★2501★ AFCOM

742 E Chapman Ave.
Orange, CA 92866
Ph: (714)997-7966   Fax: (714)997-9743
E-mail: afcom@afcom.com
URL: http://www.afcom.com

Members: Data center, networking and enterprise systems management professionals from medium and large scale mainframe, midrange and client/server data centers worldwide. **Purpose:** Works to meet the professional needs of the enterprise system management community. **Activities:** Provides information and support through educational events, research and assistance hotlines, and surveys.

★2502★ Association of Information Technology Professionals (AITP)

401 N Michigan Ave., Ste. 2400
Chicago, IL 60611-4267
Ph: (312)245-1070   Fax: (312)673-6659
Fr: 800-224-9371
E-mail: aitp_hq@aitp.org

URL: http://www.aitp.org

Members: Managerial personnel, staff, educators, and individuals interested in the management of information resources. Founder of the Certificate in Data Processing examination program, now administered by an intersociety organization. **Purpose:** Maintains Legislative Communications Network. Professional education programs include EDP-oriented business and management principles self-study courses and a series of videotaped management development seminars. Sponsors student organizations around the country interested in information technology and encourages members to serve as counselors for the Scout computer merit badge. Conducts research projects, including a business information systems curriculum for two- and four-year colleges.

★2503★ Association for Women in Computing (AWC)

41 Sutter St., Ste. 1006
San Francisco, CA 94104
Ph: (415)905-4663   Fax: (415)358-4667
E-mail: info@awc-hq.org
URL: http://www.awc-hq.org

Members: Individuals interested in promoting the education, professional development, and advancement of women in computing.

★2504★ Black Data Processing Associates (BDPA)

6301 Ivy Ln., Ste. 700
Greenbelt, MD 20770
Ph: (301)220-2180   Fax: (301)220-2185
Fr: 800-727-BDPA
E-mail: president@bdpa.org
URL: http://www.bdpa.org

Description: Represents persons employed in the information processing industry, including electronic data processing, electronic word processing, and data communications; others interested in information processing. Seeks to accumulate and share information processing knowledge and business expertise in order to increase the career and business potential of minorities in the information processing field. Conducts professional seminars, workshops, tutoring services, and community introductions to data processing. Makes annual donation to the United Negro College Fund.

★2505★ Computer Occupations

Delphi Productions
3159 6th St.
Boulder, CO 80304
Ph: (303)443-2100   Fax: (303)443-4022
Fr: 888-443-2400
E-mail: support@delphivideo.com
URL: http://www.delphivideo.com

$95.00. 50 minutes. Part of the Careers for the 21st Century Video Library.

★2506★ Information Technology Occupations

Delphi Productions
3159 6th St.
Boulder, CO 80304
Ph: (303)443-2100   Fax: (303)443-4022
Fr: 888-443-2400
E-mail: support@delphivideo.com
URL: http://www.delphivideo.com

$95.00. 52 minutes. Part of the Emerging Careers Video Library.

★2507★ Information Technology Services

Cambridge Educational
PO Box 2053
Princeton, NJ 08543-2053
Ph: 800-257-5126   Fax: (609)671-0266
Fr: 800-468-4227
E-mail: custserv@films.com
URL: http://www.cambridgeeducational.com

VHS and DVD. $89.95. 2002. 19 minutes. Part of the Career Cluster Series.

★2508★ Institute for Certification of Computing Professionals (ICCP)

2350 E Devon Ave., Ste. 115
Des Plaines, IL 60018-4610
Ph: (847)299-4227   Fax: (847)299-4280
Fr: 800-843-8227
E-mail: office@iccp.org
URL: http://www.iccp.org

Members: Professional societies. **Purpose:** Promotes the development of computer examinations which are of high quality, directed toward information technology professionals, and designed to encourage competence and professionalism. Individuals passing the exams automatically become members of the Institute for Certification of Computing Professionals and become certified as CCP or ACP. **Activities:** Has developed code of ethics and good practice to which those taking the exams promise to adhere. Maintains speakers' bureau; compiles statistics.

★2509★ Special Interest Group on Accessible Computing (SIGACCESS)

IBM T.J. Watson Research Center
19 Skyline Dr.
Hawthorne, NY 10532
Ph: (914)784-6603   Fax: (914)784-7279
E-mail: chair_sigaccess@acm.org
URL: http://www.sigaccess.org

Description: Promotes the professional interests of computing personnel with physical disabilities and the application of computing and information technology in solving relevant disability problems. Works to educate the public to support careers for the disabled.

Computer Programmers

★2510★ ACM Transactions on Graphics (TOG)
Association for Computing Machinery
2 Penn Plz., Ste. 701
New York, NY 10121-0701
Ph: (212)869-7440   Fax: (212)944-1318
Fr: 800-342-6626
URL: http://www.acm.org/tog/

Quarterly. $195.00/year for nonmembers, per year; $156.00/year for nonmembers, online; $234.00/year for nonmembers, online & print. Computer graphics journal.

★2511★ ACM Transactions on Internet Technology (ACM TOIT)
Association for Computing Machinery
2 Penn Plz., Ste. 701
New York, NY 10121-0701
Ph: (212)869-7440   Fax: (212)944-1318
Fr: 800-342-6626
URL: http://www.acm.org/pubs/periodicals/toit/

Quarterly. $35.00/year for members; $30.00/year for students; $140.00/year for nonmembers; $170.00/year for individuals, print only; $136.00 for single issue, online only; $204.00 for single issue, online & print. Publication of the Association for Computing Machinery. Brings together many computing disciplines including computer software engineering, computer programming languages, middleware, database management, security, knowledge discovery and data mining, networking and distributed systems, communications, performance and scalability, and more. Covers the results and roles of the individual disciplines and the relationships among them.

★2512★ AVIOS Journal
Applied Voice Input/Output Society
PO Box 20817
San Jose, CA 95160
Ph: (408)323-1783   Fax: (408)323-1782
E-mail: info@avios.org

URL: http://www.avios.com/
Annual. Journal covering issues in computer science.

★2513★ Communications of the ACM
Association for Computing Machinery
2 Penn Plz., Ste. 701
New York, NY 10121-0701
Ph: (212)869-7440   Fax: (212)944-1318
Fr: 800-342-6626
URL: http://www.acm.org/pubs/cacm/

Monthly. $179.00/year for nonmembers; $36.00/year for members. Computing news magazine.

★2514★ Computers and Composition
Elsevier Science Inc.
360 Park Ave. S
New York, NY 10010
Ph: (212)989-5800   Fax: (212)633-3990
URL: http://www.elsevier.com

$353.00/year for institutions; $69.00/year for individuals. Journal covering computers in writing classes, programs, and research.

★2515★ Computers Programs/PC World
IDG Communications Inc.
5 Speen St., 3rd. Fl
Framingham, MA 01701
Ph: (508)875-5000   Fax: (508)988-7888
URL: http://www.idg.com

Magazine devoted to IT specialists, covering practical questions of computing including purchase and usage of the computer technology, software, computer components and peripherals.

★2516★ Computerworld
101 Communications
9121 Oakdale Ave., Ste. 101
Chatsworth, CA 91311
Ph: (818)734-1520   Fax: (818)734-1522
URL: http://www.computerworld.com

Weekly. $99.00/year for individuals, new Australian subscribers; $99.00/year for individuals, renewals Australian; $250.00/year

for other countries, airmail; $375.00/year for other countries, overseas (airmail). Newspaper for information systems executives.

★2517★ Computerworld/Correio Informatico
IDG Communications Inc.
5 Speen St., 3rd. Fl
Framingham, MA 01701
Ph: (508)875-5000   Fax: (508)988-7888
URL: http://www.idg.com

Weekly. Magazine providing news on latest developments in computer industry.

★2518★ Computerworld Top 100
IDG Communications Inc.
5 Speen St., 3rd. Fl
Framingham, MA 01701
Ph: (508)875-5000   Fax: (508)988-7888
URL: http://www.idg.com

Annual. Magazine for analyzing trends and events of information technology business.

★2519★ Computing SA
IDG Communications Inc.
5 Speen St., 3rd. Fl
Framingham, MA 01701
Ph: (508)875-5000   Fax: (508)988-7888
URL: http://www.idg.com

Monthly. Newspaper focusing computer hardware, software, networking, telecommunications, channel management and online computing.

★2520★ Computing Surveys (CSUR)
Association for Computing Machinery
2 Penn Plz., Ste. 701
New York, NY 10121-0701
Ph: (212)869-7440   Fax: (212)944-1318
Fr: 800-342-6626
URL: http://www.acm.org/pubs/surveys/

Quarterly. $185.00 for nonmembers, print only yearly rate; $148.00/year for nonmembers, online only; $222.00 for single issue, online & print; $208.00 for single issue, print with expedited air; $245.00 for single issue, online & print with expedited air. Journal presenting surveys and tutorials in computer science.

★2521★ Consumer Electronics Lifestyles

Sandhills Publishing
120 W Harvest Dr.
Lincoln, NE 68521
Ph: (402)479-2181   Fax: (402)479-2195
Fr: 800-331-1978
E-mail: editor@ceLifestyles.com
URL: http://www.celifestyles.com/

Monthly. $12.00/year. Magazine for computer and electronic gadget enthusiasts.

★2522★ CXO

IDG Communications Inc.
5 Speen St., 3rd. Fl
Framingham, MA 01701
Ph: (508)875-5000   Fax: (508)988-7888
URL: http://www.idg.com

Monthly. Magazine providing technology information for chief officers and managers.

★2523★ Datamation

Reed Business Information
225 Wyman St.
Waltham, MA 02451-1216
URL: http://www.datamation.com

Semimonthly. Magazine on computers and information processing.

★2524★ Digital News & Review

Reed Business Information
225 Wyman St.
Waltham, MA 02451-1216

Semimonthly. Free to qualified subscribers. Covers information storage and retrieval and data systems.

★2525★ Dr. Dobb's Journal

CMP Media L.L.C.
2800 Campus Dr.
San Mateo, CA 94403
Ph: (650)513-4300   Fax: (650)513-4618
Fr: 800-842-0798
E-mail: webmaster@ercb.com
URL: http://www.ddj.com

Monthly. $25.00/year for individuals; $99.95/year for individuals, CD-ROM library. Magazine covering computer programming.

★2526★ E-Business Advisor

e-Business Advisor
PO Box 429002
San Diego, CA 92142
Ph: (858)278-5600   Fax: (858)278-0300
Fr: 800-336-6060
URL: http://www.e-businessadvisor.com

Magazine for developing strategies, practices, and innovations for e-business applications.

★2527★ Eclipse Review

BZ Media LLC
7 High St., Ste. 407
Huntington, NY 11743
Ph: (631)421-4158   Fax: (631)421-4130
URL: http://www.eclipsesource.com/contact.htm

Magazine for IT professionals.

★2528★ ENA powered by Network World

IDG Communications Inc.
5 Speen St., 3rd. Fl
Framingham, MA 01701
Ph: (508)875-5000   Fax: (508)988-7888
URL: http://www.idg.com

Monthly. Journal covering information on networking.

★2529★ Foundations of Computational Mathematics

Springer-Verlag New York Inc.
233 Spring St.
New York, NY 10013
Ph: (212)460-1500   Fax: (212)460-1575

Academic journal that publishes articles related to the connections between mathematics and computation, including the interfaces between pure and applied mathematics, numerical analysis and computer science.

★2530★ Foundations and Trends in Networking

Now Publishers
PO Box 1024
Hanover, MA 02339
Ph: (781)871-0245
URL: http://www.nowpublishers.com/product.aspx?product=NET

$315.00/year online only; $355.00/year print and online; $315.00/year online only; $355.00/year print and online. Academic journal publishing new research in computer networking.

★2531★ Government Computer News

PostNewsweek Tech Media
10 G St. NE, Ste. 500
Washington, DC 20002-4228
Ph: (202)772-2500   Fax: (202)772-2511
Fr: (866)447-6864

Semimonthly. Magazine for professionals interested in government IT.

★2532★ IEEE Computer Graphics and Applications

IEEE Computer Society
10662 Los Vaqueros Cir.
PO Box 3014
Los Alamitos, CA 90720-1314
Ph: (714)821-8380   Fax: (714)821-4010
Fr: 800-272-6657
URL: http://www.computer.org/cga/

Bimonthly. $20.00/year for members; $116.00/year for nonmembers. Magazine addressing the interests and needs of professional designers and users of computer graphics hardware, software, and systems.

★2533★ IEEE Security & Privacy Magazine

IEEE Computer Society
10662 Los Vaqueros Cir.
PO Box 3014
Los Alamitos, CA 90720-1314
Ph: (714)821-8380   Fax: (714)821-4010
Fr: 800-272-6657
URL: http://www.computer.org/portal/site/security/

Bimonthly. $24.00/year for members; $29.00/year for nonmembers; $28.00/year for members; $565.00/year for libraries, institution. Journal that aims to explore role and importance of networked infrastructure and developing lasting security solutions.

★2534★ IEEE Software

IEEE Computer Society
10662 Los Vaqueros Cir.
PO Box 3014
Los Alamitos, CA 90720-1314
Ph: (714)821-8380   Fax: (714)821-4010
Fr: 800-272-6657
E-mail: software@computer.org
URL: http://www.computer.org/software

Bimonthly. $77.00/year for nonmembers, individual; $46.00/year for members, plus online access to software articles; $76.00/year for members; $765.00/year for institutions library. Magazine covering the computer software industry for the community of leading software practitioners.

★2535★ Information Security

TechTarget
117 Kendrick St., Ste. 800
Needham, MA 02494
Ph: (781)657-1000   Fax: (781)657-1100
URL: http://searchsecurity.techtarget.com/

Monthly. Free to qualified subscribers. Magazine covering information security topics.

★2536★ InformationWeek

CMP Media L.L.C.
600 Community Dr.
Manhasset, NY 11030
Ph: (516)562-5000   Fax: (516)562-7830
URL: http://www.informationweek.com

Weekly. Free to qualified subscribers. Magazine focusing on data and information processing news and strategies.

★2537★ InfoWorld

InfoWorld Media Group
501 Second St.
San Francisco, CA 94107
Fr: 800-227-8365
E-mail: letters@infoworld.com
URL: http://www.infoworld.com/

Weekly. Free to qualified subscribers; $180.00/year for individuals. Weekly publication.

★2538★ **Intelligent Enterprise**

CMP Media L.L.C.
600 Community Dr.
Manhasset, NY 11030
Ph: (516)562-5000   Fax: (516)562-7830
E-mail: tgibb@cmp.com
URL: http://www.intelligententerprise.com

Periodic. Free. Magazine serving business and IT professionals.

★2539★ **International Journal of Computer Games Technology**

Hindawi Publishing Corp.
410 Park Ave., 15th Fl.
287 PMB
New York, NY 10022
E-mail: ijcgt@hindawi.com
URL: http://www.hindawi.com/journals/ijcgt/

$195.00/year for individuals. Journal covering research and development aspects of games technology.

★2540★ **iSeries News Magazine**

Penton Media
221 E 29th St.
Loveland, CO 80538
Ph: (970)663-4700   Fax: (970)667-2321
Fr: 800-621-1544
E-mail: service@iseriesnetwork.com
URL: http://www.systeminetwork.com/info/networkpubs/news400/about

$149.00/year for U.S. and Canada; $199.00/year for other countries. Trade magazine for programmers and data processing managers who use IBM iSeries.

★2541★ **IT Focus**

IDG Communications Inc.
5 Speen St., 3rd. Fl
Framingham, MA 01701
Ph: (508)875-5000   Fax: (508)988-7888
URL: http://www.idg.com

Online journal focusing mainly on information technology.

★2542★ **IT Solutions Guide**

SYS-CON Media
135 Chestnut Ridge Rd.
Montvale, NJ 07645
Ph: (201)802-3000   Fax: (201)782-9600
Fr: 888-303-5282
URL: http://itsolutions.sys-con.com/

Quarterly. $4.00/year for individuals, single pdf issue. Magazine for IT professionals.

★2543★ **Journal of Computer Science**

Science Publications
Vails Gate Heights Dr.
PO Box 879
Vails Gate, NY 12584
URL: http://www.scipub.us/

Bimonthly. $3,500.00/year for individuals; $300.00/year for single issue. Scholarly journal covering many areas of computer science, including: concurrent, parallel and distributed processing; artificial intelligence; image and voice processing; quality software and metrics; computer-aided education; wireless communication; real time processing; evaluative computation; and data bases and information recovery and neural networks.

★2544★ **Journal of Computer Systems, Networks, and Communications**

Hindawi Publishing Corp.
410 Park Ave., 15th Fl.
287 PMB
New York, NY 10022
E-mail: jcsnc@hindawi.com
URL: http://www.hindawi.com/journals/jcsnc/

$195.00/year for individuals. Journal covering important areas of information technology.

★2545★ **Kompiuterija PC World**

IDG Communications Inc.
5 Speen St., 3rd. Fl
Framingham, MA 01701
Ph: (508)875-5000   Fax: (508)988-7888
URL: http://www.idg.com

Monthly. Journal providing professionals, business people and users with up-to-date information on computers and the internet.

★2546★ **Mikro PC**

IDG Communications Inc.
5 Speen St., 3rd. Fl
Framingham, MA 01701
Ph: (508)875-5000   Fax: (508)988-7888
URL: http://www.idg.com

Monthly. Magazine focusing on information technology and digital lifestyle.

★2547★ **Monitor**

Capital PC User Group
19209 Mt. Airey Rd.
Brookeville, MD 20833
Ph: (301)560-6442   Fax: (301)760-3303
URL: http://monitor.cpcug.org/index.html

Quarterly. Magazine covering computer hardware and software reviews, special interest user group news, advertisers and author/subject index, and calendar of events.

★2548★ **NetWorld**

IDG Communications Inc.
5 Speen St., 3rd. Fl
Framingham, MA 01701
Ph: (508)875-5000   Fax: (508)988-7888
URL: http://www.idg.com

Monthly. Magazine focusing on networks, security, infrastructure management, wireless, mobile and VOIP technologies.

★2549★ **PC Magazine**

Ziff-Davis Publishing Co.
28 East 28th St.
New York, NY 10016
Ph: (212)503-3500
E-mail: pcmag@ziffdavis.com
URL: http://www.ziffdavisinternet.com/websites/pcmag

Biweekly. $19.97/year for individuals, 25 issues. Tabloid featuring microcomputer products and developments.

★2550★ **PC Today**

Sandhills Publishing
120 W Harvest Dr.
Lincoln, NE 68521
Ph: (402)479-2181   Fax: (402)479-2195
Fr: 800-331-1978
URL: http://www.sandhills.com

Monthly. $29.00/year for U.S. $37.00/year for Canada; $64.00/year for Canada, print; $2.42/year for U.S., print; $2.42 for single issue, in U.S. Magazine for personal computer users.

★2551★ **PC WORLD**

101 Communications
9121 Oakdale Ave., Ste. 101
Chatsworth, CA 91311
Ph: (818)734-1520   Fax: (818)734-1522
URL: http://www.pcworld.com

Quarterly. $20.00/year for individuals, 12 issues; $30.00/year for individuals, 24 issues. Technology or business magazine meeting the informational needs of tech-savvy managers, both at work and at home.

★2552★ **Queue**

Association for Computing Machinery
2 Penn Plz., Ste. 701
New York, NY 10121-0701
Ph: (212)869-7440   Fax: (212)944-1318
Fr: 800-342-6626
URL: http://www.acmqueue.org/

Monthly. Free, U.S./Canadian residents and all members. Online magazine aimed at the computer professional. Magazine editorial does not provide solutions for the "here-and-now," but instead helps decision-makers plan future projects by examining the challenges and problems they are most likely to face.

★2553★ **Revenue**

Montgomery Media International
300 Montgomery St., Ste. 1135
San Francisco, CA 94104
Ph: (415)397-2400   Fax: (415)397-2420
URL: http://www.revenuetoday.com/

$30.00/year for individuals. Magazine covering internet marketing strategies.

★2554★ **SMB Data**

IDG Communications Inc.
5 Speen St., 3rd. Fl
Framingham, MA 01701
Ph: (508)875-5000   Fax: (508)988-7888
URL: http://www.idg.com

Magazine focusing on information technology systems at small and medium-size businesses.

★2555★ SME World

IDG Communications Inc.
5 Speen St., 3rd. Fl
Framingham, MA 01701
Ph: (508)875-5000　　Fax: (508)988-7888
URL: http://www.idg.com

Magazine covering articles on technology, technology investments, IT products and services.

★2556★ Software Development

CMP Media L.L.C.
600 Community Dr.
Manhasset, NY 11030
Ph: (516)562-5000　　Fax: (516)562-7830
E-mail: aweber@cmp.com
URL: http://www.cmp.com/pubinfo?pubid=68

Monthly. $19.95/year for individuals. Magazine for the computer programming industry.

★2557★ TecCHANNEL Compact

IDG Communications Inc.
5 Speen St., 3rd. Fl
Framingham, MA 01701
Ph: (508)875-5000　　Fax: (508)988-7888
URL: http://www.idg.com

Quarterly. Magazine covering issues of information technology.

★2558★ Tips & Trucs

IDG Communications Inc.
5 Speen St., 3rd. Fl
Framingham, MA 01701
Ph: (508)875-5000　　Fax: (508)988-7888
URL: http://www.idg.com

Monthly. Magazine covering topics on computer hardware, software and the internet.

★2559★ Top 100

IDG Communications Inc.
5 Speen St., 3rd. Fl
Framingham, MA 01701
Ph: (508)875-5000　　Fax: (508)988-7888
URL: http://www.idg.com

Annual. Magazine providing analyses, assessments and statistics on information technology industry.

★2560★ Ubiquity

Association for Computing Machinery
2 Penn Plz., Ste. 701
New York, NY 10121-0701
Ph: (212)869-7440　　Fax: (212)944-1318
Fr: 800-342-6626
URL: http://www.acm.org/ubiquity/

Weekly. Free to members; $163.00/year for nonmembers, 12 issues. Web-based magazine of the Association for Computing Machinery dedicated to fostering critical analysis and in-depth commentary, including book reviews, on issues relating to the nature, constitution, structure, science, engineering, cognition, technology, practices and paradigms of the IT profession.

★2561★ WebLogic Pro

Fawcette Technical Publications
2600 S El Camino Real, Ste. 300
San Mateo, CA 94403-2332
Ph: (650)378-7100　　Fax: (650)570-6307
Fr: 800-848-5523
URL: http://www.weblogicpro.com

Bimonthly. Free to qualified subscribers. Magazine that aims to provides IT solutions for developers, architects, and administrators.

★2562★ WITI FastTrack

CMP Media L.L.C.
600 Community Dr.
Manhasset, NY 11030
Ph: (516)562-5000　　Fax: (516)562-7830
URL: http://www.witi.com/corporate/fasttrack.php

Semiannual. Semiannual publication featuring in-depth content on the issues facing today's women professionals in technology.

★2563★ The World Wide Web Journal of Biology

Epress, Inc.
130 Union Terrace Ln.
Plymouth, MN 55441
URL: http://www.epress.com/w3jbio/

Journal on Bio-informatics.

PLACEMENT AND JOB REFERRAL SERVICES

★2564★ American Indian Science and Engineering Society (AISES)

PO Box 9828
Albuquerque, NM 87119-9828
Ph: (505)765-1052　　Fax: (505)765-5608
E-mail: info@aises.org
URL: http://www.aises.org

Description: Represents American Indian and non-Indian students and professionals in science, technology, and engineering fields; corporations representing energy, mining, aerospace, electronic, and computer fields. Seeks to motivate and encourage students to pursue undergraduate and graduate studies in science, engineering, and technology. Sponsors science fairs in grade schools, teacher training workshops, summer math/science sessions for 8th-12th graders, professional chapters, and student chapters in colleges. Offers scholarships. Adult members serve as role models, advisers, and mentors for students. Operates placement service.

EMPLOYER DIRECTORIES AND NETWORKING LISTS

★2565★ Careers in Focus: Computer & Video Game Design

Facts On File Inc.
132 W 31st St., 17th Fl.
New York, NY 10001
Ph: (212)967-8800　　Fax: 800-678-3633
Fr: 800-322-8755
URL: http://www.factsonfile.com

Published 2005. $29.95 for individuals; $26.95 for libraries. Covers an overview of computer and video game design, followed by a selection of jobs profiled in detail, including the nature of the job, earnings, prospects for employment, what kind of training and skills it requires, and sources for further information.

★2566★ Careers in Focus: Computers

Facts On File Inc.
132 W 31st St., 17th Fl.
New York, NY 10001
Ph: (212)967-8800　　Fax: 800-678-3633
Fr: 800-322-8755
URL: http://www.factsonfile.com

Latest edition 4th, 2004. $29.95 for individuals; $26.95 for libraries. Covers an overview of computers, followed by a selection of jobs profiled in detail, including the nature of the job, earnings, prospects for employment, what kind of training and skills it requires, and sources for further information.

★2567★ Computer Directory

Computer Directories Inc.
23815 Nichols Sawmill Rd.
Hockley, TX 77447
Ph: (281)356-7880　　Fr: 800-234-4353
URL: http://www.compdirinc.com

Annual, fall. Covers approximately 130,000 computer installation companies; 19 separate volumes for Alaska/Hawaii, Connecticut/New Jersey, Dallas/Ft. Worth, Eastern Seaboard, Far Midwest, Houston, Illinois, Midatlantic, Midcentral, Mideast, Minnesota/Wisconsin, North Central, New England, New York Metro, Northwest, Ohio, Pennsylvania/West Virginia, Southeast, and Southwest Texas. Entries include: Company name, address, phone, fax, e-mail, name and title of contact, hardware used, software application, operating system, programming language, computer graphics, networking system. Arrangement: Geographical. Indexes: Alphabetical; industry; hardware.

★2568★ Directory of Top Computer Executives

Applied Computer Research
PO Box 41730
Phoenix, AZ 85080-1730
Ph: (602)216-9100　　Fax: (602)548-4800
Fr: 800-234-2227
URL: http://www.itmarketintelligence.com

Semiannual, June and December. Covers, in

three volumes, over 55,000 U.S. and Canadian executives with major information technology or communications responsibilities in over 30,000 U.S. and Canadian companies. Entries include: Company name, address, phone, subsidiary and/or division names, major systems installed, names and titles of top information system executives, number of IT employees, number of PCs, and web address. Arrangement: Geographical within separate eastern, western, and Canadian volumes. Indexes: Industry; alphabetical by company name.

★2569★ **Discovering Careers for Your Future: Computers**

Facts On File Inc.
132 W 31st Fl., 17th Fl.
New York, NY 10001
Ph: (212)967-8800   Fax: 800-678-3633
Fr: 800-322-8755
URL: http://www.factsonfile.com

Published 2001. $21.95 for individuals; $19.75 for libraries. Covers computer operators, programmers, database specialists, and software engineers; links career education to curriculum, helping children investigate the subjects they are interested in, and the careers those subjects might lead to.

★2570★ **Peterson's Job Opportunities in Engineering and Technology**

Peterson's Guides
2000 Lenox Dr.
Box 67005
Lawrenceville, NJ 08648
Ph: (609)896-1800   Fax: (609)896-4531
Fr: 800-338-3282
E-mail: custsvc@petersons.com
URL: http://www.petersons.com

Compiled by the Peterson's staff. Fourth edition, 1996. $21.95 (paper). 379 pages. Profiles 2,000 high-tech companies looking primarily for technical personnel in such fields as biotechnology, telecommunications, software, computers and peripherals, defense, and aerospace. Contains job-search strategies and career options to help match education and expertise to the job market. Indexed geographically, by industry, and by hiring needs.

HANDBOOKS AND MANUALS

★2571★ **America's Top 101 Computer and Technical Jobs**

Jist Publishing
875 Montreal Way
St. Paul, MN 55102
Fr: 800-648-5478
E-mail: info@jist.com
URL: http://www.jist.com

Michael J. Farr. 2004. $26.20. 359 pages. Job hunting in computer and technical industries.

★2572★ **Career Opportunities in Computers and Cyberspace**

Facts On File Inc.
132 W. 31st St., 17th Fl.
New York, NY 10001-2006
Ph: (212)967-8800   Fax: 800-678-3633
Fr: 800-322-8755
E-mail: custserv@factsonfile.com
URL: http://www.factsonfile.com

Harry Henderson. Second edition, 2004. $18.95 (paper). Part of the Career Opportunities Series. 256 pages.

★2573★ **Careers for Computer Buffs and Other Technological Types**

The McGraw-Hill Companies
PO Box 182604
Columbus, OH 43272
Fax: (614)759-3749   Fr: 877-883-5524
E-mail: customer.service@mcgraw-hill.com
URL: http://www.mcgraw-hill.com

Marjorie Eberts and Margaret Gisler. Third edition, 2006. $13.95 (paper). 160 pages. Suggested jobs in a wide range of settings, from the office to the outdoors.

★2574★ **Careers in the Computer Game Industry**

The Rosen Publishing Group Inc.
29 E. 21st St.
New York, NY 10010
Ph: (212)777-3017   Fax: (212)777-0277
Fr: 800-237-9932
URL: http://www.rosenpublishing.com/

Peter Suciu, David Gerardi. 2005. $31.95. 144 pages. Careers in mathematics.

★2575★ **Careers in Computers**

The McGraw-Hill Companies
PO Box 182604
Columbus, OH 43272
Fax: (614)759-3749   Fr: 877-883-5524
E-mail: customer.service@mcgraw-hill.com
URL: http://www.mcgraw-hill.com

Lila B. Stair and Leslie Stair. 2002. $19.95; $14.95 (paper). 192 pages. Describes trends affecting computer careers and explores a wide range of job opportunities from programming to consulting. Provides job qualifications, salary data, job market information, personal and educational requirements, career paths, and the place of the job in the organizational structure. Offers advice on education, certification, and job search.

★2576★ **Careers Inside the World of Technology**

Pearson Learning Group
135 S. Mt. Zion Rd.
PO Box 2500
Lebanon, IN 46052
Fax: 800-393-3156   Fr: 800-526-9907
URL: http://www.pearsonatschool.com

Jean W. Spencer. Revised edition, 2000. $13.50. 64 pages. Describes computer-related careers for reluctant readers.

★2577★ **Careers for Number Crunchers and Other Quantitative Types**

The McGraw-Hill Companies
PO Box 182604
Columbus, OH 43272
Fax: (614)759-3749   Fr: 877-883-5524
E-mail: customer.service@mcgraw-hill.com
URL: http://www.mcgraw-hill.com

Rebecca Burnett. Second edition, 2002. $22.95 (paper). 192 pages. Provides information to math-oriented job hunters on how to become statisticians, field researchers, computer programmers, stock analysts, investment managers, bankers, engineers, accountants, underwriters, economists, market analysts, mathematicians, systems analysts, and more.

★2578★ **Choosing a Career in Computers**

Rosen Publishing Group, Inc.
29 E. 21st St.
New York, NY 10010
Ph: (212)777-3017   Fax: (212)777-0277
Fr: 800-237-9932
URL: http://www.rosenpublishing.com/

Weigant, Chris. 2000. $29.25. Presents many of the options available to people interested in the technical side of the computer world-from designing and building computers to writing manuals explaining how to use them.

★2579★ **The Digital Frontier Job & Opportunity Finder**

Moon Lake Media
PO Box 251466
Los Angeles, CA 90025
Ph: (310)535-2453

Don B. Altman. 1996. $19.95 (paper). 245 pages.

★2580★ **Expert Resumes for Computer and Web Jobs**

Jist Publishing
875 Montreal Way
St. Paul, MN 55102
Fr: 800-648-5478
E-mail: info@jist.com
URL: http://www.jist.com

Wendy Enelow and Louis Kursmark. Second edition, 2005. $16.95 (paper). 286 pages.

★2581★ **Get Your IT Career in Gear!**

The McGraw-Hill Companies
PO Box 182604
Columbus, OH 43272
Fax: (614)759-3749   Fr: 877-883-5524
E-mail: customer.service@mcgraw-hill.com
URL: http://www.mcgraw-hill.com

Leslie Goff. 2001. $24.99 (paper). 401 pages.

★2582★ Great Jobs for Computer Science Majors

The McGraw-Hill Companies
PO Box 182604
Columbus, OH 43272
Fax: (614)759-3749   Fr: 877-883-5524
E-mail: customer.service@mcgraw-hill.com
URL: http://www.mcgraw-hill.com

Jan Goldberg, Stephen Lambert, Julie De-Galan. Second edition, 2002. $14.95 (paper). 224 pages.

★2583★ Job Seekers Guide to Silicon Valley Recruiters

John Wily and Sons, Inc.
605 Third Ave., 4th Fl.
New York, NY 10158-0012
Ph: (212)850-6276   Fax: (212)850-8641

Christopher W. Hunt, Scott A. Scanlon. First edition, 1998. $19.95 (paper). 371 pages. Includes a list of 2,400 recruiters specializing in high technology positions and explains how to work with them.

★2584★ The JobBank Guide to Computer and High-Tech Companies

Adams Media Corp.
57 Littlefield St.
Avon, MA 02322
Ph: (508)427-7100   Fax: (508)427-6790
Fr: 800-872-5627
URL: http://www.adamsmedia.com

Steven Graber, Marcie Dipietro, and Michelle Roy Kelly. Second edition, 1999. $17.95 (paper). 700 pages. Contains profiles of more than 4,500 high-tech employers.

★2585★ Opportunities in Computer Careers

The McGraw-Hill Companies
PO Box 182604
Columbus, OH 43272
Fax: (614)759-3749   Fr: 877-883-5524
E-mail: customer.service@mcgraw-hill.com
URL: http://www.mcgraw-hill.com

Julie Kling Burns. $12.95 (netLibrary). 160 pages. 2001. Computer vocational guidance and counseling.

★2586★ Opportunities in High Tech Careers

The McGraw-Hill Companies
PO Box 182604
Columbus, OH 43272
Fax: (614)759-3749   Fr: 877-883-5524
E-mail: customer.service@mcgraw-hill.com
URL: http://www.mcgraw-hill.com

Gary Colter and Deborah Yanuck. 1999. $14.95; $11.95 (paper). 160 pages. Explores high technology careers. Describes job opportunities, how to make a career decision, how to prepare for high technology jobs, job hunting techniques, and future trends.

★2587★ Opportunities in Office Occupations

The McGraw-Hill Companies
PO Box 182604
Columbus, OH 43272
Fax: (614)759-3749   Fr: 877-883-5524
E-mail: customer.service@mcgraw-hill.com
URL: http://www.mcgraw-hill.com

Blanche Ettinger. 1995. $14.95; $11.95 (paper). 146 pages. Covers a variety of office positions and discusses trends for the next decade. Describes the job market, opportunities, job duties, educational preparation, the work environment, and earnings.

★2588★ Practices of an Agile Developer: Working in the Real World

Pragamatic Bookshelf
9650 Strickland Rd., Ste. 103, PMB 255
Raleigh, NC 27615
Ph: (919)847-3884

Venkat Subramaniam and Andy Hunt. 2006. $29.95. Provides expertise in the areas of development processes, coding techniques, developer attitudes, project and team management, and iterative and incremental learning techniques in the field of computer programming.

★2589★ Preparing for an Outstanding Career in Computers: Questions and Answers for Professionals and Students

Rafi Systems, Incorporated
750 N. Diamond Bar Blvd., Ste. 224
Diamond Bar, CA 91765
Ph: (909)593-8124   Fax: (909)629-1034
Fr: 800-584-6706
E-mail: rafisystems@rafisystems.com
URL: http://www.rafisystems.com/

Mohamed Rafiquzzaman. 2001. $19.95. 204 pages. Book contains over 300 questions and answers on various important aspects of computers. Topics include basic and state-of-the-art concepts from digital logic to the design of a complete microcomputer.

★2590★ Unlocking the Clubhouse: Women in Computing

MIT Press
55 Hayward St.
Cambridge, MA 02142-1493
Ph: (617)253-5646   Fax: (617)258-6779
Fr: 800-405-1619
URL: http://mitpress.mit.edu/main/home/default.asp

Jane Margolis and Allan Fisher. 2003. $15.00. 182 pages.

★2591★ The Unofficial Guide to Getting a Job at Microsoft

The McGraw-Hill Companies
PO Box 182604
Columbus, OH 43272
Fax: (614)759-3749   Fr: 877-883-5524
E-mail: customer.service@mcgraw-hill.com
URL: http://www.mcgraw-hill.com

Rebecca Smith. 2000. $16.95 (paper). 192 pages.

★2592★ Winning Resumes for Computer Personnel

Barron's Educational Series, Inc.
250 Wireless Blvd.
Hauppauge, NY 11788-3917
Ph: (631)434-3311   Fax: (631)434-3723
Fr: 800-645-3476
E-mail: fbrown@barronseduc.com
URL: http://barronseduc.com

Anne Hart. Second edition, 1998. $14.95 (paper). 260 pages.

★2593★ Your Resume: Key to a Better Job

Arco Pub.
200 Old Tappan Rd.
Old Tappan, NJ 07675
Fr: 800-428-5331

Leonard Corwen. Sixth edition, 1996. $10.95 (paper). 176 pages. Provides guidelines for resume writing; explains what employers look for in a resume, including contents and style. Includes model resumes for high-demand careers such as computer programmers, health administrators, and high-tech professionals. Notes basic job-getting information and strategies.

EMPLOYMENT AGENCIES AND SEARCH FIRMS

★2594★ The Aspire Group

52 Second Ave, 1st Fl
Waltham, MA 02451-1129
Fax: (718)890-1810   Fr: 800-487-2967
URL: http://www.bmanet.com

Employment agency.

★2595★ C Associates

1619 G St.,SE
PO Box 73868
Washington, DC 20056-3868
Ph: (202)518-8595   Fax: (202)387-7033
E-mail: john@cassociates.com
URL: http://www.cassociates.com

Personnel consultants specialize in the placement of computer professionals, concentrating in UNIX/C+ candidates. Serves private industries as well as government contractors. Also focus on oracle, ASP, and visual basic developers, programmers, system administrators and web developers.

★2596★ Carol Maden Group

2019 Cunningham Dr., Ste. 218
Hampton, VA 23666-3316
Ph: (757)827-9010   Fax: (757)827-9081
E-mail: cmaden@hroads.net

Personnel consultants offering placement

service in computer technology and engineering; servicing manufacturing and private industries nationwide. Temporary placement servicing clerical and light industrial.

★2597★ **Data Systems Search Consultants**

1615 Bonanza St., Ste. 405
Walnut Creek, CA 94596
Ph: (925)256-0635   Fax: (925)256-9099
E-mail: dsscinfo@dssc.com
URL: http://www.dssc.com

Employment agency. Executive search firm.

★2598★ **The Datafinders Group, Inc.**

25 E. Spring Valley Ave.
Maywood, NJ 07607
Ph: (201)845-7700   Fax: (201)845-7365
E-mail: info@datafinders.net
URL: http://www.datafinders.net

Executive search firm.

★2599★ **Dean Associates**

PO Box 1079
Santa Cruz, CA 95061
Ph: (831)423-2931
E-mail: marydearn@deanassociates.com
URL: http://www.deanassociates.com

Executive search firm focused on the high technology industry.

★2600★ **DillonGray**

1796 Equestrian Dr., Ste. 112
Pleasanton, CA 94588
Ph: (925)743-4444   Fax: (925)743-1144
E-mail: info@dillongray.com
URL: http://www.dillongray.com

Executive search firm focused on technology related companies.

★2601★ **Dynamic Search Systems Inc.**

220 W Campus Dr.
Arlington Heights, IL 60004
Ph: (847)259-3444   Fax: (847)259-3480
E-mail: candidate@dssjobs.com
URL: http://www.dssjobs.com

Provides executive and professional search services to the IT community. Firm specializes in the placement of developers, programmers, programmer analysts, systems analysts, project leaders, project managers, systems programmers, data processing consultants, IT directors, and other information technology related candidates. Industries served: all.

★2602★ **Huntington Personnel Consultants, Inc.**

PO Box 1077
Huntington, NY 11743-0640
Ph: (516)549-8888

Executive search firm and employment agency.

★2603★ **KForce**

Fr: 888-663-3626
URL: http://www.kforce.com

Executive search firm. More than 30 locations throughout the United States.

★2604★ **Michael Anthony Associates Inc.**

42 Washington St., Ste. 301
Wellesley, MA 02481-1802
Ph: (781)237-4950   Fax: (781)237-6811
Fr: 800-337-4950
E-mail: saymes@maainc.com
URL: http://www.maainc.com

Applications development, systems programming, communications, and database specialists servicing the IBM mainframe, midrange, and PC marketplace. Provides technical expertise of conversions, system software installation and upgrades, performance and tuning, capacity planning, and data communications. In addition to contract services also provide retained search and contingency placement of computer professionals ranging from senior staff to senior management. Also act as brokers for independent consultants and small consulting firms requiring the services of marketing specialists. Industries served: banking, financial services, hospitals, HMO's, manufacturers, software development, universities, defense, and consulting firms.

★2605★ **Strategic Staffing Solutions Inc.**

Penobscot Bldg., 645 Griswold, Ste. 2900
645 Griswold, Ste. 2900
Detroit, MI 48226-4216
Ph: (313)596-6900   Fax: (313)596-6905
Fr: 888-738-3261
E-mail: s3corporate@strategicstaff.com
URL: http://www.strategicstaff.com

Provides staffing for customized systems development, contract programming, customer specific training programs, and alternate staffing options. Industries served: banking, retail, health-care, manufacturing, telecommunications, and automotive.

★2606★ **Technical Talent Locators Ltd.**

5570 Sterrett Pl., Ste. 208
Columbia, MD 21044
Ph: (410)740-0091
E-mail: steve@ttlgroup.com
URL: http://www.ttlgroup.com

Permanent employment agency working within the following fields: software and database engineering; computer, communication, and telecommunication system engineering; and other computer-related disciplines.

★2607★ **TRC Staffing Services Inc.**

100 Ashford Ctr. N, Ste. 500
Atlanta, GA 30338
Ph: (770)392-1411   Fax: (770)393-2742
E-mail: info@trcstaff.com
URL: http://www.trcstaff.com

A full-service executive search company with permanent placements encompassing engineering, industrial sales, financial and computer science positions. Screen, interview, and verify past employment for all candidates prior to referral. Also assist personnel staffs in the attainment of their EEO/AAP goals with the placement of talented individuals in positions which are underutilized with minorities and/or women. Industries served: all.

★2608★ **Tri-Serv Inc.**

22 W. Padonia Rd., Ste. C-353
Timonium, MD 21093
Ph: (410)561-1740   Fax: (410)252-7417
E-mail: info@tri-serv.coom
URL: http://www.tri-serv.com

Employment agency for technical personnel.

★2609★ **Wallach Associates Inc.**

7811 Montrose Rd., Ste. 505
Potomac, MD 20854
Ph: (301)340-0300   Fax: (301)340-8008
Fr: 800-296-2084
E-mail: jobs@wallach.org
URL: http://www.wallach.org

Specialists in recruitment of professional personnel, primarily in information technology and electronic systems and engineering, energy research and development, management consulting, operations research, computers, defense systems, and programmers. Specializes in Internet and software engineer for intelligence community.

★2610★ **Worlco Computer Resources, Inc.**

997 Old Eagle School Rd., Ste. 219
Wayne, PA 19087
Ph: (610)293-9070   Fax: (610)293-1027
E-mail: parisi@worlco.com
URL: http://www.worlco.com

Employment agency and executive search firm. Second location in Cherry Hill, New Jersey.

ONLINE JOB SOURCES AND SERVICES

★2611★ **ComputerJobs.com**

280 Interstate North Cir., SE, Ste. 300
Atlanta, GA 30339-2411
Ph: 800-850-0045
URL: http://www.computerjobs.com

Description: The site is an employment tool for technology professionals. Information on positions is updated hourly for seekers. Jobs may be searched by skill, or by location nationally or in a specific state or city job market. Contains thousands of job postings. National jobs may be posted for free. Also career resources for IT professionals.

★2612★ Computerwork.com
Fr: 800-691-8413
E-mail: contactus@computerwork.com
URL: http://www.computerwork.com/

Description: Job search and resume submission service for professionals in information technology.

★2613★ Computerworld Careers
URL: http://www.computerworld.com/careertopics/careers

Description: Offers career opportunities for IT (information technology) professionals. Job seekers may search the jobs database, register at the site, and read about job surveys and employment trends. Employers may post jobs.

★2614★ Computing Research Association Job Announcements
1100 17th St., NW
Washington, DC 20036-4632
Ph: (202)234-2111   Fax: (202)667-1066
URL: http://www.cra.org/main/cra.jobs.html

Description: Contains dated links to national college and university computer technology positions.

★2615★ Dice.com
4101 NW Urbandale Dr.
Urbandale, IA 50322
Fax: (515)280-1452   Fr: 877-386-3323
URL: http://www.dice.com

Description: Job search database for computer consultants and high-tech professionals, listing thousands of high tech permanent contract and consulting jobs for programmers, software engineers, systems administrators, web developers, and hardware engineers. Also free career advice e-mail newsletter and job posting e-alerts.

★2616★ Guru.com
5001 Baum Blvd., Ste. 760
Pittsburgh, PA 15213
Ph: (412)687-1316   Fax: (412)687-4466
URL: http://www.guru.com

Description: Job board specializing in contract jobs for creative and information technology professionals. Also provides online incorporation and educational opportunities for independent contractors along with articles and advice.

★2617★ Ittalent.com
E-mail: ewsmith@ITtalent.com
URL: http://www.ittalent.com

Description: Job search and resume submission service for professionals in information technology.

★2618★ Jobs for Programmers
E-mail: prgjobs@jfpresources.com
URL: http://www.prgjobs.com
Description: Job board site for computer programmers that allows them to browse through thousands of programming jobs, even search for special jobs with sign-on bonuses, relocation funding, and 4-day work weeks. Resume posting is free.

★2619★ Softwarejobs.com
E-mail: info@softwarejobs.com
URL: http://www.softwarejobs.com

Description: Job search website for software programmers. Registrants can post their resume and search available positions, review career resources, and activate e-mail job alerts. Registration is free.

★2620★ ZDNet Tech Jobs
URL: http://www.zdnet.com/

Description: Site houses a listing of national employment opportunities for professionals in high tech fields. Also contains resume building tips and relocation resources.

TRADESHOWS

★2621★ Computer & Technology Showcase - Tulsa
Event Management Services
519 Cleveland St., Ste. 205
Clearwater, FL 33755
Ph: (503)234-1552   Fax: (503)234-4253
Fr: 800-422-0251
E-mail: mfriedman@event-management.com
URL: http://www.event-management.com

Annual. **Primary Exhibits:** Products and services for computers, imaging, wireless communication, networking, application development, and e-commerce.

★2622★ XPLOR Conference
XPLOR International
24238 Hawthorne Blvd.
Torrance, CA 90505-6505
Ph: (310)373-3633   Fax: (310)375-4240
Fr: 800-669-7567
E-mail: info@xplor.org
URL: http://www.xplor.org

Annual. **Primary Exhibits:** Equipment, supplies, and services for users and manufacturers of advanced electronic document systems.

OTHER SOURCES

★2623★ Association of Information Technology Professionals (AITP)
401 N Michigan Ave., Ste. 2400
Chicago, IL 60611-4267
Ph: (312)245-1070   Fax: (312)673-6659
Fr: 800-224-9371
E-mail: aitp_hq@aitp.org
URL: http://www.aitp.org

Members: Managerial personnel, staff, educators, and individuals interested in the management of information resources. Founder of the Certificate in Data Processing examination program, now administered by an intersociety organization. **Purpose:** Maintains Legislative Communications Network. Professional education programs include EDP-oriented business and management principles self-study courses and a series of videotaped management development seminars. Sponsors student organizations around the country interested in information technology and encourages members to serve as counselors for the Scout computer merit badge. Conducts research projects, including a business information systems curriculum for two- and four-year colleges.

★2624★ Association for Women in Computing (AWC)
41 Sutter St., Ste. 1006
San Francisco, CA 94104
Ph: (415)905-4663   Fax: (415)358-4667
E-mail: info@awc-hq.org
URL: http://www.awc-hq.org

Members: Individuals interested in promoting the education, professional development, and advancement of women in computing.

★2625★ Black Data Processing Associates (BDPA)
6301 Ivy Ln., Ste. 700
Greenbelt, MD 20770
Ph: (301)220-2180   Fax: (301)220-2185
Fr: 800-727-BDPA
E-mail: president@bdpa.org
URL: http://www.bdpa.org

Description: Represents persons employed in the information processing industry, including electronic data processing, electronic word processing, and data communications; others interested in information processing. Seeks to accumulate and share information processing knowledge and business expertise in order to increase the career and business potential of minorities in the information processing field. Conducts professional seminars, workshops, tutoring services, and community introductions to data processing. Makes annual donation to the United Negro College Fund.

★2626★ COIN Career Guidance System
COIN Educational Products
3361 Executive Pky., Ste. 302
Toledo, OH 43606
Ph: (419)536-5353   Fax: (419)536-7056
Fr: 800-274-8515
URL: http://www.coinedu.com/

CD-ROM. Provides career information through seven cross-referenced files covering postsecondary schools, college majors, vocational programs, military service, apprenticeship programs, financial aid, and scholarships. Apprenticeship file describes national apprenticeship training programs, including information on how to apply, contact agencies, and program content. Military file describes more than 200 military occupations and training opportunities related to civilian employment.

★2627★ **Computer Occupations**
Delphi Productions
3159 6th St.
Boulder, CO 80304
Ph: (303)443-2100   Fax: (303)443-4022
Fr: 888-443-2400
E-mail: support@delphivideo.com
URL: http://www.delphivideo.com

$95.00. 50 minutes. Part of the Careers for the 21st Century Video Library.

★2628★ **IEEE Computer Society (CS)**
1730 Massachusetts Ave. NW
Washington, DC 20036-1992
Ph: (202)371-0101   Fax: (202)728-9614
E-mail: help@computer.org
URL: http://www.computer.org

Description: Computer professionals. Promotes the development of computer and information sciences and fosters communication within the information processing community. Sponsors conferences, symposia, workshops, tutorials, technical meetings, and seminars. Operates Computer Society Press. Presents scholarships; bestows technical achievement and service awards and certificates.

★2629★ **Information Technology Occupations**
Delphi Productions
3159 6th St.
Boulder, CO 80304
Ph: (303)443-2100   Fax: (303)443-4022
Fr: 888-443-2400

E-mail: support@delphivideo.com
URL: http://www.delphivideo.com

$95.00. 52 minutes. Part of the Emerging Careers Video Library.

★2630★ **Information Technology Services**
Cambridge Educational
PO Box 2053
Princeton, NJ 08543-2053
Ph: 800-257-5126   Fax: (609)671-0266
Fr: 800-468-4227
E-mail: custserv@films.com
URL: http://www.cambridgeeducational.com

VHS and DVD. $89.95. 2002. 19 minutes. Part of the Career Cluster Series.

★2631★ **Institute for Certification of Computing Professionals (ICCP)**
2350 E Devon Ave., Ste. 115
Des Plaines, IL 60018-4610
Ph: (847)299-4227   Fax: (847)299-4280
Fr: 800-843-8227
E-mail: office@iccp.org
URL: http://www.iccp.org

Members: Professional societies. **Purpose:** Promotes the development of computer examinations which are of high quality, directed toward information technology professionals, and designed to encourage competence and professionalism. Individuals passing the exams automatically become members of the Institute for Certification of Computing Professionals and become certified as CCP or ACP. **Activities:** Has developed code of ethics and good practice to which those taking the exams promise to adhere. Maintains speakers' bureau; compiles statistics.

★2632★ **Internet Careers: College Not Required**
Cambridge Educational
PO Box 2053
Princeton, NJ 08543-2053
Fax: (609)671-0266   Fr: 800-257-5126
E-mail: custserv@films.com
URL: http://www.cambridgeeducational.com

VHS and DVD. 1998. $79.95. 28 minutes. Covers careers and job opportunities related to developing, programming, and managing Internet sites.

★2633★ **Resumes for High Tech Careers**
The McGraw-Hill Companies
PO Box 182604
Columbus, OH 43272
Fax: (614)759-3749   Fr: 877-883-5524
E-mail: customer.service@mcgraw-hill.com
URL: http://www.mcgraw-hill.com

Third edition, 2003. $10.95 (paper). 160 pages. Demonstrates how to tailor a resume that catches a high tech employer's attention. Part of "Resumes for ..." series.

★2634★ **Special Interest Group on Accessible Computing (SIGACCESS)**
IBM T.J. Watson Research Center
19 Skyline Dr.
Hawthorne, NY 10532
Ph: (914)784-6603   Fax: (914)784-7279
E-mail: chair_sigaccess@acm.org
URL: http://www.sigaccess.org

Description: Promotes the professional interests of computing personnel with physical disabilities and the application of computing and information technology in solving relevant disability problems. Works to educate the public to support careers for the disabled.

Computer Service Technicians

SOURCES OF HELP-WANTED ADS

★2635★ ACM Transactions on Internet Technology (ACM TOIT)
Association for Computing Machinery
2 Penn Plz., Ste. 701
New York, NY 10121-0701
Ph: (212)869-7440 Fax: (212)944-1318
Fr: 800-342-6626
URL: http://www.acm.org/pubs/periodicals/toit/

Quarterly. $35.00/year for members; $30.00/year for students; $140.00/year for nonmembers; $170.00/year for individuals, print only; $136.00 for single issue, online only; $204.00 for single issue, online & print. Publication of the Association for Computing Machinery. Brings together many computing disciplines including computer software engineering, computer programming languages, middleware, database management, security, knowledge discovery and data mining, networking and distributed systems, communications, performance and scalability, and more. Covers the results and roles of the individual disciplines and the relationships among them.

★2636★ AVIOS Journal
Applied Voice Input/Output Society
PO Box 20817
San Jose, CA 95160
Ph: (408)323-1783 Fax: (408)323-1782
E-mail: info@avios.org
URL: http://www.avios.com/

Annual. Journal covering issues in computer science.

★2637★ Communications of the ACM
Association for Computing Machinery
2 Penn Plz., Ste. 701
New York, NY 10121-0701
Ph: (212)869-7440 Fax: (212)944-1318
Fr: 800-342-6626
URL: http://www.acm.org/pubs/cacm/

Monthly. $179.00/year for nonmembers; $36.00/year for members. Computing news magazine.

★2638★ Computers and Composition
Elsevier Science Inc.
360 Park Ave. S
New York, NY 10010
Ph: (212)989-5800 Fax: (212)633-3990
URL: http://www.elsevier.com

$353.00/year for institutions; $69.00/year for individuals. Journal covering computers in writing classes, programs, and research.

★2639★ Computers Programs/PC World
IDG Communications Inc.
5 Speen St., 3rd. Fl
Framingham, MA 01701
Ph: (508)875-5000 Fax: (508)988-7888
URL: http://www.idg.com

Magazine devoted to IT specialists, covering practical questions of computing including purchase and usage of the computer technology, software, computer components and peripherals.

★2640★ Computerworld
101 Communications
9121 Oakdale Ave., Ste. 101
Chatsworth, CA 91311
Ph: (818)734-1520 Fax: (818)734-1522
URL: http://www.computerworld.com

Weekly. $99.00/year for individuals, new Australian subscribers; $99.00/year for individuals, renewals Australian; $250.00/year for other countries, airmail; $375.00/year for other countries, overseas (airmail). Newspaper for information systems executives.

★2641★ Computerworld/Correio Informatico
IDG Communications Inc.
5 Speen St., 3rd. Fl
Framingham, MA 01701
Ph: (508)875-5000 Fax: (508)988-7888
URL: http://www.idg.com

Weekly. Magazine providing news on latest developments in computer industry.

★2642★ Computerworld Top 100
IDG Communications Inc.
5 Speen St., 3rd. Fl
Framingham, MA 01701
Ph: (508)875-5000 Fax: (508)988-7888
URL: http://www.idg.com

Annual. Magazine for analyzing trends and events of information technology business.

★2643★ Computing SA
IDG Communications Inc.
5 Speen St., 3rd. Fl
Framingham, MA 01701
Ph: (508)875-5000 Fax: (508)988-7888
URL: http://www.idg.com

Monthly. Newspaper focusing computer hardware, software, networking, telecommunications, channel management and online computing.

★2644★ Consumer Electronics Lifestyles
Sandhills Publishing
120 W Harvest Dr.
Lincoln, NE 68521
Ph: (402)479-2181 Fax: (402)479-2195
Fr: 800-331-1978
E-mail: editor@ceLifestyles.com
URL: http://www.celifestyles.com/

Monthly. $12.00/year. Magazine for computer and electronic gadget enthusiasts.

★2645★ CXO
IDG Communications Inc.
5 Speen St., 3rd. Fl
Framingham, MA 01701
Ph: (508)875-5000 Fax: (508)988-7888
URL: http://www.idg.com

Monthly. Magazine providing technology information for chief officers and managers.

★2646★ Eclipse Review

BZ Media LLC
7 High St., Ste. 407
Huntington, NY 11743
Ph: (631)421-4158   Fax: (631)421-4130
URL: http://www.eclipsesource.com/contact.htm

Magazine for IT professionals.

★2647★ ENA powered by Network World

IDG Communications Inc.
5 Speen St., 3rd. Fl
Framingham, MA 01701
Ph: (508)875-5000   Fax: (508)988-7888
URL: http://www.idg.com

Monthly. Journal covering information on networking.

★2648★ Foundations of Computational Mathematics

Springer-Verlag New York Inc.
233 Spring St.
New York, NY 10013
Ph: (212)460-1500   Fax: (212)460-1575

Academic journal that publishes articles related to the connections between mathematics and computation, including the interfaces between pure and applied mathematics, numerical analysis and computer science.

★2649★ Foundations and Trends in Networking

Now Publishers
PO Box 1024
Hanover, MA 02339
Ph: (781)871-0245
URL: http://www.nowpublishers.com/product.aspx?product=NET

$315.00/year online only; $355.00/year print and online; $315.00/year online only; $355.00/year print and online. Academic journal publishing new research in computer networking.

★2650★ Government Computer News

PostNewsweek Tech Media
10 G St. NE, Ste. 500
Washington, DC 20002-4228
Ph: (202)772-2500   Fax: (202)772-2511
Fr: (866)447-6864

Semimonthly. Magazine for professionals interested in government IT.

★2651★ IEEE Security & Privacy Magazine

IEEE Computer Society
10662 Los Vaqueros Cir.
PO Box 3014
Los Alamitos, CA 90720-1314
Ph: (714)821-8380   Fax: (714)821-4010
Fr: 800-272-6657
URL: http://www.computer.org/portal/site/security/

Bimonthly. $24.00/year for members; $29.00/year for nonmembers; $28.00/year

for members; $565.00/year for libraries, institution. Journal that aims to explore role and importance of networked infrastructure and developing lasting security solutions.

★2652★ Information Security

TechTarget
117 Kendrick St., Ste. 800
Needham, MA 02494
Ph: (781)657-1000   Fax: (781)657-1100
URL: http://searchsecurity.techtarget.com/

Monthly. Free to qualified subscribers. Magazine covering information security topics.

★2653★ IT Focus

IDG Communications Inc.
5 Speen St., 3rd. Fl
Framingham, MA 01701
Ph: (508)875-5000   Fax: (508)988-7888
URL: http://www.idg.com

Online journal focusing mainly on information technology.

★2654★ IT Solutions Guide

SYS-CON Media
135 Chestnut Ridge Rd.
Montvale, NJ 07645
Ph: (201)802-3000   Fax: (201)782-9600
Fr: 888-303-5282
URL: http://itsolutions.sys-con.com/

Quarterly. $4.00/year for individuals, single pdf issue. Magazine for IT professionals.

★2655★ Journal of Computer Science

Science Publications
Vails Gate Heights Dr.
PO Box 879
Vails Gate, NY 12584
URL: http://www.scipub.us/

Bimonthly. $3,500.00/year for individuals; $300.00/year for single issue. Scholarly journal covering many areas of computer science, including: concurrent, parallel and distributed processing; artificial intelligence; image and voice processing; quality software and metrics; computer-aided education; wireless communication; real time processing; evaluative computation; and data bases and information recovery and neural networks.

★2656★ Journal of Computer Systems, Networks, and Communications

Hindawi Publishing Corp.
410 Park Ave., 15th Fl.
287 PMB
New York, NY 10022
E-mail: jcsnc@hindawi.com
URL: http://www.hindawi.com/journals/jcsnc/

$195.00/year for individuals. Journal covering important areas of information technology.

★2657★ Kompiuterija PC World

IDG Communications Inc.
5 Speen St., 3rd. Fl
Framingham, MA 01701
Ph: (508)875-5000   Fax: (508)988-7888
URL: http://www.idg.com

Monthly. Journal providing professionals, business people and users with up-to-date information on computers and the internet.

★2658★ Machine Design

Penton Media Inc.
1300 E 9th St.
Cleveland, OH 44114
Ph: (216)696-7000   Fax: (216)696-1752
E-mail: mdeditor@penton.com
URL: http://www.machinedesign.com

Semimonthly. $144.00/year for Canada, 21 issues; $160.00/year for Canada, regular; $108.00/year for other countries, 21 issues; $120.00/year for other countries, regular; $157.00/year for students, 21 issues; $175.00/year for students, regular. Magazine on design engineering function.

★2659★ Mikro PC

IDG Communications Inc.
5 Speen St., 3rd. Fl
Framingham, MA 01701
Ph: (508)875-5000   Fax: (508)988-7888
URL: http://www.idg.com

Monthly. Magazine focusing on information technology and digital lifestyle.

★2660★ Monitor

Capital PC User Group
19209 Mt. Airey Rd.
Brookeville, MD 20833
Ph: (301)560-6442   Fax: (301)760-3303
URL: http://monitor.cpcug.org/index.html

Quarterly. Magazine covering computer hardware and software reviews, special interest user group news, advertisers and author/subject index, and calendar of events.

★2661★ NetWorld

IDG Communications Inc.
5 Speen St., 3rd. Fl
Framingham, MA 01701
Ph: (508)875-5000   Fax: (508)988-7888
URL: http://www.idg.com

Monthly. Magazine focusing on networks, security, infrastructure management, wireless, mobile and VOIP technologies.

★2662★ PC Magazine

Ziff-Davis Publishing Co.
28 East 28th St.
New York, NY 10016
Ph: (212)503-3500
E-mail: pcmag@ziffdavis.com
URL: http://www.ziffdavisinternet.com/websites/pcmag

Biweekly. $19.97/year for individuals, 25 issues. Tabloid featuring microcomputer products and developments.

★2663★ PC WORLD

101 Communications
9121 Oakdale Ave., Ste. 101
Chatsworth, CA 91311
Ph: (818)734-1520   Fax: (818)734-1522
URL: http://www.pcworld.com

Quarterly. $20.00/year for individuals, 12 issues; $30.00/year for individuals, 24 issues. Technology or business magazine meeting the informational needs of tech-savvy managers, both at work and at home.

★2664★ Queue

Association for Computing Machinery
2 Penn Plz., Ste. 701
New York, NY 10121-0701
Ph: (212)869-7440   Fax: (212)944-1318
Fr: 800-342-6626
URL: http://www.acmqueue.org/

Monthly. Free, U.S./Canadian residents and all members. Online magazine aimed at the computer professional. Magazine editorial does not provide solutions for the "here-and-now," but instead helps decision-makers plan future projects by examining the challenges and problems they are most likely to face.

★2665★ Revenue

Montgomery Media International
300 Montgomery St., Ste. 1135
San Francisco, CA 94104
Ph: (415)397-2400   Fax: (415)397-2420
URL: http://www.revenuetoday.com/

$30.00/year for individuals. Magazine covering internet marketing strategies.

★2666★ SMB Data

IDG Communications Inc.
5 Speen St., 3rd. Fl
Framingham, MA 01701
Ph: (508)875-5000   Fax: (508)988-7888
URL: http://www.idg.com

Magazine focusing on information technology systems at small and medium-size businesses.

★2667★ SME World

IDG Communications Inc.
5 Speen St., 3rd. Fl
Framingham, MA 01701
Ph: (508)875-5000   Fax: (508)988-7888
URL: http://www.idg.com

Magazine covering articles on technology, technology investments, IT products and services.

★2668★ TecCHANNEL Compact

IDG Communications Inc.
5 Speen St., 3rd. Fl
Framingham, MA 01701
Ph: (508)875-5000   Fax: (508)988-7888
URL: http://www.idg.com

Quarterly. Magazine covering issues of information technology.

★2669★ Tips & Trucs

IDG Communications Inc.
5 Speen St., 3rd. Fl
Framingham, MA 01701
Ph: (508)875-5000   Fax: (508)988-7888
URL: http://www.idg.com

Monthly. Magazine covering topics on computer hardware, software and the internet.

★2670★ Top 100

IDG Communications Inc.
5 Speen St., 3rd. Fl
Framingham, MA 01701
Ph: (508)875-5000   Fax: (508)988-7888
URL: http://www.idg.com

Annual. Magazine providing analyses, assessments and statistics on information technology industry.

★2671★ Ubiquity

Association for Computing Machinery
2 Penn Plz., Ste. 701
New York, NY 10121-0701
Ph: (212)869-7440   Fax: (212)944-1318
Fr: 800-342-6626
URL: http://www.acm.org/ubiquity/

Weekly. Free to members; $163.00/year for nonmembers, 12 issues. Web-based magazine of the Association for Computing Machinery dedicated to fostering critical analysis and in-depth commentary, including book reviews, on issues relating to the nature, constitution, structure, science, engineering, cognition, technology, practices and paradigms of the IT profession.

★2672★ WebLogic Pro

Fawcette Technical Publications
2600 S El Camino Real, Ste. 300
San Mateo, CA 94403-2332
Ph: (650)378-7100   Fax: (650)570-6307
Fr: 800-848-5523
URL: http://www.weblogicpro.com

Bimonthly. Free to qualified subscribers. Magazine that aims to provides IT solutions for developers, architects, and administrators.

★2673★ WITI FastTrack

CMP Media L.L.C.
600 Community Dr.
Manhasset, NY 11030
Ph: (516)562-5000   Fax: (516)562-7830
URL: http://www.witi.com/corporate/fast-track.php

Semiannual. Semiannual publication featuring in-depth content on the issues facing today's women professionals in technology.

PLACEMENT AND JOB REFERRAL SERVICES

★2674★ ETA International - Electronics Technicians Association, International (ETA)

5 Depot St.
Greencastle, IN 46135
Ph: (765)653-8262   Fax: (765)653-4287
Fr: 800-288-3824
E-mail: eta@eta-i.org
URL: http://www.eta-i.org

Description: Skilled electronics technicians. Provides placement service; offers certification examinations for electronics technicians and satellite, fiber optics, and data cabling installers. Compiles wage and manpower statistics. Administers FCC Commercial License examinations and certification of computer network systems technicians and web and internet specialists.

EMPLOYER DIRECTORIES AND NETWORKING LISTS

★2675★ Computer Directory

Computer Directories Inc.
23815 Nichols Sawmill Rd.
Hockley, TX 77447
Ph: (281)356-7880   Fr: 800-234-4353
URL: http://www.compdirinc.com

Annual, fall. Covers approximately 130,000 computer installation companies; 19 separate volumes for Alaska/Hawaii, Connecticut/New Jersey, Dallas/Ft. Worth, Eastern Seaboard, Far Midwest, Houston, Illinois, Midatlantic, Midcentral, Mideast, Minnesota/Wisconsin, North Central, New England, New York Metro, Northwest, Ohio, Pennsylvania/West Virginia, Southeast, and Southwest Texas. Entries include: Company name, address, phone, fax, e-mail, name and title of contact, hardware used, software application, operating system, programming language, computer graphics, networking system. Arrangement: Geographical. Indexes: Alphabetical; industry; hardware.

★2676★ Directory of Top Computer Executives

Applied Computer Research
PO Box 41730
Phoenix, AZ 85080-1730
Ph: (602)216-9100   Fax: (602)548-4800
Fr: 800-234-2227
URL: http://www.itmarketintelligence.com

Semiannual, June and December. Covers, in three volumes, over 55,000 U.S. and Canadian executives with major information technology or communications responsibilities in over 30,000 U.S. and Canadian companies. Entries include: Company name, address, phone, subsidiary and/or division names, major systems installed, names and titles of top information system executives, number of IT employees, number of PCs, and web address. Arrangement: Geographical within separate eastern, western, and Canadian volumes. Indexes: Industry; alphabetical by company name.

HANDBOOKS AND MANUALS

★2677★ **America's Top 101 Computer and Technical Jobs**
Jist Publishing
875 Montreal Way
St. Paul, MN 55102
Fr: 800-648-5478
E-mail: info@jist.com
URL: http://www.jist.com

Michael J. Farr. 2004. $26.20. 359 pages. Job hunting in computer and technical industries.

★2678★ **Career Opportunities in Computers and Cyberspace**
Facts On File Inc.
132 W. 31st St., 17th Fl.
New York, NY 10001-2006
Ph: (212)967-8800   Fax: 800-678-3633
Fr: 800-322-8755
E-mail: custserv@factsonfile.com
URL: http://www.factsonfile.com

Harry Henderson. Second edition, 2004. $18.95 (paper). Part of the Career Opportunities Series. 256 pages.

★2679★ **Careers for Computer Buffs and Other Technological Types**
The McGraw-Hill Companies
PO Box 182604
Columbus, OH 43272
Fax: (614)759-3749   Fr: 877-883-5524
E-mail: customer.service@mcgraw-hill.com
URL: http://www.mcgraw-hill.com

Marjorie Eberts and Margaret Gisler. Third edition, 2006. $13.95 (paper). 160 pages. Suggested jobs in a wide range of settings, from the office to the outdoors.

★2680★ **Careers in Computers**
The McGraw-Hill Companies
PO Box 182604
Columbus, OH 43272
Fax: (614)759-3749   Fr: 877-883-5524
E-mail: customer.service@mcgraw-hill.com
URL: http://www.mcgraw-hill.com

Lila B. Stair and Leslie Stair. 2002. $19.95; $14.95 (paper). 192 pages. Describes trends affecting computer careers and explores a wide range of job opportunities from programming to consulting. Provides job qualifications, salary data, job market information, personal and educational requirements, career paths, and the place of the job in the organizational structure. Offers advice on education, certification, and job search.

★2681★ **Choosing a Career in Computers**
Rosen Publishing Group, Inc.
29 E. 21st St.
New York, NY 10010
Ph: (212)777-3017   Fax: (212)777-0277
Fr: 800-237-9932
URL: http://www.rosenpublishing.com/

Weigant, Chris. 2000. $29.25. Presents many of the options available to people interested in the technical side of the computer world-from designing and building computers to writing manuals explaining how to use them.

★2682★ **Computer Support Technician**
National Learning Corp.
212 Michael Dr.
Syosset, NY 11791
Ph: (516)921-8888   Fax: (516)921-8743
Fr: 800-645-6337
URL: http://www.passbooks.com

Jack Rudman. 1997. $29.95. Part of the Career Examination Series.

★2683★ **Computer Technician Career Starter**
LearningExpress, LLC
55 Broadway, 8th Fl.
New York, NY 10006
Ph: (212)995-2566   Fax: (212)995-5512
Fr: 800-295-9556
E-mail: customerservice@learningexpressllc.com
URL: http://www.learningexpressllc.com

Joan Vaughn. Second edition, 2001. 168 pages. Part of the Career Starters Series.

★2684★ **The Digital Frontier Job & Opportunity Finder**
Moon Lake Media
PO Box 251466
Los Angeles, CA 90025
Ph: (310)535-2453

Don B. Altman. 1996. $19.95 (paper). 245 pages.

★2685★ **Expert Resumes for Computer and Web Jobs**
Jist Publishing
875 Montreal Way
St. Paul, MN 55102
Fr: 800-648-5478
E-mail: info@jist.com
URL: http://www.jist.com

Wendy Enelow and Louis Kursmark. Second edition, 2005. $16.95 (paper). 286 pages.

★2686★ **Get Your IT Career in Gear!**
The McGraw-Hill Companies
PO Box 182604
Columbus, OH 43272
Fax: (614)759-3749   Fr: 877-883-5524
E-mail: customer.service@mcgraw-hill.com
URL: http://www.mcgraw-hill.com

Leslie Goff. 2001. $24.99 (paper). 401 pages.

★2687★ **Great Jobs for Computer Science Majors**
The McGraw-Hill Companies
PO Box 182604
Columbus, OH 43272
Fax: (614)759-3749   Fr: 877-883-5524
E-mail: customer.service@mcgraw-hill.com
URL: http://www.mcgraw-hill.com

Jan Goldberg, Stephen Lambert, Julie De-Galan. Second edition, 2002. $14.95 (paper). 224 pages.

★2688★ **The JobBank Guide to Computer and High-Tech Companies**
Adams Media Corp.
57 Littlefield St.
Avon, MA 02322
Ph: (508)427-7100   Fax: (508)427-6790
Fr: 800-872-5627
URL: http://www.adamsmedia.com

Steven Graber, Marcie Dipietro, and Michelle Roy Kelly. Second edition, 1999. $17.95 (paper). 700 pages. Contains profiles of more than 4,500 high-tech employers.

★2689★ **Opportunities in Computer Careers**
The McGraw-Hill Companies
PO Box 182604
Columbus, OH 43272
Fax: (614)759-3749   Fr: 877-883-5524
E-mail: customer.service@mcgraw-hill.com
URL: http://www.mcgraw-hill.com

Julie Kling Burns. $12.95 (netLibrary). 160 pages. 2001. Computer vocational guidance and counseling.

★2690★ **Opportunities in Computer Maintenance Careers**
The McGraw-Hill Companies
PO Box 182604
Columbus, OH 43272
Fax: (614)759-3749   Fr: 877-883-5524
E-mail: customer.service@mcgraw-hill.com
URL: http://www.mcgraw-hill.com

Elliott Kanter and Jonathan Yaeger. 1995. $14.95; $11.95 (paper). 144 pages. Offers advice on job hunting and where the jobs are. Illustrated.

★2691★ **Opportunities in High Tech Careers**
The McGraw-Hill Companies
PO Box 182604
Columbus, OH 43272
Fax: (614)759-3749   Fr: 877-883-5524
E-mail: customer.service@mcgraw-hill.com
URL: http://www.mcgraw-hill.com

Gary Colter and Deborah Yanuck. 1999. $14.95; $11.95 (paper). 160 pages. Explores high technology careers. Describes job opportunities, how to make a career decision,

how to prepare for high technology jobs, job hunting techniques, and future trends.

★2692★ Preparing for an Outstanding Career in Computers: Questions and Answers for Professionals and Students

Rafi Systems, Incorporated
750 N. Diamond Bar Blvd., Ste. 224
Diamond Bar, CA 91765
Ph: (909)593-8124   Fax: (909)629-1034
Fr: 800-584-6706
E-mail: rafisystems@rafisystems.com
URL: http://www.rafisystems.com/

Mohamed Rafiquzzaman. 2001. $19.95. 204 pages. Book contains over 300 questions and answers on various important aspects of computers. Topics include basic and state-of-the-art concepts from digital logic to the design of a complete microcomputer.

★2693★ Unlocking the Clubhouse: Women in Computing

MIT Press
55 Hayward St.
Cambridge, MA 02142-1493
Ph: (617)253-5646   Fax: (617)258-6779
Fr: 800-405-1619
URL: http://mitpress.mit.edu/main/home/default.asp

Jane Margolis and Allan Fisher. 2003. $15.00. 182 pages.

★2694★ The Unofficial Guide to Getting a Job at Microsoft

The McGraw-Hill Companies
PO Box 182604
Columbus, OH 43272
Fax: (614)759-3749   Fr: 877-883-5524
E-mail: customer.service@mcgraw-hill.com
URL: http://www.mcgraw-hill.com

Rebecca Smith. 2000. $16.95 (paper). 192 pages.

★2695★ Winning Resumes for Computer Personnel

Barron's Educational Series, Inc.
250 Wireless Blvd.
Hauppauge, NY 11788-3917
Ph: (631)434-3311   Fax: (631)434-3723
Fr: 800-645-3476
E-mail: fbrown@barronseduc.com
URL: http://barronseduc.com

Anne Hart. Second edition, 1998. $14.95 (paper). 260 pages.

EMPLOYMENT AGENCIES AND SEARCH FIRMS

★2696★ Jim Ward Associates

35 Browning Ave.
Toronto, ON, Canada M4K 1V8
Ph: (416)463-1661   Fax: (416)463-1688
Fr: 888-384-8884
E-mail: wardassociates@on.aibn.com

Placement service provides careers and contract positions and professionals specifically related to the computing field. Providing personnel from operations to senior management within the information systems world. Industries served: various industries from government to small business; including banking, service, retail, distribution, manufacturing that use central, distributed or network computing facilities.

★2697★ The Murphy Group

245 W Roosevelt Rd., Bldg.15, Ste.101
Chicago, IL 60605
Ph: (630)639-5110   Fax: (630)639-5113
E-mail: info@murphygroup.com
URL: http://www.murphygroup.com

Employment agency. Places personnel in a variety of positions. Additional offices located in Napierville, Park Ridge, and OakBrook.

ONLINE JOB SOURCES AND SERVICES

★2698★ ComputerJobs.com

280 Interstate North Cir., SE, Ste. 300
Atlanta, GA 30339-2411
Ph: 800-850-0045
URL: http://www.computerjobs.com

Description: The site is an employment tool for technology professionals. Information on positions is updated hourly for seekers. Jobs may be searched by skill, or by location nationally or in a specific state or city job market. Contains thousands of job postings. National jobs may be posted for free. Also career resources for IT professionals.

★2699★ Computerwork.com

Fr: 800-691-8413
E-mail: contactus@computerwork.com
URL: http://www.computerwork.com/

Description: Job search and resume submission service for professionals in information technology.

★2700★ Computerworld Careers

URL: http://www.computerworld.com/careertopics/careers

Description: Offers career opportunities for IT (information technology) professionals. Job seekers may search the jobs database, register at the site, and read about job

surveys and employment trends. Employers may post jobs.

★2701★ Computing Research Association Job Announcements

1100 17th St., NW
Washington, DC 20036-4632
Ph: (202)234-2111   Fax: (202)667-1066
URL: http://www.cra.org/main/cra.jobs.html

Description: Contains dated links to national college and university computer technology positions.

★2702★ Guru.com

5001 Baum Blvd., Ste. 760
Pittsburgh, PA 15213
Ph: (412)687-1316   Fax: (412)687-4466
URL: http://www.guru.com

Description: Job board specializing in contract jobs for creative and information technology professionals. Also provides online incorporation and educational opportunities for independent contractors along with articles and advice.

★2703★ Ittalent.com

E-mail: ewsmith@ITtalent.com
URL: http://www.ittalent.com

Description: Job search and resume submission service for professionals in information technology.

★2704★ ZDNet Tech Jobs

URL: http://www.zdnet.com/

Description: Site houses a listing of national employment opportunities for professionals in high tech fields. Also contains resume building tips and relocation resources.

OTHER SOURCES

★2705★ Association of Information Technology Professionals (AITP)

401 N Michigan Ave., Ste. 2400
Chicago, IL 60611-4267
Ph: (312)245-1070   Fax: (312)673-6659
Fr: 800-224-9371
E-mail: aitp_hq@aitp.org
URL: http://www.aitp.org

Members: Managerial personnel, staff, educators, and individuals interested in the management of information resources. Founder of the Certificate in Data Processing examination program, now administered by an intersociety organization. **Purpose:** Maintains Legislative Communications Network. Professional education programs include EDP-oriented business and management principles self-study courses and a series of videotaped management development seminars. Sponsors student organizations around the country interested in information technology and encourages members to serve as counselors for the Scout computer merit badge. Conducts research projects, including a business information systems curriculum for two- and four-year colleges.

★2706★ **Association for Women in Computing (AWC)**

41 Sutter St., Ste. 1006
San Francisco, CA 94104
Ph: (415)905-4663   Fax: (415)358-4667
E-mail: info@awc-hq.org
URL: http://www.awc-hq.org

Members: Individuals interested in promoting the education, professional development, and advancement of women in computing.

★2707★ **Computer Occupations**

Delphi Productions
3159 6th St.
Boulder, CO 80304
Ph: (303)443-2100   Fax: (303)443-4022
Fr: 888-443-2400
E-mail: support@delphivideo.com
URL: http://www.delphivideo.com

$95.00. 50 minutes. Part of the Careers for the 21st Century Video Library.

★2708★ **Institute for Certification of Computing Professionals (ICCP)**

2350 E Devon Ave., Ste. 115
Des Plaines, IL 60018-4610
Ph: (847)299-4227   Fax: (847)299-4280
Fr: 800-843-8227
E-mail: office@iccp.org
URL: http://www.iccp.org

Members: Professional societies. **Purpose:** Promotes the development of computer examinations which are of high quality, directed toward information technology professionals, and designed to encourage competence and professionalism. Individuals passing the exams automatically become members of the Institute for Certification of Computing Professionals and become certified as CCP or ACP. **Activities:** Has developed code of ethics and good practice to which those taking the exams promise to adhere. Maintains speakers' bureau; compiles statistics.

★2709★ **International Society of Certified Electronics Technicians (ISCET)**

3608 Pershing Ave.
Fort Worth, TX 76107-4527
Ph: (817)921-9101   Fax: (817)921-3741
Fr: 800-946-0201
E-mail: info@iscet.org
URL: http://www.iscet.org

Description: Technicians in 50 countries who have been certified by the society. Seeks to provide a fraternal bond among certified electronics technicians, raise their public image, and improve the effectiveness of industry education programs for technicians. Offers training programs in new electronics information. Maintains library of service literature for consumer electronic equipment, including manuals and schematics for out-of-date equipment. Offers all FCC licenses. Sponsors testing program for certification of electronics technicians in the fields of audio, communications, computer, consumer, industrial, medical electronics, radar, radio-television, and video.

★2710★ **National Electronics Service Dealers Association (NESDA)**

3608 Pershing Ave.
Fort Worth, TX 76107-4527
Ph: (817)921-9061   Fax: (817)921-3741
E-mail: info@nesda.com
URL: http://www.nesda.com

Description: Local and state electronic service associations and companies representing 4200 individuals. Provides educational assistance in electronic training to public schools; supplies technical service information on business management training to electronic service dealers. Offers certification, apprenticeship, and training programs through International Society of Certified Electronics Technicians. Compiles statistics on electronics service business; conducts technical service and business management seminars.

★2711★ **Special Interest Group on Accessible Computing (SIGACCESS)**

IBM T.J. Watson Research Center
19 Skyline Dr.
Hawthorne, NY 10532
Ph: (914)784-6603   Fax: (914)784-7279
E-mail: chair_sigaccess@acm.org
URL: http://www.sigaccess.org

Description: Promotes the professional interests of computing personnel with physical disabilities and the application of computing and information technology in solving relevant disability problems. Works to educate the public to support careers for the disabled.

★2712★ **Technical & Related Occupations**

Delphi Productions
3159 6th St.
Boulder, CO 80304
Ph: (303)443-2100   Fax: (303)443-4022
Fr: 888-443-2400
E-mail: support@delphivideo.com
URL: http://www.delphivideo.com

$95.00. 49 minutes. Part of the Careers for the 21st Century Video Library.

Computer Support Specialists

URL: http://www.idg.com

Monthly. Magazine providing technology information for chief officers and managers.

★2724★ **Eclipse Review**
BZ Media LLC
7 High St., Ste. 407
Huntington, NY 11743
Ph: (631)421-4158   Fax: (631)421-4130
URL: http://www.eclipsesource.com/contact.htm

Magazine for IT professionals.

★2725★ **ENA powered by Network World**
IDG Communications Inc.
5 Speen St., 3rd. Fl
Framingham, MA 01701
Ph: (508)875-5000   Fax: (508)988-7888
URL: http://www.idg.com

Monthly. Journal covering information on networking.

★2726★ **Foundations of Computational Mathematics**
Springer-Verlag New York Inc.
233 Spring St.
New York, NY 10013
Ph: (212)460-1500   Fax: (212)460-1575

Academic journal that publishes articles related to the connections between mathematics and computation, including the interfaces between pure and applied mathematics, numerical analysis and computer science.

★2727★ **Foundations and Trends in Networking**
Now Publishers
PO Box 1024
Hanover, MA 02339
Ph: (781)871-0245
URL: http://www.nowpublishers.com/product.aspx?product=NET

$315.00/year online only; $355.00/year print and online; $315.00/year online only; $355.00/year print and online. Academic journal publishing new research in computer networking.

★2728★ **Government Computer News**
PostNewsweek Tech Media
10 G St. NE, Ste. 500
Washington, DC 20002-4228
Ph: (202)772-2500   Fax: (202)772-2511
Fr: (866)447-6864

Semimonthly. Magazine for professionals interested in government IT.

★2729★ **IEEE Security & Privacy Magazine**
IEEE Computer Society
10662 Los Vaqueros Cir.
PO Box 3014
Los Alamitos, CA 90720-1314
Ph: (714)821-8380   Fax: (714)821-4010
Fr: 800-272-6657
URL: http://www.computer.org/portal/site/security/

Bimonthly. $24.00/year for members; $29.00/year for nonmembers; $28.00/year for members; $565.00/year for libraries, institution. Journal that aims to explore role and importance of networked infrastructure and developing lasting security solutions.

★2730★ **Information Security**
TechTarget
117 Kendrick St., Ste. 800
Needham, MA 02494
Ph: (781)657-1000   Fax: (781)657-1100
URL: http://searchsecurity.techtarget.com/

Monthly. Free to qualified subscribers. Magazine covering information security topics.

★2731★ **IT Focus**
IDG Communications Inc.
5 Speen St., 3rd. Fl
Framingham, MA 01701
Ph: (508)875-5000   Fax: (508)988-7888
URL: http://www.idg.com

Online journal focusing mainly on information technology.

★2732★ **IT Solutions Guide**
SYS-CON Media
135 Chestnut Ridge Rd.
Montvale, NJ 07645
Ph: (201)802-3000   Fax: (201)782-9600
Fr: 888-303-5282
URL: http://itsolutions.sys-con.com/

Quarterly. $4.00/year for individuals, single pdf issue. Magazine for IT professionals.

★2733★ **Journal of Computer Science**
Science Publications
Vails Gate Heights Dr.
PO Box 879
Vails Gate, NY 12584
URL: http://www.scipub.us/

Bimonthly. $3,500.00/year for individuals; $300.00/year for single issue. Scholarly journal covering many areas of computer science, including: concurrent, parallel and distributed processing; artificial intelligence; image and voice processing; quality software and metrics; computer-aided education; wireless communication; real time processing; evaluative computation; and data bases and information recovery and neural networks.

★2734★ **Journal of Computer Systems, Networks, and Communications**
Hindawi Publishing Corp.
410 Park Ave., 15th Fl.
287 PMB
New York, NY 10022
E-mail: jcsnc@hindawi.com
URL: http://www.hindawi.com/journals/jcsnc/

$195.00/year for individuals. Journal covering important areas of information technology.

★2735★ **Kompiuterija PC World**
IDG Communications Inc.
5 Speen St., 3rd. Fl
Framingham, MA 01701
Ph: (508)875-5000   Fax: (508)988-7888
URL: http://www.idg.com

Monthly. Journal providing professionals, business people and users with up-to-date information on computers and the internet.

★2736★ **Mikro PC**
IDG Communications Inc.
5 Speen St., 3rd. Fl
Framingham, MA 01701
Ph: (508)875-5000   Fax: (508)988-7888
URL: http://www.idg.com

Monthly. Magazine focusing on information technology and digital lifestyle.

★2737★ **Monitor**
Capital PC User Group
19209 Mt. Airey Rd.
Brookeville, MD 20833
Ph: (301)560-6442   Fax: (301)760-3303
URL: http://monitor.cpcug.org/index.html

Quarterly. Magazine covering computer hardware and software reviews, special interest user group news, advertisers and author/subject index, and calendar of events.

★2738★ **NetWorld**
IDG Communications Inc.
5 Speen St., 3rd. Fl
Framingham, MA 01701
Ph: (508)875-5000   Fax: (508)988-7888
URL: http://www.idg.com

Monthly. Magazine focusing on networks, security, infrastructure management, wireless, mobile and VOIP technologies.

★2739★ **PC Today**
Sandhills Publishing
120 W Harvest Dr.
Lincoln, NE 68521
Ph: (402)479-2181   Fax: (402)479-2195
Fr: 800-331-1978
URL: http://www.sandhills.com

Monthly. $29.00/year for U.S. $37.00/year for Canada; $64.00/year for Canada, print; $2.42/year for U.S., print; $2.42 for single issue, in U.S. Magazine for personal computer users.

★2740★ PC WORLD

101 Communications
9121 Oakdale Ave., Ste. 101
Chatsworth, CA 91311
Ph: (818)734-1520   Fax: (818)734-1522
URL: http://www.pcworld.com

Quarterly. $20.00/year for individuals, 12 issues; $30.00/year for individuals, 24 issues. Technology or business magazine meeting the informational needs of tech-savvy managers, both at work and at home.

★2741★ Queue

Association for Computing Machinery
2 Penn Plz., Ste. 701
New York, NY 10121-0701
Ph: (212)869-7440   Fax: (212)944-1318
Fr: 800-342-6626
URL: http://www.acmqueue.org/

Monthly. Free, U.S./Canadian residents and all members. Online magazine aimed at the computer professional. Magazine editorial does not provide solutions for the "here-and-now," but instead helps decision-makers plan future projects by examining the challenges and problems they are most likely to face.

★2742★ Revenue

Montgomery Media International
300 Montgomery St., Ste. 1135
San Francisco, CA 94104
Ph: (415)397-2400   Fax: (415)397-2420
URL: http://www.revenuetoday.com/

$30.00/year for individuals. Magazine covering internet marketing strategies.

★2743★ SMB Data

IDG Communications Inc.
5 Speen St., 3rd. Fl
Framingham, MA 01701
Ph: (508)875-5000   Fax: (508)988-7888
URL: http://www.idg.com

Magazine focusing on information technology systems at small and medium-size businesses.

★2744★ SME World

IDG Communications Inc.
5 Speen St., 3rd. Fl
Framingham, MA 01701
Ph: (508)875-5000   Fax: (508)988-7888
URL: http://www.idg.com

Magazine covering articles on technology, technology investments, IT products and services.

★2745★ TecCHANNEL Compact

IDG Communications Inc.
5 Speen St., 3rd. Fl
Framingham, MA 01701
Ph: (508)875-5000   Fax: (508)988-7888
URL: http://www.idg.com

Quarterly. Magazine covering issues of information technology.

★2746★ Tips & Trucs

IDG Communications Inc.
5 Speen St., 3rd. Fl
Framingham, MA 01701
Ph: (508)875-5000   Fax: (508)988-7888
URL: http://www.idg.com

Monthly. Magazine covering topics on computer hardware, software and the internet.

★2747★ Top 100

IDG Communications Inc.
5 Speen St., 3rd. Fl
Framingham, MA 01701
Ph: (508)875-5000   Fax: (508)988-7888
URL: http://www.idg.com

Annual. Magazine providing analyses, assessments and statistics on information technology industry.

★2748★ Ubiquity

Association for Computing Machinery
2 Penn Plz., Ste. 701
New York, NY 10121-0701
Ph: (212)869-7440   Fax: (212)944-1318
Fr: 800-342-6626
URL: http://www.acm.org/ubiquity/

Weekly. Free to members; $163.00/year for nonmembers, 12 issues. Web-based magazine of the Association for Computing Machinery dedicated to fostering critical analysis and in-depth commentary, including book reviews, on issues relating to the nature, constitution, structure, science, engineering, cognition, technology, practices and paradigms of the IT profession.

★2749★ WebLogic Pro

Fawcette Technical Publications
2600 S El Camino Real, Ste. 300
San Mateo, CA 94403-2332
Ph: (650)378-7100   Fax: (650)570-6307
Fr: 800-848-5523
URL: http://www.weblogicpro.com

Bimonthly. Free to qualified subscribers. Magazine that aims to provides IT solutions for developers, architects, and administrators.

★2750★ WITI FastTrack

CMP Media L.L.C.
600 Community Dr.
Manhasset, NY 11030
Ph: (516)562-5000   Fax: (516)562-7830
URL: http://www.witi.com/corporate/fast-track.php

Semiannual. Semiannual publication featuring in-depth content on the issues facing today's women professionals in technology.

EMPLOYER DIRECTORIES AND NETWORKING LISTS

★2751★ A-Z of Computer Scientists

Facts On File Inc.
132 W 31st St., 17th Fl.
New York, NY 10001
Ph: (212)967-8800   Fax: 800-678-3633
Fr: 800-322-8755
URL: http://www.factsonfile.com

Published 2003. $45.00 for individuals; $40.50 for libraries. Covers the lives, work, and enduring influence of more than 150 computer pioneers and investigates the way individuals developed their ideas, overcame technical and institutional challenges, collaborated with colleagues, and created products or institutions of lasting importance.

★2752★ Career Opportunities in Computers and Cyberspace

Facts On File Inc.
132 W 31st St., 17th Fl.
New York, NY 10001
Ph: (212)967-8800   Fax: 800-678-3633
Fr: 800-322-8755
URL: http://www.factsonfile.com

Published 2004. $49.50 for individuals; $44.55 for libraries. Covers nearly 200 professions, clustering them by skill, objectives, and work conditions. Entries include: Education, salaries, employment prospects.

★2753★ Careers in Focus: Computers

Facts On File Inc.
132 W 31st St., 17th Fl.
New York, NY 10001
Ph: (212)967-8800   Fax: 800-678-3633
Fr: 800-322-8755
URL: http://www.factsonfile.com

Latest edition 4th, 2004. $29.95 for individuals; $26.95 for libraries. Covers an overview of computers, followed by a selection of jobs profiled in detail, including the nature of the job, earnings, prospects for employment, what kind of training and skills it requires, and sources for further information.

★2754★ Computer Directory

Computer Directories Inc.
23815 Nichols Sawmill Rd.
Hockley, TX 77447
Ph: (281)356-7880   Fr: 800-234-4353
URL: http://www.compdirinc.com

Annual, fall. Covers approximately 130,000 computer installation companies; 19 separate volumes for Alaska/Hawaii, Connecticut/New Jersey, Dallas/Ft. Worth, Eastern Seaboard, Far Midwest, Houston, Illinois, Midatlantic, Midcentral, Mideast, Minnesota/Wisconsin, North Central, New England, New York Metro, Northwest, Ohio, Pennsylvania/West Virginia, Southeast, and Southwest Texas. Entries include: Company name, address, phone, fax, e-mail, name and title of contact, hardware used, software application, operating system, programming language, computer graphics, networking system. Arrangement: Geographical. Indexes: Alphabetical; industry; hardware.

HANDBOOKS AND MANUALS

★2755★ America's Top 101 Computer and Technical Jobs
Jist Publishing
875 Montreal Way
St. Paul, MN 55102
Fr: 800-648-5478
E-mail: info@jist.com
URL: http://www.jist.com

Michael J. Farr. 2004. $26.20. 359 pages. Job hunting in computer and technical industries.

★2756★ Career Opportunities in Computers and Cyberspace
Facts On File Inc.
132 W. 31st St., 17th Fl.
New York, NY 10001-2006
Ph: (212)967-8800   Fax: 800-678-3633
Fr: 800-322-8755
E-mail: custserv@factsonfile.com
URL: http://www.factsonfile.com

Harry Henderson. Second edition, 2004. $18.95 (paper). Part of the Career Opportunities Series. 256 pages.

★2757★ Careers Inside the World of Technology
Pearson Learning Group
135 S. Mt. Zion Rd.
PO Box 2500
Lebanon, IN 46052
Fax: 800-393-3156   Fr: 800-526-9907
URL: http://www.pearsonatschool.com

Jean W. Spencer. Revised edition, 2000. $13.50. 64 pages. Describes computer-related careers for reluctant readers.

★2758★ Choosing a Career in Computers
Rosen Publishing Group, Inc.
29 E. 21st St.
New York, NY 10010
Ph: (212)777-3017   Fax: (212)777-0277
Fr: 800-237-9932
URL: http://www.rosenpublishing.com/

Weigant, Chris. 2000. $29.25. Presents many of the options available to people interested in the technical side of the computer world-from designing and building computers to writing manuals explaining how to use them.

★2759★ Computer Support Technician
National Learning Corporation
212 Michael Dr.
Syosset, NY 11791
Ph: (516)921-8888   Fax: (516)921-8743
Fr: 800-632-8888

URL: http://www.passbooks.com/

National Learning Corporation. 1997. $29.95 (Trade paper).

★2760★ The Digital Frontier Job & Opportunity Finder
Moon Lake Media
PO Box 251466
Los Angeles, CA 90025
Ph: (310)535-2453

Don B. Altman. 1996. $19.95 (paper). 245 pages.

★2761★ The JobBank Guide to Computer and High-Tech Companies
Adams Media Corp.
57 Littlefield St.
Avon, MA 02322
Ph: (508)427-7100   Fax: (508)427-6790
Fr: 800-872-5627
URL: http://www.adamsmedia.com

Steven Graber, Marcie Dipietro, and Michelle Roy Kelly. Second edition, 1999. $17.95 (paper). 700 pages. Contains profiles of more than 4,500 high-tech employers.

★2762★ Opportunities in Computer Careers
The McGraw-Hill Companies
PO Box 182604
Columbus, OH 43272
Fax: (614)759-3749   Fr: 877-883-5524
E-mail: customer.service@mcgraw-hill.com
URL: http://www.mcgraw-hill.com

Julie Kling Burns. $12.95 (netLibrary). 160 pages. 2001. Computer vocational guidance and counseling.

★2763★ Opportunities in Computer Systems Careers
The McGraw-Hill Companies
PO Box 182604
Columbus, OH 43272
Fax: (614)759-3749   Fr: 877-883-5524
E-mail: customer.service@mcgraw-hill.com
URL: http://www.mcgraw-hill.com

Julie King Burns. 1996. $14.95; $11.95 (paper). 160 pages.

★2764★ Winning Resumes for Computer Personnel
Barron's Educational Series, Inc.
250 Wireless Blvd.
Hauppauge, NY 11788-3917
Ph: (631)434-3311   Fax: (631)434-3723
Fr: 800-645-3476
E-mail: fbrown@barronseduc.com
URL: http://barronseduc.com

Anne Hart. Second edition, 1998. $14.95 (paper). 260 pages.

EMPLOYMENT AGENCIES AND SEARCH FIRMS

★2765★ Carol Maden Group
2019 Cunningham Dr., Ste. 218
Hampton, VA 23666-3316
Ph: (757)827-9010   Fax: (757)827-9081
E-mail: cmaden@hroads.net

Personnel consultants offering placement service in computer technology and engineering; servicing manufacturing and private industries nationwide. Temporary placement servicing clerical and light industrial.

★2766★ Chaves & Associates
222 Post Road E.
Westport, CT 06880
Ph: (203)222-2222   Fax: (203)259-5200
E-mail: admin@insitesearch.com
URL: http://www.insitesearch.com

Executive search firm.

★2767★ CNR Search & Services
30752 Via Conquista
San Juan Capistrano, CA 92675
Ph: (949)488-0065
E-mail: cnrkenmiller@juno.com
URL: http://www.cnrsearch.com

Provides staffing services of permanent and temporary employees. Works primarily on a retained basis. Contingency on a limited basis. Services include human resources consulting, mergers and acquisitions in high-technology firms. Industries served: computer; information services; insurance, pharmaceutical and healthcare.

★2768★ Doleman Enterprises
11160-F S Lakes Dr., Ste. 326
Reston, VA 20191
Ph: (703)742-5454   Fax: (703)708-6992
E-mail: doleman@patriot.net

Human resources firm specializes in recruiting for the high-tech, data and computer engineering and pharmaceutical industries.

★2769★ George Houchens Associates
11356 Tall Shadows Ct.
Pinckney, MI 48169-8471
Ph: (734)649-9250   Fax: (734)665-4961
E-mail: houchens@techie.com
URL: http://www.houchens.com

Specializes in recruiting top quality executive, technical, and sales/marketing professionals for permanent positions in the computer, electronics, biomedical, and other high technology industries. Positions handled include: computer product engineering, (software and hardware), management information systems, office automation and related systems, computer networking and communications, Wireless/RF/Mobile, computer aided engineering, expert systems, quality assurance, CIM/CAM, industrial control, robotics, image processing, motion control, automated inspection, material handling, and other related specialties. served: Primarily Midwest.

★2770★ Louis Rudzinsky Associates Inc.

394 Lowell St., Ste. 17
PO Box 640
Lexington, MA 02420
Ph: (781)862-6727   Fax: (781)862-6868
E-mail: lra@lra.com
URL: http://www.lra.com

Provides recruitment, placement, and executive search to industry (software, electronics, optics) covering positions in general management, manufacturing, engineering, and marketing. Personnel consulting activities include counsel to small and startup companies. Industries served: electronics, aerospace, optical, laser, computer, software, imaging, electro-optics, biotechnology, advanced materials, and solid-state/semiconductor.

★2771★ Michael Anthony Associates Inc.

42 Washington St., Ste. 301
Wellesley, MA 02481-1802
Ph: (781)237-4950   Fax: (781)237-6811
Fr: 800-337-4950
E-mail: saymes@maainc.com
URL: http://www.maainc.com

Applications development, systems programming, communications, and database specialists servicing the IBM mainframe, midrange, and PC marketplace. Provides technical expertise of conversions, system software installation and upgrades, performance and tuning, capacity planning, and data communications. In addition to contract services also provide retained search and contingency placement of computer professionals ranging from senior staff to senior management. Also act as brokers for independent consultants and small consulting firms requiring the services of marketing specialists. Industries served: banking, financial services, hospitals, HMO's, manufacturers, software development, universities, defense, and consulting firms.

★2772★ Professional Computer Resources Inc.

1500 South Blvd., No. 201B
Charlotte, NC 28203
Ph: (704)332-7226   Fax: (704)332-7288
Fr: 888-727-2458
E-mail: resumes@pcr.net
URL: http://www.pcr.net

Executive search firm.

★2773★ Wallach Associates Inc.

7811 Montrose Rd., Ste. 505
Potomac, MD 20854
Ph: (301)340-0300   Fax: (301)340-8008
Fr: 800-296-2084
E-mail: jobs@wallach.org
URL: http://www.wallach.org

Specialists in recruitment of professional

personnel, primarily in information technology and electronic systems and engineering, energy research and development, management consulting, operations research, computers, defense systems, and programmers. Specializes in Internet and software engineer for intelligence community.

ONLINE JOB SOURCES AND SERVICES

★2774★ ComputerJobs.com

280 Interstate North Cir., SE, Ste. 300
Atlanta, GA 30339-2411
Ph: 800-850-0045
URL: http://www.computerjobs.com

Description: The site is an employment tool for technology professionals. Information on positions is updated hourly for seekers. Jobs may be searched by skill, or by location nationally or in a specific state or city job market. Contains thousands of job postings. National jobs may be posted for free. Also career resources for IT professionals.

★2775★ Computerwork.com

Fr: 800-691-8413
E-mail: contactus@computerwork.com
URL: http://www.computerwork.com/

Description: Job search and resume submission service for professionals in information technology.

★2776★ Computerworld Careers

URL: http://www.computerworld.com/careertopics/careers

Description: Offers career opportunities for IT (information technology) professionals. Job seekers may search the jobs database, register at the site, and read about job surveys and employment trends. Employers may post jobs.

★2777★ Computing Research Association Job Announcements

1100 17th St., NW
Washington, DC 20036-4632
Ph: (202)234-2111   Fax: (202)667-1066
URL: http://www.cra.org/main/cra.jobs.html

Description: Contains dated links to national college and university computer technology positions.

★2778★ Guru.com

5001 Baum Blvd., Ste. 760
Pittsburgh, PA 15213
Ph: (412)687-1316   Fax: (412)687-4466
URL: http://www.guru.com

Description: Job board specializing in contract jobs for creative and information technology professionals. Also provides online incorporation and educational opportunities

for independent contractors along with articles and advice.

★2779★ Ittalent.com

E-mail: ewsmith@ITtalent.com
URL: http://www.ittalent.com

Description: Job search and resume submission service for professionals in information technology.

★2780★ ZDNet Tech Jobs

URL: http://www.zdnet.com/

Description: Site houses a listing of national employment opportunities for professionals in high tech fields. Also contains resume building tips and relocation resources.

TRADESHOWS

★2781★ The CSI Computer Security Conference and Exhibition

CMP Media LLC (San Mateo)
2800 Campus Dr.
San Mateo, CA 94403
Ph: (650)513-4300
E-mail: cmp@cmp.com
URL: http://www.cmp.com

Annual. **Primary Exhibits:** Computer products and services and information security equipment, supplies and services.

★2782★ XPLOR Conference

XPLOR International
24238 Hawthorne Blvd.
Torrance, CA 90505-6505
Ph: (310)373-3633   Fax: (310)375-4240
Fr: 800-669-7567
E-mail: info@xplor.org
URL: http://www.xplor.org

Annual. **Primary Exhibits:** Equipment, supplies, and services for users and manufacturers of advanced electronic document systems.

OTHER SOURCES

★2783★ Association of Information Technology Professionals (AITP)

401 N Michigan Ave., Ste. 2400
Chicago, IL 60611-4267
Ph: (312)245-1070   Fax: (312)673-6659
Fr: 800-224-9371
E-mail: aitp_hq@aitp.org
URL: http://www.aitp.org

Members: Managerial personnel, staff, educators, and individuals interested in the management of information resources. Founder of the Certificate in Data Processing examination program, now administered by an intersociety organization. **Purpose:**

Maintains Legislative Communications Network. Professional education programs include EDP-oriented business and management principles self-study courses and a series of videotaped management development seminars. Sponsors student organizations around the country interested in information technology and encourages members to serve as counselors for the Scout computer merit badge. Conducts research projects, including a business information systems curriculum for two- and four-year colleges.

★2784★ Association for Women in Computing (AWC)

41 Sutter St., Ste. 1006
San Francisco, CA 94104
Ph: (415)905-4663   Fax: (415)358-4667
E-mail: info@awc-hq.org
URL: http://www.awc-hq.org

Members: Individuals interested in promoting the education, professional development, and advancement of women in computing.

★2785★ Computer Occupations

Delphi Productions
3159 6th St.
Boulder, CO 80304
Ph: (303)443-2100   Fax: (303)443-4022
Fr: 888-443-2400
E-mail: support@delphivideo.com
URL: http://www.delphivideo.com

$95.00. 50 minutes. Part of the Careers for the 21st Century Video Library.

★2786★ Information Technology Services

Cambridge Educational
PO Box 2053
Princeton, NJ 08543-2053
Ph: 800-257-5126   Fax: (609)671-0266
Fr: 800-468-4227
E-mail: custserv@films.com
URL: http://www.cambridgeeducational.com

VHS and DVD. $89.95. 2002. 19 minutes. Part of the Career Cluster Series.

★2787★ Institute for Certification of Computing Professionals (ICCP)

2350 E Devon Ave., Ste. 115
Des Plaines, IL 60018-4610
Ph: (847)299-4227   Fax: (847)299-4280
Fr: 800-843-8227
E-mail: office@iccp.org
URL: http://www.iccp.org

Members: Professional societies. **Purpose:** Promotes the development of computer examinations which are of high quality, directed toward information technology professionals, and designed to encourage competence and professionalism. Individuals passing the exams automatically become members of the Institute for Certification of Computing Professionals and become certified as CCP or ACP. **Activities:** Has developed code of ethics and good practice to which those taking the exams promise to adhere. Maintains speakers' bureau; compiles statistics.

Computer Systems Analysts

★2788★ ACM Transactions on Internet Technology (ACM TOIT)

Association for Computing Machinery
2 Penn Plz., Ste. 701
New York, NY 10121-0701
Ph: (212)869-7440   Fax: (212)944-1318
Fr: 800-342-6626
URL: http://www.acm.org/pubs/periodicals/toit/

Quarterly. $35.00/year for members; $30.00/year for students; $140.00/year for nonmembers; $170.00/year for individuals, print only; $136.00 for single issue, online only; $204.00 for single issue, online & print. Publication of the Association for Computing Machinery. Brings together many computing disciplines including computer software engineering, computer programming languages, middleware, database management, security, knowledge discovery and data mining, networking and distributed systems, communications, performance and scalability, and more. Covers the results and roles of the individual disciplines and the relationships among them.

★2789★ AVIOS Journal

Applied Voice Input/Output Society
PO Box 20817
San Jose, CA 95160
Ph: (408)323-1783   Fax: (408)323-1782
E-mail: info@avios.org
URL: http://www.avios.com/

Annual. Journal covering issues in computer science.

★2790★ Communications of the ACM

Association for Computing Machinery
2 Penn Plz., Ste. 701
New York, NY 10121-0701
Ph: (212)869-7440   Fax: (212)944-1318
Fr: 800-342-6626
URL: http://www.acm.org/pubs/cacm/

Monthly. $179.00/year for nonmembers; $36.00/year for members. Computing news magazine.

★2791★ Computers and Composition

Elsevier Science Inc.
360 Park Ave. S
New York, NY 10010
Ph: (212)989-5800   Fax: (212)633-3990
URL: http://www.elsevier.com

$353.00/year for institutions; $69.00/year for individuals. Journal covering computers in writing classes, programs, and research.

★2792★ Computers Programs/PC World

IDG Communications Inc.
5 Speen St., 3rd. Fl
Framingham, MA 01701
Ph: (508)875-5000   Fax: (508)988-7888
URL: http://www.idg.com

Magazine devoted to IT specialists, covering practical questions of computing including purchase and usage of the computer technology, software, computer components and peripherals.

★2793★ Computerworld

101 Communications
9121 Oakdale Ave., Ste. 101
Chatsworth, CA 91311
Ph: (818)734-1520   Fax: (818)734-1522
URL: http://www.computerworld.com

Weekly. $99.00/year for individuals, new Australian subscribers; $99.00/year for individuals, renewals Australian; $250.00/year for other countries, airmail; $375.00/year for other countries, overseas (airmail). Newspaper for information systems executives.

★2794★ Computerworld/Correio Informatico

IDG Communications Inc.
5 Speen St., 3rd. Fl
Framingham, MA 01701
Ph: (508)875-5000   Fax: (508)988-7888
URL: http://www.idg.com

Weekly. Magazine providing news on latest developments in computer industry.

★2795★ Computerworld Top 100

IDG Communications Inc.
5 Speen St., 3rd. Fl
Framingham, MA 01701
Ph: (508)875-5000   Fax: (508)988-7888
URL: http://www.idg.com

Annual. Magazine for analyzing trends and events of information technology business.

★2796★ Computing SA

IDG Communications Inc.
5 Speen St., 3rd. Fl
Framingham, MA 01701
Ph: (508)875-5000   Fax: (508)988-7888
URL: http://www.idg.com

Monthly. Newspaper focusing computer hardware, software, networking, telecommunications, channel management and online computing.

★2797★ Computing Surveys (CSUR)

Association for Computing Machinery
2 Penn Plz., Ste. 701
New York, NY 10121-0701
Ph: (212)869-7440   Fax: (212)944-1318
Fr: 800-342-6626
URL: http://www.acm.org/pubs/surveys/

Quarterly. $185.00 for nonmembers, print only yearly rate; $148.00/year for nonmembers, online only; $222.00 for single issue, online & print; $208.00 for single issue, print with expedited air; $245.00 for single issue, online & print with expedited air. Journal presenting surveys and tutorials in computer science.

★2798★ Consumer Electronics Lifestyles

Sandhills Publishing
120 W Harvest Dr.
Lincoln, NE 68521
Ph: (402)479-2181   Fax: (402)479-2195
Fr: 800-331-1978
E-mail: editor@ceLifestyles.com

URL: http://www.celifestyles.com/

Monthly. $12.00/year. Magazine for computer and electronic gadget enthusiasts.

★2799★ **CXO**

IDG Communications Inc.
5 Speen St., 3rd. Fl
Framingham, MA 01701
Ph: (508)875-5000   Fax: (508)988-7888
URL: http://www.idg.com

Monthly. Magazine providing technology information for chief officers and managers.

★2800★ **Datamation**

Reed Business Information
225 Wyman St.
Waltham, MA 02451-1216
URL: http://www.datamation.com

Semimonthly. Magazine on computers and information processing.

★2801★ **Digital News & Review**

Reed Business Information
225 Wyman St.
Waltham, MA 02451-1216

Semimonthly. Free to qualified subscribers. Covers information storage and retrieval and data systems.

★2802★ **E-Business Advisor**

e-Business Advisor
PO Box 429002
San Diego, CA 92142
Ph: (858)278-5600   Fax: (858)278-0300
Fr: 800-336-6060
URL: http://www.e-businessadvisor.com

Magazine for developing strategies, practices, and innovations for e-business applications.

★2803★ **Eclipse Review**

BZ Media LLC
7 High St., Ste. 407
Huntington, NY 11743
Ph: (631)421-4158   Fax: (631)421-4130
URL: http://www.eclipsesource.com/contact.htm

Magazine for IT professionals.

★2804★ **ENA powered by Network World**

IDG Communications Inc.
5 Speen St., 3rd. Fl
Framingham, MA 01701
Ph: (508)875-5000   Fax: (508)988-7888
URL: http://www.idg.com

Monthly. Journal covering information on networking.

★2805★ **Foundations of Computational Mathematics**

Springer-Verlag New York Inc.
233 Spring St.
New York, NY 10013
Ph: (212)460-1500   Fax: (212)460-1575

Academic journal that publishes articles related to the connections between mathematics and computation, including the interfaces between pure and applied mathematics, numerical analysis and computer science.

★2806★ **Foundations and Trends in Networking**

Now Publishers
PO Box 1024
Hanover, MA 02339
Ph: (781)871-0245
URL: http://www.nowpublishers.com/product.aspx?product=NET

$315.00/year online only; $355.00/year print and online; $315.00/year online only; $355.00/year print and online. Academic journal publishing new research in computer networking.

★2807★ **Government Computer News**

PostNewsweek Tech Media
10 G St. NE, Ste. 500
Washington, DC 20002-4228
Ph: (202)772-2500   Fax: (202)772-2511
Fr: (866)447-6864

Semimonthly. Magazine for professionals interested in government IT.

★2808★ **IEEE Security & Privacy Magazine**

IEEE Computer Society
10662 Los Vaqueros Cir.
PO Box 3014
Los Alamitos, CA 90720-1314
Ph: (714)821-8380   Fax: (714)821-4010
Fr: 800-272-6657
URL: http://www.computer.org/portal/site/security/

Bimonthly. $24.00/year for members; $29.00/year for nonmembers; $28.00/year for members; $565.00/year for libraries, institution. Journal that aims to explore role and importance of networked infrastructure and developing lasting security solutions.

★2809★ **IEEE Software**

IEEE Computer Society
10662 Los Vaqueros Cir.
PO Box 3014
Los Alamitos, CA 90720-1314
Ph: (714)821-8380   Fax: (714)821-4010
Fr: 800-272-6657
E-mail: software@computer.org
URL: http://www.computer.org/software

Bimonthly. $77.00/year for nonmembers, individual; $46.00/year for members, plus online access to software articles; $76.00/year for members; $765.00/year for institutions, library. Magazine covering the computer software industry for the community of leading software practitioners.

★2810★ **Information Security**

TechTarget
117 Kendrick St., Ste. 800
Needham, MA 02494
Ph: (781)657-1000   Fax: (781)657-1100
URL: http://searchsecurity.techtarget.com/

Monthly. Free to qualified subscribers. Magazine covering information security topics.

★2811★ **InformationWeek**

CMP Media L.L.C.
600 Community Dr.
Manhasset, NY 11030
Ph: (516)562-5000   Fax: (516)562-7830
URL: http://www.informationweek.com

Weekly. Free to qualified subscribers. Magazine focusing on data and information processing news and strategies.

★2812★ **InfoWorld**

InfoWorld Media Group
501 Second St.
San Francisco, CA 94107
Fr: 800-227-8365
E-mail: letters@infoworld.com
URL: http://www.infoworld.com/

Weekly. Free to qualified subscribers; $180.00/year for individuals. Weekly publication.

★2813★ **Intelligent Enterprise**

CMP Media L.L.C.
600 Community Dr.
Manhasset, NY 11030
Ph: (516)562-5000   Fax: (516)562-7830
E-mail: tgibb@cmp.com
URL: http://www.intelligententerprise.com

Periodic. Free. Magazine serving business and IT professionals.

★2814★ **IT Focus**

IDG Communications Inc.
5 Speen St., 3rd. Fl
Framingham, MA 01701
Ph: (508)875-5000   Fax: (508)988-7888
URL: http://www.idg.com

Online journal focusing mainly on information technology.

★2815★ **IT Solutions Guide**

SYS-CON Media
135 Chestnut Ridge Rd.
Montvale, NJ 07645
Ph: (201)802-3000   Fax: (201)782-9600
Fr: 888-303-5282
URL: http://itsolutions.sys-con.com/

Quarterly. $4.00/year for individuals, single pdf issue. Magazine for IT professionals.

★2816★ **Journal of Computer Science**

Science Publications
Vails Gate Heights Dr.
PO Box 879
Vails Gate, NY 12584
URL: http://www.scipub.us/

Bimonthly. $3,500.00/year for individuals; $300.00/year for single issue. Scholarly journal covering many areas of computer science, including: concurrent, parallel and distributed processing; artificial intelligence; image and voice processing; quality software and metrics; computer-aided education; wireless communication; real time processing; evaluative computation; and data bases and information recovery and neural networks.

★2817★ Journal of Computer Systems, Networks, and Communications
Hindawi Publishing Corp.
410 Park Ave., 15th Fl.
287 PMB
New York, NY 10022
E-mail: jcsnc@hindawi.com
URL: http://www.hindawi.com/journals/jcsnc/

$195.00/year for individuals. Journal covering important areas of information technology.

★2818★ Kompiuterija PC World
IDG Communications Inc.
5 Speen St., 3rd. Fl
Framingham, MA 01701
Ph: (508)875-5000   Fax: (508)988-7888
URL: http://www.idg.com

Monthly. Journal providing professionals, business people and users with up-to-date information on computers and the internet.

★2819★ Mikro PC
IDG Communications Inc.
5 Speen St., 3rd. Fl
Framingham, MA 01701
Ph: (508)875-5000   Fax: (508)988-7888
URL: http://www.idg.com

Monthly. Magazine focusing on information technology and digital lifestyle.

★2820★ Monitor
Capital PC User Group
19209 Mt. Airey Rd.
Brookeville, MD 20833
Ph: (301)560-6442   Fax: (301)760-3303
URL: http://monitor.cpcug.org/index.html

Quarterly. Magazine covering computer hardware and software reviews, special interest user group news, advertisers and author/subject index, and calendar of events.

★2821★ NetWorld
IDG Communications Inc.
5 Speen St., 3rd. Fl
Framingham, MA 01701
Ph: (508)875-5000   Fax: (508)988-7888
URL: http://www.idg.com

Monthly. Magazine focusing on networks, security, infrastructure management, wireless, mobile and VOIP technologies.

★2822★ PC Magazine
Ziff-Davis Publishing Co.
28 East 28th St.
New York, NY 10016
Ph: (212)503-3500
E-mail: pcmag@ziffdavis.com
URL: http://www.ziffdavisinternet.com/websites/pcmag

Biweekly. $19.97/year for individuals, 25 issues. Tabloid featuring microcomputer products and developments.

★2823★ PC Today
Sandhills Publishing
120 W Harvest Dr.
Lincoln, NE 68521
Ph: (402)479-2181   Fax: (402)479-2195
Fr: 800-331-1978
URL: http://www.sandhills.com

Monthly. $29.00/year for U.S. $37.00/year for Canada; $64.00/year for Canada, print; $2.42/year for U.S., print; $2.42 for single issue, in U.S. Magazine for personal computer users.

★2824★ PC WORLD
101 Communications
9121 Oakdale Ave., Ste. 101
Chatsworth, CA 91311
Ph: (818)734-1520   Fax: (818)734-1522
URL: http://www.pcworld.com

Quarterly. $20.00/year for individuals, 12 issues; $30.00/year for individuals, 24 issues. Technology or business magazine meeting the informational needs of tech-savvy managers, both at work and at home.

★2825★ Queue
Association for Computing Machinery
2 Penn Plz., Ste. 701
New York, NY 10121-0701
Ph: (212)869-7440   Fax: (212)944-1318
Fr: 800-342-6626
URL: http://www.acmqueue.org/

Monthly. Free, U.S./Canadian residents and all members. Online magazine aimed at the computer professional. Magazine editorial does not provide solutions for the "here-and-now," but instead helps decision-makers plan future projects by examining the challenges and problems they are most likely to face.

★2826★ Revenue
Montgomery Media International
300 Montgomery St., Ste. 1135
San Francisco, CA 94104
Ph: (415)397-2400   Fax: (415)397-2420
URL: http://www.revenuetoday.com/

$30.00/year for individuals. Magazine covering internet marketing strategies.

★2827★ SMB Data
IDG Communications Inc.
5 Speen St., 3rd. Fl
Framingham, MA 01701
Ph: (508)875-5000   Fax: (508)988-7888

URL: http://www.idg.com

Magazine focusing on information technology systems at small and medium-size businesses.

★2828★ SME World
IDG Communications Inc.
5 Speen St., 3rd. Fl
Framingham, MA 01701
Ph: (508)875-5000   Fax: (508)988-7888
URL: http://www.idg.com

Magazine covering articles on technology, technology investments, IT products and services.

★2829★ TecCHANNEL Compact
IDG Communications Inc.
5 Speen St., 3rd. Fl
Framingham, MA 01701
Ph: (508)875-5000   Fax: (508)988-7888
URL: http://www.idg.com

Quarterly. Magazine covering issues of information technology.

★2830★ Tips & Trucs
IDG Communications Inc.
5 Speen St., 3rd. Fl
Framingham, MA 01701
Ph: (508)875-5000   Fax: (508)988-7888
URL: http://www.idg.com

Monthly. Magazine covering topics on computer hardware, software and the internet.

★2831★ Top 100
IDG Communications Inc.
5 Speen St., 3rd. Fl
Framingham, MA 01701
Ph: (508)875-5000   Fax: (508)988-7888
URL: http://www.idg.com

Annual. Magazine providing analyses, assessments and statistics on information technology industry.

★2832★ Ubiquity
Association for Computing Machinery
2 Penn Plz., Ste. 701
New York, NY 10121-0701
Ph: (212)869-7440   Fax: (212)944-1318
Fr: 800-342-6626
URL: http://www.acm.org/ubiquity/

Weekly. Free to members; $163.00/year for nonmembers, 12 issues. Web-based magazine of the Association for Computing Machinery dedicated to fostering critical analysis and in-depth commentary, including book reviews, on issues relating to the nature, constitution, structure, science, engineering, cognition, technology, practices and paradigms of the IT profession.

★2833★ WebLogic Pro

Fawcette Technical Publications
2600 S El Camino Real, Ste. 300
San Mateo, CA 94403-2332
Ph: (650)378-7100   Fax: (650)570-6307
Fr: 800-848-5523
URL: http://www.weblogicpro.com

Bimonthly. Free to qualified subscribers. Magazine that aims to provides IT solutions for developers, architects, and administrators.

★2834★ WITI FastTrack

CMP Media L.L.C.
600 Community Dr.
Manhasset, NY 11030
Ph: (516)562-5000   Fax: (516)562-7830
URL: http://www.witi.com/corporate/fast-track.php

Semiannual. Semiannual publication featuring in-depth content on the issues facing today's women professionals in technology.

PLACEMENT AND JOB REFERRAL SERVICES

★2835★ American Indian Science and Engineering Society (AISES)

PO Box 9828
Albuquerque, NM 87119-9828
Ph: (505)765-1052   Fax: (505)765-5608
E-mail: info@aises.org
URL: http://www.aises.org

Description: Represents American Indian and non-Indian students and professionals in science, technology, and engineering fields; corporations representing energy, mining, aerospace, electronic, and computer fields. Seeks to motivate and encourage students to pursue undergraduate and graduate studies in science, engineering, and technology. Sponsors science fairs in grade schools, teacher training workshops, summer math/science sessions for 8th-12th graders, professional chapters, and student chapters in colleges. Offers scholarships. Adult members serve as role models, advisers, and mentors for students. Operates placement service.

EMPLOYER DIRECTORIES AND NETWORKING LISTS

★2836★ Career Opportunities in Computers and Cyberspace

Facts On File Inc.
132 W 31st St., 17th Fl.
New York, NY 10001
Ph: (212)967-8800   Fax: 800-678-3633
Fr: 800-322-8755
URL: http://www.factsonfile.com

Published 2004. $49.50 for individuals; $44.55 for libraries. Covers nearly 200 professions, clustering them by skill, objectives, and work conditions. Entries include: Education, salaries, employment prospects.

★2837★ Computer Directory

Computer Directories Inc.
23815 Nichols Sawmill Rd.
Hockley, TX 77447
Ph: (281)356-7880   Fr: 800-234-4353
URL: http://www.compdirinc.com

Annual, fall. Covers approximately 130,000 computer installation companies; 19 separate volumes for Alaska/Hawaii, Connecticut/New Jersey, Dallas/Ft. Worth, Eastern Seaboard, Far Midwest, Houston, Illinois, Midatlantic, Midcentral, Mideast, Minnesota/Wisconsin, North Central, New England, New York Metro, Northwest, Ohio, Pennsylvania/West Virginia, Southeast, and Southwest Texas. Entries include: Company name, address, phone, fax, e-mail, name and title of contact, hardware used, software application, operating system, programming language, computer graphics, networking system. Arrangement: Geographical. Indexes: Alphabetical; industry; hardware.

★2838★ Directory of Top Computer Executives

Applied Computer Research
PO Box 41730
Phoenix, AZ 85080-1730
Ph: (602)216-9100   Fax: (602)548-4800
Fr: 800-234-2227
URL: http://www.itmarketintelligence.com

Semiannual, June and December. Covers, in three volumes, over 55,000 U.S. and Canadian executives with major information technology or communications responsibilities in over 30,000 U.S. and Canadian companies. Entries include: Company name, address, phone, subsidiary and/or division names, major systems installed, names and titles of top information system executives, number of IT employees, number of PCs, and web address. Arrangement: Geographical within separate eastern, western, and Canadian volumes. Indexes: Industry; alphabetical by company name.

★2839★ Discovering Careers for Your Future: Computers

Facts On File Inc.
132 W 31st St., 17th Fl.
New York, NY 10001
Ph: (212)967-8800   Fax: 800-678-3633
Fr: 800-322-8755
URL: http://www.factsonfile.com

Published 2001. $21.95 for individuals; $19.75 for libraries. Covers computer operators, programmers, database specialists, and software engineers; links career education to curriculum, helping children investigate the subjects they are interested in, and the careers those subjects might lead to.

★2840★ Peterson's Job Opportunities in Engineering and Technology

Peterson's Guides
2000 Lenox Dr.
Box 67005
Lawrenceville, NJ 08648
Ph: (609)896-1800   Fax: (609)896-4531
Fr: 800-338-3282
E-mail: custsvc@petersons.com
URL: http://www.petersons.com

Compiled by the Peterson's staff. Fourth edition, 1996. $21.95 (paper). 379 pages. Profiles 2,000 high-tech companies looking primarily for technical personnel in such fields as biotechnology, telecommunications, software, computers and peripherals, defense, and aerospace. Contains job-search strategies and career options to help match education and expertise to the job market. Indexed geographically, by industry, and by hiring needs.

HANDBOOKS AND MANUALS

★2841★ America's Top 101 Computer and Technical Jobs

Jist Publishing
875 Montreal Way
St. Paul, MN 55102
Fr: 800-648-5478
E-mail: info@jist.com
URL: http://www.jist.com

Michael J. Farr. 2004. $26.20. 359 pages. Job hunting in computer and technical industries.

★2842★ Career Opportunities in Computers and Cyberspace

Facts On File Inc.
132 W. 31st St., 17th Fl.
New York, NY 10001-2006
Ph: (212)967-8800   Fax: 800-678-3633
Fr: 800-322-8755
E-mail: custserv@factsonfile.com
URL: http://www.factsonfile.com

Harry Henderson. Second edition, 2004. $18.95 (paper). Part of the Career Opportunities Series. 256 pages.

★2843★ Careers for Computer Buffs and Other Technological Types

The McGraw-Hill Companies
PO Box 182604
Columbus, OH 43272
Fax: (614)759-3749   Fr: 877-883-5524
E-mail: customer.service@mcgraw-hill.com
URL: http://www.mcgraw-hill.com

Marjorie Eberts and Margaret Gisler. Third edition, 2006. $13.95 (paper). 160 pages. Suggested jobs in a wide range of settings, from the office to the outdoors.

★2844★ Careers in Computers

The McGraw-Hill Companies
PO Box 182604
Columbus, OH 43272
Fax: (614)759-3749   Fr: 877-883-5524
E-mail: customer.service@mcgraw-hill.com
URL: http://www.mcgraw-hill.com

Lila B. Stair and Leslie Stair. 2002. $19.95; $14.95 (paper). 192 pages. Describes trends affecting computer careers and explores a wide range of job opportunities from programming to consulting. Provides job qualifications, salary data, job market information, personal and educational requirements, career paths, and the place of the job in the organizational structure. Offers advice on education, certification, and job search.

★2845★ Careers Inside the World of Technology

Pearson Learning Group
135 S. Mt. Zion Rd.
PO Box 2500
Lebanon, IN 46052
Fax: 800-393-3156   Fr: 800-526-9907
URL: http://www.pearsonatschool.com

Jean W. Spencer. Revised edition, 2000. $13.50. 64 pages. Describes computer-related careers for reluctant readers.

★2846★ Careers for Number Crunchers and Other Quantitative Types

The McGraw-Hill Companies
PO Box 182604
Columbus, OH 43272
Fax: (614)759-3749   Fr: 877-883-5524
E-mail: customer.service@mcgraw-hill.com
URL: http://www.mcgraw-hill.com

Rebecca Burnett. Second edition, 2002. $22.95 (paper). 192 pages. Provides information to math-oriented job hunters on how to become statisticians, field researchers, computer programmers, stock analysts, investment managers, bankers, engineers, accountants, underwriters, economists, market analysts, mathematicians, systems analysts, and more.

★2847★ Choosing a Career in Computers

Rosen Publishing Group, Inc.
29 E. 21st St.
New York, NY 10010
Ph: (212)777-3017   Fax: (212)777-0277
Fr: 800-237-9932
URL: http://www.rosenpublishing.com/

Weigant, Chris. 2000. $29.25. Presents many of the options available to people interested in the technical side of the computer world-from designing and building computers to writing manuals explaining how to use them.

★2848★ Coordinator of Computer Services

National Learning Corp.
212 Michael Dr.
Syosset, NY 11791
Ph: (516)921-8888   Fax: (516)921-8743
Fr: 800-645-6337
URL: http://www.passbooks.com/

Jack Rudman. 1997. $39.95 (paper). Part of the Career Examination Series.

★2849★ The Digital Frontier Job & Opportunity Finder

Moon Lake Media
PO Box 251466
Los Angeles, CA 90025
Ph: (310)535-2453

Don B. Altman. 1996. $19.95 (paper). 245 pages.

★2850★ Expert Resumes for Computer and Web Jobs

Jist Publishing
875 Montreal Way
St. Paul, MN 55102
Fr: 800-648-5478
E-mail: info@jist.com
URL: http://www.jist.com

Wendy Enelow and Louis Kursmark. Second edition, 2005. $16.95 (paper). 286 pages.

★2851★ Get Your IT Career in Gear!

The McGraw-Hill Companies
PO Box 182604
Columbus, OH 43272
Fax: (614)759-3749   Fr: 877-883-5524
E-mail: customer.service@mcgraw-hill.com
URL: http://www.mcgraw-hill.com

Leslie Goff. 2001. $24.99 (paper). 401 pages.

★2852★ Great Jobs for Computer Science Majors

The McGraw-Hill Companies
PO Box 182604
Columbus, OH 43272
Fax: (614)759-3749   Fr: 877-883-5524
E-mail: customer.service@mcgraw-hill.com
URL: http://www.mcgraw-hill.com

Jan Goldberg, Stephen Lambert, Julie De-Galan. Second edition, 2002. $14.95 (paper). 224 pages.

★2853★ Job Seekers Guide to Silicon Valley Recruiters

John Wily and Sons, Inc.
605 Third Ave., 4th Fl.
New York, NY 10158-0012
Ph: (212)850-6276   Fax: (212)850-8641

Christopher W. Hunt, Scott A. Scanlon. First edition, 1998. $19.95 (paper). 371 pages. Includes a list of 2,400 recruiters specializing in high technology positions and explains how to work with them.

★2854★ The JobBank Guide to Computer and High-Tech Companies

Adams Media Corp.
57 Littlefield St.
Avon, MA 02322
Ph: (508)427-7100   Fax: (508)427-6790
Fr: 800-872-5627
URL: http://www.adamsmedia.com

Steven Graber, Marcie Dipietro, and Michelle Roy Kelly. Second edition, 1999. $17.95 (paper). 700 pages. Contains profiles of more than 4,500 high-tech employers.

★2855★ Opportunities in Computer Careers

The McGraw-Hill Companies
PO Box 182604
Columbus, OH 43272
Fax: (614)759-3749   Fr: 877-883-5524
E-mail: customer.service@mcgraw-hill.com
URL: http://www.mcgraw-hill.com

Julie Kling Burns. $12.95 (netLibrary). 160 pages. 2001. Computer vocational guidance and counseling.

★2856★ Opportunities in Computer Systems Careers

The McGraw-Hill Companies
PO Box 182604
Columbus, OH 43272
Fax: (614)759-3749   Fr: 877-883-5524
E-mail: customer.service@mcgraw-hill.com
URL: http://www.mcgraw-hill.com

Julie King Burns. 1996. $14.95; $11.95 (paper). 160 pages.

★2857★ Opportunities in High Tech Careers

The McGraw-Hill Companies
PO Box 182604
Columbus, OH 43272
Fax: (614)759-3749   Fr: 877-883-5524
E-mail: customer.service@mcgraw-hill.com
URL: http://www.mcgraw-hill.com

Gary Colter and Deborah Yanuck. 1999. $14.95; $11.95 (paper). 160 pages. Explores high technology careers. Describes job opportunities, how to make a career decision, how to prepare for high technology jobs, job hunting techniques, and future trends.

★2858★ Opportunities in Office Occupations

The McGraw-Hill Companies
PO Box 182604
Columbus, OH 43272
Fax: (614)759-3749   Fr: 877-883-5524
E-mail: customer.service@mcgraw-hill.com
URL: http://www.mcgraw-hill.com

Blanche Ettinger. 1995. $14.95; $11.95 (paper). 146 pages. Covers a variety of office positions and discusses trends for the next decade. Describes the job market, opportunities, job duties, educational preparation, the work environment, and earnings.

★2859★ Preparing for an Outstanding Career in Computers: Questions and Answers for Professionals and Students

Rafi Systems, Incorporated
750 N. Diamond Bar Blvd., Ste. 224
Diamond Bar, CA 91765
Ph: (909)593-8124   Fax: (909)629-1034
Fr: 800-584-6706
E-mail: rafisystems@rafisystems.com
URL: http://www.rafisystems.com/

Mohamed Rafiquzzaman. 2001. $19.95. 204 pages. Book contains over 300 questions and answers on various important aspects of computers. Topics include basic and state-of-the-art concepts from digital logic to the design of a complete microcomputer.

★2860★ Unlocking the Clubhouse: Women in Computing

MIT Press
55 Hayward St.
Cambridge, MA 02142-1493
Ph: (617)253-5646   Fax: (617)258-6779
Fr: 800-405-1619
URL: http://mitpress.mit.edu/main/home/default.asp

Jane Margolis and Allan Fisher. 2003. $15.00. 182 pages.

★2861★ The Unofficial Guide to Getting a Job at Microsoft

The McGraw-Hill Companies
PO Box 182604
Columbus, OH 43272
Fax: (614)759-3749   Fr: 877-883-5524
E-mail: customer.service@mcgraw-hill.com
URL: http://www.mcgraw-hill.com

Rebecca Smith. 2000. $16.95 (paper). 192 pages.

★2862★ Winning Resumes for Computer Personnel

Barron's Educational Series, Inc.
250 Wireless Blvd.
Hauppauge, NY 11788-3917
Ph: (631)434-3311   Fax: (631)434-3723
Fr: 800-645-3476
E-mail: fbrown@barronseduc.com
URL: http://barronseduc.com

Anne Hart. Second edition, 1998. $14.95 (paper). 260 pages.

EMPLOYMENT AGENCIES AND SEARCH FIRMS

★2863★ Ashton Computer Professionals Inc.

15 Chesterfield Pl., Unit C
North Vancouver, BC, Canada V6E 3V7
Ph: (604)904-0304   Fax: (604)904-0305
E-mail: acp@axionet.com
URL: http://www.acprecruit.com

Provides personnel recruitment and tempo-rary contract services, specializing in advanced computer technology based fields, i.e., management information services, software engineering, product manufacturing, telecommunications, management personnel in all technology based disciplines. Serves private industries as well as government agencies.

★2864★ The Aspire Group

52 Second Ave, 1st Fl
Waltham, MA 02451-1129
Fax: (718)890-1810   Fr: 800-487-2967
URL: http://www.bmanet.com

Employment agency.

★2865★ Data Systems Search Consultants

1615 Bonanza St., Ste. 405
Walnut Creek, CA 94596
Ph: (925)256-0635   Fax: (925)256-9099
E-mail: dsscinfo@dssc.com
URL: http://www.dssc.com

Employment agency. Executive search firm.

★2866★ The Datafinders Group, Inc.

25 E. Spring Valley Ave.
Maywood, NJ 07607
Ph: (201)845-7700   Fax: (201)845-7365
E-mail: info@datafinders.net
URL: http://www.datafinders.net

Executive search firm.

★2867★ Dean Associates

PO Box 1079
Santa Cruz, CA 95061
Ph: (831)423-2931
E-mail: marydearn@deanassociates.com
URL: http://www.deanassociates.com

Executive search firm focused on the high technology industry.

★2868★ Dynamic Search Systems Inc.

220 W Campus Dr.
Arlington Heights, IL 60004
Ph: (847)259-3444   Fax: (847)259-3480
E-mail: candidate@dssjobs.com
URL: http://www.dssjobs.com

Provides executive and professional search services to the IT community. Firm specializes in the placement of developers, programmers, programmer analysts, systems analysts, project leaders, project managers, systems programmers, data processing consultants, IT directors, and other information technology related candidates. Industries served: all.

★2869★ JES Search Firm Inc.

1021 Stovall Blvd., Ste. 600
950 E Paces Ferry Rd., Ste. 2245
Atlanta, GA 30319
Ph: (404)812-0622   Fax: (404)812-1910
E-mail: bde1@jessearch.com
URL: http://www.jessearch.com

Contract and permanent information technology search firm specializing in placing software developers as well as other information systems professionals.

★2870★ KForce

Fr: 888-663-3626
URL: http://www.kforce.com

Executive search firm. More than 30 locations throughout the United States.

★2871★ Michael Anthony Associates Inc.

42 Washington St., Ste. 301
Wellesley, MA 02481-1802
Ph: (781)237-4950   Fax: (781)237-6811
Fr: 800-337-4950
E-mail: saymes@maainc.com
URL: http://www.maainc.com

Applications development, systems programming, communications, and database specialists servicing the IBM mainframe, midrange, and PC marketplace. Provides technical expertise of conversions, system software installation and upgrades, performance and tuning, capacity planning, and data communications. In addition to contract services also provide retained search and contingency placement of computer professionals ranging from senior staff to senior management. Also act as brokers for independent consultants and small consulting firms requiring the services of marketing specialists. Industries served: banking, financial services, hospitals, HMO's, manufacturers, software development, universities, defense, and consulting firms.

★2872★ Sullivan and Cogliano

230 2nd Ave
Waltham, MA 02451
Ph: (781)890-7890   Fr: 888-785-2641
E-mail: contract@sullivansogliano.com
URL: http://www.sullivancogliano.com

Technical staffing firm.

★2873★ Technical Talent Locators Ltd.

5570 Sterrett Pl., Ste. 208
Columbia, MD 21044
Ph: (410)740-0091
E-mail: steve@ttlgroup.com
URL: http://www.ttlgroup.com

Permanent employment agency working within the following fields: software and database engineering; computer, communication, and telecommunication system engineering; and other computer-related disciplines.

★2874★ TRC Staffing Services Inc.

100 Ashford Ctr. N, Ste. 500
Atlanta, GA 30338
Ph: (770)392-1411   Fax: (770)393-2742
E-mail: info@trcstaff.com
URL: http://www.trcstaff.com

A full-service executive search company with permanent placements encompassing engineering, industrial sales, financial and computer science positions. Screen, interview, and verify past employment for all candidates prior to referral. Also assist personnel staffs in the attainment of their EEO/AAP goals with the placement of talented individuals in positions which are underutilized with minorities and/or women. Industries served: all.

★2875★ Tri-Serv Inc.

22 W. Padonia Rd., Ste. C-353
Timonium, MD 21093
Ph: (410)561-1740   Fax: (410)252-7417
E-mail: info@tri-serv.coom
URL: http://www.tri-serv.com

Employment agency for technical personnel.

★2876★ Wallach Associates Inc.

7811 Montrose Rd., Ste. 505
Potomac, MD 20854
Ph: (301)340-0300   Fax: (301)340-8008
Fr: 800-296-2084
E-mail: jobs@wallach.org
URL: http://www.wallach.org

Specialists in recruitment of professional personnel, primarily in information technology and electronic systems and engineering, energy research and development, management consulting, operations research, computers, defense systems, and programmers. Specializes in Internet and software engineer for intelligence community.

★2877★ Worlco Computer Resources, Inc.

997 Old Eagle School Rd., Ste. 219
Wayne, PA 19087
Ph: (610)293-9070   Fax: (610)293-1027
E-mail: parisi@worlco.com
URL: http://www.worlco.com

Employment agency and executive search firm. Second location in Cherry Hill, New Jersey.

ONLINE JOB SOURCES AND SERVICES

★2878★ ComputerJobs.com

280 Interstate North Cir., SE, Ste. 300
Atlanta, GA 30339-2411
Ph: 800-850-0045
URL: http://www.computerjobs.com

Description: The site is an employment tool for technology professionals. Information on positions is updated hourly for seekers. Jobs may be searched by skill, or by location nationally or in a specific state or city job market. Contains thousands of job postings. National jobs may be posted for free. Also career resources for IT professionals.

★2879★ Computerwork.com

Fr: 800-691-8413
E-mail: contactus@computerwork.com
URL: http://www.computerwork.com/

Description: Job search and resume submission service for professionals in information technology.

★2880★ Computerworld Careers

URL: http://www.computerworld.com/careertopics/careers

Description: Offers career opportunities for IT (information technology) professionals. Job seekers may search the jobs database, register at the site, and read about job surveys and employment trends. Employers may post jobs.

★2881★ Computing Research Association Job Announcements

1100 17th St., NW
Washington, DC 20036-4632
Ph: (202)234-2111   Fax: (202)667-1066
URL: http://www.cra.org/main/cra.jobs.html

Description: Contains dated links to national college and university computer technology positions.

★2882★ Guru.com

5001 Baum Blvd., Ste. 760
Pittsburgh, PA 15213
Ph: (412)687-1316   Fax: (412)687-4466
URL: http://www.guru.com

Description: Job board specializing in contract jobs for creative and information technology professionals. Also provides online incorporation and educational opportunities for independent contractors along with articles and advice.

★2883★ Jobs for Programmers

E-mail: prgjobs@jfpresources.com
URL: http://www.prgjobs.com

Description: Job board site for computer programmers that allows them to browse through thousands of programming jobs, even search for special jobs with sign-on bonuses, relocation funding, and 4-day work weeks. Resume posting is free.

★2884★ ZDNet Tech Jobs

URL: http://www.zdnet.com/

Description: Site houses a listing of national employment opportunities for professionals in high tech fields. Also contains resume building tips and relocation resources.

TRADESHOWS

★2885★ Computer & Technology Showcase - Tulsa

Event Management Services
519 Cleveland St., Ste. 205
Clearwater, FL 33755
Ph: (503)234-1552   Fax: (503)234-4253
Fr: 800-422-0251
E-mail: mfriedman@event-management.com
URL: http://www.event-management.com

Annual. **Primary Exhibits:** Products and services for computers, imaging, wireless communication, networking, application development, and e-commerce.

★2886★ XPLOR Conference

XPLOR International
24238 Hawthorne Blvd.
Torrance, CA 90505-6505
Ph: (310)373-3633   Fax: (310)375-4240
Fr: 800-669-7567
E-mail: info@xplor.org
URL: http://www.xplor.org

Annual. **Primary Exhibits:** Equipment, supplies, and services for users and manufacturers of advanced electronic document systems.

OTHER SOURCES

★2887★ Association of Information Technology Professionals (AITP)

401 N Michigan Ave., Ste. 2400
Chicago, IL 60611-4267
Ph: (312)245-1070   Fax: (312)673-6659
Fr: 800-224-9371
E-mail: aitp_hq@aitp.org
URL: http://www.aitp.org

Members: Managerial personnel, staff, educators, and individuals interested in the management of information resources. Founder of the Certificate in Data Processing examination program, now administered by an intersociety organization. **Purpose:** Maintains Legislative Communications Network. Professional education programs include EDP-oriented business and management principles self-study courses and a series of videotaped management development seminars. Sponsors student organizations around the country interested in information technology and encourages members to serve as counselors for the Scout computer merit badge. Conducts research projects, including a business information systems curriculum for two- and four-year colleges.

★2888★ Association for Women in Computing (AWC)

41 Sutter St., Ste. 1006
San Francisco, CA 94104
Ph: (415)905-4663   Fax: (415)358-4667

E-mail: info@awc-hq.org
URL: http://www.awc-hq.org

Members: Individuals interested in promoting the education, professional development, and advancement of women in computing.

★2889★ **Black Data Processing Associates (BDPA)**

6301 Ivy Ln., Ste. 700
Greenbelt, MD 20770
Ph: (301)220-2180   Fax: (301)220-2185
Fr: 800-727-BDPA
E-mail: president@bdpa.org
URL: http://www.bdpa.org

Description: Represents persons employed in the information processing industry, including electronic data processing, electronic word processing, and data communications; others interested in information processing. Seeks to accumulate and share information processing knowledge and business expertise in order to increase the career and business potential of minorities in the information processing field. Conducts professional seminars, workshops, tutoring services, and community introductions to data processing. Makes annual donation to the United Negro College Fund.

★2890★ **Computer Occupations**

Delphi Productions
3159 6th St.
Boulder, CO 80304
Ph: (303)443-2100   Fax: (303)443-4022
Fr: 888-443-2400
E-mail: support@delphivideo.com
URL: http://www.delphivideo.com

$95.00. 50 minutes. Part of the Careers for the 21st Century Video Library.

★2891★ **IEEE Computer Society (CS)**

1730 Massachusetts Ave. NW
Washington, DC 20036-1992
Ph: (202)371-0101   Fax: (202)728-9614

E-mail: help@computer.org
URL: http://www.computer.org

Description: Computer professionals. Promotes the development of computer and information sciences and fosters communication within the information processing community. Sponsors conferences, symposia, workshops, tutorials, technical meetings, and seminars. Operates Computer Society Press. Presents scholarships; bestows technical achievement and service awards and certificates.

★2892★ **Information Technology Occupations**

Delphi Productions
3159 6th St.
Boulder, CO 80304
Ph: (303)443-2100   Fax: (303)443-4022
Fr: 888-443-2400
E-mail: support@delphivideo.com
URL: http://www.delphivideo.com

$95.00. 52 minutes. Part of the Emerging Careers Video Library.

★2893★ **Information Technology Services**

Cambridge Educational
PO Box 2053
Princeton, NJ 08543-2053
Ph: 800-257-5126   Fax: (609)671-0266
Fr: 800-468-4227
E-mail: custserv@films.com
URL: http://www.cambridgeeducational.com

VHS and DVD. $89.95. 2002. 19 minutes. Part of the Career Cluster Series.

★2894★ **Institute for Certification of Computing Professionals (ICCP)**

2350 E Devon Ave., Ste. 115
Des Plaines, IL 60018-4610
Ph: (847)299-4227   Fax: (847)299-4280
Fr: 800-843-8227
E-mail: office@iccp.org

URL: http://www.iccp.org

Members: Professional societies. **Purpose:** Promotes the development of computer examinations which are of high quality, directed toward information technology professionals, and designed to encourage competence and professionalism. Individuals passing the exams automatically become members of the Institute for Certification of Computing Professionals and become certified as CCP or ACP. **Activities:** Has developed code of ethics and good practice to which those taking the exams promise to adhere. Maintains speakers' bureau; compiles statistics.

★2895★ *Resumes for High Tech Careers*

The McGraw-Hill Companies
PO Box 182604
Columbus, OH 43272
Fax: (614)759-3749   Fr: 877-883-5524
E-mail: customer.service@mcgraw-hill.com
URL: http://www.mcgraw-hill.com

Third edition, 2003. $10.95 (paper). 160 pages. Demonstrates how to tailor a resume that catches a high tech employer's attention. Part of "Resumes for ..." series.

★2896★ **Special Interest Group on Accessible Computing (SIGACCESS)**

IBM T.J. Watson Research Center
19 Skyline Dr.
Hawthorne, NY 10532
Ph: (914)784-6603   Fax: (914)784-7279
E-mail: chair_sigaccess@acm.org
URL: http://www.sigaccess.org

Description: Promotes the professional interests of computing personnel with physical disabilities and the application of computing and information technology in solving relevant disability problems. Works to educate the public to support careers for the disabled.

Construction and Building Inspectors

SOURCES OF HELP-WANTED ADS

★2897★ American City and County
Primedia Business
6151 Powers Ferry Rd., Ste. 200
Atlanta, GA 30339
Ph: (770)955-2500   Fax: (770)618-0204
URL: http://
www.americancityandcounty.com

Monthly. $67.00/year for individuals. Municipal and county administration magazine.

★2898★ American Professional Constructor
American Institute of Constructors
PO Box 26334
Alexandria, VA 22314
Ph: (703)683-4999   Fax: (703)683-5480
URL: http://www.aicnet.org/store/
proddetail6da9.asp?CFID=10706514

Biennial. Subscription included in membership; $100.00/year for nonmembers. Journal covering general interest and technical articles for construction professionals.

★2899★ BIA News
Brick Industry Association
1850 Centennial Park Dr., Ste. 301
Reston, VA 20191-1525
Ph: (703)620-0010   Fax: (703)620-3928

Monthly. $30.00/year for individuals. Trade publication covering issues for the brick industry.

★2900★ Builder
Hanley-Wood L.L.C.
1 Thomas Cir., NW, Ste. 600
Washington, DC 20005
Ph: (202)452-0800   Fax: (202)785-1974
URL: http://www.hanleywood.com/de-fault.aspx?page=b2bbd

$29.95/year for individuals, 13 issues; $54.95/year for Canada, 26 issues; $192.00/year for out of country, 13 issues. Magazine covering housing and construction industry.

★2901★ Building Systems Magazine
Active Interest Media
300 Continental Blvd., Ste. 650
El Segundo, CA 90245
Ph: (310)356-4100   Fax: (310)356-4110
Fr: 800-423-4880
URL: http://www.buildingsystems.com/

Bimonthly. Magazine featuring innovative construction technologies for builders, developers and general contractors.

★2902★ Civil Engineering-ASCE
American Society of Civil Engineers
1801 Alexander Bell Dr.
Reston, VA 20191-4400
Ph: (703)295-6300   Fax: (703)295-6222
Fr: 800-548-2723
URL: http://www.asce.org/cemagazine/
1006/

Monthly. Professional magazine.

★2903★ Construction
Reed Business Information
360 Park Ave. S
New York, NY 10010
Ph: (646)746-6400   Fax: (646)746-7431
URL: http://www.acppubs.com/community/
835.html

Semimonthly. $106.00/year for individuals; $126.00/year for Canada; $166.00/year for other countries. Regional construction publication covering Maryland, the District of Columbia, Virginia, North Carolina and South Carolina. Geared toward those engaged in engineering (heavy and highway), non-residential building construction and allied fields relating to construction or requiring the use of construction equipment. Containing "how to" job stories, product news, industry news and bid and award information.

★2904★ Construction Business Owner
Cahaba Media Group
PO Box 530067
Birmingham, AL 35253
Ph: (205)212-9402
URL: http://
www.constructionbusinessowner.com/

Monthly. Free. Magazine that provides information for construction management and industry business information.

★2905★ Construction Claims Monthly
Business Publishers Inc.
PO Box 17592
Baltimore, MD 21297
Fr: 800-274-6737
E-mail: custserv@bpinews.com
URL: http://www.bpinews.com/

Description: Monthly. Covers significant legal developments governing contract payment and performance. Features an article on construction claims law; summaries of recent decisions with expert commentary; and highlights of actions by the federal boards of contract appeals and the Comptroller General.

★2906★ Constructor
Associated General Contractors of America
2300 Wilson Blvd., Ste. 400
Arlington, VA 22201
Ph: (703)548-3118   Fax: (703)548-3119
URL: http://www.agc.org

Monthly. Management magazine for the Construction Industry.

★2907★ Consulting-Specifying Engineer
Reed Business Information
360 Park Ave. S
New York, NY 10010
Ph: (646)746-6400   Fax: (646)746-7431
URL: http://www.csemag.com

The integrated engineering magazine of the building construction industry.

★2908★ Engineering Times
National Society of Professional Engineers
1420 King St.
Alexandria, VA 22314
Ph: (703)684-2800
URL: http://www.nspe.org

Monthly. Magazine (tabloid) covering professional, legislative, and techology issues for an engineering audience.

★2909★ **ENR: Engineering News-Record**

McGraw-Hill Inc.
221 Ave. of the Americas
New York, NY 10020-1095
Ph: (212)512-2000   Fax: (212)512-3840
Fr: 877-833-5524
E-mail: enr_web_editors@mcgraw-hill.com
URL: http://www.mymags.com/morein-o.php?itemID=20012

Weekly. $94.00/year for individuals, print. Magazine focusing on engineering and construction.

★2910★ **ISHN**

BNP Media
2401 W Big Beaver Rd., Ste. 700
Troy, MI 48084-3333
Ph: (248)786-1642   Fax: (248)786-1388
URL: http://www.ishn.com/

Monthly. Free. Business-to-business magazine for safety and health managers at high-hazard worksites in manufacturing, construction, health facilities, and service industries. Content covering OSHA and EPA regulations, how-to features, safety and health management topics, and the latest product news.

★2911★ **Kitchen and Bath Business**

The Nielsen Co.
770 Broadway
New York, NY 10003
Ph: (646)654-5000   Fax: (646)654-5002
URL: http://www.kitchen-bath.com/kbb/index.jsp

Monthly. $10.00/year for individuals, cover; $79.00/year for individuals, domestic; $94.00/year for Canada and Mexico; $142.00/year for other countries. Trade magazine on kitchen and bath remodeling and construction.

★2912★ **Landscape Construction**

Moose River Publishing
374 Emerson Falls Rd.
St. Johnsbury, VT 05819-9083
Ph: (802)748-8908   Fax: (802)748-1866
Fr: 800-422-7147
URL: http://www.lcmmagazine.com/

Monthly. Magazine featuring landscaping.

★2913★ **MetalMag**

Spiderweb Publishing Inc.
1415 Hwy. 54 W, Ste. 105
Durham, NC 27707
Ph: (919)482-9300   Fax: (919)402-9302
E-mail: mtm@omeda.com
URL: http://www.metalmag.com/

Bimonthly. Free to qualified subscribers. Magazine for industrial construction professionals.

★2914★ **The Municipality**

League of Wisconsin Municipalities
122 W Washington Ave., Ste. 300
Madison, WI 53703-2718
Ph: (608)267-2380   Fax: (608)267-0645
Fr: 800-991-5502
URL: http://www.lwm-info.org/index.asp?Type=B_BASIC&SEC=¢0702EE8F

Monthly. Magazine for officials of Wisconsin's local municipal governments.

★2915★ **NAHRO Monitor**

National Association of Housing and
  Redevelopment Officials
630 Eye St. NW
Washington, DC 20001
Ph: (202)289-3500   Fax: (202)289-8181
Fr: 877-866-2476
E-mail: nahro@nahro.org
URL: http://www.nahro.org/publications/monitor.cfm

Description: Semimonthly. Disseminates news on low-income housing and community development issues. Intended for member professionals and government officials.

★2916★ **The NAWIC Image**

National Association of Women in
  Construction
327 S. Adams St.
Fort Worth, TX 76104
Ph: (817)877-5551   Fax: (817)877-0324
Fr: 800-552-3506
E-mail: nawic@nawic.org
URL: http://www.nawic.org

Description: Six issues/year. Fosters career advancement for women in construction. Features women business owners, training for construction trades and educational programs. Recurring features include columns titled "Issues and Trends," "Road to Success," "Chapter Highlights," "Members on the Move," and "Q&A."

★2917★ **Professional Builder**

Reed Business Information
360 Park Ave. S
New York, NY 10010
Ph: (646)746-6400   Fax: (646)746-7431
E-mail: ncrum@reedbusiness.com
URL: http://www.housingzone.com/toc-ar-chive-pbx

Monthly. Free. The integrated engineering magazine of the building construction industry.

★2918★ **Remodeling**

Hanley-Wood L.L.C.
1 Thomas Cir., NW, Ste. 600
Washington, DC 20005
Ph: (202)452-0800   Fax: (202)785-1974
URL: http://www.hanleywood.com/default.aspx?page=b2brm

$25.00/year for individuals; $40.00/year for individuals, Canadian residents; $192.00/year for individuals, international residents. Trade magazine for the professional remodeling industry.

★2919★ **Residential Architect**

Hanley-Wood L.L.C.
1 Thomas Cir., NW, Ste. 600
Washington, DC 20005
Ph: (202)452-0800   Fax: (202)785-1974
URL: http://www.hanleywood.com/default.aspx?page=b2bra

Magazine for architects, designers, and building professionals.

★2920★ **Residential Concrete**

Hanley-Wood L.L.C.
1 Thomas Cir., NW, Ste. 600
Washington, DC 20005
Ph: (202)452-0800   Fax: (202)785-1974
URL: http://www.hanleywood.com/default.aspx?page=b2bresconcrete

Bimonthly. Magazine featuring the use of concrete in residential concrete construction.

★2921★ **Retail Construction**

Retail Construction Magazine
PO Box 1589
Cumming, GA 30028
Ph: (770)781-2501   Fax: (770)781-6303
URL: http://www.retailconstructionmag.com

Free. Magazine that covers design, construction, renovation and operation of retail businesses.

★2922★ **Roofing Contractor**

BNP Media
2401 W Big Beaver Rd., Ste. 700
Troy, MI 48084-3333
Ph: (248)786-1642   Fax: (248)786-1388
URL: http://www.roofingcontractor.com/

Monthly. Trade publication covering roofing and the construction industry.

★2923★ **Tools of the Trade**

Hanley-Wood L.L.C.
1 Thomas Cir., NW, Ste. 600
Washington, DC 20005
Ph: (202)452-0800   Fax: (202)785-1974
URL: http://www.hanleywood.com/default.aspx?page=b2btt

Bimonthly. Magazine featuring tools for commercial and residential construction.

★2924★ **Western City**

League of California Cities
1400 K St., Ste. 400
Sacramento, CA 95814
Ph: (916)658-8200   Fax: (916)658-8240
Fr: 800-262-1801
URL: http://www.westerncity.com

Monthly. $39.00/year for individuals; $63.00 for two years; $52.00/year for other countries; $26.50/year for students. Municipal interest magazine.

PLACEMENT AND JOB REFERRAL SERVICES

★2925★ Building Officials and Code Administrators International (BOCA)

Chicago District Office
4051 W Flossmoor Rd.
Country Club Hills, IL 60478
Fr: 888-422-7233
E-mail: webmaster@iccsafe.org
URL: http://www.iccsafe.org

Members: Governmental officials and agencies and other interests concerned with administering or formulating building, fire, mechanical, plumbing, zoning, housing regulations. **Purpose:** Promulgates the BOCA National Codes and the ICC International Codes suitable for adoption by reference by governmental entities. **Activities:** Provides services for maintaining the codes up-to-date. Maintains services for all members in connection with codes and their administration; provides consulting, training and education, plan review, and other advisory services; conducts correspondence courses; prepares in-service training programs and assists local organizations in such activities. Maintains placement services.

★2926★ National Association of Home Builders (NAHB)

1201 15th St. NW
Washington, DC 20005
Ph: (202)266-8200　　Fax: (202)266-8400
Fr: 800-368-5242
E-mail: info@nahb.com
URL: http://www.nahb.org

Description: Single and multifamily home builders, commercial builders, and others associated with the building industry. Lobbies on behalf of the housing industry and conducts public affairs activities to increase public understanding of housing and the economy. Collects and disseminates data on current developments in home building and home builders' plans through its Economics Department and nationwide Metropolitan Housing Forecast. Maintains NAHB Research Center, which functions as the research arm of the home building industry. Sponsors seminars and workshops on construction, mortgage credit, labor relations, cost reduction, land use, remodeling, and business management. Compiles statistics; offers charitable program, spokesman training, and placement service; maintains speakers' bureau, and Hall of Fame. Subsidiaries include the National Council of the Housing Industry. Maintains over 50 committees in many areas of construction; operates National Commercial Builders Council, National Council of the Multifamily Housing Industry, National Remodelers Council, and National Sales and Marketing Council.

★2927★ Professional Women in Construction (PWC)

315 E 56th St.
New York, NY 10022-3730
Ph: (212)486-7745　　Fax: (212)486-0228

E-mail: pwcusa1@aol.com
URL: http://www.pwcusa.org

Description: Management-level women and men in construction and allied industries; owners, suppliers, architects, engineers, field personnel, office personnel, and bonding/surety personnel. Provides a forum for exchange of ideas and promotion of political and legislative action, education, and job opportunities for women in construction and related fields; forms liaisons with other trade and professional groups; develops research programs. Strives to reform abuses and to assure justice and equity within the construction industry. Sponsors mini-workshops. Maintains Action Line, which provides members with current information on pertinent legislation and on the association's activities and job referrals.

EMPLOYER DIRECTORIES AND NETWORKING LISTS

★2928★ ABC Today-Associated Builders and Contractors National Membership Directory Issue

Associated Builders & Contractors Inc.
4250 N Fairfax Dr., 9th Fl.
Arlington, VA 22203-1607
Ph: (703)812-2000　　Fax: (703)812-8203
URL: http://www.abc.org/wmspage.cfm?parm1=2033

Annual, December. $150.00. Publication includes: List of approximately 19,000 member construction contractors and suppliers. Entries include: Company name, address, phone, name of principal executive, code to volume of business, business specialty. Arrangement: Classified by chapter, then by work specialty.

★2929★ Constructor-AGC Directory of Membership and Services Issue

AGC Information Inc.
2300 Wilson Blvd., Ste. 400
Arlington, VA 22201
Ph: (703)548-3118　　Fax: (703)548-3119
Fr: 800-282-1423
URL: http://www.agc.org

Annual, August; latest edition 2004 edition. Publication includes: List of over 8,500 member firms and 24,000 national associate member firms engaged in building, highway, heavy, industrial, municipal utilities, and railroad construction (SIC 1541, 1542, 1611, 1622, 1623, 1629); listing of state and local chapter officers. Entries include: For firms–Company name, address, phone, fax, names of principal executives, and code indicating type of construction undertaken. For officers–Name, title, address. Arrangement: Geographical, alphabetical. Indexes: Company name.

★2930★ ENR-Top 400 Construction Contractors Issue

McGraw-Hill Inc.
1221 Ave. of the Americas
New York, NY 10020-1095
Ph: (212)512-2000　　Fax: (212)512-3840
Fr: 877-833-5524
URL: http://construction.ecnext.com/coms2/summary_0249-137077_ITM

Annual; 22nd, May 2006. $35.00 for individuals. Publication includes: List of 400 United States contractors receiving largest dollar volumes of contracts in preceding calendar year. Separate lists of 50 largest design construction management firms; 50 largest program and construction managers; 25 building contractors; 25 heavy contractors. Entries include: Company name, headquarters location, total value of contracts received in preceding year, value of foreign contracts, countries in which operated, construction specialities. Arrangement: By total value of contracts received.

HANDBOOKS AND MANUALS

★2931★ Building Professionals: Creating a Successful Portfolio

Prentice Hall PTR
1 Lake St.
Upper Saddle River, NJ 07458
Ph: (201)236-7000　　Fax: 800-835-5327
Fr: 800-428-5331
URL: http://www.phptr.com/index.asp?rl=1

Diane J. Orton, Tammy Freelin, Fresa J. Jacobs, Robin R. Wingo. 2002. 80 pages. $10.67.

★2932★ Exploring Careers in Construction

Prentice Hall PTR
1 Lake St.
Upper Saddle River, NJ 07458
Ph: (201)236-7000　　Fax: 800-445-6991
Fr: 800-428-5331
URL: http://www.phptr.com/index.asp?rl=1

National Center for Construction Educ. 1998. $18.67. 92 pages.

★2933★ Opportunities in Building Construction Trades

The McGraw-Hill Companies
PO Box 182604
Columbus, OH 43272
Fax: (614)759-3749　　Fr: 877-883-5524
E-mail: customer.service@mcgraw-hill.com
URL: http://www.mcgraw-hill.com

Michael Sumichrast. Second edition, 1998. $14.95; $11.95 (paper). 104 pages. From custom builder to rehabber, the many kinds of companies that employ craftspeople and contractors are explored. Includes job descriptions, requirements, and salaries for dozens of specialties within the construction industry. Contains a complete list of Bureau of Apprenticeship and Training state and area offices. Illustrated.

★2934★ **Opportunities in State and Local Government Careers**

The McGraw-Hill Companies
PO Box 182604
Columbus, OH 43272
Fax: (614)759-3749   Fr: 877-883-5524
E-mail: customer.service@mcgraw-hill.com
URL: http://www.mcgraw-hill.com

Neale J. Baxter. Revised edition, 1992. $14.95; $10.95 (paper). 148 pages. Points out the incentives and drawbacks of a government career. Describes hiring procedures and provides tips on filling out applications, taking physical and aptitude tests, handling interviews, and finding jobs. Describes the jobs in which 75% of all state and local government workers are employed. For each occupation, covers the nature of the work and the training required.

EMPLOYMENT AGENCIES AND SEARCH FIRMS

★2935★ **20-20 Foresight Executive Search Inc.**

One Lincoln Center, Fl. 15
Oakbrook Terrace, IL 60181
Ph: (708)246-2100
E-mail: bcavoto@202-4.com
URL: http://www.2020-4.com

Executive search firm. Affiliate offices in California and Washington DC.

★2936★ **Callaghan International Inc.**

119 W. 57th St., Ste. 1220
New York, NY 10019
Ph: (212)265-9200   Fax: (212)265-0024
E-mail: kmc@callaghan-international.com
URL: http://www.callaghan-international.com

Executive search firm.

★2937★ **Construction Executives Inc.**

1201 N. Orange St., Ste.747
Wilmington, DE 19801
Ph: 888-800-6952   Fax: (302)288-5656
E-mail: info@constructionexecutive.com
URL: http://www.constructionexecutive.com

Executive search firm specifically for construction.

★2938★ **Cook Associates Inc.**

212 W Kinzie St.
Chicago, IL 60610
Ph: (312)329-0900   Fax: (312)329-1528
E-mail: info@cookassociates.com
URL: http://www.cookassociates.com

Management and executive recruiting specialists offering a commitment to clients to find the best candidates and to find those candidates as efficiently as possible. Approach provides a flexible and effective structure that serves the special needs of both large and small companies. Serves the following industries: industrial, equipment manufacturer, food processing, graphic arts, chemical process, retailing, mechanical products, healthcare services, financial and professional services, legal, consumer products, construction and engineering, packaging, pulp and paper.

★2939★ **Frank Palma Associates**

27 Glacier Dr.
Morris Plains, NJ 07950
Ph: (973)884-1498   Fax: (973)884-1499
E-mail: fpalma@fpassocs.com
URL: http://www.fpalmaassoc.com

Executive search firm with additional location in Duluth, GA.

★2940★ **Real Estate Executive Search, Inc.**

306 SE 4th St.
Dania Beach, FL 33004
Ph: (954)927-6000   Fax: (954)927-6003
E-mail: reesearch954@aol.com
URL: http://reesearchinc.com

Executive search firm for the real estate and finance fields.

★2941★ **Specialized Search Associates**

7780 Dundee Ln.
Delray Beach, FL 33446
Ph: (561)499-3711   Fax: (561)499-3770
Fr: 888-405-2650

Executive search firm that specializes in construction, engineering, and sales.

ONLINE JOB SOURCES AND SERVICES

★2942★ **Construction Education.com**
E-mail: ceo@constructioneducation.com
URL: http://www.constructioneducation.com

Description: Includes link page with list of professional resources, employment opportunities listed by company, and construction-related recruiters' pages, as well as general job search websites. Also contains on-site job bank.

TRADESHOWS

★2943★ **AEC-ST**

Ecobuild Federal, LCC
1645 Falmouth Rd., Ste. 1A
Centerville, MA 02632
Ph: (508)790-4751   Fax: (508)790-4750

URL: http://www.ecobuildamerica.com/

Annual. **Primary Exhibits:** Sustainable and environmental design, energy efficiency, green building, best practices and expert strategies, building information modeling, future of IT trends. **Dates and Locations:** 2008 Jun 16-20; Anaheim, CA; 2008 Dec 08-12; Washington, DC.

★2944★ **SBCCI Research and Education Conference**

International Code Council
5203 Leesburg Pike, Ste. 600
Falls Church, VA 22041
Ph: (703)931-4533   Fax: (703)379-1546
URL: http://www.iccsafe.org

Annual. **Primary Exhibits:** Exhibits relating to uniformity in building regulations.

OTHER SOURCES

★2945★ **American Society of Home Inspectors (ASHI)**

932 Lee St., Ste. 101
Des Plaines, IL 60016-6546
Ph: (847)759-2820   Fax: (847)759-1620
Fr: 800-743-2744
E-mail: robp@ashi.org
URL: http://www.ashi.org

Description: Professional home inspectors whose goals are to: establish home inspector qualifications; set standards of practice for home inspections; adhere to a code of ethics; keep the concept of "objective third party" intact; inform members of the most advanced methods and techniques, and educate consumers on the value of home inspections. Conducts seminars through local chapters.

★2946★ **Associated Builders and Contractors (ABC)**

4250 N Fairfax Dr., 9th Fl.
Arlington, VA 22203-1607
Ph: (703)812-2000   Fax: (703)812-8200
E-mail: gotquestions@abc.org
URL: http://www.abc.org

Description: Construction contractors, subcontractors, suppliers, and associates. Aims to foster and perpetuate the principles of rewarding construction workers and management on the basis of merit. Sponsors management education programs and craft training; also sponsors apprenticeship and skill training programs. Disseminates technological and labor relations information.

★2947★ **Associated General Contractors of America (AGC)**

2300 Wilson Blvd., Ste. 400
Arlington, VA 22201
Ph: (703)548-3118   Fax: (703)548-3119
Fr: 800-242-1767
E-mail: info@agc.org
URL: http://www.agc.org

Description: General construction contractors; subcontractors; industry suppliers; service firms. Provides market services through its divisions. Conducts special conferences and seminars designed specifically for construction firms. Compiles statistics on job accidents reported by member firms. Maintains 65 committees, including joint cooperative committees with other associations and liaison committees with federal agencies.

★2948★ International Conference of Building Officials (ICBO)

Los Angeles District Office
5360 Workman Mill Rd.
Whittier, CA 90601
Fax: (562)908-5524   Fr: 888-422-7233
E-mail: webmaster@iccsafe.org
URL: http://www.iccsafe.org

Description: Representatives of local, regional, and state governments. Seeks to publish, maintain, and promote the Uniform Building Code and related documents; investigate and research principles underlying safety to life and property in the construction, use, and location of buildings and related structures; develop and promulgate uniformity in regulations pertaining to building construction; educate the building official; formulate guidelines for the administration of building inspection departments. Conducts training programs, courses, and certification programs for code enforcement inspectors. Maintains speakers' bureau.

★2949★ National Association of Women in Construction (NAWIC)

327 S Adams St.
Fort Worth, TX 76104
Ph: (817)877-5551   Fax: (817)877-0324
Fr: 800-552-3506
E-mail: nawic@nawic.org
URL: http://www.nawic.org

Description: Seeks to enhance the success of women in the construction industry.

★2950★ National Center for Construction Education and Research (NCCER)

3600 NW 43rd St., Bldg. G
Gainesville, FL 32606
Ph: (352)334-0911   Fax: (352)334-0932
Fr: 888-622-3720
URL: http://www.nccer.org

Description: Education foundation committed to the development and publication of Contren(TM) Learning Series, the source of craft training, management education and safety resources for the construction industry.

★2951★ Southern Building Code Congress International (SBCCI)

500 New Jersey Ave. NW, 6th Fl.
Washington, DC 20001-2070
Fax: (703)379-2348   Fr: 888-422-7233
E-mail: webmaster@iccsafe.org
URL: http://www.iccsafe.org

Members: Active members are state, county, municipal, or other government subdivisions; associate members are trade associations, architects, engineers, contractors, and related groups or persons. **Purpose:** Seeks to develop, maintain, and promote the adoption of the International Building, Residential, Gas, Plumbing, Mechanical, Fire, and property maintenance Codes. Encourages uniformity in building regulations through the International Codes and their application and enforcement. **Activities:** Provides technical and educational services to members and others; participates in the development of nationally recognized consensus standards. Provides research on new materials and methods of construction; conducts seminars on code enforcement, inspection, and special topics.

★2952★ Women in Building Construction

Her Own Words
PO Box 5264
Madison, WI 53705-0264
Ph: (608)271-7083   Fax: (608)271-0209
E-mail: herownword@aol.com
URL: http://www.herownwords.com/

Video. Jocelyn Riley. $95.00. 15 minutes. Resource guide also available for $45.00.

★2953★ Women in Nontraditional Careers: An Introduction

Her Own Words
PO Box 5264
Madison, WI 53705
Ph: (608)271-7083   Fax: (608)271-0209
E-mail: herownword@aol.com
URL: http://www.herownwords.com/

Video. Jocelyn Riley. $95.00. 15 minutes. Resource guide also available for $45.00.

Construction Managers

★2954★ ABC Newsline

Associated Builders & Contractors Inc.
4250 N Fairfax Dr., 9th Fl.
Arlington, VA 22203-1607
Ph: (703)812-2000   Fax: (703)812-8203
E-mail: gotquestions@abc.org
URL: http://www.abc.org/

Description: Weekly. Designed to keep readers alerted to important changes within ABC and the construction industry. Reports on legislative issues, construction trends, conferences and meetings, and ABC services. Recurring features include news of members and columns titled Labor Relations, Construction Law, Computer Corner, Bottom Line, and Chapter News.

★2955★ American Institute of Constructors Newsletter

American Institute of Constructors
PO Box 26334
Alexandria, VA 22314
Ph: (703)683-4999   Fax: (703)683-5480
URL: http://www.aicnet.org/

Description: Bimonthly. Concerned with construction practice, design, administration, and teaching. Carries news of members, listings of job opportunities, local chapter reports, notices of new publications, and conferences on construction topics.

★2956★ American Professional Constructor

American Institute of Constructors
PO Box 26334
Alexandria, VA 22314
Ph: (703)683-4999   Fax: (703)683-5480
URL: http://www.aicnet.org/store/proddetail6da9.asp?CFID=10706514

Biennial. Subscription included in membership; $100.00/year for nonmembers. Journal covering general interest and technical articles for construction professionals.

★2957★ Asphalt Roofing Manufacturers Association Newsletter

Asphalt Roofing Manufacturers
 Association
1156 15th St. NW, Ste. 900
Washington, DC 20005
Ph: (202)207-0917   Fax: (202)223-9741
URL: http://www.asphaltroofing.org/

Description: Quarterly. Reports news and information of interest to professionals in the asphalt roofing industry. Highlights Association activities and discusses developments in the industry, including occupational safety and health measures, changes in industry codes and standards, environmental issues, and legislative and regulatory actions.

★2958★ BIA News

Brick Industry Association
1850 Centennial Park Dr., Ste. 301
Reston, VA 20191-1525
Ph: (703)620-0010   Fax: (703)620-3928

Monthly. $30.00/year for individuals. Trade publication covering issues for the brick industry.

★2959★ Builder and Developer

Peninsula Publishing
1602 Monrovia Ave.
Newport Beach, CA 92663
Ph: (949)631-0308   Fax: (949)631-2475
URL: http://www.bdmag.com/new_site/

Magazine for homebuilders.

★2960★ Building Concerns

National Association of Minority
 Contractors
1300 Pennsylvania Ave, Ste. 700
Washington, DC 20001
Ph: (202)347-8259   Fax: (202)789-7349
E-mail: national@namcline.org
URL: http://www.namcline.org/

Description: Monthly. Concentrates on national and regional news regarding minority construction contractors. Contains articles on issues generally affecting the industry, especially issues affecting minorities, including topics such as legislative and regulatory activity and reports on major corporation developments. Recurring features include reports of meetings, news of educational opportunities, a calendar of events, and news of NAMC chapters, affiliates, and members.

★2961★ Building Industry Technology

National Technical Information Service
5285 Port Royal Rd.
Springfield, VA 22161
Ph: (703)605-6585   Fax: (703)605-6900
Fr: 800-553-6847
E-mail: info@ntis.gov.
URL: http://www.ntis.gov/new/alerts_printed.asp

Description: Biweekly. Consists of abstracts of reports on architectural and environmental design, building standards, construction materials and equipment, and structural analyses. Recurring features include a form for ordering reports from NTIS. Also available via e-mail.

★2962★ Building Standards

International Conference of Building
 Officials
5360 Workman Mill Rd.
Whittier, CA 90601
Ph: (562)699-0543   Fax: (562)695-4694
Fr: 800-423-6587
URL: http://www.iccsafe.org

Description: Six issues/year. Provides articles of interest to building officials, architects, engineers, and others in the construction industry. The newsletter is part of Building Standards magazine subscription.

★2963★ Building Systems Magazine

Active Interest Media
300 Continental Blvd., Ste. 650
El Segundo, CA 90245
Ph: (310)356-4100   Fax: (310)356-4110
Fr: 800-423-4880
URL: http://www.buildingsystems.com/

Bimonthly. Magazine featuring innovative construction technologies for builders, developers and general contractors.

★2964★ CM Advisor

Construction Management Association of America Inc.
7926 Jones Branch Dr., Ste. 800
Mc Lean, VA 22102
Ph: (703)356-2622   Fax: (703)356-6388
E-mail: info@cmaanet.org
URL: http://www.cmaanet.org

Description: Bimonthly. Provides information on construction management and its technical, legal, and legislative issues. Recurring features include letters to the editor, news of research, a calendar of events, reports of meetings, news of educational opportunities, book reviews, notices of publications available, and columns titled Government Affairs and For Your Information

★2965★ Concrete & Masonry Construction Products

Hanley-Wood LLC
One Thomas Cir. NW, Ste. 600
Washington, DC 20005
Ph: (202)452-0800   Fax: (202)785-1974
E-mail: cmcp@omeda.com
URL: http://www.hanleywood.com/default.aspx?page=cdconmas

Bimonthly. Free. Publication that covers carpenter tips, tools, and up keep.

★2966★ Construction

Reed Business Information
360 Park Ave. S
New York, NY 10010
Ph: (646)746-6400   Fax: (646)746-7431
URL: http://www.acppubs.com/community/835.html

Semimonthly. $106.00/year for individuals; $126.00/year for Canada; $166.00/year for other countries. Regional construction publication covering Maryland, the District of Columbia, Virginia, North Carolina and South Carolina. Geared toward those engaged in engineering (heavy and highway), non-residential building construction and allied fields relating to construction or requiring the use of construction equipment. Containing "how to" job stories, product news, industry news and bid and award information.

★2967★ Construction Business Owner

Cahaba Media Group
PO Box 530067
Birmingham, AL 35253
Ph: (205)212-9402
URL: http://www.constructionbusinessowner.com/

Monthly. Free. Magazine that provides information for construction management and industry business information.

★2968★ Construction Claims Monthly

Business Publishers Inc.
PO Box 17592
Baltimore, MD 21297
Fr: 800-274-6737
E-mail: custserv@bpinews.com

URL: http://www.bpinews.com/

Description: Monthly. Covers significant legal developments governing contract payment and performance. Features an article on construction claims law; summaries of recent decisions with expert commentary; and highlights of actions by the federal boards of contract appeals and the Comptroller General.

★2969★ Construction Division Newsletter

NSC Press
1121 Spring Lake Dr.
Itasca, IL 60143-3201
Ph: (630)285-1121   Fax: (630)285-1315
Fr: 800-621-7615
URL: http://www.nsc.org

Description: Bimonthly. Focuses on industrial and occupational safety in the construction industry. Carries items on such topics as safe work practices and products; accident prevention; and successful industrial safety programs and policies. Available online only.

★2970★ Construction Specifications Institute-Newsdigest

The Construction Specifications Institute
289 - 266 Elmwood Ave.
Buffalo, NY 14222
Fax: (866)572-5677   Fr: (866)572-5633
E-mail: sales@constructionspecifier.com
URL: http://www.constructionspecifier.com

Description: Monthly. Covers the technical and certification programs offered by the Institute, which is "dedicated to the advancement of construction technology through service, education, and research." Also reports on regional and chapter activities and carries items on educational programs related to the construction industry. Recurring features include news of members, a calendar of events, listings of new publications available through the Institute, and columns titled Board Flash, Convention Briefs, and T.I.E. (Technical Information and Education Activities).

★2971★ CRCP: The Ultimate Solution for Pavements

Concrete Reinforcing Steel Institute (CRSI)
933 N. Plum Grove Rd.
Schaumburg, IL 60173-4758
Ph: (847)517-1200   Fax: (847)517-1206
Fr: 800-328-6306
URL: http://www.crsi.org

Description: Biennial. Focuses on developments in the reinforced concrete construction industry. Reports on advances and applications of the fusion-bonded coating system for corrosion prevention. Recurring features include profiles of successful construction projects, news of the Institute and its members, and a calendar of events.

★2972★ Design Cost Data

DC & D Technologies Inc.
8602 North 40th St.
Tampa, FL 33604-2434
Ph: (813)989-9300   Fax: (813)980-3982
Fr: 800-533-5680
E-mail: webmaster@dcd.com
URL: http://www.dcd.com

Bimonthly. $89.40/year for individuals; $149.28 for two years. Publication providing real cost data case studies of various types completed around the country for design and building professionals.

★2973★ The Enterprise

Dodson Publications Inc.
546 Court St.
Reno, NV 89501
Ph: (775)333-1080   Fax: (775)333-1081
E-mail: info@westernroofing.net
URL: http://www.westernroofing.net

Description: Bimonthly. Contains information for the construction and manufacturing industries. Recurring features include news of research and a calendar of events.

★2974★ Environmental Building News

Building Green Inc.
122 Birge St., Ste. 30
Brattleboro, VT 05301-3206
Ph: (802)257-7300   Fax: (802)257-7304
Fr: 800-861-0954
E-mail: info@buildinggreen.com
URL: http://www.buildinggreen.com

Description: Monthly. Covers the building trade with an environmental slant. Covers nontoxic materials, better landscaping and water use, and resources for energy conservation in a technical manner.

★2975★ EUCA Magazine

Engineering & Utility Contractors Association
17 Crow Canyon Ct., Ste. 100
San Ramon, CA 94583
Ph: (925)855-7900   Fax: (925)855-7909
E-mail: dramirez@euca.com
URL: http://www.euca.com

Description: Monthly. Supports the Association in its efforts to "provide innovative ideas and strong leadership" to those in the contracting industry. Focuses on various issues pertinent to members and industry executives, including legislative and regulatory developments, occupational safety concerns, new products and technologies, and industry trends and developments. Recurring features include interviews, news of research, reports of meetings, news of educational opportunities, notices of publications available, and a calendar of events. Contains member profiles and news of members, Association elections, and administrative decisions.

★2976★ FM Data Monthly

Tradeline Inc.
PO Box 1568
Orinda, CA 94563
Ph: (925)254-1744   Fax: (925)254-1093
E-mail: info@fmdata.com
URL: http://www.tradelineinc.com

Description: Monthly. Provides current field data on the planning, design, construction, and renovation of a variety of corporate and institutional projects. Analyzes management strategies and budgetary priorities. Recurring features include interviews, news of research, and notices of publications available. Includes columns titled Facilities Planning News.

★2977★ Green Home Builder

Peninsula Publishing
1602 Monrovia Ave.
Newport Beach, CA 92663
Ph: (949)631-0308   Fax: (949)631-2475
URL: http://
www.greenhomebuildermag.com/

Quarterly. Magazine for home builders and home building industry.

★2978★ ISHN

BNP Media
2401 W Big Beaver Rd., Ste. 700
Troy, MI 48084-3333
Ph: (248)786-1642   Fax: (248)786-1388
URL: http://www.ishn.com/

Monthly. Free. Business-to-business magazine for safety and health managers at high-hazard worksites in manufacturing, construction, health facilities, and service industries. Content covering OSHA and EPA regulations, how-to features, safety and health management topics, and the latest product news.

★2979★ Kitchen and Bath Business

The Nielsen Co.
770 Broadway
New York, NY 10003
Ph: (646)654-5000   Fax: (646)654-5002
URL: http://www.kitchen-bath.com/kbb/index.jsp

Monthly. $10.00/year for individuals, cover; $79.00/year for individuals, domestic; $94.00/year for Canada and Mexico; $142.00/year for other countries. Trade magazine on kitchen and bath remodeling and construction.

★2980★ Landscape Construction

Moose River Publishing
374 Emerson Falls Rd.
St. Johnsbury, VT 05819-9083
Ph: (802)748-8908   Fax: (802)748-1866
Fr: 800-422-7147
URL: http://www.lcmmagazine.com/

Monthly. Magazine featuring landscaping.

★2981★ MetalMag

Spiderweb Publishing Inc.
1415 Hwy. 54 W, Ste. 105
Durham, NC 27707
Ph: (919)482-9300   Fax: (919)402-9302
E-mail: mtm@omeda.com
URL: http://www.metalmag.com/

Bimonthly. Free to qualified subscribers. Magazine for industrial construction professionals.

★2982★ NEA Notes

The Association of Union Constructors
1501 Lee Hwy.
Ste. 202
Arlington, VA 22209-1109
Ph: (703)524-3336   Fax: (703)524-3364
URL: http://www.nea-online.org

Description: Monthly. Publishes news of the construction industry and the Association, as well as the safety and industrial maintenance fields. Recurring features include news of members.

★2983★ Offshore Field Development International

Offshore Data Services Inc.
3200 Wilcrest Dr., Ste. 170
Houston, TX 77042
Ph: (832)463-3000   Fax: (832)463-3100
URL: http://www.offshore-data.com

Description: Monthly. Reports on petroleum-related offshore construction projects worldwide, from the planning stage through final installation. Covers platforms, pipelines, subsea completions, and mooring terminals. Recurring features include sections on construction barge locations and possible areas for future development.

★2984★ Remodeling

Hanley-Wood L.L.C.
1 Thomas Cir., NW, Ste. 600
Washington, DC 20005
Ph: (202)452-0800   Fax: (202)785-1974
URL: http://www.hanleywood.com/default.aspx?page=b2brm

$25.00/year for individuals; $40.00/year for individuals, Canadian residents; $192.00/year for individuals, international residents. Trade magazine for the professional remodeling industry.

★2985★ Replacement Contractor

Hanley-Wood LLC
One Thomas Cir. NW, Ste. 600
Washington, DC 20005
Ph: (202)452-0800   Fax: (202)785-1974
URL: http://www.omeda.com/rcon/

Bimonthly. Magazine for contractors engaged in roofing, siding, decking and window replacement.

★2986★ Residential Architect

Hanley-Wood L.L.C.
1 Thomas Cir., NW, Ste. 600
Washington, DC 20005
Ph: (202)452-0800   Fax: (202)785-1974
URL: http://www.hanleywood.com/default.aspx?page=b2bra

Magazine for architects, designers, and building professionals.

★2987★ Residential Concrete

Hanley-Wood L.L.C.
1 Thomas Cir., NW, Ste. 600
Washington, DC 20005
Ph: (202)452-0800   Fax: (202)785-1974
URL: http://www.hanleywood.com/default.aspx?page=b2bresconcrete

Bimonthly. Magazine featuring the use of concrete in residential concrete construction.

★2988★ Residential Contractor

Peninsula Publishing
1602 Monrovia Ave.
Newport Beach, CA 92663
Ph: (949)631-0308   Fax: (949)631-2475
URL: http://
www.residentialcontractormag.com/

Quarterly. Magazine for small volume residential builders, contractors, and specialty trades.

★2989★ Residential Design & Build

Cygnus Business Media Inc.
3 Huntington Quadrangle, Ste. 301 N
Melville, NY 11747
Ph: (631)845-2700   Fax: (631)845-7109
Fr: 800-308-6397
URL: http://www.rdbmagazine.com

Magazine providing advice and insight on the design/build project delivery method, as well as information on the latest design trends, new products and home building professionals.

★2990★ Retail Construction

Retail Construction Magazine
PO Box 1589
Cumming, GA 30028
Ph: (770)781-2501   Fax: (770)781-6303
URL: http://www.retailconstructionmag.com

Free. Magazine that covers design, construction, renovation and operation of retail businesses.

★2991★ Roofing Contractor

BNP Media
2401 W Big Beaver Rd., Ste. 700
Troy, MI 48084-3333
Ph: (248)786-1642   Fax: (248)786-1388
URL: http://www.roofingcontractor.com/

Monthly. Trade publication covering roofing and the construction industry.

★2992★ Tools of the Trade

Hanley-Wood L.L.C.
1 Thomas Cir., NW, Ste. 600
Washington, DC 20005
Ph: (202)452-0800   Fax: (202)785-1974
URL: http://www.hanleywood.com/default.aspx?page=b2btt

Bimonthly. Magazine featuring tools for commercial and residential construction.

★2993★ Words From Woody

David W. Wood
503 E. Deering Rd.
Deering, NH 03244
Ph: (603)529-2355   Fax: (603)529-3180
Fr: 800-439-9663
E-mail: woody@wordsfromwoody.com
URL: http://www.wordsfromwoody.com/

Description: Quarterly. Contains information of interest to construction-related firms. Also includes business and marketing tips.

EMPLOYER DIRECTORIES AND NETWORKING LISTS

★2994★ Athletic Business-Professional Directory Section

Athletic Business Publications Inc.
4130 Lien Rd.
Madison, WI 53704
Ph: (608)249-0186   Fax: (608)249-1153
Fr: 800-722-8764

Monthly. $8.00. Publication includes: List of architects, engineers, contractors, and consultants in athletic facility planning and construction; all listings are paid. Entries include: Company name, address, phone, fax and short description of company. Arrangement: Alphabetical.

★2995★ Career Ideas for Teens in Architecture and Construction

Facts On File Inc.
132 W 31st St., 17th Fl.
New York, NY 10001
Ph: (212)967-8800   Fax: 800-678-3633
Fr: 800-322-8755
URL: http://www.factsonfile.com

Published 2005. $40.00 for individuals; $36.00 for libraries. Covers a multitude of career possibilities based on a teenager's specific interests and skills and links his/her talents to a wide variety of actual professions.

★2996★ Careers in Focus: Construction

Facts On File Inc.
132 W 31st St., 17th Fl.
New York, NY 10001
Ph: (212)967-8800   Fax: 800-678-3633
Fr: 800-322-8755
URL: http://www.factsonfile.com

Latest edition 4th, 2004. $29.95 for individuals; $26.95 for libraries. Covers an overview of construction, followed by a selection of jobs profiled in detail, including the nature of the job, earnings, prospects for employment, what kind of training and skills it requires, and sources for further information.

★2997★ Contractor's Directory

Government Data Publications Inc.
2300 M St. NW
Washington, DC 20037
Ph: (718)627-0819   Fax: (718)998-5960
Fr: 800-275-4688
URL: http://www.govdata.com

Annual, February. Covers contractors who have received government contract under Public Law 95-507, which requires preferential treatment of small business for subcontracts. Entries include: Contractor name and address. Supplementary to 'Small Business Preferential Subcontracts Opportunities Monthly,' which lists companies with government contracts over $500,000 ($1,000,000 for construction). Arrangement: Same information given alphabetically and by ZIP code.

★2998★ Discovering Careers for Your Future: Construction

Facts On File Inc.
132 W 31st St., 17th Fl.
New York, NY 10001
Ph: (212)967-8800   Fax: 800-678-3633
Fr: 800-322-8755
URL: http://www.factsonfile.com

Published 2001. $21.95 for individuals; $19.75 for libraries. Covers architects, carpenters, drafters, engineers, painters and roofers; links career education to curriculum, helping children investigate the subjects they are interested in, and the careers those subjects might lead to.

HANDBOOKS AND MANUALS

★2999★ Building Professionals: Creating a Successful Portfolio

Prentice Hall PTR
1 Lake St.
Upper Saddle River, NJ 07458
Ph: (201)236-7000   Fax: 800-835-5327
Fr: 800-428-5331
URL: http://www.phptr.com/index.asp?rl=1

Diane J. Orton, Tammy Freelin, Fresa J. Jacobs, Robin R. Wingo. 2002. 80 pages. $10.67.

★3000★ Construction Manager

National Learning Corporation
212 Michael Dr.
Syosset, NY 11791
Ph: (516)921-8888   Fax: (516)921-8743
Fr: 800-632-8888
URL: http://www.passbooks.com/

Rudman, Jack. 1994. $34.95 (Trade paper).

★3001★ Information Technologies for Construction Managers, Architects, and Engineers

Cengage Learning
PO Box 6904
Florence, KY 41022
Fax: 800-487-8488   Fr: 800-354-9706
URL: http://www.cengage.com/

Trefor Williams. 2006. $77.50. Profiles information technology applications in construction trades, from traditional computer applications to emerging Web-based and mobile technologies.

★3002★ Preparing for Design-Build Projects: A Primer for Owners, Engineers, and Contractors

American Society of Civil Engineers
1801 Alexander Bell Dr.
Reston, VA 20191-4400
Ph: (703)295-6300   Fax: (703)295-6222
Fr: 800-548-2723
URL: http://www.asce.org/asce.cfm

Douglas D. Gransberg, James A. Koch and Keith R. Molenaar. 2006. $64.00

EMPLOYMENT AGENCIES AND SEARCH FIRMS

★3003★ 20-20 Foresight Executive Search Inc.

One Lincoln Center, Fl. 15
Oakbrook Terrace, IL 60181
Ph: (708)246-2100
E-mail: bcavoto@202-4.com
URL: http://www.2020-4.com

Executive search firm. Affiliate offices in California and Washington DC.

★3004★ Adams Executive Search

3416 Fairfield Trail
Clearwater, FL 33761
Ph: (727)772-1536   Fax: (815)328-3792
E-mail: info@axsearch.com
URL: http://www.axsearch.com

Executive search firm.

★3005★ Adams Partners

205 W. Wacker Dr., Ste. 620
Chicago, IL 60606
Ph: (312)673-0389   Fax: (312)673-0390
URL: http://www.adamspartners.com

Executive search firm.

★3006★ AET Advisors LLC

4875 Olde Towne Pkwy., Ste. 150
Marietta, GA 30068
Ph: (770)578-6556
E-mail: aetadvisors@mindspring.com

Executive search and consultant firm. Focuses on the real estate industry.

★3007★ The Cherbonnier Group Inc.
1 Riverway, Ste. 1700
Houston, TX 77056
Ph: (713)688-4701
E-mail: consult@chergroup.com
URL: http://www.thecherbonniergroup.com

Executive search firm.

★3008★ Construction Executives Inc.
1201 N. Orange St., Ste.747
Wilmington, DE 19801
Ph: 888-800-6952   Fax: (302)288-5656
E-mail: info@constructionexecutive.com
URL: http://www.constructionexecutive.com

Executive search firm specifically for construction.

★3009★ The Consulting Group
757 Third Ave., 23rd Fl.
New York, NY 10017
Ph: (212)751-8484   Fax: (212)692-9290
E-mail: research@consultinggroupny.com
URL: http://www.consultinggroupny.com

Executive search firm.

★3010★ Contractor Marketing
346 Dayton St.
Dayton, OH 45387-1704
Ph: (937)767-2876   Fax: (937)767-7281
E-mail: larry@contractormarketing.com
URL: http://www.contractormarketing.com

Executive search firm.

★3011★ Cook Associates Inc.
212 W Kinzie St.
Chicago, IL 60610
Ph: (312)329-0900   Fax: (312)329-1528
E-mail: info@cookassociates.com
URL: http://www.cookassociates.com

Management and executive recruiting specialists offering a commitment to clients to find the best candidates and to find those candidates as efficiently as possible. Approach provides a flexible and effective structure that serves the special needs of both large and small companies. Serves the following industries: industrial, equipment manufacturer, food processing, graphic arts, chemical process, retailing, mechanical products, healthcare services, financial and professional services, legal, consumer products, construction and engineering, packaging, pulp and paper.

★3012★ Crown Advisors Inc.
30 Isabella St., Ste. 203
Pittsburgh, PA 15212
Ph: (412)566-1100   Fax: (412)566-1256
E-mail: info@crownsearch.com
URL: http://www.crownsearch.com

Executive search firm.

★3013★ Edward Dellon Associates Inc.
450 N. Brand Blvd., Ste. 600
Glendale, CA 91203
Ph: (310)286-0625   Fax: (818)291-6205
E-mail: Edward_dellon@yahoo.com
URL: http://edwarddellonassociatesinc.com

Executive search firm.

★3014★ HardHatJobs Inc.
1200 Executive Dr. E, Ste. 127A
Richardson, TX 75081
Ph: (972)808-9200   Fax: (972)808-9203
E-mail: bill@hardhatjobs.com
URL: http://www.hardhatjobs.com

Executive search and consulting for Commercial Construction, Construction Engineering and Construction Management professionals. Presidents, CEO's, COO's, Business Development, Executive Vice Presidents, VP, CFO's, Program, Project and Construction Managers, Superintendents, Schedulers, Project Accountants, Cost Controllers and Safety Engineers.

★3015★ McNichol Associates
620 Chestnut St., Ste. 1031
Philadelphia, PA 19106
Ph: (215)922-4142   Fax: (215)922-0178
E-mail: mailbox@mcnicholassoc.com
URL: http://www.mcnicholassoc.com

Performs executive search for middle and senior-level management, marketing, and technical personnel for professional design firms; construction, management, and general contractors; engineering-construction organizations; environmental firms, and others needing technical management personnel.

★3016★ Oliver & Rozner Associates
598 Madison Ave., Ste. 11
New York, NY 10022
Ph: (212)688-1850

Performs executive search for top tiers of management including presidents, general management, advertising account management, division management, group executive and vice presidential line positions in such areas as marketing, research, operations, sales, finance, human resources, and others; hard-to-find specialists including specific marketing/advertising executives, research and development expertise, computer/data processing knowledge, scientific, physicians-product efficacy and occupational medicine, and engineering. Industries served include pharmaceutical, healthcare, hospital, advertising, consumer products and packaged goods, housewares, direct selling, cosmetics/toiletries, industrial products, high technology products, forest products, engineering, construction, environment/resource recovery, graphic arts, chemical, and government agencies.

★3017★ Robert Howe and Associates
35 Glenlake Pky. NE
Atlanta, GA 30328
Ph: (770)390-0030   Fax: (770)270-1209

Provides consulting services in the area of executive search and recruitment. Industries served: healthcare, hospitality, chemical, metals, electronics, construction, and food processing.

★3018★ The Sharrow Group
254 Empire Blvd.
Rochester, NY 14609
Ph: (585)697-0056   Fax: (810)759-6914
Fr: 877-759-6910
E-mail: jobs@sharrowgroup.com
URL: http://www.sharrowgroup.com

Executive search firm offers specialized placement in areas of rubber, adhesives, plastic, coatings, paint, information technology, patent and trademark attorneys, and construction executives.

★3019★ Specialty Consultants Inc.
2710 Gateway Towers
Pittsburgh, PA 15222-1189
Ph: (412)355-8200   Fax: (412)355-0498
E-mail: info@specon.com
URL: http://www.specon.com

Provides executive recruiting services for companies in the construction and real estate industry. Identifies candidates through an extensive research database and industry contacts. Services also include compensation surveys, organizational development and executive coaching.

ONLINE JOB SOURCES AND SERVICES

★3020★ Construction Education.com
E-mail: ceo@constructioneducation.com
URL: http://www.constructioneducation.com

Description: Includes link page with list of professional resources, employment opportunities listed by company, and construction-related recruiters' pages, as well as general job search websites. Also contains on-site job bank.

★3021★ Construction Management Association of America
7918 Jones Branch Dr., Ste. 540
McLean, VA 22102
Ph: (703)356-2622   Fax: (703)356-6388
E-mail: info@cmaanet.org
URL: http://cmaanet.org

Description: Association website contains a job databank, professional resources books for sale, and career development seminars to attend. Must be a member to fully utilize site, which also includes more project leads, discussion forums, and more.

TRADESHOWS

★3022★ AGC/CONSTRUCTOR Exhibition

Associated General Contractors of
  America Information
10 Airline Dr., Ste. 203
Albany, NY 12205
Ph: (518)456-1134   Fax: (518)456-1198
E-mail: agcadmin@agcnys.org
URL: http://www.agcnys.org

Annual. **Primary Exhibits:** Heavy and light
construction equipment, trucks, building materials, and management services.

★3023★ American Institute of Constructors Annual Forum

American Institute of Constructors
466 94th Ave. North
St. Petersburg, FL 33702
Ph: (727)578-0317   Fax: (727)578-9982
E-mail: admin@aicnet.org
URL: http://www.aicnet.org/

Annual. **Primary Exhibits:** Exhibits related
to professionals engaged in construction
practice, education and research.

★3024★ The Builders' Show

National Association of Home Builders of
  the United States
1201 15th St. NW
Washington, DC 20005
Ph: (202)266-8200   Fax: (202)266-8223
Fr: 800-368-5242
E-mail: exposales@nahb.com
URL: http://www.nahb.org

Annual. **Primary Exhibits:** Building products, equipment, and services. **Dates and
Locations:** 2008 Feb 06-09; Atlanta, GA;
2009 Feb 20-23; Las Vegas, NV; 2010 Jan
19 - Feb 22; Las Vegas, NV; 2011 Jan 14 -
Feb 17; Orlando, FL; 2012 Jan 13-16; Orlando, FL.

★3025★ The Building Industry Show

Building Industry Association of Southern
  California
1330 S. Valley Vista Dr.
Diamond Bar, CA 91765
Ph: (909)396-9993   Fax: (909)396-1571
E-mail: jharders@biasc.org
URL: http://www.biasc.org

Annual. **Primary Exhibits:** Products and
services for the building industry.

★3026★ Buildings Show

Merchandise Mart Properties Inc.
Merchandise Mart, Ste. 470
Chicago, IL 60654
Ph: 800-677-MART   Fax: (312)527-7782
Fr: 800-677-6278
URL: http://www.merchandisemart.com

Annual. **Primary Exhibits:** Building products, commercial furnishings, and finishes.

★3027★ Central Pennsylvania Industrial and Construction Show

Cygnus Expositions
3167 Skyway Ct.
Fremont, CA 94538
Ph: (510)354-3131   Fax: (510)354-3159
Fr: 800-548-1407
E-mail: john.wright@cygnusexpos.com
URL: http://www.proshows.com

Annual. **Primary Exhibits:** Industrial and
construction equipment, supplies, and services.

★3028★ CONEXPO-CON/AGG

Association of Equipment Manufacturers
  (AEM)
6737 W. Washington St., Ste. 2400
Milwaukee, WI 53214-5647
Ph: (414)272-0943   Fax: (414)272-1170
Fr: (866)AEM-0442
E-mail: info@conexpoconagg.com
URL: http://www.aem.org

Annual. **Primary Exhibits:** Construction and
construction materials industry equipment,
supplies, and services. **Dates and Locations:** 2008 Mar 11-15; Las Vegas, NV.

★3029★ Construction Expo West

Construction Association of Michigan
43636 Woodward Ave.
PO Box 3204
Bloomfield Hills, MI 48302
Ph: (248)972-1000   Fax: (248)972-1001
E-mail: marketing@cam-online.com
URL: http://www.cam-online.com

Annual. **Primary Exhibits:** Construction
equipment, products, and services.

★3030★ Construction Financial Management Association Annual Conference and Exhibition

Construction Financial Management
  Association
29 Emmons Dr., Ste. F-50
Princeton, NJ 08540
Ph: (609)452-8000   Fax: (609)452-0474
E-mail: info@cfma.org
URL: http://www.cfma.org

Annual. **Primary Exhibits:** Equipment, supplies, and services for the construction industry. **Dates and Locations:** 2008 May 17-
21; Orlando, FL; Caesars Palace; 2009 May;
Las Vegas, NV.

★3031★ Construction Specifications Institute Annual Convention Exhibit

Construction Specifications Institute
99 Canal Center Plz., Ste. 300
Alexandria, VA 22314
Fax: (703)684-8436   Fr: 800-689-2900
E-mail: csi@csinet.org
URL: http://www.csinet.org

Annual. **Primary Exhibits:** Products and
services used in non-residential construction.

★3032★ Constructo - International Exhibition of the Construction Industry

APEX
207 E Franklin Ave., Ste. B
El Segundo, CA 90245
E-mail: anyapex@cintermex.com.mx
URL: http://www.apex.org

Annual. **Primary Exhibits:** Construction
equipment, supplies, and services.

★3033★ Contractors & Builders Supply Show

Cygnus Expositions
801 Cliff Rd., Ste. 201
Burnsville, MN 55337
Ph: (952)894-8007   Fax: (952)894-8252
Fr: 800-827-8009
E-mail: info@farmshows.com
URL: http://www.cygnusexpos.com

Annual. **Primary Exhibits:** Equipment, materials, tools, products, and services for
exterior and interior construction, remodeling, and landscaping for commercial and
residential projects.

★3034★ Design & Construction Expo

Construction Association of Michigan
43636 Woodward Ave.
PO Box 3204
Bloomfield Hills, MI 48302
Ph: (248)972-1000   Fax: (248)972-1001
E-mail: marketing@cam-online.com
URL: http://www.cam-online.com

Annual. **Primary Exhibits:** Construction industry equipment, supplies, and services.

★3035★ ICUEE - International Construction and Utility Equipment Exposition

Association of Equipment Manufacturers
  (AEM)
6737 W. Washington St., Ste. 2400
Milwaukee, WI 53214-5647
Ph: (414)272-0943   Fax: (414)272-1170
Fr: (866)AEM-0442
E-mail: info@conexpoconagg.com
URL: http://www.aem.org

Biennial. **Primary Exhibits:** Utility and construction equipment, supplies, and services.

★3036★ International Convention

National Association of Women in
  Construction, Albany Chapter
500 Whipporwill Rd.
Albany, GA 31707
Ph: (912)435-9659   Fax: (912)435-9659
E-mail: mbmvb@mindspring.com

Annual. **Primary Exhibits:** Women in all
areas of construction.

★3037★ JLC LIVE Residential Construction Show - Pacific Northwest

Hanley-Wood Exhibitions
8600 Freeport Parkway
Irving, TX 75063
Ph: (972)536-6300   Fax: (972)536-6301
Fr: 800-869-8522
URL: http://www.hanley-wood.com

Annual. **Primary Exhibits:** Housing and construction industry equipment, supplies, and services.

★3038★ MIACON - Miami International Construction Show/Expo

MIACON Construction Show, Inc.
2921 Coral Way
Miami, FL 33145
Ph: (305)441-2865   Fax: (305)529-9217
E-mail: mail@miacon.com
URL: http://www.miacon.com

Annual. **Primary Exhibits:** Equipment, machinery, building supplies, and services for the construction industry.

★3039★ National Association of Demolition Contractors Annual Convention

National Association of Demolition Contractors
16 N. Franklin St., Ste. 203
Doylestown, PA 18901-3536
Ph: (215)348-4949   Fax: (215)348-8422
Fr: 800-541-2412
E-mail: info@demolitionassociation.com
URL: http://www.demolitionassociation.com

Annual. **Primary Exhibits:** Demolition equipment, supplies, and services.

★3040★ NeoCon New York

Merchandise Mart Properties Inc.
Merchandise Mart, Ste. 470
Chicago, IL 60654
Ph: 800-677-MART   Fax: (312)527-7782
Fr: 800-677-6278
URL: http://www.merchandisemart.com

Annual. **Primary Exhibits:** Contract and residential furnishing and construction exhibition.

★3041★ Northwest Industrial, Construction & Plant Maintenance Show

Trade Shows West
2880 S. Main, Ste. 110
Salt Lake City, UT 84115
Ph: (801)485-0176   Fax: (801)485-0241
Fr: 800-794-3706

Biennial. **Primary Exhibits:** Industrial systems, construction materials and plant maintenance.

★3042★ Power Show Ohio

Ohio-Michigan Equipment Dealers Association
6124 Avery Rd.
PO Box 68
Dublin, OH 43017
Ph: (614)889-1309   Fax: (614)889-0463
E-mail: ostaff@omeda.org
URL: http://www.omeda.org

Annual. **Primary Exhibits:** Construction equipment, agricultural equipment, and outdoor power equipment.

★3043★ SBCCI Research and Education Conference

International Code Council
5203 Leesburg Pike, Ste. 600
Falls Church, VA 22041
Ph: (703)931-4533   Fax: (703)379-1546
URL: http://www.iccsafe.org

Annual. **Primary Exhibits:** Exhibits relating to uniformity in building regulations.

★3044★ Southeast Roofing and Sheet Metal Spectacular Trade Exposition

Florida Roofing, Sheet Metal, and Air Conditioning Contractors Association FRSA
4111, Metric Dr., Ste. 6
Winter Park, FL 32792
Ph: (407)671-3772   Fax: (407)679-0010
E-mail: frsa@floridaroof.com
URL: http://www.floridaroof.com

Annual. **Primary Exhibits:** Roofing and sheet metal supplies, products and services.

★3045★ Sunbelt Builders Show

National Association of Home Builders of the United States
1201 15th St. NW
Washington, DC 20005
Ph: (202)266-8200   Fax: (202)266-8223
Fr: 800-368-5242
E-mail: exposales@nahb.com
URL: http://www.nahb.org

Annual. **Primary Exhibits:** Residential building industry exhibits.

★3046★ World Congress of the World Federation of Building Service Contractors

World Federation of Building Service Contractors
10201 Lee Hwy., Ste. 225
Fairfax, VA 22030
Ph: (703)359-7090   Fax: (703)352-0493
E-mail: cdean@bscai.org
URL: http://www.wfbsc.org

Biennial. **Primary Exhibits:** Floor care and carpet care equipment, building service contracting equipment, supplies, and services.
Dates and Locations: 2008 Dates and location not set.

★3047★ World of Masonry

Ecobuild Federal, LCC
1645 Falmouth Rd., Ste. 1A
Centerville, MA 02632
Ph: (508)790-4751   Fax: (508)790-4750
URL: http://www.ecobuildamerica.com/

Annual. **Primary Exhibits:** Concrete and masonry construction products and equipment.

OTHER SOURCES

★3048★ Administration and Management Occupations

Delphi Productions
3159 6th St.
Boulder, CO 80304
Ph: (303)443-2100   Fax: (303)443-4022
Fr: 888-443-2400
E-mail: support@delphivideo.com
URL: http://www.delphivideo.com

$95.00. 50 minutes. Part of the Careers for the 21st Century Video Library.

★3049★ American Society of Home Inspectors (ASHI)

932 Lee St., Ste. 101
Des Plaines, IL 60016-6546
Ph: (847)759-2820   Fax: (847)759-1620
Fr: 800-743-2744
E-mail: robp@ashi.org
URL: http://www.ashi.org

Description: Professional home inspectors whose goals are to: establish home inspector qualifications; set standards of practice for home inspections; adhere to a code of ethics; keep the concept of "objective third party" intact; inform members of the most advanced methods and techniques, and educate consumers on the value of home inspections. Conducts seminars through local chapters.

★3050★ American Society of Professional Estimators (ASPE)

2525 Perimeter Place Dr., Ste. 103
Nashville, TN 37214
Ph: (615)316-9200   Fax: (615)316-9800
Fr: 888-EST-MATE
E-mail: info@aspenational.com
URL: http://www.aspenational.org

Description: Construction cost estimators. Develops professional and ethical standards in construction estimating. Offers continuing education to established professionals; provides certification for estimators.

★3051★ Associated Builders and Contractors (ABC)

4250 N Fairfax Dr., 9th Fl.
Arlington, VA 22203-1607
Ph: (703)812-2000   Fax: (703)812-8200
E-mail: gotquestions@abc.org
URL: http://www.abc.org

Description: Construction contractors, subcontractors, suppliers, and associates. Aims to foster and perpetuate the principles of rewarding construction workers and management on the basis of merit. Sponsors management education programs and craft training; also sponsors apprenticeship and skill training programs. Disseminates technological and labor relations information.

★3052★ **Associated General Contractors of America (AGC)**
2300 Wilson Blvd., Ste. 400
Arlington, VA 22201
Ph: (703)548-3118   Fax: (703)548-3119
Fr: 800-242-1767
E-mail: info@agc.org
URL: http://www.agc.org

Description: General construction contractors; subcontractors; industry suppliers; service firms. Provides market services through its divisions. Conducts special conferences and seminars designed specifically for construction firms. Compiles statistics on job accidents reported by member firms. Maintains 65 committees, including joint cooperative committees with other associations and liaison committees with federal agencies.

★3053★ **Construction Industry Round Table (CIRT)**
1101 17th St. NW, Ste. 608
Washington, DC 20036-4734
Ph: (202)466-6777   Fax: (202)466-6767
E-mail: cirt@cirt.org
URL: http://www.cirt.org

Description: Represents the interests of CEOs from architectural, engineering and construction firms doing business in the United States. Enhances and develops strong management approaches through networking and peer interaction. Seeks to improve the industry's image and relationships with public and private clients.

★3054★ **Roofing Industry Educational Institute (RIEI)**
10255 W Higgins Rd., Ste. 600
Rosemont, IL 60018-5607
Ph: (847)299-9070   Fax: (847)299-1183
E-mail: nrca@nrca.net
URL: http://www.nrca.net/rp/related/riei

Members: Participants are contractors, architects, specifiers, owners, consultants, and others involved in the roofing industry. **Activities:** Conducts seminars and educational programs covering all aspects of roofing, highlighting design, installation, and maintenance including topics such as thermal insulation, vapors and condensation, and fire and codes. Provides referral service and presents diplomas.

★3055★ **Women in Building Construction**
Her Own Words
PO Box 5264
Madison, WI 53705-0264
Ph: (608)271-7083   Fax: (608)271-0209
E-mail: herownword@aol.com
URL: http://www.herownwords.com/

Video. Jocelyn Riley. $95.00. 15 minutes. Resource guide also available for $45.00.

★3056★ **Women in Highway Construction**
Her Own Words
PO Box 5264
Madison, WI 53705-0264
Ph: (608)271-7083   Fax: (608)271-0209
E-mail: herownword@aol.com
URL: http://www.herownwords.com/

Video. Jocelyn Riley. $95.00. 15 minutes. Resource guide also available for $45.00.

★3057★ **Women in Nontraditional Careers: An Introduction**
Her Own Words
PO Box 5264
Madison, WI 53705
Ph: (608)271-7083   Fax: (608)271-0209
E-mail: herownword@aol.com
URL: http://www.herownwords.com/

Video. Jocelyn Riley. $95.00. 15 minutes. Resource guide also available for $45.00.

Correction Officers and Parole Officers

SOURCES OF HELP-WANTED ADS

★3058★ ACJS Today
Academy of Criminal Justice Sciences
  (ACJS)
PO Box 960
Greenbelt, MD 20768-0960
Ph: (301)446-6300   Fax: (301)446-2819
Fr: 800-757-2257
URL: http://www.acjs.org/
Description: Four issues/year. Contains criminal justice information.

★3059★ American City and County
Primedia Business
6151 Powers Ferry Rd., Ste. 200
Atlanta, GA 30339
Ph: (770)955-2500   Fax: (770)618-0204
URL: http://
www.americancityandcounty.com
Monthly. $67.00/year for individuals. Municipal and county administration magazine.

★3060★ Law and Order
Hendon Publishing
130 Waukegan Rd. N., Ste. 202
Deerfield, IL 60015
Ph: (847)444-3300   Fax: (847)444-3333
Fr: 800-843-9764
URL: http://www.hendonpub.com/publications/lawandorder/
Monthly. $22.00/year for individuals. Law enforcement trade magazine.

★3061★ The Municipality
League of Wisconsin Municipalities
122 W Washington Ave., Ste. 300
Madison, WI 53703-2718
Ph: (608)267-2380   Fax: (608)267-0645
Fr: 800-991-5502
URL: http://www.lwm-info.org/index.asp?Type=B_BASIC&SEC=¢0702EE8F
Monthly. Magazine for officials of Wisconsin's local municipal governments.

★3062★ On the Line
American Correctional Association
206 N. Washington St.
Alexandria, VA 22314
Ph: (703)224-0000   Fax: (703)224-0179
Fr: 800-222-5646
URL: http://www.aca.org/
Description: Five issues/year. Provides updates on the Association's efforts to improve correctional standards and to develop adequate physical facilities. Presents national news of the corrections field. Recurring features include job listings, news of research, notices of publications available, reports of meetings, and a calendar of events.

★3063★ Western City
League of California Cities
1400 K St., Ste. 400
Sacramento, CA 95814
Ph: (916)658-8200   Fax: (916)658-8240
Fr: 800-262-1801
URL: http://www.westerncity.com
Monthly. $39.00/year for individuals; $63.00 for two years; $52.00/year for other countries; $26.50/year for students. Municipal interest magazine.

PLACEMENT AND JOB REFERRAL SERVICES

★3064★ American Society of Criminology (ASC)
1314 Kinnear Rd., Ste. 212
Columbus, OH 43212-1156
Ph: (614)292-9207   Fax: (614)292-6767
E-mail: asc@osu.edu
URL: http://www.asc41.com
Description: Represents professional and academic criminologists, students of criminology in accredited universities, psychiatrists, psychologists, and sociologists. Develops criminology as a science and academic discipline. Aids in the construction of criminological curricula in accredited universities.

Upgrades the practitioner in criminological fields (police, prisons, probation, parole, delinquency workers). Conducts research programs and sponsors three student paper competitions. Provides placement service at annual convention.

★3065★ Nine Lives Associates (NLA)
Executive Protection Institute
PO Box 802
Berryville, VA 22611-0802
Ph: (540)554-2540   Fax: (540)554-2558
E-mail: info@personalprotection.com
URL: http://www.personalprotection.com
Description: Law enforcement, correctional, military, and security professionals who have been granted Personal Protection Specialist Certification through completion of the protective services program offered by the Executive Protection Institute; conducts research; EPI programs emphasize personal survival skills and techniques for the protection of others. Provides professional recognition for qualified individuals engaged in executive protection assignments. Maintains placement service. Operates speakers' bureau; compiles statistics.

EMPLOYER DIRECTORIES AND NETWORKING LISTS

★3066★ Directory of Juvenile and Adult Correctional Departments, Institutions, Agencies, and Probation and Parole Authorities
American Correctional Association
206 N Washington St., Ste. 200
Alexandria, VA 22314
Ph: (703)224-0000   Fax: (703)224-0179
Fr: 800-ACA-JOIN
URL: http://www.aca.org
2006. $95.00 for individuals. Covers more than 4,000 adult and juvenile state, federal, provincial, correctional departments, institutions, agencies, programs, paroling authorities, and military correctional facilities in the United States, its territories and Canada.

Entries include: Agency name, address, phone, fax, e-mail, web address, name of administrative officers (and other personnel for agencies), length of operation, average number and types of inmates, cost of care, security level, number of staff, accreditation status, and other information. Arrangement: Geographical within authority by states, federal military, Canada. Indexes: correctional personnel (U.S. & Canada); institutions (U.S. & Canada).

★3067★ **National Directory of Law Enforcement Administrators, Correctional Institutions & Related Agencies**

National Public Safety Information Bureau
601 Main St., Ste. 201
PO Box 365
Stevens Point, WI 54481
Ph: (715)345-2772   Fax: (715)345-7288
Fr: 800-647-7579
URL: http://www.safetysource.com

Annual; latest edition 43rd, published 2007. $139.00 for individuals. Covers police departments, sheriffs, coroners, criminal prosecutors, child support agencies, state law enforcement and criminal investigation agencies; federal criminal investigation and related agencies; state and federal correctional institutions; campus law enforcement departments; county jails, airport and harbor police, Bureau of Indian Affairs officials; plus new homeland security section. Entries include: Name, address, phone, fax, names and titles of key personnel, number of officers, population served. Arrangement: Separate geographical sections for police chiefs, coroners, sheriffs, prosecutors, prisons and state criminal investigation agencies; also separate sections for federal agencies and miscellaneous law enforcement and related agencies. Indexes: Departments.

HANDBOOKS AND MANUALS

★3068★ **Career Planning in Criminal Justice**

Anderson Publishing Co.
2035 Reading Rd.
Cincinnati, OH 45202-1576
Ph: (513)421-4142   Fax: (513)562-8116
Fr: 800-582-7295

Robert C. DeLucia and Thomas J. Doyle. Third edition, 1998. 225 pages. $21.95. Surveys a wide range of career and employment opportunities in law enforcement, the courts, corrections, forensic science, and private security. Contains career planning and job hunting advice.

★3069★ **The Changing Career of the Correctional Officer**

Butterworth-Heinemann
11830 Westline Industrial Dr.
St. Louis, MO 63146
Ph: (314)453-7010   Fax: (314)453-7095
Fr: 800-545-2522
E-mail: usbkinfo@elsevier.com
URL: http://www.elsevier.com

Don A. Josi and Dale K. Sechrest. 1998. $46.95 (paper). 192 pages. Contains information for students considering the profession as well as career develoment issues for administrators, management personnel, and supervisors.

★3070★ **Opportunities in Law Enforcement and Criminal Justice Careers**

The McGraw-Hill Companies
PO Box 182604
Columbus, OH 43272
Fax: (614)759-3749   Fr: 877-883-5524
E-mail: customer.service@mcgraw-hill.com
URL: http://www.mcgraw-hill.com

James Stinchcomb. Second edition, 2002. $13.95 (paper). 160 pages. Offers information on opportunities at the city, county, state, military, and federal levels. Contains bibliography and illustrations.

★3071★ **Probation Officer, Parole Officer**

Arco Pub.
10475 Crosspoint Blvd.
Indianapolis, IN 46256
Ph: (317)572-3000   Fax: (317)572-4000
Fr: 800-667-1115

Hy Hammer. Fifth edition, 2006. $19.99. 254 pages.

★3072★ **Real People Working in Law**

The McGraw-Hill Companies
PO Box 182604
Columbus, OH 43272
Fax: (614)759-3749   Fr: 877-883-5524
E-mail: customer.service@mcgraw-hill.com
URL: http://www.mcgraw-hill.com

Blythe Camenson, Jan Goldberg. 1997. $12.95 (paper). 160 pages. Interviews and profiles of working professionals capture a range of opportunities in this field.

TRADESHOWS

★3073★ **American Jail Association Training Conference & Jail Expo**

American Jail Association
1135, Professional Ct.
Hagerstown, MD 21740-5853
Ph: (301)790-3930   Fax: (301)790-2941
E-mail: stevei@aja.org
URL: http://www.aja.org

Annual. **Primary Exhibits:** Jail supplies & services for correctional facilities; construction design; training; officer equipment and correctional equipment, supplies, and services. **Dates and Locations:** 2008 May 04-08; Sacramento, CA ; 2009 Apr 26-30; Louisville, KY; 2010 May 23-27; Portland, OR ; 2011 May 15-19; Cincinnati, OH.

OTHER SOURCES

★3074★ **American Correctional Association (ACA)**

206 N Washington St., Ste. 200
Alexandria, VA 22314
Ph: (301)918-1800   Fax: (301)918-0557
Fr: 800-222-5646
E-mail: execoffice@aca.org
URL: http://www.aca.org

Description: Correctional administrators, wardens, superintendents, members of prison and parole boards, probation officers, psychologists, educators, sociologists, and other individuals; institutions and associations involved in the correctional field. Promotes improved correctional standards, including selection of personnel, care, supervision, education, training, employment, treatment, and post-release adjustment of inmates. Studies causes of crime and juvenile delinquency and methods of crime control and prevention through grants and contracts. Compiles statistics. Conducts research programs and training of correctional professionals. Offers accreditation of institutions and certification for correctional executive, manager, supervisor, and officer.

★3075★ **Careers in Criminal Justice**

Cambridge Educational
PO Box 2053
Princeton, NJ 08543-2053
Ph: 800-257-5126   Fax: (609)671-0266
Fr: 800-468-4227
E-mail: custserv@films.com
URL: http://www.cambridgeeducational.com

VHS and DVD. $79.95. 2002. 22 minutes. Program looks at a number of different occupations, ranging from entry-level positions to those requiring a four-year degree. Experts and people on the job share first-hand information about what their work is like.

★3076★ **Human Services Occupations**

Delphi Productions
3159 6th St.
Boulder, CO 80304
Ph: (303)443-2100   Fax: (303)443-4022
Fr: 888-443-2400
E-mail: support@delphivideo.com
URL: http://www.delphivideo.com

$95.00. 50 minutes. Part of the Careers for the 21st Century Video Library.

Cosmetologists and Hairdressers

★3077★ Beauty Launchpad

Creative Age Publications Inc.
7628 Densmore Ave.
Van Nuys, CA 91406-2042
Ph: (818)782-7328   Fax: (818)782-7450
Fr: 800-442-5667
URL: http://www.beautylaunchpad.com/index.php

$24.00/year for U.S., 12 issues; $48.00/year for Canada, 12 issues. Fashion magazine.

★3078★ Beauty Store Business

Creative Age Publications Inc.
7628 Densmore Ave.
Van Nuys, CA 91406-2042
Ph: (818)782-7328   Fax: (818)782-7450
Fr: 800-442-5667
URL: http://www.beautystorebusiness.com/index.htm

Monthly. Business magazine for beauty industry professionals and beauty store owners.

★3079★ Cosmetics & Toiletries

Allured Publishing Corp.
336 Gundersen Dr.
Carol Stream, IL 60188-2403
Ph: (630)653-2155   Fax: (630)653-2192
E-mail: lhince@allured.com
URL: http://www.cosmeticsandtoiletries.com

Monthly. $98.00/year for individuals; $137.00/year for Canada; $189.00/year for other countries; $169.00 for two years; $231.00 for Canada, 2 years; $330.00 for other countries, 2 years. Trade magazine on cosmetic and toiletries manufacturing with an emphasis on product research and development issues.

★3080★ Global Cosmetic Industry

Allured Publishing Corp.
336 Gundersen Dr.
Carol Stream, IL 60188-2403
Ph: (630)653-2155   Fax: (630)653-2192

URL: http://www.globalcosmetic.com

Monthly. Free to qualified subscribers, U.S. and Canada; $98.00/year for other countries; $176.00/year for other countries, 2 years. Trade publication covering the cosmetics industry worldwide.

★3081★ Hair Gallery

Multi-Media International
13915 W 107th St.
Lenexa, KS 66215
Ph: (913)469-6800   Fax: (913)469-6805
URL: http://mmimags.com/HairGallery.html

$9.99 for single issue; $12.99 for single issue, Canada. Magazine featuring gallery of hairstyles.

★3082★ Live Design

Penton Media Inc.
9800 Metcalf Ave.
Overland Park, KS 66212
Ph: (913)341-1300   Fax: (913)967-1898
URL: http://www.etecnyc.net

Monthly. $36.00/year for individuals; $72.00 for two years; $75.00/year for Canada; $150.00 for two years; $102.00/year for other countries; $204.00 for two years. The business of entertainment technology and design.

★3083★ Modern Salon

Vance Publishing Corp.
400 Knightsbridge Pky.
Lincolnshire, IL 60069
Ph: (847)634-2600   Fax: (847)634-4379
URL: http://www.modernsalon.com/

Monthly. $25.00/year for individuals; $34.00/year for Canada; $95.00/year for other countries; $20.00/year for individuals, digital; $37.00 for two years; $54.00 for two years, Canada; $32.00/year for two years, digital; $47.01/year for individuals, 3 years; $69.99/year for Canada, 3 years; $42.00/year for individuals, digital 3 years. Magazine focusing on hairstyling salons for men and women.

★3084★ Nailpro

Creative Age Publications Inc.
7628 Densmore Ave.
Van Nuys, CA 91406-2042
Ph: (818)782-7328   Fax: (818)782-7450
Fr: 800-442-5667
E-mail: nailpro@creativeage.com
URL: http://www.nailpro.com

Monthly. $21.95/year for individuals; $45.00/year for Canada and Mexico; $89.00/year for other countries. Salon owners and nail technicians read Nailpro for continuing education in techniques and services, marketing and management tips, product information and industry news.

★3085★ Renew

Vance Publishing Corp.
400 Knightsbridge Pky.
Lincolnshire, IL 60069
Ph: (847)634-2600   Fax: (847)634-4379
URL: http://www.vancepublishing.com

Bimonthly. Free to qualified subscribers. Magazine for salon, spa, and skin care professionals.

★3086★ Skin Inc.

Allured Publishing Corp.
336 Gundersen Dr.
Carol Stream, IL 60188-2403
Ph: (630)653-2155   Fax: (630)653-2192
E-mail: customerservice@allured.com
URL: http://www.skininc.com/

Monthly. $49.00/year for individuals; $57.00/year for Canada; $98.00/year for other countries. The complete business guide for face and body care.

★3087★ Soap and Cosmetics

Chemical Week Associates
110 Williams St.
New York, NY 10038
Ph: (212)621-4900   Fax: (212)621-4800
URL: http://www.chemweek.com/verticals/sc/

Monthly. Trade publication covering the cosmetics industry.

★3088★ Soap/Cosmetics/Chemical Specialties

Cygnus Business Media Inc.
3 Huntington Quadrangle, Ste. 301 N
Melville, NY 11747
Ph: (631)845-2700   Fax: (631)845-7109
Fr: 800-308-6397

Monthly. Trade magazine for household and personal care products.

★3089★ Spa 20/20

Virgo Publishing Inc.
PO Box 40079
Phoenix, AZ 85067-0079
Ph: (480)990-1101   Fax: (480)990-0819
URL: http://www.spa20-20.com

Bimonthly. $14.00/year for individuals, in U.S.; $26.00/year for Canada; $82.00/year for elsewhere. Magazine covering the spa industry, including skin care, cosmetics, and sunless tanning.

PLACEMENT AND JOB REFERRAL SERVICES

★3090★ World International Nail and Beauty Association (WINBA)

1221 N Lake View Ave.
Anaheim, CA 92807
Ph: (714)779-9892   Fax: (714)779-9971
Fr: 800-541-9838
E-mail: dkellenberger@inmnails.com

Members: Professionals in the nail and skin care industries. **Purpose:** Objectives are to: represent the manicure and skin care industry; promote the effective use and application of manicuring and skin care products and equipment; provide a means for mutual communication and joint study; represent the industry before state boards, the Food and Drug Administration, and other regulatory agencies. **Activities:** Conducts seminars; secures discounts on supplies; offers special conducts public relations program; sponsors research and educational programs; compiles statistics. Maintains speakers' bureau and placement service.

EMPLOYER DIRECTORIES AND NETWORKING LISTS

★3091★ American Salon's Green Book

Advanstar Communications
641 Lexington Ave.
8th Fl.
New York, NY 10022
Ph: (212)951-6600   Fax: (212)951-6793
Fr: 800-225-4569
E-mail: directories@advanstar.com
URL: http://web.advanstar.com/

Annual, November; latest edition 2007.

$225.00 for individuals. Covers about 1,300 manufacturers of supplies and equipment for salons and spas; 130 manufacturers' representatives; 3,200 distributors; employment agencies, show management companies, and related trade organizations. Entries include: For manufacturers and agents–Company name, address, phone, names of principal executives, products available. For distributors–Company name, address, phone, branches, name of owner or president, number of sales representatives, trade association affiliation, Metropolitan Statistical Area (MSA) in which located. For representatives–Company name, address, phone, territory covered. Arrangement: Manufacturers are alphabetical; agents, distributors, representatives are geographical. Indexes: Product, trade name.

★3092★ Careers in Focus: Cosmetology

Facts On File Inc.
132 W 31st St., 17th Fl.
New York, NY 10001
Ph: (212)967-8800   Fax: 800-678-3633
Fr: 800-322-8755
URL: http://www.factsonfile.com

Latest edition 3rd, 2002. $29.95 for individuals; $26.95 for libraries. Covers an overview of cosmetology, followed by a selection of jobs profiled in detail, including the nature of the job, earnings, prospects for employment, what kind of training and skills it requires, and sources for further information.

★3093★ Official Show Directory

Beauty and Barber Supply Institute
1roof Community
15825 N 71St. St., No. 100
Scottsdale, AZ 85254
Ph: (480)281-0424   Fr: 800-468-2274

Semiannual. Covers wholesalers and manufacturers of beauty and barber salon equipment and supplies. Includes exhibit listings, Beauty and Barber Supply Institute membership updates, and trade show agenda.

HANDBOOKS AND MANUALS

★3094★ Career After Cosmetology School: Step-by-Step Guide to a Lucrative Career and Salon Ownership

Step-by-Step Publications
1645 Westmont Ave.
Campbell, CA 95008
Ph: (408)376-0276   Fax: (408)376-0396
Fr: 800-305-2205

Jessica Brooks. 1998. $29.95. 320 pages.

★3095★ Careers for Film Buffs and Other Hollywood Types

The McGraw-Hill Companies
PO Box 182604
Columbus, OH 43272
Fax: (614)759-3749   Fr: 877-883-5524
E-mail: customer.service@mcgraw-hill.com
URL: http://www.mcgraw-hill.com

Jaq Greenspon. Second edition, 2003. $13.95; $9.95 (paper). 208 pages. Describes job descriptions in production, camera, sound, special effects, grips, electrical, makeup, costumes, etc.

★3096★ Cosmetology Career Starter

LearningExpress, LLC
55 Broadway, 8th Fl.
New York, NY 10006
Ph: (212)995-2566   Fax: (212)995-5512
Fr: 800-295-9556
E-mail: customerservice@learningexpressllc.com
URL: http://www.learningexpressllc.com

Lorraine Korman. Second edition, 2002. $15.95. 224 pages.

★3097★ Hair, Makeup & Styling Career Guide

Set the Pace Publishing Group
1870 N. Vermont Ave., Ste. 529
Los Angeles, CA 90027
Ph: (213)913-0773   Fax: (213)913-0900

Crystal A. Wright. 2002. $39.95 (paper). 400 pages.

★3098★ How to Get a Job with a Cruise Line

Ticket to Adventure, Inc.
PO Box 41005
St. Petersburg, FL 33743-1005
Ph: (727)822-5029   Fax: (727)821-3409
Fr: 800-929-7447

Mary Fallon Miller. Fifth edition, 2001. $16.95 (paper). 352 pages. Explores jobs with cruise ships, describing duties, responsibilities, benefits, and training. Lists cruise ship lines and schools offering cruise line training. Offers job hunting advice.

★3099★ Opportunities in Beauty Culture Careers

The McGraw-Hill Companies
PO Box 182604
Columbus, OH 43272
Fax: (614)759-3749   Fr: 877-883-5524
E-mail: customer.service@mcgraw-hill.com
URL: http://www.mcgraw-hill.com

Susan Wood Gearhart. 1998. $14.95; $11.95 (paper). 160 pages. Outlines how to enter the field and build a career. Independent salon ownership in also covered. Contains bibliography and illustrations.

★3100★ *Planning Your Cosmetology Career*

Prentice Hall PTR
1 Lake St.
Upper Saddle River, NJ 07458
Ph: (201)236-7000   Fax: 800-445-6991
Fr: 800-428-5331
URL: http://www.phptr.com/index.asp?rl=1

Mary Murphy-Martin. 1993. $26.60 (paper). 108 pages.

★3101★ *The Transition, How to Become a Salon Professional*

Milady
5 Maxwell Dr.
Clifton Park, NY 12065
Fax: (859)647-5963   Fr: 800-998-7498
E-mail: milady@delmar.com
URL: http://www.milady.com

Louise Cotter and Frances L. DuBose. First edition 1996. $40.95. Part of the Cosmetology Series. 352 pages.

TRADESHOWS

★3102★ **American Association of Cosmetology Schools Annual Conference-AACS Annual Convention & Expo**

American Association of Cosmetology Schools
15825 N. 71st St., Ste. 100
Scottsdale, AZ 85254-1521
Ph: (480)281-0431   Fax: (480)905-0993
Fr: 800-831-1086
E-mail: dilsah@beautyschools.org
URL: http://www.beautyschools.org

Annual. **Primary Exhibits:** Beauty supplies and products, and cosmetology services.

★3103★ **American Electrology Association Annual Convention**

American Electrology Association
PO Box 687
Bodega Bay, CA 94923
Ph: (707)875-9135   Fax: (203)372-7134
E-mail: infoaea@electrology.com
URL: http://www.electrology.com

Annual. **Primary Exhibits:** Electrology equipment, supplies, and services.

★3104★ **Beauty Fusion**

TTCB Events Management Inc.
20225 N, 29th St.
Phoenix, AZ 85050
Ph: (602)569-9039   Fr: 888-561-8822
URL: http://www.ttcbevents.com

Annual. **Primary Exhibits:** Equipment, supplies, and services for the beauty industry.

★3105★ **Day Spa Expo**

Day Spa Association
310 - 17th St.
Union City, NJ 07087
Ph: (201)865-2065   Fax: (201)865-3961
E-mail: info@dayspaassociation.com
URL: http://www.dayspaassociation.com/

Annual. **Primary Exhibits:** Exhibits relating to skin care, massage, spas, and alternative and holistic health care. **Dates and Locations:** 2008 Feb 05-07; Las Vegas, NV; Sands Expo & Convention Center.

★3106★ **IBS - International Beauty Show, New York**

Advanstar Communications Inc.
One Park Ave.
New York, NY 10016
Ph: (212)951-6600   Fax: (212)951-6793
E-mail: info@advantstar.com
URL: http://www.advanstar.com

Annual. **Primary Exhibits:** Beauty and health related equipment, supplies, and services.

★3107★ **Midwest Beauty Show**

Chicago Cosmetologists Association
401 N. Michigan Ave., Ste. 2200
Chicago, IL 60611
Ph: (312)321-6809   Fax: (312)245-1080
Fr: 800-648-2505
E-mail: info@isnow.com
URL: http://www.isnow.com

Annual. **Primary Exhibits:** Goods and services for the beauty trade.

★3108★ **National Beauty Show - HAIRWORLD**

National Cosmetology Association
401 N Michigan Ave., 22nd Fl.
Chicago, IL 60611-4255
Ph: (312)527-6765   Fax: (312)464-6118
Fr: 800-527-1683
E-mail: nca1@ncacares.org
URL: http://
www.behindthechairexchange.com/nca

Annual. **Primary Exhibits:** Hair products, cosmetics, and jewelry.

★3109★ **Premiere Orlando**

Premiere Shows, Inc.
1607 Park Lake St.
Orlando, FL 32803-4154
Ph: (407)228-0208   Fax: (407)228-0260
E-mail: sales@premiereshows.com
URL: http://www.premiereshows.com

Annual. **Primary Exhibits:** Products and services for hair, nail, and skin care professionals and the beauty industry.

OTHER SOURCES

★3110★ **American Association of Cosmetology Schools/Cosmetology Educators of America (AACS/CEA)**

15825 N 71st St., Ste. 100
Scottsdale, AZ 85254
Ph: (480)281-0431   Fax: (480)905-0993
Fr: 800-831-1086
E-mail: jim@beautyschools.org
URL: http://www.beautyschools.org

Description: Owners and teachers in cosmetology schools.

★3111★ **Intercoiffure America**

154 Rte. 206
Chester, NJ 07930
Ph: (908)879-6211   Fax: (908)879-3286
Fr: 800-442-3007
E-mail: ebersohlady@aol.com
URL: http://www.intercoiffure.us

Members: Owners of beauty salons in the United States and Canada who meet the ethical standards set down by Intercoiffure. **Purpose:** Seeks to "make the women of America the best in hair fashion".

★3112★ **International Chain Salon Association (ICSA)**

207 E Ohio St., No. 361
Chicago, IL 60611
Fax: (815)609-5139   Fr: (866)444-ICSA
E-mail: mmelaniphy@icsa.cc
URL: http://www.icsa.cc

Members: Beauty salon chains. **Activities:** Collects and processes data on industry standards; proactively works to affect the outcome of pending legislation and regulations governing the cosmetology industry; provides continuing education programs on management issues to members; works for free exchange of corporate information, solutions to common problems, advertising ideas, and incentive programs amongst members; takes part in and supports other industry associations.

★3113★ **National Beauty Culturists' League (NBCL)**

25 Logan Cir. NW
Washington, DC 20005-3725
Ph: (202)332-2695   Fax: (202)332-0940
E-mail: nbcl@bellsouth.net
URL: http://www.nbcl.org

Members: Beauticians, cosmetologists, and beauty products manufacturers. **Purpose:** Encourages standardized, scientific, and approved methods of hair, scalp, and skin treatments. **Activities:** Offers scholarships and plans to establish a research center. Sponsors: National Institute of Cosmetology, a training course in operating and designing and business techniques; National Beauty Week. Maintains hall of fame; conducts research programs; compiles statistics.

★3114★ National Cosmetology Association (NCA)

401 N Michigan Ave., 22nd Fl.
Chicago, IL 60611
Ph: (312)527-6765   Fax: (312)464-6118
E-mail: nca1@ncacares.org
URL: http://www.ncacares.org

Members: Owners of cosmetology salons; cosmetologists. **Activities:** Sponsors: National Cosmetology Month; National Beauty Show. Provides special sections for estheticians, school owners, salon owners, and nail technicians. Maintains hall of fame. Conducts educational and charitable programs.

★3115★ Personal & Building Service Occupations

Delphi Productions
3159 6th St.
Boulder, CO 80304
Ph: (303)443-2100   Fax: (303)443-4022
Fr: 888-443-2400
E-mail: support@delphivideo.com
URL: http://www.delphivideo.com

$95.00. 48 minutes. Part of the Careers for the 21st Century Video Library.

★3116★ Professional Beauty Association (PBA)

15825 N 71st St., Ste. 100
Scottsdale, AZ 85254
Ph: (480)281-0424   Fax: (480)905-0708
Fr: 800-468-2274
E-mail: info@probeauty.org
URL: http://www.probeauty.org

Members: Manufacturers and manufacturers' representatives of beauty and barber products, cosmetics, equipment, and supplies used in or resold by beauty salons or barbershops. **Purpose:** Promotes the beauty industry; works to ensure product safety; disseminates information. **Activities:** Holds educational seminars; organizes charity events.

Cost Estimators

SOURCES OF HELP-WANTED ADS

★3117★ Builder

Hanley-Wood L.L.C.
1 Thomas Cir., NW, Ste. 600
Washington, DC 20005
Ph: (202)452-0800   Fax: (202)785-1974
URL: http://www.hanleywood.com/default.aspx?page=b2bbd

$29.95/year for individuals, 13 issues; $54.95/year for Canada, 26 issues; $192.00/year for out of country, 13 issues. Magazine covering housing and construction industry.

★3118★ Constructor

Associated General Contractors of America
2300 Wilson Blvd., Ste. 400
Arlington, VA 22201
Ph: (703)548-3118   Fax: (703)548-3119
URL: http://www.agc.org

Monthly. Management magazine for the Construction Industry.

★3119★ Cost Engineering

AACE International
209 Prairie Ave., Ste. 100
Morgantown, WV 26501
Ph: (304)296-8444   Fax: (304)291-5728
Fr: 800-858-2678
URL: http://www.aacei.org

Monthly. $65.00/year for individuals; $82.00/year for other countries; $8.00 for single issue, for members; $12.00/year for non-members. Magazine.

★3120★ Design Cost Data

DC & D Technologies Inc.
8602 North 40th St.
Tampa, FL 33604-2434
Ph: (813)989-9300   Fax: (813)980-3982
Fr: 800-533-5680
E-mail: webmaster@dcd.com
URL: http://www.dcd.com

Bimonthly. $89.40/year for individuals;

$149.28 for two years. Publication providing real cost data case studies of various types completed around the country for design and building professionals.

★3121★ ENR: Engineering News-Record

McGraw-Hill Inc.
1221 Ave. of the Americas
New York, NY 10020-1095
Ph: (212)512-2000   Fax: (212)512-3840
Fr: 877-833-5524
E-mail: enr_web_editors@mcgraw-hill.com
URL: http://www.mymags.com/moreinfo.php?itemID=20012

Weekly. $94.00/year for individuals, print. Magazine focusing on engineering and construction.

★3122★ Professional Builder

Reed Business Information
360 Park Ave. S
New York, NY 10010
Ph: (646)746-6400   Fax: (646)746-7431
E-mail: ncrum@reedbusiness.com
URL: http://www.housingzone.com/toc-archive-pbx

Monthly. Free. The integrated engineering magazine of the building construction industry.

PLACEMENT AND JOB REFERRAL SERVICES

★3123★ AACE International

209 Prairie Ave., Ste. 100
Morgantown, WV 26501
Ph: (304)296-8444   Fax: (304)291-5728
Fr: 800-858-2678
E-mail: info@aacei.org
URL: http://www.aacei.org

Description: Professional society of cost managers, cost engineers, estimators, schedulers and planners, project managers, educators, representatives of all branches of

engineering, engineering students, and others. Conducts technical and educational programs. Offers placement service. Compiles statistics. Operates certification program for Certified Cost Engineers (CCE); Certified Cost Consultants (CCC); Interim Cost Consultants (ICC); Planning & Scheduling Professionals (PSP); and Earned Value Professionals (EVP).

★3124★ International Society of Parametric Analysts (ISPA)

527 Maple Ave. E, Ste. 301
Vienna, VA 22180
Ph: (703)938-5090   Fax: (703)938-5091
E-mail: ispa@sceaonline.net
URL: http://www.ispa-cost.org

Members: Engineers, designers, statisticians, estimators, and managers in industry, the military, and government who develop and use computerized, parametric cost-estimating models. **Activities:** Conducts educational activities to promote usage of parametric modeling techniques for purposes of cost estimating, risk analysis, and technology forecasting. Sponsors placement service.

★3125★ National Association of Home Builders (NAHB)

1201 15th St. NW
Washington, DC 20005
Ph: (202)266-8200   Fax: (202)266-8400
Fr: 800-368-5242
E-mail: info@nahb.com
URL: http://www.nahb.org

Description: Single and multifamily home builders, commercial builders, and others associated with the building industry. Lobbies on behalf of the housing industry and conducts public affairs activities to increase public understanding of housing and the economy. Collects and disseminates data on current developments in home building and home builders' plans through its Economics Department and nationwide Metropolitan Housing Forecast. Maintains NAHB Research Center, which functions as the research arm of the home building industry. Sponsors seminars and workshops on construction, mortgage credit, labor relations, cost reduction, land use, remodeling, and business management. Compiles statistics; offers charitable program, spokesman training, and placement service; maintains speakers' bureau, and Hall of Fame. Subsidiaries include the National Council of the Housing Industry. Maintains over 50 committees in many areas of construction; operates National Commercial Builders Council, National Council of the Multifamily Housing Industry, National Remodelers Council, and National Sales and Marketing Council.

★3126★ **Professional Women in Construction (PWC)**
315 E 56th St.
New York, NY 10022-3730
Ph: (212)486-7745   Fax: (212)486-0228
E-mail: pwcusa1@aol.com
URL: http://www.pwcusa.org

Description: Management-level women and men in construction and allied industries; owners, suppliers, architects, engineers, field personnel, office personnel, and bonding/surety personnel. Provides a forum for exchange of ideas and promotion of political and legislative action, education, and job opportunities for women in construction and related fields; forms liaisons with other trade and professional groups; develops research programs. Strives to reform abuses and to assure justice and equity within the construction industry. Sponsors mini-workshops. Maintains Action Line, which provides members with current information on pertinent legislation and on the association's activities and job referrals.

EMPLOYER DIRECTORIES AND NETWORKING LISTS

★3127★ *ABC Today-Associated Builders and Contractors National Membership Directory Issue*
Associated Builders & Contractors Inc.
4250 N Fairfax Dr., 9th Fl.
Arlington, VA 22203-1607
Ph: (703)812-2000   Fax: (703)812-8203
URL: http://www.abc.org/wmspage.cfm?parm1=2033

Annual, December. $150.00. Publication includes: List of approximately 19,000 member construction contractors and suppliers. Entries include: Company name, address, phone, name of principal executive, code to volume of business, business specialty. Arrangement: Classified by chapter, then by work specialty.

★3128★ *Constructor-AGC Directory of Membership and Services Issue*
AGC Information Inc.
2300 Wilson Blvd., Ste. 400
Arlington, VA 22201
Ph: (703)548-3118   Fax: (703)548-3119
Fr: 800-282-1423
URL: http://www.agc.org

Annual, August; latest edition 2004 edition. Publication includes: List of over 8,500 member firms and 24,000 national associate member firms engaged in building, highway, heavy, industrial, municipal utilities, and railroad construction (SIC 1541, 1542, 1611, 1622, 1623, 1629); listing of state and local chapter officers. Entries include: For firms–Company name, address, phone, fax, names of principal executives, and code indicating type of construction undertaken. For officers–Name, title, address. Arrangement: Geographical, alphabetical. Indexes: Company name.

★3129★ *ENR-Top 400 Construction Contractors Issue*
McGraw-Hill Inc.
1221 Ave. of the Americas
New York, NY 10020-1095
Ph: (212)512-2000   Fax: (212)512-3840
Fr: 877-833-5524
URL: http://construction.ecnext.com/coms2/summary_0249-137077_ITM

Annual; 22nd, May 2006. $35.00 for individuals. Publication includes: List of 400 United States contractors receiving largest dollar volumes of contracts in preceding calendar year. Separate lists of 50 largest design/construction management firms; 50 largest program and construction managers; 25 building contractors; 25 heavy contractors. Entries include: Company name, headquarters location, total value of contracts received in preceding year, value of foreign contracts, countries in which operated, construction specialities. Arrangement: By total value of contracts received.

★3130★ *ENR-Top 500 Design Firms Issue*
McGraw-Hill Inc.
1221 Ave. of the Americas
New York, NY 10020-1095
Ph: (212)512-2000   Fax: (212)512-3840
Fr: 877-833-5524
URL: http://enr.construction.com/people/sourcebooks/top500Design/

Annual, latest edition 2007. $50.00 for individuals. Publication includes: List of 500 leading architectural, engineering, and specialty design firms selected on basis of annual billings. Entries include: Company name, headquarters location, type of firm, current and prior year rank in billings, types of services, countries in which operated in preceding year. Arrangement: Ranked by billings.

HANDBOOKS AND MANUALS

★3131★ *From Product Description to Cost: A Practical Approach for Cost Estimators*
Springer Publishing Co.
11 West 42nd St., 15th Fl.
New York, NY 10036
Ph: (212)460-1500   Fax: (212)473-6272
Fr: 877-687-7476
E-mail: contactus@springerpub.com
URL: http://www.springerpub.com/

Pierre Foussier. 2006. $199.00. Profiles cost estimating, covering data preparation, general cost estimating, the use of cost models, and risk analysis used in cost estimations.

EMPLOYMENT AGENCIES AND SEARCH FIRMS

★3132★ **Real Estate Executive Search, Inc.**
306 SE 4th St.
Dania Beach, FL 33004
Ph: (954)927-6000   Fax: (954)927-6003
E-mail: reesearch954@aol.com
URL: http://reesearchinc.com

Executive search firm for the real estate and finance fields.

★3133★ **Specialized Search Associates**
7780 Dundee Ln.
Delray Beach, FL 33446
Ph: (561)499-3711   Fax: (561)499-3770
Fr: 888-405-2650

Executive search firm that specializes in construction, engineering, and sales.

OTHER SOURCES

★3134★ **American Society of Professional Estimators (ASPE)**
2525 Perimeter Place Dr., Ste. 103
Nashville, TN 37214
Ph: (615)316-9200   Fax: (615)316-9800
Fr: 888-EST-MATE
E-mail: info@aspenational.com
URL: http://www.aspenational.org

Description: Construction cost estimators. Develops professional and ethical standards in construction estimating. Offers continuing education to established professionals; provides certification for estimators.

★3135★ Associated Builders and Contractors (ABC)

4250 N Fairfax Dr., 9th Fl.
Arlington, VA 22203-1607
Ph: (703)812-2000   Fax: (703)812-8200
E-mail: gotquestions@abc.org
URL: http://www.abc.org

Description: Construction contractors, subcontractors, suppliers, and associates. Aims to foster and perpetuate the principles of rewarding construction workers and management on the basis of merit. Sponsors management education programs and craft training; also sponsors apprenticeship and skill training programs. Disseminates technological and labor relations information.

★3136★ Associated General Contractors of America (AGC)

2300 Wilson Blvd., Ste. 400
Arlington, VA 22201
Ph: (703)548-3118   Fax: (703)548-3119
Fr: 800-242-1767
E-mail: info@agc.org
URL: http://www.agc.org

Description: General construction contractors; subcontractors; industry suppliers; service firms. Provides market services through its divisions. Conducts special conferences and seminars designed specifically for construction firms. Compiles statistics on job accidents reported by member firms. Maintains 65 committees, including joint cooperative committees with other associations and liaison committees with federal agencies.

★3137★ Financial Occupations

Delphi Productions
3159 6th St.
Boulder, CO 80304
Ph: (303)443-2100   Fax: (303)443-4022
Fr: 888-443-2400
E-mail: support@delphivideo.com
URL: http://www.delphivideo.com

$95.00. 50 minutes. Part of the Careers for the 21st Century Video Library.

★3138★ National Association of Women in Construction (NAWIC)

327 S Adams St.
Fort Worth, TX 76104
Ph: (817)877-5551   Fax: (817)877-0324
Fr: 800-552-3506
E-mail: nawic@nawic.org
URL: http://www.nawic.org

Description: Seeks to enhance the success of women in the construction industry.

★3139★ National Center for Construction Education and Research (NCCER)

3600 NW 43rd St., Bldg. G
Gainesville, FL 32606
Ph: (352)334-0911   Fax: (352)334-0932
Fr: 888-622-3720
URL: http://www.nccer.org

Description: Education foundation committed to the development and publication of Contren(TM) Learning Series, the source of craft training, management education and safety resources for the construction industry.

★3140★ Society of Cost Estimating and Analysis (SCEA)

527 Maple Ave. E, Ste. 301
Vienna, VA 22180
Ph: (703)938-5090   Fax: (703)938-5091
E-mail: scea@sceaonline.net
URL: http://www.sceaonline.net

Description: Works to improve cost estimating and analysis in government and industry and to enhance the professional competence and achievements of its members. Administers a professional certification program leading to the designation of Certified Cost Estimator/Analyst; offers extensive literature in the field through its Professional Development Program. Goals of the Society include enhancing the profession of cost estimating and analysis, fostering the professional growth of its members, enhancing the understanding and application of cost estimating, analysis and related disciplines throughout government and industry and providing forums and media through which current issues of interest to the profession can be addressed and advances in the state-of-the-art can be shared.

Counselors

search studies on alcoholism and alcohol-induced organ damage.

SOURCES OF HELP-WANTED ADS

★3141★ AAEE Connections
American Association for Employment in Education
3040 Riverside Dr., Ste. 125
Columbus, OH 43221
Ph: (614)485-1111 Fax: (614)485-9609
E-mail: office@aaee.org
URL: http://www.aaee.org/

Description: Quarterly. Publishes news of the Association, whose aim is "to enhance and promote the concept of career planning and placement as an integral part of the educational process and to undertake activities designed to help schools, colleges, and universities meet their educational staffing needs." Also concerned with teacher education and the supply of/demand for teachers. Recurring features include news of members, state and regional news, and announcements of upcoming conferences and meetings.

★3142★ Addiction Professional
Manisses Communications Group Inc.
208 Governor St.
Providence, RI 02906
Ph: (401)831-6020 Fax: (401)861-6370
Fr: 800-333-7771
URL: http://www.manisses.com/AP/AP.htm

Monthly. $67.00/year for individuals. Magazine that publishes innovations and trends in the clinical care of persons with substance use and dependence disorders.

★3143★ Alcoholism
Wiley-Blackwell
350 Main St. Commerce Pl.
Malden, MA 02148
Ph: (781)388-8200 Fax: (781)388-8210
Fr: 800-759-6120
E-mail: mnewcomb-acer@earthlink.net
URL: http://www.blackwellpublishing.com/journal.asp?ref=0145-6008

Monthly. Publishing original clinical and re-

★3144★ American Annals of the Deaf
Conference of Educational Administrators Serving the Deaf
Gallaudet University Press
Denison House
Washington, DC 20002
Ph: (202)651-5488 Fax: (202)651-5489
URL: http://gupress.gallaudet.edu/annals/

Quarterly. $55.00/year for individuals; $35.00 for single issue, foreign except Canada; $95.00/year for institutions; $50.00/year for members. Journal focusing on education of the deaf.

★3145★ Career Planning & Adult Development Network Newsletter
Career Planning & Adult Development Network
543 Vista Mar Ave.
Pacifica, CA 94044
Ph: (650)359-6911 Fax: (650)359-3089
E-mail: admin@careernetwork.org
URL: http://www.careernetwork.org

Description: BIM. Contains features and news items on career development and human resources: theory, methodology, research, practices, and techniques. Deals with manpower, organizational planning, counseling, training, equal opportunity, career transition, marketing skills, and adult learning. Recurring features include notices of resources, materials, publications of interest, conferences, workshops, seminars, employment opportunities, book reviews, network news, and a column on publishers of career development books.

★3146★ The Chronicle of Higher Education
The Chronicle of Higher Education
1255 23rd St. NW 7th Fl.
Washington, DC 20037-1125
Ph: (202)466-1050 Fax: (202)452-1033
Fr: 800-728-2803
URL: http://chronicle.com

Weekly. $82.50/year for individuals, 49 is-

sues; $45.00/year for individuals, 24 issues; $41.25/year for students, 49 issues; $22.50/year for students, 24 issues. Higher education magazine (tabloid).

★3147★ Counseling Today
American Counseling Association
5999 Stevenson Ave.
Alexandria, VA 22304
Ph: (703)823-6862 Fax: (703)823-0252
Fr: 800-347-6647
E-mail: ct@counseling.org
URL: http://www.counseling.org/ctonline

Description: Monthly. Covers news and issues relevant to the counseling profession.

★3148★ Counselor Education and Supervision
American Counseling Association
5999 Stevenson Ave.
Alexandria, VA 22304
Ph: (703)823-6862 Fax: 800-473-2329
Fr: 800-347-6647
URL: http://www.counseling.org/

Quarterly. $50.00/year for individuals, nonmember; $80.00/year for institutions, nonmember. Journal covering research in counselor teaching, training, and trends.

★3149★ Journal of Career Development
Sage Publications Inc.
2455 Teller Rd.
Thousand Oaks, CA 91320
Ph: (805)499-0721 Fax: (805)499-8096
URL: http://www.sagepub.com/journalsProdDesc.nav?prodId=Journal20

Quarterly. $94.00/year for individuals, print and online; $490.00/year for institutions, print and e-access; $441.00/year for institutions, e-access; $480.00/year for institutions, print only; $132.00 for institutions, single print; $31.00 for individuals, single print. Journal for professionals in counseling, psychology, education, student personnel, human resources, and business management.

★3150★ Journal of Career Planning & Employment

National Association of Colleges and
Employers
62 Highland Ave.
Bethlehem, PA 18017-9085
Ph: (610)868-1421   Fax: (610)868-0208
Fr: 800-544-5272
URL: http://www.naceweb.org/info_public/
journal_archives.htm

Quarterly. $70.00/year for individuals, per
year; $20.00/year for single issue; $25.00/
year for other countries, airmail postage;
$12.50/year for individuals, additional cop-
ies. Journal on career planning, and recruitment of the college educated work force.

★3151★ Journal of Counseling Psychology

American Psychological Association
750 1st St. NE
Washington, DC 20002-4242
Ph: (202)336-5540   Fax: (202)336-5549
Fr: 800-374-2721
E-mail: journals@apa.org
URL: http://www.apa.org/journals/cou.html

Quarterly. $50.00/year for members, domes-
tic; $66.00/year for members, foreign, sur-
face freight; $78.00/year for members, for-
eign, air mail; $29.00/year for students,
domestic; $45.00/year for students, foreign,
surface freight; $57.00/year for students,
foreign, air mail; $98.00/year for nonmem-
bers, domestic; $119.00/year for nonmem-
bers, foreign, surface freight; $129.00/year
for nonmembers, foreign, air mail; $267.00/
year for institutions, domestic. Journal presenting empirical studies about counseling
processes and interventions, theoretical articles about counseling, and studies dealing
with evaluation of counseling applications
and programs.

★3152★ Journal of Family Issues

Sage Publications Inc.
2455 Teller Rd.
Thousand Oaks, CA 91320
Ph: (805)499-0721   Fax: (805)499-8096
E-mail: advertising@sagepub.com
URL: http://www.sagepub.com/jour-
nal.aspx?pid=163

Monthly. $146.00/year for individuals, print
only; $1,077.00/year for institutions, com-
bined (print & e-access); $1,131.00/year for
institutions, backfile lease, combined plus
backfile, print; $969.00/year for institutions,
e-access; $1,023.00/year for institutions, all
online; $1,565.00/year for institutions, back-
file purchase, e-access; $1,055.00/year for
institutions, print only; $146.00/year for insti-
tutions, single print issue; $24.00/year for
individuals, single print issue. Family studies
journal.

★3153★ Journal of Family Psychology

American Psychological Association
750 1st St. NE
Washington, DC 20002-4242
Ph: (202)336-5540   Fax: (202)336-5549
Fr: 800-374-2721

E-mail: journals@apa.org
URL: http://www.apa.org/journals/fam.html

Quarterly. $55.00/year for members, domes-
tic; $71.00/year for members, foreign surface
freight; $83.00/year for members, foreign air
freight; $36.00/year for students, domestic;
$52.00/year for students, foreign, surface
freight; $64.00/year for students, foreign, air
freight; $120.00/year for nonmembers, do-
mestic; $141.00/year for nonmembers, for-
eign, surface freight; $151.00/year for non-
members, foreign, air freight; $298.00/year
for institutions, domestic. Journal reporting
on theory, research, and clinical practice in
family psychology; including articles on family and marital theory and concepts, research
and evaluation, therapeutic frameworks and
methods, and policies and legal matters
concerning family and marriage.

★3154★ Journal of Family Psychotherapy

The Haworth Press Inc.
10 Alice St.
Binghamton, NY 13904
Ph: (607)722-5857   Fr: 800-429-6784
URL: http://www.haworthpress.com/store/
product.asp?sid=3CXTKNPDX

Quarterly. Journal includes case studies,
treatment reports, and strategies in clinical
practice for psychotherapists.

★3155★ Monitor on Psychology

American Psychological Association
750 1st St. NE
Washington, DC 20002-4242
Ph: (202)336-5540   Fax: (202)336-5549
Fr: 800-374-2721
E-mail: journals@apa.org
URL: http://www.apa.org/monitor/

Monthly. $46.00/year for nonmembers;
$86.00/year for individuals, foreign, surface
freight; $113.00/year for individuals, foreign,
air freight; $87.00/year for institutions, non-
member, foreign, surface freight; $168.00/
year for institutions, foreign, air freight;
$195.00/year for institutions, air freight;
$3.00/year for single issue. Magazine of the
APA. Reports on the science, profession,
and social responsibility of psychology, including latest legislative developments affecting mental health, education, and research support.

★3156★ National Association of Advisors for the Health Professions-Advisor

National Association of Advisors for the
Health Professions Inc.
PO Box 1518
Champaign, IL 61824-1518
Ph: (217)355-0063   Fax: (217)355-1287
E-mail: naahpja@aol.com
URL: http://www.naahp.org/

Description: Quarterly. Intended for college
and university faculty who advise undergraduate students on health careers. Focuses on
manpower statistics, financial aid, admission
procedures, curriculum, advising, recruitment, counseling practice, and ethics. Cov-

ers Association and legislative news and
announcements from affiliated organizations. Recurring features include interviews,
statistics, book reviews, news of research,
editorials, opinion, and items on awards,
meetings, and membership.

★3157★ NCC

National Board for Certified Counselors
3 Terrace Way, Ste. D
PO Box 77699
Greensboro, NC 27417-7699
Ph: (336)547-0607   Fax: (336)547-0017
Fr: 800-398-5389
URL: http://www.nbcc.org

Description: Three issues/year. Includes
updates on counselor licensure and continuing education information.

★3158★ The New Social Worker

White Hat Communications
PO Box 5390
Harrisburg, PA 17110-0390
Ph: (717)238-3787   Fax: (717)238-2090
URL: http://www.socialworker.com

Quarterly. $15.00/year for individuals. Publi-
cation offering career guidance for social
work students.

★3159★ The NonProfit Times

NPT Publishing Group Inc.
120 Littleton Rd., Ste. 120
Parsippany, NJ 07054-1803
Ph: (973)394-1800   Fax: (973)394-2888
E-mail: ednchief@nptimes.com
URL: http://www.nptimes.com/

Biweekly. $69.00/year for individuals, sub-
scribe at the one year rate; $49.00/year for
individuals, digital only; $100.00/year for
individuals, print & digital; $122.00 for two
years, (48 issues); $101.00/year for Canada
and Mexico; $137.00/year for other coun-
tries, international. Trade journal serving
nonprofit organizations.

★3160★ Spectrum

Association for Counselor Education and
Supervision (ACES)
1678 Asylum Ave
West Hartford, CT 06117
Ph: (860)231-6778   Fax: (860)231-5774
Fr: 800-347-6647
E-mail: jdurham@sjc.edu
URL: http://www.acesonline.net/

Description: Quarterly. Focuses on "the
need for quality education and supervision of
counselors in all work settings," the accreditation process, and professional development activities for counselors. Recurring
features include news of the activities, programs, and members of ACES and related
organizations.

★3161★ Washington Counseletter

Chronicle Guidance Publications Inc.
66 Aurora St.
Moravia, NY 13118-3569
Ph: (315)497-0330   Fax: (315)497-0359
Fr: 800-899-0454
URL: http://www.chronicleguidance.com/

Description: monthly, October-May. Provides information on new developments in education and the behavioral sciences for guidance counselors. Emphasizes government materials, actions, and issues affecting education. Recurring features include items concerning scholarships, financial aid, and educational and employment opportunities.

PLACEMENT AND JOB REFERRAL SERVICES

★3162★ Alliance for Children and Families (ACF)

11700 W Lake Park Dr.
Milwaukee, WI 53224-3099
Ph: (414)359-1040   Fax: (414)359-1074
E-mail: info@alliance1.org
URL: http://www.alliance1.org

Description: Membership organization of local agencies in more than 1,000 communities providing family counseling, family life education and family advocacy services, and other programs to help families with parent-child, marital, mental health, and other problems of family living. Assists member agencies in developing and providing effective family services. Works with the media, government, and corporations to promote strong family life. Compiles statistics; conducts research. Maintains extensive files of unpublished materials from member agencies. Offers career placement services.

★3163★ American College Personnel Association (ACPA)

1 Dupont Cir. NW, Ste. 300
Washington, DC 20036-1188
Ph: (202)835-2272   Fax: (202)296-3286
E-mail: info@acpa.nche.edu
URL: http://www.acpa.nche.edu

Description: Represents individuals employed in higher education and involved in student personnel work, including administration, counseling, research, and teaching. Fosters student development in higher education in areas of service, advocacy, and standards by offering professional programs for educators committed to the overall development of post-secondary students. Sponsors professional and educational activities in cooperation with other organizations. Offers placement services.

★3164★ Association for Multicultural Counseling and Development (AMCD)

1285 Cheyenne Blvd.
Madison, TN 37115
Ph: (615)876-5117

E-mail: empower@aol.com
URL: http://www.bgsu.edu/colleges/edhd/programs/AMCD/HomePage.html

Description: Represents professionals involved in counseling careers in educational settings, social services, and community agencies; interested individuals and students. Seeks to develop programs aimed at improving ethnic and racial empathy and understanding; foster personal growth and improve educational opportunities for all minorities in the U.S.; defend human and civil rights; provide in-service and pre-service training for members and others in the profession. Works to enhance members' ability to serve as behavioral change agents. Offers placement service.

★3165★ Association for Specialists in Group Work (ASGW)

University of Buffalo, SUNY
Counseling, School and Educational
  Psychology
409 Baldy Hall
Buffalo, NY 14260
Ph: (716)645-2484   Fax: (716)645-6616
E-mail: jdelucia@buffalo.edu
URL: http://www.asgw.org

Description: A division of the American Counseling Association. Individuals interested in group counseling holding master's or doctoral degrees, and engaged in practice, teaching, or research in group work; persons holding undergraduate degrees who are interested in group work, but not actively engaged in practice, teaching, or research; students. Seeks to assist and further interests of children, youth, and adults by providing effective services through the group medium, preventing problems, providing maximum development, and remediating disabling behaviors. Sponsors programs to advance group work in schools, clinics, universities, private practice, and mental health institutions. Conducts placement service.

★3166★ International Association of Counselors and Therapists (IACT)

RR No. 2, Box 2468
Laceyville, PA 18623
Ph: (570)869-1021   Fax: (570)869-1249
Fr: 800-553-6886
E-mail: info@iact.org
URL: http://www.iact.org

Description: Mental health professionals, medical professionals, social workers, clergy, educators, hypnotherapists, counselors, and individuals interested in the helping professions. Promotes enhanced professional image and prestige for complementary therapy. Provides a forum for exchange of information and ideas among practitioners of traditional and nontraditional therapies and methodologies; fosters unity among "grassroots" practitioners and those with advanced academic credentials. Facilitates the development of new therapy programs. Conducts educational, research, and charitable programs. Awards credits for continuing education. Maintains speakers' bureau and library; operates referral and placement services;

compiles statistics. Assists in the development of local chapters.

★3167★ International Educator's Institute (TIE)

PO Box 513
Cummaquid, MA 02637
Ph: (508)790-1990   Fax: (508)790-1922
Fr: 877-375-6668
E-mail: tie@tieonline.com
URL: http://www.tieonline.com

Description: Facilitates the placement of teachers and administrators in American, British, and international schools. Seeks to create a network that provides for professional development opportunities and improved financial security of members. Offers advice and information on international school news, recent educational developments, job placement, and investment, consumer, and professional development opportunities. Makes available insurance and travel benefits. Operates International Schools Internship Program.

★3168★ National Academic Advising Association (NACADA)

Kansas State University
2323 Anderson Ave., Ste. 225
Manhattan, KS 66502-2912
Ph: (785)532-5717   Fax: (785)532-7732
E-mail: nacada@ksu.edu
URL: http://www.nacada.ksu.edu

Members: Academic program advisors, faculty, administrators, counselors, and others concerned with the intellectual, personal, and career development of students in all types of postsecondary educational institutions. **Purpose:** Works to support and promotes professional growth of academic advising and academic advisers. Provides a forum for discussion, debate, and exchange of ideas regarding academic advising. Serves as advocate for standards and quality programs in academic advising. **Activities:** Operates consultants' bureau to assist advising services on college campuses. Maintains placement service, speakers' bureau, and information clearinghouse.

★3169★ National Council on Rehabilitation Education (NCRE)

2012 W Norwood Dr.
Carbondale, IL 62901
Ph: (618)549-3267   Fax: (618)457-3632
E-mail: sbenshoff@ncre-admin.org
URL: http://www.rehabeducators.org

Description: Represents academic institutions and organizations, professional educators, researchers, and students. Goals are to: assist in the documentation of the effect of education in improving services to persons with disability; determine the skills and training necessary for effective rehabilitation services; develop models, standards, and uniform licensure and certification requirements for rehabilitation personnel; interact with consumers and public and private sector policy makers. Disseminates information and provides forum for discussion. Sponsors specialized education and placement service. Compiles statistics. Works closely with agencies and associations serving persons with disabilities.

EMPLOYER DIRECTORIES AND NETWORKING LISTS

★3170★ 50 State Educational Directories

Career Guidance Foundation
8090 Engineer Rd.
San Diego, CA 92111
Ph: (858)560-8051   Fax: (858)278-8960
Fr: 800-854-2670
URL: http://www.cgf.org

Annual. Microfiche. Collection consists of reproductions of the state educational directories published by the departments of education of individual 50 states. Directory contents vary, but the majority contain listings of elementary and secondary schools, colleges and universities, and state education officials. Amount of detail in each also varies. Entries include: Usually, institution name, address, and name of one executive.

★3171★ American Association for Correctional Psychology-Directory

American Association for Correctional Psychology
c/o Robert Smith, Ed.D.
Marshall University Graduate College
100 Angus E Peyton Dr.
South Charleston, WV 25303-1600
Ph: (304)746-1929   Fax: (304)746-1942

Continuously updated. Covers 400 mental health professionals engaged in correctional and rehabilitative work in prisons, reformatories, juvenile institutions, probation and parole agencies, and in other aspects of criminal justice. Entries include: Name, affiliation, address, phone. Arrangement: Alphabetical.

★3172★ American Group Psychotherapy Association-Membership Directory

American Group Psychotherapy Association Inc.
25 E 21st St., 6th Fl.
New York, NY 10010
Ph: (212)477-2677   Fax: (212)979-6627
Fr: 877-668-2472
URL: http://www.agpa.org

Covers 4,500 physicians, psychologists, clinical social workers, psychiatric nurses, and other mental health professionals interested in treatment of emotional problems by group methods. Entries include: Name, office or home address, highest degree held, office or home phone number. Arrangement: Alphabetical. Indexes: Geographical.

★3173★ American Society for Adolescent Psychiatry-Membership Directory

American Society for Adolescent Psychiatry
PO Box 570218
Dallas, TX 75357-0218
Ph: (972)613-0985   Fax: (972)613-5532
URL: http://www.adolpsych.org

Covers 1,500 members. Entries include: Name, office address and phone, fax, home address and phone (when given). Arrangement: Alphabetical. Indexes: Geographical, chapter.

★3174★ Boarding Schools Directory

Association of Boarding Schools
2141 Wisconsin Ave. NW, Ste. H
Washington, DC 20007
Ph: (202)965-8982   Fax: (202)965-8988
URL: http://www.schools.com/

Annual; latest edition 2007-2008. For U.S. and Canada. Covers boarding schools that are members of the Association of Boarding Schools. Entries include: School name, address, phone, e-mail and URL, grades for which boarding students are accepted, enrollment, brief description. Arrangement: Classified by type of school. Indexes: Geographical; program; alphabetical.

★3175★ Christian Association for Psychological Studies International-Membership Directory

Christian Association for Psychological Studies
PO Box 365
Batavia, IL 60510-0365
Ph: (630)639-9478   Fax: (630)454-3799

Annual, June. $12.00 for Canada; $12.00 for other countries. Covers 2,300 Christians involved in psychology, psychiatry, counseling, sociology, social work, ministry, and nursing. Entries include: Name, office address and phone number, highest degree held, area of occupational specialization, and career data. Arrangement: Geographical. Indexes: Alphabetical.

★3176★ Christian Schools International-Directory

Christian Schools International
3350 E Paris Ave. SE
Grand Rapids, MI 49512
Ph: (616)957-1070   Fax: (616)957-5022
Fr: 800-635-8288
URL: http://store.csionline.org

Annual; 2007-2008. $15.00 for members; $72.00 for nonmembers. Covers nearly 450 Reformed Christian elementary and secondary schools; related associations; societies without schools. Entries include: For schools–School name, address, phone; name, title, and address of officers; names of faculty members. Arrangement: Geographical.

★3177★ Directory of Counseling Services

International Association of Counseling Services
101 S Whiting St., Ste. 211
Alexandria, VA 22304-3416
Ph: (703)823-9840   Fax: (703)823-9843
URL: http://iacsinc.org/iacsmem.html

Annual, September. $50.00. Covers about 200 accredited services in the United States and Canada concerned with psychological, educational, and vocational counseling, including those at colleges and universities and public and private agencies. Entries include: Name, address, phone, hours of operation, director's name, service, clientele served. Arrangement: Geographical.

★3178★ Directory of Public School Systems in the U.S.

American Association for Employment in Education
3040 Riverside Dr., Ste. 125
Columbus, OH 43221
Ph: (614)485-1111   Fax: (614)485-9609
URL: http://www.aaee.org/

Annual, winter; latest edition 2004-2005 edition. $10.00 for members (plus $2.00/copy for mailing); $20.00 for nonmembers (plus $2.00/copy for mailing). Covers about 14,500 public school systems in the United States and their administrative personnel. Entries include: System name, address, phone, website address, name and title of personnel administrator, levels taught and approximate student population. Arrangement: Geographical by state.

★3179★ Directory of Refugee Mental Health Professionals and Paraprofessionals

Refugee Assistance Program–Mental Health Technical Assistance Center
University of Minnesota
Mayo MC 85
420 Delaware St. SE
Minneapolis, MN 55455

$99.95 for individuals. Covers professionals who specialize in refugee mental health. Entries include: Name, address, phone, geographical area served and area of specialty. Arrangement: Geographical.

★3180★ The Encyclopedia of Suicide

Facts On File Inc.
132 W 31st St., 17th Fl.
New York, NY 10001
Ph: (212)967-8800   Fax: 800-678-3633
Fr: 800-322-8755
URL: http://www.factsonfile.com

Latest edition 2nd, 2003. $75.00 for individuals; $67.50 for libraries. Publication includes: List of national organizations and suicide prevention/crisis intervention groups in the United States and Canada. Principal content of publication is detailed information about the problem and history of suicide. Indexes: Alphabetical.

★3181★ Handbook of Private Schools

Porter Sargent Publishers Inc.
11 Beacon St., Ste. 1400
Boston, MA 02108-3099
Ph: (617)523-1670   Fax: (617)523-1021
Fr: 800-342-7470
E-mail: orders@portersargent.com
URL: http://www.portersargent.com

Annual, latest edition 87th, 2006 edition. $99.00 for individuals. Covers more than 1,600 elementary and secondary boarding and day schools in the United States. Entries include: School name, address, phone, fax, e-mail, URL, type of school (boarding or day), sex and age range, names and titles of administrators, grades offered, academic orientation, curriculum, new admissions yearly, tests required for admission, enrollment and faculty, graduate record, number of alumni, tuition and scholarship figures, summer session, plant evaluation and endowment, date of establishment, calendar, association membership, description of school's offerings and history, test score averages, uniform requirements, and geographical and demographic data. Arrangement: Geographical. Indexes: Alphabetical by school name, cross indexed by state, region, grade range, sexes accepted, school features and enrollment.

★3182★ MDR's School Directories

Market Data Retrieval
1 Forest Pkwy.
Shelton, CT 06484-0947
Ph: (203)926-4800   Fax: (203)926-1826
Fr: 800-333-8802
URL: http://www.schooldata.com

Annual, October. Covers over 90,000 public, 8,000 Catholic, and 15,000 other private schools (grades K-12) in the United States; over 15,000 school district offices, 76,000 school librarians, 27,000 media specialists, and 33,000 technology coordinators. Includes names of over 165,000 school district administrators and staff members in county and state education administration. Entries include: District name and address; telephone and fax number; number of schools; number of teachers in the district; district enrollment; special education students; limited-english proficient students; minority percentage by race; percentage of college bound students; expenditures per student for instructional materials; poverty level; title 1 dollars; site-based management; district open/close dates; construction indicator; technologies and quantities; district-level administrators, (new superintendents shaded); school name and address (new public shaded); telephone and fax number; principal (new principal shaded); librarian, media specialist and technology coordinator; grade span; special programs and school type; student enrollment; technologies and quantities (instructional computer brand, noting predominant brand); Multi-Media Computers; Internet connection or access; Tech Sophistication Index. Arrangement: Geographical. Indexes: District county; district personnel; principal; new public schools and key personnel; district and school telephone; district URLs.

★3183★ Mental Help Net

CenterSite L.L.C.
PO Box 20709
Columbus, OH 43220
Ph: (614)448-4055   Fax: (614)448-4055
URL: http://www.mentalhelp.net

Covers resources for finding mental help, including local therapists and self-help groups, as well as services such as upcoming conferences, professional education, and universities offering degrees in mental health fields.

★3184★ National Directory for Employment in Education

American Association for Employment in Education
3040 Riverside Dr., Ste. 125
Columbus, OH 43221
Ph: (614)485-1111   Fax: (614)485-9609
URL: http://www.aaee.org/

Annual, winter; latest edition 2005 edition. $20.00 for nonmembers; $10.00 for members. Covers about 600 placement offices maintained by teacher-training institutions and 300 school district personnel officers and/or superintendents responsible for hiring profesional staff. Entries include: Institution name, address, phone, contact name, email address, and website. Arrangement: Geographical. Indexes: Personal name; subject-field of teacher training; institutions that provide vacancy bulletins and placement services to non-enrolled students.

★3185★ National Register

American Association of Sex Educators, Counselors, and Therapists
PO Box 1960
Ashland, VA 23005-1960
Ph: (804)752-0026   Fax: (804)752-0056
E-mail: aasect@worldnet.att.net

Annual. Covers about 1,600 association members. Entries include: Name, address, phone, highest degree, certification status. Arrangement: Separate geographical sections for educators, therapists, and counselors.

★3186★ Opportunities Abroad for Educators

Fulbright Teacher and Administrator Exchange Program
600 Maryland Ave. SW, Ste. 320
Washington, DC 20024-2520
Ph: (202)314-3527   Fax: (202)479-6806
Fr: 800-726-0479
URL: http://www.fulbrightexchanges.org

Annual. Covers opportunities available for elementary and secondary teachers, two-year college instructors, and school administrators to attend seminars or to teach abroad under the Mutual Educational and Cultural Exchange Act of 1961. Entries include: Countries of placement, dates, eligibility requirements, teaching assignments. Arrangement: Geographical.

★3187★ Private Independent Schools

Bunting and Lyon Inc.
238 N Main St.
Wallingford, CT 06492
Ph: (203)269-3333   Fax: (203)269-5697
URL: http://www.buntingandlyon.com

Annual; latest edition 60th, January 2007. $115.00 for individuals. Covers 1,200 English-speaking elementary and secondary private schools and summer programs in North America and abroad. Entries include: School name, address, phone, fax, e-mail, website, enrollment, tuition and other fees, financial aid information, administrator's name and educational background, director of admission, regional accreditation, description of programs, curriculum, activities, learning differences grid. Arrangement: Geographical. Indexes: school name; geographical.

★3188★ Public Human Services Directory

American Public Human Services Association
810 1st St. NE, Ste. 500
Washington, DC 20002
Ph: (202)682-0100   Fax: (202)289-6555
E-mail: pubs@aphsa.org
URL: http://www.aphsa.org

Annual, September. $110.00 for members; $149.00 for nonmembers. Covers federal, state, territorial, county, and major municipal public human service agencies. Entries include: Agency name, address, phone, fax, e-mail address, web site address, names of key personnel, program area. Arrangement: Geographical.

★3189★ Requirements for Certification of Teachers, Counselors, Librarians, Administrators for Elementary and Secondary Schools

University of Chicago Press
Journals Division
1427 E 60th St.
Chicago, IL 60637-2954
Ph: (773)702-7600   Fax: (773)702-0694
Fr: 877-705-1878

Annual, June; latest edition 71st, 2006-07. $47.00. Publication includes: List of state and local departments of education. Entries include: Office name, address, phone. Principal content of publication consists of summaries of each state's teaching and administrative certification requirements. Arrangement: Geographical.

★3190★ State Vocational Rehabilitation Agencies

U.S. Office of Special Education and Rehabilitative Services
U.S. Department of Education
400 Maryland Ave. SW
Washington, DC 20202-2800
Ph: (202)245-7488   Fax: (202)245-7591
Fr: (866)889-6737
URL: http://www.ed.gov/index.jhtml

Quarterly. Covers state government agencies responsible for vocational rehabilitation activities. Entries include: Agency name, address, phone, name and title of director, federal Rehabilitation Services Administration region number, fax, TTY, and e-mail address. Arrangement: Geographical.

HANDBOOKS AND MANUALS

★3191★ Career Counseling in Schools: Multicultural and Developmental Perspectives

American Counseling Association
5999 Stevenson Ave.
Alexandria, VA 22304-3300
Ph: (703)823-9800   Fax: 800-473-2329
Fr: 800-347-6647
URL: http://www.counseling.org/

Roger D. Herring. 1998. $67.57 (paper). 348 pages.

★3192★ Careers for Good Samaritans and Other Humanitarian Types

The McGraw-Hill Companies
PO Box 182604
Columbus, OH 43272
Fax: (614)759-3749   Fr: 877-883-5524
E-mail: customer.service@mcgraw-hill.com
URL: http://www.mcgraw-hill.com

Marjorie Eberts and Margaret Gisler. Third edition, 2006. $13.95 (paper). 160 pages. Contains hundreds of ideas for turning good work into paid work. Inventories opportunities in service organizations like the Red Cross, Goodwill, and the Salvation Army; religious groups, VISTA, the Peace Corps, and UNICEF; and agencies at all levels of the government. Part of Careers for You series.

★3193★ Careers in Health Care

The McGraw-Hill Companies
PO Box 182604
Columbus, OH 43272
Fax: (614)759-3749   Fr: 877-883-5524
E-mail: customer.service@mcgraw-hill.com
URL: http://www.mcgraw-hill.com

Barbara M. Swanson. Fifth edition, 2005. $15.95 (paper). 192 pages. Describes job duties, work settings, salaries, licensing and certification requirements, educational preparation, and future outlook. Gives ideas on how to secure a job.

★3194★ Careers in Social and Rehabilitation Services

The McGraw-Hill Companies
PO Box 182604
Columbus, OH 43272
Fax: (614)759-3749   Fr: 877-883-5524
E-mail: customer.service@mcgraw-hill.com
URL: http://www.mcgraw-hill.com

Geraldine O. Garner. 2001. $19.95; 14.95 (paper). 128 pages.

★3195★ Clinical Supervision in Alcohol and Drug Abuse Counseling: Principles, Models, Methods

Jossey-Bass
989 Market St.
San Francisco, CA 94103
Ph: (415)433-1740   Fax: (415)433-0499
Fr: 800-255-5945
E-mail: custserv@wiley.com
URL: http://www.josseybass.com/WileyCDA/

David J. Powell, Archie Brodsky. 2004. $45.00. 448 pages.

★3196★ Employment and Training Counselor

National Learning Corporation
212 Michael Dr.
Syosset, NY 11791
Ph: (516)921-8888   Fax: (516)921-8743
Fr: 800-632-8888
URL: http://www.passbooks.com/

Jack Rudman. 2005. $29.95. Career explorations.

★3197★ Great Jobs for Liberal Arts Majors

The McGraw-Hill Companies
PO Box 182604
Columbus, OH 43272
Fax: (614)759-3749   Fr: 877-883-5524
E-mail: customer.service@mcgraw-hill.com
URL: http://www.mcgraw-hill.com

Blythe Camenson. Second edition, 2001. $14.95 (paper). 256 pages.

★3198★ Guidance Counselor, Elementary School

National Learning Corporation
212 Michael Dr.
Syosset, NY 11791
Ph: (516)921-8888   Fax: (516)921-8743
Fr: 800-632-8888
URL: http://www.passbooks.com/

Jack Rudman. 2005. $23.95. 204 pages

★3199★ Handbook of Career Counseling Theory and Practice

Davies-Black Publishing Inc.
1055 Joaquin Rd., 2nd Fl.
Mountain View, CA 94043
Ph: (650)969-8901   Fax: (650)969-8608
Fr: 800-624-1765
URL: http://www.cpp.com/products/db/index.asp

Mark L. Savickas and W. Bruce Walsh, editors. 1996. $69.95. 459 pages.

★3200★ The Helping Professions: A Careers Sourcebook

Wadsworth Publishing
PO Box 6904
Florence, KY 41022
Fax: 800-487-8488   Fr: 800-354-9706
URL: http://www.cengage.com

William Burger and Merrill Youkeles. 1999.

$41.95. 176 pages. Part of the Counseling Series. Describes nine major professions in the human services field including a vignette illustrating actual work activities. Gives a realistic picture of the challenges of each profession, salary levels and duties at various levels of training, educational requirements, licensing, certification and an estimated job outlook.

★3201★ Non-Profits and Education Job Finder

Planning Communications
7215 Oak Ave.
River Forest, IL 60305-1935
Ph: (708)366-5200   Fax: (708)366-5280
Fr: 888-366-5200
E-mail: info@planningcommunications.com
URL: http://jobfindersonline.com

Daniel Lauber. 1997. $32.95; $16.95 (paper). 340 pages. Covers 1600 sources. Discusses how to use sources of non-profit sector job vacancies in a number of specialties and state-by-state, including job-matching services, job hotlines, specialty periodicals with job ads, salary surveys, and directories. Covers a variety of fields from education to religion. Includes chapters on resume and cover letter preparation and interviewing.

★3202★ Opportunities in Counseling and Development Careers

The McGraw-Hill Companies
PO Box 182604
Columbus, OH 43272
Fax: (614)759-3749   Fr: 877-883-5524
E-mail: customer.service@mcgraw-hill.com
URL: http://www.mcgraw-hill.com

Neale J.Baxter, Mark U. Toch, and Philip A. Perry. 1997. $14.95; $11.95 (paper). 160 pages. A guide to planning for and seeking opportunities in this challenging field. Illustrated.

★3203★ Opportunities in Health and Medical Careers

The McGraw-Hill Companies
PO Box 182604
Columbus, OH 43272
Fax: (614)759-3749   Fr: 877-883-5524
E-mail: customer.service@mcgraw-hill.com
URL: http://www.mcgraw-hill.com

I. Donald Snook, Jr. and Leo D'Orazio. 2004. $13.95 (paper). 157 pages. Covers the full range of medical and health occupations. Illustrated.

★3204★ Opportunities in Mental Health Careers

The McGraw-Hill Companies
PO Box 182604
Columbus, OH 43272
Fax: (614)759-3749   Fr: 877-883-5524
E-mail: customer.service@mcgraw-hill.com
URL: http://www.mcgraw-hill.com

Philip A. Perry. 1996. $14.95; $11.95 (paper) 160 pages. Part of the "Opportunities in ..." Series.

★3205★ Therapy's Best: Practical Advice and Gems of Wisdom from Twenty Accomplished Counselors and Therapists

Haworth Press, Inc.
10 Alice St.
Binghamton, NY 13904-1580
Ph: (607)722-5857   Fax: 800-895-0582
Fr: 800-429-6784
E-mail: getinfo@haworthpress.com
URL: http://www.haworthpressinc.com/

Howard Rosenthal. 2006. $29.95. Interviews with leading therapists and counselors, including Albert Ellis, Robert Alberti, Al Mahrer, and William Glasser.

EMPLOYMENT AGENCIES AND SEARCH FIRMS

★3206★ Educational Placement Service

6510-A S. Academy Blvd.
Colorado Springs, CO 80906
Ph: (719)579-9911   Fax: (719)579-5050
E-mail: accounting@educatorjobs.com
URL: http://www.educatorjobs.com

Employment agency. Focuses on teaching, administrative, and education-related openings.

ONLINE JOB SOURCES AND SERVICES

★3207★ Delta T Group

E-mail: pa@deltatg.com
URL: http://www.delta-tgroup.com

Description: Specialized contract temporary staffing source for healthcare professionals in the fields of social service, psychiatry, mental health, and substance abuse. Organizations may request services and staffing; job seekers may view services provided, submit a resume, or peruse jobs available.

★3208★ RehabWorld

URL: http://www.rehabworld.com

Description: Site for rehabilitation professionals to learn about the profession and locate jobs. Includes user groups, salary surveys, and chat capabilities. **Main files include:** Physical Therapy, Occupational Therapy, Speech Therapy, Mental Health, Employer World, Student World, International World, Forum.

TRADESHOWS

★3209★ American Counseling Association World Conference

American Counseling Association
5999 Stevenson Ave.
Alexandria, VA 22304-3300
Ph: (703)823-9800   Fax: (703)823-6862
Fr: 800-347-6647
E-mail: meetings@counseling.org
URL: http://www.counseling.org

Annual. **Primary Exhibits:** Books, career development information, college selection, student financial aid, testing and measurement techniques, practice management companies, software, rehabilitation aids, and community agencies and private clinics specializing in substance abuse and mental health.

★3210★ Association for Counselor Education and Supervision National Conference

Association for Counselor Education and Supervision
c/o American Counseling Association
PO Box 791006
Baltimore, MD 21279-1006
Ph: (703)823-9800   Fax: (703)823-0252
Fr: 800-347-6647
E-mail: feitstep@isu.edu
URL: http://www.acesonline.net

Annual. **Primary Exhibits:** Exhibits relating to the professional preparation of counselors.

★3211★ California Association for Counseling and Development Convention

California Association for Counseling and Development
543 Vista Mar Ave.
Pacifica, CA 94044
Ph: (650)359-6916   Fax: (650)359-3089
E-mail: cacd@cacd.org
URL: http://www.cacd.org

Primary Exhibits: Publications, testing materials, equipment, college representatives, and military and civil service employers.

OTHER SOURCES

★3212★ American Association of Psychiatric Technicians (AAPT)

1220 S St., Ste. 100
Sacramento, CA 95811-7138
Ph: (916)443-1701   Fax: (916)329-9145
Fr: 800-391-7589
E-mail: loger@psychtechs.net
URL: http://www.psychtechs.org

Description: Administers the Nationally Certified Psychiatric Technician examination to non-licensed direct-care workers in the fields of mental illness, developmental disabilities and substance abuse.

★3213★ American College Counseling Association (ACCA)

PO Box 791006
Baltimore, MD 21279-1006
Ph: (703)823-9800   Fax: (703)461-9260
Fr: 800-347-6647
E-mail: pfornell@csulb.edu
URL: http://www.collegecounseling.org

Purpose: Works to advance the practice of college counseling. **Activities:** Promotes ethical practice and communication among members; encourages cooperation with other related organizations; provides advocacy for the profession.

★3214★ American College of Counselors (ACC)

2750 E Sunshine St.
Springfield, MO 65804-2047
Ph: (317)826-3168   Fax: (317)826-3168
Fr: 800-205-9165
E-mail: wmsloane@widener.edu
URL: http://www.freewebs.com/counselors

Description: Represents individuals who are active in counseling in related fields of human services. Fosters values that enrich human growth and development. Works to establish guidelines and standards that will be in common with all specialties. Aims to increase knowledge and awareness of complex behavioral and emotional problems. Promotes objectivity and integrity; high standards of inquiry and communication; responsibility and competence in objectively reporting findings.

★3215★ American Counseling Association (ACA)

5999 Stevenson Ave.
Alexandria, VA 22304
Fax: 800-473-2329   Fr: 800-347-6647
E-mail: ryep@counseling.org
URL: http://www.counseling.org

Description: Counseling professionals in elementary and secondary schools, higher education, community agencies and organizations, rehabilitation programs, government, industry, business, private practice, career counseling, and mental health counseling. Conducts professional development institutes and provides liability insurance. Maintains Counseling and Human Development Foundation to fund counseling projects.

★3216★ American Family Therapy Academy (AFTA)

1608 20th St. NW, 4th Fl.
Washington, DC 20009
Ph: (202)483-8001   Fax: (202)483-8002
E-mail: afta@afta.org
URL: http://www.afta.org

Description: Family therapy teachers, researchers, and practitioners working to advance theory and therapy that regards the family as a unit. Promotes research and professional education in family therapy and allied fields. Disseminates information to practitioners, scientists, and the public. Focuses on improving the knowledge of how families function and how to treat them.

★3217★ **American Mental Health Alliance (AMHA)**

PO Box 4075
Portland, OR 97208-4075
Ph: (503)279-8160   Fr: 888-577-3386
E-mail: memberinfo@americanmentalhealth.com
URL: http://www.americanmentalhealth.com

Description: Represents mental health professionals licensed or certified for independen t practice. Creates a professional community that provides therapy of the highes t quality and ethical standards. Supports and markets competent, ethical mental health services that preserve privacy and confidentiality. Supports education, s upervision, and research opportunities for members. Opposes legislation and regu lations that invade patient privacy and confidentiality.

★3218★ **American Mental Health Counselors Association (AMHCA)**

801 N Fairfax St., Ste. 304
Alexandria, VA 22314
Ph: (703)548-6002   Fax: (703)548-4775
Fr: 800-326-2642
E-mail: mhamilton@amhca.org
URL: http://www.amhca.org

Description: Professional counselors employed in mental health services; students. Aims to: deliver quality mental health services to children, youth, adults, families, and organizations; improve the availability and quality of counseling services through licensure and certification, training standards, and consumer advocacy. Supports specialty and special interest networks. Fosters communication among members. A division of the American Counseling Association.

★3219★ **American Psychological Association (APA)**

750 First St. NE
Washington, DC 20002-4242
Ph: (202)336-5500   Fax: (202)336-6069
Fr: 800-374-2721
E-mail: president@apa.org
URL: http://www.apa.org

Description: Scientific and professional society of psychologists; students participate as affiliates. Advances psychology as a science, a profession, and as a means of promoting health, education and the human welfare.

★3220★ **American School Counselor Association (ASCA)**

1101 King St., Ste. 625
Alexandria, VA 22314
Ph: (703)683-2722   Fax: (703)683-1619
Fr: 800-306-4722
E-mail: asca@schoolcounselor.org
URL: http://www.schoolcounselor.org

Description: Supports school counselors' efforts to help students focus on academic, personal/social and career development so they not only achieve success in school but are prepared to lead fulfilling lives as responsible members of society; provides professional development, publications and other resources, research and advocacy, governmental and public relations. Serves as liaison among members and counselors in other settings; disseminates educational, professional, and scientific materials.

★3221★ **Association for Counselor Education and Supervision (ACES)**

St. Joseph College
Dept. of Counselor Education
1678 Asylum Ave.
West Hartford, CT 06117
Ph: (860)231-6778   Fax: (860)231-5774
Fr: 800-347-6647
E-mail: jdurham@sjc.edu
URL: http://www.acesonline.net

Description: Represents the interests of persons engaged in the professional preparation of counselors or who are responsible for supervising professional counselors in a wide variety of work settings. Works to improve the education, credentialing and supervision of counselors through accreditation and professional development activities. Disseminates information on current and relevant research, practices, ethical standards and problems related to the profession. Maintains archives on counselor education and supervision.

★3222★ **Association for Counselors and Educators in Government (ACEG)**

5999 Stevenson Ave.
Alexandria, VA 22304-3300
Fax: 800-473-2329   Fr: 800-347-6647
E-mail: dwilliams14@hot.rr.com
URL: http://www.dantes.doded.mil/dantes_web/organizations/aceg/index.htm

Description: Professional counselors who work in the U.S. Armed Services. Encourages and provides counseling to individuals in the service and their dependents, veterans, and civilians employed by the military. Promotes and maintains improved communication with the non-military community. Provides representation for counseling and education professionals working in and for the U.S. Department of Defense. Offers programs to enhance individual growth and development.

★3223★ **Association on Higher Education and Disability (AHEAD)**

107 Commerce Center Dr., Ste. 204
Huntersville, NC 28078
Ph: (704)947-7779   Fax: (704)948-7779
E-mail: ahead@ahead.org
URL: http://www.ahead.org

Description: Individuals interested in promoting the equal rights and opportunities of disabled postsecondary students, staff, faculty, and graduates. Provides an exchange of communication for those professionally involved with disabled students; collects, evaluates, and disseminates information; encourages and supports legislation for the benefit of disabled students. Conducts surveys on issues pertinent to college students with disabilities; offers resource referral system and employment exchange for positions in disability student services. Conducts research programs; compiles statistics.

★3224★ **Counseling Association for Humanistic Education and Development (C-AHEAD)**

PO Box 791006
Baltimore, MD 21279-1006
Ph: (703)823-9800   Fax: 800-473-2329
Fr: 800-347-6647
E-mail: lleech@gw.mp.sc.edu
URL: http://www.c-ahead.com

Description: A division of the American Counseling Association. Teachers, educational administrators, community agency workers, counselors, school social workers, and psychologists; others interested in the area of human development. Aims to assist individuals in improving their quality of life. Provides forum for the exchange of information about humanistically-oriented administrative and instructional practices. Supports humanistic practices and research on instructional and organizational methods for facilitating humanistic education; encourages cooperation among related professional groups.

★3225★ **Employee Assistance Society of North America (EASNA)**

2001 Jefferson Davis Hwy., Ste. 1004
Arlington, VA 22202-3617
Ph: (703)416-0060   Fax: (703)416-0014
E-mail: info@easna.org
URL: http://www.easna.org

Description: Individuals in the field of employee assistance, including psychiatrists, psychologists, and managers. Facilitates communication among members; provides resource information; serves as a network for employee assistance programs nationwide. Conducts research.

★3226★ **Family Therapy Section of the National Council on Family Relations (FTSNCFR)**

3989 Central Ave. NE, No. 550
Minneapolis, MN 55421
Ph: (248)370-3069   Fax: (763)781-9348
Fr: 888-781-9331
E-mail: colleen.peterson@unlv.edu
URL: http://www.oakland.edu/~blume/ncfr

Description: A section of the National Council on Family Relations. Practicing family therapists and family therapy supervisors, educators, and researchers. Seeks to improve the practice of family therapy through the development of theory, research, and training. Promotes communication between family therapy researchers and clinicians; functions as a network for family therapy research projects; conducts educational programs.

★3227★ International Alliance of Holistic Lawyers (IAHL)

PO Box 371
Milton, DE 19968
Fax: (302)684-5644
E-mail: info@iahl.org
URL: http://iahl.org

Description: Represents and promotes the interests of holistic lawyers. Seeks to transform the practice of law through education and support of holistic practices. Provides a forum for networking, progress and new vision in the legal profession.

★3228★ International Association of Biblical Counselors (IABC)

11500 Sheridan Blvd.
Westminster, CO 80020
Ph: (303)469-4222   Fax: (303)469-1787
E-mail: information@iabc.net
URL: http://www.iabc.net

Description: Represents organizations and individuals who saw the need for basic standards, beliefs and practices in counseling. Promotes Biblical Counseling through seminars, conferences and workshops. Encourages the development of Biblical research and offers a counselor network for the exchange of information and client referral.

★3229★ International Mentoring Network Organization (IMNO)

766 E 560 N, No. 206
Provo, UT 84606
Ph: (801)361-9942
E-mail: contact@imno.org
URL: http://www.imno.org

Description: Aims to solve the worldwide need for professional mentoring. Serves as an open source mentoring movement. Gives help and direction to the career development of aspiring professionals.

★3230★ National Association of State Directors of Special Education (NASDSE)

1800 Diagonal Rd., Ste. 320
Alexandria, VA 22314
Ph: (703)519-3800   Fax: (703)519-3808
E-mail: nasdse@nasdse.org

Members: Professional society of state directors; consultants, supervisors, and administrators who have statewide responsibilities for administering special education programs. **Purpose:** Provides services to state agencies to facilitate their efforts to maximize educational outcomes for individuals with disabilities.

★3231★ National Career Development Association (NCDA)

305 N Beech Cir.
Broken Arrow, OK 74012
Ph: (918)663-7060   Fax: (918)663-7058
Fr: (866)367-6232
E-mail: dpenn@ncda.org

URL: http://www.ncda.org

Description: Represents professionals and others interested in career development or counseling in various work environments. Supports counselors, education and training personnel, and allied professionals working in schools, colleges, business/industry, community and government agencies, and in private practice. Provides publications, support for state and local activities, human equity programs, and continuing education and training for these professionals. Provides networking opportunities for career professionals in business, education, and government.

★3232★ National Council for Accreditation of Teacher Education (NCATE)

2010 Massachusetts Ave. NW, Ste. 500
Washington, DC 20036
Ph: (202)466-7496   Fax: (202)296-6620
E-mail: ncate@ncate.org
URL: http://www.ncate.org

Members: Representatives from constituent colleges and universities, state departments of education, school boards, teacher, and other professional groups. **Purpose:** Voluntary accrediting body devoted exclusively to: evaluation and accreditation of institutions for preparation of elementary and secondary school teachers; preparation of school service personnel, including school principals, supervisors, superintendents, school psychologists, instructional technologists, and other specialists for school-oriented positions.

★3233★ National Employment Counseling Association (NECA)

PO Box 791006
Baltimore, MD 21279-1006
Fax: 800-473-2329   Fr: 800-347-6647
E-mail: jobfields@aol.com
URL: http://www.employmentcounseling.org/neca.html

Description: Serves as a division of the American Counseling Association. Represents individuals who are engaged in employment counseling, counselor education, research, administration or supervision in business and industry, colleges and universities, and federal and state governments; students. Offers professional leadership and development services; provides opportunities for professional growth through workshops and special projects.

★3234★ National Rehabilitation Association (NRA)

633 S Washington St.
Alexandria, VA 22314
Ph: (703)836-0850   Fax: (703)836-0848
E-mail: info@nationalrehab.org
URL: http://www.nationalrehab.org/website/index.html

Description: Provides opportunities through knowledge and diversity for professionals in the fields of rehabilitation of people with disabilities.

★3235★ National Rehabilitation Counseling Association (NRCA)

PO Box 4480
Manassas, VA 20108
Ph: (703)361-2077   Fax: (703)361-2489
E-mail: nrcaoffice@aol.com
URL: http://nrca-net.org

Description: An independent Association of Professional and student rehabilitation counselors. Works to expand the role of counselors in the rehabilitation process and seeks to advance members' professional development. Supports legislation favoring the profession.

★3236★ *Overseas Employment Opportunities for Educators: Department of Defense Dependents Schools*

DIANE Publishing Co.
PO Box 617
Darby, PA 19023-0617
Ph: (610)461-6200   Fax: (610)461-6130
Fr: 800-782-3833
URL: http://www.dianepublishingcentral.com

Barry Leonard, editor. 2000. $15.00. 54 pages. An introduction to teachings positions in the Dept. of Defense Dependents Schools (DoDDS), a worldwide school system, operated by the DoD in 14 countries.

★3237★ Society for Vocational Psychology (SVP)

University of Iowa
Division of Psychological and Quantitative Foundations
361 Lindquist Ctr.
Iowa City, IA 52242
Ph: (319)335-5495
E-mail: saba-ali@uiowa.edu
URL: http://www.div17.org/vocpsych

Description: Encourages, promotes and facilitates contributions to research, teaching, practice and public interest in vocational psychology and career interventions. Promotes quality research and practice of vocational psychology and career counseling. Supports the diversity of characteristics, work settings, roles and activities of counseling psychologists involved in vocational psychology and career intervention.

★3238★ Teaching & Related Occupations

Delphi Productions
3159 6th St.
Boulder, CO 80304
Ph: (303)443-2100   Fax: (303)443-4022
Fr: 888-443-2400
E-mail: support@delphivideo.com
URL: http://www.delphivideo.com

$95.00. 50 minutes. Part of the Careers for the 21st Century Video Library.

Counterterrorism and Intelligence Analysts

SOURCES OF HELP-WANTED ADS

★3239★ Armed Forces and Society

Sage Publications Inc.
2455 Teller Rd.
Thousand Oaks, CA 91320
Ph: (805)499-0721   Fax: (805)499-8096
URL: http://www.sagepub.com/journal-sproddesc.nav?prodid=journal20

Quarterly. $373.00/year for institutions, for print and online; $336.00/year for institutions, e-access; $366.00/year for institutions, for print; $97.00/year for individuals, for print; $101.00/year for institutions, single print; $32.00/year for individuals, single print; $392.00/year for institutions, current volume print and all online content; $354.00/year for institutions, all online content; $685.00/year for institutions, online content thru 1999. Journal focusing on such topics as civil military relations, military organizations, conflict resolution, terrorism, ethics, and security.

★3240★ International Counterterrorism & Security

Counterterrorism & Security Inc.
PO Box 10265
Arlington, VA 22210
Ph: (703)243-0993   Fax: (703)243-1197
URL: http://www.iacsp.com/publications.html

Quarterly. Journal covering terrorism and security analysis.

★3241★ Studies in Conflict and Terrorism

Taylor & Francis Group Journals
325 Chestnut St., Ste. 800
Philadelphia, PA 19106
Ph: (215)625-8900   Fax: (215)625-8914
Fr: 800-354-1420
URL: http://www.tandf.co.uk/journals/titles/1057610x.asp

$390.00/year for individuals, print only; $1,040.00/year for institutions, online only; $1,095.00/year for institutions, print and on-line. Journal publishing research on all forms of conflict and terrorism.

PLACEMENT AND JOB REFERRAL SERVICES

★3242★ Austin McGregor Executive Search

2121 Cooperative Way, Ste. 210
Herndon, VA 20171
Ph: (703)707-2208
E-mail: Jeremy@austinmcgregor.com
URL: http://www.austinmcgregor.com

Intelligence and surveillance professionals for both commercial and Federal markets.

★3243★ Security and Investigative Placement

5257 River Rd., Ste. 605
Bethesda, MD 20817
Ph: (301)229-6360   Fax: (301)263-0907
E-mail: info@siplacement.com
URL: http://www.siplacement.com

Places professionals in security and investigation positions within corporate, financial, legal, accounting and consulting firms. Candidates possess backgrounds in financial investigation, fraud, anti-money laundering, forensic accounting, investigative research, computer forensics and cyber investigation, security management, threat assessment, and global risk mitigation.

EMPLOYER DIRECTORIES AND NETWORKING LISTS

★3244★ Counterterrorism: A Reference Handbook

ABC-CLIO
130 Cremona Dr.
PO Box 1911
Santa Barbara, CA 93117
Ph: (805)968-1911   Fax: (805)685-9685
Fr: 800-368-6868
URL: http://www.abc-clio.com/products/overview.aspx?productid=109

Latest edition, 2004. $27.50 for individuals. Covers the wave of terrorism in the post-Cold War era and the ways in which states and societies are responding.

HANDBOOKS AND MANUALS

★3245★ Counterterrorism Handbook: Tactics, Procedures, and Techniques, 3rd Ed.

6000 Broken Sound Pkwy., Ste. 300
Boca Raton, FL 33487
Ph: (561)994-0555   Fax: 800-374-3401
Fr: 800-272-7737
URL: http://www.crcpress.com/

Frank Bolz, Jr., Kenneth J. Dudonis, and David P. Schulz. 2005. $93.95. Experts provide information to assist in understanding tactics, strategies and techniques to counter terrorism; topics include all aspects of terrorism, bomb threats, risk assessment, hostage situations, and weapons of mass destruction. Part of the Practical Aspects of Criminal and Forensic Investigations series, Volume 41.

★3246★ Democracy and Counterterrorism: Lessons from the Past

1200 17th St. NW
Washington, DC 20036
Ph: (202)457-1700   Fax: (202)429-6063

URL: http://bookstore.usip.org/

Robert J. Art and Louise Richardson. January 2007. $65.00 hardcopy, $28 (paper). A comparative study of the policies, strategies, and instruments used by various democratic governments in the fight against terrorism.

★3247★ First Responder Chem-Bio Handbook

PO Box 22572
Alexandria, VA 22304-9257
Ph: (703)370-2962   Fax: (703)370-1571
E-mail: info@tempestpublishing.com
URL: http://www.chem-bio.com/

$49.00 CD-ROM. Provides critical information to help analysts counter chem-bio terrorism threats. Also available in CD-ROM which contains fully searchable and indexed electronic versions of the handbook.

★3248★ On Intelligence: Spies and Secrecy in an Open World

AFCEA International Press
4400 Fair Lakes Ct.
Fairfax, VA 22033
Fr: 800-336-4583

Robert David Steele. Works as a primer for the reinvention of national defense and business intelligence within the larger context of an open world where transportation, power, financial, and communications infrastructures are so open, thus increasing the vulnerability of America to trans-continental epidemics, anonymous information terrorism, and nationwide power blackouts and financial meltdowns.

★3249★ Terror on the Internet: The New Arena, the New Challenges

1200 17th St. NW
Washington, DC 20036
Ph: (202)457-1700   Fax: (202)429-6063
URL: http://bookstore.usip.org/

Gabriel Weimann. April 2006. $20.00. 320 pages. Examination of the new psychology of terrorists and the ways in which they use the Internet to accomplish their goals.

★3250★ The War of Ideas: Jihadism against Democracy

PO Box 11221
Alexandria, VA 22312
Ph: (703)642-7450   Fax: (703)642-7451
Fr: 800-779-4007
URL: http://cicentre.com/BOOKS.htm

Required reading for senior intelligence managers to help understand the game plan, goals and denial and deception of Jihadism against the U.S.

ONLINE JOB SOURCES AND SERVICES

★3251★ Adguide Publications, Inc.: CollegeRecruiter.com

3109 W 50th St., Ste. 121
Minneapolis, MN 55410
Ph: (952)848-2211
URL: http://www.collegerecruiter.com

Online resource lists jobs, particularly those in the field of counterintelligence.

★3252★ Clearancejobs.com

4101 NW Urbandale Dr.
Urbandale, IA 50322
Fr: 877-386-3323
E-mail: support@clearancejobs.com
URL: http://www.clearancejobs.com

Online resource lists jobs for those security-cleared professionals including counterintelligence specialists.

★3253★ ClearedConnections

12020 Sunrise Valley Dr., Ste. 100
Reston, VA 20191
Ph: (703)860-2246
URL: http://www.clearedconnections.com

Online resource lists jobs for those security-cleared professionals including counterintelligence specialists.

★3254★ Cyberscientific.com

320 Goddard, Ste. 100
Irvine, CA 92618
Ph: (949)885-5121   Fax: (949)885-5152
E-mail: lance@cybercoders.com
URL: http://www.cyberscientific.com

Online resource lists jobs, particularly those in the counterintelligence industry. Also allows users to post resumes.

★3255★ IntelligenceCareers.com

Fax: (703)995-0863   Fr: 800-919-8284
E-mail: customerservice@intelligencecareers.com
URL: http://www.intelligencecareers.com/

Provides an online job search for intelligence positions by state, U.S. Forces overseas, and worldwide.

★3256★ US Army Recruiting Command: GoArmy.com

Bldg. 1307
3rd Ave.
Fort Knox, KY 40121
Ph: (502)626-0623
E-mail: gary.bishop@usarec.army.mil
URL: http://www.goarmy.com

Online resource lists jobs, particularly those in the field of counterintelligence.

★3257★ USADefenseIndustryJobs.com

Ph: (703)897-5063   Fax: (703)995-086
Fr: 800-919-8284
E-mail: action@intelligencecareers.com
URL: http://www.USADefenseIndustryJobs.com

Provides an online job search for intelligence positions with the American defense industry.

TRADESHOWS

★3258★ AFCEA Intelligence Annual Fall and Spring Classified Symposia

4400 Fair Lakes Ct.
Fairfax, VA 22033
Ph: (703)631-6219
E-mail: eschlickenmeyer@afcea.org
URL: http://www.afcea.org/

U.S. intelligence professionals in government and industry explore issues involving the challenges and opportunities in the intelligence community as well as national security issues.

★3259★ ICTOA Annual Conference

350 5th Ave., Ste. 3304-No. 16P
New York, NY 10118
Ph: (212)564-5048   Fax: (718)661-404
E-mail: info@ictoa.org
URL: http://www.ictoa.org/events.html

Public transportation safety and security Narco-Terrorism, kidnapping and torture bombs and explosive devices, terrorist surveillance, immigration and terrorist threats.

★3260★ International Association of Crime Analysts Annual Training Conference

9218 Metcalf Ave., Ste. 364
Overland Park, KS 66212
Fr: 800-609-3419
E-mail: iaca@iaca.net
URL: http://www.iaca.net/

Annual. Focuses on training in the areas of analysis and law enforcement and offers the IACA Certification Exam.

OTHER SOURCES

★3261★ AFCEA Intelligence

4400 Fair Lakes Ct.
Fairfax, VA 22033-3899
Ph: (703)631-6219   Fax: (703)631-6133
E-mail: sritchey@afcea.org
URL: http://www.afcea.org/mission/intel/

As part of the AFCEA International, the Association was established in 1981 to enhance outreach to the U.S. Intelligence Community and to support intelligence proessionals in the government, military and private sector.

★3262★ **Association of Former Intelligence Officers (AFIO)**
5723 Whittier Ave., Ste. 303 A
McLean, VA 22101
Ph: (703)790-0320   Fax: (703)991-1278
E-mail: afio@afio.com
URL: http://www.afio.com

Description: Represents educational association of current and former intelligence professionals, security and counterterrorism practitioners and some U.S. citizens. Enhances public understanding of the role and importance of intelligence for national security, counterterrorism and to deal with threats in the contemporary world. Engages in career guidance for young people who are interested in intelligence or homeland security careers.

★3263★ **Bay Area Crime and Intelligence Analysts Association**
E-mail: slawson@ci.santa-clara.ca.us
URL: http://www.baciaa.org/

Advocates for crime and intelligence analysis professionals through continuing education, networking opportunities, and professional resources.

★3264★ **California Crime and Intelligence Analysts Association**
E-mail: info@crimeanalyst.org
URL: http://www.crimeanalyst.org/

Promotes exchange of crime and intelligence analysis information and encourages increased professionalism in the crime and intelligence analysis field through learning and training opportunities for all members.

★3265★ **Central Intelligence Agency**
Office of Public Affairs
Washington, DC 20505
Ph: (703)482-0623   Fax: (703)482-1739
URL: http://www.cia.gov/careers/jobs/counterterrorism-analyst.html

Independent United States government agency providing national security intelligence to senior U.S. policymakers.

★3266★ **Central Valley Crime and Intelligence Analysts Association**
c/o Kim Miller, Pres.
PO Box 20756
Bakersfield, CA 93390
Ph: (661)391-7466
E-mail: info@cvciaa.org
URL: http://www.cvciaa.org/

Works to enhance crime and intelligence analysis as a tool in law enforcement.

★3267★ **Centre for Counterintelligence and Security Studies**
PO Box 11221
Alexandria, VA 22312
Ph: (703)642-7450   Fax: (703)642-7451
Fr: 800-779-4007
URL: http://cicentre.com/

Provides advanced counterintelligence, counterterrorism and security training, analysis and consulting.

★3268★ **Inland Empire Crime and Intelligence Analysts Association**
Ph: (909)387-3485   Fax: (909)387-0329
E-mail: ksmith@redlandspolice.org
URL: http://www.ieciaa.org/

Law enforcement professionals sharing crime analysis and intelligence knowledge, techniques and expertise.

★3269★ **IntelCenter**
PO Box 22572
Alexandria, VA 22304-9257
Ph: (703)370-2962   Fax: (703)370-1571
E-mail: info@intelcenter.com
URL: http://www.intelcenter.com/

Assists intelligence, counterterrorism and first responder professionals to prevent every act of terrorism, including the use of biological agents, chemical weapons, dirty devices or hijacked airliners. The firm studies terrorist groups and other threat actors as well as capabilities and intentions, warnings and indicators, operational characteristics and other points to better understand how to interdict terrorist operations and reduce the likelihood of future attacks.

★3270★ **International Association for Counterterrorism and Security Professionals**
Washington, DC
Ph: (703)933-3383
E-mail: info@redteamone.com
URL: http://www.redteamone.com/

Advocates on behalf of counterterrorism and security professionals for the purpose of identifying potential targets and tactics associated with an adversary or adversarial situation.

★3271★ **International Association of Crime Analysts**
9218 Metcalf Ave., Ste. 364
Overland Park, KS 66212
Fr: 800-609-3419
E-mail: iaca@iaca.net
URL: http://www.iaca.net

Crime analysts, intelligence analysts, police officers of all ranks, educators and students.

★3272★ **International Association of Law Enforcement Intelligence Analysts**
PO Box 13857
Richmond, VA 23225
Fax: (804)565-2059

E-mail: admin@ialeia.org
URL: http://www.ialeia.org/

Promotes the development and enhancement of law enforcement intelligence analysts.

★3273★ **International Counter-Terrorism Officers Association (ICTOA)**
Empire State Bldg.
350 5th Ave., Ste. 3304 - No. 16P
New York, NY 10118
Ph: (212)564-5048   Fax: (718)661-4044
E-mail: info@ictoa.org
URL: http://www.ictoa.org

Description: Promotes unity to combat and understand terrorism. Provides training, education and networking to enhance terrorism awareness. Supports members with advanced counter-terrorism measures. Ensures safety and security through international networking.

★3274★ **Law Enforcement Intelligence Unit**
4949 Broadway
Sacramento, CA 95820
Fr: 800-824-3860
E-mail: leiu@doj.ca.gov
URL: http://www.leiu-homepage.org/index.php

Provides leadership and promotes professionalism in the criminal intelligence community.

★3275★ **Memorial Institute for the Prevention of Terrorism**
621 N Robinson Ave., 4th Fl.
PO Box 889
Oklahoma City, OK 73102
Ph: (405)278-6300   Fax: (405)232-5132
URL: http://www.mipt.org/

Works to provide information about terrorism prevention and responder preparedness to better understand existing and growing terrorist threats.

★3276★ **Nathan Hale Institute (NHI)**
24 Harbor River Cir.
PMB 223
St. Helena Island, SC 29920-0192
Ph: (843)838-0191   Fax: (843)838-0192
E-mail: sulc@islc.net
URL: http://www.nathanhaleinstitute.org

Description: Seeks to increase public awareness of the "need for a strong intelligence community" and to stimulate scholarly pursuit of intelligence-related issues. Conducts research on domestic and foreign intelligence, particularly counterterrorism and the role of intelligence in a free society. Maintains speakers' bureau. Conducts interviews and briefings; provides counseling. Named for Nathan Hale (1755-76), U.S. intelligence officer famed for his comment: I only regret that I have but one life to lose for my country.

★3277★ National Geospatial-Intelligence Agency

4600 Sangamore Rd.
Bethesda, MD 20816-5003
Ph: (301)227-3132
E-mail: susan.h.meisner@nga.mil
URL: http://www.nga.mil/

Provides timely, relevant and accurate geospatial intelligence in support of national security.

★3278★ Northern Valley Crime and Intelligence Analyst Association

Ph: (530)889-7875
E-mail: novciaa@sbcglobal.net
URL: http://www.novciaa.org/

Provides a regional crime and intelligence analysis information network in the Northern California Valley area; promotes exchange of crime and intelligence analysis information to encourage increased professionalism in the field and to provide learning and training opportunities for members.

★3279★ San Diego Crime and Intelligence Analysis Association

4199 Normal St.
San Diego, CA 92103
URL: http://www.sdciaa.org/

Promotes development and enhancement of crime and intelligence analysis as a tool in law enforcement.

★3280★ Southern California Crime and Intelligence Analysts' Association

c/o Louise Ramirez
27050 Agoura Rd.
Agoura, CA 91301
URL: http://www.scciaa.net/

Promotes the development and enhancement of crime and intelligence analysis as a tool for effective law enforcement.

★3281★ Student Association on Terrorism and Security Analysis

McNaughton Hall, Ste. 402
Syracuse, NY 13244-1030
Ph: (315)443-2284   Fax: (315)443-4141
E-mail: satsa@maxwell.syr.edu
URL: http://student.maxwell.syr.edu/satsa/

Dedicated to the critical analysis of terrorism, counterterrorism policy, and national and international security issues.

★3282★ Texas Association of Crime and Intelligence Analysts

16526 Battlecreek Dr.
Houston, TX 77095
URL: http://www.tacia.org/

Crime and intelligence analysts, trainers, law enforcement officers, academia, the private sector, and others at the local, county, state or federal levels; provides guidance and assistance in order to ensure that the crime and intelligence analysis field benefits from effectual training, progressive education and a high degree of professionalism.

★3283★ United States Institute of Peace

1200 17th St. NW
Washington, DC 20036
Ph: (202)457-1700   Fax: (202)429-606?
URL: http://www.usip.org/

Independent, nonpartisan, national institution funded by Congress to help prevent manage and resolve threats to security and development worldwide, including interstate wars, internal armed conflicts, ethnic and religious strife, extremism, terrorism, and the proliferation of weapons of mass destruction

★3284★ United States Intelligence Community

Office of the Director of National
Intelligence
Washington, DC 20511
Ph: (703)733-8600
URL: http://www.intelligence.gov

Seeks to foster collaboration between the intelligence and counterintelligence agencies.

Couriers and Messengers

SOURCES OF HELP-WANTED ADS

★3285★ American Shipper

American Shipper
PO Box 4728
300 W Adams St., Ste. 600
Jacksonville, FL 32201-4728
Ph: (904)355-2601   Fax: (904)791-8836
Fr: 800-874-6422
URL: http://www.americanshipper.com

Monthly. $36.00/year for individuals. Transportation and shipping magazine.

★3286★ OAG Air Cargo Guide

OAG Worldwide
3025 Highland Pky., Ste. 200
Downers Grove, IL 60515-5561
Ph: (630)515-5300   Fax: (630)515-5301
Fr: 888-589-6340
URL: http://www.oag.com

Monthly. Guide to shipping freight by air containing current domestic, international and combination passenger cargo flight schedules.

EMPLOYER DIRECTORIES AND NETWORKING LISTS

★3287★ Air Cargo World-Express Delivery Guide Issue

Air Cargo World
1080 Holcomb Bridge Rd., Roswell
  Summit, Bldg. 200, Ste. 255
Roswell, GA 30076
Ph: (770)642-9170   Fax: (770)642-9982
URL: http://www.aircargoworld.com

Annual, March. Publication includes: List of approximately 200 air and truck express carriers. Entries include: Company name, address, contact person, phone, telex, services offered, mode of transportation, maximum size of package, method of payment, areas served. Arrangement: Alphabetical. Indexes: Organization name.

★3288★ Air Cargo World-Guide to Scheduled Air Carriers

Air Cargo World
1080 Holcomb Bridge Rd., Roswell
  Summit, Bldg. 200, Ste. 255
Roswell, GA 30076
Ph: (770)642-9170   Fax: (770)642-9982
URL: http://www.aircargoworld.com

Annual, January. Publication includes: Over 100 national and international carriers of air cargo. Entries include: Company name and location, phone, geographical area served, maximum size per item, type of delivery service, type of fleet, estimated cargo volume, and scheduling information. Arrangement: Alphabetical.

★3289★ DACA Directory

Distributors & Consolidators of America
2240 Bernays Dr.
York, PA 17404
Fr: 888-519-9195
URL: http://www.dacacarriers.com

Covers firms and individuals active in the shipping, warehousing, receiving, distribution, or consolidation of freight shipments.

★3290★ International Air Cargo Association Membership Directory

5600 NW 36th St., Ste. 620
Miami, FL 33122
Ph: (786)265-7011   Fax: (786)265-7012
E-mail: secgen@tiaca.org
URL: http://www.tiaca.org/

Directory of membership organizations listed alphabetically by category and industry.

★3291★ Messenger Courier Association of America-Network Guide and Membership Directory

Messenger Courier Association of
  America
1156 Fifteenth St. NW, Ste. 900
Washington, DC 20005
Ph: (202)785-3298   Fax: (202)223-9741
URL: http://www.mcaa.com/

Annual, January. $235.00. Covers approximately 500 member air courier companies. Entries include: Company name, office personnel, warehouse facilities area served. Arrangement: Geographical by airport city.

★3292★ Smart Mail

Pitney-Bowes
1 Elmcroft Rd.
Stamford, CT 06926-0700
Ph: (203)356-5000   Fax: (203)351-6835
Fr: 800-338-9115
URL: http://www.pitneybowes.com

Quarterly. Covers courier companies that provide same day, overnight and second-day delivery service of small packages throughout the United States. Entries include: Courier name, rates, phone, destinations, delivery times, types of service, hours of operation, company profile. Arrangement: Geographical.

★3293★ To Your Door Directory

To Your Door Enterprises, Inc.
PO Box 7116
Grayslake, IL 60030
Ph: (847)673-9653   Fax: (847)329-9653

Free. Covers Chicagoland businesses that deliver products/services to homes. Entries include: Company or service name, address, phone.

HANDBOOKS AND MANUALS

★3294★ Common Support Data Dictionary (CSDD)

Air Transport Association of America
Publications Department
1301 Pennsylvania Ave. NW, Ste, 1100
Washington, DC 20004
Ph: (202)626-4062   Fax: (202)626-4079
E-mail: pubs@airlines.org
URL: http://www.airlines.org/products/pubs/
product-detail.htm?Product=52

CD-ROM single user: $255.00 member, $365.00 non-member; CD-ROM multi user: $550.00 member, $785 non-member. Catalog of all data elements, terms, and tags that are used in association specifications; provides standardized names, definitions, and properties for data used within the air transport industry.

ONLINE JOB SOURCES AND SERVICES

★3295★ Jobkabob
300 Satellite Blvd.
Suwanee, GA 30024
E-mail: info@jobkabob.com
URL: http://www.jobkabob.com/

Online job source connecting job seekers with jobs using a proprietary search based on skills and experience, including positions for messengers and couriers.

OTHER SOURCES

★3296★ Air Cargo Annual Conference
Express Delivery & Logistics Association
14 W 3rd St., No. 200
Kansas City, MO 64105
Ph: (816)221-0254 Fax: (816)472-7765
Fr: 888-838-0761
E-mail: Kristy@robstan.com
URL: http://www.expressassociation.org/content.asp?contentID=53

Conference held annually in March in cooperation with the Air and Expedited Motor Carriers Association and the Airforwarders Association.

★3297★ Air and Expedited Motor Carriers Association
9532 Liberia Ave., Ste. 705
Manassas, VA 20110
Ph: (703)361-5208 Fax: (703)361-5028
E-mail: info@aemca.org
URL: http://aemca.org/

Advocates for air and expedited cargo trucking companies that provide ground transportation services, including airport-to-airport connecting runs and local air and expedited cargo pickup and delivery. Members include firms using a variety of equipment including tractor-trailers and straight trucks while serving an entire region or group of states or provinces; firms using mainly straight trucks and vans, serving metropolitan areas around one major regional airport; firms working with airports nationwide, running line hauls day and night providing connecting service; and ancillary providers of goods and services to the air and expedited freight trucking industry, such as computer software, communications equipment, roller bed equipment, truck bodies, insurance, legal counsel, etc.

★3298★ Air Transport Association of America
1301 Pennsylvania Ave. NW, Ste. 1100
Washington, DC 20004
Ph: (202)626-4000
E-mail: ata@airlines.org
URL: http://www.airlines.org

Trade organization representing principle U.S. airlines and their affiliates responsible for transporting airline passenger and cargo traffic.

★3299★ Airforwarders Association
1156 15th St. NW, Ste. 900
Washington, DC 20005
Ph: (202)393-2818 Fax: (202)223-9741
E-mail: bfried@airforwarders.org
URL: http://www.airforwarders.org/

Works as an alliance for the airforwarding industry, including indirect air carriers, cargo airlines, and affiliated businesses located in the U.S.

★3300★ Bicycle Courier Association of the District of Columbia
1220 L St. NW, Ste. 100-399
Washington, DC 20005
Ph: (202)521-5225
URL: http://dcbca.org/

Dedicated to protecting the rights of bicycle couriers in Washington, DC; works to ensure the future of the bike courier industry by establishing equitable understanding between couriers, the businesses they serve, and the communities in which they work; also promotes the bicycle as an alternative means of transportation.

★3301★ Courier Association of Seattle
756 Garfield St.
Seattle, WA 98109
Ph: (206)969-2267
E-mail: el_gato@speakeasy.org
URL: http://www.scn.org/

Promotes the interests of the bicycle messenger industry in Seattle, Washington.

★3302★ Express Delivery and Logistics Association (XLA)
14 W Third St., No. 200
Kansas City, MO 64105
Ph: (816)221-0254 Fax: (816)472-7765
Fr: 888-838-0761
E-mail: info@expressassociation.org
URL: http://www.expressassociation.org

Description: Represents air couriers, small package express delivery companies, airlines and associated industry members (75); supports companies and facilities such as airlines and airports. Seeks to: provide industry forum for ideas, educate members about new technologies within the industry; represent air couriers before governmental bodies; inform members of legislation affecting the industry; develop and maintain relationships among members. Conducts seminars and workshops.

★3303★ International Air Cargo Association
5600 NW 36th St., Ste. 620
Miami, FL 33122
Ph: (786)265-7011 Fax: (786)265-7012
E-mail: secgen@tiaca.org
URL: http://www.tiaca.org/

Supports and assists the air cargo industry and works to improve its role in world trade expansion.

★3304★ International Federation of Bike Messenger Associations (IFBMA)
PO Box 191443
San Francisco, CA 94119-1443
E-mail: ifbma@messengers.org
URL: http://www.messengers.org/ifbma

Description: Ensures the successful realization of an annual Cycle Messenger World Championships. Fosters a spirit of cooperation and community amongst bicycle messengers worldwide. Promotes the use of pedal power for commercial purposes.

★3305★ Messenger Courier Association of the Americas (MCAA)
1156 15th St. NW, Ste. 900
Washington, DC 20005
Ph: (202)785-3298 Fax: (202)223-9741
E-mail: bdecaprio@kellencompany.com
URL: http://www.mcaa.com

Description: Trade organization of local and international messenger courier companies. Addresses issues facing the industry, including municipal traffic ordinances that impede industry operations. Works to establish driver pools and to develop centralized core computer service bureaus for smaller courier companies. Provides training, discount purchasing programs, and legislative and regulatory issue monitoring. Conducts educational and research programs; compiles statistics.

★3306★ Minneapolis Bicycle Messenger Association
Minneapolis, MN
URL: http://www.mbma.blogspot.com/

Promotes the interests of bicycle messengers in the Minneapolis, Minnesota area.

★3307★ New York Bike Messenger Foundation
303 W 42nd St., Ste. 316
New York, NY 10036
URL: http://www.nybmf.org/

Supports bicycle messengers in New York City by providing assistance and financial support to injured messengers and promoting programs that assist in the research and advancement of the messenger workforce.

★3308★ New York State Messenger and Courier Association
150 Main St.
Port Washington, NY 11050
Ph: (516)883-1583
E-mail: info@nysmca.org
URL: http://www.nysmca.org/

Promotes the interests of the messenger and courier industry in New York.

★3309★ Philadelphia Bicycle Messenger Association
Philadelphia, PA
E-mail: danny@phillybma.org
URL: http://www.phillybma.org/

Promotes the interests of bicycle messengers in the Philadelphia, Pennsylvania area.

★3310★ Pittsburgh Bicycle Messenger Association
Pittsburgh, PA
URL: http://pittsburghmessenger.tripod.com/

Promotes the interests of bicycle messengers in the Pittsburgh, Pennsylvania area.

★3311★ San Francisco Bike Messenger Association
255 9th St.
San Francisco, CA 94103
E-mail: naccc07@nacc07sf.com
URL: http://www.ahalenia.com/sfbma/

Promotes unity and solidarity among bicycle messengers in the San Francisco Bay Area and to raise the status of the profession.

Credit Analysts

SOURCES OF HELP-WANTED ADS

★3312★ Accounting Horizons

American Accounting Association
5717 Bessie Dr.
Sarasota, FL 34233-2399
Ph: (941)921-7747   Fax: (941)923-4093
URL: http://aaahq.org/index.cfm

Quarterly. $265.00/year for individuals, print only; $265.00/year for individuals, online, vol.13 through current issue; $290.00/year for individuals, online and print. Publication covering the banking, finance, and accounting industries.

★3313★ American Banker

American Banker/Bond Buyer Inc.
1 State St. Plz. 27 Fl.
New York, NY 10004
Ph: (212)803-8200   Fax: (212)843-9600
Fr: 800-221-1809
URL: http://www.americanbanker.com

Daily. $995.00/year for individuals. Newspaper for senior executives in banking and other financial services industries. Coverage includes trends, analysis, and statistics of the legislative scene in Washington; finance; mortgages; technology; small business; and regional banking.

★3314★ Brookings Papers on Economic Activity

Brookings Institution Press
1775 Massashusetts Ave. NW
Washington, DC 20036-2188
Ph: (202)536-3600   Fax: (202)536-3623
Fr: 800-275-1447
URL: http://www.brookings.edu/press/journals.htm#bpea

Semiannual. $70.00/year for individuals; $84.00/year for institutions, other countries; $50.00/year for individuals; $64.00/year for individuals, foreign. Publication covering economics and business.

★3315★ Business Credit

National Association of Credit Management
8840 Columbia 100 Pkwy.
Columbia, MD 21045-2158
Ph: (410)740-5560   Fax: (410)740-5574
URL: http://www.nacm.org/bcmag/bcm_index.shtml

$54.00/year for individuals, business; $48.00/year for libraries; $60.00/year for Canada; $65.00/year for other countries. Magazine covering finance, business risk management, providing information for the extension of credit, maintenance of accounts receivable, and cash asset management.

★3316★ Commercial Lending Review

Aspen Publishers Inc.
76 Ninth Ave., 7th Fl.
New York, NY 10011
Ph: (212)771-0600   Fax: (212)771-0885
Fr: 800-638-8437
URL: http://www.commerciallendingreview.com/

Bimonthly. Journal covering all aspects of lending for commercial banks, community and regional banks and other financial institutions.

★3317★ Financial Management

Financial Management Association International
4202 East Fowler Ave.
BSN 3331
Tampa, FL 33620-5500
Ph: (813)974-2084   Fax: (813)974-3318
E-mail: fma@coba.usf.edu
URL: http://www.fma.org/fm.htm

Quarterly. $95.00/year for individuals; $20.00 for single issue. Journal covering business, economics, finance and management.

★3318★ Northwestern Financial Review

NFR Communications Inc.
7400 Metro Blvd., Ste. 217
Minneapolis, MN 55439
Ph: (952)835-2275
E-mail: web@nfrcom.com

URL: http://www.nfrcom.com

$94.00/year for individuals. Trade publication covering commercial banking.

★3319★ U.S. Banker

Thomson Financial
195 Broadway
New York, NY 10007
Ph: (646)822-2000   Fax: (646)822-3230
Fr: 888-605-3385
URL: http://www.americanbanker.com/usb.html

Monthly. $109.00/year for individuals; $139.00/year for individuals, Canada; $139.00/year for individuals, outside North America; $179.00/year for two years; $239.00 for two years, Canada; $239.00/year for two years, outside North America. Magazine serving the financial services industry.

PLACEMENT AND JOB REFERRAL SERVICES

★3320★ Commercial Finance Association (CFA)

225 W 34th St., Ste. 1815
New York, NY 10122
Ph: (212)594-3490   Fax: (212)564-6053
E-mail: info@cfa.com
URL: http://www.cfa.com

Members: Organizations engaged in asset-based financial services including commercial financing and factoring and lending money on a secured basis to small- and medium-sized business firms. **Purpose:** Acts as a forum for information and consideration about ideas, opportunities, and legislation concerning asset-based financial services. Seeks to improve the industry's legal and operational procedures. **Activities:** Offers job placement and reference services for members. Sponsors School for Field Examiners and other educational programs. Compiles statistics; conducts seminars and surveys; maintains Speaker's Bureau and 21 committees.

★3321★ National Association of Federal Credit Unions (NAFCU)

3138 10th St. N
Arlington, VA 22201-2149
Ph: (703)522-4770   Fax: (703)524-1082
Fr: 800-336-4644
E-mail: fbecker@nafcu.org
URL: http://www.nafcu.org

Description: Serves as federally chartered credit unions united for financial reform legislation and regulations impacting members. Provides information on the latest industry developments and proposed and final regulations issued by the National Credit Union Administration, the Federal Reserve, and other regulatory agencies. Represents members' interests before federal regulatory bodies and Congress. Maintains speakers' bureau and research information service; offers placement service; compiles statistics and holds educational conferences.

★3322★ National Bankers Association (NBA)

1513 P St. NW
Washington, DC 20005
Ph: (202)588-5432   Fax: (202)588-5443
E-mail: nahart@nationalbankers.org
URL: http://www.nationalbankers.org

Members: Minority banking institutions owned by minority individuals and institutions. **Purpose:** Serves as an advocate for the minority banking industry. Organizes banking services, government relations, marketing, scholarship, and technical assistance programs. **Activities:** Offers placement services; compiles statistics.

★3323★ Society of Certified Credit Executives (SCCE)

PO Box 390106
Minneapolis, MN 55439
Ph: (952)926-6547   Fax: (952)926-1624
E-mail: scce@collector.com
URL: http://www.acainternational.org

Description: A division of the International Credit Association. Credit executives who have been certified through SCCE's professional certification programs. Seeks to improve industry operations while expanding the knowledge of its members. Maintains placement service.

EMPLOYER DIRECTORIES AND NETWORKING LISTS

★3324★ Branches of Your State

Sheshunoff Information Services
807 Las Cimas Pkwy., Ste. 300
Austin, TX 78746-6597
Ph: (512)472-2244   Fax: (512)305-6575
Fr: 800-456-2340

Annual, February. $475.00. Covers, in separate state editions, banks, savings and loan branches, and credit unions. For those states without branch banking, individual banks, savings and loan institutions, and credit unions are listed. Entries include: Institution name, address, institution type, deposit totals, percent change over 12 months, percentage share of parent company's total deposits. Arrangement: Geographical.

★3325★ Career Opportunities in Banking, Finance, and Insurance

Facts On File Inc.
132 W 31st St., 17th Fl.
New York, NY 10001
Ph: (212)967-8800   Fax: 800-678-3633
Fr: 800-322-8755
URL: http://www.factsonfile.com/

Latest edition 2nd, February 2007. $49.50 for individuals; $44.45 for libraries. Publication includes: Lists of colleges with programs supporting banking, finance, and industry; professional associations; professional certifications; regulatory agencies; and Internet resources for career planning. Principal content of publication consists of job descriptions for professions in the banking, finance, and insurance industries. Indexes: Alphabetical.

★3326★ Corporate Finance Sourcebook

LexisNexis Group
PO Box 933
Dayton, OH 45401-0933
Ph: (937)865-6800   Fax: (518)487-3584
Fr: 800-543-6862
E-mail: nrpsales@marquiswhoswho.com
URL: http://www.financesourcebook.com

Annual; latest edition 2008. $695.00; $625.00 for standing orders. Covers securities research analysts; major private lenders; investment banking firms; commercial banks; United States-based foreign banks; commercial finance firms; leasing companies; foreign investment bankers in the United States; pension managers; banks that offer master trusts; cash managers; business insurance brokers; business real estate specialists. Lists about 3,400 firms; 14,500 key financial experts. Entries include: Firm name, address, phone, e-mail, and names and titles of officers, contacts, or specialists in corporate finance. Additional details are given as appropriate, including names of major clients, number of companies served, services, total assets, branch locations, years in business. Arrangement: Classified by line of business and then alphabetized within that line of business. Indexes: Firm name; personnel name; geographical.

★3327★ Credit Union Directory

National Credit Union Administration
1775 Duke St.
Alexandria, VA 22314-3428
Ph: (703)518-6300   Fax: (703)518-6660
URL: http://www.ncua.gov/data/directory/cudir.html

Annual, summer. Covers federal credit unions and state-chartered credit unions that are insured by the National Credit Union Share Insurance Fund; coverage includes United States possessions. Entries include: Credit union name, address, phone, charter number, principal operating officer, year-end total assets, number of members. Arrangement: Geographical.

★3328★ Employment Opportunities, USA

Washington Research Associates
1090 Vermont Ave. NW, Ste. 800
Washington, DC 20005
Ph: (202)408-7025

Annual, quarterly updates. Publication includes: List of over 1,000 employment contacts in companies and agencies in banking, arts, telecommunications, education, and 14 other industries and professions, including federal government. Entries include: Company name, name of representative, address, description of products or services, hiring and recruiting practices, training programs, and year established. Principal content is industry overviews, career news, employment opportunity information on 14 different job markets, and comprehensive guidance to career resources on the Internet. Arrangement: Classified by industry. Indexes: Occupation.

★3329★ National Bankers Association-Roster of Minority Banking Institutions

National Bankers Association
1513 P St. NW
Washington, DC 20005
Ph: (202)588-5432   Fax: (202)588-5443

Annual, October. Covers about 140 banks owned or controlled by minority group persons or women. Entries include: Bank name, address, phone, name of one executive. Arrangement: Geographical.

★3330★ NFCC Directory of Members

National Foundation for Credit Counseling
801 Roeder Rd., Ste. 900
Silver Spring, MD 20910
Ph: (301)589-5600   Fax: (301)495-5623

$5.00 for members; $10.50 for nonmembers. Covers about 1,300 affiliated non-profit consumer credit counseling services in the United States, Puerto Rico, and Canada, which provide non-profit education, counseling, and debt management programs for financial and housing issues. Entries include: Member name, address, phone, fax, name and title of contact, subsidiary and branch names and locations, names and titles of key personnel, description. Arrangement: Geographical. Indexes: Agency name, name of personnel.

★3331★ Roster of Minority Financial Institutions

U.S. Department of the Treasury
1500 Pennsylvania Ave. NW
Washington, DC 20220
Ph: (202)622-2000

Free. Covers about 170 commercial, minority-owned and controlled financial institutions participating in the Department of the Treasury's Minority Bank Deposit Program. Entries include: Name of institution, name and title of chief officer, address, phone, fax. Arrangement: Geographical.

★3332★ Thomson Bank Directory

Accuity
4709 W Golf Rd., Ste. 600
Skokie, IL 60076
Ph: (847)676-9600   Fax: (847)933-8101
Fr: 800-321-3373
URL: http://www.accuitysolutions.com/

Semiannual, June and December. $702.00 for individuals. Covers, in five volumes, about 11,000 banks and 50,000 branches of United States banks, and 60,000 foreign banks and branches engaged in foreign banking; Federal Reserve system and other United States government and state government banking agencies; the 500 largest North American and International commercial banks; paper and automated clearinghouses. Volumes 1 and 2 contain North American listings; volumes 3 and 4, international listings (also cited as "Thomson International Bank Directory"); volume 5, Worldwide Correspondents Guide containing key correspondent data to facilitate funds transfer. Entries include: For domestic banks–Bank name, address, phone, telex, cable, date established, routing number, charter type, bank holding company affiliation, memberships in Federal Reserve System and other banking organizations, principal officers by function performed, principal correspondent banks, and key financial data (deposits, etc.). For international banks–Bank name, address, phone, fax, telex, cable, SWIFT address, transit or sort codes within home country, ownership, financial data, names and titles of key personnel, branch locations. For branches–Bank name, address, phone, charter type, ownership and other details comparable to domestic bank listings. Arrangement: Geographical. Indexes: Alphabetical, geographical.

★3333★ Thomson North American Financial Institutions Directory

Accuity
4709 W Golf Rd., Ste. 600
Skokie, IL 60076
Ph: (847)676-9600   Fax: (847)933-8101
Fr: 800-321-3373
URL: http://www.tfp.com

Semiannual, January and July. $512.00 for individuals. Covers 15,000 banks and their branches; over 2,000 head offices, and 15,500 branches of savings and loan associations; over 5,500 credit unions with assets over $5 million; Federal Reserve System and other U.S. government and state government banking agencies; bank holding, commercial finance, and leasing companies; coverage includes the United States, Canada, Mexico, and Central America. Entries include: Bank name, address, phone, fax, telex, principal officers and directors, date established, financial data, association memberships, attorney or counsel, correspondent banks, out-of-town branch, holding company affiliation, ABA transit number and

routing symbol, MICR number with check digit, credit card(s) issued, trust powers, current par value and dividend of common stock, kind of charter. Arrangement: Geographical. Indexes: Alphabetical.

★3334★ Who's Who in Finance and Business

Marquis Who's Who L.L.C.
890 Mountain Ave., Ste. 300
New Providence, NJ 07974-1218
Ph: (908)673-1001   Fax: (908)673-1189
Fr: 800-473-7020
E-mail: finance@marquiswhoswho.com
URL: http://www.marquiswhoswho.com

Biennial; latest edition 36th, September 2007. $349.00 for individuals. Covers over 18,000 individuals. Entries include: Name, home and office addresses, personal, career, and family data; civic and political activities; memberships, publications, awards. Arrangement: Alphabetical.

HANDBOOKS AND MANUALS

★3335★ Careers in Banking and Finance

Rosen Publishing Group, Inc.
29 E. 21st St.
New York, NY 10010
Ph: (212)777-3017   Fax: 888-436-4643
Fr: 800-237-9932
URL: http://www.rosenpublishing.com/

Patricia Haddock. Revised edition, 2001. $31.95. 139 pages. Offers advice on job hunting. Describes jobs at all levels in banking and finance. Contains information about the types of financial organizations where the jobs are found, educational requirements, job duties, and salaries.

★3336★ Opportunities in Banking Careers

The McGraw-Hill Companies
PO Box 182604
Columbus, OH 43272
Fax: (614)759-3749   Fr: 877-883-5524
E-mail: customer.service@mcgraw-hill.com
URL: http://www.mcgraw-hill.com

Philip Perry. 1994. $15.95; $12.95 (paper). 146 pages. Discusses banking opportunities in a variety of settings: commercial banks, savings and loans, finance companies, and mortgage banks.

★3337★ Opportunities in Hospital Administration Careers

The McGraw-Hill Companies
PO Box 182604
Columbus, OH 43272
Fax: (614)759-3749   Fr: 877-883-5524
E-mail: customer.service@mcgraw-hill.com
URL: http://www.mcgraw-hill.com

I. Donald Snook. 2006. $13.95. 160 pages. Discusses opportunities for administrators in

a variety of management settings: hospital, department, clinic, group practice, HMO, mental health, and extended care facilities.

EMPLOYMENT AGENCIES AND SEARCH FIRMS

★3338★ Alfred Daniels & Associates Inc.

5795 Waverly Ave.
La Jolla, CA 92037
Ph: (858)459-4009
URL: http://www.alfreddaniels.com

Executive search firm.

★3339★ Bell Wishingrad Partners Inc.

230 Park Ave., Ste. 1000
New York, NY 10169
Ph: (212)949-6666

Executive search firm focused on the financial industry.

★3340★ Butterfass, Pepe & MacCallan Inc.

PO Box 721
Mahwah, NJ 07430
Ph: (201)560-9500   Fax: (201)560-9506
E-mail: staff@bpmi.com
URL: http://www.bpmi.com

Executive search firm.

★3341★ Cheryl Alexander & Associates

8588 Shadow Creek Dr.
Maple Grove, MN 55311
Ph: (763)416-4570
E-mail: cherylalexander@cherylalexander.com
URL: http://www.cherylalexander.com

Executive search firm.

★3342★ Cross Hill Partners LLC

245 Park Ave., Fl. 24
New York, NY 10167
Ph: (212)672-1604   Fax: (212)202-6316
E-mail: info@crosshillpartners.com
URL: http://www.crosshillpartners.com

Executive search firm.

★3343★ D. E. Foster Partners

230 W 41st St., Ste. 1550
New York, NY 10036
Ph: (646)452-4601   Fax: (212)893-2309
E-mail: recruiting@fosterpartners.com
URL: http://www.fosterpartners.com

Executive search firm affiliated with Daubenspeck and Associates Ltd. Branches in Washington, DC and Dallas.

★3344★ DBL Associates
1334 Park View Ave., Ste. 100
Manhattan Beach, CA 90266
Ph: (310)546-8121   Fax: (310)546-8122
E-mail: dlong@dblsearch.com
URL: http://www.dblsearch.com
Executive search firm focused on the financial industry.

★3345★ Douglas-Allen Inc.
Tower Square, 24th Fl.
PO Box 15368
Springfield, MA 01115
Ph: (413)739-0900
E-mail: research@douglas-allen.com
URL: http://www.douglas-allen.com
Executive search firm.

★3346★ Employment Advisors
815 Nicollet Mall
Minneapolis, MN 55402
Ph: (612)339-0521
Employment agency. Places candidates in variety of fields.

★3347★ Financial Professionals
4100 Spring Valley Rd., Ste. 307
Dallas, TX 75244
Ph: (972)991-8999   Fax: (972)702-0776
URL: http://www.fpstaff.net/
Executive search consultants with additional offices in Forth Worth and Houston.

★3348★ The Murphy Group
245 W Roosevelt Rd., Bldg.15, Ste.101
Chicago, IL 60605
Ph: (630)639-5110   Fax: (630)639-5113
E-mail: info@murphygroup.com
URL: http://www.murphygroup.com
Employment agency. Places personnel in a variety of positions. Additional offices located in Napierville, Park Ridge, and OakBrook.

★3349★ People Management International
E-mail: info@peoplemanagement.org
URL: http://www.esearchgroup.com
Executive search firm with 2 dozens offices around the world.

TRADESHOWS

★3350★ Pennsylvania Association of Community Bankers Convention
Pennsylvania Association of Community Bankers
2405 N. Front St.
Harrisburg, PA 17110
Ph: (717)231-7447   Fax: (717)231-7445
E-mail: pacb@pacb.org
URL: http://www.pacb.org

Annual. **Primary Exhibits:** Equipment, supplies, and services for community banks, thrifts, and associate firms.

OTHER SOURCES

★3351★ American Bankers Association (ABA)
1120 Connecticut Ave. NW
Washington, DC 20036
Ph: (202)663-5000   Fax: (202)663-7543
Fr: 800-BAN-KERS
E-mail: custserv@aba.com
URL: http://www.aba.com
Members: Members are principally commercial banks and trust companies; combined assets of members represent approximately 90% of the U.S. banking industry; approximately 94% of members are community banks with less than $500 million in assets. **Purpose:** Seeks to enhance the role of commercial bankers as preeminent providers of financial services through communications, research, legal action, lobbying of federal legislative and regulatory bodies, and education and training programs. Serves as spokesperson for the banking industry; facilitates exchange of information among members. Maintains the American Institute of Banking, an industry-sponsored adult education program. **Activities:** Conducts educational and training programs for bank employees and officers through a wide range of banking schools and national conferences. Maintains liaison with federal bank regulators; lobbies Congress on issues affecting commercial banks; testifies before congressional committees; represents members in U.S. postal rate proceedings. Serves as secretariat of the International Monetary Conference and the Financial Institutions Committee for the American National Standards Institute. Files briefs and lawsuits in major court cases affecting the industry. Conducts teleconferences with state banking associations on such issues as regulatory compliance; works to build consensus and coordinate activities of leading bank and financial service trade groups. Provides services to members including: public advocacy; news media contact; insurance program providing directors and officers with liability coverage, financial institution bond, and trust errors and omissions coverage; research service operated through ABA Center for Banking Information; fingerprint set processing in conjunction with the Federal Bureau of Investigation; discounts on operational and income-producing projects through the Corporation for American Banking. Conducts conferences, forums, and workshops covering subjects such as small business, consumer credit, agricultural and community banking, trust management, bank operations, and automation. Sponsors ABA Educational Foundation and the Personal Economics Program, which educates schoolchildren and the community on banking, economics, and personal finance.

★3352★ American Credit Union Mortgage Association (ACUMA)
PO Box 400955
Las Vegas, NV 89140
Ph: (702)933-2007   Fax: (702)949-3590
Fr: 877-442-2862
E-mail: bdorsa@acuma.org
URL: http://www.acuma.org
Members: Credit unions providing real estate lending services. **Purpose:** Promotes adherence to high standards of ethics and practice in the issuing of mortgage loans. **Activities:** Represents members' interests before regulatory agencies and industrial associations; conducts research and educational programs; maintains speakers' bureau; compiles statistics.

★3353★ American Financial Services Association (AFSA)
919 18th St. NW, Ste. 300
Washington, DC 20006-5517
Ph: (202)296-5544   Fax: (202)223-0321
E-mail: cstinebert@afsamail.org
URL: http://www.afsaonline.org
Description: Represents companies whose business is primarily direct credit lending to consumers and/or the purchase of sales finance paper on consumer goods. Has members that have insurance and retail subsidiaries; some are themselves subsidiaries of highly diversified parent corporations. Encourages the business of financing individuals and families for necessary and useful purposes at reasonable charges, including interest; promotes consumer understanding of basic money management principles as well as constructive uses of consumer credit. Includes educational services such as films, textbooks, and study units for the classroom and budgeting guides for individuals and families. Compiles statistical reports; offers seminars.

★3354★ Association for Financial Professionals (AFP)
4520 E West Hwy., Ste. 750
Bethesda, MD 20814
Ph: (301)907-2862   Fax: (301)907-2864
E-mail: afp@afponline.org
URL: http://www.afponline.org
Purpose: Seeks to establish a national forum for the exchange of concepts and techniques related to improving the management of treasury and the careers of professionals through research, education, publications, and recognition of the treasury management profession through a certification program. **Activities:** Conducts educational programs. Operates career center.

★3355★ Consumer Data Industry Association (CDIA)
1090 Vermont Ave. NW, Ste. 200
Washington, DC 20005-4905
Ph: (202)371-0910   Fax: (202)371-0134
Fr: (866)696-7227
E-mail: cdia@cdiaonline.org
URL: http://www.cdiaonline.org
Description: Serves as international associ-

ation of credit reporting and collection service offices. Maintains hall of fame and biographical archives; conducts specialized educational programs. Offers computerized services and compiles statistics.

★3356★ Credit Professionals International (CPI)

525 B N Laclede Station Rd.
St. Louis, MO 63119
Ph: (314)961-0031   Fax: (314)961-0040
E-mail: creditpro@creditprofessionals.org
URL: http://www.creditprofessionals.org

Description: Represents individuals employed in credit or collection departments of business firms or professional offices. Conducts educational program in credit work. Sponsors Career Club composed of members who have been involved in credit work for at least 25 years.

★3357★ Credit Union Executives Society (CUES)

PO Box 14167
Madison, WI 53708-0167
Ph: (608)271-2664   Fax: (608)271-2303
Fr: 800-252-2664
E-mail: cues@cues.org
URL: http://www.cues.org

Description: Advances the professional development of credit union CEOs, senior management and directors. Serves as an international membership association dedicated to the professional development of credit union CEOs, senior management and directors.

★3358★ Financial Occupations

Delphi Productions
3159 6th St.
Boulder, CO 80304
Ph: (303)443-2100   Fax: (303)443-4022
Fr: 888-443-2400
E-mail: support@delphivideo.com
URL: http://www.delphivideo.com

$95.00. 50 minutes. Part of the Careers for the 21st Century Video Library.

★3359★ National Association of Credit Management (NACM)

8840 Columbia 100 Pkwy.
Columbia, MD 21045
Ph: (410)740-5560   Fax: (410)740-5574
Fr: 800-955-8815
E-mail: robins@nacm.org
URL: http://www.nacm.org

Description: Credit and financial executives representing manufacturers, wholesalers, financial institutions, insurance companies, utilities, and other businesses interested in business credit. Promotes sound credit practices and legislation. Conducts Graduate School of Credit and Financial Management at Dartmouth College, Hanover, NH.

★3360★ National Association of Credit Union Services Organizations (NACUSO)

PMB 3419 Via Lido, No. 135
Newport Beach, CA 92663
Ph: (949)645-5296   Fax: (949)645-5297
Fr: 888-462-2870
E-mail: info@nacuso.org
URL: http://www.nacuso.org

Members: Credit union service organizations and their employees. **Purpose:** Promotes professional advancement of credit union service organization staff; seeks to insure adherence to high standards of ethics and practice among members. **Activities:** Conducts research and educational programs; formulates and enforces standards of conduct and practice; maintains speakers' bureau; compiles statistics.

★3361★ Risk Management Association

1801 Market St., Ste. 300
Philadelphia, PA 19103-1628
Ph: (215)446-4000   Fax: (215)446-4101
Fr: 800-677-7621
E-mail: member@rmahq.org
URL: http://www.rmahq.org/RMA

Members: Commercial and savings banks, and savings and loan, and other financial services companies. **Activities:** Conducts research and professional development activities in areas of loan administration, asset management, and commercial lending and credit to increase professionalism.

Dancers and Choreographers

SOURCES OF HELP-WANTED ADS

★3362★ AAHPERD Update

American Alliance for Health, Physical Education, Recreation & Dance
1900 Association Dr.
Reston, VA 20191
Ph: (703)476-3400   Fax: (703)476-9527
Fr: 800-213-7193
E-mail: info@aahperd.org
URL: http://www.aahperd.org

Description: Six issues/year. Provides news and information on the Alliance. Discusses current issues and research in the areas of health, physical education, recreation, dance, fitness, and adapted physical education. Recurring features include a calendar of events, reports of meetings, news of educational opportunities, job listings, notices of publications available, and columns titled President's Message, Membership Corner, and From the EVP's Desk.

★3363★ ArtSEARCH

Theatre Communications Group
520 8th Ave., 24th Fl.
New York, NY 10018-4156
Ph: (212)609-5900   Fax: (212)609-5901
E-mail: tcg@tcg.org
URL: http://www.tcg.org

Description: Biweekly. Publishes classified listings for job opportunities in the arts, especially theatre, dance, music, and educational institutions. Listings include opportunities in administration, artistic, education, production, and career development.

★3364★ Daily Variety

Reed Business Information
5700 Wilshire Blvd., Ste. 120
Los Angeles, CA 90036
Ph: (323)857-6600   Fax: (323)857-0494
URL: http://www.reedbusiness.com/index.asp?layout=theListProfile&

Daily. Global entertainment newspaper (tabloid).

★3365★ Dance Chronicle

Taylor & Francis Group Journals
325 Chestnut St., Ste. 800
Philadelphia, PA 19106
Ph: (215)625-8900   Fax: (215)625-8914
Fr: 800-354-1420
URL: http://www.tandf.co.uk/journals/titles/01472526.asp

$951.00/year for institutions, print and online; $903.00/year for institutions, online only; $115.00/year for individuals, print only. Journal covering a wide variety of topics, including dance and music, theater, film, literature, painting, and aesthetics.

★3366★ Dance Magazine

Dance Magazine Inc.
110 William St. 23rd Fl.
PO Box 2115
New York, NY 10038
Ph: (646)459-4800   Fax: (646)674-0102
URL: http://www.dancemagazine.com

Monthly. $65.00 for two years; $47.00/year for Canada; $67.00/year for other countries; $100.00/year for other countries, airmail; $35.00/year for individuals. Performing arts magazine featuring all forms of dance with profiles, news, photos, reviews of performances, and information on books, videos, films, schools, health, and technique.

★3367★ Music and Media

VNU Business Media USA
770 Broadway
New York, NY 10003
Ph: (646)654-4500
URL: http://www.vnubusinessmedia.com

Weekly. Publication covering the music and entertainment industries.

★3368★ Ross Reports Television and Film

VNU Business Media USA
770 Broadway
New York, NY 10003
Ph: (646)654-4500
URL: http://www.vnubusinessmedia.com/box/bp/div_fpa_pa_rossr.html

Bimonthly. $65.00/year for individuals; $10.00/year for individuals. Trade publication covering talent agents and casting directors in New York and Los Angeles, as well as television and film production. Special national issue of agents and casting directors is published annually. Sister publication to Back Stage, Back Stage West.

★3369★ Strategies

American Alliance for Health, Physical Education, Recreation & Dance
1900 Association Dr.
Reston, VA 20191-1598
Ph: (703)476-3400   Fax: (703)476-9527
Fr: 800-213-7193
E-mail: strategies@aahperd.org
URL: http://www.aahperd.org/naspe/template.cfm?template=strategie

Bimonthly. $115.00/year for U.S. and Canada, institution; $45.00/year for nonmembers, U.S. and Canada, individual; $127.00/year for institutions, other countries; $57.00/year for nonmembers, foreign, individual. Journal providing practical, hands-on information to physical educators and coaches.

★3370★ Variety

Reed Business Information
5700 Wilshire Blvd., Ste. 120
Los Angeles, CA 90036
Ph: (323)857-6600   Fax: (323)857-0494
URL: http://www.variety.com

Weekly. $259.00/year for individuals, year; $25.00/year for individuals, monthly. Newspaper reporting on theatre, television, radio, music, records, and movies.

PLACEMENT AND JOB REFERRAL SERVICES

★3371★ Dance Notation Bureau (DNB)

151 W 30th St., Ste. 202
New York, NY 10001-4007
Ph: (212)564-0985   Fax: (212)216-9027
E-mail: dnbinfo@dancenotation.org

URL: http://www.dancenotation.org

Description: Documents and preserves dance works through the use of graphic notation. Conducts research into movement-related analysis techniques and programs. Maintains extension at Ohio State University, Columbus. Maintains placement service; assists choreographers in copyrighting, licensing, and restaging of their dance works. Offers service for dance reconstructors and circulating library materials to members. Maintains archive of original Labanotated dance scores in the world.

★3372★ Institute of American Indian Arts (IAIA)

83 Avan Nu Po Rd.
Santa Fe, NM 87508
Ph: (505)424-2300   Fax: (505)424-3900
Fr: 800-804-6423
E-mail: setzel@iaia.edu
URL: http://www.iaia.edu

Description: Federally chartered private institution. Offers learning opportunities in the arts and crafts to Native American youth (Indian, Eskimo, or Aleut). Emphasis is placed upon Indian traditions as the basis for creative expression in fine arts including painting, sculpture, museum studies, creative writing, printmaking, photography, communications, design, and dance, as well as training in metal crafts, jewelry, ceramics, textiles, and various traditional crafts. Students are encouraged to identify with their heritage and to be aware of themselves as members of a race rich in architecture, the fine arts, music, pageantry, and the humanities. All programs are based on elements of the Native American cultural heritage that emphasizes differences between Native American and non-Native American cultures. Sponsors Indian arts-oriented junior college offering Associate of Fine Arts degrees in various fields as well as seminars, an exhibition program, and traveling exhibits. Maintains extensive library, museum, and biographical archives. Provides placement service.

★3373★ Texas International Theatrical Arts Society (TITAS)

3625 N Hall St., Ste. 740
Dallas, TX 75219
Ph: (214)528-6112   Fax: (214)528-2617
E-mail: csantos@titas.org
URL: http://www.titas.org

Description: Theatrical agencies working to book entertainers and international acts into all live music venues. Provides placement service; conducts educational seminars.

★3374★ United States National Institute of Dance (USNID)

38 S Arlington Ave.
PO Box 245
East Orange, NJ 07019
Ph: (973)673-9225

Members: Participants include dance teachers, students, colleges and universities, dance companies, and local and internation-

al dance teachers' organizations. **Purpose:** Seeks to: provide dance teachers with international variations and techniques for improving artistic qualities and teaching methods; establish a uniform method of teaching all forms of dance at the highest professional level; provide an international network of consultation and counseling services for dance teachers and dancers. **Activities:** Maintains speakers' bureau; offers placement and children's services; sponsors competitions. Conducts demonstrations, lectures, and certificate correspondence courses. Produces new correspondence course "How to Prevent and Care for Dance Injuries".

EMPLOYER DIRECTORIES AND NETWORKING LISTS

★3375★ Contemporary Theatre, Film, and Television

Gale, Cengage Learning
27500 Drake Rd.
Farmington Hills, MI 48331-3535
Ph: (248)699-4253   Fax: (248)699-8065
Fr: 800-877-4253
URL: http://www.gale.com

Bimonthly, volume 72; published December, 2006. $215.00 for individuals. Covers more than 15,000 leading and up-and-coming performers, directors, writers, producers, designers, managers, choreographers, technicians, composers, executives, and dancers in the United States, Canada, Great Britain and the rest of the world. Each volume includes updated biographies for people listed in previous volumes and in "Who's Who in the Theatre," which this series has superseded. Entries include: Name, agent and/or office addresses, personal and career data; stage, film, and television credits; writings, awards, other information. Arrangement: Alphabetical. Indexes: Cumulative name index also covers entries in "Who's Who in the Theatre" editions 1-17 and in "Who Was Who in the Theatre.".

★3376★ Employment Opportunities, USA

Washington Research Associates
1090 Vermont Ave. NW, Ste. 800
Washington, DC 20005
Ph: (202)408-7025

Annual, quarterly updates. Publication includes: List of over 1,000 employment contacts in companies and agencies in banking, arts, telecommunications, education, and 14 other industries and professions, including federal government. Entries include: Company name, name of representative, address, description of products or services, hiring and recruiting practices, training programs, and year established. Principal content is industry overviews, career news, employment opportunity information on 14 different job markets, and comprehensive guidance to career resources on the Internet. Arrange-

ment: Classified by industry. Indexes: Occupation.

★3377★ Musical America International Directory of the Performing Arts

Commonwealth Business Media Inc.
400 Windsor Corporate Pk.
50 Millstone Rd., Ste. 200
East Windsor, NJ 08520-1415
Ph: (609)371-7700   Fr: 800-221-5488
E-mail: info@musicalamerican.com
URL: http://www.musicalamerica.com

Annual, December; latest edition 2001. Covers U.S., Canadian, and international orchestras, musicians, singers, performing arts series, dance and opera companies, festivals, contests, foundations and awards, publishers of music, artist managers, booking agents, music magazines, and service and professional music organizations. Section for U.S. and Canada also includes listings of choral groups, music schools and departments, and newspaper music critics; international directory section also lists concert managers. Entries include: Name of organization, institution, address, phone, fax, URL, e-mail addresses, key personnel; most entries include name of contact, manager, conductor, etc. For schools–Number of students and faculty. For orchestras–Number of concerts and seats. Other entries show similar details as appropriate. Arrangement: Geographical. Indexes: Alphabetical and by category.

★3378★ National Directory of Arts Internships

National Network for Artist Placement
935 W Ave. 37
Los Angeles, CA 90065
Ph: (323)222-4035   Fax: (323)225-5711
Fr: 800-354-5348
URL: http://www.artistplacement.com

Biennial, odd years; latest edition 10th. $95.00 for individuals. Covers over 5,000 internship opportunities in dance, music, theater, art, design, film, and video & over 1,250 host organizations. Entries include: Name of sponsoring organization, address, name of contact; description of positions available, eligibility requirements, stipend or salary (if any), application procedures. Arrangement: Classified by discipline, then geographical.

★3379★ Regional Theater Directory

American Theatre Works Inc.
2349 W. Rd.
PO Box 159
Dorset, VT 05251
Ph: (802)867-9333   Fax: (802)867-2297
URL: http://www.theatredirectories.com

Annual, May. $29.50 for individuals. Covers regional theater companies and dinner theatres with employment opportunities in acting, design, production, and management. Entries include: Company name, address, phone, name and title of contact; type of company, activities, and size of house; whether union affiliated, whether nonprofit or commercial; year established; hiring procedure and number of positions hired annually/seasonally; description of stage; internships; description of artistic policy and audience. Arrangement: Geographical. Indexes: Company name, type of plays produced.

★3380★ *Stern's Directory*

Dance Magazine Inc.
110 William St. 23rd Fl.
PO Box 2115
New York, NY 10038
Ph: (646)459-4800   Fax: (646)674-0102
E-mail: sterns@dancemagazine.com
URL: http://www.dancemagazine.com/

Annual, September, latest edition 2002. Covers over 10,000 dance companies, managers and artists' representatives; support services presenting organizations, festivals, funding sources, dance schools, and dance merchandise. Entries include: Company, institution or personal name, address, phone, cable, telex, fax, e-mail address, names of key personnel, and brief descriptions of services offered. Arrangement: Classified by performing arts category as well as product or service. Indexes: Advertisers.

★3381★ *Summer Theater Directory*

American Theatre Works Inc.
2349 W. Rd.
PO Box 159
Dorset, VT 05251
Ph: (802)867-9333   Fax: (802)867-2297
URL: http://www.theatredirectories.com

Annual, December. $29.50 for individuals. Covers summer theater companies, theme parks and cruise lines that offer employment opportunities in acting, design, production, and management; summer theater training programs. Entries include: Company name, address, phone, name and title of contact; type of company, activities and size of house; whether union affiliated, whether nonprofit or commercial; year established; hiring procedure and number of positions hired annually/seasonally; description of stage; internships; description of company's artistic goals and audience. Arrangement: Geographical. Indexes: Company name.

HANDBOOKS AND MANUALS

★3382★ *The Art of Making Dances*

Textbook Publishers
27315 Jefferson J2
Temecula, CA 92590
Fax: (909)767-0133   Fr: (866)230-7238

Doris Humphrey. January 2003. $21.95.(paperback) 192 pages.

★3383★ *Ballet Dancers in Career Transition: Sixteen Success Stories*

McFarland & Company, Inc. Publishers
PO Box 611
Jefferson, NC 28640
Ph: (336)246-4460   Fax: (336)246-5018
Fr: 800-253-2187
E-mail: info@mcfarlandpub.com
URL: http://www.mcfarlandpub.com/

Nancy Upper. May 2004. $39.95 (paper). Illustrated. 272 Pages.

★3384★ *Career Opportunities in Theater and the Performing Arts*

Checkmark Books
132 W. 31st St., 17th Fl.
New York, NY 10001-2006
Ph: (212)967-8800   Fax: (212)967-9196
Fr: 800-322-8755

Shelly Field. Third edition, 2006. $18.95 (paper). 320 pages. Offers a complete range of information about job opportunities in the performing arts. Part of Career Opportunities Series.

★3385★ *Careers for Night Owls and Other Insomniacs*

The McGraw-Hill Companies
PO Box 182604
Columbus, OH 43272
Fax: (614)759-3749   Fr: 877-883-5524
E-mail: customer.service@mcgraw-hill.com
URL: http://www.mcgraw-hill.com

Louise Miller. Second edition, 2002. $12.95 (paper). 160 pages.

★3386★ *Careers for the Stagestruck and Other Dramatic Types*

The McGraw-Hill Companies
PO Box 182604
Columbus, OH 43272
Fax: (614)759-3749   Fr: 877-883-5524
E-mail: customer.service@mcgraw-hill.com
URL: http://www.mcgraw-hill.com

Lucia Mauro. Second edition, 2004. $12.95 (paper). 160 pages. Includes bibliographical references.

★3387★ *Opportunities in Entertainment Careers*

The McGraw-Hill Companies
PO Box 182604
Columbus, OH 43272
Fax: (614)759-3749   Fr: 877-883-5524
E-mail: customer.service@mcgraw-hill.com
URL: http://www.mcgraw-hill.com

Jan Goldberg. 1999. $11.95 (paper). 148 pages.

★3388★ *Resumes for Performing Arts Careers*

The McGraw-Hill Companies
PO Box 182604
Columbus, OH 43272
Fax: (614)759-3749   Fr: 877-883-5524
E-mail: customer.service@mcgraw-hill.com

URL: http://www.mcgraw-hill.com

2004. $10.95 (paper). 160 pages.

TRADESHOWS

★3389★ *International Society for the Performing Arts Foundation Annual Conference*

International Society for the Performing Arts Foundation
17 Purdy Ave.
PO Box 909
Rye, NY 10580
Ph: (914)921-1550   Fax: (914)921-1593
E-mail: info@ispa.org
URL: http://www.ispa.org

Annual, and December. **Primary Exhibits:** Information of performing artists, agents and managers. **Dates and Locations:** 2008 Jan 08-10; New York, NY.

★3390★ *Texas Association for Health, Physical Education, Recreation, and Dance Annual State Convention*

Texas Association for Health, Physical Education, Recreation, and Dance
6300 La Calma Dr., Ste. 410
Austin, TX 78752-3890
Ph: (512)459-1299   Fax: (512)459-1290
Fr: 800-880-7300
E-mail: tahperd@tahperd.org
URL: http://www.tahperd.org

Annual. **Primary Exhibits:** Publications, equipment, and supplies for health, physical education, recreation, and dance.

OTHER SOURCES

★3391★ *American Dance Guild (ADG)*

PO Box 2006
Lenox Hill Sta.
New York, NY 10021
Ph: (212)932-2789
E-mail: info@americandanceguild.org
URL: http://www.americandanceguild.org

Description: Serves the dance professional by providing: a networking system between dance artists and dance educators; an informed voice on behalf of the dance field to governmental, educational and corporate institutions and the general public; international dance festivals, conferences and dance film festivals; educational publications and videos; the ADG Fannie Weiss Scholarship; the ADG Harkness Resource for Dance Study.

★3392★ International Tap Association (ITA)

PO Box 356
Boulder, CO 80306
Ph: (303)443-7989   Fax: (303)443-7992
E-mail: ita@tapdance.org
URL: http://www.tapdance.org/tap/ita/index.html

Description: Represents the interests of tap dancers, performers, studios, choreographers, teachers, scholars, historians, students, and other tap enthusiasts. Promotes understanding, preservation, and development of tap dance as an art form. Encourages the creation of new tap performance venues and touring circuits. Preserves the history of tap through archival documentation and research. Establishes support mechanisms and communication networks for tap.

★3393★ Media and the Arts Occupations

Delphi Productions
3159 6th St.
Boulder, CO 80304
Ph: (303)443-2100   Fax: (303)443-4022
Fr: 888-443-2400
E-mail: support@delphivideo.com
URL: http://www.delphivideo.com

$95.00. 50 minutes. Part of the Careers for the 21st Century Video Library.

★3394★ National Dance Association (NDA)

1900 Association Dr.
Reston, VA 20191
Ph: (703)476-3400   Fax: (703)476-9527
Fr: 800-213-7193
E-mail: nda@aahperd.org
URL: http://www.aahperd.org/nda

Description: Dance educators, choreographers, schools and dance/arts administrators, researchers, performers, dance medicine/science specialists, technologists, therapists and others associated with dance/arts education. Works with 160 federal and state agencies, arts and education associations, foundations, and businesses and corporations to ensure that: (1) quality dance/arts education is available to all Americans regardless of age, sex, ability, interest, or culture; and (2) quality dance/arts education becomes a part of U.S. education for all children.

Database Administrators

SOURCES OF HELP-WANTED ADS

★3395★ Communications of the ACM

Association for Computing Machinery
2 Penn Plz., Ste. 701
New York, NY 10121-0701
Ph: (212)869-7440   Fax: (212)944-1318
Fr: 800-342-6626
URL: http://www.acm.org/pubs/cacm/

Monthly. $179.00/year for nonmembers; $36.00/year for members. Computing news magazine.

★3396★ Computerworld

101 Communications
9121 Oakdale Ave., Ste. 101
Chatsworth, CA 91311
Ph: (818)734-1520   Fax: (818)734-1522
URL: http://www.computerworld.com

Weekly. $99.00/year for individuals, new Australian subscribers; $99.00/year for individuals, renewals Australian; $250.00/year for other countries, airmail; $375.00/year for other countries, overseas (airmail). Newspaper for information systems executives.

★3397★ Computing Surveys (CSUR)

Association for Computing Machinery
2 Penn Plz., Ste. 701
New York, NY 10121-0701
Ph: (212)869-7440   Fax: (212)944-1318
Fr: 800-342-6626
URL: http://www.acm.org/pubs/surveys/

Quarterly. $185.00 for nonmembers, print only yearly rate; $148.00/year for nonmembers, online only; $222.00 for single issue, online & print; $208.00 for single issue, print with expedited air; $245.00 for single issue, online & print with expedited air. Journal presenting surveys and tutorials in computer science.

★3398★ Datamation

Reed Business Information
225 Wyman St.
Waltham, MA 02451-1216
URL: http://www.datamation.com

Semimonthly. Magazine on computers and information processing.

★3399★ Digital News & Review

Reed Business Information
225 Wyman St.
Waltham, MA 02451-1216

Semimonthly. Free to qualified subscribers. Covers information storage and retrieval and data systems.

★3400★ InformationWeek

CMP Media L.L.C.
600 Community Dr.
Manhasset, NY 11030
Ph: (516)562-5000   Fax: (516)562-7830
URL: http://www.informationweek.com

Weekly. Free to qualified subscribers. Magazine focusing on data and information processing news and strategies.

★3401★ InfoWorld

InfoWorld Media Group
501 Second St.
San Francisco, CA 94107
Fr: 800-227-8365
E-mail: letters@infoworld.com
URL: http://www.infoworld.com/

Weekly. Free to qualified subscribers; $180.00/year for individuals. Weekly publication.

★3402★ Intelligent Enterprise

CMP Media L.L.C.
600 Community Dr.
Manhasset, NY 11030
Ph: (516)562-5000   Fax: (516)562-7830
E-mail: tgibb@cmp.com
URL: http://www.intelligententerprise.com

Periodic. Free. Magazine serving business and IT professionals.

★3403★ iSeries News Magazine

Penton Media
221 E 29th St.
Loveland, CO 80538
Ph: (970)663-4700   Fax: (970)667-2321
Fr: 800-621-1544
E-mail: service@iseriesnetwork.com
URL: http://www.systeminetwork.com/info/networkpubs/news400/about

$149.00/year for U.S. and Canada; $199.00/year for other countries. Trade magazine for programmers and data processing managers who use IBM iSeries.

EMPLOYER DIRECTORIES AND NETWORKING LISTS

★3404★ Computer Directory

Computer Directories Inc.
23815 Nichols Sawmill Rd.
Hockley, TX 77447
Ph: (281)356-7880   Fr: 800-234-4353
URL: http://www.compdirinc.com

Annual, fall. Covers approximately 130,000 computer installation companies; 19 separate volumes for Alaska/Hawaii, Connecticut/New Jersey, Dallas/Ft. Worth, Eastern Seaboard, Far Midwest, Houston, Illinois, Midatlantic, Midcentral, Mideast, Minnesota/Wisconsin, North Central, New England, New York Metro, Northwest, Ohio, Pennsylvania/West Virginia, Southeast, and Southwest Texas. Entries include: Company name, address, phone, fax, e-mail, name and title of contact, hardware used, software application, operating system, programming language, computer graphics, networking system. Arrangement: Geographical. Indexes: Alphabetical; industry; hardware.

★3405★ Information Sources

Software & Information Industry Association
1090 Vermont Ave. NW, 6th Fl.
Washington, DC 20005-4095
Ph: (202)289-7442   Fax: (202)289-7097
Fr: 800-388-7478

URL: http://www.siia.net/

Continuous. Covers more than 800 companies involved in the creation, distribution, and use of information products, services, and technology. Entries are prepared by companies described. Entries include: Company name, address, phone, names of executives, international partners, regional offices, trade and brand names, and description of products and services. Arrangement: Alphabetical. Indexes: Product; personal name; trade name; geographical; corporate parents; international and niche markets.

★3406★ Signal Magazine-AFCEA Source Book Issue

Armed Forces Communications & Electronics Association (AFCEA)
4400 Fair Lakes Ct.
Fairfax, VA 22033
Ph: (703)631-6100   Fax: (703)631-6169
Fr: 800-336-4583
E-mail: signal@afcea.org
URL: http://www.afcea.org/sourcebook

Annual; latest edition 2007. Publication includes: List of member companies concerned with communications, design, production, maintenance and operation of communications, electronics, command and control, computers, intelligence systems and imagery. Entries include: Company name, address, phone, names and titles of key personnel, financial keys, trade and brand names, products or services, affiliations, description of organizational purpose, objectives. Arrangement: Alphabetical. Indexes: By disciplines.

HANDBOOKS AND MANUALS

★3407★ Careers for Computer Buffs and Other Technological Types

The McGraw-Hill Companies
PO Box 182604
Columbus, OH 43272
Fax: (614)759-3749   Fr: 877-883-5524
E-mail: customer.service@mcgraw-hill.com
URL: http://www.mcgraw-hill.com

Marjorie Eberts and Margaret Gisler. Third edition, 2006. $13.95 (paper). 160 pages. Suggested jobs in a wide range of settings, from the office to the outdoors.

★3408★ Careers in Computers

The McGraw-Hill Companies
PO Box 182604
Columbus, OH 43272
Fax: (614)759-3749   Fr: 877-883-5524
E-mail: customer.service@mcgraw-hill.com
URL: http://www.mcgraw-hill.com

Lila B. Stair and Leslie Stair. 2002. $19.95; $14.95 (paper). 192 pages. Describes trends affecting computer careers and explores a wide range of job opportunities from programming to consulting. Provides job qualifications, salary data, job market information,

personal and educational requirements, career paths, and the place of the job in the organizational structure. Offers advice on education, certification, and job search.

★3409★ Careers in Electronic Information: An Insider's Guide to the Information Job Market

National Federation of Abstracting and Information Services
1518 Walnut St., Ste. 1004
Philadelphia, PA 19102
Ph: (215)893-1561   Fax: (215)893-1564
E-mail: NFAIS@nfais.org
URL: http://www.nfais.org/

Wendy K. Wicks. 1997. $39.00 (paper). 184 pages.

★3410★ The Digital Frontier Job & Opportunity Finder

Moon Lake Media
PO Box 251466
Los Angeles, CA 90025
Ph: (310)535-2453

Don B. Altman. 1996. $19.95 (paper). 245 pages.

★3411★ Great Jobs for Computer Science Majors

The McGraw-Hill Companies
PO Box 182604
Columbus, OH 43272
Fax: (614)759-3749   Fr: 877-883-5524
E-mail: customer.service@mcgraw-hill.com
URL: http://www.mcgraw-hill.com

Jan Goldberg, Stephen Lambert, Julie De-Galan. Second edition, 2002. $14.95 (paper). 224 pages.

★3412★ Job Seekers Guide to Silicon Valley Recruiters

John Wily and Sons, Inc.
605 Third Ave., 4th Fl.
New York, NY 10158-0012
Ph: (212)850-6276   Fax: (212)850-8641

Christopher W. Hunt, Scott A. Scanlon. First edition, 1998. $19.95 (paper). 371 pages. Includes a list of 2,400 recruiters specializing in high technology positions and explains how to work with them.

★3413★ The JobBank Guide to Computer and High-Tech Companies

Adams Media Corp.
57 Littlefield St.
Avon, MA 02322
Ph: (508)427-7100   Fax: (508)427-6790
Fr: 800-872-5627
URL: http://www.adamsmedia.com

Steven Graber, Marcie Dipietro, and Michelle Roy Kelly. Second edition, 1999. $17.95 (paper). 700 pages. Contains profiles of more than 4,500 high-tech employers.

★3414★ Peterson's Job Opportunities in Engineering and Technology

Peterson's Guides
2000 Lenox Dr.
Box 67005
Lawrenceville, NJ 08648
Ph: (609)896-1800   Fax: (609)896-4531
Fr: 800-338-3282
E-mail: custsvc@petersons.com
URL: http://www.petersons.com

Compiled by the Peterson's staff. Fourth edition, 1996. $21.95 (paper). 379 pages. Profiles 2,000 high-tech companies looking primarily for technical personnel in such fields as biotechnology, telecommunications, software, computers and peripherals, defense, and aerospace. Contains job-search strategies and career options to help match education and expertise to the job market. Indexed geographically, by industry, and by hiring needs.

EMPLOYMENT AGENCIES AND SEARCH FIRMS

★3415★ Cardinal Mark Inc.

17113 Minnetonka Blvd., Ste. 112
Minnetonka, MN 55345
Ph: (952)314-4636   Fax: (610)228-7390
E-mail: jimz@cardinalmark.com
URL: http://www.cardinalmark.com

Executive search firm concentrated on telecommunication industry.

★3416★ Career Development Services

150 State St.
Rochester, NY 14614
Ph: (585)244-0765   Fax: (585)244-7115
Fr: 800-736-6710
E-mail: info@careerdev.org
URL: http://www.careerdev.org

Employment agency.

★3417★ Huntington Personnel Consultants, Inc.

PO Box 1077
Huntington, NY 11743-0640
Ph: (516)549-8888

Executive search firm and employment agency.

ONLINE JOB SOURCES AND SERVICES

★3418★ ComputerJobs.com

280 Interstate North Cir., SE, Ste. 300
Atlanta, GA 30339-2411
Ph: 800-850-0045
URL: http://www.computerjobs.com

Description: The site is an employment tool for technology professionals. Information on positions is updated hourly for seekers. Jobs may be searched by skill, or by location nationally or in a specific state or city job market. Contains thousands of job postings. National jobs may be posted for free. Also career resources for IT professionals.

★3419★ **Computerwork.com**
Fr: 800-691-8413
E-mail: contactus@computerwork.com
URL: http://www.computerwork.com/

Description: Job search and resume submission service for professionals in information technology.

★3420★ **Guru.com**
5001 Baum Blvd., Ste. 760
Pittsburgh, PA 15213
Ph: (412)687-1316   Fax: (412)687-4466
URL: http://www.guru.com

Description: Job board specializing in contract jobs for creative and information technology professionals. Also provides online incorporation and educational opportunities for independent contractors along with articles and advice.

★3421★ **Ittalent.com**
E-mail: ewsmith@ITtalent.com
URL: http://www.ittalent.com

Description: Job search and resume submission service for professionals in information technology.

★3422★ **ZDNet Tech Jobs**
URL: http://www.zdnet.com/

Description: Site houses a listing of national employment opportunities for professionals in high tech fields. Also contains resume building tips and relocation resources.

OTHER SOURCES

★3423★ **Computer Occupations**
Delphi Productions
3159 6th St.
Boulder, CO 80304
Ph: (303)443-2100   Fax: (303)443-4022
Fr: 888-443-2400
E-mail: support@delphivideo.com
URL: http://www.delphivideo.com

$95.00. 50 minutes. Part of the Careers for the 21st Century Video Library.

★3424★ **Information Technology Occupations**
Delphi Productions
3159 6th St.
Boulder, CO 80304
Ph: (303)443-2100   Fax: (303)443-4022
Fr: 888-443-2400
E-mail: support@delphivideo.com
URL: http://www.delphivideo.com

$95.00. 52 minutes. Part of the Emerging Careers Video Library.

★3425★ **Information Technology Services**
Cambridge Educational
PO Box 2053
Princeton, NJ 08543-2053
Ph: 800-257-5126   Fax: (609)671-0266
Fr: 800-468-4227
E-mail: custserv@films.com
URL: http://www.cambridgeeducational.com

VHS and DVD. $89.95. 2002. 19 minutes. Part of the Career Cluster Series.

Dental Assistants

SOURCES OF HELP-WANTED ADS

★3426★ American Dental Hygienists' Association Access

American Dental Hygienists' Association
444 North Michigan Ave., Ste. 3400
Chicago, IL 60611
Ph: (312)440-8904   Fr: 800-243-ADHA
URL: http://www.adha.org/publications

$48.00/year for individuals; $85.00 for two years; $120.00/year for individuals, for 3 years. Magazine covering current dental hygiene topics, regulatory and legislative developments, and association news.

★3427★ Bulletin of Dental Education

American Dental Education Association
1400 K St., NW, Ste. 1100
Washington, DC 20005
Ph: (202)289-7201   Fax: (202)289-7204
URL: http://www.adea.org

Description: Monthly. Contains news and information on dental education. Recurring features include a calendar of events, reports of meetings, news of educational opportunities, job listings, and notices of publications available.

★3428★ CDS Review

Chicago Dental Society
401 N Michigan Ave., Ste. 200
Chicago, IL 60611
Ph: (312)836-7300   Fax: (312)836-7337
URL: http://www.cds.org/cds_review/abstracts/index.wu4

$25.00/year for individuals, 1 year; $50.00 for individuals, 2 years; $75.00 for individuals, 3 years; $100.00 for individuals, 4 years; $125.00 for individuals, 5 years. Dental journal.

★3429★ Contemporary Oral Hygiene

Ascend Media
7015 College Blvd., Ste. 600
Overland Park, KS 66211
Ph: (913)469-1110   Fax: (913)469-0806

E-mail: medentcirc@ascendmedia.com
URL: http://www.contemporaryoralhygieneonline.com/

Magazine that publishes educational articles for dental hygienists and others in the profession.

★3430★ Dental Economics

PennWell Corp.
1421 S Sheridan Rd.
Tulsa, OK 74112
Ph: (918)835-3161   Fr: 800-331-4463
URL: http://de.pennnet.com

Monthly. $104.00/year for individuals, 1 year; $143.00/year for Canada and Mexico, 1 year; $199.00/year for other countries, 1 year, air expedited service; $169.00 for two years; $250.00/year for two years, Mexico/Canada; $343.00 for two years, other countries, air expedited service; $12.00 for single issue; $18.00 for single issue, Mexico/Canada; $20.00 for single issue, other countries, air expedited service;. Free, online. Magazine featuring business-related articles for dentists.

★3431★ Dental Town

Dental Town
10850 South 48th St.
Phoenix, AZ 85044
Ph: (480)598-0001   Fax: (480)598-3450
URL: http://www.dentaltown.com/

Monthly. Free to qualified subscribers. Magazine that offers information on the dental industry and latest dental equipment.

★3432★ The Explorer

National Association of Dental Assistants
900 S Washington St., No. G13
Falls Church, VA 22046-4020
Ph: (703)237-8616   Fax: (703)533-1153

Description: Monthly, except Nov/Dec combined. Reflects the Association's goal of improving the professional and personal lives of dental assistants and other staff. Provides information relating to the field of dentistry.

★3433★ Hawaii Dental Journal

Hawaii Medical Journal
1360 S Beretania St., Ste. 200
Honolulu, HI 96814
Ph: (808)536-7702   Fax: (808)536-2376
E-mail: hda@hawaiidentalassociation.net
URL: http://www.hawaiidentalassociation.net

Bimonthly. $25.00/year for individuals; $30.00/year for other countries. Dental journal.

★3434★ Illinois Dental Journal

Illinois State Dental Society
1010 South Second St.
Springfield, IL 62704
Ph: (217)525-1406

Monthly. $25.00/year for members; $45.00/year for nonmembers; $75.00/year for nonmembers, other countries; $5.00/year for single issue. Dental magazine.

★3435★ Journal of the American Dental Association

ADA Publishing
211 East Chicago Ave.
Chicago, IL 60611-2678
Ph: (312)440-2500
URL: http://www.ada.org

Monthly. $122.00/year for individuals, U.S. and Mexico; $153.00/year for institutions, U.S. and Mexico; $15.00 for single issue, U.S. and Mexico; $134.00/year for individuals, Canada; $174.00/year for institutions, Canada, plus airmail; $23.00 for single issue, Canada, plus airmail; $153.00/year for individuals, international, plus airmail; $194.00/year for institutions, international, plus airmail; $23.00 for single issue, international, plus airmail. Trade journal for the dental profession.

★3436★ Journal of the California Dental Association

California Dental Association
1201 K St.
Sacramento, CA 95814
Ph: (916)443-3382   Fax: (916)443-2943
Fr: 800-232-7645

URL: http://www.cda.org/publications/journal_of_the_california_de

Monthly. $18.00/year for members; $40.00/year for members, domestic; $75.00/year for nonmembers, ADA; $80.00/year for other countries. Professional magazine for dentists.

★3437★ **Journal of Dental Education**
American Dental Education Association
1400 K St. NW, Ste. 1100
Washington, DC 20005-2403
Ph: (202)289-7201   Fax: (202)289-7204
URL: http://www.adea.org

Monthly. $100.00/year; $125.00/year for Canada; $125.00/year for other countries. Peer-reviewed journal for scholarly research and reviews on dental education.

★3438★ **Journal of Dental Hygiene**
American Dental Hygienists' Association
444 North Michigan Ave., Ste. 3400
Chicago, IL 60611
Ph: (312)440-8904   Fr: 800-243-ADHA
E-mail: communications@adha.net
URL: http://www.adha.org/publications

Quarterly. $45.00/year for individuals, 1 year, 4 issues; $65.00/year for individuals for two years, 8 issues; $90.00/year for individuals, 3 years, 12 issues. Professional journal on dental hygiene.

★3439★ **Journal of Dental Research**
International and American Associations
 for Dental Research
1619 Duke St.
Alexandria, VA 22314-3406
Ph: (703)548-0066   Fax: (703)548-1883
URL: http://www.iadr.org

Monthly. $116.00/year for institutions; $436.00/year for individuals, print-only; $66.00/year for members, IADR Member Rate; $41.00/year for members, IADR Student Member Rate. Dental science journal.

★3440★ **Journal of Operative Dentistry**
American Academy of Gold Foil
 Operators
17922 Tallgrass Ct.
Noblesville, IN 46060
URL: http://operativedentistry.com/journal.html

Bimonthly. Professional journal covering issues in dentistry.

★3441★ **Maryland State Dental
Association Newsletter**
Maryland State Dental Association
6410F Dobbin Rd.
Columbia, MD 21045
Ph: (410)964-2880   Fax: (410)964-0583
E-mail: mddent@msda.com
URL: http://www.msda.com

Description: Monthly. Reports on health, legislative, economic, and medical issues that are pertinent to dentistry. Recurring

features include letters to the editor, interviews, news of research, a calendar of events, reports of meetings, news of educational opportunities, and job listings.

★3442★ **MDS News**
Massachusetts Dental Society
Two Willow St., No. 200
Southborough, MA 01745-1027
Ph: (508)480-9797   Fax: (508)480-0002
Fr: 800-342-8747
E-mail: madental@massdental.org
URL: http://www.massdental.org/

Description: Bimonthly. Provides news on the Society's activities and articles on the dental profession. Recurring features include reports of meetings, news of educational opportunities, job listings, and notices of publications available.

★3443★ **Pennsylvania Dental Journal**
Pennsylvania Dental Association
PO Box 3341
3501 North Front St.
Harrisburg, PA 17105
Ph: (717)234-5941   Fax: (717)234-2186

Bimonthly. Professional dentistry magazine containing treatment/procedure news, PDA activities information, continuing education courses, and legislation updates.

★3444★ **RDH**
PennWell Publishing Co.
1421 South Sheridan Rd.
Tulsa, OK 74112
Ph: (918)835-3161   Fr: 800-331-4463
URL: http://rdh.pennnet.com/home.cfm

Monthly. $69.00/year for individuals; $97.00/year for Canada; $122.00/year for other countries. Magazine for dental hygiene professionals covering practice management, patient motivation, practice options, financial planning, personal development, preventive oral health care and treatment, home care instruction, radiology, anesthesia, nutrition, and new products.

★3445★ **Washington State Dental
Laboratory Association Newsletter**
PO Box 385
Graham, WA 98338
Ph: (360)832-2471   Fax: (360)832-2471
Fr: 800-652-2212
E-mail: peg2@mashell.com
URL: http://www.wsdla.com

Association newsletter featuring articles of interest to dental laboratory technicians as well as classified advertising for technical positions available.

PLACEMENT AND JOB REFERRAL SERVICES

★3446★ **American Public Health
Association (APHA)**
800 I St. NW
Washington, DC 20001
Ph: (202)777-2742   Fax: (202)777-2534
E-mail: comments@apha.org
URL: http://www.apha.org

Members: Professional organization of physicians, nurses, educators, academicians, environmentalists, epidemiologists, new professionals, social workers, health administrators, optometrists, podiatrists, pharmacists, dentists, nutritionists, health planners, other community and mental health specialists, and interested consumers. **Purpose:** Seeks to protect and promote personal, mental, and environmental health. **Activities:** Services include: promulgation of standards; establishment of uniform practices and procedures; development of the etiology of communicable diseases; research in public health; exploration of medical care programs and their relationships to public health. Sponsors job placement service.

EMPLOYER DIRECTORIES AND NETWORKING LISTS

★3447★ **American Academy of
Pediatric Dentistry-Membership
Directory**
American Academy of Pediatric Dentistry
211 E Chicago Ave., Ste. 1700
Chicago, IL 60611-2663
Ph: (312)337-2169   Fax: (312)337-6329
URL: http://www.aapd.org

Annual, November. Covers 5,600 pediatric dentists and several dentists in practice, teaching, and research. Entries include: Name, address, phone. Arrangement: Alphabetical. Indexes: Geographical.

★3448★ **International Association for
Orthodontics-Membership Directory**
International Association for Orthodontics
750 North Lincoln Memorial Dr., Ste. 422
Milwaukee, WI 53202
Ph: (414)272-2757   Fax: (414)272-2754
Fr: 800-447-8770
URL: http://www.iaortho.com/iaopubl.htm

Annual, June. $75.00 for individuals. Covers 2,500 general and children's dentists who also work to correct facial and jaw irregularities. Entries include: Name, office address and phone, orthodontic techniques practiced. Arrangement: Geographical. Indexes: Personal name.

★3449★ Washington Physicians Directory

The Washington Physicians Directory
PO Box 4436
Silver Spring, MD 20914-4436
Ph: (301)384-1506   Fax: (301)384-6854
E-mail: wpd@wpdnetwork.com
URL: http://www.wpdnetwork.com

Annual, March 31. Covers 9,800 physicians in private practice or on full-time staff at hospitals in the Washington, D.C., metropolitan area. Entries include: Name, medical school and year of graduation; up to four office addresses with phone numbers for each; up to four medical specialties (indicating board certifications); Unique Physician Identification Numbers (UPIN); and e-mail. Arrangement: Alphabetical. Indexes: Geographical (within medical specialty); foreign language.

★3450★ Worldwide Online Search Directory

5401 World Dairy Dr.
Madison, WI 53718
Ph: (608)543-9220   Fax: (608)222-9540
Fr: 800-543-9220
E-mail: info@aacd.com
URL: http://www.aacd.com/professional/membershipbenefits.asp#4

Provides a worldwide listing of members of the American Academy of Cosmetic Dentistry.

HANDBOOKS AND MANUALS

★3451★ Careers in Health Care

The McGraw-Hill Companies
PO Box 182604
Columbus, OH 43272
Fax: (614)759-3749   Fr: 877-883-5524
E-mail: customer.service@mcgraw-hill.com
URL: http://www.mcgraw-hill.com

Barbara M. Swanson. Fifth edition, 2005. $15.95 (paper). 192 pages. Describes job duties, work settings, salaries, licensing and certification requirements, educational preparation, and future outlook. Gives ideas on how to secure a job.

★3452★ Clinical Primer for Dental Assistants

Lippincott Williams & Wilkins
PO Box 61
Henrico, NC 27842-0061
Ph: (252)535-5993   Fax: (252)535-1004
Fr: 800-638-3030
E-mail: customerservice@lww.com
URL: http://www.lww.com

Melanie Mitchell. 2006. $37.95. Help you learn and retain important information you need as a dental assistant

★3453★ Competency Skills for the Dental Assistant

Cengage Learning
PO Box 6904
Florence, KY 41022
Fax: 800-487-8488   Fr: 800-354-9706
URL: http://www.cengage.com

Charline M. Dofka. 1995. $80.95. 576 pages.

★3454★ Dental Assisting: A Comprehensive Approach

Cengage Learning
PO Box 6904
Florence, KY 41022
Fax: 800-487-8488   Fr: 800-354-9706
URL: http://www.cengage.com

Donna J. Phinney, Judy H. Halstead. Third edition, 2007. $98.95. Designed to help you prepare for and pass the DANB certification exam, as well as to manage the challenges of working in the modern day dental office. Illustrated. 1040 pages.

★3455★ Materials and Procedures for Today's Dental Assistant

Cengage Learning
PO Box 6904
Florence, KY 41022
Fax: 800-487-8488   Fr: 800-354-9706
URL: http://www.cengage.com/

Ellen Dietz-Bourguignon. 2005. $59.95. Profiles training and skills for individuals interested in a career as a dental assistant.

★3456★ Opportunities in Health and Medical Careers

The McGraw-Hill Companies
PO Box 182604
Columbus, OH 43272
Fax: (614)759-3749   Fr: 877-883-5524
E-mail: customer.service@mcgraw-hill.com
URL: http://www.mcgraw-hill.com

I. Donald Snook, Jr. and Leo D'Orazio. 2004. $13.95 (paper). 157 pages. Covers the full range of medical and health occupations. Illustrated.

★3457★ Opportunities in Paramedical Careers

The McGraw-Hill Companies
PO Box 182604
Columbus, OH 43272
Fax: (614)759-3749   Fr: 877-883-5524
E-mail: customer.service@mcgraw-hill.com
URL: http://www.mcgraw-hill.com

Alex Kacen. 1999. 14.95 (hardcover). 160 pages. Discusses a variety of opportunities in this field and how to pursue them. Illustrated.

★3458★ Resumes for Health and Medical Careers

The McGraw-Hill Companies
PO Box 182604
Columbus, OH 43272
Fax: (614)759-3749   Fr: 877-883-5524

E-mail: customer.service@mcgraw-hill.com
URL: http://www.mcgraw-hill.com

Third edition, 2003. $11.95 (paper). 160 pages.

★3459★ Textbook for Dental Nurses

Blackwell Publishers
350 Main St., 6th Fl.
Malden, MA 02148-5018
Ph: (781)388-8200   Fax: (781)388-8210
URL: http://www.blackwellpublishing.com/

H. Levinson. Ninth edition, 2004. Illustrated. $44.99. 448 Pages. Educational.

EMPLOYMENT AGENCIES AND SEARCH FIRMS

★3460★ Colucci, Blendow & Johnson

643 Main St., Ste. 7
PO Box 10
Half Moon Bay, CA 94019-1988
Ph: (650)712-0103   Fax: (650)712-0105
E-mail: exsearch@ix.netcom.com

Executive search consultants in the medical technology area that includes pharmaceuticals, medical equipment and device manufacturers, biotechnology, therapeutic supplies, diagnostic laboratory equipment and supplies, diagnostic imaging equipment and supplies, medical services, chemicals, cosmetic and toiletries, dental, veterinarian, and agricultural genetics companies.

★3461★ DDS Staffing Resources, Inc.

9755 Dogwood Rd., Ste. 200
Roswell, GA 30075
Ph: (770)998-7779   Fax: (770)552-0176
Fr: 888-668-7779
E-mail: ddsstaffing@ddsstaffing.com
URL: http://www.ddsstaffing.com

Dental staffing agency.

★3462★ Legal Medical Urgent Staffing Solutions

The 1605 Bldg., 1605 Evesham Rd.
Voorhees, NJ 08043
Ph: (856)795-0909   Fax: (856)795-0922
Fr: 877-674-4464
URL: http://www.legalmedicalstaffing.com

Offers a specialized service providing temporary and full-time support exclusively to the legal, dental, and medical professions.

★3463★ Team Placement Service, Inc.

1414 Prince St., Ste. 202
Alexandria, VA 22314
Ph: (703)820-8618   Fax: (703)820-3368
Fr: 800-495-6767
E-mail: 4jobs@teamplace.com
URL: http://www.teamplace.com

Full-service personnel consultants provide placement for healthcare staff, physician and dentist, private practice, and hospitals. Conduct interviews, tests, and reference checks to select the top 20% of applicants. Survey applicants' skill levels, provide backup information on each candidate, select compatible candidates for consideration, and insure the hiring process minimizes potential legal liability. Industries served: healthcare and government agencies providing medical, dental, biotech, laboratory, hospitals, and physician search.

ONLINE JOB SOURCES AND SERVICES

★3464★ Medhunters.com
Fr: 800-664-0278
E-mail: info@medhunters.com
URL: http://www.medhunters.com

Description: Career search site for jobs in all health care specialties; educational resources; visa and licensing information for relocation; interesting articles; relocation tools; links to professional organizations and general resources.

★3465★ ProHealthJobs
Fr: 800-796-1738
E-mail: Info@prohealthedujobs.com
URL: http://www.prohealthjobs.com

Description: Career resources site for the medical and health care field. Lists professional opportunities, product information, continuing education and open positions.

TRADESHOWS

★3466★ American Academy of Pediatric Dentistry Annual Meeting
American Academy of Pediatric Dentistry
211 E. Chicago Ave., Ste. 1700
Chicago, IL 60611-2663
Ph: (312)337-2169   Fax: (312)337-6329
URL: http://www.aapd.org

Annual. **Primary Exhibits:** Dental products and publications. **Dates and Locations:** 2008 May 22-26; Washington, DC; Marriott Wardman Park; 2009 May 21-25; Honolulu, HI; Hawaii Convention Center; 2010 May 27-31; Chicago, IL; Hilton Towers.

★3467★ American Dental Association Annual Session & Technical Exhibition
American Dental Association
211 E. Chicago Ave.
Chicago, IL 60611-2678
Ph: (312)440-2500
URL: http://www.ada.org

Annual. **Primary Exhibits:** Dental equip-

ment, instruments, materials, therapeutics, and services.

★3468★ Star of the North Meeting
Minnesota Dental Association
2236 Marshall Ave., Ste. 200
St. Paul, MN 55104
Ph: (651)646-7454   Fax: (651)646-8246
E-mail: info@mndental.org
URL: http://www.mndental.org

Annual. **Primary Exhibits:** Dental equipment and supplies, dental laboratory equipment, office equipment, and service organizations. **Dates and Locations:** 2008 Apr 12-14; St. Paul, MN; RiverCentre.

★3469★ Thomas P. Hinman Dental Meeting & Exhibits
Thomas P. Hinman Dental Society of Atlanta
33 Lenox Pte.
Atlanta, GA 30324-3172
Ph: (404)231-1663   Fax: (404)231-9638
E-mail: info@hinman.org
URL: http://www.hinman.org

Annual. **Primary Exhibits:** Dental equipment, supplies, and services. **Dates and Locations:** 2008 Mar 13-15; Atlanta, GA; Georgia World Congress Center.

★3470★ Yankee Dental Congress
Massachusetts Dental Society
2 Willow St., No. 200
Southborough, MA 01745-1027
Ph: (508)480-9797   Fax: (508)480-0002
Fr: 800-342-8747
E-mail: madental@massdental.org
URL: http://www.massdental.org

Annual. **Primary Exhibits:** Dental products, equipment, and services.

OTHER SOURCES

★3471★ American Academy of Cosmetic Dentistry
5401 World Dairy Dr.
Madison, WI 53718
Ph: (608)543-9220   Fax: (608)222-9540
Fr: 800-543-9220
E-mail: info@aacd.com
URL: http://www.aacd.com/

Members include more than 8,000 cosmetic and reconstructive dentists, dental laboratory technicians, dental auxiliaries, dental hygienists, educators, researchers and students. Membership benefits include AACD accreditation, registration to AACD's Annual Scientific Session, publications, online search directory, marketing materials, and more. Membership categories include: Doctors, Lab Technicians or Owners, and Supporting Members $425/one year, $745/two years, $1,050/three years. Other categories are: Corporate Gold $2,500; Faculty $115; Residents $95; Hygienists $95; Recent

Graduate Dentists $95; Dental Students $95; and Students $20.

★3472★ American College of Prosthodontists
211 E Chicago Ave., Ste. 1000
Chicago, IL 60611
Ph: (312)573-1260   Fax: (312)573-1257
URL: http://www.prosthodontics.org/

Membership includes more than 3,000 prosthodontists, dental technicians, dental students and other dental professionals contributing to the specialty. Committed to the esthetic restoration of teeth, including bridges, crowns/caps, dental implants, dentures, partial dentures, whitening and veneers. Membership includes free subscriptions to the Journal of Prosthodontics, the Messenger, and e-blasts. Five categories of membership include: Member/Fellow: (Diplomats of the American Board of Prosthodontics) $632/join before July 1; $316/join after July 1; $125 non-refundable application/reinstatement fee. Student: (students enrolled in an advanced prosthodontic training program accredited by the American Dental Association) Students pay a discounted annual session registration fee but may not hold voting membership on committees or hold elective or appointed office or serve in the House of Delegates. Dental Technician Alliance: (Certified dental technician with proof of formal training in dental technology and one current ACP member-sponsor) $250/before July 1; $125/after July 1; $125 non-refundable application/reinstatement fee. Academic Alliance: (individuals holding an academic teaching appointment within an ADA accredited prosthodontic program or an undergraduate training position in the discipline of prosthodontics) $450/before July 1; $225/after July 1; $125 non-refundable application/reinstatement fee.

★3473★ American Dental Assistants Association (ADAA)
35 E Wacker Dr., Ste. 1730
Chicago, IL 60601-2211
Ph: (312)541-1550   Fax: (312)541-1496
E-mail: lsepin@adaa1.com
URL: http://www.dentalassistant.org

Description: Individuals employed as dental assistants in dental offices, clinics, hospitals, or institutions; instructors of dental assistants; dental students. Sponsors workshops and seminars; maintains governmental liaison. Offers group insurance; maintains scholarship trust fund. Dental Assisting National Board examines members who are candidates for title of Certified Dental Assistant.

★3474★ American Dental Association (ADA)
211 E Chicago Ave.
Chicago, IL 60611-2678
Ph: (312)440-2500   Fax: (312)440-2800
E-mail: publicinfo@ada.org
URL: http://www.ada.org

Description: Professional society of dentists. Encourages the improvement of the health of the public and promotes the art and science of dentistry in matters of legislation and regulations. Inspects and accredits dental schools and schools for dental hygienists, assistants, and laboratory technicians. Conducts research programs at ADA Foundation Research Institute. Produces most of the dental health education material used in the U.S. Sponsors National Children's Dental Health Month and Give Kids a Smile Day. Compiles statistics on personnel, practice, and dental care needs and attitudes of patients with regard to dental health. Sponsors 13 councils.

★3475★ **American Dental Education Association (ADEA)**
1400 K St. NW, Ste. 1100
Washington, DC 20005
Ph: (202)289-7201   Fax: (202)289-7204
E-mail: valachovicr@adea.org
URL: http://www.adea.org
Description: Individuals interested in dental education; schools of dentistry, advanced dental and allied dental education in the U.S., Canada, and Puerto Rico; affiliated institutions of the federal government and corporations. Works to promote better teaching and education in dentistry and dental research and to facilitate exchange of ideas among dental educators. Sponsors meetings, conferences, and workshops; conducts surveys, studies, and special projects and publishes their results. Maintains 37 sections and 8 special interest groups representing many different aspects of dental education.

★3476★ **American Medical Technologists (AMT)**
10700 W Higgins Rd.
Rosemont, IL 60018
Ph: (847)823-5169   Fax: (847)823-0458
Fr: 800-275-1268
URL: http://www.amt1.com
Description: Represents medical technologists, medical laboratory technicians, medical assistants, medical administrative specialists, dental assistants, office laboratory technicians, phlebotomy technicians, laboratory consultants, and allied health instructors. Provides allied health professionals with professional certification services and membership programs to enhance their professional and personal growth. Aims to issue certification credentials to medical and dental assistants, clinical laboratory personnel, laboratory consultants, and allied health instructors.

★3477★ **American School Health Association (ASHA)**
PO Box 708
Kent, OH 44240
Ph: (330)678-1601   Fax: (330)678-4526
E-mail: asha@ashaweb.org
URL: http://www.ashaweb.org
Description: School physicians, school nurses, counsellors, nutritionists, psychologists, social workers, administrators, school health coordinators, health educators, and physical educators working in schools, professional preparation programs, public health, and community-based organizations. Promotes coordinated school health programs that include health education, health services, a healthful school environment, physical education, nutrition services, and psycho-social health services offered in schools collaboratively with families and other members of the community. Offers professional reference materials and professional development opportunities. Conducts pilot programs that inform materials development, provides technical assistance to school professionals, advocates for school health.

★3478★ **Exploring Health Occupations**
Cambridge Educational
PO Box 2053
Princeton, NJ 08543-2053
Ph: 800-257-5126   Fax: (609)671-0266
Fr: 800-468-4227
E-mail: custserv@films.com
URL: http://www.cambridgeeducational.com
VHS and DVD. $159.90. 1999. Two-part series provides a detailed view of the field of medical technicians and technologists, EMTs, nurses, therapists, and assistants.

★3479★ **Health Service Occupations**
Delphi Productions
3159 6th St.
Boulder, CO 80304
Ph: (303)443-2100   Fax: (303)443-4022
Fr: 888-443-2400
E-mail: support@delphivideo.com
URL: http://www.delphivideo.com
$95.00. 50 minutes. Part of the Careers for the 21st Century Video Library.

★3480★ **Holistic Dental Association (HDA)**
PO Box 151444
San Diego, CA 92175
Ph: (619)923-3120   Fax: (619)615-2228
E-mail: info@holisticdental.org
URL: http://www.holisticdental.org
Description: Represents dentists, chiropractors, dental hygienists, physical therapists, and medical doctors. Aims to provide a holistic approach to better dental care for patients, and to expand techniques, medications, and philosophies that pertain to extractions, anesthetics, fillings, crowns, and orthodontics. Encourages the use of homeopathic medications, acupuncture, cranial osteopathy, nutritional techniques, and physical therapy in treating patients in addition to conventional treatments. Sponsors training and educational seminars.

★3481★ **Medical Technicians and Technologists**
Cambridge Educational
PO Box 2053
Princeton, NJ 08543-2053
Ph: 800-257-5126   Fax: (609)671-0266
Fr: 800-468-4227
E-mail: custserv@films.com
URL: http://www.cambridgeeducational.com
VHS and DVD. $79.95. 18 minutes. 2000. Part of the Exploring Health Occupations Series.

★3482★ **Medicine & Related Occupations**
Delphi Productions
3159 6th St.
Boulder, CO 80304
Ph: (303)443-2100   Fax: (303)443-4022
Fr: 888-443-2400
E-mail: support@delphivideo.com
URL: http://www.delphivideo.com
$95.00. 45 minutes. Part of the Careers for the 21st Century Video Library.

★3483★ **National Association of Dental Assistants (NADA)**
900 S Washington St., No. G-13
Falls Church, VA 22046
Ph: (703)237-8616   Fax: (703)533-1153
Members: Professional dental auxiliaries. **Purpose:** Seeks to: bring added stature and purpose to the profession through continuing education; make available to dental assistants, the special benefits normally limited to members of specialized professional and fraternal groups.

★3484★ **National Dental Assistants Association (NDAA)**
3517 16th St. NW
Washington, DC 20010
Ph: (202)588-1697   Fax: (202)588-1244
E-mail: grannycml@bellsouth.net
URL: http://www.ndaonline.org
Description: An auxiliary of the National Dental Association. Works to encourage education and certification among dental assistants. Conducts clinics and workshops to further the education of members. Bestows annual Humanitarian Award; offers scholarships.

★3485★ **National Rural Health Association (NRHA)**
Administrative Office
521 E 63rd St.
Kansas City, MO 64110-3329
Ph: (816)756-3140   Fax: (816)756-3144
E-mail: mail@nrharural.org
URL: http://www.nrharural.org
Description: Administrators, physicians, nurses, physician assistants, health planners, academicians, and others interested or involved in rural health care. Creates a better understanding of health care problems unique to rural areas; utilizes a collective approach in finding positive solutions; articulates and represents the health care needs of rural America; supplies current information to rural health care providers; serves as a liaison between rural health care programs throughout the country. Offers continuing education credits for medical, dental, nursing, and management courses.

★3486★ **Women in Dentistry**
Her Own Words
PO Box 5264

Madison, WI 53705-0264
Ph: (608)271-7083   Fax: (608)271-0209
E-mail: herownword@aol.com

URL: http://www.herownwords.com/
Video. Jocelyn Riley. $95.00. 15 minutes.
Resource guide also available for $45.00.

Dental Hygienists

SOURCES OF HELP-WANTED ADS

★3487★ American Dental Hygienists' Association Access

American Dental Hygienists' Association
444 North Michigan Ave., Ste. 3400
Chicago, IL 60611
Ph: (312)440-8904   Fr: 800-243-ADHA
URL: http://www.adha.org/publications

$48.00/year for individuals; $85.00 for two years; $120.00/year for individuals, for 3 years. Magazine covering current dental hygiene topics, regulatory and legislative developments, and association news.

★3488★ Bulletin of Dental Education

American Dental Education Association
1400 K St., NW, Ste. 1100
Washington, DC 20005
Ph: (202)289-7201   Fax: (202)289-7204
URL: http://www.adea.org

Description: Monthly. Contains news and information on dental education. Recurring features include a calendar of events, reports of meetings, news of educational opportunities, job listings, and notices of publications available.

★3489★ CDS Review

Chicago Dental Society
401 N Michigan Ave., Ste. 200
Chicago, IL 60611
Ph: (312)836-7300   Fax: (312)836-7337
URL: http://www.cds.org/cds_review/abstracts/index.wu4

$25.00/year for individuals, 1 year; $50.00 for individuals, 2 years; $75.00 for individuals, 3 years; $100.00 for individuals, 4 years; $125.00 for individuals, 5 years. Dental journal.

★3490★ Contemporary Oral Hygiene

Ascend Media
7015 College Blvd., Ste. 600
Overland Park, KS 66211
Ph: (913)469-1110   Fax: (913)469-0806
E-mail: medentcirc@ascendmedia.com
URL: http://www.contemporaryoralhygieneonline.com/

Magazine that publishes educational articles for dental hygienists and others in the profession.

★3491★ Dental Economics

PennWell Corp.
1421 S Sheridan Rd.
Tulsa, OK 74112
Ph: (918)835-3161   Fr: 800-331-4463
URL: http://de.pennnet.com

Monthly. $104.00/year for individuals, 1 year; $143.00/year for Canada and Mexico, 1 year; $199.00/year for other countries, 1 year, air expedited service; $169.00 for two years; $250.00/year for two years, Mexico/Canada; $343.00 for two years, other countries, air expedited service; $12.00 for single issue; $18.00 for single issue, Mexico/Canada; $20.00 for single issue, other countries, air expedited service;. Free, online. Magazine featuring business-related articles for dentists.

★3492★ Dental Town

Dental Town
10850 South 48th St.
Phoenix, AZ 85044
Ph: (480)598-0001   Fax: (480)598-3450
URL: http://www.dentaltown.com/

Monthly. Free to qualified subscribers. Magazine that offers information on the dental industry and latest dental equipment.

★3493★ Hawaii Dental Journal

Hawaii Medical Journal
1360 S Beretania St., Ste. 200
Honolulu, HI 96814
Ph: (808)536-7702   Fax: (808)536-2376
E-mail: hda@hawaiidentalassociation.net
URL: http://www.hawaiidentalassociation.net

Bimonthly. $25.00/year for individuals; $30.00/year for other countries. Dental journal.

★3494★ Illinois Dental Journal

Illinois State Dental Society
1010 South Second St.
Springfield, IL 62704
Ph: (217)525-1406

Monthly. $25.00/year for members; $45.00/year for nonmembers; $75.00/year for nonmembers, other countries; $5.00/year for single issue. Dental magazine.

★3495★ Journal of the American Dental Association

ADA Publishing
211 East Chicago Ave.
Chicago, IL 60611-2678
Ph: (312)440-2500
URL: http://www.ada.org

Monthly. $122.00/year for individuals, U.S. and Mexico; $153.00/year for institutions, U.S. and Mexico; $15.00 for single issue, U.S. and Mexico; $134.00/year for individuals, Canada; $174.00/year for institutions, Canada, plus airmail; $23.00 for single issue, Canada, plus airmail; $153.00/year for individuals, international, plus airmail; $194.00/year for institutions, international, plus airmail; $23.00 for single issue, international, plus airmail. Trade journal for the dental profession.

★3496★ Journal of the California Dental Association

California Dental Association
1201 K St.
Sacramento, CA 95814
Ph: (916)443-3382   Fax: (916)443-2943
Fr: 800-232-7645
URL: http://www.cda.org/publications/journal_of_the_california_de

Monthly. $18.00/year for members; $40.00/year for members, domestic; $75.00/year for nonmembers, ADA; $80.00/year for other countries. Professional magazine for dentists.

★3497★ Journal of Dental Education

American Dental Education Association
1400 K St. NW, Ste. 1100
Washington, DC 20005-2403
Ph: (202)289-7201   Fax: (202)289-7204

URL: http://www.adea.org

Monthly. $100.00/year; $125.00/year for Canada; $125.00/year for other countries. Peer-reviewed journal for scholarly research and reviews on dental education.

★3498★ *Journal of Dental Hygiene*

American Dental Hygienists' Association
444 North Michigan Ave., Ste. 3400
Chicago, IL 60611
Ph: (312)440-8904   Fr: 800-243-ADHA
E-mail: communications@adha.net
URL: http://www.adha.org/publications

Quarterly. $45.00/year for individuals, 1 year, 4 issues; $65.00/year for individuals for two years, 8 issues; $90.00/year for individuals, 3 years, 12 issues. Professional journal on dental hygiene.

★3499★ *Journal of Dental Research*

International and American Associations for Dental Research
1619 Duke St.
Alexandria, VA 22314-3406
Ph: (703)548-0066   Fax: (703)548-1883
URL: http://www.iadr.org

Monthly. $116.00/year for institutions; $436.00/year for individuals, print-only; $66.00/year for members, IADR Member Rate; $41.00/year for members, IADR Student Member Rate. Dental science journal.

★3500★ *Journal of Operative Dentistry*

American Academy of Gold Foil Operators
17922 Tallgrass Ct.
Noblesville, IN 46060
URL: http://operativedentistry.com/journal.html

Bimonthly. Professional journal covering issues in dentistry.

★3501★ *Maryland State Dental Association Newsletter*

Maryland State Dental Association
6410F Dobbin Rd.
Columbia, MD 21045
Ph: (410)964-2880   Fax: (410)964-0583
E-mail: mddent@msda.com
URL: http://www.msda.com

Description: Monthly. Reports on health, legislative, economic, and medical issues that are pertinent to dentistry. Recurring features include letters to the editor, interviews, news of research, a calendar of events, reports of meetings, news of educational opportunities, and job listings.

★3502★ *MDS News*

Massachusetts Dental Society
Two Willow St., No. 200
Southborough, MA 01745-1027
Ph: (508)480-9797   Fax: (508)480-0002
Fr: 800-342-8747
E-mail: madental@massdental.org
URL: http://www.massdental.org/

Description: Bimonthly. Provides news on the Society's activities and articles on the dental profession. Recurring features include reports of meetings, news of educational opportunities, job listings, and notices of publications available.

★3503★ *Pennsylvania Dental Journal*

Pennsylvania Dental Association
PO Box 3341
3501 North Front St.
Harrisburg, PA 17105
Ph: (717)234-5941   Fax: (717)234-2186

Bimonthly. Professional dentistry magazine containing treatment/procedure news, PDA activities information, continuing education courses, and legislation updates.

★3504★ *RDH*

PennWell Publishing Co.
1421 South Sheridan Rd.
Tulsa, OK 74112
Ph: (918)835-3161   Fr: 800-331-4463
URL: http://rdh.pennnet.com/home.cfm

Monthly. $69.00/year for individuals; $97.00/year for Canada; $122.00/year for other countries. Magazine for dental hygiene professionals covering practice management, patient motivation, practice options, financial planning, personal development, preventive oral health care and treatment, home care instruction, radiology, anesthesia, nutrition, and new products.

★3505★ *Washington State Dental Laboratory Association Newsletter*

PO Box 385
Graham, WA 98338
Ph: (360)832-2471   Fax: (360)832-2471
Fr: 800-652-2212
E-mail: peg2@mashell.com
URL: http://www.wsdla.com

Association newsletter featuring articles of interest to dental laboratory technicians as well as classified advertising for technical positions available.

★3506★ *WSDA News*

Washington State Dental Association (WSDA)
1001 Fourth Ave,, Ste. 3800
Seattle, WA 98154
Ph: (206)448-1914   Fax: (206)443-9266
E-mail: wsda@wsda.org
URL: http://www.wsda.org/news/subscription.view

Description: Monthly, except October. Contains information of interest to dentists on legislation, regulations, state boards and government, and business of the association. Recurring features include letters to the editor, editorial and op-ed columns, President's message, obituraries, practice opportunities, news of educational opportunities, and job listings.

PLACEMENT AND JOB REFERRAL SERVICES

★3507★ **American Public Health Association (APHA)**

800 I St. NW
Washington, DC 20001
Ph: (202)777-2742   Fax: (202)777-2534
E-mail: comments@apha.org
URL: http://www.apha.org

Members: Professional organization of physicians, nurses, educators, academicians, environmentalists, epidemiologists, new professionals, social workers, health administrators, optometrists, podiatrists, pharmacists, dentists, nutritionists, health planners, other community and mental health specialists, and interested consumers. **Purpose:** Seeks to protect and promote personal, mental, and environmental health. **Activities:** Services include: promulgation of standards; establishment of uniform practices and procedures; development of the etiology of communicable diseases; research in public health; exploration of medical care programs and their relationships to public health. Sponsors job placement service.

EMPLOYER DIRECTORIES AND NETWORKING LISTS

★3508★ *American Academy of Pediatric Dentistry-Membership Directory*

American Academy of Pediatric Dentistry
211 E Chicago Ave., Ste. 1700
Chicago, IL 60611-2663
Ph: (312)337-2169   Fax: (312)337-6329
URL: http://www.aapd.org

Annual, November. Covers 5,600 pediatric dentists and several dentists in practice, teaching, and research. Entries include: Name, address, phone. Arrangement: Alphabetical. Indexes: Geographical.

★3509★ *International Association for Orthodontics-Membership Directory*

International Association for Orthodontics
750 North Lincoln Memorial Dr., Ste. 422
Milwaukee, WI 53202
Ph: (414)272-2757   Fax: (414)272-2754
Fr: 800-447-8770
URL: http://www.iaortho.com/iaopubl.htm

Annual, June. $75.00 for individuals. Covers 2,500 general and children's dentists who also work to correct facial and jaw irregularities. Entries include: Name, office address and phone, orthodontic techniques practiced. Arrangement: Geographical. Indexes: Personal name.

★3510★ **Washington Physicians Directory**

The Washington Physicians Directory
PO Box 4436
Silver Spring, MD 20914-4436
Ph: (301)384-1506　Fax: (301)384-6854
E-mail: wpd@wpdnetwork.com
URL: http://www.wpdnetwork.com

Annual, March 31. Covers 9,800 physicians in private practice or on full-time staff at hospitals in the Washington, D.C., metropolitan area. Entries include: Name, medical school and year of graduation; up to four office addresses with phone numbers for each; up to four medical specialties (indicating board certifications); Unique Physician Identification Numbers (UPIN); and e-mail. Arrangement: Alphabetical. Indexes: Geographical (within medical specialty); foreign language.

★3511★ **Worldwide Online Search Directory**

5401 World Dairy Dr.
Madison, WI 53718
Ph: (608)543-9220　Fax: (608)222-9540
Fr: 800-543-9220
E-mail: info@aacd.com
URL: http://www.aacd.com/professional/membershipbenefits.asp#4

Provides a worldwide listing of members of the American Academy of Cosmetic Dentistry.

HANDBOOKS AND MANUALS

★3512★ **Careers in Health Care**

The McGraw-Hill Companies
PO Box 182604
Columbus, OH 43272
Fax: (614)759-3749　Fr: 877-883-5524
E-mail: customer.service@mcgraw-hill.com
URL: http://www.mcgraw-hill.com

Barbara M. Swanson. Fifth edition, 2005. $15.95 (paper). 192 pages. Describes job duties, work settings, salaries, licensing and certification requirements, educational preparation, and future outlook. Gives ideas on how to secure a job.

★3513★ **Dental Assisting: A Comprehensive Approach**

Cengage Learning
PO Box 6904
Florence, KY 41022
Fax: 800-487-8488　Fr: 800-354-9706
URL: http://www.cengage.com

Donna J. Phinney, Judy H. Halstead. Third edition, 2007. $98.95. Designed to help you prepare for and pass the DANB certification exam, as well as to manage the challenges of working in the modern day dental office. Illustrated. 1040 pages.

★3514★ **Kaplan Dental Hygienist Licensure Exam**

Kaplan Publishing
1 Liberty Plaza, 24th Fl.
New York, NY 10006
Ph: (212)698-7000　Fax: (212)698-7007
Fr: 800-527-4836
URL: http://www.kaplanpublishing.com/

Paula Tomko. 2007. $49.95. Provides a complete review for individuals taking the National Dental Hygienist Licensure exam, including a full-length simulated test and explanations of answers.

★3515★ **Opportunities in Health and Medical Careers**

The McGraw-Hill Companies
PO Box 182604
Columbus, OH 43272
Fax: (614)759-3749　Fr: 877-883-5524
E-mail: customer.service@mcgraw-hill.com
URL: http://www.mcgraw-hill.com

I. Donald Snook, Jr. and Leo D'Orazio. 2004. $13.95 (paper). 157 pages. Covers the full range of medical and health occupations. Illustrated.

★3516★ **Opportunities in Medical Technology Careers**

The McGraw-Hill Companies
PO Box 182604
Columbus, OH 43272
Fax: (614)759-3749　Fr: 877-883-5524
E-mail: customer.service@mcgraw-hill.com
URL: http://www.mcgraw-hill.com

Karen R. Karni. Revised, 1996. $14.95; $11.95 (paper). 148 pages. Details opportunities for various technical medical personnel and supplies up-to-date information on salary levels and employment outlook. Appendices list associations and unions in each field. Illustrated.

★3517★ **Opportunities in Paramedical Careers**

The McGraw-Hill Companies
PO Box 182604
Columbus, OH 43272
Fax: (614)759-3749　Fr: 877-883-5524
E-mail: customer.service@mcgraw-hill.com
URL: http://www.mcgraw-hill.com

Alex Kacen. 1999. 14.95 (hardcover). 160 pages. Discusses a variety of opportunities in this field and how to pursue them. Illustrated.

★3518★ **Practice Management for Dental Hygienists**

Lippincott Williams & Wilkins
PO Box 61
Henrico, NC 27842-0061
Ph: (252)535-5993　Fax: (252)535-1004
Fr: 800-638-3030
URL: http://www.lww.com

Esther Andrews. 2006. $46.95. Prepares dental hygiene students and dental hygienists to handle the business and operational aspects of the dental office.

★3519★ **Resumes for Health and Medical Careers**

The McGraw-Hill Companies
PO Box 182604
Columbus, OH 43272
Fax: (614)759-3749　Fr: 877-883-5524
E-mail: customer.service@mcgraw-hill.com
URL: http://www.mcgraw-hill.com

Third edition, 2003. $11.95 (paper). 160 pages.

★3520★ **Textbook for Dental Nurses**

Blackwell Publishers
350 Main St., 6th Fl.
Malden, MA 02148-5018
Ph: (781)388-8200　Fax: (781)388-8210
URL: http://www.blackwellpublishing.com/

H. Levinson. Ninth edition, 2004. Illustrated. $44.99. 448 Pages. Educational.

EMPLOYMENT AGENCIES AND SEARCH FIRMS

★3521★ **DDS Staffing Resources, Inc.**

9755 Dogwood Rd., Ste. 200
Roswell, GA 30075
Ph: (770)998-7779　Fax: (770)552-0176
Fr: 888-668-7779
E-mail: ddsstaffing@ddsstaffing.com
URL: http://www.ddsstaffing.com

Dental staffing agency.

★3522★ **Team Placement Service, Inc.**

1414 Prince St., Ste. 202
Alexandria, VA 22314
Ph: (703)820-8618　Fax: (703)820-3368
Fr: 800-495-6767
E-mail: 4jobs@teamplace.com
URL: http://www.teamplace.com

Full-service personnel consultants provide placement for healthcare staff, physician and dentist, private practice, and hospitals. Conduct interviews, tests, and reference checks to select the top 20% of applicants. Survey applicants' skill levels, provide backup information on each candidate, select compatible candidates for consideration, and insure the hiring process minimizes potential legal liability. Industries served: healthcare and government agencies providing medical, dental, biotech, laboratory, hospitals, and physician search.

ONLINE JOB SOURCES AND SERVICES

★3523★ **Medhunters.com**

Fr: 800-664-0278
E-mail: info@medhunters.com
URL: http://www.medhunters.com

Description: Career search site for jobs in all health care specialties; educational resources; visa and licensing information for relocation; interesting articles; relocation tools; links to professional organizations and general resources.

★3524★ ProHealthJobs
Fr: 800-796-1738
E-mail: Info@prohealthedujobs.com
URL: http://www.prohealthjobs.com

Description: Career resources site for the medical and health care field. Lists professional opportunities, product information, continuing education and open positions.

TRADESHOWS

★3525★ American Academy of Pediatric Dentistry Annual Meeting
American Academy of Pediatric Dentistry
211 E. Chicago Ave., Ste. 1700
Chicago, IL 60611-2663
Ph: (312)337-2169   Fax: (312)337-6329
URL: http://www.aapd.org

Annual. **Primary Exhibits:** Dental products and publications. **Dates and Locations:** 2008 May 22-26; Washington, DC; Marriott Wardman Park; 2009 May 21-25; Honolulu, HI; Hawaii Convention Center; 2010 May 27-31; Chicago, IL; Hilton Towers.

★3526★ American Dental Association Annual Session & Technical Exhibition
American Dental Association
211 E. Chicago Ave.
Chicago, IL 60611-2678
Ph: (312)440-2500
URL: http://www.ada.org

Annual. **Primary Exhibits:** Dental equipment, instruments, materials, therapeutics, and services.

★3527★ American Dental Hygienists' Association Convention
American Dental Hygienist Association
444 N. Michigan Ave., Ste. 3400
Chicago, IL 60611
Ph: (312)440-8900   Fax: (312)440-8929
E-mail: mail@adha.net
URL: http://www.adha.org

Annual. **Primary Exhibits:** Dental hygiene products and services.

★3528★ National Dental Association Annual Convention
National Dental Association, Inc.
3517 16th St., NW
Washington, DC 20010
Ph: (202)588-1697   Fax: (202)588-1244
E-mail: admin@ndaonline.org
URL: http://www.ndaonline.org

Annual. **Primary Exhibits:** Dental and Pharmaceutical equipment, supplies, and services.

★3529★ Star of the North Meeting
Minnesota Dental Association
2236 Marshall Ave., Ste. 200
St. Paul, MN 55104
Ph: (651)646-7454   Fax: (651)646-8246
E-mail: info@mndental.org
URL: http://www.mndental.org

Annual. **Primary Exhibits:** Dental equipment and supplies, dental laboratory equipment, office equipment, and service organizations. **Dates and Locations:** 2008 Apr 12-14; St. Paul, MN; RiverCentre.

★3530★ Thomas P. Hinman Dental Meeting & Exhibits
Thomas P. Hinman Dental Society of Atlanta
33 Lenox Pte.
Atlanta, GA 30324-3172
Ph: (404)231-1663   Fax: (404)231-9638
E-mail: info@hinman.org
URL: http://www.hinman.org

Annual. **Primary Exhibits:** Dental equipment, supplies, and services. **Dates and Locations:** 2008 Mar 13-15; Atlanta, GA; Georgia World Congress Center.

★3531★ Three Rivers Dental Conference
Dental Society of Western Pennsylvania
900 Cedar Ave.
Pittsburgh, PA 15212
Ph: (412)321-5810   Fax: (412)321-7719
URL: http://www.dswp.org

Annual. **Primary Exhibits:** Dental products and equipment, computers, office equipment, and insurance.

★3532★ Yankee Dental Congress
Massachusetts Dental Society
2 Willow St., No. 200
Southborough, MA 01745-1027
Ph: (508)480-9797   Fax: (508)480-0002
Fr: 800-342-8747
E-mail: madental@massdental.org
URL: http://www.massdental.org

Annual. **Primary Exhibits:** Dental products, equipment, and services.

OTHER SOURCES

★3533★ American Academy of Cosmetic Dentistry
5401 World Dairy Dr.
Madison, WI 53718
Ph: (608)543-9220   Fax: (608)222-9540
Fr: 800-543-9220
E-mail: info@aacd.com
URL: http://www.aacd.com/

Members include more than 8,000 cosmetic and reconstructive dentists, dental laboratory technicians, dental auxiliaries, dental hygienists, educators, researchers and students. Membership benefits include AACD accreditation, registration to AACD's Annual Scientific Session, publications, online search directory, marketing materials, and more. Membership categories include: Doctors, Lab Technicians or Owners, and Supporting Members $425/one year, $745/two years, $1,050/three years. Other categories are: Corporate Gold $2,500; Faculty $115; Residents $95; Hygienists $95; Recent Graduate Dentists $95; Dental Students $95; and Students $20.

★3534★ American Association of Dental Examiners (AADE)
211 E Chicago Ave., Ste. 760
Chicago, IL 60611
Ph: (312)440-7464   Fax: (312)440-3525
E-mail: info@aadexam.org
URL: http://www.aadexam.org

Description: Represents present and past members of state dental examining boards and board administrators. Assists member agencies with problems related to state dental board examinations and licensure, and enforcement of the state dental practice act. Conducts research; compiles statistics.

★3535★ American College of Prosthodontists
211 E Chicago Ave., Ste. 1000
Chicago, IL 60611
Ph: (312)573-1260   Fax: (312)573-1257
URL: http://www.prosthodontics.org/

Membership includes more than 3,000 prosthodontists, dental technicians, dental students and other dental professionals contributing to the specialty. Committed to the esthetic restoration of teeth, including bridges, crowns/caps, dental implants, dentures, partial dentures, whitening and veneers. Membership includes free subscriptions to the Journal of Prosthodontics, the Messenger, and e-blasts. Five categories of membership include: Member/Fellow: (Diplomats of the American Board of Prosthodontics) $632/join before July 1; $316/join after July 1; $125 non-refundable application/reinstatement fee. Student: (students enrolled in an advanced prosthodontic training program accredited by the American Dental Association) Students pay a discounted annual session registration fee but may not hold voting membership on committees or hold elective or appointed office or serve in the House of Delegates. Dental Technician Alliance: (Certified dental technician with proof of formal training in dental technology and one current ACP member-sponsor) $250/before July 1; $125/after July 1; $125 non-refundable application/reinstatement fee. Academic Alliance: (individuals holding an academic teaching appointment within an ADA accredited prosthodontic program or an undergraduate training position in the discipline of prosthodontics) $450/before July 1; $225/after July 1; $125 non-refundable application/reinstatement fee.

★3536★ American Dental Association (ADA)

211 E Chicago Ave.
Chicago, IL 60611-2678
Ph: (312)440-2500   Fax: (312)440-2800
E-mail: publicinfo@ada.org
URL: http://www.ada.org

Description: Professional society of dentists. Encourages the improvement of the health of the public and promotes the art and science of dentistry in matters of legislation and regulations. Inspects and accredits dental schools and schools for dental hygienists, assistants, and laboratory technicians. Conducts research programs at ADA Foundation Research Institute. Produces most of the dental health education material used in the U.S. Sponsors National Children's Dental Health Month and Give Kids a Smile Day. Compiles statistics on personnel, practice, and dental care needs and attitudes of patients with regard to dental health. Sponsors 13 councils.

★3537★ American Dental Education Association (ADEA)

1400 K St. NW, Ste. 1100
Washington, DC 20005
Ph: (202)289-7201   Fax: (202)289-7204
E-mail: valachovicr@adea.org
URL: http://www.adea.org

Description: Individuals interested in dental education; schools of dentistry, advanced dental and allied dental education in the U.S., Canada, and Puerto Rico; affiliated institutions of the federal government and corporations. Works to promote better teaching and education in dentistry and dental research and to facilitate exchange of ideas among dental educators. Sponsors meetings, conferences, and workshops; conducts surveys, studies, and special projects and publishes their results. Maintains 37 sections and 8 special interest groups representing many different aspects of dental education.

★3538★ American Dental Hygienists' Association (ADHA)

444 N Michigan Ave., Ste. 3400
Chicago, IL 60611
Ph: (312)440-8911   Fax: (312)467-1806
Fr: 800-243-ADHA
E-mail: mail@adha.net
URL: http://www.adha.org

Description: Professional organization of licensed dental hygienists possessing a degree or certificate in dental hygiene granted by an accredited school of dental hygiene. Makes available scholarships, research grants, and continuing education programs. Maintains accrediting service through the American Dental Association's Commission on Dental Accreditation. Compiles statistics.

★3539★ American School Health Association (ASHA)

PO Box 708
Kent, OH 44240
Ph: (330)678-1601   Fax: (330)678-4526
E-mail: asha@ashaweb.org

URL: http://www.ashaweb.org

Description: School physicians, school nurses, counsellors, nutritionists, psychologists, social workers, administrators, school health coordinators, health educators, and physical educators working in schools, professional preparation programs, public health, and community-based organizations. Promotes coordinated school health programs that include health education, health services, a healthful school environment, physical education, nutrition services, and psycho-social health services offered in schools collaboratively with families and other members of the community. Offers professional reference materials and professional development opportunities. Conducts pilot programs that inform materials development, provides technical assistance to school professionals, advocates for school health.

★3540★ Exploring Health Occupations

Cambridge Educational
PO Box 2053
Princeton, NJ 08543-2053
Ph: 800-257-5126   Fax: (609)671-0266
Fr: 800-468-4227
E-mail: custserv@films.com
URL: http://www.cambridgeeducational.com

VHS and DVD. $159.90. 1999. Two-part series provides a detailed view of the field of medical technicians and technologists, EMTs, nurses, therapists, and assistants.

★3541★ Health Service Occupations

Delphi Productions
3159 6th St.
Boulder, CO 80304
Ph: (303)443-2100   Fax: (303)443-4022
Fr: 888-443-2400
E-mail: support@delphivideo.com
URL: http://www.delphivideo.com

$95.00. 50 minutes. Part of the Careers for the 21st Century Video Library.

★3542★ Health Technologists & Technicians

Delphi Productions
3159 6th St.
Boulder, CO 80304
Ph: (303)443-2100   Fax: (303)443-4022
Fr: 888-443-2400
E-mail: support@delphivideo.com
URL: http://www.delphivideo.com

$95.00. 50 minutes. Part of the Careers for the 21st Century Video Library.

★3543★ Holistic Dental Association (HDA)

PO Box 151444
San Diego, CA 92175
Ph: (619)923-3120   Fax: (619)615-2228
E-mail: info@holisticdental.org
URL: http://www.holisticdental.org

Description: Represents dentists, chiropractors, dental hygienists, physical therapists, and medical doctors. Aims to provide a holistic approach to better dental care for patients, and to expand techniques, medications, and philosophies that pertain to extractions, anesthetics, fillings, crowns, and orthodontics. Encourages the use of homeopathic medications, acupuncture, cranial osteopathy, nutritional techniques, and physical therapy in treating patients in addition to conventional treatments. Sponsors training and educational seminars.

★3544★ Medical Technicians and Technologists

Cambridge Educational
PO Box 2053
Princeton, NJ 08543-2053
Ph: 800-257-5126   Fax: (609)671-0266
Fr: 800-468-4227
E-mail: custserv@films.com
URL: http://www.cambridgeeducational.com

VHS and DVD. $79.95. 18 minutes. 2000. Part of the Exploring Health Occupations Series.

★3545★ Medicine & Related Occupations

Delphi Productions
3159 6th St.
Boulder, CO 80304
Ph: (303)443-2100   Fax: (303)443-4022
Fr: 888-443-2400
E-mail: support@delphivideo.com
URL: http://www.delphivideo.com

$95.00. 45 minutes. Part of the Careers for the 21st Century Video Library.

★3546★ National Dental Hygienists' Association (NDHA)

PO Box 22463
Tampa, FL 33622
Fr: 800-234-1096
E-mail: forndha@aol.com
URL: http://ndhaonline.org

Members: Minority dental hygienists. **Purpose:** Cultivates and promotes the art and science of dental hygiene and enhances the professional image of dental hygienists. Attempts to meet the needs of society through educational, political, and social activities while giving the minority dental hygienist a voice in shaping the profession. Encourages cooperation and mutual support among minority professionals. Seeks to increase opportunities for continuing education and employment in the field of dental hygiene. Works to improve individual and community dental health. **Activities:** Sponsors annual seminar, fundraising events, and scholarship programs; participates in career orientation programs; counsels and assists students applying for or enrolled in dental hygiene programs. Maintains liaison with American Dental Hygienists' Association.

★3547★ National Rural Health Association (NRHA)

Administrative Office
521 E 63rd St.
Kansas City, MO 64110-3329
Ph: (816)756-3140   Fax: (816)756-3144

E-mail: mail@nrharural.org
URL: http://www.nrharural.org

Description: Administrators, physicians, nurses, physician assistants, health planners, academicians, and others interested or involved in rural health care. Creates a better understanding of health care problems unique to rural areas; utilizes a collective approach in finding positive solutions; articulates and represents the health care needs of rural America; supplies current information to rural health care providers; serves as a liaison between rural health care programs throughout the country. Offers continuing education credits for medical, dental, nursing, and management courses.

★3548★ **Women in Dentistry**
Her Own Words
PO Box 5264
Madison, WI 53705-0264
Ph: (608)271-7083   Fax: (608)271-0209
E-mail: herownword@aol.com
URL: http://www.herownwords.com/

Video. Jocelyn Riley. $95.00. 15 minutes. Resource guide also available for $45.00.

Dental Lab Technicians

★3549★ American Dental Hygienists' Association Access

American Dental Hygienists' Association
444 North Michigan Ave., Ste. 3400
Chicago, IL 60611
Ph: (312)440-8904   Fr: 800-243-ADHA
URL: http://www.adha.org/publications

$48.00/year for individuals; $85.00 for two years; $120.00/year for individuals, for 3 years. Magazine covering current dental hygiene topics, regulatory and legislative developments, and association news.

★3550★ Bulletin of Dental Education

American Dental Education Association
1400 K St., NW, Ste. 1100
Washington, DC 20005
Ph: (202)289-7201   Fax: (202)289-7204
URL: http://www.adea.org

Description: Monthly. Contains news and information on dental education. Recurring features include a calendar of events, reports of meetings, news of educational opportunities, job listings, and notices of publications available.

★3551★ CDS Review

Chicago Dental Society
401 N Michigan Ave., Ste. 200
Chicago, IL 60611
Ph: (312)836-7300   Fax: (312)836-7337
URL: http://www.cds.org/cds_review/abstracts/index.wu4

$25.00/year for individuals, 1 year; $50.00 for individuals, 2 years; $75.00 for individuals, 3 years; $100.00 for individuals, 4 years; $125.00 for individuals, 5 years. Dental journal.

★3552★ Contemporary Oral Hygiene

Ascend Media
7015 College Blvd., Ste. 600
Overland Park, KS 66211
Ph: (913)469-1110   Fax: (913)469-0806

E-mail: medentcirc@ascendmedia.com
URL: http://www.contemporaryoralhygieneonline.com/

Magazine that publishes educational articles for dental hygienists and others in the profession.

★3553★ Dental Economics

PennWell Corp.
1421 S Sheridan Rd.
Tulsa, OK 74112
Ph: (918)835-3161   Fr: 800-331-4463
URL: http://de.pennnet.com

Monthly. $104.00/year for individuals, 1 year; $143.00/year for Canada and Mexico, 1 year; $199.00/year for other countries, 1 year, air expedited service; $169.00 for two years; $250.00/year for two years, Mexico/Canada; $343.00 for two years, other countries, air expedited service; $12.00 for single issue; $18.00 for single issue, Mexico/Canada; $20.00 for single issue, other countries, air expedited service;. Free, online. Magazine featuring business-related articles for dentists.

★3554★ Dental Laboratory Association of Texas

PO Box 140769
Dallas, TX 75214
Ph: (214)321-5428   Fax: (214)321-9942
Fr: 877-689-8848
E-mail: aurex@swbell.net
URL: http://www.dlat.org

Allows individuals seeking employment as a dental laboratory technician to submit their service, contact information, and resume.

★3555★ Dental Town

Dental Town
10850 South 48th St.
Phoenix, AZ 85044
Ph: (480)598-0001   Fax: (480)598-3450
URL: http://www.dentaltown.com/

Monthly. Free to qualified subscribers. Magazine that offers information on the dental industry and latest dental equipment.

★3556★ Hawaii Dental Journal

Hawaii Medical Journal
1360 S Beretania St., Ste. 200
Honolulu, HI 96814
Ph: (808)536-7702   Fax: (808)536-2376
E-mail: hda@hawaiidentalassociation.net
URL: http://www.hawaiidentalassociation.net

Bimonthly. $25.00/year for individuals; $30.00/year for other countries. Dental journal.

★3557★ Illinois Dental Journal

Illinois State Dental Society
1010 South Second St.
Springfield, IL 62704
Ph: (217)525-1406

Monthly. $25.00/year for members; $45.00/year for nonmembers; $75.00/year for nonmembers, other countries; $5.00/year for single issue. Dental magazine.

★3558★ Journal of the California Dental Association

California Dental Association
1201 K St.
Sacramento, CA 95814
Ph: (916)443-3382   Fax: (916)443-2943
Fr: 800-232-7645
URL: http://www.cda.org/publications/journal_of_the_california_de

Monthly. $18.00/year for members; $40.00/year for members, domestic; $75.00/year for nonmembers, ADA; $80.00/year for other countries. Professional magazine for dentists.

★3559★ Journal of Dental Education

American Dental Education Association
1400 K St. NW, Ste. 1100
Washington, DC 20005-2403
Ph: (202)289-7201   Fax: (202)289-7204
URL: http://www.adea.org

Monthly. $100.00/year; $125.00/year for Canada; $125.00/year for other countries. Peer-reviewed journal for scholarly research and reviews on dental education.

★3560★ **Journal of Dental Hygiene**

American Dental Hygienists' Association
444 North Michigan Ave., Ste. 3400
Chicago, IL 60611
Ph: (312)440-8904   Fr: 800-243-ADHA
E-mail: communications@adha.net
URL: http://www.adha.org/publications

Quarterly. $45.00/year for individuals, 1 year, 4 issues; $65.00/year for individuals for two years, 8 issues; $90.00/year for individuals, 3 years, 12 issues. Professional journal on dental hygiene.

★3561★ **Journal of Dental Research**

International and American Associations for Dental Research
1619 Duke St.
Alexandria, VA 22314-3406
Ph: (703)548-0066   Fax: (703)548-1883
URL: http://www.iadr.org

Monthly. $116.00/year for institutions; $436.00/year for individuals, print-only; $66.00/year for members, IADR Member Rate; $41.00/year for members, IADR Student Member Rate. Dental science journal.

★3562★ **Journal of Dental Technology**

Bldg. L103
325 John Knox Rd.
Tallahassee, FL 32303
Fax: (850)222-0053   Fr: 800-950-1150
E-mail: jdt@nadl.org
URL: http://www.nadl.org/jdtunbound/index.htm

Serves dental laboratory professionals through articles, industry and product news, classified advertising for laboratory technicians and more (8 issues/year).

★3563★ **Journal of Operative Dentistry**

American Academy of Gold Foil Operators
17922 Tallgrass Ct.
Noblesville, IN 46060
URL: http://operativedentistry.com/journal.html

Bimonthly. Professional journal covering issues in dentistry.

★3564★ **The Journal of Prosthetic Dentistry**

Mosby Inc.
11830 Westline Industrial Dr.
St. Louis, MO 63146
Ph: (314)872-8370   Fax: (314)432-1380
Fr: 800-325-4177
URL: http://www.us.elsevierhealth.com/product.jsp?isbn=00223913

Monthly. $206.00/year for individuals; $479.00/year for institutions; $102.00/year for students; $255.00/year for individuals, other countries; $534.00/year for institutions, other countries; $127.00/year for students, other countries. Journal emphasizing new techniques, evaluation of dental materials, pertinent basic science concepts, and patient psychology in restorative dentistry.

★3565★ **Maryland State Dental Association Newsletter**

Maryland State Dental Association
6410F Dobbin Rd.
Columbia, MD 21045
Ph: (410)964-2880   Fax: (410)964-0583
E-mail: mddent@msda.com
URL: http://www.msda.com

Description: Monthly. Reports on health, legislative, economic, and medical issues that are pertinent to dentistry. Recurring features include letters to the editor, interviews, news of research, a calendar of events, reports of meetings, news of educational opportunities, and job listings.

★3566★ **MDS News**

Massachusetts Dental Society
Two Willow St., No. 200
Southborough, MA 01745-1027
Ph: (508)480-9797   Fax: (508)480-0002
Fr: 800-342-8747
E-mail: madental@massdental.org
URL: http://www.massdental.org/

Description: Bimonthly. Provides news on the Society's activities and articles on the dental profession. Recurring features include reports of meetings, news of educational opportunities, job listings, and notices of publications available.

★3567★ **Minnesota Dental Laboratory Association Inc.**

1711 W County Rd. B, Ste. 30N
Roseville, MN 55113
Ph: (651)635-0306   Fax: (651)635-0307
E-mail: oei@assocmgmt.org
URL: http://www.mndentallab.org/advertising4520.php

Website provides a link to online advertising for dental technician positions, both wanted and available.

★3568★ **Pennsylvania Dental Journal**

Pennsylvania Dental Association
PO Box 3341
3501 North Front St.
Harrisburg, PA 17105
Ph: (717)234-5941   Fax: (717)234-2186

Bimonthly. Professional dentistry magazine containing treatment/procedure news, PDA activities information, continuing education courses, and legislation updates.

★3569★ **Washington State Dental Laboratory Association Newsletter**

PO Box 385
Graham, WA 98338
Ph: (360)832-2471   Fax: (360)832-2471
Fr: 800-652-2212
E-mail: peg2@mashell.com
URL: http://www.wsdla.com

Association newsletter featuring articles of interest to dental laboratory technicians as well as classified advertising for technical positions available.

EMPLOYER DIRECTORIES AND NETWORKING LISTS

★3570★ **Who's Who In Dental Technology**

National Association of Dental Laboratories
325 John Knox Rd., Nol. L103
Tallahassee, FL 32303
Ph: (850)205-5626   Fax: (850)222-0053
Fr: 800-950-1150
E-mail: membership@nadl.org
URL: http://www.nadl.org/scr/dir/index.cfm

Directory includes lab owners, technicians, suppliers, education members and components.

HANDBOOKS AND MANUALS

★3571★ **Careers in Health Care**

The McGraw-Hill Companies
PO Box 182604
Columbus, OH 43272
Fax: (614)759-3749   Fr: 877-883-5524
E-mail: customer.service@mcgraw-hill.com
URL: http://www.mcgraw-hill.com

Barbara M. Swanson. Fifth edition, 2005. $15.95 (paper). 192 pages. Describes job duties, work settings, salaries, licensing and certification requirements, educational preparation, and future outlook. Gives ideas on how to secure a job.

★3572★ **Opportunities in Health and Medical Careers**

The McGraw-Hill Companies
PO Box 182604
Columbus, OH 43272
Fax: (614)759-3749   Fr: 877-883-5524
E-mail: customer.service@mcgraw-hill.com
URL: http://www.mcgraw-hill.com

I. Donald Snook, Jr. and Leo D'Orazio. 2004. $13.95 (paper). 157 pages. Covers the full range of medical and health occupations. Illustrated.

★3573★ **Opportunities in Medical Technology Careers**

The McGraw-Hill Companies
PO Box 182604
Columbus, OH 43272
Fax: (614)759-3749   Fr: 877-883-5524
E-mail: customer.service@mcgraw-hill.com
URL: http://www.mcgraw-hill.com

Karen R. Karni. Revised, 1996. $14.95; $11.95 (paper). 148 pages. Details opportunities for various technical medical personnel and supplies up-to-date information on salary levels and employment outlook. Appendices list associations and unions in each field. Illustrated.

★3574★ Opportunities in Paramedical Careers

The McGraw-Hill Companies
PO Box 182604
Columbus, OH 43272
Fax: (614)759-3749   Fr: 877-883-5524
E-mail: customer.service@mcgraw-hill.com
URL: http://www.mcgraw-hill.com

Alex Kacen. 1999. 14.95 (hardcover). 160 pages. Discusses a variety of opportunities in this field and how to pursue them. Illustrated.

★3575★ Resumes for Health and Medical Careers

The McGraw-Hill Companies
PO Box 182604
Columbus, OH 43272
Fax: (614)759-3749   Fr: 877-883-5524
E-mail: customer.service@mcgraw-hill.com
URL: http://www.mcgraw-hill.com

Third edition, 2003. $11.95 (paper). 160 pages.

EMPLOYMENT AGENCIES AND SEARCH FIRMS

★3576★ Colucci, Blendow & Johnson

643 Main St., Ste. 7
PO Box 10
Half Moon Bay, CA 94019-1988
Ph: (650)712-0103   Fax: (650)712-0105
E-mail: exsearch@ix.netcom.com

Executive search consultants in the medical technology area that includes pharmaceuticals, medical equipment and device manufacturers, biotechnology, therapeutic supplies, diagnostic laboratory equipment and supplies, diagnostic imaging equipment and supplies, medical services, chemicals, cosmetic and toiletries, dental, veterinarian, and agricultural genetics companies.

★3577★ DDS Staffing Resources, Inc.

9755 Dogwood Rd., Ste. 200
Roswell, GA 30075
Ph: (770)998-7779   Fax: (770)552-0176
Fr: 888-668-7779
E-mail: ddsstaffing@ddsstaffing.com
URL: http://www.ddsstaffing.com

Dental staffing agency.

ONLINE JOB SOURCES AND SERVICES

★3578★ Medhunters.com

Fr: 800-664-0278
E-mail: info@medhunters.com
URL: http://www.medhunters.com

Description: Career search site for jobs in all health care specialties; educational resources; visa and licensing information for relocation; interesting articles; relocation tools; links to professional organizations and general resources.

★3579★ ProHealthJobs

Fr: 800-796-1738
E-mail: Info@prohealthedujobs.com
URL: http://www.prohealthjobs.com

Description: Career resources site for the medical and health care field. Lists professional opportunities, product information, continuing education and open positions.

TRADESHOWS

★3580★ Chicago Dental Society Midwinter Meeting

Chicago Dental Society
401 N. Michigan Ave., Ste. 200
Chicago, IL 60611-4205
Ph: (312)836-7300   Fax: (312)836-7337
URL: http://www.cds.org

Annual. **Primary Exhibits:** Dental equipment, services, and related business services.

★3581★ Fun'n Sun Weekend

PO Box 206
Elkin, NC 28621
Ph: (336)835-9251   Fax: (336)835-9243
URL: http://www.fun-n-sun-weekend.com/

Annual seminar sponsored by Louisiana Dental Laboratory Association Inc. and the Mississippi Dental Laboratory Association, offering programs and exhibits of interest to dental technicians.

★3582★ Mid-West Spring Technical Meeting

PO Box 376
New Albany, IN 47151
Ph: (812)542-0730   Fax: (866)429-5044
Fr: 800-366-1161
E-mail: mjacobi@mwstm.com
URL: http://mwstm.com/

Trade show offering more than sixty clinics and hands-on courses promoting all fields of dental laboratory technology.

★3583★ NADL Vision 21

325 John Knox Rd., No. L-103
Tallahassee, FL 32303
Ph: (850)205-5626   Fax: (850)222-0053
Fr: 800-950-1150
URL: http://www.nadl.org/V21/

Annual conference of the National Association of Dental Laboratories provides dental laboratory technicians, owners and managers with information on the technology, education, and tools required to address issues in the dental technology arena.

★3584★ Southeastern Conference of Dental Laboratories

PO Box 206
Elkin, SC 28621
Ph: (336)835-9251   Fax: (336)835-924
E-mail: contactus@scdl-online.org
URL: http://www.scdl-online.org

Annual conference promoting the profession of dental laboratory technician and industry

★3585★ Star of the North Meeting

Minnesota Dental Association
2236 Marshall Ave., Ste. 200
St. Paul, MN 55104
Ph: (651)646-7454   Fax: (651)646-824
E-mail: info@mndental.org
URL: http://www.mndental.org

Annual. **Primary Exhibits:** Dental equipment and supplies, dental laboratory equipment, office equipment, and service organizations. **Dates and Locations:** 2008 Apr 12-14; St. Paul, MN; RiverCentre.

★3586★ Yankee Dental Congress

Massachusetts Dental Society
2 Willow St., No. 200
Southborough, MA 01745-1027
Ph: (508)480-9797   Fax: (508)480-0002
Fr: 800-342-8747
E-mail: madental@massdental.org
URL: http://www.massdental.org

Annual. **Primary Exhibits:** Dental products, equipment, and services.

OTHER SOURCES

★3587★ American Academy of Cosmetic Dentistry

5401 World Dairy Dr.
Madison, WI 53718
Ph: (608)543-9220   Fax: (608)222-9540
Fr: 800-543-9220
E-mail: info@aacd.com
URL: http://www.aacd.com/

Members include more than 8,000 cosmetic and reconstructive dentists, dental laboratory technicians, dental auxiliaries, dental hygienists, educators, researchers and students. Membership benefits include AACD accreditation, registration to AACD's Annual Scientific Session, publications, online search directory, marketing materials, and more. Membership categories include: Doctors, Lab Technicians or Owners, and Supporting Members $425/one year, $745/two years, $1,050/three years. Other categories are: Corporate Gold $2,500; Faculty $115; Residents $95; Hygienists $95; Recent Graduate Dentists $95; Dental Students $95; and Students $20.

★3588★ American College of Prosthodontists

211 E Chicago Ave., Ste. 1000
Chicago, IL 60611
Ph: (312)573-1260   Fax: (312)573-1257
URL: http://www.prosthodontics.org/

Membership includes more than 3,000 prosthodontists, dental technicians, dental students and other dental professionals contributing to the specialty. Committed to the esthetic restoration of teeth, including bridges, crowns/caps, dental implants, dentures, partial dentures, whitening and veneers. Membership includes free subscriptions to the Journal of Prosthodontics, the Messenger, and e-blasts. Five categories of membership include: Member/Fellow: (Diplomats of the American Board of Prosthodontics) $632/join before July 1; $316/join after July 1; $125 non-refundable application/reinstatement fee. Student: (students enrolled in an advanced prosthodontic training program accredited by the American Dental Association) Students pay a discounted annual session registration fee but may not hold voting membership on committees or hold elective or appointed office or serve in the House of Delegates. Dental Technician Alliance: (Certified dental technician with proof of formal training in dental technology and one current ACP member-sponsor) $250/before July 1; $125/after July 1; $125 non-refundable application/reinstatement fee. Academic Alliance: (individuals holding an academic teaching appointment within an ADA accredited prosthodontic program or an undergraduate training position in the discipline of prosthodontics) $450/before July 1; $225/after July 1; $125 non-refundable application/reinstatement fee.

★3589★ American Dental Association (ADA)

211 E Chicago Ave.
Chicago, IL 60611-2678
Ph: (312)440-2500   Fax: (312)440-2800
E-mail: publicinfo@ada.org
URL: http://www.ada.org

Description: Professional society of dentists. Encourages the improvement of the health of the public and promotes the art and science of dentistry in matters of legislation and regulations. Inspects and accredits dental schools and schools for dental hygienists, assistants, and laboratory technicians. Conducts research programs at ADA Foundation Research Institute. Produces most of the dental health education material used in the U.S. Sponsors National Children's Dental Health Month and Give Kids a Smile Day. Compiles statistics on personnel, practice, and dental care needs and attitudes of patients with regard to dental health. Sponsors 13 councils.

★3590★ American Dental Education Association (ADEA)

1400 K St. NW, Ste. 1100
Washington, DC 20005
Ph: (202)289-7201   Fax: (202)289-7204
E-mail: valachovicr@adea.org
URL: http://www.adea.org

Description: Individuals interested in dental education; schools of dentistry, advanced dental and allied dental education in the U.S., Canada, and Puerto Rico; affiliated institutions of the federal government and corporations. Works to promote better teaching and education in dentistry and dental research and to facilitate exchange of ideas among dental educators. Sponsors meetings, conferences, and workshops; conducts surveys, studies, and special projects and publishes their results. Maintains 37 sections and 8 special interest groups representing many different aspects of dental education.

★3591★ Exploring Health Occupations

Cambridge Educational
PO Box 2053
Princeton, NJ 08543-2053
Ph: 800-257-5126   Fax: (609)671-0266
Fr: 800-468-4227
E-mail: custserv@films.com
URL: http://www.cambrideeducational.com

VHS and DVD. $159.90. 1999. Two-part series provides a detailed view of the field of medical technicians and technologists, EMTs, nurses, therapists, and assistants.

★3592★ Florida Dental Laboratory Association

PO Box 328
Tallahassee, FL 32302
Ph: (850)224-0711   Fax: (850)224-3019
E-mail: fdla@executiveoffice.org
URL: http://www.fdla.org

Represents operators and technicians of dental laboratories and to advance standards of service to the dental profession.

★3593★ Health Service Occupations

Delphi Productions
3159 6th St.
Boulder, CO 80304
Ph: (303)443-2100   Fax: (303)443-4022
Fr: 888-443-2400
E-mail: support@delphivideo.com
URL: http://www.delphivideo.com

$95.00. 50 minutes. Part of the Careers for the 21st Century Video Library.

★3594★ Health Technologists & Technicians

Delphi Productions
3159 6th St.
Boulder, CO 80304
Ph: (303)443-2100   Fax: (303)443-4022
Fr: 888-443-2400
E-mail: support@delphivideo.com
URL: http://www.delphivideo.com

$95.00. 50 minutes. Part of the Careers for the 21st Century Video Library.

★3595★ Holistic Dental Association (HDA)

PO Box 151444
San Diego, CA 92175
Ph: (619)923-3120   Fax: (619)615-2228

E-mail: info@holisticdental.org
URL: http://www.holisticdental.org

Description: Represents dentists, chiropractors, dental hygienists, physical therapists, and medical doctors. Aims to provide a holistic approach to better dental care for patients, and to expand techniques, medications, and philosophies that pertain to extractions, anesthetics, fillings, crowns, and orthodontics. Encourages the use of homeopathic medications, acupuncture, cranial osteopathy, nutritional techniques, and physical therapy in treating patients in addition to conventional treatments. Sponsors training and educational seminars.

★3596★ Louisiana Dental Laboratory Association Inc.

PO Box 206
Elkin, LA 28621
Ph: (336)835-9251   Fax: (336)835-9243
E-mail: contactus@ldla.org
URL: http://www.ldla.org

Serves dental laboratory technicians in Louisiana and surrounding areas; sponsors a spring meeting annually.

★3597★ Medical Technicians and Technologists

Cambridge Educational
PO Box 2053
Princeton, NJ 08543-2053
Ph: 800-257-5126   Fax: (609)671-0266
Fr: 800-468-4227
E-mail: custserv@films.com
URL: http://www.cambrideeducational.com

VHS and DVD. $79.95. 18 minutes. 2000. Part of the Exploring Health Occupations Series.

★3598★ Medicine & Related Occupations

Delphi Productions
3159 6th St.
Boulder, CO 80304
Ph: (303)443-2100   Fax: (303)443-4022
Fr: 888-443-2400
E-mail: support@delphivideo.com
URL: http://www.delphivideo.com

$95.00. 45 minutes. Part of the Careers for the 21st Century Video Library.

★3599★ Michigan Association of Commercial Dental Laboratories

22800 Stair Dr.
Clinton Township, MI 48036
Ph: (586)469-1121   Fax: (586)469-1147
URL: http://www.macdl.org

Serves 800 members; promotes the dental laboratory profession through excellence, education, integrity, ethics and standards. Membership categories include: Laboratory, $190, plus $16/each additional owner, technician (maximum fee $500); Associate Technologist, $63; Associate II, $250; Associate III, $75; Clinical Dental Technician, $75; International, $500.

★3600★ National Association of Dental Assistants (NADA)

900 S Washington St., No. G-13
Falls Church, VA 22046
Ph: (703)237-8616   Fax: (703)533-1153
Members: Professional dental auxiliaries. **Purpose:** Seeks to: bring added stature and purpose to the profession through continuing education; make available to dental assistants, the special benefits normally limited to members of specialized professional and fraternal groups.

★3601★ National Association of Dental Laboratories (NADL)

325 John Knox Rd., No. L103
Tallahassee, FL 32303
Ph: (850)205-5626   Fax: (850)222-0053
Fr: 800-950-1150
E-mail: nadl@nadl.org
URL: http://www.nadl.org
Description: Represents 2,900 commercial dental laboratories, manufacturers/suppliers and educators serving the dental profession. **Purpose:** Develops criteria for ethical dental laboratories. **Activities:** Offers business and personal insurance programs, Hazardous Materials Training Program, and an infectious disease prevention training program, business management and technical education programs. Compiles statistics; conducts educational and charitable programs.

★3602★ National Board for Certification in Dental Laboratory Technology

325 John Knox Rd., No. L103
Tallahassee, FL 32303
Ph: (850)205-5627   Fax: (850)222-0053
Fr: 800-684-5310
E-mail: liz@nbccert.org

URL: http://www.nbccert.org/
Certification program setting the standard in dental laboratory technology.

★3603★ North Carolina Dental Laboratory Association Inc.

PO Box 206
Elkin, NC 28621
Ph: (336)835-9251   Fax: (336)835-9243
E-mail: contactus@ncdla.org
URL: http://www.ncdla.org
Represents dental laboratory technicians and offers two meetings per year to promote educational opportunities for members. Membership categories include: Laboratory, $199; Technical, $70; Non-resident, $70, and life.

★3604★ Oregon Association of Dental Laboratories

707 13th St., Ste. 275
Salem, OR 97301
Ph: (503)485-1670   Fr: 800-952-2751
E-mail: oregonlabs@aol.com
URL: http://www.oadl.net
Serves owners of dental laboratories and dental laboratory technicians; seeks to advance the professional status of those engaged in the field of dental laboratory technology. Membership categories and annual dues include: Active, $250, plus $7/dental technician employed; Affiliate, $150; Associate, $52.

★3605★ Production Occupations

Delphi Productions
3159 6th St.
Boulder, CO 80304
Ph: (303)443-2100   Fax: (303)443-4022
Fr: 888-443-2400

E-mail: support@delphivideo.com
URL: http://www.delphivideo.com
$95.00. 49 minutes. Part of the Careers for the 21st Century Video Library.

★3606★ South Carolina Dental Laboratory Association

PO Box 2721
Spartanburg, SC 29304
Ph: (864)585-7330   Fax: (864)591-1643
E-mail: tulare@charter.net
URL: http://www.scdla.org
Promotes the art and science of dental laboratory operations; seeks to further the interests of dental laboratory owners and technicians. Membership categories and annual fees include: Regular (Lab owners or designated managers) $300 (invoiced $75/quarter); Associate (Individuals, except lab owners, actively engaged in dental lab technology), $35; Vendor (Manufacturers, dental companies and representatives), $150.

★3607★ Technical & Related Occupations

Delphi Productions
3159 6th St.
Boulder, CO 80304
Ph: (303)443-2100   Fax: (303)443-4022
Fr: 888-443-2400
E-mail: support@delphivideo.com
URL: http://www.delphivideo.com
$95.00. 49 minutes. Part of the Careers for the 21st Century Video Library.

Dentists

★3608★ AAOMS Surgical Update
American Association of Oral and
Maxillofacial Surgeons (AAOMS)
9700 W. Bryn Mawr Ave.
Rosemont, IL 60018-5701
Ph: (847)678-6200   Fax: (847)678-6286
Fr: 800-822-6637
E-mail: mhynes@aaoms.org
URL: http://www.aaoms.org

Description: 2/year. Provides the dental
profession and others with current information on the speciality of oral and maxillofacial
surgery and patient care.

★3609★ ACP Messenger
American College of Prosthodontists
211 E Chicago Ave., Ste. 1000
Chicago, IL 60611
Ph: (312)573-1260   Fax: (312)573-1257
URL: http://www.prosthodontics.org/prod-
ucts/Messenger.asp

Quarterly newsletter featuring industry news
as well as classified advertising.

★3610★ ADSA Pulse
American Dental Society of
Anesthesiology
211 E Chicago Ave., Ste. 780
Chicago, IL 60611
Ph: (312)664-8270   Fax: (312)224-8624
Fr: 877-255-3742
E-mail: adsahome@mac.com
URL: http://www.adsahome.org/

Description: Bimonthly. Features articles on
developments in dental anesthesiology. Includes news of research, editorials, news of
the Society and its members, and a calendar
of events.

★3611★ AGD Impact
Academy of General Dentistry
211 E. Chicago Ave., Ste. 900
Chicago, IL 60611-1999
Ph: (312)440-4300   Fax: (312)440-0559
Fr: 888-AGD-DENT
E-mail: agdimpact@agd.org
URL: http://www.agd.org/library/2005/feb/
impact.asp

Description: Eleven issues/year. Covers
the issues and trends that impact on general
dentists and the profession. Includes CDE
course list and fact sheets for patients.

**★3612★ American Academy of Implant
Dentistry Newsletter**
American Academy of Implant Dentistry
211 E. Chicago Ave., Ste. 750
Chicago, IL 60611
Ph: (312)335-1550   Fax: (312)335-9090
Fr: 877-335-AAID
URL: http://www.aaid-implant.org

Description: Quarterly. Covers current activities in the field of implant dentistry, particularly the educational programs of the Academy.

**★3613★ American Association of
Hospital Dentists-InterFace**
American Association of Hospital Dentists
401 North Michigan Ave.
Chicago, IL 60611
Ph: (312)527-6764   Fax: (312)673-6663
E-mail: scda@scdaonline.org
URL: http://www.SCDonline.org

Description: Bimonthly. Carries information
about trends, legislation, policy changes,
and issues that affect the practices of hospital dentists. Recurring features include Association news, news of research, a calendar
of events, and columns titled Fellowships,
Funding, Sources, In Brief, and What to
Write For.

**★3614★ American Association of
Women Dentists-Chronicle**
American Association of Women Dentists
216 W. Jackson Blvd, Ste. 625
Chicago, IL 60606
Ph: (312)280-9296   Fax: (312)750-1203
Fr: 800-920-2293
E-mail: info@aawd.org
URL: http://www.aawd.org/

Description: Quarterly. Includes articles of
interest on dentistry, nutrition, research, education, and federal services. Provides information on the association, the practice of
dentistry, and women in dentistry.

**★3615★ American Dental Hygienists'
Association Access**
American Dental Hygienists' Association
444 North Michigan Ave., Ste. 3400
Chicago, IL 60611
Ph: (312)440-8904   Fr: 800-243-ADHA
URL: http://www.adha.org/publications

$48.00/year for individuals; $85.00 for two
years; $120.00/year for individuals, for 3
years. Magazine covering current dental
hygiene topics, regulatory and legislative
developments, and association news.

**★3616★ American Journal of
Orthodontics and Dentofacial
Orthopedics**
Mosby Inc.
11830 Westline Industrial Dr.
St. Louis, MO 63146
Ph: (314)872-8370   Fax: (314)432-1380
Fr: 800-325-4177
URL: http://www2.us.elsevierhealth.com

Monthly. $527.00/year for institutions;
$277.00/year for individuals; $116.00/year
for students; $458.00/year for institutions,
within U.S.; $218.00/year for individuals,
within U.S.; $136.00/year for students. Jour-
nal for orthodontists and dentists who include orthodontics as a portion of their
practice.

★3617★ American Society for Dental Aesthetics Newsletter

American Society for Dental Aesthetics
635 Madison Ave., 12th Fl.
New York, NY 10022
Ph: (212)751-3263   Fax: (212)308-5182
Fr: 888-988-ASDA
URL: http://www.asdatoday.com

Description: Quarterly. Focuses on upcoming meetings and lectures of interest to ASDA members. Includes contributed items of a technical nature from members, discussing current projects, techniques, and products. Recurring features include interviews, news of research, a calendar of events, and columns titled But Paul You Can't Do That, Implants, Photography, The President Speaks, and Office Management.

★3618★ ASDA News

Alliance of the American Dental Association
211 E Chicago Ave., Ste. 730
Chicago, IL 60611
Ph: (312)440-2795   Fax: (312)440-2587
Fr: 800-621-8099
E-mail: editor@asdanet.org
URL: http://www.allianceada.org

Description: Monthly. Covers dentistry and association news. Recurring features include letters to the editor, news of research, a calendar of events, columns, Q&As, and reports of meetings.

★3619★ Bulletin of Dental Education

American Dental Education Association
1400 K St., NW, Ste. 1100
Washington, DC 20005
Ph: (202)289-7201   Fax: (202)289-7204
URL: http://www.adea.org

Description: Monthly. Contains news and information on dental education. Recurring features include a calendar of events, reports of meetings, news of educational opportunities, job listings, and notices of publications available.

★3620★ CDS Review

Chicago Dental Society
401 N Michigan Ave., Ste. 200
Chicago, IL 60611
Ph: (312)836-7300   Fax: (312)836-7337
URL: http://www.cds.org/cds_review/abstracts/index.wu4

$25.00/year for individuals, 1 year; $50.00 for individuals, 2 years; $75.00 for individuals, 3 years; $100.00 for individuals, 4 years; $125.00 for individuals, 5 years. Dental journal.

★3621★ Contemporary Oral Hygiene

Ascend Media
7015 College Blvd., Ste. 600
Overland Park, KS 66211
Ph: (913)469-1110   Fax: (913)469-0806
E-mail: medentcirc@ascendmedia.com
URL: http://
www.contemporaryoralhygieneonline.com/

Magazine that publishes educational articles for dental hygienists and others in the profession.

★3622★ The Cranial Letter

The Cranial Academy
8202 Clearvista Pkwy., No. 9-D
Indianapolis, IN 46256
Ph: (317)594-0411   Fax: (317)594-9299
E-mail: info@cranialacademy.org
URL: http://www.cranialacademy.org/

Description: Quarterly. Provides information about osteopathy in the cranio-sacral field for doctors of osteopathy, dentistry, and medicine. Carries news of reports, papers, seminars, courses offered by the Academy, and research projects. Recurring features include obituaries, a calendar of events, and columns titled President's Message, The Dental Corner, and Scientific Section.

★3623★ Dental Economics

PennWell Corp.
1421 S Sheridan Rd.
Tulsa, OK 74112
Ph: (918)835-3161   Fr: 800-331-4463
URL: http://de.pennnet.com

Monthly. $104.00/year for individuals, 1 year; $143.00/year for Canada and Mexico, 1 year; $199.00/year for other countries, 1 year, air expedited service; $169.00 for two years; $250.00/year for two years, Mexico/Canada; $343.00 for two years, other countries, air expedited service; $12.00 for single issue; $18.00 for single issue, Mexico/Canada; $20.00 for single issue, other countries, air expedited service;. Free, online. Magazine featuring business-related articles for dentists.

★3624★ Dental Implantology Update

American Health Consultants Inc.
PO Box 740056
Atlanta, GA 30374
Ph: (404)262-7436   Fr: 800-688-2421
URL: http://www.ahcpub.com/

Description: Monthly. Monitors clinical techniques and technologies in dental implants and treating patients.

★3625★ Dental Town

Dental Town
10850 South 48th St.
Phoenix, AZ 85044
Ph: (480)598-0001   Fax: (480)598-3450
URL: http://www.dentaltown.com/

Monthly. Free to qualified subscribers. Magazine that offers information on the dental industry and latest dental equipment.

★3626★ Dentistry in South Dakota

South Dakota Dental Association
804 N Euclid Ave., Ste. 103
PO Box 1194
Pierre, SD 57501
Ph: (605)224-9133   Fax: (605)224-9168
E-mail: info@sddental.org

URL: http://www.sddental.org

Description: Quarterly. Provides updates on dental profession issues, small business, employer/employee relations, nutrition, and safe workplace practices. Recurring features include letters to the editor, a calendar of events, reports of meetings, news of educational opportunities, and a column titled President's Corner.

★3627★ Facets

San Diego County Dental Society
1275 W Morena Blvd., Ste. B
San Diego, CA 92110-1562
Ph: (619)275-0244   Fax: (619)275-0640
Fr: 800-201-0244
URL: http://www.sdcds.org/

Description: Ten issues/year. Reports in-house information on the Society. Recurring features include a calendar of events and columns titled New Applicants, New Members, Classified Advertising, and Continuing Education.

★3628★ Hawaii Dental Journal

Hawaii Medical Journal
1360 S Beretania St., Ste. 200
Honolulu, HI 96814
Ph: (808)536-7702   Fax: (808)536-2376
E-mail: hda@hawaiidentalassociation.net
URL: http://
www.hawaiidentalassociation.net

Bimonthly. $25.00/year for individuals; $30.00/year for other countries. Dental journal.

★3629★ The Holistic Dental Digest Plus

Once Daily Inc.
263 W End Ave., No. 2A
New York, NY 10023
Ph: (212)874-4212

Description: Bimonthly. Deals with holistic dental practices. Discusses keeping your teeth for a life-time and preventive dentistry. Offers referral service.

★3630★ Illinois Dental Journal

Illinois State Dental Society
1010 South Second St.
Springfield, IL 62704
Ph: (217)525-1406

Monthly. $25.00/year for members; $45.00/year for nonmembers; $75.00/year for nonmembers, other countries; $5.00/year for single issue. Dental magazine.

★3631★ InterFace

American Society for Geriatric Dentistry
401 North Michigan Ave.
Chicago, IL 60611
Ph: (312)527-6764   Fax: (312)673-6663
E-mail: scda@scdaonline.org
URL: http://www.scdonline.org/displaynewsletter.cfm

Description: Quarterly. Publishes news of

geriatric dentistry as well as the Society, its members and activities. Recurring features include legislative updates, a calendar of events, news of members, book reviews, editorials, a message from the president, bibliographies, and biographies.

★3632★ **Journal of the American Dental Association**

ADA Publishing
211 East Chicago Ave.
Chicago, IL 60611-2678
Ph: (312)440-2500
URL: http://www.ada.org

Monthly. $122.00/year for individuals, U.S. and Mexico; $153.00/year for institutions, U.S. and Mexico; $15.00 for single issue, U.S. and Mexico; $134.00/year for individuals, Canada; $174.00/year for institutions, Canada, plus airmail; $23.00 for single issue, Canada, plus airmail; $153.00/year for individuals, international, plus airmail; $194.00/year for institutions, international, plus airmail; $23.00 for single issue, international, plus airmail. Trade journal for the dental profession.

★3633★ **Journal of the California Dental Association**

California Dental Association
1201 K St.
Sacramento, CA 95814
Ph: (916)443-3382   Fax: (916)443-2943
Fr: 800-232-7645
URL: http://www.cda.org/publications/journal_of_the_california_de

Monthly. $18.00/year for members; $40.00/year for members, domestic; $75.00/year for nonmembers, ADA; $80.00/year for other countries. Professional magazine for dentists.

★3634★ **Journal of Dental Education**

American Dental Education Association
1400 K St. NW, Ste. 1100
Washington, DC 20005-2403
Ph: (202)289-7201   Fax: (202)289-7204
URL: http://www.adea.org

Monthly. $100.00/year; $125.00/year for Canada; $125.00/year for other countries. Peer-reviewed journal for scholarly research and reviews on dental education.

★3635★ **Journal of Dental Hygiene**

American Dental Hygienists' Association
444 North Michigan Ave., Ste. 3400
Chicago, IL 60611
Ph: (312)440-8904   Fr: 800-243-ADHA
E-mail: communications@adha.net
URL: http://www.adha.org/publications

Quarterly. $45.00/year for individuals, 1 year, 4 issues; $65.00/year for individuals for two years, 8 issues; $90.00/year for individuals, 3 years, 12 issues. Professional journal on dental hygiene.

★3636★ **Journal of Dental Research**

International and American Associations for Dental Research
1619 Duke St.
Alexandria, VA 22314-3406
Ph: (703)548-0066   Fax: (703)548-1883
URL: http://www.iadr.org

Monthly. $116.00/year for institutions; $436.00/year for individuals, print-only; $66.00/year for members, IADR Member Rate; $41.00/year for members, IADR Student Member Rate. Dental science journal.

★3637★ **Journal of Operative Dentistry**

American Academy of Gold Foil Operators
17922 Tallgrass Ct.
Noblesville, IN 46060
URL: http://operativedentistry.com/journal.html

Bimonthly. Professional journal covering issues in dentistry.

★3638★ **The Journal of Prosthetic Dentistry**

Mosby Inc.
11830 Westline Industrial Dr.
St. Louis, MO 63146
Ph: (314)872-8370   Fax: (314)432-1380
Fr: 800-325-4177
URL: http://www.us.elsevierhealth.com/product.jsp?isbn=00223913

Monthly. $206.00/year for individuals; $479.00/year for institutions; $102.00/year for students; $255.00/year for individuals, other countries; $534.00/year for institutions, other countries; $127.00/year for students, other countries. Journal emphasizing new techniques, evaluation of dental materials, pertinent basic science concepts, and patient psychology in restorative dentistry.

★3639★ **Keynotes**

The USA Section of the International College of Dentists
51 Monroe St., Ste. 1400
Rockville, MD 20850-2408
Ph: (301)251-8861   Fax: (301)738-9143
E-mail: reg-sg@icd.org
URL: http://www.usa-icd.org/information/publications.htm

Description: Semiannual. Contains news of the activities and projects of the organization, which provides networking and educational opportunities for professionals in the dental field. Recurring features include a calendar of events, reports of meetings, news of educational opportunities, and a column titled the History Corner.

★3640★ **Maryland State Dental Association Newsletter**

Maryland State Dental Association
6410F Dobbin Rd.
Columbia, MD 21045
Ph: (410)964-2880   Fax: (410)964-0583
E-mail: mddent@msda.com
URL: http://www.msda.com

Description: Monthly. Reports on health, legislative, economic, and medical issues that are pertinent to dentistry. Recurring features include letters to the editor, interviews, news of research, a calendar of events, reports of meetings, news of educational opportunities, and job listings.

★3641★ **MDS News**

Massachusetts Dental Society
Two Willow St., No. 200
Southborough, MA 01745-1027
Ph: (508)480-9797   Fax: (508)480-0002
Fr: 800-342-8747
E-mail: madental@massdental.org
URL: http://www.massdental.org/

Description: Bimonthly. Provides news on the Society's activities and articles on the dental profession. Recurring features include reports of meetings, news of educational opportunities, job listings, and notices of publications available.

★3642★ **Momentum**

Eastman Dental Center
625 Elmwood Ave.
Rochester, NY 14620
Ph: (585)275-5051
URL: http://www.urmc.rochester.edu/dentistry/news_events/newsletter.cfm

Description: Quarterly. Contains news of interest to Center alumni and friends. Recurring features include interviews, news of research, a calendar of events, and a message from the director.

★3643★ **News From The NIDCR**

National Institute of Dental and Craniofacial Research
National Institutes of Health
Bethesda, MD 20892-2190
Ph: (301)496-4261   Fax: (301)496-9988
E-mail: nidcrinfo@mail.nih.gov
URL: http://www.nidcr.nih.gov/

Description: Bimonthly. Includes the latest news about funding opportunities, training and career development opportunities, NIDCR and NIH news, and science advances.

★3644★ **News & Views**

American College of Dentists
839J Quince Orchard Blvd.
Gaithersburg, MD 20878-1614
Ph: (301)977-3223   Fax: (301)977-3330
URL: http://www.facd.org

Description: Quarterly. Presents accounts of College meetings, as well as remarks from the College's president. Publishes notices of scheduled events, spotlights individuals recognized or given awards by the College, and profiles convocation speakers, and other dental organizations. Recurring features include reports of meetings.

★3645★ Pediatric Dentistry Today

American Academy of Pediatric Dentistry
211 E. Chicago Ave., Ste. 1700
Chicago, IL 60611-2637
Ph: (312)337-2169   Fax: (312)337-6329
E-mail: abmpbp@ln.com
URL: http://www.aapd.org

Description: Bimonthly. Reports on the activities of the Academy, which seeks to advance the specialty of pediatric dentistry through practice, education, and research. Recurring features include news of research, profiles of members, and legislative updates.

★3646★ Pennsylvania Dental Journal

Pennsylvania Dental Association
PO Box 3341
3501 North Front St.
Harrisburg, PA 17105
Ph: (717)234-5941   Fax: (717)234-2186

Bimonthly. Professional dentistry magazine containing treatment/procedure news, PDA activities information, continuing education courses, and legislation updates.

★3647★ RDH

PennWell Publishing Co.
1421 South Sheridan Rd.
Tulsa, OK 74112
Ph: (918)835-3161   Fr: 800-331-4463
URL: http://rdh.pennnet.com/home.cfm

Monthly. $69.00/year for individuals; $97.00/year for Canada; $122.00/year for other countries. Magazine for dental hygiene professionals covering practice management, patient motivation, practice options, financial planning, personal development, preventive oral health care and treatment, home care instruction, radiology, anesthesia, nutrition, and new products.

★3648★ Washington State Dental Laboratory Association Newsletter

PO Box 385
Graham, WA 98338
Ph: (360)832-2471   Fax: (360)832-2471
Fr: 800-652-2212
E-mail: peg2@mashell.com
URL: http://www.wsdla.com

Association newsletter featuring articles of interest to dental laboratory technicians as well as classified advertising for technical positions available.

★3649★ Westviews

Western Los Angeles Dental Society
14722 Hawthorne Blvd., No. B
Lawndale, CA 90260
Ph: (310)349-2199   Fax: (310)349-2175
E-mail: wlads@pacbell.net.
URL: http://www.westernlads.org/

Description: Six issues/year. Carries items relating to organized dentistry and the clinical aspects of dentistry. Covers local community events involving the organization or the profession; provides updates of states agency actions affecting dentistry.

★3650★ WSDA News

Washington State Dental Association (WSDA)
1001 Fourth Ave,, Ste. 3800
Seattle, WA 98154
Ph: (206)448-1914   Fax: (206)443-9266
E-mail: wsda@wsda.org
URL: http://www.wsda.org/news/subscription.view

Description: Monthly, except October. Contains information of interest to dentists on legislation, regulations, state boards and government, and business of the association. Recurring features include letters to the editor, editorial and op-ed columns, President's message, obituraries, practice opportunities, news of educational opportunities, and job listings.

PLACEMENT AND JOB REFERRAL SERVICES

★3651★ American Public Health Association (APHA)

800 I St. NW
Washington, DC 20001
Ph: (202)777-2742   Fax: (202)777-2534
E-mail: comments@apha.org
URL: http://www.apha.org

Members: Professional organization of physicians, nurses, educators, academicians, environmentalists, epidemiologists, new professionals, social workers, health administrators, optometrists, podiatrists, pharmacists, dentists, nutritionists, health planners, other community and mental health specialists, and interested consumers. **Purpose:** Seeks to protect and promote personal, mental, and environmental health. **Activities:** Services include: promulgation of standards; establishment of uniform practices and procedures; development of the etiology of communicable diseases; research in public health; exploration of medical care programs and their relationships to public health. Sponsors job placement service.

★3652★ Ukrainian Medical Association of North America (UMANA)

2247 W Chicago Ave.
Chicago, IL 60622
Fax: (773)278-6962   Fr: 888-RXU-MANA
E-mail: umana@umana.org
URL: http://www.umana.org

Description: Physicians, surgeons, dentists, and persons in related professions who are of Ukrainian descent. Provides assistance to members; sponsors lectures. Maintains placement service, museum, biographical and medical archives.

EMPLOYER DIRECTORIES AND NETWORKING LISTS

★3653★ American Academy of Implant Dentistry

American Academy of Implant Dentistry
211 E Chicago Ave., Ste. 750
Chicago, IL 60611
Ph: (312)335-1550   Fax: (312)335-9090
Fr: 877-335-2243
URL: http://www.aaid-implant.org

Annual. Covers implant dentists.

★3654★ American Academy of Pediatric Dentistry-Membership Directory

American Academy of Pediatric Dentistry
211 E Chicago Ave., Ste. 1700
Chicago, IL 60611-2663
Ph: (312)337-2169   Fax: (312)337-6329
URL: http://www.aapd.org

Annual, November. Covers 5,600 pediatric dentists and several dentists in practice, teaching, and research. Entries include: Name, address, phone. Arrangement: Alphabetical. Indexes: Geographical.

★3655★ International Association for Orthodontics-Membership Directory

International Association for Orthodontics
750 North Lincoln Memorial Dr., Ste. 422
Milwaukee, WI 53202
Ph: (414)272-2757   Fax: (414)272-2754
Fr: 800-447-8770
URL: http://www.iaortho.com/iaopubl.htm

Annual, June. $75.00 for individuals. Covers 2,500 general and children's dentists who also work to correct facial and jaw irregularities. Entries include: Name, office address and phone, orthodontic techniques practiced. Arrangement: Geographical. Indexes: Personal name.

★3656★ Physicians and Dentists Database

Firstmark Inc.
25 Vintinner Rd.
PO Box 1270
Campton, NH 03223-1270
Ph: (603)726-4800   Fax: (603)726-4840
Fr: 800-729-2600
URL: http://www.firstmark.com

Updated continuously; printed on request. Database covers: Over 500,000 physicians and 160,000 dentists nationwide. Entries include: Individual name, address, phone, medical specialty, whether in single or group practice.

★3657★ Washington Physicians Directory

The Washington Physicians Directory
PO Box 4436
Silver Spring, MD 20914-4436
Ph: (301)384-1506   Fax: (301)384-6854
E-mail: wpd@wpdnetwork.com

URL: http://www.wpdnetwork.com

Annual, March 31. Covers 9,800 physicians in private practice or on full-time staff at hospitals in the Washington, D.C., metropolitan area. Entries include: Name, medical school and year of graduation; up to four office addresses with phone numbers for each; up to four medical specialties (indicating board certifications); Unique Physician Identification Numbers (UPIN); and e-mail. Arrangement: Alphabetical. Indexes: Geographical (within medical specialty); foreign language.

★3658★ **Worldwide Online Search Directory**

5401 World Dairy Dr.
Madison, WI 53718
Ph: (608)543-9220   Fax: (608)222-9540
Fr: 800-543-9220
E-mail: info@aacd.com
URL: http://www.aacd.com/professional/membershipbenefits.asp#4

Provides a worldwide listing of members of the American Academy of Cosmetic Dentistry.

HANDBOOKS AND MANUALS

★3659★ **The Art and Science of Being a Dentist: Leading Dentists Reveal the Secrets to Professional and Personal Success**

Aspatore Books, Incorporated
400 Commonwealth Ave., 2nd Fl.
Boston, MA 02115
Ph: (617)249-1960   Fax: (617)249-1970
Fr: (866)277-2863
URL: http://www.aspatore.com/

Jeffrey May. August 2003. $37.95. 160 pages.

★3660★ **Barron's Guide to Medical and Dental Schools**

Barron's Educational Series, Inc.
250 Wireless Blvd.
Hauppauge, NY 11788-3917
Ph: (631)434-3311   Fax: (631)434-3723
Fr: 800-645-3476
E-mail: fbrown@barronseduc.com
URL: http://barronseduc.com

Saul Wischnitzer and Edith Wischnitzer. Eleventh edition, 2000. $18.99. 625 pages. Updated with the latest facts and figures, this school directory and guidance manual presents profiles of all accredited medical, dental, and osteopathic schools in the United States and Canada.

★3661★ **Breakthrough Marketing: A Dentist's Guide to Getting and Keeping Patients**

Aardvark Publishing Company
9587 S Grandview Dr.
Sandy, UT 84092

Joel Harris. 2006. $29.95. Methods for growing and positioning your dental practice that he has implemented in hundreds of practices across the country.

★3662★ **Dental Business Strategies and Setting up for Success**

Dental Communication Unlimited
PO Box 6405
Santa Maria, CA 93456
Ph: (805)937-8711   Fax: (805)937-3035
Fr: 800-563-1454

Reece Franklin and Gordon Burgett. 2000. $50.00.

★3663★ **Opportunities in Health and Medical Careers**

The McGraw-Hill Companies
PO Box 182604
Columbus, OH 43272
Fax: (614)759-3749   Fr: 877-883-5524
E-mail: customer.service@mcgraw-hill.com
URL: http://www.mcgraw-hill.com

I. Donald Snook, Jr. and Leo D'Orazio. 2004. $13.95 (paper). 157 pages. Covers the full range of medical and health occupations. Illustrated.

★3664★ **Power Publicity for Dentists**

Clifford Publishing
PO Box 43596
Upper Montclair, NJ 07043-0596
Ph: (973)857-4142

Paul Hartunian. 2006. $79.00. Outlines ideas for stories and press releases for dental offices seeking publicity.

★3665★ **REA's Authoritative Guide to Medical Dental School**

Research and Education Association
61 Ethel Rd., W
Piscataway, NJ 08854
Ph: (732)819-8800   Fax: (732)819-8808
Fr: 800-822-0830
E-mail: info@rea.com
URL: http://www.rea.com/

1997. $21.95 (paper). 564 pages.

★3666★ **Resumes for Health and Medical Careers**

The McGraw-Hill Companies
PO Box 182604
Columbus, OH 43272
Fax: (614)759-3749   Fr: 877-883-5524
E-mail: customer.service@mcgraw-hill.com
URL: http://www.mcgraw-hill.com

Third edition, 2003. $11.95 (paper). 160 pages.

EMPLOYMENT AGENCIES AND SEARCH FIRMS

★3667★ **Colucci, Blendow & Johnson**

643 Main St., Ste. 7
PO Box 10
Half Moon Bay, CA 94019-1988
Ph: (650)712-0103   Fax: (650)712-0105
E-mail: exsearch@ix.netcom.com

Executive search consultants in the medical technology area that includes pharmaceuticals, medical equipment and device manufacturers, biotechnology, therapeutic supplies, diagnostic laboratory equipment and supplies, diagnostic imaging equipment and supplies, medical services, chemicals, cosmetic and toiletries, dental, veterinarian, and agricultural genetics companies.

★3668★ **DDS Staffing Resources, Inc.**

9755 Dogwood Rd., Ste. 200
Roswell, GA 30075
Ph: (770)998-7779   Fax: (770)552-0176
Fr: 888-668-7779
E-mail: ddsstaffing@ddsstaffing.com
URL: http://www.ddsstaffing.com

Dental staffing agency.

★3669★ **Team Placement Service, Inc.**

1414 Prince St., Ste. 202
Alexandria, VA 22314
Ph: (703)820-8618   Fax: (703)820-3368
Fr: 800-495-6767
E-mail: 4jobs@teamplace.com
URL: http://www.teamplace.com

Full-service personnel consultants provide placement for healthcare staff, physician and dentist, private practice, and hospitals. Conduct interviews, tests, and reference checks to select the top 20% of applicants. Survey applicants' skill levels, provide backup information on each candidate, select compatible candidates for consideration, and insure the hiring process minimizes potential legal liability. Industries served: healthcare and government agencies providing medical, dental, biotech, laboratory, hospitals, and physician search.

ONLINE JOB SOURCES AND SERVICES

★3670★ **Medhunters.com**

Fr: 800-664-0278
E-mail: info@medhunters.com
URL: http://www.medhunters.com

Description: Career search site for jobs in all health care specialties; educational resources; visa and licensing information for relocation; interesting articles; relocation tools; links to professional organizations and general resources.

★3671★ Medzilla

URL: http://www.medzilla.com

Description: General medical website which matches employers and job hunters to their ideal employees and jobs through search capabilities. **Main files include:** Post Jobs, Search Resumes, Post Resumes, Search Jobs, Head Hunters, Articles, Salary Survey.

★3672★ Monster Healthcare

URL: http://healthcare.monster.com/

Description: Delivers nationwide access to healthcare recruiting. Employers can post job listings or ads. Job seekers can post and code resumes, and search over 150,000 healthcare job listings, healthcare career advice columns, career resources information, and member employer profiles and services.

★3673★ ProHealthJobs

Fr: 800-796-1738
E-mail: Info@prohealthedujobs.com
URL: http://www.prohealthjobs.com

Description: Career resources site for the medical and health care field. Lists professional opportunities, product information, continuing education and open positions.

TRADESHOWS

★3674★ Academy of General Dentistry Annual Meeting

Academy of General Dentistry
211 E. Chicago Ave., Ste. 900
Chicago, IL 60611-1999
Ph: (312)440-4300   Fax: (312)440-0559
Fr: 888-243-3368
E-mail: agdmeet@agd.org
URL: http://www.agd.org

Annual. **Primary Exhibits:** Dental products and services.

★3675★ Alabama Dental Association Annual Session

Alabama Dental Association
836 Washington Ave.
Montgomery, AL 36104
Ph: (334)265-1684   Fax: (334)262-6218
E-mail: Waren@aldaonline.org
URL: http://www.aldaonline.org/main.htm

Annual. **Primary Exhibits:** Dental equipment, sundry dental supplies, computer software, and pharmaceutical and dental instruments.

★3676★ American Academy of Fixed Prosthodontics Scientific Session

American Academy of Fixed
 Prosthodontics
1930 Sea Way
PO Box 1409
Bodega Bay, CA 94923-1409
Ph: (707)875-3040   Fax: (707)875-2927
Fr: 800-785-9188

Annual. **Primary Exhibits:** Prosthodontics equipment, supplies, and services.

★3677★ American Academy of Implant Dentistry Annual Meeting

American Academy of Implant Dentistry
211 E. Chicago Ave., Ste. 750
Chicago, IL 60611
Ph: (312)335-1550   Fax: (312)335-9090
E-mail: info@aaid-implant.org
URL: http://www.aaid-implant.org

Annual. **Primary Exhibits:** Dental equipment, supplies, and services. **Dates and Locations:** 2008 Oct 29 - Nov 02; San Diego, CA.

★3678★ American Academy of Pediatric Dentistry Annual Meeting

American Academy of Pediatric Dentistry
211 E. Chicago Ave., Ste. 1700
Chicago, IL 60611-2663
Ph: (312)337-2169   Fax: (312)337-6329
URL: http://www.aapd.org

Annual. **Primary Exhibits:** Dental products and publications. **Dates and Locations:** 2008 May 22-26; Washington, DC; Marriott Wardman Park; 2009 May 21-25; Honolulu, HI; Hawaii Convention Center; 2010 May 27-31; Chicago, IL; Hilton Towers.

★3679★ American Association of Dental Schools Annual Session and Exposition

American Dental Education Association
1400 K St., NW, Ste. 1100
Washington, DC 20005
Ph: (202)289-7201   Fax: (202)289-7204
URL: http://www.adea.org

Annual. **Primary Exhibits:** Dental equipment and supplies, publications, video equipment, and computers.

★3680★ American Association of Endodontists Annual Convention and Trade Show

American Association of Endodontists
211 E. Chicago Ave., Ste. 1100
Chicago, IL 60611-2691
Ph: (312)266-7255   Fax: (312)266-9867
Fr: 800-872-3636
E-mail: info@aae.org
URL: http://www.aae.org/

Annual. **Primary Exhibits:** Industry related equipment, supplies, and services. **Dates and Locations:** 2008 Apr 09-12; Vancouver, BC, Canada; Vancouver Convention and Exhibition Centre.

★3681★ American Association of Orthodontists Trade Show and Scientific Session

American Association of Orthodontists
401 N. Lindbergh Blvd.
St. Louis, MO 63141-7816
Ph: (314)993-1700   Fax: (314)997-1745
Fr: 800-424-2841
E-mail: info@aaortho.org
URL: http://www.aaomembers.org/

Annual. **Primary Exhibits:** Orthodontic equipment and materials. **Dates and Locations:** 2008 May 16-20; Denver, CO; 2009 May 01-05; Boston, MA; 2010 Apr 30 - May 04; Washington, DC; 2010 May 13-17; Honolulu, HI.

★3682★ American Dental Association Annual Session & Technical Exhibition

American Dental Association
211 E. Chicago Ave.
Chicago, IL 60611-2678
Ph: (312)440-2500
URL: http://www.ada.org

Annual. **Primary Exhibits:** Dental equipment, instruments, materials, therapeutics, and services.

★3683★ American Dental Society of Anesthesiology Scientific Meeting

American Dental Society of
 Anesthesiology
211 E. Chicago Ave.
Chicago, IL 60611
Ph: 877-255-3742   Fax: (312)642-9713
Fr: 800-722-7788
URL: http://www.adsahome.org

Annual. **Primary Exhibits:** Anesthetics and anesthesia monitoring equipment. **Dates and Locations:** 2008 May 01-03; Monterey, PR; Westin Rio Mar Resort.

★3684★ Annual Scientific Sessions

5401 World Dairy Dr.
Madison, WI 53718
Ph: (608)543-9220   Fax: (608)222-9540
Fr: 800-543-9220
E-mail: info@aacd.com
URL: http://www.aacd.com/

Annual conference allowing members to exchange new ideas and network on the latest in clinical procedures, cosmetic practice development and self-enrichment.

★3685★ Chicago Dental Society Midwinter Meeting

Chicago Dental Society
401 N. Michigan Ave., Ste. 200
Chicago, IL 60611-4205
Ph: (312)836-7300   Fax: (312)836-7337
URL: http://www.cds.org

Annual. **Primary Exhibits:** Dental equipment, services, and related business services.

★3686★ Detroit Dental Review

Detroit District Dental Society
3011 W. Grand Blvd., Ste. 460
Detroit, MI 48202
Ph: (313)817-3503   Fax: (313)871-3500
E-mail: teeth@provide.net
URL: http://detroitdentalsociety.org

Annual. **Primary Exhibits:** Dental equipment, supplies, and services, including office systems.

★3687★ General Session and Exhibition of the IADR

International Association for Dental
    Research
1619 Duke St.
Alexandria, VA 22314-3406
Ph: (703)548-0066   Fax: (703)548-1883
E-mail: research@iadr.org
URL: http://www.dentalresearch.org

Annual. **Primary Exhibits:** Dentistry equipment, supplies, and services. **Dates and Locations:** 2008 Jul 02-05; Toronto, ON, Canada; 2009 Apr 01-04; Miami, FL.

★3688★ Greater New York Dental Meeting

Greater New York Dental Meeting
518 Fifth Ave., 3rd Fl.
New York, NY 10036-7503
Ph: (212)398-6922   Fax: (212)398-6934
E-mail: info@gnydm.com
URL: http://www.gnydm.com

Annual. **Primary Exhibits:** Dental products and services. **Dates and Locations:** 2008 Nov 28 - Dec 03.

★3689★ International Education Congress of Dental Technology

Dental Laboratory Association of the
    State of New York
6935 Lakeshore Dr.
Dallas, TX 75214
E-mail: dlany@aol.com
URL: http://www.dlany.org

Annual. **Primary Exhibits:** Dental laboratory supplies and services.

★3690★ International Medical and Dental Hypnotherapy Association (IMDHA)

International Medical and Dental
    Hypnotherapy Association (IMDHA)
4110 Edgeland, Ste. 800
Royal Oak, MI 48073-2285
Ph: (248)549-5594   Fax: (248)549-5421
Fr: 800-257-5467
E-mail: aspencer@infinityinst.com
URL: http://www.infinityinst.com

Annual. **Primary Exhibits:** Hypnotherapy and Holistic Health.

★3691★ Jewel of the Great Lakes-Wisconsin Dental Meeting

Wisconsin Dental Association
6737 W. Washington St. Ste. 2360
West Allis, WI 53214
Ph: (414)276-4520   Fax: (414)276-8431
URL: http://www.wda.org

Annual. **Primary Exhibits:** Dental equipment and supplies, office supplies, publications, and data processing.

★3692★ Michigan Dental Association Annual Session

Michigan Dental Association
Public Relations Dept.
230 N. Washington Sq., Ste. 208
Lansing, MI 48933-1392
Ph: (517)372-9070   Fax: (517)372-0008
Fr: 800-589-2632
URL: http://www.michigandental.org

Annual. **Primary Exhibits:** Dental equipment, materials, and instruments; computers; software; uniforms; and estate planners.

★3693★ Mid-Continent Dental Congress

Greater St. Louis Dental Society
13667 Manchester Rd.
St. Louis, MO 63131-1616
Ph: (314)965-5960   Fax: (314)965-4746
E-mail: gslds@gslds.org
URL: http://www.gslds.org

Annual. **Primary Exhibits:** Dental equipment, supplies, and services.

★3694★ Mid-West Spring Technical Meeting

PO Box 376
New Albany, IN 47151
Ph: (812)542-0730   Fax: (866)429-5044
Fr: 800-366-1161
E-mail: mjacobi@mwstm.com
URL: http://mwstm.com/

Trade show offering more than sixty clinics and hands-on courses promoting all fields of dental laboratory technology.

★3695★ National Dental Association Annual Convention

National Dental Association, Inc.
3517 16th St., NW
Washington, DC 20010
Ph: (202)588-1697   Fax: (202)588-1244
E-mail: admin@ndaonline.org
URL: http://www.ndaonline.org

Annual. **Primary Exhibits:** Dental and Pharmaceutical equipment, supplies, and services.

★3696★ Nation's Capital Dental Meeting

District of Columbia Dental Society
502 C St., NE
Washington, DC 20002-5810
Ph: (202)547-7613   Fax: (202)546-1482
URL: http://www.dcdental.org

Annual. **Primary Exhibits:** Equipment, clothing, dental supplies, office management systems, and publications.

★3697★ Ohio Dental Association Annual Session

Ohio Dental Association
1370 Dublin Rd.
Columbus, OH 43215-1098
Ph: (614)486-2700   Fax: (614)486-0381
E-mail: dentist@oda.org
URL: http://www.oda.org

Annual. **Primary Exhibits:** Dental equipment, supplies, and services, computers, and insurance.

★3698★ Pacific Northwest Dental Conference

Washington State Dental Association
1001 Fourth Ave., Ste. 3800
Seattle, WA 98154
Ph: (206)448-1914   Fax: (206)443-9266
E-mail: wsda@wsda.org
URL: http://www.wsda.org

Annual. **Primary Exhibits:** Dental supplies, instruments, and equipment.

★3699★ Star of the North Meeting

Minnesota Dental Association
2236 Marshall Ave., Ste. 200
St. Paul, MN 55104
Ph: (651)646-7454   Fax: (651)646-8246
E-mail: info@mndental.org
URL: http://www.mndental.org

Annual. **Primary Exhibits:** Dental equipment and supplies, dental laboratory equipment, office equipment, and service organizations. **Dates and Locations:** 2008 Apr 12-14; St. Paul, MN; RiverCentre.

★3700★ Star of the South Dental Meeting

Greater Houston Dental Society
1 Greenway Plz., Ste. 110
Houston, TX 77046
Ph: (713)961-4337   Fax: (713)961-3617
URL: http://www.ghds.com

Annual. **Primary Exhibits:** Dental equipment, supplies, and dental office amenities.

★3701★ Thomas P. Hinman Dental Meeting & Exhibits

Thomas P. Hinman Dental Society of
    Atlanta
33 Lenox Pte.
Atlanta, GA 30324-3172
Ph: (404)231-1663   Fax: (404)231-9638
E-mail: info@hinman.org
URL: http://www.hinman.org

Annual. **Primary Exhibits:** Dental equipment, supplies, and services. **Dates and Locations:** 2008 Mar 13-15; Atlanta, GA; Georgia World Congress Center.

★3702★ Three Rivers Dental Conference

Dental Society of Western Pennsylvania
900 Cedar Ave.
Pittsburgh, PA 15212
Ph: (412)321-5810   Fax: (412)321-7719
URL: http://www.dswp.org

Annual. **Primary Exhibits:** Dental products and equipment, computers, office equipment, and insurance.

★3703★ Western Regional Dental Convention

Arizona State Dental Association
3193 N. Drinkwater Blvd.
Scottsdale, AZ 85251-6491
Ph: (480)344-5777   Fax: (480)344-1442
Fr: 800-866-2732
URL: http://www.azda.org

Annual. **Primary Exhibits:** Dental supplies and services. **Dates and Locations:** 2008 Apr 03-05; Phoenix, AZ.

★3704★ Yankee Dental Congress

Massachusetts Dental Society
2 Willow St., No. 200
Southborough, MA 01745-1027
Ph: (508)480-9797   Fax: (508)480-0002
Fr: 800-342-8747
E-mail: madental@massdental.org
URL: http://www.massdental.org

Annual. **Primary Exhibits:** Dental products, equipment, and services.

OTHER SOURCES

★3705★ Academy of General Dentistry (AGD)

211 E Chicago Ave., Ste. 900
Chicago, IL 60611-1999
Ph: (312)440-4345   Fax: (312)440-0559
Fr: 888-243-3368
E-mail: membership@agd.org
URL: http://www.agd.org

Description: Seeks to serve the needs and represent the interest of general dentists. Fosters their dentists' continued proficiency through quality continuing dental education to better serves the public.

★3706★ Academy of Operative Dentistry (AOD)

PO Box 14996
Gainesville, FL 32604-2996
E-mail: greg679@cox.net
URL: http://operativedentistry.com

Description: Dentists and persons in allied industries. Seeks to ensure quality in all of operative dentistry, teaching, service and research.

★3707★ Academy of Oral Dynamics (AOD)

134 E Church Rd.
Elkins Park, PA 19027-2208
Ph: (215)635-2336
URL: http://www.ada.org/ada/organizations

Description: Represents dentists. Promotes the study of oral dynamics, especially as it applies to the use of natural teeth in restoring and maintaining a healthy, functioning mouth; disseminates information gained through research. Conducts educational programs.

★3708★ American Academy of Cosmetic Dentistry

5401 World Dairy Dr.
Madison, WI 53718
Ph: (608)543-9220   Fax: (608)222-9540
Fr: 800-543-9220
E-mail: info@aacd.com
URL: http://www.aacd.com/

Members include more than 8,000 cosmetic and reconstructive dentists, dental laboratory technicians, dental auxiliaries, dental hygienists, educators, researchers and students. Membership benefits include AACD accreditation, registration to AACD's Annual Scientific Session, publications, online search directory, marketing materials, and more. Membership categories include: Doctors, Lab Technicians or Owners, and Supporting Members $425/one year, $745/two years, $1,050/three years. Other categories are: Corporate Gold $2,500; Faculty $115; Residents $95; Hygienists $95; Recent Graduate Dentists $95; Dental Students $95; and Students $20.

★3709★ American Academy of Dental Group Practice (AADGP)

2525 E Arizona Biltmore Cir., Ste. 127
Phoenix, AZ 85016
Ph: (602)381-1185   Fax: (602)381-1093
E-mail: info@aadgp.org
URL: http://www.aadgp.org

Description: Represents active dentists and dental group practices. Aims to improve the level of dental service provided by members through exchanging and expanding of ideas and techniques for patient treatment and practice administration. Promotes group practice and research; accumulates and disseminates information; seeks to achieve the proper recognition for the aims and goals of group practice. Helps support an accreditation program as a system of voluntary peer review.

★3710★ American Association of Dental Examiners (AADE)

211 E Chicago Ave., Ste. 760
Chicago, IL 60611
Ph: (312)440-7464   Fax: (312)440-3525
E-mail: info@aadexam.org
URL: http://www.aadexam.org

Description: Represents present and past members of state dental examining boards and board administrators. Assists member agencies with problems related to state

dental board examinations and licensure, and enforcement of the state dental practice act. Conducts research; compiles statistics.

★3711★ American Association of Women Dentists (AAWD)

216 W Jackson Blvd., Ste. 625
Chicago, IL 60606
Fax: (312)750-1203   Fr: 800-920-2293
E-mail: info@aawd.org
URL: http://www.aawd.org

Description: Represents dental students or dentists who are interested in dentistry and advancing women in dentistry. Dedicates itself to enhancing and promoting unique participation and leadership for women in organized dentistry.

★3712★ American College of Dentists (ACD)

839J Quince Orchard Blvd.
Gaithersburg, MD 20878-1614
Ph: (301)977-3223   Fax: (301)977-3330
E-mail: office@acd.org
URL: http://acd.org

Members: Dentists and others serving in capacities related to the dental profession. **Purpose:** Seeks to advance the standards of the profession of dentistry. **Activities:** Conducts educational and research programs. Maintains speakers' bureau and charitable programs.

★3713★ American College of Prosthodontists

211 E Chicago Ave., Ste. 1000
Chicago, IL 60611
Ph: (312)573-1260   Fax: (312)573-1257
URL: http://www.prosthodontics.org/

Membership includes more than 3,000 prosthodontists, dental technicians, dental students and other dental professionals contributing to the specialty. Committed to the esthetic restoration of teeth, including bridges, crowns/caps, dental implants, dentures, partial dentures, whitening and veneers. Membership includes free subscriptions to the Journal of Prosthodontics, the Messenger, and e-blasts. Five categories of membership include: Member/Fellow: (Diplomats of the American Board of Prosthodontics) $632/join before July 1; $316/join after July 1; $125 non-refundable application/reinstatement fee. Student: (students enrolled in an advanced prosthodontic training program accredited by the American Dental Association) Students pay a discounted annual session registration fee but may not hold voting membership on committees or hold elective or appointed office or serve in the House of Delegates. Dental Technician Alliance: (Certified dental technician with proof of formal training in dental technology and one current ACP member-sponsor) $250/before July 1; $125/after July 1; $125 non-refundable application/reinstatement fee. Academic Alliance: (individuals holding an academic teaching appointment within an ADA accredited prosthodontic program or an undergraduate training position in the discipline of prosthodontics) $450/before July 1; $225/

after July 1; $125 non-refundable application/reinstatement fee.

★3714★ **American Dental Association (ADA)**

211 E Chicago Ave.
Chicago, IL 60611-2678
Ph: (312)440-2500   Fax: (312)440-2800
E-mail: publicinfo@ada.org
URL: http://www.ada.org

Description: Professional society of dentists. Encourages the improvement of the health of the public and promotes the art and science of dentistry in matters of legislation and regulations. Inspects and accredits dental schools and schools for dental hygienists, assistants, and laboratory technicians. Conducts research programs at ADA Foundation Research Institute. Produces most of the dental health education material used in the U.S. Sponsors National Children's Dental Health Month and Give Kids a Smile Day. Compiles statistics on personnel, practice, and dental care needs and attitudes of patients with regard to dental health. Sponsors 13 councils.

★3715★ **American Dental Education Association (ADEA)**

1400 K St. NW, Ste. 1100
Washington, DC 20005
Ph: (202)289-7201   Fax: (202)289-7204
E-mail: valachovicr@adea.org
URL: http://www.adea.org

Description: Individuals interested in dental education; schools of dentistry, advanced dental and allied dental education in the U.S., Canada, and Puerto Rico; affiliated institutions of the federal government and corporations. Works to promote better teaching and education in dentistry and dental research and to facilitate exchange of ideas among dental educators. Sponsors meetings, conferences, and workshops; conducts surveys, studies, and special projects and publishes their results. Maintains 37 sections and 8 special interest groups representing many different aspects of dental education.

★3716★ **American School Health Association (ASHA)**

PO Box 708
Kent, OH 44240
Ph: (330)678-1601   Fax: (330)678-4526
E-mail: asha@ashaweb.org
URL: http://www.ashaweb.org

Description: School physicians, school nurses, counsellors, nutritionists, psychologists, social workers, administrators, school health coordinators, health educators, and physical educators working in schools, professional preparation programs, public health, and community-based organizations. Promotes coordinated school health programs that include health education, health services, a healthful school environment, physical education, nutrition services, and psycho-social health services offered in schools collaboratively with families and other members of the community. Offers professional reference materials and professional development opportunities. Conducts pilot programs that inform materials development, provides technical assistance to school professionals, advocates for school health.

★3717★ **American Student Dental Association (ASDA)**

211 E Chicago Ave., Ste. 700
Chicago, IL 60611-2687
Ph: (312)440-2795   Fax: (312)440-2820
Fr: 800-621-8099
E-mail: nancy@asdanet.org
URL: http://www.asdanet.org

Description: Predoctoral and postdoctoral dental students organized to improve the quality of dental education and to promote the accessibility of oral health care; additional membership categories include predental, postdoctoral, international and associate. Represents dental students before legislative bodies, organizations, and associations that affect dental students. Disseminates information to dental students. Sponsors advocacy program and "externships" including Washington National Health Policy, Chicago Administrative, State Government Affairs, and Research.

★3718★ **Dental Group Management Association (DGMA)**

2525 E Arizona Biltmore Cir., Ste. 127
Phoenix, AZ 85016
Ph: (602)381-8980   Fax: (602)381-1093
E-mail: dgma@aadgp.org
URL: http://www.dgma.org

Description: Represents dental group business managers and others interested in group practice management.

★3719★ **Exploring Health Occupations**

Cambridge Educational
PO Box 2053
Princeton, NJ 08543-2053
Ph: 800-257-5126   Fax: (609)671-0266
Fr: 800-468-4227
E-mail: custserv@films.com
URL: http://www.cambridgeeducational.com

VHS and DVD. $159.90. 1999. Two-part series provides a detailed view of the field of medical technicians and technologists, EMTs, nurses, therapists, and assistants.

★3720★ **Health Service Occupations**

Delphi Productions
3159 6th St.
Boulder, CO 80304
Ph: (303)443-2100   Fax: (303)443-4022
Fr: 888-443-2400
E-mail: support@delphivideo.com
URL: http://www.delphivideo.com

$95.00. 50 minutes. Part of the Careers for the 21st Century Video Library.

★3721★ **Holistic Dental Association (HDA)**

PO Box 151444
San Diego, CA 92175
Ph: (619)923-3120   Fax: (619)615-2228
E-mail: info@holisticdental.org
URL: http://www.holisticdental.org

Description: Represents dentists, chiropractors, dental hygienists, physical therapists, and medical doctors. Aims to provide a holistic approach to better dental care for patients, and to expand techniques, medications, and philosophies that pertain to extractions, anesthetics, fillings, crowns, and orthodontics. Encourages the use of homeopathic medications, acupuncture, cranial osteopathy, nutritional techniques, and physical therapy in treating patients in addition to conventional treatments. Sponsors training and educational seminars.

★3722★ **International Congress of Oral Implantologists (ICOI)**

248 Lorraine Ave., Ste. 3
Upper Montclair, NJ 07043
Ph: (973)783-6300   Fax: (973)783-1175
Fr: 800-442-0525
E-mail: icoi@dentalimplants.com
URL: http://www.icoi.org

Description: Dentists and oral surgeons dedicated to the teaching of and research in oral implantology (branch of dentistry dealing with dental implants placed into or on top of the jaw bone). Offers fellowship, mastership, and diplomate certification programs. Compiles statistics and maintains registry of current research in the field. Sponsors classes, seminars, and workshops at universities, hospitals, and societies worldwide. Provides consultation and patient information/referral services.

★3723★ **Medicine & Related Occupations**

Delphi Productions
3159 6th St.
Boulder, CO 80304
Ph: (303)443-2100   Fax: (303)443-4022
Fr: 888-443-2400
E-mail: support@delphivideo.com
URL: http://www.delphivideo.com

$95.00. 45 minutes. Part of the Careers for the 21st Century Video Library.

★3724★ **National Dental Association (NDA)**

3517 16th St. NW
Washington, DC 20010
Ph: (202)588-1697   Fax: (202)588-1244
Fr: 877-628-3368
E-mail: admin@ndaonline.org
URL: http://www.ndaonline.org

Description: Professional society for dentists. **Purpose:** Aims to provide quality dental care to the unserved and underserved public and promote knowledge of the art and science of dentistry. Advocates the inclusion of dental care services in health care programs on local, state, and national levels. Fosters the integration of minority dental health care providers in the profession, and promotes dentistry as a viable career for minorities through support programs. **Activities:** Conducts research programs. Group is distinct from the former name of the American Dental Association.

★3725★ National Rural Health Association (NRHA)

Administrative Office
521 E 63rd St.
Kansas City, MO 64110-3329
Ph: (816)756-3140   Fax: (816)756-3144
E-mail: mail@nrharural.org
URL: http://www.nrharural.org

Description: Administrators, physicians, nurses, physician assistants, health planners, academicians, and others interested or involved in rural health care. Creates a better understanding of health care problems unique to rural areas; utilizes a collective approach in finding positive solutions; articulates and represents the health care needs of rural America; supplies current information to rural health care providers; serves as a liaison between rural health care programs throughout the country. Offers continuing education credits for medical, dental, nursing, and management courses.

★3726★ North American Sikh Medical and Dental Association (NASMDA)

13801 Allied Rd.
Chester, VA 23836
Ph: (804)691-1906
E-mail: gurmitchilana@yahoo.com
URL: http://sikhdocs.org

Description: Promotes the interests of Sikh physicians and dentists in the United States, Canada and elsewhere. Supports Sikh physicians, dentists and other Sikh professionals pursuing their careers in those fields or any other fields. Assists Sikh medical and dental graduates to establish practices and help them obtain adequate post-graduate training. Seeks to improve the medical education and delivery of medical care in the parent homeland. Compiles a comprehensive directory of Sikh physicians and dentists residing in North America.

★3727★ Society for Executive Leadership in Academic Medicine International (SELAM)

PO Box 72
Jenkintown, PA 19046
Ph: (215)842-6473   Fax: (215)842-1041
E-mail: selam@selaminternational.org
URL: http://selaminternational.org

Description: Advocates for the advancement and promotion of women to executive positions in academic health professions. Supports programs designed for individuals interested in careers in academic medicine and dentistry. Promotes collaborations and networking among members and other organizations that share common goals.

★3728★ Women in Dentistry

Her Own Words
PO Box 5264
Madison, WI 53705-0264
Ph: (608)271-7083   Fax: (608)271-0209
E-mail: herownword@aol.com
URL: http://www.herownwords.com/

Video. Jocelyn Riley. $95.00. 15 minutes. Resource guide also available for $45.00.

★3729★ Women in Nontraditional Careers: An Introduction

Her Own Words
PO Box 5264
Madison, WI 53705
Ph: (608)271-7083   Fax: (608)271-0209
E-mail: herownword@aol.com
URL: http://www.herownwords.com/

Video. Jocelyn Riley. $95.00. 15 minutes. Resource guide also available for $45.00.

Designers

E-mail: ncrum@reedbusiness.com
URL: http://www.housingzone.com/toc-archive-pbx

Monthly. Free. The integrated engineering magazine of the building construction industry.

★3741★ Society for Environmental Graphic Design-Messages

Society for Environmental Graphic Design
1230 Avenue of the Americas, 7th Fl.
Rockefeller Plaza Center
New York, NY 10020
Ph: (917)639-4074   Fax: (917)639-4005
E-mail: editor@dexigner.com
URL: http://www.dexigner.com/graphic/links-g665.html

Description: Bimonthly. Reports on Society program news, member services, resources, and product news.

★3742★ Visual Merchandising and Store Design

ST Media Group International Inc.
407 Gilbert Ave.
Cincinnati, OH 45202
Ph: (513)421-2050   Fax: (513)421-5144
Fr: 800-925-1110
E-mail: vmsd@stmediagroup.com
URL: http://www.stmediagroup.com/index.php3?d=pubs&p=vm

Monthly. $42.00/year for individuals, U.S.; $66.00/year for individuals, 2 years, U.S.; $62.00/year for individuals, Canada (surface); $100.00/year for individuals, 2 years, Canada (surface); $65.00/year for individuals, Mexico/Foreign (surface); $105.00/year for individuals, 2 years, Mexico/Foreign (surface); $100.00/year for individuals, Mexico, 1st Class; $175.00/year for individuals, 2 years, Mexico 1st Class; $115.00/year for individuals, Central/South America; $205.00/year for individuals, 2 years, Central/South America. The leading magazine of the retail design industry covering the latest trends in retail design, store planning, and merchandise presentation.

★3743★ Voice: AIGA Journal of Design

American Institute of Graphic Arts
164 5th Ave.
New York, NY 10010
Ph: (212)807-1990   Fax: (212)807-1799

Free to members. Online journal for the discussion of design matters, including interviews, essays, and criticism.

★3744★ Wire & Cable Technology International

Initial Publications Inc.
3869 Darrow Rd., Ste. 109
Stow, OH 44224
Ph: (330)686-9544   Fax: (330)686-9563
E-mail: info@wiretech.com
URL: http://www.wiretech.com/

Bimonthly. Magazine for manufacturers of ferrous, nonferrous, bare, and insulated wire.

PLACEMENT AND JOB REFERRAL SERVICES

★3745★ American Society of Furniture Designers (ASFD)

144 Woodland Dr.
New London, NC 28127
Ph: (910)576-1273   Fax: (910)576-1573
E-mail: info@asfd.com
URL: http://www.asfd.com

Members: Represents professional furniture designers, teachers, students, corporate suppliers of products and services; others who supply products and services related to furniture design. Seeks to promote the profession of furniture design. Conducts and cooperates in educational courses and seminars for furniture designers and persons planning to enter the field. Maintains placement service.

★3746★ Broadcast Designer's Association (BDA)

9000 W Sunset Blvd., Ste. 900
Los Angeles, CA 90069
Ph: (310)788-7600   Fax: (310)788-7616
E-mail: brett@ashyagency.com
URL: http://www.bda.tv

Members: Designers, artists, art directors, illustrators, photographers, animators, and other motion graphic professionals in the electronic media industry; educators and students; commercial and industrial companies that manufacture products related to design. **Purpose:** Seeks to promote understanding between designers, clients, and management; to stimulate innovative ideas and techniques; to encourage and provide a resource for young talents; and to provide a forum for discussion on industry issues and concerns. **Activities:** Maintains placement service; conducts surveys and compiles statistics.

★3747★ Professional Services Management Association (PSMA)

99 Canal Center Plz., Ste. 330
Alexandria, VA 22314
Ph: (703)739-0277   Fax: (703)549-2498
Fr: (866)739-0277
E-mail: info@psmanet.org
URL: http://www.psmanet.org

Members: Individuals responsible for any or all aspects of business management in a professional design firm. **Purpose:** Aims to improve the effectiveness of professional design firms through the growth and development of business management skills. Seeks to: provide a forum for the exchange of ideas and information and discussion and resolution of common problems and issues; establish guidelines for approaches to common management concerns; initiate and maintain professional relationships among members; improve recognition and practice of management as a science in professional design firms; advance and improve reputable service to clients; offer a variety of comprehensive educational programs and

opportunities. **Activities:** Maintains speakers' bureau and placement service. Holds seminars. Conducts surveys and research programs. Compiles statistics.

★3748★ University and College Designers Association (UCDA)

199 W Enon Spring Rd., Ste. 300
Smyrna, TN 37167
Ph: (615)459-4559   Fax: (615)459-5229
E-mail: info@ucda.com
URL: http://www.ucda.com

Description: Represents colleges, universities, junior colleges, or technical institutions that have an interest in visual communication design; individuals who are involved in the active production of such communication design or as teachers or students of these related disciplines. Improves members' skills and techniques in communication and design areas such as graphics, photography, signage, films, and other related fields of communication design. Aids and assists members in their efforts to be professionals in their respective fields through programs of education and information. Maintains placement service.

EMPLOYER DIRECTORIES AND NETWORKING LISTS

★3749★ Black Book Photography

Black Book Marketing Group
740 Broadway, Ste. 202
New York, NY 10003
Ph: (212)979-6700   Fax: (212)673-4321
Fr: 800-841-1246
URL: http://www.BlackBook.com

Annual; latest edition 2007. $88.00 for individuals. Publication includes: Over 19,000 art directors, creative directors, photographers and photographic services, design firms, advertising agencies, and other firms whose products or services are used in advertising. Entries include: Company name, address, phone. Principal content of publication consists of 4-color samples from the leading commercial photographers. Arrangement: Classified by product/service.

★3750★ Career Opportunities in the Fashion Industry

Facts On File Inc.
132 W 31st St., 17th Fl.
New York, NY 10001
Ph: (212)967-8800   Fax: 800-678-3633
Fr: 800-322-8755
URL: http://www.factsonfile.com/

Latest edition 2nd, 2007. $49.50 for individuals; $44.55 for libraries. Publication includes: Lists of internet resources, educational institutions, organizations, and associations related to the fashion industry. Principal content of publication is information on careers in the fashion world. Indexes: Alphabetical.

★3751★ Careers in Focus: Design

Facts On File Inc.
132 W 31st St., 17th Fl.
New York, NY 10001
Ph: (212)967-8800   Fax: 800-678-3633
Fr: 800-322-8755
URL: http://www.factsonfile.com

Latest edition 2nd, 2005. $29.95 for individuals; $26.95 for libraries. Covers an overview of design, followed by a selection of jobs profiled in detail, including the nature of the job, earnings, prospects for employment, what kind of training and skills it requires, and sources for further information.

★3752★ ENR-Top 500 Design Firms Issue

McGraw-Hill Inc.
1221 Ave. of the Americas
New York, NY 10020-1095
Ph: (212)512-2000   Fax: (212)512-3840
Fr: 877-833-5524
URL: http://enr.construction.com/people/sourcebooks/top500Design/

Annual, latest edition 2007. $50.00 for individuals. Publication includes: List of 500 leading architectural, engineering, and specialty design firms selected on basis of annual billings. Entries include: Company name, headquarters location, type of firm, current and prior year rank in billings, types of services, countries in which operated in preceding year. Arrangement: Ranked by billings.

HANDBOOKS AND MANUALS

★3753★ 50 Designers/50 Costumes: Concept to Character

University of California Press/Journals
2120 Berkeley Way
Berkeley, CA 94704-1012
Ph: (510)642-4247   Fax: (510)643-7127
E-mail: askucp@ucpress.edu
URL: http://www.ucpress.edu/

Jeffrey Kurland, Deborah Nadoolman Landis, and Academy of Motion Picture Arts and Sciences. 2005. $24.95. Costume designers discuss the challenges involved in creating designs for motion pictures.

★3754★ 100 Habits of Successful Graphic Designers: Insider Secrets from the World's Top Talent

Rockport Publishers
100 Cummings Center, Ste., 406-L
Beverly, MA 01915
Ph: (978)282-9590   Fax: (978)283-2742
URL: http://www.rockpub.com/

Josh Berger. 2005. $25.00. Illustrated. 192 pages.

★3755★ An A-Z of Type Designers

Yale University Press
PO Box 209040
New Haven, CT 06520
Ph: (203)432-0960   Fax: (203)432-0948
URL: http://yalepress.yale.edu

Neil Macmillan. 2006. $35.00.

★3756★ Business and Legal Forms for Graphic Designers

Allworth Press
10 E. 23rd St., Ste. 510
New York, NY 10010
Ph: (212)777-8395   Fax: (212)777-8261
Fr: 800-491-2808
URL: http://www.allworth.com/

Tad Crawford, Eva Doman Bruck. Third edition, 2003. $35.00 (CD-ROM, trade cloth). 160 pages.

★3757★ Career Opportunities in Theater and the Performing Arts

Checkmark Books
132 W. 31st St., 17th Fl.
New York, NY 10001-2006
Ph: (212)967-8800   Fax: (212)967-9196
Fr: 800-322-8755

Shelly Field. Third edition, 2006. $18.95 (paper). 320 pages. Offers a complete range of information about job opportunities in the performing arts. Part of Career Opportunities Series.

★3758★ Careers for Color Connoisseurs and Other Visual Types

The McGraw-Hill Companies
PO Box 182604
Columbus, OH 43272
Fax: (614)759-3749   Fr: 877-883-5524
E-mail: customer.service@mcgraw-hill.com
URL: http://www.mcgraw-hill.com

Jan Goldberg. Second edition, 2005. $13.95 (paper). 176 pages.

★3759★ Careers for Crafty People and Other Dexterous Types

The McGraw-Hill Companies
PO Box 182604
Columbus, OH 43272
Fax: (614)759-3749   Fr: 877-883-5524
E-mail: customer.service@mcgraw-hill.com
URL: http://www.mcgraw-hill.com

Mark Rowh. Third edition, 2006. $13.95; $9.95 (paper). 160 pages.

★3760★ Careers for Fashion Plates and Other Trendsetters

The McGraw-Hill Companies
PO Box 182604
Columbus, OH 43272
Fax: (614)759-3749   Fr: 877-883-5524
E-mail: customer.service@mcgraw-hill.com
URL: http://www.mcgraw-hill.com

Lucia Mauro. Second edition, 2002. $14.95 (Hardcover); $9.95 (paper). 160 pages. Describes career opportunities in fashion, entertainment, retail, and promotion, with advice from fashion professionals.

★3761★ Careers for Film Buffs and Other Hollywood Types

The McGraw-Hill Companies
PO Box 182604
Columbus, OH 43272
Fax: (614)759-3749   Fr: 877-883-5524
E-mail: customer.service@mcgraw-hill.com
URL: http://www.mcgraw-hill.com

Jaq Greenspon. Second edition, 2003. $13.95; $9.95 (paper). 208 pages. Describes job descriptions in production, camera, sound, special effects, grips, electrical, makeup, costumes, etc.

★3762★ Careers Without College: Fashion

Peterson's Guides
2000 Lenox Dr.
Box 67005
Lawrenceville, NJ 08648
Ph: (609)896-1800   Fax: (609)896-4531
Fr: 800-338-3282
E-mail: custsvc@petersons.com
URL: http://www.petersons.com

Peggy Schmidt. Second edition, 1999. $34.95 (paper). Part of Careers Without College series.

★3763★ The Creative Business Guide to Running a Graphic Design Business

W. W. Norton & Company, Incorporated
500 Fifth Ave.
New York, NY 10110-0017
Ph: (212)354-5500   Fax: (212)869-0856
Fr: 800-223-2584
URL: http://www.wwnorton.com/

Cameron Foote. 2004. $29.95. 496 pages.

★3764★ Design Secrets: Products 2: 50 Real-Life Product Design Projects Uncovered

Rockport Publishers
100 Cummings Center. Ste. 406-L
Beverly, MA 01915
Ph: (978)282-9590   Fax: (978)283-2742
URL: http://www.rockpub.com

Lynn Haller and Cheryl Dangel Cullen. 2006. $30.00. 208 pages. Fifty winners of the Industrial Designers Society of America's IDEA Awards are profiled.

★3765★ Design Secrets: Products: 50 Real-Life Product Design Projects Uncovered

Rockport Publishers
100 Cummings Center. Ste. 406-L
Beverly, MA 01915
Ph: (978)282-9590   Fax: (978)283-2742
URL: http://www.rockpub.com

Cheryl Dangel Cullen and Lynn Haller. 2006. $50.00. Fifty design projects are presented from conception to completion.

★3766★ The Designer's Commonsense Business Book

North Light Books
4700 E Galbraith Rd.
Cincinnati, OH 45236
Ph: (513)531-2690   Fax: (513)531-4082
Fr: 800-289-0963
E-mail: ntcpub@tribune.com

Barbara Ganim. Revised, 1995. $29.95; $27.99 (paper). 244 pages.

★3767★ Fashion Designer Survival Guide: An Insider's Look at Starting and Running Your Own Fashion Business

Kaplan Publishing
1 Liberty Plz., 24th Fl.
New York, NY 10006
Fax: 800-943-9831   Fr: 800-223-2336
URL: http://www.kaplanpublishing.com

Mary Gehlar. 2005. $22.95. Advice is given to help designers create their own fashion line.

★3768★ Fashion Now, Volume 2

Taschen America, LLC
6671 Sunset Blvd., Ste. 1508
Los Angeles, CA 90028
Ph: (323)463-4441   Fax: (323)463-4442
E-mail: contact-us@taschen.com
URL: http://www.taschen.com/

Terry Jones and Susie Rushton. 2006. Encyclopedia of fashion personalities as well as a guide to the contemporary fashion industry.

★3769★ Fresh Dialogue 6: Friendly Fire

Princeton Architectural Press
37 E 7th St.
New York, NY 10003
Ph: (212)995-9620   Fax: (212)995-9454
Fr: 800-722-6657
E-mail: sales@papress.com
URL: http://www.papress.com/

American Institute of Graphic Arts Staff. 2006. $16.95. 127 pages.

★3770★ Great Jobs for Art Majors

The McGraw-Hill Companies
PO Box 182604
Columbus, OH 43272
Fax: (614)759-3749   Fr: 877-883-5524
E-mail: customer.service@mcgraw-hill.com
URL: http://www.mcgraw-hill.com

Blythe Camenson, Stephen Lambert, Julie DeGalan. Second edition, 2003. $15.95 (paper). 248 pages. Includes bibliographical references and index.

★3771★ Great Jobs for Theater Majors

The McGraw-Hill Companies
PO Box 182604
Columbus, OH 43272
Fax: (614)759-3749   Fr: 877-883-5524
E-mail: customer.service@mcgraw-hill.com
URL: http://www.mcgraw-hill.com

Jan Goldberg and Julie DeGalan. 2005. $15.95 (paper). 192 pages.

★3772★ Managing to Make It

University of Chicago Press
1427 E. 60th St.
Chicago, IL 60637
Ph: (773)702-7700   Fax: (773)702-9756

Frank F. Furstenberg. 2000. $21.00. 320 pages.

★3773★ New Media Careers for Artists and Designers

AuthorHouse
1663 Liberty Dr., Ste. 200
Bloomington, IN 47403
Ph: (812)961-1023   Fax: (812)339-8654
Fr: 888-519-5121
URL: http://www.authorhouse.com

Brenda S. Faison. February 2003. $13.95. 136 pages.

★3774★ Opportunities in Arts and Crafts Careers

The McGraw-Hill Companies
PO Box 182604
Columbus, OH 43272
Fax: (614)759-3749   Fr: 877-883-5524
E-mail: customer.service@mcgraw-hill.com
URL: http://www.mcgraw-hill.com

Elizabeth Gardner. 2005. $13.95 (paper). 211 pages.

★3775★ Opportunities in Commercial Art and Graphic Design Careers

The McGraw-Hill Companies
PO Box 182604
Columbus, OH 43272
Fax: (614)759-3749   Fr: 877-883-5524
E-mail: customer.service@mcgraw-hill.com
URL: http://www.mcgraw-hill.com

Barbara Gordon. 2003. $13.95; $11.95 (paper). 160 pages. Provides a survey of job opportunities in advertising and public relations, publishing, fashion, architecture, and newspapers, as well as in a variety of specialty markets. Illustrated.

★3776★ Opportunities in Museum Careers

The McGraw-Hill Companies
PO Box 182604
Columbus, OH 43272
Fax: (614)759-3749   Fr: 877-883-5524
E-mail: customer.service@mcgraw-hill.com
URL: http://www.mcgraw-hill.com

Blythe Camenson. 2006. $13.95; $11.95 (paper). 160 pages.

★3777★ Opportunities in Publishing Careers

The McGraw-Hill Companies
PO Box 182604
Columbus, OH 43272
Fax: (614)759-3749   Fr: 877-883-5524

E-mail: customer.service@mcgraw-hill.com
URL: http://www.mcgraw-hill.com

Robert A. Carter and S. William Pattis. 2000. $12.95 (paper). 160 pages. Covers all positions in book and magazine publishing, including new opportunities in multimedia publishing.

★3778★ Opportunities in Visual Arts Careers

The McGraw-Hill Companies
PO Box 182604
Columbus, OH 43272
Fax: (614)759-3749   Fr: 877-883-5524
E-mail: customer.service@mcgraw-hill.com
URL: http://www.mcgraw-hill.com

Mark Salmon and Bill Barrett. 2001. $12.95; $11.95 (paper). 160 pages. Points the way to a career in the visual arts, examining opportunities for designers, painters, sculptors, illustrators, animators, photographers, art therapists, educators, and others. Offers a view of the pros and cons of working for an art or design company or on your own.

★3779★ Power Freelancing: Home-Based Careers for Writers, Designers, & Consultants

Mid-List Press
4324 12th Ave., S
Minneapolis, MN 55407-3218
Ph: (612)822-3733   Fax: (612)823-8387
Fr: 888-543-1138
E-mail: guide@midlist.org
URL: http://www.midlist.org/

George Sorenson. 1995. $14.95 (paper). 198 pages.

★3780★ Savvy Designers Guide to Success

F & W Publications Inc.
4700 E. Galbraith Rd.
Cincinnati, OH 45236
Ph: (513)531-2690   Fax: (513)531-4082
Fr: 800-289-0963
URL: http://www.fwpublications.com/

Jeff Fisher. December 2004. $24.99. 192 pages.

★3781★ Talent Is Not Enough: Business Secrets for Designers

Peachpit Press
1249 8th St.
Berkeley, CA 94710-1413
Fr: 800-428-5331
URL: http://www.peachpit.com

Shel Perkins. 2006. $26.99. Guide for any designer whether working for someone else to becoming an independent design firm.

★3782★ What Designers Know

Architectural Press
30 Corporate Dr., Ste. 400
Burlington, MA 01803
Ph: (781)313-4700   Fax: (781)221-1615
E-mail: usbkinfo@elsevier.com
URL: http://www.elsevier.com

Bryan Lawson. 2004. $34.95. Design skills, knowledge and understanding are explored, with each chapter focusing on a different technique.

EMPLOYMENT AGENCIES AND SEARCH FIRMS

★3783★ ARI International
1501 Ocean Ave.
Seal Beach, CA 90740
Ph: (562)795-5111   Fax: (562)596-9794
E-mail: ari.ron@att.net
URL: http://www.ariinternationalsearch.com

International executive search firm.

★3784★ The Aspire Group
52 Second Ave, 1st Fl
Waltham, MA 02451-1129
Fax: (718)890-1810   Fr: 800-487-2967
URL: http://www.bmanet.com

Employment agency.

★3785★ Capitol Search
215 E. Ridgewood Ave., Ste. 205
Ridgewood, NJ 07450
Ph: (201)444-6666

Employment agency.

★3786★ Claremont-Branan, Inc.
1298 Rockbridge Rd., Ste. B
Stone Mountain, GA 30087
Ph: (770)925-2915   Fax: (770)925-2601
Fr: 800-875-1292
E-mail: ohil@cbisearch.com
URL: http://cbisearch.com

Employment agency. Executive search firm.

★3787★ Colli Associates
414 Caboose Ln.
Valrico, FL 33594
Ph: (813)681-2145   Fax: (813)661-5217
E-mail: colli@gte.net

Employment agency. Executive search firm.

★3788★ Gene Kaufman Associates Ltd.
450 Fashion Ave.
New York, NY 10123-0101
Ph: (212)643-0625   Fax: (212)643-8598

Personnel consultant specializing in recruiting on all levels for the apparel industry in the areas of design, sales, merchandising, production, operations and administration.

★3789★ Randolph Associates, Inc.
950 Massachusetts Ave., Ste. 105
Cambridge, MA 02139-3174
Ph: (617)441-8777   Fax: (617)441-8778
E-mail: jobs@greatjobs.com
URL: http://www.greatjobs.com

Employment agency. Provides regular or temporary placement of staff.

★3790★ RitaSue Siegel Resources, Inc.
162 Fifth Ave., 11th Fl.
New York, NY 10010-5969
Ph: (212)682-2100   Fax: (212)682-2946
E-mail: ritasues@ritasue.com
URL: http://www.ritasuesiegelresources.com

Executive search firm specializing in industrial and product design.

★3791★ Search and Recruit International
4455 South Blvd. Ste. 110
Virginia Beach, VA 23452
Ph: (757)625-2121   Fr: 800-800-5627

Employment agency. Headquartered in Virginia Beach. Other offices in Bremerton, WA; Charleston, SC; Jacksonville, FL; Memphis, TN; Pensacola, FL; Sacramento, CA; San Bernardino, CA; San Diego, CA.

ONLINE JOB SOURCES AND SERVICES

★3792★ Aquent.com
711 Boylston St.
Boston, MA 02116
Ph: (617)535-5000   Fax: (617)535-5005
E-mail: questions@aquent.com
URL: http://www.aquent.com/FindWork/

Description: Aquent finds contract, project-based, and permanent work for a broad range of creative and information technology professionals. Applicants submit their applications, which are reviewed by an Aquent agent and, if qualifications match job opportunities, they will be called in for an interview and skills assessment. If skills and experience are appropriate, then will then be assigned an Aquent agent who will get to work finding contract or permanent jobs. Also offers free career resources.

★3793★ Guru.com
5001 Baum Blvd., Ste. 760
Pittsburgh, PA 15213
Ph: (412)687-1316   Fax: (412)687-4466
URL: http://www.guru.com

Description: Job board specializing in contract jobs for creative and information technology professionals. Also provides online incorporation and educational opportunities for independent contractors along with articles and advice.

TRADESHOWS

★3794★ American Textile Machinery Exhibition International
Textile Hall Corp.
PO Box 5823
Greenville, SC 29606
Ph: (864)331-2277   Fax: (864)331-2282
E-mail: atmei@textilehall.com

Monthly. **Primary Exhibits:** Machinery and supplies for yarn, fiber, and nonwoven manufacturing, weaving, knitting and finishing, and plant maintenance.

★3795★ DesigNation
DesigNation, Inc.
300 M St., SW, Ste. N110
Washington, DC 20024
Ph: (202)488-1530   Fax: (202)488-3838
E-mail: info@designation.net
URL: http://www.designation.net

Annual. **Primary Exhibits:** Exhibits of interest to designers holding college degrees who are practicing graphic, industrial, fashion, textile, and interior design.

★3796★ Industrial Fabrics Association International Expo
Industrial Fabrics Association International
1801 County Rd. B W
Roseville, MN 55113-4061
Ph: (651)222-2508   Fax: (651)631-9334
Fr: 800-225-4324
E-mail: generalinfo@ifai.com
URL: http://www.ifai.com

Annual. **Primary Exhibits:** Industrial and commercial fabric equipment, supplies, and services.

OTHER SOURCES

★3797★ American Design Drafting Association (ADDA)
105 E Main St.
Newbern, TN 38059
Ph: (731)627-0802   Fax: (731)627-9321
E-mail: cadboss@comcast.net
URL: http://www.adda.org

Members: Designers, drafters, drafting managers, chief drafters, supervisors, administrators, instructors, and students of design and drafting. **Purpose:** Encourages a continued program of education for self-improvement and professionalism in design and drafting and computer-aided design/drafting. Informs members of effective techniques and materials used in drawings and other graphic presentations. **Activities:** Evaluates curriculum of educational institutions through certification program; sponsors drafter certification program.

★3798★ Home Economics Careers

Cambridge Educational
PO Box 2053
Princeton, NJ 08543-2053
Ph: 800-257-5126   Fax: (609)671-0266
Fr: 800-468-4227
E-mail: custserv@films.com
URL: http://www.cambridgeeducational.com

VHS and DVD. $79.95. 47 minutes. 1990. Includes student manual. Interviews with persons working in each field explores careers in dietetics, foods and nutrition, child development, interior design, and fashion. Working with cooperative extension, in education, and with business and industry, are among the career profiles

★3799★ Industrial Designers Society of America (IDSA)

45195 Business Ct., Ste. 250
Dulles, VA 20166-6717
Ph: (703)707-6000
E-mail: cooperw@idsa.org
URL: http://www.idsa.org

Members: Professional society of industrial designers. **Purpose:** Represents the profession in its relations with business, education, government, and international designers; promotes the industrial design profession. Conducts research, educational, and charitable programs. Compiles statistics.

★3800★ Media and the Arts Occupations

Delphi Productions
3159 6th St.
Boulder, CO 80304
Ph: (303)443-2100   Fax: (303)443-4022
Fr: 888-443-2400
E-mail: support@delphivideo.com
URL: http://www.delphivideo.com

$95.00. 50 minutes. Part of the Careers for the 21st Century Video Library.

Desktop Publishers

SOURCES OF HELP-WANTED ADS

★3801★ ACM Transactions on Internet Technology (ACM TOIT)
Association for Computing Machinery
2 Penn Plz., Ste. 701
New York, NY 10121-0701
Ph: (212)869-7440   Fax: (212)944-1318
Fr: 800-342-6626
URL: http://www.acm.org/pubs/periodicals/toit/

Quarterly. $35.00/year for members; $30.00/year for students; $140.00/year for nonmembers; $170.00/year for individuals, print only; $136.00 for single issue, online only; $204.00 for single issue, online & print. Publication of the Association for Computing Machinery. Brings together many computing disciplines including computer software engineering, computer programming languages, middleware, database management, security, knowledge discovery and data mining, networking and distributed systems, communications, performance and scalability, and more. Covers the results and roles of the individual disciplines and the relationships among them.

★3802★ AVIOS Journal
Applied Voice Input/Output Society
PO Box 20817
San Jose, CA 95160
Ph: (408)323-1783   Fax: (408)323-1782
E-mail: info@avios.org
URL: http://www.avios.com/

Annual. Journal covering issues in computer science.

★3803★ Computers and Composition
Elsevier Science Inc.
360 Park Ave. S
New York, NY 10010
Ph: (212)989-5800   Fax: (212)633-3990
URL: http://www.elsevier.com

$353.00/year for institutions; $69.00/year for individuals. Journal covering computers in writing classes, programs, and research.

★3804★ Computers Programs/PC World
IDG Communications Inc.
5 Speen St., 3rd. Fl
Framingham, MA 01701
Ph: (508)875-5000   Fax: (508)988-7888
URL: http://www.idg.com

Magazine devoted to IT specialists, covering practical questions of computing including purchase and usage of the computer technology, software, computer components and peripherals.

★3805★ Computerworld/Correio Informatico
IDG Communications Inc.
5 Speen St., 3rd. Fl
Framingham, MA 01701
Ph: (508)875-5000   Fax: (508)988-7888
URL: http://www.idg.com

Weekly. Magazine providing news on latest developments in computer industry.

★3806★ Computerworld Top 100
IDG Communications Inc.
5 Speen St., 3rd. Fl
Framingham, MA 01701
Ph: (508)875-5000   Fax: (508)988-7888
URL: http://www.idg.com

Annual. Magazine for analyzing trends and events of information technology business.

★3807★ Computing SA
IDG Communications Inc.
5 Speen St., 3rd. Fl
Framingham, MA 01701
Ph: (508)875-5000   Fax: (508)988-7888
URL: http://www.idg.com

Monthly. Newspaper focusing computer hardware, software, networking, telecommunications, channel management and online computing.

★3808★ Consumer Electronics Lifestyles
Sandhills Publishing
120 W Harvest Dr.
Lincoln, NE 68521
Ph: (402)479-2181   Fax: (402)479-2195
Fr: 800-331-1978
E-mail: editor@ceLifestyles.com
URL: http://www.celifestyles.com/

Monthly. $12.00/year. Magazine for computer and electronic gadget enthusiasts.

★3809★ CXO
IDG Communications Inc.
5 Speen St., 3rd. Fl
Framingham, MA 01701
Ph: (508)875-5000   Fax: (508)988-7888
URL: http://www.idg.com

Monthly. Magazine providing technology information for chief officers and managers.

★3810★ Eclipse Review
BZ Media LLC
7 High St., Ste. 407
Huntington, NY 11743
Ph: (631)421-4158   Fax: (631)421-4130
URL: http://www.eclipsesource.com/contact.htm

Magazine for IT professionals.

★3811★ The Editorial Eye
EEI Press
66 Canal Center Plz., Ste. 200
Alexandria, VA 22314
Ph: (703)683-0683   Fax: (703)683-4915
Fr: 800-683-8380
E-mail: eye@eeicom.com
URL: http://www.eeicommunications.com/eye/

Description: Monthly. Contains articles, tests, and columns that treat the full range of editorial questions, including editing, writing, and style.

★3812★ ENA powered by Network World

IDG Communications Inc.
5 Speen St., 3rd. Fl
Framingham, MA 01701
Ph: (508)875-5000 Fax: (508)988-7888
URL: http://www.idg.com

Monthly. Journal covering information on networking.

★3813★ Foundations of Computational Mathematics

Springer-Verlag New York Inc.
233 Spring St.
New York, NY 10013
Ph: (212)460-1500 Fax: (212)460-1575

Academic journal that publishes articles related to the connections between mathematics and computation, including the interfaces between pure and applied mathematics, numerical analysis and computer science.

★3814★ Foundations and Trends in Networking

Now Publishers
PO Box 1024
Hanover, MA 02339
Ph: (781)871-0245
URL: http://www.nowpublishers.com/product.aspx?product=NET

$315.00/year online only; $355.00/year print and online; $315.00/year online only; $355.00/year print and online. Academic journal publishing new research in computer networking.

★3815★ Government Computer News

PostNewsweek Tech Media
10 G St. NE, Ste. 500
Washington, DC 20002-4228
Ph: (202)772-2500 Fax: (202)772-2511
Fr: (866)447-6864

Semimonthly. Magazine for professionals interested in government IT.

★3816★ IEEE Security & Privacy Magazine

IEEE Computer Society
10662 Los Vaqueros Cir.
PO Box 3014
Los Alamitos, CA 90720-1314
Ph: (714)821-8380 Fax: (714)821-4010
Fr: 800-272-6657
URL: http://www.computer.org/portal/site/security/

Bimonthly. $24.00/year for members; $29.00/year for nonmembers; $28.00/year for members; $565.00/year for libraries, institution. Journal that aims to explore role and importance of networked infrastructure and developing lasting security solutions.

★3817★ Independent Publisher Online

Jenkins Group Inc.
1129 Woodmere Ave., Ste. B
Traverse City, MI 49684-2206
Ph: (231)933-0445 Fax: (231)933-0448
Fr: 800-706-4636
URL: http://www.independentpublisher.com/

Monthly. Free. Online magazine containing book reviews and articles about independent publishing.

★3818★ Information Security

TechTarget
117 Kendrick St., Ste. 800
Needham, MA 02494
Ph: (781)657-1000 Fax: (781)657-1100
URL: http://searchsecurity.techtarget.com/

Monthly. Free to qualified subscribers. Magazine covering information security topics.

★3819★ IT Focus

IDG Communications Inc.
5 Speen St., 3rd. Fl
Framingham, MA 01701
Ph: (508)875-5000 Fax: (508)988-7888
URL: http://www.idg.com

Online journal focusing mainly on information technology.

★3820★ IT Solutions Guide

SYS-CON Media
135 Chestnut Ridge Rd.
Montvale, NJ 07645
Ph: (201)802-3000 Fax: (201)782-9600
Fr: 888-303-5282
URL: http://itsolutions.sys-con.com/

Quarterly. $4.00/year for individuals, single pdf issue. Magazine for IT professionals.

★3821★ Journal of Computer Science

Science Publications
Vails Gate Heights Dr.
PO Box 879
Vails Gate, NY 12584
URL: http://www.scipub.us/

Bimonthly. $3,500.00/year for individuals; $300.00/year for single issue. Scholarly journal covering many areas of computer science, including: concurrent, parallel and distributed processing; artificial intelligence; image and voice processing; quality software and metrics; computer-aided education; wireless communication; real time processing; evaluative computation; and data bases and information recovery and neural networks.

★3822★ Kompiuterija PC World

IDG Communications Inc.
5 Speen St., 3rd. Fl
Framingham, MA 01701
Ph: (508)875-5000 Fax: (508)988-7888
URL: http://www.idg.com

Monthly. Journal providing professionals, business people and users with up-to-date information on computers and the internet.

★3823★ Mikro PC

IDG Communications Inc.
5 Speen St., 3rd. Fl
Framingham, MA 01701
Ph: (508)875-5000 Fax: (508)988-7888
URL: http://www.idg.com

Monthly. Magazine focusing on information technology and digital lifestyle.

★3824★ Monitor

Capital PC User Group
19209 Mt. Airey Rd.
Brookeville, MD 20833
Ph: (301)560-6442 Fax: (301)760-3303
URL: http://monitor.cpcug.org/index.html

Quarterly. Magazine covering computer hardware and software reviews, special interest user group news, advertisers and author/subject index, and calendar of events.

★3825★ NetWorld

IDG Communications Inc.
5 Speen St., 3rd. Fl
Framingham, MA 01701
Ph: (508)875-5000 Fax: (508)988-7888
URL: http://www.idg.com

Monthly. Magazine focusing on networks, security, infrastructure management, wireless, mobile and VOIP technologies.

★3826★ PMA Independent

Publishers Marketing Association
627 Aviation Way
Manhattan Beach, CA 90266
Ph: (310)372-2732 Fax: (310)374-3342
E-mail: info@pma-online.org
URL: http://www.pma-online.org

Description: Monthly. Informs member entrepreneurial book publishers about upcoming marketing programs and other Association activities aimed at helping independent publishers succeed. Also carries articles on topics such as desktop publishing and typesetting systems. Recurring features include member, committee, and research news, notices of educational and cooperative marketing opportunities, a calendar of events, and columns titled News from the "Net" and From the Director's Desk.

★3827★ Queue

Association for Computing Machinery
2 Penn Plz., Ste. 701
New York, NY 10121-0701
Ph: (212)869-7440 Fax: (212)944-1318
Fr: 800-342-6626
URL: http://www.acmqueue.org/

Monthly. Free, U.S./Canadian residents and all members. Online magazine aimed at the computer professional. Magazine editorial does not provide solutions for the "here-and-now," but instead helps decision-makers plan future projects by examining the challenges and problems they are most likely to face.

★3828★ Revenue

Montgomery Media International
300 Montgomery St., Ste. 1135
San Francisco, CA 94104
Ph: (415)397-2400   Fax: (415)397-2420
URL: http://www.revenuetoday.com/

$30.00/year for individuals. Magazine covering internet marketing strategies.

★3829★ SMB Data

IDG Communications Inc.
5 Speen St., 3rd. Fl
Framingham, MA 01701
Ph: (508)875-5000   Fax: (508)988-7888
URL: http://www.idg.com

Magazine focusing on information technology systems at small and medium-size businesses.

★3830★ SME World

IDG Communications Inc.
5 Speen St., 3rd. Fl
Framingham, MA 01701
Ph: (508)875-5000   Fax: (508)988-7888
URL: http://www.idg.com

Magazine covering articles on technology, technology investments, IT products and services.

★3831★ TecCHANNEL Compact

IDG Communications Inc.
5 Speen St., 3rd. Fl
Framingham, MA 01701
Ph: (508)875-5000   Fax: (508)988-7888
URL: http://www.idg.com

Quarterly. Magazine covering issues of information technology.

★3832★ Tips & Trucs

IDG Communications Inc.
5 Speen St., 3rd. Fl
Framingham, MA 01701
Ph: (508)875-5000   Fax: (508)988-7888
URL: http://www.idg.com

Monthly. Magazine covering topics on computer hardware, software and the internet.

★3833★ Top 100

IDG Communications Inc.
5 Speen St., 3rd. Fl
Framingham, MA 01701
Ph: (508)875-5000   Fax: (508)988-7888
URL: http://www.idg.com

Annual. Magazine providing analyses, assessments and statistics on information technology industry.

★3834★ WebLogic Pro

Fawcette Technical Publications
2600 S El Camino Real, Ste. 300
San Mateo, CA 94403-2332
Ph: (650)378-7100   Fax: (650)570-6307
Fr: 800-848-5523
URL: http://www.weblogicpro.com

Bimonthly. Free to qualified subscribers. Magazine that aims to provides IT solutions for developers, architects, and administrators.

★3835★ WITI FastTrack

CMP Media L.L.C.
600 Community Dr.
Manhasset, NY 11030
Ph: (516)562-5000   Fax: (516)562-7830
URL: http://www.witi.com/corporate/fast-track.php

Semiannual. Semiannual publication featuring in-depth content on the issues facing today's women professionals in technology.

EMPLOYER DIRECTORIES AND NETWORKING LISTS

★3836★ The Information Professional's Guide to Career Development Online

Information Today Inc.
143 Old Marlton Pke.
Medford, NJ 08055-8750
Ph: (609)654-6266   Fax: (609)654-4309
Fr: 800-300-9868
URL: http://books.infotoday.com/

Latest edition Jan. 2002. $29.50 for individuals. Covers Web sites, professional associations, and conferences for the career development of information professionals. Indexes: Alphabetical.

HANDBOOKS AND MANUALS

★3837★ Career Opportunities in Computers and Cyberspace

Facts On File Inc.
132 W. 31st St., 17th Fl.
New York, NY 10001-2006
Ph: (212)967-8800   Fax: 800-678-3633
Fr: 800-322-8755
E-mail: custserv@factsonfile.com
URL: http://www.factsonfile.com

Harry Henderson. Second edition, 2004. $18.95 (paper). Part of the Career Opportunities Series. 256 pages.

★3838★ Choosing a Career in Desktop Publishing

Rosen Publishing Group, Inc.
29 E. 21st St.
New York, NY 10010
Ph: (212)777-3017   Fax: (212)777-0277
Fr: 800-237-9932
URL: http://www.rosenpublishing.com/

Ross, Allison J. 2001. $29.25. 64 pages. Describes the salary, professional requirements, and personal characteristics of those interested in the field of desktop publishing

and how the job is changing due to advances in computer software and technology.

★3839★ The Complete Help Book for Authors and Publishers

Hannacroix Creek Books, Incorporated
1127 High Ridge Rd., No. 110B
Stamford, CT 06905-1203
Ph: (203)321-8674   Fax: (203)968-0193
E-mail: hannacroix@aol.com
URL: http://www.hannacroixcreekbooks.com/

Jan Yeager. 2007. $29.95. Explores self-publishing for authors.

★3840★ How to Start a Home-Based Desktop Publishing Business

Globe Pequot Press
246 Goose Ln.
Guilford, CT 06437
Ph: (203)458-4500   Fax: 800-820-2329
Fr: 888-249-7586
E-mail: info@globepequot.com
URL: http://www.globepequot.com/

Louise Kursmark. 2002. 240 pages.

★3841★ Opportunities in Publishing Careers

The McGraw-Hill Companies
PO Box 182604
Columbus, OH 43272
Fax: (614)759-3749   Fr: 877-883-5524
E-mail: customer.service@mcgraw-hill.com
URL: http://www.mcgraw-hill.com

Pattis, S. William, Robert A. Carter, and Blythe Camenson. 2000. $12.95 (Trade paper). 160 pages.

★3842★ Second Lives: Becoming a Desktop Publisher

St. Martin's Press LLC
175 Fifth Ave.
New York, NY 10010
Ph: (212)726-0200   Fax: (212)686-9491
Fr: 800-470-4767
URL: http://www.stmartins.com

Bill Harris. 1999. 117 pages. $9.95.

ONLINE JOB SOURCES AND SERVICES

★3843★ DesktopPublishing.com

URL: http://www.desktoppublishing.com

Description: General resource website contains job bank and list of links to resume enhancing and distributing software available for download on the Internet.

★3844★ Graphic Artists Guild

93 John St., Ste. 403
New York, NY 10038
Ph: (212)791-3400
E-mail: communications@gag.org
URL: http://www.gag.org

Description: JOBLine News section of Guild Resources page contains weekly e-mail newsletter of job listings. **Fee:** Must subscribe to e-mail newsletter non-member six-month rates start at $80. Visitors may download a free sample.

★3845★ Guru.com

5001 Baum Blvd., Ste. 760
Pittsburgh, PA 15213
Ph: (412)687-1316   Fax: (412)687-4466
URL: http://www.guru.com

Description: Job board specializing in contract jobs for creative and information technology professionals. Also provides online incorporation and educational opportunities for independent contractors along with articles and advice.

★3846★ National Association of Photoshop Professionals

33 Douglas Rd., E.
Oldsmar, FL 34677
Fr: 800-738-8513
URL: http://www.photoshopuser.com

Description: Membership website includes member job bank where visitors can search for available jobs or post their resumes for employer review, along with other career-related resources. **Fee:** Must be member of association to access; dues are $99 for a one-year membership.

★3847★ Publish.com

Ziff Davis Enterprise
28 E. 28th St.
New York, NY 10016
Ph: (212)503-5772
E-mail: customerservice@ziffdavisenterprise.com
URL: http://www.publish.com

Description: Offers a variety of resources for desktop publishers.

OTHER SOURCES

★3848★ Association for Women in Computing (AWC)

41 Sutter St., Ste. 1006
San Francisco, CA 94104
Ph: (415)905-4663   Fax: (415)358-4667
E-mail: info@awc-hq.org
URL: http://www.awc-hq.org

Members: Individuals interested in promoting the education, professional development, and advancement of women in computing.

Dietitians and Nutritionists

★3849★ American Journal of Clinical Nutrition

The American Society for Clinical Nutrition
9650 Rockville Pke.
L-2407A
Bethesda, MD 20814-3998
Ph: (301)634-7038   Fax: (301)634-7351
E-mail: dbier@nutrition.org
URL: http://www.ajcn.org

Annual. $470.00/year for institutions, print and online U.S.; $455.00/year for institutions, online U.S.; $200.00/year for individuals, print and online U.S.; $175.00/year for individuals, online U.S.; $85.00/year for students, print and online U.S.; $60.00/year for students, online U.S.; $495.00/year for Canada and Mexico, print and online; $455.00/year for Canada and Mexico, online only; $520.00/year for elsewhere, print and online; $455.00/year for elsewhere, online only. Journal of basic and clinical studies relevant to human nutrition.

★3850★ Bountiful Health

JNE Publishing, Inc.
PO Box 5647
Huntsville, AL 35814
Ph: (256)837-3035   Fr: 800-313-7751
URL: http://www.jnepublishing.com/bountifulhealth.php?page=public

Magazine focusing on complementary and alternative medicine, exercise, vitamins and supplements, healthy eating, and green living.

★3851★ Chef

Talcott Communications Corp.
20 W Kinzie, Ste. 1200
Chicago, IL 60610
Ph: (312)849-2220   Fax: (312)849-2174
E-mail: chef@talcott.com
URL: http://www.chefmagazine.com

$32.00/year for individuals; $47.00 for two years; $64.00 for individuals, 3 years; $43.00/year for Canada; $96.00/year for other countries. Food information for chefs.

★3852★ Cooking Smart

Coincide Publishing LLC
7944 E Beck Ln., Ste. 230
Scottsdale, AZ 85260-1664
Ph: (480)237-7100   Fax: (480)237-7103
URL: http://cookingsmartmagazine.com/aboutus.htm

$17.95/year for individuals; $24.95/year for individuals; $29.94/year for individuals, newsstand, 6 issues; $59.88/year for individuals, newsstand. Magazine features articles about healthy cooking as well as recipes.

★3853★ Dietary Manager Magazine

Dietary Managers Association
406 Surrey Woods Dr.
St. Charles, IL 60174
Ph: (630)587-6336   Fax: (630)587-6308
Fr: 800-323-1908

Monthly. $40.00/year for individuals, one year (10 issues). Professional magazine focusing on nutrition and management issues encountered by dietary managers in non-commerical food service.

★3854★ EatingWell

Eating Well Inc.
823A Ferry Rd.
PO Box 1010
Charlotte, VT 05445
Ph: (802)425-5700   Fax: (802)425-3700
Fr: 800-337-0402
URL: http://www.eatingwell.com/

Bimonthly. $14.97/year for individuals. Magazine of food & health that includes nutritional recipes.

★3855★ Field & Feast

Field & Feast
PO Box 205
Four Lakes, WA 99014
URL: http://www.fieldandfeast.net

Quarterly. $19.00/year for individuals. Magazine that offers information on organic food cultivation and its health benefits.

★3856★ Food Management

Penton Media Inc.
1300 E 9th St.
Cleveland, OH 44114
Ph: (216)696-7000   Fax: (216)696-1752
URL: http://www.food-management.com/

Monthly. Magazine for foodservice professionals in the onsite 'noncommercial' market.

★3857★ FoodService Director

Ideal Media LLC
303 E Wacker Dr., 21st Fl.
Chicago, IL 60601
Ph: (312)456-2822   Fax: (312)240-0742
URL: http://www.fsdmag.com

Monthly. $79.00/year for individuals; $99.00/year for Canada; $235.00/year for out of country. Tabloid newspaper of the noncommercial foodservice market.

★3858★ Foodservice East

The Newbury Street Group Inc.
165 New Boston St., No. 236
Woburn, MA 01801
Ph: (781)376-9080   Fax: (781)376-0010
Fr: 800-852-5212
E-mail: fdsvceast@.aol.com

Bimonthly. $30.00/year for individuals. Compact tabloid covering trends and analysis of the foodservice industry in the Northeast. A business-to-business publication featuring news, analysis and trends for the Northeast food service professional.

★3859★ Genes and Nutrition

New Century Health Publishers LLC
PO Box 50702
New Orleans, LA 70150-0702
Fax: (504)305-3762
URL: http://www.newcenturyhealthpublishers.com/genes_and_nutritio

Quarterly. $428.00/year for institutions;

$228.00/year for individuals. International, interdisciplinary peer reviewed scientific journal for critical evaluation of research on the relationship between genetics & nutrition with the goal of improving human health.

★3860★ **Herbs for Health**
Echo Media
900 Cir. 75 Pky., Ste. 1600
Atlanta, GA 30339
Ph: (770)955-3535   Fax: (770)955-3599
URL: http://www.echo-media.com

Bimonthly. Magazine covering topics ranging from recent scientific research to consumer guides, medicinal recipes, and legislative updates.

★3861★ **The IHS Primary Care Provider**
Indian Health Service (HQ)
The Reyes Bldg.
801 Thompson Ave., Ste. 400
Rockville, MD 20852-1627
URL: http://www.ihs.gov/PublicInfo/Publications/HealthProvider/Pr

Monthly. Journal for health care professionals, physicians, nurses, pharmacists, dentists, and dietitians.

★3862★ **Journal of the American College of Nutrition**
American College of Nutrition
300 S Duncan Ave., Ste. 225
Clearwater, FL 33755
Ph: (727)446-6086   Fax: (727)446-6202
URL: http://www.jacn.org

Bimonthly. Journal on nutrition.

★3863★ **Journal of the American Dietetic Association**
American Dietetic Association
120 S Riverside Plz., Ste. 2000
Chicago, IL 60606-6995
Fax: (312)899-4817   Fr: 800-877-1600
URL: http://www.eatright.org/cps/rde/xchg/ada/hs.xsl/home_7018_en

Monthly. Journal reporting original research on nutrition, diet therapy, education and administration.

★3864★ **Nutrition Notes**
American Society for Nutrition
9650 Rockville Pike, Ste. 4500
Bethesda, MD 20814
Ph: (301)634-7050   Fax: (301)634-7892
E-mail: nnotes@asns.faser.org
URL: http://www.nutrition.org/

Description: Quarterly. Contains updates on nutrition legislation, public affairs, and public information policies. Reviews the results of nutritional research conducted by members of the Institute, which is comprised of nutrition scientists from universities, government, and industry. Recurring features include news of members, letters to the editor, job listings, notices of publications

available, information on awards and fellowships, and news of scientific meetings.

★3865★ **Nutritional Outlook**
Canon Communications L.L.C.
11444 W Olympic Blvd., Ste. 900
Los Angeles, CA 90064
Ph: (310)445-4200   Fax: (310)445-4299
E-mail: info@nutritionaloutlook.com
URL: http://www.nutritionaloutlook.com/

Magazine for manufacturer's resource for dietary supplements and healthy foods and beverages.

★3866★ **Real Food**
Greenspring Media Group
600 US Trust Bldg.
730 2nd Ave. S
Minneapolis, MN 55402
Ph: (612)371-5800   Fax: (612)371-5801
Fr: 800-933-4398
URL: http://www.realfoodmag.com/

Quarterly. Magazine featuring food choices.

★3867★ **Southeast Food Service News**
Southeast Publishing Company Inc.
5672 Peachtree Pky., Ste. E
Norcross, GA 30092
Ph: (770)499-9800   Fax: (770)499-9802

Monthly. $36.00/year for individuals, per year; $5.00 for individuals, per single copy; $59.00/year for individuals, per directory issue. Magazine (tabloid) serving the food industry.

★3868★ **Sunbelt Foodservice**
Shelby Publishing Company Inc.
517 Green St.
Gainesville, GA 30501
Ph: (770)534-8380   Fax: (770)535-0110
URL: http://www.shelbypublishing.com

Monthly. $36.00/year for individuals; $60.00 for two years. Trade newspaper (tabloid) covering the food industry; geared toward restaurant operators.

★3869★ **Vegetarian Times**
Active Interest Media
300 Continental Blvd., Ste. 650
El Segundo, CA 90245
Ph: (310)356-4100   Fax: (310)356-4110
Fr: 800-423-4880
URL: http://www.vegetariantimes.com/

Monthly. $14.95/year for individuals; $31.95/year for Canada, 9 issues; $59.95/year for Canada, 18 issues; $43.95/year for other countries, 9 issues; $83.95/year for other countries, 18 issues. Magazine devoted to plant-based foods sand related topics such as health, fitness, and the environment.

★3870★ **Wellness Bound**
Community Wellness Alliance Inc.
507 2nd Ave. S
Clanton, AL 35045
Fr: 888-755-9005
URL: http://www.wellnessbound.com/

Bimonthly. Magazine that offers information and resources that encourage wellness lifestyles.

★3871★ **Your Health Now**
Merck & Co. Inc.
One Merck Dr.
PO Box 100
Whitehouse Station, NJ 08889-0100
Ph: (908)423-1000
URL: http://www.merck.com/yourhealthnow/volume2-7/

Bimonthly. Consumer health magazine.

PLACEMENT AND JOB REFERRAL SERVICES

★3872★ **American Public Health Association (APHA)**
800 I St. NW
Washington, DC 20001
Ph: (202)777-2742   Fax: (202)777-2534
E-mail: comments@apha.org
URL: http://www.apha.org

Members: Professional organization of physicians, nurses, educators, academicians, environmentalists, epidemiologists, new professionals, social workers, health administrators, optometrists, podiatrists, pharmacists, dentists, nutritionists, health planners, other community and mental health specialists, and interested consumers. **Purpose:** Seeks to protect and promote personal, mental, and environmental health. **Activities:** Services include: promulgation of standards; establishment of uniform practices and procedures; development of the etiology of communicable diseases; research in public health; exploration of medical care programs and their relationships to public health. Sponsors job placement service.

★3873★ **Dietary Managers Association (DMA)**
406 Surrey Woods Dr.
St. Charles, IL 60174
Ph: (630)587-6336   Fax: (630)587-6308
Fr: 800-323-1908
E-mail: info@dmaonline.org
URL: http://www.dmaonline.org/index.html

Description: Dietary managers united to maintain a high level of competency and quality in dietary departments through continuing education. Provides educational programs and placement service.

EMPLOYER DIRECTORIES AND NETWORKING LISTS

★3874★ AHA Guide to the Health Care Field

American Hospital Association
1 N Franklin
Chicago, IL 60606
Ph: (312)422-2050   Fax: (312)422-4700
Fr: 800-424-4301

Annual, August. Covers hospitals, networks, multi-health care systems, freestanding ambulatory surgery centers, psychiatric facilities, long-term care facilities, substance abuse programs, and other health-related organizations. Entries include: For hospitals—Facility name, address, phone, administrator's name, number of beds, facilities and services, number of employees, expenses, other statistics. For other organizations—Name, address, phone, fax, name and title of contact. Arrangement: Geographical. Indexes: Hospital name.

★3875★ Directory of Hospital Personnel

Grey House Publishing
185 Millerton Rd.
PO Box 860
Millerton, NY 12546
Ph: (518)789-8700   Fax: (518)789-0556
Fr: 800-562-2139
URL: http://www.greyhouse.com/hospital_personnel.htm

Annual. $325.00 for print product; $545.00 for online database subscription; $650.00 for online database subscription and print product combined. Covers 200,000 executives at 7,000 U.S. hospitals. Entries include: Name of hospital, address, phone; number of beds; type and JCAHO status of hospital; names and titles of key department heads and staff; medical and nursing school affiliations; number of residents, interns, and nursing students. Arrangement: Geographical. Indexes: Hospital name, personnel, hospital size.

★3876★ Directory of the National Association of Advisors for the Health Professions

National Association of Advisors for the Health Professions
PO Box 1518
Champaign, IL 61824-1518
Ph: (217)355-0063   Fax: (217)355-1287

Annual. $25.00. Covers college and university faculty who advise and counsel students on health careers.

★3877★ Discovering Careers for Your Future: Health

Facts On File Inc.
132 W 31st St., 17th Fl.
New York, NY 10001
Ph: (212)967-8800   Fax: 800-678-3633
Fr: 800-322-8755
URL: http://www.factsonfile.com

Latest edition 2nd, 2004. $21.95 for individuals; $19.75 for libraries. Covers dietitians and nutritionists, fitness experts, massage therapists, nurses, occupational therapists, pharmacists, and sports trainers; links career education to curriculum, helping children investigate the subjects they are interested in and the careers those subjects might lead to.

★3878★ Hospital Blue Book

Billian Publishing Inc./Transworld Publishing Inc.
2100 Powers Ferry Rd. SE
Atlanta, GA 30339
Ph: (770)955-5656   Fax: (770)952-0669
Fr: 800-533-8484
E-mail: blu-book@billian.com

2005. $300.00 for individuals. Covers more than 6,687 hospitals; some listings also appear in a separate southern edition of this publication. Entries include: Name of hospital, accreditation, mailing address, phone, fax, number of beds, type of facility (nonprofit, general, state, etc.); list of administrative personnel and chiefs of medical services, with specific titles. Arrangement: Geographical.

★3879★ Medical and Health Information Directory

Gale, Cengage Learning
27500 Drake Rd.
Farmington Hills, MI 48331-3535
Ph: (248)699-4253   Fax: (248)699-8065
Fr: 800-877-4253
E-mail: businessproducts@gale.com
URL: http://www.gale.com

Annual; latest edition 20th, July 2007. $375.00/volume. Covers in Volume 1, more than 26,500 medical and health oriented associations, organizations, institutions, and government agencies, including health maintenance organizations (HMOs), preferred provider organizations (PPOs), insurance companies, pharmaceutical companies, research centers, and medical and allied health schools. In Volume 2, over 12,000 medical book publishers; medical periodicals, directories, audiovisual producers and services, medical libraries and information centers, electronic resources, and health-related internet search engines. In Volume 3, more than 35,500 clinics, treatment centers, care programs, and counseling/diagnostic services for 34 subject areas. Entries include: Institution, service, or firm name, address, phone, fax, email and URL; many include names of key personnel and, when pertinent, descriptive annotations. Volume 3 was formerly listed separately as Health Services Directory. Arrangement: Classified by organization activity, service, etc. Indexes: Each volume has a complete alphabetical name and keyword index.

HANDBOOKS AND MANUALS

★3880★ Ask the Nutritionists

AuthorHouse
1663 Liberty Dr., Ste. 200
Bloomington, IN 47403
Ph: (812)339-6554   Fr: 888-519-5121
URL: http://www.authorhouse.com/

Kathy Thames and George Rapitis. 2005. $12.95.

★3881★ Career Opportunities in the Food and Beverage Industry

Facts on File, Inc.
132 W. 31st St., 17th Fl.
New York, NY 10001-2006
Ph: (212)967-8800   Fax: 800-678-3633
Fr: 800-322-8755
E-mail: custserv@factsonfile.com
URL: http://www.factsonfile.com

Barbara Sims-Bell. Second edition, 2001. $18.95 (paper). 223 pages. Provides the job seeker with information about locating and landing 80 skilled and unskilled jobs in the industry. Includes detailed job descriptions for many specific positions and lists trade associations, recruiting organizations, and major agencies. Contains index and bibliography.

★3882★ Careers in Health Care

The McGraw-Hill Companies
PO Box 182604
Columbus, OH 43272
Fax: (614)759-3749   Fr: 877-883-5524
E-mail: customer.service@mcgraw-hill.com
URL: http://www.mcgraw-hill.com

Barbara M. Swanson. Fifth edition, 2005. $15.95 (paper). 192 pages. Describes job duties, work settings, salaries, licensing and certification requirements, educational preparation, and future outlook. Gives ideas on how to secure a job.

★3883★ Careers Inside the World of Health Care

Pearson Learning Group
135 S. Mt. Zion Rd.
PO Box 2500
Lebanon, IN 46052
Fax: 800-393-3156   Fr: 800-526-9907
URL: http://www.pearsonatschool.com

Beth Wilkinson. Revised edition, 1999. $21.30. 64 pages.

★3884★ Careers in Social and Rehabilitation Services

The McGraw-Hill Companies
PO Box 182604
Columbus, OH 43272
Fax: (614)759-3749   Fr: 877-883-5524
E-mail: customer.service@mcgraw-hill.com
URL: http://www.mcgraw-hill.com

Geraldine O. Garner. 2001. $19.95; 14.95 (paper). 128 pages.

★3885★ Opportunities in Health and Medical Careers

The McGraw-Hill Companies
PO Box 182604
Columbus, OH 43272
Fax: (614)759-3749   Fr: 877-883-5524
E-mail: customer.service@mcgraw-hill.com
URL: http://www.mcgraw-hill.com

I. Donald Snook, Jr. and Leo D'Orazio. 2004. $13.95 (paper). 157 pages. Covers the full range of medical and health occupations. Illustrated.

★3886★ Opportunities in Sports Medicine Careers

The McGraw-Hill Companies
PO Box 182604
Columbus, OH 43272
Fax: (614)759-3749   Fr: 877-883-5524
E-mail: customer.service@mcgraw-hill.com
URL: http://www.mcgraw-hill.com

William Ray Heitzmann. 1992. $11.95 (paper). 160 pages. Discusses a variety of opportunities in this field and how to pursue them. Contains bibliography and illustrations.

★3887★ Resumes for Health and Medical Careers

The McGraw-Hill Companies
PO Box 182604
Columbus, OH 43272
Fax: (614)759-3749   Fr: 877-883-5524
E-mail: customer.service@mcgraw-hill.com
URL: http://www.mcgraw-hill.com

Third edition, 2003. $11.95 (paper). 160 pages.

EMPLOYMENT AGENCIES AND SEARCH FIRMS

★3888★ Harper Associates

3100 NW Hwy., Ste. 240
Farmington Hills, MI 48334
Ph: (248)932-1170   Fax: (248)932-1214
E-mail: info@harperjobs.com
URL: http://www.harperjobs.com

Executive search firm and employment agency.

★3889★ Professional Placement Associates, Inc.

287 Bowman Ave., Ste. 309
Purchase, NY 10577-2517
Ph: (914)251-1000   Fax: (914)251-1055
E-mail: careers@ppasearch.com
URL: http://www.ppasearch.com

Executive search firm specializing in the health and medical field.

★3890★ Ritt-Ritt and Associates, Inc.

5105 Tollview Dr., Ste. 110
Rolling Meadows, IL 60008
Ph: (847)483-9330   Fax: (847)483-9331
E-mail: info@rittsearch.com

Food service and hospitality employment agency and executive search firm.

ONLINE JOB SOURCES AND SERVICES

★3891★ Institute of Food Technologists - IFT Career Center

525 W. Van Buren, Ste. 1000
Chicago, IL 60607
Ph: (312)782-8424   Fr: (312)782-8348
E-mail: info@atsift.org
URL: http://www.ift.org

Description: Offers job information and resources for those considering the Food Science and Technology field. Employers may post for full- or part-time positions and have the option of receiving a resume file of current job seekers. IFT members may register for a six-month confidential service to have their credentials reviewed by food industry employers. Job seekers who list credentials will receive the monthly Jobs Available bulletin. **Main files include:** Employment and Salary Information, How to Find Your First Job in the Food Sciences, Resources for Non-US Job Seekers, and more.

★3892★ Medhunters.com

Fr: 800-664-0278
E-mail: info@medhunters.com
URL: http://www.medhunters.com

Description: Career search site for jobs in all health care specialties; educational resources; visa and licensing information for relocation; interesting articles; relocation tools; links to professional organizations and general resources.

★3893★ ProHealthJobs

Fr: 800-796-1738
E-mail: Info@prohealthedujobs.com
URL: http://www.prohealthjobs.com

Description: Career resources site for the medical and health care field. Lists professional opportunities, product information, continuing education and open positions.

TRADESHOWS

★3894★ American Dietetic Association Annual Meeting and Exhibition

American Dietetic Association
120 S Riverside Plaza, Ste. 2000
Chicago, IL 60606-6995
Ph: (312)899-0040   Fr: 800-877-1600
E-mail: foundation@eatright.org
URL: http://www.eatright.org

Annual. **Primary Exhibits:** Food products, food service equipment, nutrition supplements, healthcare books, resource materials, and computers. **Dates and Locations:** 2008 Oct 25-28; Chicago, IL; McCormick Place; 2009 Oct 17-20; Denver, CO; 2010 Nov 06-09; Boston, MA; 2011 Sep 24-27; San Diego, CA.

★3895★ California Dietetic Association Meeting

California Dietetic Association
7740 Manchester Ave., Ste. 102
Playa Del Rey, CA 90293-8499
Ph: (310)822-0177   Fax: (310)823-0264
E-mail: PatSmith@dietitian.org
URL: http://www.dietitian.org

Annual. **Primary Exhibits:** Food and nutrition services.

★3896★ Dietary Managers Association Meeting and Expo

Dietary Managers Association
406 Surrey Woods Dr.
St. Charles, IL 60174-2386
Ph: (630)587-6336   Fax: (630)587-6308
E-mail: info@dmaonline.org
URL: http://www.dmaonline.org

Annual. **Primary Exhibits:** Dietary management equipment, supplies, and services.

OTHER SOURCES

★3897★ American Association of Nutritional Consultants (AANC)

401 Kings Hwy.
Winona Lake, IN 46590
Ph: (574)267-6165   Fax: (574)268-2120
Fr: 888-828-2262
E-mail: registrar@aanc.net
URL: http://www.aanc.net

Description: Professional nutritional consultants. Seeks to create a forum for exchange of nutritional information. Offers benefits such as car rental and laboratory discounts.

★3898★ American Dietetic Association (ADA)

120 S Riverside Plz., Ste. 2000
Chicago, IL 60606-6995
Ph: (312)899-0040   Fax: (312)899-1979
Fr: 800-877-1600

E-mail: rmoen@eatright.org
URL: http://www.eatright.org

Members: Represents food and nutrition professionals. Promotes nutrition, health and well-being.

★3899★ American School Health Association (ASHA)
PO Box 708
Kent, OH 44240
Ph: (330)678-1601   Fax: (330)678-4526
E-mail: asha@ashaweb.org
URL: http://www.ashaweb.org

Description: School physicians, school nurses, counsellors, nutritionists, psychologists, social workers, administrators, school health coordinators, health educators, and physical educators working in schools, professional preparation programs, public health, and community-based organizations. Promotes coordinated school health programs that include health education, health services, a healthful school environment, physical education, nutrition services, and psycho-social health services offered in schools collaboratively with families and other members of the community. Offers professional reference materials and professional development opportunities. Conducts pilot programs that inform materials development, provides technical assistance to school professionals, advocates for school health.

★3900★ Exploring Health Occupations
Cambridge Educational
PO Box 2053
Princeton, NJ 08543-2053
Ph: 800-257-5126   Fax: (609)671-0266
Fr: 800-468-4227

E-mail: custserv@films.com
URL: http://www.cambridgeeducational.com
VHS and DVD. $159.90. 1999. Two-part series provides a detailed view of the field of medical technicians and technologists, EMTs, nurses, therapists, and assistants.

★3901★ Health Assessment & Treating Occupations
Delphi Productions
3159 6th St.
Boulder, CO 80304
Ph: (303)443-2100   Fax: (303)443-4022
Fr: 888-443-2400
E-mail: support@delphivideo.com
URL: http://www.delphivideo.com

$95.00. 50 minutes. Part of the Careers for the 21st Century Video Library.

★3902★ Health Service Occupations
Delphi Productions
3159 6th St.
Boulder, CO 80304
Ph: (303)443-2100   Fax: (303)443-4022
Fr: 888-443-2400
E-mail: support@delphivideo.com
URL: http://www.delphivideo.com

$95.00. 50 minutes. Part of the Careers for the 21st Century Video Library.

★3903★ Home Economics Careers
Cambridge Educational
PO Box 2053
Princeton, NJ 08543-2053
Ph: 800-257-5126   Fax: (609)671-0266
Fr: 800-468-4227
E-mail: custserv@films.com

URL: http://www.cambridgeeducational.com
VHS and DVD. $79.95. 47 minutes. 1990. Includes student manual. Interviews with persons working in each field explores careers in dietetics, foods and nutrition, child development, interior design, and fashion. Working with cooperative extension, in education, and with business and industry, are among the career profiles

★3904★ IDEA Health and Fitness Association
10455 Pacific Center Ct.
San Diego, CA 92121-3773
Ph: (858)535-8979   Fax: (858)535-8234
Fr: 800-999-IDEA
E-mail: contact@ideafit.com
URL: http://www.ideafit.com

Purpose: Provides continuing education for fitness professionals including; fitness instructors, personal trainers, program directors, and club/studio owners. **Activities:** Offers workshops for continuing education credits.

★3905★ Medicine & Related Occupations
Delphi Productions
3159 6th St.
Boulder, CO 80304
Ph: (303)443-2100   Fax: (303)443-4022
Fr: 888-443-2400
E-mail: support@delphivideo.com
URL: http://www.delphivideo.com

$95.00. 45 minutes. Part of the Careers for the 21st Century Video Library.

Disc Jockeys

★3906★ **AFTRA Magazine**
American Federation of Television and
  Radio Artists
260 Madison Ave.
New York, NY 10016-2401
Ph: (212)532-0800   Fax: (212)532-2242

$3.00/year for individuals, per year. Membership magazine covering issues in television and radio broadcasting.

★3907★ **Billboard Radio Monitor**
VNU Business Media USA
770 Broadway
New York, NY 10003
Ph: (646)654-4500
URL: http://www.billboardradiomonitor.com/
radiomonitor/index.jsp

Weekly. $299.00 for individuals, per year; $6.99 for single issue. Magazine covering every format of music radio, regulatory developments, news radio, talk radio, and satellite radio.

★3908★ **Community Radio News**
National Federation of Community
  Broadcasters
1970 Broadway, Ste. 1000
Oakland, CA 94612
Ph: (510)451-8200   Fax: (510)451-8208
E-mail: newsletter@nfcb.org
URL: http://www.nfcb.org

Description: Monthly. Serves as a medium of communication for independent, community-licensed radio stations. Contains brief articles and news items on such topics as public broadcasting and programming, legislative developments, activities of the Federal Communications Commission, and local stations. Recurring features include notices of grants and awards, job openings, and a calendar of events/conferences for noncommercial broadcasters.

★3909★ **Country Airplay Monitor**
VNU Business Media USA
770 Broadway
New York, NY 10003
Ph: (646)654-4500

Weekly (Sun.). Trade publication covering the radio and music industry.

★3910★ **Feminist Media Studies**
Taylor & Francis Group Journals
325 Chestnut St., Ste. 800
Philadelphia, PA 19106
Ph: (215)625-8900   Fax: (215)625-8914
Fr: 800-354-1420
URL: http://www.tandf.co.uk/journals/titles/
14680777.asp

Quarterly. $552.00/year for institutions, print and online; $106.00/year for individuals, print only; $524.00/year for institutions, online only. Journal covering media and communication studies.

★3911★ **Rock Airplay Monitor**
VNU Business Media USA
770 Broadway
New York, NY 10003
Ph: (646)654-4500

Weekly. Trade publication covering the music and radio industries.

★3912★ **GMA'S Online Christian Music Networking Guide**
Gospel Music Association
1205 Division St.
Nashville, TN 37203
Ph: (615)242-0303   Fax: (615)254-9755
E-mail: info@gospelmusic.org
URL: http://www.gospelmusic.org/re-
sources/networkingGuide.aspx

Continuous; latest edition 2007. Covers gospel musicians, composers, and artists; recording companies, studios, and production companies; booking agencies; publishers; performing rights organizations; television and radio broadcasting stations; book stores, Bible supply stores, and other retailers/managers; publications; ministry organizations, artist managers, industry related services, christian clubs, concert promoters, distributors. Entries include: Name, contact address, phone, fax, e-mail. Broadcasting station listings include contact, program title, format. Arrangement: Search engine is flexible.

★3913★ **100 Best Careers in Entertainment**
Arco Pub.
200 Old Tappan Rd.
Old Tappan, NJ 07675
Fr: 800-428-5331

Shelly Field. 1995. $15.00 (paper). 340 pages.

★3914★ **Build and Manage Your Music Career**
artistpro.com, LLC
236 Georgia St., Ste. 100
Vallejo, CA 94590
Ph: (707)554-1935   Fax: (707)554-9751

Maurice Johnson. 1999. $24.95. 180 pages.

★3915★ **Career Opportunities in Radio**
Checkmark Books
132 W. 31st St., 17th Fl.
New York, NY 10001-2006
Ph: (212)967-8800   Fax: (212)967-9196
Fr: 800-322-8755

Shelly Field Scherer. May 2004. $18.95 (paper). Illustrated. 288 pages.

★3916★ Careers as a Disc Jockey

Rosen Publishing Group, Inc.
29 E. 21st St.
New York, NY 10010
Ph: (212)777-3017   Fax: 888-436-4643
Fr: 800-237-9932
URL: http://www.rosenpublishing.com/

Chris Weigant. 1999. $31.95. 163 pages. Provides information on getting started and being successful.

★3917★ Careers for Music Lovers and Other Tuneful Types

The McGraw-Hill Companies
PO Box 182604
Columbus, OH 43272
Fax: (614)759-3749   Fr: 877-883-5524
E-mail: customer.service@mcgraw-hill.com
URL: http://www.mcgraw-hill.com

Jeff Johnson. 2003. $13.95 (paper). 208 pages. Describes hundreds of music industry jobs and careers.

★3918★ Careers for Talkative Types and Others with the Gift of Gab

The McGraw-Hill Companies
PO Box 182604
Columbus, OH 43272
Fax: (614)759-3749   Fr: 877-883-5524
E-mail: customer.service@mcgraw-hill.com
URL: http://www.mcgraw-hill.com

Marjorie Eberts and Margaret Gisler. Second edition, 2006. $13.95 (paper). 160 pages.

★3919★ Freelance Dee-Jaying: How to Become a Successful Discotheque and Radio Jock

Trans-Atlantic Publications, Inc.
311 Bainbridge St.
Philadelphia, PA 19147
Ph: (215)925-5083   Fax: (215)925-1912
E-mail: jeffgolds@comcast.net
URL: http://www.transatlanticpub.com/

John Clancy. 1997. 174 pages. Part of the Jobs and Careers Series.

★3920★ The Gigs Handbook: A Beginner's Guide to Playing Professionally

Benny Publishing
9403 Lincolnwood Dr.
Evanston, IL 60203
Ph: (847)673-2039

Sharon Black. 2000. $18.95 (paper). 200 pages. "The Gigs Handbook" is for music students who want to earn money through performing and for amateurs who want to play professionally. The book will help readers learn how to get gigs and become professional musicians, make contacts and promote themselves, deal with problems on the job, play weddings and other special events and begin playing by ear.

★3921★ Great Jobs for Music Majors

The McGraw-Hill Companies
PO Box 182604
Columbus, OH 43272
Fax: (614)759-3749   Fr: 877-883-5524
E-mail: customer.service@mcgraw-hill.com
URL: http://www.mcgraw-hill.com

Jan Goldberg, Stephen Lambert, Julie De-Galan. Second edition, 2004. $15.95 (paper). 180 pages.

★3922★ How to Be a DJ

Course Technology, Inc.
25 Thomson Pl.
Boston, MA 02210
Ph: (617)757-7900   Fax: (617)757-7985
Fr: 800-648-7450
URL: http://www.course.com/

Chuck Fresh and Charles A. Graudins. 2004. $19.99. Tips for working as a successful disc jockey in radio, bars and clubs, or private parties. Advice is given for choosing hardware and software equipment.

★3923★ How to Become a Radio DJ: A Guide to Breaking and Entering

Happy Communications
PO Box 443
Troy, MI 48099
Ph: (248)577-0777

Mike Staff. 1998. $39.95 (paper). 140 pages.

★3924★ Inside Broadcasting

Routledge
270 Madison Ave.
New York, NY 10016
Ph: (212)216-7800   Fax: (212)563-2269
URL: http://www.routledge.com/

1997. $24.99. 232 pages. Part of the Career Builders Guide Series.

★3925★ The Lost Soul Companion: Comfort & Constructive Advice for Struggling Actors, Musicians, Artists, Writers & Other Free Spirits

Dell
1745 Broadway
New York, NY 10019
Ph: (212)782-9000   Fax: (212)572-6066
Fr: 800-733-3000
URL: http://www.randomhouse.com/bantamdell

Susan M. Brackney. 2001. $10.00. 176 pages.

★3926★ Making It in Broadcasting: An Insider's Guide to Career Opportunities

Macmillan Publishing Company
175 Fifth Ave.
New York, NY 10010
Ph: (646)307-5151   Fr: 800-428-5331
URL: http://www.macmillan.com/

Leonard Mogel. 1994. $15.00 (paper). 322 pages.

★3927★ The Mobile DJ Handbook: How to Start and Run a Profitable Mobile Disc Jockey Service

Elsevier
11830 Westline Industrial Dr.
St. Louis, MO 63146
Ph: (314)453-7010   Fax: (314)453-7095
Fr: 800-545-2522
E-mail: usbkinfo@elsevier.com
URL: http://www.elsevier.com

Stacy Zemon. Second edition, 2002. $24.95 (paper). 208 pages.

★3928★ Moving up in the Music Business

Allworth Press
10 E. 23rd St., Ste. 510
New York, NY 10010
Ph: (212)777-8395   Fax: (212)777-8261
Fr: 800-491-2808
URL: http://www.allworth.com/

Jodi Summers. 2000. $18.95 (paper). 213 pages.

★3929★ On-the-Air Anywhere: A Beginner's Guide to Broadcasting

Dorrance Publishing Company, Inc.
701 Smithfield St., Ste. 301
Pittsburgh, PA 15222
Ph: (412)288-4543   Fax: (412)288-1786
Fr: 800-788-7654
URL: http://www.dorrancepublishing.com/

Charlie Pullen. 1996. $8.00 (paper). 80 pages.

★3930★ Opportunities in Broadcasting Careers

The McGraw-Hill Companies
PO Box 182604
Columbus, OH 43272
Fax: (614)759-3749   Fr: 877-883-5524
E-mail: customer.service@mcgraw-hill.com
URL: http://www.mcgraw-hill.com

Elmo I. Ellis. 2004. $14.95; $11.95 (paper). 176 pages. Discusses opportunities and job search techniques in broadcasting, television, and radio. Illustrated.

★3931★ Opportunities in Music Careers

The McGraw-Hill Companies
PO Box 182604
Columbus, OH 43272
Fax: (614)759-3749   Fr: 877-883-5524
E-mail: customer.service@mcgraw-hill.com
URL: http://www.mcgraw-hill.com

Robert Gerardi. Fourth edition, 2002. $13.95 (paper). 175 pages. Describes the job market and where to find work. Covers careers in performing, writing, musical directing, management, and technical areas. Illustrated.

★3932★ Ruthless Self-Promotion in the Music Industry

artistpro.com, LLC
236 Georgia St., Ste. 100
Vallejo, CA 94590
Ph: (707)554-1935   Fax: (707)554-9751

Jeffrey P. Fisher. Second edition, 2005. $24.99. 320 pages.

★3933★ Secrets of Negotiating a Record Contract: The Musician's Guide to Understanding & Avoiding Sneaky Lawyer Tricks

Backbeat Books
600 Harrison St.
San Francisco, CA 94107
Ph: (408)848-5294   Fax: (408)848-5784
Fr: (866)222-5232
E-mail: custserv@musicdispatch.com
URL: http://www.backbeatbooks.com/

Moses Avalon. 2001. $22.95 (paper). 303 pages.

★3934★ This Business of Music Marketing and Promotion

Billboard Books
770 Broadway
New York, NY 10003
Ph: (646)654-5400   Fax: (646)654-5486
Fr: 800-323-9432

Tad Lathrop and Jim Pettigrew, Jr. Rev edition, 2003. $24.95. 308 pages.

★3935★ What's up Dawg: How to Become a Superstar in the Music Business

Hyperion Books
77 West 66th St., 11 Fl.
New York, NY 10023
Ph: (212)522-8700   Fr: 800-759-0190
URL: http://www.hyperionbooks.com

Randy Jackson. 2004. $19.95 (paper). 208 pages.

OTHER SOURCES

★3936★ American Disc Jockey Association (ADJA)

20118 N 67th Ave., Ste. 300-605
Glendale, AZ 85308
Ph: (623)882-8048   Fax: (623)362-953
Fr: 888-723-5776
E-mail: office@adja.org
URL: http://www.adja.org

Members: Mobile and night club disc jockeys. **Purpose:** Seeks to promote the disc jockey as a professional form of entertainment; improves the industry by establishing standards, procedures, and benefits. **Activities:** Assists and trains members; provides forums for professional disc jockeys; conducts educational, charitable, and research programs.

Dispensing Opticians

★3937★ *American Optician*

Opticians Association of America
441 Carlisle Dr.
Herndon, VA 20170
Ph: (703)437-8780   Fax: (703)437-0727
Fr: 800-443-8997

Quarterly. Subscription included in membership. Professional journal covering optometry.

★3938★ *EyeNet*

American Academy of Ophthalmology
PO Box 7424
San Francisco, CA 94120
Ph: (415)561-8500   Fax: (415)561-8533
E-mail: eyenet@aao.org
URL: http://www.eyenetmagazine.org

Monthly. $128.00/year for nonmembers, within U.S. $180.00/year for nonmembers, outside US; $76.00/year for members, international; included in membership, in USA. Professional magazine of the American Academy of Ophthalmology covering clinical, socioeconomic and political trends affecting their practice for members.

★3939★ *Investigative Ophthalmology & Visual Science*

Association for Research in Vision and
Ophthalmology
12300 Twinbrook Pkwy., Ste. 250
Rockville, MD 20852-1606
Ph: (240)221-2900   Fax: (240)221-0370
E-mail: iovs@arvo.org
URL: http://www.iovs.org/

Monthly. $710.00/year for institutions, within USA; $865.00/year for institutions, outside USA; $485.00/year for nonmembers, within USA; $685.00/year for nonmembers, outside USA; $320.00/year for students, non-member + within USA; $520.00/year for students, non-member + outside USA. Journal dealing with all aspects of vision and ophthalmology.

★3940★ *Journal of Electronic Imaging*

SPIE - The International Society for
Optical Engineering
1000 20th St.
PO Box 10
Bellingham, WA 98225-6705
Ph: (360)676-3290   Fax: (360)647-1445
Fr: 888-504-8171
URL: http://spie.org/x620.xml

Quarterly. $45.00/year for individuals, online; $90.00/year for individuals, print; $430.00/year for individuals, other countries, print and online; $390.00/year for individuals, print and online; $325.00/year for individuals, other countries, online. Journal covering issues in optical engineering.

★3941★ *Journal of Optical Networking*

Optical Society of America
2010 Massachusetts Ave. NW
Washington, DC 20036-1012
Ph: (202)223-8130   Fax: (202)223-1096
URL: http://www.osa-jon.org/journal/jon/about.cfm

Monthly. $1,695.00/year for individuals, online. Online journal covering issues concerning the optical networking community.

★3942★ *Ophthalmology*

Mosby Inc.
11830 Westline Industrial Dr.
St. Louis, MO 63146
Ph: (314)872-8370   Fax: (314)432-1380
Fr: 800-325-4177
URL: http://www.ophsource.org/periodicals/ophtha

Monthly. $298.00/year for individuals, U.S.; $298.00/year for individuals, Canada; $448.00/year for individuals, Mexico; $448.00/year for individuals, international. Journal publishing original, peer-reviewed reports of research in ophthalmology, including basic science investigations and clinical studies.

★3943★ *Optometry*

American Optometric Association
243 North Lindbergh Blvd.
St. Louis, MO 63141
Ph: (314)991-4100   Fax: (314)991-4101
Fr: 800-365-2219
URL: http://www.aoanews.org/

Monthly. $238.00/year for institutions; $201.00/year for individuals; $101.00/year for students; $66.00/year for students; $179.00/year for individuals; $134.00/year for individuals; $205.00/year for individuals. Clinical journal for members of the American Optometric Association.

★3944★ *Optometry and Vision Science*

Lippincott Williams & Wilkins
351 W Camden St.
Baltimore, MD 21201
Ph: (410)528-4000   Fax: (410)528-4305
Fr: 800-399-3110
URL: http://www.optvissci.com/

Monthly. $331.00/year for individuals; $429.00/year for institutions; $429.00/year for individuals, international; $526.00/year for institutions, international. Journal providing current developments and research in optometry, physiological optics, and vision science.

★3945★ *Review of Optometry*

Jobson Professional Publications Group
11 Campus Blvd., Ste. 100
Newtown Square, PA 19073
Ph: (610)492-1000   Fax: (610)492-1039
URL: http://www.revoptom.com/

Monthly. Journal for the optometric profession and optical industry.

PLACEMENT AND JOB REFERRAL SERVICES

★3946★ American Optometric Association (AOA)

243 N Lindbergh Blvd., 1st Fl.
St. Louis, MO 63141-7881
Ph: (314)991-4100   Fax: (314)991-4101
Fr: 800-365-2219
E-mail: klalexander@aoa.org
URL: http://www.aoa.org

Members: Professional association of optometrists, students of optometry, and paraoptometric assistants and technicians. **Purpose:** Purposes are: to improve the quality, availability, and accessibility of eye and vision care; to represent the optometric profession; to help members conduct their practices; to promote the highest standards of patient care. **Activities:** Monitors and promotes legislation concerning the scope of optometric practice, alternate health care delivery systems, health care cost containment, Medicare, and other issues relevant to eye/vision care. Supports the International Library, Archives and Museum of Optometry which includes references on ophthalmic and related sciences with emphasis on the history and socioeconomic aspects of optometry. Operates Vision U.S.A. program, which provides free eye care to the working poor, and the InfantSEE program, which provides free vision assessments for infants between six and twelve months of age. Conducts specialized education programs; operates placement service; compiles statistics. Maintains museum. Conducts Seal of Acceptance Program.

★3947★ Association of University Professors of Ophthalmology (AUPO)

PO Box 420369
San Francisco, CA 94142-0369
Ph: (415)561-8548   Fax: (415)561-8531
E-mail: aupo@aao.org
URL: http://www.aupo.org

Members: Heads of departments or divisions of ophthalmology in accredited medical schools throughout the U.S. and Canada; directors of ophthalmology residency programs in institutions not connected to medical schools. **Purpose:** Promotes medical education, research, and patient care relating to ophthalmology. **Activities:** Operates Ophthalmology Matching Program and faculty placement service, which aids ophthalmologists interested in being associated with university ophthalmology programs to locate such programs.

EMPLOYER DIRECTORIES AND NETWORKING LISTS

★3948★ Contact Lenses-Retail Directory

infoUSA Inc.
5711 S 86th Cir.
PO Box 27347
Omaha, NE 68127-0347
Ph: (402)593-4593   Fax: (402)596-7688
Fr: 800-555-6124
URL: http://www.infousa.com

Annual. Number of listings: 13,108. Entries include: Name, address, phone (including area code), size of advertisement, year first in "Yellow Pages," name of owner or manager, number of employees. Compiled from telephone company "Yellow Pages," nationwide. Arrangement: Geographical.

★3949★ Guild of Prescription Opticians of America-Guild Reference Directory

Guild of Prescription Opticians of
America, Div.
411 Carlisle Dr. Herdon
Herndon, VA 20170
Ph: (703)437-8780   Fax: (703)437-0727
Fr: 800-443-8997
URL: http://www.oaa.org/

Annual, January. $60.00. Covers 250 member firms with a total of 350 retail locations. Entries include: Company name, address, name of manager, services. Arrangement: Geographical.

★3950★ Opticians Directory

infoUSA Inc.
5711 S 86th Cir.
PO Box 27347
Omaha, NE 68127-0347
Ph: (402)593-4593   Fax: (402)596-7688
Fr: 800-555-6124
URL: http://www.infousa.com

Annual. Number of listings: 13,642. Entries include: Company name, address, phone (including area code), size of advertisement, year first in "Yellow Pages," name of owner or manager, number of employees. Compiled from telephone company "Yellow Pages," nationwide. Arrangement: Geographical.

HANDBOOKS AND MANUALS

★3951★ Careers in Health Care

The McGraw-Hill Companies
PO Box 182604
Columbus, OH 43272
Fax: (614)759-3749   Fr: 877-883-5524
E-mail: customer.service@mcgraw-hill.com
URL: http://www.mcgraw-hill.com

Barbara M. Swanson. Fifth edition, 2005.

$15.95 (paper). 192 pages. Describes jo duties, work settings, salaries, licensing an certification requirements, educational prep aration, and future outlook. Gives ideas o how to secure a job.

★3952★ Opportunities in Eye Care Careers

The McGraw-Hill Companies
PO Box 182604
Columbus, OH 43272
Fax: (614)759-3749   Fr: 877-883-552
E-mail: customer.service@mcgraw-hill.com
URL: http://www.mcgraw-hill.com

Kathleen Belkoff. 2003. $12.95; $11.95 (pa per). 160 pages. Explores careers in oph thalmology, optometry, and support posi tions. Describes the work, salary, and em ployment outlook and opportunities.

★3953★ Opportunities in Health and Medical Careers

The McGraw-Hill Companies
PO Box 182604
Columbus, OH 43272
Fax: (614)759-3749   Fr: 877-883-552
E-mail: customer.service@mcgraw-hill.com
URL: http://www.mcgraw-hill.com

I. Donald Snook, Jr. and Leo D'Orazio. 2004 $13.95 (paper). 157 pages. Covers the ful range of medical and health occupations Illustrated.

EMPLOYMENT AGENCIES AND SEARCH FIRMS

★3954★ Retail Recruiters

2189 Silas Deane Hwy.
Rocky Hill, CT 06067
Ph: (860)721-9550   Fax: (860)257-8813
E-mail: careers@retailrecruitersusa.com
URL: http://www.retailrecruitersusa.com

Employment agency. Affiliate offices in many locations across the country.

ONLINE JOB SOURCES AND SERVICES

★3955★ Medhunters.com
Fr: 800-664-0278
E-mail: info@medhunters.com
URL: http://www.medhunters.com

Description: Career search site for jobs in all health care specialties; educational resources; visa and licensing information for relocation; interesting articles; relocation tools; links to professional organizations and general resources.

3956★ ProHealthJobs

r: 800-796-1738
-mail: Info@prohealthedujobs.com
RL: http://www.prohealthjobs.com

Description: Career resources site for the medical and health care field. Lists professional opportunities, product information, continuing education and open positions.

TRADESHOWS

3957★ American Academy of Optometry

American Academy of Optometry
110 Executive Blvd., Ste. 506
Rockville, MD 20852
h: (301)984-1441   Fax: (301)984-4737
-mail: AAOptom@daol.com
RL: http://www.aaopt.org

Annual. Primary Exhibits: Exhibits focusing on the latest research and patient treatments relating to clinical practice standards, optometric education, and experimental research in visual problems. **Dates and Locations:** 008 Oct 22-25; Anaheim, CA; Anaheim Marriott Hotel.

3958★ International Vision Expo and Conference/East

Association Expositions and Services
83 Main Ave.
Norwalk, CT 06851
Ph: (203)840-5427   Fax: (203)840-9442
E-mail: czahn@reedexpo.com
URL: http://www.reedexpo.com

Annual. Primary Exhibits: Equipment, supplies and services for the vision industry. **Dates and Locations:** 2008 Apr 11-13; New York, NY; Jacob K. Javits Convention Center.

OTHER SOURCES

★3959★ American Academy of Optometry (AAO)

6110 Executive Blvd., Ste. 506
Rockville, MD 20852
Ph: (301)984-1441   Fax: (301)984-4737
E-mail: aaoptom@aaoptom.org
URL: http://www.aaopt.org

Description: Represents optometrists, educators, and scientists interested in optometric education, and standards of care in visual problems. Conducts continuing education for optometrists and visual scientists. Sponsors 4-day annual meeting.

★3960★ American Board of Opticianry (ABO)

6506 Loisdale Rd., Ste. 209
Springfield, VA 22150-1815
Ph: (703)719-5800   Fax: (703)719-9144
Fr: 800-296-1379
E-mail: mail@abo-ncle.org
URL: http://www.abo.org

Description: Provides uniform standards for dispensing opticians by administering the National Opticianry Competency Examination and by issuing the Certified Optician Certificate to those passing the exam. Administers the Master in Ophthalmic Optics Examination and issues certificates to opticians at the advanced level passing the exam. Maintains records of persons certified for competency in eyeglass dispensing. Adopts and enforces continuing education requirements; assists and encourages state licensing boards in the use of the National Opticianry Competency Examination for licensure purposes.

★3961★ Exploring Health Occupations

Cambridge Educational
PO Box 2053
Princeton, NJ 08543-2053
Ph: 800-257-5126   Fax: (609)671-0266
Fr: 800-468-4227
E-mail: custserv@films.com
URL: http://www.cambridgeeducational.com

VHS and DVD. $159.90. 1999. Two-part series provides a detailed view of the field of medical technicians and technologists, EMTs, nurses, therapists, and assistants.

★3962★ Health Service Occupations

Delphi Productions
3159 6th St.
Boulder, CO 80304
Ph: (303)443-2100   Fax: (303)443-4022
Fr: 888-443-2400
E-mail: support@delphivideo.com
URL: http://www.delphivideo.com

$95.00. 50 minutes. Part of the Careers for the 21st Century Video Library.

★3963★ Health Technologists & Technicians

Delphi Productions
3159 6th St.
Boulder, CO 80304
Ph: (303)443-2100   Fax: (303)443-4022
Fr: 888-443-2400
E-mail: support@delphivideo.com
URL: http://www.delphivideo.com

$95.00. 50 minutes. Part of the Careers for the 21st Century Video Library.

★3964★ Medicine & Related Occupations

Delphi Productions
3159 6th St.
Boulder, CO 80304
Ph: (303)443-2100   Fax: (303)443-4022
Fr: 888-443-2400
E-mail: support@delphivideo.com

URL: http://www.delphivideo.com

$95.00. 45 minutes. Part of the Careers for the 21st Century Video Library.

★3965★ National Academy of Opticianry (NAO)

8401 Corporate Dr., Ste. 605
Landover, MD 20785
Ph: (301)577-4828   Fax: (301)577-3880
Fr: 800-229-4828
E-mail: info@nao.org
URL: http://www.nao.org

Description: Offers review courses for national certification and state licensure examinations to members. Maintains speakers' bureau and Career Progression Program.

★3966★ National Association of Optometrists and Opticians (NAOO)

PO Box 459
Marblehead, OH 43440
Ph: (419)798-2031   Fax: (419)798-8548
E-mail: fdrozak@cros.net

Description: Licensed optometrists, opticians, and corporations. Conducts public affairs programs of mutual importance to members; serves as an organizational center for special purpose programs; acts as a clearinghouse for information affecting the retail optical industry.

★3967★ National Contact Lens Examiners (NCLE)

6506 Loisdale Rd., Ste. 209
Springfield, VA 22150-1815
Ph: (703)719-5800   Fax: (703)719-9144
Fr: 800-296-1379
E-mail: mail@abo-ncle.org
URL: http://www.abo.org

Description: Serves as National certifying agency promoting continued development of opticians and technicians as contact lens fitters by formulating standards and procedures for determination of entry-level competency. Assists in the continuation, development, administration, and monitoring of a national Contact Lens Registry Examination (CLRE), which verifies entry-level competency of contact lens fitters. Issues certificates. Activities include: maintaining records of those certified in contact lens fitting; encouraging state occupational licensing and credentialing agencies to use the CLRE for licensure purposes; identifying contact lens dispensing education needs as a result of findings of examination programs; disseminating information to sponsors of contact lens continuing education programs.

★3968★ Opticians Association of America (OAA)

441 Carlisle Dr.
Herndon, VA 20170
Ph: (703)437-8780   Fax: (703)437-0727
Fr: 800-433-8997
E-mail: oaa@oaa.org
URL: http://www.oaa.org

Members: Retail dispensing opticians who

fill prescriptions for glasses or contact lenses written by a vision care specialist. **Purpose:**

Works to advance the science of ophthalmic optics. **Activities:** Conducts research and

educational programs. Maintains museum and speakers' bureau. Compiles statistics.

Drafters

Sources of Help-Wanted Ads

★3969★ Architectural Record

McGraw-Hill Inc.
221 Ave. of the Americas
New York, NY 10020-1095
Ph: (212)512-2000   Fax: (212)512-3840
Fr: 877-833-5524
URL: http://archrecord.construction.com

Monthly. $49.00/year for individuals. Magazine focusing on architecture.

★3970★ Builder

Hanley-Wood L.L.C.
1 Thomas Cir., NW, Ste. 600
Washington, DC 20005
Ph: (202)452-0800   Fax: (202)785-1974
URL: http://www.hanleywood.com/default.aspx?page=b2bbd

$29.95/year for individuals, 13 issues; $54.95/year for Canada, 26 issues; $192.00/year for out of country, 13 issues. Magazine covering housing and construction industry.

★3971★ Civil Engineering-ASCE

American Society of Civil Engineers
1801 Alexander Bell Dr.
Reston, VA 20191-4400
Ph: (703)295-6300   Fax: (703)295-6222
Fr: 800-548-2723
URL: http://www.asce.org/cemagazine/1006/

Monthly. Professional magazine.

★3972★ Constructor

Associated General Contractors of America
2300 Wilson Blvd., Ste. 400
Arlington, VA 22201
Ph: (703)548-3118   Fax: (703)548-3119
URL: http://www.agc.org

Monthly. Management magazine for the Construction Industry.

★3973★ Design News

Reed Business Information
225 Wyman St.
Waltham, MA 02451-1216
URL: http://www.designnews.com

Magazine covering design engineering.

★3974★ ENR: Engineering News-Record

McGraw-Hill Inc.
1221 Ave. of the Americas
New York, NY 10020-1095
Ph: (212)512-2000   Fax: (212)512-3840
Fr: 877-833-5524
E-mail: enr_web_editors@mcgraw-hill.com
URL: http://www.mymags.com/moreinfo.php?itemID=20012

Weekly. $94.00/year for individuals, print. Magazine focusing on engineering and construction.

★3975★ High Technology Careers Magazine

HTC
4701 Patrick Henry Dr., No. 1901
Santa Clara, CA 95054-1847
Fax: (408)567-0242
URL: http://www.hightechcareers.com

Bimonthly. $29.00/year; $35.00/year for Canada; $85.00/year for out of country. Magazine (tabloid) containing employment opportunity information for the engineering and technical community.

★3976★ NSBE Magazine

NSBE Publications
205 Daingerfield Rd.
Alexandria, VA 22314
Ph: (703)549-2207   Fax: (703)683-5312
URL: http://www.nsbe.org/publications/premieradvertisers.php

Journal providing information on engineering careers, self-development, and cultural issues for recent graduates with technical majors.

★3977★ Professional Builder

Reed Business Information
360 Park Ave. S
New York, NY 10010
Ph: (646)746-6400   Fax: (646)746-7431
E-mail: ncrum@reedbusiness.com
URL: http://www.housingzone.com/toc-archive-pbx

Monthly. Free. The integrated engineering magazine of the building construction industry.

Employer Directories and Networking Lists

★3978★ Directory of Contract Staffing Firms

C.E. Publications Inc.
PO Box 3006
Bothell, WA 98041-3006
Ph: (425)806-5200   Fax: (425)806-5585
URL: http://www.cjhunter.com/dcsf/overview.html

Covers nearly 1,300 contract firms actively engaged in the employment of engineering, IT/IS, and technical personnel for 'temporary' contract assignments throughout the world. Entries include: Company name, address, phone, name of contact, email, web address. Arrangement: Alphabetical. Indexes: Geographical.

★3979★ ENR-Top 500 Design Firms Issue

McGraw-Hill Inc.
1221 Ave. of the Americas
New York, NY 10020-1095
Ph: (212)512-2000   Fax: (212)512-3840
Fr: 877-833-5524
URL: http://enr.construction.com/people/sourcebooks/top500Design/

Annual, latest edition 2007. $50.00 for individuals. Publication includes: List of 500 leading architectural, engineering, and specialty design firms selected on basis of annual billings. Entries include: Company name, headquarters location, type of firm, current and prior year rank in billings, types of services, countries in which operated in preceding year. Arrangement: Ranked by billings.

★3980★ **Peterson's Job Opportunities in Engineering and Technology**

Peterson's Guides
2000 Lenox Dr.
Box 67005
Lawrenceville, NJ 08648
Ph: (609)896-1800   Fax: (609)896-4531
Fr: 800-338-3282
E-mail: custsvc@petersons.com
URL: http://www.petersons.com

Compiled by the Peterson's staff. Fourth edition, 1996. $21.95 (paper). 379 pages. Profiles 2,000 high-tech companies looking primarily for technical personnel in such fields as biotechnology, telecommunications, software, computers and peripherals, defense, and aerospace. Contains job-search strategies and career options to help match education and expertise to the job market. Indexed geographically, by industry, and by hiring needs.

★3981★ **ProFile**

Reed Construction Data
30 Technology Pkwy. S, Ste. 100
Norcross, GA 30092
Fr: 800-424-3996
E-mail: profile@reedbusiness.com
URL: http://www.reedfirstsource.com

Annual. Covers more than 27,000 architectural firms. Entries include: For firms–Firm name, address, phone, fax, year established, key staff and their primary responsibilities (for design, specification, etc.), number of staff personnel by discipline, types of work, geographical area served, projects. "ProFile" is an expanded version of, and replaces, the "Firm Directory." Arrangement: Firms are geographical. Indexes: Firm name; key individuals; specialization by category; consultants.

HANDBOOKS AND MANUALS

★3982★ **Opportunities in Drafting Careers**

The McGraw-Hill Companies
PO Box 182604
Columbus, OH 43272
Fax: (614)759-3749   Fr: 877-883-5524

E-mail: customer.service@mcgraw-hill.com
URL: http://www.mcgraw-hill.com

Mark Rowh. 1994. $13.95; $11.95 (paper). 146 pages. Provides information on opportunities in mechanical, landscape, marine, and topographical drafting in civil service, architecture, electronics, and other fields. Contains index and illustrations.

★3983★ **Opportunities in High Tech Careers**

The McGraw-Hill Companies
PO Box 182604
Columbus, OH 43272
Fax: (614)759-3749   Fr: 877-883-5524
E-mail: customer.service@mcgraw-hill.com
URL: http://www.mcgraw-hill.com

Gary Colter and Deborah Yanuck. 1999. $14.95; $11.95 (paper). 160 pages. Explores high technology careers. Describes job opportunities, how to make a career decision, how to prepare for high technology jobs, job hunting techniques, and future trends.

EMPLOYMENT AGENCIES AND SEARCH FIRMS

★3984★ **Agra Placements, Ltd.**

8435 University Ave., Ste. 6
Des Moines, IA 50325
Ph: (515)225-6563   Fax: (515)225-7733
Fr: 888-696-5624
E-mail: careers@agrapl.com
URL: http://www.agraplacements.com

Executive search firm. Branch offices in Peru, IN, Lincoln, IL, Andover, KS and Madison, SD.

★3985★ **The Aspire Group**

52 Second Ave, 1st Fl
Waltham, MA 02451-1129
Fax: (718)890-1810   Fr: 800-487-2967
URL: http://www.bmanet.com

Employment agency.

★3986★ **Global Employment Solutions**

10375 Park Meadows Dr., Ste. 375
Littleton, CO 80124
Ph: (303)216-9500   Fax: (303)216-9533
E-mail: careers@global
URL: http://www.gesnetwork.com

Employment agency.

★3987★ **International Staffing Consultants**

17310 Redhill Ave., No. 140
Irvine, CA 92614
Ph: (949)255-5857   Fax: (949)767-595
E-mail: iscinc@iscworld.com
URL: http://www.iscworld.com

Employment agency. Provides placement o regular or temporary basis. Affiliate office i London.

★3988★ **Tri-Serv Inc.**

22 W. Padonia Rd., Ste. C-353
Timonium, MD 21093
Ph: (410)561-1740   Fax: (410)252-741
E-mail: info@tri-serv.coom
URL: http://www.tri-serv.com

Employment agency for technical personne

OTHER SOURCES

★3989★ **American Design Drafting Association (ADDA)**

105 E Main St.
Newbern, TN 38059
Ph: (731)627-0802   Fax: (731)627-932
E-mail: cadboss@comcast.net
URL: http://www.adda.org

Members: Designers, drafters, draftin managers, chief drafters, supervisors, ad ministrators, instructors, and students c design and drafting. **Purpose:** Encourages continued program of education for self-im provement and professionalism in design and drafting and computer-aided design drafting. Informs members of effective tech niques and materials used in drawings and other graphic presentations. **Activities** Evaluates curriculum of educational institu tions through certification program; sponsor drafter certification program.

★3990★ **Technical & Related Occupations**

Delphi Productions
3159 6th St.
Boulder, CO 80304
Ph: (303)443-2100   Fax: (303)443-402
Fr: 888-443-2400
E-mail: support@delphivideo.com
URL: http://www.delphivideo.com

$95.00. 49 minutes. Part of the Careers fo the 21st Century Video Library.

Economists

SOURCES OF HELP-WANTED ADS

★3991★ Brookings Papers on Economic Activity

Brookings Institution Press
1775 Massachusetts Ave. NW
Washington, DC 20036-2188
Ph: (202)536-3600   Fax: (202)536-3623
Fr: 800-275-1447
URL: http://www.brookings.edu/press/journals.htm#bpea

Semiannual. $70.00/year for individuals; $84.00/year for institutions, other countries; $50.00/year for individuals; $64.00/year for individuals, foreign. Publication covering economics and business.

★3992★ Bulletin of Economic Research

Wiley-Blackwell
350 Main St. Commerce Pl.
Malden, MA 02148
Ph: (781)388-8200   Fax: (781)388-8210
Fr: 800-759-6120
URL: http://www.blackwellpublishing.com/journal.asp?ref=0307-3378

Quarterly. $74.00/year for individuals, print and online; $845.00/year for institutions, print and premium online; $768.00/year for institutions, print and standard online; $730.00/year for institutions, premium online only. Journal focusing on the entire field of economics, econometrics and economic history.

★3993★ Business Insurance

Crain Communications Inc.
1155 Gratiot Ave.
Detroit, MI 48207-2997
Ph: (313)446-6000
URL: http://www.businessinsurance.com

Weekly. $97.00/year for individuals; $173.00 for two years; $200.00/year for individuals, daily online only; $130.00/year for Canada and Mexico; $234.00 for Canada and Mexico, two years; $230.00/year for individuals, includes expedited airmail other countries; $436.00 for two years, includes expedited airmail other countries. International newsweekly reporting on corporate risk and employee benefit management news.

★3994★ Econometrica

Wiley-Blackwell
350 Main St. Commerce Pl.
Malden, MA 02148
Ph: (781)388-8200   Fax: (781)388-8210
Fr: 800-759-6120
URL: http://www.econometricsociety.org/subs.asp

Bimonthly. $520.00/year for institutions, premium print plus online; $480.00/year for institutions, online only; $302.00/year for institutions, other countries, premium print plus online; $278.00/year for institutions, other countries, online only; $40.00/year for institutions, concessionary rate. Journal publishing articles in all branches of economics.

★3995★ Economic Journal

Wiley-Blackwell
350 Main St. Commerce Pl.
Malden, MA 02148
Ph: (781)388-8200   Fax: (781)388-8210
Fr: 800-759-6120
URL: http://www.blackwellpublishing.com/journal.asp?ref=0013-0133

$595.00/year for institutions, print and premium online; $541.00/year for institutions, print and standard online; $514.00/year for institutions, premium online only; $414.00/year for institutions, other countries, print and premium online; $376.00/year for institutions, other countries, print and standard online; $357.00/year for institutions, other countries, premium online only; $389.00/year for institutions, print and premium online, Europe; $354.00/year for institutions, print and standard online, Europe; $336.00/year for institutions, premium online only, Europe. Journal focusing on economic issues.

★3996★ Economic Perspectives

Federal Reserve Bank of Chicago
230 South LaSalle St.
Chicago, IL 60604-1413
Ph: (312)322-5322   Fax: (312)322-5515
URL: http://www.chicagofed.org/economic_research_and_data/economi

Quarterly. Publication covering the field of economics.

★3997★ Economic Policy

Wiley-Blackwell
350 Main St. Commerce Pl.
Malden, MA 02148
Ph: (781)388-8200   Fax: (781)388-8210
Fr: 800-759-6120
URL: http://www.blackwellpublishing.com/journal.asp?ref=0266-4658

Quarterly. $74.00/year for individuals, print and online; $40.00/year for students, print and online; $540.00/year for institutions, print and premium online; $491.00/year for institutions, print and standard online; $466.00/year for institutions, premium online only. Journal publishing articles from economists and experts in the policy field all over the world.

★3998★ Economica

Wiley-Blackwell
350 Main St. Commerce Pl.
Malden, MA 02148
Ph: (781)388-8200   Fax: (781)388-8210
Fr: 800-759-6120
URL: http://www.blackwellpublishing.com/journal.asp?ref=0013-0427

Quarterly. $64.00/year for individuals, print and online; $45.00/year for students, print and online; $391.00/year for institutions, print and premium online; $355.00/year for institutions, print and standard online; $337.00/year for institutions, premium online only. Journal publishing research in all branches of economics.

★3999★ The Economists' Voice

Berkeley Electronic Press
2809 Telegraph Ave., Ste. 202
Berkeley, CA 94705
Ph: (510)665-1200   Fax: (510)665-1201
URL: http://www.bepress.com/ev/

Annual. $75.00/year for individuals; $300.00/year academic; $900.00/year corporate. Journal focusing on current economic issues. Its readership mainly comprises of economists of various hues, and from other professions such as lawyers, policy makers etc.

★4000★ Employment Opportunities for Business Economists

National Association for Business Economics
1233 20th St. NW, Ste. 505
Washington, DC 20036
Ph: (202)463-6223   Fax: (202)463-6239
E-mail: nabe@nabe.com
URL: http://www.nabe.com

Description: Bimonthly. Features listings of job openings for business economists and analysts.

★4001★ The Engineering Economist

Taylor & Francis Group Journals
325 Chestnut St., Ste. 800
Philadelphia, PA 19106
Ph: (215)625-8900   Fax: (215)625-8914
Fr: 800-354-1420
URL: http://www.informaworld.com/smpp/title~content=t713723642

Quarterly. $76.00/year for individuals, print only; $136.00/year for institutions, online only; $144.00/year for institutions, print and online. Journal covering capital investment analysis, cost estimation and accounting, cost of capital, design economics, economic decision analysis, education, policy analysis, and research and development.

★4002★ Financial Management

Financial Management Association International
4202 East Fowler Ave.
BSN 3331
Tampa, FL 33620-5500
Ph: (813)974-2084   Fax: (813)974-3318
E-mail: fma@coba.usf.edu
URL: http://www.fma.org/fm.htm

Quarterly. $95.00/year for individuals; $20.00 for single issue. Journal covering business, economics, finance and management.

★4003★ International Regional Science Review

Sage Publications Inc.
2455 Teller Rd.
Thousand Oaks, CA 91320
Ph: (805)499-0721   Fax: (805)499-8096
URL: http://www.sagepub.com/journalsProdDesc.nav?prodId=Journal20

Quarterly. $407.00/year for institutions, print & e-access; $427.00/year for institutions (current volume print & all online content); $366.00/year for institutions, e-access; $386.00/year for institutions, all online content; $653.00/year for institutions, backfile purchase, e-access (content through 1999); $399.00/year for institutions, print only; $97.00/year for individuals, print only; $110.00 for institutions, single print; $32.00 for individuals, single print. Journal of econo-

mists, geographers, planners, and other social scientists.

★4004★ Journal of International Business and Economics

Academy of International Business and Economics
PO Box 2536
Ceres, CA 95307
URL: http://www.AIBE.org

Peer-reviewed journal publishing theoretical, conceptual, and applied research on topics related to research, practice and teaching in all areas of business, economics, e-commerce, and related subjects.

★4005★ OECD Observer

Organization for Economic Cooperation and Development
2001 L St., NW, Ste. 650
Washington, DC 20036-4922
Ph: (202)785-6323   Fax: (202)785-0350
Fr: 800-456-6323
E-mail: observer@oecd.org
URL: http://www.oecdobserver.org

Bimonthly. $75.00/year for individuals; $105.00 for individuals, two years. Magazine on economic affairs, science, and technology.

★4006★ The Review of Network Economics

CRA International
John Hancock Tower
200 Clarendon St., T-33
Boston, MA 02116-5092
Ph: (617)425-3000   Fax: (617)425-3132
URL: http://www.rnejournal.com/

Quarterly. Journal covering new research in network economics and related subjects, including topics in the economics of networks, regulation, competition law, industrial organization etc.

★4007★ Topics in Macroeconomics

Berkeley Electronic Press
2809 Telegraph Ave., Ste. 202
Berkeley, CA 94705
Ph: (510)665-1200   Fax: (510)665-1201
URL: http://www.bepress.com/bejm/topics/

Irregular. $35.00/year for individuals; $500.00/year for institutions. Academic journal covering macroeconomics.

PLACEMENT AND JOB REFERRAL SERVICES

★4008★ African Studies Association (ASA)

Douglass Campus
132 George St.
New Brunswick, NJ 08901-1400
Ph: (732)932-8173   Fax: (732)932-3394

E-mail: asaed@rci.rutgers.edu
URL: http://www.africanstudies.org

Members: Persons specializing in teaching, writing, or research on Africa including political scientists, historians, geographers, anthropologists, economists, librarians, linguists, and government officials; persons who are studying African subjects; institutional members are universities, libraries, government agencies, and others interested in receiving information about Africa. **Purpose:** Seeks to foster communication and to stimulate research among scholars on Africa. **Activities:** Sponsors placement service; conducts panels and discussion groups; presents exhibits and films.

★4009★ American Agricultural Economics Association (AAEA)

555 E Wells, Ste. 1100
Milwaukee, WI 53202
Ph: (414)918-3190   Fax: (414)276-3349
E-mail: info@aaea.org
URL: http://www.aaea.org

Members: Professional society of agricultural economists. **Purpose:** Serves to enhance the skills, knowledge and professional contribution of those economists who serve society by solving problems related to agriculture, food, resources and economic development. **Activities:** Offers placement service.

★4010★ National Association for Business Economics (NABE)

1233 20th St. NW, Ste. 505
Washington, DC 20036
Ph: (202)463-6223   Fax: (202)463-6239
E-mail: nabe@nabe.com
URL: http://www.nabe.com

Description: Professional society of institutions, businesses, and students with an active interest in business economics and individuals who are employed by academic, private, or governmental concerns in the area of business-related economic issues. Maintains placement service for members; conducts several seminars per year. Maintains speakers' bureau.

★4011★ Southern Economic Association (SEA)

University of Tennessee at Chattanooga
313 Fletcher Hall, Department 6106
615 McCallie Ave.
Chattanooga, TN 37403-2598
Ph: (423)425-4118   Fax: (423)425-5218
E-mail: ashley-harrison@utc.edu
URL: http://www.southerneconomic.org

Description: Professional economists in government, business, and academic institutions. Provides placement service for economists.

EMPLOYER DIRECTORIES AND NETWORKING LISTS

★4012★ Business Economics-Membership Directory Issue

National Association for Business Economics
1233 20th St. NW, Ste. 505
Washington, DC 20036
Ph: (202)463-6223   Fax: (202)463-6239
E-mail: nabe@nabe.com
URL: http://www.nabe.com

Annual, March. Publication includes: List of about 3,000 members of the association, including students. Entries include: Name, address, phone, corporate affiliation, economic specialization, industries of research specialization, NABE activities, educational background, work experience. Arrangement: Alphabetical by member name, company, and roundtable affiliation. Indexes: Company, roundtable, and students.

★4013★ National Association for Business Economics-Membership Directory

National Association for Business Economics
1233 20th St. NW, Ste. 505
Washington, DC 20036
Ph: (202)463-6223   Fax: (202)463-6239
URL: http://www.nabe.com

Annual, March. Covers about 3,600 members internationally. Entries include: Name, address, phone, company affiliation, educational background, prior employment history, areas of specialization and industries of research specialization, roundtable affiliation, Standard Industrial Classification (SIC) code. Arrangement: Alphabetical. Indexes: Company name; association roundtable affiliation.

★4014★ National Economists Club-Membership Directory

National Economists Club
Box 19281
Washington, DC 20036
Ph: (703)739-9404   Fax: (703)739-9405
URL: http://www.national-economists.org/

Biennial. Covers nearly 800 professional economists and others having an interest in economic subjects. Entries include: Name, address, phone. Arrangement: Alphabetical by organization.

★4015★ Roster of Minority Financial Institutions

U.S. Department of the Treasury
1500 Pennsylvania Ave. NW
Washington, DC 20220
Ph: (202)622-2000

Free. Covers about 170 commercial, minority-owned and controlled financial institutions participating in the Department of the Treasury's Minority Bank Deposit Program. Entries include: Name of institution, name and title of chief officer, address, phone, fax. Arrangement: Geographical.

★4016★ Roster of Women Economists

Committee on the Status of Women in the Economics Profession
4901 Tower Ct.
Tallahassee, FL 32303
Ph: (850)562-1211   Fax: (850)562-3838
URL: http://www.cswep.org

Biennial, odd years. Covers 6,000 women in economics. Entries include: Name, address, phone, title, affiliation, degrees, honors, specialty, number of articles and books published, e-mail, fax. Publisher is a standing committee of the American Economic Association. Arrangement: Alphabetical. Indexes: Geographical; employer; fields of specialization.

★4017★ Thomson Bank Directory

Accuity
4709 W Golf Rd., Ste. 600
Skokie, IL 60076
Ph: (847)676-9600   Fax: (847)933-8101
Fr: 800-321-3373
URL: http://www.accuitysolutions.com/

Semiannual, June and December. $702.00 for individuals. Covers, in five volumes, about 11,000 banks and 50,000 branches of United States banks, and 60,000 foreign banks and branches engaged in foreign banking; Federal Reserve system and other United States government and state government banking agencies; the 500 largest North American and International commercial banks; paper and automated clearinghouses. Volumes 1 and 2 contain North American listings; volumes 3 and 4, international listings (also cited as "Thomson International Bank Directory"); volume 5, Worldwide Correspondents Guide containing key correspondent data to facilitate funds transfer. Entries include: For domestic banks–Bank name, address, phone, telex, cable, date established, routing number, charter type, bank holding company affiliation, memberships in Federal Reserve System and other banking organizations, principal officers by function performed, principal correspondent banks, and key financial data (deposits, etc.). For international banks–Bank name, address, phone, fax, telex, cable, SWIFT address, transit or sort codes within home country, ownership, financial data, names and titles of key personnel, branch locations. For branches–Bank name, address, phone, charter type, ownership and other details comparable to domestic bank listings. Arrangement: Geographical. Indexes: Alphabetical, geographical.

★4018★ Thomson North American Financial Institutions Directory

Accuity
4709 W Golf Rd., Ste. 600
Skokie, IL 60076
Ph: (847)676-9600   Fax: (847)933-8101
Fr: 800-321-3373
URL: http://www.tfp.com

Semiannual, January and July. $512.00 for individuals. Covers 15,000 banks and their branches; over 2,000 head offices, and 15,500 branches of savings and loan associations; over 5,500 credit unions with assets over $5 million; Federal Reserve System and other U.S. government and state government banking agencies; bank holding, commercial finance, and leasing companies; coverage includes the United States, Canada, Mexico, and Central America. Entries include: Bank name, address, phone, fax, telex, principal officers and directors, date established, financial data, association memberships, attorney or counsel, correspondent banks, out-of-town branch, holding company affiliation, ABA transit number and routing symbol, MICR number with check digit, credit card(s) issued, trust powers, current par value and dividend of common stock, kind of charter. Arrangement: Geographical. Indexes: Alphabetical.

★4019★ Top Careers for Economics Graduates

Facts On File Inc.
132 W 31st St., 17th Fl.
New York, NY 10001
Ph: (212)967-8800   Fax: 800-678-3633
Fr: 800-322-8755
URL: http://www.factsonfile.com

Published 2004. $14.95 for individuals; $13.45 for libraries. Covers what it takes to transform the skills and experience gained from an economics degree into a great job.

★4020★ Who's Who in Finance and Business

Marquis Who's Who L.L.C.
890 Mountain Ave., Ste. 300
New Providence, NJ 07974-1218
Ph: (908)673-1001   Fax: (908)673-1189
Fr: 800-473-7020
E-mail: finance@marquiswhoswho.com
URL: http://www.marquiswhoswho.com

Biennial; latest edition 36th, September 2007. $349.00 for individuals. Covers over 18,000 individuals. Entries include: Name, home and office addresses, personal, career, and family data; civic and political activities; memberships, publications, awards. Arrangement: Alphabetical.

HANDBOOKS AND MANUALS

★4021★ Careers for Number Crunchers and Other Quantitative Types

The McGraw-Hill Companies
PO Box 182604
Columbus, OH 43272
Fax: (614)759-3749   Fr: 877-883-5524
E-mail: customer.service@mcgraw-hill.com
URL: http://www.mcgraw-hill.com

Rebecca Burnett. Second edition, 2002. $22.95 (paper). 192 pages. Provides information to math-oriented job hunters on how to become statisticians, field researchers, computer programmers, stock analysts, investment managers, bankers, engineers, accountants, underwriters, economists, market analysts, mathematicians, systems analysts, and more.

★4022★ Opportunities in Research and Development Careers

The McGraw-Hill Companies
PO Box 182604
Columbus, OH 43272
Fax: (614)759-3749   Fr: 877-883-5524
E-mail: customer.service@mcgraw-hill.com
URL: http://www.mcgraw-hill.com

Jan Goldberg. 1996. $11.95 (paper). 146 pages.

★4023★ Opportunities in Social Science Careers

The McGraw-Hill Companies
PO Box 182604
Columbus, OH 43272
Fax: (614)759-3749   Fr: 877-883-5524
E-mail: customer.service@mcgraw-hill.com
URL: http://www.mcgraw-hill.com

Rosanne J. Marek. 2004. $13.95. 160 Pages. VGM Opportunities Series.

EMPLOYMENT AGENCIES AND SEARCH FIRMS

★4024★ Choi & Burns LLC

152 W. 57th St., Fl. 32
New York, NY 10019
Ph: (212)755-7051   Fax: (212)335-2610
E-mail: info@choiburns.com
URL: http://www.choiburns.com

Executive search firm focuses on the financial industry.

★4025★ Cook & Company

12 Masterton Rd.
Bronxville, NY 10708
Ph: (914)779-4838   Fax: (914)793-1885
E-mail: search@cook-co.com
URL: http://www.cook-co.com

Executive search firm dedicated to the financial industry.

★4026★ Cromwell Partners Inc.

305 Madison Ave.
New York, NY 10165
Ph: (212)953-3220   Fax: (212)953-4688
E-mail: recruiters@cromwell-partners.com
URL: http://www.cromwell-partners.com

Executive search firm.

★4027★ Dussick Management Associates

White Birch Rd., Ste. 28
Madison, CT 06443
Ph: (203)245-9311   Fax: (203)245-1648
E-mail: vince@dussick.com
URL: http://www.dussick.com

Executive search firm.

★4028★ Halbrecht & Co.

10195 Main St., Ste. L
PO Box 2601
Fairfax, VA 22031
Ph: (703)359-2880   Fax: (703)359-2933
E-mail: halbrechtandco@aol.com
URL: http://www.halbrecht.com

Performs professional recruiting in data processing and operations research, economics, corporate planning, market research, telecommunications, and decision support systems.

★4029★ Hawkes Peers

224 Fifth Ave., Fl. 6
New York, NY 10001
Ph: (646)415-7812
E-mail: noah@hawkespeers.com
URL: http://www.hawkespeers.com

Executive search firm specializing in the areas of banking and sales.

★4030★ International Staffing Consultants

17310 Redhill Ave., No. 140
Irvine, CA 92614
Ph: (949)255-5857   Fax: (949)767-5959
E-mail: iscinc@iscworld.com
URL: http://www.iscworld.com

Employment agency. Provides placement on regular or temporary basis. Affiliate office in London.

★4031★ The Murphy Group

245 W Roosevelt Rd., Bldg.15, Ste.101
Chicago, IL 60605
Ph: (630)639-5110   Fax: (630)639-5113
E-mail: info@murphygroup.com
URL: http://www.murphygroup.com

Employment agency. Places personnel in a variety of positions. Additional offices located in Napierville, Park Ridge, and OakBrook.

★4032★ Ritt-Ritt and Associates, Inc.

5105 Tollview Dr., Ste. 110
Rolling Meadows, IL 60008
Ph: (847)483-9330   Fax: (847)483-9331
E-mail: info@rittsearch.com

Food service and hospitality employment agency and executive search firm.

★4033★ Sales Executives Inc.

33900 W. 8 Mile Rd., Ste. 171
Farmington Hills, MI 48335
Ph: (248)615-0100
E-mail: dale@salesexecutives.com
URL: http://www.salesexecutives.com

Employment agency. Executive search firm.

★4034★ Werbin Associates Executive Search, Inc.

521 Fifth Ave., Rm. 1749
New York, NY 10175
Ph: (212)953-0909
E-mail: swerb@bellatlantic.net

Employment agency. Executive search firm.

OTHER SOURCES

★4035★ American Almanac of Jobs and Salaries

HarperCollins
10 E. 53rd St.
New York, NY 10022
Ph: (212)207-7000   Fr: 800-242-7737
URL: http://www.harpercollins.com/

John W. Wright. Revised edition, 2000. $20.00 (paper). 672 pages. This is a comprehensive guide to the wages of hundreds of occupations in a wide variety of industries and organizations.

★4036★ American Economic Association (AEA)

2014 Broadway, Ste. 305
Nashville, TN 37203
Ph: (615)322-2595   Fax: (615)343-7590
E-mail: aeainfo@vanderbilt.edu
URL: http://www.vanderbilt.edu/AEA

Members: Educators, business executives, government administrators, journalists, lawyers, and others interested in economics and its application to present-day problems. **Purpose:** Encourages historical and statistical research into actual conditions of industrial life and provides a nonpartisan forum for economic discussion.

★4037★ Committee on the Status of Women in the Economics Profession (CSWEP)

Economic Affairs
Fletcher School of Law and Diplomacy
Tufts University
160 Packard Ave.
Medford, MA 02155
E-mail: cswep@tufts.edu

Description: A standing committee of American Economic Association. Women economists in the U.S. Aims to support and facilitate equality of opportunity for women economists. Disseminates information about job opportunities, research funding, and research related to the status of women in economics. Sponsors technical sessions.

★4038★ **Economic Policy Institute (EPI)**

1333 H St. NW, Ste. 300
East Tower
Washington, DC 20005-4707
Ph: (202)775-8810   Fax: (202)775-0819
E-mail: epi@epi.org
URL: http://www.epinet.org

Purpose: Conducts research and provides a forum for the exchange of information on economic policy issues. Promotes educational programs to encourage discussion of economic policy and economic issues, particularly the economics of poverty, unemployment, inflation, American industry, international competitiveness, and problems of economic adjustment as they affect the community and the individual. **Activities:** Sponsors seminars for economists and citizens.

★4039★ **Institute for Economic Analysis (IEA)**

262 Harvard St., No. 12
Cambridge, MA 02139
Ph: (617)864-9933   Fax: (617)864-9944
E-mail: info@iea-macro-economics.org
URL: http://iea-macro-economics.org

Purpose: Seeks to develop tools for macroeconomic analysis and policy that can maintain stable full employment growth, low inflation, low interest rates and equitable distribution of income and wealth. Integrates GDP and financial accounts for more systematic coordination of monetary and fiscal policy. Focuses on federal monetary policy, federal budget deficit/surplus, social security, consumer credit, and world economic recovery.

★4040★ **International Studies Association (ISA)**

University of Arizona
324 Social Sciences Bldg.
Tucson, AZ 85721
Ph: (520)621-7715   Fax: (520)621-5780
E-mail: isa@u.arizona.edu
URL: http://www.isanet.org

Members: Social scientists and other scholars from a wide variety of disciplines who are specialists in international affairs and cross-cultural studies; academicians; government officials; officials in international organizations; business executives; students. **Purpose:** Promotes research, improved teaching, and the orderly growth of knowledge in the field of international studies; emphasizes a multidisciplinary approach to problems. **Activities:** Conducts conventions, workshops and discussion groups.

★4041★ **National Council on Economic Education (NCEE)**

1140 Ave. of the Americas, 2nd Fl.
New York, NY 10036
Ph: (212)730-7007   Fax: (212)730-1793
Fr: 800-338-1192
E-mail: rduvall@ncee.net
URL: http://www.ncee.net

Description: Economists, educators, and representatives from business, labor, and finance dedicated to improving economic education by improving the quality and increasing the quantity of economics being taught in all levels of schools and colleges. Initiates curriculum development and research; experiments with new economics courses and ways to prepare teachers and students; provides updated teacher-pupil materials; coordinates national and local programs in economics education. Provides consulting services to educators; sponsors workshops; tests new methods in practical school situations.

★4042★ **Professional Specialty Occupations**

Delphi Productions
3159 6th St.
Boulder, CO 80304
Ph: (303)443-2100   Fax: (303)443-4022
Fr: 888-443-2400
E-mail: support@delphivideo.com
URL: http://www.delphivideo.com

$95.00. 53 minutes. Part of the Careers for the 21st Century Video Library.

Education Administrators

SOURCES OF HELP-WANTED ADS

★4043★ AABC Newsletter

Association for Biblical Higher Education
5575 S Semoran Blvd., Ste. 26
Orlando, FL 32822-1781
Ph: (407)207-0808
URL: http://www.aabc.org

Description: Five issues/year (always January, April, June, September, and November). Provides information on issues, events, and resources for Bible college administrators and others interested in Christian higher education. Recurring features include a calendar of events, reports of meetings, news of educational opportunities, book reviews, and notices of publications available.

★4044★ AAEE Connections

American Association for Employment in Education
3040 Riverside Dr., Ste. 125
Columbus, OH 43221
Ph: (614)485-1111   Fax: (614)485-9609
E-mail: office@aaee.org
URL: http://www.aaee.org/

Description: Quarterly. Publishes news of the Association, whose aim is "to enhance and promote the concept of career planning and placement as an integral part of the educational process and to undertake activities designed to help schools, colleges, and universities meet their educational staffing needs." Also concerned with teacher education and the supply of/demand for teachers. Recurring features include news of members, state and regional news, and announcements of upcoming conferences and meetings.

★4045★ About Campus

John Wiley & Sons Inc.
111 River St.
Hoboken, NJ 07030-5774
Ph: (201)748-6000   Fax: (201)748-6088
Fr: 800-825-7550
URL: http://www3.interscience.wiley.com/

cgi-bin/jhome/86513696

Bimonthly. $60.00/year for individuals, for print; $60.00/year for Canada and Mexico, for print; $96.00/year for individuals, for print (rest of world); $159.00/year for institutions, for print; $219.00/year for institutions, Canada and Mexico, for print; $270.00/year for institutions, for print (rest of world); $175.00/year for institutions, for print and online; $235.00/year for institutions, Canada and Mexico, for print and online; $286.00/year for institutions, for print and online, (rest of world); $111.00/year for individuals, print only. Journal focused on the critical issues faced by both student affairs and academic affairs staff as they work on helping students learn.

★4046★ American Academic

American Federation of Teachers
555 New Jersey Ave. NW
Washington, DC 20001
Ph: (202)879-4400
URL: http://www.aft.org/pubs-reports/american_academic/index.htm

Higher education policy journal.

★4047★ The American School Board Journal

American School Board Journal
1680 Duke St.
Alexandria, VA 22314
Ph: (703)838-6722   Fax: (703)683-7590
URL: http://www.asbj.com

Monthly. $47.00/year for individuals, print and online version; $36.00/year for individuals, online. Magazine serving school board members, superintendents, and other administrative officials.

★4048★ American School & University

Penton Media Inc.
9800 Metcalf Ave.
Overland Park, KS 66212
Ph: (913)341-1300   Fax: (913)967-1898
URL: http://www.primediabusiness.com

Monthly. Trade magazine.

★4049★ Annals of Medicine

Taylor & Francis Group Journals
325 Chestnut St., Ste. 800
Philadelphia, PA 19106
Ph: (215)625-8900   Fax: (215)625-8914
Fr: 800-354-1420
URL: http://www.ingentaconnect.com

$418.00/year for institutions, print and online; $397.00/year for institutions, online only; $155.00/year for individuals. Journal covering health science and medical education.

★4050★ ASBSD-Bulletin

Associated School Boards of South Dakota
306 E. Capitol Ave.
Pierre, SD 57501
Ph: (605)773-2500   Fax: (605)773-2501
E-mail: info@asbsd.org
URL: http://www.asbsd.org

Description: Semimonthly. Deals with policymaking, financing, and innovation in public education. Seeks to promote reorganization and adequate financing. Recurring features include letters to the editor, news of research, reports of meetings, news of educational opportunities, job listings, notices of publications available, and columns titled On the Line, Check This, and Board Policies.

★4051★ Assessment & Evaluation in Higher Education

Taylor & Francis Group Journals
325 Chestnut St., Ste. 800
Philadelphia, PA 19106
Ph: (215)625-8900   Fax: (215)625-8914
Fr: 800-354-1420
E-mail: aehe@bath.ac.uk
URL: http://www.tandf.co.uk/journals/titles/02602938.asp

Bimonthly. $1,982.00/year for institutions, print and online; $1,882.00/year for institutions, online only; $466.00/year for individuals. Journal focusing on publishing papers and reports on all aspects of assessment and evaluation within higher education.

★4052★ Brookings Papers on Education Policy

Brookings Institution Press
1775 Massahusetts Ave. NW
Washington, DC 20036-2188
Ph: (202)536-3600   Fax: (202)536-3623
Fr: 800-275-1447
URL: http://www.brookings.edu/press/journals.htm

$46.00/year for institutions; $35.00/year for individuals. Journal dealing with all aspects of American education.

★4053★ Change

Heldref Publications
1319 18th St., NW
Washington, DC 20036-1802
Ph: (202)296-6267   Fr: 800-365-9753
E-mail: ch@heldref.org
URL: http://www.heldref.org/change.php

Bimonthly. $58.00/year for individuals, print only; $144.00/year for institutions, print only; $62.00/year for individuals, print and online; $173.00/year for institutions, print and online. Magazine dealing with contemporary issues in higher learning.

★4054★ The Chronicle of Higher Education

The Chronicle of Higher Education
1255 23rd St. NW 7th Fl.
Washington, DC 20037-1125
Ph: (202)466-1050   Fax: (202)452-1033
Fr: 800-728-2803
URL: http://chronicle.com

Weekly. $82.50/year for individuals, 49 issues; $45.00/year for individuals, 24 issues; $41.25/year for students, 49 issues; $22.50/year for students, 24 issues. Higher education magazine (tabloid).

★4055★ Communication Quarterly

MetaPress
PO Box 1943
Birmingham, AL 35201
Fr: 877-773-3833

Periodical focusing on research, criticism, communication theory, and excellence in teaching.

★4056★ Community College Journal of Research & Practice

Taylor & Francis Group Journals
325 Chestnut St., Ste. 800
Philadelphia, PA 19106
Ph: (215)625-8900   Fax: (215)625-8914
Fr: 800-354-1420
URL: http://www.tandf.co.uk/journals/titles/10668926.aspttp://www

Monthly. $778.00/year for institutions, print and online; $739.00/year for institutions, online only; $208.00/year for individuals. Journal focusing on exchange of ideas, research, and empirically tested educational innovations.

★4057★ Community Colleges Journal

American Association of Community Colleges
1 Dupont Cir. NW, Ste. 410
Washington, DC 20036
Ph: (202)728-0200   Fax: (202)833-2467
URL: http://www.aacc.nche.edu

Bimonthly. $28.00/year for nonmembers; $5.50 for single issue. Educational magazine.

★4058★ E-Journal of Teaching and Learning in Diverse Settings

Southern University at Baton Rouge
PO Box 9942
Baton Rouge, LA 70813
Ph: (225)771-3184   Fax: (225)771-4400
URL: http://www.subr.edu/coeducation/ejournal

Online academic journal that publishes research and scholarly articles in the field of education and learning.

★4059★ Education & Treatment of Children

West Virginia University Press
44 Stansbury Hall
PO Box 6295
Morgantown, WV 26506
Ph: (304)293-8400   Fax: (304)293-6585
Fr: (866)988-7737
URL: http://www.educationandtreatmentofchildren.net

Quarterly. $85.00/year for institutions; $45.00/year for individuals; $100.00/year for institutions, elsewhere; $60.00/year for individuals, elsewhere. Periodical featuring information concerning the development of services for children and youth. Includes reports written for educators and other child care and mental health providers focused on teaching, training, and treatment effectiveness.

★4060★ Education Week

Editorial Projects in Education Inc.
6935 Arlington Rd., Ste. 100
Bethesda, MD 20814-5233
Ph: (301)280-3100   Fax: (301)280-3200
Fr: 800-346-1834
E-mail: ew@epe.org
URL: http://www.edweek.org/ew

Weekly. $79.94/year for individuals, print plus online; $69.94/year for individuals, online; $135.94/year for Canada, online Monthly; $208.84/year for out of country. Professional newspaper for elementary and secondary school educators.

★4061★ Educational Administration Quarterly

Sage Publications Inc.
2455 Teller Rd.
Thousand Oaks, CA 91320
Ph: (805)499-0721   Fax: (805)499-8096
URL: http://eaq.sagepub.com/

$611.00/year for institutions, combined (print & e-access); $642.00/year for institutions,

backfile lease, combined plus backfile; $550.00/year for institutions, e-access; $581.00/year for institutions, backfile lease, e-access plus backfile; $1,590.00/year for institutions, backfile purchase, e-access; $599.00/year for institutions, print only; $131.00/year for individuals, print only; $132.00 for institutions, single print; $34.00 for individuals, single print. Journal focusing on timely and critical leadership and policy issues of educational organizations.

★4062★ Educational Management Administration & Leadership

Sage Publications Inc.
2455 Teller Rd.
Thousand Oaks, CA 91320
Ph: (805)499-0721   Fax: (805)499-8096
URL: http://ema.sagepub.com

Quarterly. $774.00/year for institutions, combined (print & e-access); $813.00/year for institutions, current volume print & all online content; $697.00/year for institutions, e-access; $736.00/year for institutions, e-access plus backfile (all online content); $1,540.00/year for institutions, backfile purchase, e-access (content through 1999); $759.00/year for institutions, print only; $387.00/year for individuals, school, combined (print & e-access); $93.00/year for individuals, print only; $209.00 for single issue, institutional; $30.00 for single issue, individual. Journal focusing on all aspects of leadership, management, administration and policy in education.

★4063★ Educational Policy

Sage Publications Inc.
2455 Teller Rd.
Thousand Oaks, CA 91320
Ph: (805)499-0721   Fax: (805)499-8096
URL: http://www.sagepub.com/journalsProdDesc.nav?prodId=Journal20

Annual. $749.00/year for institutions, combined (print & e-access); $824.00/year for institutions, backfile lease, combined plus backfile; $674.00/year for institutions, e-access; $749.00/year for institutions, backfile lease, e-access plus backfile; $687.48/year for institutions, backfile puchase, e-access (content through 1999); $734.00/year for institutions, print only; $159.00/year for individuals, print only; $135.00 for institutions, single print; $34.00 for individuals, single print. Journal for educators, policy makers, administrators, researchers, teachers, and graduate students.

★4064★ Educational Research and Evaluation

Taylor & Francis Group Journals
325 Chestnut St., Ste. 800
Philadelphia, PA 19106
Ph: (215)625-8900   Fax: (215)625-8914
Fr: 800-354-1420
URL: http://www.tandf.co.uk/journals/titles/13803611.asp

Bimonthly. $616.00/year for institutions, print and online; $585.00/year for institutions, online only; $239.00/year for individuals. Journal on theory and practice.

★4065★ Educational Researcher

American Educational Research
 Association
1230 17th St. NW
Washington, DC 20036
Ph: (202)223-9485   Fax: (202)775-1824
URL: http://www.aera.net/publications/
?id=317

Monthly. $48.00/year for individuals, plus
foreign mailing charges; $150.00/year for
institutions, plus foreign mailing charges.
Educational research journal.

**★4066★ Environmental Education
 Research**

Taylor & Francis Group Journals
325 Chestnut St., Ste. 800
Philadelphia, PA 19106
Ph: (215)625-8900   Fax: (215)625-8914
Fr: 800-354-1420
URL: http://www.tandf.co.uk/journals/titles/
13504622.asp

Journal covering all aspects of environmental education.

★4067★ Essays in Education

University of South Carolina
471 University Pky.
Aiken, SC 29801
Ph: (803)648-6851   Fax: (803)641-3461
Fr: 888-969-8722
URL: http://www.usca.edu/essays/

Monthly. Journal covering issues that impact
and influence education.

★4068★ Hematology

American Society of Hematology
1900 M St. NW, Ste. 200
Washington, DC 20036
Ph: (202)776-0544   Fax: (202)776-0545
URL: http://asheducation-
book.hematologylibrary.org

Semiweekly. $60.00/year for members;
$90.00/year for nonmembers. Journal pro-
viding continuing medical education for physicians.

**★4069★ The International Electronic
 Journal of Health Education**

American Alliance for Health, Physical
 Education, Recreation & Dance
1900 Association Dr.
Reston, VA 20191-1598
Ph: (703)476-3400   Fax: (703)476-9527
Fr: 800-213-7193
URL: http://www.aahperd.org/iejhe/temp-
late.cfm?template=about.htm

Annual. Free to health education professionals and students. Journal promoting health
through education and other systematic
strategies.

**★4070★ International Journal of Early
 Years Education**

Taylor & Francis Group Journals
325 Chestnut St., Ste. 800
Philadelphia, PA 19106
Ph: (215)625-8900   Fax: (215)625-8914
Fr: 800-354-1420
URL: http://www.tandf.co.uk/journals/titles/
09669760.asp

$512.00/year for institutions, print and on-
line; $486.00/year for institutions, online
only; $184.00/year for individuals. Journal
focusing on education world-wide.

**★4071★ International Journal of
 Inclusive Education**

Taylor & Francis Group Journals
325 Chestnut St., Ste. 800
Philadelphia, PA 19106
Ph: (215)625-8900   Fax: (215)625-8914
Fr: 800-354-1420
URL: http://www.tandf.co.uk/journals/titles/
13603116.asp

Bimonthly. $320.00/year for individuals, print
only; $616.00/year for institutions, online
only; $649.00/year for individuals, print and
online; $193.00/year for individuals, print
only; $376.00/year for institutions, online
only; $396.00/year for institutions, print and
online. Journal providing information on the
nature of schools, universities and technical
colleges for the educators and educational
policy-makers.

**★4072★ International Journal of
 Leadership in Education**

Taylor & Francis Group Journals
325 Chestnut St., Ste. 800
Philadelphia, PA 19106
Ph: (215)625-8900   Fax: (215)625-8914
Fr: 800-354-1420
E-mail: ijle@txstate.edu
URL: http://www.tandf.co.uk/journals/tf/
13603124.html

Quarterly. $196.00/year for individuals;
$536.00/year for institutions, print and on-
line; $509.00/year for institutions, online
only; Journal dealing with leadership in education.

**★4073★ International Journal of
 Progressive Education**

International Journal of Progressive
 Education
c/o Mustafa Yunus Eryaman, Mng. Ed.
2108 S Orchard St., No. D
Urbana, IL 61801
URL: http://www.inased.org/ijpe.htm

$35.00/year for members; $45.00/year for
individuals; $140.00/year for institutions, li-
brary; $35.00/year for students; $25.00/year
for single issue, U.S. Peer reviewed online
journal that aims to create an open and
continuing dialogue about current educational issues and future conceptions of educational theory.

**★4074★ International Journal of
 Research & Method in Education**

Taylor & Francis Group Journals
325 Chestnut St., Ste. 800
Philadelphia, PA 19106
Ph: (215)625-8900   Fax: (215)625-8914
Fr: 800-354-1420
URL: http://www.tandf.co.uk/journals/titles/
1743727x.asp

$1809.00/year for institutions, print and on-
line; $1718.00/year for institutions, online
only; $271.00/year for individuals. Profes-
sional journal to further international discourse in education with particular focus on
method.

**★4075★ International Journal of Whole
 Schooling**

Whole Schooling Press
Wayne State University
217 Education
Detroit, MI 48202
URL: http://www.wholeschooling.net/Jour-
nal_of_Whole_Schooling/IJW

Free to qualified subscribers. International,
refereed academic journal dedicated to exploring ways to improve learning and schooling for all children.

**★4076★ Journal of Academic
 Leadership**

Academic Leadership
600 Park St.
Rarick Hall 219
Hays, KS 67601-4099
Ph: (785)628-4547
URL: http://www.academicleadership.org/

Journal focusing on the leadership issues in
the academic world.

**★4077★ Journal of Career Planning &
 Employment**

National Association of Colleges and
 Employers
62 Highland Ave.
Bethlehem, PA 18017-9085
Ph: (610)868-1421   Fax: (610)868-0208
Fr: 800-544-5272
URL: http://www.naceweb.org/info_public/
journal_archives.htm

Quarterly. $70.00/year for individuals, per
year; $20.00/year for single issue; $25.00/
year for other countries, airmail postage;
$12.50/year for individuals, additional cop-
ies. Journal on career planning, and recruitment of the college educated work force.

**★4078★ Journal of Cases in
 Educational Leadership**

Sage Publications Inc.
2455 Teller Rd.
Thousand Oaks, CA 91320
Ph: (805)499-0721   Fax: (805)499-8096
URL: http://www.sagepub.com/journal-
sProdDesc.nav?prodId=Journal20

Quarterly. $319.00/year for institutions, e-
access; $83.00/year for individuals, e-ac-
cess. Journal covering cases appropriate for

use in programs that prepare educational leaders.

★4079★ Journal of College Teaching & Learning

The Clute Institute for Academic Research
PO Box 620760
Littleton, CO 80162
Ph: (303)904-4750   Fax: (303)978-0413
URL: http://www.cluteinstitute.com/JCTLMain.htm

Monthly. $100.00/year for individuals; $200.00/year for other countries, with postage; $495.00/year for institutions. Refereed academic journal covering all areas of college level teaching, learning and administration.

★4080★ Journal of Curriculum and Supervision

Association for Supervision and Curriculum Development
1703 N Beauregard St.
Alexandria, VA 22311-1714
Ph: (703)578-9600   Fax: (703)575-5400
Fr: 800-933-2723
URL: http://www.ascd.org/portal/site/ascd/menuitem.0545410c9839aa

Scholarly journal focusing on curriculum and supervision.

★4081★ Journal of Direct Instruction

Association for Direct Instruction
PO Box 10252
Eugene, OR 97440
Ph: (541)485-1293   Fax: (541)683-7543
Fr: 800-995-2464
URL: http://www.adihome.org/phpshop/articles/articles.php?type=JD

Quarterly. Subscription included in membership. Journal covering education.

★4082★ Journal of Higher Education Outreach and Engagement (JHEOE)

Institute of Higher Education
Meigs Hall
Athens, GA 30602
Ph: (706)542-3464   Fax: (706)542-7588
E-mail: jheoe@uga.edu
URL: http://www.uga.edu/jheoe/

Semiannual. $35.00/year for individuals; $45.00/year for Canada; $60.00/year for elsewhere, surface mail; $70.00/year for elsewhere, airmail; $95.00/year for institutions; $105.00/year for institutions, Canada; $110.00/year for institutions, other countries, surface mail; $120.00/year for institutions, other countries, airmail. Journal covering higher education outreach and engagement for scholars, practitioners, and professionals.

★4083★ Journal of Language, Identity, and Education

Lawrence Erlbaum Associates Inc.
10 Industrial Ave.
Mahwah, NJ 07430
Ph: (201)258-2200   Fax: (201)236-0072
Fr: 800-926-6579
E-mail: journals@erlbaum.com
URL: http://www.erlbaum.com

Quarterly. $50.00/year for U.S. and Canada, individual, online and print; $80.00/year for elsewhere, individual, online and print; $360.00/year for U.S. and Canada, institution, online and print; $390.00/year for elsewhere, institution, online and print; $290.00/year for U.S. and Canada, institution, online only; $290.00/year for elsewhere, institution, online only; $325.00/year for U.S. and Canada, institution, print only; $355.00/year for elsewhere, institution, print only. Scholarly, interdisciplinary journal covering issues in language, identity and education worldwide for academics, educators and policy specialists in a variety of disciplines, and others.

★4084★ Journal of Latinos and Education

Lawrence Erlbaum Associates Inc.
10 Industrial Ave.
Mahwah, NJ 07430
Ph: (201)258-2200   Fax: (201)236-0072
Fr: 800-926-6579
URL: http://www.erlbaum.com/

Quarterly. $50.00/year for individuals, online and print - U.S./Canada; $80.00/year for individuals, online and print - all other countries; $360.00/year for institutions, online and print - U.S./Canada; $390.00/year for institutions, online and print - all other countries; $290.00/year for institutions, online only - U.S./Canada; $290.00/year for institutions, online only - all other countries; $325.00/year for institutions, print only - U.S./Canada; $355.00/year for institutions, print only - all other countries. Scholarly, multidisciplinary journal covering educational issues that impact Latinos for researchers, teaching professionals, academics, scholars, institutions, and others.

★4085★ Journal of STEM Education

Auburn University
9088 Haley Ctr.
Auburn, AL 36849
Ph: (334)844-4000   Fax: (334)844-9027
URL: http://www.auburn.edu/research/litee/jstem/index.php

Semiannual. Journal for educators in Science, Technology, Engineering, and Mathematics (STEM) education.

★4086★ Journal of Teacher Education

Boston College
140 Commonwealth Ave.
Chestnut Hill, MA 02467
URL: http://www.sagepub.com

$403.00/year for institutions, print & e-access; $423.00/year for institutions, volume print & all online; $363.00/year for institutions, e-access; $383.00/year for institutions,

all online content; $1,512.00/year for institutions, backfile purchase, e-access; $395.00/year for institutions, print; $99.00/year for individuals, print; $87.00/year for institutions, single print; $26.00/year for individuals, single print. Magazine of interest to educators.

★4087★ Leadership and Policy in Schools

Taylor & Francis Group Journals
325 Chestnut St., Ste. 800
Philadelphia, PA 19106
Ph: (215)625-8900   Fax: (215)625-8914
Fr: 800-354-1420
URL: http://www.tandf.co.uk/journals/titles/15700763.asp

Quarterly. $477.00/year for institutions, print and online; $453.00/year for institutions, online only; $227.00/year for individuals; $60.00/year for ICSEI members. Journal providing information about leadership and policy in primary and secondary education.

★4088★ NJEA Review

New Jersey Education Association
180 West State St.
PO Box 1211
Trenton, NJ 08607-1211
Ph: (609)599-4561   Fax: (609)599-1201

Monthly. Educational journal for public school employees.

★4089★ Oxford Review of Education

Taylor & Francis Group Journals
325 Chestnut St., Ste. 800
Philadelphia, PA 19106
Ph: (215)625-8900   Fax: (215)625-8914
Fr: 800-354-1420
URL: http://www.tandf.co.uk/journals/titles/03054985.asp

$1,031.00/year for institutions, print and online; $979.00/year for institutions, online only; $396.00/year for individuals. Journal covering advance study of education.

★4090★ The Physics Teacher

American Association of Physics Teachers
1 Physics Ellipse
College Park, MD 20740-3845
Ph: (301)209-3300   Fax: (301)209-0845
E-mail: tpt@appstate.edu
URL: http://www.aapt.org/Publications/

$335.00/year for nonmembers, international; $105.00/year for members, regular. Scientific education magazine.

★4091★ Research Strategies

Elsevier Science Inc.
360 Park Ave. S
New York, NY 10010
Ph: (212)989-5800   Fax: (212)633-3990
URL: http://www.elsevier.com

Journal covering library literature and the educational mission of the library.

★4092★ School and Community

Missouri State Teachers Association
407 South Sixth St.
PO Box 458
Columbia, MO 65205
Ph: (573)442-3127   Fax: (573)443-5079
Fr: 800-392-0532

Quarterly. Education magazine.

★4093★ School Effectiveness and School Improvement

Taylor & Francis Group Journals
325 Chestnut St., Ste. 800
Philadelphia, PA 19106
Ph: (215)625-8900   Fax: (215)625-8914
Fr: 800-354-1420
URL: http://www.tandf.co.uk/journals/titles/09243453.asp

Quarterly. $305.00/year for institutions, print and online; $231.00/year for institutions, online only; $153.00/year for individuals, print only; $520.00/year for institutions, print and online; $494.00/year for institutions, online only; $255.00/year for individuals, print only. Journal focusing on educational progress of all students.

★4094★ Teaching and Learning in Nursing

Elsevier Science Inc.
360 Park Ave. S
New York, NY 10010
Ph: (212)989-5800   Fax: (212)633-3990
URL: http://www.elsevier.com

Quarterly. $119.00/year for institutions, U.S. $167.00/year for institutions, other countries; $75.00/year for individuals, U.S. $104.00/year for individuals, other countries. Journal devoted to associate degree nursing education and practice.

★4095★ Tech Directions

Prakken Publications Inc.
832 Phoenix Dr.
PO Box 8623
Ann Arbor, MI 48108
Ph: (734)975-2800   Fax: (734)975-2787
Fr: 800-530-9673
E-mail: tdedit@techdirections.com
URL: http://www.techdirections.com

Monthly. $30.00/year for individuals, U.S.; $20.00/year for students; $40.00/year for elsewhere; $55.00 for two years, U.S.; $75.00 for two years, elsewhere. Free to qualified subscribers. Magazine covering issues, programs, and projects in industrial education, technology education, trade and industry, and vocational-technical career education. Articles are geared toward teacher and administrator use and reference from elementary school through postsecondary levels.

★4096★ Theory and Research in Education

Sage Publications Inc.
2455 Teller Rd.
Thousand Oaks, CA 91320
Ph: (805)499-0721   Fax: (805)499-8096

URL: http://tre.sagepub.com/

$459.00/year for institutions, print and online; $413.00/year for institutions, online only; $450.00/year for institutions, print only; $77.00/year for individuals, print only. Interdisciplinary journal covering normative and theoretical issues concerning education including multi-faceted philosophical analysis of moral, social, political and epistemological problems and issues arising from educational practice.

★4097★ Women in Higher Education

Wenniger Co.
5376 Farmco Dr.
Madison, WI 53704
Ph: (608)251-3232   Fax: (608)284-0601
E-mail: career@wihe.com
URL: http://www.wihe.com/

Description: Monthly. Focuses on leadership, career strategies, gender equity, and harassment of women administrators. Recurring features include interviews, news of research, reports of meetings and presentations, news of educational opportunities, job listings, book reviews, notices of publications available, columns titled Profile, Research Briefs, Newswatch, What Should She Do?, Moveable Type, and The Last Laugh.

PLACEMENT AND JOB REFERRAL SERVICES

★4098★ American Association of Christian Schools (AACS)

National Office
602 Belvoir Ave.
East Ridge, TN 37412
Ph: (423)629-4280   Fax: (423)622-7461
E-mail: national@aacs.org
URL: http://www.aacs.org

Description: Maintains teacher/administrator certification program and placement service. Participates in school accreditation program. Sponsors National Academic Tournament. Maintains American Christian Honor Society. Compiles statistics; maintains speakers' bureau and placement service.

★4099★ American Association of School Administrators (AASA)

801 N Quincy St., Ste. 700
Arlington, VA 22203
Ph: (703)528-0700   Fax: (703)841-1543
E-mail: info@aasa.org
URL: http://www.aasa.org

Description: Professional association of administrators and executives of school systems and educational service agencies; school district superintendents; central, building, and service unit administrators; presidents of colleges, deans, and professors of educational administration; placement officers; executive directors and administrators of education associations. Sponsors

numerous professional development conferences annually.

★4100★ American College Personnel Association (ACPA)

1 Dupont Cir. NW, Ste. 300
Washington, DC 20036-1188
Ph: (202)835-2272   Fax: (202)296-3286
E-mail: info@acpa.nche.edu
URL: http://www.acpa.nche.edu

Description: Represents individuals employed in higher education and involved in student personnel work, including administration, counseling, research, and teaching. Fosters student development in higher education in areas of service, advocacy, and standards by offering professional programs for educators committed to the overall development of post-secondary students. Sponsors professional and educational activities in cooperation with other organizations. Offers placement services.

★4101★ American Education Finance Association (AEFA)

PO Box 117049
Gainesville, FL 32611-7049
Ph: (352)392-2391
E-mail: aefa@coe.ufl.edu
URL: http://www.aefa.cc

Members: State and national teacher organizations, university personnel, school administrators, state educational agency personnel, legislators and legislative staff, federal agency personnel, and interested foundations and students. **Purpose:** Facilitates communication among groups and individuals in the field of educational finance including academicians, researchers, and policy-makers. Main interests include traditional school finance concepts, public policy issues, and the review and debate of emerging issues of educational finance. **Activities:** Conducts workshop. Compiles statistics. Maintains placement service.

★4102★ Association of College and University Housing Officers International (ACUHO-I)

941 Chatham Ln., Ste. 318
Columbus, OH 43221-2416
Ph: (614)292-0099   Fax: (614)292-3205
E-mail: office@acuho-i.org
URL: http://www.acuho-i.org

Description: Officials of educational institutions in 13 countries concerned with all aspects of student housing and food service operation. Supports and conducts research. Organizes seminars and workshops. Offers internships. Maintains biographical archives; offers placement service. Compiles statistics.

★4103★ College Media Advisers (CMA)

University of Memphis
Department of Journalism
3711 Veterans Ave., Rm. 300
Memphis, TN 38152-6661
Ph: (901)678-2403   Fax: (901)678-4798

E-mail: rsplbrgr@memphis.edu
URL: http://www.collegemedia.org

Members: Professional association serving advisers, directors, and chairmen of boards of college student media (newspapers, yearbooks, magazines, handbooks, directories, and radio and television stations); heads of schools and departments of journalism; and others interested in junior college, college, and university student media. **Purpose:** Serves as a clearinghouse for student media; acts as consultant on student theses and dissertations on publications. Encourages high school journalism and examines its relationships to college and professional journalism. **Activities:** Conducts national survey of student media in rotation each year by type: newspapers, magazines, and yearbooks; radio and television stations. Compiles statistics. Maintains placement service and speakers' bureau.

★4104★ Council of Educational Facility Planners, International (CEFPI)

9180 E Desert Cove Dr., Ste. 104
Scottsdale, AZ 85260-6231
Ph: (480)391-0840   Fax: (480)391-0940
E-mail: contact@cefpi.org
URL: http://www.cefpi.org

Members: Individuals and firms who are responsible for planning, designing, creating, maintaining, and equipping the physical environment of education. **Purpose:** Sponsors an exchange of information, professional experiences, best practices research results, and other investigative techniques concerning educational facility planning. **Activities:** Activities include publication and review of current and emerging practices in educational facility planning; identification and execution of needed research; development of professional training programs; strengthening of planning services on various levels of government and in institutions of higher learning; leadership in the development of higher standards for facility design and the physical environment of education. Operates speakers' bureau; sponsors placement service; compiles statistics.

★4105★ Council for Jewish Education (CJE)

11 Olympia Ln.
Monsey, NY 10952
Ph: (845)368-8657   Fax: (845)369-6538
E-mail: mjscje@aol.com

Description: Teachers of Hebrew in universities; heads of Bureaus of Jewish Education and their administrative departments; faculty members of Jewish teacher training schools. Seeks to: further the cause of Jewish education in America; raise professional standards and practices; promote the welfare and growth of Jewish educational workers; improve and strengthen Jewish life. Conducts educational programs; cosponsors a Personnel Placement Committee with Jewish Education Service of North America.

★4106★ International Association of Baptist Colleges and Universities (IABCU)

8120 Sawyer Brown Rd., Ste. 108
Nashville, TN 37221-1410
Ph: (615)673-1896   Fax: (615)662-1396
E-mail: tim_fields@baptistschools.org
URL: http://www.baptistschools.org

Members: Southern Baptist senior colleges, universities, junior colleges, academies, and Bible schools. **Purpose:** Promotes Christian education through literature, faculty workshops, student recruitment, teacher placement, trustee orientation, statistical information, and other assistance to members.

★4107★ International Educator's Institute (TIE)

PO Box 513
Cummaquid, MA 02637
Ph: (508)790-1990   Fax: (508)790-1922
Fr: 877-375-6668
E-mail: tie@tieonline.com
URL: http://www.tieonline.com

Description: Facilitates the placement of teachers and administrators in American, British, and international schools. Seeks to create a network that provides for professional development opportunities and improved financial security of members. Offers advice and information on international school news, recent educational developments, job placement, and investment, consumer, and professional development opportunities. Makes available insurance and travel benefits. Operates International Schools Internship Program.

★4108★ Jesuit Association of Student Personnel Administrators (JASPA)

2500 California Plz.
Omaha, NE 68178
Ph: (402)280-2717   Fax: (402)280-1275
E-mail: waynejr@creighton.edu
URL: http://jaspa.creighton.edu

Description: Represents administrators of student personnel programs in 28 Jesuit colleges and universities in the United States. Sponsors institutes and seminars for personnel in Jesuit colleges. Cooperates with Catholic and non-Catholic educational associations in various projects. Maintains placement service and conducts workshops. Operates organizational archives and compiles statistics.

★4109★ Jewish Educators Assembly (JEA)

PO Box 413
Cedarhurst, NY 11516
Ph: (516)569-2537   Fax: (516)295-9039
E-mail: jewisheducators@jewisheducators.org
URL: http://www.jewisheducators.org

Members: Educational and supervisory personnel serving Jewish educational institutions. **Purpose:** Seeks to: advance the development of Jewish education in the congregation on all levels in consonance with the philosophy of the Conservative Movement; cooperate with the United Synagogue of America Commission on Jewish Education as the policy-making body of the educational enterprise; join in cooperative effort with other Jewish educational institutions and organizations; establish and maintain professional standards for Jewish educators; serve as a forum for the exchange of ideas; promote the values of Jewish education as a basis for the creative continuity of the Jewish people. **Activities:** Maintains placement service and speaker's bureau.

★4110★ National Academic Advising Association (NACADA)

Kansas State University
2323 Anderson Ave., Ste. 225
Manhattan, KS 66502-2912
Ph: (785)532-5717   Fax: (785)532-7732
E-mail: nacada@ksu.edu
URL: http://www.nacada.ksu.edu

Members: Academic program advisors, faculty, administrators, counselors, and others concerned with the intellectual, personal, and career development of students in all types of postsecondary educational institutions. **Purpose:** Works to support and promotes professional growth of academic advising and academic advisers. Provides a forum for discussion, debate, and exchange of ideas regarding academic advising. Serves as advocate for standards and quality programs in academic advising. **Activities:** Operates consultants' bureau to assist advising services on college campuses. Maintains placement service, speakers' bureau, and information clearinghouse.

★4111★ National Alliance of Black School Educators (NABSE)

310 Pennsylvania Ave.
Washington, DC 20003
Ph: (202)608-6310   Fax: (202)608-6319
Fr: 800-221-2654
E-mail: lavette@nabse.org
URL: http://www.nabse.org

Description: Black educators from all levels; others indirectly involved in the education of black youth. Promotes awareness, professional expertise, and commitment among black educators. Goals are to: eliminate and rectify the results of racism in education; work with state, local, and national leaders to raise the academic achievement level of all black students; increase members' involvement in legislative activities; facilitate the introduction of a curriculum that more completely embraces black America; improve the ability of black educators to promote problem resolution; create a meaningful and effective network of strength, talent, and professional support. Sponsors workshops, commission meetings, and special projects. Encourages research, especially as it relates to blacks, and the presentation of papers during national conferences. Plans to establish a National Black Educators Data Bank and offer placement service.

★4112★ National Association of Teachers' Agencies (NATA)

797 Kings Hwy.
Fairfield, CT 06825
Ph: (203)333-0611   Fax: (203)334-7224
E-mail: info@jobsforteachers.com

Description: Private employment agencies engaged primarily in the placement of teaching and administration personnel. Works to standardize records and promote a strong ethical sense in the placement field. Maintains speakers' bureau.

★4113★ National Association of Temple Educators (NATE)

633 Third Ave., 7th Fl.
New York, NY 10017-6778
Ph: (212)452-6510   Fax: (212)452-6512
E-mail: nateoff@aol.com
URL: http://nate.rj.org

Members: Directors of education in Reform Jewish religious schools, principals, heads of departments, supervisors, educational consultants, students, and authors. **Purpose:** Purposes are to: assist in the growth and development of Jewish religious education consistent with the aims of Reform Judaism; stimulate communal interest in Jewish religious education; represent and encourage the profession of temple educator. **Activities:** Conducts surveys on personnel practices, confirmation practices, religious school organization and administration, curricular practices, and other aspects of religious education. Sponsors institutes for principals and educational directors; maintains placement service.

★4114★ National Council of Secondary School Athletic Directors (NCSSAD)

1900 Association Dr.
Reston, VA 20191-1598
Ph: (703)476-3400   Fax: (703)476-8316
Fr: 800-213-7193
E-mail: naspe@aahperd.org
URL: http://www.aahperd.org/naspe

Description: A council of the National Association for Sport and Physical Education, which is a division of the American Alliance for Health, Physical Education, Recreation and Dance. Professional athletic directors in secondary schools. Purposes are to improve the educational aspects of interscholastic athletics; to provide for an exchange of ideas; to establish closer working relationships with related professional groups and promote greater unity; to establish and implement standards for the professional preparation of secondary school athletic directors. Provides in-service training programs. Maintains placement service and speakers' bureau.

★4115★ Solomon Schechter Day School Association (SSDSA)

155 5th Ave., 5th Fl.
New York, NY 10010-6802
Ph: (212)533-7800
E-mail: abramson@uscj.org
URL: http://www.ssdsa.org

Description: A division of the United Synagogue of Conservative Judaism Commission on Jewish Education. Jewish elementary day schools and high schools with a total of over 21,500 students. Named for Solomon Schecher (1850-1915), scholar of Talmud and rabbinical literature at Cambridge and founder of the United Synagogue of America and the Jewish Theological Seminary. Provides visitations and consultations regarding education, governance and administration; publication of advisories and position papers, biennial conferences for lay leaders, annual conferences of the principals council, Shibboley Schechter newsletter, listserves for presidents, School heads, Business managers, and development directors. Also provides dissemination of demographics and statistics, chartering and accreditation of schools, seminars and board training for lay leaders, Schechter website, SHAR''R, 7th and 8th grade trips to Israel, placement service, MaToK-TaNaKH curriculum development project for Solomon Schecter Day schools, residency fellowship program to prepare professional leadership (SREL) and a listing of consultants.

★4116★ University Council for Educational Administration (UCEA)

1 University Sta. D5400
Department of Educational Administration
University of Texas at Austin
Austin, TX 78712-0374
Ph: (512)475-8592   Fax: (512)471-5975
E-mail: michelleyoung@austin.utexas.edu
URL: http://www.ucea.org

Members: Consortium of departments of educational administration in universities. **Purpose:** Promotes and disseminates information on the improvement of pre-service and in-service training of school and higher education administrators. **Activities:** Conducts research and development in educational administration through inter-university cooperation. Operates placement service.

EMPLOYER DIRECTORIES AND NETWORKING LISTS

★4117★ 50 State Educational Directories

Career Guidance Foundation
8090 Engineer Rd.
San Diego, CA 92111
Ph: (858)560-8051   Fax: (858)278-8960
Fr: 800-854-2670
URL: http://www.cgf.org

Annual. Microfiche. Collection consists of reproductions of the state educational directories published by the departments of education of individual 50 states. Directory contents vary, but the majority contain listings of elementary and secondary schools, colleges and universities, and state education officials. Amount of detail in each also varies. Entries include: Usually, institution name, address, and name of one executive.

★4118★ Accredited Institutions of Postsecondary Education

Oryx Press
4041 N Central Ave., Ste. 700
PO Box 33889
Phoenix, AZ 85021-3397
Ph: (602)265-2651   Fax: 800-279-4663
Fr: 800-279-6799
URL: http://isbndb.com

Annual, latest edition 2006-2007. Covers more than 7,000 accredited institutions and programs of postsecondary education in the United States and U.S.-chartered schools in 14 countries. Entries include: Institution name, address, phone, whether public or private, any religious affiliation, type of institution and student body, branch campuses or affiliated institutions, date of first accreditation and latest reaffirmation of accrediting body, accredited programs in professional fields, level of degrees offered, name of chief executive officer, size and composition of enrollment, type of academic calendar. Arrangement: Geographical. Indexes: Institution.

★4119★ Boarding Schools Directory

Association of Boarding Schools
2141 Wisconsin Ave. NW, Ste. H
Washington, DC 20007
Ph: (202)965-8982   Fax: (202)965-8988
URL: http://www.schools.com/

Annual; latest edition 2007-2008. For U.S. and Canada. Covers boarding schools that are members of the Association of Boarding Schools. Entries include: School name, address, phone, e-mail and URL, grades for which boarding students are accepted, enrollment, brief description. Arrangement: Classified by type of school. Indexes: Geographical; program; alphabetical.

★4120★ Career Ideas for Teens in Education and Training

Facts On File Inc.
132 W 31st St., 17th Fl.
New York, NY 10001
Ph: (212)967-8800   Fax: 800-678-3633
Fr: 800-322-8755
URL: http://www.factsonfile.com

Published 2005. $40.00 for individuals; $36.00 for libraries. Covers a multitude of career possibilities based on a teenager's specific interests and skills and links his/her talents to a wide variety of actual professions.

★4121★ Christian Schools International-Directory

Christian Schools International
3350 E Paris Ave. SE
Grand Rapids, MI 49512
Ph: (616)957-1070   Fax: (616)957-5022
Fr: 800-635-8288
URL: http://store.csionline.org

Annual; 2007-2008. $15.00 for members; $72.00 for nonmembers. Covers nearly 450 Reformed Christian elementary and secondary schools; related associations; societies without schools. Entries include: For schools–School name, address, phone; name, title, and address of officers; names of faculty members. Arrangement: Geographical.

★4122★ College and University Professional Association-Membership Directory

College and University Professional Association for Human Resources
Tyson Pl.
2607 Kingston Pke., Ste. 250
Knoxville, TN 37919
Ph: (865)637-7673   Fax: (865)637-7674
E-mail: membership@cupahr.org
URL: http://www.search.cupahr.org/members/search.cfm

Online; continually updated; access restricted to members. Covers more than 7,000 members interested in college and university human resource administration; over 1,700 institutions. Entries include: For members–Personal name, title, affiliation, address, fax, e-mail, phone. For institutions–Organization name, address, phone, and names/titles of representatives. Arrangement: Members are alphabetical; institutions are geographical.

★4123★ Directory of Public Elementary and Secondary Education Agencies

National Center for Education Statistics
1990 K St. NW
Washington, DC 20006
Ph: (202)502-7300
URL: http://nces.ed.gov/ccd/

Annual; latest edition 2002-2003. Covers about 17,000 local education agencies in the United States, the District of Columbia, and five territories that operate their own schools or pay tuition to other local education agencies. Also lists intermediate education agencies. Entries include: Agency name, address, phone, county, description of district, grade span, membership, special education students, metropolitan status, number of high school graduates, teachers, and schools. Also available from Superintendent of Documents, U.S. Government Printing Office. Arrangement: Geographical, then by type of agency.

★4124★ Directory of Public School Systems in the U.S.

American Association for Employment in Education
3040 Riverside Dr., Ste. 125
Columbus, OH 43221
Ph: (614)485-1111   Fax: (614)485-9609
URL: http://www.aaee.org/

Annual, winter; latest edition 2004-2005 edition. $10.00 for members (plus $2.00/copy for mailing); $20.00 for nonmembers (plus $2.00/copy for mailing). Covers about 14,500 public school systems in the United States and their administrative personnel. Entries include: System name, address, phone, website address, name and title of personnel administrator, levels taught and approximate student population. Arrangement: Geographical by state.

★4125★ Educational Leadership

ABC-CLIO
130 Cremona Dr.
PO Box 1911
Santa Barbara, CA 93117
Ph: (805)968-1911   Fax: (805)685-9685
Fr: 800-368-6868
URL: http://www.abc-clio.com

Apr 2002. $27.50 for individuals. Publication includes: Directory of organizations, institutes, associations, government agencies, and leadership academies. Principal content of publication is a discussion of educational leadership styles and applications. Indexes: Alphabetical.

★4126★ Employment Opportunities, USA

Washington Research Associates
1090 Vermont Ave. NW, Ste. 800
Washington, DC 20005
Ph: (202)408-7025

Annual, quarterly updates. Publication includes: List of over 1,000 employment contacts in companies and agencies in banking, arts, telecommunications, education, and 14 other industries and professions, including federal government. Entries include: Company name, name of representative, address, description of products or services, hiring and recruiting practices, training programs, and year established. Principal content is industry overviews, career news, employment opportunity information on 14 different job markets, and comprehensive guidance to career resources on the Internet. Arrangement: Classified by industry. Indexes: Occupation.

★4127★ Encyclopedia of Education

Macmillan/McGraw-Hill
2 Penn Plz., 5th Fl.
New York, NY 10121-2298
Ph: (212)904-3834   Fax: (212)904-4878
URL: http://www.mheducation.com/home/index.shtml

Publication includes: List of assessment and achievement tests with contact information; list of state departments of education; list of Internet resources. Principal content of publication consists of a variety of topics within the field of education, including policy, curriculum, learning, assessment, legislation, history, and standards. Indexes: Alphabetical.

★4128★ Ganley's Catholic Schools in America-Elementary/Secondary/College & University

Fisher Publishing Co.
PO Box 15070
Scottsdale, AZ 85267-5070
Ph: (480)657-9422   Fax: (480)657-9422
Fr: 800-759-7615
URL: http://www.ganleyscatholicschools.com

Annual, summer; latest edition 34th, 2007 edition. $60.00 for individuals. Covers over 8,400 Catholic K-12 Schools. Arrangement: Geographical by state, then alphabetical by Diocese name.

★4129★ Guide to Technical, Trade, & Business Schools (TTB)

Riverside Publishing/Wintergreen Orchard House
425 Springlake Dr.
Itasca, IL 60143-2079
Ph: (630)467-7000   Fax: (630)467-7192
Fr: 800-323-9540

Biennial, even years. $175.53 for individuals. Covers over 3,800 accredited public and proprietary post-secondary schools offering programs in auto mechanics, aviation, business, electronics, and other technical, trade, or business fields. Available in a four-volume national edition or as four regional editions. Entries include: School name, address, phone, accrediting body, admissions contact, course offerings, placement services, and profile. Arrangement: Geographical. Indexes: Subject, special programs, sports, professional accreditations.

★4130★ Handbook of Private Schools

Porter Sargent Publishers Inc.
11 Beacon St., Ste. 1400
Boston, MA 02108-3099
Ph: (617)523-1670   Fax: (617)523-1021
Fr: 800-342-7470
E-mail: orders@portersargent.com
URL: http://www.portersargent.com

Annual, latest edition 87th, 2006 edition. $99.00 for individuals. Covers more than 1,600 elementary and secondary boarding and day schools in the United States. Entries include: School name, address, phone, fax, e-mail, URL, type of school (boarding or day), sex and age range, names and titles of administrators, grades offered, academic orientation, curriculum, new admissions yearly, tests required for admission, enrollment and faculty, graduate record, number of alumni, tuition and scholarship figures, summer session, plant evaluation and endowment, date of establishment, calendar, association membership, description of school's offerings and history, test score averages, uniform requirements, and geographical and demographic data. Arrangement: Geographical. Indexes: Alphabetical by school name, cross indexed by state, region, grade range, sexes accepted, school features and enrollment.

★4131★ Independent School Guide for Washington DC and Surrounding Area

Lift Hill Press Inc.
c/o Washington Book Distributors
4930-A Eisenhower Ave.
Alexandria, VA 22304-4809
Ph: (703)212-9113   Fax: (703)212-9114
Fr: 800-699-9113
URL: http://www.washingtonbk.com

Biennial; latest edition 2004. Covers over 525 independent schools (including parochial schools) in the Washington, DC, area, including Maryland and Virginia. Entries include: School name, address, phone, name and title of contact, number of faculty, geographical area served, tuition, courses, admission procedures, summer programs, LD/ED programs, scholarships available. Arrangement: Alphabetical. Indexes: Geographical.

★4132★ **Independent Schools Association of the Southwest-Membership List**

Independent Schools Association of the Southwest
Energy Sq., Ste 406
505 North Big Spring St.
Midland, TX 79701
Ph: (432)684-9550   Fax: (432)684-9401
URL: http://www.isasw.org

Annual, August. Covers over 84 schools located in Arizona, Kansas, Louisiana, Mexico, New Mexico, Oklahoma, and Texas enrolling over 38,000 students. Entries include: School name, address, phone, chief administrative officer, structure, and enrollment. Arrangement: Geographical. Indexes: Alphabetical.

★4133★ **MDR's School Directories**

Market Data Retrieval
1 Forest Pkwy.
Shelton, CT 06484-0947
Ph: (203)926-4800   Fax: (203)926-1826
Fr: 800-333-8802
URL: http://www.schooldata.com

Annual, October. Covers over 90,000 public, 8,000 Catholic, and 15,000 other private schools (grades K-12) in the United States; over 15,000 school district offices, 76,000 school librarians, 27,000 media specialists, and 33,000 technology coordinators. Includes names of over 165,000 school district administrators and staff members in county and state education administration. Entries include: District name and address; telephone and fax number; number of schools; number of teachers in the district; district enrollment; special education students; limited-english proficient students; minority percentage by race; percentage of college bound students; expenditures per student for instructional materials; poverty level; title 1 dollars; site-based management; district open/close dates; construction indicator; technologies and quantities; district-level administrators, (new superintendents shaded); school name and address (new public shaded); telephone and fax number; principal (new principal shaded); librarian, media specialist and technology coordinator; grade span; special programs and school type; student enrollment; technologies and quantities (instructional computer brand, noting predominant brand); Multi-Media Computers; Internet connection or access; Tech Sophistication Index. Arrangement: Geographical. Indexes: District county; district personnel; principal; new public schools and key personnel; district and school telephone; district URLs.

★4134★ **National Association of College Deans, Registrars and Admissions Officers-Directory**

National Association of College Deans, Registrars and Admissions Officers
Albany State University
504 College Dr.
Albany, GA 31705
Ph: (912)430-4638   Fax: (912)430-2953

Annual, February. Covers about 325 member deans, registrars, and admissions officers at nearly 90 predominantly Black schools. Entries include: Institution name, address, phone, names and titles of key personnel, enrollment, and whether a public or private institution. Arrangement: Alphabetical.

★4135★ **National Association of College and University Business Officers-Membership Directory**

National Association of College and University Business Officers
2501 M St. NW, Ste. 400
Washington, DC 20037
Ph: (202)861-2500   Fax: (202)861-2583
Fr: 800-462-4916
URL: http://www.nacubo.org

Annual; latest edition 2006. Number of listings: 2,800 institutions; 22,00 people. Entries include: Name of institution, address, names of primary representatives. Arrangement: Alphabetical and regional.

★4136★ **National Directory for Employment in Education**

American Association for Employment in Education
3040 Riverside Dr., Ste. 125
Columbus, OH 43221
Ph: (614)485-1111   Fax: (614)485-9609
URL: http://www.aaee.org/

Annual, winter; latest edition 2005 edition. $20.00 for nonmembers; $10.00 for members. Covers about 600 placement offices maintained by teacher-training institutions and 300 school district personnel officers and/or superintendents responsible for hiring profesional staff. Entries include: Institution name, address, phone, contact name, email address, and website. Arrangement: Geographical. Indexes: Personal name; subject-field of teacher training; institutions that provide vacancy bulletins and placement services to non-enrolled students.

★4137★ **National School Public Relations Association-Directory**

National School Public Relations Association
15948 Derwood Rd.
Rockville, MD 20855-2123
Ph: (301)519-0496   Fax: (301)519-0494
URL: http://www.nspra.org

Annual, January. Covers approximately 2,000 school system public relations directors, school administrators, principals, and others who are members of the National School Public Relations Association. Entries include: Name, affiliation, address, phone. Arrangement: Geographical.

★4138★ **Opportunities Abroad for Educators**

Fulbright Teacher and Administrator Exchange Program
600 Maryland Ave. SW, Ste. 320
Washington, DC 20024-2520
Ph: (202)314-3527   Fax: (202)479-6806
Fr: 800-726-0479
URL: http://www.fulbrightexchanges.org

Annual. Covers opportunities available for elementary and secondary teachers, two-year college instructors, and school administrators to attend seminars or to teach abroad under the Mutual Educational and Cultural Exchange Act of 1961. Entries include: Countries of placement, dates, eligibility requirements, teaching assignments. Arrangement: Geographical.

★4139★ **Patterson's American Education**

Educational Directories Inc.
PO Box 68097
Schaumburg, IL 60168
Ph: (847)891-1250   Fax: (847)891-0945
Fr: 800-357-6183
URL: http://www.ediusa.com

Annual; latest edition October 2007. $94.00 for individuals. Covers over 11,400 school districts in the United States; more than 34,000 public, private, and Catholic high schools, middle schools, and junior high schools; Approximately 300 parochial superintendents; 400 state department of education personnel. Entries include: For school districts and schools–District and superintendent name, address, phone, fax; grade ranges, enrollment; school names, addresses, phone numbers, names of principals. For postsecondary schools–School name, address, phone number, URL, e-mail, names of administrator or director of admissions. For private and Catholic high schools–name, address, phone, fax, enrollment, grades offered, name of principal. Postsecondary institutions are also covered in 'Patterson's Schools Classified.' Arrangement: Geographical by state, then alphabetical by city.

★4140★ **Patterson's Schools Classified**

Educational Directories Inc.
PO Box 68097
Schaumburg, IL 60168
Ph: (847)891-1250   Fax: (847)891-0945
Fr: 800-357-6183
URL: http://www.ediusa.com

Annual; latest edition 2007, volume 57. $18.00 for individuals. Covers over 7,000 accredited colleges, universities, community colleges, junior colleges, career schools and teaching hospitals. Entries include: School name, address, phone, URL, e-mail, name of administrator or admissions officer, description, professional accreditation (where applicable). Updated from previous year's edition of 'Patterson's American Education'. Arrangement: Classified by area of study, then geographical by state. Indexes: Alphabetical by name.

★4141★ Private Independent Schools

Bunting and Lyon Inc.
238 N Main St.
Wallingford, CT 06492
Ph: (203)269-3333   Fax: (203)269-5697
URL: http://www.buntingandlyon.com

Annual; latest edition 60th, January 2007. $115.00 for individuals. Covers 1,200 English-speaking elementary and secondary private schools and summer programs in North America and abroad. Entries include: School name, address, phone, fax, e-mail, website, enrollment, tuition and other fees, financial aid information, administrator's name and educational background, director of admission, regional accreditation, description of programs, curriculum, activities, learning differences grid. Arrangement: Geographical. Indexes: school name; geographical.

★4142★ Requirements for Certification of Teachers, Counselors, Librarians, Administrators for Elementary and Secondary Schools

University of Chicago Press
Journals Division
1427 E 60th St.
Chicago, IL 60637-2954
Ph: (773)702-7600   Fax: (773)702-0694
Fr: 877-705-1878

Annual, June; latest edition 71st, 2006-07. $47.00. Publication includes: List of state and local departments of education. Entries include: Office name, address, phone. Principal content of publication consists of summaries of each state's teaching and administrative certification requirements. Arrangement: Geographical.

★4143★ School Guide

School Guide Publications
210 N Ave.
New Rochelle, NY 10801
Ph: (914)632-7771   Fax: (914)632-3412
Fr: 800-433-7771
URL: http://distance.schoolguides.com/

Annual, September. Covers over 3,000 colleges, vocational schools, and nursing schools in the United States. Entries include: Institution name, address, phone, courses offered, degrees awarded. Arrangement: Classified by type of institution, then geographical. Indexes: Subject.

★4144★ Understanding Educational Reform

ABC-CLIO
130 Cremona Dr.
PO Box 1911
Santa Barbara, CA 93117
Ph: (805)968-1911   Fax: (805)685-9685
Fr: 800-368-6868
URL: http://www.abc-clio.com

Nov 2002. $25.00 for individuals. Publication includes: List of print and nonprint resources with Web site information regarding educational reform. Principal content of publication is a discussion of a variety of aspects of educational reform, including history and politics.

HANDBOOKS AND MANUALS

★4145★ Careers in Education

The McGraw-Hill Companies
PO Box 182604
Columbus, OH 43272
Fax: (614)759-3749   Fr: 877-883-5524
E-mail: customer.service@mcgraw-hill.com
URL: http://www.mcgraw-hill.com

Roy A. Edelfelt, Alan Reiman. Fourth edition, 2003. $15.95. 192 pages E-book, netLibrary.

★4146★ Non-Profits and Education Job Finder

Planning Communications
7215 Oak Ave.
River Forest, IL 60305-1935
Ph: (708)366-5200   Fax: (708)366-5280
Fr: 888-366-5200
E-mail: info@planningcommunications.com
URL: http://jobfindersonline.com

Daniel Lauber. 1997. $32.95; $16.95 (paper). 340 pages. Covers 1600 sources. Discusses how to use sources of non-profit sector job vacancies in a number of specialties and state-by-state, including job-matching services, job hotlines, specialty periodicals with job ads, salary surveys, and directories. Covers a variety of fields from education to religion. Includes chapters on resume and cover letter preparation and interviewing.

★4147★ Opportunities in State and Local Government Careers

The McGraw-Hill Companies
PO Box 182604
Columbus, OH 43272
Fax: (614)759-3749   Fr: 877-883-5524
E-mail: customer.service@mcgraw-hill.com
URL: http://www.mcgraw-hill.com

Neale J. Baxter. Revised edition, 1992. $14.95; $10.95 (paper). 148 pages. Points out the incentives and drawbacks of a government career. Describes hiring procedures and provides tips on filling out applications, taking physical and aptitude tests, handling interviews, and finding jobs. Describes the jobs in which 75% of all state and local government workers are employed. For each occupation, covers the nature of the work and the training required.

★4148★ Real People Working in Education

The McGraw-Hill Companies
PO Box 182604
Columbus, OH 43272
Fax: (614)759-3749   Fr: 877-883-5524

E-mail: customer.service@mcgraw-hill.com
URL: http://www.mcgraw-hill.com

Blythe Camenson, Jan Goldberg. 1997. $17.95; $12.95 (paper). 160 pages/ Interviews and profiles of working professionals capture a range of opportunities in this field.

★4149★ Who Is Leading Our Schools?: An Overview of School Administrators and their Careers

Rand Corp.
PO Box 2138
Santa Monica, CA 90407-2138
Ph: (310)393-0411   Fax: (310)393-4818
URL: http://www.rand.org/

Susan Gates, Karen Ross. June 2003. $28.50. Illustrated. 174 pages. Presents what is known about attracting and retaining school administrators.

EMPLOYMENT AGENCIES AND SEARCH FIRMS

★4150★ Auerbach Associates Inc.

385 Concord Ave., Ste. 103
Belmont, MA 02478
Ph: (617)451-0095   Fax: (617)489-9111
E-mail: info@auerbach-assc.com
URL: http://www.auerbach-assc.com

Executive search firm focused on non-profit and higher education industries.

★4151★ Berardi & Associates

1140 Ave. of the Americas, Fl. 8
New York, NY 10036
Ph: (212)403-6180   Fax: (212)764-9690
E-mail: jmiranda@spges.com
URL: http://www.spgjobs.com

Executive search firm.

★4152★ Educational Placement Service

6510-A S. Academy Blvd.
Colorado Springs, CO 80906
Ph: (719)579-9911   Fax: (719)579-5050
E-mail: accounting@educatorjobs.com
URL: http://www.educatorjobs.com

Employment agency. Focuses on teaching, administrative, and education-related openings.

★4153★ Institutional Advantage L.L.C.

340 Lothrop Rd.
Grosse Pointe Farms, MI 48236
Ph: (313)886-6349   Fax: (313)557-1331
E-mail: kts@ia-llc.com
URL: http://www.ia-llc.com

Retained executive search for higher education and not-for-profit clients.

★4154★ King & King Consulting

10287 Grayfox Dr.
San Diego, CA 92131
Ph: (858)566-8985   Fax: (858)566-8985

Offers services in the following areas: needs assessment, career development, writing skills and communication, organizational development, management development, employee development, team building, office management skills, and mid-life crisis management. Industries served: aviation, education, and scientific.

★4155★ Perez-Arton Consultants Inc.

23 Spring St., Ste. 204B
Ossining, NY 10562
Ph: (914)762-2103   Fax: (914)762-7834
E-mail: perezart@bestweb.net

Provides executive searches for major academic and administrative units. Conducts institutional evaluations and executive staff assessments. Firm works for colleges, universities and education-related non-profits only.

TRADESHOWS

★4156★ American Association of School Administrators Annual Conference and Exposition

American Association of School Administrators (AASA)
801 N. Quincy St., Ste. 700
Arlington, VA 22203-1730
Ph: (703)528-0700   Fax: (703)841-1543
E-mail: Info@aasa.org
URL: http://www.aasa.org

Annual. **Primary Exhibits:** Educational equipment and services.

★4157★ Association for Biblical Higher Education Annual Meeting

Association for Biblical Higher Education
5575 S. Semoran Blvd., Ste. 26
Orlando, FL 32822-1781
Ph: (407)207-0808   Fax: (407)207-0840
E-mail: info@abhe.org
URL: http://www.abhe.org/

Annual. **Primary Exhibits:** Publications, office equipment, travel information, educational resources, fundraising services, computers, Bible literature, films, and related material for educational institutions. **Dates and Locations:** 2008 Feb 21-23; Orlando, FL; Florida Mall Hotel and Conference Center.

★4158★ Association of School Business Officials International Annual Meeting and Exhibits

Association of School Business Officials International
11401 N. Shore Dr.
Reston, VA 20190-4200
Ph: (703)478-0405   Fax: (703)478-0205
Fr: (866)682-2729
URL: http://www.asbointl.org

Annual. **Primary Exhibits:** Equipment, supplies, and services for school districts.

★4159★ National Association of Elementary School Principals Annual Convention and Exposition

National Association of Elementary School Principals
1615 Duke St.
Alexandria, VA 22314
Ph: (703)684-3345   Fax: (703)518-6281
Fr: 800-386-2877
E-mail: naesp@naesp.org
URL: http://www.naesp.org

Annual. **Primary Exhibits:** Textbooks publishers, classroom supplies and equipment; playground equipment; incentive/fundraising programs; curriculum; technology; professional/staff development. **Dates and Locations:** 2008 Apr 04-08; Nashville, TX; Gaylord Opryland Resort & Convention Center.

★4160★ National Association of Secondary School Principals Annual Convention

National Association of Secondary School Principals
1904 Association Dr.
Reston, VA 20191-1537
Ph: (703)860-0200   Fax: (703)476-5490
Fr: 800-253-1746
URL: http://www.nassp.org

Annual. **Primary Exhibits:** School furnishings, supplies and equipment; fund raising, school jewelry, awards, yearbooks; textbooks. **Dates and Locations:** 2008 Feb 22-24; San Antonio, TX.

★4161★ National Rural Education Research Forum and Conference

National Rural Education Association
c/o Bob Mooneyham
820 Van Vleet Oval, Rm. 227
University of Oklahoma
Norman, OK 73019
Ph: (405)325-7959   Fax: (405)325-7959
E-mail: bmooneyham@ou.edu
URL: http://www.nrea.net

Annual. **Primary Exhibits:** Exhibits for rural education programs.

★4162★ Southwestern Federation of Administrative Disciplines Convention

Southwestern Federation of Administrative Disciplines
2700 Bay Area Blvd.
Houston, TX 77058
Ph: (713)283-3122   Fax: (713)283-3951

Annual. **Primary Exhibits:** Educational materials and services.

★4163★ UCEA Convention

University Council for Educational Administration
205 Hill Hall
Columbia, MO 65211-2185
Ph: (573)884-8300   Fax: (573)884-8302
E-mail: plbf9@mizzou.edu
URL: http://www.ucea.org

Annual. **Primary Exhibits:** Publications related to educational administration in universities.

OTHER SOURCES

★4164★ ACE Fellows Program

1 Dupont Cir. NW
Washington, DC 20036-1193
Ph: (202)939-9300   Fax: (202)785-8056
E-mail: fellows@ace.nche.edu
URL: http://www.acenet.edu/AM/Template.cfm?Section=Fellows_Program1

Description: Service arm of the American Council on Education to strengthen leadership in American postsecondary education by identifying and preparing individuals who have shown promise for responsible positions in higher education administration. **Purpose:** Objectives are: to encourage and prepare individuals making higher education administration their professional career; to provide opportunities for planned observation and experience in decision-making; to identify and develop potential leaders. Arranges internships whereby senior faculty and administrators are given the opportunity to study higher education leadership as an intern at a host institution. The stipulations are that the fellow will do certain assigned reading in higher education administration, focus on a strategic learning project and serve at the home institution for the academic year following the internship. Provides services for alumni of the program.

★4165★ Administration and Management Occupations

Delphi Productions
3159 6th St.
Boulder, CO 80304
Ph: (303)443-2100   Fax: (303)443-4022
Fr: 888-443-2400
E-mail: support@delphivideo.com
URL: http://www.delphivideo.com

$95.00. 50 minutes. Part of the Careers for the 21st Century Video Library.

★4166★ American Almanac of Jobs and Salaries

HarperCollins
10 E. 53rd St.
New York, NY 10022
Ph: (212)207-7000   Fr: 800-242-7737
URL: http://www.harpercollins.com/

John W. Wright. Revised edition, 2000. $20.00 (paper). 672 pages. This is a comprehensive guide to the wages of hundreds of occupations in a wide variety of industries and organizations.

★4167★ American Association of Collegiate Registrars and Admissions Officers (AACRAO)

1 Dupont Cir. NW, Ste. 520
Washington, DC 20036
Ph: (202)293-9161   Fax: (202)872-8857
E-mail: info@aacrao.org
URL: http://www.aacrao.org

Members: Degree-granting postsecondary institutions, government agencies, and higher education coordinating boards, private educational organizations, and education-oriented businesses. **Purpose:** Promotes higher education and furthers the professional development of members working in admissions, enrollment management, institutional research, records, and registration.

★4168★ American Association for Women in Community Colleges (AAWCC)

PO Box 336603
Greeley, CO 80633-0611
Ph: (970)352-2079   Fax: (970)352-2080
E-mail: aawcc@comcast.net
URL: http://www.aawccnatl.org

Description: Women faculty members, administrators, staff members, students, and trustees of community colleges. Objectives are to: develop communication and disseminate information among women in community, junior, and technical colleges; encourage educational program development; obtain grants for educational projects for community college women. Disseminates information on women's issues and programs. Conducts regional and state professional development workshops and forums. Recognizes model programs that assist women in community colleges. An affiliate council of the American Association of Community Colleges.

★4169★ American Federation of School Administrators (AFSA)

1101 17th St. NW, Ste. 408
Washington, DC 20036
Ph: (202)986-4209   Fax: (202)986-4211
Fr: 800-354-AFSA
E-mail: afsa@admin.org
URL: http://www.admin.org

Description: Principals, vice-principals, directors, supervisors, and administrators involved in pedagogical education. Purposes are to: achieve the highest goals in education; maintain and improve standards, benefits, and conditions for personnel without regard to color, race, sex, background, or national origin; obtain job security; protect seniority and merit; cooperate with all responsible organizations in education; promote understanding, participation, and support of the public, communities, and agencies; be alert to resist attacks and campaigns that would create or entrench a spoils system; promote democratic society by supporting full educational opportunities for every child and student in the nation.

★4170★ Association of Christian Schools International (ACSI)

PO Box 65130
Colorado Springs, CO 80962-5130
Ph: (719)528-6906   Fax: (719)531-0631
Fr: 800-367-0798
E-mail: info@acsi.org
URL: http://www.acsi.org

Description: Seeks to enable Christian educators and schools worldwide to effectively prepare students for life.

★4171★ Association of Departments of English (ADE)

26 Broadway, 3rd Fl.
New York, NY 10004-1789
Ph: (646)576-5130   Fax: (646)835-4056
E-mail: dlaurence@mla.org
URL: http://www.ade.org

Description: Administrators of college and university departments of English, humanities, rhetoric, and communications. Works to improve the teaching of English and the administration of English departments. Conducts studies and surveys of literature and writing courses. Sponsors sessions at major English conventions and conferences nationwide. Sponsored by Modern Language Association of America.

★4172★ Association on Higher Education and Disability (AHEAD)

107 Commerce Center Dr., Ste. 204
Huntersville, NC 28078
Ph: (704)947-7779   Fax: (704)948-7779
E-mail: ahead@ahead.org
URL: http://www.ahead.org

Description: Individuals interested in promoting the equal rights and opportunities of disabled postsecondary students, staff, faculty, and graduates. Provides an exchange of communication for those professionally involved with disabled students; collects, evaluates, and disseminates information; encourages and supports legislation for the benefit of disabled students. Conducts surveys on issues pertinent to college students with disabilities; offers resource referral system and employment exchange for positions in disability student services. Conducts research programs; compiles statistics.

★4173★ Association for the Study of Higher Education (ASHE)

Michigan State University
424 Erickson Hall
East Lansing, MI 48824
Ph: (517)432-8805   Fax: (517)432-8806
E-mail: ashemsu@msu.edu
URL: http://www.ashe.ws

Description: Professors, researchers, administrators, policy analysts, graduate students, and others concerned with the study of higher education. Aims to advance the study of higher education and facilitate and encourage discussion of priority issues for research in the study of higher education.

★4174★ Council of American Instructors of the Deaf (CAID)

PO Box 377
Bedford, TX 76095-0377
Ph: (817)354-8414
E-mail: caid@swbell.net
URL: http://www.caid.org

Members: Professional organization of teachers, administrators, and professionals in allied fields related to education of the deaf and hard-of-hearing. **Purpose:** Provides opportunities for a free interchange of views concerning methods and means of educating the deaf and hard-of-hearing. Promotes such education by the publication of reports, essays, and other information. Develops more effective methods of teaching deaf and hard-of-hearing children.

★4175★ Counseling Association for Humanistic Education and Development (C-AHEAD)

PO Box 791006
Baltimore, MD 21279-1006
Ph: (703)823-9800   Fax: 800-473-2329
Fr: 800-347-6647
E-mail: lleech@gw.mp.sc.edu
URL: http://www.c-ahead.com

Description: A division of the American Counseling Association. Teachers, educational administrators, community agency workers, counselors, school social workers, and psychologists; others interested in the area of human development. Aims to assist individuals in improving their quality of life. Provides forum for the exchange of information about humanistically-oriented administrative and instructional practices. Supports humanistic practices and research on instructional and organizational methods for facilitating humanistic education; encourages cooperation among related professional groups.

★4176★ Education and Training

Cambridge Educational
PO Box 2053
Princeton, NJ 08543-2053
Ph: 800-257-5126   Fax: (609)671-0266
Fr: 800-468-4227
E-mail: custserv@films.com
URL: http://www.cambridgeeducational.com

VHS and DVD. $89.95. 2002. 18 minutes. Presents four distinct occupations in the field: elementary teachers, teacher's aides, administrators, and librarians. People working in these jobs discuss their responsibilities.

★4177★ Friends Council on Education (FCE)

1507 Cherry St.
Philadelphia, PA 19102
Ph: (215)241-7245   Fax: (215)241-7299
E-mail: info@friendscouncil.org
URL: http://www.friendscouncil.org

Members: Representatives appointed by Friends Yearly Meetings; heads of Quaker secondary and elementary schools and colleges; members-at-large. **Purpose:** Acts as a clearinghouse for information on Quaker schools and colleges. **Activities:** Holds meetings and conferences on education and provides in-service training for teachers, administrators and trustees in Friends schools.

★4178★ NAFSA/Association of International Educators (NAFSA)

1307 New York Ave. NW, 8th Fl.
Washington, DC 20005-4701
Ph: (202)737-3699   Fax: (202)737-3657
E-mail: inbox@nafsa.org
URL: http://www.nafsa.org

Description: Individuals, organizations, and institutions dealing with international educational exchange, including foreign student advisers, overseas educational advisers, credentials and admissions officers, administrators and teachers of English as a second language, community support personnel, study-abroad administrators, and embassy cultural or educational personnel. Promotes self-regulation standards and responsibilities in international educational exchange; offers professional development opportunities primarily through publications, workshops, grants, and regional and national conferences. Advocates for increased awareness and support of international education and exchange on campuses, in government, and in communities. Offers services including: a job registry for employers and professionals involved with international education; a consultant referral service. Sponsors joint liaison activities with a variety of other educational and government organizations to conduct a census of foreign student enrollment in the U.S.; conducts workshops about specific subjects and countries.

★4179★ National Association of College and University Business Officers (NACUBO)

1110 Vermont Ave. NW, Ste. 800
Washington, DC 20005
Ph: (202)861-2500   Fax: (202)861-2583
Fr: 800-462-4916
E-mail: john.walda@nacubo.org
URL: http://www.nacubo.org

Members: Colleges, universities, and companies that are members of a regional association. **Purpose:** Develops and maintains national interest in improving the principles and practices of business and financial administration in higher education. **Activities:** Sponsors workshops in fields such as cash management, grant and contract maintenance, accounting, investment, student loan administration, and costing. Conducts research and information exchange programs between college and university personnel; compiles statistics.

★4180★ National Association of Elementary School Principals (NAESP)

1615 Duke St.
Alexandria, VA 22314
Ph: (703)684-3345   Fax: (703)549-5568
Fr: 800-386-2377
E-mail: naesp@naesp.org
URL: http://www.naesp.org

Description: Professional association of principals, assistant or vice principals, and aspiring principals; persons engaged in educational research and in the professional education of elementary and middle school administrators. Sponsors National Distinguished Principals Program, President's Award for Educational Excellence, American Student Council Association. Offers annual national convention and exhibition, on-site and internet professional development workshops throughout the year. Recently expanded professional publications offered through the National Principals' Resource Center.

★4181★ National Association of Episcopal Schools (NAES)

815 2nd Ave., Ste. 819
New York, NY 10017-4594
Ph: (212)716-6134   Fax: (212)286-9366
Fr: 800-334-7626
E-mail: info@episcopalschools.org
URL: http://www.episcopalschools.org

Description: Represents episcopal day and boarding schools and preschools. Promotes the educational ministry of the Episcopal Church. Provides publications, consultation services and conference focusing on Episcopal identity of schools, worship, religious education, spirituality, leadership development and governance for heads/directors, administrators, chaplains and teachers of religion, trustees, rectors and other church and school leaders.

★4182★ National Association of Independent Schools (NAIS)

1620 L St. NW, Ste. 1100
Washington, DC 20036-5695
Ph: (202)973-9700   Fax: (202)973-9790
Fr: 800-793-6701
E-mail: info@nais.org
URL: http://www.nais.org

Description: Independent elementary and secondary school members; regional associations of independent schools and related associations. Provides curricular and administrative research and services. Conducts educational programs; compiles statistics.

★4183★ National Association of Secondary School Principals (NASSP)

1904 Association Dr.
Reston, VA 20191-1537
Ph: (703)860-0200   Fax: (703)860-3422
Fr: 800-253-7746
URL: http://www.principals.org

Description: Middle level and high school principals, assistant principals, and aspiring school leaders, others engaged in secondary school administration and/or supervision; college professors teaching courses in secondary education. Sponsors National Association of Student Councils (NASC), National Honor Society (NHS), and National Junior Honor Society (NJHS).

★4184★ National Association of State Directors of Special Education (NASDSE)

1800 Diagonal Rd., Ste. 320
Alexandria, VA 22314
Ph: (703)519-3800   Fax: (703)519-3808
E-mail: nasdse@nasdse.org

Members: Professional society of state directors; consultants, supervisors, and administrators who have statewide responsibilities for administering special education programs. **Purpose:** Provides services to state agencies to facilitate their efforts to maximize educational outcomes for individuals with disabilities.

★4185★ National Association of Student Personnel Administrators (NASPA)

1875 Connecticut Ave. NW, Ste. 418
Washington, DC 20009
Ph: (202)265-7500   Fax: (202)797-1157
E-mail: office@naspa.org
URL: http://www.naspa.org

Description: Representatives of degree-granting institutions of higher education which have been fully accredited. Works to enrich the educational experience of all students. Serves colleges and universities by providing leadership and professional growth opportunities for the senior student affairs officer and other professionals who consider higher education and student affairs issues from an institutional perspective. Provides professional development; improves information and research; acts as an advocate for students in higher education. Maintains career service and conducts the Richard F. Stevens Institute. Supports minority undergraduate fellows program.

★4186★ National Community Education Association (NCEA)

3929 Old Lee Hwy., No. 91-A
Fairfax, VA 22030-2421
Ph: (703)359-8973   Fax: (703)359-0972
E-mail: ncea@ncea.com
URL: http://www.ncea.com

Description: Community school directors, principals, superintendents, professors, teachers, students, and laypeople. **Purpose:** Promotes and establishes community schools as an integral part of the educational plan of every community. Emphasizes community and parent involvement in the schools, lifelong learning, and enrichment of K-12 and adult education. Serves as a clearinghouse for the exchange of ideas and information, and the sharing of efforts. **Activities:** Offers leadership training.

★4187★ National Council for Accreditation of Teacher Education (NCATE)
2010 Massachusetts Ave. NW, Ste. 500
Washington, DC 20036
Ph: (202)466-7496   Fax: (202)296-6620
E-mail: ncate@ncate.org
URL: http://www.ncate.org

Members: Representatives from constituent colleges and universities, state departments of education, school boards, teacher, and other professional groups. **Purpose:** Voluntary accrediting body devoted exclusively to: evaluation and accreditation of institutions for preparation of elementary and secondary school teachers; preparation of school service personnel, including school principals, supervisors, superintendents, school psychologists, instructional technologists, and other specialists for school-oriented positions.

★4188★ Overseas Employment Opportunities for Educators: Department of Defense Dependents Schools
DIANE Publishing Co.
PO Box 617
Darby, PA 19023-0617
Ph: (610)461-6200   Fax: (610)461-6130
Fr: 800-782-3833
URL: http://www.dianepublishingcentral.com

Barry Leonard, editor. 2000. $15.00. 54 pages. An introduction to teachings positions in the Dept. of Defense Dependents Schools (DoDDS), a worldwide school system, operated by the DoD in 14 countries.

★4189★ Teaching & Related Occupations
Delphi Productions
3159 6th St.
Boulder, CO 80304
Ph: (303)443-2100   Fax: (303)443-4022
Fr: 888-443-2400
E-mail: support@delphivideo.com
URL: http://www.delphivideo.com

$95.00. 50 minutes. Part of the Careers for the 21st Century Video Library.

EEG Technologists and Technicians

SOURCES OF HELP-WANTED ADS

★4190★ **ADVANCE for Respiratory Care Practitioners**

Merion Publications Inc.
2900 Horizon Dr.
PO Box 61556
King of Prussia, PA 19406
Ph: (610)278-1400   Fr: 800-355-5627
URL: http://www.advanceweb.com/publications.asp?pub=RC

Biweekly. Magazine for RRT's, CRTT's, and cardiopulmonary technologists across the country.

EMPLOYER DIRECTORIES AND NETWORKING LISTS

★4191★ **AHA Guide to the Health Care Field**

American Hospital Association
1 N Franklin
Chicago, IL 60606
Ph: (312)422-2050   Fax: (312)422-4700
Fr: 800-424-4301

Annual, August. Covers hospitals, networks, multi-health care systems, freestanding ambulatory surgery centers, psychiatric facilities, long-term care facilities, substance abuse programs, and other health-related organizations. Entries include: For hospitals–Facility name, address, phone, administrator's name, number of beds, facilities and services, number of employees, expenses, other statistics. For other organizations–Name, address, phone, fax, name and title of contact. Arrangement: Geographical. Indexes: Hospital name.

★4192★ **Directory of Hospital Personnel**

Grey House Publishing
185 Millerton Rd.
PO Box 860
Millerton, NY 12546
Ph: (518)789-8700   Fax: (518)789-0556
Fr: 800-562-2139
URL: http://www.greyhouse.com/hospital_personnel.htm

Annual. $325.00 for print product; $545.00 for online database subscription; $650.00 for online database subscription and print product combined. Covers 200,000 executives at 7,000 U.S. hospitals. Entries include: Name of hospital, address, phone; number of beds; type and JCAHO status of hospital; names and titles of key department heads and staff; medical and nursing school affiliations; number of residents, interns, and nursing students. Arrangement: Geographical. Indexes: Hospital name, personnel, hospital size.

★4193★ **Guide to Careers in the Health Professions**

The Princeton Review
2315 Broadway
New York, NY 10024
Ph: (212)874-8282   Fax: (212)874-0775
Fr: 800-733-3000
URL: http://www.princetonreview.com/

Published January, 2001. $24.95 for individuals. Presents advice and information for those searching for satisfying careers in the health professions. Publication includes: Directory of schools and academic programs. Entries include: Name, address, phone, tuition, program details, employment profiles.

★4194★ **Hospital Blue Book**

Billian Publishing Inc./Transworld Publishing Inc.
2100 Powers Ferry Rd. SE
Atlanta, GA 30339
Ph: (770)955-5656   Fax: (770)952-0669
Fr: 800-533-8484
E-mail: blu-book@billian.com

2005. $300.00 for individuals. Covers more than 6,687 hospitals; some listings also appear in a separate southern edition of this publication. Entries include: Name of hospital, accreditation, mailing address, phone, fax, number of beds, type of facility (nonprofit, general, state, etc.); list of administrative personnel and chiefs of medical services, with specific titles. Arrangement: Geographical.

★4195★ **Medical and Health Information Directory**

Gale, Cengage Learning
27500 Drake Rd.
Farmington Hills, MI 48331-3535
Ph: (248)699-4253   Fax: (248)699-8065
Fr: 800-877-4253
E-mail: businessproducts@gale.com
URL: http://www.gale.com

Annual; latest edition 20th, July 2007. $375.00/volume. Covers in Volume 1, more than 26,500 medical and health oriented associations, organizations, institutions, and government agencies, including health maintenance organizations (HMOs), preferred provider organizations (PPOs), insurance companies, pharmaceutical companies, research centers, and medical and allied health schools. In Volume 2, over 12,000 medical book publishers; medical periodicals, directories, audiovisual producers and services, medical libraries and information centers, electronic resources, and health-related internet search engines. In Volume 3, more than 35,500 clinics, treatment centers, care programs, and counseling/diagnostic services for 34 subject areas. Entries include: Institution, service, or firm name, address, phone, fax, email and URL; many include names of key personnel and, when pertinent, descriptive annotations. Volume 3 was formerly listed separately as Health Services Directory. Arrangement: Classified by organization activity, service, etc. Indexes: Each volume has a complete alphabetical name and keyword index.

HANDBOOKS AND MANUALS

★4196★ Careers in Health Care

The McGraw-Hill Companies
PO Box 182604
Columbus, OH 43272
Fax: (614)759-3749   Fr: 877-883-5524
E-mail: customer.service@mcgraw-hill.com
URL: http://www.mcgraw-hill.com

Barbara M. Swanson. Fifth edition, 2005. $15.95 (paper). 192 pages. Describes job duties, work settings, salaries, licensing and certification requirements, educational preparation, and future outlook. Gives ideas on how to secure a job.

★4197★ Exploring Health Care Careers, Second Edition

JIST Publishing
875 Montreal Way
St. Paul, MN 55102
Fax: 800-547-8329   Fr: 800-648-5478
E-mail: info@jist.com
URL: http://www.jist.com

2002. $89.95. 984 pages. Information about careers in the health industry, including education and certification requirements, earnings, and job outlook.

★4198★ Opportunities in Health and Medical Careers

The McGraw-Hill Companies
PO Box 182604
Columbus, OH 43272
Fax: (614)759-3749   Fr: 877-883-5524
E-mail: customer.service@mcgraw-hill.com
URL: http://www.mcgraw-hill.com

I. Donald Snook, Jr. and Leo D'Orazio. 2004. $13.95 (paper). 157 pages. Covers the full range of medical and health occupations. Illustrated.

★4199★ Opportunities in Medical Imaging Careers

The McGraw-Hill Companies
PO Box 182604
Columbus, OH 43272
Fax: (614)759-3749   Fr: 877-883-5524
E-mail: customer.service@mcgraw-hill.com
URL: http://www.mcgraw-hill.com

Clifford J. Sherry. 2006. $13.95. 160 pages.

★4200★ Opportunities in Medical Technology Careers

The McGraw-Hill Companies
PO Box 182604
Columbus, OH 43272
Fax: (614)759-3749   Fr: 877-883-5524
E-mail: customer.service@mcgraw-hill.com
URL: http://www.mcgraw-hill.com

Karen R. Karni. Revised, 1996. $14.95; $11.95 (paper). 148 pages. Details opportunities for various technical medical personnel and supplies up-to-date information on salary levels and employment outlook. Append-

ices list associations and unions in each field. Illustrated.

★4201★ Resumes for Health and Medical Careers

The McGraw-Hill Companies
PO Box 182604
Columbus, OH 43272
Fax: (614)759-3749   Fr: 877-883-5524
E-mail: customer.service@mcgraw-hill.com
URL: http://www.mcgraw-hill.com

Third edition, 2003. $11.95 (paper). 160 pages.

EMPLOYMENT AGENCIES AND SEARCH FIRMS

★4202★ Shiloh Careers International, Inc.

7105 Peach Ct., Ste. 102
PO Box 831
Brentwood, TN 37024-0831
Ph: (615)373-3090   Fax: (615)373-3480
E-mail: maryann@shilohcareers.com
URL: http://www.shilohcareers.com

Employment agency serving the industry field.

ONLINE JOB SOURCES AND SERVICES

★4203★ Medhunters.com

Fr: 800-664-0278
E-mail: info@medhunters.com
URL: http://www.medhunters.com

Description: Career search site for jobs in all health care specialties; educational resources; visa and licensing information for relocation; interesting articles; relocation tools; links to professional organizations and general resources.

★4204★ ProHealthJobs

Fr: 800-796-1738
E-mail: Info@prohealthedujobs.com
URL: http://www.prohealthjobs.com

Description: Career resources site for the medical and health care field. Lists professional opportunities, product information, continuing education and open positions.

TRADESHOWS

★4205★ American Association of Neuromuscular and Electrodiagnostic Medicine Annual Scientific Meeting

American Association of Neuromuscular and Electrodiagnostic Medicine (AANEM)
2621 Superior Dr., NW /
Rochester, MN 55901
Ph: (507)288-0100   Fax: (507)288-1225
E-mail: aanem@aanem.org
URL: http://www.aanem.org

Annual. **Primary Exhibits:** Electromyographic and electrodiagnostic equipment and accessories, pharmaceutical companies, and publishers.

★4206★ American Clinical Neurophysiology Society Annual Meeting and Short Courses

American Clinical Neurophysiology Society
PO Box 30
Bloomfield, CT 06002
Ph: (860)243-3977   Fax: (860)286-0787
E-mail: acns@ssmgt.com
URL: http://www.acns.org

Annual. **Primary Exhibits:** Electroencephalographic and neurophysiology equipment, supplies, and services.

OTHER SOURCES

★4207★ American Society of Electroneurodiagnostic Technologists (ASET)

6501 E Commerce Ave., Ste. 120
Kansas City, MO 64120
Ph: (816)931-1120   Fax: (816)931-1145
E-mail: info@aset.org
URL: http://www.aset.org

Members: Persons engaged in clinical electroencephalographic (EEG) technology, evoked potential responses, nerve conduction studies, and polysomnography (sleep studies). **Purpose:** Works for the advancement of electroneurodiagnostic technology education and practice standards.

★4208★ Exploring Health Occupations

Cambridge Educational
PO Box 2053
Princeton, NJ 08543-2053
Ph: 800-257-5126   Fax: (609)671-0266
Fr: 800-468-4227
E-mail: custserv@films.com
URL: http://www.cambridgeeducational.com

VHS and DVD. $159.90. 1999. Two-part series provides a detailed view of the field of medical technicians and technologists, EMTs, nurses, therapists, and assistants.

★4209★ Health Service Occupations

Delphi Productions
3159 6th St.
Boulder, CO 80304
Ph: (303)443-2100   Fax: (303)443-4022
Fr: 888-443-2400
E-mail: support@delphivideo.com
URL: http://www.delphivideo.com

$95.00. 50 minutes. Part of the Careers for the 21st Century Video Library.

★4210★ Health Technologists & Technicians

Delphi Productions
3159 6th St.
Boulder, CO 80304
Ph: (303)443-2100   Fax: (303)443-4022
Fr: 888-443-2400

E-mail: support@delphivideo.com
URL: http://www.delphivideo.com

$95.00. 50 minutes. Part of the Careers for the 21st Century Video Library.

★4211★ Medical Technicians and Technologists

Cambridge Educational
PO Box 2053
Princeton, NJ 08543-2053
Ph: 800-257-5126   Fax: (609)671-0266
Fr: 800-468-4227
E-mail: custserv@films.com
URL: http://www.cambridgeeducational.com

VHS and DVD. $79.95. 18 minutes. 2000. Part of the Exploring Health Occupations Series.

★4212★ Medicine & Related Occupations

Delphi Productions
3159 6th St.
Boulder, CO 80304
Ph: (303)443-2100   Fax: (303)443-4022
Fr: 888-443-2400
E-mail: support@delphivideo.com
URL: http://www.delphivideo.com

$95.00. 45 minutes. Part of the Careers for the 21st Century Video Library.

EKG Technicians

Sources of Help-Wanted Ads

★4213★ *American Heart Journal*
Mosby
1600 John F. Kennedy Blvd., Ste. 1800
Philadelphia, PA 19103-2899
Ph: (215)239-3276 Fax: (215)239-3286
URL: http://www3.us.elsevierhealth.com/ahj/

Monthly. $258.00/year for individuals; $320.00/year for institutions; $258.00/year for other countries, Includes air speed delivery; $509.00/year for institutions, other countries, Includes air speed delivery. Medical journal serving practicing cardiologists, university-affiliated clinicians, and physicians keeping abreast of developments in the diagnosis and management of cardiovascular disease.

★4214★ *The American Journal of Cardiology*
Excerpta Medica Inc.
685 US-202
Bridgewater, NJ 08807
Ph: (908)547-2100 Fax: (908)547-2200
URL: http://www.ajconline.org/

Semimonthly. $414.00/year for institutions, domestic; $132.00/year for individuals, domestic; $73.00/year for students, domestic; $625.00/year for institutions, international; $337.00/year for individuals, international; $77.00/year for students, international. Journal for heart specialists.

★4215★ *Clinical Cardiology*
Clinical Cardiology Publishing Company Inc.
PO Box 832
Mahwah, NJ 07430-0832
Ph: (201)818-1010 Fax: (201)818-0086
Fr: 800-443-0263
E-mail: clinicalcardiology@fams.org

Monthly. $120.00/year for individuals; $150.00/year for institutions, no online access; $166.50/year for individuals, foreign; $400.00/year for institutions, foreign; institutional with online access; $446.50/year for institutions, other countries, foreign; $196.50/year for institutions, no online access. Peer-reviewed indexed medical journal.

★4216★ *Heart and Lung*
Mosby
1600 John F. Kennedy Blvd., Ste. 1800
Philadelphia, PA 19103-2899
Ph: (215)239-3276 Fax: (215)239-3286
URL: http://www.elsevier.com/wps/find/journaleditorialboard.cws_h

Bimonthly. $111.00/year for individuals; $321.00/year for institutions; $34.00/year for students; $99.00/year for other countries; $50.00/year for students, other countries; $289.00/year for institutions, other countries. Journal offering articles prepared by nurse and physician members of the critical care team, recognizing the nurse's role in the care and management of major organ-system conditions in critically ill patients.

★4217★ *Journal of the American Society of Echocardiography*
Mosby
1600 John F. Kennedy Blvd., Ste. 1800
Philadelphia, PA 19103-2899
Ph: (215)239-3276 Fax: (215)239-3286
URL: http://www.elsevier.com/wps/find/journalbibliographicinfo.cw

Monthly. $260.00/year for other countries, print & online; $390.00/year for institutions, other countries, print & online; $243.00/year for individuals, print & online; $402.00/year for institutions, print & online; $127.00/year for students, other countries; $116.00/year for students. Official journal of the American Society of Echocardiography serving as a source of information on the technical basis and clinical application of echocardiography. Peer-reviewed publication featuring research, reviews, and case studies.

★4218★ *Journal of Cardiopulmonary Rehabilitation (JCR)*
Lippincott Williams & Wilkins
530 Walnut St.
Philadelphia, PA 19106-3621
Ph: (215)521-8300 Fax: (215)521-8902
Fr: 800-638-3030
E-mail: jcr@sba.com
URL: http://www.jcrjournal.com/

Bimonthly. $108.91/year for individuals, U.S.; $298.96/year for institutions, U.S.; $222.94/year for individuals, international; $375.94/year for institutions, international; $37.49/year for U.S., in-training. Medical journal.

Employer Directories and Networking Lists

★4219★ *AHA Guide to the Health Care Field*
American Hospital Association
1 N Franklin
Chicago, IL 60606
Ph: (312)422-2050 Fax: (312)422-4700
Fr: 800-424-4301

Annual, August. Covers hospitals, networks, multi-health care systems, freestanding ambulatory surgery centers, psychiatric facilities, long-term care facilities, substance abuse programs, and other health-related organizations. Entries include: For hospitals–Facility name, address, phone, administrator's name, number of beds, facilities and services, number of employees, expenses, other statistics. For other organizations–Name, address, phone, fax, name and title of contact. Arrangement: Geographical. Indexes: Hospital name.

★4220★ Directory of Hospital Personnel

Grey House Publishing
185 Millerton Rd.
PO Box 860
Millerton, NY 12546
Ph: (518)789-8700   Fax: (518)789-0556
Fr: 800-562-2139
URL: http://www.greyhouse.com/hospital_personnel.htm

Annual. $325.00 for print product; $545.00 for online database subscription; $650.00 for online database subscription and print product combined. Covers 200,000 executives at 7,000 U.S. hospitals. Entries include: Name of hospital, address, phone; number of beds; type and JCAHO status of hospital; names and titles of key department heads and staff; medical and nursing school affiliations; number of residents, interns, and nursing students. Arrangement: Geographical. Indexes: Hospital name, personnel, hospital size.

★4221★ Guide to Careers in the Health Professions

The Princeton Review
2315 Broadway
New York, NY 10024
Ph: (212)874-8282   Fax: (212)874-0775
Fr: 800-733-3000
URL: http://www.princetonreview.com/

Published January, 2001. $24.95 for individuals. Presents advice and information for those searching for satisfying careers in the health professions. Publication includes: Directory of schools and academic programs. Entries include: Name, address, phone, tuition, program details, employment profiles.

★4222★ Hospital Blue Book

Billian Publishing Inc./Transworld
  Publishing Inc.
2100 Powers Ferry Rd. SE
Atlanta, GA 30339
Ph: (770)955-5656   Fax: (770)952-0669
Fr: 800-533-8484
E-mail: blu-book@billian.com

2005. $300.00 for individuals. Covers more than 6,687 hospitals; some listings also appear in a separate southern edition of this publication. Entries include: Name of hospital, accreditation, mailing address, phone, fax, number of beds, type of facility (nonprofit, general, state, etc.); list of administrative personnel and chiefs of medical services, with specific titles. Arrangement: Geographical.

★4223★ Medical and Health Information Directory

Gale, Cengage Learning
27500 Drake Rd.
Farmington Hills, MI 48331-3535
Ph: (248)699-4253   Fax: (248)699-8065
Fr: 800-877-4253
E-mail: businessproducts@gale.com
URL: http://www.gale.com

Annual; latest edition 20th, July 2007. $375.00/volume. Covers in Volume 1, more than 26,500 medical and health oriented associations, organizations, institutions, and government agencies, including health maintenance organizations (HMOs), preferred provider organizations (PPOs), insurance companies, pharmaceutical companies, research centers, and medical and allied health schools. In Volume 2, over 12,000 medical book publishers; medical periodicals, directories, audiovisual producers and services, medical libraries and information centers, electronic resources, and health-related internet search engines. In Volume 3, more than 35,500 clinics, treatment centers, care programs, and counseling/diagnostic services for 34 subject areas. Entries include: Institution, service, or firm name, address, phone, fax, email and URL; many include names of key personnel and, when pertinent, descriptive annotations. Volume 3 was formerly listed separately as Health Services Directory. Arrangement: Classified by organization activity, service, etc. Indexes: Each volume has a complete alphabetical name and keyword index.

HANDBOOKS AND MANUALS

★4224★ Careers in Health Care

The McGraw-Hill Companies
PO Box 182604
Columbus, OH 43272
Fax: (614)759-3749   Fr: 877-883-5524
E-mail: customer.service@mcgraw-hill.com
URL: http://www.mcgraw-hill.com

Barbara M. Swanson. Fifth edition, 2005. $15.95 (paper). 192 pages. Describes job duties, work settings, salaries, licensing and certification requirements, educational preparation, and future outlook. Gives ideas on how to secure a job.

★4225★ Exploring Health Care Careers, Second Edition

JIST Publishing
875 Montreal Way
St. Paul, MN 55102
Fax: 800-547-8329   Fr: 800-648-5478
E-mail: info@jist.com
URL: http://www.jist.com

2002. $89.95. 984 pages. Information about careers in the health industry, including education and certification requirements, earnings, and job outlook.

★4226★ The Only EKG Book You'll Ever Need

Lippincott Williams & Wilkins
530 Walnut St.
Philadelphia, PA 19106
Ph: (215)521-8300   Fax: (215)521-8902
Fr: 800-346-7844
URL: http://www.lww.com

Malcolm S Thaler. Fifth edition, 2006. $59.95. 342 pages.

★4227★ Opportunities in Health and Medical Careers

The McGraw-Hill Companies
PO Box 182604
Columbus, OH 43272
Fax: (614)759-3749   Fr: 877-883-5524
E-mail: customer.service@mcgraw-hill.com
URL: http://www.mcgraw-hill.com

I. Donald Snook, Jr. and Leo D'Orazio. 2004. $13.95 (paper). 157 pages. Covers the full range of medical and health occupations. Illustrated.

★4228★ Opportunities in Medical Imaging Careers

The McGraw-Hill Companies
PO Box 182604
Columbus, OH 43272
Fax: (614)759-3749   Fr: 877-883-5524
E-mail: customer.service@mcgraw-hill.com
URL: http://www.mcgraw-hill.com

Clifford J. Sherry. 2006. $13.95. 160 pages.

★4229★ Opportunities in Medical Technology Careers

The McGraw-Hill Companies
PO Box 182604
Columbus, OH 43272
Fax: (614)759-3749   Fr: 877-883-5524
E-mail: customer.service@mcgraw-hill.com
URL: http://www.mcgraw-hill.com

Karen R. Karni. Revised, 1996. $14.95; $11.95 (paper). 148 pages. Details opportunities for various technical medical personnel and supplies up-to-date information on salary levels and employment outlook. Appendices list associations and unions in each field. Illustrated.

★4230★ Resumes for Health and Medical Careers

The McGraw-Hill Companies
PO Box 182604
Columbus, OH 43272
Fax: (614)759-3749   Fr: 877-883-5524
E-mail: customer.service@mcgraw-hill.com
URL: http://www.mcgraw-hill.com

Third edition, 2003. $11.95 (paper). 160 pages.

EMPLOYMENT AGENCIES AND SEARCH FIRMS

★4231★ Shiloh Careers International, Inc.

7105 Peach Ct., Ste. 102
PO Box 831
Brentwood, TN 37024-0831
Ph: (615)373-3090   Fax: (615)373-3480
E-mail: maryann@shilohcareers.com
URL: http://www.shilohcareers.com

Employment agency serving the industry field.

★4232★ Team Placement Service, Inc.

1414 Prince St., Ste. 202
Alexandria, VA 22314
Ph: (703)820-8618   Fax: (703)820-3368
Fr: 800-495-6767
E-mail: 4jobs@teamplace.com
URL: http://www.teamplace.com

Full-service personnel consultants provide placement for healthcare staff, physician and dentist, private practice, and hospitals. Conduct interviews, tests, and reference checks to select the top 20% of applicants. Survey applicants' skill levels, provide backup information on each candidate, select compatible candidates for consideration, and insure the hiring process minimizes potential legal liability. Industries served: healthcare and government agencies providing medical, dental, biotech, laboratory, hospitals, and physician search.

ONLINE JOB SOURCES AND SERVICES

★4233★ Medhunters.com

Fr: 800-664-0278
E-mail: info@medhunters.com
URL: http://www.medhunters.com

Description: Career search site for jobs in all health care specialties; educational resources; visa and licensing information for relocation; interesting articles; relocation tools; links to professional organizations and general resources.

★4234★ ProHealthJobs

Fr: 800-796-1738
E-mail: Info@prohealthedujobs.com
URL: http://www.prohealthjobs.com

Description: Career resources site for the medical and health care field. Lists professional opportunities, product information, continuing education and open positions.

TRADESHOWS

★4235★ American Association of Neuromuscular and Electrodiagnostic Medicine Annual Scientific Meeting

American Association of Neuromuscular and Electrodiagnostic Medicine (AANEM)
2621 Superior Dr., NW /
Rochester, MN 55901
Ph: (507)288-0100   Fax: (507)288-1225
E-mail: aanem@aanem.org

URL: http://www.aanem.org

Annual. **Primary Exhibits:** Electromyographic and electrodiagnostic equipment and accessories, pharmaceutical companies, and publishers.

★4236★ American Clinical Neurophysiology Society Annual Meeting and Short Courses

American Clinical Neurophysiology Society
PO Box 30
Bloomfield, CT 06002
Ph: (860)243-3977   Fax: (860)286-0787
E-mail: acns@ssmgt.com
URL: http://www.acns.org

Annual. **Primary Exhibits:** Electroencephalographic and neurophysiology equipment, supplies, and services.

★4237★ American College of Cardiology Annual Scientific Session

American College of Cardiology
Heart House
2400 N. St., NW
Washington, DC 20037
Ph: (202)375-6000   Fax: (202)375-7000
URL: http://www.acc.org

Annual. **Primary Exhibits:** Products and services related to cardiovascular medicine.

OTHER SOURCES

★4238★ Alliance of Cardiovascular Professionals (ACVP)

PO Box 2007
Midlothian, VA 23113
Ph: (804)632-0078   Fax: (804)639-9212
E-mail: peggymcelgunn@comcast.net

Description: Strives to meet educational needs. Develops programs to meet those needs. Provides a structure to offer the cardiovascular and pulmonary technology professional a key to the future as a valuable member of the medical team. Seeks advancement for members through communication and education. Provides coordinated programs to orient the newer professional to his field and continuing educational opportunities for technologist personnel; has established guidelines for educational programs in the hospital and university setting. Works with educators and physicians to provide basic, advanced, and in-service programs for technologists. Sponsors registration and certification programs which provide technology professionals with further opportunity to clarify their level of expertise. Compiles statistics.

★4239★ Exploring Health Occupations

Cambridge Educational
PO Box 2053
Princeton, NJ 08543-2053
Ph: 800-257-5126   Fax: (609)671-0266
Fr: 800-468-4227
E-mail: custserv@films.com
URL: http://www.cambridgeeducational.com

VHS and DVD. $159.90. 1999. Two-part series provides a detailed view of the field of medical technicians and technologists, EMTs, nurses, therapists, and assistants.

★4240★ Health Service Occupations

Delphi Productions
3159 6th St.
Boulder, CO 80304
Ph: (303)443-2100   Fax: (303)443-4022
Fr: 888-443-2400
E-mail: support@delphivideo.com
URL: http://www.delphivideo.com

$95.00. 50 minutes. Part of the Careers for the 21st Century Video Library.

★4241★ Health Technologists & Technicians

Delphi Productions
3159 6th St.
Boulder, CO 80304
Ph: (303)443-2100   Fax: (303)443-4022
Fr: 888-443-2400
E-mail: support@delphivideo.com
URL: http://www.delphivideo.com

$95.00. 50 minutes. Part of the Careers for the 21st Century Video Library.

★4242★ Medical Technicians and Technologists

Cambridge Educational
PO Box 2053
Princeton, NJ 08543-2053
Ph: 800-257-5126   Fax: (609)671-0266
Fr: 800-468-4227
E-mail: custserv@films.com
URL: http://www.cambridgeeducational.com

VHS and DVD. $79.95. 18 minutes. 2000. Part of the Exploring Health Occupations Series.

★4243★ Medicine & Related Occupations

Delphi Productions
3159 6th St.
Boulder, CO 80304
Ph: (303)443-2100   Fax: (303)443-4022
Fr: 888-443-2400
E-mail: support@delphivideo.com
URL: http://www.delphivideo.com

$95.00. 45 minutes. Part of the Careers for the 21st Century Video Library.

Electrical and Electronic Equipment Repairers

PLACEMENT AND JOB REFERRAL SERVICES

★4253★ **ETA International - Electronics Technicians Association, International (ETA)**
5 Depot St.
Greencastle, IN 46135
Ph: (765)653-8262   Fax: (765)653-4287
Fr: 800-288-3824
E-mail: eta@eta-i.org
URL: http://www.eta-i.org

Description: Skilled electronics technicians. Provides placement service; offers certification examinations for electronics technicians and satellite, fiber optics, and data cabling installers. Compiles wage and manpower statistics. Administers FCC Commercial License examinations and certification of computer network systems technicians and web and internet specialists.

EMPLOYER DIRECTORIES AND NETWORKING LISTS

★4254★ **American Electronics Association-Member Directory**
AEA
601 Pennsylvania Ave. NW
North Bldg., Ste. 600
Washington, DC 20004
Ph: (202)682-9110   Fax: (202)682-9111
Fr: 800-284-4232
URL: http://www.aeanet.org/members/

Covers over 3,000 member electronics and high-technology companies and 500 associate member firms including financial institutions, law firms, and accounting firms. Entries include: Company name, address, phone, Web address, cable address, fax, names of executives, number of employees, list of products or services, date founded, whether a public or private company, stock market where traded, ticker symbol. Arrangement: Alphabetical. Indexes: Geographical, product.

★4255★ **Appliance Design-Buyers Guide**
Business News Publishing Co.
5900 Harper Rd., No. 105
Solon, OH 44139-1835
Ph: (440)349-3060   Fax: (440)498-9121
URL: http://www.ammagazine.com

Annual, December. Publication includes: Directory of manufacturers and suppliers of equipment, material, and components to the appliance industry; trade associations. Entries include: Company name, address, phone, fax, website, and e-mail. Arrangement: Classified by product or service, and by company name. Indexes: Product/service, company.

HANDBOOKS AND MANUALS

★4256★ **The Complete Guide to Electronics Troubleshooting**
Cengage Learning
PO Box 6904
Florence, KY 41022
Fax: 800-487-8488   Fr: 800-354-9706
URL: http://www.cengage.com

James Perozzo. 1994. $57.50. 850 pages.

★4257★ **Opportunities in Electrical Trades**
The McGraw-Hill Companies
PO Box 182604
Columbus, OH 43272
Fax: (614)759-3749   Fr: 877-883-5524
E-mail: customer.service@mcgraw-hill.com
URL: http://www.mcgraw-hill.com

Robert Wood and Kenneth R. Edwards. 1996. $14.95; $11.95 (paper). 145 pages. Offers advice on job hunting and where the jobs are. Includes index, bibliography, and illustrations.

★4258★ **Opportunities in Electronics Careers**
The McGraw-Hill Companies
PO Box 182604
Columbus, OH 43272
Fax: (614)759-3749   Fr: 877-883-5524
E-mail: customer.service@mcgraw-hill.com
URL: http://www.mcgraw-hill.com

Mark Rowh. 2007. $13.95; $11.95 (paper). 221 pages. Discusses career opportunities in commercial and industrial electronics equipment repair, electronics home entertainment repair, electronics engineering, and engineering technology. Includes job outlook and how to get off to a good start on the job.

★4259★ **Opportunities in High Tech Careers**
The McGraw-Hill Companies
PO Box 182604
Columbus, OH 43272
Fax: (614)759-3749   Fr: 877-883-5524
E-mail: customer.service@mcgraw-hill.com
URL: http://www.mcgraw-hill.com

Gary Colter and Deborah Yanuck. 1999. $14.95; $11.95 (paper). 160 pages. Explores high technology careers. Describes job opportunities, how to make a career decision, how to prepare for high technology jobs, job hunting techniques, and future trends.

★4260★ **Opportunities in Installation and Repair Careers**
The McGraw-Hill Companies
PO Box 182604
Columbus, OH 43272
Fax: (614)759-3749   Fr: 877-883-5524
E-mail: customer.service@mcgraw-hill.com
URL: http://www.mcgraw-hill.com

Mark Rowh. 1995. $11.95 (paper). 144 pages.

★4261★ **Troubleshooting Electrical/ Electronic Systems**
American Technical Publishers, Inc.
1155 W. 175th St.
Homewood, IL 60430
Ph: (708)957-1100   Fax: (708)957-1101
Fr: 800-323-3471
URL: http://www.americantech.org/

Glen A. Mazur and Thomas E. Proctor. Second edition, 2002. $66.00. Step-by-step applications show how to troubleshoot electrical and electronic systems. 553 pages.

★4262★ **Troubleshooting and Repairing Major Appliances**
McGraw-Hill Companies
PO Box 182604
Columbus, OH 43272
Fax: (614)759-3749   Fr: 877-883-5524
E-mail: customer.service@mcgraw-hill.com
URL: http://www.mcgraw-hill.com

Eric Kleinert. 2007. $59.95; $39.95 (paper). 744 pages.

EMPLOYMENT AGENCIES AND SEARCH FIRMS

★4263★ **Omni Recruiting Group, Inc.**
227 Sandy Springs Pl., Ste D-370
Atlanta, GA 30328
Ph: (404)256-1575   Fax: (404)256-1585
E-mail: info@omnirecruiting.com
URL: http://www.omnirecruiting.com

Executive search firm specializing in sales.

★4264★ **S.D. Kelly and Associates, Inc.**
300 Crown Colony Dr., Ste. 106
Quincy, MA 02169
Ph: (781)794-9800   Fax: (781)794-9809
E-mail: info@sdkelly.com
URL: http://www.sdkelly.com

Employment agency.

TRADESHOWS

★4265★ **E3 - Electronic Entertainment Expo**
IDG Expo Management Co.
PO Box 620
Medfield, MA 02052-0620
URL: http://www.idgexpos.com

Annual. **Primary Exhibits:** Interactive entertainment equipment, supplies, and services.

★4266★ Electronic Distribution Show and Conference

Electronic Distribution Show Corp.
222 S. Riverside Plaza, Ste. 2160
Chicago, IL 60606
Ph: (312)648-1140   Fax: (312)648-4282
E-mail: eds@edsc.org
URL: http://www.edsc.org

Annual. **Primary Exhibits:** Electronic products. **Dates and Locations:** 2008 May 06-08; Las Vegas, NV; Paris Hotel.

★4267★ International CES

CEMA - Consumer Electronics
   Manufacturers Association
2500 Wilson Blvd.
Arlington, VA 22201-3834
Ph: (703)907-7600   Fax: (703)907-7675
Fr: (866)233-7968
E-mail: cea@ce.org
URL: http://www.cesweb.org

Annual. **Primary Exhibits:** Electronic equipment, supplies, and services.

★4268★ NUCA - National Utility Contractors Association Convention

VNU Expositions, Inc. - Bill
   Communications, Inc.
1199 S. Belt Line Rd., Ste. 100
Coppell, TX 75019
Ph: (972)906-6500   Fax: (972)906-6501
E-mail: jlerner@vnuemedia.com
URL: http://www.vnuexpo.com

Annual. **Primary Exhibits:** Equipment, supplies, and services for the construction of utility lines (pipes for storm and sanitary sewers and drainage, water lines, cables, ducts, conduits, and other utility work).

★4269★ POWER-GEN International

PennWell Conferences and Exhibitions
   (Oklahoma)
1421 S Sheridan Rd.
Tulsa, OK 74112
Ph: (918)835-3161   Fax: (918)831-9497
Fr: 800-331-4463
E-mail: Headquarters@PennWell.com
URL: http://www.pennwell.com

Annual. **Primary Exhibits:** Equipment and services for power generation industries.

OTHER SOURCES

★4270★ COIN Career Guidance System

COIN Educational Products
3361 Executive Pky., Ste. 302
Toledo, OH 43606
Ph: (419)536-5353   Fax: (419)536-7056
Fr: 800-274-8515
URL: http://www.coinedu.com/

CD-ROM. Provides career information through seven cross-referenced files covering postsecondary schools, college majors, vocational programs, military service, apprenticeship programs, financial aid, and scholarships. Apprenticeship file describes national apprenticeship training programs, including information on how to apply, contact agencies, and program content. Military file describes more than 200 military occupations and training opportunities related to civilian employment.

★4271★ Electronic Industries Alliance (EIA)

2500 Wilson Blvd.
Arlington, VA 22201
Ph: (703)907-7500
E-mail: mflanigan@eia.org
URL: http://www.eia.org

Description: Seeks for the competitiveness of the American producer, represents all companies involved in the design and manufacture of electronic components, parts, systems and equipment for communications, industrial, government and consumer uses.

★4272★ International Society of Certified Electronics Technicians (ISCET)

3608 Pershing Ave.
Fort Worth, TX 76107-4527
Ph: (817)921-9101   Fax: (817)921-3741
Fr: 800-946-0201
E-mail: info@iscet.org
URL: http://www.iscet.org

Description: Technicians in 50 countries who have been certified by the society. Seeks to provide a fraternal bond among certified electronics technicians, raise their public image, and improve the effectiveness of industry education programs for technicians. Offers training programs in new elec-

tronics information. Maintains library of service literature for consumer electronic equipment, including manuals and schematics for out-of-date equipment. Offers all FCC licenses. Sponsors testing program for certification of electronics technicians in the fields of audio, communications, computer, consumer, industrial, medical electronics, radar, radio-television, and video.

★4273★ Mechanics & Repairers

Delphi Productions
3159 6th St.
Boulder, CO 80304
Ph: (303)443-2100   Fax: (303)443-4022
Fr: 888-443-2400
E-mail: support@delphivideo.com
URL: http://www.delphivideo.com

$95.00. 50 minutes. Part of the Careers for the 21st Century Video Library.

★4274★ National Electronics Service Dealers Association (NESDA)

3608 Pershing Ave.
Fort Worth, TX 76107-4527
Ph: (817)921-9061   Fax: (817)921-3741
E-mail: info@nesda.com
URL: http://www.nesda.com

Description: Local and state electronic service associations and companies representing 4200 individuals. Provides educational assistance in electronic training to public schools; supplies technical service information on business management training to electronic service dealers. Offers certification, apprenticeship, and training programs through International Society of Certified Electronics Technicians. Compiles statistics on electronics service business; conducts technical service and business management seminars.

★4275★ Scientific, Engineering, and Technical Services

Cambridge Educational
PO Box 2053
Princeton, NJ 08543-2053
Ph: 800-257-5126   Fax: (609)671-0266
Fr: 800-468-4227
E-mail: custserv@films.com
URL: http://www.cambridgeeducational.com

VHS and DVD. $89.95. 2002. 18 minutes. 2002. Part of the Career Cluster Series.

Electrical and Electronics Engineers

★4276★ AWIS Magazine

Association for Women in Science
1200 New York Ave. NW, Ste. 650
Washington, DC 20005
Ph: (202)326-8940   Fax: (202)326-8960
Fr: (866)657-2947
E-mail: awis@awis.org
URL: http://www.awis.org/

Description: Bimonthly. Covers issues, legislation, and trends related to science education for girls, women, and minorities. Includes information on grants and fellowships, job openings, educational programs, events, and notices of publications available.

★4277★ Circuits Assembly

UP Media Group Inc.
2400 Lake Park Dr., Ste. 440
Smyrna, GA 30080
Ph: (678)589-8800   Fax: (678)589-8850
E-mail: ca@up-mediagroup.com
URL: http://www.circuitsassembly.com

Monthly. Serves the PCB assembly marketplace.

★4278★ Communications of the ACM

Association for Computing Machinery
2 Penn Plz., Ste. 701
New York, NY 10121-0701
Ph: (212)869-7440   Fax: (212)944-1318
Fr: 800-342-6626
URL: http://www.acm.org/pubs/cacm/

Monthly. $179.00/year for nonmembers; $36.00/year for members. Computing news magazine.

★4279★ Community Radio News

National Federation of Community Broadcasters
1970 Broadway, Ste. 1000
Oakland, CA 94612
Ph: (510)451-8200   Fax: (510)451-8208
E-mail: newsletter@nfcb.org

URL: http://www.nfcb.org

Description: Monthly. Serves as a medium of communication for independent, community-licensed radio stations. Contains brief articles and news items on such topics as public broadcasting and programming, legislative developments, activities of the Federal Communications Commission, and local stations. Recurring features include notices of grants and awards, job openings, and a calendar of events/conferences for noncommercial broadcasters.

★4280★ Consulting-Specifying Engineer

Reed Business Information
360 Park Ave. S
New York, NY 10010
Ph: (646)746-6400   Fax: (646)746-7431
URL: http://www.csemag.com

The integrated engineering magazine of the building construction industry.

★4281★ ECN (Electronic Component News)

Advantage Business Media
100 Enterprise Dr., Ste. 600
Box 912
Rockaway, NJ 07866-0912
Ph: (973)920-7000
URL: http://www.ecnmag.com/

Monthly. Free; $93.00/year for individuals, 1 year; $112.00/year for Canada and Mexico, 1 year; $175.00/year for other countries, 1 year. Magazine for electronics design engineers and engineering management.

★4282★ EE Evaluation Engineering

Nelson Publishing Inc.
2500 Tamiami Trl. N
Nokomis, FL 34275
Ph: (941)966-9521   Fax: (941)966-2590
URL: http://
www.evaluationengineering.com/

Monthly. Free. Trade magazine covering electronic engineering, evaluation and test.

★4283★ Electric Light & Power

PennWell Corp.
1421 S Sheridan Rd.
Tulsa, OK 74112
Ph: (918)835-3161   Fr: 800-331-4463
URL: http://uaelp.pennnet.com

Bimonthly. $76.00/year for individuals, 1 year; $129.00/year for two years; $85.00/year for Canada and Mexico, 1 year; $143.00/year for Canada and Mexico, 2 years; $210.00/year for other countries, 1 year; $374.00/year for other countries, 2 years; $12.00/year for single issue; $20.00 for single issue, Canada/Mexico; $20.00/year for single issue, international; $60.00/year for individuals, schools & public libraries. Provides broad view of electric utility industry with in-depth analysis of key business issues for executives and management.

★4284★ The Electrochemical Society Interface

The Electrochemical Society Inc.
65 S Main St., Bldg. D
Pennington, NJ 08534-2839
Ph: (609)737-1902   Fax: (609)737-2743
E-mail: interface@electrochem.org
URL: http://www.electrochem.org/dl/interface/

Quarterly. $15.00/year for members; $68.00/year for nonmembers; $15.00 for single issue, members; $20.00 for single issue, nonmembers. Publication featuring news and articles of interest to members of the Electrochemical Society.

★4285★ Electronic Design

Penton Technology and Lifestyle Media Inc.
249 W 17th St.
New York, NY 10011
Ph: (212)204-4200   Fr: 800-526-6052
URL: http://www.elecdesign.com

Biweekly. $95.00/year for individuals; $105.00/year for individuals; $166.00/year for individuals, 2 years; $185.00/year for individuals, 2 years; $158.00/year for Canada; $175.00/year for Canada; $270.00/year for Canada, 2 years; $300.00/year for Canada, 2 years; $180.00/year for out of country;

$306.00/year for out of country, 2 years. Professional magazine covering current information in the field of electronic design.

★4286★ **Electronic Engineering Times**

CMP Media L.L.C.
600 Community Dr.
Manhasset, NY 11030
Ph: (516)562-5000   Fax: (516)562-7830
URL: http://www.cmp.com/products/pr_det_elecengtimesasia.jhtml

Semimonthly. Weekly trade newspaper.

★4287★ **Electronic Markets**

Taylor & Francis Group Journals
325 Chestnut St., Ste. 800
Philadelphia, PA 19106
Ph: (215)625-8900   Fax: (215)625-8914
Fr: 800-354-1420
URL: http://www.tandf.co.uk/journals/titles/10196781.asp

$683.00/year for institutions, print and online; $648.00/year for institutions, online only; $189.00/year for individuals. Journal covering all system concepts of electronic commerce.

★4288★ **Electronic Products**

Hearst Business Communications/
  Electronics Group
50 Charles Lindbergh Blvd., Ste. 100
Uniondale, NY 11553
Ph: (516)227-1383
E-mail: lens@electronicproducts.com
URL: http://www.electronicproducts.com

Monthly. $12.00/year for individuals. Magazine for electronic design engineers and management.

★4289★ **Engineering Economist**

Institute of Industrial Engineers
3577 Parkway Ln., Ste. 200
Norcross, GA 30092
Ph: (770)449-0460   Fax: (770)441-3295
Fr: 800-494-0460
URL: http://www.iienet2.org/Details.aspx?id=1486

Quarterly. $73.00/year for individuals; $129.00/year for institutions, online only; $136.00/year for institutions, print & online; $82.00/year for institutions, print + online; $77.00/year for institutions, online only. Publication covering business issues in the energy, petroleum and mining industries.

★4290★ **Engineering Times**

National Society of Professional
  Engineers
1420 King St.
Alexandria, VA 22314
Ph: (703)684-2800
URL: http://www.nspe.org

Monthly. Magazine (tabloid) covering professional, legislative, and techology issues for an engineering audience.

★4291★ **ENR: Engineering News-Record**

McGraw-Hill Inc.
1221 Ave. of the Americas
New York, NY 10020-1095
Ph: (212)512-2000   Fax: (212)512-3840
Fr: 877-833-5524
E-mail: enr_web_editors@mcgraw-hill.com
URL: http://www.mymags.com/moreinfo.php?itemID=20012

Weekly. $94.00/year for individuals, print. Magazine focusing on engineering and construction.

★4292★ **Graduating Engineer & Computer Careers**

Career Recruitment Media
211 W Wacker Dr., Ste. 900
Chicago, IL 60606
Ph: (312)525-3100
URL: http://www.graduatingengineer.com

Quarterly. $15.00/year for individuals. Magazine focusing on employment, education, and career development for entry-level engineers and computer scientists.

★4293★ **The High-Tech News**

ETA International
5 Depot St.
Greencastle, IN 46135
Ph: (765)653-8262   Fax: (765)653-4287
Fr: 800-288-3824
E-mail: eta@eta-i.org
URL: http://www.eta-i.org

Description: Monthly. Serves member technicians with news of the Association and the electronics industry, including items on service, education, employment, management, and events. Contains information on membership, management, telecommunications, and business and technical training programs. Recurring features include editorials, news of research, letters to the editor, book reviews, and a calendar of events.

★4294★ **High Technology Careers Magazine**

HTC
4701 Patrick Henry Dr., No. 1901
Santa Clara, CA 95054-1847
Fax: (408)567-0242
URL: http://www.hightechcareers.com

Bimonthly. $29.00/year; $35.00/year for Canada; $85.00/year for out of country. Magazine (tabloid) containing employment opportunity information for the engineering and technical community.

★4295★ **IEEE Spectrum**

Institute of Electrical and Electronics
  Engineers Inc.
3 Park Ave., 17th Fl.
New York, NY 10016-5997
Ph: (212)419-7900   Fax: (212)752-4929
URL: http://www.spectrum.ieee.org/mc_online

Monthly. $29.95/year for individuals, U.S. & Canada; $99.95/year for out of country,

international. Magazine for the scientific and engineering professional. Provides information on developments and trends in engineering, physics, mathematics, chemistry, medicine/biology, and the nuclear sciences.

★4296★ **IEEE Transactions on Electron Devices**

IEEE Electron Devices Society
445 Hoes Ln.
Piscataway, NJ 08855-1331
Ph: (732)981-0060   Fax: (732)981-1721
URL: http://ieeexplore.ieee.org/xpl/RecentIssue.jsp?punumber=16

Monthly. Included in membership, online. Journal covering theory, design, performance and reliability of electron devices.

★4297★ **Journal of Active and Passive Electronic Devices**

Old City Publishing
628 N 2nds St.
Philadelphia, PA 19123
Ph: (215)925-4390   Fax: (215)925-4371
URL: http://www.oldcitypublishing.com/JAPED/JAPED.html

Quarterly. $412.00/year for institutions; $122.00/year for individuals. International journal devoted to the science and technology of all types of electronic components.

★4298★ **Journal of Electronic Materials**

IEEE Electron Devices Society
445 Hoes Ln.
Piscataway, NJ 08855-1331
Ph: (732)981-0060   Fax: (732)981-1721

Monthly. Professional journal covering electronics engineering issues.

★4299★ **Machine Design**

Penton Media Inc.
1300 E 9th St.
Cleveland, OH 44114
Ph: (216)696-7000   Fax: (216)696-1752
E-mail: mdeditor@penton.com
URL: http://www.machinedesign.com

Semimonthly. $144.00/year for Canada, 21 issues; $160.00/year for Canada, regular; $108.00/year for other countries, 21 issues; $120.00/year for other countries, regular; $157.00/year for students, 21 issues; $175.00/year for students, regular. Magazine on design engineering function.

★4300★ **Microwave Journal**

Horizon House Publications Inc.
685 Canton St.
Norwood, MA 02062
Ph: (781)769-9750   Fax: (781)769-5037
Fr: 800-966-8526
E-mail: mwj@mwjournal.com
URL: http://www.mwjournal.com

Monthly. Electronic engineering magazine.

★4301★ NSBE Magazine

NSBE Publications
205 Daingerfield Rd.
Alexandria, VA 22314
Ph: (703)549-2207   Fax: (703)683-5312
URL: http://www.nsbe.org/publications/premieradvertisers.php

Journal providing information on engineering careers, self-development, and cultural issues for recent graduates with technical majors.

★4302★ PE & RS Photogrammetric Engineering & Remote Sensing

The Imaging and Geospatial Information Society
5410 Grosvenor Ln., Ste. 210
Bethesda, MD 20814-2160
Ph: (301)493-0290   Fax: (301)493-0208
E-mail: asprs@asprs.org
URL: http://www.asprs.org/

Monthly. $250.00/year for individuals, U.S.D 15 discount per subscp. off the base rate; $120.00/year for individuals, active; $80.00/year for individuals, associate; $45.00/year for students, domestic. Journal covering photogrammetry, remote sensing, geographic information systems, cartography, and surveying, global positioning systems, digital photogrammetry.

★4303★ Power

McGraw-Hill Inc.
1221 Ave. of the Americas
New York, NY 10020-1095
Ph: (212)512-2000   Fax: (212)512-3840
Fr: 877-833-5524
E-mail: robert_peltier@platts.com
URL: http://online.platts.com/PPS/P=m&s=1029337384756.1478827&e=1

Monthly. Magazine for engineers in electric utilities, process and manufacturing plants, commercial and service establishments, and consulting, design, and construction engineering firms working in the power technology field.

★4304★ Printed Circuit Design & Manufacture

UP Media Group Inc.
2400 Lake Park Dr., Ste. 440
Smyrna, GA 30080
Ph: (678)589-8800   Fax: (678)589-8850
URL: http://www.pcdandm.com/pcdmag

Monthly. Magazine for engineers and designers of PCBs and related technologies.

★4305★ RF Design

Penton Media Inc.
9800 Metcalf Ave.
Overland Park, KS 66212
Ph: (913)341-1300   Fax: (913)967-1898
URL: http://www.rfdesign.com/

Monthly. Free. Magazine covering the R.F. engineering field.

★4306★ Semiconductor International

Reed Business Information
360 Park Ave. S
New York, NY 10010
Ph: (646)746-6400   Fax: (646)746-7431
URL: http://www.reedbusiness.com/

Monthly. Free. Magazine profiling semiconductor manufacturing issues.

★4307★ SMT

PennWell Corp.
1421 S Sheridan Rd.
Tulsa, OK 74112
Ph: (918)835-3161   Fr: 800-331-4463
URL: http://smt.pennnet.com

Monthly. $109.00/year for U.S. and Canada; $198.00/year for other countries; $14.00 for single issue, US; $20.00/year for single issue, Canada; $20.00 for single issue, foreign. Trade magazine for professional engineers involved in surface mount technology circuit design and board assembly.

★4308★ Solid State Technology

PennWell Corp.
98 Spit Brook Rd.
Nashua, NH 03062-5737
Ph: (603)891-0123
URL: http://sst.pennnet.com

Monthly. $234.00/year for individuals; $327.00/year for Canada, print; $393.00/year for other countries, print. Magazine containing electronic and semiconductor engineering news and information.

★4309★ SWE, Magazine of the Society of Women Engineers

Society of Women Engineers
230 East Ohio St., Ste. 400
Chicago, IL 60611-3265
Ph: (312)596-5223
E-mail: hq@swe.org
URL: http://www.swe.org

Quarterly. $30.00/year for nonmembers. Magazine for engineering students and for women and men working in the engineering and technology fields. Covers career guidance, continuing development and topical issues.

★4310★ Test & Measurement World

Reed Business Information
225 Wyman St.
Waltham, MA 02451-1216
E-mail: tmw@reedbusiness.com
URL: http://www.tmworld.com

Monthly. Free. Electronic engineering magazine specializing in test, measurement, and inspection of electronic products.

★4311★ Transmission and Distribution World

Penton Media Inc.
9800 Metcalf Ave.
Overland Park, KS 66212
Ph: (913)341-1300   Fax: (913)967-1898

URL: http://www.tdworld.com

Monthly. Magazine about powerline construction, transmission, and distribution.

★4312★ WEPANEWS

Women in Engineering Programs & Advocates Network
1901 E. Asbury Ave., Ste. 220
Denver, CO 80208
Ph: (303)871-4643   Fax: (303)871-6833
E-mail: dmatt@wepan.org
URL: http://www.wepan.org

Description: 2/year. Seeks to provide greater access for women to careers in engineering. Includes news of graduate, undergraduate, freshmen, pre-college, and re-entry engineering programs for women. Recurring features include job listings, faculty, grant, and conference news, international engineering program news, action group news, notices of publications available, and a column titled Kudos.

PLACEMENT AND JOB REFERRAL SERVICES

★4313★ American Indian Science and Engineering Society (AISES)

PO Box 9828
Albuquerque, NM 87119-9828
Ph: (505)765-1052   Fax: (505)765-5608
E-mail: info@aises.org
URL: http://www.aises.org

Description: Represents American Indian and non-Indian students and professionals in science, technology, and engineering fields; corporations representing energy, mining, aerospace, electronic, and computer fields. Seeks to motivate and encourage students to pursue undergraduate and graduate studies in science, engineering, and technology. Sponsors science fairs in grade schools, teacher training workshops, summer math/science sessions for 8th-12th graders, professional chapters, and student chapters in colleges. Offers scholarships. Adult members serve as role models, advisers, and mentors for students. Operates placement service.

★4314★ American Society of Test Engineers (ASTE)

PO Box 389
Nutting Lake, MA 01865-0389
E-mail: aste@earthlink.net
URL: http://www.astetest.org

Members: Companies involved in the electronic testing industry and instrumentation are corporate members; engineers who work in test engineering related fields are regular members. **Purpose:** Seeks to foster improved communication among individuals and companies in the testing industry. **Activities:** Offers job referral service.

★4315★ Association for the Advancement of Medical Instrumentation (AAMI)

1110 N Glebe Rd., Ste. 220
Arlington, VA 22201-4795
Ph: (703)525-4890   Fax: (703)276-0793
Fr: 800-332-2264
E-mail: membership@aami.org
URL: http://www.aami.org

Description: Clinical engineers, biomedical equipment technicians, physicians, hospital administrators, consultants, engineers, manufacturers of medical devices, nurses, researchers and others interested in medical instrumentation. Works to improve the quality of medical care through the application, development, and management of technology. Maintains placement service. Offers certification programs for biomedical equipment technicians and clinical engineers. Produces numerous standards and recommended practices on medical devices and procedures. Offers educational programs.

★4316★ Engineering Society of Detroit (ESD)

2000 Town Ctr., Ste. 2610
Southfield, MI 48075
Ph: (248)353-0735   Fax: (248)353-0736
E-mail: esd@esd.org
URL: http://esd.org

Description: Engineers from all disciplines; scientists and technologists. Conducts technical programs and engineering refresher courses; sponsors conferences and expositions. Maintains speakers' bureau; offers placement services; although based in Detroit, MI, society membership is international.

★4317★ Korean-American Scientists and Engineers Association (KSEA)

1952 Gallows Rd., Ste. 300
Vienna, VA 22182
Ph: (703)748-1221   Fax: (703)748-1331
E-mail: admin@ksea.org
URL: http://www.ksea.org

Description: Represents scientists and engineers holding single or advanced degrees. Promotes friendship and mutuality among Korean and American scientists and engineers; contributes to Korea's scientific, technological, industrial, and economic developments; strengthens the scientific, technological, and cultural bonds between Korea and the U.S. Sponsors symposium. Maintains speakers' bureau, placement service, and biographical archives. Compiles statistics.

★4318★ Robotics Tech Group of the Society of Manufacturing Engineers (RI/SME)

PO Box 930
Dearborn, MI 48121
Ph: (313)271-1500   Fax: (313)425-3404
Fr: 800-733-4763
E-mail: techcommunities@sme.org
URL: http://www.sme.org/cgi-bin/communities.pl?/communities/ri/ri-home.htm&&SME&

Description: Represents engineers, manag-

ers, educators, and government officials in 50 countries working or interested in the field of robotics. Promotes efficient and effective use of current and future robot technology. Serves as a clearinghouse for the industry trends and developments. Includes areas of interest such as: aerospace; assembly systems; casting and forging; education and training; human factors and safety; human and food service; material handling; military systems; nontraditional systems; research and development; small shop applications; welding. Offers professional certification. Operates placement service; compiles statistics. Maintains speakers' bureau.

★4319★ Society of Hispanic Professional Engineers (SHPE)

5400 E Olympic Blvd., Ste. 210
Los Angeles, CA 90022
Ph: (323)725-3970   Fax: (323)725-0316
E-mail: shpenational@shpe.org
URL: http://oneshpe.shpe.org/wps/portal/national

Description: Represents engineers, student engineers, and scientists. Aims to increase the number of Hispanic engineers by providing motivation and support to students. Sponsors competitions and educational programs. Maintains placement service and speakers' bureau; compiles statistics.

EMPLOYER DIRECTORIES AND NETWORKING LISTS

★4320★ American Electronics Association-Member Directory

AEA
601 Pennsylvania Ave. NW
North Bldg., Ste. 600
Washington, DC 20004
Ph: (202)682-9110   Fax: (202)682-9111
Fr: 800-284-4232
URL: http://www.aeanet.org/members/

Covers over 3,000 member electronics and high-technology companies and 500 associate member firms including financial institutions, law firms, and accounting firms. Entries include: Company name, address, phone, Web address, cable address, fax, names of executives, number of employees, list of products or services, date founded, whether a public or private company, stock market where traded, ticker symbol. Arrangement: Alphabetical. Indexes: Geographical, product.

★4321★ American Men and Women of Science

Gale, Cengage Learning
27500 Drake Rd.
Farmington Hills, MI 48331-3535
Ph: (248)699-4253   Fax: (248)699-8065
Fr: 800-877-4253
URL: http://www.gale.com

Biennial, latest edition 23rd, October 2006;

new edition expected 24th, January 2008. $1,075.00 for individuals. Covers over 129,700 U.S. and Canadian scientists active in the physical, biological, mathematical, computer science, and engineering fields; includes references to previous edition for deceased scientists and nonrespondents. Entries include: Name, address, education, personal and career data, memberships, honors and awards, research interest. Arrangement: Alphabetical. Indexes: Discipline (in separate volume).

★4322★ Careers in Focus: Engineering

Facts On File Inc.
132 W 31st St., 17th Fl.
New York, NY 10001
Ph: (212)967-8800   Fax: 800-678-3633
Fr: 800-322-8755
URL: http://www.factsonfile.com

3rd edition, 2007. $29.95 for individuals; $26.95 for libraries. Publication includes: List of resources to consult for more information. Principal content of publication consists of job descriptions, advancement opportunities, educational requirements, employment outlook, salary information, and working conditions for careers in the field of engineering. Indexes: Alphabetical.

★4323★ Design News OEM Directory

Reed Business Information
225 Wyman St.
Waltham, MA 02451-1216
E-mail: dn@cahners.com
URL: http://www.reedbusiness.com

Annual, November. Covers about 5,000 manufacturers and suppliers of power transmission products, fluid power products, and electrical/electronic components to the OEM (original equipment manufacturer) market in SIC groups 34-39. Entries include: Company name, address, phone, fax, URL, e-mail. Arrangement: Alphabetical. Indexes: Product locator, trade Name, supplier locator.

★4324★ Directory of Contract Staffing Firms

C.E. Publications Inc.
PO Box 3006
Bothell, WA 98041-3006
Ph: (425)806-5200   Fax: (425)806-5585
URL: http://www.cjhunter.com/dcsf/overview.html

Covers nearly 1,300 contract firms actively engaged in the employment of engineering, IT/IS, and technical personnel for 'temporary' contract assignments throughout the world. Entries include: Company name, address, phone, name of contact, email, web address. Arrangement: Alphabetical. Indexes: Geographical.

★4325★ Indiana Society of Professional Engineers-Directory

Indiana Society of Professional Engineers
PO Box 20806
Indianapolis, IN 46220
Ph: (317)255-2267   Fax: (317)255-2530

URL: http://www.indspe.org

Annual, fall. Covers member registered engineers, land surveyors, engineering students, and engineers in training. Entries include: Member name, address, phone, type of membership, business information, specialty. Arrangement: Alphabetical by chapter area.

★4326★ **International Association of Electrical Inspectors-Membership Directory**
International Association of Electrical Inspectors
901 Waterfall Way, Ste. 602
Richardson, TX 75080-7702
Ph: (972)235-1455   Fax: (972)235-6858
URL: http://www.iaei.org/

Annual, April. Covers 26,000 state and federal government, industrial, utility, and insurance electrical inspectors, and, as associate members, electricians, manufacturers, engineers, architects, and wiremen. Entries include: Name, title, type of member, address, company affiliation. Arrangement: Geographical, then by division, chapter, or section, and type of membership, then alphabetical. Indexes: Committees; personal name.

★4327★ **Peterson's Job Opportunities in Engineering and Technology**
Peterson's Guides
2000 Lenox Dr.
Box 67005
Lawrenceville, NJ 08648
Ph: (609)896-1800   Fax: (609)896-4531
Fr: 800-338-3282
E-mail: custsvc@petersons.com
URL: http://www.petersons.com

Compiled by the Peterson's staff. Fourth edition, 1996. $21.95 (paper). 379 pages. Profiles 2,000 high-tech companies looking primarily for technical personnel in such fields as biotechnology, telecommunications, software, computers and peripherals, defense, and aerospace. Contains job-search strategies and career options to help match education and expertise to the job market. Indexed geographically, by industry, and by hiring needs.

Handbooks and Manuals

★4328★ **The Best Resumes for Scientists and Engineers**
John Wiley & Sons Inc.
1 Wiley Dr.
Somerset, NJ 08873
Ph: (732)469-4400   Fax: (732)302-2300
Fr: 800-225-5945
E-mail: custserv@wiley.com
URL: http://www.wiley.com/WileyCDA/

Adele Lewis and David J. Moore. Second edition, 1993. $37.50; $19.95 (paper). 224 pages. Presents an extensive collection of scientific and engineering resumes, high-

lighting the important differences between these and resumes written for other occupations.

★4329★ **The I Hate Selling Book: Business-Building Advice for Consultants, Attorneys, Accountants, Engineers, Architects, and Other Professionals**
AMACOM
1601 Broadway, 12th Fl.
New York, NY 10019-7420
Ph: (212)586-8100   Fax: (212)903-8168
Fr: 800-262-9699
URL: http://www.amanet.org

Allan S. Boress. 2001. $29.95. 240 pages.

★4330★ **Keys to Engineering Success**
Prentice Hall PTR
One Lake St.
Upper Saddle River, NJ 07458
Ph: (201)236-7000   Fr: 800-428-5331
URL: http://www.phptr.com/index.asp?rl=1

Jill S. Tietjen, Kristy A. Schloss, Carol Carter, Joyce Bishop, and Sarah Lyman. 2000. $46.00 (paper). 288 pages.

★4331★ **The New Engineer's Guide to Career Growth & Professional Awareness**
Institute of Electrical & Electronics Engineers
445 Hoes Lane
Piscataway, NJ 08854
Ph: (732)981-0060   Fax: (732)981-9667
Fr: 800-678-4333
URL: http://www.ieee.org

Irving J. Gabelman, editor. 1996. $39.95 (paper). 275 pages.

★4332★ **On Becoming an Engineer: A Guide to Career Paths**
Institute of Electrical & Electronics Engineers
445 Hoes Lane
Piscataway, NJ 08854
Ph: (732)981-0060   Fax: (732)981-9667
Fr: 800-678-4333
URL: http://www.ieee.org

J. David Irwin. 1996. $19.95. 152 pages.

★4333★ **Opportunities in Electronics Careers**
The McGraw-Hill Companies
PO Box 182604
Columbus, OH 43272
Fax: (614)759-3749   Fr: 877-883-5524
E-mail: customer.service@mcgraw-hill.com
URL: http://www.mcgraw-hill.com

Mark Rowh. 2007. $13.95; $11.95 (paper). 221 pages. Discusses career opportunities in commercial and industrial electronics equipment repair, electronics home entertainment repair, electronics engineering, and engineering technology. Includes job outlook and how to get off to a good start on the job.

★4334★ **Opportunities in Engineering Careers**
The McGraw-Hill Companies
PO Box 182604
Columbus, OH 43272
Fax: (614)759-3749   Fr: 877-883-5524
E-mail: customer.service@mcgraw-hill.com
URL: http://www.mcgraw-hill.com

Nicholas Basta. Revised second edition, 2002. $13.95; $11.95 (paper). 160 pages. Outlines typical job titles, salaries, career paths, and employment prospects.

★4335★ **Opportunities in High Tech Careers**
The McGraw-Hill Companies
PO Box 182604
Columbus, OH 43272
Fax: (614)759-3749   Fr: 877-883-5524
E-mail: customer.service@mcgraw-hill.com
URL: http://www.mcgraw-hill.com

Gary Colter and Deborah Yanuck. 1999. $14.95; $11.95 (paper). 160 pages. Explores high technology careers. Describes job opportunities, how to make a career decision, how to prepare for high technology jobs, job hunting techniques, and future trends.

★4336★ **Opportunities in Research and Development Careers**
The McGraw-Hill Companies
PO Box 182604
Columbus, OH 43272
Fax: (614)759-3749   Fr: 877-883-5524
E-mail: customer.service@mcgraw-hill.com
URL: http://www.mcgraw-hill.com

Jan Goldberg. 1996. $11.95 (paper). 146 pages.

★4337★ **Real People Working in Engineering**
The McGraw-Hill Companies
PO Box 182604
Columbus, OH 43272
Fax: (614)759-3749   Fr: 877-883-5524
E-mail: customer.service@mcgraw-hill.com
URL: http://www.mcgraw-hill.com

Blythe Camenson, Jan Goldberg. 1997. $17.95 (paper). 160 pages. Interviews and profiles of working professionals capture a range of opportunities in this field.

★4338★ **Resumes for Engineering Careers**
The McGraw-Hill Companies
PO Box 182604
Columbus, OH 43272
Fax: (614)759-3749   Fr: 877-883-5524
E-mail: customer.service@mcgraw-hill.com
URL: http://www.mcgraw-hill.com

Third edition, 2005. $11.95 (paper). 144 pages. Contains sample resumes and cover letters applicable to any engineering field.

★4339★ Resumes for Scientific and Technical Careers

The McGraw-Hill Companies
PO Box 182604
Columbus, OH 43272
Fax: (614)759-3749   Fr: 877-883-5524
E-mail: customer.service@mcgraw-hill.com
URL: http://www.mcgraw-hill.com

Third edition, 2007. $12.95 (paper). 144 pages. Provides resume advice for individuals interested in working in scientific and technical careers. Includes sample resumes and cover letters.

EMPLOYMENT AGENCIES AND SEARCH FIRMS

★4340★ The Aspire Group

52 Second Ave, 1st Fl
Waltham, MA 02451-1129
Fax: (718)890-1810   Fr: 800-487-2967
URL: http://www.bmanet.com

Employment agency.

★4341★ The Bedford Group

3343 Peachtree Rd. NE, Ste. 333
Atlanta, GA 30326
Ph: (404)237-7471   Fax: (404)846-2172
E-mail: bed-ford@bedfordgroupconsulting.com
URL: http://www.bedfordgroupconsulting.com

Executive search firm.

★4342★ Bell Oaks Co.

10 Glenlake Pkwy., Ste. 300
Atlanta, GA 30328
Ph: (678)287-2000   Fax: (678)287-2002
E-mail: info@belloaks.com
URL: http://www.belloaks.com

Personnel service firm.

★4343★ Claremont-Branan, Inc.

1298 Rockbridge Rd., Ste. B
Stone Mountain, GA 30087
Ph: (770)925-2915   Fax: (770)925-2601
Fr: 800-875-1292
E-mail: ohil@cbisearch.com
URL: http://cbisearch.com

Employment agency. Executive search firm.

★4344★ Colli Associates

414 Caboose Ln.
Valrico, FL 33594
Ph: (813)681-2145   Fax: (813)661-5217
E-mail: colli@gte.net

Employment agency. Executive search firm.

★4345★ Electronic Careers

21355 Pacific Coast Hwy., Ste. 100
Malibu, CA 90265
Ph: (310)317-6113   Fax: (310)317-6119
E-mail: E-Careers@ElectronicCareers.com
URL: http://www.electroniccareers.com

Executive search firm.

★4346★ Engineer One, Inc.

PO Box 23037
Knoxville, TN 37933
Fax: (865)691-0110
E-mail: engineerone@engineerone.com
URL: http://www.engineerone.com

Engineering employment service specializes in engineering and management in the chemical process, power utilities, manufacturing, mechanical, electrical, and electronic industries. Established an Information Technology Division in 1998 that works nationwide across all industries. Also provides systems analysis consulting services specializing in VAX based systems.

★4347★ Executive Recruiters Agency

14 Office Park Dr., Ste. 100
PO Box 21810
Little Rock, AR 72221-1810
Ph: (501)224-7000   Fax: (501)224-8534
E-mail: jobs@execrecruit.com
URL: http://www.execrecruit.com

Personnel service firm.

★4348★ Global Employment Solutions

10375 Park Meadows Dr., Ste. 375
Littleton, CO 80124
Ph: (303)216-9500   Fax: (303)216-9533
E-mail: careers@global
URL: http://www.gesnetwork.com

Employment agency.

★4349★ James Bangert & Associates Inc.

15500 Wayzata Blvd.
Wayzata, MN 55391
Ph: (952)475-3454   Fax: (952)473-4306
E-mail: jab@bangertassoc.com

Executive search firm.

★4350★ Rand Personnel

1200 Truxtun Ave., Ste. 130
Bakersfield, CA 93301
Ph: (805)325-0751   Fax: (805)325-4120

Personnel service firm serving a variety of fields.

★4351★ Search and Recruit International

4455 South Blvd. Ste. 110
Virginia Beach, VA 23452
Ph: (757)625-2121   Fr: 800-800-5627

Employment agency. Headquartered in Virginia Beach. Other offices in Bremerton, WA; Charleston, SC; Jacksonville, FL; Memphis,

TN; Pensacola, FL; Sacramento, CA; San Bernardino, CA; San Diego, CA.

★4352★ Technical Talent Locators Ltd.

5570 Sterrett Pl., Ste. 208
Columbia, MD 21044
Ph: (410)740-0091
E-mail: steve@ttlgroup.com
URL: http://www.ttlgroup.com

Permanent employment agency working within the following fields: software and database engineering; computer, communication, and telecommunication system engineering; and other computer-related disciplines.

★4353★ Trambley the Recruiter

5325 Wyoming Blvd. NE
Albuquerque, NM 87109-3132
Ph: (505)821-5440   Fax: (505)821-8509

Personnel consultancy firm recruits and places engineering professionals in specific areas of off-road equipment design and manufacturing. Industries served: construction, agricultural, lawn and garden, oil exploration and mining equipment manufacturing.

★4354★ Tri-Serv Inc.

22 W. Padonia Rd., Ste. C-353
Timonium, MD 21093
Ph: (410)561-1740   Fax: (410)252-7417
E-mail: info@tri-serv.coom
URL: http://www.tri-serv.com

Employment agency for technical personnel.

★4355★ TSS Consulting Ltd.

14700 N Airport Dr., Ste. 117
Scottsdale, AZ 85260
Fax: (480)951-6261   Fr: 800-489-2425
E-mail: john@tss-consulting.com
URL: http://www.tss-consulting.com

A technical executive search and consulting firm as a boutique executive search firm, specializes in technical contributor and management or executive level electrical engineer searches for venture-backed start-ups. A requirement-driven search organization specializing in critical-need response.

ONLINE JOB SOURCES AND SERVICES

★4356★ Spherion

2050 Spectrum Blvd.
Fort Lauderdale, FL 33309
Ph: (954)308-7600
E-mail: help@spherion.com
URL: http://www.spherion.com

Description: Recruitment firm specializing in accounting and finance, sales and marketing, interim executives, technology, engineering, retail and human resources.

TRADESHOWS

★4357★ American Society for Engineering Education Annual Conference and Exposition

American Society for Engineering Education
1818 N. St. NW, Ste. 600
Washington, DC 20036-2479
Ph: (202)331-3500   Fax: (202)265-8504
E-mail: conferences@asee.org
URL: http://www.asee.org

Annual. **Primary Exhibits:** Publications, engineering supplies and equipment, computers, software, and research companies all products and services related to engineering education.

★4358★ Electronic Imaging International - part of Photonics East

SPIE - International Society for Optical Engineering
PO Box 10
Bellingham, WA 98227-0010
Ph: (360)676-3290   Fax: (360)647-1445
E-mail: spie@spie.org
URL: http://www.spie.org

Annual. **Primary Exhibits:** Equipment, supplies, and services for image processing computer graphics, fiber optics, high definition television, electronic printing and publishing, military electronics, medical tomography industries, and electronic imaging products.

★4359★ PCB Design Conference West

CMP Media LLC (San Mateo)
2800 Campus Dr.
San Mateo, CA 94403
Ph: (650)513-4300
E-mail: cmp@cmp.com
URL: http://www.cmp.com

Annual. **Primary Exhibits:** To provide circuit board designers education and information about the industry, including tools and techniques.

OTHER SOURCES

★4360★ Aircraft Electronics Association (AEA)

4217 S Hocker
Independence, MO 64055-0963
Ph: (816)373-6565   Fax: (816)478-3100
E-mail: info@aea.net
URL: http://www.aea.net

Members: Companies engaged in the sales, engineering, installation, and service of electronic aviation equipment and systems. **Purpose:** Seeks to: advance the science of aircraft electronics; promote uniform and stable regulations and uniform standards of performance; establish and maintain a code of ethics; gather and disseminate technical data; advance the education of members and the public in the science of aircraft electronics. **Activities:** Offers supplement type certificates, test equipment licensing, temporary FCC licensing for new installations, spare parts availability and pricing, audiovisual technician training, equipment and spare parts loan, profitable installation, and service facility operation. Provides employment information, equipment exchange information and service assistance on member installations anywhere in the world.

★4361★ American Almanac of Jobs and Salaries

HarperCollins
10 E. 53rd St.
New York, NY 10022
Ph: (212)207-7000   Fr: 800-242-7737
URL: http://www.harpercollins.com/

John W. Wright. Revised edition, 2000. $20.00 (paper). 672 pages. This is a comprehensive guide to the wages of hundreds of occupations in a wide variety of industries and organizations.

★4362★ American Association of Engineering Societies (AAES)

1620 I St. NW, Ste. 210
Washington, DC 20006
Ph: (202)296-2237   Fax: (202)296-1151
Fr: 888-400-2237
E-mail: dbateson@aaes.org
URL: http://www.aaes.org

Description: Coordinates the efforts of the member societies in the provision of reliable and objective information to the general public concerning issues which affect the engineering profession and the field of engineering as a whole; collects, analyzes, documents, and disseminates data which will inform the general public of the relationship between engineering and the national welfare; provides a forum for the engineering societies to exchange and discuss their views on matters of common interest; and represents the U.S. engineering community abroad through representation in WFEO and UPADI.

★4363★ ASPRS - The Imaging and Geospatial Information Society

5410 Grosvenor Ln., Ste. 210
Bethesda, MD 20814-2160
Ph: (301)493-0290   Fax: (301)493-0208
E-mail: asprs@asprs.org
URL: http://www.asprs.org

Members: Firms, individuals, government employees and academicians engaged in photogrammetry, photointerpretation, remote sensing, and geographic information systems and their application to such fields as archaeology, geographic information systems, military reconnaissance, urban planning, engineering, traffic surveys, meteorological observations, medicine, geology, forestry, agriculture, construction and topographic mapping. Mission is to advance knowledge and improve understanding of these sciences and to promote responsible applications. **Activities:** Offers voluntary certification program open to persons associated with one or more functional area of photogrammetry, remote sensing and GIS. Surveys the profession of private firms in photogrammetry and remote sensing in the areas of products and services.

★4364★ Association for International Practical Training (AIPT)

10400 Little Patuxent Pkwy., Ste. 250
Columbia, MD 21044-3519
Ph: (410)997-2200   Fax: (410)992-3924
E-mail: aipt@aipt.org
URL: http://www.aipt.org

Description: Providers worldwide of on-the-job training programs for students and professionals seeking international career development and life-changing experiences. Arranges workplace exchanges in hundreds of professional fields, bringing employers and trainees together from around the world. Client list ranges from small farming communities to Fortune 500 companies.

★4365★ Electronic Industries Alliance (EIA)

2500 Wilson Blvd.
Arlington, VA 22201
Ph: (703)907-7500
E-mail: mflanigan@eia.org
URL: http://www.eia.org

Description: Seeks for the competitiveness of the American producer, represents all companies involved in the design and manufacture of electronic components, parts, systems and equipment for communications, industrial, government and consumer uses.

★4366★ Engineering Occupations

Delphi Productions
3159 6th St.
Boulder, CO 80304
Ph: (303)443-2100   Fax: (303)443-4022
Fr: 888-443-2400
E-mail: support@delphivideo.com
URL: http://www.delphivideo.com

$95.00. 50 minutes. Part of the Careers for the 21st Century Video Library.

★4367★ Institute of Electrical and Electronics Engineers (IEEE)

445 Hoes Ln.
Piscataway, NJ 08854
Ph: (732)981-0060   Fax: (732)981-1721
Fr: 800-678-4333
E-mail: corporate-communications@ieee.org
URL: http://www.ieee.org

Description: Promotes the advancement of technology. Consists of engineers and scientists in electrical engineering, electronics, computer sciences and allied fields. Publishes 30 percent of the world's literature in the electrical and electronics engineering and computer science fields, and has developed nearly 900 active industry standards.

★4368★ International Microelectronic and Packaging Society (IMAPS)

611 2nd St. NE
Washington, DC 20002-4909
Ph: (202)548-4001   Fax: (202)548-6115
E-mail: imaps@imaps.org
URL: http://www.imaps.org

Description: Electronics engineers and specialists in industry, business, and education. Encourages the exchange of information across boundaries of fields of specialization; supports close interactions between the complementary technologies of ceramics, thick and thin films, semiconductor packaging, discrete semiconductor devices, and monolithic circuits. Promotes and assists in the development and expansion of microelectronics instruction in schools and departments of electrical and electronic engineering. Conducts seminars at international, national, regional, and chapter levels.

★4369★ ISA - Instrumentation, Systems, and Automation Society

67 Alexander Dr.
PO Box 12277
Research Triangle Park, NC 27709
Ph: (919)549-8411   Fax: (919)549-8288
E-mail: info@isa.org
URL: http://www.isa.org

Description: Sets the standard for automation by helping over 30,000 worldwide members and other professionals solve difficult technical problems, while enhancing their leadership and personal career capabilities. Develops standards; certifies industry professionals; provides education and training; publishes books and technical articles; and hosts the largest conference and exhibition for automation professionals in the Western Hemisphere. Is the founding sponsor of The Automation Federation.

★4370★ National Action Council for Minorities in Engineering (NACME)

440 Hamilton Ave., Ste. 302
White Plains, NY 10601-1813
Ph: (914)539-4010   Fax: (914)539-4032

E-mail: webmaster@nacme.org
URL: http://www.nacme.org

Description: Leads the national effort to increase access to careers in engineering and other science-based disciplines. Conducts research and public policy analysis, develops and operates national demonstration programs at precollege and university levels, and disseminates information through publications, conferences and electronic media. Serves as a privately funded source of scholarships for minority students in engineering.

★4371★ National Society of Professional Engineers (NSPE)

1420 King St.
Alexandria, VA 22314-2794
Ph: (703)684-2800   Fax: (703)836-4875
Fr: 888-285-6773
E-mail: memserv@nspe.org
URL: http://www.nspe.org

Description: Represents professional engineers and engineers-in-training in all fields registered in accordance with the laws of states or territories of the U.S. or provinces of Canada; qualified graduate engineers, student members, and registered land surveyors. Is concerned with social, professional, ethical, and economic considerations of engineering as a profession; encompasses programs in public relations, employment practices, ethical considerations, education, and career guidance. Monitors legislative and regulatory actions of interest to the engineering profession.

★4372★ Scientific, Engineering, and Technical Services

Cambridge Educational
PO Box 2053
Princeton, NJ 08543-2053
Ph: 800-257-5126   Fax: (609)671-0266
Fr: 800-468-4227
E-mail: custserv@films.com
URL: http://www.cambridgeeducational.com

VHS and DVD. $89.95. 2002. 18 minutes. 2002. Part of the Career Cluster Series.

★4373★ Society of Women Engineers (SWE)

230 E Ohio St., Ste. 400
Chicago, IL 60611-3265
Ph: (312)596-5223   Fax: (312)596-5252
Fr: 877-SWE-INFO
E-mail: hq@swe.org
URL: http://www.swe.org

Description: Educational and service organization representing both students and professional women in engineering and technical fields.

★4374★ SPIE - The International Society for Optical Engineering (SPIE)

PO Box 10
Bellingham, WA 98227-0010
Ph: (360)676-3290   Fax: (360)647-1445
Fr: 888-504-8171
E-mail: customerservice@spie.org
URL: http://www.spie.org

Description: Advances scientific research and engineering applications of optical, photonic, imaging and optoelectronic technologies through meetings, education programs and publications.

★4375★ Women in Engineering

Her Own Words
PO Box 5264
Madison, WI 53705-0264
Ph: (608)271-7083   Fax: (608)271-0209
E-mail: herownword@aol.com
URL: http://www.herownwords.com/

Video. Jocelyn Riley. $95.00. 15 minutes. Resource guide also available for $45.00.

Electricians

SOURCES OF HELP-WANTED ADS

★4376★ Builder
Hanley-Wood L.L.C.
1 Thomas Cir., NW, Ste. 600
Washington, DC 20005
Ph: (202)452-0800   Fax: (202)785-1974
URL: http://www.hanleywood.com/default.aspx?page=b2bbd

$29.95/year for individuals, 13 issues; $54.95/year for Canada, 26 issues; $192.00/year for out of country, 13 issues. Magazine covering housing and construction industry.

★4377★ Constructor
Associated General Contractors of America
2300 Wilson Blvd., Ste. 400
Arlington, VA 22201
Ph: (703)548-3118   Fax: (703)548-3119
URL: http://www.agc.org

Monthly. Management magazine for the Construction Industry.

★4378★ Electric Light & Power
PennWell Corp.
1421 S Sheridan Rd.
Tulsa, OK 74112
Ph: (918)835-3161   Fr: 800-331-4463
URL: http://uaelp.pennnet.com

Bimonthly. $76.00/year for individuals, 1 year; $129.00/year for two years; $85.00/year for Canada and Mexico, 1 year; $143.00/year for Canada and Mexico, 2 years; $210.00/year for other countries, 1 year; $374.00/year for other countries, 2 years; $12.00/year for single issue; $20.00 for single issue, Canada/Mexico; $20.00/year for single issue, international; $60.00/year for individuals, schools & public libraries. Provides broad view of electric utility industry with in-depth analysis of key business issues for executives and management.

★4379★ Engineering Economist
Institute of Industrial Engineers
3577 Parkway Ln., Ste. 200
Norcross, GA 30092
Ph: (770)449-0460   Fax: (770)441-3295
Fr: 800-494-0460
URL: http://www.iienet2.org/Details.aspx?id=1486

Quarterly. $73.00/year for individuals; $129.00/year for institutions, online only; $136.00/year for institutions, print & online; $82.00/year for institutions, print + online; $77.00/year for institutions, online only. Publication covering business issues in the energy, petroleum and mining industries.

★4380★ The High-Tech News
ETA International
5 Depot St.
Greencastle, IN 46135
Ph: (765)653-8262   Fax: (765)653-4287
Fr: 800-288-3824
E-mail: eta@eta-i.org
URL: http://www.eta-i.org

Description: Monthly. Serves member technicians with news of the Association and the electronics industry, including items on service, education, employment, management, and events. Contains information on membership, management, telecommunications, and business and technical training programs. Recurring features include editorials, news of research, letters to the editor, book reviews, and a calendar of events.

★4381★ Professional Builder
Reed Business Information
360 Park Ave. S
New York, NY 10010
Ph: (646)746-6400   Fax: (646)746-7431
E-mail: ncrum@reedbusiness.com
URL: http://www.housingzone.com/toc-archive-pbx

Monthly. Free. The integrated engineering magazine of the building construction industry.

★4382★ WIT
Vermont Works for Women
51 Park St.
Essex Junction, VT 05452
Ph: (802)878-0004   Fax: (802)878-0050
Fr: 800-639-1472
URL: http://www.nnetw.org/

Description: Three issues/year. Provides a network of support, information, and skill sharing for women in skilled trades professions.

PLACEMENT AND JOB REFERRAL SERVICES

★4383★ National Association of Home Builders (NAHB)
1201 15th St. NW
Washington, DC 20005
Ph: (202)266-8200   Fax: (202)266-8400
Fr: 800-368-5242
E-mail: info@nahb.com
URL: http://www.nahb.org

Description: Single and multifamily home builders, commercial builders, and others associated with the building industry. Lobbies on behalf of the housing industry and conducts public affairs activities to increase public understanding of housing and the economy. Collects and disseminates data on current developments in home building and home builders' plans through its Economics Department and nationwide Metropolitan Housing Forecast. Maintains NAHB Research Center, which functions as the research arm of the home building industry. Sponsors seminars and workshops on construction, mortgage credit, labor relations, cost reduction, land use, remodeling, and business management. Compiles statistics; offers charitable program, spokesman training, and placement service; maintains speakers' bureau, and Hall of Fame. Subsidiaries include the National Council of the Housing Industry. Maintains over 50 committees in many areas of construction; operates National Commercial Builders Council, National Council of the Multifamily Housing

Industry, National Remodelers Council, and National Sales and Marketing Council.

EMPLOYER DIRECTORIES AND NETWORKING LISTS

★4384★ ABC Today-Associated Builders and Contractors National Membership Directory Issue

Associated Builders & Contractors Inc.
4250 N Fairfax Dr., 9th Fl.
Arlington, VA 22203-1607
Ph: (703)812-2000   Fax: (703)812-8203
URL: http://www.abc.org/
wmspage.cfm?parm1=2033

Annual, December. $150.00. Publication includes: List of approximately 19,000 member construction contractors and suppliers. Entries include: Company name, address, phone, name of principal executive, code to volume of business, business specialty. Arrangement: Classified by chapter, then by work specialty.

★4385★ Buyer's Guide & Membership Directory

Independent Electrical Contractors Inc.
4401 Ford Ave., Ste. 1100
Alexandria, VA 22302-1432
Ph: (703)549-7351   Fax: (703)549-7448
Fr: 800-456-4324
URL: http://www.ieci.org

Annual. Covers member electrical contracting firms, electrical manufacturers, and distributors. Entries include: Name of company, address, names of principals. Arrangement: Geographical.

★4386★ Constructor-AGC Directory of Membership and Services Issue

AGC Information Inc.
2300 Wilson Blvd., Ste. 400
Arlington, VA 22201
Ph: (703)548-3118   Fax: (703)548-3119
Fr: 800-282-1423
URL: http://www.agc.org

Annual, August; latest edition 2004 edition. Publication includes: List of over 8,500 member firms and 24,000 national associate member firms engaged in building, highway, heavy, industrial, municipal utilities, and railroad construction (SIC 1541, 1542, 1611, 1622, 1623, 1629); listing of state and local chapter officers. Entries include: For firms–Company name, address, phone, fax, names of principal executives, and code indicating type of construction undertaken. For officers–Name, title, address. Arrangement: Geographical, alphabetical. Indexes: Company name.

★4387★ ENR-Top 400 Construction Contractors Issue

McGraw-Hill Inc.
1221 Ave. of the Americas
New York, NY 10020-1095
Ph: (212)512-2000   Fax: (212)512-3840
Fr: 877-833-5524
URL: http://construction.ecnext.com/coms2/
summary_0249-137077_ITM

Annual; 22nd, May 2006. $35.00 for individuals. Publication includes: List of 400 United States contractors receiving largest dollar volumes of contracts in preceding calendar year. Separate lists of 50 largest design/construction management firms; 50 largest program and construction managers; 25 building contractors; 25 heavy contractors. Entries include: Company name, headquarters location, total value of contracts received in preceding year, value of foreign contracts, countries in which operated, construction specialities. Arrangement: By total value of contracts received.

★4388★ International Association of Electrical Inspectors-Membership Directory

International Association of Electrical Inspectors
901 Waterfall Way, Ste. 602
Richardson, TX 75080-7702
Ph: (972)235-1455   Fax: (972)235-6858
URL: http://www.iaei.org/

Annual, April. Covers 26,000 state and federal government, industrial, utility, and insurance electrical inspectors, and, as associate members, electricians, manufacturers, engineers, architects, and wiremen. Entries include: Name, title, type of member, address, company affiliation. Arrangement: Geographical, then by division, chapter, or section, and type of membership, then alphabetical. Indexes: Committees; personal name.

HANDBOOKS AND MANUALS

★4389★ Audel Questions and Answers for Electricians' Examinations

Hungry Minds, Inc.
10475 Crosspoint Blvd.
Indianapolis, IN 46256
Fax: (317)572-4000   Fr: 800-667-1115
Paul Rosenberg. Revised, 2003. $24.99. 312 pages.

★4390★ Electrician's Exam Preparation Guide

Craftsman Book Co.
6058 Corte del Cedro
Carlsbad, CA 92011
Ph: (760)438-7828   Fax: (760)438-0398
Fr: 800-829-8123
URL: http://www.craftsman-book.com/
John E. Traister, updated by Dale Brickner. 2005. $39.50 (paper). 352 pages. Covers every area of electrical installation: electrical

drawings, services and systems, transformers, capacitors, distribution equipment branch circuits, feeders, calculations, measuring and testing, and more. Updated to the 2005 NEC.

★4391★ Electricity for the Trades

McGraw-Hill
PO Box 182604
Columbus, OH 43272
Fax: (614)759-3749   Fr: 877-833-5524
E-mail: customer.service@mcgraw-hill.com
URL: http://www.mcgraw-hill.com/edu/default.shtml

Frank D. Petruzella. 2005. $61.25. Resource for students in basic electricity trades.

★4392★ Exploring Careers as an Electrician

Rosen Publishing Group Inc.
29 E. 21st St.
New York, NY 10010
Ph: (212)777-3017   Fax: 888-436-4643
Fr: 800-237-9932
URL: http://www.rosenpublishing.com/

Elizabeth S. Lytle. Revised edition, 1999. $18.95. 114 pages. Details the steps one takes in becoming an electrician, starting with apprenticeship and ending with full-time electrician work.

★4393★ Opportunities in Building Construction Trades

The McGraw-Hill Companies
PO Box 182604
Columbus, OH 43272
Fax: (614)759-3749   Fr: 877-883-5524
E-mail: customer.service@mcgraw-hill.com
URL: http://www.mcgraw-hill.com

Michael Sumichrast. Second edition, 1998. $14.95; $11.95 (paper). 104 pages. From custom builder to rehabber, the many kinds of companies that employ craftspeople and contractors are explored. Includes job descriptions, requirements, and salaries for dozens of specialties within the construction industry. Contains a complete list of Bureau of Apprenticeship and Training state and area offices. Illustrated.

★4394★ Opportunities in Electrical Trades

The McGraw-Hill Companies
PO Box 182604
Columbus, OH 43272
Fax: (614)759-3749   Fr: 877-883-5524
E-mail: customer.service@mcgraw-hill.com
URL: http://www.mcgraw-hill.com

Robert Wood and Kenneth R. Edwards. 1996. $14.95; $11.95 (paper). 145 pages. Offers advice on job hunting and where the jobs are. Includes index, bibliography, and illustrations.

TRADESHOWS

★4395★ **AMRA International Symposium**

Automatic Meter Reading Association
60 Revere Dr., Ste. 500
Northbrook, IL 60062
Ph: (847)480-9628   Fax: (847)480-9282
Fr: 888-612-2672
E-mail: amra@amra-intl.org
URL: http://www.amra-intl.org

Annual. **Primary Exhibits:** Utilities meter reading equipment, supplies, and services.

★4396★ **Edison Electric Institute Convention and Expo**

Edison Electric Institute
701 Pennsylvania Ave. NW
Washington, DC 20004-2696
Ph: (202)508-5714   Fax: (202)508-5759
E-mail: eblume@eei.org
URL: http://www.eei.org

Annual. **Primary Exhibits:** Exhibits directed to investor-owned electric utility companies operating in the U.S. and abroad.

★4397★ **Electric Expo**

Comprehensive Show Management, Inc.
PO Box 297
Springfield, PA 19064
Ph: (610)544-5775   Fax: (610)544-9808
E-mail: sally.oshea@verizon.net

Biennial. **Primary Exhibits:** Electrical equipment, supplies, and services.

★4398★ **Electri...FYI - Upstate Electrical Show**

Electrical Association of Rochester
PO Box 20219
Rochester, NY 14602
Ph: (585)538-6350   Fax: (585)538-6166
E-mail: info@earoch.com
URL: http://www.earoch.com

Triennial. **Primary Exhibits:** Electrical supplies and services.

★4399★ **ICCON - International Commercial Construction Exposition**

National Association of Home Builders of the United States
1201 15th St. NW
Washington, DC 20005
Ph: (202)266-8200   Fax: (202)266-8223
Fr: 800-368-5242
E-mail: exposales@nahb.com
URL: http://www.nahb.org

Annual. **Primary Exhibits:** Equipment, supplies, and services for the construction industries.

★4400★ **Independent Electrical Contractors Annual Convention and Expo**

Independent Electrical Contractors' Association
4401 Ford Ave. Ste 1100
Alexandria, VA 22302
Ph: (703)549-7351   Fax: (703)549-7448
Fr: 800-456-4324
E-mail: info@ieci.org
URL: http://www.ieci.org

Annual. **Primary Exhibits:** Equipment, supplies, and services for independent electrical contractors.

★4401★ **The NECA Show**

National Electrical Contractors Association
3 Bethesda Metro Center, Ste. 1100
Bethesda, MD 20814
Ph: (301)657-3110   Fax: (301)215-4500
URL: http://www.necanet.org

Annual. **Primary Exhibits:** Electrical products, publications, computers, software, tools, and equipment.

★4402★ **Upper Midwest Electrical Expo**

North Central Electrical League
2901 Metro Dr. Ste. 203
Bloomington, MN 55425-1556
Ph: (952)854-4405   Fax: (952)854-7076
Fr: 800-925-4985
E-mail: dale@ncel.org
URL: http://www.ncel.org

Biennial. **Primary Exhibits:** Electrical equipment, supplies, and services.

OTHER SOURCES

★4403★ **Associated Builders and Contractors (ABC)**

4250 N Fairfax Dr., 9th Fl.
Arlington, VA 22203-1607
Ph: (703)812-2000   Fax: (703)812-8200
E-mail: gotquestions@abc.org
URL: http://www.abc.org

Description: Construction contractors, subcontractors, suppliers, and associates. Aims to foster and perpetuate the principles of rewarding construction workers and management on the basis of merit. Sponsors management education programs and craft training; also sponsors apprenticeship and skill training programs. Disseminates technological and labor relations information.

★4404★ **Associated General Contractors of America (AGC)**

2300 Wilson Blvd., Ste. 400
Arlington, VA 22201
Ph: (703)548-3118   Fax: (703)548-3119
Fr: 800-242-1767
E-mail: info@agc.org
URL: http://www.agc.org

Description: General construction contractors; subcontractors; industry suppliers; service firms. Provides market services through its divisions. Conducts special conferences and seminars designed specifically for construction firms. Compiles statistics on job accidents reported by member firms. Maintains 65 committees, including joint cooperative committees with other associations and liaison committees with federal agencies.

★4405★ **Associated Specialty Contractors (ASC)**

3 Bethesda Metro Ctr., Ste. 1100
Bethesda, MD 20814
Ph: (703)548-3118
E-mail: dgw@necanet.org
URL: http://www.assoc-spec-con.org

Description: Works to promote efficient management and productivity. Coordinates the work of specialized branches of the industry in management information, research, public information, government relations and construction relations. Serves as a liaison among specialty trade associations in the areas of public relations, government relations, and with other organizations. Seeks to avoid unnecessary duplication of effort and expense or conflicting programs among affiliates. Identifies areas of interest and problems shared by members, and develops positions and approaches on such problems.

★4406★ **Building Trades**

Delphi Productions
3159 6th St.
Boulder, CO 80304
Ph: (303)443-2100   Fax: (303)443-4022
Fr: 888-443-2400
E-mail: support@delphivideo.com
URL: http://www.delphivideo.com

$95.00. 46 minutes. Part of the Careers for the 21st Century Video Library.

★4407★ **COIN Career Guidance System**

COIN Educational Products
3361 Executive Pky., Ste. 302
Toledo, OH 43606
Ph: (419)536-5353   Fax: (419)536-7056
Fr: 800-274-8515
URL: http://www.coinedu.com/

CD-ROM. Provides career information through seven cross-referenced files covering postsecondary schools, college majors, vocational programs, military service, apprenticeship programs, financial aid, and scholarships. Apprenticeship file describes national apprenticeship training programs, including information on how to apply, contact agencies, and program content. Military file describes more than 200 military occupations and training opportunities related to civilian employment.

★4408★ Independent Electrical Contractors (IEC)

4401 Ford Ave., Ste. 1100
Alexandria, VA 22302-1432
Ph: (703)549-7351 Fax: (703)549-7448
Fr: 800-456-4324
E-mail: info@ieci.org
URL: http://www.ieci.org

Members: Independent electrical contractors, small and large, primarily open shop. **Purpose:** Promotes the interests of members; works to eliminate "unwise and unfair business practices" and to protect its members against "unfair or unjust taxes and legislative enactments." **Activities:** Sponsors electrical apprenticeship programs; conducts educational programs on cost control and personnel motivation. Represents independent electrical contractors to the National Electrical Code panel. Conducts surveys on volume of sales and purchases and on type of products used. Has formulated National Pattern Standards for Apprentice Training for Electricians.

★4409★ National Association of Women in Construction (NAWIC)

327 S Adams St.
Fort Worth, TX 76104
Ph: (817)877-5551 Fax: (817)877-0324
Fr: 800-552-3506
E-mail: nawic@nawic.org
URL: http://www.nawic.org

Description: Seeks to enhance the success of women in the construction industry.

★4410★ National Electrical Contractors Association (NECA)

3 Bethesda Metro Ctr., Ste. 1100
Bethesda, MD 20814
Ph: (301)657-3110 Fax: (301)215-4500
E-mail: webmaster@necanet.org
URL: http://www.necanet.org

Members: Contractors erecting, installing, repairing, servicing, and maintaining electric wiring, equipment, and appliances. **Activities:** Provides management services and labor relations programs for electrical contractors; conducts seminars for contractor sales and training. Conducts research and educational programs; compiles statistics. Sponsors honorary society, the Academy of Electrical Contracting.

★4411★ Women in Building Construction

Her Own Words
PO Box 5264
Madison, WI 53705-0264
Ph: (608)271-7083 Fax: (608)271-0209
E-mail: herownword@aol.com
URL: http://www.herownwords.com/

Video. Jocelyn Riley. $95.00. 15 minutes. Resource guide also available for $45.00.

Emergency Medical Technicians

★4422★ Hospitals & Health Networks

Health Forum L.L.C.
1 N Franklin, 29th Fl.
Chicago, IL 60606
Ph: (312)893-6800   Fax: (312)422-4506
Fr: 800-821-2039
URL: http://www.hhnmag.com

Weekly. Publication covering the health care industry.

★4423★ The IHS Primary Care Provider

Indian Health Service (HQ)
The Reyes Bldg.
801 Thompson Ave., Ste. 400
Rockville, MD 20852-1627
URL: http://www.ihs.gov/PublicInfo/Publications/HealthProvider/Pr

Monthly. Journal for health care professionals, physicians, nurses, pharmacists, dentists, and dietitians.

★4424★ Injury

Mosby Inc.
11830 Westline Industrial Dr.
St. Louis, MO 63146
Ph: (314)872-8370   Fax: (314)432-1380
Fr: 800-325-4177
URL: http://www.elsevier.com/wps/find/journaldescription.cws_home

Monthly. $1,106.00/year for institutions, all countries except Europe, Japan and Iran; $169.00/year for individuals, all countries except Europe, Japan and Iran. Journal publishing articles and research related to the treatment of injuries such as trauma systems and management; surgical procedures; epidemiological studies; surgery (of all tissues); resuscitation; biomechanics; rehabilitation; anaesthesia; radiology and wound management.

★4425★ Intensive and Critical Care Nursing

Mosby Inc.
11830 Westline Industrial Dr.
St. Louis, MO 63146
Ph: (314)872-8370   Fax: (314)432-1380
Fr: 800-325-4177
URL: http://www.us.elsevierhealth.com/product.jsp?isbn=09643397&r

Bimonthly. $92.00/year for individuals, international; $422.00/year for institutions, international; $92.00/year for individuals; $422.00/year for institutions. Journal for nurses in intensive and critical care nursing.

★4426★ The Internet Journal of Emergency Medicine

Internet Scientific Publications L.L.C.
23 Rippling Creek Dr.
Sugar Land, TX 77479
Ph: (832)443-1193   Fax: (281)240-1532
URL: http://www.ispub.com/ostia/index.php?xmlFilePath=journals/ij

Free, online. Electronic journal for medical professionals focusing on the field of emergency medicine.

★4427★ Journal of the American Society of Podiatric Medical Assistants

American Society of Podiatric Medical Assistants
2124 S Austin Blvd.
Cicero, IL 60804
Ph: (708)863-6303   Fr: 888-882-7762
URL: http://www.aspma.org

Quarterly. Subscription included in membership. Professional journal covering issues in podiatry.

★4428★ Journal of Health Law

American Health Lawyers Association
1025 Connecticut Ave., NW, Ste. 600
Washington, DC 20036-5405
Ph: (202)833-1100   Fax: (202)833-1105
URL: http://www.healthlawyers.org

Quarterly. Professional journal covering healthcare issues and cases and their impact on the health care arena.

★4429★ Journal of Hospital Medicine

John Wiley & Sons Inc.
111 River St.
Hoboken, NJ 07030-5774
Ph: (201)748-6000   Fax: (201)748-6088
Fr: 800-825-7550
URL: http://www.wiley.com/WileyCDA/WileyTitle/productCd-JHM.html

Bimonthly. $110.00/year for individuals, print only; Online version available with subscription. Journal on hospital medicine.

★4430★ Medical Risks

Taylor & Francis Group Journals
325 Chestnut St., Ste. 800
Philadelphia, PA 19106
Ph: (215)625-8900   Fax: (215)625-8914
Fr: 800-354-1420
URL: http://www.tandf.co.uk

Monthly. Journal covering articles on medical risks.

★4431★ Medical Staff Development Professional

American Academy of Medical Management
Crossville Commons
560 W Crossville Rd., Ste. 103
Roswell, GA 30075
Ph: (770)649-7150   Fax: (770)649-7552

Periodic. Professional journal covering medical education.

★4432★ The Municipality

League of Wisconsin Municipalities
122 W Washington Ave., Ste. 300
Madison, WI 53703-2718
Ph: (608)267-2380   Fax: (608)267-0645
Fr: 800-991-5502
URL: http://www.lwm-info.org/index.asp?Type=B_BASIC&SEC=¢0702EE8F

Monthly. Magazine for officials of Wisconsin's local municipal governments.

★4433★ NAFAC News

National Association for Ambulatory Urgent Care
2000 Plymouth Rd., Ste. 130
Hopkins, MN 55305
Ph: (612)476-0015   Fax: (612)476-0646
Fr: (866)793-1396
URL: http://www.urgentcare.org

Description: Reports on issues current to the ambulatory urgent care industry, including government activity, national developments, and trends in health care. Recurring features include editorials, news of research, letters to the editor, and Association news. Available online only.

★4434★ Same-Day Surgery

American Health Consultants Inc.
PO Box 1556
Pearl River, NY 10965
Fax: (845)620-9035   Fr: 800-688-2421
E-mail: customerservice@same-daysurgery.com
URL: http://www.ahcpub.com/ahc_root_html/products/newsletters/sds.html

Description: Monthly. Focuses on the management, structure, and legal and medical aspects of ambulatory surgery. Carries expert opinions and recommendations on policies and procedures.

★4435★ USA Body Psychotherapy Journal

United States Association for Body Psychotherapy
7831 Woodmont Ave.
Bethesda, MD 20814
URL: http://www.usabp.org/displaycommon.cfm?an=4

Semiannual. Academic journal that seeks to support, promote and stimulate the exchange of ideas, scholarship and research within the field of body psychotherapy as well as an interdisciplinary exchange with related fields of clinical practice and inquiry.

★4436★ Year Book of Critical Care Medicine

Elsevier Science Inc.
360 Park Ave. S
New York, NY 10010
Ph: (212)989-5800   Fax: (212)633-3990
URL: http://www.elsevier.com

$180.00/year for institutions, U.S. $191.00/year for institutions, other countries; $121.00/year for individuals, U.S. $134.00/year for individuals, other countries; $59.00/year for students, U.S. $71.00/year for students, other countries. Journal focused on treatment of severe sepsis and septic shock, echocardiography in the evaluation of hemodynamically unstable patients & mechanical ventilation of acute respiratory distress syndrome.

EMPLOYER DIRECTORIES AND NETWORKING LISTS

★4437★ **AHA Guide to the Health Care Field**

American Hospital Association
1 N Franklin
Chicago, IL 60606
Ph: (312)422-2050   Fax: (312)422-4700
Fr: 800-424-4301

Annual, August. Covers hospitals, networks, multi-health care systems, freestanding ambulatory surgery centers, psychiatric facilities, long-term care facilities, substance abuse programs, and other health-related organizations. Entries include: For hospitals–Facility name, address, phone, administrator's name, number of beds, facilities and services, number of employees, expenses, other statistics. For other organizations–Name, address, phone, fax, name and title of contact. Arrangement: Geographical. Indexes: Hospital name.

★4438★ **Directory of Hospital Personnel**

Grey House Publishing
185 Millerton Rd.
PO Box 860
Millerton, NY 12546
Ph: (518)789-8700   Fax: (518)789-0556
Fr: 800-562-2139
URL: http://www.greyhouse.com/hospital_personnel.htm

Annual. $325.00 for print product; $545.00 for online database subscription; $650.00 for online database subscription and print product combined. Covers 200,000 executives at 7,000 U.S. hospitals. Entries include: Name of hospital, address, phone; number of beds; type and JCAHO status of hospital; names and titles of key department heads and staff; medical and nursing school affiliations; number of residents, interns, and nursing students. Arrangement: Geographical. Indexes: Hospital name, personnel, hospital size.

★4439★ **Guide to Careers in the Health Professions**

The Princeton Review
2315 Broadway
New York, NY 10024
Ph: (212)874-8282   Fax: (212)874-0775
Fr: 800-733-3000
URL: http://www.princetonreview.com/

Published January, 2001. $24.95 for individuals. Presents advice and information for those searching for satisfying careers in the health professions. Publication includes: Directory of schools and academic programs. Entries include: Name, address, phone, tuition, program details, employment profiles.

★4440★ **Hospital Blue Book**

Billian Publishing Inc./Transworld Publishing Inc.
2100 Powers Ferry Rd. SE
Atlanta, GA 30339
Ph: (770)955-5656   Fax: (770)952-0669
Fr: 800-533-8484
E-mail: blu-book@billian.com

2005. $300.00 for individuals. Covers more than 6,687 hospitals; some listings also appear in a separate southern edition of this publication. Entries include: Name of hospital, accreditation, mailing address, phone, fax, number of beds, type of facility (nonprofit, general, state, etc.); list of administrative personnel and chiefs of medical services, with specific titles. Arrangement: Geographical.

★4441★ **The JobBank Guide to Health Care Companies**

Adams Media Corp.
57 Littlefield St.
Avon, MA 02322
Ph: (508)427-7100   Fax: (508)427-6790
Fr: 800-872-5627
URL: http://www.amazon.com/Jobbank-Guide-Health-Care-Companies/dp

Biennial. Covers jobs nationwide in health care companies. Entries include: Firm or organization name, address, phone, name and title of contact; description of organization, headquarters location, typical titles for entry- and middle-level positions, educational backgrounds desired, fringe benefits offered, stock exchange listing, training programs, internships, parent company, number of employees, revenues, e-mail and web addresses, projected number of hires. Indexes: Alphabetical.

★4442★ **Medical and Health Information Directory**

Gale, Cengage Learning
27500 Drake Rd.
Farmington Hills, MI 48331-3535
Ph: (248)699-4253   Fax: (248)699-8065
Fr: 800-877-4253
E-mail: businessproducts@gale.com
URL: http://www.gale.com

Annual; latest edition 20th, July 2007. $375.00/volume. Covers in Volume 1, more than 26,500 medical and health oriented associations, organizations, institutions, and government agencies, including health maintenance organizations (HMOs), preferred provider organizations (PPOs), insurance companies, pharmaceutical companies, research centers, and medical and allied health schools. In Volume 2, over 12,000 medical book publishers; medical periodicals, directories, audiovisual producers and services, medical libraries and information centers, electronic resources, and health-related internet search engines. In Volume 3, more than 35,500 clinics, treatment centers, care programs, and counseling/diagnostic services for 34 subject areas. Entries include: Institution, service, or firm name, address, phone, fax, email and URL; many include names of key personnel and, when pertinent, descriptive annotations. Volume 3

was formerly listed separately as Health Services Directory. Arrangement: Classified by organization activity, service, etc. Indexes: Each volume has a complete alphabetical name and keyword index.

★4443★ **National Directory of Fire Chiefs & EMS Administrators**

National Public Safety Information Bureau
601 Main St., Ste. 201
PO Box 365
Stevens Point, WI 54481
Ph: (715)345-2772   Fax: (715)345-7288
Fr: 800-647-7579
URL: http://www.safetysource.com

Annual; latest edition 16th edition, 2007. $149.00 for print product; $189.00 for print and online, combined. Covers over 36,000 fire and emergency departments in the U.S. Entries include: Department name, address, phone, fax, county, name of chief, type of department, financial structure. Arrangement: Geographical.

★4444★ **Registry of Ambulance Services**

Emergency Medical Services Div.
1000 NE., 10th St.,Rm. 1104
Oklahoma City, OK 73117
Ph: (405)271-4027

Irregular; latest edition 2006. Covers approximately 200 licensed ambulance services in Oklahoma. Entries include: Company, name, address, phone, geographical area served, names and titles of key personnel, number of employees, number of vehicles, description of service, number of primary hospitals. An abridged version containing only names and addresses is available for $38.50. Arrangement: Alphabetical by county and city.

HANDBOOKS AND MANUALS

★4445★ **Careers in the Emergency Medical Response Team's Search and Rescue Unit**

The Rosen Publishing Group, Inc.
29 E. 21st St.
New York, NY 10010
Ph: (212)777-3017   Fax: (212)777-0277
Fr: 800-237-9932
URL: http://www.rosenpublishing.com/

Jeri Freedman. December 2002. $29.25. Illustrated. 64 pages.

★4446★ **Careers in Health Care**

The McGraw-Hill Companies
PO Box 182604
Columbus, OH 43272
Fax: (614)759-3749   Fr: 877-883-5524
E-mail: customer.service@mcgraw-hill.com
URL: http://www.mcgraw-hill.com

Barbara M. Swanson. Fifth edition, 2005. $15.95 (paper). 192 pages. Describes job duties, work settings, salaries, licensing and certification requirements, educational preparation, and future outlook. Gives ideas on how to secure a job.

★4447★ Careers for Night Owls and Other Insomniacs

The McGraw-Hill Companies
PO Box 182604
Columbus, OH 43272
Fax: (614)759-3749   Fr: 877-883-5524
E-mail: customer.service@mcgraw-hill.com
URL: http://www.mcgraw-hill.com

Louise Miller. Second edition, 2002. $12.95 (paper). 160 pages.

★4448★ Exploring Health Care Careers, Second Edition

JIST Publishing
875 Montreal Way
St. Paul, MN 55102
Fax: 800-547-8329   Fr: 800-648-5478
E-mail: info@jist.com
URL: http://www.jist.com

2002. $89.95. 984 pages. Information about careers in the health industry, including education and certification requirements, earnings, and job outlook.

★4449★ Opportunities in Health and Medical Careers

The McGraw-Hill Companies
PO Box 182604
Columbus, OH 43272
Fax: (614)759-3749   Fr: 877-883-5524
E-mail: customer.service@mcgraw-hill.com
URL: http://www.mcgraw-hill.com

I. Donald Snook, Jr. and Leo D'Orazio. 2004. $13.95 (paper). 157 pages. Covers the full range of medical and health occupations. Illustrated.

★4450★ Opportunities in Paramedical Careers

The McGraw-Hill Companies
PO Box 182604
Columbus, OH 43272
Fax: (614)759-3749   Fr: 877-883-5524
E-mail: customer.service@mcgraw-hill.com
URL: http://www.mcgraw-hill.com

Alex Kacen. 1999. 14.95 (hardcover). 160 pages. Discusses a variety of opportunities in this field and how to pursue them. Illustrated.

★4451★ Opportunities in State and Local Government Careers

The McGraw-Hill Companies
PO Box 182604
Columbus, OH 43272
Fax: (614)759-3749   Fr: 877-883-5524
E-mail: customer.service@mcgraw-hill.com
URL: http://www.mcgraw-hill.com

Neale J. Baxter. Revised edition, 1992. $14.95; $10.95 (paper). 148 pages. Points out the incentives and drawbacks of a government career. Describes hiring procedures and provides tips on filling out applications,

taking physical and aptitude tests, handling interviews, and finding jobs. Describes the jobs in which 75% of all state and local government workers are employed. For each occupation, covers the nature of the work and the training required.

★4452★ The Paramedic Review

Cengage Learning
PO Box 6904
Florence, KY 41022
Fax: 800-487-8488   Fr: 800-354-9706
URL: http://www.cengage.com

Bob Elling and Kirsten Elling. 2007. $35.95. 464 pages.

★4453★ Resumes for Health and Medical Careers

The McGraw-Hill Companies
PO Box 182604
Columbus, OH 43272
Fax: (614)759-3749   Fr: 877-883-5524
E-mail: customer.service@mcgraw-hill.com
URL: http://www.mcgraw-hill.com

Third edition, 2003. $11.95 (paper). 160 pages.

EMPLOYMENT AGENCIES AND SEARCH FIRMS

★4454★ JPM International

26034 Acero
Mission Viejo, CA 92691
Ph: (949)699-4300   Fax: (949)699-4333
Fr: 800-685-7856
E-mail: trish@jpmintl.com
URL: http://www.jpmintl.com

Executive search firm and employment agency.

ONLINE JOB SOURCES AND SERVICES

★4455★ Medhunters.com

Fr: 800-664-0278
E-mail: info@medhunters.com
URL: http://www.medhunters.com

Description: Career search site for jobs in all health care specialties; educational resources; visa and licensing information for relocation; interesting articles; relocation tools; links to professional organizations and general resources.

★4456★ ProHealthJobs

Fr: 800-796-1738
E-mail: Info@prohealthedujobs.com
URL: http://www.prohealthjobs.com

Description: Career resources site for the

medical and health care field. Lists professional opportunities, product information, continuing education and open positions.

TRADESHOWS

★4457★ American Ambulance Association Annual Conference and Trade Show

Executive Management Services
3800 Auburn Blvd.,
Sacramento, CA 95821
Ph: (916)974-0139   Fr: 800-523-4447

Annual. **Primary Exhibits:** Ambulance equipment, supplies, and services.

★4458★ American College of Emergency Physicians Scientific Assembly

American College of Emergency Physicians
1125 Executive Cir.
PO Box 619911
Irving, TX 75038-2522
Ph: (972)550-0911   Fax: (214)580-2816
Fr: 800-798-1822
URL: http://www.acep.org

Annual. **Primary Exhibits:** Products and services related to emergency medicine. **Dates and Locations:** 2008 Oct 27-30; Chicago, IL.

★4459★ Federated Ambulatory Surgery Association - Annual Meeting

Federated Ambulatory Surgery Association
1012 Cameron St.
Alexandria, VA 22314
Ph: (703)836-8808   Fax: (703)549-0976
E-mail: FASA@fasa.org
URL: http://www.fasa.org

Annual. **Primary Exhibits:** Ambulatory equipment, supplies, and services. **Dates and Locations:** 2008 May 14-17; San Antonio, TX; Marriott Rivercenter.

★4460★ National Association of Emergency Medical Technicians Annual Conference and Exposition

National Association of Emergency Medical Technicians
PO Box 1400
Clinton, MS 39060-1400
Ph: (601)924-7744   Fax: (601)924-7325
Fr: 800-34-NAEMT
E-mail: INFO@NAEMT.ORG
URL: http://www.naemt.org

Annual. **Primary Exhibits:** Emergency medical supplies, ambulances, publications, and clothing.

★4461★ **Society for Academic Emergency Medicine Annual Meeting**

Society for Academic Emergency Medicine
901 N Washington Ave.
Lansing, MI 48906-5137
Ph: (517)485-5484   Fax: (517)485-0801
E-mail: saem@saem.org
URL: http://www.saem.org

Annual. **Primary Exhibits:** Emergency medicine equipment, supplies, and services. **Dates and Locations:** 2008 May 29 - Jun 01; Washington, DC; 2009 May 14-17; New Orleans, LA; 2010 Jun 03-06; Phoenix, AZ.

★4462★ **Trends in Urgent Care**

North American Association for Ambulatory Urgent Care
2000 Plymouth Rd., Ste. 130
Minneapolis, MN 55411
Ph: (612)868-8417   Fax: (952)476-0646
Fr: (866)793-1396
E-mail: rungirlbb@aol.com
URL: http://www.nafac.com

Annual. **Primary Exhibits:** Governing body for urgent care in North America.

OTHER SOURCES

★4463★ **Commission on Accreditation of Allied Health Education Programs (CAAHEP)**

1361 Park St.
Clearwater, FL 33756
Ph: (727)210-2350   Fax: (727)210-2354
E-mail: megivern@caahep.org
URL: http://www.caahep.org

Description: Serves as a nationally recognized accrediting agency for allied health programs in 18 occupational areas.

★4464★ **EMTs, Nurses, Therapists, and Assistants**

Cambridge Educational
PO Box 2053
Princeton, NJ 08543-2053
Ph: 800-257-5126   Fax: (609)671-0266
Fr: 800-468-4227
E-mail: custserv@films.com
URL: http://www.cambridgeeducational.com

VHS and DVD. $79.95. 2000. 18 minutes. Part of the series "Exploring Health Occupations."

★4465★ **Exploring Health Occupations**

Cambridge Educational
PO Box 2053
Princeton, NJ 08543-2053
Ph: 800-257-5126   Fax: (609)671-0266
Fr: 800-468-4227
E-mail: custserv@films.com
URL: http://www.cambridgeeducational.com

VHS and DVD. $159.90. 1999. Two-part series provides a detailed view of the field of medical technicians and technologists, EMTs, nurses, therapists, and assistants.

★4466★ **Health Service Occupations**

Delphi Productions
3159 6th St.
Boulder, CO 80304
Ph: (303)443-2100   Fax: (303)443-4022
Fr: 888-443-2400
E-mail: support@delphivideo.com
URL: http://www.delphivideo.com

$95.00. 50 minutes. Part of the Careers for the 21st Century Video Library.

★4467★ **Health Technologists & Technicians**

Delphi Productions
3159 6th St.
Boulder, CO 80304
Ph: (303)443-2100   Fax: (303)443-4022
Fr: 888-443-2400
E-mail: support@delphivideo.com
URL: http://www.delphivideo.com

$95.00. 50 minutes. Part of the Careers for the 21st Century Video Library.

★4468★ **Medical Technicians and Technologists**

Cambridge Educational
PO Box 2053
Princeton, NJ 08543-2053
Ph: 800-257-5126   Fax: (609)671-0266
Fr: 800-468-4227
E-mail: custserv@films.com
URL: http://www.cambridgeeducational.com

VHS and DVD. $79.95. 18 minutes. 2000. Part of the Exploring Health Occupations Series.

★4469★ **Medicine & Related Occupations**

Delphi Productions
3159 6th St.
Boulder, CO 80304
Ph: (303)443-2100   Fax: (303)443-4022
Fr: 888-443-2400
E-mail: support@delphivideo.com
URL: http://www.delphivideo.com

$95.00. 45 minutes. Part of the Careers for the 21st Century Video Library.

★4470★ **National Association of Emergency Medical Technicians (NAEMT)**

PO Box 1400
Clinton, MS 39060-1400
Ph: (601)924-7744   Fax: (601)924-7325
Fr: 800-34N-AEMT
E-mail: info@naemt.org
URL: http://www.naemt.org

Description: Represents and supports EMTS, paramedics and other professionals working in pre-hospital emergency medicine working in all sectors of EMS, including government third-service agencies, fire departments, hospital-based ambulance services, private companies, industrial, special operations settings, and in the military. Acts as a voice for EMS personnel in Washington, DC regarding decisions affecting EMS; speaks on behalf of all EMS providers; representatives sit on boards, associations, expert panels, and commissions to ensure that EMS is represented in decisions affecting health care and public safety; works on behalf of members in the areas of compensation and recognition, recruitment and retention, safety, and education and training.

★4471★ **National Registry of Emergency Medical Technicians (NREMT)**

Rocco V. Morando Bldg.
6610 Busch Blvd.
PO Box 29233
Columbus, OH 43229
Ph: (614)888-4484   Fax: (614)888-8920
E-mail: webmaster@nremt.org
URL: http://www.nremt.org

Purpose: Promotes the improved delivery of emergency medical services. **Activities:** Assists in the development and evaluation of educational programs to train emergency medical technicians; establishes qualifications for eligibility to apply for registration; prepares and conducts examinations designed to assure the competency of emergency medical technicians and paramedics; establishes a system for biennial registration; establishes procedures for revocation of certificates of registration for cause; maintains a directory of registered emergency medical technicians.

★4472★ **Women in Firefighting**

Her Own Words
PO Box 5264
Madison, WI 53705-0264
Ph: (608)271-7083   Fax: (608)271-0209
E-mail: herownword@aol.com
URL: http://www.herownwords.com/

Video. Jocelyn Riley. $95.00. 15 minutes. Resource guide also available for $45.00.

Employment Interviewers

SOURCES OF HELP-WANTED ADS

★4473★ Advances in Developing Human Resources

Sage Publications Inc.
2455 Teller Rd.
Thousand Oaks, CA 91320
Ph: (805)499-0721   Fax: (805)499-8096
URL: http://www.sagepub.com/journalsProdDesc.nav?prodId=Journal20

Quarterly. $408.00/year for institutions, print & e-access; $367.00/year for institutions, e-access; $400.00/year for institutions, print only; $93.00/year for individuals, print only; $110.00 for institutions, single print issue; $30.00 for individuals, single print issue. Journal for professionals working in the field of human resource development.

★4474★ International Journal of Selection and Assessment

Wiley-Blackwell
350 Main St. Commerce Pl.
Malden, MA 02148
Ph: (781)388-8200   Fax: (781)388-8210
Fr: 800-759-6120
URL: http://www.blackwellpublishing.com/journal.asp?ref=0965-075X

Quarterly. $104.00/year for individuals, print and online; $81.00/year for students, print and online; $732.00/year for institutions, print and premium online; $665.00/year for institutions, print and standard online; $632.00/year for institutions, premium online only; $435.00/year for institutions, other countries, print and premium online; $395.00/year for institutions, other countries, print and standard online; $375.00/year for institutions, other countries, premium online only; $93.00/year for individuals, print and online, Europe; $62.00/year for individuals, print and online. Journal publishing articles related to all aspects of personnel selection, staffing, and assessment in organizations.

★4475★ Journal of Business and Psychology

Springer-Verlag New York Inc.
233 Spring St.
New York, NY 10013
Ph: (212)460-1500   Fax: (212)460-1575
URL: http://www.springer.com/journal/10869/

Journal covering all aspects of psychology that apply to the business segment. Includes topics such as personnel selection and training, organizational assessment and development, risk management and loss control, marketing and consumer behavior research.

★4476★ Journal of Job Placement

National Rehabilitation Association
633 S Washington St.
Alexandria, VA 22314
Ph: (703)836-0850   Fax: (703)836-0848
E-mail: info@natioanlrehab.org
URL: http://www.nationalrehab.org

Periodic. Employment journal.

★4477★ Recruiting Trends

Kennedy Information Inc.
1 Phoenix Mill Ln., 3rd Fl.
Peterborough, NH 03458
Ph: (603)924-1006   Fax: (603)924-4460
Fr: 800-531-0007
E-mail: support@kennedyinfo.com
URL: http://www.kennedyinfo.com/rt/rec-trends.html

Description: Bimonthly. Provides strategies and tactics for creating and maintaining a competitive work force.

★4478★ SI Review

Staffing Industry Analysts Inc.
881 Fremont Ave.
Los Altos, CA 94024
Ph: (650)232-2350   Fax: (650)232-2360
Fr: 800-950-9496
URL: http://www.staffingindustry.com/ME2/dirsect.asp?sid=52854874

Monthly. $99.00/year for individuals. Online news publication covering news and developments in employment and staffing.

★4479★ Staffing Industry Employment Bulletin

Staffing Industry Analysts Inc.
881 Fremont Ave.
Los Altos, CA 94024
Ph: (650)232-2350   Fax: (650)232-2360
Fr: 800-950-9496
URL: http://www.staffingindustry.com/pub/siemployment

Irregular. Online news publication covering key events in employment and staffing.

★4480★ Staffing Industry Healthcare News

Staffing Industry Analysts Inc.
881 Fremont Ave.
Los Altos, CA 94024
Ph: (650)232-2350   Fax: (650)232-2360
Fr: 800-950-9496

Weekly. $10.00 for single issue. Online publication covering key events in health care staffing.

★4481★ Staffing Industry News Bulletin

Staffing Industry Analysts Inc.
881 Fremont Ave.
Los Altos, CA 94024
Ph: (650)232-2350   Fax: (650)232-2360
Fr: 800-950-9496
URL: http://www.staffingindustry.com/pub/sinewsbulletin

Daily. $10.00 for single issue. Online publication covering key events in all sectors of the staffing industry.

★4482★ Workforce Managment

Crain Communications, Inc.
4 Executive Cir., Ste. 185
Irvine, CA 92614
Ph: (949)255-5340
E-mail: mailroom@workforcemag.com
URL: http://www.workforceonline.com

Biweekly. $79.00/year for individuals, U.S. domestic rate; $129.00/year for Canada; $199.00/year for other countries, all other international. A business magazine for human resources management leaders.

★4483★ Young Professional

IDG Communications Inc.
5 Speen St., 3rd. Fl
Framingham, MA 01701
Ph: (508)875-5000   Fax: (508)988-7888
URL: http://www.idg.com

Magazine focusing on technology issues, job market information for students, post-graduates and young professionals.

PLACEMENT AND JOB REFERRAL SERVICES

★4484★ Association of Career Management Consulting Firms International (AOCFI)

204 E St. NE
Washington, DC 20002
Ph: (202)547-6344   Fax: (202)547-6348
E-mail: acf@acfinternational.org
URL: http://www.aocfi.org

Members: Represents firms providing displaced employees, who are sponsored by their organization, with counsel and assistance in job searching and the techniques and practices of choosing a career. **Purpose:** Develops, improves and encourages the art and science of outplacement consulting and the professional standards of competence, objectivity, and integrity in the service of clients. Cooperates with other industrial, technical, educational, professional, and governmental bodies in areas of mutual interest and concern.

★4485★ International Association of Workforce Professionals (IAWP)

1801 Louisville Rd.
Frankfort, KY 40601
Ph: (502)223-4459   Fax: (502)223-4127
Fr: 888-898-9960
E-mail: iapes@iapes.org
URL: http://www.iawponline.org

Description: Officials and others engaged in job placement, unemployment compensation, and labor market information administration through municipal, state, provincial, and federal government employment agencies and unemployment compensation agencies. Conducts workshops and research. Offers professional development program of study guides and tests.

EMPLOYER DIRECTORIES AND NETWORKING LISTS

★4486★ The Directory of Executive Recruiters

Kennedy Information Inc.
1 Phoenix Mill Lane, 3rd Fl.
Peterborough, NH 03458
Ph: (603)924-1006   Fax: (603)924-4460
Fr: 800-531-0007
E-mail: bookstore@kennedyinfo.com
URL: http://www.kennedyinfo.com/

2006. $59.95 (paper). 2,100 pages. Lists and describes more than 5,600 firms in North America and indexes these by function, industry, and geographic area. Names key principals of recruiting firms. Includes narrative section on executive search and how it affects job candidates. Also available: Corporate Edition, expanded for use by corporate staffs, $299.00 (paper).

★4487★ Executive Search Research Directory

Recruiting & Search Report
PO Box 9433
Panama City Beach, FL 32417
Ph: (850)235-3733   Fax: (850)233-9695
Fr: 800-634-4548
URL: http://www.rsronline.com

Latest edition 10th. $15.00 for individuals. Covers 389 freelance executive search researchers that specialize in candidate locating, screening, and development for executive recruiters and corporate (in-house) recruiters; publishers of directories, books, periodicals, and other resources related to recruitment research. Entries include: For researchers–Name, address, phone, rates, year established, first year listed, a description of services and specialties, hourly rates. Arrangement: Researchers are geographical by zip code. Indexes: Geographical; means of industry or functional concentration; unusual expertise; specialty.

★4488★ National Directory of Personnel Service Firms

National Association of Personnel Services
The Village At Banner Elk, Ste. 108
PO Box 2128
Banner Elk, NC 28604
Ph: (828)898-4929   Fax: (828)898-8098
URL: http://www.recruitinglife.com

Annual, spring. Covers over 1,100 member private (for-profit) personnel service firms and temporary service firms. Entries include: Firm name, address, phone, fax, contact, area of specialization. Arrangement: Same information given geographically by employment specialty.

HANDBOOKS AND MANUALS

★4489★ 96 Great Interview Questions to Ask Before You Hire

AMACOM
1601 Broadway, 12th Fl.
New York, NY 10019-7420
Ph: (212)586-8100   Fax: (212)903-8168
Fr: 800-262-9699
URL: http://www.amanet.org

Paul Falcone. 2000. $17.95. 224 pages.

★4490★ Hiring: More Than a Gut Feeling (Build Your Business)

Career Press, Inc.
3 Tice Rd.
Franklin Lakes, NJ 07417-1322
Ph: (201)848-0310   Fax: (201)848-1727
Fr: 800-227-3371
URL: http://www.careerpress.com

Richard S. Deems. 1995. $12.99 (paper). 127 pages.

★4491★ How to Become a Skillful Interviewer (Worksmart Series)

AMACOM
1601 Broadway, 12th Fl.
New York, NY 10019-7420
Ph: (212)586-8100   Fax: (212)903-8168
Fr: 800-262-9699
URL: http://www.amanet.org

Randi Toler Sachs. 1994. $12.95 (paper). 83 pages.

★4492★ How to Spot a Liar in a Job Interview

Management Advantage, Incorporated
PO Box 3708
Walnut Creek, CA 94598-0708
Ph: (925)671-0404   Fax: (925)825-3930
Fr: 888-671-0404
URL: http://www.management-advantage.com/

Wayne D. Ford. 1999. $14.95 (paper). 125 pages.

★4493★ How to Succeed in Employee Development: Moving from Vision to Results

The McGraw-Hill Companies
PO Box 182604
Columbus, OH 43272
Fax: (614)759-3749   Fr: 877-883-5524
E-mail: customer.service@mcgraw-hill.com
URL: http://www.mcgraw-hill.com

Edward Moorby. Third edition, 1998. 193 pages. Part of the Training Series.

★4494★ The Human Resource Professional's Career Guide: Building a Position of Strength
John Wiley & Sons, Inc.
1 Wiley Dr.
Somerset, NJ 08873
Ph: (732)469-4400   Fax: (732)302-2300
Fr: 800-526-5368
E-mail: custserv@wiley.com
URL: http://www.wiley.com/WileyCDA/

Jeanne Palmer, Martha I. Finney. June 2004. $38.00. 264 pages.

★4495★ Interviewer Approaches
Dartmouth Publishing Group
101 Cherry St.
Ste. 420
Burlington, VT 05401-4405
Ph: (802)865-7641   Fax: (802)865-7847
URL: http://www.ashgate.com

Jean Morton-Williams. 1993. $119.95. 239 pages.

★4496★ Interviewing the World's Top Interviewers: The Inside Story of Journalism's Most Momentous Revelations
S.P.I. Books
99 Spring St., 3rd Fl.
New York, NY 10012
Ph: (212)431-5011   Fax: (212)431-8646
URL: http://www.spibooks.com/

Jack Huper and Dean Diggins. Reprint edition, 1992. $5.50 (paper)

★4497★ Real-Resumes for Human-Resources and Personnel Jobs: Including Real Resumes Used to Change Careers and Transfer Skills to Other Industries
PREP Publishing
1110 1/2 Hay St., PMB 66
Fayetteville, NC 28305
Ph: (910)483-6611   Fax: (910)483-2439
Fr: 800-533-2814

Anne McKinney. September 2002. $16.95. 192 pages.

★4498★ Up Is Not the Only Way: A Guide to Developing Workforce Talent
Prentice Hall PTR
1 Lake St.
Upper Saddle River, NJ 07458
Ph: (201)236-7000   Fax: 800-445-6991
Fr: 800-428-5331
URL: http://www.phptr.com/index.asp?rl=1

Beverly L. Kaye. Second Edition. 1982. $22.95. 293 pages.

EMPLOYMENT AGENCIES AND SEARCH FIRMS

★4499★ Abbott Smith Associates, Inc.
11697 W. Grand Ave.
Northlake, IL 60164
Ph: (708)223-1191
E-mail: contactus@abbottsmith.com
URL: http://www.abbottsmith.com

Human Resources executive search firm.

★4500★ Abel Fuller & Zedler LLC
440 Benmar, Ste. 1085
Houston, TX 77060
Ph: (281)447-3334   Fax: (281)447-3334
E-mail: agarcia@execufirm.com
URL: http://www.execufirm.com

Executive search firm.

★4501★ The Andre Group Inc.
1220 Valley Forge Rd., Ste. 19
Phoenixville, PA 19460
Ph: (610)917-2212   Fax: (610)917-0551
E-mail: info@theandregroup.com

Executive search firm. Focused on the human resource field.

★4502★ The Aspire Group
52 Second Ave, 1st Fl
Waltham, MA 02451-1129
Fax: (718)890-1810   Fr: 800-487-2967
URL: http://www.bmanet.com

Employment agency.

★4503★ Campbell/Carlson LLC
831 E. Morehead St., Ste. 750
Charlotte, NC 28202
Ph: (704)373-0234
E-mail: recruiting@campbellcarlson.com
URL: http://www.campbellcarlson.com

Executive search firm.

★4504★ Dankowski and Associates, Inc.
13089 Root Rd.
The Woods, Ste. 200 SE
Columbia Station, OH 44028
Ph: (440)236-3088   Fax: (440)236-9621
Fr: 800-326-5694
E-mail: info@dankowskiassocites.com
URL: http://www.dankowskiassociates.com

Executive search firm.

★4505★ The Enfield Company
106 E. 6th St., Ste. 900
Austin, TX 78701
Ph: (512)444-9921
E-mail: enfieldco@yahoo.com
URL: http://members.aol.com/enfieldco/

Executive search firm.

★4506★ FM Industries
10125 Crosstown Cir.
Eden Prairie, MN 55344-3319
Ph: (952)941-0966   Fax: (952)941-4462
E-mail: fmindustries@fmindustries.net
URL: http://www.fmindustries.net

Executive search firm.

★4507★ John J. Davis & Associates Inc.
30 Chatham Road
PO Box G
Short Hills, NJ 07078
Ph: (973)467-8339   Fax: (973)467-3706
E-mail: jdavis@1013@aol.com
URL: http://www.johnjdavisandassoc.com

Executive search firm.

★4508★ Karras Personnel, Inc.
2 Central Ave.
Madison, NJ 07940
Ph: (208)238-6190
E-mail: amy.kakalec@karraspersonnel.com
URL: http://www.karraspersonnel.com

Executive search firm specializing in human resources recruiting.

★4509★ Philip Conway Management
320 Hampton Place
Hinsdale, IL 60521-3823
Ph: (630)655-4566

Executive search firm.

★4510★ Protocol Agency Inc.
2659 Townsgate Rd., Ste.203
Westlake Village, CA 91361-2774
Ph: (805)371-0069   Fax: (805)371-0048
E-mail: corp@protocolexec.com
URL: http://www.protocolagency.com

Executive search firm focusing on a variety of placements.

★4511★ Williams Executive Search Inc.
90 S. 7th St., Ste. 4200
Minneapolis, MN 55402
Ph: (612)339-2900   Fax: (612)305-5040
URL: http://www.williams-exec.com/

Executive search firm.

★4512★ Willmott and Associates, Inc.
922 Waltham St., Ste. 103
Lexington, MA 02421
Ph: (781)863-5400   Fax: (781)863-8000
E-mail: willmont@willmont.com
URL: http://www.willmott.com

Executive search firm and permanent employment agency. Also fills some temporary placements.

ONLINE JOB SOURCES AND SERVICES

★4513★ Spherion
2050 Spectrum Blvd.
Fort Lauderdale, FL 33309
Ph: (954)308-7600
E-mail: help@spherion.com
URL: http://www.spherion.com

Description: Recruitment firm specializing in accounting and finance, sales and marketing, interim executives, technology, engineering, retail and human resources.

OTHER SOURCES

★4514★ American Almanac of Jobs and Salaries
HarperCollins
10 E. 53rd St.
New York, NY 10022
Ph: (212)207-7000   Fr: 800-242-7737
URL: http://www.harpercollins.com/

John W. Wright. Revised edition, 2000. $20.00 (paper). 672 pages. This is a comprehensive guide to the wages of hundreds of occupations in a wide variety of industries and organizations.

★4515★ American Staffing Association (ASA)
277 S Washington St., Ste. 200
Alexandria, VA 22314-3675
Ph: (703)253-2020   Fax: (703)253-2053
E-mail: asa@americanstaffing.net
URL: http://www.americanstaffing.net

Description: Promotes and represents the staffing industry through legal and legislative advocacy, public relations, education, and the establishment of high standards of ethical conduct.

★4516★ Employment Support Center (ESC)
1556 Wisconsin Ave. NW
Washington, DC 20007
Ph: (202)628-2919   Fax: (202)628-2919
E-mail: jobclubs@hotmail.com
URL: http://www.angelfire.com/biz/jobclubs

Description: Trains individuals to facilitate support groups for job-seekers. Operates a job bank for employment assistance; helps people learn to network for job contacts; provides technical assistance to employment support self help groups. Maintains speakers' bureau. Provides job-search skills training.

★4517★ HR Policy Association
1015 15th St. NW, Ste. 1200
Washington, DC 20005-2605
Ph: (202)789-8670   Fax: (202)789-0064
E-mail: info@hrpolicy.org
URL: http://www.hrpolicy.org

Description: Senior human resource executives of Fortune 500 companies. Conducts research and publishes findings on matters relating to federal human resources policy and its application and effects. Maintains task forces to study pending employment issues; conducts seminars, and offers a suite of labor relations and HR effectiveness training courses.

★4518★ National Association of Personnel Services (NAPS)
The Village at Banner Elk, Ste. 108
PO Box 2128
Banner Elk, NC 28604
Ph: (828)898-4929   Fax: (828)898-8098
E-mail: conrad.taylor@recruitinglife.com
URL: http://www.recruitinglife.com

Description: Private employment and temporary service firms. Compiles statistics on professional agency growth and development; conducts certification program and educational programs. Association is distinct from former name of National Association of Personnel Consultants.

Engineering Technicians

SOURCES OF HELP-WANTED ADS

★4519★ AIE Perspectives Newsmagazine

American Institute of Engineers
4630 Appian Way, Ste. 206
El Sobrante, CA 94803-1875
Ph: (510)758-6240   Fax: (510)758-6240

Monthly. Professional magazine covering engineering.

★4520★ Chemical & Engineering News

American Chemical Society
1155 16th St. NW
Washington, DC 20036
Ph: (202)872-4600   Fax: (202)872-4615
Fr: 800-227-5558
URL: http://pubs.acs.org/cen/about.html

Weekly. Magazine on chemical and engineering news.

★4521★ EE Evaluation Engineering

Nelson Publishing Inc.
2500 Tamiami Trl. N
Nokomis, FL 34275
Ph: (941)966-9521   Fax: (941)966-2590
URL: http://
www.evaluationengineering.com/

Monthly. Free. Trade magazine covering electronic engineering, evaluation and test.

★4522★ Electronic Engineering Times

CMP Media L.L.C.
600 Community Dr.
Manhasset, NY 11030
Ph: (516)562-5000   Fax: (516)562-7830
URL: http://www.cmp.com/products/pr_det_
elecengtimesasia.jhtml

Semimonthly. Weekly trade newspaper.

★4523★ Electronic Products

Hearst Business Communications/
  Electronics Group
50 Charles Lindbergh Blvd., Ste. 100
Uniondale, NY 11553
Ph: (516)227-1383
E-mail: lens@electronicproducts.com
URL: http://www.electronicproducts.com

Monthly. $12.00/year for individuals. Magazine for electronic design engineers and management.

★4524★ Engineering Conferences International Symposium Series

Berkeley Electronic Press
2809 Telegraph Ave., Ste. 202
Berkeley, CA 94705
Ph: (510)665-1200   Fax: (510)665-1201
URL: http://services.bepress.com/eci/

Journal focusing on advance engineering science.

★4525★ Engineering Times

National Society of Professional
  Engineers
1420 King St.
Alexandria, VA 22314
Ph: (703)684-2800
URL: http://www.nspe.org

Monthly. Magazine (tabloid) covering professional, legislative, and techology issues for an engineering audience.

★4526★ ENR: Engineering News-Record

McGraw-Hill Inc.
1221 Ave. of the Americas
New York, NY 10020-1095
Ph: (212)512-2000   Fax: (212)512-3840
Fr: 877-833-5524
E-mail: enr_web_editors@mcgraw-hill.com
URL: http://www.mymags.com/morein-
fo.php?itemID=20012

Weekly. $94.00/year for individuals, print. Magazine focusing on engineering and construction.

★4527★ High Technology Careers Magazine

HTC
4701 Patrick Henry Dr., No. 1901
Santa Clara, CA 95054-1847
Fax: (408)567-0242
URL: http://www.hightechcareers.com

Bimonthly. $29.00/year; $35.00/year for Canada; $85.00/year for out of country. Magazine (tabloid) containing employment opportunity information for the engineering and technical community.

★4528★ InterJournal

New England Complex Systems Institute
24 Mt. Auburn St.
Cambridge, MA 02138
Ph: (617)547-4100   Fax: (617)661-7711
URL: http://www.interjournal.org/

Journal covering the fields of science and engineering.

★4529★ International Archives of Bioscience

International Archives of Bioscience
PO Box 737254
Elmhurst, NY 11373-9997
URL: http://www.iabs.us/jdoc/aboutiabs.htm

Free, online only. Journal reporting multidisciplinary coverage and interaction between scientists in biology, informatics, mathematics, physics, engineering and other sciences.

★4530★ Journal of Engineering Education

American Society for Engineering
  Education
1818 North St., NW, Ste. 600
Washington, DC 20036-2479
Ph: (202)331-3500
URL: http://www.asee.org/publications/jee/
index.cfm

Quarterly. Journal covering scholarly research in engineering education.

★4531★ *Mechanical Engineering*

American Society of Mechanical
 Engineers
3 Park Ave.
New York, NY 10016-5990
Ph: (212)591-7158   Fax: (212)591-7739
E-mail: memag@asme.org

Monthly. $25.00 for single issue; $28.50 for
single issue, international surface. Mechanical Engineering featuring technical and industry related technological advancements
and news.

★4532★ *Metal Producing & Processing*

Penton Media Inc.
1300 E 9th St.
Cleveland, OH 44114
Ph: (216)696-7000   Fax: (216)696-1752
URL: http://www.metalproducing.com/

Bimonthly. $40.00/year for individuals;
$43.00/year for Canada; $48.00/year for
other countries. Magazine covering the met-
al-producing industry.

★4533★ *Microwave Journal*

Horizon House Publications Inc.
685 Canton St.
Norwood, MA 02062
Ph: (781)769-9750   Fax: (781)769-5037
Fr: 800-966-8526
E-mail: mwj@mwjournal.com
URL: http://www.mwjournal.com

Monthly. Electronic engineering magazine.

★4534★ *Modern Metals*

Trend Publishing
625 N Michigan Ave., Ste. 15
Chicago, IL 60611
Ph: (312)654-2300   Fax: (312)654-2323
Fr: 800-278-7363
URL: http://www.modernmetals.com

Monthly. $180.00/year for individuals, 1
year; $270.00/year for individuals, 2 years;
$260.00/year for individuals, 1 year;
$430.00/year for individuals, 2 years. Metals
fabrication magazine.

★4535★ *NSBE Magazine*

NSBE Publications
205 Daingerfield Rd.
Alexandria, VA 22314
Ph: (703)549-2207   Fax: (703)683-5312
URL: http://www.nsbe.org/publications/
premieradvertisers.php

Journal providing information on engineering
careers, self-development, and cultural issues for recent graduates with technical
majors.

★4536★ *Power*

McGraw-Hill Inc.
1221 Ave. of the Americas
New York, NY 10020-1095
Ph: (212)512-2000   Fax: (212)512-3840
Fr: 877-833-5524

E-mail: robert_peltier@platts.com
URL: http://online.platts.com/PPS/
P=m&s=1029337384756.1478827&e=1

Monthly. Magazine for engineers in electric
utilities, process and manufacturing plants,
commercial and service establishments, and
consulting, design, and construction engineering firms working in the power technology field.

★4537★ *Printed Circuit Design &
Manufacture*

UP Media Group Inc.
2400 Lake Park Dr., Ste. 440
Smyrna, GA 30080
Ph: (678)589-8800   Fax: (678)589-8850
URL: http://www.pcdandm.com/pcdmag

Monthly. Magazine for engineers and designers of PCBs and related technologies.

★4538★ *SMT*

PennWell Corp.
1421 S Sheridan Rd.
Tulsa, OK 74112
Ph: (918)835-3161   Fr: 800-331-4463
URL: http://smt.pennnet.com

Monthly. $109.00/year for U.S. and Canada;
$198.00/year for other countries; $14.00 for
single issue, US; $20.00/year for single
issue, Canada; $20.00 for single issue,
foreign. Trade magazine for professional
engineers involved in surface mount technology circuit design and board assembly.

★4539★ *SPE Technical Journals*

Society of Petroleum Engineers
222 Palisades Creek Dr.
Richardson, TX 75080
Ph: (972)952-9393   Fax: (972)952-9435
Fr: 800-456-6863
URL: http://www.spe.org

Journal devoted to engineers and scientists.

★4540★ *Structure Magazine*

American Consulting Engineers Council
1015 15th St. NW, 8th Fl.
Washington, DC 20005-2605
Ph: (202)347-7474   Fax: (202)898-0068
URL: http://www.structuremag.org

Annual. $65.00/year for nonmembers;
$35.00/year for students; $90.00/year for
Canada; $125.00/year for other countries.
Magazine focused on providing tips, tools,
techniques, and innovative concepts for
structural engineers.

★4541★ *SWE, Magazine of the Society
of Women Engineers*

Society of Women Engineers
230 East Ohio St., Ste. 400
Chicago, IL 60611-3265
Ph: (312)596-5223
E-mail: hq@swe.org
URL: http://www.swe.org

Quarterly. $30.00/year for nonmembers.
Magazine for engineering students and for

women and men working in the engineering
and technology fields. Covers career guidance, continuing development and topical
issues.

★4542★ *The Technology Interface*

New Mexico State University
College of Engineering
PO Box 30001
Las Cruces, NM 88003-8001
Ph: (505)646-0111
URL: http://engr.nmsu.edu/etti/

Journal for the engineering technology profession serving education and industry.

★4543★ *Test & Measurement World*

Reed Business Information
225 Wyman St.
Waltham, MA 02451-1216
E-mail: tmw@reedbusiness.com
URL: http://www.tmworld.com

Monthly. Free. Electronic engineering magazine specializing in test, measurement, and
inspection of electronic products.

★4544★ *Tooling & Production*

Nelson Publishing Inc.
2500 Tamiami Trl. N
Nokomis, FL 34275
Ph: (941)966-9521   Fax: (941)966-2590
URL: http://www.manufacturingcenter.com

Monthly. Magazine concerning metalworking.

★4545★ *Uratie*

IDG Communications Inc.
5 Speen St., 3rd. Fl
Framingham, MA 01701
Ph: (508)875-5000   Fax: (508)988-7888
URL: http://www.idg.com

Magazine providing job offers for graduates,
engineers and information technology professionals.

PLACEMENT AND JOB
REFERRAL SERVICES

★4546★ **American Indian Science and
Engineering Society (AISES)**

PO Box 9828
Albuquerque, NM 87119-9828
Ph: (505)765-1052   Fax: (505)765-5608
E-mail: info@aises.org
URL: http://www.aises.org

Description: Represents American Indian
and non-Indian students and professionals in
science, technology, and engineering fields;
corporations representing energy, mining,
aerospace, electronic, and computer fields.
Seeks to motivate and encourage students
to pursue undergraduate and graduate studies in science, engineering, and technology.

Sponsors science fairs in grade schools, teacher training workshops, summer math/science sessions for 8th-12th graders, professional chapters, and student chapters in colleges. Offers scholarships. Adult members serve as role models, advisers, and mentors for students. Operates placement service.

★4547★ **Engineering Society of Detroit (ESD)**

2000 Town Ctr., Ste. 2610
Southfield, MI 48075
Ph: (248)353-0735   Fax: (248)353-0736
E-mail: esd@esd.org
URL: http://esd.org

Description: Engineers from all disciplines; scientists and technologists. Conducts technical programs and engineering refresher courses; sponsors conferences and expositions. Maintains speakers' bureau; offers placement services; although based in Detroit, MI, society membership is international.

★4548★ **ETA International - Electronics Technicians Association, International (ETA)**

5 Depot St.
Greencastle, IN 46135
Ph: (765)653-8262   Fax: (765)653-4287
Fr: 800-288-3824
E-mail: eta@eta-i.org
URL: http://www.eta-i.org

Description: Skilled electronics technicians. Provides placement service; offers certification examinations for electronics technicians and satellite, fiber optics, and data cabling installers. Compiles wage and manpower statistics. Administers FCC Commercial License examinations and certification of computer network systems technicians and web and internet specialists.

★4549★ **Robotics Tech Group of the Society of Manufacturing Engineers (RI/SME)**

PO Box 930
Dearborn, MI 48121
Ph: (313)271-1500   Fax: (313)425-3404
Fr: 800-733-4763
E-mail: techcommunities@sme.org
URL: http://www.sme.org/cgi-bin/communities.pl?/communities/ri/ri-home.htm&&&SME&

Description: Represents engineers, managers, educators, and government officials in 50 countries working or interested in the field of robotics. Promotes efficient and effective use of current and future robot technology. Serves as a clearinghouse for the industry trends and developments. Includes areas of interest such as: aerospace; assembly systems; casting and forging; education and training; human factors and safety; human and food service; material handling; military systems; nontraditional systems; research and development; small shop applications; welding. Offers professional certification. Operates placement service; compiles statistics. Maintains speakers' bureau.

★4550★ **Society of Hispanic Professional Engineers (SHPE)**

5400 E Olympic Blvd., Ste. 210
Los Angeles, CA 90022
Ph: (323)725-3970   Fax: (323)725-0316
E-mail: shpenational@shpe.org
URL: http://oneshpe.shpe.org/wps/portal/national

Description: Represents engineers, student engineers, and scientists. Aims to increase the number of Hispanic engineers by providing motivation and support to students. Sponsors competitions and educational programs. Maintains placement service and speakers' bureau; compiles statistics.

★4551★ **Society for Mining, Metallurgy, and Exploration (SME)**

8307 Shaffer Pkwy.
Littleton, CO 80127-4102
Ph: (303)973-9550   Fax: (303)973-3845
Fr: 800-763-3132
E-mail: cs@smenet.org
URL: http://www.smenet.org

Description: A member society of the American Institute of Mining, Metallurgical and Petroleum Engineers. Persons engaged in the finding, exploitation, treatment, and marketing of all classes of minerals (metal ores, industrial minerals, and solid fuels) except petroleum. Promotes the arts and sciences connected with the production of useful minerals and metals. Offers specialized education programs; compiles enrollment and graduation statistics from schools offering engineering degrees in mining, mineral, mineral processing/metallurgical, geological, geophysical, and mining technology. Provides placement service and sponsors charitable programs.

EMPLOYER DIRECTORIES AND NETWORKING LISTS

★4552★ *Careers in Focus: Technicians*

Facts On File Inc.
132 W 31st St., 17th Fl.
New York, NY 10001
Ph: (212)967-8800   Fax: 800-678-3633
Fr: 800-322-8755
URL: http://www.factsonfile.com

Latest edition 2nd, 2004. $29.95 for individuals; $26.95 for libraries. Covers an overview of technicians, followed by a selection of jobs profiled in detail, including the nature of the job, earnings, prospects for employment, what kind of training and skills it requires, and sources for further information.

★4553★ *Directory of Contract Staffing Firms*

C.E. Publications Inc.
PO Box 3006
Bothell, WA 98041-3006
Ph: (425)806-5200   Fax: (425)806-5585
URL: http://www.cjhunter.com/dcsf/over-

view.html

Covers nearly 1,300 contract firms actively engaged in the employment of engineering, IT/IS, and technical personnel for 'temporary' contract assignments throughout the world. Entries include: Company name, address, phone, name of contact, email, web address. Arrangement: Alphabetical. Indexes: Geographical.

★4554★ *ENR-Top 500 Design Firms Issue*

McGraw-Hill Inc.
1221 Ave. of the Americas
New York, NY 10020-1095
Ph: (212)512-2000   Fax: (212)512-3840
Fr: 877-833-5524
URL: http://enr.construction.com/people/sourcebooks/top500Design/

Annual, latest edition 2007. $50.00 for individuals. Publication includes: List of 500 leading architectural, engineering, and specialty design firms selected on basis of annual billings. Entries include: Company name, headquarters location, type of firm, current and prior year rank in billings, types of services, countries in which operated in preceding year. Arrangement: Ranked by billings.

★4555★ *Peterson's Job Opportunities for Engineering and Computer Science Majors*

Peterson's
Princeton Pke. Corporate Ctr., 2000 Lenox Dr.
PO Box 67005
Lawrenceville, NJ 08648
Ph: (609)896-1800   Fax: (609)896-4531
Fr: 800-338-3282
URL: http://www.petersons.com

Annual; latest edition 1999. $18.95 for individuals. Covers approximately 2,000 research, consulting, manufacturing, government, and technical services organizations hiring colleges graduates in the fields of engineering, telecommunications, biotechnology, software, and consumer electronics. Entries include: Organization name, address, phone, name and title of contact, type of organization, number of employees, Standard Industrial Classification (SIC) code, description of opportunities available, level of education required, starting salary, location, level of experience accepted, benefits.

★4556★ *Peterson's Job Opportunities in Engineering and Technology*

Peterson's Guides
2000 Lenox Dr.
Box 67005
Lawrenceville, NJ 08648
Ph: (609)896-1800   Fax: (609)896-4531
Fr: 800-338-3282
E-mail: custsvc@petersons.com
URL: http://www.petersons.com

Compiled by the Peterson's staff. Fourth edition, 1996. $21.95 (paper). 379 pages. Profiles 2,000 high-tech companies looking primarily for technical personnel in such fields as biotechnology, telecommunications, software, computers and peripherals, defense, and aerospace. Contains job-search strategies and career options to help match education and expertise to the job market. Indexed geographically, by industry, and by hiring needs.

★4557★ *Profiles of Engineering and Engineering Technology Colleges*

American Society for Engineering Education
1818 North St., NW, Ste. 600
Washington, DC 20036-2479
Ph: (202)331-3500

$75.00 for nonmembers; $50.00 for members; $25.00 for students. Covers U.S. and Canadian schools offering undergraduate and graduate engineering and engineering technology programs. Entries include: Name, address, phone, fax.

HANDBOOKS AND MANUALS

★4558★ *Opportunities in Electronics Careers*

The McGraw-Hill Companies
PO Box 182604
Columbus, OH 43272
Fax: (614)759-3749   Fr: 877-883-5524
E-mail: customer.service@mcgraw-hill.com
URL: http://www.mcgraw-hill.com

Mark Rowh. 2007. $13.95; $11.95 (paper). 221 pages. Discusses career opportunities in commercial and industrial electronics equipment repair, electronics home entertainment repair, electronics engineering, and engineering technology. Includes job outlook and how to get off to a good start on the job.

★4559★ *Opportunities in Science Technician Careers*

The McGraw-Hill Companies
PO Box 182604
Columbus, OH 43272
Fax: (614)759-3749   Fr: 877-883-5524
E-mail: customer.service@mcgraw-hill.com
URL: http://www.mcgraw-hill.com

JoAnn Chirico and Jan Goldberg 1996. $14.95 (paper). 160 pages. Part of "Opportunities in ..." Series.

★4560★ *Real People Working in Engineering*

The McGraw-Hill Companies
PO Box 182604
Columbus, OH 43272
Fax: (614)759-3749   Fr: 877-883-5524
E-mail: customer.service@mcgraw-hill.com
URL: http://www.mcgraw-hill.com

Blythe Camenson, Jan Goldberg. 1997. $17.95 (paper). 160 pages. Interviews and profiles of working professionals capture a range of opportunities in this field.

★4561★ *Resumes for Engineering Careers*

The McGraw-Hill Companies
PO Box 182604
Columbus, OH 43272
Fax: (614)759-3749   Fr: 877-883-5524
E-mail: customer.service@mcgraw-hill.com
URL: http://www.mcgraw-hill.com

Third edition, 2005. $11.95 (paper). 144 pages. Contains sample resumes and cover letters applicable to any engineering field.

★4562★ *Resumes for Scientific and Technical Careers*

The McGraw-Hill Companies
PO Box 182604
Columbus, OH 43272
Fax: (614)759-3749   Fr: 877-883-5524
E-mail: customer.service@mcgraw-hill.com
URL: http://www.mcgraw-hill.com

Third edition, 2007. $12.95 (paper). 144 pages. Provides resume advice for individuals interested in working in scientific and technical careers. Includes sample resumes and cover letters.

EMPLOYMENT AGENCIES AND SEARCH FIRMS

★4563★ **Andrew Associates Executive Search Inc.**

4000 Kruse Way Place
Bldg. 2 Ste 225
PO Box 2029
Lake Oswego, OR 97035
Ph: (503)635-7222   Fax: (503)635-5236
E-mail: AAES@andysrch.com
URL: http://www.andysrch.com

Executive search firm.

★4564★ **The Aspire Group**

52 Second Ave, 1st Fl
Waltham, MA 02451-1129
Fax: (718)890-1810   Fr: 800-487-2967
URL: http://www.bmanet.com

Employment agency.

★4565★ **Brandywine Management Group**

8 Drawbridge Rd.
Berlin, MD 21811
Ph: (410)208-9791   Fax: (410)208-9792
Fr: 800-860-8812
E-mail: brandywinemgmt@optonline.net
URL: http://
www.brandywineconsultants.com/

Executive search firm.

★4566★ **Colli Associates**

414 Caboose Ln.
Valrico, FL 33594
Ph: (813)681-2145   Fax: (813)661-5217

E-mail: colli@gte.net

Employment agency. Executive search firm.

★4567★ **Emplex Associates**

10051 E. Highland Rd. Ste. 29-353
Howell, MI 48843
Ph: (517)548-2800   Fr: 888-203-1010
E-mail: emplex@emplexcorp.com
URL: http://www.emplexcorp.com

Executive search firm.

★4568★ **Ethos Consulting LLC**

3219 E. Camelback Rd., Ste. 515
Phoenix, AZ 85018
Ph: (480)296-3801   Fax: (480)664-7270
E-mail: resumes@ethosconsulting.com
URL: http://www.ethoscounsulting.com

Executive search firm. Second branch in Scottsdale, AZ.

★4569★ **Executive Directions Inc.**

PO Box 223
Foxboro, MA 02035
Ph: (508)698-3030   Fax: (508)543-6047
URL: http://www.execdir.com

Executive search firm.

★4570★ **Global Employment Solutions**

10375 Park Meadows Dr., Ste. 375
Littleton, CO 80124
Ph: (303)216-9500   Fax: (303)216-9533
E-mail: careers@global
URL: http://www.gesnetwork.com

Employment agency.

★4571★ **Search and Recruit International**

4455 South Blvd. Ste. 110
Virginia Beach, VA 23452
Ph: (757)625-2121   Fr: 800-800-5627

Employment agency. Headquartered in Virginia Beach. Other offices in Bremerton, WA; Charleston, SC; Jacksonville, FL; Memphis, TN; Pensacola, FL; Sacramento, CA; San Bernardino, CA; San Diego, CA.

★4572★ **Tri-Serv Inc.**

22 W. Padonia Rd., Ste. C-353
Timonium, MD 21093
Ph: (410)561-1740   Fax: (410)252-7417
E-mail: info@tri-serv.coom
URL: http://www.tri-serv.com

Employment agency for technical personnel.

OTHER SOURCES

★4573★ Aircraft Electronics Association (AEA)

4217 S Hocker
Independence, MO 64055-0963
Ph: (816)373-6565   Fax: (816)478-3100
E-mail: info@aea.net
URL: http://www.aea.net

Members: Companies engaged in the sales, engineering, installation, and service of electronic aviation equipment and systems. **Purpose:** Seeks to: advance the science of aircraft electronics; promote uniform and stable regulations and uniform standards of performance; establish and maintain a code of ethics; gather and disseminate technical data; advance the education of members and the public in the science of aircraft electronics. **Activities:** Offers supplement type certificates, test equipment licensing, temporary FCC licensing for new installations, spare parts availability and pricing, audiovisual technician training, equipment and spare parts loan, profitable installation, and service facility operation. Provides employment information, equipment exchange information and service assistance on member installations anywhere in the world.

★4574★ American Association of Engineering Societies (AAES)

1620 I St. NW, Ste. 210
Washington, DC 20006
Ph: (202)296-2237   Fax: (202)296-1151
Fr: 888-400-2237
E-mail: dbateson@aaes.org
URL: http://www.aaes.org

Description: Coordinates the efforts of the member societies in the provision of reliable and objective information to the general public concerning issues which affect the engineering profession and the field of engineering as a whole; collects, analyzes, documents, and disseminates data which will inform the general public of the relationship between engineering and the national welfare; provides a forum for the engineering societies to exchange and discuss their views on matters of common interest; and represents the U.S. engineering community abroad through representation in WFEO and UPADI.

★4575★ American Engineering Association (AEA)

4116 S Carrier Pkwy., Ste. 280-809
Grand Prairie, TX 75052
Ph: (201)664-6954
E-mail: info@aea.org
URL: http://www.aea.org

Description: Members consist of Engineers and engineering professionals. Purpose to advance the engineering profession and U.S. engineering capabilities. Issues of concern include age discrimination, immigration laws, displacement of U.S. Engineers by foreign workers, trade agreements, off shoring of U.S. Engineering and manufacturing jobs, loss of U.S. manufacturing and engineering capability, and recruitment of foreign students. Testifies before Congress. Holds local Chapter meetings.

★4576★ American Society of Certified Engineering Technicians (ASCET)

PO Box 1536
Brandon, MS 39043
Ph: (601)824-8991   Fax: (913)890-1021
E-mail: general-manager@ascet.org
URL: http://www.ascet.org

Description: Represents certified and non-certified engineering technicians and technologists. Works to obtain recognition of the contribution of engineering technicians and engineering technologists as an essential part of the engineering-scientific team. Cooperates with engineering and scientific societies. Improves the utilization of the engineering technician and technologist. Assists the educational, social, economic, and ethical development of the engineering technician and technologist. **Activities:** Conducts triennial survey among members to determine employer support, pay scales, and fringe benefits. Offers referral service.

★4577★ Association for International Practical Training (AIPT)

10400 Little Patuxent Pkwy., Ste. 250
Columbia, MD 21044-3519
Ph: (410)997-2200   Fax: (410)992-3924
E-mail: aipt@aipt.org
URL: http://www.aipt.org

Description: Providers worldwide of on-the-job training programs for students and professionals seeking international career development and life-changing experiences. Arranges workplace exchanges in hundreds of professional fields, bringing employers and trainees together from around the world. Client list ranges from small farming communities to Fortune 500 companies.

★4578★ International Society of Certified Electronics Technicians (ISCET)

3608 Pershing Ave.
Fort Worth, TX 76107-4527
Ph: (817)921-9101   Fax: (817)921-3741
Fr: 800-946-0201
E-mail: info@iscet.org
URL: http://www.iscet.org

Description: Technicians in 50 countries who have been certified by the society. Seeks to provide a fraternal bond among certified electronics technicians, raise their public image, and improve the effectiveness of industry education programs for technicians. Offers training programs in new electronics information. Maintains library of service literature for consumer electronic equipment, including manuals and schematics for out-of-date equipment. Offers all FCC licenses. Sponsors testing program for certification of electronics technicians in the fields of audio, communications, computer, consumer, industrial, medical electronics, radar, radio-television, and video.

★4579★ ISA - Instrumentation, Systems, and Automation Society

67 Alexander Dr.
PO Box 12277
Research Triangle Park, NC 27709
Ph: (919)549-8411   Fax: (919)549-8288
E-mail: info@isa.org
URL: http://www.isa.org

Description: Sets the standard for automation by helping over 30,000 worldwide members and other professionals solve difficult technical problems, while enhancing their leadership and personal career capabilities. Develops standards; certifies industry professionals; provides education and training; publishes books and technical articles; and hosts the largest conference and exhibition for automation professionals in the Western Hemisphere. Is the founding sponsor of The Automation Federation.

★4580★ National Institute for Certification in Engineering Technologies (NICET)

1420 King St.
Alexandria, VA 22314-2794
Ph: (703)548-1518   Fax: (703)682-2756
Fr: 888-IS-NICET
E-mail: test@nicet.org
URL: http://www.nicet.org

Description: Grants and issues certificates to engineering technicians and technologists who voluntarily apply for certification and satisfy competency criteria through examinations and verification of work experience. Requirements for certification involve work experience in terms of job task proficiency and length of progressively more responsible experience. Levels of certification are Technician Trainee, Associate Engineering Technician, Engineering Technician, Senior Engineering Technician, Associate Engineering Technologist, and Certified Engineering Technologist.

★4581★ Scientific, Engineering, and Technical Services

Cambridge Educational
PO Box 2053
Princeton, NJ 08543-2053
Ph: 800-257-5126   Fax: (609)671-0266
Fr: 800-468-4227
E-mail: custserv@films.com
URL: http://www.cambridgeeducational.com

VHS and DVD. $89.95. 2002. 18 minutes. 2002. Part of the Career Cluster Series.

★4582★ Society of Women Engineers (SWE)

230 E Ohio St., Ste. 400
Chicago, IL 60611-3265
Ph: (312)596-5223   Fax: (312)596-5252
Fr: 877-SWE-INFO
E-mail: hq@swe.org
URL: http://www.swe.org

Description: Educational and service organization representing both students and professional women in engineering and technical fields.

★4583★ **Technical & Related Occupations**

Delphi Productions
3159 6th St.
Boulder, CO 80304
Ph: (303)443-2100   Fax: (303)443-4022
Fr: 888-443-2400
E-mail: support@delphivideo.com
URL: http://www.delphivideo.com

$95.00. 49 minutes. Part of the Careers for the 21st Century Video Library.

★4584★ **Women in Engineering**

Her Own Words
PO Box 5264
Madison, WI 53705-0264
Ph: (608)271-7083   Fax: (608)271-0209
E-mail: herownword@aol.com
URL: http://www.herownwords.com/

Video. Jocelyn Riley. $95.00. 15 minutes. Resource guide also available for $45.00.

Environmental Engineers

★4585★ AIE Perspectives Newsmagazine

American Institute of Engineers
4630 Appian Way, Ste. 206
El Sobrante, CA 94803-1875
Ph: (510)758-6240   Fax: (510)758-6240

Monthly. Professional magazine covering engineering.

★4586★ Applied Occupational & Environmental Hygiene

Applied Industrial Hygiene Inc.
1330 Kemper Meadow Dr., Ste. 600
Cincinnati, OH 45240
Ph: (513)742-2020   Fax: (513)742-3355
URL: http://www.acgih.org

Monthly. $223.00/year for individuals, individual membership; $623.00/year for institutions, institution or organization. Peer-reviewed journal presenting applied solutions for the prevention of occupational and environmental disease and injury.

★4587★ AWIS Magazine

Association for Women in Science
1200 New York Ave. NW, Ste. 650
Washington, DC 20005
Ph: (202)326-8940   Fax: (202)326-8960
Fr: (866)657-2947
E-mail: awis@awis.org
URL: http://www.awis.org/

Description: Bimonthly. Covers issues, legislation, and trends related to science education for girls, women, and minorities. Includes information on grants and fellowships, job openings, educational programs, events, and notices of publications available.

★4588★ Drinking Water & Backflow Prevention

IAPMO
5001 E Philadelphia St.
Ontario, CA 91761-2816
Ph: (909)472-4100   Fax: (909)472-4150
Fr: 800-854-2766
E-mail: backflow@dwbp-online.com
URL: http://www.dwbp-online.com

Description: Monthly. Presents articles directed toward "individuals, companies, organizations, agencies, and municipalities with an interest in drinking water protection and backflow prevention." Contains information on safety standards, water system protection, training programs, cross-connection control, and all issues related to preventing the contamination of potable drinking water supplies with backflow prevention devices. Recurring features include case studies, letters to the editor, news of research, columns titled Test Your Investigative Skills and Backflow Prevention Device Repairs, and reports of meetings. Also carries news of educational opportunities, job listings, notices of publications available, and a calendar of events.

★4589★ Earth Work

Student Conservation Association
689 River Rd.
PO Box 550
Charlestown, NH 03603
Ph: (603)543-1700   Fax: (603)543-1828
E-mail: earthwork@sca-inc.org
URL: http://www.thesca.org/

Description: Monthly. Contains listings of environmental positions, ranging from internships and administrative assistants for environmental groups to camp directors, state natural resource managers, and biologists.

★4590★ Engineering Conferences International Symposium Series

Berkeley Electronic Press
2809 Telegraph Ave., Ste. 202
Berkeley, CA 94705
Ph: (510)665-1200   Fax: (510)665-1201
URL: http://services.bepress.com/eci/

Journal focusing on advance engineering science.

★4591★ Environmental Business Journal

Environmental Business International Inc.
ZweigWhite Information Services
One Apple Hill Dr., Ste. 2
Natick, MA 01760
Ph: 800-466-6275   Fax: (508)653-6522
E-mail: info@zweigwhite.com
URL: http://www.ebiusa.com

Description: Six issues/year. Provides research and articles on various segments of the environmental business industry. Recurring features include news of research.

★4592★ Environmental Education Research

Taylor & Francis Group Journals
325 Chestnut St., Ste. 800
Philadelphia, PA 19106
Ph: (215)625-8900   Fax: (215)625-8914
Fr: 800-354-1420
URL: http://www.tandf.co.uk/journals/titles/13504622.asp

Journal covering all aspects of environmental education.

★4593★ Environmental Pollution

Elsevier Science Inc.
360 Park Ave. S
New York, NY 10010
Ph: (212)989-5800   Fax: (212)633-3990
URL: http://www.elsevier.com

$4,689.00/year for institutions, for all countries except Europe, Japan and Iran; $136.00/year for individuals, for all countries except Europe, Japan and Iran. Journal covering issues relevant to chemical pollutants in air, soil and water.

★4594★ Environmental Progress

John Wiley & Sons Inc.
111 River St.
Hoboken, NJ 07030-5774
Ph: (201)748-6000   Fax: (201)748-6088
Fr: 800-825-7550
URL: http://www.wiley.com/WileyCDA/WileyTitle/productCd-EP.html

Quarterly. $445.00/year for institutions, print, U.S.; $493.00/year for institutions, Canada and Mexico, print; $521.00/year for institutions, print, rest of world; $490.00/year for institutions, print & online, U.S.; $538.00/year for institutions, Canada and Mexico, print & online; $566.00/year for institutions, print & online, rest of world. Journal reporting technological advances vital to engineering professionals whose responsibility includes or is related to environmental issues.

★4595★ **Graduating Engineer & Computer Careers**
Career Recruitment Media
211 W Wacker Dr., Ste. 900
Chicago, IL 60606
Ph: (312)525-3100
URL: http://www.graduatingengineer.com

Quarterly. $15.00/year for individuals. Magazine focusing on employment, education, and career development for entry-level engineers and computer scientists.

★4596★ **High Technology Careers Magazine**
HTC
4701 Patrick Henry Dr., No. 1901
Santa Clara, CA 95054-1847
Fax: (408)567-0242
URL: http://www.hightechcareers.com

Bimonthly. $29.00/year; $35.00/year for Canada; $85.00/year for out of country. Magazine (tabloid) containing employment opportunity information for the engineering and technical community.

★4597★ **Infogram**
Engineering Resource Center
Box 2201
Brookings, SD 57007
Ph: (605)688-4121   Fax: (605)688-6891
Fr: 800-952-3541
URL: http://www3.sdstate.edu/

Description: Semiannual. Provides information on Center activities, programs, and technology transfer items to improve the industry and solve technical problems.

★4598★ **InterJournal**
New England Complex Systems Institute
24 Mt. Auburn St.
Cambridge, MA 02138
Ph: (617)547-4100   Fax: (617)661-7711
URL: http://www.interjournal.org/

Journal covering the fields of science and engineering.

★4599★ **International Archives of Bioscience**
International Archives of Bioscience
PO Box 737254
Elmhurst, NY 11373-9997
URL: http://www.iabs.us/jdoc/aboutiabs.htm

Free, online only. Journal reporting multidisciplinary coverage and interaction between scientists in biology, informatics, mathematics, physics, engineering and other sciences.

★4600★ **The Job Seeker**
The Job Seeker
403 Oakwood St.
Warrens, WI 54666
Ph: (608)378-4450   Fax: (267)295-2005
URL: http://www.thejobseeker.net

Description: Semimonthly. Specializes "in environmental and natural resource vacancies nationwide." Lists current vacancies from federal, state, local, private, and non-profit employers. Also available via e-mail.

★4601★ **Journal of the American Water Works Association**
American Water Works Association
6666 W Quincy Ave.
Denver, CO 80235
Ph: (303)794-7711   Fax: (303)347-0804
Fr: 800-926-7337
URL: http://www.awwa.org

Monthly. Subscription included in membership. Magazine dealing with water supply resources, treatment, and distribution.

★4602★ **Journal of Engineering Education**
American Society for Engineering Education
1818 North St., NW, Ste. 600
Washington, DC 20036-2479
Ph: (202)331-3500
URL: http://www.asee.org/publications/jee/index.cfm

Quarterly. Journal covering scholarly research in engineering education.

★4603★ **Journal of Environmental Engineering**
American Society of Civil Engineers
1801 Alexander Bell Dr.
Reston, VA 20191-4400
Ph: (703)295-6300   Fax: (703)295-6222
Fr: 800-548-2723
E-mail: ztrem@ce.udel.edu
URL: http://www.pubs.asce.org/journals/ee.html

Monthly. $234.00/year for members, domestic; $585.00/year for individuals, domestic; $936.00/year for institutions, domestic; $211.00/year for members, print only; $527.00/year for individuals, print only; $843.00/year for institutions, print only; $282.00/year for members, print only; $633.00/year for individuals, print only; $984.00/year for institutions, print only; $259.00/year for individuals, print & online. Journal on the practice and status of research in environmental engineering science, systems engineering, and sanitation.

★4604★ **Journal of Environmental Health**
National Environmental Health Association
720 S Colorado Blvd., Ste. 1000-N
Denver, CO 80246-1925
Ph: (303)756-9090   Fax: (303)691-9490
URL: http://www.umi.com/proquest

Monthly. Journal presenting environmental health and protection issues.

★4605★ **MainStream**
American Water Works Association
6666 W Quincy Ave.
Denver, CO 80235
Ph: (303)794-7711   Fax: (303)347-0804
Fr: 800-926-7337
URL: http://www.awwa.org/communications/mainstream/

Description: Biweekly, online; print issue is quarterly. Carries news of the Association and features about the drinking water industry, including regulations, legislation, conservation, treatment, quality, distribution, management, and utility operations. Recurring features include letters to the editor, a calendar of events, reports of meetings, news of educational opportunities, notices of publications available, education and job opportunities in the industry and legislative news.

★4606★ **NAAEE Communicator**
North American Association for Environmental Education
2000 P St. NW
Ste. 540
Washington, DC 20036
Ph: (202)419-0412   Fax: (202)419-0415
URL: http://www.naaee.org

Description: Bimonthly. Concerned with environmental education, training services, and activities on local, national, and international levels. Encourages and supports creative thinking about environmental issues. Recognizes outstanding contributions to environmental education. Recurring features include news of members, news of educational listings, job listings, notices of publications available, association and Affiliate news, and a message from the president.

★4607★ **SPE Technical Journals**
Society of Petroleum Engineers
222 Palisades Creek Dr.
Richardson, TX 75080
Ph: (972)952-9393   Fax: (972)952-9435
Fr: 800-456-6863
URL: http://www.spe.org

Journal devoted to engineers and scientists.

★4608★ **Structure Magazine**
American Consulting Engineers Council
1015 15th St. NW, 8th Fl.
Washington, DC 20005-2605
Ph: (202)347-7474   Fax: (202)898-0068
URL: http://www.structuremag.org

Annual. $65.00/year for nonmembers; $35.00/year for students; $90.00/year for Canada; $125.00/year for other countries. Magazine focused on providing tips, tools, techniques, and innovative concepts for structural engineers.

★4609★ SWE, Magazine of the Society of Women Engineers

Society of Women Engineers
230 East Ohio St., Ste. 400
Chicago, IL 60611-3265
Ph: (312)596-5223
E-mail: hq@swe.org
URL: http://www.swe.org

Quarterly. $30.00/year for nonmembers. Magazine for engineering students and for women and men working in the engineering and technology fields. Covers career guidance, continuing development and topical issues.

★4610★ Uratie

IDG Communications Inc.
5 Speen St., 3rd. Fl
Framingham, MA 01701
Ph: (508)875-5000   Fax: (508)988-7888
URL: http://www.idg.com

Magazine providing job offers for graduates, engineers and information technology professionals.

★4611★ Water Environment Research

Water Environment Federation
601 Wythe St.
Alexandria, VA 22314-1994
Ph: (703)684-2452   Fax: (703)684-2492
Fr: 800-666-0206
E-mail: msc@wef.org
URL: http://www.wef.org

Bimonthly. $125.00/year for individuals, WEF Member, print plus online; $308.00/year for individuals, print plus online; $780.00/year for institutions, print plus online; $200.00/year for individuals, WEF Member, print plus online; $350.00/year for individuals, print plus online; $830.00/year for institutions, print plus online; $812.00/year for institutions, Domestic; $883.00/year for institutions, international. Technical journal covering municipal and industrial water pollution control, water quality, and hazardous wastes.

★4612★ WEPANEWS

Women in Engineering Programs & Advocates Network
1901 E. Asbury Ave., Ste. 220
Denver, CO 80208
Ph: (303)871-4643   Fax: (303)871-6833
E-mail: dmatt@wepan.org
URL: http://www.wepan.org

Description: 2/year. Seeks to provide greater access for women to careers in engineering. Includes news of graduate, undergraduate, freshmen, pre-college, and re-entry engineering programs for women. Recurring features include job listings, faculty, grant, and conference news, international engineering program news, action group news, notices of publications available, and a column titled Kudos.

PLACEMENT AND JOB REFERRAL SERVICES

★4613★ American Indian Science and Engineering Society (AISES)

PO Box 9828
Albuquerque, NM 87119-9828
Ph: (505)765-1052   Fax: (505)765-5608
E-mail: info@aises.org
URL: http://www.aises.org

Description: Represents American Indian and non-Indian students and professionals in science, technology, and engineering fields; corporations representing energy, mining, aerospace, electronic, and computer fields. Seeks to motivate and encourage students to pursue undergraduate and graduate studies in science, engineering, and technology. Sponsors science fairs in grade schools, teacher training workshops, summer math/science sessions for 8th-12th graders, professional chapters, and student chapters in colleges. Offers scholarships. Adult members serve as role models, advisers, and mentors for students. Operates placement service.

★4614★ Engineering Society of Detroit (ESD)

2000 Town Ctr., Ste. 2610
Southfield, MI 48075
Ph: (248)353-0735   Fax: (248)353-0736
E-mail: esd@esd.org
URL: http://esd.org

Description: Engineers from all disciplines; scientists and technologists. Conducts technical programs and engineering refresher courses; sponsors conferences and expositions. Maintains speakers' bureau; offers placement services; although based in Detroit, MI, society membership is international.

★4615★ Environmental Careers Organization (ECO)

30 Winter St., 6th Fl.
Boston, MA 02108-4720
Ph: (617)426-4375   Fax: (617)423-0998
E-mail: kdoyle@eco.org
URL: http://www.eco.org

Description: Seeks to protect and enhance the environment through the development of professionals, the promotion of careers, and the inspiration of individual action. Offers paid internships, career development educational programs and related publications. Participants in programs are mostly upper-level undergraduate, graduate, and doctoral students, or recent graduates seeking professional experience relevant to careers in the environmental fields. Individual subject areas of placement service include biology, chemistry, community development, hazardous waste, natural resources, pollution, public/occupational health, transportation, and wildlife.

★4616★ Society of Hispanic Professional Engineers (SHPE)

5400 E Olympic Blvd., Ste. 210
Los Angeles, CA 90022
Ph: (323)725-3970   Fax: (323)725-031(
E-mail: shpenational@shpe.org
URL: http://oneshpe.shpe.org/wps/portal/national

Description: Represents engineers, student engineers, and scientists. Aims to increase the number of Hispanic engineers by providing motivation and support to students. Sponsors competitions and educational programs. Maintains placement service and speakers' bureau; compiles statistics.

EMPLOYER DIRECTORIES AND NETWORKING LISTS

★4617★ American Men and Women of Science

Gale, Cengage Learning
27500 Drake Rd.
Farmington Hills, MI 48331-3535
Ph: (248)699-4253   Fax: (248)699-8065
Fr: 800-877-4253
URL: http://www.gale.com

Biennial, latest edition 23rd, October 2006; new edition expected 24th, January 2008. $1,075.00 for individuals. Covers over 129,700 U.S. and Canadian scientists active in the physical, biological, mathematical, computer science, and engineering fields; includes references to previous edition for deceased scientists and nonrespondents. Entries include: Name, address, education, personal and career data, memberships, honors and awards, research interest. Arrangement: Alphabetical. Indexes: Discipline (in separate volume).

★4618★ Association of Conservation Engineers-Membership Directory

Association of Conservation Engineers
Missouri Department of Conservation
PO Box 180
Jefferson City, MO 65102-0180
Ph: (573)522-4115
URL: http://conservationengineers.org

Annual, June. Covers 280 persons with administrative or engineering background in conservation. Entries include: Member name, address, phone, company or institution name. Arrangement: Alphabetical.

★4619★ Careers in Focus: Environment

Facts On File Inc.
132 W 31st St., 17th Fl.
New York, NY 10001
Ph: (212)967-8800   Fax: 800-678-3633
Fr: 800-322-8755
URL: http://www.factsonfile.com

Latest edition 3rd, 2004. $29.95 for individuals; $26.95 for libraries. Covers an overview of environmental jobs, followed by a selection of jobs profiled in detail, including the nature of the job, earnings, prospects for employment, what kind of training and skills it requires, and sources for further information.

★4620★ **Directory of Contract Staffing Firms**

C.E. Publications Inc.
PO Box 3006
Bothell, WA 98041-3006
Ph: (425)806-5200   Fax: (425)806-5585
URL: http://www.cjhunter.com/dcsf/overview.html

Covers nearly 1,300 contract firms actively engaged in the employment of engineering, IT/IS, and technical personnel for 'temporary' contract assignments throughout the world. Entries include: Company name, address, phone, name of contact, email, web address. Arrangement: Alphabetical. Indexes: Geographical.

★4621★ **Indiana Society of Professional Engineers-Directory**

Indiana Society of Professional Engineers
PO Box 20806
Indianapolis, IN 46220
Ph: (317)255-2267   Fax: (317)255-2530
URL: http://www.indspe.org

Annual, fall. Covers member registered engineers, land surveyors, engineering students, and engineers in training. Entries include: Member name, address, phone, type of membership, business information, specialty. Arrangement: Alphabetical by chapter area.

★4622★ **What Can I Do Now**

Facts On File Inc.
132 W 31st St., 17th Fl.
New York, NY 10001
Ph: (212)967-8800   Fax: 800-678-3633
Fr: 800-322-8755
URL: http://www.factsonfile.com

Published 1998. $22.95 for individuals; $20.65 for libraries. Covers ecologists, hazardous waste management technicians, national park service employees, and oceanographers.

★4623★ **Who's Who in Environmental Engineering**

American Academy of Environmental Engineers
130 Holiday Ct., Ste. 100
Annapolis, MD 21401
Ph: (410)266-3311   Fax: (410)266-7653
URL: http://www.aaee.net

Annual, April. $75.00 for individuals. Covers about 2,400 licensed professional environmental engineers who have been certified by examination in one or more of seven specialties: air pollution control, general environmental engineering, industrial hygiene, hazardous waste management, radiation protection, solid waste management, and water supply and wastewater. Entries include: Name, affiliation, address, phone, area of specialization, biographical data. Arrangement: Alphabetical, geographical, area of specialization.

HANDBOOKS AND MANUALS

★4624★ **The Best Resumes for Scientists and Engineers**

John Wiley & Sons Inc.
1 Wiley Dr.
Somerset, NJ 08873
Ph: (732)469-4400   Fax: (732)302-2300
Fr: 800-225-5945
E-mail: custserv@wiley.com
URL: http://www.wiley.com/WileyCDA/

Adele Lewis and David J. Moore. Second edition, 1993. $37.50; $19.95 (paper). 224 pages. Presents an extensive collection of scientific and engineering resumes, highlighting the important differences between these and resumes written for other occupations.

★4625★ **Careers in the Environment**

The McGraw-Hill Companies
PO Box 182604
Columbus, OH 43272
Fax: (614)759-3749   Fr: 877-883-5524
E-mail: customer.service@mcgraw-hill.com
URL: http://www.mcgraw-hill.com

Michael Fasulo and Paul Walker. Second edition, 2000. $17.95; $13.95 (paper). 290 pages. Comprehensive information on the diverse career opportunities available in environmental services.

★4626★ **Careers in Environmental Geoscience**

AAPG Publications
PO Box 979
Tulsa, OK 74101-0979
Ph: (918)584-2555   Fax: (918)560-2694
Fr: 800-364-2274
E-mail: postmaster@aapg.org
URL: http://www.aapg.org/index.cfm

Robert R. Jordan, Rima Petrossian, and William J. Murphy. 1996. $5.00 (paper). DEP Publications Series. 54 pages.

★4627★ **Careers for Environmental Types and Others Who Respect the Earth**

The McGraw-Hill Companies
PO Box 182604
Columbus, OH 43272
Fax: (614)759-3749   Fr: 877-883-5524
E-mail: customer.service@mcgraw-hill.com
URL: http://www.mcgraw-hill.com

Jane Kinney and Mike Fasulo. Second edition, 2001. $13.95; $10.74 (paper). 192 pages. Describes environmentally friendly positions with corporations, government, and environmental organizations.

★4628★ **Careers Inside the World of Environmental Science**

Pearson Learning Group
135 S. Mt. Zion Rd.
PO Box 2500
Lebanon, IN 46052
Fax: 800-393-3156   Fr: 800-526-9907
URL: http://www.pearsonatschool.com

Robert Gartner. 1996. $21.30. 64 pages. Describes jobs in environmental studies and related fields for reluctant readers.

★4629★ **Careers in Science and Engineering**

National Academies Press
500 5th St. NW
Lockbox 285
Washington, DC 20055
Ph: (202)334-3313   Fax: (202)334-2793
Fr: 888-624-8373
URL: http://www.nap.edu/

1996. $11.95. 134 pages. Covers planning for graduate school and beyond.

★4630★ **The Complete Guide to Environmental Careers in the 21st Century**

Island Press
1718 Connecticut Ave. NW, Ste. 300
Washington, DC 20009
Ph: (202)232-7933   Fax: (202)234-1328
Fr: 800-621-2736
URL: http://www.islandpress.org/

Environmental Careers Organization. 1998. Third edition. $28.50 (paper). 463 pages. A completely revised and updated edition of the standard reference on environmental careers.

★4631★ **Great Jobs for Engineering Majors**

The McGraw-Hill Companies
PO Box 182604
Columbus, OH 43272
Fax: (614)759-3749   Fr: 877-883-5524
E-mail: customer.service@mcgraw-hill.com
URL: http://www.mcgraw-hill.com

Geraldine O. Garner. Second edition, 2002. $14.95. 256 pages. Covers all the career options open to students majoring in engineering.

★4632★ **Hidden Job Market**

Peterson's Guides
2000 Lenox Dr.
Box 67005
Lawrenceville, NJ 08648
Ph: (609)896-1800   Fax: (609)896-4531
Fr: 800-338-3282
E-mail: custsvc@petersons.com
URL: http://www.petersons.com

Ninth edition, 1999. $18.95 (paper). 319 pages. Guide to 2,000 fast-growing companies that are hiring now. Focuses on high technology companies in such fields as environmental consulting, genetic engineering, home health care, telecommunications, alternative energy systems, and others. Part of Peterson's Hidden Job Market series.

★4633★ How to Succeed as an Engineer: A Practical Guide to Enhance Your Career

Institute of Electrical & Electronics Engineers
445 Hoes Lane
Piscataway, NJ 08854
Ph: (732)981-0060   Fax: (732)981-9667
Fr: 800-678-4333
URL: http://www.ieee.org

Todd Yuzuriha. 1999. $29.95 (paper). 367 pages.

★4634★ Keys to Engineering Success

Prentice Hall PTR
One Lake St.
Upper Saddle River, NJ 07458
Ph: (201)236-7000   Fr: 800-428-5331
URL: http://www.phptr.com/index.asp?rl=1

Jill S. Tietjen, Kristy A. Schloss, Carol Carter, Joyce Bishop, and Sarah Lyman. 2000. $46.00 (paper). 288 pages.

★4635★ Nature (Career Portraits)

The McGraw-Hill Companies
PO Box 182604
Columbus, OH 43272
Fax: (614)759-3749   Fr: 877-883-5524
E-mail: customer.service@mcgraw-hill.com
URL: http://www.mcgraw-hill.com

Marjorie Eberts. 1996. $13.95. 96 pages. Highlights a range of careers that focus on the environment, with descriptions of a typical day on the job and interactive exercises for readers.

★4636★ The New Engineer's Guide to Career Growth & Professional Awareness

Institute of Electrical & Electronics Engineers
445 Hoes Lane
Piscataway, NJ 08854
Ph: (732)981-0060   Fax: (732)981-9667
Fr: 800-678-4333
URL: http://www.ieee.org

Irving J. Gabelman, editor. 1996. $39.95 (paper). 275 pages.

★4637★ Opportunities in Engineering Careers

The McGraw-Hill Companies
PO Box 182604
Columbus, OH 43272
Fax: (614)759-3749   Fr: 877-883-5524
E-mail: customer.service@mcgraw-hill.com
URL: http://www.mcgraw-hill.com

Nicholas Basta. Revised second edition, 2002. $13.95; $11.95 (paper). 160 pages. Outlines typical job titles, salaries, career paths, and employment prospects.

★4638★ Opportunities in Environmental Careers

The McGraw-Hill Companies
PO Box 182604
Columbus, OH 43272
Fax: (614)759-3749   Fr: 877-883-5524
E-mail: customer.service@mcgraw-hill.com
URL: http://www.mcgraw-hill.com

Odom Fanning. Revised, 2002. $12.95 (paper). 174 pages. Describes a broad range of opportunities in fields such as environmental health, recreation, physics, and hygiene, and provides job search advice. Part of the "Opportunities in ..." Series.

★4639★ Peterson's Job Opportunities in Engineering and Technology

Peterson's Guides
2000 Lenox Dr.
Box 67005
Lawrenceville, NJ 08648
Ph: (609)896-1800   Fax: (609)896-4531
Fr: 800-338-3282
E-mail: custsvc@petersons.com
URL: http://www.petersons.com

Compiled by the Peterson's staff. Fourth edition, 1996. $21.95 (paper). 379 pages. Profiles 2,000 high-tech companies looking primarily for technical personnel in such fields as biotechnology, telecommunications, software, computers and peripherals, defense, and aerospace. Contains job-search strategies and career options to help match education and expertise to the job market. Indexed geographically, by industry, and by hiring needs.

★4640★ Real People Working in Engineering

The McGraw-Hill Companies
PO Box 182604
Columbus, OH 43272
Fax: (614)759-3749   Fr: 877-883-5524
E-mail: customer.service@mcgraw-hill.com
URL: http://www.mcgraw-hill.com

Blythe Camenson, Jan Goldberg. 1997. $17.95 (paper). 160 pages. Interviews and profiles of working professionals capture a range of opportunities in this field.

★4641★ Resumes for Engineering Careers

The McGraw-Hill Companies
PO Box 182604
Columbus, OH 43272
Fax: (614)759-3749   Fr: 877-883-5524
E-mail: customer.service@mcgraw-hill.com
URL: http://www.mcgraw-hill.com

Third edition, 2005. $11.95 (paper). 144 pages. Contains sample resumes and cover letters applicable to any engineering field.

★4642★ Resumes for Environmental Careers

The McGraw-Hill Companies
PO Box 182604
Columbus, OH 43272
Fax: (614)759-3749   Fr: 877-883-5524

E-mail: customer.service@mcgraw-hill.com
URL: http://www.mcgraw-hill.com

Second edition, 2002. $10.95 (paper). 160 pages. Provides resume advice tailored to people pursuing careers focusing on the environment. Includes sample resumes and cover letters.

★4643★ Resumes for Scientific and Technical Careers

The McGraw-Hill Companies
PO Box 182604
Columbus, OH 43272
Fax: (614)759-3749   Fr: 877-883-5524
E-mail: customer.service@mcgraw-hill.com
URL: http://www.mcgraw-hill.com

Third edition, 2007. $12.95 (paper). 144 pages. Provides resume advice for individuals interested in working in scientific and technical careers. Includes sample resumes and cover letters.

EMPLOYMENT AGENCIES AND SEARCH FIRMS

★4644★ Amtec Engineering Corp.

2749 Saturn St.
Brea, CA 92821
Ph: (714)993-1900   Fax: (714)993-2419
E-mail: info@amtechc.com
URL: http://www.amtec-eng.com

Employment agency.

★4645★ The Angus Group Ltd.

5080 Wooster Rd., Ste. 300
Cincinnati, OH 45226
Ph: (513)961-5575   Fax: (513)961-5616
E-mail: angus@angusgroup.com
URL: http://www.angusgroup.com

Executive search firm.

★4646★ Bell Oaks Co.

10 Glenlake Pkwy., Ste. 300
Atlanta, GA 30328
Ph: (678)287-2000   Fax: (678)287-2002
E-mail: info@belloaks.com
URL: http://www.belloaks.com

Personnel service firm.

★4647★ The Borton Wallace Company

PO Box 8816
Asheville, NC 28814-0989
Ph: (828)258-1831   Fax: (828)251-0989
E-mail: mes@boone-scaturro.com
URL: http://www.bortonwallace.com

Executive search firm.

★4648★ Career Center, Inc.
194 Passaic St.
Hackensack, NJ 07601
Ph: (201)342-1777   Fax: (201)342-1776
Fr: 800-227-3379
E-mail: career@careercenterinc.com
URL: http://www.careercenterinc.com

Employment agency.

★4649★ The Carter Group LLC
PO Box 850303
Mobile, AL 36685-0303
Ph: (251)342-0999   Fax: (251)342-7999
E-mail: info@thecartergroup.com
URL: http://www.thecartergroup.com

Executive search firm. Branch in Alpharetta GA.

★4650★ COBA Executive Search
14947 E. Wagontrail Pl.
Aurora, CO 80015
Ph: (303)693-8382
E-mail: mekiken43256@comcast.net

Executive search firm.

★4651★ Corporate Environment Ltd.
PO Box 798
Crystal Lake, IL 60039-0798
Ph: (815)455-6070   Fax: (815)455-0124
E-mail: tomsearch@consultant.com

Executive search firm.

★4652★ The Elliot Company
Ph: (202)521-5300
E-mail: suppt.staff@elliottco.net
URL: http://www.elliottco.net

Executive search firm.

★4653★ Erspamer Associates
4010 W. 65th St., Ste. 100
Edina, MN 55435
Ph: (952)925-3747   Fax: (952)925-4022
E-mail: hdhuntrel@aol.com

Executive search firm specializing in technical management.

★4654★ Executive Recruiters Agency
14 Office Park Dr., Ste. 100
PO Box 21810
Little Rock, AR 72221-1810
Ph: (501)224-7000   Fax: (501)224-8534
E-mail: jobs@execrecruit.com
URL: http://www.execrecruit.com

Personnel service firm.

★4655★ JPM International
26034 Acero
Mission Viejo, CA 92691
Ph: (949)699-4300   Fax: (949)699-4333
Fr: 800-685-7856
E-mail: trish@jpmintl.com
URL: http://www.jpmintl.com

Executive search firm and employment agency.

★4656★ McNichol Associates
620 Chestnut St., Ste. 1031
Philadelphia, PA 19106
Ph: (215)922-4142   Fax: (215)922-0178
E-mail: mailbox@mcnicholassoc.com
URL: http://www.mcnicholassoc.com

Performs executive search for middle and senior-level management, marketing, and technical personnel for professional design firms; construction, management, and general contractors; engineering-construction organizations; environmental firms, and others needing technical management personnel.

★4657★ Rand Personnel
1200 Truxtun Ave., Ste. 130
Bakersfield, CA 93301
Ph: (805)325-0751   Fax: (805)325-4120

Personnel service firm serving a variety of fields.

★4658★ Randolph Associates, Inc.
950 Massachusetts Ave., Ste. 105
Cambridge, MA 02139-3174
Ph: (617)441-8777   Fax: (617)441-8778
E-mail: jobs@greatjobs.com
URL: http://www.greatjobs.com

Employment agency. Provides regular or temporary placement of staff.

★4659★ Roberson & Co.
10751 Parfet St.
Broomfield, CO 80021
Ph: (303)410-6510
E-mail: roberson@recruiterpro.com
URL: http://www.recruiterpro.com

A contingency professional and executive recruiting firm working the national and international marketplace. Specialize in accounting, finance, data processing and information services, healthcare, environmental and mining, engineering, manufacturing, human resources, and sales and marketing.

★4660★ Search North America Inc.
PO Box 3577
Sunriver, OR 97707-0577
Ph: (503)222-6461   Fax: (503)227-2804
E-mail: mylinda@searchna.com
URL: http://www.searchna.com

An executive search and recruiting firm whose focus is placing engineers, operations and maintenance managers, sales and marketing management, financial and general management executives (both domestic and international). Industries served: forest products, pulp and paper, waste to energy, environmental services, consulting and equipment suppliers for above related industries.

★4661★ Winters Technical Staffing Services
6 Lansing Sq., Ste. 101
Toronto, ON, Canada M2J 1T5
Ph: (416)495-7422   Fax: (416)495-8479
E-mail: brian@winterstaffing.com
URL: http://www.winterstaffing.com

Technical staffing service for permanent and contract positions in all facets of engineering. Serves government agencies, consulting engineers, and all areas of manufacturing in Canada and northeast United States.

ONLINE JOB SOURCES AND SERVICES

★4662★ Spherion
2050 Spectrum Blvd.
Fort Lauderdale, FL 33309
Ph: (954)308-7600
E-mail: help@spherion.com
URL: http://www.spherion.com

Description: Recruitment firm specializing in accounting and finance, sales and marketing, interim executives, technology, engineering, retail and human resources.

TRADESHOWS

★4663★ Air and Waste Management Association Annual Conference and Exhibition
Air and Waste Management Association
One Gateway Center, 3rd Fl.
420 Fort Duquesne Blvd
Pittsburgh, PA 15222-1435
Ph: (412)232-3444   Fax: (412)232-3450
Fr: 800-270-3444
E-mail: info@awma.org
URL: http://www.awma.org

Annual. **Primary Exhibits:** Instrumentation, environmental control products, and services. **Dates and Locations:** 2008 Jun 24-27; Portland, OR; 2009 Jun 23-26; Detroit, MI; 2010 Jun 22-25; Calgary, AB, Canada.

★4664★ American Society for Engineering Education Annual Conference and Exposition
American Society for Engineering Education
1818 N. St. NW, Ste. 600
Washington, DC 20036-2479
Ph: (202)331-3500   Fax: (202)265-8504
E-mail: conferences@asee.org
URL: http://www.asee.org

Annual. **Primary Exhibits:** Publications, engineering supplies and equipment, computers, software, and research companies all products and services related to engineering education.

★4665★ National Water Resources Association Annual Conference

National Water Resources Association
3800 N Fairfax Dr., Ste. 4
Arlington, VA 22203
Ph: (703)524-1544   Fax: (703)524-1548
URL: http://www.nwra.org

Annual. **Primary Exhibits:** Exhibits relating to the development, control, conservation, and utilization of water resources in the reclamation states (17 western states). **Dates and Locations:** 2008 Nov 28 - Dec 01; San Diego, CA; Hotel del Coronado.

★4666★ NGWA Annual Convention/ Exposition

National Ground Water Association
601 Dempsey Rd.
Westerville, OH 43081-8978
Ph: (614)898-7791   Fax: (614)898-7786
Fr: 800-551-7379
E-mail: ngwa@ngwa.org
URL: http://www.ngwa.org

Annual. **Primary Exhibits:** Equipment, products and technology for the ground water industry.

★4667★ Texas Ground Water Association Trade Show and Convention

Texas Ground Water Association (TGWA)
221 E. 9th St., Ste. 206
San Jacinto Bldg.
Austin, TX 78701
Ph: (512)472-7437   Fax: (512)472-0537
E-mail: goodson@twca.org
URL: http://www.tgwa.org

Annual. **Primary Exhibits:** Water well equipment, including drills.

★4668★ Water Quality Association Convention

Water Quality Association
4151 Naperville Rd.
Lisle, IL 60532-1088
Ph: (630)505-0160   Fax: (630)505-9637
E-mail: info@wqa.org
URL: http://www.wqa.org

Annual. **Primary Exhibits:** Water treatment equipment and related articles.

★4669★ WEFTEC

Water Environment Federation
601 Wythe St.
Alexandria, VA 22314-1994
Ph: (703)684-2452   Fax: (703)684-2492
Fr: 800-666-0206
E-mail: csc@wef.org
URL: http://www.wef.org

Annual. **Primary Exhibits:** Water treatment equipment, supplies, and services.

OTHER SOURCES

★4670★ Air and Waste Management Association (A&WMA)

1 Gateway Ctr., 3rd Fl.
420 Ft. Duquesne Blvd.
Pittsburgh, PA 15222-1435
Ph: (412)232-3444   Fax: (412)232-3450
Fr: 800-270-3444
E-mail: info@awma.org
URL: http://www.awma.org

Description: Serves as environmental, educational, and technical organization. **Purpose:** Seeks to provide a neutral forum for the exchange of technical information on a wide variety of environmental topics.

★4671★ American Academy of Environmental Engineers (AAEE)

130 Holiday Ct., Ste. 100
Annapolis, MD 21401
Ph: (410)266-3311   Fax: (410)266-7653
E-mail: info@aaee.net
URL: http://www.aaee.net

Members: Environmentally oriented registered professional engineers certified by examination as Diplomates of the Academy. **Purpose:** Seeks to improve the standards of environmental engineering. Certifies those with special knowledge of environmental engineering. Furnishes lists of those certified to the public. **Activities:** Maintains speakers' bureau. Recognizes areas of specialization: Air Pollution Control; General Environmental; Hazardous Waste Management; Industrial Hygiene; Radiation Protection; Solid Waste Management; Water Supply and Wastewater. Requires written and oral examinations for certification. Works with other professional organizations on environmentally oriented activities. Identifies potential employment candidates through Talent Search Service.

★4672★ American Association of Engineering Societies (AAES)

1620 I St. NW, Ste. 210
Washington, DC 20006
Ph: (202)296-2237   Fax: (202)296-1151
Fr: 888-400-2237
E-mail: dbateson@aaes.org
URL: http://www.aaes.org

Description: Coordinates the efforts of the member societies in the provision of reliable and objective information to the general public concerning issues which affect the engineering profession and the field of engineering as a whole; collects, analyzes, documents, and disseminates data which will inform the general public of the relationship between engineering and the national welfare; provides a forum for the engineering societies to exchange and discuss their views on matters of common interest; and represents the U.S. engineering community abroad through representation in WFEO and UPADI.

★4673★ American Engineering Association (AEA)

4116 S Carrier Pkwy., Ste. 280-809
Grand Prairie, TX 75052
Ph: (201)664-6954
E-mail: info@aea.org
URL: http://www.aea.org

Description: Members consist of Engineers and engineering professionals. Purpose to advance the engineering profession and U.S. engineering capabilities. Issues of concern include age discrimination, immigration laws, displacement of U.S. Engineers by foreign workers, trade agreements, off shoring of U.S. Engineering and manufacturing jobs, loss of U.S. manufacturing and engineering capability, and recruitment of foreign students. Testifies before Congress. Holds local Chapter meetings.

★4674★ Environmental Industry Associations (EIA)

4301 Connecticut Ave. NW, Ste. 300
Washington, DC 20008-2304
Ph: (202)244-4700   Fax: (202)966-4818
Fr: 800-424-2869
E-mail: membership@envasns.org
URL: http://www.envasns.org

Activities: Compiles statistics; conducts research and educational programs.

★4675★ Environmental Occupations: Professional

Delphi Productions
3159 6th St.
Boulder, CO 80304
Ph: (303)443-2100   Fax: (303)443-4022
Fr: 888-443-2400
E-mail: support@delphivideo.com
URL: http://www.delphivideo.com

$95.00. 49 minutes. Part of the Emerging Careers Video Library.

★4676★ Environmental Occupations: Technical

Delphi Productions
3159 6th St.
Boulder, CO 80304
Ph: (303)443-2100   Fax: (303)443-4022
Fr: 888-443-2400
E-mail: support@delphivideo.com
URL: http://www.delphivideo.com

$95.00. 48 minutes. Part of the Emerging Careers Video Library.

★4677★ National Action Council for Minorities in Engineering (NACME)

440 Hamilton Ave., Ste. 302
White Plains, NY 10601-1813
Ph: (914)539-4010   Fax: (914)539-4032
E-mail: webmaster@nacme.org
URL: http://www.nacme.org

Description: Leads the national effort to increase access to careers in engineering and other science-based disciplines. Conducts research and public policy analysis, develops and operates national demonstration programs at precollege and university evels, and disseminates information through publications, conferences and electronic media. Serves as a privately funded source of scholarships for minority students in engineering.

★4678★ National Society of Professional Engineers (NSPE)

1420 King St.
Alexandria, VA 22314-2794
Ph: (703)684-2800   Fax: (703)836-4875
Fr: 888-285-6773
E-mail: memserv@nspe.org
URL: http://www.nspe.org

Description: Represents professional engineers and engineers-in-training in all fields registered in accordance with the laws of states or territories of the U.S. or provinces of Canada; qualified graduate engineers, student members, and registered land surveyors. Is concerned with social, professional, ethical, and economic considerations of engineering as a profession; encompasses programs in public relations, employment practices, ethical considerations, education, and career guidance. Monitors legislative and regulatory actions of interest to the engineering profession.

★4679★ *Resumes for High Tech Careers*

The McGraw-Hill Companies
PO Box 182604
Columbus, OH 43272
Fax: (614)759-3749   Fr: 877-883-5524
E-mail: customer.service@mcgraw-hill.com
URL: http://www.mcgraw-hill.com

Third edition, 2003. $10.95 (paper). 160 pages. Demonstrates how to tailor a resume that catches a high tech employer's attention. Part of "Resumes for ..." series.

★4680★ Scientific, Engineering, and Technical Services

Cambridge Educational
PO Box 2053
Princeton, NJ 08543-2053
Ph: 800-257-5126   Fax: (609)671-0266
Fr: 800-468-4227
E-mail: custserv@films.com
URL: http://www.cambridgeeducational.com

VHS and DVD. $89.95. 2002. 18 minutes. 2002. Part of the Career Cluster Series.

★4681★ Society of Women Engineers (SWE)

230 E Ohio St., Ste. 400
Chicago, IL 60611-3265
Ph: (312)596-5223   Fax: (312)596-5252
Fr: 877-SWE-INFO
E-mail: hq@swe.org
URL: http://www.swe.org

Description: Educational and service organization representing both students and professional women in engineering and technical fields.

★4682★ Women in Engineering

Her Own Words
PO Box 5264
Madison, WI 53705-0264
Ph: (608)271-7083   Fax: (608)271-0209
E-mail: herownword@aol.com
URL: http://www.herownwords.com/

Video. Jocelyn Riley. $95.00. 15 minutes. Resource guide also available for $45.00.

Epidemiologists

SOURCES OF HELP-WANTED ADS

★4683★ American Journal of Epidemiology

Oxford University Press
2001 Evans Rd.
Cary, NC 27513
Ph: (919)677-0977   Fax: (919)677-1714
Fr: 800-852-7323
URL: http://aje.oupjournals.org

Semimonthly. $473.00/year for institutions, print & online; $709.00/year for institutions, print & online; $709.00/year for institutions, print & online; $449.00/year for individuals, online; $674.00/year for individuals, online; $674.00/year for individuals, online; $449.00/year for institutions, print; $674.00/year for institutions, print; $674.00/year for institutions, print. Science research and medical journal.

★4684★ Annals of Medicine

Taylor & Francis Group Journals
325 Chestnut St., Ste. 800
Philadelphia, PA 19106
Ph: (215)625-8900   Fax: (215)625-8914
Fr: 800-354-1420
URL: http://www.ingentaconnect.com

$418.00/year for institutions, print and online; $397.00/year for institutions, online only; $155.00/year for individuals. Journal covering health science and medical education.

★4685★ Clinical Medicine & Research

Marshfield Clinic
1000 North Oak Ave.
Marshfield, WI 54449
Ph: (715)387-5511   Fr: 800-782-8581
URL: http://www.clinmedres.org/

Monthly. Journal that publishes scientific medical research that is relevant to a broad audience of medical researchers and healthcare professionals.

★4686★ CME Supplement to Emergency Medicine Clinics of North America

Elsevier Science Inc.
360 Park Ave. S
New York, NY 10010
Ph: (212)989-5800   Fax: (212)633-3990
URL: http://www.elsevier.com

Quarterly. $190.00/year for individuals. Journal covering emergency medicine clinics.

★4687★ Discovery Medicine

Discovery Medicine
2245 Chapel Valley Ln.
Timonium, MD 21093
Ph: (410)560-9007   Fax: (410)560-9000
URL: http://www.discoverymedicine.com

Bimonthly. $39.95/year for individuals; $49.95/year for individuals, digital edition and online access; $69.95 for two years, online access; $84.95 for two years, digital edition and online access; $99.95/year for individuals, 3 years, online access; $119.95/year for individuals, 3 years, digital and online access; $299.00/year for individuals, medical report (PMR); $99.00/year for individuals, medical report update. Online journal that publishes articles on diseases, biology, new diagnostics, and treatments for medical professionals.

★4688★ Education & Treatment of Children

West Virginia University Press
44 Stansbury Hall
PO Box 6295
Morgantown, WV 26506
Ph: (304)293-8400   Fax: (304)293-6585
Fr: (866)988-7737
URL: http://www.educationandtreatmentofchildren.net

Quarterly. $85.00/year for institutions; $45.00/year for individuals; $100.00/year for institutions, elsewhere; $60.00/year for individuals, elsewhere. Periodical featuring information concerning the development of services for children and youth. Includes reports written for educators and other child care and mental health providers focused on teaching, training, and treatment effectiveness.

★4689★ Epidemiology

Lippincott Williams & Wilkins
530 Walnut St.
Philadelphia, PA 19106-3621
Ph: (215)521-8300   Fax: (215)521-8902
Fr: 800-638-3030
URL: http://www.epidem.com/

Bimonthly. $262.00/year for individuals, U.S.; $563.00/year for institutions, U.S.; $135.00/year U.S., in-training; $334.00/year for individuals, international; $569.00/year for institutions, international; $135.00/year international, in-training. Professional medical journal for epidemiologists and related disciplines.

★4690★ Epidemiology Bulletin

Communicable Diseases Div.
1000 NE 10th St., Rm. 605
Oklahoma City, OK 73117-1299
Ph: (405)271-4060   Fax: (405)271-6680
URL: http://www.health.state.ok.us/program/qies/mds/newsletter/index.html*PRJ NIP

Description: Quarterly. Reports on communicable diseases, outbreaks, immunizations, and injuries.

★4691★ Genetic Epidemiology

John Wiley & Sons Inc.
111 River St.
Hoboken, NJ 07030-5774
Ph: (201)748-6000   Fax: (201)748-6088
Fr: 800-825-7550
URL: http://as.wiley.com/WileyCDA/WileyTitle/productCd-GEPI.html

$2,780.00/year for U.S., print only rates; $2,876.00/year for Canada and Mexico, print only rates; $2,932.00/year for other countries, print only rates; $3,058.00/year for U.S., combined print with online access rates; $3,154.00/year for Canada and Mexico, combined print with online access rates; $3,210.00/year for other countries, combined print with online access rates. Medical research journal.

★4692★ The IHS Primary Care Provider

Indian Health Service (HQ)
The Reyes Bldg.
801 Thompson Ave., Ste. 400
Rockville, MD 20852-1627
URL: http://www.ihs.gov/PublicInfo/Publications/HealthProvider/Pr

Monthly. Journal for health care professionals, physicians, nurses, pharmacists, dentists, and dietitians.

★4693★ Infection Control and Hospital Epidemiology

SLACK Inc.
6900 Grove Rd.
Thorofare, NJ 08086-9447
Ph: (856)848-1000   Fax: (856)853-5991
URL: http://www.journals.uchicago.edu/ICHE/home.html

Monthly. $164.00/year for individuals, print & electronic; $82.00/year for institutions, electronic; $295.00 for individuals, print & electronic, 2 years; $442.00 for individuals, print & electronic, 3 years. Medical journal that covers all areas of infection control and epidemiology for physicians and nurses.

★4694★ Infection Control Today

Virgo Publishing
3300 N. Central Ave., Ste. 300
Phoenix, AZ 85012
Ph: (480)990-1101   Fax: (602)567-6855
E-mail: kpyrek@vpico.com
URL: http://www.infectioncontroltoday.com

Monthly. Online publication listing job opportunities in the field of epidemiology.

★4695★ Infectious Diseases in Children

SLACK Inc.
6900 Grove Rd.
Thorofare, NJ 08086-9447
Ph: (856)848-1000   Fax: (856)853-5991
E-mail: idc@slackinc.com
URL: http://www.idinchildren.com

Monthly. $269.00/year for individuals; $429.00/year for institutions; $457.00/year for individuals, two years; $729.00/year for institutions, two years; $605.00/year for individuals, three years; $965.00/year for institutions, three years; $36.00 for single issue, resident. Newspapers for physician.

★4696★ Injury

Mosby Inc.
11830 Westline Industrial Dr.
St. Louis, MO 63146
Ph: (314)872-8370   Fax: (314)432-1380
Fr: 800-325-4177
URL: http://www.elsevier.com/wps/find/journaldescription.cws_home

Monthly. $1,106.00/year for institutions, all countries except Europe, Japan and Iran; $169.00/year for individuals, all countries except Europe, Japan and Iran. Journal publishing articles and research related to the treatment of injuries such as trauma

systems and management; surgical procedures; epidemiological studies; surgery (of all tissues); resuscitation; biomechanics; rehabilitation; anaesthesia; radiology and wound management.

★4697★ Journal of Hospital Medicine

John Wiley & Sons Inc.
111 River St.
Hoboken, NJ 07030-5774
Ph: (201)748-6000   Fax: (201)748-6088
Fr: 800-825-7550
URL: http://www.wiley.com/WileyCDA/WileyTitle/productCd-JHM.html

Bimonthly. $110.00/year for individuals, print only; Online version available with subscription. Journal on hospital medicine.

★4698★ Medical Risks

Taylor & Francis Group Journals
325 Chestnut St., Ste. 800
Philadelphia, PA 19106
Ph: (215)625-8900   Fax: (215)625-8914
Fr: 800-354-1420
URL: http://www.tandf.co.uk

Monthly. Journal covering articles on medical risks.

★4699★ New Epidemiology Monitor

Epidemiology Monitor
2560 Whisper Wind Ct.
Roswell, GA 30076
Ph: (770)594-1613   Fax: (770)594-0997
E-mail: epimon@aol.com
URL: http://www.epimonitor.net/EpidemiologyMonitor/Index.htm

Description: Monthly. Covers people, events, and developments in epidemiology.

★4700★ Pacifica Review

Taylor & Francis Group Journals
325 Chestnut St., Ste. 800
Philadelphia, PA 19106
Ph: (215)625-8900   Fax: (215)625-8914
Fr: 800-354-1420
URL: http://www.tandf.co.uk/

$462.00/year for individuals; $279.00/year for individuals; $487.00/year for individuals; $294.00/year for individuals; $123.00/year for individuals; $86.00/year for individuals. Journal promoting physical therapy and integration.

★4701★ Public Health Jobs Worldwide
URL: http://www.jobspublichealth.com

Biweekly. Electronic newspaper with current public health job openings in the United States and worldwide.

★4702★ PublicHealthJobs.net

Association of Schools of Public Health
1101 15th St. NW
Washington, DC 20005
Ph: (202)296-1099   Fax: (202)296-1252
E-mail: publichealthjobs@asph.org

URL: http://www.publichealthjobs.net

Online service that provides links to epidemiology job postings in the private sector, not-for-profit sector, and the federal government.

★4703★ USA Body Psychotherapy Journal

United States Association for Body Psychotherapy
7831 Woodmont Ave.
Bethesda, MD 20814
URL: http://www.usabp.org/displaycommon.cfm?an=4

Semiannual. Academic journal that seeks to support, promote and stimulate the exchange of ideas, scholarship and research within the field of body psychotherapy as well as an interdisciplinary exchange with related fields of clinical practice and inquiry.

★4704★ Year Book of Critical Care Medicine

Elsevier Science Inc.
360 Park Ave. S
New York, NY 10010
Ph: (212)989-5800   Fax: (212)633-3990
URL: http://www.elsevier.com

$180.00/year for institutions, U.S. $191.00/year for institutions, other countries; $121.00/year for individuals, U.S. $134.00/year for individuals, other countries; $59.00/year for students, U.S. $71.00/year for students, other countries. Journal focused on treatment of severe sepsis and septic shock, echocardiography in the evaluation of hemodynamically unstable patients & mechanical ventilation of acute respiratory distress syndrome.

HANDBOOKS AND MANUALS

★4705★ Managerial Epidemiology and Theory and Practice

Jones & Bartlett Publishers Inc.
40 Tall Pine Dr.
Sudbury, MA 01776
Ph: (978)443-5000   Fax: (978)443-8000
Fr: 800-832-0034
E-mail: info@jbpub.com
URL: http://www.jbpub.com/

G.E. Alan Dever. 2005. $83.95. 598 pages.

★4706★ A Practical Handbook for Healthcare Epidemiology

SLACK, Inc.
6900 Grove Rd.
Thorofare, NJ 08086
Ph: (856)848-1000   Fax: (856)853-5991
Fr: 800-257-8290
URL: http://www.slackbooks.com

Ebbing Lautenbach and Keith Woeltje. 2004. $114.95 (CD-ROM). Covers all facets of the field of epidemiology in the healthcare arena.

ONLINE JOB SOURCES AND SERVICES

★4707★ Epidemiologist.com
URL: http://www.epidemiologist.com
Description: Serves as an online source of information for professional epidemiologists, including job listings in the field.

TRADESHOWS

★4708★ Society for Epidemiologic Research Conference

Society for Epidemiologic Research
PO Box 990
Clearfield, UT 84089
Ph: (801)525-0231   Fax: (801)774-9211
E-mail: membership@epiresearch.org
URL: http://www.epiresearch.org

Annual. **Primary Exhibits:** Epidemiology equipment, supplies, and services.

OTHER SOURCES

★4709★ American College of Epidemiology

1500 Sunday Dr., Ste. 102
Raleigh, NC 27607
Ph: (919)861-5573   Fax: (919)787-4916
E-mail: fkenan@firstpointresources.com
URL: http://www.acepidemiology2.org

Members: Professional epidemiologists. **Purpose:** Promotes the professional development of epidemiologists through educational initiatives; advocates for policies and actions that enhance the science and practice of epidemiology; recognizes excellence in epidemiology; and develops and maintains an active membership representing all aspects of epidemiology. **Activities:** Provides job-listing services for epidemiologists.

★4710★ Association for Professionals in Infection Control and Epidemiology

1275 K St. NW, Ste. 1000
Washington, DC 20005-4006
Ph: (202)789-1890   Fax: (202)789-1899
E-mail: apicinfo@apic.org
URL: http://www.apic.org

Members: Professionals working in the field of infection control and epidemiology. **Purpose:** Promotes excellence in the prevention and control of infections and related adverse outcomes. **Activities:** Provides a forum for members to network, offers educational opportunities, produces publications, and serves as an advocate in governmental policymaking.

★4711★ Council of State and Territorial Epidemiologists (CSTE)

2872 Woodcock Blvd., Ste. 303
Atlanta, GA 30341
Ph: (770)458-3811   Fax: (770)458-8516
E-mail: pmcconnon@cste.org
URL: http://www.cste.org

Description: State epidemiologists. Works to establish closer working relationships among members; consults with and advises appropriate disciplines in other health agencies; provides technical advice and assistance to the Association of State and Territorial Health Officials ; works closely with Centers for Disease Control on epidemiology, surveillance, and prevention activities.

★4712★ Emergency Management Insitute

16825 S. Seton Ave.
Emmitsburg, MD 21727
Ph: (301)447-1000   Fax: (301)447-1658
URL: http://training.fema.gov/EMIWeb/

Description: Offers access to listed employment opportunities in emergency management, including epidemiology, via the website.

★4713★ International Society for Environmental Epidemiology

44 Farnsworth St.
Boston, MA 02210
Ph: (617)482-9485   Fax: (617)482-0617
E-mail: iseepi@jsi.org
URL: http://www.iseepi.org

Members: Environmental epidemiologists and scientists worldwide. **Purpose:** Provides a forum for the discussion of problems unique to the study of health and the environment. **Activities:** Holds meetings and workshops, publishes newsletter, acts as liaison with academic, governmental, intergovernmental, non-profit, and business institutions. Serves as a forum for networking among its members.

★4714★ Society for Epidemiologic Research (SER)

PO Box 990
Clearfield, UT 84089
Ph: (801)525-0231   Fax: (801)774-9211
E-mail: membership@epiresearch.org
URL: http://www.epiresearch.org

Description: Epidemiologists, researchers, public health administrators, educators, mathematicians, statisticians, and others interested in epidemiological research. Stimulates scientific interest in and promotes the exchange of information about epidemiological research.

★4715★ Society for Healthcare Epidemiology of America

1300 Wilson Blvd., Ste. 300
Arlington, VA 22209
Ph: (703)684-1006   Fax: (703)684-1009
E-mail: info@shea-online.org
URL: http://www.shea-online.org

Members: Professionals in all branches of medicine, public health, and healthcare epidemiology. **Purpose:** Advances the application of the science of healthcare epidemiology and works to maintain the quality of patient care and healthcare worker safety in all healthcare settings. **Activities:** Hosts meetings and provides a forum for networking among its members.

★4716★ Society for Pediatric and Perinatal Epidemiologic Research

2C402 SOM, 50 N. Medical Dr.
Salt Lake City, UT 84132
Ph: (801)257-0566   Fax: (801)257-0572
E-mail: marcia.feldkamp@hsc.utah.edu
URL: http://www.sper.org

Members: Professionals interested in the epidemiology of pregnancy, infancy, and childhood. **Purpose:** Fosters pediatric and perinatal epidemiologic research. **Activities:** Produces a newsletter and offers opportunities for networking among its members.

Event Planners

SOURCES OF HELP-WANTED ADS

★4717★ Association News

Schneider Publishing Company Inc.
11835 W Olympic Blvd., 12th Fl.
Los Angeles, CA 90064
Ph: (310)577-3700   Fax: (310)577-3715
Fr: 877-577-3700
URL: http://www.associationnews.com/

Monthly. Free. Magazine containing management and meeting plan information for association executives and meeting planners.

★4718★ Event Management

Cognizant Communications Corp.
3 Hartsdale Rd.
Elmsford, NY 10523-3701
Ph: (914)592-7720   Fax: (914)592-8981
URL: http://
www.cognizantcommunication.com/filecabi-net/EventManag

Quarterly. $325.00/year for institutions, library; $360.00/year for institutions, rest of the world, library; $585.00/year for institutions, library, 2 years; $648.00/year for institutions, rest if the world, library, 2 years; $45.00/year professional; $52.00/year for other countries, professional. Journal covering research and analytic needs of a rapidly growing profession focused on events.

★4719★ Meeting News

The Nielsen Co.
770 Broadway
New York, NY 10003
Ph: (646)654-5000   Fax: (646)654-5002
URL: http://www.meetingnews.com/

$89.00/year for individuals; $99.00/year for Canada; $205.00/year for other countries, by airmail. The newspaper for conventions, meetings, incentive travel and trade show professionals.

★4720★ Special Events

Miramar Communications Inc.
23805 Stuart Ranch Rd., Ste. 235
PO Box 8987
Malibu, CA 90265-8987
Ph: (310)317-4522   Fax: (310)317-9644
Fr: 800-543-4116
E-mail: secs@pbsub.com
URL: http://www.specialevents.com

Monthly. $59.00/year. Free to qualified subscribers; $110.00/year for Canada; $106.00/year for other countries; $200.00 for Canada, two years; $200.00 for other countries, two years. Magazine for special event professionals.

PLACEMENT AND JOB REFERRAL SERVICES

★4721★ Association for Convention Operations Management (ACOM)

191 Clarksville Rd.
Princeton Junction, NJ 08550
Ph: (609)799-3712   Fax: (609)799-7032
E-mail: info@acomonline.org
URL: http://www.acomonline.org

Description: Convention service directors and managers of hotels, convention centers, and convention bureaus; suppliers of services and products to the convention and meetings industry are affiliate members. Works to increase the effectiveness, productivity, and quality of meetings, conventions, and exhibitions. Works to establish high ethical standards, improve professional management techniques, and increase awareness of client, employer, and provider needs. Maintains speakers' bureau, resource center, and placement services; compiles statistics. Conducts research and educational programs.

★4722★ Connected International Meeting Professionals Association (CIMPA)

9200 Bayard Pl.
Fairfax, VA 22032
Ph: (512)684-0889   Fax: (267)390-5193
E-mail: susan2@cimpa.org
URL: http://www.cimpa.org

Members: Meeting planners, incentive organizers, travel agents, tour operators, and seminar organizers in 42 countries. **Purpose:** Works to improve the skills of professional conference and convention planners. Serves as a clearinghouse of information on new travel destinations and planning technologies, techniques, and strategies. **Activities:** Facilitates exchange of information among Internet professionals. Produces a television program on travel and meetings. Conducts educational courses and awards Certified Internet Meeting Professional designation. Conducts research programs and placement service. Sponsors training courses on the Internet.

★4723★ National Coalition of Black Meeting Planners (NCBMP)

8630 Fenton St., Ste. 126
Silver Spring, MD 20910
Ph: (202)628-3952   Fax: (301)588-0011
E-mail: jmardis.richards@yahoo.com
URL: http://www.ncbmp.com

Description: Black meeting planners. Purposes are to: act as liaison with hotels, airlines, convention centers, and bureaus in an effort to assess the impact of minorities in these fields; assess the needs of the convention industry and how best to meet these needs; enhance members' sophistication in planning meetings; maximize employment of minorities in the convention industry. Maintains speakers' bureau. Conducts educational and research programs and compiles statistics on demographic employment of minorities in the convention industry. Maintains placement service.

EMPLOYER DIRECTORIES AND NETWORKING LISTS

★4724★ Meeting Professionals International Membership Directory

Meeting Professionals International
3030 LBJ Fwy., Ste. 1700
Dallas, TX 75234-2759
Ph: (972)702-3000   Fax: (972)702-3070

Annual. $155.00 for nonmembers. Covers profiles of the members of Meeting Professionals International.

HANDBOOKS AND MANUALS

★4725★ Association Meeting and Event Planners

Douglas Publications, Inc.
2807 N Parham Rd., Ste. 200
Richmond, VA 23294
Ph: (804)762-9600   Fax: (804)217-8999
Fr: 800-223-1797
E-mail: info@douglaspublications.com
URL: http://www.douglaspublications.com/

Patrick Snyder. 2004. $650.00.

★4726★ The Business of Event Planning: Behind-the-Scenes Secrets of Successful Special Events

John Wiley & Sons Inc.
1 Wiley Dr.
Somerset, NJ 08875-1272
Ph: (732)469-4400   Fax: (732)302-2300
Fr: 800-225-5945
E-mail: custserv@wiley.com
URL: http://www.wiley.com/WileyCDA/

Judy Allen. 2002. 320 pages. $34.95. Provides expert advice for professional event planners.

★4727★ How to Start a Home-Based Event Planning Business

Globe Pequot Press
246 Goose Lane
Guilford, CT 06437
Ph: (203)458-4500   Fr: 800-820-2329
E-mail: info@globepequot.com
URL: http://www.globepequot.com

Jill Moran. 2004. $17.95. 197 pages. This insider's handbook reveals how to start a successful business planning a wide variety of events from home.

★4728★ Opportunities in Event Planning Careers

McGraw-Hill Companies
2 Penn Plaza
New York, NY 10121
Ph: 877-833-5524   Fax: (614)759-3749
Fr: 800-722-4729
E-mail: customer.service@mcgraw-hill.com
URL: http://www.mcgraw-hill.com

Blyth Camenson. $13.95. 2002. 160 pages. Details how to get started as an independent or corporate event planner. Includes training advice and salary statistics.

★4729★ Time Management for Event Planners

John Wiley & Sons, Inc.
111 River St.
Hoboken, NJ 07030
Ph: (201)748-6000   Fax: (201)748-6088
E-mail: info@wiley.com
URL: http://www.wiley.com/WileyCDA/

Judy Allen. 2005. $34.95. Time management skills to help event planners balance personal and professional lives.

ONLINE JOB SOURCES AND SERVICES

★4730★ Event Planner

893 Chinquapin Rd.
McLean, VA 22102
Ph: (703)757-0653   Fax: (703)757-0654
E-mail: eventpln@mindspring.com
URL: http://www.event-planner.com

Description: Industry news and employment opportunities.

★4731★ Event Planner Directory 123

Fr: 800-379-4626
URL: http://www.eventplannerdirectory123.com

Description: Vendor resources.

OTHER SOURCES

★4732★ Association of Collegiate Conference and Events Directors-International (ACCED-I)

Colorado State University
8037 Campus Delivery
Fort Collins, CO 80523-8037
Ph: (970)491-3772   Fax: (970)491-0667
Fr: 877-50-ACCED
E-mail: acced@colostate.edu
URL: http://www.acced-i.org

Members: University conference and special events directors; professionals who design, coordinate, and market conferences and special events on college and university campuses. **Purpose:** Dedicated to the professional development of the members; promotes the growth and distinction of the profession by uniting personnel and encouraging camaraderie. Promotes high standards of business and ethical conduct; works to foster communication, cooperation, and information sharing. **Activities:** Conducts research programs; collaborates with sister associations. Provides leadership opportunities through committee and board participation. Acts as an information clearinghouse compiles statistics.

★4733★ GCG Event Partners

125 Main St., Ste. H
Stoneham, MA 02180-1600
Ph: (781)279-9887   Fax: (781)279-9875
E-mail: info@gcgeventpartners.com
URL: http://www.gcgeventpartners.com

Description: Network of event planning professionals.

★4734★ Golf Tournament Association of America (GTAA)

PO Box 47405
Phoenix, AZ 85068
Ph: (602)667-3250   Fax: (480)704-4785
E-mail: info@gtaaweb.org
URL: http://www.gtaaweb.org

Description: Represents the interests of golf tournament planners and coordinators. Provides golf tournament planning tips, education and resources to golf tournament planners and coordinators. Conducts golf tournament planning seminars across the country.

★4735★ International Association of Fairs and Expositions

PO Box 985
Springfield, MO 65801
Ph: (417)862-5771   Fax: (417)862-0156
Fr: 800-516-0313
E-mail: iafe@fairsandexpos.com
URL: http://www.fairsandexpos.com

Description: Individuals, corporations, and organizations involved with the planning and management of fairs, expositions.

★4736★ International Festivals and Events Association

2603 Eastover Terrace
Boise, ID 83706
Ph: (208)433-0950   Fax: (208)433-9812
URL: http://www.ifea.com

Description: Provides professional development opportunities and fundraising ideas for individuals involved in the special events industry.

★4737★ International Society of Meeting Planners (ISMP)

1224 N Nokomis NE
Alexandria, MN 56308-5072
Ph: (320)763-4919   Fax: (320)763-9290
E-mail: ismp@iami.org
URL: http://www.iami.org/ismp.cfm

Members: Meeting planners and related industries. **Purpose:** Works to improve professionalism and competency in the industry as well as create new business opportunities for members. **Activities:** Provides networking opportunities. Offers professional designations: the RMP - Registered Meeting Planner, CDS - Certified Destination Specialist, ITS - Incentive Travel Specialist, and CEP - Certified Event Planner.

★4738★ International Special Events Society

401 N. Michigan Ave.
Chicago, IL 60611-4267
Ph: (312)321-6853   Fax: (312)673-6953
Fr: 800-688-4737
URL: http://www.ises.com

Description: Fosters performance through education. Represents special event producers.

★4739★ Meeting Professionals International (MPI)

3030 Lyndon B. Johnson Fwy., Ste. 1700
Dallas, TX 75234-2759
Ph: (972)702-3000   Fax: (972)702-3070
E-mail: feedback@mpiweb.org
URL: http://www.mpiweb.org

Members: Meeting planners, full meeting consultants, and suppliers of goods and services. **Purpose:** Works to: improve meeting method education; create an "open platform" for research and experimentation. Provides survey results, statistics, supply sources, and technical information; offers members assistance with specific problems; encourages information and idea exchange. Maintains professional code; standardizes

terminology; monitors legislation affecting the industry. **Activities:** Maintains resource center. Conducts educational, charitable, and research programs.

★4740★ Professional Convention Management Association (PCMA)

2301 S Lake Shore Dr., Ste. 1001
Chicago, IL 60616-1419
Ph: (312)423-7262   Fax: (312)423-7222
Fr: 877-827-7262
E-mail: president@pcma.org
URL: http://www.pcma.org

Description: Represents the interests of meeting management executives from associations, non-profit organizations, corporations, independent meeting planning companies, and multi-management firms who recognize the importance of meetings to their organization. Provides education, research and advocacy to advance the meetings and hospitality industry. Empowers members with the tools they need to succeed as meeting professionals and to promote the value of the industry to their organizations and the general public.

★4741★ Religious Conference Management Association (RCMA)

1 RCA Dome, Ste. 120
Indianapolis, IN 46225
Ph: (317)632-1888   Fax: (317)632-7909

E-mail: rcma@rcmaweb.org
URL: http://www.rcmaweb.org

Description: Represents persons responsible for planning and/or managing religious conventions, meetings, and assemblies; associate members are individuals who directly support the logistics of religious meetings. Promotes professional excellence through exchange of ideas, techniques, and methods of management.

★4742★ Society of Government Meeting Professionals (SGMP)

908 King St., Lower Level
Alexandria, VA 22314
Ph: (703)549-0892   Fax: (703)549-0708
Fr: 800-827-8916
E-mail: carl.c.thompson@sgmp.org
URL: http://www.sgmp.org

Description: Individuals involved in planning government meetings on a full- or part-time basis; suppliers of services to government planners. Provides education in basic and advanced areas of meeting planning and facilitates professional contact with other government planners and suppliers knowledgeable in government contracting. Maintains referral network of planning resources, information on latest techniques, and opportunities to inspect conference facilities.

Fashion Models

SOURCES OF HELP-WANTED ADS

★4743★ Beauty Launchpad

Creative Age Publications Inc.
7628 Densmore Ave.
Van Nuys, CA 91406-2042
Ph: (818)782-7328   Fax: (818)782-7450
Fr: 800-442-5667
URL: http://www.beautylaunchpad.com/index.php

$24.00/year for U.S., 12 issues; $48.00/year for Canada, 12 issues. Fashion magazine.

★4744★ Clear

Clear Magazine
433 N Washington
Royal Oak, MI 48067
Ph: (248)544-2532   Fax: (248)544-0008
URL: http://www.clearmag.com

Bimonthly. $22.00/year for individuals. Contemporary fashion and design journal.

★4745★ Daily Variety

Reed Business Information
5700 Wilshire Blvd., Ste. 120
Los Angeles, CA 90036
Ph: (323)857-6600   Fax: (323)857-0494
URL: http://www.reedbusiness.com/index.asp?layout=theListProfile&

Daily. Global entertainment newspaper (tabloid).

★4746★ JQ

Adams Business Media
420 S Palm Canyon Dr., 2nd Fl.
Palm Springs, CA 92262
Ph: (760)318-7000   Fax: (760)323-4310
URL: http://www.retailmerchandising.net/jq/

Bimonthly. $30.00/year for individuals; $50.00 for two years; $45.00/year for Canada; $110.00/year for out of country. Trade publication covering the fashion and retail industries.

★4747★ New York Moves

New York Moves Magazine
PO Box 4097
Lexington Ave.
New York, NY 10163
Ph: (212)396-2394   Fax: (212)202-7615
URL: http://www.newyorkmoves.com

Monthly. $16.00/year for individuals. Fashion and lifestyle magazine for professional women in and around New York City.

★4748★ Supermodels Unlimited

Supermodel Productions
24 West 30 St., Fl. 11
New York, NY 10001
Ph: (917)992-4084
URL: http://www.supermodelsunlimited.com/

Quarterly. $18.00/year for individuals. Magazine covering fashion, health and beauty, modeling, talent, fitness & health, entertainment and teen and women's issues.

EMPLOYER DIRECTORIES AND NETWORKING LISTS

★4749★ Black Book Photography

Black Book Marketing Group
740 Broadway, Ste. 202
New York, NY 10003
Ph: (212)979-6700   Fax: (212)673-4321
Fr: 800-841-1246
URL: http://www.BlackBook.com

Annual; latest edition 2007. $88.00 for individuals. Publication includes: Over 19,000 art directors, creative directors, photographers and photographic services, design firms, advertising agencies, and other firms whose products or services are used in advertising. Entries include: Company name, address, phone. Principal content of publication consists of 4-color samples from the leading commercial photographers. Arrangement: Classified by product/service.

★4750★ Careers in Focus: Fashion

Facts On File Inc.
132 W 31st St., 17th Fl.
New York, NY 10001
Ph: (212)967-8800   Fax: 800-678-3633
Fr: 800-322-8755
URL: http://www.factsonfile.com

Latest edition 3rd, 2006. $29.95 for individuals; $26.95 for libraries. Covers an overview of fashion, followed by a selection of jobs profiled in detail, including the nature of the job, earnings, prospects for employment, what kind of training and skills it requires, and sources for further information.

★4751★ Discovering Careers for Your Future: Fashion

Facts On File Inc.
132 W 31st St., 17th Fl.
New York, NY 10001
Ph: (212)967-8800   Fax: 800-678-3633
Fr: 800-322-8755
URL: http://www.factsonfile.com

Published 2004. $21.95 for individuals; $19.75 for libraries. Covers buyers, costume designers, fashion illustrators, fashion models, makeup artists, tailors and dressmakers, and textile manufacturing workers; links career education to curriculum, helping children investigate the subjects they are interested in, and the careers those subjects might lead to.

★4752★ Model & Talent Directory

Peter Glenn Publications
235 SE 5th Ave., Ste. R
Delray Beach, FL 33483
Ph: (561)404-4275   Fax: (561)279-4672
Fr: 888-332-6700
URL: http://www.pgdirect.com

Annual; latest edition 25th, 2007. $29.95 for individuals. Covers over 2,200 listings of model and talent agencies worldwide. Arrangement: Geographical.

★4753★ **New York City Model Agency Directory**

Peter Glenn Publications
235 SE 5th Ave., Ste. R
Delray Beach, FL 33483
Ph: (561)404-4275 Fax: (561)279-4672
Fr: 888-332-6700
URL: http://www.pgdirect.com

Annual. $59.95 for individuals. Covers about 80 modeling agencies in New York City. Entries include: Company name, address, phone, fax, name and title of contact, type of modeling work handled, interview information, years of operation. Arrangement: Alphabetical. Indexes: Name.

HANDBOOKS AND MANUALS

★4754★ **Beginner's Guide to Model Photography: Techniques for the Photographer and Tips for the Aspiring Model**

Reference Desk Books
430 Quintana Rd., Ste. 146
Morro Bay, CA 93442
Ph: (805)772-8806 Fax: (805)528-0218

Valentine DelVecchio. 1993. $29.95 (paper). 128 pages.

★4755★ **Careers for Fashion Plates and Other Trendsetters**

The McGraw-Hill Companies
PO Box 182604
Columbus, OH 43272
Fax: (614)759-3749 Fr: 877-883-5524
E-mail: customer.service@mcgraw-hill.com
URL: http://www.mcgraw-hill.com

Lucia Mauro. Second edition, 2002. $14.95 (Hardcover); $9.95 (paper). 160 pages. Describes career opportunities in fashion, entertainment, retail, and promotion, with advice from fashion professionals.

★4756★ **Hollywood, Here I Come!: An Insider's Guide to a Successful Acting & Modeling Career in Los Angeles**

Yellow Deer Press
PO Box 7309A
Santa Monica, CA 90406-7309
Ph: (213)871-8755 Fr: 800-437-3267

Cynthia Hunter. 2001. $19.95. 275 pages.

★4757★ **Opportunities in Beauty and Modeling Careers**

The McGraw-Hill Companies
PO Box 182604
Columbus, OH 43272
Fax: (614)759-3749 Fr: 877-883-5524
E-mail: customer.service@mcgraw-hill.com
URL: http://www.mcgraw-hill.com

Susan Wood Gearhart. 2004. $13.95. 163 pages.

★4758★ **Opportunities in Modeling Careers**

The McGraw-Hill Companies
PO Box 182604
Columbus, OH 43272
Fax: (614)759-3749 Fr: 877-883-5524
E-mail: customer.service@mcgraw-hill.com
URL: http://www.mcgraw-hill.com

Susan Wood Gearhart. 1999. $14.95; $11.95 (paper). 160 pages. Addresses opportunities in modeling, ranging from artist's model to photographic model. Includes bibliography and illustrations.

★4759★ **Real-Resumes for Retailing, Modeling, Fashion and Beauty Jobs: Including Real Resumes Used to Change Careers and Transfer Skills to Other Industries**

PREP Publishing
1110 1/2 Hay St., PMB 66
Fayetteville, NC 28305
Ph: (910)483-6611 Fax: (910)483-2439
Fr: 800-533-2814

Anne McKinney. 2002. $16.95. 192 pages

★4760★ **So, You Want to Be a Fashion Model?**

InterScout, LLC
PO Box 965
Estes Park, CO 80517

Marcia Rothschild Moellers. 2003. $27.50. 166 Pages.

★4761★ **Your Modeling Career: You Don't Have to Be a Superstar to Succeed**

Allworth Press
10 E. 23rd St., Ste. 510
New York, NY 10010
Ph: (212)777-8395 Fax: (212)777-8261
Fr: 800-491-2808
URL: http://www.allworth.com/

Debbie Press and Skip Press. Second edition, 2004. $19.95 (paper). 288 pages.

ONLINE JOB SOURCES AND SERVICES

★4762★ **Talent Networks.com**

127 W. 25th St., 5th Fl.
New York, NY 10001
Ph: (212)929-3633 Fr: (801)681-5914
E-mail: info@talentnetworks.com
URL: http://www.photographynetwork.com/

Description: A business-to-business portal for the fashion, arts, and entertainment industries. Online site contains a industry listings, portfolios and news items.

Financial Managers

SOURCES OF HELP-WANTED ADS

★4763★ Accounting Horizons

American Accounting Association
5717 Bessie Dr.
Sarasota, FL 34233-2399
Ph: (941)921-7747   Fax: (941)923-4093
URL: http://aaahq.org/index.cfm

Quarterly. $265.00/year for individuals, print only; $265.00/year for individuals, online, vol.13 through current issue; $290.00/year for individuals, online and print. Publication covering the banking, finance, and accounting industries.

★4764★ American Banker

American Banker/Bond Buyer Inc.
1 State St. Plz. 27 Fl.
New York, NY 10004
Ph: (212)803-8200   Fax: (212)843-9600
Fr: 800-221-1809
URL: http://www.americanbanker.com

Daily. $995.00/year for individuals. Newspaper for senior executives in banking and other financial services industries. Coverage includes trends, analysis, and statistics of the legislative scene in Washington; finance; mortgages; technology; small business; and regional banking.

★4765★ Barron's

Dow Jones & Company Inc.
1 World Financial Ctr.
200 Liberty St.
New York, NY 10281
Ph: (212)416-2000
E-mail: editors@barrons.com
URL: http://online.barrons.com/public/main

Weekly (Mon.). $245.00 for two years; $145.00/year for individuals, 52 weeks; $74.00/year for individuals, 26 weeks; $39.00/year for individuals, 13 weeks. Business and finance magazine.

★4766★ Boomer Market Advisor

Wiesner Publishing L.L.C.
7009 South Potomac St., Ste. 200
Centennial, CO 80112
Ph: (303)397-7600   Fax: (303)397-7619
URL: http://www.boomermarketadvisor.com

Monthly. Magazine for financial planners who work with variable products.

★4767★ Business Credit

National Association of Credit
  Management
8840 Columbia 100 Pkwy.
Columbia, MD 21045-2158
Ph: (410)740-5560   Fax: (410)740-5574
URL: http://www.nacm.org/bcmag/bcm_index.shtml

$54.00/year for individuals, business; $48.00/year for libraries; $60.00/year for Canada; $65.00/year for other countries. Magazine covering finance, business risk management, providing information for the extension of credit, maintenance of accounts receivable, and cash asset management.

★4768★ Business Insurance

Crain Communications Inc.
1155 Gratiot Ave.
Detroit, MI 48207-2997
Ph: (313)446-6000
URL: http://www.businessinsurance.com

Weekly. $97.00/year for individuals; $173.00 for two years; $200.00/year for individuals, daily online only; $130.00/year for Canada and Mexico; $234.00 for Canada and Mexico, two years; $230.00/year for individuals, includes expedited airmail other countries; $436.00 for two years, includes expedited airmail other countries. International newsweekly reporting on corporate risk and employee benefit management news.

★4769★ CFO

CFO Publishing
253 Summer St.
Boston, MA 02210
Ph: (617)345-9700
URL: http://www.cfo.com/magazine/?f=header

Monthly. Business magazine for small to mid-sized companies.

★4770★ Financial Management

Financial Management Association
  International
4202 East Fowler Ave.
BSN 3331
Tampa, FL 33620-5500
Ph: (813)974-2084   Fax: (813)974-3318
E-mail: fma@coba.usf.edu
URL: http://www.fma.org/fm.htm

Quarterly. $95.00/year for individuals; $20.00 for single issue. Journal covering business, economics, finance and management.

★4771★ Forbes

Forbes Magazine
90 5th Ave.
New York, NY 10011
Ph: (212)366-8900   Fr: 800-295-0893
URL: http://www.forbes.com

Biweekly. $30.00/year for individuals, per year; $1.00/year for single issue. Magazine reporting on industry, business and finance management.

★4772★ Journal of Accountancy

The American Institute of Certified Public
  Accountants
1211 Ave. of the Americas
New York, NY 10036-8775
Ph: (212)596-6200   Fax: (212)596-6213
URL: http://www.aicpa.org/

Monthly. $75.00/year for individuals; $60.00/year for members. Accounting journal.

★4773★ Journal of Financial and Quantitative Analysis

Journal of Financial & Quantitative
  Analysis
University of Washington
School of Business Administration
115 Lewis Hall
PO Box 353200
Seattle, WA 98195-3200
Ph: (206)543-4598   Fax: (206)616-1894

E-mail: jfqa@u.washington.edu

Quarterly. $70.00/year for individuals, U.S. and Canada; $80.00/year for other countries; $150.00/year for institutions; $160.00/year for institutions, other countries; $25.00/year for students; $30.00/year for students, other countries. Journal on research in finance.

★4774★ **The Journal of Taxation**

RIA Group
395 Hudson St., 4th Fl.
New York, NY 10014
Ph: (212)367-6300   Fax: (212)367-6314
Fr: 800-431-9025
URL: http://ria.thomson.com/estore/detail.aspx?ID=JTAX

Monthly. $300.00/year for individuals, print; $450.00/year for individuals, online/print bundle; $345.00/year for individuals, online. Journal for sophisticated tax practitioners.

★4775★ **Mortgage Banking Magazine**

Mortgage Bankers Association of America
1919 Pennsylvania Ave. NW
Washington, DC 20006-3404
Ph: (202)557-2700   Fax: (202)721-0245
Fr: 800-793-MBAA

Monthly. $80.00/year for individuals. Magazine of the real estate finance industry.

★4776★ **National Mortgage News**

Thomson Financial
195 Broadway
New York, NY 10007
Ph: (646)822-2000   Fax: (646)822-3230
Fr: 888-605-3385
E-mail: custserv@sourcemedia.com
URL: http://
www.nationalmortgagenews.com

Weekly. Newspaper for mortgage lenders and investment bankers.

★4777★ **Northwestern Financial Review**

NFR Communications Inc.
7400 Metro Blvd., Ste. 217
Minneapolis, MN 55439
Ph: (952)835-2275
E-mail: web@nfrcom.com
URL: http://www.nfrcom.com

$94.00/year for individuals. Trade publication covering commercial banking.

★4778★ **Pensions & Investments**

Crain Communications Inc.
1155 Gratiot Ave.
Detroit, MI 48207-2997
Ph: (313)446-6000
URL: http://www.pionline.com

Biweekly. $239.00/year for individuals; $595.00/year for individuals, daily email; $695.00/year for individuals. Magazine containing news and features on investment management, pension management, corporate finance, and cash management.

★4779★ **Servicing Management**

Zackin Publications Inc.
PO Box 2180
Waterbury, CT 06722
Ph: (203)262-4670   Fax: (203)262-4680
Fr: 800-325-6745
URL: http://www.sm-online.com/sm

Monthly. $48.00/year for individuals; $72.00 for two years. Trade magazine for mortgage professionals involved with mortgage loan servicing.

★4780★ **Strategic Finance**

Institute of Management Accountants
10 Paragon Dr.
Montvale, NJ 07645-1718
Ph: (201)573-9000   Fax: (201)474-1603
Fr: 800-638-4427
E-mail: sfmag@imanet.org
URL: http://www.imanet.org

Monthly. $195.00/year for individuals; $195.00/year for other countries; $195.00/year for individuals, corporate libraries; $195.00/year for individuals, international libraries; $98.00/year for individuals, nonprofit U.S. libraries only. Magazine reporting on corporate finance, accounting, cash management, and budgeting.

★4781★ **U.S. Banker**

Thomson Financial
195 Broadway
New York, NY 10007
Ph: (646)822-2000   Fax: (646)822-3230
Fr: 888-605-3385
URL: http://www.americanbanker.com/usb.html

Monthly. $109.00/year for individuals; $139.00/year for individuals, Canada; $139.00/year for individuals, outside North America; $179.00/year for two years; $239.00 for two years, Canada; $239.00/year for two years, outside North America. Magazine serving the financial services industry.

PLACEMENT AND JOB REFERRAL SERVICES

★4782★ **Commercial Finance Association (CFA)**

225 W 34th St., Ste. 1815
New York, NY 10122
Ph: (212)594-3490   Fax: (212)564-6053
E-mail: info@cfa.com
URL: http://www.cfa.com

Members: Organizations engaged in asset-based financial services including commercial financing and factoring and lending money on a secured basis to small- and medium-sized business firms. **Purpose:** Acts as a forum for information and consideration about ideas, opportunities, and legislation concerning asset-based financial services. Seeks to improve the industry's legal and operational procedures. **Activities:** Offers job placement and reference services for members. Sponsors School for Field Examiners and other educational programs. Compiles statistics; conducts seminars and surveys; maintains Speaker's Bureau and 21 committees.

★4783★ **Financial Management Association International (FMA)**

University of South Florida
College of Business Administration
4202 E Fowler Ave., BSN 3331
Tampa, FL 33620-5500
Ph: (813)974-2084   Fax: (813)974-3318
E-mail: fma@coba.usf.edu
URL: http://www.fma.org

Members: Professors of financial management; corporate financial officers. **Purpose:** Facilitates exchange of ideas among persons involved in financial management or the study thereof. **Activities:** Conducts workshops for comparison of current research projects and development of cooperative ventures in writing and research. Sponsors honorary society for superior students at 300 colleges and universities. Offers placement services.

★4784★ **Financial Women's Association of New York (FWA)**

215 Park Ave. S, Ste. 1713
New York, NY 10003
Ph: (212)533-2141   Fax: (212)982-3008
E-mail: fwaoffice@fwa.org
URL: http://www.fwa.org

Members: Persons of professional status in the field of finance in the New York metropolitan area. **Purpose:** Works to promote and maintain high professional standards in the financial and business communities; provide an opportunity for members to enhance one another's professional contacts; achieve recognition of the contribution of women to the financial and business communities; encourage other women to seek professional positions within the financial and business communities. **Activities:** Activities include educational trips to foreign countries; college internship program including foreign student exchange; high school mentorship program; Washington and international briefings; placement service for members. Maintains speakers' bureau.

★4785★ **International Newspaper Financial Executives (INFE)**

21525 Ridgetop Cir., Ste. 200
Sterling, VA 20166
Ph: (703)421-4060   Fax: (703)421-4068
E-mail: infehq@infe.org
URL: http://www.infe.org

Members: Controllers, chief accountants, auditors, business managers, treasurers, secretaries and related newspaper executives, educators, and public accountants. **Activities:** Conducts research projects on accounting methods and procedures for newspapers. Offers placement service; maintains Speaker's Bureau. Produces conferences and seminars.

★4786★ National Bankers Association (NBA)

1513 P St. NW
Washington, DC 20005
Ph: (202)588-5432   Fax: (202)588-5443
E-mail: nahart@nationalbankers.org
URL: http://www.nationalbankers.org

Members: Minority banking institutions owned by minority individuals and institutions. **Purpose:** Serves as an advocate for the minority banking industry. Organizes banking services, government relations, marketing, scholarship, and technical assistance programs. **Activities:** Offers placement services; compiles statistics.

EMPLOYER DIRECTORIES AND NETWORKING LISTS

★4787★ America's Corporate Finance Directory

LexisNexis Group
PO Box 933
Dayton, OH 45401-0933
Ph: (937)865-6800   Fax: (518)487-3584
Fr: 800-543-6862
URL: http://www.lexisnexis.com

Annual, September. $1,069.00 for individuals. Covers financial personnel and outside financial services relationships of 5,000 leading United States corporations and their wholly-owned United States subsidiaries. Entries include: Company name, address, phone, fax, telex, e-mail addresses, stock exchange information, earnings, total assets, size of pension/profit-sharing fund portfolio, number of employees, description of business, wholly-owned U.S. subsidiaries of parent company; name and title of key executives; outside suppliers of financial services. Arrangement: Alphabetical. Indexes: Financial responsibilities, Standard Industrial Classification (SIC) code, geographical, personnel, private companies, company name.

★4788★ Association for Investment Management & Research-Membership Directory

CFA Institute
560 Ray C Hunt Dr.
PO Box 3668
Charlottesville, VA 22903-2981
Ph: (434)951-5499   Fax: (434)951-5262
Fr: 800-247-8132
URL: http://www.cfainstitute.org/

Annual, January. $150.00. Covers 38,000 security and financial analysts who are practicing investment analysis. Entries include: Name, firm affiliation and address, phone, fax, e-mail. Arrangement: Alphabetical.

★4789★ Branches of Your State

Sheshunoff Information Services
807 Las Cimas Pkwy., Ste. 300
Austin, TX 78746-6597
Ph: (512)472-2244   Fax: (512)305-6575
Fr: 800-456-2340

Annual, February. $475.00. Covers, in separate state editions, banks, savings and loan branches, and credit unions. For those states without branch banking, individual banks, savings and loan institutions, and credit unions are listed. Entries include: Institution name, address, institution type, deposit totals, percent change over 12 months, percentage share of parent company's total deposits. Arrangement: Geographical.

★4790★ Career Opportunities in Banking, Finance, and Insurance

Facts On File Inc.
132 W 31st St., 17th Fl.
New York, NY 10001
Ph: (212)967-8800   Fax: 800-678-3633
Fr: 800-322-8755
URL: http://www.factsonfile.com/

Latest edition 2nd, February 2007. $49.50 for individuals; $44.45 for libraries. Publication includes: Lists of colleges with programs supporting banking, finance, and industry; professional associations; professional certifications; regulatory agencies; and Internet resources for career planning. Principal content of publication consists of job descriptions for professions in the banking, finance, and insurance industries. Indexes: Alphabetical.

★4791★ Corporate Finance Sourcebook

LexisNexis Group
PO Box 933
Dayton, OH 45401-0933
Ph: (937)865-6800   Fax: (518)487-3584
Fr: 800-543-6862
E-mail: nrpsales@marquiswhoswho.com
URL: http://www.financesourcebook.com

Annual; latest edition 2008. $695.00; $625.00 for standing orders. Covers securities research analysts; major private lenders; investment banking firms; commercial banks; United States-based foreign banks; commercial finance firms; leasing companies; foreign investment bankers in the United States; pension managers; banks that offer master trusts; cash managers; business insurance brokers; business real estate specialists. Lists about 3,400 firms; 14,500 key financial experts. Entries include: Firm name, address, phone, e-mail, and names and titles of officers, contacts, or specialists in corporate finance. Additional details are given as appropriate, including names of major clients, number of companies served, services, total assets, branch locations, years in business. Arrangement: Classified by line of business and then alphabetized within that line of business. Indexes: Firm name; personnel name; geographical.

★4792★ Employment Opportunities, USA

Washington Research Associates
1090 Vermont Ave. NW, Ste. 800
Washington, DC 20005
Ph: (202)408-7025

Annual, quarterly updates. Publication includes: List of over 1,000 employment contacts in companies and agencies in banking, arts, telecommunications, education, and 14 other industries and professions, including federal government. Entries include: Company name, name of representative, address, description of products or services, hiring and recruiting practices, training programs, and year established. Principal content is industry overviews, career news, employment opportunity information on 14 different job markets, and comprehensive guidance to career resources on the Internet. Arrangement: Classified by industry. Indexes: Occupation.

★4793★ National Bankers Association-Roster of Minority Banking Institutions

National Bankers Association
1513 P St. NW
Washington, DC 20005
Ph: (202)588-5432   Fax: (202)588-5443

Annual, October. Covers about 140 banks owned or controlled by minority group persons or women. Entries include: Bank name, address, phone, name of one executive. Arrangement: Geographical.

★4794★ NFCC Directory of Members

National Foundation for Credit Counseling
801 Roeder Rd., Ste. 900
Silver Spring, MD 20910
Ph: (301)589-5600   Fax: (301)495-5623

$5.00 for members; $10.50 for nonmembers. Covers about 1,300 affiliated non-profit consumer credit counseling services in the United States, Puerto Rico, and Canada, which provide non-profit education, counseling, and debt management programs for financial and housing issues. Entries include: Member name, address, phone, fax, name and title of contact, subsidiary and branch names and locations, names and titles of key personnel, description. Arrangement: Geographical. Indexes: Agency name, name of personnel.

★4795★ Peterson's Job Opportunities for Business Majors

Peterson's
Princeton Pke. Corporate Ctr., 2000 Lenox Dr.
PO Box 67005
Lawrenceville, NJ 08648
Ph: (609)896-1800   Fax: (609)896-4531
Fr: 800-338-3282
URL: http://www.petersons.com/

Irregular; latest edition 16th, 2000. Covers the 2,000 largest U.S. employers hiring in several fields, including financial services, management consulting, consumer products, and media/entertainment. Entries include: Organization name, address, phone, name and title of contact, number of employees, type of organization. Arrangement: Alphabetical. Indexes: Type of organization.

★4796★ Roster of Minority Financial Institutions

U.S. Department of the Treasury
1500 Pennsylvania Ave. NW
Washington, DC 20220
Ph: (202)622-2000

Free. Covers about 170 commercial, minority-owned and controlled financial institutions participating in the Department of the Treasury's Minority Bank Deposit Program. Entries include: Name of institution, name and title of chief officer, address, phone, fax. Arrangement: Geographical.

★4797★ Thomson Bank Directory

Accuity
4709 W Golf Rd., Ste. 600
Skokie, IL 60076
Ph: (847)676-9600   Fax: (847)933-8101
Fr: 800-321-3373
URL: http://www.accuitysolutions.com/

Semiannual, June and December. $702.00 for individuals. Covers, in five volumes, about 11,000 banks and 50,000 branches of United States banks, and 60,000 foreign banks and branches engaged in foreign banking; Federal Reserve system and other United States government and state government banking agencies; the 500 largest North American and International commercial banks; paper and automated clearinghouses. Volumes 1 and 2 contain North American listings; volumes 3 and 4, international listings (also cited as "Thomson International Bank Directory"); volume 5, Worldwide Correspondents Guide containing key correspondent data to facilitate funds transfer. Entries include: For domestic banks–Bank name, address, phone, telex, cable, date established, routing number, charter type, bank holding company affiliation, memberships in Federal Reserve System and other banking organizations, principal officers by function performed, principal correspondent banks, and key financial data (deposits, etc.). For international banks–Bank name, address, phone, fax, telex, cable, SWIFT address, transit or sort codes within home country, ownership, financial data, names and titles of key personnel, branch locations. For branches–Bank name, address, phone, charter type, ownership and other details comparable to domestic bank listings. Arrangement: Geographical. Indexes: Alphabetical, geographical.

★4798★ Thomson North American Financial Institutions Directory

Accuity
4709 W Golf Rd., Ste. 600
Skokie, IL 60076
Ph: (847)676-9600   Fax: (847)933-8101
Fr: 800-321-3373
URL: http://www.tfp.com

Semiannual, January and July. $512.00 for individuals. Covers 15,000 banks and their branches; over 2,000 head offices, and 15,500 branches of savings and loan associations; over 5,500 credit unions with assets over $5 million; Federal Reserve System and other U.S. government and state government banking agencies; bank holding, commercial finance, and leasing companies; coverage includes the United States, Canada, Mexico, and Central America. Entries include: Bank name, address, phone, fax, telex, principal officers and directors, date established, financial data, association memberships, attorney or counsel, correspondent banks, out-of-town branch, holding company affiliation, ABA transit number and routing symbol, MICR number with check digit, credit card(s) issued, trust powers, current par value and dividend of common stock, kind of charter. Arrangement: Geographical. Indexes: Alphabetical.

★4799★ Top Careers for Business Graduates

Facts On File Inc.
132 W 31st St., 17th Fl.
New York, NY 10001
Ph: (212)967-8800   Fax: 800-678-3633
Fr: 800-322-8755

Published November 2003. $14.95 for individuals. Covers what it takes to transform a major in business into a job that pays well, is expected to grow, offers a sense of security and opportunity for advancement, and is likely to provide a sense of job satisfaction.

★4800★ Who's Who in Finance and Business

Marquis Who's Who L.L.C.
890 Mountain Ave., Ste. 300
New Providence, NJ 07974-1218
Ph: (908)673-1001   Fax: (908)673-1189
Fr: 800-473-7020
E-mail: finance@marquiswhoswho.com
URL: http://www.marquiswhoswho.com

Biennial; latest edition 36th, September 2007. $349.00 for individuals. Covers over 18,000 individuals. Entries include: Name, home and office addresses, personal, career, and family data; civic and political activities; memberships, publications, awards. Arrangement: Alphabetical.

★4801★ Women in Insurance and Financial Services-Membership Directory

Women in Insurance and Financial Services
6748 Wauconda Dr.
Larkspur, CO 80118
Ph: (303)681-9777   Fr: (866)264-9437
URL: http://www.w-wifs.org

Covers list of contact information of WIFS' members who are devoted to helping women succeed in both insurance and financial services.

HANDBOOKS AND MANUALS

★4802★ Accountants' Handbook, Set

John Wiley & Sons, Inc.
111 River St.
Hoboken, NJ 07030
Ph: (201)748-6000   Fax: (201)748-6088
E-mail: info@wiley.com
URL: http://www.wiley.com/WileyCDA/

D.R. Carmichael and Paul H. Rosenfield. 2007. $95.00. Series covering accounting and financial reporting of interest to accountants, auditors, financial analysts, and users of accounting information.

★4803★ Best Websites for Financial Professionals, Business Appraisers, & Accountants

John Wiley & Sons Inc.
111 River St.
Hoboken, NJ 07030-5774
Ph: (201)748-6000   Fax: (201)748-5774
E-mail: custserv@wiley.com
URL: http://www.wiley.com/WileyCDA/

Eva M. Lang and Jan Davis Tudor. Second edition, 2003. $49.95 (paper). 256 pages.

★4804★ Careers in Banking and Finance

Rosen Publishing Group, Inc.
29 E. 21st St.
New York, NY 10010
Ph: (212)777-3017   Fax: 888-436-4643
Fr: 800-237-9932
URL: http://www.rosenpublishing.com/

Patricia Haddock. Revised edition, 2001. $31.95. 139 pages. Offers advice on job hunting. Describes jobs at all levels in banking and finance. Contains information about the types of financial organizations where the jobs are found, educational requirements, job duties, and salaries.

★4805★ Careers in Finance

The McGraw-Hill Companies
PO Box 182604
Columbus, OH 43272
Fax: (614)759-3749   Fr: 877-883-5524
E-mail: customer.service@mcgraw-hill.com
URL: http://www.mcgraw-hill.com

Trudy Ring. Third edition, 2004. $15.95 (paper). 182 pages. Vocational guidance in the banking and financial industries.

★4806★ Careers for Financial Mavens and Other Money Movers

The McGraw-Hill Companies
PO Box 182604
Columbus, OH 43272
Fax: (614)759-3749   Fr: 877-883-5524
E-mail: customer.service@mcgraw-hill.com
URL: http://www.mcgraw-hill.com

Marjorie Eberts and Margaret Gisler. Second edition, 2004. $13.95; $9.95 (paper). 153 pages.

★4807★ Careers for Number Crunchers and Other Quantitative Types

The McGraw-Hill Companies
PO Box 182604
Columbus, OH 43272
Fax: (614)759-3749   Fr: 877-883-5524
E-mail: customer.service@mcgraw-hill.com
URL: http://www.mcgraw-hill.com

Rebecca Burnett. Second edition, 2002. $22.95 (paper). 192 pages. Provides information to math-oriented job hunters on how to become statisticians, field researchers, computer programmers, stock analysts, investment managers, bankers, engineers, accountants, underwriters, economists, market analysts, mathematicians, systems analysts, and more.

★4808★ Great Jobs for Business Majors

The McGraw-Hill Companies
PO Box 182604
Columbus, OH 43272
Fax: (614)759-3749   Fr: 877-883-5524
E-mail: customer.service@mcgraw-hill.com
URL: http://www.mcgraw-hill.com

Stephen Lambert. Second edition, 2003. $15.95 (paper). 240 pages.

★4809★ Job Seekers Guide to Wall Street Recruiters

John Wiley & Sons Inc.
1 Wiley Dr.
Somerset, NJ 08873
Ph: (732)469-4400   Fax: (732)302-2300
Fr: 800-225-5945
E-mail: custserv@wiley.com
URL: http://www.wiley.com/WileyCDA/

Christopher W. Hunt and Scott A. Scanlon. 1998. $26.95 (paper). 344 pages. Lists recruiters covering investment banking, investment management, and the securities industry.

★4810★ Opportunities in Banking Careers

The McGraw-Hill Companies
PO Box 182604
Columbus, OH 43272
Fax: (614)759-3749   Fr: 877-883-5524
E-mail: customer.service@mcgraw-hill.com
URL: http://www.mcgraw-hill.com

Philip Perry. 1994. $15.95; $12.95 (paper). 146 pages. Discusses banking opportunities in a variety of settings: commercial banks, savings and loans, finance companies, and mortgage banks.

★4811★ Opportunities in Financial Careers

The McGraw-Hill Companies
PO Box 182604
Columbus, OH 43272
Fax: (614)759-3749   Fr: 877-883-5524
E-mail: customer.service@mcgraw-hill.com
URL: http://www.mcgraw-hill.com

Michael Sumichrast. 2004. $13.95; $11.95

(paper). 160 pages. A guide to planning for and seeking opportunities in this challenging field.

★4812★ Opportunities in Hospital Administration Careers

The McGraw-Hill Companies
PO Box 182604
Columbus, OH 43272
Fax: (614)759-3749   Fr: 877-883-5524
E-mail: customer.service@mcgraw-hill.com
URL: http://www.mcgraw-hill.com

I. Donald Snook. 2006. $13.95. 160 pages. Discusses opportunities for administrators in a variety of management settings: hospital, department, clinic, group practice, HMO, mental health, and extended care facilities.

★4813★ Reinventing the CFO: How Financial Managers Can Reinvent Their Roles and Add Greater Value

Harvard Business School Press
60 Harvard Way
Boston, MA 02163
Ph: (617)783-7500   Fax: (617)783-7555
Fr: 800-988-0886
URL: http://www.hbsp.harvard.edu

Jeremy Hope. 2006. $29.95. Outlines seven critical roles for CFOs to follow in order to streamline processes and regulate risk.

★4814★ Resumes for Banking and Financial Careers

The McGraw-Hill Companies
PO Box 182604
Columbus, OH 43272
Fax: (614)759-3749   Fr: 877-883-5524
E-mail: customer.service@mcgraw-hill.com
URL: http://www.mcgraw-hill.com

Second edition, 2001. $11.95 (paper). 160 pages.

EMPLOYMENT AGENCIES AND SEARCH FIRMS

★4815★ 20-20 Foresight Executive Search Inc.

One Lincoln Center, Fl. 15
Oakbrook Terrace, IL 60181
Ph: (708)246-2100
E-mail: bcavoto@202-4.com
URL: http://www.2020-4.com

Executive search firm. Affiliate offices in California and Washington DC.

★4816★ 306 Search Advisors Inc.

230 Park Ave., Ste. 1000
New York, NY 10169
Ph: (646)435-5751
E-mail: info@360advisors.com
URL: http://www.360advisors.com

Executive search firm.

★4817★ A-L Associates Inc.

546 5th Ave., Fl. 6
New York, NY 10036
Ph: (212)878-9000   Fax: (212)878-9096
Fr: 800-292-1390
URL: http://www.alassoc.com

Executive search firm.

★4818★ Abel Fuller & Zedler LLC

440 Benmar, Ste. 1085
Houston, TX 77060
Ph: (281)447-3334   Fax: (281)447-3334
E-mail: agarcia@execufirm.com
URL: http://www.execufirm.com

Executive search firm.

★4819★ AKS Associates Ltd.

175 Derby St., Ste. 27
Hingham, MA 02043
Ph: (781)740-1704   Fax: (781)740-4383
E-mail: aks@akssearch.com
URL: http://www.akssearch.com

Senior search firm. Concentrates on the financial industry.

★4820★ Alfred Daniels & Associates Inc.

5795 Waverly Ave.
La Jolla, CA 92037
Ph: (858)459-4009
URL: http://www.alfreddaniels.com

Executive search firm.

★4821★ Allard Associates Inc.

425 Market St., Ste. 2200
San Francisco, CA 94105
Ph: (415)433-0500   Fax: 800-526-7791
Fr: 800-291-5279
E-mail: resourcing@allardassociates.com
URL: http://www.allardinstitute.com

Executive recruiters in card, consumer credit, financial services and related emerging markets.

★4822★ Allen Evans Klein International

305 Madison Ave., Ste. 2228
New York, NY 10165
Ph: (212)983-9300   Fax: (212)983-9272
E-mail: info@allenevans.com
URL: http://www.allenevans.com

Global Executive search firm.

★4823★ Allen Personnel Agency Inc.

160 Broadway Lbby, Ste. 200
New York, NY 10038-4201
Ph: (212)571-1150   Fax: (212)766-1015
Fr: 800-486-1150

Personnel consultants specializing in business and finance recruitment, specifically insurance, banking, stock brokerage, law and accounting. Industries served: all.

★4824★ Allerton Heneghan & O'Neill
1 Tower Ln., Ste. 1700
Oakbrook Terrace, IL 60181
Ph: (630)645-2294   Fax: (630)645-2298
E-mail: info@ahosearch.com
URL: http://www.ahosearch.com

Executive search firm.

★4825★ Ambler Associates
14881 Quorum Dr., Ste. 450
Dallas, TX 75254
Ph: (972)404-8712   Fax: (972)404-8761
Fr: 800-728-8712

Executive search firm.

★4826★ American Executive Management Inc.
30 Federal St., Ste. 102
Salem, MA 01970
Ph: (978)477-5923
E-mail: execsearch@americanexecutive.us
URL: http://www.americanexecutive.us

Executive search firm. Second location in Boston.

★4827★ American Human Resources Associates Ltd. (AHRA)
PO Box 18269
Cleveland, OH 44118-0269
Ph: (440)995-7120   Fr: 877-342-5833
E-mail: inquiry@ahrasearch.com
URL: http://www.ahrasearch.com

Executive search firm. Focused on real estate, banking and credit & collection.

★4828★ The Angus Group Ltd.
5080 Wooster Rd., Ste. 300
Cincinnati, OH 45226
Ph: (513)961-5575   Fax: (513)961-5616
E-mail: angus@angusgroup.com
URL: http://www.angusgroup.com

Executive search firm.

★4829★ Arlene Clapp Ltd.
4250 Park Glen Rd.
Minneapolis, MN 55416
Ph: (952)928-7474   Fax: (952)928-7475
E-mail: arlene@arleneclapp.com
URL: http://www.arleneclapp.com/

Executive search firm.

★4830★ The Bankers Register
1140 Avenue of the Americas
New York, NY 10036
Ph: (212)840-0800   Fax: (212)840-7039
E-mail: recruiter@spgbankingjobs.com
URL: http://www.tbrspg.com

Specialists in the recruitment and placement of men and women in the banking community. Committed exclusively to: commercial banking, international banking, trust/investments, and thrift/mortgage banking.

★4831★ Barger & Sargeant Inc.
131 Windermere Rd., Ste. 600
PO Box 1460
Center Harbor, NH 03226-1460
Ph: (603)253-4700

Retained executive search consultants. Works only with companies performing very focused executive searches and Board of Director Recruiting. Industries served: financial services, manufacturing, healthcare, retailing and service businesses.

★4832★ Barkston Group LLC
113 South St.
PO Box 218
Litchfield, CT 06759-0218
Ph: (860)567-2400   Fax: (860)567-1466
E-mail: dpatenge@barkstongroup.com
URL: http://www.barkstongroup.com

Executive search firm focused on the banking industry.

★4833★ Bartholdi Partners
12020 Sunrise Valley Dr., Ste. 160
Reston, VA 20191
Ph: (703)476-5519   Fax: (703)391-0029
URL: http://www.bartholdisearch.com

Executive search firm. Affiliates in San Francisco; San Jose; Phoenix; Scottsdale; Parker, CO; and Framingham, MA.

★4834★ The Beam Group
1835 Market St., Ste. 502
Philadelphia, PA 19103
Ph: (215)988-2100   Fax: (215)988-1558
E-mail: info@beamgroup.com
URL: http://www.beamgroup.com

Executive search firm.

★4835★ Bell Wishingrad Partners Inc.
230 Park Ave., Ste. 1000
New York, NY 10169
Ph: (212)949-6666

Executive search firm focused on the financial industry.

★4836★ Bialecki Inc.
780 3rd Ave., Ste. 4203
New York, NY 10017
Ph: (212)755-1090
E-mail: search@bialecki.com
URL: http://www.bialecki.com

Senior executive search firm focused on the financial industry.

★4837★ Bonell Ryan Inc.
415 Madison Ave., 15th Fl.
New York, NY 10017
Ph: (646)673-8620   Fax: (702)995-9935
E-mail: info@bonellryan.com
URL: http://www.bonellryan.com

Executive search firm.

★4838★ Brandjes & Associates
721 Cliveden Rd.
PO Box 5971
Pikesville, MD 21208-4715
Ph: (410)484-5423   Fax: (410)484-6140
Fr: 877-485-8193

Executive Recruiting for the Financial Services Industry.

★4839★ Brush Creek Partners
14512 Horton
Overland Park, KS 66223
Ph: (816)228-9192   Fax: (816)228-6740
E-mail: jlunn@brushcreekpartners.com

Executive search firm.

★4840★ The Burling Group Ltd.
191 N. Wacker Dr., Ste. 2300
Chicago, IL 60606
Ph: (312)346-0888
E-mail: web@burlinggroup.com
URL: http://www.burlinggroup.com

Executive search firm.

★4841★ Butterfass, Pepe & MacCallan Inc.
PO Box 721
Mahwah, NJ 07430
Ph: (201)560-9500   Fax: (201)560-9506
E-mail: staff@bpmi.com
URL: http://www.bpmi.com

Executive search firm.

★4842★ Buxbaum/Rink Consulting L.L.C.
1 Bradley Rd., Ste. 901
Woodbridge, CT 06525-2296
Ph: (203)389-5949   Fax: (203)397-0615
E-mail: gen@buxbaumrink.com
URL: http://www.buxbaumrink.com

Personnel consulting firms offer contingency search, recruitment and placement of accounting and finance, as well as other business management positions. In addition to serving these two major career areas, also provides similar services to operations, marketing and human resources executives. Industries served: manufacturing, financial services, and service.

★4843★ Cannellos-Smartt Associates
23 Davenport Way
Hillsborough, NJ 08844-2923
Ph: (908)359-8319   Fax: (908)369-OO41
E-mail: rudysmartt@csa-search.com
URL: http://www.csa-search.com

Executive search firm with another office in Hillborough.

★4844★ Canny, Bowen Inc.
400 Madison Ave., Rm. 11D
New York, NY 10017
Ph: (212)949-6611   Fax: (212)949-5191
E-mail: main@cannybowen.com

URL: http://www.cannybowen.com

Executive search firm.

★4845★ Career Specialists Inc.

155 108th Ave. NE, Ste. 200
Bellevue, WA 98004
Ph: (425)455-0582   Fax: (425)646-9738
E-mail: prolfe@qwest.net

Executive search firm.

★4846★ Carrington & Carrington Ltd

4354 Town Center Blvd., Ste. 114-248
El Dorado Hills, CA 95762
Ph: (312)606-0015   Fax: (312)606-0501
E-mail: info@carnegiepartners.com
URL: http://www.carnegiepartners.com

Executive search firm.

★4847★ CarterBaldwin

200 Mansell Ct. E., Ste. 450
Roswell, GA 30076
Ph: (678)448-0000   Fax: (770)552-1088
E-mail: info@carterbaldwin.com
URL: http://www.carterbaldwin.com

Executive search firm.

★4848★ Caruthers & Company LLC

1175 Post Rd., E.
Westport, CT 06880
Ph: (203)221-3234   Fax: (203)221-7300

Executive search firm.

★4849★ Chanko-Ward Ltd.

2 W 45th St., Ste. 1201
New York, NY 10036
Ph: (212)869-4040   Fax: (212)869-0281
E-mail: info@chankoward.com
URL: http://www.chankoward.com

Primarily engaged in executive recruiting for individuals and corporations, where disciplines of accounting, planning, mergers and acquisitions, finance, or MIS are required. In addition will function as the internal personnel department of a corporation, either to augment present staff or in a situation where there is no formal personnel department. Serves private industries as well as government agencies.

★4850★ Chicago Consulting Partners Ltd.

930 4th Ave. S
Libertyville, IL 60048
Ph: (847)680-0416   Fax: (847)680-1046
E-mail: blichty@ccpltd.com
URL: http://www.ccpltd.com

Executive search firm concentrated in the financial industry.

★4851★ Chiron Advisors Inc.

420 Lexington Ave., Ste. 2736
New York, NY 10170
Ph: (212)867-6969   Fax: (212)867-7449

E-mail: mstone@cchironadvisors.com
URL: http://www.chironadvisors.com

Executive search firm focused on the financial industry.

★4852★ Choi & Burns LLC

152 W. 57th St., Fl. 32
New York, NY 10019
Ph: (212)755-7051   Fax: (212)335-2610
E-mail: info@choiburns.com
URL: http://www.choiburns.com

Executive search firm focuses on the financial industry.

★4853★ Christian & Timbers

28601 Chagrin Blvd, Ste. 600
Cleveland, OH 44122
Ph: (216)682-3200   Fax: (216)464-6172
Fr: 800-380-9444
E-mail: comments@ctnet.com
URL: http://www.ctnet.com

Executive search firm. Eight branches spanning the USA.

★4854★ Coffou Partners Inc.

1 IBM Plaza
330 N. Wabash Ave., Ste. 2111
Chicago, IL 60611
Ph: (312)464-0896   Fax: (312)464-0322
E-mail: info@coffou.com
URL: http://www.coffou.com

Executive search firm.

★4855★ Consultants to Executive Management Company Ltd.

20 S Clark St., Ste. 610
Chicago, IL 60603
Ph: (312)855-1500   Fax: (312)855-1510
Fr: 800-800-2362
E-mail: cemco@cemcoltd.com
URL: http://www.cemcoltd.com

National personnel consultancy specializes in executive search with focus on accounting and finance, management information systems, professional medical, and real estate fields. Industries served: all.

★4856★ The Consulting Group

757 Third Ave., 23rd Fl.
New York, NY 10017
Ph: (212)751-8484   Fax: (212)692-9290
E-mail: research@consultinggroupny.com
URL: http://www.consultinggroupny.com

Executive search firm.

★4857★ Cook & Company

12 Masterton Rd.
Bronxville, NY 10708
Ph: (914)779-4838   Fax: (914)793-1885
E-mail: search@cook-co.com
URL: http://www.cook-co.com

Executive search firm dedicated to the financial industry.

★4858★ Cornell Global

PO Box 7113
Wilton, CT 06897
Ph: (203)762-0730   Fax: (203)761-9507
E-mail: infor@cornellglobal.com
URL: http://www.cornellglobal.com

Executive search firm.

★4859★ Cornell Group

4017 Williamsburg Ct.
Fairfax, VA 22032
Ph: (703)877-2080   Fax: (703)877-2081
E-mail: parora@thecornellgroup.com
URL: http://www.thecornellgroup.com

Executive search firm.

★4860★ The Corporate Source Group Inc.

280 S. Main St.
Andover, MA 01810
Ph: (987)475-6400   Fax: (987)475-6800
E-mail: inquiry@csg-search.com
URL: http://www.csg-search.com

Executive search firm branches in Phoenix, AZ; Tampa, Fl; North Potomac, MD; McMurray, PA.

★4861★ CP Consulting

674 Hideout
Lake Ariel, PA 18436
Ph: (570)698-8321   Fax: (570)698-8321
E-mail: PhillipsConsult@echoes.net

Executive search firm.

★4862★ Deerfield Associates

572 Washington St., Ste. 15
Wellesley, MA 02482
Ph: (781)237-2800   Fax: (781)237-5600
E-mail: jobs@deerfieldassociates.com
URL: http://www.deerfieldassociates.com

Executive search firm.

★4863★ Dellosso and Greenberg

525 E. 82nd St., Ste. 2B
New York, NY 10028
Ph: (212)570-5350   Fax: (212)327-0613
E-mail:
esearch@dellossoandgreenberg.com
URL: http://
www.dellossoandgreenberg.com

Executive search firm.

★4864★ DGL Consultants

189 S. Main St.
PO Box 450
Richford, VT 05476
Ph: (802)848-7764   Fax: (802)848-3117
E-mail: info@dglconsultants.com
URL: http://www.dglconsultants.com

Executive search firm.

★4865★ **DLG Associates Inc.**
1515 Mockingbird Ln., Ste. 560
Charlotte, NC 28209
Ph: (704)522-9993   Fax: (704)522-7730
E-mail: dguilford@dlgassociates.com
URL: http://www.dlgassociates.com
Executive search firm.

★4866★ **Dotson & Associates**
412 E. 55th St., Ste. 8A
New York, NY 10022
Ph: (212)593-4274
Executive search firm.

★4867★ **Douglas-Allen Inc.**
Tower Square, 24th Fl.
PO Box 15368
Springfield, MA 01115
Ph: (413)739-0900
E-mail: research@douglas-allen.com
URL: http://www.douglas-allen.com
Executive search firm.

★4868★ **Eileen Finn & Associates Inc.**
230 Park Ave., Fl. 10
New York, NY 10169
Ph: (212)687-1260   Fax: (212)551-1473
E-mail: eileen@eileenfinn.com
URL: http://www.eileenfinn.com
Executive search firm.

★4869★ **Epsen, Fuller & Associates LLC**
10 Park Pl., Ste. 420
Morristown, NJ 07960
Ph: (973)359-9929   Fax: (973)359-9928
E-mail: info@epsenfuller.com
URL: http://www.epsenfuller.com
Executive search firm.

★4870★ **Essex Consulting Group Inc.**
PO Box 550
Essex, MA 01929
Ph: (978)337-6633
E-mail: brad@essexsearch.com
URL: http://www.essexsearch.com/
Executive search firm.

★4871★ **Ethos Consulting LLC**
3219 E. Camelback Rd., Ste. 515
Phoenix, AZ 85018
Ph: (480)296-3801   Fax: (480)664-7270
E-mail: resumes@ethosconsulting.com
URL: http://www.ethoscounsulting.com
Executive search firm. Second branch in Scottsdale, AZ.

★4872★ **Executive Dimensions**
PO Box 801
Williamsville, NY 14231
Ph: (716)632-9034   Fax: (716)632-2889

E-mail: execu-search@executivedimensions.com
URL: http://www.executivedimensions.com
Executive search firm.

★4873★ **Executive Search Consultants Ltd.**
3030 N Josey Ln., Ste. 101
Carrollton, TX 75007
Ph: (972)394-4131   Fax: (972)394-2111
Firm offers executive recruitment to the transportation, computer manufacturing, health and beauty aids, consumer package goods, and financial service industries.

★4874★ **The Executive Source Inc.**
55 5th Ave., Ste. 1900
New York, NY 10003
Ph: (212)691-5505   Fax: (212)691-9839
E-mail: tes@executivesource.com
URL: http://www.executivesource.com
Executive search firm.

★4875★ **Fagan & Company**
416 Franklin St.
Ligonier, PA 15658
Ph: (724)238-9571
E-mail: faganco@laurelweb.net
Executive search firm.

★4876★ **Faircastle Technology Group LLC**
27 Wells Rd., Ste. 1117
Monroe, CT 06468-1266
Ph: (203)459-0631   Fax: (203)459-0778
E-mail: resumes@faircastle.com
URL: http://www.faircastle.com
Executive search firm focused on high technology.

★4877★ **Fast Start Inc.**
15 Pelican Pl.
Belleair, FL 33756-1512
Ph: (727)581-2224   Fax: (727)581-4743
E-mail: carolacfp@aol.com
Small consulting firm offering consulting, and broker/dealer referral services for the registered representative and the broker dealer. Offers assistance in areas of: practice management, broker/dealer selection, start-up interfacing, and career guidance. Start-up services include: starting an independent financial planning firm and feasibility studies on starting a broker/dealer and/or registered investment advisory firm. We match buyers and sellers of an RIA's Book of Business. We offer search services for mid-level and executive positions in financial services firms.

★4878★ **Ferrari Search Group**
200 East End Ave., Ste. 5N
New York, NY 10128
Ph: (212)289-5099   Fax: (716)386-2367
E-mail: contactus@ferrarisearchgroup.com

URL: http://www.ferrarisearchgroup.com/
Executive search firm.

★4879★ **Financial Professionals**
4100 Spring Valley Rd., Ste. 307
Dallas, TX 75244
Ph: (972)991-8999   Fax: (972)702-0776
URL: http://www.fpstaff.net/
Executive search consultants with additional offices in Forth Worth and Houston.

★4880★ **Flagship Global Inc.**
6308 Reserve Dr.
Boulder, CO 80303
Ph: (303)440-0280
E-mail: ac@flagshipboston.com
URL: http://www.flagshipglobal.com
Executive search firm focused on the financial industry.

★4881★ **Flynn, Hannock Inc.**
1001 Farmington Ave.
West Hartford, CT 06107-2121
Ph: (860)521-5005   Fax: (860)561-5294
E-mail: search@flynnhannock.com
URL: http://www.flynnhannock.com
Executive search firm.

★4882★ **Fogec Consultants Inc.**
PO Box 28806
Milwaukee, WI 53228
Ph: (414)427-0690   Fax: (414)427-0691
E-mail: tfogec@fogec.com
URL: http://www.fogec.com/fci/
Executive search firm focused on the financial industry.

★4883★ **Frank Palma Associates**
27 Glacier Dr.
Morris Plains, NJ 07950
Ph: (973)884-1498   Fax: (973)884-1499
E-mail: fpalma@fpassocs.com
URL: http://www.fpalmaassoc.com
Executive search firm with additional location in Duluth, GA.

★4884★ **Gans, Gans and Associates**
7445 Quail Meadow Rd.
Plant City, FL 33565-3314
Ph: (813)986-4441   Fax: (813)986-4775
E-mail: simone@gansgans.com
URL: http://www.gansgans.com
A human resources firm that specializes in executive search, human resources, management consulting, diversity consulting, and resume assessment. Takes a personal approach in the development of tailored programs that consider the corporate culture, history, and objectives of client. Industries served: consulting, financial services, legal, insurance, engineering, healthcare, manufacturing, utilities, and the public sector.

★4885★ Graystone Partners L.L.C.

62 Southfield Ave., Ste. 204
Stamford, CT 06902-7229
Ph: (203)323-0023   Fax: (203)353-9035
E-mail: contact@graystonepartners.com
URL: http://www.graystonepartners.com

A retainer-based, executive search firm providing professional consulting services in the area of executive recruitment and management selection. Functional areas of expertise include senior level general management, financial officers, technology officers, marketing and human resource executives.

★4886★ The Hanover Consulting Group

11707 Hunters Run Dr.
Hunt Valley, MD 21030
Ph: (410)785-1912   Fax: (410)785-1913
Fr: 800-785-1912
E-mail: info@thehanovergroup.net
URL: http://www.thehanovergroup.net

Specializes in finding, evaluating, and selecting top talent for the banking and trust industries.

★4887★ International Insurance Consultants Inc.

1191 E Newport Center Dr., Ste. 206
Deerfield Beach, FL 33442
Ph: (954)421-0122   Fax: (954)421-3332
E-mail: info@insurancerecruitersusa.com
URL: http://
www.insurancerecruitersusa.com

Offers executive search to the insurance industry. Clients include insurance companies, brokers, consultants and investment banks. Industries served: insurance and financial services industries.

★4888★ J Nicolas Arthur

77 Franklin St., Fl. 10
Boston, MA 02110
Ph: (617)204-9000   Fax: (617)303-8934
E-mail: nicholas.bogard@jnicholasarthur.com
URL: http://www.jnicholasarthur.com/

Executive search firm specializing in the finance industry.

★4889★ J.R. Scott and Associates

1 S Wacker Dr., Ste. 1616
Chicago, IL 60606-4616
Ph: (312)795-9999   Fax: (312)795-4329
E-mail: mark@esquirestaffing.com
URL: http://www.esquirestaffing.com

Executive search firm specializing in retail securities sales, investment banking, and equity and debt trading. A division of Esquire Personnel Services, Inc.

★4890★ Karen Dexter & Associates Inc.

2012 Chestnut
Wilmette, IL 60091-1512
Ph: (847)853-9500   Fax: (847)256-7108

Training and development consultant offering interpersonal skills training and one-on-one performance counseling for employees of large organizations. Industries served: advertising, banking and finance, consumer products, entertainment, food and beverage, healthcare, legal profession, manufacturing, government agencies, publishing and broadcasting.

★4891★ KForce

Fr: 888-663-3626
URL: http://www.kforce.com

Executive search firm. More than 30 locations throughout the United States.

★4892★ Milo Research

305 Madison Ave., Ste. 1762
New York, NY 10017
Ph: (212)972-2780   Fax: (212)983-5854
E-mail: miloresearch@compuserve.com

Human resources firm helps executives find work in the publishing, finance, telecommunications, direct mail, and consumer products fields.

★4893★ The Murphy Group

245 W Roosevelt Rd., Bldg.15, Ste.101
Chicago, IL 60605
Ph: (630)639-5110   Fax: (630)639-5113
E-mail: info@murphygroup.com
URL: http://www.murphygroup.com

Employment agency. Places personnel in a variety of positions. Additional offices located in Napierville, Park Ridge, and OakBrook.

★4894★ Neal Management Inc.

450 7th Ave., Ste. 923
New York, NY 10123
Ph: (212)686-1686   Fax: (212)686-1590
E-mail: info@nealmanagement.com
URL: http://nealmanagement.com

An executive search firm dedicated to the placement of financial professionals.

★4895★ Oliver & Rozner Associates

598 Madison Ave., Ste. 11
New York, NY 10022
Ph: (212)688-1850

Performs executive search for top tiers of management including presidents, general management, advertising account management, division management, group executive and vice presidential line positions in such areas as marketing, research, operations, sales, finance, human resources, and others; hard-to-find specialists including specific marketing/advertising executives, research and development expertise, computer/data processing knowledge, scientific, physicians-product efficacy and occupational medicine, and engineering. Industries served include pharmaceutical, healthcare, hospital, advertising, consumer products and packaged goods, housewares, direct selling, cosmetics/toiletries, industrial products, high technology products, forest products, engineering, construction, environment/resource recovery, graphic arts, chemical, and government agencies.

★4896★ Pate Resources Group Inc.

595 Orleans, Ste. 707
Beaumont, TX 77701
Ph: (409)833-4514   Fax: (409)833-4646
Fr: 800-669-4514
E-mail: opportunities@pateresourcesgroup.com
URL: http://www.pateresourcesgroup.com

Offers executive search and recruiting services to professionals who include physicians, healthcare administrators, engineers, accounting and financial disciplines, legal, outplacement, sales and marketing. Industries served: healthcare, petrochemicals, accounting, utility, legal, and municipalities.

★4897★ Paul Falcone Associates

PO Box 115
Mount Freedom, NJ 07970
Ph: (973)895-5200   Fax: (973)895-5266
E-mail: pfasearch@yahoo.com

Executive pharmaceutical search firm.

★4898★ Penn Hill Associates Inc.

14323 Ocean Hwy., Ste. 4131
PO Box 1367
Pawleys Island, SC 29585
Ph: (843)237-8988   Fax: (843)237-9220
E-mail: janette@pennhillassociates.com
URL: http://www.pennhillassociates.com

Offers executive search services for consumer finance companies. Industries served: consumer finance, home equity, and auto financing.

★4899★ Penn Search Inc.

1045 1st Ave., Ste. 110
PO Box 688
Wayne, PA 19087
Ph: (610)964-8820   Fax: (610)964-8916
E-mail: charlied@pennsearch.com
URL: http://www.pennsearch.com

Assists in recruiting and hiring accounting and financial professionals from staff accountant to chief financial officer. Industries served: all.

★4900★ Princeton Executive Search

1 Eves Dr., Ste. 115
Marlton, NJ 08053
Ph: (609)584-1100   Fax: (856)596-8866
E-mail: info@bonifield.com
URL: http://
www.princetonexecutivesearch.com

Provides search and placement for management level professions. Specializes in accounting, banking, engineering and human resources. Industries served: financial, research and development, insurance, manufacturing, banking, and government agencies.

★4901★ Quirk-Corporon and Associates Inc.
1229 N Jackson St., Ste. 205
Milwaukee, WI 53202
Ph: (414)224-9399   Fax: (414)224-9472
E-mail: quirkrecruiters@sbcglobal.net
URL: http://www.quirkinsrecruiters.com

Employment agency specializing in all disciplines of the insurance and financial industries.

★4902★ Raines International Inc.
250 Park Ave., 17th Fl.
New York, NY 10177
Ph: (212)997-1100   Fax: (212)997-0196
E-mail: contact@rainesinternational.com
URL: http://www.rainesinternational.com

International generalist firm specializing in middle to upper management executives. Concentrations include general management, finance and accounting, information technology, operations/procurement, strategic planning, investment banking, real estate/finance, human resources, insurance, and legal.

★4903★ Raymond Alexander Associates
97 Lackawanna Ave., Ste. 102
Totowa, NJ 07512
Ph: (973)256-1000   Fax: (973)256-5871
E-mail: raa@raymondalexander.com
URL: http://www.raymondalexander.com

Personnel consulting firm conducts executive search services in the specific areas of accounting, tax and finance. Industries served: manufacturing, financial services, and public accounting.

★4904★ Roberson & Co.
10751 Parfet St.
Broomfield, CO 80021
Ph: (303)410-6510
E-mail: roberson@recruiterpro.com
URL: http://www.recruiterpro.com

A contingency professional and executive recruiting firm working the national and international marketplace. Specialize in accounting, finance, data processing and information services, healthcare, environmental and mining, engineering, manufacturing, human resources, and sales and marketing.

★4905★ Rocky Mountain Recruiters, Inc.
1776 S. Jackson St., Ste. 412
Denver, CO 80210
Ph: (303)296-2000   Fax: (303)296-2223
E-mail: resumes@rmrecruiters.com
URL: http://www.rmrecruiters.com

Accounting, financial, and executive search firm.

★4906★ Search North America Inc.
PO Box 3577
Sunriver, OR 97707-0577
Ph: (503)222-6461   Fax: (503)227-2804
E-mail: mylinda@searchna.com
URL: http://www.searchna.com

An executive search and recruiting firm whose focus is placing engineers, operations and maintenance managers, sales and marketing management, financial and general management executives (both domestic and international). Industries served: forest products, pulp and paper, waste to energy, environmental services, consulting and equipment suppliers for above related industries.

★4907★ Techtronix Technical Search
4805 N 24th Pl.
PO Box 17713
Milwaukee, WI 53217-0173
Ph: (414)466-3100   Fax: (414)466-3598

Firm specializes in recruiting executives for the engineering, information systems, manufacturing, marketing, finance, and human resources industries.

★4908★ Terry Taylor & Associates
459 Bechman St.
Springdale, PA 15144-1170
Ph: (724)274-5627
E-mail: tdtassoc@comcast.net

An executive search consulting firm specializing in financial, litigation support, performance improvement and management information systems recruitment.

★4909★ TRC Staffing Services Inc.
100 Ashford Ctr. N, Ste. 500
Atlanta, GA 30338
Ph: (770)392-1411   Fax: (770)393-2742
E-mail: info@trcstaff.com
URL: http://www.trcstaff.com

A full-service executive search company with permanent placements encompassing engineering, industrial sales, financial and computer science positions. Screen, interview, and verify past employment for all candidates prior to referral. Also assist personnel staffs in the attainment of their EEO/AAP goals with the placement of talented individuals in positions which are underutilized with minorities and/or women. Industries served: all.

★4910★ Val Executive Resources Group
100 Merrick Rd., Ste. 302E
Rockville Centre, NY 11570-4801
Ph: (516)764-9000   Fax: (516)764-9122
E-mail: info@val-group.com

Personnel consultants recruiting on contingency and retained search basis specializing in Banking and Finance, to include: Corporate, Commercial and Consumer Banking, Private Banking, Trust, Investments, Human Resources, Marketing, focusing on lower, middle, and senior management positions.

Industries served: banking, finance, brokerage, insurance.

ONLINE JOB SOURCES AND SERVICES

★4911★ American Association of Finance and Accounting
E-mail: feedback@aafa.com
URL: http://www.aafa.com

Description: AAFA is the largest and oldest alliance of executive search firms specializing in the recruitment and placement of finance and accounting professionals. Contains career opportunities site with job board for both job seekers and hiring employers. One does not have to be a member to search for jobs.

★4912★ The Digital Financier
URL: http://www.dfin.com

Description: Job postings from financial companies. Offers links to major job search websites. Has leads for further training and allows companies to post their own job links.

★4913★ Financial Executives International
200 Campus Dr.
Florham Park, NJ 07932
Ph: (973)765-1000   Fax: (973)965-1018
URL: http://www.financialexecutives.org

Description: Member site for financial executive professional association. Contains job board and field-related information. **Fee:** Must be member to access services. Annual membership dues $475.

★4914★ Financial Job Network
15030 Ventura Blvd., No. 378
Sherman Oaks, CA 91403
E-mail: info@fjn.com
URL: http://www.fjn.com

Description: Contains information on international and national employment opportunities for those in the financial job market. Job listings may be submitted, as well as resumes. **Main files include:** Testimonials, Calendar, Corporate Listings, FJN Clients, more. **Fee:** Free to candidates.

★4915★ Spherion
2050 Spectrum Blvd.
Fort Lauderdale, FL 33309
Ph: (954)308-7600
E-mail: help@spherion.com
URL: http://www.spherion.com

Description: Recruitment firm specializing in accounting and finance, sales and marketing, interim executives, technology, engineering, retail and human resources.

TRADESHOWS

★4916★ Pennsylvania Association of Community Bankers Convention

Pennsylvania Association of Community
Bankers
2405 N. Front St.
Harrisburg, PA 17110
Ph: (717)231-7447   Fax: (717)231-7445
E-mail: pacb@pacb.org
URL: http://www.pacb.org

Annual. **Primary Exhibits:** Equipment, supplies, and services for community banks, thrifts, and associate firms.

OTHER SOURCES

★4917★ Administration and Management Occupations

Delphi Productions
3159 6th St.
Boulder, CO 80304
Ph: (303)443-2100   Fax: (303)443-4022
Fr: 888-443-2400
E-mail: support@delphivideo.com
URL: http://www.delphivideo.com

$95.00. 50 minutes. Part of the Careers for the 21st Century Video Library.

★4918★ American Bankers Association (ABA)

1120 Connecticut Ave. NW
Washington, DC 20036
Ph: (202)663-5000   Fax: (202)663-7543
Fr: 800-BAN-KERS
E-mail: custserv@aba.com
URL: http://www.aba.com

Members: Members are principally commercial banks and trust companies; combined assets of members represent approximately 90% of the U.S. banking industry; approximately 94% of members are community banks with less than $500 million in assets. **Purpose:** Seeks to enhance the role of commercial bankers as preeminent providers of financial services through communications, research, legal action, lobbying of federal legislative and regulatory bodies, and education and training programs. Serves as spokesperson for the banking industry; facilitates exchange of information among members. Maintains the American Institute of Banking, an industry-sponsored adult education program. **Activities:** Conducts educational and training programs for bank employees and officers through a wide range of banking schools and national conferences. Maintains liaison with federal bank regulators; lobbies Congress on issues affecting commercial banks; testifies before congressional committees; represents members in U.S. postal rate proceedings. Serves as secretariat of the International Monetary Conference and the Financial Institutions Committee for the American National Standards Institute. Files briefs and lawsuits in major court cases affecting the industry. Conducts teleconferences with state banking associations on such issues as regulatory compliance; works to build consensus and coordinate activities of leading bank and financial service trade groups. Provides services to members including: public advocacy; news media contact; insurance program providing directors and officers with liability coverage, financial institution bond, and trust errors and omissions coverage; research service operated through ABA Center for Banking Information; fingerprint set processing in conjunction with the Federal Bureau of Investigation; discounts on operational and income-producing projects through the Corporation for American Banking. Conducts conferences, forums, and workshops covering subjects such as small business, consumer credit, agricultural and community banking, trust management, bank operations, and automation. Sponsors ABA Educational Foundation and the Personal Economics Program, which educates schoolchildren and the community on banking, economics, and personal finance.

★4919★ American Financial Services Association (AFSA)

919 18th St. NW, Ste. 300
Washington, DC 20006-5517
Ph: (202)296-5544   Fax: (202)223-0321
E-mail: cstinebert@afsamail.org
URL: http://www.afsaonline.org

Description: Represents companies whose business is primarily direct credit lending to consumers and/or the purchase of sales finance paper on consumer goods. Has members that have insurance and retail subsidiaries; some are themselves subsidiaries of highly diversified parent corporations. Encourages the business of financing individuals and families for necessary and useful purposes at reasonable charges, including interest; promotes consumer understanding of basic money management principles as well as constructive uses of consumer credit. Includes educational services such as films, textbooks, and study units for the classroom and budgeting guides for individuals and families. Compiles statistical reports; offers seminars.

★4920★ Association for Financial Professionals (AFP)

4520 E West Hwy., Ste. 750
Bethesda, MD 20814
Ph: (301)907-2862   Fax: (301)907-2864
E-mail: afp@afponline.org
URL: http://www.afponline.org

Purpose: Seeks to establish a national forum for the exchange of concepts and techniques related to improving the management of treasury and the careers of professionals through research, education, publications, and recognition of the treasury management profession through a certification program. **Activities:** Conducts educational programs. Operates career center.

★4921★ Bank Administration Institut(e) (BAI)

1 N Franklin St., Ste. 1000
Chicago, IL 60606-3421
Ph: (312)683-2464   Fax: (312)683-2(
Fr: 888-284-4078
E-mail: info@bai.org
URL: http://www.bai.org

Description: Works to improve the comp(
tive position of banking companies thro(
strategic research and educational offerin(

★4922★ Eastern Finance Association (EFA)

Auburn Montgomery
School of Business
PO Box 244023
Montgomery, AL 36124-4023
E-mail: membershipservices@blackwellpublishers.co.uk
URL: http://www.easternfinance.org

Description: College and university prof(
sors and financial officers; libraries. Provi(
a meeting place for persons interested in (
aspect of finance, including financial m(
agement, investments, and banking. Sp(
sors research competitions.

★4923★ Financial Executives International (FEI)

200 Campus Dr.
Florham Park, NJ 07932-0674
Ph: (973)765-1000   Fax: (973)765-10
E-mail: mcangemi@fei.org
URL: http://www.fei.org

Members: Professional organization of c(
porate financial executives performing du(
of chief financial officer, controller, treasu(
or vice-president-finance. **Activities:** Sp(
sors research activities through its affilia(
Financial Executives Research Foundati(
Maintains offices in Toronto, Canada, (
Washington, DC.

★4924★ Financial Managers Society (FMS)

100 W Monroe, Ste. 810
Chicago, IL 60603
Ph: (312)578-1300   Fax: (312)578-1(
Fr: 800-275-4367
E-mail: info@fmsinc.org
URL: http://www.fmsinc.org

Description: Works for the needs of finan(
and accounting professionals from ban(
thrifts and credit unions. Offers career-(
hancing education, specialized publicatio(
national leadership opportunities, and wor(
wide connections with other industry prof(
sionals.

★4925★ Financial Occupations

Delphi Productions
3159 6th St.
Boulder, CO 80304
Ph: (303)443-2100   Fax: (303)443-4(
Fr: 888-443-2400
E-mail: support@delphivideo.com
URL: http://www.delphivideo.com

$95.00. 50 minutes. Part of the Careers for the 21st Century Video Library.

★4926★ National Association of Black Accountants (NABA)
7249-A Hanover Pkwy.
Greenbelt, MD 20770
Ph: (301)474-6222   Fax: (301)474-3114
Fr: 888-571-2939
E-mail: customerservice@nabainc.org
URL: http://www.nabainc.org
Description: Minority students and professionals currently working, or interested in the fields of accounting, finance, technology, consulting or general business. Seeks, promotes, develops, and represents the interests of current and future minority business professionals.

★4927★ National Association of Corporate Treasurers (NACT)
12100 Sunset Hills Rd., Ste. 130
Reston, VA 20190
Ph: (703)437-4377   Fax: (703)435-4390
E-mail: nact@nact.org
URL: http://www.nact.org
Description: Serves as a forum for high-level finance executives who perform all or a substantial part of the duties of corporate treasurership. Seeks to produce and facilitate the exchange of information relevant to the management of corporate treasury operations. Sponsors general sessions on such topics as Cash Management Issues for the 90's, Corporate Finance, Data Processing/Electronic Services, International Liquidity Management. Offers job clearinghouse services.

★4928★ Risk and Insurance Management Society (RIMS)
1065 Ave. of the Americas, 13th Fl.
New York, NY 10018
Ph: (212)286-9292   Fax: (212)655-7423
E-mail: membership@rims.org
URL: http://www.rims.org
Description: Business association serving corporate risk and insurance managers. Dedicated to advancing the practice of risk management, a discipline that protects physical, financial, and human resources.

★4929★ Risk Management Association
1801 Market St., Ste. 300
Philadelphia, PA 19103-1628
Ph: (215)446-4000   Fax: (215)446-4101
Fr: 800-677-7621
E-mail: member@rmahq.org
URL: http://www.rmahq.org/RMA
Members: Commercial and savings banks, and savings and loan, and other financial services companies. **Activities:** Conducts research and professional development activities in areas of loan administration, asset management, and commercial lending and credit to increase professionalism.

★4930★ Society of Cost Estimating and Analysis (SCEA)
527 Maple Ave. E, Ste. 301
Vienna, VA 22180
Ph: (703)938-5090   Fax: (703)938-5091
E-mail: scea@sceaonline.net
URL: http://www.sceaonline.net
Description: Works to improve cost estimating and analysis in government and industry and to enhance the professional competence and achievements of its members. Administers a professional certification program leading to the designation of Certified Cost Estimator/Analyst; offers extensive literature in the field through its Professional Development Program. Goals of the Society include enhancing the profession of cost estimating and analysis, fostering the professional growth of its members, enhancing the understanding and application of cost estimating, analysis and related disciplines throughout government and industry and providing forums and media through which current issues of interest to the profession can be addressed and advances in the state-of-the-art can be shared.

Fire Fighters

SOURCES OF HELP-WANTED ADS

★4931★ American City and County

Primedia Business
6151 Powers Ferry Rd., Ste. 200
Atlanta, GA 30339
Ph: (770)955-2500   Fax: (770)618-0204
URL: http://
www.americancityandcounty.com

Monthly. $67.00/year for individuals. Municipal and county administration magazine.

★4932★ Firehouse Magazine

Cygnus Business Media Inc.
3 Huntington Quadrangle, Ste. 301 N
Melville, NY 11747
Ph: (631)845-2700   Fax: (631)845-7109
Fr: 800-308-6397
URL: http://www.firehouse.com

Monthly. $30.00/year for individuals; $49.00 for two years. Magazine focusing on fire protection.

★4933★ Homeland First Response

Jems Communications
525 B St., Ste. 1900
San Diego, CA 92101
Fax: (619)699-6396   Fr: 800-266-5367
URL: http://www.jems.com/Columnists/homelandfirstresponse

Bimonthly. Magazine for first responders including police, fire fighters, and emergency medical technicians.

★4934★ ICHIEFS On Scene

International Association of Fire Chiefs
4025 Fair Ridge Dr., Ste. 300
Fairfax, VA 22033-2868
Ph: (703)273-0911   Fax: (703)273-9363
E-mail: onscene@ichiefs.org
URL: http://www.iafc.org/onscene/index.asp

Description: Semimonthly. Covers management, technical, and legislative issues that affect fire fighting professionals, including volunteers. Recurring features include letters to the editor, interviews, news of research, reports of meetings, news of educational opportunities, job listings, notices of publications available, and columns titled Executive Director's Column, Comm Center, Announcements, Section News, President's Column, and Staying Out of Trouble-A Case Study.

★4935★ International Fire Fighter

International Association of Fire Fighters
1750 New York Ave. NW
Washington, DC 20006
Ph: (202)737-8484   Fax: (202)737-8418
URL: http://www.iffmag.com/

Bimonthly. $35.00/year for individuals, sterling; $70.00/year for individuals. Union tabloid.

★4936★ The Municipality

League of Wisconsin Municipalities
122 W Washington Ave., Ste. 300
Madison, WI 53703-2718
Ph: (608)267-2380   Fax: (608)267-0645
Fr: 800-991-5502
URL: http://www.lwm-info.org/index.asp?Type=B_BASIC&SEC=¢0702EE8F

Monthly. Magazine for officials of Wisconsin's local municipal governments.

★4937★ Necdigest

National Fire Protection Association
1 Batterymarch Pk.
Quincy, MA 02169-7471
Ph: (617)770-3000   Fax: (617)770-0700
Fr: 800-344-3555
URL: http://www.necdigest.org

Monthly. Free to qualified subscribers. Magazine that features articles on all aspects of fire safety.

★4938★ NFPA Journal

National Fire Protection Association
1 Batterymarch Pk.
Quincy, MA 02169-7471
Ph: (617)770-3000   Fax: (617)770-0700
Fr: 800-344-3555
URL: http://www.nfpa.org

Bimonthly. Magazine concerning fire protection, prevention.

★4939★ Turn Out

International Fire Buff Associates Inc.
115 Glenmont Ave.
955 Regina Dr.
Glen Burnie, MD 21061
Ph: (410)242-8672   Fax: (410)242-4688
E-mail: info@bublitzcreative.com
URL: http://www.ifba.org/

Description: Semiannual. Concerned with the firefighting activities of fire departments across the nation. Includes historical accounts and news of association and member activities.

★4940★ Western City

League of California Cities
1400 K St., Ste. 400
Sacramento, CA 95814
Ph: (916)658-8200   Fax: (916)658-8240
Fr: 800-262-1801
URL: http://www.westerncity.com

Monthly. $39.00/year for individuals; $63.00 for two years; $52.00/year for other countries; $26.50/year for students. Municipal interest magazine.

★4941★ Wyoming Fire & Electrical Safety News

Wyoming State Department of Fire
  Prevention & Electrical Safety
Herschler Bldg., 1 W
122 W 25th St.
Cheyenne, WY 82002
Ph: (307)777-7288   Fax: (307)777-7119
URL: http://wyofire.state.wy.us/

Description: Quarterly. Covers state developments in fire protection and electrical safety administration and training, including news and studies from the National Fire Protection Association. Recurring features include a calendar of events.

EMPLOYER DIRECTORIES AND NETWORKING LISTS

★4942★ *Fellowship of Christian Firefighters International-Directory*

Fellowship of Christian Firefighters International
PO Box 901
Fort Collins, CO 80522-0901
Fax: (970)416-9076   Fr: 800-322-9848
URL: http://www.fellowshipofchristianfirefighters.com

Biennial, Odd years. Covers about 2,000 member Christian firefighters. Entries include: Name, address, phone. Arrangement: Alphabetical. Indexes: Local chapter.

★4943★ *National Directory of Fire Chiefs & EMS Administrators*

National Public Safety Information Bureau
601 Main St., Ste. 201
PO Box 365
Stevens Point, WI 54481
Ph: (715)345-2772   Fax: (715)345-7288
Fr: 800-647-7579
URL: http://www.safetysource.com

Annual; latest edition 16th edition, 2007. $149.00 for print product; $189.00 for print and online, combined. Covers over 36,000 fire and emergency departments in the U.S. Entries include: Department name, address, phone, fax, county, name of chief, type of department, financial structure. Arrangement: Geographical.

★4944★ *What Can I Do Now*

Facts On File Inc.
132 W 31st St., 17th Fl.
New York, NY 10001
Ph: (212)967-8800   Fax: 800-678-3633
Fr: 800-322-8755
URL: http://www.factsonfile.com

$22.95 for individuals; $20.65 for libraries. Covers border patrol officers, corrections officers, crime analysts, emergency medical technicians, FBI agents, firefighters, and police officers.

HANDBOOKS AND MANUALS

★4945★ *Firefighter Career Starter*

LearningExpress, LLC
55 Broadway, 8th Fl.
New York, NY 10006
Ph: (212)995-2566   Fax: (212)995-5512
Fr: 800-295-9556
E-mail: customerservice@learningexpressllc.com
URL: http://www.learningexpressllc.com

Mary Masi and Lauren B. Starkey. Second edition, 2001. $15.95 (paper). 208 pages. Part of the Career Starters Series.

★4946★ *Opportunities in Fire Protection Services*

The McGraw-Hill Companies
PO Box 182604
Columbus, OH 43272
Fax: (614)759-3749   Fr: 877-883-5524
E-mail: customer.service@mcgraw-hill.com
URL: http://www.mcgraw-hill.com

Ronny J. Coleman. 2003. $11.95 (paper). 160 pages. Surveys opportunities in local, state, and federal fire departments and forestry services, as well as with fire equipment and fire insurance companies. Contains bibliography and illustrations.

★4947★ *Real-Resumes for Firefighting Jobs*

PREP Publishing
1110 1/2 Hay St., PMB 66
Fayetteville, NC 28305
Ph: (910)483-6611   Fax: (910)483-2439
Fr: 800-533-2814

Anne McKinney. 2004. $16.95. Illustrated. 192 pages. Firefighting careers.

TRADESHOWS

★4948★ *Fire - Rescue International*

International Association of Fire Chiefs
4025 Fair Ridge Dr.
Fairfax, VA 22033-2868
Ph: (703)273-0911   Fax: (703)273-9363
E-mail: cafc@igs.net
URL: http://www.iafc.org

Annual. **Primary Exhibits:** Fire safety and emergency medical service equipment, supplies, and services; related training and support materials.

OTHER SOURCES

★4949★ *Human Services Occupations*

Delphi Productions
3159 6th St.
Boulder, CO 80304
Ph: (303)443-2100   Fax: (303)443-4022
Fr: 888-443-2400
E-mail: support@delphivideo.com
URL: http://www.delphivideo.com

$95.00. 50 minutes. Part of the Careers for the 21st Century Video Library.

★4950★ *International Association of Fire Chiefs (IAFC)*

4025 Fair Ridge Dr., Ste. 300
Fairfax, VA 22033-2868
Ph: (703)273-0911   Fax: (703)273-9363
Fr: 800-661-3336
E-mail: membership@iafc.org
URL: http://www.iafc.org

Members: Fire Department chief officers, emergency services administrators and emergency medical services directors/managers and supervisors, career, volunteer, municipal and private, who are interested in improving fire, rescue, and EMS coverage to the general public. **Purpose:** Provides leadership to career and volunteer chiefs, chief fire officers and managers of emergency service organizations throughout the international community through vision, information, education, services and representation to enhance their professionalism and capabilities.

★4951★ *Math at Work: Women in Nontraditional Careers*

Her Own Words
PO Box 5264
Madison, WI 53705-0264
Ph: (608)271-7083   Fax: (608)271-0209
E-mail: herownword@aol.com
URL: http://www.herownwords.com/

Video. Jocelyn Riley. $95.00. 15 minutes. Resource guide also available for $45.00.

★4952★ *Women in Firefighting*

Her Own Words
PO Box 5264
Madison, WI 53705-0264
Ph: (608)271-7083   Fax: (608)271-0209
E-mail: herownword@aol.com
URL: http://www.herownwords.com/

Video. Jocelyn Riley. $95.00. 15 minutes. Resource guide also available for $45.00.

★4953★ *Women in Nontraditional Careers: An Introduction*

Her Own Words
PO Box 5264
Madison, WI 53705
Ph: (608)271-7083   Fax: (608)271-0209
E-mail: herownword@aol.com
URL: http://www.herownwords.com/

Video. Jocelyn Riley. $95.00. 15 minutes. Resource guide also available for $45.00.

Fitness Trainers

SOURCES OF HELP-WANTED ADS

★4954★ AAHPERD Update

American Alliance for Health, Physical Education, Recreation & Dance
1900 Association Dr.
Reston, VA 20191
Ph: (703)476-3400   Fax: (703)476-9527
Fr: 800-213-7193
E-mail: info@aahperd.org
URL: http://www.aahperd.org

Description: Six issues/year. Provides news and information on the Alliance. Discusses current issues and research in the areas of health, physical education, recreation, dance, fitness, and adapted physical education. Recurring features include a calendar of events, reports of meetings, news of educational opportunities, job listings, notices of publications available, and columns titled President's Message, Membership Corner, and From the EVP's Desk.

★4955★ ACE FitnessMatters

American Council on Exercise
4851 Paramont Dr.
San Diego, CA 92123
Ph: (858)279-8227   Fax: (858)279-8064
Fr: 800-825-3636
E-mail: conted@acefitness.org

Bimonthly. $14.95/year for individuals. Consumer magazine covering health and fitness news.

★4956★ Bountiful Health

JNE Publishing, Inc.
PO Box 5647
Huntsville, AL 35814
Ph: (256)837-3035   Fr: 800-313-7751
URL: http://www.jnepublishing.com/bountifulhealth.php?page=public

Magazine focusing on complementary and alternative medicine, exercise, vitamins and supplements, healthy eating, and green living.

★4957★ The IHS Primary Care Provider

Indian Health Service (HQ)
The Reyes Bldg.
801 Thompson Ave., Ste. 400
Rockville, MD 20852-1627
URL: http://www.ihs.gov/PublicInfo/Publications/HealthProvider/Pr

Monthly. Journal for health care professionals, physicians, nurses, pharmacists, dentists, and dietitians.

★4958★ NSCA Bulletin

National Strength & Conditioning Association
1885 Bob Johnson Dr.
Colorado Springs, CO 80906
Ph: (719)632-6722   Fax: (719)632-6367
Fr: 800-815-6826
E-mail: nsca@nsca-lift.org
URL: http://www.nsca-lift.org/Publications/

Description: Bimonthly. Tracks Association activities. Recurring features include interviews, a calendar of events, reports of meetings, news of educational opportunities, job listings, book reviews, and notices of publications available.

★4959★ Nutritional Outlook

Canon Communications L.L.C.
11444 W Olympic Blvd., Ste. 900
Los Angeles, CA 90064
Ph: (310)445-4200   Fax: (310)445-4299
E-mail: info@nutritionaloutlook.com
URL: http://www.nutritionaloutlook.com/

Magazine for manufacturer's resource for dietary supplements and healthy foods and beverages.

PLACEMENT AND JOB REFERRAL SERVICES

★4960★ American Athletic Trainers Association and Certification Board (AATA)

146 E Duarte Rd.
Arcadia, CA 91006
Ph: (626)445-1978   Fax: (626)574-1999
E-mail: americansportsmedicine@hotmail.com

Purpose: Aims to qualify and certify active athletic trainers; establish minimum competence standards for individuals participating in the prevention and care of athletic injuries; to inform communities nationwide of the importance of having competent leadership in the area of athletic training. **Activities:** Conducts continuing education and charitable programs; maintains placement service.

★4961★ Exercise Safety Association (ESA)

PO Box 547916
Orlando, FL 32854-7916
Ph: (407)246-5090
E-mail: askesa@aol.com
URL: http://www.exercisesafety.com

Description: Fitness instructors, personal trainers, health spas, YMCAs, community recreation departments, and hospital wellness programs. Purposes are: to improve the qualifications of exercise instructors; to train instructors to develop safe exercise programs that will help people avoid injury while exercising; to prepare instructors for national certification. Offers training in aerobics and exercise and on the physiological aspects of exercise. Conducts exercise safety and research programs. Sponsors charitable program; maintains speakers' bureau. Offers instructor placement services.

★4962★ National Athletic Trainers' Association (NATA)

2952 Stemmons Fwy., No. 200
Dallas, TX 75247-6196
Ph: (214)637-6282   Fax: (214)637-2206
Fr: 800-879-6282
E-mail: mjalbohm@aol.com
URL: http://www.nata.org

Members: Athletic trainers from universities, colleges, and junior colleges; professional football, baseball, basketball, and ice hockey; high schools, preparatory schools, military establishments, sports medicine clinics, and business/industrial health programs. **Activities:** Maintains hall of fame and placement service. Conducts research programs; compiles statistics.

HANDBOOKS AND MANUALS

★4963★ Athlete's Guide to Career Planning

Human Kinetics Publishers
PO Box 5076
Champaign, IL 61825-5076
Ph: (217)351-5076   Fax: (217)351-1549
Fr: 800-747-4457
E-mail: info@hkusa.com
URL: http://www.humankinetics.com/

Delight Champagne, Judy Chartrand, Steven Danish, and Shane M. Murphy. 1997. $17.95 (paper). 240 pages.

★4964★ Careers for Health Nuts and Others Who Like to Stay Fit

The McGraw-Hill Companies
PO Box 182604
Columbus, OH 43272
Fax: (614)759-3749   Fr: 877-883-5524
E-mail: customer.service@mcgraw-hill.com
URL: http://www.mcgraw-hill.com

Blythe Camenson. Second edition, 2005. $13.95 (paper). 208 pages.

★4965★ Certified Fitness Instructor Career Starter: Finding and Getting a Great Job

LearningExpress, LLC
55 Broadway, 8th Fl.
New York, NY 10006
Ph: (212)995-2566   Fax: (212)995-5512
Fr: 800-295-9556
E-mail: customerservice@learningexpressllc.com
URL: http://www.learningexpressllc.com

Lauren B. Starkey. December 2002. $16.95. Illustrated. 224 Pages. Career Starters Series.

★4966★ It's More Than Just Making Them Sweat: A Career Training Guide for Personal Fitness Trainers

Robert D. Reed Publishers
PO Box 1992
Bandon, OR 97411
Ph: (541)347-9882   Fax: (541)347-9883
E-mail: 4bobreed@msn.com
URL: http://www.rdrpublishers.com/home.html

Ed Thornton. 2001 (paper). $11.95. 120 pages.

★4967★ Opportunities in Fitness Careers

The McGraw-Hill Companies
PO Box 182604
Columbus, OH 43272
Fax: (614)759-3749   Fr: 877-883-5524
E-mail: customer.service@mcgraw-hill.com
URL: http://www.mcgraw-hill.com

Mary Miller. 2003. $12.95 (paper). 146 pages. Surveys fitness related careers. Describes career opportunities, education and experience needed, how to get into entry-level jobs and what income to expect. Schools are listed in the appendix.

OTHER SOURCES

★4968★ American College of Sports Medicine (ACSM)

401 W Michigan St.
Indianapolis, IN 46202-3233
Ph: (317)637-9200   Fax: (317)634-7817
E-mail: publicinfo@acsm.org
URL: http://www.acsm.org

Purpose: Promotes and integrates scientific research, education, and practical applications of sports medicine and exercise science to maintain and enhance physical performance, fitness, health, and quality of life. **Activities:** Certifies fitness leaders, fitness instructors, exercise test technologists, exercise specialists, health/fitness program directors, and U.S. military fitness personnel. Grants Continuing Medical Education (CME) and Continuing Education Credits (CEC). Operates more than 50 committees.

★4969★ American Council on Exercise (ACE)

4851 Paramount Dr.
San Diego, CA 92123
Ph: (858)279-8227   Fax: (858)279-8064
Fr: 888-825-3636
E-mail: support@acefitness.org
URL: http://www.acefitness.org

Description: Promotes the benefits of physical activity and protects consumers against unsafe and ineffective fitness products and instruction. Sponsors university-based exercise science research and testing that targets fitness products and trends. Sets standards for fitness professionals.

★4970★ American Senior Fitness Association (SFA)

PO Box 2575
New Smyrna Beach, FL 32170
Ph: (386)423-6634   Fax: (386)427-0613
Fr: 800-243-1478
E-mail: sfa@ucnsb.net
URL: http://www.seniorfitness.net

Description: Promotes excellence in older adult fitness. Provides comprehensive training, recognized certification, professional resources and member support for fitness professionals who serve older adults. Offers senior fitness specialist courses for colleges and universities.

★4971★ IDEA Health and Fitness Association

10455 Pacific Center Ct.
San Diego, CA 92121-3773
Ph: (858)535-8979   Fax: (858)535-8234
Fr: 800-999-IDEA
E-mail: contact@ideafit.com
URL: http://www.ideafit.com

Purpose: Provides continuing education for fitness professionals including; fitness instructors, personal trainers, program directors, and club/studio owners. **Activities:** Offers workshops for continuing education credits.

★4972★ National Federation of Professional Trainers (NFPT)

PO Box 4579
Lafayette, IN 47903-4579
Ph: (765)471-4514   Fax: (765)471-7369
Fr: 800-729-6378
E-mail: info@nfpt.com
URL: http://www.nfpt.com

Purpose: Offers affordable, convenient, comprehensive, and applicable information to those seeking personal fitness trainer certification. Offers organizational certification credentials for consumer recognition of competence; provides certified affiliates with ongoing education; establishes a network of support, and provides professional products and services to trainers and consumers; and facilitates and encourages the exchange of ideas, knowledge, business experiences, and financial opportunities between all fitness administrators internationally. **Activities:** Offers educational programs.

★4973★ Personal & Building Service Occupations

Delphi Productions
3159 6th St.
Boulder, CO 80304
Ph: (303)443-2100   Fax: (303)443-4022
Fr: 888-443-2400
E-mail: support@delphivideo.com
URL: http://www.delphivideo.com

$95.00. 48 minutes. Part of the Careers for the 21st Century Video Library.

Flight Attendants

SOURCES OF HELP-WANTED ADS

★4974★ Airport Highlights
Airports Council International-North
  America
1775 K St. NW, No. 500
Washington, DC 20006-1502
Ph: (202)293-8500   Fax: (202)331-1362
Fr: 888-424-7767
E-mail: publicaffairs@aci-na.org
URL: http://www.aci-na.org/

Description: Monthly. Spotlights airport news, regulatory and Congressional developments, domestic and international aviation news, industry issues, and employment and business opportunities.

★4975★ Flying
Hachette Filipacchi Media U.S. Inc.
1633 Broadway
New York, NY 10019
Ph: (212)767-6000   Fax: (212)767-5631
URL: http://www.hfmus.com/

Monthly. $17.00/year for individuals, add 8 per year for Canada & other countries; $29.00 for two years, add 8 per year for Canada & other countries; $22.00/year for individuals; $12.00 for two years. General aviation magazine.

★4976★ Regional Aviation News
Access Intelligence L.L.C.
4 Choke Cherry Rd.
Rockville, MD 20850
Ph: (301)354-2000   Fax: (301)309-3847
Fr: 800-777-5006
E-mail: info@accessintel.com
URL: http://www.accessintel.com

Description: Weekly. Covers the commuter/regional airline industry, including airline management, marketing, labor, personnel changes, aircraft acquisitions, new products, and the financial and operational environment. Recurring features include interviews, news of research, a calendar of events, reports of meetings, job listings, and notices of publications available.

EMPLOYER DIRECTORIES AND NETWORKING LISTS

★4977★ National Air Transportation Association-Aviation Business Resource Book and Official Membership Directory
National Air Transportation Association
4226 King St.
Alexandria, VA 22302
Ph: (703)845-9000   Fax: (703)845-8176
Fr: 800-808-6282
URL: http://www.nata.aero/lo-gin.jsp?uri=%2Fdirectory%2Fmember%2F

Annual, October. $50.00 for nonmembers; $25.00 for members. Covers more than 1,000 regular, associate, and affiliate members; regular members include airport service organizations, air taxi operators, and commuter airlines. Entries include: Company name, address, phone, fax number, name and title of contact. Arrangement: Regular members are classified by service; associate and affiliate members are alphabetical in separate sections. Indexes: Geographical.

★4978★ World Aviation Directory & Aerospace Database (WAD&AD)
Aviation Week
1200 G St. NW, Ste. 200
Washington, DC 20005
Ph: (202)383-2484   Fax: (202)383-2478
Fr: 800-551-2015
E-mail: wad@mcgraw-hill.com
URL: http://a1.ecom01.com/aw_marketda-tacenter?s_id=7

Semiannual, March and September. $269.00 for U.S. Database covers: 19,000 airlines, manufacturers, MRO stations, airports military/government and distributors/suppliers; 6,000 product/service categories and 150,000 listings; 60,000 aviation/aerospace professionals; 500,000 users across all 3 platforms/formats; and commercial, military & business aviation fleet data. Arrangement: Classified by major activity (manufacturers, airlines, etc.). Indexes: Company and organization, personnel, product, trade name.

HANDBOOKS AND MANUALS

★4979★ Careers as a Flight Attendant: Flight to the Future
Rosen Publishing Group, Inc.
29 E. 21st St.
New York, NY 10010
Ph: (212)777-3017   Fax: 888-436-464?
Fr: 800-237-9932
URL: http://www.rosenpublishing.com/

Catherine Okray Lobus. Revised edition, 1995. $16.95. Discusses the work, persona characteristics of successful flight atten dants, physical and educational qualifica tions, the application process, and airline training programs. Lists major airlines and outlines their application processes, policie and benefits, and training programs.

★4980★ Careers for Night Owls and Other Insomniacs
The McGraw-Hill Companies
PO Box 182604
Columbus, OH 43272
Fax: (614)759-3749   Fr: 877-883-552
E-mail: customer.service@mcgraw-hill.com
URL: http://www.mcgraw-hill.com

Louise Miller. Second edition, 2002. $12.9 (paper). 160 pages.

★4981★ Careers in Travel, Tourism, and Hospitality
The McGraw-Hill Companies
PO Box 182604
Columbus, OH 43272
Fax: (614)759-3749   Fr: 877-883-552
E-mail: customer.service@mcgraw-hill.com
URL: http://www.mcgraw-hill.com

Marjorie Eberts, Linda Brothers, and Ar Gisler. Second edition, 2005. $15.95 (pa per). 224 pages.

★4982★ The Flight Attendant Career Guide

TK Enterprises
PO Box 6455
Delray Beach, FL 33482-6455
Ph: (561)495-4604   Fax: (561)495-5027
Fr: 800-735-4448
URL: http://jobfindersonline.com

Tim Kirkwood. 2002. $16.95. 178 pages. This step-by-step guide, written by a flight attendant, explains the real-life aspects of the job, and helps the applicant decide if this is the career for them. Chapter topics include: History of Flight Attendants, Minimum Requirements, Types of Airlines, Applying and Interviewing, Training, Scheduling, A Typical 3-Day Trip. In addition, the guide lists the hiring requirements of over 75 US airlines, including salary, languages, age, domiciles, and application addresses for each.

★4983★ Flight Attendant Career: Your Key to Your Office in the Skies

Tom's Midnight Flight
3212 E. Hwy. 30
PO Box 2110
Kearney, NE 68847
Ph: (308)236-7888   Fax: (308)237-0263
Fr: 800-650-7888

Tom Janovsky. 1998. $14.95 (paper). 228 pages.

★4984★ Flight Attendant Job Finder and Career Guide

Planning Communications
7215 Oak Ave.
River Forest, IL 60305-1935
Ph: (708)366-5200   Fax: (708)366-5280
Fr: 888-366-5200

Tim Kirkwood. Seventh, edition. 2002. $16.95. 178 pages.

★4985★ Follow Your Dreams?: Secrets to Getting Hired As a Flight Attendant

AuthorHouse
1663 Liberty Dr., Ste. 200
Bloomington, IN 47403
Ph: (812)961-1023   Fax: (812)339-8654
Fr: 888-519-5121
URL: http://www.authorhouse.com

Tammy Clark. January 2003. $13.95. 108 pages.

★4986★ Opportunities in Airline Careers

The McGraw-Hill Companies
PO Box 182604
Columbus, OH 43272
Fax: (614)759-3749   Fr: 877-883-5524
E-mail: customer.service@mcgraw-hill.com
URL: http://www.mcgraw-hill.com

Adrian A. Paradis. 1997. $14.95; $11.95 (paper). 148 pages.

★4987★ Opportunities in Travel Careers

The McGraw-Hill Companies
PO Box 182604
Columbus, OH 43272
Fax: (614)759-3749   Fr: 877-883-5524
E-mail: customer.service@mcgraw-hill.com
URL: http://www.mcgraw-hill.com

Robert Scott Milne. Second edition, 2003. $14.95 (paper). 141 pages. Discusses what the jobs are and where to find them in airlines, shipping lines, and railroads. Discusses related opportunities in hotels, motels, resorts, travel agencies, public relation firms, and recreation departments. Illustrated.

★4988★ Ready to Fly: An Insider's Guide to Becoming a Flight Attendant

iUniverse Inc.
2021 Pine Lake Rd., Ste. 100
Lincoln, NE 68512
Ph: (402)323-7800   Fax: (402)323-7824
Fr: 877-288-4677
URL: http://www.iuniverse.com/

Peter Conrad Joseph. November 2002. $13.95. 141 pages.

★4989★ Vault Guide to Flight Attendant Careers

Vault, Inc.
150 W 22nd St., 5th Fl.
New York, NY 10011
Ph: (212)366-4212   Fax: (212)366-6117
Fr: 888-562-8285
URL: http://www.vault.com/index.jsp

Mark Gazdik. 2005. $29.95. 128 pages. Profiles training programs, unions, crew schedules, and perks for individuals interested in a career as a flight attendant.

★4990★ Welcome Aboard!: Your Career As a Flight Attendant

Aviation Supplies & Academics, Inc.
7005 132nd Pl. SE
Newcastle, WA 98059
Ph: (425)235-1500   Fr: 800-272-2359
URL: http://www.asa2fly.com/

Becky S. Bock. 2005. $19.95 (paper). 126 pages.

ONLINE JOB SOURCES AND SERVICES

★4991★ AirlineCareer.com

Ph: (978)615-3190
E-mail: jbelotti@airlinecareer.com
URL: http://www.airlinecareer.com

Web-based training center. Provides flight attendant job placement services.

OTHER SOURCES

★4992★ Association of Flight Attendants - CWA (AFA)

501 3rd St., NW
Washington, DC 20001
Ph: (202)434-1300
E-mail: afatalk@afanet.org
URL: http://www.afanet.org

Description: Labor union organized by flight attendants. AFA represents over 50,000 flight attendants at 26 airlines, serving as a voice for flight attendants at their workplace, in the industry, and in the media.

★4993★ Personal & Building Service Occupations

Delphi Productions
3159 6th St.
Boulder, CO 80304
Ph: (303)443-2100   Fax: (303)443-4022
Fr: 888-443-2400
E-mail: support@delphivideo.com
URL: http://www.delphivideo.com

$95.00. 48 minutes. Part of the Careers for the 21st Century Video Library.

Florists

SOURCES OF HELP-WANTED ADS

★4994★ The Extra Touch Online
Extra Touch Florists
197 Ste. 104-280
Woodlawn Pky.
San Marcos, CA 92069
Fax: (323)657-5379   Fr: 888-419-1515
URL: http://www.etfa.org

Monthly. Online publication for retail florists.

★4995★ Florists' Review
PO Box 4368
Topeka, KS 66604
Ph: (785)266-0888   Fax: (785)266-0333
Fr: 800-367-4708
URL: http://www.floristsreview.com

Monthly guidebook for operating a successful floral business.

★4996★ Grower Talks
Ball Publishing
335 N River St.
PO Box 9
Batavia, IL 60510-0009
Ph: (630)208-9080   Fax: (630)208-9350
URL: http://www.growertalks.com

Monthly. $29.00/year for U.S. $39.00/year for Canada and Mexico; $79.00/year for other countries, air mail; $52.00 for two years; $68.00/year for Canada and Mexico, 2 years; $148.00/year for other countries, air mail; $72.00/year 3 years; $97.00/year for Canada and Mexico, 3 years; $212.00/year for other countries, airmail, 3 years. Trade magazine covering issues for commercial greenhouse growers with a focus on North American production.

EMPLOYER DIRECTORIES AND NETWORKING LISTS

★4997★ Michigan Florist-Membership Directory
Michigan Floral Association
1152 Haslett Rd.
Haslett, MI 48840
Ph: (517)575-0110   Fax: (517)575-0115
URL: http://www.michiganfloral.org/findflorist.htm

Annual, fall. Publication includes: List of about 1,100 member floral retailers and wholesalers, nurseries and garden centers, and individual members. Entries include: Company name, owner's name, address, phone, type of business. Arrangement: Separate geographical and alphabetical lists.

★4998★ Professional Floral Communicators-International-Directory
Professional Floral Communicators-International
1601 Duke St.
Alexandria, VA 22314
Ph: (703)836-8700   Fax: (703)836-8705
Fr: 800-336-4743
E-mail: keidam@safnow.org
URL: http://alliedfloristsofhouston.org/memberdirectory.htm

Covers about 80 member floral presenters and educators. Entries include: Name, address, phone, professional affiliation, education, career data, interests, design and presentation techniques. Arrangement: Alphabetical; geographical; area of expertise.

★4999★ Wholesale Florist & Florist Supplier Association-Membership Directory
Wholesale Florists & Florist Supplier Association
147 Old Solomons Island Rd., Ste. 302
Annapolis, MD 21401
Ph: (410)573-0400   Fax: (410)573-5001
Fr: 888-289-3372
URL: http://www.wffsa.org/

Semiannual, summer/winter. Number of listings: 1,275. Entries include: Company name, address, phone, names of executives, list of products or services. Arrangement: Geographical. Indexes: Alphabetical.

HANDBOOKS AND MANUALS

★5000★ Careers in Horticulture and Botany
The McGraw-Hill Companies
PO Box 182604
Columbus, OH 43272
Fax: (614)759-3749   Fr: 877-883-5524
E-mail: customer.service@mcgraw-hill.com
URL: http://www.mcgraw-hill.com

Jerry Garner. 2006. 15.95 (paper). 192 pages. Includes bibliographical references.

★5001★ Careers for Plant Lovers and Other Green Thumb Types
The McGraw-Hill Companies
PO Box 182604
Columbus, OH 43272
Fax: (614)759-3749   Fr: 877-883-5524
E-mail: customer.service@mcgraw-hill.com
URL: http://www.mcgraw-hill.com

Blythe Camenson. Second edition, 2004. $13.95; $9.95 (paper). 160 pages. Describes careers for people who love working with plants and flowers.

★5002★ FabJob Guide to Become a Florist
FabJob.com
4616 25 Ave. NE
Seattle, WA 98105
Ph: (403)949-4980
URL: http://www.fabjob.com

2004. $29.95. 275 pages. Offers a step-by-step guide to becoming a florist.

★5003★ How to Start and Manage a Flower and Plant Store Business

Lewis & Renn Associates
4860 E. Main St., No. A128
Mesa, AZ 85205
Fax: (480)830-1187

Jerre G. Lewis and Leslie Renn. 1999. $21.95 (paper).

★5004★ How to Start and Manage a Retail Florist Business: Step by Step Guide to Starting and Managing Your Own Business

Lewis & Renn Associates
4860 E. Main St., No. A128
Mesa, AZ 85205
Fax: (480)830-1187

Jerre G. Lewis and Leslie Renn. 2004. $21.95 (paper). 120 pages.

★5005★ Opportunities in Horticulture Careers

The McGraw-Hill Companies
PO Box 182604
Columbus, OH 43272
Fax: (614)759-3749   Fr: 877-883-5524
E-mail: customer.service@mcgraw-hill.com
URL: http://www.mcgraw-hill.com

Jan Goldberg. 1995. $14.95; $11.95 (paper). 146 pages. Describes careers in horticulture, the nursery industry, and floriculture, among others.

★5006★ Power Publicity for Florists

Clifford Publishing
PO Box 43596
Upper Montclair, NJ 07043-0596
Ph: (973)857-4142

Paul Hartunian. 2006. $79.00. Profiles marketing ideas for florists using press releases as a tool for publicity; includes a full year calendar with story ideas and headlines for each month.

★5007★ The Profit Minded Florist

American Floral Services, Inc.
PO Box 12309
Oklahoma City, OK 73157-2309
Ph: (405)947-3373   Fax: (405)943-7131
Fr: 800-456-7890

American Floral Services, Inc. Staff, Paul Goodman, and Marie Ackerman. 2000. $99.95 (paper).

★5008★ The Retail Florist Business

Interstate Publishers, Inc.
PO Box 50
Danville, IL 61834-0050
Ph: (217)446-0500   Fax: (217)446-9706
Fr: 800-843-4774

Peter B. Pfahl. Fifth edition, 1994. $48.75. 336 pages.

★5009★ Start Your Own Florist Shop and Five Other Floral Businesses

Entrepreneur Press
PO Box 432
Newburgh, NY 12551
Fax: (845)457-5029   Fr: 800-215-7814
E-mail: epresscs@etcdata.com
URL: http://www.entrepreneurpress.com/

Cheryl Kimball. 2006. $14.95. 116 pages. Guide for starting a florist shop, office plant care, pick-your-own flower business, and other creative businesses.

OTHER SOURCES

★5010★ American Floral Industry Association (AFIA)

PO Box 420244
Dallas, TX 75342-0244
Ph: (214)742-2747   Fax: (214)742-2648
E-mail: afia@afia.net
URL: http://www.afia.net

Purpose: Strives to act as the national organization for importers, domestic manufacturers, wholesalers, retailers, overseas suppliers, manufacturers sales representatives, etc., of artificial, botanical, Christmas and floral products and accessories.

★5011★ American Institute of Floral Designers (AIFD)

720 Light St.
Baltimore, MD 21230
Ph: (410)752-3318   Fax: (410)752-8295
E-mail: aifd@assnhqtrs.com
URL: http://www.aifd.org

Description: Active floral designers, associates, retired floral designers, and other individuals. Works to promote the profession and art of floral design. Maintains student chapter.

★5012★ Florist

Cambridge Educational
PO Box 2053
Princeton, NJ 08543-2053
Ph: 800-257-5126   Fax: (609)671-0266
Fr: 800-468-4227
E-mail: custserv@films.com

URL: http://www.cambridgeeducational.com
VHS and DVD. $39.95. 12 minutes. 1990. Part of the Vocational Visions Career series.

★5013★ International Freeze-Dry Floral Association (IFDFA)

320 Scandia Ave.
Des Moines, IA 50315
Ph: (515)953-2211   Fr: 888-554-9706
E-mail: gardensoftheheart@yahoo.com
URL: http://www.ifdfa.org

Members: Growers, freeze-dry processors, retail florists, home-based crafters, students, educators, suppliers, researchers, and interested individuals. **Purpose:** Promotes the interest and improvement in freeze-dried product industry. **Activities:** Encourages the interaction between the different service industries. Compiles and disseminates information on the production of freeze-drieds. Conducts research on the production and marketing of freeze-dried florals and botanicals.

★5014★ Society of American Florists (SAF)

1601 Duke St.
Alexandria, VA 22314-3406
Ph: (703)836-8700   Fax: (703)836-8705
Fr: 800-336-4743
E-mail: info@safnow.org

Description: Growers, wholesalers, retailers, and allied tradesmen in the floral industry. Lobbies Congress on behalf of the industry; sponsors educational programs; promotes the floral industry; prepares materials for consumers and for high school and college students; provides business resources. Sponsors Floricultural Hall of Fame, American Academy of Floriculture, and Professional Floral Commentators International. Compiles statistics; sponsors competitions.

★5015★ Wholesale Florist and Florist Supplier Association (WF&FSA)

147 Old Solomons Island Rd., Ste. 302
Annapolis, MD 21401
Ph: (410)573-0400   Fax: (410)573-5001
Fr: 888-289-3372
E-mail: info@wffsa.org
URL: http://www.wffsa.org

Description: Proprietorships, partnerships or corporations conducting wholesale businesses in fresh flowers, greens, or plants, or engaged in the manufacture and/or wholesaling of florist supplies; others actively engaged in the floral industry are associate members. Preserves and strengthens the wholesale florists' position in the floral industry. Provides a unified voice to promote the wholesalers' contributions to the industry.

Forensic Scientists

SOURCES OF HELP-WANTED ADS

★5016★ AWIS Magazine
Association for Women in Science
1200 New York Ave., NW, Ste. 650
Washington, DC 20005
Ph: (202)326-8940   Fax: (202)326-8960
Fr: (866)657-2947
URL: http://www.awis.org/

Quarterly. $7.00 for nonmembers, price per issue; $5.00 for members, price per issue. Professional magazine covering the status of women in science.

★5017★ Current Opinion in Pharmacology
Elsevier Science Inc.
360 Park Ave. S
New York, NY 10010
Ph: (212)989-5800   Fax: (212)633-3990
URL: http://www.elsevier.com

$1,603.00/year for institutions, other countries; $198,900.00/year for institutions; $1,434.00/year for institutions; $317.00/year for elsewhere; $35,500.00/year for individuals; $292.00/year for individuals. Journal covering current advances in pharmacology.

★5018★ Forensic Science, Medicine and Pathology
Humana Press Inc.
999 Riverview Dr., Ste. 208
Totowa, NJ 07512
Ph: (973)256-1699   Fax: (973)256-8341
URL: http://www.humanapress.com/index.php?option=com_journalshome

Journal focusing on forensic science, medicine, and pathology.

★5019★ Harvard Science Review
Harvard University Press
79 Garden St.
Cambridge, MA 02138
Ph: (401)531-2800   Fax: 800-406-9145
Fr: 800-405-1619

E-mail: hsr@hcs.harvard.edu
URL: http://www.harvardsciencereview.org
Semiannual. A science journal.

★5020★ InterJournal
New England Complex Systems Institute
24 Mt. Auburn St.
Cambridge, MA 02138
Ph: (617)547-4100   Fax: (617)661-7711
URL: http://www.interjournal.org/

Journal covering the fields of science and engineering.

★5021★ The Internet Journal of Forensic Science
Internet Scientific Publications L.L.C.
23 Rippling Creek Dr.
Sugar Land, TX 77479
Ph: (832)443-1193   Fax: (281)240-1532
URL: http://www.ispub.com/ostia/index.php?xmlFilePath=journals/ij

Free, online. Electronic journal for medical professionals focusing on the field of forensic science.

★5022★ Journal of the American Society of Questioned Document Examiners
American Society of Questioned
  Document Examiners
PO Box 18298
Long Beach, CA 90807
Ph: (562)901-3376   Fax: (562)901-3376
URL: http://www.asqde.org

Semiannual. $70.00/year for U.S. and Canada; $110.00/year for U.S. and Canada, institution, agency; $85.00/year for other countries, individual; $125.00/year for institutions, other countries, agency. Professional journal covering forensic sciences.

★5023★ Journal of Forensic Identification
International Association for Identification
2535 Pilot Knob Rd., Ste. 117
Mendota Heights, MN 55120-1120
Ph: (651)681-8566   Fr: (651)681-8443

URL: http://www.theiai.org

A scientific journal that provides over 115 pages of articles related to forensics. Also offers information regarding training and educational events, job postings and announcements. Yearly subscriptions: $130.00 for individuals, $155.00 for institutions and libraries.

★5024★ Oxymag
Elsevier Science Inc.
360 Park Ave. S
New York, NY 10010
Ph: (212)989-5800   Fax: (212)633-3990
URL: http://www.elsevier.com

Bimonthly. $190.00/year for institutions in all countries except Europe, Japan and Iran; $89.00/year for individuals in all countries except Europe, Japan and Iran; $63.00/year for students in all countries except Europe, Japan and Iran. Journal related to the construction field covering information in the manufacture of commercial, industrial, spark proof and decorative terrazzo floors, flooring for railroad boxcars, industrial fireproof coatings, fire-resistant marine interior deckings and a variety of building units.

★5025★ Psychology Journal
Psychological Publishing
PO Box 176
Natchitoches, LA 71458
URL: http://www.psychologicalpublishing.com/

$40.00/year for individuals; $75.00/year for institutions. Journal dedicated to all areas of the science and practice of counseling and clinical psychology.

★5026★ Science
American Association for the
  Advancement of Science
1200 New York Ave. NW
Washington, DC 20005
Ph: (202)326-6400   Fax: (202)371-9227
URL: http://www.scienceonline.org

Weekly (Fri.). $142.00/year for members, professional; $119.00/year for individuals, NPA postdoctoral; $99.00/year for individus, postdoctoral/resident; $75.00/year for tudents; $142.00/year for individuals, k-12 eacher; $310.00/year for individuals, patron; 110.00/year for individuals, emeritus. Magzine devoted to science, scientific research, nd public policy.

EMPLOYER DIRECTORIES AND NETWORKING LISTS

★5027★ American Academy of Forensic Sciences-Membership Directory

American Academy of Forensic Sciences
10 North 21St St.
Colorado Springs, CO 80904-2798
Ph: (719)636-1100   Fax: (719)636-1993
URL: http://www.aafs.org/

Annual, May. Covers 3,800 persons qualified n forensic sciences, including law, patholoy, biology, odontology, physical anthropoloy, psychiatry, questioned documents, crimialistics, engineering, and toxicology. Enries include: Name, office address and hone, highest degree held, professional tle, type of certification. Arrangement: Alhabetical. Indexes: Geographical, subject.

★5028★ Career Opportunities in Science

Facts On File Inc.
32 W 31st St., 17th Fl.
New York, NY 10001
Ph: (212)967-8800   Fax: 800-678-3633
Fr: 800-322-8755
URL: http://www.factsonfile.com

Published 2003. $49.50 for individuals; $44.55 for libraries. Covers more than 80 obs, such as biochemist, molecular biologist, bioinformatic specialist, pharmacologist, computer engineer, geographic information systems specialist, science teacher, forensic scientist, patent agent, as well as physicist, astronomer, chemist, zoologist, oceanographer, and geologist.

★5029★ Encyclopedia of Forensic Science

Oryx Press
4041 N Central Ave., Ste. 700
PO Box 33889
Phoenix, AZ 85021-3397
Ph: (602)265-2651   Fax: 800-279-4663
Fr: 800-279-6799
URL: http://www.greenwood.com

Published June 30, 2002. $76.95 for individuals. Publication includes: List of Web sites elated to forensic science. Principal content of publication consists of entries on people and events dealing with forensic science. Arrangement: Alphabetical. Indexes: Alphabetical.

★5030★ Forensic Services Directory

National Forensic Center
17 Temple Ter.
Lawrenceville, NJ 08648-3254
Ph: (609)883-0550   Fax: (609)883-7622
Fr: 800-526-5177
URL: http://expertindex.com

Annual, January. Covers about 5,000 individuals willing to serve as expert witnesses or consultants during litigation; also associations, societies, and institutes with specialized information. Entries include: For individuals–Name, address, phone, degrees, affiliation, professional license (if any), specialties; many listings include biographical data. For organizations–Name, address, phone, areas of interest, information service available. Arrangement: Alphabetical by individual or organization name, then by consulting field or specialty.

★5031★ International Association for Identification-Membership Directory

International Association for Identification
2535 Pilot Knob Rd., Ste. 117
Mendota Heights, MN 55120-1120
Ph: (651)681-8566   Fax: (651)681-8443
URL: http://www.theiai.org

Annual, December. Covers about 4,600 police officials, identification personnel, and others engaged in forensic identification, investigation, and scientific crime detection. Entries include: Name, preferred mailing address. Arrangement: Geographical. Indexes: Alphabetical.

★5032★ Opportunities in Forensic Science

The McGraw-Hill Cos.
PO Box 182604
Columbus, OH 43272
Fax: (614)759-3749   Fr: 877-833-5524
URL: http://www.mcgraw-hill.com/

$13.95 for individuals; $10.36 for individuals. Publication includes: A list of colleges and universities offering graduate programs and internships in the field of forensic science. Principal content of publication consists of information on career opportunities in the forensic sciences, including educational requirements, qualifications needed, and salary. Publisher also offers a catalog card kit for this title.

HANDBOOKS AND MANUALS

★5033★ Career Planning in Criminal Justice

Anderson Publishing Co.
2035 Reading Rd.
Cincinnati, OH 45202-1576
Ph: (513)421-4142   Fax: (513)562-8116
Fr: 800-582-7295

Robert C. DeLucia and Thomas J. Doyle. Third edition, 1998. 225 pages. $21.95. Surveys a wide range of career and employ-

ment opportunities in law enforcement, the courts, corrections, forensic science, and private security. Contains career planning and job hunting advice.

★5034★ Forensic Science Handbook

Prentice Hall PTR
1 Lake St.
Upper Saddle River, NJ 07458
Ph: (201)236-7616   Fax: (201)236-7696
URL: http://www.prenhall.com

Second edition, 2001. 767 pages. Reference source for the field of criminalistics. Each chapter offers a review of a particular aspect of the field written by noted experts.

★5035★ Guide to Nontraditional Careers in Science

Taylor & Francis
325 Chestnut St., 8th Fl.
Philadelphia, PA 19106
Ph: (215)625-8900   Fax: (215)269-0363
Fr: 800-821-8312
URL: http://www.taylorandfrancis.com

Karen Young Kreeger. 1998. $45.95 (paper). Guidebook aids the reader in evaluating and finding career opportunities in non-academic research fields. 263 pages.

★5036★ Principles and Practice of Criminalistics: The Profession of Forensic Science

CRC Press LLC
6000 Broken Sound Pkwy NW, Ste. 300
Boca Raton, FL 33487
Ph: (561)994-0555   Fax: (561)989-9732
Fr: 800-272-7737
URL: http://www.crcpress.com

Keith Inman and Norah Rudin. 2000. $89.95. 392 pages. Outlines a logical framework for the examination of physical evidence in a criminalistics laboratory.

TRADESHOWS

★5037★ American Academy of Forensic Sciences Annual Scientific Meeting

American Academy of Forensic Sciences
410 N. 21st St., Ste. 203
PO Box 669
Colorado Springs, CO 80901-0669
Ph: (719)636-1100   Fax: (719)636-1993
E-mail: sdoolittle@aafs.org
URL: http://www.aafs.org

Annual. **Primary Exhibits:** Scientific instruments.

OTHER SOURCES

★5038★ American Academy of Forensic Sciences (AAFS)

410 N 21st St.
Colorado Springs, CO 80904-2712
Ph: (719)636-1100   Fax: (719)636-1993
E-mail: awarren@aafs.org
URL: http://www.aafs.org

Description: Represents criminalists, scientists, members of the bench and bar, pathologists, biologists, psychiatrists, examiners of questioned documents, toxicologists, odontologists, anthropologists, and engineers. Works to: encourage the study, improve the practice, elevate the standards, and advance the cause of the forensic sciences; improve the quality of scientific techniques, tests, and criteria; plan, organize, and administer meetings, reports, and other projects for the stimulation and advancement of these and related purposes. Maintains Forensic Sciences Job Listing; conducts selected research for the government; offers forensic expert referral service.

★5039★ American Board of Criminalistics (ABC)

PO Box 1123
Wausau, WI 54402-1123
Ph: (715)845-3684   Fax: (715)845-4156
E-mail: abcreg@dwave.net
URL: http://www.criminalistics.com

Members: Regional and national organizations of forensic scientists and criminalists. **Purpose:** Offers certificates of Professional Competency in Criminalistics as well as in specialty disciplines of forensic biology, drug chemistry, fire debris analysis, and various areas of trace evidence examination. Works to establish professional standards and promote growth within the industry. **Activities:** Answers questions regarding the certification process.

★5040★ American Board of Forensic Toxicology (ABFT)

410 N. 21st St.
Colorado Springs, CO 80904
Ph: (719)636-1100   Fax: (719)636-1993
E-mail: abftox@aol.com
URL: http://www.abft.org/

Description: Works to establish, enhance, and revise as necessary, standards of qualification for those who practice forensic toxicology, and to certify as qualified specialists those applicants who comply with the requirements of the Board.

★5041★ American College of Forensic Examiners International (ACFEI)

2750 E Sunshine
Springfield, MO 65804
Ph: (417)881-3818   Fax: (417)881-4702
Fr: 800-423-9737
E-mail: cao@acfei.com
URL: http://www.acfei.com

Members: Professionals in the field of foren-sic examination, including the following disciplines: accounting, accident reconstruction, criminology, crisis intervention, counselors, social work, nursing and law enforcement hypnosis, all medical fields, physics, psychiatry, psychology, and toxicology. **Purpose:** Works to advance the profession of forensic examination through education, training, and certification.

★5042★ American Society of Crime Laboratory Directors

139K Technology Dr.
Garner, NC 27529
Ph: (919)773-2044   Fax: (919)773-2602
URL: http://www.ascld.org

Description: Nonprofit professional society dedicated to providing excellence in forensic science analysis through leadership in the management of forensic science. The purpose of the organization is to foster professional interests; assist the development of laboratory management principles and techniques; acquire, preserve and disseminate forensic based information; maintain and improve communications among crime laboratory directors; and to promote, encourage and maintain the highest standards of practice in the field.

★5043★ Association of Forensic Document Examiners (AFDE)

PO Box 31402
Cleveland, OH 44131
E-mail: expert@afde.org
URL: http://www.afde.org

Description: Represents forensic document examiners and students of document examination. Sponsors annual continuing education conferences and offers a certification program.

★5044★ Evidence Photographers International Council (EPIC)

229 Peachtree St. NE, No. 2200
Atlanta, GA 30303
Ph: (404)614-6406   Fr: (866)868-EPIC
E-mail: cwerner@evidencephotographers.com
URL: http://www.epic-photo.org

Members: Law enforcement and civil evidence photographers; others in related fields. **Purpose:** Objectives are to: aid in the worldwide advancement of forensic photography; assist in research and development of new techniques; enhance professional education; inform members of new procedures. **Activities:** Maintains speakers' bureau. Offers certification upon satisfactory completion of an oral or written examination by a three-member panel, receipt of a minimum of 30 prints for review, and a $150 application fee. Provides an honors program to recognize those who have shown expertise in the field of forensic photography, and service to the Council. Sponsors the EPIC Witness Referral Service.

★5045★ Forensic Sciences Foundation (FSF)

410 N 21st St.
Colorado Springs, CO 80904
Ph: (719)636-1100   Fax: (719)636-1993
E-mail: awarren@aafs.org
URL: http://www.aafs.org

Purpose: Purposes are to: conduct research in the procedures and standards utilized in the practice of forensic sciences; develop and implement useful educational and training programs and methods of benefit to forensic sciences; conduct programs of public education concerning issues of importance to the forensic sciences; engage in activities which will promote, encourage, and assist the development of the forensic sciences. **Activities:** Provides referral service for forensic scientists. Compiles statistics. Operates the Forensic Sciences Foundation Press.

★5046★ International Association of Computer Investigative Specialists (IACIS)

PO Box 1728
Fairmont, WV 26555
Fr: 888-884-2247
URL: http://www.iacis.info

Description: Provides education and certification of law enforcement professionals in the field of computer forensic science. Creates and establishes procedures, trains personnel, and certifies forensic examiners in the recovery of evidence from computer systems. Offers professional training in the seizure and processing computer systems. Provides an opportunity to network with other law enforcement officers trained in computer forensics, and to share and learn from others.

★5047★ International Association for Identification (IAI)

2535 Pilot Knob Rd., Ste. 117
Mendota Heights, MN 55120-1120
Ph: (651)681-8566   Fax: (651)681-8443
E-mail: iaisecty@theiai.org
URL: http://www.theiai.org

Description: Individuals engaged in forensic identification, investigation, and scientific crime detection. Strives to improve methods of scientific identification techniques used in criminal investigations.

★5048★ Law Enforcement and Emergency Services Video Association (LEVA)

PO Box 547
Midlothian, TX 76065
Ph: (972)291-5888   Fax: (972)291-5888
E-mail: president@leva.org
URL: http://www.leva.org

Description: Serves as a key resource to the global public safety community by focusing on the needs of video production and forensic imaging disciplines. Provides opportunities for professional development through quality training and informational xchange. Offers forensic video analysis raining to law enforcement professionals.

★5049★ National Forensic Center (NFC)

PO Box 270529
San Diego, CA 92198-2529
Fax: (858)487-7747   Fr: 800-735-6660
E-mail: info@national-experts.com
URL: http://www.national-experts.com

Description: Expert witnesses and litigation consultants who serve attorneys, insurance companies, and government agencies. Trains consultants to work with attorneys and to testify in court; trains individuals to serve as expert witnesses and litigation consultants. Makes speakers available upon request. Compiles statistics on experts' fees.

★5050★ National Forensic Science Technology Center

7881 114th Ave. North
Largo, FL 33773
Ph: (727)549-6067   Fax: (727)549-6070
E-mail: info@nfstc.org
URL: http://www.nfstc.org/index.htm

Description: Provides systems support, training and education to the forensic science community in the United States.

★5051★ Society of Forensic Toxicologists (SOFT)

One MacDonald Center
1 N MacDonald St., Ste. 15
Mesa, AZ 85201
Ph: (480)839-9106   Fax: (480)839-9106
Fr: 888-866-7638
E-mail: trohrig@sedgwick.gov
URL: http://www.soft-tox.org

Description: Scientists who analyze tissue and body fluids for drugs and poisons and interpret the information for judicial purposes. Objectives are to establish uniform qualifications and requirements for certification of forensic toxicologists and promote support mechanisms for continued certification; to stimulate research and development; to provide review board for cases involving differences of professional opinion; to act on administrative and career problems affecting forensic toxicologists. Serves as clearinghouse; conducts proficiency testing programs; provides information on case histories and job opportunities. Sponsors American Board of Forensic Toxicology.

Foresters and Conservation Scientists

★5052★ Appalachian Trailway News

Appalachian Trail Conservancy
799 Washington St.
PO Box 807
Harpers Ferry, WV 25425-0807
Ph: (304)535-6331   Fax: (304)535-2667
URL: http://www.appalachiantrail.org/site/
c.jkLXJ8MQKtH/b.850199/

$15.00/year for individuals. Magazine on hiking, Appalachian Trail protection, and general conservation issues.

★5053★ Archives of Nature Conservation & Landscape Research

Taylor & Francis Group Journals
325 Chestnut St., Ste. 800
Philadelphia, PA 19106
Ph: (215)625-8900   Fax: (215)625-8914
Fr: 800-354-1420
URL: http://www.tandf.co.uk/

Quarterly. Journal focusing on research of nature conservation and landscape.

★5054★ AWIS Magazine

Association for Women in Science
1200 New York Ave. NW, Ste. 650
Washington, DC 20005
Ph: (202)326-8940   Fax: (202)326-8960
Fr: (866)657-2947
E-mail: awis@awis.org
URL: http://www.awis.org/

Description: Bimonthly. Covers issues, legislation, and trends related to science education for girls, women, and minorities. Includes information on grants and fellowships, job openings, educational programs, events, and notices of publications available.

★5055★ Capital Ideas

Alabama Forest Owners' Association
c/o R. Lee Laechelt, Exec.VP
PO Box 361434
Birmingham, AL 35236
Ph: (205)987-8811   Fax: (205)987-9824
E-mail: AlaFOA@aol.com
URL: http://www.alabamaforestowners.com

Description: Monthly. Covers activities of Alabama Forest Owners' Association. Contains calendar of forestry events and forestry related news.

★5056★ Carolina Forestry Journal

South Carolina Forestry Association
PO Box 21303
Columbia, SC 29221-1303
Ph: (803)798-4170   Fax: (803)798-2340
URL: http://www.scforestry.org

Monthly. Journal containing information for the forestry industry, including forest conservation and preservation.

★5057★ CINTRAFOR News

Center for International Trade in Forest Products
College of Forest Resources
Box 352100
Seattle, WA 98195-2100
Ph: (206)543-8684   Fax: (206)685-0790
E-mail: eastin@u.washington.edu
URL: http://www.cintrafor.org

Description: Biennial. Summarizes research and related activities in the area of forest products trade, including international symposiums, workshops, publications, and new technology trends sponsored by the Center.

★5058★ City Trees

Society of Municipal Arborists
5 Monson Dr.
Peabody, MA 01960
Ph: (978)535-0373   Fax: (978)535-3899
URL: http://www.urban-forestry.com

Description: Bimonthly. Addresses all aspects of municipal (urban) forestry. Contains technical articles on species of trees, pest control, conservation, planning, design, and equipment. Recurring features include lists of new publications, statistics, news of research, letters to the editor, announcements of meetings, and columns titled President's Column, Professor's Column, City of the Month, Park of the Month, Tree of the Month, and Editor's Column.

★5059★ Corporate Social Responsibility and Environmental Management

John Wiley & Sons Inc.
111 River St.
Hoboken, NJ 07030-5774
Ph: (201)748-6000   Fax: (201)748-608
Fr: 800-825-7550
URL: http://www3.interscience.wiley.com/
cgi-bin/jhome/90513547

$165.00/year for individuals, U.S. print only; $290.00/year for individuals, print only, other countries; $1,000.00/year for institutions print only; $1,100.00/year for institutions print and online. Journal providing a resource for organizations concerned with social and environmental responsibilities in the context of sustainable development.

★5060★ Drinking Water & Backflow Prevention

IAPMO
5001 E Philadelphia St.
Ontario, CA 91761-2816
Ph: (909)472-4100   Fax: (909)472-415
Fr: 800-854-2766
E-mail: backflow@dwbp-online.com
URL: http://www.dwbp-online.com

Description: Monthly. Presents articles directed toward "individuals, companies, organizations, agencies, and municipalities with an interest in drinking water protection and backflow prevention." Contains information on safety standards, water system protection, training programs, cross-connection control, and all issues related to preventing the contamination of potable drinking water supplies with backflow prevention devices. Recurring features include case studies, letters to the editor, news of research, columns titled Test Your Investigative Skills and Backflow Prevention Device Repairs, and reports of meetings. Also carries news of educational opportunities, job listings, notices of publications available, and a calendar of events.

★5061★ Ecological Entomology

Wiley-Blackwell
350 Main St. Commerce Pl.
Malden, MA 02148
Ph: (781)388-8200   Fax: (781)388-8210
Fr: 800-759-6120
URL: http://www.blackwellpublishing.com/
journal.asp?ref=0307-6946

Bimonthly. $328.00/year for individuals, print plus online; $1,629.00/year for institutions, print plus premium online; $1,481.00/year for institutions, print plus standard online; $1,407.00/year for institutions, premium online. Journal publishing articles on conversation issues.

★5062★ Environment (News)

Global Information Network
146 W. 29th St., Ste. No. 7E
New York, NY 10001
Ph: (212)244-3123   Fax: (212)244-3522
URL: http://www.globalinfo.org/eng/topicto-day.asp?TopicId=4

Daily. Free. Publication covering environmental issues.

★5063★ Environmental Conservation

Cambridge University Press
32 Ave. of the Americas
New York, NY 10013-2473
Ph: (212)924-3900   Fax: (212)691-3239
Fr: 800-221-4512
URL: http://www.cambridge.org/journals/
journal_catalogue.asp?mnem

$484.00/year for institutions, print & online; $416.00/year for institutions, online; $136.00/year for individuals, print only; $20.00/year for individuals, article price. Journal covering environmental policy, practice, and natural and social science of environmental concern at a global level. Topics covered include issues in human institutions, pollution and habitat degradation, resource exploitation, terrestrial biomes, atmospheric and oceanic processes, and coastal and land management.

★5064★ Environmental Education Research

Taylor & Francis Group Journals
325 Chestnut St., Ste. 800
Philadelphia, PA 19106
Ph: (215)625-8900   Fax: (215)625-8914
Fr: 800-354-1420
URL: http://www.tandf.co.uk/journals/titles/
13504622.asp

Journal covering all aspects of environmental education.

★5065★ Fisheries

American Fisheries Society
5410 Grosvenor Ln., Ste. 110
Bethesda, MD 20814
Ph: (301)897-8616   Fax: (301)897-8096
URL: http://www.fisheries.org

Monthly. $76.00/year for individuals; $76.00/year for Canada and Mexico; $88.00/year for elsewhere; $22.00/year for students; $22.00/

year for Canada and Mexico, students and retirees; $44.00/year for elsewhere, students and retirees; $38.00/year for students, retirees also; $38.00/year for Canada and Mexico, students and retirees. Magazine covering fisheries management and aquatic resource issues.

★5066★ Forest Log

Oregon Department of Forestry
2600 State St.
Salem, OR 97310
Ph: (503)945-7200   Fax: (503)945-7212
Fr: 800-437-4490
URL: http://egov.oregon.gov/ODF/

Description: Quarterly. Discusses forestry issues on state and private lands, laws reguarding forest management, and practices. Recurring features include interviews, news of research, report of meetings, and notices of publications available.

★5067★ Forest Pathology

Wiley-Blackwell
350 Main St. Commerce Pl.
Malden, MA 02148
Ph: (781)388-8200   Fax: (781)388-8210
Fr: 800-759-6120
URL: http://www.blackwellpublishing.com/
journal.asp?ref=1437-4781

Bimonthly. $277.00/year for individuals, U.S. print and online; $1,047.00/year for institutions, U.S. print and premium online; $952.00/year for institutions, U.S. print and standard online; $904.00/year for institutions, U.S. premium online only. Journal focusing on forest pathological problems occurring in any part of the world.

★5068★ FRA Bulletin

Forest Resources Association
600 Jefferson Plaza, Ste. 350
Rockville, MD 20852
Ph: (301)838-9385   Fax: (301)838-9481
URL: http://www.forestresources.org/

Description: Monthly. Electronic newsletter covering current events and policy in wood supply and forest management. Recurring features include a calendar of events, news of educational opportunities, job listings, and notices of publications available.

★5069★ FYI

Washington Forest Protection Association
724 Columbia St., NW, Ste. 250
Olympia, WA 98501
Ph: (360)352-1500   Fax: (360)352-4621
E-mail: info@wfpa.org
URL: http://www.wfpa.org

Description: Quarterly. Covers activities of Washington Forest Protection Association. Contains research summary.

★5070★ Hardwood Research Bulletin

National Hardwood Lumber Association
6830 Raleigh La Grange Rd.
Memphis, TN 38134-0518
Ph: (901)377-1818   Fax: (901)382-6419

E-mail: info@nhla.com.
URL: http://www.natlhardwood.org

Description: Monthly. Provides abstracts and digests of current research information concerning hardwood forest management, silviculture, insects, diseases, resource utilization, product development, manufacturing technology, and economics. Lists upcoming events, workshops, short courses, and seminars of interest to members.

★5071★ ISTF News

International Society of Tropical Foresters Inc.
5400 Grosvenor Ln.
Bethesda, MD 20814-2161
Ph: (301)897-8720   Fax: (301)897-3690
E-mail: istf.bethesda@verizon.com
URL: http://www.istf-bethesda.org/

Description: Quarterly. Covers developments in tropical forestry. Recurring features include book reviews, notices of upcoming meetings, lists of members, and notes on member activities.

★5072★ The Job Seeker

The Job Seeker
403 Oakwood St.
Warrens, WI 54666
Ph: (608)378-4450   Fax: (267)295-2005
URL: http://www.thejobseeker.net

Description: Semimonthly. Specializes "in environmental and natural resource vacancies nationwide." Lists current vacancies from federal, state, local, private, and non-profit employers. Also available via e-mail.

★5073★ Journal of Applied Ecology

Wiley-Blackwell
350 Main St. Commerce Pl.
Malden, MA 02148
Ph: (781)388-8200   Fax: (781)388-8210
Fr: 800-759-6120
URL: http://www.blackwellpublishing.com/
journal.asp?ref=0021-8901

Bimonthly. $1,234.00/year for institutions, U.S. print and premium online; $1,122.00/year for institutions, U.S. print and standard online; $1,066.00/year for institutions, U.S. premium online only. Journal focusing on ecological science and environmental management.

★5074★ The Journal of Environment and Development

Sage Publications Inc.
2455 Teller Rd.
Thousand Oaks, CA 91320
Ph: (805)499-0721   Fax: (805)499-8096
E-mail: envdev@irpsmail.ucsd.edu
URL: http://www-irps.ucsd.edu/~jed

Quarterly. $479.00/year for institutions, print & e-access; $503.00/year for institutions, current volume print & all online content; $431.00/year for institutions, e-access; $455.00/year for institutions, e-access; $469.00/year for institutions, print only; $106.00/year for individuals, print only;

$129.00 for institutions, single print; $34.00 for individuals, single print; $431.00/year for institutions, backfile e-content thru 1999. Journal covering for anyone concerned with environment and development issues at the local, national, regional and international levels.

★5075★ Journal of Forest Products Business Research

Forest Products Society
2801 Marshall Ct.
Madison, WI 53705-2295
Ph: (608)231-1361   Fax: (608)231-2152
URL: http://www.forestprod.org/jfpbr.html

Annual. $25.00/year for members; $50.00/year for nonmembers; $100.00/year for libraries. Journal that publishes research manuscripts that focus on the forest industry.

★5076★ Journal of Forestry

Society of American Foresters
5400 Grosvenor Ln.
Bethesda, MD 20814-2198
Ph: (301)897-8720   Fax: (301)897-3690
Fr: (866)897-8720
E-mail: journal@safnet.org
URL: http://www.safnet.org/periodicals/jof/

$85.00/year for nonmembers, U.S./Canada, print only; $185.00/year for institutions, U.S./Canada, print only; $70.00/year for nonmembers, online only; $116.00/year for institutions, online only; $94.00/year for nonmembers, U.S./Canada, print and online; $204.00/year for institutions, U.S./Canada, print and online; $115.00/year for nonmembers, foreign, print only; $215.00/year for institutions, foreign, print only; $127.00/year for nonmembers, foreign, print and online; $237.00/year for institutions, other countries, print and online. Journal of forestry serves to advance the profession by keeping professionals informed about significant developments and ideas in forest science, natural resource management, and forest policy.

★5077★ Journal of Soil Contamination

Association for the Environmental Health of Soils
150 Fearing St.
Amherst, MA 01002
Ph: (413)549-5170   Fax: (413)549-0579
Fr: 888-540-2347
URL: http://www.aehs.com

Bimonthly. Journal covering environmental issues and soil.

★5078★ Nature International Weekly Journal of Science

Nature Publishing Group
75 Varick St., 9th Fl.
New York, NY 10013-1917
Ph: (212)726-9200   Fax: (212)696-9006
Fr: 888-331-6288
E-mail: nature@natureny.com
URL: http://www.nature.com

Weekly. $145.00/year for individuals; $49.00/year for institutions. Magazine covering science and technology, including the

fields of biology, biochemistry, genetics, medicine, earth sciences, physics, pharmacology, and behavioral sciences.

★5079★ New Growth

New England Forestry Foundation Inc.
PO Box 1346
Littleton, MA 01460
Ph: (978)952-6856
E-mail: info@newenglandforestry.org
URL: http://www.neforestry.org

Description: Quarterly. Contains forestry-related articles.

★5080★ The Northeastern Naturalist

Humboldt Field Research Institute
59 Eagle Hill Rd.
PO Box 9
Steuben, ME 04680-0009
Ph: (207)546-2821   Fax: (207)546-3042
URL: http://www.eaglehill.us/jngeninf.html

Quarterly. $40.00/year for individuals; $30.00/year for students; $60.00/year for institutions. Peer-reviewed interdisciplinary scientific journal covering field ecology, biology, behavior, biogeography, taxonomy, anatomy, physiology, geology and related fields in the northeastern United States.

★5081★ Northern Logger and Timber Processor

N.L. Publishing Inc.
3311 State Rte. 28
PO Box 69
Old Forge, NY 13420
Ph: (315)369-3078   Fax: (315)369-3736
Fr: 800-318-7561

Monthly. $12.00/year for individuals. Magazine for the logging and lumber industries.

★5082★ Ornithological Newsletter

Ornithological Societies of North America
5400 Bosque Blvd., Ste. 680
Waco, TX 76710
Ph: (254)399-9636   Fax: (254)776-3767
E-mail: business@osnabirds.org
URL: http://birds.cornell.edu/OSNA/orn-newsl.htm

Description: Bimonthly. Provides information of interest to ornithologists. Recurring features include listings of available grants and awards, news of members, a calendar of events, activities of sponsoring societies, and notices of publications available. Notices of employment opportunities are also available on the Web version.

★5083★ P2

John Wiley & Sons Inc.
111 River St.
Hoboken, NJ 07030-5774
Ph: (201)748-6000   Fax: (201)748-6088
Fr: 800-825-7550
URL: http://as.wiley.com/WileyCDA/WileyTitle/productCd-PPR.html

Quarterly. Journal discussing source reduction and waste minimization, and focusing on

the tactics, techniques, and answers fo solving pollution problems before they begir

★5084★ PALAIOS

SEPM Publications
6128 E 38th St., Ste. 308
Tulsa, OK 74135-5814
Ph: (918)610-3361   Fax: (918)621-168:
Fr: 800-865-9765
URL: http://www.sepm.org/

Bimonthly. $200.00/year for individuals, fo U.S. online version with CD-ROM; $235.00 year for individuals, for U.S. print and onlin version with CD-ROM; $200.00/year for oth er countries, online version with CD-ROM $245.00/year for other countries, print an online version with CD-ROM. Journal provid ing information on the impact of life on Eart history as recorded in the paleontologica and sedimentological records. Covers area such as biogeochemistry, ichnology, sedi mentology, stratigraphy, paleoecology, pa leoclimatology, and paleoceanography.

★5085★ PE & RS Photogrammetric Engineering & Remote Sensing

The Imaging and Geospatial Information Society
5410 Grosvenor Ln., Ste. 210
Bethesda, MD 20814-2160
Ph: (301)493-0290   Fax: (301)493-020:
E-mail: asprs@asprs.org
URL: http://www.asprs.org/

Monthly. $250.00/year for individuals, U.S.[15 discount per subscp. off the base rate $120.00/year for individuals, active; $80.00 year for individuals, associate; $45.00/yea for students, domestic. Journal covering photogrammetry, remote sensing, geograph ic information systems, cartography, an surveying, global positioning systems, digita photogrammetry.

★5086★ Seedling News

TreePeople
12601 Mulholland Dr.
Beverly Hills, CA 90210
Ph: (818)753-4600   Fax: (818)753-463£
E-mail: info@treepeople.org
URL: http://www.treepeople.org

Description: Quarterly. Covers environmen tal topics, such as urban forestry and sus tainable communities. Recurring feature: include a collection and reports of meetings

★5087★ SFPA Newsletter

Southern Forest Products Association
2900 Indiana Ave.
Kenner, LA 70065
Ph: (504)443-4464   Fax: (504)443-6612
E-mail: Mail@sfpa.org
URL: http://www.sfpa.org

Description: Weekly. Covers activities o Southern Forest Products Association. Cov ers forest products, timber resources, marke development activities, transportation, lum ber manufacturing, and business and associ ation news.

★5088★ The Southeastern Naturalist

Humboldt Field Research Institute
59 Eagle Hill Rd.
PO Box 9
Steuben, ME 04680-0009
Ph: (207)546-2821   Fax: (207)546-3042
E-mail: office@eaglehill.us
URL: http://www.eaglehill.us/jsgeninf.html

Quarterly. $45.00/year for individuals; $35.00/year for students; $75.00/year for institutions. Peer-reviewed interdisciplinary scientific journal covering field ecology, biology, behavior, biogeography, taxonomy, anatomy, physiology, geology and related fields in the southeastern United States.

★5089★ Under the Canopy-Forestry & Forest Products Newsletter

Alaska Cooperative Extension
PO Box 756180
University of Alaska Fairbanks
Fairbanks, AK 99775-6180
Ph: (907)474-7246   Fax: (907)474-6971
URL: http://www.uaf.edu/coop-ext/forestry/

Description: Three issues/year. Focuses on forestry in Alaska, including legislation, tree diseases, forest fires, wood use, and tree farms. Recurring features include news from the Board of Forestry, the 4-H Forestry Camp, and state forests in Alaska and a list of free publications from the Cooperative Extension Service.

★5090★ Wetlands

Society of Wetland Scientists
1313 Dolley Madison Blvd., Ste. 402
Mc Lean, VA 22101
Ph: (703)790-1745   Fax: (703)790-2672
URL: http://www.sws.org/wetlands/index.mgi

Quarterly. $100.00/year for individuals; $35.00/year for students; $500.00/year for institutions; $200.00/year for libraries. Scholarly journal covering all aspects of wetlands biology, ecology, hydrology, water chemistry, soil and sediment characteristics, management, and laws and regulations.

★5091★ The Wildlifer

The Wildlife Society Inc.
5410 Grosvenor Ln., Ste. 200
Bethesda, MD 20814-2144
Ph: (301)897-9770   Fax: (301)530-2471
URL: http://www.wildlife.org/publications

Description: Bimonthly. Serves as the Society's official publication of record. Contains items on section and chapter activities, meetings of interest, career notes, job opportunities, and timely articles on significant developments in conservation issues. Recurring features include editorials, news of members, letters to the editor, a calendar of events, and a column titled Call for Papers.

★5092★ The Woodland Steward

Massachusetts Forestry Association
PO Box 1096
Belchertown, MA 01007-1096
Ph: (413)323-7326   Fax: (413)339-5526

E-mail: info@massforests.org
URL: http://www.massforests.org/

Description: Five issues/year. Presents issues, facts, and events concerning Massachusetts forests, trees, and ecology. Advocates sustainable forest use. Recurring features include news of research, a calendar of events, and columns titled Forest Health, Practical Management, Tree Farm News, and Legislation & Policy.

★5093★ Woods, Water & Wildlife

Grand View Media Group Inc.
200 Croft St., Ste. 1
Birmingham, AL 35242
Ph: (205)408-3797   Fax: (205)408-3797
Fr: 888-431-2877

Semiannual. Magazine that aims to give information that shows responsible forest and land management and ethical hunting and outdoor behavior.

PLACEMENT AND JOB REFERRAL SERVICES

★5094★ Korean-American Scientists and Engineers Association (KSEA)

1952 Gallows Rd., Ste. 300
Vienna, VA 22182
Ph: (703)748-1221   Fax: (703)748-1331
E-mail: admin@ksea.org
URL: http://www.ksea.org

Description: Represents scientists and engineers holding single or advanced degrees. Promotes friendship and mutuality among Korean and American scientists and engineers; contributes to Korea's scientific, technological, industrial, and economic developments; strengthens the scientific, technological, and cultural bonds between Korea and the U.S. Sponsors symposium. Maintains speakers' bureau, placement service, and biographical archives. Compiles statistics.

EMPLOYER DIRECTORIES AND NETWORKING LISTS

★5095★ American Men and Women of Science

Gale, Cengage Learning
27500 Drake Rd.
Farmington Hills, MI 48331-3535
Ph: (248)699-4253   Fax: (248)699-8065
Fr: 800-877-4253
URL: http://www.gale.com

Biennial, latest edition 23rd, October 2006; new edition expected 24th, January 2008. $1,075.00 for individuals. Covers over 129,700 U.S. and Canadian scientists active in the physical, biological, mathematical, computer science, and engineering fields; includes references to previous edition for

deceased scientists and nonrespondents. Entries include: Name, address, education, personal and career data, memberships, honors and awards, research interest. Arrangement: Alphabetical. Indexes: Discipline (in separate volume).

★5096★ Association of Consulting Foresters-Membership Specialization Directory

Association of Consulting Foresters
312 Montgomery St., Ste. 208
Alexandria, VA 22314
Ph: (703)548-0990   Fax: (703)548-6395
URL: http://www.acf-foresters.org

Annual, August. Free. Covers nearly 500 member forestry consulting firms and professional foresters who earn the largest part of their income from consulting. Entries include: Name, address, phone, specialties, background, career data, staff (if a consulting firm), geographic area served, capabilities, including equipment available and foreign language proficiency. Arrangement: Alphabetical. Indexes: Name, office location, language, international capability.

★5097★ Conservation Directory

National Wildlife Federation
11100 Wildlife Center Dr.
Reston, VA 20190-5362
Ph: (703)638-6000   Fax: (703)438-6061
Fr: 800-822-9919
E-mail: admin@nwf.org
URL: http://www.nwf.org/conservationdirectory/

Annual; latest edition March 2007. $80.00 for individuals. Covers over 4,000 organizations, agencies, colleges and universities with conservation programs and more than 18,000 officials concerned with environmental conservation, education, and natural resource use and management. Entries include: Agency name, address, branch or subsidiary office name and address, names and titles of key personnel, descriptions of program areas, size of membership (where appropriate), telephone, fax, e-mail and URL addresses. Arrangement: Classified by type of organization. Indexes: Personal name, keyword, geographic, organization.

★5098★ National Parks

U.S. National Park Service
Harpers Ferry Center
PO Box 50
Harpers Ferry, WV 25425-0050
Ph: (202)208-4747   Fax: (304)535-6144
URL: http://www.nps.gov/

Biennial, odd years. Covers over 379 areas administered by the National Park Service, including parks, shores, historic sites, 80 national trails, and wild and scenic rivers. Entries include: Name, location, address, acreage (federal, non-federal, and gross), federal facilities, brief description. Arrangement: Most areas are alphabetical by state; geographical and historical by state; wild and scenic rivers and national trails are alphabetical by state. Indexes: Alphabetical by state.

★5099★ Peterson's Job Opportunities in Engineering and Technology

Peterson's Guides
2000 Lenox Dr.
Box 67005
Lawrenceville, NJ 08648
Ph: (609)896-1800   Fax: (609)896-4531
Fr: 800-338-3282
E-mail: custsvc@petersons.com
URL: http://www.petersons.com

Compiled by the Peterson's staff. Fourth edition, 1996. $21.95 (paper). 379 pages. Profiles 2,000 high-tech companies looking primarily for technical personnel in such fields as biotechnology, telecommunications, software, computers and peripherals, defense, and aerospace. Contains job-search strategies and career options to help match education and expertise to the job market. Indexed geographically, by industry, and by hiring needs.

HANDBOOKS AND MANUALS

★5100★ The Best Resumes for Scientists and Engineers

John Wiley & Sons Inc.
1 Wiley Dr.
Somerset, NJ 08873
Ph: (732)469-4400   Fax: (732)302-2300
Fr: 800-225-5945
E-mail: custserv@wiley.com
URL: http://www.wiley.com/WileyCDA/

Adele Lewis and David J. Moore. Second edition, 1993. $37.50; $19.95 (paper). 224 pages. Presents an extensive collection of scientific and engineering resumes, highlighting the important differences between these and resumes written for other occupations.

★5101★ Careers in the Environment

The McGraw-Hill Companies
PO Box 182604
Columbus, OH 43272
Fax: (614)759-3749   Fr: 877-883-5524
E-mail: customer.service@mcgraw-hill.com
URL: http://www.mcgraw-hill.com

Michael Fasulo and Paul Walker. Second edition, 2000. $17.95; $13.95 (paper). 290 pages. Comprehensive information on the diverse career opportunities available in environmental services.

★5102★ Careers for Environmental Types and Others Who Respect the Earth

The McGraw-Hill Companies
PO Box 182604
Columbus, OH 43272
Fax: (614)759-3749   Fr: 877-883-5524
E-mail: customer.service@mcgraw-hill.com
URL: http://www.mcgraw-hill.com

Jane Kinney and Mike Fasulo. Second edition, 2001. $13.95; $10.74 (paper). 192 pages. Describes environmentally friendly

positions with corporations, government, and environmental organizations.

★5103★ Careers for Health Nuts and Others Who Like to Stay Fit

The McGraw-Hill Companies
PO Box 182604
Columbus, OH 43272
Fax: (614)759-3749   Fr: 877-883-5524
E-mail: customer.service@mcgraw-hill.com
URL: http://www.mcgraw-hill.com

Blythe Camenson. Second edition, 2005. $13.95 (paper). 208 pages.

★5104★ The Complete Guide to Environmental Careers in the 21st Century

Island Press
1718 Connecticut Ave. NW, Ste. 300
Washington, DC 20009
Ph: (202)232-7933   Fax: (202)234-1328
Fr: 800-621-2736
URL: http://www.islandpress.org/

Environmental Careers Organization. 1998. Third edition. $28.50 (paper). 463 pages. A completely revised and updated edition of the standard reference on environmental careers.

★5105★ Nature (Career Portraits)

The McGraw-Hill Companies
PO Box 182604
Columbus, OH 43272
Fax: (614)759-3749   Fr: 877-883-5524
E-mail: customer.service@mcgraw-hill.com
URL: http://www.mcgraw-hill.com

Marjorie Eberts. 1996. $13.95. 96 pages. Highlights a range of careers that focus on the environment, with descriptions of a typical day on the job and interactive exercises for readers.

★5106★ Opportunities in Agriculture Careers

The McGraw-Hill Companies
PO Box 182604
Columbus, OH 43272
Fax: (614)759-3749   Fr: 877-883-5524
E-mail: customer.service@mcgraw-hill.com
URL: http://www.mcgraw-hill.com

William C. White and Donald N. Collins. 1987. $13.95. 150 pages.

★5107★ Opportunities in Biological Science Careers

The McGraw-Hill Companies
PO Box 182604
Columbus, OH 43272
Fax: (614)759-3749   Fr: 877-883-5524
E-mail: customer.service@mcgraw-hill.com
URL: http://www.mcgraw-hill.com

Charles A. Winter. 2004. $13.95; $11.95 (paper). 160 pages. Identifies employers and outlines opportunities in plant and animal biology, biological specialties, biomedical sciences, applied biology, and other areas. Illustrated.

★5108★ Opportunities in Environmental Careers

The McGraw-Hill Companies
PO Box 182604
Columbus, OH 43272
Fax: (614)759-3749   Fr: 877-883-5524
E-mail: customer.service@mcgraw-hill.com
URL: http://www.mcgraw-hill.com

Odom Fanning. Revised, 2002. $12.95 (paper). 174 pages. Describes a broad range of opportunities in fields such as environmental health, recreation, physics, and hygiene, and provides job search advice. Part of the "Opportunities in ..." Series.

★5109★ Opportunities in Forestry Careers

The McGraw-Hill Companies
PO Box 182604
Columbus, OH 43272
Fax: (614)759-3749   Fr: 877-883-5524
E-mail: customer.service@mcgraw-hill.com
URL: http://www.mcgraw-hill.com

Christopher M. Wille. 2003. $11.95 (paper). 160 pages. Describes the forestry opportunities available in governmental agencies, commercial enterprises, education, and private conservation association, and how to pursue openings. Illustrated. Part of the "Opportunities in ..." Series.

★5110★ Opportunities in State and Local Government Careers

The McGraw-Hill Companies
PO Box 182604
Columbus, OH 43272
Fax: (614)759-3749   Fr: 877-883-5524
E-mail: customer.service@mcgraw-hill.com
URL: http://www.mcgraw-hill.com

Neale J. Baxter. Revised edition, 1992. $14.95; $10.95 (paper). 148 pages. Points out the incentives and drawbacks of a government career. Describes hiring procedures and provides tips on filling out applications, taking physical and aptitude tests, handling interviews, and finding jobs. Describes the jobs in which 75% of all state and local government workers are employed. For each occupation, covers the nature of the work and the training required.

★5111★ Resumes for Environmental Careers

The McGraw-Hill Companies
PO Box 182604
Columbus, OH 43272
Fax: (614)759-3749   Fr: 877-883-5524
E-mail: customer.service@mcgraw-hill.com
URL: http://www.mcgraw-hill.com

Second edition, 2002. $10.95 (paper). 160 pages. Provides resume advice tailored to people pursuing careers focusing on the environment. Includes sample resumes and cover letters.

★5112★ *Resumes for Scientific and Technical Careers*

The McGraw-Hill Companies
PO Box 182604
Columbus, OH 43272
Fax: (614)759-3749   Fr: 877-883-5524
E-mail: customer.service@mcgraw-hill.com
URL: http://www.mcgraw-hill.com

Third edition, 2007. $12.95 (paper). 144 pages. Provides resume advice for individuals interested in working in scientific and technical careers. Includes sample resumes and cover letters.

TRADESHOWS

★5113★ **Forest Products Machinery & Equipment Exposition**

Southern Forest Products Association
PO Box 641700
Kenner, LA 70064
Ph: (504)443-4464   Fax: (504)443-6612
E-mail: tkessler@sfpa.org
URL: http://www.sfpa.org

Biennial. **Primary Exhibits:** Equipment, supplies, and services for the forest products industry. Including lumber, panels, engineered wood products, plywood, secondary processing, forestry and land management.

★5114★ **Forestry, Conservation Communications Association Annual Meeting**

Forestry, Conservation Communications Association
PO Box 3217
444 N. Capitol St.
Gettysburg, PA 17325
Ph: (202)624-8474   Fax: (202)624-5407
E-mail: nfc@fcca-usa.org
URL: http://www.fcca.info

Annual. **Primary Exhibits:** Forestry and conservation communications equipment, systems, and procedures.

★5115★ **New Hampshire Farm and Forest Exposition**

New Hampshire Department of Agriculture
PO Box 2042
Concord, NH 03302
Ph: (603)271-3551   Fax: (603)271-1109
URL: http://agriculture.nh.gov

Annual. **Primary Exhibits:** Agricultural and forest technology, products, and services.

★5116★ **Northeastern Forest Products Equipment Expo**

Northeastern Loggers Association
PO Box 69
Old Forge, NY 13420
Ph: (315)369-3078   Fax: (315)369-3736
URL: http://www.loggertraining.com

Annual. **Primary Exhibits:** Forest industry services, equipment, and associated products.

★5117★ **Pacific Logging Congress**

Pacific Logging Congress
PO Box 1281
Maple Valley, WA 98038
Ph: (425)413-2808   Fax: (425)413-1359
E-mail: pacificlogging@aol.com
URL: http://www.pacificloggingcongress.com

Annual. **Primary Exhibits:** Logging and allied industry equipment.

★5118★ **Redwood Region Logging Conference**

Redwood Region Logging Conference
5601 S Broadway
Eureka, CA 95502-7127
Ph: (707)443-4091   Fax: (707)443-0926
E-mail: rrlc@rrlc.net
URL: http://www.rrlc.net

Annual. **Primary Exhibits:** Logging equipment supplies and services.

★5119★ **Society of American Foresters National Convention**

Society of American Foresters
5400 Grosvenor Ln.
Bethesda, MD 20814-2198
Ph: (301)897-8720   Fax: (301)897-3690
E-mail: safweb@safnet.org
URL: http://www.safnet.org

Annual. **Primary Exhibits:** Forestry equipment, publications, hardware and software, chemicals, machinery, and geographic information systems.

OTHER SOURCES

★5120★ **American Forests**

PO Box 2000
Washington, DC 20013
Ph: (202)737-1944   Fax: (202)737-2457
E-mail: info@amfor.org
URL: http://www.americanforests.org

Description: Works to advance the intelligent management and use of forests, soil, water, wildlife, and all other natural resources. Promotes public appreciation of natural resources, helps plant trees to restore areas damaged by wildfire.

★5121★ **ASPRS - The Imaging and Geospatial Information Society**

5410 Grosvenor Ln., Ste. 210
Bethesda, MD 20814-2160
Ph: (301)493-0290   Fax: (301)493-0208
E-mail: asprs@asprs.org
URL: http://www.asprs.org

Members: Firms, individuals, government employees and academicians engaged in photogrammetry, photointerpretation, remote sensing, and geographic information systems and their application to such fields as archaeology, geographic information systems, military reconnaissance, urban planning, engineering, traffic surveys, meteorological observations, medicine, geology, forestry, agriculture, construction and topographic mapping. Mission is to advance knowledge and improve understanding of these sciences and to promote responsible applications. **Activities:** Offers voluntary certification program open to persons associated with one or more functional area of photogrammetry, remote sensing and GIS. Surveys the profession of private firms in photogrammetry and remote sensing in the areas of products and services.

★5122★ **Association of Consulting Foresters of America (ACF)**

312 Montgomery St., Ste. 208
Alexandria, VA 22314
Ph: (703)548-0990   Fax: (703)548-6395
E-mail: director@acf-foresters.org
URL: http://www.acf-foresters.org

Members: Professional foresters in the field of applied forestry and forest utilization who work for private landowners or industry on a contract or contingency basis. Members must be graduates of an association-approved forestry school and have five years experience in forest administration and management. **Activities:** Provides client referral service. Compiles statistics.

★5123★ **Association for International Practical Training (AIPT)**

10400 Little Patuxent Pkwy., Ste. 250
Columbia, MD 21044-3519
Ph: (410)997-2200   Fax: (410)992-3924
E-mail: aipt@aipt.org
URL: http://www.aipt.org

Description: Providers worldwide of on-the-job training programs for students and professionals seeking international career development and life-changing experiences. Arranges workplace exchanges in hundreds of professional fields, bringing employers and trainees together from around the world. Client list ranges from small farming communities to Fortune 500 companies.

★5124★ **Environmental Occupations: Professional**

Delphi Productions
3159 6th St.
Boulder, CO 80304
Ph: (303)443-2100   Fax: (303)443-4022
Fr: 888-443-2400
E-mail: support@delphivideo.com
URL: http://www.delphivideo.com

$95.00. 49 minutes. Part of the Emerging Careers Video Library.

★5125★ Environmental Occupations: Technical

Delphi Productions
3159 6th St.
Boulder, CO 80304
Ph: (303)443-2100   Fax: (303)443-4022
Fr: 888-443-2400
E-mail: support@delphivideo.com
URL: http://www.delphivideo.com

$95.00. 48 minutes. Part of the Emerging Careers Video Library.

★5126★ Minority Women In Science (MWIS)

Directorate for Education and Human
Resources Programs
1200 New York Ave. NW
Washington, DC 20005
Ph: (202)326-7019   Fax: (202)371-9849
E-mail: ygeorge@aaas.org

Description: A national network group of the American association for the Advancement of Science (AAAS), Education and Human Resources Directorate. The objectives of this group are: to identify and share information on resources and programs that could help in mentoring young women and minorities interested in science and engineering careers, and to strengthen communication among women and minorities in science and education.

★5127★ National Association of Conservation Districts (NACD)

509 Capitol Ct. NE
Washington, DC 20002-4937
Ph: (202)547-6223   Fax: (202)547-6450
E-mail: krysta-harden@nacdnet.org
URL: http://www.nacdnet.org

Description: Soil and water conservation districts organized by the citizens of watersheds, counties, or communities under provisions of state laws. Directs and coordinates, through local self-government efforts, the conservation and development of soil, water, and related natural resources. Includes districts over 90% of the nation's privately owned land. Conducts educational programs and children's services.

★5128★ Scientific, Engineering, and Technical Services

Cambridge Educational
PO Box 2053
Princeton, NJ 08543-2053
Ph: 800-257-5126   Fax: (609)671-0266
Fr: 800-468-4227
E-mail: custserv@films.com
URL: http://www.cambridgeeducational.com

VHS and DVD. $89.95. 2002. 18 minutes. 2002. Part of the Career Cluster Series.

★5129★ Scientific Occupations

Delphi Productions
3159 6th St.
Boulder, CO 80304
Ph: (303)443-2100   Fax: (303)443-4022
Fr: 888-443-2400
E-mail: support@delphivideo.com
URL: http://www.delphivideo.com

$95.00. 60 minutes. Part of the Careers for the 21st Century Video Library.

★5130★ Society of American Foresters (SAF)

5400 Grosvenor Ln.
Bethesda, MD 20814-2198
Ph: (301)897-8720   Fax: (301)897-3690
Fr: (866)897-8720
E-mail: safweb@safnet.org
URL: http://www.safnet.org

Description: National scientific and educational organization representing forestry in the United States. Aims to advance the science, education, technology, and practice of forestry. Supports 28 subject-oriented working groups.

★5131★ Society for Range Management (SRM)

10030 W 27th Ave.
Wheat Ridge, CO 80215-6601
Ph: (303)986-3309   Fax: (303)986-3892
E-mail: info@rangelands.org
URL: http://www.rangelands.org

Description: Professional international society of scientists, technicians, ranchers, administrators, teachers, and students interested in the study, use, and management of rangeland resources for livestock, wildlife, watershed, and recreation.

★5132★ Student Conservation Association (SCA)

PO Box 550
Charlestown, NH 03603-0550
Ph: (603)543-1700   Fax: (603)543-1828
E-mail: ask-us@thesca.org
URL: http://www.thesca.org

Description: Works to build the next generation of conservation leaders and inspire lifelong stewardship of the environment and communities by engaging young people in hands-on service to the land. Provides conservation service opportunities, outdoor education and leadership development for young people. Offers college and graduate students, as well as older adults expense-paid conservation internships, these positions includes wildlife research, wilderness patrols and interpretive opportunities and provide participants with valuable hands-on career experience. Places 15-19 year old high school students in four-week volunteer conservation crews in national parks forests and refuges across the country each summer to accomplish a range of trail building and habitat conservation projects. Offers year-round diversity conservation programs for young women and young persons of color in leading metropolitan areas of U.S.

Fuel Cell Engineers

SOURCES OF HELP-WANTED ADS

★5133★ **Advanced Fuel Cell Technology**
Seven Mountains Scientific Inc.
PO Box 650
913 Tressler St.
Boalsburg, PA 16827
Ph: (814)466-6559   Fr: (814)466-2777
E-mail: mail@7ms.com
URL: http://www.7ms.com

Monthly. Covers research on fuel cell technology and the people and companies involved with the development of such technology.

★5134★ **AIE Perspectives Newsmagazine**
American Institute of Engineers
4630 Appian Way, Ste. 206
El Sobrante, CA 94803-1875
Ph: (510)758-6240   Fax: (510)758-6240

Monthly. Professional magazine covering engineering.

★5135★ **Energy User News**
BNP Media
2401 W Big Beaver Rd., Ste. 700
Troy, MI 48084-3333
Ph: (248)786-1642   Fax: (248)786-1388
URL: http://www.energyusernews.com

Monthly. Magazine reporting on the energy management market as it relates to commercial, industrial, and institutional facilities.

★5136★ **Engineering Conferences International Symposium Series**
Berkeley Electronic Press
2809 Telegraph Ave., Ste. 202
Berkeley, CA 94705
Ph: (510)665-1200   Fax: (510)665-1201
URL: http://services.bepress.com/eci/

Journal focusing on advance engineering science.

★5137★ **Engineering Times**
National Society of Professional Engineers
1420 King St.
Alexandria, VA 22314
Ph: (703)684-2800
URL: http://www.nspe.org

Monthly. Magazine (tabloid) covering professional, legislative, and techology issues for an engineering audience.

★5138★ **ENR: Engineering News-Record**
McGraw-Hill Inc.
1221 Ave. of the Americas
New York, NY 10020-1095
Ph: (212)512-2000   Fax: (212)512-3840
Fr: 877-833-5524
E-mail: enr_web_editors@mcgraw-hill.com
URL: http://www.mymags.com/morein-fo.php?itemID=20012

Weekly. $94.00/year for individuals, print. Magazine focusing on engineering and construction.

★5139★ **Fuel Cell Industry Report**
Alexander Communications Group
28 West 25th St., 8th Fl.
New York, NY 10010
Ph: (212)228-0246   Fax: (212)228-0376
Fr: (866)285-7215
E-mail: info@fcellreport.com
URL: http://www.sanewsletters.com/FCIR/FCIRinfo.asp

Information for manufacturers, integrators, suppliers, and end users.

★5140★ **Fuel Cell Magazine**
Webcom Communications Corp.
7355 E. Orchard Road, Ste. 100
Greenwood Village, CO 80111
Fr: 800-803-9488
E-mail: softpub@infowebcom.com
URL: http://www.fuelcell-magazine.com

Trade journal with a distribution of 10,000 copies worldwide.

★5141★ **High Technology Careers Magazine**
HTC
4701 Patrick Henry Dr., No. 1901
Santa Clara, CA 95054-1847
Fax: (408)567-0242
URL: http://www.hightechcareers.com

Bimonthly. $29.00/year; $35.00/year for Canada; $85.00/year for out of country. Magazine (tabloid) containing employment opportunity information for the engineering and technical community.

★5142★ **InterJournal**
New England Complex Systems Institute
24 Mt. Auburn St.
Cambridge, MA 02138
Ph: (617)547-4100   Fax: (617)661-7711
URL: http://www.interjournal.org/

Journal covering the fields of science and engineering.

★5143★ **International Archives of Bioscience**
International Archives of Bioscience
PO Box 737254
Elmhurst, NY 11373-9997
URL: http://www.iabs.us/jdoc/aboutiabs.htm

Free, online only. Journal reporting multidisciplinary coverage and interaction between scientists in biology, informatics, mathematics, physics, engineering and other sciences.

★5144★ **National Fuel Cell Research Center Journal**
National Fuel Cell Research Center
University of California Irvine
221 Engineering Lab Facility, Bldg. 323
Irvine, CA 92697-3550
Ph: (949)824-1999   Fax: (949)824-7423
URL: http://www.nfcr.uci.edu

Quarterly. $60/year. Provides a forum for the discussion of information related to high efficiency, environmentally sensitive energy and power technologies.

★5145★ NSBE Magazine

NSBE Publications
205 Daingerfield Rd.
Alexandria, VA 22314
Ph: (703)549-2207   Fax: (703)683-5312
URL: http://www.nsbe.org/publications/
premieradvertisers.php

Journal providing information on engineering careers, self-development, and cultural issues for recent graduates with technical majors.

★5146★ SWE, Magazine of the Society of Women Engineers

Society of Women Engineers
230 East Ohio St., Ste. 400
Chicago, IL 60611-3265
Ph: (312)596-5223
E-mail: hq@swe.org
URL: http://www.swe.org

Quarterly. $30.00/year for nonmembers. Magazine for engineering students and for women and men working in the engineering and technology fields. Covers career guidance, continuing development and topical issues.

★5147★ Uratie

IDG Communications Inc.
5 Speen St., 3rd. Fl
Framingham, MA 01701
Ph: (508)875-5000   Fax: (508)988-7888
URL: http://www.idg.com

Magazine providing job offers for graduates, engineers and information technology professionals.

★5148★ WEPANEWS

Women in Engineering Programs &
 Advocates Network
1901 E. Asbury Ave., Ste. 220
Denver, CO 80208
Ph: (303)871-4643   Fax: (303)871-6833
E-mail: dmatt@wepan.org
URL: http://www.wepan.org

Description: 2/year. Seeks to provide greater access for women to careers in engineering. Includes news of graduate, undergraduate, freshmen, pre-college, and re-entry engineering programs for women. Recurring features include job listings, faculty, grant, and conference news, international engineering program news, action group news, notices of publications available, and a column titled Kudos.

PLACEMENT AND JOB REFERRAL SERVICES

★5149★ Engineering Society of Detroit (ESD)

2000 Town Ctr., Ste. 2610
Southfield, MI 48075
Ph: (248)353-0735   Fax: (248)353-0736

E-mail: esd@esd.org
URL: http://esd.org

Description: Engineers from all disciplines; scientists and technologists. Conducts technical programs and engineering refresher courses; sponsors conferences and expositions. Maintains speakers' bureau; offers placement services; although based in Detroit, MI, society membership is international.

★5150★ Society of Hispanic Professional Engineers (SHPE)

5400 E Olympic Blvd., Ste. 210
Los Angeles, CA 90022
Ph: (323)725-3970   Fax: (323)725-0316
E-mail: shpenational@shpe.org
URL: http://oneshpe.shpe.org/wps/portal/
national

Description: Represents engineers, student engineers, and scientists. Aims to increase the number of Hispanic engineers by providing motivation and support to students. Sponsors competitions and educational programs. Maintains placement service and speakers' bureau; compiles statistics.

EMPLOYER DIRECTORIES AND NETWORKING LISTS

★5151★ Careers in Focus: Engineering

Facts On File Inc.
132 W 31st St., 17th Fl.
New York, NY 10001
Ph: (212)967-8800   Fax: 800-678-3633
Fr: 800-322-8755
URL: http://www.factsonfile.com

3rd edition, 2007. $29.95 for individuals; $26.95 for libraries. Publication includes: List of resources to consult for more information. Principal content of publication consists of job descriptions, advancement opportunities, educational requirements, employment outlook, salary information, and working conditions for careers in the field of engineering. Indexes: Alphabetical.

HANDBOOKS AND MANUALS

★5152★ The Best Resumes for Scientists and Engineers

John Wiley & Sons Inc.
1 Wiley Dr.
Somerset, NJ 08873
Ph: (732)469-4400   Fax: (732)302-2300
Fr: 800-225-5945
E-mail: custserv@wiley.com
URL: http://www.wiley.com/WileyCDA/

Adele Lewis and David J. Moore. Second edition, 1993. $37.50; $19.95 (paper). 224 pages. Presents an extensive collection of scientific and engineering resumes, highlighting the important differences between

these and resumes written for other occupations.

★5153★ Great Jobs for Engineering Majors

The McGraw-Hill Companies
PO Box 182604
Columbus, OH 43272
Fax: (614)759-3749   Fr: 877-883-5524
E-mail: customer.service@mcgraw-hill.com
URL: http://www.mcgraw-hill.com

Geraldine O. Garner. Second edition, 2002. $14.95. 256 pages. Covers all the career options open to students majoring in engineering.

★5154★ Keys to Engineering Success

Prentice Hall PTR
One Lake St.
Upper Saddle River, NJ 07458
Ph: (201)236-7000   Fr: 800-428-5331
URL: http://www.phptr.com/index.asp?rl=1

Jill S. Tietjen, Kristy A. Schloss, Carol Carter, Joyce Bishop, and Sarah Lyman. 2000. $46.00 (paper). 288 pages.

★5155★ The New Engineer's Guide to Career Growth & Professional Awareness

Institute of Electrical & Electronics
 Engineers
445 Hoes Lane
Piscataway, NJ 08854
Ph: (732)981-0060   Fax: (732)981-9667
Fr: 800-678-4333
URL: http://www.ieee.org

Irving J. Gabelman, editor. 1996. $39.95 (paper). 275 pages.

★5156★ Resumes for Engineering Careers

The McGraw-Hill Companies
PO Box 182604
Columbus, OH 43272
Fax: (614)759-3749   Fr: 877-883-5524
E-mail: customer.service@mcgraw-hill.com
URL: http://www.mcgraw-hill.com

Third edition, 2005. $11.95 (paper). 144 pages. Contains sample resumes and cover letters applicable to any engineering field.

EMPLOYMENT AGENCIES AND SEARCH FIRMS

★5157★ Aureus Group

13609 California St.
Omaha, NE 68154
Ph: (402)891-6900   Fax: (402)891-1290
Fr: 888-239-5993
E-mail: info@aureusgroup.com
URL: http://www.aureusgroup.com

Provides human capital management services in a wide variety of industries. Executive search and recruiting consultants specializing in six areas: accounting and finance, data processing, aerospace, engineering, manufacturing and medical professionals. Industries served: hospitals, all mainframe computer shops and all areas of accounting.

★5158★ The Corban Group

5050 Research Ct., Ste. 600
Johns Creek, GA 30024
Ph: (678)638-6000   Fax: (678)638-6001
Fr: (866)426-7226
E-mail: info@corbangroup.com
URL: http://www.corbangroup.com

Executive search firm.

ONLINE JOB SOURCES AND SERVICES

★5159★ Fuel Cells 2000

1100 H. St. NW, Ste. 800
Washington, DC 20005
Ph: (202)785-4222   Fax: (202)785-4313
E-mail: marleen@fuelcells.org
URL: http://www.fuelcells.org

Description: Provides news, educational resources, and job postings.

TRADESHOWS

★5160★ American Society for Engineering Education Annual Conference and Exposition

American Society for Engineering Education
1818 N. St. NW, Ste. 600
Washington, DC 20036-2479
Ph: (202)331-3500   Fax: (202)265-8504
E-mail: conferences@asee.org
URL: http://www.asee.org

Annual. **Primary Exhibits:** Publications, engineering supplies and equipment, computers, software, and research companies all products and services related to engineering education.

OTHER SOURCES

★5161★ American Association of Blacks in Energy (AABE)

927 15th St. NW, Ste. 200
Washington, DC 20005-2321
Ph: (202)371-9530   Fax: (202)371-9218
Fr: 800-466-0204
E-mail: aabe@aabe.org

URL: http://www.aabe.org

Description: Seeks to increase the knowledge, understanding, and awareness of the minority community in energy issues by serving as an energy information source for policymakers, recommending blacks and other minorities to appropriate energy officials and executives, encouraging students to pursue professional careers in the energy industry, and advocating the participation of blacks and other minorities in energy programs and policymaking activities. Updates members on key legislation and regulations being developed by the Department of Energy, the Department of Interior, the Department of Commerce, the Small Business Administration, and other federal and state agencies.

★5162★ American Association of Engineering Societies (AAES)

1620 I St. NW, Ste. 210
Washington, DC 20006
Ph: (202)296-2237   Fax: (202)296-1151
Fr: 888-400-2237
E-mail: dbateson@aaes.org
URL: http://www.aaes.org

Description: Coordinates the efforts of the member societies in the provision of reliable and objective information to the general public concerning issues which affect the engineering profession and the field of engineering as a whole; collects, analyzes, documents, and disseminates data which will inform the general public of the relationship between engineering and the national welfare; provides a forum for the engineering societies to exchange and discuss their views on matters of common interest; and represents the U.S. engineering community abroad through representation in WFEO and UPADI.

★5163★ American Engineering Association (AEA)

4116 S Carrier Pkwy., Ste. 280-809
Grand Prairie, TX 75052
Ph: (201)664-6954
E-mail: info@aea.org
URL: http://www.aea.org

Description: Members consist of Engineers and engineering professionals. Purpose to advance the engineering profession and U.S. engineering capabilities. Issues of concern include age discrimination, immigration laws, displacement of U.S. Engineers by foreign workers, trade agreements, off shoring of U.S. Engineering and manufacturing jobs, loss of U.S. manufacturing and engineering capability, and recruitment of foreign students. Testifies before Congress. Holds local Chapter meetings.

★5164★ American Hydrogen Association

2350 W. Shangri La
Phoenix, AZ 85029
Ph: (602)328-4238
URL: http://www.clean-air.org

Description: Seeks to stimulate interest and help establish the renewable hydrogen energy economy.

★5165★ American Institute of Engineers (AIE)

4630 Appian Way, Ste. 206
El Sobrante, CA 94803-1875
Ph: (510)758-6240   Fax: (510)758-6240
E-mail: aie@members-aie.org
URL: http://www.members-aie.org

Description: Professional association for engineers, scientists, and mathematicians. Multi-disciplined, non-technical association who aims to improve the stature and image of engineers, scientists, and mathematicians. Provides endorsements, awards and opportunities for small business start-ups within the AIE Councils. Sponsors "LA Engineer", a comedy-drama television series; produces annual "Academy Hall of FAME (TV)".

★5166★ Association of Energy Engineers

4025 Pleasantdale Rd., Ste. 420
Atlanta, GA 30340
Ph: (770)447-5083   Fax: (770)446-3969
E-mail: Jennifer@aeecenter.org
URL: http://www.aeecenter.org

Description: Provides information on energy efficiency, utility deregulation, facility management, plant engineering, and environmental compliance. Offers resources such as seminars, tradeshows, and certification programs.

★5167★ California Fuel Cell Partnership

3300 Industrial Blvd., Ste. 1000
West Sacramento, CA 95691
Ph: (916)371-2870   Fax: (916)375-2008
E-mail: info@cafcp.org
URL: http://www.fuelcellpartnership.org

Description: Auto manufacturers, energy companies, fuel cell technology companies, and government agencies striving to advance new vehicle technology.

★5168★ Engineering Occupations

Delphi Productions
3159 6th St.
Boulder, CO 80304
Ph: (303)443-2100   Fax: (303)443-4022
Fr: 888-443-2400
E-mail: support@delphivideo.com
URL: http://www.delphivideo.com

$95.00. 50 minutes. Part of the Careers for the 21st Century Video Library.

★5169★ Engineering Workforce Commission (EWC)

1620 I St. NW, Ste. 210
Washington, DC 20006
Ph: (202)296-2237   Fax: (202)296-1151
Fr: 888-400-2237
E-mail: dbateson@aaes.org
URL: http://www.ewc-online.org

Description: Represents commissioners appointed by member societies of the American Association of Engineering Societies to engage in studies and analyses of the supply, demand, use and remuneration of engineering and technical personnel. Provides representation to government groups dealing with professional manpower policy; consults with industry. Gathers and disseminates information on the engineering profession. Conducts surveys of engineering school enrollments, degrees, and salaries; monitors federal labor statistics.

★5170★ International Federation of Professional and Technical Engineers (IFPTE)

8630 Fenton St., Ste. 400
Silver Spring, MD 20910-3803
Ph: (301)565-9016   Fax: (301)565-0018
E-mail: gjunemann@ifpte.org
URL: http://www.ifpte.org

Description: Represents engineers, scientists, architects and technicians.

★5171★ National Action Council for Minorities in Engineering (NACME)

440 Hamilton Ave., Ste. 302
White Plains, NY 10601-1813
Ph: (914)539-4010   Fax: (914)539-4032
E-mail: webmaster@nacme.org
URL: http://www.nacme.org

Description: Leads the national effort to increase access to careers in engineering and other science-based disciplines. Conducts research and public policy analysis, develops and operates national demonstration programs at precollege and university levels, and disseminates information through publications, conferences and electronic media. Serves as a privately funded source of scholarships for minority students in engineering.

★5172★ National Society of Professional Engineers (NSPE)

1420 King St.
Alexandria, VA 22314-2794
Ph: (703)684-2800   Fax: (703)836-4875
Fr: 888-285-6773

E-mail: memserv@nspe.org
URL: http://www.nspe.org

Description: Represents professional engineers and engineers-in-training in all fields registered in accordance with the laws of states or territories of the U.S. or provinces of Canada; qualified graduate engineers, student members, and registered land surveyors. Is concerned with social, professional, ethical, and economic considerations of engineering as a profession; encompasses programs in public relations, employment practices, ethical considerations, education, and career guidance. Monitors legislative and regulatory actions of interest to the engineering profession.

★5173★ Scientific, Engineering, and Technical Services

Cambridge Educational
PO Box 2053
Princeton, NJ 08543-2053
Ph: 800-257-5126   Fax: (609)671-0266
Fr: 800-468-4227
E-mail: custserv@films.com
URL: http://www.cambridgeeducational.com

VHS and DVD. $89.95. 2002. 18 minutes. 2002. Part of the Career Cluster Series.

★5174★ Society of Engineering Science (SES)

Pennsylvania State University
Dept. of Engineering Science and
  Mechanics
212 EES Bldg.
University Park, PA 16802
E-mail: jtodd@psu.edu
URL: http://www.sesinc.org

Members: Individuals with at least a baccalaureate degree who are engaged in any aspect of engineering science or in other pursuits that contributes to the advancement of engineering science. **Purpose:** Fosters and promotes the interchange of ideas and information among the various fields of engineering science and among engineering science and the fields of theoretical and applied physics, chemistry, and mathematics. Is dedicated to the advancement of interdisciplinary research and to the estab-

lishment of a bridge between science and engineering.

★5175★ Society of Women Engineers (SWE)

230 E Ohio St., Ste. 400
Chicago, IL 60611-3265
Ph: (312)596-5223   Fax: (312)596-5252
Fr: 877-SWE-INFO
E-mail: hq@swe.org
URL: http://www.swe.org

Description: Educational and service organization representing both students and professional women in engineering and technical fields.

★5176★ United Engineering Foundation (UEF)

PO Box 70
Mount Vernon, VA 22121-0070
Ph: (973)244-2328   Fax: (973)882-5155
E-mail: engfnd@aol.com
URL: http://www.uefoundation.org

Description: Federation of 5 major national engineering societies: American Institute of Chemical Engineers; American Institute of Mining, Metallurgical and Petroleum Engineers; American Society of Civil Engineers; American Society of Mechanical Engineers; Institute of Electrical and Electronics Engineers. Supports research in engineering and advances the engineering arts and sciences through its conference program.

★5177★ US Fuel Cell Council

1100 H St. NW, Ste. 800
Washington, DC 20005
Ph: (202)293-5500   Fr: (202)785-4313
E-mail: sarah@usfcc.com
URL: http://www.usfcc.com

Description: Dedicated to fostering the commercialization of fuel cells in the United States. Provides technical advice, collects information and issues reports on the industry, and raises public awareness of fuel cells and their potential.

Fund Raisers

★5178★ The Chronicle of Philanthropy

The Chronicle of Philanthropy
1255 23rd St. NW, Ste. 700
Washington, DC 20037
Ph: (202)466-1200
E-mail: editor@philanthropy.com
URL: http://philanthropy.com

$72.00/year for individuals; $125.00 for two years; $72.00/year for individuals, online access only; $99.75/year for Canada; $72.00/year for Canada, online access only; $135.00/year for other countries; $72.00/year for other countries, online access only. Magazine covering fundraising, philanthropy, and non-profit organizations. Includes information on tax rulings, new grants, and statistics, reports on grant makers, and profiles of foundations.

★5179★ Community Radio News

National Federation of Community
  Broadcasters
1970 Broadway, Ste. 1000
Oakland, CA 94612
Ph: (510)451-8200   Fax: (510)451-8208
E-mail: newsletter@nfcb.org
URL: http://www.nfcb.org

Description: Monthly. Serves as a medium of communication for independent, community-licensed radio stations. Contains brief articles and news items on such topics as public broadcasting and programming, legislative developments, activities of the Federal Communications Commission, and local stations. Recurring features include notices of grants and awards, job openings, and a calendar of events/conferences for noncommercial broadcasters.

★5180★ DM News

DM News
114 W 26th St., 4th Fl.
New York, NY 10001
Ph: (646)638-6000   Fax: (646)638-6159
E-mail: inquiry@dmnews.com
URL: http://www.dmnews.com/

Weekly. $49.00/year for U.S. $99.00/year for Canada and Mexico; $149.00/year for other countries. Tabloid newspaper for publishers, fund raisers, financial marketers, catalogers, package goods advertisers and their agencies, and other marketers who use direct mail, mail order advertising, catalogs, or other direct response media to sell their products or services.

★5181★ The NonProfit Times

NPT Publishing Group Inc.
120 Littleton Rd., Ste. 120
Parsippany, NJ 07054-1803
Ph: (973)394-1800   Fax: (973)394-2888
E-mail: ednchief@nptimes.com
URL: http://www.nptimes.com/

Biweekly. $69.00/year for individuals, subscribe at the one year rate; $49.00/year for individuals, digital only; $100.00/year for individuals, print & digital; $122.00 for two years, (48 issues); $101.00/year for Canada and Mexico; $137.00/year for other countries, international. Trade journal serving nonprofit organizations.

★5182★ American Association of Fund-Raising Counsel Membership Directory

American Association of Fund-Raising
  Counsel Inc.
4700 W Lake Ave.
Glenview, IL 60025
Ph: (847)375-4709   Fr: 800-462-2372
URL: http://www.aafrc.org/

Annual. Covers member fund-raising consulting firms. Entries include: Company name, address, phone, fax, geographical area served, types of clients, description of services. Arrangement: Alphabetical.

★5183★ National Directory of Nonprofit Organizations

The Taft Group
27500 Drake Rd.
Farmington Hills, MI 48331-3535
Ph: (248)699-4253   Fax: 800-414-5043
Fr: 800-877-4253
E-mail: businessproducts@gale.com
URL: http://www.gale.com

Annual; latest edition 21, December 2007. $750.00 for individuals. Covers over 265,000 nonprofit organizations; volume 1 covers organizations with annual incomes of over $100,000; volume 2 covers organizations with incomes between $25,000 and $99,999. Entries include: Organization name, address, phone, annual income, IRS filing status, employer identification number, tax deductible status, activity description. Arrangement: Alphabetical. Indexes: Area of activity, geographical.

★5184★ NSFRE Directory

National Society of Fund Raising
  Executives
1101 King St., Ste. 700
Alexandria, VA 22314
Ph: (703)684-0410   Fax: (703)684-0540

Annual, January. Database covers: About 18,000 fund raisers and development officers for private and public not-for-profit organizations. Entries include: Name, organization name, address, phone, fax, e-mail. Database is housed in the members-only section of web site. Arrangement: Classified by chapter, then alphabetical.

★5185★ Careers for Good Samaritans and Other Humanitarian Types

The McGraw-Hill Companies
PO Box 182604
Columbus, OH 43272
Fax: (614)759-3749   Fr: 877-883-5524
E-mail: customer.service@mcgraw-hill.com
URL: http://www.mcgraw-hill.com

Marjorie Eberts and Margaret Gisler. Third edition, 2006. $13.95 (paper). 160 pages. Contains hundreds of ideas for turning good work into paid work. Inventories opportunities in service organizations like the Red Cross, Goodwill, and the Salvation Army; religious groups, VISTA, the Peace Corps, and UNICEF; and agencies at all levels of the government. Part of Careers for You series.

★5186★ Fund Raisers: Their Careers, Stories, Concerns, and Accomplishments

Jossey-Bass
989 Market St.
San Francisco, CA 94103
Ph: (415)433-1740   Fax: (415)433-0499
Fr: 800-255-5945
E-mail: custserv@wiley.com
URL: http://www.josseybass.com/WileyCDA/

Margaret A. Duronio and Eugene R. Temple. 1996. $42.00. 221 pages. Part of the Non-profit Sector Series. Helps professional fund raisers examine their work environment and make smarter choices about their careers. Based on results from a three-year national study that included a survey of 1,700 professional fund raisers and 82 personal interviews. Reveals compensation practices, factors involved in entering and advancing in the field, the status of women and minorities in fund raising, and reasons for turnover. Other areas discussed include accountability, ethical practice, and licensing and regulation.

★5187★ Fund Raising 101: How to Raise Money for Charities

John Wiley and Sons, Inc.
1 Wiley Dr.
Somerset, NJ 08875-1272
Ph: (732)469-4400   Fax: (732)302-2300
Fr: 800-225-5945
E-mail: custserv@wiley.com
URL: http://www.wiley.com/WileyCDA/

William L. Doyle. 1993. $34.50. 237 pages.

★5188★ Fund-Raising Fundamentals: A Guide to Annual Giving for Professionals and Volunteers

John Wiley & Sons Inc.
1 Wiley Dr.
Somerset, NJ 08873
Ph: (732)469-4400   Fax: (732)302-2300
Fr: 800-225-5945
E-mail: custserv@wiley.com
URL: http://www.wiley.com/WileyCDA/

James M. Greenfield. 1994. $47.00 (paper). 432 pages.

★5189★ Fundraising As a Profession: Advancements and Challenges in the Field

Jossey-Bass
989 Market St.
San Francisco, CA 94103
Ph: (415)433-1740   Fax: (415)433-0499
Fr: 800-255-5945
E-mail: custserv@wiley.com
URL: http://www.josseybass.com/WileyCDA/

Lilya D. Wagner and Patrick Ryan. January 2004. $29.00. 104 pages. Part of the J-B PF Single Issue Philanthropic Fundraising Series.

★5190★ Great Jobs for Liberal Arts Majors

The McGraw-Hill Companies
PO Box 182604
Columbus, OH 43272
Fax: (614)759-3749   Fr: 877-883-5524
E-mail: customer.service@mcgraw-hill.com
URL: http://www.mcgraw-hill.com

Blythe Camenson. Second edition, 2001. $14.95 (paper). 256 pages.

★5191★ How to Successfully Start a Grassroots Non-Profit Organization

Achievement U.S.A. Corporation
PO Box 9328
Washington, DC 20005
Ph: (202)319-9057   Fr: 800-891-3296

Darryl Webster. 2001. $20.00 The author provides a unique grassroots perspective on the pros and cons of getting started in the non-profit world. This book was written to save its reader's money, time and energy looking for information to help them start a non-profit organization. Some of the subjects covered in the book are: incorporating, obtaining tax exemption, garnering community support, marketing, proposal writing for grants, fundraising, getting publicity, giving interviews, and also comments on the significance and impact that grass-roots' citizens are having in the non-profit sector.

★5192★ Non-Profits and Education Job Finder

Planning Communications
7215 Oak Ave.
River Forest, IL 60305-1935
Ph: (708)366-5200   Fax: (708)366-5280
Fr: 888-366-5200
E-mail: info@planningcommunications.com
URL: http://jobfindersonline.com

Daniel Lauber. 1997. $32.95; $16.95 (paper). 340 pages. Covers 1600 sources. Discusses how to use sources of non-profit sector job vacancies in a number of specialties and state-by-state, including job-matching services, job hotlines, specialty periodicals with job ads, salary surveys, and directories. Covers a variety of fields from education to religion. Includes chapters on resume and cover letter preparation and interviewing.

★5193★ Opportunities in Nonprofit Organizations

The McGraw-Hill Companies
PO Box 182604
Columbus, OH 43272
Fax: (614)759-3749   Fr: 877-883-5524
E-mail: customer.service@mcgraw-hill.com
URL: http://www.mcgraw-hill.com

Adrian Paradis. 1994. $14.95; $11.95 (paper). 151 pages. Covers a range of career opportunities with nonprofit organizations.

EMPLOYMENT AGENCIES AND SEARCH FIRMS

★5194★ Thomas R. Moore Executive Search L.L.C.

Bank of America Bldg., 2000 E Lamar Blvd., Ste. 600
Arlington, TX 76006
Ph: (817)548-8766   Fax: (817)588-3099
E-mail: trm@trmexecsearch.com
URL: http://www.trmexecsearch.com

Search firm focusing on the recruitment of experienced fundraising professionals for institutions, organizations and firms associated with the not-for-profit industry.

OTHER SOURCES

★5195★ Association of Professional Researchers for Advancement (APRA)

401 N Michigan Ave., Ste. 2200
Chicago, IL 60611
Ph: (312)321-5196   Fax: (312)673-6966
E-mail: info@aprahome.org
URL: http://www.aprahome.org

Description: Individuals involved in educational, medical, cultural, and religious organizations; fundraising consultants. Facilitates education and dissemination of information about prospect research; encourages professional development and cooperative relationships among members. Prospect research is aimed at securing gifts, grants, and charitable donations for nonprofit organizations.

★5196★ Society for Nonprofit Organizations (SNPO)

5820 Canton Center Rd., Ste. 165
Canton, MI 48187-2683
Ph: (734)451-3582   Fax: (734)451-5935
E-mail: info@snpo.org
URL: http://www.snpo.org

Description: Brings together those who serve in the nonprofit world in order to build a strong network of professionals throughout the country; provides a forum for the exchange of information, knowledge, and ideas on strengthening and increasing productivity within nonprofit organizations and among their leaders. Mission is accomplished through the publication of Nonprofit World magazine, educational programs offered by the Learning Institute, and other communications with its members.

Funeral Directors

SOURCES OF HELP-WANTED ADS

★5197★ *Funeral Monitor*
Abbott & Hast Publications
2361 Horseshoe Dr.
West Bloomfield, MI 48322
Ph: (248)737-9294   Fax: (248)737-9296
Fr: 800-453-1199
E-mail: info@abbottandhast.com
URL: http://www.funeralmonitor.com

Description: Weekly. Provides information on the funeral industry.

★5198★ *Funeral Service "Insider"*
United Communications Group
11300 Rockville Pike, Ste. 1100
Rockville, MD 20852-3030
Ph: (301)287-2326   Fax: (301)287-2904
E-mail: mgrossma@ucg.com
URL: http://www.ucg.com/products.html

Description: Weekly. Covers the latest trends in funeral service education, legislation, franchising, marketing, and consumer purchasing. Recurring features include editorials, news of research, letters to the editor, and a calendar of events.

★5199★ *NFDA Bulletin*
National Funeral Directors Association
13625 Bishop's Dr.
Brookfield, WI 53005-6607
Ph: (262)789-1880   Fax: (262)789-6977
Fr: 800-228-6332
E-mail: nfda@nfda.org
URL: http://www.nfda.org

Description: Monthly. Covers association activities and funeral business management topics. Reports on association news, government regulation, public relations issues, and local developments.

PLACEMENT AND JOB REFERRAL SERVICES

★5200★ **FuneralStaff**
4430 Wade Green Rd., Ste. 180-138
Kennesaw, GA 30144
Ph: (770)966-8048   Fax: (770)966-8049
Fr: (866)386-7823
E-mail: funeralstaff@bellsouth.net
URL: http://www.funeralstaff.com

Full service staffing and consulting firm specializing in placing funeral service professionals, administrators and support staff.

EMPLOYER DIRECTORIES AND NETWORKING LISTS

★5201★ *Associated Funeral Directors Service International-Shipping Directory*
Associated Funeral Directors International
PO Box 1347
Kingsport, TN 37662-1347
Ph: (423)392-1985   Fax: (423)392-1179
Fr: 800-346-7151

Annual. Covers funeral service field. Includes obituaries and directory and member list.

HANDBOOKS AND MANUALS

★5202★ *Choosing a Career in Mortuary Science & the Funeral Industry*
Rosen Publishing Group, Inc.
29 E. 21st St.
New York, NY 10010
Ph: (212)777-3017   Fax: (212)777-0277
Fr: 800-237-9932
URL: http://www.rosenpublishing.com/

Stair, Nancy L. 2002. $29.25. 64 pages. Descriptions of each job, qualities needed to do the job, education, training, salary, and outlook are all outlined.

★5203★ *Opportunities in Funeral Services Careers*
The McGraw-Hill Companies
PO Box 182604
Columbus, OH 43272
Fax: (614)759-3749   Fr: 877-883-5524
E-mail: customer.service@mcgraw-hill.com
URL: http://www.mcgraw-hill.com

Sacks, Terence J. 1997. $11.95 (Trade paper). 152 pages.

ONLINE JOB SOURCES AND SERVICES

★5204★ **FuneralNet.com**
E-mail: info@funeralnet.com
URL: http://www.funeralnet.com

Description: General mortuary science information site contains Funeral Careers section with information on continuing education and classifieds section with postings for internship and employment opportunities.

★5205★ **National Funeral Directors Association**
13625 Bishop's Dr.
Brookfield, WI 53005-6607
Ph: (262)789-1880   Fax: (262)789-6977
Fr: 800-228-6332
E-mail: nfda@nfda.org
URL: http://www.nfda.org

Description: Contains employment classifieds and career resources such as licensing and educational requirements, continuing education credit opportunities and more for those interested in finding a position as a funeral director.

TRADESHOWS

★5206★ Monument Builders of North America Conference

Monument Builders of North America
401 N. Michigan Ave., Ste. 2200
Chicago, IL 60611-4267
Ph: (708)803-8800   Fax: (312)673-6732
Fr: 800-233-4472
E-mail: info@monumentbuilders.org
URL: http://www.monumentbuilders.org

Annual. **Primary Exhibits:** Equipment, supplies, and services for modern and religious memorial designs.

★5207★ National Funeral Directors Association Annual Convention & Expo

National Funeral Directors Association
13625 Bishop's Dr.
Brookfield, WI 53005-6607
Ph: (262)789-1880   Fax: (262)789-6977
Fr: 800-228-6332
E-mail: nfda@nfda.org
URL: http://www.nfda.org

Annual. **Primary Exhibits:** Equipment, supplies, and services for funeral directors and morticians.

★5208★ New Jersey State Funeral Directors Association Convention

New Jersey State Funeral Directors
  Association
PO Box L
Manasquan, NJ 08736
Ph: (732)974-9444   Fax: (732)974-8144

E-mail: njsfda@njsfda.org
URL: http://www.njsfda.org

Annual. **Primary Exhibits:** Funeral industry equipment, supplies, and services.

★5209★ South Dakota Funeral Directors Association Annual Convention

South Dakota Funeral Directors
  Association
106 W Capitol Ave.
PO Box 1037
Pierre, SD 57501-1037
Ph: (605)224-1353   Fax: (605)224-7426
URL: http://www.nfda.org

Annual. **Primary Exhibits:** Caskets, chemical supplies, publications, clothing, coaches, accounting services, computer services, vaults, funeral vehicles, and cemetery monument dealers. **Dates and Locations:** 2008 May 12-13; Sioux Falls, SD; Ramkota Hotel and Convention Center; 2009 May 11-12; Sioux Falls, SD; Ramkota Hotel and Convention Center.

OTHER SOURCES

★5210★ Illinois Funeral Directors Association

215 S Grand Ave W
Springfield, IL 62704-3838
Ph: (217)525-2000   Fax: (217)525-8342
Fr: 800-240-4332
E-mail: info@ifda.org

URL: http://www.ifda.org

Members: Funeral Directors seeking a common voice, a way to share information, ideas and methods, and to protect themselves and consumers through legislation. **Activities:** Offers services to members and the public, including a credit union, funeral financing, legislative lobbying, and a job location service.

★5211★ New York State Funeral Directors Association, Inc.

426 New Karner Rd.
Albany, NY 12205
Ph: (518)452-8230   Fax: (518)452-8667
Fr: 800-291-2629
E-mail: info@nysfda.org
URL: http://www.nysfda.org

Description: Aims to enhance the environment in which the members operate and to promote the highest standards of funeral service to the public.

★5212★ Texas Funeral Directors Association

1513 S I H 35
Austin, TX 78741-2598
Fax: (512)443-3559   Fr: 800-460-8332
E-mail: admin@tfda.com
URL: http://www.tfda.com

Professional association for the funeral industry providing personal contact, group meetings and publications.

Gaming Services Workers

SOURCES OF HELP-WANTED ADS

★5213★ Gaming Morning Report

Fantini's Gaming Report
PO Box 1676
Dover, DE 19903
Ph: (302)730-3793   Fr: (866)683-4357

Daily. News, research, and analysis for industry executives.

PLACEMENT AND JOB REFERRAL SERVICES

★5214★ Gaming Search Associates, Inc.

23798 Via Sergovia
Murrieta, CA 92562
Ph: (951)698-9944   Fax: (951)698-5410
E-mail: jodi@gsainc.net
URL: http://gsainc.net

An exective search firm specializing in the casino and hotel industries.

EMPLOYER DIRECTORIES AND NETWORKING LISTS

★5215★ American Casino Guide

Casino Vacations
PO Box 703
Dania, FL 33004
Ph: (954)989-2766   Fax: (954)966-7048
URL: http://www.americancasinoguide.com

Annual, November; latest edition 2007. $16.95. Covers more than 700 casino/resorts, including riverboat casinos and Indian casinos, in the U.S. Entries include: Casino name, address, phone, toll-free number, room rates, dining information, games of-

fered, features, web site addresses. Arrangement: Geographical. Indexes: Name.

★5216★ Career Opportunities in Casinos and Casino Hotels

Facts On File Inc.
132 W 31st St., 17th Fl.
New York, NY 10001
Ph: (212)967-8800   Fax: 800-678-3633
Fr: 800-322-8755
URL: http://www.factsonfile.com

Irregular; Latest edition 2000. $49.50 for individuals; $44.55 for libraries. Publication includes: A directory of casinos and cruise lines, gaming conferences and expos, seminars, workshops, and industry Web sites. Principal content of publication consists of information on 100 occupations in 10 employment sections regarding careers in gaming, administration, management, security, entertainment, hotel management, and food and beverage service in the casino industry.

★5217★ Casino Vendors Guide

Casino City Press
95 Wells Ave.
Newton, MA 02459
Ph: (617)332-2850   Fax: (617)964-2280
Fr: 800-490-1715
URL: http://www.casinocitypress.com

$49.95. Covers 10,000 industry suppliers, manufacturers, and distributors, 1,000 gaming products and services, 1,500 gaming properties around the world, gaming associations, analysts, attorneys, trade shows, and trade publications. Entries include: company name, address, branch office locations, phone and fax numbers, email and website addresses, executive contacts and company description.

★5218★ Gambler's Digest

Krause Publications Inc.
700 E State St.
Iola, WI 54990-0001
Ph: (715)445-2214   Fax: (715)445-4087
Fr: 800-258-0929
URL: http://www.collect.com

$14.94 for individuals. Lists more than 1,200

gaming destinations in the U.S., including casinos, horse tracks, dog tracks, riverboats and gambling cruises. Offers articles and tips on gaming success as well as a list of gaming-related books, magazines, videos, gaming web sites and other reference sources. Publication includes: Directory details for each destination, including name, address, phone, prices, entertainment, restaurants and hotel accommodations.

★5219★ Gaming Business Directory

Casino City Press
95 Wells Ave.
Newton, MA 02459
Ph: (617)332-2850   Fax: (617)964-2280
Fr: 800-490-1715
URL: http://www.casinocitypress.com

$169.95. Covers information on more than 4,500 casinos, card rooms, horse tracks, dog tracks, and casino cruises and cruise ships, around the world, 650 major gaming property owners, and 2,000 gaming properties owned and operated. Entries include: 25,000 executive contacts, names and titles by department, property name, location and mailing addresses, and phone and fax numbers. Indexes: Alphabetical by size; alphabetical by property type.

★5220★ Gaming Products and Services-Buyers Guide Issue

RCM Enterprises Inc.
2233 University Ave. W, Ste. 410
PO Box 14268
St. Paul, MN 55114-1629
Ph: (612)473-5088   Fax: (612)473-7068
Fr: 800-451-9278

Annual, May. $25.00. Publication includes: List of companies providing products and services for the gaming industry; international coverage. Entries include: Company name, address, phone, fax, sales office location, description, geographical area served, product/service. Principal content of publication is information on gaming products. Arrangement: Alphabetical by company name. Indexes: Product/service; trade name.

★5221★ International Gaming Resource Guide

Gem Communications
1771 E Flamingo Rd., No. 208A
Las Vegas, NV 89119
Ph: (702)794-0718   Fax: (702)794-0799

Annual. Publication includes: Lists of 1,800 organizations concerned with gaming and wagering establishments, including casinos, lotteries, racing commissions, race tracks, jai alai frontons, etc., and regulatory agencies. Entries include: Listings in the 'Corporate Profiles' section (which expand selected listings) include name, parent company name, address, mailing address (if different), phone, names and titles of key personnel. Other listings show name, address, and phone only. Arrangement: Alphabetical.

★5222★ Thoroughbred Racing Associations of North America-Directory and Record Book

Thoroughbred Racing Associations
420 Fair Hill Dr., Ste. 1
Elkton, MD 21921-2573
Ph: (410)392-9200   Fax: (410)398-1366

Annual, April. $18.00 for individuals. Covers features on member thoroughbred race-tracks in the United States and Canada and the Eclipse Awards. Entries include: For member tracks—Corporate name, track name, address, phone, names of officers and staff, track data, equipment data, capacity, prices, and brief history of the track. Listings for nonmember tracks do not include descriptive data or history. Arrangement: Alphabetical by track name.

EMPLOYMENT AGENCIES AND SEARCH FIRMS

★5223★ The IMC Group of Companies Ltd.

120 White Plains Rd., Ste. 405
Tarrytown, NY 10591
Ph: (914)468-7050   Fax: (914)468-7051
E-mail: herbert.regehly@the-imc.com
URL: http://www.the-imc.com

International executive recruiting and man-agement consulting company providing leading-edge services for the hospitality, leisure, entertainment, gaming and new media industries throughout the United States, Europe, Africa, Asia Pacific and Latin America.

TRADESHOWS

★5224★ North American Association of State and Provincial Lotteries Conference and Trade Show

North American Association of State and Provincial Lotteries
2775 Bishop Rd., Ste. B
Willoughby Hills, OH 44092
Ph: (216)241-2310   Fax: (216)241-4350
E-mail: NASPLHQ@aol.com
URL: http://www.naspl.org

Annual. **Primary Exhibits:** Lottery equipment, supplies, and services.

★5225★ World Gaming Congress and Expo

Ascend Media Gaming Group
1771 E Flamingo Rd., Ste.208A
Las Vegas, NV 89119
Fax: (702)794-0799
E-mail: sgibbs@ascendmedia.com
URL: http://www.ascendgaming.com

Primary Exhibits: Casino operations equipment, supplies, and services. Hotel, & resort systems, services. Decorative furnishings and fixtures.

OTHER SOURCES

★5226★ American Gaming Association

1299 Pennsylvania Ave. NW, Ste. 1175
Washington, DC 20004
Ph: (202)552-2675   Fax: (202)552-2676
E-mail: info@americangaming.org
URL: http://www.americangaming.org

Description: Represents the commercial casino entertainment industry by addressing federal legislative and regulatory issues affecting its members and their employees and customers, such as federal taxation, regulatory issues, and travel and tourism matters.

★5227★ Gaming Standards Association (GSA)

39355 California St., Ste. 307
Fremont, CA 94538
Ph: (510)774-4007   Fax: (510)608-5917
E-mail: info@gamingstandards.com
URL: http://www.gamingstandards.com

Description: Gaming manufacturers, suppliers and operators. Promotes identification, definition, development, and implementation of open standards to facilitate innovation, education and communication for the gaming industry.

★5228★ International Simulation and Gaming Association (ISAGA)

George Washington University
School of Business and Public Mgt.
Monroe Hall
Washington, DC 20052
Ph: (202)994-6918
E-mail: lobuts@gwu.edu
URL: http://www.isaga.info

Description: Individuals interested in any facet of simulation and gaming. Maintains resource lists; conducts specialized education; sponsors workshops, symposia, and research activities.

★5229★ North American Gaming Regulators Association

333 Ravenswood Ave.
Menlo Park, CA 94025-3493
Ph: (651)203-7244   Fax: (651)290-2266
E-mail: info@nagra.org
URL: http://www.nagra.org

Description: Brings together agencies that regulate gaming activities and provides a forum for the mutual exchange of regulatory information and techniques. Collects and disseminates regulatory and enforcement information, procedures, and experiences from all jurisdictions provided on-going gaming education and training for all members.

General Managers and Top Executives

SOURCES OF HELP-WANTED ADS

★5230★ Academy of Management Journal

Academy of Management
PO Box 3020
Briarcliff Manor, NY 10510-8020
Ph: (914)923-2607   Fax: (914)923-2615
URL: http://www.aom.pace.edu/amr

Bimonthly. Professional journal covering management.

★5231★ Academy of Management Learning & Education

Academy of Management
PO Box 3020
Briarcliff Manor, NY 10510-8020
Ph: (914)923-2607   Fax: (914)923-2615
URL: http://journals.aomonline.org/amle

Quarterly. $80.00/year for individuals, print; $130.00/year for individuals, print & online; $165.00/year for libraries, print; $215.00/year for libraries, print and online; $100.00/year for individuals, other countries, print; $150.00/year for individuals, other countries, print & online; $185.00/year for other countries, print, corporate library; $235.00/year for other countries, print & online, corporate library. Journal covering management issues for professionals.

★5232★ AMI Bulletin

Association for Management Information in Financial Services (AMI)
3895 Fairfax Court
Atlanta, GA 30339
Ph: (770)444-3557   Fax: (770)444-9084
E-mail: ami@amifs.org
URL: http://www.amifs.org/

Description: Quarterly. Monitors events and profiles members and committees. Recurring features include reports of meetings and workshops and a calendar of events.

★5233★ Association News

Schneider Publishing Company Inc.
11835 W Olympic Blvd., 12th Fl.
Los Angeles, CA 90064
Ph: (310)577-3700   Fax: (310)577-3715
Fr: 877-577-3700
URL: http://www.associationnews.com/

Monthly. Free. Magazine containing management and meeting plan information for association executives and meeting planners.

★5234★ Business Performance Management

Penton Media Inc.
249 W 17th St.
New York, NY 10011
Ph: (212)204-4200
URL: http://www.bpmmag.net/

Free to qualified subscribers. Magazine for business managers. Covers organizing, automating, and analyzing of business methodologies and processes.

★5235★ CFO

CFO Publishing
253 Summer St.
Boston, MA 02210
Ph: (617)345-9700
URL: http://www.cfo.com/magazine/?f=header

Monthly. Business magazine for small to mid-sized companies.

★5236★ CXO

IDG Communications Inc.
5 Speen St., 3rd. Fl
Framingham, MA 01701
Ph: (508)875-5000   Fax: (508)988-7888
URL: http://www.idg.com

Monthly. Magazine providing technology information for chief officers and managers.

★5237★ D & O Advisor

American Lawyer Media L.P.
345 Pk. Ave. S
New York, NY 10010
Ph: (212)779-9200   Fax: (212)481-8110
Fr: 800-888-8300
URL: http://www.alm.com

Quarterly. Magazine that offers advice and perspective on corporate oversight responsibilities for directors and officers.

★5238★ E Journal of Organizational Learning and Leadership

WeLEAD Inc.
PO Box 202
Litchfield, OH 44253
Fr: 877-778-5494
URL: http://www.weleadinlearning.org/ejournal.htm

Continuous. Free. Online academic journal about organizational leadership.

★5239★ Executive Leadership

National Institute of Business Management
PO Box 906
Williamsport, PA 17703-9933
Ph: 800-433-0622   Fax: (570)567-0166
Fr: 800-543-2049
E-mail: customer@nibm.net
URL: http://www.nibm.net/newsletter.asp?pub=EL

Description: Monthly. Shows the reader how to become a better leader. Contains information on taking charge in the workplace, enjoying a wider business perspective, leading organizations to more efficiency and greater success, and rising faster in the field of management.

★5240★ Executive Legal Adviser

American Lawyer Media L.P.
345 Pk. Ave. S
New York, NY 10010
Ph: (212)779-9200   Fax: (212)481-8110
Fr: 800-888-8300
URL: http://www.executivelegaladviser.com

Bimonthly. Free to qualified subscribers.

Magazine that offers legal advice for corporate executives.

★5241★ Fleet Maintenance

Cygnus Business Media Inc.
3 Huntington Quadrangle, Ste. 301 N
Melville, NY 11747
Ph: (631)845-2700   Fax: (631)845-7109
Fr: 800-308-6397
URL: http://www.fleetmag.com

Bimonthly. Business tabloid magazine offering a chapterized curriculum of technical, regulatory and managerial information designed to help maintenance managers, directors and supervisors better perform their jobs and reduce their overall cost-per-mile.

★5242★ Forbes

Forbes Magazine
90 5th Ave.
New York, NY 10011
Ph: (212)366-8900   Fr: 800-295-0893
URL: http://www.forbes.com

Biweekly. $30.00/year for individuals, per year; $1.00/year for single issue. Magazine reporting on industry, business and finance management.

★5243★ Forrester

Forrester Research Inc.
400 Technology Sq.
Cambridge, MA 02139
Ph: (617)613-6000   Fax: (617)613-5000
URL: http://www.forrester.com/mag

Free. Journal that aims to provide ideas and advice that are relevant to today's CEOs.

★5244★ Franchising World

International Franchise Association
1501 K St. NW, Ste. 350
Washington, DC 20005
Ph: (202)628-8000   Fax: (202)628-0812
Fr: 800-543-1038
URL: http://www.franchise.org/

Monthly. $50.00/year for individuals. Trade magazine covering topics of interest to franchise company executives and the business world.

★5245★ IndustryWeek

Penton Media Inc.
1300 E 9th St.
Cleveland, OH 44114
Ph: (216)696-7000   Fax: (216)696-1752
E-mail: iwinfo@industryweek.com
URL: http://www.industryweek.com

Monthly. Magazine containing articles to help industry executives sharpen their managerial skills and increase their effectiveness.

★5246★ International Journal of Business Research

Academy of International Business and
    Economics
PO Box 2536
Ceres, CA 95307
URL: http://www.aibe.org

Peer-reviewed journal publishing theoretical, conceptual, and applied research on topics related to research, practice and teaching in all areas of business, management, and marketing.

★5247★ Journal of Academic Leadership

Academic Leadership
600 Park St.
Rarick Hall 219
Hays, KS 67601-4099
Ph: (785)628-4547
URL: http://www.academicleadership.org/

Journal focusing on the leadership issues in the academic world.

★5248★ Journal of Business and Psychology

Springer-Verlag New York Inc.
233 Spring St.
New York, NY 10013
Ph: (212)460-1500   Fax: (212)460-1575
URL: http://www.springer.com/journal/10869/

Journal covering all aspects of psychology that apply to the business segment. Includes topics such as personnel selection and training, organizational assessment and development, risk management and loss control, marketing and consumer behavior research.

★5249★ Journal of International Business Strategy

Academy of International Business and
    Economics
PO Box 2536
Ceres, CA 95307
URL: http://www.AIBE.org

Peer-reviewed journal publishing theoretical, conceptual, and applied research on topics related to strategy in international business.

★5250★ The Los Angeles Business Journal

The Los Angeles Business Journal
5700 Wilshire, No. 170
Los Angeles, CA 90036
Ph: (213)549-5225   Fax: (213)549-5255
URL: http://www.labusinessjournal.com

Weekly (Mon.). $99.95/year for individuals; $179.95 for two years. Newspaper (tabloid) covering local business news, business trends, executive profiles, and information for the Los Angeles area executive.

★5251★ Management Research

M.E. Sharpe Inc.
80 Business Pk. Dr.
Armonk, NY 10504
Ph: (914)273-1800   Fax: (914)273-2106
Fr: 800-541-6563
URL: http://www.mesharpe.com/mall/
results1.asp?ACR=JMR

$72.00/year for individuals; $349.00/year for institutions; $84.00/year for other countries, individual; $391.00/year for institutions, other countries. International journal dedicated to advancing the understanding of management in private and public sector organizations through empirical investigation and theoretical analysis. Attempts to promote an international dialogue between researchers, improve the understanding of the nature of management in different settings, and achieve a reasonable transfer of research results to management practice in several contexts. Receptive to research across a broad range of management topics such as human resource management, organizational behavior, organizational theory, and strategic management. While not regional in nature, articles dealing with Iberoamerican issues are particularly welcomed.

★5252★ The Organization Development Institute

International Registry of Organization
    Development Professionals
11234 Walnut Ridge Rd.
Chesterland, OH 44026
Ph: (440)729-7419
URL: http://www.odinstitute.org

Description: Monthly. Serves organization development professionals, teachers of organizational behavior, management consultants, personnel directors and executives by carrying news items, interest surveys, economic information, and committee reports. Recurring features include announcements of conferences, meetings, publications, consulting opportunities, and employment openings. Subscription includes annual publication titled The International Registry of Organization Development Professionals and Organization Development Handbook, and copies of The Organizational Development Journal.

★5253★ Organization Management Journal

Eastern Academy of Management
c/o Craig Tunwall, VP
Empire State College
2805 State Hwy. 67
Johnstown, NY 12095
Ph: (518)762-4651   Fax: (518)736-1716
URL: http://www1.wnec.edu/omj

Free to qualified subscribers. Refereed, online journal focusing on organization management issues.

★5254★ Public Performance and Management Review

M.E. Sharpe Inc.
80 Business Pk. Dr.
Armonk, NY 10504
Ph: (914)273-1800   Fax: (914)273-2106
Fr: 800-541-6563
URL: http://www.mesharpe.com/mall/results1.asp?ACR=pmr

Quarterly. $85.00/year for individuals; $399.00/year for institutions; $101.00/year for other countries, individual; $431.00/year for institutions, other countries. Journal addressing a broad range of factors influencing the performance of public and nonprofit organizations and agencies. Aims to facilitate the development of innovative techniques and encourage a wider application of those already established; stimulate research and critical thinking about the relationship between public and private management theories; present integrated analyses of theories, concepts, strategies and techniques dealing with productivity, measurement and related questions of performance improvement; and provide a forum for practitioner-academic exchange. Continuing themes include managing for productivity, measuring and evaluating performance, improving budget strategies, managing human resources, building partnerships, and applying new technologies.

★5255★ Regional Aviation News

Access Intelligence L.L.C.
4 Choke Cherry Rd.
Rockville, MD 20850
Ph: (301)354-2000   Fax: (301)309-3847
Fr: 800-777-5006
E-mail: info@accessintel.com
URL: http://www.accessintel.com

Description: Weekly. Covers the commuter/regional airline industry, including airline management, marketing, labor, personnel changes, aircraft acquisitions, new products, and the financial and operational environment. Recurring features include interviews, news of research, a calendar of events, reports of meetings, job listings, and notices of publications available.

★5256★ San Diego Business Journal

San Diego Business Journal
4909 Murphy Canyon Rd., Ste. 200
San Diego, CA 92123
Ph: (858)277-6359
URL: http://www.sdbj.com

Weekly (Mon.). Metropolitan business newspaper specializing in investigative and enterprise reporting on San Diego County businesses and related issues.

★5257★ San Diego Daily Transcript

San Diego Daily Transcript
2131 3rd Ave.
San Diego, CA 92101
Ph: (619)232-4381   Fax: (619)236-8126
E-mail: webmaster@sddt.com
URL: http://www.sddt.com

Daily (morn.). $200.00/year for individuals,

print + online; $337.50 for two years, print + online. Local business newspaper.

★5258★ San Francisco Business Times

American City Business Journals Inc.
120 W Morehead St., Ste. 200
Charlotte, NC 28202
Ph: (704)973-1000   Fax: (704)973-1001
E-mail: sanfrancisco@bizjournals.com
URL: http://sanfrancisco.bizjournals.com/sanfrancisco

Weekly. $93.00/year for individuals; $158.00 for individuals, for two years; $188.00/year for individuals, for three years. Local business newspaper (tabloid) serving the San Francisco Bay Area.

★5259★ Supply Chain Management Review

Reed Business Information
225 Wyman St.
Waltham, MA 02451-1216
URL: http://www.scmr.com

$199.00/year for U.S. and Canada; $241.00/year for other countries. Publication covering business and management.

PLACEMENT AND JOB REFERRAL SERVICES

★5260★ The International Alliance for Women (TIAW)

8405 Greensboro Dr., Ste. 800
McLean, VA 22102-5120
Ph: (703)506-3284   Fax: (905)305-1548
Fr: (866)533-8429
E-mail: info@tiaw.org
URL: http://www.tiaw.org

Members: Local networks comprising 50,000 professional and executive women in 12 countries; individual businesswomen without a network affiliation are alliance associates. **Purpose:** Promotes recognition of the achievements of women in business. Encourages placement of women in senior executive positions. Maintains high standards of professional competence among members. Facilitates communication on an international scale among professional women's networks and their members. Represents members' interests before policymaking business and government. **Activities:** Sponsors programs that support equal opportunity and enhance members' business and professional skills. Operates appointments and directors service. Maintains speakers' bureau.

★5261★ National Black MBA Association (NBMBAA)

180 N Michigan Ave., Ste. 1400
Chicago, IL 60601
Ph: (312)236-2622   Fax: (312)236-0390
E-mail: mail@nbmbaa.org

URL: http://www.nbmbaa.org

Description: Business professionals, lawyers, accountants, and engineers concerned with the role of blacks who hold advanced management degrees. Works to create economic and intellectual wealth for the black community. Encourages blacks to pursue continuing business education; assists students preparing to enter the business world. Provides programs for minority youths, students, and professionals, and entrepreneurs including workshops, panel discussions, and Destination MBA seminar. Sponsors job fairs. Works with graduate schools. Operates job placement service.

EMPLOYER DIRECTORIES AND NETWORKING LISTS

★5262★ Careers in Focus: Business

Facts On File Inc.
132 W 31st St., 17th Fl.
New York, NY 10001
Ph: (212)967-8800   Fax: 800-678-3633
Fr: 800-322-8755
URL: http://www.factsonfile.com

Latest edition 2nd, 2005. $29.95 for individuals; $26.95 for libraries. Covers an overview of business, followed by a selection of jobs profiled in detail, including the nature of the job, earnings, prospects for employment, what kind of training and skills it requires, and sources for further information.

★5263★ Careers in Focus: Business Managers

Facts On File Inc.
132 W 31st St., 17th Fl.
New York, NY 10001
Ph: (212)967-8800   Fax: 800-678-3633
Fr: 800-322-8755
URL: http://www.factsonfile.com

Published 2003. $29.95 for individuals; $26.95 for libraries. Covers an overview of business managers, followed by a selection of jobs profiled in detail, including the nature of the job, earnings, prospects for employment, what kind of training and skills it requires, and sources for further information.

★5264★ D & B Million Dollar Directory

Dun & Bradstreet Corp.
103 JFK Pkwy.
Short Hills, NJ 07078
Ph: (973)921-5500   Fax: (973)921-6056
Fr: 800-234-3867
URL: http://www.dnbmdd.com

Annual. Covers 1,600,000 public and private businesses with either a net worth of $500,000 or more, 250 or more employees at that location, or $25,000,000 or more in sales volume; includes industrial corporations, utilities, transportation companies, bank and trust companies, stock brokers, mutual and stock insurance companies, wholesalers, retailers, and domestic subsidiaries of foreign corporations. Entries include: Company name, address, phone, state of incorporation; annual sales; number of employees, company ticker symbol on stock exchange, Standard Industrial Classification (SIC) number, line of business; principal bank, accounting firm; parent company name, current ownership date, division names and functions, directors or trustees; names, titles, functions of principal executives; number of employees; import/export designation. Arrangement: Alphabetical, cross referenced geographically and by industry classification. Indexes: Geographical (with address and SIC); product by SIC (with address).

★5265★ **Financial Managers Society-Membership and Peer Consulting Directory**

Financial Managers Society
100 W Monroe, Ste. 810
Chicago, IL 60603
Ph: (312)578-1300   Fax: (312)578-1308
Fr: 800-275-4367
URL: http://www.fmsinc.org

Annual. Covers executives and managers of financial institutions.

★5266★ **Forbes-Up-and-Comers 200**

Forbes Magazine
90 5th Ave.
New York, NY 10011
Ph: (212)366-8900   Fr: 800-295-0893
URL: http://www.forbes.com

Weekly. Publication includes: List of 200 small companies judged to be high quality and fast-growing on the basis of 5-year return on equity and other qualitative measurements. Also includes a list of the 100 best small companies outside the U.S. Note: Issue does not carry address or CEO information for the foreign companies. Entries include: Company name, shareholdings data on chief executive officer; financial data. Arrangement: Alphabetical. Indexes: Ranking.

★5267★ **Inc.-The Inc. 500 Issue**

Gruner & Jahr USA Publishing
375 Lexington Ave. 10th Fl.
New York, NY 10017-4024
URL: http://www.inc.com

Annual, October. Publication includes: List of 500 fastest-growing privately held companies based on percentage increase in sales over the five year period prior to compilation of current year's list. Entries include: Company name, headquarters city, description of business, year founded, number of employees, sales five years earlier and currently, profitability range, and growth statistics. Arrangement: Ranked by sales growth.

★5268★ **MBA Employment Guide Report**

Association of MBA Executives Inc.
5 Summit Pl.
Branford, CT 06405-3527
Ph: (203)315-5221   Fax: (203)483-6186

Continuous. Database covers: More than 4,000 firms that employ persons with Master of Business Administration degrees. More detailed profiles are given for 100 firms selected on the basis of their on-campus recruitment activity. Custom reports are issued upon request at $10.00 per report. Database includes: For companies covered in detail–Name, headquarters location, description of business, current recruitment objectives, employment policies, benefits offered, name and address of employment representative, financial data. For others–Name, location, contact person and telephone number, parent company (if any), code for primary line of business.

★5269★ **Peterson's Job Opportunities for Business Majors**

Peterson's
Princeton Pke. Corporate Ctr., 2000 Lenox Dr.
PO Box 67005
Lawrenceville, NJ 08648
Ph: (609)896-1800   Fax: (609)896-4531
Fr: 800-338-3282
URL: http://www.petersons.com/

Irregular; latest edition 16th, 2000. Covers the 2,000 largest U.S. employers hiring in several fields, including financial services, management consulting, consumer products, and media/entertainment. Entries include: Organization name, address, phone, name and title of contact, number of employees, type of organization. Arrangement: Alphabetical. Indexes: Type of organization.

★5270★ **Standard & Poor's Register of Corporations, Directors and Executives**

Standard & Poor's
55 Water St.
New York, NY 10041
Ph: (212)438-1000   Fax: (212)438-2000
Fr: 800-852-1641
URL: http://www2.standardandpoors.com/

Annual, January; supplements in April, July, and October. Covers over 55,000 public and privately held corporations in the United States, including names and titles of over 400,000 officials (Volume 1); 70,000 biographies of directors and executives (Volume 2). Entries include: For companies–Name, address, phone, names of principal executives and accountants; primary bank, primary law firm, number of employees, estimated annual sales, outside directors, Standard Industrial Classification (SIC) code, product or service provided. For directors and executives–Name, home and principal business addresses, date and place of birth, fraternal organization memberships, business affiliations. Arrangement: Alphabetical. Indexes: Volume 3 indexes companies geographically, by Standard Industrial Classification (SIC) code, and by corporate family groups.

HANDBOOKS AND MANUALS

★5271★ **Better Resumes for Executives and Professionals**

Barron's Educational Series, Inc.
250 Wireless Blvd.
PO Box 8040
Hauppauge, NY 11788-3917
Ph: (631)434-3311   Fax: (631)434-3723
Fr: 800-645-3476
E-mail: fbrown@barronseduc.com
URL: http://barronseduc.com

Robert F. Wilson and Adele Lewis. Fourth edition, 2000. $16.95 (paper). 280 pages. Explains how to write resumes and cover letters for executives and professionals in most fields.

★5272★ **Careers in International Business**

The McGraw-Hill Companies
PO Box 182604
Columbus, OH 43272
Fax: (614)759-3749   Fr: 877-883-5524
E-mail: customer.service@mcgraw-hill.com
URL: http://www.mcgraw-hill.com

Ed Halloran. Second edition, 2003. $14.95 (paper). 192 pages.

★5273★ **The Directory of Executive Recruiters**

Kennedy Information Inc.
1 Phoenix Mill Lane, 3rd Fl.
Peterborough, NH 03458
Ph: (603)924-1006   Fax: (603)924-4460
Fr: 800-531-0007
E-mail: bookstore@kennedyinfo.com
URL: http://www.kennedyinfo.com/

2006. 1200 pages. Contains detailed contact information for over 5,000 search firms located in the United States, Canada, and Mexico.

★5274★ **The Executive Job Search: A Comprehensive Handbook for Seasoned Professionals**

The McGraw-Hill Companies
PO Box 182604
Columbus, OH 43272
Fax: (614)759-3749   Fr: 877-883-5524
E-mail: customer.service@mcgraw-hill.com
URL: http://www.mcgraw-hill.com

Orrin G. Wood. $15.95 (paper). Illustrated. 256 pages. 2003. Executive job search manual.

★5275★ **Executive Search Firms and Employment Agencies in Seattle: Job-Search Resources for the Executive, Manager and Professional**

Barrett Street Productions
PO Box 99642
Seattle, WA 98199
Ph: (206)284-8202   Fax: (206)352-0944

Linda Carlson. 1998. $21.95 (paper). 192 pages. Contains information regarding employment agencies, recruiting and job hunting in Seattle, Washington area.

★5276★ Expert Resumes for Managers and Executives

Jist Works
875 Montreal Way
St. Paul, MN 55102
Fr: 800-648-5478
E-mail: info@jist.com
URL: http://www.jist.com

Wendy S. Enelow, Louise M. Kursmark. 2007. $16.95. 274 pages.

★5277★ Job Seekers Guide to Executive Recruiters

John Wiley & Sons Inc.
1 Wiley Dr.
Somerset, NJ 08873
Ph: (732)469-4400   Fax: (732)302-2300
Fr: 800-225-5945
E-mail: custserv@wiley.com
URL: http://www.wiley.com/WileyCDA/

Christopher W. Hunt. Scott A. Scanlon. 1997. $34.95 (paper). 516 pages. The authors give a complete guide and listing of over 5,200 recruiters, including names, addresses, phone numbers, as well as lowest and average salary ranges, industry specialization, function specialization, and recruiter classification.

★5278★ Making a Life, Making a Living: Reclaiming Your Purpose and Passion in Business and in Life

Hachette Book Group
237 Park Ave.
New York, NY 10017
Ph: (212)522-7200
URL: http://www.hachettebookgroupusa.com/

Mark Albion. 2000. $28.00. 304 pages.

★5279★ Opportunities in Business Management Careers

The McGraw-Hill Companies
PO Box 182604
Columbus, OH 43272
Fax: (614)759-3749   Fr: 877-883-5524
E-mail: customer.service@mcgraw-hill.com
URL: http://www.mcgraw-hill.com

Irene Place and Lewis Baratz. 1997. $11.95 (paper). 148 pages. Provides guidance on the most effective channels to management positions.

★5280★ The Secrets of Executive Search: Professional Strategies for Managing Your personal Job Search

John Wiley & Sons, Inc.
111 River St.
Hoboken, NJ 07030
Ph: (201)748-6000   Fax: (201)748-6088
Fr: 800-255-5945
E-mail: custserv@wiley.com
URL: http://www.wiley.com/WileyCDA/

Robert Melancon. September 2002. $16.95. 208 pages.

EMPLOYMENT AGENCIES AND SEARCH FIRMS

★5281★ 306 Search Advisors Inc.

230 Park Ave., Ste. 1000
New York, NY 10169
Ph: (646)435-5751
E-mail: info@360advisors.com
URL: http://www.360advisors.com

Executive search firm.

★5282★ A-L Associates Inc.

546 5th Ave., Fl. 6
New York, NY 10036
Ph: (212)878-9000   Fax: (212)878-9096
Fr: 800-292-1390
URL: http://www.alassoc.com

Executive search firm.

★5283★ Abeln, Magy & Associates

800 E. Wayzata Blvd., Ste. 200
Wayzata, MN 55391
Ph: (952)476-4938   Fax: (952)404-7470
E-mail: info@abelnmagy.com
URL: http://www.abelnmagy.com

Executive search firm.

★5284★ ADA Executive Search Inc.

945 Ben Franklin Dr., Ste. 1
Sarasota, FL 34236
Ph: (941)388-5343   Fax: (941)388-5343
E-mail: adaeziman@adaexecutivesearch.com
URL: http://www.adaexecutivesearch.com/

Executive search firm.

★5285★ Adams & Associates International

520 Shorely Dr. 201
PO Box 129
Barrington, IL 60011-0129
Ph: (847)304-5300   Fax: (847)400-0798
URL: http://www.leanthinking.net

Global executive search firm.

★5286★ Adams Executive Search

3416 Fairfield Trail
Clearwater, FL 33761
Ph: (727)772-1536   Fax: (815)328-3792
E-mail: info@axsearch.com
URL: http://www.axsearch.com

Executive search firm.

★5287★ Adams Partners

205 W. Wacker Dr., Ste. 620
Chicago, IL 60606
Ph: (312)673-0389   Fax: (312)673-0390
URL: http://www.adamspartners.com

Executive search firm.

★5288★ The Adkins Group Inc.

3105 Manchaca Rd., Ste. A
Austin, TX 78704
Ph: (512)916-9600   Fax: (512)916-9665
Fr: (866)916-9600
E-mail: info@theadkinsgroup.com
URL: http://www.theadkinsgroup.com

Executive search firm.

★5289★ Adler Management Inc.

66 Witherspoon St., Ste. 315
Princeton, NJ 08542
Ph: (609)443-3300   Fax: (609)443-4439
E-mail: jadler@amiconsulting.com
URL: http://www.amiconsulting.com

Executive search firm.

★5290★ Advantage Partners Inc.

29225 Chagrin Blvd., Ste. 300
Cleveland, OH 44122
Ph: (216)514-1212   Fax: (216)514-1213
E-mail: resume@advantagepartnersinc.com
URL: http://www.advantagepartnersinc.com

Executive search firm.

★5291★ Aegis Group Search Consultants LLC

41451 W. 11 Mile Rd.
Novi, MI 48375-1855
Ph: (248)344-1450   Fax: (248)347-2231
E-mail: resume@aegis-group.com
URL: http://www.aegis-group.com

Executive search and consultant firm. Focuses on the medical industry.

★5292★ AET Advisors LLC

4875 Olde Towne Pkwy., Ste. 150
Marietta, GA 30068
Ph: (770)578-6556
E-mail: aetadvisors@mindspring.com

Executive search and consultant firm. Focuses on the real estate industry.

★5293★ AGORA Consulting

1880 Office Club Pointe
Colorado Springs, CO 80920
Ph: (719)219-0360   Fax: (719)272-8361
E-mail: agora@agoraconsulting.com
URL: http://www.agoraconsulting.com

An executive search firm that recruits for senior-level management positions, primarily in the high-tech industry. Consultants research target companies and candidates, set up interviews, perform reference checks, and assist with salary negotiations. Provides a range of other consulting services, including providing competitive intelligence and market research services, as well as advising on staffing strategy and organizational design.

★5294★ Ahern Search Partners
3982 Powell Rd. Ste. 205
Powell, OH 43065
Ph: (614)436-4126   Fax: (614)436-4125
E-mail: mahern@ahernsearch.com
URL: http://www.ahernsearch.com/
Executive search firm. Concentrates on the healthcare market.

★5295★ AKS Associates Ltd.
175 Derby St., Ste. 27
Hingham, MA 02043
Ph: (781)740-1704   Fax: (781)740-4383
E-mail: aks@akssearch.com
URL: http://www.akssearch.com
Senior search firm. Concentrates on the financial industry.

★5296★ Alexander Associates
993 Lenox Dr., Ste. 200
Lawrenceville, NJ 08648
Ph: (609)844-7597   Fax: (609)844-7589
E-mail: info@alexassociates.com
URL: http://www.alexassociates.com
Executive search firm for the Boston to DC area.

★5297★ The Alexander Group
2700 Post Oak Blvd., Ste. 2400
Houston, TX 77056
Ph: (713)993-7900   Fax: (713)993-7979
E-mail: info@thealexandergroup.com
URL: http://www.thealexandergroup.com
Executive search firm. Second location in San Francisco.

★5298★ Alexander Ross & Company
100 Park Ave., 34th Fl.
New York, NY 10017
Ph: (212)889-9333   Fax: (212)843-3411
E-mail: info@alexanderross.com
URL: http://www.alexanderross.com
Executive search firm.

★5299★ The Alfus Group Inc.
353 Lexington Ave., Fl. 8
New York, NY 10016
Ph: (212)599-1000   Fax: (212)599-1523
E-mail: mail@thealfusgroup.com
URL: http://www.thealfusgroup.com
Executive search firm. Specializes in the hospitality industry.

★5300★ Allen Associates
4555 Lake Forest Dr., 6th Fl.
Cincinnati, OH 45242
Ph: (513)563-3040
E-mail: feedback@allensearch.com

URL: http://www.allensearch.com
Executive senior-level search firm.

★5301★ Allen Austin
4543 Post Oak Place Dr., Ste. 217
Houston, TX 77027
Ph: (713)355-1900   Fax: (713)355-1901
E-mail: randrews@allenaustinsearch.com
URL: http://www.allenaustinsearch.com
Executive search firm. Branches in North Carolina and Dallas.

★5302★ Allen Evans Klein International
305 Madison Ave., Ste. 2228
New York, NY 10165
Ph: (212)983-9300   Fax: (212)983-9272
E-mail: info@allenevans.com
URL: http://www.allenevans.com
Global Executive search firm.

★5303★ Allerton Heneghan & O'Neill
1 Tower Ln., Ste. 1700
Oakbrook Terrace, IL 60181
Ph: (630)645-2294   Fax: (630)645-2298
E-mail: info@ahosearch.com
URL: http://www.ahosearch.com
Executive search firm.

★5304★ Alliance Search Management Inc.
594 Sawdust Rd., Ste. 194
The Woodlands, TX 77380
Ph: (281)367-8630   Fr: 800-444-0573
E-mail: kathy@alliancesearch.com
URL: http://www.alliancesearch.com
Employment agency.

★5305★ AllianceSource LLC
865 United Nations Plaza, Fl. 13A
New York, NY 10017
Ph: (212)308-1095
E-mail: execsearch@att.net
URL: http://www.alliancesource.net
Executive search firm.

★5306★ Ambler Associates
14881 Quorum Dr., Ste. 450
Dallas, TX 75254
Ph: (972)404-8712   Fax: (972)404-8761
Fr: 800-728-8712
Executive search firm.

★5307★ American Executive Management Inc.
30 Federal St., Ste. 102
Salem, MA 01970
Ph: (978)477-5923
E-mail: execsearch@americanexecutive.us
URL: http://www.americanexecutive.us
Executive search firm. Second location in Boston.

★5308★ American Incite
917 Hillfield Ct., Ste. 4
Oceanside, CA 92054-7013
Ph: (760)754-2444   Fax: (760)754-2453
E-mail: search@americanincite.com
URL: http://www.americanincite.com
Executive search firm.

★5309★ American Physician Network Inc.
2794 Tennis Club Dr., Ste. 204
PO Box 222352
West Palm Beach, FL 33422-2352
Ph: (561)688-2999   Fax: 888-699-5512
Fr: 800-245-8227
E-mail: apn12345@aol.com
Employment agency focused on the healthcare industry.

★5310★ Anderson & Associates
112 S. Tryon St., Ste. 700
Charlotte, NC 28284
Ph: (704)347-0090   Fax: (704)347-0064
E-mail: info@andersonexecsearch.com
URL: http://www.andersonexecsearch.com
Executive search firm. Branch in Cumming, Georgia.

★5311★ Anderson Bradshaw Associates Inc.
444 Benmar, Ste. 1017
Houston, TX 77060
Ph: (713)869-6789
E-mail: aba@hal-pc.org
URL: http://www.andersonbradshaw.com/
Domestic and international search firm.

★5312★ Andre David & Associates Inc.
PO Box 700967
Dallas, TX 75370
Ph: (972)250-1986   Fax: (972)250-2243
E-mail: info@andredavid.com
URL: http://www.andredavid.com/
Executive search firm.

★5313★ The Andre Group Inc.
1220 Valley Forge Rd., Ste. 19
Phoenixville, PA 19460
Ph: (610)917-2212   Fax: (610)917-0551
E-mail: info@theandregroup.com
Executive search firm. Focused on the human resource field.

★5314★ Andrew Associates Executive Search Inc.
4000 Kruse Way Place
Bldg. 2 Ste 225
PO Box 2029
Lake Oswego, OR 97035
Ph: (503)635-7222   Fax: (503)635-5236
E-mail: AAES@andysrch.com
URL: http://www.andysrch.com
Executive search firm.

★5315★ The Angus Group Ltd.
5080 Wooster Rd., Ste. 300
Cincinnati, OH 45226
Ph: (513)961-5575   Fax: (513)961-5616
E-mail: angus@angusgroup.com
URL: http://www.angusgroup.com
Executive search firm.

★5316★ APA Search Inc.
1 Byram Brook Pl., Ste. 201
Armonk, NY 10504
Ph: (914)273-6000   Fax: (914)273-8025
E-mail: info@apasearch.com
URL: http://www.apasearch.com
Employment agency specializing in the automotive, retail, and hardware industries.

★5317★ The Arcus Group Inc.
5001 LBJ Freeway, Ste. 875
Dallas, TX 75244
Ph: (214)294-0516   Fax: (214)871-1338
URL: http://www.arcusgroup.com
Executive search firm. Branch in Chicago.

★5318★ Argus National Inc.
98 Mill Plain Rd., Ste. 301
Danbury, CT 06811-6101
Ph: (203)790-8420
E-mail: argusnat@aol.com
Executive search firm.

★5319★ ARI International
1501 Ocean Ave.
Seal Beach, CA 90740
Ph: (562)795-5111   Fax: (562)596-9794
E-mail: ari.ron@att.net
URL: http://www.ariinternationalsearch.com
International executive search firm.

★5320★ Ariel Associates
159-34 Riverside Dr. W., Apt. 5J
New York, NY 10032-1155
Ph: (212)923-1155
E-mail: info@arielassociates.com
URL: http://www.arielassociates.com
Executive search firm specializing in media, advertising and publishing.

★5321★ Arthur Diamond Associates Inc.
4630 Montgomery Ave., Ste. 200
Bethesda, MD 20814-3436
Ph: (301)657-8866   Fax: (301)657-8876
E-mail: bribakow@arthurdiamond.com
URL: http://www.arthurdiamond.com
Executive search firm.

★5322★ Ashworth Consultants Inc.
53 Fulton St.
Boston, MA 02109-1415
Ph: (617)720-0350

E-mail: ashworthcp@aol.com
Executive search firm.

★5323★ Asset Group Inc.
PO Box 211
Verona, NJ 07044
Ph: (973)641-0967   Fax: (973)571-1387
E-mail: ralley@assetgroupsearch.com
URL: http://www.assetgroupsearch.com
International executive search firm.

★5324★ Association Executive Resources Group
PO Box 3880
Gaithersburg, MD 20885-3880
Ph: (301)417-7045   Fax: (301)417-7049
E-mail: Jhurley@aerg.org
URL: http://www.aerg.org
Executive search firm. Concentrates on non-profits.

★5325★ Association Strategies
1111 N. Fairfax St.
Alexandria, VA 22314
Ph: (703)683-0580   Fax: (703)683-1006
URL: http://www.assnstrategies.com
Employment agency.

★5326★ Aster Search Group
555 Madison Ave
New York, NY 10022
Ph: (212)888-6182   Fax: (212)826-3436
E-mail: ecohen@astersearch.com
URL: http://www.astersearch.com
Executive search firm focused on the healthcare industry.

★5327★ Atlanta Partners Inc.
PO Box W
Teaticket, MA 02536
Ph: (508)495-4300
E-mail: aep@mindspring.com
URL: http://www.atlantapartners.com/
Executive search firm.

★5328★ Auguston and Associates Inc.
1010 S. Ocean Blvd., Ste. 601
Pompano Beach, FL 33062
Ph: (954)943-0503   Fax: (954)784-1660
Fr: 888-244-5598
URL: http://www.augustonandassociates.com/
Executive search firm focused on medical devices.

★5329★ Austin-McGregor International
3500 Oak Lawn Ave., Ste. 550
Dallas, TX 75219
Ph: (972)488-0500   Fax: (972)488-0535
E-mail: info@austinmcgregor.com
URL: http://www.austinmcgregor.com

Executive search firm. Branch located in Mattoon, IL.

★5330★ Avery Associates
3 1/2 N. Santa Cruz Ave., Ste. A
Los Gatos, CA 95030
Ph: (408)399-4424   Fax: (408)399-4423
E-mail: jobs@averyassoc.net
URL: http://www.averyassoc.net
Administration search firm.

★5331★ Avery James Inc.
6601 Center Dr. W., Ste. 500
Los Angeles, CA 90045
Ph: (310)342-8224   Fax: (310)348-8150
URL: http://www.averyjames.com
Executive search firm.

★5332★ The Ayers Group
405 Lexington Ave., Fl. 16
New York, NY 10174
Ph: (212)889-7788   Fax: (212)697-0682
URL: http://www.ayers.com
Executive search firm. Location in Norwalk, CT and two locations in New Jersey.

★5333★ The Baer Group
53 Perimeter Center E., Ste. 100
Atlanta, GA 30346
Ph: (770)557-4900   Fax: (770)557-3499
URL: http://www.baergroup.com
Executive search firm.

★5334★ Baker Montgomery
980 N. Michigan Ave., Ste. 930
Chicago, IL 60611
Ph: (312)397-8808   Fax: (312)397-9631
E-mail: contact@bakermontgomery.com
URL: http://www.bakermontgomery.com
Executive search firm.

★5335★ Baker, Parker & Associates Inc.
5 Concourse Pkwy., Ste. 2440
Atlanta, GA 30328
Ph: (770)804-1996   Fax: (770)804-1917
E-mail: confidential@bpasearch.com
URL: http://www.bpasearch.com
Executive search firm.

★5336★ Bales Partners Inc.
980 N. Michigan Ave., Ste. 1400
Chicago, IL 60611
Ph: (312)214-3998   Fax: (312)214-3981
E-mail: pbales@balespartners.com
Executive search firm.

★5337★ Ballein Search Partners
PO Box 5204
Oak Brook, IL 60522
Ph: (630)322-9220   Fax: (630)322-9221

E-mail: kathybsp@xnet.com
URL: http://www.concentrichealth.net/BSP.htm

Executive search firm focused in the healthcare industry.

★5338★ **Ballos & Company Inc.**
45 Fieldstone Dr.
Morristown, NJ 07960-2634
Ph: (973)538-4609   Fax: (973)538-4753
E-mail: ballosscj@aol.com

Executive search firm.

★5339★ **Banyan Group ESC Ltd.**
6 Courseview Rd.
Bronxville, NY 10708
Ph: (914)337-7159   Fax: (914)337-7164
URL: http://www.banyan-group.com/

Executive search firm.

★5340★ **The Barack Group Inc.**
Grand Central Station
PO Box 4407
New York, NY 10163
Ph: (212)867-9700   Fax: (212)681-9555
URL: http://www.barackgroup.com

Executive search firm.

★5341★ **Barger & Sargeant Inc.**
131 Windermere Rd., Ste. 600
PO Box 1460
Center Harbor, NH 03226-1460
Ph: (603)253-4700

Retained executive search consultants. Works only with companies performing very focused executive searches and Board of Director Recruiting. Industries served: financial services, manufacturing, healthcare, retailing and service businesses.

★5342★ **Barkston Group LLC**
113 South St.
PO Box 218
Litchfield, CT 06759-0218
Ph: (860)567-2400   Fax: (860)567-1466
E-mail: dpatenge@barkstongroup.com
URL: http://www.barkstongroup.com

Executive search firm focused on the banking industry.

★5343★ **Barnes Development Group LLC**
1045 W. Glen Oak Lane, Ste. 4
Mequon, WI 53092
Ph: (262)241-8468   Fr: (262)241-8438
E-mail: resume@barnesdevelopment.com
URL: http://www.barnesdevelopment.com

Executive search firm.

★5344★ **Barone-O'Hara Associates Inc.**
34 Fackler Rd.
Princeton, NJ 08540
Ph: (609)683-5566   Fax: (609)683-8077

URL: http://www.baroneohara.com

Executive search firm focused on medical devices.

★5345★ **Barro Global Search Inc.**
10951 Pico Blvd., Ste. 316
Los Angeles, CA 90064
Ph: (310)441-5305
E-mail: resumes@barroglobal.com
URL: http://www.barroglobal.com

Executive search firm focused on healthcare and hospitals.

★5346★ **Bartholdi Partners**
12020 Sunrise Valley Dr., Ste. 160
Reston, VA 20191
Ph: (703)476-5519   Fax: (703)391-0029
URL: http://www.bartholdisearch.com

Executive search firm. Affiliates in San Francisco; San Jose; Phoenix; Scottsdale; Parker, CO; and Framingham, MA.

★5347★ **Barton Associates Inc.**
4314 Yoakum Blvd.
Houston, TX 77006
Ph: (713)961-9111   Fax: (713)993-9399
E-mail: info@bartona.com
URL: http://www.bartona.com

Executive search firm. Affiliate in Houston, TX.

★5348★ **Battalia Winston International**
555 Madison Ave.
New York, NY 10022
Ph: (212)308-8080   Fax: (212)308-1309
E-mail: info@battaliawinston.com
URL: http://www.battaliawinston.com

Executive search firm. Branches in Los Angeles; Chicago; Wellesley Hills, MA; Edison, NJ.

★5349★ **Beach Executive Search Inc.**
11324 NW 12th Ct.
Coral Springs, FL 33071-6494
Ph: (954)340-7337
E-mail: wlbeach@bellsouth.net

Executive search firm.

★5350★ **The Beam Group**
1835 Market St., Ste. 502
Philadelphia, PA 19103
Ph: (215)988-2100   Fax: (215)988-1558
E-mail: info@beamgroup.com
URL: http://www.beamgroup.com

Executive search firm.

★5351★ **The Bedford Group**
3343 Peachtree Rd. NE, Ste. 333
Atlanta, GA 30326
Ph: (404)237-7471   Fax: (404)846-2172
E-mail: bedford@bedfordgroupconsulting.com
URL: http://

www.bedfordgroupconsulting.com

Executive search firm.

★5352★ **Bell Wishingrad Partners Inc.**
230 Park Ave., Ste. 1000
New York, NY 10169
Ph: (212)949-6666

Executive search firm focused on the financial industry.

★5353★ **Bench International Search Inc.**
120 S. Doheny Dr.
Beverly Hills, CA 90211
Ph: (310)854-9900   Fax: (310)854-9000
E-mail: contact@benchinternational.com
URL: http://www.benchinternational.com

Executive search firm.

★5354★ **Bender Executive Search Management Consulting**
45 N. Station Plaza, Ste. 315
Great Neck, NY 11021
Ph: (516)773-4300   Fax: (516)482-5355
E-mail: benderexec@aol.com
URL: http://www.marketingexecsearch.com

Executive search firm.

★5355★ **Bennett Search & Consulting Company Inc.**
285-1 W. Naomi Dr.
Naples, FL 34104
Ph: (239)352-0219   Fax: (239)353-7719
E-mail: robertbennett3@comcast.net
URL: http://www.bscinc.org

Executive search firm.

★5356★ **Bennett Wheelless Group Ltd.**
33 W. Monroe, Ste. 2110
Chicago, IL 60603
Ph: (312)252-8883   Fax: (801)697-5227
URL: http://www.bennettwheelless.com

Executive search firm focused on direct marketing positions.

★5357★ **Berkana International Ltd.**
20021 Ballinger Way NE, Ste. C
Seattle, WA 98155
Ph: (206)363-6970   Fax: (206)547-3843
E-mail: sonja@headhunters.com
URL: http://www.berkanainternational.com

Executive search firm.

★5358★ **Berkhemer Clayton Inc.**
241 S. Figueroa St., Ste. 300
Los Angeles, CA 90012
Ph: (213)621-2300   Fax: (213)621-2309
E-mail: info@berkhemerclayton.com
URL: http://www.berkhemerclayton.com

Executive search firm.

★5359★ Bert Davis Executive Search Inc.
425 Madison Ave., Fl. 14
New York, NY 10017
Ph: (212)838-4000   Fax: (212)935-3291
E-mail: info@bertdavis.com
URL: http://www.bertdavis.com

Executive search firm.

★5360★ BFL Associates Ltd.
11 Greenway Plaza, Ste. 545
Houston, TX 77046
Ph: (713)965-2112   Fax: (713)965-2114
E-mail: bjorn@bflassociates.com
URL: http://www.bflassociates.com

Executive search firm.

★5361★ Bialecki Inc.
780 3rd Ave., Ste. 4203
New York, NY 10017
Ph: (212)755-1090
E-mail: search@bialecki.com
URL: http://www.bialecki.com

Senior executive search firm focused on the financial industry.

★5362★ Bill Young & Associates
6901A Baltimore National Pike
Frederick, MD 21702
Ph: (301)639-4395
E-mail: enkiho@gmail.com
URL: http://www.billyoung.com/

Executive search firm.

★5363★ Bishop Partners
708 3rd Ave., Ste. 2200
New York, NY 10017
Ph: (212)986-3419   Fax: (212)986-3350
E-mail: info@bishoppartners.com
URL: http://www.bishoppartners.com

A retainer-based executive search firm specializing in media and communications. This includes cable, broadcasting, publishing, Internet and interactive media, entertainment. Consulting closely with clients, finds the right person to fill a specific need and/or solve a specific business issue in functional areas which include CEO and COO, sales, marketing, finance, human resources, programming and production, and e-commerce.

★5364★ Blackshaw, Olmstead, Lynch & Koenig
3414 Peachtree Rd. NE, Ste. 730
Atlanta, GA 30326
Ph: (404)261-7770   Fax: (404)261-4469
E-mail: resumes@bolksearch.com
URL: http://www.bolksearch.com

Executive search firm. Branches in Woodland Hills, CA; Fairfield, CT; and Chicago, IL.

★5365★ Blake/Hansen & Schmidt Ltd.
5514 Ridgeway Ct.
Westlake Village, CA 91362
Ph: (818)879-1192
E-mail: contact@blakehansenschmidt.com
URL: http://www.blakehansenschmidt.com

Executive search firm specializing in plastics, rubber and packaging.

★5366★ Blaney Executive Search
9 Damonmill Sq.
Concord, MA 01742
Ph: (978)371-2192   Fax: (978)371-2193
E-mail: jblaney@blaneyinc.com
URL: http://www.blaneyinc.com

Executive search firm.

★5367★ Blumenthal-Hart LLC
53 W. Jackson Blvd., Ste. 426
Chicago, IL 60604-3413
Ph: (312)663-0090   Fax: (312)663-0405
E-mail: resumes@blumenthal-hart.com
URL: http://www.blumenthal-hart.com

Executive search firm.

★5368★ Boettcher Associates
120 Bishops Way, Ste. 126
Brookfield, WI 53005
Ph: (262)782-2205

Executive search firm.

★5369★ Bonell Ryan Inc.
415 Madison Ave., 15th Fl.
New York, NY 10017
Ph: (646)673-8620   Fax: (702)995-9935
E-mail: info@bonellryan.com
URL: http://www.bonellryan.com

Executive search firm.

★5370★ Bonnell Associates Ltd.
1499 Post Rd., 2nd Fl.
Fairfield, CT 06824
Ph: (203)319-7214   Fax: (203)319-7219
E-mail: wbonnell@bonnellassociates.com
URL: http://www.bonnellassociates.com

Executive search firm.

★5371★ Boston Search Group Inc.
224 Clarendon St., Ste. 41
Boston, MA 02116-3729
Ph: (617)266-4333   Fax: (781)735-0562
E-mail: rprotsik@bostonsearchgroup.com
URL: http://www.bostonsearchgroup.com

Executive search firm.

★5372★ The Boulware Group, Inc.
625 N. Michigan Ave., Ste. 422
Chicago, IL 60611
Ph: (312)322-0088   Fax: (312)322-0092
E-mail: Resume@boulwareinc.com
URL: http://www.boulwareinc.com

Executive search firm.

★5373★ Boyden
360 Lexington Ave., Ste. 1300
New York, NY 10017
Ph: (212)949-9400   Fax: (212)949-5905
E-mail: jbranthover@boyden.com
URL: http://www.boyden.com

Executive search firm. Affiliate offices across the country and abroad.

★5374★ Boyle & Associates Retained Search Group
PO Box 16658
St. Paul, MN 55116
Ph: (651)223-5050   Fax: (651)699-5378
E-mail: paul@talenthunt.com
URL: http://www.talenthunt.com

Executive search firm.

★5375★ The Bradbury Group Inc.
2112 Vizcaya Way, Ste. 200
Campbell, CA 95008
Ph: (408)377-5400   Fax: (408)377-1112
E-mail: paul@ifindem.com
URL: http://www.thebradburygroup.net

Executive search firm.

★5376★ Brady Associates International Inc.
PO Box 1892
New York, NY 10021
Ph: (212)396-4950

Executive search firm focused on the energy and utilities industry.

★5377★ Brandywine Consulting Group
1398 Morstein Rd.
West Chester, PA 19380
Ph: (610)696-5872   Fax: (610)429-1954
Fr: 800-555-1668
URL: http://brandywineconsulting.com/html/index.php

Executive search firm. An Affiliate of Brandywine Management Group in Berlin, MD.

★5378★ Brandywine Management Group
8 Drawbridge Rd.
Berlin, MD 21811
Ph: (410)208-9791   Fax: (410)208-9792
Fr: 800-860-8812
E-mail: brandywinemgmt@optonline.net
URL: http://www.brandywineconsultants.com/

Executive search firm.

★5379★ Brault & Associates Ltd.
11703 Bowman Green Dr.
Reston, VA 20190
Ph: (703)471-0920
E-mail: jean-pierre@mindspring.com

Executive search firm.

★5380★ The Brazik Group LLC

14862 Crescent Cove Dr.
Fort Myers, FL 33908
Ph: (239)249-1003   Fr: 800-838-5701
E-mail: chuck@brazikgroup.com
URL: http://www.brazikgroup.com

Executive search firm. Branches in Tinley Park, IL and Union Pier, MI.

★5381★ The Brentwood Group Inc.

170 Kinnelon Rd., Ste. 7
Kinnelon, NJ 07405
Ph: (973)283-1000   Fax: (973)283-1220
E-mail: info@thebrentwoodgroup.com
URL: http://www.thebrentwoodgroup.com

Executive search firm.

★5382★ The Brentwood Group Ltd.

4949 SW Meadows Rd., Ste. 140
Lake Oswego, OR 97035
Ph: (503)697-8136   Fax: (503)697-8161
E-mail: contact@brentwoodgroup.com
URL: http://www.brentwoodgroup.com

Executive search firm focused on the high technology industry.

★5383★ Brentwood International

9841 Airport Blvd., Ste. 420
Los Angeles, CA 90045
Ph: (310)338-5470   Fax: (310)338-5484
E-mail: postmaster@brentwoodintl.com
URL: http://www.brentwoodintl.com

Executive search firm with focus on information technology. Branch in Fairfield, CA.

★5384★ Briant Associates Inc.

18 E. Dundee Rd. Bldg 2, Ste. 202
Barrington, IL 60010
Ph: (847)382-5725   Fax: (847)382-7265
E-mail: rbingham@briantassociates.com
URL: http://www.briantassociates.com

Executive search firm.

★5385★ BridgeGate LLC

17701 Cowan Ave., Ste. 240
Irvine, CA 92614
Ph: (949)553-9200   Fax: (949)660-1810
E-mail: info@bridgegate.com
URL: http://www.bridgegate.com

Executive search firm.

★5386★ The Brimeyer Group Inc.

50 9th Ave. S., Ste. 101
Hopkins, MN 55343
Ph: (952)945-0246   Fax: (952)945-0102
E-mail: brimgroup@aol.com
URL: http://www.brimgroup.com

Executive search firm.

★5387★ Brindisi Search

10751 Falls Rd., Greenspring Sta., Ste. 250
Greenspring Stn.
Lutherville, MD 21093
Ph: (410)339-7673   Fax: (410)823-0146
E-mail: tbrindisi@aol.com
URL: http://www.brindisisearch.com

Specializes in contemporary human resource and select strategic leadership assignments, ranging from manager to senior vice president level.

★5388★ Brooke Chase Associates Inc.

1543 2ND St., Ste. 201
Sarasota, FL 34236
Ph: (941)358-3111   Fax: (866)851-5693
Fr: 877-374-0039
E-mail: jmcelmeel@brookechase.com
URL: http://www.brookechase.com

Executive search firm. Branches in San Rafael, CA; Chicago; and Charlotte, NC.

★5389★ Brown Venture Associates Inc.

2500 Sand Hill Rd., Ste. 110
Menlo Park, CA 94025
Ph: (650)233-0205   Fax: (650)233-1902
E-mail: Brown@bva.com
URL: http://www.bva.com

Executive search firm.

★5390★ Brownson & Associates LP

2825 Wilcrest, Ste. 530
Houston, TX 77042
Ph: (713)626-4790   Fax: (713)877-1745
E-mail: brownsonassoc@brownson.com
URL: http://www.brownson.com

Executive search firm.

★5391★ Bruce Edwards & Associates Inc.

1502 W NC Highway 54, Ste. 610
Durham, NC 27707
Ph: (919)489-5368   Fax: (919)604-3157
E-mail: brucedwar@aol.com

Executive search firm.

★5392★ Brush Creek Partners

14512 Horton
Overland Park, KS 66223
Ph: (816)228-9192   Fax: (816)228-6740
E-mail: jlunn@brushcreekpartners.com

Executive search firm.

★5393★ Buffkin & Associates LLC

730 Cool Springs Blvd., Ste. 120
Franklin, TN 37067
Ph: (615)771-0098   Fax: (615)771-0099
E-mail: info@buffkinassociates.com
URL: http://www.buffkinassociates.com

Executive search firm.

★5394★ Burke, O'Brien & Bishop, LLC

33 Richard Ct.
Princeton, NJ 08540
Ph: (609)921-3510   Fax: (609)683-1578

Executive search firm.

★5395★ The Burling Group Ltd.

191 N. Wacker Dr., Ste. 2300
Chicago, IL 60606
Ph: (312)346-0888
E-mail: web@burlinggroup.com
URL: http://www.burlinggroup.com

Executive search firm.

★5396★ Burton & Grove Executive Search.

1320 Tower Rd.
Schaumburg, IL 60173
Ph: (847)919-8880
E-mail: support@burtonandgrove.com
URL: http://www.burtonandgrove.com

Executive search firm.

★5397★ Busch International

1000 Fremont Ave., Ste. 195
Los Altos, CA 94024
Ph: (650)949-6500
E-mail: olga@buschint.com
URL: http://www.buschint.com

Executive search firm focused solely on high-technology electronics.

★5398★ Buxbaum/Rink Consulting L.L.C.

1 Bradley Rd., Ste. 901
Woodbridge, CT 06525-2296
Ph: (203)389-5949   Fax: (203)397-0615
E-mail: gen@buxbaumrink.com
URL: http://www.buxbaumrink.com

Personnel consulting firms offer contingency search, recruitment and placement of accounting and finance, as well as other business management positions. In addition to serving these two major career areas, also provides similar services to operations, marketing and human resources executives. Industries served: manufacturing, financial services, and service.

★5399★ Byron Leonard International

99 Long Ct., Ste. 201
Thousand Oaks, CA 91360
Ph: (805)373-7500   Fax: (805)373-5531
Fr: (818)222-2744
E-mail: swolf@bli-inc.com
URL: http://www.bli-inc.com

Executive search firm.

★5400★ CAA Search

5469 Sunbird Dr.
Loves Park, IL 61111
Ph: (815)654-8535   Fax: (815)654-0469
E-mail: christian@caasearch.com

URL: http://www.caasearch.com

Executive search firm.

★5401★ Cabot Consultants

1750 Tysons Blvd., Ste. 400
McLean, VA 22102
Ph: (703)744-1081   Fax: (703)744-1001
E-mail: info@cabotinc.com
URL: http://www.cabotinc.com

A retained executive search firm specializing in filling senior-level positions.

★5402★ The Caler Group

23337 Lago Mar Cir.
Boca Raton, FL 33433
Ph: (561)394-8045   Fax: (561)394-4645
E-mail: caler@calergroup.com
URL: http://www.calergroup.com

Executive search firm.

★5403★ Caliber Associates

6336 Greenwich Dr., Ste. C
San Diego, CA 92122
Ph: (858)551-7880   Fax: (858)551-7887
E-mail: info@caliberassociates.com
URL: http://www.caliberassociates.com

Executive search firm.

★5404★ Callaghan International Inc.

119 W. 57th St., Ste. 1220
New York, NY 10019
Ph: (212)265-9200   Fax: (212)265-0024
E-mail: kmc@callaghan-international.com
URL: http://www.callaghan-international.com

Executive search firm.

★5405★ Callan Associates Ltd.

2215 York Rd., Ste. 510
Oak Brook, IL 60523
Ph: (630)574-9300   Fax: (630)574-3099
E-mail: info@callanassociates.com
URL: http://www.callanassociates.com

Executive search firm.

★5406★ Calland & Company

2296 Henderson Mill Rd., Ste. 222
Atlanta, GA 30345
Ph: (770)270-9100   Fax: (770)270-9300
E-mail: bob@callandcompany.com
URL: http://www.callandcompany.com

Executive search firm focused on senior management and healthcare.

★5407★ Campbell/Carlson LLC

831 E. Morehead St., Ste. 750
Charlotte, NC 28202
Ph: (704)373-0234
E-mail: recruiting@campbellcarlson.com
URL: http://www.campbellcarlson.com

Executive search firm.

★5408★ Cannellos-Smartt Associates

23 Davenport Way
Hillsborough, NJ 08844-2923
Ph: (908)359-8319   Fax: (908)369-OO41
E-mail: rudysmartt@csa-search.com
URL: http://www.csa-search.com

Executive search firm with another office in Hillborough.

★5409★ Cantor Executive Search Solutions Inc.

250 W. 57 St., Ste. 1632
New York, NY 10107-1609
Ph: (212)333-3000   Fax: (212)245-1012
E-mail: requests@cantorconcern.com
URL: http://www.cantorconcern.com

Executive search firm. Branch in Fairfield, CT.

★5410★ Capodice & Associates

Midtown Plaza
1243 S. Tamiami Trail
Sarasota, FL 34239
Ph: (941)906-1990   Fax: (941)906-1991
E-mail: peter@capodice.com
URL: http://www.capodice.com

Executive search firm. Branch in Carlisle, MA.

★5411★ Caprio & Associates Inc.

1415 W. 22nd St., Tower Fl.
Oak Brook, IL 60523
Ph: (630)705-9101   Fax: (630)705-9102
E-mail: jerry@caprioassociates.com
URL: http://www.caprioassociates.com

Executive search firm.

★5412★ Capstone Consulting Inc.

723 S. Dearborn St.
Chicago, IL 60605
Ph: (312)922-9556   Fax: (312)922-9558
E-mail: Lori@CapstoneConsulting.com
URL: http://www.capstoneconsulting.com

Executive search firm.

★5413★ Capstone Inc.

971 Albany Shaker Rd.
Latham, NY 12110
Ph: (518)783-9300   Fax: (518)783-9328
E-mail: info@capstone-inc.com
URL: http://www.capstone-inc.com

Executive search firm.

★5414★ Career Specialists Inc.

155 108th Ave. NE, Ste. 200
Bellevue, WA 98004
Ph: (425)455-0582   Fax: (425)646-9738
E-mail: prolfe@qwest.net

Executive search firm.

★5415★ Carlson Research Group

5051 Castello Dr., Ste. 211
Naples, FL 34103
Ph: (239)649-7576   Fax: (239)649-805
E-mail: info@carlsonresearch.com
URL: http://www.carlsonresearch.com

Executive search firm.

★5416★ Carrington & Carrington Ltd

4354 Town Center Blvd., Ste. 114-248
El Dorado Hills, CA 95762
Ph: (312)606-0015   Fax: (312)606-050
E-mail: info@carnegiepartners.com
URL: http://www.carnegiepartners.com

Executive search firm.

★5417★ CarterBaldwin

200 Mansell Ct. E., Ste. 450
Roswell, GA 30076
Ph: (678)448-0000   Fax: (770)552-108
E-mail: info@carterbaldwin.com
URL: http://www.carterbaldwin.com

Executive search firm.

★5418★ Caruso & Associates Inc.

990 Stinson Way, Ste. 201
West Palm Beach, FL 33411
Ph: (561)683-2336
E-mail: info@carusoassociates.com
URL: http://www.carusoassociates.com

Executive search firm.

★5419★ Cary & Associates

PO Box 2043
Winter Park, FL 32790-2043
Ph: (407)647-1145
E-mail: concary@caryassociates.com
URL: http://www.caryassociates.com

Executive search firm.

★5420★ Catalyx Group

303 W. 42nd St., Ste. 607
New York, NY 10036
Ph: (212)956-3525
E-mail: lposter@catalyx.com
URL: http://www.catalyx.com

Executive search firm.

★5421★ Cendea

8002 Weldon Springs Ct., Ste. 200
Austin, TX 78726
Ph: (512)219-6000
E-mail: info.kd@cendea.com
URL: http://www.cendea.com

Executive search firm.

★5422★ Chaitin & Associates Inc.

22543 Ventura Blvd., Ste. 220
Woodland Hills, CA 91364
Ph: (818)225-8655   Fax: (818)225-8660
E-mail: execpro2@aol.com

Executive search firm.

★5423★ **Chase Hunter Group Inc.**
143 W. North Shore Ave.
Chicago, IL 60626
Ph: (773)338-7865   Fax: (773)338-1389
E-mail: bdouglas@chase-hunter.com
URL: http://www.chase-hunter.com
Executive search firm focused around the healthcare industry.

★5424★ **The Cherbonnier Group Inc.**
1 Riverway, Ste. 1700
Houston, TX 77056
Ph: (713)688-4701
E-mail: consult@chergroup.com
URL: http://www.thecherbonniergroup.com
Executive search firm.

★5425★ **Cheryl Alexander & Associates**
3588 Shadow Creek Dr.
Maple Grove, MN 55311
Ph: (763)416-4570
E-mail: cherylalexander@cherylalexander.com
URL: http://www.cherylalexander.com
Executive search firm.

★5426★ **Chicago Research Group Inc.**
PO Box 3757
Chapel Hill, NC 27515-3757
Ph: (919)968-0120
E-mail: infoplease@chicagoresearch.com
URL: http://www.chicagoresearch.com
Executive search firm.

★5427★ **Chiron Advisors Inc.**
420 Lexington Ave., Ste. 2736
New York, NY 10170
Ph: (212)867-6969   Fax: (212)867-7449
E-mail: mstone@cchironadvisors.com
URL: http://www.chironadvisors.com
Executive search firm focused on the financial industry.

★5428★ **Chrisman & Company Inc.**
350 S. Figueroa St., Ste. 550
Los Angeles, CA 90071
Ph: (213)620-1192   Fax: (213)620-1693
E-mail: info@chrismansearch.com
URL: http://www.chrismansearch.com
Executive search firm.

★5429★ **Christian & Timbers**
28601 Chagrin Blvd, Ste. 600
Cleveland, OH 44122
Ph: (216)682-3200   Fax: (216)464-6172
Fr: 800-380-9444
E-mail: comments@ctnet.com
URL: http://www.ctnet.com
Executive search firm. Eight branches spanning the USA.

★5430★ **Clarey Andrews & Klein Inc.**
1200 Shermer Rd., Ste. 108
Northbrook, IL 60062
Ph: (847)498-2870
E-mail: cak@clarey-a-klein.com
URL: http://www.penrhyn.com
Executive search firm.

★5431★ **Cole, Warren & Long Inc.**
Two Penn Center Plaza, Ste. 312
Philadelphia, PA 19102
Ph: (215)563-0701   Fax: (215)563-2907
Fr: 800-394-8517
E-mail: cwlserch@cwl-inc.com
URL: http://www.cwl-inc.com
Executive search firm with international placement.

★5432★ **Coleman Lew & Associates Inc.**
326 W. 10th St.
Charlotte, NC 28202
Ph: (704)377-0362   Fax: (704)377-0424
Fr: 800-533-9523
E-mail: mail@colemanlew.com
URL: http://www.colemanlew.com
Executive search firm.

★5433★ **Columbia Consulting Group**
5525 Twin Knolls Rd., Ste. 331
Columbia, MD 21045
Ph: (443)276-2525   Fax: (410)276-2536
E-mail: info@ccgsearch.com
URL: http://www.ccgsearch.com
Executive search firm. Branches in Ft. Lauderdale, FL; Jupiter, FL; and New York, NY.

★5434★ **Compton Graham International Inc.**
9986 Horse Creek Road
Fort Myers, FL 33913
Ph: (239)433-4660   Fr: 800-218-2031
E-mail: jac@comptongraham.com
URL: http://www.comptongraham.com
Executive search firm. Second location in Toronto, Canada.

★5435★ **Conard Associates Inc.**
74 Northeastern Blvd., Unit 22A
Nashua, NH 03062
Ph: (603)886-0600   Fax: (603)804-0421
E-mail: rod@conard.com
URL: http://www.conard.com
Executive search firm.

★5436★ **Conex**
575 Madison Ave., 10th Fl.
New York, NY 10022
Ph: (212)371-3737   Fax: (212)371-3897
E-mail: mail@conex-usa.com
URL: http://www.conex-usa.com
Executive search firm.

★5437★ **Conway & Associates**
1007 Church St., Ste. 307
Evanston, IL 60201
Ph: (847)866-6832   Fax: (847)866-6265
E-mail: Conway@sisna.com
Executive search firm.

★5438★ **The Cooke Group Inc.**
1001 W. Glen Oaks Lane, Ste. 102
Mequon, WI 53092
Ph: (262)241-9842   Fax: (262)241-1004
Fr: 888-432-7800
E-mail: rmarshall@cookegroup.net
URL: http://www.cookegroup.net/
Executive search firm.

★5439★ **The Cooper Executive Search Group Inc.**
PO Box 375
Wales, WI 53183-0375
Ph: (262)968-9049   Fax: (262)968-9059
E-mail: cesgroup@aol.com
Executive search firm.

★5440★ **Core Management Search LLC**
5130 Saratoga Ln. N., Ste. 201
Minneapolis, MN 55442
Ph: (763)559-0977   Fax: (763)559-1664
E-mail: jlentner@coremanage.com
URL: http://www.coremanage.com
Executive search firm.

★5441★ **Cornell Group**
4017 Williamsburg Ct.
Fairfax, VA 22032
Ph: (703)877-2080   Fax: (703)877-2081
E-mail: parora@thecornellgroup.com
URL: http://www.thecornellgroup.com
Executive search firm.

★5442★ **Corporate Moves Inc.**
PO Box 1638
Williamsville, NY 14231-1638
Ph: (716)633-0234
E-mail: info@CMISearch.com
URL: http://www.corporatemovesinc.com
Executive search & recruitment specialist firm with emphasis on Sales, Marketing and Senior Management generally in the $70,000 and above income levels. Industries served: medical, biotech, scientific, pharmaceutical, industrial, business products.

★5443★ **Courtright & Associates Inc.**
PO Box 236
Scranton, PA 18504
Ph: (570)961-5450
E-mail: rjcx@comcast.net
URL: http://www.courtrightassoc.com
Executive search firm.

★5444★ CraigSearch
1130 E. Arapaho Rd., Ste. 180
Richardson, TX 75081
Ph: (972)644-3264   Fax: (972)644-3265
E-mail: search@craigsearch.com
URL: http://www.craigsearch.com
Executive search firm.

★5445★ Creative-Leadership Inc.
445 Hutchinson Ave., Ste. 800
Columbus, OH 43235
Ph: (614)410-6505   Fax: (614)760-0737
Fr: 800-875-5323
E-mail: info@clci.com
URL: http://www.clci.com
Executive search firm.

★5446★ Crist Associates
21 W. 2nd St. Ste. 3
Hinsdale, IL 60521
Ph: (630)321-1110   Fax: (630)321-1112
URL: http://www.cristassociates.com
Executive search firm.

★5447★ Cross Hill Partners LLC
245 Park Ave., Fl. 24
New York, NY 10167
Ph: (212)672-1604   Fax: (212)202-6316
E-mail: info@crosshillpartners.com
URL: http://www.crosshillpartners.com
Executive search firm.

★5448★ Crown Advisors Inc.
30 Isabella St., Ste. 203
Pittsburgh, PA 15212
Ph: (412)566-1100   Fax: (412)566-1256
E-mail: info@crownsearch.com
URL: http://www.crownsearch.com
Executive search firm.

★5449★ CTR Group
11843-C Canon Blvd.
Newport News, CA 23606
Ph: (757)462-5900   Fax: (757)873-6724
Fr: 800-462-5309
URL: http://www.ctrc.com/jobs/
Executive search firm.

★5450★ Cullen International Executive Search Inc.
50 North Crest Dr.
Newnan, GA 30265-1200
Ph: (678)230-5475   Fax: (678)423-1718
E-mail: info@cullenexecutivesearch.com
Executive search firm.

★5451★ Curran Partners Inc.
1 Landmark Sq., Ste. 525
Stamford, CT 06901
Ph: (203)363-5350   Fax: (203)363-5353
E-mail: research@curranpartners.com

URL: http://www.curranpartners.com
Executive search firm.

★5452★ Custom Research Solutions
16400 Pacific Coast Hwy., Ste. 221
Huntington Beach, CA 92649
Ph: (562)431-6690   Fr: 800-829-5870
E-mail: arodrique@custom-research.com
URL: http://www.custom-research.com
Executive search firm.

★5453★ Cyntal International Ltd.
405 Lexington Ave., Ste. 2600-19
New York, NY 10174
Ph: (917)368-8181
E-mail: cynthia@cyntal.com
Executive search firm.

★5454★ D. E. Foster Partners
230 W 41st St., Ste. 1550
New York, NY 10036
Ph: (646)452-4601   Fax: (212)893-2309
E-mail: recruiting@fosterpartners.com
URL: http://www.fosterpartners.com
Executive search firm affiliated with Daubenspeck and Associates Ltd. Branches in Washington, DC and Dallas.

★5455★ Dahl-Morrow International
11260 Roger Bacon Dr., Ste. 204
Reston, VA 20190
Ph: (703)787-8117   Fax: (703)787-8114
E-mail: dmi@dahl-morrowintl.com
URL: http://www.dahl-morrowintl.com/
Executive search firm specializes in high technology.

★5456★ DAL Partners
501 Kings Highway E., Ste. 101
Fairfield, CT 06825
Ph: (203)256-3777   Fax: (203)256-8294
E-mail: resumes@dalpartners.com
URL: http://www.dalpartners.com
Executive search firm.

★5457★ Daly & Company Inc.
175 Federal St.
Boston, MA 02110-2210
Ph: (617)262-2800   Fax: (617)728-4477
E-mail: info@dalyco.com
URL: http://www.dalyco.com
Executive search firm.

★5458★ David Allen Associates
PO Box 56
Haddonfield, NJ 08033-0048
Ph: (856)795-6470   Fax: (856)795-0175
E-mail: david@davidallenassoc.com
URL: http://www.davidallenassoc.com
Executive search firm.

★5459★ Derba & Derba
7 Whispering Pines
Andover, MA 01810
Ph: (978)470-8270   Fax: (978)470-459
E-mail: info@derbaandderba.com
URL: http://derbaandderba.com/
Executive search firm focused on the hospitality industry.

★5460★ DHR International
10 S. Riverside Plaza, Ste. 2220
Chicago, IL 60606
Ph: (312)782-1581   Fax: (312)782-209
URL: http://www.dhrinternational.com
Executive search firm. International organization with a variety of affiliate offices.

★5461★ The Dieck Group Inc.
30 Rough Lee Court
Madison, WI 53705
Ph: (608)238-1000
E-mail: dan.dieck@dieckgroup.com
URL: http://www.dieckgroup.com
Executive search firm focused on pulp, paper and the packaging industries.

★5462★ The Diestel Group
2755 E. Cottonwood Pkwy., Ste. 580
Salt Lake City, UT 84121
Ph: (801)365-0400   Fax: (801)365-040
E-mail: info@diestel.com
URL: http://www.diestel.com
Executive search firm.

★5463★ Dinte Resources Inc.
8300 Greensboro Dr., Ste. 750
McLean, VA 22102
Ph: (703)448-3300   Fax: (703)448-021£
E-mail: DRI@dinte.com
URL: http://www.dinte.com
Executive search firm.

★5464★ DLB Associates
2403 State Route 66
Ocean, NJ 07712
Ph: (732)774-2000   Fax: (732)774-500(
E-mail: info@dlbassociates.com
URL: http://www.dlbassociates.com/
Executive search firm.

★5465★ DNPitchon Associates
60 W. Ridgewood Ave.
Ridgewood, NJ 07450
Ph: (201)612-8350
E-mail: info@dnpitchon.com
URL: http://www.dnpitchon.com
Executive search firm.

★5466★ Doherty International Inc.
899 Skokie Blvd., Ste. 430
Northbrook, IL 60062
Ph: (847)564-1753   Fax: (847)564-1763

E-mail: doherty_int@ameritech.net

Executive search firm.

★5467★ **Donahue/Patterson Associates**
3 N. LaSalle St., Ste. 2600
Chicago, IL 60602
Ph: (312)732-0999
E-mail: info@donahuepatterson.com
URL: http://www.donahuepatterson.com

Executive search firm.

★5468★ **Dressler Associates**
524 University Ave.
Palo Alto, CA 94301
Ph: (650)458-8737
E-mail: kathyn@ullrichassociates.com
URL: http://www.dresslerassociates.com

Executive search firm.

★5469★ **Drinkwater & Associates**
67 West St.
Beverly, MA 01915
Ph: (978)922-3676
E-mail: wendydrinkwater@comcast.com

Executive search firm.

★5470★ **Dunhill Professional Search**
150 Motor Pkwy.
Hauppauge, NY 11788-5111
Ph: (631)952-3000   Fax: (631)952-3500
E-mail: info@dunhillstaff.com
URL: http://www.dunhillstaff.com

Executive search firm. Over 180 affiliated locations coast-to-coast.

★5471★ **Dunlap & Sullivan Associates**
29 Pearl St. NW, Ste. 227
Grand Rapids, MI 49503
Ph: (616)458-4142   Fax: (616)458-4203
E-mail: dunsul@aol.com

Executive search firm with second location in Hobe Sound, FL.

★5472★ **DuVall & Associates**
4203 Costa Salada
San Clemente, CA 92673
Ph: (949)488-8790   Fax: (949)488-8793
E-mail: Karen@ducall.com
URL: http://www.duvall.com

Executive search firm specializing in management team placement.

★5473★ **Dynamic Synergy Corp.**
600 Entrada Dr., Fl. 2
Santa Monica, CA 90402
Ph: (650)493-2000
E-mail: info@dynamicsynergy.com
URL: http://www.dynamicsynergy.com

Executive search firm.

★5474★ **E/Search International**
PO Box 408
West Suffield, CT 06093-0408
Ph: (860)668-5848   Fax: (860)668-5125
Fr: 800-300-0477
E-mail: esearch@esearchintl.com
URL: http://www.esearchinternational.net

Executive search firm for companies needing highly successful, industry-specific executives. A database of executives and sales people in sales, operations, manufacturing, engineering, and supply chain management.

★5475★ **Eastman & Beaudine Inc.**
7201 Bishop Rd., Ste. 220
Plano, TX 75024
Ph: (972)312-1012   Fax: (972)312-1020
URL: http://www.eastman-beaudine.com/

Executive search firm. Second location in Alpharetta, GA.

★5476★ **EFL Associates**
7101 College Blvd., Ste. 550
Overland Park, KS 66210-2075
Ph: (913)451-8866   Fax: (913)451-7490
E-mail: eflinfo@eflassociates.com
URL: http://www.eflassociates.com

Executive search firm. Locations in Englewood, CO and Lake Forest, IL.

★5477★ **Egan & Associates Inc.**
White House Ctr.
1784 Barton Ave., Ste. 10
West Bend, WI 53095
Ph: (262)335-0707   Fax: (262)335-0625
E-mail: info@eganassociates.com
URL: http://www.eganassociates.com

Executive search firm.

★5478★ **The Elliot Company**
Ph: (202)521-5300
E-mail: suppt.staff@elliottco.net
URL: http://www.elliottco.net

Executive search firm.

★5479★ **Elwell & Associates Inc.**
3100 W. Liberty Rd., Ste. E
Ann Arbor, MI 48103
Ph: (734)662-8775   Fax: (734)662-2045
E-mail: elwallas@elwellassociates.com
URL: http://www.elwellassociates.com

Executive search firm.

★5480★ **ESA Professional Consultants**
141 Durham Rd., Ste. 16
Madison, CT 06443
Ph: (203)245-1983   Fax: (203)245-8428

Executive search firm.

★5481★ **ET Search Inc.**
1250 Prospect St., Ste. 101
La Jolla, CA 92037-3618
Ph: (858)459-3443   Fax: (858)459-4147

E-mail: ets@esearch.com
URL: http://www.etsearch.com

Executive search firm focused on the tax industry.

★5482★ **ETI Search International**
990 Hammond Dr., Ste. 825
Atlanta, GA 30328
Ph: (770)399-8492   Fax: (770)399-8487

Executive search firm.

★5483★ **Executive Careers Ltd.**
1801 Century Park E., Ste. 2400
Los Angeles, CA 90067
Ph: (310)552-3455   Fax: (310)578-7524
E-mail: eclresumes@att.net

Executive search firm.

★5484★ **Executive Resources International LLC**
Boston Harbor
63 Atlantic Ave.
Boston, MA 02110-3722
Ph: (617)742-8970   Fax: (617)523-9093
E-mail: resume@erisearch.net
URL: http://www.erisearch.net

Executive search firm.

★5485★ **The Executive Roundtable**
483 Godshall Rd.
Souderton, PA 18964
Ph: (215)721-1650   Fax: (215)721-8650
Fr: 888-315-1150
E-mail: execrt@verizon.net

Executive search firm.

★5486★ **Executive Search World**
Harbor Ct.
66 Queen St., Ste. 1802
Honolulu, HI 96813
Ph: (808)526-3812   Fax: (808)523-9356
E-mail: info@executivesearchworld.com
URL: http://www.executivesearchworld.com

Executive search firm for Hawaii.

★5487★ **Executives Unlimited Inc.**
5000 E. Spring St., Ste. 395
Long Beach, CA 90803
Ph: (562)627-3800   Fax: (562)627-1092
Fr: (866)957-4466
E-mail: resumes@executives-unlimited.com
URL: http://www.executives-unlimited.com

Executive search firm. Branches in Western Springs, IL; Scotch Plains, NJ; Long Beach, CA.

★5488★ **Ferneborg & Associates Inc.**
160 Bovet Rd., Ste. 403
San Mateo, CA 94402
Ph: (650)577-0100   Fax: (650)577-0122
E-mail: mailbox@execsearch.com

URL: http://www.execsearch.com

Executive search firm.

★5489★ FM Industries
10125 Crosstown Cir.
Eden Prairie, MN 55344-3319
Ph: (952)941-0966   Fax: (952)941-4462
E-mail: fmindustries@fmindustries.net
URL: http://www.fmindustries.net

Executive search firm.

★5490★ Fox-Morris
1617 JFK Blvd., Ste. 210
Philadelphia, PA 19103
Ph: (215)561-6300   Fax: (215)561-7518

Executive search firm. Branch locations in many states throughout the U.S.

★5491★ Francis & Associates
6923 Vista Dr.
West Des Moines, IA 50266
Ph: (515)221-9800   Fax: (515)221-9806
E-mail: knovak@francisassociates.com
URL: http://www.francisassociates.com

Executive search firm.

★5492★ Graystone Partners L.L.C.
62 Southfield Ave., Ste. 204
Stamford, CT 06902-7229
Ph: (203)323-0023   Fax: (203)353-9035
E-mail: contact@graystonepartners.com
URL: http://www.graystonepartners.com

A retainer-based, executive search firm providing professional consulting services in the area of executive recruitment and management selection. Functional areas of expertise include senior level general management, financial officers, technology officers, marketing and human resource executives.

★5493★ Harvey Bell & Associates
700 Lindsay Ave.
Rohnert Park, CA 94928
Ph: (707)795-0650   Fax: (707)795-0655
E-mail: harveybell@aol.com

Executive search firm.

★5494★ Heidrick and Struggles, Inc.
233 S. Wacker Dr., Ste. 4200
Sears Tower
Chicago, IL 60606-6303
Ph: (312)496-1200   Fax: (312)496-1290
URL: http://www.heidrick.com

Executive search firm. International organization with a variety of affiliate offices.

★5495★ Integrated Search Solutions Group
33 Main St.
Port Washington, NY 11050
Ph: (516)767-3030
E-mail: info@issg.net
URL: http://www.issg.net

A retainer based executive search firm that has been successful in attracting top talent in the areas of outsourcing, consulting and traditional IT functions.

★5496★ J. Burkey Associates
900 Laurel Ave.
River Edge, NJ 07661
Ph: (201)262-7990   Fax: (201)262-7955
E-mail: jburkey@erols.com

Executive search firm.

★5497★ J H Dugan & Company
431 El Camino Real, Ste. 5302
Santa Clara, CA 95050
Ph: (408)920-7700   Fax: (408)920-7701
E-mail: info@jhdugan.com
URL: http://www.jhdugan.com

Executive search firm.

★5498★ J Nicolas Arthur
77 Franklin St., Fl. 10
Boston, MA 02110
Ph: (617)204-9000   Fax: (617)303-8934
E-mail: nicholas.bogard@jnicholasarthur.com
URL: http://www.jnicholasarthur.com/

Executive search firm specializing in the finance industry.

★5499★ James Bangert & Associates Inc.
15500 Wayzata Blvd.
Wayzata, MN 55391
Ph: (952)475-3454   Fax: (952)473-4306
E-mail: jab@bangertassoc.com

Executive search firm.

★5500★ James Drury Partners
875 N. Michigan Ave., Ste. 3805
Chicago, IL 60611
Ph: (312)654-6708   Fax: (312)654-6710
E-mail: jdrury@drurypartners.com
URL: http://www.jdrurypartners.com

Executive search firm.

★5501★ John J. Davis & Associates Inc.
30 Chatham Road
PO Box G
Short Hills, NJ 07078
Ph: (973)467-8339   Fax: (973)467-3706
E-mail: jdavis@1013@aol.com
URL: http://www.johnjdavisandassoc.com

Executive search firm.

★5502★ Joseph R. Burns & Associates Inc.
2 Shunpike Rd
Madison, NJ 07940
Ph: (973)377-1350   Fax: (973)377-9350

E-mail: burnsassc@aol.com

Executive search firm.

★5503★ Joy Reed Belt Search Consultants Inc.
PO Box 54410
Oklahoma City, OK 73154
Ph: (405)842-5155   Fax: (405)842-635
E-mail: executiverecruiter@joyreedbelt.com
URL: http://www.joyreedbeltsearch.com

Executive search firm. Branch in Tulsa, OK

★5504★ J.R. Bechtle & Company
67 S. Bedford St., Ste. 400W
Burlington, MA 01803-5177
Ph: (781)229-5804   Fax: (781)359-182
E-mail: jrb.boston@jrbechtle.com
URL: http://www.jrbechtle.com

Executive search firm.

★5505★ JT Brady & Associates
10900 Perry Hwy. 12203
Wexford, PA 15090
Ph: (412)934-2228   Fax: (724)935-805
E-mail: jack@jtbrady.net
URL: http://www.jtbrady.net

Executive search firm.

★5506★ Judith Cushman & Associates
15600 NE 8th St., Ste. B1
Bellevue, WA 98008
Ph: (425)392-8660   Fax: (425)746-862
E-mail: jcushman@jc-a.com
URL: http://www.jc-a.com

Executive search firm.

★5507★ JW Barleycorn & Associates Inc.
1614 Lancaster Ave.
Reynoldsburg, OH 43068
Ph: (614)861-4400   Fax: (614)861-555

Executive search firm.

★5508★ Kinser & Baillou L.L.C.
590 Madison Ave.
New York, NY 10022
Ph: (212)588-8801   Fax: (212)588-880
E-mail: search@kinserbaillou.com
URL: http://www.kinserbaillou.com

A general executive search firm with special ties in boards, management consulting and communications/marketing communications

★5509★ Korn/Ferry International
200 Park Ave., 37 Fl.
New York, NY 10166
Ph: (212)687-1834   Fax: (212)986-568
URL: http://www.kornferry.com

Executive search firm. International organization with a variety of affiliate offices.

★5510★ Lancaster Associates

35 W High St.
Somerville, NJ 08876-2114
Ph: (908)526-5440   Fax: (908)526-1992
E-mail: rfl@lancasterinc.net
URL: http://www.lancasterassociates.net

Personnel consulting firm focuses recruitment on information systems, voice and data communications, managers, telecommunications, client server technology, data warehouse, project leaders, and systems programmers. Industries served: pharmaceutical, consumer products, manufacturing, transportation, financial services and insurance.

★5511★ Management Architects

6484 Washington St., Ste. B
Yountville, CA 94599
Ph: (707)945-1340   Fax: (707)945-1345
E-mail: doug@managementarchitects.net
URL: http://www.caywood.com

Executive search firm. Focuses on networking industries.

★5512★ Management Recruiters International, Inc.

1717 Arch St., 36th Fl.
Philadelphia, PA 19103
Ph: (866)836-9890   Fax: (215)751-1757
Fr: 800-836-9890
URL: http://www.mrinetwork.com

Executive search firm. More than 300 offices throughout the U.S.

★5513★ Martin H. Bauman Associates LLC

150 E. 58th St.
New York, NY 10155
Ph: (212)752-6580   Fax: (212)755-1096
E-mail: mhb@baumanassociates.com
URL: http://
www.martinbaumanassociates.com

Executive search firm.

★5514★ Neil Frank & Company

PO Box 3570
Redondo Beach, CA 90277-1570
Ph: (310)543-1611   Fax: (310)540-2639
E-mail: neilnick@aol.com
URL: http://www.neilfrank.com

Executive search firm.

★5515★ Norman Broadbent International

233 S Wacker Dr., Ste. 6850
Chicago, IL 60606
Ph: (312)876-3300   Fax: (312)876-3640
E-mail: info@nbisearch.com

Consultants specializing in the recruitment of management professionals.

★5516★ Oliver & Rozner Associates

598 Madison Ave., Ste. 11
New York, NY 10022
Ph: (212)688-1850

Performs executive search for top tiers of management including presidents, general management, advertising account management, division management, group executive and vice presidential line positions in such areas as marketing, research, operations, sales, finance, human resources, and others; hard-to-find specialists including specific marketing/advertising executives, research and development expertise, computer/data processing knowledge, scientific, physicians-product efficacy and occupational medicine, and engineering. Industries served include pharmaceutical, healthcare, hospital, advertising, consumer products and packaged goods, housewares, direct selling, cosmetics/toiletries, industrial products, high technology products, forest products, engineering, construction, environment/resource recovery, graphic arts, chemical, and government agencies.

★5517★ Pacific Crest Associates LLC

4695 MacArthur Ct., 11th Fl.
Newport Beach, CA 92660
Ph: (949)798-6204   Fax: (949)798-5549
E-mail: Careers@pacificcrestassociates.com
URL: http://www.pacificcrestassociates.com

Executive search firm.

★5518★ Paul Bodner & Associates Inc.

260 Stoney Ridge Dr.
Alpharetta, GA 30022
Ph: (678)907-6239
E-mail: pbodner@lvcm.com
URL: http://
www.paulbodnerassociates.com/index.html

Executive search firm. Second branch in Denver, CO.

★5519★ Paul Falcone Associates

PO Box 115
Mount Freedom, NJ 07970
Ph: (973)895-5200   Fax: (973)895-5266
E-mail: pfasearch@yahoo.com

Executive pharmaceutical search firm.

★5520★ Paul J. Biestek Associates Inc.

800 E. NW Hwy., Ste. 700
PO Box 101
Palatine, IL 60074
Ph: (847)825-5131
E-mail: search@biestek-associates.com
URL: http://www.biestek-associates.com

Executive search firm.

★5521★ Personnel Management Associates

48433 Sparta Line
Aylmer, ON, Canada N5H 2R4
Ph: (519)765-3788   Fax: (519)765-3788

Human resource consulting. Specialties include organizational review, employee compensation, pay equity, job descriptions, staff selection procedures, personnel policy manuals, outplacement counseling, and management training.

★5522★ Philip Conway Management

320 Hampton Place
Hinsdale, IL 60521-3823
Ph: (630)655-4566

Executive search firm.

★5523★ Phillips Personnel/Search; Phillips Temps

1675 Broadway, Ste. 2410
Denver, CO 80202
Ph: (303)893-1850   Fax: (303)893-0639
E-mail: info@phillipspersonnel.com
URL: http://www.phillipspersonnel.com

Personnel recruiting and staffing consultants in: accounting/finance, MIS, sales/marketing, engineering, administration and general/executive management. Industries served: telecommunications, distribution, financial services, and general business.

★5524★ Polly Brown Associates Inc.

230 Park Ave., Ste. 1152
New York, NY 10169
Ph: (212)661-7575   Fax: (212)808-4126
E-mail: pbrown@pollybrownassociates.com
URL: http://www.pollybrownassociates.com

Executive search firm.

★5525★ Princeton Executive Search

1 Eves Dr., Ste. 115
Marlton, NJ 08053
Ph: (609)584-1100   Fax: (856)596-8866
E-mail: info@bonifield.com
URL: http://
www.princetonexecutivesearch.com

Provides search and placement for management level professions. Specializes in accounting, banking, engineering and human resources. Industries served: financial, research and development, insurance, manufacturing, banking, and government agencies.

★5526★ R Gaines Baty Associates Inc.

12750 Merit Dr., Ste. 990
Dallas, TX 75251
Ph: (972)386-7900   Fax: (972)387-2224
E-mail: gbaty@rgba.com
URL: http://www.rgba.com

Executive search firm.

★5527★ Raines International Inc.

250 Park Ave., 17th Fl.
New York, NY 10177
Ph: (212)997-1100 Fax: (212)997-0196
E-mail: contact@rainesinternational.com
URL: http://www.rainesinternational.com

International generalist firm specializing in middle to upper management executives. Concentrations include general management, finance and accounting, information technology, operations/procurement, strategic planning, investment banking, real estate/finance, human resources, insurance, and legal.

★5528★ Robert W. Dingman Company Inc.

650 Hampshire Rd., Ste. 116
Westlake Village, CA 91361
Ph: (805)778-1777 Fax: (805)778-9288
E-mail: info@dingman.com
URL: http://www.dingman.com

Executive search firm with a second office in Black Forest, CO.

★5529★ Robohm Management Group Inc.

3 Goose Cove Rd.
Bath, ME 04530-4017
Ph: (207)442-7070 Fax: (207)442-8995
E-mail: baldwinsearch@aol.com

Executive search firm focused on the high-technology industry.

★5530★ Roth Young of Milwaukee

5215 Noth Ironwood Rd., Ste. 201
Milwaukee, WI 53217
Ph: (414)962-7684 Fax: (414)962-6261
E-mail: rothyong@execpc.com
URL: http://www.rothyoungmilwaukee.com

Executive search firm. Over 25 affiliated offices across the nation.

★5531★ Russell Reynolds Associates, Inc.

200 Park Ave., Ste. 2300
New York, NY 10166-0002
Ph: (212)351-2000 Fax: (212)370-0896
E-mail: info@russellreynolds.com
URL: http://www.russellreynolds.com

Executive search firm. Affiliate offices across the country and abroad.

★5532★ Sanford Rose Associates

3737 Embassy Pkwy, Ste. 200
Akron, OH 44333-8369
Ph: (330)670-9797 Fax: (330)670-9798
Fr: 800-731-7724
E-mail: hw@sanfordrose.com
URL: http://www.sanfordrose.com

Executive search firm. Over 80 franchised office locations nationwide.

★5533★ Search North America Inc.

PO Box 3577
Sunriver, OR 97707-0577
Ph: (503)222-6461 Fax: (503)227-2804
E-mail: mylinda@searchna.com
URL: http://www.searchna.com

An executive search and recruiting firm whose focus is placing engineers, operations and maintenance managers, sales and marketing management, financial and general management executives (both domestic and international). Industries served: forest products, pulp and paper, waste to energy, environmental services, consulting and equipment suppliers for above related industries.

★5534★ Snelling Personnel Services

6555 NW 9th Ave., Ste. 203
Fort Lauderdale, FL 33309
Ph: (954)771-0090 Fax: (954)771-8583
Fr: 800-393-0090
E-mail: ellie@snellingfl.com
URL: http://www.snelling.com/ftlauderdale

Employment agency. Over 50 offices across the country.

★5535★ Sunny Bates Associates

1123 Broadway, Ste. 311
New York, NY 10010
Ph: (212)691-5252 Fax: (212)691-3133
E-mail: info@sunnybates.com
URL: http://www.sunnybates.com

Executive search firm.

★5536★ TeamWork Consulting Inc.

22550 McCauley Rd.
Shaker Heights, OH 44122
Ph: (216)360-1790 Fax: (216)292-9265
E-mail: info@teamworkonline.com
URL: http://www.teamworkconsulting.com

A retained executive search firm retained by professional sports and live event organizations to fill open executive-level positions.

★5537★ Valerie Fredrickson & Company

800 Menlo Ave., Ste. 220
Menlo Park, CA 94025
Ph: (650)614-0220 Fax: (650)614-0223
E-mail: andrew@vfandco.com
URL: http://www.vfandco.com

Executive search firm.

★5538★ William B. Arnold Associates Inc.

2303 S. Holly St., Unit A
Denver, CO 80222
Ph: (303)393-6662
URL: http://www.wbarnold.com

Executive search firm.

★5539★ William J. Christopher Associates Inc.

307 N. Walnut St.
West Chester, PA 19380
Ph: (610)696-4397 Fax: (610)692-517?
E-mail: wjc@wjca.com
URL: http://www.wjca.com

Executive search firm.

★5540★ Williams Executive Search Inc.

90 S. 7th St., Ste. 4200
Minneapolis, MN 55402
Ph: (612)339-2900 Fax: (612)305-504(
URL: http://www.williams-exec.com/

Executive search firm.

ONLINE JOB SOURCES AND SERVICES

★5541★ 6Figurejobs.com
E-mail: info@6figurejobs.com
URL: http://www.6figurejobs.com

Description: 6FigureJobs provides executives and experienced professionals with access to some of the most exclusive executive jobs, executive recruiters and career management tools available. Includes tools for both posting and viewing jobs, resume refinement, company research and more.

★5542★ American Society of Association Executives
E-mail: career@asaenet.org
URL: http://www.asaecenter.org/YourCareer/

Description: Membership site for executives of non-profit associations. "Career Headquarters" section contains resources both for searching for employees and new positions. Executives can also search resumes and review a list of executive recruiters, plus read information on a number of employment-related issues. You do not have to be a member to view job boards.

★5543★ A.T. Kearney Executive Search
E-mail: executive_search@atkearney.com
URL: http://www.atkearney.com

Description: A.T. Kearney is an innovative, corporate-focused management consulting firm that ensures clients receive superior value in the digital economy. Executives may also submit their resumes through e-mail for consideration for present and future searches conducted by Kearney.

★5544★ Christian & Timbers
E-mail: comments@ctnet.com
URL: http://www.ctnet.com

Description: Focusing on CEO, Board director and senior-level executive search and election, clients span high-profile early-stage companies to the Fortune 50 and EuroTop 500. Site contains information on recent job trends and articles on choosing an executive level recruiter.

★5545★ ExecuNet
295 Westport Ave.
Norwalk, CT 06851
Fr: 800-637-3126
URL: http://www.execunet.com

Description: Job site dedicated to the $100,000+ executive job seeker. Members may access job bank, recruiter and employer information, have their resumes reviewed, attend networking meetings, and access cutting-edge career information and references. **Fee:** Must become member to access services, cost is $219 for six-month membership.

★5546★ ExecutivesOnly.com, Inc.
Jefferson Executive Bldg.
55 Jefferson Blvd.
Warwick, RI 02888
Ph: (401)223-0256   Fax: (401)223-0276
E-mail: support@executivesonly.com
URL: http://Executivesonly.com

Description: Job site specializing in executive positions netting an annual salary of $100K or more. Members can view job bank and set up daily e-mail alerts. They may also choose to recruit the help of a senior adviser who can help review resumes and distribute them to recruiters. **Fee:** Must become member to access services.

★5547★ Heidrick & Struggles Management Search
233 S. Wacker Dr.
Sears Tower, Ste. 4200
Chicago, IL 60606-6303
Ph: (312)496-1200
URL: http://www.heidrick.com/default.aspx

Description: Executive search firm that will distribute registered resumes to recruiters with suitable positions available.

★5548★ MBA Careers
3934 SW Corbett Ave.
Portland, OR 97239
Ph: (503)221-7779   Fax: (503)221-7780
E-mail: eric@careerexposure.com
URL: http://www.mbacareers.com

Description: Job site that provides resume posting, databank search and e-mail alert services to MBA and other advanced graduate degree holders.

★5549★ NetShare.com
83 Hamilton Dr., Ste. 202
Novato, CA 94949
Fr: 800-241-5642
E-mail: netshare@netshare.com
URL: http://www.netshare.com

Description: Members-only resource for $100,000+ executives who are actively searching for new positions or passively tracking the job market. Listings that match posted profile will be e-mailed. **Fee:** Fees vary by level of service; annual basic level dues are $360.

★5550★ Ray & Berndtson
E-mail: marketing@rayberndtson.com
URL: http://www.rayberndtson.com/

Description: Ray & Berndtson is an international executive search firm, specializing in recruiting services for top-level executives in the automotive, business and professional services, consumer products and services, e-business, energy and utilities, financial services, healthcare and life sciences, industrial products and services, education/not-for-profit, and technology industries.

★5551★ SpencerStuart.com
E-mail: contact@spenserstuart.com
URL: http://www.spencerstuart.com

Description: Executive search firm; contains professionalism resources and assessment tools for career management. Seekers can post their resume online and receive e-mail alerts about newly posted positions, along with industry news and event announcements. Must sign up for membership to take full advantage of resources.

★5552★ Spherion
2050 Spectrum Blvd.
Fort Lauderdale, FL 33309
Ph: (954)308-7600
E-mail: help@spherion.com
URL: http://www.spherion.com

Description: Recruitment firm specializing in accounting and finance, sales and marketing, interim executives, technology, engineering, retail and human resources.

★5553★ Transearch.com
E-mail: contact@transearch.com
URL: http://www.transearch.com

Description: International executive search firm concentrating in searches for executives in retail, real estate, information technology, industry, life sciences and financial services. Seekers may search job board and submit their resume for recruiter review.

★5554★ WSA Executive Job Search Center
E-mail: info@execcoachkc.com
URL: http://www.wsacorp.com

Description: A site intended for $50K-$700K range executives. Offers resume preparation, critiques and distribution, and interview preparation.

OTHER SOURCES

★5555★ Administration and Management Occupations
Delphi Productions
3159 6th St.
Boulder, CO 80304
Ph: (303)443-2100   Fax: (303)443-4022
Fr: 888-443-2400
E-mail: support@delphivideo.com
URL: http://www.delphivideo.com

$95.00. 50 minutes. Part of the Careers for the 21st Century Video Library.

★5556★ American Almanac of Jobs and Salaries
HarperCollins
10 E. 53rd St.
New York, NY 10022
Ph: (212)207-7000   Fr: 800-242-7737
URL: http://www.harpercollins.com/

John W. Wright. Revised edition, 2000. $20.00 (paper). 672 pages. This is a comprehensive guide to the wages of hundreds of occupations in a wide variety of industries and organizations.

★5557★ American Chamber of Commerce Executives (ACCE)
4875 Eisenhower Ave., Ste. 250
Alexandria, VA 22304
Ph: (703)998-0072   Fax: (703)212-9512
E-mail: mfleming@acce.org
URL: http://www.acce.org

Members: Professional society of chamber of commerce executives and staff members.

★5558★ American Management Association (AMA)
1601 Broadway
New York, NY 10019-7420
Ph: (212)586-8100   Fax: (212)903-8168
Fr: 800-262-9699
E-mail: membership@amanet.org
URL: http://www.amanet.org

Description: Provides educational forums worldwide where members and their colleagues learn superior, practical business skills and explore best practices of world-class organizations through interaction with each other and expert faculty practitioners. **Purpose:** Maintains a publishing program providing tools individuals use to extend learning beyond the classroom in a process of life-long professional growth and development through education.

★5559★ American Society of Association Executives (ASAE)
1575 I St. NW
Washington, DC 20005
Ph: (202)371-0940   Fax: (202)371-8315
Fr: 888-950-2723
E-mail: pr@asaenet.org
URL: http://www.asaecenter.org

Members: Professional society of paid executives of international, national, state, and local trade, professional, and philanthropic associations. **Purpose:** Seeks to educate association executives on effective management, including: the proper objectives, functions, and activities of associations; the basic principles of association management; the legal aspects of association activity; policies relating to association management; efficient methods, procedures, and techniques of association management; the responsibilities and professional standards of association executives. Maintains information resource center. **Activities:** Conducts resume, guidance, and consultation services; compiles statistics in the form of reports, surveys, and studies; carries out research and education. Maintains ASAE Services Corporation to provide special services and ASAE Foundation to do future-oriented research and make grant awards. Offers executive search services and insurance programs. Provides CEO center for chief staff executives. Conducts Certified Association Executive (CAE) program.

★5560★ **Center for Creative Leadership (CCL)**

PO Box 26300
Greensboro, NC 27438-6300
Ph: (336)545-2810   Fax: (336)282-3284
E-mail: info@leaders.ccl.org
URL: http://www.ccl.org

Description: Promotes behavioral science research and leadership education.

★5561★ **National Association of Corporate Directors (NACD)**

2 Lafayette Centre
1133 21st St. NW, Ste. 700
Washington, DC 20036
Ph: (202)775-0509   Fax: (202)775-4857
E-mail: info@nacdonline.org
URL: http://www.nacdonline.org

Members: Corporate directors and boards of directors; chief executive officers, presidents, accountants, lawyers, consultants, and other executives are members. **Activities:** Conducts research, surveys, and seminars.

★5562★ **National Management Association (NMA)**

2210 Arbor Blvd.
Dayton, OH 45439
Ph: (937)294-0421   Fax: (937)294-2374
E-mail: nma@nma1.org
URL: http://www.nma1.org

Description: Business and industrial management personnel; membership comes from supervisory level, with the remainder from middle management and above. Seeks to develop and recognize management as a profession and to promote the free enterprise system. Prepares chapter programs on basic management, management policy and practice, communications, human behavior, industrial relations, economics, political education, and liberal education. Maintains speakers' bureau and hall of fame. Maintains

educational, charitable, and research programs. Sponsors charitable programs.

★5563★ **National Society of Hispanic MBAs (NSHMBA)**

1303 Walnut Hill Ln., Ste. 100
Irving, TX 75038
Ph: (214)596-9338   Fax: (214)596-9325
Fr: 877-467-4622
E-mail: lhassler@nshmba.org
URL: http://www.nshmba.org

Description: Hispanic MBA professional business network dedicated to economic and philanthropic advancement.

★5564★ **Women in Management (WIM)**

PO Box 1032
Dundee, IL 60118-7032
Ph: (708)386-0496   Fax: (847)683-3751
Fr: 877-946-6285
E-mail: nationalwim@wimonline.org
URL: http://www.wimonline.org

Description: Supports network of women in professional and management positions that facilitate the exchange of experience and ideas. Promotes self-growth in management; provides speakers who are successful in management; sponsors workshops and special interest groups to discuss problems and share job experiences.

Genetic Counselors

SOURCES OF HELP-WANTED ADS

★5565★ **The American Journal of Human Genetics**

University of Chicago Press
1427 E 60th St.
Chicago, IL 60637
Ph: (773)702-7700   Fax: (773)702-9756
Fr: 877-705-1878
E-mail: ajhg@ajhg.net
URL: http://www.ajhg.org

Monthly. $1,100.00/year for individuals, print and electronic; $990.00/year for individuals, electronic only; $990.00/year for individuals, print only; $1,100.00/year for institutions, print and electronic; $990.00/year for institutions, electronic only; $990.00/year for institutions, print only; $110.00/year for institutions, single copy; $1,190.00/year for institutions, Canada, print and electronic; $1,049.40/year for institutions, Canada, electronic only; $1,073.40/year for institutions, Canada, print only. Journal devoted to research and review on heredity in man and the application of genetic principles in medicine, psychology, anthropology, and social sciences.

★5566★ **Annals of Human Genetics**

Cambridge University Press
32 Ave. of the Americas
New York, NY 10013-2473
Ph: (212)924-3900   Fax: (212)691-3239
Fr: 800-221-4512
E-mail: customerservices@oxon.blackwellpublishing.com
URL: http://www.journals.cup.org

Bimonthly. $10.00/year for individuals, article price. Journal focusing on research of human genetics and human inheritance.

★5567★ **Annual Review of Genetics**

Annual Reviews Inc.
4139 El Camino Way
PO Box 10139
Palo Alto, CA 94303-0139
Ph: (650)493-4400   Fax: (650)424-0910
Fr: 800-523-8635

URL: http://www.annualreviews.org/

Annual. $80.00/year for individuals, print & online; $80.00/year for out of country, print & online; $226.00/year for institutions, print & online; $226.00/year for institutions, other countries, print & online. Periodical covering issues in genetics and the biological sciences.

★5568★ **Clinical Genetics**

Wiley-Blackwell
350 Main St. Commerce Pl.
Malden, MA 02148
Ph: (781)388-8200   Fax: (781)388-8210
Fr: 800-759-6120
E-mail: clingen@interchg.ubc.ca
URL: http://www.blackwellpublishing.com/journal.asp?ref=0009-9163

Monthly. $410.00/year for individuals, print and online; $390.00/year for individuals, online only; $1,136.00/year for institutions, print and standard online; $1,250.00/year for institutions, print and premium online; $1,079.00/year for institutions, premium online only; $293.00/year for members, print and online; $249.00/year for members, online only; $744.00/year for institutions, other countries, print and premium online; $676.00/year for institutions, other countries, print and standard online; $642.00/year for institutions, other countries, premium online only. Journal focusing on research related to molecular approaches to genetic disease and the translation of these advances for the practicing geneticist.

★5569★ **Genetic Alliance Community Job Postings**

4301 Connecticut Ave. NW, Ste. 404
Washington, DC 20008
Ph: (202)966-5557   Fax: (202)966-8553
E-mail: network@geneticalliance.org
URL: http://www.geneticalliance.org/ws_display.asp?filter=job.board

Presents job postings in the genetics community at no cost for non profit and not-for-profit organizations; for-profits companies can post want ads for $50/month.

★5570★ **Genetical Research**

Cambridge University Press
32 Ave. of the Americas
New York, NY 10013-2473
Ph: (212)924-3900   Fax: (212)691-3239
Fr: 800-221-4512
E-mail: journals_advertising@cup.org
URL: http://journals.cambridge.org

$770.00/year for institutions, print only; $950.00/year for institutions, online and print. Science journal on all aspects of genetics.

★5571★ **Genetics**

Genetics Society of America
9650 Rockville Pke.
Bethesda, MD 20814-3998
Ph: (301)634-7300   Fax: (301)530-7079
Fr: (866)486-4363
E-mail: genetics-gsa@andrew.cmu.edu
URL: http://www.genetics.org

Monthly. $620.00/year for nonmembers, institution + postage; $640.00/year for other countries, non-members & institutions. Journal on genetics.

★5572★ **HelpWantedSanDiego.com**

1 Civic Center Plz., Ste. 506
Poughkeepsie, NY 12601
Ph: (845)485-8398
URL: http://regionalhelpwanted.com

Online job source for genetics professionals highlighting help wanted ads on the Internet and local radio stations. Resumes are sent to the advertiser's private online account.

★5573★ **Human Biology**

Wayne State University Press
Leonard N Simons Bldg., 4809 Woodward Ave.
Detroit, MI 48201-1309
Ph: (313)577-6120   Fax: (313)577-6131
Fr: 800-978-7323
E-mail: humbiol@sfbrgenetics.org
URL: http://www.humbiol.org/

Bimonthly. $95.00/year for individuals; $200.00/year for institutions; $40.00/year for students, seniors also. Journal on population genetics, evolutionary and genetic demography, and behavioral genetics.

★5574★ **Job Line**
Association of Genetic Technologists
PO Box 15945-288
Lenexa, KS 66285
Ph: (913)895-4605   Fax: (913)895-4652
E-mail: agt-info@goAMP.com
URL: http://www.agt-info.org/

Association Website offering classified job advertising for careers in genetics, posted by region.

★5575★ **Perspectives in Genetic Counseling Newsletter**
National Society of Genetic Counselors
4061 Paysphere Cir.
Chicago, IL 60674
URL: http://www.nsgc.org/resources/pgc_newsletter.cfm

Quarterly newsletter spotlighting new legislation regarding genetics issues and genetic counselors, marketing strategies for organizations, media reporting on medical genetics, meeting announcements and job listings in the field of genetics counseling.

★5576★ **PLoS Genetics**
Public Library of Science
185 Berry St., Ste. 3100
San Francisco, CA 94107
Ph: (415)624-1200   Fax: (415)546-4090
E-mail: plosgenetics@plos.org
URL: http://journals.plos.org/plosgenetics/guidelines.php

Free, online. Open access, peer-reviewed journal that publishes research and case studies in the field of genetics.

★5577★ **RetirementJobs.com, Inc.**
204 2nd Ave.
Waltham, MA 02451
Ph: (781)890-5050
E-mail: support@retirementjobs.com
URL: http://www.retirement.jobs.com/retirementstories/dreamJobs/Dream_Job_GeneticCounselor.html

Identifies companies best-suited to older workers and matches them with active, productive, conscientious, mature adults seeking jobs or projects matching their lifestyles, particularly in the genetics industry.

EMPLOYER DIRECTORIES AND NETWORKING LISTS

★5578★ **AGT International Membership Directory**
PO Box 15945-288
Lenexa, KS 66285
Ph: (913)895-4605   Fax: (913)895-4652
E-mail: agt-info@goAMP.com

URL: http://www.agt-info.org
Electronic membership directory, updated monthly; includes a collection of cytogenetics, molecular, and biochemical laboratories located throughout the U.S. and internationally.

★5579★ **American Board of Genetic Counseling-Membership Directory**
American Board of Genetic Counseling
18000 W 105th St.
Olathe, KS 66061
Ph: (913)895-4617   Fax: (913)895-4652
URL: http://www.abgc.net

Covers individuals who have passed the Board examination and includes the ABGC, Genetics Society of America, American Society of Human Genetics, American College of Medical Genetics, and the American Board of Medical Genetics.

★5580★ **American Society of Human Genetics-Membership Directory**
Genetics Society of America
9650 Rockville Pke.
Bethesda, MD 20814-3998
Ph: (301)634-7300   Fax: (301)530-7079
Fr: (866)486-4363
URL: http://www.genetics-gsa.org/cgi-bin/Search-GSA

Biennial, even years. Covers about 10,000 teachers, physicians, researchers, genetic counselors, and others interested in human genetics. Lists members of the American Society of Human Genetics, the American Board of Medical Genetics, the Genetics Society of America, the American College of Medical Genetics, and the American Board of Genetic Counseling. Entries include: Name, degree(s), institution name, department name, address, phone; type of membership and society of which a member. Arrangement: Alphabetical. Indexes: Geographical, subspecialty (American Board of Medical Genetics Members and American Board of Genetic Counseling Members) and American College of Medical Genetics.

★5581★ **Directory of Genetic Services**
Mountain States Genetics Network
8129 W Fremont Ave.
Littleton, CO 80128
Ph: (303)978-0125   Fax: (303)948-1890

Covers medical genetics service providers in the Mountain States region.

★5582★ **Genetic Disorders Sourcebook**
Omnigraphics Inc.
615 Griswold St.
PO Box 31-1640
Detroit, MI 48226
Ph: (313)961-1340   Fax: (313)961-1383
Fr: 800-234-1340
URL: http://www.omnigraphics.com

Irregular, latest edition 3rd; Published 2004. $78.00 for individuals. Covers information about genetic disorders and related organi-

zations. Entries include: Contact information. Indexes: General.

★5583★ **International Directory of Genetic Advocacy Organizations and Related Resources**
Genetic Alliance
4301 Connecticut Ave. NW, Ste. 404
Washington, DC 20008-2369
Ph: (202)966-5557   Fax: (202)966-8553
Fr: 800-336-GENE
URL: http://www.geneticalliance.org

Triennial, latest edition 2001. $37.00 for individuals. Covers more than 300 mutual support groups focused on genetic and congenital conditions, such as Alzheimer's disease, arthritis, autism, cerebral palsy, cystic fibrosis, Down syndrome, epilepsy, hemophilia, Huntington's disease, hydrocephalus, leukemia, lupus, multiple sclerosis, neurofibromatosis, Parkinson's disease, scoliosis, spina bifida, and others. Entries include: Organization name, address, phone, director name, contact, chapters, purpose, publications, audiovisuals, newsletters. Arrangement: Classified by disorder. Indexes: Subject, title.

★5584★ **National Society of Genetic Counselors E-Blast**
401 N Michigan Ave.
Chicago, IL 60611
Ph: (312)321-6834   Fax: (312)673-6972
E-mail: nsgc@nsgc.org
URL: http://www.nsgc.org/resources/eb-last.cfm

Allows members to email announcements and messages to the desktops of other members; it is recommended announcements include salary information in the text. Each announcement will have the subject line: NSGC INFORMATION to ensure prominence to each message.

ONLINE JOB SOURCES AND SERVICES

★5585★ **Employment Spot**
13 Elm St.
Birmingham, AL 35213
URL: http://www.employmentspot.com

Help wanted advertisements for professional positions, including those in the genetics field. Users can search for positions by city, state or industry.

★5586★ **National Society of Genetic Counselors Job Connection Service**
401 N Michigan Ave.
Chicago, IL 60611
Ph: (312)321-6834   Fax: (312)673-6972
E-mail: nsgc@nsgc.org
URL: http://www.nsgc.org/resources/orders_landing.cfm

Services includes a three month posting on the Society's Member's Only Website as well as a one-time posting on its General Listserv, reaching more than 85 percent of the society's full and associated members. The Listserv allows users to target a select audience of members in the following specialties: cancer, prenatal, pediatric, cardiovascular, industry, psychiatric disorders, and general.

OTHER SOURCES

★5587★ **Alstrom Syndrome International (ASI)**
14 Whitney Farm Rd.
Mount Desert, ME 04660
Ph: (207)288-6385   Fax: (207)288-6078
Fr: 800-371-3628
E-mail: asisandra@eastlink.ca
URL: http://www.jax.org/alstrom

Members: Individuals with Alstrom's syndrome (a genetic disorder resulting in multiple organ failures) and their families; health care professionals with an interest in the syndrome and its diagnosis and treatment. **Purpose:** Seeks to improve the quality of life of people with Alstrom's syndrome. **Activities:** Serves as a clearinghouse on the syndrome and its treatment; functions as a support group for people with Alstrom's syndrome and their families. Encourages and fosters genetic and clinical research on Alstrom Syndrome.

★5588★ **American Board of Genetic Counseling (ABGC)**
PO Box 14216
Lenexa, KS 66285
Ph: (913)895-4617   Fax: (913)895-4652
E-mail: info@abgc.net
URL: http://www.abgc.net

Description: Comprised only of individuals who have passed the certification examination. Certifies individuals for the delivery of genetic counseling services and accredits genetic counseling master's degree granting programs.

★5589★ **American Board of Medical Genetics (ABMG)**
9650 Rockville Pike
Bethesda, MD 20814-3998
Ph: (301)634-7315   Fax: (301)634-7320
E-mail: abmg@abmg.org
URL: http://www.abmg.org

Description: Certifies individuals and accredits training programs in the field of human genetics.

★5590★ **American College of Medical Genetics (ACMG)**
9650 Rockville Pike
Bethesda, MD 20814-3999
Ph: (301)634-7127   Fax: (301)634-7275

E-mail: acmg@acmg.net
URL: http://www.acmg.net

Members: Physicians and others with an interest in genetics and the delivery of medical genetics services to the public. **Purpose:** Works to insure the availability of genetic services without regard to considerations of race, gender, sexual orientation, disability, or ability to pay. Promotes and supports genetics research. **Activities:** Establishes and maintains scientific and professional standards for medical genetics education, research, and practice. Lobbies for effective and fair health policies and legislation; provides information and technical assistance to government agencies engaged in health care regulation or policy formation. Makes available continuing professional education programs; represents members' interests. Conducts advocacy campaigns for people with genetic problems; sponsors public education programs.

★5591★ **American Genetic Association (AGA)**
PO Box 257
Buckeystown, MD 21717-0257
Ph: (301)695-9292   Fax: (301)695-9292
E-mail: agajoh@mail.ncifcrf.gov
URL: http://www.theaga.org

Description: Represents biologists, zoologists, geneticists, botanists, and others engaged in basic and applied research in genetics. Explores transmission genetics of plants and animals.

★5592★ **American Society of Human Genetics (ASHG)**
9650 Rockville Pike
Bethesda, MD 20814-3998
Ph: (301)634-7300   Fax: (301)634-7079
Fr: (866)HUM-GENE
E-mail: society@ashg.org
URL: http://www.ashg.org

Members: Professional society of physicians, researchers, genetic counselors, and others interested in human genetics.

★5593★ **Association of Genetic Technologists**
PO Box 15945-288
Lenexa, KS 66285
Ph: (913)895-4605   Fax: (913)895-4652
E-mail: agt-info@goAMP.com
URL: http://www.agt-info.org/

Professional organization of 1,200 technologists, supervisors and laboratory directors dedicated to promoting these professionals engaged in classical cytogenetics and molecular and biochemical genetics; and to stimulate interest in genetics as a career.

★5594★ **Association of Professors of Human and Medical Genetics (APHMG)**
Wayne State University School of Medicine
Molecular Medicine and Genetics Dept.
540 E Canfield St.
3216 Scott Hall
Detroit, MI 48201-1928
Ph: (313)577-6298   Fax: (313)577-9137
E-mail: glfeldman@genetics.wayne.edu
URL: http://genetics.faseb.org/genetics/aphmg/aphmg1.htm

Description: Promotes human and medical genetics educational programs in North American medical and graduate schools. Conducts academic activities and workshops that deal with medical genetics.

★5595★ **Behavior Genetics Association (BGA)**
University of Colorado
Institute for Behavioral Genetics
447 UCB
Boulder, CO 80309-0447
E-mail: treasurer@bga.org
URL: http://www.bga.org

Description: Individuals engaged in teaching or research in some area of behavior genetics. Purposes are: to promote the scientific study of the interrelationship of genetic mechanisms and human and animal behavior through sponsorship of scientific meetings, publications, and communications among and by members; to encourage and aid the education and training of research workers in the field of behavior genetics; to aid in public dissemination and interpretation of information concerning the interrelationship of genetics and behavior and its implications for health, human development, and education.

★5596★ **Genetic Counseling Foundation**
401 N Michigan Ave., Ste. 2200
Chicago, IL 60611
Ph: (312)321-5163   Fax: (312)673-6972
E-mail: info@geneticcounselingfoundation.org
URL: http://www.nsgc.org/

Seeks to improve quality education and research in the field of genetic counseling and to enhance the value, availability and awareness of genetic information and counseling in the medical community as well as the general public.

★5597★ **Genetics Society of America (GSA)**
9650 Rockville Pike
Bethesda, MD 20814-3998
Ph: (301)634-7300   Fax: (301)530-7079
Fr: (866)486-GENE
E-mail: society@genetics-gsa.org
URL: http://www.genetics-gsa.org

Members: Individuals and organizations interested in any field of genetics. **Purpose:** Provides facilities for association and conferences of students in heredity; encourages communication among workers in genetics and those in related sciences.

★5598★ **International Federation of Human Genetics Societies**
9650 Rockville Pike
Bethesda, MD 20814-3998
Ph: (301)634-7300   Fax: (301)634-7079
E-mail: estrass@ashg.org
URL: http://www.ifhgs.org

Description: Supports human genetics research and practice.

★5599★ **International Society of Nurses in Genetics (ISONG)**
461 Cochran Rd.
Box 246
Pittsburgh, PA 15228
Ph: (412)344-1414   Fax: (412)344-0599
E-mail: isonghq@msn.com
URL: http://www.isong.org

Description: Represents case managers, administrators, coordinators of public and private programs, educators in the field of nursing and/or genetics, genetic counselors, researchers. Committed to incorporating the knowledge of human genetics into nursing practice, education and research activities.

★5600★ **Mountain States Genetics Network (MostGene)**
8129 W Fremont Ave.
Littleton, CO 80128
Ph: (303)978-0125   Fax: (303)948-1890

E-mail: mostgenes@msn.com
URL: http://www.mostgene.org

Description: Advocates and supports education, awareness and access to medical genetics information.

★5601★ **National Board for Certified Counselors and Affiliates (NBCC)**
3 Terrace Way
Greensboro, NC 27403-3660
Ph: (336)547-0607   Fax: (336)547-0017
E-mail: nbcc@nbcc.org
URL: http://www.nbcc.org

Purpose: Establishes and monitors professional credentialing standards for counselors. Identifies individuals who have obtained voluntary certification as a National Certified Counselor, one who assists persons with aging, vocational development, adolescence, family, and marital concerns, or a National Certified School Counselor, one who specializes in counseling within the school setting, or a Certified Clinical Mental Health Counselor, one who specializes in working in clinical settings, or a Master Addictions Counselor, one who specializes in addictions counseling. Maintains a database of nearly 37,000 certified counselors.

★5602★ **National Coalition for Health Professional Education in Genetics (NCHPEG)**
2360 W Joppa Rd., Ste. 320
Lutherville, MD 21093
Ph: (410)583-0600   Fax: (410)583-0520

E-mail: info@nchpeg.org
URL: http://www.nchpeg.org

Description: Promotes advances in health professional education and access to human genetics information.

★5603★ **National Society of Genetic Counselors (NSGC)**
401 N Michigan Ave., Ste. 2200
Chicago, IL 60611
Ph: (312)321-6834   Fax: (312)673-6972
E-mail: fyi@nsgc.org
URL: http://www.nsgc.org

Description: Promotes the genetic counseling profession as a recognized and integral part of health care delivery, education, research and public policy.

★5604★ **Professional Status Survey**
National Society of Genetic Counselors
401 N Michigan Ave.
Chicago, IL 60611
Ph: (312)321-6834   Fax: (312)673-6972
E-mail: nsgc@nsgc.org
URL: http://www.nsgc.org/career/pss_index.cfm

Bi-annual survey presenting an overview of genetics professions; includes information regarding salary ranges, work environments, faculty status, and job satisfaction.

Geographers

SOURCES OF HELP-WANTED ADS

★5605★ AAG Newsletter
Association of American Geographers
1710 16th St. NW
Washington, DC 20009-3198
Ph: (202)234-1450   Fax: (202)234-2744
URL: http://www.aag.org/Publications/
NewsLetter.html

Description: Monthly. Publishes items of interest to Association members and persons in related disciplines. Contains news of research, news of members, listings of publications, information on grant and employment opportunities, notices of field courses and seminars, calls for papers, and a calendar of events.

★5606★ Base Line
Map and Geography Round Table
c/o James A. Coombs
SW Missiouri State Univ.
Maps Library
Springfield, MO 65804-0095
Ph: (417)280-3205   Fax: (417)280-3257
Fr: 800-545-2433
E-mail: library@ala.org
URL: http://www.ala.org/ala/alalibrary/ala-periodicals/alaperiodicals.htm

Description: Bimonthly. Provides current information on cartographic materials, publications of interest to map and geography librarians, related government activities, and map librarianship. Recurring features include conference and meeting information, news of research, job listings, and columns by the Division chair and the editor.

★5607★ Geographical Analysis
Wiley-Blackwell
350 Main St. Commerce Pl.
Malden, MA 02148
Ph: (781)388-8200   Fax: (781)388-8210
Fr: 800-759-6120
URL: http://www.blackwellpublishing.com/
journal.asp?ref=0016-7363

Quarterly. $54.00/year for individuals, print and online; $29.00/year for students, print and online; $272.00/year for institutions, print and premium online; $247.00/year for institutions, print and standard online; $235.00/year for institutions, premium online only. Journal focusing on significant advances in geographical theory, model building, and quantitative methods to geographers and scholars in a wide spectrum of related fields.

★5608★ Geographical Journal
Wiley-Blackwell
350 Main St. Commerce Pl.
Malden, MA 02148
Ph: (781)388-8200   Fax: (781)388-8210
Fr: 800-759-6120
URL: http://www.blackwellpublishing.com/
journal.asp?ref=0016-7398

Quarterly. $263.00/year for institutions, print and premium online; $239.00/year for institutions, print and standard online; $227.00/year for institutions, premium online only; $156.00/year for institutions, other countries, print and premium online; $142.00/year for institutions, other countries, print and standard online; $135.00/year for institutions, other countries, premium online only. Journal focusing on original research and scholarship in physical and human geography.

★5609★ Geographical Research
Wiley-Blackwell
350 Main St. Commerce Pl.
Malden, MA 02148
Ph: (781)388-8200   Fax: (781)388-8210
Fr: 800-759-6120
URL: http://www.blackwellpublishing.com/
journal.asp?ref=1745-5863

Quarterly. $49.00/year for individuals, print and online, Australia & New Zealand; $37.00/year for members, print and online, Australia & New Zealand; $135.00/year for institutions, print and premium online, Australia & New Zealand; $123.00/year for institutions, print and standard online, Australia & New Zealand; $117.00/year for institutions, premium online only, Australia & New Zealand; $71.00/year for individuals, print and online; $50.00/year for members, print and online; $376.00/year for institutions, other countries, print and premium online; $342.00/year for institutions, other countries, print and standard online; $325.00/year for institutions, other countries, premium online only. Journal focusing on advancing geographical research across the discipline.

★5610★ International Regional Science Review
Sage Publications Inc.
2455 Teller Rd.
Thousand Oaks, CA 91320
Ph: (805)499-0721   Fax: (805)499-8096
URL: http://www.sagepub.com/journal-sProdDesc.nav?prodId=Journal20

Quarterly. $407.00/year for institutions, print & e-access; $427.00/year for institutions (current volume print & all online content); $366.00/year for institutions, e-access; $386.00/year for institutions, all online content; $653.00/year for institutions, backfile purchase, e-access (content through 1999); $399.00/year for institutions, print only; $97.00/year for individuals, print only; $110.00 for institutions, single print; $32.00 for individuals, single print. Journal of economists, geographers, planners, and other social scientists.

★5611★ Journal of Latin American Geography
University of Texas Press
2100 Comal
PO Box 7819
Austin, TX 78722
Ph: (512)471-7233   Fax: (512)232-7178
Fr: 800-252-3206
URL: http://www.utexas.edu/utpress/journals/jlag.html

Semiannual. $60.00/year for individuals; $72.00/year for individuals, Canada; $20.00/year for individuals, Latin America; $75.00/year for individuals, other countries; $15.00/year for students; $27.00/year for students, Canada; $30.00/year for students, other countries; $100.00/year for institutions; $112.00/year for institutions, Canada; $20.00/year for institutions, Latin America. Journal of the Conference of Latin American Geographists containing articles of interest to professionals in the field.

★5612★ PALAIOS

SEPM Publications
6128 E 38th St., Ste. 308
Tulsa, OK 74135-5814
Ph: (918)610-3361   Fax: (918)621-1685
Fr: 800-865-9765
URL: http://www.sepm.org/

Bimonthly. $200.00/year for individuals, for U.S. online version with CD-ROM; $235.00/year for individuals, for U.S. print and online version with CD-ROM; $200.00/year for other countries, online version with CD-ROM; $245.00/year for other countries, print and online version with CD-ROM. Journal providing information on the impact of life on Earth history as recorded in the paleontological and sedimentological records. Covers areas such as biogeochemistry, ichnology, sedimentology, stratigraphy, paleoecology, paleoclimatology, and paleoceanography.

★5613★ PE & RS Photogrammetric Engineering & Remote Sensing

The Imaging and Geospatial Information Society
5410 Grosvenor Ln., Ste. 210
Bethesda, MD 20814-2160
Ph: (301)493-0290   Fax: (301)493-0208
E-mail: asprs@asprs.org
URL: http://www.asprs.org/

Monthly. $250.00/year for individuals, U.S.D 15 discount per subscp. off the base rate; $120.00/year for individuals, active; $80.00/year for individuals, associate; $45.00/year for students, domestic. Journal covering photogrammetry, remote sensing, geographic information systems, cartography, and surveying, global positioning systems, digital photogrammetry.

★5614★ Population, Space and Place

John Wiley & Sons Inc.
111 River St.
Hoboken, NJ 07030-5774
Ph: (201)748-6000   Fax: (201)748-6088
Fr: 800-825-7550
URL: http://www3.interscience.wiley.com/cgi-bin/jhome/106562735

Bimonthly. $465.00/year for individuals, for print; $945.00/year for institutions, for print; $1,040.00/year for elsewhere, for combined print with online. Journal focusing on research in the field of geographical population studies.

★5615★ The Professional Geographer

San Diego State University
BAM-2
San Diego, CA 92182-7800
Ph: (619)594-4199   Fax: (619)594-7277
URL: http://www.aag.org/Publications/pgweb1.html

Quarterly. $840.00/year for institutions, print + premium online; $931.00/year for Canada and Mexico, print + premium online; $764.00/year for institutions, print + standard online; $846.00/year for Canada and Mexico, institutional: print + standard online; $726.00/year for institutions, premium online only; $804.00/year for Canada and Mexico,

premium online only; $655.00/year for institutions, other countries, print + premium online; $595.00/year for institutions, other countries, institutional: print + standard online; $655.00/year for institutions, Europe, print and premium online; $595.00/year for institutions, Europe, print + standard online. Geographical journal.

PLACEMENT AND JOB REFERRAL SERVICES

★5616★ African Studies Association (ASA)

Douglass Campus
132 George St.
New Brunswick, NJ 08901-1400
Ph: (732)932-8173   Fax: (732)932-3394
E-mail: asaed@rci.rutgers.edu
URL: http://www.africanstudies.org

Members: Persons specializing in teaching, writing, or research on Africa including political scientists, historians, geographers, anthropologists, economists, librarians, linguists, and government officials; persons who are studying African subjects; institutional members are universities, libraries, government agencies, and others interested in receiving information about Africa. **Purpose:** Seeks to foster communication and to stimulate research among scholars on Africa. **Activities:** Sponsors placement service; conducts panels and discussion groups; presents exhibits and films.

EMPLOYER DIRECTORIES AND NETWORKING LISTS

★5617★ Guide to Programs in Geography in the United States and Canada/AAG Handbook and Directory of Geographers

Association of American Geographers
1710 16th St. NW
Washington, DC 20009-3198
Ph: (202)234-1450   Fax: (202)234-2744
E-mail: aagguide@aag.org

Annual; latest edition February 2005. $60.00 for nonmembers; $25.00 for students; $35.00 for members. Covers institutions offering undergraduate and graduate geography programs; and government agencies, private firms and research institutions that employ geographers in the U.S., Canada and Mexico. Entries include: For institutions–Department, address, and phone, contact person, requirements, programs, facilities, financial aid, faculty, titles of dissertations and theses completed. For individuals–Name, address, birth date, degrees received, place of employment. Arrangement: Geographical. Indexes: Department specialty; ZIP code.

HANDBOOKS AND MANUALS

★5618★ Opportunities in Social Science Careers

The McGraw-Hill Companies
PO Box 182604
Columbus, OH 43272
Fax: (614)759-3749   Fr: 877-883-5524
E-mail: customer.service@mcgraw-hill.com
URL: http://www.mcgraw-hill.com

Rosanne J. Marek. 2004. $13.95. 160 Pages. VGM Opportunities Series.

TRADESHOWS

★5619★ Association of American Geographers Annual Meeting

Association of American Geographers
1710 16th St., NW
Washington, DC 20009-3198
Ph: (202)234-1450   Fax: (202)234-2744
E-mail: gaia@aag.org
URL: http://www.aag.org/

Annual. **Primary Exhibits:** Publications, geographic information systems, and technical equipment. **Dates and Locations:** 2008 Apr 15-19; Boston, MA.

OTHER SOURCES

★5620★ American Geographical Society

120 Wall St., Ste. 100
New York, NY 10005-3904
Ph: (212)422-5456   Fax: (212)422-5480
E-mail: ags@amergeog.org
URL: http://www.amergeog.org

Description: Industry professionals and other interested individuals.

★5621★ ASPRS - The Imaging and Geospatial Information Society

5410 Grosvenor Ln., Ste. 210
Bethesda, MD 20814-2160
Ph: (301)493-0290   Fax: (301)493-0208
E-mail: asprs@asprs.org
URL: http://www.asprs.org

Members: Firms, individuals, government employees and academicians engaged in photogrammetry, photointerpretation, remote sensing, and geographic information systems and their application to such fields as archaeology, geographic information systems, military reconnaissance, urban planning, engineering, traffic surveys, meteorological observations, medicine, geology, forestry, agriculture, construction and topographic mapping. Mission is to advance knowledge and improve understanding of these sciences and to promote responsible applications. **Activities:** Offers voluntary certification program open to persons associated with one or more functional area of photogrammetry, remote sensing and GIS. Surveys the profession of private firms in photogrammetry and remote sensing in the areas of products and services.

★5622★ **Association of American Geographers (AAG)**
1710 16th St. NW
Washington, DC 20009-3198
Ph: (202)234-1450   Fax: (202)234-2744
E-mail: gaia@aag.org
URL: http://www.aag.org

Description: Professional society of educators and scientists in the field of geography. Seeks to further professional investigations in geography and to encourage the application of geographic research in education, government, and business. Conducts research; compiles statistics.

★5623★ **Geography Education National Implementation Project**
Texas A & M University
College Station, TX 77843-3147
Ph: (979)845-1579   Fax: (979)862-4487
E-mail: s-bednarz@tamu.edu
URL: http://genip.tamu.edu

Description: Consortium of geographic associations committed to improving the status and quality of geography education.

★5624★ **National Council for Geographic Education (NCGE)**
206A Martin Hall
Jacksonville State University
Jacksonville, AL 36265-1602
Ph: (256)782-5293   Fax: (256)782-5336
E-mail: ncge@ncge.org
URL: http://www.ncge.org

Description: Teachers of geography and social studies in elementary and secondary schools, colleges and universities; geogra-

phers in governmental agencies and private businesses. Encourages the training of teachers in geographic concepts, practices, teaching methods and techniques; works to develop effective geographic educational programs in schools and colleges and with adult groups; stimulates the production and use of accurate and understandable geographic teaching aids and materials.

★5625★ **Scientific, Engineering, and Technical Services**
Cambridge Educational
PO Box 2053
Princeton, NJ 08543-2053
Ph: 800-257-5126   Fax: (609)671-0266
Fr: 800-468-4227
E-mail: custserv@films.com
URL: http://www.cambridgeeducational.com
VHS and DVD. $89.95. 2002. 18 minutes. 2002. Part of the Career Cluster Series.

Geologists and Geophysicists

SOURCES OF HELP-WANTED ADS

★5626★ AAPG Bulletin
American Association of Petroleum
  Geologists
1444 S Boulder
PO Box 979
Tulsa, OK 74101-0979
Ph: (918)584-2555   Fax: (918)560-2694
Fr: 800-364-AAPG
E-mail: bulletin@aapg.org
URL: http://www.aapg.org

Monthly. $99.00/year for individuals. Peer-reviewed journal on the application of geological and geophysical principles to exploration and production for the development of energy resources. Subjects include petroleum geology, oil shale, coal, uranium, and geothermal energy.

★5627★ AAPG Explorer
American Association of Petroleum
  Geologists
1444 S Boulder
PO Box 979
Tulsa, OK 74101-0979
Ph: (918)584-2555   Fax: (918)560-2694
Fr: 800-364-AAPG
URL: http://www.aapg.org

Monthly. $63.00/year for nonmembers; $60.00/year for individuals, airmail service. Magazine containing articles about energy issues with an emphasis on exploration for hydrocarbons and energy minerals.

★5628★ AEG News
Association of Engineering Geologists
PO Box 460518
Denver, CO 80246
Ph: (303)757-2926   Fax: (303)757-2969
E-mail: aeg@aegweb.org
URL: http://www.aegweb.org

Description: Bimonthly. Covers news of the engineering geology profession and the Association, whose members are engineering geologists and geological engineers worldwide. Recurring features include letters to the editor, a calendar of events, news of research, and short articles of technical interest.

★5629★ AWIS Magazine
Association for Women in Science
1200 New York Ave. NW, Ste. 650
Washington, DC 20005
Ph: (202)326-8940   Fax: (202)326-8960
Fr: (866)657-2947
E-mail: awis@awis.org
URL: http://www.awis.org/

Description: Bimonthly. Covers issues, legislation, and trends related to science education for girls, women, and minorities. Includes information on grants and fellowships, job openings, educational programs, events, and notices of publications available.

★5630★ Engineering and Mining Journal
Penton Media Inc.
9800 Metcalf Ave.
Overland Park, KS 66212
Ph: (913)341-1300   Fax: (913)967-1898
URL: http://www.e-mj.com

Monthly. Provides professionals in metallic and nonmetallic ores and minerals industries with news and technical economic information.

★5631★ Geological Abstracts
Elsevier Science Inc.
360 Park Ave. S
New York, NY 10010
Ph: (212)989-5800   Fax: (212)633-3990
URL: http://www.elsevier.com

$3,402.00/year for institutions in all countries except Europe, Japan and Iran. Journal relating to geological literature.

★5632★ Geology
Geological Society of America Inc.
3300 Penrose Pl.
PO Box 9140
Boulder, CO 80301-1806
Ph: (303)357-1000   Fax: (303)357-1070
Fr: 888-443-4472

E-mail: pubs@geocociety.org
URL: http://www.gsajournals.org/perlserv/
?request=index-html

Monthly. Geology journal.

★5633★ Geophysical Journal International
Wiley-Blackwell
350 Main St. Commerce Pl.
Malden, MA 02148
Ph: (781)388-8200   Fax: (781)388-8210
Fr: 800-759-6120
URL: http://www.blackwellpublishing.com/
journal.asp?ref=0956-540X

Monthly. $393.00/year for individuals, print and online; $359.00/year for individuals, online only; $191.00/year for members, print and online; $2,404.00/year for institutions, print and premium online; $2,185.00/year for institutions, print and standard online; $2,076.00/year for institutions, premium online only. Journal focusing on research in geophysics.

★5634★ Nature International Weekly Journal of Science
Nature Publishing Group
75 Varick St., 9th Fl.
New York, NY 10013-1917
Ph: (212)726-9200   Fax: (212)696-9006
Fr: 888-331-6288
E-mail: nature@natureny.com
URL: http://www.nature.com

Weekly. $145.00/year for individuals; $49.00/year for institutions. Magazine covering science and technology, including the fields of biology, biochemistry, genetics, medicine, earth sciences, physics, pharmacology, and behavioral sciences.

★5635★ Oil & Gas Journal
PennWell Publishing Co.
1421 S Sheridan Rd.
Tulsa, OK 74112
Ph: (918)835-3161   Fr: 800-331-4463
URL: http://www.ogjonline.com

Weekly. $89.00/year for individuals; $94.00/year for Canada, Latin America; $139.00/year for other countries; $150.00 for two years; $160.00 for two years, Canada/Latin America; $238.00/year for other countries, 2 years; $215.00/year for individuals, 3 years; $220.00/year for Canada, Latin America, 3 years; $332.00/year for other countries, 3 years; $60.00/year for individuals. Trade magazine serving engineers and managers in international petroleum operations.

★5636★ *PALAIOS*

SEPM Publications
6128 E 38th St., Ste. 308
Tulsa, OK 74135-5814
Ph: (918)610-3361   Fax: (918)621-1685
Fr: 800-865-9765
URL: http://www.sepm.org/

Bimonthly. $200.00/year for individuals, for U.S. online version with CD-ROM; $235.00/year for individuals, for U.S. print and online version with CD-ROM; $200.00/year for other countries, online version with CD-ROM; $245.00/year for other countries, print and online version with CD-ROM. Journal providing information on the impact of life on Earth history as recorded in the paleontological and sedimentological records. Covers areas such as biogeochemistry, ichnology, sedimentology, stratigraphy, paleoecology, paleoclimatology, and paleoceanography.

★5637★ *PE & RS Photogrammetric Engineering & Remote Sensing*

The Imaging and Geospatial Information Society
5410 Grosvenor Ln., Ste. 210
Bethesda, MD 20814-2160
Ph: (301)493-0290   Fax: (301)493-0208
E-mail: asprs@asprs.org
URL: http://www.asprs.org/

Monthly. $250.00/year for individuals, U.S.D 15 discount per subscp. off the base rate; $120.00/year for individuals, active; $80.00/year for individuals, associate; $45.00/year for students, domestic. Journal covering photogrammetry, remote sensing, geographic information systems, cartography, and surveying, global positioning systems, digital photogrammetry.

★5638★ *The Scientist*

The Scientist Inc.
400 Market St., No. 1250
Philadelphia, PA 19106
Ph: (215)351-1660   Fax: (215)351-1146
URL: http://www.the-scientist.com

Bimonthly. $49.95/year for individuals, online; $74.95/year for individuals, online plus print edition; $124.95/year for out of country, online plus print edition (air freight); $29.95/year for individuals, 6 months; $14.95 for individuals, 1 month; $9.95 for individuals, 1 week; $4.95 for individuals, 1 week. News journal (tabloid) for life scientists featuring news, opinions, research, and professional section.

PLACEMENT AND JOB REFERRAL SERVICES

★5639★ American Geophysical Union (AGU)

2000 Florida Ave. NW
Washington, DC 20009-1277
Ph: (202)462-6900   Fax: (202)328-0566
Fr: 800-966-2481
E-mail: service@agu.org
URL: http://www.agu.org

Members: Individuals professionally associated with the field of geophysics; supporting institutional members are companies and other organizations whose work involves geophysics. **Purpose:** Promotes the study of problems concerned with the figure and physics of the earth; initiates and coordinates research that depends upon national and international cooperation and provides for scientific discussion of research results. **Activities:** Sponsors placement service at semiannual meeting.

★5640★ Association of Ground Water Scientists and Engineers - A Division of National Ground Water Association (AGWSE)

601 Dempsey Rd.
Westerville, OH 43081-8978
Ph: (614)898-7791   Fax: (614)898-7786
Fr: 800-551-7379
E-mail: smasters@ngwa.org
URL: http://www.ngwa.org/agwse/index.aspx

Description: A technical division of the National Ground Water Association. Hydrogeologists, geologists, hydrologists, civil and environmental engineers, geochemists, biologists, and scientists in related fields. Seeks to: provide leadership and guidance for scientific, economical, and beneficial groundwater development; promote the use, protection, and management of the world's groundwater resources. Conducts educational programs, seminars, short courses, symposia, and field research projects. Maintains speakers' bureau and museum; offers placement service; sponsors competitions; compiles statistics.

★5641★ Geological Society of America (GSA)

PO Box 9140
Boulder, CO 80301-9140
Ph: (303)357-1000   Fax: (303)357-1070
Fr: 888-443-4472
E-mail: gsaservice@geosociety.org
URL: http://www.geosociety.org

Description: Serves as professional society of earth scientists. Promotes the science of geology. Maintains placement service.

★5642★ National Ground Water Association (NGWA)

601 Dempsey Rd.
Westerville, OH 43081-8978
Ph: (614)898-7791   Fax: (614)898-7786
Fr: 800-551-7379

E-mail: ngwa@ngwa.org
URL: http://www.ngwa.org

Description: Ground water drilling contractors; manufacturers and suppliers of drilling equipment; ground water scientists such as geologists, engineers, public health officials, and others interested in the problems of locating, developing, preserving, and using ground water supplies. Conducts seminars, and continuing education programs. Encourages scientific education, research, and the development of standards; offers placement services; compiles market statistics. Offers charitable program. Maintains speakers' bureau.

EMPLOYER DIRECTORIES AND NETWORKING LISTS

★5643★ *American Men and Women of Science*

Gale, Cengage Learning
27500 Drake Rd.
Farmington Hills, MI 48331-3535
Ph: (248)699-4253   Fax: (248)699-8065
Fr: 800-877-4253
URL: http://www.gale.com

Biennial, latest edition 23rd, October 2006; new edition expected 24th, January 2008. $1,075.00 for individuals. Covers over 129,700 U.S. and Canadian scientists active in the physical, biological, mathematical, computer science, and engineering fields; includes references to previous edition for deceased scientists and nonrespondents. Entries include: Name, address, education, personal and career data, memberships, honors and awards, research interest. Arrangement: Alphabetical. Indexes: Discipline (in separate volume).

★5644★ *Directory of Certified Petroleum Geologists*

American Association of Petroleum Geologists
1444 S Boulder Ave.
PO Box 979
Tulsa, OK 74101-0979
Ph: (918)584-2555   Fax: (918)560-2665
Fr: 800-364-2274
URL: http://www.aapg.org/dpadirectory/

Covers about 3,400 members of the association. Entries include: Name, address; education and career data; whether available for consulting. Arrangement: Alphabetical. Indexes: Geographical.

★5645★ *Directory of Physics, Astronomy, and Geophysics Staff*

American Institute of Physics
1 Physics Ellipse
College Park, MD 20740-3843
Ph: (301)209-3100
URL: http://www.aip.org/pubs/books/dpags.html

Biennial; latest edition 2006. $82.00 for

individuals. Covers 31,000 staff members at 2,300 colleges, universities, and laboratories throughout North America that employ physicists and astronomers; list of foreign organizations. Entries include: Name, address, phone, fax, e-mail address. Arrangement: Separate alphabetical sections for individuals, academic institutions, and laboratories. Indexes: Academic institution location, type of laboratory.

★5646★ **The Geophysical Directory**

Geophysical Directory Inc.
PO Box 130508
Houston, TX 77219
Ph: (713)529-8789   Fax: (713)529-3646
Fr: 800-929-2462
E-mail: info@geophysicaldirectory.com
URL: http://www.geophysicaldirectory.com

Annual; latest edition 62nd. $140.00 for individuals; $155.00 for individuals. Covers about 4,000 companies that provide geophysical equipment, supplies, or services, and mining and petroleum companies that use geophysical techniques; international coverage. Entries include: Company name, address, phone, fax, names of principal executives, operations, and sales personnel; similar information for branch locations. Arrangement: Classified by product or service. Indexes: Company name, personal name.

★5647★ **Geophysicists**

American Geophysical Union
2000 Florida Ave. NW
Washington, DC 20009-1277
Ph: (202)462-6900   Fax: (202)328-0566
Fr: 800-966-2481
URL: http://www.agu.org

Covers 40,000 member geophysicists. Entries include: Name, address, office and home phone numbers, fax, electronic mail address, type of membership, year joined, and section affiliation. Arrangement: Alphabetical.

★5648★ **The Oil & Gas Directory**

Geophysical Directory Inc.
PO Box 130508
Houston, TX 77219
Ph: (713)529-8789   Fax: (713)529-3646
Fr: 800-929-2462
URL: http://www.geophysicaldirectory.com

Annual, October; latest edition 37th. $130.00 for individuals; $145.00 for individuals. Covers about 9,000 companies worldwide involved in petroleum exploration, drilling, and production, and suppliers to the industry. Entries include: Company name, address, phone, fax, names of principal personnel; branch office addresses, phone, and names of key personnel. Arrangement: Classified by activity. Indexes: Company name, personal name and regional.

★5649★ **Peterson's Job Opportunities in Engineering and Technology**

Peterson's Guides
2000 Lenox Dr.
Box 67005
Lawrenceville, NJ 08648
Ph: (609)896-1800   Fax: (609)896-4531
Fr: 800-338-3282
E-mail: custsvc@petersons.com
URL: http://www.petersons.com

Compiled by the Peterson's staff. Fourth edition, 1996. $21.95 (paper). 379 pages. Profiles 2,000 high-tech companies looking primarily for technical personnel in such fields as biotechnology, telecommunications, software, computers and peripherals, defense, and aerospace. Contains job-search strategies and career options to help match education and expertise to the job market. Indexed geographically, by industry, and by hiring needs.

★5650★ **Society of Exploration Geophysicists-Yearbook**

Society of Exploration Geophysicists
8801 S Yale
PO Box 702740
Tulsa, OK 74170-2740
Ph: (918)497-5500   Fax: (918)497-5557
URL: http://seg.org/publications/yearbook/

Annual, May. Publication includes: Membership roster of nearly 14,500 geophysicists, corporations, and students. Entries include: Name, address, phone, fax, e-mail type of member; affiliation given for individuals. Arrangement: Alphabetical; geographical.

HANDBOOKS AND MANUALS

★5651★ **Becoming an Independent Geologist: Thriving in Good Times & Bad**

American Association of Petroleum Geologist
PO Box 979
Tulsa, OK 74101-9979
Fax: (918)560-2632
URL: http://www.aapg.org/

James A. Gibbs. 1999. $12.00 (paper). 40 pages.

★5652★ **The Best Resumes for Scientists and Engineers**

John Wiley & Sons Inc.
1 Wiley Dr.
Somerset, NJ 08873
Ph: (732)469-4400   Fax: (732)302-2300
Fr: 800-225-5945
E-mail: custserv@wiley.com
URL: http://www.wiley.com/WileyCDA/

Adele Lewis and David J. Moore. Second edition, 1993. $37.50; $19.95 (paper). 224 pages. Presents an extensive collection of scientific and engineering resumes, highlighting the important differences between

these and resumes written for other occupations.

★5653★ **Careers in Environmental Geoscience**

American Association of Petroleum Geologists
PO Box 979
Tulsa, OK 74101-0979
Ph: (918)584-2555   Fax: (918)560-2652
Fr: 800-364-2274
URL: http://www.aapg.org

Robert R. Jordan, Rima Petrossian and William J. Murphy. 1996. $5.00 (paper). 54 pages.

★5654★ **Guide to Nontraditional Careers in Science**

Taylor & Francis
325 Chestnut St., 8th Fl.
Philadelphia, PA 19106
Ph: (215)625-8900   Fax: (215)269-0363
Fr: 800-821-8312
URL: http://www.taylorandfrancis.com

Karen Young Kreeger. 1998. $45.95 (paper). Guidebook aids the reader in evaluating and finding career opportunities in non-academic research fields. 263 pages.

★5655★ **Guiding Your Career As a Professional Geologist**

American Association of Petroleum Geologists
PO Box 979
Tulsa, OK 74101-0979
Ph: (918)584-2555   Fax: (918)560-2652
Fr: 800-364-2274
URL: http://www.aapg.org

Peter R. Rose, editor. 1994. $5.00 (paper). 78 pages.

★5656★ **Opportunities in Research and Development Careers**

The McGraw-Hill Companies
PO Box 182604
Columbus, OH 43272
Fax: (614)759-3749   Fr: 877-883-5524
E-mail: customer.service@mcgraw-hill.com
URL: http://www.mcgraw-hill.com

Jan Goldberg. 1996. $11.95 (paper). 146 pages.

★5657★ **Resumes for Scientific and Technical Careers**

The McGraw-Hill Companies
PO Box 182604
Columbus, OH 43272
Fax: (614)759-3749   Fr: 877-883-5524
E-mail: customer.service@mcgraw-hill.com
URL: http://www.mcgraw-hill.com

Third edition, 2007. $12.95 (paper). 144 pages. Provides resume advice for individuals interested in working in scientific and technical careers. Includes sample resumes and cover letters.

★5658★ To Boldly Go: A Practical Career Guide for Scientists

Amer Global Pub
2000 Florida Ave., NW
Washington, DC 20009
Ph: (202)462-6900   Fax: (202)328-0566
Fr: 800-966-2481

Peter S. Fiske. 1996. $19.00 (paper). 188 pages.

TRADESHOWS

★5659★ Geological Society of America Annual Meeting and GeoScience Expo

Geological Society of America
3300 Penrose Pl.
PO Box 9140
Boulder, CO 80301-1806
Ph: (303)447-2020   Fax: (303)357-1070
E-mail: gsaservice@geosociety.org
URL: http://www.geosociety.org

Annual. **Primary Exhibits:** Geology equipment, supplies, and services including instrumentation and computer hardware and software. **Dates and Locations:** 2008 Oct 26-30; Chicago, IL.

★5660★ Society of Exploration Geophysicists Annual International Meeting and Exposition

Society of Exploration Geophysicists
8801 S Yale
PO Box 702740
Tulsa, OK 74170-2740
Ph: (918)497-5500   Fax: (918)497-5557
E-mail: web@seg.org
URL: http://www.seg.org

Annual. **Primary Exhibits:** Geophysical products and services, computer hardware and software, data storage, visualization technology.

OTHER SOURCES

★5661★ American Almanac of Jobs and Salaries

HarperCollins
10 E. 53rd St.
New York, NY 10022
Ph: (212)207-7000   Fr: 800-242-7737
URL: http://www.harpercollins.com/

John W. Wright. Revised edition, 2000. $20.00 (paper). 672 pages. This is a comprehensive guide to the wages of hundreds of occupations in a wide variety of industries and organizations.

★5662★ American Geological Institute (AGI)

4220 King St.
Alexandria, VA 22302-1502
Ph: (703)379-2480   Fax: (703)379-7563
E-mail: agi@agiweb.org
URL: http://www.agiweb.org

Members: Federation of national scientific and technical societies in the Earth sciences. **Purpose:** Seeks to: stimulate public understanding of Geological sciences; improve teaching of the geological sciences in schools, colleges, and universities; maintain high standards of professional training and conduct; work for the general welfare of members. **Activities:** Provides career guidance program.

★5663★ American Institute of Professional Geologists (AIPG)

1400 W 122nd Ave., Ste. 250
Westminster, CO 80234
Ph: (303)412-6205   Fax: (303)253-9220
E-mail: aipg@aipg.org
URL: http://www.aipg.org

Members: Geologists. **Purpose:** Provides certification to geologists attesting to their competence and integrity. Represents the geologic profession before government bodies and the public.

★5664★ ASPRS - The Imaging and Geospatial Information Society

5410 Grosvenor Ln., Ste. 210
Bethesda, MD 20814-2160
Ph: (301)493-0290   Fax: (301)493-0208
E-mail: asprs@asprs.org
URL: http://www.asprs.org

Members: Firms, individuals, government employees and academicians engaged in photogrammetry, photointerpretation, remote sensing, and geographic information systems and their application to such fields as archaeology, geographic information systems, military reconnaissance, urban planning, engineering, traffic surveys, meteorological observations, medicine, geology, forestry, agriculture, construction and topographic mapping. Mission is to advance knowledge and improve understanding of these sciences and to promote responsible applications. **Activities:** Offers voluntary certification program open to persons associated with one or more functional area of photogrammetry, remote sensing and GIS. Surveys the profession of private firms in photogrammetry and remote sensing in the areas of products and services.

★5665★ Association of Environmental and Engineering Geologists (AEG)

PO Box 460518
Denver, CO 80246
Ph: (303)757-2926   Fax: (303)757-2969
E-mail: aeg@aegweb.org
URL: http://www.aegweb.org

Members: Represents graduate geologists and geological engineers; full members must have five years experience in the field of engineering geology. **Purpose:** Promotes professional success by providing leadership, advocacy, and applied research in environmental and engineering geology. Seeks to provide a forum for the discussion and dissemination of technical and scientific information. Encourages the advancement of professional recognition, scientific research, and high ethical and professional standards. Compiles information on engineering geology curricula of colleges and universities. Promotes public understanding, health, safety and welfare, and acceptance of the engineering geology profession. **Activities:** Conducts technical sessions, symposia, abstracts, and short courses; cosponsors seminars and conferences with other professional and technical societies and organizations.

★5666★ Association for International Practical Training (AIPT)

10400 Little Patuxent Pkwy., Ste. 250
Columbia, MD 21044-3519
Ph: (410)997-2200   Fax: (410)992-3924
E-mail: aipt@aipt.org
URL: http://www.aipt.org

Description: Providers worldwide of on-the-job training programs for students and professionals seeking international career development and life-changing experiences. Arranges workplace exchanges in hundreds of professional fields, bringing employers and trainees together from around the world. Client list ranges from small farming communities to Fortune 500 companies.

★5667★ Association for Women Geoscientists (AWG)

PO Box 30645
Lincoln, NE 68503-0645
Ph: (402)489-8122
E-mail: office@awg.org
URL: http://www.awg.org

Members: Represents men and women geologists, geophysicists, petroleum engineers, geological engineers, hydrogeologists, paleontologists, geochemists, and other geoscientists. **Purpose:** Aims to encourage the participation of women in the geosciences. Exchanges educational, technical, and professional information. Enhances the professional growth and advancement of women in the geosciences. Provides information through web site on opportunities and careers available to women in the geosciences. **Activities:** Sponsors educational booths and programs at geological society conventions. Operates charitable program. Maintains speaker's bureau, and Association for Women Geoscientists Foundation (educational arm).

★5668★ Environmental Occupations: Professional

Delphi Productions
3159 6th St.
Boulder, CO 80304
Ph: (303)443-2100   Fax: (303)443-4022
Fr: 888-443-2400
E-mail: support@delphivideo.com
URL: http://www.delphivideo.com

$95.00. 49 minutes. Part of the Emerging Careers Video Library.

★5669★ **Environmental Occupations: Technical**

Delphi Productions
3159 6th St.
Boulder, CO 80304
Ph: (303)443-2100   Fax: (303)443-4022
Fr: 888-443-2400
E-mail: support@delphivideo.com
URL: http://www.delphivideo.com

$95.00. 48 minutes. Part of the Emerging Careers Video Library.

★5670★ **Marine Technology Society (MTS)**

5565 Sterrett Pl., Ste. 108
Columbia, MD 21044
Ph: (410)884-5330   Fax: (410)884-9060
E-mail: mtsmbrship@erols.com
URL: http://www.mtsociety.org

Description: Scientists, engineers, educators, and others with professional interest in the marine sciences or related fields; includes institutional and corporate members. Disseminates marine scientific and technical information, including institutional, environmental, physical, and biological aspects; fosters a deeper understanding of the world's seas and attendant technologies. Maintains 13 sections and 29 professional committees. Conducts tutorials.

★5671★ **Minority Women In Science (MWIS)**

Directorate for Education and Human Resources Programs
1200 New York Ave. NW
Washington, DC 20005
Ph: (202)326-7019   Fax: (202)371-9849
E-mail: ygeorge@aaas.org

Description: A national network group of the American association for the Advancement of Science (AAAS), Education and Human Resources Directorate. The objectives of this group are: to identify and share information on resources and programs that could help in mentoring young women and minorities interested in science and engineering careers, and to strengthen communication among women and minorities in science and education.

★5672★ **Scientific, Engineering, and Technical Services**

Cambridge Educational
PO Box 2053
Princeton, NJ 08543-2053
Ph: 800-257-5126   Fax: (609)671-0266
Fr: 800-468-4227
E-mail: custserv@films.com
URL: http://www.cambridgeeducational.com

VHS and DVD. $89.95. 2002. 18 minutes. 2002. Part of the Career Cluster Series.

★5673★ **Scientific Occupations**

Delphi Productions
3159 6th St.
Boulder, CO 80304
Ph: (303)443-2100   Fax: (303)443-4022
Fr: 888-443-2400
E-mail: support@delphivideo.com
URL: http://www.delphivideo.com

$95.00. 60 minutes. Part of the Careers for the 21st Century Video Library.

★5674★ **Society of Exploration Geophysicists (SEG)**

PO Box 702740
Tulsa, OK 74170-2740
Ph: (918)497-5500   Fax: (918)497-5557
E-mail: mfleming@seg.org
URL: http://www.seg.org

Description: Individuals having eight years of education and experience in exploration geophysics or geology. Promotes the science of geophysics, especially as it applies to the exploration for petroleum and other minerals. Encourages high professional standards among members; supports the common interests of members. Maintains SEG Foundation, which receives contributions from companies and individuals and distributes them in the form of scholarships to students of geophysics and related subjects. Offers short continuing education courses to geophysicists and geologists. Maintains 37 committees, including: Development and Production; Engineering and Groundwater Geophysics; Mining and Geothermal; Offshore Exploration and Oceanography.

Graphic Artists

SOURCES OF HELP-WANTED ADS

★5675★ ACM Transactions on Graphics (TOG)
Association for Computing Machinery
2 Penn Plz., Ste. 701
New York, NY 10121-0701
Ph: (212)869-7440   Fax: (212)944-1318
Fr: 800-342-6626
URL: http://www.acm.org/tog/

Quarterly. $195.00/year for nonmembers, per year; $156.00/year for nonmembers, online; $234.00/year for nonmembers, online & print. Computer graphics journal.

★5676★ APC Newsletter
Advertising Production Club of New York
428 East State St.
Long Beach, NY 11561
Ph: (212)671-2975   Fax: (718)228-8202
E-mail: admin@apc-ny.org
URL: http://www.apc-ny.org

Description: Quarterly. Covers activities of Advertising Production Club of New York. Keeps club members informed of new technology and techniques in advertising production and includes profiles of print production persons and vendors.

★5677★ CAP&Design
IDG Communications Inc.
5 Speen St., 3rd. Fl
Framingham, MA 01701
Ph: (508)875-5000   Fax: (508)988-7888
URL: http://www.idg.com

Monthly. Professional magazine providing information for professional graphic designers and illustrators.

★5678★ Computer Graphics World
PennWell Corp.
98 Spit Brook Rd.
Nashua, NH 03062-5737
Ph: (603)891-0123
URL: http://cgw.pennnet.com/home.cfm

Monthly. $55.00/year for individuals, U.S.; $75.00/year for Canada; $115.00/year for other countries; $90.00 for two years, U.S.; $104.00 for two years, Canada; $160.00 for two years, other countries; $27.00/year digital distribution; $10.00 for single issue. Publication reporting on the use of modeling, animation, and multimedia in the areas of science and engineering, art and entertainment, and presentation and training.

★5679★ Creative Business
Creative Business
101 Tremont St., Ste. 300
Boston, MA 02108
Ph: (617)451-0041   Fax: (617)338-6570
E-mail: mail@creativebusiness.com
URL: http://www.creativebusiness.com/newsletter.lasso

Description: Ten issues/year. Provides business information for freelance graphic designers and studio principals.

★5680★ Design Perspectives
Industrial Designers Society of America
45195 Business Ct., Ste. 250
Dulles, VA 20166-6717
Ph: (703)707-6000   Fax: (703)759-7679
URL: http://www.idsa.org

Description: Ten issues/year. The largest newsletter examining the news and trends of industrial design. Recurring features include: new and cutting-edge products, news of people and events in industrial design, resource section, reports of chapter and national activities of IDSA, and a calendar of events.

★5681★ Digital Design Newsletter
Step-By-Step Publishing
c/o Dynamic Graphics Inc.
1015 Atlantic Ave.
Alameda, CA 94501
Ph: (510)522-0700   Fax: (510)522-5670
Fr: 888-698-8544
E-mail: dgi@dgi.com
URL: http://www.dgi.com/

Description: Monthly. Contains how-to arti-cles on electronic illustration, graphic design, and production via real-world projects.

★5682★ The Eagle
Fitzpatrick Management Inc.
1522 Lilac Rd.
Charlotte, NC 28209
Ph: (704)334-2047   Fax: (704)334-0220
E-mail: robertf765@aol.com.
URL: http://members.whattheythink.com/home/theeagle.cfm

Description: Three issues/year. Serves as a publication about issues pertaining to dealer/manufacturer relations in the graphic arts industry. Recurring features include interviews, reports of meetings, and the analysis and interpretation of topical issues in North America and internationally.

★5683★ Graphic Arts Monthly Magazine
Reed Business Information
360 Park Ave. S
New York, NY 10010
Ph: (646)746-6400   Fax: (646)746-7431
URL: http://www.reedbusiness.com

Monthly. Free. Magazine featuring commercial printing and graphic arts, including digital technologies.

★5684★ Graphic Communications Today
International Digital Enterprise Alliance.
1421 Prince St., Ste. 230
Alexandria, VA 22314-2805
Ph: (703)837-1070   Fax: (703)837-1072
E-mail: info@idealliance.org
URL: http://www.idealliance.org/

Description: Daily. Provides current information on the graphic communications industry. Available online only.

★5685★ Graphic Communicator
Graphic Communications International Union
1900 L St. NW
Washington, DC 20036
Ph: (202)462-1400   Fax: (202)721-0600

URL: http://www.gciu.org

Periodic. $12.00/year for U.S. and Canada; $15.00/year for other countries. Trade newspaper of the Graphic Communications International Union.

★5686★ **Graphic & Design Business**

North American Publishing Co.
1500 Spring Garden St., Ste. 1200
Philadelphia, PA 19130
Ph: (215)238-5482   Fax: (215)238-5412
Fr: 800-777-8074
URL: http://www.gdbmag.com/

Free to qualified subscribers. Magazine covering the graphic design and creative arts industry for managers and executives.

★5687★ **Graphics Update**

Printing Association of Florida Inc.
6275 Hazeltine National Dr.
Orlando, FL 32822
Ph: (407)240-8009   Fax: (407)240-8333
Fr: 800-331-0461
URL: http://www.pafgraf.org/Benefits.aspx

Description: Monthly. Concerned with developments within the field of graphic arts. Covers aspects of the industry with an emphasis on Florida, including news of exhibitions, statistics, new technologies and products, and events affecting the ancillary industries. Recurring features include letters to the editor, reports of meetings, news of educational opportunities, seminars, notices of publications available, news of members, and a calendar of events.

★5688★ **I.D. Magazine**

F & W Publications Inc.
4700 E Galbraith Rd.
Cincinnati, OH 45236
Ph: (513)531-2690   Fax: (513)531-0798
Fr: 800-289-0963
URL: http://www.fwmagazines.com/category/id

$30.00/year for individuals; $45.00/year for Canada; $60.00/year for other countries. Magazine covering art, business and culture of design.

★5689★ **IEEE Computer Graphics and Applications**

IEEE Computer Society
10662 Los Vaqueros Cir.
PO Box 3014
Los Alamitos, CA 90720-1314
Ph: (714)821-8380   Fax: (714)821-4010
Fr: 800-272-6657
URL: http://www.computer.org/cga/

Bimonthly. $20.00/year for members; $116.00/year for nonmembers. Magazine addressing the interests and needs of professional designers and users of computer graphics hardware, software, and systems.

★5690★ **Inside Illustrator**

Eli Journals
500 Canal View Blvd.
Rochester, NY 14623-2800
Ph: 877-203-5248   Fax: (585)292-4392
Fr: 800-223-8720
URL: http://www.elementkjournals.com/

Monthly. Journal publishing recent developments in the techniques, functions and tips for designing and producing good looking images for every medium.

★5691★ **Jobline News**

Graphic Artists Guild
32 Broadway, Ste. 1114
New York, NY 10004
Ph: (212)791-3400   Fax: (212)791-0333
E-mail: jobline@gag.org
URL: http://www.gag.org/jobline/index.html

Description: Weekly. Lists jobs for freelance and staff artists in areas such as graphic design, illustration, and art education. Lists jobs from across the country; quantity and locales vary weekly.

★5692★ **Journal of Mathematics and the Arts**

Taylor & Francis Group Journals
325 Chestnut St., Ste. 800
Philadelphia, PA 19106
Ph: (215)625-8900   Fax: (215)625-8914
Fr: 800-354-1420
URL: http://www.tandf.co.uk/journals/titles/17513472.asp

$330.00/year for institutions, print and online; $314.00/year for institutions, online only; $72.00/year for individuals, print only. Journal focusing on the challenges and opportunities presented by new media and information technology.

★5693★ **SEGDesign**

Society for Environmental Graphic Design
401 F St. NW, Ste. 333
Washington, DC 20001-2728
Ph: (202)638-5555

Quarterly. $200.00/year for individuals, in U.S. $275.00/year for elsewhere. Publication that covers environmental graphics, exhibit and industrial design, architecture, interiors, landscape architecture, and communication arts.

★5694★ **Society for Environmental Graphic Design-Messages**

Society for Environmental Graphic Design
1000 Vermont Ave., Ste. 400
Washington, DC 20005
Ph: (202)638-5555   Fax: (202)638-0891
E-mail: segd@segd.org
URL: http://www.segd.org/

Description: Bimonthly. Reports on Society program news, member services, resources, and product news.

★5695★ **TAGA Newsletter**

TAGA (Technical Association of the Graphic Arts)
200 Deer Run Rd.
Sewickley, PA 15143
Ph: (412)741-6860   Fax: (412)741-2311
E-mail: hbarcalow@piagatf.org
URL: http://www.taga.org

Description: Quarterly. Disseminates information in the graphic arts industry to members. Recurring features include interviews, news of research, reports of meetings, news of educational opportunities, and standards updates.

★5696★ **Voice: AIGA Journal of Design**

American Institute of Graphic Arts
164 5th Ave.
New York, NY 10010
Ph: (212)807-1990   Fax: (212)807-1799

Free to members. Online journal for the discussion of design matters, including interviews, essays, and criticism.

PLACEMENT AND JOB REFERRAL SERVICES

★5697★ **Advertising Production Club of New York (APC)**

428 E State St.
Long Beach, NY 11561
Ph: (212)671-2975   Fax: (718)228-8202
E-mail: admin@apc-ny.org
URL: http://www.apc-ny.org

Description: Production and traffic department personnel from advertising agencies, corporate or retail advertising departments, and publishing companies; college level graphic arts educators. Meetings include educational programs on graphic arts procedures and plant tours. Maintains employment service for members.

EMPLOYER DIRECTORIES AND NETWORKING LISTS

★5698★ **American Showcase Illustration**

American Showcase Inc.
915 Broadway, 14th Fl.
New York, NY 10010
Ph: (212)673-6600   Fax: (212)673-9795
Fr: 800-894-7469

Annual. $29.90 for individuals. Covers illustrators and graphic designers. Entries include: Name, address, phone, sample of work. Arrangement: Geographical.

★5699★ Discovering Careers for Your Future: Art

Facts On File Inc.
132 W 31st St., 17th Fl.
New York, NY 10001
Ph: (212)967-8800   Fax: 800-678-3633
Fr: 800-322-8755
URL: http://www.factsonfile.com

Published 2001. $21.95 for individuals; $19.75 for libraries. Covers artists, cartoonists, graphic designers, illustrators, and photographers; links career education to curriculum, helping children investigate the subjects they are interested in and the careers those subjects might lead to.

★5700★ Graphics Products Source Book

Graphic Products Association
4709 N El Capitan Ave., Ste. 103
Fresno, CA 93722
Ph: (559)276-8494   Fax: (559)276-8496
Fr: 800-276-8428

Annual. $55.00 for individuals. Covers equipment, tools, materials, services, and blank products for all types of businesses that put graphics onto products.

★5701★ Klik! Showcase Photography

American Showcase Inc.
915 Broadway, 14th Fl.
New York, NY 10010
Ph: (212)673-6600   Fax: (212)673-9795
Fr: 800-894-7469
URL: http://www.americanshowcase.com/pages/k9_branding.html

Annual. $45.00 for individuals. Covers 9,500 photographers and related companies. Entries include: Name, address, phone, sample of work. Illustrators and graphic designers are described in 'American Showcase Illustration.' Arrangement: Geographical. Indexes: Specialty.

★5702★ Printworld Directory of Contemporary Prints and Prices

Printworld International Inc.
PO Box 1957
West Chester, PA 19380
Ph: (610)431-6654   Fax: (610)431-6653
Fr: 800-788-9101
URL: http://www.printworlddirectory.com

Irregular; latest edition 2006, 11th edition. Publication includes: Biographical data on 5,000 international artists in contemporary printmaking; thousands of galleries that handle prints and hundreds of print publishers; and 600,000 print/price listings. Entries include: For artists–Name, address, personal and educational data, major exhibits, collections, publishers, printers, galleries, awards, teaching positions and documentation of prints. For galleries and publishers–Name, address. Arrangement: Alphabetical. Indexes: Artist name, printer/print workshop, publisher, gallery, art appraiser.

★5703★ RSVP

RSVP: The Directory of Illustration and Design
PO Box 050314
Brooklyn, NY 11205
Ph: (718)857-9267   Fax: (718)783-2376
URL: http://www.rsvpdirectory.com/

Annual, January/February; latest edition 2005. $20.00 for individuals. Covers about 250 illustrators and designers in the graphic arts industry. All listings are paid. Entries include: Name, address, phone, sample of work. Arrangement: Separate sections for illustrators and designers; each subdivided into color and black and white. Indexes: Specialty (with phone), geographical, alphabetical.

★5704★ Self-Employed Writers and Artists Network-Directory

Self-Employed Writers and Artists Network Inc.
PO Box 440
Paramus, NJ 07653
Ph: (201)967-1313
URL: http://www.swan-net.com

Annual, spring. Covers over 135 freelance writers, graphic designers, illustrators, photographers, and other graphic arts professionals in northern New Jersey and New York city providing services in advertising, marketing, sales promotion, public relations, and telecommunications. Entries include: Name, address, phone, biographical data, description of services provided. Arrangement: Alphabetical. Indexes: Line of business.

★5705★ Society for Environmental Graphic Design-Messages

Society for Environmental Graphic Design
1230 Avenue of the Americas, 7th Fl.
Rockefeller Plaza Center
New York, NY 10020
Ph: (917)639-4074   Fax: (917)639-4005
E-mail: editor@dexigner.com
URL: http://www.dexigner.com/graphic/links-g665.html

Description: Bimonthly. Reports on Society program news, member services, resources, and product news.

★5706★ Who's Who in SGIA

Screenprinting and Graphic Imaging Association International
10015 Main St.
Fairfax, VA 22031
Ph: (703)385-1335   Fax: (703)273-0456
Fr: 888-385-3588

Annual, August. Covers about 3,800 screen printers and graphic imaging companies, suppliers of screen printing equipment and graphic imaging materials, and investors in the Screen Printing Technical Foundation; international coverage. Entries include: Company name, address, phone, fax, e-mail, name of contact, products or services. Arrangement: Classified by type of business, then geographical. Indexes: Alphabetical by company, within state or country.

★5707★ The Workbook

Scott & Daughters Publishing Inc.
940 N Highland Ave.
Los Angeles, CA 90038
Ph: (213)856-0008   Fax: (323)856-4368
Fr: 800-547-2688
URL: http://www.workbook.com

Annual, February. Covers 49,000 advertising agencies, art directors, photographers, freelance illustrators and designers, artists' representatives, interactive designers, prepress services, and other graphic arts services in the U.S. Entries include: Company or individual name, address, phone, specialty. National in scope. Arrangement: Classified by product or service.

HANDBOOKS AND MANUALS

★5708★ 100 Best Careers for Writers and Artists

Macmillan Publishing Company
175 Fifth Ave.
New York, NY 10010
Ph: (646)307-5151   Fr: 800-428-5331
URL: http://www.macmillan.com/

Shelly Field. 1997. $15.95 (paper). 274 pages. Identifies job opportunities in communications and the arts.

★5709★ 100 Habits of Successful Graphic Designers: Insider Secrets on Working Smart and Staying Creative

Rockport Publishers
100 Cummings Center. Ste. 406-L
Beverly, MA 01915
Ph: (978)282-9590   Fax: (978)283-2742
URL: http://www.rockpub.com

Sarah Dougher and Josh Berger. 2005. $25.00. Designers from the graphic design, fashion, architecture, typography, and industrial design fields address topics ranging from deadlines, inspiration, competition, rules, respect, education, and criticism.

★5710★ 2007 Artists and Graphic Designers Market

Writers Digest Books
4700 E Galbraith Rd.
Cincinnati, OH 45236
Ph: (513)531-2690   Fax: (513)531-7185
Fr: 800-289-0963

Mary Cox and Michael Schweer. 2006. $26.99.

★5711★ All Access: The Making of Thirty Extraordinary Graphic Designers

Rockport Publishers
100 Cummings Center. Ste. 406-L
Beverly, MA 01915
Ph: (978)282-9590   Fax: (978)283-2742
URL: http://www.rockpub.com

Stefan G. Bucher. 2006. $25.00. Features the work of top graphic designers along with profiles of 20 newcomers.

★5712★ Becoming a Computer Graphics Designer Artist

John Wiley and Sons, Inc.
1 Wiley Dr.
Somerset, NJ 08875-1272
Ph: (732)469-4400   Fax: (732)302-2300
Fr: 800-225-5945
E-mail: custserv@wiley.com
URL: http://www.wiley.com/WileyCDA/

Gardner. 2007. $29.95 (paper). 288 pages. Part of Design and Graphic Design series.

★5713★ Becoming a Graphic Designer

John Wiley and Sons, Inc.
1 Wiley Dr.
Somerset, NJ 08875-1272
Ph: (732)469-4400   Fax: (732)302-2300
Fr: 800-225-5945
E-mail: custserv@wiley.com
URL: http://www.wiley.com/WileyCDA/

Steven Heller and Teresa Fernandes. Third edition, 2005. $35.00 (paper). 368 pages.

★5714★ Becoming a Successful Artist

North Light Books
4700 E Galbraith Rd.
Cincinnati, OH 45236
Ph: (513)531-2690   Fax: (513)531-4082
Fr: 800-289-0963

Lewis B. Lehrman. 1996. $24.99 (paper). 138 pages.

★5715★ Careers for Color Connoisseurs and Other Visual Types

The McGraw-Hill Companies
PO Box 182604
Columbus, OH 43272
Fax: (614)759-3749   Fr: 877-883-5524
E-mail: customer.service@mcgraw-hill.com
URL: http://www.mcgraw-hill.com

Jan Goldberg. Second edition, 2005. $13.95 (paper). 176 pages.

★5716★ Careers for Crafty People and Other Dexterous Types

The McGraw-Hill Companies
PO Box 182604
Columbus, OH 43272
Fax: (614)759-3749   Fr: 877-883-5524
E-mail: customer.service@mcgraw-hill.com
URL: http://www.mcgraw-hill.com

Mark Rowh. Third edition, 2006. $13.95; $9.95 (paper). 160 pages.

★5717★ Careers by Design: A Headhunter's Secrets for Success and Survival in Graphic Design

Allworth Press
10 E. 23rd St., Ste. 510
New York, NY 10010
Ph: (212)777-8395   Fax: (212)777-8261
Fr: 800-491-2808
URL: http://www.allworth.com/

Roz Goldfarb. Third edition, 2002. $18.95. 223 pages.

★5718★ Careers for Film Buffs and Other Hollywood Types

The McGraw-Hill Companies
PO Box 182604
Columbus, OH 43272
Fax: (614)759-3749   Fr: 877-883-5524
E-mail: customer.service@mcgraw-hill.com
URL: http://www.mcgraw-hill.com

Jaq Greenspon. Second edition, 2003. $13.95; $9.95 (paper). 208 pages. Describes job descriptions in production, camera, sound, special effects, grips, electrical, makeup, costumes, etc.

★5719★ Careers in Graphic Communications: A Resource Book

GATF Press
PO Box 1020
Sewickley, PA 15143-1020
Ph: (412)741-5733   Fax: (412)741-0609
Fr: 800-662-3916

Sally A. Flecker and Pamela J. Groff. 1998. $35.00 (paper). 200 pages.

★5720★ Careers for Night Owls and Other Insomniacs

The McGraw-Hill Companies
PO Box 182604
Columbus, OH 43272
Fax: (614)759-3749   Fr: 877-883-5524
E-mail: customer.service@mcgraw-hill.com
URL: http://www.mcgraw-hill.com

Louise Miller. Second edition, 2002. $12.95 (paper). 160 pages.

★5721★ Chronicle Artistic Occupations Guidebook

Chronicle Guidance Publications Inc.
66 Aurora St.
Moravia, NY 13118-3569
Fax: (315)497-3359   Fr: 800-899-0454
URL: http://www.chronicleguidance.com/

Paul Downes, editor. Revised, 1986. $81.80. 250 pages.

★5722★ The Education of a Graphic Designer

Allworth Press
10 E. 23rd St., Ste. 510
New York, NY 10010
Ph: (212)777-8395   Fax: (212)777-8261
Fr: 800-491-2808
URL: http://www.allworth.com/

Steven Heller, editor. Second edition, 2005.

$24.95 (paper). 352 pages. Designers discuss how they acquired knowledge of design and then succeeded in applying this academic training to practical solutions in their careers.

★5723★ Fresh Dialogue 4: New Voices in Graphic Design

Princeton Architectural Press
37 E 7th St.
New York, NY 10003
Ph: (212)995-9620   Fax: (212)995-9454
Fr: 800-722-6657
E-mail: sales@papress.com
URL: http://www.papress.com/

Veronique Vienne and Seamus Mullarkey. 2004. $24.95. Three graphic designers offer insight into the work of publishing and self-publishing from a graphics perspective.

★5724★ Fresh Dialogue 6: Friendly Fire

Princeton Architectural Press
37 E 7th St.
New York, NY 10003
Ph: (212)995-9620   Fax: (212)995-9454
Fr: 800-722-6657
E-mail: sales@papress.com
URL: http://www.papress.com/

American Institute of Graphic Arts Staff. 2006. $16.95. 127 pages.

★5725★ Graphic Designer's Ultimate Resource Directory

North Light Books
4700 E Galbraith Rd.
Cincinnati, OH 45236
Ph: (513)531-2690   Fax: (513)531-4082
Fr: 800-289-0963

Poppy Evans. 1999. $28.99 (paper). 192 pages.

★5726★ Great Jobs for Art Majors

The McGraw-Hill Companies
PO Box 182604
Columbus, OH 43272
Fax: (614)759-3749   Fr: 877-883-5524
E-mail: customer.service@mcgraw-hill.com
URL: http://www.mcgraw-hill.com

Blythe Camenson, Stephen Lambert, Julie DeGalan. Second edition, 2003. $15.95 (paper). 248 pages. Includes bibliographical references and index.

★5727★ How to Be a Successful Cartoonist

North Light Books
4700 E Galbraith Rd.
Cincinnati, OH 45236
Ph: (513)531-2690   Fax: (513)531-4082
Fr: 800-289-0963

Randy Glasbergen. 1996. $19.99. 122 pages. Explains how to get started and what the opportunities are, among other topics.

★5728★ How to Start and Operate Your Own Design Firm

The McGraw-Hill Companies
PO Box 182604
Columbus, OH 43272
Fax: (614)759-3749   Fr: 877-883-5524
E-mail: customer.service@mcgraw-hill.com
URL: http://www.mcgraw-hill.com

Albert W. Rubeling, Jr. 2007. $24.95. 256 pages.

★5729★ How to Survive and Prosper as an Artist: Selling Yourself Without Selling Your Soul

Holt Paperbacks
175 Fifth Ave.
New York, NY 10010
Ph: (646)307-5095   Fax: (212)633-0748
Fr: 800-672-2054
URL: http://www.henryholt.com

Caroll Michels. 5 Revised edition, 2001. $18.00. 369 pages. Includes index and bibliographical references.

★5730★ New Media Careers for Artists and Designers

AuthorHouse
1663 Liberty Dr., Ste. 200
Bloomington, IN 47403
Ph: (812)961-1023   Fax: (812)339-8654
Fr: 888-519-5121
URL: http://www.authorhouse.com

Brenda S. Faison. February 2003. $13.95. 136 pages.

★5731★ Opportunities in Arts and Crafts Careers

The McGraw-Hill Companies
PO Box 182604
Columbus, OH 43272
Fax: (614)759-3749   Fr: 877-883-5524
E-mail: customer.service@mcgraw-hill.com
URL: http://www.mcgraw-hill.com

Elizabeth Gardner. 2005. $13.95 (paper). 211 pages.

★5732★ Opportunities in Commercial Art and Graphic Design Careers

The McGraw-Hill Companies
PO Box 182604
Columbus, OH 43272
Fax: (614)759-3749   Fr: 877-883-5524
E-mail: customer.service@mcgraw-hill.com
URL: http://www.mcgraw-hill.com

Barbara Gordon. 2003. $13.95; $11.95 (paper). 160 pages. Provides a survey of job opportunities in advertising and public relations, publishing, fashion, architecture, and newspapers, as well as in a variety of specialty markets. Illustrated.

★5733★ Opportunities in Drafting Careers

The McGraw-Hill Companies
PO Box 182604
Columbus, OH 43272
Fax: (614)759-3749   Fr: 877-883-5524

E-mail: customer.service@mcgraw-hill.com
URL: http://www.mcgraw-hill.com

Mark Rowh. 1994. $13.95; $11.95 (paper). 146 pages. Provides information on opportunities in mechanical, landscape, marine, and topographical drafting in civil service, architecture, electronics, and other fields. Contains index and illustrations.

★5734★ Opportunities in Visual Arts Careers

The McGraw-Hill Companies
PO Box 182604
Columbus, OH 43272
Fax: (614)759-3749   Fr: 877-883-5524
E-mail: customer.service@mcgraw-hill.com
URL: http://www.mcgraw-hill.com

Mark Salmon and Bill Barrett. 2001. $12.95; $11.95 (paper). 160 pages. Points the way to a career in the visual arts, examining opportunities for designers, painters, sculptors, illustrators, animators, photographers, art therapists, educators, and others. Offers a view of the pros and cons of working for an art or design company or on your own.

★5735★ Power Freelancing: Home-Based Careers for Writers, Designers, & Consultants

Mid-List Press
4324 12th Ave., S
Minneapolis, MN 55407-3218
Ph: (612)822-3733   Fax: (612)823-8387
Fr: 888-543-1138
E-mail: guide@midlist.org
URL: http://www.midlist.org/

George Sorenson. 1995. $14.95 (paper). 198 pages.

★5736★ Resumes for Advertising Careers

The McGraw-Hill Companies
PO Box 182604
Columbus, OH 43272
Fax: (614)759-3749   Fr: 877-883-5524
E-mail: customer.service@mcgraw-hill.com
URL: http://www.mcgraw-hill.com

Third edition, 2003. $10.95 (paper). 160 pages. Aimed at job seekers trying to enter or advance in advertising. Provides sample resumes for copywriters, art directors, account managers, ad managers, and media people at all levels of experience. Furnishes sample cover letters.

★5737★ Taking the Leap: Building a Career as a Visual Artist

Chronicle Books LLC
680 Second St.
San Francisco, CA 94107
Ph: (415)537-4200   Fax: (415)537-4460
Fr: 800-722-6657
E-mail: frontdesk@chroniclebooks.com
URL: http://www.chroniclebooks.com

Cay Lang. 2006. $19.95. 256 pages.

EMPLOYMENT AGENCIES AND SEARCH FIRMS

★5738★ Brattle Temps

50 Congress St., Ste. 935
Boston, MA 02109-4008
Ph: (617)523-4600   Fax: (617)523-3939
E-mail: temps@brattletemps.com
URL: http://www.brattletemps.com

Personnel consulting firm specializes in providing temporary consultants. Skill areas available include: computer operators, secretaries, editors, librarians, graphic artists, and marketing professionals. Industries served: universities, publishing, engineering, manufacturing, and government agencies.

★5739★ Caprio & Associates Inc.

1415 W. 22nd St., Tower Fl.
Oak Brook, IL 60523
Ph: (630)705-9101   Fax: (630)705-9102
E-mail: jerry@caprioassociates.com
URL: http://www.caprioassociates.com

Executive search firm.

★5740★ Cook Associates Inc.

212 W Kinzie St.
Chicago, IL 60610
Ph: (312)329-0900   Fax: (312)329-1528
E-mail: info@cookassociates.com
URL: http://www.cookassociates.com

Management and executive recruiting specialists offering a commitment to clients to find the best candidates and to find those candidates as efficiently as possible. Approach provides a flexible and effective structure that serves the special needs of both large and small companies. Serves the following industries: industrial, equipment manufacturer, food processing, graphic arts, chemical process, retailing, mechanical products, healthcare services, financial and professional services, legal, consumer products, construction and engineering, packaging, pulp and paper.

★5741★ Gordon Wahls Executive Search Co.

450 Parkway Blvd., Ste. 104
PO Box 386
Broomall, PA 19008-0386
Fax: (610)359-8803   Fr: 800-523-7112
E-mail: search@gwahls.com

Offers executive search services for the printing, packaging, publishing and graphic arts industry.

★5742★ Graphic Arts Employment Service, Inc.

409 N Pacific Coast Hwy., Ste.455
Redondo Beach, CA 90277
Ph: (818)499-9722   Fax: (310)937-3760
Fr: 888-499-9722
E-mail: info@gaes.com
URL: http://www.gaes.com

Employment agency specializing in the publishing and packaging industries.

★5743★ Graphic Search Associates Inc.

1217 W. Chester Pike, Ste. 203
West Chester, PA 19382
Ph: (610)429-8077   Fax: (610)429-1355
Fr: 800-342-1777
E-mail: info@graphsrch.com
URL: http://www.graphsrch.com

Executive search firm for the graphic arts industry.

★5744★ LandaJob Advertising Staffing Specialists

8177 Wornall Rd.
Kansas City, MO 64114
Ph: (816)523-1881   Fax: (816)523-1876
Fr: 800-931-8806
E-mail: adstaff@landajobnow.com
URL: http://www.landajobnow.com

Personnel consultants and recruiters for advertising, marketing, and communications positions. Industries served: advertising, communications, marketing, graphic arts, printing and publishing.

★5745★ Lloyd Staffing

445 Broadhollow Rd., Ste. 119
Melville, NY 11747
Ph: (631)777-7600   Fax: (631)777-7626
Fr: 888-292-6678
E-mail: info@lloydstaffing.com
URL: http://www.lloydstaffing.com

Personnel agency and search firm.

★5746★ Max Brown

3208 Q St. NW
Washington, DC 20007
Ph: (202)338-2727   Fax: (202)338-3131

Executive recruiter to the magazine and book publishing industries. Employment placements in all publishing disciplines, including operation and financial management, new product development, marketing, advertising sales, editorial, graphic design, production, manufacturing, circulation, distribution, corporate communications, promotion and administration. Secondary concentrations include management advising for publishers, providing the following services: marketing and product positioning for new and existing publications, market research and development, business planning and financial projections, publishing models, launch strategies and start-up operations and acquisitions and mergers counsel.

★5747★ Printemps

18 Avery Pl.
Westport, CT 06880
Ph: (203)226-6869   Fax: (203)226-1594
E-mail: printemps7@aol.com

Specializes in providing temporary support for graphic design, document management

and the electronic printing industry. Provides permanent placement for professionals and production personnel. Consults with printers and in-house printshops for greater production efficiency. Handles personnel management and policy programs as well. Industries served: printing, advertising, manufacturing, insurance, banking, and government agencies.

ONLINE JOB SOURCES AND SERVICES

★5748★ Graphic Artists Guild

93 John St., Ste. 403
New York, NY 10038
Ph: (212)791-3400
E-mail: communications@gag.org
URL: http://www.gag.org

Description: JOBLine News section of Guild Resources page contains weekly e-mail newsletter of job listings. **Fee:** Must subscribe to e-mail newsletter non-member six-month rates start at $80. Visitors may download a free sample.

★5749★ PrintJobs.com

Newhouse Associates
PO Box 135
Bowmansville, NY 14026
Ph: (716)686-9251   Fax: (716)686-9258
E-mail: printjobs@roadrunner.com
URL: http://www.printjobs.com

Description: Aims to find suitable graphic arts jobs for qualified candidates. Over a hundred jobs are maintained and updated on the site. **Fee:** Must be paid by employers using the site; no registration charge for job hunters.

TRADESHOWS

★5750★ Graph Expo and Converting Expo

Graphic Arts Show Co. (GASC)
1899 Preston White Dr.
Reston, VA 20191-4367
Ph: (703)264-7200   Fax: (703)620-9187
E-mail: info@gasc.org
URL: http://www.gasc.org

Annual. **Primary Exhibits:** Graphic art equipment, supplies, and services. Printing, publishing, and converting equipment. **Dates and Locations:** 2008 Oct 26-29; Chicago, IL; McCormick Place South.

★5751★ Graphic Arts/Awards Exhibition

Association of Graphic Communications
330 Seventh Ave., 9th Fl.
New York, NY 10001-5010
Ph: (212)279-2100   Fax: (212)279-5381

E-mail: info@agcomm.org
URL: http://www.agcomm.org

Annual. **Primary Exhibits:** A network for industry information and idea exchange; a provider for graphic arts education and training; a vehicle for industry promotion and marketing; an advocate on legislative and environmental issues and a source for bottom-line savings for the benefit of its New York/New Jersey membership.

★5752★ Graphics of the Americas

Printing Association of Florida, Inc.
6275 Hazeltine National Dr.
Orlando, FL 32822
Ph: (407)240-8009   Fax: (407)240-8333
Fr: 800-749-4855
E-mail: agaither@pafgraf.org
URL: http://www.pafgraf.org

Annual. **Primary Exhibits:** Graphic arts and specialty printing equipment, supplies, and services.

★5753★ Gutenberg Festival

Graphic Arts Show Co. (GASC)
1899 Preston White Dr.
Reston, VA 20191-4367
Ph: (703)264-7200   Fax: (703)620-9187
E-mail: info@gasc.org
URL: http://www.gasc.org

Annual. **Primary Exhibits:** Printing, graphic arts and digital imaging equipment, services, and supplies. **Dates and Locations:** 2008 Oct 26-29; Chicago, IL; McCormick Place South.

★5754★ Midwest Graphics

Graphic Arts Show Co. (GASC)
1899 Preston White Dr.
Reston, VA 20191-4367
Ph: (703)264-7200   Fax: (703)620-9187
E-mail: info@gasc.org
URL: http://www.gasc.org

Annual. **Primary Exhibits:** Graphics expo.

★5755★ NEXPO

Newspaper Association of America
1921 Gallows Rd. Ste. 600
Vienna, VA 22182-3900
Ph: (703)902-1600   Fax: (703)917-0636
E-mail: sales@nna.org
URL: http://www.naa.org

Annual. **Primary Exhibits:** Newspaper publishing graphic arts systems and equipment and electronic publishing, ranging from computerized systems to newspaper presses to post press systems. **Dates and Locations:** 2008 Apr 12-15; Washington, DC.

OTHER SOURCES

★5756★ American Artists Professional League (AAPL)

47 5th Ave.
New York, NY 10003
Ph: (212)645-1345   Fax: (212)645-1345
E-mail: aapl@verizon.com
URL: http://www.americanartistsprofessionalleague.org

Description: Advances the cause of fine arts in America through the promotion of high standards of beauty, integrity and craftsmanship in painting, sculpture and the graphic arts.

★5757★ American Institute of Graphic Arts (AIGA)

164 5th Ave.
New York, NY 10010
Ph: (212)807-1990   Fax: (212)807-1799
E-mail: comments@aiga.org
URL: http://www.aiga.org

Description: Graphic designers, art directors, illustrators and packaging designers. Sponsors exhibits and projects in the public interest. Sponsors traveling exhibitions. Operates gallery. Maintains library of design books and periodicals; offers slide archives.

★5758★ Animators Unite

525 85th St.
Brooklyn, NY 11209
E-mail: rkohr@animatorsunite.com
URL: http://www.animatorsunite.com

Description: Cultivates interest in all forms of animation. Provides educational, informational and promotional services to individuals who are interested in pursuing a career in the animation industry. Provides an online forum for its members to interact and exchange information.

★5759★ Art Directors Club (ADC)

106 W 29th St.
New York, NY 10001
Ph: (212)643-1440   Fax: (212)643-4266
E-mail: info@adcglobal.org
URL: http://www.adcglobal.org

Members: Art directors of advertising magazines and agencies, visual information specialists, and graphic designers; associate members are artists, cinematographers, photographers, copywriters, educators, journalists, and critics. **Purpose:** Promotes and stimulates interest in the practice of art direction. **Activities:** Sponsors Annual Exhibition of Advertising, Editorial and Television Art and Design; International Traveling Exhibition. Provides educational, professional, and entertainment programs; on-premise art exhibitions; portfolio review program. Conducts panels for students and faculty.

★5760★ Association for Graphic Arts Training (AGAT)

McNaughton and Gunn, Inc.
960 Woodland Dr.
Saline, MI 48176
Ph: (734)429-5411   Fax: 800-677-2665
E-mail: albertl@mcnaughton-gunn.com
URL: http://www.agatweb.org

Members: Full- and part-time graphic arts trainers at printing and pre-press companies; graphic arts teachers; and other interested individuals and companies. **Purpose:** Seeks to increase the productivity of graphic arts trainers through effective, efficient education and training with support from suppliers, educational institutions, associations, non-profit organizations, and consultants. Aims to: establish networking opportunities for trainers; share performance challenges, solutions, and resources; improve members' skills, knowledge, and professionalism; align training with corporate strategies; increase awareness of the importance of training; and create guidelines for training materials used in the industry.

★5761★ Design Management Institute (DMI)

29 Temple Pl., 2nd Fl.
Boston, MA 02111-1350
Ph: (617)338-6380   Fax: (617)338-6570
E-mail: dmistaff@dmi.org
URL: http://www.dmi.org

Description: In-house design groups and consultant design firms; individuals involved in the management of designers with in-house corporate design groups or consultant design firms. Aims to share management techniques as applied to design groups, and to facilitate better understanding by business management of the role design can play in achieving business goals. Design disciplines included are: architecture, advertising, communications, exhibit design, graphics, interior design, packaging and product design. Develops and distributes design management education materials. Sponsors seminars for design professionals. Identifies critical areas of design management study; conducts surveys and research on corporate design management. Maintains design management archive. Operates Center for Research, Center for Education, and Center for Design and Management Resources.

★5762★ Graphic Arts Employers of America (GAE)

200 Deer Run Rd.
Sewickley, PA 15143
Ph: (412)741-6860   Fax: (412)741-2311
Fr: 800-910-4283
E-mail: jkyger@piagatf.org
URL: http://www.gain.net

Description: Serves as a division of Printing Industries of America. Represents graphic communications, imaging, and printing companies who have at least some unionization or are interested in keeping informed on industrial relations issues. Assists management in functioning at optimal efficiency in a unionized environment. Compiles statistics and assists companies that deal with the major printing unions in the U.S. and Canada. Compiles statistics.

★5763★ Graphic Arts Technical Foundation (GATF)

200 Deer Run Rd.
Sewickley, PA 15143-2600
Fax: (412)741-2311   Fr: 800-910-GATF
E-mail: info@piagatf.org
URL: http://www.gain.net

Description: Scientific, research, technical, and educational organization serving the international graphic communications industries. Conducts research in all graphic processes and their commercial applications. Conducts seminars, workshops, and forums on graphic arts and environmental subjects. Conducts educational programs, including the publishing of graphic arts textbooks and learning modules, videotapes and CD-ROMs and broadcast video seminars. Conducts training and certification program in sheet-fed offset press operating, Web Offset press operating, Image Assembly, and desktop publishing. Produces test images and quality control devices for the industry. Performs technical services for the graphic arts industry, including problem-solving, material evaluation, and plant audits.

★5764★ Gravure Education Foundation (GEF)

1200-A Scottsville Rd.
Rochester, NY 14624
Ph: (585)436-2150   Fax: (585)436-7689
E-mail: rbsheridan@gaa.org
URL: http://www.gaa.org/gef/index.htm

Purpose: Aims to establish gravure curricula with graphic arts educational facilities at all educational levels; provides financial assistance to students; develops new resources for conducting educational programs; encourages postgraduate projects and research within the graphic arts; provides career orientation at the high school level; provides for internships throughout the gravure industry. Seeks to serve as a catalyst within the framework of established institutions and to provide encouragement to enterprising individuals.

★5765★ International Association of Printing House Craftsmen (IAPHC)

7042 Brooklyn Blvd.
Minneapolis, MN 55429-1370
Ph: (763)560-1620   Fax: (763)560-1350
Fr: 800-466-4274
E-mail: kkeane1069@aol.com
URL: http://www.iaphc.org

Members: Individuals world-wide employed or interested in any facet of the graphic arts. **Activities:** Conducts field trips; maintains Speaker's Bureau; sponsors educational programs. Sponsors International Printing Week and International Gallery of Superb Printing.

★5766★ International Graphic Arts Education Association (IGAEA)

1899 Preston White Dr.
Reston, VA 20191-4367
Ph: (703)758-0595
E-mail: dw.dailey@eku.edu
URL: http://www.igaea.org

Description: Graphic arts and printing teachers. Develops an integrated and comprehensive system of graphic arts education in schools and colleges of the U.S. Assists organizations in arranging lectures or other programs relating to graphic arts. Sponsors annual Graphic Communications Week; Visual Communication Journal; conducts research programs.

★5767★ Media and the Arts Occupations

Delphi Productions
3159 6th St.
Boulder, CO 80304
Ph: (303)443-2100   Fax: (303)443-4022
Fr: 888-443-2400
E-mail: support@delphivideo.com
URL: http://www.delphivideo.com

$95.00. 50 minutes. Part of the Careers for the 21st Century Video Library.

★5768★ North American Graphic Arts Suppliers Association (NAGASA)

PO Box 934483
Margate, FL 33093
Ph: (954)971-1383   Fax: (954)971-4362
E-mail: nagasa4info@nagasa.org
URL: http://www.nagasa.org

Members: Graphic communications dealers and manufacturers. **Purpose:** Works to advance the interests of graphic arts dealers and manufacturers, and improve the partnership between them. Seeks to streamline costs and increase efficiency. Fosters communication between dealers and manufacturers. Produces technical and business performance information through standards, statistical, educational, and publishing services.

★5769★ Photo Imaging Education Association (PIEA)

Arlington Independent School District
1203 W Pioneer Pkwy.
Arlington, TX 76013
Ph: (817)229-2237
E-mail: consultant@pieapma.org
URL: http://www.pieapma.org

Description: Represents photo imaging education practitioners and students. Builds a network where educators and students can create resources, solve problems and discuss issues relating to photo industry. Inspires members to be successful and to become better teachers of photo imaging.

★5770★ Society of American Graphic Artists (SAGA)

32 Union Sq., Rm. 1214
New York, NY 10003
E-mail: tbaker@monmouth.edu
URL: http://www.clt.astate.edu/elind/saga-main.htm

Description: Workers in the print media (etching, lithography, engraving, woodcut, wood engraving); also offers associate membership. Sponsors exhibitions and traveling shows.

★5771★ Technical Association of the Graphic Arts (TAGA)

200 Deer Run Rd.
Sewickley, PA 15143
Ph: (412)259-1706   Fax: (412)741-2311
Fr: 800-910-4283
E-mail: cmeyers@piagatf.org
URL: http://www.gain.net

Description: Professional society of individuals interested in or engaged in research or technical control of graphic arts processes or related industries. Promotes advanced technical study and research in the graphic arts.

★5772★ Type Directors Club (TDC)

127 W 25th St., 8th Fl.
New York, NY 10001
Ph: (212)633-8943   Fax: (212)633-8944
E-mail: director@tdc.org
URL: http://www.tdc.org

Description: Serves as a professional society of typographic designers, type directors, and teachers of typography; sustaining members are individuals with interests in typographic education. Seeks to stimulate research and disseminate information. Provides speakers, classes and offers presentations on history and new developments in typography.

★5773★ Typophiles

30 E 23rd St., 8th Fl.
New York, NY 10010
E-mail: info@typophiles.org
URL: http://www.typophiles.org

Description: Represents designers, printers, book collectors, artists, calligraphers, private press owners, wood engravers, librarians and others interested in graphic arts. Promotes the love and appreciation of fine graphic design and printing. Conducts quarterly meeting-luncheons and maintains publications.

Hazardous Waste Management Specialists

SOURCES OF HELP-WANTED ADS

★5774★ BioCycle
The JG Press Inc.
419 State Ave.
Emmaus, PA 18049
Ph: (610)967-4135
URL: http://www.biocycle.net/

Monthly. $69.00/year for individuals; $113.00 for two years; $89.00/year for Canada; $153.00 for Canada, two years; $97.00/year for other countries; $169.00 for other countries, two years. Magazine focusing on management of city and industrial wastes by recycling and composting.

★5775★ Drinking Water & Backflow Prevention
IAPMO
5001 E Philadelphia St.
Ontario, CA 91761-2816
Ph: (909)472-4100   Fax: (909)472-4150
Fr: 800-854-2766
E-mail: backflow@dwbp-online.com
URL: http://www.dwbp-online.com

Description: Monthly. Presents articles directed toward "individuals, companies, organizations, agencies, and municipalities with an interest in drinking water protection and backflow prevention." Contains information on safety standards, water system protection, training programs, cross-connection control, and all issues related to preventing the contamination of potable drinking water supplies with backflow prevention devices. Recurring features include case studies, letters to the editor, news of research, columns titled Test Your Investigative Skills and Backflow Prevention Device Repairs, and reports of meetings. Also carries news of educational opportunities, job listings, notices of publications available, and a calendar of events.

★5776★ Industrial Hygiene News
Rimbach Publishing Inc.
8650 Babcock Blvd.
Pittsburgh, PA 15237
Ph: (412)364-5366   Fax: (412)369-9720
Fr: 800-245-3182
URL: http://www.rimbach.com

Bimonthly. Free to qualified subscribers. Magazine covering industrial hygiene, occupational health, and safety.

★5777★ Journal of Applied Ground Water Protection
Ground Water Protection Council
13308 North Macarthur Blvd.
Oklahoma City, OK 73142
Ph: (405)516-4972   Fax: (405)516-4973
URL: http://www.gwpc.org/

Semiannual. Journal covering issues in water and waste management.

★5778★ Occupational Hazards
Penton Media Inc.
1300 E 9th St.
Cleveland, OH 44114
Ph: (216)696-7000   Fax: (216)696-1752
URL: http://www.occupationalhazards.com

Monthly. $72.00/year for individuals, Canada; $126.00 for two years, Canada; $50.00/year for individuals, Canada; $99.00/year for other countries; $162.00 for two years, international; $80.00/year for other countries, #. Monthly publication for safety professionals featuring information to meet OSHA and EPA compliance requirements, improve management of safety, industrial hygiene and environmental programs and find products and services to protect employees and property.

★5779★ Onsite Installer
Cole Publishing Inc.
PO Box 220
1720 Maple Lake Dam Rd.
Three Lakes, WI 54562
Ph: (715)546-3346   Fax: (715)546-3786
Fr: 800-257-7222
E-mail: info@onsiteinstaller.com
URL: http://www.onsiteinstaller.com/

Monthly. Free to qualified subscribers in U.S. Magazine that offers information for professionals who design and install septic systems and other onsite wastewater treatment systems serving single-family homes, small businesses, and small communities.

★5780★ Operations Forum
Water Environment Federation
601 Wythe St.
Alexandria, VA 22314-1994
Ph: (703)684-2452   Fax: (703)684-2492
Fr: 800-666-0206
URL: http://www.wef.org

Monthly. $79.00/year for nonmembers. Magazine covering operation/maintenance of WWTPs and wastewater collections systems.

★5781★ Pollution Engineering
BNP Media
2401 W Big Beaver Rd., Ste. 700
Troy, MI 48084-3333
Ph: (248)786-1642   Fax: (248)786-1388
URL: http://www.pollutionengineering.com/

Magazine focusing on pollution control, air, water, solid waste, and toxic/hazardous waste.

★5782★ Pollution Equipment News
Rimbach Publishing Inc.
8650 Babcock Blvd.
Pittsburgh, PA 15237
Ph: (412)364-5366   Fax: (412)369-9720
Fr: 800-245-3182
URL: http://www.rimbach.com

Bimonthly. Free to qualified subscribers. Pollution control equipment and products magazine.

★5783★ Public Works
Hanley-Wood LLC
One Thomas Cir. NW, Ste. 600
Washington, DC 20005
Ph: (202)452-0800   Fax: (202)785-1974
URL: http://www.pwmag.com

$60.00/year for individuals; $75.00/year for

individuals, Canada; $90.00/year for individuals, international. Trade magazine covering the public works industry nationwide for city, county, and state.

★5784★ **Stormwater**
Forester Communications Inc.
2946 De La Vina
Santa Barbara, CA 93105
Ph: (805)682-1300   Fax: (805)682-0200
URL: http://www.stormh2o.com/sw.html

Journal devoted to surface water quality professionals.

★5785★ **Water Environment Research**
Water Environment Federation
601 Wythe St.
Alexandria, VA 22314-1994
Ph: (703)684-2452   Fax: (703)684-2492
Fr: 800-666-0206
E-mail: msc@wef.org
URL: http://www.wef.org

Bimonthly. $125.00/year for individuals, WEF Member, print plus online; $308.00/year for individuals, print plus online; $780.00/year for institutions, print plus online; $200.00/year for individuals, WEF Member, print plus online; $350.00/year for individuals, print plus online; $830.00/year for institutions, print plus online; $812.00/year for institutions, Domestic; $883.00/year for institutions, international. Technical journal covering municipal and industrial water pollution control, water quality, and hazardous wastes.

★5786★ **Water & Wastes Digest**
Scranton Gillette Communications Inc.
3030 W Salt Creek Ln., Ste. 201
Arlington Heights, IL 60005-5025
Ph: (847)391-1000   Fax: (847)390-0408
URL: http://www.wwdmag.com

Monthly. Magazine (tabloid) featuring product news for decision makers in the municipal and industrial water and water pollution control industries.

PLACEMENT AND JOB REFERRAL SERVICES

★5787★ **Environmental Technology Council (ETC)**
734 15th St. NW, Ste. 720
Washington, DC 20005-1013
Ph: (202)783-0870
E-mail: comments@etc.org
URL: http://www.etc.org

Description: Firms dedicated to the use of high technology treatment in the management of hazardous wastes and to the restricted use of land disposal facilities in the interests of protecting human health and the environment. Advocates minimization of hazardous wastes and the use of alternative

technologies in their treatment, including chemical and biological treatments, fixation, neutralization, reclamation, recycling, and thermal treatments such as incineration. Encourages land disposal prohibitions. Promotes reductions in the volume of hazardous waste generated annually and expansion of EPA hazardous waste list. Advocates use of treatment technology as a more cost-effective approach to Superfund site cleanups. Works with state, national, and international officials and firms to assist in development of programs that utilize treatment and minimize land disposal. Provides technical and placement assistance to members; sponsors special studies, technical seminars, and workshops; participates in federal legislation, litigation, and regulatory development. Maintains library of materials on new technologies; operates speakers' bureau; compiles statistics and mailing list.

★5788★ **Spill Control Association of America (SCAA)**
2105 Laurel Bush Rd., Ste. 200
Bel Air, MD 21015
Ph: (443)640-1085   Fax: (443)640-1086
E-mail: info@scaa-spill.org
URL: http://www.scaa-spill.org

Description: Third party contractors; manufacturers or suppliers of pollution control and containment equipment; individuals in private or governmental capacities involved with spill clean-up and containment operations; associate companies. Aims to provide information on the oil and hazardous material emergency response and remediation industry's practices, trends, and achievements; to establish liaison with local, state, and federal government agencies responsible for laws and regulations regarding pollution caused by oil and hazardous materials; to cooperate in the development of industry programs and efforts so that pollutants are properly controlled and removed from land and water. Provides certification for hazardous material technicians. Maintains Spill Control Institute, Technical Services Division; collects and disseminates educational and technical information. Operates speakers' bureau; conducts research. Maintains placement service.

EMPLOYER DIRECTORIES AND NETWORKING LISTS

★5789★ **EI Environmental Services Directory**
Environmental Information Ltd.
PO Box 390266
Edina, MN 55439
Ph: (952)831-2473   Fax: (952)831-6550
URL: http://www.envirobiz.com

Biennial; latest edition 2007. $1,250.00 for individuals. Covers over 8,000 environmental services businesses, including waste-handling facilities, transportation firms, spill response firms, consultants, laboratories,

soil boring/well drilling firms; also includes incineration services, polychlorinated biphenyl (PCB) detoxification and mobile solvent-recovery services, asbestos services and underground tank services, and summaries of states' regulatory programs. Entries include: Company name, address, phone, description of services, regulatory status, on and off site processes used, type of waste handled. Arrangement: Geographical. Indexes: Service.

★5790★ **Hazardous Materials Advisory Council-Directory**
Hazardous Materials Advisory Council
1101 H St. NW, Ste. 740
Washington, DC 20005-3521
Ph: (202)289-4550   Fax: (202)289-4074
URL: http://www.hmac.org/

Annual; latest edition 2007. Covers about 300 members, shippers, and carriers of hazardous materials; manufacturers of hazardous materials containers; and related organizations. Entries include: Company name, address, phone, fax, representative name. Arrangement: Classified by line of business. Indexes: Geographical; member representative.

★5791★ **Hazardous Waste Consultant-Directory of Commercial Hazardous Waste Management Facilities Issue**
Elsevier Science
PO Box 945
New York, NY 10159-0945
Ph: (212)989-5800   Fax: (212)633-3680
Fr: 888-615-4500

Semiannual. Publication includes: List of 170 licensed commercial facilities that treat and/or dispose of hazardous waste in North America. Entries include: Facility name, address, phone, contact name, type of waste handled, methods of on-site treatment and/or disposal, Environmental Protection Agency permit status and identification number, restrictions, description of other services. Arrangement: Geographical. Indexes: Organization name.

★5792★ **Peterson's Job Opportunities in Engineering and Technology**
Peterson's Guides
2000 Lenox Dr.
Box 67005
Lawrenceville, NJ 08648
Ph: (609)896-1800   Fax: (609)896-4531
Fr: 800-338-3282
E-mail: custsvc@petersons.com
URL: http://www.petersons.com

Compiled by the Peterson's staff. Fourth edition, 1996. $21.95 (paper). 379 pages. Profiles 2,000 high-tech companies looking primarily for technical personnel in such fields as biotechnology, telecommunications, software, computers and peripherals, defense, and aerospace. Contains job-search strategies and career options to help match education and expertise to the job market. Indexed geographically, by industry, and by hiring needs.

★5793★ Who's Who in Environmental Engineering

American Academy of Environmental Engineers
130 Holiday Ct., Ste. 100
Annapolis, MD 21401
Ph: (410)266-3311   Fax: (410)266-7653
URL: http://www.aaee.net

Annual, April. $75.00 for individuals. Covers about 2,400 licensed professional environmental engineers who have been certified by examination in one or more of seven specialties: air pollution control, general environmental engineering, industrial hygiene, hazardous waste management, radiation protection, solid waste management, and water supply and wastewater. Entries include: Name, affiliation, address, phone, area of specialization, biographical data. Arrangement: Alphabetical, geographical, area of specialization.

HANDBOOKS AND MANUALS

★5794★ The Best Resumes for Scientists and Engineers

John Wiley & Sons Inc.
1 Wiley Dr.
Somerset, NJ 08873
Ph: (732)469-4400   Fax: (732)302-2300
Fr: 800-225-5945
E-mail: custserv@wiley.com
URL: http://www.wiley.com/WileyCDA/

Adele Lewis and David J. Moore. Second edition, 1993. $37.50; $19.95 (paper). 224 pages. Presents an extensive collection of scientific and engineering resumes, highlighting the important differences between these and resumes written for other occupations.

★5795★ Hazardous Materials & Waste Management: A Guide for the Professional Hazards Manager

William Andrew Publishing
13 Eaton Ave.
Norwich, NY 13815
Ph: (607)337-5080   Fax: (607)337-5090
Fr: 800-932-7045
E-mail: sales@williamandrew.com
URL: http://www.williamandrew.com

Paul N. Cheremisinoff and Nicholas P. Cheremisinoff. 1995. $116.00. 277 pages. Volume has been written as a desk reference for the Professional Hazards Manager (PHM).

★5796★ Opportunities in Waste Management Careers

The McGraw-Hill Companies
PO Box 182604
Columbus, OH 43272
Fax: (614)759-3749   Fr: 877-883-5524
E-mail: customer.service@mcgraw-hill.com
URL: http://www.mcgraw-hill.com

Mark Rowh. 1994. $14.95; $11.95 (paper).

145 pages. Outlines the diverse opportunities in waste management and examines the duties, working conditions, salaries, and future of a variety of positions. Profiles jobs and opportunities in solid waste and waste water management, environmental engineering, soil and wildlife conservation, and related career areas.

EMPLOYMENT AGENCIES AND SEARCH FIRMS

★5797★ The Energists

10260 Westheimer Blvd., Ste. 300
Houston, TX 77042
Ph: (713)781-6881   Fax: (713)781-2998
E-mail: search@energists.com
URL: http://www.energists.com

Executive search firm.

★5798★ Intech Summit Group, Inc.

3450 Bonita Rd., Ste. 203
Chula Vista, CA 91910
Ph: (619)862-2720   Fax: (619)862-2699
Fr: 800-750-8100
E-mail: isg@isgsearch.com
URL: http://www.isgsearch.com

Employment agency and executive recruiter with a branch in Carlsbad, CA.

★5799★ Lybrook Associates, Inc.

266 N. Farm Dr.
Bristol, RI 02809
Ph: (401)254-5840

Executive search firm specializing in the field of chemistry.

★5800★ Search Consultants International, Inc.

4545 Post Oak Pl., Ste. 208
Houston, TX 77027
Ph: (713)622-9188   Fax: (713)622-9186
E-mail: info@searchconsultants.com
URL: http://www.searchconsultants.com

Management executive search firm.

OTHER SOURCES

★5801★ Air and Waste Management Association (A&WMA)

1 Gateway Ctr., 3rd Fl.
420 Ft. Duquesne Blvd.
Pittsburgh, PA 15222-1435
Ph: (412)232-3444   Fax: (412)232-3450
Fr: 800-270-3444
E-mail: info@awma.org
URL: http://www.awma.org

Description: Serves as environmental, educational, and technical organization. **Pur-**

pose: Seeks to provide a neutral forum for the exchange of technical information on a wide variety of environmental topics.

★5802★ American Academy of Environmental Engineers (AAEE)

130 Holiday Ct., Ste. 100
Annapolis, MD 21401
Ph: (410)266-3311   Fax: (410)266-7653
E-mail: info@aaee.net
URL: http://www.aaee.net

Members: Environmentally oriented registered professional engineers certified by examination as Diplomates of the Academy. **Purpose:** Seeks to improve the standards of environmental engineering. Certifies those with special knowledge of environmental engineering. Furnishes lists of those certified to the public. **Activities:** Maintains speakers' bureau. Recognizes areas of specialization: Air Pollution Control; General Environmental; Hazardous Waste Management; Industrial Hygiene; Radiation Protection; Solid Waste Management; Water Supply and Wastewater. Requires written and oral examinations for certification. Works with other professional organizations on environmentally oriented activities. Identifies potential employment candidates through Talent Search Service.

★5803★ Environmental Industry Associations (EIA)

4301 Connecticut Ave. NW, Ste. 300
Washington, DC 20008-2304
Ph: (202)244-4700   Fax: (202)966-4818
Fr: 800-424-2869
E-mail: membership@envasns.org
URL: http://www.envasns.org

Activities: Compiles statistics; conducts research and educational programs.

★5804★ Environmental Occupations: Professional

Delphi Productions
3159 6th St.
Boulder, CO 80304
Ph: (303)443-2100   Fax: (303)443-4022
Fr: 888-443-2400
E-mail: support@delphivideo.com
URL: http://www.delphivideo.com

$95.00. 49 minutes. Part of the Emerging Careers Video Library.

★5805★ Environmental Occupations: Technical

Delphi Productions
3159 6th St.
Boulder, CO 80304
Ph: (303)443-2100   Fax: (303)443-4022
Fr: 888-443-2400
E-mail: support@delphivideo.com
URL: http://www.delphivideo.com

$95.00. 48 minutes. Part of the Emerging Careers Video Library.

★5806★ Scientific, Engineering, and Technical Services

Cambridge Educational
PO Box 2053
Princeton, NJ 08543-2053
Ph: 800-257-5126   Fax: (609)671-0266
Fr: 800-468-4227
E-mail: custserv@films.com
URL: http://www.cambridgeeducational.com

VHS and DVD. $89.95. 2002. 18 minutes. 2002. Part of the Career Cluster Series.

★5807★ Water Environment Federation (WEF)

601 Wythe St.
Alexandria, VA 22314-1994
Ph: (703)684-2400   Fax: (703)684-2492
Fr: 800-666-0206
E-mail: csc@wef.org
URL: http://www.wef.org

Description: Technical societies representing chemists, biologists, ecologists, geologists, operators, educational and research personnel, industrial wastewater engineers, consultant engineers, municipal officials, equipment manufacturers, and university professors and students dedicated to the enhancement and preservation of water quality and resources. Seeks to advance fundamental and practical knowledge concerning the nature, collection, treatment, and disposal of domestic and industrial wastewaters, and the design, construction, operation, and management of facilities for these purposes. Disseminates technical information; and promotes good public relations and regulations that improve water quality and the status of individuals working in this field. Conducts educational and research programs.

Health Services Managers and Hospital Administrators

SOURCES OF HELP-WANTED ADS

★5808★ AABB Weekly Report

American Association of Blood Banks
8101 Glenbrook Rd.
Bethesda, MD 20814-2749
Ph: (301)907-6977   Fax: (301)907-6895
E-mail: aabb@aabb.org
URL: http://www.aabb.org

Description: 4 issues/year. Reports on developments in the area of blood banking and transfusion medicine. Covers scientific, regulatory, legislative, and legal information. Recurring features include news summaries and notices of employment positions.

★5809★ AAOHN News

American Association of Occupational
    Health Nurses Inc.
2920 Brandywine Rd., Ste. 100
Atlanta, GA 30341
Ph: (770)455-7757   Fax: (770)455-7271
URL: http://www.aaohn.org/member_services/newsletter/index.cfm

Description: Monthly. Covers Association events as well as trends and legislation affecting occupational and enivornmental health nursing. Recurring features include news of research, a calendar of events, reports of meetings, news of educational opportunities, job listings, notices of publications available, resources for career-building, briefs on governmental issues concerning occupational and environment health, and a President's column.

**★5810★ Advisor for Medical and
    Professional Staff Services**

Medical Staff Solutions
32 Wood St.
Nashua, NH 03064
Ph: (603)886-0444   Fax: (810)277-0578
E-mail: info@medicalstaffsolutions.net
URL: http://www.medicalstaffsolutions.net

Description: Monthly. Offers news and advice for medical office staff. Recurring features include interviews, notices of publications available.

**★5811★ American Academy of Medical
    Administrators-Executive**

American Academy of Medical
    Administrators
701 Lee St., Ste. 600
Des Plaines, IL 60016-4516
Ph: (847)759-8601   Fax: (847)759-8602
E-mail: info@aameda.org
URL: http://www.aameda.org

Description: Quarterly. Covers membership activities. Contains article abstracts and book reviews.

**★5812★ American Dental Hygienists'
    Association Access**

American Dental Hygienists' Association
444 North Michigan Ave., Ste. 3400
Chicago, IL 60611
Ph: (312)440-8904   Fr: 800-243-ADHA
URL: http://www.adha.org/publications

$48.00/year for individuals; $85.00 for two years; $120.00/year for individuals, for 3 years. Magazine covering current dental hygiene topics, regulatory and legislative developments, and association news.

**★5813★ Applied Occupational &
    Environmental Hygiene**

Applied Industrial Hygiene Inc.
1330 Kemper Meadow Dr., Ste. 600
Cincinnati, OH 45240
Ph: (513)742-2020   Fax: (513)742-3355
URL: http://www.acgih.org

Monthly. $223.00/year for individuals, individual membership; $623.00/year for institutions, institution or organization. Peer-reviewed journal presenting applied solutions for the prevention of occupational and environmental disease and injury.

★5814★ CAP Today

College of American Pathologists
325 Waukegan Rd.
Northfield, IL 60093-2750
Ph: (847)832-7000   Fax: (847)832-8000
Fr: 800-323-4040
URL: http://www.cap.org

Monthly. $95.00/year for individuals; $30.00/year for U.S. and Canada, single copy; $190.00/year for other countries; $120.00/year for Canada; $40.00/year for other countries, single copy. Magazine covering advances in pathology tests and equipment, clinical lab management and operations trends, and related regulatory and legislative changes.

★5815★ Catholic Health World

Catholic Health Association of the United
    States
4455 Woodson Rd.
St. Louis, MO 63134-3797
Ph: (314)427-2500
URL: http://www.chausa.org

Semimonthly. $40.00/year for individuals; $45.00/year for other countries. Tabloid containing national and regional news stories, human interest items, healthcare legislation articles, and photos of interest to administrators of U.S. Catholic hospitals, medical centers, and long-term care facilities.

**★5816★ CCH Monitor-The Newsletter
    of Managed Care**

CCH Inc.
4025 W Peterson Ave.
Chicago, IL 60646-6085
Ph: (847)267-7000   Fax: (773)866-3895
Fr: 888-224-7377
URL: http://www.cch.com

Description: Semimonthly. Provides coverage of issues facing managed care providers, with practical advice on managed care plans, including "how to" tips on compliance, coverage, and certification requirements, and analysis of legal developments affecting managed care systems. Recurring features include a calendar of events and reports of meetings.

★5817★ CME Supplement to Emergency Medicine Clinics of North America

Elsevier Science Inc.
360 Park Ave. S
New York, NY 10010
Ph: (212)989-5800   Fax: (212)633-3990
URL: http://www.elsevier.com

Quarterly. $190.00/year for individuals. Journal covering emergency medicine clinics.

★5818★ COR Healthcare Market Strategist

COR Health L.L.C.
200 Hoods Lane
Marblehead, MA 01945
Fax: 800-639-8511   Fr: 877-727-1728
URL: http://www.corhealth.com

Description: Monthly. Provides information on healthcare industry.

★5819★ Diversity

Career Recruitment Media
211 W Wacker Dr., Ste. 900
Chicago, IL 60606
Ph: (312)525-3100
URL: http://www.diversityalliedhealth.com/

Magazine focus on multicultural career and educational development magazine for allied health students and professionals.

★5820★ Ethnicity and Health

Taylor & Francis Group Journals
325 Chestnut St., Ste. 800
Philadelphia, PA 19106
Ph: (215)625-8900   Fax: (215)625-8914
Fr: 800-354-1420
URL: http://www.tandf.co.uk/journals/titles/13557858.asp

Journal covering ethnicity and health.

★5821★ Group Practice Journal

American Medical Group Association
1422 Duke St.
Alexandria, VA 22314-3403
Ph: (703)838-0033   Fax: (703)548-1890
E-mail: srozga@amga.org
URL: http://www.amga.org

Monthly. $95.00/year; $176.00/year; $180.00/year for individuals; $278.00 for two years; $180.00/year for out of country; $278.00 for two years, foreign. Magazine covering the business of medicine.

★5822★ Health Care Registration

Aspen Publishers Inc.
76 Ninth Ave., 7th Fl.
New York, NY 10011
Ph: (212)771-0600   Fax: (212)771-0885
Fr: 800-234-1660
URL: http://www.aspenpublishers.com/

Description: Monthly. Provides information and tips for health care administrators on how to run their departments more effectively. Topics include patient relations, collec-

tions, admissions, employee management, productivity, and others.

★5823★ Health Facilities Management

Health Forum L.L.C.
1 N Franklin, 29th Fl.
Chicago, IL 60606
Ph: (312)893-6800   Fax: (312)422-4506
Fr: 800-821-2039
URL: http://www.hfmmagazine.com

Monthly. Magazine covering health care.

★5824★ Health & Place

Mosby Inc.
11830 Westline Industrial Dr.
St. Louis, MO 63146
Ph: (314)872-8370   Fax: (314)432-1380
Fr: 800-325-4177
URL: http://www.us.elsevierhealth.com

Quarterly. $650.00/year for institutions, for all countries except European countries, Japan and Iran; $126.00/year for individuals, personal. Journal publishing articles for health care professionals.

★5825★ Health Policy, Economics and Management

Elsevier Science Inc.
360 Park Ave. S
New York, NY 10010
Ph: (212)989-5800   Fax: (212)633-3990
URL: http://www.elsevier.com

Monthly. $2,427.00/year for institutions in all countries except Europe, Japan and Iran. $404.00/year for individuals in all countries except Europe, Japan and Iran. Journal covering the economic, social and political aspects of health care and its organization includes hospital management, health care marketing, hospital automation, and the assessment of new technology for the health care industry.

★5826★ Health Progress

Catholic Health Association of the United States
4455 Woodson Rd.
St. Louis, MO 63134-3797
Ph: (314)427-2500
URL: http://www.chausa.org

Bimonthly. $50.00/year   for   members; $61.00/year for others; $61.00/year for out of country, foreign and Canada; $3.00/year for nonmembers,   special   section   reprints; $10.00/year for nonmembers, single copy. Magazine for administrative-level and other managerial personnel in Catholic healthcare and related organizations. Featured are articles on management concepts, legislative and regulatory trends, and theological, sociological, ethical, legal, and technical issues.

★5827★ Healthcare Purchasing News

Nelson Publishing Inc.
2500 Tamiami Trl. N
Nokomis, FL 34275
Ph: (941)966-9521   Fax: (941)966-2590

E-mail: hpn@hpnonline.com
URL: http://www.hpnonline.com

Monthly. $72.00/year   for   individuals, $110.00/year for Canada; $130.00/year for other countries. Magazine for healthcare material management, central services, operating room and infection control professionals, and others involved in supply chain issues with hospitals and outpatient settings.

★5828★ HIMSS News

Healthcare Information and Management Systems Society
230 E. Ohio St., Ste. 500
Chicago, IL 60611-3269
Ph: (312)664-4467   Fax: (312)664-6143
E-mail: himss@himss.org
URL: http://www.himss.org/asp/himss_news_list.asp

Description: Monthly. Tracks developments in the health care information and management systems field. Provides latest management trends in information systems, management engineering, and telecommunications.

★5829★ Hospital Outlook

Federation of American Hospitals
801 Pennsylvania Ave. NW, Ste. 245
Washington, DC 20004-2604
Ph: (202)624-1500   Fax: (202)737-6462
E-mail: info@fah.org
URL: http://www.americashospitals.com/

Description: Bimonthly. Monitors health legislation, regulatory and reimbursement matters and developments of interest to the investor-owned hospital industry.

★5830★ Hospitals & Health Networks

Health Forum L.L.C.
1 N Franklin, 29th Fl.
Chicago, IL 60606
Ph: (312)893-6800   Fax: (312)422-4506
Fr: 800-821-2039
URL: http://www.hhnmag.com

Weekly. Publication covering the health care industry.

★5831★ The IHS Primary Care Provider

Indian Health Service (HQ)
The Reyes Bldg.
801 Thompson Ave., Ste. 400
Rockville, MD 20852-1627
URL: http://www.ihs.gov/PublicInfo/Publications/HealthProvider/Pr

Monthly. Journal for health care professionals, physicians, nurses, pharmacists, dentists, and dietitians.

★5832★ The International Electronic Journal of Health Education

American Alliance for Health, Physical Education, Recreation & Dance
1900 Association Dr.
Reston, VA 20191-1598
Ph: (703)476-3400   Fax: (703)476-9527
Fr: 800-213-7193

URL: http://www.aahperd.org/iejhe/template.cfm?template=about.htm

Annual. Free to health education professionals and students. Journal promoting health through education and other systematic strategies.

★5833★ **International Journal of Healthcare Information Systems and Informatics**

Idea Group Publishing
701 E Chocolate Ave., Ste. 200
Hershey, PA 17033
Ph: (717)533-8845   Fax: (717)533-8661
Fr: (866)342-6657
URL: http://www.igi-pub.com/journals/details.asp?id=4835

Quarterly. $90.00/year for individuals, print only; $395.00/year for institutions, print and free online; $345.00/year for institutions, online only. Journal covering advance health care and clinical practices and research.

★5834★ **JONA's Healthcare Law, Ethics, and Regulation**

Lippincott Williams & Wilkins
351 W Camden St.
Baltimore, MD 21201
Ph: (410)528-4000   Fax: (410)528-4305
Fr: 800-399-3110
URL: http://www.jonalaw.com/

Quarterly. $55.00/year for individuals; $82.00/year for institutions; $97.00/year for individuals, international; $117.00/year for institutions, international. Journal covering the legal, ethical and regulatory issues facing nursing care management.

★5835★ **Journal of the American Society of Podiatric Medical Assistants**

American Society of Podiatric Medical Assistants
2124 S Austin Blvd.
Cicero, IL 60804
Ph: (708)863-6303   Fr: 888-882-7762
URL: http://www.aspma.org

Quarterly. Subscription included in membership. Professional journal covering issues in podiatry.

★5836★ **Journal of Health Administration Education**

Association of University Programs in Health Administration
2000 N 14th St., Ste. 780
Arlington, VA 22201
Ph: (703)894-0940   Fax: (703)894-0941
URL: http://www.aupha.org/i4a/pages/index.cfm?pageid=3321#top

Quarterly. $100.00/year for individuals; $120.00/year for individuals, international; $25.00/year for members, back issues; $30.00/year for nonmembers, back issues; $150.00/year for members, set of entire series; $250.00/year for nonmembers, set of entire series. Journal covering health administration education.

★5837★ **Journal of Health Law**

American Health Lawyers Association
1025 Connecticut Ave., NW, Ste. 600
Washington, DC 20036-5405
Ph: (202)833-1100   Fax: (202)833-1105
URL: http://www.healthlawyers.org

Quarterly. Professional journal covering healthcare issues and cases and their impact on the health care arena.

★5838★ **Journal of Health Management**

Sage Publications Inc.
2455 Teller Rd.
Thousand Oaks, CA 91320
Ph: (805)499-0721   Fax: (805)499-8096
URL: http://www.sagepub.com/journalsProdAdv.nav?prodId=Journal200

$287.00/year for institutions, print & e-access; $258.00/year for institutions, e-access; $281.00/year for institutions, print only; $88.00/year for individuals, print only; $104.00 for institutions, single print; $38.00 for individuals, single print. Journal focusing on health management and policy.

★5839★ **Journal for Healthcare Quality**

National Association for Healthcare Quality
4700 West Lake Ave.
Glenview, IL 60025
Ph: (847)375-4720   Fr: 800-966-9392
E-mail: jhq@nahq.org
URL: http://www.nahq.org/journal/online/

Bimonthly. $115.00/year for individuals; $170.00/year for institutions; $190.00/year for individuals, other countries; $190.00/year for institutions, other countries. Professional publication that explores safe, cost-effective, quality healthcare.

★5840★ **Journal of Hospital Medicine**

John Wiley & Sons Inc.
111 River St.
Hoboken, NJ 07030-5774
Ph: (201)748-6000   Fax: (201)748-6088
Fr: 800-825-7550
URL: http://www.wiley.com/WileyCDA/WileyTitle/productCd-JHM.html

Bimonthly. $110.00/year for individuals, print only; Online version available with subscription. Journal on hospital medicine.

★5841★ **Journal of Nursing Care Quality**

Lippincott Williams & Wilkins
351 W Camden St.
Baltimore, MD 21201
Ph: (410)528-4000   Fax: (410)528-4305
Fr: 800-399-3110
URL: http://www.lww.com/product/?1057-3631

Quarterly. $98.00/year for individuals; $263.00/year for institutions; $168.00/year for individuals, other countries; $351.00/year for institutions, other countries. Journal keeping practicing nurses and those who play leadership roles in nursing care quality programs fully current on the utilization of quality principles and concepts in the practice setting.

★5842★ **Journal of Nursing Scholarship**

Wiley-Blackwell
350 Main St. Commerce Pl.
Malden, MA 02148
Ph: (781)388-8200   Fax: (781)388-8210
Fr: 800-759-6120
URL: http://www.blackwellpublishing.com/journal.asp?ref=1527-6546

Quarterly. $51.00/year for individuals, print and online; $185.00/year for institutions, print and premium online; $168.00/year for institutions, print and standard online; $160.00/year for institutions, premium online only; $59.00/year for individuals, print and online; $135.00/year for institutions, other countries, print and premium online; $123.00/year for institutions, other countries, print and standard online; $117.00/year for institutions, other countries, premium online only; $39.00/year for individuals, print and online. Peer-reviewed journal covering nursing.

★5843★ **LDI Health Policy & Research Quarterly**

Leonard Davis Institute of Health Economics
3641 Locust Walk
Colonial Penn Center
Philadelphia, PA 19104
Ph: (215)898-5611   Fax: (215)898-0229
URL: http://www.upenn.edu/ldi/

Description: Quarterly. Reports on the Institute's research and policy activities on medical, behavioral, economic, social and ethical issues that influence how health care is organized, financed, managed, and delivered in the U.S. and worldwide. Recurring features include cover story on published research of major health policy significance, guest commentary on cover story, interviews, abstracts of recent publications and new grants, national health policy conference reports, newsmakers, and calendar of events.

★5844★ **Magnetic Resonance Imaging Clinics**

Mosby Inc.
11830 Westline Industrial Dr.
St. Louis, MO 63146
Ph: (314)872-8370   Fax: (314)432-1380
Fr: 800-325-4177
URL: http://www.mri.theclinics.com

Quarterly. $345.00/year for individuals, international; $463.00/year for institutions, international; $167.00/year for students, international; $253.00/year for individuals; $376.00/year for institutions; $123.00/year for students. Journal publishing articles and research on the latest trends in magnetic resonance imagining clinics and patient management.

★5845★ Medical Care

Lippincott Williams & Wilkins
351 W Camden St.
Baltimore, MD 21201
Ph: (410)528-4000   Fax: (410)528-4305
Fr: 800-399-3110
URL: http://www.lww-medicalcare.com/

Monthly. $373.00/year for individuals; $813.00/year for institutions; $475.00/year for individuals, other countries; $869.00/year for institutions, other countries; $207.00/year for individuals, in-training. Journal focusing on all aspects of the administration and delivery of healthcare.

★5846★ Medical Records Briefing

HCPro Inc.
200 Hoods Ln.
PO Box 1168
Marblehead, MA 01945
Ph: 877-727-1728   Fax: 800-639-8511
Fr: 800-639-8511
URL: http://www.hcmarketplace.com/Prod.cfm?id=140

Description: Monthly. Provides news and advice of interest to medical records professionals, including reimbursement, coding, legalities, regulations, and reviews. Recurring features include interviews, book reviews, and columns titled Computer Chronicle, Focus on JCAHO, Benchmarking Report, In Brief, and This Month's Idea. Subscription includes bimonthly "A Minute for the Medical Staff."

★5847★ Medical Staff Development Professional

American Academy of Medical Management
Crossville Commons
560 W Crossville Rd., Ste. 103
Roswell, GA 30075
Ph: (770)649-7150   Fax: (770)649-7552

Periodic. Professional journal covering medical education.

★5848★ MEEN Imaging Technology News

Reilly Communications Group
16 E Schaumburg Rd.
Schaumburg, IL 60194-3536
Ph: (847)882-6336   Fax: (847)882-0631
URL: http://www.itnonline.net

Trade magazine (tabloid) serving users and buyers of medical imaging technologies and services.

★5849★ Minnesota Medicine

Minnesota Medical Association
1300 Godward St. NE, Ste. 2500
Minneapolis, MN 55413
Ph: (612)378-1875   Fax: (612)378-3875
Fr: 800-342-5662
URL: http://www.minnesotamedicine.com/

Monthly. $45.00/year for individuals; $81.00 for two years; $80.00/year for other countries; $144.00/year for other countries, two years. Magazine on medical, socioeconom-

ic, public health, medical-legal, and biomedical ethics issues of interest to physicians.

★5850★ Modern Healthcare

Crain Communications Inc.
360 N Michigan Ave.
Chicago, IL 60601
Ph: (312)649-5411   Fax: (312)280-3150
Fr: 888-909-9111
E-mail: subs@crain.com
URL: http://www.modernhealthcare.com

Weekly. $154.00/year for individuals; $244.00/year for Canada; $208.00/year for other countries. Weekly business news magazine for healthcare management.

★5851★ Neuroimaging Clinics of North America

Mosby Inc.
11830 Westline Industrial Dr.
St. Louis, MO 63146
Ph: (314)872-8370   Fax: (314)432-1380
Fr: 800-325-4177
URL: http://www.neuroimaging.theclinics.com

Quarterly. $454.00/year for institutions, international; $332.00/year for individuals, international; $166.00/year for students, international; $370.00/year for institutions, U.S.; $123.00/year for students, U.S.; $277.00/year for individuals, Canada; $166.00/year for students, Canada; $454.00/year for institutions, Canada. Journal publishing articles on newest advances in neuroimaging and patient treatment options.

★5852★ Nursing Administration Quarterly

Lippincott Williams & Wilkins
351 W Camden St.
Baltimore, MD 21201
Ph: (410)528-4000   Fax: (410)528-4305
Fr: 800-399-3110
URL: http://www.lww.com/product/?0363-9568

Quarterly. $105.96/year for individuals; $282.96/year for institutions; $62.96/year for individuals in-training; $169.96/year for individuals, international; $340.94/year for institutions, international. Journal providing nursing administrators with information on the effective management of nursing services in all health care settings.

★5853★ Nursing Economics

Jannetti Publications Inc.
East Holly Ave., Box 56
Pitman, NJ 08071-0056
Ph: (856)256-2300
E-mail: nejrnl@ajj.com
URL: http://www.ajj.com

Bimonthly. $65.00/year for individuals; $110.00 for individuals, 2 years; $80.00/year for institutions; $130.00 for institutions, 2 years; $89.00/year for individuals, other countries; $158.00 for individuals, other countries, 2 years; $104.00/year for institutions, other countries; $178.00 for institu-

tions, other countries, 2 years. Business magazine for nursing administrators.

★5854★ Nutrition Business Journal

Penton Media Inc.
249 W 17th St.
New York, NY 10011
Ph: (212)204-4200
E-mail: info@nutritionbusiness.com
URL: http://www.nutritionbusiness.com/

Monthly. $995.00/year for individuals; $299.00/year for individuals, for 3 months. Journal catering to nutrition, natural products and alternative health care industries. Publishes information regarding business activities, market size/growth, trends, and opportunities, with a particular emphasis on the nutrition industry.

★5855★ Organizational Ethics

University Publishing Group Inc.
219 W Washington St.
Hagerstown, MD 21740
Ph: (240)420-0036   Fax: (240)420-0037
Fr: 800-654-8188
URL: http://www.organizationalethics.com

Semiannual. $127.00/year for institutions; $65.00/year for individuals. Magazine covering business and healthcare policy.

★5856★ Patient Education and Counseling

Mosby Inc.
11830 Westline Industrial Dr.
St. Louis, MO 63146
Ph: (314)872-8370   Fax: (314)432-1380
Fr: 800-325-4177
URL: http://www.elsevier.com/wps/find/journaldescription.cws_home

Monthly. $229.00/year for individuals; $2,169.00/year for institutions. Journal publishing articles on patient education and health promotion researchers, managers, physicians, nurses and other health care providers.

★5857★ Patient Safety & Quality Healthcare

Lionheart Publishing Inc.
506 Roswell St., Ste. 220
Marietta, GA 30060
Ph: (770)431-0867   Fax: (770)432-6969
URL: http://www.psqh.com

Bimonthly. $49.00/year for individuals; $69.00/year for Canada and Mexico, individual; $89.00/year for other countries, individual; $10.00 for single issue. Publication that provides information about patient safety and quality healthcare for patients, doctors, hospital administrators, and others in the healthcare industry.

★5858★ Public Health Forum

Elsevier Science Inc.
360 Park Ave. S
New York, NY 10010
Ph: (212)989-5800   Fax: (212)633-3990

URL: http://www.elsevier.com

$38.00/year for institutions, for all countries except Europe, Japan and Iran; $12.00/year for students, for all countries except Japan. Journal focused on research methods, and program evaluation in the field of public health.

★5859★ Public Health Law & Policy Journal

University of Hawaii
1859 E.-W. Rd., No. 106
Honolulu, HI 96822-2322
Ph: (808)956-9424   Fax: (808)956-5983
E-mail: phlo@hawaii.edu
URL: http://www.hawaii.edu/phlo/phlpj/

Free, online. Open access academic journal covering worldwide public health issues.

★5860★ Public Health, Social Medicine and Epidemiology

Elsevier Science Inc.
360 Park Ave. S
New York, NY 10010
Ph: (212)989-5800   Fax: (212)633-3990
URL: http://www.elsevier.com

Semimonthly. $5,682.00/year for institutions, for all countries except Europe, Japan and Iran. Journal covering public health and social medicine, and includes health planning and education, epidemiology and prevention of communicable disease, public health aspects of risk populations.

★5861★ Quality Management in Health Care

Lippincott Williams & Wilkins
351 W Camden St.
Baltimore, MD 21201
Ph: (410)528-4000   Fax: (410)528-4305
Fr: 800-399-3110
URL: http://www.lww.com/product/?1063-8628

Quarterly. $104.96/year for individuals; $289.96/year for institutions; $62.96/year for individuals, in-training; $172.96/year for international individuals; $372.96/year for international institutions. Journal providing a forum to explore the theoretical, technical, and strategic elements of total quality management in health care.

★5862★ Russ Coile's Health Trends

Aspen Publishers Inc.
76 Ninth Ave., 7th Fl.
New York, NY 10011
Ph: (212)771-0600   Fax: (212)771-0885
Fr: 800-234-1660
URL: http://www.aspenpublishers.com

Description: Monthly. Provides information on trends in healthcare, with advice on how executives can position their organizations to take advantage of those trends.

★5863★ Staffing Industry Healthcare News

Staffing Industry Analysts Inc.
881 Fremont Ave.
Los Altos, CA 94024
Ph: (650)232-2350   Fax: (650)232-2360
Fr: 800-950-9496

Weekly. $10.00 for single issue. Online publication covering key events in health care staffing.

★5864★ Topics in Emergency Medicine

Lippincott Williams & Wilkins
351 W Camden St.
Baltimore, MD 21201
Ph: (410)528-4000   Fax: (410)528-4305
Fr: 800-399-3110
URL: http://www.lww.com/product/?0164-2340

Quarterly. $91.95/year for individuals; $241.95/year for institutions; $141.95/year for other countries. Journal offering information that encompasses the coordinated responsibilities of emergency physicians, nurses, and paramedics.

★5865★ Trustee

Health Forum L.L.C.
1 N Franklin, 29th Fl.
Chicago, IL 60606
Ph: (312)893-6800   Fax: (312)422-4506
Fr: 800-821-2039
URL: http://www.trusteemag.com

Monthly. Magazine for hospital and health care system governing board members containing information about events and issues affecting the health care industry.

PLACEMENT AND JOB REFERRAL SERVICES

★5866★ American Academy of Medical Administrators Research and Educational Foundation (AAMA)

701 Lee St., Ste. 600
Des Plaines, IL 60016
Ph: (847)759-8601   Fax: (847)759-8602
E-mail: info@aameda.org
URL: http://www.aameda.org/aboutaama/aboutfoundation.html

Description: Individuals with health care backgrounds. Conducts research in the health care field and seminars geared toward professional development. Maintains placement services.

★5867★ American College Health Association (ACHA)

PO Box 28937
Baltimore, MD 21240-8937
Ph: (410)859-1500   Fax: (410)859-1510
E-mail: contact@acha.org
URL: http://www.acha.org

Purpose: Provides an organization in which institutions of higher education and interested individuals may work together to promote health in its broadest aspects for students and all other members of the college community. Activities: Offers continuing education programs for health professionals. Maintains placement listings for physicians and other personnel seeking positions in college health. Compiles statistics. Conducts seminars and training programs.

★5868★ American College of Health Care Administrators (ACHCA)

300 N Lee St., Ste. 301
Alexandria, VA 22314
Ph: (703)739-7900   Fax: (703)739-7901
E-mail: mgrachek@achca.org
URL: http://www.achca.org

Members: Persons actively engaged in the administration of long-term care facilities, such as nursing homes, retirement communities, assisted living facilities, and sub-acute care programs. Purpose: Administers professional certification programs for assisted living, sub-acute and nursing home administrators. Works to elevate the standards in the field and to develop and promote a code of ethics and standards of education and training. Seeks to inform allied professions and the public that good administration of long-term care facilities calls for special formal academic training and experience. Encourages research in all aspects of geriatrics, the chronically ill, and administration. Activities: Maintains placement service. Holds special education programs; facilitates networking among administrators.

★5869★ American College of Health Plan Management (ACHPM)

701 Lee St., No. 600
Des Plaines, IL 60016-4516
Ph: (847)759-8601   Fax: (847)759-8602
E-mail: kevin.franke@usaf.af.mil
URL: http://www.aameda.org

Description: Serves as specialty college of the American Academy of Medical Administrators. Represents managers of professionals who are directly or indirectly providing managed healthcare. Works to promote the advancement of members' professional standing, education, and personal achievement and develop innovative concepts in managed care administration. Conducts an employment referral and educational programs.

★5870★ American Correctional Health Services Association (ACHSA)

250 Gatsby Pl.
Alpharetta, GA 30022-6161
Fax: (770)650-5789   Fr: 877-918-1842
E-mail: admin@achsa.org
URL: http://www.achsa.org

Members: Represents individuals interested in improving the quality of correctional health services. Purpose: Aims to promote the provision of health services to incarcerated persons consistent in quality and quantity with acceptable health care practices. Promotes and encourages continuing education and provides technical and professional guidance for correctional health care personnel. Establishes a forum for the sharing and discussion of correctional health care issues. **Activities:** Conducts conferences on correctional health care management, nursing, mental health, juvenile corrections, dentistry and related subjects. Maintains placement service.

★5871★ American Public Health Association (APHA)

800 I St. NW
Washington, DC 20001
Ph: (202)777-2742   Fax: (202)777-2534
E-mail: comments@apha.org
URL: http://www.apha.org

Members: Professional organization of physicians, nurses, educators, academicians, environmentalists, epidemiologists, new professionals, social workers, health administrators, optometrists, podiatrists, pharmacists, dentists, nutritionists, health planners, other community and mental health specialists, and interested consumers. **Purpose:** Seeks to protect and promote personal, mental, and environmental health. **Activities:** Services include: promulgation of standards; establishment of uniform practices and procedures; development of the etiology of communicable diseases; research in public health; exploration of medical care programs and their relationships to public health. Sponsors job placement service.

★5872★ American Society of Ophthalmic Administrators (ASOA)

4000 Legato Rd., Ste. 700
Fairfax, VA 22033
Ph: (703)591-2220   Fax: (703)591-0614
Fr: 800-451-1339
E-mail: kkrzmarzick@asoa.org
URL: http://www.asoa.org

Description: Serves as a division of the American Society of Cataract and Refractive Surgery. Represents persons involved with the administration of an ophthalmic office or clinic. Facilitates the exchange of ideas and information in order to improve management practices and working conditions. Offers placement services.

★5873★ Association for the Advancement of Medical Instrumentation (AAMI)

1110 N Glebe Rd., Ste. 220
Arlington, VA 22201-4795
Ph: (703)525-4890   Fax: (703)276-0793
Fr: 800-332-2264
E-mail: membership@aami.org
URL: http://www.aami.org

Description: Clinical engineers, biomedical equipment technicians, physicians, hospital administrators, consultants, engineers, manufacturers of medical devices, nurses, researchers and others interested in medical instrumentation. Works to improve the quality of medical care through the application, development, and management of technolo-

gy. Maintains placement service. Offers certification programs for biomedical equipment technicians and clinical engineers. Produces numerous standards and recommended practices on medical devices and procedures. Offers educational programs.

★5874★ Society for Radiation Oncology Administrators (SROA)

5272 River Rd., Ste. 630
Bethesda, MD 20816
Ph: (301)718-6510   Fax: (301)656-0989
Fr: (866)458-7762
E-mail: sroa@paimgmt.com
URL: http://www.sroa.org

Members: Individuals with managerial responsibilities in radiation oncology at the executive, divisional, or departmental level, and whose functions include personnel, budget, and development of operational procedures and guidelines for therapeutic radiology departments. **Purpose:** Strives to improve the administration of the business and nonmedical management aspects of therapeutic radiology, to promote the field of therapeutic radiology administration, to provide a forum for communication among members, and to disseminate information among members. **Activities:** Maintains speakers' bureau; offers placement service.

EMPLOYER DIRECTORIES AND NETWORKING LISTS

★5875★ AHA Guide to the Health Care Field

American Hospital Association
1 N Franklin
Chicago, IL 60606
Ph: (312)422-2050   Fax: (312)422-4700
Fr: 800-424-4301

Annual, August. Covers hospitals, networks, multi-health care systems, freestanding ambulatory surgery centers, psychiatric facilities, long-term care facilities, substance abuse programs, and other health-related organizations. Entries include: For hospitals–Facility name, address, phone, administrator's name, number of beds, facilities and services, number of employees, expenses, other statistics. For other organizations–Name, address, phone, fax, name and title of contact. Arrangement: Geographical. Indexes: Hospital name.

★5876★ Directory of Hospital Personnel

Grey House Publishing
185 Millerton Rd.
PO Box 860
Millerton, NY 12546
Ph: (518)789-8700   Fax: (518)789-0556
Fr: 800-562-2139
URL: http://www.greyhouse.com/hospital_
personnel.htm

Annual. $325.00 for print product; $545.00

for online database subscription; $650.00 for online database subscription and print product combined. Covers 200,000 executives at 7,000 U.S. hospitals. Entries include: Name of hospital, address, phone; number of beds; type and JCAHO status of hospital; names and titles of key department heads and staff; medical and nursing school affiliations; number of residents, interns, and nursing students. Arrangement: Geographical. Indexes: Hospital name, personnel, hospital size.

★5877★ Directory of Personnel Responsible for Radiological Health Programs

Conference of Radiation Control Program Directors Inc.
205 Capital Ave.
Frankfort, KY 40601-2832
Ph: (502)227-4543   Fax: (502)227-7862
URL: http://www.crcpd.org

Annual, January. $50.00. Covers about 350 individuals who conduct radiological health program activities in federal, state, and local government agencies; members of the conferences. Entries include: For directors–Name and title, name of agency address, phone; office hours listed with state heading. For members–name, address, phone, affiliation, department, and title. Arrangement: Directors are by level of agency and geographical. Indexes: Personal name, agency, state.

★5878★ Guide to Careers in the Health Professions

The Princeton Review
2315 Broadway
New York, NY 10024
Ph: (212)874-8282   Fax: (212)874-0775
Fr: 800-733-3000
URL: http://www.princetonreview.com/

Published January, 2001. $24.95 for individuals. Presents advice and information for those searching for satisfying careers in the health professions. Publication includes: Directory of schools and academic programs. Entries include: Name, address, phone, tuition, program details, employment profiles.

★5879★ Health Professions Career and Education Directory

American Medical Association
515 N State St.
Chicago, IL 60610
Fr: 800-621-8335
E-mail: dorothy-grant@ama-assn.org
URL: http://www.ama-assn.org

Annual; latest edition 2007-2008. $52.50 for members; $70.00 for nonmembers. Covers more than 6,500 health career educational programs in over 64 health occupations at 2,800 sponsoring institutions. Entries include: Occupational descriptions, employment characteristics, and information on education programs, such as length, curriculum, and prerequisites. Arrangement: Classified by occupation, then geographical. Indexes: Institution name, program name.

★5880★ *Hospital Blue Book*

Billian Publishing Inc./Transworld
Publishing Inc.
2100 Powers Ferry Rd. SE
Atlanta, GA 30339
Ph: (770)955-5656   Fax: (770)952-0669
Fr: 800-533-8484
E-mail: blu-book@billian.com

2005. $300.00 for individuals. Covers more than 6,687 hospitals; some listings also appear in a separate southern edition of this publication. Entries include: Name of hospital, accreditation, mailing address, phone, fax, number of beds, type of facility (nonprofit, general, state, etc.); list of administrative personnel and chiefs of medical services, with specific titles. Arrangement: Geographical.

★5881★ *The JobBank Guide to Health Care Companies*

Adams Media Corp.
57 Littlefield St.
Avon, MA 02322
Ph: (508)427-7100   Fax: (508)427-6790
Fr: 800-872-5627
URL: http://www.amazon.com/Jobbank-Guide-Health-Care-Companies/dp

Biennial. Covers jobs nationwide in health care companies. Entries include: Firm or organization name, address, phone, name and title of contact; description of organization, headquarters location, typical titles for entry- and middle-level positions, educational backgrounds desired, fringe benefits offered, stock exchange listing, training programs, internships, parent company, number of employees, revenues, e-mail and web addresses, projected number of hires. Indexes: Alphabetical.

★5882★ *Medical and Health Information Directory*

Gale, Cengage Learning
27500 Drake Rd.
Farmington Hills, MI 48331-3535
Ph: (248)699-4253   Fax: (248)699-8065
Fr: 800-877-4253
E-mail: businessproducts@gale.com
URL: http://www.gale.com

Annual; latest edition 20th, July 2007. $375.00/volume. Covers in Volume 1, more than 26,500 medical and health oriented associations, organizations, institutions, and government agencies, including health maintenance organizations (HMOs), preferred provider organizations (PPOs), insurance companies, pharmaceutical companies, research centers, and medical and allied health schools. In Volume 2, over 12,000 medical book publishers; medical periodicals, directories, audiovisual producers and services, medical libraries and information centers, electronic resources, and health-related internet search engines. In Volume 3, more than 35,500 clinics, treatment centers, care programs, and counseling/diagnostic services for 34 subject areas. Entries include: Institution, service, or firm name, address, phone, fax, email and URL; many include names of key personnel and, when pertinent, descriptive annotations. Volume 3

was formerly listed separately as Health Services Directory. Arrangement: Classified by organization activity, service, etc. Indexes: Each volume has a complete alphabetical name and keyword index.

HANDBOOKS AND MANUALS

★5883★ *Career Opportunities in Health Care (Career Opportunities)*

Facts On File Inc.
132 W. 31st St., 17th Fl.
New York, NY 10001-2006
Ph: (212)967-8800   Fax: 800-678-3633
Fr: 800-322-8755
E-mail: custserv@factsonfile.com
URL: http://www.factsonfile.com

Shelly Field. Arthur E. Weintraub. 2002. Reprint. $49.50. 243 pages. Part of the Career Opportunities Series.

★5884★ *Great Jobs for Business Majors*

The McGraw-Hill Companies
PO Box 182604
Columbus, OH 43272
Fax: (614)759-3749   Fr: 877-883-5524
E-mail: customer.service@mcgraw-hill.com
URL: http://www.mcgraw-hill.com

Stephen Lambert. Second edition, 2003. $15.95 (paper). 240 pages.

★5885★ *Opportunities in Health and Medical Careers*

The McGraw-Hill Companies
PO Box 182604
Columbus, OH 43272
Fax: (614)759-3749   Fr: 877-883-5524
E-mail: customer.service@mcgraw-hill.com
URL: http://www.mcgraw-hill.com

I. Donald Snook, Jr. and Leo D'Orazio. 2004. $13.95 (paper). 157 pages. Covers the full range of medical and health occupations. Illustrated.

★5886★ *Opportunities in Hospital Administration Careers*

The McGraw-Hill Companies
PO Box 182604
Columbus, OH 43272
Fax: (614)759-3749   Fr: 877-883-5524
E-mail: customer.service@mcgraw-hill.com
URL: http://www.mcgraw-hill.com

I. Donald Snook. 2006. $13.95. 160 pages. Discusses opportunities for administrators in a variety of management settings: hospital, department, clinic, group practice, HMO, mental health, and extended care facilities.

★5887★ *Resumes for Health and Medical Careers*

The McGraw-Hill Companies
PO Box 182604
Columbus, OH 43272
Fax: (614)759-3749   Fr: 877-883-5524
E-mail: customer.service@mcgraw-hill.com
URL: http://www.mcgraw-hill.com

Third edition, 2003. $11.95 (paper). 160 pages.

★5888★ *Your Resume: Key to a Better Job*

Arco Pub.
200 Old Tappan Rd.
Old Tappan, NJ 07675
Fr: 800-428-5331

Leonard Corwen. Sixth edition, 1996. $10.95 (paper). 176 pages. Provides guidelines for resume writing; explains what employers look for in a resume, including contents and style. Includes model resumes for high-demand careers such as computer programmers, health administrators, and high-tech professionals. Notes basic job-getting information and strategies.

EMPLOYMENT AGENCIES AND SEARCH FIRMS

★5889★ *Aegis Group Search Consultants LLC*

41451 W. 11 Mile Rd.
Novi, MI 48375-1855
Ph: (248)344-1450   Fax: (248)347-2231
E-mail: resume@aegis-group.com
URL: http://www.aegis-group.com

Executive search and consultant firm. Focuses on the medical industry.

★5890★ *Ahern Search Partners*

3982 Powell Rd. Ste. 205
Powell, OH 43065
Ph: (614)436-4126   Fax: (614)436-4125
E-mail: mahern@ahernsearch.com
URL: http://www.ahernsearch.com/

Executive search firm. Concentrates on the healthcare market.

★5891★ *Alan Darling Consulting*

374 Dover Rd., Ste. 18
South Newfane, VT 05351-7901
Ph: (802)348-6365   Fax: (802)348-7826
URL: http://www.alandarling.com

Executive search firm focused on the healthcare industry.

★5892★ *Alliance Search Management Inc.*

594 Sawdust Rd., Ste. 194
The Woodlands, TX 77380
Ph: (281)367-8630   Fr: 800-444-0573

E-mail: kathy@alliancesearch.com
URL: http://www.alliancesearch.com

Employment agency.

★5893★ American Group Practice

1016 5th Ave.
New York, NY 10028
Ph: (212)371-3170   Fax: (212)401-4752
E-mail: agp420@aol.com

Employment agency focused on the health-care industry.

★5894★ American Physician Network Inc.

2794 Tennis Club Dr., Ste. 204
PO Box 222352
West Palm Beach, FL 33422-2352
Ph: (561)688-2999   Fax: 888-699-5512
Fr: 800-245-8227
E-mail: apn12345@aol.com

Employment agency focused on the health-care industry.

★5895★ Anderson & Associates

112 S. Tryon St., Ste. 700
Charlotte, NC 28284
Ph: (704)347-0090   Fax: (704)347-0064
E-mail: info@andersonexecsearch.com
URL: http://www.andersonexecsearch.com

Executive search firm. Branch in Cumming, Georgia.

★5896★ Aster Search Group

555 Madison Ave
New York, NY 10022
Ph: (212)888-6182   Fax: (212)826-3436
E-mail: ecohen@astersearch.com
URL: http://www.astersearch.com

Executive search firm focused on the health-care industry.

★5897★ Ballein Search Partners

PO Box 5204
Oak Brook, IL 60522
Ph: (630)322-9220   Fax: (630)322-9221
E-mail: kathybsp@xnet.com
URL: http://www.concentrichealth.net/BSP.htm

Executive search firm focused in the health-care industry.

★5898★ Barro Global Search Inc.

10951 Pico Blvd., Ste. 316
Los Angeles, CA 90064
Ph: (310)441-5305
E-mail: resumes@barroglobal.com
URL: http://www.barroglobal.com

Executive search firm focused on healthcare and hospitals.

★5899★ The Bauman Group

350 Second St., Ste. 2
Los Altos, CA 94022
Ph: (650)941-0800   Fax: (650)941-1729
E-mail: info@thebaumangroup.com
URL: http://www.thebaumangroup.com

Executive search firm.

★5900★ Boone-Scaturro Associates Inc.

8831 S. Somerset Lane
Alpharetta, GA 30004
Ph: (770)740-9737   Fax: (770)475-5055
Fr: 800-749-1884
E-mail: mes@boone-scaturro.com
URL: http://www.boone-scaturro.com

Executive search firm focused on the health-care industry.

★5901★ Bowen & Briggs Inc.

646 Turner Ave.
Drexel Hill, PA 19026
Ph: (610)284-6631   Fax: (610)284-6651
Fr: 877-853-9611
E-mail: solutions@bowenbriggs.com
URL: http://www.bowenbriggs.com

Specializes in executive search, coaching and consulting for children's health-care.

★5902★ The Brazik Group LLC

14862 Crescent Cove Dr.
Fort Myers, FL 33908
Ph: (239)249-1003   Fr: 800-838-5701
E-mail: chuck@brazikgroup.com
URL: http://www.brazikgroup.com

Executive search firm. Branches in Tinley Park, IL and Union Pier, MI.

★5903★ Breitner Clark & Hall Inc.

1017 Turnpike St., Ste. 22A
Canton, MA 02021
Ph: (781)828-6411   Fax: (781)828-6431
Fr: 800-331-7004
E-mail: info@breitner.com
URL: http://breitnerclarkandhall.com/site/a-bout/default.asp

Executive search firm focused on the health-care industry.

★5904★ Calland & Company

2296 Henderson Mill Rd., Ste. 222
Atlanta, GA 30345
Ph: (770)270-9100   Fax: (770)270-9300
E-mail: bob@callandcompany.com
URL: http://www.callandcompany.com

Executive search firm focused on senior management and healthcare.

★5905★ Caplan Associates Inc.

77 Bull Path
PO Box 4227
East Hampton, NY 11937
Ph: (631)907-9700   Fax: (631)907-0444
E-mail: info@caplanassoc.com

URL: http://www.caplanassoc.com

Executive search firm.

★5906★ The Caplan Taylor Group

550 Bear Canyon Ln.
Arroyo Grande, CA 93420
Ph: (805)481-3000
E-mail: jcaplan@caplantaylorgroup.com

Executive search firm.

★5907★ Capodice & Associates

Midtown Plaza
1243 S. Tamiami Trail
Sarasota, FL 34239
Ph: (941)906-1990   Fax: (941)906-1991
E-mail: peter@capodice.com
URL: http://www.capodice.com

Executive search firm. Branch in Carlisle, MA.

★5908★ Carson Kolb Healthcare Group Inc.

20301 Birch St., Ste. 101
Newport Beach, CA 92660-1754
Ph: (949)476-2988   Fax: (949)476-2155
Fr: 800-606-9439
E-mail: info@carsonkolb.com
URL: http://www.carsonkolb.com

Executive search firm focused on the health-care industry.

★5909★ The Cassie-Shipherd Group

26 Main St.
Toms River, NJ 08753
Ph: (732)473-1779   Fax: (732)473-1023
E-mail: cassiegroup@cassie.com
URL: http://www.cassie.com

Executive search firm. Branches in San Diego; Bridgewater, NJ; New Bern, NC; and Salt Lake City.

★5910★ Cejka Search

4 CityPlace Dr., Ste. 300
St. Louis, MO 63141
Ph: (314)726-1603   Fax: (314)726-0026
Fr: 800-678-7858
E-mail: info@cejkasearch.com
URL: http://www.cejkasearch.com

Executive search firm for the healthcare industry. Branch in Norcross, GA.

★5911★ Celia D. Crossley & Associates Ltd.

3011 Bethel Rd., Ste. 201
Columbus, OH 43220
Ph: (614)538-2808   Fax: (614)442-8886
E-mail: crosworks@aol.com
URL: http://www.crosworks.com

Firm specializes in career planning and development, executive and organizational career coaching, assessment, key employee selection and team integration. Also offers career transition services, including in-place-ment, outplacement, and career coaching.

Serves government, nonprofit, health-care, higher education and service industries.

★5912★ **Chase Hunter Group Inc.**
1143 W. North Shore Ave.
Chicago, IL 60626
Ph: (773)338-7865   Fax: (773)338-1389
E-mail: bdouglas@chase-hunter.com
URL: http://www.chase-hunter.com

Executive search firm focused around the healthcare industry.

★5913★ **CNR Search & Services**
30752 Via Conquista
San Juan Capistrano, CA 92675
Ph: (949)488-0065
E-mail: cnrkenmiller@juno.com
URL: http://www.cnrsearch.com

Provides staffing services of permanent and temporary employees. Works primarily on a retained basis. Contingency on a limited basis. Services include human resources consulting, mergers and acquisitions in high-technology firms. Industries served: computer; information services; insurance, pharmaceutical and healthcare.

★5914★ **Compass Group Ltd.**
Birmingham Place Bldg.
401 S. Old Woodward, Ste. 460
Birmingham, MI 48009-6613
Ph: (248)540-9110   Fax: (248)647-8288
E-mail: executiveserach@compassgroup.com
URL: http://www.compassgroup.com

Executive search firm. Second location in Oak Brook, IL.

★5915★ **Conyngham Partners LLC**
PO Box 94
Ridgewood, NJ 07451
Ph: (201)652-3444   Fax: (201)652-6357
E-mail: info@conynghampartners.com
URL: http://www.conynghampartners.com

Executive search firm.

★5916★ **Cook Associates Inc.**
212 W Kinzie St.
Chicago, IL 60610
Ph: (312)329-0900   Fax: (312)329-1528
E-mail: info@cookassociates.com
URL: http://www.cookassociates.com

Management and executive recruiting specialists offering a commitment to clients to find the best candidates and to find those candidates as efficiently as possible. Approach provides a flexible and effective structure that serves the special needs of both large and small companies. Serves the following industries: industrial, equipment manufacturer, food processing, graphic arts, chemical process, retailing, mechanical products, healthcare services, financial and professional services, legal, consumer products, construction and engineering, packaging, pulp and paper.

★5917★ **Criterion Search Group Inc.**
PO Box 466
Wayne, PA 19087
Ph: (610)581-0590   Fax: (610)581-0594
E-mail: hare@criterionsg.com
URL: http://www.criterionsg.com

Executive search firm.

★5918★ **The Custer Group**
6005 Tattersall Ct.
Brentwood, TN 37027
Ph: (615)309-0577
E-mail: general@custergroup.com
URL: http://www.custergroup.com

Executive search firm.

★5919★ **D'Antoni Partners Inc.**
122 W. John Carpenter Fwy., Ste. 525
Irving, TX 75039
Ph: (972)719-4400   Fax: (972)719-4401
E-mail: richard@dantonipartners.com
URL: http://www.dantonipartners.com

Executive search firm.

★5920★ **Daudlin, De Beaupre & Company Inc.**
18530 Mack Ave., Ste. 315
Grosse Pointe Farms, MI 48236
Ph: (313)885-1235   Fax: (313)885-1247
URL: http://www.daudlindebeaupre.com/

Executive search firm focused on the healthcare industry.

★5921★ **Diversified Health Resources Inc.**
875 N Michigan Ave., Ste. 3250
Chicago, IL 60611-1901
Ph: (312)266-0466   Fax: (312)266-0715
E-mail: yablon@ix.netcom.com
URL: http://www.diversifiedhealth.net

Offers healthcare consulting for hospitals, nursing homes (including homes for the aged), and other health-related facilities and companies. Specializes in planning and marketing. Also conducts executive searches for top level healthcare administrative positions. Serves private industries as well as government agencies.

★5922★ **Drew Associates International**
77 Park St.
Montclair, NJ 07042
Ph: (201)746-8877

Executive search firm focused on the healthcare industry.

★5923★ **Eton Partners**
1 Baltimore Pl., Ste. 130
Atlanta, GA 30308
Ph: (404)685-9088   Fax: (404)685-9208
E-mail: ebirchfield@etonpartners.com
URL: http://etonpartners.com

Executive search firm.

★5924★ **Executive Dimensions**
PO Box 801
Williamsville, NY 14231
Ph: (716)632-9034   Fax: (716)632-2889
E-mail: execu-search@executivedimensions.com
URL: http://www.executivedimensions.com

Executive search firm.

★5925★ **Fitzgerald Associates**
21 Muzzey St.
Lexington, MA 02421-5259
Ph: (781)863-1945   Fax: (781)863-8872
E-mail: info@fizsearch.com
URL: http://www.fitzsearch.com

Executive search firm specifically for the healthcare industry.

★5926★ **Flannery, Sarna & Associates LLC**
N14 W23953 Paul Rd., Ste. 204
Pewaukee, WI 53072
Ph: (262)523-1206   Fax: (262)523-1873
E-mail: shari@flannerysearch.com
URL: http://www.flannerysearch.com

Executive search firm.

★5927★ **Foley Proctor Yoskowitz LLC**
1 Cattano Ave.
Morristown, NJ 07960
Ph: (973)605-1000   Fax: (973)605-1020
Fr: 800-238-1123
E-mail: fpy@fpysearch.com
URL: http://www.fpysearch.com

Executive search firm for the healthcare industry. Second location in New York, NY.

★5928★ **Forager**
1516 Sudeenew Dr.
McHenry, IL 60051
Ph: (815)344-0006
E-mail: aaforager@comcast.net

Executive search firm. Branches in Alta Loma, CA; and Littleton, CO.

★5929★ **The Ford Group Inc.**
295 E. Swedesford Rd., Ste. 282
Wayne, PA 19087
Ph: (610)296-5205
E-mail: info@thefordgroup.com
URL: http://www.thefordgroup.com

Executive search firm.

★5930★ **Gans, Gans and Associates**
7445 Quail Meadow Rd.
Plant City, FL 33565-3314
Ph: (813)986-4441   Fax: (813)986-4775
E-mail: simone@gansgans.com
URL: http://www.gansgans.com

A human resources firm that specializes in executive search, human resources, management consulting, diversity consulting, and resume assessment. Takes a personal approach in the development of tailored programs that consider the corporate culture, history, and objectives of client. Industries served: consulting, financial services, legal, insurance, engineering, healthcare, manufacturing, utilities, and the public sector.

★5931★ Joseph R. Burns & Associates Inc.

2 Shunpike Rd
Madison, NJ 07940
Ph: (973)377-1350   Fax: (973)377-9350
E-mail: burnsassc@aol.com

Executive search firm.

★5932★ JPM International

26034 Acero
Mission Viejo, CA 92691
Ph: (949)699-4300   Fax: (949)699-4333
Fr: 800-685-7856
E-mail: trish@jpmintl.com
URL: http://www.jpmintl.com

Executive search firm and employment agency.

★5933★ Karen Dexter & Associates Inc.

2012 Chestnut
Wilmette, IL 60091-1512
Ph: (847)853-9500   Fax: (847)256-7108

Training and development consultant offering interpersonal skills training and one-on-one performance counseling for employees of large organizations. Industries served: advertising, banking and finance, consumer products, entertainment, food and beverage, healthcare, legal profession, manufacturing, government agencies, publishing and broadcasting.

★5934★ Lee Calhoon & Company Inc.

1621 Birchrun Rd.
PO Box 201
Birchrunville, PA 19421
Ph: (610)469-9000   Fax: (610)469-0398
Fr: 800-469-0896
E-mail: info@leecalhoon.com
URL: http://www.leecalhoon.com

Executive search firm.

★5935★ McCormack & Farrow Co.

949 S Coast Dr., Ste. 620
Costa Mesa, CA 92626
Ph: (714)549-7222   Fax: (714)549-7227
E-mail: resumes@mfsearch.com
URL: http://www.mfsearch.com

General practice retained search in most industries. Special emphasis on high-technology, start-up and emerging companies, manufacturing, healthcare, financial services, nonprofit and privately owned businesses.

★5936★ MedSearch Staffing Services Inc.

7530 Lucerne Dr., Islander 2, Ste. 208
Plaza S 3
Middleburg Heights, OH 44130
Ph: (440)243-5300   Fax: (440)243-9117
E-mail: info@medicalreserves.com
URL: http://www.medicalreserves.com

Provides specialized recruitment of sales, marketing and management personnel. Also involved in top-level hospital management consulting and physician recruitment, interim/temporary staffing. Industries served: healthcare manufacturers and institutions.

★5937★ Minority Executive Search Inc.

PO Box 18063
Cleveland, OH 44118
Ph: (216)932-2022   Fax: (216)932-7988
E-mail: info@minorityexecsearch.com
URL: http://www.minorityexecsearch.com

Firm specializes in finding executives for the consumer, financial, military, automotive, medical, legal, and telecommunications industries.

★5938★ Noyes & Associates Ltd.

5179 NE Sullivan Rd.
Bainbridge Island, WA 98110-2002
Ph: (206)780-8142   Fax: (206)780-8144
E-mail: info@noyesconsult.com
URL: http://www.noyesconsult.com

Provides nationwide consulting services to health care clients. Major services include management education course and skill assessment survey; departmental performance reviews; and temporary and permanent management/executive search.

★5939★ Pate Resources Group Inc.

595 Orleans, Ste. 707
Beaumont, TX 77701
Ph: (409)833-4514   Fax: (409)833-4646
Fr: 800-669-4514
E-mail: opportunities@pateresourcesgroup.com
URL: http://www.pateresourcesgroup.com

Offers executive search and recruiting services to professionals who include physicians, healthcare administrators, engineers, accounting and financial disciplines, legal, outplacement, sales and marketing. Industries served: healthcare, petrochemicals, accounting, utility, legal, and municipalities.

★5940★ Paul Bodner & Associates Inc.

260 Stoney Ridge Dr.
Alpharetta, GA 30022
Ph: (678)907-6239
E-mail: pbodner@lvcm.com
URL: http://www.paulbodnerassociates.com/index.html

Executive search firm. Second branch in Denver, CO.

★5941★ Roberson & Co.

10751 Parfet St.
Broomfield, CO 80021
Ph: (303)410-6510
E-mail: roberson@recruiterpro.com
URL: http://www.recruiterpro.com

A contingency professional and executive recruiting firm working the national and international marketplace. Specialize in accounting, finance, data processing and information services, healthcare, environmental and mining, engineering, manufacturing, human resources, and sales and marketing.

★5942★ Robert Howe and Associates

35 Glenlake Pky. NE
Atlanta, GA 30328
Ph: (770)390-0030   Fax: (770)270-1209

Provides consulting services in the area of executive search and recruitment. Industries served: healthcare, hospitality, chemical, metals, electronics, construction, and food processing.

★5943★ Skott/Edwards Consultants

7 Royal Dr.
Brick, NJ 08723
Ph: (732)920-1883   Fax: (732)477-1541
E-mail: search@skottedwards.com
URL: http://www.skottedwards.com

Firm specializes in providing executive search services to clients in the health care, biotechnology, medical device and pharmaceutical industries. Offers are strategic organizational development advice, corporate governance, employee appraisal and related services.

★5944★ Theken Associates Inc.

Ridge Rd.
PO Box 307
Randolph, VT 05060
Ph: (802)728-5811   Fax: (802)728-5996

Executive search firm for nursing administrators. Consulting services include emphasis on organizational development in the healthcare field and interim leadership in patient care services across the continuum.

★5945★ Tyler & Co.

375 Northridge Rd., Ste. 400
Atlanta, GA 30350-3299
Ph: (770)396-3939   Fax: (770)396-6693
Fr: 800-989-6789
E-mail: art@tylerandco.com
URL: http://www.tylerandco.com

Retained executive search for the healthcare, food, market research, manufacturing and insurance industries.

★5946★ Vine and Associates

225 W Broadway., Ste. 120
Glendale, CA 91204
Ph: (818)550-9802   Fax: (818)550-9806
E-mail: info@vineassociates.com
URL: http://www.vineassociates.com

Engaged in executive search and management consulting for healthcare in both the United States and overseas. In addition, the company develops feasibility and strategic planning for its clients who are primarily engaged in staffing, joint ventures and operations of institutions connected with the health industry.

★5947★ Weatherby Locums
6451 N Federal Hwy., Ste. 800
Fort Lauderdale, FL 33308
Ph: (954)343-3050   Fax: 800-463-2985
Fr: (866)906-1636
E-mail: jobs@weatherbylocums.com
URL: http://www.weatherbylocums.com

Executive search firm for physicians. Branch office in Fairfax, VA.

★5948★ Witt/Kieffer, Ford, Hadelman & Lloyd
2015 Spring Rd., Ste. 510
Oak Brook, IL 60523
Ph: (630)990-1370   Fax: (630)990-1382
E-mail: claudiat@wittkieffer.com
URL: http://www.wittkieffer.com

A leading national executive search firm and the single largest that specializes in hospitals and health systems, including those with faith-based sponsors, as well as managed care and insurance companies; specialty, venture-capital-backed and e-Health corporations; physician group practices; colleges and universities and not-for-profit community service and cultural organizations. The firm has 13 offices across the country, an extensive database of executive talent nationwide and a variety of online networking resources.

ONLINE JOB SOURCES AND SERVICES

★5949★ Health Care Job Store
395 South End Ave., Ste. 15-D
New York, NY 10280
Ph: (561)630-5201
E-mail: jobs@healthcarejobstore.com
URL: http://www.healthcarejobstore.com/

Description: Job sites include every job title in the healthcare industry, every healthcare industry and every geographic location in the U.S.

★5950★ HealthCareerWeb
URL: http://www.healthcareerweb.com/

Description: Advertises jobs for healthcare professionals. **Main files include:** Jobs, Employers, Resumes, Jobwire. Relocation tools and career guidance resources available.

★5951★ Medhunters.com
Fr: 800-664-0278

E-mail: info@medhunters.com
URL: http://www.medhunters.com

Description: Career search site for jobs in all health care specialties; educational resources; visa and licensing information for relocation; interesting articles; relocation tools; links to professional organizations and general resources.

★5952★ Medzilla
URL: http://www.medzilla.com

Description: General medical website which matches employers and job hunters to their ideal employees and jobs through search capabilities. **Main files include:** Post Jobs, Search Resumes, Post Resumes, Search Jobs, Head Hunters, Articles, Salary Survey.

★5953★ ProHealthJobs
Fr: 800-796-1738
E-mail: Info@prohealthedujobs.com
URL: http://www.prohealthjobs.com

Description: Career resources site for the medical and health care field. Lists professional opportunities, product information, continuing education and open positions.

TRADESHOWS

★5954★ American Academy of Medical Administrators Annual Conference and Convocation
American Academy of Medical Administrators
701 Lee St., Ste. 600
Des Plaines, IL 60016
Ph: (847)759-8601   Fax: (847)759-8602
E-mail: info@aameda.org
URL: http://www.aameda.org

Annual. **Primary Exhibits:** Equipment, supplies, and services related to health care. **Dates and Locations:** 2008 Nov 19-21; San Antonio, TX; Hyatt Regency.

★5955★ American Health Care Association Annual Convention and Exposition
American Health Care Association
1201 L St. NW
Washington, DC 20005
Ph: (202)842-4444   Fax: (202)842-3860
URL: http://www.ahca.org

Annual. **Primary Exhibits:** Supplies for the long-term health care industry.

★5956★ Joint Clinical Conference on Hospice & Palliative Care
National Hospice Organization
1700 Diagonal Rd., Ste. 625
Alexandria, VA 22314
Ph: (703)837-1500   Fax: (703)837-1233
E-mail: nhpco_info@nhpco.org

URL: http://www.nhpco.org

Annual. **Primary Exhibits:** equipment, supplies, and services for hospice organizations.

OTHER SOURCES

★5957★ Administration and Management Occupations
Delphi Productions
3159 6th St.
Boulder, CO 80304
Ph: (303)443-2100   Fax: (303)443-4022
Fr: 888-443-2400
E-mail: support@delphivideo.com
URL: http://www.delphivideo.com

$95.00. 50 minutes. Part of the Careers for the 21st Century Video Library.

★5958★ American Academy of Medical Administrators (AAMA)
701 Lee St., Ste. 600
Des Plaines, IL 60016-4516
Ph: (847)759-8601   Fax: (847)759-8602
E-mail: info@aameda.org
URL: http://www.aameda.org

Description: Serves healthcare management at all levels, within all types of healthcare organizations by providing solid solutions, unique connections, resources and professional recognition that healthcare professionals need to navigate today's complex healthcare environment and stay competitive. Has 7 specialty groups: American College of Cardiovascular Administrators; American College of Oncology Administrators; American College of Contingency Planners; Federal Sector; Small or Rural Healthcare; American College of Managed Care Administrators; and American College of Healthcare Information Administrators.

★5959★ American Almanac of Jobs and Salaries
HarperCollins
10 E. 53rd St.
New York, NY 10022
Ph: (212)207-7000   Fr: 800-242-7737
URL: http://www.harpercollins.com/

John W. Wright. Revised edition, 2000. $20.00 (paper). 672 pages. This is a comprehensive guide to the wages of hundreds of occupations in a wide variety of industries and organizations.

★5960★ American College of Healthcare Executives (ACHE)
1 N Franklin, Ste. 1700
Chicago, IL 60606
Ph: (312)424-2800   Fax: (312)424-0023
E-mail: geninfo@ache.org
URL: http://www.ache.org

Description: Healthcare executives. Conducts credentialing and educational programs and an annual Congress on Healthcare Management. Conducts groundbreaking research and career development and public policy programs. Publishing division, Health Administration Press, publishes books and journals on health services management and textbooks for use in college and university courses. Works to improve the health status of society by advancing healthcare leadership management excellence.

★5961★ American College of Medical Quality (ACMQ)

4334 Montgomery Ave., Ste. B
Bethesda, MD 20814
Ph: (301)913-9149   Fax: (301)913-9142
Fr: 800-924-2149
E-mail: acmq@acmq.org
URL: http://www.acmq.org

Members: Physicians, affiliates, and institutions. **Purpose:** Seeks to educate and set standards of competence in the field of quality improvement and management. Offers a core curriculum in quality. Maintains Speaker's Bureau.

★5962★ American Health Care Association (AHCA)

1201 L St. NW
Washington, DC 20005
Ph: (202)842-4444   Fax: (202)842-3860
E-mail: hr@ahca.org
URL: http://www.ahca.org

Description: Federation of state associations of long-term health care facilities. Promotes standards for professionals in long-term health care delivery and quality care for patients and residents in a safe environment. Focuses on issues of availability, quality, affordability, and fair payment. Operates as liaison with governmental agencies, Congress, and professional associations. Compiles statistics.

★5963★ American Hospital Association (AHA)

1 N Franklin
Chicago, IL 60606-3421
Ph: (312)422-3000   Fax: (312)422-4796
URL: http://www.aha.org

Description: Represents health care provider organizations. Seeks to advance the health of individuals and communities. Leads, represents, and serves health care provider organizations that are accountable to the community and committed to health improvement.

★5964★ American Society for Healthcare Environmental Services of the American Hospital Association (ASHES)

1 N Franklin St., Ste. 2800
Chicago, IL 60606
Ph: (312)422-3860   Fax: (312)422-4578
E-mail: ashes@aha.org
URL: http://www.ashes.org

Description: Managers and directors of hospital environmental services, laundry and linen services, as well as housekeeping departments and waste management (non-hazardous and hazardous), in government or university settings. Provides a forum for discussion among members of common challenges, Professional development, and career advancement. Maintains liaison between members and governmental and standards setting bodies. Certified Healthcare Environmental Services Professional (CHESP) available through education and Examination.

★5965★ Association of Healthcare Internal Auditors (AHIA)

10200 W 44th Ave., Ste. 304
Wheat Ridge, CO 80033
Ph: (303)327-7546   Fax: (303)422-8894
Fr: 888-ASK-AHIA
E-mail: ahia@ahia.org
URL: http://www.ahia.org

Members: Health care internal auditors and other interested individuals. **Purpose:** Promotes cost containment and increased productivity in health care institutions through internal auditing. Serves as a forum for the exchange of experience, ideas, and information among members; provides continuing professional education courses and informs members of developments in health care internal auditing. **Activities:** Offers employment clearinghouse services.

★5966★ Food and Drug Law Institute (FDLI)

1155 15 St. NW, Ste. 800
Washington, DC 20005-4903
Ph: (202)371-1420   Fax: (202)371-0649
Fr: 800-956-6293
E-mail: comments@fdli.org
URL: http://www.fdli.org

Description: Provides forum regarding laws, regulations and policies related to drugs, medical devices, and other health care technologies.

★5967★ Health Service Occupations

Delphi Productions
3159 6th St.
Boulder, CO 80304
Ph: (303)443-2100   Fax: (303)443-4022
Fr: 888-443-2400
E-mail: support@delphivideo.com
URL: http://www.delphivideo.com

$95.00. 50 minutes. Part of the Careers for the 21st Century Video Library.

★5968★ International Executive Housekeepers Association (IEHA)

1001 Eastwind Dr., Ste. 301
Westerville, OH 43081-3361
Ph: (614)895-7166   Fax: (614)895-1248
Fr: 800-200-6342
E-mail: excel@ieha.org
URL: http://www.ieha.org

Description: Persons engaged in facility housekeeping management in hospitals, hotels and motels, schools, and industrial establishments. Established educational standards. Sponsors certificate and collegiate degree programs. Holds annual International Housekeepers Week celebration.

★5969★ International Medical Spa Association (IMSA)

310 17th St.
Union City, NJ 07087
Ph: (201)865-2065   Fax: (201)865-3961
E-mail: medspaassn@aol.com
URL: http://www.medicalspaassociation.org

Description: Promotes innovation and co-operation within the medical spa industry. Seeks to develop and implement programs that will help shape and enhance the future of the medical spa industry. Promotes education, communication and standards of excellence for the medical spa profession.

★5970★ Medical Group Management Association (MGMA)

104 Inverness Terr. E
Englewood, CO 80112-5306
Ph: (303)799-1111   Fax: (303)643-4439
Fr: 877-275-6462
E-mail: service@mgma.com
URL: http://www.mgma.com

Description: Represents professionals involved in the management of medical group practices and administration of other ambulatory healthcare facilities. Provides products and services that includes education, benchmarking, surveys, national advocacy and networking opportunities for members.

★5971★ Medicine & Related Occupations

Delphi Productions
3159 6th St.
Boulder, CO 80304
Ph: (303)443-2100   Fax: (303)443-4022
Fr: 888-443-2400
E-mail: support@delphivideo.com
URL: http://www.delphivideo.com

$95.00. 45 minutes. Part of the Careers for the 21st Century Video Library.

★5972★ National Association of Health Services Executives (NAHSE)

8630 Fenton St., Ste. 126
Silver Spring, MD 20910
Ph: (202)628-3953   Fax: (301)588-0011
E-mail: nahsehq@nahse.org
URL: http://www.nahse.org

Description: Black health care executive managers, planners, educators, advocates, providers, organizers, researchers, and consumers participating in academic ventures, educational forums, seminars, workshops, systems design, legislation, and other activities. Conducts National Work-Study Program and sponsors educational programs.

★5973★ **National Association for Healthcare Quality (NAHQ)**

4700 W Lake Ave.
Glenview, IL 60025
Ph: (847)375-4720   Fax: 877-218-7939
Fr: 800-966-9392
E-mail: heidi_benson@northcrest.com
URL: http://www.nahq.org

Description: Healthcare professionals in quality assessment and improvement, utilization and risk management, case management, infection control, managed care, nursing, and medical records. Objectives are: to encourage, develop, and provide continuing education for all persons involved in health care quality; to give the patient primary consideration in all actions affecting his or her health and welfare; to promote the sharing of knowledge and encourage a high degree of professional ethics in health care quality. Offers accredited certification in the field of healthcare quality, utilization, and risk management. Facilitates communication and cooperation among members, medical staff, and health care government agencies. Conducts educational seminars and conferences.

★5974★ **National Health Council (NHC)**

1730 M St. NW, Ste. 500
Washington, DC 20036
Ph: (202)785-3910   Fax: (202)785-5923
E-mail: info@nhcouncil.org

URL: http://www.nhcouncil.org

Description: National association of voluntary and professional societies in the health field; national organizations and business groups with strong health interests. Seeks to improve the health of patients, particularly those with chronic diseases, through conferences, publications, policy briefings and special projects. Distributes printed material on health careers and related subjects. Promotes standardization of financial reporting for voluntary health groups.

★5975★ **National Rural Health Association (NRHA)**

Administrative Office
521 E 63rd St.
Kansas City, MO 64110-3329
Ph: (816)756-3140   Fax: (816)756-3144
E-mail: mail@nrharural.org
URL: http://www.nrharural.org

Description: Administrators, physicians, nurses, physician assistants, health planners, academicians, and others interested or involved in rural health care. Creates a better understanding of health care problems unique to rural areas; utilizes a collective approach in finding positive solutions; articulates and represents the health care needs of rural America; supplies current information to rural health care providers; serves as a liaison between rural health care programs throughout the country. Offers continuing education credits for medical, dental, nursing, and management courses.

★5976★ **National Society of Certified Healthcare Business Consultants (NSCHBC)**

12100 Sunset Hills Rd., Ste. 130
Reston, VA 20190
Ph: (703)234-4099   Fax: (703)435-4390
E-mail: info@nschbc.org
URL: http://www.healthcon.org

Description: Advances the profession of healthcare business consultants through education, certification and professional interaction. Provides education and training to assist members in fulfilling the requirements of certification.

★5977★ **Radiology Business Management Association (RBMA)**

10300 Eaton Pl., Ste. 460
Fairfax, VA 22030
Ph: (703)621-3355   Fax: (703)621-3356
Fr: 888-224-7262
E-mail: info@rbma.org
URL: http://www.rbma.org

Description: Provides education, resources and solutions to manage the business of radiology. Offers an online course in radiology coding.

Heating, Air-Conditioning, and Refrigeration Mechanics

SOURCES OF HELP-WANTED ADS

★5978★ Air Conditioning, Heating and Refrigeration News

BNP Media
2401 W Big Beaver Rd., Ste. 700
Troy, MI 48084-3333
Ph: (248)786-1642   Fax: (248)786-1388
URL: http://www.achrnews.com/

$59.00/year for individuals; $91.00 for individuals, 2 years; $118.00 for individuals, 3 years. Tabloid for HVAC and commercial refrigeration contractors, wholesalers, manufacturers, engineers, and owners/managers.

★5979★ ASHRAE Journal

American Society of Heating,
  Refrigerating and Air-Conditioning
  Engineers Inc.
1791 Tullie Cir. NE
Atlanta, GA 30329
Ph: (404)636-8400   Fax: (404)321-5478
Fr: 800-527-4723
URL: http://www.ashrae.org/publications/
page/540

Monthly. $59.00/year for nonmembers; $79.00/year for Canada; $149.00/year for other countries; Subscription included in membership. Magazine for the heating, refrigeration, and air conditioning trade.

★5980★ Contractor Magazine

Penton Media Inc.
2700 South River Rd., Ste. 109
Des Plaines, IL 60018
Ph: (847)299-3101   Fax: (847)299-3018
URL: http://www.contractormag.com

Monthly. $90.00/year for other countries; $157.50 for two years, international. Free, to U.S. and Canadian residents. Industry news and management how-to magazine for heating, plumbing, piping, fire sprinkler, and other mechanical specialties contracting firms.

★5981★ Heating/Piping/Air Conditioning Engineering (HPAC)

Penton Media Inc.
1300 E 9th St.
Cleveland, OH 44114
Ph: (216)696-7000   Fax: (216)696-1752
URL: http://www.penton.com/

Monthly. $99.00/year for individuals, 1 year - 12 issues, international; $110.00/year for individuals, regular price, 1 year - 12 issues, international; $158.00 for two years, 2 years - 24 issues,international; $175.00 for two years, 2 years - 24 issues, regular price, international. Business magazine serving the growing mechanical engineered systems market in the areas of building construction, renovation, and retrofit.

★5982★ Industrial Heating

Business News Publishing Co.
2401 W Big Beaver Rd., Ste. 700
Troy, MI 48084-3333
URL: http://www.industrialheating.com/
Monthly. Magazine.

★5983★ Snips Magazine

Snips Magazine
2401 West Big Beaver., Ste. 700
Troy, MI 48084
Ph: (248)362-3700   Fax: (248)362-0317
URL: http://www.snipsmag.com/

Monthly. Free. Magazine for the sheet metal, warm-air heating, ventilating, and air conditioning industry.Provides helpful hints for contractors.

★5984★ Southern PHC Magazine

Southern Trade Publications Inc.
Box 7344
Greensboro, NC 27417
Ph: (336)454-3516   Fax: (336)454-3649

Bimonthly. $10.00/year. Free to qualified subscribers; $10.00/year others. Trade magazine covering plumbing, heating, and air conditioning, targeted to contractors and wholesalers in 14 southern states.

★5985★ WIT

Vermont Works for Women
51 Park St.
Essex Junction, VT 05452
Ph: (802)878-0004   Fax: (802)878-0050
Fr: 800-639-1472
URL: http://www.nnetw.org/

Description: Three issues/year. Provides a network of support, information, and skill sharing for women in skilled trades professions.

PLACEMENT AND JOB REFERRAL SERVICES

★5986★ National Association of Home Builders (NAHB)

1201 15th St. NW
Washington, DC 20005
Ph: (202)266-8200   Fax: (202)266-8400
Fr: 800-368-5242
E-mail: info@nahb.com
URL: http://www.nahb.org

Description: Single and multifamily home builders, commercial builders, and others associated with the building industry. Lobbies on behalf of the housing industry and conducts public affairs activities to increase public understanding of housing and the economy. Collects and disseminates data on current developments in home building and home builders' plans through its Economics Department and nationwide Metropolitan Housing Forecast. Maintains NAHB Research Center, which functions as the research arm of the home building industry. Sponsors seminars and workshops on construction, mortgage credit, labor relations, cost reduction, land use, remodeling, and business management. Compiles statistics; offers charitable program, spokesman training, and placement service; maintains speakers' bureau, and Hall of Fame. Subsidiaries include the National Council of the Housing Industry. Maintains over 50 committees in many areas of construction; operates National Commercial Builders Council, National Council of the Multifamily Housing

Industry, National Remodelers Council, and National Sales and Marketing Council.

EMPLOYER DIRECTORIES AND NETWORKING LISTS

★5987★ ABC Today-Associated Builders and Contractors National Membership Directory Issue

Associated Builders & Contractors Inc.
4250 N Fairfax Dr., 9th Fl.
Arlington, VA 22203-1607
Ph: (703)812-2000   Fax: (703)812-8203
URL: http://www.abc.org/wmspage.cfm?parm1=2033

Annual, December. $150.00. Publication includes: List of approximately 19,000 member construction contractors and suppliers. Entries include: Company name, address, phone, name of principal executive, code to volume of business, business specialty. Arrangement: Classified by chapter, then by work specialty.

★5988★ Air Conditioning Contractors of America-Membership Directory

Air Conditioning Contractors of America
2800 Shirlington Rd., Ste. 300
Arlington, VA 22206
Ph: (703)575-4477
URL: http://www.acca.org/

Annual, summer. Covers member air conditioning and heating contractors, manufacturers, vocational technical schools. Entries include: Company name, address, phone, fax, names and titles of key personnel, description of fields, and types of work performed. Arrangement: Geographical. Indexes: Alphabetical.

★5989★ Air Conditioning, Heating & Refrigeration News-Directory Issue

BNP Media
2401 W Big Beaver Rd., Ste. 700
Troy, MI 48084-3333
Ph: (248)786-1642   Fax: (248)786-1388
E-mail: wraym@astbnp.com
URL: http://www.achrnews.com

Annual, January. Publication includes: Lists of about 2,086 manufacturers, 4,383 wholesalers and factory outlets, 1,667 HVACR products; exporters specializing in the industry; related trade organizations; manufacturers representatives, consultants, services; videos and software. Entries include: For manufacturers–Company Name, address, phone, fax, e-mail, URL, names of key personnel, brand names, list of products; similar information for other categories. Arrangement: Manufacturers and exporters are alphabetical; wholesalers and representatives are geographical. Indexes: Product, trade name.

★5990★ Constructor-AGC Directory of Membership and Services Issue

AGC Information Inc.
2300 Wilson Blvd., Ste. 400
Arlington, VA 22201
Ph: (703)548-3118   Fax: (703)548-3119
Fr: 800-282-1423
URL: http://www.agc.org

Annual, August; latest edition 2004 edition. Publication includes: List of over 8,500 member firms and 24,000 national associate member firms engaged in building, highway, heavy, industrial, municipal utilities, and railroad construction (SIC 1541, 1542, 1611, 1622, 1623, 1629); listing of state and local chapter officers. Entries include: For firms–Company name, address, phone, fax, names of principal executives, and code indicating type of construction undertaken. For officers–Name, title, address. Arrangement: Geographical, alphabetical. Indexes: Company name.

★5991★ ENR-Top 400 Construction Contractors Issue

McGraw-Hill Inc.
1221 Ave. of the Americas
New York, NY 10020-1095
Ph: (212)512-2000   Fax: (212)512-3840
Fr: 877-833-5524
URL: http://construction.ecnext.com/coms2/summary_0249-137077_ITM

Annual; 22nd, May 2006. $35.00 for individuals. Publication includes: List of 400 United States contractors receiving largest dollar volumes of contracts in preceding calendar year. Separate lists of 50 largest design/construction management firms; 50 largest program and construction managers; 25 building contractors; 25 heavy contractors. Entries include: Company name, headquarters location, total value of contracts received in preceding year, value of foreign contracts, countries in which operated, construction specialities. Arrangement: By total value of contracts received.

★5992★ Michigan Plumbing and Mechanical Contractors Association-Membership Directory

Michigan Plumbing and Mechanical Contractors Association
400 N Walnut St.
Lansing, MI 48933
Ph: (517)484-5500   Fax: (517)484-5225
URL: http://www.mpmca.org

Annual. Covers member firms, industry and auxiliary associations, legislative and regulatory agencies in the plumbing and heating industry of Michigan. Entries include: Organization name, address, phone, names and titles of key personnel. Arrangement: Separate sections for members, industry associations, legislative and regulatory agencies, and auxiliaries; members are geographical. Indexes: Company name (members), president name (members).

★5993★ North American Heating, Refrigeration & Airconditioning Wholesaler Association-Membership Directory

Heating, Airconditioning, & Refrigeration Distributors International
1389 Dublin Rd.
Columbus, OH 43215-1084
Ph: (614)488-1835   Fax: (614)488-0482
Fr: 888-253-2128
URL: http://209.235.200.147/member_search.html

Annual, spring. Covers about 2,000 wholesalers and distributors. Entries include: Company name, address, phone and names of executives. Arrangement: Alphabetical.

HANDBOOKS AND MANUALS

★5994★ Opportunities in Building Construction Trades

The McGraw-Hill Companies
PO Box 182604
Columbus, OH 43272
Fax: (614)759-3749   Fr: 877-883-5524
E-mail: customer.service@mcgraw-hill.com
URL: http://www.mcgraw-hill.com

Michael Sumichrast. Second edition, 1998. $14.95; $11.95 (paper). 104 pages. From custom builder to rehabber, the many kinds of companies that employ craftspeople and contractors are explored. Includes job descriptions, requirements, and salaries for dozens of specialties within the construction industry. Contains a complete list of Bureau of Apprenticeship and Training state and area offices. Illustrated.

★5995★ Opportunities in Plumbing and Pipefitting Careers

The McGraw-Hill Companies
PO Box 182604
Columbus, OH 43272
Fax: (614)759-3749   Fr: 877-883-5524
E-mail: customer.service@mcgraw-hill.com
URL: http://www.mcgraw-hill.com

Patrick J. Galvin. Reprint edition, 1995. $14.95; $10.95 (paper). 160 pages. Provides information on getting into the trade, apprenticeship programs, and how to build a career in a variety of settings. Illustrated.

TRADESHOWS

★5996★ AHR Expo - International Air-Conditioning, Heating, Refrigerating Exposition

International Exposition Co., Inc.
15 Franklin St.
Westport, CT 06880-5958
Ph: (203)221-9232   Fax: (203)221-9260
E-mail: info@chemshow.com
URL: http://www.chemshow.com

Annual. **Primary Exhibits:** Industrial, commercial, and residential heating, refrigeration, air conditioning, and ventilation equipment and components. **Dates and Locations:** 2008 Jan 22-24; New York, NY; Javits Convention Center.

★5997★ Massachusetts Association of Plumbing/Heating/Cooling Contractors Convention and Tradeshow

Massachusetts Association of Plumbing/ Heating/Cooling Contractors
178 Forbes Rd., Ste. 218
Braintree, MA 02184-2610
Ph: (781)843-3800   Fax: (781)843-1178
Fr: 800-542-7422
E-mail: phcc.ma@verizon.net
URL: http://www.phccma.org

Annual. **Primary Exhibits:** Plumbing, heating and cooling equipment, supplies, and services.

★5998★ NEX - North American Exposition

American Supply Association
222 Merchandise Mart Plaza, Ste. 1400
Chicago, IL 60654-1202
Ph: (312)464-0090   Fax: (312)464-0091
Fr: 800-464-0314
E-mail: info@asa.net
URL: http://www.asa.net

Biennial. **Primary Exhibits:** Plumbing, heating, and cooling, piping, hydronic heating, tools, software.

★5999★ North American Heating and Air Conditioning Wholesalers Association

North American Heating and Air Conditioning Wholesalers Association
1389 Dublin Rd.
Columbus, OH 43215-1084
Ph: (614)488-1835   Fax: (614)488-0482
Fr: 888-253-2128
E-mail: HARDImail@HARDInet.org

Annual. **Primary Exhibits:** Heating and air conditioning equipment, supplies, and services.

★6000★ Refrigeration Service Engineers Society Educational Conference

Refrigeration Service Engineers Society
1666 Rand Rd.
Des Plaines, IL 60016
Ph: 800-297-5660   Fax: (847)297-5038
URL: http://www.rses.org

Annual. **Primary Exhibits:** Equipment, supplies, and services for refrigeration, air-conditioning and heating installation, service, sales, and maintenance.

OTHER SOURCES

★6001★ Air Conditioning Contractors of America (ACCA)

2800 Shirlington Rd., Ste. 300
Arlington, VA 22206
Ph: (703)575-4477   Fax: (703)575-4449
E-mail: info@acca.org
URL: http://www.acca.org

Members: Contractors involved in installation and service of heating, air conditioning, and refrigeration systems. Associate members are utilities, manufacturers, wholesalers, and other market-oriented businesses. **Purpose:** Monitors utility competition and operating practices of HVAC manufacturers and wholesalers. **Activities:** Provides consulting services, technical training, and instructor certification program; offers management seminars. Operates annual educational institute.

★6002★ Associated Builders and Contractors (ABC)

4250 N Fairfax Dr., 9th Fl.
Arlington, VA 22203-1607
Ph: (703)812-2000   Fax: (703)812-8200
E-mail: gotquestions@abc.org
URL: http://www.abc.org

Description: Construction contractors, subcontractors, suppliers, and associates. Aims to foster and perpetuate the principles of rewarding construction workers and management on the basis of merit. Sponsors management education programs and craft training; also sponsors apprenticeship and skill training programs. Disseminates technological and labor relations information.

★6003★ Associated Specialty Contractors (ASC)

3 Bethesda Metro Ctr., Ste. 1100
Bethesda, MD 20814
Ph: (703)548-3118
E-mail: dgw@necanet.org
URL: http://www.assoc-spec-con.org

Description: Works to promote efficient management and productivity. Coordinates the work of specialized branches of the industry in management information, research, public information, government relations and construction relations. Serves as a liaison among specialty trade associations in the areas of public relations, government relations, and with other organizations. Seeks to avoid unnecessary duplication of effort and expense or conflicting programs among affiliates. Identifies areas of interest and problems shared by members, and develops positions and approaches on such problems.

★6004★ Building Trades

Delphi Productions
3159 6th St.
Boulder, CO 80304
Ph: (303)443-2100   Fax: (303)443-4022
Fr: 888-443-2400

E-mail: support@delphivideo.com
URL: http://www.delphivideo.com

$95.00. 46 minutes. Part of the Careers for the 21st Century Video Library.

★6005★ COIN Career Guidance System

COIN Educational Products
3361 Executive Pky., Ste. 302
Toledo, OH 43606
Ph: (419)536-5353   Fax: (419)536-7056
Fr: 800-274-8515
URL: http://www.coinedu.com/

CD-ROM. Provides career information through seven cross-referenced files covering postsecondary schools, college majors, vocational programs, military service, apprenticeship programs, financial aid, and scholarships. Apprenticeship file describes national apprenticeship training programs, including information on how to apply, contact agencies, and program content. Military file describes more than 200 military occupations and training opportunities related to civilian employment.

★6006★ Mechanical Contractors Association of America (MCAA)

1385 Piccard Dr.
Rockville, MD 20850-4329
Ph: (301)869-5800   Fax: (301)990-9690
Fr: 800-556-3653
E-mail: membership@mcaa.org
URL: http://www.mcaa.org

Members: Contractors who furnish, install, and service piping systems and related equipment for heating, cooling, refrigeration, ventilating, and air conditioning systems. **Purpose:** Works to standardize materials and methods used in the industry. Conducts business overhead, labor wage, and statistical surveys. Maintains dialogue with key officials in building trade unions. Promotes apprenticeship training programs. Conducts seminars on contracts, labor estimating, job cost control, project management, marketing, collective bargaining, contractor insurance, and other management topics. Promotes methods to conserve energy in new and existing buildings. Sponsors Industrial Relations Council for the Plumbing and Pipe Fitting Industry.

★6007★ Mechanics & Repairers

Delphi Productions
3159 6th St.
Boulder, CO 80304
Ph: (303)443-2100   Fax: (303)443-4022
Fr: 888-443-2400
E-mail: support@delphivideo.com
URL: http://www.delphivideo.com

$95.00. 50 minutes. Part of the Careers for the 21st Century Video Library.

★6008★ National Association of Women in Construction (NAWIC)
327 S Adams St.
Fort Worth, TX 76104
Ph: (817)877-5551   Fax: (817)877-0324
Fr: 800-552-3506
E-mail: nawic@nawic.org
URL: http://www.nawic.org
Description: Seeks to enhance the success of women in the construction industry.

★6009★ Plumbing-Heating-Cooling Contractors Association (PHCC)
PO Box 6808
Falls Church, VA 22046
Ph: (703)237-8100   Fax: (703)237-7442
Fr: 800-533-7694
E-mail: naphcc@naphcc.org
URL: http://www.phccweb.org
Members: Federation of state and local associations of plumbing, heating, and cooling contractors. **Purpose:** Seeks to advance sanitation, encourage sanitary laws, and generally improve the plumbing, heating, ventilating, and air conditioning industries. **Activities:** Conducts apprenticeship training programs, workshops, seminars, political action committee, educational and research programs.

★6010★ Refrigeration Service Engineers Society (RSES)
1666 Rand Rd.
Des Plaines, IL 60016-3552
Ph: (847)297-6464   Fax: (847)297-5038
Fr: 800-297-5660
E-mail: general@rses.org
URL: http://www.rses.org
Members: Persons engaged in refrigeration, air-conditioning and heating installation, service, sales, and maintenance. **Activities:** Conducts training courses and certification testing. Maintains a hall of fame and a speakers' bureau.

Historians

SOURCES OF HELP-WANTED ADS

★6011★ American Antiquarian Society Proceedings

American Antiquarian Society
185 Salisbury St.
Worcester, MA 01609-1634
Ph: (508)755-5221   Fax: (508)753-3311
URL: http://www.americanantiquarian.org/proceedings.htm

Semiannual. $45.00/year for U.S. $53.00/year for other countries. Journal covering bibliographies, research aids, and edited primary documents covering early American history and culture.

★6012★ American Nineteenth Century History

Taylor & Francis Group Journals
325 Chestnut St., Ste. 800
Philadelphia, PA 19106
Ph: (215)625-8900   Fax: (215)625-8914
Fr: 800-354-1420
URL: http://www.tandf.co.uk/journals/titles/14664658.asp

$279.00/year for institutions, print and online; $265.00/year for institutions, online only; $85.00/year for individuals, print only. Journal covering topics of the history of the United States during the nineteenth century.

★6013★ American Periodicals

Ohio State University Press
180 Pressey Hall, 1070 Carmack Rd.
Columbus, OH 43210-1002
Ph: (614)292-6930   Fax: (614)292-2065
URL: http://muse.jhu.edu/journals/american_periodicals/

Monthly. A Journal of History, Criticism, and Bibliography.

★6014★ American Studies Association Newsletter

American Studies Association
1120 19th St. NW, Ste. 301
Washington, DC 20036
Ph: (202)467-4783   Fax: (202)467-4786
E-mail: asastaff@theasa.net
URL: http://www.theasa.net/

Description: Quarterly. Promotes the interdisciplinary study of American culture. Presents news of research, publications, and conferences. Also includes information on grants, employment opportunities, and Association activities.

★6015★ Classical Antiquity

University of California Press/Journals
2120 Berkeley Way
Berkeley, CA 94704-1012
Ph: (510)642-4247   Fax: (510)643-7127
URL: http://www.ucpress.edu/journals/ca

Biennial. $45.00/year   for   individuals; $158.00/year for institutions, print & electronic; $25.00/year for students; $135.00/year for institutions, electronic only; $22.00 for single issue, individuals/students; $87.00 for single issue, institutions. Scholarly journal covering interdisciplinary research and issues in Classics-Greek and Roman literature, history, art, philosophy, archaeology, and philology.

★6016★ Common-place

American Antiquarian Society
185 Salisbury St.
Worcester, MA 01609-1634
Ph: (508)755-5221   Fax: (508)753-3311
URL: http://www.common-place.org/

Quarterly. Journal on early American history and culture.

★6017★ Dispatch

American Association for State & Local History
1717 Church St.
Nashville, TN 37203-2991
Ph: (615)320-3203   Fax: (615)327-9013
E-mail: membership@AASLH.org
URL: http://www.aaslh.org/pdispatch.htm

Description: Monthly. Offers general information about state and local historical societies and the study of state and local history in the U.S. and Canada. Informs members of new training programs, seminars, and exhibits in the field. Recurring features include information on grant opportunities, updates on legislation, Association activities, and historical society personnel, interviews, job listings, and notices of publications available.

★6018★ The Historian

Wiley-Blackwell
350 Main St. Commerce Pl.
Malden, MA 02148
Ph: (781)388-8200   Fax: (781)388-8210
Fr: 800-759-6120
URL: http://www.blackwellpublishing.com/journal.asp?ref=0018-2370

Quarterly. $48.00/year for individuals, U.S. print and online; $158.00/year for institutions, U.S. print and premium online; $144.00/year for institutions, U.S. print and standard online; $137.00/year for institutions, U.S. premium online only. Journal focusing on contemporary and relevant historical scholarship.

★6019★ History News

American Association for State & Local History
1717 Church St.
Nashville, TN 37203-2991
Ph: (615)320-3203   Fax: (615)327-9013
URL: http://www.aaslh.org/historynews.htm

Quarterly. Magazine for employees of historic sites, museums, and public history agencies. Coverage includes museum education programs and techniques for working with volunteers.

★6020★ Journal of the American Institute for Conservation

American Institute for Conservation of Historic & Artistic Works
1156 15th St. NW, Ste. 320
Washington, DC 20005
Ph: (202)452-9545   Fax: (202)452-9328
URL: http://aic.stanford.edu/jaic/

$100.00/year for U.S. $130.00/year for other countries. Journal covering historic preservation issues.

★6021★ *Journal of America's Military Past*

Council on America's Military Past
PO Box 1151
Fort Myer, VA 22211
URL: http://www.campjamp.org/The%20Journal.htm

Quarterly. Subscription included in membership. Journal covering military history in the U.S., including famous battles, military personnel, and the bases where they served.

★6022★ *Journal of Contemporary History*

Sage Publications Inc.
2455 Teller Rd.
Thousand Oaks, CA 91320
Ph: (805)499-0721   Fax: (805)499-8096
URL: http://www.sagepub.com/journalsProdAdv.nav?prodId=Journal200

Quarterly. $718.00/year for institutions, print & e-access; $790.00/year for institutions, print & all online; $646.00/year for institutions, e-access; $704.00/year for institutions, print only; $99.00/year for individuals, print only; $194.00 for institutions, single print; $32.00 for individuals, single print; $1,812.03/year for institutions, e-access content thru 1999. Journal covering a range of historical approaches including social, economic, political, diplomatic, intellectual, and cultural.

★6023★ *The Minnesota History Interpreter*

Minnesota Historical Society
345 Kellogg Blvd. W
St. Paul, MN 55102-1906
Ph: (651)259-3000   Fax: (651)282-2374
URL: http://www.mnhs.org/about/publications/interpreter.html

Description: Nine issues/year. Promotes the preservation of Minnesota history. Explores statewide Historical Society activities, providing news of exhibits, programs, seminars, conferences, and research findings. Recurring features include news of meetings, Heritage Preservation Commission News, news of members, job listings, book reviews, individual/organization profiles, and "how to" articles on topics such as museum work.

★6024★ *Oral History Review*

University of California Press/Journals
2120 Berkeley Way
Berkeley, CA 94704-1012
Ph: (510)642-4247   Fax: (510)643-7127
URL: http://www.ucpress.edu/journals/ohr

Biennial. $65.00/year for individuals; $35.00/year for students; $80.00/year for individuals, contributing individuals; $140.00/year for institutions, member print & electronic; $116.00/year for individuals, electronic;

$34.00 for single issue, individuals/students/retired; $69.00 for single issue, institutions. Scholarly journal of the Oral History Association covering oral history of people who have participated in important political, cultural, and economic social developments in modern times.

★6025★ *Preservation*

National Trust for Historic Preservation
1785 Massachusetts Ave. NW
Washington, DC 20036
Ph: (202)588-6000   Fax: (202)588-6038
Fr: 800-944-6847
URL: http://www.nationaltrust.org

Bimonthly. $20.00/year for individuals; $30.00/year for family membership. Magazine featuring historic preservation.

★6026★ *Presidential Studies Quarterly*

Wiley-Blackwell
350 Main St. Commerce Pl.
Malden, MA 02148
Ph: (781)388-8200   Fax: (781)388-8210
Fr: 800-759-6120
URL: http://www.blackwell-synergy.com

Quarterly. $355.00/year for institutions, print and premium online; $323.00/year for institutions, print and standard online; $307.00/year for institutions, premium online only; $266.00/year for institutions, other countries, print and premium online; $242.00/year for institutions, other countries, print and standard online; $230.00/year for institutions, other countries, premium online only. Publication covering political science and history.

★6027★ *Sea History Gazette*

National Maritime Historical Society
5 John Walsh Blvd.
PO Box 68
Peekskill, NY 10566
Ph: (914)737-7878   Fax: (914)737-7816
Fr: 800-221-6647
E-mail: editorial@seahistory.org
URL: http://www.seahistory.org/public_html/pblctn.htm

Description: Quarterly. Carries news from the fields of maritime history and preservation, including items on ship preservation, marine archaeology, sail training, and museum and exhibit openings. Designed for the layman and professional involved with the maritime heritage community. Recurring features include a calendar of events, reports of meetings, job listings, and book reviews.

★6028★ *Southern Association for Women Historians Newsletter*

Southern Association for Women Historians
c/o Dr. Melissa Walker
Dept. of History and Politics
310 Auditorium Bldg.
East Lansing, MI 48824
Ph: (517)432-5134   Fax: (517)355-8363
E-mail: h-sawh@h-net.msu.edu
URL: http://www.h-net.org/~sawh/newsletters/index.htm

Description: Three issues/year. Informs members of the Association's activities aimed at advancing the professional development of women historians and historians of women. Carries minutes of the annual meeting, announcements of awards and prizes available for work published in a variety of areas, and calls for papers at various conferences. Recurring features include notices of publications available, job listings, and member updates.

★6029★ *White House Studies*

Nova Science Publishers Inc.
400 Oser Ave., Ste. 1600
Hauppauge, NY 11788-3619
Ph: (631)231-7269   Fax: (631)231-8175
URL: http://www.novapublishers.com/catalog/product_info.php?cPat

Quarterly. $245.00/year for individuals. Publication covering political science and history.

★6030★ *World History Connected*

University of Illinois Press
1325 S Oak St.
Champaign, IL 61820-6903
Ph: (217)333-0950   Fax: (217)244-8082
Fr: 800-537-5487
URL: http://worldhistoryconnected.press.uiuc.edu

Journal covering a variety of global history topics for teachers and students.

PLACEMENT AND JOB REFERRAL SERVICES

★6031★ **African Studies Association (ASA)**

Douglass Campus
132 George St.
New Brunswick, NJ 08901-1400
Ph: (732)932-8173   Fax: (732)932-3394
E-mail: asaed@rci.rutgers.edu
URL: http://www.africanstudies.org

Members: Persons specializing in teaching, writing, or research on Africa including political scientists, historians, geographers, anthropologists, economists, librarians, linguists, and government officials; persons who are studying African subjects; institutional members are universities, libraries, government agencies, and others interested in receiving information about Africa. **Purpose:** Seeks to foster communication and to stimulate research among scholars on Africa. **Activities:** Sponsors placement service; conducts panels and discussion groups; presents exhibits and films.

★6032★ **Flag Research Center (FRC)**

PO Box 580
Winchester, MA 01890-0880
Ph: (781)729-9410   Fax: (781)721-4817
E-mail: vexor@comcast.net

URL: http://www.crwflags.com/fotw/flags/vex-frc.html

Description: Professional and amateur vexillologists (flag historians) seeking to coordinate flag research activities and promote vexillology as a historical discipline and hobby and to increase knowledge of and appreciation for flags of all kinds. Provides data and gives lectures on flag history, etiquette, design, symbolism, and uses. Operates speakers' bureau; offers children's services and placement service; compiles statistics. Plans to establish museum.

EMPLOYER DIRECTORIES AND NETWORKING LISTS

★6033★ Directory of Federal Historical Programs and Activities

American Historical Association
400 A St. SE
Washington, DC 20003-3889
Ph: (202)544-2422   Fax: (202)544-8307
URL: http://www.historians.org

Triennial; latest edition 7th, 2003. $10.00 for nonmembers; $8.00 for members. Covers about 1,700 federally employed historians and federal government agencies operating historical programs. Entries include: For historians–Name, phone, area of expertise, historical program. For programs–Name, address, functions of historians.

★6034★ Discovering Careers for Your Future: History

Facts On File Inc.
132 W 31st St., 17th Fl.
New York, NY 10001
Ph: (212)967-8800   Fax: 800-678-3633
Fr: 800-322-8755
URL: http://www.factsonfile.com

Published 2001. $21.95 for individuals; $19.75 for libraries. Covers archaeologists, genealogists, historians, museum curators, and sociologists; links career education to curriculum, helping children investigate the subjects they are interested in and the careers those subjects might lead to.

★6035★ Grants, Fellowships, and Prizes of Interest to Historians

American Historical Association
400 A St. SE
Washington, DC 20003-3889
Ph: (202)544-2422   Fax: (202)544-8307
E-mail: grantguide@theaha.org
URL: http://www.historians.org

Annual; latest edition 2006. For American Historical Association members. Covers over 450 sources of funding (scholarships, fellowships, internships, awards, and book and essay prizes) in the United States and abroad for graduate students, postdoctoral researchers, and institutions in the humanities. Entries include: Name of source, institution name or contact, address, phone, eligibility and proposal requirements, award or stipend amount, location requirements for research, application deadlines. Arrangement: Alphabetical in three categories: support for individual research and teaching; grants for groups and organizations for research and education; and book, article, essay, and manuscript prizes.

★6036★ Newsletter-Society for Historical Archaeology Membership Directory Issue

Society for Historical Archaeology
15245 Shady Grove Rd., Ste. 130
Rockville, MD 20850
Ph: (301)990-2454   Fax: (301)990-9771
URL: http://www.sha.org

Annual, June. Publication includes: List of about 2,100 member archaeologists, historians, anthropologists, and ethnohistorians, and other individuals and institutions having an interest in historical archaeology or allied fields. Entries include: Name, address. Arrangement: Alphabetical.

★6037★ Official Museum Directory

LexisNexis Group
PO Box 933
Dayton, OH 45401-0933
Ph: (937)865-6800   Fax: (518)487-3584
Fr: 800-543-6862

Annual, December. Covers approximately 7,850 institutions of art, history, and science in the United States, including general museums, college and university museums, children's and junior museums, company museums, national park and nature center displays, and highly specialized museums. Also includes a separate volume of 2,000 suppliers of services and products to museums. Entries include: For museums–Name, address, phone, date established, personnel, governing authority, brief description of museum and type of collections, facilities, activities, publications, hours of operation, admission prices, membership fees, attendance figures. For suppliers–Company name, address, phone, name and title of contact. Arrangement: Museums are geographical; suppliers are by specialty. Indexes: Museum personnel (with name, title, affiliation, city, and state); type of museum (with name, city, and state); alphabetical; special collection.

★6038★ Perspectives-Employment Information Section

American Historical Association
400 A St. SE
Washington, DC 20003-3889
Ph: (202)544-2422   Fax: (202)544-8307
URL: http://www.historians.org

Monthly, during the academic year. Publication includes: List of over 1,000 job openings per year for historians; international coverage. Entries include: Institution or organization name, address, department name, name and title of contact, responsibilities, application deadline. Arrangement: Geographical.

★6039★ Top Careers for History Graduates

Facts On File Inc.
132 W 31st St., 17th Fl.
New York, NY 10001
Ph: (212)967-8800   Fax: 800-678-3633
Fr: 800-322-8755

Published 2004. $14.95 for individuals. Covers the information needed to transform a history degree into a satisfying job, exploring everything from reasons to major in history to what types of jobs are available and how much they pay.

HANDBOOKS AND MANUALS

★6040★ Careers for History Buffs & Others Who Learn from the Past

The McGraw-Hill Companies
PO Box 182604
Columbus, OH 43272
Fax: (614)759-3749   Fr: 877-883-5524
E-mail: customer.service@mcgraw-hill.com
URL: http://www.mcgraw-hill.com

Blythe Camenson. Second edition, 2002. $12.95 (paper). 192 pages.

★6041★ Great Jobs for History Majors

The McGraw-Hill Companies
PO Box 182604
Columbus, OH 43272
Fax: (614)759-3749   Fr: 877-883-5524
E-mail: customer.service@mcgraw-hill.com
URL: http://www.mcgraw-hill.com

Julie DeGalan and Stephen Lambert. 2001. $15.95 (paper). 256 pages.

★6042★ Opportunities in Social Science Careers

The McGraw-Hill Companies
PO Box 182604
Columbus, OH 43272
Fax: (614)759-3749   Fr: 877-883-5524
E-mail: customer.service@mcgraw-hill.com
URL: http://www.mcgraw-hill.com

Rosanne J. Marek. 2004. $13.95. 160 Pages. VGM Opportunities Series.

TRADESHOWS

★6043★ American Association for State and Local History Annual Meeting

American Association for State and Local History
1717 Church St.
Nashville, TN 37203-2991
Ph: (615)320-3203   Fax: (615)327-9013
E-mail: membership@AASLH.org
URL: http://www.aaslh.org

Annual. **Primary Exhibits:** Products and services directed toward the museum and history field, including: publications, fundraising devices, software, exhibit design, historic preservation, historic research and technical information.

★6044★ **American Historical Association Annual Meeting**

American Historical Association
400 A St. SE
Washington, DC 20003-3889
Ph: (202)544-2422   Fax: (202)544-8307
E-mail: info@historians.org
URL: http://www.historians.org

Annual. **Primary Exhibits:** Books and journals from commercial publishers and university presses. **Dates and Locations:** 2008 Jan 03-06; Washington, DC; Marriott Wardman Park & Omni Shoreham; 2009 Jan 02-05; New York, NY; Hilton New York, Sheraton New York; 2010 Jan 07-10; San Diego, CA; Manchester Grand Hyatt and San Diego Marriott; 2011 Jan 06-09; Boston, MA; Boston Marriott, Sheraton Boston, and Westin Boston.

★6045★ **American Society for Ethnohistory Conference**

American Society for Ethnohistory
c/o R. David Edmunds, Pres.
University of Texas at Dallas
2601 N Floyd Rd.
Richardson, TX 75080
URL: http://ethnohistory.org

Annual. **Primary Exhibits:** Exhibits relating to the cultural history of ethnic groups worldwide.

★6046★ **Congress of the International Society for Human Ethology**

International Society for Human Ethology
PO Box 418
Nyack, NY 10960
Ph: (207)581-2044   Fax: (207)581-6128
E-mail: karl.grammer@univie.ac.at

Biennial. **Primary Exhibits:** Books, journals, and equipment for observational research.

★6047★ **Oral History Association Conference**

Oral History Association
Dickinson College
PO Box 1773
Carlisle, PA 17013
Ph: (717)245-1036   Fax: (717)245-1046
E-mail: oha@dickinson.edu
URL: http://omega.dickinson.edu

Annual. **Primary Exhibits:** Equipment, supplies, and services related to recording, transcribing, and preserving conversations constituting oral history.

★6048★ **Organization of American Historians Annual Meeting**

Organization of American Historians
112 N Bryan Ave.
PO Box 5457
Bloomington, IN 47408-5457
Ph: (812)855-7311   Fax: (812)855-0696
E-mail: oah@oah.org
URL: http://www.oah.org

Annual. **Primary Exhibits:** Equipment, supplies, and services of interest to historians, including textbooks and computer software.

★6049★ **Southern Historical Association Meeting**

Southern Historical Association
220 LeConte Hall
Athens, GA 30602-1602
Ph: (706)542-2053   Fax: (706)542-2455
E-mail: osfa@uga.edu
URL: http://www.uga.edu

Annual. **Primary Exhibits:** Publications. **Dates and Locations:** 2008 Nov 06-09; Birmingham, AL; Sheraton Birmingham Hotel.

OTHER SOURCES

★6050★ **American Association for State and Local History (AASLH)**

1717 Church St.
Nashville, TN 37203-2921
Ph: (615)320-3203   Fax: (615)327-9013
E-mail: membership@aaslh.org
URL: http://www.aaslh.org

Description: Works to preserve and promote history. Ensures the highest-quality expressions of state and local history in publications, exhibitions, and public programs through its diverse services. Represents more than 6,400 individual and institutional members.

★6051★ **American Catholic Historical Association (ACHA)**

Mullen Library, Rm. 320
Catholic University of America
Washington, DC 20064
Ph: (202)319-5079   Fax: (202)319-5079
E-mail: cua-chracha@cua.edu
URL: http://research.cua.edu/acha

Description: Professional society of historians, educators, students, and others interested in the history of the Catholic Church in the United States and abroad and in the promotion of historical scholarship among Catholics. Has sponsored the publication of the papers of John Carroll, first Bishop and Archbishop of Baltimore, MD.

★6052★ **American Historical Association (AHA)**

400 A St. SE
Washington, DC 20003-3889
Ph: (202)544-2422   Fax: (202)544-8307

E-mail: info@historians.org
URL: http://www.historians.org

Members: Professional historians, educators, and others interested in promoting historical studies and collecting and preserving historical manuscripts. **Activities:** Conducts research and educational programs.

★6053★ **American Institute for Conservation of Historic and Artistic Works (AIC)**

1717 K St. NW, Ste. 200
Washington, DC 20036
Ph: (202)452-9545   Fax: (202)452-9328
E-mail: info@aic-faic.org
URL: http://www.aic-faic.org

Members: Professionals, scientists, administrators, and educators in the field of art conservation; interested individuals. **Purpose:** Advances the practice and promotes the importance of the preservation of cultural property. **Activities:** Coordinates the exchange of knowledge, research, and publications. Establishes and upholds professional standards. Publishes conservation literature. Compiles statistics. Represents membership to allied professional associations and advocates on conservation-related issues. Solicits and dispenses money exclusively for charitable, scientific, and educational objectives.

★6054★ **American Society for Eighteenth-Century Studies (ASECS)**

Wake Forest University
PO Box 7867
Winston-Salem, NC 27109
Ph: (336)727-4694   Fax: (336)727-4697
E-mail: asecs@wfu.edu
URL: http://asecs.press.jhu.edu

Description: Scholars and others interested in the cultural history of the 18th century. Encourages and advances study and research in this area; promotes the interchange of information and ideas among scholars from different disciplines (such as librarianship and bibliography) who are interested in the 18th century. Co-sponsors seven fellowship programs; sponsors Graduate Student Caucus.

★6055★ **American Society of Psychopathology of Expression (ASPE)**

74 Lawton St.
Brookline, MA 02446
Ph: (617)738-9821   Fax: (617)975-0411

Description: Psychiatrists, psychologists, art therapists, sociologists, art critics, artists, social workers, linguists, educators, criminologists, writers, and historians. At least two-thirds of the members must be physicians. Fosters collaboration among specialists in the United States who are interested in the problems of expression and in the artistic activities connected with psychiatric, sociological, and psychological research. Disseminates information about research and clinical applications in the field of psychopathology of expression. Sponsors consultations, seminars, and lectures on art therapy.

★6056★ **International Studies Association (ISA)**

University of Arizona
324 Social Sciences Bldg.
Tucson, AZ 85721
Ph: (520)621-7715   Fax: (520)621-5780
E-mail: isa@u.arizona.edu
URL: http://www.isanet.org

Members: Social scientists and other scholars from a wide variety of disciplines who are specialists in international affairs and cross-cultural studies; academicians; government officials; officials in international organizations; business executives; students. **Purpose:** Promotes research, improved teaching, and the orderly growth of knowledge in the field of international studies; emphasizes a multidisciplinary approach to problems. **Activities:** Conducts conventions, workshops and discussion groups.

★6057★ **National Coalition for History (NCH)**

400 A St. SE
Washington, DC 20003
Ph: (202)544-2422   Fax: (202)544-8307
E-mail: lwhite@historycoalition.org
URL: http://historycoalition.org

Description: Archival and historical organizations such as: American Historical Association; Organization of American Historians; Phi Alpha Theta; Society of American Archivists; Western History Association. Serves as central advocacy office and information clearinghouse for history/archival related topics affecting government agencies, legislative aides, and professional history and archival associations; develops network of constituent contacts in districts and states; testifies before congressional committees; monitors employment opportunities.

★6058★ **National Council on Public History (NCPH)**

327 Cavanaugh Hall - IUPUI
425 University Blvd.
Indianapolis, IN 46202
Ph: (317)274-2716   Fax: (317)278-5230
E-mail: ncph@iupui.edu
URL: http://www.ncph.org

Description: Aims to encourage a broader interest in professional history and to stimulate national interest in public history by promoting its use at all levels of society. (Public history deals with nonacademic history. History is brought to the public rather than the classroom through museum work, public displays, and federal, local, and corporate historians.) Serves as an information clearinghouse; sponsors training programs, local and regional colloquia, projects, and panels. Offers advice to departments of history, historical associations, and others seeking information on public history, professional standards, opportunities, and internships. Conducts surveys and analyses.

★6059★ **Newcomen Society of the United States (NSUS)**

211 Welsh Pool Rd., Ste. 240
Exton, PA 19341-1321
Ph: (610)363-6600   Fax: (610)363-0612
Fr: 800-466-7604
E-mail: info@newcomen.org
URL: http://www.newcomen.org

Members: Business and professional people in education and industry in the United States and Canada. **Purpose:** Studies material history, as distinguished from political history, in terms of the beginnings, growth, and contributions of industry, transportation, communication, mining, agriculture, banking, insurance, medicine, education, invention, law, and related historical fields. Maintains Thomas Newcomen Memorial Museum in Steam Technology and Industrial History in Chester County, PA. Society named for Thomas Newcomen (1663-1729), British pi-

oneer who invented the first atmospheric steam engine.

★6060★ **Organization of American Historians (OAH)**

PO Box 5457
Bloomington, IN 47407-5457
Ph: (812)855-9852   Fax: (812)855-0696
E-mail: oah@oah.org
URL: http://www.oah.org

Description: Professional historians, including college faculty members, secondary school teachers, graduate students, and other individuals in related fields; institutional subscribers are college, university, high school and public libraries, and historical agencies. Promotes historical research and study. Sponsors 12 prize programs for historical writing; maintains speakers' bureau. Conducts educational programs.

★6061★ **United States Capitol Historical Society (USCHS)**

200 Maryland Ave. NE
Washington, DC 20002
Ph: (202)543-8919   Fax: (202)544-8244
Fr: 800-887-9318
E-mail: uschs@uschs.org
URL: http://www.uschs.org

Description: Preserves and communicates the history and heritage of the U.S. Capital, its institutions, and the individuals who have served in Congress. Activities include educational programs, popular and scholarly symposia and publications, enhancement of the Capitol's collection of art and artifacts, and research in the U.S. Capitol and the U.S. Congress.

Home Health Aides

SOURCES OF HELP-WANTED ADS

★6062★ Addiction Professional

Manisses Communications Group Inc.
208 Governor St.
Providence, RI 02906
Ph: (401)831-6020   Fax: (401)861-6370
Fr: 800-333-7771
URL: http://www.manisses.com/AP/AP.htm

Monthly. $67.00/year for individuals. Magazine that publishes innovations and trends in the clinical care of persons with substance use and dependence disorders.

★6063★ ADVANCE for Nurse Practitioners

Merion Publications Inc.
2900 Horizon Dr.
PO Box 61556
King of Prussia, PA 19406
Ph: (610)278-1400   Fr: 800-355-5627
URL: http://nurse-practition-ers.advanceweb.com/main.aspx

Monthly. For practicing nurse practitioner students with senior status.

★6064★ American Dental Hygienists' Association Access

American Dental Hygienists' Association
444 North Michigan Ave., Ste. 3400
Chicago, IL 60611
Ph: (312)440-8904   Fr: 800-243-ADHA
URL: http://www.adha.org/publications

$48.00/year for individuals; $85.00 for two years; $120.00/year for individuals, for 3 years. Magazine covering current dental hygiene topics, regulatory and legislative developments, and association news.

★6065★ American Journal of Nursing

American Journal of Nursing
c/o Lippincott, Williams & Wilkins
530 Walnut St.
Philadelphia, PA 19106-3621
Ph: (215)521-8300   Fax: (215)521-8902
Fr: 800-627-0484

URL: http://www.nursingcenter.com

Monthly. $32.90/year   for   individuals; $159.00/year for institutions; $69.00/year for individuals, other countries; $199.00/year for institutions, other countries. Journal for staff nurses, nurse managers, and clinical nurse specialists. Focuses on patient care in hospitals, hospital ICUs and homes. Provides news coverage of health care from the nursing perspective.

★6066★ The American Nurse

American Nurses Association
8515 Georgia Ave., Ste. 400
Silver Spring, MD 20910
Ph: (301)628-5000   Fax: (301)628-5001
Fr: 800-274-4262
E-mail: adsales@ana.org
URL: http://nursingworld.org/tan/

Monthly. Newspaper (tabloid) for the nursing profession.

★6067★ Bountiful Health

JNE Publishing, Inc.
PO Box 5647
Huntsville, AL 35814
Ph: (256)837-3035   Fr: 800-313-7751
URL: http://www.jnepublishing.com/bounti-fulhealth.php?page=public

Magazine focusing on complementary and alternative medicine, exercise, vitamins and supplements, healthy eating, and green living.

★6068★ Cancer Nursing

Lippincott Williams & Wilkins
530 Walnut St.
Philadelphia, PA 19106-3621
Ph: (215)521-8300   Fax: (215)521-8902
Fr: 800-638-3030
E-mail: bguthy@lww.com
URL: http://www.cancernursingonline.com/

Bimonthly. $94.43/year   for   individuals; $243.48/year for institutions; $49.48/year for other countries, in-training; $167.46/year for individuals; $284.46/year   for   institutions. Medical journal covering problems arising in the care and support of cancer patients.

★6069★ Diversity

Career Recruitment Media
211 W Wacker Dr., Ste. 900
Chicago, IL 60606
Ph: (312)525-3100
URL: http://www.diversityalliedhealth.com/

Magazine focus on multicultural career and educational development magazine for allied health students and professionals.

★6070★ Environmental Pollution

Elsevier Science Inc.
360 Park Ave. S
New York, NY 10010
Ph: (212)989-5800   Fax: (212)633-3990
URL: http://www.elsevier.com

$4,689.00/year for institutions, for all countries except Europe, Japan and Iran; $136.00/year for individuals, for all countries except Europe, Japan and Iran. Journal covering issues relevant to chemical pollutants in air, soil and water.

★6071★ Ethnicity and Health

Taylor & Francis Group Journals
325 Chestnut St., Ste. 800
Philadelphia, PA 19106
Ph: (215)625-8900   Fax: (215)625-8914
Fr: 800-354-1420
URL: http://www.tandf.co.uk/journals/titles/13557858.asp

Journal covering ethnicity and health.

★6072★ Geriatric Nursing

Mosby Inc.
10801 Executive Center Dr., Ste. 509
Little Rock, AR 72211
Ph: (501)223-5165   Fax: (501)223-0519
URL: http://journals.elsevierhealth.com/peri-odicals/ymgn

Bimonthly. $63.00/year   for   individuals; $113.00/year   for   individuals,   Canada; $113.00/year   for   individuals,   Mexico; $113.00/year for individuals, international. Magazine for nurses in geriatric and gerontologic nursing practice, the primary professional providers of care for the aging. Provides news on issues affecting elders and clinical information on techniques and procedures.

★6073★ Health & Place

Mosby Inc.
11830 Westline Industrial Dr.
St. Louis, MO 63146
Ph: (314)872-8370   Fax: (314)432-1380
Fr: 800-325-4177
URL: http://www.us.elsevierhealth.com

Quarterly. $650.00/year for institutions, for all countries except European countries, Japan and Iran; $126.00/year for individuals, personal. Journal publishing articles for health care professionals.

★6074★ Health Policy, Economics and Management

Elsevier Science Inc.
360 Park Ave. S
New York, NY 10010
Ph: (212)989-5800   Fax: (212)633-3990
URL: http://www.elsevier.com

Monthly. $2,427.00/year for institutions in all countries except Europe, Japan and Iran. $404.00/year for individuals in all countries except Europe, Japan and Iran. Journal covering the economic, social and political aspects of health care and its organization includes hospital management, health care marketing, hospital automation, and the assessment of new technology for the health care industry.

★6075★ Home Healthcare Nurse

Lippincott Williams & Wilkins
530 Walnut St.
Philadelphia, PA 19106-3621
Ph: (215)521-8300   Fax: (215)521-8902
Fr: 800-638-3030
URL: http://www.homehealthcarenurseonline.com/

Monthly. $56.43/year for individuals, U.S.; $202.95/year for institutions, U.S.; $126.46/year for individuals, other countries; $252.95/year for institutions, other countries; $43.48/year for U.S., in-training. Magazine for the practicing professional nurse working in the home health, community health, and public health areas.

★6076★ HomeCare Magazine

Miramar Communications Inc.
23805 Stuart Ranch Rd., Ste. 235
PO Box 8987
Malibu, CA 90265-8987
Ph: (310)317-4522   Fax: (310)317-9644
Fr: 800-543-4116
URL: http://www.homecaremag.com

Monthly. Free, in US; $135.00/year for Canada; $150.00/year for two years, Canada; $250.00/year for other countries; $250.00/year for two years, other countries. Magazine serving home medical equipment suppliers, including independent and chain centers specializing in home care, pharmacies or chain drug stores with home care products, and joint-ventured hospital home health care businesses. Contains industry news

and new product launches and marketing strategies.

★6077★ Hospitals & Health Networks

Health Forum L.L.C.
1 N Franklin, 29th Fl.
Chicago, IL 60606
Ph: (312)893-6800   Fax: (312)422-4506
Fr: 800-821-2039
URL: http://www.hhnmag.com

Weekly. Publication covering the health care industry.

★6078★ The IHS Primary Care Provider

Indian Health Service (HQ)
The Reyes Bldg.
801 Thompson Ave., Ste. 400
Rockville, MD 20852-1627
URL: http://www.ihs.gov/PublicInfo/Publications/HealthProvider/Pr

Monthly. Journal for health care professionals, physicians, nurses, pharmacists, dentists, and dietitians.

★6079★ The International Electronic Journal of Health Education

American Alliance for Health, Physical Education, Recreation & Dance
1900 Association Dr.
Reston, VA 20191-1598
Ph: (703)476-3400   Fax: (703)476-9527
Fr: 800-213-7193
URL: http://www.aahperd.org/iejhe/template.cfm?template=about.htm

Annual. Free to health education professionals and students. Journal promoting health through education and other systematic strategies.

★6080★ JONA's Healthcare Law, Ethics, and Regulation

Lippincott Williams & Wilkins
351 W Camden St.
Baltimore, MD 21201
Ph: (410)528-4000   Fax: (410)528-4305
Fr: 800-399-3110
URL: http://www.jonalaw.com/

Quarterly. $55.00/year for individuals; $82.00/year for institutions; $97.00/year for individuals, international; $117.00/year for institutions, international. Journal covering the legal, ethical and regulatory issues facing nursing care management.

★6081★ Journal of the American College of Nutrition

American College of Nutrition
300 S Duncan Ave., Ste. 225
Clearwater, FL 33755
Ph: (727)446-6086   Fax: (727)446-6202
URL: http://www.jacn.org

Bimonthly. Journal on nutrition.

★6082★ Journal of the American Society of Podiatric Medical Assistants

American Society of Podiatric Medical Assistants
2124 S Austin Blvd.
Cicero, IL 60804
Ph: (708)863-6303   Fr: 888-882-7762
URL: http://www.aspma.org

Quarterly. Subscription included in membership. Professional journal covering issues in podiatry.

★6083★ Journal of Gerontological Nursing

SLACK Inc.
6900 Grove Rd.
Thorofare, NJ 08086-9447
Ph: (856)848-1000   Fax: (856)853-5991
E-mail: jgn@slackinc.com
URL: http://www.jognonline.com

Monthly. $84.00/year for individuals; $142.00 for individuals, two years; $189.00 for individuals, three years; $169.00/year for institutions; $287.00 for institutions, two years; $380.00 for institutions, three years; $21.00 for single issue. Gerontological nursing journal.

★6084★ Journal of Health Law

American Health Lawyers Association
1025 Connecticut Ave., NW, Ste. 600
Washington, DC 20036-5405
Ph: (202)833-1100   Fax: (202)833-1105
URL: http://www.healthlawyers.org

Quarterly. Professional journal covering healthcare issues and cases and their impact on the health care arena.

★6085★ Journal of Nursing Care Quality

Lippincott Williams & Wilkins
351 W Camden St.
Baltimore, MD 21201
Ph: (410)528-4000   Fax: (410)528-4305
Fr: 800-399-3110
URL: http://www.lww.com/product/?1057-3631

Quarterly. $98.00/year for individuals; $263.00/year for institutions; $168.00/year for individuals, other countries; $351.00/year for institutions, other countries. Journal keeping practicing nurses and those who play leadership roles in nursing care quality programs fully current on the utilization of quality principles and concepts in the practice setting.

★6086★ Journal of Nursing Scholarship

Wiley-Blackwell
350 Main St. Commerce Pl.
Malden, MA 02148
Ph: (781)388-8200   Fax: (781)388-8210
Fr: 800-759-6120
URL: http://www.blackwellpublishing.com/journal.asp?ref=1527-6546

Quarterly. $51.00/year for individuals, print

and online; $185.00/year for institutions, print and premium online; $168.00/year for institutions, print and standard online; $160.00/year for institutions, premium online only; $59.00/year for individuals, print and online; $135.00/year for institutions, other countries, print and premium online; $123.00/year for institutions, other countries, print and standard online; $117.00/year for institutions, other countries, premium online only; $39.00/year for individuals, print and online. Peer-reviewed journal covering nursing.

★6087★ **McKnight's Long-Term Care News**

McKnight's Long-Term Care News
1 Northfield Plz., Ste. 521
Northfield, IL 60093-1216
Ph: (847)784-8706   Fax: (847)784-9346
Fr: 800-558-1703
E-mail: ltcn-webmaster@mltcn.com
URL: http://www.mcknightsonline.com/home

Professional magazine.

★6088★ **Medical Care**

Lippincott Williams & Wilkins
351 W Camden St.
Baltimore, MD 21201
Ph: (410)528-4000   Fax: (410)528-4305
Fr: 800-399-3110
URL: http://www.lww-medicalcare.com/

Monthly. $373.00/year for individuals; $813.00/year for institutions; $475.00/year for individuals, other countries; $869.00/year for institutions, other countries; $207.00/year for individuals, in-training. Journal focusing on all aspects of the administration and delivery of healthcare.

★6089★ **Medical Staff Development Professional**

American Academy of Medical
  Management
Crossville Commons
560 W Crossville Rd., Ste. 103
Roswell, GA 30075
Ph: (770)649-7150   Fax: (770)649-7552

Periodic. Professional journal covering medical education.

★6090★ **Modern Healthcare**

Crain Communications Inc.
360 N Michigan Ave.
Chicago, IL 60601
Ph: (312)649-5411   Fax: (312)280-3150
Fr: 888-909-9111
E-mail: subs@crain.com
URL: http://www.modernhealthcare.com

Weekly. $154.00/year for individuals; $244.00/year for Canada; $208.00/year for other countries. Weekly business news magazine for healthcare management.

★6091★ **Nursing Administration Quarterly**

Lippincott Williams & Wilkins
351 W Camden St.
Baltimore, MD 21201
Ph: (410)528-4000   Fax: (410)528-4305
Fr: 800-399-3110
URL: http://www.lww.com/product/?0363-9568

Quarterly. $105.96/year for individuals; $282.96/year for institutions; $62.96/year for individuals in-training; $169.96/year for individuals, international; $340.94/year for institutions, international. Journal providing nursing administrators with information on the effective management of nursing services in all health care settings.

★6092★ **Nursing Outlook**

Mosby Inc.
10801 Executive Center Dr., Ste. 509
Little Rock, AR 72211
Ph: (501)223-5165   Fax: (501)223-0519
URL: http://journals.elsevierhealth.com/periodicals/ymno

Bimonthly. $65.00/year for individuals; $106.00/year for individuals, Canada; $106.00/year for individuals, other countries. Official journal of the American Academy of Nursing, reporting on trends and issues in nursing.

★6093★ **Nutrition Business Journal**

Penton Media Inc.
249 W 17th St.
New York, NY 10011
Ph: (212)204-4200
E-mail: info@nutritionbusiness.com
URL: http://www.nutritionbusiness.com/

Monthly. $995.00/year for individuals; $299.00/year for individuals, for 3 months. Journal catering to nutrition, natural products and alternative health care industries. Publishes information regarding business activities, market size/growth, trends, and opportunities, with a particular emphasis on the nutrition industry.

★6094★ **Organizational Ethics**

University Publishing Group Inc.
219 W Washington St.
Hagerstown, MD 21740
Ph: (240)420-0036   Fax: (240)420-0037
Fr: 800-654-8188
URL: http://www.organizationalethics.com

Semiannual. $127.00/year for institutions; $65.00/year for individuals. Magazine covering business and healthcare policy.

★6095★ **Patient Education and Counseling**

Mosby Inc.
11830 Westline Industrial Dr.
St. Louis, MO 63146
Ph: (314)872-8370   Fax: (314)432-1380
Fr: 800-325-4177
URL: http://www.elsevier.com/wps/find/journaldescription.cws_home

Monthly. $229.00/year for individuals; $2,169.00/year for institutions. Journal publishing articles on patient education and health promotion researchers, managers, physicians, nurses and other health care providers.

★6096★ **Physical & Occupational Therapy in Geriatrics**

The Haworth Press Inc.
10 Alice St.
Binghamton, NY 13904
Ph: (607)722-5857   Fr: 800-429-6784
URL: http://www.haworthpress.com

Quarterly. $99.00/year for individuals; $145.00/year for Canada, individual; $152.00/year for other countries, individual; $660.00/year for institutions, agency, library; $949.00/year for institutions, Canada, agency, library; $1,011.00/year for institutions, other countries, agency, library. Journal for allied health professionals focusing on current practice and emerging issues in the health care of and rehabilitation of the older client.

★6097★ **Provider**

American Health Care Association
1201 L St. NW
Washington, DC 20005
Ph: (202)842-4444   Fax: (202)842-3860
E-mail: sales@ahca.org
URL: http://www.providermagazine.com

Monthly. $48.00/year for U.S.; $61.00/year for Canada and Mexico; $85.00/year for other countries. Provider Magazine.

★6098★ **Public Health Forum**

Elsevier Science Inc.
360 Park Ave. S
New York, NY 10010
Ph: (212)989-5800   Fax: (212)633-3990
URL: http://www.elsevier.com

$38.00/year for institutions, for all countries except Europe, Japan and Iran; $12.00/year for students, for all countries except Japan. Journal focused on research methods, and program evaluation in the field of public health.

★6099★ **Public Health Law & Policy Journal**

University of Hawaii
1859 E.-W. Rd., No. 106
Honolulu, HI 96822-2322
Ph: (808)956-9424   Fax: (808)956-5983
E-mail: phlo@hawaii.edu
URL: http://www.hawaii.edu/phlo/phlpj/

Free, online. Open access academic journal covering worldwide public health issues.

★6100★ **Public Health, Social Medicine and Epidemiology**

Elsevier Science Inc.
360 Park Ave. S
New York, NY 10010
Ph: (212)989-5800   Fax: (212)633-3990

URL: http://www.elsevier.com

Semimonthly. $5,682.00/year for institutions, for all countries except Europe, Japan and Iran. Journal covering public health and social medicine, and includes health planning and education, epidemiology and prevention of communicable disease, public health aspects of risk populations.

★6101★ Quality Management in Health Care

Lippincott Williams & Wilkins
351 W Camden St.
Baltimore, MD 21201
Ph: (410)528-4000   Fax: (410)528-4305
Fr: 800-399-3110
URL: http://www.lww.com/product/?1063-8628

Quarterly. $104.96/year for individuals; $289.96/year for institutions; $62.96/year for individuals, in-training; $172.96/year for international individuals; $372.96/year for international institutions. Journal providing a forum to explore the theoretical, technical, and strategic elements of total quality management in health care.

★6102★ Rehabilitation Nursing

Rehabilitation Nursing
4700 West Lake Ave.
Glenview, IL 60025
Ph: (847)375-4710   Fr: 800-229-7530
E-mail: info@rehabnurse.org
URL: http://www.rehabnurse.org/index.html

Bimonthly. $95.00/year for individuals; $125.00/year for institutions; $135.00/year for other countries; $18.00 for single issue; $125.00/year for Canada. Magazine focusing on rehabilitation nursing involving clinical practice, research, education, and administration.

★6103★ Staffing Industry Healthcare News

Staffing Industry Analysts Inc.
881 Fremont Ave.
Los Altos, CA 94024
Ph: (650)232-2350   Fax: (650)232-2360
Fr: 800-950-9496

Weekly. $10.00 for single issue. Online publication covering key events in health care staffing.

★6104★ Topics in Emergency Medicine

Lippincott Williams & Wilkins
351 W Camden St.
Baltimore, MD 21201
Ph: (410)528-4000   Fax: (410)528-4305
Fr: 800-399-3110
URL: http://www.lww.com/product/?0164-2340

Quarterly. $91.95/year for individuals; $241.95/year for institutions; $141.95/year for other countries. Journal offering information that encompasses the coordinated responsibilities of emergency physicians, nurses, and paramedics.

PLACEMENT AND JOB REFERRAL SERVICES

★6105★ American Public Health Association (APHA)

800 I St. NW
Washington, DC 20001
Ph: (202)777-2742   Fax: (202)777-2534
E-mail: comments@apha.org
URL: http://www.apha.org

Members: Professional organization of physicians, nurses, educators, academicians, environmentalists, epidemiologists, new professionals, social workers, health administrators, optometrists, podiatrists, pharmacists, dentists, nutritionists, health planners, other community and mental health specialists, and interested consumers. **Purpose:** Seeks to protect and promote personal, mental, and environmental health. **Activities:** Services include: promulgation of standards; establishment of uniform practices and procedures; development of the etiology of communicable diseases; research in public health; exploration of medical care programs and their relationships to public health. Sponsors job placement service.

EMPLOYER DIRECTORIES AND NETWORKING LISTS

★6106★ American Journal of Nursing-Career Guide

American Journal of Nursing
c/o Lippincott, Williams & Wilkins
530 Walnut St.
Philadelphia, PA 19106-3621
Ph: (215)521-8300   Fax: (215)521-8902
Fr: 800-627-0484
URL: http://www.ajnonline.com

Annual, April. $34.90 for individuals; $234.95 for institutions; $26.95 for individuals, in-training; $87.00 for individuals, international; $299.00 for institutions, international. Publication includes: List of nursing organizations and agencies. Entries include: Name, address, names of officers or nursing representatives. Arrangement: Classified by type of organization.

★6107★ Careers in Focus: Geriatric Care

Facts On File Inc.
132 W 31st St., 17th Fl.
New York, NY 10001
Ph: (212)967-8800   Fax: 800-678-3633
Fr: 800-322-8755
URL: http://www.factsonfile.com

Latest edition 2nd, 2005. $29.95 for individuals; $26.95 for libraries. Covers an overview of geriatric care, followed by a selection of jobs profiled in detail, including the nature of the job, earnings, prospects for employment, what kind of training and skills it requires, and sources for further information.

★6108★ The JobBank Guide to Health Care Companies

Adams Media Corp.
57 Littlefield St.
Avon, MA 02322
Ph: (508)427-7100   Fax: (508)427-6790
Fr: 800-872-5627
URL: http://www.amazon.com/Jobbank-Guide-Health-Care-Companies/dp

Biennial. Covers jobs nationwide in health care companies. Entries include: Firm or organization name, address, phone, name and title of contact; description of organization, headquarters location, typical titles for entry- and middle-level positions, educational backgrounds desired, fringe benefits offered, stock exchange listing, training programs, internships, parent company, number of employees, revenues, e-mail and web addresses, projected number of hires. Indexes: Alphabetical.

★6109★ Medical and Health Information Directory

Gale, Cengage Learning
27500 Drake Rd.
Farmington Hills, MI 48331-3535
Ph: (248)699-4253   Fax: (248)699-8065
Fr: 800-877-4253
E-mail: businessproducts@gale.com
URL: http://www.gale.com

Annual; latest edition 20th, July 2007. $375.00/volume. Covers in Volume 1, more than 26,500 medical and health oriented associations, organizations, institutions, and government agencies, including health maintenance organizations (HMOs), preferred provider organizations (PPOs), insurance companies, pharmaceutical companies, research centers, and medical and allied health schools. In Volume 2, over 12,000 medical book publishers; medical periodicals, directories, audiovisual producers and services, medical libraries and information centers, electronic resources, and health-related internet search engines. In Volume 3, more than 35,500 clinics, treatment centers, care programs, and counseling/diagnostic services for 34 subject areas. Entries include: Institution, service, or firm name, address, phone, fax, email and URL; many include names of key personnel and, when pertinent, descriptive annotations. Volume 3 was formerly listed separately as Health Services Directory. Arrangement: Classified by organization activity, service, etc. Indexes: Each volume has a complete alphabetical name and keyword index.

★6110★ Peterson's Job Opportunities for Health and Science Majors

Peterson's
Princeton Pke. Corporate Ctr., 2000 Lenox Dr.
PO Box 67005
Lawrenceville, NJ 08648
Ph: (609)896-1800   Fax: (609)896-4531
Fr: 800-338-3282
URL: http://www.petersons.com

Irregular; latest edition 1999. Covers about 1,300 research, consulting, government, and non-profit and profit service organizations that hire college and university graduates in science and health-related majors. Entries include: Organization name, address, phone, name and title of contact, type of organization, number of employees, Standard Industrial Classification (SIC) code; description of opportunities available including disciplines, level of education required, starting locations and salaries, level of experience accepted, benefits.

HANDBOOKS AND MANUALS

★6111★ Being a Long-Term Care Nursing Assistant

Prentice Hall PTR
1 Lake St.
Upper Saddle River, NJ 07458
Ph: (201)236-7000   Fax: 800-445-6991
Fr: 800-428-5331
URL: http://www.phptr.com/index.asp?rl=1

Connie A. Will-Black and Judith B. Eighmy. Fifth edition, 2002. $62.20 (paper). 534 pages.

★6112★ Being a Nursing Assistant

Prentice Hall PTR
1 Lake St.
Upper Saddle River, NJ 07458
Ph: (201)236-7000   Fax: 800-445-6991
Fr: 800-428-5331
URL: http://www.phptr.com/index.asp?rl=1

Francie Wolgin. Ninth edition, 2004. $60.80 (paper). 800 pages.

★6113★ Careers for Caring People and Other Sensitive Types

The McGraw-Hill Companies
PO Box 182604
Columbus, OH 43272
Fax: (614)759-3749   Fr: 877-883-5524
E-mail: customer.service@mcgraw-hill.com
URL: http://www.mcgraw-hill.com

Adrian Paradis. Second edition, 2003. $13.95 (paper). 208 pages.

★6114★ Careers in Health Care

The McGraw-Hill Companies
PO Box 182604
Columbus, OH 43272
Fax: (614)759-3749   Fr: 877-883-5524
E-mail: customer.service@mcgraw-hill.com
URL: http://www.mcgraw-hill.com

Barbara M. Swanson. Fifth edition, 2005. $15.95 (paper). 192 pages. Describes job duties, work settings, salaries, licensing and certification requirements, educational preparation, and future outlook. Gives ideas on how to secure a job.

★6115★ Core Curriculum for the Licensed Practical/Vocational Hospice and Palliative Nurse

Kendall/Hunt Publishing Company
4050 Westmark Dr.
Dubuque, IA 52004
Ph: (563)589-1000   Fax: (563)589-1046
Fr: 800-228-0810
URL: http://www.kendallhunt.com/

Hospice & Palliative Nurses Association. 2005. $55.00.

★6116★ The Long-Term Care Nursing Assistant Training Manual

Health Professions Press
PO Box 10624
Baltimore, MD 21285-0624
Ph: (410)337-9585   Fax: (410)337-8539
Fr: 888-337-8808
E-mail: custserv@healthpropress.com
URL: http://www.healthpropress.com/

Mary A. Anderson, Karen W. Beaver and Kathleen R. Culliton, editors. Second edition, 1996. $29.95 (paper). 316 pages.

★6117★ The Nurses' Career Guide: Discovering New Horizons in Health Care

Sovereignty Press
1241 Johnson Ave., No. 353
San Luis Obispo, CA 93401
Ph: (805)543-6100   Fax: (805)543-1085
Fr: 888-201-2501

Zardoya E. Eagles and Marti Kock. 1999. $17.95 (paper). 118 pages. Helps the reader identify work skills and achievements, clarify values and goals, explore career options, develop a personal action plan, prepare cover letters and resumes, and conduct informational and job interviews. Also addresses the dramatic changes that nurses currently face in the workplace. Includes a 65-page resource section which lists references, samples of resumes and letters, professional magazines, organizations, and online resources.

★6118★ Nursing Today: Transition and Trends

W. B. Saunders Co.
6277 Sea Harbor Dr.
Orlando, FL 32887
Fr: 800-654-2452
URL: http://www.elsevier.com

JoAnn Zerwekh and Jo C. Claborn, editors. Fifth edition, 2005. $47.95 (paper). 688 pages.

★6119★ Opportunities in Health and Medical Careers

The McGraw-Hill Companies
PO Box 182604
Columbus, OH 43272
Fax: (614)759-3749   Fr: 877-883-5524
E-mail: customer.service@mcgraw-hill.com
URL: http://www.mcgraw-hill.com

I. Donald Snook, Jr. and Leo D'Orazio. 2004. $13.95 (paper). 157 pages. Covers the full

range of medical and health occupations. Illustrated.

★6120★ Opportunities in Homecare Services Careers

The McGraw-Hill Companies
PO Box 182604
Columbus, OH 43272
Fax: (614)759-3749   Fr: 877-883-5524
E-mail: customer.service@mcgraw-hill.com
URL: http://www.mcgraw-hill.com

Anna deSola Cardoza. 1994. $14.95; $11.95 (paper). 150 pages. Professional child care careers, including various types of therapy and post-intensive surgery assistance.

★6121★ Opportunities in Mental Health Careers

The McGraw-Hill Companies
PO Box 182604
Columbus, OH 43272
Fax: (614)759-3749   Fr: 877-883-5524
E-mail: customer.service@mcgraw-hill.com
URL: http://www.mcgraw-hill.com

Philip A. Perry. 1996. $14.95; $11.95 (paper) 160 pages. Part of the "Opportunities in ..." Series.

★6122★ Real People Working in Health Care

The McGraw-Hill Companies
PO Box 182604
Columbus, OH 43272
Fax: (614)759-3749   Fr: 877-883-5524
E-mail: customer.service@mcgraw-hill.com
URL: http://www.mcgraw-hill.com

Blythe Camenson, Jan Goldberg. 1996. $12.95 (paper). 144 pages. Interviews and profiles of working professionals capture a range of opportunities in this field.

★6123★ Real People Working in the Helping Professions

The McGraw-Hill Companies
PO Box 182604
Columbus, OH 43272
Fax: (614)759-3749   Fr: 877-883-5524
E-mail: customer.service@mcgraw-hill.com
URL: http://www.mcgraw-hill.com

Blythe Camenson, Jan Goldberg. 1997. $12.95 (paper). 192 pages. Interviews and profiles of working professionals capture a range of opportunities in this field.

★6124★ Reinventing Your Nursing Career: A Handbook for Success in the Age of Managed Care

Aspen Publishers
1 Lake St.
Upper Saddle River, NJ 07458
Ph: (201)236-7000   Fax: 800-445-6991
Fr: 800-638-8437
URL: http://www.aspenpublishers.com/

Michael Newell and Mario Pinardo. 1998. $53.95 (paper). 253 pages. Helps nurses identify career goals and take practical steps to realize them using self-surveys, goal-setting methods, personal action plans, and networking techniques.

★6125★ Resumes for Health and Medical Careers

The McGraw-Hill Companies
PO Box 182604
Columbus, OH 43272
Fax: (614)759-3749   Fr: 877-883-5524
E-mail: customer.service@mcgraw-hill.com
URL: http://www.mcgraw-hill.com

Third edition, 2003. $11.95 (paper). 160 pages.

EMPLOYMENT AGENCIES AND SEARCH FIRMS

★6126★ Boone-Scaturro Associates Inc.

8831 S. Somerset Lane
Alpharetta, GA 30004
Ph: (770)740-9737   Fax: (770)475-5055
Fr: 800-749-1884
E-mail: mes@boone-scaturro.com
URL: http://www.boone-scaturro.com

Executive search firm focused on the healthcare industry.

★6127★ Medical Personnel Services, Inc.

1748 N St., NW
Washington, DC 20036
Ph: (202)466-2955   Fax: (202)452-1818
E-mail: jobs@medicalpersonnel.com
URL: http://www.medicalpersonnel.com

Employment agency specializing in permanent health/medical placements.

★6128★ Professional Placement Associates, Inc.

287 Bowman Ave., Ste. 309
Purchase, NY 10577-2517
Ph: (914)251-1000   Fax: (914)251-1055
E-mail: careers@ppasearch.com
URL: http://www.ppasearch.com

Executive search firm specializing in the health and medical field.

ONLINE JOB SOURCES AND SERVICES

★6129★ HealthCareerWeb

URL: http://www.healthcareerweb.com/

Description: Advertises jobs for healthcare professionals. **Main files include:** Jobs, Employers, Resumes, Jobwire. Relocation tools and career guidance resources available.

★6130★ Medhunters.com

Fr: 800-664-0278
E-mail: info@medhunters.com
URL: http://www.medhunters.com

Description: Career search site for jobs in all health care specialties; educational resources; visa and licensing information for relocation; interesting articles; relocation tools; links to professional organizations and general resources.

★6131★ ProHealthJobs

Fr: 800-796-1738
E-mail: Info@prohealthedujobs.com
URL: http://www.prohealthjobs.com

Description: Career resources site for the medical and health care field. Lists professional opportunities, product information, continuing education and open positions.

TRADESHOWS

★6132★ HOMECARExpo

National Association for Home Care
228 7th St. SE
Washington, DC 20003
Ph: (202)547-7424   Fax: (202)547-3540
URL: http://www.nahc.org

Annual. **Primary Exhibits:** General home health products, emergency response systems, computers, uniforms, publications, surgical and medical supplies, pharmaceuticals, durable and home medical equipment.

OTHER SOURCES

★6133★ American Assembly for Men in Nursing (AAMN)

PO Box 130220
Birmingham, AL 35213
Ph: (205)802-7551   Fax: (205)802-7553
E-mail: aamn@aamn.org
URL: http://aamn.org

Members: Registered nurses. **Purpose:** Works to: help eliminate prejudice in nursing; interest men in the nursing profession; provide opportunities for the discussion of common problems; encourage education and promote further professional growth; advise and assist in areas of professional inequity; help develop sensitivities to various social needs; promote the principles and practices of positive health care. **Activities:** Acts as a clearinghouse for information on men in nursing. Conducts educational programs. Promotes education and research about men's health issues.

★6134★ American Health Care Association (AHCA)

1201 L St. NW
Washington, DC 20005
Ph: (202)842-4444   Fax: (202)842-3860
E-mail: hr@ahca.org
URL: http://www.ahca.org

Description: Federation of state associations of long-term health care facilities. Promotes standards for professionals in long-term health care delivery and quality care for patients and residents in a safe environment. Focuses on issues of availability, quality, affordability, and fair payment. Operates as liaison with governmental agencies, Congress, and professional associations. Compiles statistics.

★6135★ Exploring Health Occupations

Cambridge Educational
PO Box 2053
Princeton, NJ 08543-2053
Ph: 800-257-5126   Fax: (609)671-0266
Fr: 800-468-4227
E-mail: custserv@films.com
URL: http://www.cambridgeeducational.com

VHS and DVD. $159.90. 1999. Two-part series provides a detailed view of the field of medical technicians and technologists, EMTs, nurses, therapists, and assistants.

★6136★ Health Service Occupations

Delphi Productions
3159 6th St.
Boulder, CO 80304
Ph: (303)443-2100   Fax: (303)443-4022
Fr: 888-443-2400
E-mail: support@delphivideo.com
URL: http://www.delphivideo.com

$95.00. 50 minutes. Part of the Careers for the 21st Century Video Library.

★6137★ Medicine & Related Occupations

Delphi Productions
3159 6th St.
Boulder, CO 80304
Ph: (303)443-2100   Fax: (303)443-4022
Fr: 888-443-2400
E-mail: support@delphivideo.com
URL: http://www.delphivideo.com

$95.00. 45 minutes. Part of the Careers for the 21st Century Video Library.

★6138★ National Association of Professional Geriatric Care Managers (GCM)

1604 N Country Club Rd.
Tucson, AZ 85716
Ph: (520)881-8008   Fax: (520)325-7925
E-mail: kboothroyd@kellencompany.com
URL: http://www.caremanager.org

Description: Promotes quality services and care for elderly citizens. Provides referral service and distributes information to individuals interested in geriatric care management. Maintains referral network.

★6139★ National League for Nursing (NLN)

61 Broadway, 33rd Fl.
New York, NY 10006
Ph: (212)363-5555   Fax: (212)812-0393
Fr: 800-669-1656
E-mail: generalinfo@nln.org
URL: http://www.nln.org

Description: Champions the pursuit of quality nursing education. A professional association of nursing faculty, education agencies, health care agencies, allied/public agencies, and public members whose mission is to advance quality nursing education that prepares the nursing workforce to meet the needs of diverse populations in an ever-changing health care environment. Serves as the primary source of information about every type of nursing education program, from the LVN and LPN to the EdD and PhD. There are 20 affiliated constituent leagues that provide a local forum for members. The National League for Nursing Accrediting Commission is an independent corporate affiliate of the NLN, responsible for providing accreditation services to all levels of nursing education.

★6140★ National Rural Health Association (NRHA)

Administrative Office
521 E 63rd St.
Kansas City, MO 64110-3329
Ph: (816)756-3140   Fax: (816)756-3144
E-mail: mail@nrharural.org
URL: http://www.nrharural.org

Description: Administrators, physicians, nurses, physician assistants, health planners, academicians, and others interested or involved in rural health care. Creates a better understanding of health care problems unique to rural areas; utilizes a collective approach in finding positive solutions; articulates and represents the health care needs of rural America; supplies current information to rural health care providers; serves as a liaison between rural health care programs throughout the country. Offers continuing education credits for medical, dental, nursing, and management courses.

★6141★ Visiting Nurse Associations of America (VNAA)

Administration Office
99 Summer St., Ste. 1700
Boston, MA 02110
Ph: (617)737-3200   Fax: (617)737-1144
Fr: 800-426-2547
E-mail: vnaa@vnaa.org
URL: http://www.vnaa.org

Members: Home health care agencies. **Purpose:** Develops competitive strength among community-based nonprofit visiting nurse organizations; works to strengthen business resources and economic programs through contracting, marketing, governmental affairs and publications.

Hotel Managers and Assistants

SOURCES OF HELP-WANTED ADS

★6142★ Hotel F & B Executive
Hotel Forums LLC
5455 N Sheridan Rd., Ste. 2802
Chicago, IL 60640
Ph: (773)728-4995   Fax: (773)728-4996
URL: http://www.hfbexecutive.com/

Bimonthly. $49.00/year for individuals; $25.00/year for students; $76.00/year for institutions. Magazine that addresses the needs of the hospitality F&B markets, which include hotels, resorts, cruise lines and conference, and convention & meeting centers.

★6143★ Hotel & Motel Management
Questex Media Group
275 Grove St., 2-130
Newton, MA 02466
Ph: (617)219-8300   Fax: (617)219-8310
Fr: 888-552-4346
URL: http://www.hotelmotel.com

$53.50/year for individuals; $74.00/year for individuals, Canada and Mexico; $130.00/year for individuals, all other countries; $75.00/year for individuals, all other countries. Free to qualified subscribers. Magazine covering the global lodging industry.

★6144★ HOTELS
Reed Business Information
360 Park Ave. S
New York, NY 10010
Ph: (646)746-6400   Fax: (646)746-7431
URL: http://www.reedbusiness.com/

Monthly. Free. Magazine covering management and operations as well as foodservice and design in the hospitality industry.

★6145★ Lodging Hospitality
Penton Media Inc.
1300 E 9th St.
Cleveland, OH 44114
Ph: (216)696-7000   Fax: (216)696-1752

URL: http://www.lhonline.com

Monthly. Free to qualified subscribers. Magazine serving managers of independent, franchise, chain-owned, and referral groups in the hospitality industry.

★6146★ Restaurants & Institutions
Reed Business Information
360 Park Ave. S
New York, NY 10010
Ph: (646)746-6400   Fax: (646)746-7431
URL: http://www.reedbusiness.com/

Semimonthly. Free. Magazine focusing on foodservice and lodging management.

PLACEMENT AND JOB REFERRAL SERVICES

★6147★ Association for Convention Operations Management (ACOM)
191 Clarksville Rd.
Princeton Junction, NJ 08550
Ph: (609)799-3712   Fax: (609)799-7032
E-mail: info@acomonline.org
URL: http://www.acomonline.org

Description: Convention service directors and managers of hotels, convention centers, and convention bureaus; suppliers of services and products to the convention and meetings industry are affiliate members. Works to increase the effectiveness, productivity, and quality of meetings, conventions, and exhibitions. Works to establish high ethical standards, improve professional management techniques, and increase awareness of client, employer, and provider needs. Maintains speakers' bureau, resource center, and placement services; compiles statistics. Conducts research and educational programs.

EMPLOYER DIRECTORIES AND NETWORKING LISTS

★6148★ Career Opportunities in Casinos and Casino Hotels
Facts On File Inc.
132 W 31st St., 17th Fl.
New York, NY 10001
Ph: (212)967-8800   Fax: 800-678-3633
Fr: 800-322-8755
URL: http://www.factsonfile.com

Irregular; Latest edition 2000. $49.50 for individuals; $44.55 for libraries. Publication includes: A directory of casinos and cruise lines, gaming conferences and expos, seminars, workshops, and industry Web sites. Principal content of publication consists of information on 100 occupations in 10 employment sections regarding careers in gaming, administration, management, security, entertainment, hotel management, and food and beverage service in the casino industry.

★6149★ Official Hotel Guide
Northstar Travel Media L.L.C.
100 Lighting Way, 2nd Fl.
Secaucus, NJ 07094
Ph: (201)902-2000   Fax: (201)902-2045
Fr: 800-446-6551
URL: http://www.northstartravelmedia.com/

Annual. Covers, in four volumes, 29,000 hotels, motels, and resorts worldwide. Volume 1 covers most of the U.S.; Volume 2 covers the rest of the U.S. and the Western Hemisphere; Volume 3 covers Europe, the Middle East, Asia, and Africa. Volume 4, specialty travel guide, includes listings of golf resorts and tennis resorts; health spas, dude ranches, bed and breakfasts, and casino and hotels in the United States; also includes lists of hotels in the Caribbean with golf facilities, tennis facilities, casinos, and all-inclusive offers. Entries include: Hotel/motel/resort name, address, phone, fax, CRS's, number of rooms or units, rates, brief description of facilities, ratings, codes indicating credit cards accepted, email and website addresses, and travel agent's commission, if any. Arrangement: Geographical.

★6150★ **Peterson's Job Opportunities for Business Majors**

Peterson's
Princeton Pke. Corporate Ctr., 2000 Lenox Dr.
PO Box 67005
Lawrenceville, NJ 08648
Ph: (609)896-1800   Fax: (609)896-4531
Fr: 800-338-3282
URL: http://www.petersons.com/

Irregular; latest edition 16th, 2000. Covers the 2,000 largest U.S. employers hiring in several fields, including financial services, management consulting, consumer products, and media/entertainment. Entries include: Organization name, address, phone, name and title of contact, number of employees, type of organization. Arrangement: Alphabetical. Indexes: Type of organization.

HANDBOOKS AND MANUALS

★6151★ **Best Impressions in Hospitality: Your Professional Image for Excellence**

Cengage Learning
PO Box 6904
Florence, KY 41022
Fax: 800-487-8488   Fr: 800-354-9706
URL: http://www.cengage.com

Angie Michael. 1999. $63.95 (paper). 240 pages.

★6152★ **Career Opportunities in Travel and Tourism**

Facts On File Inc.
132 W. 31st St., 17th Fl.
New York, NY 10001-2006
Ph: (212)967-8800   Fax: 800-678-3633
Fr: 800-322-8755
E-mail: custserv@factsonfile.com
URL: http://www.factsonfile.com

John K. Hawks. 1996. $18.95 (paper). 224 pages. Includes detailed job descriptions, educational requirements, salary ranges, and advancement prospects for 70 different job opportunities in this fast-paced industry. Contains index and bibliography.

★6153★ **Careers for Night Owls and Other Insomniacs**

The McGraw-Hill Companies
PO Box 182604
Columbus, OH 43272
Fax: (614)759-3749   Fr: 877-883-5524
E-mail: customer.service@mcgraw-hill.com
URL: http://www.mcgraw-hill.com

Louise Miller. Second edition, 2002. $12.95 (paper). 160 pages.

★6154★ **Careers in Travel, Tourism, and Hospitality**

The McGraw-Hill Companies
PO Box 182604
Columbus, OH 43272
Fax: (614)759-3749   Fr: 877-883-5524
E-mail: customer.service@mcgraw-hill.com
URL: http://www.mcgraw-hill.com

Marjorie Eberts, Linda Brothers, and Ann Gisler. Second edition, 2005. $15.95 (paper). 224 pages.

★6155★ **Hospitality and Tourism Careers: A Blueprint for Success**

The McGraw-Hill Companies
PO Box 182604
Columbus, OH 43272
Fax: (614)759-3749   Fr: 877-883-5524
E-mail: customer.service@mcgraw-hill.com
URL: http://www.mcgraw-hill.com

Melissa Dallas and Carl Riegel. Second edition, 1997. $57.00 (paper). 252 pages.

★6156★ **How to Get a Job with a Cruise Line**

Ticket to Adventure, Inc.
PO Box 41005
St. Petersburg, FL 33743-1005
Ph: (727)822-5029   Fax: (727)821-3409
Fr: 800-929-7447

Mary Fallon Miller. Fifth edition, 2001. $16.95 (paper). 352 pages. Explores jobs with cruise ships, describing duties, responsibilities, benefits, and training. Lists cruise ship lines and schools offering cruise line training. Offers job hunting advice.

★6157★ **Opportunities in Hotel and Motel Careers**

The McGraw-Hill Companies
PO Box 182604
Columbus, OH 43272
Fax: (614)759-3749   Fr: 877-883-5524
E-mail: customer.service@mcgraw-hill.com
URL: http://www.mcgraw-hill.com

Shepard Henkin. 2006. $13.95 (paper). 160 pages.

★6158★ **Opportunities in Travel Careers**

The McGraw-Hill Companies
PO Box 182604
Columbus, OH 43272
Fax: (614)759-3749   Fr: 877-883-5524
E-mail: customer.service@mcgraw-hill.com
URL: http://www.mcgraw-hill.com

Robert Scott Milne. Second edition, 2003. $14.95 (paper). 141 pages. Discusses what the jobs are and where to find them in airlines, shipping lines, and railroads. Discusses related opportunities in hotels, motels, resorts, travel agencies, public relation firms, and recreation departments. Illustrated.

★6159★ **Purchasing for Chefs: A Concise Guide**

John Wiley & Sons, Inc.
111 River St.
Hoboken, NJ 07030
Ph: (201)748-6000   Fax: (201)748-6088
E-mail: info@wiley.com
URL: http://www.wiley.com/WileyCDA/

Andrew H. Feinstein and John M. Stefanelli. 2006. $45.00. Guide details purchasing principles to chefs and hospitality managers for obtaining goods and services for their business.

★6160★ **Quality Service: What Every Hospitality Manager Needs to Know**

Prentice Hall, PTR
One Lake St.
Upper Saddle River, NJ 07458
Ph: (201)236-7000   Fr: 800-428-5331
URL: http://www.phptr.com/index.asp?rl=1

Martin. 2002. $52.00. 202 pages.

★6161★ **Real-Resumes for Restaurant Food Service and Hotel Jobs: Including Real Resumes Used to Change Careers and Transfer Skills to Other Industries**

PREP Publishing
1110 1/2 Hay St., PMB 66
Fayetteville, NC 28305
Ph: (910)483-2439   Fax: (910)483-2439
Fr: 800-533-2814

Anne McKinney. September 2002. $16.95. Real-Resumes Series. 181 pages.

★6162★ **So-You Want to Be an Innkeeper**

Chronicle Books LLC
680 Second St.
San Francisco, CA 94107
Ph: (415)537-4200   Fax: (415)537-4460
Fr: 800-722-6657
E-mail: frontdesk@chroniclebooks.com
URL: http://www.chroniclebooks.com

Jo Ann M. Bell, Susan Brown, Mary Davies, and Pat Hardy, et al. Fourth edition, 2004. $16.95 (paper). 336 pages.

★6163★ **Working in Hotels and Catering**

Cengage Learning
PO Box 6904
Florence, KY 41022
Fax: 800-487-8488   Fr: 800-354-9706
URL: http://www.cengage.com

Roy Woods. Second edition, 1997. $46.99 (paper). 252 pages.

★6164★ **Working in Hotels and Catering: How to Find Great Employment Opportunities Worldwide**

Trans-Atlantic Publications, Inc.
311 Bainbridge St.
Philadelphia, PA 19147
Ph: (215)925-5083   Fax: (215)925-1912

E-mail: jeffgolds@comcast.net
URL: http://www.transatlanticpub.com/

Mark Hempshell. 1997. $19.95 (paper). Part of the Jobs and Careers Series. 174 pages.

EMPLOYMENT AGENCIES AND SEARCH FIRMS

★6165★ The Alfus Group Inc.
353 Lexington Ave., Fl. 8
New York, NY 10016
Ph: (212)599-1000   Fax: (212)599-1523
E-mail: mail@thealfusgroup.com
URL: http://www.thealfusgroup.com

Executive search firm. Specializes in the hospitality industry.

★6166★ Bowman & Associates
1660 S Amphlett Blvd., Ste. 245
San Mateo, CA 94402
Ph: (650)573-0188   Fax: (650)573-8209
E-mail: contact@bowmansearch.com
URL: http://www.bowmansearch.com

Executive search firm specializes in the hospitality industry.

★6167★ ChaseAmerica Inc.
6231 PGA Blvd., Ste. 104
Palm Beach Gardens, FL 33418
Ph: (561)491-5000   Fax: (561)491-5001
E-mail: davidstefanjr@chaseamericainc
URL: http://www.chaseamericainc.com

Executive search firm.

★6168★ Classic Consultants Inc.
8051 N. Tamiami Trail
Sarasota, FL 34243
Ph: (941)351-3500   Fax: (941)351-8156
Fr: 800-949-6107
E-mail: cci3513500@aol.com
URL: http://www.classicconsultants.com

Executive search firm.

★6169★ Dixie Search Associates
670 Village Trace, Bldg. 19, Ste. D
Marietta, GA 30067
Ph: (770)850-0250   Fax: (770)850-9295
E-mail: dsa@dixiesearch.com
URL: http://www.dixiesearch.com

Recruiting firm specializing exclusively in all segments of the food, beverage and hospitality industries both domestically and internationally.

★6170★ Eastman & Beaudine Inc.
7201 Bishop Rd., Ste. 220
Plano, TX 75024
Ph: (972)312-1012   Fax: (972)312-1020
URL: http://www.eastman-beaudine.com/

Executive search firm. Second location in Alpharetta, GA.

★6171★ The Elliot Group LLC
505 White Plains Rd., Ste. 228
Tarrytown, NY 10591
Ph: (914)631-4904   Fax: (914)631-6481
URL: http://www.theelliotgroup.com

Executive search firm. Six locations throughout the United States.

★6172★ Employment Advisors
815 Nicollet Mall
Minneapolis, MN 55402
Ph: (612)339-0521

Employment agency. Places candidates in variety of fields.

★6173★ Harper Associates
3100 NW Hwy., Ste. 240
Farmington Hills, MI 48334
Ph: (248)932-1170   Fax: (248)932-1214
E-mail: info@harperjobs.com
URL: http://www.harperjobs.com

Executive search firm and employment agency.

★6174★ Hospitality International
23 W 73rd St., Ste.100
New York, NY 10023
Ph: (212)769-8800   Fax: (212)769-2138
E-mail: jar@hospitalityinternational.com
URL: http://www.hospitalityinternational.com

Executive search firm. Branch office in New York, NY.

★6175★ The IMC Group of Companies Ltd.
120 White Plains Rd., Ste. 405
Tarrytown, NY 10591
Ph: (914)468-7050   Fax: (914)468-7051
E-mail: herbert.regehly@the-imc.com
URL: http://www.the-imc.com

International executive recruiting and management consulting company providing leading-edge services for the hospitality, leisure, entertainment, gaming and new media industries throughout the United States, Europe, Africa, Asia Pacific and Latin America.

★6176★ J.D. Hersey and Associates
8 E. Poplar Ave.
Columbus, OH 43215
Ph: (614)228-4022   Fax: (614)228-4085
E-mail: requests@jdhersey.com
URL: http://www.jdhersey.com

Executive search firm for permanent and contingency placements.

★6177★ The Personnel Network, Inc.
1246 Lake Murray Blvd.
PO Box 1426
Irmo, SC 29063
Ph: (803)781-2087   Fax: (803)732-7986
E-mail: chuckirmo@aol.com

Executive search firm.

★6178★ Ritt-Ritt and Associates, Inc.
5105 Tollview Dr., Ste. 110
Rolling Meadows, IL 60008
Ph: (847)483-9330   Fax: (847)483-9331
E-mail: info@rittsearch.com

Food service and hospitality employment agency and executive search firm.

★6179★ Robert Howe and Associates
35 Glenlake Pky. NE
Atlanta, GA 30328
Ph: (770)390-0030   Fax: (770)270-1209

Provides consulting services in the area of executive search and recruitment. Industries served: healthcare, hospitality, chemical, metals, electronics, construction, and food processing.

★6180★ Robert W. Dingman Company Inc.
650 Hampshire Rd., Ste. 116
Westlake Village, CA 91361
Ph: (805)778-1777   Fax: (805)778-9288
E-mail: info@dingman.com
URL: http://www.dingman.com

Executive search firm with a second office in Black Forest, CO.

★6181★ Travel People Personnel
1199 Park Ave., Ste. 3E
New York, NY 10128-1762
Ph: (212)348-6942   Fax: (617)542-0070
E-mail: sue@travelpeople.com
URL: http://www.travelpeople.com

Provides temporary and regular placement to travel related companies. Industries served: travel and hospitality.

ONLINE JOB SOURCES AND SERVICES

★6182★ Bristol Associates, Inc.
5757 W. Century Blvd., Ste. 62B
Los Angeles, CA 90045
Ph: (310)670-0525   Fax: (310)670-4075
E-mail: lstern@bristolassoc.com
URL: http://www.bristolassoc.com

Description: Executive search firm specializing in direct marketing, hospitality and food industries. Applicants can post their resumes online for recruiters' viewing and search current job databank. Also contains job tools and resources.

★6183★ Hotel Jobs Network

10019 Reisterstown Rd.
Owings Mills, MD 21117
Ph: (410)342-8630
E-mail: info@hoteljobsnetwork.com
URL: http://www.hoteljobsnetwork.com

Online job site for the hospitality industry.

TRADESHOWS

★6184★ American Hotel and Motel Association Annual Conference and Leadership Forum

American Hotel and Lodging Association
1201 New York Ave. NW, Ste. 600
Washington, DC 20005-3931
Ph: (202)289-3100   Fax: (202)289-3199
E-mail: info@ahla.com
URL: http://www.ahma.com

Annual. **Primary Exhibits:** Hotel and motel supplies and equipment.

★6185★ Annual Hotel, Motel, and Restaurant Supply Show of the Southeast

Leisure Time Unlimited, Inc.
708 Main St.
PO Box 332
Myrtle Beach, SC 29577
Ph: (843)448-9483   Fax: (843)626-1513
Fr: 800-261-5591
E-mail: dickensshow@sc.rr.com

Annual. **Primary Exhibits:** Carpeting, furniture, coffee makers, produce companies, wine and beer and food companies, and services to motels, hotels, and restaurants.

★6186★ Florida Restaurant Association - International U.S. Foodservice Expo

Florida Restaurant Association
230 S Adams St.
Tallahassee, FL 32301
Ph: (850)224-2250   Fax: (850)224-9213
Fr: 888-372-9119
URL: http://www.flra.com

Annual. **Primary Exhibits:** Products and services pertaining to the foodservice/hospitality industry.

★6187★ Hospitality Design

VNU Expositions
14685 Avion Pkwy., Ste. 400
Chantilly, VA 20151
Ph: (703)488-2700   Fax: (703)488-2800
Fr: 800-765-7615
URL: http://www.vnuexpo.com

Annual. **Primary Exhibits:** Hospitality industry equipment, supplies, and services.

★6188★ IH/M & RS - International Hotel/Motel & Restaurant Show

George Little Management, LLC (New York)
10 Bank St.
White Plains, NY 10606-1954
Ph: (914)421-3200   Fax: (914)948-6180
Fr: 800-272-SHOW
E-mail: cathy_steel@glmshows.com
URL: http://www.glmshows.com

Annual. **Primary Exhibits:** Products and services for lodging and food serving properties, including: technology, uniforms, linens and bedding, tabletop accessories, guest amenities and services, food and beverages, cleaning maintenance, foodservice equipment and supplies, franchising information, finance and management furnishings and fixtures, fitness equipment, and leisure and entertainment services.

★6189★ Mid-Atlantic Food, Beverage & Lodging Expo

Restaurant Association of Maryland, Inc.
6301 Hillside Court
Columbia, MD 21046
Ph: (410)290-6800   Fax: (410)290-6882
Fr: 800-874-1313
E-mail: kwhitting-ton@marylandrestaurants.com
URL: http://www.midatlanticexpo.com

Annual. **Primary Exhibits:** Food, equipment, beverages, and related services for the hospitality industry.

★6190★ Upper Midwest Hospitality, Restaurant, and Lodging Show - UP Show

Hospitality Minnesota - Minnesota's Restaurant, Hotel, and Resort Associations
305 E Roselawn Ave.
St. Paul, MN 55117-2031
Ph: (651)778-2400   Fax: (651)778-2424
E-mail: info@hospitalitymn.com
URL: http://www.hospitalitymn.com

Annual. **Primary Exhibits:** Food, beverages, hospitality business services, lodging supplies, and foodservice equipment.

★6191★ Virginia Travel Conference and Hospitality Expo

Virginia Hospitality and Travel Association
2101 Libbie Ave.
Richmond, VA 23230-2621
Ph: (804)288-3065   Fax: (804)285-3093
Fr: 800-552-2225
URL: http://www.vhta.org

Annual. **Primary Exhibits:** Products and services geared toward restaurant/foodservice; lodging and travel attraction industries.

★6192★ Washington Restaurant and Hospitality Show

TJS Productions
6017 Tower Ct.
Alexandria, VA 22304
Ph: (703)823-7960   Fax: (703)823-1515

E-mail: tjsevents@aol.com
URL: http://www.tjsproductions.com

Annual. **Primary Exhibits:** Food equipment, food products, and related products and services for the food service, hospitality, and hotel industries.

★6193★ West Ex: The Rocky Mountain Regional Hospitality Exposition

Colorado Restaurant Association
430 E. 7th Ave.
Denver, CO 80203
Ph: (303)830-2972   Fax: (303)830-2973
Fr: 800-522-2972
E-mail: info@coloradorestaurant.com
URL: http://www.coloradorestaurant.com

Annual. **Primary Exhibits:** Food service and lodging products, equipment, and services.

★6194★ Western Food Service & Hospitality Expo Los Angeles

California Restaurant Association
1011 10th St.
Sacramento, CA 95814
Ph: (916)447-5793   Fax: (916)447-6182
Fr: 800-765-4842
URL: http://www.calrest.org

Primary Exhibits: Food, equipment, supplies, and services for foodservice and lodging industries.

OTHER SOURCES

★6195★ Administration and Management Occupations

Delphi Productions
3159 6th St.
Boulder, CO 80304
Ph: (303)443-2100   Fax: (303)443-4022
Fr: 888-443-2400
E-mail: support@delphivideo.com
URL: http://www.delphivideo.com

$95.00. 50 minutes. Part of the Careers for the 21st Century Video Library.

★6196★ American Almanac of Jobs and Salaries

HarperCollins
10 E. 53rd St.
New York, NY 10022
Ph: (212)207-7000   Fr: 800-242-7737
URL: http://www.harpercollins.com/

John W. Wright. Revised edition, 2000. $20.00 (paper). 672 pages. This is a comprehensive guide to the wages of hundreds of occupations in a wide variety of industries and organizations.

★6197★ American Hotel and Lodging Association (AH&LA)

1201 New York Ave. NW, No. 600
Washington, DC 20005-3931
Ph: (202)289-3100   Fax: (202)289-3199

E-mail: info@ahla.com
URL: http://www.ahla.com

Description: Represents state lodging associations throughout the United States with some 13,000 property members worldwide, representing more than 1.7 million guest rooms. Provides its members with assistance in operations, education and communications and lobbies on Capitol Hill to provide a business climate in which the industry can continue to prosper. Individual state associations provide representation at the state level and offer many additional cost-saving benefits.

★6198★ Association for International Practical Training (AIPT)

10400 Little Patuxent Pkwy., Ste. 250
Columbia, MD 21044-3519
Ph: (410)997-2200   Fax: (410)992-3924
E-mail: aipt@aipt.org
URL: http://www.aipt.org

Description: Providers worldwide of on-the-job training programs for students and professionals seeking international career development and life-changing experiences. Arranges workplace exchanges in hundreds of professional fields, bringing employers and trainees together from around the world. Client list ranges from small farming communities to Fortune 500 companies.

★6199★ Behind the Scenes: Hospitality/Hotels

Cambridge Educational
PO Box 2053
Princeton, NJ 08543-2053
Ph: 800-257-5126   Fax: (609)671-0266
Fr: 800-468-4227

E-mail: custserv@films.com
URL: http://www.cambridgeeducational.com
VHS and DVD. $69.95. 20 minutes. 2001
Part of the series "Behind the Scenes: Industrial Field Trips."

★6200★ Club Managers Association of America (CMAA)

1733 King St.
Alexandria, VA 22314
Ph: (703)739-9500   Fax: (703)739-0124
E-mail: cmaa@cmaa.org
URL: http://www.cmaa.org

Members: Professional managers and assistant managers of private golf, yacht, athletic, city, country, luncheon, university, and military clubs. **Purpose:** Encourages education and advancement of members and promotes efficient and successful club operations. **Activities:** Provides reprints of articles on club management. Supports courses in club management. Compiles statistics; maintains management referral service.

★6201★ International Council on Hotel, Restaurant, and Institutional Education (CHRIE)

2810 N Parham Rd., Ste. 230
Richmond, VA 23294
Ph: (804)346-4800   Fax: (804)346-5009
E-mail: kmccarty@chrie.org
URL: http://www.chrie.org

Description: Schools and colleges offering specialized education and training in hospitals, recreation, tourism and hotel, restaurant, and institutional administration; individuals, executives, and students. Provides

networking opportunities and professional development.

★6202★ International Executive Housekeepers Association (IEHA)

1001 Eastwind Dr., Ste. 301
Westerville, OH 43081-3361
Ph: (614)895-7166   Fax: (614)895-1248
Fr: 800-200-6342
E-mail: excel@ieha.org
URL: http://www.ieha.org

Description: Persons engaged in facility housekeeping management in hospitals, hotels and motels, schools, and industrial establishments. Established educational standards. Sponsors certificate and collegiate degree programs. Holds annual International Housekeepers Week celebration.

★6203★ National Association of Black Hotel Owners, Operators and Developers (NABHOOD)

3520 W Broward Blvd., Ste. 218B
Fort Lauderdale, FL 33312
Ph: (954)797-7102   Fax: (954)337-2877
E-mail: horizons@gate.net
URL: http://nabhood.com

Description: Enhances the stability and growth of the lodging industry. Aims to increase the number of African-Americans owning, developing, managing and operating hotels. Strives to create vendor opportunities and executive level jobs for minorities.

Human Services Workers

SOURCES OF HELP-WANTED ADS

★6204★ EAP Digest

Performance Resource Press Inc.
1270 Rankin Dr., Ste. F
Troy, MI 48083
Ph: (248)588-7733   Fax: (248)588-6633
URL: http://www.prponline.net/Work/EAP/eap.htm

Quarterly. $36.00/year for individuals; $82.00 for two years, Canada, Hawaii, & Alaska; $99.00 for individuals for three years, Canada, Hawaii, & Alaska; $104.00 for other countries, three years; $87.00 for other countries, two years; $54.00/year for other countries; $49.00/year for individuals, Canada, Hawaii, & Alaska; $60.00 for two years. Magazine covering planning, development, and administration of employee assistance programs.

★6205★ Journal of Career Development

Sage Publications Inc.
2455 Teller Rd.
Thousand Oaks, CA 91320
Ph: (805)499-0721   Fax: (805)499-8096
URL: http://www.sagepub.com/journal-sProdDesc.nav?prodId=Journal20

Quarterly. $94.00/year for individuals, print and online; $490.00/year for institutions, print and e-access; $441.00/year for institutions, e-access; $480.00/year for institutions, print only; $132.00 for institutions, single print; $31.00 for individuals, single print. Journal for professionals in counseling, psychology, education, student personnel, human resources, and business management.

★6206★ The Lutheran

Augsburg Fortress, Publishers
100 S 5th St., Ste. 600
PO Box 1209
Minneapolis, MN 55402-1209
Ph: (612)330-3271   Fax: (612)330-3455
Fr: 800-328-4648
E-mail: lutheran@elca.org
URL: http://www.thelutheran.org

Monthly. $15.95/year for individuals; $1.50 for single issue; $29.95 for individuals for two years; $39.95/year for individuals, 3 years. Magazine of the Evangelical Lutheran Church in America.

★6207★ The NonProfit Times

NPT Publishing Group Inc.
120 Littleton Rd., Ste. 120
Parsippany, NJ 07054-1803
Ph: (973)394-1800   Fax: (973)394-2888
E-mail: ednchief@nptimes.com
URL: http://www.nptimes.com/

Biweekly. $69.00/year for individuals, subscribe at the one year rate; $49.00/year for individuals, digital only; $100.00/year for individuals, print & digital; $122.00 for two years, (48 issues); $101.00/year for Canada and Mexico; $137.00/year for other countries, international. Trade journal serving nonprofit organizations.

PLACEMENT AND JOB REFERRAL SERVICES

★6208★ American Humanics (AH)

1100 Walnut St., Ste. 1900
Kansas City, MO 64106
Ph: (816)561-6415   Fax: (816)531-3527
Fr: 800-343-6466
E-mail: kstroup@humanics.org
URL: http://www.humanics.org

Description: Individuals, corporations, and foundations supporting AH work in preparing young people for professional leadership in youth and human service agencies. Provides leadership for co-curricular program on 71 campuses of colleges that feature specialized professional courses that lead to B.A., B.S., or M.A. degrees and prepare graduates to serve professionally with groups such as Boy Scouts of America, Boys and Girls Clubs of America, American Red Cross, Big Brothers/Big Sisters of America, Camp Fire Boys and Girls, Girl Scouts of the U.S.A., Junior Achievement, Young Men's Christian Associations of the United States of America, Young Women's Christian Association of the United States of America, and Girls, Inc., Catholic Charities United States of America, Habitat for Humanity International, National Urban League, Special Olympics, Inc., United Way of America, Volunteers of America. Sponsors field trips, workshops, and special courses; offers counseling, loan assistance, and career placement services to students; operates graduate programs in affiliation with American Humanics at Lindenwood College, Missouri Valley College, Murray State University, and University of Northern Iowa. Conducts research, compiles statistics.

★6209★ American Public Health Association (APHA)

800 I St. NW
Washington, DC 20001
Ph: (202)777-2742   Fax: (202)777-2534
E-mail: comments@apha.org
URL: http://www.apha.org

Members: Professional organization of physicians, nurses, educators, academicians, environmentalists, epidemiologists, new professionals, social workers, health administrators, optometrists, podiatrists, pharmacists, dentists, nutritionists, health planners, other community and mental health specialists, and interested consumers. **Purpose:** Seeks to protect and promote personal, mental, and environmental health. **Activities:** Services include: promulgation of standards; establishment of uniform practices and procedures; development of the etiology of communicable diseases; research in public health; exploration of medical care programs and their relationships to public health. Sponsors job placement service.

★6210★ Council for Health and Human Services Ministries, United Church of Christ (CHHSM)

700 Prospect Ave.
Cleveland, OH 44115
Fax: (216)736-2251   Fr: (866)822-8224
E-mail: sickbert@chhsm.org
URL: http://www.chhsm.org

Members: Health and human service institutions related to the United Church of Christ. **Purpose:** Seeks to study, plan, and implement a program in health and human services; assist members in developing and providing quality services and in financing institutional and non-institutional health and human service ministries; stimulate awareness of and support for these programs; inform the UCC of policies that affect the needs, problems, and conditions of patients; cooperate with interdenominational agencies and others in the field. **Activities:** Maintains placement service and hall of fame. Compiles statistics; provides specialized education programs.

EMPLOYER DIRECTORIES AND NETWORKING LISTS

★6211★ Directory of Catholic Charities USA Directories

Catholic Charities USA
1731 King St.
Alexandria, VA 22314
Ph: (703)549-1390   Fax: (703)549-1656
URL: http://www.catholiccharitiesusa.org/

Annual. $25.00 for individuals. Covers nearly 1,200 Catholic community and social service agencies. Listings include diocesan agencies and state Catholic conferences. Entries include: Organization name, address, name and title of director, phone, fax. Arrangement: Geographical by state, then classified by diocese.

★6212★ National Directory of Private Social Agencies

Croner Publications Inc.
10951 Sorrento Valley Rd., Ste. 1-D
San Diego, CA 92121-1613
Fax: 800-809-0334   Fr: 800-441-4033
URL: http://www.sdic.net/croner

$109.95 for individuals. Number of listings: Over 10,000. Entries include: Agency name, address, phone, name and title of contact, description of services. Arrangement: Geographical. Indexes: Service, agency type.

★6213★ Public Human Services Directory

American Public Human Services
Association
810 1st St. NE, Ste. 500
Washington, DC 20002
Ph: (202)682-0100   Fax: (202)289-6555
E-mail: pubs@aphsa.org
URL: http://www.aphsa.org

Annual, September. $110.00 for members; $149.00 for nonmembers. Covers federal, state, territorial, county, and major municipal public human service agencies. Entries include: Agency name, address, phone, fax, e-mail address, web site address, names of key personnel, program area. Arrangement: Geographical.

HANDBOOKS AND MANUALS

★6214★ Careers for Caring People and Other Sensitive Types

The McGraw-Hill Companies
PO Box 182604
Columbus, OH 43272
Fax: (614)759-3749   Fr: 877-883-5524
E-mail: customer.service@mcgraw-hill.com
URL: http://www.mcgraw-hill.com

Adrian Paradis. Second edition, 2003. $13.95 (paper). 208 pages.

★6215★ Careers in Counseling & Human Services

Accelerated Development
7625 Empire Dr.
Florence, KY 41042
Fr: 800-821-8312
URL: http://www.tandf.co.uk/homepages/a-dhome.html

Brooke B. Collison and Nancy J. Garfield, editors. Second edition, 1996. $32.95 (paper). 153 pages.

★6216★ Careers for Good Samaritans and Other Humanitarian Types

The McGraw-Hill Companies
PO Box 182604
Columbus, OH 43272
Fax: (614)759-3749   Fr: 877-883-5524
E-mail: customer.service@mcgraw-hill.com
URL: http://www.mcgraw-hill.com

Marjorie Eberts and Margaret Gisler. Third edition, 2006. $13.95 (paper). 160 pages. Contains hundreds of ideas for turning good work into paid work. Inventories opportunities in service organizations like the Red Cross, Goodwill, and the Salvation Army; religious groups, VISTA, the Peace Corps, and UNICEF; and agencies at all levels of the government. Part of Careers for You series.

★6217★ Careers in Health Care

The McGraw-Hill Companies
PO Box 182604
Columbus, OH 43272
Fax: (614)759-3749   Fr: 877-883-5524
E-mail: customer.service@mcgraw-hill.com
URL: http://www.mcgraw-hill.com

Barbara M. Swanson. Fifth edition, 2005. $15.95 (paper). 192 pages. Describes job duties, work settings, salaries, licensing and certification requirements, educational preparation, and future outlook. Gives ideas on how to secure a job.

★6218★ Great Jobs for Liberal Arts Majors

The McGraw-Hill Companies
PO Box 182604
Columbus, OH 43272
Fax: (614)759-3749   Fr: 877-883-5524
E-mail: customer.service@mcgraw-hill.com
URL: http://www.mcgraw-hill.com

Blythe Camenson. Second edition, 2001. $14.95 (paper). 256 pages.

★6219★ Interviewing in Health & Human Services

Wadsworth Publishing
PO Box 6904
Florence, KY 41022
Fax: 800-487-8488   Fr: 800-354-9706
URL: http://www.cengage.com

Krishna Samantrai. 1996. $19.50 (paper). 159 pages.

★6220★ Non-Profits and Education Job Finder

Planning Communications
7215 Oak Ave.
River Forest, IL 60305-1935
Ph: (708)366-5200   Fax: (708)366-5280
Fr: 888-366-5200
E-mail: info@planningcommunications.com
URL: http://jobfindersonline.com

Daniel Lauber. 1997. $32.95; $16.95 (paper). 340 pages. Covers 1600 sources. Discusses how to use sources of non-profit sector job vacancies in a number of specialties and state-by-state, including job-matching services, job hotlines, specialty periodicals with job ads, salary surveys, and directories. Covers a variety of fields from education to religion. Includes chapters on resume and cover letter preparation and interviewing.

★6221★ Opportunities in Gerontology and Aging Services Careers

The McGraw-Hill Companies
PO Box 182604
Columbus, OH 43272
Fax: (614)759-3749   Fr: 877-883-5524
E-mail: customer.service@mcgraw-hill.com
URL: http://www.mcgraw-hill.com

Ellen Williams. Second edition, 2002. $12.95 (paper). 160 pages. Covers jobs in community, health and medical programs, financial, legal, residential, travel and tourism, and counseling, and how to go after them. Includes bibliography and illustrations.

★6222★ Opportunities in Mental Health Careers

The McGraw-Hill Companies
PO Box 182604
Columbus, OH 43272
Fax: (614)759-3749   Fr: 877-883-5524
E-mail: customer.service@mcgraw-hill.com
URL: http://www.mcgraw-hill.com

Philip A. Perry. 1996. $14.95; $11.95 (paper). 160 pages. Part of the "Opportunities in ..." Series.

★6223★ Opportunities in Social Work Careers

The McGraw-Hill Companies
PO Box 182604
Columbus, OH 43272
Fax: (614)759-3749   Fr: 877-883-5524

E-mail: customer.service@mcgraw-hill.com
URL: http://www.mcgraw-hill.com

Renee Wittenberg. Second edition, 2002. 160 pages. $12.95 (paper).

★6224★ *Real-Resumes for Social Work and Counseling Jobs*
PREP Publishing
1110 1/2 Hay St., PMB 66
Fayetteville, NC 28305
Ph: (910)483-2439   Fax: (910)483-2439
Fr: 800-533-2814

Anne McKinney. April 2002. $16.95. 181 pages. Real-Resumes Series.

EMPLOYMENT AGENCIES AND SEARCH FIRMS

★6225★ Al Gates & Associates
2280A James White Blvd.
Sidney, BC, Canada V8L 1Z4
Ph: (250)656-5707   Fax: (250)654-0058
E-mail: info@cybercoaching.ca
URL: http://www.cybercoaching.ca

Specializes in executive coaching and career development. Helps organizations with ex human resource management, appraisals and human resource consulting.

TRADESHOWS

★6226★ EAPA Annual Conference
Employee Assistance Professionals
  Association
2101 Wilson Blvd., Ste. 500
Arlington, VA 22201-3062
Ph: (703)387-1000   Fax: (703)522-4585
URL: http://www.eap-association.com

Annual. **Primary Exhibits:** Exhibits geared toward persons employed full-time in the development or operation of employee assistance programs (EAPs) as administrators, consultants, or motivational counselors.

OTHER SOURCES

★6227★ Association on Higher Education and Disability (AHEAD)
107 Commerce Center Dr., Ste. 204
Huntersville, NC 28078
Ph: (704)947-7779   Fax: (704)948-7779
E-mail: ahead@ahead.org
URL: http://www.ahead.org

Description: Individuals interested in promoting the equal rights and opportunities of disabled postsecondary students, staff, faculty, and graduates. Provides an exchange of communication for those professionally involved with disabled students; collects, evaluates, and disseminates information; encourages and supports legislation for the benefit of disabled students. Conducts surveys on issues pertinent to college students with disabilities; offers resource referral system and employment exchange for positions in disability student services. Conducts research programs; compiles statistics.

★6228★ Center for the Child Care Workforce, A Project of the American Federation of Teachers Educational Foundation (CCW/AFTEF)
555 New Jersey Ave. NW
Washington, DC 20001
Ph: (202)662-8005   Fax: (202)662-8006
E-mail: ccw@aft.org
URL: http://ccw.cleverspin.com

Purpose: Purposes are: to develop innovative solutions to the child care crisis to improve salaries, working conditions, and status of child care workers; to increase public awareness about the importance of child care work and the training and skill it demands; to develop resources and create an information sharing network for child care workers nationwide. **Activities:** Gathers current information on salaries and benefits; offers consultation services. Sponsors research projects; compiles statistics; operates Speaker's Bureau. Maintains extensive file of materials on working conditions and research on child care workers.

★6229★ Child Life Council (CLC)
11820 Parklawn Dr., Ste. 240
Rockville, MD 20852-2529
Ph: (301)881-7090   Fax: (301)881-7092
Fr: 800-CLC-4515
E-mail: clcstaff@childlife.org
URL: http://www.childlife.org

Members: Professional organization representing child life personnel, patient activities

specialists, and students in the field. **Purpose:** Promotes psychological well-being and optimum development of children, adolescents, and their families in health care settings. **Activities:** Works to minimize the stress and anxiety of illness and hospitalization. Addresses professional issues such as program standards, competencies, and core curriculum. Provides resources and conducts research and educational programs. Offers a Job Bank Service listing employment openings.

★6230★ Child Welfare League of America (CWLA)
2345 Crystal Dr., Ste. 250
Arlington, VA 22202
Ph: (703)412-2400   Fax: (703)412-2401
E-mail: register@cwla.org
URL: http://www.cwla.org

Purpose: Works to improve care and services for abused, dependent, or neglected children, youth, and their families. **Activities:** Provides training and consultation; conducts research; maintains information service and develops standards for child welfare practice.

★6231★ Human Services Occupations
Delphi Productions
3159 6th St.
Boulder, CO 80304
Ph: (303)443-2100   Fax: (303)443-4022
Fr: 888-443-2400
E-mail: support@delphivideo.com
URL: http://www.delphivideo.com

$95.00. 50 minutes. Part of the Careers for the 21st Century Video Library.

★6232★ National Organization for Human Services (NOHS)
90 Madison St., Ste. 206
Denver, CO 80206
Ph: (303)320-5430   Fax: (303)322-1455
E-mail: info@nationalhumanservices.org
URL: http://www.nationalhumanservices.org

Description: Human service professionals, faculty, and students. Fosters excellence in teaching, research and curriculum planning in the human service area. Encourages and supports the development of local, state, and national human services organizations. Aids faculty and professional members in their career development. Provides a medium for cooperation and communication among members. Maintains registry of qualified consultants in human service education. Conducts professional development workshop. Operates speakers' bureau.

Image Consultants

HANDBOOKS AND MANUALS

★6233★ Careers for Fashion Plates and Other Trendsetters

The McGraw-Hill Companies
PO Box 182604
Columbus, OH 43272
Fax: (614)759-3749   Fr: 877-883-5524
E-mail: customer.service@mcgraw-hill.com
URL: http://www.mcgraw-hill.com

Lucia Mauro. Second edition, 2002. $14.95 (Hardcover); $9.95 (paper). 160 pages. Describes career opportunities in fashion, entertainment, retail, and promotion, with advice from fashion professionals.

★6234★ Careers for Film Buffs and Other Hollywood Types

The McGraw-Hill Companies
PO Box 182604
Columbus, OH 43272
Fax: (614)759-3749   Fr: 877-883-5524
E-mail: customer.service@mcgraw-hill.com
URL: http://www.mcgraw-hill.com

Jaq Greenspon. Second edition, 2003. $13.95; $9.95 (paper). 208 pages. Describes job descriptions in production, camera, sound, special effects, grips, electrical, makeup, costumes, etc.

OTHER SOURCES

★6235★ Anderson Research Center for Image and Etiquette

304 Park Ave. S., 11th Fl.
New York, NY 10010
Ph: (917)842-6675   Fax: (646)219-1447
Fr: (866)203-6670
E-mail: image2etiquette@yahoo.com
URL: http://www.image2etiquette.com

Description: Offers a full range of services to assess image and create a personal style strategy that coincides with an individual's body type, lifestyle and goals. Services are available as personalized, one-to-one consultations and coaching, or as seminars and workshops for groups of all sizes, corporate or personal.

★6236★ Association of Image Consultants International (AICI)

100 E Grand Ave., Ste. 330
Des Moines, IA 50309
Ph: (515)282-5500   Fax: (515)243-2049
E-mail: info@aici.org
URL: http://www.aici.org

Description: Personal color, style, wardrobe, and image planning consultants. Promotes quality service for clients; aids in establishing working relations between retail stores and consultants; assists community colleges in offering accredited image consulting programs; maintains standards of professionalism for members in the image consulting industry. Provides continuing education and training; maintains speakers' bureau.

★6237★ Image Industry Council International/Institute for Image Management

PO Box 190007
San Francisco, CA 94119
Ph: (415)863-2573   Fax: (415)840-0655
E-mail: marily@image360.com
URL: http://www.image360.com

Activities: Maintains speakers' bureau. Conducts educational and research programs.

★6238★ Professional Image Consulting

7633 Shore Haven Dr.
Las Vegas, NV 89128
Ph: (702)953-4772
E-mail: info@professionalimagedress.com
URL: http://www.professionalimagedress.com

Description: Provides Image Consultants to organizations throughout the United States and abroad. Offers programs, seminars, training, and consulting.

★6239★ Professional Image Management

65 Coon Rd.
Troy, NY 12180
Ph: (518)279-9388
E-mail: image3@mucap.rr.com
URL: http://www.professionalimagemgt.com

Description: Provides executive coaching in professional image.

Industrial Engineers

SOURCES OF HELP-WANTED ADS

★6240★ AIE Perspectives Newsmagazine

American Institute of Engineers
4630 Appian Way, Ste. 206
El Sobrante, CA 94803-1875
Ph: (510)758-6240   Fax: (510)758-6240

Monthly. Professional magazine covering engineering.

★6241★ Applied Occupational & Environmental Hygiene

Applied Industrial Hygiene Inc.
1330 Kemper Meadow Dr., Ste. 600
Cincinnati, OH 45240
Ph: (513)742-2020   Fax: (513)742-3355
URL: http://www.acgih.org

Monthly. $223.00/year for individuals, individual membership; $623.00/year for institutions, institution or organization. Peer-reviewed journal presenting applied solutions for the prevention of occupational and environmental disease and injury.

★6242★ AWIS Magazine

Association for Women in Science
1200 New York Ave. NW, Ste. 650
Washington, DC 20005
Ph: (202)326-8940   Fax: (202)326-8960
Fr: (866)657-2947
E-mail: awis@awis.org
URL: http://www.awis.org/

Description: Bimonthly. Covers issues, legislation, and trends related to science education for girls, women, and minorities. Includes information on grants and fellowships, job openings, educational programs, events, and notices of publications available.

★6243★ Engineering Conferences International Symposium Series

Berkeley Electronic Press
2809 Telegraph Ave., Ste. 202
Berkeley, CA 94705
Ph: (510)665-1200   Fax: (510)665-1201

URL: http://services.bepress.com/eci/
Journal focusing on advance engineering science.

★6244★ The Engineering Economist

Institute of Industrial Engineers
3577 Pkwy. Ln., Ste. 200
Norcross, GA 30092
Ph: (770)449-0460   Fax: (770)441-3295
Fr: 800-494-0460
URL: http://www.iienet2.org

Description: Quarterly. Discusses news of the Institute. Recurring features include a column titled In-Coming Director's Message. Discusses engineering economics. Articles featured have an academic slant with an emphasis on research.

★6245★ Engineering Times

National Society of Professional Engineers
1420 King St.
Alexandria, VA 22314
Ph: (703)684-2800
URL: http://www.nspe.org

Monthly. Magazine (tabloid) covering professional, legislative, and techology issues for an engineering audience.

★6246★ ENR: Engineering News-Record

McGraw-Hill Inc.
1221 Ave. of the Americas
New York, NY 10020-1095
Ph: (212)512-2000   Fax: (212)512-3840
Fr: 877-833-5524
E-mail: enr_web_editors@mcgraw-hill.com
URL: http://www.mymags.com/morein-fo.php?itemID=20012

Weekly. $94.00/year for individuals, print. Magazine focusing on engineering and construction.

★6247★ Graduating Engineer & Computer Careers

Career Recruitment Media
211 W Wacker Dr., Ste. 900
Chicago, IL 60606
Ph: (312)525-3100
URL: http://www.graduatingengineer.com

Quarterly. $15.00/year for individuals. Magazine focusing on employment, education, and career development for entry-level engineers and computer scientists.

★6248★ High Technology Careers Magazine

HTC
4701 Patrick Henry Dr., No. 1901
Santa Clara, CA 95054-1847
Fax: (408)567-0242
URL: http://www.hightechcareers.com

Bimonthly. $29.00/year; $35.00/year for Canada; $85.00/year for out of country. Magazine (tabloid) containing employment opportunity information for the engineering and technical community.

★6249★ IE News: Energy, Environment & Plant Engineering

Institute of Industrial Engineers
3577 Pkwy. Ln., Ste. 200
Norcross, GA 30092
Ph: (770)449-0460   Fax: (770)441-3295
Fr: 800-494-0460
URL: http://www.iienet2.org/

Description: Quarterly. Considers environmental and energy issues in the design and operation of plants. Features articles concerning quality standards and Institute activities.

★6250★ IE News: Ergonomics

Institute of Industrial Engineers
3577 Pkwy. Ln., Ste. 200
Norcross, GA 30092
Ph: (770)449-0460   Fax: (770)441-3295
Fr: 800-494-0460
URL: http://www.iienet2.org

Description: Quarterly. Focuses on ergonomics (human factors) in the work place, the development of ergonomic standards, and case studies. Recurring features include a calendar of events, reports of meetings, and columns titled Message from the Director, Academic Roundup: Update, and Message from the Editor.

★6251★ IIE Solutions

Institute of Industrial Engineers
3577 Parkway Ln., Ste. 200
Norcross, GA 30092
Ph: (770)449-0460   Fax: (770)441-3295
Fr: 800-494-0460
E-mail: advertising@iienet.org
URL: http://www.iienet2.org/Default.aspx

Monthly. Magazine covering industrial engineering, facilities design, systems integration, production control, material handling, quality, productivity, management, and other industrial engineering topics.

★6252★ InterJournal

New England Complex Systems Institute
24 Mt. Auburn St.
Cambridge, MA 02138
Ph: (617)547-4100   Fax: (617)661-7711
URL: http://www.interjournal.org/

Journal covering the fields of science and engineering.

★6253★ International Archives of Bioscience

International Archives of Bioscience
PO Box 737254
Elmhurst, NY 11373-9997
URL: http://www.iabs.us/jdoc/aboutiabs.htm

Free, online only. Journal reporting multidisciplinary coverage and interaction between scientists in biology, informatics, mathematics, physics, engineering and other sciences.

★6254★ Journal of Engineering Education

American Society for Engineering Education
1818 North St., NW, Ste. 600
Washington, DC 20036-2479
Ph: (202)331-3500
URL: http://www.asee.org/publications/jee/index.cfm

Quarterly. Journal covering scholarly research in engineering education.

★6255★ Managing Automation

Thomas Publishing Co.
5 Penn Plz.
New York, NY 10001
Ph: (212)695-0500   Fax: (212)290-7362
E-mail: contact@thomaspublishing.com
URL: http://www.managingautomation.com/maonline/

Monthly. $60.00/year for individuals; $8.00 for single issue; $75.00/year for Canada and Mexico; $125.00/year for other countries. Managing Automation covers advanced manufacturing technology including automation, integrated manufacturing, enterprise applications, and IT and e-business for the manufacturing enterprise.

★6256★ NSBE Magazine

NSBE Publications
205 Daingerfield Rd.
Alexandria, VA 22314
Ph: (703)549-2207   Fax: (703)683-5312
URL: http://www.nsbe.org/publications/premieradvertisers.php

Journal providing information on engineering careers, self-development, and cultural issues for recent graduates with technical majors.

★6257★ Plant Engineering

Reed Business Information
360 Park Ave. S
New York, NY 10010
Ph: (646)746-6400   Fax: (646)746-7431
URL: http://www.plantengineering.com/info/CA6287653.html

Monthly. Free. Magazine focusing on engineering support and maintenance in industry.

★6258★ Power

McGraw-Hill Inc.
1221 Ave. of the Americas
New York, NY 10020-1095
Ph: (212)512-2000   Fax: (212)512-3840
Fr: 877-833-5524
E-mail: robert_peltier@platts.com
URL: http://online.platts.com/PPS/P=m&s=1029337384756.1478827&e=1

Monthly. Magazine for engineers in electric utilities, process and manufacturing plants, commercial and service establishments, and consulting, design, and construction engineering firms working in the power technology field.

★6259★ SPE Technical Journals

Society of Petroleum Engineers
222 Palisades Creek Dr.
Richardson, TX 75080
Ph: (972)952-9393   Fax: (972)952-9435
Fr: 800-456-6863
URL: http://www.spe.org

Journal devoted to engineers and scientists.

★6260★ Structure Magazine

American Consulting Engineers Council
1015 15th St. NW, 8th Fl.
Washington, DC 20005-2605
Ph: (202)347-7474   Fax: (202)898-0068
URL: http://www.structuremag.org

Annual. $65.00/year for nonmembers; $35.00/year for students; $90.00/year for Canada; $125.00/year for other countries. Magazine focused on providing tips, tools, techniques, and innovative concepts for structural engineers.

★6261★ SWE, Magazine of the Society of Women Engineers

Society of Women Engineers
230 East Ohio St., Ste. 400
Chicago, IL 60611-3265
Ph: (312)596-5223
E-mail: hq@swe.org
URL: http://www.swe.org

Quarterly. $30.00/year for nonmembers. Magazine for engineering students and for women and men working in the engineering and technology fields. Covers career guidance, continuing development and topical issues.

★6262★ The Technology Interface

New Mexico State University
College of Engineering
PO Box 30001
Las Cruces, NM 88003-8001
Ph: (505)646-0111
URL: http://engr.nmsu.edu/etti/

Journal for the engineering technology profession serving education and industry.

★6263★ Uratie

IDG Communications Inc.
5 Speen St., 3rd. Fl
Framingham, MA 01701
Ph: (508)875-5000   Fax: (508)988-7888
URL: http://www.idg.com

Magazine providing job offers for graduates, engineers and information technology professionals.

★6264★ WEPANEWS

Women in Engineering Programs & Advocates Network
1901 E. Asbury Ave., Ste. 220
Denver, CO 80208
Ph: (303)871-4643   Fax: (303)871-6833
E-mail: dmatt@wepan.org
URL: http://www.wepan.org

Description: 2/year. Seeks to provide greater access for women to careers in engineering. Includes news of graduate, undergraduate, freshmen, pre-college, and re-entry engineering programs for women. Recurring features include job listings, faculty, grant, and conference news, international engineering program news, action group news, notices of publications available, and a column titled Kudos.

★6265★ Wire & Cable Technology International

Initial Publications Inc.
3869 Darrow Rd., Ste. 109
Stow, OH 44224
Ph: (330)686-9544   Fax: (330)686-9563
E-mail: info@wiretech.com
URL: http://www.wiretech.com/

Bimonthly. Magazine for manufacturers of ferrous, nonferrous, bare, and insulated wire.

PLACEMENT AND JOB REFERRAL SERVICES

★6266★ American Indian Science and Engineering Society (AISES)
PO Box 9828
Albuquerque, NM 87119-9828
Ph: (505)765-1052   Fax: (505)765-5608
E-mail: info@aises.org
URL: http://www.aises.org

Description: Represents American Indian and non-Indian students and professionals in science, technology, and engineering fields; corporations representing energy, mining, aerospace, electronic, and computer fields. Seeks to motivate and encourage students to pursue undergraduate and graduate studies in science, engineering, and technology. Sponsors science fairs in grade schools, teacher training workshops, summer math/science sessions for 8th-12th graders, professional chapters, and student chapters in colleges. Offers scholarships. Adult members serve as role models, advisers, and mentors for students. Operates placement service.

★6267★ Association for Finishing Processes of the Society of Manufacturing Engineers (AFP/SME)
1 SME Dr.
PO Box 930
Dearborn, MI 48121
Ph: (313)271-1500   Fax: (313)425-3401
Fr: 800-733-4763
E-mail: service@sme.org
URL: http://www.sme.org/cgi-bin/communities.pl?/communities/afp/af-phome.htm&&&SME

Description: Promotes the technology, process, and management aspects of the cleaning and coating of metal or plastic manufactured products and trade organizations concerned with the dissemination of knowledge related to industrial finishing. Conducts clinics and expositions. Offers professional certification. Maintains placement service with free listings for members.

★6268★ Engineering Society of Detroit (ESD)
2000 Town Ctr., Ste. 2610
Southfield, MI 48075
Ph: (248)353-0735   Fax: (248)353-0736
E-mail: esd@esd.org
URL: http://esd.org

Description: Engineers from all disciplines; scientists and technologists. Conducts technical programs and engineering refresher courses; sponsors conferences and expositions. Maintains speakers' bureau; offers placement services; although based in Detroit, MI, society membership is international.

★6269★ Korean-American Scientists and Engineers Association (KSEA)
1952 Gallows Rd., Ste. 300
Vienna, VA 22182
Ph: (703)748-1221   Fax: (703)748-1331
E-mail: admin@ksea.org
URL: http://www.ksea.org

Description: Represents scientists and engineers holding single or advanced degrees. Promotes friendship and mutuality among Korean and American scientists and engineers; contributes to Korea's scientific, technological, industrial, and economic developments; strengthens the scientific, technological, and cultural bonds between Korea and the U.S. Sponsors symposium. Maintains speakers' bureau, placement service, and biographical archives. Compiles statistics.

★6270★ Society of Hispanic Professional Engineers (SHPE)
5400 E Olympic Blvd., Ste. 210
Los Angeles, CA 90022
Ph: (323)725-3970   Fax: (323)725-0316
E-mail: shpenational@shpe.org
URL: http://oneshpe.shpe.org/wps/portal/national

Description: Represents engineers, student engineers, and scientists. Aims to increase the number of Hispanic engineers by providing motivation and support to students. Sponsors competitions and educational programs. Maintains placement service and speakers' bureau; compiles statistics.

★6271★ SOLE - The International Society of Logistics (SOLE)
8100 Professional Pl., Ste. 111
Hyattsville, MD 20785-2229
Ph: (301)459-8446   Fax: (301)459-1522
E-mail: solehq@erols.com
URL: http://www.sole.org

Description: Represents corporate and individual management and technical practitioners in the field of logistics, including scientists, engineers, educators, managers, and other specialists in commerce, aerospace, and other industries, government, and the military. (Logistics is the art and science of management engineering and technical activities concerned with requirements, and designing, supplying, and maintaining resources to support objectives, plans, and operations.) Covers every logistics specialty, including reliability, maintainability, systems and equipment maintenance, maintenance support equipment, human factors, training and training equipment, spare parts, overhaul and repair, handbooks, field site activation and operation, field engineering, facilities, packaging, supply chain management, materials handling, and transportation. Sponsors on-line job referral service; conducts specialized education programs.

EMPLOYER DIRECTORIES AND NETWORKING LISTS

★6272★ American Men and Women of Science
Gale, Cengage Learning
27500 Drake Rd.
Farmington Hills, MI 48331-3535
Ph: (248)699-4253   Fax: (248)699-8065
Fr: 800-877-4253
URL: http://www.gale.com

Biennial, latest edition 23rd, October 2006; new edition expected 24th, January 2008. $1,075.00 for individuals. Covers over 129,700 U.S. and Canadian scientists active in the physical, biological, mathematical, computer science, and engineering fields; includes references to previous edition for deceased scientists and nonrespondents. Entries include: Name, address, education, personal and career data, memberships, honors and awards, research interest. Arrangement: Alphabetical. Indexes: Discipline (in separate volume).

★6273★ Careers in Focus: Engineering
Facts On File Inc.
132 W 31st St., 17th Fl.
New York, NY 10001
Ph: (212)967-8800   Fax: 800-678-3633
Fr: 800-322-8755
URL: http://www.factsonfile.com

3rd edition, 2007. $29.95 for individuals; $26.95 for libraries. Publication includes: List of resources to consult for more information. Principal content of publication consists of job descriptions, advancement opportunities, educational requirements, employment outlook, salary information, and working conditions for careers in the field of engineering. Indexes: Alphabetical.

★6274★ Directory of Contract Staffing Firms
C.E. Publications Inc.
PO Box 3006
Bothell, WA 98041-3006
Ph: (425)806-5200   Fax: (425)806-5585
URL: http://www.cjhunter.com/dcsf/overview.html

Covers nearly 1,300 contract firms actively engaged in the employment of engineering, IT/IS, and technical personnel for 'temporary' contract assignments throughout the world. Entries include: Company name, address, phone, name of contact, email, web address. Arrangement: Alphabetical. Indexes: Geographical.

★6275★ Peterson's Job Opportunities in Engineering and Technology
Peterson's Guides
2000 Lenox Dr.
Box 67005
Lawrenceville, NJ 08648
Ph: (609)896-1800   Fax: (609)896-4531
Fr: 800-338-3282
E-mail: custsvc@petersons.com

URL: http://www.petersons.com

Compiled by the Peterson's staff. Fourth edition, 1996. $21.95 (paper). 379 pages. Profiles 2,000 high-tech companies looking primarily for technical personnel in such fields as biotechnology, telecommunications, software, computers and peripherals, defense, and aerospace. Contains job-search strategies and career options to help match education and expertise to the job market. Indexed geographically, by industry, and by hiring needs.

HANDBOOKS AND MANUALS

★6276★ The Best Resumes for Scientists and Engineers
John Wiley & Sons Inc.
1 Wiley Dr.
Somerset, NJ 08873
Ph: (732)469-4400   Fax: (732)302-2300
Fr: 800-225-5945
E-mail: custserv@wiley.com
URL: http://www.wiley.com/WileyCDA/

Adele Lewis and David J. Moore. Second edition, 1993. $37.50; $19.95 (paper). 224 pages. Presents an extensive collection of scientific and engineering resumes, highlighting the important differences between these and resumes written for other occupations.

★6277★ Great Jobs for Engineering Majors
The McGraw-Hill Companies
PO Box 182604
Columbus, OH 43272
Fax: (614)759-3749   Fr: 877-883-5524
E-mail: customer.service@mcgraw-hill.com
URL: http://www.mcgraw-hill.com

Geraldine O. Garner. Second edition, 2002. $14.95. 256 pages. Covers all the career options open to students majoring in engineering.

★6278★ The I Hate Selling Book: Business-Building Advice for Consultants, Attorneys, Accountants, Engineers, Architects, and Other Professionals
AMACOM
1601 Broadway, 12th Fl.
New York, NY 10019-7420
Ph: (212)586-8100   Fax: (212)903-8168
Fr: 800-262-9699
URL: http://www.amanet.org

Allan S. Boress. 2001. $29.95. 240 pages.

★6279★ Opportunities in Engineering Careers
The McGraw-Hill Companies
PO Box 182604
Columbus, OH 43272
Fax: (614)759-3749   Fr: 877-883-5524
E-mail: customer.service@mcgraw-hill.com

URL: http://www.mcgraw-hill.com

Nicholas Basta. Revised second edition, 2002. $13.95; $11.95 (paper). 160 pages. Outlines typical job titles, salaries, career paths, and employment prospects.

★6280★ Opportunities in High Tech Careers
The McGraw-Hill Companies
PO Box 182604
Columbus, OH 43272
Fax: (614)759-3749   Fr: 877-883-5524
E-mail: customer.service@mcgraw-hill.com
URL: http://www.mcgraw-hill.com

Gary Colter and Deborah Yanuck. 1999. $14.95; $11.95 (paper). 160 pages. Explores high technology careers. Describes job opportunities, how to make a career decision, how to prepare for high technology jobs, job hunting techniques, and future trends.

★6281★ Opportunities in Research and Development Careers
The McGraw-Hill Companies
PO Box 182604
Columbus, OH 43272
Fax: (614)759-3749   Fr: 877-883-5524
E-mail: customer.service@mcgraw-hill.com
URL: http://www.mcgraw-hill.com

Jan Goldberg. 1996. $11.95 (paper). 146 pages.

★6282★ Real People Working in Engineering
The McGraw-Hill Companies
PO Box 182604
Columbus, OH 43272
Fax: (614)759-3749   Fr: 877-883-5524
E-mail: customer.service@mcgraw-hill.com
URL: http://www.mcgraw-hill.com

Blythe Camenson, Jan Goldberg. 1997. $17.95 (paper). 160 pages. Interviews and profiles of working professionals capture a range of opportunities in this field.

★6283★ Resumes for Engineering Careers
The McGraw-Hill Companies
PO Box 182604
Columbus, OH 43272
Fax: (614)759-3749   Fr: 877-883-5524
E-mail: customer.service@mcgraw-hill.com
URL: http://www.mcgraw-hill.com

Third edition, 2005. $11.95 (paper). 144 pages. Contains sample resumes and cover letters applicable to any engineering field.

★6284★ Resumes for Scientific and Technical Careers
The McGraw-Hill Companies
PO Box 182604
Columbus, OH 43272
Fax: (614)759-3749   Fr: 877-883-5524
E-mail: customer.service@mcgraw-hill.com
URL: http://www.mcgraw-hill.com

Third edition, 2007. $12.95 (paper). 144 pages. Provides resume advice for individuals interested in working in scientific and technical careers. Includes sample resumes and cover letters.

EMPLOYMENT AGENCIES AND SEARCH FIRMS

★6285★ The Aspire Group
52 Second Ave, 1st Fl
Waltham, MA 02451-1129
Fax: (718)890-1810   Fr: 800-487-2967
URL: http://www.bmanet.com

Employment agency.

★6286★ Auguston and Associates Inc.
1010 S. Ocean Blvd., Ste. 601
Pompano Beach, FL 33062
Ph: (954)943-0503   Fax: (954)784-1660
Fr: 888-244-5598
URL: http://www.augustonandassociates.com/

Executive search firm focused on medical devices.

★6287★ Bell Oaks Co.
10 Glenlake Pkwy., Ste. 300
Atlanta, GA 30328
Ph: (678)287-2000   Fax: (678)287-2002
E-mail: info@belloaks.com
URL: http://www.belloaks.com

Personnel service firm.

★6288★ CEO Resources Inc.
PO Box 2883
Framingham, MA 01703-2883
Ph: (508)877-2775   Fax: (508)877-8433
E-mail: info@ceoresourcesinc.com
URL: http://ceoresourcesinc.com

Executive search firm.

★6289★ C.H. Cowles Associates
93 W Alyssa Canyon Pl.
PO Box 89291
Tucson, AZ 85737-1636
Ph: (520)297-7608   Fax: (520)297-7608

Firm provides services in industrial engineering and industrial management including long-range planning, facilities planning, work improvement, profit improvement, executive search, quality assurance, manufacturing engineering and staff reorganization, site search and site planning.

★6290★ Cizek Associates Inc.
2415 E. Camelback Rd., Ste. 700
Phoenix, AZ 85016
Ph: (602)553-1066   Fax: (602)553-1166
E-mail: phx@cizekassociates.com
URL: http://www.cizekassociates.com/

Executive search firm. Also offices in Chicago and San Francisco.

★6291★ **Colli Associates**
414 Caboose Ln.
Valrico, FL 33594
Ph: (813)681-2145   Fax: (813)661-5217
E-mail: colli@gte.net

Employment agency. Executive search firm.

★6292★ **Dean Associates**
PO Box 1079
Santa Cruz, CA 95061
Ph: (831)423-2931
E-mail: marydearn@deanassociates.com
URL: http://www.deanassociates.com

Executive search firm focused on the high technology industry.

★6293★ **Dinte Resources Inc.**
8300 Greensboro Dr., Ste. 750
McLean, VA 22102
Ph: (703)448-3300   Fax: (703)448-0215
E-mail: DRI@dinte.com
URL: http://www.dinte.com

Executive search firm.

★6294★ **Electronic Careers**
21355 Pacific Coast Hwy., Ste. 100
Malibu, CA 90265
Ph: (310)317-6113   Fax: (310)317-6119
E-mail: E-Careers@ElectronicCareers.com
URL: http://www.electroniccareers.com

Executive search firm.

★6295★ **Elite Resources Group**
1239 Stetson Lane
Sevierville, TN 37876
Ph: (865)774-8228   Fax: (865)774-8229
E-mail: search@elite-rg.com
URL: http://www.elite-rg.com

Executive search firm.

★6296★ **Engineer One, Inc.**
PO Box 23037
Knoxville, TN 37933
Fax: (865)691-0110
E-mail: engineerone@engineerone.com
URL: http://www.engineerone.com

Engineering employment service specializes in engineering and management in the chemical process, power utilities, manufacturing, mechanical, electrical, and electronic industries. Established an Information Technology Division in 1998 that works nationwide across all industries. Also provides systems analysis consulting services specializing in VAX based systems.

★6297★ **Executive Recruiters Agency**
14 Office Park Dr., Ste. 100
PO Box 21810
Little Rock, AR 72221-1810
Ph: (501)224-7000   Fax: (501)224-8534
E-mail: jobs@execrecruit.com
URL: http://www.execrecruit.com

Personnel service firm.

★6298★ **Executive Resource Group Inc.**
1330 Cedar Point, Ste. 201
Amelia, OH 45102
Ph: (513)947-1447   Fax: (513)752-3026
E-mail: hrjobs4@executiveresource.net
URL: http://www.executiveresource.net

Executive search firm.

★6299★ **Executive Search Services (ESS)**
2925 4th St., Ste. 11
Santa Monica, CA 90405
Ph: (310)392-3244
E-mail: ess@exec.nu
URL: http://www.exec.nu

Executive search firm.

★6300★ **Fischer Group International Inc.**
296 Country Club Rd., Fl 2
Avon, CT 06001
Ph: (860)404-7700   Fax: (860)404-7799
E-mail: info@fischergroupintl.com
URL: http://www.fischergroupintl.com

Executive search firm.

★6301★ **Fisher Personnel Management Services**
2351 N. Filbert Rd.
Exeter, CA 93221
Ph: (559)594-5774   Fax: (559)594-5777
E-mail: hookme@fisheads.net
URL: http://www.fisheads.net

Executive search firm.

★6302★ **Global Employment Solutions**
10375 Park Meadows Dr., Ste. 375
Littleton, CO 80124
Ph: (303)216-9500   Fax: (303)216-9533
E-mail: careers@global
URL: http://www.gesnetwork.com

Employment agency.

★6303★ **International Staffing Consultants**
17310 Redhill Ave., No. 140
Irvine, CA 92614
Ph: (949)255-5857   Fax: (949)767-5959
E-mail: iscinc@iscworld.com
URL: http://www.iscworld.com

Employment agency. Provides placement on regular or temporary basis. Affiliate office in London.

★6304★ **Mfg/Search, Inc.**
431 E Colfax Ave., Ste.120
South Bend, IN 46617
Ph: (574)282-2547   Fr: 800-782-7976
E-mail: mfg@mfgsearch.com
URL: http://www.mfgsearch.com

Executive search firm. Offices in GA, IL, MI, NY.

★6305★ **Rand Personnel**
1200 Truxtun Ave., Ste. 130
Bakersfield, CA 93301
Ph: (805)325-0751   Fax: (805)325-4120

Personnel service firm serving a variety of fields.

★6306★ **Search and Recruit International**
4455 South Blvd. Ste. 110
Virginia Beach, VA 23452
Ph: (757)625-2121   Fr: 800-800-5627

Employment agency. Headquartered in Virginia Beach. Other offices in Bremerton, WA; Charleston, SC; Jacksonville, FL; Memphis, TN; Pensacola, FL; Sacramento, CA; San Bernardino, CA; San Diego, CA.

★6307★ **Tri-Serv Inc.**
22 W. Padonia Rd., Ste. C-353
Timonium, MD 21093
Ph: (410)561-1740   Fax: (410)252-7417
E-mail: info@tri-serv.coom
URL: http://www.tri-serv.com

Employment agency for technical personnel.

ONLINE JOB SOURCES AND SERVICES

★6308★ **Spherion**
2050 Spectrum Blvd.
Fort Lauderdale, FL 33309
Ph: (954)308-7600
E-mail: help@spherion.com
URL: http://www.spherion.com

Description: Recruitment firm specializing in accounting and finance, sales and marketing, interim executives, technology, engineering, retail and human resources.

TRADESHOWS

★6309★ **American Society for Engineering Education Annual Conference and Exposition**
American Society for Engineering Education
1818 N. St. NW, Ste. 600
Washington, DC 20036-2479
Ph: (202)331-3500   Fax: (202)265-8504

E-mail: conferences@asee.org
URL: http://www.asee.org

Annual. **Primary Exhibits:** Publications, engineering supplies and equipment, computers, software, and research companies all products and services related to engineering education.

OTHER SOURCES

★6310★ American Almanac of Jobs and Salaries

HarperCollins
10 E. 53rd St.
New York, NY 10022
Ph: (212)207-7000   Fr: 800-242-7737
URL: http://www.harpercollins.com/

John W. Wright. Revised edition, 2000. $20.00 (paper). 672 pages. This is a comprehensive guide to the wages of hundreds of occupations in a wide variety of industries and organizations.

★6311★ American Association of Engineering Societies (AAES)

1620 I St. NW, Ste. 210
Washington, DC 20006
Ph: (202)296-2237   Fax: (202)296-1151
Fr: 888-400-2237
E-mail: dbateson@aaes.org
URL: http://www.aaes.org

Description: Coordinates the efforts of the member societies in the provision of reliable and objective information to the general public concerning issues which affect the engineering profession and the field of engineering as a whole; collects, analyzes, documents, and disseminates data which will inform the general public of the relationship between engineering and the national welfare; provides a forum for the engineering societies to exchange and discuss their views on matters of common interest; and represents the U.S. engineering community abroad through representation in WFEO and UPADI.

★6312★ American Engineering Association (AEA)

4116 S Carrier Pkwy., Ste. 280-809
Grand Prairie, TX 75052
Ph: (201)664-6954
E-mail: info@aea.org
URL: http://www.aea.org

Description: Members consist of Engineers and engineering professionals. Purpose to advance the engineering profession and U.S. engineering capabilities. Issues of concern include age discrimination, immigration laws, displacement of U.S. Engineers by foreign workers, trade agreements, off shoring of U.S. Engineering and manufacturing jobs, loss of U.S. manufacturing and engineering capability, and recruitment of foreign students. Testifies before Congress. Holds local Chapter meetings.

★6313★ American Supplier Institute (ASI)

38705 7 Mile Rd., Ste. 345
Livonia, MI 48152
Ph: (734)464-1395   Fax: (734)464-1399
Fr: 800-462-4500
E-mail: asi@asiusa.com
URL: http://www.amsup.com

Description: Seeks to encourage change in U.S. industry through development and implementation of advanced manufacturing and engineering technologies such as Taguchi Methods, Quality Function Deployment, Statistical Process Control, and Total Quality Management. Offers educational courses, training seminars, and workshops to improve quality, reduce cost, and enhance competitive position of U.S. products. Maintains international network of affiliates for developing training specialists and technologies curriculum. Provides training services to government supplier companies.

★6314★ Association for International Practical Training (AIPT)

10400 Little Patuxent Pkwy., Ste. 250
Columbia, MD 21044-3519
Ph: (410)997-2200   Fax: (410)992-3924
E-mail: aipt@aipt.org
URL: http://www.aipt.org

Description: Providers worldwide of on-the-job training programs for students and professionals seeking international career development and life-changing experiences. Arranges workplace exchanges in hundreds of professional fields, bringing employers and trainees together from around the world. Client list ranges from small farming communities to Fortune 500 companies.

★6315★ Engineering Occupations

Delphi Productions
3159 6th St.
Boulder, CO 80304
Ph: (303)443-2100   Fax: (303)443-4022
Fr: 888-443-2400
E-mail: support@delphivideo.com
URL: http://www.delphivideo.com

$95.00. 50 minutes. Part of the Careers for the 21st Century Video Library.

★6316★ Institute of Industrial Engineers (IIE)

3577 Parkway Ln., Ste. 200
Norcross, GA 30092
Ph: (770)449-0460   Fax: (770)441-3295
Fr: 800-494-0460
E-mail: execoffice@iienet.org
URL: http://www.iienet2.org/Default.aspx

Description: Serves as professional society of industrial engineers. Concerned with the design, improvement, and installation of integrated systems of people, materials, equipment, and energy. Draws upon specialized knowledge and skill in the mathematical, physical, and social sciences together with the principles and methods of engineering analysis and design, to specify, predict, and evaluate the results obtained from such

systems. Maintains technical societies and divisions.

★6317★ National Action Council for Minorities in Engineering (NACME)

440 Hamilton Ave., Ste. 302
White Plains, NY 10601-1813
Ph: (914)539-4010   Fax: (914)539-4032
E-mail: webmaster@nacme.org
URL: http://www.nacme.org

Description: Leads the national effort to increase access to careers in engineering and other science-based disciplines. Conducts research and public policy analysis, develops and operates national demonstration programs at precollege and university levels, and disseminates information through publications, conferences and electronic media. Serves as a privately funded source of scholarships for minority students in engineering.

★6318★ National Society of Professional Engineers (NSPE)

1420 King St.
Alexandria, VA 22314-2794
Ph: (703)684-2800   Fax: (703)836-4875
Fr: 888-285-6773
E-mail: memserv@nspe.org
URL: http://www.nspe.org

Description: Represents professional engineers and engineers-in-training in all fields registered in accordance with the laws of states or territories of the U.S. or provinces of Canada; qualified graduate engineers, student members, and registered land surveyors. Is concerned with social, professional, ethical, and economic considerations of engineering as a profession; encompasses programs in public relations, employment practices, ethical considerations, education, and career guidance. Monitors legislative and regulatory actions of interest to the engineering profession.

★6319★ Scientific, Engineering, and Technical Services

Cambridge Educational
PO Box 2053
Princeton, NJ 08543-2053
Ph: 800-257-5126   Fax: (609)671-0266
Fr: 800-468-4227
E-mail: custserv@films.com
URL: http://www.cambridgeeducational.com

VHS and DVD. $89.95. 2002. 18 minutes. 2002. Part of the Career Cluster Series.

★6320★ Society of Women Engineers (SWE)

230 E Ohio St., Ste. 400
Chicago, IL 60611-3265
Ph: (312)596-5223   Fax: (312)596-5252
Fr: 877-SWE-INFO
E-mail: hq@swe.org
URL: http://www.swe.org

Description: Educational and service organization representing both students and professional women in engineering and technical fields.

★6321★ Women in Engineering
Her Own Words
PO Box 5264
Madison, WI 53705-0264
Ph: (608)271-7083   Fax: (608)271-0209
E-mail: herownword@aol.com
URL: http://www.herownwords.com/
Video. Jocelyn Riley. $95.00. 15 minutes.
Resource guide also available for $45.00.

Industrial Production Managers

Free. Journal that aims to provide ideas and advice that are relevant to today's CEOs.

★6333★ **Industrial Distribution**

Reed Business Information
225 Wyman St.
Waltham, MA 02451-1216
URL: http://www.inddist.com

Monthly. $121.00/year for individuals; $145.00/year for Canada; $140.00/year for individuals, for Mexico; $280.00/year for other countries. Magazine covering industrial supplies marketing, management, sales, telecommunications, computers, inventory, and warehouse management.

★6334★ **International Journal of Business Research**

Academy of International Business and Economics
PO Box 2536
Ceres, CA 95307
URL: http://www.aibe.org

Peer-reviewed journal publishing theoretical, conceptual, and applied research on topics related to research, practice and teaching in all areas of business, management, and marketing.

★6335★ **Journal of Academic Leadership**

Academic Leadership
600 Park St.
Rarick Hall 219
Hays, KS 67601-4099
Ph: (785)628-4547
URL: http://www.academicleadership.org/

Journal focusing on the leadership issues in the academic world.

★6336★ **Journal of Business and Psychology**

Springer-Verlag New York Inc.
233 Spring St.
New York, NY 10013
Ph: (212)460-1500   Fax: (212)460-1575
URL: http://www.springer.com/journal/10869/

Journal covering all aspects of psychology that apply to the business segment. Includes topics such as personnel selection and training, organizational assessment and development, risk management and loss control, marketing and consumer behavior research.

★6337★ **Journal of International Business Strategy**

Academy of International Business and Economics
PO Box 2536
Ceres, CA 95307
URL: http://www.AIBE.org

Peer-reviewed journal publishing theoretical, conceptual, and applied research on topics related to strategy in international business.

★6338★ **Management Research**

M.E. Sharpe Inc.
80 Business Pk. Dr.
Armonk, NY 10504
Ph: (914)273-1800   Fax: (914)273-2106
Fr: 800-541-6563
URL: http://www.mesharpe.com/mall/results1.asp?ACR=JMR

$72.00/year for individuals; $349.00/year for institutions; $84.00/year for other countries, individual; $391.00/year for institutions, other countries. International journal dedicated to advancing the understanding of management in private and public sector organizations through empirical investigation and theoretical analysis. Attempts to promote an international dialogue between researchers, improve the understanding of the nature of management in different settings, and achieve a reasonable transfer of research results to management practice in several contexts. Receptive to research across a broad range of management topics such as human resource management, organizational behavior, organizational theory, and strategic management. While not regional in nature, articles dealing with Iberoamerican issues are particularly welcomed.

★6339★ **Organization Management Journal**

Eastern Academy of Management
c/o Craig Tunwall, VP
Empire State College
2805 State Hwy. 67
Johnstown, NY 12095
Ph: (518)762-4651   Fax: (518)736-1716
URL: http://www1.wnec.edu/omj

Free to qualified subscribers. Refereed, online journal focusing on organization management issues.

★6340★ **Public Performance and Management Review**

M.E. Sharpe Inc.
80 Business Pk. Dr.
Armonk, NY 10504
Ph: (914)273-1800   Fax: (914)273-2106
Fr: 800-541-6563
URL: http://www.mesharpe.com/mall/results1.asp?ACR=pmr

Quarterly. $85.00/year for individuals; $399.00/year for institutions; $101.00/year for other countries, individual; $431.00/year for institutions, other countries. Journal addressing a broad range of factors influencing the performance of public and nonprofit organizations and agencies. Aims to facilitate the development of innovative techniques and encourage a wider application of those already established; stimulate research and critical thinking about the relationship between public and private management theories; present integrated analyses of theories, concepts, strategies and techniques dealing with productivity, measurement and related questions of performance improvement; and provide a forum for practitioner-academic exchange. Continuing themes include managing for productivity, measuring and evaluating performance, improving budget strategies, managing human

resources, building partnerships, and applying new technologies.

★6341★ **Supply Chain Management Review**

Reed Business Information
225 Wyman St.
Waltham, MA 02451-1216
URL: http://www.scmr.com

$199.00/year for U.S. and Canada; $241.00/year for other countries. Publication covering business and management.

HANDBOOKS AND MANUALS

★6342★ **Getting and Keeping the Job: Success in Business and Technical Careers**

Prentice Hall PTR
One Lake St.
Upper Saddle River, NJ 07458
Ph: (201)236-7000   Fax: 800-445-6991
Fr: 800-567-3800
URL: http://www.phptr.com/index.asp?rl=1

Clark, Val. Second edition, 2002. $38.05 (Trade paper). 196 pages.

★6343★ **Materials Manager**

National Learning Corporation
212 Michael Dr.
Syosset, NY 11791
Ph: (516)921-8888   Fax: (516)921-8743
Fr: 800-632-8888
URL: http://www.passbooks.com/

Rudman, Jack. 1994. $39.95 (Trade paper).

EMPLOYMENT AGENCIES AND SEARCH FIRMS

★6344★ **1 Exec Street**

201 Post St., Ste. 401
San Francisco, CA 94108
Ph: (415)982-0555   Fax: (415)982-0550
Fr: 888-554-6845
E-mail: contactus@1execstreet.com
URL: http://www.1execstreet.com

Executive search firm.

★6345★ **Abel Fuller & Zedler LLC**

440 Benmar, Ste. 1085
Houston, TX 77060
Ph: (281)447-3334   Fax: (281)447-3334
E-mail: agarcia@execufirm.com
URL: http://www.execufirm.com

Executive search firm.

★6346★ APA Search Inc.
1 Byram Brook Pl., Ste. 201
Armonk, NY 10504
Ph: (914)273-6000   Fax: (914)273-8025
E-mail: info@apasearch.com
URL: http://www.apasearch.com
Employment agency specializing in the automotive, retail, and hardware industries.

★6347★ Blake/Hansen & Schmidt Ltd.
5514 Ridgeway Ct.
Westlake Village, CA 91362
Ph: (818)879-1192
E-mail: contact@blakehansenschmidt.com
URL: http://www.blakehansenschmidt.com
Executive search firm specializing in plastics, rubber and packaging.

★6348★ Boyden
360 Lexington Ave., Ste 1300
New York, NY 10017
Ph: (212)949-9400   Fax: (212)949-5905
E-mail: jbranthover@boyden.com
URL: http://www.boyden.com
Executive search firm.

★6349★ Boyle Ogata Bregman
17461 Derian Ave., Ste. 202
Irvine, CA 92614
Ph: (949)474-0115   Fax: (949)474-2204
E-mail: info@bobsearch.com
URL: http://www.bobsearch.com
Executive search firm.

★6350★ Cochran, Cochran & Yale LLC
955 E. Henrietta Rd.
Rochester, NY 14623
Ph: (585)424-6060   Fax: (585)424-6069
E-mail: roch@ccy.com
URL: http://www.ccy.com
Executive search firm. Branches in Denver, CO and Williamsville, NY.

★6351★ Conboy, Sur & Associates Inc.
15 E. Churchville Rd., Ste. 170
Bel Air, MD 21014-3837
Ph: (410)925-4122
E-mail: wksur@conboysur.com
URL: http://www.conboysur.com
Executive search firm.

★6352★ The Corban Group
5050 Research Ct., Ste. 600
Johns Creek, GA 30024
Ph: (678)638-6000   Fax: (678)638-6001
Fr: (866)426-7226
E-mail: info@corbangroup.com
URL: http://www.corbangroup.com
Executive search firm.

★6353★ Crowder & Company
40950 Woodward Ave., Ste. 335
Bloomfield Hills, MI 48304
Ph: (248)645-0909   Fax: (248)645-2366
E-mail: ewc@crowdercompany.com
URL: http://www.crowdercompany.com
Executive search firm.

★6354★ The Dieck Group Inc.
30 Rough Lee Court
Madison, WI 53705
Ph: (608)238-1000
E-mail: dan.dieck@dieckgroup.com
URL: http://www.dieckgroup.com
Executive search firm focused on pulp, paper and the packaging industries.

★6355★ Ferneborg & Associates Inc.
160 Bovet Rd., Ste. 403
San Mateo, CA 94402
Ph: (650)577-0100   Fax: (650)577-0122
E-mail: mailbox@execsearch.com
URL: http://www.execsearch.com
Executive search firm.

★6356★ First Call Temporary and Professional Services
6960 Hillsdale Ct.
Indianapolis, IN 46250
Ph: (317)596-3280   Fax: (317)596-3258
Executive search firm.

★6357★ Fortune Personnel Consultants of Southwest Missouri
5309 S Golden Ave.
Springfield, MO 65810
Ph: (417)887-6737   Fax: (417)887-6955
E-mail: info@fpcswmo.com
URL: http://www.fpcswmo.com
Executive search firm.

★6358★ FPC of Savannah
145 Bull St.
Savannah, GA 31401
Ph: (912)233-4556   Fax: (912)223-8633
E-mail: execsearch@fpcsav.com
URL: http://www.fpcnational.com/savannah
Executive search firm.

★6359★ Heller Kil Associates Inc.
2060 S Halifax Dr.
Daytona Beach, FL 32118
Ph: (386)761-5100   Fax: (386)761-7206
E-mail: pheller@bellsouth.net
Executive search firm.

★6360★ JB Linde & Associates
1415 Elbridge Payne Rd.
Chesterfield, MO 63017
Ph: (314)532-8040
E-mail: jblinde@inlink.com
Executive search firm.

★6361★ John Wylie Associates Inc.
1727 E 71st St.
Tulsa, OK 74136
Ph: (918)496-2100
E-mail: jlwylie@inetmail.att.net
Executive search firm.

★6362★ K.S. Frary & Associates
16 Schooner Ridge, Ste. 301
Marblehead, MA 01945
Ph: (781)631-2464   Fax: (781)631-2465
E-mail: ksfrary@comcast.net
URL: http://www.ksfrary.com
Executive search firm.

★6363★ Lange & Associates
499 Bristol Dr.
Wabash, IN 46992
Ph: (260)563-7402   Fax: (260)563-3897
E-mail: langeassoc@ctlnet.com
Executive search firm.

★6364★ Miller Personnel Consultants Inc.
931 E 86th St., Ste. 103
Indianapolis, IN 46240
Ph: (317)251-5938   Fax: (317)251-5762
Fr: 800-851-5938
E-mail: markmiller@netdirect.net
URL: http://www.millerpersonnel.com
Executive search firm.

★6365★ MRI Network CompuSearch of Dearborn
3 Parklane Blvd., Ste. 1210W
Dearborn, MI 48126
Ph: (313)336-6650   Fax: (313)336-7436
URL: http://www.mrinetwork.com
Executive search firm.

★6366★ Recruiting Services Group Inc.
3107 E Corporate Edge Dr.
Germantown, TN 38138
Ph: (901)367-0778   Fax: (901)367-0868
E-mail: info@rsghunt.com
URL: http://www.rsghunt.com
Executive search firm.

★6367★ RGT Associates Inc.
2 Greenleaf Woods Dr., Ste.101
PO Box 1032
Portsmouth, NH 03802
Ph: (603)431-9500   Fax: (603)431-6984
E-mail: recruitrgt@aol.com
Executive search firm.

★6368★ Riley Cole Professional Recruiters
PO Box 10635
Oakland, CA 94610
Ph: (510)336-2333   Fax: (510)336-2777

E-mail: riled@pacbell.net

Executive search firm.

★6369★ RN Eyler Associates Inc.

2923 Vine St., Ste. 170
West Des Moines, IA 50265
Ph: (515)245-4244
E-mail: mreyler@msn.com

Executive search firm.

★6370★ Ronald Dukes Associates LLC

20 North Wacker, Ste. 2010
Chicago, IL 60606
Ph: (312)357-2895   Fax: (312)357-2897
E-mail: ron@rdukesassociates.com
URL: http://www.rdukesassociates.com

Executive search firm focused on the industrial and automotive industries.

★6371★ Russ Hadick & Associates Inc.

77 W Elmwood Dr., Ste 100
Dayton, OH 45459
Ph: (937)439-7700   Fax: (937)439-7705
E-mail: rhadick@rharecruiters.com
URL: http://www.rharecruiters.com

Executive search firm.

★6372★ Sanford Rose Associates

635 E. Bay St., Ste. A
Charleston, SC 29403
Ph: (843)579-3077   Fax: (843)579-3055
E-mail: tjtolan@sanfordrose.com
URL: http://www.sanfordrose.com

Executive search firm.

★6373★ Southern Recruiters & Consultants Inc.

PO Box 2745
Aiken, SC 29802
Ph: (803)648-7834   Fax: (803)642-2770
E-mail: recruiters@southernrecruiters.com
URL: http://www.southernrecruiters.com

Executive search firm.

★6374★ Stiles Associates LLC

276 Newport Rd., Ste. 206
New London, NH 03257
Ph: (603)526-6566   Fax: (603)526-6185
Fr: 800-322-5185
E-mail: tberio@leanexecs.com
URL: http://www.leanexecs.com

Executive search firm.

★6375★ Summit Group Consultants Inc.

16 Voight Ln.
Lafayette, NJ 07848
Ph: (973)875-3300
E-mail: garyp@nac.net

Executive search firm.

★6376★ Teknon Employment Resources Inc.

17 S. St. Clair St., Ste. 300
Dayton, OH 45402-2137
Ph: (937)222-5300   Fax: (937)222-6311
E-mail: teknon@teknongroup.cp
URL: http://www.teknongroup.com

Executive search firm.

★6377★ Thorsen Associates Inc.

2020 Grand Ave.
Baldwin, NY 11510
Ph: (516)868-6500   Fax: (516)868-7842
E-mail: info@thorsenassociates.com
URL: http://www.thorsenassociates.com

Executive search firm.

★6378★ William J. Christopher Associates Inc.

307 N. Walnut St.
West Chester, PA 19380
Ph: (610)696-4397   Fax: (610)692-5177
E-mail: wjc@wjca.com
URL: http://www.wjca.com

Executive search firm.

TRADESHOWS

★6379★ ITSC - International Thermal Spray Conference and Exposition

ASM International
9639 Kinsman Rd.
Materials Park, OH 44073-0002
Ph: (440)338-5151   Fax: (440)338-4634
Fr: 800-336-5152
E-mail: CustomerService@asminternational.org
URL: http://www.asminternational.org

Annual. **Primary Exhibits:** Thermal spray and welding equipment, supplies, and services. **Dates and Locations:** 2008 Jun 02-04; Maastricht, Netherlands.

OTHER SOURCES

★6380★ Administration and Management Occupations

Delphi Productions
3159 6th St.
Boulder, CO 80304
Ph: (303)443-2100   Fax: (303)443-4022
Fr: 888-443-2400
E-mail: support@delphivideo.com
URL: http://www.delphivideo.com

$95.00. 50 minutes. Part of the Careers for the 21st Century Video Library.

★6381★ Production Occupations

Delphi Productions
3159 6th St.
Boulder, CO 80304
Ph: (303)443-2100   Fax: (303)443-4022
Fr: 888-443-2400
E-mail: support@delphivideo.com
URL: http://www.delphivideo.com

$95.00. 49 minutes. Part of the Careers for the 21st Century Video Library.

Inspectors and Compliance Officers, except Construction

SOURCES OF HELP-WANTED ADS

★6382★ American City and County
Primedia Business
6151 Powers Ferry Rd., Ste. 200
Atlanta, GA 30339
Ph: (770)955-2500   Fax: (770)618-0204
URL: http://
www.americancityandcounty.com

Monthly. $67.00/year for individuals. Municipal and county administration magazine.

★6383★ American Industrial Hygiene Association Journal
American Industrial Hygiene Association
2700 Prosperity Ave., Ste. 250
Fairfax, VA 22031
Ph: (703)849-8888   Fax: (703)207-3561
URL: http://www.aiha.org

Monthly. Journal providing a forum for peer-reviewed articles in the field of industrial hygiene.

★6384★ Applied Occupational & Environmental Hygiene
Applied Industrial Hygiene Inc.
1330 Kemper Meadow Dr., Ste. 600
Cincinnati, OH 45240
Ph: (513)742-2020   Fax: (513)742-3355
URL: http://www.acgih.org

Monthly. $223.00/year for individuals, individual membership; $623.00/year for institutions, institution or organization. Peer-reviewed journal presenting applied solutions for the prevention of occupational and environmental disease and injury.

★6385★ Cal-OSHA Reporter
Providence Publications
PO Box 2610
Granite Bay, CA 95746
Ph: (916)780-5200   Fax: (916)781-6444
E-mail: newsdesk@cal-osha.com
URL: http://www.cal-osha.com/

Description: 48/year. Reports on laws, regulations, court cases, and other issues of interest to occupational safety and health professionals. Recurring features include a calendar of events, reports of meetings, news of educational opportunities, job listings, and notices of publications available. Reviews all Cal-OSHA cases.

★6386★ Food Production Management
CTI Publications Inc.
2 Oakway Rd.
Timonium, MD 21093-4247
Ph: (410)308-2080   Fax: (410)308-2079
Fr: 800-468-6770
E-mail: fpmeditorial@ctipubs.com

Monthly. $40.00/year for individuals; $70.00 for two years; $60.00/year for other countries; $110.00 for two years, other countries. Magazine on food processing and individual packing news for management, sales, and production personnel in the canning, glass packing, aseptic, and frozen food industries.

★6387★ Industrial Hygiene News
Rimbach Publishing Inc.
8650 Babcock Blvd.
Pittsburgh, PA 15237
Ph: (412)364-5366   Fax: (412)369-9720
Fr: 800-245-3182
URL: http://www.rimbach.com

Bimonthly. Free to qualified subscribers. Magazine covering industrial hygiene, occupational health, and safety.

★6388★ Journal of Occupational and Environmental Medicine
Lippincott Williams & Wilkins
530 Walnut St.
Philadelphia, PA 19106-3621
Ph: (215)521-8300   Fax: (215)521-8902
Fr: 800-638-3030
URL: http://www.lww.com/product/?1076-2752

Monthly. $319.00/year for individuals, U.S.; $432.00/year for institutions, U.S.; $435.00/year for individuals, other countries; $531.00/year for institutions, other countries. Occupational and environmental medicine journal.

★6389★ Occupational Health & Safety
Stevens Publishing Corp.
5151 Beltline Rd., 10th Fl.
Dallas, TX 75254
Ph: (972)687-6700   Fax: (972)687-6799
E-mail: jlaws@stevenspublishing.com
URL: http://www.ohsonline.com

Monthly. $99.00/year for individuals. Magazine covering federal and state regulation of occupational health and safety.

★6390★ Pharmaceutical Technology
Advanstar Communications
485 Rte. 1 S
Bldg. F, 1st Fl.
Iselin, NJ 08830
Ph: (732)596-0276   Fax: (732)596-0003
E-mail: ptpress@advanstar.com
URL: http://www.pharmtech.com

Monthly. $185.00/year for individuals; $331.00 for two years; $263.00/year for individuals, Canada and Mexico; $458.00/year for two years, Canada and Mexico; $55.00/year for individuals, back issue; $85.00 for two years, Can/Intl back issue. Magazine on applied technology for pharmaceutical firms.

★6391★ SafetyHealth
National Safety Council
1121 Spring Lake Dr.
Itasca, IL 60143-3201
Ph: (630)285-1121   Fax: (630)285-1315
Fr: 800-621-7615

Monthly. $56.00/year; $5.00 for single issue. Publication focusing on workplace safety and health issues.

PLACEMENT AND JOB REFERRAL SERVICES

★6392★ American Public Health Association (APHA)

800 I St. NW
Washington, DC 20001
Ph: (202)777-2742   Fax: (202)777-2534
E-mail: comments@apha.org
URL: http://www.apha.org

Members: Professional organization of physicians, nurses, educators, academicians, environmentalists, epidemiologists, new professionals, social workers, health administrators, optometrists, podiatrists, pharmacists, dentists, nutritionists, health planners, other community and mental health specialists, and interested consumers. **Purpose:** Seeks to protect and promote personal, mental, and environmental health. **Activities:** Services include: promulgation of standards; establishment of uniform practices and procedures; development of the etiology of communicable diseases; research in public health; exploration of medical care programs and their relationships to public health. Sponsors job placement service.

★6393★ American Society of Safety Engineers (ASSE)

1800 E Oakton St.
Des Plaines, IL 60018
Ph: (847)699-2929   Fax: (847)768-3434
E-mail: customerservice@asse.org
URL: http://www.asse.org

Description: Professional society of safety engineers, safety directors, and others concerned with accident prevention, environmental protection and safety and health programs. Sponsors National Safety Month and conducts research and educational programs. Develops/publishes ANSI safety-related standards and other technical literature. Compiles statistics; maintains job placement service.

EMPLOYER DIRECTORIES AND NETWORKING LISTS

★6394★ American Industrial Hygiene Association-Directory

American Industrial Hygiene Association
2700 Prosperity, Ste. 250
Fairfax, VA 22031
Ph: (703)849-8888   Fax: (703)207-3561
URL: http://www.aiha.org

Annual, September. Covers approximately 12,000 members concerned with the study and control of environmental factors affecting people at work. Entries include: Name, address, phone, affiliation. Arrangement: Alphabetical. Indexes: Employer, geographical.

★6395★ Carroll's State Directory

Carroll Publishing
4701 Sangamore Rd., Ste. S-155
Bethesda, MD 20816
Ph: (301)263-9800   Fax: (301)263-9801
Fr: 800-336-4240
URL: http://www.carrollpub.com/state-print.asp

3x/yr. $385.00 for individuals. Covers about 73,000 state government officials in all branches of government; officers, committees and members of state legislatures; managers of boards and authorities. Entries include: Name, address, phone, fax, title. Arrangement: Geographical; separate sections for state offices and legislatures. Indexes: Personal name (with phone and e-mail address), organizational, keyword.

★6396★ Federal Staff Directory

CQ Press
1255 22nd St. NW, Ste. 400
Washington, DC 20037
Ph: (202)729-1800   Fax: 800-380-3810
Fr: (866)427-7737
URL: http://www.staffdirectories.com/

Latest edition 52, April 2007. $450.00 for individuals. Covers approximately 45,000 persons in federal government offices and independent agencies, with biographies of 2,600 key executives; includes officials at policy level in agencies of the Office of the President, Cabinet-level departments, independent and regulatory agencies, military commands, federal information centers, and libraries, and United States attorneys, marshals, and ambassadors. Entries include: Name, title, location (indicating building, address, and/or room), phone, fax, e-mail address, website, symbols indicating whether position is a presidential appointment and whether senate approval is required. Arrangement: Classified by department/agency. Indexes: Office locator page; extensive subject/keyword; individual name.

HANDBOOKS AND MANUALS

★6397★ Opportunities in State and Local Government Careers

The McGraw-Hill Companies
PO Box 182604
Columbus, OH 43272
Fax: (614)759-3749   Fr: 877-883-5524
E-mail: customer.service@mcgraw-hill.com
URL: http://www.mcgraw-hill.com

Neale J. Baxter. Revised edition, 1992. $14.95; $10.95 (paper). 148 pages. Points out the incentives and drawbacks of a government career. Describes hiring procedures and provides tips on filling out applications, taking physical and aptitude tests, handling interviews, and finding jobs. Describes the jobs in which 75% of all state and local government workers are employed. For each occupation, covers the nature of the work and the training required.

★6398★ Start Your Own Home Inspection Service

The McGraw-Hill Companies
PO Box 182604
Columbus, OH 43272
Fax: (614)759-3749   Fr: 877-883-5524
E-mail: customer.service@mcgraw-hill.com
URL: http://www.mcgraw-hill.com

December 2007. $15.95. Illustrated. 120 pages. Entrepreneur Magazine's Start Up Series.

EMPLOYMENT AGENCIES AND SEARCH FIRMS

★6399★ Summit Executive Search Consultants, Inc.

245 SE 1st St., Ste. 319
Miami, FL 33131
Ph: (305)379-5008   Fax: (305)379-5150
E-mail: summitsearch@compuserve.com

Executive search firm serving a variety of industries.

TRADESHOWS

★6400★ National Safety Council Congress and Expo

National Safety Council
1121 Spring Lake Dr.
Itasca, IL 60143
Ph: (630)285-1121   Fax: (630)285-1315
Fr: 800-621-7619
URL: http://www.nsc.org

Annual. **Primary Exhibits:** Safety- and health-related products and services, including protective clothing, footwear, consulting services, breathing apparatuses, educational materials, films and related equipment, supplies, and services.

OTHER SOURCES

★6401★ National Environmental Health Association (NEHA)

720 S Colorado Blvd., Ste. 1000-N
Denver, CO 80246-1926
Ph: (303)756-9090   Fax: (303)691-9490
E-mail: staff@neha.org
URL: http://www.neha.org

Description: Represents all professionals in environmental health and protection, including Registered Sanitarians, Registered Environmental Health Specialists, Registered Environmental Technicians, Certified Environmental Health Technicians, Registered Hazardous Substances Professionals and Registered Hazardous Substances Specialists. Advances the environmental health and protection profession for the purpose of providing a healthful environment for all. Provides educational materials, publications, credentials and meetings to members and non-member professionals who strive to improve the environment.

★6402★ Production Occupations

Delphi Productions
3159 6th St.
Boulder, CO 80304
Ph: (303)443-2100   Fax: (303)443-4022
Fr: 888-443-2400

E-mail: support@delphivideo.com
URL: http://www.delphivideo.com

$95.00. 49 minutes. Part of the Careers for the 21st Century Video Library.

Insurance Sales Agents

SOURCES OF HELP-WANTED ADS

★6403★ ASCnet Quarterly

Applied Systems Client Network
801 Douglas Ave., Ste. 205
Altamonte Springs, FL 32714
Ph: (407)869-0404   Fax: (407)869-0418
Fr: 800-605-1045
URL: http://www.ascnetquarterly.org/

Quarterly. Subscription included in membership. Professional magazine covering technical information, association news, and industry information for insurance professionals.

★6404★ Best's Review

A.M. Best Company, Inc.
Ambest Rd.
Oldwick, NJ 08858
Ph: (908)439-2200
E-mail: editor_br@ambest.com
URL: http://www.ambest.com/sales/news-overview.asp#br

Monthly. Magazine covering issues and trends for the management personnel of life/health insurers, the agents, and brokers who market their products.

★6405★ Business Insurance

Crain Communications Inc.
1155 Gratiot Ave.
Detroit, MI 48207-2997
Ph: (313)446-6000
URL: http://www.businessinsurance.com

Weekly. $97.00/year for individuals; $173.00 for two years; $200.00/year for individuals, daily online only; $130.00/year for Canada and Mexico; $234.00 for Canada and Mexico, two years; $230.00/year for individuals, includes expedited airmail other countries; $436.00 for two years, includes expedited airmail other countries. International newsweekly reporting on corporate risk and employee benefit management news.

★6406★ Claims

Claims
15112 64th Ave. W
Edmonds, WA 98026
Ph: (425)745-6394
E-mail: editor@claimsmag.com
URL: http://www.claimsmag.com

Monthly. $54.00/year for individuals; $75.00/year for Canada; $113.00/year for other countries. Magazine for the property-casualty insurance claims industry.

★6407★ Insurance & Technology

CMP Media L.L.C.
600 Community Dr.
Manhasset, NY 11030
Ph: (516)562-5000   Fax: (516)562-7830
URL: http://www.insurancetech.com

Monthly. Publication for insurance professionals covering the role of the Internet in financial services organizations.

★6408★ National Underwriter Property and Casualty/Risk and Benefits Management

National Underwriter Co.
5081 Olympic Blvd.
Erlanger, KY 41018
Ph: (859)692-2100   Fr: 800-543-0874
E-mail: nup&c@nuco.com
URL: http://www.nunews.com/pandc/subscribe/

Weekly. $94.00/year for individuals, 2nd class; $133.00/year for Canada, air mail; $178.00/year for U.S. and Canada, air mail; $211.00/year for other countries, air mail. Newsweekly for agents, brokers, executives, and managers in risk and benefit insurance.

★6409★ The Standard

Standard Publishing Corp.
155 Federal St., 13th Fl.
Boston, MA 02110
Ph: (617)457-0600   Fax: (617)457-0608
E-mail: stnd@earthlink.net
URL: http://www.spcpub.com

Weekly (Fri.). $85.00/year for individuals, U.S. Trade newspaper covering insurance events, legislation, regulatory hearings, and court sessions for independent insurance agents in New England.

★6410★ Today's Insurance Professionals

National Association of Insurance Women (International)
1847 East 15th St.
Tulsa, OK 74104-4610
Ph: (918)744-5195   Fax: (918)743-1968
Fr: 800-766-6249
URL: http://www.naiw.org

Quarterly. Magazine on insurance and professional development topics for men and women in the risk and insurance field.

PLACEMENT AND JOB REFERRAL SERVICES

★6411★ American Association of Insurance Management Consultants (AAIMCO)

8980 Lakes at 610 Dr., Ste. 100
Houston, TX 77054
Ph: (713)664-6424   Fax: (713)524-3350
E-mail: thomas@aaimco.com
URL: http://www.aaimco.com

Description: Consists of individuals who devote a substantial portion of their services to insurance consulting, risk management activities, legal representation relating to insurance issues; as well as education and professional development training, employment consulting, and other technical and management advice to the insurance industry. Advises and assists the insurance industry and seeks to achieve professional recognition for insurance management consultants. Mediates the exchange of ideas; sets standards of service and performance; maintains a code of ethics; offers a referral service and a series of educational conferences and seminars. Operates speakers' bureau; offers placement services; compiles statistics.

EMPLOYER DIRECTORIES AND NETWORKING LISTS

★6412★ Best's Insurance Reports

A.M. Best Co.
Ambest Rd.
Oldwick, NJ 08858
Ph: (908)439-2200   Fax: (908)439-2688
URL: http://www.ambest.com

Annual, latest edition 2007. $1,295.00 for individuals. Published in three editions–Life-health insurance, covering about 1,750 companies; property-casualty insurance, covering over 3,200 companies; and international, covering more than 1,200 insurers. Each edition lists state insurance commissioners and related companies and agencies (mutual funds, worker compensation funds, underwriting agencies, etc.). Entries include: For each company–Company name, address, phone; history; states in which licensed; names of officers and directors; financial data; financial analysis and Best's rating. Arrangement: Alphabetical.

★6413★ Business Insurance-Agent/ Broker Profiles Issue

Business Insurance
360 N Michigan Ave.
Chicago, IL 60601-3806
Ph: (312)649-5319   Fax: (312)280-3174
Fr: 800-678-2724
URL: http://www.businessinsurance.com

Annual; latest edition 2007. Publication includes: List of top 10 insurance agents/brokers worldwide specializing in commercial insurance. Entries include: Firm name, address, phone, fax, branch office locations, year established, names of subsidiaries, gross revenues, premium volume, number of employees, principal officers, percent of revenue generated by commercial retail brokerage, acquisitions. Arrangement: Alphabetical by company. Indexes: Geographical.

★6414★ Insurance Phone Book and Directory

Douglas Publications L.L.C.
2807 N Parham Rd., Ste. 200
Richmond, VA 23294
Ph: (804)762-9600   Fax: (804)217-8999
Fr: 800-794-6086
URL: http://www.douglaspublications.com/

Annual; latest edition 2006-2007. $195.00 for print product; $249.00 for print product/ CD, combined. Covers about 3,500 life, accident and health, worker's compensation, auto, fire and casualty, marine, surety, and other insurance companies; 2,100 executive contacts, from presidents and CEOs to claims and customer service managers. Entries include: Company name, address, phone, fax, toll-free number, type of insurance provided. Arrangement: Alphabetical.

★6415★ Kirshner's Insurance Directories

National Underwriter Co.
5081 Olympic Blvd.
Erlanger, KY 41018
Ph: (859)692-2100   Fr: 800-543-0874
URL: http://www.nationalunderwriter.com/ kirschners/

Annual; latest edition 2007. Covers insurance agents and agencies in all 50 states and the District of Columbia. Published in separate editions for Southern California, Northern California, Pacific Northwest (AK, ID, HI, OR, WA, MT), Michigan, Illinois, New England states (CT, ME, MA, NH, RI, VT), Ohio, Rocky Mountain states (AZ, CO, NV, NM, UT, WY), South Central states (GA, AL, MS), Indiana, Texas, Kentucky/Tennessee, East Central states (VA, WV, NC, SC), South Central West states (AR, OK, LA), Wisconsin, Central states (KS, MO, NE), North Central states (IA, MN, ND, SD), Mid-Atlantic states (DE, MD, NJ, DC), Pennsylvania, Florida. Entries include: For companies–Name, address, key personnel (with addresses and phone numbers). Arrangement: Separate alphabetical sections for insurance companies, wholesalers, field agents, and agencies. Indexes: Type of insurance.

★6416★ National Insurance Association-Member Roster

National Insurance Association
411 Chapel Hill Dr., Ste. 633
Durham, NC 27701
Ph: (919)683-5328

Annual, June. Covers about 13 insurance companies owned or controlled by African-Americans. Entries include: Company name, address, phone, date founded, states in which licensed, officers. Arrangement: Alphabetical.

★6417★ Who's Who in Insurance

Underwriter Printing and Publishing Co.
50 E Palisade Ave.
Englewood, NJ 07631
Ph: (201)569-8808   Fr: 800-526-4700

Annual, February. Covers over 5,000 insurance officials, brokers, agents, and buyers. Entries include: Name, title, company name, address, home address, educational background, professional club and association memberships, personal and career data. Arrangement: Alphabetical.

★6418★ Women in Insurance and Financial Services-Membership Directory

Women in Insurance and Financial Services
6748 Wauconda Dr.
Larkspur, CO 80118
Ph: (303)681-9777   Fr: (866)264-9437
URL: http://www.w-wifs.org

Covers list of contact information of WIFS' members who are devoted to helping women succeed in both insurance and financial services.

★6419★ Yearbook

American Association of Managing General Agents
150 S Warner Rd., Ste. 156
King of Prussia, PA 19406
Ph: (610)225-1999   Fax: (610)225-1996
URL: http://www.aamga.org/

Annual, spring. Covers 250 managing general agents of insurance companies and their more than 500 branch offices; coverage includes Canada. Entries include: Name, address, names and titles of principal figures and contact, insurance companies represented. Arrangement: Geographical.

HANDBOOKS AND MANUALS

★6420★ The Adjuster: Making Insurance Claims Pay

Cargo Publishing Co.
PO Box 75146
Houston, TX 77234
Ph: (713)484-1880   Fax: (713)484-8887
Fr: 800-725-2468

Gordon G. Smith. 1998. $39.95 (paper). 356 pages.

★6421★ Opportunities in Insurance Careers

The McGraw-Hill Companies
PO Box 182604
Columbus, OH 43272
Fax: (614)759-3749   Fr: 877-883-5524
E-mail: customer.service@mcgraw-hill.com
URL: http://www.mcgraw-hill.com

Robert M. Schrayer. Revised, 2007. $14.95 (paper). 160 pages. A guide to planning for and seeking opportunities in the field. Contains bibliography and illustrations.

EMPLOYMENT AGENCIES AND SEARCH FIRMS

★6422★ Burkholder Group Inc.

985 Pico Pt.
Colorado Springs, CO 80906
Ph: (719)867-1222   Fax: (719)623-0033
E-mail: info@burkholdergroup.com
URL: http://www.burkholdergroup.com

Executive search firm focused on the insurance industry.

★6423★ Eggers Consulting Company Inc.

11272 Elm St., Eggers Plz.
Omaha, NE 68144
Ph: (402)333-3480   Fax: (402)333-9759
E-mail: admin@eggersconsulting.com
URL: http://www.eggersconsulting.com

Executive search consulting firm. Industries

served: insurance, data processing, retail and banking.

★6424★ Employment Advisors

815 Nicollet Mall
Minneapolis, MN 55402
Ph: (612)339-0521

Employment agency. Places candidates in variety of fields.

★6425★ Godfrey Personnel Inc.

300 W. Adams, Ste. 612
Chicago, IL 60606-5194
Ph: (312)236-4455   Fax: (312)580-6292
E-mail: jim@godfreypersonnel.com
URL: http://www.godfreypersonnel.com

Search firm specializing in insurance industry.

★6426★ Insurance Consultants Inc.

9607 Page Ave.
Bethesda, MD 20814
Ph: (301)493-5115   Fax: (301)493-5696

Personnel consultants specializing in insurance job placement and management consulting. Industries served: insurance (property and casualty, and life and health).

★6427★ International Insurance Consultants Inc.

1191 E Newport Center Dr., Ste. 206
Deerfield Beach, FL 33442
Ph: (954)421-0122   Fax: (954)421-3332
E-mail: info@insurancerecruitersusa.com
URL: http://www.insurancerecruitersusa.com

Offers executive search to the insurance industry. Clients include insurance companies, brokers, consultants and investment banks. Industries served: insurance and financial services industries.

★6428★ International Insurance Personnel, Inc.

300 W. Wieuca Rd., Bldg. 2, Ste. 101
Atlanta, GA 30342
Ph: (404)255-9710   Fax: (404)255-9864
E-mail: info@intlinspersonnel.com
URL: http://yp.bellsouth.com/sites/intlinspersonnel/index.html

Employment agency specializing in the area of insurance.

★6429★ Questor Consultants, Inc.

2515 N. Broad St.
Colmar, PA 18915
Ph: (215)997-9262   Fax: (215)997-9226
E-mail: sbevivino@questorconsultants.com
URL: http://www.questorconsultants.com

Executive search firm specializing in the insurance and legal fields.

★6430★ Quirk-Corporon and Associates Inc.

1229 N Jackson St., Ste. 205
Milwaukee, WI 53202
Ph: (414)224-9399   Fax: (414)224-9472
E-mail: quirkrecruiters@sbcglobal.net
URL: http://www.quirkinsrecruiters.com

Employment agency specializing in all disciplines of the insurance and financial industries.

★6431★ SHS of Cherry Hill

496 N Kings Hwy., Ste. 125
Cherry Hill, NJ 08034
Ph: (856)779-9030   Fax: (856)779-0898
E-mail: shs@shsofcherryhill.com
URL: http://www.shsofcherryhill.com

Personnel recruiters operating in the disciplines of accounting, sales, insurance, engineering, and administration. Industries served: insurance, distribution, manufacturing, and service.

★6432★ Tyler & Co.

375 Northridge Rd., Ste. 400
Atlanta, GA 30350-3299
Ph: (770)396-3939   Fax: (770)396-6693
Fr: 800-989-6789
E-mail: art@tylerandco.com
URL: http://www.tylerandco.com

Retained executive search for the healthcare, food, market research, manufacturing and insurance industries.

ONLINE JOB SOURCES AND SERVICES

★6433★ Great Insurance Jobs

Fr: 800-818-4898
URL: http://www.greatinsurancejobs.com

Description: Contains varied insurance positions. Job seekers may browse employee profiles, post resumes, and read descriptions of hundreds of recently-posted insurance jobs.

★6434★ National Insurance Recruiters Association

URL: http://www.insurancerecruiters.com

Description: Contains lists of recruiters (listed by department and line of business) and available insurance positions.

★6435★ Premier Careers, Inc.

117 Main Ave. N.
Fayetteville, TN 37334
Ph: (931)438-7070
E-mail: info@atspremiercareers.com
URL: http://www.premiercareers.com

Description: Contains a database with information on candidates searching for jobs in the property and casualty insurance industry

and with national sales organizations. Houses resumes and letters of reference. Candidate searches may be run by industry, geography, job title, years of experience, compensation, education, and/or accreditation. Also offers resume writing and interviewing tips to job hunters.

TRADESHOWS

★6436★ Annual NAIW Convention - National Association of Insurance Women International

National Association of Insurance Women - International
6528 E. 101st St. PMB No. 750
Tulsa, OK 74133
Fax: (918)743-1968   Fr: 800-766-6249
URL: http://www.naiw.org

Annual. **Primary Exhibits:** Equipment, supplies, and services for insurance industry professionals.

★6437★ Independent Insurance Agents of Indiana Annual Convention

Independent Insurance Agents of Indiana
3435 W, 96th St.
Indianapolis, IN 46268
Ph: (317)824-3780   Fax: (317)824-3786
Fr: 800-438-4424
E-mail: mason@bigi.org
URL: http://www.iiaa.org

Annual. **Primary Exhibits:** Small business supplies, automation equipment, solutions, insurance service, coverage providers and carriers.

★6438★ Insurance Accounting and Systems Association Conference

Insurance Accounting and Systems Association
PO Box 51340
4705 University Dr., Ste. 280
Durham, NC 27717-3409
Ph: (919)489-0991   Fax: (919)489-1994
E-mail: info@iasa.org
URL: http://www.iasa.org

Annual. **Primary Exhibits:** Insurance equipment, supplies, and services.

★6439★ Insurance Claim Conference

Eastern Claims Conference
PO Box 2730
Stamford, CT 06906
Ph: (212)615-7424   Fax: (212)615-7345
E-mail: stan.brzozowski@pfsfhg.com
URL: http://www.easternclaimsconference.com

Annual. **Primary Exhibits:** Participants include claim examiners of life, health, disability, and group claims of the insurance industry; travel, investigators, data base, consulting.

★6440★ Massachusetts Association of Insurance Agents Convention

Massachusetts Association of Insurance
Agents
137 Pennsylvania Ave.
Framingham, MA 01701
Ph: (508)628-5452   Fax: (508)628-5444
Fr: 800-742-6363
E-mail: info@massagent.com
URL: http://www.massagent.com

Annual. **Primary Exhibits:** Computers and related services, office equipment, financial consultation services, managerial services, car rental, restoration, premium finance companies.

★6441★ Missouri Association of Insurance Agents Exhibition - Annual Convention

Missouri Association of Insurance Agents
2701 Industrial Dr.
PO Box 1785,
Jefferson City, MO 65102
Ph: (573)893-4301   Fax: (573)893-3708
Fr: 800-617-3658
E-mail: maia@moagent.org

Annual. **Primary Exhibits:** Insurance related equipment, supplies, and services.

★6442★ National Association of Independent Life Brokerage Agencies Conference

National Association of Independent Life
Brokerage Agencies
12150 Monument Dr., Ste. 125
Fairfax, VA 22033
Ph: (703)383-3081   Fax: (703)383-6942
E-mail: jmn@nailba.com
URL: http://www.nailba.org

Annual. **Primary Exhibits:** Equipment, supplies, and services for licensed independent life brokerage agencies that represent at least 3 insurance companies, but are not controlled or owned by an underwriting company.

★6443★ National Association of Mutual Insurance Companies Annual Convention and Exposition

National Association of Mutual Insurance
Companies
3601 Vincennes Rd.
PO Box 68700
Indianapolis, IN 46268
Ph: (317)875-5250   Fax: (317)879-8408
Fr: 800-33-NAMIC
E-mail: service@namic.org
URL: http://www.namic.org

Annual. **Primary Exhibits:** Mutual property and casualty insurance Equipment, supplies, and services.

★6444★ Professional Independent Insurance Agents of Illinois Annual Convention

Professional Independent Insurance
Agents of Illinois
4360 Wabash Ave.
Springfield, IL 62711
Ph: (217)793-6660   Fax: (217)793-6744
Fr: 800-628-6436
E-mail: info@piiai.org
URL: http://www.piiai.org

Annual. **Primary Exhibits:** Insurance-related products, including computers and office supplies, restoration services and cell phones.

★6445★ Public Agency Risk Managers Association Convention

Public Agency Risk Managers Association
PO Box 6810
San Jose, CA 95150
Ph: 888-907-2762   Fax: 888-412-5913
Fr: 888-90-PARMA
E-mail: brenda.reisinger@parma.com
URL: http://www.parma.com

Annual. **Primary Exhibits:** Risk management equipment, supplies, and services.

★6446★ Risk and Insurance Management Society Annual Conference

Risk and Insurance Management Society
1065 Avenue of the Americas, 13th Fl.
New York, NY 10018
Ph: (212)286-9292   Fax: (212)986-9716
URL: http://www.rims.org

Annual. **Primary Exhibits:** Insurance industry related equipment, supplies, and services. **Dates and Locations:** 2008 Apr 27 - May 01; San Diego, CA.

★6447★ Society of Insurance Trainers and Educators Conference

Society of Insurance Trainers and
Educators
2120 Market St., Ste. 108
San Francisco, CA 94114
Ph: (415)621-2830   Fax: (415)621-0889
E-mail: ed@insurancetrainers.org
URL: http://www.insurancetrainers.org

Annual. **Primary Exhibits:** Insurance education equipment, supplies, and services.

OTHER SOURCES

★6448★ American Council of Life Insurers (ACLI)

American Council of Life Insurers
101 Constitution Ave. NW
Washington, DC 20001-2133
Ph: (202)624-2000   Fax: (202)624-2319
Fr: 877-674-4659
E-mail: media@acli.com
URL: http://www.acli.com

Description: Represents the interests of

legal reserve life insurance companies in legislative, regulatory and judicial matters at the federal, state and municipal levels of government and at the NAIC. Member companies hold majority of the life insurance in force in the United States.

★6449★ American Institute for CPCU (AICPCU)

720 Providence Rd., Ste. 100
PO Box 3016
Malvern, PA 19355-0716
Ph: (610)644-2100   Fax: (610)640-9576
Fr: 800-644-2101
E-mail: customersupport@cpcuiia.org
URL: http://www.aicpcu.org

Purpose: Determines qualifications for professional certification of insurance personnel; conducts examinations and awards designation of Chartered Property Casualty Underwriter (CPCU).

★6450★ APIW

Sherman Think Tank
15 Hopkins Dr.
Lawrenceville, NJ 08648
Ph: (609)896-2280   Fax: (609)896-0063
E-mail: info@apiw.org
URL: http://www.apiw.org

Members: Professional women from the insurance/reinsurance industry. **Purpose:** Promotes cooperation and understanding among members; maintains high professional standards in the insurance industry; provides a strong network of professional contacts and educational aid; recognizes the contributions of women to insurance; encourages women to seek employment in the insurance community.

★6451★ Business and Administration Support Occupations

Delphi Productions
3159 6th St.
Boulder, CO 80304
Ph: (303)443-2100   Fax: (303)443-4022
Fr: 888-443-2400
E-mail: support@delphivideo.com
URL: http://www.delphivideo.com

$95.00. 42 minutes. Part of the Careers for the 21st Century Video Library.

★6452★ GAMA International

2901 Telestar Ct., Ste. 140
Falls Church, VA 22042-1205
Ph: (703)770-8184   Fax: (703)770-8182
Fr: 800-345-2687
E-mail: gamamail@gama.naifa.org
URL: http://www.gamaweb.com

Description: Provides world-class education and training resources for individuals, companies and organizations involved with the recruitment and development of field managers, representatives and staff in the life insurance and financial services industry; advocates of the value-added role of field management and representatives in the ethical distribution of life insurance and financial products and services industry.

★6453★ Independent Insurance Agents and Brokers of America (IIABA)

127 S Peyton St.
Alexandria, VA 22314
Ph: (703)683-4422   Fax: (703)683-7556
Fr: 800-221-7917
E-mail: info@iiaba.org
URL: http://www.iiaba.net

Description: Sales agencies handling property, fire, casualty, and surety insurance. Organizes technical and sales courses for new and established agents. Sponsors Independent Insurance Agent Junior Classic Golf Tournament.

★6454★ Insurance Agent

Cambridge Educational
PO Box 2053
Princeton, NJ 08543-2053
Ph: 800-257-5126   Fax: (609)671-0266
Fr: 800-468-4227
E-mail: custserv@films.com
URL: http://www.cambridgeeducational.com

VHS and DVD. $39.95. 11 minutes. 1989. Part of the Vocational Visions Career Series.

★6455★ Insurance Information Institute (III)

110 William St.
New York, NY 10038
Ph: (212)346-5500   Fr: 800-331-9146
E-mail: johns@iii.org
URL: http://www.iii.org

Description: Property and casualty insurance companies. Provides information and educational services to mass media, educational institutions, trade associations, businesses, government agencies, and the public.

★6456★ LOMA

2300 Windy Ridge Pkwy., Ste. 600
Atlanta, GA 30339-8443
Ph: (770)951-1770   Fax: (770)984-0441
Fr: 800-275-5662
E-mail: askloma@loma.org
URL: http://www.loma.org

Description: Life and health insurance companies and financial services in the U.S. and Canada; and overseas in 45 countries; affiliate members are firms that provide professional support to member companies. Provides research, information, training, and educational activities in areas of operations and systems, human resources, financial planning and employee development. Administers FLMI Insurance Education Program, which awards FLMI (Fellow, Life Management Institute) designation to those who complete the ten-examination program.

★6457★ Marketing & Sales Occupations

Delphi Productions
3159 6th St.
Boulder, CO 80304
Ph: (303)443-2100   Fax: (303)443-4022
Fr: 888-443-2400
E-mail: support@delphivideo.com
URL: http://www.delphivideo.com

$95.00. 50 minutes. Part of the Careers for the 21st Century Video Library.

★6458★ National Association of Health Underwriters (NAHU)

2000 N 14th St., Ste. 450
Arlington, VA 22201
Ph: (703)276-0220   Fax: (703)841-7797
E-mail: info@nahu.org
URL: http://www.nahu.org

Description: Insurance agents and brokers engaged in the promotion, sale, and administration of disability income and health insurance. Sponsors advanced health insurance underwriting and research seminars. Testifies before federal and state committees on pending health insurance legislation. Sponsors Leading Producers Roundtable Awards for leading salesmen. Maintains a speakers' bureau and a political action committee.

★6459★ National Association of Insurance Women International (NAIW)

6528 E 101st St., Ste. D-1
PMB No. 750
Tulsa, OK 74133
Fax: (918)743-1968   Fr: 800-766-6249
E-mail: joinnaiw@naiw.org
URL: http://www.naiw.org

Members: Insurance industry professionals. **Purpose:** Promotes continuing education and networking for the professional advancement of its members. **Activities:** Offers education programs, meetings, services, and leadership opportunities. Provides a forum to learn about other disciplines in the insurance industry.

★6460★ National Association of Professional Insurance Agents (PIA)

400 N Washington St.
Alexandria, VA 22314
Ph: (703)836-9340   Fax: (703)836-1279
E-mail: piaweb@pianet.org
URL: http://www.pianet.com

Description: Represents independent agents in all 50 states, Puerto Rico and the District of Columbia. Represents members' interests in government and industry; provides educational programs; compiles statistics; conducts research programs; develops products/services unique to independent agencies; provides information and networking opportunities.

★6461★ Society of Financial Service Professionals (SFSP)

17 Campus Blvd., Ste. 201
Newtown Square, PA 19073-3230
Ph: (215)321-9662   Fax: (610)527-1499
Fr: 800-927-2427
E-mail: mpepe@financialpro.org
URL: http://www.financialpro.org

Description: Represents the interests of financial advisers. Fosters the development of professional responsibility. Assists clients to achieve personal and business-related financial goals. Offers educational programs, online professional resources and networking opportunities.

Interior Designers

★6473★ PLANET News

Professional Landcare Network
950 Herndon Pky., Ste. 450
Herndon, VA 20170
Ph: (703)736-9666   Fax: (703)736-9668
Fr: 800-395-2522
URL: http://www.landcarenetwork.org/

Description: Monthly. Serves specialists interested in the design, installation, and maintenance of interior and exterior landscapes, with emphasis on artistic and healthful results. Carries technical information and tips on subjects such as pricing work to make money. Recurring features include news of research, book reviews, award winning landscapes, and a calendar of events.

★6474★ Portfolio

Interior Design Society
3910 Tinsley Dr., Ste. 101
High Point, NC 27265
Fax: (336)801-6110   Fr: 800-888-9590
E-mail: info@interiordesignsociety.org
URL: http://www.interiordesignsociety.org

Description: Quarterly. Reports on society activities and news of the interior design industry.

★6475★ Qualified Remodeler Magazine

Cygnus Business Media
1233 Janesville Ave.
Fort Atkinson, WI 53538
Fr: 800-547-7377
URL: http://www.qualifiedremodeler.com

Monthly. Magazine for remodeling contractor/distributors.

★6476★ Remodeling

Hanley-Wood L.L.C.
1 Thomas Cir., NW, Ste. 600
Washington, DC 20005
Ph: (202)452-0800   Fax: (202)785-1974
URL: http://www.hanleywood.com/default.aspx?page=b2brm

$25.00/year for individuals; $40.00/year for individuals, Canadian residents; $192.00/year for individuals, international residents. Trade magazine for the professional remodeling industry.

★6477★ Visual Merchandising and Store Design

ST Media Group International Inc.
407 Gilbert Ave.
Cincinnati, OH 45202
Ph: (513)421-2050   Fax: (513)421-5144
Fr: 800-925-1110
E-mail: vmsd@stmediagroup.com
URL: http://www.stmediagroup.com/index.php3?d=pubs&p=vm

Monthly. $42.00/year for individuals, U.S.; $66.00/year for individuals, 2 years, U.S.; $62.00/year for individuals, Canada (surface); $100.00/year for individuals, 2 years, Canada (surface); $65.00/year for individuals, Mexico/Foreign (surface); $105.00/year for individuals, 2 years, Mexico/Foreign (sur-

face); $100.00/year for individuals, Mexico, 1st Class; $175.00/year for individuals, 2 years, Mexico 1st Class; $115.00/year for individuals, Central/South America; $205.00/year for individuals, 2 years, Central/South America. The leading magazine of the retail design industry covering the latest trends in retail design, store planning, and merchandise presentation.

★6478★ Walls, Windows, and Floors

Hachette Filipacchi Media U.S. Inc.
1633 Broadway
New York, NY 10019
Ph: (212)767-6000   Fax: (212)767-5631

Special interest home and garden magazine focusing on decorating the home.

PLACEMENT AND JOB REFERRAL SERVICES

★6479★ Council of Educational Facility Planners, International (CEFPI)

9180 E Desert Cove Dr., Ste. 104
Scottsdale, AZ 85260-6231
Ph: (480)391-0840   Fax: (480)391-0940
E-mail: contact@cefpi.org
URL: http://www.cefpi.org

Members: Individuals and firms who are responsible for planning, designing, creating, maintaining, and equipping the physical environment of education. **Purpose:** Sponsors an exchange of information, professional experiences, best practices research results, and other investigative techniques concerning educational facility planning. **Activities:** Activities include publication and review of current and emerging practices in educational facility planning; identification and execution of needed research; development of professional training programs; strengthening of planning services on various levels of government and in institutions of higher learning; leadership in the development of higher standards for facility design and the physical environment of education. Operates speakers' bureau; sponsors placement service; compiles statistics.

★6480★ Institute of Store Planners (ISP)

25 N Broadway
Tarrytown, NY 10591-3221
Ph: (914)332-0040   Fax: (914)332-1541
E-mail: info@ispo.org
URL: http://ww3.ispo.org

Description: Persons active in store planning and design; visual merchandisers, students, and educators; contractors and suppliers to the industry; dedicated to the professional growth of members while providing service to the public through improvement of the retail environment. Provides forum for debate and discussion by store design experts, retailers, and public figures. Makes available speakers for store planning and

design courses at the college level; develops programs for store planning courses. Sponsors student design competitions and annual international store design competition with awards in 10 categories. Maintains placement service.

EMPLOYER DIRECTORIES AND NETWORKING LISTS

★6481★ Almanac of Architecture and Design

Greenway Consulting
25 Technology Pkwy. S, Ste. 101
Norcross, GA 30092
Ph: (678)879-0929   Fax: (678)879-0930
URL: http://www.greenway.us

Annual, latest edition 8, 2007. $49.50 for individuals. Publication includes: Lists of professional organizations, degree programs, and leading firms in architecture and design. Principal content of publication is a collection of information regarding architecture and design.

★6482★ Directory of Interior Design Programs Accredited by FIDER

Council for Interior Design Accreditation
146 Monroe Ctr. NW, Ste. 1318
Grand Rapids, MI 49503
Ph: (616)458-0400   Fax: (616)458-0460
URL: http://www.fider.org

Semiannual, June and November. Covers 128 interior design programs in the United States and Canada in conformance with the accreditation standards of the foundation. Entries include: Type of program, name of institution, name of department chair or program head, phone, dates of last and next accreditation review, degrees offered, e-mail and web addresses. Arrangement: Geographical, degree level offered, then alphabetical by institution name.

★6483★ ENR-Top 500 Design Firms Issue

McGraw-Hill Inc.
1221 Ave. of the Americas
New York, NY 10020-1095
Ph: (212)512-2000   Fax: (212)512-3840
Fr: 877-833-5524
URL: http://enr.construction.com/people/sourcebooks/top500Design/

Annual, latest edition 2007. $50.00 for individuals. Publication includes: List of 500 leading architectural, engineering, and specialty design firms selected on basis of annual billings. Entries include: Company name, headquarters location, type of firm, current and prior year rank in billings, types of services, countries in which operated in preceding year. Arrangement: Ranked by billings.

★6484★ **International Directory of Design**

Penrose Press
1333 Gough, Ste. 8B
PO Box 470925
San Francisco, CA 94109
Ph: (415)567-4157   Fax: (415)567-4165
URL: http://penrose-press.com/idd/search_db.php

Covers design colleges and universities worldwide. Entries include: Links to complete name, address, phone, fax and other contact information. Arrangement: Alphabetical by major of study, then alphabetical by country (U.S. alphabetical by state), then alphabetical by university.

HANDBOOKS AND MANUALS

★6485★ **77 Habits of Highly Creative Interior Designers: Insider Secrets from the World's Top Design Professionals**

Quarry Books
100 Cummings Center, Ste. 406-L
Beverly, MA 01915
Ph: (978)282-9590   Fax: (978)283-2742
Fr: 800-328-0590
URL: http://www.quarrybooks.com/

Sarah Lynch. 2005. $15.99. Designers provide tips on 77 key design elements covering style, decor and furnishings.160 pages

★6486★ **Careers for Color Connoisseurs and Other Visual Types**

The McGraw-Hill Companies
PO Box 182604
Columbus, OH 43272
Fax: (614)759-3749   Fr: 877-883-5524
E-mail: customer.service@mcgraw-hill.com
URL: http://www.mcgraw-hill.com

Jan Goldberg. Second edition, 2005. $13.95 (paper). 176 pages.

★6487★ **The Creative Business Guide to Running a Graphic Design Business**

W. W. Norton & Company, Incorporated
500 Fifth Ave.
New York, NY 10110-0017
Ph: (212)354-5500   Fax: (212)869-0856
Fr: 800-223-2584
URL: http://www.wwnorton.com/

Cameron Foote. 2004. $29.95. 496 pages.

★6488★ **Managing to Make It**

University of Chicago Press
1427 E. 60th St.
Chicago, IL 60637
Ph: (773)702-7700   Fax: (773)702-9756

Frank F. Furstenberg. 2000. $21.00. 320 pages.

★6489★ **Opportunities in Interior Design and Decorating Careers**

The McGraw-Hill Companies
PO Box 182604
Columbus, OH 43272
Fax: (614)759-3749   Fr: 877-883-5524
E-mail: customer.service@mcgraw-hill.com
URL: http://www.mcgraw-hill.com

Victoria Kloss Ball and David Stearns. Second edition, revised, 2001. $13.95 (paper). 144 pages. Covers opportunities and job search techniques in interior design. Addresses working for a design house, contract work, and starting a business. Illustrated.

★6490★ **Professional Interior Design: A Career Guide**

iUniverse, Inc.
2021 Pine Lake Rd. Ste. 100
Lincoln, NE 68512
Ph: (402)323-7800   Fax: (402)323-7824
Fr: 877-288-4677
URL: http://www.iuniverse.com/

Jason Znoy, ASID Illinois Association. May 2004. $9.95 (paper). 64 pages.

★6491★ **Residential Planning: A Guide for Interior Designers**

John Wiley & Sons, Inc.
111 River St.
Hoboken, NJ 07030
Ph: (201)748-6000   Fax: (201)748-6088
E-mail: info@wiley.com
URL: http://www.wiley.com/WileyCDA/

Maureen Mitton and Courtney Nystuen. 2007. $45.00. Fundamental skills for designers working in any type of home or decorative style, focusing on planning, human factors, code and building systems, storage and exterior spaces.

★6492★ **Start Your Own Interior Design Business and Keep It Growing!**

Touch of Design
5342 Elsinore St.
Oceanside, CA 92056
Ph: (619)945-7909   Fax: (619)945-4283

Linda M. Ramsay. 1994. $39.99 (paper). 367 pages.

EMPLOYMENT AGENCIES AND SEARCH FIRMS

★6493★ **Claremont-Branan, Inc.**

1298 Rockbridge Rd., Ste. B
Stone Mountain, GA 30087
Ph: (770)925-2915   Fax: (770)925-2601
Fr: 800-875-1292
E-mail: ohil@cbisearch.com
URL: http://cbisearch.com

Employment agency. Executive search firm.

★6494★ **Randolph Associates, Inc.**

950 Massachusetts Ave., Ste. 105
Cambridge, MA 02139-3174
Ph: (617)441-8777   Fax: (617)441-8778
E-mail: jobs@greatjobs.com
URL: http://www.greatjobs.com

Employment agency. Provides regular or temporary placement of staff.

★6495★ **RitaSue Siegel Resources, Inc.**

162 Fifth Ave., 11th Fl.
New York, NY 10010-5969
Ph: (212)682-2100   Fax: (212)682-2946
E-mail: ritasues@ritasue.com
URL: http://www.ritasuesiegelresources.com

Executive search firm specializing in industrial and product design.

TRADESHOWS

★6496★ **American Society of Interior Designers National Conference and International Exposition of Designer Sources**

American Society of Interior Designers
608 Massachusetts Ave., NE
Washington, DC 20002-6006
Ph: (202)546-3480   Fax: (202)546-3240
E-mail: asid@asid.org
URL: http://www.asid.org

Annual. **Primary Exhibits:** Interior design merchandise, including wall coverings, laminates, lighting fixtures, plumbing fixtures, carpets, furniture, office systems, and fabrics.

★6497★ **Annual Home Decorating and Remodeling Show**

Show Pros International, LLC.
PO Box 230669
Las Vegas, NV 89123-0012
Ph: (702)450-7984   Fr: 800-343-8344
E-mail: spvandy@cox.net
URL: http://www.showprosintl.com/

Annual. **Primary Exhibits:** Home products.

★6498★ **Chicago Design Show**

Merchandise Mart Properties Inc.
Merchandise Mart, Ste. 470
Chicago, IL 60654
Ph: 800-677-MART   Fax: (312)527-7782
Fr: 800-677-6278
URL: http://www.merchandisemart.com

Annual. **Primary Exhibits:** Contemporary design in furniture, fashion, food.

★6499★ Coverings

National Trade Productions, Inc.
313 S Patrick St.
Alexandria, VA 22314-3567
Ph: (703)683-8500   Fax: (703)836-4486
Fr: 800-687-7469
E-mail: ntpinfo@ntpshow.com
URL: http://www.ntpshow.com

Annual. **Primary Exhibits:** Residential and commercial covering industries: flooring, ceramic tile, natural stone and related products and services. Also hardwood flooring, laminate flooring, resilient flooring and related adhesives, grouts, sealants, tools and allied products. **Dates and Locations:** 2008 Apr 29 - May 02; Orlando, FL; Orange County Convention Center.

★6500★ Design Show Los Angeles

Merchandise Mart Properties Inc.
Merchandise Mart, Ste. 470
Chicago, IL 60654
Ph: 800-677-MART   Fax: (312)527-7782
Fr: 800-677-6278
URL: http://www.merchandisemart.com

Primary Exhibits: Contemporary design exhibition.

★6501★ DesigNation

DesigNation, Inc.
300 M St., SW, Ste. N110
Washington, DC 20024
Ph: (202)488-1530   Fax: (202)488-3838
E-mail: info@designation.net
URL: http://www.designation.net

Annual. **Primary Exhibits:** Exhibits of interest to designers holding college degrees who are practicing graphic, industrial, fashion, textile, and interior design.

★6502★ DesignFest

Merchandise Mart Properties Inc.
Merchandise Mart, Ste. 470
Chicago, IL 60654
Ph: 800-677-MART   Fax: (312)527-7782
Fr: 800-677-6278
URL: http://www.merchandisemart.com

Annual. **Primary Exhibits:** Interior design, contract furnishings, lighting, flooring, wall coverings.

★6503★ Fall Home and Decorating Expo

Tower Show Productions, Inc.
800 Roosevelt Rd., Ste. A-109
Bldg. A
Glen Ellyn, IL 60137
Ph: (630)469-4611   Fax: (630)469-4811
Fr: 800-946-4611
E-mail: info@towershow.com
URL: http://www.towershow.com

Annual. **Primary Exhibits:** Home improvement equipment, supplies, and services.

★6504★ NeoCon New York

Merchandise Mart Properties Inc.
Merchandise Mart, Ste. 470
Chicago, IL 60654
Ph: 800-677-MART   Fax: (312)527-7782
Fr: 800-677-6278
URL: http://www.merchandisemart.com

Annual. **Primary Exhibits:** Contract and residential furnishing and construction exhibition.

★6505★ Old House/New House Home Show

Kennedy Productions, Inc.
1208 Lisle Pl.
Lisle, IL 60532-2262
Ph: (630)515-1160   Fax: (630)515-1165
E-mail: kp@corecomm.net
URL: http://www.kennedyproductions.com

Semiannual. **Primary Exhibits:** Products and services for home remodeling, improvement, enhancement, decorating, landscaping and more. Hundreds of ideas to improve and beautify every home.

★6506★ Sacramento Home Improvement and Decorating Show

Bakarich Presents, Inc.
PO Box 448
834-A Jefferson Blvd.
Sacramento, CA 95812
Ph: (916)371-0560   Fax: (916)371-0624
Fr: 800-372-0560

Primary Exhibits: Interior design products, and home furnishing equipment, supplies, and services.

★6507★ Surfaces

World Floor Covering Association
2211 E Howell Ave.
Anaheim, CA 92806
Ph: (714)978-6440   Fax: (714)978-6066
Fr: 800-624-6880
E-mail: wfca@wfca.org
URL: http://www.wfca.org

Annual. **Primary Exhibits:** Floor covering equipment, supplies, and services.

OTHER SOURCES

★6508★ Home Economics Careers

Cambridge Educational
PO Box 2053
Princeton, NJ 08543-2053
Ph: 800-257-5126   Fax: (609)671-0266
Fr: 800-468-4227
E-mail: custserv@films.com
URL: http://www.cambridgeeducational.com

VHS and DVD. $79.95. 47 minutes. 1990.

Includes student manual. Interviews with persons working in each field explores careers in dietetics, foods and nutrition, child development, interior design, and fashion. Working with cooperative extension, in education, and with business and industry, are among the career profiles

★6509★ Interior Design Society (IDS)

3910 Tinsley Dr., Ste. 101
High Point, NC 27265
Fax: (336)801-6110   Fr: 800-888-9590
E-mail: info@interiordesignsociety.org
URL: http://www.interiordesignsociety.org

Description: Represents independent designers and decorators, retail designers and sales people, design-oriented firms, and manufacturers. Grants accreditation and recognition to qualified residential interior designers and retail home furnishing stores. Conducts educational seminars in design, sales training, and marketing. Offers products and publications for designers and a correspondence course for home furnishing sales people.

★6510★ International Design Guild (IDG)

670 Commercial St.
Manchester, NH 03101
Fr: 800-205-4345
E-mail: info@design-guild.com
URL: http://www.design-guild.com

Description: Brings together interior designers to share and gain insight for business development and networking. Provides members with customizable marketing, merchandising, educational and operational tools. Aims to help members operate their businesses more profitably.

★6511★ International Interior Design Association (IIDA)

222 Merchandise Mart Plz., Ste. 1540
Chicago, IL 60654
Ph: (312)467-1950   Fax: (312)467-0779
Fr: 888-799-4432
E-mail: iidahq@iida.org
URL: http://www.iida.org

Purpose: Represents professional interior designers, including designers of commercial, healthcare, hospitality, government, retail, residential facilities; educators; researchers; representatives of allied manufacturing sources. **Activities:** Conducts research, student programs, and continuing education programs for members. Has developed a code of ethics for the professional design membership.

Jewelers

SOURCES OF HELP-WANTED ADS

★6512★ Couture International Jeweler
VNU Business Media USA
770 Broadway
New York, NY 10003
Ph: (646)654-4500
URL: http://www.vnubusinessmedia.com/
box/bp/div_ret_j_cij.html

Bimonthly. $60.00/year for U.S. $105.00/year for other countries. Trade magazine covering the jewelry and retail industry.

★6513★ Diamond Intelligence Briefs
VNU Business Media USA
770 Broadway
New York, NY 10003
Ph: (646)654-4500

Trade publication for the diamond and jewelry industry.

★6514★ Fashion Accessories
S.C.M. Publications Inc.
PO Box 859
Mahwah, NJ 07430
Ph: (201)684-9222   Fax: (201)684-9228

Monthly. $24.00/year for individuals. Magazine focusing on fashion jewelry & accessories for women and men.

★6515★ JCK's High-Volume Jeweler
Reed Business Information
360 Park Ave. S
New York, NY 10010
Ph: (646)746-6400   Fax: (646)746-7431
URL: http://www.reedbusiness.com

Bimonthly. Professional publication covering the jewelry industry.

★6516★ Jewelers' Circular-Keystone
Reed Business Information
360 Park Ave. S
New York, NY 10010
Ph: (646)746-6400   Fax: (646)746-7431

URL: http://www.jckonline.com/
Monthly. Retail jewelers trade magazine.

★6517★ National Jeweler
The Nielsen Co.
770 Broadway
New York, NY 10003
Ph: (646)654-5000   Fax: (646)654-5002
URL: http://
www.nationaljewelernetwork.com/njn/index.jsp

Semimonthly. $10.00 for single issue, cover; $89.00/year for U.S. $104.00/year for Canada; $330.00/year for other countries, airmail only. Jewelry industry magazine.

★6518★ New York Diamonds
Reed Business Information
360 Park Ave. S
New York, NY 10010
Ph: (646)746-6400   Fax: (646)746-7431
URL: http://www.reedbusiness.com

Bimonthly. Publication covering the jewelry trade.

★6519★ Watch & Clock Review
Golden Bell Press
2403 Champa St.
Denver, CO 80205
Ph: (303)296-1600   Fax: (303)295-2159

Monthly. $19.50/year for individuals, 1 year; $35.00/year for individuals, 2 years. Magazine on watches and clocks.

PLACEMENT AND JOB REFERRAL SERVICES

★6520★ Gemological Institute of America (GIA)
5345 Armada Dr.
The Robert Mouawad Campus
Carlsbad, CA 92008
Ph: (760)603-4000   Fax: (760)603-4003
Fr: 800-421-7250
E-mail: donna.baker@gia.edu
URL: http://www.gia.edu

Description: Works to ensure the public trust in gems and jewelry by upholding the highest standards of integrity, academics, science, and professionalism through research, education, gemological laboratory services, and instrument development; alumni are sustaining members. Conducts home study programs, resident courses, online classes and traveling seminars in identification and quality analysis of diamonds and other gemstones and pearls, and in jewelry making and repair, jewelry designing, and jewelry sales. Manufactures and sells gem testing, diamond grading equipment and audiovisual gemstone presentations through subsidiaries. Maintains gem testing and research laboratories in Carlsbad, CA and New York City. Offers job placement service; organizes gemological study tours. Awards diplomas and operates speakers' bureau.

EMPLOYER DIRECTORIES AND NETWORKING LISTS

★6521★ Israel Jewelry Industry Export-Import Directory
International Business Publications, USA
PO Box 15343
Washington, DC 20003
Ph: (202)546-2103   Fax: (202)546-3275

$99.95. Covers strategic business opportunities, contact information and basic info for conducting business in the country.

★6522★ Jewelers Board of Trade-Confidential Reference Book

Jewelers Board of Trade
95 Jefferson Blvd.
Warwick, RI 02888-1046
Ph: (401)467-0055   Fax: (401)467-1199
URL: http://www.jewelersboard.com

Semiannual, March and September. Covers about 45,000 jewelry manufacturers, importers, distributors, and retailers. Entries include: Company name, address, phone, whether a wholesaler, retailer, or manufacturer, credit rating. Arrangement: Geographical.

★6523★ National Association of Jewelry Appraisers-Membership Directory

National Association of Jewelry Appraisers Inc.
PO Box 18
Rego Park, NY 11374-0018
Ph: (718)896-1536   Fax: (718)997-9057
URL: http://www.najaappraisers.com

Annual, April. Covers nearly 750 members. Entries include: Name, address, phone, business affiliation, area of specialization. Arrangement: Alphabetical, with separate geographical listing. Indexes: Specialty.

HANDBOOKS AND MANUALS

★6524★ How to Be Successful in the Bead Jewelry Business

Kate Drew-Wilkinson Designs
PO Box 1803
Bisbee, AZ 85603
Ph: (520)432-7818   Fax: (520)432-7117
E-mail: robson@drobson.info

Kate Drew-Wilkinson. 1994. $24.00; $9.95 (paper). 103 pages.

TRADESHOWS

★6525★ AKS Summer Bead & Gem Fest

AKS Gem Shows
PO Box 24552
New Orleans, LA 70184
Ph: (504)455-6101   Fax: (504)455-6157
Fr: (866)AKS-SHOW
E-mail: info@aksshow.com
URL: http://aksshow.com

Primary Exhibits: Full spectrum of gems, jewelry, beads, rocks, and minerals.

★6526★ Atlanta Jewelry Show

Southern Jewelry Travelers Association
4 Executive Park Dr. NE, Ste. 1202
Atlanta, GA 30329-2235
Ph: (404)634-3434   Fax: (404)634-4663
Fr: 800-241-0399
E-mail: info@atlantajewelryshow.com
URL: http://www.atlantajewelryshow.com/

Semiannual, and August. **Primary Exhibits:** Fine jewelry, diamonds, pearls, gemstones, watches, jewelry boxes, safes, store fixtures, and jewelry computer programming. **Dates and Locations:** 2008 Mar 01-03; Atlanta, GA; Cobb Galleria Centre.

★6527★ Columbus Jewelry Show

Ohio Jewelers Association
50 W Broad St., Ste. 2020
Columbus, OH 43215
Ph: (614)221-2237   Fax: (614)221-7020
Fr: 800-652-6257
E-mail: reg@walcom.com
URL: http://www.ohiojewelers.org

Annual. **Primary Exhibits:** Fine jewelry, display units, security systems, gems, diamonds, and other accessories and equipment for the retail jeweler.

★6528★ Gem Fair

American Gem Trade Association
3030 LBJ Freeway, Ste. 840
Dallas, TX 75234
Ph: (214)742-4367   Fax: (214)742-7334
Fr: 800-972-1162
E-mail: info@agta.org
URL: http://www.agta.org

Annual. **Primary Exhibits:** Suppliers of natural colored gemstones; retail jewelers and jewelry manufacturers.

★6529★ JA International Jewelry Show

CMP Media LLC (New York City)
600 Community Dr.
Manhasset, NY 11030
Ph: (516)562-5000   Fax: (212)378-2160
E-mail: cmp@cmp.com
URL: http://www.cmp.com

Semiannual. **Primary Exhibits:** Fine jewelry, watches, gems, precious stones, and jewelry services.

★6530★ The JCK International Jewelry Show/Las Vegas

Reed Exhibitions (North American Headquarters)
383 Main Ave.
Norwalk, CT 06851
Ph: (203)840-5337   Fax: (203)840-9570
E-mail: export@reedexpo.com
URL: http://www.reedexpo.com

Annual. **Primary Exhibits:** Trade event only for high end jewelry manufacturers, related products and services. **Dates and Locations:** 2008 May 30 - Jun 03; Las Vegas, NV.

★6531★ Jewelers International Showcase

Jewelers International Showcase, Inc.
17th St. & Convention Center Dr.; 1901 Convention Center Dr.
Miami Beach, FL 33139
Ph: (561)998-0205   Fax: (561)998-0209
E-mail: jisshow@aol.com
URL: http://www.jisshow.com

3/year. **Primary Exhibits:** Fine jewelry, fashion jewelry, and related products and services to jewelry trade members.

★6532★ The Jewelry Show

Mahone Associates
800 Briarcreek Rd., Ste. BB503
Charlotte, NC 28205
Ph: (704)377-5881   Fax: (704)358-9115
E-mail: mahoneassociates@aol.com
URL: http://www.charlottegiftshow.com

Semiannual. **Primary Exhibits:** Jewelry equipment, supplies, and services.

★6533★ Memphis Gift and Jewelry Show Spring

Helen Brett Enterprises, Inc.
5111 Academy Dr.
Lisle, IL 60532-2171
Ph: (630)241-9865   Fax: (630)241-9870
Fr: 800-541-8171
URL: http://www.gift2jewelry.com

Semiannual. **Primary Exhibits:** Giftware and jewelry, apparel, home decor, novelties, silk flowers, fine/costume jewelry and accessories.

★6534★ MJSA Expo Providence

Manufacturing Jewelers and Suppliers of America
45 Royal Little Dr.
Providence, RI 02904
Ph: (401)274-3840   Fax: (401)274-0265
Fr: 800-444-MJSA
E-mail: mjsa@mjsainc.com
URL: http://www.mjsainc.com

Biennial. **Primary Exhibits:** Jewelry manufacturing equipment, supplies, machinery and tools, components, and business services.

OTHER SOURCES

★6535★ American Watchmakers-Clockmakers Institute (AWI)

701 Enterprise Dr.
Harrison, OH 45030
Ph: (513)367-9800   Fax: (513)367-1414
Fr: (866)367-2924
E-mail: jlubic@awci.com
URL: http://www.awci.com

Members: Jewelers, watchmakers, clockmakers, watch and clock engineers, scientists, repairmen, and others in the watch, clock, and jewelry industry. **Purpose:** Examines and certifies master watchmakers and clockmakers. Maintains a museum displaying horological items, and the National Watch Mark Identification Bureau. Conducts home study course in clock repairing and bench courses for watchmakers in most major U.S. cities. Disseminates career information to vocational counselors in the form of brochures and filmstrips.

★6536★ Jewelers of America (JA)

52 Vanderbilt Ave., 19th Fl.
New York, NY 10017-3827
Ph: (646)658-0246   Fax: (646)658-0256
Fr: 800-223-0673
E-mail: info@jewelers.org
URL: http://www.jewelers.org

Members: Retailers of jewelry, watches, silver, and allied merchandise. **Activities:** Conducts surveys and compiles statistics. Conducts educational programs. Provides information to consumers.

★6537★ Manufacturing Jewelers and Suppliers of America (MJSA)

45 Royal Little Dr.
Providence, RI 02904
Ph: (401)274-3840   Fax: (401)274-0265
Fr: 800-444-MJSA
E-mail: info@mjsa.org
URL: http://www.mjsa.org

Description: Represents American manufacturers and suppliers within the jewelry industry. Seeks to foster long-term stability and prosperity of the jewelry industry. Provides leadership in government affairs and industry education.

★6538★ National Association of Jewelry Appraisers (NAJA)

PO Box 18
Rego Park, NY 11374-0018
Ph: (718)896-1536   Fax: (718)997-9057
E-mail: naja.appraisers@netzero.net
URL: http://www.najaappraisers.com

Members: Gem and jewelry appraisers, jewelers, importers, brokers, manufacturers, gemological students, and others professionally interested in jewelry appraisal. **Purpose:** Seeks to recognize and make available to the public the services of highly

qualified, experienced, independent, and reliable jewelry appraisers. Conducts seminars on jewelry appraisal techniques, methods, and pricing for members and the public. Supports legislation to establish minimum standards of competency and licensing of jewelry appraisers; maintains code of professional ethics. **Activities:** Operates appraiser referral program; sponsors ongoing public relations campaign. Offers equipment discounts, new appraisal forms, travel discounts, insurance, and professional aids for members only. Compiles statistics.

★6539★ Women's Jewelry Association (WJA)

19 Mantua Rd.
Mount Royal, NJ 08061-1006
Ph: (856)423-3156   Fax: (856)423-3420
E-mail: info@womensjewelry.org
URL: http://www.womensjewelry.org

Description: Represents those involved in jewelry design, manufacture, retail, and advertising. Aims to: enhance the status of women in the jewelry industry; make known the contribution of women to the industry; provide a network for women involved with fine jewelry. Maintains hall of fame.

Kindergarten and Elementary School Teachers

SOURCES OF HELP-WANTED ADS

★6540★ AAEE Connections

American Association for Employment in Education
3040 Riverside Dr., Ste. 125
Columbus, OH 43221
Ph: (614)485-1111   Fax: (614)485-9609
E-mail: office@aaee.org
URL: http://www.aaee.org/

Description: Quarterly. Publishes news of the Association, whose aim is "to enhance and promote the concept of career planning and placement as an integral part of the educational process and to undertake activities designed to help schools, colleges, and universities meet their educational staffing needs." Also concerned with teacher education and the supply of/demand for teachers. Recurring features include news of members, state and regional news, and announcements of upcoming conferences and meetings.

★6541★ About Campus

John Wiley & Sons Inc.
111 River St.
Hoboken, NJ 07030-5774
Ph: (201)748-6000   Fax: (201)748-6088
Fr: 800-825-7550
URL: http://www3.interscience.wiley.com/cgi-bin/jhome/86513696

Bimonthly. $60.00/year for individuals, for print; $60.00/year for Canada and Mexico, for print; $96.00/year for individuals, for print (rest of world); $159.00/year for institutions, for print; $219.00/year for institutions, Canada and Mexico, for print; $270.00/year for institutions, for print (rest of world); $175.00/year for institutions, for print and online; $235.00/year for institutions, Canada and Mexico, for print and online; $286.00/year for institutions, for print and online, (rest of world); $111.00/year for individuals, print only. Journal focused on the critical issues faced by both student affairs and academic affairs staff as they work on helping students learn.

★6542★ American Academic

American Federation of Teachers
555 New Jersey Ave. NW
Washington, DC 20001
Ph: (202)879-4400
URL: http://www.aft.org/pubs-reports/american_academic/index.htm

Higher education policy journal.

★6543★ The American Biology Teacher

National Association of Biology Teachers
12030 Sunrise Valley Dr., Ste. 110
Reston, VA 20191-3409
Fax: (703)264-7778   Fr: 800-406-0775
E-mail: publication@nabt.org
URL: http://www.nabt.org

Monthly. Journal featuring articles on biology, science, and education for elementary, high school and college level biology teachers. Includes audio-visual, book, computer, and research reviews.

★6544★ Annals of Medicine

Taylor & Francis Group Journals
325 Chestnut St., Ste. 800
Philadelphia, PA 19106
Ph: (215)625-8900   Fax: (215)625-8914
Fr: 800-354-1420
URL: http://www.ingentaconnect.com

$418.00/year for institutions, print and online; $397.00/year for institutions, online only; $155.00/year for individuals. Journal covering health science and medical education.

★6545★ Assessment & Evaluation in Higher Education

Taylor & Francis Group Journals
325 Chestnut St., Ste. 800
Philadelphia, PA 19106
Ph: (215)625-8900   Fax: (215)625-8914
Fr: 800-354-1420
E-mail: aehe@bath.ac.uk
URL: http://www.tandf.co.uk/journals/titles/02602938.asp

Bimonthly. $1,982.00/year for institutions, print and online; $1,882.00/year for institutions, online only; $466.00/year for individu-als. Journal focusing on publishing papers and reports on all aspects of assessment and evaluation within higher education.

★6546★ Brookings Papers on Education Policy

Brookings Institution Press
1775 Massashusetts Ave. NW
Washington, DC 20036-2188
Ph: (202)536-3600   Fax: (202)536-3623
Fr: 800-275-1447
URL: http://www.brookings.edu/press/journals.htm

$46.00/year for institutions; $35.00/year for individuals. Journal dealing with all aspects of American education.

★6547★ Communication Quarterly

MetaPress
PO Box 1943
Birmingham, AL 35201
Fr: 877-773-3833

Periodical focusing on research, criticism, communication theory, and excellence in teaching.

★6548★ Community College Journal of Research & Practice

Taylor & Francis Group Journals
325 Chestnut St., Ste. 800
Philadelphia, PA 19106
Ph: (215)625-8900   Fax: (215)625-8914
Fr: 800-354-1420
URL: http://www.tandf.co.uk/journals/titles/10668926.aspttp://www

Monthly. $778.00/year for institutions, print and online; $739.00/year for institutions, online only; $208.00/year for individuals. Journal focusing on exchange of ideas, research, and empirically tested educational innovations.

★6549★ E-Journal of Teaching and Learning in Diverse Settings

Southern University at Baton Rouge
PO Box 9942
Baton Rouge, LA 70813
Ph: (225)771-3184   Fax: (225)771-4400

URL: http://www.subr.edu/coeducation/ej-ournal

Online academic journal that publishes research and scholarly articles in the field of education and learning.

★6550★ Education & Treatment of Children

West Virginia University Press
44 Stansbury Hall
PO Box 6295
Morgantown, WV 26506
Ph: (304)293-8400   Fax: (304)293-6585
Fr: (866)988-7737
URL: http://
www.educationandtreatmentofchildren.net

Quarterly. $85.00/year for institutions; $45.00/year for individuals; $100.00/year for institutions, elsewhere; $60.00/year for individuals, elsewhere. Periodical featuring information concerning the development of services for children and youth. Includes reports written for educators and other child care and mental health providers focused on teaching, training, and treatment effectiveness.

★6551★ Education Week

Editorial Projects in Education Inc.
6935 Arlington Rd., Ste. 100
Bethesda, MD 20814-5233
Ph: (301)280-3100   Fax: (301)280-3200
Fr: 800-346-1834
E-mail: ew@epe.org
URL: http://www.edweek.org/ew

Weekly. $79.94/year for individuals, print plus online; $69.94/year for individuals, online; $135.94/year for Canada, online Monthly; $208.84/year for out of country. Professional newspaper for elementary and secondary school educators.

★6552★ Educational Policy

Sage Publications Inc.
2455 Teller Rd.
Thousand Oaks, CA 91320
Ph: (805)499-0721   Fax: (805)499-8096
URL: http://www.sagepub.com/journalsProdDesc.nav?prodId=Journal20

Annual. $749.00/year for institutions, combined (print & e-access); $824.00/year for institutions, backfile lease, combined plus backfile; $674.00/year for institutions, e-access; $749.00/year for institutions, backfile lease, e-access plus backfile; $687.48/year for institutions, backfile puchase, e-access (content through 1999); $734.00/year for institutions, print only; $159.00/year for individuals, print only; $135.00 for institutions, single print; $34.00 for individuals, single print. Journal for educators, policy makers, administrators, researchers, teachers, and graduate students.

★6553★ Educational Research and Evaluation

Taylor & Francis Group Journals
325 Chestnut St., Ste. 800
Philadelphia, PA 19106
Ph: (215)625-8900   Fax: (215)625-8914
Fr: 800-354-1420
URL: http://www.tandf.co.uk/journals/titles/13803611.asp

Bimonthly. $616.00/year for institutions, print and online; $585.00/year for institutions, online only; $239.00/year for individuals. Journal on theory and practice.

★6554★ Educational Researcher

American Educational Research Association
1230 17th St. NW
Washington, DC 20036
Ph: (202)223-9485   Fax: (202)775-1824
URL: http://www.aera.net/publications/?id=317

Monthly. $48.00/year for individuals, plus foreign mailing charges; $150.00/year for institutions, plus foreign mailing charges. Educational research journal.

★6555★ Environmental Education Research

Taylor & Francis Group Journals
325 Chestnut St., Ste. 800
Philadelphia, PA 19106
Ph: (215)625-8900   Fax: (215)625-8914
Fr: 800-354-1420
URL: http://www.tandf.co.uk/journals/titles/13504622.asp

Journal covering all aspects of environmental education.

★6556★ Essays in Education

University of South Carolina
471 University Pky.
Aiken, SC 29801
Ph: (803)648-6851   Fax: (803)641-3461
Fr: 888-969-8722
URL: http://www.usca.edu/essays/

Monthly. Journal covering issues that impact and influence education.

★6557★ Hematology

American Society of Hematology
1900 M St. NW, Ste. 200
Washington, DC 20036
Ph: (202)776-0544   Fax: (202)776-0545
URL: http://asheducation-book.hematologylibrary.org

Semiweekly. $60.00/year for members; $90.00/year for nonmembers. Journal providing continuing medical education for physicians.

★6558★ The International Electronic Journal of Health Education

American Alliance for Health, Physical Education, Recreation & Dance
1900 Association Dr.
Reston, VA 20191-1598
Ph: (703)476-3400   Fax: (703)476-9527
Fr: 800-213-7193
URL: http://www.aahperd.org/iejhe/template.cfm?template=about.htm

Annual. Free to health education professionals and students. Journal promoting health through education and other systematic strategies.

★6559★ International Journal of Early Years Education

Taylor & Francis Group Journals
325 Chestnut St., Ste. 800
Philadelphia, PA 19106
Ph: (215)625-8900   Fax: (215)625-8914
Fr: 800-354-1420
URL: http://www.tandf.co.uk/journals/titles/09669760.asp

$512.00/year for institutions, print and online; $486.00/year for institutions, online only; $184.00/year for individuals. Journal focusing on education world-wide.

★6560★ International Journal of Inclusive Education

Taylor & Francis Group Journals
325 Chestnut St., Ste. 800
Philadelphia, PA 19106
Ph: (215)625-8900   Fax: (215)625-8914
Fr: 800-354-1420
URL: http://www.tandf.co.uk/journals/titles/13603116.asp

Bimonthly. $320.00/year for individuals, print only; $616.00/year for institutions, online only; $649.00/year for individuals, print and online; $193.00/year for individuals, print only; $376.00/year for institutions, online only; $396.00/year for institutions, print and online. Journal providing information on the nature of schools, universities and technical colleges for the educators and educational policy-makers.

★6561★ International Journal of Leadership in Education

Taylor & Francis Group Journals
325 Chestnut St., Ste. 800
Philadelphia, PA 19106
Ph: (215)625-8900   Fax: (215)625-8914
Fr: 800-354-1420
E-mail: ijle@txstate.edu
URL: http://www.tandf.co.uk/journals/tf/13603124.html

Quarterly. $196.00/year for individuals; $536.00/year for institutions, print and online; $509.00/year for institutions, online only; Journal dealing with leadership in education.

★6562★ International Journal of Progressive Education

International Journal of Progressive Education
c/o Mustafa Yunus Eryaman, Mng. Ed.
2108 S Orchard St., No. D
Urbana, IL 61801
URL: http://www.inased.org/ijpe.htm

$35.00/year for members; $45.00/year for individuals; $140.00/year for institutions, library; $35.00/year for students; $25.00/year for single issue, U.S. Peer reviewed online journal that aims to create an open and continuing dialogue about current educational issues and future conceptions of educational theory.

★6563★ International Journal of Research & Method in Education

Taylor & Francis Group Journals
325 Chestnut St., Ste. 800
Philadelphia, PA 19106
Ph: (215)625-8900   Fax: (215)625-8914
Fr: 800-354-1420
URL: http://www.tandf.co.uk/journals/titles/1743727x.asp

$1809.00/year for institutions, print and online; $1718.00/year for institutions, online only; $271.00/year for individuals. Professional journal to further international discourse in education with particular focus on method.

★6564★ International Journal of Whole Schooling

Whole Schooling Press
Wayne State University
217 Education
Detroit, MI 48202
URL: http://www.wholeschooling.net/Journal_of_Whole_Schooling/IJW

Free to qualified subscribers. International, refereed academic journal dedicated to exploring ways to improve learning and schooling for all children.

★6565★ Journal of Academic Leadership

Academic Leadership
600 Park St.
Rarick Hall 219
Hays, KS 67601-4099
Ph: (785)628-4547
URL: http://www.academicleadership.org/

Journal focusing on the leadership issues in the academic world.

★6566★ Journal of Cases in Educational Leadership

Sage Publications Inc.
2455 Teller Rd.
Thousand Oaks, CA 91320
Ph: (805)499-0721   Fax: (805)499-8096
URL: http://www.sagepub.com/journalsProdDesc.nav?prodId=Journal20

Quarterly. $319.00/year for institutions, e-access; $83.00/year for individuals, e-access. Journal covering cases appropriate for use in programs that prepare educational leaders.

★6567★ Journal of Curriculum and Supervision

Association for Supervision and Curriculum Development
1703 N Beauregard St.
Alexandria, VA 22311-1714
Ph: (703)578-9600   Fax: (703)575-5400
Fr: 800-933-2723
URL: http://www.ascd.org/portal/site/ascd/menuitem.0545410c9839aa

Scholarly journal focusing on curriculum and supervision.

★6568★ Journal of Direct Instruction

Association for Direct Instruction
PO Box 10252
Eugene, OR 97440
Ph: (541)485-1293   Fax: (541)683-7543
Fr: 800-995-2464
URL: http://www.adihome.org/phpshop/articles/articles.php?type=JD

Quarterly. Subscription included in membership. Journal covering education.

★6569★ Journal of Language, Identity, and Education

Lawrence Erlbaum Associates Inc.
10 Industrial Ave.
Mahwah, NJ 07430
Ph: (201)258-2200   Fax: (201)236-0072
Fr: 800-926-6579
E-mail: journals@erlbaum.com
URL: http://www.erlbaum.com

Quarterly. $50.00/year for U.S. and Canada, individual, online and print; $80.00/year for elsewhere, individual, online and print; $360.00/year for U.S. and Canada, institution, online and print; $390.00/year for elsewhere, institution, online and print; $290.00/year for U.S. and Canada, institution, online only; $290.00/year for elsewhere, institution, online only; $325.00/year for U.S. and Canada, institution, print only; $355.00/year for elsewhere, institution, print only. Scholarly, interdisciplinary journal covering issues in language, identity and education worldwide for academics, educators and policy specialists in a variety of disciplines, and others.

★6570★ Journal of Latinos and Education

Lawrence Erlbaum Associates Inc.
10 Industrial Ave.
Mahwah, NJ 07430
Ph: (201)258-2200   Fax: (201)236-0072
Fr: 800-926-6579
URL: http://www.erlbaum.com/

Quarterly. $50.00/year for individuals, online and print - U.S./Canada; $80.00/year for individuals, online and print - all other countries; $360.00/year for institutions, online and print - U.S./Canada; $390.00/year for institutions, online and print - all other countries; $290.00/year for institutions, online only - U.S./Canada; $290.00/year for institutions, online only - all other countries; $325.00/year for institutions, print only - U.S./Canada; $355.00/year for institutions, print only - all other countries. Scholarly, multidisciplinary journal covering educational issues that impact Latinos for researchers, teaching professionals, academics, scholars, institutions, and others.

★6571★ Journal of Learning Disabilities

PRO-ED Inc.
8700 Shoal Creek Blvd.
PO Box 678370
Austin, TX 78757-6897
Ph: (512)451-3246   Fax: 800-397-7633
Fr: 800-897-3202
URL: http://www.proedinc.com

Bimonthly. $60.00/year for individuals; $96.00 for individuals, 2 years; $161.00/year for institutions; $258.00 for institutions, 2 years; $96.00/year for individuals, international; $154.00 for individuals, 2 year international; $187.00/year for institutions, international; $300.00 for institutions, 2 year international. Special education journal.

★6572★ Journal of STEM Education

Auburn University
9088 Haley Ctr.
Auburn, AL 36849
Ph: (334)844-4000   Fax: (334)844-9027
URL: http://www.auburn.edu/research/litee/jstem/index.php

Semiannual. Journal for educators in Science, Technology, Engineering, and Mathematics (STEM) education.

★6573★ Journal of Teacher Education

Boston College
140 Commonwealth Ave.
Chestnut Hill, MA 02467
URL: http://www.sagepub.com

$403.00/year for institutions, print & e-access; $423.00/year for institutions, volume print & all online; $363.00/year for institutions, e-access; $383.00/year for institutions, all online content; $1,512.00/year for institutions, backfile purchase, e-access; $395.00/year for institutions, print; $99.00/year for individuals, print; $87.00/year for institutions, single print; $26.00/year for individuals, single print. Magazine of interest to educators.

★6574★ Leadership and Policy in Schools

Taylor & Francis Group Journals
325 Chestnut St., Ste. 800
Philadelphia, PA 19106
Ph: (215)625-8900   Fax: (215)625-8914
Fr: 800-354-1420
URL: http://www.tandf.co.uk/journals/titles/15700763.asp

Quarterly. $477.00/year for institutions, print and online; $453.00/year for institutions, online only; $227.00/year for individuals; $60.00/year for ICSEI members. Journal providing information about leadership and policy in primary and secondary education.

★6575★ Learning
Education Center Inc.
PO Box 9753
Greensboro, NC 27429-0753
Fr: 800-334-0298
URL: http://www.learningmagazine.com

Quarterly. $4.95 for single issue; $14.95/year for U.S. Definitive guide to products and services for K-6 grade teachers in the classroom.

★6576★ Music Educators Journal
MENC: The National Association for Music Education
1806 Robert Fulton Dr.
Reston, VA 20191
Ph: (703)860-4000   Fax: (703)860-1531
Fr: 800-336-3768
URL: http://www.menc.org/publication/articles/journals.html

Journal covering all levels of music education. Published on alternate months with Teaching Music.

★6577★ NJEA Review
New Jersey Education Association
180 West State St.
PO Box 1211
Trenton, NJ 08607-1211
Ph: (609)599-4561   Fax: (609)599-1201

Monthly. Educational journal for public school employees.

★6578★ Oxford Review of Education
Taylor & Francis Group Journals
325 Chestnut St., Ste. 800
Philadelphia, PA 19106
Ph: (215)625-8900   Fax: (215)625-8914
Fr: 800-354-1420
URL: http://www.tandf.co.uk/journals/titles/03054985.asp

$1,031.00/year for institutions, print and online; $979.00/year for institutions, online only; $396.00/year for individuals. Journal covering advance study of education.

★6579★ The Physics Teacher
American Association of Physics Teachers
1 Physics Ellipse
College Park, MD 20740-3845
Ph: (301)209-3300   Fax: (301)209-0845
E-mail: tpt@appstate.edu
URL: http://www.aapt.org/Publications/

$335.00/year for nonmembers, international; $105.00/year for members, regular. Scientific education magazine.

★6580★ Research Strategies
Elsevier Science Inc.
360 Park Ave. S
New York, NY 10010
Ph: (212)989-5800   Fax: (212)633-3990
URL: http://www.elsevier.com

Journal covering library literature and the educational mission of the library.

★6581★ School and Community
Missouri State Teachers Association
407 South Sixth St.
PO Box 458
Columbia, MO 65205
Ph: (573)442-3127   Fax: (573)443-5079
Fr: 800-392-0532

Quarterly. Education magazine.

★6582★ School Effectiveness and School Improvement
Taylor & Francis Group Journals
325 Chestnut St., Ste. 800
Philadelphia, PA 19106
Ph: (215)625-8900   Fax: (215)625-8914
Fr: 800-354-1420
URL: http://www.tandf.co.uk/journals/titles/09243453.asp

Quarterly. $305.00/year for institutions, print and online; $231.00/year for institutions, online only; $153.00/year for individuals, print only; $520.00/year for institutions, print and online; $494.00/year for institutions, online only; $255.00/year for individuals, print only. Journal focusing on educational progress of all students.

★6583★ The Science Teacher
National Science Teachers Association
1840 Wilson Blvd.
Arlington, VA 22201
Ph: (703)243-7100   Fax: (703)243-7177
URL: http://www.nsta.org/highschool/

Journal on science education.

★6584★ Strategies
American Alliance for Health, Physical Education, Recreation & Dance
1900 Association Dr.
Reston, VA 20191-1598
Ph: (703)476-3400   Fax: (703)476-9527
Fr: 800-213-7193
E-mail: strategies@aahperd.org
URL: http://www.aahperd.org/naspe/template.cfm?template=strategie

Bimonthly. $115.00/year for U.S. and Canada, institution; $45.00/year for nonmembers, U.S. and Canada, individual; $127.00/year for institutions, other countries; $57.00/year for nonmembers, foreign, individual. Journal providing practical, hands-on information to physical educators and coaches.

★6585★ Teacher Magazine
Editorial Projects in Education Inc.
6935 Arlington Rd., Ste. 100
Bethesda, MD 20814-5233
Ph: (301)280-3100   Fax: (301)280-3200
Fr: 800-346-1834
URL: http://www.edweek.org/ew/index.html

$10.00/year for individuals; $17.00/year for individuals, two years. Professional magazine for elementary and secondary school teachers.

★6586★ Teaching Children Mathematics
National Council of Teachers of Mathematics
1906 Association Dr.
Reston, VA 20191-1502
Ph: (703)620-9840   Fax: (703)476-2970
Fr: 800-235-7566
URL: http://www.nctm.org/publications/tcm.aspx

$65.00/year for individuals; $95.00/year for institutions; $8.00/year for single issue. Journal covering mathematics content and methods for pre-service and in-service teachers of grades pre-kindergarten through 6th.

★6587★ Teaching Exceptional Children
Council for Exceptional Children
1110 N Glebe Rd., Ste. 300
Arlington, VA 22201-5704
Ph: (703)620-3660   Fax: (703)264-9494
Fr: 888-232-7733
E-mail: tec@bc.edu
URL: http://www.cec.sped.org

Bimonthly. $135.00/year for individuals; $250.00 for two years; $145.00 for two years, Canada; $270.00 for two years, Canada; $165.00/year for out of country, foreign-air printed matter; $310.00/year for out of country, two years, foreign-air printed matter; $25.00/year for institutions, single copy; $170.00/year for institutions; $290.00 for two years, institutional. Journal exploring practical methods for teaching students who have exceptionalities and those who are gifted and talented.

★6588★ Teaching/K-8
Teaching/K-8
40 Richards Ave.
Norwalk, CT 06854
Fr: 800-249-9363
E-mail: teachingk8@aol.com

$23.97/year for individuals; $4.50 for single issue; $12.00/year for institutions; $21.00 for institutions, two years; $30.00 for institutions, three years. Magazine for elementary teachers.

★6589★ Teaching and Learning in Nursing
Elsevier Science Inc.
360 Park Ave. S
New York, NY 10010
Ph: (212)989-5800   Fax: (212)633-3990
URL: http://www.elsevier.com

Quarterly. $119.00/year for institutions, U.S. $167.00/year for institutions, other countries; $75.00/year for individuals, U.S. $104.00/year for individuals, other countries. Journal devoted to associate degree nursing education and practice.

★6590★ Tech Directions

Prakken Publications Inc.
832 Phoenix Dr.
PO Box 8623
Ann Arbor, MI 48108
Ph: (734)975-2800 Fax: (734)975-2787
Fr: 800-530-9673
E-mail: tdedit@techdirections.com
URL: http://www.techdirections.com

Monthly. $30.00/year for individuals, U.S.; $20.00/year for students; $40.00/year for elsewhere; $55.00 for two years, U.S.; $75.00 for two years, elsewhere. Free to qualified subscribers. Magazine covering issues, programs, and projects in industrial education, technology education, trade and industry, and vocational-technical career education. Articles are geared toward teacher and administrator use and reference from elementary school through postsecondary levels.

★6591★ Theory and Research in Education

Sage Publications Inc.
2455 Teller Rd.
Thousand Oaks, CA 91320
Ph: (805)499-0721 Fax: (805)499-8096
URL: http://tre.sagepub.com/

$459.00/year for institutions, print and online; $413.00/year for institutions, online only; $450.00/year for institutions, print only; $77.00/year for individuals, print only. Interdisciplinary journal covering normative and theoretical issues concerning education including multi-faceted philosophical analysis of moral, social, political and epistemological problems and issues arising from educational practice.

★6592★ Uratie

IDG Communications Inc.
5 Speen St., 3rd. Fl
Framingham, MA 01701
Ph: (508)875-5000 Fax: (508)988-7888
URL: http://www.idg.com

Magazine providing job offers for graduates, engineers and information technology professionals.

PLACEMENT AND JOB REFERRAL SERVICES

★6593★ American Alliance for Health, Physical Education, Recreation and Dance (AAHPERD)

1900 Association Dr.
Reston, VA 20191-1598
Ph: (703)476-3400 Fax: (703)476-9527
Fr: 800-213-7193
E-mail: info@aahperd.org
URL: http://www.aahperd.org

Members: Students and educators in physical education, dance, health, athletics, safety education, recreation, and outdoor education. **Purpose:** Works to improve its fields of education at all levels through such services as consultation, periodicals and special publications, leadership development, determination of standards, and research. Sponsors placement service.

★6594★ American Association of Christian Schools (AACS)

National Office
602 Belvoir Ave.
East Ridge, TN 37412
Ph: (423)629-4280 Fax: (423)622-7461
E-mail: national@aacs.org
URL: http://www.aacs.org

Description: Maintains teacher/administrator certification program and placement service. Participates in school accreditation program. Sponsors National Academic Tournament. Maintains American Christian Honor Society. Compiles statistics; maintains speakers' bureau and placement service.

★6595★ American Association of Teachers of French (AATF)

Southern Illinois University
Mail Code 4510
Carbondale, IL 62901
Ph: (618)453-5731 Fax: (618)453-5733
E-mail: abrate@siu.edu
URL: http://www.frenchteachers.org

Members: Teachers of French in public and private elementary and secondary schools, colleges and universities. **Activities:** Sponsors National French Week each November to take French out of the classroom and into the schools and community. Conducts National French Contest in elementary and secondary schools and awards prizes at all levels. Maintains Materials Center with promotional and pedagogical materials; National French Honor Society (high school), Placement Bureau, summer scholarships.

★6596★ American Association of Teachers of Spanish and Portuguese (AATSP)

900 Ladd Rd.
Walled Lake, MI 48390
Ph: (248)960-2180 Fax: (248)960-9570
E-mail: corporate@aatsp.org
URL: http://www.aatsp.org

Description: Teachers of Spanish and Portuguese languages and literatures and others interested in Hispanic culture. Operates placement bureau and maintains pen pal registry. Sponsors honor society, Sociedad Honoraria Hispanica and National Spanish Examinations for secondary school students.

★6597★ American Montessori Society (AMS)

281 Park Ave. S
New York, NY 10010-6102
Ph: (212)358-1250 Fax: (212)358-1256
E-mail: info@amshq.org
URL: http://www.amshq.org

Description: School affiliates and teacher training affiliates; heads of schools, teachers, parents, non-Montessori educators, and other interested individuals dedicated to stimulating the use of the Montessori teaching approach and promoting better education for all children. Seeks to meet demands of growing interest in the Montessori approach to early learning. Assists in establishing schools; supplies information and limited services to member schools in other countries. Maintains school consultation and accreditation service; provides information service; assists research and gathers statistical data; offers placement service. Maintains Montessori and related materials exhibit.

★6598★ Association for Direct Instruction (ADI)

PO Box 10252
Eugene, OR 97440
Ph: (541)485-1293 Fax: (541)868-1397
Fr: 800-995-2464
E-mail: info@adihome.org
URL: http://www.adihome.org

Members: Public school regular and special education teachers and university instructors. **Purpose:** Encourages, promotes, and engages in research aimed at improving educational methods. Promotes dissemination of developmental information and skills that facilitate the education of adults and children. **Activities:** Administers a preschool for developmentally delayed children. Offers educational training workshops for instructors. Maintains speaker's bureau and placement service.

★6599★ Christian Schools International (CSI)

3350 E Paris Ave. SE
Grand Rapids, MI 49512-2907
Ph: (616)957-1070 Fax: (616)957-5022
Fr: 800-635-8288
E-mail: info@csionline.org
URL: http://csionline.org

Description: Christian elementary and secondary schools enrolling 100,000 pupils and employing 7,800 teachers. Aims to: provide a medium for a united witness regarding the role of Christian schools in contemporary society; promote the establishment of Christian schools; help members function more effectively in areas of promotion, organization, administration, and curriculum; help establish standards and criteria to guide the operation of its members; foster high professional ideals and economic well-being among Christian school personnel; establish and maintain communication with member schools, colleges, churches, government agencies, and the public. Encourages study, research, and writing that embodies Christian theories of education; conducts salary studies, research, and surveys on operating costs; offers expert and confidential analysis of member school programs and operation. Sponsors meetings, workshops, and seminars; offers placement service. Administers the Christian School Pension and Trust Funds, Group Insurance Plans, and Life and Insurance Plans and Trust Funds.

★6600★ International Educator's Institute (TIE)

PO Box 513
Cummaquid, MA 02637
Ph: (508)790-1990   Fax: (508)790-1922
Fr: 877-375-6668
E-mail: tie@tieonline.com
URL: http://www.tieonline.com

Description: Facilitates the placement of teachers and administrators in American, British, and international schools. Seeks to create a network that provides for professional development opportunities and improved financial security of members. Offers advice and information on international school news, recent educational developments, job placement, and investment, consumer, and professional development opportunities. Makes available insurance and travel benefits. Operates International Schools Internship Program.

★6601★ Jewish Educators Assembly (JEA)

PO Box 413
Cedarhurst, NY 11516
Ph: (516)569-2537   Fax: (516)295-9039
E-mail: jewisheducators@jewisheducators.org
URL: http://www.jewisheducators.org

Members: Educational and supervisory personnel serving Jewish educational institutions. **Purpose:** Seeks to: advance the development of Jewish education in the congregation on all levels in consonance with the philosophy of the Conservative Movement; cooperate with the United Synagogue of America Commission on Jewish Education as the policy-making body of the educational enterprise; join in cooperative effort with other Jewish educational institutions and organizations; establish and maintain professional standards for Jewish educators; serve as a forum for the exchange of ideas; promote the values of Jewish education as a basis for the creative continuity of the Jewish people. **Activities:** Maintains placement service and speaker's bureau.

★6602★ National Alliance of Black School Educators (NABSE)

310 Pennsylvania Ave.
Washington, DC 20003
Ph: (202)608-6310   Fax: (202)608-6319
Fr: 800-221-2654
E-mail: lavette@nabse.org
URL: http://www.nabse.org

Description: Black educators from all levels; others indirectly involved in the education of black youth. Promotes awareness, professional expertise, and commitment among black educators. Goals are to: eliminate and rectify the results of racism in education; work with state, local, and national leaders to raise the academic achievement level of all black students; increase members' involvement in legislative activities; facilitate the introduction of a curriculum that more completely embraces black America; improve the ability of black educators to promote problem resolution; create a meaningful and effective network of strength, talent, and professional

support. Sponsors workshops, commission meetings, and special projects. Encourages research, especially as it relates to blacks, and the presentation of papers during national conferences. Plans to establish a National Black Educators Data Bank and offer placement service.

★6603★ National Association for Sport and Physical Education (NASPE)

1900 Association Dr.
Reston, VA 20191-1598
Ph: (703)476-3400   Fax: (703)476-8316
Fr: 800-213-7193
E-mail: naspe@aahperd.org
URL: http://www.naspeinfo.org

Description: Men and women professionally involved with physical activity and sports. Seeks to improve the total sport and physical activity experience in America. Conducts research and education programs in such areas as sport psychology, curriculum development, kinesiology, history, philosophy, sport sociology, and the biological and behavioral basis of human activity. Develops and distributes public information materials which explain the value of physical education programs. Supports councils involved in organizing and supporting elementary, secondary, and college physical education and sport programs; administers the National Council of Athletic Training in conjunction with the National Association for Girls and Women in Sport; serves the professional interests of coaches, trainers, and officials. Maintains hall of fame, placement service, and media resource center for public information and professional preparation. Member benefits include group insurance and discounts.

★6604★ National Association of Teachers' Agencies (NATA)

797 Kings Hwy.
Fairfield, CT 06825
Ph: (203)333-0611   Fax: (203)334-7224
E-mail: info@jobsforteachers.com

Description: Private employment agencies engaged primarily in the placement of teaching and administration personnel. Works to standardize records and promote a strong ethical sense in the placement field. Maintains speakers' bureau.

★6605★ National Communication Association (NCA)

1765 N St. NW
Washington, DC 20036
Ph: (202)464-4622   Fax: (202)464-4600
E-mail: rsmitter@natcom.org
URL: http://www.natcom.org

Members: Elementary, secondary, college, and university teachers, speech clinicians, media specialists, communication consultants, students, theater directors, and other interested persons; libraries and other institutions. **Purpose:** Works to promote study, criticism, research, teaching, and application of the artistic, humanistic, and scientific principles of communication, particularly speech communication. Sponsors the publi-

cation of scholarly volumes in speech. **Activities:** Conducts international debate tours in the U.S. and abroad. Maintains placement service.

★6606★ U.S.-China Education Foundation (USCEF)

4140 Oceanside Blvd., Ste. 159 - No. 112
Oceanside, CA 92056-6005
Ph: (760)644-0977
E-mail: uscef@sage-usa.net
URL: http://www.sage-usa.net/uscef.htm

Purpose: Aims to promote the learning of the Chinese languages (including Mandarin, Cantonese, and minority languages such as Mongolian) by Americans, and the learning of English by Chinese. **Activities:** Conducts short-term travel-study program to prepare Americans and Chinese for stays of four, six, or eight months or one to four years in China or the U.S., respectively. Operates teacher placement service and speakers' bureau. A project of The Society for the Development of Global Education (S.A.G.E. Inc.).

EMPLOYER DIRECTORIES AND NETWORKING LISTS

★6607★ 50 State Educational Directories

Career Guidance Foundation
8090 Engineer Rd.
San Diego, CA 92111
Ph: (858)560-8051   Fax: (858)278-8960
Fr: 800-854-2670
URL: http://www.cgf.org

Annual. Microfiche. Collection consists of reproductions of the state educational directories published by the departments of education of individual 50 states. Directory contents vary, but the majority contain listings of elementary and secondary schools, colleges and universities, and state education officials. Amount of detail in each also varies. Entries include: Usually, institution name, address, and name of one executive.

★6608★ Boarding Schools Directory

Association of Boarding Schools
2141 Wisconsin Ave. NW, Ste. H
Washington, DC 20007
Ph: (202)965-8982   Fax: (202)965-8988
URL: http://www.schools.com/

Annual; latest edition 2007-2008. For U.S. and Canada. Covers boarding schools that are members of the Association of Boarding Schools. Entries include: School name, address, phone, e-mail and URL, grades for which boarding students are accepted, enrollment, brief description. Arrangement: Classified by type of school. Indexes: Geographical; program; alphabetical.

★6609★ Career Ideas for Teens in Education and Training

Facts On File Inc.
132 W 31st St., 17th Fl.
New York, NY 10001
Ph: (212)967-8800   Fax: 800-678-3633
Fr: 800-322-8755
URL: http://www.factsonfile.com

Published 2005. $40.00 for individuals; $36.00 for libraries. Covers a multitude of career possibilities based on a teenager's specific interests and skills and links his/her talents to a wide variety of actual professions.

★6610★ Christian Schools International-Directory

Christian Schools International
3350 E Paris Ave. SE
Grand Rapids, MI 49512
Ph: (616)957-1070   Fax: (616)957-5022
Fr: 800-635-8288
URL: http://store.csionline.org

Annual; 2007-2008. $15.00 for members; $72.00 for nonmembers. Covers nearly 450 Reformed Christian elementary and secondary schools; related associations; societies without schools. Entries include: For schools–School name, address, phone; name, title, and address of officers; names of faculty members. Arrangement: Geographical.

★6611★ Directory of Public Elementary and Secondary Education Agencies

National Center for Education Statistics
1990 K St. NW
Washington, DC 20006
Ph: (202)502-7300
URL: http://nces.ed.gov/ccd/

Annual; latest edition 2002-2003. Covers about 17,000 local education agencies in the United States, the District of Columbia, and five territories that operate their own schools or pay tuition to other local education agencies. Also lists intermediate education agencies. Entries include: Agency name, address, phone, county, description of district, grade span, membership, special education students, metropolitan status, number of high school graduates, teachers, and schools. Also available from Superintendent of Documents, U.S. Government Printing Office. Arrangement: Geographical, then by type of agency.

★6612★ Directory of Public School Systems in the U.S.

American Association for Employment in Education
3040 Riverside Dr., Ste. 125
Columbus, OH 43221
Ph: (614)485-1111   Fax: (614)485-9609
URL: http://www.aaee.org/

Annual, winter; latest edition 2004-2005 edition. $10.00 for members (plus $2.00/copy for mailing); $20.00 for nonmembers (plus $2.00/copy for mailing). Covers about 14,500 public school systems in the United States and their administrative personnel.

Entries include: System name, address, phone, website address, name and title of personnel administrator, levels taught and approximate student population. Arrangement: Geographical by state.

★6613★ Educators Resource Directory

Grey House Publishing
185 Millerton Rd.
PO Box 860
Millerton, NY 12546
Ph: (518)789-8700   Fax: (518)789-0556
Fr: 800-562-2139
E-mail: books@greyhouse.com
URL: http://www.greyhouse.com/education.htm

Annual; latest edition 2007/2008. $145.00 for individuals. Covers publishing opportunities, state by state information on enrollment, funding and grant resources, associations and conferences, and teaching jobs abroad all geared toward elementary and secondary school professionals. Also covers online databases, textbook publishers, school suppliers, plus state and federal agencies. Entries include: Contact name, address, phone, fax, description, publications. A compilation of over 6,500 educational resources and over 130 tables and charts of education statistics and rankings. Arrangement: By subject categories. Indexes: Entry; geographical; publisher; web sites.

★6614★ Employment Opportunities, USA

Washington Research Associates
1090 Vermont Ave. NW, Ste. 800
Washington, DC 20005
Ph: (202)408-7025

Annual, quarterly updates. Publication includes: List of over 1,000 employment contacts in companies and agencies in banking, arts, telecommunications, education, and 14 other industries and professions, including federal government. Entries include: Company name, name of representative, address, description of products or services, hiring and recruiting practices, training programs, and year established. Principal content is industry overviews, career news, employment opportunity information on 14 different job markets, and comprehensive guidance to career resources on the Internet. Arrangement: Classified by industry. Indexes: Occupation.

★6615★ Encyclopedia of Education

Macmillan/McGraw-Hill
2 Penn Plz., 5th Fl.
New York, NY 10121-2298
Ph: (212)904-3834   Fax: (212)904-4878
URL: http://www.mheducation.com/home/index.shtml

Publication includes: List of assessment and achievement tests with contact information; list of state departments of education; list of Internet resources. Principal content of publication consists of a variety of topics within the field of education, including policy, curriculum, learning, assessment, legislation, history, and standards. Indexes: Alphabetical.

★6616★ Ganley's Catholic Schools in America-Elementary/Secondary/College & University

Fisher Publishing Co.
PO Box 15070
Scottsdale, AZ 85267-5070
Ph: (480)657-9422   Fax: (480)657-9422
Fr: 800-759-7615
URL: http:// www.ganleyscatholicschools.com

Annual, summer; latest edition 34th, 2007 edition. $60.00 for individuals. Covers over 8,400 Catholic K-12 Schools. Arrangement: Geographical by state, then alphabetical by Diocese name.

★6617★ Handbook of Private Schools

Porter Sargent Publishers Inc.
11 Beacon St., Ste. 1400
Boston, MA 02108-3099
Ph: (617)523-1670   Fax: (617)523-1021
Fr: 800-342-7470
E-mail: orders@portersargent.com
URL: http://www.portersargent.com

Annual, latest edition 87th, 2006 edition. $99.00 for individuals. Covers more than 1,600 elementary and secondary boarding and day schools in the United States. Entries include: School name, address, phone, fax, e-mail, URL, type of school (boarding or day), sex and age range, names and titles of administrators, grades offered, academic orientation, curriculum, new admissions yearly, tests required for admission, enrollment and faculty, graduate record, number of alumni, tuition and scholarship figures, summer session, plant evaluation and endowment, date of establishment, calendar, association membership, description of school's offerings and history, test score averages, uniform requirements, and geographical and demographic data. Arrangement: Geographical. Indexes: Alphabetical by school name, cross indexed by state, region, grade range, sexes accepted, school features and enrollment.

★6618★ Independent School Guide for Washington DC and Surrounding Area

Lift Hill Press Inc.
c/o Washington Book Distributors
4930-A Eisenhower Ave.
Alexandria, VA 22304-4809
Ph: (703)212-9113   Fax: (703)212-9114
Fr: 800-699-9113
URL: http://www.washingtonbk.com

Biennial; latest edition 2004. Covers over 525 independent schools (including parochial schools) in the Washington, DC, area, including Maryland and Virginia. Entries include: School name, address, phone, name and title of contact, number of faculty, geographical area served, tuition, courses, admission procedures, summer programs, LD/ED programs, scholarships available. Arrangement: Alphabetical. Indexes: Geographical.

★6619★ Independent Schools Association of the Southwest-Membership List

Independent Schools Association of the Southwest
Energy Sq., Ste 406
505 North Big Spring St.
Midland, TX 79701
Ph: (432)684-9550   Fax: (432)684-9401
URL: http://www.isasw.org

Annual, August. Covers over 84 schools located in Arizona, Kansas, Louisiana, Mexico, New Mexico, Oklahoma, and Texas enrolling over 38,000 students. Entries include: School name, address, phone, chief administrative officer, structure, and enrollment. Arrangement: Geographical. Indexes: Alphabetical.

★6620★ MDR's School Directories

Market Data Retrieval
1 Forest Pkwy.
Shelton, CT 06484-0947
Ph: (203)926-4800   Fax: (203)926-1826
Fr: 800-333-8802
URL: http://www.schooldata.com

Annual, October. Covers over 90,000 public, 8,000 Catholic, and 15,000 other private schools (grades K-12) in the United States; over 15,000 school district offices, 76,000 school librarians, 27,000 media specialists, and 33,000 technology coordinators. Includes names of over 165,000 school district administrators and staff members in county and state education administration. Entries include: District name and address; telephone and fax number; number of schools; number of teachers in the district; district enrollment; special education students; limited-english proficient students; minority percentage by race; percentage of college bound students; expenditures per student for instructional materials; poverty level; title 1 dollars; site-based management; district open/close dates; construction indicator; technologies and quantities; district-level administrators, (new superintendents shaded); school name and address (new public shaded); telephone and fax number; principal (new principal shaded); librarian, media specialist and technology coordinator; grade span; special programs and school type; student enrollment; technologies and quantities (instructional computer brand, noting predominant brand); Multi-Media Computers; Internet connection or access; Tech Sophistication Index. Arrangement: Geographical. Indexes: District county; district personnel; principal; new public schools and key personnel; district and school telephone; district URLs.

★6621★ National Directory for Employment in Education

American Association for Employment in Education
3040 Riverside Dr., Ste. 125
Columbus, OH 43221
Ph: (614)485-1111   Fax: (614)485-9609
URL: http://www.aaee.org/

Annual, winter; latest edition 2005 edition. $20.00 for nonmembers; $10.00 for members. Covers about 600 placement offices maintained by teacher-training institutions and 300 school district personnel officers and/or superintendents responsible for hiring profesional staff. Entries include: Institution name, address, phone, contact name, email address, and website. Arrangement: Geographical. Indexes: Personal name; subject-field of teacher training; institutions that provide vacancy bulletins and placement services to non-enrolled students.

★6622★ Opportunities Abroad for Educators

Fulbright Teacher and Administrator Exchange Program
600 Maryland Ave. SW, Ste. 320
Washington, DC 20024-2520
Ph: (202)314-3527   Fax: (202)479-6806
Fr: 800-726-0479
URL: http://www.fulbrightexchanges.org

Annual. Covers opportunities available for elementary and secondary teachers, two-year college instructors, and school administrators to attend seminars or to teach abroad under the Mutual Educational and Cultural Exchange Act of 1961. Entries include: Countries of placement, dates, eligibility requirements, teaching assignments. Arrangement: Geographical.

★6623★ Patterson's American Education

Educational Directories Inc.
PO Box 68097
Schaumburg, IL 60168
Ph: (847)891-1250   Fax: (847)891-0945
Fr: 800-357-6183
URL: http://www.ediusa.com

Annual; latest edition October 2007. $94.00 for individuals. Covers over 11,400 school districts in the United States; more than 34,000 public, private, and Catholic high schools, middle schools, and junior high schools; Approximately 300 parochial superintendents; 400 state department of education personnel. Entries include: For school districts and schools–District and superintendent name, address, phone, fax; grade ranges, enrollment; school names, addresses, phone numbers, names of principals. For postsecondary schools–School name, address, phone number, URL, e-mail, names of administrator or director of admissions. For private and Catholic high schools–name, address, phone, fax, enrollment, grades offered, name of principal. Postsecondary institutions are also covered in 'Patterson's Schools Classified.' Arrangement: Geographical by state, then alphabetical by city.

★6624★ Patterson's Elementary Education

Educational Directories Inc.
PO Box 68097
Schaumburg, IL 60168
Ph: (847)891-1250   Fax: (847)891-0945
Fr: 800-357-6183
URL: http://www.ediusa.com/

Annual; latest edition 2007. $94.00 for individuals. Covers over 13,400 public school districts; more than 82,447 public, private, and Catholic elementary and middle schools; and 400 state departments of education personnel. Entries include: County name, city, population, public school district name, enrollment, grade range; superintendent name, address, phone, fax; names of public schools, address, phone, fax, principal's name, enrollment; private and Catholic school listings include school name, enrollment, grade ranges, principal's name, address, phone, fax. Arrangement: Geographical by state, then alphabetical by city.

★6625★ Private Independent Schools

Bunting and Lyon Inc.
238 N Main St.
Wallingford, CT 06492
Ph: (203)269-3333   Fax: (203)269-5697
URL: http://www.buntingandlyon.com

Annual; latest edition 60th, January 2007. $115.00 for individuals. Covers 1,200 English-speaking elementary and secondary private schools and summer programs in North America and abroad. Entries include: School name, address, phone, fax, e-mail, website, enrollment, tuition and other fees, financial aid information, administrator's name and educational background, director of admission, regional accreditation, description of programs, curriculum, activities, learning differences grid. Arrangement: Geographical. Indexes: school name; geographical.

★6626★ QED's State School Guides

Quality Education Data Inc.
1050 Seventeenth St, Ste. 1100
Denver, CO 80265
Ph: (303)209-9400   Fax: (303)209-9401
Fr: 800-525-5811
URL: http://www.qeddata.com/MarketKno/SchoolGuides/SchoolGuides.a

Annual, October. $1,345.00 for national print set; $3,565.00 for national online version; $4175.00 for print set and online version, combined. Covers over 100,000 public and private elementary and secondary schools in 16,000 school districts; in 52 volumes (national set). Entries include: School district name, address, phone, district enrollment, identification of site-based managed schools, number of teachers, number of schools, financial data, minority enrollment statistics, names and educational specializations of key personnel, list of member schools, including school name, address, phone, name of principal, name of librarian, grade levels taught, enrollment, services outsourced, number and brands of microcomputers used. Arrangement: Geographical - county within state. Indexes: School name, district name, geographical (county name), personal name.

★6627★ Requirements for Certification of Teachers, Counselors, Librarians, Administrators for Elementary and Secondary Schools

University of Chicago Press
Journals Division
1427 E 60th St.
Chicago, IL 60637-2954
Ph: (773)702-7600   Fax: (773)702-0694
Fr: 877-705-1878

Annual, June; latest edition 71st, 2006-07. $47.00. Publication includes: List of state and local departments of education. Entries include: Office name, address, phone. Principal content of publication consists of summaries of each state's teaching and administrative certification requirements. Arrangement: Geographical.

HANDBOOKS AND MANUALS

★6628★ The ABC's of Job-Hunting for Teachers: An A-Z Guide to Landing the Perfect Job

Kappa Delta Pi, Int'l Honor Society in Education
3707 Woodview Trace
Indianapolis, IN 46268-1158
Ph: (317)871-4900   Fax: (317)704-2323
Fr: 800-284-3167

Mary C. Clement. April 2003. $10.95 (paper). Illustrated. 82 pages.

★6629★ Becoming a Teacher

Pearson Allyn & Bacon
1 Lake St.
Upper Saddle River, NJ 07458
Ph: (201)236-7000   Fr: 800-922-0579
URL: http://www.pearsoned.com/higher-ed/

Gary Borich. 1995. $43.95 (paper). 152 pages. Part of The Falmer Press Teachers' Library Series No. 7.

★6630★ Developing a Teaching Style: Methods for Elementary School Teachers

Waveland Press
4180 IL Route 83, Ste. 101
Long Grove, IL 60047
Ph: (847)634-0081   Fax: (847)634-9501
E-mail: info@waveland.com
URL: http://www.waveland.com/

Robert D. Louisell and Jorge Descamps. Second edition, 2000. $31.95 (paper). 439 pages.

★6631★ Great Jobs for Music Majors

The McGraw-Hill Companies
PO Box 182604
Columbus, OH 43272
Fax: (614)759-3749   Fr: 877-883-5524
E-mail: customer.service@mcgraw-hill.com
URL: http://www.mcgraw-hill.com

Jan Goldberg, Stephen Lambert, Julie De-

Galan. Second edition, 2004. $15.95 (paper). 180 pages.

★6632★ Handbook for Christian EFL Teachers: Christian Teacher-Preparation Programs, Overseas Teaching Opportunities, Instructional Materials and Resources

Institute for Cross-Cultural Training, Billy Graham Center, Wheaton College; Berry Pub. Services
PO Box 794
Wheaton, IL 60189
Ph: (630)752-7158   Fax: (630)752-7155

Lonna J. Dickerson and Dianne F. Dow. 1997. $9.00 (paper). 96 pages. Part of the Monograph Series.

★6633★ How to Get the Teaching Position You Want: Teacher Candidate Guide

Educational Enterprises
PO Box 1836
Spring Valley, CA 91979
Ph: (619)660-7720

Phyllis Murton. Second edition, revised, 1996. $19.95 (paper). 110 pages. This book provides a comprehensive guide for the teacher candidate's job search, as the format offers information that includes: interview questions most often asked in the teaching interview (grade-level and subject-matter specific); sample forms for applications, cover letters, and resumes that will impact principals and district personnel; strategies on preparing for the teaching interview; interview follow-up techniques; inside tips from a superintendent, a principal and a counselor.

★6634★ The Inside Secrets of Finding a Teaching Job

Jist Works
875 Montreal Way
St. Paul, MN 55102
Fr: 800-648-5478
E-mail: info@jist.com
URL: http://www.jist.com

Jack Warner, Clyde Bryan, and Diane Warner. Third edition, 2006. $12.95. 196 pages. Tips from educators on finding an entry-level teaching position.

★6635★ Job Hunting in Education: An Insider's Guide to Success

Scarecrow Press, Inc.
4501 Forbes Blvd., Ste. 200
Lanham, MD 20706-4310
Ph: (301)459-3366   Fax: (301)429-5747

Herbert F. Pandiscio. April 2004. $41.95 (paper). 192 pages.

★6636★ The New Elementary Teacher's Handbook: (Almost) Everything You Need to Know for Your First Years of Teaching

Corwin Press, Inc.
2455 Teller Rd.
Thousand Oaks, CA 91320-2218
Ph: (805)499-5323   Fax: 800-417-2466
Fr: 800-233-9936
URL: http://www.corwinpress.com/

Kathleen F. Jonson, Ed D. Jonson. 1997. $69.95 (paper). 224 pages.

★6637★ Non-Profits and Education Job Finder

Planning Communications
7215 Oak Ave.
River Forest, IL 60305-1935
Ph: (708)366-5200   Fax: (708)366-5280
Fr: 888-366-5200
E-mail: info@planningcommunications.com
URL: http://jobfinderonline.com

Daniel Lauber. 1997. $32.95; $16.95 (paper). 340 pages. Covers 1600 sources. Discusses how to use sources of non-profit sector job vacancies in a number of specialties and state-by-state, including job-matching services, job hotlines, specialty periodicals with job ads, salary surveys, and directories. Covers a variety of fields from education to religion. Includes chapters on resume and cover letter preparation and interviewing.

★6638★ Opportunities in State and Local Government Careers

The McGraw-Hill Companies
PO Box 182604
Columbus, OH 43272
Fax: (614)759-3749   Fr: 877-883-5524
E-mail: customer.service@mcgraw-hill.com
URL: http://www.mcgraw-hill.com

Neale J. Baxter. Revised edition, 1992. $14.95; $10.95 (paper). 148 pages. Points out the incentives and drawbacks of a government career. Describes hiring procedures and provides tips on filling out applications, taking physical and aptitude tests, handling interviews, and finding jobs. Describes the jobs in which 75% of all state and local government workers are employed. For each occupation, covers the nature of the work and the training required.

★6639★ Opportunities in Teaching Careers

The McGraw-Hill Companies
PO Box 182604
Columbus, OH 43272
Fax: (614)759-3749   Fr: 877-883-5524
E-mail: customer.service@mcgraw-hill.com
URL: http://www.mcgraw-hill.com

Janet Fine. 2005. $13.95 (paper). 160 pages. Discusses licensing and accreditation programs, sources of placement information, job-seeking correspondence, selection procedures, and paths to advancement. Also covers professional associations, non-traditional teaching opportunities, and jobs abroad.

★6640★ A Practical Guide to Elementary Instruction: From Plan to Delivery

Pearson Allyn & Bacon
1 Lake St.
Upper Saddle River, NJ 07458
Ph: (201)236-7000   Fr: 800-922-0579
URL: http://www.pearsoned.com/higher-ed/

Suzanne Borman and Joel M. Levine. 1997. $100.40. 396 pages.

★6641★ Real People Working in Education

The McGraw-Hill Companies
PO Box 182604
Columbus, OH 43272
Fax: (614)759-3749   Fr: 877-883-5524
E-mail: customer.service@mcgraw-hill.com
URL: http://www.mcgraw-hill.com

Blythe Camenson, Jan Goldberg. 1997. $17.95; $12.95 (paper). 160 pages/ Interviews and profiles of working professionals capture a range of opportunities in this field.

★6642★ The Teaching Career

Teachers College Press, Teachers
College, Columbia University
1234 Amsterdam Ave.
New York, NY 10027
Ph: (212)678-3929   Fax: (212)678-4149

John I. Goodlad, Timothy J. McMannon. February 2004. $24.95 (paper). Illustrated. 240 pages. The Series in School Reform.

★6643★ Why Choose a Career in Teaching?

The Graduate Group
PO Box 370351
West Hartford, CT 06137-0351
Ph: (860)233-2330   Fax: (860)233-2330
Fr: 800-484-7280
E-mail: graduategroup@hotmail.com
URL: http://www.graduategroup.com

James Abbott. April 2004. $30.00 (paper). Book explores traditional and non-traditional routes to becoming an elementary or secondary teacher.

EMPLOYMENT AGENCIES AND SEARCH FIRMS

★6644★ Educational Placement Service

6510-A S. Academy Blvd.
Colorado Springs, CO 80906
Ph: (719)579-9911   Fax: (719)579-5050
E-mail: accounting@educatorjobs.com
URL: http://www.educatorjobs.com

Employment agency. Focuses on teaching, administrative, and education-related openings.

TRADESHOWS

★6645★ Association for Childhood Education International Annual International Conference & Exhibition

Association for Childhood Education
International
17904 Georgia Ave., Ste. 215
Olney, MD 20832
Ph: (301)570-2111   Fax: (301)570-2212
Fr: 800-423-3563
E-mail: headquarters@acei.org
URL: http://www.acei.org

Annual. **Primary Exhibits:** Commercial and educational exhibits of interest to teachers, teacher educators, college students, day care personnel and other care givers. **Dates and Locations:** 2008 Mar 26-29; Atlanta, GA; Westin Peachtree Plaza; 2009 Mar 18-21; Chicago, IL; Westin Michigan Avenue.

★6646★ National Art Education Association Convention

National Art Education Association
1916 Association Dr.
Reston, VA 20191-1590
Ph: (703)860-8000   Fax: (703)860-2960
E-mail: naea@dgs.dgsys.com
URL: http://www.naea-reston.org

Annual. **Primary Exhibits:** Art materials; art-related books and magazines; art career education information; arts and crafts supplies. **Dates and Locations:** 2008 Mar 26-30; New Orleans, LA.

★6647★ National Association for the Education of Young Children Annual Conference

National Association for the Education of
Young Children
1509 16th St., NW
Washington, DC 20036
Ph: (202)232-8777   Fax: (202)328-1846
Fr: 800-424-2460
E-mail: naeyc@naeyc.org
URL: http://www.naeyc.org

Annual. **Primary Exhibits:** Educational materials and equipment designed for children ages birth through eight years old.

OTHER SOURCES

★6648★ American Association for Health Education (AAHE)

1900 Association Dr.
Reston, VA 20191-1599
Ph: (703)476-3437   Fax: (703)476-6638
Fr: 800-213-7193
E-mail: aahe@aahperd.org
URL: http://www.aahperd.org/aahe

Members: Professionals who have responsibility for health education in schools, colleges, communities, hospitals and clinics, and industries. **Purpose:** Aims to advance the health education through program activities and federal legislation; encourage close working relationships between all health education and health service organizations; achieve good health and well-being for all Americans automatically, without conscious thought and endeavor. Member of the American Alliance for Health, Physical Education, Recreation and Dance.

★6649★ American Association of Teachers of German (AATG)

112 Haddontowne Ct., No. 104
Cherry Hill, NJ 08034-3668
Ph: (856)795-5553   Fax: (856)795-9398
E-mail: headquarters@aatg.org
URL: http://www.aatg.org

Description: Represents teachers of German at all levels; individuals interested in German language and culture. Offers in-service teacher-training workshops, materials, student honor society, national German examination and stipends/scholarships.

★6650★ American Federation of Teachers (AFT)

555 New Jersey Ave. NW
Washington, DC 20001
Ph: (202)879-4400   Fax: (202)879-4545
Fr: 800-238-1133
E-mail: online@aft.org
URL: http://www.aft.org

Description: Affiliated with the AFL-CIO. Works with teachers and other educational employees at the state and local level in organizing, collective bargaining, research, educational issues, and public relations. Conducts research in areas such as educational reform, teacher certification, and national assessments and standards. Represents members' concerns through legislative action; offers technical assistance. Serves professionals with concerns similar to those of teachers, including state employees, healthcare workers, and paraprofessionals.

★6651★ Association of Christian Schools International (ACSI)

PO Box 65130
Colorado Springs, CO 80962-5130
Ph: (719)528-6906   Fax: (719)531-0631
Fr: 800-367-0798
E-mail: info@acsi.org
URL: http://www.acsi.org

Description: Seeks to enable Christian educators and schools worldwide to effectively prepare students for life.

★6652★ Center for the Child Care Workforce, A Project of the American Federation of Teachers Educational Foundation (CCW/AFTEF)

555 New Jersey Ave. NW
Washington, DC 20001
Ph: (202)662-8005   Fax: (202)662-8006
E-mail: ccw@aft.org
URL: http://ccw.cleverspin.com

Purpose: Purposes are: to develop innovative solutions to the child care crisis to improve salaries, working conditions, and status of child care workers; to increase public awareness about the importance of child care work and the training and skill it demands; to develop resources and create an information sharing network for child care workers nationwide. **Activities:** Gathers current information on salaries and benefits; offers consultation services. Sponsors research projects; compiles statistics; operates Speaker's Bureau. Maintains extensive file of materials on working conditions and research on child care workers.

★6653★ **Council of American Instructors of the Deaf (CAID)**

PO Box 377
Bedford, TX 76095-0377
Ph: (817)354-8414
E-mail: caid@swbell.net
URL: http://www.caid.org

Members: Professional organization of teachers, administrators, and professionals in allied fields related to education of the deaf and hard-of-hearing. **Purpose:** Provides opportunities for a free interchange of views concerning methods and means of educating the deaf and hard-of-hearing. Promotes such education by the publication of reports, essays, and other information. Develops more effective methods of teaching deaf and hard-of-hearing children.

★6654★ **Education and Training**

Cambridge Educational
PO Box 2053
Princeton, NJ 08543-2053
Ph: 800-257-5126   Fax: (609)671-0266
Fr: 800-468-4227
E-mail: custserv@films.com
URL: http://www.cambridgeeducational.com

VHS and DVD. $89.95. 2002. 18 minutes. Presents four distinct occupations in the field: elementary teachers, teacher's aides, administrators, and librarians. People working in these jobs discuss their responsibilities.

★6655★ **Friends Council on Education (FCE)**

1507 Cherry St.
Philadelphia, PA 19102
Ph: (215)241-7245   Fax: (215)241-7299
E-mail: info@friendscouncil.org
URL: http://www.friendscouncil.org

Members: Representatives appointed by Friends Yearly Meetings; heads of Quaker secondary and elementary schools and colleges; members-at-large. **Purpose:** Acts as a clearinghouse for information on Quaker schools and colleges. **Activities:** Holds meetings and conferences on education and provides in-service training for teachers, administrators and trustees in Friends schools.

★6656★ **International Reading Association (IRA)**

PO Box 8139
Newark, DE 19714-8139
Ph: (302)731-1600   Fax: (302)731-1057
Fr: 800-336-7323
E-mail: pubinfo@reading.org
URL: http://www.reading.org

Description: Represents teachers, reading specialists, consultants, administrators, supervisors, researchers, psychologists, librarians, and parents interested in promoting literacy. Seeks to improve the quality of reading instruction and promote literacy worldwide. Disseminates information pertaining to research on reading, including information on adult literacy, early childhood and literacy development, international education, literature for children and adolescents, and teacher education and professional development. Maintains over 40 special interest groups and over 70 committees.

★6657★ **International Technology Education Association - Council for Supervisors (ITEA-CS)**

PO Box 144200
Salt Lake City, UT 84114-4200
Ph: (801)538-7598   Fax: (801)538-7868
E-mail: mrobinson@schools.utah.gov
URL: http://www.iteawww.net/CS

Description: Technology education supervisors from the U.S. Office of Education; local school department chairpersons; state departments of education, local school districts, territories, provinces, and foreign countries. Improves instruction and supervision of programs in technology education. Conducts research; compiles statistics. Sponsors competitions. Maintains speakers' bureau.

★6658★ **Jewish Education Service of North America (JESNA)**

111 8th Ave., 11th Fl.
New York, NY 10011
Ph: (212)284-6950   Fax: (212)284-6951
E-mail: info@jesna.org
URL: http://www.jesna.org

Description: Widely recognized leader in the areas of research and program evaluation, organizational change and innovative program design and dissemination. Operates the Mandell J. Berman Jewish Heritage Center for Research and Evaluation. Supports the Covenant Foundation, a joint venture with the Crown Family, which makes awards and grants for creativity in Jewish education.

★6659★ **NAFSA/Association of International Educators (NAFSA)**

1307 New York Ave. NW, 8th Fl.
Washington, DC 20005-4701
Ph: (202)737-3699   Fax: (202)737-3657
E-mail: inbox@nafsa.org
URL: http://www.nafsa.org

Description: Individuals, organizations, and institutions dealing with international educational exchange, including foreign student advisers, overseas educational advisers, credentials and admissions officers, administrators and teachers of English as a second language, community support personnel, study-abroad administrators, and embassy cultural or educational personnel. Promotes self-regulation standards and responsibilities in international educational exchange; offers professional development opportunities primarily through publications, workshops, grants, and regional and national conferences. Advocates for increased awareness and support of international education and exchange on campuses, in government, and in communities. Offers services including: a job registry for employers and professionals involved with international education; a consultant referral service. Sponsors joint liaison activities with a variety of other educational and government organizations to conduct a census of foreign student enrollment in the U.S.; conducts workshops about specific subjects and countries.

★6660★ **National Art Education Association (NAEA)**

1916 Association Dr.
Reston, VA 20191-1502
Ph: (703)860-8000   Fax: (703)860-2960
E-mail: info@naea-reston.org
URL: http://www.naea-reston.org

Members: Teachers of art at elementary, middle, secondary, and college levels; colleges, libraries, museums, and other educational institutions. **Purpose:** Studies problems of teaching art; encourages research and experimentation. **Activities:** Serves as a clearinghouse for information on art education programs, materials, and methods of instruction. Sponsors special institutes. Cooperates with other national organizations for the furtherance of creative art experiences for youth.

★6661★ **National Association of Blind Teachers (NABT)**

1155 15th St. NW, Ste. 1004
Washington, DC 20005
Ph: (202)467-5081   Fax: (202)467-5085
Fr: 800-424-8666
E-mail: info@acb.org
URL: http://www.acb.org

Description: Public school teachers, college and university professors, and teachers in residential schools for the blind. Promotes employment and professional goals of blind persons entering the teaching profession or those established in their respective teaching fields. Serves as a vehicle for the dissemination of information and the exchange of ideas addressing special problems of members. Compiles statistics.

★6662★ **National Association of Catholic School Teachers (NACST)**

1700 Sansom St., Ste. 903
Philadelphia, PA 19103
Ph: (215)568-4175   Fax: (215)568-8270
Fr: 800-99-NACST
E-mail: nacst.nacst@verizon.net
URL: http://www.nacst.com

Description: Catholic school teachers. Aims

to unify, advise, and assist Catholic school teachers in matters of collective bargaining. Promotes the welfare and rights of Catholic schools and teachers; determines needs of Catholic schools and teachers. Monitors legislation, trends, and statistics concerning Catholic education; promotes legislation favorable to nonpublic schools and Catholic school teachers; offers legal advice and addresses issues such as unemployment compensation; assists teachers in organizing and negotiating contracts. Maintains speakers' bureau.

★6663★ National Association for the Education of Young Children (NAEYC)

1313 L St. NW, Ste. 500
Washington, DC 20005
Ph: (202)232-8777   Fax: (202)328-1846
Fr: 800-424-2460
E-mail: naeyc@naeyc.org
URL: http://www.naeyc.org

Description: Teachers and directors of preschool and primary schools, kindergartens, child care centers, and early other learning programs for young childhood; early childhood education and child development educators, trainers, and researchers and other professionals dedicated to young children's healthy development.

★6664★ National Association of Episcopal Schools (NAES)

815 2nd Ave., Ste. 819
New York, NY 10017-4594
Ph: (212)716-6134   Fax: (212)286-9366
Fr: 800-334-7626
E-mail: info@episcopalschools.org
URL: http://www.episcopalschools.org

Description: Represents episcopal day and boarding schools and preschools. Promotes the educational ministry of the Episcopal Church. Provides publications, consultation services and conference focusing on Episcopal identity of schools, worship, religious education, spirituality, leadership development and governance for heads/directors, administrators, chaplains and teachers of religion, trustees, rectors and other church and school leaders.

★6665★ National Association of Independent Schools (NAIS)

1620 L St. NW, Ste. 1100
Washington, DC 20036-5695
Ph: (202)973-9700   Fax: (202)973-9790
Fr: 800-793-6701
E-mail: info@nais.org
URL: http://www.nais.org

Description: Independent elementary and secondary school members; regional associations of independent schools and related associations. Provides curricular and administrative research and services. Conducts educational programs; compiles statistics.

★6666★ National Association for Research in Science Teaching (NARST)

12100 Sunset Hills Rd., Ste. 130
Reston, VA 20190-3221
Ph: (703)437-4377   Fax: (703)435-4390
E-mail: info@narst.org
URL: http://www.narst.org

Description: Science teachers, supervisors, and science educators specializing in research and teacher education. Promotes and coordinates science education research and interprets and reports the results.

★6667★ National Association of State Directors of Special Education (NASDSE)

1800 Diagonal Rd., Ste. 320
Alexandria, VA 22314
Ph: (703)519-3800   Fax: (703)519-3808
E-mail: nasdse@nasdse.org

Members: Professional society of state directors; consultants, supervisors, and administrators who have statewide responsibilities for administering special education programs. **Purpose:** Provides services to state agencies to facilitate their efforts to maximize educational outcomes for individuals with disabilities.

★6668★ National Community Education Association (NCEA)

3929 Old Lee Hwy., No. 91-A
Fairfax, VA 22030-2421
Ph: (703)359-8973   Fax: (703)359-0972
E-mail: ncea@ncea.com
URL: http://www.ncea.com

Description: Community school directors, principals, superintendents, professors, teachers, students, and laypeople. **Purpose:** Promotes and establishes community schools as an integral part of the educational plan of every community. Emphasizes community and parent involvement in the schools, lifelong learning, and enrichment of K-12 and adult education. Serves as a clearinghouse for the exchange of ideas and information, and the sharing of efforts. **Activities:** Offers leadership training.

★6669★ National Council for Accreditation of Teacher Education (NCATE)

2010 Massachusetts Ave. NW, Ste. 500
Washington, DC 20036
Ph: (202)466-7496   Fax: (202)296-6620
E-mail: ncate@ncate.org
URL: http://www.ncate.org

Members: Representatives from constituent colleges and universities, state departments of education, school boards, teacher, and other professional groups. **Purpose:** Voluntary accrediting body devoted exclusively to: evaluation and accreditation of institutions for preparation of elementary and secondary school teachers; preparation of school service personnel, including school principals,

supervisors, superintendents, school psychologists, instructional technologists, and other specialists for school-oriented positions.

★6670★ National Council for Geographic Education (NCGE)

206A Martin Hall
Jacksonville State University
Jacksonville, AL 36265-1602
Ph: (256)782-5293   Fax: (256)782-5336
E-mail: ncge@ncge.org
URL: http://www.ncge.org

Description: Teachers of geography and social studies in elementary and secondary schools, colleges and universities; geographers in governmental agencies and private businesses. Encourages the training of teachers in geographic concepts, practices, teaching methods and techniques; works to develop effective geographic educational programs in schools and colleges and with adult groups; stimulates the production and use of accurate and understandable geographic teaching aids and materials.

★6671★ National Council of Teachers of Mathematics (NCTM)

1906 Association Dr.
Reston, VA 20191-1502
Ph: (703)620-9840   Fax: (703)476-2970
Fr: 800-235-7566
E-mail: inquiries@nctm.org
URL: http://www.nctm.org

Description: Aims to improve teaching and learning of mathematics.

★6672★ *Overseas Employment Opportunities for Educators: Department of Defense Dependents Schools*

DIANE Publishing Co.
PO Box 617
Darby, PA 19023-0617
Ph: (610)461-6200   Fax: (610)461-6130
Fr: 800-782-3833
URL: http://www.dianepublishingcentral.com

Barry Leonard, editor. 2000. $15.00. 54 pages. An introduction to teachings positions in the Dept. of Defense Dependents Schools (DoDDS), a worldwide school system, operated by the DoD in 14 countries.

★6673★ Teaching & Related Occupations

Delphi Productions
3159 6th St.
Boulder, CO 80304
Ph: (303)443-2100   Fax: (303)443-4022
Fr: 888-443-2400
E-mail: support@delphivideo.com
URL: http://www.delphivideo.com

$95.00. 50 minutes. Part of the Careers for the 21st Century Video Library.

Landscape Architects

SOURCES OF HELP-WANTED ADS

★6674★ American Nurseryman
American Nurseryman Publishing Co.
223 West Jackson Blvd., Ste. 500
Chicago, IL 60606-6904
Ph: (312)427-7339   Fax: (312)427-7346
Fr: 800-621-5727
E-mail: editors@amerinursery.com
URL: http://www.amerinursery.com/

Semimonthly. $48.00/year for individuals; $80.00/year for other countries; $85.60/year for Canada; $5.00 for single issue. Trade magazine containing information on commercial horticulture: nursery, landscape and garden center management.

★6675★ Arboriculture Consultant
American Society of Consulting Arborists
15245 Shady Grove Rd., Ste. 130
Rockville, MD 20850
Ph: (301)947-0483   Fax: (301)990-9771
E-mail: asca@mgmtsol.com
URL: http://www.asca-consultants.org
Description: Quarterly. Contains information on trees.

★6676★ Architectural Record
McGraw-Hill Inc.
1221 Ave. of the Americas
New York, NY 10020-1095
Ph: (212)512-2000   Fax: (212)512-3840
Fr: 877-833-5524
URL: http://archrecord.construction.com
Monthly. $49.00/year for individuals. Magazine focusing on architecture.

★6677★ Fabric Architecture
Industrial Fabrics Association International
1801 County Rd. B W
Roseville, MN 55113
Ph: (651)222-2508   Fax: (651)631-9334
Fr: 800-225-4324
URL: http://www.ifai.com/awning/fabricarchitecturemagazine.cfm

Bimonthly. Magazine specializing in interior and exterior design ideas and technical information for architectural fabric applications in architecture and the landscape.

★6678★ Interiorscape
Brantwood Publications Inc.
2430 Estancia Blvd, Ste. 100
Clearwater, FL 33761-2644
Ph: (727)724-0020   Fax: (727)724-0021
URL: http://www.interiorbiz.com/

Bimonthly. $12.00/year for U.S., 1-year; $30.00/year for U.S., 3-year; $50.00/year by mail, Canadian/foreign surface mail 1-year; $100.00/year by mail, Canada/foreign air mail 1-year; $100.00/year by mail, Canadian/foreign surface mail 3-year; $200.00/year by mail, Canada/foreign air mail 3-year. Interior landscape design magazine.

★6679★ LAND
American Society of Landscape Architects
636 Eye St., NW
Washington, DC 20001-3736
Ph: (202)898-2444   Fax: (202)898-1185
Fr: 888-999-2752
URL: http://www.asla.org

Description: Biweekly. Carries news and monitors developments in landscape architecture, environmental design, and related fields. Focuses on public policy, education, and other areas affecting landscape architecture.

★6680★ Landscape Architecture
American Society of Landscape Architects
636 Eye St., NW
Washington, DC 20001-3736
Ph: (202)898-2444   Fax: (202)898-1185
Fr: 888-999-2752
URL: http://www.asla.org

Monthly. $59.00/year for nonmembers; $99.00/year for nonmembers, international; $75.00/year for institutions, library; $125.00/year for institutions, library, international; $43.00/year for students; $70.00/year for students, international. Professional magazine covering land planning and design.

★6681★ Landscape Construction
Moose River Publishing
374 Emerson Falls Rd.
St. Johnsbury, VT 05819-9083
Ph: (802)748-8908   Fax: (802)748-1866
Fr: 800-422-7147
URL: http://www.lcmmagazine.com/

Monthly. Magazine featuring landscaping.

★6682★ The Landscape Contractor
Illinois Landscape Contractor Association
2625 Butterfield Rd., Ste. 204-W
Oak Brook, IL 60523
Ph: (630)472-2851   Fax: (630)472-3150
URL: http://www.ilca.net/publications.asp

Monthly. $65.00/year for individuals in-state (Illinois); $150.00/year for out of state. Magazine for the landscape trade.

★6683★ Landscape Management
Questex Media Group
275 Grove St., 2-130
Newton, MA 02466
Ph: (617)219-8300   Fax: (617)219-8310
Fr: 888-552-4346
URL: http://www.advanstar.com/index_all-pubs.html

$46.00/year. Free to qualified subscribers, domestic; $69.00/year for Canada and Mexico; $89.00/year for other countries. Magazine for professionals in landscape, grounds management and lawn care, construction, and maintenance.

★6684★ Landscape Superintendent and Maintenance Professional
Landscape Communications Inc.
14771 Plaza Dr., Ste. M
Tustin, CA 92780
Ph: (714)979-5276   Fax: (714)979-3543
URL: http://www.landscapeonline.com/contact/contact_mag.php?pub=l

Free to qualified subscribers. Magazine for landscape professionals.

★6685★ Nursery News

Cenflo Inc.
PO Box 44040
Rio Rancho, NM 87174
Fax: (505)867-0991   Fr: 800-732-4581
URL: http://www.cenflo.com/nursery-news.html

Biweekly. $20.00/year for individuals; $36.00 for two years; $125.00/year for other countries. Trade newspaper (tabloid) for nursery industry.

★6686★ PLANET News

Professional Landcare Network
950 Herndon Pkwy., Ste. 450
Herndon, VA 20170
Ph: (703)736-9666   Fax: (703)736-9668
Fr: 800-395-2522
URL: http://www.landcarenetwork.org

Description: Quarterly. Features articles on technical, business, legislation and safety in the field of lawn care. Includes calendar of events, new member companies, and association news.

★6687★ Qualified Remodeler Magazine

Cygnus Business Media
1233 Janesville Ave.
Fort Atkinson, WI 53538
Fr: 800-547-7377
URL: http://www.qualifiedremodeler.com

Monthly. Magazine for remodeling contractor/distributors.

★6688★ Remodeling

Hanley-Wood L.L.C.
1 Thomas Cir., NW, Ste. 600
Washington, DC 20005
Ph: (202)452-0800   Fax: (202)785-1974
URL: http://www.hanleywood.com/default.aspx?page=b2brm

$25.00/year for individuals; $40.00/year for individuals, Canadian residents; $192.00/year for individuals, international residents. Trade magazine for the professional remodeling industry.

PLACEMENT AND JOB REFERRAL SERVICES

★6689★ American Society of Landscape Architects (ASLA)

636 Eye St. NW
Washington, DC 20001-3736
Ph: (202)898-2444   Fax: (202)898-1185
Fr: 888-999-ASLA
E-mail: nsomerville@asla.org
URL: http://www.asla.org

Description: Professional society of landscape architects. Promotes the advancement of education and skill in the art of landscape architecture as an instrument in service to the public welfare. Seeks to strengthen existing and proposed university

programs in landscape architecture. Offers counsel to new and emerging programs; encourages state registration of landscape architects. Sponsors annual educational exhibit. Offers placement service; conducts specialized education and research.

EMPLOYER DIRECTORIES AND NETWORKING LISTS

★6690★ American Society of Landscape Architects-Members' Handbook

American Society of Landscape Architects
636 Eye St., NW
Washington, DC 20001-3736
Ph: (202)898-2444   Fax: (202)898-1185
Fr: 888-999-2752
E-mail: handbook@asla.org
URL: http://www.asla.org

Annual, November. $195.00 for individuals. Covers 11,000 member landscape architects and affiliates. Entries include: Name, address, phone, chapter, membership category, year joined, type of practice. Arrangement: Alphabetical. Indexes: Geographical.

★6691★ Directory of Public Garden Internships

American Association of Botanical
Gardens and Arboreta
100 W 10th St., Ste. 614
Wilmington, DE 19801
Ph: (302)655-7100   Fax: (302)655-8100
E-mail: bvincent@aabga.org
URL: http://aabga.org

Annual, November; latest edition 2005. Covers 700 student internships and summer jobs at public gardens throughout North America. Entries include: Name of institution, address, name of contact, deadline for application, number of students hired, whether internships are available, employment period, hours, rate of pay, whether housing is available, other comments. Arrangement: Alphabetical. Indexes: By position, by state/province.

★6692★ New York State Nursery/ Landscape Association-Directory

New York State Nursery/Landscape
Assoc. Inc.
PO Box 657
Baldwinsville, NY 13027
Ph: (315)635-5008   Fax: (315)635-4874
Fr: 800-647-0384
URL: http://www.nysnla.com/

Annual, January. Covers over 800 member nursery, landscape, gardening, and lawn maintenance firms in New York. Entries include: Company name, address, phone. Arrangement: Alphabetical.

★6693★ ProFile

Reed Construction Data
30 Technology Pkwy. S, Ste. 100
Norcross, GA 30092
Fr: 800-424-3996
E-mail: profile@reedbusiness.com
URL: http://www.reedfirstsource.com

Annual. Covers more than 27,000 architectural firms. Entries include: For firms–Firm name, address, phone, fax, year established, key staff and their primary responsibilities (for design, specification, etc.), number of staff personnel by discipline, types of work, geographical area served, projects. "ProFile" is an expanded version of, and replaces, the "Firm Directory." Arrangement: Firms are geographical. Indexes: Firm name; key individuals; specialization by category; consultants.

HANDBOOKS AND MANUALS

★6694★ Careers for Health Nuts and Others Who Like to Stay Fit

The McGraw-Hill Companies
PO Box 182604
Columbus, OH 43272
Fax: (614)759-3749   Fr: 877-883-5524
E-mail: customer.service@mcgraw-hill.com
URL: http://www.mcgraw-hill.com

Blythe Camenson. Second edition, 2005. $13.95 (paper). 208 pages.

★6695★ Careers in Horticulture and Botany

The McGraw-Hill Companies
PO Box 182604
Columbus, OH 43272
Fax: (614)759-3749   Fr: 877-883-5524
E-mail: customer.service@mcgraw-hill.com
URL: http://www.mcgraw-hill.com

Jerry Garner. 2006. 15.95 (paper). 192 pages. Includes bibliographical references.

★6696★ Opportunities in Environmental Careers

The McGraw-Hill Companies
PO Box 182604
Columbus, OH 43272
Fax: (614)759-3749   Fr: 877-883-5524
E-mail: customer.service@mcgraw-hill.com
URL: http://www.mcgraw-hill.com

Odom Fanning. Revised, 2002. $12.95 (paper). 174 pages. Describes a broad range of opportunities in fields such as environmental health, recreation, physics, and hygiene, and provides job search advice. Part of the "Opportunities in ..." Series.

★6697★ Opportunities in Landscape Architecture, Botanical Gardens, and Arboreta Careers

The McGraw-Hill Companies
PO Box 182604
Columbus, OH 43272
Fax: (614)759-3749   Fr: 877-883-5524
E-mail: customer.service@mcgraw-hill.com
URL: http://www.mcgraw-hill.com

Blythe Cameron. 2007. $13.95; $11.95 (paper). 160 pages. Includes bibliography.

★6698★ Opportunities in Real Estate Careers

The McGraw-Hill Companies
PO Box 182604
Columbus, OH 43272
Fax: (614)759-3749   Fr: 877-883-5524
E-mail: customer.service@mcgraw-hill.com
URL: http://www.mcgraw-hill.com

Mariwyn Evansand and Richard Mendenhal. Second edition, 2002. $12.95 (paper). 160 pages.

★6699★ The Perfect Guide to Making $ in Landscaping and Maintenance: A How-To Book

Moran Publishing
210 Lazy River
Sealy, TX 77474
Fr: 800-223-0351

Gene Yezak. 2000. $9.95 (paper). 220 pages.

★6700★ Professional Practice for Landscape Architects

Elsevier
11830 Westline Industrial Dr.
St. Louis, MO 63146
Ph: (314)453-7010   Fax: (314)453-7095
Fr: 800-545-2522
E-mail: usbkinfo@elsevier.com
URL: http://www.elsevier.com

Tennant, Garmory, and Winsch. 2002. $32.95 (paper). 192 pages.

EMPLOYMENT AGENCIES AND SEARCH FIRMS

★6701★ Claremont-Branan, Inc.

1298 Rockbridge Rd., Ste. B
Stone Mountain, GA 30087
Ph: (770)925-2915   Fax: (770)925-2601
Fr: 800-875-1292
E-mail: ohil@cbisearch.com
URL: http://cbisearch.com

Employment agency. Executive search firm.

ONLINE JOB SOURCES AND SERVICES

★6702★ American Society of Landscape Architects JobLink

American Society of Landscape Architects
636 Eye St. NW
Washington, DC 20001-3736
Ph: (202)898-2444   Fax: (202)898-1185
URL: http://www.asla.org/nonmembers/joblink.cfm

Description: A job-search site of the American Society of Landscape Architects. **Fee:** Resume postings cost $100 (nonmembers) or $10 (members) for a two-month listing. Job postings cost $560 (nonmembers) or $280 (members) for a one-month listing.

TRADESHOWS

★6703★ American Society of Landscape Architects Annual Meeting and Expo

American Society of Landscape Architects
636 Eye St., NW
Washington, DC 20001-3736
Ph: (202)898-2444   Fax: (202)898-1185
Fr: 800-787-ASLA
E-mail: AM2004@asla.org
URL: http://www.asla.org

Annual. **Primary Exhibits:** Irrigation supplies, outdoor lighting, park and playground equipment, paving and ground cover, street and park furniture, landscape maintenance equipment, computer hardware and software, architectural finishing materials, construction materials, historic preservation services, surveying and mapping equipment, and related equipment, supplies, and services. **Dates and Locations:** 2008 Oct 03-07; Philadelphia, PA; 2009 Sep 18-22; Chicago, IL; 2010 Sep 10-14; Washington, DC.

OTHER SOURCES

★6704★ American Nursery and Landscape Association (ANLA)

1000 Vermont Ave. NW, Ste. 300
Washington, DC 20005-4914
Ph: (202)789-2900   Fax: (202)789-1893
E-mail: jbardzik@anla.org
URL: http://www.anla.org

Members: Vertical organization of wholesale growers; landscape firms; garden centers; mail order nurseries; suppliers. Promotes the industry and its products. Offers management and consulting services and public relations programs. Provides government representation and bank card plan for members. Maintains hall of fame.

★6705★ American Public Gardens Association (APGA)

100 W 10th St., Ste. 614
Wilmington, DE 19801-6604
Ph: (302)655-7100   Fax: (302)655-8100
E-mail: dstark@publicgardens.org
URL: http://www.publicgardens.org

Members: Directors and staffs of botanical gardens, arboreta, institutions maintaining or conducting horticultural courses, and others. **Purpose:** Seeks to serve North American public gardens and horticultural organizations by promoting professional development through its publications and meetings, advocating the interests of public gardens in political, corporate, foundation, and community arenas, and encouraging gardens to adhere to professional standards in their programs and operations.

★6706★ International Society of Arboriculture (ISA)

PO Box 3129
Champaign, IL 61826-3129
Ph: (217)355-9411   Fax: (217)355-9516
Fr: 888-472-8733
E-mail: isa@isa-arbor.com
URL: http://www.isa-arbor.com

Description: Individuals engaged in commercial, municipal, and utility arboriculture; city, state, and national government employees; municipal and commercial arborists; others interested in shade tree welfare. Disseminates information on the care and preservation of shade and ornamental trees. Supports research projects at educational institutions.

★6707★ Landscape Architecture Foundation (LAF)

818 18th St. NW, Ste. 810
Washington, DC 20006
Ph: (202)331-7070   Fax: (202)331-7079
E-mail: rfigura@lafoundation.org
URL: http://www.lafoundation.org

Description: Serves as an education and research vehicle for the landscape architecture profession in the U.S. Combines the capabilities of landscape architects, interests of environmentalists, and needs of agencies and resource foundations. Provides for the preparation and dissemination of educational and scientific information through publications, exhibits, lectures, and seminars. Solicits and expends gifts, legacies, and grants. Established an endowment fund for professorships at colleges and universities. Sponsors California Landscape Architectural Student Scholarship Fund. Conducts a study of the profession to establish goals in terms of education, research needs, practice, and formulation of public policy.

★6708★ Professional Specialty Occupations

Delphi Productions
3159 6th St.
Boulder, CO 80304
Ph: (303)443-2100   Fax: (303)443-4022
Fr: 888-443-2400

E-mail: support@delphivideo.com
URL: http://www.delphivideo.com

$95.00. 53 minutes. Part of the Careers for

the 21st Century Video Library.

Landscapers

SOURCES OF HELP-WANTED ADS

★6709★ American City and County

Primedia Business
6151 Powers Ferry Rd., Ste. 200
Atlanta, GA 30339
Ph: (770)955-2500   Fax: (770)618-0204
URL: http://
www.americancityandcounty.com

Monthly. $67.00/year for individuals. Municipal and county administration magazine.

★6710★ American Nurseryman

American Nurseryman Publishing Co.
223 West Jackson Blvd., Ste. 500
Chicago, IL 60606-6904
Ph: (312)427-7339   Fax: (312)427-7346
Fr: 800-621-5727
E-mail: editors@amerinursery.com
URL: http://www.amerinursery.com/

Semimonthly. $48.00/year for individuals; $80.00/year for other countries; $85.60/year for Canada; $5.00 for single issue. Trade magazine containing information on commercial horticulture: nursery, landscape and garden center management.

★6711★ Grower Talks

Ball Publishing
335 N River St.
PO Box 9
Batavia, IL 60510-0009
Ph: (630)208-9080   Fax: (630)208-9350
URL: http://www.growertalks.com

Monthly. $29.00/year for U.S. $39.00/year for Canada and Mexico; $79.00/year for other countries, air mail; $52.00 for two years; $68.00/year for Canada and Mexico, 2 years; $148.00/year for other countries, air mail; $72.00/year 3 years; $97.00/year for Canada and Mexico, 3 years; $212.00/year for other countries, airmail, 3 years. Trade magazine covering issues for commercial greenhouse growers with a focus on North American production.

★6712★ Interiorscape

Brantwood Publications Inc.
2430 Estancia Blvd, Ste. 100
Clearwater, FL 33761-2644
Ph: (727)724-0020   Fax: (727)724-0021
URL: http://www.interiorbiz.com/

Bimonthly. $12.00/year for U.S., 1-year; $30.00/year for U.S., 3-year; $50.00/year by mail, Canadian/foreign surface mail 1-year; $100.00/year by mail, Canada/foreign air mail 1-year; $100.00/year by mail, Canadian/foreign surface mail 3-year; $200.00/year by mail, Canada/foreign air mail 3-year. Interior landscape design magazine.

★6713★ Job Line...and News from CPRS

California Park & Recreation Society Inc.
7971 Freeport Blvd.
Sacramento, CA 95832-9701
Ph: (916)665-2777   Fax: (916)665-9149
URL: http://www.cprs.org/publications-job-line.htm

Description: Monthly. Discusses parks and recreation news of interest.

★6714★ Landscape Construction

Moose River Publishing
374 Emerson Falls Rd.
St. Johnsbury, VT 05819-9083
Ph: (802)748-8908   Fax: (802)748-1866
Fr: 800-422-7147
URL: http://www.lcmmagazine.com/

Monthly. Magazine featuring landscaping.

★6715★ The Landscape Contractor

Illinois Landscape Contractor Association
2625 Butterfield Rd., Ste. 204-W
Oak Brook, IL 60523
Ph: (630)472-2851   Fax: (630)472-3150
URL: http://www.ilca.net/publications.asp

Monthly. $65.00/year for individuals in-state (Illinois); $150.00/year for out of state. Magazine for the landscape trade.

★6716★ Landscape Management

Questex Media Group
275 Grove St., 2-130
Newton, MA 02466
Ph: (617)219-8300   Fax: (617)219-8310
Fr: 888-552-4346
URL: http://www.advanstar.com/index_all-pubs.html

$46.00/year. Free to qualified subscribers, domestic; $69.00/year for Canada and Mexico; $89.00/year for other countries. Magazine for professionals in landscape, grounds management and lawn care, construction, and maintenance.

★6717★ Landscape Superintendent and Maintenance Professional

Landscape Communications Inc.
14771 Plaza Dr., Ste. M
Tustin, CA 92780
Ph: (714)979-5276   Fax: (714)979-3543
URL: http://www.landscapeonline.com/contact/contact_mag.php?pub=l

Free to qualified subscribers. Magazine for landscape professionals.

★6718★ Lawn & Landscape Magazine

G.I.E. Media, MC
4020 Kinross Lakes Pkwy., Ste. 201
Richfield, OH 44286
Ph: (216)961-4130   Fax: (216)925-5038
Fr: 800-456-0707
URL: http://www.lawnandlandscape.com/lockedout.asp

Monthly. $15.00/year for U.S., Canada, and Mexico; $35.00/year for individuals; $100.00/year for other countries, south America/Europe. Business management magazine for lawn and landscape contracting professionals.

★6719★ The Municipality

League of Wisconsin Municipalities
122 W Washington Ave., Ste. 300
Madison, WI 53703-2718
Ph: (608)267-2380   Fax: (608)267-0645
Fr: 800-991-5502
URL: http://www.lwm-info.org/index.asp?Type=B_BASIC&SEC=¢0702EE8F

Monthly. Magazine for officials of Wisconsin's local municipal governments.

★6720★ **NRPA Job Bulletin**

National Recreation and Park Association, Professional Services Div.
22377 Belmont Ridge Rd.
Ashburn, VA 20148
Ph: (703)858-0784   Fax: (703)858-0794
Fr: 800-626-6772
E-mail: info@nrpa.org
URL: http://www.nrpa.org

Description: Semimonthly. Provides listings of employment opportunities in the park, recreation, and leisure services field.

★6721★ **Nursery Management and Production**

Branch-Smith Inc.
120 St. Louis
PO Box 1868
Fort Worth, TX 76104
Ph: (817)882-4110   Fax: (817)882-4111
Fr: 800-433-5612
URL: http://www.greenbeam.com

Monthly. Trade journal covering nursery growing, landscape distribution and landscaping.

★6722★ **Nursery News**

Cenflo Inc.
PO Box 44040
Rio Rancho, NM 87174
Fax: (505)867-0991   Fr: 800-732-4581
URL: http://www.cenflo.com/nursery-news.html

Biweekly. $20.00/year for individuals; $36.00 for two years; $125.00/year for other countries. Trade newspaper (tabloid) for nursery industry.

★6723★ **Pro**

Cygnus Business Media
1233 Janesville Ave.
Fort Atkinson, WI 53538
Fr: 800-547-7377
URL: http://www.promagazine.com

Magazine for landscape service firms.

★6724★ **Western City**

League of California Cities
1400 K St., Ste. 400
Sacramento, CA 95814
Ph: (916)658-8200   Fax: (916)658-8240
Fr: 800-262-1801
URL: http://www.westerncity.com

Monthly. $39.00/year for individuals; $63.00 for two years; $52.00/year for other countries; $26.50/year for students. Municipal interest magazine.

★6725★ **Yard and Garden**

Cygnus Business Media
1233 Janesville Ave.
Fort Atkinson, WI 53538
Fr: 800-547-7377
URL: http://www.cygnusexpos.com/PropertyPub.cfm?PropertyID=117

Yard and garden magazine featuring product news and retailer success stories.

EMPLOYER DIRECTORIES AND NETWORKING LISTS

★6726★ **Directory of Public Garden Internships**

American Association of Botanical Gardens and Arboreta
100 W 10th St., Ste. 614
Wilmington, DE 19801
Ph: (302)655-7100   Fax: (302)655-8100
E-mail: bvincent@aabga.org
URL: http://aabga.org

Annual, November; latest edition 2005. Covers 700 student internships and summer jobs at public gardens throughout North America. Entries include: Name of institution, address, name of contact, deadline for application, number of students hired, whether internships are available, employment period, hours, rate of pay, whether housing is available, other comments. Arrangement: Alphabetical. Indexes: By position, by state/province.

★6727★ **New York State Nursery/Landscape Association-Directory**

New York State Nursery/Landscape Assoc. Inc.
PO Box 657
Baldwinsville, NY 13027
Ph: (315)635-5008   Fax: (315)635-4874
Fr: 800-647-0384
URL: http://www.nysnla.com/

Annual, January. Covers over 800 member nursery, landscape, gardening, and lawn maintenance firms in New York. Entries include: Company name, address, phone. Arrangement: Alphabetical.

★6728★ **Who's Who in Landscape Contracting**

Professional Landcare Network
950 Herndon Pky., Ste. 450
Herndon, VA 20170
Ph: (703)736-9666   Fax: (703)736-9668
Fr: 800-395-2522
E-mail: kathywemhoff@alca.org

Annual, winter. Covers 2,500 member exterior and interior landscape contractors, related suppliers, affiliates, state associations, students, and student chapters. Entries include: Company name, address, phone, fax, Web site, e-mail, and names of key personnel and specialties. Arrangement: Alphabetical. Indexes: Interior contractor location; exterior contractor location; personal name.

HANDBOOKS AND MANUALS

★6729★ **Careers in Horticulture and Botany**

The McGraw-Hill Companies
PO Box 182604
Columbus, OH 43272
Fax: (614)759-3749   Fr: 877-883-5524
E-mail: customer.service@mcgraw-hill.com
URL: http://www.mcgraw-hill.com

Jerry Garner. 2006. 15.95 (paper). 192 pages. Includes bibliographical references.

★6730★ **Opportunities in Landscape Architecture, Botanical Gardens, and Arboreta Careers**

The McGraw-Hill Companies
PO Box 182604
Columbus, OH 43272
Fax: (614)759-3749   Fr: 877-883-5524
E-mail: customer.service@mcgraw-hill.com
URL: http://www.mcgraw-hill.com

Blythe Cameron. 2007. $13.95; $11.95 (paper). 160 pages. Includes bibliography.

★6731★ **The Perfect Guide to Making $ in Landscaping and Maintenance: A How-To Book**

Moran Publishing
210 Lazy River
Sealy, TX 77474
Fr: 800-223-0351

Gene Yezak. 2000. $9.95 (paper). 220 pages.

TRADESHOWS

★6732★ **Green Industry Expo**

PLANET, The Professional Landcare Network
950 Herndon Parkway, Ste. 450
Herndon, VA 20170
Ph: (703)736-9666   Fax: (703)736-9668
Fr: 800-395-2522
E-mail: info@gieonline.com
URL: http://www.landcarenetwork.org

Annual. **Primary Exhibits:** Lawn care equipment, supplies, and services, including fertilizers, weed control materials, insurance information, and power equipment.

★6733★ **International Lawn, Garden, and Power Equipment Expo**

Sellers Expositions
222 Pearl St., Ste. 300
New Albany, IN 47150
Ph: (812)949-9200   Fax: (812)949-9600
Fr: 800-558-8767
URL: http://www.sellersexpo.com

Annual. **Primary Exhibits:** Lawn, garden, and power equipment.

★6734★ Mid-Atlantic Nursery Trade Show

The Mid-Atlantic Nursery Trade Show, Inc. (MANTS)
PO Box 818
Brooklandville, MD 21022
Ph: (410)296-6959   Fax: (410)296-8288
Fr: 800-431-0066
E-mail: info@mants.com
URL: http://www.mants.com

Annual. **Primary Exhibits:** Equipment, supplies, and services relating to all aspects of nursery, landscaping, and garden center businesses.

★6735★ The World's Showcase of Horticulture

Southern Nursery Association
1827 Powers Ferry Rd. SE, Ste. 4-100
Atlanta, GA 30339-8422
Ph: (770)953-3311   Fax: (770)953-4411
URL: http://www.sna.org

Annual. **Primary Exhibits:** Nursery products, including plants, chemicals, machinery and equipment, soil and soil supplements, and plant containers. **Dates and Locations:** 2008 Aug 07-09; Atlanta, GA; Georgia World Congress Center.

OTHER SOURCES

★6736★ American Nursery and Landscape Association (ANLA)

1000 Vermont Ave. NW, Ste. 300
Washington, DC 20005-4914
Ph: (202)789-2900   Fax: (202)789-1893
E-mail: jbardzik@anla.org
URL: http://www.anla.org

Members: Vertical organization of wholesale growers; landscape firms; garden centers; mail order nurseries; suppliers. Promotes the industry and its products. Offers management and consulting services and public relations programs. Provides government representation and bank card plan for members. Maintains hall of fame.

★6737★ American Public Gardens Association (APGA)

100 W 10th St., Ste. 614
Wilmington, DE 19801-6604
Ph: (302)655-7100   Fax: (302)655-8100
E-mail: dstark@publicgardens.org
URL: http://www.publicgardens.org

Members: Directors and staffs of botanical gardens, arboreta, institutions maintaining or conducting horticultural courses, and others. **Purpose:** Seeks to serve North American public gardens and horticultural organizations by promoting professional development through its publications and meetings, advocating the interests of public gardens in political, corporate, foundation, and community arenas, and encouraging gardens to adhere to professional standards in their programs and operations.

★6738★ International Society of Arboriculture (ISA)

PO Box 3129
Champaign, IL 61826-3129
Ph: (217)355-9411   Fax: (217)355-9516
Fr: 888-472-8733
E-mail: isa@isa-arbor.com
URL: http://www.isa-arbor.com

Description: Individuals engaged in commercial, municipal, and utility arboriculture; city, state, and national government employees; municipal and commercial arborists; others interested in shade tree welfare. Disseminates information on the care and preservation of shade and ornamental trees. Supports research projects at educational institutions.

★6739★ National Landscape Association (NLA)

1000 Vermont Ave. NW, Ste. 300
Washington, DC 20005-4914
Ph: (202)789-2900   Fax: (202)789-1893
E-mail: leagle@anla.org
URL: http://www.anla.org/about/nla/nla.htm

Members: Landscape firms. **Purpose:** Works to: enhance the professionalism of its member firms in designing, building, and maintaining quality landscapes in a profitable and environmentally responsible manner; represent the landscape perspective within the industry. **Activities:** Sponsors annual landscape tour in conjunction with American Association of Nurserymen.

★6740★ Personal & Building Service Occupations

Delphi Productions
3159 6th St.
Boulder, CO 80304
Ph: (303)443-2100   Fax: (303)443-4022
Fr: 888-443-2400
E-mail: support@delphivideo.com
URL: http://www.delphivideo.com

$95.00. 48 minutes. Part of the Careers for the 21st Century Video Library.

★6741★ Professional Grounds Management Society (PGMS)

720 Light St.
Baltimore, MD 21230-3816
Fax: (410)752-8295   Fr: 800-609-7467
E-mail: pgms@assnhqtrs.com
URL: http://www.pgms.org

Description: Professional society of grounds managers of large institutions of all sorts and independent landscape contractors. Establishes grounds management as a profession; secures opportunities for professional advancement of well-qualified grounds managers; acquaints the public with "the distinction between competent ground managers, equipped through practical experience and systematic study, and self-styled 'maintenance' personnel, lacking these essentials." Sponsors contests. Conducts research and surveys; sponsors certification program for professional grounds managers and grounds keepers. Takes action with the legislative and executive branches of government on issues affecting grounds managers; keeps members informed on matters affecting the profession.

★6742★ Professional Landcare Network (PLANET)

950 Herndon Pkwy., Ste. 450
Herndon, VA 20170
Ph: (703)736-9666   Fax: (703)736-9668
Fr: 800-395-2522
E-mail: info@landcarenetwork.org
URL: http://www.landcarenetwork.org

Members: Landscape contractors. **Purpose:** Works to represent, lead, and unify the interior and exterior landscape industry by working together on a national basis; addressing environmental and legislative issues; and creating increased opportunities in business. **Activities:** Provides forum to encourage members' profitability, personal growth, and professional advancement.

Law Enforcement Officers

SOURCES OF HELP-WANTED ADS

★6743★ ACJS Today
Academy of Criminal Justice Sciences (ACJS)
PO Box 960
Greenbelt, MD 20768-0960
Ph: (301)446-6300   Fax: (301)446-2819
Fr: 800-757-2257
URL: http://www.acjs.org/
Description: Four issues/year. Contains criminal justice information.

★6744★ American City and County
Primedia Business
6151 Powers Ferry Rd., Ste. 200
Atlanta, GA 30339
Ph: (770)955-2500   Fax: (770)618-0204
URL: http://
www.americancityandcounty.com
Monthly. $67.00/year for individuals. Municipal and county administration magazine.

★6745★ Criminal Justice Studies
Taylor & Francis Group Journals
325 Chestnut St., Ste. 800
Philadelphia, PA 19106
Ph: (215)625-8900   Fax: (215)625-8914
Fr: 800-354-1420
URL: http://www.tandf.co.uk/journals/titles/
1478601x.html
$352.00/year for institutions, print and online; $334.00/year for institutions, online only; $107.00/year for individuals. Journal covering articles on criminal justice and criminological issues.

★6746★ D & O Advisor
American Lawyer Media L.P.
345 Pk. Ave. S
New York, NY 10010
Ph: (212)779-9200   Fax: (212)481-8110
Fr: 800-888-8300
URL: http://www.alm.com
Quarterly. Magazine that offers advice and

perspective on corporate oversight responsibilities for directors and officers.

★6747★ Executive Legal Adviser
American Lawyer Media L.P.
345 Pk. Ave. S
New York, NY 10010
Ph: (212)779-9200   Fax: (212)481-8110
Fr: 800-888-8300
URL: http://www.executivelegaladviser.com
Bimonthly. Free to qualified subscribers. Magazine that offers legal advice for corporate executives.

★6748★ Institute of Justice and International Studies
Central Missouri State University
PO Box 800
Warrensburg, MO 64093
Ph: (660)543-4111   Fax: (660)543-8517
Fr: 877-729-8266
E-mail: wallace@cmsu1.cmsu.edu
Irregular. Free to qualified subscribers. Journal that publishes reports on international crime including corrections, media coverage, public policy, counter terrorism, and civil liberties.

★6749★ Journal of the American Criminal Justice Association
American Criminal Justice Association
PO Box 601047
Sacramento, CA 95860-1047
Ph: (916)484-6553   Fax: (916)488-2227
URL: http://www.acjalae.org/index.html
Semiannual. Journal covering issues in criminal justice.

★6750★ Journal of Contemporary Criminal Justice
Sage Publications Inc.
2455 Teller Rd.
Thousand Oaks, CA 91320
Ph: (805)499-0721   Fax: (805)499-8096
URL: http://www.unl.edu/eskridge/jccjab-stracts.html
Quarterly. $453.00/year for institutions, com-

bined (print & e-access); $476.00/year for institutions, current volume print & all online content; $408.00/year for institutions, e-access; $431.00/year for institutions, backfile lease, e-access plus backfile; $486.00/year for institutions, backfile e-access (content through 1999); $444.00/year for institutions, print only; $85.00/year for individuals, print only; $123.00 for institutions, single print; $28.00 for individuals, single print. Journal focusing on all aspects of criminal justice.

★6751★ Journal of Criminal Justice Education
Academy of Criminal Justice Sciences
7339 Hanover Pky., Ste. A
Greenbelt, MD 20770
Ph: (301)446-6300   Fax: (301)446-2819
Fr: 800-757-2257
URL: http://www.tandf.co.uk/journals/titles/
10511253.asp
Semiannual. Journal covering criminal justice.

★6752★ Journal of Empirical Legal Studies
Wiley-Blackwell
350 Main St. Commerce Pl.
Malden, MA 02148
Ph: (781)388-8200   Fax: (781)388-8210
Fr: 800-759-6120
URL: http://www.blackwellpublishing.com/
journal.asp?ref=1740-1453
$318.00/year for institutions, U.S. print and premium online; $289.00/year for institutions, U.S. print and standard online; $275.00/year for institutions, U.S. premium online only; $243.00/year for institutions, other countries, print and premium online; $221.00/year for institutions, other countries, print and standard online; $210.00/year for institutions, other countries, premium online only. Journal focusing on law and law-related fields, including civil justice, corporate law, criminal justice, domestic relations, economics, finance, health care, political science, psychology, public policy, securities regulation, and sociology.

★6753★ **Journal of Health Law**

American Health Lawyers Association
1025 Connecticut Ave., NW, Ste. 600
Washington, DC 20036-5405
Ph: (202)833-1100   Fax: (202)833-1105
URL: http://www.healthlawyers.org

Quarterly. Professional journal covering healthcare issues and cases and their impact on the health care arena.

★6754★ **Law Enforcement Technology**

Cygnus Business Media
1233 Janesville Ave.
Fort Atkinson, WI 53538
Fr: 800-547-7377
URL: http://www.officer.com/magazines/let

Monthly. Free. Magazine for police technology and management.

★6755★ **Law Officers Magazine**

Elsevier Science Inc.
360 Park Ave. S
New York, NY 10010
Ph: (212)989-5800   Fax: (212)633-3990
URL: http://www.elsevier.com

Monthly. $31.69/year for U.S. $52.00/year for Canada; $63.49/year for other countries. Journal for the professional law enforcement officer.

★6756★ **Law and Order**

Hendon Publishing
130 Waukegan Rd. N., Ste. 202
Deerfield, IL 60015
Ph: (847)444-3300   Fax: (847)444-3333
Fr: 800-843-9764
URL: http://www.hendonpub.com/publications/lawandorder/

Monthly. $22.00/year for individuals. Law enforcement trade magazine.

★6757★ **The Municipality**

League of Wisconsin Municipalities
122 W Washington Ave., Ste. 300
Madison, WI 53703-2718
Ph: (608)267-2380   Fax: (608)267-0645
Fr: 800-991-5502
URL: http://www.lwm-info.org/index.asp?Type=B_BASIC&SEC=¢0702EE8F

Monthly. Magazine for officials of Wisconsin's local municipal governments.

★6758★ **Police & Security News**

Days Communications
1208 Juniper St.
Quakertown, PA 18951-1520
Ph: (215)538-1240   Fax: (215)538-1208
E-mail: advertising@policeandsecuritynews.com
URL: http://www.policeandsecuritynews.com

Bimonthly. $18.00/year for by mail; $54.00/year for other countries, mail; $3.00 for single issue, mail. Tabloid for the law enforcement and private security industries.

Includes articles on training, new products, and new technology.

★6759★ **Western City**

League of California Cities
1400 K St., Ste. 400
Sacramento, CA 95814
Ph: (916)658-8200   Fax: (916)658-8240
Fr: 800-262-1801
URL: http://www.westerncity.com

Monthly. $39.00/year for individuals; $63.00 for two years; $52.00/year for other countries; $26.50/year for students. Municipal interest magazine.

PLACEMENT AND JOB REFERRAL SERVICES

★6760★ **American Society of Criminology (ASC)**

1314 Kinnear Rd., Ste. 212
Columbus, OH 43212-1156
Ph: (614)292-9207   Fax: (614)292-6767
E-mail: asc@osu.edu
URL: http://www.asc41.com

Description: Represents professional and academic criminologists, students of criminology in accredited universities, psychiatrists, psychologists, and sociologists. Develops criminology as a science and academic discipline. Aids in the construction of criminological curricula in accredited universities. Upgrades the practitioner in criminological fields (police, prisons, probation, parole, delinquency workers). Conducts research programs and sponsors three student paper competitions. Provides placement service at annual convention.

★6761★ **National Association of Investigative Specialists (NAIS)**

PO Box 82148
Austin, TX 78708
Ph: (512)719-3595   Fax: (512)719-3594
E-mail: rthomas007@aol.com
URL: http://www.pimall.com/nais

Members: Private investigators, automobile repossessors, bounty hunters, and law enforcement officers. **Purpose:** Promotes professionalism and provides for information exchange among private investigators. Lobbies for investigative regulations. Offers training programs and issues certificates of completion. **Activities:** Sponsors charitable programs; compiles statistics; maintains speakers' bureau and placement service. Operates Investigators' Hall of Fame of Private Investigators. Offers seminars on cassette tape.

★6762★ **Nine Lives Associates (NLA)**

Executive Protection Institute
PO Box 802
Berryville, VA 22611-0802
Ph: (540)554-2540   Fax: (540)554-2558

E-mail: info@personalprotection.com
URL: http://www.personalprotection.com

Description: Law enforcement, correctional, military, and security professionals who have been granted Personal Protection Specialist Certification through completion of the protective services program offered by the Executive Protection Institute; conducts research; EPI programs emphasize personal survival skills and techniques for the protection of others. Provides professional recognition for qualified individuals engaged in executive protection assignments. Maintains placement service. Operates speakers' bureau; compiles statistics.

EMPLOYER DIRECTORIES AND NETWORKING LISTS

★6763★ **Association of Former Agents of the U.S. Secret Service-Membership Directory**

Association of Former Agents of the U.S. Secret Service
PO Box 1670
Millersville, MD 21108-4670
Ph: (703)256-0188   Fr: 877-392-4368
URL: http://www.oldstar.org

Annual, March. Entries include: Name, home address. Arrangement: Alphabetical.

★6764★ **Career Opportunities in Law Enforcement, Security, and Protective Services**

Facts On File Inc.
132 W 31st St., 17th Fl.
New York, NY 10001
Ph: (212)967-8800   Fax: 800-678-3633
Fr: 800-322-8755
URL: http://www.factsonfile.com

Published 2005. $49.50 for individuals; $44.55 for libraries. Covers more than 77 profiles on a diverse range of occupations, including law enforcement, physical security, computer security, emergency services, fire protection, and air travel safety.

★6765★ **Careers in Focus: Public Safety**

Facts On File Inc.
132 W 31st St., 17th Fl.
New York, NY 10001
Ph: (212)967-8800   Fax: 800-678-3633
Fr: 800-322-8755
URL: http://www.factsonfile.com

Latest edition 3rd, 2007. $29.95 for individuals; $26.95 for libraries. Covers an overview of public safety, followed by a selection of jobs profiled in detail, including the nature of the job, earnings, prospects for employment, what kind of training and skills it requires, and sources for further information.

★6766★ International Association of Chiefs of Police Membership Directory

International Association of Chiefs of Police
515 N Washington St.
Alexandria, VA 22314
Ph: (703)836-6767   Fax: (703)836-4543
Fr: 800-843-4233
URL: http://www.theiacp.org/members/directory.htm

Annual, October. Covers 20,000 members in command and administrative positions in federal, state, and local law enforcement and related fields; includes county police and sheriffs; international, national, and regional law enforcement agencies and related organizations. Entries include: For officers–Name, title, name of law enforcement agency, address, phone. For agencies and organizations–Name, address, names and titles of key personnel, publications. Arrangement: Geographical and alphabetical.

★6767★ National Directory of Law Enforcement Administrators, Correctional Institutions & Related Agencies

National Public Safety Information Bureau
601 Main St., Ste. 201
PO Box 365
Stevens Point, WI 54481
Ph: (715)345-2772   Fax: (715)345-7288
Fr: 800-647-7579
URL: http://www.safetysource.com

Annual; latest edition 43rd, published 2007. $139.00 for individuals. Covers police departments, sheriffs, coroners, criminal prosecutors, child support agencies, state law enforcement and criminal investigation agencies; federal criminal investigation and related agencies; state and federal correctional institutions; campus law enforcement departments; county jails, airport and harbor police, Bureau of Indian Affairs officials; plus new homeland security section. Entries include: Name, address, phone, fax, names and titles of key personnel, number of officers, population served. Arrangement: Separate geographical sections for police chiefs, coroners, sheriffs, prosecutors, prisons and state criminal investigation agencies; also separate sections for federal agencies and miscellaneous law enforcement and related agencies. Indexes: Departments.

HANDBOOKS AND MANUALS

★6768★ Arco Police Officer

Hungry Minds, Inc.
909 Third Ave.
New York, NY 10022
Ph: (212)884-5000   Fax: (212)884-5400
Fr: 800-667-1115

Hugh O'Neill. 2000. $13.95. 480 pages. Part of Arco Police Officer series.

★6769★ Become an Officer in Law Enforcement: Getting the Edge

LearningExpress, LLC
55 Broadway, 8th Fl.
New York, NY 10006
Ph: (212)995-2566   Fax: (212)995-5512
Fr: 800-295-9556
E-mail: customerservice@learningexpressllc.com
URL: http://www.learningexpressllc.com

Robert J. Piel and Paul C. Van Der Linden. Second edition, 2001. $15.95 (paper). 208 pages.

★6770★ Career Planning in Criminal Justice

Anderson Publishing Co.
2035 Reading Rd.
Cincinnati, OH 45202-1576
Ph: (513)421-4142   Fax: (513)562-8116
Fr: 800-582-7295

Robert C. DeLucia and Thomas J. Doyle. Third edition, 1998. 225 pages. $21.95. Surveys a wide range of career and employment opportunities in law enforcement, the courts, corrections, forensic science, and private security. Contains career planning and job hunting advice.

★6771★ Careers in Law Enforcement: Interviewing for Results

The Graduate Group
PO Box 370351
West Hartford, CT 06137-0351
Fr: 800-484-7280

Jim Nelson. 1996. $27.50 (paper).

★6772★ Careers for Legal Eagles and Other Law-and-Order Types

The McGraw-Hill Companies
PO Box 182604
Columbus, OH 43272
Fax: (614)759-3749   Fr: 877-883-5524
E-mail: customer.service@mcgraw-hill.com
URL: http://www.mcgraw-hill.com

Blythe Camenson. Second edition, 2005. $13.95 (paper). 176 pages.

★6773★ Careers for Mystery Buffs and Other Snoops and Sleuths

The McGraw-Hill Companies
PO Box 182604
Columbus, OH 43272
Fax: (614)759-3749   Fr: 877-883-5524
E-mail: customer.service@mcgraw-hill.com
URL: http://www.mcgraw-hill.com

Blythe Camenson. Second edition, 2004. $12.95 (paper); $14.95 (cloth). 160 pages.

★6774★ Criminal Justice Career Opportunities in Ohio

Kendall Hunt Publishing Company
4050 Westmark Dr.
PO Box 1840
Dubuque, IA 52002
Ph: (319)589-1000   Fax: (319)589-1046
Fr: 800-228-0810

URL: http://www.kendallhunt.com/

Katherine Steinbeck, Daniel Ponstingle. January 2003. $20.95. Illustrated. 185 pages.

★6775★ Federal Jobs in Law Enforcement

Impact Publications
9104 Manassas Dr., Ste. N
Manassas Park, VA 20111-5211
Ph: (703)361-7300   Fax: (703)335-9486
Fr: 800-361-1055
E-mail: query@impactpublications.com
URL: http://www.impactpublications.com

Russ Smith. 1996. $14.95 (paper). 191 pages.

★6776★ Guide to Careers in Criminal Justice

Cengage Learning
PO Box 6904
Florence, KY 41022
Fax: 800-487-8488   Fr: 800-354-9706
URL: http://www.cengage.com

Wadsworth. 2003. $32.95.

★6777★ Guide to Law Enforcement Careers

Barron's Educational Series, Inc.
250 Wireless Blvd.
Hauppauge, NY 11788-3917
Ph: (631)434-3311   Fax: (631)434-3723
Fr: 800-645-3476
E-mail: fbrown@barronseduc.com
URL: http://barronseduc.com

Donald B. Hutton and Anna Mydlarz. Second edition, 2001. $14.95 (paper). 368 pages.

★6778★ How to Be a Great Cop

Prentice Hall PTR
One Lake St.
Upper Saddle River, NJ 07458
Ph: (201)236-7000   Fr: 800-428-5331
URL: http://www.phptr.com/index.asp?rl=1

Neal E. Trautman. 2001. $30.20 (paper). 204 pages.

★6779★ Law Enforcement Career Guide California

LearningExpress, LLC
55 Broadway, 8th Fl.
New York, NY 10006
Ph: (212)995-2566   Fax: (212)995-5512
Fr: 800-295-9556
E-mail: customerservice@learningexpressllc.com
URL: http://www.learningexpressllc.com

Learning Express Law. 1997. $35.00 (paper). 144 pages.

★6780★ Law Enforcement Career Guide Florida

LearningExpress, LLC
55 Broadway, 8th Fl.
New York, NY 10006
Ph: (212)995-2566   Fax: (212)995-5512
Fr: 800-295-9556
E-mail: customer-service@learningexpressllc.com
URL: http://www.learningexpressllc.com

Learning Express Law. 1996. $20.00 (paper). 144 pages.

★6781★ Law Enforcement Career Guide New Jersey

LearningExpress, LLC
55 Broadway, 8th Fl.
New York, NY 10006
Ph: (212)995-2566   Fax: (212)995-5512
Fr: 800-295-9556
E-mail: customer-service@learningexpressllc.com
URL: http://www.learningexpressllc.com

Learning Express Law. 1996. $35.00 (paper). 144 pages.

★6782★ Law Enforcement Career Guide New York

LearningExpress, LLC
55 Broadway, 8th Fl.
New York, NY 10006
Ph: (212)995-2566   Fax: (212)995-5512
Fr: 800-295-9556
E-mail: customer-service@learningexpressllc.com
URL: http://www.learningexpressllc.com

Learning Express Law. First edition, 1997. $35.00 (paper). 144 pages.

★6783★ Law Enforcement Career Guide Texas

LearningExpress, LLC
55 Broadway, 8th Fl.
New York, NY 10006
Ph: (212)995-2566   Fax: (212)995-5512
Fr: 800-295-9556
E-mail: customer-service@learningexpressllc.com
URL: http://www.learningexpressllc.com

Learning Express Law. 1996. $20.00 (paper). 144 pages.

★6784★ The Law Enforcement Manual

Princeton Educational Research Inst
34 Virginia St.
Kendall Park, NJ 08824
Ph: (732)821-8444   Fr: 800-295-9556
URL: http://www.policetesting.com/

Mark Adamson, Michael A. Petrillo and Daniel R. DelBagno. Third edition, revised, 1999. $39.95. 341 pages.

★6785★ Opportunities in Law Enforcement and Criminal Justice Careers

The McGraw-Hill Companies
PO Box 182604
Columbus, OH 43272
Fax: (614)759-3749   Fr: 877-883-5524
E-mail: customer.service@mcgraw-hill.com
URL: http://www.mcgraw-hill.com

James Stinchcomb. Second edition, 2002. $13.95 (paper). 160 pages. Offers information on opportunities at the city, county, state, military, and federal levels. Contains bibliography and illustrations.

★6786★ Real People Working in Law

The McGraw-Hill Companies
PO Box 182604
Columbus, OH 43272
Fax: (614)759-3749   Fr: 877-883-5524
E-mail: customer.service@mcgraw-hill.com
URL: http://www.mcgraw-hill.com

Blythe Camenson, Jan Goldberg. 1997. $12.95 (paper). 160 pages. Interviews and profiles of working professionals capture a range of opportunities in this field.

EMPLOYMENT AGENCIES AND SEARCH FIRMS

★6787★ Ferrari Search Group

200 East End Ave., Ste. 5N
New York, NY 10128
Ph: (212)289-5099   Fax: (716)386-2367
E-mail: contactus@ferrarisearchgroup.com
URL: http://www.ferrarisearchgroup.com/

Executive search firm.

TRADESHOWS

★6788★ International Association of Campus Law Enforcement Administrators Annual Meeting

International Association of Campus Law Enforcement Administrators
342 N. Main St.
West Hartford, CT 06117-2507
Ph: (860)586-7517   Fax: (860)586-7550
E-mail: info@iaclea.org
URL: http://www.iaclea.org

Annual. **Primary Exhibits:** Exhibits relating to the administration, planning and development, and operation and maintenance of security, police, and public safety departments of institutions of higher education.

★6789★ International Association of Chiefs of Police Annual Conference

International Association of Chiefs of Police
515 N Washington St.
Alexandria, VA 22314-2357
Ph: (703)836-6767   Fax: (703)836-4543
Fr: 800-THE-IACP
E-mail: phalenc@theiacp.org
URL: http://www.theiacp.org

Annual. **Primary Exhibits:** Law enforcement equipment, supplies, and services.

★6790★ Michigan Association of Chiefs of Police Mid-Winter Conference

Michigan Association of Chiefs of Police
2133 University Park Dr., Ste. 200
Okemos, MI 48864-3975
Ph: (517)349-9420   Fax: (517)349-5823
E-mail: info@michiganpolicechiefs.org
URL: http://www.michiganpolicechiefs.org

Annual. **Primary Exhibits:** Law enforcement equipment, supplies, and services.

★6791★ National Sheriffs' Association Annual Conference

National Sheriff Association
1450 Duke St.
Alexandria, VA 22314-3490
Ph: (703)836-7827   Fax: (703)683-6541
Fr: 800-424-7827
E-mail: nsamail@sheriffs.org
URL: http://www.sheriffs.org

Annual. **Primary Exhibits:** Exhibits of interest to local law enforcement professionals. **Dates and Locations:** 2008 Jul 27-02; Indianapolis, IN; 2009 Jun 20-24; Fort Lauderdale, FL.

★6792★ South Carolina Law Enforcement Officers Association Annual Conference and Training Session

South Carolina Law Enforcement Officers Association (SCLEOA)
PO Box 210709
Columbia, SC 29221-0709
Ph: (803)781-5913   Fax: (803)781-9208
Fr: 800-922-0038
E-mail: scleoa@scleoa.org
URL: http://www.scleoa.org

Annual. **Primary Exhibits:** Law enforcement equipment and supplies, computer equipment, specialty items, and uniforms.

OTHER SOURCES

★6793★ American Federation of Police and Concerned Citizens (AFP&CC)

6350 Horizon Dr.
Titusville, FL 32780
Ph: (305)573-0070   Fax: (305)573-9819
E-mail: info@aphf.org
URL: http://www.aphf.org

Members: Governmental and private law enforcement officers (paid, part-time, or volunteer) united for the prevention of crime and the apprehension of criminals. Offers death benefits and training programs to members and police survivors. **Activities:** Sponsors American Police Academy. Maintains hall of fame. Conducts workshops.

★6794★ **Careers in Criminal Justice**

Cambridge Educational
PO Box 2053
Princeton, NJ 08543-2053
Ph: 800-257-5126   Fax: (609)671-0266
Fr: 800-468-4227
E-mail: custserv@films.com
URL: http://www.cambridgeeducational.com

VHS and DVD. $79.95. 2002. 22 minutes. Program looks at a number of different occupations, ranging from entry-level positions to those requiring a four-year degree. Experts and people on the job share first-hand information about what their work is like.

★6795★ **Federal Criminal Investigators Association (FCIA)**

PO Box 23400
Washington, DC 20026
Ph: (630)969-8537   Fax: 800-528-3492
Fr: 800-403-3374
E-mail: fcianat@aol.com
URL: http://www.fedcia.org

Description: Serves as professional fraternal organization dedicated to the advancement of federal law enforcement officers and the citizens they serve. Aims to ensure law enforcement professionals have the tools and support network to meet the challenges of future criminal investigations while becoming more community oriented. Intends to pursue mission by promoting professionalism, enhancing the image of federal officers, fostering cooperation among all law enforcement professionals, providing a fraternal environment for the advancement of the membership and community. Helps charitable programs and organizations.

★6796★ **Federal Hispanic Law Enforcement Officers Association (FHLEOA)**

4445 Summer Oak Dr.
Tampa, FL 33618
Ph: (813)390-7532
E-mail: edirector@fhleoa.org
URL: http://www.fhleoa.org

Description: Supports equal treatment for all people in the law enforcement workplace. Acts as a collective voice and representation to address law enforcement concerns before legislative bodies, regulatory agencies, and the courts. Provides networking opportunities for its members.

★6797★ **Human Services Occupations**

Delphi Productions
3159 6th St.
Boulder, CO 80304
Ph: (303)443-2100   Fax: (303)443-4022
Fr: 888-443-2400
E-mail: support@delphivideo.com
URL: http://www.delphivideo.com

$95.00. 50 minutes. Part of the Careers for the 21st Century Video Library.

★6798★ **International Association of Campus Law Enforcement Administrators (IACLEA)**

342 N Main St., Ste. 301
West Hartford, CT 06117-2507
Ph: (860)586-7517   Fax: (860)586-7550
E-mail: info@iaclea.org
URL: http://www.iaclea.org

Description: Advances public safety for educational institutions by providing educational resources, advocacy, and professional development. Promotes professional ideals and standards in the administration of campus security/public safety/law enforcement. Works to make campus security/public safety/law enforcement an integral part of the educational community.

★6799★ **International Association of Computer Investigative Specialists (IACIS)**

PO Box 1728
Fairmont, WV 26555
Fr: 888-884-2247
URL: http://www.iacis.info

Description: Provides education and certification of law enforcement professionals in the field of computer forensic science. Creates and establishes procedures, trains personnel, and certifies forensic examiners in the recovery of evidence from computer systems. Offers professional training in the seizure and processing computer systems. Provides an opportunity to network with other law enforcement officers trained in computer forensics, and to share and learn from others.

★6800★ **International Police Work Dog Association (IPWDA)**

PO Box 7455
Greenwood, IN 46143
E-mail: k9cop496@aol.com
URL: http://www.ipwda.org

Description: Aims to unite and assist all law enforcement agencies in the training and continued progress of all police work dogs. Seeks to establish a working standard for all police work dogs, handlers, and trainers through an accreditation program. Promotes the image of the police work dog.

★6801★ **International Society of Stress Analysts (ISSA)**

9 Westchester Dr.
Kissimmee, FL 34744
Ph: (407)933-4839   Fax: (407)935-0911
E-mail: diogenesfl@aol.com

Members: Jurists, attorneys, physicians, private detectives, law enforcement personnel, security personnel, scholar/researchers, and individuals interested in stress analysis for lie detection/truth verification. **Purpose:** Purposes are to: promote the science of psychological stress evaluation and the efficient administration of justice; aid indigent persons, without cost, who may be wrongfully accused; develop and maintain high educational standards; observe and evaluate training programs for the purpose of accreditation and endorsement. **Activities:** Sponsors and certifies schools; offers workshops and research and educational programs; conducts forums. Offers expertise, consultation, and advice; invites inquiries.

★6802★ **Law Enforcement and Emergency Services Video Association (LEVA)**

PO Box 547
Midlothian, TX 76065
Ph: (972)291-5888   Fax: (972)291-5888
E-mail: president@leva.org
URL: http://www.leva.org

Description: Serves as a key resource to the global public safety community by focusing on the needs of video production and forensic imaging disciplines. Provides opportunities for professional development through quality training and informational exchange. Offers forensic video analysis training to law enforcement professionals.

★6803★ **Math at Work: Women in Nontraditional Careers**

Her Own Words
PO Box 5264
Madison, WI 53705-0264
Ph: (608)271-7083   Fax: (608)271-0209
E-mail: herownword@aol.com
URL: http://www.herownwords.com/

Video. Jocelyn Riley. $95.00. 15 minutes. Resource guide also available for $45.00.

★6804★ **National Association of Traffic Accident Reconstructionists and Investigators (NATARI)**

PO Box 2588
West Chester, PA 19382
Ph: (610)696-1919
E-mail: natari@natari.org
URL: http://www.natari.org

Description: Represents engineers, attorneys, police officers, private investigators, medical examiners, and other individuals involved in the analysis of motor vehicle traffic accidents. Gathers and disseminates information on techniques and equipment of potential use to members; reviews literature in the field. Participating Organization of the Accreditation Commission for Traffic Accident Reconstruction.

★6805★ **National Organization of Black Law Enforcement Executives (NOBLE)**

4609-F Pinecrest Office Park Dr.
Alexandria, VA 22312-1442
Ph: (703)658-1529   Fax: (703)658-9479
E-mail: jlee@noblenational.net
URL: http://www.noblenational.org

Description: Represents law enforcement executives above the rank of lieutenant; police educators; academy directors; interested individuals and organizations. Provides a platform from which the concerns and opinions of minority law enforcement executives and command-level officers can be expressed. Facilitates the exchange of programmatic information among minority law enforcement executives. Aims to eliminate racism in the field of criminal justice and to increased cooperation from criminal justice agencies. Encourages coordination between law enforcement agencies and the community to prevent and abate crime and its causes. Conducts research and training and offers technical assistance in crime victim assistance, community oriented policing, domestic violence, use of deadly force, reduction of fear of crime, airport security assessment, and minority recruitment. Offers internships; operates Speaker's Bureau.

★6806★ **Society of Professional Investigators (SPI)**

PO Box 1128
Bellmore, NY 11710
Ph: (516)781-5100   Fax: (516)783-0000
E-mail: info@spionline.org
URL: http://www.spionline.org

Description: Persons with at least 5 years' investigative experience for an official federal, state, or local government agency or for a quasi-official agency formed for law enforcement or related activities. Seeks to advance knowledge of the science and technology of professional investigation, law enforcement, and police science; maintains high standards and ethics; promotes efficiency of investigators in the services they perform.

★6807★ **Women in Nontraditional Careers: An Introduction**

Her Own Words
PO Box 5264
Madison, WI 53705
Ph: (608)271-7083   Fax: (608)271-0209
E-mail: herownword@aol.com
URL: http://www.herownwords.com/

Video. Jocelyn Riley. $95.00. 15 minutes. Resource guide also available for $45.00.

★6808★ **Women in Policing**

Her Own Words
PO Box 5264
Madison, WI 53705
Ph: (608)271-7083   Fax: (608)271-0209
E-mail: herownword@aol.com
URL: http://www.herownwords.com/

Video. Jocelyn Riley. $95.00. 15 minutes. Resource guide also available for $45.00.

Lawyers

★6809★ Annual Review of Law and Social Science

Annual Reviews Inc.
4139 El Camino Way
PO Box 10139
Palo Alto, CA 94303-0139
Ph: (650)493-4400   Fax: (650)424-0910
Fr: 800-523-8635
URL: http://arjournals.annualreviews.org/loi/lawsocsci

Annual. $75.00/year for individuals, print & online; $210.00/year for institutions, print & online; $175.00/year for institutions, print only; $175.00/year for institutions, online only. Journal covering current issues in law and the social sciences.

★6810★ Berkeley Business Law Journal

University of California, Boalt Hall School of Law
158 Boalt Hall
Berkeley, CA 94720
Ph: (510)643-6319
URL: http://www.boalt.org/bblj/index.html

Semiannual. $45.00/year for individuals; $65.00/year for elsewhere. Journal that aims to create innovative business law-oriented commentary created by professors, professionals, and students.

★6811★ Boston Bar Journal

Boston Bar Association
16 Beacon St.
Boston, MA 02108
Ph: (617)742-0615   Fax: (617)523-0127
URL: http://www.bostonbar.org/pub/index.htm

Quarterly. Journal for lawyers on important matters of legal interest.

★6812★ California Lawyer

Daily Journal Corp.
915 E 1st St.
Los Angeles, CA 90012
Ph: (213)229-5300   Fax: (213)680-3682
URL: http://www.dailyjournal.com

Monthly. $47.00 for two years; $40.00/year for individuals; $38.00/year for individuals, bulk order; $28.00/year for individuals, bulk order; $26.00/year for individuals, bulk order. Law magazine.

★6813★ Chicago Lawyer

Law Bulletin Publishing Co.
415 N State St.
Chicago, IL 60610
Ph: (312)644-7800   Fax: (312)416-1864
E-mail: displayads@lbc.com
URL: http://www.lbpc.com

Monthly. $40.00/year. Legal magazine (Tabloid).

★6814★ Columbia Journal of Law and Social Problems

Columbia Law School
435 W 116th St.
New York, NY 10027-7297
Ph: (212)854-2670
E-mail: jlsp@law.columbia.edu
URL: http://www.columbia.edu/cu/jlsp/

$40.00/year for individuals; $45.00/year for individuals, other countries; $17.50 for single issue. Journal covering economic, sociological and political laws.

★6815★ Cornerstone

National Legal Aid & Defender Association
1140 Connecticut Ave. NW, Ste. 900
Washington, DC 20036
Ph: (202)452-0620   Fax: (202)872-1031
E-mail: info@nlada.org
URL: http://www.nlada.org/

Description: Four issues/year. Monitors current issues affecting legal aid attorneys and public defenders. Recurring features include job listings, conference and training updates, news of research, book reviews, and news of members.

★6816★ Criminal Justice Studies

Taylor & Francis Group Journals
325 Chestnut St., Ste. 800
Philadelphia, PA 19106
Ph: (215)625-8900   Fax: (215)625-8914
Fr: 800-354-1420
URL: http://www.tandf.co.uk/journals/titles/1478601x.html

$352.00/year for institutions, print and online; $334.00/year for institutions, online only; $107.00/year for individuals. Journal covering articles on criminal justice and criminological issues.

★6817★ D & O Advisor

American Lawyer Media L.P.
345 Pk. Ave. S
New York, NY 10010
Ph: (212)779-9200   Fax: (212)481-8110
Fr: 800-888-8300
URL: http://www.alm.com

Quarterly. Magazine that offers advice and perspective on corporate oversight responsibilities for directors and officers.

★6818★ Executive Legal Adviser

American Lawyer Media L.P.
345 Pk. Ave. S
New York, NY 10010
Ph: (212)779-9200   Fax: (212)481-8110
Fr: 800-888-8300
URL: http://www.executivelegaladviser.com

Bimonthly. Free to qualified subscribers. Magazine that offers legal advice for corporate executives.

★6819★ Global Jurist Frontiers

Berkeley Electronic Press
2809 Telegraph Ave., Ste. 202
Berkeley, CA 94705
Ph: (510)665-1200   Fax: (510)665-1201
URL: http://www.bepress.com/gj/frontiers/

Annual. $645.00/year corporate; $215.00/year academic. Journal that publishes papers on new issues of comparative law, law and economics, international law, law and development, and legal anthropology.

★6820★ Houston Law Review

University of Houston
800 Calhoun Rd.
Houston, TX 77004
Ph: (713)743-2255
E-mail: inquiry@houstonlawreview.org
URL: http://www.houstonlawreview.org/

Quarterly. $33.00/year for individuals. Journal focusing on current issues in law. Publishes contributions from academicians, practicing lawyers, and other scholars, and selected Law Review students.

★6821★ Institute of Justice and International Studies

Central Missouri State University
PO Box 800
Warrensburg, MO 64093
Ph: (660)543-4111   Fax: (660)543-8517
Fr: 877-729-8266
E-mail: wallace@cmsu1.cmsu.edu

Irregular. Free to qualified subscribers. Journal that publishes reports on international crime including corrections, media coverage, public policy, counter terrorism, and civil liberties.

★6822★ Ius Gentium

University of Baltimore
1420 North Charles St.
Baltimore, MD 21201-5779
Ph: (410)837-4459
URL: http://law.ubalt.edu/cicl/ilt/index.html#ius

Annual. Journal that facilitates analysis and the exchange of ideas about contemporary legal issues from a comparative perspective.

★6823★ Job Announcements

National Center for State Courts
300 Newport Ave.
PO Box 8798
Williamsburg, VA 23185-4147
Ph: (757)253-2000   Fax: (757)564-2022
Fr: 800-616-6164
URL: http://www.ncsconline.org/

Description: Semimonthly. Provides lists of court-related job openings in the United States and its territories.

★6824★ Journal of the American Criminal Justice Association

American Criminal Justice Association
PO Box 601047
Sacramento, CA 95860-1047
Ph: (916)484-6553   Fax: (916)488-2227
URL: http://www.acjalae.org/index.html

Semiannual. Journal covering issues in criminal justice.

★6825★ Journal of Contemporary Criminal Justice

Sage Publications Inc.
2455 Teller Rd.
Thousand Oaks, CA 91320
Ph: (805)499-0721   Fax: (805)499-8096

URL: http://www.unl.edu/eskridge/jccjabstracts.html

Quarterly. $453.00/year for institutions, combined (print & e-access); $476.00/year for institutions, current volume print & all online content; $408.00/year for institutions, e-access; $431.00/year for institutions, backfile lease, e-access plus backfile; $486.00/year for institutions, backfile e-access (content through 1999); $444.00/year for institutions, print only; $85.00/year for individuals, print only; $123.00 for institutions, single print; $28.00 for individuals, single print. Journal focusing on all aspects of criminal justice.

★6826★ Journal of Criminal Justice Education

Academy of Criminal Justice Sciences
7339 Hanover Pky., Ste. A
Greenbelt, MD 20770
Ph: (301)446-6300   Fax: (301)446-2819
Fr: 800-757-2257
URL: http://www.tandf.co.uk/journals/titles/10511253.asp

Semiannual. Journal covering criminal justice.

★6827★ Journal of Empirical Legal Studies

Wiley-Blackwell
350 Main St. Commerce Pl.
Malden, MA 02148
Ph: (781)388-8200   Fax: (781)388-8210
Fr: 800-759-6120
URL: http://www.blackwellpublishing.com/journal.asp?ref=1740-1453

$318.00/year for institutions, U.S. print and premium online; $289.00/year for institutions, U.S. print and standard online; $275.00/year for institutions, U.S. premium online only; $243.00/year for institutions, other countries, print and premium online; $221.00/year for institutions, other countries, print and standard online; $210.00/year for institutions, other countries, premium online only. Journal focusing on law and law-related fields, including civil justice, corporate law, criminal justice, domestic relations, economics, finance, health care, political science, psychology, public policy, securities regulation, and sociology.

★6828★ Journal of Health Law

American Health Lawyers Association
1025 Connecticut Ave., NW, Ste. 600
Washington, DC 20036-5405
Ph: (202)833-1100   Fax: (202)833-1105
URL: http://www.healthlawyers.org

Quarterly. Professional journal covering healthcare issues and cases and their impact on the health care arena.

★6829★ Journal of the Missouri Bar

The Missouri Bar
326 Monroe St.
PO Box 119
Jefferson City, MO 65102-0119
Ph: (573)635-4128   Fax: (573)635-2811
URL: http://www.mobar.org/

Bimonthly. Magazine featuring short, practical articles on legal subjects for practicing attorneys.

★6830★ The Journal of Taxation

RIA Group
395 Hudson St., 4th Fl.
New York, NY 10014
Ph: (212)367-6300   Fax: (212)367-6314
Fr: 800-431-9025
URL: http://ria.thomson.com/estore/detail.aspx?ID=JTAX

Monthly. $300.00/year for individuals, print; $450.00/year for individuals, online/print bundle; $345.00/year for individuals, online. Journal for sophisticated tax practitioners.

★6831★ Jungle Law

Jungle Media Group
150 Varick St., 8th Fl.
New York, NY 10013
URL: http://www.jdjungle.com

$11.97/year. Magazine covering all aspects of law school education.

★6832★ Kentucky Bench & Bar Magazine

Kentucky Bar Association
514 West Main St.
Frankfort, KY 40601-1883
Ph: (502)564-3795   Fax: (502)564-3225

Bimonthly. $20.00/year for individuals. Kentucky law magazine.

★6833★ Law Officers Magazine

Elsevier Science Inc.
360 Park Ave. S
New York, NY 10010
Ph: (212)989-5800   Fax: (212)633-3990
URL: http://www.elsevier.com

Monthly. $31.69/year for U.S. $52.00/year for Canada; $63.49/year for other countries. Journal for the professional law enforcement officer.

★6834★ Lawyers Job E-Bulletin Board

Federal Bar Association
2011 Crystal Dr., Ste. 400
Arlington, VA 22202
Ph: (703)682-7000   Fax: (703)682-7001
E-mail: fba@fedbar.org
URL: http://www.fedbar.org/

Description: Semimonthly. Provides a listing of job openings for attorneys, usually in the federal sector. Recurring features include a calendar of events. Available only via e-mail.

★6835★ Legal Affairs

Legal Affairs
254 Elm St.
New Haven, CT 06511
Ph: (203)789-1510
URL: http://legalaffairs.org/mediakit/LegalAffairsMediaKit.pdf

Bimonthly. $39.95/year for institutions, Canada. Publication that presents critical essays about current issues in law.

★6836★ Legal Times

American Lawyer Media L.P.
1730 M St. NW, Ste. 802
Washington, DC 20036
Ph: (202)457-0686   Fax: (202)785-4539
Fr: 800-933-4317
E-mail: legaltimes@legaltimes.com
URL: http://www.law.com/dc

Weekly. $349.00/year print & online. Legal publication covering law and lobbying in the nation's capitol.

★6837★ Los Angeles Lawyer

Los Angeles County Bar Association
261 S Figueroa St., Ste. 300
PO Box 55020
Los Angeles, CA 90055-2020
Ph: (213)627-2727   Fax: (213)896-6500
URL: http://www.lacba.org/show-page.cfm?pageid=40

Monthly. $28.00/year for nonmembers; $4.00 for single issue, plus handling; subscription included in membership. Magazine featuring scholarly legal articles.

★6838★ Massachusetts Lawyers Weekly

Lawyers Weekly Publications
41 West St.
Boston, MA 02111
Ph: (617)451-7300   Fax: (617)451-1466
Fr: 800-444-5297
URL: http://www.masslaw.com

Weekly. $330.00/year for individuals, 52 issues; $195.00/year for individuals, 26 issues. Newspaper (tabloid) reporting Massachusetts legal news.

★6839★ Michigan Bar Journal

State Bar of Michigan
306 Townsend St.
Lansing, MI 48933-2083
Ph: (517)346-6300   Fax: (517)482-6248
Fr: 800-968-1442
URL: http://www.michbar.org/publications

Monthly. $45.00/year for individuals; $55.00/year for other countries. Legal magazine.

★6840★ The National Law Journal

The New York Law Journal
345 Pk. Ave. S
New York, NY 10010
Ph: (212)779-9200   Fax: (212)481-8110
Fr: 800-888-8300
URL: http://www.law.com

Weekly. $50.00/year for individuals, print subscriber rate for a 1-year; $25.00/year for individuals, for 6 months of online access. Tabloid focusing on the practice of law and trends in law.

★6841★ New Jersey Law Journal

New Jersey Law Journal
238 Mulberry St.
PO Box 20081
Newark, NJ 07101-6081
Ph: (973)642-0075   Fax: (973)642-0920
URL: http://www.law.com/jsp/nj/index.jsp

Weekly. $219.00/year for individuals. Journal containing digests of court opinions, notes, and orders to the bar from New Jersey Supreme Court and federal district court. Includes news articles on legal topics and commentary by legal specialists.

★6842★ Public Interest Employment Service Job Alert!

Public Interest Clearinghouse
47 Kearny St., Ste. 705
San Francisco, CA 94108
Ph: (415)834-0100   Fax: (415)834-0202
E-mail: pies@pic.org
URL: http://www.pic.org

Description: Semimonthly. Lists job openings in legal aid offices and public interest law organizations. Also available via e-mail.

★6843★ The Recorder

American Lawyer Media L.P.
105 Madison Ave.
New York, NY 10016
Fr: 800-603-6571
E-mail: recorder@counsel.com
URL: http://www.therecorder.com

Daily (morn.). $350.00/year for individuals. Legal newspaper.

★6844★ Texas Bar Journal

State Bar of Texas
Texas Law Center
1414 Colorado St.
PO Box 12487
Austin, TX 78701
Ph: (512)427-1463   Fax: (512)427-4100
Fr: 800-204-2222
URL: http://www.texasbar.com/template.cfm?section=texas_bar_journ

Monthly. $12.00/year for individuals; $2.50 for single issue. Legal news journal for the legal profession.

★6845★ The Washington Lawyer

The District of Columbia Bar
1250 H St. NW, 6th Fl.
Washington, DC 20005-5937
Ph: (202)737-4700   Fax: (202)626-3471
Fr: 877-333-2227
URL: http://www.dcbar.org

Monthly. Forum for articles and news items for the Washington legal community.

★6846★ Wisconsin Lawyer

State Bar of Wisconsin
PO Box 7158
Madison, WI 53707-7158
Ph: (608)257-3838   Fax: (608)257-5502
Fr: 800-728-7788

E-mail: wislawyer@wisbar.org
URL: http://www.wisbar.org/wislawmag/

Monthly. $48.00/year for individuals. Official monthly publication of the State Bar of Wisconsin.

PLACEMENT AND JOB REFERRAL SERVICES

★6847★ American Board of Professional Liability Attorneys (ABPLA)

170 Wright Ave.
Malverne, NY 11565
Ph: (516)599-7700   Fax: (516)599-7701
E-mail: info@abpla.org
URL: http://www.abpla.org

Description: Accredited by the American Bar Association to certify Attorneys in the areas of medical, legal or accounting professional. **Members:** Liability litigation attorneys who have satisfied requirements of litigation experience and who have passed the written liability examination. **Purpose:** Promotes and improves ethical and technical standards of advocacy and litigation practice in professional liability litigation; establishes basic standards for training, qualification, and recognition of specialists; fosters efficient administration of justice. **Activities:** Provides graduated training program for licensed attorneys desiring certification as specialists in the field. Offers placement service; compiles statistics. Maintains file of abstracts and program transcripts.

★6848★ Association of American Law Schools (AALS)

1201 Connecticut Ave. NW, Ste. 800
Washington, DC 20036-2717
Ph: (202)296-8851   Fax: (202)296-8869
E-mail: aals@aals.org
URL: http://www.aals.org

Description: Law schools association. Seeks to improve the legal profession through legal education. Interacts for law professors with state and federal government, other legal education and professional associations, and other national higher education and learned society organizations. Compiles statistics; sponsors teacher placement service. Presents professional development programs.

★6849★ Decalogue Society of Lawyers (DSL)

39 S LaSalle St., Ste. 410
Chicago, IL 60603
Ph: (312)263-6493   Fax: (312)263-6512
E-mail: decaloguesociety@aol.com
URL: http://decaloguesociety.com

Description: Represents lawyers of the Jewish faith. Seeks to promote and cultivate social and professional relations among members of the legal profession. Conducts a forum on topics of general and Jewish interest. Maintains placement service to help members find employment and office facilities.

★6850★ International Technology Law Association (ITechLaw)

401 Edgewater Pl., Ste. 600
Wakefield, MA 01880
Ph: (781)876-8877   Fax: (781)224-1239
E-mail: office@itechlaw.org
URL: http://www.itechlaw.org

Members: Lawyers, law students, and others interested in legal problems related to computer-communications technology. **Purpose:** Aids in: contracting for computer-communications goods and services; perfecting and protecting proprietary rights chiefly in software; and taxing computer-communications goods, services, and transactions, and liability for acquisition and use of computer-communications goods and services. **Activities:** Provides specialized educational programs; and offers limited placement service. Holds Annual Computer Law Update.

★6851★ National Counsel of Black Lawyers (NCBL)

116 W 111 St., 3rd Fl.
New York, NY 10026
Fax: (212)829-5182   Fr: (866)266-5091

Description: Attorneys throughout the U.S. and Canada united to use legal skills in the service of black and poor communities. Maintains projects in legal services to community organizations, voting rights, and international affairs; provides public education on legal issues affecting blacks and poor people. Researches racism in law schools and bar admissions. Conducts programs of continuing legal education for member attorneys. Maintains general law library. Compiles statistics; maintains lawyer referral and placement services. Provides speakers' bureau on criminal justice issues, international human rights law, and civil rights practice.

★6852★ Serbian Bar Association of America (SBAA)

260 Maple St.
Beecher, IL 60401
E-mail: kellypavich@yahoo.com
URL: http://www.serbbar.org

Description: Provides resource assistance to, and promotes the best interests of, the Serbian American community. Acts as a vehicle for making unified public pronouncements to represent and advocate the vital interests of the Serbian American community as a whole with respect to current social, political, economic, legal and other matters of vital concern. Serves as a national network of communication among members of the Serbian American legal community for purposes of networking, exchange of ideas, client referrals and career placement opportunities.

EMPLOYER DIRECTORIES AND NETWORKING LISTS

★6853★ *American Bar Association-Directory*

American Bar Association
321 N Clark St.
Chicago, IL 60610
Ph: (312)988-5000   Fax: (312)988-5177
Fr: 800-285-2221

Annual, October. $14.95. Covers approximately 7,500 lawyers active in the affairs of the Association, including officers, members of Boards of Governors and House of Delegates, section officers and council members, committee leaders, headquarters staff, state and local bars, affiliated and other legal organizations. Entries include: Section, council, or other unit name; names, addresses, and phone numbers of officers or chairpersons and members. Arrangement: Classified by position in ABA. Indexes: Alphabetical, geographical committee.

★6854★ *The American Bar Including The Canadian Bar, The Mexican Bar, and The International Bar*

Forster Long Inc.
3280 Ramos Cir.
Sacramento, CA 95827
Ph: (916)362-3276   Fax: (916)362-5643
Fr: 800-328-5091
URL: http://www.forster-long.com/

Annual; latest edition 2006. $435.00 for individuals, main volume set; $50.00 for individuals, reference handbook. Covers top law firms in the United States and 100 other countries with individual attorney biographies; selected state administrative offices. Entries include: Firm name, type of practice, address, phone, names, educational data, and memberships of partners and associates. State offices' listings include address, phone. Arrangement: Geographical, alphabetical; separate sections for Canadian, Mexican and international lawyers. Indexes: Personal name; firm name and location; practice areas.

★6855★ *American Lawyers Quarterly*

The American Lawyers Co.
853 Westpoint Pky., Ste. 710
Cleveland, OH 44145-1532
Ph: (440)871-8700   Fax: (440)871-9997
Fr: 800-843-4000
URL: http://www.alqlist.com/

Quarterly; monthly supplements. A commercial law list. Arrangement: Geographical.

★6856★ *Attorney Jobs Online*

Federal Reports Inc.
1010 Vermont Ave. NW, Ste. 408
Washington, DC 20005
Ph: (202)393-3311   Fax: (202)393-1553
Fr: 800-296-9611
URL: http://www.attorneyjobs.com

Monthly. Publication includes: Listings of approximately 600 current attorney and law-related job opportunities with the U.S. Government and other public and private employers in Washington D.C., nationwide, and abroad. Arrangement: Geographical.

★6857★ *Best Lawyers in America*

Woodward/White Inc.
129 1st Ave. SW
Aiken, SC 29801
Ph: (803)648-0300   Fax: (803)641-4794
Fr: (803)641-1710
URL: http://www.bestlawyers.com

Biennial; latest edition 2008. $225.00. Covers approximately 15,000 attorneys selected as "the best" in their specialties by a survey of their peers. Entries include: Individual or firm name, address, phone, and subspecialties of interest. Arrangement: Geographical, then classified by legal specialty. Indexes: Name index.

★6858★ *Career Ideas for Teens in Law and Public Safety*

Facts On File Inc.
132 W 31st St., 17th Fl.
New York, NY 10001
Ph: (212)967-8800   Fax: 800-678-3633
Fr: 800-322-8755
URL: http://www.factsonfile.com

Published 2005. $40.00 for individuals; $36.00 for libraries. Covers a multitude of career possibilities based on a teenager's specific interests and skills and links his/her talents to a wide variety of actual professions.

★6859★ *Career Opportunities in Law and the Legal Industry*

Facts On File Inc.
132 W 31st St., 17th Fl.
New York, NY 10001
Ph: (212)967-8800   Fax: 800-678-3633
Fr: 800-322-8755
URL: http://www.factsonfile.com/

Latest edition 2nd, 2007. $49.50 for individuals; $44.55 for libraries. Publication includes: Lists of industry associations and organizations, educational institutions, and Web sites related to the legal industry. Principal content of publication is information on careers in the legal field. Indexes: Alphabetical.

★6860★ *Careers in Focus: Law*

Facts On File Inc.
132 W 31st St., 17th Fl.
New York, NY 10001
Ph: (212)967-8800   Fax: 800-678-3633
Fr: 800-322-8755
URL: http://www.factsonfile.com

Latest edition 2nd, 2003. $29.95 for individuals; $26.95 for libraries. Covers an overview of law, followed by a selection of jobs profiled in detail, including the nature of the job, earnings, prospects for employment, what kind of training and skills it requires, and sources for further information.

★6861★ Decalogue Society of Lawyers-Directory of Members

Decalogue Society of Lawyers
39 S La Salle, No. 410
Chicago, IL 60603
Ph: (312)263-6493   Fax: (312)263-6512
URL: http://www.decaloguesociety.com

Annual. Covers about 1,500 lawyers of the Jewish faith. Entries include: Name, address, phone, fax, area of speciality. Arrangement: Alphabetical and by special area of law.

★6862★ Directory of Environmental Law Education Opportunities at American Law Schools

The Graduate Group
PO Box 370351
West Hartford, CT 06137-0351
Ph: (860)233-2330   Fax: (860)233-2330
URL: http://www.graduategroup.com/

$30.00 for individuals. Covers American Bar Association approved law schools offering opportunities in environmental law education, including degree programs, concentrations, and studies toward environmental law careers. Entries include: Contact details for schools and programs.

★6863★ Executor's Handbook

Facts On File Inc.
132 W 31st St., 17th Fl.
New York, NY 10001
Ph: (212)967-8800   Fax: 800-678-3633
Fr: 800-322-8755
URL: http://www.factsonfile.com

Latest edition 3rd, 2007. $39.50 for individuals; $35.55 for libraries. Covers guides for nonprofessional estate executors, providing clear explanations of aspects of estate law, including the responsibilities associated with being an executor, understanding the provisions of a will, managing or liquidating assets, dealing with beneficiaries and creditors, handling income and death taxes, resolving family issues and situations, and dispersing non-monetary items.

★6864★ Gale Encyclopedia of Everyday Law

Gale, Cengage Learning
27500 Drake Rd.
Farmington Hills, MI 48331-3535
Ph: (248)699-4253   Fax: (248)699-8065
Fr: 800-877-4253
URL: http://www.gale.com

Latest edition 2nd, July 2006. $352.00 for individuals. Publication includes: Listing of law-related organizations. Principal content of publication consists of approximately 200 articles covering specific legal issues of interest to a layperson in the United States and includes details on their background, historical cases, profiles of U.S. Laws and regulations, differentiation between states, and further reading information.

★6865★ International Law and Practice-Leadership Directory

International Law and Practice Section
740 15th St. NW
Washington, DC 20005-1019
Ph: (202)662-1000

Annual. Covers over 300 member lawyers, academics, law students, and international associates in leadership positions in the section. Entries include: Name, address, phone, fax and e-mail address.

★6866★ International Municipal Lawyers Association-Directory of Officers and Sections

International Municipal Lawyer Association
1110 Vermont Ave. NW, Ste. 200
Washington, DC 20005
Ph: (202)466-5424   Fax: (202)785-0152

Bimonthly, winter. Covers members of IMLA committees. Entries include: Name and title of member, address, phone, fax. Arrangement: Classified by sections, officers, and membership departments.

★6867★ Law Firms Yellow Book

Leadership Directories Inc.
104 5th Ave.
New York, NY 10011
Ph: (212)627-4140   Fax: (212)645-0931
E-mail: techsupport@leadershipdirectories.com
URL: http://www.leadershipdirectories.com/products/lyb.htm

Quarterly. $355.00 for individuals; $338.00 for individuals, standing order. Covers approximately 850 large law firms and over 24,000 attorneys and administrators at more than 3,000 domestic and foreign offices, subsidiaries, and affiliates. Entries include: Firm name, address, phone, fax, telex, year founded, description of practice; officers' names, titles, phone numbers, and law schools attended; addresses, phone numbers, and principal officials at branch offices; e-mails. Arrangement: Alphabetical by firm name. Indexes: Geographical, law school, individual name, law firm, practice area.

★6868★ Law and Legal Information Directory

Gale, Cengage Learning
27500 Drake Rd.
Farmington Hills, MI 48331-3535
Ph: (248)699-4253   Fax: (248)699-8065
Fr: 800-877-4253
E-mail: businessproducts@gale.com
URL: http://www.gale.com

Annual; latest edition 18th, published June 2007. $540.00 for individuals. Covers more than 19,000 national and international organizations, bar associations, federal and highest state courts, federal regulatory agencies, law schools, firms and organizations offering continuing legal education, paralegal education, sources of scholarships and grants, awards and prizes, special libraries, information systems and services, research centers, publishers of legal periodicals, books, and audiovisual materials, lawyer referral services, legal aid offices, public defender offices, legislature manuals and registers, small claims courts, corporation departments of state, state law enforcement agencies, state agencies, including disciplinary agencies, and state bar requirements. Entries include: All entries include institution or firm name, address, phone; many include names and titles of key personnel and, when pertinent, descriptive annotations. Contents based in part on information selected from several other Gale directories. Arrangement: Classified by type of organization, activity, service, etc. Indexes: Individual sections have special indexes as required.

★6869★ Lawyers' List

Commercial Publishing Company Inc.
8706 Commerce Dr., Ste. 4
Easton, MD 21601
Ph: (410)820-8089   Fax: (410)820-4474
Fr: 800-824-9911
URL: http://www.thelawyerslist.com/about.shtml

Annual; latest edition 97th. Covers about 2,500 lawyers in general, corporate, trial, patent, trademark, and copywrite practices internationally. Entries include: Firm name, address, phone, fax, e-mail, website, areas of practice, branch offices, names of representative clients, names of partners and associates. A general law list. Arrangement: Geographical.

★6870★ Lawyer's Register International by Specialties and Fields of Law Including a Directory of Corporate Counsel

Lawyer's Register Publishing Co.
4555 Renaissance Pkwy., Ste. 101
Cleveland, OH 44128
Ph: (216)591-1492   Fax: (216)591-0265
Fr: 800-477-6345
URL: http://www.lawyersregister.com

Annual. Covers corporate legal staffs worldwide; legal firms; independent practicing attorneys each identified as a specialist in one or more fields of law. Entries include: In corporate section–Corporation, subsidiary, and department names; address, phone, fax; names and titles of legal staff, law schools attended, specialties. In fields of law sections–Name, address, phone, fax, specialties (identified by Standard Industrial Classification, or SIC, codes), personal data. A general international/corporate law list. Arrangement: Separate sections for specializing lawyers and their firms and corporate counsel. Indexes: Lawyers and firms by areas, corporations; additional indexes included.

★6871★ Martindale-Hubbell Bar Register of Preeminent Lawyers

Martindale-Hubbell Inc.
121 Chanlon Rd.
New Providence, NJ 07974
Ph: (908)464-6800   Fax: (908)771-8704
Fr: 800-526-4902
URL: http://www.martindale.com

Annual. $195.00 for individuals. Covers over

10,000 of today's most skilled attorneys and law partnerships and firms. Entries include: Firm name, telephone, fax, e-mail, URL, members, associate clients, and name and title of contact. Arrangement: Geographical.

★6872★ **Martindale-Hubbell Law Directory**

Martindale-Hubbell Inc.
121 Chanlon Rd.
New Providence, NJ 07974
Ph: (908)464-6800   Fax: (908)771-8704
Fr: 800-526-4902
URL: http://www.martindale.com

Annual, April 2004. $1,065.00 for individuals. Covers lawyers and law firms in the United States, its possessions, and Canada, plus leading law firms worldwide; includes a biographical section by firm, and a separate list of patent lawyers, attorneys in government service, in-house counsel, and services, suppliers, and consultants to the legal profession. Entries include: For non-subscribing lawyers–Name, year of birth and of first admission to bar, code indicating college and law school attended and first degree, firm name (or other affiliation, if any) and relationship to firm, whether practicing other than as individual or in partnership. For subscribing lawyers–Above information plus complete address, phone, fax, e-mail and URL, type of practice, clients, plus additional personal details (education, certifications, etc.). A general law list. Arrangement: Geographical. Indexes: Alphabetical, area of practice.

★6873★ **National Directory of Prosecuting Attorneys**

National District Attorneys Association
99 Canal Ctr. Plz., Ste. 510
Alexandria, VA 22314
Ph: (703)549-9222   Fax: (703)836-3195
E-mail: cathy.yates@ndaa-apri.org
URL: http://www.ndaa-apri.org/publications/ndaa/index.html

Biennial; latest edition 2007. $35.00 for members; $50.00 for nonmembers. Covers about 2,800 elected or appointed local prosecuting attorneys. Entries include: Name, address, phone, jurisdiction, fax, e-mail. Arrangement: Geographical. Indexes: Alphabetical.

★6874★ **National Hispanic American Attorney Directory**

Hispanic National Bar Association
1101 Connecticut Ave. NW, Ste. 1000
Washington, DC 20036
Ph: (202)223-4777   Fax: (202)223-2324
URL: http://www.hnba.com/

Irregular. Covers approximately 8,000 Hispanic American lawyers. Entries include: Name, business address, phone, fax, home phone, area of practice. Arrangement: Alphabetical. Indexes: Geographical; area of practice.

★6875★ **National Lawyers Guild-Referral Directory**

National Lawyers Guild
132 Nassau St., Ste. 922
New York, NY 10038
Ph: (212)679-5100   Fax: (212)679-2811
URL: http://www.nlg.org/

Annual. Covers guild lawyers and their legal services.

★6876★ **NLADA Directory of Legal Aid and Defender Offices in the United States and Territories**

National Legal Aid & Defender Association
1140 Connecticut Ave. NW, Ste. 900
Washington, DC 20036
Ph: (202)452-0620   Fax: (202)872-1031
URL: http://www.nlada.org/Member_Svcs/Publications/Directory/

Biennial; latest edition 2007-08. $95.00 for nonmembers; $35.00 for members, program price; $55.00 for members, individual price. Covers approximately 3,000 civil legal aid and indigent defense organizations in the United States; includes programs for specific groups such as prisoners, senior citizens, the disabled, etc. Entries include: Agency name, address, phone, director's name. Arrangement: Geographical. Indexes: Type of service.

★6877★ **USBD-United States Bar Directory**

Attorneys National Clearing House Co.
PO Box 142828
Gainesville, FL 32614-2828
Fax: (866)859-2624   Fr: (866)860-2624
E-mail: usbd@usbardirectory.com
URL: http://www.usbardirectory.com

Annual, January. Covers over 3,000 general and specialized practice attorneys employed through correspondence (letter, phone, fax or e-mail). Entries include: Firm name, address, phone, preferred fields of practice, fax, e-mail, Web site. Arrangement: Geographical.

★6878★ **Who's Who in American Law**

Marquis Who's Who L.L.C.
890 Mountain Ave., Ste. 300
New Providence, NJ 07974-1218
Ph: (908)673-1001   Fax: (908)673-1189
Fr: 800-473-7020
E-mail: law@marquiswhoswho.com
URL: http://www.marquiswhoswho.com/

Biennial; latest edition 2007-2008. $345.00 for individuals. Covers over 15,000 lawyers, judges, law school deans and professors, and other legal professionals. Entries include: Name, home and office addresses, place and date of birth, educational background, career history, civic positions, professional memberships, publications, awards, special achievements. Arrangement: Alphabetical. Indexes: Fields of practice; professional area.

★6879★ **Wright-Holmes Law List**

Wright-Holmes Inc.
1020 8th Ave. S, Ste. 10
Naples, FL 34102-6959
Ph: (239)434-8880   Fax: (239)434-5983
Fr: 800-882-5478
URL: http://www.collectioncenter.com/index.htm

Annual, April. Free. Covers over 1,400 law firms throughout the U.S., Canada and 35 other countries. Entries include: Firm name, address, phone. A commercial law list. Arrangement: Geographical.

HANDBOOKS AND MANUALS

★6880★ **Administration of Justice: An Internship Guide to the Quest for Justice**

Kendall Hunt Publishing Company
4050 Westmark Dr.
PO Box 1840
Dubuque, IA 52002
Ph: (319)589-1000   Fax: (319)589-1046
Fr: 800-228-0810
URL: http://www.kendallhunt.com/

Carol L. Fine. 2001. $55.95 (paper). 370 pages.

★6881★ **Attorney's Career Guide**

Cengage Learning
PO Box 6904
Florence, KY 41022
Fax: 800-487-8488   Fr: 800-354-9706
URL: http://www.cengage.com

Chere B. Estrin. July 2003. $23.95 (paper). Vocational guidance in law.

★6882★ **Careers in Law**

The McGraw-Hill Companies
PO Box 182604
Columbus, OH 43272
Fax: (614)759-3749   Fr: 877-883-5524
E-mail: customer.service@mcgraw-hill.com
URL: http://www.mcgraw-hill.com

Gary Munneke. Third edition, 2003. $15.95 (paper). 192 pages. Overview of opportunities available to lawyers in private practice, corporate law, in federal, state, and local governments, and in teaching. Provides information on the typical law school curriculum plus opportunities in internships and clerkships.

★6883★ **Careers for Legal Eagles and Other Law-and-Order Types**

The McGraw-Hill Companies
PO Box 182604
Columbus, OH 43272
Fax: (614)759-3749   Fr: 877-883-5524
E-mail: customer.service@mcgraw-hill.com
URL: http://www.mcgraw-hill.com

Blythe Camenson. Second edition, 2005. $13.95 (paper). 176 pages.

★6884★ Careers for Mystery Buffs and Other Snoops and Sleuths

The McGraw-Hill Companies
PO Box 182604
Columbus, OH 43272
Fax: (614)759-3749   Fr: 877-883-5524
E-mail: customer.service@mcgraw-hill.com
URL: http://www.mcgraw-hill.com

Blythe Camenson. Second edition, 2004. $12.95 (paper); $14.95 (cloth). 160 pages.

★6885★ Great Jobs for Liberal Arts Majors

The McGraw-Hill Companies
PO Box 182604
Columbus, OH 43272
Fax: (614)759-3749   Fr: 877-883-5524
E-mail: customer.service@mcgraw-hill.com
URL: http://www.mcgraw-hill.com

Blythe Camenson. Second edition, 2001. $14.95 (paper). 256 pages.

★6886★ A Guide to a Successful Legal Internship

Anderson Publishing Co.
2035 Reading Rd.
Cincinnati, OH 45202-1576
Ph: (513)421-4142   Fax: (513)562-8116
Fr: 800-582-7295

Hedi Nasheri and Peter C. Kratcoski. 1996. $22.95 (paper). 171 pages.

★6887★ The I Hate Selling Book: Business-Building Advice for Consultants, Attorneys, Accountants, Engineers, Architects, and Other Professionals

AMACOM
1601 Broadway, 12th Fl.
New York, NY 10019-7420
Ph: (212)586-8100   Fax: (212)903-8168
Fr: 800-262-9699
URL: http://www.amanet.org

Allan S. Boress. 2001. $29.95. 240 pages.

★6888★ Law School 101: Survival Techniques from First Year to Finding the Right Job

Sphinx Publishing
1935 Brookdale Rd., Ste. 139
Naperville, IL 60563
Ph: (630)961-3900   Fax: (630)961-2168
Fr: 800-727-8866
URL: http://www.sphinxlegal.com/

R. Stephanie Good. May 2004. 232 pages. $19.95

★6889★ The Lawyer's Career Change Handbook: More Than 300 Things You Can Do with a Law Degree

HarperCollins
10 E. 53rd St.
New York, NY 10022
Ph: (212)207-7000   Fr: 800-242-7737
URL: http://www.harpercollins.com/

Hindi Greenberg. 1998. Revised and updated. $14.00 (paper). 320 pages.

★6890★ Lawyer's Desk Book

Aspen Publishers
1 Lake St.
Upper Saddle River, NJ 07458
Ph: (201)236-7000   Fax: 800-445-6991
Fr: 800-638-8437
URL: http://www.aspenpublishers.com/

Dana Shilling. First edition, supplementary. 2007. $149.00. 1,860 pages.

★6891★ Letters to a Young Lawyer

Basic Books
387 Park Ave. S., 12th Fl.
New York, NY 10016
Ph: (212)340-8100   Fax: (212)207-7703
URL: http://www.perseusbooksgroup.com/basic/

Alan Dershowitz. 2001. $22.00. 226 pages.

★6892★ My First Year As a Lawyer: Real-World Stories from America's Lawyers

Signet
375 Hudson St.
New York, NY 10014-3657
Ph: (212)366-2000   Fr: 800-847-5515
URL: http://us.penguingroup.com/

Melissa Ramsdell and Mark Simenhoff, editors. 1996. $9.95. 191 pages. Part of the First Year Career Series.

★6893★ Opportunities in Gerontology and Aging Services Careers

The McGraw-Hill Companies
PO Box 182604
Columbus, OH 43272
Fax: (614)759-3749   Fr: 877-883-5524
E-mail: customer.service@mcgraw-hill.com
URL: http://www.mcgraw-hill.com

Ellen Williams. Second edition, 2002. $12.95 (paper). 160 pages. Covers jobs in community, health and medical programs, financial, legal, residential, travel and tourism, and counseling, and how to go after them. Includes bibliography and illustrations.

★6894★ Opportunities in Law Careers

The McGraw-Hill Companies
PO Box 182604
Columbus, OH 43272
Fax: (614)759-3749   Fr: 877-883-5524
E-mail: customer.service@mcgraw-hill.com
URL: http://www.mcgraw-hill.com

Gary A. Munneke. 2001. $12.95 (paper). 160 pages. Covers the entire range of careers in law, from admission to law school to finding the job in private practice, corporate law, public interest law, or teaching.

★6895★ Opportunities in State and Local Government Careers

The McGraw-Hill Companies
PO Box 182604
Columbus, OH 43272
Fax: (614)759-3749   Fr: 877-883-5524
E-mail: customer.service@mcgraw-hill.com
URL: http://www.mcgraw-hill.com

Neale J. Baxter. Revised edition, 1992. $14.95; $10.95 (paper). 148 pages. Points out the incentives and drawbacks of a government career. Describes hiring procedures and provides tips on filling out applications, taking physical and aptitude tests, handling interviews, and finding jobs. Describes the jobs in which 75% of all state and local government workers are employed. For each occupation, covers the nature of the work and the training required.

★6896★ Real People Working in Law

The McGraw-Hill Companies
PO Box 182604
Columbus, OH 43272
Fax: (614)759-3749   Fr: 877-883-5524
E-mail: customer.service@mcgraw-hill.com
URL: http://www.mcgraw-hill.com

Blythe Camenson, Jan Goldberg. 1997. $12.95 (paper). 160 pages. Interviews and profiles of working professionals capture a range of opportunities in this field.

★6897★ Real-Resumes for Legal and Paralegal Jobs

PREP Publishing
1110 1/2 Hay St., PMB 66
Fayetteville, NC 28305
Ph: (910)483-6611   Fax: (910)483-2439
Fr: 800-533-2814

March 2004. $16.95 (paper). 192 pages. Real-Resumes Series.

★6898★ Resumes for Law Careers

The McGraw-Hill Companies
PO Box 182604
Columbus, OH 43272
Fax: (614)759-3749   Fr: 877-883-5524
E-mail: customer.service@mcgraw-hill.com
URL: http://www.mcgraw-hill.com

Third edition, 2007. $12.95 (paper). 144 pages.

★6899★ Vault Guide to Bankruptcy Law Careers

Vault.com
150 W 22nd St., 5th Fl.
New York, NY 10011
Ph: (212)366-4212   Fax: (212)366-6117
Fr: 888-562-8285
URL: http://www.vault.com

Seth A. Stuhl. December 2003. $29.95 (paper). 128 pages. Vault Career Library.

★6900★ Vault Guide to Careers in Labor and Employment Law

Vault.com
150 W. 22nd St., 5th Fl.
New York, NY 10011
Ph: (212)366-4212   Fax: (212)366-6117
Fr: 888-562-8285
URL: http://www.vault.com

Timothy Grubb. October 2003. $29.95 (paper). 96 pages. Part of the Vault Career Library series.

★6901★ Vault Guide to Careers in Litigation

Vault.com
150 W. 22nd St., 5th Fl.
New York, NY 10011
Ph: (212)366-4212   Fax: (212)366-6117
Fr: 888-562-8285
URL: http://www.vault.com

Kristin Nichols, Neeraja Viswanathan. December 2003. $29.95 (paper). 128 pages.

★6902★ Vault Guide to Corporate Law Careers

Vault.com
150 W. 22nd St., 5th Fl.
New York, NY 10011
Ph: (212)366-4212   Fax: (212)366-6117
Fr: 888-562-8285
URL: http://www.vault.com

Zahie El Kouri. December 2003. $29.95 (paper). 128 pages. Vault Career Library.

★6903★ Vault Guide to the Top Boston Law Firms

Vault.com
150 W. 22nd St., 5th Fl.
New York, NY 10011
Ph: (212)366-4212   Fax: (212)366-6117
Fr: 888-562-8285
URL: http://www.vault.com

Brook Moshan, Hussam Hamadeh, Mark Oldman, Tyya N. Turner, Marcy Lerner. March 2003. $29.95 (paper). 45 pages. Part of the Vault Career Library series.

★6904★ Vault Guide to the Top Chicago Law Firms

Vault.com
150 W. 22nd St., 5th Fl.
New York, NY 10011
Ph: (212)366-4212   Fax: (212)366-6117
Fr: 888-562-8285
URL: http://www.vault.com

Brook Moshan, Hussam Hamadeh, Mark Oldman, Tyya N. Turner, Mercy Lerner. Second edition, June 2005. $29.95 (paper). 45 pages. Part of the Vault Career Library series.

★6905★ Vault Guide to the Top Government and Non-Profit Legal Employers

Vault.com
150 W. 22nd St., 5th Fl.
New York, NY 10011
Ph: (212)366-4212   Fax: (212)366-6117
Fr: 888-562-8285
URL: http://www.vault.com

Marcy Lerner. October 2003. $29.95 (paper). 176 pages. Part of the Vault Career Library Series.

★6906★ Vault Guide to the Top Texas Law Firms

Vault.com
150 W. 22nd St., 5th Fl.
New York, NY 10011
Ph: (212)366-4212   Fax: (212)366-6117
Fr: 888-562-8285
URL: http://www.vault.com

Brook Moshan, Hussam Hamadeh, Mark Oldman, Tyya N. Turner, Marcy Lerner. March 2003. $29.95 (paper). 45 pages. Part of the Vault Career Library series.

★6907★ What Can You Do with a Law Degree?: A Lawyer's Guide to Career Alternatives Inside, Outside and Around the Law

Niche Press
PO Box 99477
Seattle, WA 98199
Ph: (206)285-5239   Fax: (206)213-0750

Deborah L. Arron. Fifth edition, 1992. $29.95 (paper). 198 pages.

EMPLOYMENT AGENCIES AND SEARCH FIRMS

★6908★ Attorney Resources, Inc.

750 North St. Paul, Ste. 540
Dallas, TX 75201
Ph: (214)922-8050   Fax: (214)871-3041
Fr: 800-324-4828
E-mail: dallas@attorneyresource.com
URL: http://www.attorneyresource.com

Employment agency. Offices in Austin, Dallas, Fort Worth, Houston and Tulsa, OK. Provides staffing assistance on regular or temporary basis.

★6909★ Bader Research Corp.

49 E. 41st St.
New York, NY 10165
Ph: (212)682-4750   Fax: (212)682-4758

Executive search firm.

★6910★ Beverly Hills Bar Association Personnel Service

300 S. Beverly Dr., Ste. 201
Beverly Hills, CA 90212-4805
Ph: (310)601-2422   Fax: (310)601-2423
URL: http://www.bhba.org

Employment agency.

★6911★ Bishop Partners

708 3rd Ave., Ste. 2200
New York, NY 10017
Ph: (212)986-3419   Fr: (212)986-3350
E-mail: info@bishoppartners.com
URL: http://www.bishoppartners.com

Executive search firm focuses on legal and accounting fields.

★6912★ Coleman Legal Search Consultants

15th & JFK Blvd., Ste. 1010
Philadelphia, PA 19102
Ph: (215)864-2700   Fax: (215)864-2709
E-mail: search@cnlegalsearch.com
URL: http://www.colemanlegal.com

Legal executive search firm.

★6913★ Combined Resources Inc.

12252 Moss Point Rd.
Strongsville, OH 44136
Ph: (440)570-2285   Fax: (440)572-2000
Fr: 877-236-9789
E-mail: info@cri-search.com
URL: http://www.cri-search.com

Executive search firm focused on the legal field.

★6914★ Early Cochran & Olson LLC

1 E. Wacker Dr., Ste. 2510
Chicago, IL 60601
Ph: (312)595-4200   Fax: (312)595-4209
E-mail: info@ecollc.com
URL: http://www.ecollc.com

Executive search firm focused specifically on the legal field.

★6915★ Fergus Partnership Consulting Inc.

1325 Avenue of the Americas, Ste. 2302
New York, NY 10019-6026
Ph: (212)767-1775   Fax: (212)315-0351
E-mail: ny@ferguslex.com
URL: http://www.ferguslex.com

An executive search firm for lawyers. Over 15 years of experience with prestigious law firms worldwide. Experienced in international business and finance.

★6916★ Gibson Arnold & Associates Inc.

1111 Washington, Ste. 220
Golden, CO 80401
Ph: (303)273-9420   Fax: (303)273-9424
Fr: 888-324-9420
E-mail: golden@gibsonarnold.com

URL: http://www.gibsonarnold.com

Legal temporary service supplies attorneys, paralegals, and production clerks to major law firms and corporations nationwide. Also maintains a full-time placement division. Assists law firms and corporations with staffing any in-house needs.

★6917★ Gillard Associates Legal Search
75 McNeil Way
Dedham, MA 02026
Ph: (781)329-4731   Fax: (617)329-1357
E-mail: gillardlgl@aol.com
Search firm.

★6918★ Houser Martin Morris
110th Ave. NE, 110 Atrium Pl., Ste. 580
110 Atrium Pl.
Bellevue, WA 98004
Ph: (425)453-2700   Fax: (425)453-8726
E-mail: info@houser.com
URL: http://www.houser.com

Focus is in the areas of retained executive search, professional and technical recruiting. Areas of specialization include software engineering, sales and marketing, information technology, legal, human resources, accounting and finance, manufacturing, factory automation, and engineering.

★6919★ Ingle-Terrell & Associates
3100 Sunset Dr.
Charlotte, NC 28209-1208
Ph: (704)333-8400

Provides assistance in recruitment and placement of personnel. Industries served: insurance and law.

★6920★ Interquest Inc.
98 Cuttermill Rd.
Great Neck, NY 11021-3006
Ph: (212)319-0790   Fax: (516)482-2114

Offers retained executive search and other consulting services for the legal profession, with primary focus being general counsel searches for corporations, law firm members and lateral movement of partners for law firms.

★6921★ Kali Consultants Inc.
420 Lexington Ave., Ste. 303
New York, NY 10170-0303
Ph: (212)682-5882   Fax: (212)697-4834

Specializing exclusively in the placement of attorneys in law firms and corporations.

★6922★ Karen Dexter & Associates Inc.
2012 Chestnut
Wilmette, IL 60091-1512
Ph: (847)853-9500   Fax: (847)256-7108

Training and development consultant offering interpersonal skills training and one-on-one performance counseling for employees of large organizations. Industries served: advertising, banking and finance, consumer products, entertainment, food and beverage, healthcare, legal profession, manufacturing, government agencies, publishing and broadcasting.

★6923★ Legal Placement Services, Inc.
6737 W. Washington St., Ste. 2390
West Allis, WI 53214
Ph: (414)276-6689   Fax: (414)276-1418
E-mail: info@legalplacementservices.com
URL: http://www.legalplacementservices.com

Employment agency. Periodically fills temporary placements, as well.

★6924★ Major, Hagen, and Africa
938 B. St.
San Rafael, CA 94901
Ph: (415)485-5111   Fax: (415)485-5110
Fr: 877-482-1010
E-mail: infosf@nhaglobal.com
URL: http://www.mhaglobal.com

Executive search firm. Affiliate offices in Atlanta, GA, Chicago, IL, and New York, NY.

★6925★ Phyllis Hawkins and Associates
7601 N. Central Ave., No. 5
Phoenix, AZ 85020
Ph: (602)263-0248   Fax: (602)678-1564
E-mail: phyllis@azlawsearch.com
URL: http://www.azlawsearch.com

Executive search firm focusing on attorney searches.

★6926★ Spherion Pacific Enterprises L.L.C.
2050 Spectrum Blvd.
Fort Lauderdale, FL 33309
Ph: (954)938-7600   Fax: (954)938-7666
Fr: 800-900-4686
E-mail: info@spherion.com
URL: http://www.spherion.com

Firm specializes in recruiting, assessing and deploying talent. It provides the widest range of services available including consulting, managed staffing, outsourcing, search/recruitment and flexible staffing. The company has expertise in industries such as information technology, outsourcing, accounting and finance, law, manufacturing and human resources; as well as clerical, administrative and light industrial.

★6927★ Synectics for Management Decisions Inc.
1901 N Moore St., Ste. 900
Arlington, VA 22209
Ph: (703)528-2772   Fax: (703)528-2857
E-mail: info@smdi.com
URL: http://www.smdi.com

Organizational analysis and development consulting firm specializing in economic and international expertise, executive search, management information systems, data processing, training, economic expertise to legal profession, business brokerage, mergers and acquisitions, and leasing services. Serves private industries as well as government agencies.

★6928★ Weiss & Associates
2422 Sweetwater Cc Place Dr.
PO Box 915656
Apopka, FL 32712
Ph: (407)774-1212   Fax: (407)774-0084

Executive and legal search consultants and recruiters for major law firms and multinational corporations throughout North America and Europe. Special expertise with tax attorneys and key tax executives in addition to experienced partners with significant portable business. Also specialize in mergers and outplacement services.

ONLINE JOB SOURCES AND SERVICES

★6929★ EmpLawyerNet.com
2331 Westwood Blvd., No. 331
Los Angeles, CA 90064
Fr: 800-270-2688
E-mail: membership@emplawyernet.com
URL: http://www.emplawyernet.com/

Description: Career resource site for lawyers. Contains career information, resume posting and job board search, along with links to CLE events, online bookstores, and recruiter directories. **Fee:** Limited access permitted with free basic membership. Premier membership is $59 or $14.95/month and includes free CLE courses, e-mail alerts, networking opportunities and personal career advice.

★6930★ Headhunt.com: The Counsel Network
Fr: 800-268-6735
E-mail: snash@headhunt.com
URL: http://www.thecounselnetwork.com/

Description: Job search and career resource site for attorneys. Search for jobs, post profile, contact recruiters and consultants, download PDF career guides, and more. Registration is free.

★6931★ Law.com: Law Jobs
URL: http://www.lawjobs.com

Description: Visitors can post job openings for attorneys, legal support staff and temporary workers. Also resources for legal recruiters and temporary staffing agencies.

★6932★ The Legal Employment Search Site
E-mail: webmaster@legalemploy.com
URL: http://www.legalemploy.com

Description: Contains links to job search and career-related websites for lawyers and legal support staff.

TRADESHOWS

★6933★ American Association of Attorney-Certified Public Accountants Annual Conference

American Association of Attorney-Certified Public Accountants
24196 Alicia Pky., Ste. K
Mission Viejo, CA 92691
Ph: (949)768-0336
URL: http://www.attorney-cpa.com

Annual. **Primary Exhibits:** Exhibits for persons licensed both as attorneys and CPAs.

★6934★ American Bar Association Annual Meeting/ABA Expo

American Bar Association
321 N. Clark St.
Chicago, IL 60610
Ph: (312)988-5000   Fax: (312)988-6338
Fr: 800-285-2221
E-mail: abamtgs@abanet.org
URL: http://www.abanet.org

Annual. **Primary Exhibits:** Law books, computers, data processing equipment, and other products and services related to the legal profession.

★6935★ American Society of International Law Meeting

American Society of International Law
2223 Massachusetts Ave. NW
Washington, DC 20008-2864
Ph: (202)939-6000   Fax: (202)797-7133
E-mail: services@asil.org
URL: http://www.asil.org

Annual. **Primary Exhibits:** Scholars, practitioners, government officials, political scientists, and specialists in subjects; international law publications and services.

★6936★ Association of American Law Schools Annual Meeting

Association of American Law Schools
1201 Connecticut Ave., NW, Ste. 800
Washington, DC 20036-2717
Ph: (202)296-8851   Fax: (202)296-8869
E-mail: aals@aals.org
URL: http://www.aals.org

Annual. **Primary Exhibits:** Law books, personal computers and hardware and software, video equipment, and communication technology. **Dates and Locations:** 2008 Jan 02-06; New York, NY.

★6937★ Association for Continuing Legal Education Meeting

Association for Continuing Legal Education
4025 Chestnut St.
Philadelphia, PA 19104-3099
Ph: (215)243-1656   Fax: (215)243-1664
E-mail: aclea@aclea.org
URL: http://www.aclea.org

Primary Exhibits: Legal education information and services.

★6938★ Association of Legal Administrators Meeting

Association of Legal Administrators
75 Tri-State International, Ste. 222
Lincolnshire, IL 60069-4435
Ph: (847)267-1252   Fax: (847)267-1329
URL: http://www.alanet.org

Annual. **Primary Exhibits:** Computers, hardware, and software; office equipment and supplies; publications, printers, and engravers; insurance; travel consultants; litigation support; facilities management; hotels; and coffee suppliers. **Dates and Locations:** 2008 May 05-08; Seattle, WA; Washington State Convention and Trade Center.

★6939★ Association of Trial Lawyers of America Convention/Exposition

Association of Trial Lawyers of America
1050 31st St., NW
Washington, DC 20007
Ph: (202)965-3500   Fax: (202)625-7313
Fr: 800-424-2725
E-mail: info@atlahq.org
URL: http://www.atlanet.org

Annual. **Primary Exhibits:** Legal product/service providers, including computer animation videos, computer software/hardware, demonstrative evidence products, expert witness services and marketing firms, as well as high end consumer gifts, online services, structured settlement services, litigation support, legal publishing. **Dates and Locations:** 2008 Jan 26-30; San Juan, PR; El Conquistador Resort and Golden Day Spa; 2008 Jul 14-18; Chicago, IL.

★6940★ Education Law Association Convention

Education Law Association
300 College Park
Dayton, OH 45469-0528
Ph: (937)229-3589   Fax: (937)229-3845
E-mail: ela@educationlaw.org
URL: http://www.educationlaw.org

Annual. **Primary Exhibits:** Law/educational books, supplies, and services.

★6941★ Federal Bar Association Convention

Federal Bar Association
2215 M St.
Washington, DC 20037
Ph: (202)785-1614   Fax: (202)785-1568
E-mail: fba@fedbar.org
URL: http://www.fedbar.org

Annual. **Primary Exhibits:** Legal publications, computer software, and insurance information.

★6942★ Florida Bar Annual Meeting

The Florida Bar
651 E Jefferson St.
Tallahassee, FL 32399-2300
Ph: (850)561-5600   Fax: (850)561-5826
Fr: 800-342-8060
E-mail: flabarwm@flabar.org
URL: http://www.flabar.org

Annual. **Primary Exhibits:** Publications, office equipment, computers, insurance, and information on investment services and overnight carriers.

★6943★ National Association for Law Placement Annual Education Conference

National Association for Law Placement
1025 Connecticut Ave., Ste. 1110
Washington, DC 20036-5413
Ph: (202)835-1001   Fax: (202)835-1112
E-mail: info@nalp.org
URL: http://www.nalp.org

Annual. **Primary Exhibits:** Exhibits relating to recruitment and placement of lawyers. **Dates and Locations:** 2008 Apr 16-19; Toronto, ON, Canada; Westin Harbour Castle Hotel ; 2009 Apr 01-04; Washington, DC; Omni Shoreham Hotel.

★6944★ National Bar Association Annual Convention & Exhibits

National Bar Association
1225 11th St., NW
Washington, DC 20001
Ph: (202)842-3900   Fax: (202)289-6170
URL: http://www.nationalbar.org

Annual. **Primary Exhibits:** Computers and legal software; office products; accounting services; financial planners, temporary employment agencies; legal publications; travel agencies; luggage and leather goods; fine arts and jewelry.

★6945★ State Bar of California Annual Meeting

State Bar of California
180 Howard St.
San Francisco, CA 94105
Ph: (415)538-2000   Fax: (415)538-2368
E-mail: feedback@calbar.ca.gov
URL: http://www.calbar.ca.gov

Annual. **Primary Exhibits:** Publications, computers, timekeeping equipment, and office equipment. **Dates and Locations:** 2008 Sep 25-28; Monterey, CA; 2009 Sep 10-13; San Diego, CA; 2010 Sep 23-26; Monterey, CA.

★6946★ State Bar of Michigan Annual Meeting

State Bar of Michigan
306 Townsend St.
Lansing, MI 48933-2083
Ph: (517)346-6300   Fax: (517)482-6248
Fr: 800-968-1442
E-mail: nbrown@mail.michbar.org
URL: http://www.michbar.org

Annual. **Primary Exhibits:** Law books, encyclopedias, telephones, stationery, legal newspapers, computers, and office equipment.

★6947★ Virginia Trial Lawyers Association Conference

Virginia Trial Lawyers Association
700 E. Main St., Ste. 1400
Richmond, VA 23219
Ph: (804)343-1143   Fax: (804)343-7124
Fr: 800-267-8852
E-mail: vtla@vtla.com
URL: http://www.vtla.com

Annual. **Primary Exhibits:** Equipment, supplies, and services for trial lawyers, including clothiers, printers, financial investors, and mediators.

OTHER SOURCES

★6948★ American Academy of Adoption Attorneys (AAAA)

PO Box 33053
Washington, DC 20033
Ph: (202)832-2222
E-mail: info@adoptionattorneys.org
URL: http://www.adoptionattorneys.org

Members: Attorneys who practice or have otherwise distinguished themselves in the field of adoption law. **Purpose:** Promotes the reform of adoption laws and disseminating information on ethical adoption practices. **Activities:** Offers educational and charitable programs and a speakers' bureau.

★6949★ American Academy of Matrimonial Lawyers (AAML)

150 N Michigan Ave., Ste. 2040
Chicago, IL 60601
Ph: (312)263-6477   Fax: (312)263-7682
E-mail: gferro@marvinandferro.com
URL: http://www.aaml.org

Description: Represents board certified attorneys specializing in the field of matrimonial and family law. Seeks to encourage the study, improve the practice, elevate the standards, and advance the cause of matrimonial law in an effort to preserve the welfare of the family and society. Conducts legal institutes. Sponsors advanced mandatory continuing legal education program.

★6950★ American Almanac of Jobs and Salaries

HarperCollins
10 E. 53rd St.
New York, NY 10022
Ph: (212)207-7000   Fr: 800-242-7737
URL: http://www.harpercollins.com/

John W. Wright. Revised edition, 2000. $20.00 (paper). 672 pages. This is a comprehensive guide to the wages of hundreds of occupations in a wide variety of industries and organizations.

★6951★ American Association for Justice (AAJ)

1050 31st St. NW
Washington, DC 20007-4405
Ph: (202)965-3500   Fax: (202)298-6849
Fr: 800-424-2725
E-mail: membership@justice.org
URL: http://www.atla.org

Description: Represents lawyers, judges, law professors, paralegals, and students engaged in civil plaintiff or criminal defense advocacy. Advances jurisprudence and the law as a profession; encouraging mutual support and cooperation among members of the bar; advancing the cause of persons seeking redress for damages against person or property; training in advocacy; upholding and improving the adversary system and trial by jury. Holds year-round educational programs. Sponsors environmental law essay contest; student trial by jury program; public interest programs; and National Student Trial Advocacy Competition. Conducts research on insurance, product liability, premises liability, environmental torts, and medical malpractice.

★6952★ American Association of Nurse Attorneys (TAANA)

PO Box 515
Columbus, OH 43216-0515
Fax: (614)221-2335   Fr: 877-538-2262
E-mail: taana@taana.org
URL: http://www.taana.org

Members: Nurse attorneys, nurses in law school, and attorneys in nursing school. **Purpose:** Aims to inform the public on matters of nursing, health care and law. Facilitates communication and information sharing between professional groups; establishes an employment network; assists new and potential nurse attorneys; develops the profession; promotes the image of nurse attorneys as experts and consultants in nursing and law. **Activities:** Maintains educational foundation.

★6953★ American Association of Visually Impaired Attorneys (AAVIA)

1155 15th St. NW, Ste. 1004
Washington, DC 20005
Ph: (202)467-5081   Fax: (202)467-5085
Fr: 800-424-8666
E-mail: austingl@bellsouth.net
URL: http://
www.visuallyimpairedattorneys.org

Description: Blind lawyers and blind law students. Seeks to: provide a forum for discussion of the special problems encountered by blind persons licensed to practice law and by blind students training for the legal profession; protect the interests of blind members of the legal profession; acquire, preserve, and maintain law libraries and periodicals of special interest to blind lawyers and blind law students; promote the production of and disseminate information concerning legal materials in Braille or recorded form; advance the legal profession. Conducts educational research, and professional training programs. Operates speakers' bureau. Maintains index of legal material in Braille and on cassette; reproduces items from the *American Bar Journal* and related publications on cassettes.

★6954★ American Bar Association (ABA)

321 N Clark St.
Chicago, IL 60610
Ph: (312)988-5000   Fr: 800-285-2221
E-mail: askaba@abanet.org
URL: http://www.abanet.org

Description: Attorneys in good standing of the bar of any state. Conducts research and educational projects and activities to: encourage professional improvement; provide public services; improve the administration of civil and criminal justice; increase the availability of legal services to the public. Sponsors Law Day USA. Administers numerous standing and special committees such as Committee on Soviet and East European Law, providing seminars and newsletters. Operates 25 sections, including Criminal Justice, Economics of Law Practice, and Family Law. Sponsors essay competitions. Maintains library.

★6955★ American Board of Trial Advocates (ABOTA)

2001 Bryan St., Bryan Tower, Ste. 3000
Dallas, TX 75201-3078
Ph: (214)871-7523   Fax: (214)871-6025
Fr: 800-932-2682
E-mail: national@abota.org
URL: http://www.abota.org

Members: Civil trial plaintiff and defense attorneys. **Purpose:** Seeks to preserve the jury system. Promotes the 7th Amendment. Fosters improvement in the ethical and technical standards of practice in the field of advocacy. Elevates the standards of integrity, honor and courtesy in the legal profession. Aids in further education and training of trial lawyers. Works for the preservation of the jury system. Improves the methods of procedure of the present trial court system.

★6956★ American College of Trial Lawyers (ACTL)

19900 MacArthur Blvd., Ste. 610
Irvine, CA 92612-8405
Ph: (949)752-1801   Fax: (949)752-1674
E-mail: nationaloffice@actl.com
URL: http://www.actl.com

Description: Maintains and improves the standards of trial practice, the administration of justice and the ethics of the profession. Brings together members of the profession who are qualified and who, by reason of probity and ability, will contribute to the accomplishments and good fellowship of the College.

★6957★ American Foreign Law Association (AFLA)

Fragomen, Del Rey, Bernsen and Loewy, LLP
515 Madison Ave.
New York, NY 10022
E-mail: mpatrick@fragomen.com
URL: http://www.afla-law.org

Description: Represents attorneys, jurists, and law professors concerned with issues in international, comparative, and foreign law. Maintains non-governmental organization status with the United Nations. Conducts research. Sponsors educational programs, monthly luncheon programs, and International Law Weekend.

★6958★ American Health Lawyers Association (AHLA)

1025 Connecticut Ave. NW, Ste. 600
Washington, DC 20036-5405
Ph: (202)833-1100   Fax: (202)833-1105
E-mail: pleibold@healthlawyers.org
URL: http://www.healthlawyers.org

Description: Focuses on the legal issues in the healthcare field. Provides resources to address the issues facing its active members who practice in law firms, government, in-house settings, and academia and who represent the entire spectrum of the health industry: physicians, hospitals and health systems, health maintenance organizations, health insurers, managed care companies, nursing facilities, home care providers, and consumers.

★6959★ American Immigration Lawyers Association (AILA)

918 F St. NW
Washington, DC 20004-1400
Ph: (202)216-2400   Fax: (202)783-7853
E-mail: executive@aila.org
URL: http://www.aila.org

Description: Lawyers specializing in the field of immigration and nationality law. Fosters and promotes the administration of justice with particular reference to the immigration and nationality laws of the United States.

★6960★ American Intellectual Property Law Association (AIPLA)

241 18th St. S, Ste. 700
Arlington, VA 22202
Ph: (703)415-0780   Fax: (703)415-0786
E-mail: aipla@aipla.org
URL: http://www.aipla.org

Description: Voluntary bar association of lawyers practicing in the fields of patents, trademarks, copyrights, and trade secrets. Aids in the operation and improvement of U.S. patent, trademark, and copyright sys-

tems, including the laws by which they are governed and rules and regulations under which federal agencies administer those laws. Sponsors moot court and legal writing competitions.

★6961★ American Law Institute (ALI)

4025 Chestnut St.
Philadelphia, PA 19104-3099
Ph: (215)243-1600   Fax: (215)243-1636
Fr: 800-253-6397
E-mail: ali@ali.org
URL: http://www.ali.org

Description: Judges, law teachers, and lawyers. Promotes the clarification and simplification of the law and its better adaptation to social needs by continuing work on the Restatement of the Law, model and uniform codes, and model statutes. Conducts a program of continuing legal education jointly with the American Bar Association called "ALI-ABA".

★6962★ Association of Defense Trial Attorneys (ADTA)

PO Box 310
Rutland, VT 05702-0310
Ph: (802)786-1045   Fax: (802)786-1100
E-mail: gsm@rsclaw.com
URL: http://www.adtalaw.com

Members: Trial lawyers who have over five years' experience in the preparation and trial of insurance cases and the handling of insurance matters, and who possess the knowledge, skill, and facilities to provide insurance companies and self-insurers a legal service of the highest standard. **Activities:** Maintains current biographical data on each member.

★6963★ Association of Family and Conciliation Courts (AFCC)

6525 Grand Teton Plz.
Madison, WI 53719-1083
Ph: (608)664-3750   Fax: (608)664-3751
E-mail: afcc@afccnet.org
URL: http://www.afccnet.org

Members: Judges, counselors, family court personnel, attorneys, mediators, researchers, and teachers concerned with the resolution of family disputes as they affect children. **Purpose:** Proposes to develop and improve the practice of dispute resolution procedure as a complement to judicial procedures. Aims to strengthen the family unit and minimize family strife by improving the process of marriage, family, and divorce counseling; and to provide an interdisciplinary forum for the exchange of ideas, for the creation of new approaches to child custody matters and solutions to problems of family discord. Collaborates with the National Council of Juvenile and Family Court Judges, National Judicial College, the National Center for State Courts, the American Bar Association and several universities, law schools, and state organizations responsible for providing ongoing training for attorneys, judges, and family therapists. **Activities:** Conducts research and offers technical assistance and training to courts, legal associations, judicial

organizations, and behavioral science professionals.

★6964★ Careers in Criminal Justice

Cambridge Educational
PO Box 2053
Princeton, NJ 08543-2053
Ph: 800-257-5126   Fax: (609)671-0266
Fr: 800-468-4227
E-mail: custserv@films.com
URL: http://www.cambridgeeducational.com

VHS and DVD. $79.95. 2002. 22 minutes. Program looks at a number of different occupations, ranging from entry-level positions to those requiring a four-year degree. Experts and people on the job share firsthand information about what their work is like.

★6965★ Center for American and International Law

5201 Democracy Dr.
Plano, TX 75024-3561
Ph: (972)244-3400   Fax: (972)244-3401
Fr: 800-409-1090
E-mail: cail@cailaw.org
URL: http://www.cailaw.org

Description: Provides continuing legal and law enforcement education, focusing primarily on continuing education programs for lawyers and management training programs for law enforcement officials.

★6966★ Croatian American Bar Association (CABA)

1850 Whittier Ave., Unit E201
Costa Mesa, CA 92627
E-mail: marko@croatianamericanbar.com
URL: http://www.croatianamericanbar.com

Description: Promotes the advancement of lawyers and law students of Croatian heritage in the legal profession. Provides a forum for professional networking, support, and exchange of ideas among its members. Supports the provision of legal services to the Croatian-American community. Fosters camaraderie among its members.

★6967★ Education Law Association (ELA)

Mail Drop 0528
300 College Park
Dayton, OH 45469
Ph: (937)229-3589   Fax: (937)229-3845
E-mail: ela@educationlaw.org
URL: http://www.educationlaw.org

Description: School attorneys, law professors, professors of education, school administrators, teachers, and school board members. Works for exchange of information on law school; seeks to stimulate research and publication in the field.

★6968★ Equal Justice Works

2120 L St. NW, Ste. 450
Washington, DC 20037-1541
Ph: (202)466-3686   Fax: (202)429-9766

E-mail: mail@equaljusticeworks.org
URL: http://www.equaljusticeworks.org

Description: Works to surmount barriers to equal justice that affect millions of low-income individuals and families. Engaged in organizing, training, and supporting public service-minded law students and creates summer and postgraduate public interest jobs.

★6969★ Federation of Defense and Corporate Counsel (FDCC)

11812 N 56th St.
Tampa, FL 33617
Ph: (813)983-0022   Fax: (813)988-5837
E-mail: mstreeper@thefederation.org
URL: http://www.thefederation.org

Members: Professional society of attorneys actively engaged in the legal aspects of the insurance industry; insurance company executives; corporate counsel involved in the defense of claims. **Activities:** Conducts research through Federation of Defense and Corporate Counsel Foundation. Sponsors annual essay competition for students at accredited law colleges. Maintains 36 law sections and committees. Conducts seminars and educational sessions.

★6970★ First Amendment Lawyers Association (FALA)

121 S Wilke Rd., No. 500
Arlington Heights, IL 60005
Ph: (847)590-8700   Fax: (847)590-9825
E-mail: wgiampietro@skdaglaw.com
URL: http://firstamendmentlawyers.org

Description: Lawyers who support and defend cases involving the First Amendment to the U.S. Constitution (i.e., freedom of religion, freedom of speech and the press, freedom to peaceably assemble, and freedom to petition the government for a redress of grievances).

★6971★ Food and Drug Law Institute (FDLI)

1155 15 St. NW, Ste. 800
Washington, DC 20005-4903
Ph: (202)371-1420   Fax: (202)371-0649
Fr: 800-956-6293
E-mail: comments@fdli.org
URL: http://www.fdli.org

Description: Provides forum regarding laws, regulations and policies related to drugs, medical devices, and other health care technologies.

★6972★ Human Rights Advocates (HRA)

PO Box 5675
Berkeley, CA 94705
E-mail: info@humanrightsadvocates.org
URL: http://www.humanrightsadvocates.org

Description: International human rights lawyers and professionals. Objectives are to provide education about the application of human rights law and to promote this body of law domestically and internationally. Orga-nizes public conferences, lectures, and seminars; submits amicus curiae briefs. Maintains library of current United Nations documents and materials on human rights organizations; has consultative status with ECO-SOC.

★6973★ Institute of Judicial Administration (IJA)

New York University School of Law
Vanderbilt Hall
40 Washington Square Park, Rm. 413
New York, NY 10012
Ph: (212)998-6217   Fax: (212)995-4881
E-mail: alison.kinney@nyu.edu
URL: http://www.law.nyu.edu/institutes/judi-cial

Members: Lawyers, judges, and laypersons with an interest in judicial administration. **Purpose:** Promotes judicial, procedural, and administrative improvements in the courts; encourages dialogue among the bench, bar, and academy. Furthers empirical research on improving the understanding of the justice system. **Activities:** Offers educational programs for appellate and trial judges.

★6974★ Inter-American Bar Association (IABA)

1211 Connecticut Ave. NW, Ste. 202
Washington, DC 20036
Ph: (202)466-5944   Fax: (202)466-5946
E-mail: iaba@iaba.org
URL: http://www.iaba.org

Members: National, regional, and special associations of attorneys; individual lawyers. **Purpose:** Purposes are to: advance the science of jurisprudence, and in particular, the study of comparative law; promote uniformity in commercial legislation; further the knowledge of laws of Western Hemisphere countries; propagate justificative administration through the creation and maintenance of independent judicial systems; protect and defend civil, human, and political rights of individuals; uphold the honor of the legal profession; encourage geniality and brotherhood among members.

★6975★ International Academy of Trial Lawyers (IATL)

5841 Cedar Lake Rd., Ste. 204
Minneapolis, MN 55416-5657
Ph: (952)546-2364   Fax: (952)545-6073
Fr: (866)823-2443
E-mail: iatl@llmsi.com
URL: http://www.iatl.net

Description: Represents the interests of attorneys who have been practicing for a minimum of 12 years and who are principally engaged in trial and appellate practice. Maintains museum-type Lincoln Library, including old and rare books. Operates charitable program.

★6976★ International Alliance of Holistic Lawyers (IAHL)

PO Box 371
Milton, DE 19968
Fax: (302)684-5644

E-mail: info@iahl.org
URL: http://iahl.org

Description: Represents and promotes the interests of holistic lawyers. Seeks to transform the practice of law through education and support of holistic practices. Provides a forum for networking, progress and new vision in the legal profession.

★6977★ International Municipal Lawyers Association (IMLA)

1110 Vermont Ave. NW, Ste. 200
Washington, DC 20005
Ph: (202)466-5424   Fax: (202)785-1052
E-mail: info@imla.org

Purpose: Seeks to promote and advance the development of local government law and. **Activities:** Serves as a clearinghouse of local law materials; collects and disseminates information; assists government agencies to prepare for litigation and develop new local laws; provides legal research and writing services; offers continuing legal education opportunities; conducts research programs.

★6978★ International Society of Barristers (ISOB)

802 Legal Research Bldg.
University of Michigan Law School
Ann Arbor, MI 48109-1215
Ph: (734)763-0165   Fax: (734)764-8309
E-mail: reedj@umich.edu
URL: http://www.internationalsocietyofbarristers.com

Description: Encourages the continuation of advocacy under the adversary system. Seeks young lawyers to enter advocacy and preserves the right of trial by jury.

★6979★ International Society of Stress Analysts (ISSA)

9 Westchester Dr.
Kissimmee, FL 34744
Ph: (407)933-4839   Fax: (407)935-0911
E-mail: diogenesfl@aol.com

Members: Jurists, attorneys, physicians, private detectives, law enforcement personnel, security personnel, scholar/researchers, and individuals interested in stress analysis for lie detection/truth verification. **Purpose:** Purposes are to: promote the science of psychological stress evaluation and the efficient administration of justice; aid indigent persons, without cost, who may be wrongfully accused; develop and maintain high educational standards; observe and evaluate training programs for the purpose of accreditation and endorsement. **Activities:** Sponsors and certifies schools; offers workshops and research and educational programs; conducts forums. Offers expertise, consultation, and advice; invites inquiries.

★6980★ Media Law Resource Center (MLRC)

North Tower, 20th Fl.
520 Eight Ave.
New York, NY 10018
Ph: (212)337-0200   Fax: (212)337-9893
E-mail: medialaw@medialaw.org
URL: http://www.medialaw.org

Description: Provides support for media defendants in libel and privacy cases, including development of statistical and empirical data, assistance in locating expert witnesses or consultants, and help in coordinating amicus curiae briefs by supporting organizations. Maintains a brief, pleading, and information bank; collects and disseminates information on pending libel and privacy cases for use in legal defense against claims. Serves as a liaison with media organizations, attorneys, and other groups working to advance the defense of libel and privacy claims. Prepares bulletins and reports on current developments and cases, legal theories, privileges, and defenses. Compiles statistics on the incidence and cost of libel and privacy litigation. Provides employment for law student interns. Conducts educational and training workshops and programs; has established fellowship program in libel law. Operates MLRC Institute.

★6981★ Minority Corporate Counsel Association (MCCA)

1111 Pennsylvania Ave. NW
Washington, DC 20004
Ph: (202)739-5901   Fax: (202)739-5999
E-mail: info@mcca.com
URL: http://www.mcca.com

Description: Advocates for the expanded hiring, retention, and promotion of minority attorneys in corporate law departments and the law firms that serve them. Collects and disseminates information about diversity in the legal profession. Creates effective professional skills development programs for minority attorneys.

★6982★ National Association of College and University Attorneys (NACUA)

1 Dupont Cir., Ste. 620
Washington, DC 20036
Ph: (202)833-8390   Fax: (202)296-8379
E-mail: nacua@nacua.org
URL: http://www.nacua.org

Description: Represents attorneys from U.S. and Canadian campuses, colleges and universities. Compiles and distributes legal decisions, opinions, and other writings and information on legal problems affecting colleges and universities.

★6983★ National Association of County Civil Attorneys (NACCA)

2501 7th St., Ste. 300
Tuscaloosa, AL 35401-1801
Ph: (205)349-3870   Fax: (205)345-9580
E-mail: rspence@hsmbb.com
URL: http://www.naco.org

Description: County civil attorneys. Aims to respond to growing organizational needs of the office of county civil attorney. Seeks to educate members in areas including environment, labor-management relations, consumer protection, land use, utilization of energy sources, traditional statutory and case law, national legislation, and Supreme Court decisions. Offers educational programs; and compiles statistics.

★6984★ National Association of Criminal Defense Lawyers (NACDL)

1150 18th St. NW, Ste. 950
Washington, DC 20036
Ph: (202)872-8600   Fax: (202)872-8690
E-mail: assist@nacdl.org
URL: http://www.criminaljustice.org

Description: Advances the mission of the nation's criminal defense lawyers to ensure justice and due process for persons accused of crime or other misconduct. A professional bar association that includes private criminal defense lawyers, public defenders, law professors, active military defense counsel and judges committed to preserving fairness within America's criminal justice system.

★6985★ National Association for Law Placement (NALP)

1025 Connecticut Ave. NW, Ste. 1110
Washington, DC 20036-5413
Ph: (202)835-1001   Fax: (202)835-1112
E-mail: info@nalp.org
URL: http://www.nalp.org

Description: Brings together law schools, legal employers, and bar associations to share information, research, and professional development opportunities. Works to facilitate legal career counseling and planning, recruitment and retention, and the professional development of law students and lawyers. Aims to cultivate ethical practices and fairness in legal career counseling and planning, recruitment, employment, and professional development; to promote the full range of legal career opportunities and to foster access to legal public interest and public sector employment; and to advocate for diversity in the legal profession and in the membership.

★6986★ National Association of Legal Investigators (NALI)

PO Box 8479
Portland, ME 04104
Fax: (207)893-1457   Fr: 888-244-5685
E-mail: info@nalionline.org
URL: http://www.nalionline.org

Description: Legal investigators, both independent and law firm staff, who specialize in investigation of personal injury matters for the plaintiff and criminal defense. Promotes professionalization of the legal investigator, accomplished by seminars and a professional certification program. Provides nationwide network of contact among members. Compiles statistics.

★6987★ National Association of Traffic Accident Reconstructionists and Investigators (NATARI)

PO Box 2588
West Chester, PA 19382
Ph: (610)696-1919
E-mail: natari@natari.org
URL: http://www.natari.org

Description: Represents engineers, attorneys, police officers, private investigators, medical examiners, and other individuals involved in the analysis of motor vehicle traffic accidents. Gathers and disseminates information on techniques and equipment of potential use to members; reviews literature in the field. Participating Organization of the Accreditation Commission for Traffic Accident Reconstruction.

★6988★ National Association of Women Lawyers (NAWL)

American Bar Center 15.2
321 N Clark St.
Chicago, IL 60610
Ph: (312)988-6186   Fax: (312)988-5491
E-mail: nawl@nawl.org
URL: http://www.abanet.org/nawl

Purpose: Membership is open to any person who is a member in good standing of the bar of any state or U.S. territory, any non-U.S. legal professional (attorney or judge), any prospective attorney currently attending law school, and any state or local bar or law school association with compatible objectives. Men are welcome and encouraged to join.

★6989★ National Bar Association (NBA)

1225 11th St. NW
Washington, DC 20001
Ph: (202)842-3900   Fax: (202)289-6170
E-mail: lf@williegary.com
URL: http://www.nationalbar.org

Members: Professional association of minority (predominantly African-American) attorneys, members of the judiciary, law students, and law faculty. **Purpose:** Represents the interests of members and the communities they serve. **Activities:** Offers continuing legal education programs. Maintains hall of fame.

★6990★ National Black Law Students Association (NBLSA)

1225 11th St. NW
Washington, DC 20001-4217
Ph: (202)210-6556   Fax: (866)518-6863
E-mail: chair@nblsa.org
URL: http://www.nblsa.org

Description: Aims to serve the needs and goals of black law students and "effectuate change" in the legal community. Includes chapters or affiliates in six different countries including the Bahamas, Nigeria, and South Africa. Conducts sessions comprising a program of prominent speakers, seminars, case study analyses, and small group discussions covering concerns, problems, issues, and opportunities in academic administration.

★6991★ National Criminal Justice Association (NCJA)

720 7th St. NW, 3rd Fl.
Washington, DC 20001
Ph: (202)628-8550   Fax: (202)628-0080
E-mail: info@ncja.org
URL: http://www.ncja.org

Description: State, tribal and local criminal justice planners, police chiefs, judges, prosecutors, defenders, corrections officials, educators, researchers, and elected officials. Promotes innovation in the criminal justice system through the focused coordination of law enforcement, the courts, corrections, and juvenile justice. Seeks to: focus attention on national issues and developments related to the control of crime; determine and effectively express the states' and tribes' collective views on pending legislative and administrative action encompassing criminal and juvenile justice; improve the states' and tribes' administration of their criminal and juvenile justice responsibilities through the development and dissemination of information to and among justice administrators and policy makers. Conducts technical assistance and training programs.

★6992★ National District Attorneys Association (NDAA)

99 Canal CN Plz., Ste. 510
Alexandria, VA 22314
Ph: (703)549-9222   Fax: (703)836-3195
E-mail: velva.walter@ndaa.org
URL: http://www.ndaa.org

Description: Elected/appointed prosecuting attorneys; associate members are assistant prosecuting attorneys, investigators, paralegals, and other prosecution office staff. Dedicated in providing information and a national forum for prosecuting attorneys. Seeks to serve prosecuting attorneys and to improve and facilitate the administration of justice in the U.S. Provides educational and informational services, technical assistance and research in areas such as vehicular crimes, juvenile justice, guns prosecution, community prosecution, DNA forensics, white collar crime, drug prosecution and child abuse prosecution through the American Prosecutors Research Institute. Prepares amicus curiae briefs.

★6993★ National Employment Lawyers Association (NELA)

44 Montgomery St., Ste. 2080
San Francisco, CA 94104
Ph: (415)296-7629   Fax: (415)677-9445
E-mail: nelahq@nela.org
URL: http://www.nela.org

Description: Attorneys who represent individual employees in cases involving employment discrimination, wrongful termination, benefits, and other employment-related matters. Promotes the professional development of members through networking, publications, technical assistance, and education. Supports the workplace rights of individual employees via lobbying and other activities. Maintains informational bank of pleadings and briefs; does not operate a lawyer referral service. Conducts regional seminars; conducts educational programs.

★6994★ National Lawyers Guild (NLG)

132 Nassau St., Rm. 922
New York, NY 10038
Ph: (212)679-5100   Fax: (212)679-2811
E-mail: nlgno@nlg.org
URL: http://www.nlg.org

Description: Lawyers, law students, legal workers, and jailhouse lawyers dedicated to seek economic justice, social equality, and the right to political dissent. Serves as national center for progressive legal work providing training programs to both members and nonmembers. Sponsors skills seminars in different areas of law. Maintains speakers' bureau and offers legal referrals.

★6995★ National Organization of Bar Counsel (NOBC)

1560 Broadway, Ste. 1800
Denver, CO 80210
Ph: (303)866-6577   Fax: (303)893-5302
E-mail: admin@nobc.org
URL: http://www.nobc.org

Members: Attorneys for bar associations and disciplinary agencies in the U.S. and Canada who are professionally involved in representing their associations in all legal matters, with emphasis on matters of professional misconduct by lawyers. **Activities:** Participates in interpreting and prosecuting professional ethics, investigating unauthorized practice of law, and initiating improved legislation.

★6996★ North American South Asian Bar Association (NASABA)

Schiffrin amd Barroway, LLP
280 King of Prussia Rd.
Radnor, PA 19087
Ph: (484)270-1456   Fax: (610)667-7056
E-mail: bsharma@sbclasslaw.com
URL: http://www.na-saba.org

Description: Promotes professional development for South Asians, attorneys and law students. Coordinates activities with other national bar associations. Provides a nationwide networking forum for all South Asian attorneys. Offers a referral network/service to the South Asian community. Seeks to educate and disseminate information to the South Asian community about the law, legal access, and relevant legal issues.

★6997★ Professional Specialty Occupations

Delphi Productions
3159 6th St.
Boulder, CO 80304
Ph: (303)443-2100   Fax: (303)443-4022
Fr: 888-443-2400
E-mail: support@delphivideo.com
URL: http://www.delphivideo.com

$95.00. 53 minutes. Part of the Careers for the 21st Century Video Library.

★6998★ Puerto Rican Legal Defense and Education Fund (PRLDEF)

99 Hudson St., 14th Fl.
New York, NY 10013-2815
Ph: (212)219-3360   Fax: (212)431-4276
Fr: 800-328-2322
E-mail: info@prldef.org
URL: http://www.prldef.org

Description: Seeks to secure, promote and protect the civil and human rights of the Puerto Rican and wider Latino community. (Three divisions, Legal, Policy and Education, carry out the core program areas - Civil and Human Rights, Civic Engagement and Empowerment, Civil Society and Culture and Equitable Educational Opportunities -the pursuit of a legal career for Puerto Ricans and other minorities via its LSAT prep course, Law Day and other programs.)

★6999★ Society of Trust and Estate Practitioners USA (STEP USA)

7 Times Sq.
New York, NY 10036-7311
Ph: (914)636-2531
E-mail: marian.kramer@step.org
URL: http://www.step.org

Description: Aims to bring together all practitioners in the field of trusts and estates. Raises the public profile of trust and estate work as a profession in its own right. Advances knowledge and learning in trusts, estates and allied subjects. Encourages and promotes the study of trusts and estate practice. Provides education, training, representation and networking for its members.

★7000★ Transportation Lawyers Association (TLA)

PO Box 15122
Lenexa, KS 66285-5122
Ph: (913)895-4615   Fax: (913)895-4652
E-mail: tla-info@goamp.com
URL: http://www.translaw.org

Description: Attorneys representing transportation interests throughout the U.S. and Canada. Assists members in the practice of transportation law through exchange of ideas, education, and participation in rule-making proceedings. Cosponsors annual Transportation Law Institute.

Legal Assistants

SOURCES OF HELP-WANTED ADS

★7001★ Annual Review of Law and Social Science

Annual Reviews Inc.
4139 El Camino Way
PO Box 10139
Palo Alto, CA 94303-0139
Ph: (650)493-4400   Fax: (650)424-0910
Fr: 800-523-8635
URL: http://arjournals.annualreviews.org/loi/lawsocsci

Annual. $75.00/year for individuals, print & online; $210.00/year for institutions, print & online; $175.00/year for institutions, print only; $175.00/year for institutions, online only. Journal covering current issues in law and the social sciences.

★7002★ Berkeley Business Law Journal

University of California, Boalt Hall School of Law
158 Boalt Hall
Berkeley, CA 94720
Ph: (510)643-6319
URL: http://www.boalt.org/bblj/index.html

Semiannual. $45.00/year for individuals; $65.00/year for elsewhere. Journal that aims to create innovative business law-oriented commentary created by professors, professionals, and students.

★7003★ Boston Bar Journal

Boston Bar Association
16 Beacon St.
Boston, MA 02108
Ph: (617)742-0615   Fax: (617)523-0127
URL: http://www.bostonbar.org/pub/index.htm

Quarterly. Journal for lawyers on important matters of legal interest.

★7004★ California Lawyer

Daily Journal Corp.
915 E 1st St.
Los Angeles, CA 90012
Ph: (213)229-5300   Fax: (213)680-3682
URL: http://www.dailyjournal.com

Monthly. $47.00 for two years; $40.00/year for individuals; $38.00/year for individuals, bulk order; $28.00/year for individuals, bulk order; $26.00/year for individuals, bulk order. Law magazine.

★7005★ Chicago Lawyer

Law Bulletin Publishing Co.
415 N State St.
Chicago, IL 60610
Ph: (312)644-7800   Fax: (312)416-1864
E-mail: displayads@lbc.com
URL: http://www.lbpc.com

Monthly. $40.00/year. Legal magazine (Tabloid).

★7006★ Columbia Journal of Law and Social Problems

Columbia Law School
435 W 116th St.
New York, NY 10027-7297
Ph: (212)854-2670
E-mail: jlsp@law.columbia.edu
URL: http://www.columbia.edu/cu/jlsp/

$40.00/year for individuals; $45.00/year for individuals, other countries; $17.50 for single issue. Journal covering economic, sociological and political laws.

★7007★ Cornerstone

National Legal Aid & Defender Association
1140 Connecticut Ave. NW, Ste. 900
Washington, DC 20036
Ph: (202)452-0620   Fax: (202)872-1031
E-mail: info@nlada.org
URL: http://www.nlada.org/

Description: Four issues/year. Monitors current issues affecting legal aid attorneys and public defenders. Recurring features include job listings, conference and training updates, news of research, book reviews, and news of members.

★7008★ Criminal Justice Studies

Taylor & Francis Group Journals
325 Chestnut St., Ste. 800
Philadelphia, PA 19106
Ph: (215)625-8900   Fax: (215)625-8914
Fr: 800-354-1420
URL: http://www.tandf.co.uk/journals/titles/1478601x.html

$352.00/year for institutions, print and online; $334.00/year for institutions, online only; $107.00/year for individuals. Journal covering articles on criminal justice and criminological issues.

★7009★ D & O Advisor

American Lawyer Media L.P.
345 Pk. Ave. S
New York, NY 10010
Ph: (212)779-9200   Fax: (212)481-8110
Fr: 800-888-8300
URL: http://www.alm.com

Quarterly. Magazine that offers advice and perspective on corporate oversight responsibilities for directors and officers.

★7010★ Executive Legal Adviser

American Lawyer Media L.P.
345 Pk. Ave. S
New York, NY 10010
Ph: (212)779-9200   Fax: (212)481-8110
Fr: 800-888-8300
URL: http://www.executivelegaladviser.com

Bimonthly. Free to qualified subscribers. Magazine that offers legal advice for corporate executives.

★7011★ Global Jurist Frontiers

Berkeley Electronic Press
2809 Telegraph Ave., Ste. 202
Berkeley, CA 94705
Ph: (510)665-1200   Fax: (510)665-1201
URL: http://www.bepress.com/gj/frontiers/

Annual. $645.00/year corporate; $215.00/year academic. Journal that publishes papers on new issues of comparative law, law and economics, international law, law and development, and legal anthropology.

★7012★ Houston Law Review
University of Houston
4800 Calhoun Rd.
Houston, TX 77004
Ph: (713)743-2255
E-mail: inquiry@houstonlawreview.org
URL: http://www.houstonlawreview.org/

Quarterly. $33.00/year for individuals. Journal focusing on current issues in law. Publishes contributions from academicians, practicing lawyers, and other scholars, and selected Law Review students.

★7013★ Institute of Justice and International Studies
Central Missouri State University
PO Box 800
Warrensburg, MO 64093
Ph: (660)543-4111   Fax: (660)543-8517
Fr: 877-729-8266
E-mail: wallace@cmsu1.cmsu.edu

Irregular. Free to qualified subscribers. Journal that publishes reports on international crime including corrections, media coverage, public policy, counter terrorism, and civil liberties.

★7014★ Ius Gentium
University of Baltimore
1420 North Charles St.
Baltimore, MD 21201-5779
Ph: (410)837-4459
URL: http://law.ubalt.edu/cicl/ilt/index.html#ius

Annual. Journal that facilitates analysis and the exchange of ideas about contemporary legal issues from a comparative perspective.

★7015★ Job Announcements
National Center for State Courts
300 Newport Ave.
PO Box 8798
Williamsburg, VA 23185-4147
Ph: (757)253-2000   Fax: (757)564-2022
Fr: 800-616-6164
URL: http://www.ncsconline.org/

Description: Semimonthly. Provides lists of court-related job openings in the United States and its territories.

★7016★ Journal of the American Criminal Justice Association
American Criminal Justice Association
PO Box 601047
Sacramento, CA 95860-1047
Ph: (916)484-6553   Fax: (916)488-2227
URL: http://www.acjalae.org/index.html

Semiannual. Journal covering issues in criminal justice.

★7017★ Journal of Contemporary Criminal Justice
Sage Publications Inc.
2455 Teller Rd.
Thousand Oaks, CA 91320
Ph: (805)499-0721   Fax: (805)499-8096

URL: http://www.unl.edu/eskridge/jccjabstracts.html

Quarterly. $453.00/year for institutions, combined (print & e-access); $476.00/year for institutions, current volume print & all online content; $408.00/year for institutions, e-access; $431.00/year for institutions, backfile lease, e-access plus backfile; $486.00/year for institutions, backfile e-access (content through 1999); $444.00/year for institutions, print only; $85.00/year for individuals, print only; $123.00 for institutions, single print; $28.00 for individuals, single print. Journal focusing on all aspects of criminal justice.

★7018★ Journal of Criminal Justice Education
Academy of Criminal Justice Sciences
7339 Hanover Pky., Ste. A
Greenbelt, MD 20770
Ph: (301)446-6300   Fax: (301)446-2819
Fr: 800-757-2257
URL: http://www.tandf.co.uk/journals/titles/10511253.asp

Semiannual. Journal covering criminal justice.

★7019★ Journal of Empirical Legal Studies
Wiley-Blackwell
350 Main St. Commerce Pl.
Malden, MA 02148
Ph: (781)388-8200   Fax: (781)388-8210
Fr: 800-759-6120
URL: http://www.blackwellpublishing.com/journal.asp?ref=1740-1453

$318.00/year for institutions, U.S. print and premium online; $289.00/year for institutions, U.S. print and standard online; $275.00/year for institutions, U.S. premium online only; $243.00/year for institutions, other countries, print and premium online; $221.00/year for institutions, other countries, print and standard online; $210.00/year for institutions, other countries, premium online only. Journal focusing on law and law-related fields, including civil justice, corporate law, criminal justice, domestic relations, economics, finance, health care, political science, psychology, public policy, securities regulation, and sociology.

★7020★ Journal of Health Law
American Health Lawyers Association
1025 Connecticut Ave., NW, Ste. 600
Washington, DC 20036-5405
Ph: (202)833-1100   Fax: (202)833-1105
URL: http://www.healthlawyers.org

Quarterly. Professional journal covering healthcare issues and cases and their impact on the health care arena.

★7021★ Journal of the Missouri Bar
The Missouri Bar
326 Monroe St.
PO Box 119
Jefferson City, MO 65102-0119
Ph: (573)635-4128   Fax: (573)635-2811
URL: http://www.mobar.org/

Bimonthly. Magazine featuring short, practical articles on legal subjects for practicing attorneys.

★7022★ The Journal of Taxation
RIA Group
395 Hudson St., 4th Fl.
New York, NY 10014
Ph: (212)367-6300   Fax: (212)367-6314
Fr: 800-431-9025
URL: http://ria.thomson.com/estore/detail.aspx?ID=JTAX

Monthly. $300.00/year for individuals, print; $450.00/year for individuals, online/print bundle; $345.00/year for individuals, online. Journal for sophisticated tax practitioners.

★7023★ Jungle Law
Jungle Media Group
150 Varick St., 8th Fl.
New York, NY 10013
URL: http://www.jdjungle.com

$11.97/year. Magazine covering all aspects of law school education.

★7024★ Kentucky Bench & Bar Magazine
Kentucky Bar Association
514 West Main St.
Frankfort, KY 40601-1883
Ph: (502)564-3795   Fax: (502)564-3225

Bimonthly. $20.00/year for individuals. Kentucky law magazine.

★7025★ Law Officers Magazine
Elsevier Science Inc.
360 Park Ave. S
New York, NY 10010
Ph: (212)989-5800   Fax: (212)633-3990
URL: http://www.elsevier.com

Monthly. $31.69/year for U.S. $52.00/year for Canada; $63.49/year for other countries. Journal for the professional law enforcement officer.

★7026★ Legal Affairs
Legal Affairs
254 Elm St.
New Haven, CT 06511
Ph: (203)789-1510
URL: http://legalaffairs.org/mediakit/LegalAffairsMediaKit.pdf

Bimonthly. $39.95/year for institutions, Canada. Publication that presents critical essays about current issues in law.

★7027★ Legal Times
American Lawyer Media L.P.
1730 M St. NW, Ste. 802
Washington, DC 20036
Ph: (202)457-0686   Fax: (202)785-4539
Fr: 800-933-4317
E-mail: legaltimes@legaltimes.com
URL: http://www.law.com/dc

Weekly. $349.00/year print & online. Legal publication covering law and lobbying in the nation's capitol.

★7028★ **Los Angeles Lawyer**
Los Angeles County Bar Association
261 S Figueroa St., Ste. 300
PO Box 55020
Los Angeles, CA 90055-2020
Ph: (213)627-2727   Fax: (213)896-6500
URL: http://www.lacba.org/show-page.cfm?pageid=40

Monthly. $28.00/year for nonmembers; $4.00 for single issue, plus handling; subscription included in membership. Magazine featuring scholarly legal articles.

★7029★ **Michigan Bar Journal**
State Bar of Michigan
306 Townsend St.
Lansing, MI 48933-2083
Ph: (517)346-6300   Fax: (517)482-6248
Fr: 800-968-1442
URL: http://www.michbar.org/publications

Monthly. $45.00/year for individuals; $55.00/year for other countries. Legal magazine.

★7030★ **The National Law Journal**
The New York Law Journal
345 Pk. Ave. S
New York, NY 10010
Ph: (212)779-9200   Fax: (212)481-8110
Fr: 800-888-8300
URL: http://www.law.com

Weekly. $50.00/year for individuals, print subscriber rate for a 1-year; $25.00/year for individuals, for 6 months of online access. Tabloid focusing on the practice of law and trends in law.

★7031★ **National Paralegal Reporter**
National Federation of Paralegal Associations Inc.
PO Box 2016
Edmonds, WA 98020
Ph: (425)967-0045   Fax: (425)771-9588
E-mail: info@paralegals.org
URL: http://www.paralegals.org

Description: Bimonthly. Focuses on issues of concern to the paralegal profession such as responsibility and ethics, new developments in the field, and educational opportunities. Promotes the recognition and advancement of paralegals and provides information on programs and help offered by paralegal associations. Reports regional NFPA news and news of paralegal associations throughout the U.S. Recurring features include book reviews, news of research, and President's Column.

★7032★ **New Jersey Law Journal**
New Jersey Law Journal
238 Mulberry St.
PO Box 20081
Newark, NJ 07101-6081
Ph: (973)642-0075   Fax: (973)642-0920

URL: http://www.law.com/jsp/nj/index.jsp

Weekly. $219.00/year for individuals. Journal containing digests of court opinions, notes, and orders to the bar from New Jersey Supreme Court and federal district court. Includes news articles on legal topics and commentary by legal specialists.

★7033★ **Public Interest Employment Service Job Alert!**
Public Interest Clearinghouse
47 Kearny St., Ste. 705
San Francisco, CA 94108
Ph: (415)834-0100   Fax: (415)834-0202
E-mail: pies@pic.org
URL: http://www.pic.org

Description: Semimonthly. Lists job openings in legal aid offices and public interest law organizations. Also available via e-mail.

★7034★ **The Recorder**
American Lawyer Media L.P.
105 Madison Ave.
New York, NY 10016
Fr: 800-603-6571
E-mail: recorder@counsel.com
URL: http://www.therecorder.com

Daily (morn.). $350.00/year for individuals. Legal newspaper.

★7035★ **The Washington Lawyer**
The District of Columbia Bar
1250 H St. NW, 6th Fl.
Washington, DC 20005-5937
Ph: (202)737-4700   Fax: (202)626-3471
Fr: 877-333-2227
URL: http://www.dcbar.org

Monthly. Forum for articles and news items for the Washington legal community.

★7036★ **Wisconsin Lawyer**
State Bar of Wisconsin
PO Box 7158
Madison, WI 53707-7158
Ph: (608)257-3838   Fax: (608)257-5502
Fr: 800-728-7788
E-mail: wislawyer@wisbar.org
URL: http://www.wisbar.org/wislawmag/

Monthly. $48.00/year for individuals. Official monthly publication of the State Bar of Wisconsin.

PLACEMENT AND JOB REFERRAL SERVICES

★7037★ **International Technology Law Association (ITechLaw)**
401 Edgewater Pl., Ste. 600
Wakefield, MA 01880
Ph: (781)876-8877   Fax: (781)224-1239
E-mail: office@itechlaw.org
URL: http://www.itechlaw.org

Members: Lawyers, law students, and others interested in legal problems related to computer-communications technology. **Purpose:** Aids in: contracting for computer-communications goods and services; perfecting and protecting proprietary rights chiefly in software; and taxing computer-communications goods, services, and transactions, and liability for acquisition and use of computer-communications goods and services. **Activities:** Provides specialized educational programs; and offers limited placement service. Holds Annual Computer Law Update.

★7038★ **National Paralegal Association (NPA)**
Box 406
Solebury, PA 18963
Ph: (215)297-8333   Fax: (215)297-8358
E-mail: admin@nationalparalegal.org
URL: http://www.nationalparalegal.org

Description: Paralegals, paralegal students, educators, supervisors, paralegal schools, administrators, law librarians, law clinics, and attorneys. Advances the paralegal profession by promoting recognition, economic benefits, and high standards. Registers paralegals; maintains speakers' bureau, job bank, and placement service; offers resume preparation assistance. Offers free job bank nationally. Sponsors commercial exhibits. Operates mail order bookstore and gift shop. Compiles statistics. Develops promotion and public relations, insurance, certification, and computer bank programs. Compiles and maintains for rental the largest list of paralegals nationwide.

EMPLOYER DIRECTORIES AND NETWORKING LISTS

★7039★ **American Bar Association-Directory**
American Bar Association
321 N Clark St.
Chicago, IL 60610
Ph: (312)988-5000   Fax: (312)988-5177
Fr: 800-285-2221

Annual, October. $14.95. Covers approximately 7,500 lawyers active in the affairs of the Association, including officers, members of Boards of Governors and House of Delegates, section officers and council members, committee leaders, headquarters staff, state and local bars, affiliated and other legal organizations. Entries include: Section, council, or other unit name; names, addresses, and phone numbers of officers or chairpersons and members. Arrangement: Classified by position in ABA. Indexes: Alphabetical, geographical committee.

★7040★ American Lawyers Quarterly

The American Lawyers Co.
853 Westpoint Pky., Ste. 710
Cleveland, OH 44145-1532
Ph: (440)871-8700   Fax: (440)871-9997
Fr: 800-843-4000
URL: http://www.alqlist.com/

Quarterly; monthly supplements. A commercial law list. Arrangement: Geographical.

★7041★ Attorney Jobs Online

Federal Reports Inc.
1010 Vermont Ave. NW, Ste. 408
Washington, DC 20005
Ph: (202)393-3311   Fax: (202)393-1553
Fr: 800-296-9611
URL: http://www.attorneyjobs.com

Monthly. Publication includes: Listings of approximately 600 current attorney and law-related job opportunities with the U.S. Government and other public and private employers in Washington D.C., nationwide, and abroad. Arrangement: Geographical.

★7042★ Career Opportunities in Law and the Legal Industry

Facts On File Inc.
132 W 31st St., 17th Fl.
New York, NY 10001
Ph: (212)967-8800   Fax: 800-678-3633
Fr: 800-322-8755
URL: http://www.factsonfile.com/

Latest edition 2nd, 2007. $49.50 for individuals; $44.55 for libraries. Publication includes: Lists of industry associations and organizations, educational institutions, and Web sites related to the legal industry. Principal content of publication is information on careers in the legal field. Indexes: Alphabetical.

★7043★ Directory of Local Paralegal Clubs

National Paralegal Association
PO Box 406
Solebury, PA 18963
Ph: (215)297-8333   Fax: (215)297-8358
URL: http://www.nationalparalegal.org/

Annual. $5.00. Covers Regional, state, and local paralegal groups.

★7044★ Gale Encyclopedia of Everyday Law

Gale, Cengage Learning
27500 Drake Rd.
Farmington Hills, MI 48331-3535
Ph: (248)699-4253   Fax: (248)699-8065
Fr: 800-877-4253
URL: http://www.gale.com

Latest edition 2nd, July 2006. $352.00 for individuals. Publication includes: Listing of law-related organizations. Principal content of publication consists of approximately 200 articles covering specific legal issues of interest to a layperson in the United States and includes details on their background, historical cases, profiles of U.S. Laws and regulations, differentiation between states, and further reading information.

★7045★ Law Firms Yellow Book

Leadership Directories Inc.
104 5th Ave.
New York, NY 10011
Ph: (212)627-4140   Fax: (212)645-0931
E-mail: techsupport@leadershipdirectories.com
URL: http://www.leadershipdirectories.com/products/lyb.htm

Quarterly. $355.00 for individuals; $338.00 for individuals, standing order. Covers approximately 850 large law firms and over 24,000 attorneys and administrators at more than 3,000 domestic and foreign offices, subsidiaries, and affiliates. Entries include: Firm name, address, phone, fax, telex, year founded, description of practice; officers' names, titles, phone numbers, and law schools attended; addresses, phone numbers, and principal officials at branch offices; e-mails. Arrangement: Alphabetical by firm name. Indexes: Geographical, law school, individual name, law firm, practice area.

★7046★ Law and Legal Information Directory

Gale, Cengage Learning
27500 Drake Rd.
Farmington Hills, MI 48331-3535
Ph: (248)699-4253   Fax: (248)699-8065
Fr: 800-877-4253
E-mail: businessproducts@gale.com
URL: http://www.gale.com

Annual; latest edition 18th, published June 2007. $540.00 for individuals. Covers more than 19,000 national and international organizations, bar associations, federal and highest state courts, federal regulatory agencies, law schools, firms and organizations offering continuing legal education, paralegal education, sources of scholarships and grants, awards and prizes, special libraries, information systems and services, research centers, publishers of legal periodicals, books, and audiovisual materials, lawyer referral services, legal aid offices, public defender offices, legislature manuals and registers, small claims courts, corporation departments of state, state law enforcement agencies, state agencies, including disciplinary agencies, and state bar requirements. Entries include: All entries include institution or firm name, address, phone; many include names and titles of key personnel and, when pertinent, descriptive annotations. Contents based in part on information selected from several other Gale directories. Arrangement: Classified by type of organization, activity, service, etc. Indexes: Individual sections have special indexes as required.

★7047★ Lawyer's Register International by Specialties and Fields of Law Including a Directory of Corporate Counsel

Lawyer's Register Publishing Co.
4555 Renaissance Pkwy., Ste. 101
Cleveland, OH 44128
Ph: (216)591-1492   Fax: (216)591-0265
Fr: 800-477-6345
URL: http://www.lawyersregister.com

Annual. Covers corporate legal staffs world-wide; legal firms; independent practicing attorneys each identified as a specialist in one or more fields of law. Entries include: In corporate section–Corporation, subsidiary, and department names; address, phone, fax; names and titles of legal staff, law schools attended, specialties. In fields of law sections–Name, address, phone, fax, specialties (identified by Standard Industrial Classification, or SIC, codes), personal data. A general international/corporate law list. Arrangement: Separate sections for specializing lawyers and their firms and corporate counsel. Indexes: Lawyers and firms by areas, corporations; additional indexes included.

★7048★ Martindale-Hubbell Law Directory

Martindale-Hubbell Inc.
121 Chanlon Rd.
New Providence, NJ 07974
Ph: (908)464-6800   Fax: (908)771-8704
Fr: 800-526-4902
URL: http://www.martindale.com

Annual, April 2004. $1,065.00 for individuals. Covers lawyers and law firms in the United States, its possessions, and Canada, plus leading law firms worldwide; includes a biographical section by firm, and a separate list of patent lawyers, attorneys in government service, in-house counsel, and services, suppliers, and consultants to the legal profession. Entries include: For non-subscribing lawyers–Name, year of birth and of first admission to bar, code indicating college and law school attended and first degree, firm name (or other affiliation, if any) and relationship to firm, whether practicing other than as individual or in partnership. For subscribing lawyers–Above information plus complete address, phone, fax, e-mail and URL, type of practice, clients, plus additional personal details (education, certifications, etc.). A general law list. Arrangement: Geographical. Indexes: Alphabetical, area of practice.

★7049★ NLADA Directory of Legal Aid and Defender Offices in the United States and Territories

National Legal Aid & Defender Association
1140 Connecticut Ave. NW, Ste. 900
Washington, DC 20036
Ph: (202)452-0620   Fax: (202)872-1031
URL: http://www.nlada.org/Member_Svcs/Publications/Directory/

Biennial; latest edition 2007-08. $95.00 for nonmembers; $35.00 for members, program price; $55.00 for members, individual price. Covers approximately 3,000 civil legal aid and indigent defense organizations in the United States; includes programs for specific groups such as prisoners, senior citizens, the disabled, etc. Entries include: Agency name, address, phone, director's name. Arrangement: Geographical. Indexes: Type of service.

★7050★ USBD-United States Bar Directory

Attorneys National Clearing House Co.
PO Box 142828
Gainesville, FL 32614-2828
Fax: (866)859-2624   Fr: (866)860-2624
E-mail: usbd@usbardirectory.com
URL: http://www.usbardirectory.com

Annual, January. Covers over 3,000 general and specialized practice attorneys employed through correspondence (letter, phone, fax or e-mail). Entries include: Firm name, address, phone, preferred fields of practice, fax, e-mail, Web site. Arrangement: Geographical.

★7051★ Who's Who in American Law

Marquis Who's Who L.L.C.
890 Mountain Ave., Ste. 300
New Providence, NJ 07974-1218
Ph: (908)673-1001   Fax: (908)673-1189
Fr: 800-473-7020
E-mail: law@marquiswhoswho.com
URL: http://www.marquiswhoswho.com/

Biennial; latest edition 2007-2008. $345.00 for individuals. Covers over 15,000 lawyers, judges, law school deans and professors, and other legal professionals. Entries include: Name, home and office addresses, place and date of birth, educational background, career history, civic positions, professional memberships, publications, awards, special achievements. Arrangement: Alphabetical. Indexes: Fields of practice; professional area.

★7052★ Wright-Holmes Law List

Wright-Holmes Inc.
1020 8th Ave. S, Ste. 10
Naples, FL 34102-6959
Ph: (239)434-8880   Fax: (239)434-5983
Fr: 800-882-5478
URL: http://www.collectioncenter.com/index.htm

Annual, April. Free. Covers over 1,400 law firms throughout the U.S., Canada and 35 other countries. Entries include: Firm name, address, phone. A commercial law list. Arrangement: Geographical.

HANDBOOKS AND MANUALS

★7053★ Basic Administrative Law for Paralegals

Aspen Publishers Inc.
76 Ninth Ave., 7th Fl.
New York, NY 10011
Ph: (212)771-0600   Fax: (212)771-0885
Fr: 800-234-1660
URL: http://www.aspenpublishers.com/

Anne Adams. Third edition, 2006. $88.95. 360 Pages. Explore the basics of Administrative Law.

★7054★ Career Opportunities for Writers

Facts On File Inc.
132 W. 31st St., 17th Fl.
New York, NY 10001-2006
Ph: (212)967-8800   Fax: 800-678-3633
Fr: 800-322-8755
E-mail: custserv@factsonfile.com
URL: http://www.factsonfile.com

Rosemary Ellen Guiley and Janet Frick. 2nd edition, 1991. $49.50. 230 pages. Part of the Career Opportunities Series. Describes more than 100 jobs in eight major fields, offering such details as duties, salaries, perquisites, employment and advancement opportunities, organizations to join, and opportunities for women and minorities.

★7055★ Careers in Law

The McGraw-Hill Companies
PO Box 182604
Columbus, OH 43272
Fax: (614)759-3749   Fr: 877-883-5524
E-mail: customer.service@mcgraw-hill.com
URL: http://www.mcgraw-hill.com

Gary Munneke. Third edition, 2003. $15.95 (paper). 192 pages. Overview of opportunities available to lawyers in private practice, corporate law, in federal, state, and local governments, and in teaching. Provides information on the typical law school curriculum plus opportunities in internships and clerkships.

★7056★ Effective Interviewing for Paralegals

Anderson Publishing Co.
2035 Reading Rd.
Cincinnati, OH 45202-1576
Ph: (513)421-4142   Fax: (513)562-8116
Fr: 800-582-7295

Fred E. Jandt. Second edition, 1994. $28.95. 300 pages.

★7057★ Everything You Need to Know About Being a Legal Assistant

Cengage Learning
PO Box 6904
Florence, KY 41022
Fax: 800-487-8488   Fr: 800-354-9706
URL: http://www.cengage.com

Chere B. Estrin. 1995. $69.95 (paper). 206 pages.

★7058★ A Guide to a Successful Legal Internship

Anderson Publishing Co.
2035 Reading Rd.
Cincinnati, OH 45202-1576
Ph: (513)421-4142   Fax: (513)562-8116
Fr: 800-582-7295

Hedi Nasheri and Peter C. Kratcoski. 1996. $22.95 (paper). 171 pages.

★7059★ How to Find a Job As a Paralegal: A Step-by-Step Job Search

Cengage Learning
PO Box 6904
Florence, KY 41022
Fax: 800-487-8488   Fr: 800-354-9706
URL: http://www.cengage.com

Marie Kisiel. 1996. $67.95. 224 pages.

★7060★ The Independent Paralegal's Handbook

Nolo.com
950 Parker St.
Berkeley, CA 94710
Ph: (510)549-1976   Fax: 800-645-0895
Fr: 800-728-3555
URL: http://www.nolo.com

Ralph E. Warner, Stephen Elias and Catherine Elias-Jermany. Sixth edition, 2004. $34.99. 360 pages. Part of the Independent Paralegal's Handbook Series.

★7061★ Introduction to Paralegalism: Perspectives, Problems, & Skills

Cengage Learning
PO Box 6904
Florence, KY 41022
Fax: 800-487-8488   Fr: 800-354-9706
URL: http://www.cengage.com

William P. Statsky. 2002. $138.95. 916 pages.

★7062★ Life Outside the Law Firm: Non-Traditional Careers for Paralegals

Cengage Learning
PO Box 6904
Florence, KY 41022
Fax: 800-487-8488   Fr: 800-354-9706
URL: http://www.cengage.com

Karen Treffinger. 1995. $26.75 (paper). 237 pages.

★7063★ Opportunities in Paralegal Careers

The McGraw-Hill Companies
PO Box 182604
Columbus, OH 43272
Fax: (614)759-3749   Fr: 877-883-5524
E-mail: customer.service@mcgraw-hill.com
URL: http://www.mcgraw-hill.com

Alice Fins. 2005. $13.95 (paper). 160 pages. Defines job opportunities and provides advice about identifying and obtaining positions. Includes bibliography and illustrations.

★7064★ Paralegal Career for Dummies

For Dummies
111 River St.
Hoboken, NJ 07030
Ph: (201)748-6000   Fax: (201)748-6817
E-mail: info@wiley.com
URL: http://www.dummies.com/WileyCDA/

Scott Hatch and Lisa Hatch. 2006. $24.99. Comprehensive guide to becoming a paralegal; includes CD-ROM with forms.

★7065★ Paralegal Career Guide

Prentice Hall PTR
1 Lake St.
Upper Saddle River, NJ 07458
Ph: (201)236-7000   Fax: 800-445-6991
Fr: 800-428-5331
URL: http://www.phptr.com/index.asp?rl=1

Chere B. Estrin. Third edition, 2001. $42.40 (paper). 442 pages. Includes information on jobhunting contacts, sample resumes, and salary data.

★7066★ Paralegal Career Starter

LearningExpress, LLC
55 Broadway, 8th Fl.
New York, NY 10006
Ph: (212)995-2566   Fax: (212)995-5512
Fr: 800-295-9556
E-mail: customerservice@learningexpressllc.com
URL: http://www.learningexpressllc.com

LearningExpress Editors. Third Updated edition, 2006. $15.95. 208 pages.

★7067★ The Paralegal Internship Manual

Prentice Hall PTR
One Lake St.
Upper Saddle River, NJ 07458
URL: http://vig.prenhall.com/

Deborah Orlik. 2006. $26.67.

★7068★ Paralegal Internships: Finding, Managing & Transitioning Your Career

Cengage Learning
PO Box 6904
Florence, KY 41022
Fax: 800-487-8488   Fr: 800-354-9706
URL: http://www.cengage.com

Ruth-Ellen Post. 1998. $51.95 (paper). 288 pages. Part of the Paralegal Series. Text covers all stages of the internship experience, including identifying learning objectives, finding the "right office," managing "office politics," self-monitoring and documentation an finally how to use the internship to land a permanent job.

★7069★ Paralegal Practice and Procedure: A Practical Guide for The Legal Assistant

Prentice Hall PTR
1 Lake St.
Upper Saddle River, NJ 07458
Ph: (201)236-7000   Fax: 800-445-6991
Fr: 800-428-5331
URL: http://www.phptr.com/index.asp?rl=1

Deborah E. Larbalestier. Third edition, 1994. $40.00 (paper). 576 pages.

★7070★ A Paralegal Primer

The Center for Legal Studies
22316 Sunset Dr.
Golden, CO 80401
Ph: (303)273-9777   Fax: (303)271-1777
Fr: 800-522-7737

E-mail: info@legalstudies.com
URL: http://www.legalstudies.com/

Scott A. Hatch. Third edition, 2006. $19.00 (paper). 182 pages.

★7071★ The Paralegal's Guide to U.S. Government Jobs: How to Land a Job in 140 Law-Related Career Fields

Federal Reports, Inc.
1010 Vermont Ave. NW, Ste. 408
Washington, DC 20005
Ph: (202)393-3311

Richard L. Hermann, Jeanette J. Sobajian and Linda P. Sutherland. Seventh edition, 1996. $19.95. 140 pages. Explains U.S. Government procedures and describes 140 law-related federal careers for which paralegals may qualify. Includes a directory of several hundred Federal Agency personnel offices that hire the most paralegal and law-related talents.

★7072★ The Practical Paralegal: Strategies for Success

Aspen Publishers Inc.
76 Ninth Ave., 7th Fl.
New York, NY 10011
Ph: (212)771-0786   Fax: (212)771-0796
Fr: 800-538-8437
URL: http://www.aspenpublishers.com

Deborah E. Bouchoux. 2005. $77.95.

★7073★ The Professional Paralegal Workbook

Cengage Learning
PO Box 6904
Florence, KY 41022
Fax: 800-487-8488   Fr: 800-354-9706
URL: http://www.cengage.com/

Elizabeth Angus. 2006. $26.95. Workbook for paralegals covering criminal, tort, and contract law.

★7074★ Real People Working in Law

The McGraw-Hill Companies
PO Box 182604
Columbus, OH 43272
Fax: (614)759-3749   Fr: 877-883-5524
E-mail: customer.service@mcgraw-hill.com
URL: http://www.mcgraw-hill.com

Blythe Camenson, Jan Goldberg. 1997. $12.95 (paper). 160 pages. Interviews and profiles of working professionals capture a range of opportunities in this field.

★7075★ Real-Resumes for Legal and Paralegal Jobs

PREP Publishing
1110 1/2 Hay St., PMB 66
Fayetteville, NC 28305
Ph: (910)483-6611   Fax: (910)483-2439
Fr: 800-533-2814

March 2004. $16.95 (paper). 192 pages. Real-Resumes Series.

★7076★ Style and Sense For the Legal Profession: A Handbook for Court Reporters, Transcribers, Paralegals and Secretaries

ETC Publications
1456 Rodeo Rd.
Palm Springs, CA 92262
Ph: (760)316-9695   Fax: (760)316-9681
Fr: (866)514-9969
URL: http://www.etcpublications.com/

Audrey Fatooh and Barbara R. Mauk. Revised, 1996. $22.95. 228 pages

★7077★ The Successful Paralegal Job Search Guide

Cengage Learning
PO Box 6904
Florence, KY 41022
Fax: 800-487-8488   Fr: 800-354-9706
URL: http://www.cengage.com

Chere B. Estrin and Stacey Hunt. 2000. $48.95. 432 pages.

★7078★ Your Opportunities in Legal Support

Energeia Publishing, Inc.
1307 Fairmount Ave., S
Salem, OR 97302-4313
Ph: (503)362-1480   Fax: (503)362-2123
Fr: 800-639-6048

Laurie Bean. 1994. $2.00 (paper). 8 pages.

EMPLOYMENT AGENCIES AND SEARCH FIRMS

★7079★ Attorney Resources, Inc.

750 North St. Paul, Ste. 540
Dallas, TX 75201
Ph: (214)922-8050   Fax: (214)871-3041
Fr: 800-324-4828
E-mail: dallas@attorneyresource.com
URL: http://www.attorneyresource.com

Employment agency. Offices in Austin, Dallas, Fort Worth, Houston and Tulsa, OK. Provides staffing assistance on regular or temporary basis.

★7080★ Beverly Hills Bar Association Personnel Service

300 S. Beverly Dr., Ste. 201
Beverly Hills, CA 90212-4805
Ph: (310)601-2422   Fax: (310)601-2423
URL: http://www.bhba.org

Employment agency.

★7081★ Bill Young and Associates

273 Oak Dale Lane
Stuarts Draft, VA 24477
Ph: (540)255-9909
E-mail: billyoung@ntelos.net
URL: http://www.billyoung.com

Employment agency. Executive recruiter.

★7082★ Bishop Partners

708 3rd Ave., Ste. 2200
New York, NY 10017
Ph: (212)986-3419   Fr: (212)986-3350
E-mail: info@bishoppartners.com
URL: http://www.bishoppartners.com

Executive search firm focuses on legal and accounting fields.

★7083★ Coleman Legal Search Consultants

15th & JFK Blvd., Ste. 1010
Philadelphia, PA 19102
Ph: (215)864-2700   Fax: (215)864-2709
E-mail: search@cnlegalsearch.com
URL: http://www.colemanlegal.com

Legal executive search firm.

★7084★ Cook Associates Inc.

212 W Kinzie St.
Chicago, IL 60610
Ph: (312)329-0900   Fax: (312)329-1528
E-mail: info@cookassociates.com
URL: http://www.cookassociates.com

Management and executive recruiting specialists offering a commitment to clients to find the best candidates and to find those candidates as efficiently as possible. Approach provides a flexible and effective structure that serves the special needs of both large and small companies. Serves the following industries: industrial, equipment manufacturer, food processing, graphic arts, chemical process, retailing, mechanical products, healthcare services, financial and professional services, legal, consumer products, construction and engineering, packaging, pulp and paper.

★7085★ Early Cochran & Olson LLC

1 E. Wacker Dr., Ste. 2510
Chicago, IL 60601
Ph: (312)595-4200   Fax: (312)595-4209
E-mail: info@ecollc.com
URL: http://www.ecollc.com

Executive search firm focused specifically on the legal field.

★7086★ Gibson Arnold & Associates Inc.

1111 Washington, Ste. 220
Golden, CO 80401
Ph: (303)273-9420   Fax: (303)273-9424
Fr: 888-324-9420
E-mail: golden@gibsonarnold.com
URL: http://www.gibsonarnold.com

Legal temporary service supplies attorneys, paralegals, and production clerks to major law firms and corporations nationwide. Also maintains a full-time placement division. Assists law firms and corporations with staffing any in-house needs.

★7087★ Gillard Associates Legal Search

75 McNeil Way
Dedham, MA 02026
Ph: (781)329-4731   Fax: (617)329-1357
E-mail: gillardlgl@aol.com

Search firm.

★7088★ Ingle-Terrell & Associates

3100 Sunset Dr.
Charlotte, NC 28209-1208
Ph: (704)333-8400

Provides assistance in recruitment and placement of personnel. Industries served: insurance and law.

★7089★ Legal Medical Urgent Staffing Solutions

The 1605 Bldg., 1605 Evesham Rd.
Voorhees, NJ 08043
Ph: (856)795-0909   Fax: (856)795-0922
Fr: 877-674-4464
URL: http://www.legalmedicalstaffing.com

Offers a specialized service providing temporary and full-time support exclusively to the legal, dental, and medical professions.

★7090★ Legal Placement Services, Inc.

6737 W. Washington St., Ste. 2390
West Allis, WI 53214
Ph: (414)276-6689   Fax: (414)276-1418
E-mail: info@legalplacementservices.com
URL: http://www.legalplacementservices.com

Employment agency. Periodically fills temporary placements, as well.

★7091★ Synectics for Management Decisions Inc.

1901 N Moore St., Ste. 900
Arlington, VA 22209
Ph: (703)528-2772   Fax: (703)528-2857
E-mail: info@smdi.com
URL: http://www.smdi.com

Organizational analysis and development consulting firm specializing in economic and international expertise, executive search, management information systems, data processing, training, economic expertise to legal profession, business brokerage, mergers and acquisitions, and leasing services. Serves private industries as well as government agencies.

ONLINE JOB SOURCES AND SERVICES

★7092★ EmpLawyerNet.com

2331 Westwood Blvd., No. 331
Los Angeles, CA 90064
Fr: 800-270-2688
E-mail: membership@emplawyernet.com
URL: http://www.emplawyernet.com/

Description: Career resource site for lawyers. Contains career information, resume posting and job board search, along with links to CLE events, online bookstores, and recruiter directories. **Fee:** Limited access permitted with free basic membership. Premier membership is $59 or $14.95/month and includes free CLE courses, e-mail alerts, networking opportunities and personal career advice.

★7093★ Law.com: Law Jobs

URL: http://www.lawjobs.com
Description: Visitors can post job openings for attorneys, legal support staff and temporary workers. Also resources for legal recruiters and temporary staffing agencies.

★7094★ The Legal Employment Search Site

E-mail: webmaster@legalemploy.com
URL: http://www.legalemploy.com
Description: Contains links to job search and career-related websites for lawyers and legal support staff.

TRADESHOWS

★7095★ American Association for Paralegal Education Convention

American Association for Paralegal Education
19 Mantua Rd.
Mount Royal, NJ 08061
Ph: (856)423-2829   Fax: (856)423-3420
E-mail: info@aafpe.org
URL: http://www.aafpe.org/

Annual. **Primary Exhibits:** Computer hardware and software; paralegal publications and educational materials; related supplies.

★7096★ Association of Legal Administrators Meeting

Association of Legal Administrators
75 Tri-State International, Ste. 222
Lincolnshire, IL 60069-4435
Ph: (847)267-1252   Fax: (847)267-1329
URL: http://www.alanet.org

Annual. **Primary Exhibits:** Computers, hardware, and software; office equipment and supplies; publications, printers, and engravers; insurance; travel consultants; litigation support; facilities management; hotels; and coffee suppliers. **Dates and Locations:** 2008 May 05-08; Seattle, WA; Washington State Convention and Trade Center.

OTHER SOURCES

★7097★ American Almanac of Jobs and Salaries

HarperCollins
10 E. 53rd St.
New York, NY 10022
Ph: (212)207-7000   Fr: 800-242-7737
URL: http://www.harpercollins.com/

John W. Wright. Revised edition, 2000. $20.00 (paper). 672 pages. This is a comprehensive guide to the wages of hundreds of occupations in a wide variety of industries and organizations.

★7098★ Media Law Resource Center (MLRC)

North Tower, 20th Fl.
520 Eight Ave.
New York, NY 10018
Ph: (212)337-0200   Fax: (212)337-9893
E-mail: medialaw@medialaw.org
URL: http://www.medialaw.org

Description: Provides support for media defendants in libel and privacy cases, including development of statistical and empirical data, assistance in locating expert witnesses or consultants, and help in coordinating amicus curiae briefs by supporting organizations. Maintains a brief, pleading, and information bank; collects and disseminates information on pending libel and privacy cases for use in legal defense against claims. Serves as a liaison with media organizations, attorneys, and other groups working to advance the defense of libel and privacy claims. Prepares bulletins and reports on current developments and cases, legal theories, privileges, and defenses. Compiles statistics on the incidence and cost of libel and privacy litigation. Provides employment for law student interns. Conducts educational and training workshops and programs; has established fellowship program in libel law. Operates MLRC Institute.

★7099★ National Association of Legal Assistants (NALA)

1516 S Boston, Ste. 200
Tulsa, OK 74119
Ph: (918)587-6828   Fax: (918)582-6772
E-mail: nalanet@nala.org
URL: http://www.nala.org

Members: Professional paralegals employed for over six months; graduates or students of legal assistant training programs; attorneys. Members subscribe to and are bound by the NALA Code of Ethics and Professional Responsibility. **Purpose:** Cooperates with local, state, and national bar associations in setting standards and guidelines for legal assistants. Promotes the profession and attempts to broaden public understanding of the function of the legal assistant. **Activities:** Offers continuing education for legal assistants both nationwide and statewide, and professional certification on a national basis to members and nonmembers who meet certain criteria.

★7100★ National Association of Legal Investigators (NALI)

PO Box 8479
Portland, ME 04104
Fax: (207)893-1457   Fr: 888-244-5685
E-mail: info@nalionline.org
URL: http://www.nalionline.org

Description: Legal investigators, both independent and law firm staff, who specialize in investigation of personal injury matters for the plaintiff and criminal defense. Promotes professionalization of the legal investigator, accomplished by seminars and a professional certification program. Provides nationwide network of contact among members. Compiles statistics.

★7101★ National Federation of Paralegal Associations (NFPA)

PO Box 2016
Edmonds, WA 98020
Ph: (425)967-0045   Fax: (425)771-9588

E-mail: info@paralegals.org
URL: http://www.paralegals.org

Members: State and local paralegal associations and other organizations supporting the goals of the federation; individual paralegals. **Purpose:** Works to serve as a national voice of the paralegal profession; to advance, foster, and promote the paralegal concept; to monitor and participate in developments in the paralegal profession; to maintain a nationwide communications network among paralegal associations and other members of the legal community. **Activities:** Provides a resource center of books, publications, and literature of the field. Monitors activities of local, state, and national bar associations and legislative bodies; presents testimony on matters affecting the profession. Developed PACE exam for Registered Paralegal credentials.

★7102★ Paralegal

Cambridge Educational
PO Box 2053
Princeton, NJ 08543-2053
Ph: 800-257-5126   Fax: (609)671-0266
Fr: 800-468-4227
E-mail: custserv@films.com
URL: http://www.cambridgeeducational.com

VHS and DVD. $39.95. 15 minutes. 1989. Part of the Vocational Visions Career Series.

★7103★ Technical & Related Occupations

Delphi Productions
3159 6th St.
Boulder, CO 80304
Ph: (303)443-2100   Fax: (303)443-4022
Fr: 888-443-2400
E-mail: support@delphivideo.com
URL: http://www.delphivideo.com

$95.00. 49 minutes. Part of the Careers for the 21st Century Video Library.

Librarians

SOURCES OF HELP-WANTED ADS

★7104★ AALL Spectrum

American Association of Law Libraries
53 W Jackson Blvd., Ste. 940
Chicago, IL 60604
Ph: (312)939-4764   Fax: (312)431-1097
URL: http://www.aallnet.org/products/pub_
spectrum.asp

Description: Ten issues/year, monthly with an exception of January and August. Presents news of interest to law libraries. Includes job listings and announcements from the Association's officers, chapters, and committees.

★7105★ The Abbey Newsletter

Abbey Publications Inc.
7105 Geneva Dr.
Austin, TX 78723
Ph: (512)929-3992   Fax: (512)929-3995
E-mail: abbeypub@grandecom.net
URL: http://palimpsest.stanford.edu/byorg/
abbey/

Description: Six issues/year. Encourages the development of library and archival conservation, particularly technical advances and cross-disciplinary research in the field. Covers book repair and the conservation of books, papers, photographs, and non-paper materials. Recurring features include book reviews, news of research, job listings, convention reports, a calendar of events, and an occasional column about equipment and supplies.

★7106★ American Theological Library Association Newsletter

American Theological Library Association
300 S. Wacker Dr., Ste. 2100
Chicago, IL 60606-6701
Ph: (312)454-5100   Fax: (312)454-5505
Fr: 888-665-2852
E-mail: atla@atla.com
URL: http://www.atla.com/member/publica-
tions/newsletter.html

Description: Quarterly. Presents news of interest to library professionals at theological schools. Recurring features include notices of publications available and job listings. Also available via e-mail.

★7107★ Base Line

Map and Geography Round Table
c/o James A. Coombs
SW Missiouri State Univ.
Maps Library
Springfield, MO 65804-0095
Ph: (417)280-3205   Fax: (417)280-3257
Fr: 800-545-2433
E-mail: library@ala.org.
URL: http://www.ala.org/ala/alalibrary/ala-
periodicals/alaperiodicals.htm

Description: Bimonthly. Provides current information on cartographic materials, publications of interest to map and geography librarians, related government activities, and map librarianship. Recurring features include conference and meeting information, news of research, job listings, and columns by the Division chair and the editor.

★7108★ Book Marks

South Dakota Library Association
PO Box 1212
Rapid City, SD 57709
Ph: (605)343-3750
E-mail: bkstand@rap.midco.net
URL: http://www.sdlibraryassociation.org

Description: Bimonthly. Carries news by and for South Dakota public, school, academic, and special libraries. Discusses statewide library issues, reviews South Dakota books, and advises members of continuing education opportunities. Recurring features include columns, a calendar of events, news from libraries, and job listings.

★7109★ Change

Heldref Publications
1319 18th St., NW
Washington, DC 20036-1802
Ph: (202)296-6267   Fr: 800-365-9753
E-mail: ch@heldref.org
URL: http://www.heldref.org/change.php

Bimonthly. $58.00/year for individuals, print only; $144.00/year for institutions, print only; $62.00/year for individuals, print and online; $173.00/year for institutions, print and online. Magazine dealing with contemporary issues in higher learning.

★7110★ Children and Libraries

American Library Association
50 E Huron St.
Chicago, IL 60611
Fr: 800-545-2433
URL: http://www.ala.org

$50.00/year for elsewhere; $40.00/year for nonmembers. Journal that focuses on the continuing education of librarians working with children.

★7111★ Choice

Association of College and Research
  Libraries
50 E Huron St.
Chicago, IL 60611-2795
Ph: (312)280-2523   Fax: (312)280-2520
Fr: 800-545-2433
URL: http://www.ala.org/ala/acrl/acrlpubs/
choice/about.htm

Online journal providing reviews of academic books, electronic media, and internet resources.

★7112★ The Chronicle of Higher Education

The Chronicle of Higher Education
1255 23rd St. NW 7th Fl.
Washington, DC 20037-1125
Ph: (202)466-1050   Fax: (202)452-1033
Fr: 800-728-2803
URL: http://chronicle.com

Weekly. $82.50/year for individuals, 49 issues; $45.00/year for individuals, 24 issues; $41.25/year for students, 49 issues; $22.50/year for students, 24 issues. Higher education magazine (tabloid).

★7113★ Computers in Libraries

Information Today Inc.
143 Old Marlton Pke.
Medford, NJ 08055-8750
Ph: (609)654-6266   Fax: (609)654-4309
Fr: 800-300-9868
URL: http://www.infotoday.com/cilmag/default.shtml

Monthly. $100.00/year for individuals, computers in libraries; $118.00 for individuals, 2 years, U.S.; $288.00 for individuals, 3 years, U.S.; $114.00/year for Canada and Mexico; $124.00/year for individuals, outside North America; $68.00/year for individuals; $128.00 for individuals, 2 years; $196.00 for individuals, 3 years; $86.00/year for individuals, Canada and Mexico; $99.00/year for individuals, outside North America. Library science magazine that provides complete coverage of the news and issues in the rapidly evolving field of library information technology.

★7114★ IFLA Journal

Sage Publications Inc.
2455 Teller Rd.
Thousand Oaks, CA 91320
Ph: (805)499-0721   Fax: (805)499-8096
URL: http://www.ifla.org

Quarterly. $315.00/year for institutions, print & e-access; $331.00/year for institutions, print & all online; $284.00/year for institutions, e-access; $300.00/year for institutions, backfile lease, e-access plus backfile all online; $579.00/year for institutions, backfile purchase, e-access (content through 1999); $309.00/year for institutions, print only; $84.00/year for individuals, print only; $85.00 for single issue, institutional; $27.00 for single issue, individual. Journal of the International Federation of Library Associations and Institutions (IFLA).

★7115★ Information Technology Newsletter

Idea Group Publishing
701 E Chocolate Ave., Ste. 200
Hershey, PA 17033-1240
Ph: (717)533-8845   Fax: (717)533-8661
Fr: (866)342-6657
E-mail: cust@igi-global.com
URL: http://www.idea-group.com/

Description: 2/year. Discusses cybrary networks, library practices, information access, and new technology product releases. Recurring features include letters to the editor, interviews, news of research, a calendar of events, news of educational opportunities, and book reviews.

★7116★ Information Today

Information Today Inc.
143 Old Marlton Pke.
Medford, NJ 08055-8750
Ph: (609)654-6266   Fax: (609)654-4309
Fr: 800-300-9868
URL: http://www.infotoday.com

Monthly. $75.00/year for individuals; $106.00/year for Canada and Mexico; $150.00 for two years, individuals; $116.00/

year for two years, outside North America. User and producer magazine (tabloid) covering electronic and optical information services.

★7117★ Inter-Com

District of Columbia Library Association
Box 14177
Benjamin Franklin Station
Washington, DC 20044
Ph: (202)872-1112
URL: http://www.dcla.org/

Description: Eleven issues/year (monthly with July/August combined). Deals with libraries and librarians in the Washington D.C., area. Recurring features include a calendar of events, reports of meetings, job listings, and notices of publications available.

★7118★ Journal of Access Services

The Haworth Press Inc.
10 Alice St.
Binghamton, NY 13904
Ph: (607)722-5857   Fr: 800-429-6784
URL: http://www.haworthpress.com/store/product.asp?sid=9EQS2STUT

Quarterly. $69.00/year for individuals; $101.00/year for individuals, Canada; $106.00/year for other countries, individual; $190.00/year for institutions, agency, library; $283.00/year for institutions, other countries, agency, library; $268.00/year for institutions, Canada, agency, library. Journal focusing on the basic business of providing library users with access to information and helping librarians stay up to date on continuing education and professional development in the field of access services.

★7119★ Journal of Classification

Classification Society of North America
c/o Stanley Sclove
IDS Dept., University of Illinois M/C 294
CSNA Business Office
601 South Morgan St.
Chicago, IL 60607-7124
Ph: (312)996-2676   Fax: (312)413-0385
URL: http://www.cs-na.org

Semiannual. Journal of the Classification Society of North America.

★7120★ Journal of Interlibrary Loan, Document Delivery & Electronic Reserve

The Haworth Press Inc.
10 Alice St.
Binghamton, NY 13904
Ph: (607)722-5857   Fr: 800-429-6784
URL: http://www.haworthpress.com/store/product.asp?sid=PC3BHEAN6

Quarterly. $40.00/year for individuals; $58.00/year for individuals, Canada; $62.00/year for individuals, elsewhere; $275.00/year for institutions, agency, library; $399.00/year for institutions, Canada, agency, library; $426.00/year for institutions, other countries, agency, library. Journal focusing on a broad spectrum of library and information center functions that rely heavily on interlibrary

loans, document delivery, and electronic reserve.

★7121★ Journal of Librarianship and Information Science

Sage Publications Inc.
2455 Teller Rd.
Thousand Oaks, CA 91320
Ph: (805)499-0721   Fax: (805)499-8096
URL: http://www.sagepub.com/journalsProdDesc.nav?prodId=Journal20

Quarterly. $539.00/year for institutions, print & e-access; $566.00/year for institutions, print & all online; $485.00/year for institutions, e-access; $512.00/year for institutions, e-access & all online; $1,237.00/year for institutions, e-access; $528.00/year for institutions, print only; $84.00/year for individuals, print only; $146.00 for institutions, single print; $27.00 for individuals, single print. Journal for librarians, information scientists, specialists, managers, and educators.

★7122★ Law Librarians' Bulletin Board

Legal Information Services
PO Box 2383
Chapel Hill, NC 27517-2383
Ph: (919)672-3035   Fax: (919)408-0267
E-mail: info@legalinformationservices.com
URL: http://www.legalinformationservices.com/Publications/librarians-newsletter.php

Description: 8/year. Tracks current events in law librarianship. Recurring features include job listings.

★7123★ Library Journal

Reed Business Information
360 Park Ave. S
New York, NY 10010
Ph: (646)746-6400   Fax: (646)746-7431
E-mail: ljinfo@reedbusiness.com
URL: http://www.libraryjournal.com

$149.99/year for U.S., per year; $199.99/year for Canada, per year; $259.99/year for individuals, international air delivery; $171.00/year for Canada, 1 year. Library management and book selection journal.

★7124★ Library Management Reports

Library Specialists Inc.
PO Box 666100
Marietta, GA 30066
Ph: (678)290-8001   Fax: (678)290-8004
E-mail: info@libraryspecialists.com
URL: http://www.libraryspecialists.com

Description: Quarterly. Devotes each issue to a single topic in law librarianship and legal information services.

★7125★ MLA News

Medical Library Association
65 E Wacker Pl., Ste. 1900
Chicago, IL 60601-7246
Ph: (312)419-9094   Fax: (312)419-8950
E-mail: info@mlahq.org
URL: http://www.mlanet.org/publications/

mlanews/index.html

Description: Monthly, except June/July and November/December, which are combined issues. Covers topics about the association, the health sciences information industry, legislation, and international events. Regular features include updates and reviews of new information technology, medical publication trends, classifieds, educational opportunities, and Internet resources.

★7126★ MLA Newsletter

Music Library Association
8551 Research Way, Ste. 180
Middleton, WI 53562
Ph: (608)836-5825   Fax: (608)831-8200
E-mail: mla@areditions.com
URL: http://www.musiclibraryassoc.org/

Description: Quarterly. Serves as an information exchange among music librarians. Published to keep members abreast of events, ideas, and trends related to music librarianship. Presents Association committee and round table updates, chapter news, and listings of music-related articles appearing in non-music journals. Recurring features include notices of publications available, a calendar of events, news of members, and columns titled The President Reports and Placement Service News.

★7127★ The One-Person Library

Information Bridges International Inc.
477 Harris Rd.
Cleveland, OH 44143-2537
Ph: (216)486-7443   Fax: (216)486-8810
E-mail: jsiess@ibi-opl.com
URL: http://www.ibi-opl.com

Description: Monthly. Provides reports on the literature, management thoughts, case studies, book reviews, and general information for the librarian who works alone. Functions as a forum for the exchange of ideas and information for the reader. Recurring features include Thinking About, Heard on the Lists, Found on the Web, Technology Matters!, An OPL Profile, OPL Management Tips, Professional Reading.

★7128★ The Outrider

Wyoming State Library
516 S. Greeley Hwy.
Cheyenne, WY 82002
Ph: (307)777-6333   Fax: (307)777-6289
URL: http://will.state.wy.us/slpub/outrider/index.html

Description: Biennial. Provides news about the activities of the Wyoming State Library, its board, other tax-supported libraries in the state, the American Library Association, and the library field in general. Recurring features include job listings, meetings, workshops, and other events; personnel news; reports on consultant activities and acquisitions news; and columns titled News Briefs, Around the State.

★7129★ The Reference Librarian

The Haworth Press Inc.
10 Alice St.
Binghamton, NY 13904
Ph: (607)722-5857   Fr: 800-429-6784
URL: http://www.haworthpress.com/store/product.asp?sid=3FVKLBCEM

Quarterly. $109.00/year for individuals; $159.00/year for Canada, individual; $168.00/year for other countries, individual; $470.00/year for institutions, agency, library; $674.00/year for institutions, Canada, agency, library; $717.00/year for institutions, other countries, agency, library. Journal for librarians and students, providing information on the changing field of reference librarianship.

★7130★ Research Strategies

Elsevier Science Inc.
360 Park Ave. S
New York, NY 10010
Ph: (212)989-5800   Fax: (212)633-3990
URL: http://www.elsevier.com

Journal covering library literature and the educational mission of the library.

★7131★ School Library Journal

Reed Business Information
360 Park Ave. S
New York, NY 10010
Ph: (646)746-6400   Fax: (646)746-7431
E-mail: slj@reedbusiness.com
URL: http://www.reedbusiness.com/

Monthly. $129.00/year for individuals, per year; $199.99/year for Canada, per year. A new Canadian Web site launched with the blessing of Microsoft Chairman Bill Gates is using games and cartoons to teach kids about the evils of online predators.

★7132★ SLA Geography & Map Division-Bulletin

Geography & Map Div.
Illinois State Univ.
Campus Box 8900
Normal, IL 61790
Ph: (309)438-3486
E-mail: vmschwa@ilstu.edu
URL: http://www.sla.org/division/dgm/index.htm

Description: Three issues/year. Provides a medium of exchange of information, news, and research in the field of geographic and cartographic bibliography, literature, and libraries. Recurring features include letters to the editor, news of research, a calendar of events, reports of meetings, news of educational opportunities, job listings, book reviews, and notices of publications available.

★7133★ TEST Engineering & Management

The Mattingley Publishing Company Inc.
3756 Grand Ave., Ste. 205
Oakland, CA 94610-1545
Ph: (510)839-0909   Fax: (510)839-2950
URL: http://www.testmagazine.biz/

Bimonthly. $40.00/year for individuals; $55.00/year for other countries; $5.00 for single issue. Trade publication that covers physical and mechanical testing and environmental simulation; edited for test engineering professionals.

PLACEMENT AND JOB REFERRAL SERVICES

★7134★ African Studies Association (ASA)

Douglass Campus
132 George St.
New Brunswick, NJ 08901-1400
Ph: (732)932-8173   Fax: (732)932-3394
E-mail: asaed@rci.rutgers.edu
URL: http://www.africanstudies.org

Members: Persons specializing in teaching, writing, or research on Africa including political scientists, historians, geographers, anthropologists, economists, librarians, linguists, and government officials; persons who are studying African subjects; institutional members are universities, libraries, government agencies, and others interested in receiving information about Africa. **Purpose:** Seeks to foster communication and to stimulate research among scholars on Africa. **Activities:** Sponsors placement service; conducts panels and discussion groups; presents exhibits and films.

★7135★ American Association of Law Libraries (AALL)

53 W Jackson Blvd., Ste. 940
Chicago, IL 60604
Ph: (312)939-4764   Fax: (312)431-1097
E-mail: aallhq@aall.org
URL: http://www.aallnet.org

Members: Librarians who serve the legal profession in the courts, bar associations, law societies, law schools, private law firms, federal, state, and county governments, and business; associate members are legal publishers and other interested persons. **Purpose:** Seeks to advance the profession of law librarianship. **Activities:** Conducts continuing professional development programs for members; maintains placement service.

★7136★ American Library Association (ALA)

50 E Huron St.
Chicago, IL 60611
Ph: (312)944-6780   Fax: (312)440-9374
Fr: 800-545-2433
E-mail: ala@ala.org
URL: http://www.ala.org

Members: Librarians, libraries, trustees, friends of libraries, and others interested in the responsibilities of libraries in the educational, social, and cultural needs of society. **Purpose:** Promotes and improves library service and librarianship. Establishes standards of service, support, education, and welfare for libraries and library personnel; promotes the adoption of such standards in libraries of all kinds; safeguards the professional status of librarians; encourages the recruiting of competent personnel for professional careers in librarianship; promotes popular understanding and public acceptance of the value of library service and librarianship. **Activities:** Works in liaison with federal agencies to initiate the enactment and administration of legislation that will extend library services. Offers placement services.

★7137★ American Society for Information Science and Technology (ASIS&T)

1320 Fenwick Ln., Ste. 510
Silver Spring, MD 20910
Ph: (301)495-0900   Fax: (301)495-0810
E-mail: asis@asis.org
URL: http://www.asis.org

Members: Information specialists, scientists, librarians, administrators, social scientists, and others interested in the use, organization, storage, retrieval, evaluation, and dissemination of recorded specialized information. **Purpose:** Seeks to improve the information transfer process through research, development, application, and education. **Activities:** Provides a forum for the discussion, publication, and critical analysis of work dealing with the theory, practice, research, and development of elements involved in communication of information. Members are engaged in a variety of activities and specialties including classification and coding systems, automatic and associative indexing, machine translation of languages, special librarianship and library systems analysis, and copyright issues. Sponsors National Auxiliary Publications Service, which provides reproduction services and a central depository for all types of information. Maintains placement service. Sponsors numerous special interest groups. Conducts continuing education programs and professional development workshops.

★7138★ Asia/Pacific American Librarians Association (APALA)

MIT Humanities Library
77 Massachusetts Ave., Rm. 14S-222
Cambridge, MA 02139
Ph: (617)253-9352   Fax: (617)253-3109
E-mail: baildon@mit.edu
URL: http://www.apalaweb.org

Description: Librarians and information specialists of Asian Pacific descent working in the U.S.; interested persons. Provides a forum for discussing problems and concerns; supports and encourages library services to Asian Pacific communities; recruits and supports Asian Pacific Americans in the library and information science professions. Offers placement service; compiles statistics. Conducts fundraising for scholarships.

★7139★ Association of College and Research Libraries (ACRL)

50 E Huron St.
Chicago, IL 60611-2795
Ph: (312)280-2523   Fax: (312)280-2520
Fr: 800-545-2433
E-mail: acrl@ala.org
URL: http://www.ala.org/acrl

Description: A division of the American Library Association. **Members:** Academic and research librarians **Purpose:** seeking to improve the quality of service in academic libraries; promotes the professional and career development of academic and research librarians; represent the interests and support the programs of academic and research libraries. **Activities:** Operates placement services; sponsors specialized education and research grants and programs; gathers, compiles, and disseminates statistics. Establishes and adopts standards; maintains publishing program; offers professional development courses.

★7140★ Association of Seventh-Day Adventist Librarians (ASDAL)

Columbia Union College Library
7600 Flower Ave.
Takoma Park, MD 20912-7796
Ph: (301)891-4222   Fax: (301)891-4204
E-mail: lwisel@cuc.edu
URL: http://www.asdal.org

Members: Librarians belonging to the Seventh-Day Adventist church. **Purpose:** Aims to: enhance communication among members; serve as a forum for discussion of mutual problems and professional concerns; promote librarianship and library services to Seventh-Day Adventist institutions. **Activities:** Sponsors D. Glenn Hilts Scholarship for graduate studies. Maintains placement service. Compiles statistics.

★7141★ Chinese American Librarians Association (CALA)

Southern Illinois University - Carbondale
Morris Library
605 Agriculture Dr.
Mailcode 6632
Carbondale, IL 62901
E-mail: shixingwen@yahoo.com
URL: http://www.cala-web.org

Purpose: Promotes better communication among Chinese American librarians in the U.S., serves as a forum for the discussion of mutual problems, and supports the development and promotion of librarianship. **Activities:** Maintains placement referral service.

★7142★ Health Science Communications Association (HeSCA)

39 Wedgewood Dr., Ste. A
Jewett City, CT 06351-2420
Ph: (860)376-5915   Fax: (860)376-6621
E-mail: hesca@hesca.org
URL: http://www.hesca.org

Description: Represents media managers, graphic artists, biomedical librarians, producers, faculty members of health science and veterinary medicine schools, health profes-

sional organizations, and industry representatives. Acts as a clearinghouse for information used by professionals engaged in health science communications. Coordinates Media Festivals Program that recognizes outstanding media productions in the health sciences. Offers placement service.

★7143★ Music Library Association (MLA)

8551 Research Way, Ste. 180
Middleton, WI 53562-3567
Ph: (608)836-5825   Fax: (608)831-8200
E-mail: mla@areditions.com
URL: http://www.musiclibraryassoc.org

Description: Promotes the establishment, growth, and use of music libraries and collection of music, musical instruments, musical literature, and audio-visual aids. Maintains placement service.

★7144★ Special Libraries Association (SLA)

331 S Patrick St.
Alexandria, VA 22314-3501
Ph: (703)647-4900   Fax: (703)647-4901
E-mail: sla@sla.org
URL: http://www.sla.org

Description: International association of information professionals who work in special libraries serving business, research, government, universities, newspapers, museums, and institutions that use or produce specialized information. Seeks to advance the leadership role of special librarians. Offers consulting services to organizations that wish to establish or expand a library or information services. Conducts strategic learning and development courses, public relations, and government relations programs. Provides employment services. Operates knowledge exchange on topics pertaining to the development and management of special libraries. Maintains Hall of Fame.

EMPLOYER DIRECTORIES AND NETWORKING LISTS

★7145★ 50 State Educational Directories

Career Guidance Foundation
8090 Engineer Rd.
San Diego, CA 92111
Ph: (858)560-8051   Fax: (858)278-8960
Fr: 800-854-2670
URL: http://www.cgf.org

Annual. Microfiche. Collection consists of reproductions of the state educational directories published by the departments of education of individual 50 states. Directory contents vary, but the majority contain listings of elementary and secondary schools, colleges and universities, and state education officials. Amount of detail in each also varies. Entries include: Usually, institution name, address, and name of one executive.

★7146★ American Library Directory

Information Today Inc.
143 Old Marlton Pke.
Medford, NJ 08055-8750
Ph: (609)654-6266   Fax: (609)654-4309
Fr: 800-300-9868
URL: http://books.infotoday.com/

Annual; latest edition 59th, 2005-2006. $299.00 for individuals. Covers over 36,000 U.S. and Canadian academic, public, county, provincial, and regional libraries; library systems; medical, law, and other special libraries; and libraries for the blind and physically handicapped. Separate section lists over 350 library networks and consortia and 220 accredited and unaccredited library school programs. Entries include: For libraries–Name, supporting or affiliated institution or firm name, address, phone, fax, e-mail address, Standard Address Number (SAN), names of librarian and department heads, income, collection size, special collections, computer hardware, automated functions, and type of catalog. For library systems–Name, location. For library schools–Name, address, phone, fax, e-mail address, director, type of training and degrees, admission requirements, tuition, faculty size. For networks and consortia–Name, address, phone, names of affiliates, name of director, function. Arrangement: Geographical. Indexes: Institution name. Library Services and Suppliers index.

★7147★ The Basic Business Library

Greenwood Publishing Group Inc.
88 Post Rd. W
Westport, CT 06881
Ph: (203)226-3571
URL: http://www.greenwood.com

Latest edition 4th. $75.00 for individuals. Publication includes: Publisher's Web site as part of each entry. Principal content of publication is list of 210 entries of suggested resources for business libraries, as well as essays on business reference sources and services. Indexes: Alphabetical.

★7148★ Career Opportunities in Library and Information Science

Facts On File Inc.
132 W 31st St., 17th Fl.
New York, NY 10001
Ph: (212)967-8800   Fax: 800-678-3633
Fr: 800-322-8755
URL: http://www.factsonfile.com

Published 2005. $49.50 for individuals; $44.55 for libraries. Covers more than 70 different jobs typically held by librarians, including academic, government, K-12, outside-the-library, public, and special positions.

★7149★ Directory of Federal Libraries

Oryx Press
4041 N Central Ave., Ste. 700
PO Box 33889
Phoenix, AZ 85021-3397
Ph: (602)265-2651   Fax: 800-279-4663
Fr: 800-279-6799

URL: http://isbndb.com/d/book/directory_of_federal_libraries.html

Irregular; latest edition December 2000. Covers nearly 3,000 libraries serving branches of the federal government. Entries include: Library name, type, address, phone, fax, e-mail, telnet, and websites, name of administrator and selected staff, special collections, database services available, depository status for documents from the Government Printing Office or other organizations, involvement with cooperative library organizations, electronic mail or cataloging networks, whether accessible to the public. Arrangement: Classified by federal establishment. Indexes: Library type; subject; geographical; alphabetical index of libraries by name.

★7150★ Directory of Public School Systems in the U.S.

American Association for Employment in Education
3040 Riverside Dr., Ste. 125
Columbus, OH 43221
Ph: (614)485-1111   Fax: (614)485-9609
URL: http://www.aaee.org/

Annual, winter; latest edition 2004-2005 edition. $10.00 for members (plus $2.00/copy for mailing); $20.00 for nonmembers (plus $2.00/copy for mailing). Covers about 14,500 public school systems in the United States and their administrative personnel. Entries include: System name, address, phone, website address, name and title of personnel administrator, levels taught and approximate student population. Arrangement: Geographical by state.

★7151★ Directory of Special Libraries and Information Centers

Gale, Cengage Learning
27500 Drake Rd.
Farmington Hills, MI 48331-3535
Ph: (248)699-4253   Fax: (248)699-8065
Fr: 800-877-4253
E-mail: businessproducts@gale.com
URL: http://www.gale.com

Annual; latest edition 33rd, April 2007. $1210.00 for individuals. Covers over 34,800 special libraries, information centers, documentation centers, etc.; about 500 networks and consortia; major special libraries abroad also included. Volume 1 part 3 contains 6 other appendices (beside networks and consortia): Regional and Subregional Libraries for the Blind and Physically Handicapped, Patent and Trademark Depository Libraries, Regional Government Depository Libraries, United Nations Depository Libraries, World Bank Depository Libraries, and European Community Depository Libraries. Entries include: Library name, address, phone, fax, e-mail address; contact; year founded; sponsoring organization; special collections; subject interests; names and titles of staff; services (copying, online searches); size of collection; subscriptions; computerized services and automated operations; Internet home page address; publications; special catalogs; special indexes. For consortia and networks–Name, address, phone, contact.

Other appendices have varying amounts of directory information. Contents of Volume 1 are available in "Subject Directory of Special Libraries and Information Centers." Arrangement: Libraries are alphabetical by name of sponsoring organization or institution; consortia and networks are geographical. Indexes: Subject. Geographic and personnel indexes constitute volume 2.

★7152★ Guide to Employment Sources in the Library & Information Professions

Office for Human Resource Development and Recruitment
50 E Huron St.
Chicago, IL 60611
Ph: (312)280-4282   Fax: (312)280-3256
Fr: 800-545-2433
URL: http://www.ala.org/hrdr/employment_guide.html

Annual, spring. Covers library job sources, such as specialized and state and regional library associations, state library agencies, federal library agencies, and overseas exchange programs. Entries include: Library, company, or organization name, address, phone; contact name, description of services, publications, etc. This is a reprint of a segment of the "Bowker Annual of Library and Book Trade Information." Arrangement: Classified by type of source.

★7153★ Handbook of Private Schools

Porter Sargent Publishers Inc.
11 Beacon St., Ste. 1400
Boston, MA 02108-3099
Ph: (617)523-1670   Fax: (617)523-1021
Fr: 800-342-7470
E-mail: orders@portersargent.com
URL: http://www.portersargent.com

Annual, latest edition 87th, 2006 edition. $99.00 for individuals. Covers more than 1,600 elementary and secondary boarding and day schools in the United States. Entries include: School name, address, phone, fax, e-mail, URL, type of school (boarding or day), sex and age range, names and titles of administrators, grades offered, academic orientation, curriculum, new admissions yearly, tests required for admission, enrollment and faculty, graduate record, number of alumni, tuition and scholarship figures, summer session, plant evaluation and endowment, date of establishment, calendar, association membership, description of school's offerings and history, test score averages, uniform requirements, and geographical and demographic data. Arrangement: Geographical. Indexes: Alphabetical by school name, cross indexed by state, region, grade range, sexes accepted, school features and enrollment.

★7154★ Higher Education Directory

Higher Education Publications Inc.
6400 Arlington Blvd., Ste. 648
Falls Church, VA 22042-2342
Ph: (703)532-2300   Fax: (703)532-2305
Fr: 888-349-7715
URL: http://www.hepinc.com/hed.htm

Annual; latest edition 2007. $75.00 for individuals. Covers over 4,364 degree granting colleges and universities accredited by approved agencies recognized by the U.S. Secretary of Education and by the Council of Higher Education Accreditation (CHEA); 103 systems offices; over 550 related associations and state government agencies; recognized accrediting agencies. Entries include: For institutions–Name, address, congressional district, phone, fax, year established; Carnegie classification; enrollment; type of student body; religious or other affiliation; undergraduate tuition and fees; type of academic calendar; highest degree offered; accreditations; IRS status; names, titles and job classification codes for academic and administrative officers. For associations and state agencies–Name, address, phone, name of chief executive officer. Same content and coverage as the base volume of the Department of Education's publication "Directory of Postsecondary Institutions". Arrangement: Geographical, alphabetical by state. Indexes: Administrator name (with phone and e-mail addresses), accreditation, FICE numbers, college or university name.

★7155★ **Independent Schools Association of the Southwest-Membership List**

Independent Schools Association of the Southwest
Energy Sq., Ste 406
505 North Big Spring St.
Midland, TX 79701
Ph: (432)684-9550   Fax: (432)684-9401
URL: http://www.isasw.org

Annual, August. Covers over 84 schools located in Arizona, Kansas, Louisiana, Mexico, New Mexico, Oklahoma, and Texas enrolling over 38,000 students. Entries include: School name, address, phone, chief administrative officer, structure, and enrollment. Arrangement: Geographical. Indexes: Alphabetical.

★7156★ **MDR's School Directories**

Market Data Retrieval
1 Forest Pkwy.
Shelton, CT 06484-0947
Ph: (203)926-4800   Fax: (203)926-1826
Fr: 800-333-8802
URL: http://www.schooldata.com

Annual, October. Covers over 90,000 public, 8,000 Catholic, and 15,000 other private schools (grades K-12) in the United States; over 15,000 school district offices, 76,000 school librarians, 27,000 media specialists, and 33,000 technology coordinators. Includes names of over 165,000 school district administrators and staff members in county and state education administration. Entries include: District name and address; telephone and fax number; number of schools; number of teachers in the district; district enrollment; special education students; limited-english proficient students; minority percentage by race; percentage of college bound students; expenditures per student for instructional materials; poverty level; title 1 dollars; site-based management; district

open/close dates; construction indicator; technologies and quantities; district-level administrators, (new superintendents shaded); school name and address (new public shaded); telephone and fax number; principal (new principal shaded); librarian, media specialist and technology coordinator; grade span; special programs and school type; student enrollment; technologies and quantities (instructional computer brand, noting predominant brand); Multi-Media Computers; Internet connection or access; Tech Sophistication Index. Arrangement: Geographical. Indexes: District county; district personnel; principal; new public schools and key personnel; district and school telephone; district URLs.

★7157★ **Midwest Archives Conference-Membership Directory**

Midwest Archives Conference
c/o Menzi Behrnd-Klodt
7422 Longmeadow Rd.
Madison, WI 53717
Ph: (608)827-5727
URL: http://www.midwestarchives.org

Annual. Covers more than 1,000 individual and institutional members, largely librarians, archivists, records managers, manuscripts curators, historians, and museum and historical society personnel, as well as about 25 archival associations in the Midwest. Entries include: For institutions–Name of archives, parent organization, address, phone. For individuals–Name, title, business address, phone. Arrangement: Separate alphabetical sections for individuals and institutions.

★7158★ **Patterson's American Education**

Educational Directories Inc.
PO Box 68097
Schaumburg, IL 60168
Ph: (847)891-1250   Fax: (847)891-0945
Fr: 800-357-6183
URL: http://www.ediusa.com

Annual; latest edition October 2007. $94.00 for individuals. Covers over 11,400 school districts in the United States; more than 34,000 public, private, and Catholic high schools, middle schools, and junior high schools; Approximately 300 parochial superintendents; 400 state department of education personnel. Entries include: For school districts and schools–District and superintendent name, address, phone, fax; grade ranges, enrollment; school names, addresses, phone numbers, names of principals. For postsecondary schools–School name, address, phone number, URL, e-mail, names of administrator or director of admissions. For private and Catholic high schools–name, address, phone, fax, enrollment, grades offered, name of principal. Postsecondary institutions are also covered in 'Patterson's Schools Classified.' Arrangement: Geographical by state, then alphabetical by city.

★7159★ **Patterson's Schools Classified**

Educational Directories Inc.
PO Box 68097
Schaumburg, IL 60168
Ph: (847)891-1250   Fax: (847)891-0945
Fr: 800-357-6183
URL: http://www.ediusa.com

Annual; latest edition 2007, volume 57. $18.00 for individuals. Covers over 7,000 accredited colleges, universities, community colleges, junior colleges, career schools and teaching hospitals. Entries include: School name, address, phone, URL, e-mail, name of administrator or admissions officer, description, professional accreditation (where applicable). Updated from previous year's edition of 'Patterson's American Education'. Arrangement: Classified by area of study, then geographical by state. Indexes: Alphabetical by name.

★7160★ **Requirements for Certification of Teachers, Counselors, Librarians, Administrators for Elementary and Secondary Schools**

University of Chicago Press
Journals Division
1427 E 60th St.
Chicago, IL 60637-2954
Ph: (773)702-7600   Fax: (773)702-0694
Fr: 877-705-1878

Annual, June; latest edition 71st, 2006-07. $47.00. Publication includes: List of state and local departments of education. Entries include: Office name, address, phone. Principal content of publication consists of summaries of each state's teaching and administrative certification requirements. Arrangement: Geographical.

HANDBOOKS AND MANUALS

★7161★ **Career Opportunities for Writers**

Facts On File Inc.
132 W. 31st St., 17th Fl.
New York, NY 10001-2006
Ph: (212)967-8800   Fax: 800-678-3633
Fr: 800-322-8755
E-mail: custserv@factsonfile.com
URL: http://www.factsonfile.com

Rosemary Ellen Guiley and Janet Frick. 2nd edition, 1991. $49.50. 230 pages. Part of the Career Opportunities Series. Describes more than 100 jobs in eight major fields, offering such details as duties, salaries, perquisites, employment and advancement opportunities, organizations to join, and opportunities for women and minorities.

★7162★ **Careers in Health Care**

The McGraw-Hill Companies
PO Box 182604
Columbus, OH 43272
Fax: (614)759-3749   Fr: 877-883-5524
E-mail: customer.service@mcgraw-hill.com
URL: http://www.mcgraw-hill.com

Barbara M. Swanson. Fifth edition, 2005. $15.95 (paper). 192 pages. Describes job duties, work settings, salaries, licensing and certification requirements, educational preparation, and future outlook. Gives ideas on how to secure a job.

★7163★ *Careers in Music Librarianship II: Traditions and Transitions*

Scarecrow Press, Inc.
4501 Forbes Blvd., Ste. 200
Lanham, MD 20706-4310
Ph: (301)459-3366   Fax: (301)429-5747

Blair, Linda. 2004. $34.95 (paper). 168 pages. Explores music librarianship.

★7164★ *Great Jobs for History Majors*

The McGraw-Hill Companies
PO Box 182604
Columbus, OH 43272
Fax: (614)759-3749   Fr: 877-883-5524
E-mail: customer.service@mcgraw-hill.com
URL: http://www.mcgraw-hill.com

Julie DeGalan and Stephen Lambert. 2001. $15.95 (paper). 256 pages.

★7165★ *Library Employment Within the Law*

Neal-Schuman Publishers, Inc.
100 William St., Ste. 2004
New York, NY 10038
Ph: (212)925-8650   Fax: (212)219-8916
E-mail: info@neal-schuman.com
URL: http://www.neal-schuman.com/

Arlene C. Bielefield and Lawrence G. Cheeseman. 1994. $75.00 (paper). 147 pages.

★7166★ *New Challenges Facing Academic Librarians Today: Electronic Journals, Archival Digitization, Document Delivery, Etc.*

Edwin Mellen Press
PO Box 450
Lewiston, NY 14092-0450
Ph: (716)754-2266   Fax: (716)754-4056
URL: http://www.mellenpress.com/index.cfm

Jean Caswell, Paul G. Haschak, and Dayne Sherman. 2006. $119.95. Collection of essays by individuals offering scholarship in library science, information science, and higher education.

★7167★ *The NextGen Librarian's Survival Guide*

Information Today Inc.
143 Old Marlton Pke.
Medford, NJ 08055-8750
Ph: (609)654-6266   Fax: (609)654-4309
Fr: 800-300-9868
E-mail: custserv@infotoday.com
URL: http://www.infotoday.com/

Rachel Singer Gordon. 2006. $29.50.

★7168★ *Opportunities in Library and Information Science Careers*

The McGraw-Hill Companies
PO Box 182604
Columbus, OH 43272
Fax: (614)759-3749   Fr: 877-883-5524
E-mail: customer.service@mcgraw-hill.com
URL: http://www.mcgraw-hill.com

Kathleen M. Heim and Margaret Myers. 2001. $13.95 (paper). 145 pages. A guide to planning for and seeking opportunities in this changing field. Includes bibliography and illustrations.

★7169★ *Opportunities in State and Local Government Careers*

The McGraw-Hill Companies
PO Box 182604
Columbus, OH 43272
Fax: (614)759-3749   Fr: 877-883-5524
E-mail: customer.service@mcgraw-hill.com
URL: http://www.mcgraw-hill.com

Neale J. Baxter. Revised edition, 1992. $14.95; $10.95 (paper). 148 pages. Points out the incentives and drawbacks of a government career. Describes hiring procedures and provides tips on filling out applications, taking physical and aptitude tests, handling interviews, and finding jobs. Describes the jobs in which 75% of all state and local government workers are employed. For each occupation, covers the nature of the work and the training required.

★7170★ *Writing Resumes That Work: A How-to-Do-It Manual for Librarians*

Neal-Schuman Publishers, Inc.
100 William St., Ste. 2004
New York, NY 10038
Ph: (212)925-8650   Fax: (212)219-8916
E-mail: info@neal-schuman.com
URL: http://www.neal-schuman.com/

Robert R. Newlen. 2006. $55.00 (paper). 206 pages. Provides ideas for alternate library careers in this new edition of a 1980 publication. Most of the 62 contributors have information science, academic, and other adult-focused backgrounds; four come from the fields of children's and elementary school media services and one from the YA ranks.

EMPLOYMENT AGENCIES AND SEARCH FIRMS

★7171★ **Brattle Temps**

50 Congress St., Ste. 935
Boston, MA 02109-4008
Ph: (617)523-4600   Fax: (617)523-3939
E-mail: temps@brattletemps.com
URL: http://www.brattletemps.com

Personnel consulting firm specializes in providing temporary consultants. Skill areas available include: computer operators, secretaries, editors, librarians, graphic artists, and marketing professionals. Industries

served: universities, publishing, engineering, manufacturing, and government agencies.

★7172★ **C. Berger Group Inc.**

327 E Gundersen Dr.
PO Box 274
Carol Stream, IL 60188
Ph: (630)653-1115   Fax: (630)653-1691
Fr: 800-382-4222
E-mail: cberger@cberger.com
URL: http://www.cberger.com

Provides consultation in library services and information and knowledge management. The firm staffs and directs projects which range from organizing, inventorying and cataloging special collections and files to installing custom PC databases. Personnel services include executive search for information specialists and supplying temporary and contract librarians, support staff and looseleaf filers on demand. Serves corporate, not for profit and academic libraries as well as government agencies.

★7173★ **Educational Placement Service**

6510-A S. Academy Blvd.
Colorado Springs, CO 80906
Ph: (719)579-9911   Fax: (719)579-5050
E-mail: accounting@educatorjobs.com
URL: http://www.educatorjobs.com

Employment agency. Focuses on teaching, administrative, and education-related openings.

★7174★ **Gossage Sager Associates**

351 Town Pl. Cir., Ste. 508
Buffalo Grove, IL 60089
Ph: (312)961-5536   Fax: (847)419-7743
E-mail: gossagesager@altavista.com
URL: http://www.gossagesager.com

Firm provides executive recruiting for public libraries, college and university libraries, corporate libraries, nonprofit libraries, information centers, archives, records management, and other information handling organizations. Offers additional expertise in library management consulting, emphasizing planning, personnel and labor relations and management and systems evaluation. Other areas of specialization include: records management consultation for corporations and nonprofit organizations and computer systems consultation for libraries, corporate and nonprofit records management and other information handling systems. Serves private industries as well as government agencies.

★7175★ **Gossage Sager Associates LLC**

351 Town Pl. Cir., Ste. 508
Buffalo Grove, IL 60089
Ph: (312)961-5536   Fax: (847)419-7743
E-mail: dsager@gossagesager.com
URL: http://www.gossagesager.com

Executive search firm. Concentrates in placement of library and information professionals on permanent basis nationwide.

ONLINE JOB SOURCES AND SERVICES

★7176★ American Library Association Education and Employment

50 E. Huron
Chicago, IL 60611
Fr: 800-545-2433
URL: http://www.ala.org

Description: Contains links to monthly job and career leads lists posted in American Libraries and College & Research Libraries NewsNet and other sources, as well as a Conference Placement Service and accreditation information.

★7177★ Library and Information Technology Association Job Listing

E-mail: lita@ala.org
URL: http://www.lita.org

Description: Contains weekly postings of available library jobs. Searchable by region.

★7178★ Library Job Postings on the Internet

E-mail: sarah@libraryjobpostings.org
URL: http://www.libraryjobpostings.org

Description: Employers may post library position announcements. Also contains links to around 250 library employment sites and links to library-related e-mail lists. Positions are searchable by region and type of library.

TRADESHOWS

★7179★ American Association of Law Libraries Meeting

American Association of Law Libraries
53 W. Jackson Blvd., Ste. 940
Chicago, IL 60604
Ph: (312)939-4764   Fax: (312)431-1097
E-mail: events@aall.org
URL: http://www.aallnet.org/

Annual. **Primary Exhibits:** Library equipment, supplies, and services, including computer hardware and software/publishers of legal materials/information. **Dates and Locations:** 2008 Jul 12-15; Portland, OR; Oregon Convention Center; 2009 Jul 25-28; Washington, DC; Washington Convention Center; 2010 Jul 10-13; Denver, CO; Colorado Convention Center; 2011 Jul 23-26; Philadelphia, PA; Pennsylvania Convention Center; 2012 Jul 21-24; Boston, MA; Hynes Veterans Memorial Convention Center; 2013 Jul 13-16; Seattle, WA; Washington State Convention & Trade Center.

★7180★ American Association of School Librarians National Conference and Exhibition

American Association of School Librarians
50 E. Huron St.
Chicago, IL 60611
Ph: (312)280-4386   Fax: (312)664-7459
Fr: 800-545-2433
E-mail: library@ala.org
URL: http://www.ala.org

Biennial. **Primary Exhibits:** Equipment, supplies, and services for school library media centers, including print and nonprint materials and other equipment.

★7181★ American Library Association Annual Conference

American Library Association
50 E. Huron St.
Chicago, IL 60611-2795
Ph: (312)944-6780   Fax: (312)280-3255
Fr: 800-545-2433
E-mail: library@ala.org
URL: http://www.ala.org

Annual. **Primary Exhibits:** Books, periodicals, reference works, audio-visual equipment, films, data processing services, computer hardware and software, library equipment and supplies. **Dates and Locations:** 2008 Jun 26 - Jul 02; Anaheim, CA.

★7182★ American Library Association Mid-Winter Meeting

American Library Association
50 E. Huron St.
Chicago, IL 60611-2795
Ph: (312)944-6780   Fax: (312)280-3255
Fr: 800-545-2433
E-mail: library@ala.org
URL: http://www.ala.org

Annual. **Primary Exhibits:** Books, periodicals, reference works, audio-visual equipment, films, data processing services, computer hardware and software, library equipment and supplies. **Dates and Locations:** 2008 Jan 11-16; Philadelphia, PA.

★7183★ Arkansas Library Association Annual Conference

Arkansas Library Association
9 Shackleford Plz., Ste.1
Little Rock, AR 72211
Ph: (501)228-0775   Fax: (501)228-5535
E-mail: arlassociation@aol.com
URL: http://www.arlib.org

Annual. **Primary Exhibits:** Products related to libraries. **Dates and Locations:** 2008 Oct 04-07; Little Rock, AR; DoubleTree Hotel.

★7184★ Association of College and Research Libraries National Conference

Association of College and Research Libraries
50 E. Huron St.
Chicago, IL 60611-2795
Ph: (312)280-2523   Fax: (312)280-2520
Fr: 800-545-2433

E-mail: acrl@ala.org
URL: http://www.ala.org/acrl

Biennial. **Primary Exhibits:** Books, computers, Web products, furniture, journals, and audiovisual publications; library materials, equipment, supplies, and services. **Dates and Locations:** 2009 Mar 12 - Apr 15; Seattle, WA; Washington State Trade and Convention Center.

★7185★ California Library Association Annual Conference

California Library Association
717 20th Ste.200
Sacramento, CA 95814-1713
Ph: (916)447-8541   Fax: (916)447-8394
E-mail: info@cla-net.org
URL: http://www.cla-net.org

Annual. **Primary Exhibits:** Publications and library equipment, supplies, and services.

★7186★ Catholic Library Association Convention

Catholic Library Association
100 North St., Ste. 224
Pittsfield, MA 01201-5109
Ph: (413)443-2252   Fax: (413)442-2252
E-mail: cla@cathla.org
URL: http://www.cathla.org

Annual. **Primary Exhibits:** Exhibits relating to Catholic libraries and their specialized problems and the writing, publishing, and distribution of Catholic literature.

★7187★ Church and Synagogue Library Association Conference

Church and Synagogue Library Association
2920 SW Dolph Ct., Ste. 3A
Portland, OR 97219-3962
Ph: (503)244-6919   Fax: (503)977-3734
Fr: 800-542-2752
E-mail: csla@worldaccessnet.com
URL: http://cslainfo.org

Annual. **Primary Exhibits:** Books, media, and library equipment, supplies, and services.

★7188★ Colorado Library Association Conference

Colorado Library Association
12081 W. Alameda Pkwy., No. 427
Lakewood, CO 80228
Ph: (303)463-6400   Fax: (303)798-2485
E-mail: executivedirector@cal-webs.org
URL: http://www.cal-webs.org

Annual. **Primary Exhibits:** Print and nonprint media, bibliographic services, computer products and services, furniture and facilities products, and database and reference services, space planners, architects and more.

★7189★ Computers in Libraries

Information Today, Inc.
143 Old Marlton Pke.
Medford, NJ 08055-8750
Ph: (609)654-6266   Fax: (609)654-4309
Fr: 800-300-9868
E-mail: custserv@infotoday.com
URL: http://www.infotoday.com

Annual. **Primary Exhibits:** Computer hardware, software, CD-ROMS, and related equipment, supplies, and services for use in libraries.

★7190★ Encyclo-Media

Oklahoma Library Association
300 Hardy Dr.
Edmond, OK 73013
Ph: (405)348-0506   Fax: (405)348-1629
E-mail: kboies@coxinet.net
URL: http://www.oklibs.org

Primary Exhibits: Library and media equipment, supplies, and services.

★7191★ Florida Library Association Annual Conference and Trade Show

Florida Library Association
1133 W Morse Blvd., Ste. 201
Winter Park, FL 32789
Ph: (407)647-8839   Fax: (407)629-2502
E-mail: mjs@crowsegal.com
URL: http://www.flalib.org

Annual. **Primary Exhibits:** Library equipment, books, binding information, and furniture.

★7192★ Idaho Library Association Annual Convention

Idaho Library Association
PO Box 8533
Moscow, ID 83843
Ph: (208)383-0165
URL: http://www.idaholibraries.org

Annual. **Primary Exhibits:** Library equipment, supplies, and services, including; computers, audiovisual equipment, and books.

★7193★ Illinois Library Association Annual Conference

Illinois Library Association
33 W Grand Ave., Ste. 301
Chicago, IL 60610-4306
Ph: (312)644-1896   Fax: (312)644-1899
E-mail: ila@ila.org
URL: http://www.ila.org

Annual. **Primary Exhibits:** Library equipment, supplies, and services.

★7194★ Illinois School Library Media Association Conference

Illinois School Library Media Association
PO Box 598
Canton, IL 61520
Ph: (309)649-0911   Fax: (309)649-0916
URL: http://www.islma.org

Annual. **Primary Exhibits:** Equipment, supplies, and services for elementary and secondary school library media specialists interested in the general improvement and extension of services for children and young people.

★7195★ International Association of Aquatic and Marine Science Libraries and Information Centers Conference

International Association of Aquatic and Marine Science Libraries and Information Centers
c/o Harbor Branch Oceanographic Institute Library
5600 U.S. 1 N.
Fort Pierce, FL 34946
Ph: (772)465-2400   Fax: (772)465-2446
Fr: 800-333-4264
E-mail: iamslic-exe@hafro.is
URL: http://www.iamslic.org

Annual. **Primary Exhibits:** Equipment, supplies, and services for marine-related libraries and information centers.

★7196★ Internet Librarian

Information Today, Inc.
143 Old Marlton Pke.
Medford, NJ 08055-8750
Ph: (609)654-6266   Fax: (609)654-4309
Fr: 800-300-9868
E-mail: custserv@infotoday.com
URL: http://www.infotoday.com

Annual. **Primary Exhibits:** Internet librarians equipment, supplies, and services.

★7197★ Iowa Library Association Annual Conference

Iowa Library Association
3636 Westown Pkwy. Ste. 202
West Des Moines, IA 50266
Ph: (515)273-5322   Fax: (515)309-4576
Fr: 800-452-5507
E-mail: executivedirector@iowalibraryassociation.org
URL: http://www.iowalibraryassociation.org

Annual. **Primary Exhibits:** Equipment, supplies, and services for libraries.

★7198★ Medical Library Association Annual Meeting

Medical Library Association
65 E Wacker Pl., Ste. 1900
Chicago, IL 60601-7246
Ph: (312)419-9094   Fax: (312)419-8950
E-mail: mlacom2@mlahq.org
URL: http://www.mlanet.org

Annual. **Primary Exhibits:** Computers, security equipment, audiovisual equipment, office equipment, publications, library suppliers, and computer vendors. **Dates and Locations:** 2008 May 16-21; Chicago, IL.

★7199★ Michigan Library Association Annual Conference

Michigan Library Association
1407 Rensen, Ste. 2
Lansing, MI 48911
Ph: (517)394-2774   Fax: (517)394-2675

E-mail: mla@mlcnet.org
URL: http://www.mla.lib.mi.us

Annual. **Primary Exhibits:** Exhibits pertaining to library and information technology. **Dates and Locations:** 2008 Oct 21-24; Kalamazoo, MI; Radisson Plaza Hotel.

★7200★ Mountain Plains Library Association Annual Conference

Mountain Plains Library Association
USD Library
414 E. Clark St.
University of South Dakota
Vermillion, SD 57069
Ph: (605)677-6082   Fax: (605)677-5488
URL: http://www.usd.edu

Annual. **Primary Exhibits:** Publications and library equipment, supplies, and services.

★7201★ New England Library Association Annual Convention

New England Library Association
PO Box 709
Marblehead, MA 01945
Ph: (781)631-1578   Fax: (781)631-1579
E-mail: office@nelib.org
URL: http://www.nelib.org

Annual. **Primary Exhibits:** Books, media, supplies, furniture, equipment, hardware, software and services used by libraries.

★7202★ New York Library Association Trade Show

New York Library Association
252 Hudson Ave.
Albany, NY 12210-1802
Ph: (518)432-6952   Fax: (518)427-1697
Fr: 800-252-6952
E-mail: info@nyla.org
URL: http://www.nyla.org

Annual. **Primary Exhibits:** New products and services of interest to the library community. **Dates and Locations:** 2008 Nov 05-08; Saratoga Springs, NY.

★7203★ North Carolina Library Association Conference

MW Bell Library
PO Box 309
Jamestown, NC 27282-0309
Ph: (336)334-4822   Fax: (336)841-4350

Biennial. **Primary Exhibits:** Library related equipment, supplies, and services.

★7204★ Pacific Northwest Library Association Conference and Exhibition

Pacific Northwest Library Association
629 Dock St.
Ketchikan, AK 99901
Ph: (907)225-0370   Fax: (907)225-0153
E-mail: charg@firstcitylibraries.org
URL: http://www.pnla.org

Annual. **Primary Exhibits:** Library supplies and services.

★7205★ Public Library Association National Conference

Public Library Association
50 E Huron St.
Chicago, IL 60611
Ph: (312)280-5752   Fax: (312)280-5029
Fr: 800-545-2433
E-mail: pla@ala.org
URL: http://www.pla.org

Biennial. **Primary Exhibits:** Books, software & hardware and other equipment, supplies, and services for libraries. **Dates and Locations:** 2008 Mar 25-29; Minneapolis, MN.

★7206★ Southeastern Library Association Biennial Conference

Southeastern Library Association
Administrative Services
PO Box 950
Rex, GA 30273
Ph: (770)961-3520   Fax: (770)961-3712

Biennial. **Primary Exhibits:** Reps of libraries, furnishings, supplies, services, publishers, and binders, jobbers, computer and networking systems, security, and film systems.

★7207★ Special Libraries Association Information Revolution

Special Libraries Association
331 South Patrick St.
Alexandria, VA 22314-3501
Ph: (703)647-4900   Fax: (703)647-4901
E-mail: sla@sla.org
URL: http://www.sla.org

Annual. **Primary Exhibits:** Library equipment, supplies, and services, including computers and software, Database information.

★7208★ Texas Library Association Conference

Texas Library Association
3355 Bee Cave Rd., Ste. 401
Austin, TX 78746-6763
Ph: (512)328-1518   Fax: (512)328-8852
Fr: 800-580-2852
E-mail: tla@txla.org
URL: http://www.txla.org

Annual. **Primary Exhibits:** Library equipment, supplies, and services, including bookbinding materials, library shelving and furniture, computers, books, audiovisual materials, small press publications, automation, hardware, software, and telecommunications.

★7209★ Wisconsin Library Association Annual Conference

Wisconsin Library Association
5250 E Terrace Dr., Ste. A1
Madison, WI 53718-8345
Ph: (608)245-3640   Fax: (608)245-3646
URL: http://www.wla.lib.wi.us

Annual. **Primary Exhibits:** Library equipment, supplies, and services, including books.

OTHER SOURCES

★7210★ American Almanac of Jobs and Salaries

HarperCollins
10 E. 53rd St.
New York, NY 10022
Ph: (212)207-7000   Fr: 800-242-7737
URL: http://www.harpercollins.com/

John W. Wright. Revised edition, 2000. $20.00 (paper). 672 pages. This is a comprehensive guide to the wages of hundreds of occupations in a wide variety of industries and organizations.

★7211★ Association of Jewish Libraries (AJL)

330 7th Ave., 21st Fl.
New York, NY 10001
Ph: (212)725-5359   Fax: (513)221-0519
E-mail: ajlibs@osu.edu
URL: http://www.jewishlibraries.org

Description: Devoted to the educational, informational, and networking needs of librarians responsible for collections of Judaica and to the promotion of Judaic librarianship.

★7212★ Association for Library and Information Science Education (ALISE)

65 E Wacker Pl., Ste. 1900
Chicago, IL 60601-7246
Ph: (312)795-0996   Fax: (312)419-8950
E-mail: contact@alise.org
URL: http://www.alise.org

Description: Graduate schools offering degree programs in library science and their faculties. Seeks to: promote excellence in education for library and information science as a means of increasing the effectiveness of library and information services; provide a forum for the active interchange of ideas and information among library educators; promote research related to teaching and to library and information science; formulate and promulgate positions on matters related to library education. Offers employment program at annual conference.

★7213★ Education and Training

Cambridge Educational
PO Box 2053
Princeton, NJ 08543-2053
Ph: 800-257-5126   Fax: (609)671-0266
Fr: 800-468-4227
E-mail: custserv@films.com
URL: http://www.cambridgeeducational.com

VHS and DVD. $89.95. 2002. 18 minutes. Presents four distinct occupations in the field: elementary teachers, teacher's aides, administrators, and librarians. People working in these jobs discuss their responsibilities.

★7214★ North American Serials Interest Group (NASIG)

PMB 214
2103 N Decatur Rd.
Decatur, GA 30033
E-mail: info@nasig.org
URL: http://www.nasig.org

Description: Promotes communication, information exchange, and continuing education about serials and the broader issues of scholarly communication. Represents librarians; subscription vendors; publishers; serial automation vendors; serials binders; library science educators; others involved in serials management. **Purpose:** Promotes educational and social networking among members.

★7215★ Teaching & Related Occupations

Delphi Productions
3159 6th St.
Boulder, CO 80304
Ph: (303)443-2100   Fax: (303)443-4022
Fr: 888-443-2400
E-mail: support@delphivideo.com
URL: http://www.delphivideo.com

$95.00. 50 minutes. Part of the Careers for the 21st Century Video Library.

Library Technicians

★7216★ AALL Spectrum

American Association of Law Libraries
53 W Jackson Blvd., Ste. 940
Chicago, IL 60604
Ph: (312)939-4764   Fax: (312)431-1097
URL: http://www.aallnet.org/products/pub_spectrum.asp

Description: Ten issues/year, monthly with an exception of January and August. Presents news of interest to law libraries. Includes job listings and announcements from the Association's officers, chapters, and committees.

★7217★ Base Line

Map and Geography Round Table
c/o James A. Coombs
SW Missiouri State Univ.
Maps Library
Springfield, MO 65804-0095
Ph: (417)280-3205   Fax: (417)280-3257
Fr: 800-545-2433
E-mail: library@ala.org.
URL: http://www.ala.org/ala/alalibrary/ala-periodicals/alaperiodicals.htm

Description: Bimonthly. Provides current information on cartographic materials, publications of interest to map and geography librarians, related government activities, and map librarianship. Recurring features include conference and meeting information, news of research, job listings, and columns by the Division chair and the editor.

★7218★ Book Marks

South Dakota Library Association
PO Box 1212
Rapid City, SD 57709
Ph: (605)343-3750
E-mail: bkstand@rap.midco.net
URL: http://www.sdlibraryassociation.org

Description: Bimonthly. Carries news by and for South Dakota public, school, academic, and special libraries. Discusses statewide library issues, reviews South Da-

kota books, and advises members of continuing education opportunities. Recurring features include columns, a calendar of events, news from libraries, and job listings.

★7219★ Children and Libraries

American Library Association
50 E Huron St.
Chicago, IL 60611
Fr: 800-545-2433
URL: http://www.ala.org

$50.00/year for elsewhere; $40.00/year for nonmembers. Journal that focuses on the continuing education of librarians working with children.

★7220★ Choice

Association of College and Research Libraries
50 E Huron St.
Chicago, IL 60611-2795
Ph: (312)280-2523   Fax: (312)280-2520
Fr: 800-545-2433
URL: http://www.ala.org/ala/acrl/acrlpubs/choice/about.htm

Online journal providing reviews of academic books, electronic media, and internet resources.

★7221★ Computers in Libraries

Information Today Inc.
143 Old Marlton Pke.
Medford, NJ 08055-8750
Ph: (609)654-6266   Fax: (609)654-4309
Fr: 800-300-9868
URL: http://www.infotoday.com/cilmag/default.shtml

Monthly. $100.00/year for individuals, computers in libraries; $118.00 for individuals, 2 years, U.S.; $288.00 for individuals, 3 years, U.S.; $114.00/year for Canada and Mexico; $124.00/year for individuals, outside North America; $68.00/year for individuals; $128.00 for individuals, 2 years; $196.00 for individuals, 3 years; $86.00/year for individuals, Canada and Mexico; $99.00/year for individuals, outside North America. Library science magazine that provides complete coverage of the news and issues in the

rapidly evolving field of library information technology.

★7222★ IFLA Journal

Sage Publications Inc.
2455 Teller Rd.
Thousand Oaks, CA 91320
Ph: (805)499-0721   Fax: (805)499-8096
URL: http://www.ifla.org

Quarterly. $315.00/year for institutions, print & e-access; $331.00/year for institutions, print & all online; $284.00/year for institutions, e-access; $300.00/year for institutions, backfile lease, e-access plus backfile all online; $579.00/year for institutions, backfile purchase, e-access (content through 1999); $309.00/year for institutions, print only; $84.00/year for individuals, print only; $85.00 for single issue, institutional; $27.00 for single issue, individual. Journal of the International Federation of Library Associations and Institutions (IFLA).

★7223★ Information Today

Information Today Inc.
143 Old Marlton Pke.
Medford, NJ 08055-8750
Ph: (609)654-6266   Fax: (609)654-4309
Fr: 800-300-9868
URL: http://www.infotoday.com

Monthly. $75.00/year for individuals; $106.00/year for Canada and Mexico; $150.00 for two years, individuals; $116.00/year for two years, outside North America. User and producer magazine (tabloid) covering electronic and optical information services.

★7224★ Journal of Access Services

The Haworth Press Inc.
10 Alice St.
Binghamton, NY 13904
Ph: (607)722-5857   Fr: 800-429-6784
URL: http://www.haworthpress.com/store/product.asp?sid=9EQS2STUT

Quarterly. $69.00/year for individuals; $101.00/year for individuals, Canada; $106.00/year for other countries, individual; $190.00/year for institutions, agency, library;

$283.00/year for institutions, other countries, agency, library; $268.00/year for institutions, Canada, agency, library. Journal focusing on the basic business of providing library users with access to information and helping librarians stay up to date on continuing education and professional development in the field of access services.

★7225★ **Journal of Classification**

Classification Society of North America
c/o Stanley Sclove
IDS Dept., University of Illinois M/C 294
CSNA Business Office
601 South Morgan St.
Chicago, IL 60607-7124
Ph: (312)996-2676   Fax: (312)413-0385
URL: http://www.cs-na.org

Semiannual. Journal of the Classification Society of North America.

★7226★ **Journal of Interlibrary Loan, Document Delivery & Electronic Reserve**

The Haworth Press Inc.
10 Alice St.
Binghamton, NY 13904
Ph: (607)722-5857   Fr: 800-429-6784
URL: http://www.haworthpress.com/store/product.asp?sid=PC3BHEAN6

Quarterly. $40.00/year for individuals; $58.00/year for individuals, Canada; $62.00/year for individuals, elsewhere; $275.00/year for institutions, agency, library; $399.00/year for institutions, Canada, agency, library; $426.00/year for institutions, other countries, agency, library. Journal focusing on a broad spectrum of library and information center functions that rely heavily on interlibrary loans, document delivery, and electronic reserve.

★7227★ **Journal of Librarianship and Information Science**

Sage Publications Inc.
2455 Teller Rd.
Thousand Oaks, CA 91320
Ph: (805)499-0721   Fax: (805)499-8096
URL: http://www.sagepub.com/journalsProdDesc.nav?prodId=Journal20

Quarterly. $539.00/year for institutions, print & e-access; $566.00/year for institutions, print & all online; $485.00/year for institutions, e-access; $512.00/year for institutions, e-access & all online; $1,237.00/year for institutions, e-access; $528.00/year for institutions, print only; $84.00/year for individuals, print only; $146.00 for institutions, single print; $27.00 for individuals, single print. Journal for librarians, information scientists, specialists, managers, and educators.

★7228★ **Law Librarians' Bulletin Board**

Legal Information Services
PO Box 2383
Chapel Hill, NC 27517-2383
Ph: (919)672-3035   Fax: (919)408-0267
E-mail: info@legalinformationservices.com
URL: http://

www.legalinformationservices.com/Publications/librarians-newsletter.php

Description: 8/year. Tracks current events in law librarianship. Recurring features include job listings.

★7229★ **Library Journal**

Reed Business Information
360 Park Ave. S
New York, NY 10010
Ph: (646)746-6400   Fax: (646)746-7431
E-mail: ljinfo@reedbusiness.com
URL: http://www.libraryjournal.com

$149.99/year for U.S., per year; $199.99/year for Canada, per year; $259.99/year for individuals, international air delivery; $171.00/year for Canada, 1 year. Library management and book selection journal.

★7230★ **MLA News**

Medical Library Association
65 E Wacker Pl., Ste. 1900
Chicago, IL 60601-7246
Ph: (312)419-9094   Fax: (312)419-8950
E-mail: info@mlahq.org
URL: http://www.mlanet.org/publications/mlanews/index.html

Description: Monthly, except June/July and November/December, which are combined issues. Covers topics about the association, the health sciences information industry, legislation, and international events. Regular features include updates and reviews of new information technology, medical publication trends, classifieds, educational opportunities, and Internet resources.

★7231★ **The Outrider**

Wyoming State Library
516 S. Greeley Hwy.
Cheyenne, WY 82002
Ph: (307)777-6333   Fax: (307)777-6289
URL: http://will.state.wy.us/slpub/outrider/index.html

Description: Biennial. Provides news about the activities of the Wyoming State Library, its board, other tax-supported libraries in the state, the American Library Association, and the library field in general. Recurring features include job listings, meetings, workshops, and other events; personnel news; reports on consultant activities and acquisitions news; and columns titled News Briefs, Around the State.

★7232★ **Research Strategies**

Elsevier Science Inc.
360 Park Ave. S
New York, NY 10010
Ph: (212)989-5800   Fax: (212)633-3990
URL: http://www.elsevier.com

Journal covering library literature and the educational mission of the library.

★7233★ **School Library Journal**

Reed Business Information
360 Park Ave. S
New York, NY 10010
Ph: (646)746-6400   Fax: (646)746-7431
E-mail: slj@reedbusiness.com
URL: http://www.reedbusiness.com/

Monthly. $129.00/year for individuals, per year; $199.99/year for Canada, per year. A new Canadian Web site launched with the blessing of Microsoft Chairman Bill Gates is using games and cartoons to teach kids about the evils of online predators.

★7234★ **SLA Geography & Map Division-Bulletin**

Geography & Map Div.
Illinois State Univ.
Campus Box 8900
Normal, IL 61790
Ph: (309)438-3486
E-mail: vmschwa@ilstu.edu
URL: http://www.sla.org/division/dgm/index.htm

Description: Three issues/year. Provides a medium of exchange of information, news, and research in the field of geographic and cartographic bibliography, literature, and libraries. Recurring features include letters to the editor, news of research, a calendar of events, reports of meetings, news of educational opportunities, job listings, book reviews, and notices of publications available.

PLACEMENT AND JOB REFERRAL SERVICES

★7235★ **American Library Association (ALA)**

50 E Huron St.
Chicago, IL 60611
Ph: (312)944-6780   Fax: (312)440-9374
Fr: 800-545-2433
E-mail: ala@ala.org
URL: http://www.ala.org

Members: Librarians, libraries, trustees, friends of libraries, and others interested in the responsibilities of libraries in the educational, social, and cultural needs of society. **Purpose:** Promotes and improves library service and librarianship. Establishes standards of service, support, education, and welfare for libraries and library personnel; promotes the adoption of such standards in libraries of all kinds; safeguards the professional status of librarians; encourages the recruiting of competent personnel for professional careers in librarianship; promotes popular understanding and public acceptance of the value of library service and librarianship. **Activities:** Works in liaison with federal agencies to initiate the enactment and administration of legislation that will extend library services. Offers placement services.

★7236★ American Society for Information Science and Technology (ASIS&T)

1320 Fenwick Ln., Ste. 510
Silver Spring, MD 20910
Ph: (301)495-0900   Fax: (301)495-0810
E-mail: asis@asis.org
URL: http://www.asis.org

Members: Information specialists, scientists, librarians, administrators, social scientists, and others interested in the use, organization, storage, retrieval, evaluation, and dissemination of recorded specialized information. **Purpose:** Seeks to improve the information transfer process through research, development, application, and education. **Activities:** Provides a forum for the discussion, publication, and critical analysis of work dealing with the theory, practice, research, and development of elements involved in communication of information. Members are engaged in a variety of activities and specialties including classification and coding systems, automatic and associative indexing, machine translation of languages, special librarianship and library systems analysis, and copyright issues. Sponsors National Auxiliary Publications Service, which provides reproduction services and a central depository for all types of information. Maintains placement service. Sponsors numerous special interest groups. Conducts continuing education programs and professional development workshops.

★7237★ Association of College and Research Libraries (ACRL)

50 E Huron St.
Chicago, IL 60611-2795
Ph: (312)280-2523   Fax: (312)280-2520
Fr: 800-545-2433
E-mail: acrl@ala.org
URL: http://www.ala.org/acrl

Description: A division of the American Library Association. **Members:** Academic and research librarians **Purpose:** seeking to improve the quality of service in academic libraries; promotes the professional and career development of academic and research librarians; represent the interests and support the programs of academic and research libraries. **Activities:** Operates placement services; sponsors specialized education and research grants and programs; gathers, compiles, and disseminates statistics. Establishes and adopts standards; maintains publishing program; offers professional development courses.

★7238★ Music Library Association (MLA)

8551 Research Way, Ste. 180
Middleton, WI 53562-3567
Ph: (608)836-5825   Fax: (608)831-8200
E-mail: mla@areditions.com
URL: http://www.musiclibraryassoc.org

Description: Promotes the establishment, growth, and use of music libraries and collection of music, musical instruments, musical literature, and audio-visual aids. Maintains placement service.

★7239★ Special Libraries Association (SLA)

331 S Patrick St.
Alexandria, VA 22314-3501
Ph: (703)647-4900   Fax: (703)647-4901
E-mail: sla@sla.org
URL: http://www.sla.org

Description: International association of information professionals who work in special libraries serving business, research, government, universities, newspapers, museums, and institutions that use or produce specialized information. Seeks to advance the leadership role of special librarians. Offers consulting services to organizations that wish to establish or expand a library or information services. Conducts strategic learning and development courses, public relations, and government relations programs. Provides employment services. Operates knowledge exchange on topics pertaining to the development and management of special libraries. Maintains Hall of Fame.

EMPLOYER DIRECTORIES AND NETWORKING LISTS

★7240★ 50 State Educational Directories

Career Guidance Foundation
8090 Engineer Rd.
San Diego, CA 92111
Ph: (858)560-8051   Fax: (858)278-8960
Fr: 800-854-2670
URL: http://www.cgf.org

Annual. Microfiche. Collection consists of reproductions of the state educational directories published by the departments of education of individual 50 states. Directory contents vary, but the majority contain listings of elementary and secondary schools, colleges and universities, and state education officials. Amount of detail in each also varies. Entries include: Usually, institution name, address, and name of one executive.

★7241★ American Library Directory

Information Today Inc.
143 Old Marlton Pke.
Medford, NJ 08055-8750
Ph: (609)654-6266   Fax: (609)654-4309
Fr: 800-300-9868
URL: http://books.infotoday.com/

Annual; latest edition 59th, 2005-2006. $299.00 for individuals. Covers over 36,000 U.S. and Canadian academic, public, county, provincial, and regional libraries; library systems; medical, law, and other special libraries; and libraries for the blind and physically handicapped. Separate section lists over 350 library networks and consortia and 220 accredited and unaccredited library school programs. Entries include: For libraries—Name, supporting or affiliated institution or firm name, address, phone, fax, e-mail address, Standard Address Number (SAN), names of librarian and department heads, income, collection size, special collections, computer hardware, automated functions, and type of catalog. For library systems—Name, location. For library schools—Name, address, phone, fax, e-mail address, director, type of training and degrees, admission requirements, tuition, faculty size. For networks and consortia—Name, address, phone, names of affiliates, name of director, function. Arrangement: Geographical. Indexes: Institution name. Library Services and Suppliers index.

★7242★ The Basic Business Library

Greenwood Publishing Group Inc.
88 Post Rd. W
Westport, CT 06881
Ph: (203)226-3571
URL: http://www.greenwood.com

Latest edition 4th. $75.00 for individuals. Publication includes: Publisher's Web site as part of each entry. Principal content of publication is list of 210 entries of suggested resources for business libraries, as well as essays on business reference sources and services. Indexes: Alphabetical.

★7243★ Directory of Federal Libraries

Oryx Press
4041 N Central Ave., Ste. 700
PO Box 33889
Phoenix, AZ 85021-3397
Ph: (602)265-2651   Fax: 800-279-4663
Fr: 800-279-6799
URL: http://isbndb.com/d/book/directory_of_federal_libraries.html

Irregular; latest edition December 2000. Covers nearly 3,000 libraries serving branches of the federal government. Entries include: Library name, type, address, phone, fax, e-mail, telnet, and websites, name of administrator and selected staff, special collections, database services available, depository status for documents from the Government Printing Office or other organizations, involvement with cooperative library organizations, electronic mail or cataloging networks, whether accessible to the public. Arrangement: Classified by federal establishment. Indexes: Library type; subject; geographical; alphabetical index of libraries by name.

★7244★ Directory of Public School Systems in the U.S.

American Association for Employment in Education
3040 Riverside Dr., Ste. 125
Columbus, OH 43221
Ph: (614)485-1111   Fax: (614)485-9609
URL: http://www.aaee.org/

Annual, winter; latest edition 2004-2005 edition. $10.00 for members (plus $2.00/copy for mailing); $20.00 for nonmembers (plus $2.00/copy for mailing). Covers about 14,500 public school systems in the United States and their administrative personnel. Entries include: System name, address, phone, website address, name and title of personnel administrator, levels taught and approximate student population. Arrangement: Geographical by state.

★7245★ Directory of Special Libraries and Information Centers

Gale, Cengage Learning
27500 Drake Rd.
Farmington Hills, MI 48331-3535
Ph: (248)699-4253   Fax: (248)699-8065
Fr: 800-877-4253
E-mail: businessproducts@gale.com
URL: http://www.gale.com

Annual; latest edition 33rd, April 2007. $1210.00 for individuals. Covers over 34,800 special libraries, information centers, documentation centers, etc.; about 500 networks and consortia; major special libraries abroad also included. Volume 1 part 3 contains 6 other appendices (beside networks and consortia): Regional and Subregional Libraries for the Blind and Physically Handicapped, Patent and Trademark Depository Libraries, Regional Government Depository Libraries, United Nations Depository Libraries, World Bank Depository Libraries, and European Community Depository Libraries. Entries include: Library name, address, phone, fax, e-mail address; contact; year founded; sponsoring organization; special collections; subject interests; names and titles of staff; services (copying, online searches); size of collection; subscriptions; computerized services and automated operations; Internet home page address; publications; special catalogs; special indexes. For consortia and networks–Name, address, phone, contact. Other appendices have varying amounts of directory information. Contents of Volume 1 are available in "Subject Directory of Special Libraries and Information Centers." Arrangement: Libraries are alphabetical by name of sponsoring organization or institution; consortia and networks are geographical. Indexes: Subject. Geographic and personnel indexes constitute volume 2.

★7246★ Guide to Employment Sources in the Library & Information Professions

Office for Human Resource Development and Recruitment
50 E Huron St.
Chicago, IL 60611
Ph: (312)280-4282   Fax: (312)280-3256
Fr: 800-545-2433
URL: http://www.ala.org/hrdr/employment_guide.html

Annual, spring. Covers library job sources, such as specialized and state and regional library associations, state library agencies, federal library agencies, and overseas exchange programs. Entries include: Library, company, or organization name, address, phone; contact name, description of services, publications, etc. This is a reprint of a segment of the "Bowker Annual of Library and Book Trade Information." Arrangement: Classified by type of source.

★7247★ Higher Education Directory

Higher Education Publications Inc.
6400 Arlington Blvd., Ste. 648
Falls Church, VA 22042-2342
Ph: (703)532-2300   Fax: (703)532-2305
Fr: 888-349-7715

URL: http://www.hepinc.com/hed.htm

Annual; latest edition 2007. $75.00 for individuals. Covers over 4,364 degree granting colleges and universities accredited by approved agencies recognized by the U.S. Secretary of Education and by the Council of Higher Education Accreditation (CHEA); 103 systems offices; over 550 related associations and state government agencies; recognized accrediting agencies. Entries include: For institutions–Name, address, congressional district, phone, fax, year established; Carnegie classification; enrollment; type of student body; religious or other affiliation; undergraduate tuition and fees; type of academic calendar; highest degree offered; accreditations; IRS status; names, titles and job classification codes for academic and administrative officers. For associations and state agencies–Name, address, phone, name of chief executive officer. Same content and coverage as the base volume of the Department of Education's publication "Directory of Postsecondary Institutions". Arrangement: Geographical, alphabetical by state. Indexes: Administrator name (with phone and e-mail addresses), accreditation, FICE numbers, college or university name.

★7248★ Midwest Archives Conference-Membership Directory

Midwest Archives Conference
c/o Menzi Behrnd-Klodt
7422 Longmeadow Rd.
Madison, WI 53717
Ph: (608)827-5727
URL: http://www.midwestarchives.org

Annual. Covers more than 1,000 individual and institutional members, largely librarians, archivists, records managers, manuscripts curators, historians, and museum and historical society personnel, as well as about 25 archival associations in the Midwest. Entries include: For institutions–Name of archives, parent organization, address, phone. For individuals–Name, title, business address, phone. Arrangement: Separate alphabetical sections for individuals and institutions.

★7249★ Patterson's American Education

Educational Directories Inc.
PO Box 68097
Schaumburg, IL 60168
Ph: (847)891-1250   Fax: (847)891-0945
Fr: 800-357-6183
URL: http://www.ediusa.com

Annual; latest edition October 2007. $94.00 for individuals. Covers over 11,400 school districts in the United States; more than 34,000 public, private, and Catholic high schools, middle schools, and junior high schools; Approximately 300 parochial superintendents; 400 state department of education personnel. Entries include: For school districts and schools–District and superintendent name, address, phone, fax; grade ranges, enrollment; school names, addresses, phone numbers, names of principals. For postsecondary schools–School name, address, phone number, URL, e-mail, names of administrator or director of admis-

sions. For private and Catholic high schools–name, address, phone, fax, enrollment, grades offered, name of principal. Postsecondary institutions are also covered in 'Patterson's Schools Classified.' Arrangement: Geographical by state, then alphabetical by city.

★7250★ Patterson's Schools Classified

Educational Directories Inc.
PO Box 68097
Schaumburg, IL 60168
Ph: (847)891-1250   Fax: (847)891-0945
Fr: 800-357-6183
URL: http://www.ediusa.com

Annual; latest edition 2007, volume 57. $18.00 for individuals. Covers over 7,000 accredited colleges, universities, community colleges, junior colleges, career schools and teaching hospitals. Entries include: School name, address, phone, URL, e-mail, name of administrator or admissions officer, description, professional accreditation (where applicable). Updated from previous year's edition of 'Patterson's American Education'. Arrangement: Classified by area of study, then geographical by state. Indexes: Alphabetical by name.

★7251★ Requirements for Certification of Teachers, Counselors, Librarians, Administrators for Elementary and Secondary Schools

University of Chicago Press
Journals Division
1427 E 60th St.
Chicago, IL 60637-2954
Ph: (773)702-7600   Fax: (773)702-0694
Fr: 877-705-1878

Annual, June; latest edition 71st, 2006-07. $47.00. Publication includes: List of state and local departments of education. Entries include: Office name, address, phone. Principal content of publication consists of summaries of each state's teaching and administrative certification requirements. Arrangement: Geographical.

HANDBOOKS AND MANUALS

★7252★ Library Employment Within the Law

Neal-Schuman Publishers, Inc.
100 William St., Ste. 2004
New York, NY 10038
Ph: (212)925-8650   Fax: (212)219-8916
E-mail: info@neal-schuman.com
URL: http://www.neal-schuman.com/

Arlene C. Bielefield and Lawrence G. Cheeseman. 1994. $75.00 (paper). 147 pages.

★7253★ *Opportunities in Library and Information Science Careers*

The McGraw-Hill Companies
PO Box 182604
Columbus, OH 43272
Fax: (614)759-3749   Fr: 877-883-5524
E-mail: customer.service@mcgraw-hill.com
URL: http://www.mcgraw-hill.com

Kathleen M. Heim and Margaret Myers. 2001. $13.95 (paper). 145 pages. A guide to planning for and seeking opportunities in this changing field. Includes bibliography and illustrations.

EMPLOYMENT AGENCIES AND SEARCH FIRMS

★7254★ **C.H. Cowles Associates**

93 W Alyssa Canyon Pl.
PO Box 89291
Tucson, AZ 85737-1636
Ph: (520)297-7608   Fax: (520)297-7608

Firm provides services in industrial engineering and industrial management including long-range planning, facilities planning, work improvement, profit improvement, executive search, quality assurance, manufacturing engineering and staff reorganization, site search and site planning.

★7255★ **Gossage Sager Associates**

351 Town Pl. Cir., Ste. 508
Buffalo Grove, IL 60089
Ph: (312)961-5536   Fax: (847)419-7743
E-mail: gossagesager@altavista.com
URL: http://www.gossagesager.com

Firm provides executive recruiting for public libraries, college and university libraries, corporate libraries, nonprofit libraries, information centers, archives, records management, and other information handling organizations. Offers additional expertise in library management consulting, emphasizing planning, personnel and labor relations and management and systems evaluation. Other areas of specialization include: records management consultation for corporations and nonprofit organizations and computer systems consultation for libraries, corporate and nonprofit records management and other information handling systems. Serves private industries as well as government agencies.

★7256★ **Gossage Sager Associates LLC**

351 Town Pl. Cir., Ste. 508
Buffalo Grove, IL 60089
Ph: (312)961-5536   Fax: (847)419-7743
E-mail: dsager@gossagesager.com
URL: http://www.gossagesager.com

Executive search firm. Concentrates in placement of library and information professionals on permanent basis nationwide.

ONLINE JOB SOURCES AND SERVICES

★7257★ **Library Job Postings on the Internet**

E-mail: sarah@libraryjobpostings.org
URL: http://www.libraryjobpostings.org

Description: Employers may post library position announcements. Also contains links to around 250 library employment sites and links to library-related e-mail lists. Positions are searchable by region and type of library.

TRADESHOWS

★7258★ **Computers in Libraries**

Information Today, Inc.
143 Old Marlton Pke.
Medford, NJ 08055-8750
Ph: (609)654-6266   Fax: (609)654-4309
Fr: 800-300-9868
E-mail: custserv@infotoday.com
URL: http://www.infotoday.com

Annual. **Primary Exhibits:** Computer hardware, software, CD-ROMS, and related equipment, supplies, and services for use in libraries.

★7259★ **Illinois School Library Media Association Conference**

Illinois School Library Media Association
PO Box 598
Canton, IL 61520
Ph: (309)649-0911   Fax: (309)649-0916
URL: http://www.islma.org

Annual. **Primary Exhibits:** Equipment, supplies, and services for elementary and secondary school library media specialists interested in the general improvement and extension of services for children and young people.

★7260★ **Michigan Library Association Annual Conference**

Michigan Library Association
1407 Rensen, Ste. 2
Lansing, MI 48911
Ph: (517)394-2774   Fax: (517)394-2675
E-mail: mla@mlcnet.org
URL: http://www.mla.lib.mi.us

Annual. **Primary Exhibits:** Exhibits pertaining to library and information technology. **Dates and Locations:** 2008 Oct 21-24; Kalamazoo, MI; Radisson Plaza Hotel.

★7261★ **Public Library Association National Conference**

Public Library Association
50 E Huron St.
Chicago, IL 60611
Ph: (312)280-5752   Fax: (312)280-5029
Fr: 800-545-2433

E-mail: pla@ala.org
URL: http://www.pla.org

Biennial. **Primary Exhibits:** Books, software & hardware and other equipment, supplies, and services for libraries. **Dates and Locations:** 2008 Mar 25-29; Minneapolis, MN.

★7262★ **Special Libraries Association Information Revolution**

Special Libraries Association
331 South Patrick St.
Alexandria, VA 22314-3501
Ph: (703)647-4900   Fax: (703)647-4901
E-mail: sla@sla.org
URL: http://www.sla.org

Annual. **Primary Exhibits:** Library equipment, supplies, and services, including computers and software, Database information.

OTHER SOURCES

★7263★ **Association of Jewish Libraries (AJL)**

330 7th Ave., 21st Fl.
New York, NY 10001
Ph: (212)725-5359   Fax: (513)221-0519
E-mail: ajlibs@osu.edu
URL: http://www.jewishlibraries.org

Description: Devoted to the educational, informational, and networking needs of librarians responsible for collections of Judaica and to the promotion of Judaic librarianship.

★7264★ **Council on Library-Media Technicians (COLT)**

28262 Chardon Rd.
PMB 168
Wickliffe, OH 44092-2793
Ph: (202)231-3836   Fax: (202)231-3838
E-mail: jmhite0@dia.mil
URL: http://colt.ucr.edu

Description: Persons involved in two-year associate degree programs for the training of library technical assistants (professional-support workers) and graduates of programs employed as library/media technical assistants (B.A. degree holders without M.L.S. degree). Membership includes junior college deans, librarians, curriculum directors, professors, employers, special libraries, university libraries, library schools, publishers, and library technical assistants. Provides a channel of communication among the institutions and personnel that have developed such training programs; attempts to standardize curriculum offerings; develops educational standards; conducts research on graduates of the programs; represents the interests of library technical assistants and support staff. The council's concerns also include development of clear job descriptions and criteria for employment of technicians and dissemination of information to the public and to prospective students. Sponsors workshops for support staff in areas such as management, supervisory skills, interpersonal communication, business writing, and media center management. Maintains speakers' bureau. Develops a program for certification of library media technicians and a continuing education program for library support staff.

★7265★ Education and Training
Cambridge Educational
PO Box 2053
Princeton, NJ 08543-2053
Ph: 800-257-5126   Fax: (609)671-0266
Fr: 800-468-4227
E-mail: custserv@films.com
URL: http://www.cambridgeeducational.com

VHS and DVD. $89.95. 2002. 18 minutes. Presents four distinct occupations in the field: elementary teachers, teacher's aides, administrators, and librarians. People working in these jobs discuss their responsibilities.

★7266★ North American Serials Interest Group (NASIG)
PMB 214
2103 N Decatur Rd.
Decatur, GA 30033
E-mail: info@nasig.org
URL: http://www.nasig.org

Description: Promotes communication, information exchange, and continuing education about serials and the broader issues of scholarly communication. Represents librarians; subscription vendors; publishers; serial automation vendors; serials binders; library science educators; others involved in serials management. **Purpose:** Promotes educational and social networking among members.

Licensed Practical Nurses

SOURCES OF HELP-WANTED ADS

★7267★ AANA Journal
AANA Publishing Inc.
222 South Prospect Ave.
Park Ridge, IL 60068
Ph: (847)692-7050   Fax: (847)518-0938
URL: http://www.aana.com

Bimonthly. $45.00/year for individuals; $10.00 for single issue. Nursing and anesthesia journal.

★7268★ AAOHN Journal
SLACK Inc.
6900 Grove Rd.
Thorofare, NJ 08086-9447
Ph: (856)848-1000   Fax: (856)853-5991
E-mail: aaohn@slackinc.com
URL: http://www.aaohnjournal.com

Monthly. $99.00/year for individuals, U.S. Official journal of the American Association of Occupational Health Nurses.

★7269★ AAOHN News
American Association of Occupational Health Nurses Inc.
2920 Brandywine Rd., Ste. 100
Atlanta, GA 30341
Ph: (770)455-7757   Fax: (770)455-7271
URL: http://www.aaohn.org/member_services/newsletter/index.cfm

Description: Monthly. Covers Association events as well as trends and legislation affecting occupational and enivornmental health nursing. Recurring features include news of research, a calendar of events, reports of meetings, news of educational opportunities, job listings, notices of publications available, resources for career-building, briefs on governmental issues concerning occupational and environment health, and a President's column.

★7270★ ADVANCE for LPNs
Merion Publications Inc.
2900 Horizon Dr.
PO Box 61556
King of Prussia, PA 19406
Ph: (610)278-1400   Fr: 800-355-5627
URL: http://lpn.advanceweb.com/

Biweekly. Free to qualified subscribers. Magazine for licensed practical nurses covering clinical information and job opportunities.

★7271★ ADVANCE for Nurse Practitioners
Merion Publications Inc.
2900 Horizon Dr.
PO Box 61556
King of Prussia, PA 19406
Ph: (610)278-1400   Fr: 800-355-5627
URL: http://nurse-practitioners.advanceweb.com/main.aspx

Monthly. For practicing nurse practitioner students with senior status.

★7272★ Advances in Nursing Science (ANS)
Lippincott Williams & Wilkins
530 Walnut St.
Philadelphia, PA 19106-3621
Ph: (215)521-8300   Fax: (215)521-8902
Fr: 800-638-3030
URL: http://www.lww.com/product/?0161-9268

Quarterly. $97.91/year for individuals, U.S.; $272.96/year for institutions, U.S.; $52.94/year for U.S., in-training; $145.94/year for individuals, international; $320.94/year for institutions, international. Academic medical journal focusing on nursing research and education.

★7273★ American Family Physician
American Academy of Family Physicians
11400 Tomahawk Creek Pkwy.
PO Box 11210
Leawood, KS 66211-2672
Ph: (913)906-6000   Fax: (913)906-6010
Fr: 800-274-2237
E-mail: afpedit@aafp.org
URL: http://www.aafp.org/afp

Semimonthly. $120.00/year for individuals, U.S.; $200.00/year for out of country, individuals; $160.00/year for Canada, individuals; $160.00/year for institutions, U.S.; $200.00/year for institutions, Canada, $240.00/year for institutions, foreign countries; $68.00/year for students, medical; $108.00/year for students, medical; $148.00/year for students, medical; $11.00 for single issue, six copies. Peer reviewed clinical journal for family physicians and others in primary care. Review articles detail the latest diagnostic and therapeutic techniques in the medical field. Department features in each issue include 'Tips from other Journals,' CME credit opportunities and course calendar.

★7274★ American Journal of Nursing
American Journal of Nursing
c/o Lippincott, Williams & Wilkins
530 Walnut St.
Philadelphia, PA 19106-3621
Ph: (215)521-8300   Fax: (215)521-8902
Fr: 800-627-0484
URL: http://www.nursingcenter.com

Monthly. $32.90/year for individuals; $159.00/year for institutions; $69.00/year for individuals, other countries; $199.00/year for institutions, other countries. Journal for staff nurses, nurse managers, and clinical nurse specialists. Focuses on patient care in hospitals, hospital ICUs and homes. Provides news coverage of health care from the nursing perspective.

★7275★ The American Nurse
American Nurses Association
8515 Georgia Ave., Ste. 400
Silver Spring, MD 20910
Ph: (301)628-5000   Fax: (301)628-5001
Fr: 800-274-4262
E-mail: adsales@ana.org
URL: http://nursingworld.org/tan/

Monthly. Newspaper (tabloid) for the nursing profession.

★7276★ Applied Nursing Research

Mountain Association for Community
  Economic Development
433 Chestnut St.
Berea, KY 40403
Ph: (859)986-2373   Fax: (859)986-1299
URL: http://www.elsevier.com/wps/find/journaldescription.cws_home

Quarterly. $298.00/year for institutions, outside U.S; $88.00/year for individuals, inside U.S.; $246.00/year for institutions, inside U.S.; $125.00/year for individuals, outside U.S. Nursing journal publishing peer-reviewed research findings for clinical applications.

★7277★ Cancer Nursing

Lippincott Williams & Wilkins
530 Walnut St.
Philadelphia, PA 19106-3621
Ph: (215)521-8300   Fax: (215)521-8902
Fr: 800-638-3030
E-mail: bguthy@lww.com
URL: http://www.cancernursingonline.com/

Bimonthly. $94.43/year for individuals; $243.48/year for institutions; $49.48/year for other countries, in-training; $167.46/year for individuals; $284.46/year for institutions. Medical journal covering problems arising in the care and support of cancer patients.

★7278★ Clinical Effectiveness in Nursing

Mosby Inc.
11830 Westline Industrial Dr.
St. Louis, MO 63146
Ph: (314)872-8370   Fax: (314)432-1380
Fr: 800-325-4177
URL: http://www.us.elsevierhealth.com/product.jsp?isbn=13619004

Quarterly. $70.00/year for individuals; $316.00/year for institutions. Journal for nurses demonstrating the impact of nursing on patients and clients; addresses the effects of interventions on patients' well-being.

★7279★ Clinical Nurse Specialist

Lippincott Williams & Wilkins
530 Walnut St.
Philadelphia, PA 19106-3621
Ph: (215)521-8300   Fax: (215)521-8902
Fr: 800-638-3030
URL: http://www.cns-journal.com

Bimonthly. $97.91/year for individuals, U.S.; $228.96/year for institutions, U.S.; $52.96/year for other countries, U.S. in-training:; $177.94/year for individuals, international; $307.94/year for institutions, international in-training. Nursing journal.

★7280★ Critical Care Nurse

Critical Care Nurse
101 Columbia
Aliso Viejo, CA 92656
Ph: (949)448-7370   Fr: 800-899-2273
URL: http://ccn.aacnjournals.org

Bimonthly. Nursing journal.

★7281★ Dialysis & Transplantation

Creative Age Publications Inc.
7628 Densmore Ave.
Van Nuys, CA 91406-2042
Ph: (818)782-7328   Fax: (818)782-7450
Fr: 800-442-5667
URL: http://www.eneph.com

Monthly. $22.00/year for individuals, 12 issues; $26.00/year for out of country; $43.00/year for Canada and Mexico, by mail; $82.00/year for other countries. Multi-disciplinary, peer-reviewed journal on clinical applications in dialysis, transplantation and nephrology for renal-care teams.

★7282★ EndoNurse

Virgo Publishing Inc.
PO Box 40079
Phoenix, AZ 85067-0079
Ph: (480)990-1101   Fax: (480)990-0819
URL: http://endonurse.com/

Bimonthly. $34.95/year in U.S.; $54.95/year for Canada; $64.95/year for elsewhere. Magazine covering endoscopic nursing.

★7283★ Heart and Lung

Mosby
1600 John F. Kennedy Blvd., Ste. 1800
Philadelphia, PA 19103-2899
Ph: (215)239-3276   Fax: (215)239-3286
URL: http://www.elsevier.com/wps/find/journaleditorialboard.cws_h

Bimonthly. $111.00/year for individuals; $321.00/year for institutions; $34.00/year for students; $99.00/year for other countries; $50.00/year for students, other countries; $289.00/year for institutions, other countries. Journal offering articles prepared by nurse and physician members of the critical care team, recognizing the nurse's role in the care and management of major organ-system conditions in critically ill patients.

★7284★ Home Healthcare Nurse

Lippincott Williams & Wilkins
530 Walnut St.
Philadelphia, PA 19106-3621
Ph: (215)521-8300   Fax: (215)521-8902
Fr: 800-638-3030
URL: http://www.homehealthcarenurseonline.com/

Monthly. $56.43/year for individuals, U.S.; $202.95/year for institutions, U.S.; $126.46/year for individuals, other countries; $252.95/year for institutions, other countries; $43.48/year for U.S., in-training. Magazine for the practicing professional nurse working in the home health, community health, and public health areas.

★7285★ HomeCare Magazine

Miramar Communications Inc.
23805 Stuart Ranch Rd., Ste. 235
PO Box 8987
Malibu, CA 90265-8987
Ph: (310)317-4522   Fax: (310)317-9644
Fr: 800-543-4116
URL: http://www.homecaremag.com

Monthly. Free, in US; $135.00/year for Canada; $150.00/year for two years, Canada; $250.00/year for other countries; $250.00/year for two years, other countries. Magazine serving home medical equipment suppliers, including independent and chain centers specializing in home care, pharmacies or chain drug stores with home care products, and joint-ventured hospital home health care businesses. Contains industry news and new product launches and marketing strategies.

★7286★ Hospitals & Health Networks

Health Forum L.L.C.
1 N Franklin, 29th Fl.
Chicago, IL 60606
Ph: (312)893-6800   Fax: (312)422-4506
Fr: 800-821-2039
URL: http://www.hhnmag.com

Weekly. Publication covering the health care industry.

★7287★ The IHS Primary Care Provider

Indian Health Service (HQ)
The Reyes Bldg.
801 Thompson Ave., Ste. 400
Rockville, MD 20852-1627
URL: http://www.ihs.gov/PublicInfo/Publications/HealthProvider/Pr

Monthly. Journal for health care professionals, physicians, nurses, pharmacists, dentists, and dietitians.

★7288★ Imprint

National Student Nurses' Association Inc.
45 Main St., Ste. 606
Brooklyn, NY 11201
Ph: (718)210-0705   Fax: (718)210-7010
E-mail: nsna@nsna.org
URL: http://www.nsna.org/

Periodic. Magazine for nursing students, focusing on issues and trends in nursing.

★7289★ Intensive and Critical Care Nursing

Mosby Inc.
11830 Westline Industrial Dr.
St. Louis, MO 63146
Ph: (314)872-8370   Fax: (314)432-1380
Fr: 800-325-4177
URL: http://www.us.elsevierhealth.com/product.jsp?isbn=09643397&r

Bimonthly. $92.00/year for individuals, international; $422.00/year for institutions, international; $92.00/year for individuals; $422.00/year for institutions. Journal for nurses in intensive and critical care nursing.

★7290★ International Journal of Nursing Education Scholarship

Berkeley Electronic Press
2809 Telegraph Ave., Ste. 202
Berkeley, CA 94705
Ph: (510)665-1200   Fax: (510)665-1201
URL: http://www.bepress.com/ijnes

Semiannual. $525.00/year corporate; $175.00/year academic. Journal that publishes original papers on nursing education issues and research.

★7291★ **International Journal of Nursing Practice**

Wiley-Blackwell
350 Main St. Commerce Pl.
Malden, MA 02148
Ph: (781)388-8200   Fax: (781)388-8210
Fr: 800-759-6120
URL: http://www.blackwellpublishing.com/journal.asp?ref=1322-7114

Bimonthly. $122.00/year for individuals, print and online; $759.00/year for institutions, print and premium online; $690.00/year for institutions, print and standard online; $656.00/year for institutions, premium online only; $469.00/year for institutions, other countries, print and premium online; $426.00/year for institutions, other countries, print and standard online; $405.00/year for institutions, other countries, premium online only; $311.00/year for institutions, print and premium online, Australia/New Zealand; $283.00/year for institutions, print and standard online, Australia/New Zealand; $269.00/year for institutions, premium online only, Australia/New Zealand. Journal publishing articles about advancing the international understanding and development of nursing, both as a profession and as an academic discipline.

★7292★ **International Nursing Review**

Wiley-Blackwell
350 Main St. Commerce Pl.
Malden, MA 02148
Ph: (781)388-8200   Fax: (781)388-8210
Fr: 800-759-6120
URL: http://www.blackwellpublishing.com/journal.asp?ref=0020-8132

Quarterly. $96.00/year for individuals, U.S. print and online; $77.00/year for individuals, print and online, Euro zone; $51.00/year for individuals, print and online, non Euro zone; $57.00/year for individuals, print and online, rest of world; $277.00/year for institutions, print and premium online; $150.00/year for institutions, print and premium online, Euro zone; $150.00/year for institutions, print and premium online, non Euro zone; $165.00/year for institutions, print and premium online, rest of world; $239.00/year for institutions, premium online only; $129.00/year for institutions, premium online only, Euro zone. Journal focusing on current concerns and issues of modern day nursing and health care from an international perspective.

★7293★ **Journal of Addictions Nursing**

Taylor & Francis Group Journals
325 Chestnut St., Ste. 800
Philadelphia, PA 19106
Ph: (215)625-8900   Fax: (215)625-8914
Fr: 800-354-1420
URL: http://www.tandf.co.uk/journals/titles/10884602.asp

$443.00/year for institutions, print and online; $421.00/year for institutions, online only; $135.00/year for individuals. Journal for nursing addiction professionals.

★7294★ **Journal of the Association of Nurses in AIDS Care**

Mosby Inc.
11830 Westline Industrial Dr.
St. Louis, MO 63146
Ph: (314)872-8370   Fax: (314)432-1380
Fr: 800-325-4177
URL: http://www.elsevier.com/wps/find/journaldescription.cws_home

Bimonthly. $428.00/year for institutions; $119.00/year for individuals; $399.00/year for U.S. institutions; $90.00/year for U.S. individuals. Journal covering the spectrum of nursing issues in HIV/AIDS: education, treatment, prevention, research, practice, clinical issues, awareness, policies and program development.

★7295★ **Journal of Clinical Nursing**

Wiley-Blackwell
350 Main St. Commerce Pl.
Malden, MA 02148
Ph: (781)388-8200   Fax: (781)388-8210
Fr: 800-759-6120
E-mail: jcn@oxon.blackwellpublishing.com
URL: http://www.blackwellpublishing.com/journal.asp?ref=0962-1067

Monthly. $307.00/year for individuals, U.S. print and online; $167.00/year for students, U.S. print and online; $1,660.00/year for institutions, U.S. print and premium online; $1,509.00/year for institutions, U.S. print and standard online; $1,434.00/year for institutions, U.S. premium online only; $251.00/year for individuals, Europe print and online; $135.00/year for students, Europe print and online; $899.00/year for institutions, Europe print and premium online; $817.00/year for institutions, Europe print and standard online; $776.00/year for institutions, Europe premium online only. Journal focusing on all spheres of nursing and midwifery practice.

★7296★ **The Journal of Continuing Education in Nursing**

SLACK Inc.
6900 Grove Rd.
Thorofare, NJ 08086-9447
Ph: (856)848-1000   Fax: (856)853-5991
URL: http://www.slackinc.com/allied/jcen

Bimonthly. $99.00/year for individuals; $245.00/year for institutions; $168.00 for individuals, two years; $416.00 for institutions, two years; $32.00 for single issue. Journal for nurses involved in planning and implementing educational programs for the practitioner and others in patient care.

★7297★ **Journal of Emergency Nursing**

Mosby
1600 John F. Kennedy Blvd., Ste. 1800
Philadelphia, PA 19103-2899
Ph: (215)239-3276   Fax: (215)239-3286
URL: http://www.elsevier.com/wps/find/journaleditorialboard.cws_h

Bimonthly. $83.00/year for individuals; $299.00/year for institutions; $88.00/year for other countries, Includes air speed delivery; $256.00/year for institutions, other countries, Includes air speed delivery. Journal containing peer-reviewed articles on clinical aspects of emergency care by, and for, emergency nurses. Presents information about professional, political, administrative, and educational aspects of emergency nursing and nursing in general.

★7298★ **Journal of Gerontological Nursing**

SLACK Inc.
6900 Grove Rd.
Thorofare, NJ 08086-9447
Ph: (856)848-1000   Fax: (856)853-5991
E-mail: jgn@slackinc.com
URL: http://www.jognonline.com

Monthly. $84.00/year for individuals; $142.00 for individuals, two years; $189.00 for individuals, three years; $169.00/year for institutions; $287.00 for institutions, two years; $380.00 for institutions, three years; $21.00 for single issue. Gerontological nursing journal.

★7299★ **Journal of Nursing Administration (JONA)**

Lippincott Williams & Wilkins
530 Walnut St.
Philadelphia, PA 19106-3621
Ph: (215)521-8300   Fax: (215)521-8902
Fr: 800-638-3030
E-mail: jonaeditor@aol.com
URL: http://jonajournal.com/

Monthly. $108.91/year for individuals, U.S.; $345.79/year for institutions, U.S.; $202.94/year for other countries; $478.75/year for institutions, other countries. Journal covering developments and advances in nursing administration and management.

★7300★ **Journal of Nursing Scholarship**

Wiley-Blackwell
350 Main St. Commerce Pl.
Malden, MA 02148
Ph: (781)388-8200   Fax: (781)388-8210
Fr: 800-759-6120
URL: http://www.blackwellpublishing.com/journal.asp?ref=1527-6546

Quarterly. $51.00/year for individuals, print and online; $185.00/year for institutions, print and premium online; $168.00/year for institutions, print and standard online; $160.00/year for institutions, premium online only; $59.00/year for individuals, print and online; $135.00/year for institutions, other countries, print and premium online; $123.00/year for institutions, other countries, print and standard online; $117.00/year for institutions, other countries, premium online only; $39.00/year for individuals, print and online. Peer-reviewed journal covering nursing.

★7301★ Journal of Obstetric, Gynecologic and Neonatal Nursing (JOGNN)

Sage Publications Inc.
2455 Teller Rd.
Thousand Oaks, CA 91320
Ph: (805)499-0721   Fax: (805)499-8096
E-mail: advertising@sagepub.com
URL: http://www.sagepub.com/journal.aspx?pid=245

Bimonthly. $97.00/year for individuals, print + online; $762.00/year for institutions, print + premium online; $724.00/year for institutions, premium online only; $81.00/year for institutions, print + online; $424.00/year for institutions, print + premium online; $402.00/year for institutions, premium online only; $54.00/year for institutions, print + online; $402.00/year; $402.00/year for institutions, premium online only-All countries. Journal covering trends, policies, and research. Official publication of the Association of Women's Health, Obstetric, and Neonatal Nurses (AWHONN).

★7302★ Journal of Orthopaedic Nursing

Mosby Inc.
11830 Westline Industrial Dr.
St. Louis, MO 63146
Ph: (314)872-8370   Fax: (314)432-1380
Fr: 800-325-4177
URL: http://http://www.elsevier.com/wps/find/journaldescription.cws_home/623057/description#description

Quarterly. $84.00/year for individuals, U.S.; $326.00/year for institutions, U.S. Journal for orthopaedic nurses.

★7303★ Journal of Pediatric Health Care

Mosby
1600 John F. Kennedy Blvd., Ste. 1800
Philadelphia, PA 19103-2899
Ph: (215)239-3276   Fax: (215)239-3286
URL: http://www.elsevier.com/wps/find/journaldescription.cws_home

Bimonthly. $99.00/year for other countries; $210.00/year for institutions, other countries; $50.00/year for students, other countries, or resident; $83.00/year for individuals; $229.00/year for institutions; $40.00/year for students, resident in USA. Official publication of the National Association of Pediatric Nurse Practitioners. Provides current information on pediatric clinical topics as well as research studies, health policy, and legislative issues applicable to pediatric clinical practice.

★7304★ Journal of PeriAnesthesia Nursing

Mosby Inc.
11830 Westline Industrial Dr.
St. Louis, MO 63146
Ph: (314)872-8370   Fax: (314)432-1380
Fr: 800-325-4177
URL: http://www.elsevier.com/wps/find/journaldescription.cws_home

Bimonthly. $359.00/year for institutions; $249.00/year for individuals; $267.00/year for U.S. institutions; $119.00/year for U.S. individuals. Journal publishing original, peer-reviewed research for a primary audience that includes nurses in perianesthesia settings, including ambulatory surgery, preadmission testing, postanesthesia (Phases I, II, and III) care, and pain management. Journal providing forum for sharing professional knowledge and experience relating to management, ethics, legislation, research, and other aspects of perianesthesia nursing.

★7305★ Journal of Practical Nursing

National Association for Practical Nurse Education and Service Inc.
PO Box 25647
Alexandria, VA 22313
Ph: (703)933-1003   Fax: (703)940-4049
URL: http://www.napnes.org/jpn/index.htm

Quarterly. $25.00/year for nonmembers; $70.00/year for nonmembers, non-U.S. Journal providing information on licensed practical nursing for LPNs, PN educators, and students.

★7306★ Journal of Psychosocial Nursing and Mental Health Services

SLACK Inc.
6900 Grove Rd.
Thorofare, NJ 08086-9447
Ph: (856)848-1000   Fax: (856)853-5991
E-mail: jpn@slackinc.com
URL: http://www.psychnurse.org

Monthly. $85.00/year for individuals; $144.00 for individuals, two years; $191.00 for individuals, three years; $259.00/year for institutions; $440.00 for institutions, two years; $582.00 for institutions, three years. Journal presenting original, peer-reviewed articles on psychiatric/mental health nursing.

★7307★ Journal of Radiology Nursing

Mosby Inc.
11830 Westline Industrial Dr.
St. Louis, MO 63146
Ph: (314)872-8370   Fax: (314)432-1380
Fr: 800-325-4177
URL: http://www.radiologynursing.org

Quarterly. $72.00/year for individuals, U.S.; $122.00/year for institutions, U.S.; $103.00/year for individuals, International; $157.00/year for institutions, International. Journal publishing articles about patient care in the diagnostic and therapeutic imaging environments.

★7308★ Journal for Specialists in Pediatric Nursing

Wiley-Blackwell
350 Main St. Commerce Pl.
Malden, MA 02148
Ph: (781)388-8200   Fax: (781)388-8210
Fr: 800-759-6120
URL: http://www.blackwellpublishing.com/journal.asp?ref=1539-0136

Quarterly. $71.00/year for individuals, U.S. print and online; $158.00/year for institutions, U.S. print and premium online; $144.00/year for institutions, U.S. print and standard online; $137.00/year for institutions, U.S. premium online only; $74.00/year for individuals, Europe, print and online; $110.00/year for institutions, Europe, print and premium online; $100.00/year for institutions, Europe, print and standard online; $95.00/year for institutions, Europe, premium online only; $49.00/year for individuals, print and online; $110.00/year for institutions, other countries, print and premium online. Journal focusing on nurses who specialize in the care of children and families.

★7309★ LPN2008

Lippincott Williams & Wilkins
530 Walnut St.
Philadelphia, PA 19106-3621
Ph: (215)521-8300   Fax: (215)521-8902
Fr: 800-638-3030
URL: http://www.lww.com/product/?1553-0582

Bimonthly. $119.96/year for institutions; $27.86/year for individuals; $21.91/year for U.S., in-training; $67.96/year for individuals, other countries; $167.96/year for institutions, other countries. Peer-reviewed journal that focuses on bedside care skills for practical nurses.

★7310★ McKnight's Long-Term Care News

McKnight's Long-Term Care News
1 Northfield Plz., Ste. 521
Northfield, IL 60093-1216
Ph: (847)784-8706   Fax: (847)784-9346
Fr: 800-558-1703
E-mail: ltcn-webmaster@mltcn.com
URL: http://www.mcknightsonline.com/home

Professional magazine.

★7311★ MCN, The American Journal of Maternal/Child Nursing

Lippincott Williams & Wilkins
530 Walnut St.
Philadelphia, PA 19106-3621
Ph: (215)521-8300   Fax: (215)521-8902
Fr: 800-638-3030
URL: http://www.mcnjournal.com/

Bimonthly. $53.91/year for individuals, U.S.; $131.95/year for institutions, U.S.; $121.94/year for other countries, individual; $161.95/year for institutions, other countries. Journal focusing on maternal/child nursing and health.

★7312★ Military Medicine

AMSUS - The Society of the Federal Health Agencies
9320 Old Georgetown Rd.
Bethesda, MD 20814
Ph: (301)897-8800   Fax: (301)503-5446
Fr: 800-761-9320
URL: http://www.amsus.org/journal/

Monthly. $132.00/year for individuals; $177.00/year for other countries; $20.00 for single issue; $27.00 for single issue, other ountries. Journal for professional personnel ffiliated with the Federal medical services.

★7313★ Minority Nurse Newsletter

ucker Publications Inc.
O Box 580
isle, IL 60532
h: (630)969-3809   Fax: (630)969-3895
-mail: drsallie@gmail.com
RL: http://www.tuckerpub.com

Description: Quarterly. Provides health are information of interest to minority nurs-ng faculty.

★7314★ Modern Healthcare

rain Communications Inc.
60 N Michigan Ave.
hicago, IL 60601
h: (312)649-5411   Fax: (312)280-3150
r: 888-909-9111
-mail: subs@crain.com
RL: http://www.modernhealthcare.com

Weekly. $154.00/year for individuals; 244.00/year for Canada; $208.00/year for ther countries. Weekly business news mag-zine for healthcare management.

7315★ Nephrology Nursing Journal

American Nephrology Nurses' Association
East Holly Ave.
O Box 56
Pitman, NJ 08071-0056
h: (856)256-2320   Fax: (856)589-7463
URL: http://www.nephrologynursing.net/
Bimonthly. Nursing journal.

★7316★ Nurse Education in Practice

Mosby Inc.
1830 Westline Industrial Dr.
St. Louis, MO 63146
h: (314)872-8370   Fax: (314)432-1380
r: 800-325-4177
URL: http://www.us.elsevierhealth.com/
product.jsp?isbn=14715953#a

Bimonthly. $77.00/year for individuals; 311.00/year for institutions. Journal en-abling lecturers and practitioners to both share and disseminate evidence that dem-onstrates the actual practice of education as t is experienced in the realities of their respective work environments.

★7317★ Nurse Leader

Mosby Inc.
11830 Westline Industrial Dr.
St. Louis, MO 63146
Ph: (314)872-8370   Fax: (314)432-1380
Fr: 800-325-4177
E-mail: roxane.spitzer@comcast.net
URL: http://www.nurseleader.com

Bimonthly. $64.00/year for individuals, do-mestic; $140.00/year for institutions, domes-tic; $219.00/year for institutions, internation-al; $100.00/year for individuals, international. Journal publishing articles on the vision, skills, and tools needed by nurses currently aspiring to leadership positions.

★7318★ The Nurse Practitioner

Lippincott Williams & Wilkins
530 Walnut St.
Philadelphia, PA 19106-3621
Ph: (215)521-8300   Fax: (215)521-8902
Fr: 800-638-3030
E-mail: npedit@wolterskluwer.com
URL: http://www.tnpj.com

Monthly. $57.95/year for individuals; $209.00/year for institutions; $29.00/year for U.S., in-training; $120.98/year for other countries, individual; $258.98/year for institu-tions. Magazine presenting clinical informa-tion to nurses in advanced primary care practice. Also covers legal, business, eco-nomic, ethical, research, and pharmaceutical issues.

★7319★ Nurse Practitioner Forum

Elsevier
1600 John F. Kennedy Blvd., Ste. 1800
Philadelphia, PA 19103-2899
Ph: (215)239-3900   Fax: (215)238-7883
URL: http://202.117.24.24/html/xjtu/ckzl/
ssci/ssci_n.htm

Quarterly. Journal for nurse practitioners.

★7320★ Nursing Clinics of North America

Mosby Inc.
11830 Westline Industrial Dr.
St. Louis, MO 63146
Ph: (314)872-8370   Fax: (314)432-1380
Fr: 800-325-4177
URL: http://www.elsevier.com/wps/find/bo-okdescription.cws_home/70

Quarterly. $55.00/year for individuals. Jour-nal publishing articles by experts in the field; provides current, practical information geared to the active nurse.

★7321★ Nursing Education Perspectives

National League for Nursing
61 Broadway, 33rd Fl.
New York, NY 10006-2701
Ph: (212)363-5555   Fax: (212)812-0391
Fr: 800-669-1656
URL: http://www.nln.org/nlnjournal/in-dex.htm

Bimonthly. $40.00/year; $70.00/year for non-members; $90.00/year for Canada; $98.00/year for other countries, non-member; $137.00/year for individuals; $157.00/year for Canada; $165.00/year for other coun-tries. Professional journal for nurses. In-cludes articles on health policy, social and economic issues affecting health care, and nursing education and practice.

★7322★ Nursing Management

Lippincott Williams & Wilkins
323 Norristown Rd., Ste. 200
Ambler, PA 19002-2758
Ph: (215)646-8700   Fax: (215)654-1328
URL: http://www.nursingmanagement.com/

Monthly. $46.95/year for individuals, U.S.; $199.00/year for institutions, U.S.; $103.00/

year for individuals, international; $258.00/year for institutions, international. Magazine focusing on nursing management.

★7323★ Nursing Outlook

Mosby Inc.
10801 Executive Center Dr., Ste. 509
Little Rock, AR 72211
Ph: (501)223-5165   Fax: (501)223-0519
URL: http://journals.elsevierhealth.com/peri-odicals/ymno

Bimonthly. $65.00/year for individuals; $106.00/year for individuals, Canada; $106.00/year for individuals, other countries. Official journal of the American Academy of Nursing, reporting on trends and issues in nursing.

★7324★ Nursing Science Quarterly

Sage Publications Inc.
2455 Teller Rd.
Thousand Oaks, CA 91320
Ph: (805)499-0721   Fax: (805)499-8096
URL: http://www.sagepub.com

Quarterly. $443.00/year for institutions, com-bined (print & e-access); $465.00/year for institutions, combined plus backfile current volume print and all; $399.00/year for institu-tions, e-access; $421.00/year for institutions, e-access plus backfile (all online content); $399.00/year for institutions, e-access (con-tent through 1999); $434.00/year for institu-tions, print only; $129.00/year for individuals, print only; $120.00 for institutions, single print; $42.00 for individuals, single print. Journal focusing on enhancement of nursing knowledge.

★7325★ Orthopaedic Nursing

National Association of Orthopaedic Nurses
401 North Michigan Ave., Ste. 2200
Chicago, IL 60611
Fax: (312)527-6658   Fr: 800-289-6266
URL: http://www.orthopaedicnursing.com

Bimonthly. Nursing magazine.

★7326★ Pediatric Nursing

Jannetti Publications Inc.
East Holly Ave., Box 56
Pitman, NJ 08071-0056
Ph: (856)256-2300
URL: http://www.pediatricnursing.net

Bimonthly. $42.00/year for individuals; $78.00 for individuals, two years; $65.00/year for institutions; $120.00 for institutions, two years; $66.00/year for individuals, for-eign; $126.00 for individuals, foreign, two years; $89.00/year for institutions, foreign; $168.00 for institutions, foreign, two years; $15.00 for single issue, current issue; $15.00 for single issue, back future issue. Profes-sional nursing magazine.

★7327★ Provider

American Health Care Association
1201 L St. NW
Washington, DC 20005
Ph: (202)842-4444   Fax: (202)842-3860
E-mail: sales@ahca.org
URL: http://www.providermagazine.com

Monthly. $48.00/year for U.S.; $61.00/year
for Canada and Mexico; $85.00/year for
other countries. Provider Magazine.

★7328★ Rehabilitation Nursing

Rehabilitation Nursing
4700 West Lake Ave.
Glenview, IL 60025
Ph: (847)375-4710   Fr: 800-229-7530
E-mail: info@rehabnurse.org
URL: http://www.rehabnurse.org/index.html

Bimonthly. $95.00/year for individuals;
$125.00/year for institutions; $135.00/year
for other countries; $18.00 for single issue;
$125.00/year for Canada. Magazine focus-
ing on rehabilitation nursing involving clinical
practice, research, education, and administration.

★7329★ Research in Nursing & Health

John Wiley & Sons Inc.
111 River St.
Hoboken, NJ 07030-5774
Ph: (201)748-6000   Fax: (201)748-6088
Fr: 800-825-7550
URL: http://as.wiley.com/WileyCDA/Wiley-
Title/productCd-NUR.html

Bimonthly. $140.00/year for individuals, print
only; $140.00/year for Canada and Mexico,
in Canada, add 7% GST print only; $176.00/
year for other countries, print only;
$1,185.00/year for institutions, print only;
$1,257.00/year for institutions, Canada and
Mexico, print only in Canada, add 7% GST;
$1,299.00/year for institutions, other coun-
tries, print only; $1,304.00/year for institu-
tions, print and online U.S.; $1,376.00/year
for institutions, Canada and Mexico, print
and online, in Canada, add 7% GST;
$1,418.00/year for institutions, other coun-
tries, print and online. Journal providing
forum for research in the areas of nursing
practice, education, and administration. Covers health issues relevant to nursing as well
as investigations of the applications of research findings in clinical settings.

★7330★ Seminars in Oncology

Elsevier
1600 John F. Kennedy Blvd., Ste. 1800
Philadelphia, PA 19103-2899
Ph: (215)239-3900   Fax: (215)238-7883
E-mail: elspcs@elsevier.com
URL: http://www.elsevier.com

$228.00/year for individuals, U.S.; $114.00/
year for students, U.S.; $311.00/year for
individuals, Canada; $156.00/year for stu-
dents, Canada; $311.00/year for individuals,
Mexico; $156.00/year for students, Mexico;
$311.00/year for individuals, international;
$156.00/year for students, international;
$510.00/year for institutions, international;
$424.00/year for institutions, U.S. Journal

reviewing current diagnostic and treatment
techniques used in oncology patient care.

★7331★ Seminars in Oncology Nursing

Mosby Inc.
11830 Westline Industrial Dr.
St. Louis, MO 63146
Ph: (314)872-8370   Fax: (314)432-1380
Fr: 800-325-4177
URL: http://www.nursingoncology.com

Quarterly. $91.00/year for individuals;
$227.00/year for institutions; $23.00 for individuals, single issue; $172.00/year for indi-
viduals, International; $298.00/year for insti-
tutions, International; $43.00 for individuals,
single issue, international. Journal publishing
material to disseminate knowledge in the
complex field of cancer nursing.

★7332★ Teaching and Learning in Nursing

Elsevier Science Inc.
360 Park Ave. S
New York, NY 10010
Ph: (212)989-5800   Fax: (212)633-3990
URL: http://www.elsevier.com

Quarterly. $119.00/year for institutions, U.S.
$167.00/year for institutions, other countries;
$75.00/year for individuals, U.S. $104.00/
year for individuals, other countries. Journal
devoted to associate degree nursing education and practice.

★7333★ Worldviews on Evidence-Based Nursing

Wiley-Blackwell
350 Main St. Commerce Pl.
Malden, MA 02148
Ph: (781)388-8200   Fax: (781)388-8210
Fr: 800-759-6120
URL: http://www.blackwellpublishing.com/
journals/WVN

Quarterly. $112.00/year for individuals, print
and online; $116.00/year for individuals,
online only; $49.00/year for members, print
and online; $47.00/year for members, online
only; $318.00/year for institutions, print and
premium online; $289.00/year for institu-
tions, print and standard online; $275.00/
year for institutions, premium online only;
$132.00/year for individuals, print and online;
$126.00/year for individuals, online only;
$53.00/year for members, print and online.
Journal that offers research, policy and
practice, education and management for
nursing.

PLACEMENT AND JOB REFERRAL SERVICES

★7334★ American Association of Occupational Health Nurses (AAOHN)

2920 Brandywine Rd., Ste. 100
Atlanta, GA 30341
Ph: (770)455-7757   Fax: (770)455-7271
E-mail: ann@aaohn.org
URL: http://www.aaohn.org

Description: Represents registered professional nurses employed by business and
industrial firms; nurse educators, nurse editors, nurse writers, and others interested in
occupational health nursing. Promotes and
sets standards for the profession. Provides
and approves continuing education; maintains governmental affairs program; offers
placement service.

★7335★ American Organization of Nurse Executives (AONE)

325 Seventh St. NW
Liberty Pl.
Washington, DC 20004
Ph: (202)626-2240   Fax: (202)638-5499
E-mail: aone@aha.org
URL: http://www.aone.org

Description: Provides leadership, professional development, advocacy, and research
to advance nursing practice and patient
care, promote nursing leadership and excellence, and shape healthcare public policy.
Supports and enhances the management,
leadership, educational, and professional
development of nursing leaders. Offers
placement service through Career Development and Referral Center.

★7336★ American Public Health Association (APHA)

800 I St. NW
Washington, DC 20001
Ph: (202)777-2742   Fax: (202)777-2534
E-mail: comments@apha.org
URL: http://www.apha.org

Members: Professional organization of physicians, nurses, educators, academicians,
environmentalists, epidemiologists, new professionals, social workers, health administrators, optometrists, podiatrists, pharmacists,
dentists, nutritionists, health planners, other
community and mental health specialists,
and interested consumers. **Purpose:** Seeks
to protect and promote personal, mental,
and environmental health. **Activities:** Services include: promulgation of standards;
establishment of uniform practices and procedures; development of the etiology of
communicable diseases; research in public
health; exploration of medical care programs
and their relationships to public health.
Sponsors job placement service.

EMPLOYER DIRECTORIES AND NETWORKING LISTS

★7337★ AHA Guide to the Health Care Field

American Hospital Association
1 N Franklin
Chicago, IL 60606
Ph: (312)422-2050   Fax: (312)422-4700
Fr: 800-424-4301

Annual, August. Covers hospitals, networks, multi-health care systems, freestanding ambulatory surgery centers, psychiatric facilities, long-term care facilities, substance abuse programs, and other health-related organizations. Entries include: For hospitals–Facility name, address, phone, administrator's name, number of beds, facilities and services, number of employees, expenses, other statistics. For other organizations–Name, address, phone, fax, name and title of contact. Arrangement: Geographical. Indexes: Hospital name.

★7338★ American Journal of Nursing-Career Guide

American Journal of Nursing
c/o Lippincott, Williams & Wilkins
530 Walnut St.
Philadelphia, PA 19106-3621
Ph: (215)521-8300   Fax: (215)521-8902
Fr: 800-627-0484
URL: http://www.ajnonline.com

Annual, April. $34.90 for individuals; $234.95 for institutions; $26.95 for individuals, in-training; $87.00 for individuals, international; $299.00 for institutions, international. Publication includes: List of nursing organizations and agencies. Entries include: Name, address, names of officers or nursing representatives. Arrangement: Classified by type of organization.

★7339★ CriticalCare Choices

Lippincott Williams & Wilkins
530 Walnut St.
Philadelphia, PA 19106-3621
Ph: (215)521-8300   Fax: (215)521-8902
Fr: 800-346-7844
URL: http://www.nursingcenter.com

Annual, May 2005. Free. Clinical and career directory for critical care nurses. Covers non-profit and investor-owned hospitals and departments of the United States government that hire critical care nurses. Arrangement: Geographical. Indexes: Geographical.

★7340★ Directory of Hospital Personnel

Grey House Publishing
185 Millerton Rd.
PO Box 860
Millerton, NY 12546
Ph: (518)789-8700   Fax: (518)789-0556
Fr: 800-562-2139
URL: http://www.greyhouse.com/hospital_personnel.htm

Annual. $325.00 for print product; $545.00 for online database subscription; $650.00 for online database subscription and print product combined. Covers 200,000 executives at 7,000 U.S. hospitals. Entries include: Name of hospital, address, phone; number of beds; type and JCAHO status of hospital; names and titles of key department heads and staff; medical and nursing school affiliations; number of residents, interns, and nursing students. Arrangement: Geographical. Indexes: Hospital name, personnel, hospital size.

★7341★ Essentials of Internet Use in Nursing

Springer Publishing Co.
11 W 42nd St., 15th Fl.
New York, NY 10036
Ph: (212)431-4370   Fax: (212)941-7342
Fr: 877-687-7476
URL: http://www.springerpub.com/prod.aspx?prod_id=15543

Latest edition August 2002. $32.95 for individuals. Publication includes: Appendix listing relevant Web sites. Principal content of publication is information on Internet usage for clinical nursing practice, for continuing nursing education, for medical research, and for nursing staff recruitment and development. Indexes: Topical.

★7342★ Guide to Careers in the Health Professions

The Princeton Review
2315 Broadway
New York, NY 10024
Ph: (212)874-8282   Fax: (212)874-0775
Fr: 800-733-3000
URL: http://www.princetonreview.com/

Published January, 2001. $24.95 for individuals. Presents advice and information for those searching for satisfying careers in the health professions. Publication includes: Directory of schools and academic programs. Entries include: Name, address, phone, tuition, program details, employment profiles.

★7343★ Hitting the Road

Lippincott Williams & Wilkins
530 Walnut St.
Philadelphia, PA 19106-3621
Ph: (215)521-8300   Fax: (215)521-8902
Fr: 800-638-3030
URL: http://www.lww.com

Published January 2003. $24.95 for individuals. Publication includes: List of 70 health care staffing agencies. Principal content of publication is discussion of and assistance in entering field of travel nursing.

★7344★ Hospital Blue Book

Billian Publishing Inc./Transworld Publishing Inc.
2100 Powers Ferry Rd. SE
Atlanta, GA 30339
Ph: (770)955-5656   Fax: (770)952-0669
Fr: 800-533-8484
E-mail: blu-book@billian.com

2005. $300.00 for individuals. Covers more than 6,687 hospitals; some listings also appear in a separate southern edition of this publication. Entries include: Name of hospital, accreditation, mailing address, phone, fax, number of beds, type of facility (nonprofit, general, state, etc.); list of administrative personnel and chiefs of medical services, with specific titles. Arrangement: Geographical.

★7345★ How to Survive and Maybe Even Love Nursing School!

F.A. Davis Co.
1915 Arch St.
Philadelphia, PA 19103
Ph: (215)568-2270   Fax: (215)568-5065
Fr: 800-523-4049

2nd edition 2004. $24.95 for individuals. Publication includes: List of resources for nursing students, such as Web sites and related organizations. Principal content of publication is information about succeeding in nursing school.

★7346★ The JobBank Guide to Health Care Companies

Adams Media Corp.
57 Littlefield St.
Avon, MA 02322
Ph: (508)427-7100   Fax: (508)427-6790
Fr: 800-872-5627
URL: http://www.amazon.com/Jobbank-Guide-Health-Care-Companies/dp

Biennial. Covers jobs nationwide in health care companies. Entries include: Firm or organization name, address, phone, name and title of contact; description of organization, headquarters location, typical titles for entry- and middle-level positions, educational backgrounds desired, fringe benefits offered, stock exchange listing, training programs, internships, parent company, number of employees, revenues, e-mail and web addresses, projected number of hires. Indexes: Alphabetical.

★7347★ Medical and Health Information Directory

Gale, Cengage Learning
27500 Drake Rd.
Farmington Hills, MI 48331-3535
Ph: (248)699-4253   Fax: (248)699-8065
Fr: 800-877-4253
E-mail: businessproducts@gale.com
URL: http://www.gale.com

Annual; latest edition 20th, July 2007. $375.00/volume. Covers in Volume 1, more than 26,500 medical and health oriented associations, organizations, institutions, and government agencies, including health maintenance organizations (HMOs), preferred provider organizations (PPOs), insurance companies, pharmaceutical companies, research centers, and medical and allied health schools. In Volume 2, over 12,000 medical book publishers; medical periodicals, directories, audiovisual producers and services, medical libraries and information centers, electronic resources, and health-related internet search engines. In Volume 3, more than 35,500 clinics, treatment centers, care programs, and counseling/diagnostic services for 34 subject areas. Entries include: Institution, service, or firm name, address, phone, fax, email and URL; many include names of key personnel and, when pertinent, descriptive annotations. Volume 3 was formerly listed separately as Health Services Directory. Arrangement: Classified by organization activity, service, etc. Indexes: Each volume has a complete alphabetical name and keyword index.

★7348★ Nursing Career Directory

Lippincott Williams & Wilkins
530 Walnut St.
Philadelphia, PA 19106-3621
Ph: (215)521-8300   Fax: (215)521-8902
Fr: 800-346-7844
URL: http://www.springnet.com

Annual, January. Covers nonprofit and investor-owned hospitals and departments of the United States government that hire nurses. Does not report specific positions available. Entries include: Unit name, location, areas of nursing specialization, educational requirements for nurses, licensing, facilities, benefits, etc. Arrangement: Geographical. Indexes: Geographical.

★7349★ The Nursing Job Search Handbook

University of Pennsylvania Press
3905 Spruce St.
Philadelphia, PA 19104-4112
Ph: (215)898-6261   Fax: (215)898-0404
Fr: 800-445-9880
URL: http://www.upenn.edu/pennpress/book/13752.html

Latest edition 2002. $18.95 for individuals; $12.50 for individuals. Publication includes: Appendix listing state licensing boards and nursing organizations. Entries include: Name, address, phone. Principal content of publication is information on obtaining a job in the field of nursing. Indexes: Alphabetical.

★7350★ Peterson's Guide to Nursing Programs

Peterson's
Princeton Pke. Corporate Ctr., 2000
  Lenox Dr.
PO Box 67005
Lawrenceville, NJ 08648
Ph: (609)896-1800   Fax: (609)896-4531
Fr: 800-338-3282
URL: http://www.petersons.com/

Annual; latest edition 12th, April 2006. $18.48 for individuals. Covers over 700 institutions offering approximately 2,000 accredited nursing programs in the U.S. and Canada. Entries include: Academic information, extracurricular issues, costs, financial aid.

★7351★ Peterson's Job Opportunities for Health and Science Majors

Peterson's
Princeton Pke. Corporate Ctr., 2000
  Lenox Dr.
PO Box 67005
Lawrenceville, NJ 08648
Ph: (609)896-1800   Fax: (609)896-4531
Fr: 800-338-3282
URL: http://www.petersons.com

Irregular; latest edition 1999. Covers about 1,300 research, consulting, government, and non-profit and profit service organizations that hire college and university graduates in science and health-related majors. Entries include: Organization name, address, phone, name and title of contact, type of organization, number of employees, Standard Industrial Classification (SIC) code; description of opportunities available including disciplines, level of education required, starting locations and salaries, level of experience accepted, benefits.

★7352★ Saunders Student Nurse Planners

W.B. Saunders Company
c/o Elsevier
30 Corporate Dr., 4th Fl.
Burlington, MA 01803
Ph: (781)313-4700   Fax: (781)313-4880
URL: http://www.elsevier.com/

Latest edition July, 2005. $10.99. Covers nursing orientation. Publication includes: telephone and address directory.

HANDBOOKS AND MANUALS

★7353★ 101 Careers in Nursing

Springer-Verlag New York, Inc.
233 Spring St.
New York, NY 10013
Ph: (212)460-1501   Fax: (212)460-1595
URL: http://www.springer.com/

Jeanne M. Novotny, Doris T. Lippman, Nicole K. Sanders, Joyce J. Fitzpatrick. June 2006. $16.00 (paper). Illustrated. 222 pages.

★7354★ Anatomy of a Job Search: A Nurse's Guide to Finding and Landing the Job You Want

Lippincott Williams & Wilkins
530 Walnut St.
Philadelphia, PA 19106
Ph: (215)521-8300   Fax: (215)521-8902
Fr: 800-346-7844
URL: http://www.lww.com

Jeanna Bozell. 1999. $25.95 (paper). 146 pages.

★7355★ Building and Managing a Career in Nursing: Strategies for Advancing Your Career

Sigma Theta Tau International, Center for Nursing Press
550 W. North St.
Indianapolis, IN 46202
Ph: (317)634-8171   Fax: (317)634-8188
Fr: 888-634-7575

Terry W. Miller. May 2003. $25.00. Illustrated. 411 pages.

★7356★ Career Opportunities in Health Care (Career Opportunities)

Facts On File Inc.
132 W. 31st St., 17th Fl.
New York, NY 10001-2006
Ph: (212)967-8800   Fax: 800-678-3633
Fr: 800-322-8755
E-mail: custserv@factsonfile.com
URL: http://www.factsonfile.com

Shelly Field. Arthur E. Weintraub. 2002. Reprint. $49.50. 243 pages. Part of the Career Opportunities Series.

★7357★ Careers in Health Care

The McGraw-Hill Companies
PO Box 182604
Columbus, OH 43272
Fax: (614)759-3749   Fr: 877-883-5524
E-mail: customer.service@mcgraw-hill.com
URL: http://www.mcgraw-hill.com

Barbara M. Swanson. Fifth edition, 2005. $15.95 (paper). 192 pages. Describes job duties, work settings, salaries, licensing and certification requirements, educational preparation, and future outlook. Gives ideas on how to secure a job.

★7358★ Careers for Night Owls and Other Insomniacs

The McGraw-Hill Companies
PO Box 182604
Columbus, OH 43272
Fax: (614)759-3749   Fr: 877-883-5524
E-mail: customer.service@mcgraw-hill.com
URL: http://www.mcgraw-hill.com

Louise Miller. Second edition, 2002. $12.95 (paper). 160 pages.

★7359★ Careers in Nursing

The McGraw-Hill Companies
PO Box 182604
Columbus, OH 43272
Fax: (614)759-3749   Fr: 877-883-5524
E-mail: customer.service@mcgraw-hill.com
URL: http://www.mcgraw-hill.com

Terence J. Sacks. Second edition, 2003. $15.95 (paper). 192 pages.

★7360★ Comprehensive Review of Practical Nursing for NCLEX-PN

Mosby
11830 Westline Industrial Dr.
St. Louis, MO 63146
Ph: (314)872-8370   Fax: 800-235-0256
Fr: 800-325-4177

URL: http://www.elsevier.com

Mary O. Eyles, editor. First edition, 2004. $34.95 (paper). 740 pages. With more than 3,500 review questions, this useful study tool covers essential nursing content from all core clinical areas.

★7361★ **Core Curriculum for the Licensed Practical/Vocational Hospice and Palliative Nurse**
Kendall/Hunt Publishing Company
4050 Westmark Dr.
Dubuque, IA 52004
Ph: (563)589-1000   Fax: (563)589-1046
Fr: 800-228-0810
URL: http://www.kendallhunt.com/
Hospice & Palliative Nurses Association. 2005. $55.00.

★7362★ **Developing Your Career in Nursing**
Sage Publications, Inc.
2455 Teller Rd.
Thousand Oaks, CA 91320-2218
Ph: (805)499-0721   Fax: (805)499-0871
E-mail: info@sagepub.com
URL: http://www.sagepub.com/
Robert Newell, editor. 2003. $37.95. 184 pages.

★7363★ **Expert Resumes for Health Care Careers**
Jist Works
875 Montreal Way
St. Paul, MN 55102
Fr: 800-648-5478
E-mail: info@jist.com
URL: http://www.jist.com
Wendy S. Enelow and Louise M. Kursmark. December 2003. $16.95. 288 pages.

★7364★ **Federal Jobs in Nursing and Health Sciences**
Impact Publications
9104 Manassas Dr., Ste. N
Manassas Park, VA 20111-5211
Ph: (703)361-7300   Fax: (703)335-9486
Fr: 800-361-1055
E-mail: query@impactpublications.com
URL: http://www.impactpublications.com
Russ Smith. 1996. Part of "Federal Jobs in ..." Series. $14.95. 130 pages.

★7365★ **Gerontological Nursing Certification Review Guide for the Generalist, Clinical Specialist & Nurse Practitioner**
Health Leadership Associates, Inc
PO Box 1784
Germantown, MD 20875
Ph: (301)983-2405   Fax: (301)983-2693
Fr: 800-435-4775
E-mail: hlacert@aol.com
URL: http://www.healthleadership.com/
Catharine Kopac and Virginia L. Millonig,

editors. Revised, 1996. $47.75 (paper). 563 pages.

★7366★ **Health Careers Today**
Elsevier
11830 Westline Industrial Dr.
St. Louis, MO 63146
Ph: (314)453-7010   Fax: (314)453-7095
Fr: 800-545-2522
E-mail: usbkinfo@elsevier.com
URL: http://www.elsevier.com
Gerdin, Judith. Fourth edition. 2007. $59.95. 496 pages. Covers more than 45 health careers. Discusses the roles and responsibilities of various occupations and provides a solid foundation in the skills needed for all health careers.

★7367★ **Mosby's Review Questions for NCLEX-RN**
Mosby
11830 Westline Industrial Dr.
St. Louis, MO 63146
Ph: (314)872-8370   Fax: 800-235-0256
Fr: 800-325-4177
URL: http://www.elsevier.com
Dolores F. Saxton, Patricia M. Nugent, Phyllis K. Pelikan, and Judith S. Green. Fourth edition, 2007. $39.95 (paper). 650 pages.

★7368★ **Mosby's Tour Guide to Nursing School: A Student's Road Survival Guide**
Mosby
11830 Westline Industrial Dr.
St. Louis, MO 63146
Ph: (314)872-8370   Fax: 800-235-0256
Fr: 800-325-4177
URL: http://www.elsevier.com
Melodie Chenevert. Fifth edition, 2006. $27.95 (paper). 256 pages.

★7369★ **The Nurses' Career Guide: Discovering New Horizons in Health Care**
Sovereignty Press
1241 Johnson Ave., No. 353
San Luis Obispo, CA 93401
Ph: (805)543-6100   Fax: (805)543-1085
Fr: 888-201-2501
Zardoya E. Eagles and Marti Kock. 1999. $17.95 (paper). 118 pages. Helps the reader identify work skills and achievements, clarify values and goals, explore career options, develop a personal action plan, prepare cover letters and resumes, and conduct informational and job interviews. Also addresses the dramatic changes that nurses currently face in the workplace. Includes a 65-page resource section which lists references, samples of resumes and letters, professional magazines, organizations, and online resources.

★7370★ **Nursing (Career Portraits)**
The McGraw-Hill Companies
PO Box 182604
Columbus, OH 43272
Fax: (614)759-3749   Fr: 877-883-5524
E-mail: customer.service@mcgraw-hill.com
URL: http://www.mcgraw-hill.com
Blythe Camenson. 1997. $13.95. 96 pages.

★7371★ **The Nursing Experience: Trends, Challenges & Transitions**
The McGraw-Hill Companies
PO Box 182604
Columbus, OH 43272
Fax: (614)759-3749   Fr: 877-883-5524
E-mail: customer.service@mcgraw-hill.com
URL: http://www.mcgraw-hill.com
Lucille A. Joel and L.Y. Kelly. Fifth edition, 2006. $44.95 (paper). 792 pages.

★7372★ **Nursing Today: Transition and Trends**
W. B. Saunders Co.
6277 Sea Harbor Dr.
Orlando, FL 32887
Fr: 800-654-2452
URL: http://www.elsevier.com
JoAnn Zerwekh and Jo C. Claborn, editors. Fifth edition, 2005. $47.95 (paper). 688 pages.

★7373★ **Opportunities in Child Care Careers**
The McGraw-Hill Companies
PO Box 182604
Columbus, OH 43272
Fax: (614)759-3749   Fr: 877-883-5524
E-mail: customer.service@mcgraw-hill.com
URL: http://www.mcgraw-hill.com
Renee Wittenberg. 2006. $13.95 (paper). 160 pages. Discusses various job opportunities and how to secure a position. Illustrated.

★7374★ **Opportunities in Environmental Careers**
The McGraw-Hill Companies
PO Box 182604
Columbus, OH 43272
Fax: (614)759-3749   Fr: 877-883-5524
E-mail: customer.service@mcgraw-hill.com
URL: http://www.mcgraw-hill.com
Odom Fanning. Revised, 2002. $12.95 (paper). 174 pages. Describes a broad range of opportunities in fields such as environmental health, recreation, physics, and hygiene, and provides job search advice. Part of the "Opportunities in ..." Series.

★7375★ **Opportunities in Health and Medical Careers**
The McGraw-Hill Companies
PO Box 182604
Columbus, OH 43272
Fax: (614)759-3749   Fr: 877-883-5524
E-mail: customer.service@mcgraw-hill.com
URL: http://www.mcgraw-hill.com

I. Donald Snook, Jr. and Leo D'Orazio. 2004. $13.95 (paper). 157 pages. Covers the full range of medical and health occupations. Illustrated.

★7376★ Opportunities in Nursing Careers

The McGraw-Hill Companies
PO Box 182604
Columbus, OH 43272
Fax: (614)759-3749   Fr: 877-883-5524
E-mail: customer.service@mcgraw-hill.com
URL: http://www.mcgraw-hill.com

Keville Frederickson and Judith A. Ryan. Second edition, 2003. $13.95 (paper). 160 pages. Discusses the employment outlook and job-seeking techniques for LVN's, LPN's, RN's, nurse practitioners, nurse anesthetists, and other nurse members of the medical team. Includes a complete list of state nurses associations, state nursing boards, and specialty nursing organizations. Contains bibliography and illustrations.

★7377★ Opportunities in Physician Assistant Careers

The McGraw-Hill Companies
PO Box 182604
Columbus, OH 43272
Fax: (614)759-3749   Fr: 877-883-5524
E-mail: customer.service@mcgraw-hill.com
URL: http://www.mcgraw-hill.com

Terence J. Sacks. 2005. $13.95 (paper). 151 pages.

★7378★ Opportunities in State and Local Government Careers

The McGraw-Hill Companies
PO Box 182604
Columbus, OH 43272
Fax: (614)759-3749   Fr: 877-883-5524
E-mail: customer.service@mcgraw-hill.com
URL: http://www.mcgraw-hill.com

Neale J. Baxter. Revised edition, 1992. $14.95; $10.95 (paper). 148 pages. Points out the incentives and drawbacks of a government career. Describes hiring procedures and provides tips on filling out applications, taking physical and aptitude tests, handling interviews, and finding jobs. Describes the jobs in which 75% of all state and local government workers are employed. For each occupation, covers the nature of the work and the training required.

★7379★ Real People Working in Health Care

The McGraw-Hill Companies
PO Box 182604
Columbus, OH 43272
Fax: (614)759-3749   Fr: 877-883-5524
E-mail: customer.service@mcgraw-hill.com
URL: http://www.mcgraw-hill.com

Blythe Camenson, Jan Goldberg. 1996. $12.95 (paper). 144 pages. Interviews and profiles of working professionals capture a range of opportunities in this field.

★7380★ Real-Resumes for Nursing Jobs: Including Real Resumes Used to Change Careers and Resumes Used to Gain Federal Employment

PREP Publishing
1110 1/2 Hay St., PMB 66
Fayetteville, NC 28305
Ph: (910)483-6611   Fax: (910)483-2439
Fr: 800-533-2814

Anne McKinney. 2003. $16.95. 181 pages. Real-Resumes Series.

★7381★ Reinventing Your Nursing Career: A Handbook for Success in the Age of Managed Care

Aspen Publishers
1 Lake St.
Upper Saddle River, NJ 07458
Ph: (201)236-7000   Fax: 800-445-6991
Fr: 800-638-8437
URL: http://www.aspenpublishers.com/

Michael Newell and Mario Pinardo. 1998. $53.95 (paper). 253 pages. Helps nurses identify career goals and take practical steps to realize them using self-surveys, goal-setting methods, personal action plans, and networking techniques.

★7382★ Resumes for the Health Care Professional

John Wiley & Sons Inc.
1 Wiley Dr.
Somerset, NJ 08873
Ph: (732)469-4400   Fax: (732)302-2300
Fr: 800-225-5945
E-mail: custserv@wiley.com
URL: http://www.wiley.com/WileyCDA/

Kim Marino. Second edition, 2000. $21.50 (paper). 224 pages.

★7383★ Resumes for Nursing Careers

The McGraw-Hill Companies
PO Box 182604
Columbus, OH 43272
Fax: (614)759-3749   Fr: 877-883-5524
E-mail: customer.service@mcgraw-hill.com
URL: http://www.mcgraw-hill.com

2001. $11.95 (paper). 144 pages.

★7384★ Your Career in Nursing: Manage Your Future in the Changing World of Healthcare

Kaplan Publishing
1 Liberty Plaza, 24th Fl.
New York, NY 10006
Ph: (312)836-4400   Fax: (312)836-1021
Fr: 800-527-4836
URL: http://www.kaplanpublishing.com

Annette Vallano. November 2006. $16.00. Illustrated. 384 Pages. Vocational guide.

★7385★ Your First Year as a Nurse: Making the Transition from Total Novice to Successful Professional

Three Rivers Press
280 Park Ave. (11-3)
New York, NY 10017
Fax: (212)940-7381   Fr: 800-726-0600
URL: http://www.primapublishing.com/crown/trp.html

Donna Cardillo. 2001. $19.95 (paper). 267 pages.

EMPLOYMENT AGENCIES AND SEARCH FIRMS

★7386★ Cross Country TravCorps

6551 Park of Commerce Blvd.
Boca Raton, FL 33487-8247
Fax: (562)998-8533   Fr: 800-530-6125
URL: http://www.crosscountrytravcorps.com

Places traveling nurses in assignments nationwide.

★7387★ Harper Associates

3100 NW Hwy., Ste. 240
Farmington Hills, MI 48334
Ph: (248)932-1170   Fax: (248)932-1214
E-mail: info@harperjobs.com
URL: http://www.harperjobs.com

Executive search firm and employment agency.

★7388★ Legal Medical Urgent Staffing Solutions

The 1605 Bldg., 1605 Evesham Rd.
Voorhees, NJ 08043
Ph: (856)795-0909   Fax: (856)795-0922
Fr: 877-674-4464
URL: http://www.legalmedicalstaffing.com

Offers a specialized service providing temporary and full-time support exclusively to the legal, dental, and medical professions.

★7389★ Medical Personnel Services, Inc.

1748 N St., NW
Washington, DC 20036
Ph: (202)466-2955   Fax: (202)452-1818
E-mail: jobs@medicalpersonnel.com
URL: http://www.medicalpersonnel.com

Employment agency specializing in permanent health/medical placements.

★7390★ Nursing Technomics

814 Sunset Hollow Rd.
West Chester, PA 19380-1848
Ph: (610)436-4551   Fax: (610)436-0255
E-mail: jimccrea@chesco.com

Administrative nursing consultants offer expertise in the design and implementation of customized software applications for departments of nursing, organizational design and implementation and executive nurse search. Also specializes in department staffing, scheduling and nurse recruitment. Serves private industries as well as government agencies.

★7391★ **Professional Placement Associates, Inc.**
287 Bowman Ave., Ste. 309
Purchase, NY 10577-2517
Ph: (914)251-1000   Fax: (914)251-1055
E-mail: careers@ppasearch.com
URL: http://www.ppasearch.com

Executive search firm specializing in the health and medical field.

★7392★ **Team Placement Service, Inc.**
1414 Prince St., Ste. 202
Alexandria, VA 22314
Ph: (703)820-8618   Fax: (703)820-3368
Fr: 800-495-6767
E-mail: 4jobs@teamplace.com
URL: http://www.teamplace.com

Full-service personnel consultants provide placement for healthcare staff, physician and dentist, private practice, and hospitals. Conduct interviews, tests, and reference checks to select the top 20% of applicants. Survey applicants' skill levels, provide backup information on each candidate, select compatible candidates for consideration, and insure the hiring process minimizes potential legal liability. Industries served: healthcare and government agencies providing medical, dental, biotech, laboratory, hospitals, and physician search.

ONLINE JOB SOURCES AND SERVICES

★7393★ **Health Care Job Store**
395 South End Ave., Ste. 15-D
New York, NY 10280
Ph: (561)630-5201
E-mail: jobs@healthcarejobstore.com
URL: http://www.healthcarejobstore.com/

Description: Job sites include every job title in the healthcare industry, every healthcare industry and every geographic location in the U.S.

★7394★ **HealthCareerWeb**
URL: http://www.healthcareerweb.com/
Description: Advertises jobs for healthcare professionals. **Main files include:** Jobs, Employers, Resumes, Jobwire. Relocation tools and career guidance resources available.

★7395★ **MedExplorer**
E-mail: medmaster@medexplorer.com
URL: http://www.medexplorer.com

Description: Employment postings make up one module of this general medical site. Other sections contain: Newsletter, Classifieds, and Discussion Forum.

★7396★ **Medhunters.com**
Fr: 800-664-0278
E-mail: info@medhunters.com
URL: http://www.medhunters.com

Description: Career search site for jobs in all health care specialties; educational resources; visa and licensing information for relocation; interesting articles; relocation tools; links to professional organizations and general resources.

★7397★ **Monster Healthcare**
URL: http://healthcare.monster.com/
Description: Delivers nationwide access to healthcare recruiting. Employers can post job listings or ads. Job seekers can post and code resumes, and search over 150,000 healthcare job listings, healthcare career advice columns, career resources information, and member employer profiles and services.

★7398★ **NursesRX.com**
13620 Reese Blvd. E., Ste. 200
Huntersville, NC 28078
Fr: 800-733-9354
E-mail: info@nursesrx.com
URL: http://www.nursesrx.com

Description: Job board site for travel nursing. In addition to traditional travel nursing, Nurses RX provides staffing possibilities from temporary-to-permanent, traditional permanent placement, staffing/recruitment outsourcing, new graduate internship programs, and a full Canadian Placement Division.

★7399★ **ProHealthJobs**
Fr: 800-796-1738
E-mail: Info@prohealthedujobs.com
URL: http://www.prohealthjobs.com

Description: Career resources site for the medical and health care field. Lists professional opportunities, product information, continuing education and open positions.

TRADESHOWS

★7400★ **American Association of Office Nurses Annual Meeting and Convention**
American Association of Office Nurses
52 Park Ave. Ste. B4
Park Ridge, NJ 07656
Ph: (201)391-2600   Fax: (201)573-8543
Fr: 800-457-7504
E-mail: aaonmail@aaon.org
URL: http://www.aaon.org

Annual. **Primary Exhibits:** Exhibits of interest to nurses.

★7401★ **AORN World Conference on Surgical Patient Care**
Association of Perioperative Registered Nurses (AORN)
2170 S. Parker Rd., Ste. 300
Denver, CO 80231-5711
Ph: (303)755-6304   Fax: (303)752-0299
Fr: 800-755-2676
E-mail: custserv@aorn.org
URL: http://www.aorn.org

Biennial. **Primary Exhibits:** Equipment, supplies, and services used in operating room suites and pre-surgical areas.

★7402★ **Conference on Classification of Nursing Diagnosis**
North American Nursing Diagnosis Association
1211 Locust St.
Philadelphia, PA 19107
Ph: (215)545-8105   Fax: (215)545-8107
Fr: 800-647-9002
E-mail: info@nanda.org
URL: http://www.nanda.org

Biennial. **Primary Exhibits:** Exhibits relating to the development of a taxonomy of diagnostic terminology for use by professional nurses. Booth publishers, electronic media publishers.

★7403★ **Conference of the National Association of Pediatric Nurse Associates and Practitioners**
National Association of Pediatric Nurse Associates and Practitioners
20 Brace Rd., Ste. 200
Cherry Hill, NJ 08034-2634
Ph: (856)857-9700   Fax: (856)857-1600
Fr: 877-662-7627
E-mail: info@napnap.org
URL: http://www.napnap.org

Annual. **Primary Exhibits:** Equipment, supplies, and services for pediatric, school, and family nurse practitioners.

★7404★ **Emergency Nurses Association Annual Meeting**
Emergency Nurses Association
915 Lee St.
Des Plaines, IL 60016-6569
Ph: (847)460-4099   Fr: 800-900-9659
URL: http://www.ena.org

Annual. **Primary Exhibits:** Exhibits relating to emergency room care. **Dates and Locations:** 2008 Sep 24-27; Minneapolis, MN.

★7405★ **House of Delegates Meeting**
American Nurses Association
8515 Georgia Ave., Ste. 400
Silver Spring, MD 20910
Ph: (301)628-5000   Fax: (301)628-5001
Fr: 800-274-4262
E-mail: convention@ana.org
URL: http://www.ana.org

Annual. **Primary Exhibits:** Equipment, supplies, and services for nurses, including publications, uniforms and shoes, computers, laboratory services, medical equipment, and nutritional products.

★7406★ International Society of Psychiatric-Mental Health Nurses Annual Conference

International Society of Psychiatric - Mental Health Nurses
7600 Terrace Ave., Ste. 203
Middleton, WI 53562-3174
Ph: (608)836-3363   Fax: (608)831-5122
Fr: 800-826-2950
E-mail: info@ispn-psych.org
URL: http://www.ispn-psych.org

Annual. **Primary Exhibits:** Psychiatric nursing equipment, supplies, and services.

★7407★ National Association of Orthopedic Nurses Annual Congress

Smith, Bucklin and Associates, Inc. (Chicago)
401 N Michigan Ave.
Chicago, IL 60611-4267
Ph: (312)321-6610   Fax: (312)673-6670
Fr: 800-289-NAON
E-mail: info@smithbucklin.com
URL: http://www.smithbucklin.com

Annual. **Primary Exhibits:** Pharmaceuticals, medical equipment, medical instruments, and publications. **Dates and Locations:** 2008 May 17-21; San Jose, CA; McEnry Convention Center; 2009 May 16-20; Tampa, FL; Tampa Convention Center; 2010 May 15-19; Seattle, WA; Washington State Convention & Trade Center.

★7408★ National Student Nurses' Association Convention

National Student Nurse Association
45 Main St., Ste., 606
Brooklyn, NY 11201
Ph: (718)210-0705   Fax: (718)210-0710
E-mail: nsna@nsna.org
URL: http://www.nsna.org

Annual. **Primary Exhibits:** Equipment, supplies, and services for the student nurse.

★7409★ North Carolina Nurses Association Convention

North Carolina Nurses Association
103 Enterprise St.
PO Box 12025
Raleigh, NC 27607
Ph: (919)821-4250   Fax: (919)829-5807
Fr: 800-626-2153
E-mail: rns@ncnurses.org
URL: http://www.ncnurses.org

Annual. **Primary Exhibits:** Nursing equipment, supplies, and services, books.

★7410★ Oncology Nursing Society Meeting

Oncology Nursing Society
125 Enterprise Dr., RIDC Park W
Pittsburgh, PA 15275-1214
Ph: (412)859-6100   Fax: 877-369-5497
Fr: (866)257-4ONS
E-mail: customer.service@ons.org
URL: http://www.ons.org

Annual. **Primary Exhibits:** Oncology nursing equipment, supplies, and services.

OTHER SOURCES

★7411★ American Almanac of Jobs and Salaries

HarperCollins
10 E. 53rd St.
New York, NY 10022
Ph: (212)207-7000   Fr: 800-242-7737
URL: http://www.harpercollins.com/

John W. Wright. Revised edition, 2000. $20.00 (paper). 672 pages. This is a comprehensive guide to the wages of hundreds of occupations in a wide variety of industries and organizations.

★7412★ American Health Care Association (AHCA)

1201 L St. NW
Washington, DC 20005
Ph: (202)842-4444   Fax: (202)842-3860
E-mail: hr@ahca.org
URL: http://www.ahca.org

Description: Federation of state associations of long-term health care facilities. Promotes standards for professionals in long-term health care delivery and quality care for patients and residents in a safe environment. Focuses on issues of availability, quality, affordability, and fair payment. Operates as liaison with governmental agencies, Congress, and professional associations. Compiles statistics.

★7413★ American Hospital Association (AHA)

1 N Franklin
Chicago, IL 60606-3421
Ph: (312)422-3000   Fax: (312)422-4796
URL: http://www.aha.org

Description: Represents health care provider organizations. Seeks to advance the health of individuals and communities. Leads, represents, and serves health care provider organizations that are accountable to the community and committed to health improvement.

★7414★ American School Health Association (ASHA)

PO Box 708
Kent, OH 44240
Ph: (330)678-1601   Fax: (330)678-4526
E-mail: asha@ashaweb.org

URL: http://www.ashaweb.org

Description: School physicians, school nurses, counsellors, nutritionists, psychologists, social workers, administrators, school health coordinators, health educators, and physical educators working in schools, professional preparation programs, public health, and community-based organizations. Promotes coordinated school health programs that include health education, health services, a healthful school environment, physical education, nutrition services, and psycho-social health services offered in schools collaboratively with families and other members of the community. Offers professional reference materials and professional development opportunities. Conducts pilot programs that inform materials development, provides technical assistance to school professionals, advocates for school health.

★7415★ Association of Staff Physician Recruiters (ASPR)

1711 W County Rd. B, Ste. 300N
Roseville, MN 55113
Fax: (651)635-0307   Fr: 800-830-2777
E-mail: admin@aspr.org
URL: http://www.aspr.org

Description: Recruits physicians and other healthcare providers to staff hospitals, clinics and managed care organizations where the members are employed. Sponsors educational programs and meetings on various recruitment issues.

★7416★ EMTs, Nurses, Therapists, and Assistants

Cambridge Educational
PO Box 2053
Princeton, NJ 08543-2053
Ph: 800-257-5126   Fax: (609)671-0266
Fr: 800-468-4227
E-mail: custserv@films.com
URL: http://www.cambridgeeducational.com

VHS and DVD. $79.95. 2000. 18 minutes. Part of the series "Exploring Health Occupations."

★7417★ Exploring Health Occupations

Cambridge Educational
PO Box 2053
Princeton, NJ 08543-2053
Ph: 800-257-5126   Fax: (609)671-0266
Fr: 800-468-4227
E-mail: custserv@films.com
URL: http://www.cambridgeeducational.com

VHS and DVD. $159.90. 1999. Two-part series provides a detailed view of the field of medical technicians and technologists, EMTs, nurses, therapists, and assistants.

★7418★ Health Service Occupations

Delphi Productions
3159 6th St.
Boulder, CO 80304
Ph: (303)443-2100   Fax: (303)443-4022
Fr: 888-443-2400
E-mail: support@delphivideo.com

URL: http://www.delphivideo.com

$95.00. 50 minutes. Part of the Careers for the 21st Century Video Library.

★7419★ Health Technologists & Technicians

Delphi Productions
3159 6th St.
Boulder, CO 80304
Ph: (303)443-2100   Fax: (303)443-4022
Fr: 888-443-2400
E-mail: support@delphivideo.com
URL: http://www.delphivideo.com

$95.00. 50 minutes. Part of the Careers for the 21st Century Video Library.

★7420★ Medicine & Related Occupations

Delphi Productions
3159 6th St.
Boulder, CO 80304
Ph: (303)443-2100   Fax: (303)443-4022
Fr: 888-443-2400
E-mail: support@delphivideo.com
URL: http://www.delphivideo.com

$95.00. 45 minutes. Part of the Careers for the 21st Century Video Library.

★7421★ National Association of Pediatric Nurse Practitioners (NAPNAP)

20 Brace Rd., Ste. 200
Cherry Hill, NJ 08034-2634
Ph: (856)857-9700   Fax: (856)857-1600
Fr: 877-662-7627
E-mail: info@napnap.org
URL: http://www.napnap.org

Members: Pediatric, school, and family nurse practitioners and interested persons. **Purpose:** Seeks to improve the quality of infant, child, and adolescent health care by making health care services accessible and providing a forum for continuing education of members. **Activities:** Facilitates and supports legislation designed to promote the role of pediatric nurse practitioners; promotes salary ranges commensurate with practitioners' responsibilities; facilitates exchange of information between prospective employers and job seekers in the field. Supports research programs; compiles statistics.

★7422★ National Association for Practical Nurse Education and Service (NAPNES)

PO Box 25647
Alexandria, VA 22314
Ph: (703)933-1003   Fax: (703)940-4089

E-mail: jbova@napnes.org
URL: http://www.napnes.org

Description: Licensed practical/vocational nurses, registered nurses, physicians, hospital and nursing home administrators, and interested others. Provides consultation service to advise schools wishing to develop a practical/vocational nursing program on facilities, equipment, policies, curriculum, and staffing. Promotes recruitment of students through preparation and distribution of recruitment materials. Sponsors seminars for directors and instructors in schools of practical/vocational nursing and continuing education programs for LPNs/LVNs; approves continuing education programs and awards contact hours; holds national certification courses in post licensure specialties such as pharmacology, long term care and gerontics.

★7423★ National Federation of Licensed Practical Nurses (NFLPN)

605 Poole Dr.
Garner, NC 27529
Ph: (919)779-0046   Fax: (919)779-5642
E-mail: cbarbour@mgmt4u.com
URL: http://www.nflpn.org

Description: Federation of state associations of licensed practical and vocational nurses. Aims to: preserve and foster the ideal of comprehensive nursing care for the ill and aged; improve standards of practice; secure recognition and effective utilization of LPNs; further continued improvement in the education of LPNs. Acts as clearinghouse for information on practical nursing and cooperates with other groups concerned with better patient care. Maintains loan program.

★7424★ National League for Nursing (NLN)

61 Broadway, 33rd Fl.
New York, NY 10006
Ph: (212)363-5555   Fax: (212)812-0393
Fr: 800-669-1656
E-mail: generalinfo@nln.org
URL: http://www.nln.org

Description: Champions the pursuit of quality nursing education. A professional association of nursing faculty, education agencies, health care agencies, allied/public agencies, and public members whose mission is to advance quality nursing education that prepares the nursing workforce to meet the needs of diverse populations in an ever-changing health care environment. Serves as the primary source of information about every type of nursing education program, from the LVN and LPN to the EdD and PhD. There are 20 affiliated constituent leagues that provide a local forum for members. The National League for Nursing Accrediting

Commission is an independent corporate affiliate of the NLN, responsible for providing accreditation services to all levels of nursing education.

★7425★ National Rural Health Association (NRHA)

Administrative Office
521 E 63rd St.
Kansas City, MO 64110-3329
Ph: (816)756-3140   Fax: (816)756-3144
E-mail: mail@nrharural.org
URL: http://www.nrharural.org

Description: Administrators, physicians, nurses, physician assistants, health planners, academicians, and others interested or involved in rural health care. Creates a better understanding of health care problems unique to rural areas; utilizes a collective approach in finding positive solutions; articulates and represents the health care needs of rural America; supplies current information to rural health care providers; serves as a liaison between rural health care programs throughout the country. Offers continuing education credits for medical, dental, nursing, and management courses.

★7426★ The Patient Care Nursing Team

Cambridge Educational
PO Box 2053
Princeton, NJ 08543-2053
Ph: 800-257-5126   Fax: (609)671-0266
Fr: 800-468-4227
E-mail: custserv@films.com
URL: http://www.cambridgeeducational.com

VHS and DVD. $89.95. 2002. 15 minutes. Program describes the challenges that nurses face in a variety of work environments, including hospitals, clinics, schools, and homes, and outlines the education and licensing process that nurses must complete.

★7427★ Visiting Nurse Associations of America (VNAA)

Administration Office
99 Summer St., Ste. 1700
Boston, MA 02110
Ph: (617)737-3200   Fax: (617)737-1144
Fr: 800-426-2547
E-mail: vnaa@vnaa.org
URL: http://www.vnaa.org

Members: Home health care agencies. **Purpose:** Develops competitive strength among community-based nonprofit visiting nurse organizations; works to strengthen business resources and economic programs through contracting, marketing, governmental affairs and publications.

Loan Officers

SOURCES OF HELP-WANTED ADS

★7428★ American Banker
American Banker/Bond Buyer Inc.
1 State St. Plz. 27 Fl.
New York, NY 10004
Ph: (212)803-8200   Fax: (212)843-9600
Fr: 800-221-1809
URL: http://www.americanbanker.com

Daily. $995.00/year for individuals. Newspaper for senior executives in banking and other financial services industries. Coverage includes trends, analysis, and statistics of the legislative scene in Washington; finance; mortgages; technology; small business; and regional banking.

★7429★ Mortgage Banking Magazine
Mortgage Bankers Association of America
1919 Pennsylvania Ave. NW
Washington, DC 20006-3404
Ph: (202)557-2700   Fax: (202)721-0245
Fr: 800-793-MBAA

Monthly. $80.00/year for individuals. Magazine of the real estate finance industry.

★7430★ National Mortgage News
Thomson Financial
195 Broadway
New York, NY 10007
Ph: (646)822-2000   Fax: (646)822-3230
Fr: 888-605-3385
E-mail: custserv@sourcemedia.com
URL: http://www.nationalmortgagenews.com

Weekly. Newspaper for mortgage lenders and investment bankers.

★7431★ Northwestern Financial Review
NFR Communications Inc.
7400 Metro Blvd., Ste. 217
Minneapolis, MN 55439
Ph: (952)835-2275
E-mail: web@nfrcom.com
URL: http://www.nfrcom.com

$94.00/year for individuals. Trade publication covering commercial banking.

★7432★ Servicing Management
Zackin Publications Inc.
PO Box 2180
Waterbury, CT 06722
Ph: (203)262-4670   Fax: (203)262-4680
Fr: 800-325-6745
URL: http://www.sm-online.com/sm

Monthly. $48.00/year for individuals; $72.00 for two years. Trade magazine for mortgage professionals involved with mortgage loan servicing.

★7433★ U.S. Banker
Thomson Financial
195 Broadway
New York, NY 10007
Ph: (646)822-2000   Fax: (646)822-3230
Fr: 888-605-3385
URL: http://www.americanbanker.com/usb.html

Monthly. $109.00/year for individuals; $139.00/year for individuals, Canada; $139.00/year for individuals, outside North America; $179.00/year for two years; $239.00 for two years, Canada; $239.00/year for two years, outside North America. Magazine serving the financial services industry.

PLACEMENT AND JOB REFERRAL SERVICES

★7434★ National Bankers Association (NBA)
1513 P St. NW
Washington, DC 20005
Ph: (202)588-5432   Fax: (202)588-5443
E-mail: nahart@nationalbankers.org
URL: http://www.nationalbankers.org

Members: Minority banking institutions owned by minority individuals and institutions. **Purpose:** Serves as an advocate for the minority banking industry. Organizes banking services, government relations, marketing, scholarship, and technical assistance programs. **Activities:** Offers placement services; compiles statistics.

EMPLOYER DIRECTORIES AND NETWORKING LISTS

★7435★ Branches of Your State
Sheshunoff Information Services
807 Las Cimas Pkwy., Ste. 300
Austin, TX 78746-6597
Ph: (512)472-2244   Fax: (512)305-6575
Fr: 800-456-2340

Annual, February. $475.00. Covers, in separate state editions, banks, savings and loan branches, and credit unions. For those states without branch banking, individual banks, savings and loan institutions, and credit unions are listed. Entries include: Institution name, address, institution type, deposit totals, percent change over 12 months, percentage share of parent company's total deposits. Arrangement: Geographical.

★7436★ Corporate Finance Sourcebook
LexisNexis Group
PO Box 933
Dayton, OH 45401-0933
Ph: (937)865-6800   Fax: (518)487-3584
Fr: 800-543-6862
E-mail: nrpsales@marquiswhoswho.com
URL: http://www.financesourcebook.com

Annual; latest edition 2008. $695.00; $625.00 for standing orders. Covers securities research analysts; major private lenders; investment banking firms; commercial banks; United States-based foreign banks; commercial finance firms; leasing companies; foreign investment bankers in the United States; pension managers; banks that offer master trusts; cash managers; business insurance brokers; business real estate specialists. Lists about 3,400 firms; 14,500 key financial experts. Entries include: Firm name, address, phone, e-mail, and names and titles of officers, contacts, or specialists in corporate finance. Additional details are given as appropriate, including names of major clients, number of companies served, services, total assets, branch locations, years in business. Arrangement: Classified by line of business and then alphabetized within that line of business. Indexes: Firm name; personnel name; geographical.

★7437★ **Employment Opportunities, USA**

Washington Research Associates
1090 Vermont Ave. NW, Ste. 800
Washington, DC 20005
Ph: (202)408-7025

Annual, quarterly updates. Publication includes: List of over 1,000 employment contacts in companies and agencies in banking, arts, telecommunications, education, and 14 other industries and professions, including federal government. Entries include: Company name, name of representative, address, description of products or services, hiring and recruiting practices, training programs, and year established. Principal content is industry overviews, career news, employment opportunity information on 14 different job markets, and comprehensive guidance to career resources on the Internet. Arrangement: Classified by industry. Indexes: Occupation.

★7438★ **National Bankers Association-Roster of Minority Banking Institutions**

National Bankers Association
1513 P St. NW
Washington, DC 20005
Ph: (202)588-5432   Fax: (202)588-5443

Annual, October. Covers about 140 banks owned or controlled by minority group persons or women. Entries include: Bank name, address, phone, name of one executive. Arrangement: Geographical.

★7439★ **Peterson's Job Opportunities for Business Majors**

Peterson's
Princeton Pke. Corporate Ctr., 2000
  Lenox Dr.
PO Box 67005
Lawrenceville, NJ 08648
Ph: (609)896-1800   Fax: (609)896-4531
Fr: 800-338-3282
URL: http://www.petersons.com/

Irregular; latest edition 16th, 2000. Covers the 2,000 largest U.S. employers hiring in several fields, including financial services, management consulting, consumer products, and media/entertainment. Entries include: Organization name, address, phone, name and title of contact, number of employees, type of organization. Arrangement: Alphabetical. Indexes: Type of organization.

★7440★ **Roster of Minority Financial Institutions**

U.S. Department of the Treasury
1500 Pennsylvania Ave. NW
Washington, DC 20220
Ph: (202)622-2000

Free. Covers about 170 commercial, minority-owned and controlled financial institutions participating in the Department of the Treasury's Minority Bank Deposit Program. Entries include: Name of institution, name and title of chief officer, address, phone, fax. Arrangement: Geographical.

★7441★ **Thomson Bank Directory**

Accuity
4709 W Golf Rd., Ste. 600
Skokie, IL 60076
Ph: (847)676-9600   Fax: (847)933-8101
Fr: 800-321-3373
URL: http://www.accuitysolutions.com/

Semiannual, June and December. $702.00 for individuals. Covers, in five volumes, about 11,000 banks and 50,000 branches of United States banks, and 60,000 foreign banks and branches engaged in foreign banking; Federal Reserve system and other United States government and state government banking agencies; the 500 largest North American and International commercial banks; paper and automated clearinghouses. Volumes 1 and 2 contain North American listings; volumes 3 and 4, international listings (also cited as "Thomson International Bank Directory"); volume 5, Worldwide Correspondents Guide containing key correspondent data to facilitate funds transfer. Entries include: For domestic banks–Bank name, address, phone, telex, cable, date established, routing number, charter type, bank holding company affiliation, memberships in Federal Reserve System and other banking organizations, principal officers by function performed, principal correspondent banks, and key financial data (deposits, etc.). For international banks–Bank name, address, phone, fax, telex, cable, SWIFT address, transit or sort codes within home country, ownership, financial data, names and titles of key personnel, branch locations. For branches–Bank name, address, phone, charter type, ownership and other details comparable to domestic bank listings. Arrangement: Geographical. Indexes: Alphabetical, geographical.

★7442★ **Thomson North American Financial Institutions Directory**

Accuity
4709 W Golf Rd., Ste. 600
Skokie, IL 60076
Ph: (847)676-9600   Fax: (847)933-8101
Fr: 800-321-3373
URL: http://www.tfp.com

Semiannual, January and July. $512.00 for individuals. Covers 15,000 banks and their branches; over 2,000 head offices, and 15,500 branches of savings and loan associations; over 5,500 credit unions with assets over $5 million; Federal Reserve System and other U.S. government and state government banking agencies; bank holding,

commercial finance, and leasing companies; coverage includes the United States, Canada, Mexico, and Central America. Entries include: Bank name, address, phone, fax, telex, principal officers and directors, date established, financial data, association memberships, attorney or counsel, correspondent banks, out-of-town branch, holding company affiliation, ABA transit number and routing symbol, MICR number with check digit, credit card(s) issued, trust powers, current par value and dividend of common stock, kind of charter. Arrangement: Geographical. Indexes: Alphabetical.

★7443★ **Who's Who in Finance and Business**

Marquis Who's Who L.L.C.
890 Mountain Ave., Ste. 300
New Providence, NJ 07974-1218
Ph: (908)673-1001   Fax: (908)673-1189
Fr: 800-473-7020
E-mail: finance@marquiswhoswho.com
URL: http://www.marquiswhoswho.com

Biennial; latest edition 36th, September 2007. $349.00 for individuals. Covers over 18,000 individuals. Entries include: Name, home and office addresses, personal, career, and family data; civic and political activities; memberships, publications, awards. Arrangement: Alphabetical.

HANDBOOKS AND MANUALS

★7444★ **Careers in Banking and Finance**

Rosen Publishing Group, Inc.
29 E. 21st St.
New York, NY 10010
Ph: (212)777-3017   Fax: 888-436-4643
Fr: 800-237-9932
URL: http://www.rosenpublishing.com/

Patricia Haddock. Revised edition, 2001. $31.95. 139 pages. Offers advice on job hunting. Describes jobs at all levels in banking and finance. Contains information about the types of financial organizations where the jobs are found, educational requirements, job duties, and salaries.

★7445★ **Opportunities in Banking Careers**

The McGraw-Hill Companies
PO Box 182604
Columbus, OH 43272
Fax: (614)759-3749   Fr: 877-883-5524
E-mail: customer.service@mcgraw-hill.com
URL: http://www.mcgraw-hill.com

Philip Perry. 1994. $15.95; $12.95 (paper). 146 pages. Discusses banking opportunities in a variety of settings: commercial banks, savings and loans, finance companies, and mortgage banks.

★7446★ Opportunities in Financial Careers

The McGraw-Hill Companies
PO Box 182604
Columbus, OH 43272
Fax: (614)759-3749   Fr: 877-883-5524
E-mail: customer.service@mcgraw-hill.com
URL: http://www.mcgraw-hill.com

Michael Sumichrast. 2004. $13.95; $11.95 (paper). 160 pages. A guide to planning for and seeking opportunities in this challenging field.

★7447★ Opportunities in Real Estate Careers

The McGraw-Hill Companies
PO Box 182604
Columbus, OH 43272
Fax: (614)759-3749   Fr: 877-883-5524
E-mail: customer.service@mcgraw-hill.com
URL: http://www.mcgraw-hill.com

Mariwyn Evansand and Richard Mendenhal. Second edition, 2002. $12.95 (paper). 160 pages.

★7448★ Resumes for Banking and Financial Careers

The McGraw-Hill Companies
PO Box 182604
Columbus, OH 43272
Fax: (614)759-3749   Fr: 877-883-5524
E-mail: customer.service@mcgraw-hill.com
URL: http://www.mcgraw-hill.com

Second edition, 2001. $11.95 (paper). 160 pages.

EMPLOYMENT AGENCIES AND SEARCH FIRMS

★7449★ Financial Professionals

4100 Spring Valley Rd., Ste. 307
Dallas, TX 75244
Ph: (972)991-8999   Fax: (972)702-0776
URL: http://www.fpstaff.net/

Executive search consultants with additional offices in Forth Worth and Houston.

★7450★ J.B. Brown and Associates

820 Terminal Twr.
Cleveland, OH 44113
Ph: (216)696-2525   Fax: (216)696-5825

Employment agency and executive recruiter.

★7451★ KForce

Fr: 888-663-3626
URL: http://www.kforce.com

Executive search firm. More than 30 locations throughout the United States.

★7452★ The Murphy Group

245 W Roosevelt Rd., Bldg.15, Ste.101
Chicago, IL 60605
Ph: (630)639-5110   Fax: (630)639-5113
E-mail: info@murphygroup.com
URL: http://www.murphygroup.com

Employment agency. Places personnel in a variety of positions. Additional offices located in Napierville, Park Ridge, and OakBrook.

OTHER SOURCES

★7453★ American Bankers Association (ABA)

1120 Connecticut Ave. NW
Washington, DC 20036
Ph: (202)663-5000   Fax: (202)663-7543
Fr: 800-BAN-KERS
E-mail: custserv@aba.com
URL: http://www.aba.com

Members: Members are principally commercial banks and trust companies; combined assets of members represent approximately 90% of the U.S. banking industry; approximately 94% of members are community banks with less than $500 million in assets. **Purpose:** Seeks to enhance the role of commercial bankers as preeminent providers of financial services through communications, research, legal action, lobbying of federal legislative and regulatory bodies, and education and training programs. Serves as spokesperson for the banking industry; facilitates exchange of information among members. Maintains the American Institute of Banking, an industry-sponsored adult education program. **Activities:** Conducts educational and training programs for bank employees and officers through a wide range of banking schools and national conferences. Maintains liaison with federal bank regulators; lobbies Congress on issues affecting commercial banks; testifies before congressional committees; represents members in U.S. postal rate proceedings. Serves as secretariat of the International Monetary Conference and the Financial Institutions Committee for the American National Standards Institute. Files briefs and lawsuits in major court cases affecting the industry. Conducts teleconferences with state banking associations on such issues as regulatory compliance; works to build consensus and coordinate activities of leading bank and financial service trade groups. Provides services to members including: public advocacy; news media contact; insurance program providing directors and officers with liability coverage, financial institution bond, and trust errors and omissions coverage; research service operated through ABA Center for Banking Information; fingerprint set processing in conjunction with the Federal Bureau of Investigation; discounts on operational and income-producing projects through the Corporation for American Banking. Conducts

conferences, forums, and workshops covering subjects such as small business, consumer credit, agricultural and community banking, trust management, bank operations, and automation. Sponsors ABA Educational Foundation and the Personal Economics Program, which educates schoolchildren and the community on banking, economics, and personal finance.

★7454★ Bank Administration Institute (BAI)

1 N Franklin St., Ste. 1000
Chicago, IL 60606-3421
Ph: (312)683-2464   Fax: (312)683-2373
Fr: 888-284-4078
E-mail: info@bai.org
URL: http://www.bai.org

Description: Works to improve the competitive position of banking companies through strategic research and educational offerings.

★7455★ Financial Managers Society (FMS)

100 W Monroe, Ste. 810
Chicago, IL 60603
Ph: (312)578-1300   Fax: (312)578-1308
Fr: 800-275-4367
E-mail: info@fmsinc.org
URL: http://www.fmsinc.org

Description: Works for the needs of finance and accounting professionals from banks, thrifts and credit unions. Offers career-enhancing education, specialized publications, national leadership opportunities, and worldwide connections with other industry professionals.

★7456★ Financial Occupations

Delphi Productions
3159 6th St.
Boulder, CO 80304
Ph: (303)443-2100   Fax: (303)443-4022
Fr: 888-443-2400
E-mail: support@delphivideo.com
URL: http://www.delphivideo.com

$95.00. 50 minutes. Part of the Careers for the 21st Century Video Library.

★7457★ Risk Management Association

1801 Market St., Ste. 300
Philadelphia, PA 19103-1628
Ph: (215)446-4000   Fax: (215)446-4101
Fr: 800-677-7621
E-mail: member@rmahq.org
URL: http://www.rmahq.org/RMA

Members: Commercial and savings banks, and savings and loan, and other financial services companies. **Activities:** Conducts research and professional development activities in areas of loan administration, asset management, and commercial lending and credit to increase professionalism.

Management Analysts and Consultants

SOURCES OF HELP-WANTED ADS

★7458★ Academy of Management Journal

Academy of Management
PO Box 3020
Briarcliff Manor, NY 10510-8020
Ph: (914)923-2607   Fax: (914)923-2615
URL: http://www.aom.pace.edu/amr

Bimonthly. Professional journal covering management.

★7459★ Academy of Management Learning & Education

Academy of Management
PO Box 3020
Briarcliff Manor, NY 10510-8020
Ph: (914)923-2607   Fax: (914)923-2615
URL: http://journals.aomonline.org/amle

Quarterly. $80.00/year for individuals, print; $130.00/year for individuals, print & online; $165.00/year for libraries, print; $215.00/year for libraries, print and online; $100.00/year for individuals, other countries, print; $150.00/year for individuals, other countries, print & online; $185.00/year for other countries, print, corporate library; $235.00/year for other countries, print & online, corporate library. Journal covering management issues for professionals.

★7460★ Business Performance Management

Penton Media Inc.
249 W 17th St.
New York, NY 10011
Ph: (212)204-4200
URL: http://www.bpmmag.net/

Free to qualified subscribers. Magazine for business managers. Covers organizing, automating, and analyzing of business methodologies and processes.

★7461★ CXO

IDG Communications Inc.
5 Speen St., 3rd. Fl
Framingham, MA 01701
Ph: (508)875-5000   Fax: (508)988-7888
URL: http://www.idg.com

Monthly. Magazine providing technology information for chief officers and managers.

★7462★ D & O Advisor

American Lawyer Media L.P.
345 Pk. Ave. S
New York, NY 10010
Ph: (212)779-9200   Fax: (212)481-8110
Fr: 800-888-8300
URL: http://www.alm.com

Quarterly. Magazine that offers advice and perspective on corporate oversight responsibilities for directors and officers.

★7463★ E Journal of Organizational Learning and Leadership

WeLEAD Inc.
PO Box 202
Litchfield, OH 44253
Fr: 877-778-5494
URL: http://www.weleadinlearning.org/ejournal.htm

Continuous. Free. Online academic journal about organizational leadership.

★7464★ Event Management

Cognizant Communications Corp.
3 Hartsdale Rd.
Elmsford, NY 10523-3701
Ph: (914)592-7720   Fax: (914)592-8981
URL: http://www.cognizantcommunication.com/filecabinet/EventManag

Quarterly. $325.00/year for institutions, library; $360.00/year for institutions, rest of the world, library; $585.00/year for institutions, library, 2 years; $648.00/year for institutions, rest if the world, library, 2 years; $45.00/year professional; $52.00/year for other countries, professional. Journal covering research and analytic needs of a rapidly growing profession focused on events.

★7465★ Executive Legal Adviser

American Lawyer Media L.P.
345 Pk. Ave. S
New York, NY 10010
Ph: (212)779-9200   Fax: (212)481-8110
Fr: 800-888-8300
URL: http://www.executivelegaladviser.com

Bimonthly. Free to qualified subscribers. Magazine that offers legal advice for corporate executives.

★7466★ Fleet Maintenance

Cygnus Business Media Inc.
3 Huntington Quadrangle, Ste. 301 N
Melville, NY 11747
Ph: (631)845-2700   Fax: (631)845-7109
Fr: 800-308-6397
URL: http://www.fleetmag.com

Bimonthly. Business tabloid magazine offering a chapterized curriculum of technical, regulatory and managerial information designed to help maintenance managers, directors and supervisors better perform their jobs and reduce their overall cost-per-mile.

★7467★ Forbes

Forbes Magazine
90 5th Ave.
New York, NY 10011
Ph: (212)366-8900   Fr: 800-295-0893
URL: http://www.forbes.com

Biweekly. $30.00/year for individuals, per year; $1.00/year for single issue. Magazine reporting on industry, business and finance management.

★7468★ Forrester

Forrester Research Inc.
400 Technology Sq.
Cambridge, MA 02139
Ph: (617)613-6000   Fax: (617)613-5000
URL: http://www.forrester.com/mag

Free. Journal that aims to provide ideas and advice that are relevant to today's CEOs.

★7469★ International Journal of Business Research

Academy of International Business and Economics
PO Box 2536
Ceres, CA 95307
URL: http://www.aibe.org

Peer-reviewed journal publishing theoretical, conceptual, and applied research on topics related to research, practice and teaching in all areas of business, management, and marketing.

★7470★ Journal of Academic Leadership

Academic Leadership
600 Park St.
Rarick Hall 219
Hays, KS 67601-4099
Ph: (785)628-4547
URL: http://www.academicleadership.org/

Journal focusing on the leadership issues in the academic world.

★7471★ Journal of Business and Psychology

Springer-Verlag New York Inc.
233 Spring St.
New York, NY 10013
Ph: (212)460-1500   Fax: (212)460-1575
URL: http://www.springer.com/journal/10869/

Journal covering all aspects of psychology that apply to the business segment. Includes topics such as personnel selection and training, organizational assessment and development, risk management and loss control, marketing and consumer behavior research.

★7472★ Journal of International Business Strategy

Academy of International Business and Economics
PO Box 2536
Ceres, CA 95307
URL: http://www.AIBE.org

Peer-reviewed journal publishing theoretical, conceptual, and applied research on topics related to strategy in international business.

★7473★ Management Research

M.E. Sharpe Inc.
80 Business Pk. Dr.
Armonk, NY 10504
Ph: (914)273-1800   Fax: (914)273-2106
Fr: 800-541-6563
URL: http://www.mesharpe.com/mall/results1.asp?ACR=JMR

$72.00/year for individuals; $349.00/year for institutions; $84.00/year for other countries, individual; $391.00/year for institutions, other countries. International journal dedicated to advancing the understanding of management in private and public sector organizations through empirical investigation and theoretical analysis. Attempts to promote an international dialogue between researchers, improve the understanding of the nature of management in different settings, and achieve a reasonable transfer of research results to management practice in several contexts. Receptive to research across a broad range of management topics such as human resource management, organizational behavior, organizational theory, and strategic management. While not regional in nature, articles dealing with Iberoamerican issues are particularly welcomed.

★7474★ The Organization Development Institute

International Registry of Organization Development Professionals
11234 Walnut Ridge Rd.
Chesterland, OH 44026
Ph: (440)729-7419
URL: http://www.odinstitute.org

Description: Monthly. Serves organization development professionals, teachers of organizational behavior, management consultants, personnel directors and executives by carrying news items, interest surveys, economic information, and committee reports. Recurring features include announcements of conferences, meetings, publications, consulting opportunities, and employment openings. Subscription includes annual publication titled The International Registry of Organization Development Professionals and Organization Development Handbook, and copies of The Organizational Development Journal.

★7475★ Organization Management Journal

Eastern Academy of Management
c/o Craig Tunwall, VP
Empire State College
2805 State Hwy. 67
Johnstown, NY 12095
Ph: (518)762-4651   Fax: (518)736-1716
URL: http://www1.wnec.edu/omj

Free to qualified subscribers. Refereed, online journal focusing on organization management issues.

★7476★ Public Performance and Management Review

M.E. Sharpe Inc.
80 Business Pk. Dr.
Armonk, NY 10504
Ph: (914)273-1800   Fax: (914)273-2106
Fr: 800-541-6563
URL: http://www.mesharpe.com/mall/results1.asp?ACR=pmr

Quarterly. $85.00/year for individuals; $399.00/year for institutions; $101.00/year for other countries, individual; $431.00/year for institutions, other countries. Journal addressing a broad range of factors influencing the performance of public and nonprofit organizations and agencies. Aims to facilitate the development of innovative techniques and encourage a wider application of those already established; stimulate research and critical thinking about the relationship between public and private management theories; present integrated analyses of theories, concepts, strategies and techniques dealing with productivity, measurement and related questions of performance improvement; and provide a forum for practitioner-academic exchange. Continuing themes include managing for productivity, measuring and evaluating performance, improving budget strategies, managing human resources, building partnerships, and applying new technologies.

★7477★ Supply Chain Management Review

Reed Business Information
225 Wyman St.
Waltham, MA 02451-1216
URL: http://www.scmr.com

$199.00/year for U.S. and Canada; $241.00/year for other countries. Publication covering business and management.

★7478★ TD Magazine

American Society for Training & Development
1640 King St.
PO Box 1443
Alexandria, VA 22313-2043
Ph: (703)683-8100   Fax: (703)683-8103
Fr: 800-628-2783
URL: http://www.astd.org/

Monthly. $99.00/year for individuals; $165.00/year for other countries; $125.00/year for Canada and Mexico; $225.00 for two years, Canada/Mexico; $165.00/year for individuals, international. Magazine on training and development.

EMPLOYER DIRECTORIES AND NETWORKING LISTS

★7479★ ASTD Buyer's Guide

ASTD
PO Box 1443
1640 King St.
Alexandria, VA 22313-2043
Ph: (703)683-8100   Fax: (703)683-1523
Fr: 800-628-2783
URL: http://www.astd.org

Annual. Covers suppliers who serve the training and development industry. Includes subject and geographical index.

★7480★ Business

Westview Press
2465 Central Ave.
Boulder, CO 80301
Ph: (303)444-3541   Fax: (720)406-7336
Fr: 800-343-4499
URL: http://www.ultimatebusinessresource.com/main.asp?lang=us

Latest edition 2nd. Covers more than 3,000 business resource Web sites, organizations, books, journals, and magazines. Indexes: Alphabetical.

★7481★ Business Management Consultants Directory

infoUSA Inc.
5711 S 86th Cir.
PO Box 27347
Omaha, NE 68127-0347
Ph: (402)593-4593   Fax: (402)596-7688
Fr: 800-555-6124
URL: http://www.infousa.com

Annual. Number of listings: 51,839. Entries include: Name, address, phone (including area code), size of advertisement, year first in "Yellow Pages," name of owner or manager, number of employees. Compiled from telephone company "Yellow Pages," nationwide. Arrangement: Geographical.

★7482★ Consultants and Consulting Organizations Directory

Gale, Cengage Learning
27500 Drake Rd.
Farmington Hills, MI 48331-3535
Ph: (248)699-4253   Fax: (248)699-8065
Fr: 800-877-4253
E-mail: businessproducts@gale.com
URL: http://www.gale.com

Annual; latest edition 30th, published March 2007. $1050.00 for individuals. Covers over 25,000 firms, individuals, and organizations active in consulting. Entries include: Individual or organization name, address, phone, fax, e-mail, URL, specialties, founding date, branch offices, names and titles of key personnel, number of employees, financial data, publications, seminars and workshops. Arrangement: By broad subject categories. Indexes: Subject; geographical; organization name.

★7483★ Consultants in the Midwest

Midwest Society of Professional
 Consultants
640 Camelot Dr.
Burr Ridge, IL 60527-6238
Ph: (630)734-0211   Fax: (630)734-0212
URL: http://www.mspc.org/

Annual. Free. Covers members of the Midwest Society of Professional Consultants. Entries include: Individual member profiles; brief descriptions of each member's background, experience, and expertise. Arrangement: Alphabetical. Indexes: Company name and area of specialization.

★7484★ D & B Consultants Directory

Dun & Bradstreet Corp.
103 JFK Pkwy.
Short Hills, NJ 07078
Ph: (973)921-5500   Fax: (973)921-6056
Fr: 800-234-3867
URL: http://www.dnb.com

Annual. Covers top 30,000 U.S. consulting firms in more than 200 areas of specialization. Entries include: Firm name, address, phone, sales, number of employees, year established, description of service, other locations, names and titles of key personnel, reference to parent company, D&B DUNS number, trade name, consulting activity, owned companies' clientele, territory served, number of accounts, stock exchange symbol and indicator for publicly owned companies. Arrangement: Complete consultants profiles appear in the consultants alphabetical section. Companies are cross-referenced geographically and by activity. Indexes: All companies with a primary or secondary Standard Industrial Classification (SIC) code of 8748 "Business Consulting Services," as well as those companies whose type of business description includes the word "consult." All companies must have a phone number and be either a headquarters or single location.

★7485★ Directory of Certified Business Counselors

Institute of Certified Business Counselors
18615 Willamette Dr.
West Linn, OR 97068
Fax: (503)292-8237   Fr: 877-422-2674
URL: http://www.i-cbc.org/directory_alphabetical.htm

Irregular; updated as necessary. Covers 160 member counselors, brokers, and attorneys qualified to act as advisors for persons with business problems. Entries include: Name, address, phone, business specialty. Arrangement: Alphabetical.

★7486★ Directory of Management Consultants

Kennedy Information
1 Phoenix Mill Ln., 3rd Fl.
Peterborough, NH 03458
Ph: (603)924-1006   Fax: (603)924-4460
Fr: 800-531-0007
URL: http://www.managementconsultants.consultingcentral.com

Biennial; latest edition 2004. Covers 2,859 management consulting firms in North America. Entries include: Firm name, address, phone, fax, e-mail, name of principal executive, date founded, staff size and revenue (in range), services offered, SIC numbers of industries served, plus brief description of firm. For commercial use requests, please contact publisher. Arrangement: Alphabetical. Indexes: Geographical; key contacts; services; industries.

★7487★ Harvard Business School Guide to Careers in Management Consulting

Harvard Business School Publishing
60 Harvard Way
Boston, MA 02163
Ph: (617)783-7500   Fax: (617)783-7555
Fr: 800-988-0886
URL: http://www.hbsp.harvard.edu

$10.83 for individuals. Publication includes: Well-known consulting firms, a mailing list of recruiting contacts, and a selective bibliography of relevant books and directories compiled by the Harvard Business School.

★7488★ MBA Employment Guide Report

Association of MBA Executives Inc.
5 Summit Pl.
Branford, CT 06405-3527
Ph: (203)315-5221   Fax: (203)483-6186

Continuous. Database covers: More than 4,000 firms that employ persons with Master of Business Administration degrees. More detailed profiles are given for 100 firms selected on the basis of their on-campus recruitment activity. Custom reports are issued upon request at $10.00 per report. Database includes: For companies covered in detail–Name, headquarters location, description of business, current recruitment objectives, employment policies, benefits offered, name and address of employment representative, financial data. For others–Name, location, contact person and telephone number, parent company (if any), code for primary line of business.

★7489★ Peterson's Job Opportunities for Business Majors

Peterson's
Princeton Pke. Corporate Ctr., 2000
 Lenox Dr.
PO Box 67005
Lawrenceville, NJ 08648
Ph: (609)896-1800   Fax: (609)896-4531
Fr: 800-338-3282
URL: http://www.petersons.com/

Irregular; latest edition 16th, 2000. Covers the 2,000 largest U.S. employers hiring in several fields, including financial services, management consulting, consumer products, and media/entertainment. Entries include: Organization name, address, phone, name and title of contact, number of employees, type of organization. Arrangement: Alphabetical. Indexes: Type of organization.

★7490★ Professional and Technical Consultants Association-Directory of Consultants

Professional and Technical Consultants
 Association
PO Box 2261
Santa Clara, CA 95055
Ph: (408)971-5902   Fax: (866)746-1053
Fr: 800-747-2822
URL: http://www.patca.org

Annual, January. Covers more than 350 consultants involved in computer technology, management, marketing, manufacturing, engineering, etc. Entries include: Individual or firm name, address, phone, specialties, degrees held. Arrangement: Alphabetical. Indexes: Specialty, geographical.

★7491★ Project Management Step-by-Step

AMACOM
1601 Broadway
New York, NY 10019-7420
Ph: (212)586-8100   Fax: (518)891-0368
Fr: 800-262-9699
URL: http://www.amanet.org/

Latest edition 2002. $27.95 for individuals.

Publication includes: List of resources for project management. Principal content of publication is information on the theory and practice of project management. Indexes: Alphabetical.

★7492★ **Turning Research into Results**
CEP Press
1100 Johnson Ferry Rd., Ste. 150
Atlanta, GA 30342
Ph: (770)458-4080   Fax: (770)458-9109
Fr: 800-558-4237
URL: http://www.cepworldwide.com

$26.95 for individuals. Publication includes: Extensive list of references in the management field. Principal content of publication is an explanation of ways to implement change in an organization's structure and operating culture. Indexes: Alphabetical.

HANDBOOKS AND MANUALS

★7493★ **How to Be Your Own Management Consultant: Consultant Tools and Techniques to Improve Your Business**
Kogan Page, Ltd.
22 Broad St., Ste. 34
Milford, CT 06460
Calvert Markham. 2002. $32.00. 224 pages.

★7494★ **Opportunities in Business Management Careers**
The McGraw-Hill Companies
PO Box 182604
Columbus, OH 43272
Fax: (614)759-3749   Fr: 877-883-5524
E-mail: customer.service@mcgraw-hill.com
URL: http://www.mcgraw-hill.com

Irene Place and Lewis Baratz. 1997. $11.95 (paper). 148 pages. Provides guidance on the most effective channels to management positions.

★7495★ **Rasputin for Hire: An Inside Look at Management Consulting Between Jobs or as a Second Career**
Dialogue Press
PO Box 657
Westport, CT 06881
Ph: (203)226-8824   Fax: (203)226-1823
E-mail: info@dialoguepress.com
URL: http://www.dialoguepress.com/

Michael A. Goodman. 2003. $19.95 (paper). 244 pages.

EMPLOYMENT AGENCIES AND SEARCH FIRMS

★7496★ **A-L Associates Inc.**
546 5th Ave., Fl. 6
New York, NY 10036
Ph: (212)878-9000   Fax: (212)878-9096
Fr: 800-292-1390
URL: http://www.alassoc.com

Executive search firm.

★7497★ **AD Check Associates Inc.**
116 Doran Dr.
Wilkes Barre, PA 18708
Ph: (570)829-5066   Fax: (570)820-8293
E-mail: check204@aol.com

Executive search firm.

★7498★ **Allerton Heneghan & O'Neill**
1 Tower Ln., Ste. 1700
Oakbrook Terrace, IL 60181
Ph: (630)645-2294   Fax: (630)645-2298
E-mail: info@ahosearch.com
URL: http://www.ahosearch.com

Executive search firm.

★7499★ **Ashworth Consultants Inc.**
53 Fulton St.
Boston, MA 02109-1415
Ph: (617)720-0350
E-mail: ashworthcp@aol.com

Executive search firm.

★7500★ **Baker Montgomery**
980 N. Michigan Ave., Ste. 930
Chicago, IL 60611
Ph: (312)397-8808   Fax: (312)397-9631
E-mail: contact@bakermontgomery.com
URL: http://www.bakermontgomery.com

Executive search firm.

★7501★ **BeechTree Partners LLC**
875 N. Michigan Ave., Ste. 3100
Chicago, IL 60611
Ph: (312)794-7808
E-mail: brad@beechtreepartners.com
URL: http://www.beechtreepartners.com

Executive search firm.

★7502★ **Boyden**
360 Lexington Ave., Ste. 1300
New York, NY 10017
Ph: (212)949-9400   Fax: (212)949-5905
E-mail: jbranthover@boyden.com
URL: http://www.boyden.com

Executive search firm. Affiliate offices across the country and abroad.

★7503★ **Callan Associates Ltd.**
2215 York Rd., Ste. 510
Oak Brook, IL 60523
Ph: (630)574-9300   Fax: (630)574-3099
E-mail: info@callanassociates.com
URL: http://www.callanassociates.com

Executive search firm.

★7504★ **Chandler Group**
4165 Shoreline Dr., Ste. 220
Spring Park, MN 55384
Ph: (952)471-3000   Fax: (952)471-3021
E-mail: info@chandgroup.com
URL: http://www.chandgroup.com

Executive search firm.

★7505★ **Charleston Partners**
2 Bellevue Ave.
Rumson, NJ 07760
Ph: (732)842-5015   Fax: (732)842-0993
E-mail: info@charlestonpartners.com
URL: http://www.charlestonpartners.com

Executive search firm concentrated on human resource services.

★7506★ **The Cheyenne Group**
60 E. 42nd St., Ste. 2821
New York, NY 10165
Ph: (212)471-5000   Fax: (212)471-5050
E-mail: contact_us@cheyennegroup.com
URL: http://www.cheyennegroup.com

Executive search firm.

★7507★ **The Cooke Group Inc.**
1001 W. Glen Oaks Lane, Ste. 102
Mequon, WI 53092
Ph: (262)241-9842   Fax: (262)241-1004
Fr: 888-432-7800
E-mail: rmarshall@cookegroup.net
URL: http://www.cookegroup.net/

Executive search firm.

★7508★ **Custom Research Solutions**
16400 Pacific Coast Hwy., Ste. 221
Huntington Beach, CA 92649
Ph: (562)431-6690   Fr: 800-829-5870
E-mail: arodrique@custom-research.com
URL: http://www.custom-research.com

Executive search firm.

★7509★ **DNPitchon Associates**
60 W. Ridgewood Ave.
Ridgewood, NJ 07450
Ph: (201)612-8350
E-mail: info@dnpitchon.com
URL: http://www.dnpitchon.com

Executive search firm.

★7510★ **Drinkwater & Associates**
167 West St.
Beverly, MA 01915
Ph: (978)922-3676

E-mail: wendydrinkwater@comcast.com

Executive search firm.

★7511★ **DuVall & Associates**

4203 Costa Salada
San Clemente, CA 92673
Ph: (949)488-8790   Fax: (949)488-8793
E-mail: Karen@ducall.com
URL: http://www.duvall.com

Executive search firm specializing in management team placement.

★7512★ **The Executive Source Inc.**

55 5th Ave., Ste. 1900
New York, NY 10003
Ph: (212)691-5505   Fax: (212)691-9839
E-mail: tes@executivesource.com
URL: http://www.executivesource.com

Executive search firm.

★7513★ **Explore Company**

1054 31st St. NW, Ste. 330
Washington, DC 20007
Ph: (202)333-3473
E-mail: explorecompany@aol.com
URL: http://www.explorecompany.com

Executive search firm.

★7514★ **Foy, Schneid & Daniel Inc.**

575 Madison Ave., Ste. 1006
New York, NY 10022
Ph: (212)980-2525   Fax: (212)639-9221
URL: http://www.fsdsearch.com

Executive search firm with a second location Ridgefield, CT.

★7515★ **Hawkes Peers**

224 Fifth Ave., Fl. 6
New York, NY 10001
Ph: (646)415-7812
E-mail: noah@hawkespeers.com
URL: http://www.hawkespeers.com

Executive search firm specializing in the areas of banking and sales.

★7516★ **Heidrick and Struggles, Inc.**

233 S. Wacker Dr., Ste. 4200
Sears Tower
Chicago, IL 60606-6303
Ph: (312)496-1200   Fax: (312)496-1290
URL: http://www.heidrick.com

Executive search firm. International organization with a variety of affiliate offices.

★7517★ **Hintz Associates, Inc.**

196 Prospect Ave.
Valhalla, NY 10595-1831
Ph: (914)761-4227   Fax: (914)948-8630
E-mail: geohintz@aol.com

Executive search firm specializing in cost reduction analysis and internal/external consultants.

★7518★ **Intech Summit Group, Inc.**

3450 Bonita Rd., Ste. 203
Chula Vista, CA 91910
Ph: (619)862-2720   Fax: (619)862-2699
Fr: 800-750-8100
E-mail: isg@isgsearch.com
URL: http://www.isgsearch.com

Employment agency and executive recruiter with a branch in Carlsbad, CA.

★7519★ **Kenmore Executives Inc.**

PO Box 66
Boca Raton, FL 33429
Ph: (561)392-0700   Fax: (561)750-0818
E-mail: inquires@kenmoreexecutives.com
URL: http://www.kenmoreexecutives.com

Executive search firm that works with consultants in a variety of fields.

★7520★ **Korn/Ferry International**

200 Park Ave., 37 Fl.
New York, NY 10166
Ph: (212)687-1834   Fax: (212)986-5684
URL: http://www.kornferry.com

Executive search firm. International organization with a variety of affiliate offices.

★7521★ **Protocol Agency Inc.**

2659 Townsgate Rd., Ste.203
Westlake Village, CA 91361-2774
Ph: (805)371-0069   Fax: (805)371-0048
E-mail: corp@protocolexec.com
URL: http://www.protocolagency.com

Executive search firm focusing on a variety of placements.

★7522★ **Ronald Dukes Associates LLC**

20 North Wacker, Ste. 2010
Chicago, IL 60606
Ph: (312)357-2895   Fax: (312)357-2897
E-mail: ron@rdukesassociates.com
URL: http://www.rdukesassociates.com

Executive search firm focused on the industrial and automotive industries.

★7523★ **Russell Reynolds Associates, Inc.**

200 Park Ave., Ste. 2300
New York, NY 10166-0002
Ph: (212)351-2000   Fax: (212)370-0896
E-mail: info@russellreynolds.com
URL: http://www.russellreynolds.com

Executive search firm. Affiliate offices across the country and abroad.

★7524★ **Systems Careers**

564 Market St., Ste. 620
San Francisco, CA 94104
Ph: (415)434-4770

Executive search firm and employment agency.

★7525★ **Valerie Fredrickson & Company**

800 Menlo Ave., Ste. 220
Menlo Park, CA 94025
Ph: (650)614-0220   Fax: (650)614-0223
E-mail: andrew@vfandco.com
URL: http://www.vfandco.com

Executive search firm.

TRADESHOWS

★7526★ **Association of Career Management Consulting Firms International Annual Conference**

Association of Career Management Consulting Firms International
204 E St., NE
Washington, DC 20002
Ph: (202)547-6344   Fax: (202)547-6348
E-mail: acf@acfinternational.org
URL: http://www.aocfi.org

Annual. **Primary Exhibits:** Exhibits relating for outplacement consultants, who counsel and assist in job searching, as well as educate about the techniques and practices of choosing a career.

★7527★ **Organization Development Network Conference**

Organization Development Network
71 Valley St., Ste. 301
South Orange, NJ 07079-2825
Ph: (973)763-7337   Fax: (973)763-7488
E-mail: odnetwork@ODNetwork.org
URL: http://www.odnetwork.org

Annual. **Primary Exhibits:** Exhibits related to organization development.

OTHER SOURCES

★7528★ **Administration and Management Occupations**

Delphi Productions
3159 6th St.
Boulder, CO 80304
Ph: (303)443-2100   Fax: (303)443-4022
Fr: 888-443-2400
E-mail: support@delphivideo.com
URL: http://www.delphivideo.com

$95.00. 50 minutes. Part of the Careers for the 21st Century Video Library.

★7529★ *American Almanac of Jobs and Salaries*

HarperCollins
10 E. 53rd St.
New York, NY 10022
Ph: (212)207-7000   Fr: 800-242-7737
URL: http://www.harpercollins.com/

John W. Wright. Revised edition, 2000.

$20.00 (paper). 672 pages. This is a comprehensive guide to the wages of hundreds of occupations in a wide variety of industries and organizations.

★7530★ Association of Management Consulting Firms (AMCF)
380 Lexington Ave., Ste. 1700
New York, NY 10168
Ph: (212)551-7887   Fax: (212)551-7934
E-mail: info@amcf.org
URL: http://www.amcf.org

Description: Trade association for consulting organizations that provide a broad range of managerial services to commercial, industrial, governmental, and other organizations and individuals. Seeks to unite management-consulting firms in order to develop and improve professional standards and practice in the field. Offers information and referral services on management consultants; administers public relations program. Conducts research. Monitors regulatory environment.

★7531★ National Society of Certified Healthcare Business Consultants (NSCHBC)
12100 Sunset Hills Rd., Ste. 130
Reston, VA 20190
Ph: (703)234-4099   Fax: (703)435-4390
E-mail: info@nschbc.org

URL: http://www.healthcon.org

Description: Advances the profession of healthcare business consultants through education, certification and professional interaction. Provides education and training to assist members in fulfilling the requirements of certification.

★7532★ Organization Development Institute
11234 Walnut Ridge Rd.
Chesterland, OH 44026
Ph: (440)729-7419   Fax: (440)729-9319
E-mail: donwcole@aol.com
URL: http://www.odinstitute.org

Description: Professionals, students, and individuals interested in organization development. Disseminates information on and promotes a better understanding of organization development worldwide. Conducts specialized education programs. Develops the International O.D. Code of Ethics and a competency test for individuals wishing to qualify as a Registered Organization Development Consultant and a statement on the knowledge and skill necessary to be competent in organization development and criteria for the accreditation of OD/OB academic programs. Maintains job and consultant information service. Sponsors International Registry of Organization Development Professionals and Research/Study Team on Nonviolent Large Systems Change. Main-

tains 18 committees including an International Advisory Board.

★7533★ Organization Development Network (ODN)
71 Valley St., Ste. 301
South Orange, NJ 07079-2825
Ph: (973)763-7337   Fax: (973)763-7448
E-mail: odnetwork@odnetwork.org
URL: http://www.odnetwork.org

Description: Represents practitioners, academics, managers, and students employed or interested in organization development. Works to enhance and provide opportunities for colleagueship and professional development.

★7534★ Professional and Technical Consultants Association (PATCA)
PO Box 2261
Santa Clara, CA 95055
Ph: (408)971-5902   Fax: (866)746-1053
Fr: 800-74-PATCA
E-mail: info@patca.org
URL: http://www.patca.org

Description: Represents Independent consultants active in the support of business, industry, and government. Serves as a referral service to aid independent consultants in marketing their services as well as to assist those seeking their services.

Manicurists and Nail Technicians

★7535★ Beauty Launchpad

Creative Age Publications Inc.
7628 Densmore Ave.
Van Nuys, CA 91406-2042
Ph: (818)782-7328   Fax: (818)782-7450
Fr: 800-442-5667
URL: http://www.beautylaunchpad.com/index.php

$24.00/year for U.S., 12 issues; $48.00/year for Canada, 12 issues. Fashion magazine.

★7536★ Beauty Store Business

Creative Age Publications Inc.
7628 Densmore Ave.
Van Nuys, CA 91406-2042
Ph: (818)782-7328   Fax: (818)782-7450
Fr: 800-442-5667
URL: http://www.beautystorebusiness.com/index.htm

Monthly. Business magazine for beauty industry professionals and beauty store owners.

★7537★ Global Cosmetic Industry

Allured Publishing Corp.
336 Gundersen Dr.
Carol Stream, IL 60188-2403
Ph: (630)653-2155   Fax: (630)653-2192
URL: http://www.globalcosmetic.com

Monthly. Free to qualified subscribers, U.S. and Canada; $98.00/year for other countries; $176.00/year for other countries, 2 years. Trade publication covering the cosmetics industry worldwide.

★7538★ Modern Salon

Vance Publishing Corp.
400 Knightsbridge Pky.
Lincolnshire, IL 60069
Ph: (847)634-2600   Fax: (847)634-4379
URL: http://www.modernsalon.com/

Monthly. $25.00/year for individuals; $34.00/year for Canada; $95.00/year for other coun-

tries; $20.00/year for individuals, digital; $37.00 for two years; $54.00 for two years, Canada; $32.00/year for two years, digital; $47.01/year for individuals, 3 years; $69.99/year for Canada, 3 years; $42.00/year for individuals, digital 3 years. Magazine focusing on hairstyling salons for men and women.

★7539★ Nailpro

Creative Age Publications Inc.
7628 Densmore Ave.
Van Nuys, CA 91406-2042
Ph: (818)782-7328   Fax: (818)782-7450
Fr: 800-442-5667
E-mail: nailpro@creativeage.com
URL: http://www.nailpro.com

Monthly. $21.95/year for individuals; $45.00/year for Canada and Mexico; $89.00/year for other countries. Salon owners and nail technicians read Nailpro for continuing education in techniques and services, marketing and management tips, product information and industry news.

★7540★ Renew

Vance Publishing Corp.
400 Knightsbridge Pky.
Lincolnshire, IL 60069
Ph: (847)634-2600   Fax: (847)634-4379
URL: http://www.vancepublishing.com

Bimonthly. Free to qualified subscribers. Magazine for salon, spa, and skin care professionals.

★7541★ Soap and Cosmetics

Chemical Week Associates
110 Williams St.
New York, NY 10038
Ph: (212)621-4900   Fax: (212)621-4800
URL: http://www.chemweek.com/verticals/sc/

Monthly. Trade publication covering the cosmetics industry.

★7542★ Spa 20/20

Virgo Publishing Inc.
PO Box 40079
Phoenix, AZ 85067-0079
Ph: (480)990-1101   Fax: (480)990-0819
URL: http://www.spa20-20.com

Bimonthly. $14.00/year for individuals, in U.S.; $26.00/year for Canada; $82.00/year for elsewhere. Magazine covering the spa industry, including skin care, cosmetics, and sunless tanning.

★7543★ World International Nail and Beauty Association (WINBA)

1221 N Lake View Ave.
Anaheim, CA 92807
Ph: (714)779-9892   Fax: (714)779-9971
Fr: 800-541-9838
E-mail: dkellenberger@inmnails.com

Members: Professionals in the nail and skin care industries. **Purpose:** Objectives are to: represent the manicure and skin care industry; promote the effective use and application of manicuring and skin care products and equipment; provide a means for mutual communication and joint study; represent the industry before state boards, the Food and Drug Administration, and other regulatory agencies. **Activities:** Conducts seminars; secures discounts on supplies; offers special conducts public relations program; sponsors research and educational programs; compiles statistics. Maintains speakers' bureau and placement service.

EMPLOYER DIRECTORIES AND NETWORKING LISTS

★7544★ Official Show Directory
Beauty and Barber Supply Institute
1roof Community
15825 N 71St. St., No. 100
Scottsdale, AZ 85254
Ph: (480)281-0424   Fr: 800-468-2274

Semiannual. Covers wholesalers and manufacturers of beauty and barber salon equipment and supplies. Includes exhibit listings, Beauty and Barber Supply Institute membership updates, and trade show agenda.

HANDBOOKS AND MANUALS

★7545★ The Art and Science of Nail Technology
Cengage Learning
PO Box 6904
Florence, KY 41022
Fax: 800-487-8488   Fr: 800-354-9706
URL: http://www.cengage.com

Second edition, revised, 1997. $52.95. Part of Nails series. 288 pages.

★7546★ Career After Cosmetology School: Step-by-Step Guide to a Lucrative Career and Salon Ownership
Step-by-Step Publications
1645 Westmont Ave.
Campbell, CA 95008
Ph: (408)376-0276   Fax: (408)376-0396
Fr: 800-305-2205

Jessica Brooks. 1998. $29.95. 320 pages.

★7547★ Cosmetology Career Starter
LearningExpress, LLC
55 Broadway, 8th Fl.
New York, NY 10006
Ph: (212)995-2566   Fax: (212)995-5512
Fr: 800-295-9556
E-mail: customerservice@learningexpressllc.com
URL: http://www.learningexpressllc.com

Lorraine Korman. Second edition, 2002. $15.95. 224 pages.

★7548★ Opportunities in Beauty Culture Careers
The McGraw-Hill Companies
PO Box 182604
Columbus, OH 43272
Fax: (614)759-3749   Fr: 877-883-5524
E-mail: customer.service@mcgraw-hill.com
URL: http://www.mcgraw-hill.com

Susan W. Gearhart. 1996. $14.95. Part of the "Opportunities in ..." Series.

★7549★ Planning Your Cosmetology Career
Prentice Hall PTR
1 Lake St.
Upper Saddle River, NJ 07458
Ph: (201)236-7000   Fax: 800-445-6991
Fr: 800-428-5331
URL: http://www.phptr.com/index.asp?rl=1

Mary Murphy-Martin. 1993. $26.60 (paper). 108 pages.

★7550★ The Transition, How to Become a Salon Professional
Milady
5 Maxwell Dr.
Clifton Park, NY 12065
Fax: (859)647-5963   Fr: 800-998-7498
E-mail: milady@delmar.com
URL: http://www.milady.com

Louise Cotter and Frances L. DuBose. First edition 1996. $40.95. Part of the Cosmetology Series. 352 pages.

TRADESHOWS

★7551★ American Association of Cosmetology Schools Annual Conference-AACS Annual Convention & Expo
American Association of Cosmetology Schools
15825 N. 71st St., Ste. 100
Scottsdale, AZ 85254-1521
Ph: (480)281-0431   Fax: (480)905-0993
Fr: 800-831-1086
E-mail: dilsah@beautyschools.org
URL: http://www.beautyschools.org

Annual. **Primary Exhibits:** Beauty supplies and products, and cosmetology services.

★7552★ American Electrology Association Annual Convention
American Electrology Association
PO Box 687
Bodega Bay, CA 94923
Ph: (707)875-9135   Fax: (203)372-7134
E-mail: infoaea@electrology.com
URL: http://www.electrology.com

Annual. **Primary Exhibits:** Electrology equipment, supplies, and services.

★7553★ IBS - International Beauty Show, New York
Advanstar Communications Inc.
One Park Ave.
New York, NY 10016
Ph: (212)951-6600   Fax: (212)951-6793

E-mail: info@advantstar.com
URL: http://www.advantstar.com

Annual. **Primary Exhibits:** Beauty and health related equipment, supplies, and services.

★7554★ Midwest Beauty Show
Chicago Cosmetologists Association
401 N. Michigan Ave., Ste. 2200
Chicago, IL 60611
Ph: (312)321-6809   Fax: (312)245-1080
Fr: 800-648-2505
E-mail: info@isnow.com
URL: http://www.isnow.com

Annual. **Primary Exhibits:** Goods and services for the beauty trade.

★7555★ National Beauty Show - HAIRWORLD
National Cosmetology Association
401 N Michigan Ave., 22nd Fl.
Chicago, IL 60611-4255
Ph: (312)527-6765   Fax: (312)464-6118
Fr: 800-527-1683
E-mail: nca1@ncacares.org
URL: http://www.behindthechairexchange.com/nca

Annual. **Primary Exhibits:** Hair products, cosmetics, and jewelry.

OTHER SOURCES

★7556★ National Cosmetology Association (NCA)
401 N Michigan Ave., 22nd Fl.
Chicago, IL 60611
Ph: (312)527-6765   Fax: (312)464-6118
E-mail: nca1@ncacares.org
URL: http://www.ncacares.org

Members: Owners of cosmetology salons; cosmetologists. **Activities:** Sponsors: National Cosmetology Month; National Beauty Show. Provides special sections for estheticians, school owners, salon owners, and nail technicians. Maintains hall of fame. Conducts educational and charitable programs.

★7557★ Personal & Building Service Occupations
Delphi Productions
3159 6th St.
Boulder, CO 80304
Ph: (303)443-2100   Fax: (303)443-4022
Fr: 888-443-2400
E-mail: support@delphivideo.com
URL: http://www.delphivideo.com

$95.00. 48 minutes. Part of the Careers for the 21st Century Video Library.

Manufacturer's Sales Representatives

SOURCES OF HELP-WANTED ADS

★7558★ AATCC Review

American Association of Textile Chemists and Colorists
PO Box 12215
Research Triangle Park, NC 27709
Ph: (919)549-8141   Fax: (919)549-8933
URL: http://www.aatcc.org

Monthly. Magazine focusing on dyeing, finishing of fibers and fabrics.

★7559★ Agency Sales Magazine

Manufacturers' Agents National Association
1 Spectrum Pointe, Ste. 150
Lake Forest, CA 92630-2283
Ph: (949)859-4040   Fax: (949)855-2973
Fr: 877-626-2776
URL: http://www.manaonline.org/html/agency_sales_magazine.html

Monthly. Magazine for manufacturers' agents and manufacturers. Includes tax developments and tips, management aids for manufacturers and agents, legal bulletins, trend-identifying market data, classified ads.

★7560★ Apparel

Bill Communications Inc.
770 Broadway
New York, NY 10003-9595
Ph: (646)654-4500   Fr: 800-845-8820
E-mail: apparelmag@halldata.com
URL: http://www.bobbin.com

Monthly. $69.00/year for U.S. $85.00/year for Canada; $190.00/year for other countries, by airmail. Trade magazine on sewn-products industry management and manufacturing. Reports on industry trends, technology, new products, etc.

★7561★ BedTimes

International Sleep Products Association
501 Wythe St.
Alexandria, VA 22314-1917
Ph: (703)683-8371   Fax: (703)683-4503

E-mail: bedtimes@sleepproducts.org
URL: http://www.sleepproducts.org/TemplateBedtimes.cfm?Section=BE

Monthly. $50.00/year for U.S. $90.00/year for U.S., 2 years; $65.00/year for other countries; $110.00/year for other countries, 2 years;. Free, for ISPA members. Trade magazine covering trends and developments in the mattress bedding industry.

★7562★ Beverage World

Beverage World
90 Broad St., Ste. 402
New York, NY 10004-3312
Ph: (646)708-7300   Fax: (646)708-7399
Fr: (866)890-8541
URL: http://www.beverageworld.com

Monthly. $99.00/year for individuals. Trade magazine for corporate, marketing, distribution, production, and purchasing top and middle management in the multi-product beverage industry.

★7563★ BtoB Magazine

Crain Communications Inc.
360 N Michigan Ave.
Chicago, IL 60601
Ph: (312)649-5411   Fax: (312)280-3150
Fr: 888-909-9111
URL: http://www.btobonline.com

Monthly. $59.00/year for individuals; $69.00/year for Canada; $89.00/year for other countries. Trade magazine on business-to-business marketing news, strategy, and tactics.

★7564★ Chemical Market Reporter

Schnell Publishing Company Inc.
360 Park Ave. S
12th Fl.
New York, NY 10010
Ph: (212)791-4200   Fax: (212)791-4321

Weekly (Mon.). International tabloid newspaper for the chemical process industries. Includes analytical reports on developments in the chemical marketplace, plant expansions, new technology, corporate mergers, finance, current chemical prices, and regulatory matters.

★7565★ Concrete Products

Penton Media Inc.
9800 Metcalf Ave.
Overland Park, KS 66212
Ph: (913)341-1300   Fax: (913)967-1898
E-mail: dmarsh@prismb2b.com
URL: http://www.concreteproducts.com/

Monthly. Free, online; $96.00/year for other countries, print. Magazine on concrete products and ready-mixed concrete.

★7566★ Cosmetics & Toiletries

Allured Publishing Corp.
336 Gundersen Dr.
Carol Stream, IL 60188-2403
Ph: (630)653-2155   Fax: (630)653-2192
E-mail: lhince@allured.com
URL: http://www.cosmeticsandtoiletries.com

Monthly. $98.00/year for individuals; $137.00/year for Canada; $189.00/year for other countries; $169.00 for two years; $231.00 for Canada, 2 years; $330.00 for other countries, 2 years. Trade magazine on cosmetic and toiletries manufacturing with an emphasis on product research and development issues.

★7567★ CRN

CMP Media L.L.C.
600 Community Dr.
Manhasset, NY 11030
Ph: (516)562-5000   Fax: (516)562-7830
URL: http://www.crn.com

Weekly. Newspaper for value added resellers, retailers, and distributors in the computer market.

★7568★ Dealernews

Advanstar Communications
641 Lexington Ave., 8th Fl.
New York, NY 10022
Ph: (212)951-6600   Fax: (212)951-6793
URL: http://www.dealernews.com

Monthly. Magazine covering dealers of motorcycles, ATV/off-road vehicles, watercraft, other powersport vehicles, and related aftermarket and apparel products.

★7569★ Electrical Wholesaling

Penton Media Inc.
9800 Metcalf Ave.
Overland Park, KS 66212
Ph: (913)341-1300   Fax: (913)967-1898
URL: http://www.ewweb.com/

Monthly. Magazine focusing on electrical wholesaling for distributors of electrical supplies.

★7570★ Feedstuffs

Miller Publishing Co.
12400 Whitewater Dr., Ste. 160
Minnetonka, MN 55343
Ph: (952)931-0211   Fax: (952)938-1832
URL: http://www.feedstuffs.com/ME2/Default.asp

Weekly. $144.00/year for individuals; $230.00 for two years; $150.00/year for Canada; $235.00/year Europe and Middle East, airmail; $280.00/year for other countries, Japan, Far East/Australia airmail; $210.00/year Mexico/Central/South America; $196.00/year print and internet version; $334.00 for two years, print and internet version; $202.00/year for Canada, print and internet version; $287.00/year Europe/Middle East by air/print and internet version. Magazine serving the grain and feed industries and animal agriculture.

★7571★ Food Production Management

CTI Publications Inc.
2 Oakway Rd.
Timonium, MD 21093-4247
Ph: (410)308-2080   Fax: (410)308-2079
Fr: 800-468-6770
E-mail: fpmeditorial@ctipubs.com

Monthly. $40.00/year for individuals; $70.00 for two years; $60.00/year for other countries; $110.00 for two years, other countries. Magazine on food processing and individual packing news for management, sales, and production personnel in the canning, glass packing, aseptic, and frozen food industries.

★7572★ Furniture Today

Reed Business Information
7025 Albert Pick Rd., Ste. 200
Greensboro, NC 27409
Ph: (336)605-0121   Fax: (336)605-1143
URL: http://www.furnituretoday.com/

Weekly (Mon.). $159.97/year for U.S., Canada, and Mexico; $279.97 for two years, US, Canada, Mexico. Furniture retailing and manufacturing magazine.

★7573★ Gases & Welding Distributor

Penton Media Inc.
1300 E 9th St.
Cleveland, OH 44114
Ph: (216)696-7000   Fax: (216)696-1752
URL: http://weldingdesign.com

$72.00/year for individuals, international; $121.50 for individuals, 2 years, international. Free to qualified subscribers, in U.S. and Canada. Distributor magazine featuring industrial, medical, specialty gases and welding supplies.

★7574★ Health Products Business

Cygnus Business Media Inc.
3 Huntington Quadrangle, Ste. 301 N
Melville, NY 11747
Ph: (631)845-2700   Fax: (631)845-7109
Fr: 800-308-6397
URL: http://www.cygnusb2b.com/PressRelease.cfm?PRID=171

Monthly. Health and nutrition magazine focusing on the natural products industry.

★7575★ Home Channel News

Lebhar-Friedman, Inc.
425 Park Ave., 6th Fl.
New York, NY 10022
Ph: (212)756-5000   Fax: (212)756-5215
URL: http://www.homechannelnews.com

$189.00/year for individuals. Business tabloid serving home center/building material retailers.

★7576★ Implement & Tractor

Scissortail Productions LLC
2302 W 4th St., Ste. 1
Cedar Falls, IA 50613-2864
Ph: (319)277-3599   Fax: (319)277-3783
E-mail: agrausa@cfu.net
URL: http://www.scissortailproductionsllc.com/ITAbout.htm

Bimonthly. $38.00/year for U.S. and Canada; $98.00/year for other countries, airmail only; $72.00/year for U.S. and Canada, 2 years; $175.00 for two years, all foreign, airmail only. Magazine about agricultural equipment and machinery.

★7577★ Industrial Distribution

Reed Business Information
225 Wyman St.
Waltham, MA 02451-1216
URL: http://www.inddist.com

Monthly. $121.00/year for individuals; $145.00/year for Canada; $140.00/year for individuals, for Mexico; $280.00/year for other countries. Magazine covering industrial supplies marketing, management, sales, telecommunications, computers, inventory, and warehouse management.

★7578★ Industrial Heating

Business News Publishing Co.
2401 W Big Beaver Rd., Ste. 700
Troy, MI 48084-3333
URL: http://www.industrialheating.com/
Monthly. Magazine.

★7579★ Kitchen and Bath Business

The Nielsen Co.
770 Broadway
New York, NY 10003
Ph: (646)654-5000   Fax: (646)654-5002

URL: http://www.kitchen-bath.com/kbb/index.jsp

Monthly. $10.00/year for individuals, cover; $79.00/year for individuals, domestic; $94.00/year for Canada and Mexico; $142.00/year for other countries. Trade magazine on kitchen and bath remodeling and construction.

★7580★ Laser Focus World

PennWell Corp.
98 Spit Brook Rd.
Nashua, NH 03062-5737
Ph: (603)891-0123
URL: http://lfw.pennnet.com

Monthly. $150.00/year for individuals; $200.00/year for individuals, Canada; $75.00/year for individuals, digital distribution; $250.00/year for other countries. Magazine covering advances and applications in optoelectronics and photonics.

★7581★ LDB Interior Textiles

E.W. Williams Publications Co.
2125 Center Ave., Ste. 305
Fort Lee, NJ 07024-5898
Ph: (201)592-7007   Fax: (201)592-7171
URL: http://www.ldbinteriortextiles.com

Monthly. $72.00/year for individuals; $125.00/year for Canada; $150.00/year for elsewhere; $100.00 for two years; $7.00/year for single issue; $12.00 for single issue, Canada; $18.00/year for single issue, elsewhere. Magazine for buyers of home fashions, including bed, bath and table linens, hard and soft window treatments, home fragrances, decorative pillows and home accessories, accent rugs, and decorative fabrics.

★7582★ Managing Automation

Thomas Publishing Co.
5 Penn Plz.
New York, NY 10001
Ph: (212)695-0500   Fax: (212)290-7362
E-mail: contact@thomaspublishing.com
URL: http://www.managingautomation.com/maonline/

Monthly. $60.00/year for individuals; $8.00 for single issue; $75.00/year for Canada and Mexico; $125.00/year for other countries. Managing Automation covers advanced manufacturing technology including automation, integrated manufacturing, enterprise applications, and IT and e-business for the manufacturing enterprise.

★7583★ Manufacturers Representatives of America-Newsline

Manufacturers Representatives of America
PO Box 150229
Arlington, TX 76015
Ph: (682)518-6008   Fax: (682)518-6476
E-mail: assnhqtrs@aol.com
URL: http://www.mra-reps.com/

Description: Monthly. Published for member independent manufacturers' representatives handling sanitary supplies and paper and plastic disposable products. Carries articles to help improve agent sales skills, market coverage, and customer service, and to help establish more effective agent/principal communications. Recurring features include news of members, a calendar of events, job listings, notices of publications available, news of educational opportunities, and a column titled President's Report.

★7584★ **Meat & Poultry**

Sosland Publishing Co.
4800 Main St., Ste. 100
Kansas City, MO 64112
Ph: (816)756-1000   Fax: (816)756-0494
Fr: 800-338-6201
URL: http://www.meatpoultry.com

Monthly. $85.00/year for Canada and Mexico; $165.00/year for other countries, surface mail; $165.00/year for other countries, air mail. Magazine serving the meat and poultry processing, distributing, and wholesaling industries in the U.S. and Canada.

★7585★ **Med Ad News**

Engel Publishing Partners
820 Bear Tavern Rd., Ste. 300
West Trenton, NJ 08628
Fax: (609)530-0207
E-mail: mwalsh@engelpub.com
URL: http://www.pharmalive.com

Monthly. $190.00/year for individuals. Pharmaceutical business and marketing magazine.

★7586★ **Milling & Baking News**

Sosland Publishing Co.
4800 Main St., Ste. 100
Kansas City, MO 64112
Ph: (816)756-1000   Fax: (816)756-0494
Fr: 800-338-6201
E-mail:
mbncirc@sosland.com?subject=mbn
URL: http://www.bakingbusiness.com

Weekly (Tues.). $128.00/year for individuals; $200.00 for individuals, 2 years; $276.00 for individuals, 3 years; $183.00/year for out of country; $310.00 for out of country, 2 years; $441.00 for out of country, 3 years. Trade magazine covering the grain-based food industries.

★7587★ **Modern Grocer**

GC Publishing Company Inc.
PO Box 2010
744 Main St., Rte. 6A
Dennis, MA 02638
Ph: (508)385-7700   Fax: (508)385-0089
URL: http://www.gccomm.net/mg.htm

Monthly. $50.00/year for individuals. Magazine for food retailers, wholesalers, distributors, brokers, manufacturers, and packers in the metro New York and New Jersey marketing area.

★7588★ **Modern Plastics**

Chemical Week Associates
110 Williams St.
New York, NY 10038
Ph: (212)621-4900   Fax: (212)621-4800
URL: http://www.modplas.com

Monthly. $59.00/year for individuals; $99.00 for two years, U.S. and possessions; $110.00/year for Canada; $199.00 for two years, for Canada; $150.00/year for other countries; $250.00 for two years. Magazine for the plastics industry.

★7589★ **Money Making Opportunities**

Success Publishing International
11071 Ventura Blvd.
Studio City, CA 91604
Ph: (818)980-9166   Fax: (818)980-7829
URL: http://www.moneymakingopps.com/

Free. Magazine Source for small business opportunity seekers.

★7590★ **Multi-Housing News**

The Nielsen Co.
770 Broadway
New York, NY 10003
Ph: (646)654-5000   Fax: (646)654-5002
URL: http://www.multi-housingnews.com/multihousing/index.jsp

Monthly. $10.00/year for individuals, cover. Trade magazine.

★7591★ **Packaging Digest**

Reed Business Information
2000 Clearwater Dr.
Oak Brook, IL 60523
Ph: (630)288-8000   Fax: (630)288-8750
E-mail: sreiss@reedbusiness.com
URL: http://www.packagingdigest.com/

Monthly. Business trade magazine for the packaging field.

★7592★ **Paperboard Packaging Worldwide**

Advanstar Communications
641 Lexington Ave.
8th Fl.
New York, NY 10022
Ph: (212)951-6600   Fax: (212)951-6793
Fr: 800-225-4569
URL: http://www.packaging-online.com

Monthly. $30.00/year for individuals. Trade magazine for the corrugated container, folding carton, and rigid box converting industry.

★7593★ **Photo Marketing**

Photo Marketing Association International
3000 Picture Pl.
Jackson, MI 49201
Ph: (517)788-8100   Fax: (517)788-8371
Fr: 800-762-9287
URL: http://www.photomarketing.com/

Monthly. $50.00/year for individuals; $55.00/year for Canada; $70.00/year for other countries; $5.00/year for single issue; $90.00 for two years; $100.00 for two years, Canada;

$130.00 for two years, other countries. Trade magazine for photo/video dealers and photo finishers.

★7594★ **RV Business**

TL Enterprises Inc.
2575 Vista Del Mar
Ventura, CA 93001
Ph: (805)667-4100   Fax: (805)667-4419
URL: http://www.rvbusiness.com

Monthly. Magazine about the business of manufacturing, distributing, and selling travel trailers, conversion vehicles, and motorhomes and related parts, accessories, and services.

★7595★ **Sales & Marketing Management**

The Nielsen Co.
770 Broadway
New York, NY 10003
Ph: (646)654-5000   Fax: (646)654-5002
URL: http://www.salesandmarketing.com

Monthly. $48.00/year for individuals. Business magazine.

★7596★ **Sporting Goods Dealer**

Bill Communications Inc.
1115 Northmeadow Pkwy.
Roswell, GA 30076
Ph: (770)569-1540   Fax: (770)569-5105
Fr: 800-241-9034
URL: http://www.sgdealer.com/sportinggoodsdealer/index.jsp

Bimonthly. Magazine that offers expert reporting on trends affecting team dealers and retailers who service schools, colleges, pro and local teams.

★7597★ **Timber Harvesting**

Hatton-Brown Publishers Inc.
225 Hanrick St.
PO Box 2268
Montgomery, AL 36104
Ph: (334)834-1170   Fax: (334)834-4525
Fr: 800-669-5613
URL: http://www.timberharvesting.com/

Monthly. $50.00/year for U.S. $60.00/year for Canada; $24.95/year for individuals, full online; $9.95/year for individuals, limited online; $95.00/year for other countries. National magazine for the U.S. logging industry.

★7598★ **Transmission Digest**

MD Publications Inc.
3057 E Cairo
PO Box 2210
Springfield, MO 65802
Ph: (417)866-3917   Fax: (417)866-2781
Fr: 800-274-7890
URL: http://www.transmissiondigest.com/

Monthly. $39.00/year for individuals; $4.75 for single issue. Automotive transmission industry news.

★7599★ TWICE

Reed Business Information
360 Park Ave. S
New York, NY 10010
Ph: (646)746-6400   Fax: (646)746-7431
E-mail: mgrand@reedbusiness.com
URL: http://www.reedbusiness.com/

Biweekly. Free. Trade tabloid covering consumer electronics, appliance, and camera industries for retailers, manufacturers, and distributors.

★7600★ UAMR Confidential Bulletin

United Association of Manufacturers'
   Representatives (UAMR)
PO Box 784
Branson, MO 65615
Ph: (417)779-1575   Fax: (417)779-1576
E-mail: info@uamr.com
URL: http://www.uamr.com/

Description: Monthly. Covers product lines offered for representation in all fields. Provides details of the company and product, type of accounts to be serviced, and the areas open for representation. Subscription includes bulletin of lines for representatives, articles on rep business, and trade show listings.

★7601★ Undercar Digest

MD Publications Inc.
3057 E Cairo
PO Box 2210
Springfield, MO 65802
Ph: (417)866-3917   Fax: (417)866-2781
Fr: 800-274-7890
URL: http://www.mdpublications.com

Monthly. $49.00/year for individuals. Magazine for the undercar service and supply industry.

★7602★ Watch & Clock Review

Golden Bell Press
2403 Champa St.
Denver, CO 80205
Ph: (303)296-1600   Fax: (303)295-2159

Monthly. $19.50/year for individuals, 1 year; $35.00/year for individuals, 2 years. Magazine on watches and clocks.

★7603★ Yard and Garden

Cygnus Business Media
1233 Janesville Ave.
Fort Atkinson, WI 53538
Fr: 800-547-7377
URL: http://www.cygnusexpos.com/PropertyPub.cfm?PropertyID=117

Yard and garden magazine featuring product news and retailer success stories.

PLACEMENT AND JOB REFERRAL SERVICES

★7604★ Sporting Goods Agents Association (SGAA)

PO Box 998
Morton Grove, IL 60053
Ph: (847)296-3670   Fax: (847)827-0196
E-mail: sgaa998@aol.com
URL: http://www.sgaaonline.org

Members: Represents manufacturers' agents whose goal is to provide free legal counsel for members and additional product lines from manufacturers, and to improve the image of the independent agent. **Activities:** Offers placement service.

EMPLOYER DIRECTORIES AND NETWORKING LISTS

★7605★ Agricultural & Industrial Manufacturers Representatives Association-Membership Directory

Agricultural & Industrial Manufacturers
   Representatives Association
7500 Flying Cloud Dr., Ste. 900
Eden Prairie, MN 55344-3756
Ph: (952)253-6230   Fax: (952)835-4774
Fr: (866)759-2467
URL: http://www.aimrareps.org

Annual, October. Covers 120 members; coverage includes Canada. Entries include: Company name, address, phone, name of principal executive, territory covered. Arrangement: Alphabetical.

★7606★ American Hardware Manufacturers Association-Rep/Factory Contact Service Directory

American Hardware Manufacturers
   Association
801 N Plz. Dr.
Schaumburg, IL 60173
Ph: (847)605-1025   Fax: (847)605-1030
URL: http://www.ahma.org/

Annual, April. Covers over 280 manufacturer representatives in the hardware industry. Entries include: Firm name, address, number of years in business, number of salespeople, territory covered, manufacturers represented, products or service offered, type of accounts currently served, whether firm has a distribution network or warehouses, whether firm provides in-store service. Arrangement: Geographical. Indexes: Product line, firm name.

★7607★ American Salon's Green Book

Advanstar Communications
641 Lexington Ave.
8th Fl.
New York, NY 10022
Ph: (212)951-6600   Fax: (212)951-6793
Fr: 800-225-4569

E-mail: directories@advanstar.com
URL: http://web.advanstar.com/

Annual, November; latest edition 2007. $225.00 for individuals. Covers about 1,300 manufacturers of supplies and equipment for salons and spas; 130 manufacturers' representatives; 3,200 distributors; employment agencies, show management companies, and related trade organizations. Entries include: For manufacturers and agents–Company name, address, phone, names of principal executives, products available. For distributors–Company name, address, phone, branches, name of owner or president, number of sales representatives, trade association affiliation, Metropolitan Statistical Area (MSA) in which located. For representatives–Company name, address, phone, territory covered. Arrangement: Manufacturers are alphabetical; agents, distributors, representatives are geographical. Indexes: Product, trade name.

★7608★ American Wholesalers and Distributors Directory

Gale, Cengage Learning
27500 Drake Rd.
Farmington Hills, MI 48331-3535
Ph: (248)699-4253   Fax: (248)699-8065
Fr: 800-877-4253
E-mail: businessproducts@gale.com
URL: http://www.gale.com

Annual; latest edition 15th, July 2006. $305.00 for individuals. Covers name and address, fax number, SIC code, principal product lines, total number of employees, estimated annual sales volume and principal officers' information of 27,000 large and small wholesalers and distributors in the U.S. and Puerto Rico. Arrangement: By broad subject from principal product line. Indexes: SIC, geographical, alphabetical.

★7609★ Bacon's Radio/TV/Cable Directory, Volume 1

Cision US Inc.
332 S Michigan Ave., Ste. 900
Chicago, IL 60604
Ph: (312)922-2400   Fax: (312)922-9387
Fr: (866)639-5087
URL: http://www.bacons.com

Annual; latest edition 2007. $450.00 for individuals. Covers over 13,500 radio and television stations, including college radio and public television stations, and cable companies. Entries include: For radio and television stations–Call letters, address, phone, names and titles of key personnel, programs, times broadcast, name of contact, network affiliation, frequency or channel number, target audience data. For cable companies–Name, address, phone, description of activities. Arrangement: Geographical.

★7610★ Career Ideas for Teens in Manufacturing

Facts On File Inc.
132 W 31st St., 17th Fl.
New York, NY 10001
Ph: (212)967-8800   Fax: 800-678-3633
Fr: 800-322-8755
URL: http://www.factsonfile.com

Published 2005. $40.00 for individuals; $36.00 for libraries. Covers a multitude of career possibilities based on a teenager's specific interests and skills and links his/her talents to a wide variety of actual professions.

★7611★ Careers in Focus: Manufacturing

Facts On File Inc.
132 W 31st St., 17th Fl.
New York, NY 10001
Ph: (212)967-8800   Fax: 800-678-3633
Fr: 800-322-8755
URL: http://www.factsonfile.com

Latest edition 2nd, 2002. $29.95 for individuals; $26.95 for libraries. Covers an overview of manufacturing, followed by a selection of jobs profiled in detail, including the nature of the job, earnings, prospects for employment, what kind of training and skills it requires, and sources for further information.

★7612★ Electrical Equipment Representatives Association-Membership Directory

Electrical Equipment Representatives Association
638 W 39th St.
PO Box 419264
Kansas City, MO 64111
Ph: (816)561-5323   Fax: (816)561-1249
URL: http://www.eera.org

Continuous. Free. Covers more than 105 manufacturers' representatives of electrical equipment companies. Entries include: Company name, address, phone, names and titles of key personnel. Arrangement: Alphabetical.

★7613★ Gift and Decorative Accessories Center Association-Directory

Gift and Decorative Accessories Center Association
1000 Technology Park Dr.
Billerica, MA 01821
Ph: (978)670-6363   Fax: (781)275-7479
URL: http://www.giftsanddec.com

Continuous. Free. Covers about 60 individuals who are giftware manufacturers' representatives in New England; also lists their manufacturers and suppliers. Entries include: For representatives–Name, address, phone, e-mail, manufacturers and products represented. Arrangement: Alphabetical.

★7614★ The Locator-The Electronics Representatives Directory/Electronics Industry Calendar

Electronics Representatives Association
444 N Michigan Ave., Ste. 1960
Chicago, IL 60611
Ph: (312)527-3050   Fax: (312)527-3783
URL: http://www.era.org

Annual, October. Covers 1,400 member and approximately 4,000 nonmember firms and 500 electronics industry trade shows; international coverage. Entries include: Firm name, address, phone; names of owners; facilities; states in territory; association divisional memberships; number of employees; branch offices' addresses, phone numbers, fax, and names of managers. Type of product handled is shown in separate tabulation at beginning of each chapter section. Arrangement: Geographical, by chapter. Indexes: Key personnel name, company.

★7615★ Manufacturers' Agents National Association-Directory of Manufacturers' Sales Agencies

Manufacturers' Agents National Association
1 Spectrum Pointe, Ste. 150
Lake Forest, CA 92630-2283
Ph: (949)859-4040   Fax: (949)855-2973
Fr: 877-626-2776
URL: http://www.manaonline.org

Online Directory. Covers 4,000 independent agents and firms representing manufacturers and other businesses in specified territories on a commission basis, including consultants and associate member firms interested in the manufacturer/agency method of marketing. Entries include: For manufacturers–Company name, address, phone, fax, e-mail, URL, name of contact, product. For agencies–Agency name, address, phone, fax, e-mail, URL, name of contact, warehouse facilities, territory covered, number of field sales representatives, branch office location, year established, date of joining association. Arrangement: Separate alphabetical sections for manufacturers and agencies. Indexes: Geographic, target industries.

★7616★ Manufacturers Representatives of America-Yearbook and Directory of Members

Manufacturers Representatives of America
PO Box 150229
Arlington, TX 76015
Ph: (682)518-6008   Fax: (682)518-6476
URL: http://www.mra-reps.com/lookup.asp

Annual, fall. Covers several hundred independent manufacturers' representatives in paper, plastic, packaging, and sanitary supplies. Entries include: Name, address, phone, distributors served, territory, number of persons in sales, branch offices, products handled, marketing services provided, warehouse locations and facilities. Arrangement: Geographical. Indexes: Organization, personal name.

★7617★ Office Products Representatives Association-Rep Locator

Office Products Representatives Association
3131 Elbee Rd.
Dayton, OH 45439-1900
Ph: (937)297-2250   Fax: (937)297-2254
URL: http://www.oprareps.org

Annual, June. Covers about 105 member manufacturers' representative firms in the office products industry. Entries include: Firm name, address, phone, names of contacts, fax, e-mail, website addresses. Arrangement: Geographical. Indexes: Market segment (business products and furniture), districts, firm listing, principal listing.

★7618★ Pharmaceutical Marketers Directory

CPS Communications Inc.
7200 W Camino Real, Ste. 215
Boca Raton, FL 33433
Ph: (561)368-9301   Fax: (561)368-7870
Fr: 800-346-2015
E-mail: pmd@cpsnet.com
URL: http://www.haymarketgroup.com

Annual; latest edition June 2004. $285.00 for individuals. Covers about 15,000 personnel of pharmaceutical, medical device and equipment manufacturers, and biotechnology companies; advertising agencies with clients in the healthcare field; health care publications; alternative media and healthcare industry suppliers. Entries include: Company name, address, list of personnel by job classification (with titles, internet and e-mail addresses, direct dial and fax numbers). Arrangement: Classified by type of business (health care company, advertising agency, healthcare journals, medical education service, and industry suppliers). Indexes: Personnel, geographical/product or service.

★7619★ Thomas Register of American Manufacturers

Thomas Publishing Co.
5 Penn Plz.
New York, NY 10001
Ph: (212)695-0500   Fax: (212)290-7362
URL: http://www.thomasregister.com

Annual, January. More than 168,000 manufacturing firms are listed in this 34 volume set. Volumes 1-23 list the firms under 68,000 product headings. Thomas Register is enhanced with over 8,000 manufacturers' catalogs and is available in print, CD-ROM, DVD or online. Logistics Guide is a reference manual for freight and shipping sourcing. Arrangement: Volumes 1-23, classified by product or service; Volumes 24-26 alphabetical by company; Volumes 27-34 company catalogs alphabetical by company. Indexes: Product/service, brand/trade name.

★7620★ The Wholesaler-'The Wholesaling 100' Issue

TMB Publishing Inc.
1838 Techny Ct.
Northbrook, IL 60062
Ph: (847)564-1127   Fax: (847)564-1264
URL: http://www.plumbingengineer.com

Annual, July; $50.00 for individuals. Publication includes: Ranks 100 leading wholesalers of plumbing, heating, air conditioning, refrigeration equipment, and industrial pipe, valves and fittings. Entries include: Company name, address, phone, fax, names and titles of key personnel, number of employees, business breakdown (percentage). Arrangement: Ranked by sales.

HANDBOOKS AND MANUALS

★7621★ America's Top Office, Management, & Sales Jobs

Jist Works
8902 Otis Ave.
Indianapolis, IN 46216-1033
Ph: (317)613-4200   Fax: (317)613-4307
Fr: 800-648-5478
E-mail: info@jist.com
URL: http://www.jist.com

Micheal J. Farr. Fifth edition, 2000. $16.95 (paper). 238 pages. Part of America's Top White-Collar Jobs Series.

★7622★ Careers for Talkative Types and Others with the Gift of Gab

The McGraw-Hill Companies
PO Box 182604
Columbus, OH 43272
Fax: (614)759-3749   Fr: 877-883-5524
E-mail: customer.service@mcgraw-hill.com
URL: http://www.mcgraw-hill.com

Marjorie Eberts and Margaret Gisler. Second edition, 2006. $13.95 (paper). 160 pages.

★7623★ Great Jobs for Business Majors

The McGraw-Hill Companies
PO Box 182604
Columbus, OH 43272
Fax: (614)759-3749   Fr: 877-883-5524
E-mail: customer.service@mcgraw-hill.com
URL: http://www.mcgraw-hill.com

Stephen Lambert. Second edition, 2003. $15.95 (paper). 240 pages.

★7624★ Loyalty-Based Selling: The Magic Formula for Becoming the No. 1 Sales Rep

AMACOM
1601 Broadway, 12th Fl.
New York, NY 10019-7420
Ph: (212)586-8100   Fax: (212)903-8168
Fr: 800-262-9699
URL: http://www.amanet.org

Tim Smith. 2001. $17.95 (paper). 162 pages.

A strategic guide for acquiring and retaining a customer base through loyalty-based selling. Focuses on practical advice on how to create lasting customer relationships.

★7625★ Opportunities in Marketing Careers

The McGraw-Hill Companies
PO Box 182604
Columbus, OH 43272
Fax: (614)759-3749   Fr: 877-883-5524
E-mail: customer.service@mcgraw-hill.com
URL: http://www.mcgraw-hill.com

Margery Steinberg. 2005. $13.95; $11.95 (paper). 176. Gives guidance on identifying and pursuing job opportunities. Illustrated.

★7626★ Opportunities in Medical Sales Careers

The McGraw-Hill Companies
PO Box 182604
Columbus, OH 43272
Fax: (614)759-3749   Fr: 877-883-5524
E-mail: customer.service@mcgraw-hill.com
URL: http://www.mcgraw-hill.com

Chad Ellis. 1997. $14.95; $11.95 (paper). 160 pages. Includes index.

★7627★ Opportunities in Sales Careers

The McGraw-Hill Companies
PO Box 182604
Columbus, OH 43272
Fax: (614)759-3749   Fr: 877-883-5524
E-mail: customer.service@mcgraw-hill.com
URL: http://www.mcgraw-hill.com

James Brescoll and Ralph Dahm. 160 pages. 2001. $12.95 (paper). Details sales in retail, wholesale and industrial sales, sales of services and intangibles, and sales management. Illustrated.

★7628★ Resumes for Sales and Marketing Careers

The McGraw-Hill Companies
PO Box 182604
Columbus, OH 43272
Fax: (614)759-3749   Fr: 877-883-5524
E-mail: customer.service@mcgraw-hill.com
URL: http://www.mcgraw-hill.com

Chuck Cochran and Donna Peerce. 1998. $13.95. 336 pages. Sample resumes and cover letters from all levels of the sales and marketing field.

★7629★ Sales Careers: The Ultimate Guide to Getting a High-Paying Sales Job

Jist Works
875 Montreal Way
St. Paul, MN 55102
Fr: 800-648-5478
E-mail: info@jist.com
URL: http://www.jist.com

Edward R. Newill, Louise Kursmark. 2003. $12.95. 196 pages.

EMPLOYMENT AGENCIES AND SEARCH FIRMS

★7630★ 1 Exec Street

201 Post St., Ste. 401
San Francisco, CA 94108
Ph: (415)982-0555   Fax: (415)982-0550
Fr: 888-554-6845
E-mail: contactus@1execstreet.com
URL: http://www.1execstreet.com

Executive search firm.

★7631★ Adams & Associates International

520 Shorely Dr. 201
PO Box 129
Barrington, IL 60011-0129
Ph: (847)304-5300   Fax: (847)400-0798
URL: http://www.leanthinking.net

Global executive search firm.

★7632★ Bender Executive Search

45 N. Station Plaza, Ste. 315
Great Neck, NY 11021
Ph: (516)773-3200   Fax: (516)482-5355
URL: http://www.marketingexecsearch.com

Executive search firm.

★7633★ The Borton Wallace Company

PO Box 8816
Asheville, NC 28814-0989
Ph: (828)258-1831   Fax: (828)251-0989
E-mail: mes@boone-scaturro.com
URL: http://www.bortonwallace.com

Executive search firm.

★7634★ The Caler Group

23337 Lago Mar Cir.
Boca Raton, FL 33433
Ph: (561)394-8045   Fax: (561)394-4645
E-mail: caler@calergroup.com
URL: http://www.calergroup.com

Executive search firm.

★7635★ Cendea

8002 Weldon Springs Ct., Ste. 200
Austin, TX 78726
Ph: (512)219-6000
E-mail: info.kd@cendea.com
URL: http://www.cendea.com

Executive search firm.

★7636★ Chaitin & Associates Inc.

22543 Ventura Blvd., Ste. 220
Woodland Hills, CA 91364
Ph: (818)225-8655   Fax: (818)225-8660
E-mail: execpro2@aol.com

Executive search firm.

★7637★ Cizek Associates Inc.
2415 E. Camelback Rd., Ste. 700
Phoenix, AZ 85016
Ph: (602)553-1066   Fax: (602)553-1166
E-mail: phx@cizekassociates.com
URL: http://www.cizekassociates.com/
Executive search firm. Also offices in Chicago and San Francisco.

★7638★ Clarey Andrews & Klein Inc.
1200 Shermer Rd., Ste. 108
Northbrook, IL 60062
Ph: (847)498-2870
E-mail: cak@clarey-a-klein.com
URL: http://www.penrhyn.com
Executive search firm.

★7639★ Crowe-Innes & Associates LLC
1120 Mar West St., Ste. D
Tiburon, CA 94920
Ph: (415)789-1422   Fax: (415)435-6867
E-mail: jenny@croweinnes.com
URL: http://www.croweinnes.com
Executive search firm.

★7640★ The Culver Group, Inc.
600 City Parkway W., Ste. 320
Orange, CA 92868
Ph: (714)939-8900
URL: http://www.culvergroup.com
Employment agency specializing in sales positions.

★7641★ Cyntal International Ltd.
405 Lexington Ave., Ste. 2600-19
New York, NY 10174
Ph: (917)368-8181
E-mail: cynthia@cyntal.com
Executive search firm.

★7642★ The Dalley Hewitt Company
3075 Howell Mill Rd., NW Unit 11
Atlanta, GA 30327
Ph: (404)992-5065   Fax: (404)355-6136
E-mail: rives@dalleyhewitt.com
URL: http://www.dalleyhewitt.com
Executive search firm.

★7643★ DMR Global Inc.
10230 W. Sample Rd.
Coral Springs, FL 33065
Ph: (954)796-5043   Fax: (954)796-5044
E-mail: rdaratany@dmrglobal.com
URL: http://www.dmrglobal.com
Executive search firm.

★7644★ Egan & Associates Inc.
White House Ctr.
1784 Barton Ave., Ste. 10
West Bend, WI 53095
Ph: (262)335-0707   Fax: (262)335-0625

E-mail: info@eganassociates.com
URL: http://www.eganassociates.com
Executive search firm.

★7645★ Executive Search International
1525 Centre St.
Newton, MA 02461-1200
Ph: (617)527-8787
E-mail: info@execsearchintl.com
URL: http://www.execsearchintl.com
Executive search firm.

★7646★ Fairfield
Trump Tower
721 5th Ave.
New York, NY 10022-2523
Ph: (212)838-0220
E-mail: newyork@fairfield.ch
URL: http://www.fairfield.ch
Executive search firm specializing in retail and apparel manufacturing.

★7647★ Highlander Search
1901 Lendew St., Ste. 9
PO Box 4163
Greensboro, NC 27404
Ph: (336)333-9886   Fax: (336)574-8305
E-mail: jphighlander@mindspring.com
Conducts retained search of technical and staff level professionals. Contingency search services available. Also provides counseling of salaried work force caught in RIF's, and job search and resume preparation. Instruction is offered on an individual basis. Industries served: manufacturing, automotive and furniture industry worldwide. Consulting services in organizational and human resource areas.

★7648★ James Drury Partners
875 N. Michigan Ave., Ste. 3805
Chicago, IL 60611
Ph: (312)654-6708   Fax: (312)654-6710
E-mail: jdrury@drurypartners.com
URL: http://www.jdrurypartners.com
Executive search firm.

★7649★ National Register Columbus, Inc.
550 Polaris Pkwy., Ste. 530
Westerville, OH 43082
Ph: (614)890-1200   Fax: (614)890-1259
E-mail: sales@nrcols.com
URL: http://www.nrcols.com
Employment agency. Offices in Akron and Toledo, OH.

★7650★ Sales Executives Inc.
33900 W. 8 Mile Rd., Ste. 171
Farmington Hills, MI 48335
Ph: (248)615-0100
E-mail: dale@salesexecutives.com
URL: http://www.salesexecutives.com
Employment agency. Executive search firm.

★7651★ Salespositions.com
450 7th Ave., Ste. 507A
New York, NY 10123
Ph: (609)407-4774
E-mail: salepositions@comcast.net
URL: http://www.salespositions.com
Employment agency.

TRADESHOWS

★7652★ Marketing Seminar Conference
Manufacturers Agents for Food Service Industry (MAFSI)
2814 Spring Rd., Ste. 211
Atlanta, GA 30339
Ph: (770)433-9844   Fax: (770)433-2450
E-mail: info@mafsi.org
URL: http://www.mafsi.org
Annual. **Primary Exhibits:** Manufacturers' representative equipment, furnishings, and supplies for dealers and users.

OTHER SOURCES

★7653★ American Wholesale Marketers Association (AWMA)
2750 Prosperity Ave., Ste. 530
Fairfax, VA 22031
Ph: (703)208-3358   Fax: (703)573-5738
Fr: 800-482-2962
E-mail: info@awmanet.org
URL: http://www.awmanet.org
Description: Represents the interests of distributors of convenience products. Its members include wholesalers, retailers, manufacturers, brokers and allied organizations from across the U.S. and abroad. Programs include strong legislative representation in Washington and a broad spectrum of targeted education, business and information services. Sponsors the country's largest show for candy and convenience related products in conjunction with its semi-annual convention.

★7654★ Asian American MultiTechnology Association (AAMA)
PO Box 7522
Menlo Park, CA 94026-7522
Ph: (650)738-1480   Fax: (650)738-1486
E-mail: aama@aamasv.com
URL: http://www.aamasv.com
Description: Promotes the success of the Asia America region's technology enterprises. Through its diverse programs ranging from monthly Speakers Series to the Asia-Silicon Valley Technology Investment Conference, the association provides a forum in which members can network, exchange ideas and share resources to promote and build one another's companies and careers,

ultimately benefiting the larger Pacific Rim technological community.

★7655★ **Association of Independent Manufacturers'/Representatives (AIM/R)**

One Spectrum Pointe, Ste. 150
Lake Forest, CA 92630-2283
Ph: (949)859-2884   Fax: (949)855-2973
Fr: (866)729-0975
E-mail: info@aimr.net
URL: http://www.aimr.net

Description: Manufacturers' representative companies in the plumbing-heating-cooling-piping industry promoting the use of independent sales representatives. Conducts educational programs and establishes a code of ethics between members and customers.

★7656★ **Automotive Aftermarket Industry Association (AAIA)**

7101 Wisconsin Ave., Ste. 1300
Bethesda, MD 20814-3415
Ph: (301)654-6664   Fax: (301)654-3299
E-mail: aaia@aftermarket.org
URL: http://www.aftermarket.org

Members: Automotive parts and accessories retailers, distributors, manufacturers, and manufacturers' representatives. **Activities:** Conducts research and compiles statistics. Conducts seminars and provides specialized education program.

★7657★ **Computing Technology Industry Association (CompTIA)**

1815 S Meyers Rd., Ste. 300
Oakbrook Terrace, IL 60181-5228
Ph: (630)678-8300   Fax: (630)678-8384
E-mail: information@comptia.org
URL: http://www.comptia.org

Description: Trade association of more than 19,000 companies and professional IT members in the rapidly converging computing and communications market. Has members in more than 89 countries and provides a unified voice for the industry in the areas of e-commerce standards, vendor-neutral certification, service metrics, public policy and workforce development. Serves as information clearinghouse and resource for the industry; sponsors educational programs.

★7658★ **Manufacturers' Agents National Association (MANA)**

1 Spectrum Pointe, Ste. 150
Lake Forest, CA 92630-2283
Ph: (949)859-4040   Fax: (949)855-2973
Fr: 877-626-2776
E-mail: mana@manaonline.org
URL: http://www.manaonline.org

Members: Manufacturers' agents in all fields representing two or more manufacturers on a commission basis; associate members are manufacturers and others interested in improving the agent-principal relationship. **Activities:** Maintains code of ethics and rules of business and professional conduct; issues model standard form of agreement.

★7659★ **Marketing & Sales Occupations**

Delphi Productions
3159 6th St.
Boulder, CO 80304
Ph: (303)443-2100   Fax: (303)443-4022
Fr: 888-443-2400
E-mail: support@delphivideo.com
URL: http://www.delphivideo.com

$95.00. 50 minutes. Part of the Careers for the 21st Century Video Library.

★7660★ **National Association of Chain Drug Stores (NACDS)**

413 N Lee St.
Alexandria, VA 22314
Ph: (703)549-3001   Fax: (703)836-4869
URL: http://www.nacds.org

Description: Represents the concerns of community pharmacies in Washington, in state capitals, and across the country. Members are more than 210 chain community pharmacy companies. Collectively, community pharmacy comprises the largest component of pharmacy practice with over 107,000 FTE pharmacists. Membership also includes more than 1000 suppliers of goods and services to chain community pharmacies. International membership consists of almost 100 members from 30 countries.

★7661★ **National Electrical Manufacturers Representatives Association (NEMRA)**

660 White Plains Rd., Ste. 600
Tarrytown, NY 10591-5172
Ph: (914)524-8650   Fax: (914)524-8655
Fr: 800-446-3672
E-mail: nemra@nemra.org
URL: http://www.nemra.org

Purpose: North American trade association dedicated to promoting continuing education, professionalism, and the use of independent manufacturers representatives in the electrical industry. Offers professional development programs in business management and sales training, and offers a proprietary computer system for independent electrical representatives. Sponsors educational programs; compiles statistics; and holds an annual networking conference for its representative members and their manufacturers.

★7662★ **National Marine Representatives Association (NMRA)**

PO Box 360
Gurnee, IL 60031
Ph: (847)662-3167   Fax: (847)336-7126
E-mail: info@nmraonline.org
URL: http://www.nmraonline.org

Description: Works to serve the marine industry independent sales representatives and the manufacturers selling through representatives. Serves as industry voice, networking tool and information source promoting benefits of utilizing independent marine representatives for sales. Aims to assist manufacturers find the right marine sales reps for product lines.

Market Research Analysts

SOURCES OF HELP-WANTED ADS

★7663★ Alert!

Marketing Research Association
110 National Dr., 2nd Fl.
Glastonbury, CT 06033-1212
Ph: (860)682-1000   Fax: (860)682-1010
URL: http://www.mra-net.org/publications/alert.cfm

Description: Monthly. Provides information about marketing industry events, trends in marketing research, management techniques, association events, and legislative activities affecting the marketing industry. Recurring features include news of research, a calendar of events, reports of meetings, news of educational opportunities, job listings, notices of publications available, business opportunities, and facilities for sale.

★7664★ BtoB Magazine

Crain Communications Inc.
360 N Michigan Ave.
Chicago, IL 60601
Ph: (312)649-5411   Fax: (312)280-3150
Fr: 888-909-9111
URL: http://www.btobonline.com

Monthly. $59.00/year for individuals; $69.00/year for Canada; $89.00/year for other countries. Trade magazine on business-to-business marketing news, strategy, and tactics.

★7665★ Direct Marketing Magazine

Hoke Communications Inc.
224 7th St.
Garden City, NY 11530
Ph: (516)746-6700

Monthly. $60.00/year for individuals; $6.00 for single issue. Direct response advertising magazine.

★7666★ DM News

DM News
114 W 26th St., 4th Fl.
New York, NY 10001
Ph: (646)638-6000   Fax: (646)638-6159

E-mail: inquiry@dmnews.com
URL: http://www.dmnews.com/

Weekly. $49.00/year for U.S. $99.00/year for Canada and Mexico; $149.00/year for other countries. Tabloid newspaper for publishers, fund raisers, financial marketers, catalogers, package goods advertisers and their agencies, and other marketers who use direct mail, mail order advertising, catalogs, or other direct response media to sell their products or services.

★7667★ Marketing News

American Marketing Association (Chicago, Illinois)
311 S Wacker Dr., Ste. 5800
Chicago, IL 60606
Ph: (312)542-9000   Fax: (312)542-9001
Fr: 800-262-1150
E-mail: news@ama.org
URL: http://www.marketingpower.com/

$35.00/year for members; $100.00/year for nonmembers; $130.00/year for institutions, libraries and corporations; $3.00 for single issue, individuals; $5.00 for single issue, institutions; $140.00/year for institutions, other countries, extra for air delivery. Business magazine focusing on current marketing trends.

★7668★ Quirk's Marketing Research Review

Quirk Enterprises Inc.
4662 Slater Rd.
Eagan, MN 55122
Ph: (952)224-1919
URL: http://www.quirks.com

$70.00/year for individuals; $100.00/year for Canada and Mexico; $119.00/year for other countries. Trade publication for the marketing research industry.

★7669★ Sales & Marketing Management

The Nielsen Co.
770 Broadway
New York, NY 10003
Ph: (646)654-5000   Fax: (646)654-5002
URL: http://www.salesandmarketing.com

Monthly. $48.00/year for individuals. Business magazine.

PLACEMENT AND JOB REFERRAL SERVICES

★7670★ American Marketing Association (AMA)

311 S Wacker Dr., Ste. 5800
Chicago, IL 60606
Ph: (312)542-9000   Fax: (312)542-9001
Fr: 800-262-1150
E-mail: info@ama.org
URL: http://www.marketingpower.com

Description: Serves as a professional society of marketing and market research executives, sales and promotion managers, advertising specialists, academics, and others interested in marketing. **Activities:** Fosters research; sponsors seminars, conferences, and student marketing clubs; provides educational placement service and doctoral consortium.

EMPLOYER DIRECTORIES AND NETWORKING LISTS

★7671★ Bradford's International Directory of Marketing Research Agencies

Business Research Services Inc.
7720 Wisconsin Ave., Ste. 213
Bethesda, MD 20814
Ph: (301)229-5561   Fax: (301)229-6133
Fr: 800-845-8420
E-mail: verify@bradfordsdirectory.com
URL: http://www.bradfordsdirectory.com/

Biennial; latest edition 29th. $95.00 for individuals, print product; $95.00 for individuals, CD-ROM; $125.00 for individuals, print product and CD-ROM, combined. Covers over 2,700 marketing research agencies worldwide. Includes domestic and international demographic data and professional association contacts. Entries include: Company name, address, phone, name and title of contact, date founded, number of employees, description of products or services, e-mail, URL. Arrangement: Geographical. Indexes: Alphabetical by company.

★7672★ **GreenBook Worldwide-Directory of Marketing Research Companies and Services**

New York AMA Communication Services Inc.
116 E 27th St., 6th Fl.
New York, NY 10016
Ph: (212)849-2752   Fax: (212)202-7920
Fr: 800-792-9202
URL: http://www.greenbook.org

Annual, March. $350.00 plus $15.00 for shipping costs (U.S. and Canada). Covers more than 2,500 marketing research companies worldwide (computer services, interviewing services, etc.) of marketing research needs; international coverage. Includes a list of computer programs for marketing research. Entries include: Company name, address, phone, name of principal executive, products and services, branch offices. Arrangement: Alphabetical. Indexes: Geographical, principal executive name, research services, market/industry served, computer program name, trademark/service-marks.

★7673★ **MRA Blue Book Research Services Directory**

Marketing Research Association
110 National Dr., 2nd Fl.
Glastonbury, CT 06033
Ph: (860)682-1000   Fax: (860)682-1010
E-mail: bluebook@mra-net.org
URL: http://www.bluebook.org

Annual; latest edition February 2007. $152.90 for nonmembers; $97.95 for members. Covers over 1,200 marketing research companies and field interviewing services. Entries include: Company name, address, phone, names of executives, services, facilities, special interviewing capabilities. Arrangement: Geographical; business type. Indexes: Geographic and by specialty.

★7674★ **Quirk's Marketing Research Review-Researcher SourceBook Issue**

Quirk Enterprises Inc.
4662 Slater Rd.
Eagan, MN 55122
Ph: (952)224-1919
URL: http://www.quirks.com

Annual, September. Covers about 7,300 organizations providing marketing research products and services. Entries include: Name, address, phone, fax, contact, research specialties, URL, e-mail. Arrangement: Geographical. Indexes: Personnel; industry specialization; research specialization; alphabetic.

HANDBOOKS AND MANUALS

★7675★ **Careers in Marketing**

The McGraw-Hill Companies
PO Box 182604
Columbus, OH 43272
Fax: (614)759-3749   Fr: 877-883-5524
E-mail: customer.service@mcgraw-hill.com
URL: http://www.mcgraw-hill.com

Lila B. Stair and Leslie Stair. Third edition, 2001. $13.95 (paper). 192 pages. Surveys career opportunities in marketing and related areas such as marketing research, product development, and sales promotion. Includes a description of the work, places of employment, employment outlook, trends, and salaries. Offers job hunting advice.

★7676★ **Careers for Number Crunchers and Other Quantitative Types**

The McGraw-Hill Companies
PO Box 182604
Columbus, OH 43272
Fax: (614)759-3749   Fr: 877-883-5524
E-mail: customer.service@mcgraw-hill.com
URL: http://www.mcgraw-hill.com

Rebecca Burnett. Second edition, 2002. $22.95 (paper). 192 pages. Provides information to math-oriented job hunters on how to become statisticians, field researchers, computer programmers, stock analysts, investment managers, bankers, engineers, accountants, underwriters, economists, market analysts, mathematicians, systems analysts, and more.

★7677★ **Great Jobs for History Majors**

The McGraw-Hill Companies
PO Box 182604
Columbus, OH 43272
Fax: (614)759-3749   Fr: 877-883-5524
E-mail: customer.service@mcgraw-hill.com
URL: http://www.mcgraw-hill.com

Julie DeGalan and Stephen Lambert. 2001. $15.95 (paper). 256 pages.

★7678★ **How to Get into Marketing and PR**

Continuum International Publishing Group, Inc.
80 Maiden Ln., Ste. 704
New York, NY 10038
Ph: (212)953-5858   Fax: (212)953-5944
URL: http://www.continuumbooks.com/

Annie Gurton. June 2003. $129.99 (hardcover). 213 pages.

★7679★ **Opportunities in Direct Marketing**

The McGraw-Hill Companies
PO Box 182604
Columbus, OH 43272
Fax: (614)759-3749   Fr: 877-883-5524
E-mail: customer.service@mcgraw-hill.com
URL: http://www.mcgraw-hill.com

Anne Basye. 2008. $14.95; $11.95 (paper). 160 pages. Examines opportunities with direct marketers, catalog companies, direct marketing agencies, telemarketing firms, mailing list brokers, and database marketing companies. Describes how to prepare for a career in direct marketing and how to break into the field. Includes sources of short-term professional training.

★7680★ **Opportunities in Marketing Careers**

The McGraw-Hill Companies
PO Box 182604
Columbus, OH 43272
Fax: (614)759-3749   Fr: 877-883-5524
E-mail: customer.service@mcgraw-hill.com
URL: http://www.mcgraw-hill.com

Margery Steinberg. 2005. $13.95; $11.95 (paper). 176. Gives guidance on identifying and pursuing job opportunities. Illustrated.

★7681★ **Resumes for Sales and Marketing Careers**

The McGraw-Hill Companies
PO Box 182604
Columbus, OH 43272
Fax: (614)759-3749   Fr: 877-883-5524
E-mail: customer.service@mcgraw-hill.com
URL: http://www.mcgraw-hill.com

Chuck Cochran and Donna Peerce. 1998. $13.95. 336 pages. Sample resumes and cover letters from all levels of the sales and marketing field.

OTHER SOURCES

★7682★ **Academy of Marketing Science (AMS)**

University of Miami
School of Business Administration
PO Box 248012
Coral Gables, FL 33124-6536
Ph: (305)284-6673   Fax: (305)284-3762
E-mail: ams.sba@miami.edu
URL: http://www.ams-web.org

Description: Marketing academicians and practitioners; individuals interested in fostering education in marketing science. Aims to promote the advancement of knowledge and the furthering of professional standards in the field of marketing. Explores the special application areas of marketing science and its responsibilities as an economic, ethical, and social force; promotes research and the widespread dissemination of findings. Facilitates exchange of information and experience among members, and the transfer of marketing knowledge and technology to developing countries; promotes marketing science on an international level. Provides a forum for discussion and refinement of concepts, methods and applications, and the opportunity to publish papers in the field. Assists member educators in the development of improved teaching methods, devices, directions, and materials. Offers guidance and direction in marketing practice and reviewer assistance on scholarly works. Contributes to the solution of marketing problems encountered by individual firms, industries, and society as a whole. Encourages members to utilize their marketing talents to the fullest through redirection, reassignment, and relocation. Sponsors competitions.

★7683★ Financial Occupations

Delphi Productions
3159 6th St.
Boulder, CO 80304
Ph: (303)443-2100   Fax: (303)443-4022
Fr: 888-443-2400
E-mail: support@delphivideo.com
URL: http://www.delphivideo.com

$95.00. 50 minutes. Part of the Careers for the 21st Century Video Library.

★7684★ Marketing Agencies Association Worldwide (MAA)

460 Summer St., 4th Fl.
Stamford, CT 06901
Ph: (203)978-1590   Fax: (203)969-1499
E-mail: keith.mccracken@maaw.org
URL: http://www.maaw.org

Description: Represents the interests of CEOs, presidents, managing directors and principals of top marketing services agencies. Provides opportunity for marketing professionals to meet with peers, raise company profile on both a national and a global platform, and influence the future of industry. Fosters networking through conferences.

★7685★ Marketing Research Association (MRA)

110 National Dr., 2nd Fl.
Glastonbury, CT 06033-1212
Ph: (860)682-1000   Fax: (860)682-1010
E-mail: larry.brownell@mra-net.org
URL: http://www.mra-net.org

Members: Companies and individuals involved in any area of opinion and marketing research, such as data collection, research, or as an end-user.

★7686★ Society for Marketing Professional Services (SMPS)

99 Canal Center Plz., Ste. 330
Alexandria, VA 22314
Ph: (703)549-6117   Fax: (703)549-2498
Fr: 800-292-7677
E-mail: info@smps.org

URL: http://www.smps.org

Members: Marketing employees of architectural, engineering, planning, interior design, landscape architectural, and construction management firms who are responsible for the new business development of their companies. **Activities:** Compiles statistics. Offers local and national educational programs; maintains certification program.

★7687★ Women in Direct Marketing International (WDMI)

200 Cir. Dr. N
Piscataway, NJ 08854
Ph: (732)469-8414
E-mail: bladden@directmaildepot.com
URL: http://www.wdmi.org

Description: Direct marketing professionals. Seeks to: advance the interests and influence of women in the direct response industry; provide for communication and career education; assist in advancement of personal career objectives; serve as professional network to develop business contacts and foster mutual goals. Maintains career talent bank. Distributes information nationally; maintains other chapters in Chicago, IL, Los Angeles, CA, Dallas, TX, Japan, UK, and Belgium.

Marketing, Advertising, and Public Relations Managers

SOURCES OF HELP-WANTED ADS

★7688★ Adweek

VNU Business Media USA
770 Broadway
New York, NY 10003
Ph: (646)654-4500
URL: http://www.adweek.com/aw/index.jsp

Weekly. $149.00/year for individuals, 12 months basic; $85.00 for individuals, 6 months basic; $135.00 for individuals, 6 months premium; $249.00/year for individuals, 12 months premium; $20.00/year for individuals, monthly online. Advertising news magazine.

★7689★ Adweek/New England

Adweek L.P.
100 Boylston St., Ste. 210
Boston, MA 02116
Ph: (617)482-9447   Fr: 800-641-2030
E-mail: info-adweek@pubservice.com
URL: http://www.adweek.com

Weekly. $249.00/year for individuals, premium; $149.00/year for individuals, basic. News magazine serving the advertising, marketing, and media industries in New England.

★7690★ Alert!

Marketing Research Association
110 National Dr., 2nd Fl.
Glastonbury, CT 06033-1212
Ph: (860)682-1000   Fax: (860)682-1010
URL: http://www.mra-net.org/publications/alert.cfm

Description: Monthly. Provides information about marketing industry events, trends in marketing research, management techniques, association events, and legislative activities affecting the marketing industry. Recurring features include news of research, a calendar of events, reports of meetings, news of educational opportunities, job listings, notices of publications available, business opportunities, and facilities for sale.

★7691★ APC Newsletter

Advertising Production Club of New York
428 East State St.
Long Beach, NY 11561
Ph: (212)671-2975   Fax: (718)228-8202
E-mail: admin@apc-ny.org
URL: http://www.apc-ny.org

Description: Quarterly. Covers activities of Advertising Production Club of New York. Keeps club members informed of new technology and techniques in advertising production and includes profiles of print production persons and vendors.

★7692★ B2B MarketingTrends

Penton Media Inc.
249 W 17th St.
New York, NY 10011
Ph: (212)204-4200
E-mail: publisher@b2bmarketingtrends.com
URL: http://www.B2BmarketingTrends.com

Quarterly. Free to qualified subscribers. Magazine that covers business-to-business marketing.

★7693★ BtoB Magazine

Crain Communications Inc.
360 N Michigan Ave.
Chicago, IL 60601
Ph: (312)649-5411   Fax: (312)280-3150
Fr: 888-909-9111
URL: http://www.btobonline.com

Monthly. $59.00/year for individuals; $69.00/year for Canada; $89.00/year for other countries. Trade magazine on business-to-business marketing news, strategy, and tactics.

★7694★ The Counselor

Advertising Specialty Institute
4800 East St. Rd.
Trevose, PA 19053
Ph: (215)953-4000   Fr: 800-326-7378

Monthly. $75.00/year for individuals; $150.00/year for other countries. Magazine.

★7695★ DIRECT

Penton Media Inc.
9800 Metcalf Ave.
Overland Park, KS 66212
Ph: (913)341-1300   Fax: (913)967-1898
URL: http://www.directmag.com/

Free to qualified subscribers. Magazine for direct marketing professionals, covering direct mail, email, and telemarketing.

★7696★ Direct Marketing Magazine

Hoke Communications Inc.
224 7th St.
Garden City, NY 11530
Ph: (516)746-6700

Monthly. $60.00/year for individuals; $6.00 for single issue. Direct response advertising magazine.

★7697★ DM News

DM News
114 W 26th St., 4th Fl.
New York, NY 10001
Ph: (646)638-6000   Fax: (646)638-6159
E-mail: inquiry@dmnews.com
URL: http://www.dmnews.com/

Weekly. $49.00/year for U.S. $99.00/year for Canada and Mexico; $149.00/year for other countries. Tabloid newspaper for publishers, fund raisers, financial marketers, catalogers, package goods advertisers and their agencies, and other marketers who use direct mail, mail order advertising, catalogs, or other direct response media to sell their products or services.

★7698★ Editor & Publisher

Editor & Publisher Magazine
770 Broadway
New York, NY 10003-9595
Ph: (646)654-5500   Fax: (646)654-5370
Fr: 800-562-2706
URL: http://www.editorandpublisher.com/eandp/index.jsp

Weekly (Mon.). $99.00/year for individuals, print and online; $159.00/year for Canada, print and online; $320.00/year for other countries; $7.95/year for individuals, monthly. Magazine focusing on newspaper journalism, advertising, printing equipment, and interactive services.

★7699★ **Event Marketer**

Red 7 Media Inc.
10 Norden Pl.
Norwalk, CT 06855
Ph: (203)854-6730   Fax: (203)854-6735
URL: http://www.eventmarketer.com

Free to qualified subscribers. Magazine for brand-side event marketers and face-to-face media agency executives.

★7700★ **Foundations and Trends in Marketing**

World Scientific Publishing Company Inc.
27 Warren St., Ste. 401-402
Hackensack, NJ 07601
Ph: (201)487-9655   Fax: (201)487-9656
Fr: 800-227-7562
URL: http://www.worldscinet.com/ftmkt/mkt/editorial.shtml

Weekly. Journal covering business to business marketing, Bayesian models, behavioral decision making, branding and brand equity, channel management, choice modeling, comparative market structure and competitive marketing strategy.

★7701★ **Franchising World**

International Franchise Association
1501 K St. NW, Ste. 350
Washington, DC 20005
Ph: (202)628-8000   Fax: (202)628-0812
Fr: 800-543-1038
URL: http://www.franchise.org/

Monthly. $50.00/year for individuals. Trade magazine covering topics of interest to franchise company executives and the business world.

★7702★ **HOW**

F & W Publications Inc.
4700 E Galbraith Rd.
Cincinnati, OH 45236
Ph: (513)531-2690   Fax: (513)531-0798
Fr: 800-289-0963
URL: http://www.howdesign.com

Bimonthly. $29.96/year for U.S. $45.00/year for Canada; $52.00/year for other countries. Instructional trade magazine.

★7703★ **Marketing News**

American Marketing Association (Chicago, Illinois)
311 S Wacker Dr., Ste. 5800
Chicago, IL 60606
Ph: (312)542-9000   Fax: (312)542-9001
Fr: 800-262-1150
E-mail: news@ama.org
URL: http://www.marketingpower.com/

$35.00/year for members; $100.00/year for nonmembers; $130.00/year for institutions, libraries and corporations; $3.00 for single issue, individuals; $5.00 for single issue, institutions; $140.00/year for institutions, other countries, extra for air delivery. Business

magazine focusing on current marketing trends.

★7704★ **Media Week**

VNU Business Media USA
770 Broadway
New York, NY 10003
Ph: (646)654-4500
URL: http://www.mediaweek.com/mw/index.jsp

Weekly. $4.00 for single issue; $149.00/year for U.S.; $199.00/year for Canada; $310.00/year for elsewhere. Weekly magazine covering the media decision-makers at the top 350 ad agencies and all top media buying services and client media departments in the U.S.

★7705★ **Multichannel Merchant**

Primedia Business
11 River Bend Dr. S
PO Box 4949
Stamford, CT 06907-0949
Ph: (203)358-9900   Fax: (203)358-5811
Fr: 800-776-1246
URL: http://multichannelmerchant.com

Monthly. Magazine for marketing and advertising professionals that covers print, web, and cross-channel marketing.

★7706★ **Package Design Magazine**

Lyons Media Inc.
20 Valley Stream Pkwy., Ste. 265
Malvern, PA 19355
URL: http://www.packagedesignmag.com/

Free to qualified subscribers. Magazine that covers marketing and branding through package design.

★7707★ **PROMO**

Penton Media Inc.
9800 Metcalf Ave.
Overland Park, KS 66212
Ph: (913)341-1300   Fax: (913)967-1898
URL: http://www.promomagazine.com/

Monthly. Free to qualified subscribers. Magazine for marketing professionals at consumer product and service companies, retail chains, and Internet businesses, as well as principals at marketing agencies and supplier companies serving the promotion industry.

★7708★ **Public Relations Career Opportunities**

Public Relations Career Opportunities
1220 L St. NW
Washington, DC 20005
Ph: (202)721-7656
E-mail: info@ceoupdate.com
URL: http://www.careeropps.com

Description: Semimonthly. Provides information about positions available in the fields of public affairs and public relations.

★7709★ **Quirk's Marketing Research Review**

Quirk Enterprises Inc.
4662 Slater Rd.
Eagan, MN 55122
Ph: (952)224-1919
URL: http://www.quirks.com

$70.00/year for individuals; $100.00/year for Canada and Mexico; $119.00/year for other countries. Trade publication for the marketing research industry.

★7710★ **Revenue**

Montgomery Media International
300 Montgomery St., Ste. 1135
San Francisco, CA 94104
Ph: (415)397-2400   Fax: (415)397-2420
URL: http://www.revenuetoday.com/

$30.00/year for individuals. Magazine covering internet marketing strategies.

★7711★ **Sales and Marketing Executive Report**

The Dartnell Corp.
2272 Airport Rd. S.
Naples, FL 34112
Fr: 800-477-4030
E-mail: customerservice@dartnellcorp.com
URL: http://www.dartnellcorp.com/

Description: Biweekly. Discusses topics of interest to managers, including motivating and training sales personnel, executive self-improvement, and advertising and public relations strategies. Recurring features include news of research, letters to the editor, book reviews, a calendar of events, and columns titled Sales/Marketing Briefs and Special Report.

★7712★ **Sales & Marketing Management**

The Nielsen Co.
770 Broadway
New York, NY 10003
Ph: (646)654-5000   Fax: (646)654-5002
URL: http://www.salesandmarketing.com

Monthly. $48.00/year for individuals. Business magazine.

★7713★ **TelevisionWeek**

Crain Communications Inc.
1155 Gratiot Ave.
PO Box 07924
Detroit, MI 48207-2997
Ph: (313)446-6000   Fax: (313)446-0347
Fr: 888-909-9111
URL: http://www.tvweek.com/

Weekly. $119.00/year for individuals; $171.00/year for Canada, including GST; $309.00/year for other countries, airmail. Newspaper covering management, programming, cable and trends in the television and the media industry.

PLACEMENT AND JOB REFERRAL SERVICES

★7714★ Advertising Production Club of New York (APC)

428 E State St.
Long Beach, NY 11561
Ph: (212)671-2975   Fax: (718)228-8202
E-mail: admin@apc-ny.org
URL: http://www.apc-ny.org

Description: Production and traffic department personnel from advertising agencies, corporate or retail advertising departments, and publishing companies; college level graphic arts educators. Meetings include educational programs on graphic arts procedures and plant tours. Maintains employment service for members.

★7715★ American Marketing Association (AMA)

311 S Wacker Dr., Ste. 5800
Chicago, IL 60606
Ph: (312)542-9000   Fax: (312)542-9001
Fr: 800-262-1150
E-mail: info@ama.org
URL: http://www.marketingpower.com

Description: Serves as a professional society of marketing and market research executives, sales and promotion managers, advertising specialists, academics, and others interested in marketing. **Activities:** Fosters research; sponsors seminars, conferences, and student marketing clubs; provides educational placement service and doctoral consortium.

★7716★ Direct Marketing Association (DMA)

1120 Ave. of the Americas
New York, NY 10036-6700
Ph: (212)768-7277   Fax: (212)302-6714
E-mail: presiden@the-dma.org
URL: http://www.the-dma.org

Members: Manufacturers, wholesalers, public utilities, retailers, mail order firms, publishers, schools, clubs, insurance companies, financial organizations, business equipment manufacturers, paper and envelope manufacturers, list brokers, compilers, managers, owners, computer service bureaus, advertising agencies, letter shops, research organizations, printers, lithographers, creators, and producers of direct mail and direct response advertising. **Purpose:** Studies consumer and business attitudes toward direct mail and related direct marketing statistics. **Activities:** Offers Mail Preference Service for consumers who wish to receive less mail advertising, Mail Order Action Line to help resolve difficulties with mail order purchases, and Telephone Preference Service for people who wish to receive fewer telephone sales calls. Maintains hall of fame; offers placement service; compiles statistics. Sponsors several three-day Basic Direct Marketing Institutes, Advanced Direct Marketing Institutes, and special interest seminars and workshops. Maintains Government Affairs office in Washington, DC. Operates Direct Marketing Educational Foundation.

★7717★ PROMAX

9000 W Sunset Blvd., Ste. 900
Los Angeles, CA 90069
Ph: (310)788-7600   Fax: (310)788-7616
E-mail: michael.d.benson@abc.com
URL: http://www.promax.tv

Members: Advertising, public relations, and promotion managers of cable, radio, and television stations, systems and networks; syndicators. **Purpose:** Seeks to: advance the role and increase the effectiveness of promotion and marketing within the industry, related industries, and educational communities. **Activities:** Conducts workshops and weekly fax service for members. Operates employment service. Maintains speakers' bureau, hall of fame, and resource center with print, audio, and visual materials.

★7718★ Trade Show Exhibitors Association (TSEA)

2301 S Lake Shore Dr., Ste. 1005
Chicago, IL 60616
Ph: (312)842-8732   Fax: (312)842-8744
E-mail: tsea@tsea.org
URL: http://www.tsea.org

Description: Exhibitors working to improve the effectiveness of trade shows as a marketing tool. Purposes are to promote the progress and development of trade show exhibiting; to collect and disseminate trade show information; conduct studies, surveys, and stated projects designed to improve trade shows; to foster good relations and communications with organizations representing others in the industry; to undertake other activities necessary to promote the welfare of member companies. Sponsors Exhibit Industry Education Foundation and professional exhibiting seminars; the forum series of educational programs on key issues affecting the industry. Maintains placement services; compiles statistics.

EMPLOYER DIRECTORIES AND NETWORKING LISTS

★7719★ Adcrafter-Roster Issue

Adcraft Club of Detroit
3011 W Grand Blvd., Ste. 1715
Detroit, MI 48202-3000
Ph: (313)872-7850   Fax: (313)872-7858
URL: http://www.adcraft.org

Annual, May. $30.00 for individuals. Covers 3,000 executives of advertising agencies, advertising media, and advertising companies in the Detroit metropolitan area, and 500 out-of-state members. Entries include: Name, title, company name, office address and phone, business classification, membership code. Arrangement: Alphabetical and classified by line of business; identical information in both sections.

★7720★ Advertiser & Agency Red Books Plus

LexisNexis Group
PO Box 933
Dayton, OH 45401-0933
Ph: (937)865-6800   Fax: (518)487-3584
Fr: 800-543-6862
URL: http://www.redbooks.com

Quarterly; latest edition January 2007. $1,895.00 for individuals. CD-ROM. Covers 15,750 of the world's top advertisers, their products and what media they use, as well as 13,900 U.S. and international ad agencies and nearly 100,000 key executives worldwide in management, creative, and media positions. Entries include: For advertisers–Company name, job function/title, product/brand name, advertising expenditures by media. For personnel–Name and title.

★7721★ Advertising Age-Advertising Agency Income Report Issue

Crain Communications Inc.
360 N Michigan Ave.
Chicago, IL 60601
Ph: (312)649-5411   Fax: (312)280-3150
Fr: 888-909-9111
URL: http://www.adage.com

Annual, April. $3.50. Publication includes: Ranked lists of about 650 U.S. advertising agencies, 1,600 foreign agencies, the world's Top 50 advertising organizations, top media services companies in the U.S. and worldwide, top U.S. healthcare agencies, and multicultural agencies, which report billings and gross incomes, or whose billings and gross incomes were ascertained through research. Entries include: U.S. and foreign agency lists from more than 120 countries include gross income and capitalized billings. Profiles of the World's Top 30 ad organizations include gross income, capitalized billings, and billings for each operating unit, subsidiary, and full service office. Arrangement: Ranked by gross income.

★7722★ The Advertising Age Encyclopedia of Advertising

Taylor and Francis Group LLC
6000 NW Broken Sound Pkwy.
Boca Raton, FL 33487
Ph: (561)994-0555   Fax: 800-374-3401
Fr: 800-272-7737
URL: http://www.taylorandfrancis.com/

Latest edition 2003. $395.00 for individuals. Publication includes: Profiles of 120 ad agencies worldwide. Principal content of publication is encyclopedic account of the advertising industry. Indexes: Alphabetical.

★7723★ The ADWEEK Directory

ADWEEK Magazines
770 Broadway, 7th Fl.
New York, NY 10003-9595
Ph: (646)654-5105   Fax: (646)654-5350
Fr: 800-562-2706
URL: http://www.adweek.com

Annual. Covers over 6,400 U.S. advertising agencies, public relations firms, media buying services, direct marketing and related organizations. Entries include: Agency name, address, phone, fax/e-mail, URL; names and titles of key personnel; major accounts; parent company; headquarters location; major subsidiaries and other operating units; year founded; number of employees; fee income; billings; percentage of billings by medium. Individual listings for each agency branch. Arrangement: Alphabetical. Indexes: Geographical; parent company, subsidiary, branch; ethnic specialities; organization, name changes, agencies opened/closed.

★7724★ **Agri Marketing-The Top 50**
Doane Agricultural Services
77 Westport Plz., Ste. 250
St. Louis, MO 63146-4193
Ph: (314)569-2700   Fax: (314)569-1083
URL: http://www.doane.com/

Annual, April or May. Publication includes: List of the top 50 U.S. and Canadian advertising agencies and public relations firms, chosen on the basis of agricultural business income. Entries include: Agency name, location, income for agricultural accounts in most recent year, branch offices, major clients served. Arrangement: Alphabetical.

★7725★ **American Marketing Association-The M Guide Directory**
American Marketing Association (Chicago, Illinois)
311 S Wacker Dr., Ste. 5800
Chicago, IL 60606
Ph: (312)542-9000   Fax: (312)542-9001
Fr: 800-262-1150
E-mail: lgil@ama.org
URL: http://www.marketingpower.com/

Annual, February. Covers 28,000 individual members and about 1,000 paid listings for member research and service firms. Entries include: For individuals–Member name, position, home and office addresses, and phone numbers. For advertisers–Company name, address, phone, names of principal executives.

★7726★ **Black Book Photography**
Black Book Marketing Group
740 Broadway, Ste. 202
New York, NY 10003
Ph: (212)979-6700   Fax: (212)673-4321
Fr: 800-841-1246
URL: http://www.BlackBook.com

Annual; latest edition 2007. $88.00 for individuals. Publication includes: Over 19,000 art directors, creative directors, photographers and photographic services, design firms, advertising agencies, and other firms whose products or services are used in advertising. Entries include: Company name, address, phone. Principal content of publication consists of 4-color samples from the leading commercial photographers. Arrangement: Classified by product/service.

★7727★ **Careers in Focus: Advertising & Marketing**
Facts On File Inc.
132 W 31st St., 17th Fl.
New York, NY 10001
Ph: (212)967-8800   Fax: 800-678-3633
Fr: 800-322-8755
URL: http://www.factsonfile.com

Published 2003. $29.95 for individuals; $26.95 for libraries. Covers an overview of advertising and marketing, followed by a selection of jobs profiled in detail, including the nature of the job, earnings, prospects for employment, what kind of training and skills it requires, and sources for further information.

★7728★ **Chicago Creative Directory**
Chicago Creative Directory
333 N Michigan Ave., Ste. 810
Chicago, IL 60601
Ph: (312)236-7337   Fax: (312)236-6078
URL: http://www.creativedir.com

Annual, March. Covers over 6,000 advertising agencies, photographers, sound studios, talent agencies, audiovisual services, and others offering creative and production services. Entries include: For most listings–Company name, address, phone, list of officers, description of services. For freelance listings–Name, talent, address, phone. Arrangement: Classified by specialty.

★7729★ **Discovering Careers for Your Future: Advertising & Marketing**
Facts On File Inc.
132 W 31st St., 17th Fl.
New York, NY 10001
Ph: (212)967-8800   Fax: 800-678-3633
Fr: 800-322-8755
URL: http://www.factsonfile.com

Published 2005. $21.95 for individuals; $19.75 for libraries. Covers advertising account executives, buyers, composers, demographers, illustrators, public opinion researchers, telemarketers, and more; links career education to curriculum, helping children investigate the subjects they are interested in and the careers those subjects might lead to.

★7730★ **Fashion & Print Directory**
Peter Glenn Publications
235 SE 5th Ave., Ste. R
Delray Beach, FL 33483
Ph: (561)404-4275   Fax: (561)279-4672
Fr: 888-332-6700
URL: http://www.pgdirect.com

Annual, November; latest edition 47th. $39.95 for individuals. Covers advertising agencies, PR firms, marketing companies, 1,000 client brand companies and related services in the U.S. and Canada. Includes photographers, marketing agencies, suppliers, sources of props and rentals, fashion houses, and beauty services. Entries include: Company name, address, phone; paid listings numbering 5,000 include description of products or services, key personnel. Arrangement: Classified by line of business.

★7731★ **IAA Membership Directory**
International Advertising Association
521 5th Ave., Ste. 1807
New York, NY 10175
Ph: (212)557-1133   Fax: (212)983-0455

Annual. Covers the advertising industry, with emphasis on the value of advertising, freedom of commercial speech, and consumer choice.

★7732★ **Job Choices for Business & Liberal Arts Students**
National Association of Colleges and Employers
62 Highland Ave.
Bethlehem, PA 18017-9085
Ph: (610)868-1421   Fax: (610)868-0208
Fr: 800-544-5272
URL: http://www.naceweb.org

Annual. $16.95 for individuals. Covers information about prospective employers, as well as career advice.

★7733★ **Medical Marketing and Media-Healthcare Agency Profiles Issue**
CPS Communications Inc.
7200 W Camino Real, Ste. 215
Boca Raton, FL 33433
Ph: (561)368-9301   Fax: (561)368-7870
Fr: 800-346-2015
URL: http://www.mmm-online.com

Monthly, July. Publication includes: List of about 130 health care advertising agencies. Entries include: Agency name, address, phone, name and title of contact, financial data, percentages of regional markets, market breakdown, current accounts, new accounts and accounts lost, number of employees, year established, special services, divisions, and best ad submissions with creative team information. Arrangement: Alphabetical.

★7734★ **O'Dwyer's Directory of Corporate Communications**
J.R. O'Dwyer Company Inc.
271 Madison Ave. No. 600
New York, NY 10016
Ph: (212)679-2471   Fax: (212)683-2750
Fr: (866)395-7710
URL: http://www.odwyerpr.com

Annual; latest edition 2005. $65.00 for individuals. Covers more than 18,000 PR professionals, including public relations departments of approximately 7,800 companies, associations, and government agencies. Entries include: Organization name, address, phone, sales, type of business; names and duties of principal public relations personnel at headquarters and other major offices, plus name and title of person to whom PR head reports; PR budget. Arrangement: Alphabetical. Indexes: Geographical, product.

★7735★ O'Dwyer's Directory of Public Relations Firms

J.R. O'Dwyer Company Inc.
271 Madison Ave., No. 600
New York, NY 10016
Ph: (212)679-2471   Fax: (212)683-2750
Fr: (866)395-7710
E-mail: sales@odwyerpr.com
URL: http://www.odwyerpr.com/

Annual; latest edition 2007 Edition. $175.00 for individuals. Covers over 1,900 public relations firms; international coverage. Entries include: Firm name, address, phone, principal executives, branch and overseas offices, billings, date founded, and 19,000+ clients, which are cross-indexed. Arrangement: Geographical by country. Indexes: Specialty (beauty and fashions, finance/investor, etc.); geographical; client.

★7736★ O'Dwyer's New York Public Relations Directory

J.R. O'Dwyer Company Inc.
271 Madison Ave., Ste. 600
New York, NY 10016
Ph: (212)679-2471   Fax: (212)683-2750
Fr: (866)395-7710

Annual. $50.00 for individuals. Covers approximately 600 public relations firms, 840 corporations, 225 trade associations, and 500 public relations service firms; over 50 executive recruiters and employment agencies. Entries include: Contact information.

★7737★ Peterson's Job Opportunities for Business Majors

Peterson's
Princeton Pke. Corporate Ctr., 2000 Lenox Dr.
PO Box 67005
Lawrenceville, NJ 08648
Ph: (609)896-1800   Fax: (609)896-4531
Fr: 800-338-3282
URL: http://www.petersons.com/

Irregular; latest edition 16th, 2000. Covers the 2,000 largest U.S. employers hiring in several fields, including financial services, management consulting, consumer products, and media/entertainment. Entries include: Organization name, address, phone, name and title of contact, number of employees, type of organization. Arrangement: Alphabetical. Indexes: Type of organization.

★7738★ Plunkett's Advertising and Branding Industry Almanac

Plunkett Research Ltd.
PO Drawer 541737
Houston, TX 77254-1737
Ph: (713)932-0000   Fax: (713)932-7080
URL: http://www.plunkettresearch.com

Published March 2007. $279.99 for individuals, book and CD-ROM database; $379.99 for individuals, book and CD-ROM database plus online subscription. Covers leading companies in advertising and marketing, including the areas of media, direct mail, online advertising, branding, and image-crafting. Entries include: Name, address, phone, fax, and key executives. Also in-cludes analysis and information on trends, technology, and statistics in the field.

★7739★ Public Relations Tactics-Member Services Directory-The Blue Book

Public Relations Society of America
33 Maiden Ln., 11th Fl.
New York, NY 10038-5150
Ph: (212)460-1400   Fax: (212)995-0757
Fr: 800-937-7772
E-mail: 74224.1456@compuserve.com
URL: http://www.prsa.org

Annual; latest edition 2007. Covers PRSA members–headquaters, staff contacts, and chapter, section, and district information. Entries include: Name, professional affiliation and title, address, phone, membership rank. Arrangement: Alphabetical. Indexes: Geographical, organizational.

★7740★ Quirk's Marketing Research Review-Researcher SourceBook Issue

Quirk Enterprises Inc.
4662 Slater Rd.
Eagan, MN 55122
Ph: (952)224-1919
URL: http://www.quirks.com

Annual, September. Covers about 7,300 organizations providing marketing research products and services. Entries include: Name, address, phone, fax, contact, research specialties, URL, e-mail. Arrangement: Geographical. Indexes: Personnel; industry specialization; research specialization; alphabetic.

★7741★ Reed's Worldwide Directory of Public Relations Organizations

Pigafetta Press
PO Box 39244
Washington, DC 20016
Ph: (202)244-2580   Fax: (202)244-2581
E-mail: 110104.1310@compuserve.com

Annual, October. $95.00. Covers approximately 225 professional public relations associations in 75 countries. Entries include: Association name, address, phone, publications, current officers, activities, and history of the organization. Arrangement: Geographical; separate section for international organizations.

★7742★ Sports Market Place

Sports Careers
2990 E Northern Ave., Ste. D107
Phoenix, AZ 85028
Ph: (602)485-5555   Fax: (602)485-5556

Annual, January. Covers manufacturers, organizations, professional sports teams, broadcasting networks, sports arenas, syndicators, publications, trade shows, marketing services, corporate sports sponsors, and other groups concerned with the business and promotional aspects of sports generally and with air sports, arm wrestling, auto sports, badminton, baseball, basketball, biathlon, bowling, boxing, curling, equestrian, exercise, fencing, field hockey, football, golf, gymnastics, ice hockey, lacrosse, martial arts, paddleball, paddle tennis, platform tennis, pentathlon, racquetball, rowing, rugby, running/jogging, skiing, soccer, softball, squash, swimming, table tennis, tennis, track and field, volleyball, water sports, weightlifting, and wrestling. Entries include: Name of company or organization, address, fax, e-mail, URL, name of key personnel with titles, and description of products or services. Arrangement: Classified by type of firm, sport, or activity. Indexes: Alphabetical; single sport; media; sport sponsors; agencies; manufacturers; brand name; facilities; executives; and geographical.

★7743★ Standard Directory of Advertising Agencies

LexisNexis Group
PO Box 933
Dayton, OH 45401-0933
Ph: (937)865-6800   Fax: (518)487-3584
Fr: 800-543-6862
URL: http://www.redbooks.com

Semiannual; latest edition January 2007. Covers nearly 10,800 advertising agencies. Entries include: Agency name, address, phone, e-mail, website, year founded, number of employees, association memberships, area of specialization, annual billing, breakdown of gross billings by media, clients, executives, special markets, and new agencies. Arrangement: Alphabetical. Indexes: Geographical (includes address); special market; agency responsibilities; and personnel.

★7744★ Standard Directory of International Advertisers and Agencies

LexisNexis Group
PO Box 933
Dayton, OH 45401-0933
Ph: (937)865-6800   Fax: (518)487-3584
Fr: 800-543-6862
URL: http://www.lexisnexis.com/

Annual; latest edition January, 2006. Covers nearly 14,000 advertiser companies and advertising agencies; international coverage. Entries include: Company name, address, phone, fax, telex, annual sales or billings, number of employees, Standard Industrial Classification (SIC) code, names and titles of key personnel, line of business; subsidiary and branch office names, address, phone, telex, key officers. Advertiser companies include their advertising agency's name, address, and description of advertising budget and strategies; advertising agencies include names of client companies and their lines of business. Arrangement: Separate alphabetical and geographical sections for advertiser companies and advertising agencies. Indexes: Geographical; company name; personal name; trade name; SIC.

★7745★ Top Careers for Communications Graduates

Facts On File Inc.
132 W 31st St., 17th Fl.
New York, NY 10001
Ph: (212)967-8800   Fax: 800-678-3633
Fr: 800-322-8755
URL: http://www.factsonfile.com

Published 2003. $14.95 for individuals; $13.45 for libraries. Covers what it takes to turn a major in communications into a good career that offers a decent salary, is projected to grow in the coming years, provides a sense of job security and advancement possibility, and is likely to be rewarding.

★7746★ The Workbook

Scott & Daughters Publishing Inc.
940 N Highland Ave.
Los Angeles, CA 90038
Ph: (213)856-0008   Fax: (323)856-4368
Fr: 800-547-2688
URL: http://www.workbook.com

Annual, February. Covers 49,000 advertising agencies, art directors, photographers, freelance illustrators and designers, artists' representatives, interactive designers, prepress services, and other graphic arts services in the U.S. Entries include: Company or individual name, address, phone, specialty. National in scope. Arrangement: Classified by product or service.

HANDBOOKS AND MANUALS

★7747★ The Advertising Age Handbook of Advertising

The McGraw-Hill Companies
PO Box 182604
Columbus, OH 43272
Fax: (614)759-3749   Fr: 877-883-5524
E-mail: customer.service@mcgraw-hill.com
URL: http://www.mcgraw-hill.com

Herschell Gordon Lewis, Carol Nelson. Contributor: Rance Crain. 1999. 240 pages. $39.95.

★7748★ A Big Life in Advertising

Alfred A. Knopf Incorporated
1745 Broadway
New York, NY 10019
Ph: (212)782-9000   Fax: (212)572-6066
Fr: 800-733-3000
URL: http://www.randomhouse.com/knopf/home.pperl

Mary Wells Lawrence. 2003. $14.00. 320 pages. Story of how Mary Wells Lawrence lived her life in advertising and helped shape her profession.

★7749★ Breaking into Advertising

Peterson's Guides
2000 Lenox Dr.
Box 67005
Lawrenceville, NJ 08648
Ph: (609)896-1800   Fax: (609)896-4531
Fr: 800-338-3282
E-mail: custsvc@petersons.com
URL: http://www.petersons.com

Smith. 1998. $14.95 (paper). 235 pages. Explains how to get a job in advertising.

★7750★ Career Opportunities for Writers

Facts On File Inc.
132 W. 31st St., 17th Fl.
New York, NY 10001-2006
Ph: (212)967-8800   Fax: 800-678-3633
Fr: 800-322-8755
E-mail: custserv@factsonfile.com
URL: http://www.factsonfile.com

Rosemary Ellen Guiley and Janet Frick. 2nd edition, 1991. $49.50. 230 pages. Part of the Career Opportunities Series. Describes more than 100 jobs in eight major fields, offering such details as duties, salaries, perquisites, employment and advancement opportunities, organizations to join, and opportunities for women and minorities.

★7751★ Career Solutions for Creative People: How to Balance Artistic Goals with Career Security

Allworth Press
10 E. 23rd St., Ste. 510
New York, NY 10010
Ph: (212)777-8395   Fax: (212)777-8261
Fr: 800-491-2808
URL: http://www.allworth.com/

Ronda Ormont. 2001. $19.95 (paper). 305 pages.

★7752★ Careers in Advertising

The McGraw-Hill Companies
PO Box 182604
Columbus, OH 43272
Fax: (614)759-3749   Fr: 877-883-5524
E-mail: customer.service@mcgraw-hill.com
URL: http://www.mcgraw-hill.com

S. William Pattis. Third Edition, 2004. $15.95 (paper). $17.95 (Hardcover). 192 pages.

★7753★ Careers in Communications

The McGraw-Hill Companies
PO Box 182604
Columbus, OH 43272
Fax: (614)759-3749   Fr: 877-883-5524
E-mail: customer.service@mcgraw-hill.com
URL: http://www.mcgraw-hill.com

Shonan Noronha. Fourth edition, 2004. $15.95 (paper). 192 pages. Examines the fields of journalism, photography, radio, television, film, public relations, and advertising. Gives concrete details on job locations and how to secure a job. Suggests many resources for job hunting.

★7754★ Careers in International Business

The McGraw-Hill Companies
PO Box 182604
Columbus, OH 43272
Fax: (614)759-3749   Fr: 877-883-5524
E-mail: customer.service@mcgraw-hill.com
URL: http://www.mcgraw-hill.com

Ed Halloran. Second edition, 2003. $14.95 (paper). 192 pages.

★7755★ Careers in Marketing

The McGraw-Hill Companies
PO Box 182604
Columbus, OH 43272
Fax: (614)759-3749   Fr: 877-883-5524
E-mail: customer.service@mcgraw-hill.com
URL: http://www.mcgraw-hill.com

Lila B. Stair and Leslie Stair. Third edition, 2001. $13.95 (paper). 192 pages. Surveys career opportunities in marketing and related areas such as marketing research, product development, and sales promotion. Includes a description of the work, places of employment, employment outlook, trends, and salaries. Offers job hunting advice.

★7756★ Careers for Writers and Others Who Have a Way with Words

The McGraw-Hill Companies
PO Box 182604
Columbus, OH 43272
Fax: (614)759-3749   Fr: 877-883-5524
E-mail: customer.service@mcgraw-hill.com
URL: http://www.mcgraw-hill.com

Robert W. Bly. Second edition, 2003. $13.95 (paper). 208 pages.

★7757★ Encyclopedia of Advertising

Routledge
270 Madison Ave.
New York, NY 10016
Ph: (212)216-7800   Fax: (212)563-2269
URL: http://www.routledge.com/

Editor: John McDonough. 2002. $550.00. 2000 pages.

★7758★ Get Noticed!: Self Promotion for Creative Professionals

North Light Books
4700 E Galbraith Rd.
Cincinnati, OH 45236
Ph: (513)531-2690   Fax: (513)531-4082
Fr: 800-289-0963

Sheree Clark, Kristin Lennert. 2000. $29.99 (paper). 143 pages.

★7759★ Great Jobs for Business Majors

The McGraw-Hill Companies
PO Box 182604
Columbus, OH 43272
Fax: (614)759-3749   Fr: 877-883-5524
E-mail: customer.service@mcgraw-hill.com
URL: http://www.mcgraw-hill.com

Stephen Lambert. Second edition, 2003. $15.95 (paper). 240 pages.

★7760★ Great Jobs for Communications Majors

The McGraw-Hill Companies
PO Box 182604
Columbus, OH 43272
Fax: (614)759-3749   Fr: 877-883-5524
E-mail: customer.service@mcgraw-hill.com
URL: http://www.mcgraw-hill.com

Blythe Camenson. Second edition, 2001. $15.95 (paper). 256 pages.

★7761★ Great Jobs for English Majors

The McGraw-Hill Companies
PO Box 182604
Columbus, OH 43272
Fax: (614)759-3749   Fr: 877-883-5524
E-mail: customer.service@mcgraw-hill.com
URL: http://www.mcgraw-hill.com

Julie DeGalan. Third edition, 2006. $15.95 (paper). 192 pages.

★7762★ Great Jobs for Liberal Arts Majors

The McGraw-Hill Companies
PO Box 182604
Columbus, OH 43272
Fax: (614)759-3749   Fr: 877-883-5524
E-mail: customer.service@mcgraw-hill.com
URL: http://www.mcgraw-hill.com

Blythe Camenson. Second edition, 2001. $14.95 (paper). 256 pages.

★7763★ Harvard Business School Guide to Careers in Marketing: A Guide to Management Careers in Marketing

Harvard Business School Press
60 Harvard Way
Boston, MA 02163
Ph: (617)783-7500   Fax: (617)783-7555
Fr: 800-988-0886
URL: http://www.hbsp.harvard.edu

Harvard Business School Press Staff. 2000. $22.95 (paper). 77 pages.

★7764★ How to Become a Marketing Superstar: Unexpected Rules That Ring the Cash Register

Hyperion Books
77 West 66th St., 11 Fl.
New York, NY 10023
Ph: (212)522-8700   Fr: 800-759-0190
URL: http://www.hyperionbooks.com

Jeffrey J. Fox. 2003. $16.95. E-book. 192 pages.

★7765★ How to Get into Marketing and PR

Continuum International Publishing Group, Inc.
80 Maiden Ln., Ste. 704
New York, NY 10038
Ph: (212)953-5858   Fax: (212)953-5944
URL: http://www.continuumbooks.com/

Annie Gurton. June 2003. $129.99 (hardcover). 213 pages.

★7766★ Opportunities in Advertising Careers

The McGraw-Hill Companies
PO Box 182604
Columbus, OH 43272
Fax: (614)759-3749   Fr: 877-883-5524
E-mail: customer.service@mcgraw-hill.com
URL: http://www.mcgraw-hill.com

S. William Pattis and Ruth Wooden. 1995. $11.95 (paper). 145 pages. A guide to planning for and seeking opportunities in this growing field. Illustrated.

★7767★ Opportunities in Direct Marketing

The McGraw-Hill Companies
PO Box 182604
Columbus, OH 43272
Fax: (614)759-3749   Fr: 877-883-5524
E-mail: customer.service@mcgraw-hill.com
URL: http://www.mcgraw-hill.com

Anne Basye. 2008. $14.95; $11.95 (paper). 160 pages. Examines opportunities with direct marketers, catalog companies, direct marketing agencies, telemarketing firms, mailing list brokers, and database marketing companies. Describes how to prepare for a career in direct marketing and how to break into the field. Includes sources of short-term professional training.

★7768★ Opportunities in International Business Careers

The McGraw-Hill Companies
PO Box 182604
Columbus, OH 43272
Fax: (614)759-3749   Fr: 877-883-5524
E-mail: customer.service@mcgraw-hill.com
URL: http://www.mcgraw-hill.com

Jeffrey Arpan. 1994. $11.95 (paper). 147 pages. Describes what types of jobs exist in international business, where they are located, what challenges and rewards they bring, and how to prepare for and obtain jobs in international business.

★7769★ Opportunities in Journalism Careers

The McGraw-Hill Companies
PO Box 182604
Columbus, OH 43272
Fax: (614)759-3749   Fr: 877-883-5524
E-mail: customer.service@mcgraw-hill.com
URL: http://www.mcgraw-hill.com

Jim Patten and Donald L. Ferguson. 2001. $12.95 (paper). 160 pages. Outlines opportunities in every field of journalism, including newspaper reporting and editing, magazine and book publishing, corporate communications, advertising and public relations, freelance writing, and teaching. Covers how to prepare for and enter each field, outlining responsibilities, salaries, benefits, and job outlook for each specialty. Illustrated.

★7770★ Opportunities in Magazine Publishing Careers

The McGraw-Hill Companies
PO Box 182604
Columbus, OH 43272
Fax: (614)759-3749   Fr: 877-883-5524
E-mail: customer.service@mcgraw-hill.com
URL: http://www.mcgraw-hill.com

S. William Pattis. 1994. $13.95; $14.95 (paper). 148 pages. Covers the scope of magazine publishing and addresses how to identify and pursue available positions. Illustrated.

★7771★ Opportunities in Marketing Careers

The McGraw-Hill Companies
PO Box 182604
Columbus, OH 43272
Fax: (614)759-3749   Fr: 877-883-5524
E-mail: customer.service@mcgraw-hill.com
URL: http://www.mcgraw-hill.com

Margery Steinberg. 2005. $13.95; $11.95 (paper). 176. Gives guidance on identifying and pursuing job opportunities. Illustrated.

★7772★ Opportunities in Public Relations Careers

The McGraw-Hill Companies
PO Box 182604
Columbus, OH 43272
Fax: (614)759-3749   Fr: 877-883-5524
E-mail: customer.service@mcgraw-hill.com
URL: http://www.mcgraw-hill.com

Morris B. Rotman. 2001. $12.95 (paper). 160 pages. Tells the reader how to enter the field and how to build a career. Contains bibliography and illustrations.

★7773★ Opportunities in Publishing Careers

The McGraw-Hill Companies
PO Box 182604
Columbus, OH 43272
Fax: (614)759-3749   Fr: 877-883-5524
E-mail: customer.service@mcgraw-hill.com
URL: http://www.mcgraw-hill.com

Robert A. Carter and S. William Pattis. 2000. $12.95 (paper). 160 pages. Covers all positions in book and magazine publishing, including new opportunities in multimedia publishing.

★7774★ Opportunities in Writing Careers

The McGraw-Hill Companies
PO Box 182604
Columbus, OH 43272
Fax: (614)759-3749   Fr: 877-883-5524

E-mail: customer.service@mcgraw-hill.com
URL: http://www.mcgraw-hill.com

Elizabeth Foote-Smith. 2006. $13.95; $11.95 (paper). 160 pages. Discusses opportunities in the print media, broadcasting, advertising or publishing. Business writing, public relations, and technical writing are among the careers covered. Contains bibliography and illustrations.

★7775★ **Real People Working in Communications**

The McGraw-Hill Companies
PO Box 182604
Columbus, OH 43272
Fax: (614)759-3749   Fr: 877-883-5524
E-mail: customer.service@mcgraw-hill.com
URL: http://www.mcgraw-hill.com

Jan Goldberg. 1996. $17.95 (paper). 133 pages. Interviews and profiles of working professionals capture a range of opportunities in this field.

★7776★ **Resumes for Advertising Careers**

The McGraw-Hill Companies
PO Box 182604
Columbus, OH 43272
Fax: (614)759-3749   Fr: 877-883-5524
E-mail: customer.service@mcgraw-hill.com
URL: http://www.mcgraw-hill.com

Third edition, 2003. $10.95 (paper). 160 pages. Aimed at job seekers trying to enter or advance in advertising. Provides sample resumes for copywriters, art directors, account managers, ad managers, and media people at all levels of experience. Furnishes sample cover letters.

★7777★ **Resumes for Communications Careers**

The McGraw-Hill Companies
PO Box 182604
Columbus, OH 43272
Fax: (614)759-3749   Fr: 877-883-5524
E-mail: customer.service@mcgraw-hill.com
URL: http://www.mcgraw-hill.com

Third edition, 2003. $10.95 (paper). 160 pages.

★7778★ **Resumes for Sales and Marketing Careers**

The McGraw-Hill Companies
PO Box 182604
Columbus, OH 43272
Fax: (614)759-3749   Fr: 877-883-5524
E-mail: customer.service@mcgraw-hill.com
URL: http://www.mcgraw-hill.com

Chuck Cochran and Donna Peerce. 1998. $13.95. 336 pages. Sample resumes and cover letters from all levels of the sales and marketing field.

★7779★ **This Business of Music Marketing and Promotion**

Billboard Books
770 Broadway
New York, NY 10003
Ph: (646)654-5400   Fax: (646)654-5486
Fr: 800-323-9432

Tad Lathrop and Jim Pettigrew, Jr. Rev edition, 2003. $24.95. 308 pages.

★7780★ **Vault Career Guide to Advertising**

Vault.com
150 W. 22nd St., 5th Fl.
New York, NY 10011
Ph: (212)366-4212   Fax: (212)366-6117
Fr: 888-562-8285
URL: http://www.vault.com

Ira Berkowitz. April 2004. $29.95 (paper). 128 pages.

★7781★ **Working in Public Relations: How to Gain the Skills and Opportunities for a Career in Public Relations**

Trans-Atlantic Publications, Inc.
311 Bainbridge St.
Philadelphia, PA 19147
Ph: (215)925-5083   Fax: (215)925-1912
E-mail: bookinquiries@earthlink.net
URL: http://www.transatlanticpub.com/

Carole Chester. 1998. $21.95 (paper). 144 pages.

EMPLOYMENT AGENCIES AND SEARCH FIRMS

★7782★ **Adler Management Inc.**
66 Witherspoon St., Ste. 315
Princeton, NJ 08542
Ph: (609)443-3300   Fax: (609)443-4439
E-mail: jadler@amiconsulting.com
URL: http://www.amiconsulting.com

Executive search firm.

★7783★ **Allen Associates**
4555 Lake Forest Dr., 6th Fl.
Cincinnati, OH 45242
Ph: (513)563-3040
E-mail: feedback@allensearch.com
URL: http://www.allensearch.com

Executive senior-level search firm.

★7784★ **Allen Austin**
4543 Post Oak Place Dr., Ste. 217
Houston, TX 77027
Ph: (713)355-1900   Fax: (713)355-1901
E-mail: randrews@allenaustinsearch.com
URL: http://www.allenaustinsearch.com

Executive search firm. Branches in North Carolina and Dallas.

★7785★ **Ambler Associates**
14881 Quorum Dr., Ste. 450
Dallas, TX 75254
Ph: (972)404-8712   Fax: (972)404-8761
Fr: 800-728-8712

Executive search firm.

★7786★ **American Executive Management Inc.**
30 Federal St., Ste. 102
Salem, MA 01970
Ph: (978)477-5923
E-mail: execsearch@americanexecutive.us
URL: http://www.americanexecutive.us

Executive search firm. Second location in Boston.

★7787★ **Ariel Associates**
159-34 Riverside Dr. W., Apt. 5J
New York, NY 10032-1155
Ph: (212)923-1155
E-mail: info@arielassociates.com
URL: http://www.arielassociates.com

Executive search firm specializing in media, advertising and publishing.

★7788★ **Banyan Group ESC Ltd.**
6 Courseview Rd.
Bronxville, NY 10708
Ph: (914)337-7159   Fax: (914)337-7164
URL: http://www.banyan-group.com/

Executive search firm.

★7789★ **The Barack Group Inc.**
Grand Central Station
PO Box 4407
New York, NY 10163
Ph: (212)867-9700   Fax: (212)681-9555
URL: http://www.barackgroup.com

Executive search firm.

★7790★ **Barton Associates Inc.**
4314 Yoakum Blvd.
Houston, TX 77006
Ph: (713)961-9111   Fax: (713)993-9399
E-mail: info@bartona.com
URL: http://www.bartona.com

Executive search firm. Affiliate in Houston, TX.

★7791★ **Bender Executive Search Management Consulting**
45 N. Station Plaza, Ste. 315
Great Neck, NY 11021
Ph: (516)773-4300   Fax: (516)482-5355
E-mail: benderexec@aol.com
URL: http://www.marketingexecsearch.com

Executive search firm.

★7792★ Bennett Wheelless Group Ltd.
33 W. Monroe, Ste. 2110
Chicago, IL 60603
Ph: (312)252-8883   Fax: (801)697-5227
URL: http://www.bennettwheelless.com

Executive search firm focused on direct marketing positions.

★7793★ Berardi & Associates
1140 Ave. of the Americas, Fl. 8
New York, NY 10036
Ph: (212)403-6180   Fax: (212)764-9690
E-mail: jmiranda@spges.com
URL: http://www.spgjobs.com

Executive search firm.

★7794★ Bert Davis Executive Search Inc.
425 Madison Ave., Fl. 14
New York, NY 10017
Ph: (212)838-4000   Fax: (212)935-3291
E-mail: info@bertdavis.com
URL: http://www.bertdavis.com

Executive search firm.

★7795★ Blumenthal-Hart LLC
53 W. Jackson Blvd., Ste. 426
Chicago, IL 60604-3413
Ph: (312)663-0090   Fax: (312)663-0405
E-mail: resumes@blumenthal-hart.com
URL: http://www.blumenthal-hart.com

Executive search firm.

★7796★ Buffkin & Associates LLC
730 Cool Springs Blvd., Ste. 120
Franklin, TN 37067
Ph: (615)771-0098   Fax: (615)771-0099
E-mail: info@buffkinassociates.com
URL: http://www.buffkinassociates.com

Executive search firm.

★7797★ Byron Leonard International
99 Long Ct., Ste. 201
Thousand Oaks, CA 91360
Ph: (805)373-7500   Fax: (805)373-5531
Fr: (818)222-2744
E-mail: swolf@bli-inc.com
URL: http://www.bli-inc.com

Executive search firm.

★7798★ Canny, Bowen Inc.
400 Madison Ave., Rm. 11D
New York, NY 10017
Ph: (212)949-6611   Fax: (212)949-5191
E-mail: main@cannybowen.com
URL: http://www.cannybowen.com

Executive search firm.

★7799★ Cantor Executive Search Solutions Inc.
250 W. 57 St., Ste. 1632
New York, NY 10107-1609
Ph: (212)333-3000   Fax: (212)245-1012
E-mail: requests@cantorconcern.com
URL: http://www.cantorconcern.com

Executive search firm. Branch in Fairfield, CT.

★7800★ Cardinal Mark Inc.
17113 Minnetonka Blvd., Ste. 112
Minnetonka, MN 55345
Ph: (952)314-4636   Fax: (610)228-7390
E-mail: jimz@cardinalmark.com
URL: http://www.cardinalmark.com

Executive search firm concentrated on tele-communication industry.

★7801★ Cardwell Enterprises Inc.
PO Box 59418
Chicago, IL 60659
Ph: (773)273-5774

Executive search firm.

★7802★ Carnegie Partners Inc.
4354 Town Center Blvd, Ste. 114-248
El Dorado Hills, CA 95762
Ph: (916)941-9053   Fax: (916)290-0312
E-mail: Support@CarnegiePartners.com
URL: http://www.carnegiepartners.com

Executive search firm. Branches in Glenview, IL; Kewadin, MI; and Westlake, OH.

★7803★ Caruthers & Company LLC
1175 Post Rd., E.
Westport, CT 06880
Ph: (203)221-3234   Fax: (203)221-7300

Executive search firm.

★7804★ cFour Partners
100 Wilshire Blvd., Ste. 1840
Santa Monica, CA 90401
Ph: (310)394-2639   Fax: (310)394-2669
E-mail: info@cfour.com
URL: http://www.cfour.com

Executive search firm.

★7805★ Chaloner Associates
36 Milford St.
Boston, MA 02118
Ph: (617)451-5170   Fax: (617)451-8160
E-mail: info@chaloner.com
URL: http://www.chaloner.com

Executive search firm.

★7806★ Cheryl Alexander & Associates
8588 Shadow Creek Dr.
Maple Grove, MN 55311
Ph: (763)416-4570

E-mail: cherylalexander@cherylalexander.com
URL: http://www.cherylalexander.com

Executive search firm.

★7807★ Churchill & Affiliates Inc.
1200 Bustleton Pike, Ste. 3
Feasterville, PA 19053
Ph: (215)364-8070   Fax: (215)322-4391
E-mail: hwasserman@churchillsearch.com
URL: http://www.churchillsearch.com

Executive search firm focusing on the tele-communications industry.

★7808★ Colton Bernard Inc.
870 Market St., Ste. 822
San Francisco, CA 94102
Ph: (415)399-8700   Fax: (415)399-0750
E-mail: inquiry@coltonbernard.com
URL: http://www.coltonbernard.com

Executive search firm focused on textiles, apparel and retail industries.

★7809★ Corporate Moves Inc.
PO Box 1638
Williamsville, NY 14231-1638
Ph: (716)633-0234
E-mail: info@CMISearch.com
URL: http://www.corporatemovesinc.com

Executive search & recruitment specialist firm with emphasis on Sales, Marketing and Senior Management generally in the $70,000 and above income levels. Industries served: medical, biotech, scientific, pharmaceutical, industrial, business products.

★7810★ Crowe-Innes & Associates LLC
1120 Mar West St., Ste. D
Tiburon, CA 94920
Ph: (415)789-1422   Fax: (415)435-6867
E-mail: jenny@croweinnes.com
URL: http://www.croweinnes.com

Executive search firm.

★7811★ David Allen Associates
PO Box 56
Haddonfield, NJ 08033-0048
Ph: (856)795-6470   Fax: (856)795-0175
E-mail: david@davidallenassoc.com
URL: http://www.davidallenassoc.com

Executive search firm.

★7812★ David Blevins & Associates Inc.
611 S. Palm Canyon Dr., Ste. 7140
Palm Springs, CA 92264
Ph: (707)495-3714
E-mail: DaveBlevins@daveblevins.com
URL: http://www.daveblevins.com/vineyards.swf

Executive search firm.

★7813★ **David M. Ellner Associates**
41 Barkers Point Rd.
Port Washington, NY 11050
Ph: (516)767-9480
E-mail: elldoda@aol.com
Executive search firm.

★7814★ **The Dinerstein Group**
45 Rockefeller Plaza, Ste. 2000
New York, NY 10111
Ph: (212)332-3224
E-mail: jm@dinersteingroup.com
URL: http://www.dinersteingroup.com
Executive search firm. Branch in Stamford, CT.

★7815★ **Dise & Company Inc.**
20600 Chagrin Blvd., Ste. 925
Tower East
Cleveland, OH 44122
Ph: (216)752-1700   Fax: (216)929-0042
E-mail: support@diseco.com
URL: http://www.diseco.com
Executive search firm.

★7816★ **DLB Associates**
2403 State Route 66
Ocean, NJ 07712
Ph: (732)774-2000   Fax: (732)774-5000
E-mail: info@dlbassociates.com
URL: http://www.dlbassociates.com/
Executive search firm.

★7817★ **Doherty International Inc.**
899 Skokie Blvd., Ste. 430
Northbrook, IL 60062
Ph: (847)564-1753   Fax: (847)564-1763
E-mail: doherty_int@ameritech.net
Executive search firm.

★7818★ **Dotson & Associates**
412 E. 55th St., Ste. 8A
New York, NY 10022
Ph: (212)593-4274
Executive search firm.

★7819★ **Dussick Management Associates**
White Birch Rd., Ste. 28
Madison, CT 06443
Ph: (203)245-9311   Fax: (203)245-1648
E-mail: vince@dussick.com
URL: http://www.dussick.com
Executive search firm.

★7820★ **Edgewood International**
3018 Edgewood Pkwy.
Woodridge, IL 60517-3720
Ph: (630)985-6067   Fax: (630)985-6069
E-mail: wocatedgewood@aol.com
Executive search firm.

★7821★ **The Enfield Company**
106 E. 6th St., Ste. 900
Austin, TX 78701
Ph: (512)444-9921
E-mail: enfieldco@yahoo.com
URL: http://members.aol.com/enfieldco/
Executive search firm.

★7822★ **Epsen, Fuller & Associates LLC**
10 Park Pl., Ste. 420
Morristown, NJ 07960
Ph: (973)359-9929   Fax: (973)359-9928
E-mail: info@epsenfuller.com
URL: http://www.epsenfuller.com
Executive search firm.

★7823★ **The Esquire Staffing Group Ltd.**
1 S. Wacker Dr., Ste. 1616
Chicago, IL 60606-4616
Ph: (312)795-4300   Fax: (312)795-4329
E-mail: d.williams@esquirestaffing.com
URL: http://www.esquirestaffing.com
Employment agency. Fills permanent as well as temporary openings.

★7824★ **The Executive Roundtable**
483 Godshall Rd.
Souderton, PA 18964
Ph: (215)721-1650   Fax: (215)721-8650
Fr: 888-315-1150
E-mail: execrt@verizon.net
Executive search firm.

★7825★ **Fairfield**
Trump Tower
721 5th Ave.
New York, NY 10022-2523
Ph: (212)838-0220
E-mail: newyork@fairfield.ch
URL: http://www.fairfield.ch
Executive search firm specializing in retail and apparel manufacturing.

★7826★ **Filcro Media Staffing**
521 5th Ave., Fl. 18
New York, NY 10175
Ph: (212)599-0909   Fax: (212)599-1023
E-mail: mail@executivesearch.tv
URL: http://www.executivesearch.tv
Executive search firm for the entertainment industry.

★7827★ **Fisher & Associates**
1063 Lenor Way
San Jose, CA 95128
Ph: (408)554-0156   Fax: (408)246-7807
E-mail: fisherassoc@aol.com
Executive search firm focused on the high technology industry.

★7828★ **Franchise Recruiters Ltd.**
Lincolnshire Country Club
3500 Innsbruck
Crete, IL 60417
Ph: (708)757-5595   Fax: (708)758-8222
Fr: 800-334-6257
E-mail: franchise@att.net
URL: http://www.franchiserecruiteer.com
Executive search firm. Second location in Toronto, Canada.

★7829★ **Gundersen Partners L.L.C.**
30 Irving Pl., 2nd Fl.
New York, NY 10003
Ph: (212)677-7660   Fax: (212)358-0275
E-mail: esteffen@gpllc.com
URL: http://www.gundersenpartners.com
Management consulting firm provides the following: marketing consulting and executive search. Industries served: marketing, marketing services, consumer packaged goods, financial services, internet/high tech, sales promotion and advertising agencies.

★7830★ **Hilleren & Associates**
3800 American Blvd. W, Ste. 880
Minneapolis, MN 55431
Ph: (952)956-9090   Fax: (952)956-9009
E-mail: jerry@hilleren.com
URL: http://www.hilleren.com
Provides executive search services in sales, marketing and management in the medical and pharmaceutical manufacturing industry.

★7831★ **Houser Martin Morris**
110th Ave. NE, 110 Atrium Pl., Ste. 580
110 Atrium Pl.
Bellevue, WA 98004
Ph: (425)453-2700   Fax: (425)453-8726
E-mail: info@houser.com
URL: http://www.houser.com
Focus is in the areas of retained executive search, professional and technical recruiting. Areas of specialization include software engineering, sales and marketing, information technology, legal, human resources, accounting and finance, manufacturing, factory automation, and engineering.

★7832★ **Howard-Sloan Professional Search Inc.**
1140 Ave. of the Americas
New York, NY 10036
Ph: (212)704-0444   Fax: (212)869-7999
Fr: 800-221-1326
E-mail: info@howardsloan.com
URL: http://www.howardsloan.com
Executive search firm.

★7833★ **Intech Summit Group Inc.**
180 Otay Lakes Rd., Ste. 106
Bonita, CA 91902
Ph: (619)931-1100   Fax: (619)931-1101
Fr: 800-750-8100
E-mail: isg@isgsearch.com
URL: http://www.isgsearch.com

Retained executive search and human resources consulting firm. Industries served: healthcare, MIS, sales and marketing, high-tech, other consulting groups, human resources, and information systems.

★7834★ **Joseph A. Davis Consultants Inc.**

104 E. 40th St., Ste. 203
New York, NY 10016
Ph: (212)682-4006   Fax: (212)661-0846
E-mail: jadci@compuserve.com

Executive search firm.

★7835★ **Joy Reed Belt Search Consultants Inc.**

PO Box 54410
Oklahoma City, OK 73154
Ph: (405)842-5155   Fax: (405)842-6357
E-mail: executiverecruiter@joyreedbelt.com
URL: http://www.joyreedbeltsearch.com

Executive search firm. Branch in Tulsa, OK.

★7836★ **JT Brady & Associates**

10900 Perry Hwy. 12203
Wexford, PA 15090
Ph: (412)934-2228   Fax: (724)935-8059
E-mail: jack@jtbrady.net
URL: http://www.jtbrady.net

Executive search firm.

★7837★ **Juan Menefee & Associates**

503 S Oak Park Ave., Ste. 206
Oak Park, IL 60304
Ph: (708)848-7722   Fax: (708)848-6008
E-mail: jmenefee@jmarecruiter.com
URL: http://www.jmarecruiter.com

Diversity Search Firm. Firm places executives in the sales, marketing, finance, engineering, medical, high tech and insurance industries.

★7838★ **Judith Cushman & Associates**

15600 NE 8th St., Ste. B1
Bellevue, WA 98008
Ph: (425)392-8660   Fax: (425)746-8629
E-mail: jcushman@jc-a.com
URL: http://www.jc-a.com

Executive search firm.

★7839★ **Karen Dexter & Associates Inc.**

2012 Chestnut
Wilmette, IL 60091-1512
Ph: (847)853-9500   Fax: (847)256-7108

Training and development consultant offering interpersonal skills training and one-on-one performance counseling for employees of large organizations. Industries served: advertising, banking and finance, consumer products, entertainment, food and beverage, healthcare, legal profession, manufacturing, government agencies, publishing and broadcasting.

★7840★ **Lamay Associates**

1465 Post Rd. E
Old Greenwich, CT 06870
Ph: (203)637-8440   Fax: (203)256-3594
E-mail: dmsearch_lamay@msn.com
URL: http://www.lamayassociates.com

Offers executive search and recruitment specializing in all areas of direct marketing-both to consumers, business-to-business, and non-profit development. Clients include advertising agencies, retailers, manufacturers of consumer goods, cataloguers, publishers, and Internet/e-commerce entities.

★7841★ **LandaJob Advertising Staffing Specialists**

8177 Wornall Rd.
Kansas City, MO 64114
Ph: (816)523-1881   Fax: (816)523-1876
Fr: 800-931-8806
E-mail: adstaff@landajobnow.com
URL: http://www.landajobnow.com

Personnel consultants and recruiters for advertising, marketing, and communications positions. Industries served: advertising, communications, marketing, graphic arts, printing and publishing.

★7842★ **Max Brown**

3208 Q St. NW
Washington, DC 20007
Ph: (202)338-2727   Fax: (202)338-3131

Executive recruiter to the magazine and book publishing industries. Employment placements in all publishing disciplines, including operation and financial management, new product development, marketing, advertising sales, editorial, graphic design, production, manufacturing, circulation, distribution, corporate communications, promotion and administration. Secondary concentrations include management advising for publishers, providing the following services: marketing and product positioning for new and existing publications, market research and development, business planning and financial projections, publishing models, launch strategies and start-up operations and acquisitions and mergers counsel.

★7843★ **MedSearch Staffing Services Inc.**

7530 Lucerne Dr., Islander 2, Ste. 208
Plaza S 3
Middleburg Heights, OH 44130
Ph: (440)243-5300   Fax: (440)243-9117
E-mail: info@medicalreserves.com
URL: http://www.medicalreserves.com

Provides specialized recruitment of sales, marketing and management personnel. Also involved in top-level hospital management consulting and physician recruitment, interim/temporary staffing. Industries served: healthcare manufacturers and institutions.

★7844★ **Neil Frank & Company**

PO Box 3570
Redondo Beach, CA 90277-1570
Ph: (310)543-1611   Fax: (310)540-2639

E-mail: neilnick@aol.com
URL: http://www.neilfrank.com

Executive search firm.

★7845★ **Normyle/Erstling Health Search Group**

350 W Passaic St.
Rochelle Park, NJ 07662
Ph: (201)843-6009   Fax: (201)843-2060
E-mail: nehsg@medpharmsales.com
URL: http://www.healthcaresales.com

Firm performs executive search and recruitment of medical device and pharmaceutical sales and marketing professionals.

★7846★ **Pacific Crest Associates LLC**

4695 MacArthur Ct., 11th Fl.
Newport Beach, CA 92660
Ph: (949)798-6204   Fax: (949)798-5549
E-mail: Careers@pacificcrestassociates.com
URL: http://www.pacificcrestassociates.com

Executive search firm.

★7847★ **Roberson & Co.**

10751 Parfet St.
Broomfield, CO 80021
Ph: (303)410-6510
E-mail: roberson@recruiterpro.com
URL: http://www.recruiterpro.com

A contingency professional and executive recruiting firm working the national and international marketplace. Specialize in accounting, finance, data processing and information services, healthcare, environmental and mining, engineering, manufacturing, human resources, and sales and marketing.

★7848★ **Sales Executives Inc.**

33900 W. 8 Mile Rd., Ste. 171
Farmington Hills, MI 48335
Ph: (248)615-0100
E-mail: dale@salesexecutives.com
URL: http://www.salesexecutives.com

Employment agency. Executive search firm.

★7849★ **Sales Recruiters International Ltd.**

2 Depot Plz., Ste. 303A
Bedford Hills, NY 10507
Ph: (914)631-0090   Fax: (914)244-3001
Fr: 800-836-0881
E-mail: info@salesrecruiters.net
URL: http://www.salesrecruiters.net

Offers management and consulting services including recruitment, selection, and retention of sales and marketing personnel, and teambuilding. Industries served: office products, telecommunications, data processing, financial, contract interiors, food service, hospitality, consumer products, and graphic arts.

★7850★ Techtronix Technical Search
4805 N 24th Pl.
PO Box 17713
Milwaukee, WI 53217-0173
Ph: (414)466-3100   Fax: (414)466-3598
Firm specializes in recruiting executives for the engineering, information systems, manufacturing, marketing, finance, and human resources industries.

★7851★ Toby Clark Associates Inc.
405 E 54th St., Ste. 6C
New York, NY 10022-3133
Ph: (212)752-5670   Fax: (212)752-5674
Executive recruiting firm specializing in marketing communications and public relations. Industries served: all.

★7852★ Todd Arro Inc.
3024 Delaware Ave.
PO Box 172
Buffalo, NY 14217
Ph: (716)871-0993   Fax: (716)871-1376
Recruiting and search consultants specializing in sales and marketing management in the industrial, commercial, consumer product, pharmaceutical and medical areas.

★7853★ Tyler & Co.
375 Northridge Rd., Ste. 400
Atlanta, GA 30350-3299
Ph: (770)396-3939   Fax: (770)396-6693
Fr: 800-989-6789
E-mail: art@tylerandco.com
URL: http://www.tylerandco.com
Retained executive search for the healthcare, food, market research, manufacturing and insurance industries.

★7854★ Wendell L. Johnson Associates Inc.
12 Grandview Dr., Ste. 1117
Danbury, CT 06811-4321
Ph: (203)743-4112   Fax: (203)778-5377
Executive search firm specializing in areas of workforce diversity, accounting/finance, human resources, marketing/sales, strategic planning, and MIS.

★7855★ Young & Thulin
555 Clover Ln.
Boulder, CO 80303
Ph: (303)499-7242   Fax: (303)499-6436
E-mail: bill@ytsearch.com
URL: http://www.ytsearch.com
A retained executive search firm formed to serve local and international technology, communications, medical and media industries. Assists in strengthening clients' management team or acquiring new talent. Works with companies that have a sound business plan, a solid market, and realistic potential for growth.

★7856★ Zachary & Sanders Inc.
Linden Ln.
East Norwich, NY 11732
Ph: (516)922-5500   Fax: (516)922-2286
Fr: 800-540-7919
E-mail: zacharyserch@earthlink.net
Serves the printing, packaging, publishing, advertising, direct marketing industries.

ONLINE JOB SOURCES AND SERVICES

★7857★ Delta Services
Ph: (281)494-9300
E-mail: contact@thesearchfirm.com
URL: http://www.thesearchfirm.com
Executive search firm.

★7858★ Omni Search, Inc.
E-mail: omni@omnisearch.biz
URL: http://www.omnisearch.biz/opps.htm
Description: Job search engine for those in the sales and marketing positions in the pharmaceutical, medical and consumer industries.

TRADESHOWS

★7859★ Annual Catalog Conference and Exhibition
Dydacomp
11 D Commerce Way
Totowa, NJ 07512-1154
Ph: (973)237-9415   Fax: (973)237-9043
Fr: 800-858-3666
E-mail: info@dydacomp.com
URL: http://www.dydacomp.com
Primary Exhibits: Marketing industry exhibition.

★7860★ Association for Convention Marketing Executives
Total Association Management Services
2965 Flowers Rd., Ste. 105
Atlanta, GA 30341
Ph: (770)454-6111   Fax: (770)458-3314
E-mail: shelby@tamshq.com
URL: http://www.acmenet.org
Annual. Primary Exhibits: Management and marketing products and services, for convention centers and convention bureaus.

★7861★ BMA Annual Marketing Forum
American Bankers Association
1120 Connecticut Ave. NW
Washington, DC 20036
Fr: 800-BAN-KERS
E-mail: custserv@aba.com
URL: http://www.aba.com

Annual. **Primary Exhibits:** Financial services marketing offering banking solutions in advertising services, bank equipment/systems, computer software, database marketing, direct marketing/sales, incentive/premium programs, insurance services, investment services, marketing consulting, merchandising, publishing, research, retail delivery, sales training, service quality, signage, and telemarketing.

★7862★ Direct Marketing Association Annual Conference & Exhibition
Direct Marketing Association
1120 Ave. of the Americas
New York, NY 10036-6700
Ph: (212)768-7277   Fax: (212)302-6714
Fr: 800-255-0006
E-mail: customerservice@the-dma.org
URL: http://www.the-dma.org
Annual. **Primary Exhibits:** Printers, list brokers, envelope manufacturers, telephone marketing companies, computers and other equipment, supplies, and services for direct marketing.

★7863★ Direct Marketing Association of Washington Conference and Expo
Direct Marketing Association of Washington
801 Roeder Rd., Ste. 575
Silver Spring, MD 20910
Ph: (301)427-0050   Fax: (301)565-9791
E-mail: dmaw@hqstaff.com
URL: http://www.dmaw.org
Annual. **Primary Exhibits:** Direct marketing information and services.

★7864★ DMD New York Conference and Expo
Direct Marketing Association
1120 Ave. of the Americas
New York, NY 10036-6700
Ph: (212)768-7277   Fax: (212)302-6714
Fr: 800-255-0006
E-mail: customerservice@the-dma.org
URL: http://www.the-dma.org
Annual. **Primary Exhibits:** Providing information covering all aspects of marketing, including internet, radio, phone, internet, TV, and mail.

★7865★ The Incentive Show
VNU Expositions
14685 Avion Pkwy., Ste. 400
Chantilly, VA 20151
Ph: (703)488-2700   Fax: (703)488-2800
Fr: 800-765-7615
URL: http://www.vnuexpo.com
Annual. **Primary Exhibits:** Provides information on incentive awards, promotion products and advertising specialties, gift certificates and debit cards, and incentive travel.

★7866★ International Advertising Association - World Advertising Congress

International Advertising Association
521 5th Ave., Ste. 1807
New York, NY 10175
Ph: (212)557-1133   Fax: (212)983-0455
URL: http://www.iaaglobal.org

Biennial. **Primary Exhibits:** Advertising services.

★7867★ International Collegiate Conference

American Marketing Association
311 S. Wacker Dr., Ste. 5800
Chicago, IL 60606
Ph: (312)542-9000   Fax: (312)542-9001
Fr: 800-AMA-1150
E-mail: info@ama.org
URL: http://www.marketingpower.com/

Annual. **Primary Exhibits:** Provides career development and chapter management information. Includes demonstrations of collegiate chapter activities.

★7868★ Marketing and Business Expo

New York/New Jersey Minority
  Purchasing Council, Inc.
1270 Broadway, Ste. 606
New York, NY 10001
Ph: (212)502-5663   Fax: (212)502-5807
URL: http://www.nynjmpc.org

Primary Exhibits: Marketing and business information, supplies, and services.

★7869★ Marketing Research Conference

American Marketing Association
311 S. Wacker Dr., Ste. 5800
Chicago, IL 60606
Ph: (312)542-9000   Fax: (312)542-9001
Fr: 800-AMA-1150
E-mail: info@ama.org
URL: http://www.marketingpower.com/

Annual. **Primary Exhibits:** Marketing research products and services.

★7870★ National Center for Database Marketing

Cowles Event Management
220 Thunderbird
El Paso, TX 79912
Ph: (915)585-2041

Primary Exhibits: Database marketing industry exhibition.

★7871★ National Marketing Conference

Society for Marketing Professional
  Services
99 Canal Center Plaza, Ste. 300
Alexandria, VA 22314
Ph: 800-292-7677   Fax: (703)549-2498
E-mail: info@smps.org
URL: http://www.smps.org

Annual. **Primary Exhibits:** New business

development equipment, supplies, and services.

★7872★ Net.Marketing Conference and Exhibition

Direct Marketing Association
1120 Ave. of the Americas
New York, NY 10036-6700
Ph: (212)768-7277   Fax: (212)302-6714
Fr: 800-255-0006
E-mail: customerservice@the-dma.org
URL: http://www.the-dma.org

Primary Exhibits: Direct marketing information, supplies and services.

★7873★ Point-of-Purchase Advertising Institute Marketplace

Point-of-Purchase Advertising Institute
1660 Duke St., Ste. 400
Alexandria, VA 22314
Ph: (703)373-8800   Fax: (703)373-8801
E-mail: info@popai.com
URL: http://www.popai.com

Annual. **Primary Exhibits:** Point-of-purchase displays for use in retail establishments, including displays of personal products and accessories, household goods, foods and paper goods, beverages, farm supplies, agricultural supplies, garden supplies, transportation items, health and beauty aids, services, hardware, and building materials.

★7874★ PPAI Expo

Promotional Products Association
  International
3125 Skyway Cir. N.
Irving, TX 75038-3526
Ph: (972)258-3100   Fax: (972)258-3003
Fr: 888-492-6890
E-mail: expo@ppa.org
URL: http://www.ppa.org

Annual. **Primary Exhibits:** Specialty advertising and business gifts.

OTHER SOURCES

★7875★ ABA Marketing Network

1120 Connecticut Ave. NW
Washington, DC 20036
Fax: (202)828-4540   Fr: 800-BAN-KERS
E-mail: marketingnetwork@aba.com
URL: http://www.aba.com/MarketingNetwork/default.htm

Members: Marketing and public relations executives for commercial and savings banks, credit unions, and savings and loans associations, and related groups such as advertising agencies and research firms. **Purpose:** Provides marketing education, information, and services to the financial services industry. **Activities:** Conducts research; cosponsors summer sessions of fundamentals and advanced courses in mar-

keting at the University of Colorado at Boulder; compiles statistics.

★7876★ Academy of Marketing Science (AMS)

University of Miami
School of Business Administration
PO Box 248012
Coral Gables, FL 33124-6536
Ph: (305)284-6673   Fax: (305)284-3762
E-mail: ams.sba@miami.edu
URL: http://www.ams-web.org

Description: Marketing academicians and practitioners; individuals interested in fostering education in marketing science. Aims to promote the advancement of knowledge and the furthering of professional standards in the field of marketing. Explores the special application areas of marketing science and its responsibilities as an economic, ethical, and social force; promotes research and the widespread dissemination of findings. Facilitates exchange of information and experience among members, and the transfer of marketing knowledge and technology to developing countries; promotes marketing science on an international level. Provides a forum for discussion and refinement of concepts, methods and applications, and the opportunity to publish papers in the field. Assists member educators in the development of improved teaching methods, devices, directions, and materials. Offers guidance and direction in marketing practice and reviewer assistance on scholarly works. Contributes to the solution of marketing problems encountered by individual firms, industries, and society as a whole. Encourages members to utilize their marketing talents to the fullest through redirection, reassignment, and relocation. Sponsors competitions.

★7877★ Administration and Management Occupations

Delphi Productions
3159 6th St.
Boulder, CO 80304
Ph: (303)443-2100   Fax: (303)443-4022
Fr: 888-443-2400
E-mail: support@delphivideo.com
URL: http://www.delphivideo.com

$95.00. 50 minutes. Part of the Careers for the 21st Century Video Library.

★7878★ Advertising Club of New York (ACNY)

235 Park Ave. S, 6th Fl.
New York, NY 10003-1405
Ph: (212)533-8080   Fax: (212)533-1929
E-mail: gina@theadvertisingclub.org
URL: http://www.theadvertisingclub.org

Members: Professionals in advertising, publishing, marketing, and business. **Purpose:** Sponsors educational and public service activities, promotional and public relations projects, and talks by celebrities and advertising persons. **Activities:** Conducts annual advertising and marketing course, which offers classes in copywriting, special graphics, verbal communication, advertising production, sale promotion, marketing and management. Sponsors competitions and charitable programs.

★7879★ **Advertising Council (AC)**
261 Madison Ave., 11th Fl.
New York, NY 10016-2303
Ph: (212)922-1500   Fax: (212)922-1676
Fr: 800-933-7727
E-mail: info@adcouncil.org
URL: http://www.adcouncil.org

Members: Founded and supported by American business, media, and advertising sectors to conduct public service advertising campaigns. **Purpose:** Encourages advertising media to contribute time and space and advertising agencies to supply creative talent and facilities to further timely national causes. **Activities:** Specific campaigns include: Drug Abuse Prevention; AIDS Prevention; Teen-Alcoholism; Child Abuse; Crime Prevention; Forest Fire Prevention.

★7880★ **Advertising and Marketing International Network (AMIN)**
12323 Nantucket
Wichita, KS 67235
Ph: (316)531-2342
E-mail: vaughn.sink@shscom.com
URL: http://www.aminworldwide.com

Members: Comprised of cooperative worldwide network of non-competing independent advertising agencies organized to provide facilities and branch office services for affiliated agencies.

★7881★ **Advertising Women of New York (AWNY)**
25 W 45th St., Ste. 403
New York, NY 10036
Ph: (212)221-7969   Fax: (212)221-8296
E-mail: awny@awny.org
URL: http://www.awny.org

Description: Women in advertising and related industries that provides a forum for professional growth, serves as catalyst for enhancement and advancement of women; promotes philanthropic endeavors. Conducts events of interest and benefit to members and non-members involved in the industry. Membership concentrated in the metropolitan New York area.

★7882★ **American Academy of Advertising (AAA)**
College of Mass Communications
Texas Tech University
Box 43082
Lubbock, TX 79409-3082
Ph: (806)742-3385   Fax: (806)742-1085
E-mail: donald.jugenheimer@ttu.edu
URL: http://www.aaasite.org

Description: Serves as a professional organization for college and university teachers of advertising.

★7883★ **American Advertising Federation (AAF)**
1101 Vermont Ave. NW, Ste. 500
Washington, DC 20005-6306
Ph: (202)898-0089   Fax: (202)898-0159
E-mail: aaf@aaf.org
URL: http://www.aaf.org

Purpose: Works to advance the business of advertising as a vital and essential part of the American economy and culture through government and public relations; professional development and recognition; community service, social responsibility and high standards; and benefits and services to members. **Activities:** Operates Advertising Hall of Fame, Hall of Achievement, and National Student Advertising Competition. Maintains Speaker's Bureau.

★7884★ **American Association of Advertising Agencies (AAAA)**
405 Lexington Ave., 18th Fl.
New York, NY 10174-1801
Ph: (212)682-2500   Fax: (212)682-8391
E-mail: tfinneran@aaaa.org
URL: http://www.aaaa.org

Purpose: Fosters development of the advertising industry; assists member agencies to operate more efficiently and profitably. **Activities:** Sponsors member information and international services. Maintains 47 committees. Conducts government relations.

★7885★ **American Society of Association Executives (ASAE)**
1575 I St. NW
Washington, DC 20005
Ph: (202)371-0940   Fax: (202)371-8315
Fr: 888-950-2723
E-mail: pr@asaenet.org
URL: http://www.asaecenter.org

Members: Professional society of paid executives of international, national, state, and local trade, professional, and philanthropic associations. **Purpose:** Seeks to educate association executives on effective management, including: the proper objectives, functions, and activities of associations; the basic principles of association management; the legal aspects of association activity; policies relating to association management; efficient methods, procedures, and techniques of association management; the responsibilities and professional standards of association executives. Maintains information resource center. **Activities:** Conducts resume, guidance, and consultation services; compiles statistics in the form of reports, surveys, and studies; carries out research and education. Maintains ASAE Services Corporation to provide special services and ASAE Foundation to do future-oriented research and make grant awards. Offers executive search services and insurance programs. Provides CEO center for chief staff executives. Conducts Certified Association Executive (CAE) program.

★7886★ **American Wholesale Marketers Association (AWMA)**
2750 Prosperity Ave., Ste. 530
Fairfax, VA 22031
Ph: (703)208-3358   Fax: (703)573-5738
Fr: 800-482-2962
E-mail: info@awmanet.org
URL: http://www.awmanet.org

Description: Represents the interests of distributors of convenience products. Its members include wholesalers, retailers, manufacturers, brokers and allied organizations from across the U.S. and abroad. Programs include strong legislative representation in Washington and a broad spectrum of targeted education, business and information services. Sponsors the country's largest show for candy and convenience related products in conjunction with its semi-annual convention.

★7887★ **ARF - Advertising Research Foundation (ARF)**
432 Park Ave. S
New York, NY 10016
Ph: (212)751-5656   Fax: (212)319-5265
E-mail: info@thearf.org
URL: http://www.thearf.org

Members: Advertisers, advertising agencies, research organizations, associations, and the media are regular members of the foundation; colleges and universities are associate members. **Purpose:** Objectives are to: further scientific practices and promote greater effectiveness of advertising and marketing by means of objective and impartial research; develop new research methods and techniques; analyze and evaluate existing methods and techniques, and define proper applications; establish research standards, criteria, and reporting methods. **Activities:** Compiles statistics and conducts research programs.

★7888★ **Association of Independent Commercial Producers (AICP)**
3 W 18th St., 5th Fl.
New York, NY 10011
Ph: (212)929-3000   Fax: (212)929-3359
E-mail: info@aicp.com
URL: http://www.aicp.com

Description: Represents the interests of companies that specialize in producing television commercials for advertisers and agencies, and the businesses that furnish supplies and services to this industry. Serves as a collective voice for the industry before government and business councils, and in union negotiations; disseminates information; works to develop industry standards and tools; provides professional development; and markets American production.

★7889★ **Association of National Advertisers (ANA)**
708 Third Ave.
New York, NY 10017-4270
Ph: (212)697-5950   Fax: (212)661-8057
E-mail: rliodice@ana.net
URL: http://www.ana.net

Description: Serves the needs of members by providing marketing and advertising industry leadership in traditional and e-marketing, legislative leadership, information resources, professional development and industry-wide networking. Maintains offices in New York City and Washington, DC.

★7890★ **Association for Women in Communications (AWC)**

3337 Duke St.
Alexandria, VA 22314
Ph: (703)370-7436   Fax: (703)370-7437
E-mail: info@womcom.org
URL: http://www.womcom.org

Description: Professional association of journalism and communications.

★7891★ **Business Marketing Association (BMA)**

401 N Michigan Ave., Ste. 1200
Chicago, IL 60611
Ph: (312)822-0005   Fax: (312)822-0054
Fr: 800-664-4262
E-mail: bma@marketing.org
URL: http://www.marketing.org

Description: Business-to-business marketing and communications professionals working in business, industry and the professions. Develops and delivers benefits, services, information, skill enhancement, and networking opportunities to help members grow, develop, and succeed throughout business-to-business careers.

★7892★ **Cabletelevision Advertising Bureau (CAB)**

830 Third Ave., 2nd Fl.
New York, NY 10022
Ph: (212)508-1200   Fax: (212)832-3268
E-mail: cynthiap@cabletvadbureau.com
URL: http://www.onetvworld.org

Members: Ad-supported cable networks.
Purpose: Provides marketing and advertising support to members and promotes the use of cable by advertisers and ad agencies locally, regionally, and nationally.

★7893★ **Direct Marketing Educational Foundation (DMEF)**

1120 Ave. of the Americas
New York, NY 10036-6700
Ph: (212)768-7277   Fax: (212)790-1561
E-mail: dmef@the-dma.org
URL: http://www.the-dma.org/dmef

Description: Represents individuals, firms, and organizations interested in furthering college-level education in direct marketing. Functions as the collegiate arm of the direct marketing profession. Sponsors a summer internship, programs for students and professors, and campaign competition for students. Provides educational materials and course outlines to faculty members; arranges for speakers for college classes and clubs. Co-sponsors academic research competitions. Maintains hall of fame.

★7894★ **Hispanic Marketing and Communication Association (HMCA)**

PO Box 565891
Miami, FL 33256-5891
Ph: (305)648-2848
E-mail: hmca@hmca.org
URL: http://www.hmca.org

Description: Represents individuals of diverse backgrounds with a common interest in the Hispanic market in the United States, Latin America and the Caribbean. Promotes excellence in Hispanic marketing. Encourages professional development. Provides opportunities to network among practitioners who practice or have an interest in the Hispanic Market.

★7895★ **Intermarket Agency Network (IAN)**

5307 S 92nd St.
Hales Corners, WI 53130
Ph: (414)425-8800   Fax: (414)425-0021
E-mail: bille@nonbox.com
URL: http://www.intermarketnetwork.com

Description: An active network of high-powered marketing/communications agencies in the United States, Canada, Central and South America, and Europe.

★7896★ **International Advertising Association (IAA)**

521 5th Ave., Ste. 1807
New York, NY 10175
Ph: (212)557-1133   Fax: (212)983-0455
E-mail: iaa@iaaglobal.org
URL: http://www.iaaglobal.org

Members: Global network of advertisers, advertising agencies, the media and related services, spanning 99 countries. **Purpose:** Demonstrates to governments and consumers the benefits of advertising as the foundation of diverse, independent media. Protects and advances freedom of commercial speech and consumer choice, encourages greater practice and acceptance of advertising self-regulation, provides a forum to debate emerging professional marketing communications issues and their consequences in the fast-changing world environment, and takes the lead in state-of-the-art professional development through education and training for the marketing communications industry of tomorrow. **Activities:** Conducts research on such topics as restrictions and taxes on advertising, advertising trade practices and related information, and advertising expenditures around the world. Sponsors IAA Education Program. Has compiled recommendations for international advertising standards and practices.

★7897★ **International Design Guild (IDG)**

670 Commercial St.
Manchester, NH 03101
Fr: 800-205-4345
E-mail: info@design-guild.com
URL: http://www.design-guild.com

Description: Brings together interior designers to share and gain insight for business

development and networking. Provides members with customizable marketing, merchandising, educational and operational tools. Aims to help members operate their businesses more profitably.

★7898★ **Los Angeles Advertising Agencies Association (LAAAA)**

4223 Glencoe Ave., Ste. C-100
Marina del Rey, CA 90292
Ph: (310)823-7320   Fax: (310)823-7325
E-mail: submissions@laaaa.com
URL: http://www.laaaa.com

Purpose: Assists heads of advertising agencies in the Western U.S. to operate their agencies more effectively and profitably. Offers assistance to agency management and staff. Provides a forum for discussion and exchange of information. Promotes members' interests.

★7899★ **Mailing and Fulfillment Service Association (MFSA)**

1421 Prince St., Ste. 410
Alexandria, VA 22314-2806
Ph: (703)836-9200   Fax: (703)548-8204
Fr: 800-333-6272
E-mail: mfsa-mail@mfsanet.org
URL: http://www.mfsanet.org

Members: Commercial direct mail producers, letter shops, mailing list houses, fulfillment operations, and advertising agencies. **Activities:** Conducts special interest group meetings. Offers specialized education; conducts research programs.

★7900★ **Marketing and Advertising Global Network (MAGNET)**

1017 Perry Hwy., Ste. 5
Pittsburgh, PA 15237
Ph: (412)366-6850   Fax: (412)366-6840
E-mail: mxdirector@verizon.net
URL: http://www.magnetglobal.org

Members: Cooperative network of non-competing advertising, marketing, merchandising, and public relations agencies. **Purpose:** Aims to bring about, through mutual cooperation, greater accomplishment and efficiency in the management of member advertising agencies. Other goals are: to raise standards of the advertising agency business through the exchange of information relative to agency management and all phases of advertising; to exchange information on all common problems, such as management, sales development, market studies, agency functions, and operations. Aims to inform the general public of current global marketing trends.

★7901★ **Marketing Agencies Association Worldwide (MAA)**

460 Summer St., 4th Fl.
Stamford, CT 06901
Ph: (203)978-1590   Fax: (203)969-1499
E-mail: keith.mccracken@maaw.org
URL: http://www.maaw.org

Description: Represents the interests of CEOs, presidents, managing directors and principals of top marketing services agencies. Provides opportunity for marketing professionals to meet with peers, raise company profile on both a national and a global platform, and influence the future of industry. Fosters networking through conferences.

★7902★ **Marketing Research Association (MRA)**

110 National Dr., 2nd Fl.
Glastonbury, CT 06033-1212
Ph: (860)682-1000   Fax: (860)682-1010
E-mail: larry.brownell@mra-net.org
URL: http://www.mra-net.org

Members: Companies and individuals involved in any area of opinion and marketing research, such as data collection, research, or as an end-user.

★7903★ **Marketing & Sales Occupations**

Delphi Productions
3159 6th St.
Boulder, CO 80304
Ph: (303)443-2100   Fax: (303)443-4022
Fr: 888-443-2400
E-mail: support@delphivideo.com
URL: http://www.delphivideo.com

$95.00. 50 minutes. Part of the Careers for the 21st Century Video Library.

★7904★ **National Alliance of Market Developers (NAMD)**

620 Sheridan Ave.
Plainfield, NJ 07060
Ph: (908)561-4062   Fax: (908)561-6827
E-mail: allenpartner@earthlink.net
URL: http://www.namdntl.org

Description: Professionals engaged in marketing, sales, sales promotion, advertising, or public relations who are concerned with the delivery of goods and services to the minority consumer market.

★7905★ **National Management Association (NMA)**

2210 Arbor Blvd.
Dayton, OH 45439
Ph: (937)294-0421   Fax: (937)294-2374
E-mail: nma@nma1.org
URL: http://www.nma1.org

Description: Business and industrial management personnel; membership comes from supervisory level, with the remainder from middle management and above. Seeks to develop and recognize management as a profession and to promote the free enterprise system. Prepares chapter programs on basic management, management policy and practice, communications, human behavior, industrial relations, economics, political education, and liberal education. Maintains speakers' bureau and hall of fame. Maintains educational, charitable, and research programs. Sponsors charitable programs.

★7906★ **National School Public Relations Association (NSPRA)**

15948 Derwood Rd.
Rockville, MD 20855-2123
Ph: (301)519-0496   Fax: (301)519-0494
E-mail: nspra@nspra.org
URL: http://www.nspra.org

Description: Represents school system public relations directors, school administrators, and others interested in furthering public understanding of the public schools. Has adopted standards for public relations professionals and programs and an accreditation program.

★7907★ **Outdoor Advertising Association of America (OAAA)**

1850 M St. NW, Ste. 1040
Washington, DC 20036
Ph: (202)833-5566   Fax: (202)833-1522
E-mail: kklein@oaaa.org
URL: http://www.oaaa.org

Members: Firms owning, erecting, and maintaining standardized poster panels and painted display advertising facilities. Aims to provide leadership, services, and standards to promote, protect and advance the outdoor advertising industry.

★7908★ **Point-of-Purchase Advertising International (POPAI)**

1600 Duke St., Ste. 400
Alexandria, VA 22314
Ph: (703)373-8800   Fax: (703)373-8801
E-mail: info@popai.com
URL: http://www.popai.com

Members: Producers and suppliers of point-of-purchase advertising signs and displays and national and regional advertisers and retailers interested in use and effectiveness of signs, displays, and other point-of-purchase media. **Activities:** Conducts student education programs; maintains speakers' bureau.

★7909★ **Polaris International North American Network (PINAN)**

3700 Crestwood Pkwy., Ste. 350
Duluth, GA 30096
Ph: (770)279-4560   Fax: (770)279-4566
E-mail: rbeilfuss@pkfnan.org
URL: http://www.pkfnan.org

Members: Independent certified public accounting firms practicing on a regional or local basis. **Purpose:** Objectives are to: strengthen accounting practices; increase competency and quality of service; provide a practice management program; maintain technical competence in accounting principles and auditing standards; make available a reservoir of specialists who are immediately accessible to members; provide for the sharing of skills, knowledge and experience. **Activities:** Offers technical, marketing, and public relations support; promotes continuing professional education; facilitates networking. Conducts 4 staff development, 2 tax training, and 3 manager/partner training courses per year; operates committees and task forces.

★7910★ **Promotion Marketing Association (PMA)**

257 Park Ave. S, 11th Fl.
New York, NY 10010-7304
Ph: (212)420-1100   Fax: (212)533-7622
E-mail: pma@pmalink.org
URL: http://www.pmalink.org

Description: Fortune 500 marketer companies, promotion agencies, and companies using promotion programs; supplier members are manufacturers of package goods, cosmetics, and pharmaceuticals, consultants, and advertising agencies. Conducts surveys and studies of industry issues.

★7911★ **Promotional Products Association International (PPAI)**

3125 Skyway Cir. N
Irving, TX 75038-3526
Ph: (972)252-0404   Fax: (972)258-3007
Fr: 888-IAM-PPAI
E-mail: steves@ppa.org
URL: http://www.ppa.org

Members: Suppliers and distributors of promotional products including incentives, imprinted ad specialties, premiums, and executive gifts. **Purpose:** Promotes industry contacts in 60 countries. **Activities:** Holds executive development and sales training seminars. Conducts research and compiles statistics. Administers industry advertising and public relations program. Maintains speakers' bureau. Conducts trade shows, regional training, publishes educational resources.

★7912★ **Public Relations Society of America (PRSA)**

33 Maiden Ln., 11th Fl.
New York, NY 10038-5150
Ph: (212)460-1400   Fax: (212)995-0757
E-mail: exec@prsa.org
URL: http://www.prsa.org

Description: Professional society of public relations practitioners in business and industry, counseling firms, government, associations, hospitals, schools, and nonprofit organizations. Conducts professional development programs. Maintains a Professional Resource Center. Offers accreditation program.

★7913★ **Retail Advertising and Marketing Association (RAMA)**

325 7th St. NW, Ste. 1100
Washington, DC 20004-2818
Ph: (202)661-3052   Fax: (202)737-2849
E-mail: perweilerp@rama-nrf.com
URL: http://www.rama-nrf.org

Members: Persons in retail sales promotion, advertising, and marketing, and persons serving retailers in promotional capacities. **Activities:** Elects one professional to the Retail Advertising Hall of Fame. Conducts research programs.

★7914★ Society for Marketing Professional Services (SMPS)
99 Canal Center Plz., Ste. 330
Alexandria, VA 22314
Ph: (703)549-6117   Fax: (703)549-2498
Fr: 800-292-7677
E-mail: info@smps.org
URL: http://www.smps.org

Members: Marketing employees of architectural, engineering, planning, interior design, landscape architectural, and construction management firms who are responsible for the new business development of their companies. **Activities:** Compiles statistics. Offers local and national educational programs; maintains certification program.

★7915★ Transworld Advertising Agency Network (TAAN)
7920 Summer Lake Ct.
Fort Myers, FL 33907
Ph: (239)433-0669   Fax: (239)433-1366
E-mail: info@taan.org
URL: http://www.taan.org

Members: Independently owned advertising agencies that cooperate for exchange of management education and information, reciprocal service, and personal local contact. **Purpose:** Allows members to seek aid of other members in campaign planning, creative services, merchandising, public relations, publicity, media, research, and test facilities. **Activities:** Conducts annual expertise audit.

★7916★ Women in Direct Marketing International (WDMI)
200 Cir. Dr. N
Piscataway, NJ 08854
Ph: (732)469-8414
E-mail: bladden@directmaildepot.com
URL: http://www.wdmi.org

Description: Direct marketing professionals. Seeks to: advance the interests and influence of women in the direct response industry; provide for communication and career education; assist in advancement of personal career objectives; serve as professional network to develop business contacts and foster mutual goals. Maintains career talent bank. Distributes information nationally; maintains other chapters in Chicago, IL, Los Angeles, CA, Dallas, TX, Japan, UK, and Belgium.

Marriage and Family Counselors

SOURCES OF HELP-WANTED ADS

★7917★ American Journal of Family Therapy

MetaPress
PO Box 1943
Birmingham, AL 35201
Fr: 877-773-3833

Quarterly. $248.00/year for individuals, one year. Periodical covering the techniques for treating families, theory on normal and dysfunctional family relationships, research on sexuality and intimacy, the effects of traditional and alternative family styles, and community approaches to family intervention. Also includes family measurement techniques, family behavioral medicine and health, family law issues in family therapy practice, and continuing education and training.

★7918★ Family Relations

National Council on Family Relations
3989 Central Ave. NE, Ste. 550
Minneapolis, MN 55421
Ph: (763)781-9331   Fax: (763)781-9348
Fr: 888-781-9331
E-mail: fr@iog.wayne.edu
URL: http://www.blackwell-synergy.com

Quarterly. $120.00/year for individuals, non-member, print and online; $50.00/year for students, print and standard online. Publication for family practitioners and academics on relationships across the life cycle with implications for intervention, education and public policy.

★7919★ Family Therapy

Libra Publishers Inc.
3089 C Clairemont Dr., Ste. 383
San Diego, CA 92117
Ph: (858)571-1414   Fax: (858)571-1414

$87.00/year for individuals; $29.00 for single issue. Journal covering clinical, family, group, and interactional therapy.

★7920★ Family Therapy News

American Association for Marriage and Family Therapy
112 S Alfred St.
Alexandria, VA 22314-3061
Ph: (703)838-9808   Fax: (703)838-9805
E-mail: central@aamft.org
URL: http://www.aamft.org

Description: Bimonthly. Provides broad coverage of news in the field of marital and family therapy. Reports legislative and other governmental and organizational developments affecting families. Recurring features include letters to the editor, interviews with leading therapists, information on workshops and conferences, and regional news.

★7921★ Journal of Counseling Psychology

American Psychological Association
750 1st St. NE
Washington, DC 20002-4242
Ph: (202)336-5540   Fax: (202)336-5549
Fr: 800-374-2721
E-mail: journals@apa.org
URL: http://www.apa.org/journals/cou.html

Quarterly. $50.00/year for members, domestic; $66.00/year for members, foreign, surface freight; $78.00/year for members, foreign, air mail; $29.00/year for students, domestic; $45.00/year for students, foreign, surface freight; $57.00/year for students, foreign, air mail; $98.00/year for nonmembers, domestic; $119.00/year for nonmembers, foreign, surface freight; $129.00/year for nonmembers, foreign, air mail; $267.00/year for institutions, domestic. Journal presenting empirical studies about counseling processes and interventions, theoretical articles about counseling, and studies dealing with evaluation of counseling applications and programs.

★7922★ Journal of Couple and Relationship Therapy

The Haworth Press Inc.
10 Alice St.
Binghamton, NY 13904
Ph: (607)722-5857   Fr: 800-429-6784
URL: http://www.haworthpress.com/store/product.asp?sku=J398

Quarterly. $48.00/year for individuals; $70.00/year for Canada, individuals; $74.00/year for other countries, individuals; $360.00/year for institutions, agency, library; $522.00/year for institutions, Canada, agency, library; $558.00/year for institutions, other countries, agency, library. Journal presenting clinical, theoretical, and research articles on a wide array of couple and adult relationship treatment issues.

★7923★ Journal of Divorce and Remarriage

The Haworth Press Inc.
10 Alice St.
Binghamton, NY 13904
Ph: (607)722-5857   Fr: 800-429-6784
URL: http://www.haworthpress.com/store/product.asp?sid=55UH6X1U2K

$84.00/year for individuals; $123.00/year for Canada, individuals; $129.00/year for other countries, individuals; $720.00/year for institutions, agency, library; $1,036.00/year for institutions, Canada, agency, library; $1,104.00/year for institutions, other countries, agency, library. Journal covering all aspects of divorce, including pre-divorce marital and family treatment, marital separation and dissolution, children's responses to divorce and separation, single parenting, remarriage, and stepfamilies.

★7924★ Journal of Family Issues

Sage Publications Inc.
2455 Teller Rd.
Thousand Oaks, CA 91320
Ph: (805)499-0721   Fax: (805)499-8096
E-mail: advertising@sagepub.com
URL: http://www.sagepub.com/journal.aspx?pid=163

Monthly. $146.00/year for individuals, print only; $1,077.00/year for institutions, combined (print & e-access); $1,131.00/year for institutions, backfile lease, combined plus backfile, print; $969.00/year for institutions, e-access; $1,023.00/year for institutions, all online; $1,565.00/year for institutions, backfile purchase, e-access; $1,055.00/year for institutions, print only; $146.00/year for institutions, single print issue; $24.00/year for individuals, single print issue. Family studies journal.

★7925★ **Journal of Family Psychology**
American Psychological Association
750 1st St. NE
Washington, DC 20002-4242
Ph: (202)336-5540   Fax: (202)336-5549
Fr: 800-374-2721
E-mail: journals@apa.org
URL: http://www.apa.org/journals/fam.html

Quarterly. $55.00/year for members, domestic; $71.00/year for members, foreign surface freight; $83.00/year for members, foreign air freight; $36.00/year for students, domestic; $52.00/year for students, foreign, surface freight; $64.00/year for students, foreign, air freight; $120.00/year for nonmembers, domestic; $141.00/year for nonmembers, foreign, surface freight; $151.00/year for nonmembers, foreign, air freight; $298.00/year for institutions, domestic. Journal reporting on theory, research, and clinical practice in family psychology; including articles on family and marital theory and concepts, research and evaluation, therapeutic frameworks and methods, and policies and legal matters concerning family and marriage.

★7926★ **Journal of Family Psychotherapy**
The Haworth Press Inc.
10 Alice St.
Binghamton, NY 13904
Ph: (607)722-5857   Fr: 800-429-6784
URL: http://www.haworthpress.com/store/product.asp?sid=3CXTKNPDX

Quarterly. Journal includes case studies, treatment reports, and strategies in clinical practice for psychotherapists.

★7927★ **Journal of Family Social Work**
The Haworth Press Inc.
10 Alice St.
Binghamton, NY 13904
Ph: (607)722-5857   Fr: 800-429-6784
URL: http://www.haworthpress.com/store/product.asp?sid=9LJ67H8WF

Quarterly. $99.00/year for U.S., individual; $145.00/year for Canada, individual; $152.00/year for other countries, individual; $255.00/year for institutions, agency, library; $362.00/year for institutions, Canada, agency, library; $383.00/year for institutions, other countries, agency, library. Journal serves as a forum for family practitioners, scholars, and educators in the field of social work.

★7928★ **Journal of Feminist Family Therapy**
The Haworth Press Inc.
10 Alice St.
Binghamton, NY 13904
Ph: (607)722-5857   Fr: 800-429-6784
URL: http://www.haworthpress.com/store/product.asp?sid=9LJ67H8WF

Quarterly. $60.00/year for individuals; $87.00/year for individuals, Canada; $93.00/year for individuals, other countries;

$495.00/year for institutions, agency, library; $718.00/year for institutions, Canada, agency, library; $767.00/year for institutions, other countries, agency, library. Journal exploring the relationship between feminist theory and family therapy practice and theory.

★7929★ **Journal of Marital & Family Therapy**
American Association for Marriage and Family Therapy
112 South Alfred St.
Alexandria, VA 22314-3061
Ph: (703)838-9808   Fax: (703)838-9805
URL: http://www.aamft.org/

Quarterly. $69.99/year for members; $119.99/year for individuals. Journal for professional therapists. Covers clinical techniques, research, and theory of marital and family therapy.

★7930★ **Journal of Marriage and Family**
National Council on Family Relations
3989 Central Ave. NE, Ste. 550
Minneapolis, MN 55421
Ph: (763)781-9331   Fax: (763)781-9348
Fr: 888-781-9331
URL: http://www.ncfr.org/jmf

Quarterly. Publication in the family field featuring original research and theory, research interpretation, and critical discussion related to marriage and the family.

★7931★ **Marriage and Family Review**
The Haworth Press Inc.
10 Alice St.
Binghamton, NY 13904
Ph: (607)722-5857   Fr: 800-429-6784
URL: http://www.haworthpress.com/store/product.asp?sid=9LJ67H8WF

$75.00/year for individuals; $600.00/year for institutions, agency, library; $109.00/year for Canada, individual; $870.00/year for institutions, Canada, agency, library; $116.00/year for other countries, individual; $930.00/year for institutions, other countries, agency, library. Journal for socially oriented and clinically oriented marriage and family specialists in a broad range of research and applied disciplines.

★7932★ **Monitor on Psychology**
American Psychological Association
750 1st St. NE
Washington, DC 20002-4242
Ph: (202)336-5540   Fax: (202)336-5549
Fr: 800-374-2721
E-mail: journals@apa.org
URL: http://www.apa.org/monitor/

Monthly. $46.00/year for nonmembers; $86.00/year for individuals, foreign, surface freight; $113.00/year for individuals, foreign, air freight; $87.00/year for institutions, nonmember, foreign, surface freight; $168.00/year for institutions, foreign, air freight; $195.00/year for institutions, air freight; $3.00/year for single issue. Magazine of the APA. Reports on the science, profession,

and social responsibility of psychology, including latest legislative developments affecting mental health, education, and research support.

★7933★ **National Council News**
National Council for Community Behavioral Healthcare
12300 Twinbrook Pkwy., Ste. 320
Rockville, MD 20852
Ph: (301)984-6200   Fax: (301)881-7159
E-mail: Communications@thenationalcouncil.org
URL: http://www.nccbh.org/SERVICE/Bookstore/nc-news.htm

Description: Monthly. Dedicated to increasing the quality and accessibility of community mental health services. Recurring features include interviews, a calendar of events, news of educational opportunities, book reviews, marketplace news, and job listings.

★7934★ **Sage Family Studies Abstracts**
Sage Publications Inc.
2455 Teller Rd.
Thousand Oaks, CA 91320
Ph: (805)499-0721   Fax: (805)499-8096
E-mail: advertising@sagepub.com
URL: http://www.sagepub.com/journal.aspx?pid=141

Quarterly. $951.00/year for institutions, print only; $209.00/year for individuals, print only; $262.00 for single issue, institutional; $68.00 for single issue, individual. Journal containing family studies abstracts.

PLACEMENT AND JOB REFERRAL SERVICES

★7935★ **Alliance for Children and Families (ACF)**
11700 W Lake Park Dr.
Milwaukee, WI 53224-3099
Ph: (414)359-1040   Fax: (414)359-1074
E-mail: info@alliance1.org
URL: http://www.alliance1.org

Description: Membership organization of local agencies in more than 1,000 communities providing family counseling, family life education and family advocacy services, and other programs to help families with parent-child, marital, mental health, and other problems of family living. Assists member agencies in developing and providing effective family services. Works with the media, government, and corporations to promote strong family life. Compiles statistics; conducts research. Maintains extensive files of unpublished materials from member agencies. Offers career placement services.

EMPLOYER DIRECTORIES AND NETWORKING LISTS

★7936★ Magill's Encyclopedia of Social Science

Salem Press Inc.
2 University Plz., Ste. 121
Hackensack, NJ 07601
Ph: (201)968-9899   Fax: (201)968-1411
Fr: 800-221-1592
URL: http://www.salempress.com

Published January 2003. $404.00 for individuals. Publication includes: Lists of Web sites, organizations, and support groups in the field of psychology. Principal content of publication consists of entries on psychology including specific disorders, diagnosis, and therapies. Indexes: Alphabetical.

★7937★ Mental Help Net

CenterSite L.L.C.
PO Box 20709
Columbus, OH 43220
Ph: (614)448-4055   Fax: (614)448-4055
URL: http://www.mentalhelp.net

Covers resources for finding mental help, including local therapists and self-help groups, as well as services such as upcoming conferences, professional education, and universities offering degrees in mental health fields.

HANDBOOKS AND MANUALS

★7938★ Careers in Counseling & Human Services

Accelerated Development
7625 Empire Dr.
Florence, KY 41042
Fr: 800-821-8312
URL: http://www.tandf.co.uk/homepages/a-dhome.html

Brooke B. Collison and Nancy J. Garfield, editors. Second edition, 1996. $32.95 (paper). 153 pages.

★7939★ Careers in Social and Rehabilitation Services

The McGraw-Hill Companies
PO Box 182604
Columbus, OH 43272
Fax: (614)759-3749   Fr: 877-883-5524
E-mail: customer.service@mcgraw-hill.com
URL: http://www.mcgraw-hill.com

Geraldine O. Garner. 2001. $19.95; 14.95 (paper). 128 pages.

★7940★ Great Jobs for Liberal Arts Majors

The McGraw-Hill Companies
PO Box 182604
Columbus, OH 43272
Fax: (614)759-3749   Fr: 877-883-5524

E-mail: customer.service@mcgraw-hill.com
URL: http://www.mcgraw-hill.com

Blythe Camenson. Second edition, 2001. $14.95 (paper). 256 pages.

★7941★ Opportunities in Counseling and Development Careers

The McGraw-Hill Companies
PO Box 182604
Columbus, OH 43272
Fax: (614)759-3749   Fr: 877-883-5524
E-mail: customer.service@mcgraw-hill.com
URL: http://www.mcgraw-hill.com

Neale J.Baxter, Mark U. Toch, and Philip A. Perry. 1997. $14.95; $11.95 (paper). 160 pages. A guide to planning for and seeking opportunities in this challenging field. Illustrated.

TRADESHOWS

★7942★ American Counseling Association World Conference

American Counseling Association
5999 Stevenson Ave.
Alexandria, VA 22304-3300
Ph: (703)823-9800   Fax: (703)823-6862
Fr: 800-347-6647
E-mail: meetings@counseling.org
URL: http://www.counseling.org

Annual. **Primary Exhibits:** Books, career development information, college selection, student financial aid, testing and measurement techniques, practice management companies, software, rehabilitation aids, and community agencies and private clinics specializing in substance abuse and mental health.

★7943★ Association for Counselor Education and Supervision National Conference

Association for Counselor Education and Supervision
c/o American Counseling Association
PO Box 791006
Baltimore, MD 21279-1006
Ph: (703)823-9800   Fax: (703)823-0252
Fr: 800-347-6647
E-mail: feitstep@isu.edu
URL: http://www.acesonline.net

Annual. **Primary Exhibits:** Exhibits relating to the professional preparation of counselors.

OTHER SOURCES

★7944★ American Association for Marriage and Family Therapy (AAMFT)

112 S Alfred St.
Alexandria, VA 22314-3061
Ph: (703)838-9808   Fax: (703)838-9805
E-mail: central@aamft.org
URL: http://www.aamft.org

Members: Professional society of marriage and family therapists. **Purpose:** Assumes a major role in developing and maintaining the highest standards of excellence in this field. **Activities:** Conducts 76 accredited training programs throughout the U.S. Sponsors educational and research programs.

★7945★ American Psychological Association (APA)

750 First St. NE
Washington, DC 20002-4242
Ph: (202)336-5500   Fax: (202)336-6069
Fr: 800-374-2721
E-mail: president@apa.org
URL: http://www.apa.org

Description: Scientific and professional society of psychologists; students participate as affiliates. Advances psychology as a science, a profession, and as a means of promoting health, education and the human welfare.

★7946★ Association of Family and Conciliation Courts (AFCC)

6525 Grand Teton Plz.
Madison, WI 53719-1083
Ph: (608)664-3750   Fax: (608)664-3751
E-mail: afcc@afccnet.org
URL: http://www.afccnet.org

Members: Judges, counselors, family court personnel, attorneys, mediators, researchers, and teachers concerned with the resolution of family disputes as they affect children. **Purpose:** Proposes to develop and improve the practice of dispute resolution procedure as a complement to judicial procedures. Aims to strengthen the family unit and minimize family strife by improving the process of marriage, family, and divorce counseling; and to provide an interdisciplinary forum for the exchange of ideas, for the creation of new approaches to child custody matters and solutions to problems of family discord. Collaborates with the National Council of Juvenile and Family Court Judges, National Judicial College, the National Center for State Courts, the American Bar Association and several universities, law schools, and state organizations responsible for providing ongoing training for attorneys, judges, and family therapists. **Activities:** Conducts research and offers technical assistance and training to courts, legal associations, judicial organizations, and behavioral science professionals.

★7947★ **Human Services Occupations**

Delphi Productions
3159 6th St.
Boulder, CO 80304
Ph: (303)443-2100   Fax: (303)443-4022
Fr: 888-443-2400
E-mail: support@delphivideo.com
URL: http://www.delphivideo.com

$95.00. 50 minutes. Part of the Careers for the 21st Century Video Library.

★7948★ **International Association for Marriage and Family Counselors (IAMFC)**

Texas A&M University - Corpus Christi
College of Education
6300 Ocean Dr.
Corpus Christi, TX 78412
Ph: (361)825-2307   Fax: (703)461-9260
Fr: 800-347-6647

E-mail: director@iamfc.com
URL: http://www.counseling.org

Description: A division of the American Counseling Association. Individuals working in the areas of marriage counseling, marital therapy, divorce counseling, mediation, and family counseling and therapy; interested others. Promotes ethical practices in marriage and family counseling/therapy. Encourages research; provides a forum for dialogue on relevant issues; facilitates the exchange of information. Assists couples and families in coping with life challenges; works to ameliorate problems confronting families and married couples.

★7949★ **National Council on Family Relations (NCFR)**

3989 Central Ave. NE, Ste. 550
Minneapolis, MN 55421
Ph: (763)781-9331   Fax: (763)781-9348
Fr: 888-781-9331
E-mail: info@ncfr.org
URL: http://www.ncfr.org

Members: Multidisciplinary group of family life professionals, including clergy, counselors, educators, home economists, lawyers, nurses, therapists, librarians, physicians, psychologists, social workers, sociologists, and researchers. **Purpose:** Seeks to provide opportunities for members to plan and act together to advance marriage and family life through consultation, conferences, and the dissemination of information and research.

Mathematicians

★7950★ Acta Mathematica

Springer-Verlag New York Inc.
233 Spring St.
New York, NY 10013
Ph: (212)460-1500   Fax: (212)460-1575
URL: http://www.springer.com

Journal for mathematics.

★7951★ Association for Women in Mathematics Newsletter

Association for Women in Mathematics
11240 Waples Mill Rd., Ste. 200
Fairfax, VA 22030
Ph: (703)934-0163   Fax: (703)359-7562
E-mail: awm@awm-math.org
URL: http://www.awm-math.org/newsletter.html

Description: Six issues/year. Concerned with the progress of women in professional fields, particularly in mathematics and related careers. Recounts facets of the history of women in mathematics, discusses issues related to education, and highlights women being honored for studies and achievements. Recurring features include letters to the editor and a section on job openings.

★7952★ AWIS Magazine

Association for Women in Science
1200 New York Ave. NW, Ste. 650
Washington, DC 20005
Ph: (202)326-8940   Fax: (202)326-8960
Fr: (866)657-2947
E-mail: awis@awis.org
URL: http://www.awis.org/

Description: Bimonthly. Covers issues, legislation, and trends related to science education for girls, women, and minorities. Includes information on grants and fellowships, job openings, educational programs, events, and notices of publications available.

★7953★ Communications in Mathematical Analysis (CMA)

Howard University Press
2225 Georgia Ave. NW, Ste. 718
Washington, DC 20059
Ph: (202)238-2570   Fax: (202)588-9849
URL: http://www.ripublication.com/cma.htm

Semiannual. $80.00/year for individuals. Journal focusing on analysis and applications of mathematics.

★7954★ Electronic Research Announcements of the American Mathematical Society

American Mathematical Society
201 Charles St.
Providence, RI 02904-2294
Ph: (401)455-4000   Fax: (401)331-3842
Fr: 800-321-4267
URL: http://www.ams.org/era

Free. Electronic journal publishing announcements of significant advances in all branches of mathematics.

★7955★ Employment Information in the Mathematical Sciences/Journal

American Mathematical Society
201 Charles St.
Providence, RI 02904-2294
Ph: (401)455-4000   Fax: (401)331-3842
Fr: 800-321-4267
E-mail: reprint-permission@ams.org
URL: http://www.ams.org/journals/

Description: Six issues/year. Provides concise listings of open positions (1,400-1,500/yr.) suitable for mathematicians with education and experience at every level beyond the Bachelor's degree. Lists positions by state.

★7956★ Foundations of Computational Mathematics

Springer-Verlag New York Inc.
233 Spring St.
New York, NY 10013
Ph: (212)460-1500   Fax: (212)460-1575

Academic journal that publishes articles related to the connections between mathematics and computation, including the interfaces between pure and applied mathematics, numerical analysis and computer science.

★7957★ Global Journal of Pure and Applied Mathematics (GJPAM)

Howard University Press
2225 Georgia Ave. NW, Ste. 718
Washington, DC 20059
Ph: (202)238-2570   Fax: (202)588-9849
URL: http://www.ripublication.com/gjpam.htm

$150.00/year for institutions, print only; $100.00/year for individuals, print only. Journal publishing research articles from pure and applied mathematics. Covers pure and applied aspects of all sub-disciplines of mathematical analysis.

★7958★ International Archives of Bioscience

International Archives of Bioscience
PO Box 737254
Elmhurst, NY 11373-9997
URL: http://www.iabs.us/jdoc/aboutiabs.htm

Free, online only. Journal reporting multidisciplinary coverage and interaction between scientists in biology, informatics, mathematics, physics, engineering and other sciences.

★7959★ International Mathematics Research Surveys

Hindawi Publishing Corp.
410 Park Ave., 15th Fl.
287 PMB
New York, NY 10022
URL: http://www.hindawi.com/journals/imrs/index.html

Annual. $195.00/year for institutions. Journal that publishes articles on the state of research in all parts of mathematics emphasizing trends and open problems.

★7960★ Journal of Applied Mathematics

Hindawi Publishing Corp.
410 Park Ave., 15th Fl.
287 PMB
New York, NY 10022
URL: http://www.hindawi.com/journals/jam/index.html

Annual. $295.00/year for institutions. Journal that publishes original Research papers and review articles in all areas of applied, computational, and industrial mathematics.

★7961★ Journal of Concrete and Applicable Mathematics

Nova Science Publishers Inc.
400 Oser Ave., Ste. 1600
Hauppauge, NY 11788-3619
Ph: (631)231-7269   Fax: (631)231-8175

Quarterly. $395.00/year. Peer-reviewed international journal that publishes high quality original research articles from all sub-areas of non-pure and/or applicable mathematics as well connections to other areas of mathematical sciences.

★7962★ Journal of Mathematics and the Arts

Taylor & Francis Group Journals
325 Chestnut St., Ste. 800
Philadelphia, PA 19106
Ph: (215)625-8900   Fax: (215)625-8914
Fr: 800-354-1420
URL: http://www.tandf.co.uk/journals/titles/17513472.asp

$330.00/year for institutions, print and online; $314.00/year for institutions, online only; $72.00/year for individuals, print only. Journal focusing on the challenges and opportunities presented by new media and information technology.

★7963★ Journal of Mathematics and Statistics

Science Publications
Vails Gate Heights Dr.
PO Box 879
Vails Gate, NY 12584
URL: http://www.scipub.us/

Quarterly. $1,100.00/year for individuals; $300.00/year for single issue. Scholarly journal covering all areas of mathematics and statistics.

★7964★ Notices of the American Mathematical Society

American Mathematical Society
201 Charles St.
Providence, RI 02904-2294
Ph: (401)455-4000   Fax: (401)331-3842
Fr: 800-321-4267
URL: http://www.ams.org/notices

Monthly. $417.00/year for individuals;. Free, members. AMS journal publishing programs, meeting reports, new publications, announcements, upcoming mathematical meetings, scientific development trends, computer software reviews, and federal funding reports.

★7965★ The Ramanujan Journal

Springer Publishing Co.
11 W 42nd St., 15th Fl.
New York, NY 10036
Ph: (212)431-4370   Fax: (212)941-7342
Fr: 877-687-7476
URL: http://www.springer.com

Journal on mathematics.

PLACEMENT AND JOB REFERRAL SERVICES

★7966★ American Geophysical Union (AGU)

2000 Florida Ave. NW
Washington, DC 20009-1277
Ph: (202)462-6900   Fax: (202)328-0566
Fr: 800-966-2481
E-mail: service@agu.org
URL: http://www.agu.org

Members: Individuals professionally associated with the field of geophysics; supporting institutional members are companies and other organizations whose work involves geophysics. **Purpose:** Promotes the study of problems concerned with the figure and physics of the earth; initiates and coordinates research that depends upon national and international cooperation and provides for scientific discussion of research results. **Activities:** Sponsors placement service at semiannual meeting.

★7967★ American Mathematical Society (AMS)

201 Charles St.
Providence, RI 02904-2213
Ph: (401)455-4000   Fax: (401)331-3842
Fr: 800-321-4AMS
E-mail: ams@ams.org
URL: http://www.ams.org

Description: Professional society of mathematicians and educators. Promotes the interests of mathematical scholarship and research. Holds institutes, seminars, short courses, and symposia to further mathematical research; awards prizes. Offers placement services; compiles statistics.

★7968★ Mathematical Association of America (MAA)

1529 18th St. NW
Washington, DC 20036-1358
Ph: (202)387-5200   Fax: (202)265-2384
Fr: 800-741-9415
E-mail: maahq@maa.org
URL: http://www.maa.org

Description: College mathematics teachers; individuals using mathematics as a tool in a business or profession. Sponsors annual high school mathematics contests and W.L. Putnam Competition for college students. Conducts faculty enhancement workshops and promotes the use of computers through classroom training. Offers college placement test program; operates speakers' bureau.

EMPLOYER DIRECTORIES AND NETWORKING LISTS

★7969★ American Men and Women of Science

Gale, Cengage Learning
27500 Drake Rd.
Farmington Hills, MI 48331-3535
Ph: (248)699-4253   Fax: (248)699-8065
Fr: 800-877-4253
URL: http://www.gale.com

Biennial, latest edition 23rd, October 2006; new edition expected 24th, January 2008. $1,075.00 for individuals. Covers over 129,700 U.S. and Canadian scientists active in the physical, biological, mathematical, computer science, and engineering fields; includes references to previous edition for deceased scientists and nonrespondents. Entries include: Name, address, education, personal and career data, memberships, honors and awards, research interest. Arrangement: Alphabetical. Indexes: Discipline (in separate volume).

★7970★ Assistantships and Graduate Fellowships in the Mathematical Sciences

American Mathematical Society
201 Charles St.
Providence, RI 02904-2294
Ph: (401)455-4000   Fax: (401)331-3842
Fr: 800-321-4267
URL: http://www.ams.org/employment/asst2001-frnt.pdf

Annual; latest edition 2006. $23.00 for individuals. Publication includes: List of assistantship and graduate fellowship opportunities in math, statistics, computer science and related fields at about 270 colleges and universities in the United States and Canada; sources of fellowship information. Entries include: For assistantships and fellowships–Title, sponsoring organization name, web site address, address, name and title of contact; description of position, including stipend (if any), duties, deadline for application; number and type of degrees awarded for previous year. For fellowship information sources–Name, address. Arrangement: Geographical. Indexes: Type of stipend.

★7971★ Careers in Focus: Mathematics and Physics

Facts On File Inc.
132 W 31st St., 17th Fl.
New York, NY 10001
Ph: (212)967-8800   Fax: 800-678-3633
Fr: 800-322-8755
URL: http://www.factsonfile.com

$29.95 for individuals; $26.95 for libraries. Covers an overview of mathematics and physics, followed by a selection of jobs profiled in detail, including the nature of the job, earnings, prospects for employment, what kind of training and skills it requires, and sources for further information.

★7972★ **Discovering Careers for Your Future: Math**

Facts On File Inc.
132 W 31st St., 17th Fl.
New York, NY 10001
Ph: (212)967-8800   Fax: 800-678-3633
Fr: 800-322-8755
URL: http://www.factsonfile.com

March 2005. $15.95 for individuals. Covers auditors, computer programmers, financial planners, and physicists; links career education to curriculum, helping children investigate the subjects they are interested in and the careers those subjects might lead to.

★7973★ **Employment Information in the Mathematical Sciences**

American Mathematical Society
201 Charles St.
Providence, RI 02904-2294
Ph: (401)455-4000   Fax: (401)331-3842
Fr: 800-321-4267
E-mail: eims-info@ams.org
URL: http://www.ams.org/eims/

Five times a year. Covers colleges and universities with departments in the mathematical sciences, and non-academic and foreign organizations with employment openings. Entries include: For departments–Name, address, name and title of contact; job title, job description, salary (if applicable). Arrangement: Classified as academic or nonacademic, then geographical.

★7974★ **Facts on File Geometry Handbook**

Facts On File Inc.
132 W 31st St., 17th Fl.
New York, NY 10001
Ph: (212)967-8800   Fax: 800-678-3633
Fr: 800-322-8755
URL: http://www.factsonfile.com/

Latest edition 2003. $35.00 for individuals; $31.50 for libraries. Publication includes: List of Web sites to consult for further information on geometry. Principal content of publication consists of over 3,000 terms covering Euclidean and non-Euclidean geometry as well as other overlapping mathematical branches. Indexes: Alphabetical.

★7975★ **Mathematical Sciences Professional Directory**

American Mathematical Society
201 Charles St.
Providence, RI 02904-2294
Ph: (401)455-4000   Fax: (401)331-3842
Fr: 800-321-4267
URL: http://www.ams.org

Annual; latest edition 2006. $55.00. Covers

37 professional organizations concerned with mathematics, government agencies, academic institutions with department in the mathematical sciences, nonacademic organizations, and individuals. Entries include: For professional organizations and government agencies–Name, address, names and titles of key personnel. For institutions–Name, address; name, title, and address of department chair. Arrangement: Classified by type of organization; institutions are then geographical; others, alphabetical. Indexes: University or college name.

HANDBOOKS AND MANUALS

★7976★ **101 Careers in Mathematics**

Mathematical Association of America
1529 18th St. NW
Washington, DC 20036
Ph: (301)617-7800   Fax: (301)206-9789
Fr: 800-331-1622
URL: http://www.maa.org/

Andrew Sterrett (Editor). Second edition January 2003. $43.50. 354 pages. Classroom Resource Materials Series.

★7977★ **Careers for Number Crunchers and Other Quantitative Types**

The McGraw-Hill Companies
PO Box 182604
Columbus, OH 43272
Fax: (614)759-3749   Fr: 877-883-5524
E-mail: customer.service@mcgraw-hill.com
URL: http://www.mcgraw-hill.com

Rebecca Burnett. Second edition, 2002. $22.95 (paper). 192 pages. Provides information to math-oriented job hunters on how to become statisticians, field researchers, computer programmers, stock analysts, investment managers, bankers, engineers, accountants, underwriters, economists, market analysts, mathematicians, systems analysts, and more.

★7978★ **Great Jobs for Math Majors**

The McGraw-Hill Companies
PO Box 182604
Columbus, OH 43272
Fax: (614)759-3749   Fr: 877-883-5524
E-mail: customer.service@mcgraw-hill.com
URL: http://www.mcgraw-hill.com

Stephen Lambert and Ruth J. DeCotis. Second edition, 2005. $15.95 (paper). 208 pages.

★7979★ **Guide to Nontraditional Careers in Science**

Taylor & Francis
325 Chestnut St., 8th Fl.
Philadelphia, PA 19106
Ph: (215)625-8900   Fax: (215)269-0363
Fr: 800-821-8312
URL: http://www.taylorandfrancis.com

Karen Young Kreeger. 1998. $45.95 (paper). Guidebook aids the reader in evaluating and finding career opportunities in non-academic research fields. 263 pages.

★7980★ **Math for Soil Scientists**

Cengage Learning
PO Box 6904
Florence, KY 41022
Fax: 800-487-8488   Fr: 800-354-9706
URL: http://www.cengage.com/

Mark S. Coyne and James A. Thompson. 2005. $31.95. Soil science students and practitioners are offered a review of basic mathematical operations in the field.

★7981★ **A Mathematician's Survival Guide: Graduate School and Early Career Development**

American Mathematical Society
201 Charles St.
Providence, RI 02904
Ph: (401)455-4157   Fax: (401)331-3842
Fr: 800-321-4267
E-mail: ams@ams.org
URL: http://www.ams.org

Steven G. Krantz. April 2003. $28.00 (paper). Illustrated. 240 pages.

★7982★ **Opportunities in Research and Development Careers**

The McGraw-Hill Companies
PO Box 182604
Columbus, OH 43272
Fax: (614)759-3749   Fr: 877-883-5524
E-mail: customer.service@mcgraw-hill.com
URL: http://www.mcgraw-hill.com

Jan Goldberg. 1996. $11.95 (paper). 146 pages.

★7983★ **Starting Our Careers: A Collection of Essays & Advice on Professional Development from the Young Mathematicians' Network**

American Mathematical Society
201 Charles St.
Providence, RI 02940-6248
Ph: (401)455-4000   Fax: (401)331-3842
Fr: 800-321-4267
E-mail: ams@ams.org
URL: http://www.ams.org

Curtis D. Bennett and Annalisa Crannell. 1999. 116 pages. $25.00.

★7984★ **To Boldly Go: A Practical Career Guide for Scientists**

Amer Global Pub
2000 Florida Ave., NW
Washington, DC 20009
Ph: (202)462-6900   Fax: (202)328-0566
Fr: 800-966-2481

Peter S. Fiske. 1996. $19.00 (paper). 188 pages.

TRADESHOWS

★7985★ American Mathematical Association of Two-Year Colleges Conference

American Mathematical Association of Two Year Colleges
5983 Macon Cove
Memphis, TN 38134
Ph: (901)333-4643   Fax: (901)333-4651
E-mail: amatyc@amatyc.org
URL: http://www.amatyc.org

Annual. **Primary Exhibits:** Exhibits relating to the improvement of mathematics education and mathematics-related experiences of students in two-year colleges or at the lower division level. **Dates and Locations:** 2008 Nov 20-23; Washington, DC.

★7986★ Joint Mathematics Meetings

American Mathematical Society
PO Box 6887
Providence, RI 02940
Ph: (401)455-4000   Fax: (401)455-4004
E-mail: meet@ams.org
URL: http://www.ams.org/meetings

Annual. **Primary Exhibits:** Software and on-line systems, books, publishers, mathematical associations, insurance companies, math related games, accessories, tee shirts, hardware.

OTHER SOURCES

★7987★ Association for International Practical Training (AIPT)

10400 Little Patuxent Pkwy., Ste. 250
Columbia, MD 21044-3519
Ph: (410)997-2200   Fax: (410)992-3924
E-mail: aipt@aipt.org
URL: http://www.aipt.org

Description: Providers worldwide of on-the-job training programs for students and professionals seeking international career development and life-changing experiences. Arranges workplace exchanges in hundreds of professional fields, bringing employers and trainees together from around the world. Client list ranges from small farming communities to Fortune 500 companies.

★7988★ Institute of Mathematical Statistics (IMS)

PO Box 22718
Beachwood, OH 44122
Ph: (216)295-2340   Fax: (216)295-5661
E-mail: ims@imstat.org
URL: http://www.imstat.org

Members: Professional society of mathematicians and others interested in mathematical statistics and probability theory. **Purpose:** Seeks to further research in mathematical statistics and probability.

★7989★ National Council of Teachers of Mathematics (NCTM)

1906 Association Dr.
Reston, VA 20191-1502
Ph: (703)620-9840   Fax: (703)476-2970
Fr: 800-235-7566
E-mail: inquiries@nctm.org
URL: http://www.nctm.org

Description: Aims to improve teaching and learning of mathematics.

★7990★ Scientific, Engineering, and Technical Services

Cambridge Educational
PO Box 2053
Princeton, NJ 08543-2053
Ph: 800-257-5126   Fax: (609)671-0266
Fr: 800-468-4227
E-mail: custserv@films.com
URL: http://www.cambridgeeducational.com

VHS and DVD. $89.95. 2002. 18 minutes. 2002. Part of the Career Cluster Series.

Mechanical Engineers

SOURCES OF HELP-WANTED ADS

★7991★ Advanced Materials & Processes

ASM Intl.
9639 Kinsman Rd.
Materials Park, OH 44073-0002
Ph: (440)338-5151   Fax: (440)338-4634
Fr: 800-336-5152
URL: http://www.asminternational.org/

Monthly. Magazine covering advances in metal, materials, testing technology and more.

★7992★ AIE Perspectives Newsmagazine

American Institute of Engineers
4630 Appian Way, Ste. 206
El Sobrante, CA 94803-1875
Ph: (510)758-6240   Fax: (510)758-6240

Monthly. Professional magazine covering engineering.

★7993★ Applied Mechanics Transactions

American Society of Mechanical Engineers
3 Park Ave.
New York, NY 10016-5990
Ph: (212)591-7158   Fax: (212)591-7739
Fr: 800-843-2763
URL: http://catalog.asme.org/Journals/PrintOnlineProduct/JOURNAL_

Quarterly. $430.00/year for nonmembers, list price; $60.00/year for members, print + online. Journal covering mechanical engineering.

★7994★ ASME News

American Society of Mechanical Engineers
3 Park Ave.
New York, NY 10016-5990
Ph: (212)591-7158   Fax: (212)591-7739
Fr: 800-843-2763

E-mail: infocentral@asme.org
URL: http://www.asmenews.org/
Monthly. Engineering tabloid.

★7995★ AWIS Magazine

Association for Women in Science
1200 New York Ave. NW, Ste. 650
Washington, DC 20005
Ph: (202)326-8940   Fax: (202)326-8960
Fr: (866)657-2947
E-mail: awis@awis.org
URL: http://www.awis.org/

Description: Bimonthly. Covers issues, legislation, and trends related to science education for girls, women, and minorities. Includes information on grants and fellowships, job openings, educational programs, events, and notices of publications available.

★7996★ Chemical Equipment

Reed Business Information
360 Park Ave. S
New York, NY 10010
Ph: (646)746-6400   Fax: (646)746-7431
URL: http://www.reedbusinessinteractive.com

Free, for qualified professionals; $72.90/year for individuals, cover price. Tabloid on the chemical process industry.

★7997★ Consulting-Specifying Engineer

Reed Business Information
360 Park Ave. S
New York, NY 10010
Ph: (646)746-6400   Fax: (646)746-7431
URL: http://www.csemag.com

The integrated engineering magazine of the building construction industry.

★7998★ Engineering Conferences International Symposium Series

Berkeley Electronic Press
2809 Telegraph Ave., Ste. 202
Berkeley, CA 94705
Ph: (510)665-1200   Fax: (510)665-1201
URL: http://services.bepress.com/eci/

Journal focusing on advance engineering science.

★7999★ Engineering Times

National Society of Professional Engineers
1420 King St.
Alexandria, VA 22314
Ph: (703)684-2800
URL: http://www.nspe.org

Monthly. Magazine (tabloid) covering professional, legislative, and techology issues for an engineering audience.

★8000★ ENR: Engineering News-Record

McGraw-Hill Inc.
1221 Ave. of the Americas
New York, NY 10020-1095
Ph: (212)512-2000   Fax: (212)512-3840
Fr: 877-833-5524
E-mail: enr_web_editors@mcgraw-hill.com
URL: http://www.mymags.com/moreinfo.php?itemID=20012

Weekly. $94.00/year for individuals, print. Magazine focusing on engineering and construction.

★8001★ Graduating Engineer & Computer Careers

Career Recruitment Media
211 W Wacker Dr., Ste. 900
Chicago, IL 60606
Ph: (312)525-3100
URL: http://www.graduatingengineer.com

Quarterly. $15.00/year for individuals. Magazine focusing on employment, education, and career development for entry-level engineers and computer scientists.

★8002★ High Technology Careers Magazine

HTC
4701 Patrick Henry Dr., No. 1901
Santa Clara, CA 95054-1847
Fax: (408)567-0242
URL: http://www.hightechcareers.com

Bimonthly. $29.00/year; $35.00/year for Canada; $85.00/year for out of country. Magazine (tabloid) containing employment opportunity information for the engineering and technical community.

★8003★ Hydraulics & Pneumatics

Penton Media Inc.
1300 E 9th St.
Cleveland, OH 44114
Ph: (216)696-7000   Fax: (216)696-1752
URL: http://www.hydraulicspneumatics.com/default.aspx

Monthly. $63.00/year for individuals; $90.00/year for individuals, 2 years; $77.00/year for Canada; $122.00/year for Canada, 2 years; $90.00/year for individuals, print version; $149.00/year for individuals, print version, 2 years; $20.00/year for individuals, digital version; $120.00/year for individuals, print and digital. Magazine of hydraulic and pneumatic systems and engineering.

★8004★ InterJournal

New England Complex Systems Institute
24 Mt. Auburn St.
Cambridge, MA 02138
Ph: (617)547-4100   Fax: (617)661-7711
URL: http://www.interjournal.org/

Journal covering the fields of science and engineering.

★8005★ International Archives of Bioscience

International Archives of Bioscience
PO Box 737254
Elmhurst, NY 11373-9997
URL: http://www.iabs.us/jdoc/aboutiabs.htm

Free, online only. Journal reporting multidisciplinary coverage and interaction between scientists in biology, informatics, mathematics, physics, engineering and other sciences.

★8006★ Journal of Engineering Education

American Society for Engineering Education
1818 North St., NW, Ste. 600
Washington, DC 20036-2479
Ph: (202)331-3500
URL: http://www.asee.org/publications/jee/index.cfm

Quarterly. Journal covering scholarly research in engineering education.

★8007★ Machine Design

Penton Media Inc.
1300 E 9th St.
Cleveland, OH 44114
Ph: (216)696-7000   Fax: (216)696-1752
E-mail: mdeditor@penton.com
URL: http://www.machinedesign.com

Semimonthly. $144.00/year for Canada, 21 issues; $160.00/year for Canada, regular; $108.00/year for other countries, 21 issues;

$120.00/year for other countries, regular; $157.00/year for students, 21 issues; $175.00/year for students, regular. Magazine on design engineering function.

★8008★ Mechanical Engineering

American Society of Mechanical Engineers
3 Park Ave.
New York, NY 10016-5990
Ph: (212)591-7158   Fax: (212)591-7739
Fr: 800-843-2763
E-mail: memag@asme.org

Monthly. $25.00 for single issue; $28.50 for single issue, international surface. Mechanical Engineering featuring technical and industry related technological advancements and news.

★8009★ NSBE Magazine

NSBE Publications
205 Daingerfield Rd.
Alexandria, VA 22314
Ph: (703)549-2207   Fax: (703)683-5312
URL: http://www.nsbe.org/publications/premieradvertisers.php

Journal providing information on engineering careers, self-development, and cultural issues for recent graduates with technical majors.

★8010★ Plumbing Engineer

TMB Publishing Inc.
1838 Techny Ct.
Northbrook, IL 60062
Ph: (847)564-1127   Fax: (847)564-1264
URL: http://www.tmbpublishing.com

Monthly. Trade journal for consulting engineering, mechanical engineering, architecture, and contracting professionals.

★8011★ Power

McGraw-Hill Inc.
1221 Ave. of the Americas
New York, NY 10020-1095
Ph: (212)512-2000   Fax: (212)512-3840
Fr: 877-833-5524
E-mail: robert_peltier@platts.com
URL: http://online.platts.com/PPS/P=m&s=1029337384756.1478827&e=1

Monthly. Magazine for engineers in electric utilities, process and manufacturing plants, commercial and service establishments, and consulting, design, and construction engineering firms working in the power technology field.

★8012★ SPE Technical Journals

Society of Petroleum Engineers
222 Palisades Creek Dr.
Richardson, TX 75080
Ph: (972)952-9393   Fax: (972)952-9435
Fr: 800-456-6863
URL: http://www.spe.org

Journal devoted to engineers and scientists.

★8013★ SWE, Magazine of the Society of Women Engineers

Society of Women Engineers
230 East Ohio St., Ste. 400
Chicago, IL 60611-3265
Ph: (312)596-5223
E-mail: hq@swe.org
URL: http://www.swe.org

Quarterly. $30.00/year for nonmembers. Magazine for engineering students and for women and men working in the engineering and technology fields. Covers career guidance, continuing development and topical issues.

★8014★ The Technology Interface

New Mexico State University
College of Engineering
PO Box 30001
Las Cruces, NM 88003-8001
Ph: (505)646-0111
URL: http://engr.nmsu.edu/etti/

Journal for the engineering technology profession serving education and industry.

★8015★ Uratie

IDG Communications Inc.
5 Speen St., 3rd. Fl
Framingham, MA 01701
Ph: (508)875-5000   Fax: (508)988-7888
URL: http://www.idg.com

Magazine providing job offers for graduates, engineers and information technology professionals.

★8016★ WEPANEWS

Women in Engineering Programs & Advocates Network
1901 E. Asbury Ave., Ste. 220
Denver, CO 80208
Ph: (303)871-4643   Fax: (303)871-6833
E-mail: dmatt@wepan.org
URL: http://www.wepan.org

Description: 2/year. Seeks to provide greater access for women to careers in engineering. Includes news of graduate, undergraduate, freshmen, pre-college, and re-entry engineering programs for women. Recurring features include job listings, faculty, grant, and conference news, international engineering program news, action group news, notices of publications available, and a column titled Kudos.

PLACEMENT AND JOB REFERRAL SERVICES

★8017★ American Indian Science and Engineering Society (AISES)

PO Box 9828
Albuquerque, NM 87119-9828
Ph: (505)765-1052   Fax: (505)765-5608
E-mail: info@aises.org
URL: http://www.aises.org

Description: Represents American Indian and non-Indian students and professionals in science, technology, and engineering fields; corporations representing energy, mining, aerospace, electronic, and computer fields. Seeks to motivate and encourage students to pursue undergraduate and graduate studies in science, engineering, and technology. Sponsors science fairs in grade schools, teacher training workshops, summer math/science sessions for 8th-12th graders, professional chapters, and student chapters in colleges. Offers scholarships. Adult members serve as role models, advisers, and mentors for students. Operates placement service.

★8018★ **Engineering Society of Detroit (ESD)**

2000 Town Ctr., Ste. 2610
Southfield, MI 48075
Ph: (248)353-0735   Fax: (248)353-0736
E-mail: esd@esd.org
URL: http://esd.org

Description: Engineers from all disciplines; scientists and technologists. Conducts technical programs and engineering refresher courses; sponsors conferences and expositions. Maintains speakers' bureau; offers placement services; although based in Detroit, MI, society membership is international.

★8019★ **Korean-American Scientists and Engineers Association (KSEA)**

1952 Gallows Rd., Ste. 300
Vienna, VA 22182
Ph: (703)748-1221   Fax: (703)748-1331
E-mail: admin@ksea.org
URL: http://www.ksea.org

Description: Represents scientists and engineers holding single or advanced degrees. Promotes friendship and mutuality among Korean and American scientists and engineers; contributes to Korea's scientific, technological, industrial, and economic developments; strengthens the scientific, technological, and cultural bonds between Korea and the U.S. Sponsors symposium. Maintains speakers' bureau, placement service, and biographical archives. Compiles statistics.

★8020★ **Robotics Tech Group of the Society of Manufacturing Engineers (RI/SME)**

PO Box 930
Dearborn, MI 48121
Ph: (313)271-1500   Fax: (313)425-3404
Fr: 800-733-4763
E-mail: techcommunities@sme.org
URL: http://www.sme.org/cgi-bin/communities.pl?/communities/ri/ri-home.htm&&&SME&

Description: Represents engineers, managers, educators, and government officials in 50 countries working or interested in the field of robotics. Promotes efficient and effective use of current and future robot technology. Serves as a clearinghouse for the industry trends and developments. Includes areas of interest such as: aerospace; assembly systems; casting and forging; education and training; human factors and safety; human and food service; material handling; military systems; nontraditional systems; research and development; small shop applications; welding. Offers professional certification. Operates placement service; compiles statistics. Maintains speakers' bureau.

★8021★ **Society of Hispanic Professional Engineers (SHPE)**

5400 E Olympic Blvd., Ste. 210
Los Angeles, CA 90022
Ph: (323)725-3970   Fax: (323)725-0316
E-mail: shpenational@shpe.org
URL: http://oneshpe.shpe.org/wps/portal/national

Description: Represents engineers, student engineers, and scientists. Aims to increase the number of Hispanic engineers by providing motivation and support to students. Sponsors competitions and educational programs. Maintains placement service and speakers' bureau; compiles statistics.

EMPLOYER DIRECTORIES AND NETWORKING LISTS

★8022★ *American Men and Women of Science*

Gale, Cengage Learning
27500 Drake Rd.
Farmington Hills, MI 48331-3535
Ph: (248)699-4253   Fax: (248)699-8065
Fr: 800-877-4253
URL: http://www.gale.com

Biennial, latest edition 23rd, October 2006; new edition expected 24th, January 2008. $1,075.00 for individuals. Covers over 129,700 U.S. and Canadian scientists active in the physical, biological, mathematical, computer science, and engineering fields; includes references to previous edition for deceased scientists and nonrespondents. Entries include: Name, address, education, personal and career data, memberships, honors and awards, research interest. Arrangement: Alphabetical. Indexes: Discipline (in separate volume).

★8023★ *Career Opportunities in the Automotive Industry*

Facts On File Inc.
132 W 31st St., 17th Fl.
New York, NY 10001
Ph: (212)967-8800   Fax: 800-678-3633
Fr: 800-322-8755
URL: http://www.factsonfile.com

Published 2005. $49.50 for individuals; $44.55 for libraries. Covers 70 jobs from pit crew mechanic to restoration expert, from mechanical engineer to parts distribution director, from RV specialist to exotic car museum director.

★8024★ *Directory of Contract Staffing Firms*

C.E. Publications Inc.
PO Box 3006
Bothell, WA 98041-3006
Ph: (425)806-5200   Fax: (425)806-5585
URL: http://www.cjhunter.com/dcsf/overview.html

Covers nearly 1,300 contract firms actively engaged in the employment of engineering, IT/IS, and technical personnel for 'temporary' contract assignments throughout the world. Entries include: Company name, address, phone, name of contact, email, web address. Arrangement: Alphabetical. Indexes: Geographical.

★8025★ *Indiana Society of Professional Engineers-Directory*

Indiana Society of Professional Engineers
PO Box 20806
Indianapolis, IN 46220
Ph: (317)255-2267   Fax: (317)255-2530
URL: http://www.indspe.org

Annual, fall. Covers member registered engineers, land surveyors, engineering students, and engineers in training. Entries include: Member name, address, phone, type of membership, business information, specialty. Arrangement: Alphabetical by chapter area.

★8026★ *Mechanical Contractors Association of America (MCAA)-Membership Directory*

National Certified Pipe Welding Bureau
1385 Piccard Dr.
Rockville, MD 20850
Ph: (301)869-5800   Fax: (301)990-9690
URL: http://www.mcaa.org/directory/

Annual, December. Covers about 600 mechanical contractors regularly engaged in the fabrication or erecting of piping systems, who employ certified pipe welders. Entries include: Firm name, address, phone, telex, fax, name of contact. Arrangement: By each chapter, then by firm name.

★8027★ *Peterson's Job Opportunities in Engineering and Technology*

Peterson's Guides
2000 Lenox Dr.
Box 67005
Lawrenceville, NJ 08648
Ph: (609)896-1800   Fax: (609)896-4531
Fr: 800-338-3282
E-mail: custsvc@petersons.com
URL: http://www.petersons.com

Compiled by the Peterson's staff. Fourth edition, 1996. $21.95 (paper). 379 pages. Profiles 2,000 high-tech companies looking primarily for technical personnel in such fields as biotechnology, telecommunications, software, computers and peripherals, defense, and aerospace. Contains job-search strategies and career options to help match education and expertise to the job market. Indexed geographically, by industry, and by hiring needs.

HANDBOOKS AND MANUALS

★8028★ The Best Resumes for Scientists and Engineers

John Wiley & Sons Inc.
1 Wiley Dr.
Somerset, NJ 08873
Ph: (732)469-4400   Fax: (732)302-2300
Fr: 800-225-5945
E-mail: custserv@wiley.com
URL: http://www.wiley.com/WileyCDA/

Adele Lewis and David J. Moore. Second edition, 1993. $37.50; $19.95 (paper). 224 pages. Presents an extensive collection of scientific and engineering resumes, highlighting the important differences between these and resumes written for other occupations.

★8029★ Great Jobs for Engineering Majors

The McGraw-Hill Companies
PO Box 182604
Columbus, OH 43272
Fax: (614)759-3749   Fr: 877-883-5524
E-mail: customer.service@mcgraw-hill.com
URL: http://www.mcgraw-hill.com

Geraldine O. Garner. Second edition, 2002. $14.95. 256 pages. Covers all the career options open to students majoring in engineering.

★8030★ How to Succeed as an Engineer: A Practical Guide to Enhance Your Career

Institute of Electrical & Electronics Engineers
445 Hoes Lane
Piscataway, NJ 08854
Ph: (732)981-0060   Fax: (732)981-9667
Fr: 800-678-4333
URL: http://www.ieee.org

Todd Yuzuriha. 1999. $29.95 (paper). 367 pages.

★8031★ The I Hate Selling Book: Business-Building Advice for Consultants, Attorneys, Accountants, Engineers, Architects, and Other Professionals

AMACOM
1601 Broadway, 12th Fl.
New York, NY 10019-7420
Ph: (212)586-8100   Fax: (212)903-8168
Fr: 800-262-9699
URL: http://www.amanet.org

Allan S. Boress. 2001. $29.95. 240 pages.

★8032★ Keys to Engineering Success

Prentice Hall PTR
One Lake St.
Upper Saddle River, NJ 07458
Ph: (201)236-7000   Fr: 800-428-5331
URL: http://www.phptr.com/index.asp?rl=1

Jill S. Tietjen, Kristy A. Schloss, Carol Car-ter, Joyce Bishop, and Sarah Lyman. 2000. $46.00 (paper). 288 pages.

★8033★ The New Engineer's Guide to Career Growth & Professional Awareness

Institute of Electrical & Electronics Engineers
445 Hoes Lane
Piscataway, NJ 08854
Ph: (732)981-0060   Fax: (732)981-9667
Fr: 800-678-4333
URL: http://www.ieee.org

Irving J. Gabelman, editor. 1996. $39.95 (paper). 275 pages.

★8034★ Opportunities in Engineering Careers

The McGraw-Hill Companies
PO Box 182604
Columbus, OH 43272
Fax: (614)759-3749   Fr: 877-883-5524
E-mail: customer.service@mcgraw-hill.com
URL: http://www.mcgraw-hill.com

Nicholas Basta. Revised second edition, 2002. $13.95; $11.95 (paper). 160 pages. Outlines typical job titles, salaries, career paths, and employment prospects.

★8035★ Opportunities in High Tech Careers

The McGraw-Hill Companies
PO Box 182604
Columbus, OH 43272
Fax: (614)759-3749   Fr: 877-883-5524
E-mail: customer.service@mcgraw-hill.com
URL: http://www.mcgraw-hill.com

Gary Colter and Deborah Yanuck. 1999. $14.95; $11.95 (paper). 160 pages. Explores high technology careers. Describes job opportunities, how to make a career decision, how to prepare for high technology jobs, job hunting techniques, and future trends.

★8036★ Opportunities in Research and Development Careers

The McGraw-Hill Companies
PO Box 182604
Columbus, OH 43272
Fax: (614)759-3749   Fr: 877-883-5524
E-mail: customer.service@mcgraw-hill.com
URL: http://www.mcgraw-hill.com

Jan Goldberg. 1996. $11.95 (paper). 146 pages.

★8037★ Real People Working in Engineering

The McGraw-Hill Companies
PO Box 182604
Columbus, OH 43272
Fax: (614)759-3749   Fr: 877-883-5524
E-mail: customer.service@mcgraw-hill.com
URL: http://www.mcgraw-hill.com

Blythe Camenson, Jan Goldberg. 1997. $17.95 (paper). 160 pages. Interviews and profiles of working professionals capture a range of opportunities in this field.

★8038★ Resumes for Engineering Careers

The McGraw-Hill Companies
PO Box 182604
Columbus, OH 43272
Fax: (614)759-3749   Fr: 877-883-5524
E-mail: customer.service@mcgraw-hill.com
URL: http://www.mcgraw-hill.com

Third edition, 2005. $11.95 (paper). 144 pages. Contains sample resumes and cover letters applicable to any engineering field.

★8039★ Resumes for Scientific and Technical Careers

The McGraw-Hill Companies
PO Box 182604
Columbus, OH 43272
Fax: (614)759-3749   Fr: 877-883-5524
E-mail: customer.service@mcgraw-hill.com
URL: http://www.mcgraw-hill.com

Third edition, 2007. $12.95 (paper). 144 pages. Provides resume advice for individuals interested in working in scientific and technical careers. Includes sample resumes and cover letters.

EMPLOYMENT AGENCIES AND SEARCH FIRMS

★8040★ The Aspire Group

52 Second Ave, 1st Fl
Waltham, MA 02451-1129
Fax: (718)890-1810   Fr: 800-487-2967
URL: http://www.bmanet.com

Employment agency.

★8041★ Bell Oaks Co.

10 Glenlake Pkwy., Ste. 300
Atlanta, GA 30328
Ph: (678)287-2000   Fax: (678)287-2002
E-mail: info@belloaks.com
URL: http://www.belloaks.com

Personnel service firm.

★8042★ The Bradbury Group Inc.

2112 Vizcaya Way, Ste. 200
Campbell, CA 95008
Ph: (408)377-5400   Fax: (408)377-1112
E-mail: paul@ifindem.com
URL: http://www.thebradburygroup.net

Executive search firm.

★8043★ Brown Venture Associates Inc.

2500 Sand Hill Rd., Ste. 110
Menlo Park, CA 94025
Ph: (650)233-0205   Fax: (650)233-1902
E-mail: Brown@bva.com
URL: http://www.bva.com

Executive search firm.

★8044★ Claremont-Branan, Inc.
1298 Rockbridge Rd., Ste. B
Stone Mountain, GA 30087
Ph: (770)925-2915   Fax: (770)925-2601
Fr: 800-875-1292
E-mail: ohil@cbisearch.com
URL: http://cbisearch.com

Employment agency. Executive search firm.

★8045★ Colli Associates
414 Caboose Ln.
Valrico, FL 33594
Ph: (813)681-2145   Fax: (813)661-5217
E-mail: colli@gte.net

Employment agency. Executive search firm.

★8046★ The Corporate Source Group Inc.
280 S. Main St.
Andover, MA 01810
Ph: (987)475-6400   Fax: (987)475-6800
E-mail: inquiry@csg-search.com
URL: http://www.csg-search.com

Executive search firm branches in Phoenix, AZ; Tampa, Fl; North Potomac, MD; McMurray, PA.

★8047★ The Coxe Group Inc.
1904 Third Ave., Ste. 229
Seattle, WA 98101-1194
Ph: (206)467-4040   Fax: (206)467-4038
E-mail: consultants@coxegroup.com
URL: http://www.coxegroup.com

Executive search firm.

★8048★ Dunlap & Sullivan Associates
29 Pearl St. NW, Ste. 227
Grand Rapids, MI 49503
Ph: (616)458-4142   Fax: (616)458-4203
E-mail: dunsul@aol.com

Executive search firm with second location in Hobe Sound, FL.

★8049★ Engineer One, Inc.
PO Box 23037
Knoxville, TN 37933
Fax: (865)691-0110
E-mail: engineerone@engineerone.com
URL: http://www.engineerone.com

Engineering employment service specializes in engineering and management in the chemical process, power utilities, manufacturing, mechanical, electrical, and electronic industries. Established an Information Technology Division in 1998 that works nationwide across all industries. Also provides systems analysis consulting services specializing in VAX based systems.

★8050★ Executive Recruiters Agency
14 Office Park Dr., Ste. 100
PO Box 21810
Little Rock, AR 72221-1810
Ph: (501)224-7000   Fax: (501)224-8534

E-mail: jobs@execrecruit.com
URL: http://www.execrecruit.com

Personnel service firm.

★8051★ Global Employment Solutions
10375 Park Meadows Dr., Ste. 375
Littleton, CO 80124
Ph: (303)216-9500   Fax: (303)216-9533
E-mail: careers@global
URL: http://www.gesnetwork.com

Employment agency.

★8052★ Modem Engineering Design Associates
1575 Lauzon Rd.
Windsor, ON, Canada N8S 3N4
Ph: (519)944-7221   Fax: (519)944-6862
Fr: 800-999-6332
E-mail: meda@medagroup.com
URL: http://www.medagroup.com

Engineering consultants offering design services principally to automotive, OEM and components manufacturing industries, including military applications. Major area of expertise is in engine, transmission and chassis design. Also provides technical personnel recruitment. Industries served: automotive, petrochemical, food, brewery, aircraft, ship building, tooling, and environmental companies.

★8053★ Rand Personnel
1200 Truxtun Ave., Ste. 130
Bakersfield, CA 93301
Ph: (805)325-0751   Fax: (805)325-4120

Personnel service firm serving a variety of fields.

★8054★ Search and Recruit International
4455 South Blvd. Ste. 110
Virginia Beach, VA 23452
Ph: (757)625-2121   Fr: 800-800-5627

Employment agency. Headquartered in Virginia Beach. Other offices in Bremerton, WA; Charleston, SC; Jacksonville, FL; Memphis, TN; Pensacola, FL; Sacramento, CA; San Bernardino, CA; San Diego, CA.

★8055★ Trambley the Recruiter
5325 Wyoming Blvd. NE
Albuquerque, NM 87109-3132
Ph: (505)821-5440   Fax: (505)821-8509

Personnel consultancy firm recruits and places engineering professionals in specific areas of off-road equipment design and manufacturing. Industries served: construction, agricultural, lawn and garden, oil exploration and mining equipment manufacturing.

★8056★ Tri-Serv Inc.
22 W. Padonia Rd., Ste. C-353
Timonium, MD 21093
Ph: (410)561-1740   Fax: (410)252-7417
E-mail: info@tri-serv.coom

URL: http://www.tri-serv.com

Employment agency for technical personnel.

ONLINE JOB SOURCES AND SERVICES

★8057★ Spherion
2050 Spectrum Blvd.
Fort Lauderdale, FL 33309
Ph: (954)308-7600
E-mail: help@spherion.com
URL: http://www.spherion.com

Description: Recruitment firm specializing in accounting and finance, sales and marketing, interim executives, technology, engineering, retail and human resources.

TRADESHOWS

★8058★ American Society for Engineering Education Annual Conference and Exposition
American Society for Engineering Education
1818 N. St. NW, Ste. 600
Washington, DC 20036-2479
Ph: (202)331-3500   Fax: (202)265-8504
E-mail: conferences@asee.org
URL: http://www.asee.org

Annual. **Primary Exhibits:** Publications, engineering supplies and equipment, computers, software, and research companies all products and services related to engineering education.

OTHER SOURCES

★8059★ American Almanac of Jobs and Salaries
HarperCollins
10 E. 53rd St.
New York, NY 10022
Ph: (212)207-7000   Fr: 800-242-7737
URL: http://www.harpercollins.com/

John W. Wright. Revised edition, 2000. $20.00 (paper). 672 pages. This is a comprehensive guide to the wages of hundreds of occupations in a wide variety of industries and organizations.

★8060★ American Association of Engineering Societies (AAES)
1620 I St. NW, Ste. 210
Washington, DC 20006
Ph: (202)296-2237   Fax: (202)296-1151
Fr: 888-400-2237
E-mail: dbateson@aaes.org

URL: http://www.aaes.org

Description: Coordinates the efforts of the member societies in the provision of reliable and objective information to the general public concerning issues which affect the engineering profession and the field of engineering as a whole; collects, analyzes, documents, and disseminates data which will inform the general public of the relationship between engineering and the national welfare; provides a forum for the engineering societies to exchange and discuss their views on matters of common interest; and represents the U.S. engineering community abroad through representation in WFEO and UPADI.

★8061★ American Society of Mechanical Engineers (ASME)

3 Park Ave.
New York, NY 10016-5990
Ph: (973)882-1170   Fax: (973)882-1717
Fr: 800-THE-ASME
E-mail: infocentral@asme.org
URL: http://www.asme.org

Members: Technical society of mechanical engineers and students. **Purpose:** Conducts research; develops boiler, pressure vessel, and power test codes. Develops safety codes and standards for equipment. Conducts short course programs, and Identifying Research Needs Program. Maintains 19 research committees and 38 divisions.

★8062★ American Society of Mechanical Engineers Auxiliary (ASMEA)

3 Park Ave., 23rd Fl.
New York, NY 10016-5990
Ph: (212)591-7846   Fax: (212)591-7739
E-mail: persaudl@asme.org
URL: http://www.asme.org

Description: Members of the American Society of Mechanical Engineers and their immediate families. Cooperates with officers and committees of the ASME. Operates a scholarship and student loan fund.

★8063★ Association for International Practical Training (AIPT)

10400 Little Patuxent Pkwy., Ste. 250
Columbia, MD 21044-3519
Ph: (410)997-2200   Fax: (410)992-3924
E-mail: aipt@aipt.org
URL: http://www.aipt.org

Description: Providers worldwide of on-the-job training programs for students and professionals seeking international career development and life-changing experiences. Arranges workplace exchanges in hundreds of professional fields, bringing employers and trainees together from around the world. Client list ranges from small farming communities to Fortune 500 companies.

★8064★ Engineering Occupations

Delphi Productions
3159 6th St.
Boulder, CO 80304
Ph: (303)443-2100   Fax: (303)443-4022
Fr: 888-443-2400
E-mail: support@delphivideo.com
URL: http://www.delphivideo.com

$95.00. 50 minutes. Part of the Careers for the 21st Century Video Library.

★8065★ ISA - Instrumentation, Systems, and Automation Society

67 Alexander Dr.
PO Box 12277
Research Triangle Park, NC 27709
Ph: (919)549-8411   Fax: (919)549-8288
E-mail: info@isa.org
URL: http://www.isa.org

Description: Sets the standard for automation by helping over 30,000 worldwide members and other professionals solve difficult technical problems, while enhancing their leadership and personal career capabilities. Develops standards; certifies industry professionals; provides education and training; publishes books and technical articles; and hosts the largest conference and exhibition for automation professionals in the Western Hemisphere. Is the founding sponsor of The Automation Federation.

★8066★ National Action Council for Minorities in Engineering (NACME)

440 Hamilton Ave., Ste. 302
White Plains, NY 10601-1813
Ph: (914)539-4010   Fax: (914)539-4032
E-mail: webmaster@nacme.org
URL: http://www.nacme.org

Description: Leads the national effort to increase access to careers in engineering and other science-based disciplines. Conducts research and public policy analysis, develops and operates national demonstration programs at precollege and university levels, and disseminates information through publications, conferences and electronic media. Serves as a privately funded source of scholarships for minority students in engineering.

★8067★ National Society of Professional Engineers (NSPE)

1420 King St.
Alexandria, VA 22314-2794
Ph: (703)684-2800   Fax: (703)836-4875
Fr: 888-285-6773
E-mail: memserv@nspe.org
URL: http://www.nspe.org

Description: Represents professional engineers and engineers-in-training in all fields registered in accordance with the laws of states or territories of the U.S. or provinces of Canada; qualified graduate engineers, student members, and registered land surveyors. Is concerned with social, professional, ethical, and economic considerations of engineering as a profession; encompasses programs in public relations, employment practices, ethical considerations, education, and career guidance. Monitors legislative and regulatory actions of interest to the engineering profession.

★8068★ Scientific, Engineering, and Technical Services

Cambridge Educational
PO Box 2053
Princeton, NJ 08543-2053
Ph: 800-257-5126   Fax: (609)671-0266
Fr: 800-468-4227
E-mail: custserv@films.com
URL: http://www.cambridgeeducational.com

VHS and DVD. $89.95. 2002. 18 minutes. 2002. Part of the Career Cluster Series.

★8069★ Society of Women Engineers (SWE)

230 E Ohio St., Ste. 400
Chicago, IL 60611-3265
Ph: (312)596-5223   Fax: (312)596-5252
Fr: 877-SWE-INFO
E-mail: hq@swe.org
URL: http://www.swe.org

Description: Educational and service organization representing both students and professional women in engineering and technical fields.

★8070★ SPIE - The International Society for Optical Engineering (SPIE)

PO Box 10
Bellingham, WA 98227-0010
Ph: (360)676-3290   Fax: (360)647-1445
Fr: 888-504-8171
E-mail: customerservice@spie.org
URL: http://www.spie.org

Description: Advances scientific research and engineering applications of optical, photonic, imaging and optoelectronic technologies through meetings, education programs and publications.

★8071★ Women in Engineering

Her Own Words
PO Box 5264
Madison, WI 53705-0264
Ph: (608)271-7083   Fax: (608)271-0209
E-mail: herownword@aol.com
URL: http://www.herownwords.com/

Video. Jocelyn Riley. $95.00. 15 minutes. Resource guide also available for $45.00.

Medical Assistants

SOURCES OF HELP-WANTED ADS

★8072★ Academic Emergency Medicine

Mosby Inc.
11830 Westline Industrial Dr.
St. Louis, MO 63146
Ph: (314)872-8370   Fax: (314)432-1380
Fr: 800-325-4177
URL: http://www.elsevier.com/wps/find/journaldescription.cws_home

Monthly. $259.00/year for institutions; $161.00/year for individuals; $77.00/year for students; $245.00/year for institutions; $151.00/year for individuals; $83.00/year for students. Journal publishing material relevant to the practice, education, and investigation of emergency medicine; reaches a wide audience of emergency care practitioners and educators.

★8073★ American Journal of Emergency Medicine

Mosby Inc.
11830 Westline Industrial Dr.
St. Louis, MO 63146
Ph: (314)872-8370   Fax: (314)432-1380
Fr: 800-325-4177
URL: http://www.elsevier.com/wps/find/journaldescription.cws_home

Bimonthly. $275.00/year for individuals; $419.00/year for institutions; $129.00/year for students; $397.00/year for individuals, international; $546.00/year for institutions, international; $198.00/year for students, international. Journal reporting on emergency medicine.

★8074★ Annals of Medicine

Taylor & Francis Group Journals
325 Chestnut St., Ste. 800
Philadelphia, PA 19106
Ph: (215)625-8900   Fax: (215)625-8914
Fr: 800-354-1420
URL: http://www.ingentaconnect.com

$418.00/year for institutions, print and online; $397.00/year for institutions, online only; $155.00/year for individuals. Journal covering health science and medical education.

★8075★ Clinical Medicine & Research

Marshfield Clinic
1000 North Oak Ave.
Marshfield, WI 54449
Ph: (715)387-5511   Fr: 800-782-8581
URL: http://www.clinmedres.org/

Monthly. Journal that publishes scientific medical research that is relevant to a broad audience of medical researchers and healthcare professionals.

★8076★ The CMA Today

American Association of Medical Assistants
20 North Wacker Dr., Ste. 1575
Chicago, IL 60606
Ph: (312)899-1500   Fax: (312)899-1259
URL: http://www.aama-ntl.org/cmatoday/about.aspx

Bimonthly. Free to members; $30.00/year for nonmembers. Professional health journal.

★8077★ CME Supplement to Emergency Medicine Clinics of North America

Elsevier Science Inc.
360 Park Ave. S
New York, NY 10010
Ph: (212)989-5800   Fax: (212)633-3990
URL: http://www.elsevier.com

Quarterly. $190.00/year for individuals. Journal covering emergency medicine clinics.

★8078★ Discovery Medicine

Discovery Medicine
2245 Chapel Valley Ln.
Timonium, MD 21093
Ph: (410)560-9007   Fax: (410)560-9000
URL: http://www.discoverymedicine.com

Bimonthly. $39.95/year for individuals; $49.95/year for individuals, digital edition and online access; $69.95 for two years, online access; $84.95 for two years, digital edition and online access; $99.95/year for individuals, 3 years, online access; $119.95/year for individuals, 3 years, digital and online access; $299.00/year for individuals, medical report (PMR); $99.00/year for individuals, medical report update. Online journal that publishes articles on diseases, biology, new diagnostics, and treatments for medical professionals.

★8079★ Education & Treatment of Children

West Virginia University Press
44 Stansbury Hall
PO Box 6295
Morgantown, WV 26506
Ph: (304)293-8400   Fax: (304)293-6585
Fr: (866)988-7737
URL: http://www.educationandtreatmentofchildren.net

Quarterly. $85.00/year for institutions; $45.00/year for individuals; $100.00/year for institutions, elsewhere; $60.00/year for individuals, elsewhere. Periodical featuring information concerning the development of services for children and youth. Includes reports written for educators and other child care and mental health providers focused on teaching, training, and treatment effectiveness.

★8080★ Genes and Nutrition

New Century Health Publishers LLC
PO Box 50702
New Orleans, LA 70150-0702
Fax: (504)305-3762
URL: http://www.newcenturyhealthpublishers.com/genes_and_nutritio

Quarterly. $428.00/year for institutions; $228.00/year for individuals. International, interdisciplinary peer reviewed scientific journal for critical evaluation of research on the relationship between genetics & nutrition with the goal of improving human health.

★8081★ Hospitals & Health Networks

Health Forum L.L.C.
1 N Franklin, 29th Fl.
Chicago, IL 60606
Ph: (312)893-6800   Fax: (312)422-4506
Fr: 800-821-2039
URL: http://www.hhnmag.com

Weekly. Publication covering the health care industry.

★8082★ The IHS Primary Care Provider

Indian Health Service (HQ)
The Reyes Bldg.
801 Thompson Ave., Ste. 400
Rockville, MD 20852-1627
URL: http://www.ihs.gov/PublicInfo/Publications/HealthProvider/Pr

Monthly. Journal for health care professionals, physicians, nurses, pharmacists, dentists, and dietitians.

★8083★ Injury

Mosby Inc.
11830 Westline Industrial Dr.
St. Louis, MO 63146
Ph: (314)872-8370   Fax: (314)432-1380
Fr: 800-325-4177
URL: http://www.elsevier.com/wps/find/journaldescription.cws_home

Monthly. $1,106.00/year for institutions, all countries except Europe, Japan and Iran; $169.00/year for individuals, all countries except Europe, Japan and Iran. Journal publishing articles and research related to the treatment of injuries such as trauma systems and management; surgical procedures; epidemiological studies; surgery (of all tissues); resuscitation; biomechanics; rehabilitation; anaesthesia; radiology and wound management.

★8084★ Intensive and Critical Care Nursing

Mosby Inc.
11830 Westline Industrial Dr.
St. Louis, MO 63146
Ph: (314)872-8370   Fax: (314)432-1380
Fr: 800-325-4177
URL: http://www.us.elsevierhealth.com/product.jsp?isbn=09643397&r

Bimonthly. $92.00/year for individuals, international; $422.00/year for institutions, international; $92.00/year for individuals; $422.00/year for institutions. Journal for nurses in intensive and critical care nursing.

★8085★ Journal of the American Society of Podiatric Medical Assistants

American Society of Podiatric Medical Assistants
2124 S Austin Blvd.
Cicero, IL 60804
Ph: (708)863-6303   Fr: 888-882-7762
URL: http://www.aspma.org

Quarterly. Subscription included in membership. Professional journal covering issues in podiatry.

★8086★ Journal of Health Law

American Health Lawyers Association
1025 Connecticut Ave., NW, Ste. 600
Washington, DC 20036-5405
Ph: (202)833-1100   Fax: (202)833-1105
URL: http://www.healthlawyers.org

Quarterly. Professional journal covering healthcare issues and cases and their impact on the health care arena.

★8087★ Journal of Hospital Medicine

John Wiley & Sons Inc.
111 River St.
Hoboken, NJ 07030-5774
Ph: (201)748-6000   Fax: (201)748-6088
Fr: 800-825-7550
URL: http://www.wiley.com/WileyCDA/WileyTitle/productCd-JHM.html

Bimonthly. $110.00/year for individuals, print only; Online version available with subscription. Journal on hospital medicine.

★8088★ Medical Risks

Taylor & Francis Group Journals
325 Chestnut St., Ste. 800
Philadelphia, PA 19106
Ph: (215)625-8900   Fax: (215)625-8914
Fr: 800-354-1420
URL: http://www.tandf.co.uk

Monthly. Journal covering articles on medical risks.

★8089★ Medical Staff Development Professional

American Academy of Medical Management
Crossville Commons
560 W Crossville Rd., Ste. 103
Roswell, GA 30075
Ph: (770)649-7150   Fax: (770)649-7552

Periodic. Professional journal covering medical education.

★8090★ Pacifica Review

Taylor & Francis Group Journals
325 Chestnut St., Ste. 800
Philadelphia, PA 19106
Ph: (215)625-8900   Fax: (215)625-8914
Fr: 800-354-1420
URL: http://www.tandf.co.uk/

$462.00/year for individuals; $279.00/year for individuals; $487.00/year for individuals; $294.00/year for individuals; $123.00/year for individuals; $86.00/year for individuals. Journal promoting physical therapy and integration.

★8091★ USA Body Psychotherapy Journal

United States Association for Body Psychotherapy
7831 Woodmont Ave.
Bethesda, MD 20814
URL: http://www.usabp.org/displaycommon.cfm?an=4

Semiannual. Academic journal that seeks to support, promote and stimulate the exchange of ideas, scholarship and research within the field of body psychotherapy as well as an interdisciplinary exchange with related fields of clinical practice and inquiry.

★8092★ Year Book of Critical Care Medicine

Elsevier Science Inc.
360 Park Ave. S
New York, NY 10010
Ph: (212)989-5800   Fax: (212)633-3990
URL: http://www.elsevier.com

$180.00/year for institutions, U.S. $191.00/year for institutions, other countries; $121.00/year for individuals, U.S. $134.00/year for individuals, other countries; $59.00/year for students, U.S. $71.00/year for students, other countries. Journal focused on treatment of severe sepsis and septic shock, echocardiography in the evaluation of hemodynamically unstable patients & mechanical ventilation of acute respiratory distress syndrome.

EMPLOYER DIRECTORIES AND NETWORKING LISTS

★8093★ AHA Guide to the Health Care Field

American Hospital Association
1 N Franklin
Chicago, IL 60606
Ph: (312)422-2050   Fax: (312)422-4700
Fr: 800-424-4301

Annual, August. Covers hospitals, networks, multi-health care systems, freestanding ambulatory surgery centers, psychiatric facilities, long-term care facilities, substance abuse programs, and other health-related organizations. Entries include: For hospitals–Facility name, address, phone, administrator's name, number of beds, facilities and services, number of employees, expenses, other statistics. For other organizations–Name, address, phone, fax, name and title of contact. Arrangement: Geographical. Indexes: Hospital name.

★8094★ Guide to Careers in the Health Professions

The Princeton Review
2315 Broadway
New York, NY 10024
Ph: (212)874-8282   Fax: (212)874-0775
Fr: 800-733-3000
URL: http://www.princetonreview.com/

Published January, 2001. $24.95 for individuals. Presents advice and information for those searching for satisfying careers in the health professions. Publication includes: Directory of schools and academic programs. Entries include: Name, address, phone, tuition, program details, employment profiles.

★8095★ **Hospital Blue Book**

Billian Publishing Inc./Transworld Publishing Inc.
2100 Powers Ferry Rd. SE
Atlanta, GA 30339
Ph: (770)955-5656   Fax: (770)952-0669
Fr: 800-533-8484
E-mail: blu-book@billian.com

2005. $300.00 for individuals. Covers more than 6,687 hospitals; some listings also appear in a separate southern edition of this publication. Entries include: Name of hospital, accreditation, mailing address, phone, fax, number of beds, type of facility (nonprofit, general, state, etc.); list of administrative personnel and chiefs of medical services, with specific titles. Arrangement: Geographical.

★8096★ **Medical and Health Information Directory**

Gale, Cengage Learning
27500 Drake Rd.
Farmington Hills, MI 48331-3535
Ph: (248)699-4253   Fax: (248)699-8065
Fr: 800-877-4253
E-mail: businessproducts@gale.com
URL: http://www.gale.com

Annual; latest edition 20th, July 2007. $375.00/volume. Covers in Volume 1, more than 26,500 medical and health oriented associations, organizations, institutions, and government agencies, including health maintenance organizations (HMOs), preferred provider organizations (PPOs), insurance companies, pharmaceutical companies, research centers, and medical and allied health schools. In Volume 2, over 12,000 medical book publishers; medical periodicals, directories, audiovisual producers and services, medical libraries and information centers, electronic resources, and health-related internet search engines. In Volume 3, more than 35,500 clinics, treatment centers, care programs, and counseling/diagnostic services for 34 subject areas. Entries include: Institution, service, or firm name, address, phone, fax, email and URL; many include names of key personnel and, when pertinent, descriptive annotations. Volume 3 was formerly listed separately as Health Services Directory. Arrangement: Classified by organization activity, service, etc. Indexes: Each volume has a complete alphabetical name and keyword index.

★8097★ **Peterson's Job Opportunities for Health and Science Majors**

Peterson's
Princeton Pke. Corporate Ctr., 2000 Lenox Dr.
PO Box 67005
Lawrenceville, NJ 08648
Ph: (609)896-1800   Fax: (609)896-4531
Fr: 800-338-3282
URL: http://www.petersons.com

Irregular; latest edition 1999. Covers about 1,300 research, consulting, government, and non-profit and profit service organizations that hire college and university graduates in science and health-related majors. Entries include: Organization name, address, phone, name and title of contact, type of organization, number of employees, Standard Industrial Classification (SIC) code; description of opportunities available including disciplines, level of education required, starting locations and salaries, level of experience accepted, benefits.

Handbooks and Manuals

★8098★ **150 Careers in the Health Care Field**

U.S. Directory Service
121 Chanlon Rd.
New Providence, NJ 07974
Ph: (908)464-6800   Fax: (908)665-3560
Fr: 800-521-8110

Janice Eldredge and Darrell Buono. Revised, 1993. $59.95. 555 pages. Book describes the occupation and training requirements of allied health personnel, administrators, assistants, auxiliary workers, technicians, therapists, technologists, and more.

★8099★ **Careers in Health Care**

The McGraw-Hill Companies
PO Box 182604
Columbus, OH 43272
Fax: (614)759-3749   Fr: 877-883-5524
E-mail: customer.service@mcgraw-hill.com
URL: http://www.mcgraw-hill.com

Barbara M. Swanson. Fifth edition, 2005. $15.95 (paper). 192 pages. Describes job duties, work settings, salaries, licensing and certification requirements, educational preparation, and future outlook. Gives ideas on how to secure a job.

★8100★ **Delmar's Comprehensive Medical Assisting: Administrative and Clinical Competencies**

Delmar, Cengage Learning
PO Box 6904
Florence, KY 41022
Fax: 800-487-8488   Fr: 800-354-9706
URL: http://www.cengage.com

Wilburta Q. Lindh. 2nd edition, 2002. $100.25. Illustrated. 1899 pages. Explores medical assisting.

★8101★ **Expert Resumes for Health Care Careers**

Jist Works
875 Montreal Way
St. Paul, MN 55102
Fr: 800-648-5478
E-mail: info@jist.com
URL: http://www.jist.com

Wendy S. Enelow and Louise M. Kursmark. December 2003. $16.95. 288 pages.

★8102★ **Exploring Health Care Careers, Second Edition**

JIST Publishing
875 Montreal Way
St. Paul, MN 55102
Fax: 800-547-8329   Fr: 800-648-5478
E-mail: info@jist.com
URL: http://www.jist.com

2002. $89.95. 984 pages. Information about careers in the health industry, including education and certification requirements, earnings, and job outlook.

★8103★ **Health Care Job Explosion! High Growth Health Care Careers and Job Locator**

Bookhaven Press LLC
249 Field Club Cir.
McKees Rocks, PA 15136
Ph: (412)494-6926   Fax: (412)494-5749
Fr: 800-782-7424
E-mail: info@bookhavenpress.com
URL: http://www.bookhavenpress.com/

Dennis V. Damp. Third edition, 2006. 320 pages. $19.95.

★8104★ **Health Careers Today**

Elsevier
11830 Westline Industrial Dr.
St. Louis, MO 63146
Ph: (314)453-7010   Fax: (314)453-7095
Fr: 800-545-2522
E-mail: usbkinfo@elsevier.com
URL: http://www.elsevier.com

Gerdin, Judith. Fourth edition. 2007. $59.95. 496 pages. Covers more than 45 health careers. Discusses the roles and responsibilities of various occupations and provides a solid foundation in the skills needed for all health careers.

★8105★ **Health Careers: Undergraduate Careers in the Health Profession**

Kendall Hunt Publishing Company
4050 Westmark Dr.
PO Box 1840
Dubuque, IA 52004-1840
Ph: (319)589-1000   Fax: (319)589-1046
Fr: 800-228-0810
URL: http://www.kendallhunt.com/

Michael Beard and Yasmen Simonian. 1996. $11.45. 80 pages.

★8106★ Medical Assisting: Administrative and Clinical Competencies

The McGraw-Hill Companies
PO Box 182604
Columbus, OH 43272
Fax: (614)759-3749   Fr: 877-883-5524
E-mail: customer.service@mcgraw-hill.com
URL: http://www.mcgraw-hill.com

Barbara Prickett-Ramutkowski. Second edition, 2004. $70.67. 1205 pages. Explores medical assisting and the competencies of it.

★8107★ Opportunities in Health and Medical Careers

The McGraw-Hill Companies
PO Box 182604
Columbus, OH 43272
Fax: (614)759-3749   Fr: 877-883-5524
E-mail: customer.service@mcgraw-hill.com
URL: http://www.mcgraw-hill.com

I. Donald Snook, Jr. and Leo D'Orazio. 2004. $13.95 (paper). 157 pages. Covers the full range of medical and health occupations. Illustrated.

★8108★ Opportunities in Paramedical Careers

The McGraw-Hill Companies
PO Box 182604
Columbus, OH 43272
Fax: (614)759-3749   Fr: 877-883-5524
E-mail: customer.service@mcgraw-hill.com
URL: http://www.mcgraw-hill.com

Alex Kacen. 1999. 14.95 (hardcover). 160 pages. Discusses a variety of opportunities in this field and how to pursue them. Illustrated.

★8109★ Resumes for the Health Care Professional

John Wiley & Sons Inc.
1 Wiley Dr.
Somerset, NJ 08873
Ph: (732)469-4400   Fax: (732)302-2300
Fr: 800-225-5945
E-mail: custserv@wiley.com
URL: http://www.wiley.com/WileyCDA/

Kim Marino. Second edition, 2000. $21.50 (paper). 224 pages.

★8110★ Resumes for Health and Medical Careers

The McGraw-Hill Companies
PO Box 182604
Columbus, OH 43272
Fax: (614)759-3749   Fr: 877-883-5524
E-mail: customer.service@mcgraw-hill.com
URL: http://www.mcgraw-hill.com

Third edition, 2003. $11.95 (paper). 160 pages.

★8111★ Top 100 Health-Care Careers, Second Edition

JIST Publishing
875 Montreal Way
St. Paul, MN 55102
Fax: 800-547-8329   Fr: 800-648-5478
E-mail: info@jist.com
URL: http://www.jist.com

Dr. Saul Wischnitzer and Edith Wischnitzer. 2005. $24.95. 464 pages. A career guidance manual that helps the reader choose the right career in the field using a self-assessment; gives the reader a detailed overview of 100 jobs, including scope, activities, educational requirements, salary range, advancement, certification, and outlook; and offers a directory of education and training programs for each of the 100 featured careers.

★8112★ VGM's Handbook of Health Care Careers

The McGraw-Hill Companies
PO Box 182604
Columbus, OH 43272
Fax: (614)759-3749   Fr: 877-883-5524
E-mail: customer.service@mcgraw-hill.com
URL: http://www.mcgraw-hill.com

VGM Career Horizons Staff. Second edition, revised, 1997. $12.95 (paper). 112 pages.

EMPLOYMENT AGENCIES AND SEARCH FIRMS

★8113★ Davis-Smith, Inc.

27656 Franklin Rd.
Southfield, MI 48034
Ph: (248)354-4100   Fax: (248)354-6702
Fr: 800-541-4672
E-mail: info@davissmith.com
URL: http://www.davissmith.com

Healthcare staffing agency. Executive search firm.

★8114★ Harper Associates

3100 NW Hwy., Ste. 240
Farmington Hills, MI 48334
Ph: (248)932-1170   Fax: (248)932-1214
E-mail: info@harperjobs.com
URL: http://www.harperjobs.com

Executive search firm and employment agency.

★8115★ Professional Placement Associates, Inc.

287 Bowman Ave., Ste. 309
Purchase, NY 10577-2517
Ph: (914)251-1000   Fax: (914)251-1055
E-mail: careers@ppasearch.com
URL: http://www.ppasearch.com

Executive search firm specializing in the health and medical field.

ONLINE JOB SOURCES AND SERVICES

★8116★ Medhunters.com

Fr: 800-664-0278
E-mail: info@medhunters.com
URL: http://www.medhunters.com

Description: Career search site for jobs in all health care specialties; educational resources; visa and licensing information for relocation; interesting articles; relocation tools; links to professional organizations and general resources.

★8117★ ProHealthJobs

Fr: 800-796-1738
E-mail: Info@prohealthedujobs.com
URL: http://www.prohealthjobs.com

Description: Career resources site for the medical and health care field. Lists professional opportunities, product information, continuing education and open positions.

TRADESHOWS

★8118★ American Association of Medical Assistants National Convention

American Association of Medical Assistants
20 N. Wacker Dr., Ste. 1575
Chicago, IL 60606-2963
Ph: (312)899-1500   Fax: (312)899-1259
Fr: 800-228-2262
URL: http://www.aama-ntl.org

Annual. **Primary Exhibits:** Data processing equipment, pharmaceuticals, publications, insurance services, text books, coding system reference guides, health care services, filing and accounting systems, and computer hardware and software.

OTHER SOURCES

★8119★ American Association of Medical Assistants (AAMA)

20 N Wacker Dr., Ste. 1575
Chicago, IL 60606
Ph: (312)899-1500   Fax: (312)899-1259
Fr: 800-228-2262
E-mail: info@aama-ntl.org
URL: http://www.aama-ntl.org

Description: Medical assistants are allied health professionals who work primarily in ambulatory (out patient) settings and perform clinical and administrative procedures. Activities include a certification program consisting of study and an examination, passage of which entitles the individual to become credentialed as a Certified Medical

Assistant. Conducts accreditation of one and two-year programs in medical assisting in conjunction with the commission on Accreditation of Allied Health Education Programs. Provides assistance and information to institutions of higher learning desirous of initiating courses for medical assistants. Awards continuing education units for selected educational programs.

★8120★ **American Medical Technologists (AMT)**
10700 W Higgins Rd.
Rosemont, IL 60018
Ph: (847)823-5169   Fax: (847)823-0458
Fr: 800-275-1268
URL: http://www.amt1.com

Description: Represents medical technologists, medical laboratory technicians, medical assistants, medical administrative specialists, dental assistants, office laboratory technicians, phlebotomy technicians, laboratory consultants, and allied health instructors. Provides allied health professionals with professional certification services and membership programs to enhance their professional and personal growth. Aims to issue certification credentials to medical and dental assistants, clinical laboratory personnel, laboratory consultants, and allied health instructors.

★8121★ **American Society of Podiatric Medical Assistants (ASPMA)**
2124 S Austin Blvd.
Cicero, IL 60804
Ph: (708)863-6303   Fr: 888-88A-SPMA
E-mail: aspmaex@aol.com
URL: http://www.aspma.org

Description: Represents podiatric assistants. Holds educational seminars and administers certification examinations.

★8122★ **Exploring Health Occupations**
Cambridge Educational
PO Box 2053
Princeton, NJ 08543-2053
Ph: 800-257-5126   Fax: (609)671-0266
Fr: 800-468-4227
E-mail: custserv@films.com
URL: http://www.cambridgeeducational.com

VHS and DVD. $159.90. 1999. Two-part series provides a detailed view of the field of medical technicians and technologists, EMTs, nurses, therapists, and assistants.

★8123★ **Health Service Occupations**
Delphi Productions
3159 6th St.
Boulder, CO 80304
Ph: (303)443-2100   Fax: (303)443-4022
Fr: 888-443-2400

E-mail: support@delphivideo.com
URL: http://www.delphivideo.com

$95.00. 50 minutes. Part of the Careers for the 21st Century Video Library.

★8124★ **Medical Technicians and Technologists**
Cambridge Educational
PO Box 2053
Princeton, NJ 08543-2053
Ph: 800-257-5126   Fax: (609)671-0266
Fr: 800-468-4227
E-mail: custserv@films.com
URL: http://www.cambridgeeducational.com

VHS and DVD. $79.95. 18 minutes. 2000. Part of the Exploring Health Occupations Series.

★8125★ **Medicine & Related Occupations**
Delphi Productions
3159 6th St.
Boulder, CO 80304
Ph: (303)443-2100   Fax: (303)443-4022
Fr: 888-443-2400
E-mail: support@delphivideo.com
URL: http://www.delphivideo.com

$95.00. 45 minutes. Part of the Careers for the 21st Century Video Library.

Medical Record Technicians

EMPLOYER DIRECTORIES AND NETWORKING LISTS

★8126★ **AHA Guide to the Health Care Field**
American Hospital Association
1 N Franklin
Chicago, IL 60606
Ph: (312)422-2050   Fax: (312)422-4700
Fr: 800-424-4301

Annual, August. Covers hospitals, networks, multi-health care systems, freestanding ambulatory surgery centers, psychiatric facilities, long-term care facilities, substance abuse programs, and other health-related organizations. Entries include: For hospitals–Facility name, address, phone, administrator's name, number of beds, facilities and services, number of employees, expenses, other statistics. For other organizations–Name, address, phone, fax, name and title of contact. Arrangement: Geographical. Indexes: Hospital name.

★8127★ **Careers in Focus: Medical Technicians**
Facts On File Inc.
132 W 31st St., 17th Fl.
New York, NY 10001
Ph: (212)967-8800   Fax: 800-678-3633
Fr: 800-322-8755
URL: http://www.factsonfile.com

Latest edition 4th, 2004. $29.95 for individuals; $26.95 for libraries. Covers an overview of medical technicians, followed by a selection of jobs profiled in detail, including the nature of the job, earnings, prospects for employment, what kind of training and skills it requires, and sources for further information.

★8128★ **Directory of Hospital Personnel**
Grey House Publishing
185 Millerton Rd.
PO Box 860
Millerton, NY 12546
Ph: (518)789-8700   Fax: (518)789-0556
Fr: 800-562-2139

URL: http://www.greyhouse.com/hospital_personnel.htm

Annual. $325.00 for print product; $545.00 for online database subscription; $650.00 for online database subscription and print product combined. Covers 200,000 executives at 7,000 U.S. hospitals. Entries include: Name of hospital, address, phone; number of beds; type and JCAHO status of hospital; names and titles of key department heads and staff; medical and nursing school affiliations; number of residents, interns, and nursing students. Arrangement: Geographical. Indexes: Hospital name, personnel, hospital size.

★8129★ **Guide to Careers in the Health Professions**
The Princeton Review
2315 Broadway
New York, NY 10024
Ph: (212)874-8282   Fax: (212)874-0775
Fr: 800-733-3000
URL: http://www.princetonreview.com/

Published January, 2001. $24.95 for individuals. Presents advice and information for those searching for satisfying careers in the health professions. Publication includes: Directory of schools and academic programs. Entries include: Name, address, phone, tuition, program details, employment profiles.

★8130★ **Hospital Blue Book**
Billian Publishing Inc./Transworld Publishing Inc.
2100 Powers Ferry Rd. SE
Atlanta, GA 30339
Ph: (770)955-5656   Fax: (770)952-0669
Fr: 800-533-8484
E-mail: blu-book@billian.com

2005. $300.00 for individuals. Covers more than 6,687 hospitals; some listings also appear in a separate southern edition of this publication. Entries include: Name of hospital, accreditation, mailing address, phone, fax, number of beds, type of facility (nonprofit, general, state, etc.); list of administrative personnel and chiefs of medical services, with specific titles. Arrangement: Geographical.

★8131★ **The JobBank Guide to Health Care Companies**
Adams Media Corp.
57 Littlefield St.
Avon, MA 02322
Ph: (508)427-7100   Fax: (508)427-6790
Fr: 800-872-5627
URL: http://www.amazon.com/Jobbank-Guide-Health-Care-Companies/dp

Biennial. Covers jobs nationwide in health care companies. Entries include: Firm or organization name, address, phone, name and title of contact; description of organization, headquarters location, typical titles for entry- and middle-level positions, educational backgrounds desired, fringe benefits offered, stock exchange listing, training programs, internships, parent company, number of employees, revenues, e-mail and web addresses, projected number of hires. Indexes: Alphabetical.

★8132★ **Medical and Health Information Directory**
Gale, Cengage Learning
27500 Drake Rd.
Farmington Hills, MI 48331-3535
Ph: (248)699-4253   Fax: (248)699-8065
Fr: 800-877-4253
E-mail: businessproducts@gale.com
URL: http://www.gale.com

Annual; latest edition 20th, July 2007. $375.00/volume. Covers in Volume 1, more than 26,500 medical and health oriented associations, organizations, institutions, and government agencies, including health maintenance organizations (HMOs), preferred provider organizations (PPOs), insurance companies, pharmaceutical companies, research centers, and medical and allied health schools. In Volume 2, over 12,000 medical book publishers; medical periodicals, directories, audiovisual producers and services, medical libraries and information centers, electronic resources, and health-related internet search engines. In Volume 3, more than 35,500 clinics, treatment centers, care programs, and counseling/diagnostic services for 34 subject areas. Entries include: Institution, service, or firm name, address, phone, fax, email and URL; many include names of key personnel and, when pertinent, descriptive annotations. Volume 3 was formerly listed separately as Health Services Directory. Arrangement: Classified by organization activity, service, etc. Indexes: Each volume has a complete alphabetical name and keyword index.

HANDBOOKS AND MANUALS

★8133★ *Careers in Health Care*
The McGraw-Hill Companies
PO Box 182604
Columbus, OH 43272
Fax: (614)759-3749   Fr: 877-883-5524
E-mail: customer.service@mcgraw-hill.com
URL: http://www.mcgraw-hill.com

Barbara M. Swanson. Fifth edition, 2005. $15.95 (paper). 192 pages. Describes job duties, work settings, salaries, licensing and certification requirements, educational preparation, and future outlook. Gives ideas on how to secure a job.

★8134★ *Expert Resumes for Health Care Careers*
Jist Works
875 Montreal Way
St. Paul, MN 55102
Fr: 800-648-5478
E-mail: info@jist.com
URL: http://www.jist.com

Wendy S. Enelow and Louise M. Kursmark. December 2003. $16.95. 288 pages.

★8135★ *Exploring Health Care Careers, Second Edition*
JIST Publishing
875 Montreal Way
St. Paul, MN 55102
Fax: 800-547-8329   Fr: 800-648-5478
E-mail: info@jist.com
URL: http://www.jist.com

2002. $89.95. 984 pages. Information about careers in the health industry, including education and certification requirements, earnings, and job outlook.

★8136★ *Health Careers Today*
Elsevier
11830 Westline Industrial Dr.
St. Louis, MO 63146
Ph: (314)453-7010   Fax: (314)453-7095
Fr: 800-545-2522
E-mail: usbkinfo@elsevier.com
URL: http://www.elsevier.com

Gerdin, Judith. Fourth edition. 2007. $59.95. 496 pages. Covers more than 45 health careers. Discusses the roles and responsibilities of various occupations and provides a solid foundation in the skills needed for all health careers.

★8137★ *Health Careers: Undergraduate Careers in the Health Profession*
Kendall Hunt Publishing Company
4050 Westmark Dr.
PO Box 1840
Dubuque, IA 52004-1840
Ph: (319)589-1000   Fax: (319)589-1046
Fr: 800-228-0810
URL: http://www.kendallhunt.com/

Michael Beard and Yasmen Simonian. 1996. $11.45. 80 pages.

★8138★ *Opportunities in Health and Medical Careers*
The McGraw-Hill Companies
PO Box 182604
Columbus, OH 43272
Fax: (614)759-3749   Fr: 877-883-5524
E-mail: customer.service@mcgraw-hill.com
URL: http://www.mcgraw-hill.com

I. Donald Snook, Jr. and Leo D'Orazio. 2004. $13.95 (paper). 157 pages. Covers the full range of medical and health occupations. Illustrated.

★8139★ *Resumes for Health and Medical Careers*
The McGraw-Hill Companies
PO Box 182604
Columbus, OH 43272
Fax: (614)759-3749   Fr: 877-883-5524
E-mail: customer.service@mcgraw-hill.com
URL: http://www.mcgraw-hill.com

Third edition, 2003. $11.95 (paper). 160 pages.

★8140★ *Top 100 Health-Care Careers, Second Edition*
JIST Publishing
875 Montreal Way
St. Paul, MN 55102
Fax: 800-547-8329   Fr: 800-648-5478
E-mail: info@jist.com
URL: http://www.jist.com

Dr. Saul Wischnitzer and Edith Wischnitzer. 2005. $24.95. 464 pages. A career guidance manual that helps the reader choose the right career in the field using a self-assesment; gives the reader a detailed overview of 100 jobs, including scope, activities, educational requirements, salary range, advancement, certification, and outlook; and offers a directory of education and training programs for each of the 100 featured careers.

★8141★ *Your Career in Administrative Medical Services*
W. B. Saunders Co.
6277 Sea Harbor Dr.
Orlando, FL 32887
Fr: 800-654-2452
URL: http://www.elsevier.com

Roberta C. Weiss. 1996. $52.95. 299 pages.

EMPLOYMENT AGENCIES AND SEARCH FIRMS

★8142★ **Davis-Smith, Inc.**
27656 Franklin Rd.
Southfield, MI 48034
Ph: (248)354-4100   Fax: (248)354-6702
Fr: 800-541-4672
E-mail: info@davissmith.com
URL: http://www.davissmith.com

Healthcare staffing agency. Executive search firm.

★8143★ **Harper Associates**
3100 NW Hwy., Ste. 240
Farmington Hills, MI 48334
Ph: (248)932-1170   Fax: (248)932-1214
E-mail: info@harperjobs.com
URL: http://www.harperjobs.com

Executive search firm and employment agency.

★8144★ **JPM International**
26034 Acero
Mission Viejo, CA 92691
Ph: (949)699-4300   Fax: (949)699-4333
Fr: 800-685-7856
E-mail: trish@jpmintl.com
URL: http://www.jpmintl.com

Executive search firm and employment agency.

★8145★ **Professional Placement Associates, Inc.**
287 Bowman Ave., Ste. 309
Purchase, NY 10577-2517
Ph: (914)251-1000   Fax: (914)251-1055
E-mail: careers@ppasearch.com
URL: http://www.ppasearch.com

Executive search firm specializing in the health and medical field.

ONLINE JOB SOURCES AND SERVICES

★8146★ **Medhunters.com**
Fr: 800-664-0278
E-mail: info@medhunters.com
URL: http://www.medhunters.com

Description: Career search site for jobs in all health care specialties; educational resources; visa and licensing information for relocation; interesting articles; relocation tools; links to professional organizations and general resources.

★8147★ **ProHealthJobs**
Fr: 800-796-1738
E-mail: Info@prohealthedujobs.com
URL: http://www.prohealthjobs.com

Description: Career resources site for the medical and health care field. Lists professional opportunities, product information, continuing education and open positions.

OTHER SOURCES

★8148★ American Health Information Management Association (AHIMA)

233 N Michigan Ave., 21st Fl.
Chicago, IL 60601
Ph: (312)233-1100   Fax: (312)233-1090
Fr: 800-335-5535
E-mail: info@ahima.org
URL: http://www.ahima.org

Description: Registered record administrators; accredited record technicians with expertise in health information management, biostatistics, classification systems, and systems analysis. Sponsors Independent Study Programs in Medical Record Technology and coding. Conducts annual qualification examinations to credential medical record personnel as Registered Record Administrators (RRA), Accredited Record Technicians (ART) and Certified Coding Specialists (CCS). Maintains Foundation of Research and Education Library, Scholarships and loans.

★8149★ ARMA International - The Association of Information Management Professionals

13725 W 109th St., Ste. 101
Lenexa, KS 66215
Ph: (913)341-3808   Fax: (913)341-3742
Fr: 800-422-2762
E-mail: hq@arma.org
URL: http://www.arma.org

Description: Provides education, research, and networking opportunities to information professionals to enable them to use their skills and experience to leverage the value of records, information and knowledge as corporate assets and as contributors to organizational success.

★8150★ Exploring Health Occupations

Cambridge Educational
PO Box 2053
Princeton, NJ 08543-2053
Ph: 800-257-5126   Fax: (609)671-0266
Fr: 800-468-4227
E-mail: custserv@films.com
URL: http://www.cambridgeeducational.com

VHS and DVD. $159.90. 1999. Two-part series provides a detailed view of the field of medical technicians and technologists, EMTs, nurses, therapists, and assistants.

★8151★ Health Service Occupations

Delphi Productions
3159 6th St.
Boulder, CO 80304
Ph: (303)443-2100   Fax: (303)443-4022
Fr: 888-443-2400
E-mail: support@delphivideo.com
URL: http://www.delphivideo.com

$95.00. 50 minutes. Part of the Careers for the 21st Century Video Library.

★8152★ Health Technologists & Technicians

Delphi Productions
3159 6th St.
Boulder, CO 80304
Ph: (303)443-2100   Fax: (303)443-4022
Fr: 888-443-2400
E-mail: support@delphivideo.com
URL: http://www.delphivideo.com

$95.00. 50 minutes. Part of the Careers for the 21st Century Video Library.

★8153★ Medical Technicians and Technologists

Cambridge Educational
PO Box 2053
Princeton, NJ 08543-2053
Ph: 800-257-5126   Fax: (609)671-0266
Fr: 800-468-4227

E-mail: custserv@films.com
URL: http://www.cambridgeeducational.com

VHS and DVD. $79.95. 18 minutes. 2000. Part of the Exploring Health Occupations Series.

★8154★ Medicine & Related Occupations

Delphi Productions
3159 6th St.
Boulder, CO 80304
Ph: (303)443-2100   Fax: (303)443-4022
Fr: 888-443-2400
E-mail: support@delphivideo.com
URL: http://www.delphivideo.com

$95.00. 45 minutes. Part of the Careers for the 21st Century Video Library.

★8155★ National Association for Healthcare Quality (NAHQ)

4700 W Lake Ave.
Glenview, IL 60025
Ph: (847)375-4720   Fax: 877-218-7939
Fr: 800-966-9392
E-mail: heidi_benson@northcrest.com
URL: http://www.nahq.org

Description: Healthcare professionals in quality assessment and improvement, utilization and risk management, case management, infection control, managed care, nursing, and medical records. Objectives are: to encourage, develop, and provide continuing education for all persons involved in health care quality; to give the patient primary consideration in all actions affecting his or her health and welfare; to promote the sharing of knowledge and encourage a high degree of professional ethics in health care quality. Offers accredited certification in the field of healthcare quality, utilization, and risk management. Facilitates communication and cooperation among members, medical staff, and health care government agencies. Conducts educational seminars and conferences.

Metallurgical, Ceramic, and Materials Engineers

SOURCES OF HELP-WANTED ADS

★8156★ Advanced Materials & Processes

ASM Intl.
9639 Kinsman Rd.
Materials Park, OH 44073-0002
Ph: (440)338-5151   Fax: (440)338-4634
Fr: 800-336-5152
URL: http://www.asminternational.org/

Monthly. Magazine covering advances in metal, materials, testing technology and more.

★8157★ AIE Perspectives Newsmagazine

American Institute of Engineers
4630 Appian Way, Ste. 206
El Sobrante, CA 94803-1875
Ph: (510)758-6240   Fax: (510)758-6240

Monthly. Professional magazine covering engineering.

★8158★ American Machinist

Penton Media Inc.
1300 E 9th St.
Cleveland, OH 44114
Ph: (216)696-7000   Fax: (216)696-1752
URL: http://www.americanmachinist.com/

Monthly. $90.00/year for Canada, individual; $153.00 for Canada, 2 years, individual; $113.00/year for individuals; $176.00/year for out of country, 2 years, individual. Magazine serving the metalworking marketplace, consisting of plants in industries primarily engaged in manufacturing durable goods and other metal products.

★8159★ The Electrochemical Society Interface

The Electrochemical Society Inc.
65 S Main St., Bldg. D
Pennington, NJ 08534-2839
Ph: (609)737-1902   Fax: (609)737-2743
E-mail: interface@electrochem.org

URL: http://www.electrochem.org/dl/interface/

Quarterly. $15.00/year for members; $68.00/year for nonmembers; $15.00 for single issue, members; $20.00 for single issue, nonmembers. Publication featuring news and articles of interest to members of the Electrochemical Society.

★8160★ Engineering Conferences International Symposium Series

Berkeley Electronic Press
2809 Telegraph Ave., Ste. 202
Berkeley, CA 94705
Ph: (510)665-1200   Fax: (510)665-1201
URL: http://services.bepress.com/eci/

Journal focusing on advance engineering science.

★8161★ Engineering Times

National Society of Professional
  Engineers
1420 King St.
Alexandria, VA 22314
Ph: (703)684-2800
URL: http://www.nspe.org

Monthly. Magazine (tabloid) covering professional, legislative, and techology issues for an engineering audience.

★8162★ ENR: Engineering News-Record

McGraw-Hill Inc.
1221 Ave. of the Americas
New York, NY 10020-1095
Ph: (212)512-2000   Fax: (212)512-3840
Fr: 877-833-5524
E-mail: enr_web_editors@mcgraw-hill.com
URL: http://www.mymags.com/morein-fo.php?itemID=20012

Weekly. $94.00/year for individuals, print. Magazine focusing on engineering and construction.

★8163★ Graduating Engineer & Computer Careers

Career Recruitment Media
211 W Wacker Dr., Ste. 900
Chicago, IL 60606
Ph: (312)525-3100
URL: http://www.graduatingengineer.com

Quarterly. $15.00/year for individuals. Magazine focusing on employment, education, and career development for entry-level engineers and computer scientists.

★8164★ High Technology Careers Magazine

HTC
4701 Patrick Henry Dr., No. 1901
Santa Clara, CA 95054-1847
Fax: (408)567-0242
URL: http://www.hightechcareers.com

Bimonthly. $29.00/year; $35.00/year for Canada; $85.00/year for out of country. Magazine (tabloid) containing employment opportunity information for the engineering and technical community.

★8165★ InterJournal

New England Complex Systems Institute
24 Mt. Auburn St.
Cambridge, MA 02138
Ph: (617)547-4100   Fax: (617)661-7711
URL: http://www.interjournal.org/

Journal covering the fields of science and engineering.

★8166★ International Archives of Bioscience

International Archives of Bioscience
PO Box 737254
Elmhurst, NY 11373-9997
URL: http://www.iabs.us/jdoc/aboutiabs.htm

Free, online only. Journal reporting multidisciplinary coverage and interaction between scientists in biology, informatics, mathematics, physics, engineering and other sciences.

★8167★ International Journal of Powder Metallurgy

APMI International
105 College Rd. E
Princeton, NJ 08540-6992
Ph: (609)452-7700   Fax: (609)987-8523
URL: http://www.mpif.org/apmi/intljournal.html

Bimonthly. Powder metallurgy journal.

★8168★ Iron & Steel Technology

Association for Iron & Steel Technology
186 Thorn Hill Rd.
Warrendale, PA 15086
Ph: (724)776-6040   Fax: (724)776-1880
URL: http://www.aist.org/contact.htm

Monthly. $115.00/year for U.S., Canada, and Mexico, members only; $145.00/year for other countries, members only. Journal offers information on metallurgical, engineering, operating and maintenance of the iron and steel industries.

★8169★ Journal of Engineering Education

American Society for Engineering Education
1818 North St., NW, Ste. 600
Washington, DC 20036-2479
Ph: (202)331-3500
URL: http://www.asee.org/publications/jee/index.cfm

Quarterly. Journal covering scholarly research in engineering education.

★8170★ Light Metal Age

Fellom Publishing Co.
170 S Spruce Ave., Ste. 120
South San Francisco, CA 94080
Ph: (650)588-8832
E-mail: lma@lightmetalage.com
URL: http://www.lightmetalage.com/

Bimonthly. $47.00/year for individuals; $62.00 for two years; $77.00 for individuals, three years; $77.00/year for out of country, seamail; $122.00 for two years, seamail; $167.00 for out of country, three years, seamail; $117.00/year for out of country, airmail; $202.00 for two years, airmail; $287.00 for out of country, three years, airmail. Magazine serving primary and semi-fabrication metal plants that produce, semi-fabricate, process or manufacture the light metals: aluminum, magnesium, titanium, beryllium and their alloys, and/or the non-ferrous metals copper and zinc.

★8171★ Materials Performance

NACE International
1440 S Creek Dr.
Houston, TX 77084-4906
Ph: (281)228-6200   Fax: (281)228-6300
Fr: 800-797-6223
E-mail: pubs@mail.nace.org
URL: http://www.nace.org/

Monthly. $115.00/year for nonmembers, USA; $205.00/year for libraries; $130.00/year for nonmembers, foreign; $220.00/year for libraries, foreign;. Free, for members. Magazine on performance and protection of materials in a corrosive environment.

★8172★ Metal Producing & Processing

Penton Media Inc.
1300 E 9th St.
Cleveland, OH 44114
Ph: (216)696-7000   Fax: (216)696-1752
URL: http://www.metalproducing.com/

Bimonthly. $40.00/year for individuals; $43.00/year for Canada; $48.00/year for other countries. Magazine covering the metal-producing industry.

★8173★ Metalforming

Precision Metalforming Association
6363 Oak Tree Blvd.
Independence, OH 44131-2500
Ph: (216)901-8800   Fax: (216)901-9190
E-mail: metalforming@pma.org
URL: http://www.metalformingmagazine.com

Monthly. $40.00/year for individuals, North America; $225.00/year for other countries;. Free to qualified subscribers, Canada, Mexico, USA. Serving those who add value to sheetmetal.

★8174★ MetalMag

Spiderweb Publishing Inc.
1415 Hwy. 54 W, Ste. 105
Durham, NC 27707
Ph: (919)482-9300   Fax: (919)402-9302
E-mail: mtm@omeda.com
URL: http://www.metalmag.com/

Bimonthly. Free to qualified subscribers. Magazine for industrial construction professionals.

★8175★ Modern Casting Magazine

American Foundry Society
1695 N Penny Ln.
Schaumburg, IL 60173-4555
Ph: (847)824-0181   Fax: (847)824-7848
Fr: 800-537-4237
URL: http://www.moderncasting.com/

Monthly. $40.00/year for individuals; $5.00 for single issue; $50.00/year for individuals, year; $75.00/year for by mail. Magazine on metal casting plants and pattern shops.

★8176★ Modern Metals

Trend Publishing
625 N Michigan Ave., Ste. 15
Chicago, IL 60611
Ph: (312)654-2300   Fax: (312)654-2323
Fr: 800-278-7363
URL: http://www.modernmetals.com

Monthly. $180.00/year for individuals, 1 year; $270.00/year for individuals, 2 years; $260.00/year for individuals, 1 year; $430.00/year for individuals, 2 years. Metals fabrication magazine.

★8177★ NSBE Magazine

NSBE Publications
205 Daingerfield Rd.
Alexandria, VA 22314
Ph: (703)549-2207   Fax: (703)683-5312
URL: http://www.nsbe.org/publications/premieradvertisers.php

Journal providing information on engineering careers, self-development, and cultural issues for recent graduates with technical majors.

★8178★ Snips Magazine

Snips Magazine
2401 West Big Beaver., Ste. 700
Troy, MI 48084
Ph: (248)362-3700   Fax: (248)362-0317
URL: http://www.snipsmag.com/

Monthly. Free. Magazine for the sheet metal, warm-air heating, ventilating, and air conditioning industry.Provides helpful hints for contractors.

★8179★ SWE, Magazine of the Society of Women Engineers

Society of Women Engineers
230 East Ohio St., Ste. 400
Chicago, IL 60611-3265
Ph: (312)596-5223
E-mail: hq@swe.org
URL: http://www.swe.org

Quarterly. $30.00/year for nonmembers. Magazine for engineering students and for women and men working in the engineering and technology fields. Covers career guidance, continuing development and topical issues.

★8180★ Tooling & Production

Nelson Publishing Inc.
2500 Tamiami Trl. N
Nokomis, FL 34275
Ph: (941)966-9521   Fax: (941)966-2590
URL: http://www.manufacturingcenter.com

Monthly. Magazine concerning metalworking.

★8181★ Uratie

IDG Communications Inc.
5 Speen St., 3rd. Fl
Framingham, MA 01701
Ph: (508)875-5000   Fax: (508)988-7888
URL: http://www.idg.com

Magazine providing job offers for graduates, engineers and information technology professionals.

★8182★ WEPANEWS

Women in Engineering Programs & Advocates Network
1901 E. Asbury Ave., Ste. 220
Denver, CO 80208
Ph: (303)871-4643   Fax: (303)871-6833
E-mail: dmatt@wepan.org
URL: http://www.wepan.org

Description: 2/year. Seeks to provide greater access for women to careers in engineering. Includes news of graduate, undergraduate, freshmen, pre-college, and re-entry engineering programs for women. Recurring features include job listings, faculty, grant, and conference news, international engineering program news, action group news, notices of publications available, and a column titled Kudos.

PLACEMENT AND JOB REFERRAL SERVICES

★8183★ American Ceramic Society (ACerS)

735 Ceramic Pl., Ste. 100
Westerville, OH 43081-8728
Ph: (614)794-5855   Fax: (301)206-9789
Fr: (866)721-3322
E-mail: customerservice@ceramics.org
URL: http://www.ceramics.org

Description: Professional society of scientists, engineers, educators, plant operators, and others interested in the glass, cements, refractories, nuclear ceramics, whitewares, electronics, engineering, and structural clay products industries. Disseminates scientific and technical information through its publications and technical meetings. Conducts continuing education courses and training such as the Precollege Education Program. Sponsors over 10 meetings yearly; encourages high school and college students' interest in ceramics. Maintains Ross C. Purdy Museum of Ceramics; offers placement service and speakers' bureau.

★8184★ American Indian Science and Engineering Society (AISES)

PO Box 9828
Albuquerque, NM 87119-9828
Ph: (505)765-1052   Fax: (505)765-5608
E-mail: info@aises.org
URL: http://www.aises.org

Description: Represents American Indian and non-Indian students and professionals in science, technology, and engineering fields; corporations representing energy, mining, aerospace, electronic, and computer fields. Seeks to motivate and encourage students to pursue undergraduate and graduate studies in science, engineering, and technology. Sponsors science fairs in grade schools, teacher training workshops, summer math/science sessions for 8th-12th graders, professional chapters, and student chapters in colleges. Offers scholarships. Adult members serve as role models, advisers, and mentors for students. Operates placement service.

★8185★ APMI International

105 College Rd. E
Princeton, NJ 08540-6692
Ph: (609)452-7700   Fax: (609)987-8523
E-mail: apmi@mpif.org
URL: http://www.mpif.org/apmi/index_

frame.html

Description: Technical society for powder metallurgists and others interested in powder metallurgy and particulate materials, and their applications. Maintains speakers' bureau and placement service.

★8186★ Engineering Society of Detroit (ESD)

2000 Town Ctr., Ste. 2610
Southfield, MI 48075
Ph: (248)353-0735   Fax: (248)353-0736
E-mail: esd@esd.org
URL: http://esd.org

Description: Engineers from all disciplines; scientists and technologists. Conducts technical programs and engineering refresher courses; sponsors conferences and expositions. Maintains speakers' bureau; offers placement services; although based in Detroit, MI, society membership is international.

★8187★ Korean-American Scientists and Engineers Association (KSEA)

1952 Gallows Rd., Ste. 300
Vienna, VA 22182
Ph: (703)748-1221   Fax: (703)748-1331
E-mail: admin@ksea.org
URL: http://www.ksea.org

Description: Represents scientists and engineers holding single or advanced degrees. Promotes friendship and mutuality among Korean and American scientists and engineers; contributes to Korea's scientific, technological, industrial, and economic developments; strengthens the scientific, technological, and cultural bonds between Korea and the U.S. Sponsors symposium. Maintains speakers' bureau, placement service, and biographical archives. Compiles statistics.

★8188★ Metal Powder Industries Federation (MPIF)

105 College Rd. E
Princeton, NJ 08540-6692
Ph: (609)452-7700   Fax: (609)987-8523
E-mail: info@mpif.org
URL: http://www.mpif.org

Members: Manufacturers of metal powders, powder metallurgy processing equipment and tools, powder metallurgy products, and refractory and reactive metals. Member associations are: Metal Injection Molding Association; Metal Powder Producers Association; Advanced Particulate Materials Association; Powder Metallurgy Equipment Association; Powder Metallurgy Parts Association; Refractory Metals Association. **Purpose:** Promotes the science and industry of powder metallurgy and metal powder application through: sponsorship of technical meetings, seminars, and exhibits; establishment of standards; compilation of statistics; public relations; publications. **Activities:** Maintains speakers' bureau and placement service; conducts research.

★8189★ National Institute of Ceramic Engineers (NICE)

735 Ceramic Pl., Ste. 100
Westerville, OH 43081-8728
Ph: (614)794-5858   Fax: (614)794-5882
E-mail: ggeiger@ceramics.org
URL: http://www.ceramics.org/membership/NICE/home.asp

Purpose: Promotes the profession of ceramic engineering, accreditation of educational programs in ceramic and glass engineering and science, and in materials science and engineering and high ethical engineering standards and practices. **Activities:** Sponsors continuing education courses. Offers employment service and promotes professional engineer registration. Responsible for Professional Engineering exams in Ceramic Engineering.

★8190★ Society for the Advancement of Material and Process Engineering (SAMPE)

1161 Park View Dr., Ste. 200
Covina, CA 91724
Ph: (626)331-0616   Fax: (626)332-8929
Fr: 800-562-7360
E-mail: sampeibo@sampe.org
URL: http://www.sampe.org

Description: Material and process engineers, scientists, and other professionals engaged in development of advanced materials and processing technology in airframe, missile, aerospace, propulsion, electronics, life sciences, management, and related industries. International and local chapters sponsor scholarships for science students seeking financial assistance. Provides placement service for members.

★8191★ Society of Hispanic Professional Engineers (SHPE)

5400 E Olympic Blvd., Ste. 210
Los Angeles, CA 90022
Ph: (323)725-3970   Fax: (323)725-0316
E-mail: shpenational@shpe.org
URL: http://oneshpe.shpe.org/wps/portal/national

Description: Represents engineers, student engineers, and scientists. Aims to increase the number of Hispanic engineers by providing motivation and support to students. Sponsors competitions and educational programs. Maintains placement service and speakers' bureau; compiles statistics.

★8192★ Society for Mining, Metallurgy, and Exploration (SME)

8307 Shaffer Pkwy.
Littleton, CO 80127-4102
Ph: (303)973-9550   Fax: (303)973-3845
Fr: 800-763-3132
E-mail: cs@smenet.org
URL: http://www.smenet.org

Description: A member society of the American Institute of Mining, Metallurgical and Petroleum Engineers. Persons engaged in the finding, exploitation, treatment, and marketing of all classes of minerals (metal ores, industrial minerals, and solid fuels) except petroleum. Promotes the arts and sciences connected with the production of useful minerals and metals. Offers specialized education programs; compiles enrollment and graduation statistics from schools offering engineering degrees in mining, mineral, mineral processing/metallurgical, geological, geophysical, and mining technology. Provides placement service and sponsors charitable programs.

EMPLOYER DIRECTORIES AND NETWORKING LISTS

★8193★ American Men and Women of Science

Gale, Cengage Learning
27500 Drake Rd.
Farmington Hills, MI 48331-3535
Ph: (248)699-4253   Fax: (248)699-8065
Fr: 800-877-4253
URL: http://www.gale.com

Biennial, latest edition 23rd, October 2006; new edition expected 24th, January 2008. $1,075.00 for individuals. Covers over 129,700 U.S. and Canadian scientists active in the physical, biological, mathematical, computer science, and engineering fields; includes references to previous edition for deceased scientists and nonrespondents. Entries include: Name, address, education, personal and career data, memberships, honors and awards, research interest. Arrangement: Alphabetical. Indexes: Discipline (in separate volume).

★8194★ Careers in Focus: Engineering

Facts On File Inc.
132 W 31st St., 17th Fl.
New York, NY 10001
Ph: (212)967-8800   Fax: 800-678-3633
Fr: 800-322-8755
URL: http://www.factsonfile.com

3rd edition, 2007. $29.95 for individuals; $26.95 for libraries. Publication includes: List of resources to consult for more information. Principal content of publication consists of job descriptions, advancement opportunities, educational requirements, employment outlook, salary information, and working conditions for careers in the field of engineering. Indexes: Alphabetical.

★8195★ Directory of Contract Staffing Firms

C.E. Publications Inc.
PO Box 3006
Bothell, WA 98041-3006
Ph: (425)806-5200   Fax: (425)806-5585
URL: http://www.cjhunter.com/dcsf/overview.html

Covers nearly 1,300 contract firms actively engaged in the employment of engineering, IT/IS, and technical personnel for 'temporary' contract assignments throughout the world. Entries include: Company name, address,

phone, name of contact, email, web address. Arrangement: Alphabetical. Indexes: Geographical.

★8196★ The Minerals, Metals & Materials Society Membership Directory

American Institute of Mining, Metallurgical and Petroleum Engineers
184 Thorn Hill Rd.
Warrendale, PA 15086
Ph: (724)776-9000   Fax: (724)776-3770
Fr: 800-759-4867
E-mail: csc@tms.org
URL: http://www.tms.org/Business/TD/TDsearch.asp

Annual, July. Covers 8,300 metallurgists, metallurgical engineers, and materials scientists, worldwide. Entries include: Name, office address, career data, telephone number. Arrangement: Alphabetical; geographical. Indexes: Geographical.

★8197★ Peterson's Job Opportunities in Engineering and Technology

Peterson's Guides
2000 Lenox Dr.
Box 67005
Lawrenceville, NJ 08648
Ph: (609)896-1800   Fax: (609)896-4531
Fr: 800-338-3282
E-mail: custsvc@petersons.com
URL: http://www.petersons.com

Compiled by the Peterson's staff. Fourth edition, 1996. $21.95 (paper). 379 pages. Profiles 2,000 high-tech companies looking primarily for technical personnel in such fields as biotechnology, telecommunications, software, computers and peripherals, defense, and aerospace. Contains job-search strategies and career options to help match education and expertise to the job market. Indexed geographically, by industry, and by hiring needs.

HANDBOOKS AND MANUALS

★8198★ The Best Resumes for Scientists and Engineers

John Wiley & Sons Inc.
1 Wiley Dr.
Somerset, NJ 08873
Ph: (732)469-4400   Fax: (732)302-2300
Fr: 800-225-5945
E-mail: custserv@wiley.com
URL: http://www.wiley.com/WileyCDA/

Adele Lewis and David J. Moore. Second edition, 1993. $37.50; $19.95 (paper). 224 pages. Presents an extensive collection of scientific and engineering resumes, highlighting the important differences between these and resumes written for other occupations.

★8199★ Great Jobs for Engineering Majors

The McGraw-Hill Companies
PO Box 182604
Columbus, OH 43272
Fax: (614)759-3749   Fr: 877-883-5524
E-mail: customer.service@mcgraw-hill.com
URL: http://www.mcgraw-hill.com

Geraldine O. Garner. Second edition, 2002. $14.95. 256 pages. Covers all the career options open to students majoring in engineering.

★8200★ The I Hate Selling Book: Business-Building Advice for Consultants, Attorneys, Accountants, Engineers, Architects, and Other Professionals

AMACOM
1601 Broadway, 12th Fl.
New York, NY 10019-7420
Ph: (212)586-8100   Fax: (212)903-8168
Fr: 800-262-9699
URL: http://www.amanet.org

Allan S. Boress. 2001. $29.95. 240 pages.

★8201★ Keys to Engineering Success

Prentice Hall PTR
One Lake St.
Upper Saddle River, NJ 07458
Ph: (201)236-7000   Fr: 800-428-5331
URL: http://www.phptr.com/index.asp?rl=1

Jill S. Tietjen, Kristy A. Schloss, Carol Carter, Joyce Bishop, and Sarah Lyman. 2000. $46.00 (paper). 288 pages.

★8202★ Opportunities in Engineering Careers

The McGraw-Hill Companies
PO Box 182604
Columbus, OH 43272
Fax: (614)759-3749   Fr: 877-883-5524
E-mail: customer.service@mcgraw-hill.com
URL: http://www.mcgraw-hill.com

Nicholas Basta. Revised second edition, 2002. $13.95; $11.95 (paper). 160 pages. Outlines typical job titles, salaries, career paths, and employment prospects.

★8203★ Opportunities in High Tech Careers

The McGraw-Hill Companies
PO Box 182604
Columbus, OH 43272
Fax: (614)759-3749   Fr: 877-883-5524
E-mail: customer.service@mcgraw-hill.com
URL: http://www.mcgraw-hill.com

Gary Colter and Deborah Yanuck. 1999. $14.95; $11.95 (paper). 160 pages. Explores high technology careers. Describes job opportunities, how to make a career decision, how to prepare for high technology jobs, job hunting techniques, and future trends.

★8204★ Real People Working in Engineering

The McGraw-Hill Companies
PO Box 182604
Columbus, OH 43272
Fax: (614)759-3749   Fr: 877-883-5524
E-mail: customer.service@mcgraw-hill.com
URL: http://www.mcgraw-hill.com

Blythe Camenson, Jan Goldberg. 1997. $17.95 (paper). 160 pages. Interviews and profiles of working professionals capture a range of opportunities in this field.

★8205★ Resumes for Engineering Careers

The McGraw-Hill Companies
PO Box 182604
Columbus, OH 43272
Fax: (614)759-3749   Fr: 877-883-5524
E-mail: customer.service@mcgraw-hill.com
URL: http://www.mcgraw-hill.com

Third edition, 2005. $11.95 (paper). 144 pages. Contains sample resumes and cover letters applicable to any engineering field.

★8206★ Resumes for Scientific and Technical Careers

The McGraw-Hill Companies
PO Box 182604
Columbus, OH 43272
Fax: (614)759-3749   Fr: 877-883-5524
E-mail: customer.service@mcgraw-hill.com
URL: http://www.mcgraw-hill.com

Third edition, 2007. $12.95 (paper). 144 pages. Provides resume advice for individuals interested in working in scientific and technical careers. Includes sample resumes and cover letters.

EMPLOYMENT AGENCIES AND SEARCH FIRMS

★8207★ Colli Associates

414 Caboose Ln.
Valrico, FL 33594
Ph: (813)681-2145   Fax: (813)661-5217
E-mail: colli@gte.net

Employment agency. Executive search firm.

★8208★ Edgewood International

3018 Edgewood Pkwy.
Woodridge, IL 60517-3720
Ph: (630)985-6067   Fax: (630)985-6069
E-mail: wocatedgewood@aol.com

Executive search firm.

★8209★ Elite Resources Group

1239 Stetson Lane
Sevierville, TN 37876
Ph: (865)774-8228   Fax: (865)774-8229
E-mail: search@elite-rg.com

URL: http://www.elite-rg.com

Executive search firm.

★8210★ Empire International

1147 Lancaster Ave.
Berwyn, PA 19312
Ph: (610)647-7976   Fax: (610)647-8488
E-mail: emhunter@empire-internl.com
URL: http://www.empire-internl.com

Executive search firm.

★8211★ Engineer One, Inc.

PO Box 23037
Knoxville, TN 37933
Fax: (865)691-0110
E-mail: engineerone@engineerone.com
URL: http://www.engineerone.com

Engineering employment service specializes in engineering and management in the chemical process, power utilities, manufacturing, mechanical, electrical, and electronic industries. Established an Information Technology Division in 1998 that works nationwide across all industries. Also provides systems analysis consulting services specializing in VAX based systems.

★8212★ Evenium Inc.

520 Marquette Ave.
Minneapolis, MN 55402
Ph: (612)436-3200   Fax: (612)436-3157
URL: http://www.eveniumgroup.com/

Executive search firm.

★8213★ Executive Directions

PO Box 223
Foxboro, MA 02035
Ph: (505)698-3030   Fax: (508)543-6047
E-mail: info@execdir.com
URL: http://www.executivedirections.com

Executive search firm.

★8214★ Executive Resource Group Inc.

1330 Cedar Point, Ste. 201
Amelia, OH 45102
Ph: (513)947-1447   Fax: (513)752-3026
E-mail: hrjobs4@executiveresource.net
URL: http://www.executiveresource.net

Executive search firm.

★8215★ Executives Unlimited Inc.

5000 E. Spring St., Ste. 395
Long Beach, CA 90803
Ph: (562)627-3800   Fax: (562)627-1092
Fr: (866)957-4466
E-mail: resumes@executives-unlimited.com
URL: http://www.executives-unlimited.com

Executive search firm. Branches in Western Springs, IL; Scotch Plains, NJ; Long Beach, CA.

★8216★ First Choice Search

PO Box 946
Danville, WA 94526
Ph: (925)552-9985
E-mail: info@firstchoicesearch.com
URL: http://www.firstchoicesearch.com

Executive search firm.

★8217★ Fischer Group International Inc.

296 Country Club Rd., Fl 2
Avon, CT 06001
Ph: (860)404-7700   Fax: (860)404-7799
E-mail: info@fischergroupintl.com
URL: http://www.fischergroupintl.com

Executive search firm.

★8218★ Global Employment Solutions

10375 Park Meadows Dr., Ste. 375
Littleton, CO 80124
Ph: (303)216-9500   Fax: (303)216-9533
E-mail: careers@global
URL: http://www.gesnetwork.com

Employment agency.

★8219★ International Staffing Consultants

17310 Redhill Ave., No. 140
Irvine, CA 92614
Ph: (949)255-5857   Fax: (949)767-5959
E-mail: iscinc@iscworld.com
URL: http://www.iscworld.com

Employment agency. Provides placement on regular or temporary basis. Affiliate office in London.

★8220★ National Recruiting Service

1832 Hart St.
PO Box 218
Dyer, IN 46311-1564
Ph: (219)865-2373   Fax: (219)865-2375
E-mail: info@nationalrecruitingservice.com
URL: http://www.nationalrecruitingservice.com

A privately held Midwestern human resource firm, which specializes in the identification and screening of personnel exclusively to the pipe and tubing industry. In addition to the recruiting function the firm also offers a comprehensive outplacement and employee termination service, which can be used for all levels of management. Through executive search, psychological evaluations, contingency methods, consulting and outplacement services, firm helps organizations to fully utilize client personnel as a cost effective asset. Industries served: metals.

★8221★ RN Eyler Associates Inc.

2923 Vine St., Ste. 170
West Des Moines, IA 50265
Ph: (515)245-4244
E-mail: mreyler@msn.com

Executive search firm.

★8222★ Search and Recruit International

4455 South Blvd. Ste. 110
Virginia Beach, VA 23452
Ph: (757)625-2121   Fr: 800-800-5627

Employment agency. Headquartered in Virginia Beach. Other offices in Bremerton, WA; Charleston, SC; Jacksonville, FL; Memphis, TN; Pensacola, FL; Sacramento, CA; San Bernardino, CA; San Diego, CA.

ONLINE JOB SOURCES AND SERVICES

★8223★ Spherion

2050 Spectrum Blvd.
Fort Lauderdale, FL 33309
Ph: (954)308-7600
E-mail: help@spherion.com
URL: http://www.spherion.com

Description: Recruitment firm specializing in accounting and finance, sales and marketing, interim executives, technology, engineering, retail and human resources.

TRADESHOWS

★8224★ American Ceramic Society Annual Meeting and Exposition

American Ceramic Society
735 Ceramic Place, Ste. 100
Westerville, OH 43086-6136
Ph: (614)890-4700   Fax: (614)899-6109
Fr: (866)721-3322
E-mail: info@ceramics.org
URL: http://www.ceramics.org/

Annual. **Primary Exhibits:** Manufacturing equipment, supplies, raw materials, and advanced products.

★8225★ METALFORM

Precision Metalforming Association
6363 Oak Tree Blvd.
Independence, OH 44131-2500
Ph: (216)901-8800   Fax: (216)901-9190
E-mail: pma@pma.org
URL: http://www.metalforming.com

Annual. **Primary Exhibits:** Presses and stamping equipment, tooling and fabricating machines, management aids, and related materials.

★8226★ The NGA Show: America's Glass Expo (GlassBuild)

National Glass Association
8200 Greensboro Dr., Ste. 302
McLean, VA 22102-3881
Ph: (703)442-4890   Fax: (703)442-0630
Fr: (866)342-5642
E-mail: nga@glass.org

URL: http://www.glass.org

Annual. **Primary Exhibits:** Glass and glass-related products, supplies, equipment, tools, and machinery, automotive glazing, equipment/machinery, curtain wall, store front systems, doors/hardware, windows, mirrors, shower/tub enclosures, and tools.

★8227★ TMS Annual Meeting and Exhibition

TMS - Minerals, Metals and Materials Society
184 Thorn Hill Rd.
Warrendale, PA 15086-7514
Ph: (724)776-9000   Fax: (724)776-3770
Fr: 800-759-4867
E-mail: tmsgeneral@tms.org
URL: http://www.tms.org

Annual. **Primary Exhibits:** Equipment, supplies, and services for those involved in the scientific and technological aspects of the minerals, metals, and materials industries.

★8228★ WELDEX - International Welding, Cutting, and Metal Fabrication Exhibition

Reed Exhibitions (North American Headquarters)
383 Main Ave.
Norwalk, CT 06851
Ph: (203)840-5337   Fax: (203)840-9570
E-mail: export@reedexpo.com
URL: http://www.reedexpo.com

Quadrennial. **Primary Exhibits:** Plant, equipment, and consumables for welding, brazing, soldering, and surfacing; equipment for safety and fume extraction, gases and gas, industrial robots and automated welding, metal working and machinery, and inspection; fasteners, and hand and power tools.

OTHER SOURCES

★8229★ American Almanac of Jobs and Salaries

HarperCollins
10 E. 53rd St.
New York, NY 10022
Ph: (212)207-7000   Fr: 800-242-7737
URL: http://www.harpercollins.com/

John W. Wright. Revised edition, 2000. $20.00 (paper). 672 pages. This is a comprehensive guide to the wages of hundreds of occupations in a wide variety of industries and organizations.

★8230★ American Association of Engineering Societies (AAES)

1620 I St. NW, Ste. 210
Washington, DC 20006
Ph: (202)296-2237   Fax: (202)296-1151
Fr: 888-400-2237
E-mail: dbateson@aaes.org
URL: http://www.aaes.org

Description: Coordinates the efforts of the member societies in the provision of reliable and objective information to the general public concerning issues which affect the engineering profession and the field of engineering as a whole; collects, analyzes, documents, and disseminates data which will inform the general public of the relationship between engineering and the national welfare; provides a forum for the engineering societies to exchange and discuss their views on matters of common interest; and represents the U.S. engineering community abroad through representation in WFEO and UPADI.

★8231★ ASM International (ASM)

9639 Kinsman Rd.
Novelty, OH 44073-0002
Ph: (440)338-5151   Fax: (440)338-4634
Fr: 800-336-5152
E-mail: customerservice@asminternational.org
URL: http://www.asminternational.org

Description: Metallurgists, materials engineers, executives in materials producing and consuming industries; teachers and students. Disseminates technical information about the manufacture, use, and treatment of engineered materials. Offers in-plant, home study, and intensive courses through Materials Engineering Institute. Conducts career development program. Established ASM Foundation for Education and Research.

★8232★ Association for International Practical Training (AIPT)

10400 Little Patuxent Pkwy., Ste. 250
Columbia, MD 21044-3519
Ph: (410)997-2200   Fax: (410)992-3924
E-mail: aipt@aipt.org
URL: http://www.aipt.org

Description: Providers worldwide of on-the-job training programs for students and professionals seeking international career development and life-changing experiences. Arranges workplace exchanges in hundreds of professional fields, bringing employers and trainees together from around the world. Client list ranges from small farming communities to Fortune 500 companies.

★8233★ Engineering Occupations

Delphi Productions
3159 6th St.
Boulder, CO 80304
Ph: (303)443-2100   Fax: (303)443-4022
Fr: 888-443-2400
E-mail: support@delphivideo.com
URL: http://www.delphivideo.com

$95.00. 50 minutes. Part of the Careers for the 21st Century Video Library.

★8234★ ISA - Instrumentation, Systems, and Automation Society

67 Alexander Dr.
PO Box 12277
Research Triangle Park, NC 27709
Ph: (919)549-8411   Fax: (919)549-8288
E-mail: info@isa.org
URL: http://www.isa.org

Description: Sets the standard for automation by helping over 30,000 worldwide members and other professionals solve difficult technical problems, while enhancing their leadership and personal career capabilities. Develops standards; certifies industry professionals; provides education and training; publishes books and technical articles; and hosts the largest conference and exhibition for automation professionals in the Western Hemisphere. Is the founding sponsor of The Automation Federation.

★8235★ National Action Council for Minorities in Engineering (NACME)

440 Hamilton Ave., Ste. 302
White Plains, NY 10601-1813
Ph: (914)539-4010   Fax: (914)539-4032
E-mail: webmaster@nacme.org
URL: http://www.nacme.org

Description: Leads the national effort to increase access to careers in engineering and other science-based disciplines. Conducts research and public policy analysis, develops and operates national demonstration programs at precollege and university levels, and disseminates information through publications, conferences and electronic media. Serves as a privately funded source of scholarships for minority students in engineering.

★8236★ National Society of Professional Engineers (NSPE)

1420 King St.
Alexandria, VA 22314-2794
Ph: (703)684-2800   Fax: (703)836-4875
Fr: 888-285-6773
E-mail: memserv@nspe.org
URL: http://www.nspe.org

Description: Represents professional engineers and engineers-in-training in all fields registered in accordance with the laws of states or territories of the U.S. or provinces of Canada; qualified graduate engineers, student members, and registered land surveyors. Is concerned with social, professional, ethical, and economic considerations of engineering as a profession; encompasses programs in public relations, employment practices, ethical considerations, education, and career guidance. Monitors legislative and regulatory actions of interest to the engineering profession.

★8237★ Scientific, Engineering, and Technical Services

Cambridge Educational
PO Box 2053
Princeton, NJ 08543-2053
Ph: 800-257-5126   Fax: (609)671-0266
Fr: 800-468-4227
E-mail: custserv@films.com
URL: http://www.cambridgeeducational.com
VHS and DVD. $89.95. 2002. 18 minutes. 2002. Part of the Career Cluster Series.

★8238★ Society of Women Engineers (SWE)

230 E Ohio St., Ste. 400
Chicago, IL 60611-3265
Ph: (312)596-5223   Fax: (312)596-5252
Fr: 877-SWE-INFO
E-mail: hq@swe.org
URL: http://www.swe.org

Description: Educational and service organization representing both students and professional women in engineering and technical fields.

★8239★ Women in Engineering

Her Own Words
PO Box 5264
Madison, WI 53705-0264
Ph: (608)271-7083   Fax: (608)271-0209
E-mail: herownword@aol.com
URL: http://www.herownwords.com/

Video. Jocelyn Riley. $95.00. 15 minutes. Resource guide also available for $45.00.

Meteorologists

★8248★ *National Weather Service Offices and Stations*

U.S. National Weather Service
1325 East-W Hwy.
Silver Spring, MD 20910
Ph: (301)713-1698
URL: http://www.nws.noaa.gov/

Annual, September. Covers offices and stations operated by or under the supervision of the National Weather Service in the United States, Mexico, the Caribbean, Central and South America, and Oceania. Entries include: Station and airport name, type of station, call letters, International Index Number, latitude, longitude, elevation, and number, type, and frequency of weather observations. Arrangement: Geographical.

★8249★ *Peterson's Job Opportunities in Engineering and Technology*

Peterson's Guides
2000 Lenox Dr.
Box 67005
Lawrenceville, NJ 08648
Ph: (609)896-1800   Fax: (609)896-4531
Fr: 800-338-3282
E-mail: custsvc@petersons.com
URL: http://www.petersons.com

Compiled by the Peterson's staff. Fourth edition, 1996. $21.95 (paper). 379 pages. Profiles 2,000 high-tech companies looking primarily for technical personnel in such fields as biotechnology, telecommunications, software, computers and peripherals, defense, and aerospace. Contains job-search strategies and career options to help match education and expertise to the job market. Indexed geographically, by industry, and by hiring needs.

HANDBOOKS AND MANUALS

★8250★ *The Best Resumes for Scientists and Engineers*

John Wiley & Sons Inc.
1 Wiley Dr.
Somerset, NJ 08873
Ph: (732)469-4400   Fax: (732)302-2300
Fr: 800-225-5945
E-mail: custserv@wiley.com
URL: http://www.wiley.com/WileyCDA/

Adele Lewis and David J. Moore. Second edition, 1993. $37.50; $19.95 (paper). 224 pages. Presents an extensive collection of scientific and engineering resumes, highlighting the important differences between these and resumes written for other occupations.

★8251★ *Opportunities in Research and Development Careers*

The McGraw-Hill Companies
PO Box 182604
Columbus, OH 43272
Fax: (614)759-3749   Fr: 877-883-5524
E-mail: customer.service@mcgraw-hill.com
URL: http://www.mcgraw-hill.com

Jan Goldberg. 1996. $11.95 (paper). 146 pages.

TRADESHOWS

★8252★ *AMS Annual Meeting*

American Meteorological Society
45 Beacon St.
Boston, MA 02108-3693
Ph: (617)227-2425   Fax: (617)742-8718
E-mail: amsmtgs@ametsoc.org
URL: http://www.ametsoc.org

Annual. **Primary Exhibits:** Satellite weather data systems, meteorological data integration systems, hydro-meteorological instruments, and aerostatic vehicles.

OTHER SOURCES

★8253★ *American Almanac of Jobs and Salaries*

HarperCollins
10 E. 53rd St.
New York, NY 10022
Ph: (212)207-7000   Fr: 800-242-7737
URL: http://www.harpercollins.com/

John W. Wright. Revised edition, 2000. $20.00 (paper). 672 pages. This is a comprehensive guide to the wages of hundreds of occupations in a wide variety of industries and organizations.

★8254★ *American Meteorological Society (AMS)*

45 Beacon St.
Boston, MA 02108-3693
Ph: (617)227-2425   Fax: (617)742-8718
E-mail: amsinfo@ametsoc.org
URL: http://www.ametsoc.org

Description: Professional meteorologists, oceanographers, and hydrologists; interested students and nonprofessionals. Develops and disseminates information on the atmospheric and related oceanic and hydrospheric sciences; seeks to advance professional applications. Activities include guidance service, scholarship programs, career information, certification of consulting meteorologists, and a seal of approval program to recognize competence in radio and television weathercasting. Issues statements of policy to assist public understanding on subjects such as weather modification, forecasting, tornadoes, hurricanes, flash floods, and meteorological satellites. Provides abstracting services. Prepares educational films, filmstrips, and slides for a new curriculum in meteorology at the ninth grade level. Issues monthly announcements of job openings for meteorologists.

★8255★ *ASPRS - The Imaging and Geospatial Information Society*

5410 Grosvenor Ln., Ste. 210
Bethesda, MD 20814-2160
Ph: (301)493-0290   Fax: (301)493-0208
E-mail: asprs@asprs.org
URL: http://www.asprs.org

Members: Firms, individuals, government employees and academicians engaged in photogrammetry, photointerpretation, remote sensing, and geographic information systems and their application to such fields as archaeology, geographic information systems, military reconnaissance, urban planning, engineering, traffic surveys, meteorological observations, medicine, geology, forestry, agriculture, construction and topographic mapping. Mission is to advance knowledge and improve understanding of these sciences and to promote responsible applications. **Activities:** Offers voluntary certification program open to persons associated with one or more functional area of photogrammetry, remote sensing and GIS. Surveys the profession of private firms in photogrammetry and remote sensing in the areas of products and services.

★8256★ *Association for International Practical Training (AIPT)*

10400 Little Patuxent Pkwy., Ste. 250
Columbia, MD 21044-3519
Ph: (410)997-2200   Fax: (410)992-3924
E-mail: aipt@aipt.org
URL: http://www.aipt.org

Description: Providers worldwide of on-the-job training programs for students and professionals seeking international career development and life-changing experiences. Arranges workplace exchanges in hundreds of professional fields, bringing employers and trainees together from around the world. Client list ranges from small farming communities to Fortune 500 companies.

★8257★ *Minority Women In Science (MWIS)*

Directorate for Education and Human Resources Programs
1200 New York Ave. NW
Washington, DC 20005
Ph: (202)326-7019   Fax: (202)371-9849
E-mail: ygeorge@aaas.org

Description: A national network group of the American association for the Advancement of Science (AAAS), Education and Human Resources Directorate. The objectives of this group are: to identify and share information on resources and programs that could help in mentoring young women and minorities interested in science and engineering careers, and to strengthen communication among women and minorities in science and education.

★8258★ Scientific, Engineering, and Technical Services

Cambridge Educational
PO Box 2053
Princeton, NJ 08543-2053
Ph: 800-257-5126   Fax: (609)671-0266
Fr: 800-468-4227
E-mail: custserv@films.com
URL: http://www.cambridgeeducational.com

VHS and DVD. $89.95. 2002. 18 minutes. 2002. Part of the Career Cluster Series.

★8259★ Scientific Occupations

Delphi Productions
3159 6th St.
Boulder, CO 80304
Ph: (303)443-2100   Fax: (303)443-4022
Fr: 888-443-2400
E-mail: support@delphivideo.com
URL: http://www.delphivideo.com

$95.00. 60 minutes. Part of the Careers for the 21st Century Video Library.

Mining Engineers

SOURCES OF HELP-WANTED ADS

★8260★ AEG News
Association of Engineering Geologists
PO Box 460518
Denver, CO 80246
Ph: (303)757-2926   Fax: (303)757-2969
E-mail: aeg@aegweb.org
URL: http://www.aegweb.org

Description: Bimonthly. Covers news of the engineering geology profession and the Association, whose members are engineering geologists and geological engineers worldwide. Recurring features include letters to the editor, a calendar of events, news of research, and short articles of technical interest.

★8261★ Coal Age
Mining Media Inc.
751 East Hampden Ave., Ste. B-1
Denver, CO 80231
Ph: (303)283-0640   Fax: (303)283-0641
URL: http://www.coalage.com

Monthly. Coal production magazine.

★8262★ Energy User News
NP Media
401 W Big Beaver Rd., Ste. 700
Troy, MI 48084-3333
Ph: (248)786-1642   Fax: (248)786-1388
URL: http://www.energyusernews.com

Monthly. Magazine reporting on the energy management market as it relates to commercial, industrial, and institutional facilities.

★8263★ Engineering Economist
Institute of Industrial Engineers
3577 Parkway Ln., Ste. 200
Norcross, GA 30092
Ph: (770)449-0460   Fax: (770)441-3295
Fr: 800-494-0460
URL: http://www.iienet2.org/De-tails.aspx?id=1486
Quarterly. $73.00/year   for   individuals;

$129.00/year for institutions, online only; $136.00/year for institutions, print & online; $82.00/year for institutions, print + online; $77.00/year for institutions, online only. Publication covering business issues in the energy, petroleum and mining industries.

★8264★ Engineering and Mining Journal
Penton Media Inc.
9800 Metcalf Ave.
Overland Park, KS 66212
Ph: (913)341-1300   Fax: (913)967-1898
URL: http://www.e-mj.com

Monthly. Provides professionals in metallic and nonmetallic ores and minerals industries with news and technical economic information.

★8265★ Engineering Times
National Society of Professional Engineers
1420 King St.
Alexandria, VA 22314
Ph: (703)684-2800
URL: http://www.nspe.org

Monthly. Magazine (tabloid) covering professional, legislative, and techology issues for an engineering audience.

★8266★ ENR: Engineering News-Record
McGraw-Hill Inc.
1221 Ave. of the Americas
New York, NY 10020-1095
Ph: (212)512-2000   Fax: (212)512-3840
Fr: 877-833-5524
E-mail: enr_web_editors@mcgraw-hill.com
URL: http://www.mymags.com/morein-fo.php?itemID=20012

Weekly. $94.00/year for individuals, print. Magazine focusing on engineering and construction.

★8267★ Graduating Engineer & Computer Careers
Career Recruitment Media
211 W Wacker Dr., Ste. 900
Chicago, IL 60606
Ph: (312)525-3100
URL: http://www.graduatingengineer.com

Quarterly. $15.00/year for individuals. Magazine focusing on employment, education, and career development for entry-level engineers and computer scientists.

★8268★ High Technology Careers Magazine
HTC
4701 Patrick Henry Dr., No. 1901
Santa Clara, CA 95054-1847
Fax: (408)567-0242
URL: http://www.hightechcareers.com

Bimonthly. $29.00/year; $35.00/year for Canada; $85.00/year for out of country. Magazine (tabloid) containing employment opportunity information for the engineering and technical community.

★8269★ International California Mining Journal
International California Mining Journal
PO Box 2260
Aptos, CA 95001-2260
Ph: (831)479-1500   Fax: (831)479-4385
URL: http://www.icmj.com

Monthly. $25.95/year for U.S.; $67.85 for U.S., 2-years; $46.90 for U.S., 3-years; $39.50/year for Canada; $72.50 for Canada, 2-years; $105.00 for Canada, 3-years; $43.50/year for out of country; $79.00 for out of country, 2-years; $114.50 for out of country, 3-years. Mining trade magazine covering prospecting and mining throughout the world.

★8270★ The Mining Record
Howell International Enterprises
PO Box 1630
Castle Rock, CO 80104-6130
Ph: (303)663-7820   Fax: (303)663-7823
Fr: 800-441-4748
URL: http://www.miningrecord.com/

Monthly. $55.00/year for individuals; $90.00 for individuals, 2 years; $125.00 for individuals, 3 years. International mining industry newspaper. Features reporting on exploration, discovery, development, production, joint ventures, operating results, legislation, government reports, and metals prices.

★8271★ **Monthly Energy Review**

U.S. Government Printing Office and
  Superintendent of Documents
PO Box 371954
Pittsburgh, PA 15250-7954
Ph: (202)512-1800   Fax: (202)512-2104
URL: http://bookstore.gpo.gov/

Monthly. $147.00/year for individuals; $205.80/year for other countries. Publication covering the petroleum, energy and mining industries.

★8272★ **NSBE Magazine**

NSBE Publications
205 Daingerfield Rd.
Alexandria, VA 22314
Ph: (703)549-2207   Fax: (703)683-5312
URL: http://www.nsbe.org/publications/
premieradvertisers.php

Journal providing information on engineering careers, self-development, and cultural issues for recent graduates with technical majors.

★8273★ **Pay Dirt Magazine**

Copper Queen Publishing Company Inc.
PO Box 48
Bisbee, AZ 85603
Ph: (520)432-2244   Fax: (520)432-2247
E-mail: paydirt@theriver.com

Monthly. $30.00/year for individuals; $3.00 for single issue. Magazine bringing mining developments, government mining policies, environmental issues, and mining heritage to the U.S. and around the world.

★8274★ **SWE, Magazine of the Society of Women Engineers**

Society of Women Engineers
230 East Ohio St., Ste. 400
Chicago, IL 60611-3265
Ph: (312)596-5223
E-mail: hq@swe.org
URL: http://www.swe.org

Quarterly. $30.00/year for nonmembers. Magazine for engineering students and for women and men working in the engineering and technology fields. Covers career guidance, continuing development and topical issues.

★8275★ **WEPANEWS**

Women in Engineering Programs &
  Advocates Network
1901 E. Asbury Ave., Ste. 220
Denver, CO 80208
Ph: (303)871-4643   Fax: (303)871-6833
E-mail: dmatt@wepan.org
URL: http://www.wepan.org

Description: 2/year. Seeks to provide greater access for women to careers in engineering. Includes news of graduate, undergraduate, freshmen, pre-college, and re-entry engineering programs for women. Recurring features include job listings, faculty, grant, and conference news, international engineering program news, action group news, notices of publications available, and a column titled Kudos.

PLACEMENT AND JOB REFERRAL SERVICES

★8276★ **American Indian Science and Engineering Society (AISES)**

PO Box 9828
Albuquerque, NM 87119-9828
Ph: (505)765-1052   Fax: (505)765-5608
E-mail: info@aises.org
URL: http://www.aises.org

Description: Represents American Indian and non-Indian students and professionals in science, technology, and engineering fields; corporations representing energy, mining, aerospace, electronic, and computer fields. Seeks to motivate and encourage students to pursue undergraduate and graduate studies in science, engineering, and technology. Sponsors science fairs in grade schools, teacher training workshops, summer math/science sessions for 8th-12th graders, professional chapters, and student chapters in colleges. Offers scholarships. Adult members serve as role models, advisers, and mentors for students. Operates placement service.

★8277★ **Engineering Society of Detroit (ESD)**

2000 Town Ctr., Ste. 2610
Southfield, MI 48075
Ph: (248)353-0735   Fax: (248)353-0736
E-mail: esd@esd.org
URL: http://esd.org

Description: Engineers from all disciplines; scientists and technologists. Conducts technical programs and engineering refresher courses; sponsors conferences and expositions. Maintains speakers' bureau; offers placement services; although based in Detroit, MI, society membership is international.

★8278★ **Korean-American Scientists and Engineers Association (KSEA)**

1952 Gallows Rd., Ste. 300
Vienna, VA 22182
Ph: (703)748-1221   Fax: (703)748-1331
E-mail: admin@ksea.org
URL: http://www.ksea.org

Description: Represents scientists and engineers holding single or advanced degrees. Promotes friendship and mutuality among Korean and American scientists and engineers; contributes to Korea's scientific, technological, industrial, and economic developments; strengthens the scientific, technological, and cultural bonds between Korea and the U.S. Sponsors symposium. Maintains speakers' bureau, placement service, and biographical archives. Compiles statistics.

★8279★ **Society of Hispanic Professional Engineers (SHPE)**

5400 E Olympic Blvd., Ste. 210
Los Angeles, CA 90022
Ph: (323)725-3970   Fax: (323)725-0316
E-mail: shpenational@shpe.org
URL: http://oneshpe.shpe.org/wps/portal/
national

Description: Represents engineers, student engineers, and scientists. Aims to increase the number of Hispanic engineers by providing motivation and support to students. Sponsors competitions and educational programs. Maintains placement service and speakers' bureau; compiles statistics.

★8280★ **Society for Mining, Metallurgy, and Exploration (SME)**

8307 Shaffer Pkwy.
Littleton, CO 80127-4102
Ph: (303)973-9550   Fax: (303)973-3845
Fr: 800-763-3132
E-mail: cs@smenet.org
URL: http://www.smenet.org

Description: A member society of the American Institute of Mining, Metallurgical and Petroleum Engineers. Persons engaged in the finding, exploitation, treatment, and marketing of all classes of minerals (metal ores, industrial minerals, and solid fuels) except petroleum. Promotes the arts and sciences connected with the production of useful minerals and metals. Offers specialized education programs; compiles enrollment and graduation statistics from schools offering engineering degrees in mining, mineral, mineral processing/metallurgical, geological, geophysical, and mining technology. Provides placement service and sponsors charitable programs.

EMPLOYER DIRECTORIES AND NETWORKING LISTS

★8281★ **American Men and Women of Science**

Gale, Cengage Learning
27500 Drake Rd.
Farmington Hills, MI 48331-3535
Ph: (248)699-4253   Fax: (248)699-8065
Fr: 800-877-4253
URL: http://www.gale.com

Biennial, latest edition 23rd, October 2006; new edition expected 24th, January 2008. $1,075.00 for individuals. Covers over 129,700 U.S. and Canadian scientists active in the physical, biological, mathematical, computer science, and engineering fields; includes references to previous edition for deceased scientists and nonrespondents.

Entries include: Name, address, education, personal and career data, memberships, honors and awards, research interest. Arrangement: Alphabetical. Indexes: Discipline (in separate volume).

★8282★ **Careers in Focus: Engineering**
Facts On File Inc.
132 W 31st St., 17th Fl.
New York, NY 10001
Ph: (212)967-8800   Fax: 800-678-3633
Fr: 800-322-8755
URL: http://www.factsonfile.com

3rd edition, 2007. $29.95 for individuals; $26.95 for libraries. Publication includes: List of resources to consult for more information. Principal content of publication consists of job descriptions, advancement opportunities, educational requirements, employment outlook, salary information, and working conditions for careers in the field of engineering. Indexes: Alphabetical.

★8283★ **Directory of Contract Staffing Firms**
C.E. Publications Inc.
PO Box 3006
Bothell, WA 98041-3006
Ph: (425)806-5200   Fax: (425)806-5585
URL: http://www.cjhunter.com/dcsf/overview.html

Covers nearly 1,300 contract firms actively engaged in the employment of engineering, IT/IS, and technical personnel for 'temporary' contract assignments throughout the world. Entries include: Company name, address, phone, name of contact, email, web address. Arrangement: Alphabetical. Indexes: Geographical.

★8284★ **The Geophysical Directory**
Geophysical Directory Inc.
PO Box 130508
Houston, TX 77219
Ph: (713)529-8789   Fax: (713)529-3646
Fr: 800-929-2462
E-mail: info@geophysicaldirectory.com
URL: http://www.geophysicaldirectory.com

Annual; latest edition 62nd. $140.00 for individuals; $155.00 for individuals. Covers about 4,000 companies that provide geophysical equipment, supplies, or services, and mining and petroleum companies that use geophysical techniques; international coverage. Entries include: Company name, address, phone, fax, names of principal executives, operations, and sales personnel; similar information for branch locations. Arrangement: Classified by product or service. Indexes: Company name, personal name.

★8285★ **Indiana Society of Professional Engineers-Directory**
Indiana Society of Professional Engineers
PO Box 20806
Indianapolis, IN 46220
Ph: (317)255-2267   Fax: (317)255-2530
URL: http://www.indspe.org

Annual, fall. Covers member registered engineers, land surveyors, engineering students, and engineers in training. Entries include: Member name, address, phone, type of membership, business information, specialty. Arrangement: Alphabetical by chapter area.

★8286★ **Peterson's Job Opportunities in Engineering and Technology**
Peterson's Guides
2000 Lenox Dr.
Box 67005
Lawrenceville, NJ 08648
Ph: (609)896-1800   Fax: (609)896-4531
Fr: 800-338-3282
E-mail: custsvc@petersons.com
URL: http://www.petersons.com

Compiled by the Peterson's staff. Fourth edition, 1996. $21.95 (paper). 379 pages. Profiles 2,000 high-tech companies looking primarily for technical personnel in such fields as biotechnology, telecommunications, software, computers and peripherals, defense, and aerospace. Contains job-search strategies and career options to help match education and expertise to the job market. Indexed geographically, by industry, and by hiring needs.

★8287★ **SME Mining Reference Handbook**
Society for Mining, Metallurgy and Exploration Inc.
8307 Shaffer Pkwy.
PO Box 277002
Littleton, CO 80127-4102
Ph: (303)973-9550   Fax: (303)973-3845
Fr: 800-763-3132
URL: http://www.smenet.org

Latest edition 2002. $139.00 for individuals. Publication includes: List of Web sites for further mining information. Principal content of publication is detailed information helpful for mining engineers working in the field. Indexes: Alphabetical.

★8288★ **Western Mining Directory**
Howell International Enterprises
PO Box 1630
Castle Rock, CO 80104-6130
Ph: (303)663-7820   Fax: (303)663-7823
Fr: 800-441-4748
URL: http://www.miningrecord.com

Annual, March. $49.00 for U.S. and Canada; $55.00 for other countries. Covers about 300 mining firms and organizations in the mining industry of the western United States, including active hardrock and coal mines, uranium and vanadium mines; mining firms, consultants, contractors-developers, suppliers of equipment and services, exploration and drilling companies; educational institutions; mining associations; related government agencies; mining exhibitions and conferences. Entries include: For mining companies–Name, corporate, regional, and exploration office addresses; information regarding companies that are privately or publicly held; stock exchange information; trading symbol. For mines–Names of managers, location, type of mine (open pit or underground), type of recovery, product, operator, reserves, grade, mining rates, number of employees. Arrangement: Alphabetical and geographical. Indexes: Mining location.

HANDBOOKS AND MANUALS

★8289★ **The Best Resumes for Scientists and Engineers**
John Wiley & Sons Inc.
1 Wiley Dr.
Somerset, NJ 08873
Ph: (732)469-4400   Fax: (732)302-2300
Fr: 800-225-5945
E-mail: custserv@wiley.com
URL: http://www.wiley.com/WileyCDA/

Adele Lewis and David J. Moore. Second edition, 1993. $37.50; $19.95 (paper). 224 pages. Presents an extensive collection of scientific and engineering resumes, highlighting the important differences between these and resumes written for other occupations.

★8290★ **The I Hate Selling Book: Business-Building Advice for Consultants, Attorneys, Accountants, Engineers, Architects, and Other Professionals**
AMACOM
1601 Broadway, 12th Fl.
New York, NY 10019-7420
Ph: (212)586-8100   Fax: (212)903-8168
Fr: 800-262-9699
URL: http://www.amanet.org

Allan S. Boress. 2001. $29.95. 240 pages.

★8291★ **Opportunities in Engineering Careers**
The McGraw-Hill Companies
PO Box 182604
Columbus, OH 43272
Fax: (614)759-3749   Fr: 877-883-5524
E-mail: customer.service@mcgraw-hill.com
URL: http://www.mcgraw-hill.com

Nicholas Basta. Revised second edition, 2002. $13.95; $11.95 (paper). 160 pages. Outlines typical job titles, salaries, career paths, and employment prospects.

★8292★ **Real People Working in Engineering**
The McGraw-Hill Companies
PO Box 182604
Columbus, OH 43272
Fax: (614)759-3749   Fr: 877-883-5524
E-mail: customer.service@mcgraw-hill.com
URL: http://www.mcgraw-hill.com

Blythe Camenson, Jan Goldberg. 1997. $17.95 (paper). 160 pages. Interviews and profiles of working professionals capture a range of opportunities in this field.

★8293★ Resumes for Engineering Careers

The McGraw-Hill Companies
PO Box 182604
Columbus, OH 43272
Fax: (614)759-3749   Fr: 877-883-5524
E-mail: customer.service@mcgraw-hill.com
URL: http://www.mcgraw-hill.com

Third edition, 2005. $11.95 (paper). 144 pages. Contains sample resumes and cover letters applicable to any engineering field.

★8294★ Resumes for Scientific and Technical Careers

The McGraw-Hill Companies
PO Box 182604
Columbus, OH 43272
Fax: (614)759-3749   Fr: 877-883-5524
E-mail: customer.service@mcgraw-hill.com
URL: http://www.mcgraw-hill.com

Third edition, 2007. $12.95 (paper). 144 pages. Provides resume advice for individuals interested in working in scientific and technical careers. Includes sample resumes and cover letters.

★8295★ Study Guide for the Professional Registration of Mining/Mineral Engineers

Random House Trade
1745 Broadway
New York, NY 10019
Ph: (212)782-9000   Fax: (212)572-6066
Fr: 800-733-3000
URL: http://www.randomhouse.com

Fifth edition. 1996. $25.00 (paper). 120 pages.

EMPLOYMENT AGENCIES AND SEARCH FIRMS

★8296★ Engineer One, Inc.

PO Box 23037
Knoxville, TN 37933
Fax: (865)691-0110
E-mail: engineerone@engineerone.com
URL: http://www.engineerone.com

Engineering employment service specializes in engineering and management in the chemical process, power utilities, manufacturing, mechanical, electrical, and electronic industries. Established an Information Technology Division in 1998 that works nationwide across all industries. Also provides systems analysis consulting services specializing in VAX based systems.

★8297★ Global Employment Solutions

10375 Park Meadows Dr., Ste. 375
Littleton, CO 80124
Ph: (303)216-9500   Fax: (303)216-9533
E-mail: careers@global
URL: http://www.gesnetwork.com

Employment agency.

★8298★ Search and Recruit International

4455 South Blvd. Ste. 110
Virginia Beach, VA 23452
Ph: (757)625-2121   Fr: 800-800-5627

Employment agency. Headquartered in Virginia Beach. Other offices in Bremerton, WA; Charleston, SC; Jacksonville, FL; Memphis, TN; Pensacola, FL; Sacramento, CA; San Bernardino, CA; San Diego, CA.

ONLINE JOB SOURCES AND SERVICES

★8299★ Spherion

2050 Spectrum Blvd.
Fort Lauderdale, FL 33309
Ph: (954)308-7600
E-mail: help@spherion.com
URL: http://www.spherion.com

Description: Recruitment firm specializing in accounting and finance, sales and marketing, interim executives, technology, engineering, retail and human resources.

TRADESHOWS

★8300★ American Society of Mining and Reclamation

American Society of Mining and
Reclamation
3134 Montevesta Rd.
Lexington, KY 40502
Ph: (859)335-6529   Fax: (859)335-6529
E-mail: asmr@insightbb.com
URL: http://ces.ca.uky.edu/asmr

Annual. **Primary Exhibits:** Exhibits relating to the protection and enhancement of land disturbed by mining.

★8301★ Rapid Excavation & Tunneling Conference

Society for Mining, Metallurgy, and
Exploration, Inc.
8307 Shaffer Pkwy.
PO Box 277002
Littleton, CO 80127
Ph: (303)973-9550   Fax: (303)973-3845
Fr: 800-763-3132
URL: http://www.smenet.org

Biennial. **Primary Exhibits:** Excavation equipment.

OTHER SOURCES

★8302★ American Almanac of Jobs and Salaries

HarperCollins
10 E. 53rd St.
New York, NY 10022
Ph: (212)207-7000   Fr: 800-242-7737
URL: http://www.harpercollins.com/

John W. Wright. Revised edition, 2000. $20.00 (paper). 672 pages. This is a comprehensive guide to the wages of hundreds of occupations in a wide variety of industries and organizations.

★8303★ American Association of Blacks in Energy (AABE)

927 15th St. NW, Ste. 200
Washington, DC 20005-2321
Ph: (202)371-9530   Fax: (202)371-9218
Fr: 800-466-0204
E-mail: aabe@aabe.org
URL: http://www.aabe.org

Description: Seeks to increase the knowledge, understanding, and awareness of the minority community in energy issues by serving as an energy information source for policymakers, recommending blacks and other minorities to appropriate energy officials and executives, encouraging students to pursue professional careers in the energy industry, and advocating the participation of blacks and other minorities in energy programs and policymaking activities. Updates members on key legislation and regulations being developed by the Department of Energy, the Department of Interior, the Department of Commerce, the Small Business Administration, and other federal and state agencies.

★8304★ American Association of Engineering Societies (AAES)

1620 I St. NW, Ste. 210
Washington, DC 20006
Ph: (202)296-2237   Fax: (202)296-1151
Fr: 888-400-2237
E-mail: dbateson@aaes.org
URL: http://www.aaes.org

Description: Coordinates the efforts of the member societies in the provision of reliable and objective information to the general public concerning issues which affect the engineering profession and the field of engineering as a whole; collects, analyzes, documents, and disseminates data which will inform the general public of the relationship between engineering and the national welfare; provides a forum for the engineering societies to exchange and discuss their views on matters of common interest; and represents the U.S. engineering community abroad through representation in WFEO and UPADI.

★8305★ **American Engineering Association (AEA)**

4116 S Carrier Pkwy., Ste. 280-809
Grand Prairie, TX 75052
Ph: (201)664-6954
E-mail: info@aea.org
URL: http://www.aea.org

Description: Members consist of Engineers and engineering professionals. Purpose to advance the engineering profession and U.S. engineering capabilities. Issues of concern include age discrimination, immigration laws, displacement of U.S. Engineers by foreign workers, trade agreements, off shoring of U.S. Engineering and manufacturing jobs, loss of U.S. manufacturing and engineering capability, and recruitment of foreign students. Testifies before Congress. Holds local Chapter meetings.

★8306★ **Association for International Practical Training (AIPT)**

10400 Little Patuxent Pkwy., Ste. 250
Columbia, MD 21044-3519
Ph: (410)997-2200   Fax: (410)992-3924
E-mail: aipt@aipt.org
URL: http://www.aipt.org

Description: Providers worldwide of on-the-job training programs for students and professionals seeking international career development and life-changing experiences. Arranges workplace exchanges in hundreds of professional fields, bringing employers and trainees together from around the world. Client list ranges from small farming communities to Fortune 500 companies.

★8307★ **Engineering Occupations**

Delphi Productions
3159 6th St.
Boulder, CO 80304
Ph: (303)443-2100   Fax: (303)443-4022
Fr: 888-443-2400

E-mail: support@delphivideo.com
URL: http://www.delphivideo.com

$95.00. 50 minutes. Part of the Careers for the 21st Century Video Library.

★8308★ **National Action Council for Minorities in Engineering (NACME)**

440 Hamilton Ave., Ste. 302
White Plains, NY 10601-1813
Ph: (914)539-4010   Fax: (914)539-4032
E-mail: webmaster@nacme.org
URL: http://www.nacme.org

Description: Leads the national effort to increase access to careers in engineering and other science-based disciplines. Conducts research and public policy analysis, develops and operates national demonstration programs at precollege and university levels, and disseminates information through publications, conferences and electronic media. Serves as a privately funded source of scholarships for minority students in engineering.

★8309★ **National Society of Professional Engineers (NSPE)**

1420 King St.
Alexandria, VA 22314-2794
Ph: (703)684-2800   Fax: (703)836-4875
Fr: 888-285-6773
E-mail: memserv@nspe.org
URL: http://www.nspe.org

Description: Represents professional engineers and engineers-in-training in all fields registered in accordance with the laws of states or territories of the U.S. or provinces of Canada; qualified graduate engineers, student members, and registered land surveyors. Is concerned with social, professional, ethical, and economic considerations of engineering as a profession; encompasses programs in public relations, employment practices, ethical considerations, education, and career guidance. Monitors legislative and regulatory actions of interest to the engineering profession.

★8310★ **Scientific, Engineering, and Technical Services**

Cambridge Educational
PO Box 2053
Princeton, NJ 08543-2053
Ph: 800-257-5126   Fax: (609)671-0266
Fr: 800-468-4227
E-mail: custserv@films.com
URL: http://www.cambridgeeducational.com

VHS and DVD. $89.95. 2002. 18 minutes. 2002. Part of the Career Cluster Series.

★8311★ **Society of Women Engineers (SWE)**

230 E Ohio St., Ste. 400
Chicago, IL 60611-3265
Ph: (312)596-5223   Fax: (312)596-5252
Fr: 877-SWE-INFO
E-mail: hq@swe.org
URL: http://www.swe.org

Description: Educational and service organization representing both students and professional women in engineering and technical fields.

★8312★ **Women in Engineering**

Her Own Words
PO Box 5264
Madison, WI 53705-0264
Ph: (608)271-7083   Fax: (608)271-0209
E-mail: herownword@aol.com
URL: http://www.herownwords.com/

Video. Jocelyn Riley. $95.00. 15 minutes. Resource guide also available for $45.00.

Ministers and Christian Religious Professionals

SOURCES OF HELP-WANTED ADS

★8313★ The Lutheran

Augsburg Fortress, Publishers
100 S 5th St., Ste. 600
PO Box 1209
Minneapolis, MN 55402-1209
Ph: (612)330-3271   Fax: (612)330-3455
Fr: 800-328-4648
E-mail: lutheran@elca.org
URL: http://www.thelutheran.org

Monthly. $15.95/year for individuals; $1.50 for single issue; $29.95 for individuals for two years; $39.95/year for individuals, 3 years. Magazine of the Evangelical Lutheran Church in America.

★8314★ Panorama

Pittsburgh Theological Seminary
616 N. Highland Ave.
Pittsburgh, PA 15206-2596
Ph: (412)362-5610   Fax: (412)363-3260
URL: http://www.pts.edu/

Description: Quarterly. Provides news for Semimary faculty, staff. Recurring features include Interviews, news of research, calendar of events, news of educational opportunities, job listings, book reviews, notices of publications available.

★8315★ Sojourners

Sojourners
2401 15th St. NW
Washington, DC 20009
Ph: (202)328-8842   Fax: (202)328-8757
Fr: 800-714-7474
URL: http://www.sojo.net/

Monthly. $39.95/year for individuals; $49.95/ year for Canada; $59.95/year for other countries; $60.00/year for individuals, supporting; $110.00/year for individuals, partnership. Independent, ecumenical Christian magazine which analyzes faith, politics, and culture from a progressive, justice-oriented perspective.

★8316★ United Church News

United Church of Christ
700 Prospect Ave.
Cleveland, OH 44115
Ph: (216)736-2222   Fax: (216)736-2223
E-mail: guessb@ucc.org
URL: http://www.ucc.org/ucnews

Description: Ten issues/year. Concerned with the programs and activities of the United Church of Christ. Reports news of the UCC's 39 regional groupings and carries notices of pastoral changes within the UCC. Recurring features include letters to the editor, interviews, reports of meetings, news of resources and educational opportunities, and job listings. Also includes columns titled Focus on Faith, Heart Warmers, As I See It, and Current Comment.

★8317★ Vision

National Association of Catholic Chaplains
5007 S. Howell Ave., Ste. 120
Milwaukee, WI 53207-0473
Ph: (414)483-4898   Fax: (414)483-6712
E-mail: info@nacc.org
URL: http://www.nacc.org/vision/

Description: Ten issues/year. Serves Catholic lay persons, priests, and religious personnel in professional health care, related institutional ministries and parishes. Recurring features include book reviews of publications on pastoral care, employment opportunities, and notices of conferences and meetings.

PLACEMENT AND JOB REFERRAL SERVICES

★8318★ American Association of Christian Schools (AACS)

National Office
602 Belvoir Ave.
East Ridge, TN 37412
Ph: (423)629-4280   Fax: (423)622-7461
E-mail: national@aacs.org
URL: http://www.aacs.org

Description: Maintains teacher/administrator certification program and placement service. Participates in school accreditation program. Sponsors National Academic Tournament. Maintains American Christian Honor Society. Compiles statistics; maintains speakers' bureau and placement service.

★8319★ Association of North American Missions (ANAM)

PO Box 8667
Longview, TX 75607-8667
Ph: (903)234-2075
E-mail: info@anamissions.org
URL: http://www.anamissions.org

Description: Missions of more than five missionaries operating in North America. Aims to make missions more credible and visible; to promote unity and cooperation among members; to collect, organize, and disseminate information relating to missionary work to the public and to act as clearinghouse for members. Offers referral and placement service to qualified missionaries not serving with member missions. Provides information about missions to pastors and schools. Offers workshops and in-depth seminars for mission leaders and missionaries.

★8320★ Association of Unity Churches

PO Box 610
Lee's Summit, MO 64063
Ph: (816)524-7414   Fax: (816)525-4020
E-mail: info@mail.unity.org
URL: http://www.unity.org

Description: Ministers and interested members of Unity Churches and study groups. Serves and supports member ministries by providing human resources, administrative and educational programs, and consultation in accordance with the teachings of the Unity School of Christianity founded by Charles and Myrtle Fillmore. Trains and licenses teachers, ministers, and youth advisors; offers continuing education programs and minister employment service. Holds skills development seminars and workshops; sponsors retreats. Offers media service consultation. Assists with the development of local groups.

★8321★ Catholic Campus Ministry Association (CCMA)

1118 Pendleton St., Ste. 300
Cincinnati, OH 45202-8805
Ph: (513)842-0167   Fax: (513)842-0171
Fr: 888-714-6631
E-mail: info@ccmanet.org

Purpose: Purposes are: to form a strong and coordinated voice for the church's ministry in higher education; to provide continuing education programs for members; to provide liaison with other individuals and agencies of the church interested in campus ministry and the role of the church in higher education; to advance ecumenical and interfaith understanding and cooperation; to provide guidelines for, and assistance in, developing effective campus ministries. Maintains placement service and speakers' bureau; offers colleague consultation service.

★8322★ Chinese Christian Mission (CCM)

PO Box 750759
Petaluma, CA 94975-0759
Ph: (707)762-1314   Fax: (707)762-1713
E-mail: ccm@ccmusa.org
URL: http://www.ccmusa.org

Purpose: Serves as an evangelical faith mission dedicated to reaching Chinese people around the world with the gospel of Jesus Christ. Broadcasts radio programs to foster Christianity in China. **Activities:** Operates placement service providing ministers with churches. Sponsors short-term mission trips to Latin America and East Asia.

★8323★ Christian Chiropractors Association (CCA)

2550 Stover, No. B-102
Fort Collins, CO 80525
Ph: (970)482-1404   Fax: (970)482-1538
Fr: 800-999-1970
E-mail: bkaseman@gmail.com
URL: http://www.christianchiropractors.org

Description: Works to spread the Gospel of Christ throughout the U.S. and abroad. Offers Christian fellowship and works to unify Christian chiropractors around the essentials of the faith, "leaving minor points of doctrine to the conscience of the individual believer." Focuses on world missions; organizing short-term trips and aiding in the placement of Christian chiropractors as missionaries.

★8324★ Christian Management Association (CMA)

PO Box 4090
San Clemente, CA 92674
Ph: (949)487-0900   Fax: (949)487-0927
Fr: 800-727-4CMA
E-mail: cma@cmaonline.org
URL: http://sites.silaspartners.com/cma

Description: Represents CEO's, key leaders and managers who serve Christian organizations and churches. Provides management information, leadership training and strategic networking management through its annual national conference, the Christian Management Institute. Holds bimonthly fellowship meeting for training and information reports. Provides job referral and professional referral service to assist Christian management personnel.

★8325★ Christian Schools International (CSI)

3350 E Paris Ave. SE
Grand Rapids, MI 49512-2907
Ph: (616)957-1070   Fax: (616)957-5022
Fr: 800-635-8288
E-mail: info@csionline.org
URL: http://csionline.org

Description: Christian elementary and secondary schools enrolling 100,000 pupils and employing 7,800 teachers. Aims to: provide a medium for a united witness regarding the role of Christian schools in contemporary society; promote the establishment of Christian schools; help members function more effectively in areas of promotion, organization, administration, and curriculum; help establish standards and criteria to guide the operation of its members; foster high professional ideals and economic well-being among Christian school personnel; establish and maintain communication with member schools, colleges, churches, government agencies, and the public. Encourages study, research, and writing that embodies Christian theories of education; conducts salary studies, research, and surveys on operating costs; offers expert and confidential analysis of member school programs and operation. Sponsors meetings, workshops, and seminars; offers placement service. Administers the Christian School Pension and Trust Funds, Group Insurance Plans, and Life and Insurance Plans and Trust Funds.

★8326★ Conservative Baptist Association of America

3686 Stagecoach Rd., Ste. F
Longmont, CO 80504-5660
Ph: (720)283-3030   Fax: (303)772-5690
Fr: 888-366-3010
E-mail: info@cbamerica.org
URL: http://www.cbamerica.org

Description: Provides leadership, fellowship, counseling services, and specialized support ministries to 1200 member churches in an effort "to advance the cause of Christ through worship, evangelism, instruction, and service throughout the world". Conducts charitable program; offers placement service, chaplaincy endorsement.

★8327★ Council for Health and Human Services Ministries, United Church of Christ (CHHSM)

700 Prospect Ave.
Cleveland, OH 44115
Fax: (216)736-2251   Fr: (866)822-8224
E-mail: sickbert@chhsm.org
URL: http://www.chhsm.org

Members: Health and human service institutions related to the United Church of Christ. **Purpose:** Seeks to study, plan, and implement a program in health and human services; assist members in developing and providing quality services and in financing institutional and non-institutional health and human service ministries; stimulate awareness of and support for these programs; inform the UCC of policies that affect the needs, problems, and conditions of patients; cooperate with interdenominational agencies and others in the field. **Activities:** Maintains placement service and hall of fame. Compiles statistics; provides specialized education programs.

★8328★ Evangelical Press Association (EPA)

PO Box 28129
Crystal, MN 55428
Ph: (763)535-4793   Fax: (763)535-4794
E-mail: director@epassoc.org
URL: http://www.epassoc.org

Members: Editors and publishers of Christian periodicals. **Activities:** Maintains placement service.

★8329★ International Catholic Stewardship Council (ICSC)

1275 K St. NW, Ste. 880
Washington, DC 20005-4077
Ph: (202)289-1093   Fax: (202)682-9018
E-mail: info@catholicstewardship.org
URL: http://www.catholicstewardship.org

Description: Commits to promote the right use of God's gifts of time, talent, and treasure through diocesan and parish leadership. Encourages the adoption of the holistic stewardship concept which stresses that everything is a gift from God, and that gratitude for gifts received is best expressed in right management and ministry to others. Fosters the exchange of ideas and materials among dioceses, parishes, and other church organizations. Maintains Speaker's Bureau and placement service. Compiles statistics.

★8330★ Jesuit Association of Student Personnel Administrators (JASPA)

2500 California Plz.
Omaha, NE 68178
Ph: (402)280-2717   Fax: (402)280-1275
E-mail: waynejr@creighton.edu
URL: http://jaspa.creighton.edu

Description: Represents administrators of student personnel programs in 28 Jesuit colleges and universities in the United States. Sponsors institutes and seminars for personnel in Jesuit colleges. Cooperates with Catholic and non-Catholic educational associations in various projects. Maintains placement service and conducts workshops. Operates organizational archives and compiles statistics.

★8331★ National Association of Church Business Administration (NACBA)

100 N Central Expy., Ste. 914
Richardson, TX 75080-5326
Ph: (972)699-7555   Fax: (972)699-7617
Fr: 800-898-8085
E-mail: info@nacba.net
URL: http://www.nacba.net

Description: Represents business administrators and managers employed by local churches or institutions of the Christian church. Aims to train, certify and provide resources for those serving in the field of church administration. Offers placement service; conducts research programs; and compiles statistics. Maintains hall of fame.

★8332★ National Association of Congregational Christian Churches (NACCC)

8473 S Howell Ave.
PO Box 288
Oak Creek, WI 53154-0288
Ph: (414)764-1620   Fax: (414)764-0319
Fr: 800-262-1620
E-mail: naccc@naccc.org
URL: http://www.naccc.org

Purpose: Aims to provide a means whereby Congregational Christian churches may consult and exchange advise on spiritual and temporal matters of common concern; and to encourage the continuance of Christian purposes and practices that have been the historic and accepted characteristics of Congregational Christian churches. **Activities:** Supports the education of ministers through its Congregational Foundation for Theological Studies. Compiles statistics. Operates placement service and mission program. Provides a variety of financial services. Supports youth programming from coast to coast and hosts annual meeting.

★8333★ National Conference for Catechetical Leadership (NCCL)

125 Michigan Ave. NE
Washington, DC 20017
Ph: (202)884-9753   Fax: (202)884-9756
E-mail: nccl@nccl.org
URL: http://www.nccl.org

Members: Diocesan directors of religious education and their staff; publishers, academics, Diocesan religious education, Associations, and individuals interested in religious education. **Purpose:** Fosters communication and unity among members. Addresses the special responsibility to provide lifelong religious education within the Catholic Church; assists members with increasing religious education needs; coordinates religious education and helps to supply needed materials. **Activities:** Aids in formal religious education for children, adults, and handicapped persons. Compiles statistics; provides placement service; operates research programs; conducts charitable program; maintains speakers' bureau.

★8334★ National Lutheran Outdoors Ministry Association (NLOMA)

275 N Syndicate St.
St. Paul, MN 55104
Ph: (651)603-6165
E-mail: nloma@nloma.org
URL: http://www.nloma.org

Description: Individuals and camps joined to aid in the mission of the Lutheran church and to promote Christian camping and relat-

ed experience. Provides support for all areas of outdoor ministry. Serves as resource base for camps in the areas of personnel development, site evaluation, program development, and staff recruitment. Conducts seminars and training sessions. Maintains placement service for individuals seeking employment at a member camp.

★8335★ North American Maritime Ministry Association (NAMMA)

PO Box 2434
Niagara Falls, NY 14302
Ph: (905)892-8818
E-mail: namma@cogeco.ca
URL: http://www.namma.org

Description: Spiritual and social welfare agencies from the U.S., Canada, and the Caribbean providing facilities and services for merchant seafarers. Sponsors Chaplain Training School; operates placement service. Maintains archives; conducts research programs.

★8336★ Presbyterian Association of Musicians (PAM)

100 Witherspoon St.
Louisville, KY 40202-1396
Ph: (502)569-5288   Fax: (502)569-8465
Fr: 888-728-7228
E-mail: abarthel@ctr.pcusa.org
URL: http://www.pam.pcusa.org

Description: Represents organists, choir directors, singers, churches, clergy, directors of Christian education, and interested persons of all denominations. Aims to develop the use of music and the arts in the life and worship of individual congregations. Offers assistance in the areas of worship, music, and the arts. Conducts continuing education. Acts as a clearinghouse for job referrals; promotes the professional status of church musicians and recommends salaries and benefits to churches; certifies church musicians.

★8337★ Presbyterians for Renewal

8134 New LaGrange Rd., Ste. 227
Louisville, KY 40222-4673
Ph: (502)425-4630   Fax: (502)423-8329
E-mail: pfroffice@pfrenewal.org
URL: http://www.pfrenewal.org

Description: Supporters are individuals, congregations, and foundations. Trains church officers. Conducts renewal weekends, officer retreats, and marriage enrichment programs. Provides placement service; bestows awards; compiles statistics. Operates charitable program and speakers' bureau.

★8338★ Society of Biblical Literature (SBL)

Luce Center
825 Houston Mill Rd.
Atlanta, GA 30329
Ph: (404)727-3100   Fax: (404)727-3101
Fr: (866)727-9955
E-mail: sblexec@sbl-site.org

URL: http://www.sbl-site.org

Members: Professors and persons interested in biblical studies, ancient world and religious studies. **Purpose:** Seeks to "stimulate the critical investigation of classical biblical literature, together with other related literature, by the exchange of scholarly research both in published form and in public forum". Endeavors to support those disciplines and sub disciplines pertinent to the illumination of the literatures and religions of the ancient Near Eastern and Mediterranean regions, including the study of ancient languages, textual criticism, history, and archaeology. **Activities:** Supports and cooperates with several national and international groups. Conducts research programs; offers placement services.

★8339★ Teen Missions International (TMI)

885 E Hall Rd.
Merritt Island, FL 32953
Ph: (321)453-0350   Fax: (321)452-7988
E-mail: info@teenmissions.org
URL: http://www.teenmissions.org

Description: Organizes interdenominational evangelical missionary work projects in areas such as agriculture and community development; programs have operated in 60 countries, including Australia, Brazil, Mongolia, India, Indonesia, Mexico, South Africa, and Zimbabwe. Trains teen and adult missionaries through camps and conferences; operates placement service. Promotes the Christian gospel through the production of films, videos, printed materials, and media presentations. Assists in establishing local teen mission clubs in an effort to encourage evangelical outreach.

★8340★ Youth for Christ/U.S.A. (YFC/USA)

PO Box 4478
Englewood, CO 80155
Ph: (303)843-9000   Fax: (303)843-9002
E-mail: info@yfc.net
URL: http://www.yfc.net/Brix?pageID=2941

Description: Fights juvenile delinquency through counseling and Youth Guidance programs for youth penal institutions. Carries on projects in various countries through Youth for Christ International. Maintains placement service. Programs for staff are: area refreshers; college training; intern training; and summer training. Programs for youth are: camps; Campus Life Clubs; counseling; short-term missions and work projects overseas; and Youth Guidance work with troubled teenagers. Sponsors "Lighten Up!" radio.

EMPLOYER DIRECTORIES AND NETWORKING LISTS

★8341★ Christian Schools International-Directory

Christian Schools International
3350 E Paris Ave. SE
Grand Rapids, MI 49512
Ph: (616)957-1070   Fax: (616)957-5022
Fr: 800-635-8288
URL: http://store.csionline.org

Annual; 2007-2008. $15.00 for members; $72.00 for nonmembers. Covers nearly 450 Reformed Christian elementary and secondary schools; related associations; societies without schools. Entries include: For schools–School name, address, phone; name, title, and address of officers; names of faculty members. Arrangement: Geographical.

★8342★ Directory of Catholic Charities USA Directories

Catholic Charities USA
1731 King St.
Alexandria, VA 22314
Ph: (703)549-1390   Fax: (703)549-1656
URL: http://www.catholiccharitiesusa.org/

Annual. $25.00 for individuals. Covers nearly 1,200 Catholic community and social service agencies. Listings include diocesan agencies and state Catholic conferences. Entries include: Organization name, address, name and title of director, phone, fax. Arrangement: Geographical by state, then classified by diocese.

★8343★ Ganley's Catholic Schools in America-Elementary/Secondary/College & University

Fisher Publishing Co.
PO Box 15070
Scottsdale, AZ 85267-5070
Ph: (480)657-9422   Fax: (480)657-9422
Fr: 800-759-7615
URL: http://www.ganleyscatholicschools.com

Annual, summer; latest edition 34th, 2007 edition. $60.00 for individuals. Covers over 8,400 Catholic K-12 Schools. Arrangement: Geographical by state, then alphabetical by Diocese name.

★8344★ Official Traditional Catholic Directory

iUniverse Inc.
2021 Pine Lake Rd., Ste. 100
Lincoln, NE 68512
Ph: (402)323-7800   Fax: (402)323-7824
Fr: 800-288-4677
URL: http://www.iuniverse.com/bookstore/book_detail.asp?isbn=0-59

$15.95 for individuals. Publication includes: Listing of over 600 traditional Latin masses regularly and publicly celebrated in the United States and Canada. Also provides extensive lists of traditional resources, including traditional Catholic organizations, seminaries, religious orders, lay societies, periodicals, suppliers, retreats, and schooling, as well as contacts for traditional Latin masses outside the United States and Canada. Indexes: Alphabetical.

HANDBOOKS AND MANUALS

★8345★ Becoming a Minister

Baker Books House
2768 E. Paris Ave. SE
Grand Rapids, MI 49546
Ph: (616)957-3110   Fax: (616)957-0965
Fr: (866)241-6733
E-mail: retail@bakerbookretail.com
URL: http://www.bakerbooksretail.com/

Thomas C. Oden. Reprint, 2000. $16.99 (paper). 200 pages. Part of Classical Pastoral Care Series Volume One. Out of print.

★8346★ Careers in Social and Rehabilitation Services

The McGraw-Hill Companies
PO Box 182604
Columbus, OH 43272
Fax: (614)759-3749   Fr: 877-883-5524
E-mail: customer.service@mcgraw-hill.com
URL: http://www.mcgraw-hill.com

Geraldine O. Garner. 2001. $19.95; 14.95 (paper). 128 pages.

★8347★ Non-Profits and Education Job Finder

Planning Communications
7215 Oak Ave.
River Forest, IL 60305-1935
Ph: (708)366-5200   Fax: (708)366-5280
Fr: 888-366-5200
E-mail: info@planningcommunications.com
URL: http://jobfindersonline.com

Daniel Lauber. 1997. $32.95; $16.95 (paper). 340 pages. Covers 1600 sources. Discusses how to use sources of non-profit sector job vacancies in a number of specialties and state-by-state, including job-matching services, job hotlines, specialty periodicals with job ads, salary surveys, and directories. Covers a variety of fields from education to religion. Includes chapters on resume and cover letter preparation and interviewing.

★8348★ Opportunities in Religious Service Careers

The McGraw-Hill Companies
PO Box 182604
Columbus, OH 43272
Fax: (614)759-3749   Fr: 877-883-5524
E-mail: customer.service@mcgraw-hill.com
URL: http://www.mcgraw-hill.com

John Oliver Nelson. 2003. $12.95; $11.95 (paper). 160 pages.

★8349★ What Shall I Say? Discerning God's Call to Ministry

Augsburg Fortress Publishers
PO Box 1209
Minneapolis, MN 55440
Fr: 800-328-4648
URL: http://www.augsburgfortress.org/

Walter R. Bouman and Sue M. Setzer. 1995. $6.95 (paper). 86 pages.

★8350★ Who Will Go for Us?: An Invitation to Ordained Ministry

Abingdon Press
PO Box 801
Nashville, TN 37202
Ph: (615)749-6409   Fax: (615)749-6056
Fr: 800-251-3320
E-mail: orders@abingdonpress.com
URL: http://www.abingdonpress.com/

Dennis M. Campbell. 1994. $16.00 (paper). 128 pages.

TRADESHOWS

★8351★ Society for the Scientific Study of Religion Annual Meeting

Exhibit Promotions Plus
11620 Vixens Path
Ellicott City, MD 21042-1539
Ph: (410)997-0763   Fax: (410)997-0764
E-mail: exhibit@epponline.com
URL: http://www.epponline.com

Annual. **Primary Exhibits:** Publications and films and other resources in the fields of religion, philosophy, sociology, psychology and anthropology.

OTHER SOURCES

★8352★ American Association of Pastoral Counselors (AAPC)

9504A Lee Hwy.
Fairfax, VA 22031-2303
Ph: (703)385-2967   Fax: (703)352-7725
E-mail: info@aapc.org
URL: http://www.aapc.org

Description: Pastoral counseling is a form of psychotherapy which uses spiritual resources as well as psychological understanding for healing and growth. Counselors are certified mental health professionals who have had in-depth religious and/or theological training. Represents and sets standards for the profession around the world. Certifies counselors, accredits pastoral counseling centers and approves training programs. "Is a non-sectarian and respects the spiritual commitments and religious traditions of those who needs assistance without imposing counselor beliefs onto the client." Members may join through a process of consultation and review of academic and clinical education. Offers members continuing education opportunities, encourages networks of members for professional support and enrichment, facilitates growth and innovation in the ministry of pastoral counseling and provides both specialized in-service training and supervision in pastoral counseling.

★8353★ American Orff-Schulwerk Association (AOSA)

PO Box 391089
Cleveland, OH 44139-8089
Ph: (440)543-5366   Fax: (440)543-2687
E-mail: info@aosa.org
URL: http://www.aosa.org

Description: Music and movement educators, music therapists, and church choir directors united to promote and encourage the philosophy of Carl Orff's (1895-1982, German composer) Schulwerk (Music for Children) in America. Distributes information on the activities and growth of Orff Schulwerk in America. Conducts research; offers information on teacher training. Operates clearinghouse.

★8354★ Association of Christian Schools International (ACSI)

PO Box 65130
Colorado Springs, CO 80962-5130
Ph: (719)528-6906   Fax: (719)531-0631
Fr: 800-367-0798
E-mail: info@acsi.org
URL: http://www.acsi.org

Description: Seeks to enable Christian educators and schools worldwide to effectively prepare students for life.

★8355★ Association of Southern Baptist Campus Ministers (ASBCM)

PO Box 25118
Baton Rouge, LA 70894
Ph: (225)343-0408   Fax: (225)343-0424
E-mail: lsubcm@eatel.net
URL: http://www.lsubcm.org

Description: Full-time campus ministers with a graduate degree or five years experience in ministry (125); part-time and volunteer ministers, students, and interested individuals are affiliate members (25). Aims to: strengthen the individual's commitment and expertise in the ministry through fellowship and programs; enhance the minister's view of campus and church; promote professional competence among campus ministers; develop and encourage fellowship among members; act as a liaison between campus ministers seeking employment or reassignment and employers seeking campus ministers; share knowledge, personnel, and material resources. Cooperates with seminaries in continuing education.

★8356★ Baptist Women in Ministry/ Folio (BWIM/FOLIO)

3001 Mercer University Dr.
Atlanta, GA 30341
E-mail: rtshapard@msn.com
URL: http://www.bwim.info

Members: Ordained and unordained female Baptist ministers; students of the Baptist ministry; interested individuals. **Purpose:** Promotes the image of women as ministers. Fosters support and communication among members. **Activities:** Conducts educational and research programs.

★8357★ Catholic Press Association (CPA)

3555 Veterans Memorial Hwy., Unit O
Ronkonkoma, NY 11779
Ph: (631)471-4730   Fax: (631)471-4804
E-mail: cathjourn@catholicpress.org
URL: http://www.catholicpress.org

Description: Consists of Catholic writers and publishers of Catholic newspapers, magazines, newsletters and books. Maintains 25 committees, including Freedom of Information, Fair Publishing Practices Code, Catholic News Service Liaison.

★8358★ A Christian Ministry in the National Parks (ACMNP)

10 Justin's Way
Freeport, ME 04032
Ph: (207)865-6436   Fax: (207)865-6852
Fr: 800-786-3450
E-mail: info@acmnp.com
URL: http://www.acmnp.com

Description: Recommends employment for seminary and college students with private concessionaires operating lodges, inns, restaurants, and stores within national parks; aims to offer students the opportunity to conduct interdenominational worship services and Bible studies for park employees and visitors.

★8359★ Division of Higher Education, Christian Church-Disciples of Christ

11477 Olde Cabin Rd., Ste. 310
St. Louis, MO 63141-7137
Ph: (314)991-3000   Fax: (314)991-2957
E-mail: helm@helmdisciples.org
URL: http://dhedisciples.org

Description: Elected administrative board working to advance the concerns of the Christian Church - Disciples of Christ in higher education and interpret issues in higher education to CCDC leadership. Maintains affiliation with 17 liberal arts colleges and 7 theological seminaries throughout the U.S.

★8360★ Forward in Faith North America

PO Box 210248
Bedford, TX 76095-7248
Fax: (817)735-1351   Fr: 800-225-3661
E-mail: ed.denblaauwen@gmail.com
URL: http://www.forwardinfaith.com

Description: Dioceses, parishes, institutions, and societies of Anglican laity and clergy in North America, Central America, South America and the Caribbean who "embrace the Gospel of Jesus Christ and uphold evangelical faith and order, laboring with zeal for the reform and renewal of the church." Promotes the establishment and implementation of cooperative programs.

★8361★ Human Services Occupations

Delphi Productions
3159 6th St.
Boulder, CO 80304
Ph: (303)443-2100   Fax: (303)443-4022
Fr: 888-443-2400
E-mail: support@delphivideo.com
URL: http://www.delphivideo.com

$95.00. 50 minutes. Part of the Careers for the 21st Century Video Library.

★8362★ IFCA International

PO Box 810
Grandville, MI 49468-0810
Ph: (616)531-1840   Fr: 800-347-1840
E-mail: office@ifca.org
URL: http://www.ifca.org

Members: Ministers, missionaries, youth leaders, musicians, and ministerial students; churches and organizations. **Purpose:** Seeks to offer independent churches the benefits of unity, while allowing them to keep their autonomy. **Activities:** Supports active evangelism; encourages churches to extend their ministry into neighboring communities, the military, and other Christian churches, which the group believes are in harmony with the Word of God. Serves to reinforce members' doctrinal beliefs; provides interchurch fellowship and the sharing of ministers; trains pastors and lay workers.

★8363★ Intercristo

19303 Fremont Ave. N
MS No. 20
Seattle, WA 98133
Fax: (206)546-7375
E-mail: careerhelp@intercristo.com
URL: http://intercristo.searchease.com

Members: Division of CRISTA Ministries. **Purpose:** Provides job exploration and job information service with computerized referrals on current openings with Christian organizations. Has career counseling, which is available through The Birkman Method Assessment Tool.

★8364★ International Council of Community Churches (ICCC)

21116 Washington Pkwy.
Frankfort, IL 60423
Ph: (815)464-5690   Fax: (815)464-5692
E-mail: iccc60423@sbcglobal.net
URL: http://www.icccusa.com

Description: Promotes the fellowship of community churches, provides an annual meeting for worship, study, fellowship; relates to the larger church through membership in the NCCCUSA and the WCC. Assists congregations in pastoral search process. Provides pension plan and health benefits for members.

★8365★ Lutheran Deaconess Conference (LDC)

1304 LaPorte Ave.
Valparaiso, IN 46383
Ph: (219)464-6925   Fax: (219)464-6928
E-mail: deacserv@valpo.edu
URL: http://www.valpo.edu/lda

Members: Consecrated deaconesses having completed the educational requirements of the Lutheran Deaconess Association; students in training. **Purpose:** Seeks to: develop sisterhood and community among deaconesses; present an opportunity for renewed inspiration and personal and professional growth; encourage women in the church to use their full potential and to shape, promote, and support the total deaconess program.

★8366★ National Association of Episcopal Schools (NAES)

815 2nd Ave., Ste. 819
New York, NY 10017-4594
Ph: (212)716-6134   Fax: (212)286-9366
Fr: 800-334-7626
E-mail: info@episcopalschools.org
URL: http://www.episcopalschools.org

Description: Represents episcopal day and boarding schools and preschools. Promotes the educational ministry of the Episcopal Church. Provides publications, consultation services and conference focusing on Episcopal identity of schools, worship, religious education, spirituality, leadership development and governance for heads/directors, administrators, chaplains and teachers of religion, trustees, rectors and other church and school leaders.

★8367★ National Association of Parish Catechetical Directors (NPCD)

1077 30th St. NW, Ste. 100
Washington, DC 20007-3852
Ph: (202)337-6232   Fax: (202)333-6706
E-mail: npcd@ncea.org
URL: http://www.ncea.org/departments/npcd

Members: A subdivision of the National Catholic Educational Association. Directors, coordinators and administrators of religious education/catechesis in Roman Catholic parishes; students considering careers as catechetical leaders; clergy, laity, and others involved in the religious community. **Purpose:** Works to act as a representative and advocate for professionals who administer parish catechetical programs; foster cooperation and communication among organizations serving parish catechesis including other NCEA groups and independent associations; promote the spiritual, personal, and professional growth of parish DREs and encourage careers in catechetical ministry. **Activities:** Supports and develops the practice of family catechesis and encourages efforts in adult religious education; urges cooperation among parish leadership, especially parish staff members; promotes competency standards. Provides guidelines for members' contracts, salaries, benefits, and job descriptions. Disseminates information on members' jobs, educational background, salaries, and benefits; reports on parish program activities and surveys. Conducts research.

★8368★ National Association of Pastoral Musicians (NPM)

962 Wayne Ave., Ste. 210
Silver Spring, MD 20910-4461
Ph: (240)247-3000   Fax: (240)247-3001
E-mail: npmsing@npm.org
URL: http://www.npm.org

Description: Fosters the art of musical liturgy. Members serve the Catholic Church in the United States as musicians, clergy, liturgists, and other leaders of prayer. Provides ongoing formation for musicians and clergy through annual conventions, educational institutes, and events in more than 70 diocesan chapters. Also provides certification programs for cantors, organists, and directors of music ministries.

★8369★ North American Association of Christians in Social Work (NACSW)

PO Box 121
Botsford, CT 06404-0121
Fax: (203)270-8780   Fr: 888-426-4712
E-mail: info@nacsw.org
URL: http://www.nacsw.org

Description: Professional social workers and related professionals, students, interested individuals. Supports the integration of Christian faith and professional social work practice in the lives of its members, the profession and the church, promoting love and justice in social service and social reform. Provides opportunities for Christian fellowship, education and service opportunities; articulates informed Christian voice on social welfare practice and policy to the social work profession; provides professional understanding and help for the social ministry of the church; and promotes social welfare services and policies in society that bring about greater justice and meet basic human needs.

★8370★ OMF International - USA

10 W Dry Creek Cir.
Littleton, CO 80120-4413
Ph: (303)730-4160   Fax: (303)730-4165
Fr: 800-422-5330
E-mail: info@omf.org
URL: http://www.us.omf.org

Description: Protestant missionaries. American office of international missionary society, which originated in England in 1865 for work in inland China. Church planting, evangelism, training and development work now carried out in most countries of East Asia. Through its publications, the group seeks to mobilize new missionaries and supporters, and educate the public.

★8371★ Presbyterian-Reformed Ministries International (PRMI)

PO Box 429
Black Mountain, NC 28711-0429
Ph: (828)669-7373   Fax: (828)669-4880
E-mail: prmi@prmi.org
URL: http://www.prmi.org

Description: Aims to ignite the Church in the power of the Holy Spirit through prayer, leadership development, congregational renewal, and mission outreach. Seeks to call the church to prayer and teach the work of prayer, equip clergy and laity for Holy Spirit-empowered ministry, assist congregations in their renewal process and promote the Holy Spirit for the advancement of the Kingdom of God.

★8372★ United Church of Christ Justice and Witness Ministries

700 Prospect Ave.
Cleveland, OH 44115-1110
Ph: (216)736-3704   Fax: (216)736-3703
E-mail: fordjond@ucc.org
URL: http://www.ucc.org/justice/index.html

Description: Represents ministers of United Church of Christ who work to maximize the impact of African American and other people of color constituencies within the UCC.

Musicians

SOURCES OF HELP-WANTED ADS

★8373★ ArtSEARCH

Theatre Communications Group
520 8th Ave., 24th Fl.
New York, NY 10018-4156
Ph: (212)609-5900   Fax: (212)609-5901
E-mail: tcg@tcg.org
URL: http://www.tcg.org

Description: Biweekly. Publishes classified listings for job opportunities in the arts, especially theatre, dance, music, and educational institutions. Listings include opportunities in administration, artistic, education, production, and career development.

★8374★ Country Airplay Monitor

VNU Business Media USA
770 Broadway
New York, NY 10003
Ph: (646)654-4500

Weekly (Sun.). Trade publication covering the radio and music industry.

★8375★ Daily Variety

Reed Business Information
5700 Wilshire Blvd., Ste. 120
Los Angeles, CA 90036
Ph: (323)857-6600   Fax: (323)857-0494
URL: http://www.reedbusiness.com/index.asp?layout=theListProfile&

Daily. Global entertainment newspaper (tabloid).

★8376★ Down Beat

Maher Publications Inc.
102 N Haven Rd.
Elmhurst, IL 60126
Ph: (630)941-2030   Fax: (630)941-3210
Fr: 800-535-7496
URL: http://www.downbeat.com

Monthly. $55.00/year for individuals, two years; $52.00/year for out of country; $77.00 for two years, Canada; $99.00 for two years, outside U.S. and Canada; $41.00/year for

Canada; $30.00/year for individuals. Magazine edited for the learning musician.

★8377★ Electronic Musician

Penton Media
249 W 17th St.
New York, NY 10011
Ph: (212)204-4200
E-mail: emeditorial@prismb2b.com
URL: http://emusician.com/

Monthly. $24.00/year for individuals. Magazine on music and home or personal recording industry technology.

★8378★ Future Music

Future Network USA
150 North Hill Dr., Ste. 40
Brisbane, CA 94005
Ph: (415)468-4684   Fax: (415)468-4686
URL: http://www.futuremusicmag.com

Monthly. $24.95/year for individuals. Magazine that offers information on creating and distributing music using digital technology.

★8379★ IAWM Journal

International Alliance for Women in Music
Department of Music
Indiana University of Pennsylvania
1011 South Dr.
Indiana, PA 15705
Ph: (724)357-2100
E-mail: kilst001@tc.umn.edu.
URL: http://www.iawm.org/

Description: 3/year (Feb, Jun, Oct). Concerned with women in music. Features scholarly articles, reviews, reports, announcements, press releases and member activities. Recurring features include letters to the editor, interviews, news of research, news of educational opportunities, job listings, and notices of publications available.

★8380★ Jelly

Peppercorn Press
PO Box 693
Snow Camp, NC 27349
Ph: (336)574-1634   Fax: (336)376-9099
Fr: 877-574-1634

URL: http://www.jellyroll.com/

Magazine covering blues, jazz, country, soul and rock'n'roll music.

★8381★ Journal of the AMIS

American Musical Instrument Society
The Guild Associates, Inc.
389 Main St., Ste. 202
Malden, MA 02148
Ph: (781)397-8870   Fax: (781)397-8887
URL: http://www.amis.org/publications/journal

Annual. Journal covering all aspects of musical instruments.

★8382★ Music Educators Journal

MENC: The National Association for
  Music Education
1806 Robert Fulton Dr.
Reston, VA 20191
Ph: (703)860-4000   Fax: (703)860-1531
Fr: 800-336-3768
URL: http://www.menc.org/publication/articles/journals.html

Journal covering all levels of music education. Published on alternate months with Teaching Music.

★8383★ Music and Media

VNU Business Media USA
770 Broadway
New York, NY 10003
Ph: (646)654-4500
URL: http://www.vnubusinessmedia.com

Weekly. Publication covering the music and entertainment industries.

★8384★ Music Trades

Music Trades Corp.
80 West St.
Englewood, NJ 07631
Ph: (201)871-1965   Fax: (201)871-0455
Fr: 800-423-6530
URL: http://www.musictrades.com/

Monthly. $23.00/year for individuals, foreign; $23.00 for two years, domestic; $16.00/year for individuals, domestic. Music trade magazine.

★8385★ Musical News

Musicians Union Local 6
116 Ninth St.
San Francisco, CA 94103
Ph: (415)575-0777   Fax: (415)863-6173
URL: http://www.afm6.org/Musical-News.htm

Description: Monthly. Contains union news and information of importance to members of the American Federation of Musicians.

★8386★ Paste

Paste Media Group LLC
PO Box 1606
Decatur, GA 30031
Ph: (404)664-4320   Fax: (404)377-4508
Fr: (866)370-9067
URL: http://www.pastemagazine.com

Monthly. $19.95/year for individuals; $39.90 for two years; $50.00/year for other countries. Music magazine.

★8387★ Quarternote

American Musicians Union
1501 Broadway, Ste.600
New York, NY 10036
Ph: (212)869-1330   Fax: (212)764-6134
URL: http://www.afm.org

Description: Quarterly. Includes information on music and instruments, obituaries, new member information, and Drummers Corner.

★8388★ Rock Airplay Monitor

VNU Business Media USA
770 Broadway
New York, NY 10003
Ph: (646)654-4500

Weekly. Trade publication covering the music and radio industries.

★8389★ The Sinfonian

Phi Mu Alpha - Sinfonia
National Headquarters
10600 Old State Rd.
Evansville, IN 47711
Ph: (812)867-2433   Fax: (812)867-0633
Fr: 800-473-2649
E-mail: lyrecrest@sinfonia.org
URL: http://www.sinfonia.org

Description: 2/year. Announces and reviews activities and programs of this fraternity for professional musicians. Profiles members and their careers. Discusses major developments in the music industry and education.

★8390★ Sounding Board

American Composers Forum
332 Minnesota St., Ste. E. 145
St. Paul, MN 55101
Ph: (651)251-2833   Fax: (651)291-7978
E-mail: dwolff@composersforum.org

URL: http://www.composersforum.org/old-site/programs/soundingboard

Description: Bimonthly. Features news and updates on Forum programming, articles of interest to composers, musicians, and others in the new music community. Provides a listing of opportunities including grants, fellowships, and calls for scores.

★8391★ SYMPHONY

American Symphony Orchestra League
33 West 60th St., 5th Fl.
New York, NY 10023-7905
Ph: (212)262-5161   Fax: (212)262-5198
E-mail: league@symphony.org

Bimonthly. $22.00/year for individuals; $50.00/year for members, individual membership; $100.00/year for members, professional membership; $25.00/year for students. Magazine with news and articles for symphony orchestra managers, trustees, conductors, volunteers, and musicians.

★8392★ THE DIAPASON

Scranton Gillette Communications Inc.
3030 W Salt Creek Ln., Ste. 201
Arlington Heights, IL 60005-5025
Ph: (847)391-1000   Fax: (847)390-0408
URL: http://www.thediapason.com

Monthly. $70.00/year for individuals, 3 years; $55.00/year for two years; $35.00/year for individuals; $85.00/year for other countries, 3 years; $65.00/year for other countries, 2 years; $45.00/year for other countries. Magazine devoted to pipe organ building, organ and church music performance, and repertoire.

★8393★ UMS Notes

University Musical Society (UMS)
Burton Memorial Tower
881 N. University Ave.
Ann Arbor, MI 48109-1011
Ph: (734)764-2538   Fax: (734)647-1171
URL: http://www.ums.org/

Features articles and news of events involving classical music and musicians. Covers festivals, concerts, and other programs. Includes a calendar of events, a column titled Remembrances, and news of Society activities.

★8394★ Variety

Reed Business Information
5700 Wilshire Blvd., Ste. 120
Los Angeles, CA 90036
Ph: (323)857-6600   Fax: (323)857-0494
URL: http://www.variety.com

Weekly. $259.00/year for individuals, year; $25.00/year for individuals, monthly. Newspaper reporting on theatre, television, radio, music, records, and movies.

PLACEMENT AND JOB REFERRAL SERVICES

★8395★ American Symphony Orchestra League

33 W 60th St., 5th Fl.
New York, NY 10023
Ph: (212)262-5161   Fax: (212)262-5198
E-mail: league@symphony.org
URL: http://www.symphony.org

Members: Symphony orchestras; associate members include educational institutions, arts councils, public libraries, business firms, orchestra professionals, and individuals interested in symphony orchestras. **Purpose:** Engages in extensive research on diverse facets of symphony orchestra operations and development. Provides consulting services for orchestras, their boards, and volunteer organizations. **Activities:** Sponsors management seminars and workshops for professional symphony orchestra administrative and artistic staff, volunteers, and prospective management personnel. Maintains employment services; collects and distributes resource materials, financial data, and statistical reports on many aspects of orchestra operations. Compiles statistics; sponsors educational programs; maintains resource center.

★8396★ Association of Anglican Musicians (AAM)

PO Box 7530
Little Rock, AR 72217
Ph: (828)274-2681
E-mail: cr273@aol.com
URL: http://www.anglicanmusicians.org

Description: Represents church musicians (laypersons or clergy) serving Episcopal and Anglican churches. Seeks to promote excellence in church music. Fosters a relationship of mutual respect and trust between clergy and musicians actively encouraging and supporting composers and other artists to create works for the church. Maintains communication with and supporting the work of the Standing Commission on Liturgy and Church. Encourages equitable compensation and benefits for professional church musicians. Works closely with seminaries toward the establishment and continuation of courses in music and the allied arts as they relate to worship and theology. Maintains placement service.

★8397★ Jazz World Society (JWS)

PO Box 35
New York, NY 10018
Fax: (212)253-4160
E-mail: jws@jazzsociety.com
URL: http://www.jazzsociety.com

Description: Professionals involved in jazz, including musicians, composers, record producers, distributors, collectors, and journalists; individuals actively supporting jazz music. Promotes the development of jazz music in its various interpretations and fosters communication among jazz participants. Operates library of records, publications, books, and photographs. Organizes competitions; offers specialized education programs, seminars, and placement service. Maintains hall of fame and biographical archives.

★8398★ National Traditional Country Music Association (NTCMA)

PO Box 492
Anita, IA 50020
Ph: (712)762-4363
E-mail: bobeverhart@yahoo.com
URL: http://www.oldtimemusic.bigstep.com

Description: Individuals interested in the preservation, presentation, and perpetuation of traditional acoustic country, folk, honky-tonk, ragtime, mountain, and bluegrass music celebrating contributions of U.S. settlers and pioneers; country music associations. Supports what the association views as related, traditional values. Holds jam sessions; sponsors booths and offers hands-on music and craft experiences; operates charitable program; offers children's services; maintains placement service. Sponsors championship contests in numerous categories, including: Great Plains Story Telling; Hank Williams Songwriting; International Country Singer; Jimmie Rodgers Yodeling; National Bluegrass Band; National Harmonica Playing. Programs are taped and televised by various local, national, and international stations. Established the "Old-Time Music Hour" radio program at the Walnut Country Opera House, Pioneer Music Museum, America Old-Time Fiddlers Hall of Fame, and America Country Music Hall of Fame.

★8399★ Presbyterian Association of Musicians (PAM)

100 Witherspoon St.
Louisville, KY 40202-1396
Ph: (502)569-5288   Fax: (502)569-8465
Fr: 888-728-7228
E-mail: abarthel@ctr.pcusa.org
URL: http://www.pam.pcusa.org

Description: Represents organists, choir directors, singers, churches, clergy, directors of Christian education, and interested persons of all denominations. Aims to develop the use of music and the arts in the life and worship of individual congregations. Offers assistance in the areas of worship, music, and the arts. Conducts continuing education. Acts as a clearinghouse for job referrals; promotes the professional status of church musicians and recommends salaries and benefits to churches; certifies church musicians.

★8400★ Texas International Theatrical Arts Society (TITAS)

3625 N Hall St., Ste. 740
Dallas, TX 75219
Ph: (214)528-6112   Fax: (214)528-2617
E-mail: csantos@titas.org
URL: http://www.titas.org

Description: Theatrical agencies working to book entertainers and international acts into

all live music venues. Provides placement service; conducts educational seminars.

EMPLOYER DIRECTORIES AND NETWORKING LISTS

★8401★ AMG's All Music Guide

All Media Guide L.L.C.
1168 Oak Valley Dr.
Ann Arbor, MI 48108
Ph: (734)887-5600   Fax: (734)827-2492

Database covers: Information on musical artists. Entries include: Birth year, biography, list of recordings, genre, years in the business, instruments played, tone, labels, and where to buy sheet music.

★8402★ Careers in Focus: Music

Facts On File Inc.
132 W 31st St., 17th Fl.
New York, NY 10001
Ph: (212)967-8800   Fax: 800-678-3633
Fr: 800-322-8755
URL: http://www.factsonfile.com

Published 2004. $29.95 for individuals; $26.95 for libraries. Covers an overview of music, followed by a selection of jobs profiled in detail, including the nature of the job, earnings, prospects for employment, what kind of training and skills it requires, and sources for further information.

★8403★ Chamber Music America-Membership Directory

Chamber Music America
305 7th Ave., 5th Fl.
New York, NY 10001
Ph: (212)242-2022   Fax: (212)242-7955
URL: http://www.chamber-music.org

Annual, in the September issue of Chamber Music Magazine. Covers over 800 member ensembles, presenters, festivals, and training programs; over 4,000 associate members, including managers, publishers, arts organizations, instrument manufacturers, libraries and individuals. Entries include: For members–Name, address, phone, name of contact, activities, awards, year established. For associates–Name, address, phone. Arrangement: Separate geographical sections for ensembles, presenters, festivals and training programs; associate members are classified by type of organization, then alphabetical. Indexes: General, subject.

★8404★ Chicago Creative Directory

Chicago Creative Directory
333 N Michigan Ave., Ste. 810
Chicago, IL 60601
Ph: (312)236-7337   Fax: (312)236-6078
URL: http://www.creativedir.com

Annual, March. Covers over 6,000 advertising agencies, photographers, sound studios, talent agencies, audiovisual services, and

others offering creative and production services. Entries include: For most listings–Company name, address, phone, list of officers, description of services. For freelance listings–Name, talent, address, phone. Arrangement: Classified by specialty.

★8405★ Directory of Festivals and Workshops

Chamber Music America
305 7th Ave., 5th Fl.
New York, NY 10001
Ph: (212)242-2022   Fax: (212)242-7955
URL: http://www.chamber-music.org/

Annual, in the March/April issue of Chamber Music Magazine. Covers over 150 chamber music workshops and schools for students, young professionals, and adult amateurs; international listings. Entries include: Name, location or address, description of program and participants sought, procedure for auditions, type of accommodations and recreational facilities, dates, age requirements, and fees. Arrangement: Geographical. Indexes: Alphabetical by state; alphabetical by program.

★8406★ Employment Opportunities, USA

Washington Research Associates
1090 Vermont Ave. NW, Ste. 800
Washington, DC 20005
Ph: (202)408-7025

Annual, quarterly updates. Publication includes: List of over 1,000 employment contacts in companies and agencies in banking, arts, telecommunications, education, and 14 other industries and professions, including federal government. Entries include: Company name, name of representative, address, description of products or services, hiring and recruiting practices, training programs, and year established. Principal content is industry overviews, career news, employment opportunity information on 14 different job markets, and comprehensive guidance to career resources on the Internet. Arrangement: Classified by industry. Indexes: Occupation.

★8407★ GMA'S Online Christian Music Networking Guide

Gospel Music Association
1205 Division St.
Nashville, TN 37203
Ph: (615)242-0303   Fax: (615)254-9755
E-mail: info@gospelmusic.org
URL: http://www.gospelmusic.org/resources/networkingGuide.aspx

Continuous; latest edition 2007. Covers gospel musicians, composers, and artists; recording companies, studios, and production companies; booking agencies; publishers; performing rights organizations; television and radio broadcasting stations; book stores, Bible supply stores, and other retailers/managers; publications; ministry organizations, artist managers, industry related services, christian clubs, concert promoters, distributors. Entries include: Name, contact address, phone, fax, e-mail. Broadcasting station listings include contact, program title, format. Arrangement: Search engine is flexible.

★8408★ *Instrumentalist-Directory of Summer Music Camps, Clinics, and Workshops Issue*

Instrumentalist Co.
200 Northfield Rd.
Northfield, IL 60093
Ph: (847)446-5600   Fax: (847)446-6263
Fr: 888-446-6888
URL: http://www.instrumentalistmagazine.com/

Annual, March. $2.50. Publication includes: List of nearly 250 summer music camps, clinics, and workshops in the United States; limited Canadian and foreign coverage. Entries include: Camp name, location, name of director, opening and closing dates, tuition fees, courses offered. Arrangement: Geographical.

★8409★ *Musical America International Directory of the Performing Arts*

Commonwealth Business Media Inc.
400 Windsor Corporate Pk.
50 Millstone Rd., Ste. 200
East Windsor, NJ 08520-1415
Ph: (609)371-7700   Fr: 800-221-5488
E-mail: info@musicalamerica.com
URL: http://www.musicalamerica.com

Annual, December; latest edition 2001. Covers U.S., Canadian, and international orchestras, musicians, singers, performing arts series, dance and opera companies, festivals, contests, foundations and awards, publishers of music, artist managers, booking agents, music magazines, and service and professional music organizations. Section for U.S. and Canada also includes listings of choral groups, music schools and departments, and newspaper music critics; international directory section also lists concert managers. Entries include: Name of organization, institution, address, phone, fax, URL, e-mail addresses, key personnel; most entries include name of contact, manager, conductor, etc. For schools–Number of students and faculty. For orchestras–Number of concerts and seats. Other entries show similar details as appropriate. Arrangement: Geographical. Indexes: Alphabetical and by category.

★8410★ *National Directory of Arts Internships*

National Network for Artist Placement
935 W Ave. 37
Los Angeles, CA 90065
Ph: (323)222-4035   Fax: (323)225-5711
Fr: 800-354-5348
URL: http://www.artistplacement.com

Biennial, odd years; latest edition 10th. $95.00 for individuals. Covers over 5,000 internship opportunities in dance, music, theater, art, design, film, and video & over 1,250 host organizations. Entries include: Name of sponsoring organization, address, name of contact; description of positions available, eligibility requirements, stipend or salary (if any), application procedures. Ar-

rangement: Classified by discipline, then geographical.

★8411★ *The R & R Directory*

Radio and Records Inc.
2049 Century Pk. E, 41St. Fl.
Los Angeles, CA 90067-4004
Ph: (310)553-4330   Fax: (310)203-9763
E-mail: moreinfo@rronline.com
URL: http://www.radioandrecords.com/RRDirectory/Directory_Main.as

Semiannual, spring and fall. $75.00. Covers more than 3,000 radio group owners, equipment manufacturers, jingle producers, TV production houses and spot producers, record companies, representative firms, research companies, consulting firms, media brokers, networks, program suppliers, trade associations, and other organizations involved in the radio and record industry. Entries include: Organization name, address, phone, fax, e-mail, name and title of contacts, branch offices or subsidiary names and locations. Arrangement: Alphabetical; classified by subject. Indexes: Company.

★8412★ *Regional Theater Directory*

American Theatre Works Inc.
2349 W. Rd.
PO Box 159
Dorset, VT 05251
Ph: (802)867-9333   Fax: (802)867-2297
URL: http://www.theatredirectories.com

Annual, May. $29.50 for individuals. Covers regional theater companies and dinner theatres with employment opportunities in acting, design, production, and management. Entries include: Company name, address, phone, name and title of contact; type of company, activities, and size of house; whether union affiliated, whether nonprofit or commercial; year established; hiring procedure and number of positions hired annually/seasonally; description of stage; internships; description of artistic policy and audience. Arrangement: Geographical. Indexes: Company name, type of plays produced.

★8413★ *Songwriter's Market*

Writer's Digest Books
1507 Dana Ave.
PO Box 420235
Cincinnati, OH 45207
Fr: 800-221-5831
E-mail: songmarket@fwpubs.com
URL: http://www.writersdigest.com

Annual; latest edition 2007. $26.99 for individuals. Covers 2,000 music publishers, jingle writers, advertising agencies, audiovisual firms, radio and television stations, booking agents, and other buyers of musical compositions and lyrics; also lists contests, competitions, and workshops. Entries include: Buyer's name and address, phone, payment rates, submission requirements, etc. Arrangement: Classified by type of market. Indexes: Geographical.

★8414★ *Summer Theater Directory*

American Theatre Works Inc.
2349 W. Rd.
PO Box 159
Dorset, VT 05251
Ph: (802)867-9333   Fax: (802)867-2297
URL: http://www.theatredirectories.com

Annual, December. $29.50 for individuals. Covers summer theater companies, theme parks and cruise lines that offer employment opportunities in acting, design, production, and management; summer theater training programs. Entries include: Company name, address, phone, name and title of contact; type of company, activities and size of house; whether union affiliated, whether nonprofit or commercial; year established; hiring procedure and number of positions hired annually/seasonally; description of stage; internships; description of company's artistic goals and audience. Arrangement: Geographical. Indexes: Company name.

★8415★ *Women and Music in America Since 1900*

Oryx Press
4041 N Central Ave., Ste. 700
PO Box 33889
Phoenix, AZ 85021-3397
Ph: (602)265-2651   Fax: 800-279-4663
Fr: 800-279-6799
URL: http://greenwood.com

Published December 2002. $172.95 for individuals. Publication includes: Women's organizations, women's subcommittees in other organizations, and groups in which women have historically been underrepresented. Principal content of publication consists of entries on issues and individuals highlighting women's impact on music. Arrangement: Alphabetical. Indexes: Alphabetical.

HANDBOOKS AND MANUALS

★8416★ *All You Need to Know About the Music Business*

Free Press
1230 Ave. of the Americas
New York, NY 10020
Ph: (212)698-7000   Fax: (212)698-7007
Fr: 800-897-7650

Donald S. Passman. Sixth edition, 2006. $30.00. 464 pages.

★8417★ *Build and Manage Your Music Career*

artistpro.com, LLC
236 Georgia St., Ste. 100
Vallejo, CA 94590
Ph: (707)554-1935   Fax: (707)554-9751

Maurice Johnson. 1999. $24.95. 180 pages.

★8418★ The Business of Getting More Gigs as a Professional Musician

Hal Leonard Corporation
PO Box 13819
Milwaukee, WI 53213
Ph: (414)774-3630   Fax: (414)774-3259
Fr: 800-524-4425
URL: http://www.halleonard.com/

Bob Popyk. June 2003. $14.95. 144 pages. Music Business Series.

★8419★ Career Opportunities in the Music Industry

Facts On File Inc.
132 W. 31st St., 17th Fl.
New York, NY 10001-2006
Ph: (212)967-8800   Fax: 800-678-3633
Fr: 800-322-8755
E-mail: custserv@factsonfile.com
URL: http://www.factsonfile.com

Shelly Field. Fifth edition, 2005. $49.50. 310 pages

★8420★ Career Opportunities in Theater and the Performing Arts

Checkmark Books
132 W. 31st St., 17th Fl.
New York, NY 10001-2006
Ph: (212)967-8800   Fax: (212)967-9196
Fr: 800-322-8755

Shelly Field. Third edition, 2006. $18.95 (paper). 320 pages. Offers a complete range of information about job opportunities in the performing arts. Part of Career Opportunities Series.

★8421★ Careers for Music Lovers and Other Tuneful Types

The McGraw-Hill Companies
PO Box 182604
Columbus, OH 43272
Fax: (614)759-3749   Fr: 877-883-5524
E-mail: customer.service@mcgraw-hill.com
URL: http://www.mcgraw-hill.com

Jeff Johnson. 2003. $13.95 (paper). 208 pages. Describes hundreds of music industry jobs and careers.

★8422★ Careers for Night Owls and Other Insomniacs

The McGraw-Hill Companies
PO Box 182604
Columbus, OH 43272
Fax: (614)759-3749   Fr: 877-883-5524
E-mail: customer.service@mcgraw-hill.com
URL: http://www.mcgraw-hill.com

Louise Miller. Second edition, 2002. $12.95 (paper). 160 pages.

★8423★ Careers Without College: Music

Peterson's Guides
2000 Lenox Dr.
Box 67005
Lawrenceville, NJ 08648
Ph: (609)896-1800   Fax: (609)896-4531
Fr: 800-338-3282

E-mail: custsvc@petersons.com
URL: http://www.petersons.com

Ted Greenwald. 1997. $7.95 (paper). 98 pages.

★8424★ The Garage Band Cookbook: How to Operate a Band for Success and Profit

Juice Gallery Multimedia
2042 Big Oak Ave.
Chino Hills, CA 91709
Ph: (909)597-0791   Fax: (909)597-0791
Fr: 800-710-0163
E-mail: info@juicegallery.com
URL: http://www.juicegallery.com/

$34.95. 2002. 178 pages. Part of the VM business Series.

★8425★ Getting Radio Airplay: The Guide to Getting Your Music Played on College, Public and Commercial

Music Books Plus
4600 Witmer Industrial Estates, Ste. 6
Niagara Falls, NY 14305
Ph: (905)641-0552   Fax: (905)641-1648
Fr: 800-265-8481
E-mail: order@nor.com
URL: http://www.musicbooksplus.com

Gary Hustwit. Second edition, 1998. $19.95 (paper). 128 pages

★8426★ The Gigs Handbook: A Beginner's Guide to Playing Professionally

Benny Publishing
9403 Lincolnwood Dr.
Evanston, IL 60203
Ph: (847)673-2039

Sharon Black. 2000. $18.95 (paper). 200 pages. "The Gigs Handbook" is for music students who want to earn money through performing and for amateurs who want to play professionally. The book will help readers learn how to get gigs and become professional musicians, make contacts and promote themselves, deal with problems on the job, play weddings and other special events and begin playing by ear.

★8427★ Great Jobs for Music Majors

The McGraw-Hill Companies
PO Box 182604
Columbus, OH 43272
Fax: (614)759-3749   Fr: 877-883-5524
E-mail: customer.service@mcgraw-hill.com
URL: http://www.mcgraw-hill.com

Jan Goldberg, Stephen Lambert, Julie DeGalan. Second edition, 2004. $15.95 (paper). 180 pages.

★8428★ How to Be Your Own Booking Agent and Save Thousands of Dollars: A Performing Artist's Guide to a Successful Touring Career

New Music Times, Inc.
PO Box 1105
Charlottesville, VA 22902-1105
Ph: (804)977-8979   Fax: (804)977-6914

Jeri Goldstein. 2004. $29.97 (paper). 492 pages.

★8429★ How to Make It in the New Music Business: Lessons, Tips and Inspiration from Music's Biggest and Best

Watson-Guptill Publications
770 Broadway
New York, NY 10003
Ph: (646)654-5400   Fax: (646)654-5487
Fr: 800-278-8477
E-mail: info@watsonguptill.com
URL: http://www.watsonguptill.com

Robert Wolff. April 2004. $19.95 (paper). Illustrated. 288 pages.

★8430★ How to Make a Living as a Musician: So You Never Have to Have a Day Job Again

Sonata Publishing
1277 S. Adams St.
Glendale, CA 91205
Ph: (818)380-7155   Fax: (818)242-5551
Fr: (866)348-4893
URL: http://www.sonatapublishing.com/

Marty Buttwinick. 1994. $29.95 (paper). 272 pages. This book covers the day-to-day activities, truths and myths of how to actually make a living, directly answers the thousands of questions asked of the author over the past twenty-five years, and emphasizes professionalism and goal achievement.

★8431★ In Concert: The Freelance Musician's Keys to Financial Success

Thimbleberry Press
1506 E. Fox. Ln.
Milwaukee, WI 53217-2853
Ph: (414)241-9711

Gail Nelson and Pamela Foard. 1994. $16.95 (paper). 91 pages.

★8432★ The Lost Soul Companion: Comfort & Constructive Advice for Struggling Actors, Musicians, Artists, Writers & Other Free Spirits

Dell
1745 Broadway
New York, NY 10019
Ph: (212)782-9000   Fax: (212)572-6066
Fr: 800-733-3000
URL: http://www.randomhouse.com/bantamdell

Susan M. Brackney. 2001. $10.00. 176 pages.

★8433★ **Making Money Teaching Music**

Writers Digest Books
4700 E. Galbraith Rd.
Cincinnati, OH 45236
Ph: (513)531-2690   Fax: (513)531-4082
Fr: 800-289-0963
E-mail: writersdig@fwpubs.com
URL: http://www.writersdigest.com

Barbara Newsam and David Newsam. 2002. $18.99 (paper). 244 pages.

★8434★ **Making Music Your Business: A Guide for Young Musicians**

Sphinx Publishing
1935 Brookdale Rd., Ste. 139
Naperville, IL 60563
Ph: (630)961-3900   Fax: (630)961-2168
Fr: 800-432-7444
URL: http://www.sphinxlegal.com

David Ellefson. 2005. $14.95. 142 pages. Covers many aspects of the music business.

★8435★ **Making Your Living As a String Player: Career Guidance from the Experts at Strings Magazine**

String Letter Publishing
255 W. End Ave.
San Rafael, CA 94901
Ph: (415)485-6946   Fax: (415)485-0831
URL: http://www.stringletter.com/

Greg Cahill. January 2004. $12.95. 96 pages.

★8436★ **Monsters and Angels: Surviving a Career in Music**

Manduca Music
861 Washington Ave.
Portland, ME 04103
Ph: (207)773-7012   Fax: (207)773-6597
Fr: 800-626-3822
URL: http://www.manducamusic.com/

Seymour Bernstein. March 2004. $22.95. 507 pages.

★8437★ **More About This Business of Music**

Watson-Guptill Publications
770 Broadway
New York, NY 10003
Ph: (646)654-5400   Fax: (646)654-5487
Fr: 800-278-8477
E-mail: info@watsonguptill.com
URL: http://www.watsonguptill.com

M. William Krasilovsky and Sidney Shemel. Fifth edition, 1994. $18.95. 224 pages.

★8438★ **Moving up in the Music Business**

Allworth Press
10 E. 23rd St., Ste. 510
New York, NY 10010
Ph: (212)777-8395   Fax: (212)777-8261
Fr: 800-491-2808
URL: http://www.allworth.com/

Jodi Summers. 2000. $18.95 (paper). 213 pages.

★8439★ **Music Business Made Simple: A Guide to Becoming a Recording Artist**

Music Sales Corporation
257 Park Ave., S., 20th Fl.
New York, NY 10010
Ph: (212)254-2100   Fax: (212)254-2103

J. Scott Rudsenke and James P. Denk. April 2004. $14.95. Illustrated. 144 pages. Music Business Made Simpler Series.

★8440★ **Music Business Primer**

Prentice Hall PTR
1 Lake St.
Upper Saddle River, NJ 07458
Ph: (201)236-7000   Fax: 800-835-5327
Fr: 800-428-5331
URL: http://www.phptr.com/index.asp?rl=1

Diane Sward Rapaport. September 2002. $34.60 (paper). 329 pages. Illustrated.

★8441★ **The Musician's Guide to Making and Selling Your Own CDs and Cassettes**

Writer's Digest Books
4700 Galbraith Rd.
Cincinnati, OH 45236
Ph: (513)531-2690   Fax: (513)531-4082
Fr: 800-289-0963
E-mail: writersdig@fwpubs.com
URL: http://www.writersdigest.com

Jana Stanfield. 1997. $18.99 (paper). 170 pages.

★8442★ **Opportunities in Entertainment Careers**

The McGraw-Hill Companies
PO Box 182604
Columbus, OH 43272
Fax: (614)759-3749   Fr: 877-883-5524
E-mail: customer.service@mcgraw-hill.com
URL: http://www.mcgraw-hill.com

Jan Goldberg. 1999. $11.95 (paper). 148 pages.

★8443★ **Opportunities in Music Careers**

The McGraw-Hill Companies
PO Box 182604
Columbus, OH 43272
Fax: (614)759-3749   Fr: 877-883-5524
E-mail: customer.service@mcgraw-hill.com
URL: http://www.mcgraw-hill.com

Robert Gerardi. Fourth edition, 2002. $13.95 (paper). 175 pages. Describes the job market and where to find work. Covers careers in performing, writing, musical directing, management, and technical areas. Illustrated.

★8444★ **Resumes for Performing Arts Careers**

The McGraw-Hill Companies
PO Box 182604
Columbus, OH 43272
Fax: (614)759-3749   Fr: 877-883-5524
E-mail: customer.service@mcgraw-hill.com
URL: http://www.mcgraw-hill.com

2004. $10.95 (paper). 160 pages.

★8445★ **The Rock Band Handbook: Everything You Need to Know to Get a Band Together and Take It on the Road**

Penguin Books
375 Hudson St.
New York, NY 10014
Ph: (212)366-2000   Fax: (212)366-2385
Fr: 800-788-6262
URL: http://us.penguingroup.com/

Kathryn Lineberger. 1996. $10.00 (paper). 180 pages.

★8446★ **Ruthless Self-Promotion in the Music Industry**

artistpro.com, LLC
236 Georgia St., Ste. 100
Vallejo, CA 94590
Ph: (707)554-1935   Fax: (707)554-9751

Jeffrey P. Fisher. Second edition, 2005. $24.99. 320 pages.

★8447★ **Secrets of Negotiating a Record Contract: The Musician's Guide to Understanding & Avoiding Sneaky Lawyer Tricks**

Backbeat Books
600 Harrison St.
San Francisco, CA 94107
Ph: (408)848-5294   Fax: (408)848-5784
Fr: (866)222-5232
E-mail: custserv@musicdispatch.com
URL: http://www.backbeatbooks.com/

Moses Avalon. 2001. $22.95 (paper). 303 pages.

★8448★ **Songwriting Success: How to Write Songs for Fun and (Maybe) Profit**

Routledge
270 Madison Ave.
New York, NY 10016
Ph: (212)216-7800   Fax: (212)563-2269
URL: http://www.routledge.com/

Michael Lydon. Book & CD edition. May 2004. $20.95 (paper). Illustrated. 208 pages.

★8449★ **Stage Writers Handbook: A Complete Business Guide for Playwrights, Composers, Lyricists, and Librettists**

Theatre Communications Group
520 Eighth Ave., 24th Fl.
New York, NY 10018-4156
Ph: (212)609-5900   Fax: (212)609-5901
E-mail: custserv@tcg.org

URL: http://www.tcg.org/

Dana Singer. 1997. $22.95 (paper). 302 pages.

★8450★ Star Tracks: Principles for Success in the Music and Entertainment Business

Thumbs Up Publishing
1700 Falcon Ct.
Mount Juliet, TN 37122-7425
Ph: (615)269-7412

Larry E. Wacholtz. 1997. $33.00 (paper). 284 pages. Discusses copyright law, music publishing, songwriting, record labels, recording studios, studio musicians, recording artists, audio engineers, record producers, marketing, radio promotion, artist management, concert promotion, distribution, budgets, and music business economics.

★8451★ This Business of Music Marketing and Promotion

Billboard Books
770 Broadway
New York, NY 10003
Ph: (646)654-5400   Fax: (646)654-5486
Fr: 800-323-9432

Tad Lathrop and Jim Pettigrew, Jr. Rev edition, 2003. $24.95. 308 pages.

★8452★ What's up Dawg: How to Become a Superstar in the Music Business

Hyperion Books
77 West 66th St., 11 Fl.
New York, NY 10023
Ph: (212)522-8700   Fr: 800-759-0190
URL: http://www.hyperionbooks.com

Randy Jackson. 2004. $19.95 (paper). 208 pages.

EMPLOYMENT AGENCIES AND SEARCH FIRMS

★8453★ NMC Inc.

24 Music Sq. W
Nashville, TN 37203
Ph: (615)345-4976

Consults aspiring country music singers and songwriters by listening to their works and prior to submission to record labels and publishing companies. Singers and songwriters who the firm feels are not ready will be given the opportunity to resubmit material after six months at no additional charge.

TRADESHOWS

★8454★ American Harp Society National Conference

American Harp Society
PO Box 38334
Los Angeles, CA 90038-0334
Ph: (323)469-3050
URL: http://www.harpsociety.org

Annual. **Primary Exhibits:** Harps and related materials. **Dates and Locations:** 2008 Jun 23-26; Plymouth, MI; St. John Golf and Conference Center.

★8455★ American Orff-Schulwerk Association National Conference

American Orff-Schulwerk Association Inc.
PO Box 391089
Cleveland, OH 44139-8089
Ph: (440)543-5366   Fax: (440)543-2687
E-mail: info@aosa.org
URL: http://www.aosa.org

Annual. **Primary Exhibits:** Music, music books, instruments, pitched and unpitched percussion, early music instruments, records and music gifts, computer music software.

★8456★ Chamber Music America Conference

Chamber Music America
305 7th Ave., 5th Fl.
New York, NY 10001-6008
Ph: (212)242-2022   Fax: (212)242-7955
E-mail: info@chamber-music.org
URL: http://www.chamber-music.org

Annual. **Primary Exhibits:** Professional chamber music ensembles and presenters; organizations, foundations, and individuals actively supporting chamber music performances.

★8457★ College Music Society Annual Meeting

The College Music Society
312 E. Pine St.
Missoula, MT 59802
Ph: (406)721-9616   Fax: (406)721-9419
Fr: 800-729-0235
E-mail: cms@music.org
URL: http://www.music.org

Annual. **Primary Exhibits:** Music publishers, instrument manufacturers, music retailers, non-profit associations, music hardware and software manufacturers.

★8458★ International Association for Jazz Education Conference

International Association for Jazz Educators
PO Box 724
Manhattan, KS 66505
Ph: (785)776-8744   Fax: (785)776-6190
E-mail: info@iaje.org
URL: http://www.iaje.org

Annual. **Primary Exhibits:** Music, musical instruments, accessories, apparel, electron-

ics, travel information, and other services for musicians and educators.

★8459★ Mid-West Band and Orchestra Conference

National Band Association
118 College Dr., No. 5032
Hattiesburg, MS 39406-0001
Ph: (601)297-8168   Fax: (601)266-6185
E-mail: info@nationalbandassociation.org
URL: http://www.nationalbandassoc.org

Annual. **Primary Exhibits:** Directors of school, college, professional, military, and community bands; music publishers; manufacturers of musical instruments and others interested in development of bands and band music.

★8460★ The Midwest Clinic An International Band and Orchestra Conference

The Midwest Clinic
828 Davis St., Ste. 100
Evanston, IL 60201
Ph: (847)424-4163   Fax: (847)424-5185
E-mail: info@midwestclinic.org
URL: http://www.midwestclinic.org

Annual. **Primary Exhibits:** Music instruments and publications, supplies, and services, universities, military org., fund raisers, music publishers.

★8461★ Music Teachers National Association Convention

Music Teachers National Association
441 Vine St., Ste. 505
Cincinnati, OH 45202-2811
Ph: (513)421-1420   Fax: (513)421-2503
E-mail: mtnanet@mtna.org
URL: http://www.mtna.org

Annual. **Primary Exhibits:** Musical equipment, supplies, and services.

★8462★ MUSICORA - Classical and Jazz Music Show

Secession
E-mail: secession@secession.fr
URL: http://www.secession.at

Annual. **Primary Exhibits:** Instruments, records, scores, books, and antiques related to classical music.

★8463★ NAMM - Summer Session

NAMM - International Music Products Association
5790 Armada Dr.
Carlsbad, CA 92008
Ph: (760)438-8001   Fax: (760)438-7327
Fr: 800-767-6266
E-mail: info@namm.com
URL: http://www.namm.com

Annual. **Primary Exhibits:** Musical instruments and accessories, acoustical equipment, and sheet music publications.

★8464★ National Association of Pastoral Musicians National Convention

National Association of Pastoral Musicians
962 Wayne Ave., Ste. 210
Silver Spring, MD 20910-4461
Ph: (240)247-3000 Fax: (240)247-3001
E-mail: npmsing@npm.org
URL: http://npm.org

Annual. **Primary Exhibits:** Music, musical instruments, books, church furnishings and art.

★8465★ National Opera Association Conference

National Opera Association
c/o Robert Hansen
PO Box 60869
Canyon, TX 79016-0869
Ph: (806)651-2857 Fax: (806)651-2958
URL: http://www.noa.org

Annual. **Primary Exhibits:** Opera-related music, CDs and equipment, supplies, and services.

★8466★ Violin Society of America Convention

Violin Society of America
48 Academy St.
614 Lerew Rd.
Poughkeepsie, NY 12601
Ph: (845)452-7557
E-mail: edwardcampbell@sprintmail.com
URL: http://www.vsa.to

Annual. **Primary Exhibits:** Violins, violas, cellos, and their bows, strings, and other accessories; books; tone and bow woods.

★8467★ Western Division Choral Directors Association Convention

American Choral Directors Association
545 Couch Dr.
PO Box 2720
Oklahoma City, OK 73101-2720
Ph: (405)232-8161 Fax: (405)232-8162
E-mail: acda@acdaonline.org
URL: http://www.acdaonline.org

Biennial. **Primary Exhibits:** Exhibits of interest to choral directors.

OTHER SOURCES

★8468★ *American Almanac of Jobs and Salaries*

HarperCollins
10 E. 53rd St.
New York, NY 10022
Ph: (212)207-7000 Fr: 800-242-7737
URL: http://www.harpercollins.com/

John W. Wright. Revised edition, 2000. $20.00 (paper). 672 pages. This is a comprehensive guide to the wages of hundreds of occupations in a wide variety of industries and organizations.

★8469★ American Federation of Musicians of the United States and Canada (AFM)

1501 Broadway, Ste. 600
New York, NY 10036
Ph: (212)869-1330 Fax: (212)764-6134
E-mail: presoffice@afm.org
URL: http://www.afm.org

Description: Union representing the interests of professional musicians through collective bargaining, benefits, and services.

★8470★ American Guild of Musical Artists (AGMA)

1430 Broadway, 14th Fl.
New York, NY 10018
Ph: (212)265-3687 Fax: (212)262-9088
E-mail: agma@musicalartists.org
URL: http://www.musicalartists.org

Description: AFL-CIO. Represents opera and classical concert singers, classical ballet and modern dance performers, and affiliated stage directors, stage managers and choreographers.

★8471★ American Guild of Organists (AGO)

475 Riverside Dr., Ste. 1260
New York, NY 10115
Ph: (212)870-2310 Fax: (212)870-2163
Fr: 800-AGO-5115
E-mail: info@agohq.org
URL: http://www.agohq.org

Purpose: Educational and service organization organized to advance the cause of organ and choral music and to maintain standards of artistic excellence of organists and choral conductors. **Activities:** Offers professional certification in organ playing, choral and instrumental training, and theory and general knowledge of music.

★8472★ Association of Music Writers and Photographers (AMWP)

PO Box 79
Oak Lawn, IL 60454
Fax: (801)327-4735
E-mail: amwp@amwp.org
URL: http://www.musicpressreport.com

Description: Defends the interests of music writers and photographers. Establishes the first music press community. Offers networking opportunities, job listings, industry directories, guides and contests.

★8473★ Band Director

Cambridge Educational
PO Box 2053
Princeton, NJ 08543-2053
Fax: (609)671-0266 Fr: 800-257-5126
E-mail: custserv@films.com
URL: http://www.cambridgeeducational.com

VHS and DVD. $39.95. 15 minutes. 1989. Part of the Vocational Visions Career series.

★8474★ Country Music Showcase International (CMSI)

PO Box 368
Carlisle, IA 50047-0368
Ph: (515)989-3748
E-mail: haroldl@cmshowcase.org
URL: http://www.cmshowcase.org

Purpose: Helps songwriters and entertainers learn more about songwriting and the general music industry. **Activities:** Sponsors Song Evaluation and Critiques Service, songwriting seminars and workshops and songwriter showcases. Operates a BMI Music Publishing Company for the benefit of members whose songs qualify for publishing. Configures specially made computers for songwriters, musicians, and entertainers to use. Owns and operates: Country Music Showcase International, Inc.; Attraction Booking Agency, which serves fairs, festivals, and corporate fund raising events providing them access to all 14 Art Forms of Country Music Entertainers and Stage Shows. Serves as the trustee for the Iowa/Midwest Country Music Heritage "Virtual" Museum, Library and Hall Of Fame.

★8475★ Media and the Arts Occupations

Delphi Productions
3159 6th St.
Boulder, CO 80304
Ph: (303)443-2100 Fax: (303)443-4022
Fr: 888-443-2400
E-mail: support@delphivideo.com
URL: http://www.delphivideo.com

$95.00. 50 minutes. Part of the Careers for the 21st Century Video Library.

★8476★ MENC: The National Association for Music Education (MENC)

1806 Robert Fulton Dr.
Reston, VA 20191
Ph: (703)860-4000 Fax: (703)860-1531
Fr: 800-336-3768
E-mail: executive@menc.org
URL: http://www.menc.org

Description: Comprised of music educators, administrators, supervisors, consultants, and music education majors in colleges. Publishes materials for music educators, presents conferences, compiles statistics.

★8477★ Music Teachers National Association (MTNA)

441 Vine St., Ste. 3100
Cincinnati, OH 45202-3004
Ph: (513)421-1420 Fax: (513)421-2503
Fr: 888-512-5278
E-mail: mtnanet@mtna.org
URL: http://www.mtna.org

Description: Professional society of independent and collegiate music teachers committed to furthering the art of music through programs that encourage and support teaching, performance, composition, and scholarly research.

★8478★ National Association of Pastoral Musicians (NPM)

962 Wayne Ave., Ste. 210
Silver Spring, MD 20910-4461
Ph: (240)247-3000   Fax: (240)247-3001
E-mail: npmsing@npm.org
URL: http://www.npm.org

Description: Fosters the art of musical liturgy. Members serve the Catholic Church in the United States as musicians, clergy, liturgists, and other leaders of prayer. Provides ongoing formation for musicians and clergy through annual conventions, educational institutes, and events in more than 70 diocesan chapters. Also provides certification programs for cantors, organists, and directors of music ministries.

★8479★ National Association of Teachers of Singing (NATS)

9957 Moorings Dr., Ste. 401
Jacksonville, FL 32257
Ph: (904)992-9101   Fax: (904)262-2587
Fr: 888-262-2065
E-mail: info@nats.org
URL: http://www.nats.org

Description: Serves as a professional society of teachers of singing. Encourages the highest standards of the vocal art and of ethical principles in the teaching of singing. Promotes vocal education and research at all levels, both for the enrichment of the general public and for the professional advancement of the talented.

★8480★ Organization of American Kodaly Educators (OAKE)

1612 29th Ave. S
Moorhead, MN 56560
Ph: (218)227-6253   Fax: (218)277-6254
E-mail: oakeoffice@oake.org
URL: http://www.oake.org

Description: Represents music educators, students, organizations, schools, and libraries interested in the Kodaly concept of music education. Zoltan Kodaly (1882-1967), Hungarian composer and educator, originated a concept of music education that seeks to develop the sensibilities, intellectual facilities, and skills of children, with the intention of creating a musically educated public. Objectives are: to encourage communication and cooperation among Kodaly educators; to encourage musical and human growth; to provide a forum for comment on the impact of the Kodaly concept; to recognize, identify, and convey the multicultural musical heritage of American society; to contribute to and encourage the aesthetic education of the child. Conducts clinics and other small unit activities.

★8481★ Professional Women Singers Association (PWSA)

PO Box 884
New York, NY 10159
Ph: (212)969-0590
E-mail: info@womensingers.org
URL: http://www.womensingers.org

Members: Professional women singers. **Purpose:** Promotes career advancement of women singers. **Activities:** Serves as a network for singers looking for career support.

Nuclear Engineers

SOURCES OF HELP-WANTED ADS

★8482★ AWIS Magazine

Association for Women in Science
1200 New York Ave. NW, Ste. 650
Washington, DC 20005
Ph: (202)326-8940   Fax: (202)326-8960
Fr: (866)657-2947
E-mail: awis@awis.org
URL: http://www.awis.org/

Description: Bimonthly. Covers issues, legislation, and trends related to science education for girls, women, and minorities. Includes information on grants and fellowships, job openings, educational programs, events, and notices of publications available.

★8483★ Energy User News

BNP Media
2401 W Big Beaver Rd., Ste. 700
Troy, MI 48084-3333
Ph: (248)786-1642   Fax: (248)786-1388
URL: http://www.energyusernews.com

Monthly. Magazine reporting on the energy management market as it relates to commercial, industrial, and institutional facilities.

★8484★ Engineering Economist

Institute of Industrial Engineers
3577 Parkway Ln., Ste. 200
Norcross, GA 30092
Ph: (770)449-0460   Fax: (770)441-3295
Fr: 800-494-0460
URL: http://www.iienet2.org/Details.aspx?id=1486

Quarterly. $73.00/year for individuals; $129.00/year for institutions, online only; $136.00/year for institutions, print & online; $82.00/year for institutions, print + online; $77.00/year for institutions, online only. Publication covering business issues in the energy, petroleum and mining industries.

★8485★ Engineering Times

National Society of Professional
  Engineers
1420 King St.
Alexandria, VA 22314
Ph: (703)684-2800
URL: http://www.nspe.org

Monthly. Magazine (tabloid) covering professional, legislative, and techology issues for an engineering audience.

★8486★ ENR: Engineering News-Record

McGraw-Hill Inc.
1221 Ave. of the Americas
New York, NY 10020-1095
Ph: (212)512-2000   Fax: (212)512-3840
Fr: 877-833-5524
E-mail: enr_web_editors@mcgraw-hill.com
URL: http://www.mymags.com/moreinfo.php?itemID=20012

Weekly. $94.00/year for individuals, print. Magazine focusing on engineering and construction.

★8487★ Graduating Engineer & Computer Careers

Career Recruitment Media
211 W Wacker Dr., Ste. 900
Chicago, IL 60606
Ph: (312)525-3100
URL: http://www.graduatingengineer.com

Quarterly. $15.00/year for individuals. Magazine focusing on employment, education, and career development for entry-level engineers and computer scientists.

★8488★ High Technology Careers Magazine

HTC
4701 Patrick Henry Dr., No. 1901
Santa Clara, CA 95054-1847
Fax: (408)567-0242
URL: http://www.hightechcareers.com

Bimonthly. $29.00/year; $35.00/year for Canada; $85.00/year for out of country. Magazine (tabloid) containing employment opportunity information for the engineering and technical community.

★8489★ IEEE Spectrum

Institute of Electrical and Electronics
  Engineers Inc.
3 Park Ave., 17th Fl.
New York, NY 10016-5997
Ph: (212)419-7900   Fax: (212)752-4929
URL: http://www.spectrum.ieee.org/mc_online

Monthly. $29.95/year for individuals, U.S. & Canada; $99.95/year for out of country, international. Magazine for the scientific and engineering professional. Provides information on developments and trends in engineering, physics, mathematics, chemistry, medicine/biology, and the nuclear sciences.

★8490★ NSBE Magazine

NSBE Publications
205 Daingerfield Rd.
Alexandria, VA 22314
Ph: (703)549-2207   Fax: (703)683-5312
URL: http://www.nsbe.org/publications/premieradvertisers.php

Journal providing information on engineering careers, self-development, and cultural issues for recent graduates with technical majors.

★8491★ Nuclear Plant Journal

Nuclear Plant Journal
799 Roosevelt Rd., Bldg. 6, Ste. 208
Glen Ellyn, IL 60137
Ph: (630)858-6161   Fax: (630)858-8787
E-mail: npj@goinfo.com
URL: http://www.npjonline.com

Bimonthly. Free, to industry professionals. Magazine focusing on nuclear power plants.

★8492★ Power

McGraw-Hill Inc.
1221 Ave. of the Americas
New York, NY 10020-1095
Ph: (212)512-2000   Fax: (212)512-3840
Fr: 877-833-5524
E-mail: robert_peltier@platts.com
URL: http://online.platts.com/PPS/P=m&s=1029337384756.1478827&e=1

Monthly. Magazine for engineers in electric utilities, process and manufacturing plants, commercial and service establishments, and consulting, design, and construction engineering firms working in the power technology field.

★8493★ Power Engineering

PennWell Corp.
1421 S Sheridan Rd.
Tulsa, OK 74112
Ph: (918)835-3161   Fr: 800-331-4463
E-mail: pe@pennwell.com
URL: http://pepei.pennnet.com

Monthly. $76.00/year for U.S. $85.00/year for Canada and Mexico; $210.00/year for other countries. Magazine focusing on power generation.

★8494★ Radwaste Solutions

American Nuclear Society
555 N Kensington Ave.
La Grange Park, IL 60526
Ph: (708)352-6611   Fax: (708)352-0499
URL: http://www.ans.org/pubs/magazines/rs/

Bimonthly. $460.00/year for individuals. Magazine promoting awareness and understanding of the application of nuclear science and technology.

★8495★ SWE, Magazine of the Society of Women Engineers

Society of Women Engineers
230 East Ohio St., Ste. 400
Chicago, IL 60611-3265
Ph: (312)596-5223
E-mail: hq@swe.org
URL: http://www.swe.org

Quarterly. $30.00/year for nonmembers. Magazine for engineering students and for women and men working in the engineering and technology fields. Covers career guidance, continuing development and topical issues.

★8496★ Weapons Complex Monitor

ExchangeMonitor Publications,Inc.
4455 Connecticut Ave NW, Ste. A700
Washington, DC 20008
Ph: (202)296-2814   Fax: (202)296-2805
Fr: 800-776-1314
E-mail: helminski@exchangemonitor.com
URL: http://www.exchangemonitor.com

Description: Weekly. Devoted exclusively to providing intelligence and inside information on the largest environmental program in the world–the cleanup of the Department of Energy's nuclear weapons comples. Includes special bi-weekly report Post-Soviet States & Eastern Europe Monitor, which covers radioactive waste management and nuclear facilities cleanup in Russia and the post-Soviet States.

★8497★ WEPANEWS

Women in Engineering Programs & Advocates Network
1901 E. Asbury Ave., Ste. 220
Denver, CO 80208
Ph: (303)871-4643   Fax: (303)871-6833
E-mail: dmatt@wepan.org
URL: http://www.wepan.org

Description: 2/year. Seeks to provide greater access for women to careers in engineering. Includes news of graduate, undergraduate, freshmen, pre-college, and re-entry engineering programs for women. Recurring features include job listings, faculty, grant, and conference news, international engineering program news, action group news, notices of publications available, and a column titled Kudos.

PLACEMENT AND JOB REFERRAL SERVICES

★8498★ American Indian Science and Engineering Society (AISES)

PO Box 9828
Albuquerque, NM 87119-9828
Ph: (505)765-1052   Fax: (505)765-5608
E-mail: info@aises.org
URL: http://www.aises.org

Description: Represents American Indian and non-Indian students and professionals in science, technology, and engineering fields; corporations representing energy, mining, aerospace, electronic, and computer fields. Seeks to motivate and encourage students to pursue undergraduate and graduate studies in science, engineering, and technology. Sponsors science fairs in grade schools, teacher training workshops, summer math/science sessions for 8th-12th graders, professional chapters, and student chapters in colleges. Offers scholarships. Adult members serve as role models, advisers, and mentors for students. Operates placement service.

★8499★ Engineering Society of Detroit (ESD)

2000 Town Ctr., Ste. 2610
Southfield, MI 48075
Ph: (248)353-0735   Fax: (248)353-0736
E-mail: esd@esd.org
URL: http://esd.org

Description: Engineers from all disciplines; scientists and technologists. Conducts technical programs and engineering refresher courses; sponsors conferences and expositions. Maintains speakers' bureau; offers placement services; although based in Detroit, MI, society membership is international.

★8500★ Korean-American Scientists and Engineers Association (KSEA)

1952 Gallows Rd., Ste. 300
Vienna, VA 22182
Ph: (703)748-1221   Fax: (703)748-1331

E-mail: admin@ksea.org
URL: http://www.ksea.org

Description: Represents scientists and engineers holding single or advanced degrees. Promotes friendship and mutuality among Korean and American scientists and engineers; contributes to Korea's scientific, technological, industrial, and economic developments; strengthens the scientific, technological, and cultural bonds between Korea and the U.S. Sponsors symposium. Maintains speakers' bureau, placement service, and biographical archives. Compiles statistics.

★8501★ Society of Hispanic Professional Engineers (SHPE)

5400 E Olympic Blvd., Ste. 210
Los Angeles, CA 90022
Ph: (323)725-3970   Fax: (323)725-0316
E-mail: shpenational@shpe.org
URL: http://oneshpe.shpe.org/wps/portal/national

Description: Represents engineers, student engineers, and scientists. Aims to increase the number of Hispanic engineers by providing motivation and support to students. Sponsors competitions and educational programs. Maintains placement service and speakers' bureau; compiles statistics.

EMPLOYER DIRECTORIES AND NETWORKING LISTS

★8502★ American Men and Women of Science

Gale, Cengage Learning
27500 Drake Rd.
Farmington Hills, MI 48331-3535
Ph: (248)699-4253   Fax: (248)699-8065
Fr: 800-877-4253
URL: http://www.gale.com

Biennial, latest edition 23rd, October 2006; new edition expected 24th, January 2008. $1,075.00 for individuals. Covers over 129,700 U.S. and Canadian scientists active in the physical, biological, mathematical, computer science, and engineering fields; includes references to previous edition for deceased scientists and nonrespondents. Entries include: Name, address, education, personal and career data, memberships, honors and awards, research interest. Arrangement: Alphabetical. Indexes: Discipline (in separate volume).

★8503★ Careers in Focus: Engineering

Facts On File Inc.
132 W 31st St., 17th Fl.
New York, NY 10001
Ph: (212)967-8800   Fax: 800-678-3633
Fr: 800-322-8755
URL: http://www.factsonfile.com

3rd edition, 2007. $29.95 for individuals; $26.95 for libraries. Publication includes: List of resources to consult for more information. Principal content of publication consists of job descriptions, advancement opportunities, educational requirements, employment outlook, salary information, and working conditions for careers in the field of engineering. Indexes: Alphabetical.

★8504★ **Directory of Contract Staffing Firms**

C.E. Publications Inc.
PO Box 3006
Bothell, WA 98041-3006
Ph: (425)806-5200   Fax: (425)806-5585
URL: http://www.cjhunter.com/dcsf/overview.html

Covers nearly 1,300 contract firms actively engaged in the employment of engineering, IT/IS, and technical personnel for 'temporary' contract assignments throughout the world. Entries include: Company name, address, phone, name of contact, email, web address. Arrangement: Alphabetical. Indexes: Geographical.

★8505★ **Indiana Society of Professional Engineers-Directory**

Indiana Society of Professional Engineers
PO Box 20806
Indianapolis, IN 46220
Ph: (317)255-2267   Fax: (317)255-2530
URL: http://www.indspe.org

Annual, fall. Covers member registered engineers, land surveyors, engineering students, and engineers in training. Entries include: Member name, address, phone, type of membership, business information, specialty. Arrangement: Alphabetical by chapter area.

★8506★ **Peterson's Job Opportunities in Engineering and Technology**

Peterson's Guides
2000 Lenox Dr.
Box 67005
Lawrenceville, NJ 08648
Ph: (609)896-1800   Fax: (609)896-4531
Fr: 800-338-3282
E-mail: custsvc@petersons.com
URL: http://www.petersons.com

Compiled by the Peterson's staff. Fourth edition, 1996. $21.95 (paper). 379 pages. Profiles 2,000 high-tech companies looking primarily for technical personnel in such fields as biotechnology, telecommunications, software, computers and peripherals, defense, and aerospace. Contains job-search strategies and career options to help match education and expertise to the job market. Indexed geographically, by industry, and by hiring needs.

HANDBOOKS AND MANUALS

★8507★ **The Best Resumes for Scientists and Engineers**

John Wiley & Sons Inc.
1 Wiley Dr.
Somerset, NJ 08873
Ph: (732)469-4400   Fax: (732)302-2300
Fr: 800-225-5945
E-mail: custserv@wiley.com
URL: http://www.wiley.com/WileyCDA/

Adele Lewis and David J. Moore. Second edition, 1993. $37.50; $19.95 (paper). 224 pages. Presents an extensive collection of scientific and engineering resumes, highlighting the important differences between these and resumes written for other occupations.

★8508★ **Great Jobs for Engineering Majors**

The McGraw-Hill Companies
PO Box 182604
Columbus, OH 43272
Fax: (614)759-3749   Fr: 877-883-5524
E-mail: customer.service@mcgraw-hill.com
URL: http://www.mcgraw-hill.com

Geraldine O. Garner. Second edition, 2002. $14.95. 256 pages. Covers all the career options open to students majoring in engineering.

★8509★ **How to Succeed as an Engineer: A Practical Guide to Enhance Your Career**

Institute of Electrical & Electronics Engineers
445 Hoes Lane
Piscataway, NJ 08854
Ph: (732)981-0060   Fax: (732)981-9667
Fr: 800-678-4333
URL: http://www.ieee.org

Todd Yuzuriha. 1999. $29.95 (paper). 367 pages.

★8510★ **The I Hate Selling Book: Business-Building Advice for Consultants, Attorneys, Accountants, Engineers, Architects, and Other Professionals**

AMACOM
1601 Broadway, 12th Fl.
New York, NY 10019-7420
Ph: (212)586-8100   Fax: (212)903-8168
Fr: 800-262-9699
URL: http://www.amanet.org

Allan S. Boress. 2001. $29.95. 240 pages.

★8511★ **Keys to Engineering Success**

Prentice Hall PTR
One Lake St.
Upper Saddle River, NJ 07458
Ph: (201)236-7000   Fr: 800-428-5331
URL: http://www.phptr.com/index.asp?rl=1

Jill S. Tietjen, Kristy A. Schloss, Carol Carter, Joyce Bishop, and Sarah Lyman. 2000. $46.00 (paper). 288 pages.

★8512★ **The New Engineer's Guide to Career Growth & Professional Awareness**

Institute of Electrical & Electronics Engineers
445 Hoes Lane
Piscataway, NJ 08854
Ph: (732)981-0060   Fax: (732)981-9667
Fr: 800-678-4333
URL: http://www.ieee.org

Irving J. Gabelman, editor. 1996. $39.95 (paper). 275 pages.

★8513★ **Opportunities in Engineering Careers**

The McGraw-Hill Companies
PO Box 182604
Columbus, OH 43272
Fax: (614)759-3749   Fr: 877-883-5524
E-mail: customer.service@mcgraw-hill.com
URL: http://www.mcgraw-hill.com

Nicholas Basta. Revised second edition, 2002. $13.95; $11.95 (paper). 160 pages. Outlines typical job titles, salaries, career paths, and employment prospects.

★8514★ **Opportunities in High Tech Careers**

The McGraw-Hill Companies
PO Box 182604
Columbus, OH 43272
Fax: (614)759-3749   Fr: 877-883-5524
E-mail: customer.service@mcgraw-hill.com
URL: http://www.mcgraw-hill.com

Gary Colter and Deborah Yanuck. 1999. $14.95; $11.95 (paper). 160 pages. Explores high technology careers. Describes job opportunities, how to make a career decision, how to prepare for high technology jobs, job hunting techniques, and future trends.

★8515★ **Opportunities in Research and Development Careers**

The McGraw-Hill Companies
PO Box 182604
Columbus, OH 43272
Fax: (614)759-3749   Fr: 877-883-5524
E-mail: customer.service@mcgraw-hill.com
URL: http://www.mcgraw-hill.com

Jan Goldberg. 1996. $11.95 (paper). 146 pages.

★8516★ **Real People Working in Engineering**

The McGraw-Hill Companies
PO Box 182604
Columbus, OH 43272
Fax: (614)759-3749   Fr: 877-883-5524
E-mail: customer.service@mcgraw-hill.com
URL: http://www.mcgraw-hill.com

Blythe Camenson, Jan Goldberg. 1997. $17.95 (paper). 160 pages. Interviews and profiles of working professionals capture a range of opportunities in this field.

★8517★ Resumes for Engineering Careers

The McGraw-Hill Companies
PO Box 182604
Columbus, OH 43272
Fax: (614)759-3749   Fr: 877-883-5524
E-mail: customer.service@mcgraw-hill.com
URL: http://www.mcgraw-hill.com

Third edition, 2005. $11.95 (paper). 144 pages. Contains sample resumes and cover letters applicable to any engineering field.

★8518★ Resumes for Scientific and Technical Careers

The McGraw-Hill Companies
PO Box 182604
Columbus, OH 43272
Fax: (614)759-3749   Fr: 877-883-5524
E-mail: customer.service@mcgraw-hill.com
URL: http://www.mcgraw-hill.com

Third edition, 2007. $12.95 (paper). 144 pages. Provides resume advice for individuals interested in working in scientific and technical careers. Includes sample resumes and cover letters.

EMPLOYMENT AGENCIES AND SEARCH FIRMS

★8519★ Engineer One, Inc.

PO Box 23037
Knoxville, TN 37933
Fax: (865)691-0110
E-mail: engineerone@engineerone.com
URL: http://www.engineerone.com

Engineering employment service specializes in engineering and management in the chemical process, power utilities, manufacturing, mechanical, electrical, and electronic industries. Established an Information Technology Division in 1998 that works nationwide across all industries. Also provides systems analysis consulting services specializing in VAX based systems.

★8520★ Global Employment Solutions

10375 Park Meadows Dr., Ste. 375
Littleton, CO 80124
Ph: (303)216-9500   Fax: (303)216-9533
E-mail: careers@global
URL: http://www.gesnetwork.com

Employment agency.

★8521★ International Staffing Consultants

17310 Redhill Ave., No. 140
Irvine, CA 92614
Ph: (949)255-5857   Fax: (949)767-5959
E-mail: iscinc@iscworld.com
URL: http://www.iscworld.com

Employment agency. Provides placement on regular or temporary basis. Affiliate office in London.

★8522★ Search and Recruit International

4455 South Blvd. Ste. 110
Virginia Beach, VA 23452
Ph: (757)625-2121   Fr: 800-800-5627

Employment agency. Headquartered in Virginia Beach. Other offices in Bremerton, WA; Charleston, SC; Jacksonville, FL; Memphis, TN; Pensacola, FL; Sacramento, CA; San Bernardino, CA; San Diego, CA.

ONLINE JOB SOURCES AND SERVICES

★8523★ NuclearMarket.com

E-mail: info@nuclearmarket.com
URL: http://www.nuclearmarket.com

Description: Nuclear Market's Career Center allows seekers to search a database of Nuclear Jobs in the United States, Europe and beyond. Candidates also have the option of registering their profile in database in order to receive email notification of any relevant vacancies.

★8524★ Spherion

2050 Spectrum Blvd.
Fort Lauderdale, FL 33309
Ph: (954)308-7600
E-mail: help@spherion.com
URL: http://www.spherion.com

Description: Recruitment firm specializing in accounting and finance, sales and marketing, interim executives, technology, engineering, retail and human resources.

OTHER SOURCES

★8525★ American Almanac of Jobs and Salaries

HarperCollins
10 E. 53rd St.
New York, NY 10022
Ph: (212)207-7000   Fr: 800-242-7737
URL: http://www.harpercollins.com/

John W. Wright. Revised edition, 2000. $20.00 (paper). 672 pages. This is a comprehensive guide to the wages of hundreds of occupations in a wide variety of industries and organizations.

★8526★ American Association of Blacks in Energy (AABE)

927 15th St. NW, Ste. 200
Washington, DC 20005-2321
Ph: (202)371-9530   Fax: (202)371-9218
Fr: 800-466-0204
E-mail: aabe@aabe.org
URL: http://www.aabe.org

Description: Seeks to increase the knowledge, understanding, and awareness of the minority community in energy issues by serving as an energy information source for policymakers, recommending blacks and other minorities to appropriate energy officials and executives, encouraging students to pursue professional careers in the energy industry, and advocating the participation of blacks and other minorities in energy programs and policymaking activities. Updates members on key legislation and regulations being developed by the Department of Energy, the Department of Interior, the Department of Commerce, the Small Business Administration, and other federal and state agencies.

★8527★ American Association of Engineering Societies (AAES)

1620 I St. NW, Ste. 210
Washington, DC 20006
Ph: (202)296-2237   Fax: (202)296-1151
Fr: 888-400-2237
E-mail: dbateson@aaes.org
URL: http://www.aaes.org

Description: Coordinates the efforts of the member societies in the provision of reliable and objective information to the general public concerning issues which affect the engineering profession and the field of engineering as a whole; collects, analyzes, documents, and disseminates data which will inform the general public of the relationship between engineering and the national welfare; provides a forum for the engineering societies to exchange and discuss their views on matters of common interest; and represents the U.S. engineering community abroad through representation in WFEO and UPADI.

★8528★ American Engineering Association (AEA)

4116 S Carrier Pkwy., Ste. 280-809
Grand Prairie, TX 75052
Ph: (201)664-6954
E-mail: info@aea.org
URL: http://www.aea.org

Description: Members consist of Engineers and engineering professionals. Purpose to advance the engineering profession and U.S. engineering capabilities. Issues of concern include age discrimination, immigration laws, displacement of U.S. Engineers by foreign workers, trade agreements, off shoring of U.S. Engineering and manufacturing jobs, loss of U.S. manufacturing and engineering capability, and recruitment of foreign students. Testifies before Congress. Holds local Chapter meetings.

★8529★ American Nuclear Society (ANS)

555 N Kensington Ave.
La Grange Park, IL 60526
Ph: (708)352-6611   Fax: (708)352-0499
Fr: 800-323-3044
URL: http://www.ans.org

Description: Physicists, chemists, educators, mathematicians, life scientists, engineers, metallurgists, managers, and administrators with professional experience in nuclear science or nuclear engineering. Works to advance science and engineering in the nuclear industry. Disseminates information; promotes research; conducts meetings devoted to scientific and technical papers; works with government agencies, educational institutions, and other organizations dealing with nuclear issues.

★8530★ **Association for International Practical Training (AIPT)**
10400 Little Patuxent Pkwy., Ste. 250
Columbia, MD 21044-3519
Ph: (410)997-2200   Fax: (410)992-3924
E-mail: aipt@aipt.org
URL: http://www.aipt.org

Description: Providers worldwide of on-the-job training programs for students and professionals seeking international career development and life-changing experiences. Arranges workplace exchanges in hundreds of professional fields, bringing employers and trainees together from around the world. Client list ranges from small farming communities to Fortune 500 companies.

★8531★ **Engineering Occupations**
Delphi Productions
3159 6th St.
Boulder, CO 80304
Ph: (303)443-2100   Fax: (303)443-4022
Fr: 888-443-2400
E-mail: support@delphivideo.com
URL: http://www.delphivideo.com

$95.00. 50 minutes. Part of the Careers for the 21st Century Video Library.

★8532★ **National Action Council for Minorities in Engineering (NACME)**
440 Hamilton Ave., Ste. 302
White Plains, NY 10601-1813
Ph: (914)539-4010   Fax: (914)539-4032
E-mail: webmaster@nacme.org
URL: http://www.nacme.org

Description: Leads the national effort to increase access to careers in engineering and other science-based disciplines. Conducts research and public policy analysis, develops and operates national demonstration programs at precollege and university levels, and disseminates information through publications, conferences and electronic media. Serves as a privately funded source of scholarships for minority students in engineering.

★8533★ **National Society of Professional Engineers (NSPE)**
1420 King St.
Alexandria, VA 22314-2794
Ph: (703)684-2800   Fax: (703)836-4875
Fr: 888-285-6773
E-mail: memserv@nspe.org
URL: http://www.nspe.org

Description: Represents professional engineers and engineers-in-training in all fields registered in accordance with the laws of states or territories of the U.S. or provinces of Canada; qualified graduate engineers, student members, and registered land surveyors. Is concerned with social, professional, ethical, and economic considerations of engineering as a profession; encompasses programs in public relations, employment practices, ethical considerations, education, and career guidance. Monitors legislative

and regulatory actions of interest to the engineering profession.

★8534★ **Scientific, Engineering, and Technical Services**
Cambridge Educational
PO Box 2053
Princeton, NJ 08543-2053
Ph: 800-257-5126   Fax: (609)671-0266
Fr: 800-468-4227
E-mail: custserv@films.com
URL: http://www.cambridgeeducational.com

VHS and DVD. $89.95. 2002. 18 minutes. 2002. Part of the Career Cluster Series.

★8535★ **Society of Women Engineers (SWE)**
230 E Ohio St., Ste. 400
Chicago, IL 60611-3265
Ph: (312)596-5223   Fax: (312)596-5252
Fr: 877-SWE-INFO
E-mail: hq@swe.org
URL: http://www.swe.org

Description: Educational and service organization representing both students and professional women in engineering and technical fields.

★8536★ **Women in Engineering**
Her Own Words
PO Box 5264
Madison, WI 53705-0264
Ph: (608)271-7083   Fax: (608)271-0209
E-mail: herownword@aol.com
URL: http://www.herownwords.com/

Video. Jocelyn Riley. $95.00. 15 minutes. Resource guide also available for $45.00.

Nuclear Medicine Technologists

★8537★ Applied Radiation and Isotopes

Mosby Inc.
11830 Westline Industrial Dr.
St. Louis, MO 63146
Ph: (314)872-8370   Fax: (314)432-1380
Fr: 800-325-4177
URL: http://www.elsevier.com/wps/find/journaldescription.cws_home

Monthly. $3,117.00/year for institutions (price for all countries except European countries, Japan and Iran). Journal for radiologists.

★8538★ ASTRO News

American Society for Therapeutic Radiology and Oncology
8280 Willow Oaks Corporate Dr., Ste. 500
Fairfax, VA 22031
Ph: (703)502-1550   Fax: (703)502-7876
Fr: 800-962-7876
URL: http://www.astro.org/Publications/ASTROnews/index.asp

Quarterly. Subscription included in membership. Professional magazine covering radiology.

★8539★ Clinical Nuclear Medicine

Lippincott Williams & Wilkins
530 Walnut St.
Philadelphia, PA 19106-3621
Ph: (215)521-8300   Fax: (215)521-8902
Fr: 800-638-3030
E-mail: cnm@pond.com
URL: http://www.nuclearmed.com

Monthly. $329.00/year for individuals, U.S.; $613.00/year for institutions, U.S.; $436.00/year for other countries; $691.00/year for institutions, other countries; $186.00/year for other countries, in-training; $169.00/year for U.S., in-training. Journal publishing original manuscripts about scanning, imaging, and related subjects.

★8540★ CME Supplement to Radiologic Clinics of North America

Elsevier Science Inc.
360 Park Ave. S
New York, NY 10010
Ph: (212)989-5800   Fax: (212)633-3990
URL: http://www.elsevier.com

$431.00/year for institutions, U.S. $530.00/year for institutions, Canada; $290.00/year for individuals, U.S. $339.00/year for individuals, Canada; $142.00/year for students, U.S. 192.00/year for students, Canada. Journal covering radiology, nuclear medicine and medical imaging.

★8541★ Diagnostic Imaging

CMP Media L.L.C.
600 Community Dr.
Manhasset, NY 11030
Ph: (516)562-5000   Fax: (516)562-7830
URL: http://www.diagnosticimaging.com/

Monthly. News and analysis on clinical and economic developments in medical imaging.

★8542★ Journal of Nuclear Medicine Technology

Society of Nuclear Medicine Inc.
1850 Samuel Morse Dr.
Reston, VA 20190-5316
Ph: (703)708-9000   Fax: (703)708-9015
URL: http://tech.snmjournals.org

Quarterly. $210.00/year for nonmembers; $252.00/year for individuals, overseas. Peer-reviewed scientific journal for technologists presenting original research, clinical reports, continuing education articles, and commentary on scientific trends and discoveries in nuclear medicine.

★8543★ Magnetic Resonance Imaging Clinics

Mosby Inc.
11830 Westline Industrial Dr.
St. Louis, MO 63146
Ph: (314)872-8370   Fax: (314)432-1380
Fr: 800-325-4177
URL: http://www.mri.theclinics.com

Quarterly. $345.00/year for individuals, international; $463.00/year for institutions, international; $167.00/year for students, international; $253.00/year for individuals; $376.00/year for institutions; $123.00/year for students. Journal publishing articles and research on the latest trends in magnetic resonance imagining clinics and patient management.

★8544★ Magnetic Resonance in Medicine

International Society for Magnetic Resonance in Medicine
2118 Milvia St., Ste. 201
Berkeley, CA 94704
Ph: (510)841-1899   Fax: (510)841-2340
URL: http://www.ismrm.org

Monthly. $850.00/year for individuals, U.S.; $850.00/year for individuals, Canada and Mexico; $892.00/year for individuals, rest of world; $1,795.00/year for institutions, U.S.; $1,795.00/year for institutions, Canada and Mexico; $1,867.00/year for institutions, rest of world; $1,975.00/year for U.S., combined print with online; $1,975.00/year for Canada and Mexico, combined print with online; $2,047.00/year for rest of world, combined print with online. Journal covering radiology worldwide.

★8545★ Neuroimaging Clinics of North America

Mosby Inc.
11830 Westline Industrial Dr.
St. Louis, MO 63146
Ph: (314)872-8370   Fax: (314)432-1380
Fr: 800-325-4177
URL: http://www.neuroimaging.theclinics.com

Quarterly. $454.00/year for institutions, international; $332.00/year for individuals, international; $166.00/year for students, international; $370.00/year for institutions, U.S.; $123.00/year for students, U.S.; $277.00/year for individuals, Canada; $166.00/year for students, Canada; $454.00/year for institutions, Canada. Journal publishing articles on newest advances in neuroimaging and patient treatment options.

★8546★ Radiologic Clinics of North America

Mountain Association for Community Economic Development
433 Chestnut St.
Berea, KY 40403
Ph: (859)986-2373   Fax: (859)986-1299
URL: http://www.radiologic.theclinics.com

Bimonthly. $259.00/year for individuals; $385.00/year for institutions; $127.00/year for students; $43.00 for individuals, single issue; $64.00 for institutions, single issue; $21.00 for students, single issue; $79.00 for single issue, non-subscribers; $352.00/year for individuals, international; $473.00/year for institutions, international; $171.00/year for students, international. Journal publishing articles written by leading experts, along with high-quality reproductions of radiographs, MR images, CT scans and sonograms.

★8547★ Radiologic Technology

American Society of Radiologic Technologists
15000 Central Ave. SE
Albuquerque, NM 87123-3909
Ph: (505)298-4500   Fax: (505)298-5063
Fr: 800-444-2778
E-mail: pubsdept@asrt.org
URL: http://www.asrt.org

Bimonthly. $60.00/year for individuals; $90.00/year for other countries; $108.00 for two years; $162.00 for two years, other countries. Medical imaging technology. Includes annual index.

★8548★ Seminars in Roentgenology

Mosby Inc.
11830 Westline Industrial Dr.
St. Louis, MO 63146
Ph: (314)872-8370   Fax: (314)432-1380
Fr: 800-325-4177
URL: http://www.seminarsinroentgenology.com/

Quarterly. $240.00/year for individuals, U.S.; $120.00/year for students, U.S.; $345.00/year for individuals, Canada; $173.00/year for students, Canada; $345.00/year for individuals, Mexico; $173.00/year for students, Mexico; $345.00/year for individuals, international; $173.00/year for students, international. Journal covering issues concerning the practicing radiologist and for the resident.

EMPLOYER DIRECTORIES AND NETWORKING LISTS

★8549★ AHA Guide to the Health Care Field

American Hospital Association
1 N Franklin
Chicago, IL 60606
Ph: (312)422-2050   Fax: (312)422-4700
Fr: 800-424-4301

Annual, August. Covers hospitals, networks, multi-health care systems, freestanding ambulatory surgery centers, psychiatric facilities, long-term care facilities, substance abuse programs, and other health-related organizations. Entries include: For hospitals–Facility name, address, phone, administrator's name, number of beds, facilities and services, number of employees, expenses, other statistics. For other organizations–Name, address, phone, fax, name and title of contact. Arrangement: Geographical. Indexes: Hospital name.

★8550★ Directory of Hospital Personnel

Grey House Publishing
185 Millerton Rd.
PO Box 860
Millerton, NY 12546
Ph: (518)789-8700   Fax: (518)789-0556
Fr: 800-562-2139
URL: http://www.greyhouse.com/hospital_personnel.htm

Annual. $325.00 for print product; $545.00 for online database subscription; $650.00 for online database subscription and print product combined. Covers 200,000 executives at 7,000 U.S. hospitals. Entries include: Name of hospital, address, phone; number of beds; type and JCAHO status of hospital; names and titles of key department heads and staff; medical and nursing school affiliations; number of residents, interns, and nursing students. Arrangement: Geographical. Indexes: Hospital name, personnel, hospital size.

★8551★ Guide to Careers in the Health Professions

The Princeton Review
2315 Broadway
New York, NY 10024
Ph: (212)874-8282   Fax: (212)874-0775
Fr: 800-733-3000
URL: http://www.princetonreview.com/

Published January, 2001. $24.95 for individuals. Presents advice and information for those searching for satisfying careers in the health professions. Publication includes: Directory of schools and academic programs. Entries include: Name, address, phone, tuition, program details, employment profiles.

★8552★ Hospital Blue Book

Billian Publishing Inc./Transworld Publishing Inc.
2100 Powers Ferry Rd. SE
Atlanta, GA 30339
Ph: (770)955-5656   Fax: (770)952-0669
Fr: 800-533-8484
E-mail: blu-book@billian.com

2005. $300.00 for individuals. Covers more than 6,687 hospitals; some listings also appear in a separate southern edition of this publication. Entries include: Name of hospital, accreditation, mailing address, phone, fax, number of beds, type of facility (nonprofit, general, state, etc.); list of administrative personnel and chiefs of medical services, with specific titles. Arrangement: Geographical.

★8553★ The JobBank Guide to Health Care Companies

Adams Media Corp.
57 Littlefield St.
Avon, MA 02322
Ph: (508)427-7100   Fax: (508)427-6790
Fr: 800-872-5627
URL: http://www.amazon.com/Jobbank-Guide-Health-Care-Companies/dp

Biennial. Covers jobs nationwide in health care companies. Entries include: Firm or organization name, address, phone, name and title of contact; description of organization, headquarters location, typical titles for entry- and middle-level positions, educational backgrounds desired, fringe benefits offered, stock exchange listing, training programs, internships, parent company, number of employees, revenues, e-mail and web addresses, projected number of hires. Indexes: Alphabetical.

★8554★ Medical and Health Information Directory

Gale, Cengage Learning
27500 Drake Rd.
Farmington Hills, MI 48331-3535
Ph: (248)699-4253   Fax: (248)699-8065
Fr: 800-877-4253
E-mail: businessproducts@gale.com
URL: http://www.gale.com

Annual; latest edition 20th, July 2007. $375.00/volume. Covers in Volume 1, more than 26,500 medical and health oriented associations, organizations, institutions, and government agencies, including health maintenance organizations (HMOs), preferred provider organizations (PPOs), insurance companies, pharmaceutical companies, research centers, and medical and allied health schools. In Volume 2, over 12,000 medical book publishers; medical periodicals, directories, audiovisual producers and services, medical libraries and information centers, electronic resources, and health-related internet search engines. In Volume 3, more than 35,500 clinics, treatment centers, care programs, and counseling/diagnostic services for 34 subject areas. Entries include: Institution, service, or firm name, address, phone, fax, email and URL; many include names of key personnel and, when pertinent, descriptive annotations. Volume 3 was formerly listed separately as Health Services Directory. Arrangement: Classified by organization activity, service, etc. Indexes: Each volume has a complete alphabetical name and keyword index.

HANDBOOKS AND MANUALS

★8555★ Cardiac Nuclear Medicine

McGraw-Hill Professional
PO Box 182604
Columbus, OH 43272
Fax: (614)759-3749   Fr: 877-883-5524
E-mail: customer.service@mcgraw-hill.com
URL: http://www.mcgraw-hill.com

Myron C. Gerson, editor. Third edition, 1996. $169.00. 830 pages.

★8556★ Careers in Health Care

The McGraw-Hill Companies
PO Box 182604
Columbus, OH 43272
Fax: (614)759-3749   Fr: 877-883-5524
E-mail: customer.service@mcgraw-hill.com
URL: http://www.mcgraw-hill.com

Barbara M. Swanson. Fifth edition, 2005. $15.95 (paper). 192 pages. Describes job duties, work settings, salaries, licensing and certification requirements, educational preparation, and future outlook. Gives ideas on how to secure a job.

★8557★ Expert Resumes for Health Care Careers

Jist Works
875 Montreal Way
St. Paul, MN 55102
Fr: 800-648-5478
E-mail: info@jist.com
URL: http://www.jist.com

Wendy S. Enelow and Louise M. Kursmark. December 2003. $16.95. 288 pages.

★8558★ Health Careers Today

Elsevier
11830 Westline Industrial Dr.
St. Louis, MO 63146
Ph: (314)453-7010   Fax: (314)453-7095
Fr: 800-545-2522
E-mail: usbkinfo@elsevier.com
URL: http://www.elsevier.com

Gerdin, Judith. Fourth edition. 2007. $59.95. 496 pages. Covers more than 45 health careers. Discusses the roles and responsibilities of various occupations and provides a solid foundation in the skills needed for all health careers.

★8559★ Opportunities in Health and Medical Careers

The McGraw-Hill Companies
PO Box 182604
Columbus, OH 43272
Fax: (614)759-3749   Fr: 877-883-5524
E-mail: customer.service@mcgraw-hill.com
URL: http://www.mcgraw-hill.com

I. Donald Snook, Jr. and Leo D'Orazio. 2004. $13.95 (paper). 157 pages. Covers the full range of medical and health occupations. Illustrated.

★8560★ Opportunities in High Tech Careers

The McGraw-Hill Companies
PO Box 182604
Columbus, OH 43272
Fax: (614)759-3749   Fr: 877-883-5524
E-mail: customer.service@mcgraw-hill.com
URL: http://www.mcgraw-hill.com

Gary Colter and Deborah Yanuck. 1999. $14.95; $11.95 (paper). 160 pages. Explores high technology careers. Describes job opportunities, how to make a career decision, how to prepare for high technology jobs, job hunting techniques, and future trends.

★8561★ Opportunities in Medical Technology Careers

The McGraw-Hill Companies
PO Box 182604
Columbus, OH 43272
Fax: (614)759-3749   Fr: 877-883-5524
E-mail: customer.service@mcgraw-hill.com
URL: http://www.mcgraw-hill.com

Karen R. Karni. Revised, 1996. $14.95; $11.95 (paper). 148 pages. Details opportunities for various technical medical personnel and supplies up-to-date information on salary levels and employment outlook. Appendices list associations and unions in each field. Illustrated.

★8562★ Resumes for Health and Medical Careers

The McGraw-Hill Companies
PO Box 182604
Columbus, OH 43272
Fax: (614)759-3749   Fr: 877-883-5524
E-mail: customer.service@mcgraw-hill.com
URL: http://www.mcgraw-hill.com

Third edition, 2003. $11.95 (paper). 160 pages.

EMPLOYMENT AGENCIES AND SEARCH FIRMS

★8563★ JPM International

26034 Acero
Mission Viejo, CA 92691
Ph: (949)699-4300   Fax: (949)699-4333
Fr: 800-685-7856
E-mail: trish@jpmintl.com
URL: http://www.jpmintl.com

Executive search firm and employment agency.

ONLINE JOB SOURCES AND SERVICES

★8564★ Medhunters.com

Fr: 800-664-0278
E-mail: info@medhunters.com
URL: http://www.medhunters.com

Description: Career search site for jobs in all health care specialties; educational resources; visa and licensing information for relocation; interesting articles; relocation tools; links to professional organizations and general resources.

★8565★ ProHealthJobs

Fr: 800-796-1738
E-mail: Info@prohealthedujobs.com
URL: http://www.prohealthjobs.com

Description: Career resources site for the medical and health care field. Lists professional opportunities, product information, continuing education and open positions.

TRADESHOWS

★8566★ American Association of Physicists in Medicine Annual Meeting

American Association of Physicists in Medicine
1 Physics Ellipse
College Park, MD 20740-3846
Ph: (301)209-3350   Fax: (301)209-0862
E-mail: aapm@aapm.org
URL: http://www.aapm.org

Annual. **Primary Exhibits:** Radiation therapy, diagnostic radiology, radiation protection, hyperthermia, nuclear medicine, and magnetic resonance imaging. **Dates and Locations:** 2008 Jul 27-31; Houston, TX; 2009 Jul 26-30; Anaheim, CA; 2010 Jul 18-22; Philadelphia, PA.

★8567★ Society of Nuclear Medicine Annual Meeting

Society of Nuclear Medicine
1850 Samuel Morse Dr.
Reston, VA 20190-5316
Ph: (703)708-9000   Fax: (703)708-9015
URL: http://interactive.snm.org

Annual. **Primary Exhibits:** Nuclear medicine equipment, supplies, and services and radiopharmaceuticals. **Dates and Locations:** 2008 Jun 14-18; New Orleans, LA.

★8568★ Southwestern Chapter - Society of Nuclear Medicine Exhibition

Southwestern Chapter - Society of Nuclear Medicine
910 Pecan St.
Kerrville, TX 78028
Ph: (830)257-0112   Fax: (830)257-0119
URL: http://www.swcsnm.org

Annual. **Primary Exhibits:** Industry related technology and pharmaceuticals.

OTHER SOURCES

★8569★ American Registry of Radiologic Technologists (ARRT)

1255 Northland Dr.
St. Paul, MN 55120-1155
Ph: (651)687-0048
URL: http://www.arrt.org

Description: Radiologic technologist certification board that administers examinations, issues certificates of registration to radiographers, nuclear medicine technologists, and radiation therapists, and investigates the qualifications of practicing radiologic technologists. Governed by trustees appointed from American College of Radiology and American Society of Radiologic Technologists.

★8570★ **American Society of Radiologic Technologists (ASRT)**

15000 Central Ave. SE
Albuquerque, NM 87123-3909
Ph: (505)298-4500   Fax: (505)298-5063
Fr: 800-444-2778
E-mail: customerinfo@asrt.org
URL: http://www.asrt.org

Description: Serves as professional society of diagnostic radiography, radiation therapy, ultrasound, and nuclear medicine technologists. Advances the science of radiologic technology; establishes and maintains high standards of education; evaluates the quality of patient care; improves the welfare and socioeconomics of radiologic technologists. Operates ASRT Education and Research Foundation, which provides educational materials to radiologic technologists.

★8571★ **Exploring Health Occupations**

Cambridge Educational
PO Box 2053
Princeton, NJ 08543-2053
Ph: 800-257-5126   Fax: (609)671-0266
Fr: 800-468-4227
E-mail: custserv@films.com
URL: http://www.cambridgeeducational.com

VHS and DVD. $159.90. 1999. Two-part series provides a detailed view of the field of medical technicians and technologists, EMTs, nurses, therapists, and assistants.

★8572★ **Health Service Occupations**

Delphi Productions
3159 6th St.
Boulder, CO 80304
Ph: (303)443-2100   Fax: (303)443-4022
Fr: 888-443-2400
E-mail: support@delphivideo.com
URL: http://www.delphivideo.com

$95.00. 50 minutes. Part of the Careers for the 21st Century Video Library.

★8573★ **Health Technologists & Technicians**

Delphi Productions
3159 6th St.
Boulder, CO 80304
Ph: (303)443-2100   Fax: (303)443-4022
Fr: 888-443-2400
E-mail: support@delphivideo.com
URL: http://www.delphivideo.com

$95.00. 50 minutes. Part of the Careers for the 21st Century Video Library.

★8574★ **Medical Technicians and Technologists**

Cambridge Educational
PO Box 2053
Princeton, NJ 08543-2053
Ph: 800-257-5126   Fax: (609)671-0266
Fr: 800-468-4227
E-mail: custserv@films.com
URL: http://www.cambridgeeducational.com

VHS and DVD. $79.95. 18 minutes. 2000. Part of the Exploring Health Occupations Series.

★8575★ **Medicine & Related Occupations**

Delphi Productions
3159 6th St.
Boulder, CO 80304
Ph: (303)443-2100   Fax: (303)443-4022
Fr: 888-443-2400
E-mail: support@delphivideo.com
URL: http://www.delphivideo.com

$95.00. 45 minutes. Part of the Careers for the 21st Century Video Library.

★8576★ **Nuclear Medicine Technology Certification Board (NMTCB)**

3558 Habersham at Northlake, Bldg. I
Tucker, GA 30084
Ph: (404)315-1739   Fax: (404)315-6502
E-mail: board@nmtcb.org
URL: http://www.nmtcb.org

Description: Aims to provide for the certification of nuclear medical technologists and to develop, assess, and administer basic and specialty examinations relevant to nuclear medicine technology.

★8577★ **Society of Nuclear Medicine (SNM)**

1850 Samuel Morse Dr.
Reston, VA 20190-5316
Ph: (703)708-9000   Fax: (703)708-9015
E-mail: vpappas@snm.org
URL: http://www.snm.org

Description: Serves as professional society of physicians, physicists, chemists, radiopharmacists, nuclear medicine technologists, and others interested in nuclear medicine, nuclear magnetic resonance, and the use of radioactive isotopes in clinical practice, research, and teaching. Disseminates information concerning the utilization of nuclear phenomena in the diagnosis and treatment of disease. Oversees the Technologist Section of the Society of Nuclear Medicine.

Nursing Aides and Psychiatric Aides

SOURCES OF HELP-WANTED ADS

★8578★ AAAP News

American Academy of Addiction
  Psychiatry
345 Blackstone Blvd., 2nd Fl. RCH
Providence, RI 02906
Ph: (401)524-3076   Fax: (401)272-0922
URL: http://www.aaap.org/pulications.htm

$45.00/year for individuals; $15.00 for individuals, per issue; $50.00/year for individuals, international; $20.00 for individuals, per issue, international. Professional journal covering addiction psychiatry.

★8579★ AANA Journal

AANA Publishing Inc.
222 South Prospect Ave.
Park Ridge, IL 60068
Ph: (847)692-7050   Fax: (847)518-0938
URL: http://www.aana.com

Bimonthly. $45.00/year for individuals; $10.00 for single issue. Nursing and anesthesia journal.

★8580★ AAOHN Journal

SLACK Inc.
6900 Grove Rd.
Thorofare, NJ 08086-9447
Ph: (856)848-1000   Fax: (856)853-5991
E-mail: aaohn@slackinc.com
URL: http://www.aaohnjournal.com

Monthly. $99.00/year for individuals, U.S. Official journal of the American Association of Occupational Health Nurses.

★8581★ Academic Psychiatry

American Psychiatric Publishing Inc.
1000 Wilson Blvd., Ste. 1825
Arlington, VA 22209-3901
Ph: (703)907-7322   Fax: (703)907-1091
Fr: 800-368-5777
URL: http://ap.psychiatryonline.org/

$132.00/year for members, 1 year; $168.00/year for members, 1 year; $187.00/year for nonmembers, 1 year; $211.00/year for members, 1 year; $281.00/year for nonmembers, 1 year. Journal contributing to the efforts in furthering psychiatry as a profession and to knowledge pool of medicine.

★8582★ ADVANCE for Nurse Practitioners

Merion Publications Inc.
2900 Horizon Dr.
PO Box 61556
King of Prussia, PA 19406
Ph: (610)278-1400   Fr: 800-355-5627
URL: http://nurse-practitioners.advanceweb.com/main.aspx

Monthly. For practicing nurse practitioner students with senior status.

★8583★ Advances in Nursing Science (ANS)

Lippincott Williams & Wilkins
530 Walnut St.
Philadelphia, PA 19106-3621
Ph: (215)521-8300   Fax: (215)521-8902
Fr: 800-638-3030
URL: http://www.lww.com/product/?0161-9268

Quarterly. $97.91/year for individuals, U.S.; $272.96/year for institutions, U.S.; $52.94/year for U.S., in-training; $145.94/year for individuals, international; $320.94/year for institutions, international. Academic medical journal focusing on nursing research and education.

★8584★ American Journal of Geriatric Psychiatry

American Association for Geriatric
  Psychiatry
7910 Woodmont Ave., Ste. 1050
Bethesda, MD 20814-3004
Ph: (301)654-7850   Fax: (301)654-4137
URL: http://ajgponline.org

Monthly. $351.00/year for individuals; $965.00/year for institutions; $491.00/year for individuals, other countries; $849.00/year for institutions, other countries; $201.00/year for individuals, in-training; $253.00/year for individuals, other countries, in-training. Professional journal covering geriatric psychiatry.

★8585★ American Journal of Nursing

American Journal of Nursing
c/o Lippincott, Williams & Wilkins
530 Walnut St.
Philadelphia, PA 19106-3621
Ph: (215)521-8300   Fax: (215)521-8902
Fr: 800-627-0484
URL: http://www.nursingcenter.com

Monthly. $32.90/year for individuals; $159.00/year for institutions; $69.00/year for individuals, other countries; $199.00/year for institutions, other countries. Journal for staff nurses, nurse managers, and clinical nurse specialists. Focuses on patient care in hospitals, hospital ICUs and homes. Provides news coverage of health care from the nursing perspective.

★8586★ American Journal of Psychology

University of Illinois Press
1325 S Oak St.
Champaign, IL 61820-6903
Ph: (217)333-0950   Fax: (217)244-8082
Fr: 800-537-5487
URL: http://www.press.uillinois.edu/journals/ajp.html

Quarterly. $70.00/year for individuals; $126.00/year for individuals, two years; $178.00/year for individuals, three years; $190.00/year for institutions; $342.00/year for institutions, two years; $484.00/year for institutions, three years; $80.00/year for individuals, outside U.S.; $146.00/year for individuals, outside U.S., two years; $208.00/year for individuals, outside U.S., three years; $40.00 for single issue. Journal dealing with experimental psychology and basic principles of psychology.

★8587★ The American Nurse

American Nurses Association
8515 Georgia Ave., Ste. 400
Silver Spring, MD 20910
Ph: (301)628-5000   Fax: (301)628-5001
Fr: 800-274-4262
E-mail: adsales@ana.org

URL: http://nursingworld.org/tan/

Monthly. Newspaper (tabloid) for the nursing profession.

★8588★ Annals of Behavioral Medicine

Society of Behavioral Medicine
10 Industrial Ave.
Mahwah, NJ 07430
Ph: (201)258-2238   Fax: (201)760-3735
Fr: 800-926-6579

Quarterly. Journal describing the interactions of behavior and health.

★8589★ Annual Review of Psychology

Annual Reviews Inc.
4139 El Camino Way
PO Box 10139
Palo Alto, CA 94303-0139
Ph: (650)493-4400   Fax: (650)424-0910
Fr: 800-523-8635

Annual. $75.00/year for individuals, print and online; $181.00/year for institutions, print only; $181.00/year for institutions, online only; $217.00/year for institutions, print and online. Publication covering psychology and mental health issues.

★8590★ Applied Nursing Research

Mountain Association for Community
  Economic Development
433 Chestnut St.
Berea, KY 40403
Ph: (859)986-2373   Fax: (859)986-1299
URL: http://www.elsevier.com/wps/find/journaldescription.cws_home

Quarterly. $298.00/year for institutions, outside U.S; $88.00/year for individuals, inside U.S.; $246.00/year for institutions, inside U.S.; $125.00/year for individuals, outside U.S. Nursing journal publishing peer-reviewed research findings for clinical applications.

★8591★ Archives of Psychiatric Nursing

Mosby Inc.
11830 Westline Industrial Dr.
St. Louis, MO 63146
Ph: (314)872-8370   Fax: (314)432-1380
Fr: 800-325-4177
URL: http://www.us.elsevierhealth.com/product.jsp?isbn=08839417&r

Bimonthly. $177.00/year for individuals, other countries; $261.00/year for institutions, other countries; $98.00/year for individuals; $194.00/year for institutions. Journal for psychiatric nurses.

★8592★ Cancer Nursing

Lippincott Williams & Wilkins
530 Walnut St.
Philadelphia, PA 19106-3621
Ph: (215)521-8300   Fax: (215)521-8902
Fr: 800-638-3030
E-mail: bguthy@lww.com
URL: http://www.cancernursingonline.com/

Bimonthly. $94.43/year for individuals; $243.48/year for institutions; $49.48/year for other countries, in-training; $167.46/year for individuals; $284.46/year for institutions. Medical journal covering problems arising in the care and support of cancer patients.

★8593★ Children & Society

John Wiley & Sons Inc.
111 River St.
Hoboken, NJ 07030-5774
Ph: (201)748-6000   Fax: (201)748-6088
Fr: 800-825-7550
E-mail: children&society@ncb.org.uk
URL: http://www3.interscience.wiley.com/cgi-bin/jhome/4805

$655.00/year for institutions, print and online; $566.00/year for institutions, online only; $194.00/year for individuals, print and online. Journal focusing on children and services for children.

★8594★ Clinical Effectiveness in Nursing

Mosby Inc.
11830 Westline Industrial Dr.
St. Louis, MO 63146
Ph: (314)872-8370   Fax: (314)432-1380
Fr: 800-325-4177
URL: http://www.us.elsevierhealth.com/product.jsp?isbn=13619004

Quarterly. $70.00/year for individuals; $316.00/year for institutions. Journal for nurses demonstrating the impact of nursing on patients and clients; addresses the effects of interventions on patients' well-being.

★8595★ Clinical Nurse Specialist

Lippincott Williams & Wilkins
530 Walnut St.
Philadelphia, PA 19106-3621
Ph: (215)521-8300   Fax: (215)521-8902
Fr: 800-638-3030
URL: http://www.cns-journal.com

Bimonthly. $97.91/year for individuals, U.S.; $228.96/year for institutions, U.S.; $52.96/year for other countries, U.S. in-training:; $177.94/year for individuals, international; $307.94/year for institutions, international in-training. Nursing journal.

★8596★ Clinical Psychiatry News

International Medical News Group
60-B Columbia Rd.
Morristown, NJ 07960
Ph: (973)290-8200   Fax: (973)290-8250
URL: http://journals.elsevierhealth.com/periodicals/cpnews

Monthly. $90.00/year for individuals; $144.00/year for other countries, surface mail. Medical and psychiatry tabloid.

★8597★ Counselling Psychology Quarterly

Taylor & Francis Group Journals
325 Chestnut St., Ste. 800
Philadelphia, PA 19106
Ph: (215)625-8900   Fax: (215)625-8914
Fr: 800-354-1420
URL: http://www.tandf.co.uk/journals/titles/09515070.asp

Quarterly. $1,067.00/year for institutions, print and online; $1,013.00/year for institutions, online only; $303.00/year for individuals; $66.00/year for BPS and APA members. Journal covering practical counseling, clinical, occupational and medical psychology.

★8598★ Ethical Human Psychology and Psychiatry

Springer Publishing Co.
11 W 42nd St., 15th Fl.
New York, NY 10036
Ph: (212)431-4370   Fax: (212)941-7342
Fr: 877-687-7476
URL: http://www.springerpub.com/

$70.00/year for individuals; $105.00/year for individuals, print and online; $200.00/year for institutions; $300.00/year for institutions, print and online. Books on nursing, psychology, gerontology, geriatrics, social work, counseling, public health, rehabilitation and medical education.

★8599★ GradPsych

American Psychoanalytic Association
309 E 49th St.
New York, NY 10017
Ph: (212)752-0450   Fax: (212)593-0571
E-mail: gradpsych@apa.org
URL: http://www.gradpsych.apags.org

Quarterly. $18.00/year for members, domestic; $35.00/year for individuals, non-members; $70.00/year for institutions; $18.00/year for other countries, international affiliates; $18.00/year for individuals, high school teacher affiliates; $28.00/year for members, international surface; $50.00/year for individuals, international surface; $40.00/year for members, international air mail; $60.00/year for individuals, international air mail; $115.00/year for institutions, international air mail. Magazine that offers information about psychology careers, finance, and emerging trends in psychology practice, research, and education.

★8600★ Home Healthcare Nurse

Lippincott Williams & Wilkins
530 Walnut St.
Philadelphia, PA 19106-3621
Ph: (215)521-8300   Fax: (215)521-8902
Fr: 800-638-3030
URL: http://www.homehealthcarenurseonline.com/

Monthly. $56.43/year for individuals, U.S.; $202.95/year for institutions, U.S.; $126.46/year for individuals, other countries; $252.95/year for institutions, other countries; $43.48/year for U.S., in-training. Magazine for the practicing professional nurse working in the home health, community health, and public health areas.

★8601★ HomeCare Magazine

Miramar Communications Inc.
23805 Stuart Ranch Rd., Ste. 235
PO Box 8987
Malibu, CA 90265-8987
Ph: (310)317-4522   Fax: (310)317-9644
Fr: 800-543-4116
URL: http://www.homecaremag.com

Monthly. Free, in US; $135.00/year for Canada; $150.00/year for two years, Canada; $250.00/year for other countries; $250.00/year for two years, other countries. Magazine serving home medical equipment suppliers, including independent and chain centers specializing in home care, pharmacies or chain drug stores with home care products, and joint-ventured hospital home health care businesses. Contains industry news and new product launches and marketing strategies.

★8602★ Hospitals & Health Networks

Health Forum L.L.C.
1 N Franklin, 29th Fl.
Chicago, IL 60606
Ph: (312)893-6800   Fax: (312)422-4506
Fr: 800-821-2039
URL: http://www.hhnmag.com

Weekly. Publication covering the health care industry.

★8603★ The IHS Primary Care Provider

Indian Health Service (HQ)
The Reyes Bldg.
801 Thompson Ave., Ste. 400
Rockville, MD 20852-1627
URL: http://www.ihs.gov/PublicInfo/Publications/HealthProvider/Pr

Monthly. Journal for health care professionals, physicians, nurses, pharmacists, dentists, and dietitians.

★8604★ Intensive and Critical Care Nursing

Mosby Inc.
11830 Westline Industrial Dr.
St. Louis, MO 63146
Ph: (314)872-8370   Fax: (314)432-1380
Fr: 800-325-4177
URL: http://www.us.elsevierhealth.com/product.jsp?isbn=09643397&r

Bimonthly. $92.00/year for individuals, international; $422.00/year for institutions, international; $92.00/year for individuals; $422.00/year for institutions. Journal for nurses in intensive and critical care nursing.

★8605★ International Journal of Nursing Education Scholarship

Berkeley Electronic Press
2809 Telegraph Ave., Ste. 202
Berkeley, CA 94705
Ph: (510)665-1200   Fax: (510)665-1201

URL: http://www.bepress.com/ijnes
Semiannual. $525.00/year corporate; $175.00/year academic. Journal that publishes original papers on nursing education issues and research.

★8606★ International Journal of Nursing Practice

Wiley-Blackwell
350 Main St. Commerce Pl.
Malden, MA 02148
Ph: (781)388-8200   Fax: (781)388-8210
Fr: 800-759-6120
URL: http://www.blackwellpublishing.com/journal.asp?ref=1322-7114

Bimonthly. $122.00/year for individuals, print and online; $759.00/year for institutions, print and premium online; $690.00/year for institutions, print and standard online; $656.00/year for institutions, premium online only; $469.00/year for institutions, other countries, print and premium online; $426.00/year for institutions, other countries, print and standard online; $405.00/year for institutions, other countries, premium online only; $311.00/year for institutions, print and premium online, Australia/New Zealand; $283.00/year for institutions, print and standard online, Australia/New Zealand; $269.00/year for institutions, premium online only, Australia/New Zealand. Journal publishing articles about advancing the international understanding and development of nursing, both as a profession and as an academic discipline.

★8607★ International Journal of Psychiatry in Clinical Practice

Taylor & Francis Group Journals
325 Chestnut St., Ste. 800
Philadelphia, PA 19106
Ph: (215)625-8900   Fax: (215)625-8914
Fr: 800-354-1420
URL: http://www.tandf.co.uk/journals/titles/13651501.asp

Quarterly. Journal for health professionals with clinical, academic, and research interests in psychiatry.

★8608★ International Journal of Psychology

Psychology Press
270 Madison Ave.
New York, NY 10016
Ph: (212)216-7800   Fax: (212)563-2269
Fr: 800-634-7064
URL: http://www.tandf.co.uk/journals/titles/00207594.asp

$735.00/year for institutions, print and online; $698.00/year for institutions, online only; $171.00/year for individuals. Journal dealing with all aspects of development of international psychological science.

★8609★ International Nursing Review

Wiley-Blackwell
350 Main St. Commerce Pl.
Malden, MA 02148
Ph: (781)388-8200   Fax: (781)388-8210
Fr: 800-759-6120
URL: http://www.blackwellpublishing.com/journal.asp?ref=0020-8132

Quarterly. $96.00/year for individuals, U.S. print and online; $77.00/year for individuals, print and online, Euro zone; $51.00/year for individuals, print and online, non Euro zone; $57.00/year for individuals, print and online, rest of world; $277.00/year for institutions, print and premium online; $150.00/year for institutions, print and premium online, Euro zone; $150.00/year for institutions, print and premium online, non Euro zone; $165.00/year for institutions, print and premium online, rest of world; $239.00/year for institutions, premium online only; $129.00/year for institutions, premium online only, Euro zone. Journal focusing on current concerns and issues of modern day nursing and health care from an international perspective.

★8610★ Journal of Addictions Nursing

Taylor & Francis Group Journals
325 Chestnut St., Ste. 800
Philadelphia, PA 19106
Ph: (215)625-8900   Fax: (215)625-8914
Fr: 800-354-1420
URL: http://www.tandf.co.uk/journals/titles/10884602.asp

$443.00/year for institutions, print and online; $421.00/year for institutions, online only; $135.00/year for individuals. Journal for nursing addiction professionals.

★8611★ Journal of the American Psychiatric Nurses Association

Sage Publications Inc.
2455 Teller Rd.
Thousand Oaks, CA 91320
Ph: (805)499-0721   Fax: (805)499-8096
URL: http://www.apna.org

Bimonthly. $391.00/year for institutions, for print and online; $411.00/year for institutions, for online; $352.00/year for institutions, e-access; $372.00/year for individuals, e-access; $383.00/year; $136.00/year for individuals, print only; $71.00/year for individuals, print only; $29.00/year for institutions, single print issue; $29.00/year for individuals, single print issue. Journal focusing on psychiatric nursing.

★8612★ Journal of the Association of Nurses in AIDS Care

Mosby Inc.
11830 Westline Industrial Dr.
St. Louis, MO 63146
Ph: (314)872-8370   Fax: (314)432-1380
Fr: 800-325-4177
URL: http://www.elsevier.com/wps/find/journaldescription.cws_home

Bimonthly. $428.00/year for institutions; $119.00/year for individuals; $399.00/year for U.S. institutions; $90.00/year for U.S. individuals. Journal covering the spectrum of nursing issues in HIV/AIDS: education, treatment, prevention, research, practice, clinical issues, awareness, policies and program development.

★8613★ **Journal of Business and Psychology**

Springer-Verlag New York Inc.
233 Spring St.
New York, NY 10013
Ph: (212)460-1500   Fax: (212)460-1575
URL: http://www.springer.com/journal/10869/

Journal covering all aspects of psychology that apply to the business segment. Includes topics such as personnel selection and training, organizational assessment and development, risk management and loss control, marketing and consumer behavior research.

★8614★ **Journal of Clinical Nursing**

Wiley-Blackwell
350 Main St. Commerce Pl.
Malden, MA 02148
Ph: (781)388-8200   Fax: (781)388-8210
Fr: 800-759-6120
E-mail: jcn@oxon.blackwellpublishing.com
URL: http://www.blackwellpublishing.com/journal.asp?ref=0962-1067

Monthly. $307.00/year for individuals, U.S. print and online; $167.00/year for students, U.S. print and online; $1,660.00/year for institutions, U.S. print and premium online; $1,509.00/year for institutions, U.S. print and standard online; $1,434.00/year for institutions, U.S. premium online only; $251.00/year for individuals, Europe print and online; $135.00/year for students, Europe print and online; $899.00/year for institutions, Europe print and premium online; $817.00/year for institutions, Europe print and standard online; $776.00/year for institutions, Europe premium online only. Journal focusing on all spheres of nursing and midwifery practice.

★8615★ **Journal of Clinical Psychology**

John Wiley & Sons Inc.
111 River St.
Hoboken, NJ 07030-5774
Ph: (201)748-6000   Fax: (201)748-6088
Fr: 800-825-7550
URL: http://www3.interscience.wiley.com/cgi-bin/jhome/31171

Monthly. $115.00/year for individuals, for print (U.S., Canada, and Mexico); $187.00/year for individuals, for print (rest of world); $725.00/year for institutions, print only; $809.00/year for institutions, other countries, print only; $798.00/year for institutions, combined print with online access rates; $882.00/year for Canada and Mexico, combined print with online access rates; $882.00/year for other countries, combined print with online access rates. Journal for professionals in the field of psychology.

★8616★ **The Journal of Continuing Education in Nursing**

SLACK Inc.
6900 Grove Rd.
Thorofare, NJ 08086-9447
Ph: (856)848-1000   Fax: (856)853-5991
URL: http://www.slackinc.com/allied/jcen

Bimonthly. $99.00/year for individuals; $245.00/year for institutions; $168.00 for individuals, two years; $416.00 for institutions, two years; $32.00 for single issue. Journal for nurses involved in planning and implementing educational programs for the practitioner and others in patient care.

★8617★ **Journal of Gerontological Nursing**

SLACK Inc.
6900 Grove Rd.
Thorofare, NJ 08086-9447
Ph: (856)848-1000   Fax: (856)853-5991
E-mail: jgn@slackinc.com
URL: http://www.jognonline.com

Monthly. $84.00/year for individuals; $142.00 for individuals, two years; $189.00 for individuals, three years; $169.00/year for institutions; $287.00 for institutions, two years; $380.00 for institutions, three years; $21.00 for single issue. Gerontological nursing journal.

★8618★ **Journal of Nursing Administration (JONA)**

Lippincott Williams & Wilkins
530 Walnut St.
Philadelphia, PA 19106-3621
Ph: (215)521-8300   Fax: (215)521-8902
Fr: 800-638-3030
E-mail: jonaeditor@aol.com
URL: http://jonajournal.com/

Monthly. $108.91/year for individuals, U.S.; $345.79/year for institutions, U.S.; $202.94/year for other countries; $478.75/year for institutions, other countries. Journal covering developments and advances in nursing administration and management.

★8619★ **Journal of Nursing Scholarship**

Wiley-Blackwell
350 Main St. Commerce Pl.
Malden, MA 02148
Ph: (781)388-8200   Fax: (781)388-8210
Fr: 800-759-6120
URL: http://www.blackwellpublishing.com/journal.asp?ref=1527-6546

Quarterly. $51.00/year for individuals, print and online; $185.00/year for institutions, print and premium online; $168.00/year for institutions, print and standard online; $160.00/year for institutions, premium online only; $59.00/year for individuals, print and online; $135.00/year for institutions, other countries, print and premium online; $123.00/year for institutions, other countries, print and standard online; $117.00/year for institutions, other countries, premium online only; $39.00/year for individuals, print and online. Peer-reviewed journal covering nursing.

★8620★ **Journal of Obstetric, Gynecologic and Neonatal Nursing (JOGNN)**

Sage Publications Inc.
2455 Teller Rd.
Thousand Oaks, CA 91320
Ph: (805)499-0721   Fax: (805)499-8096
E-mail: advertising@sagepub.com
URL: http://www.sagepub.com/journal.aspx?pid=245

Bimonthly. $97.00/year for individuals, print + online; $762.00/year for institutions, print + premium online; $724.00/year for institutions, premium online only; $81.00/year for institutions, print + online; $424.00/year for institutions, print + premium online; $402.00/year for institutions, premium online only; $54.00/year for institutions, print + online; $402.00/year; $402.00/year for institutions, premium online only-All countries. Journal covering trends, policies, and research. Official publication of the Association of Women's Health, Obstetric, and Neonatal Nurses (AWHONN).

★8621★ **Journal of Orthopaedic Nursing**

Mosby Inc.
11830 Westline Industrial Dr.
St. Louis, MO 63146
Ph: (314)872-8370   Fax: (314)432-1380
Fr: 800-325-4177
URL: http://http://www.elsevier.com/wps/find/journaldescription.cws_home/623057/description#description

Quarterly. $84.00/year for individuals, U.S.; $326.00/year for institutions, U.S. Journal for orthopaedic nurses.

★8622★ **Journal of Positive Behavior Interventions**

PRO-ED Inc.
8700 Shoal Creek Blvd.
PO Box 678370
Austin, TX 78757-6897
Ph: (512)451-3246   Fax: 800-397-7633
Fr: 800-897-3202
URL: http://www.proedinc.com

Quarterly. $48.00/year for individuals, North America,1 year; $78.00/year for individuals, North America,2 year; $128.00/year for institutions, North America, 1 year; $205.00/year for institutions, North America,2 year; $78.00/year for individuals, foreign subscriptions,1 year; $125.00/year for individuals, foreign subscriptions, 2 year; $161.00/year for institutions, foreign subscriptions,1 year; $258.00/year for institutions, foreign subscriptions, 2 year; $46.00/year for individuals, North America; $124.00/year for institutions, North America. Journal covering issues in mental health and psychology.

★8623★ **Journal of Psychosocial Nursing and Mental Health Services**

SLACK Inc.
6900 Grove Rd.
Thorofare, NJ 08086-9447
Ph: (856)848-1000   Fax: (856)853-5991
E-mail: jpn@slackinc.com

URL: http://www.psychnurse.org

Monthly. $85.00/year for individuals; $144.00 for individuals, two years; $191.00 for individuals, three years; $259.00/year for institutions; $440.00 for institutions, two years; $582.00 for institutions, three years. Journal presenting original, peer-reviewed articles on psychiatric/mental health nursing.

★8624★ **Journal of Radiology Nursing**

Mosby Inc.
11830 Westline Industrial Dr.
St. Louis, MO 63146
Ph: (314)872-8370 Fax: (314)432-1380
Fr: 800-325-4177
URL: http://www.radiologynursing.org

Quarterly. $72.00/year for individuals, U.S.; $122.00/year for institutions, U.S.; $103.00/year for individuals, International; $157.00/year for institutions, International. Journal publishing articles about patient care in the diagnostic and therapeutic imaging environments.

★8625★ **LPN2008**

Lippincott Williams & Wilkins
530 Walnut St.
Philadelphia, PA 19106-3621
Ph: (215)521-8300 Fax: (215)521-8902
Fr: 800-638-3030
URL: http://www.lww.com/product/?1553-0582

Bimonthly. $119.96/year for institutions; $27.86/year for individuals; $21.91/year for U.S., in-training; $67.96/year for individuals, other countries; $167.96/year for institutions, other countries. Peer-reviewed journal that focuses on bedside care skills for practical nurses.

★8626★ **McKnight's Long-Term Care News**

McKnight's Long-Term Care News
1 Northfield Plz., Ste. 521
Northfield, IL 60093-1216
Ph: (847)784-8706 Fax: (847)784-9346
Fr: 800-558-1703
E-mail: ltcn-webmaster@mltcn.com
URL: http://www.mcknightsonline.com/home

Professional magazine.

★8627★ **MCN, The American Journal of Maternal/Child Nursing**

Lippincott Williams & Wilkins
530 Walnut St.
Philadelphia, PA 19106-3621
Ph: (215)521-8300 Fax: (215)521-8902
Fr: 800-638-3030
URL: http://www.mcnjournal.com/

Bimonthly. $53.91/year for individuals, U.S.; $131.95/year for institutions, U.S.; $121.94/year for other countries, individual; $161.95/year for institutions, other countries. Journal focusing on maternal/child nursing and health.

★8628★ **Minority Nurse Newsletter**

Tucker Publications Inc.
PO Box 580
Lisle, IL 60532
Ph: (630)969-3809 Fax: (630)969-3895
E-mail: drsallie@gmail.com
URL: http://www.tuckerpub.com

Description: Quarterly. Provides health care information of interest to minority nursing faculty.

★8629★ **Modern Healthcare**

Crain Communications Inc.
360 N Michigan Ave.
Chicago, IL 60601
Ph: (312)649-5411 Fax: (312)280-3150
Fr: 888-909-9111
E-mail: subs@crain.com
URL: http://www.modernhealthcare.com

Weekly. $154.00/year for individuals; $244.00/year for Canada; $208.00/year for other countries. Weekly business news magazine for healthcare management.

★8630★ **Monitor on Psychology**

American Psychological Association
750 1st St. NE
Washington, DC 20002-4242
Ph: (202)336-5540 Fax: (202)336-5549
Fr: 800-374-2721
E-mail: journals@apa.org
URL: http://www.apa.org/monitor/

Monthly. $46.00/year for nonmembers; $86.00/year for individuals, foreign, surface freight; $113.00/year for individuals, foreign, air freight; $87.00/year for institutions, non-member, foreign, surface freight; $168.00/year for institutions, foreign, air freight; $195.00/year for institutions, air freight; $3.00/year for single issue. Magazine of the APA. Reports on the science, profession, and social responsibility of psychology, including latest legislative developments affecting mental health, education, and research support.

★8631★ **Nurse Education in Practice**

Mosby Inc.
11830 Westline Industrial Dr.
St. Louis, MO 63146
Ph: (314)872-8370 Fax: (314)432-1380
Fr: 800-325-4177
URL: http://www.us.elsevierhealth.com/product.jsp?isbn=14715953#a

Bimonthly. $77.00/year for individuals; $311.00/year for institutions. Journal enabling lecturers and practitioners to both share and disseminate evidence that demonstrates the actual practice of education as it is experienced in the realities of their respective work environments.

★8632★ **Nurse Practitioner Forum**

Elsevier
1600 John F. Kennedy Blvd., Ste. 1800
Philadelphia, PA 19103-2899
Ph: (215)239-3900 Fax: (215)238-7883
URL: http://202.117.24.24/html/xjtu/ckzl/

ssci/ssci_n.htm

Quarterly. Journal for nurse practitioners.

★8633★ **Nursing Clinics of North America**

Mosby Inc.
11830 Westline Industrial Dr.
St. Louis, MO 63146
Ph: (314)872-8370 Fax: (314)432-1380
Fr: 800-325-4177
URL: http://www.elsevier.com/wps/find/bookdescription.cws_home/70

Quarterly. $55.00/year for individuals. Journal publishing articles by experts in the field; provides current, practical information geared to the active nurse.

★8634★ **Nursing Education Perspectives**

National League for Nursing
61 Broadway, 33rd Fl.
New York, NY 10006-2701
Ph: (212)363-5555 Fax: (212)812-0391
Fr: 800-669-1656
URL: http://www.nln.org/nlnjournal/index.htm

Bimonthly. $40.00/year; $70.00/year for non-members; $90.00/year for Canada; $98.00/year for other countries, non-member; $137.00/year for individuals; $157.00/year for Canada; $165.00/year for other countries. Professional journal for nurses. Includes articles on health policy, social and economic issues affecting health care, and nursing education and practice.

★8635★ **Nursing Management**

Lippincott Williams & Wilkins
323 Norristown Rd., Ste. 200
Ambler, PA 19002-2758
Ph: (215)646-8700 Fax: (215)654-1328
URL: http://www.nursingmanagement.com/

Monthly. $46.95/year for individuals, U.S.; $199.00/year for institutions, U.S.; $103.00/year for individuals, international; $258.00/year for institutions, international. Magazine focusing on nursing management.

★8636★ **Nursing Outlook**

Mosby Inc.
10801 Executive Center Dr., Ste. 509
Little Rock, AR 72211
Ph: (501)223-5165 Fax: (501)223-0519
URL: http://journals.elsevierhealth.com/periodicals/ymno

Bimonthly. $65.00/year for individuals; $106.00/year for individuals, Canada; $106.00/year for individuals, other countries. Official journal of the American Academy of Nursing, reporting on trends and issues in nursing.

★8637★ **Nursing Science Quarterly**

Sage Publications Inc.
2455 Teller Rd.
Thousand Oaks, CA 91320
Ph: (805)499-0721 Fax: (805)499-8096

URL: http://www.sagepub.com

Quarterly. $443.00/year for institutions, combined (print & e-access); $465.00/year for institutions, combined plus backfile current volume print and all; $399.00/year for institutions, e-access; $421.00/year for institutions, e-access plus backfile (all online content); $399.00/year for institutions, e-access (content through 1999); $434.00/year for institutions, print only; $129.00/year for individuals, print only; $120.00 for institutions, single print; $42.00 for individuals, single print. Journal focusing on enhancement of nursing knowledge.

★8638★ Patient Education and Counseling

Mosby Inc.
11830 Westline Industrial Dr.
St. Louis, MO 63146
Ph: (314)872-8370   Fax: (314)432-1380
Fr: 800-325-4177
URL: http://www.elsevier.com/wps/find/journaldescription.cws_home

Monthly. $229.00/year for individuals; $2,169.00/year for institutions. Journal publishing articles on patient education and health promotion researchers, managers, physicians, nurses and other health care providers.

★8639★ Provider

American Health Care Association
1201 L St. NW
Washington, DC 20005
Ph: (202)842-4444   Fax: (202)842-3860
E-mail: sales@ahca.org
URL: http://www.providermagazine.com

Monthly. $48.00/year for U.S.; $61.00/year for Canada and Mexico; $85.00/year for other countries. Provider Magazine.

★8640★ Psychiatric Annals

SLACK Inc.
6900 Grove Rd.
Thorofare, NJ 08086-9447
Ph: (856)848-1000   Fax: (856)853-5991
E-mail: psyann@slackinc.com
URL: http://www.psychiatricannalsonline.com

Monthly. $219.00/year for individuals; $438.00 for individuals, two years; $657.00 for individuals, three years; $373.00/year for institutions; $746.00 for institutions, two years; $1119.00 for institutions, three years; $109.00/year for individuals, resident; $48.00 for single issue. Journal analyzing concepts and practices in every area of psychiatry.

★8641★ Psychiatric News

American Psychiatric Publishing Inc.
1000 Wilson Blvd., Ste. 1825
Arlington, VA 22209-3901
Ph: (703)907-7322   Fax: (703)907-1091
Fr: 800-368-5777
URL: http://pn.psychiatryonline.org/

Semimonthly. $93.00/year for individuals,

U.S.; $126.00/year for members, international member; $140.00/year for nonmembers, international; $19.00 for single issue, U.S.; $31.00/year for single issue, international. Professional magazine of the American Psychiatric Assn.

★8642★ Psychiatric Services

Association of Partners for Public Lands
2401 Blueridge Ave., Ste. 303
Wheaton, MD 20902
Ph: (301)946-9475   Fax: (301)946-9478

Monthly. Interdisciplinary mental health journal covering clinical, legal, and public policy issues.

★8643★ Psychiatric Times

CMP Media L.L.C.
600 Community Dr.
Manhasset, NY 11030
Ph: (516)562-5000   Fax: (516)562-7830
URL: http://www.psychiatrictimes.com

Monthly. $54.95/year for individuals; $120.00/year for institutions, library; $120.00/year for individuals, other countries; $90.00 for individuals, 2 years. Monthly magazine publishing features, clinical news, special reports and career opportunities in the field of psychiatry.

★8644★ Psychiatry

Elsevier Science Inc.
360 Park Ave. S
New York, NY 10010
Ph: (212)989-5800   Fax: (212)633-3990
URL: http://www.elsevier.com

$464.00/year for institutions in all countries except Europe, Japan and Iran. $243.00/year for individuals in all countries except Europe, Japan and Iran. $135.00/year for students in all countries except Europe, Japan and Iran. $87.00/year for nurses in all countries except Europe, Japan and Iran. Journal covering medical specialties dealing with diagnosis, treatment, and rehabilitation of mental illness.

★8645★ Psychological Bulletin

American Psychological Association
750 1st St. NE
Washington, DC 20002-4242
Ph: (202)336-5540   Fax: (202)336-5549
Fr: 800-374-2721
E-mail: journals@apa.org
URL: http://www.apa.org/journals/bul.html

Bimonthly. $93.00/year for members, domestic; $111.00/year for members, foreign, surface freight; $129.00/year for members, foreign, air mail; $59.00/year for students, domestic; $77.00/year for students, foreign, surface freight; $95.00/year for students, foreign, air mail; $198.00/year for nonmembers, domestic; $224.00/year for nonmembers, foreign, surface freight; $238.00/year for nonmembers, foreign, air mail; $555.00/year for institutions, domestic. Journal presenting comprehensive and integrative reviews and interpretations of critical substantive and methodological issues and practical

problems from all the diverse areas of psychology.

★8646★ Psychological Services

American Psychological Association
750 1st St. NE
Washington, DC 20002-4242
Ph: (202)336-5540   Fax: (202)336-5549
Fr: 800-374-2721
URL: http://www.apa.org/journals/ser

Quarterly. $55.00/year for members, domestic; $71.00/year for members, international surface; $83.00/year for members, international airmail; $55.00/year for students, domestic; $71.00/year for students, international surface; $83.00/year for students, international airmail; $80.00/year for nonmembers, domestic; $101.00/year for nonmembers, international surface; $111.00/year for nonmembers, international airmail; $289.00/year for institutions, domestic. Journal of the Division of Psychologists in Public Service, publishing data-based articles on the broad range of psychological services.

★8647★ Psychology Journal

Psychological Publishing
PO Box 176
Natchitoches, LA 71458
URL: http://www.psychologicalpublishing.com/

$40.00/year for individuals; $75.00/year for institutions. Journal dedicated to all areas of the science and practice of counseling and clinical psychology.

★8648★ Rehabilitation Nursing

Rehabilitation Nursing
4700 West Lake Ave.
Glenview, IL 60025
Ph: (847)375-4710   Fr: 800-229-7530
E-mail: info@rehabnurse.org
URL: http://www.rehabnurse.org/index.html

Bimonthly. $95.00/year for individuals; $125.00/year for institutions; $135.00/year for other countries; $18.00 for single issue; $125.00/year for Canada. Magazine focusing on rehabilitation nursing involving clinical practice, research, education, and administration.

★8649★ Research in Nursing & Health

John Wiley & Sons Inc.
111 River St.
Hoboken, NJ 07030-5774
Ph: (201)748-6000   Fax: (201)748-6088
Fr: 800-825-7550
URL: http://as.wiley.com/WileyCDA/WileyTitle/productCd-NUR.html

Bimonthly. $140.00/year for individuals, print only; $140.00/year for Canada and Mexico, in Canada, add 7% GST print only; $176.00/year for other countries, print only; $1,185.00/year for institutions, print only; $1,257.00/year for institutions, Canada and Mexico, print only in Canada, add 7% GST; $1,299.00/year for institutions, other countries, print only; $1,304.00/year for institutions, print and online U.S.; $1,376.00/year for institutions, Canada and Mexico, print and online, in Canada, add 7% GST; $1,418.00/year for institutions, other countries, print and online. Journal providing forum for research in the areas of nursing practice, education, and administration. Covers health issues relevant to nursing as well as investigations of the applications of research findings in clinical settings.

★8650★ Review of General Psychology

American Psychological Association
750 1st St. NE
Washington, DC 20002-4242
Ph: (202)336-5540   Fax: (202)336-5549
Fr: 800-374-2721
URL: http://www.apa.org/journals/gpr.html

Quarterly. $55.00/year for members, domestic; $55.00/year for students, domestic; $80.00/year for nonmembers, domestic; $279.00/year for institutions, domestic; $71.00/year for members, surface mail; $71.00/year for students, surface mail; $101.00/year for nonmembers, surface mail; $317.00/year for institutions, surface mail; $83.00/year for members, airmail; $83.00/year for students, airmail. Journal including a wide variety of psychological research-related articles.

★8651★ Seminars in Oncology

Elsevier
1600 John F. Kennedy Blvd., Ste. 1800
Philadelphia, PA 19103-2899
Ph: (215)239-3900   Fax: (215)238-7883
E-mail: elspcs@elsevier.com
URL: http://www.elsevier.com

$228.00/year for individuals, U.S.; $114.00/year for students, U.S.; $311.00/year for individuals, Canada; $156.00/year for students, Canada; $311.00/year for individuals, Mexico; $156.00/year for students, Mexico; $311.00/year for individuals, international; $156.00/year for students, international; $510.00/year for institutions, international; $424.00/year for institutions, U.S. Journal reviewing current diagnostic and treatment techniques used in oncology patient care.

★8652★ Seminars in Oncology Nursing

Mosby Inc.
11830 Westline Industrial Dr.
St. Louis, MO 63146
Ph: (314)872-8370   Fax: (314)432-1380
Fr: 800-325-4177
URL: http://www.nursingoncology.com

Quarterly. $91.00/year for individuals; $227.00/year for institutions; $23.00 for individuals, single issue; $172.00/year for individuals, International; $298.00/year for institutions, International; $43.00 for individuals, single issue, international. Journal publishing material to disseminate knowledge in the complex field of cancer nursing.

★8653★ Teaching and Learning in Nursing

Elsevier Science Inc.
360 Park Ave. S
New York, NY 10010
Ph: (212)989-5800   Fax: (212)633-3990
URL: http://www.elsevier.com

Quarterly. $119.00/year for institutions, U.S. $167.00/year for institutions, other countries; $75.00/year for individuals, U.S. $104.00/year for individuals, other countries. Journal devoted to associate degree nursing education and practice.

★8654★ USA Body Psychotherapy Journal

United States Association for Body
  Psychotherapy
7831 Woodmont Ave.
Bethesda, MD 20814
URL: http://www.usabp.org/displaycommon.cfm?an=4

Semiannual. Academic journal that seeks to support, promote and stimulate the exchange of ideas, scholarship and research within the field of body psychotherapy as well as an interdisciplinary exchange with related fields of clinical practice and inquiry.

★8655★ Worldviews on Evidence-Based Nursing

Wiley-Blackwell
350 Main St. Commerce Pl.
Malden, MA 02148
Ph: (781)388-8200   Fax: (781)388-8210
Fr: 800-759-6120
URL: http://www.blackwellpublishing.com/journals/WVN

Quarterly. $112.00/year for individuals, print and online; $116.00/year for individuals, online only; $49.00/year for members, print and online; $47.00/year for members, online only; $318.00/year for institutions, print and premium online; $289.00/year for institutions, print and standard online; $275.00/year for institutions, premium online only; $132.00/year for individuals, print and online; $126.00/year for individuals, online only; $53.00/year for members, print and online. Journal that offers research, policy and practice, education and management for nursing.

PLACEMENT AND JOB REFERRAL SERVICES

★8656★ American Association for Geriatric Psychiatry (AAGP)

7910 Woodmont Ave., Ste. 1050
Bethesda, MD 20814-3069
Ph: (301)654-7850   Fax: (301)654-4137
E-mail: main@aagponline.org
URL: http://www.aagpgpa.org

Description: Psychiatrists interested in promoting better mental health care for the elderly. Maintains placement service and speakers' bureau.

★8657★ American Public Health Association (APHA)

800 I St. NW
Washington, DC 20001
Ph: (202)777-2742   Fax: (202)777-2534
E-mail: comments@apha.org
URL: http://www.apha.org

Members: Professional organization of physicians, nurses, educators, academicians, environmentalists, epidemiologists, new professionals, social workers, health administrators, optometrists, podiatrists, pharmacists, dentists, nutritionists, health planners, other community and mental health specialists, and interested consumers. **Purpose:** Seeks to protect and promote personal, mental, and environmental health. **Activities:** Services include: promulgation of standards; establishment of uniform practices and procedures; development of the etiology of communicable diseases; research in public health; exploration of medical care programs and their relationships to public health. Sponsors job placement service.

EMPLOYER DIRECTORIES AND NETWORKING LISTS

★8658★ AHA Guide to the Health Care Field

American Hospital Association
1 N Franklin
Chicago, IL 60606
Ph: (312)422-2050   Fax: (312)422-4700
Fr: 800-424-4301

Annual, August. Covers hospitals, networks, multi-health care systems, freestanding ambulatory surgery centers, psychiatric facilities, long-term care facilities, substance abuse programs, and other health-related organizations. Entries include: For hospitals–Facility name, address, phone, administrator's name, number of beds, facilities and services, number of employees, expenses, other statistics. For other organizations–Name, address, phone, fax, name and title of contact. Arrangement: Geographical. Indexes: Hospital name.

★8659★ American Journal of Nursing-Career Guide

American Journal of Nursing
c/o Lippincott, Williams & Wilkins
530 Walnut St.
Philadelphia, PA 19106-3621
Ph: (215)521-8300   Fax: (215)521-8902
Fr: 800-627-0484
URL: http://www.ajnonline.com

Annual, April. $34.90 for individuals; $234.95 for institutions; $26.95 for individuals, in-training; $87.00 for individuals, international; $299.00 for institutions, international. Publication includes: List of nursing organizations and agencies. Entries include: Name, address, names of officers or nursing representatives. Arrangement: Classified by type of organization.

★8660★ *Careers in Focus: Geriatric Care*

Ferguson Publishing Co.
200 W Jackson Blvd.
Chicago, IL 60606-6941
Fax: 800-306-9942   Fr: 800-306-9941
URL: http://www.fergpubco.com/

Latest edition 2nd, 2005. $29.95 for individuals; $26.95 for libraries. Publication includes: List of resources to consult for more information. Principal content of publication consists of job descriptions, advancement opportunities, educational requirements, employment outlook, salary information, and working conditions for careers in the field of geriatric care. Indexes: Alphabetical.

★8661★ *Directory of Hospital Personnel*

Grey House Publishing
185 Millerton Rd.
PO Box 860
Millerton, NY 12546
Ph: (518)789-8700   Fax: (518)789-0556
Fr: 800-562-2139
URL: http://www.greyhouse.com/hospital_personnel.htm

Annual. $325.00 for print product; $545.00 for online database subscription; $650.00 for online database subscription and print product combined. Covers 200,000 executives at 7,000 U.S. hospitals. Entries include: Name of hospital, address, phone; number of beds; type and JCAHO status of hospital; names and titles of key department heads and staff; medical and nursing school affiliations; number of residents, interns, and nursing students. Arrangement: Geographical. Indexes: Hospital name, personnel, hospital size.

★8662★ *Hospital Blue Book*

Billian Publishing Inc./Transworld
   Publishing Inc.
2100 Powers Ferry Rd. SE
Atlanta, GA 30339
Ph: (770)955-5656   Fax: (770)952-0669
Fr: 800-533-8484
E-mail: blu-book@billian.com

2005. $300.00 for individuals. Covers more than 6,687 hospitals; some listings also appear in a separate southern edition of this publication. Entries include: Name of hospital, accreditation, mailing address, phone, fax, number of beds, type of facility (nonprofit, general, state, etc.); list of administrative personnel and chiefs of medical services, with specific titles. Arrangement: Geographical.

★8663★ *How to Survive and Maybe Even Love Nursing School!*

F.A. Davis Co.
1915 Arch St.
Philadelphia, PA 19103
Ph: (215)568-2270   Fax: (215)568-5065
Fr: 800-523-4049

2nd edition 2004. $24.95 for individuals. Publication includes: List of resources for nursing students, such as Web sites and related organizations. Principal content of publication is information about succeeding in nursing school.

★8664★ *The JobBank Guide to Health Care Companies*

Adams Media Corp.
57 Littlefield St.
Avon, MA 02322
Ph: (508)427-7100   Fax: (508)427-6790
Fr: 800-872-5627
URL: http://www.amazon.com/Jobbank-Guide-Health-Care-Companies/dp

Biennial. Covers jobs nationwide in health care companies. Entries include: Firm or organization name, address, phone, name and title of contact; description of organization, headquarters location, typical titles for entry- and middle-level positions, educational backgrounds desired, fringe benefits offered, stock exchange listing, training programs, internships, parent company, number of employees, revenues, e-mail and web addresses, projected number of hires. Indexes: Alphabetical.

★8665★ *Legal and Ethical Dictionary for Mental Health Professionals*

University Press of America
4501 Forbes Blvd., Ste. 200
Lanham, MD 20706
Ph: (301)459-3366   Fax: (301)429-5748
Fr: 800-462-6420
URL: http://www.univpress.com/

$76.50 for print product, cloth-bound; $47.50 for print product, paperback. Publication includes: Lists of state licensure boards and Web sites for mental health organizations. Principal content of publication is a dictionary of legal and ethical responsibilities for mental health professionals.

★8666★ *Medical and Health Information Directory*

Gale, Cengage Learning
27500 Drake Rd.
Farmington Hills, MI 48331-3535
Ph: (248)699-4253   Fax: (248)699-8065
Fr: 800-877-4253
E-mail: businessproducts@gale.com
URL: http://www.gale.com

Annual; latest edition 20th, July 2007. $375.00/volume. Covers in Volume 1, more than 26,500 medical and health oriented associations, organizations, institutions, and government agencies, including health maintenance organizations (HMOs), preferred provider organizations (PPOs), insurance companies, pharmaceutical companies, research centers, and medical and allied

health schools. In Volume 2, over 12,000 medical book publishers; medical periodicals, directories, audiovisual producers and services, medical libraries and information centers, electronic resources, and health-related internet search engines. In Volume 3, more than 35,500 clinics, treatment centers, care programs, and counseling/diagnostic services for 34 subject areas. Entries include: Institution, service, or firm name, address, phone, fax, email and URL; many include names of key personnel and, when pertinent, descriptive annotations. Volume 3 was formerly listed separately as Health Services Directory. Arrangement: Classified by organization activity, service, etc. Indexes: Each volume has a complete alphabetical name and keyword index.

★8667★ *Nursing Career Directory*

Lippincott Williams & Wilkins
530 Walnut St.
Philadelphia, PA 19106-3621
Ph: (215)521-8300   Fax: (215)521-8902
Fr: 800-346-7844
URL: http://www.springnet.com

Annual, January. Covers nonprofit and investor-owned hospitals and departments of the United States government that hire nurses. Does not report specific positions available. Entries include: Unit name, location, areas of nursing specialization, educational requirements for nurses, licensing, facilities, benefits, etc. Arrangement: Geographical. Indexes: Geographical.

★8668★ *Online Resources for Senior Citizens*

McFarland & Company Inc., Publishers
960 NC Hwy. 88 W
PO Box 611
Jefferson, NC 28640
Ph: (336)246-4460   Fax: (336)246-5018
Fr: 800-253-2187
URL: http://www.mcfarlandpub.com

Latest edition 2nd, published 2006. $39.95 for individuals. Covers federal government resources, general resources, and resources listed by topics, such as caregivers, death and dying, volunteering, employment, grandparenting, health care, and travel.

★8669★ *Peterson's Job Opportunities for Health and Science Majors*

Peterson's
Princeton Pke. Corporate Ctr., 2000
   Lenox Dr.
PO Box 67005
Lawrenceville, NJ 08648
Ph: (609)896-1800   Fax: (609)896-4531
Fr: 800-338-3282
URL: http://www.petersons.com

Irregular; latest edition 1999. Covers about 1,300 research, consulting, government, and non-profit and profit service organizations that hire college and university graduates in science and health-related majors. Entries include: Organization name, address, phone, name and title of contact, type of organization, number of employees, Standard Industrial Classification (SIC) code;

description of opportunities available including disciplines, level of education required, starting locations and salaries, level of experience accepted, benefits.

HANDBOOKS AND MANUALS

★8670★ Being a Long-Term Care Nursing Assistant

Prentice Hall PTR
1 Lake St.
Upper Saddle River, NJ 07458
Ph: (201)236-7000   Fax: 800-445-6991
Fr: 800-428-5331
URL: http://www.phptr.com/index.asp?rl=1

Connie A. Will-Black and Judith B. Eighmy. Fifth edition, 2002. $62.20 (paper). 534 pages.

★8671★ Being a Nursing Assistant

Prentice Hall PTR
1 Lake St.
Upper Saddle River, NJ 07458
Ph: (201)236-7000   Fax: 800-445-6991
Fr: 800-428-5331
URL: http://www.phptr.com/index.asp?rl=1

Francie Wolgin. Ninth edition, 2004. $60.80 (paper). 800 pages.

★8672★ Careers for Caring People and Other Sensitive Types

The McGraw-Hill Companies
PO Box 182604
Columbus, OH 43272
Fax: (614)759-3749   Fr: 877-883-5524
E-mail: customer.service@mcgraw-hill.com
URL: http://www.mcgraw-hill.com

Adrian Paradis. Second edition, 2003. $13.95 (paper). 208 pages.

★8673★ Careers in Health Care

The McGraw-Hill Companies
PO Box 182604
Columbus, OH 43272
Fax: (614)759-3749   Fr: 877-883-5524
E-mail: customer.service@mcgraw-hill.com
URL: http://www.mcgraw-hill.com

Barbara M. Swanson. Fifth edition, 2005. $15.95 (paper). 192 pages. Describes job duties, work settings, salaries, licensing and certification requirements, educational preparation, and future outlook. Gives ideas on how to secure a job.

★8674★ Developing Your Career in Nursing

Sage Publications, Inc.
2455 Teller Rd.
Thousand Oaks, CA 91320-2218
Ph: (805)499-0721   Fax: (805)499-0871
E-mail: info@sagepub.com
URL: http://www.sagepub.com/

Robert Newell, editor. 2003. $37.95. 184 pages.

★8675★ Expert Resumes for Health Care Careers

Jist Works
875 Montreal Way
St. Paul, MN 55102
Fr: 800-648-5478
E-mail: info@jist.com
URL: http://www.jist.com

Wendy S. Enelow and Louise M. Kursmark. December 2003. $16.95. 288 pages.

★8676★ Federal Jobs in Nursing and Health Sciences

Impact Publications
9104 Manassas Dr., Ste. N
Manassas Park, VA 20111-5211
Ph: (703)361-7300   Fax: (703)335-9486
Fr: 800-361-1055
E-mail: query@impactpublications.com
URL: http://www.impactpublications.com

Russ Smith. 1996. Part of "Federal Jobs in ..." Series. $14.95. 130 pages.

★8677★ From Nursing Assistant to Clinical Care Associate

Prentice Hall PTR
1 Lake St.
Upper Saddle River, NJ 07458
Ph: (201)236-7000   Fax: 800-445-6991
Fr: 800-428-5331
URL: http://www.phptr.com/index.asp?rl=1

Carole Miele and Teresa England 1998. $65.00 (paper). 512 pages.

★8678★ From Nursing Assistant to Patient Care Technician: New Roles, New Knowledge, New Skills

W. B. Saunders Co.
6277 Sea Harbor Dr.
Orlando, FL 32887
Fr: 800-654-2452
URL: http://www.elsevier.com

Donna J. Brust and Joyce A. Foster. 1997. 408 pages.

★8679★ Gerontological Nursing Certification Review Guide for the Generalist, Clinical Specialist & Nurse Practitioner

Health Leadership Associates, Inc
PO Box 1784
Germantown, MD 20875
Ph: (301)983-2405   Fax: (301)983-2693
Fr: 800-435-4775
E-mail: hlacert@aol.com
URL: http://www.healthleadership.com/

Catharine Kopac and Virginia L. Millonig, editors. Revised, 1996. $47.75 (paper). 563 pages.

★8680★ Health Careers Today

Elsevier
11830 Westline Industrial Dr.
St. Louis, MO 63146
Ph: (314)453-7010   Fax: (314)453-7095
Fr: 800-545-2522
E-mail: usbkinfo@elsevier.com
URL: http://www.elsevier.com

Gerdin, Judith. Fourth edition. 2007. $59.95. 496 pages. Covers more than 45 health careers. Discusses the roles and responsibilities of various occupations and provides a solid foundation in the skills needed for all health careers.

★8681★ The Long-Term Care Nursing Assistant Training Manual

Health Professions Press
PO Box 10624
Baltimore, MD 21285-0624
Ph: (410)337-9585   Fax: (410)337-8539
Fr: 888-337-8808
E-mail: custserv@healthpropress.com
URL: http://www.healthpropress.com/

Mary A. Anderson, Karen W. Beaver and Kathleen R. Culliton, editors. Second edition, 1996. $29.95 (paper). 316 pages.

★8682★ The Nurses' Career Guide: Discovering New Horizons in Health Care

Sovereignty Press
1241 Johnson Ave., No. 353
San Luis Obispo, CA 93401
Ph: (805)543-6100   Fax: (805)543-1085
Fr: 888-201-2501

Zardoya E. Eagles and Marti Kock. 1999. $17.95 (paper). 118 pages. Helps the reader identify work skills and achievements, clarify values and goals, explore career options, develop a personal action plan, prepare cover letters and resumes, and conduct informational and job interviews. Also addresses the dramatic changes that nurses currently face in the workplace. Includes a 65-page resource section which lists references, samples of resumes and letters, professional magazines, organizations, and online resources.

★8683★ Nursing Assistant: A Nursing Process Approach

Cengage Learning
PO Box 6904
Florence, KY 41022
Fax: 800-487-8488   Fr: 800-354-9706
URL: http://www.cengage.com

Barbara Hegner, Barbara Acello and Esther Caldwell. Eighth edition, 2007. $76.95 (paper). 1,024 pages.

★8684★ Nursing Assistants: A Basic Study Guide

First Class Books, Inc.
113 E. Magnesium Rd., Ste. C
Spokane, WA 99208
Ph: (509)466-6847   Fax: (509)466-6896
Fr: 800-524-6911

URL: http://www.longtermcareprovider.com/storefronts/firstclass.html

Beverly Robertson. Seventh edition, 2005. $16.00 (paper). 184 pages.

★8685★ **Nursing (Career Portraits)**
The McGraw-Hill Companies
PO Box 182604
Columbus, OH 43272
Fax: (614)759-3749   Fr: 877-883-5524
E-mail: customer.service@mcgraw-hill.com
URL: http://www.mcgraw-hill.com

Blythe Camenson. 1997. $13.95. 96 pages.

★8686★ **The Nursing Experience: Trends, Challenges & Transitions**
The McGraw-Hill Companies
PO Box 182604
Columbus, OH 43272
Fax: (614)759-3749   Fr: 877-883-5524
E-mail: customer.service@mcgraw-hill.com
URL: http://www.mcgraw-hill.com

Lucille A. Joel and L.Y. Kelly. Fifth edition, 2006. $44.95 (paper). 792 pages.

★8687★ **Nursing Today: Transition and Trends**
W. B. Saunders Co.
6277 Sea Harbor Dr.
Orlando, FL 32887
Fr: 800-654-2452
URL: http://www.elsevier.com

JoAnn Zerwekh and Jo C. Claborn, editors. Fifth edition, 2005. $47.95 (paper). 688 pages.

★8688★ **Opportunities in Health and Medical Careers**
The McGraw-Hill Companies
PO Box 182604
Columbus, OH 43272
Fax: (614)759-3749   Fr: 877-883-5524
E-mail: customer.service@mcgraw-hill.com
URL: http://www.mcgraw-hill.com

I. Donald Snook, Jr. and Leo D'Orazio. 2004. $13.95 (paper). 157 pages. Covers the full range of medical and health occupations. Illustrated.

★8689★ **Opportunities in Mental Health Careers**
The McGraw-Hill Companies
PO Box 182604
Columbus, OH 43272
Fax: (614)759-3749   Fr: 877-883-5524
E-mail: customer.service@mcgraw-hill.com
URL: http://www.mcgraw-hill.com

Philip A. Perry. 1996. $14.95; $11.95 (paper) 160 pages. Part of the "Opportunities in ..." Series.

★8690★ **Opportunities in Nursing Careers**
The McGraw-Hill Companies
PO Box 182604
Columbus, OH 43272
Fax: (614)759-3749   Fr: 877-883-5524
E-mail: customer.service@mcgraw-hill.com
URL: http://www.mcgraw-hill.com

Keville Frederickson and Judith A. Ryan. Second edition, 2003. $13.95 (paper). 160 pages. Discusses the employment outlook and job-seeking techniques for LVN's, LPN's, RN's, nurse practitioners, nurse anesthetists, and other nurse members of the medical team. Includes a complete list of state nurses associations, state nursing boards, and specialty nursing organizations. Contains bibliography and illustrations.

★8691★ **Psychiatric Therapy Aide**
National Learning Corp.
212 Michael Dr.
Syosset, NY 11791
Ph: (516)921-8888   Fax: (516)921-8743
Fr: 800-645-6337
URL: http://www.passbooks.com

Jack Rudman. 1994. $23.95 (paper). Part of the Career Examination Series.

★8692★ **Real People Working in Health Care**
The McGraw-Hill Companies
PO Box 182604
Columbus, OH 43272
Fax: (614)759-3749   Fr: 877-883-5524
E-mail: customer.service@mcgraw-hill.com
URL: http://www.mcgraw-hill.com

Blythe Camenson, Jan Goldberg. 1996. $12.95 (paper). 144 pages. Interviews and profiles of working professionals capture a range of opportunities in this field.

★8693★ **Real People Working in the Helping Professions**
The McGraw-Hill Companies
PO Box 182604
Columbus, OH 43272
Fax: (614)759-3749   Fr: 877-883-5524
E-mail: customer.service@mcgraw-hill.com
URL: http://www.mcgraw-hill.com

Blythe Camenson, Jan Goldberg. 1997. $12.95 (paper). 192 pages. Interviews and profiles of working professionals capture a range of opportunities in this field.

★8694★ **Reinventing Your Nursing Career: A Handbook for Success in the Age of Managed Care**
Aspen Publishers
1 Lake St.
Upper Saddle River, NJ 07458
Ph: (201)236-7000   Fax: 800-445-6991
Fr: 800-638-8437
URL: http://www.aspenpublishers.com/

Michael Newell and Mario Pinardo. 1998. $53.95 (paper). 253 pages. Helps nurses identify career goals and take practical steps to realize them using self-surveys, goal-set-

ting methods, personal action plans, and networking techniques.

★8695★ **Resumes for Health and Medical Careers**
The McGraw-Hill Companies
PO Box 182604
Columbus, OH 43272
Fax: (614)759-3749   Fr: 877-883-5524
E-mail: customer.service@mcgraw-hill.com
URL: http://www.mcgraw-hill.com

Third edition, 2003. $11.95 (paper). 160 pages.

EMPLOYMENT AGENCIES AND SEARCH FIRMS

★8696★ **Cross Country TravCorps**
6551 Park of Commerce Blvd.
Boca Raton, FL 33487-8247
Fax: (562)998-8533   Fr: 800-530-6125
URL: http://www.crosscountrytravcorps.com

Places traveling nurses in assignments nationwide.

★8697★ **Daudlin, De Beaupre & Company Inc.**
18530 Mack Ave., Ste. 315
Grosse Pointe Farms, MI 48236
Ph: (313)885-1235   Fax: (313)885-1247
URL: http://www.daudlindebeaupre.com/

Executive search firm focused on the health-care industry.

★8698★ **Davis-Smith, Inc.**
27656 Franklin Rd.
Southfield, MI 48034
Ph: (248)354-4100   Fax: (248)354-6702
Fr: 800-541-4672
E-mail: info@davissmith.com
URL: http://www.davissmith.com

Healthcare staffing agency. Executive search firm.

★8699★ **Harper Associates**
3100 NW Hwy., Ste. 240
Farmington Hills, MI 48334
Ph: (248)932-1170   Fax: (248)932-1214
E-mail: info@harperjobs.com
URL: http://www.harperjobs.com

Executive search firm and employment agency.

★8700★ **Legal Medical Urgent Staffing Solutions**
The 1605 Bldg., 1605 Evesham Rd.
Voorhees, NJ 08043
Ph: (856)795-0909   Fax: (856)795-0922
Fr: 877-674-4464
URL: http://www.legalmedicalstaffing.com

Offers a specialized service providing temporary and full-time support exclusively to the legal, dental, and medical professions.

★8701★ MEDCareerNET
23072 Lake Center Dr., Ste. 210
Lake Forest, CA 92630
Ph: (949)380-4800   Fax: (949)380-7477
E-mail: vic@medcareernet.com
URL: http://www.medcareernet.com

Firm provides medical career professionals with a choice of career alternatives that extend their reach within their respective disciplines.

★8702★ Medical Personnel Services, Inc.
1748 N St., NW
Washington, DC 20036
Ph: (202)466-2955   Fax: (202)452-1818
E-mail: jobs@medicalpersonnel.com
URL: http://www.medicalpersonnel.com

Employment agency specializing in permanent health/medical placements.

★8703★ Professional Placement Associates, Inc.
287 Bowman Ave., Ste. 309
Purchase, NY 10577-2517
Ph: (914)251-1000   Fax: (914)251-1055
E-mail: careers@ppasearch.com
URL: http://www.ppasearch.com

Executive search firm specializing in the health and medical field.

ONLINE JOB SOURCES AND SERVICES

★8704★ Delta T Group
E-mail: pa@deltatg.com
URL: http://www.delta-tgroup.com

Description: Specialized contract temporary staffing source for healthcare professionals in the fields of social service, psychiatry, mental health, and substance abuse. Organizations may request services and staffing; job seekers may view services provided, submit a resume, or peruse jobs available.

★8705★ Medhunters.com
Fr: 800-664-0278
E-mail: info@medhunters.com
URL: http://www.medhunters.com

Description: Career search site for jobs in all health care specialties; educational resources; visa and licensing information for relocation; interesting articles; relocation tools; links to professional organizations and general resources.

★8706★ Medzilla
URL: http://www.medzilla.com

Description: General medical website which matches employers and job hunters to their ideal employees and jobs through search capabilities. **Main files include:** Post Jobs, Search Resumes, Post Resumes, Search Jobs, Head Hunters, Articles, Salary Survey.

★8707★ ProHealthJobs
Fr: 800-796-1738
E-mail: Info@prohealthedujobs.com
URL: http://www.prohealthjobs.com

Description: Career resources site for the medical and health care field. Lists professional opportunities, product information, continuing education and open positions.

TRADESHOWS

★8708★ American Association of Office Nurses Annual Meeting and Convention
American Association of Office Nurses
52 Park Ave. Ste. B4
Park Ridge, NJ 07656
Ph: (201)391-2600   Fax: (201)573-8543
Fr: 800-457-7504
E-mail: aaonmail@aaon.org
URL: http://www.aaon.org

Annual. **Primary Exhibits:** Exhibits of interest to nurses.

★8709★ American Psychiatric Association Annual Meeting
American Psychiatric Association
1000 Wilson Blvd., Ste. 1825
Arlington, VA 22209-3901
Ph: (703)907-7300   Fax: (202)682-6132
E-mail: apa@psych.org
URL: http://www.psych.org

Annual. **Primary Exhibits:** Computer software online service, media product, criminal justice, diagnostic tool, ECT educational, insurance, market research, professional/support organizations, publishers, recruitment, store/federal and pharmaceuticals. **Dates and Locations:** 2008 May 03-08; Washington, DC.

★8710★ Association for Gerontology in Higher Education Annual Meeting
Association for Gerontology in Higher Education
1220 L St., Ste. 901
Washington, DC 20005-1503
Ph: (202)289-9806   Fax: (202)289-9824
E-mail: info@aghe.org
URL: http://www.aghe.org

Annual. **Primary Exhibits:** Publications and education programs related to gerontology. **Dates and Locations:** 2008 Feb 21-24.

★8711★ Florida Nurses Association Annual Convention
Florida Nurses Association
1235 E. Concord St.
PO Box 536985
Orlando, FL 32853-6985
Ph: (407)896-3261   Fax: (407)896-9042
E-mail: info@floridanurse.org
URL: http://www.floridanurse.org

Annual. **Primary Exhibits:** Hospital and health care agency information; hospital products and supplies; pharmaceuticals; insurance information; employment information; textbooks and related publications; nursing school information; and graduate program information for the health care industry.

★8712★ Illinois Health Care Association Convention and Trade Show
Illinois Health Care Association
1029 S Fourth St.
Springfield, IL 62703-2224
Ph: (217)528-6455   Fax: (217)528-0452
Fr: 800-252-8988
E-mail: info@ihca.com
URL: http://www.ihca.com

Annual. **Primary Exhibits:** Long-term (nursing homes) healthcare industry and assisted living industry service providers and suppliers.

★8713★ International Society of Psychiatric-Mental Health Nurses Annual Conference
International Society of Psychiatric - Mental Health Nurses
7600 Terrace Ave., Ste. 203
Middleton, WI 53562-3174
Ph: (608)836-3363   Fax: (608)831-5122
Fr: 800-826-2950
E-mail: info@ispn-psych.org
URL: http://www.ispn-psych.org

Annual. **Primary Exhibits:** Psychiatric nursing equipment, supplies, and services.

★8714★ New York State Nurses Association Annual Convention & Exhibits
New York State Nurses Association
11 Cornell Rd.
Latham, NY 12110
Ph: (518)782-9400   Fr: 800-724-6974
E-mail: info@nysna.org
URL: http://www.nysna.org

Annual. **Primary Exhibits:** Nursing equipment, supplies, and services.

★8715★ South Carolina Nurses Association Convention
South Carolina Nurses Association
1821 Gadsden St.
Columbia, SC 29201
Ph: (803)252-4781   Fax: (803)779-3870
E-mail: info@scnurses.org
URL: http://www.scnurses.org

Annual. **Primary Exhibits:** Medical supplies

and services, including schools, hospital recruiters, pharmaceuticals, and textbooks.

OTHER SOURCES

★8716★ American Academy of Addiction Psychiatry (AAAP)

345 Blackstone Blvd., 2nd Fl. - RCH
Providence, RI 02906
Ph: (401)524-3076   Fax: (401)272-0922
E-mail: cj@aaap.org
URL: http://www.aaap.org

Members: Psychiatrists and other health care and mental health professionals treating people with addictive behaviors. **Purpose:** Promotes accessibility to highest quality treatment for all who need it; promotes excellence in clinical practice in addiction psychiatry; educates the public to influence public policy regarding addictive illness; provides continuing education for addiction professionals; disseminates new information in the field of addiction psychiatry; and encourages research on the etiology, prevention, identification, and treatment of the addictions.

★8717★ American Association of Psychiatric Technicians (AAPT)

1220 S St., Ste. 100
Sacramento, CA 95811-7138
Ph: (916)443-1701   Fax: (916)329-9145
Fr: 800-391-7589
E-mail: loger@psychtechs.net
URL: http://www.psychtechs.org

Description: Administers the Nationally Certified Psychiatric Technician examination to non-licensed direct-care workers in the fields of mental illness, developmental disabilities and substance abuse.

★8718★ American Health Care Association (AHCA)

1201 L St. NW
Washington, DC 20005
Ph: (202)842-4444   Fax: (202)842-3860
E-mail: hr@ahca.org
URL: http://www.ahca.org

Description: Federation of state associations of long-term health care facilities. Promotes standards for professionals in long-term health care delivery and quality care for patients and residents in a safe environment. Focuses on issues of availability, quality, affordability, and fair payment. Operates as liaison with governmental agencies, Congress, and professional associations. Compiles statistics.

★8719★ American Hospital Association (AHA)

1 N Franklin
Chicago, IL 60606-3421
Ph: (312)422-3000   Fax: (312)422-4796
URL: http://www.aha.org

Description: Represents health care provider organizations. Seeks to advance the health of individuals and communities. Leads, represents, and serves health care provider organizations that are accountable to the community and committed to health improvement.

★8720★ American Mental Health Alliance (AMHA)

PO Box 4075
Portland, OR 97208-4075
Ph: (503)279-8160   Fr: 888-577-3386
E-mail: memberinfo@americanmentalhealth.com
URL: http://www.americanmentalhealth.com

Description: Represents mental health professionals licensed or certified for independen t practice. Creates a professional community that provides therapy of the highes t quality and ethical standards. Supports and markets competent, ethical mental health services that preserve privacy and confidentiality. Supports education, s upervision, and research opportunities for members. Opposes legislation and regu lations that invade patient privacy and confidentiality.

★8721★ American School Health Association (ASHA)

PO Box 708
Kent, OH 44240
Ph: (330)678-1601   Fax: (330)678-4526
E-mail: asha@ashaweb.org
URL: http://www.ashaweb.org

Description: School physicians, school nurses, counsellors, nutritionists, psychologists, social workers, administrators, school health coordinators, health educators, and physical educators working in schools, professional preparation programs, public health, and community-based organizations. Promotes coordinated school health programs that include health education, health services, a healthful school environment, physical education, nutrition services, and psycho-social health services offered in schools collaboratively with families and other members of the community. Offers professional reference materials and professional development opportunities. Conducts pilot programs that inform materials development, provides technical assistance to school professionals, advocates for school health.

★8722★ Association of Black Nursing Faculty (ABNF)

PO Box 589
Lisle, IL 60532
Ph: (630)969-3809   Fax: (630)969-3895
E-mail: clay@tuckerpub.com

Members: Black nursing faculty teaching in nursing programs accredited by the National League for Nursing. **Purpose:** Works to promote health-related issues and educational concerns of interest to the black community and ABNF. **Activities:** Serves as a forum for communication and the exchange of information among members; develops strategies for expressing concerns to other individuals, institutions, and communities. Assists members in professional development; develops and sponsors continuing education activities; fosters networking and guidance in employment and recruitment activities. Promotes health-related issues of legislation, government programs, and community activities. Supports black consumer advocacy issues. Encourages research. Maintains speakers' bureau and hall of fame.

★8723★ Exploring Health Occupations

Cambridge Educational
PO Box 2053
Princeton, NJ 08543-2053
Ph: 800-257-5126   Fax: (609)671-0266
Fr: 800-468-4227
E-mail: custserv@films.com
URL: http://www.cambridgeeducational.com

VHS and DVD. $159.90. 1999. Two-part series provides a detailed view of the field of medical technicians and technologists, EMTs, nurses, therapists, and assistants.

★8724★ Health Service Occupations

Delphi Productions
3159 6th St.
Boulder, CO 80304
Ph: (303)443-2100   Fax: (303)443-4022
Fr: 888-443-2400
E-mail: support@delphivideo.com
URL: http://www.delphivideo.com

$95.00. 50 minutes. Part of the Careers for the 21st Century Video Library.

★8725★ Institute on Psychiatric Services/American Psychiatric Association

1000 Wilson Blvd., Ste. 1825
Arlington, VA 22209-3901
Ph: (703)907-7300   Fax: (703)907-1085
Fr: 888-357-7924
E-mail: apa@psych.org
URL: http://www.psych.org

Description: Annual meeting sponsored by the American Psychiatric Association. Open to Physicians and all mental health professionals of all psychiatric and related health and educational facilities. Includes lectures by experts in the field and workshops and accredited courses on problems, programs, and trends. Offers on-site Job Bank, which lists opportunities for mental health professionals. Organized scientific exhibits.

★8726★ Medicine & Related Occupations

Delphi Productions
3159 6th St.
Boulder, CO 80304
Ph: (303)443-2100   Fax: (303)443-4022
Fr: 888-443-2400
E-mail: support@delphivideo.com
URL: http://www.delphivideo.com

$95.00. 45 minutes. Part of the Careers for the 21st Century Video Library.

★8727★ National League for Nursing (NLN)

61 Broadway, 33rd Fl.
New York, NY 10006
Ph: (212)363-5555   Fax: (212)812-0393
Fr: 800-669-1656
E-mail: generalinfo@nln.org
URL: http://www.nln.org

Description: Champions the pursuit of quality nursing education. A professional association of nursing faculty, education agencies, health care agencies, allied/public agencies, and public members whose mission is to advance quality nursing education that prepares the nursing workforce to meet the needs of diverse populations in an ever-changing health care environment. Serves as the primary source of information about every type of nursing education program, from the LVN and LPN to the EdD and PhD. There are 20 affiliated constituent leagues that provide a local forum for members. The National League for Nursing Accrediting Commission is an independent corporate affiliate of the NLN, responsible for providing accreditation services to all levels of nursing education.

★8728★ National Rural Health Association (NRHA)

Administrative Office
521 E 63rd St.
Kansas City, MO 64110-3329
Ph: (816)756-3140   Fax: (816)756-3144
E-mail: mail@nrharural.org
URL: http://www.nrharural.org

Description: Administrators, physicians, nurses, physician assistants, health planners, academicians, and others interested or involved in rural health care. Creates a better understanding of health care problems unique to rural areas; utilizes a collective approach in finding positive solutions; articulates and represents the health care needs of rural America; supplies current information to rural health care providers; serves as a liaison between rural health care programs throughout the country. Offers continuing education credits for medical, dental, nursing, and management courses.

★8729★ Visiting Nurse Associations of America (VNAA)

Administration Office
99 Summer St., Ste. 1700
Boston, MA 02110
Ph: (617)737-3200   Fax: (617)737-1144
Fr: 800-426-2547
E-mail: vnaa@vnaa.org
URL: http://www.vnaa.org

Members: Home health care agencies. **Purpose:** Develops competitive strength among community-based nonprofit visiting nurse organizations; works to strengthen business resources and economic programs through contracting, marketing, governmental affairs and publications.

Occupational Health and Safety Specialists and Technicians

SOURCES OF HELP-WANTED ADS

★8730★ BNA's SafetyNet

Bureau of National Affairs Inc.
1801 S. Bell St.
Arlington, VA 22202
Fr: 800-372-1033
E-mail: customercare@bna.com
URL: http://www.bna.com/products/ens/josh.htm

Description: Biweekly. Designed to help employers deal with occupational safety and health regulations, policies, standards, and practices, and to understand the effects of compliance on employee relations. Covers the establishment, management, evaluation, maintenance, and administration of health and safety programs. Carries information on recordkeeping, inspections, enforcement, employer defenses, and training.

★8731★ Cal-OSHA Reporter

Providence Publications
PO Box 2610
Granite Bay, CA 95746
Ph: (916)780-5200   Fax: (916)781-6444
E-mail: newsdesk@cal-osha.com
URL: http://www.cal-osha.com/

Description: 50/year. Reports on laws, regulations, court cases, and other issues of interest to occupational safety and health professionals. Recurring features include a calendar of events, reports of meetings, news of educational opportunities, job listings, and notices of publications available. Reviews all Cal-OSHA cases.

★8732★ Conflict, Security and Development

Taylor & Francis Group Journals
325 Chestnut St., Ste. 800
Philadelphia, PA 19106
Ph: (215)625-8900   Fax: (215)625-8914
Fr: 800-354-1420
URL: http://www.tandf.co.uk/journals/titles/14678802.asp

Quarterly. $466.00/year for institutions, print

and online; $442.00/year for institutions, online only; $135.00/year for individuals. Journal focusing on traditional development and security studies.

★8733★ Construction Division Newsletter

NSC Press
1121 Spring Lake Dr.
Itasca, IL 60143-3201
Ph: (630)285-1121   Fax: (630)285-1315
Fr: 800-621-7615
URL: http://www.nsc.org

Description: Bimonthly. Focuses on industrial and occupational safety in the construction industry. Carries items on such topics as safe work practices and products; accident prevention; and successful industrial safety programs and policies. Available online only.

★8734★ CTD News

LRP Publications
747 Dresher Rd., Ste. 500
PO Box 980
Horsham, PA 19044
Ph: (215)784-0860   Fax: (215)784-9639
Fr: 800-341-7874
URL: http://www.ctdnews.com/

Description: Monthly. Concerned with occupational health hazards that result in Cumulative Trauma Disorders (CTD) such as carpal tunnel syndrome, RSI, stress, and back discomfort. Covers prevention, treatment, litigation, and worker's compensation related to CTD.

★8735★ Inside OSHA

Inside Washington Publishers
1225 S. Clark St. Ste. 1400
Arlington, VA 22202
Ph: (703)416-8500   Fax: (703)415-8543
Fr: 800-424-9068
E-mail: custsvc@iwpnews.com
URL: http://www.iwpnews.com/

Description: Biweekly, every other Monday. Reports on news of the Occupational Safety and Health Administration.

★8736★ ISHN

BNP Media
2401 W Big Beaver Rd., Ste. 700
Troy, MI 48084-3333
Ph: (248)786-1642   Fax: (248)786-1388
URL: http://www.ishn.com/

Monthly. Free. Business-to-business magazine for safety and health managers at high-hazard worksites in manufacturing, construction, health facilities, and service industries. Content covering OSHA and EPA regulations, how-to features, safety and health management topics, and the latest product news.

★8737★ Job Safety and Health Quarterly

Occupational Safety and Health Administration
200 Constitution Ave.
Washington, DC 20210
Ph: (202)693-1999   Fax: (202)693-1634
Fr: 800-321-OSHA
URL: http://www.osha.gov

Description: Quarterly. Informs readers of changes, developments, and new rulings made by the Occupational Safety and Health Administration (OSHA).

★8738★ Journal of Safety Management

National Safety Management Society
PO Box 4460
Walnut Creek, CA 94596-0460
Fr: 800-321-2910

Quarterly. Journal covering issues in the field of safety.

★8739★ Keller's Industrial Safety Report

J.J. Keller & Associates Inc.
3003 W Breezewood Ln.
PO Box 368
Neenah, WI 54957
Ph: 877-564-2333   Fax: 800-727-7516
Fr: 800-346-4812
E-mail: kellersoft@jjkeller.com
URL: http://www.jjkeller.com/

Description: Monthly. Concerned with activities of the Occupational Safety and Health

Administration (OSHA) and all aspects of safety in an industrial setting. Recurring features include includes sections titles OSHA Activity, Safety Issues, and State Activity.

★8740★ Labor Division Newsletter

NSC Press
1121 Spring Lake Dr.
Itasca, IL 60143-3201
Ph: (630)285-1121   Fax: (630)285-1315
Fr: 800-621-7615
URL: http://www.nsc.org

Description: Bimonthly. Concerned with industrial and occupational safety, safe work practices, and products. Covers industrial safety programs and relevant legislation and regulations. Reports on conferences and seminars centered on safety. Available online only.

★8741★ Occupational Safety & Health Reporter

Bureau of National Affairs Inc.
1801 S. Bell St.
Arlington, VA 22202
Fax: 800-253-0332   Fr: 800-372-1033
E-mail: customercare@bna.com
URL: http://www.bna.com/products/ens/oshr.htm

Description: Weekly, except week preceding Labor Day and last week of year. Provides a notification and reference service covering federal and state regulation of occupational safety and health, standards, legislation, enforcement activities, research, and legal decisions. Recurring features include a calendar of meetings and seminars and the full text of selected administrative rulings, proposed standards, criteria documents, variance notices, and compliance manuals.

★8742★ Safety Focus

NSC Press
1121 Spring Lake Dr.
Itasca, IL 60143-3201
Ph: (630)285-1121   Fax: (630)285-1315
Fr: 800-621-7615
E-mail: info@nsc.org
URL: http://www.nsc.org

Description: Bimonthly. Concerned with occupational safety, safety products, hazard control, and accident prevention in the following industries and sectors: chemical, metals, heath care, marine, air transport, public employment, rubber/plastics, laboratories/emerging technology, and retail trades and services. Recurring features include news of research and announcements of related conferences.

EMPLOYER DIRECTORIES AND NETWORKING LISTS

★8743★ The JobBank Guide to Health Care Companies

Adams Media Corp.
57 Littlefield St.
Avon, MA 02322
Ph: (508)427-7100   Fax: (508)427-6790
Fr: 800-872-5627
URL: http://www.amazon.com/Jobbank-Guide-Health-Care-Companies/dp

Biennial. Covers jobs nationwide in health care companies. Entries include: Firm or organization name, address, phone, name and title of contact; description of organization, headquarters location, typical titles for entry- and middle-level positions, educational backgrounds desired, fringe benefits offered, stock exchange listing, training programs, internships, parent company, number of employees, revenues, e-mail and web addresses, projected number of hires. Indexes: Alphabetical.

HANDBOOKS AND MANUALS

★8744★ Career Guide to the Safety Profession

Board of Certified Safety Professionals
208 Burwash Ave.
Savoy, IL 61874
Ph: (217)359-9263   Fax: (217)359-0055
URL: http://www.bcsp.org

1997. 68 pages.

★8745★ Labor Safety Technician

National Learning Corporation
212 Michael Dr.
Syosset, NY 11791
Ph: (516)921-8888   Fax: (516)921-8743
Fr: 800-632-8888
URL: http://www.passbooks.com/

Rudman, Jack. 1994. $29.95 (Trade paper).

★8746★ Principal Safety Coordinator

National Learning Corporation
212 Michael Dr.
Syosset, NY 11791
Ph: (516)921-8888   Fax: (516)921-8743
Fr: 800-632-8888
URL: http://www.passbooks.com/

Rudman, Jack. 1994. $34.95 (Trade paper).

★8747★ Safety Consultant

National Learning Corporation
212 Michael Dr.
Syosset, NY 11791
Ph: (516)921-8888   Fax: (516)921-8743
Fr: 800-632-8888
URL: http://www.passbooks.com/

National Learning Corporation (editor). 2005. $34.95 (Trade paper).

Occupational Therapists

SOURCES OF HELP-WANTED ADS

★8748★ **ADVANCE for Occupational Therapy Practitioners**
Merion Publications Inc.
2900 Horizon Dr.
PO Box 61556
King of Prussia, PA 19406
Ph: (610)278-1400   Fr: 800-355-5627
E-mail: advance@merion.com
URL: http://www.advanceforot.com

Biweekly. Serves licensed and registered occupational therapists, certified occupational therapy assistants, and senior OT students nationwide.

★8749★ **The American Journal of Occupational Therapy**
American Occupational Therapy
  Association Inc.
4720 Montgomery Ln.
PO Box 31220
Bethesda, MD 20824-1220
Ph: (301)652-2682   Fax: (301)652-7711
Fr: 800-377-8555
E-mail: ajotsis@aota.org
URL: http://www.aota.org/

Bimonthly. $114.00/year for individuals, U.S.; $182.00/year for institutions, U.S.; $159.75/year for individuals, Canada; $214.00/year for institutions, Canada; $285.00/year for individuals, foreign (via airmail); $310.00/year for institutions, foreign (via airmail). Journal providing a forum for occupational therapy personnel to share research, case studies, and new theory.

★8750★ **American Journal of Physical Medicine and Rehabilitation**
Lippincott Williams & Wilkins
530 Walnut St.
Philadelphia, PA 19106-3621
Ph: (215)521-8300   Fax: (215)521-8902
Fr: 800-638-3030
E-mail: jmulliga@lww.com
URL: http://www.amjphysmedrehab.com/

Monthly. Medical journal.

★8751★ **Journal of Learning Disabilities**
PRO-ED Inc.
8700 Shoal Creek Blvd.
PO Box 678370
Austin, TX 78757-6897
Ph: (512)451-3246   Fax: 800-397-7633
Fr: 800-897-3202
URL: http://www.proedinc.com

Bimonthly. $60.00/year for individuals; $96.00 for individuals, 2 years; $161.00/year for institutions; $258.00 for institutions, 2 years; $96.00/year for individuals, international; $154.00 for individuals, 2 year international; $187.00/year for institutions, international; $300.00 for institutions, 2 year international. Special education journal.

★8752★ **Occupational Therapy in Health Care**
The Haworth Press Inc.
10 Alice St.
Binghamton, NY 13904
Ph: (607)722-5857   Fr: 800-429-6784
URL: http://www.haworthpress.com/store/product.asp?sid=31TPBXNBB

Quarterly. $109.00/year for individuals; $159.00/year for Canada, individual; $168.00/year for other countries, individual; $420.00/year for institutions, agency, library; $601.00/year for institutions, Canada, agency, library; $639.00/year for institutions, other countries, agency, library. Journal for occupational therapists.

★8753★ **Occupational Therapy in Mental Health**
The Haworth Press Inc.
10 Alice St.
Binghamton, NY 13904
Ph: (607)722-5857   Fr: 800-429-6784
E-mail: info@haworthpress.com
URL: http://www.haworthpress.com/store/product.asp?sid=3CXTKNPDX

Quarterly. $60.00/year for individuals; $465.00/year for institutions, agency, library; $87.00/year for Canada, individual; $674.00/year for institutions, Canada, agency, library; $93.00/year for other countries, individual; $721.00/year for institutions, other countries,

agency, library. Journal for occupational therapists working in the mental health field.

★8754★ **OT Practice**
American Occupational Therapy
  Association Inc.
4720 Montgomery Ln.
PO Box 31220
Bethesda, MD 20824-1220
Ph: (301)652-2682   Fax: (301)652-7711
Fr: 800-377-8555
URL: http://www.aota.org

Semimonthly. Professional magazine for occupational therapy practitioners.

★8755★ **Physical and Occupational Therapy in Pediatrics**
The Haworth Press Inc.
10 Alice St.
Binghamton, NY 13904
Ph: (607)722-5857   Fr: 800-429-6784
URL: http://www.haworthpress.com/store/product.asp?sid=RGDXP14RA

Quarterly. $75.00/year for U.S., individual; $109.00/year for Canada, individual; $116.00/year for other countries, individual; $640.00/year for institutions, agency, library; $928.00/year for institutions, Canada, agency, library; $992.00/year for institutions, other countries, agency, library. Journal for therapists involved in developmental and physical rehabilitation of infants and children.

★8756★ **Teaching Exceptional Children**
Council for Exceptional Children
1110 N Glebe Rd., Ste. 300
Arlington, VA 22201-5704
Ph: (703)620-3660   Fax: (703)264-9494
Fr: 888-232-7733
E-mail: tec@bc.edu
URL: http://www.cec.sped.org

Bimonthly. $135.00/year for individuals; $250.00 for two years; $145.00 for two years, Canada; $270.00 for two years, Canada; $165.00/year for out of country, foreign-air printed matter; $310.00/year for out of country, two years, foreign-air printed matter; $25.00/year for institutions, single copy; $170.00/year for institutions; $290.00 for two years, institutional. Journal exploring practical methods for teaching students who have exceptionalities and those who are gifted and talented.

PLACEMENT AND JOB REFERRAL SERVICES

★8757★ American Public Health Association (APHA)

800 I St. NW
Washington, DC 20001
Ph: (202)777-2742   Fax: (202)777-2534
E-mail: comments@apha.org
URL: http://www.apha.org

Members: Professional organization of physicians, nurses, educators, academicians, environmentalists, epidemiologists, new professionals, social workers, health administrators, optometrists, podiatrists, pharmacists, dentists, nutritionists, health planners, other community and mental health specialists, and interested consumers. **Purpose:** Seeks to protect and promote personal, mental, and environmental health. **Activities:** Services include: promulgation of standards; establishment of uniform practices and procedures; development of the etiology of communicable diseases; research in public health; exploration of medical care programs and their relationships to public health. Sponsors job placement service.

EMPLOYER DIRECTORIES AND NETWORKING LISTS

★8758★ AHA Guide to the Health Care Field

American Hospital Association
1 N Franklin
Chicago, IL 60606
Ph: (312)422-2050   Fax: (312)422-4700
Fr: 800-424-4301

Annual, August. Covers hospitals, networks, multi-health care systems, freestanding ambulatory surgery centers, psychiatric facilities, long-term care facilities, substance abuse programs, and other health-related organizations. Entries include: For hospitals–Facility name, address, phone, administrator's name, number of beds, facilities and services, number of employees, expenses, other statistics. For other organizations–Name, address, phone, fax, name and title of contact. Arrangement: Geographical. Indexes: Hospital name.

★8759★ Careers in Focus:Therapists

Facts On File Inc.
132 W 31st St., 17th Fl.
New York, NY 10001
Ph: (212)967-8800   Fax: 800-678-3633
Fr: 800-322-8755

URL: http://www.factsonfile.com

Published 2003. $29.95 for individuals; $26.95 for libraries. Covers an overview of therapists, followed by a selection of jobs profiled in detail, including the nature of the job, earnings, prospects for employment, what kind of training and skills it requires, and sources for further information.

★8760★ Directory of Hospital Personnel

Grey House Publishing
185 Millerton Rd.
PO Box 860
Millerton, NY 12546
Ph: (518)789-8700   Fax: (518)789-0556
Fr: 800-562-2139
URL: http://www.greyhouse.com/hospital_personnel.htm

Annual. $325.00 for print product; $545.00 for online database subscription; $650.00 for online database subscription and print product combined. Covers 200,000 executives at 7,000 U.S. hospitals. Entries include: Name of hospital, address, phone; number of beds; type and JCAHO status of hospital; names and titles of key department heads and staff; medical and nursing school affiliations; number of residents, interns, and nursing students. Arrangement: Geographical. Indexes: Hospital name, personnel, hospital size.

★8761★ Hospital Blue Book

Billian Publishing Inc./Transworld Publishing Inc.
2100 Powers Ferry Rd. SE
Atlanta, GA 30339
Ph: (770)955-5656   Fax: (770)952-0669
Fr: 800-533-8484
E-mail: blu-book@billian.com

2005. $300.00 for individuals. Covers more than 6,687 hospitals; some listings also appear in a separate southern edition of this publication. Entries include: Name of hospital, accreditation, mailing address, phone, fax, number of beds, type of facility (nonprofit, general, state, etc.); list of administrative personnel and chiefs of medical services, with specific titles. Arrangement: Geographical.

★8762★ The JobBank Guide to Health Care Companies

Adams Media Corp.
57 Littlefield St.
Avon, MA 02322
Ph: (508)427-7100   Fax: (508)427-6790
Fr: 800-872-5627
URL: http://www.amazon.com/Jobbank-Guide-Health-Care-Companies/dp

Biennial. Covers jobs nationwide in health care companies. Entries include: Firm or organization name, address, phone, name and title of contact; description of organization, headquarters location, typical titles for entry- and middle-level positions, educational backgrounds desired, fringe benefits offered, stock exchange listing, training programs, internships, parent company, number of employees, revenues, e-mail and web

addresses, projected number of hires. Indexes: Alphabetical.

★8763★ Medical and Health Information Directory

Gale, Cengage Learning
27500 Drake Rd.
Farmington Hills, MI 48331-3535
Ph: (248)699-4253   Fax: (248)699-8065
Fr: 800-877-4253
E-mail: businessproducts@gale.com
URL: http://www.gale.com

Annual; latest edition 20th, July 2007. $375.00/volume. Covers in Volume 1, more than 26,500 medical and health oriented associations, organizations, institutions, and government agencies, including health maintenance organizations (HMOs), preferred provider organizations (PPOs), insurance companies, pharmaceutical companies, research centers, and medical and allied health schools. In Volume 2, over 12,000 medical book publishers; medical periodicals, directories, audiovisual producers and services, medical libraries and information centers, electronic resources, and health-related internet search engines. In Volume 3, more than 35,500 clinics, treatment centers, care programs, and counseling/diagnostic services for 34 subject areas. Entries include: Institution, service, or firm name, address, phone, fax, email and URL; many include names of key personnel and, when pertinent, descriptive annotations. Volume 3 was formerly listed separately as Health Services Directory. Arrangement: Classified by organization activity, service, etc. Indexes: Each volume has a complete alphabetical name and keyword index.

HANDBOOKS AND MANUALS

★8764★ Careers in Health Care

The McGraw-Hill Companies
PO Box 182604
Columbus, OH 43272
Fax: (614)759-3749   Fr: 877-883-5524
E-mail: customer.service@mcgraw-hill.com
URL: http://www.mcgraw-hill.com

Barbara M. Swanson. Fifth edition, 2005. $15.95 (paper). 192 pages. Describes job duties, work settings, salaries, licensing and certification requirements, educational preparation, and future outlook. Gives ideas on how to secure a job.

★8765★ Careers for Health Nuts and Others Who Like to Stay Fit

The McGraw-Hill Companies
PO Box 182604
Columbus, OH 43272
Fax: (614)759-3749   Fr: 877-883-5524
E-mail: customer.service@mcgraw-hill.com
URL: http://www.mcgraw-hill.com

Blythe Camenson. Second edition, 2005. $13.95 (paper). 208 pages.

★8766★ **Careers in Social and Rehabilitation Services**

The McGraw-Hill Companies
PO Box 182604
Columbus, OH 43272
Fax: (614)759-3749   Fr: 877-883-5524
E-mail: customer.service@mcgraw-hill.com
URL: http://www.mcgraw-hill.com

Geraldine O. Garner. 2001. $19.95; 14.95 (paper). 128 pages.

★8767★ **Opportunities in Fitness Careers**

The McGraw-Hill Companies
PO Box 182604
Columbus, OH 43272
Fax: (614)759-3749   Fr: 877-883-5524
E-mail: customer.service@mcgraw-hill.com
URL: http://www.mcgraw-hill.com

Mary Miller. 2003. $12.95 (paper). 146 pages. Surveys fitness related careers. Describes career opportunities, education and experience needed, how to get into entry-level jobs and what income to expect. Schools are listed in the appendix.

★8768★ **Opportunities in Health and Medical Careers**

The McGraw-Hill Companies
PO Box 182604
Columbus, OH 43272
Fax: (614)759-3749   Fr: 877-883-5524
E-mail: customer.service@mcgraw-hill.com
URL: http://www.mcgraw-hill.com

I. Donald Snook, Jr. and Leo D'Orazio. 2004. $13.95 (paper). 157 pages. Covers the full range of medical and health occupations. Illustrated.

★8769★ **Opportunities in Occupational Therapy Careers**

The McGraw-Hill Companies
PO Box 182604
Columbus, OH 43272
Fax: (614)759-3749   Fr: 877-883-5524
E-mail: customer.service@mcgraw-hill.com
URL: http://www.mcgraw-hill.com

Zona R. Weeks, Marie Louise Franciscus, and Marguerite Abbott. 2006. $13.95. 160 pages. Provides an overview of opportunities in clinical positions, government and non-profit agencies, rehabilitation centers, hospices, and other areas, and provides job-hunting guidance. Illustrated.

★8770★ **Opportunities in Paramedical Careers**

The McGraw-Hill Companies
PO Box 182604
Columbus, OH 43272
Fax: (614)759-3749   Fr: 877-883-5524
E-mail: customer.service@mcgraw-hill.com
URL: http://www.mcgraw-hill.com

Alex Kacen. 1999. 14.95 (hardcover). 160 pages. Discusses a variety of opportunities in this field and how to pursue them. Illustrated.

★8771★ **Real People Working in Health Care**

The McGraw-Hill Companies
PO Box 182604
Columbus, OH 43272
Fax: (614)759-3749   Fr: 877-883-5524
E-mail: customer.service@mcgraw-hill.com
URL: http://www.mcgraw-hill.com

Blythe Camenson, Jan Goldberg. 1996. $12.95 (paper). 144 pages. Interviews and profiles of working professionals capture a range of opportunities in this field.

★8772★ **Real People Working in the Helping Professions**

The McGraw-Hill Companies
PO Box 182604
Columbus, OH 43272
Fax: (614)759-3749   Fr: 877-883-5524
E-mail: customer.service@mcgraw-hill.com
URL: http://www.mcgraw-hill.com

Blythe Camenson, Jan Goldberg. 1997. $12.95 (paper). 192 pages. Interviews and profiles of working professionals capture a range of opportunities in this field.

EMPLOYMENT AGENCIES AND SEARCH FIRMS

★8773★ **Cross Country TravCorps**

6551 Park of Commerce Blvd.
Boca Raton, FL 33487-8247
Fax: (562)998-8533   Fr: 800-530-6125
URL: http://www.crosscountrytravcorps.com

Places traveling nurses in assignments nationwide.

★8774★ **Harper Associates**

3100 NW Hwy., Ste. 240
Farmington Hills, MI 48334
Ph: (248)932-1170   Fax: (248)932-1214
E-mail: info@harperjobs.com
URL: http://www.harperjobs.com

Executive search firm and employment agency.

★8775★ **J.B. Brown and Associates**

820 Terminal Twr.
Cleveland, OH 44113
Ph: (216)696-2525   Fax: (216)696-5825

Employment agency and executive recruiter.

★8776★ **JPM International**

26034 Acero
Mission Viejo, CA 92691
Ph: (949)699-4300   Fax: (949)699-4333
Fr: 800-685-7856
E-mail: trish@jpmintl.com
URL: http://www.jpmintl.com

Executive search firm and employment agency.

★8777★ **Professional Placement Associates, Inc.**

287 Bowman Ave., Ste. 309
Purchase, NY 10577-2517
Ph: (914)251-1000   Fax: (914)251-1055
E-mail: careers@ppasearch.com
URL: http://www.ppasearch.com

Executive search firm specializing in the health and medical field.

ONLINE JOB SOURCES AND SERVICES

★8778★ **Medhunters.com**
Fr: 800-664-0278
E-mail: info@medhunters.com
URL: http://www.medhunters.com

Description: Career search site for jobs in all health care specialties; educational resources; visa and licensing information for relocation; interesting articles; relocation tools; links to professional organizations and general resources.

★8779★ **Medzilla**
URL: http://www.medzilla.com

Description: General medical website which matches employers and job hunters to their ideal employees and jobs through search capabilities. **Main files include:** Post Jobs, Search Resumes, Post Resumes, Search Jobs, Head Hunters, Articles, Salary Survey.

★8780★ **ProHealthJobs**
Fr: 800-796-1738
E-mail: Info@prohealthedujobs.com
URL: http://www.prohealthjobs.com

Description: Career resources site for the medical and health care field. Lists professional opportunities, product information, continuing education and open positions.

★8781★ **RehabJobs Online**
PO Box 480536
Los Angeles, CA 90048
Ph: (213)938-7718   Fax: (213)938-9609
Fr: 800-43-REHAB
E-mail: support@atsrehabjobs.com
URL: http://www.rehabjobs.com

Description: Resource center for the professional therapist. **Main files include:** Therapists Only, Therapy Forums, Nationwide Job Search (database), Therapy Job Outlook, Therapy Job Search Utilities, Therapy Links, Information for Employers and Recruiters.

★8782★ **RehabWorld**
URL: http://www.rehabworld.com

Description: Site for rehabilitation professionals to learn about the profession and locate jobs. Includes user groups, salary surveys, and chat capabilities. **Main files include:** Physical Therapy, Occupational Therapy, Speech Therapy, Mental Health, Employer World, Student World, International World, Forum.

TRADESHOWS

★8783★ American Occupational Health Conference & Exhibits

Slack, Inc.
6900 Grove Rd.
Thorofare, NJ 08086-9447
Ph: (856)848-1000   Fax: (856)853-5991
URL: http://www.slackinc.com

Annual. **Primary Exhibits:** Pharmaceuticals, medical equipment, computer software packages for medical offices, lab services, diagnostic testing, and EAP's., ergonomics, environmental products and services. **Dates and Locations:** 2008 Apr 13-16; New York, NY; Marriott Marquis.

★8784★ American Society of Hand Therapists and American Society for Surgery of the Hand Annual Meeting

Smith, Bucklin and Associates, Inc.
 (Chicago)
401 N Michigan Ave.
Chicago, IL 60611-4267
Ph: (312)321-6610   Fax: (312)673-6670
Fr: 800-289-NAON
E-mail: info@smithbucklin.com
URL: http://www.smithbucklin.com

Annual. **Primary Exhibits:** Hand therapy equipment and products.

★8785★ National Rehabilitation Association Annual Training Conference and Exhibit

National Rehabilitation Association
633 S Washington St.
Alexandria, VA 22314-4109
Ph: (703)836-0850   Fax: (703)836-0848
E-mail: info@nationalrehab.org
URL: http://www.nationalrehab.org

Annual. **Primary Exhibits:** Rehabilitation equipment, supplies, and services, educational computer systems for the disabled, cars and vans featuring accessible equipment.

★8786★ Occupational Therapy Association of California Conference

Occupational Therapy Association of
 California
1401 El Camino Ave., Ste. 230
Sacramento, CA 95815
Ph: (916)567-7000   Fax: (916)567-7001
E-mail: info@otaconline.org
URL: http://www.otaconline.org

Annual. **Primary Exhibits:** Occupational therapy equipment, supplies, and services.

OTHER SOURCES

★8787★ American Almanac of Jobs and Salaries

HarperCollins
10 E. 53rd St.
New York, NY 10022
Ph: (212)207-7000   Fr: 800-242-7737
URL: http://www.harpercollins.com/

John W. Wright. Revised edition, 2000. $20.00 (paper). 672 pages. This is a comprehensive guide to the wages of hundreds of occupations in a wide variety of industries and organizations.

★8788★ American Health Care Association (AHCA)

1201 L St. NW
Washington, DC 20005
Ph: (202)842-4444   Fax: (202)842-3860
E-mail: hr@ahca.org
URL: http://www.ahca.org

Description: Federation of state associations of long-term health care facilities. Promotes standards for professionals in long-term health care delivery and quality care for patients and residents in a safe environment. Focuses on issues of availability, quality, affordability, and fair payment. Operates as liaison with governmental agencies, Congress, and professional associations. Compiles statistics.

★8789★ American Kinesiotherapy Association (AKTA)

118 College Dr., No. 5142
Hattiesburg, MS 39406
Fr: 800-296-AKTA
E-mail: info@akta.org
URL: http://www.akta.org

Members: Professional society of kinesiotherapists, associate and student members with interest in therapeutic exercise and education. Kinesiotherapy is the application of scientifically-based exercise principles adapted to enhance the strength, endurance and mobility of individuals with functional limitations of those requiring extended physical reconditioning. Seeks to serve the interest of members and represent the profession to the public through the promotion of continuing competency and continuing educational opportunities.

★8790★ American Occupational Therapy Association (AOTA)

4720 Montgomery Ln.
PO Box 31220
Bethesda, MD 20824-1220
Ph: (301)652-2682   Fax: (301)652-7711
Fr: 800-377-8555
E-mail: execdept@aota.org
URL: http://www.aota.org

Members: Occupational therapists and occupational therapy assistants. **Purpose:** Provides services to people whose lives have been disrupted by physical injury or illness, developmental problems, the aging

process, or social or psychological difficulties. Occupational therapy focuses on the active involvement of the patient in specially designed therapeutic tasks and activities to improve function, performance capacity, and the ability to cope with demands of daily living.

★8791★ American Society of Hand Therapists (ASHT)

401 N Michigan Ave.
Chicago, IL 60611-4267
Ph: (312)321-6866   Fax: (312)673-6670
E-mail: info@asht.org
URL: http://www.asht.org

Members: Registered and licensed occupational and physical therapists specializing in hand therapy and committed to excellence and professionalism in hand rehabilitation. **Purpose:** Works to promote research, publish information, improve treatment techniques, and standardize hand evaluation and care. Fosters education and communication between therapists in the U.S. and abroad. **Activities:** Compiles statistics; conducts research and education programs and continuing education seminars.

★8792★ Association on Higher Education and Disability (AHEAD)

107 Commerce Center Dr., Ste. 204
Huntersville, NC 28078
Ph: (704)947-7779   Fax: (704)948-7779
E-mail: ahead@ahead.org
URL: http://www.ahead.org

Description: Individuals interested in promoting the equal rights and opportunities of disabled postsecondary students, staff, faculty, and graduates. Provides an exchange of communication for those professionally involved with disabled students; collects, evaluates, and disseminates information; encourages and supports legislation for the benefit of disabled students. Conducts surveys on issues pertinent to college students with disabilities; offers resource referral system and employment exchange for positions in disability student services. Conducts research programs; compiles statistics.

★8793★ EMTs, Nurses, Therapists, and Assistants

Cambridge Educational
PO Box 2053
Princeton, NJ 08543-2053
Ph: 800-257-5126   Fax: (609)671-0266
Fr: 800-468-4227
E-mail: custserv@films.com
URL: http://www.cambridgeeducational.com

VHS and DVD. $79.95. 2000. 18 minutes. Part of the series "Exploring Health Occupations."

★8794★ Exploring Health Occupations

Cambridge Educational
PO Box 2053
Princeton, NJ 08543-2053
Ph: 800-257-5126   Fax: (609)671-0266
Fr: 800-468-4227

E-mail: custserv@films.com
URL: http://www.cambridgeeducational.com
VHS and DVD. $159.90. 1999. Two-part series provides a detailed view of the field of medical technicians and technologists, EMTs, nurses, therapists, and assistants.

★8795★ **Health Assessment & Treating Occupations**
Delphi Productions
3159 6th St.
Boulder, CO 80304
Ph: (303)443-2100   Fax: (303)443-4022
Fr: 888-443-2400
E-mail: support@delphivideo.com
URL: http://www.delphivideo.com
$95.00. 50 minutes. Part of the Careers for the 21st Century Video Library.

★8796★ **Health Service Occupations**
Delphi Productions
3159 6th St.
Boulder, CO 80304
Ph: (303)443-2100   Fax: (303)443-4022
Fr: 888-443-2400
E-mail: support@delphivideo.com
URL: http://www.delphivideo.com
$95.00. 50 minutes. Part of the Careers for the 21st Century Video Library.

★8797★ **Medicine & Related Occupations**
Delphi Productions
3159 6th St.
Boulder, CO 80304
Ph: (303)443-2100   Fax: (303)443-4022
Fr: 888-443-2400
E-mail: support@delphivideo.com
URL: http://www.delphivideo.com

$95.00. 45 minutes. Part of the Careers for the 21st Century Video Library.

★8798★ **National Board for Certification in Occupational Therapy (NBCOT)**
The Eugene B. Casey Bldg.
800 S Frederick Ave., Ste. 200
Gaithersburg, MD 20877-4150
Ph: (301)990-7979   Fax: (301)869-8492
E-mail: info@nbcot.org
URL: http://www.nbcot.org

Members: Participants are occupational therapists and occupational therapy assistants. **Activities:** Administers certification program and maintains certification records of certificants; operates disciplinary mechanisms.

★8799★ **National Rehabilitation Association (NRA)**
633 S Washington St.
Alexandria, VA 22314
Ph: (703)836-0850   Fax: (703)836-0848
E-mail: info@nationalrehab.org
URL: http://www.nationalrehab.org/website/index.html

Description: Provides opportunities through knowledge and diversity for professionals in the fields of rehabilitation of people with disabilities.

★8800★ **Neuro-Developmental Treatment Association (NDTA)**
1540 S Coast Hwy., Ste. 203
Laguna Beach, CA 92651
Fax: (949)376-3456   Fr: 800-869-9295
E-mail: info@ndta.org
URL: http://www.ndta.org

Members: Physical and occupational therapists, speech pathologists, special educators, physicians, parents, and others interested in neurodevelopmental treatment. (NDT is a form of therapy for individuals who suffer from central nervous system disorders resulting in abnormal movement. Treatment attempts to initiate or refine normal stages and processes in the development of movement.) **Purpose:** Informs members of new developments in the field and with ideas that will eventually improve fundamental independence. **Activities:** Locates articles related to NDT.

★8801★ **Project Magic (PM)**
3707 SW 6th Ave.
Topeka, KS 66606
Ph: (785)270-4610   Fax: (785)232-8545
Fr: 888-221-8199
URL: http://www.dcopperfield.com

Description: Provides information and facilitates communication between magicians, occupational therapists, and patients with physical, psychosocial, and developmental disabilities. Created by television magician David Copperfield, the project works to rehabilitate patients by teaching them magic tricks instead of, or in addition to, traditional therapy techniques. Seeks to motivate patients to develop new skills and improve their self-image by demonstrating magical tricks. Tricks such as sleight-of-hand teach physical dexterity and mental puzzles help people to improve memory, concentration, and the ability to think sequentially. Provides interested magicians and occupational therapists with information and written material on the therapeutic value of magic for disabled persons. Sponsors educational seminars and workshops for rehabilitation facilities and health professionals.

Occupational Therapy Assistants and Aides

SOURCES OF HELP-WANTED ADS

★8802★ ADVANCE for Occupational Therapy Practitioners

Merion Publications Inc.
2900 Horizon Dr.
PO Box 61556
King of Prussia, PA 19406
Ph: (610)278-1400   Fr: 800-355-5627
E-mail: advance@merion.com
URL: http://www.advanceforot.com

Biweekly. Serves licensed and registered occupational therapists, certified occupational therapy assistants, and senior OT students nationwide.

★8803★ The American Journal of Occupational Therapy

American Occupational Therapy
  Association Inc.
4720 Montgomery Ln.
PO Box 31220
Bethesda, MD 20824-1220
Ph: (301)652-2682   Fax: (301)652-7711
Fr: 800-377-8555
E-mail: ajotsis@aota.org
URL: http://www.aota.org/

Bimonthly. $114.00/year for individuals, U.S.; $182.00/year for institutions, U.S.; $159.75/year for individuals, Canada; $214.00/year for institutions, Canada; $285.00/year for individuals, foreign (via airmail); $310.00/year for institutions, foreign (via airmail). Journal providing a forum for occupational therapy personnel to share research, case studies, and new theory.

★8804★ American Journal of Physical Medicine and Rehabilitation

Lippincott Williams & Wilkins
530 Walnut St.
Philadelphia, PA 19106-3621
Ph: (215)521-8300   Fax: (215)521-8902
Fr: 800-638-3030
E-mail: jmulliga@lww.com
URL: http://www.amjphysmedrehab.com/

Monthly. Medical journal.

★8805★ Occupational Therapy in Health Care

The Haworth Press Inc.
10 Alice St.
Binghamton, NY 13904
Ph: (607)722-5857   Fr: 800-429-6784
URL: http://www.haworthpress.com/store/product.asp?sid=31TPBXNBB

Quarterly. $109.00/year for individuals; $159.00/year for Canada, individual; $168.00/year for other countries, individual; $420.00/year for institutions, agency, library; $601.00/year for institutions, Canada, agency, library; $639.00/year for institutions, other countries, agency, library. Journal for occupational therapists.

★8806★ Occupational Therapy in Mental Health

The Haworth Press Inc.
10 Alice St.
Binghamton, NY 13904
Ph: (607)722-5857   Fr: 800-429-6784
E-mail: info@haworthpress.com
URL: http://www.haworthpress.com/store/product.asp?sid=3CXTKNPDX

Quarterly. $60.00/year for individuals; $465.00/year for institutions, agency, library; $87.00/year for Canada, individual; $674.00/year for institutions, Canada, agency, library; $93.00/year for other countries, individual; $721.00/year for institutions, other countries, agency, library. Journal for occupational therapists working in the mental health field.

★8807★ OT Practice

American Occupational Therapy
  Association Inc.
4720 Montgomery Ln.
PO Box 31220
Bethesda, MD 20824-1220
Ph: (301)652-2682   Fax: (301)652-7711
Fr: 800-377-8555
URL: http://www.aota.org

Semimonthly. Professional magazine for occupational therapy practitioners.

★8808★ Physical & Occupational Therapy in Geriatrics

The Haworth Press Inc.
10 Alice St.
Binghamton, NY 13904
Ph: (607)722-5857   Fr: 800-429-6784
URL: http://www.haworthpress.com

Quarterly. $99.00/year for individuals; $145.00/year for Canada, individual; $152.00/year for other countries, individual; $660.00/year for institutions, agency, library; $949.00/year for institutions, Canada, agency, library; $1,011.00/year for institutions, other countries, agency, library. Journal for allied health professionals focusing on current practice and emerging issues in the health care of and rehabilitation of the older client.

★8809★ Physical and Occupational Therapy in Pediatrics

The Haworth Press Inc.
10 Alice St.
Binghamton, NY 13904
Ph: (607)722-5857   Fr: 800-429-6784
URL: http://www.haworthpress.com/store/product.asp?sid=RGDXP14RA

Quarterly. $75.00/year for U.S., individual; $109.00/year for Canada, individual; $116.00/year for other countries, individual; $640.00/year for institutions, agency, library; $928.00/year for institutions, Canada, agency, library; $992.00/year for institutions, other countries, agency, library. Journal for therapists involved in developmental and physical rehabilitation of infants and children.

EMPLOYER DIRECTORIES AND NETWORKING LISTS

★8810★ Careers in Focus:Therapists

Facts On File Inc.
132 W 31st St., 17th Fl.
New York, NY 10001
Ph: (212)967-8800   Fax: 800-678-3633
Fr: 800-322-8755
URL: http://www.factsonfile.com

Published 2003. $29.95 for individuals; $26.95 for libraries. Covers an overview of therapists, followed by a selection of jobs profiled in detail, including the nature of the job, earnings, prospects for employment, what kind of training and skills it requires, and sources for further information.

★8811★ **Health Professions Career and Education Directory**
American Medical Association
515 N State St.
Chicago, IL 60610
Fr: 800-621-8335
E-mail: dorothy-grant@ama-assn.org
URL: http://www.ama-assn.org

Annual; latest edition 2007-2008. $52.50 for members; $70.00 for nonmembers. Covers more than 6,500 health career educational programs in over 64 health occupations at 2,800 sponsoring institutions. Entries include: Occupational descriptions, employment characteristics, and information on education programs, such as length, curriculum, and prerequisites. Arrangement: Classified by occupation, then geographical. Indexes: Institution name, program name.

★8812★ **The JobBank Guide to Health Care Companies**
Adams Media Corp.
57 Littlefield St.
Avon, MA 02322
Ph: (508)427-7100   Fax: (508)427-6790
Fr: 800-872-5627
URL: http://www.amazon.com/Jobbank-Guide-Health-Care-Companies/dp

Biennial. Covers jobs nationwide in health care companies. Entries include: Firm or organization name, address, phone, name and title of contact; description of organization, headquarters location, typical titles for entry- and middle-level positions, educational backgrounds desired, fringe benefits offered, stock exchange listing, training programs, internships, parent company, number of employees, revenues, e-mail and web addresses, projected number of hires. Indexes: Alphabetical.

★8813★ **Occupational Therapy Educational Programs List**
American Occupational Therapy Association Inc.
4720 Montgomery Ln.
PO Box 31220
Bethesda, MD 20824-1220
Ph: (301)652-2682   Fax: (301)652-7711
Fr: 800-377-8555
E-mail: accred@aota.org
URL: http://www.aota.org

Database covers: Approximately 150 accredited, developing, and applicant programs in occupational therapy and 149 accredited, developing, and applicant occupational therapy assistant programs. Database includes: Institution name, address, phone, URL, level of program. Telecommunications Device for the Deaf, 800-377-8555. Arrangement: Geographical, then classified by educational institution. Separate listings for accredited, developing, and applicant OT and OTA programs.

HANDBOOKS AND MANUALS

★8814★ **Careers for Health Nuts and Others Who Like to Stay Fit**
The McGraw-Hill Companies
PO Box 182604
Columbus, OH 43272
Fax: (614)759-3749   Fr: 877-883-5524
E-mail: customer.service@mcgraw-hill.com
URL: http://www.mcgraw-hill.com

Blythe Camenson. Second edition, 2005. $13.95 (paper). 208 pages.

★8815★ **Careers Inside the World of Health Care**
Pearson Learning Group
135 S. Mt. Zion Rd.
PO Box 2500
Lebanon, IN 46052
Fax: 800-393-3156   Fr: 800-526-9907
URL: http://www.pearsonatschool.com

Beth Wilkinson. Revised edition, 1999. $21.30. 64 pages.

★8816★ **Careers in Social and Rehabilitation Services**
The McGraw-Hill Companies
PO Box 182604
Columbus, OH 43272
Fax: (614)759-3749   Fr: 877-883-5524
E-mail: customer.service@mcgraw-hill.com
URL: http://www.mcgraw-hill.com

Geraldine O. Garner. 2001. $19.95; 14.95 (paper). 128 pages.

★8817★ **Opportunities in Health and Medical Careers**
The McGraw-Hill Companies
PO Box 182604
Columbus, OH 43272
Fax: (614)759-3749   Fr: 877-883-5524
E-mail: customer.service@mcgraw-hill.com
URL: http://www.mcgraw-hill.com

I. Donald Snook, Jr. and Leo D'Orazio. 2004. $13.95 (paper). 157 pages. Covers the full range of medical and health occupations. Illustrated.

★8818★ **Opportunities in Occupational Therapy Careers**
The McGraw-Hill Companies
PO Box 182604
Columbus, OH 43272
Fax: (614)759-3749   Fr: 877-883-5524
E-mail: customer.service@mcgraw-hill.com
URL: http://www.mcgraw-hill.com

Zona R. Weeks, Marie Louise Franciscus, and Marguerite Abbott. 2006. $13.95. 160 pages. Provides an overview of opportunities in clinical positions, government and non-profit agencies, rehabilitation centers, hospices, and other areas, and provides job-hunting guidance. Illustrated.

★8819★ **Real People Working in Health Care**
The McGraw-Hill Companies
PO Box 182604
Columbus, OH 43272
Fax: (614)759-3749   Fr: 877-883-5524
E-mail: customer.service@mcgraw-hill.com
URL: http://www.mcgraw-hill.com

Blythe Camenson, Jan Goldberg. 1996. $12.95 (paper). 144 pages. Interviews and profiles of working professionals capture a range of opportunities in this field.

★8820★ **Real People Working in the Helping Professions**
The McGraw-Hill Companies
PO Box 182604
Columbus, OH 43272
Fax: (614)759-3749   Fr: 877-883-5524
E-mail: customer.service@mcgraw-hill.com
URL: http://www.mcgraw-hill.com

Blythe Camenson, Jan Goldberg. 1997. $12.95 (paper). 192 pages. Interviews and profiles of working professionals capture a range of opportunities in this field.

★8821★ **Resumes for the Health Care Professional**
John Wiley & Sons Inc.
1 Wiley Dr.
Somerset, NJ 08873
Ph: (732)469-4400   Fax: (732)302-2300
Fr: 800-225-5945
E-mail: custserv@wiley.com
URL: http://www.wiley.com/WileyCDA/

Kim Marino. Second edition, 2000. $21.50 (paper). 224 pages.

EMPLOYMENT AGENCIES AND SEARCH FIRMS

★8822★ **Cross Country TravCorps**
6551 Park of Commerce Blvd.
Boca Raton, FL 33487-8247
Fax: (562)998-8533   Fr: 800-530-6125
URL: http://www.crosscountrytravcorps.com

Places traveling nurses in assignments nationwide.

★8823★ **Team Placement Service, Inc.**
1414 Prince St., Ste. 202
Alexandria, VA 22314
Ph: (703)820-8618   Fax: (703)820-3368
Fr: 800-495-6767
E-mail: 4jobs@teamplace.com
URL: http://www.teamplace.com

Full-service personnel consultants provide

placement for healthcare staff, physician and dentist, private practice, and hospitals. Conduct interviews, tests, and reference checks to select the top 20% of applicants. Survey applicants' skill levels, provide backup information on each candidate, select compatible candidates for consideration, and insure the hiring process minimizes potential legal liability. Industries served: healthcare and government agencies providing medical, dental, biotech, laboratory, hospitals, and physician search.

ONLINE JOB SOURCES AND SERVICES

★8824★ RehabJobs Online
PO Box 480536
Los Angeles, CA 90048
Ph: (213)938-7718   Fax: (213)938-9609
Fr: 800-43-REHAB
E-mail: support@atsrehabjobs.com
URL: http://www.rehabjobs.com

Description: Resource center for the professional therapist. **Main files include:** Therapists Only, Therapy Forums, Nationwide Job Search (database), Therapy Job Outlook, Therapy Job Search Utilities, Therapy Links, Information for Employers and Recruiters.

★8825★ RehabWorld
URL: http://www.rehabworld.com

Description: Site for rehabilitation professionals to learn about the profession and locate jobs. Includes user groups, salary surveys, and chat capabilities. **Main files include:** Physical Therapy, Occupational Therapy, Speech Therapy, Mental Health, Employer World, Student World, International World, Forum.

TRADESHOWS

★8826★ American Society of Hand Therapists and American Society for Surgery of the Hand Annual Meeting
Smith, Bucklin and Associates, Inc. (Chicago)
401 N Michigan Ave.
Chicago, IL 60611-4267
Ph: (312)321-6610   Fax: (312)673-6670
Fr: 800-289-NAON
E-mail: info@smithbucklin.com
URL: http://www.smithbucklin.com

Annual. **Primary Exhibits:** Hand therapy equipment and products.

★8827★ Occupational Therapy Association of California Conference
Occupational Therapy Association of California
1401 El Camino Ave., Ste. 230
Sacramento, CA 95815
Ph: (916)567-7000   Fax: (916)567-7001
E-mail: info@otaconline.org
URL: http://www.otaconline.org

Annual. **Primary Exhibits:** Occupational therapy equipment, supplies, and services.

OTHER SOURCES

★8828★ American Occupational Therapy Association (AOTA)
4720 Montgomery Ln.
PO Box 31220
Bethesda, MD 20824-1220
Ph: (301)652-2682   Fax: (301)652-7711
Fr: 800-377-8555
E-mail: execdept@aota.org
URL: http://www.aota.org

Members: Occupational therapists and occupational therapy assistants. **Purpose:** Provides services to people whose lives have been disrupted by physical injury or illness, developmental problems, the aging process, or social or psychological difficulties. Occupational therapy focuses on the active involvement of the patient in specially designed therapeutic tasks and activities to improve function, performance capacity, and the ability to cope with demands of daily living.

★8829★ EMTs, Nurses, Therapists, and Assistants
Cambridge Educational
PO Box 2053
Princeton, NJ 08543-2053
Ph: 800-257-5126   Fax: (609)671-0266
Fr: 800-468-4227
E-mail: custserv@films.com
URL: http://www.cambridgeeducational.com

VHS and DVD. $79.95. 2000. 18 minutes. Part of the series "Exploring Health Occupations."

★8830★ Exploring Health Occupations
Cambridge Educational
PO Box 2053
Princeton, NJ 08543-2053
Ph: 800-257-5126   Fax: (609)671-0266
Fr: 800-468-4227
E-mail: custserv@films.com
URL: http://www.cambridgeeducational.com

VHS and DVD. $159.90. 1999. Two-part series provides a detailed view of the field of medical technicians and technologists, EMTs, nurses, therapists, and assistants.

★8831★ Health Assessment & Treating Occupations
Delphi Productions
3159 6th St.
Boulder, CO 80304
Ph: (303)443-2100   Fax: (303)443-4022
Fr: 888-443-2400
E-mail: support@delphivideo.com
URL: http://www.delphivideo.com

$95.00. 50 minutes. Part of the Careers for the 21st Century Video Library.

★8832★ Health Service Occupations
Delphi Productions
3159 6th St.
Boulder, CO 80304
Ph: (303)443-2100   Fax: (303)443-4022
Fr: 888-443-2400
E-mail: support@delphivideo.com
URL: http://www.delphivideo.com

$95.00. 50 minutes. Part of the Careers for the 21st Century Video Library.

★8833★ Medicine & Related Occupations
Delphi Productions
3159 6th St.
Boulder, CO 80304
Ph: (303)443-2100   Fax: (303)443-4022
Fr: 888-443-2400
E-mail: support@delphivideo.com
URL: http://www.delphivideo.com

$95.00. 45 minutes. Part of the Careers for the 21st Century Video Library.

★8834★ National Board for Certification in Occupational Therapy (NBCOT)
The Eugene B. Casey Bldg.
800 S Frederick Ave., Ste. 200
Gaithersburg, MD 20877-4150
Ph: (301)990-7979   Fax: (301)869-8492
E-mail: info@nbcot.org
URL: http://www.nbcot.org

Members: Participants are occupational therapists and occupational therapy assistants. **Activities:** Administers certification program and maintains certification records of certificants; operates disciplinary mechanisms.

★8835★ Neuro-Developmental Treatment Association (NDTA)
1540 S Coast Hwy., Ste. 203
Laguna Beach, CA 92651
Fax: (949)376-3456   Fr: 800-869-9295
E-mail: info@ndta.org
URL: http://www.ndta.org

Members: Physical and occupational therapists, speech pathologists, special educators, physicians, parents, and others interested in neurodevelopmental treatment. (NDT is a form of therapy for individuals who suffer from central nervous system disorders resulting in abnormal movement. Treatment attempts to initiate or refine normal stages and processes in the development of movement.) **Purpose:** Informs members of new developments in the field and with ideas that will eventually improve fundamental independence. **Activities:** Locates articles related to NDT.

★8836★ **Project Magic (PM)**
3707 SW 6th Ave.
Topeka, KS 66606
Ph: (785)270-4610   Fax: (785)232-8545
Fr: 888-221-8199

URL: http://www.dcopperfield.com

Description: Provides information and facilitates communication between magicians, occupational therapists, and patients with physical, psychosocial, and developmental disabilities. Created by television magician David Copperfield, the project works to rehabilitate patients by teaching them magic tricks instead of, or in addition to, traditional therapy techniques. Seeks to motivate patients to develop new skills and improve their self-image by demonstrating magical tricks. Tricks such as sleight-of-hand teach physical dexterity and mental puzzles help people to improve memory, concentration, and the ability to think sequentially. Provides interested magicians and occupational therapists with information and written material on the therapeutic value of magic for disabled persons. Sponsors educational seminars and workshops for rehabilitation facilities and health professionals.

Office and Administrative Support Worker Supervisors and Managers

★8837★ Academy of Management Journal

Academy of Management
PO Box 3020
Briarcliff Manor, NY 10510-8020
Ph: (914)923-2607   Fax: (914)923-2615
URL: http://www.aom.pace.edu/amr

Bimonthly. Professional journal covering management.

★8838★ Academy of Management Learning & Education

Academy of Management
PO Box 3020
Briarcliff Manor, NY 10510-8020
Ph: (914)923-2607   Fax: (914)923-2615
URL: http://journals.aomonline.org/amle

Quarterly. $80.00/year for individuals, print; $130.00/year for individuals, print & online; $165.00/year for libraries, print; $215.00/year for libraries, print and online; $100.00/year for individuals, other countries, print; $150.00/year for individuals, other countries, print & online; $185.00/year for other countries, print, corporate library; $235.00/year for other countries, print & online, corporate library. Journal covering management issues for professionals.

★8839★ Business Performance Management

Penton Media Inc.
249 W 17th St.
New York, NY 10011
Ph: (212)204-4200
URL: http://www.bpmmag.net/

Free to qualified subscribers. Magazine for business managers. Covers organizing, automating, and analyzing of business methodologies and processes.

★8840★ CXO

IDG Communications Inc.
5 Speen St., 3rd. Fl
Framingham, MA 01701
Ph: (508)875-5000   Fax: (508)988-7888
URL: http://www.idg.com

Monthly. Magazine providing technology information for chief officers and managers.

★8841★ D & O Advisor

American Lawyer Media L.P.
345 Pk. Ave. S
New York, NY 10010
Ph: (212)779-9200   Fax: (212)481-8110
Fr: 800-888-8300
URL: http://www.alm.com

Quarterly. Magazine that offers advice and perspective on corporate oversight responsibilities for directors and officers.

★8842★ E Journal of Organizational Learning and Leadership

WeLEAD Inc.
PO Box 202
Litchfield, OH 44253
Fr: 877-778-5494
URL: http://www.weleadinlearning.org/ejournal.htm

Continuous. Free. Online academic journal about organizational leadership.

★8843★ Event Management

Cognizant Communications Corp.
3 Hartsdale Rd.
Elmsford, NY 10523-3701
Ph: (914)592-7720   Fax: (914)592-8981
URL: http://www.cognizantcommunication.com/filecabinet/EventManag

Quarterly. $325.00/year for institutions, library; $360.00/year for institutions, rest of the world, library; $585.00/year for institutions, library, 2 years; $648.00/year for institutions, rest if the world, library, 2 years; $45.00/year professional; $52.00/year for other countries, professional. Journal covering research and analytic needs of a rapidly growing profession focused on events.

★8844★ Executive Legal Adviser

American Lawyer Media L.P.
345 Pk. Ave. S
New York, NY 10010
Ph: (212)779-9200   Fax: (212)481-8110
Fr: 800-888-8300
URL: http://www.executivelegaladviser.com

Bimonthly. Free to qualified subscribers. Magazine that offers legal advice for corporate executives.

★8845★ Fleet Maintenance

Cygnus Business Media Inc.
3 Huntington Quadrangle, Ste. 301 N
Melville, NY 11747
Ph: (631)845-2700   Fax: (631)845-7109
Fr: 800-308-6397
URL: http://www.fleetmag.com

Bimonthly. Business tabloid magazine offering a chapterized curriculum of technical, regulatory and managerial information designed to help maintenance managers, directors and supervisors better perform their jobs and reduce their overall cost-per-mile.

★8846★ Forrester

Forrester Research Inc.
400 Technology Sq.
Cambridge, MA 02139
Ph: (617)613-6000   Fax: (617)613-5000
URL: http://www.forrester.com/mag

Free. Journal that aims to provide ideas and advice that are relevant to today's CEOs.

★8847★ International Journal of Business Research

Academy of International Business and Economics
PO Box 2536
Ceres, CA 95307
URL: http://www.aibe.org

Peer-reviewed journal publishing theoretical, conceptual, and applied research on topics related to research, practice and teaching in all areas of business, management, and marketing.

★8848★ Journal of Academic Leadership

Academic Leadership
600 Park St.
Rarick Hall 219
Hays, KS 67601-4099
Ph: (785)628-4547
URL: http://www.academicleadership.org/

Journal focusing on the leadership issues in the academic world.

★8849★ Journal of Business and Psychology

Springer-Verlag New York Inc.
233 Spring St.
New York, NY 10013
Ph: (212)460-1500   Fax: (212)460-1575
URL: http://www.springer.com/journal/10869/

Journal covering all aspects of psychology that apply to the business segment. Includes topics such as personnel selection and training, organizational assessment and development, risk management and loss control, marketing and consumer behavior research.

★8850★ Journal of International Business Strategy

Academy of International Business and Economics
PO Box 2536
Ceres, CA 95307
URL: http://www.AIBE.org

Peer-reviewed journal publishing theoretical, conceptual, and applied research on topics related to strategy in international business.

★8851★ Management Research

M.E. Sharpe Inc.
80 Business Pk. Dr.
Armonk, NY 10504
Ph: (914)273-1800   Fax: (914)273-2106
Fr: 800-541-6563
URL: http://www.mesharpe.com/mall/results1.asp?ACR=JMR

$72.00/year for individuals; $349.00/year for institutions; $84.00/year for other countries, individual; $391.00/year for institutions, other countries. International journal dedicated to advancing the understanding of management in private and public sector organizations through empirical investigation and theoretical analysis. Attempts to promote an international dialogue between researchers, improve the understanding of the nature of management in different settings, and achieve a reasonable transfer of research results to management practice in several contexts. Receptive to research across a broad range of management topics such as human resource management, organizational behavior, organizational theory, and strategic management. While not regional in nature, articles dealing with Iberoamerican issues are particularly welcomed.

★8852★ OfficePRO

Stratton Publishing and Marketing Inc.
5285 Shawnee Rd., Ste. 510
Alexandria, VA 22312-2334
Ph: (703)914-9200   Fax: (703)914-6777

Magazine for administrative assistants, office managers, and secretaries featuring information on trends in business, technology, career development, and management.

★8853★ Organization Management Journal

Eastern Academy of Management
c/o Craig Tunwall, VP
Empire State College
2805 State Hwy. 67
Johnstown, NY 12095
Ph: (518)762-4651   Fax: (518)736-1716
URL: http://www1.wnec.edu/omj

Free to qualified subscribers. Refereed, online journal focusing on organization management issues.

★8854★ Public Performance and Management Review

M.E. Sharpe Inc.
80 Business Pk. Dr.
Armonk, NY 10504
Ph: (914)273-1800   Fax: (914)273-2106
Fr: 800-541-6563
URL: http://www.mesharpe.com/mall/results1.asp?ACR=pmr

Quarterly. $85.00/year for individuals; $399.00/year for institutions; $101.00/year for other countries, individual; $431.00/year for institutions, other countries. Journal addressing a broad range of factors influencing the performance of public and nonprofit organizations and agencies. Aims to facilitate the development of innovative techniques and encourage a wider application of those already established; stimulate research and critical thinking about the relationship between public and private management theories; present integrated analyses of theories, concepts, strategies and techniques dealing with productivity, measurement and related questions of performance improvement; and provide a forum for practitioner-academic exchange. Continuing themes include managing for productivity, measuring and evaluating performance, improving budget strategies, managing human resources, building partnerships, and applying new technologies.

★8855★ Supply Chain Management Review

Reed Business Information
225 Wyman St.
Waltham, MA 02451-1216
URL: http://www.scmr.com

$199.00/year for U.S. and Canada; $241.00/year for other countries. Publication covering business and management.

HANDBOOKS AND MANUALS

★8856★ Administrative Manager

National Learning Corporation
212 Michael Dr.
Syosset, NY 11791
Ph: (516)921-8888   Fax: (516)921-8743
Fr: 800-632-8888
URL: http://www.passbooks.com/

Rudman, Jack. 2005. $34.95 (Trade paper).

★8857★ Real-Resumes for Administrative Support, Office and Secretarial Jobs

PREP Publishing
1110 1/2 Hay St., PMB 66
Fayetteville, NC 28305
Ph: (910)483-6611   Fax: (910)483-2439
Fr: 800-533-2814

Anne McKinney (Editor). March 2004. $16.95. Illustrated. 192 pages. Part of the Real-Resumes Series.

★8858★ Supervising for Success: A Guide for Supervisors

Crisp Publications, Inc.
1200 Hamilton Ct.
Menlo Park, CA 94025
Ph: (650)323-6100   Fax: (650)323-5800
Fr: 800-442-7477

Tony Moglia. 1997. $13.95. 88 pages.

EMPLOYMENT AGENCIES AND SEARCH FIRMS

★8859★ Ambassador Personnel Services Inc.

1541 Fording Island Rd., Ste. 4
PO Box 22448
Hilton Head Island, SC 29925
Ph: (843)837-9066   Fax: (843)837-6477
E-mail: k.wilson@ambassadorpersonnel.com
URL: http://www.teamambassador.com

Full service employment agency that includes local temporary and permanent placements, medical home health provider and regional and national hospitality placement. Industries served: locally: administrative and clerical, home health; regionally: food and beverage and hospitality.

★8860★ Barrett Business Services Inc.

4505 Pacific Hwy. E, Ste. C5
Fife, WA 98424
Ph: (253)896-0635   Fax: (253)896-0637
Fr: 800-251-7251
E-mail: webcreations123@cs.com
URL: http://www.barrettbusiness.com

Offers temporary and long-term staffing. Services focus primarily on light industrial businesses; clerical and technical staffing account for the rest. Also does business as a professional employment organization, providing outsourced human resource services, such as payroll management, benefits administration, recruiting, and placement.

★8861★ Brattle Temps
50 Congress St., Ste. 935
Boston, MA 02109-4008
Ph: (617)523-4600   Fax: (617)523-3939
E-mail: temps@brattletemps.com
URL: http://www.brattletemps.com

Personnel consulting firm specializes in providing temporary consultants. Skill areas available include: computer operators, secretaries, editors, librarians, graphic artists, and marketing professionals. Industries served: universities, publishing, engineering, manufacturing, and government agencies.

★8862★ Churchill & Affiliates Inc.
1200 Bustleton Pike, Ste. 3
Feasterville, PA 19053
Ph: (215)364-8070   Fax: (215)322-4391
E-mail: hwasserman@churchillsearch.com
URL: http://www.churchillsearch.com

Executive search firm focusing on the telecommunications industry.

★8863★ Metropolitan Personnel Inc.
1260 Valley Forge Rd., Ste. 109
PO Box 641
Phoenixville, PA 19460
Ph: (610)933-4000   Fax: (610)933-4670
E-mail: office@metpersnl.com
URL: http://www.metpersnl.com

Offers permanent placement services and specializes in office support, medical and technological staffing. Industries served: multi-industry oriented including government agencies. Firm also provides temporary staffing services and is a PEO.

★8864★ Spherion Pacific Enterprises L.L.C.
2050 Spectrum Blvd.
Fort Lauderdale, FL 33309
Ph: (954)938-7600   Fax: (954)938-7666
Fr: 800-900-4686

E-mail: info@spherion.com
URL: http://www.spherion.com

Firm specializes in recruiting, assessing and deploying talent. It provides the widest range of services available including consulting, managed staffing, outsourcing, search/recruitment and flexible staffing. The company has expertise in industries such as information technology, outsourcing, accounting and finance, law, manufacturing and human resources; as well as clerical, administrative and light industrial.

★8865★ The Underwood Group Inc.
1209-A Brooks Ave.
Raleigh, NC 27607
Ph: (919)782-3024   Fax: (919)782-2811
Fr: 800-409-4498
E-mail: consulting@underwoodgroup.com
URL: http://www.underwoodgroup.com

Personnel consultants provide data processing placement services, both permanent and temporary. Industries served: data processing and engineering. Solutions and project delivery.

ONLINE JOB SOURCES AND SERVICES

★8866★ Admin Exchange
E-mail: info@adminexchange.com
URL: http://www.adminexchange.com
Description: Contains links to job search and career-related websites.

★8867★ Career One Stop
Ph: 877-348-0502
E-mail: info@careeronestop.org
URL: http://www.careeronestop.org
Description: Career resources for administrative staff. Job seekers can post their resume and search for job openings.

★8868★ Office Team
Fr: 800-804-8367
URL: http://www.officeteam.com

Description: Job search site for administrative support staff. Contains resume submission and job databank, plus resources and e-mail notification of available jobs.

OTHER SOURCES

★8869★ Administration and Management Occupations
Delphi Productions
3159 6th St.
Boulder, CO 80304
Ph: (303)443-2100   Fax: (303)443-4022
Fr: 888-443-2400
E-mail: support@delphivideo.com
URL: http://www.delphivideo.com

$95.00. 50 minutes. Part of the Careers for the 21st Century Video Library.

★8870★ Business and Administration Support Occupations
Delphi Productions
3159 6th St.
Boulder, CO 80304
Ph: (303)443-2100   Fax: (303)443-4022
Fr: 888-443-2400
E-mail: support@delphivideo.com
URL: http://www.delphivideo.com

$95.00. 42 minutes. Part of the Careers for the 21st Century Video Library.

★8871★ International Association of Administrative Professionals (IAAP)
10502 NW Ambassador Dr.
PO Box 20404
Kansas City, MO 64195-0404
Ph: (816)891-6600   Fax: (816)891-9118
E-mail: aensminger@iaap-hq.org
URL: http://www.iaap-hq.org/

Description: IAAP is the world's largest association of administrative support staff, with over 600 chapters and 40,000 members and affiliates worldwide. Provides up-to-date research on office trends, publications, seminars and conferences, and resources to help administrative professionals enhance their skills and become more effective contributors to their employers.

Operations Research Analysts

HANDBOOKS AND MANUALS

★8872★ Great Jobs for Computer Science Majors
The McGraw-Hill Companies
PO Box 182604
Columbus, OH 43272
Fax: (614)759-3749   Fr: 877-883-5524
E-mail: customer.service@mcgraw-hill.com
URL: http://www.mcgraw-hill.com

Jan Goldberg, Stephen Lambert, Julie De-Galan. Second edition, 2002. $14.95 (paper). 224 pages.

★8873★ The Information System Consultant's Handbook: Systems Analysis and Design
CRC Press LLC
6000 Broken Sound Parkway, NW, Ste 300
Boca Raton, FL 33487
Fax: 800-374-3401   Fr: 800-272-7737
URL: http://www.crcpress.com

William S. Davis and David C. Yen. 1998. $159.95. 800 pages. This book familiarizes systems analysts, systems designers, and information systems consultants with underlying principles, specific documentation, and methodologies.

★8874★ Next Generation Product Development: How to Increase Productivity, Cut Costs, and Reduce Cycle Times
McGraw-Hill Companies
PO Box 182604
Columbus, OH 43272
Ph: 877-833-5524   Fax: (614)759-3749
Fr: 800-722-4729
E-mail: customer.service@mcgraw-hill.com
URL: http://www.mcgraw-hill.com

Michael E. McGrath. 2004. $39.95. 379 pages. A guide to making the most of today's product development breakthroughs.

★8875★ Opportunities in Research and Development Careers
The McGraw-Hill Companies
PO Box 182604
Columbus, OH 43272
Fax: (614)759-3749   Fr: 877-883-5524
E-mail: customer.service@mcgraw-hill.com
URL: http://www.mcgraw-hill.com

Jan Goldberg. 1996. $11.95 (paper). 146 pages.

EMPLOYMENT AGENCIES AND SEARCH FIRMS

★8876★ Analytic Recruiting, Inc.
144 E. 44th St., 3rd Fl.
New York, NY 10017
Ph: (212)545-8511   Fax: (212)545-8520
E-mail: email@analyticrecruiting.com
URL: http://www.analyticrecruiting.com

Executive search firm.

★8877★ The Aspire Group
52 Second Ave, 1st Fl
Waltham, MA 02451-1129
Fax: (718)890-1810   Fr: 800-487-2967
URL: http://www.bmanet.com

Employment agency.

★8878★ Colli Associates
414 Caboose Ln.
Valrico, FL 33594
Ph: (813)681-2145   Fax: (813)661-5217
E-mail: colli@gte.net

Employment agency. Executive search firm.

★8879★ Data Systems Search Consultants
1615 Bonanza St., Ste. 405
Walnut Creek, CA 94596
Ph: (925)256-0635   Fax: (925)256-9099
E-mail: dsscinfo@dssc.com

URL: http://www.dssc.com

Employment agency. Executive search firm.

★8880★ Mfg/Search, Inc.
431 E Colfax Ave., Ste.120
South Bend, IN 46617
Ph: (574)282-2547   Fr: 800-782-7976
E-mail: mfg@mfgsearch.com
URL: http://www.mfgsearch.com

Executive search firm. Offices in GA, IL, MI, NY.

★8881★ Placemart Personnel Service
80 Haines St.
Lanoka Harbor, NJ 08734
Ph: (732)212-0144   Fax: (609)242-4347
Fr: 800-394-7522
E-mail: info@placemart.com
URL: http://www.placemart.com

Executive search firm focusing on the field of clinical research.

★8882★ Tri-Serv Inc.
22 W. Padonia Rd., Ste. C-353
Timonium, MD 21093
Ph: (410)561-1740   Fax: (410)252-7417
E-mail: info@tri-serv.coom
URL: http://www.tri-serv.com

Employment agency for technical personnel.

★8883★ Werbin Associates Executive Search, Inc.
521 Fifth Ave., Rm. 1749
New York, NY 10175
Ph: (212)953-0909
E-mail: swerb@bellatlantic.net

Employment agency. Executive search firm.

TRADESHOWS

★8884★ Organization Development Network Conference

Organization Development Network
71 Valley St., Ste. 301
South Orange, NJ 07079-2825
Ph: (973)763-7337   Fax: (973)763-7488
E-mail: odnetwork@ODNetwork.org
URL: http://www.odnetwork.org

Annual. **Primary Exhibits:** Exhibits related to organization development.

OTHER SOURCES

★8885★ American Supplier Institute (ASI)

38705 7 Mile Rd., Ste. 345
Livonia, MI 48152
Ph: (734)464-1395   Fax: (734)464-1399
Fr: 800-462-4500
E-mail: asi@asiusa.com
URL: http://www.amsup.com

Description: Seeks to encourage change in U.S. industry through development and implementation of advanced manufacturing and engineering technologies such as Taguchi Methods, Quality Function Deployment, Statistical Process Control, and Total Quality Management. Offers educational courses, training seminars, and workshops to improve quality, reduce cost, and enhance competitive position of U.S. products. Maintains international network of affiliates for developing training specialists and technologies curriculum. Provides training services to government supplier companies.

★8886★ Military Operations Research Society (MORS)

1703 N Beauregard St., Ste. 450
Alexandria, VA 22311-1717
Ph: (703)933-9070   Fax: (703)933-9066
E-mail: morsoffice@mors.org
URL: http://www.mors.org

Description: Works to improve the quality and effectiveness of military operations research. Sponsors colloquia; facilitates exchange of information and peer criticism among students, theoreticians, practitioners, and users of military operations research. Does not make or advocate official policy nor attempts to influence policy formulation.

Ophthalmic Laboratory Technicians

SOURCES OF HELP-WANTED ADS

★8887★ American Optician

Opticians Association of America
441 Carlisle Dr.
Herndon, VA 20170
Ph: (703)437-8780   Fax: (703)437-0727
Fr: 800-443-8997

Quarterly. Subscription included in membership. Professional journal covering optometry.

★8888★ Archives of Ophthalmology

American Medical Association
515 N State St.
Chicago, IL 60610
Fr: 800-621-8335
URL: http://archopht.ama-assn.org/

Monthly. $215.00/year for individuals. Educational/clinical journal for ophthalmologists.

★8889★ EyeNet

American Academy of Ophthalmology
PO Box 7424
San Francisco, CA 94120
Ph: (415)561-8500   Fax: (415)561-8533
E-mail: eyenet@aao.org
URL: http://www.eyenetmagazine.org

Monthly. $128.00/year for nonmembers, within U.S. $180.00/year for nonmembers, outside US; $76.00/year for members, international; included in membership, in USA. Professional magazine of the American Academy of Ophthalmology covering clinical, socioeconomic and political trends affecting their practice for members.

★8890★ Investigative Ophthalmology & Visual Science

Association for Research in Vision and Ophthalmology
12300 Twinbrook Pkwy., Ste. 250
Rockville, MD 20852-1606
Ph: (240)221-2900   Fax: (240)221-0370
E-mail: iovs@arvo.org

URL: http://www.iovs.org/

Monthly. $710.00/year for institutions, within USA; $865.00/year for institutions, outside USA; $485.00/year for nonmembers, within USA; $685.00/year for nonmembers, outside USA; $320.00/year for students, non-member + within USA; $520.00/year for students, non-member + outside USA. Journal dealing with all aspects of vision and ophthalmology.

★8891★ Journal of Electronic Imaging

SPIE - The International Society for Optical Engineering
1000 20th St.
PO Box 10
Bellingham, WA 98225-6705
Ph: (360)676-3290   Fax: (360)647-1445
Fr: 888-504-8171
URL: http://spie.org/x620.xml

Quarterly. $45.00/year for individuals, online; $90.00/year for individuals, print; $430.00/year for individuals, other countries, print and online; $390.00/year for individuals, print and online; $325.00/year for individuals, other countries, online. Journal covering issues in optical engineering.

★8892★ Journal of Optical Networking

Optical Society of America
2010 Massachusetts Ave. NW
Washington, DC 20036-1012
Ph: (202)223-8130   Fax: (202)223-1096
URL: http://www.osa-jon.org/journal/jon/about.cfm

Monthly. $1,695.00/year for individuals, online. Online journal covering issues concerning the optical networking community.

★8893★ Ophthalmology

Mosby Inc.
11830 Westline Industrial Dr.
St. Louis, MO 63146
Ph: (314)872-8370   Fax: (314)432-1380
Fr: 800-325-4177
URL: http://www.ophsource.org/periodicals/ophtha

Monthly. $298.00/year for individuals, U.S.; $298.00/year for individuals, Canada; $448.00/year for individuals, Mexico;

$448.00/year for individuals, international. Journal publishing original, peer-reviewed reports of research in ophthalmology, including basic science investigations and clinical studies.

★8894★ Ophthalmology Journal

American Academy of Ophthalmology
PO Box 7424
San Francisco, CA 94120
Ph: (415)561-8500   Fax: (415)561-8533

Monthly. $261.00/year for individuals; $440.00/year for institutions; $365.00/year for individuals, other countries; $562.00/year for institutions, other countries. Medical journal on ophthalmology.

★8895★ Optometry

American Optometric Association
243 North Lindbergh Blvd.
St. Louis, MO 63141
Ph: (314)991-4100   Fax: (314)991-4101
Fr: 800-365-2219
URL: http://www.aoanews.org/

Monthly. $238.00/year for institutions; $201.00/year for individuals; $101.00/year for students; $66.00/year for students; $179.00/year for individuals; $134.00/year for individuals; $205.00/year for individuals. Clinical journal for members of the American Optometric Association.

★8896★ Optometry and Vision Science

Lippincott Williams & Wilkins
351 W Camden St.
Baltimore, MD 21201
Ph: (410)528-4000   Fax: (410)528-4305
Fr: 800-399-3110
URL: http://www.optvissci.com/

Monthly. $331.00/year for individuals; $429.00/year for institutions; $429.00/year for individuals, international; $526.00/year for institutions, international. Journal providing current developments and research in optometry, physiological optics, and vision science.

★8897★ Review of Optometry

Jobson Professional Publications Group
11 Campus Blvd., Ste. 100
Newtown Square, PA 19073
Ph: (610)492-1000   Fax: (610)492-1039
URL: http://www.revoptom.com/

Monthly. Journal for the optometric profession and optical industry.

PLACEMENT AND JOB REFERRAL SERVICES

★8898★ Association for Research in Vision and Ophthalmology (ARVO)

12300 Twinbrook Pkwy., Ste. 250
Rockville, MD 20852-1606
Ph: (240)221-2900   Fax: (240)221-0370
E-mail: arvo@arvo.org
URL: http://www.arvo.org

Members: Professional society of researchers in vision and ophthalmology. **Purpose:** Encourages ophthalmic research in the field of blinding eye disease. **Activities:** Operates placement service. Maintains 13 scientific sections.

★8899★ Association of University Professors of Ophthalmology (AUPO)

PO Box 420369
San Francisco, CA 94142-0369
Ph: (415)561-8548   Fax: (415)561-8531
E-mail: aupo@aao.org
URL: http://www.aupo.org

Members: Heads of departments or divisions of ophthalmology in accredited medical schools throughout the U.S. and Canada; directors of ophthalmology residency programs in institutions not connected to medical schools. **Purpose:** Promotes medical education, research, and patient care relating to ophthalmology. **Activities:** Operates Ophthalmology Matching Program and faculty placement service, which aids ophthalmologists interested in being associated with university ophthalmology programs to locate such programs.

EMPLOYER DIRECTORIES AND NETWORKING LISTS

★8900★ Eye Care Sourcebook

Omnigraphics Inc.
615 Griswold St.
PO Box 31-1640
Detroit, MI 48226
Ph: (313)961-1340   Fax: (313)961-1383
Fr: 800-234-1340
URL: http://www.omnigraphics.com

Latest edition 2nd; published 2003. $78.00 for individuals. Publication includes: List of eye care organizations. Principal content of

publication is information on various eye-related problems and solutions. Indexes: Alphabetical.

HANDBOOKS AND MANUALS

★8901★ Careers in Health Care

The McGraw-Hill Companies
PO Box 182604
Columbus, OH 43272
Fax: (614)759-3749   Fr: 877-883-5524
E-mail: customer.service@mcgraw-hill.com
URL: http://www.mcgraw-hill.com

Barbara M. Swanson. Fifth edition, 2005. $15.95 (paper). 192 pages. Describes job duties, work settings, salaries, licensing and certification requirements, educational preparation, and future outlook. Gives ideas on how to secure a job.

★8902★ Certified Ophthalmic Technician Exam Review Manual

SLACK, Inc.
6900 Grove Rd.
Thorofare, NJ 08086-9447
Ph: (856)848-1000   Fax: (856)853-5991
Fr: 800-257-8290
URL: http://www.slackinc.com/

Janice K. Ledford. Second edition, 2004. $40.95 (paper). 272 pages. Part of the Basic Bookshelf for Eyecare Professionals Series.

★8903★ Expert Resumes for Health Care Careers

Jist Works
875 Montreal Way
St. Paul, MN 55102
Fr: 800-648-5478
E-mail: info@jist.com
URL: http://www.jist.com

Wendy S. Enelow and Louise M. Kursmark. December 2003. $16.95. 288 pages.

★8904★ Health Careers Today

Elsevier
11830 Westline Industrial Dr.
St. Louis, MO 63146
Ph: (314)453-7010   Fax: (314)453-7095
Fr: 800-545-2522
E-mail: usbkinfo@elsevier.com
URL: http://www.elsevier.com

Gerdin, Judith. Fourth edition. 2007. $59.95. 496 pages. Covers more than 45 health careers. Discusses the roles and responsibilities of various occupations and provides a solid foundation in the skills needed for all health careers.

★8905★ Opportunities in Eye Care Careers

The McGraw-Hill Companies
PO Box 182604
Columbus, OH 43272
Fax: (614)759-3749   Fr: 877-883-5524

E-mail: customer.service@mcgraw-hill.com
URL: http://www.mcgraw-hill.com

Kathleen Belkoff. 2003. $12.95; $11.95 (paper). 160 pages. Explores careers in ophthalmology, optometry, and support positions. Describes the work, salary, and employment outlook and opportunities.

★8906★ Resumes for Health and Medical Careers

The McGraw-Hill Companies
PO Box 182604
Columbus, OH 43272
Fax: (614)759-3749   Fr: 877-883-5524
E-mail: customer.service@mcgraw-hill.com
URL: http://www.mcgraw-hill.com

Third edition, 2003. $11.95 (paper). 160 pages.

EMPLOYMENT AGENCIES AND SEARCH FIRMS

★8907★ Retail Recruiters

2189 Silas Deane Hwy.
Rocky Hill, CT 06067
Ph: (860)721-9550   Fax: (860)257-8813
E-mail: careers@retailrecruitersusa.com
URL: http://www.retailrecruitersusa.com

Employment agency. Affiliate offices in many locations across the country.

ONLINE JOB SOURCES AND SERVICES

★8908★ American Academy of Ophthalmology Professional Choices Career Center

American Academy of Ophthalmology
655 Beach St.
PO Box 7424
San Francisco, CA 94120-7424
Ph: (415)561-8500   Fax: (415)561-8533
E-mail: pchoices@atsaao.org
URL: http://www.aao.org/careers/

Description: A site providing regularly updated ophthalmology positions. Applicants for jobs contact the AAO with resume, cover letter, and listing reference number. Job hunters may post resumes for free. Employers may post 90-day job listings at the rate of $335 for members, $535 for nonmembers.

★8909★ Medhunters.com

Fr: 800-664-0278
E-mail: info@medhunters.com
URL: http://www.medhunters.com

Description: Career search site for jobs in all health care specialties; educational resources; visa and licensing information for relocation; interesting articles; relocation tools; links to professional organizations and general resources.

★8910★ ProHealthJobs
Fr: 800-796-1738
E-mail: Info@prohealthedujobs.com
URL: http://www.prohealthjobs.com

Description: Career resources site for the medical and health care field. Lists professional opportunities, product information, continuing education and open positions.

TRADESHOWS

★8911★ Annual Meeting of the American Academy of Ophthalmology
American Academy of Ophthalmology
655 Beach St.
PO Box 7424
San Francisco, CA 94120-7424
Ph: (415)561-8500   Fax: (415)561-8533
E-mail: meetings@aao.org
URL: http://www.aao.org

Annual. Primary Exhibits: Ophthalmic equipment and instruments.

★8912★ International Vision Expo and Conference/East
Association Expositions and Services
383 Main Ave.
Norwalk, CT 06851
Ph: (203)840-5427   Fax: (203)840-9442
E-mail: czahn@reedexpo.com
URL: http://www.reedexpo.com

Annual. Primary Exhibits: Equipment, supplies and services for the vision industry. Dates and Locations: 2008 Apr 11-13; New York, NY; Jacob K. Javits Convention Center.

★8913★ The OLA
Optical Laboratories Association
11096-B Lee Hwy, Ste. 101
Fairfax, VA 22030-5014
Ph: (703)359-2830   Fax: (703)359-2834
E-mail: ola@ola-labs.org
URL: http://www.ola-labs.org

Annual. Primary Exhibits: Ophthalmic laboratory equipment, supplies, and services.

★8914★ Pan-American Congress of Ophthalmology
Pan-American Association of Ophthalmology
1301 S Bowen Rd., Ste. 365
Arlington, TX 76013
Ph: (817)275-7553   Fax: (817)275-3961
E-mail: info@paao.org
URL: http://www.paao.org

Biennial. Primary Exhibits: Ophthalmology equipment, supplies, and services.

★8915★ Symposium of the New Orleans Academy of Ophthalmology
New Orleans Academy of Ophthalmology
7733 Maple St.
New Orleans, LA 70118
Ph: (504)861-2550   Fax: (504)861-2549
E-mail: noao@noao.org
URL: http://www.noao.org

Annual. Primary Exhibits: Medical instruments, drug companies, and medical publishers.

★8916★ Washington Academy of Eye Physicians and Surgeons Trade Show
Washington Academy of Eye Physicians and Surgeons
2033 6th Ave., Ste. 1100
Seattle, WA 98121
Ph: (206)441-9762   Fax: (206)441-5863
Fr: 800-552-0612

Annual. Primary Exhibits: Ophthalmic, technical, and scientific equipment, supplies, and services.

OTHER SOURCES

★8917★ American Academy of Optometry (AAO)
6110 Executive Blvd., Ste. 506
Rockville, MD 20852
Ph: (301)984-1441   Fax: (301)984-4737
E-mail: aaoptom@aaoptom.org
URL: http://www.aaopt.org

Description: Represents optometrists, educators, and scientists interested in optometric education, and standards of care in visual problems. Conducts continuing education for optometrists and visual scientists. Sponsors 4-day annual meeting.

★8918★ Association of Technical Personnel in Ophthalmology (ATPO)
2025 Woodlane Dr.
St. Paul, MN 55125-2998
Ph: (651)731-7239   Fax: (651)731-0410
Fr: 800-482-4858
E-mail: atpomembership@jcahpo.org
URL: http://www.atpo.org

Members: Ophthalmic assistants, technicians, technologists, surgical and keratorefractive techs, photographers, nurses, and orthoptists. Purpose: Promotes high standards and professional ethics dedicated to quality ophthalmic medical care under the direction of an ophthalmologist. Recognizes the utilization of ophthalmic medical personnel to perform certain non-medical procedures or tests as a means of enhancing the productivity of ophthalmologists and thereby increasing the availability of ophthalmologists to provide the highest level of medical service and comprehensive vision care to their patients.

★8919★ Exploring Health Occupations
Cambridge Educational
PO Box 2053
Princeton, NJ 08543-2053
Ph: 800-257-5126   Fax: (609)671-0266
Fr: 800-468-4227
E-mail: custserv@films.com
URL: http://www.cambridgeeducational.com

VHS and DVD. $159.90. 1999. Two-part series provides a detailed view of the field of medical technicians and technologists, EMTs, nurses, therapists, and assistants.

★8920★ Health Service Occupations
Delphi Productions
3159 6th St.
Boulder, CO 80304
Ph: (303)443-2100   Fax: (303)443-4022
Fr: 888-443-2400
E-mail: support@delphivideo.com
URL: http://www.delphivideo.com

$95.00. 50 minutes. Part of the Careers for the 21st Century Video Library.

★8921★ Health Technologists & Technicians
Delphi Productions
3159 6th St.
Boulder, CO 80304
Ph: (303)443-2100   Fax: (303)443-4022
Fr: 888-443-2400
E-mail: support@delphivideo.com
URL: http://www.delphivideo.com

$95.00. 50 minutes. Part of the Careers for the 21st Century Video Library.

★8922★ Medical Technicians and Technologists
Cambridge Educational
PO Box 2053
Princeton, NJ 08543-2053
Ph: 800-257-5126   Fax: (609)671-0266
Fr: 800-468-4227
E-mail: custserv@films.com
URL: http://www.cambridgeeducational.com

VHS and DVD. $79.95. 18 minutes. 2000. Part of the Exploring Health Occupations Series.

★8923★ Medicine & Related Occupations
Delphi Productions
3159 6th St.
Boulder, CO 80304
Ph: (303)443-2100   Fax: (303)443-4022
Fr: 888-443-2400
E-mail: support@delphivideo.com
URL: http://www.delphivideo.com

$95.00. 45 minutes. Part of the Careers for the 21st Century Video Library.

★8924★ Production Occupations
Delphi Productions
3159 6th St.
Boulder, CO 80304
Ph: (303)443-2100   Fax: (303)443-4022
Fr: 888-443-2400

E-mail: support@delphivideo.com
URL: http://www.delphivideo.com

$95.00. 49 minutes. Part of the Careers for the 21st Century Video Library.

★8925★ Technical & Related Occupations

Delphi Productions
3159 6th St.
Boulder, CO 80304
Ph: (303)443-2100   Fax: (303)443-4022

Fr: 888-443-2400
E-mail: support@delphivideo.com
URL: http://www.delphivideo.com

$95.00. 49 minutes. Part of the Careers for the 21st Century Video Library.

Optometrists

★8926★ American Optician
Opticians Association of America
441 Carlisle Dr.
Herndon, VA 20170
Ph: (703)437-8780   Fax: (703)437-0727
Fr: 800-443-8997

Quarterly. Subscription included in membership. Professional journal covering optometry.

★8927★ AOSA Foresight
American Optometric Association
243 N. Lindbergh Blvd.
St. Louis, MO 63141
Ph: (314)991-4100   Fax: (314)991-4101
Fr: 800-365-2219
URL: http://www.aoa.org/

Description: Semiannual. Reports news of AOSA and allied organizations and provides information concerning scholarships, grants, internships, and other educational issues related to the study of optometry. Recurring features include a calendar of events, news of research, editorials, and a President's Column.

★8928★ Archives of Ophthalmology
American Medical Association
515 N State St.
Chicago, IL 60610
Fr: 800-621-8335
URL: http://archopht.ama-assn.org/

Monthly. $215.00/year for individuals. Educational/clinical journal for ophthalmologists.

★8929★ Eye World Online
New York State Optometric Association
119 Washington Ave., 2nd Fl.
Albany, NY 12210
Ph: (518)449-7300   Fax: (518)432-5902
Fr: 800-342-9836
E-mail: nysoa2020@aol.com.
URL: http://www.nysoa.org

Description: Covers activities of New York State Optometric Association. Provides a news service for eye professionals.

★8930★ EyeNet
American Academy of Ophthalmology
PO Box 7424
San Francisco, CA 94120
Ph: (415)561-8500   Fax: (415)561-8533
E-mail: eyenet@aao.org
URL: http://www.eyenetmagazine.org

Monthly. $128.00/year for nonmembers, within U.S. $180.00/year for nonmembers, outside US; $76.00/year for members, international; included in membership, in USA. Professional magazine of the American Academy of Ophthalmology covering clinical, socioeconomic and political trends affecting their practice for members.

★8931★ Eyewitness
Contact Lens Society of America
441 Carlisle Dr.
Herndon, VA 20170
Ph: (703)437-5100   Fax: (703)437-0727
Fr: 800-296-9776
E-mail: clsa@clsa.info
URL: http://www.clsa.info/MemberServices/index.shtml

Description: Quarterly. Informs members of developments in the contact lens industry. Also reports on related educational information and technical papers. Recurring features include news of research, calendar of events, reports of meetings, and associate member listing.

★8932★ Investigative Ophthalmology & Visual Science
Association for Research in Vision and Ophthalmology
12300 Twinbrook Pkwy., Ste. 250
Rockville, MD 20852-1606
Ph: (240)221-2900   Fax: (240)221-0370
E-mail: iovs@arvo.org
URL: http://www.iovs.org/

Monthly. $710.00/year for institutions, within USA; $865.00/year for institutions, outside USA; $485.00/year for nonmembers, within USA; $685.00/year for nonmembers, outside USA; $320.00/year for students, non-member + within USA; $520.00/year for students, non-member + outside USA. Journal dealing with all aspects of vision and ophthalmology.

★8933★ Journal of Electronic Imaging
SPIE - The International Society for Optical Engineering
1000 20th St.
PO Box 10
Bellingham, WA 98225-6705
Ph: (360)676-3290   Fax: (360)647-1445
Fr: 888-504-8171
URL: http://spie.org/x620.xml

Quarterly. $45.00/year for individuals, online; $90.00/year for individuals, print; $430.00/year for individuals, other countries, print and online; $390.00/year for individuals, print and online; $325.00/year for individuals, other countries, online. Journal covering issues in optical engineering.

★8934★ Journal of Optical Networking
Optical Society of America
2010 Massachusetts Ave. NW
Washington, DC 20036-1012
Ph: (202)223-8130   Fax: (202)223-1096
URL: http://www.osa-jon.org/journal/jon/about.cfm

Monthly. $1,695.00/year for individuals, online. Online journal covering issues concerning the optical networking community.

★8935★ oemagazine
SPIE - The International Society for Optical Engineering
1000 20th St.
PO Box 10
Bellingham, WA 98225-6705
Ph: (360)676-3290   Fax: (360)647-1445
Fr: 888-504-8171
E-mail: info@oemagazine.com
URL: http://oemagazine.com

Monthly. Magazine publishing technical articles and interviews with recognized leaders in optical and optoelectronic applied science and engineering. Includes information about the industry, technological advances, upcoming symposia, and other news. Official magazine of SPIE-The International Society for Optical Engineering.

★8936★ Ophthalmology

Mosby Inc.
11830 Westline Industrial Dr.
St. Louis, MO 63146
Ph: (314)872-8370   Fax: (314)432-1380
Fr: 800-325-4177
URL: http://www.ophsource.org/periodicals/ophtha

Monthly. $298.00/year for individuals, U.S.; $298.00/year for individuals, Canada; $448.00/year for individuals, Mexico; $448.00/year for individuals, international. Journal publishing original, peer-reviewed reports of research in ophthalmology, including basic science investigations and clinical studies.

★8937★ Ophthalmology Journal

American Academy of Ophthalmology
PO Box 7424
San Francisco, CA 94120
Ph: (415)561-8500   Fax: (415)561-8533

Monthly. $261.00/year for individuals; $440.00/year for institutions; $365.00/year for individuals, other countries; $562.00/year for institutions, other countries. Medical journal on ophthalmology.

★8938★ Optometric Management

Lippincott Williams & Wilkins VisionCare Group
1300 Virginia Dr., Ste. 400
Fort Washington, PA 19034
Ph: (215)643-8000
E-mail: om@boucher1.com
URL: http://www.optometric.com

Monthly. Medical professional journal.

★8939★ The Optometrist's Patient Newsletter

Newsletters Ink
450 N Prince St.
PO Box 4008
Lancaster, PA 17604-4008
Ph: (717)393-1000   Fax: (717)393-4702
Fr: 800-379-5585
E-mail: info@newslettersink.com
URL: http://www.newslettersink.com

Description: Quarterly. Carries patient-oriented articles on vision and eye health topics such as prevention and detection of eye disease, new vision products and technologies, and eye safety. May be customized to include the name of the optometrist or practice on the masthead; space is available for articles by the practice.

★8940★ Optometry

American Optometric Association
243 North Lindbergh Blvd.
St. Louis, MO 63141
Ph: (314)991-4100   Fax: (314)991-4101
Fr: 800-365-2219

URL: http://www.aoanews.org/

Monthly. $238.00/year for institutions; $201.00/year for individuals; $101.00/year for students; $66.00/year for students; $179.00/year for individuals; $134.00/year for individuals; $205.00/year for individuals. Clinical journal for members of the American Optometric Association.

★8941★ Optometry and Vision Science

Lippincott Williams & Wilkins
351 W Camden St.
Baltimore, MD 21201
Ph: (410)528-4000   Fax: (410)528-4305
Fr: 800-399-3110
URL: http://www.optvissci.com/

Monthly. $331.00/year for individuals; $429.00/year for institutions; $429.00/year for individuals, international; $526.00/year for institutions, international. Journal providing current developments and research in optometry, physiological optics, and vision science.

★8942★ RETINA

Lippincott Williams & Wilkins
530 Walnut St.
Philadelphia, PA 19106-3621
Ph: (215)521-8300   Fax: (215)521-8902
Fr: 800-638-3030
E-mail: brucker@retinajournal.com
URL: http://www.retinajournal.com

Monthly. $299.00/year for individuals; $653.00/year for institutions; $153.00/year for U.S., in-training; $400.00/year for other countries; $697.00/year for institutions, other countries; $153.00/year for other countries, in-training. Journal publishing clinically oriented articles for the general ophthalmologist and vitreoretinal specialist.

★8943★ Review of Optometry

Jobson Professional Publications Group
11 Campus Blvd., Ste. 100
Newtown Square, PA 19073
Ph: (610)492-1000   Fax: (610)492-1039
URL: http://www.revoptom.com/

Monthly. Journal for the optometric profession and optical industry.

PLACEMENT AND JOB REFERRAL SERVICES

★8944★ American Optometric Association (AOA)

243 N Lindbergh Blvd., 1st Fl.
St. Louis, MO 63141-7881
Ph: (314)991-4100   Fax: (314)991-4101
Fr: 800-365-2219
E-mail: klalexander@aoa.org
URL: http://www.aoa.org

Members: Professional association of optometrists, students of optometry, and paraoptometric assistants and technicians. **Pur-**

pose: Purposes are: to improve the quality, availability, and accessibility of eye and vision care; to represent the optometric profession; to help members conduct their practices; to promote the highest standards of patient care. **Activities:** Monitors and promotes legislation concerning the scope of optometric practice, alternate health care delivery systems, health care cost containment, Medicare, and other issues relevant to eye/vision care. Supports the International Library, Archives and Museum of Optometry which includes references on ophthalmic and related sciences with emphasis on the history and socioeconomic aspects of optometry. Operates Vision U.S.A. program, which provides free eye care to the working poor, and the InfantSEE program, which provides free vision assessments for infants between six and twelve months of age. Conducts specialized education programs; operates placement service; compiles statistics. Maintains museum. Conducts Seal of Acceptance Program.

★8945★ American Public Health Association (APHA)

800 I St. NW
Washington, DC 20001
Ph: (202)777-2742   Fax: (202)777-2534
E-mail: comments@apha.org
URL: http://www.apha.org

Members: Professional organization of physicians, nurses, educators, academicians, environmentalists, epidemiologists, new professionals, social workers, health administrators, optometrists, podiatrists, pharmacists, dentists, nutritionists, health planners, other community and mental health specialists, and interested consumers. **Purpose:** Seeks to protect and promote personal, mental, and environmental health. **Activities:** Services include: promulgation of standards; establishment of uniform practices and procedures; development of the etiology of communicable diseases; research in public health; exploration of medical care programs and their relationships to public health. Sponsors job placement service.

★8946★ National Optometric Association (NOA)

3723 Main St.
PO Box F
East Chicago, IN 46312
Ph: (219)398-4483   Fax: (219)398-1077
Fr: 877-394-2020
E-mail: ddodpc@verizon.net
URL: http://www.natoptassoc.org

Description: Represents optometrists dedicated to increasing awareness of the status of eye/vision health in the minority community and the national community at-large. Strives to make known the impact of the eye/vision dysfunction on the effectiveness and productivity of citizens and the academic proficiency of students. Conducts national minority recruiting programs, job placement, assistance programs for graduates, practitioners, and optometric organizations, and the promotion of delivery of care. Maintains speakers' bureau. Offers specialized education program.

EMPLOYER DIRECTORIES AND NETWORKING LISTS

★8947★ College of Optometrists in Vision Development-Membership Directory

College of Optometrists in Vision Development
243 North Lindbergh Blvd., Ste. 310
St. Louis, MO 63141
Ph: (314)991-4007   Fax: (314)991-1167
Fr: 888-268-3770
URL: http://www.covd.org/

Annual, April. Covers about 1,500 members. Entries include: Name, address, phone, fax, e-mail. Arrangement: Geographical.

★8948★ Directory of Boards of Optometry

Association of Regulatory Boards of Optometry
1750 S Brentwood Blvd., Ste. 503
St. Louis, MO 63144-1341
Ph: (314)785-6000   Fax: (314)785-6002
URL: http://www.arbo.org/

Annual. Covers North American regulatory boards of optometry.

★8949★ Eye Care Sourcebook

Omnigraphics Inc.
615 Griswold St.
PO Box 31-1640
Detroit, MI 48226
Ph: (313)961-1340   Fax: (313)961-1383
Fr: 800-234-1340
URL: http://www.omnigraphics.com

Latest edition 2nd; published 2003. $78.00 for individuals. Publication includes: List of eye care organizations. Principal content of publication is information on various eye-related problems and solutions. Indexes: Alphabetical.

★8950★ HMO/PPO Directory

Grey House Publishing
185 Millerton Rd.
PO Box 860
Millerton, NY 12546
Ph: (518)789-8700   Fax: (518)789-0556
Fr: 800-562-2139
URL: http://www.greyhouse.com/hmo_ppo.htm

Annual; latest edition November 2006. $325.00 for individuals, print product; $495.00 for individuals, online database subscription; $600.00 for individuals, print product and online database subscription,combined. Covers over 600 health maintenance organizations (HMOs) and more than 1,000 preferred provider organizations (PPOs). Entries include: Name of organization, address, phone, number of members, names of officers, employer references, geographical area served, parent company, average fees and co-payments, financial data, and cost control procedures. Arrangement: Geographical. Indexes: Organization name, personnel name, HMOs and PPOs by state, and number of members enrolled.

★8951★ Medical and Health Information Directory

Gale, Cengage Learning
27500 Drake Rd.
Farmington Hills, MI 48331-3535
Ph: (248)699-4253   Fax: (248)699-8065
Fr: 800-877-4253
E-mail: businessproducts@gale.com
URL: http://www.gale.com

Annual; latest edition 20th, July 2007. $375.00/volume. Covers in Volume 1, more than 26,500 medical and health oriented associations, organizations, institutions, and government agencies, including health maintenance organizations (HMOs), preferred provider organizations (PPOs), insurance companies, pharmaceutical companies, research centers, and medical and allied health schools. In Volume 2, over 12,000 medical book publishers; medical periodicals, directories, audiovisual producers and services, medical libraries and information centers, electronic resources, and health-related internet search engines. In Volume 3, more than 35,500 clinics, treatment centers, care programs, and counseling/diagnostic services for 34 subject areas. Entries include: Institution, service, or firm name, address, phone, fax, email and URL; many include names of key personnel and, when pertinent, descriptive annotations. Volume 3 was formerly listed separately as Health Services Directory. Arrangement: Classified by organization activity, service, etc. Indexes: Each volume has a complete alphabetical name and keyword index.

★8952★ Optometry and Vision Science-Geographical Directory, American Academy of Optometry Issue

American Academy of Optometry
6110 Executive Blvd., Ste. 506
Rockville, MD 20852
Ph: (301)984-1441   Fax: (301)984-4737
URL: http://www.aaopt.org/membersearch/

Biennial, odd years. $25.00. Publication includes: List of 3,400 members; international coverage. Entries include: Name, title, affiliation; office address, phone, fax, e-mail. Arrangement: Geographical and alphabetical. Indexes: Name, specialty.

HANDBOOKS AND MANUALS

★8953★ Business Awareness for Optometrists: A Primer

Elsevier
11830 Westline Industrial Dr.
St. Louis, MO 63146
Ph: (314)453-7010   Fax: (314)453-7095
Fr: 800-545-2522
E-mail: usbkinfo@elsevier.com
URL: http://www.elsevier.com

Nizar K. Hirji. 1999. $50.95. 114 pages.

★8954★ Expert Resumes for Health Care Careers

Jist Works
875 Montreal Way
St. Paul, MN 55102
Fr: 800-648-5478
E-mail: info@jist.com
URL: http://www.jist.com

Wendy S. Enelow and Louise M. Kursmark. December 2003. $16.95. 288 pages.

★8955★ Health Careers Today

Elsevier
11830 Westline Industrial Dr.
St. Louis, MO 63146
Ph: (314)453-7010   Fax: (314)453-7095
Fr: 800-545-2522
E-mail: usbkinfo@elsevier.com
URL: http://www.elsevier.com

Gerdin, Judith. Fourth edition. 2007. $59.95. 496 pages. Covers more than 45 health careers. Discusses the roles and responsibilities of various occupations and provides a solid foundation in the skills needed for all health careers.

★8956★ Opportunities in Eye Care Careers

The McGraw-Hill Companies
PO Box 182604
Columbus, OH 43272
Fax: (614)759-3749   Fr: 877-883-5524
E-mail: customer.service@mcgraw-hill.com
URL: http://www.mcgraw-hill.com

Kathleen Belkoff. 2003. $12.95; $11.95 (paper). 160 pages. Explores careers in ophthalmology, optometry, and support positions. Describes the work, salary, and employment outlook and opportunities.

★8957★ Opportunities in Paramedical Careers

The McGraw-Hill Companies
PO Box 182604
Columbus, OH 43272
Fax: (614)759-3749   Fr: 877-883-5524
E-mail: customer.service@mcgraw-hill.com
URL: http://www.mcgraw-hill.com

Alex Kacen. 1999. 14.95 (hardcover). 160 pages. Discusses a variety of opportunities in this field and how to pursue them. Illustrated.

★8958★ Resumes for Health and Medical Careers

The McGraw-Hill Companies
PO Box 182604
Columbus, OH 43272
Fax: (614)759-3749   Fr: 877-883-5524
E-mail: customer.service@mcgraw-hill.com
URL: http://www.mcgraw-hill.com

Third edition, 2003. $11.95 (paper). 160 pages.

EMPLOYMENT AGENCIES AND SEARCH FIRMS

★8959★ Retail Recruiters

2189 Silas Deane Hwy.
Rocky Hill, CT 06067
Ph: (860)721-9550   Fax: (860)257-8813
E-mail: careers@retailrecruitersusa.com
URL: http://www.retailrecruitersusa.com

Employment agency. Affiliate offices in many locations across the country.

ONLINE JOB SOURCES AND SERVICES

★8960★ American Academy of Ophthalmology Professional Choices Career Center

American Academy of Ophthalmology
655 Beach St.
PO Box 7424
San Francisco, CA 94120-7424
Ph: (415)561-8500   Fax: (415)561-8533
E-mail: pchoices@atsaao.org
URL: http://www.aao.org/careers/

Description: A site providing regularly updated ophthalmology positions. Applicants for jobs contact the AAO with resume, cover letter, and listing reference number. Job hunters may post resumes for free. Employers may post 90-day job listings at the rate of $335 for members, $535 for nonmembers.

★8961★ Medhunters.com

Fr: 800-664-0278
E-mail: info@medhunters.com
URL: http://www.medhunters.com

Description: Career search site for jobs in all health care specialties; educational resources; visa and licensing information for relocation; interesting articles; relocation tools; links to professional organizations and general resources.

★8962★ ProHealthJobs

Fr: 800-796-1738
E-mail: Info@prohealthedujobs.com
URL: http://www.prohealthjobs.com

Description: Career resources site for the medical and health care field. Lists professional opportunities, product information, continuing education and open positions.

TRADESHOWS

★8963★ American Academy of Optometry

American Academy of Optometry
6110 Executive Blvd., Ste. 506
Rockville, MD 20852
Ph: (301)984-1441   Fax: (301)984-4737
E-mail: AAOptom@daol.com
URL: http://www.aaopt.org

Annual. **Primary Exhibits:** Exhibits focusing on the latest research and patient treatments relating to clinical practice standards, optometric education, and experimental research in visual problems. **Dates and Locations:** 2008 Oct 22-25; Anaheim, CA; Anaheim Marriott Hotel.

★8964★ American Optometric Association Congress

American Optometric Association
243 N Lindbergh Blvd.
St. Louis, MO 63141
Ph: (314)991-4100   Fax: (314)991-4101
Fr: 800-365-2219
URL: http://www.aoanet.org

Annual. **Primary Exhibits:** Optometry equipment, supplies, and services.

★8965★ College of Optometrists in Vision Development Annual Meeting

College of Optometrists in Vision Development
243 N Lindbergh Blvd., Ste. 310
St. Louis, MO 63141
Ph: (314)991-4007   Fax: (314)991-1167
E-mail: info@covd.org
URL: http://www.covd.org

Annual. **Primary Exhibits:** Exhibits relating to orthoptics and optometric vision therapy with emphasis on visual information processing in visually related learning problems.

★8966★ International Vision Expo and Conference/East

Association Expositions and Services
383 Main Ave.
Norwalk, CT 06851
Ph: (203)840-5427   Fax: (203)840-9442
E-mail: czahn@reedexpo.com
URL: http://www.reedexpo.com

Annual. **Primary Exhibits:** Equipment, supplies and services for the vision industry. **Dates and Locations:** 2008 Apr 11-13; New York, NY; Jacob K. Javits Convention Center.

★8967★ Pan-American Congress of Ophthalmology

Pan-American Association of Ophthalmology
1301 S Bowen Rd., Ste. 365
Arlington, TX 76013
Ph: (817)275-7553   Fax: (817)275-3961
E-mail: info@paao.org
URL: http://www.paao.org

Biennial. **Primary Exhibits:** Ophthalmology equipment, supplies, and services.

★8968★ SECO International (Southern Council of Optometrists)

Southern Council of Optometrists
4661 N. Shallowford Rd.
Atlanta, GA 30338
Ph: (770)451-8206   Fax: (770)451-3156
URL: http://www.secointernational.com

Annual. **Primary Exhibits:** Ophthalmic supplies, diagnostic equipment, reference books, frames for glasses, office equipment, computers, contact lenses, and ophthalmic pharmaceuticals. **Dates and Locations:** 2008 Feb 27 - Mar 02.

OTHER SOURCES

★8969★ American Academy of Optometry (AAO)

6110 Executive Blvd., Ste. 506
Rockville, MD 20852
Ph: (301)984-1441   Fax: (301)984-4737
E-mail: aaoptom@aaoptom.org
URL: http://www.aaopt.org

Description: Represents optometrists, educators, and scientists interested in optometric education, and standards of care in visual problems. Conducts continuing education for optometrists and visual scientists. Sponsors 4-day annual meeting.

★8970★ American Almanac of Jobs and Salaries

HarperCollins
10 E. 53rd St.
New York, NY 10022
Ph: (212)207-7000   Fr: 800-242-7737
URL: http://www.harpercollins.com/

John W. Wright. Revised edition, 2000. $20.00 (paper). 672 pages. This is a comprehensive guide to the wages of hundreds of occupations in a wide variety of industries and organizations.

★8971★ American Optometric Student Association (AOSA)

243 N Lindbergh
St. Louis, MO 63141
Fax: (314)991-4101   Fr: 800-365-2291
E-mail: marburle@aol.com
URL: http://www.theaosa.org

Members: Optometric students, state optometric associations, and family members of optometric students. **Activities:** Collects updated information on progress in the optometry field. Provides members with opportunities to work in areas of health care need such as local community health projects, school curriculum changes, and health manpower legislation. Works to improve optometric education and health care for the general population. Maintains active liaison with other optometric associations. Conducts communications program.

★8972★ **Exploring Health Occupations**
Cambridge Educational
PO Box 2053
Princeton, NJ 08543-2053
Ph: 800-257-5126   Fax: (609)671-0266
Fr: 800-468-4227
E-mail: custserv@films.com
URL: http://www.cambridgeeducational.com

VHS and DVD. $159.90. 1999. Two-part series provides a detailed view of the field of medical technicians and technologists, EMTs, nurses, therapists, and assistants.

★8973★ **Health Service Occupations**
Delphi Productions
3159 6th St.
Boulder, CO 80304
Ph: (303)443-2100   Fax: (303)443-4022
Fr: 888-443-2400
E-mail: support@delphivideo.com
URL: http://www.delphivideo.com

$95.00. 50 minutes. Part of the Careers for the 21st Century Video Library.

★8974★ **Medicine & Related Occupations**
Delphi Productions
3159 6th St.
Boulder, CO 80304
Ph: (303)443-2100   Fax: (303)443-4022
Fr: 888-443-2400

E-mail: support@delphivideo.com
URL: http://www.delphivideo.com

$95.00. 45 minutes. Part of the Careers for the 21st Century Video Library.

★8975★ **National Association of Optometrists and Opticians (NAOO)**
PO Box 459
Marblehead, OH 43440
Ph: (419)798-2031   Fax: (419)798-8548
E-mail: fdrozak@cros.net

Description: Licensed optometrists, opticians, and corporations. Conducts public affairs programs of mutual importance to members; serves as an organizational center for special purpose programs; acts as a clearinghouse for information affecting the retail optical industry.

Orthotic and Prosthetic Technicians

SOURCES OF HELP-WANTED ADS

★8976★ The Journal of Arthroplasty
Elsevier
1600 John F. Kennedy Blvd., Ste. 1800
Philadelphia, PA 19103-2899
Ph: (215)239-3900   Fax: (215)238-7883
E-mail: elspcs@elsevier.com
URL: http://www.us.elsevierhealth.com/product.jsp?isbn=08835403

$777.00/year for institutions, outside U.S.; $172.00/year for students; $638.00/year for institutions; $390.00/year for individuals; $200.00/year for students, outside U.S.; $512.00/year for individuals, outside U.S. Medical journal for orthopaedic surgeons. Covering clinical and basic science research on arthroplasty including surgical techniques, prosthetic design, biomechanics, biomaterials, and metallurgy.

★8977★ Journal of Prosthetics and Orthotics
Lippincott Williams & Wilkins
530 Walnut St.
Philadelphia, PA 19106
Ph: (215)521-8300   Fax: (215)521-8902
URL: http://www.lww.com/index.html

Four issues/year. $168.00 for individuals. Industry publication provides information concerning the latest research and clinical thinking in orthotics and prosthetics, including information on new devices, fitting techniques and patient management experiences.

★8978★ O&P Business News
SLACK Inc.
6900 Grove Rd.
Thorofare, NJ 08086-9447
Ph: (856)848-1000   Fax: (856)853-5991
URL: http://www.oandpbiznews.com

Semimonthly. $139.00/year for individuals; $229.00/year for institutions; $278.00/two years for individuals; $458.00/two years for institutions; $417.00/three years for individuals; $697.00/three years for institutions. Professional magazine covering technical, business, professional and reimbursement activities of the orthotics and prosthetics industry.

★8979★ The O&P Edge
Western Media LLC
11698 Huron St., Ste. 102
Northglenn, CO 80234
Ph: (303)255-0843   Fax: (303)255-0844
Fr: (866)613-0257
E-mail: edge@oandp.com
URL: http://www.oandp.com

Monthly. Free to individuals in the United States; $36/year in Canada; $96/year in other countries. Magazine covers news and cutting edge technology in the orthotics and prosthetics industry.

EMPLOYMENT AGENCIES AND SEARCH FIRMS

★8980★ Jordan Medical Consultants
743 Spirit 40 Park Dr., Ste. 233
Chesterfield, MO 63005
Ph: (636)519-4793   Fax: (636)519-4798
URL: http://www.jordanmc.com/

Employment agency serving medical professionals, particularly orthotic and prosthetic technicians; aims to match recruits with geographic and practical preferences such as family needs.

ONLINE JOB SOURCES AND SERVICES

★8981★ American Orthotic and Prosthetic Association
330 John Carlyle St., Ste. 200
Alexandria, VA 22314
Ph: (571)431-0876   Fax: (571)431-0899
E-mail: info@aopanet.org
URL: http://www.aopanet.org/

American Orthotic and Prosthetic Association's online membership directory, searchable by name, city, state or zip code.

★8982★ Employment Spot
13 Elm St.
Birmingham, AL 35213
Ph: (205)668-6868
E-mail: dns@employmentspot.com
URL: http://www.employmentspot.com/

Online resource provides job listings, particularly for orthotic and prosthetic technicians. Also includes articles and information about salary negotiation, interviewing and career fairs.

★8983★ Guidetohealthcareschools.com
123 Lake St. S, B-1
Kirkland, WA 98033
E-mail: privacy@degreepages.com
URL: http://www.guidetohealthcareschools.com/

Online resource provides information concerning orthotic and prosthetic technicians such as career and salary outlook, training and education, career overviews and related fields.

★8984★ O&P Digital Technologies: OandP.com
6800 NW 9th Blvd., Ste. 3
Gainesville, FL 32605
Ph: (352)331-3741   Fax: (352)332-8074
Fr: 800-876-7740
E-mail: info@oandp.com

Online resource provides comprehensive information and services to the orthotics and prosthetics profession including news, articles, job listings, a calendar of events and a directory of products and services.

★8985★ PayScale, Inc.
316 Occidental Ave., Ste. 310
Seattle, WA 98104
E-mail: service@payscale.com
URL: http://www.payscale.com/research/

US/Job=Orthotic_and_Prosthetic_Technician_(O_and_P_Technician)/Hourly_Rate

Online resource provides detailed information for orthotic and prosthetic technicians concerning salary, vacation time, bonuses and commute time. Also gives tips for salary negotiation and career planning.

★8986★ Pedorthic Footwear
Association

2025 M St. NW, Ste. 800
Washington, DC 20036
Ph: (202)367-1145   Fax: (202)367-2145
Fr: 800-673-8447
E-mail: info@pedorthics.org
URL: http://www.pedorthics.org/

Represents the interests of certified and/or licensed pedorthists, the design, manufacture, modification, and fit of shoes and foot orthoses to alleviate problems caused by disease, congenital condition, overuse or injury. Website provides listings of help wanted classified for individuals in the pedorthic industry.

OTHER SOURCES

★8987★ American Academy of
Orthotists and Prosthetists

526 King St., Ste. 201
Alexandria, VA 22314
Ph: (703)836-0788   Fax: (703)836-0737
E-mail: prosenstein@oandp.org
URL: http://www.oandp.org/

Promotes professionalism of orthotists and prosthetists and works to advance the standards of patient care through education, literature, research, advocacy and collaboration. Memberships include Active: practitioners in orthotics and/or prosthetics; Associate: practitioners not meeting the criteria for Active; Affiliate: technicians, fitters, assistants and CPeds; Professional: individuals in other professional fields related to orthotics and prosthetics; International Affiliate: international practitioners; Candidate: individuals in orthotics and/or prosthetics who have completed an NCOPE-accredited program; Resident: individuals currently enrolled in an NCOPE-accredited residency program; Student: individuals currently enrolled in a AAH-EP accredited practitioner program; Emeritus: members awarded the title; Honorary: individuals in recognition of their contribution to the profession of orthotics and/or prosthetics. Membership benefits include access to the Academy's Member Directory, newsletters and journals, as well as papers from the Thranhardt Lecture Series and discounts on meetings and publications.

★8988★ California Orthotics and
Prosthetics Association

236 W Elm Ave.
Galt, CA 95632
Ph: (209)744-2672
E-mail: copamail@oandp.com

URL: http://www.oandp.com/copa/

Represents orthodists and prosthetists as well as orthotic and prosthetic companies in the State of California; offers annual newsletter to members. Individual membership includes: Certified, Technician/Fitter, Associate, and Student; Corporate and Organizational membership includes: Corporate Patient Care, Corporate Supplier, Corporate Allied Health, and Corporate Associate.

★8989★ Florida Association of
Orthotists and Prosthetists

PO Box 340507
Tampa, FL 33694
Ph: (813)265-3267
E-mail: faopoffice@verizon.net
URL: http://www.faop.org/

Aims to ensure the highest standard of orthotic and prosthetic care for persons with disabilities by actively promoting the professional development of members and supporting excellence in business practices. Also provides educational opportunities and sponsors seminars relating to the advancement of the field.

★8990★ Florida Chapter of the
American Academy of Orthotists and
Prosthetists

6152 Nicole Dr.
Sarasota, FL 34243
Ph: (941)359-3550   Fax: (941)313-1333
E-mail: dan.drowne@comcast.net
URL: http://www.oandp.org/membership/chapters/florida/

Promotes professionalism of orthotists and prosthetists in Florida; also works to advance the standards of patient care through education, literature, research, advocacy and collaboration. Membership dues are $35/year. Members must be within the geographical boundaries and in good standing with the American Academy of Orthotists and Prosthetists.

★8991★ Midwest Chapter of the
American Academy of Orthotists and
Prosthetists

5027 Green Bay Rd., Ste. 120
Kenosha, WI 53144
Ph: (262)654-4300   Fax: (262)654-4305
E-mail: dougreichertcp@aol.com
URL: http://www.oandp.org/membership/chapters/midwest/

Promotes professionalism of orthotists and prosthetists in Wisconsin, Illinois and Indiana; also works to advance the standards of patient care through education, literature, research, advocacy and collaboration. Members must be in good standing with the American Academy of Orthotists and Prosthetists.

★8992★ National Commission on
Orthotic and Prosthetic Education

330 John Carlyle St., Ste. 200
Alexandria, VA 22314
Ph: (703)836-7114   Fax: (703)836-0838

E-mail: info@ncope.org
URL: http://www.ncope.org/

Aims to promote education in the field of orthotics and prosthetics and raise the standards of education in the field; establish accreditation and evaluation procedures; aid in the development of new programs and ensure people entering the field receive formal preparation related to current requirements for professional practice.

★8993★ New England Chapter of the
American Academy of Orthotists and
Prosthetists

1985 Barnum Ave.
Stratford, CT 06615
Ph: (203)377-8820   Fax: (203)380-0675
E-mail: nseversky@hanger.com
URL: http://www.oandp.org/membership/chapters/new_england/

Promotes professionalism of orthotists and prosthetists in Massachusetts, Maine, New Hampshire, Vermont, Connecticut, and Rhode Island; also works to advance the standards of patient care through education, literature, research, advocacy and collaboration. Members must be within the geographical boundaries and in good standing with the American Academy of Orthotists and Prosthetists.

★8994★ North Carolina Chapter of the
American Academy of Orthotists and
Prosthetists

PO Box 1481
New Bern, NC 28563
Ph: (252)638-1312   Fax: (252)638-4648
E-mail: cpo1758@cconnect.net
URL: http://www.oandp.org/membership/chapters/north_carolina/

Promotes professionalism of orthotists and prosthetists in North Carolina; also works to advance the standards of patient care through education, literature, research, advocacy and collaboration. Members must be within the geographical boundaries and in good standing with the American Academy of Orthotists and Prosthetists.

★8995★ Northern Plains Chapter of
the American Academy of Orthotists
and Prosthetists

Shriner's Hospital for Children
2025 E River Pkwy.
Minneapolis, MN 55414
Ph: (612)596-6205   Fax: (612)339-5954
E-mail: mmorel@shrinenet.org
URL: http://www.oandp.org/membership/chapters/northern_plains/

Promotes professionalism of orthotists and prosthetists in North Dakota, South Dakota, Minnesota and Iowa; also works to advance the standards of patient care through education, literature, research, advocacy and collaboration.

★8996★ Northwest Chapter of the American Academy of Orthotists and Prosthetists

University of Washington Medical Center
P&O
1959 NE Pacific St.
PO Box 356490
Seattle, WA 98195
Ph: (206)543-6339   Fax: (206)593-4761
E-mail: ayamane@u.washing.edu
URL: http://www.oandp.org/membership/chapters/northwest/

Promotes professionalism of orthotists and prosthetists in Alaska, Washington, Montana, Oregon and Idaho; also works to advance the standards of patient care through education, literature, research, advocacy and collaboration. Members receive discounted registration fees for Northwest Chapter meetings.

★8997★ Ohio Chapter of the American Academy of Orthotists and Prosthetists

Acor Orthopaedic Inc.
18530 S Miles Rd.
Cleveland, OH 44128
Ph: (216)662-4500   Fax: (216)662-4547
E-mail: fiz@acor.com
URL: http://www.oandp.org/membership/chapters/ohio/

Promotes professionalism of orthotists and prosthetists in Ohio, Michigan, Kentucky and West Virginia; also works to advance the standards of patient care through education, literature, research, advocacy and collaboration. Members must be within the geographical boundaries and in good standing with the American Academy of Orthotists and Prosthetists.

★8998★ Pennsylvania/MD/DC/VA Chapter of the American Academy of Orthotists and Prosthetists

3435 Box Hill Corporate Center Dr., Ste. D
Abingdon, MD 21009
Ph: (410)569-0606   Fax: (410)569-7477
E-mail: gmichalov@hotmail.com
URL: http://www.oandp.org/membership/chapters/maryland/

Promotes professionalism of orthotists and prosthetists in Pennsylvania, Maryland, Virginia and the District of Columbia; also works to advance the standards of patient care through education, literature, research, advocacy and collaboration; 130 members. Dues are $45 annually. Members must practice within the geographical boundaries and be in good standing with the American Academy of Orthotists and Prosthetists.

★8999★ Southwest Chapter of the American Academy of Orthotists and Prosthetists

3737 Moraga Ave., Ste. B107
San Diego, CA 92117
Ph: (858)270-9972   Fax: (858)270-6560
E-mail: bionics@utm.net
URL: http://www.oandp.org/membership/chapters/southwest_regional/

Promotes professionalism of orthotists and prosthetists in California, Nevada, Arizona, Utah, New Mexico and Hawaii; also works to advance the standards of patient care through education, literature, research, advocacy and collaboration.

★9000★ Texas Chapter of the American Academy of Orthotists and Prosthetists

519 Bryan St.
Denton, TX 76201
Ph: (940)243-4198   Fax: (940)591-9017
E-mail: walcin@airmail.net
URL: http://www.oandp.org/membership/chapters/texas/

Promotes professionalism of orthotists and prosthetists in Texas; also works to advance the standards of patient care through education, literature, research, advocacy and collaboration. Chapter currently consists of 105 members with annual dues of $50. Active members include any orthotist and/or prosthetist within the geographical boundaries and in good standing with the American Academy of Orthotists and Prosthetists; Affiliate members include any ABC registered orthotic or prosthetic technician within the geographical boundaries and in good standing with the American Academy of Orthotists and Prosthetists.

Outdoor Guides

SOURCES OF HELP-WANTED ADS

★9001★ Adventure Travel Business

Adventure Media Inc.
PO Box 3210
Incline Village, NV 89451
Ph: (775)832-3700   Fax: (775)832-3775
Fr: (866)214-6164

Quarterly. $24.95/year for individuals, 6 issues a year. Business magazine for the adventure travel tour operator.

★9002★ Tourism, Culture & Communication

Cognizant Communications Corp.
3 Hartsdale Rd.
Elmsford, NY 10523-3701
Ph: (914)592-7720   Fax: (914)592-8981
URL: http://www.cognizantcommunication.com/filecabinet/Tourism_Cu

$250.00/year for institutions, library; $275.00/year for institutions, rest of the world, library; $40.00/year professional; $55.00/year for other countries, professional. Journal covering tourism, culture, and communication.

★9003★ Workamper News

Workamper News
709 West Searcy St.
Heber Springs, AR 72543-3761
Ph: (501)362-2637   Fax: (501)362-6769
E-mail: info@workamper.com
URL: http://www.workamper.com/WorkamperNews/WNIndex.cfm

Description: Bimonthly. Provides a list of information on seasonal and full-time job openings at campgrounds, forests, public and private resort areas, and motorsports events.

EMPLOYER DIRECTORIES AND NETWORKING LISTS

★9004★ Alaskaguidesdirectory.com

Kenai River Professional Guide
  Association
PO Box 3667
Homer, AK 99603
Fr: 800-478-7777
URL: http://alaskaguidesdirectory.com

Online directory lists guides and lodges throughout Alaska.

★9005★ Discovering Careers for Your Future

Facts On File Inc.
132 W 31st St., 17th Fl.
New York, NY 10001
Ph: (212)967-8800   Fax: 800-678-3633
Fr: 800-322-8755
URL: http://www.factsonfile.com

Published 2001. $21.95 for individuals; $19.75 for libraries. Covers adventure travel specialists, astronauts, detectives, police officers, and spies; links career education to curriculum, helping children investigate the subjects they are interested in and the careers those subjects might lead to.

★9006★ Gray's Sporting Journal Expeditions and Guides Book

Morris Communications Corp.
725 Broad St.
Augusta, GA 30901
Ph: (706)724-0851   Fr: 800-622-6358
URL: http://grayssportingjournal.com/ExpedGuides05/index.shtml

Annual, December. $6.95. Covers approximately 200 hunting, fishing, and wilderness adventure guides, outfitters, and lodges worldwide. Entries include: Company name, address, phone; descriptions of services provided, nearby activities and attractions, location; season of operation, rates, transportation access. Arrangement: Geographical. Indexes: Guide name, type of camp, size of camp, activities available.

★9007★ Outside-Active Travel Directory

Mariah Media Inc.
400 Market St.
Santa Fe, NM 87501
Ph: (505)989-7100   Fax: (505)989-4700

Monthly. Publication includes: List of about 275 wilderness trip guides, licensed outfitters, and active travel companies in each issue. Entries include: Personal or company name, address, phone, description of specialties or services. Arrangement: Geographical.

ONLINE JOB SOURCES AND SERVICES

★9008★ Infinite Outdoors
URL: http://www.infiniteoutdoors.com

Description: Online directory of outdoor related web sites including, manufacturers, guides, clubs, and organizations.

★9009★ Outdoor Guides and Preserves in Alaska
E-mail: guide@crosstel.net
URL: http://www.outdoorguides.com

Description: Online directory to guide services and outfitters in the state of Alaska.

TRADESHOWS

★9010★ Adventures in Travel Expos

Unicomm, LLC
472 Wheelers Farms Rd', 3rd Fl.
Milford, CT 06461
Ph: (203)878-2577   Fax: (203)878-2154
E-mail: info@adventureexpo.com
URL: http://www.adventureexpo.com

Primary Exhibits: Adventure, active travel, eco, nature, cultural, and outdoor travel.

OTHER SOURCES

★9011★ Acadia Mountain Guides

PO Box 121
92 Main St.
Orono, ME 04473
Ph: (207)288-8186   Fax: (207)866-7562
E-mail: climb@acadiamountainguides.com
URL: http://www.acadiamountainguides.com

Activities: Operates the Acadia Mountain Guides Climbing School that provides career development for professional guides. Offers a variety of courses for professional guides and is accredited by the American Mountain Guides Association for its certification program.

★9012★ Adventure Travel Trade Association

601 Union St., 42nd Fl.
Seattle, WA 98101
Ph: (360)805-3131   Fax: (360)805-0649
E-mail: info@adventuretravel.biz
URL: http://www.adventuretravel.biz

Description: Serves the adventure travel industry as a membership organization. Aims to grow the adventure travel industry overall and to help build up its member organizations. Provides exposure, marketing expertise, education, research, and discount to its members.

★9013★ American Mountain Guides Association

PO Box 1739
Boulder, CO 80306
Ph: (303)271-0984   Fax: (303)271-1377
URL: http://www.amga.com

Members: Professional mountain guides. **Purpose:** Provides support, education, and standards to its membership. **Activities:** Establishes and maintains certification guidelines for professional guides, sponsors educational opportunities, provides a guide finding service to the public, and offers scholarships and grants.

★9014★ Idaho Outfitters and Guides Association

PO Box 95
Boise, ID 83701
Ph: (208)342-1438   Fax: (208)338-7830
Fr: 800-494-3246
E-mail: gsimonds@cableone.net
URL: http://www.ioga.org

Members: Full-time licensed outfitters and guides. **Activities:** Disseminates information on the licensing requirements of guides. Maintains an outfitter directory listing its members.

★9015★ Maine Professional Guides Association

PO Box 336
Augusta, ME 04332-0336
E-mail: info@maineguides.org
URL: http://www.maineguides.org

Members: Registered Maine guides. **Purpose:** Promotes a quality, ethical, and legal outdoor experience for all. **Activities:** Monitors new and proposed legislation that affects the guiding industry. Issues guide licenses. Provides an online searchable database of members.

★9016★ Mississippi Outfitters and Guides Association

E-mail: jaco9865@bellsouth.net
URL: http://www.outfittersandguides.com/mississippi.htm

Members: Professional outfitters and guides. **Purpose:** Promotes the commercial hunting, fishing, and wildlife viewing industry in Mississippi. **Activities:** Provides information about hunting seasons and how to obtain hunting and fishing licenses. Publishes the Mississippi Outfitter's Directory.

★9017★ Montana Outfitters and Guides Association (MOGA)

2033 11th Ave., No. 8
Helena, MT 59601
Ph: (406)449-3578   Fax: (406)449-9769
E-mail: macminard@imt.net
URL: http://www.montanaoutfitters.org

Description: Represents outfitters and guides who operate outdoor trips in Montana for hunting, fishing, float boating, and sightseeing parties using saddle and pack animals, boats, and motorized equipment; operators of dude ranches, wagon trains, and cattle drives. Supports standards of service to be provided by members set by licensing board; encourages preservation of back country and wise use of resources, fish, and game. Is conducting a study of the economic impact of industry on Montana. Maintains speaker's bureau.

★9018★ New York State Outdoor Guides Association

1936 Saranac Ave., Ste. 2
Lake Placid, NY 12946
Fr: (866)469-7642
E-mail: info@nysoga.org
URL: http://www.nysoga.com

Members: Professional guides. **Activities:** Maintains a searchable membership list. Provides outdoor training and licensing information for its members.

★9019★ Oregon Guides and Packers

531 SW 13th St.
Bend, OR 97702
Ph: (541)617-2876   Fr: 800-747-9552
E-mail: info@ogpa.org

URL: http://www.ogpa.org

Members: Professional outdoor recreation service providers. **Purpose:** Assist outdoor enthusiasts from all walks-of-life to have a safe and rewarding outdoor experience. **Activities:** Provides a listing of member guides.

★9020★ Outdoor Guides Association of North America

1323 Lehigh Dr.
Tallahassee, FL 32301
Ph: (850)212-8366   Fax: (904)212-1524
E-mail: info@outdoorguidesassociation.com
URL: http://199.44.235.18/oga/

Members: Professional guides and outfitters. **Purpose:** Provides group based benefits to its membership and offers a way for independent guides to employ a unified voice in building, promoting, and protecting the business of professional guiding. **Activities:** Maintains the Guides & Outfitters List, provides insurance for its members, and offers discounts from outdoor retailers.

★9021★ Rogue Sportsmen and Guides Association

PO Box 1258
Eagle Point, OR 97524
Ph: (541)878-2100
E-mail: oatp@scwi.us
URL: http://www.rsga.us

Members: Professional guides. **Purpose:** Works to upgrade guiding standards and the quality of service offered to clients. **Activities:** Maintains a membership list, publishes a newsletter, and posts classified advertisements.

★9022★ Vermont Outdoor Guide Association

PO Box 10
North Ferrisburg, VT 05473
Ph: (802)425-6211   Fr: 800-425-8747
E-mail: info@voga.org
URL: http://www.voga.org

Members: Outdoor leaders, educators, guides, and related services. **Purpose:** Provides support and promotion for outdoor travel services, including guides and outfitters. **Activities:** Maintains a membership directory and provides a forum for networking.

★9023★ Western Montana School for Guides

c/o Scott Boulanger
PO Box 733
Darby, MT 59829
Ph: (406)821-0017
E-mail: elkhunter@montana.com
URL: http://www.guidetraining.com

Purpose: Offers training in every aspect of the guide and outfitter profession. **Activities:** Provides information on starting a guide business and offers job placement services.

PC Network Administrators

★9035★ Foundations of Computational Mathematics

Springer-Verlag New York Inc.
233 Spring St.
New York, NY 10013
Ph: (212)460-1500   Fax: (212)460-1575

Academic journal that publishes articles related to the connections between mathematics and computation, including the interfaces between pure and applied mathematics, numerical analysis and computer science.

★9036★ Foundations and Trends in Networking

Now Publishers
PO Box 1024
Hanover, MA 02339
Ph: (781)871-0245
URL: http://www.nowpublishers.com/product.aspx?product=NET

$315.00/year online only; $355.00/year print and online; $315.00/year online only; $355.00/year print and online. Academic journal publishing new research in computer networking.

★9037★ Government Computer News

PostNewsweek Tech Media
10 G St. NE, Ste. 500
Washington, DC 20002-4228
Ph: (202)772-2500   Fax: (202)772-2511
Fr: (866)447-6864

Semimonthly. Magazine for professionals interested in government IT.

★9038★ IEEE Security & Privacy Magazine

IEEE Computer Society
10662 Los Vaqueros Cir.
PO Box 3014
Los Alamitos, CA 90720-1314
Ph: (714)821-8380   Fax: (714)821-4010
Fr: 800-272-6657
URL: http://www.computer.org/portal/site/security/

Bimonthly. $24.00/year for members; $29.00/year for nonmembers; $28.00/year for members; $565.00/year for libraries, institution. Journal that aims to explore role and importance of networked infrastructure and developing lasting security solutions.

★9039★ Information Security

TechTarget
117 Kendrick St., Ste. 800
Needham, MA 02494
Ph: (781)657-1000   Fax: (781)657-1100
URL: http://searchsecurity.techtarget.com/

Monthly. Free to qualified subscribers. Magazine covering information security topics.

★9040★ IT Focus

IDG Communications Inc.
5 Speen St., 3rd. Fl
Framingham, MA 01701
Ph: (508)875-5000   Fax: (508)988-7888

URL: http://www.idg.com

Online journal focusing mainly on information technology.

★9041★ IT Solutions Guide

SYS-CON Media
135 Chestnut Ridge Rd.
Montvale, NJ 07645
Ph: (201)802-3000   Fax: (201)782-9600
Fr: 888-303-5282
URL: http://itsolutions.sys-con.com/

Quarterly. $4.00/year for individuals, single pdf issue. Magazine for IT professionals.

★9042★ Journal of Computer Science

Science Publications
Vails Gate Heights Dr.
PO Box 879
Vails Gate, NY 12584
URL: http://www.scipub.us/

Bimonthly. $3,500.00/year for individuals; $300.00/year for single issue. Scholarly journal covering many areas of computer science, including: concurrent, parallel and distributed processing; artificial intelligence; image and voice processing; quality software and metrics; computer-aided education; wireless communication; real time processing; evaluative computation; and data bases and information recovery and neural networks.

★9043★ Journal of Computer Systems, Networks, and Communications

Hindawi Publishing Corp.
410 Park Ave., 15th Fl.
287 PMB
New York, NY 10022
E-mail: jcsnc@hindawi.com
URL: http://www.hindawi.com/journals/jcsnc/

$195.00/year for individuals. Journal covering important areas of information technology.

★9044★ Kompiuterija PC World

IDG Communications Inc.
5 Speen St., 3rd. Fl
Framingham, MA 01701
Ph: (508)875-5000   Fax: (508)988-7888
URL: http://www.idg.com

Monthly. Journal providing professionals, business people and users with up-to-date information on computers and the internet.

★9045★ Mikro PC

IDG Communications Inc.
5 Speen St., 3rd. Fl
Framingham, MA 01701
Ph: (508)875-5000   Fax: (508)988-7888
URL: http://www.idg.com

Monthly. Magazine focusing on information technology and digital lifestyle.

★9046★ Monitor

Capital PC User Group
19209 Mt. Airey Rd.
Brookeville, MD 20833
Ph: (301)560-6442   Fax: (301)760-3303
URL: http://monitor.cpcug.org/index.html

Quarterly. Magazine covering computer hardware and software reviews, special interest user group news, advertisers and author/subject index, and calendar of events.

★9047★ NetWorld

IDG Communications Inc.
5 Speen St., 3rd. Fl
Framingham, MA 01701
Ph: (508)875-5000   Fax: (508)988-7888
URL: http://www.idg.com

Monthly. Magazine focusing on networks, security, infrastructure management, wireless, mobile and VOIP technologies.

★9048★ Optimize

CMP Media L.L.C.
600 Community Dr.
Manhasset, NY 11030
Ph: (516)562-5000   Fax: (516)562-7830
URL: http://www.optimizemag.com

Monthly. Monthly business technology publication providing business strategies to IT Executives.

★9049★ PC Magazine

Ziff-Davis Publishing Co.
28 East 28th St.
New York, NY 10016
Ph: (212)503-3500
E-mail: pcmag@ziffdavis.com
URL: http://www.ziffdavisinternet.com/websites/pcmag

Biweekly. $19.97/year for individuals, 25 issues. Tabloid featuring microcomputer products and developments.

★9050★ PC Today

Sandhills Publishing
120 W Harvest Dr.
Lincoln, NE 68521
Ph: (402)479-2181   Fax: (402)479-2195
Fr: 800-331-1978
URL: http://www.sandhills.com

Monthly. $29.00/year for U.S. $37.00/year for Canada; $64.00/year for Canada, print; $2.42/year for U.S., print; $2.42 for single issue, in U.S. Magazine for personal computer users.

★9051★ PC WORLD

101 Communications
9121 Oakdale Ave., Ste. 101
Chatsworth, CA 91311
Ph: (818)734-1520   Fax: (818)734-1522
URL: http://www.pcworld.com

Quarterly. $20.00/year for individuals, 12 issues; $30.00/year for individuals, 24 issues. Technology or business magazine meeting the informational needs of tech-savvy managers, both at work and at home.

★9052★ **Queue**

Association for Computing Machinery
2 Penn Plz., Ste. 701
New York, NY 10121-0701
Ph: (212)869-7440   Fax: (212)944-1318
Fr: 800-342-6626
URL: http://www.acmqueue.org/

Monthly. Free, U.S./Canadian residents and all members. Online magazine aimed at the computer professional. Magazine editorial does not provide solutions for the "here-and-now," but instead helps decision-makers plan future projects by examining the challenges and problems they are most likely to face.

★9053★ **Revenue**

Montgomery Media International
300 Montgomery St., Ste. 1135
San Francisco, CA 94104
Ph: (415)397-2400   Fax: (415)397-2420
URL: http://www.revenuetoday.com/

$30.00/year for individuals. Magazine covering internet marketing strategies.

★9054★ **SMB Data**

IDG Communications Inc.
5 Speen St., 3rd. Fl
Framingham, MA 01701
Ph: (508)875-5000   Fax: (508)988-7888
URL: http://www.idg.com

Magazine focusing on information technology systems at small and medium-size businesses.

★9055★ **SME World**

IDG Communications Inc.
5 Speen St., 3rd. Fl
Framingham, MA 01701
Ph: (508)875-5000   Fax: (508)988-7888
URL: http://www.idg.com

Magazine covering articles on technology, technology investments, IT products and services.

★9056★ **TecCHANNEL Compact**

IDG Communications Inc.
5 Speen St., 3rd. Fl
Framingham, MA 01701
Ph: (508)875-5000   Fax: (508)988-7888
URL: http://www.idg.com

Quarterly. Magazine covering issues of information technology.

★9057★ **Tips & Trucs**

iDG Communications Inc.
5 Speen St., 3rd. Fl
Framingham, MA 01701
Ph: (508)875-5000   Fax: (508)988-7888
URL: http://www.idg.com

Monthly. Magazine covering topics on computer hardware, software and the internet.

★9058★ **Top 100**

IDG Communications Inc.
5 Speen St., 3rd. Fl
Framingham, MA 01701
Ph: (508)875-5000   Fax: (508)988-7888
URL: http://www.idg.com

Annual. Magazine providing analyses, assessments and statistics on information technology industry.

★9059★ **Ubiquity**

Association for Computing Machinery
2 Penn Plz., Ste. 701
New York, NY 10121-0701
Ph: (212)869-7440   Fax: (212)944-1318
Fr: 800-342-6626
URL: http://www.acm.org/ubiquity/

Weekly. Free to members; $163.00/year for nonmembers, 12 issues. Web-based magazine of the Association for Computing Machinery dedicated to fostering critical analysis and in-depth commentary, including book reviews, on issues relating to the nature, constitution, structure, science, engineering, cognition, technology, practices and paradigms of the IT profession.

★9060★ **WebLogic Pro**

Fawcette Technical Publications
2600 S El Camino Real, Ste. 300
San Mateo, CA 94403-2332
Ph: (650)378-7100   Fax: (650)570-6307
Fr: 800-848-5523
URL: http://www.weblogicpro.com

Bimonthly. Free to qualified subscribers. Magazine that aims to provides IT solutions for developers, architects, and administrators.

★9061★ **WITI FastTrack**

CMP Media L.L.C.
600 Community Dr.
Manhasset, NY 11030
Ph: (516)562-5000   Fax: (516)562-7830
URL: http://www.witi.com/corporate/fast-track.php

Semiannual. Semiannual publication featuring in-depth content on the issues facing today's women professionals in technology.

EMPLOYER DIRECTORIES AND NETWORKING LISTS

★9062★ **Career Opportunities in Computers and Cyberspace**

Facts On File Inc.
132 W 31st St., 17th Fl.
New York, NY 10001
Ph: (212)967-8800   Fax: 800-678-3633
Fr: 800-322-8755
URL: http://www.factsonfile.com

Published 2004. $49.50 for individuals; $44.55 for libraries. Covers nearly 200 professions, clustering them by skill, objectives,

and work conditions. Entries include: Education, salaries, employment prospects.

★9063★ **Computer Directory**

Computer Directories Inc.
23815 Nichols Sawmill Rd.
Hockley, TX 77447
Ph: (281)356-7880   Fr: 800-234-4353
URL: http://www.compdirinc.com

Annual, fall. Covers approximately 130,000 computer installation companies; 19 separate volumes for Alaska/Hawaii, Connecticut/New Jersey, Dallas/Ft. Worth, Eastern Seaboard, Far Midwest, Houston, Illinois, Midatlantic, Midcentral, Mideast, Minnesota/Wisconsin, North Central, New England, New York Metro, Northwest, Ohio, Pennsylvania/West Virginia, Southeast, and Southwest Texas. Entries include: Company name, address, phone, fax, e-mail, name and title of contact, hardware used, software application, operating system, programming language, computer graphics, networking system. Arrangement: Geographical. Indexes: Alphabetical; industry; hardware.

★9064★ **Peterson's Job Opportunities for Engineering and Computer Science Majors**

Peterson's
Princeton Pke. Corporate Ctr., 2000 Lenox Dr.
PO Box 67005
Lawrenceville, NJ 08648
Ph: (609)896-1800   Fax: (609)896-4531
Fr: 800-338-3282
URL: http://www.petersons.com

Annual; latest edition 1999. $18.95 for individuals. Covers approximately 2,000 research, consulting, manufacturing, government, and technical services organizations hiring colleges graduates in the fields of engineering, telecommunications, biotechnology, software, and consumer electronics. Entries include: Organization name, address, phone, name and title of contact, type of organization, number of employees, Standard Industrial Classification (SIC) code, description of opportunities available, level of education required, starting salary, location, level of experience accepted, benefits.

HANDBOOKS AND MANUALS

★9065★ **The Digital Frontier Job & Opportunity Finder**

Moon Lake Media
PO Box 251466
Los Angeles, CA 90025
Ph: (310)535-2453

Don B. Altman. 1996. $19.95 (paper). 245 pages.

★9066★ Great Jobs for Computer Science Majors

The McGraw-Hill Companies
PO Box 182604
Columbus, OH 43272
Fax: (614)759-3749   Fr: 877-883-5524
E-mail: customer.service@mcgraw-hill.com
URL: http://www.mcgraw-hill.com

Jan Goldberg, Stephen Lambert, Julie De-Galan. Second edition, 2002. $14.95 (paper). 224 pages.

★9067★ Job Seekers Guide to Silicon Valley Recruiters

John Wily and Sons, Inc.
605 Third Ave., 4th Fl.
New York, NY 10158-0012
Ph: (212)850-6276   Fax: (212)850-8641

Christopher W. Hunt, Scott A. Scanlon. First edition, 1998. $19.95 (paper). 371 pages. Includes a list of 2,400 recruiters specializing in high technology positions and explains how to work with them.

★9068★ The JobBank Guide to Computer and High-Tech Companies

Adams Media Corp.
57 Littlefield St.
Avon, MA 02322
Ph: (508)427-7100   Fax: (508)427-6790
Fr: 800-872-5627
URL: http://www.adamsmedia.com

Steven Graber, Marcie Dipietro, and Michelle Roy Kelly. Second edition, 1999. $17.95 (paper). 700 pages. Contains profiles of more than 4,500 high-tech employers.

★9069★ Opportunities in Computer Systems Careers

The McGraw-Hill Companies
PO Box 182604
Columbus, OH 43272
Fax: (614)759-3749   Fr: 877-883-5524
E-mail: customer.service@mcgraw-hill.com
URL: http://www.mcgraw-hill.com

Julie King Burns. 1996. $14.95; $11.95 (paper). 160 pages.

★9070★ Opportunities in High Tech Careers

The McGraw-Hill Companies
PO Box 182604
Columbus, OH 43272
Fax: (614)759-3749   Fr: 877-883-5524
E-mail: customer.service@mcgraw-hill.com
URL: http://www.mcgraw-hill.com

Gary Colter and Deborah Yanuck. 1999. $14.95; $11.95 (paper). 160 pages. Explores high technology careers. Describes job opportunities, how to make a career decision, how to prepare for high technology jobs, job hunting techniques, and future trends.

★9071★ Opportunities in Telecommunications Careers

The McGraw-Hill Companies
PO Box 182604
Columbus, OH 43272
Fax: (614)759-3749   Fr: 877-883-5524
E-mail: customer.service@mcgraw-hill.com
URL: http://www.mcgraw-hill.com

Jan Bone, Suzanne Nagle. 1995. $11.95 (paper).

★9072★ Winning Resumes for Computer Personnel

Barron's Educational Series, Inc.
250 Wireless Blvd.
Hauppauge, NY 11788-3917
Ph: (631)434-3311   Fax: (631)434-3723
Fr: 800-645-3476
E-mail: fbrown@barronseduc.com
URL: http://barronseduc.com

Anne Hart. Second edition, 1998. $14.95 (paper). 260 pages.

EMPLOYMENT AGENCIES AND SEARCH FIRMS

★9073★ Data Systems Search Consultants

1615 Bonanza St., Ste. 405
Walnut Creek, CA 94596
Ph: (925)256-0635   Fax: (925)256-9099
E-mail: dsscinfo@dssc.com
URL: http://www.dssc.com

Employment agency. Executive search firm.

★9074★ Huntington Personnel Consultants, Inc.

PO Box 1077
Huntington, NY 11743-0640
Ph: (516)549-8888

Executive search firm and employment agency.

★9075★ Intech Summit Group, Inc.

3450 Bonita Rd., Ste. 203
Chula Vista, CA 91910
Ph: (619)862-2720   Fax: (619)862-2699
Fr: 800-750-8100
E-mail: isg@isgsearch.com
URL: http://www.isgsearch.com

Employment agency and executive recruiter with a branch in Carlsbad, CA.

★9076★ O'Keefe and Partners

4 Corporate Dr., Ste 490
Shelton, CT 06484
Ph: (203)929-4222   Fax: (203)926-0073
E-mail: smoore@okeefepartners.com
URL: http://www.okeefepartners.com

Executive search firm.

★9077★ Sullivan and Cogliano

230 2nd Ave
Waltham, MA 02451
Ph: (781)890-7890   Fr: 888-785-2641
E-mail: contract@sullivansogliano.com
URL: http://www.sullivancogliano.com

Technical staffing firm.

★9078★ Technical Talent Locators Ltd.

5570 Sterrett Pl., Ste. 208
Columbia, MD 21044
Ph: (410)740-0091
E-mail: steve@ttlgroup.com
URL: http://www.ttlgroup.com

Permanent employment agency working within the following fields: software and database engineering; computer, communication, and telecommunication system engineering; and other computer-related disciplines.

★9079★ Worlco Computer Resources, Inc.

997 Old Eagle School Rd., Ste. 219
Wayne, PA 19087
Ph: (610)293-9070   Fax: (610)293-1027
E-mail: parisi@worlco.com
URL: http://www.worlco.com

Employment agency and executive search firm. Second location in Cherry Hill, New Jersey.

ONLINE JOB SOURCES AND SERVICES

★9080★ ComputerJobs.com

280 Interstate North Cir., SE, Ste. 300
Atlanta, GA 30339-2411
Ph: 800-850-0045
URL: http://www.computerjobs.com

Description: The site is an employment tool for technology professionals. Information on positions is updated hourly for seekers. Jobs may be searched by skill, or by location nationally or in a specific state or city job market. Contains thousands of job postings. National jobs may be posted for free. Also career resources for IT professionals.

★9081★ Computerwork.com

Fr: 800-691-8413
E-mail: contactus@computerwork.com
URL: http://www.computerwork.com/

Description: Job search and resume submission service for professionals in information technology.

★9082★ Computerworld Careers

URL: http://www.computerworld.com/careertopics/careers

Description: Offers career opportunities for IT (information technology) professionals.

Job seekers may search the jobs database, register at the site, and read about job surveys and employment trends. Employers may post jobs.

★9083★ Computing Research Association Job Announcements

1100 17th St., NW
Washington, DC 20036-4632
Ph: (202)234-2111   Fax: (202)667-1066
URL: http://www.cra.org/main/cra.jobs.html

Description: Contains dated links to national college and university computer technology positions.

★9084★ Dice.com

4101 NW Urbandale Dr.
Urbandale, IA 50322
Fax: (515)280-1452   Fr: 877-386-3323
URL: http://www.dice.com

Description: Job search database for computer consultants and high-tech professionals, listing thousands of high tech permanent contract and consulting jobs for programmers, software engineers, systems administrators, web developers, and hardware engineers. Also free career advice e-mail newsletter and job posting e-alerts.

★9085★ Ittalent.com

E-mail: ewsmith@ITtalent.com
URL: http://www.ittalent.com

Description: Job search and resume submission service for professionals in information technology.

★9086★ ZDNet Tech Jobs

URL: http://www.zdnet.com/

Description: Site houses a listing of national employment opportunities for professionals in high tech fields. Also contains resume building tips and relocation resources.

OTHER SOURCES

★9087★ Computer Occupations

Delphi Productions
3159 6th St.
Boulder, CO 80304
Ph: (303)443-2100   Fax: (303)443-4022
Fr: 888-443-2400
E-mail: support@delphivideo.com
URL: http://www.delphivideo.com

$95.00. 50 minutes. Part of the Careers for the 21st Century Video Library.

★9088★ Information Technology Occupations

Delphi Productions
3159 6th St.
Boulder, CO 80304
Ph: (303)443-2100   Fax: (303)443-4022
Fr: 888-443-2400
E-mail: support@delphivideo.com
URL: http://www.delphivideo.com

$95.00. 52 minutes. Part of the Emerging Careers Video Library.

Personal Service Providers

SOURCES OF HELP-WANTED ADS

★9089★ CRM Buyer
NewsFactor Network
21700 Oxnard St., Ste. 2040
Woodland Hills, CA 91367
Ph: (818)713-2500
URL: http://www.crmbuyer.com/

Monthly. Magazine covering customer relationship management solutions.

★9090★ Service Revenue
Center for Services Marketing Inc.
300 Hess Ave., Bldg. II
Golden, CO 80401
Ph: (720)746-1900   Fax: (720)746-0599
URL: http://www.csmhub.com/

Semiannual. $129.00/year for individuals. Newsletter giving information on marketing and sales knowledge for the service industry.

PLACEMENT AND JOB REFERRAL SERVICES

★9091★ International Nanny Association (INA)
3801 Kirby Dr., Ste. 540
Houston, TX 77098
Ph: (713)526-2670   Fax: (713)526-2667
Fr: 888-878-1477
E-mail: ina@nanny.org
URL: http://www.nanny.org

Description: An educational association for nannies and those who educate, place, employ, and support professional in-home child care. Membership is open to those who are directly involved with the in-home child care profession, including nannies, nanny employers, nanny placement agency owners (and staff), nanny educators, and providers of special services related to the nanny profession.

EMPLOYER DIRECTORIES AND NETWORKING LISTS

★9092★ Careers in Focus: Personal Services
Facts On File Inc.
132 W 31st St., 17th Fl.
New York, NY 10001
Ph: (212)967-8800   Fax: 800-678-3633
Fr: 800-322-8755
URL: http://www.factsonfile.com

$29.95 for individuals; $26.95 for libraries. Covers an overview of personal services, followed by a selection of jobs profiled in detail, including the nature of the job, earnings, prospects for employment, what kind of training and skills it requires, and sources for further information.

HANDBOOKS AND MANUALS

★9093★ Career Information Center: Consumer, Homemaking, and Personal Services
Cengage Learning
PO Box 6904
Florence, KY 41022
Fax: 800-487-8488   Fr: 800-354-9706
URL: http://www.cengage.com

Darryl Kestler.

★9094★ Household Careers: Nannies, Butlers, Maids and More: The Complete Guide for Finding Household Employment or 'If the Dog Likes You, You're Hired!'
Five Star Publications, Inc.
PO Box 6698
Chandler, AZ 85246-6698
Ph: (480)940-8182   Fax: (480)940-8787
Fr: (866)471-0777
URL: http://www.fivestarpublications.com/

Linda F. Radke. 2001. 120 pages. $14.95.

★9095★ How to Start and Operate an Errand Service
Legacy Marketing
403 Hobart Dr.
Laurel Springs, NJ 08021
Ph: (609)346-0276   Fax: (609)346-2994
Fr: 888-725-2639

Rob Spina. Second edition, 2002. $29.95. 70 pages.

TRADESHOWS

★9096★ IEHA Convention & Trade Show
International Executive Housekeepers Association Inc.
University of South Carolina, Campus Services
720 College St.
Columbia, SC 29208
Ph: (803)777-4878   Fax: (803)777-7334
Fr: 800-200-6342
E-mail: har@fmc.sc.edu
URL: http://www.ieha.org

Annual. **Primary Exhibits:** Cleaning, maintenance, and sterilization supplies and equipment, including chemicals, cleaners, paper products, linens, and amenities.

OTHER SOURCES

★9097★ Association of Residential Cleaning Services International
931 Monroe Dr., Ste. A102-349
Atlanta, GA 30308
Fax: (866)642-9562   Fr: (866)880-5914
E-mail: perry@arcsi.org
URL: http://www.arcsi.org

Description: Assists residential cleaning service owners and professionals in starting, promoting, building, and expanding their businesses.

★9098★ National Association of Nannies

4604 N. Lakefront Dr.
Glen Allen, VA 23060
Ph: (843)548-0105   Fr: 800-344-6266
E-mail: apn@hargray.com
URL: http://www.nannyassociation.com

Description: Promotes the nanny as a legitimate career choice.

★9099★ National Association of Professional Organizers (NAPO)

15000 Commerce Pkwy, Ste. C
Mount Laurel, NJ 08054
Ph: (856)380-6828   Fax: (856)439-0525
E-mail: hq@napo.net
URL: http://www.napo.net/

Description: Educational association whose members include organizing consultants, speakers, trainers, authors, and manufacturers of organizing people.

★9100★ National Association of Professional Pet Sitters (NAPPS)

15000 Commerce Pkwy., Ste. C
Mount Laurel, NJ 08054
Ph: (856)439-0324   Fax: (856)439-0525
E-mail: napps@ahint.com
URL: http://www.petsitters.org

Description: Owners or employees of pet-sitting services; professionals or businesses in related fields. Promotes professional and ethical standards in pet sitting and fosters cooperation among members of the pet-care industry. Serves as a network for the exchange of ideas and information on pet sitting and current industry practices. Disseminates information educating the pet-owning public on the advantages of leaving pets in a home environment and how to choose a reliable sitter.

★9101★ Personal & Building Service Occupations

Delphi Productions
3159 6th St.
Boulder, CO 80304
Ph: (303)443-2100   Fax: (303)443-4022
Fr: 888-443-2400
E-mail: support@delphivideo.com
URL: http://www.delphivideo.com

$95.00. 48 minutes. Part of the Careers for the 21st Century Video Library.

★9102★ Pet Sitters International

201 E King St.
King, NC 27021
Ph: (336)983-9222
E-mail: info@petsit.com
URL: http://www.petsit.com

Members: Represents professional pet sitters. Serves as an educational organization for professional pet sitters and advocates of at-home pet care. Promotes, recognizes and supports excellence in pet sitting. **Purpose:** Provides a forum of communication for members who share a common vision of excellence in at-home pet care.

★9103★ United States Personal Chef Association

610 Quantum Road NE
Rio Rancho, NM 87124
Ph: (505)994-6372   Fr: 800-995-2138
URL: http://www.uspca.com

Description: The largest organization dedicated to the personal service industry.

Personnel, Training, and Labor Relations Specialists and Managers

SOURCES OF HELP-WANTED ADS

★9104★ Business Insurance

Crain Communications Inc.
1155 Gratiot Ave.
Detroit, MI 48207-2997
Ph: (313)446-6000
URL: http://www.businessinsurance.com

Weekly. $97.00/year for individuals; $173.00 for two years; $200.00/year for individuals, daily online only; $130.00/year for Canada and Mexico; $234.00 for Canada and Mexico, two years; $230.00/year for individuals, includes expedited airmail other countries; $436.00 for two years, includes expedited airmail other countries. International newsweekly reporting on corporate risk and employee benefit management news.

★9105★ Human Resource Executive

LRP Publications
747 Dresher Rd., Ste. 500
PO Box 980
Horsham, PA 19044-0980
Ph: (215)784-0860   Fax: (215)784-9639
Fr: 800-341-7874
URL: http://www.hrexecutive.com

Business magazine (tabloid) for human resource executives in corporations, non-profit organizations, and government agencies.

★9106★ Journal of Labor Research

Transaction Publishers
Rutgers - The State University of New Jersey
35 Berrue Cir.
Piscataway, NJ 08854-8042
Ph: (732)445-2280   Fax: (732)445-3138
URL: http://www.transactionpub.com/cgi-bin/transactionpublishers.

Quarterly. $70.00/year for individuals, one-year online subscription; $70.00/year for individuals, one-year print subscription; $75.00/year for individuals, one-year print and online subscription; $328.00/year for institutions, one-year online subscription; $328.00/year for institutions, one-year print subscription; $345.00/year for institutions, one-year print and online subscription. Journal publishing articles on issues related to employment practices and policies, with specific interest in new types of employment relationships, emerging economic and institutional arrangements with respect to labor issues, and objective analyses of employee-related issues.

★9107★ The Organization Development Institute

International Registry of Organization Development Professionals
11234 Walnut Ridge Rd.
Chesterland, OH 44026
Ph: (440)729-7419
URL: http://www.odinstitute.org

Description: Monthly. Serves organization development professionals, teachers of organizational behavior, management consultants, personnel directors and executives by carrying news items, interest surveys, economic information, and committee reports. Recurring features include announcements of conferences, meetings, publications, consulting opportunities, and employment openings. Subscription includes annual publication titled The International Registry of Organization Development Professionals and Organization Development Handbook, and copies of The Organizational Development Journal.

★9108★ Pensions & Investments

Crain Communications Inc.
1155 Gratiot Ave.
Detroit, MI 48207-2997
Ph: (313)446-6000
URL: http://www.pionline.com

Biweekly. $239.00/year for individuals; $595.00/year for individuals, daily email; $695.00/year for individuals. Magazine containing news and features on investment management, pension management, corporate finance, and cash management.

★9109★ TD Magazine

American Society for Training & Development
1640 King St.
PO Box 1443
Alexandria, VA 22313-2043
Ph: (703)683-8100   Fax: (703)683-8103
Fr: 800-628-2783
URL: http://www.astd.org/

Monthly. $99.00/year for individuals; $165.00/year for other countries; $125.00/year for Canada and Mexico; $225.00 for two years, Canada/Mexico; $165.00/year for individuals, international. Magazine on training and development.

★9110★ Workforce Managment

Crain Communications, Inc.
4 Executive Cir., Ste. 185
Irvine, CA 92614
Ph: (949)255-5340
E-mail: mailroom@workforcemag.com
URL: http://www.workforceonline.com

Biweekly. $79.00/year for individuals, U.S. domestic rate; $129.00/year for Canada; $199.00/year for other countries, all other international. A business magazine for human resources management leaders.

★9111★ Workforce Performance Solutions

MediaTec Publishing
444 N Michigan Ave., Ste. 3530
Chicago, IL 60611
Ph: (312)828-2800   Fax: (312)828-1105
URL: http://www.wpsmag.com/content/templates/wps_home.asp?article

Monthly. Free to qualified subscribers. Magazine covering workplace performance and effectiveness.

PLACEMENT AND JOB REFERRAL SERVICES

★9112★ American Society for Healthcare Human Resources Administration (ASHHRA)

1 N Franklin, 31st Fl.
Chicago, IL 60606
Ph: (312)422-3720   Fax: (312)422-4577
E-mail: ashhra@aha.org
URL: http://www.ashhra.org

Description: Provides effective and continuous leadership in the field of health care human resources administration. Promotes cooperation with hospitals and allied associations in matters pertaining to hospital human resources administration. Works to further the professional and educational development of members. Encourages and assists local groups in chapter formation through regular programs and institutes on health care human resources issues. Offers placement service.

★9113★ International Registry of Organization Development Professionals (IRODP)

11234 Walnut Ridge Rd.
Chesterland, OH 44026
Ph: (440)729-7419   Fax: (440)729-9319
E-mail: donwcole@aol.com
URL: http://members.aol.com/odinst

Description: Educational subsidiary of the Organization Development Institute. **Members:** Organization development professionals, students, and persons interested in improving the way organizations function. **Purpose:** Promotes a better understanding of and disseminates information about organization development. **Activities:** Maintains job placement service. Conducts specialized education.

EMPLOYER DIRECTORIES AND NETWORKING LISTS

★9114★ College and University Professional Association-Membership Directory

College and University Professional Association for Human Resources
Tyson Pl.
2607 Kingston Pke., Ste. 250
Knoxville, TN 37919
Ph: (865)637-7673   Fax: (865)637-7674
E-mail: membership@cupahr.org
URL: http://www.search.cupahr.org/members/search.cfm

Online; continually updated; access restricted to members. Covers more than 7,000 members interested in college and university human resource administration; over 1,700 institutions. Entries include: For members–Personal name, title, affiliation, address, fax, e-mail, phone. For institutions–Organization name, address, phone, and names/titles of representatives. Arrangement: Members are alphabetical; institutions are geographical.

★9115★ Peterson's Job Opportunities for Business Majors

Peterson's
Princeton Pke. Corporate Ctr., 2000 Lenox Dr.
PO Box 67005
Lawrenceville, NJ 08648
Ph: (609)896-1800   Fax: (609)896-4531
Fr: 800-338-3282
URL: http://www.petersons.com/

Irregular; latest edition 16th, 2000. Covers the 2,000 largest U.S. employers hiring in several fields, including financial services, management consulting, consumer products, and media/entertainment. Entries include: Organization name, address, phone, name and title of contact, number of employees, type of organization. Arrangement: Alphabetical. Indexes: Type of organization.

★9116★ Skills and Training Directory

World View Forum
55 W 17th St., 5th Fl.
New York, NY 10011-5513
Ph: (212)627-2994   Fax: (212)675-7869

Latest edition 4th, 2003. $40.00 for individuals. Covers Over 1,000 occupational training and business education providers for professionals in human resource development. Entries include: Name, address, phone.

HANDBOOKS AND MANUALS

★9117★ 96 Great Interview Questions to Ask Before You Hire

AMACOM
1601 Broadway, 12th Fl.
New York, NY 10019-7420
Ph: (212)586-8100   Fax: (212)903-8168
Fr: 800-262-9699
URL: http://www.amanet.org

Paul Falcone. 2000. $17.95. 224 pages.

★9118★ How to Succeed in Employee Development: Moving from Vision to Results

The McGraw-Hill Companies
PO Box 182604
Columbus, OH 43272
Fax: (614)759-3749   Fr: 877-883-5524
E-mail: customer.service@mcgraw-hill.com
URL: http://www.mcgraw-hill.com

Edward Moorby. Third edition, 1998. 193 pages. Part of the Training Series.

★9119★ Management Development: Strategy and Practice

John Wiley & Sons Inc.
1 Wiley Dr.
Somerset, NJ 08873
Ph: (732)469-4400   Fax: (732)302-2300
Fr: 800-225-5945
E-mail: custserv@wiley.com
URL: http://www.wiley.com/WileyCDA/

Jean Woodall and Diana Winstanley. 1998. $64.95 (paper). 290 pages.

★9120★ Opportunities in Hospital Administration Careers

The McGraw-Hill Companies
PO Box 182604
Columbus, OH 43272
Fax: (614)759-3749   Fr: 877-883-5524
E-mail: customer.service@mcgraw-hill.com
URL: http://www.mcgraw-hill.com

I. Donald Snook. 2006. $13.95. 160 pages. Discusses opportunities for administrators in a variety of management settings: hospital, department, clinic, group practice, HMO, mental health, and extended care facilities.

★9121★ Opportunities in Insurance Careers

The McGraw-Hill Companies
PO Box 182604
Columbus, OH 43272
Fax: (614)759-3749   Fr: 877-883-5524
E-mail: customer.service@mcgraw-hill.com
URL: http://www.mcgraw-hill.com

Robert M. Schrayer. Revised, 2007. $14.95 (paper). 160 pages. A guide to planning for and seeking opportunities in the field. Contains bibliography and illustrations.

★9122★ Opportunities in International Business Careers

The McGraw-Hill Companies
PO Box 182604
Columbus, OH 43272
Fax: (614)759-3749   Fr: 877-883-5524
E-mail: customer.service@mcgraw-hill.com
URL: http://www.mcgraw-hill.com

Jeffrey Arpan. 1994. $11.95 (paper). 147 pages. Describes what types of jobs exist in international business, where they are located, what challenges and rewards they bring, and how to prepare for and obtain jobs in international business.

★9123★ Real-Resumes for Human-Resources and Personnel Jobs: Including Real Resumes Used to Change Careers and Transfer Skills to Other Industries

PREP Publishing
1110 1/2 Hay St., PMB 66
Fayetteville, NC 28305
Ph: (910)483-6611   Fax: (910)483-2439
Fr: 800-533-2814

Anne McKinney. September 2002. $16.95. 192 pages.

★9124★ Up Is Not the Only Way: A Guide to Developing Workforce Talent
Prentice Hall PTR
1 Lake St.
Upper Saddle River, NJ 07458
Ph: (201)236-7000   Fax: 800-445-6991
Fr: 800-428-5331
URL: http://www.phptr.com/index.asp?rl=1

Beverly L. Kaye. Second Edition. 1982. $22.95. 293 pages.

EMPLOYMENT AGENCIES AND SEARCH FIRMS

★9125★ Abbott Smith Associates, Inc.
11697 W. Grand Ave.
Northlake, IL 60164
Ph: (708)223-1191
E-mail: contactus@abbottsmith.com
URL: http://www.abbottsmith.com

Human Resources executive search firm.

★9126★ The Alexander Group
2700 Post Oak Blvd., Ste. 2400
Houston, TX 77056
Ph: (713)993-7900   Fax: (713)993-7979
E-mail: info@thealexandergroup.com
URL: http://www.thealexandergroup.com

Executive search firm. Second location in San Francisco.

★9127★ The Aspire Group
52 Second Ave, 1st Fl
Waltham, MA 02451-1129
Fax: (718)890-1810   Fr: 800-487-2967
URL: http://www.bmanet.com

Employment agency.

★9128★ Boettcher Associates
120 Bishops Way, Ste. 126
Brookfield, WI 53005
Ph: (262)782-2205

Executive search firm.

★9129★ Brindisi Search
10751 Falls Rd., Greenspring Sta., Ste. 250
Greenspring Stn.
Lutherville, MD 21093
Ph: (410)339-7673   Fax: (410)823-0146
E-mail: tbrindisi@aol.com
URL: http://www.brindisisearch.com

Specializes in contemporary human resource and select strategic leadership assignments, ranging from manager to senior vice president level.

★9130★ Charleston Partners
2 Bellevue Ave.
Rumson, NJ 07760
Ph: (732)842-5015   Fax: (732)842-0993
E-mail: info@charlestonpartners.com
URL: http://www.charlestonpartners.com

Executive search firm concentrated on human resource services.

★9131★ CJA Executive Search
17852 17th St., Ste. 209
Tustin, CA 92780
Ph: (714)573-1820   Fax: (714)731-3952
Fr: 800-559-2559
E-mail: lindas@cjapower.com

Executive search firm. Second location in Los Angeles.

★9132★ Dankowski and Associates, Inc.
13089 Root Rd.
The Woods, Ste. 200 SE
Columbia Station, OH 44028
Ph: (440)236-3088   Fax: (440)236-9621
Fr: 800-326-5694
E-mail: info@dankowskiassocites.com
URL: http://www.dankowskiassociates.com

Executive search firm.

★9133★ Daubenspeck and Associates Ltd.
Two Prudential Plaza
180 N. Stetson Ave., Ste. 1935
Chicago, IL 60611
Ph: (312)297-4100
E-mail: rd@daubenspeck.com
URL: http://www.daubenspeck.com

Executive search firm specializes in team building.

★9134★ Elinvar
1804 Hillsborough St.
Raleigh, NC 27605
Ph: (919)878-4454
E-mail: info@elinvar.com
URL: http://www.elinvar.com

Executive search firm.

★9135★ The Esquire Staffing Group Ltd.
1 S. Wacker Dr., Ste. 1616
Chicago, IL 60606-4616
Ph: (312)795-4300   Fax: (312)795-4329
E-mail: d.williams@esquirestaffing.com
URL: http://www.esquirestaffing.com

Employment agency. Fills permanent as well as temporary openings.

★9136★ ExecuGroup Inc.
142 S. Main St.
PO Box 5040
Grenada, MS 38901
Ph: (662)226-9025   Fax: (662)226-9090
E-mail: tray@execugroup.com

URL: http://www.execugroup.com

Executive search firm. Second location in Bethlehem, PA.

★9137★ The Executive Management Consulting Organization (TEMCO)
Ph: (262)367-4240

Executive search firm.

★9138★ Houser Martin Morris
110th Ave. NE, 110 Atrium Pl., Ste. 580
110 Atrium Pl.
Bellevue, WA 98004
Ph: (425)453-2700   Fax: (425)453-8726
E-mail: info@houser.com
URL: http://www.houser.com

Focus is in the areas of retained executive search, professional and technical recruiting. Areas of specialization include software engineering, sales and marketing, information technology, legal, human resources, accounting and finance, manufacturing, factory automation, and engineering.

★9139★ HRD Consultants Inc.
1199 Rte. 22 E
Mountainside, NJ 07092
Ph: (908)228-5500   Fax: (908)228-7415
E-mail: hrd@aol.com
URL: http://www.hrdconsultants.com

Specializes exclusively on the placement of executive level human resource professionals. Assesses a candidate's professional and personal competencies for a leadership role in human resources.

★9140★ James Farris Associates
909 NW 63rd St.
Oklahoma City, OK 73116
Ph: (405)525-5061   Fax: (405)525-5069
E-mail: james@jamesfarris.com
URL: http://www.jamesfarris.com

Executive search firm.

★9141★ Karras Personnel, Inc.
2 Central Ave.
Madison, NJ 07940
Ph: (208)238-6190
E-mail: amy.kakalec@karraspersonnel.com
URL: http://www.karraspersonnel.com

Executive search firm specializing in human resources recruiting.

★9142★ Protocol Agency Inc.
2659 Townsgate Rd., Ste.203
Westlake Village, CA 91361-2774
Ph: (805)371-0069   Fax: (805)371-0048
E-mail: corp@protocolexec.com
URL: http://www.protocolagency.com

Executive search firm focusing on a variety of placements.

★9143★ **R.A. Clark Consulting Ltd.**
3400 Peachtree Rd. NE, Ste. 645
Atlanta, GA 30326
Ph: (404)231-0005   Fax: (404)231-1030
Fr: 800-251-0041
E-mail: info@raclark.com
URL: http://www.raclark.com

National and international executive search focusing exclusively in the human resource field. Also contracts human resource executives for temporary assignments.

★9144★ **Techtronix Technical Search**
4805 N 24th Pl.
PO Box 17713
Milwaukee, WI 53217-0173
Ph: (414)466-3100   Fax: (414)466-3598

Firm specializes in recruiting executives for the engineering, information systems, manufacturing, marketing, finance, and human resources industries.

★9145★ **Willmott and Associates, Inc.**
922 Waltham St., Ste. 103
Lexington, MA 02421
Ph: (781)863-5400   Fax: (781)863-8000
E-mail: willmont@willmont.com
URL: http://www.willmott.com

Executive search firm and permanent employment agency. Also fills some temporary placements.

TRADESHOWS

★9146★ **Annual Employee Benefits Conference**
International Foundation of Employee
  Benefit Plans
18700 W. Bluemound Rd.
PO Box 69
Brookfield, WI 53008-0069
Ph: (262)786-6710   Fax: (262)786-6647
E-mail: av@ifebp.org
URL: http://www.ifebp.org

Annual. **Primary Exhibits:** Products and services relating to accounting services, alternative medicine, banking/financial, communication, computer software, consulting services, health services, insurance, investments, legal services, preretirement planning.

★9147★ **EAPA Annual Conference**
Employee Assistance Professionals
  Association
2101 Wilson Blvd., Ste. 500
Arlington, VA 22201-3062
Ph: (703)387-1000   Fax: (703)522-4585
URL: http://www.eap-association.com

Annual. **Primary Exhibits:** Exhibits geared toward persons employed full-time in the development or operation of employee assistance programs (EAPs) as administrators, consultants, or motivational counselors.

★9148★ **Education Technology**
Society for Applied Learning Technology
50 Culpeper St.
Warrenton, VA 20186
Ph: (540)347-0055   Fax: (540)349-3169
E-mail: info@salt.org
URL: http://www.salt.org

Annual. **Primary Exhibits:** Distance learning, web-based training systems, knowledge management systems, instructional systems design, and e-learning technology.

★9149★ **Society for Human Resource Management (SHRM) The HRM Marketplace Exposition**
Society for Human Resource
  Management
1800 Duke St.
Alexandria, VA 22314
Ph: (703)548-3440   Fax: (703)535-6490
Fr: 800-283-SHRM
E-mail: shrm@shrm.org
URL: http://www.shrm.org

Annual. **Primary Exhibits:** Human resource management products and services; including relocation human resource information systems, recruitment, executive search, temporary/contact personnel employee compensation and benefits, incentive program information, childcare/eldercare, and drug testing information.

★9150★ **Training Conference and Expo**
VNU Expositions
14685 Avion Pkwy., Ste. 400
Chantilly, VA 20151
Ph: (703)488-2700   Fax: (703)488-2800
Fr: 800-765-7615
URL: http://www.vnuexpo.com

Annual. **Primary Exhibits:** Training and personnel materials, equipment, and services.

OTHER SOURCES

★9151★ **Administration and Management Occupations**
Delphi Productions
3159 6th St.
Boulder, CO 80304
Ph: (303)443-2100   Fax: (303)443-4022
Fr: 888-443-2400
E-mail: support@delphivideo.com
URL: http://www.delphivideo.com

$95.00. 50 minutes. Part of the Careers for the 21st Century Video Library.

★9152★ **American Almanac of Jobs and Salaries**
HarperCollins
10 E. 53rd St.
New York, NY 10022
Ph: (212)207-7000   Fr: 800-242-7737
URL: http://www.harpercollins.com/

John W. Wright. Revised edition, 2000. $20.00 (paper). 672 pages. This is a comprehensive guide to the wages of hundreds of occupations in a wide variety of industries and organizations.

★9153★ **American Society of Pension Professionals and Actuaries (ASPPA)**
4245 N Fairfax Dr., Ste. 750
Arlington, VA 22203
Ph: (703)516-9300   Fax: (703)516-9308
E-mail: asppa@asppa.org
URL: http://www.aspa.org

Description: Aims to educate pension actuaries, consultants, administrators, and other benefits professionals. Seeks to preserve and enhance the private pension system as part of the development of a cohesive and coherent national retirement income policy.

★9154★ **American Staffing Association (ASA)**
277 S Washington St., Ste. 200
Alexandria, VA 22314-3675
Ph: (703)253-2020   Fax: (703)253-2053
E-mail: asa@americanstaffing.net
URL: http://www.americanstaffing.net

Description: Promotes and represents the staffing industry through legal and legislative advocacy, public relations, education, and the establishment of high standards of ethical conduct.

★9155★ **ASTD**
Box 1443
1640 King St.
Alexandria, VA 22313-2043
Ph: (703)683-8100   Fax: (703)683-8103
Fr: 800-628-2783
E-mail: memberservices@astd.org
URL: http://www.astd.org

Description: Represents workplace learning and performance professionals.

★9156★ **College and University Professional Association for Human Resources (CUPA-HR)**
2607 Kingston Pike, Ste. 250
Knoxville, TN 37919
Ph: (865)637-7673   Fax: (865)637-7674
E-mail: abrantley@cupahr.org
URL: http://www.cupahr.org

Members: Professional organization made up of colleges and universities interested in the improvement of campus Human Resource administration. **Activities:** Carries out special research projects and surveys, including annual administrative compensation survey for higher education. Sponsors training seminars to meet members' technical, professional, and developmental needs in human resource management. Disseminates information to members regarding federal legislation and regulations affecting higher education institutions. Compiles statistics.

★9157★ Employee Assistance Society of North America (EASNA)

2001 Jefferson Davis Hwy., Ste. 1004
Arlington, VA 22202-3617
Ph: (703)416-0060   Fax: (703)416-0014
E-mail: info@easna.org
URL: http://www.easna.org

Description: Individuals in the field of employee assistance, including psychiatrists, psychologists, and managers. Facilitates communication among members; provides resource information; serves as a network for employee assistance programs nationwide. Conducts research.

★9158★ Human Resource Certification Institute (HRCI)

1800 Duke St.
Alexandria, VA 22314
Ph: (703)548-3440   Fr: (866)898-4724
E-mail: info@hrci.org
URL: http://www.hrci.org

Description: Promotes the establishment of standards for the profession. Recognizes human resource professionals who have met, through demonstrated professional experience and the passing of a comprehensive written examination, the Institute's requirements for mastering the codified HR body of knowledge. Offers three professional certifications: Professional in Human Resources (PHR), Senior Professional in Human Resources (SPHR), and Global Professional in Human Resources (GPHR).

★9159★ Human Resource Planning Society (HRPS)

317 Madison Ave., Ste. 1509
New York, NY 10017
Ph: (212)490-6387   Fax: (212)682-6851
E-mail: info@hrps.org
URL: http://www.hrps.org

Members: Human resource planning professionals representing 160 corporations and 3000 individual members, including strategic human resources planning and development specialists, staffing analysts, business planners, line managers, and others who function as business partners in the application of strategic human resource management practices. **Purpose:** Seeks to increase the impact of human resource planning and management on business and organizational performance. **Activities:** Sponsors program of professional development in human resource planning concepts, techniques, and practices. Offers networking opportunities.

★9160★ International Association for Human Resource Information Management (IHRIM)

PO Box 1086
Burlington, MA 01803-6086
Fax: (781)998-8011   Fr: 800-804-3983
E-mail: moreinfo@ihrim.org
URL: http://www.ihrim.org

Description: Human resource, payroll, and data processing professionals; others concerned with the development, maintenance, and operation of automated human resource systems. Provides a forum for exchanging experiences, acquiring information, and discussing common needs and problems relating to human resource systems. Works to enhance capabilities for effective and efficient human resource management. Conducts activities on the local, national, and international level. Offers programs and job posting services. Operates resource center, member referral network, and vendor fairs.

★9161★ International Public Management Association for Human Resources (IPMA-HR)

1617 Duke St.
Alexandria, VA 22314
Ph: (703)549-7100   Fax: (703)684-0948
E-mail: ipma@ipma-hr.org
URL: http://www.ipma-hr.org

Description: Seeks to improve human resource practices in government through provision of testing services, advisory service, conferences, professional development programs, research, and publications. Sponsors seminars, conferences, and workshops on various phases of public personnel administration. Compiles statistics.

★9162★ Labor and Employment Relations Association (LERA)

University of Illinois
121 LIR Bldg.
504 E Armory Ave.
Champaign, IL 61820
Ph: (217)333-0072   Fax: (217)265-5130
E-mail: leraoffice@uiuc.edu
URL: http://www.lera.uiuc.edu

Description: Businesspersons, union leaders, government officials, lawyers, arbitrators, academics, and others interested in research and exchange of ideas on social, political, economic, legal, and psychological aspects of labor and employment relations.

★9163★ Organization Development Institute

11234 Walnut Ridge Rd.
Chesterland, OH 44026
Ph: (440)729-7419   Fax: (440)729-9319
E-mail: donwcole@aol.com
URL: http://www.odinstitute.org

Description: Professionals, students, and individuals interested in organization development. Disseminates information on and promotes a better understanding of organization development worldwide. Conducts specialized education programs. Develops the International O.D. Code of Ethics and a competency test for individuals wishing to qualify as a Registered Organization Development Consultant and a statement on the knowledge and skill necessary to be competent in organization development and criteria for the accreditation of OD/OB academic programs. Maintains job and consultant information service. Sponsors International Registry of Organization Development Professionals and Research/Study Team on Nonviolent Large Systems Change. Maintains 18 committees including an International Advisory Board.

★9164★ Organization Development Network (ODN)

71 Valley St., Ste. 301
South Orange, NJ 07079-2825
Ph: (973)763-7337   Fax: (973)763-7448
E-mail: odnetwork@odnetwork.org
URL: http://www.odnetwork.org

Description: Represents practitioners, academics, managers, and students employed or interested in organization development. Works to enhance and provide opportunities for colleagueship and professional development.

★9165★ Society for Human Resource Management (SHRM)

1800 Duke St.
Alexandria, VA 22314-3499
Ph: (703)548-3440   Fax: (703)535-6490
Fr: 800-283-7476
E-mail: shrm@shrm.org
URL: http://www.shrm.org

Members: Professional organization of human resource, personnel, and industrial relations professionals and executives. **Purpose:** Promotes the advancement of human resource management. **Activities:** Sponsors SHRM Foundation. Offers certification through the Human Resource Certification Institute.

★9166★ Team and Workplace Excellence Forum

PO Box 3005
Milwaukee, WI 53201-3005
Ph: (414)272-1734   Fax: (414)272-1734
Fr: 800-248-1946
E-mail: help@aqp.org
URL: http://www.asq.org/teamwork

Description: Works to promote the ideas of involvement, empowerment and workplace democracy. Disseminates information to members through the internet, publications, conferences and educational events.

★9167★ WorldatWork

14040 N Northsight Blvd.
Scottsdale, AZ 85260
Ph: (480)951-9191   Fax: (480)483-8352
Fr: 877-951-9191
E-mail: customerrelations@worldatwork.org
URL: http://www.worldatwork.org

Description: Dedicated to knowledge leadership in compensation, benefits and total rewards, focusing on disciplines associated with attracting, retaining and motivating employees. Offers CCP, CBP, and GRP certification and education programs, conducts surveys, research and provides networking opportunities.

Pest Control Workers

SOURCES OF HELP-WANTED ADS

★9168★ *AMCA Newsletter*

American Mosquito Control Association Inc.
15000 Commerce Parkway, Ste. C
Mount Laurel, NJ 08054
Ph: (856)439-9222   Fax: (856)439-0525
Fr: 800-663-0301
E-mail: amca@mosquito.org
URL: http://www.mosquito.org/

Description: Six issues/year. Reports new products and developments in the mosquito control industry. Recurring features include Association news, listings of job openings and of new publications, and a calendar of events.

★9169★ *Common Sense Pest Control Quarterly*

Bio-Integral Resource Center
PO Box 7414
Berkeley, CA 94707
Ph: (510)524-2567   Fax: (510)524-1758
E-mail: birc@igc.org
URL: http://www.birc.org

Features descriptions of the latest research, products, resources, and book reviews.

★9170★ *Home, Yard & Garden Pest Newsletter*

University of Illinois at Urbana-Champaign
1401 West Green St.
Urbana, IL 61801
Ph: (217)333-4666   Fr: 800-345-6087
URL: http://www.uiuc.edu/

Description: 20/year. Discusses insect, weed, and plant disease pests of the yard and garden. Covers current pest controls, application equipment and methods, and storage and disposal of pesticides for the yard and garden.

★9171★ *Hort Notes*

UMass Extension
French Hall
230 Stockbridge Rd.
University of Massachusetts
Amherst, MA 01003-9316
Ph: (413)545-0895   Fax: (413)577-1620
E-mail: kcarroll@umext.umass.edu
URL: http://www.umassextension.org/on-line_services/newsletters.html

Description: Biweekly, March-October. Contains information highlighting new approaches in integrated pest management and plant maintenance. Includes updates on pest outbreaks, a calendar of educational programs, and insect/disease monitoring checklists.

★9172★ *The IPM Practitioner*

Bio-Integral Resource Center
PO Box 7414
Berkeley, CA 94707
Ph: (510)524-2567   Fax: (510)524-1758
E-mail: birc@igc.org
URL: http://www.birc.org/

Description: Ten issues/year. Supports the Center in its efforts to publish information "on all aspects of environmentally-sound pest control." Investigates the least-toxic methods of controlling pests in agriculture, urban landscapes and structures, greenhouse and general horticulture, forestry, medical/veterinary, range, and other settings. Recurring features include letters to the editor, interviews, news of research, reports of meetings, news of educational opportunities and job listings, notices and reviews of publications available, and a calendar of events. Contains yearly listings of products and services in the area of integrated pest management; listings of suppliers of beneficial insects.

★9173★ *Nebraska Pest Control Association Newsletter*

Nebraska State Pest Control Association Inc.
1335 H St., Ste. 100
Lincoln, NE 68508-3784
Ph: (402)476-1528   Fax: (402)476-1259
E-mail: info@nspca.org

URL: http://www.nspca.org/

Description: Quarterly. Features news and information for those working in pest control.

★9174★ *Pest Control Technology*

GIE Media
4020 Kinross Lakes Pkwy, Ste. 201
Richfield, OH 44286
Fax: (216)925-5038   Fr: 800-456-0707
E-mail: bharbison@gie.net
URL: http://www.pctonline.com

Industry news.

★9175★ *Resistant Pest Management*

Insecticide Resistance Action Committee
Michigan State University
107 Center for Integrated Plant Systems
East Lansing, MI 48824-1311
Ph: (517)353-9430   Fax: (517)353-5598
E-mail: aporter@intraspin.com
URL: http://www.irac-online.org/

Description: Biennial. Provides information about pest control. Recurring features include news of research, a calendar of events, reports of meetings, news of educational opportunities, book reviews, and notices of publications available.

★9176★ *Techletter*

Pinto & Associates Inc.
1576 Willow St.
San Diego, CA 92106
Ph: (619)223-2233   Fax: (619)223-2253
E-mail: pintoinc@aol.com
URL: http://www.pintoinc.com/

Description: Biweekly. Covers topics of interest to pest control technicians.

PLACEMENT AND JOB REFERRAL SERVICES

★9177★ Association of Applied IPM Ecologists (AAIE)

PO Box 12181
Fresno, CA 93776
Ph: (559)907-4897
E-mail: director@aaie.net

Description: Professional agricultural pest management consultants, entomologists, and field personnel. Promotes the implementation of integrated pest management in agricultural and urban environments. Provides a forum for the exchange of technical information on pest control. Offers placement service.

HANDBOOKS AND MANUALS

★9178★ Insect Pest Management: Field and Protected Crops

Springer-Verlag New York, Inc.
233 Spring St.
New York, NY 10013
Ph: (212)460-1501   Fax: (212)460-1595
URL: http://www.springer.com/

A. Rami Horowitz, I. Ishaaya. May 2004. $229.00. Illustrated. 344 pages.

★9179★ Introduction to Insect Pest Management

John Wiley & Sons Inc.
111 River St.
Hoboken, NJ 07030-5774
Ph: (201)748-6000   Fax: (201)748-6088
Fr: 800-225-5945
E-mail: info@wiley.com
URL: http://www.wiley.com

Robert L. Metcalf and William H. Luckmann. Third edition. 1994. $210.00. 672 pages. ISBN: 0471589578. Presents the philosophy and practice, ecological and economic background, as well as strategies and techniques of pest management, including the use of chemical pesticides. Also addresses biological, genetic and cultural methods to manage the harm done by insect pests.

★9180★ Pests of Landscape Trees and Shrubs: An Integrated Pest Management Guide

University of California Statewide Integrated Pest Management Program
One Shields Ave.
Davis, CA 95616-8621
Ph: (530)752-8350   Fax: (530)752-6004
URL: http://www.ipm.ucdavis.edu

Steve H. Dreistadt. 2004. $42.00. Second Edition. Compiled by scientists at the University of California's Statewide Integrated Pest Management Project, this guide is aimed at homeowners and gardeners as well as landscape and pest management professionals.

TRADESHOWS

★9181★ American Mosquito Control Association Convention

American Mosquito Control Association
15000 Commerce Parkway
Ste. C
N. House
Mount Laurel, NJ 08054
Ph: (856)439-9222   Fax: (856)439-0525
E-mail: amca@mosquito.org
URL: http://www.mosquito.org

Annual. **Primary Exhibits:** Equipment, supplies, and services related to mosquito control, including chemicals. **Dates and Locations:** 2008 Mar 02-06; Sparks, NV; John Ascuaga's Nugget.

★9182★ Florida Pest Management Association Convention and Exposition

Florida Pest Management Association
14055 SW 142nd Ave., Ste. 40
Miami, FL 33186
Ph: (305)233-7222   Fax: (305)235-9783
Fr: 800-426-4829
URL: http://www.fpca.org

Annual. **Primary Exhibits:** Equipment, services, and supplies for the chemical industry.

★9183★ Pest Control Operators of California Convention

Pest Control Operators of California
3031 Beacon Blvd.
West Sacramento, CA 95691
Ph: (916)372-4363   Fax: (916)372-5437
URL: http://www.pcoc.org

Annual. **Primary Exhibits:** Equipment, supplies, and services for owners and operators of structural pest control companies in California.

OTHER SOURCES

★9184★ American Mosquito Control Association (AMCA)

15000 Commerce Pkwy., Ste. C
Mount Laurel, NJ 08054
Ph: (856)439-9222   Fax: (856)439-0525
E-mail: amca@mosquito.org
URL: http://www.mosquito.org

Members: Entomologists, biologists, medical personnel, engineers, public health officials, military personnel, and others interested in mosquito control and related work.

★9185★ Association of American Pesticide Control Officials (AAPCO)

PO Box 466
Milford, DE 19963
Ph: (302)422-8152   Fax: (302)422-2435
E-mail: aapco-sfireg@comcast.net
URL: http://aapco.ceris.purdue.edu

Description: State agencies controlling the sale, use, and distribution of pesticides. Promotes uniform laws, regulations, and policies of enforcement.

★9186★ Bio-Integral Resource Center (BIRC)

PO Box 7414
Berkeley, CA 94707
Ph: (510)524-2567   Fax: (510)524-1758
E-mail: birc@igc.org
URL: http://www.birc.org

Purpose: Provides publications and consultations for pest management professionals, farmers, foresters, park service resource managers, environmentalists, and interested individuals. Provides practical information on methods of managing pests and land resource problems. Evaluates and disseminates information on the least toxic method of managing weed, vertebrate, insect, and microbe pests in urban, agricultural, forestall, and veterinary environments. Develops integrated pest management programs for community groups, public agencies, and private institutions. (IPM involves integrating biological, horticultural, mechanical, and chemical strategies to suppress pest populations below levels causing economic, medical, or aesthetic damage.) **Activities:** Areas of technical assistance include: consultation of community pest problems; identification of pests and their natural enemies; pest control program evaluation; development of contract specifications; landscape design and design plan review; integration of IPM methods and sustainable agriculture. Reports on educational opportunities; sponsors workshops and lectures.

★9187★ Interstate Professional Applicators Association (IPAA)

PO Box 13262
Salem, OR 97309
Ph: (503)363-7205   Fax: (503)378-0864
E-mail: ipaa2002@hotmail.com

Description: Companies engaged in the application of horticultural spraying. Aims to insure a healthy and safe environment through proper pesticide usage. Works to acquire and disseminate technological information regarding the safe application of pesticides. Contributes to state research facilities. Sponsors seminars on entomology, pathology, safety, soils, business management, and employee relations.

★9188★ National Animal Damage Control Association (NADCA)

Dept. of Game, Fish and Parks
523 E Capitol Ave.
Pierre, SD 57501
Ph: (402)472-8961   Fax: (402)472-8390

E-mail: svantassel2@unl.edu
URL: http://nadca.unl.edu

Description: Vertebrate pest controllers; nuisance wildlife control operators; trappers; federal, state, and local directors, managers, and employees concerned with wildlife management; individuals concerned with creating a more favorable attitude toward vertebrate pest management. Strives to increase public awareness and understanding of the purposes and principles of animal damage control. Supports the use of vertebrate pest management programs as a wildlife management tool. Promotes the animal damage control profession as it relates to the agribusiness community, wildlife resource management, and various government and private entities. Conducts educational and informational programs designed to aid in public and private decision-making concerning animal damage control. Maintains information center on animal damage control problems; sponsors seminars and workshops on vertebrate pest management.

★9189★ National Pest Management Association International (NPMA)
9300 Lee Hwy., Ste. 301
Fairfax, VA 22031
Ph: (703)352-6762   Fax: (703)352-3031
Fr: 800-678-6722
E-mail: info@pestworld.org

URL: http://www.pestworld.org

Description: Represents firms engaged in control of insects, rodents, birds, and other pests, in or around structures, through use of insecticides, rodenticides, miticides, fumigants, and non-chemical methods. Provides advisory services on control procedures, new products, and safety and business administration practices. Promotes June as National Pest Control Month. Sponsors research, periodic technical and management seminars.

★9190★ Pesticide Applicators Professional Association (PAPA)
PO Box 80095
Salinas, CA 93912-0095
Ph: (831)442-3536   Fax: (831)442-2351
E-mail: stephanie@papaseminars.com
URL: http://www.papaseminars.com

Purpose: Seeks to provide continuing education for members to be able to renew state licenses.

★9191★ Responsible Industry for a Sound Environment (RISE)
1156 15th St. NW, Ste. 400
Washington, DC 20005
Ph: (202)872-3860   Fax: (202)355-1467
E-mail: margulies@bluepumpkingroup.com

URL: http://www.pestfacts.org

Members: Manufacturers, formulators, distributors, and representatives of the specialty pesticides industry. **Purpose:** Promotes the environmental, health, and safety benefits of the proper use of specialty pesticides.

★9192★ Safer Pest Control Project
4611 N. Ravenswood Ave., Ste. 107
Chicago, IL 60640
Ph: (773)878-7378   Fax: (773)878-8250
E-mail: info@spcpweb.org
URL: http://www.spcpweb.org/

Description: Non-profit organization dedicated to reducing the public health risks and environmental impacts of pesticide use and promoting safer alternatives.

★9193★ The Structural Pest Control Board
1418 Howe Ave., Ste. 18
Sacramento, CA 95825
Ph: (916)561-8700   Fax: (916)263-2469
E-mail: pestboard@dca.ca.gov
URL: http://www.pestboard.ca.gov/

Description: Strives to be the national leader in creating an environment where the public is fully protected and well informed, and where structural pest control industry operates without unreasonable restraint.

Petroleum Engineers

year for Canada, Latin America; $139.00/year for other countries; $150.00 for two years; $160.00 for two years, Canada/Latin America; $238.00/year for other countries, 2 years; $215.00/year for individuals, 3 years; $220.00/year for Canada, Latin America, 3 years; $332.00/year for other countries, 3 years; $60.00/year for individuals. Trade magazine serving engineers and managers in international petroleum operations.

★9205★ *SWE, Magazine of the Society of Women Engineers*

Society of Women Engineers
230 East Ohio St., Ste. 400
Chicago, IL 60611-3265
Ph: (312)596-5223
E-mail: hq@swe.org
URL: http://www.swe.org

Quarterly. $30.00/year for nonmembers. Magazine for engineering students and for women and men working in the engineering and technology fields. Covers career guidance, continuing development and topical issues.

★9206★ *WEPANEWS*

Women in Engineering Programs & Advocates Network
1901 E. Asbury Ave., Ste. 220
Denver, CO 80208
Ph: (303)871-4643   Fax: (303)871-6833
E-mail: dmatt@wepan.org
URL: http://www.wepan.org

Description: 2/year. Seeks to provide greater access for women to careers in engineering. Includes news of graduate, undergraduate, freshmen, pre-college, and re-entry engineering programs for women. Recurring features include job listings, faculty, grant, and conference news, international engineering program news, action group news, notices of publications available, and a column titled Kudos.

★9207★ *World Oil*

Gulf Publishing Co.
PO Box 2608
Houston, TX 77252-2608
Ph: (713)529-4301   Fax: (713)520-4433
E-mail: editorial@worldoil.com
URL: http://www.gulfpub.com

Monthly. $149.00/year for individuals, domestic; $345.00/year for individuals, domestic, 3 years;. Free, qualifiers; $261.00/year for two years. Trade magazine on oil and gas exploration, drilling, and production.

PLACEMENT AND JOB REFERRAL SERVICES

★9208★ American Indian Science and Engineering Society (AISES)

PO Box 9828
Albuquerque, NM 87119-9828
Ph: (505)765-1052   Fax: (505)765-5608
E-mail: info@aises.org
URL: http://www.aises.org

Description: Represents American Indian and non-Indian students and professionals in science, technology, and engineering fields; corporations representing energy, mining, aerospace, electronic, and computer fields. Seeks to motivate and encourage students to pursue undergraduate and graduate studies in science, engineering, and technology. Sponsors science fairs in grade schools, teacher training workshops, summer math/science sessions for 8th-12th graders, professional chapters, and student chapters in colleges. Offers scholarships. Adult members serve as role models, advisers, and mentors for students. Operates placement service.

★9209★ Engineering Society of Detroit (ESD)

2000 Town Ctr., Ste. 2610
Southfield, MI 48075
Ph: (248)353-0735   Fax: (248)353-0736
E-mail: esd@esd.org
URL: http://esd.org

Description: Engineers from all disciplines; scientists and technologists. Conducts technical programs and engineering refresher courses; sponsors conferences and expositions. Maintains speakers' bureau; offers placement services; although based in Detroit, MI, society membership is international.

★9210★ Korean-American Scientists and Engineers Association (KSEA)

1952 Gallows Rd., Ste. 300
Vienna, VA 22182
Ph: (703)748-1221   Fax: (703)748-1331
E-mail: admin@ksea.org
URL: http://www.ksea.org

Description: Represents scientists and engineers holding single or advanced degrees. Promotes friendship and mutuality among Korean and American scientists and engineers; contributes to Korea's scientific, technological, industrial, and economic developments; strengthens the scientific, technological, and cultural bonds between Korea and the U.S. Sponsors symposium. Maintains speakers' bureau, placement service, and biographical archives. Compiles statistics.

★9211★ Society of Hispanic Professional Engineers (SHPE)

5400 E Olympic Blvd., Ste. 210
Los Angeles, CA 90022
Ph: (323)725-3970   Fax: (323)725-0316
E-mail: shpenational@shpe.org
URL: http://oneshpe.shpe.org/wps/portal/

national

Description: Represents engineers, student engineers, and scientists. Aims to increase the number of Hispanic engineers by providing motivation and support to students. Sponsors competitions and educational programs. Maintains placement service and speakers' bureau; compiles statistics.

★9212★ Society of Petroleum Engineers (SPE)

222 Palisades Creek Dr.
PO Box 833836
Richardson, TX 75083-3836
Ph: (972)952-9393   Fax: (972)952-9435
Fr: 800-456-6863
E-mail: spedal@spe.org
URL: http://www.spe.org

Members: Worldwide technical society of engineers, scientists, managers, and operating personnel in the upstream petroleum industry Activities: Offers distance learning, continuing education short courses, and distinguished lecturer program; sponsors contests; offers placement service and Internet Career Center.

EMPLOYER DIRECTORIES AND NETWORKING LISTS

★9213★ *American Men and Women of Science*

Gale, Cengage Learning
27500 Drake Rd.
Farmington Hills, MI 48331-3535
Ph: (248)699-4253   Fax: (248)699-8065
Fr: 800-877-4253
URL: http://www.gale.com

Biennial, latest edition 23rd, October 2006; new edition expected 24th, January 2008. $1,075.00 for individuals. Covers over 129,700 U.S. and Canadian scientists active in the physical, biological, mathematical, computer science, and engineering fields; includes references to previous edition for deceased scientists and nonrespondents. Entries include: Name, address, education, personal and career data, memberships, honors and awards, research interest. Arrangement: Alphabetical. Indexes: Discipline (in separate volume).

★9214★ *Careers in Focus: Engineering*

Facts On File Inc.
132 W 31st St., 17th Fl.
New York, NY 10001
Ph: (212)967-8800   Fax: 800-678-3633
Fr: 800-322-8755
URL: http://www.factsonfile.com

3rd edition, 2007. $29.95 for individuals; $26.95 for libraries. Publication includes: List of resources to consult for more information. Principal content of publication consists of job descriptions, advancement opportunities, educational requirements, employment outlook, salary information, and working conditions for careers in the field of engineering. Indexes: Alphabetical.

★9215★ Directory of Certified Petroleum Geologists

American Association of Petroleum Geologists
1444 S Boulder Ave.
PO Box 979
Tulsa, OK 74101-0979
Ph: (918)584-2555   Fax: (918)560-2665
Fr: 800-364-2274
URL: http://www.aapg.org/dpadirectory/

Covers about 3,400 members of the association. Entries include: Name, address; education and career data; whether available for consulting. Arrangement: Alphabetical. Indexes: Geographical.

★9216★ Directory of Contract Staffing Firms

C.E. Publications Inc.
PO Box 3006
Bothell, WA 98041-3006
Ph: (425)806-5200   Fax: (425)806-5585
URL: http://www.cjhunter.com/dcsf/overview.html

Covers nearly 1,300 contract firms actively engaged in the employment of engineering, IT/IS, and technical personnel for 'temporary' contract assignments throughout the world. Entries include: Company name, address, phone, name of contact, email, web address. Arrangement: Alphabetical. Indexes: Geographical.

★9217★ The Geophysical Directory

Geophysical Directory Inc.
PO Box 130508
Houston, TX 77219
Ph: (713)529-8789   Fax: (713)529-3646
Fr: 800-929-2462
E-mail: info@geophysicaldirectory.com
URL: http://www.geophysicaldirectory.com

Annual; latest edition 62nd. $140.00 for individuals; $155.00 for individuals. Covers about 4,000 companies that provide geophysical equipment, supplies, or services, and mining and petroleum companies that use geophysical techniques; international coverage. Entries include: Company name, address, phone, fax, names of principal executives, operations, and sales personnel; similar information for branch locations. Arrangement: Classified by product or service. Indexes: Company name, personal name.

★9218★ Indiana Society of Professional Engineers-Directory

Indiana Society of Professional Engineers
PO Box 20806
Indianapolis, IN 46220
Ph: (317)255-2267   Fax: (317)255-2530
URL: http://www.indspe.org

Annual, fall. Covers member registered engineers, land surveyors, engineering students, and engineers in training. Entries include: Member name, address, phone, type of membership, business information, special-

ty. Arrangement: Alphabetical by chapter area.

★9219★ The Oil & Gas Directory

Geophysical Directory Inc.
PO Box 130508
Houston, TX 77219
Ph: (713)529-8789   Fax: (713)529-3646
Fr: 800-929-2462
URL: http://www.geophysicaldirectory.com

Annual, October; latest edition 37th. $130.00 for individuals; $145.00 for individuals. Covers about 9,000 companies worldwide involved in petroleum exploration, drilling, and production, and suppliers to the industry. Entries include: Company name, address, phone, fax, names of principal personnel; branch office addresses, phone, and names of key personnel. Arrangement: Classified by activity. Indexes: Company name, personal name and regional.

★9220★ Peterson's Job Opportunities in Engineering and Technology

Peterson's Guides
2000 Lenox Dr.
Box 67005
Lawrenceville, NJ 08648
Ph: (609)896-1800   Fax: (609)896-4531
Fr: 800-338-3282
E-mail: custsvc@petersons.com
URL: http://www.petersons.com

Compiled by the Peterson's staff. Fourth edition, 1996. $21.95 (paper). 379 pages. Profiles 2,000 high-tech companies looking primarily for technical personnel in such fields as biotechnology, telecommunications, software, computers and peripherals, defense, and aerospace. Contains job-search strategies and career options to help match education and expertise to the job market. Indexed geographically, by industry, and by hiring needs.

HANDBOOKS AND MANUALS

★9221★ The Best Resumes for Scientists and Engineers

John Wiley & Sons Inc.
1 Wiley Dr.
Somerset, NJ 08873
Ph: (732)469-4400   Fax: (732)302-2300
Fr: 800-225-5945
E-mail: custserv@wiley.com
URL: http://www.wiley.com/WileyCDA/

Adele Lewis and David J. Moore. Second edition, 1993. $37.50; $19.95 (paper). 224 pages. Presents an extensive collection of scientific and engineering resumes, highlighting the important differences between these and resumes written for other occupations.

★9222★ Careers in Environmental Geoscience

AAPG Publications
PO Box 979
Tulsa, OK 74101-0979
Ph: (918)584-2555   Fax: (918)560-2694
Fr: 800-364-2274
E-mail: postmaster@aapg.org
URL: http://www.aapg.org/index.cfm

Robert R. Jordan, Rima Petrossian, and William J. Murphy. 1996. $5.00 (paper). DEP Publications Series. 54 pages.

★9223★ How to Succeed as an Engineer: A Practical Guide to Enhance Your Career

Institute of Electrical & Electronics Engineers
445 Hoes Lane
Piscataway, NJ 08854
Ph: (732)981-0060   Fax: (732)981-9667
Fr: 800-678-4333
URL: http://www.ieee.org

Todd Yuzuriha. 1999. $29.95 (paper). 367 pages.

★9224★ The I Hate Selling Book: Business-Building Advice for Consultants, Attorneys, Accountants, Engineers, Architects, and Other Professionals

AMACOM
1601 Broadway, 12th Fl.
New York, NY 10019-7420
Ph: (212)586-8100   Fax: (212)903-8168
Fr: 800-262-9699
URL: http://www.amanet.org

Allan S. Boress. 2001. $29.95. 240 pages.

★9225★ The New Engineer's Guide to Career Growth & Professional Awareness

Institute of Electrical & Electronics Engineers
445 Hoes Lane
Piscataway, NJ 08854
Ph: (732)981-0060   Fax: (732)981-9667
Fr: 800-678-4333
URL: http://www.ieee.org

Irving J. Gabelman, editor. 1996. $39.95 (paper). 275 pages.

★9226★ Opportunities in Engineering Careers

The McGraw-Hill Companies
PO Box 182604
Columbus, OH 43272
Fax: (614)759-3749   Fr: 877-883-5524
E-mail: customer.service@mcgraw-hill.com
URL: http://www.mcgraw-hill.com

Nicholas Basta. Revised second edition, 2002. $13.95; $11.95 (paper). 160 pages. Outlines typical job titles, salaries, career paths, and employment prospects.

★9227★ **Opportunities in Petroleum Careers**

The McGraw-Hill Companies
PO Box 182604
Columbus, OH 43272
Fax: (614)759-3749   Fr: 877-883-5524
E-mail: customer.service@mcgraw-hill.com
URL: http://www.mcgraw-hill.com

Gretchen Krueger. 1999. $11.95 (paper). 160 pages. Outlines jobs in looking for oil; drilling and producing oil; and transporting, refining, and marketing oil. Discusses job seeking, opportunities for advancement, and employment outlook.

★9228★ **Real People Working in Engineering**

The McGraw-Hill Companies
PO Box 182604
Columbus, OH 43272
Fax: (614)759-3749   Fr: 877-883-5524
E-mail: customer.service@mcgraw-hill.com
URL: http://www.mcgraw-hill.com

Blythe Camenson, Jan Goldberg. 1997. $17.95 (paper). 160 pages. Interviews and profiles of working professionals capture a range of opportunities in this field.

★9229★ **Resumes for Engineering Careers**

The McGraw-Hill Companies
PO Box 182604
Columbus, OH 43272
Fax: (614)759-3749   Fr: 877-883-5524
E-mail: customer.service@mcgraw-hill.com
URL: http://www.mcgraw-hill.com

Third edition, 2005. $11.95 (paper). 144 pages. Contains sample resumes and cover letters applicable to any engineering field.

★9230★ **Resumes for Scientific and Technical Careers**

The McGraw-Hill Companies
PO Box 182604
Columbus, OH 43272
Fax: (614)759-3749   Fr: 877-883-5524
E-mail: customer.service@mcgraw-hill.com
URL: http://www.mcgraw-hill.com

Third edition, 2007. $12.95 (paper). 144 pages. Provides resume advice for individuals interested in working in scientific and technical careers. Includes sample resumes and cover letters.

EMPLOYMENT AGENCIES AND SEARCH FIRMS

★9231★ **Anderson Bradshaw Associates Inc.**

444 Benmar, Ste. 1017
Houston, TX 77060
Ph: (713)869-6789
E-mail: aba@hal-pc.org

URL: http://www.andersonbradshaw.com/
Domestic and international search firm.

★9232★ **Dunn Associates**

229 Limberline Dr.
Greensburg, PA 15601
Ph: (724)832-9822   Fax: (724)832-9836
Fr: 877-586-2538
E-mail: maddunn@aol.com
URL: http://www.dunnassociatesinc.com/

Executive search firm.

★9233★ **Engineer One, Inc.**

PO Box 23037
Knoxville, TN 37933
Fax: (865)691-0110
E-mail: engineerone@engineerone.com
URL: http://www.engineerone.com

Engineering employment service specializes in engineering and management in the chemical process, power utilities, manufacturing, mechanical, electrical, and electronic industries. Established an Information Technology Division in 1998 that works nationwide across all industries. Also provides systems analysis consulting services specializing in VAX based systems.

★9234★ **First Choice Search**

PO Box 946
Danville, WA 94526
Ph: (925)552-9985
E-mail: info@firstchoicesearch.com
URL: http://www.firstchoicesearch.com

Executive search firm.

★9235★ **Global Employment Solutions**

10375 Park Meadows Dr., Ste. 375
Littleton, CO 80124
Ph: (303)216-9500   Fax: (303)216-9533
E-mail: careers@global
URL: http://www.gesnetwork.com

Employment agency.

★9236★ **International Staffing Consultants**

17310 Redhill Ave., No. 140
Irvine, CA 92614
Ph: (949)255-5857   Fax: (949)767-5959
E-mail: iscinc@iscworld.com
URL: http://www.iscworld.com

Employment agency. Provides placement on regular or temporary basis. Affiliate office in London.

★9237★ **Search and Recruit International**

4455 South Blvd. Ste. 110
Virginia Beach, VA 23452
Ph: (757)625-2121   Fr: 800-800-5627

Employment agency. Headquartered in Virginia Beach. Other offices in Bremerton, WA; Charleston, SC; Jacksonville, FL; Memphis,

TN; Pensacola, FL; Sacramento, CA; San Bernardino, CA; San Diego, CA.

★9238★ **Winters Technical Staffing Services**

6 Lansing Sq., Ste. 101
Toronto, ON, Canada M2J 1T5
Ph: (416)495-7422   Fax: (416)495-8479
E-mail: brian@winterstaffing.com
URL: http://www.winterstaffing.com

Technical staffing service for permanent and contract positions in all facets of engineering. Serves government agencies, consulting engineers, and all areas of manufacturing in Canada and northeast United States.

TRADESHOWS

★9239★ **International Thermal and Heavy Oil Symposium**

Society of Petroleum Engineers (Texas)
222 Palisades Creek Dr.
PO Box 833836
Richardson, TX 75080-2040
Ph: (972)952-9494   Fax: (972)952-9435
E-mail: service@otcnet.org
URL: http://www.otcnet.org

Biennial. **Primary Exhibits:** Equipment, supplies, and services for thermal operations, new recovery techniques, cold pumping, and application of horizontal drilling.

OTHER SOURCES

★9240★ **American Association of Blacks in Energy (AABE)**

927 15th St. NW, Ste. 200
Washington, DC 20005-2321
Ph: (202)371-9530   Fax: (202)371-9218
Fr: 800-466-0204
E-mail: aabe@aabe.org
URL: http://www.aabe.org

Description: Seeks to increase the knowledge, understanding, and awareness of the minority community in energy issues by serving as an energy information source for policymakers, recommending blacks and other minorities to appropriate energy officials and executives, encouraging students to pursue professional careers in the energy industry, and advocating the participation of blacks and other minorities in energy programs and policymaking activities. Updates members on key legislation and regulations being developed by the Department of Energy, the Department of Interior, the Department of Commerce, the Small Business Administration, and other federal and state agencies.

★9241★ American Association of Engineering Societies (AAES)

1620 I St. NW, Ste. 210
Washington, DC 20006
Ph: (202)296-2237   Fax: (202)296-1151
Fr: 888-400-2237
E-mail: dbateson@aaes.org
URL: http://www.aaes.org

Description: Coordinates the efforts of the member societies in the provision of reliable and objective information to the general public concerning issues which affect the engineering profession and the field of engineering as a whole; collects, analyzes, documents, and disseminates data which will inform the general public of the relationship between engineering and the national welfare; provides a forum for the engineering societies to exchange and discuss their views on matters of common interest; and represents the U.S. engineering community abroad through representation in WFEO and UPADI.

★9242★ Association for International Practical Training (AIPT)

10400 Little Patuxent Pkwy., Ste. 250
Columbia, MD 21044-3519
Ph: (410)997-2200   Fax: (410)992-3924
E-mail: aipt@aipt.org
URL: http://www.aipt.org

Description: Providers worldwide of on-the-job training programs for students and professionals seeking international career development and life-changing experiences. Arranges workplace exchanges in hundreds of professional fields, bringing employers and trainees together from around the world. Client list ranges from small farming communities to Fortune 500 companies.

★9243★ Association for Women Geoscientists (AWG)

PO Box 30645
Lincoln, NE 68503-0645
Ph: (402)489-8122
E-mail: office@awg.org
URL: http://www.awg.org

Members: Represents men and women geologists, geophysicists, petroleum engineers, geological engineers, hydrogeologists, paleontologists, geochemists, and other geoscientists. **Purpose:** Aims to encourage the participation of women in the geosciences. Exchanges educational, technical, and professional information. Enhances the professional growth and advancement of women in the geosciences. Provides information through web site on opportunities and careers available to women in the geosciences. **Activities:** Sponsors educational booths and programs at geological society conventions. Operates charitable program. Maintains speaker's bureau, and Association for Women Geoscientists Foundation (educational arm).

★9244★ Engineering Occupations

Delphi Productions
3159 6th St.
Boulder, CO 80304
Ph: (303)443-2100   Fax: (303)443-4022
Fr: 888-443-2400
E-mail: support@delphivideo.com
URL: http://www.delphivideo.com

$95.00. 50 minutes. Part of the Careers for the 21st Century Video Library.

★9245★ National Action Council for Minorities in Engineering (NACME)

440 Hamilton Ave., Ste. 302
White Plains, NY 10601-1813
Ph: (914)539-4010   Fax: (914)539-4032
E-mail: webmaster@nacme.org
URL: http://www.nacme.org

Description: Leads the national effort to increase access to careers in engineering and other science-based disciplines. Conducts research and public policy analysis, develops and operates national demonstration programs at precollege and university levels, and disseminates information through publications, conferences and electronic media. Serves as a privately funded source of scholarships for minority students in engineering.

★9246★ National Society of Professional Engineers (NSPE)

1420 King St.
Alexandria, VA 22314-2794
Ph: (703)684-2800   Fax: (703)836-4875
Fr: 888-285-6773
E-mail: memserv@nspe.org
URL: http://www.nspe.org

Description: Represents professional engineers and engineers-in-training in all fields registered in accordance with the laws of states or territories of the U.S. or provinces of Canada; qualified graduate engineers, student members, and registered land surveyors. Is concerned with social, professional, ethical, and economic considerations of engineering as a profession; encompasses programs in public relations, employment practices, ethical considerations, education, and career guidance. Monitors legislative and regulatory actions of interest to the engineering profession.

★9247★ Scientific, Engineering, and Technical Services

Cambridge Educational
PO Box 2053
Princeton, NJ 08543-2053
Ph: 800-257-5126   Fax: (609)671-0266
Fr: 800-468-4227
E-mail: custserv@films.com
URL: http://www.cambridgeeducational.com

VHS and DVD. $89.95. 2002. 18 minutes. 2002. Part of the Career Cluster Series.

★9248★ Society of Women Engineers (SWE)

230 E Ohio St., Ste. 400
Chicago, IL 60611-3265
Ph: (312)596-5223   Fax: (312)596-5252
Fr: 877-SWE-INFO
E-mail: hq@swe.org
URL: http://www.swe.org

Description: Educational and service organization representing both students and professional women in engineering and technical fields.

★9249★ Women in Engineering

Her Own Words
PO Box 5264
Madison, WI 53705-0264
Ph: (608)271-7083   Fax: (608)271-0209
E-mail: herownword@aol.com
URL: http://www.herownwords.com/

Video. Jocelyn Riley. $95.00. 15 minutes. Resource guide also available for $45.00.

Pharmacists

SOURCES OF HELP-WANTED ADS

★9250★ AACP News

American Association of Colleges of
  Pharmacy
1426 Prince St.
Alexandria, VA 22314
Ph: (703)739-2330   Fax: (703)836-8982
Fr: 800-510-2227
E-mail: mail@aacp.org
URL: http://www.aacp.org/site/
page.asp?TRACKID=&VID=1&CID=111&DID=3118

Description: Monthly. Discusses issues relating to pharmaceutical education. Carries
legislative information, feature stories on
award winners, and Association news. Recurring features include news of research,
notices of continuing education and employment opportunities, and listings of publications.

★9251★ AAPS Newsmagazine

American Association of Pharmaceutical
  Scientists
2107 Wilson Blvd. Ste. 700
Arlington, VA 22201-3042
Ph: (703)243-2800   Fax: (703)243-9650
URL: http://www.aapspharmaceutica.com

Monthly. Subscription included in membership. Professional magazine covering issues
of interest to pharmaceutical scientists.

★9252★ AAPS PharmSciTech

American Association of Pharmaceutical
  Scientists
2107 Wilson Blvd. Ste. 700
Arlington, VA 22201-3042
Ph: (703)243-2800   Fax: (703)243-9650
URL: http://www.aapspharmscitech.org/

Quarterly. Journal covering pharmaceuticals
in health care, with particular emphasis on
drug marketing and management.

**★9253★ American College of
Apothecaries Newsletter**

American College of Apothecaries
Research & Education Resource Center
PO Box 341266
Memphis, TN 38184
Ph: (901)383-8119   Fax: (901)383-8882
Fr: 800-828-5933
E-mail: aca@acainfo.org
URL: http://
www.americancollegeofapothecaries.com

Description: Monthly. Presents national
pharmacy news designed to assist Association members in their professional practices.
Covers Association news, including items on
membership, chapters, committees, elections, and conferences. Recurring features
include book reviews and a necrology.

**★9254★ American Journal of Health-
System Pharmacy**

American Society of Health-System
  Pharmacists
7272 Wisconsin Ave.
Bethesda, MD 20814
Ph: (301)664-8700   Fr: (866)279-0681
E-mail: ajhp@ashp.org
URL: http://www.ajhp.org

Semimonthly. Journal for pharmacists practicing in health-systems (acute care, ambulatory care, homecare, long term care, HMO's,
PPOs, & PBMs).

**★9255★ The Annals of
Pharmacotherapy**

Harvey Whitney Books Co.
8044 Montgomery Rd., Ste. 415
PO Box 42696
Cincinnati, OH 45236-2919
Ph: (513)793-3555   Fax: (513)793-3600
Fr: 877-742-7631
E-mail: customer-service@theannals.com
URL: http://www.theannals.com

Monthly. $446.00/year for U.S., Canada, and
Mexico, online only; $588.00/year for U.S.,
Canada, and Mexico, online only; $782.00/
year for U.S., Canada, and Mexico, online
only; $465.00/year for U.S., Canada, and
Mexico, online & print; $621.00/year for U.S.,
Canada, and Mexico, online & print;
$825.00/year for U.S., Canada, and Mexico,

online & print; $446.00/year for U.S., Cana-
da, and Mexico, print only; $562.00/year for
U.S., Canada, and Mexico, print only. Journal covering drug therapy, new drugs, and
pharmacotherapy.

★9256★ BioPharm International

Advanstar Communications
641 Lexington Ave.
8th Fl.
New York, NY 10022
Ph: (212)951-6600   Fax: (212)951-6793
Fr: 800-225-4569
URL: http://www.biopharminternational.com

Monthly. $70.00/year for U.S.; $95.00/year
for Canada and Mexico; $135.00/year for
other countries. Periodical publishing professional practice news and care reports, research development and manufacturing.

**★9257★ Christian Pharmacists
Fellowship International-Newsletter**

Christian Pharmacists Fellowship
  International
PO Box 24708
West Palm Beach, FL 33416-4708
Ph: (561)803-2737   Fax: (561)803-2738
Fr: 888-253-6885
URL: http://cpfi.org/

Description: Bimonthly. Reports on the activities of members and the fellowship, as
well as Christian events in pharmacy. Includes book reviews and directory.

★9258★ Community Pharmacist

ELF Publications Inc.
5285 W Louisiana Ave.
Lakewood, CO 80232-5976
Ph: (303)975-0075   Fax: (303)975-0132
Fr: 800-922-8513
E-mail: elfedit@qwest.net
URL: http://www.elfpublications.com

Bimonthly. National magazine addressing
the professional and business needs, concerns and continuing education of retail
pharmacists practicing in independent, chain
and supermarket pharmacies.

★9259★ Current Opinion in Pharmacology

Elsevier Science Inc.
360 Park Ave. S
New York, NY 10010
Ph: (212)989-5800   Fax: (212)633-3990
URL: http://www.elsevier.com

$1,603.00/year for institutions, other countries; $198,900.00/year for institutions; $1,434.00/year for institutions; $317.00/year for elsewhere; $35,500.00/year for individuals; $292.00/year for individuals. Journal covering current advances in pharmacology.

★9260★ Drug Topics

Advanstar Communications Inc.
641 Lexington Ave., 8th Fl.
New York, NY 10022
Ph: (212)951-6600   Fax: (212)951-6793
E-mail: fulfill@superfill.com
URL: http://www.drugtopics.com/drugtopics

Bimonthly. $61.00/year for individuals; $30.50/year for students; $109.00/year for out of country; $10.00 for single issue; $10.00 for Canada and Mexico, for single issue; $15.00 for other countries, for single issue. Newsmagazine for pharmacists.

★9261★ Journal of the American Pharmacists Association

American Pharmaceutical Association
1100 15th St. NW, Ste. 400
Washington, DC 20037-2985
Ph: (202)628-4410   Fax: (202)783-2351
Fr: 800-237-2742
URL: http://www.aphanet.org/

Bimonthly. $495.00/year for institutions, per year, print and online; $395.00/year for institutions, per year, online only. Journal for pharmacy professionals.

★9262★ MAPS Bulletin

Multidisciplinary Association for
  Psychedelic Studies
2105 Robinson Ave.
Sarasota, FL 34232
Ph: (941)924-6277   Fax: (941)924-6265
URL: http://www.maps.org/news-letters/

Quarterly. Professional magazine covering issues in drugs and pharmacy for association members.

★9263★ McKnight's Long-Term Care News

McKnight's Long-Term Care News
1 Northfield Plz., Ste. 521
Northfield, IL 60093-1216
Ph: (847)784-8706   Fax: (847)784-9346
Fr: 800-558-1703
E-mail: ltcn-webmaster@mltcn.com
URL: http://www.mcknightsonline.com/home

Professional magazine.

★9264★ Med Ad News

Engel Publishing Partners
820 Bear Tavern Rd., Ste. 300
West Trenton, NJ 08628
Fax: (609)530-0207
E-mail: mwalsh@engelpub.com
URL: http://www.pharmalive.com

Monthly. $190.00/year for individuals. Pharmaceutical business and marketing magazine.

★9265★ NCPA Newsletter

National Community Pharmacists
  Association
100 Daingerfield Rd.
Alexandria, VA 22314
Ph: (703)683-8200   Fax: (703)683-3619
Fr: 800-544-7447
E-mail: info@ncpanet.org
URL: http://www.ncpanet.org/about/ncpa_periodicals.shtml

Description: Semimonthly. Reports on topics affecting independents, including developments within the pharmaceutical industry, regulatory and legislative activity, and pricing and import information. Recurring features include reports of meetings, news of educational opportunities, notices of publications available, and news of NARD activities and events.

★9266★ The Nurse Practitioner

Lippincott Williams & Wilkins
530 Walnut St.
Philadelphia, PA 19106-3621
Ph: (215)521-8300   Fax: (215)521-8902
Fr: 800-638-3030
E-mail: npedit@wolterskluwer.com
URL: http://www.tnpj.com

Monthly. $57.95/year for individuals; $209.00/year for institutions; $29.00/year for U.S., in-training; $120.98/year for other countries, individual; $258.98/year for institutions. Magazine presenting clinical information to nurses in advanced primary care practice. Also covers legal, business, economic, ethical, research, and pharmaceutical issues.

★9267★ NYCPS-Newsletter

New York City Pharmacists Society
41 E. 11th St., 11th Fl.
New York, NY 10003
Ph: (212)905-8919   Fax: (718)665-2123
E-mail: keos1@aol.com
URL: http://www.nycps.org

Description: Nine issues/year. Provides news, research, and developments relating to pharmacists and pharmaceutical products. Includes information on the New York City Pharmacists Society. Recurring features include letters to the editor, news of research, and lists of job opportunities.

★9268★ Ohio Society of Health System Pharmacists-Bulletin

Ohio Society of Health-System
  Pharmacists
50 Greenwood Cir.
Marietta, OH 45750
Ph: (740)373-8595   Fax: (740)373-8595
E-mail: ohioshp@ohioshp.org
URL: http://www.ohioshp.org/

Description: Six issues/year. Presents news of the Society and information on pharmacy rulings from the state board. Recurring features include news of research, a calendar of events, reports of meetings, news of educational opportunities, job listings, notices of publications available, a column titled News from Members, and clinical articles.

★9269★ The PDA Journal of Pharmaceutical Science & Technology

PDA
4350 E West Hwy., Ste. 200
Bethesda, MD 20814
Ph: (301)656-5900   Fax: (301)986-1093
E-mail: pda-journal@uiowa.edu
URL: http://www.pda.org/journal/index.html

Bimonthly. $270.00/year for institutions, worldwide. Professional journal covering pharmaceutical science.

★9270★ Pharmaceutical Engineering

International Society for Pharmaceutical
  Engineering Inc.
3109 West Dr. Martin Luther King Jr.
  Blvd., Ste. 250
Tampa, FL 33607
Ph: (813)960-2105   Fax: (813)264-2816
URL: http://www.ispe.org

Bimonthly. Subscription included in membership. Magazine on the health care manufacturing industry.

★9271★ Pharmaceutical Executive

Advanstar Communications
641 Lexington Ave., 8th Fl.
New York, NY 10022
Ph: (212)951-6600   Fax: (212)951-6793
Fr: 800-225-4569
URL: http://www.pharmexec.com/pharmexec

Monthly. Free to qualified subscribers. Periodical covering all aspects of pharmaceutical business strategy and marketing.

★9272★ Pharmaceutical Technology

Advanstar Communications
485 Rte. 1 S
Bldg. F, 1st Fl.
Iselin, NJ 08830
Ph: (732)596-0276   Fax: (732)596-0003
E-mail: ptpress@advanstar.com
URL: http://www.pharmtech.com

Monthly. $185.00/year for individuals; $331.00 for two years; $263.00/year for individuals, Canada and Mexico; $458.00/year for two years, Canada and Mexico; $55.00 for individuals, back issue;

$85.00 for two years, Can/Intl back issue. Magazine on applied technology for pharmaceutical firms.

★9273★ **Pharmacy Now**

Now Publishing Inc.
1026 Chestnut St., First Fl.
West Bend, WI 53095
Ph: (262)334-4112   Fax: (262)334-4112
URL: http://www.pharmacynow.com

Continuous. Free, online. Online resource for pharmaceutical professionals. Features career advice and employment listings.

★9274★ **Pharmacy Times**

Pharmacy Times
103 College Rd. E
Princeton, NJ 08540-6612
Ph: (609)524-9560   Fax: (609)524-9699
URL: http://www.pharmacytimes.com

Monthly. $65.00/year; $115.00/year for individuals; $115.00/year for two years; $210.00/year for institutions; $39.00/year for institutions, two years; $25.00/year for students, retired; $120.00/year for two years, student/retired; $220.00/year for Canada, student/retired; $220.00 for two years, Canada, student/retired. Journal providing information on health items (including prescription and over-the-counter drugs and surgical supplies) to independent, chain, and hospital pharmacists.

★9275★ **Pharmacy Today**

American Pharmaceutical Association
1100 15th St. NW, Ste. 400
Washington, DC 20037-2985
Ph: (202)628-4410   Fax: (202)783-2351
Fr: 800-237-2742
E-mail: pt@aphanet.org
URL: http://www.aphanet.org

Monthly. $200.00/year for individuals, one year; $250.00/year for out of country, one year. Reports on current news and opinions for pharmacists.

★9276★ **Pharmacy Week**

Pharmacy Week
7780 Elmwood Ave. Ste. 210
Middleton, WI 53562
Ph: (608)828-4400   Fax: (608)828-4401
E-mail: info@pharmacyweek.com
URL: http://www.pharmacyweek.com

Description: Weekly. Employment newsletter for pharmacists.

★9277★ **Voice of the Pharmacist Newsletter**

American College of Apothecaries
Research & Education Resource Center
PO Box 341266
Memphis, TN 38184
Ph: (901)383-8119   Fax: (901)383-8882
Fr: 800-828-5933
E-mail: aca@acainfo.org
URL: http://
www.americancollegeofapothecaries.com

Description: Quarterly. Examines current issues and opportunities affecting the retail, hospital, and consultant practices of pharmacy. Discusses controversial issues, often with commentary by pharmacists. Recurring features include editorials, news of research, and letters to the editor.

PLACEMENT AND JOB REFERRAL SERVICES

★9278★ **American Association of Pharmaceutical Scientists (AAPS)**

2107 Wilson Blvd., Ste. 700
Arlington, VA 22201-3042
Ph: (703)243-2800   Fax: (703)243-9650
E-mail: mays@aaps.org
URL: http://www.aapspharmaceutica.com

Description: Pharmaceutical scientists. Provides a forum for exchange of scientific information; serves as a resource in forming public policies to regulate pharmaceutical sciences and related issues of public concern. Promotes pharmaceutical sciences and provides for recognition of individual achievement; works to foster career growth and the development of members. Offers placement service.

★9279★ **American College of Clinical Pharmacy (ACCP)**

13000 W 87th St. Pkwy.
Lenexa, KS 66215-4530
Ph: (913)492-3311   Fax: (913)492-0088
E-mail: accp@accp.com
URL: http://www.accp.com

Description: Clinical pharmacists dedicated to: promoting rational use of drugs in society; advancing the practice of clinical pharmacy and interdisciplinary health care; assuring high quality clinical pharmacy by establishing and maintaining standards in education and training at advanced levels. Encourages research and recognizes excellence in clinical pharmacy. Offers educational programs, symposia, research forums, fellowship training, and college-funded grants through competitions. Maintains placement service.

★9280★ **American Public Health Association (APHA)**

800 I St. NW
Washington, DC 20001
Ph: (202)777-2742   Fax: (202)777-2534
E-mail: comments@apha.org
URL: http://www.apha.org

Members: Professional organization of physicians, nurses, educators, academicians, environmentalists, epidemiologists, new professionals, social workers, health administrators, optometrists, podiatrists, pharmacists, dentists, nutritionists, health planners, other community and mental health specialists, and interested consumers. **Purpose:** Seeks to protect and promote personal, mental, and environmental health. **Activities:** Ser-

vices include: promulgation of standards; establishment of uniform practices and procedures; development of the etiology of communicable diseases; research in public health; exploration of medical care programs and their relationships to public health. Sponsors job placement service.

★9281★ **American Society of Health System Pharmacists (ASHP)**

7272 Wisconsin Ave.
Bethesda, MD 20814
Ph: (301)657-3000   Fax: (301)664-8867
Fr: (866)279-0681
E-mail: membership@ashp.org
URL: http://www.ashp.org

Description: Professional society of pharmacists employed by hospitals, HMOs, clinics, and other health systems. Provides personnel placement service for members; sponsors professional and personal liability program. Conducts educational and exhibit programs. Has 30 practice interest areas, special sections for home care practitioners and clinical specialists, and research and education foundation.

EMPLOYER DIRECTORIES AND NETWORKING LISTS

★9282★ **AHA Guide to the Health Care Field**

American Hospital Association
1 N Franklin
Chicago, IL 60606
Ph: (312)422-2050   Fax: (312)422-4700
Fr: 800-424-4301

Annual, August. Covers hospitals, networks, multi-health care systems, freestanding ambulatory surgery centers, psychiatric facilities, long-term care facilities, substance abuse programs, and other health-related organizations. Entries include: For hospitals–Facility name, address, phone, administrator's name, number of beds, facilities and services, number of employees, expenses, other statistics. For other organizations–Name, address, phone, fax, name and title of contact. Arrangement: Geographical. Indexes: Hospital name.

★9283★ **Directory of Drug Store & HBC Chains**

Chain Store Guide
3922 Coconut Palm Dr.
Tampa, FL 33619
Fax: (813)627-6883   Fr: 800-778-9794
URL: http://www.csgis.com

Annual, May. Covers more than 1,700 drug store chains operations of two or more units, including mass merchants and grocers with pharmacies; 215 wholesale drug companies in the United States and Canada. Entries include: For retailers–company name; phone and fax numbers; physical and mailing addresses; company e-mail and web addresses; listing type; number of stores; product lines; percentage of sales by product line; total sales; prescription drug sales; percentage of prescriptions filled with generic drugs; number of prescriptions filled daily; percentage of prescriptions filled with private third party, cash, and Medicaid; number of stores by type; mail order pharmacy indicator; managed care division indicator; projected openings and remodelings; store prototype sizes; total selling square footage; trading area; franchise group headquarters' name and location; distribution center and primary wholesaler names and locations; number of specialty departments; packaged liquor indicators; private label indicators; computerized pharmacy indicator; average number of checkouts; year founded; public company indicator; parent company name and location; regional and divisional office locations; headquarters personnel with titles. For wholesalers–company name, address, phone, and fax; e-mail and web addresses; listing type; product lines; percentage of sales by product line; total sales; percentage of sales by customer type; total stores served; number of member and non-member stores served; trading area; group store trading names; wholesaler type; distribution center locations; private label indicator; year founded; public company indicator; headquarters personnel with titles. Arrangement: Separate geographical sections for retailers and wholesalers. Indexes: Alphabetical, exclusions.

★9284★ **Directory of Hospital Personnel**

Grey House Publishing
185 Millerton Rd.
PO Box 860
Millerton, NY 12546
Ph: (518)789-8700   Fax: (518)789-0556
Fr: 800-562-2139
URL: http://www.greyhouse.com/hospital_
personnel.htm

Annual. $325.00 for print product; $545.00 for online database subscription; $650.00 for online database subscription and print product combined. Covers 200,000 executives at 7,000 U.S. hospitals. Entries include: Name of hospital, address, phone; number of beds; type and JCAHO status of hospital; names and titles of key department heads and staff; medical and nursing school affiliations; number of residents, interns, and nursing students. Arrangement: Geographical. Indexes: Hospital name, personnel, hospital size.

★9285★ **Federation of American Societies for Experimental Biology-Directory of Members**

Federation of American Societies for Experimental Biology
9650 Rockville Pke.
Bethesda, MD 20814-3998
Ph: (301)634-7100   Fax: (301)634-7809
Fr: 800-433-2732
URL: http://www.faseb.org/directory/

Annual, fall. Covers about 63,000 members of The American Physiological Society, American Society for Biochemistry and Molecular Biology, American Society for Phar-

macology and Experimental Therapeutics, American Society for Investigative Pathology, American Society for Nutritional Sciences, The American Association of Immunologists, Biophysical Society, American Association of Anatomists, The Protein Society, The American Society for Bone and Mineral Research, American Society for Clinical Investigation, The Endocrine Society, The American Society of Human Genetics, Society for Developmental Biology, American Peptide Society, Society for the Study of Reproduction and Radiation Research Society. Entries include: Name, address, title, affiliation, memberships in federation societies, highest degree, year elected to membership, phone, fax and electronic mail address. Membership directories of the Biophysical Society, The Protein Society, The American Society for Bone and Mineral Research, and American Society for Clinical Investigation are also available separately. Arrangement: Alphabetical. Indexes: Geographical.

★9286★ **Hospital Blue Book**

Billian Publishing Inc./Transworld Publishing Inc.
2100 Powers Ferry Rd. SE
Atlanta, GA 30339
Ph: (770)955-5656   Fax: (770)952-0669
Fr: 800-533-8484
E-mail: blu-book@billian.com

2005. $300.00 for individuals. Covers more than 6,687 hospitals; some listings also appear in a separate southern edition of this publication. Entries include: Name of hospital, accreditation, mailing address, phone, fax, number of beds, type of facility (nonprofit, general, state, etc.); list of administrative personnel and chiefs of medical services, with specific titles. Arrangement: Geographical.

★9287★ **Medical and Health Information Directory**

Gale, Cengage Learning
27500 Drake Rd.
Farmington Hills, MI 48331-3535
Ph: (248)699-4253   Fax: (248)699-8065
Fr: 800-877-4253
E-mail: businessproducts@gale.com
URL: http://www.gale.com

Annual; latest edition 20th, July 2007. $375.00/volume. Covers in Volume 1, more than 26,500 medical and health oriented associations, organizations, institutions, and government agencies, including health maintenance organizations (HMOs), preferred provider organizations (PPOs), insurance companies, pharmaceutical companies, research centers, and medical and allied health schools. In Volume 2, over 12,000 medical book publishers; medical periodicals, directories, audiovisual producers and services, medical libraries and information centers, electronic resources, and health-related internet search engines. In Volume 3, more than 35,500 clinics, treatment centers, care programs, and counseling/diagnostic services for 34 subject areas. Entries include: Institution, service, or firm name, address, phone, fax, email and URL; many

include names of key personnel and, when pertinent, descriptive annotations. Volume 3 was formerly listed separately as Health Services Directory. Arrangement: Classified by organization activity, service, etc. Indexes: Each volume has a complete alphabetical name and keyword index.

★9288★ **Peterson's Job Opportunities for Health and Science Majors**

Peterson's
Princeton Pke. Corporate Ctr., 2000 Lenox Dr.
PO Box 67005
Lawrenceville, NJ 08648
Ph: (609)896-1800   Fax: (609)896-4531
Fr: 800-338-3282
URL: http://www.petersons.com

Irregular; latest edition 1999. Covers about 1,300 research, consulting, government, and non-profit and profit service organizations that hire college and university graduates in science and health-related majors. Entries include: Organization name, address, phone, name and title of contact, type of organization, number of employees, Standard Industrial Classification (SIC) code; description of opportunities available including disciplines, level of education required, starting locations and salaries, level of experience accepted, benefits.

HANDBOOKS AND MANUALS

★9289★ **Careers in Health Care**

The McGraw-Hill Companies
PO Box 182604
Columbus, OH 43272
Fax: (614)759-3749   Fr: 877-883-5524
E-mail: customer.service@mcgraw-hill.com
URL: http://www.mcgraw-hill.com

Barbara M. Swanson. Fifth edition, 2005. $15.95 (paper). 192 pages. Describes job duties, work settings, salaries, licensing and certification requirements, educational preparation, and future outlook. Gives ideas on how to secure a job.

★9290★ **Discovering New Medicines: Careers in Pharmaceutical Research & Development**

John Wiley & Sons Inc.
1 Wiley Dr.
Somerset, NJ 08873
Ph: (732)469-4400   Fax: (732)302-2300
Fr: 800-225-5945
E-mail: custserv@wiley.com
URL: http://www.wiley.com/WileyCDA/

Peter D. Stonier, editor. 1995. $65.00 (paper). 406 pages. An overview of the diverse opportunities in this field including the scientific, medical or specialist training necessary to attain them.

★9291★ Expert Resumes for Health Care Careers

Jist Works
875 Montreal Way
St. Paul, MN 55102
Fr: 800-648-5478
E-mail: info@jist.com
URL: http://www.jist.com

Wendy S. Enelow and Louise M. Kursmark. December 2003. $16.95. 288 pages.

★9292★ Health Careers Today

Elsevier
11830 Westline Industrial Dr.
St. Louis, MO 63146
Ph: (314)453-7010   Fax: (314)453-7095
Fr: 800-545-2522
E-mail: usbkinfo@elsevier.com
URL: http://www.elsevier.com

Gerdin, Judith. Fourth edition. 2007. $59.95. 496 pages. Covers more than 45 health careers. Discusses the roles and responsibilities of various occupations and provides a solid foundation in the skills needed for all health careers.

★9293★ Inside Pharmacy: The Anatomy of a Profession

Technomic Publishing Company
6000 Broken Sounds Pkwy. NW, Ste. 300
Boca Raton, FL 33487
Ph: (561)994-0555   Fax: 800-374-3401
Fr: 800-272-7737
E-mail: orders@crcpress.com

M. Christine Gosselin and Jack Robbins. 1999. $59.95. 134 pages.

★9294★ Introduction to Public Health in Pharmacy

Jones & Bartlett Publishers, Inc.
40 Tall Pine Dr.
Sudbury, MA 01776-2256
Ph: (978)443-5000   Fax: (978)443-8000
Fr: 800-832-0034
URL: http://www.jbpub.com

Lubotsky Levin, Peter D. Hurd, and Artis Hanson. 2008. $59.95. Two-part introduction to public health from a pharmacy perspective.

★9295★ Opportunities in Health and Medical Careers

The McGraw-Hill Companies
PO Box 182604
Columbus, OH 43272
Fax: (614)759-3749   Fr: 877-883-5524
E-mail: customer.service@mcgraw-hill.com
URL: http://www.mcgraw-hill.com

I. Donald Snook, Jr. and Leo D'Orazio. 2004. $13.95 (paper). 157 pages. Covers the full range of medical and health occupations. Illustrated.

★9296★ The Pharmacy Student Companion: Your Road Map to Pharmacy Education and Careers

American Pharmaceutical Association
1100 15th St. NW, Ste. 400
Washington, DC 20005
Ph: (202)628-4410   Fax: (202)783-2351
Fr: 800-878-0729
URL: http://www.pharmacyandyou.org/

Daniel H. Albrant and Linda R. Harteker, authors. Vicki L. Meade, editor. Third edition, revised, 1999. $20.00 (paper). 157 pages.

★9297★ Resumes for Health and Medical Careers

The McGraw-Hill Companies
PO Box 182604
Columbus, OH 43272
Fax: (614)759-3749   Fr: 877-883-5524
E-mail: customer.service@mcgraw-hill.com
URL: http://www.mcgraw-hill.com

Third edition, 2003. $11.95 (paper). 160 pages.

★9298★ Road Map to a Profession's Future: The Millis Study Commission on Pharmacy

Pharmaceutical Products Press
10 Alice St.
Binghamton, NY 13904
Ph: (607)722-5857   Fax: 800-895-0582
Fr: 800-429-6784
E-mail: getinfo@haworthpress.com
URL: http://www.haworthpressinc.com

Dennis B. Worthen. 2006. $39.95. 264 pages.

EMPLOYMENT AGENCIES AND SEARCH FIRMS

★9299★ Allerton Heneghan & O'Neill

1 Tower Ln., Ste. 1700
Oakbrook Terrace, IL 60181
Ph: (630)645-2294   Fax: (630)645-2298
E-mail: info@ahosearch.com
URL: http://www.ahosearch.com

Executive search firm.

★9300★ BioQuest

100 Spear St., Ste. 1125
San Francisco, CA 94105-1526
Ph: (415)777-4363
E-mail: info@bioquestinc.com
URL: http://www.bioquestinc.com

Executive search firm focused in healthcare and life sciences.

★9301★ Brandywine Consulting Group

1398 Morstein Rd.
West Chester, PA 19380
Ph: (610)696-5872   Fax: (610)429-1954
Fr: 800-555-1668

URL: http://brandywineconsulting.com/html/index.php

Executive search firm. An Affiliate of Brandywine Management Group in Berlin, MD.

★9302★ Caplan Associates Inc.

77 Bull Path
PO Box 4227
East Hampton, NY 11937
Ph: (631)907-9700   Fax: (631)907-0444
E-mail: info@caplanassoc.com
URL: http://www.caplanassoc.com

Executive search firm.

★9303★ Clark Executive Search Inc.

135 N. Ferry Rd.
PO Box 560
Shelter Island, NY 11964
Ph: (631)749-3540   Fax: (631)749-3539
E-mail: mail@clarksearch.com
URL: http://www.clarksearch.com

Executive search firm.

★9304★ CNR Search & Services

30752 Via Conquista
San Juan Capistrano, CA 92675
Ph: (949)488-0065
E-mail: cnrkenmiller@juno.com
URL: http://www.cnrsearch.com

Provides staffing services of permanent and temporary employees. Works primarily on a retained basis. Contingency on a limited basis. Services include human resources consulting, mergers and acquisitions in high-technology firms. Industries served: computer; information services; insurance, pharmaceutical and healthcare.

★9305★ Colucci, Blendow & Johnson

643 Main St., Ste. 7
PO Box 10
Half Moon Bay, CA 94019-1988
Ph: (650)712-0103   Fax: (650)712-0105
E-mail: exsearch@ix.netcom.com

Executive search consultants in the medical technology area that includes pharmaceuticals, medical equipment and device manufacturers, biotechnology, therapeutic supplies, diagnostic laboratory equipment and supplies, diagnostic imaging equipment and supplies, medical services, chemicals, cosmetic and toiletries, dental, veterinarian, and agricultural genetics companies.

★9306★ Conyngham Partners LLC

PO Box 94
Ridgewood, NJ 07451
Ph: (201)652-3444   Fax: (201)652-6357
E-mail: info@conynghampartners.com
URL: http://www.conynghampartners.com

Executive search firm.

★9307★ Courtright & Associates Inc.

PO Box 236
Scranton, PA 18504
Ph: (570)961-5450
E-mail: rjcx@comcast.net
URL: http://www.courtrightassoc.com

Executive search firm.

★9308★ Cromwell Partners Inc.

305 Madison Ave.
New York, NY 10165
Ph: (212)953-3220   Fax: (212)953-4688
E-mail: recruiters@cromwell-partners.com
URL: http://www.cromwell-partners.com

Executive search firm.

★9309★ Day & Associates

577 Airport Blvd., Ste. 130
Burlingame, CA 94010
Ph: (650)343-2660   Fax: (650)344-8460
E-mail: info@dayassociates.net
URL: http://www.dayassociates.net

Executive search firm.

★9310★ Doleman Enterprises

11160-F S Lakes Dr., Ste. 326
Reston, VA 20191
Ph: (703)742-5454   Fax: (703)708-6992
E-mail: doleman@patriot.net

Human resources firm specializes in recruiting for the high-tech, data and computer engineering and pharmaceutical industries.

★9311★ Emerging Medical Technologies Inc.

7784 S. Addison Way
Aurora, CO 80016
Ph: (303)699-1990
E-mail: tcmemt@aol.com

Executive search firm focused on the medical devices industry.

★9312★ Franklin Allen Consultants Ltd.

1205 Franklin Ave., Ste. 350
Garden City, NY 11530-1629
Ph: (516)248-4511   Fax: (516)294-6646
E-mail: hroher@frankinallen.com

Executive search firm.

★9313★ J. Blakslee International Inc.

336 Bon Air Shopping Ctr., Ste. 369
Greenbrae, CA 94904-3208
Ph: (415)389-7300   Fax: (415)389-7302
E-mail: resumes@jblakslee.com

Executive search firm.

★9314★ J. Burkey Associates

900 Laurel Ave.
River Edge, NJ 07661
Ph: (201)262-7990   Fax: (201)262-7955
E-mail: jburkey@erols.com

Executive search firm.

★9315★ JPM International

26034 Acero
Mission Viejo, CA 92691
Ph: (949)699-4300   Fax: (949)699-4333
Fr: 800-685-7856
E-mail: trish@jpmintl.com
URL: http://www.jpmintl.com

Executive search firm and employment agency.

★9316★ Ken Clark International

2000 Lenox Dr., Ste. 200
Lawrenceville, NJ 08648
Ph: (609)308-5200   Fax: (609)308-5250
E-mail: info-princeton@kenclark.com
URL: http://www.kenclark.com

Executive search firm. Branches in Newport Beach, CA; Deerfield, IL; Waltham, MA; and Wayne, PA.

★9317★ Med Exec International

100 N Brand Blvd., Ste. 306-308
Glendale, CA 91203
Ph: (818)552-2036   Fax: (818)552-2475
Fr: 800-507-5277
E-mail: info@medexecintl.com
URL: http://www.medexecintl.com

Firm provides customized executive recruitment services in a rapidly growing competitive pharmaceutical, medical device, biologics, diagnostics, and biotech market. Expertise include clinical research; regulatory affairs; quality assurance and compliance; medical affairs.

★9318★ Rosemary Cass Ltd.

175 Post Rd. W
Westport, CT 06880
Ph: (203)454-2920   Fax: (203)454-4643
E-mail: resumes@rosemarycassltd.com
URL: http://www.rosemarycassltd.com/

Executive search firm.

ONLINE JOB SOURCES AND SERVICES

★9319★ MedExplorer
E-mail: medmaster@medexplorer.com
URL: http://www.medexplorer.com

Description: Employment postings make up one module of this general medical site. Other sections contain: Newsletter, Classifieds, and Discussion Forum.

★9320★ Medhunters.com
Fr: 800-664-0278
E-mail: info@medhunters.com
URL: http://www.medhunters.com

Description: Career search site for jobs in all health care specialties; educational resources; visa and licensing information for relocation; interesting articles; relocation tools; links to professional organizations and general resources.

★9321★ ProHealthJobs
Fr: 800-796-1738
E-mail: Info@prohealthedujobs.com
URL: http://www.prohealthjobs.com

Description: Career resources site for the medical and health care field. Lists professional opportunities, product information, continuing education and open positions.

TRADESHOWS

★9322★ American Association of Pharmaceutical Scientists Annual Meeting and Exposition

American Association of Pharmaceutical Scientists
2107 Wilson Blvd., Ste. 700
Arlington, VA 22201-3042
Ph: (703)243-2800   Fax: (703)243-9650
E-mail: aaps@aaps.org
URL: http://www.aaps.org

Annual. **Primary Exhibits:** Raw materials, supplies, equipment, contract research & contract service labs, computer software, packaging, and other suppliers to pharmaceutical scientists. **Dates and Locations:** 2008 Nov 16-20; Atlanta, GA; Georgia World Congress Center; 2009 Nov 08-12; Los Angeles, CA; Los Angeles Convention Center; 2010 Nov 14-18; New Orleans, LA; Ernest N. Morial Convention Center; 2011 Oct 23-27; Washington, DC; Washington Convention Center.

★9323★ American Society of Consultant Pharmacists Annual Meeting and Exhibition

American Society of Consultant Pharmacists
1321 Duke St.
Alexandria, VA 22314-3563
Ph: (703)739-1300   Fax: (703)739-1321
Fr: 800-355-2727
E-mail: info@ascp.com
URL: http://www.ascp.com

Annual. **Primary Exhibits:** Pharmaceuticals, drug distribution systems, packaging equipment, computers, durable medical equipment, and medical supplies. **Dates and Locations:** 2008 Nov 09-12; New Orleans, LA; Ernest E. Morial Convention Center; 2009 Nov 17-20; Anaheim, CA; Anaheim Convention Center.

★9324★ **Texas Pharmacy Association Annual Meeting and Exhibit**

Texas Pharmacy Association
PO Box 14709
Austin, TX 78761-4709
Ph: (512)836-8350   Fax: (512)836-0308
Fr: 800-505-5463
URL: http://www.txpharmacy.com

Annual. **Primary Exhibits:** Pharmaceuticals and various services provided to pharmacists.

★9325★ **Western Pharmacy Education Faire**

California Pharmacists Association/
  Pharmacy California
4030 Lennane Dr.
Sacramento, CA 95834
Ph: (916)779-1400   Fax: (916)779-1401
Fr: 800-444-3851
E-mail: info@pharmacyfoundation.org
URL: http://www.pharmacyfoundation.org

Annual. **Primary Exhibits:** Pharmaceutical equipment, supplies, and services.

OTHER SOURCES

★9326★ **American Academy of Clinical Toxicology (AACT)**

777 E Park Dr.
PO Box 8820
Harrisburg, PA 17105-8820
Ph: (717)558-7847   Fax: (717)558-7841
Fr: 888-633-5784
E-mail: swilson@pamedsoc.org
URL: http://www.clintox.org

Members: Physicians, veterinarians, pharmacists, nurses research scientists, and analytical chemists. **Purpose:** Objectives are to: unite medical scientists and facilitate the exchange of information; encourage the development of therapeutic methods and technology; **Activities:** Conducts professional training in poison information and emergency service personnel.

★9327★ *American Almanac of Jobs and Salaries*

HarperCollins
10 E. 53rd St.
New York, NY 10022
Ph: (212)207-7000   Fr: 800-242-7737
URL: http://www.harpercollins.com/

John W. Wright. Revised edition, 2000. $20.00 (paper). 672 pages. This is a comprehensive guide to the wages of hundreds of occupations in a wide variety of industries and organizations.

★9328★ **American Hospital Association (AHA)**

1 N Franklin
Chicago, IL 60606-3421
Ph: (312)422-3000   Fax: (312)422-4796
URL: http://www.aha.org

Description: Represents health care provider organizations. Seeks to advance the health of individuals and communities. Leads, represents, and serves health care provider organizations that are accountable to the community and committed to health improvement.

★9329★ **American Pharmacists Association - Academy of Pharmacy Practice and Management (APhA-APPM)**

1100 15th St. NW, Ste. 400
Washington, DC 20005-1707
Ph: (202)628-4410   Fax: (202)783-2351
Fr: 800-237-APHA
E-mail: apha-appm@aphanet.org
URL: http://www.pharmacist.com/AM/
Template.cfm?Section=Practitioners

Description: Pharmacists concerned with rendering professional services directly to the public, without regard for status of employment or environment of practice. Aims to provide a forum and mechanism whereby pharmacists may meet to discuss and implement programs and activities relevant and helpful to the practitioner of pharmacy; to recommend programs and courses of action which should be undertaken or implemented by the profession; to coordinate academy efforts so as to be an asset to the progress of the profession. Provides and co-sponsors continuing education meetings, seminars, and workshops; produces audiovisual materials.

★9330★ **American Society of Consultant Pharmacists (ASCP)**

1321 Duke St., Ste. 400
Alexandria, VA 22314-3563
Ph: (703)739-1300   Fax: (703)739-1321
Fr: 800-355-2727
E-mail: info@ascp.com
URL: http://www.ascp.com

Description: Provides leadership, education, advocacy and resources enabling consultant and senior care pharmacists to enhance quality of care and quality of life for older individuals through the provision of pharmaceutical care and the promotion of healthy aging. Excels in the areas of: knowledge and skills in geriatric pharmacotherapy; expertise in long-term care settings for the frail at-risk elderly and other residents; and patient-centered advocate for seniors at-risk for medication related problems. Improves drug therapy and quality of life of geriatric patients and other individuals residing in a variety of environments, including nursing facilities, subacute care and assisted living facilities, psychiatric hospitals, hospice programs, and in home and community settings.

★9331★ **Exploring Health Occupations**

Cambridge Educational
PO Box 2053
Princeton, NJ 08543-2053
Ph: 800-257-5126   Fax: (609)671-0266
Fr: 800-468-4227
E-mail: custserv@films.com
URL: http://www.cambridgeeducational.com

VHS and DVD. $159.90. 1999. Two-part series provides a detailed view of the field of medical technicians and technologists, EMTs, nurses, therapists, and assistants.

★9332★ **Health Assessment & Treating Occupations**

Delphi Productions
3159 6th St.
Boulder, CO 80304
Ph: (303)443-2100   Fax: (303)443-4022
Fr: 888-443-2400
E-mail: support@delphivideo.com
URL: http://www.delphivideo.com

$95.00. 50 minutes. Part of the Careers for the 21st Century Video Library.

★9333★ **Health Service Occupations**

Delphi Productions
3159 6th St.
Boulder, CO 80304
Ph: (303)443-2100   Fax: (303)443-4022
Fr: 888-443-2400
E-mail: support@delphivideo.com
URL: http://www.delphivideo.com

$95.00. 50 minutes. Part of the Careers for the 21st Century Video Library.

★9334★ **Medicine & Related Occupations**

Delphi Productions
3159 6th St.
Boulder, CO 80304
Ph: (303)443-2100   Fax: (303)443-4022
Fr: 888-443-2400
E-mail: support@delphivideo.com
URL: http://www.delphivideo.com

$95.00. 45 minutes. Part of the Careers for the 21st Century Video Library.

★9335★ **National Association of Boards of Pharmacy (NABP)**

1600 Feehanville Dr.
Mount Prospect, IL 60056
Ph: (847)391-4406   Fax: (847)391-4502
E-mail: custserv@nabp.net
URL: http://www.nabp.net

Members: Pharmacy boards of several states, District of Columbia, Puerto Rico, Virgin Islands, several Canadian provinces, the states of Victoria, Australia, and New South Wales, the Pharmaceutical Society of New Zealand, and the South African Pharmacy Council. **Purpose:** Provides for interstate reciprocity in pharmaceutic licensure based upon a uniform minimum standard of pharmaceutic education and uniform legislation; improves the standards of pharmaceutical education licensure and practice. **Activities:** Provides legislative information; sponsors uniform licensure examination; also provides information on accredited school and college requirements. Maintains pharmacy and drug law statistics.

★9336★ National Association of Chain Drug Stores (NACDS)

413 N Lee St.
Alexandria, VA 22314
Ph: (703)549-3001   Fax: (703)836-4869
URL: http://www.nacds.org

Description: Represents the concerns of community pharmacies in Washington, in state capitals, and across the country. Members are more than 210 chain community pharmacy companies. Collectively, community pharmacy comprises the largest component of pharmacy practice with over 107,000 FTE pharmacists. Membership also includes more than 1000 suppliers of goods and services to chain community pharmacies. International membership consists of almost 100 members from 30 countries.

★9337★ National Pharmaceutical Association (NPhA)

107 Kilmayne Dr., Ste. C
Cary, NC 27511
Fax: (919)469-5870   Fr: 800-944-NPHA
E-mail: npha@npha.net
URL: http://www.npha.net

Description: State and local associations of professional minority pharmacists. Provides a means whereby members may "contribute to their common improvement, share their experiences, and contribute to the public good".

★9338★ Pharmaceutical Care Management Association (PCMA)

601 Pennsylvania Ave. NW, 7th Fl.
Washington, DC 20004-2601
Ph: (202)207-3610   Fax: (202)207-3623
E-mail: info@pcmanet.org
URL: http://www.pcmanet.org

Description: Represents managed care pharmacy, Pharmaceutical Benefits Management companies (PBMs) and their healthcare partners in pharmaceutical care. Promotes education, legislation, practice standards, and research to foster quality, affordable pharmaceutical care.

Pharmacy Assistants

SOURCES OF HELP-WANTED ADS

★9339★ AACP News

American Association of Colleges of Pharmacy
1426 Prince St.
Alexandria, VA 22314
Ph: (703)739-2330   Fax: (703)836-8982
Fr: 800-510-2227
E-mail: mail@aacp.org
URL: http://www.aacp.org/site/
page.asp?TRACKID=&VID=1&CID=111&DID=3

Description: Monthly. Discusses issues relating to pharmaceutical education. Carries legislative information, feature stories on award winners, and Association news. Recurring features include news of research, notices of continuing education and employment opportunities, and listings of publications.

★9340★ AAPS Newsmagazine

American Association of Pharmaceutical Scientists
2107 Wilson Blvd. Ste. 700
Arlington, VA 22201-3042
Ph: (703)243-2800   Fax: (703)243-9650
URL: http://www.aapspharmaceutica.com

Monthly. Subscription included in membership. Professional magazine covering issues of interest to pharmaceutical scientists.

★9341★ American Journal of Health-System Pharmacy

American Society of Health-System Pharmacists
7272 Wisconsin Ave.
Bethesda, MD 20814
Ph: (301)664-8700   Fr: (866)279-0681
E-mail: ajhp@ashp.org
URL: http://www.ajhp.org

Semimonthly. Journal for pharmacists practicing in health-systems (acute care, ambulatory care, homecare, long term care, HMO's, PPOs, & PBMs).

★9342★ The Annals of Pharmacotherapy

Harvey Whitney Books Co.
8044 Montgomery Rd., Ste. 415
PO Box 42696
Cincinnati, OH 45236-2919
Ph: (513)793-3555   Fax: (513)793-3600
Fr: 877-742-7631
E-mail: customer-service@theannals.com
URL: http://www.theannals.com

Monthly. $446.00/year for U.S., Canada, and Mexico, online only; $588.00/year for U.S., Canada, and Mexico, online only; $782.00/year for U.S., Canada, and Mexico, online only; $465.00/year for U.S., Canada, and Mexico, online & print; $621.00/year for U.S., Canada, and Mexico, online & print; $825.00/year for U.S., Canada, and Mexico, online & print; $446.00/year for U.S., Canada, and Mexico, print only; $562.00/year for U.S., Canada, and Mexico, print only. Journal covering drug therapy, new drugs, and pharmacotherapy.

★9343★ BioPharm International

Advanstar Communications
641 Lexington Ave.
8th Fl.
New York, NY 10022
Ph: (212)951-6600   Fax: (212)951-6793
Fr: 800-225-4569
URL: http://www.biopharminternational.com

Monthly. $70.00/year for U.S.; $95.00/year for Canada and Mexico; $135.00/year for other countries. Periodical publishing professional practice news and care reports, research development and manufacturing.

★9344★ Community Pharmacist

ELF Publications Inc.
5285 W Louisiana Ave.
Lakewood, CO 80232-5976
Ph: (303)975-0075   Fax: (303)975-0132
Fr: 800-922-8513
E-mail: elfedit@qwest.net
URL: http://www.elfpublications.com

Bimonthly. National magazine addressing the professional and business needs, concerns and continuing education of retail pharmacists practicing in independent, chain and supermarket pharmacies.

★9345★ Journal of the American Pharmacists Association

American Pharmaceutical Association
1100 15th St. NW, Ste. 400
Washington, DC 20037-2985
Ph: (202)628-4410   Fax: (202)783-2351
Fr: 800-237-2742
URL: http://www.aphanet.org/

Bimonthly. $495.00/year for institutions, per year, print and online; $395.00/year for institutions, per year, online only. Journal for pharmacy professionals.

★9346★ MAPS Bulletin

Multidisciplinary Association for Psychedelic Studies
2105 Robinson Ave.
Sarasota, FL 34232
Ph: (941)924-6277   Fax: (941)924-6265
URL: http://www.maps.org/news-letters/

Quarterly. Professional magazine covering issues in drugs and pharmacy for association members.

★9347★ Med Ad News

Engel Publishing Partners
820 Bear Tavern Rd., Ste. 300
West Trenton, NJ 08628
Fax: (609)530-0207
E-mail: mwalsh@engelpub.com
URL: http://www.pharmalive.com

Monthly. $190.00/year for individuals. Pharmaceutical business and marketing magazine.

★9348★ The PDA Journal of Pharmaceutical Science & Technology

PDA
4350 E West Hwy., Ste. 200
Bethesda, MD 20814
Ph: (301)656-5900   Fax: (301)986-1093
E-mail: pda-journal@uiowa.edu
URL: http://www.pda.org/journal/index.html

Bimonthly. $270.00/year for institutions, worldwide. Professional journal covering pharmaceutical science.

★9349★ Pharmaceutical Engineering

International Society for Pharmaceutical
  Engineering Inc.
3109 West Dr. Martin Luther King Jr.
  Blvd., Ste. 250
Tampa, FL 33607
Ph: (813)960-2105   Fax: (813)264-2816
URL: http://www.ispe.org

Bimonthly. Subscription included in membership. Magazine on the health care manufacturing industry.

★9350★ Pharmaceutical Executive

Advanstar Communications
641 Lexington Ave., 8th Fl.
New York, NY 10022
Ph: (212)951-6600   Fax: (212)951-6793
Fr: 800-225-4569
URL: http://www.pharmexec.com/pharmexec

Monthly. Free to qualified subscribers. Periodical covering all aspects of pharmaceutical business strategy and marketing.

★9351★ Pharmacy Now

Now Publishing Inc.
1026 Chestnut St., First Fl.
West Bend, WI 53095
Ph: (262)334-4112   Fax: (262)334-4112
URL: http://www.pharmacynow.com

Continuous. Free, online. Online resource for pharmaceutical professionals. Features career advice and employment listings.

★9352★ Pharmacy Times

Pharmacy Times
103 College Rd. E
Princeton, NJ 08540-6612
Ph: (609)524-9560   Fax: (609)524-9699
URL: http://www.pharmacytimes.com

Monthly. $65.00/year; $115.00/year for individuals; $115.00/year for two years; $210.00/year for institutions; $39.00/year for institutions, two years; $25.00/year for students, retired; $120.00/year for two years, student/retired; $220.00/year for Canada, student/retired; $220.00 for two years, Canada, student/retired. Journal providing information on health items (including prescription and over-the-counter drugs and surgical supplies) to independent, chain, and hospital pharmacists.

★9353★ Pharmacy Today

American Pharmaceutical Association
1100 15th St. NW, Ste. 400
Washington, DC 20037-2985
Ph: (202)628-4410   Fax: (202)783-2351
Fr: 800-237-2742
E-mail: pt@aphanet.org
URL: http://www.aphanet.org

Monthly. $200.00/year for individuals, one year; $250.00/year for out of country, one year. Reports on current news and opinions for pharmacists.

PLACEMENT AND JOB REFERRAL SERVICES

★9354★ American Public Health Association (APHA)

800 I St. NW
Washington, DC 20001
Ph: (202)777-2742   Fax: (202)777-2534
E-mail: comments@apha.org
URL: http://www.apha.org

Members: Professional organization of physicians, nurses, educators, academicians, environmentalists, epidemiologists, new professionals, social workers, health administrators, optometrists, podiatrists, pharmacists, dentists, nutritionists, health planners, other community and mental health specialists, and interested consumers. **Purpose:** Seeks to protect and promote personal, mental, and environmental health. **Activities:** Services include: promulgation of standards; establishment of uniform practices and procedures; development of the etiology of communicable diseases; research in public health; exploration of medical care programs and their relationships to public health. Sponsors job placement service.

EMPLOYER DIRECTORIES AND NETWORKING LISTS

★9355★ AHA Guide to the Health Care Field

American Hospital Association
1 N Franklin
Chicago, IL 60606
Ph: (312)422-2050   Fax: (312)422-4700
Fr: 800-424-4301

Annual, August. Covers hospitals, networks, multi-health care systems, freestanding ambulatory surgery centers, psychiatric facilities, long-term care facilities, substance abuse programs, and other health-related organizations. Entries include: For hospitals–Facility name, address, phone, administrator's name, number of beds, facilities and services, number of employees, expenses, other statistics. For other organizations–Name, address, phone, fax, name and title of contact. Arrangement: Geographical. Indexes: Hospital name.

★9356★ Directory of Drug Store & HBC Chains

Chain Store Guide
3922 Coconut Palm Dr.
Tampa, FL 33619
Fax: (813)627-6883   Fr: 800-778-9794
URL: http://www.csgis.com

Annual, May. Covers more than 1,700 drug store chains operations of two or more units, including mass merchants and grocers with pharmacies; 215 wholesale drug companies in the United States and Canada. Entries include: For retailers–company name; phone and fax numbers; physical and mailing addresses; company e-mail and web addresses; listing type; number of stores; product lines; percentage of sales by product line; total sales; prescription drug sales; percentage of prescriptions filled with generic drugs; number of prescriptions filled daily; percentage of prescriptions filled with private third party, cash, and Medicaid; number of stores by type; mail order pharmacy indicator; managed care division indicator; projected openings and remodelings; store prototype sizes; total selling square footage; trading area; franchise group headquarters' name and location; distribution center and primary wholesaler names and locations; number of specialty departments; packaged liquor indicators; private label indicators; computerized pharmacy indicator; average number of checkouts; year founded; public company indicator; parent company name and location; regional and divisional office locations; headquarters personnel with titles. For wholesalers–company name, address, phone, and fax; e-mail and web addresses; listing type; product lines; percentage of sales by product line; total sales; percentage of sales by customer type; total stores served; number of member and non-member stores served; trading area; group store trading names; wholesaler type; distribution center locations; private label indicator; year founded; public company indicator; headquarters personnel with titles. Arrangement: Separate geographical sections for retailers and wholesalers. Indexes: Alphabetical, exclusions.

★9357★ Directory of Hospital Personnel

Grey House Publishing
185 Millerton Rd.
PO Box 860
Millerton, NY 12546
Ph: (518)789-8700   Fax: (518)789-0556
Fr: 800-562-2139
URL: http://www.greyhouse.com/hospital_personnel.htm

Annual. $325.00 for print product; $545.00 for online database subscription; $650.00 for online database subscription and print product combined. Covers 200,000 executives at 7,000 U.S. hospitals. Entries include: Name of hospital, address, phone; number of beds; type and JCAHO status of hospital; names and titles of key department heads and staff; medical and nursing school affiliations; number of residents, interns, and nursing students. Arrangement: Geographical. Indexes: Hospital name, personnel, hospital size.

★9358★ Hospital Blue Book

Billian Publishing Inc./Transworld
  Publishing Inc.
2100 Powers Ferry Rd. SE
Atlanta, GA 30339
Ph: (770)955-5656   Fax: (770)952-0669
Fr: 800-533-8484
E-mail: blu-book@billian.com

2005. $300.00 for individuals. Covers more than 6,687 hospitals; some listings also appear in a separate southern edition of this publication. Entries include: Name of hospital, accreditation, mailing address, phone, fax, number of beds, type of facility (nonprofit, general, state, etc.); list of administrative personnel and chiefs of medical services, with specific titles. Arrangement: Geographical.

★9359★ **Medical and Health Information Directory**

Gale, Cengage Learning
27500 Drake Rd.
Farmington Hills, MI 48331-3535
Ph: (248)699-4253   Fax: (248)699-8065
Fr: 800-877-4253
E-mail: businessproducts@gale.com
URL: http://www.gale.com

Annual; latest edition 20th, July 2007. $375.00/volume. Covers in Volume 1, more than 26,500 medical and health oriented associations, organizations, institutions, and government agencies, including health maintenance organizations (HMOs), preferred provider organizations (PPOs), insurance companies, pharmaceutical companies, research centers, and medical and allied health schools. In Volume 2, over 12,000 medical book publishers; medical periodicals, directories, audiovisual producers and services, medical libraries and information centers, electronic resources, and health-related internet search engines. In Volume 3, more than 35,500 clinics, treatment centers, care programs, and counseling/diagnostic services for 34 subject areas. Entries include: Institution, service, or firm name, address, phone, fax, email and URL; many include names of key personnel and, when pertinent, descriptive annotations. Volume 3 was formerly listed separately as Health Services Directory. Arrangement: Classified by organization activity, service, etc. Indexes: Each volume has a complete alphabetical name and keyword index.

★9360★ **Peterson's Job Opportunities for Health and Science Majors**

Peterson's
Princeton Pke. Corporate Ctr., 2000 Lenox Dr.
PO Box 67005
Lawrenceville, NJ 08648
Ph: (609)896-1800   Fax: (609)896-4531
Fr: 800-338-3282
URL: http://www.petersons.com

Irregular; latest edition 1999. Covers about 1,300 research, consulting, government, and non-profit and profit service organizations that hire college and university graduates in science and health-related majors. Entries include: Organization name, address, phone, name and title of contact, type of organization, number of employees, Standard Industrial Classification (SIC) code; description of opportunities available including disciplines, level of education required, starting locations and salaries, level of experience accepted, benefits.

HANDBOOKS AND MANUALS

★9361★ **Discovering New Medicines: Careers in Pharmaceutical Research & Development**

John Wiley & Sons Inc.
1 Wiley Dr.
Somerset, NJ 08873
Ph: (732)469-4400   Fax: (732)302-2300
Fr: 800-225-5945
E-mail: custserv@wiley.com
URL: http://www.wiley.com/WileyCDA/

Peter D. Stonier, editor. 1995. $65.00 (paper). 406 pages. An overview of the diverse opportunities in this field including the scientific, medical or specialist training necessary to attain them.

★9362★ **Expert Resumes for Health Care Careers**

Jist Works
875 Montreal Way
St. Paul, MN 55102
Fr: 800-648-5478
E-mail: info@jist.com
URL: http://www.jist.com

Wendy S. Enelow and Louise M. Kursmark. December 2003. $16.95. 288 pages.

★9363★ **Health Careers Today**

Elsevier
11830 Westline Industrial Dr.
St. Louis, MO 63146
Ph: (314)453-7010   Fax: (314)453-7095
Fr: 800-545-2522
E-mail: usbkinfo@elsevier.com
URL: http://www.elsevier.com

Gerdin, Judith. Fourth edition. 2007. $59.95. 496 pages. Covers more than 45 health careers. Discusses the roles and responsibilities of various occupations and provides a solid foundation in the skills needed for all health careers.

★9364★ **Inside Pharmacy: The Anatomy of a Profession**

Technomic Publishing Company
6000 Broken Sounds Pkwy. NW, Ste. 300
Boca Raton, FL 33487
Ph: (561)994-0555   Fax: 800-374-3401
Fr: 800-272-7737
E-mail: orders@crcpress.com

M. Christine Gosselin and Jack Robbins. 1999. $59.95. 134 pages.

★9365★ **The Pharmacy Student Companion: Your Road Map to Pharmacy Education and Careers**

American Pharmaceutical Association
1100 15th St. NW, Ste. 400
Washington, DC 20005
Ph: (202)628-4410   Fax: (202)783-2351
Fr: 800-878-0729
URL: http://www.pharmacyandyou.org/

Daniel H. Albrant and Linda R. Harteker,

authors. Vicki L. Meade, editor. Third edition, revised, 1999. $20.00 (paper). 157 pages.

★9366★ **Resumes for Health and Medical Careers**

The McGraw-Hill Companies
PO Box 182604
Columbus, OH 43272
Fax: (614)759-3749   Fr: 877-883-5524
E-mail: customer.service@mcgraw-hill.com
URL: http://www.mcgraw-hill.com

Third edition, 2003. $11.95 (paper). 160 pages.

★9367★ **Resumes for Science Careers**

The McGraw-Hill Companies
PO Box 182604
Columbus, OH 43272
Fax: (614)759-3749   Fr: 877-883-5524
E-mail: customer.service@mcgraw-hill.com
URL: http://www.mcgraw-hill.com

1997. $11.95 (paper). 144 pages.

OTHER SOURCES

★9368★ **American Society of Consultant Pharmacists (ASCP)**

1321 Duke St., Ste. 400
Alexandria, VA 22314-3563
Ph: (703)739-1300   Fax: (703)739-1321
Fr: 800-355-2727
E-mail: info@ascp.com
URL: http://www.ascp.com

Description: Provides leadership, education, advocacy and resources enabling consultant and senior care pharmacists to enhance quality of care and quality of life for older individuals through the provision of pharmaceutical care and the promotion of healthy aging. Excels in the areas of: knowledge and skills in geriatric pharmacotherapy; expertise in long-term care settings for the frail at-risk elderly and other residents; and patient-centered advocate for seniors at-risk for medication related problems. Improves drug therapy and quality of life of geriatric patients and other individuals residing in a variety of environments, including nursing facilities, subacute care and assisted living facilities, psychiatric hospitals, hospice programs, and in home and community settings.

★9369★ **Exploring Health Occupations**

Cambridge Educational
PO Box 2053
Princeton, NJ 08543-2053
Ph: 800-257-5126   Fax: (609)671-0266
Fr: 800-468-4227
E-mail: custserv@films.com
URL: http://www.cambridgeeducational.com

VHS and DVD. $159.90. 1999. Two-part series provides a detailed view of the field of medical technicians and technologists, EMTs, nurses, therapists, and assistants.

★9370★ Health Service Occupations
Delphi Productions
3159 6th St.
Boulder, CO 80304
Ph: (303)443-2100   Fax: (303)443-4022
Fr: 888-443-2400
E-mail: support@delphivideo.com
URL: http://www.delphivideo.com

$95.00. 50 minutes. Part of the Careers for the 21st Century Video Library.

★9371★ Medicine & Related Occupations
Delphi Productions
3159 6th St.
Boulder, CO 80304
Ph: (303)443-2100   Fax: (303)443-4022
Fr: 888-443-2400
E-mail: support@delphivideo.com
URL: http://www.delphivideo.com

$95.00. 45 minutes. Part of the Careers for the 21st Century Video Library.

★9372★ National Association of Boards of Pharmacy (NABP)
1600 Feehanville Dr.
Mount Prospect, IL 60056
Ph: (847)391-4406   Fax: (847)391-4502
E-mail: custserv@nabp.net
URL: http://www.nabp.net

Members: Pharmacy boards of several states, District of Columbia, Puerto Rico, Virgin Islands, several Canadian provinces, the states of Victoria, Australia, and New South Wales, the Pharmaceutical Society of New Zealand, and the South African Pharmacy Council. **Purpose:** Provides for interstate reciprocity in pharmaceutic licensure based upon a uniform minimum standard of pharmaceutic education and uniform legislation; improves the standards of pharmaceutical education licensure and practice. **Activities:** Provides legislative information; sponsors uniform licensure examination; also provides information on accredited school and college requirements. Maintains pharmacy and drug law statistics.

★9373★ National Association of Chain Drug Stores (NACDS)
413 N Lee St.
Alexandria, VA 22314
Ph: (703)549-3001   Fax: (703)836-4869
URL: http://www.nacds.org

Description: Represents the concerns of community pharmacies in Washington, in state capitals, and across the country. Members are more than 210 chain community pharmacy companies. Collectively, community pharmacy comprises the largest component of pharmacy practice with over 107,000 FTE pharmacists. Membership also includes more than 1000 suppliers of goods and services to chain community pharmacies. International membership consists of almost 100 members from 30 countries.

★9374★ National Pharmaceutical Association (NPhA)
107 Kilmayne Dr., Ste. C
Cary, NC 27511
Fax: (919)469-5870   Fr: 800-944-NPHA
E-mail: npha@npha.net
URL: http://www.npha.net

Description: State and local associations of professional minority pharmacists. Provides a means whereby members may "contribute to their common improvement, share their experiences, and contribute to the public good".

★9375★ Pharmaceutical Care Management Association (PCMA)
601 Pennsylvania Ave. NW, 7th Fl.
Washington, DC 20004-2601
Ph: (202)207-3610   Fax: (202)207-3623
E-mail: info@pcmanet.org
URL: http://www.pcmanet.org

Description: Represents managed care pharmacy, Pharmaceutical Benefits Management companies (PBMs) and their healthcare partners in pharmaceutical care. Promotes education, legislation, practice standards, and research to foster quality, affordable pharmaceutical care.

★9376★ Pharmacy Technician
Cambridge Educational
PO Box 2053
Princeton, NJ 08543-2053
Ph: 800-257-5126   Fax: (609)671-0266
Fr: 800-468-4227
E-mail: custserv@films.com
URL: http://www.cambridgeeducational.com

VHS and DVD. $89.95. 2002. 15 minutes. Part of the series "Working in Health Care: Opportunities for Life."

Photographers and Camera Operators

SOURCES OF HELP-WANTED ADS

★9377★ Advanced Imaging
Cygnus Business Media Inc.
3 Huntington Quadrangle, Ste. 301 N
Melville, NY 11747
Ph: (631)845-2700   Fax: (631)845-7109
Fr: 800-308-6397
URL: http://www.cygnusb2b.com
Magazine covering the full range of electronic imaging technology and its uses.

★9378★ Adweek
VNU Business Media USA
770 Broadway
New York, NY 10003
Ph: (646)654-4500
URL: http://www.adweek.com/aw/index.jsp
Weekly. $149.00/year for individuals, 12 months basic; $85.00 for individuals, 6 months basic; $135.00 for individuals, 6 months premium; $249.00/year for individuals, 12 months premium; $20.00/year for individuals, monthly online. Advertising news magazine.

★9379★ AeroSpaceNews.com
AeroSpaceNews.com
PO Box 1748
Ojai, CA 93024-1748
Ph: (805)985-2320
URL: http://www.aerospacenews.com/content/view/41/33/
Monthly. $19.95/year for individuals, private; $53.95/year for two years, individual, private; $79.95/year for individuals, trade; $143.95 for two years, individual. Journal reporting on the insights, impressions and images of tomorrow's technological wonders in the field of aerospace.

★9380★ Afterimage
Visual Studies Workshop Press
31 Prince St.
Rochester, NY 14607
Ph: (585)442-8676
E-mail: afterimage@vsw.org
URL: http://www.vsw.org/afterimage/index.html
Bimonthly. $33.00/year for individuals; $61.00 for two years; $90.00/year for institutions, library. Publication providing independent critical commentary on issues in media arts, including scholarly research, in-depth reviews, investigative journalism, interviews, and the largest list of exhibitions, festivals, position announcements and calls for work of its kind.

★9381★ AV Video & Multimedia Producer
Access Intelligence L.L.C.
4 Choke Cherry Rd., 2nd Fl.
Rockville, MD 20850
Ph: (301)354-2000   Fax: (301)309-3847
Fr: 800-777-5006
Monthly. Magazine covering audio-visual, video and multimedia production, presentation, people, technology and techniques.

★9382★ Broadcasting & Cable
Reed Business Information
360 Park Ave. S
New York, NY 10010
Ph: (646)746-6400   Fax: (646)746-7431
URL: http://www.reedbusiness.com
Weekly. $199.99/year for individuals. News magazine covering The Fifth Estate (radio, TV, cable, and satellite), and the regulatory commissions involved.

★9383★ Columbia Journalism Review
Columbia Journalism Review
2950 Broadway, Journalism Bldg.
Columbia University
New York, NY 10027
Ph: (212)854-1881   Fax: (212)854-8580
Fr: 888-425-7782
E-mail: cjr@columbia.edu
URL: http://www.cjr.org/
Bimonthly. $19.95/year for U.S. $27.95 for single issue, Canadian & international orders. Magazine focusing on journalism.

★9384★ Digital Imaging Techniques
Cygnus Business Media Inc.
3 Huntington Quadrangle, Ste. 301 N
Melville, NY 11747
Ph: (631)845-2700   Fax: (631)845-7109
Fr: 800-308-6397
URL: http://www.imaginginfo.com
Bimonthly. Magazine serving digital imaging professionals. Concentrating on digital image creation with technical editorial provided by leading experts; covering new products launches, imaging techniques, industry trends, business development and more.

★9385★ Editor & Publisher
Editor & Publisher Magazine
770 Broadway
New York, NY 10003-9595
Ph: (646)654-5500   Fax: (646)654-5370
Fr: 800-562-2706
URL: http://www.editorandpublisher.com/eandp/index.jsp
Weekly (Mon.). $99.00/year for individuals, print and online; $159.00/year for Canada, print and online; $320.00/year for other countries; $7.95/year for individuals, monthly. Magazine focusing on newspaper journalism, advertising, printing equipment, and interactive services.

★9386★ Entertainment Employment Journal
Studiolot Publishing
5632 Van Nuys Blvd., Ste. 320
Van Nuys, CA 91401-4600
Ph: (818)776-2800   Fr: 800-335-4335
E-mail: support@eejonline.com
URL: http://www.eej.com
Semimonthly. Subscription included in membership. Trade magazine covering business and technical careers in broadcast, electronic media, and motion pictures.

★9387★ Film History
Indiana University Press
601 N Morton St.
Bloomington, IN 47404-3797
Ph: (812)855-6657   Fax: (812)855-8817
Fr: 800-842-6796

E-mail: filmhist@aol.com
URL: http://inscribe.iupress.org/loi/fil

Quarterly. $77.00/year for individuals, print and online, for U.S. $63.00/year for individuals, electronic only, for U.S. Journal tracing the history of the motion picture with reference to social, technological, and economic aspects, covering various aspects of motion pictures such as production, distribution, exhibition, and reception.

★9388★ **The Hollywood Reporter**

The Nielsen Co.
770 Broadway
New York, NY 10003
Ph: (646)654-5000   Fax: (646)654-5002
URL: http://www.hollywoodreporter.com/thr/index.jsp

Daily (morn.). $3.00 for single issue; $6.00/year for U.S., weekly; $299.00/year for individuals, print; $175.00/year for U.S., weekly print; $299.00/year for U.S., print/online combination; $265.00/year for U.S., weekly print/online combination. Film, TV, and entertainment trade newspaper.

★9389★ **HOW**

F & W Publications Inc.
4700 E Galbraith Rd.
Cincinnati, OH 45236
Ph: (513)531-2690   Fax: (513)531-0798
Fr: 800-289-0963
URL: http://www.howdesign.com

Bimonthly. $29.96/year for U.S. $45.00/year for Canada; $52.00/year for other countries. Instructional trade magazine.

★9390★ **News Photographer**

National Press Photographers Association
3200 Croasdaile Dr., Ste. 306
Durham, NC 27705
Ph: (919)383-7246   Fax: (919)383-7261
URL: http://www.nppa.org./news_and_events/magazine/

Monthly. $60.00/year for nonmembers, retail price, Canada; $65.00/year for nonmembers, international; $48.00/year for nonmembers, USA. Magazine featuring still and television photojournalism.

★9391★ **PDN (Photo District News)**

VNU Business Media USA
770 Broadway
New York, NY 10003
Ph: (646)654-4500
URL: http://www.vnubusinessmedia.com/box/bp/div_mma_art_pdn.html

Monthly. $8.00 per issue, cover price; $65.00 for individuals, one year domestic; $105.00 for Canada, one year; $125.00 for institutions, one year foreign. Monthly magazine for professional photographers emphasizing the business aspects of advertising, corporate, editorial, fine-art and stock photography.

★9392★ **Photo Trade News**

Cygnus Business Media Inc.
3 Huntington Quadrangle, Ste. 301 N
Melville, NY 11747
Ph: (631)845-2700   Fax: (631)845-7109
Fr: 800-308-6397
URL: http://www.cygnusb2b.com

Monthly. Trade publication covering the photography business.

★9393★ **Producers Masterguide**

Producers Masterguide
60 E 8th St., 34th Fl.
New York, NY 10003-6514
Ph: (212)777-4002   Fax: (212)777-4101
URL: http://www.producers.masterguide.com

Annual. $155.00/year for U.S. $165.00/year for Canada; $195.00/year for other countries. An international film and TV production directory and guide for the professional motion picture, broadcast television, feature film, TV commercial, cable/satellite, digital and videotape industries in the U.S., Canada, the UK, the Caribbean Islands, Mexico, Australia, New Zealand, Europe, Israel, Morocco, the Far East, and South America.

★9394★ **Professional Photographer**

Professional Photographers of America Inc.
229 Peachtree St. NE, Ste. 2200
Atlanta, GA 30303
Ph: (404)522-8600   Fax: (404)614-6400
E-mail: ppaeditor@aol.com
URL: http://www.ppa.com/

Monthly. $19.95/year for individuals, print (U.S.); $35.95/year for individuals, print (Canada). Magazine for photographers.

★9395★ **The Rangefinder**

The Rangefinder Publishing Company Inc.
1312 Lincoln Blvd.
Santa Monica, CA 90406
Ph: (310)451-8506   Fax: (310)395-9058
URL: http://www.rangefindermag.com

Monthly. $18.00/year for individuals. Free to qualified subscribers. Trade publication for portrait, commercial and wedding photographers.

★9396★ **SMPTE Journal**

Society of Motion Picture and Television Engineers
3 Barker Ave.
White Plains, NY 10601
Ph: (914)761-1100
URL: http://www.smpte.org

Monthly. $130.00/year for individuals. Journal containing articles pertaining to new developments in motion picture and television technology; standards and recommended practices; general news of the industry.

★9397★ **Studio Photography & Design Magazine (SP & D)**

Cygnus Business Media Inc.
3 Huntington Quadrangle, Ste. 301 N
Melville, NY 11747
Ph: (631)845-2700   Fax: (631)845-7109
Fr: 800-308-6397
URL: http://www.imaginginfo.com

Monthly. Magazine for the professional photographer. Highlights industry professionals working in today's photographic applications. Showcases portrait, wedding, commercial, digital, and travel photographers and includes a monthly selection of supplementary guides, tech tips, tutorials, and product round-ups.

★9398★ **TelevisionWeek**

Crain Communications Inc.
1155 Gratiot Ave.
PO Box 07924
Detroit, MI 48207-2997
Ph: (313)446-6000   Fax: (313)446-0347
Fr: 888-909-9111
URL: http://www.tvweek.com/

Weekly. $119.00/year for individuals; $171.00/year for Canada, including GST; $309.00/year for other countries, airmail. Newspaper covering management, programming, cable and trends in the television and the media industry.

★9399★ **Video Systems**

Penton Media Inc.
9800 Metcalf Ave.
Overland Park, KS 66212
Ph: (913)341-1300   Fax: (913)967-1898
URL: http://digitalcontentproducer.com

Monthly. Magazine for users of professional video equipment.

PLACEMENT AND JOB REFERRAL SERVICES

★9400★ **Broadcast Designer's Association (BDA)**

9000 W Sunset Blvd., Ste. 900
Los Angeles, CA 90069
Ph: (310)788-7600   Fax: (310)788-7616
E-mail: brett@ashyagency.com
URL: http://www.bda.tv

Members: Designers, artists, art directors, illustrators, photographers, animators, and other motion graphic professionals in the electronic media industry; educators and students; commercial and industrial companies that manufacture products related to design. **Purpose:** Seeks to promote understanding between designers, clients, and management; to stimulate innovative ideas and techniques; to encourage and provide a resource for young talents; and to provide a forum for discussion on industry issues and concerns. **Activities:** Maintains placement service; conducts surveys and compiles statistics.

★9401★ Health Science Communications Association (HeSCA)

39 Wedgewood Dr., Ste. A
Jewett City, CT 06351-2420
Ph: (860)376-5915   Fax: (860)376-6621
E-mail: hesca@hesca.org
URL: http://www.hesca.org

Description: Represents media managers, graphic artists, biomedical librarians, producers, faculty members of health science and veterinary medicine schools, health professional organizations, and industry representatives. Acts as a clearinghouse for information used by professionals engaged in health science communications. Coordinates Media Festivals Program that recognizes outstanding media productions in the health sciences. Offers placement service.

★9402★ Institute of American Indian Arts (IAIA)

83 Avan Nu Po Rd.
Santa Fe, NM 87508
Ph: (505)424-2300   Fax: (505)424-3900
Fr: 800-804-6423
E-mail: setzel@iaia.edu
URL: http://www.iaia.edu

Description: Federally chartered private institution. Offers learning opportunities in the arts and crafts to Native American youth (Indian, Eskimo, or Aleut). Emphasis is placed upon Indian traditions as the basis for creative expression in fine arts including painting, sculpture, museum studies, creative writing, printmaking, photography, communications, design, and dance, as well as training in metal crafts, jewelry, ceramics, textiles, and various traditional crafts. Students are encouraged to identify with their heritage and to be aware of themselves as members of a race rich in architecture, the fine arts, music, pageantry, and the humanities. All programs are based on elements of the Native American cultural heritage that emphasizes differences between Native American and non-Native American cultures. Sponsors Indian arts-oriented junior college offering Associate of Fine Arts degrees in various fields as well as seminars, an exhibition program, and traveling exhibits. Maintains extensive library, museum, and biographical archives. Provides placement service.

★9403★ National Association of Broadcasters (NAB)

1771 N St. NW
Washington, DC 20036
Ph: (202)429-5300   Fax: (202)429-4199
E-mail: nab@nab.org
URL: http://www.nab.org

Description: Representatives of radio and television stations and networks; associate members include producers of equipment and programs. Seeks to ensure the viability, strength, and success of free, over-the-air broadcasters; serves as an information resource to the industry. Monitors and reports on events regarding radio and television broadcasting. Maintains Broadcasting Hall of Fame. Offers minority placement service and employment clearinghouse.

★9404★ University Photographers Association of America (UPAA)

SUNY Brockport
350 New Campus Dr.
Brockport, NY 14420-2931
Ph: (585)395-2133
E-mail: jdusen@brockport.edu
URL: http://www.upaa.org

Description: College and university personnel engaged professionally in photography, audiovisual work, or journalism for universities. Seeks to advance applied photography and the profession through the exchange of thoughts and opinions among its members. Awards fellowship for exceptional work in the advancement of photography. Provides a medium for exchange of ideas and technical information on photography, especially university photographic work. Sponsors exhibits. Provides placement service for members.

EMPLOYER DIRECTORIES AND NETWORKING LISTS

★9405★ American Society of Media Photographers-Membership Directory

American Society of Media Photographers Inc.
150 N Second St.
Philadelphia, PA 19106
Ph: (215)451-2767   Fax: (215)451-0880
URL: http://www.asmp.org/tips/

Covers 5,000 professional photographers for publications. Entries include: Name, address, phone, fax, e-mail address, specialty.

★9406★ Black Book Photography

Black Book Marketing Group
740 Broadway, Ste. 202
New York, NY 10003
Ph: (212)979-6700   Fax: (212)673-4321
Fr: 800-841-1246
URL: http://www.BlackBook.com

Annual; latest edition 2007. $88.00 for individuals. Publication includes: Over 19,000 art directors, creative directors, photographers and photographic services, design firms, advertising agencies, and other firms whose products or services are used in advertising. Entries include: Company name, address, phone. Principal content of publication consists of 4-color samples from the leading commercial photographers. Arrangement: Classified by product/service.

★9407★ Bowker's News Media Directory

R.R. Bowker L.L.C.
630 Central Ave.
New Providence, NJ 07974
Ph: (908)286-1090   Fr: 888-269-5372
E-mail: wpn@bowker.com
URL: http://www.bowker.com

Annual; latest edition November 2006. $635.00 for individuals, set; $385.00 for individuals, per volume. Covers, in three separate volumes, syndicates and over 8,500 daily and weekly newspapers; 1,750 newsletters; over 16,800 radio and television stations; 5,500 magazines; 1,000 internal publications. Entries include: Name of publication or station, address, phone, fax, e-mail and URL, names of executives, editors, writers, etc., as appropriate. Broadcasting and magazine volumes include data on kinds of material accepted. Technical and mechanical requirements for publications are given. Arrangement: Magazines are classified by subject; newspapers and broadcasting stations geographical. Indexes: Newspaper department/editor by interest, metro area, feature syndicate subject; magazine subject, publication title; television director/personnel by subject, radio personnel and director by subject.

★9408★ Broadcasting & Cable Yearbook

R.R. Bowker L.L.C.
630 Central Ave.
New Providence, NJ 07974
Ph: (908)286-1090   Fr: 888-269-5372
URL: http://www.bowker.com

Annual; latest edition 2007, published October 2006. $235.00 for individuals. Covers over 17,000 television and radio stations in the United States, its territories, and Canada; cable MSOs and their individual systems; television and radio networks, broadcast and cable group owners, station representatives, satellite networks and services, film companies, advertising agencies, government agencies, trade associations, schools, and suppliers of professional and technical services, including books, serials, and videos; communications lawyers. Entries include: Company name, address, phone, fax, names of executives. Station listings include broadcast power, other operating details. Arrangement: Stations and systems are geographical, others are alphabetical. Indexes: Alphabetical.

★9409★ Careers in Focus: Photography

Facts On File Inc.
132 W 31st St., 17th Fl.
New York, NY 10001
Ph: (212)967-8800   Fax: 800-678-3633
Fr: 800-322-8755
URL: http://www.factsonfile.com

Published 2004. $29.95 for individuals; $26.95 for libraries. Covers an overview of photography, followed by a selection of jobs profiled in detail, including the nature of the job, earnings, prospects for employment, what kind of training and skills it requires, and sources for further information.

★9410★ Chicago Creative Directory

Chicago Creative Directory
333 N Michigan Ave., Ste. 810
Chicago, IL 60601
Ph: (312)236-7337   Fax: (312)236-6078
URL: http://www.creativedir.com

Annual, March. Covers over 6,000 advertising agencies, photographers, sound studios, talent agencies, audiovisual services, and others offering creative and production services. Entries include: For most listings–Company name, address, phone, list of officers, description of services. For freelance listings–Name, talent, address, phone. Arrangement: Classified by specialty.

★9411★ CPB Public Broadcasting Directory

Corporation for Public Broadcasting
401 9th St. NW
Washington, DC 20004-2129
Ph: (202)879-9600   Fax: (202)879-9700
Fr: 800-272-2190
URL: http://www.cpb.org/stations/publicdirectory/

Annual. Covers public television and radio stations, national and regional public broadcasting organizations and networks, state government agencies and commissions, and other related organizations. Entries include: For radio and television stations–Station call letters, frequency or channel, address, phone, licensee name, licensee type, date on air, antenna height, area covered, names and titles of key personnel. For organizations–Name, address, phone, name and title of key personnel. Arrangement: National and regional listings are alphabetical; state groups and the public radio and television stations are each geographical; other organizations and agencies are alphabetical. Indexes: Geographical, personnel, call letter, licensee type (all in separate indexes for radio and television).

★9412★ Fashion & Print Directory

Peter Glenn Publications
235 SE 5th Ave., Ste. R
Delray Beach, FL 33483
Ph: (561)404-4275   Fax: (561)279-4672
Fr: 888-332-6700
URL: http://www.pgdirect.com

Annual, November; latest edition 47th. $39.95 for individuals. Covers advertising agencies, PR firms, marketing companies, 1,000 client brand companies and related services in the U.S. and Canada. Includes photographers, marketing agencies, suppliers, sources of props and rentals, fashion houses, and beauty services. Entries include: Company name, address, phone; paid listings numbering 5,000 include description of products or services, key personnel. Arrangement: Classified by line of business.

★9413★ The Guide to Photography, Film & New Media Schools

ShawGuides Inc., Educational Publishers
PO Box 231295, Ansonia Sta.
New York, NY 10023
Ph: (212)799-6464   Fax: (212)724-9287
URL: http://photoschools.shawguides.com/

Continuously updated. Free. Covers listings for more than 250 educational programs for photography, film and new media in the U.S. and abroad, searchable by date, state or country, or by type. Entries include: Name of school or program, description of education-

al offerings, fees, locations, enrollment details, degrees conferred, contact name, address, phone, fax, e-mail, web site.

★9414★ The Guide to Photography, Film & New Media Workshops

ShawGuides Inc., Educational Publishers
PO Box 231295, Ansonia Sta.
New York, NY 10023
Ph: (212)799-6464   Fax: (212)724-9287
URL: http://photoworkshops.shawguides.com/

Continuously updated. Free. Covers listings for more than 2,400 photography, film and new media educational workshops in the U.S. and abroad, searchable by date, state or country, or by type. Entries include: Name of workshop, description of programs, fees, locations, contact name, address, phone, fax, e-mail, web site.

★9415★ International Television and Video Almanac

Quigley Publishing Company Inc.
64 Wintergreen Ln.
Groton, MA 01450-4129
Ph: (860)228-0247   Fax: (860)228-0157
Fr: 800-231-8239
URL: http://hometown.aol.com/quigleypub/mp.html

Annual, January; latest edition 2007. $175.00 for individuals. Covers "Who's Who in Motion Pictures and Television and Home Video," television networks, major program producers, major group station owners, cable television companies, distributors, firms serving the television and home video industry, equipment manufacturers, casting agencies, literary agencies, advertising and publicity representatives, television stations, associations, list of feature films produced for television, statistics, industry's year in review, award winners, satellite and wireless cable providers, primetime programming, video producers, distributors, wholesalers. Entries include: Generally, company name, address, phone; manufacturer and service listings may include description of products and services and name of contact; producing, distributing, and station listings include additional details and contacts for cable and broadcast networks. Arrangement: Classified by service or activity. Indexes: Full.

★9416★ Klik! Showcase Photography

American Showcase Inc.
915 Broadway, 14th Fl.
New York, NY 10010
Ph: (212)673-6600   Fax: (212)673-9795
Fr: 800-894-7469
URL: http://www.americanshowcase.com/pages/k9_branding.html

Annual. $45.00 for individuals. Covers 9,500 photographers and related companies. Entries include: Name, address, phone, sample of work. Illustrators and graphic designers are described in 'American Showcase Illustration.' Arrangement: Geographical. Indexes: Specialty.

★9417★ National Directory of Arts Internships

National Network for Artist Placement
935 W Ave. 37
Los Angeles, CA 90065
Ph: (323)222-4035   Fax: (323)225-5711
Fr: 800-354-5348
URL: http://www.artistplacement.com

Biennial, odd years; latest edition 10th. $95.00 for individuals. Covers over 5,000 internship opportunities in dance, music, theater, art, design, film, and video & over 1,250 host organizations. Entries include: Name of sponsoring organization, address, name of contact; description of positions available, eligibility requirements, stipend or salary (if any), application procedures. Arrangement: Classified by discipline, then geographical.

★9418★ National Directory of Magazines

Oxbridge Communications Inc.
186 5th Ave.
New York, NY 10010
Ph: (212)741-0231   Fax: (212)633-2938
Fr: 800-955-0231
E-mail: custserv@oxbridge.com
URL: http://www.oxbridge.com/

Latest edition September 2007. $995.00 for individuals, print product; $1,195.00 for individuals, CD-ROM; $1,995.00 for individuals, print product and CD-ROM. Covers over 19,000 magazines; coverage includes Canada. Entries include: Title, publisher name, address, phone, fax number, names and titles of contact and key personnel, financial data, editorial and advertising information, circulation. Arrangement: Classified by subject. Indexes: Title; geographical; publisher.

★9419★ Photographer's Market

Writer's Digest Books
1507 Dana Ave.
PO Box 420235
Cincinnati, OH 45207
Fr: 800-221-5831
E-mail: photomarket@fwpubs.com
URL: http://www.writersdigest.com

Annual; latest edition 2007. $26.99 for individuals. Covers 2,000 companies and publications that purchase original photographs, including advertising agencies, public relations agencies, book and periodical publishers, stock photo agencies, photographic workshops, galleries, and competitions. Entries include: Name of buyer, address, phone, payment rates, requirements, reporting time, how to break in. Arrangement: Classified by type of market. Indexes: Digital markets, subject.

★9420★ PhotoSource Book

PhotoSource International
Pine Lake Farm
1910 35th Rd.
Osceola, WI 54020-5602
Ph: (715)248-3800   Fax: (715)248-7394
Fr: 800-624-0266
E-mail: web@photosource.com

URL: http://www.photosource.com

Bimonthly. Covers magazine and book publishers, public relations firms, advertising and government agencies currently soliciting photographs for publication; 6-12 listings per issue. Entries include: Company name, name of contact, address, phone, project title, and nature of photos sought. Indexes: CD-ROM editors.

★9421★ Self-Employed Writers and Artists Network-Directory

Self-Employed Writers and Artists Network Inc.
PO Box 440
Paramus, NJ 07653
Ph: (201)967-1313
URL: http://www.swan-net.com

Annual, spring. Covers over 135 freelance writers, graphic designers, illustrators, photographers, and other graphic arts professionals in northern New Jersey and New York city providing services in advertising, marketing, sales promotion, public relations, and telecommunications. Entries include: Name, address, phone, biographical data, description of services provided. Arrangement: Alphabetical. Indexes: Line of business.

★9422★ Television & Cable Factbook

Warren Communications News Inc.
2115 Ward Ct. NW
Washington, DC 20037
Ph: (202)872-9202   Fax: (202)318-8350
Fr: 800-771-9202
URL: http://www.warren-news.com/factbook.htm

Annual. $925.00 for individuals, print product; $995.00 for individuals, full online database. Covers commercial and noncommercial television stations and networks, including educational, low-power and instructional TV stations, as well as translators; United States cable television systems; cable and television group owners; program and service suppliers; and brokerage and financing companies. Entries include: For stations–Call letters, licensee name and address, studio address and phone; identification of owners, sales and legal representatives and chief station personnel; rates, technical data, map of service area, and Nielsen circulation data. For cable systems–Name, address, basic and pay subscribers, programming and fees, physical plant; names of personnel and ownership. Arrangement: Geographical by state, province, city, county, or country. Indexes: Call letters; product/service; name; general subject.

★9423★ Who's Who in Photographic Management

Photo Marketing Association International
3000 Picture Pl.
Jackson, MI 49201
Ph: (517)788-8100   Fax: (517)788-8371
Fr: 800-762-9287

Annual. Covers over 15,500 members of the

association and manufacturers and suppliers of photographic equipment; also members of the National Association of Photo Equipment Technicians and of the Professional School Photographers of America. Entries include: Name of firm, address, phone, name of contact. Arrangement: Separate alphabetical sections for each association and for the companies. Indexes: Geographical; product.

★9424★ Who's Who in Professional Imaging

Professional Photographers of America Inc.
229 Peachtree St. NE, Ste. 2200
Atlanta, GA 30303
Ph: (404)522-8600   Fax: (404)614-6400
URL: http://www.ppa.com/splash.cfm

Annual, April. Covers over 18,000 members, including portrait, commercial, wedding, and industrial photographers; also includes guide to photographic equipment and supply manufacturers and distributors. Entries include: For members–Name, office address, phone, show specialties; listings for members available for assignments. For suppliers–Company name, address, phone, product/service. Arrangement: Geographical.

★9425★ The Workbook

Scott & Daughters Publishing Inc.
940 N Highland Ave.
Los Angeles, CA 90038
Ph: (213)856-0008   Fax: (323)856-4368
Fr: 800-547-2688
URL: http://www.workbook.com

Annual, February. Covers 49,000 advertising agencies, art directors, photographers, freelance illustrators and designers, artists' representatives, interactive designers, prepress services, and other graphic arts services in the U.S. Entries include: Company or individual name, address, phone, specialty. National in scope. Arrangement: Classified by product or service.

HANDBOOKS AND MANUALS

★9426★ ASMP Professional Business Practices in Photography

Watson-Guptill Publications
770 Broadway
New York, NY 10003
Ph: (646)654-5400   Fax: (646)654-5487
Fr: 800-278-8477
E-mail: info@watsonguptill.com
URL: http://www.watsonguptill.com

American Society of Media Photographers Seventh edition. 2007. $29.95. 416 pages.

★9427★ Breaking into Film

Peterson's Guides
2000 Lenox Dr.
Box 67005
Lawrenceville, NJ 08648
Ph: (609)896-1800   Fax: (609)896-4531
Fr: 800-338-3282
E-mail: custsvc@petersons.com
URL: http://www.petersons.com

Kenna Mchugh. 1998. $14.95 (paper). 240 pages. Provides insight into jobs dealing with film and video and explains how to get a job in the film industry, with a list of key employers. Also offers advice from industry insiders and internship information.

★9428★ Breaking into Television

Peterson's Guides
2000 Lenox Dr.
Box 67005
Lawrenceville, NJ 08648
Ph: (609)896-1800   Fax: (609)896-4531
Fr: 800-338-3282
E-mail: custsvc@petersons.com
URL: http://www.petersons.com

Dan Weaver. 1998. $14.95 (paper). 244 pages. Explains how to get a job in the television industry, with a list of internship opportunities.

★9429★ Business of Wedding Photography

Watson-Guptill Publications
770 Broadway
New York, NY 10003
Ph: (646)654-5400   Fax: (646)654-5487
Fr: 800-278-8477
E-mail: info@watsonguptill.com
URL: http://www.watsonguptill.com

Ann Monteith. 1996. $35.00 (paper). 192 pages. Subtitled, "A Professional's Guide to Marketing and Managing a Successful Studio With Profiles of 30 Top Portrait Photographers."

★9430★ Careers in Communications

The McGraw-Hill Companies
PO Box 182604
Columbus, OH 43272
Fax: (614)759-3749   Fr: 877-883-5524
E-mail: customer.service@mcgraw-hill.com
URL: http://www.mcgraw-hill.com

Shonan Noronha. Fourth edition, 2004. $15.95 (paper). 192 pages. Examines the fields of journalism, photography, radio, television, film, public relations, and advertising. Gives concrete details on job locations and how to secure a job. Suggests many resources for job hunting.

★9431★ Careers for Film Buffs and Other Hollywood Types

The McGraw-Hill Companies
PO Box 182604
Columbus, OH 43272
Fax: (614)759-3749   Fr: 877-883-5524
E-mail: customer.service@mcgraw-hill.com
URL: http://www.mcgraw-hill.com

Jaq Greenspon. Second edition, 2003. $13.95; $9.95 (paper). 208 pages. Describes job descriptions in production, camera, sound, special effects, grips, electrical, makeup, costumes, etc.

★9432★ Careers in Health Care

The McGraw-Hill Companies
PO Box 182604
Columbus, OH 43272
Fax: (614)759-3749   Fr: 877-883-5524
E-mail: customer.service@mcgraw-hill.com
URL: http://www.mcgraw-hill.com

Barbara M. Swanson. Fifth edition, 2005. $15.95 (paper). 192 pages. Describes job duties, work settings, salaries, licensing and certification requirements, educational preparation, and future outlook. Gives ideas on how to secure a job.

★9433★ Careers for Night Owls and Other Insomniacs

The McGraw-Hill Companies
PO Box 182604
Columbus, OH 43272
Fax: (614)759-3749   Fr: 877-883-5524
E-mail: customer.service@mcgraw-hill.com
URL: http://www.mcgraw-hill.com

Louise Miller. Second edition, 2002. $12.95 (paper). 160 pages.

★9434★ Careers for Shutterbugs: And Other Candid Types

The McGraw-Hill Companies
PO Box 182604
Columbus, OH 43272
Fax: (614)759-3749   Fr: 877-883-5524
E-mail: customer.service@mcgraw-hill.com
URL: http://www.mcgraw-hill.com

Cheryl McLean. 1995. $14.95 (paper). 236 pages.

★9435★ International Directory of Film, Photography, Video and Television

Penrose Press
PO Box 470925
San Francisco, CA 94147
Ph: (415)567-4157   Fax: (415)567-4165

Raymond Lavzzana and Denise Penrose, editors. Fifth edition, 1996. $70.00 (paper). 200 pages. Part of the International Directory of Design Series. Includes references for educational programs, professional organizations and periodical publications. The subjects covered span the range of subjects of interest to photographers, cinematographers and videographers practicing in entertainment and documentation industries, including photography, cinematography, filmaking, videography and electronic imaging. Contact information includes street addresses, telephone and fax numbers, e-mail addresses and URL links to home pages. This directory is one of ten supplemental directories that are domain-specific guides to educational programs, professional societies, trade organizations, scholarly journals, and trade magazines throughout the world.

★9436★ Make Money with Your Camera

Amherst Media, Inc.
PO Box 586
Buffalo, NY 14226
Ph: (716)874-4450   Fax: (716)874-4508
Fr: 800-622-3278
URL: http://www.amherstmedia.com/

David Neil Arndt. 1999. $29.95 (paper). 123 pages.

★9437★ Master Guide for Professional Photographers

Amherst Media, Inc.
175 Rano St., Ste. 200
Buffalo, NY 14207
Ph: (716)874-4450   Fax: (716)874-4508
Fr: 800-622-3278
URL: http://www.amherstmedia.com/

Patrick Rice. 2006. $34.95. Comprehensive guide for photographers, covering techniques from shooting basics to image editing.

★9438★ On Being a Photographer: A Practical Guide

Lenswork Publishing
909 Third St.
Anacortes, OR 98221-1502
Fax: (503)905-6111   Fr: 800-659-2130

David Hurn and Bill Jay. Third Edition, 2001. $12.95 (paper). 95 pages.

★9439★ Opportunities in Film Careers

The McGraw-Hill Companies
PO Box 182604
Columbus, OH 43272
Fax: (614)759-3749   Fr: 877-883-5524
E-mail: customer.service@mcgraw-hill.com
URL: http://www.mcgraw-hill.com

Jan Bone and Ana Fernandez. 2004. $12.95 (paper). 160 pages. Provides advice on obtaining a job in film and in corporate non-broadcast film/video production. Illustrated.

★9440★ Opportunities in Journalism Careers

The McGraw-Hill Companies
PO Box 182604
Columbus, OH 43272
Fax: (614)759-3749   Fr: 877-883-5524
E-mail: customer.service@mcgraw-hill.com
URL: http://www.mcgraw-hill.com

Jim Patten and Donald L. Ferguson. 2001. $12.95 (paper). 160 pages. Outlines opportunities in every field of journalism, including newspaper reporting and editing, magazine and book publishing, corporate communications, advertising and public relations, freelance writing, and teaching. Covers how to prepare for and enter each field, outlining responsibilities, salaries, benefits, and job outlook for each specialty. Illustrated.

★9441★ Opportunities in Magazine Publishing Careers

The McGraw-Hill Companies
PO Box 182604
Columbus, OH 43272
Fax: (614)759-3749   Fr: 877-883-552₄
E-mail: customer.service@mcgraw-hill.com
URL: http://www.mcgraw-hill.com

S. William Pattis. 1994. $13.95; $14.95 (paper). 148 pages. Covers the scope o₁ magazine publishing and addresses how t₀ identify and pursue available positions. Illus₁ trated.

★9442★ Opportunities in Publishing Careers

The McGraw-Hill Companies
PO Box 182604
Columbus, OH 43272
Fax: (614)759-3749   Fr: 877-883-552₄
E-mail: customer.service@mcgraw-hill.com
URL: http://www.mcgraw-hill.com

Robert A. Carter and S. William Pattis. 2000₁ $12.95 (paper). 160 pages. Covers all positions in book and magazine publishing including new opportunities in multimedia publishing.

★9443★ Opportunities in Sports and Athletics Careers

The McGraw-Hill Companies
PO Box 182604
Columbus, OH 43272
Fax: (614)759-3749   Fr: 877-883-5524
E-mail: customer.service@mcgraw-hill.com
URL: http://www.mcgraw-hill.com

William Ray Heitzmann. 1993. 160 pages₁ $11.95 (paper). A guide to planning for anc seeking opportunities in this growing field. Illustrated.

★9444★ Opportunities in Television and Video Careers

The McGraw-Hill Companies
PO Box 182604
Columbus, OH 43272
Fax: (614)759-3749   Fr: 877-883-5524
E-mail: customer.service@mcgraw-hill.com
URL: http://www.mcgraw-hill.com

Shonan Noronha. Second edition, 2003₁ $12.95 (paper). 160 pages. Details the employment opportunities open in television, cable, corporate video, institutional and government media, including independent production, and discusses how to land a job. Illustrated.

★9445★ Opportunities in Visual Arts Careers

The McGraw-Hill Companies
PO Box 182604
Columbus, OH 43272
Fax: (614)759-3749   Fr: 877-883-5524
E-mail: customer.service@mcgraw-hill.com
URL: http://www.mcgraw-hill.com

Mark Salmon and Bill Barrett. 2001. $12.95; $11.95 (paper). 160 pages. Points the way to a career in the visual arts, examining opporinities for designers, painters, sculptors, illustrators, animators, photographers, art therapists, educators, and others. Offers a view of the pros and cons of working for an art or design company or on your own.

9446★ The Photographer's Market Guide to Photo Submission and Portfolio Formats

Writers Digest Books
1700 E. Galbraith Rd.
Cincinnati, OH 45236
Ph: (513)531-2690   Fax: (513)531-4082
Fr: 800-289-0963
E-mail: writersdig@fwpubs.com
URL: http://www.writersdigest.com

Michael Willins. 1997. $18.99 (paper). 152 pages. Includes steps for amateur and professional photographers to successfully market their work.

★9447★ Photography Your Way: A Career Guide to Satisfaction and Success

Allworth Press
10 E. 23rd St., Ste. 510
New York, NY 10010
Ph: (212)777-8395   Fax: (212)777-8261
Fr: 800-491-2808
URL: http://www.allworth.com/

Chuck Delaney. Second edition, 2005. $22.95 (paper). 352 pages.

★9448★ Photos That Sell: The Art of Successful Freelance Photography

Watson-Guptill Publications
770 Broadway
New York, NY 10003
Ph: (646)654-5400   Fax: (646)654-5487
Fr: 800-278-8477
E-mail: info@watsonguptill.com
URL: http://www.watsonguptill.com

Lee Frost. 2004. $27.95 (paper). 192 pages.

TRADESHOWS

★9449★ Mid-East States Regional Print Competition and Exhibition and Trade Show

Professional Photographers of Ohio
37 W. Broad St. Ste. 480
Columbus, OH 43215
Ph: (614)228-6703   Fax: (614)241-2215
E-mail: Carol@ppofohio.org
URL: http://www.ppofohio.org

Annual. **Primary Exhibits:** Photographic equipment, supplies, and services; to include office equipment, computers and phone systems.

★9450★ Photohistory

Photographic Historical Society
One Lomb Memorial Dr.
Rochester, NY 14623-5603
Ph: (585)475-2411
URL: http://www.rit.edu

Triennial. **Primary Exhibits:** Cameras and photographic images.

★9451★ PMA - Photo Marketing Association International Annual Convention and Trade Show

Photo Marketing Association International
3000 Picture Pl.
Jackson, MI 49201
Ph: (517)788-8100   Fax: (517)788-8371
E-mail: PMA_Trade_Exhibits@pmai.org
URL: http://www.pmai.org

Annual. **Primary Exhibits:** Profile of exhibitors: film, cameras and photo accessory manufacturers and distributors; photo processing equipment and materials suppliers; digital imaging hardware and software marketers; studio imaging equipment distributors; and original equipment manufacturers (OEMs).

★9452★ PMAI Imaging Conference & Mini-Trade Show

Photo Marketing Association International
3000 Picture Pl.
Jackson, MI 49201
Ph: (517)788-8100   Fax: (517)788-8371
E-mail: PMA_Trade_Exhibits@pmai.org
URL: http://www.pmai.org

Annual. **Primary Exhibits:** People-oriented, educational event for photo-imaging industry executives and their suppliers. Profile of exhibition: Manufacturers and distributors of consumer photo, video, optics, and digital picture products; photo processing equipment and supplies; professional photo services; and digital imaging systems and supplies.

OTHER SOURCES

★9453★ American Almanac of Jobs and Salaries

HarperCollins
10 E. 53rd St.
New York, NY 10022
Ph: (212)207-7000   Fr: 800-242-7737
URL: http://www.harpercollins.com/

John W. Wright. Revised edition, 2000. $20.00 (paper). 672 pages. This is a comprehensive guide to the wages of hundreds of occupations in a wide variety of industries and organizations.

★9454★ American Society of Media Photographers (ASMP)

150 N 2nd St.
Philadelphia, PA 19106
Ph: (215)451-2767   Fax: (215)451-0880

E-mail: mopsik@asmp.org
URL: http://www.asmp.org

Members: Professional society of freelance photographers. **Purpose:** Works to evolve trade practices for photographers in communications fields. Provides business information to photographers and their potential clients; promotes ethics and rights of members. **Activities:** Holds educational programs and seminars. Compiles statistics.

★9455★ Art Directors Club (ADC)

106 W 29th St.
New York, NY 10001
Ph: (212)643-1440   Fax: (212)643-4266
E-mail: info@adcglobal.org
URL: http://www.adcglobal.org

Members: Art directors of advertising magazines and agencies, visual information specialists, and graphic designers; associate members are artists, cinematographers, photographers, copywriters, educators, journalists, and critics. **Purpose:** Promotes and stimulates interest in the practice of art direction. **Activities:** Sponsors Annual Exhibition of Advertising, Editorial and Television Art and Design; International Traveling Exhibition. Provides educational, professional, and entertainment programs; on-premise art exhibitions; portfolio review program. Conducts panels for students and faculty.

★9456★ Association of Music Writers and Photographers (AMWP)

PO Box 79
Oak Lawn, IL 60454
Fax: (801)327-4735
E-mail: amwp@amwp.org
URL: http://www.musicpressreport.com

Description: Defends the interests of music writers and photographers. Establishes the first music press community. Offers networking opportunities, job listings, industry directories, guides and contests.

★9457★ BioCommunications Association (BCA)

220 Southwind Ln.
Hillsborough, NC 27278
Ph: (919)245-0906   Fax: (919)245-0906
E-mail: office@bca.org
URL: http://www.bca.org

Description: Photographers, technicians, doctors, scientists, educators, and individuals concerned with photography in the health sciences and related fields. Seeks to advance the techniques of biophotography and biomedical communications through meetings, seminars, and workshops.

★9458★ Corporation for Public Broadcasting (CPB)

401 9th St. NW
Washington, DC 20004-2129
Ph: (202)879-9600   Fax: (202)879-9700
Fr: 800-272-2190
E-mail: comments@cpb.org
URL: http://www.cpb.org

Description: Promotes and finances the growth and development of noncommercial radio and television. Makes grants to local public television and radio stations, program producers, and program distribution networks; studies emerging technologies; works to provide adequate long-range financing from the U.S. government and other sources for public broadcasting. Supports children's services; compiles statistics; sponsors training programs.

★9459★ Editorial Photographers (EP)

PO Box 591811
San Francisco, CA 94159-1811
E-mail: info@editorialphoto.com
URL: http://www.editorialphoto.com

Description: Aims to improve the health and profitability of editorial photography. Seeks to educate photographers and photography buyers about business issues affecting the industry, and to raise the level of business practices in the profession. Promotes healthy relationships between photographers and publishers.

★9460★ Media Alliance (MA)

1904 Franklin St., Ste. 500
Oakland, CA 94612
Ph: (510)832-9000   Fax: (510)238-8557
E-mail: information@media-alliance.org
URL: http://www.media-alliance.org

Description: Writers, photographers, editors, broadcast workers, public relations practitioners, videographers, filmmakers, commercial artists and other media workers and aspiring media workers. Supports free press and independent, alternative journalism that services progressive politics and social justice.

★9461★ Media and the Arts Occupations

Delphi Productions
3159 6th St.
Boulder, CO 80304
Ph: (303)443-2100   Fax: (303)443-4022
Fr: 888-443-2400
E-mail: support@delphivideo.com
URL: http://www.delphivideo.com

$95.00. 50 minutes. Part of the Careers for the 21st Century Video Library.

★9462★ National Press Photographers Association (NPPA)

3200 Croasdaile Dr., Ste. 306
Durham, NC 27705-2588
Ph: (919)383-7246   Fax: (919)383-7261
E-mail: info@nppa.org
URL: http://www.nppa.org

Purpose: Professional news photographers and others whose occupation has a direct professional relationship with photojournalism, the art of news communication by photographic image through publication, television film, or theater screen. **Activities:** Sponsors annual television-news film workshop and annual cross-country (five locations) short course. Conducts annual competition for news photos and for television-news film, and monthly contest for still clipping and television-news film.

★9463★ Professional Photographers of America (PPA)

229 Peachtree St. NE, Ste. 2200
Atlanta, GA 30303-1608
Ph: (404)522-8600   Fax: (404)614-6400
Fr: 800-786-6277
E-mail: csc@ppa.com
URL: http://www.ppa.com

Description: Strives to create a global perspective that promotes business first, creativity foremost and excellence always. Aims to be the leader in the dissemination of knowledge in the areas of professional business practices and creative image-making, and to define and maintain the industry's standards of excellence. Represents portrait, wedding, commercial, industrial, and specialized photographers. Sponsors PPA International School of Professional Photography. Maintains speakers' bureau.

★9464★ Professional School Photographers Association International (PSPA)

26 W Broad St.
Bethlehem, PA 18018-5732
Ph: (610)694-8825   Fax: (610)694-0930
E-mail: royal@schoolportraits.com
URL: http://pspa.pmai.org

Description: A section of the Photo Marketing Association International. Firms engaged in the photographing and/or processing of school photographs. Purposes are: to encourage the exchange of production ideas and economies; to cooperate in the overall promotion of photography; to work for better relations and understanding with schools; to act as a group in making manufacturers of sensitized goods and photographic equipment aware of the specialized needs of school photography; to maintain a close watch on any legislation that may affect school photography; to promote career possibilities and personnel training and recruitment for school photography; to foster the well-being of the member firms by providing some of the advantages of a large-scale operation.

★9465★ Wedding and Portrait Photographers International (WPPI)

1312 Lincoln Blvd.
PO Box 2003
Santa Monica, CA 90406-2003
Ph: (310)451-0090   Fax: (310)395-9058
URL: http://www.wppinow.com/index2.tml

Description: Represents wedding portrait and digital photographers and photographers employed at general photography studios. Promotes high artistic and technical standards in wedding photography. Serves as a forum for the exchange of technical knowledge and experience; makes available the expertise of top professionals in the field of photographic arts and technology, advertising, sales promotion, marketing, public relations, accounting, business management, tax, and profit planning. Members are offered the opportunity to purchase special products and services.

★9466★ Women in Cable Telecommunications (WICT)

PO Box 791305
Baltimore, MD 21279-1305
Ph: (703)234-9810   Fax: (703)817-1595
E-mail: bfmosley@wict.org
URL: http://www.wict.org

Description: Empowers and educates women to achieve their professional goals by providing opportunities for leadership, networking and advocacy.

Physical Therapists

★9476★ Pediatric Physical Therapy

Lippincott Williams & Wilkins
530 Walnut St.
Philadelphia, PA 19106-3621
Ph: (215)521-8300   Fax: (215)521-8902
Fr: 800-638-3030
URL: http://www.pedpt.com/

Quarterly. $149.00/year for individuals, U.S.; $249.00/year for institutions, U.S.; $98.00/year for institutions, U.S. in-training; $202.00/year for individuals, international; $307.00/year for institutions, international; $142.00/year for institutions, international, in-training. Journal reporting on new clinical care for pediatric patients.

★9477★ Physical & Occupational Therapy in Geriatrics

The Haworth Press Inc.
10 Alice St.
Binghamton, NY 13904
Ph: (607)722-5857   Fr: 800-429-6784
URL: http://www.haworthpress.com

Quarterly. $99.00/year for individuals; $145.00/year for Canada, individual; $152.00/year for other countries, individual; $660.00/year for institutions, agency, library; $949.00/year for institutions, Canada, agency, library; $1,011.00/year for institutions, other countries, agency, library. Journal for allied health professionals focusing on current practice and emerging issues in the health care of and rehabilitation of the older client.

★9478★ Physical and Occupational Therapy in Pediatrics

The Haworth Press Inc.
10 Alice St.
Binghamton, NY 13904
Ph: (607)722-5857   Fr: 800-429-6784
URL: http://www.haworthpress.com/store/product.asp?sid=RGDXP14RA

Quarterly. $75.00/year for U.S., individual; $109.00/year for Canada, individual; $116.00/year for other countries, individual; $640.00/year for institutions, agency, library; $928.00/year for institutions, Canada, agency, library; $992.00/year for institutions, other countries, agency, library. Journal for therapists involved in developmental and physical rehabilitation of infants and children.

★9479★ Physical Therapy

American Physical Therapy Association
1111 N Fairfax St.
Alexandria, VA 22314-1488
Ph: (703)684-2782   Fax: (703)684-7343
Fr: 800-999-2782
E-mail: ptjourn@apta.org
URL: http://www.ptjournal.org/

Monthly. $80.00/year for nonmembers, U.S.; $110.00/year for institutions, non-members; $105.00/year for nonmembers, international; $135.00/year for institutions, other countries, non-members; included free with membership. Journal of the American Physical Therapy Association.

★9480★ Physical Therapy Products

Novicom Inc.
6100 Center Dr., Ste. 1000
Los Angeles, CA 90045
Ph: (310)642-4400
URL: http://www.ptproductsonline.com/

Monthly. Free to qualified subscribers. Magazine featuring new products and services available in the physical therapy field.

★9481★ PT, Magazine of Physical Therapy

American Physical Therapy Association
1111 N Fairfax St.
Alexandria, VA 22314-1488
Ph: (703)684-2782   Fax: (703)684-7343
Fr: 800-999-2782
URL: http://www.apta.org

Monthly. $75.00/year for individuals, non-members; $95.00/year for individuals, international, non-members; $100.00/year for institutions, non-members; $125.00/year for institutions, other countries, international, non-members; Subscription included in membership. Magazine for physical therapy professionals.

★9482★ Teaching Exceptional Children

Council for Exceptional Children
1110 N Glebe Rd., Ste. 300
Arlington, VA 22201-5704
Ph: (703)620-3660   Fax: (703)264-9494
Fr: 888-232-7733
E-mail: tec@bc.edu
URL: http://www.cec.sped.org

Bimonthly. $135.00/year for individuals; $250.00 for two years; $145.00 for two years, Canada; $270.00 for two years, Canada; $165.00/year for out of country, foreign-air printed matter; $310.00/year for out of country, two years, foreign-air printed matter; $25.00/year for institutions, single copy; $170.00/year for institutions; $290.00 for two years, institutional. Journal exploring practical methods for teaching students who have exceptionalities and those who are gifted and talented.

PLACEMENT AND JOB REFERRAL SERVICES

★9483★ American Physical Therapy Association (APTA)

1111 N Fairfax St.
Alexandria, VA 22314-1488
Ph: (703)684-2782   Fax: (703)684-7343
Fr: 800-999-2782
E-mail: frankmallon@apta.org
URL: http://www.apta.org

Members: Professional organization of physical therapists and physical therapist assistants and students. **Purpose:** Fosters the development and improvement of physical therapy service, education, and research; evaluates the organization and administration of curricula; directs the maintenance of

standards and promotes scientific research. Acts as an accrediting body for educational programs in physical therapy. Establishes standards. **Activities:** Offers advisory and consultation services to schools of physical therapy and facilities offering physical therapy services; provides placement services at conference.

★9484★ American Public Health Association (APHA)

800 I St. NW
Washington, DC 20001
Ph: (202)777-2742   Fax: (202)777-2534
E-mail: comments@apha.org
URL: http://www.apha.org

Members: Professional organization of physicians, nurses, educators, academicians, environmentalists, epidemiologists, new professionals, social workers, health administrators, optometrists, podiatrists, pharmacists, dentists, nutritionists, health planners, other community and mental health specialists, and interested consumers. **Purpose:** Seeks to protect and promote personal, mental, and environmental health. **Activities:** Services include: promulgation of standards; establishment of uniform practices and procedures; development of the etiology of communicable diseases; research in public health; exploration of medical care programs and their relationships to public health. Sponsors job placement service.

EMPLOYER DIRECTORIES AND NETWORKING LISTS

★9485★ AHA Guide to the Health Care Field

American Hospital Association
1 N Franklin
Chicago, IL 60606
Ph: (312)422-2050   Fax: (312)422-4700
Fr: 800-424-4301

Annual, August. Covers hospitals, networks, multi-health care systems, freestanding ambulatory surgery centers, psychiatric facilities, long-term care facilities, substance abuse programs, and other health-related organizations. Entries include: For hospitals–Facility name, address, phone, administrator's name, number of beds, facilities and services, number of employees, expenses, other statistics. For other organizations–Name, address, phone, fax, name and title of contact. Arrangement: Geographical. Indexes: Hospital name.

★9486★ Directory of Hospital Personnel

Grey House Publishing
185 Millerton Rd.
PO Box 860
Millerton, NY 12546
Ph: (518)789-8700   Fax: (518)789-0556
Fr: 800-562-2139
URL: http://www.greyhouse.com/hospital_

personnel.htm

Annual. $325.00 for print product; $545.00 for online database subscription; $650.00 for online database subscription and print product combined. Covers 200,000 executives at 7,000 U.S. hospitals. Entries include: Name of hospital, address, phone; number of beds; type and JCAHO status of hospital; names and titles of key department heads and staff; medical and nursing school affiliations; number of residents, interns, and nursing students. Arrangement: Geographical. Indexes: Hospital name, personnel, hospital size.

★9487★ **Hospital Blue Book**
Billian Publishing Inc./Transworld
    Publishing Inc.
2100 Powers Ferry Rd. SE
Atlanta, GA 30339
Ph: (770)955-5656   Fax: (770)952-0669
Fr: 800-533-8484
E-mail: blu-book@billian.com

2005. $300.00 for individuals. Covers more than 6,687 hospitals; some listings also appear in a separate southern edition of this publication. Entries include: Name of hospital, accreditation, mailing address, phone, fax, number of beds, type of facility (nonprofit, general, state, etc.); list of administrative personnel and chiefs of medical services, with specific titles. Arrangement: Geographical.

★9488★ **The JobBank Guide to Health Care Companies**
Adams Media Corp.
57 Littlefield St.
Avon, MA 02322
Ph: (508)427-7100   Fax: (508)427-6790
Fr: 800-872-5627
URL: http://www.amazon.com/Jobbank-Guide-Health-Care-Companies/dp

Biennial. Covers jobs nationwide in health care companies. Entries include: Firm or organization name, address, phone, name and title of contact; description of organization, headquarters location, typical titles for entry- and middle-level positions, educational backgrounds desired, fringe benefits offered, stock exchange listing, training programs, internships, parent company, number of employees, revenues, e-mail and web addresses, projected number of hires. Indexes: Alphabetical.

★9489★ **Medical and Health Information Directory**
Gale, Cengage Learning
27500 Drake Rd.
Farmington Hills, MI 48331-3535
Ph: (248)699-4253   Fax: (248)699-8065
Fr: 800-877-4253
E-mail: businessproducts@gale.com
URL: http://www.gale.com

Annual; latest edition 20th, July 2007. $375.00/volume. Covers in Volume 1, more than 26,500 medical and health oriented associations, organizations, institutions, and government agencies, including health maintenance organizations (HMOs), preferred

provider organizations (PPOs), insurance companies, pharmaceutical companies, research centers, and medical and allied health schools. In Volume 2, over 12,000 medical book publishers; medical periodicals, directories, audiovisual producers and services, medical libraries and information centers, electronic resources, and health-related internet search engines. In Volume 3, more than 35,500 clinics, treatment centers, care programs, and counseling/diagnostic services for 34 subject areas. Entries include: Institution, service, or firm name, address, phone, fax, email and URL; many include names of key personnel and, when pertinent, descriptive annotations. Volume 3 was formerly listed separately as Health Services Directory. Arrangement: Classified by organization activity, service, etc. Indexes: Each volume has a complete alphabetical name and keyword index.

★9490★ **Private Practice Section of the American Physical Therapy Association-Membership Directory**
American Physical Therapy Association
1055 N Fairfax St., Ste. 100
Alexandria, VA 22314-1488
Ph: (703)299-2410   Fax: (703)299-2411
Fr: 800-999-2782
URL: http://www.ppsapta.org

Biennial; fall of even years. Covers about 4,700 member physical therapists in private practice. Entries include: Firm name, home address, business address and phone, fax, names and titles of key personnel, specialty, type of practice, congressional district. Arrangement: Same information is listed alphabetically and geographically. Indexes: Geographical, personal name.

Handbooks and Manuals

★9491★ **Careers in Health Care**
The McGraw-Hill Companies
PO Box 182604
Columbus, OH 43272
Fax: (614)759-3749   Fr: 877-883-5524
E-mail: customer.service@mcgraw-hill.com
URL: http://www.mcgraw-hill.com

Barbara M. Swanson. Fifth edition, 2005. $15.95 (paper). 192 pages. Describes job duties, work settings, salaries, licensing and certification requirements, educational preparation, and future outlook. Gives ideas on how to secure a job.

★9492★ **Careers for Health Nuts and Others Who Like to Stay Fit**
The McGraw-Hill Companies
PO Box 182604
Columbus, OH 43272
Fax: (614)759-3749   Fr: 877-883-5524
E-mail: customer.service@mcgraw-hill.com
URL: http://www.mcgraw-hill.com

Blythe Camenson. Second edition, 2005. $13.95 (paper). 208 pages.

★9493★ **Careers in Physical Therapy**
Rosen Publishing Group, Inc.
29 E 21st St.
New York, NY 10010
Ph: (212)777-3017   Fax: 888-436-4643
Fr: 800-237-9932
URL: http://www.rosenpublishing.com/

Trish Hawkins. 2001. $31.95. Profiles opportunities for individuals considering a profession in physical therapy.

★9494★ **Careers in Social and Rehabilitation Services**
The McGraw-Hill Companies
PO Box 182604
Columbus, OH 43272
Fax: (614)759-3749   Fr: 877-883-5524
E-mail: customer.service@mcgraw-hill.com
URL: http://www.mcgraw-hill.com

Geraldine O. Garner. 2001. $19.95; 14.95 (paper). 128 pages.

★9495★ **Expert Resumes for Health Care Careers**
Jist Works
875 Montreal Way
St. Paul, MN 55102
Fr: 800-648-5478
E-mail: info@jist.com
URL: http://www.jist.com

Wendy S. Enelow and Louise M. Kursmark. December 2003. $16.95. 288 pages.

★9496★ **Handbook of Teaching for Physical Therapists**
Butterworth-Heinemann
11830 Westline Industrial Dr.
St. Louis, MO 63146
Ph: (314)453-7010   Fax: (314)453-7095
Fr: 800-545-2522
E-mail: usbkinfo@elsevier.com
URL: http://www.elsevier.com

Katherine F. Shepard and Gail M. Jensen. Second edition, 2002. $49.95 (paper). 430 pages.

★9497★ **Health Careers Today**
Elsevier
11830 Westline Industrial Dr.
St. Louis, MO 63146
Ph: (314)453-7010   Fax: (314)453-7095
Fr: 800-545-2522
E-mail: usbkinfo@elsevier.com
URL: http://www.elsevier.com

Gerdin, Judith. Fourth edition. 2007. $59.95. 496 pages. Covers more than 45 health careers. Discusses the roles and responsibilities of various occupations and provides a solid foundation in the skills needed for all health careers.

★9498★ How to Become a Physical Therapist

Skip Hunter Enterprises
PO Box 61
Clemson, SC 29633
Ph: (803)654-3800   Fax: (803)654-4006

Skip Hunter. 1995. $19.95 (paper). 115 pages.

★9499★ Marketing Techniques for Physical Therapists

Aspen Publishers Inc.
76 Ninth Ave., 7th Fl.
New York, NY 10011
Ph: (212)771-0786   Fax: (212)771-0796
Fr: 800-538-8437
URL: http://www.aspenpublishers.com

Kathryn Schaefer. 2005. $68.00.

★9500★ Opportunities in Fitness Careers

The McGraw-Hill Companies
PO Box 182604
Columbus, OH 43272
Fax: (614)759-3749   Fr: 877-883-5524
E-mail: customer.service@mcgraw-hill.com
URL: http://www.mcgraw-hill.com

Mary Miller. 2003. $12.95 (paper). 146 pages. Surveys fitness related careers. Describes career opportunities, education and experience needed, how to get into entry-level jobs and what income to expect. Schools are listed in the appendix.

★9501★ Opportunities in Health and Medical Careers

The McGraw-Hill Companies
PO Box 182604
Columbus, OH 43272
Fax: (614)759-3749   Fr: 877-883-5524
E-mail: customer.service@mcgraw-hill.com
URL: http://www.mcgraw-hill.com

I. Donald Snook, Jr. and Leo D'Orazio. 2004. $13.95 (paper). 157 pages. Covers the full range of medical and health occupations. Illustrated.

★9502★ Opportunities in Paramedical Careers

The McGraw-Hill Companies
PO Box 182604
Columbus, OH 43272
Fax: (614)759-3749   Fr: 877-883-5524
E-mail: customer.service@mcgraw-hill.com
URL: http://www.mcgraw-hill.com

Alex Kacen. 1999. 14.95 (hardcover). 160 pages. Discusses a variety of opportunities in this field and how to pursue them. Illustrated.

★9503★ Opportunities in Physical Therapy Careers

The McGraw-Hill Companies
PO Box 182604
Columbus, OH 43272
Fax: (614)759-3749   Fr: 877-883-5524

E-mail: customer.service@mcgraw-hill.com
URL: http://www.mcgraw-hill.com

Bernice R. Krumhansl. 2005. $13.95 (paper). 160 pages. Defines what the jobs are, where they are, and how to pursue them. Contains bibliography and illustrations.

★9504★ Opportunities in Sports and Athletics Careers

The McGraw-Hill Companies
PO Box 182604
Columbus, OH 43272
Fax: (614)759-3749   Fr: 877-883-5524
E-mail: customer.service@mcgraw-hill.com
URL: http://www.mcgraw-hill.com

William Ray Heitzmann. 1993. 160 pages. $11.95 (paper). A guide to planning for and seeking opportunities in this growing field. Illustrated.

★9505★ Opportunities in Sports Medicine Careers

The McGraw-Hill Companies
PO Box 182604
Columbus, OH 43272
Fax: (614)759-3749   Fr: 877-883-5524
E-mail: customer.service@mcgraw-hill.com
URL: http://www.mcgraw-hill.com

William Ray Heitzmann. 1992. $11.95 (paper). 160 pages. Discusses a variety of opportunities in this field and how to pursue them. Contains bibliography and illustrations.

★9506★ Real People Working in Health Care

The McGraw-Hill Companies
PO Box 182604
Columbus, OH 43272
Fax: (614)759-3749   Fr: 877-883-5524
E-mail: customer.service@mcgraw-hill.com
URL: http://www.mcgraw-hill.com

Blythe Camenson, Jan Goldberg. 1996. $12.95 (paper). 144 pages. Interviews and profiles of working professionals capture a range of opportunities in this field.

★9507★ Real People Working in the Helping Professions

The McGraw-Hill Companies
PO Box 182604
Columbus, OH 43272
Fax: (614)759-3749   Fr: 877-883-5524
E-mail: customer.service@mcgraw-hill.com
URL: http://www.mcgraw-hill.com

Blythe Camenson, Jan Goldberg. 1997. $12.95 (paper). 192 pages. Interviews and profiles of working professionals capture a range of opportunities in this field.

★9508★ Resumes for Health and Medical Careers

The McGraw-Hill Companies
PO Box 182604
Columbus, OH 43272
Fax: (614)759-3749   Fr: 877-883-5524
E-mail: customer.service@mcgraw-hill.com

URL: http://www.mcgraw-hill.com

Third edition, 2003. $11.95 (paper). 160 pages.

EMPLOYMENT AGENCIES AND SEARCH FIRMS

★9509★ Cross Country TravCorps

6551 Park of Commerce Blvd.
Boca Raton, FL 33487-8247
Fax: (562)998-8533   Fr: 800-530-6125
URL: http://www.crosscountrytravcorps.com

Places traveling nurses in assignments nationwide.

★9510★ Harper Associates

3100 NW Hwy., Ste. 240
Farmington Hills, MI 48334
Ph: (248)932-1170   Fax: (248)932-1214
E-mail: info@harperjobs.com
URL: http://www.harperjobs.com

Executive search firm and employment agency.

★9511★ J.B. Brown and Associates

820 Terminal Twr.
Cleveland, OH 44113
Ph: (216)696-2525   Fax: (216)696-5825

Employment agency and executive recruiter.

★9512★ JPM International

26034 Acero
Mission Viejo, CA 92691
Ph: (949)699-4300   Fax: (949)699-4333
Fr: 800-685-7856
E-mail: trish@jpmintl.com
URL: http://www.jpmintl.com

Executive search firm and employment agency.

★9513★ Professional Placement Associates, Inc.

287 Bowman Ave., Ste. 309
Purchase, NY 10577-2517
Ph: (914)251-1000   Fax: (914)251-1055
E-mail: careers@ppasearch.com
URL: http://www.ppasearch.com

Executive search firm specializing in the health and medical field.

★9514★ Team Placement Service, Inc.

1414 Prince St., Ste. 202
Alexandria, VA 22314
Ph: (703)820-8618   Fax: (703)820-3368
Fr: 800-495-6767
E-mail: 4jobs@teamplace.com
URL: http://www.teamplace.com

Full-service personnel consultants provide placement for healthcare staff, physician and dentist, private practice, and hospitals. Conduct interviews, tests, and reference checks to select the top 20% of applicants. Survey applicants' skill levels, provide backup information on each candidate, select compatible candidates for consideration, and insure the hiring process minimizes potential legal liability. Industries served: healthcare and government agencies providing medical, dental, biotech, laboratory, hospitals, and physician search.

ONLINE JOB SOURCES AND SERVICES

★9515★ **Medhunters.com**
Fr: 800-664-0278
E-mail: info@medhunters.com
URL: http://www.medhunters.com

Description: Career search site for jobs in all health care specialties; educational resources; visa and licensing information for relocation; interesting articles; relocation tools; links to professional organizations and general resources.

★9516★ **ProHealthJobs**
Fr: 800-796-1738
E-mail: Info@prohealthedujobs.com
URL: http://www.prohealthjobs.com

Description: Career resources site for the medical and health care field. Lists professional opportunities, product information, continuing education and open positions.

★9517★ **RehabJobs Online**
PO Box 480536
Los Angeles, CA 90048
Ph: (213)938-7718   Fax: (213)938-9609
Fr: 800-43-REHAB
E-mail: support@atsrehabjobs.com
URL: http://www.rehabjobs.com

Description: Resource center for the professional therapist. **Main files include:** Therapists Only, Therapy Forums, Nationwide Job Search (database), Therapy Job Outlook, Therapy Job Search Utilities, Therapy Links, Information for Employers and Recruiters.

★9518★ **RehabWorld**
URL: http://www.rehabworld.com

Description: Site for rehabilitation professionals to learn about the profession and locate jobs. Includes user groups, salary surveys, and chat capabilities. **Main files include:** Physical Therapy, Occupational Therapy, Speech Therapy, Mental Health, Employer World, Student World, International World, Forum.

TRADESHOWS

★9519★ **American Physical Therapy Association Annual Conference**
American Physical Therapy Association
1111 N Fairfax St.
Alexandria, VA 22314-1488
Ph: (703)683-6748   Fax: (703)684-7343
Fr: 800-999-2782
URL: http://www.apta.org

Annual. **Primary Exhibits:** Physical therapy products, equipment, and services. **Dates and Locations:** 2008 Jun 11-14; San Antonio, TX.

★9520★ **American Society of Hand Therapists and American Society for Surgery of the Hand Annual Meeting**
Smith, Bucklin and Associates, Inc. (Chicago)
401 N Michigan Ave.
Chicago, IL 60611-4267
Ph: (312)321-6610   Fax: (312)673-6670
Fr: 800-289-NAON
E-mail: info@smithbucklin.com
URL: http://www.smithbucklin.com

Annual. **Primary Exhibits:** Hand therapy equipment and products.

OTHER SOURCES

★9521★ *American Almanac of Jobs and Salaries*
HarperCollins
10 E. 53rd St.
New York, NY 10022
Ph: (212)207-7000   Fr: 800-242-7737
URL: http://www.harpercollins.com/

John W. Wright. Revised edition, 2000. $20.00 (paper). 672 pages. This is a comprehensive guide to the wages of hundreds of occupations in a wide variety of industries and organizations.

★9522★ **American Health Care Association (AHCA)**
1201 L St. NW
Washington, DC 20005
Ph: (202)842-4444   Fax: (202)842-3860
E-mail: hr@ahca.org
URL: http://www.ahca.org

Description: Federation of state associations of long-term health care facilities. Promotes standards for professionals in long-term health care delivery and quality care for patients and residents in a safe environment. Focuses on issues of availability, quality, affordability, and fair payment. Operates as liaison with governmental agencies, Congress, and professional associations. Compiles statistics.

★9523★ **American Kinesiotherapy Association (AKTA)**
118 College Dr., No. 5142
Hattiesburg, MS 39406
Fr: 800-296-AKTA
E-mail: info@akta.org
URL: http://www.akta.org

Members: Professional society of kinesiotherapists, associate and student members with interest in therapeutic exercise and education. Kinesiotherapy is the application of scientifically-based exercise principles adapted to enhance the strength, endurance and mobility of individuals with functional limitations of those requiring extended physical reconditioning. Seeks to serve the interest of members and represent the profession to the public through the promotion of continuing competency and continuing educational opportunities.

★9524★ **American Society of Hand Therapists (ASHT)**
401 N Michigan Ave.
Chicago, IL 60611-4267
Ph: (312)321-6866   Fax: (312)673-6670
E-mail: info@asht.org
URL: http://www.asht.org

Members: Registered and licensed occupational and physical therapists specializing in hand therapy and committed to excellence and professionalism in hand rehabilitation. **Purpose:** Works to promote research, publish information, improve treatment techniques, and standardize hand evaluation and care. Fosters education and communication between therapists in the U.S. and abroad. **Activities:** Compiles statistics; conducts research and education programs and continuing education seminars.

★9525★ **Association on Higher Education and Disability (AHEAD)**
107 Commerce Center Dr., Ste. 204
Huntersville, NC 28078
Ph: (704)947-7779   Fax: (704)948-7779
E-mail: ahead@ahead.org
URL: http://www.ahead.org

Description: Individuals interested in promoting the equal rights and opportunities of disabled postsecondary students, staff, faculty, and graduates. Provides an exchange of communication for those professionally involved with disabled students; collects, evaluates, and disseminates information; encourages and supports legislation for the benefit of disabled students. Conducts surveys on issues pertinent to college students with disabilities; offers resource referral system and employment exchange for positions in disability student services. Conducts research programs; compiles statistics.

★9526★ **EMTs, Nurses, Therapists, and Assistants**
Cambridge Educational
PO Box 2053
Princeton, NJ 08543-2053
Ph: 800-257-5126   Fax: (609)671-0266
Fr: 800-468-4227

E-mail: custserv@films.com
URL: http://www.cambridgeeducational.com
VHS and DVD. $79.95. 2000. 18 minutes. Part of the series "Exploring Health Occupations."

★9527★ **Exploring Health Occupations**
Cambridge Educational
PO Box 2053
Princeton, NJ 08543-2053
Ph: 800-257-5126   Fax: (609)671-0266
Fr: 800-468-4227
E-mail: custserv@films.com
URL: http://www.cambridgeeducational.com
VHS and DVD. $159.90. 1999. Two-part series provides a detailed view of the field of medical technicians and technologists, EMTs, nurses, therapists, and assistants.

★9528★ **Foundation for Physical Therapy (FPT)**
1111 N Fairfax St.
Alexandria, VA 22314-1488
Ph: (703)684-2782   Fax: (703)684-7343
Fr: 800-875-1378
E-mail: foundation@apta.org
URL: http://www.apta.org/Foundation
Description: Supports the physical therapy profession's research needs by funding scientific and clinically-relevant physical therapy research.

★9529★ **Health Assessment & Treating Occupations**
Delphi Productions
3159 6th St.
Boulder, CO 80304
Ph: (303)443-2100   Fax: (303)443-4022
Fr: 888-443-2400
E-mail: support@delphivideo.com
URL: http://www.delphivideo.com
$95.00. 50 minutes. Part of the Careers for the 21st Century Video Library.

★9530★ **Health Service Occupations**
Delphi Productions
3159 6th St.
Boulder, CO 80304
Ph: (303)443-2100   Fax: (303)443-4022
Fr: 888-443-2400

E-mail: support@delphivideo.com
URL: http://www.delphivideo.com
$95.00. 50 minutes. Part of the Careers for the 21st Century Video Library.

★9531★ **Holistic Dental Association (HDA)**
PO Box 151444
San Diego, CA 92175
Ph: (619)923-3120   Fax: (619)615-2228
E-mail: info@holisticdental.org
URL: http://www.holisticdental.org
Description: Represents dentists, chiropractors, dental hygienists, physical therapists, and medical doctors. Aims to provide a holistic approach to better dental care for patients, and to expand techniques, medications, and philosophies that pertain to extractions, anesthetics, fillings, crowns, and orthodontics. Encourages the use of homeopathic medications, acupuncture, cranial osteopathy, nutritional techniques, and physical therapy in treating patients in addition to conventional treatments. Sponsors training and educational seminars.

★9532★ **Inter-American Conductive Education Association (IACEA)**
PO Box 3169
Toms River, NJ 08756-3169
Ph: (732)797-2566   Fax: (732)797-2599
Fr: 800-824-2232
E-mail: info@iacea.org
URL: http://www.iacea.org
Description: Promotes and disseminates the principles of conductive education using the services of parents, conductors, therapists, teachers, and other related health care professionals. Qualifies trained conductors as new professionals to obtain health care, Medicare, Medicaid, and private health insurance reimbursement. Trains and certifies conductive education practitioners working in the United States and Canada.

★9533★ **Medicine & Related Occupations**
Delphi Productions
3159 6th St.
Boulder, CO 80304
Ph: (303)443-2100   Fax: (303)443-4022
Fr: 888-443-2400

E-mail: support@delphivideo.com
URL: http://www.delphivideo.com
$95.00. 45 minutes. Part of the Careers for the 21st Century Video Library.

★9534★ **National Rehabilitation Association (NRA)**
633 S Washington St.
Alexandria, VA 22314
Ph: (703)836-0850   Fax: (703)836-0848
E-mail: info@nationalrehab.org
URL: http://www.nationalrehab.org/website/index.html
Description: Provides opportunities through knowledge and diversity for professionals in the fields of rehabilitation of people with disabilities.

★9535★ **National Strength and Conditioning Association (NSCA)**
1885 Bob Johnson Dr.
Colorado Springs, CO 80906
Ph: (719)632-6722   Fax: (719)632-6367
Fr: 800-815-6826
E-mail: nsca@nsca-lift.org
URL: http://www.nsca-lift.org
Description: Represents professionals in the sports science, athletic, and fitness industries. Promotes the total conditioning of athletes to a level of optimum performance, with the belief that a better conditioned athlete not only performs better but is less prone to injury. Gathers and disseminates information on strength and conditioning techniques and benefits. Conducts national, regional, state, and local clinics and workshops. Operates professional certification program.

★9536★ **Physical Therapist**
Cambridge Educational
PO Box 2053
Princeton, NJ 08543-2053
Ph: 800-257-5126   Fax: (609)671-0266
Fr: 800-468-4227
E-mail: custserv@films.com
URL: http://www.cambridgeeducational.com
VHS and DVD. $39.95. 15 minutes. 1990. Part of the Vocational Visions Career Series.

Physical Therapy Assistants and Aides

SOURCES OF HELP-WANTED ADS

★9537★ ADVANCE for Physical Therapists and PT Assistants

Merion Publications Inc.
2900 Horizon Dr.
PO Box 61556
King of Prussia, PA 19406
Ph: (610)278-1400   Fr: 800-355-5627
URL: http://www.advanceforpt.com

Biweekly. Reaches active, qualified physical therapists, physical therapist assistants, and senior students in PT and PTA programs.

★9538★ American Journal of Physical Medicine and Rehabilitation

Lippincott Williams & Wilkins
530 Walnut St.
Philadelphia, PA 19106-3621
Ph: (215)521-8300   Fax: (215)521-8902
Fr: 800-638-3030
E-mail: jmulliga@lww.com
URL: http://www.amjphysmedrehab.com/

Monthly. Medical journal.

★9539★ The Journal of Orthopaedic and Sports Physical Therapy (JOSPT)

Lippincott Williams & Wilkins
530 Walnut St.
Philadelphia, PA 19106-3621
Ph: (215)521-8300   Fax: (215)521-8902
Fr: 800-638-3030
URL: http://www.jospt.org/

Monthly. $170.00/year for individuals, U.S.; $285.00/year for institutions, U.S.; $95.00/year for students, U.S.; $240.00/year for individuals, other countries; $365.00/year for institutions, other countries; $160.00/year for students, other countries, other countries; $60.00/year for other countries, airmail. Medical journal.

★9540★ Massage Therapy Journal

American Massage Therapy Association
500 Davis St., Ste. 900
Evanston, IL 60201-4695
Ph: (847)864-0123   Fax: (847)864-1178
Fr: 877-905-2700
E-mail: info@amtamassage.org
URL: http://www.amtamassage.org/journal/home.html

Annual. $25.00 for U.S. and Canada, per year; $45.00 for two years; $70.00 for elsewhere, per year; $120.00 for elsewhere, 2 years. Magazine focusing on professional massage therapy benefits, techniques, research, news, and practitioners.

★9541★ Pediatric Physical Therapy

Lippincott Williams & Wilkins
530 Walnut St.
Philadelphia, PA 19106-3621
Ph: (215)521-8300   Fax: (215)521-8902
Fr: 800-638-3030
URL: http://www.pedpt.com/

Quarterly. $149.00/year for individuals, U.S.; $249.00/year for institutions, U.S.; $98.00/year for institutions, U.S. in-training; $202.00/year for individuals, international; $307.00/year for institutions, international; $142.00/year for institutions, international, in-training. Journal reporting on new clinical care for pediatric patients.

★9542★ Physical & Occupational Therapy in Geriatrics

The Haworth Press Inc.
10 Alice St.
Binghamton, NY 13904
Ph: (607)722-5857   Fr: 800-429-6784
URL: http://www.haworthpress.com

Quarterly. $99.00/year for individuals; $145.00/year for Canada, individual; $152.00/year for other countries, individual; $660.00/year for institutions, agency, library; $949.00/year for institutions, Canada, agency, library; $1,011.00/year for institutions, other countries, agency, library. Journal for allied health professionals focusing on current practice and emerging issues in the health care of and rehabilitation of the older client.

★9543★ Physical and Occupational Therapy in Pediatrics

The Haworth Press Inc.
10 Alice St.
Binghamton, NY 13904
Ph: (607)722-5857   Fr: 800-429-6784
URL: http://www.haworthpress.com/store/product.asp?sid=RGDXP14RA

Quarterly. $75.00/year for U.S., individual; $109.00/year for Canada, individual; $116.00/year for other countries, individual; $640.00/year for institutions, agency, library; $928.00/year for institutions, Canada, agency, library; $992.00/year for institutions, other countries, agency, library. Journal for therapists involved in developmental and physical rehabilitation of infants and children.

★9544★ Physical Therapy

American Physical Therapy Association
1111 N Fairfax St.
Alexandria, VA 22314-1488
Ph: (703)684-2782   Fax: (703)684-7343
Fr: 800-999-2782
E-mail: ptjourn@apta.org
URL: http://www.ptjournal.org/

Monthly. $80.00/year for nonmembers, U.S.; $110.00/year for institutions, non-members; $105.00/year for nonmembers, international; $135.00/year for institutions, other countries, non-members; included free with membership. Journal of the American Physical Therapy Association.

★9545★ Physical Therapy Products

Novicom Inc.
6100 Center Dr., Ste. 1000
Los Angeles, CA 90045
Ph: (310)642-4400
URL: http://www.ptproductsonline.com/

Monthly. Free to qualified subscribers. Magazine featuring new products and services available in the physical therapy field.

★9546★ PT, Magazine of Physical Therapy

American Physical Therapy Association
1111 N Fairfax St.
Alexandria, VA 22314-1488
Ph: (703)684-2782   Fax: (703)684-7343
Fr: 800-999-2782
URL: http://www.apta.org

Monthly. $75.00/year for individuals, non-members; $95.00/year for individuals, international, non-members; $100.00/year for institutions, non-members; $125.00/year for institutions, other countries, international, non-members; Subscription included in membership. Magazine for physical therapy professionals.

PLACEMENT AND JOB REFERRAL SERVICES

★9547★ American Physical Therapy Association (APTA)

1111 N Fairfax St.
Alexandria, VA 22314-1488
Ph: (703)684-2782   Fax: (703)684-7343
Fr: 800-999-2782
E-mail: frankmallon@apta.org
URL: http://www.apta.org

Members: Professional organization of physical therapists and physical therapist assistants and students. **Purpose:** Fosters the development and improvement of physical therapy service, education, and research; evaluates the organization and administration of curricula; directs the maintenance of standards and promotes scientific research. Acts as an accrediting body for educational programs in physical therapy. Establishes standards. **Activities:** Offers advisory and consultation services to schools of physical therapy and facilities offering physical therapy services; provides placement services at conference.

EMPLOYER DIRECTORIES AND NETWORKING LISTS

★9548★ The JobBank Guide to Health Care Companies

Adams Media Corp.
57 Littlefield St.
Avon, MA 02322
Ph: (508)427-7100   Fax: (508)427-6790
Fr: 800-872-5627
URL: http://www.amazon.com/Jobbank-Guide-Health-Care-Companies/dp

Biennial. Covers jobs nationwide in health care companies. Entries include: Firm or organization name, address, phone, name and title of contact; description of organization, headquarters location, typical titles for entry- and middle-level positions, educational backgrounds desired, fringe benefits of-fered, stock exchange listing, training programs, internships, parent company, number of employees, revenues, e-mail and web addresses, projected number of hires. Indexes: Alphabetical.

HANDBOOKS AND MANUALS

★9549★ Careers for Health Nuts and Others Who Like to Stay Fit

The McGraw-Hill Companies
PO Box 182604
Columbus, OH 43272
Fax: (614)759-3749   Fr: 877-883-5524
E-mail: customer.service@mcgraw-hill.com
URL: http://www.mcgraw-hill.com

Blythe Camenson. Second edition, 2005. $13.95 (paper). 208 pages.

★9550★ Careers Inside the World of Health Care

Pearson Learning Group
135 S. Mt. Zion Rd.
PO Box 2500
Lebanon, IN 46052
Fax: 800-393-3156   Fr: 800-526-9907
URL: http://www.pearsonatschool.com

Beth Wilkinson. Revised edition, 1999. $21.30. 64 pages.

★9551★ Careers in Social and Rehabilitation Services

The McGraw-Hill Companies
PO Box 182604
Columbus, OH 43272
Fax: (614)759-3749   Fr: 877-883-5524
E-mail: customer.service@mcgraw-hill.com
URL: http://www.mcgraw-hill.com

Geraldine O. Garner. 2001. $19.95; 14.95 (paper). 128 pages.

★9552★ Expert Resumes for Health Care Careers

Jist Works
875 Montreal Way
St. Paul, MN 55102
Fr: 800-648-5478
E-mail: info@jist.com
URL: http://www.jist.com

Wendy S. Enelow and Louise M. Kursmark. December 2003. $16.95. 288 pages.

★9553★ Handbook of Teaching for Physical Therapists

Butterworth-Heinemann
11830 Westline Industrial Dr.
St. Louis, MO 63146
Ph: (314)453-7010   Fax: (314)453-7095
Fr: 800-545-2522
E-mail: usbkinfo@elsevier.com
URL: http://www.elsevier.com

Katherine F. Shepard and Gail M. Jensen.

Second edition, 2002. $49.95 (paper). 430 pages.

★9554★ Health Careers Today

Elsevier
11830 Westline Industrial Dr.
St. Louis, MO 63146
Ph: (314)453-7010   Fax: (314)453-7095
Fr: 800-545-2522
E-mail: usbkinfo@elsevier.com
URL: http://www.elsevier.com

Gerdin, Judith. Fourth edition. 2007. $59.95. 496 pages. Covers more than 45 health careers. Discusses the roles and responsibilities of various occupations and provides a solid foundation in the skills needed for all health careers.

★9555★ How to Become a Physical Therapist

Skip Hunter Enterprises
PO Box 61
Clemson, SC 29633
Ph: (803)654-3800   Fax: (803)654-4006

Skip Hunter. 1995. $19.95 (paper). 115 pages.

★9556★ Opportunities in Health and Medical Careers

The McGraw-Hill Companies
PO Box 182604
Columbus, OH 43272
Fax: (614)759-3749   Fr: 877-883-5524
E-mail: customer.service@mcgraw-hill.com
URL: http://www.mcgraw-hill.com

I. Donald Snook, Jr. and Leo D'Orazio. 2004. $13.95 (paper). 157 pages. Covers the full range of medical and health occupations. Illustrated.

★9557★ Opportunities in Physical Therapy Careers

The McGraw-Hill Companies
PO Box 182604
Columbus, OH 43272
Fax: (614)759-3749   Fr: 877-883-5524
E-mail: customer.service@mcgraw-hill.com
URL: http://www.mcgraw-hill.com

Bernice R. Krumhansl. 2005. $13.95 (paper). 160 pages. Defines what the jobs are, where they are, and how to pursue them. Contains bibliography and illustrations.

★9558★ Pediatric Physical Therapy: A Guide for the Physical Therapy Team

Mosby
11830 Westline Industrial Dr.
St. Louis, MO 63146
Ph: (314)872-8370   Fax: 800-235-0256
Fr: 800-325-4177
URL: http://www.elsevier.com

Katherine Ratliffe. 1997. $51.95. 464 pages. Focuses on clinical skills and strategies including educational and family environments.

★9559★ **Real People Working in Health Care**

The McGraw-Hill Companies
PO Box 182604
Columbus, OH 43272
Fax: (614)759-3749   Fr: 877-883-5524
E-mail: customer.service@mcgraw-hill.com
URL: http://www.mcgraw-hill.com

Blythe Camenson, Jan Goldberg. 1996. $12.95 (paper). 144 pages. Interviews and profiles of working professionals capture a range of opportunities in this field.

★9560★ **Real People Working in the Helping Professions**

The McGraw-Hill Companies
PO Box 182604
Columbus, OH 43272
Fax: (614)759-3749   Fr: 877-883-5524
E-mail: customer.service@mcgraw-hill.com
URL: http://www.mcgraw-hill.com

Blythe Camenson, Jan Goldberg. 1997. $12.95 (paper). 192 pages. Interviews and profiles of working professionals capture a range of opportunities in this field.

★9561★ **Resumes for the Health Care Professional**

John Wiley & Sons Inc.
1 Wiley Dr.
Somerset, NJ 08873
Ph: (732)469-4400   Fax: (732)302-2300
Fr: 800-225-5945
E-mail: custserv@wiley.com
URL: http://www.wiley.com/WileyCDA/

Kim Marino. Second edition. 2000. $21.50 (paper). 224 pages.

EMPLOYMENT AGENCIES AND SEARCH FIRMS

★9562★ **Cross Country TravCorps**

6551 Park of Commerce Blvd.
Boca Raton, FL 33487-8247
Fax: (562)998-8533   Fr: 800-530-6125
URL: http://www.crosscountrytravcorps.com

Places traveling nurses in assignments nationwide.

★9563★ **Team Placement Service, Inc.**

1414 Prince St., Ste. 202
Alexandria, VA 22314
Ph: (703)820-8618   Fax: (703)820-3368
Fr: 800-495-6767
E-mail: 4jobs@teamplace.com
URL: http://www.teamplace.com

Full-service personnel consultants provide placement for healthcare staff, physician and dentist, private practice, and hospitals. Conduct interviews, tests, and reference checks to select the top 20% of applicants. Survey applicants' skill levels, provide backup information on each candidate, select compatible candidates for consideration, and insure the hiring process minimizes potential legal liability. Industries served: healthcare and government agencies providing medical, dental, biotech, laboratory, hospitals, and physician search.

ONLINE JOB SOURCES AND SERVICES

★9564★ **Medhunters.com**

Fr: 800-664-0278
E-mail: info@medhunters.com
URL: http://www.medhunters.com

Description: Career search site for jobs in all health care specialties; educational resources; visa and licensing information for relocation; interesting articles; relocation tools; links to professional organizations and general resources.

★9565★ **ProHealthJobs**

Fr: 800-796-1738
E-mail: Info@prohealthedujobs.com
URL: http://www.prohealthjobs.com

Description: Career resources site for the medical and health care field. Lists professional opportunities, product information, continuing education and open positions.

★9566★ **RehabJobs Online**

PO Box 480536
Los Angeles, CA 90048
Ph: (213)938-7718   Fax: (213)938-9609
Fr: 800-43-REHAB
E-mail: support@atsrehabjobs.com
URL: http://www.rehabjobs.com

Description: Resource center for the professional therapist. **Main files include:** Therapists Only, Therapy Forums, Nationwide Job Search (database), Therapy Job Outlook, Therapy Job Search Utilities, Therapy Links, Information for Employers and Recruiters.

★9567★ **RehabWorld**

URL: http://www.rehabworld.com

Description: Site for rehabilitation professionals to learn about the profession and locate jobs. Includes user groups, salary surveys, and chat capabilities. **Main files include:** Physical Therapy, Occupational Therapy, Speech Therapy, Mental Health, Employer World, Student World, International World, Forum.

TRADESHOWS

★9568★ **American Physical Therapy Association Annual Conference**

American Physical Therapy Association
1111 N Fairfax St.
Alexandria, VA 22314-1488
Ph: (703)683-6748   Fax: (703)684-7343
Fr: 800-999-2782
URL: http://www.apta.org

Annual. **Primary Exhibits:** Physical therapy products, equipment, and services. **Dates and Locations:** 2008 Jun 11-14; San Antonio, TX.

★9569★ **American Society of Hand Therapists and American Society for Surgery of the Hand Annual Meeting**

Smith, Bucklin and Associates, Inc. (Chicago)
401 N Michigan Ave.
Chicago, IL 60611-4267
Ph: (312)321-6610   Fax: (312)673-6670
Fr: 800-289-NAON
E-mail: info@smithbucklin.com
URL: http://www.smithbucklin.com

Annual. **Primary Exhibits:** Hand therapy equipment and products.

OTHER SOURCES

★9570★ **EMTs, Nurses, Therapists, and Assistants**

Cambridge Educational
PO Box 2053
Princeton, NJ 08543-2053
Ph: 800-257-5126   Fax: (609)671-0266
Fr: 800-468-4227
E-mail: custserv@films.com
URL: http://www.cambridgeeducational.com

VHS and DVD. $79.95. 2000. 18 minutes. Part of the series "Exploring Health Occupations."

★9571★ **Exploring Health Occupations**

Cambridge Educational
PO Box 2053
Princeton, NJ 08543-2053
Ph: 800-257-5126   Fax: (609)671-0266
Fr: 800-468-4227
E-mail: custserv@films.com
URL: http://www.cambridgeeducational.com

VHS and DVD. $159.90. 1999. Two-part series provides a detailed view of the field of medical technicians and technologists, EMTs, nurses, therapists, and assistants.

★9572★ **Foundation for Physical Therapy (FPT)**

1111 N Fairfax St.
Alexandria, VA 22314-1488
Ph: (703)684-2782   Fax: (703)684-7343
Fr: 800-875-1378

E-mail: foundation@apta.org
URL: http://www.apta.org/Foundation

Description: Supports the physical therapy profession's research needs by funding scientific and clinically-relevant physical therapy research.

★9573★ Health Assessment & Treating Occupations

Delphi Productions
3159 6th St.
Boulder, CO 80304
Ph: (303)443-2100   Fax: (303)443-4022
Fr: 888-443-2400
E-mail: support@delphivideo.com
URL: http://www.delphivideo.com

$95.00. 50 minutes. Part of the Careers for the 21st Century Video Library.

★9574★ Health Service Occupations

Delphi Productions
3159 6th St.
Boulder, CO 80304
Ph: (303)443-2100   Fax: (303)443-4022
Fr: 888-443-2400
E-mail: support@delphivideo.com
URL: http://www.delphivideo.com

$95.00. 50 minutes. Part of the Careers for the 21st Century Video Library.

★9575★ Medicine & Related Occupations

Delphi Productions
3159 6th St.
Boulder, CO 80304
Ph: (303)443-2100   Fax: (303)443-4022
Fr: 888-443-2400
E-mail: support@delphivideo.com

URL: http://www.delphivideo.com

$95.00. 45 minutes. Part of the Careers for the 21st Century Video Library.

★9576★ National Association of Rehabilitation Providers and Agencies (NARA)

PO Box 1440
Oldsmar, FL 34677-1440
Ph: (813)855-9168   Fax: (813)855-6449
E-mail: info@naranet.org
URL: http://www.naranet.org

Members: Members are rehabilitation companies servicing patients (including Medicare recipients) with physical therapy, occupational therapy and speech pathology services in outpatient and long-term care settings. Associate members are rehabilitation vendors.

Physician Assistants

SOURCES OF HELP-WANTED ADS

★9577★ AAPA News

American Academy of Physician
 Assistants
950 N. Washington St.
Alexandria, VA 22314-1552
Ph: (703)836-2272   Fax: (703)684-1924
E-mail: aapa@aapa.org
URL: http://www.aapa.org

Description: Biweekly. Updates physician assistants on professional, legislative, and academy issues. Profiles members. Recurring features include news of research, a calendar of events, news of educational opportunities, available resource materials, and news affecting physician profession and practice.

★9578★ Academic Emergency Medicine

Mosby Inc.
11830 Westline Industrial Dr.
St. Louis, MO 63146
Ph: (314)872-8370   Fax: (314)432-1380
Fr: 800-325-4177
URL: http://www.elsevier.com/wps/find/journaldescription.cws_home

Monthly. $259.00/year for institutions; $161.00/year for individuals; $77.00/year for students; $245.00/year for institutions; $151.00/year for individuals; $83.00/year for students. Journal publishing material relevant to the practice, education, and investigation of emergency medicine; reaches a wide audience of emergency care practitioners and educators.

★9579★ ADVANCE for Physician Assistants

Merion Publications Inc.
2900 Horizon Dr.
PO Box 61556
King of Prussia, PA 19406
Ph: (610)278-1400   Fr: 800-355-5627
URL: http://physician-assistant.advanceweb.com/main.aspx

Monthly. Targets practicing physician assistants and physician assistant students with senior status.

★9580★ American Family Physician

American Academy of Family Physicians
11400 Tomahawk Creek Pkwy.
PO Box 11210
Leawood, KS 66211-2672
Ph: (913)906-6000   Fax: (913)906-6010
Fr: 800-274-2237
E-mail: afpedit@aafp.org
URL: http://www.aafp.org/afp

Semimonthly. $120.00/year for individuals, U.S.; $200.00/year for out of country, individuals; $160.00/year for Canada, individuals; $160.00/year for institutions, U.S.; $200.00/year for institutions, Canada; $240.00/year for institutions, foreign countries; $68.00/year for students, medical; $108.00/year for students, medical; $148.00/year for students, medical; $11.00 for single issue, six copies. Peer reviewed clinical journal for family physicians and others in primary care. Review articles detail the latest diagnostic and therapeutic techniques in the medical field. Department features in each issue include 'Tips from other Journals,' CME credit opportunities and course calendar.

★9581★ American Journal of Emergency Medicine

Mosby Inc.
11830 Westline Industrial Dr.
St. Louis, MO 63146
Ph: (314)872-8370   Fax: (314)432-1380
Fr: 800-325-4177
URL: http://www.elsevier.com/wps/find/journaldescription.cws_home

Bimonthly. $275.00/year for individuals; $419.00/year for institutions; $129.00/year for students; $397.00/year for individuals, international; $546.00/year for institutions, international; $198.00/year for students, international. Journal reporting on emergency medicine.

★9582★ Annals of Medicine

Taylor & Francis Group Journals
325 Chestnut St., Ste. 800
Philadelphia, PA 19106
Ph: (215)625-8900   Fax: (215)625-8914
Fr: 800-354-1420
URL: http://www.ingentaconnect.com

$418.00/year for institutions, print and online; $397.00/year for institutions, online only; $155.00/year for individuals. Journal covering health science and medical education.

★9583★ APAP Update

Physician Assistant Education Association
300 N. Washington St., Ste. 505
Alexandria, VA 22314-2544
Ph: (703)548-5538   Fax: (703)548-5539
E-mail: info@PAEAonline.org
URL: http://www.paeaonline.org/

Description: Monthly. Presents news of interest to members. Recurring features include interviews, a calendar of events, job listings, news of recent events and meetings, articles on APAP award winners, updates on member services.

★9584★ Clinical Medicine & Research

Marshfield Clinic
1000 North Oak Ave.
Marshfield, WI 54449
Ph: (715)387-5511   Fr: 800-782-8581
URL: http://www.clinmedres.org/

Monthly. Journal that publishes scientific medical research that is relevant to a broad audience of medical researchers and healthcare professionals.

★9585★ The CMA Today

American Association of Medical
 Assistants
20 North Wacker Dr., Ste. 1575
Chicago, IL 60606
Ph: (312)899-1500   Fax: (312)899-1259
URL: http://www.aama-ntl.org/cmatoday/about.aspx

Bimonthly. Free to members; $30.00/year for nonmembers. Professional health journal.

★9586★ CME Supplement to Emergency Medicine Clinics of North America

Elsevier Science Inc.
360 Park Ave. S
New York, NY 10010
Ph: (212)989-5800   Fax: (212)633-3990
URL: http://www.elsevier.com

Quarterly. $190.00/year for individuals. Journal covering emergency medicine clinics.

★9587★ Discovery Medicine

Discovery Medicine
2245 Chapel Valley Ln.
Timonium, MD 21093
Ph: (410)560-9007   Fax: (410)560-9000
URL: http://www.discoverymedicine.com

Bimonthly. $39.95/year for individuals; $49.95/year for individuals, digital edition and online access; $69.95 for two years, online access; $84.95 for two years, digital edition and online access; $99.95/year for individuals, 3 years, online access; $119.95/year for individuals, 3 years, digital and online access; $299.00/year for individuals, medical report (PMR); $99.00/year for individuals, medical report update. Online journal that publishes articles on diseases, biology, new diagnostics, and treatments for medical professionals.

★9588★ Education & Treatment of Children

West Virginia University Press
44 Stansbury Hall
PO Box 6295
Morgantown, WV 26506
Ph: (304)293-8400   Fax: (304)293-6585
Fr: (866)988-7737
URL: http://
www.educationandtreatmentofchildren.net

Quarterly. $85.00/year for institutions; $45.00/year for individuals; $100.00/year for institutions, elsewhere; $60.00/year for individuals, elsewhere. Periodical featuring information concerning the development of services for children and youth. Includes reports written for educators and other child care and mental health providers focused on teaching, training, and treatment effectiveness.

★9589★ Genes and Nutrition

New Century Health Publishers LLC
PO Box 50702
New Orleans, LA 70150-0702
Fax: (504)305-3762
URL: http://
www.newcenturyhealthpublishers.com/
genes_and_nutritio

Quarterly. $428.00/year for institutions; $228.00/year for individuals. International, interdisciplinary peer reviewed scientific journal for critical evaluation of research on the relationship between genetics & nutrition with the goal of improving human health.

★9590★ Hospitals & Health Networks

Health Forum L.L.C.
1 N Franklin, 29th Fl.
Chicago, IL 60606
Ph: (312)893-6800   Fax: (312)422-4506
Fr: 800-821-2039
URL: http://www.hhnmag.com

Weekly. Publication covering the health care industry.

★9591★ The IHS Primary Care Provider

Indian Health Service (HQ)
The Reyes Bldg.
801 Thompson Ave., Ste. 400
Rockville, MD 20852-1627
URL: http://www.ihs.gov/PublicInfo/Publications/HealthProvider/Pr

Monthly. Journal for health care professionals, physicians, nurses, pharmacists, dentists, and dietitians.

★9592★ Injury

Mosby Inc.
11830 Westline Industrial Dr.
St. Louis, MO 63146
Ph: (314)872-8370   Fax: (314)432-1380
Fr: 800-325-4177
URL: http://www.elsevier.com/wps/find/journaldescription.cws_home

Monthly. $1,106.00/year for institutions, all countries except Europe, Japan and Iran; $169.00/year for individuals, all countries except Europe, Japan and Iran. Journal publishing articles and research related to the treatment of injuries such as trauma systems and management; surgical procedures; epidemiological studies; surgery (of all tissues); resuscitation; biomechanics; rehabilitation; anaesthesia; radiology and wound management.

★9593★ Journal of the American Society of Podiatric Medical Assistants

American Society of Podiatric Medical Assistants
2124 S Austin Blvd.
Cicero, IL 60804
Ph: (708)863-6303   Fr: 888-882-7762
URL: http://www.aspma.org

Quarterly. Subscription included in membership. Professional journal covering issues in podiatry.

★9594★ Journal of Health Law

American Health Lawyers Association
1025 Connecticut Ave., NW, Ste. 600
Washington, DC 20036-5405
Ph: (202)833-1100   Fax: (202)833-1105
URL: http://www.healthlawyers.org

Quarterly. Professional journal covering healthcare issues and cases and their impact on the health care arena.

★9595★ Journal of Hospital Medicine

John Wiley & Sons Inc.
111 River St.
Hoboken, NJ 07030-5774
Ph: (201)748-6000   Fax: (201)748-6088
Fr: 800-825-7550
URL: http://www.wiley.com/WileyCDA/WileyTitle/productCd-JHM.html

Bimonthly. $110.00/year for individuals, print only; Online version available with subscription. Journal on hospital medicine.

★9596★ Laboratory Medicine

American Society for Clinical Pathology
33 West Monroe, Ste. 1600
Chicago, IL 60603
Ph: (312)541-4999   Fax: (312)541-4998
Fr: 800-267-2727
E-mail: labmed@ascp.org
URL: http://www.labmedicine.com/

Monthly. $105.00/year for individuals, print and online; $105.00/year for other countries, print and online, individual; $140.00/year for other countries, print and online, individual expedited; $116.00/year for institutions, other countries, print and online, individual expedited; $20.00 for single issue, print and online; $15.00 for single issue, print and online, rest of world; $130.00/year for institutions, print and online; $130.00/year for institutions, other countries, print and online; $165.00/year for institutions, other countries, print and online, expedited. Professional journal covering medical technology and pathology.

★9597★ Medical Risks

Taylor & Francis Group Journals
325 Chestnut St., Ste. 800
Philadelphia, PA 19106
Ph: (215)625-8900   Fax: (215)625-8914
Fr: 800-354-1420
URL: http://www.tandf.co.uk

Monthly. Journal covering articles on medical risks.

★9598★ Medical Staff Development Professional

American Academy of Medical Management
Crossville Commons
560 W Crossville Rd., Ste. 103
Roswell, GA 30075
Ph: (770)649-7150   Fax: (770)649-7552

Periodic. Professional journal covering medical education.

★9599★ Minnesota Medicine

Minnesota Medical Association
1300 Godward St. NE, Ste. 2500
Minneapolis, MN 55413
Ph: (612)378-1875   Fax: (612)378-3875
Fr: 800-342-5662
URL: http://www.minnesotamedicine.com/

Monthly. $45.00/year for individuals; $81.00 for two years; $80.00/year for other countries; $144.00/year for other countries, two years. Magazine on medical, socioeconomic, public health, medical-legal, and biomedical ethics issues of interest to physicians.

★9600★ **Pacifica Review**

Taylor & Francis Group Journals
325 Chestnut St., Ste. 800
Philadelphia, PA 19106
Ph: (215)625-8900   Fax: (215)625-8914
Fr: 800-354-1420
URL: http://www.tandf.co.uk/

$462.00/year for individuals; $279.00/year for individuals; $487.00/year for individuals; $294.00/year for individuals; $123.00/year for individuals; $86.00/year for individuals. Journal promoting physical therapy and integration.

★9601★ **USA Body Psychotherapy Journal**

United States Association for Body
  Psychotherapy
7831 Woodmont Ave.
Bethesda, MD 20814
URL: http://www.usabp.org/displaycommon.cfm?an=4

Semiannual. Academic journal that seeks to support, promote and stimulate the exchange of ideas, scholarship and research within the field of body psychotherapy as well as an interdisciplinary exchange with related fields of clinical practice and inquiry.

★9602★ **Year Book of Critical Care Medicine**

Elsevier Science Inc.
360 Park Ave. S
New York, NY 10010
Ph: (212)989-5800   Fax: (212)633-3990
URL: http://www.elsevier.com

$180.00/year for institutions, U.S. $191.00/year for institutions, other countries; $121.00/year for individuals, U.S. $134.00/year for individuals, other countries; $59.00/year for students, U.S. $71.00/year for students, other countries. Journal focused on treatment of severe sepsis and septic shock, echocardiography in the evaluation of hemodynamically unstable patients & mechanical ventilation of acute respiratory distress syndrome.

PLACEMENT AND JOB REFERRAL SERVICES

★9603★ **Physician Assistant Education Association (PAEA)**

300 N Washington St., Ste. 505
Alexandria, VA 22314-2544
Ph: (703)548-5538   Fax: (703)548-5539
E-mail: info@paeaonline.org
URL: http://www.paeaonline.org

Description: Represents physician assistant (PA) educational programs in the United States. Assists PA educational programs-in-stitutions with training programs for physician assistants to primary care and surgical physicians. Assists in the development and organization of educational curricula for PA programs to assure the public of competent PA's. Contributes to defining the roles of PA's in the field of medicine to maximize their benefit to the public; serves as a public information center on the profession; coordinates program logistics such as admissions and career placements; and is currently initiating a centralized application service for PA applicants. Sponsors the Annual Survey of Physician Assistant Educational Programs in the United States. Conducts and sponsors research projects; compiles statistics; offers ongoing training for PA leadership and faculty.

EMPLOYER DIRECTORIES AND NETWORKING LISTS

★9604★ **AHA Guide to the Health Care Field**

American Hospital Association
1 N Franklin
Chicago, IL 60606
Ph: (312)422-2050   Fax: (312)422-4700
Fr: 800-424-4301

Annual, August. Covers hospitals, networks, multi-health care systems, freestanding ambulatory surgery centers, psychiatric facilities, long-term care facilities, substance abuse programs, and other health-related organizations. Entries include: For hospitals—Facility name, address, phone, administrator's name, number of beds, facilities and services, number of employees, expenses, other statistics. For other organizations—Name, address, phone, fax, name and title of contact. Arrangement: Geographical. Indexes: Hospital name.

★9605★ **Association of Physician's Assistants in Cardiovascular Surgery-Membership Directory**

Association of Physician's Assistants in
  Cardiovascular Surgery
PO Box 4834
Englewood, CA 80155
Ph: (303)221-5651   Fax: (303)771-2550
Fr: 877-221-5651
URL: http://www.apacvs.org/

Annual. Covers about 800 physician's assistants who work with cardiovascular surgeons. Entries include: Name, address, phone. Arrangement: Alphabetical.

★9606★ **Directory of Hospital Personnel**

Grey House Publishing
185 Millerton Rd.
PO Box 860
Millerton, NY 12546
Ph: (518)789-8700   Fax: (518)789-0556
Fr: 800-562-2139
URL: http://www.greyhouse.com/hospital_

personnel.htm

Annual. $325.00 for print product; $545.00 for online database subscription; $650.00 for online database subscription and print product combined. Covers 200,000 executives at 7,000 U.S. hospitals. Entries include: Name of hospital, address, phone; number of beds; type and JCAHO status of hospital; names and titles of key department heads and staff; medical and nursing school affiliations; number of residents, interns, and nursing students. Arrangement: Geographical. Indexes: Hospital name, personnel, hospital size.

★9607★ **Guide to Careers in the Health Professions**

The Princeton Review
2315 Broadway
New York, NY 10024
Ph: (212)874-8282   Fax: (212)874-0775
Fr: 800-733-3000
URL: http://www.princetonreview.com/

Published January, 2001. $24.95 for individuals. Presents advice and information for those searching for satisfying careers in the health professions. Publication includes: Directory of schools and academic programs. Entries include: Name, address, phone, tuition, program details, employment profiles.

★9608★ **Hospital Blue Book**

Billian Publishing Inc./Transworld
  Publishing Inc.
2100 Powers Ferry Rd. SE
Atlanta, GA 30339
Ph: (770)955-5656   Fax: (770)952-0669
Fr: 800-533-8484
E-mail: blu-book@billian.com

2005. $300.00 for individuals. Covers more than 6,687 hospitals; some listings also appear in a separate southern edition of this publication. Entries include: Name of hospital, accreditation, mailing address, phone, fax, number of beds, type of facility (nonprofit, general, state, etc.); list of administrative personnel and chiefs of medical services, with specific titles. Arrangement: Geographical.

★9609★ **The JobBank Guide to Health Care Companies**

Adams Media Corp.
57 Littlefield St.
Avon, MA 02322
Ph: (508)427-7100   Fax: (508)427-6790
Fr: 800-872-5627
URL: http://www.amazon.com/Jobbank-Guide-Health-Care-Companies/dp

Biennial. Covers jobs nationwide in health care companies. Entries include: Firm or organization name, address, phone, name and title of contact; description of organization, headquarters location, typical titles for entry- and middle-level positions, educational backgrounds desired, fringe benefits offered, stock exchange listing, training programs, internships, parent company, number of employees, revenues, e-mail and web addresses, projected number of hires. Indexes: Alphabetical.

★9610★ Medical and Health Information Directory

Gale, Cengage Learning
27500 Drake Rd.
Farmington Hills, MI 48331-3535
Ph: (248)699-4253   Fax: (248)699-8065
Fr: 800-877-4253
E-mail: businessproducts@gale.com
URL: http://www.gale.com

Annual; latest edition 20th, July 2007. $375.00/volume. Covers in Volume 1, more than 26,500 medical and health oriented associations, organizations, institutions, and government agencies, including health maintenance organizations (HMOs), preferred provider organizations (PPOs), insurance companies, pharmaceutical companies, research centers, and medical and allied health schools. In Volume 2, over 12,000 medical book publishers; medical periodicals, directories, audiovisual producers and services, medical libraries and information centers, electronic resources, and health-related internet search engines. In Volume 3, more than 35,500 clinics, treatment centers, care programs, and counseling/diagnostic services for 34 subject areas. Entries include: Institution, service, or firm name, address, phone, fax, email and URL; many include names of key personnel and, when pertinent, descriptive annotations. Volume 3 was formerly listed separately as Health Services Directory. Arrangement: Classified by organization activity, service, etc. Indexes: Each volume has a complete alphabetical name and keyword index.

★9611★ Peterson's Job Opportunities for Health and Science Majors

Peterson's
Princeton Pke. Corporate Ctr., 2000 Lenox Dr.
PO Box 67005
Lawrenceville, NJ 08648
Ph: (609)896-1800   Fax: (609)896-4531
Fr: 800-338-3282
URL: http://www.petersons.com

Irregular; latest edition 1999. Covers about 1,300 research, consulting, government, and non-profit and profit service organizations that hire college and university graduates in science and health-related majors. Entries include: Organization name, address, phone, name and title of contact, type of organization, number of employees, Standard Industrial Classification (SIC) code; description of opportunities available including disciplines, level of education required, starting locations and salaries, level of experience accepted, benefits.

★9612★ Physician Assistant Directory

Association of Physician Assistant Programs
950 N Washington St.
Alexandria, VA 22314-1552
Ph: (703)548-5538   Fax: (703)684-1924
URL: http://www.apap.org

Annual. Covers over 100 accredited programs that educate physician assistants. Entries include: Program name, institution name, address, phone; description of program, including curriculum, selection criteria, degrees of certificates offered. Arrangement: Geographical.

HANDBOOKS AND MANUALS

★9613★ Career Opportunities in Health Care (Career Opportunities)

Facts On File Inc.
132 W. 31st St., 17th Fl.
New York, NY 10001-2006
Ph: (212)967-8800   Fax: 800-678-3633
Fr: 800-322-8755
E-mail: custserv@factsonfile.com
URL: http://www.factsonfile.com

Shelly Field. Arthur E. Weintraub. 2002. Reprint. $49.50. 243 pages. Part of the Career Opportunities Series.

★9614★ Careers in Health Care

The McGraw-Hill Companies
PO Box 182604
Columbus, OH 43272
Fax: (614)759-3749   Fr: 877-883-5524
E-mail: customer.service@mcgraw-hill.com
URL: http://www.mcgraw-hill.com

Barbara M. Swanson. Fifth edition, 2005. $15.95 (paper). 192 pages. Describes job duties, work settings, salaries, licensing and certification requirements, educational preparation, and future outlook. Gives ideas on how to secure a job.

★9615★ Careers for Night Owls and Other Insomniacs

The McGraw-Hill Companies
PO Box 182604
Columbus, OH 43272
Fax: (614)759-3749   Fr: 877-883-5524
E-mail: customer.service@mcgraw-hill.com
URL: http://www.mcgraw-hill.com

Louise Miller. Second edition, 2002. $12.95 (paper). 160 pages.

★9616★ Expert Resumes for Health Care Careers

Jist Works
875 Montreal Way
St. Paul, MN 55102
Fr: 800-648-5478
E-mail: info@jist.com
URL: http://www.jist.com

Wendy S. Enelow and Louise M. Kursmark. December 2003. $16.95. 288 pages.

★9617★ Federal Jobs in Nursing and Health Sciences

Impact Publications
9104 Manassas Dr., Ste. N
Manassas Park, VA 20111-5211
Ph: (703)361-7300   Fax: (703)335-9486
Fr: 800-361-1055
E-mail: query@impactpublications.com

URL: http://www.impactpublications.com

Russ Smith. 1996. Part of "Federal Jobs in ..." Series. $14.95. 130 pages.

★9618★ Health Careers Today

Elsevier
11830 Westline Industrial Dr.
St. Louis, MO 63146
Ph: (314)453-7010   Fax: (314)453-7095
Fr: 800-545-2522
E-mail: usbkinfo@elsevier.com
URL: http://www.elsevier.com

Gerdin, Judith. Fourth edition. 2007. $59.95. 496 pages. Covers more than 45 health careers. Discusses the roles and responsibilities of various occupations and provides a solid foundation in the skills needed for all health careers.

★9619★ Opportunities in Health and Medical Careers

The McGraw-Hill Companies
PO Box 182604
Columbus, OH 43272
Fax: (614)759-3749   Fr: 877-883-5524
E-mail: customer.service@mcgraw-hill.com
URL: http://www.mcgraw-hill.com

I. Donald Snook, Jr. and Leo D'Orazio. 2004. $13.95 (paper). 157 pages. Covers the full range of medical and health occupations. Illustrated.

★9620★ Opportunities in Paramedical Careers

The McGraw-Hill Companies
PO Box 182604
Columbus, OH 43272
Fax: (614)759-3749   Fr: 877-883-5524
E-mail: customer.service@mcgraw-hill.com
URL: http://www.mcgraw-hill.com

Alex Kacen. 1999. 14.95 (hardcover). 160 pages. Discusses a variety of opportunities in this field and how to pursue them. Illustrated.

★9621★ Opportunities in Physician Assistant Careers

The McGraw-Hill Companies
PO Box 182604
Columbus, OH 43272
Fax: (614)759-3749   Fr: 877-883-5524
E-mail: customer.service@mcgraw-hill.com
URL: http://www.mcgraw-hill.com

Terence J. Sacks. 2005. $13.95 (paper). 151 pages.

★9622★ Physician Assistant: A Guide to Clinical Practice

W. B. Saunders Co.
6277 Sea Harbor Dr.
Orlando, FL 32887
Fr: 800-654-2452
URL: http://www.elsevier.com

Ruth Ballweg, Edward M. Sullivan and Sherry Stolberg (editors). Third edition, 2003. $89.95. 1,072 pages. The first and only comprehensive physician assistant text, this up-to-date edition covers all aspects of the physician assistant profession, the PA curriculum, and the PA's role in practice.

★9623★ **Physician Assistants in American Medicine**

Churchill Livingstone
6277 Sea Harbor Dr.
Orlando, FL 32887
Ph: (407)345-4020   Fax: (407)363-1354
Fr: 877-839-7126
E-mail: usjcs@elsevier.com
URL: http://intl.elsevierhealth.com/cl/

Roderick S. Hooker and James F. Cawley. Second Edition, 2002. $46.95 (paper). 384 pages.

★9624★ **Physician Assistant's Business Practice and Legal Guide**

Jones & Bartlett Publishers, Inc.
40 Tall Pine Dr.
Sudbury, MA 01776-2256
Ph: (978)443-5000   Fax: (978)443-8000
Fr: 800-832-0034
E-mail: info@jbpub.com
URL: http://www.jbpub.com/

Michele Roth-Kauffman. 2005. $82.95. Medical resource for physician assistants, covering the role the physician assistant plays in patient care.

★9625★ **Physician Assistants: Who They Are**

Jones & Bartlett Publishers, Inc.
40 Tall Pine Dr.
Sudbury, MA 01776-2256
Ph: (978)443-5000   Fax: (978)443-8000
Fr: 800-832-0034
E-mail: info@jbpub.com
URL: http://www.jbpub.com/

J. Jeffrey Heinrich. 2008. $24.95.

★9626★ **Real People Working in Health Care**

The McGraw-Hill Companies
PO Box 182604
Columbus, OH 43272
Fax: (614)759-3749   Fr: 877-883-5524
E-mail: customer.service@mcgraw-hill.com
URL: http://www.mcgraw-hill.com

Blythe Camenson, Jan Goldberg. 1996. $12.95 (paper). 144 pages. Interviews and profiles of working professionals capture a range of opportunities in this field.

★9627★ **Resumes for the Health Care Professional**

John Wiley & Sons Inc.
1 Wiley Dr.
Somerset, NJ 08873
Ph: (732)469-4400   Fax: (732)302-2300
Fr: 800-225-5945
E-mail: custserv@wiley.com
URL: http://www.wiley.com/WileyCDA/

Kim Marino. Second edition, 2000. $21.50 (paper). 224 pages.

★9628★ **Resumes for Health and Medical Careers**

The McGraw-Hill Companies
PO Box 182604
Columbus, OH 43272
Fax: (614)759-3749   Fr: 877-883-5524
E-mail: customer.service@mcgraw-hill.com
URL: http://www.mcgraw-hill.com

Third edition, 2003. $11.95 (paper). 160 pages.

★9629★ **Surgical Review for Physician Assistants**

Lippincott Williams & Wilkins
PO Box 61
Henrico, NC 27842-0061
Ph: (252)535-5993   Fax: (252)535-1004
Fr: 800-638-3030
E-mail: customerservice@lww.com
URL: http://www.lww.com

American Academy of Physician Assistants, Association of Physician Assistant Programs Staff. 2008. $43.95.

EMPLOYMENT AGENCIES AND SEARCH FIRMS

★9630★ **Davis-Smith, Inc.**

27656 Franklin Rd.
Southfield, MI 48034
Ph: (248)354-4100   Fax: (248)354-6702
Fr: 800-541-4672
E-mail: info@davissmith.com
URL: http://www.davissmith.com

Healthcare staffing agency. Executive search firm.

★9631★ **MEDCareerNET**

23072 Lake Center Dr., Ste. 210
Lake Forest, CA 92630
Ph: (949)380-4800   Fax: (949)380-7477
E-mail: vic@medcareernet.com
URL: http://www.medcareernet.com

Firm provides medical career professionals with a choice of career alternatives that extend their reach within their respective disciplines.

★9632★ **Professional Placement Associates, Inc.**

287 Bowman Ave., Ste. 309
Purchase, NY 10577-2517
Ph: (914)251-1000   Fax: (914)251-1055
E-mail: careers@ppasearch.com
URL: http://www.ppasearch.com

Executive search firm specializing in the health and medical field.

ONLINE JOB SOURCES AND SERVICES

★9633★ **American Academy of Physician Assistants Career Opportunities**

950 N. Washington St.
Alexandria, VA 22314-1352
Ph: (703)836-2272   Fax: (703)684-1924
E-mail: aapa@aapa.org
URL: http://www.aapa.org

Description: Online newsletter of the AAPA. Job opportunities may be searched by state or type. Members may also post position wanted on AAPA website.

★9634★ **Medhunters.com**

Fr: 800-664-0278
E-mail: info@medhunters.com
URL: http://www.medhunters.com

Description: Career search site for jobs in all health care specialties; educational resources; visa and licensing information for relocation; interesting articles; relocation tools; links to professional organizations and general resources.

★9635★ **ProHealthJobs**

Fr: 800-796-1738
E-mail: Info@prohealthedujobs.com
URL: http://www.prohealthjobs.com

Description: Career resources site for the medical and health care field. Lists professional opportunities, product information, continuing education and open positions.

TRADESHOWS

★9636★ **Annual Academy of Physician Assistants Conference**

American Academy of Physician Assistants
950 N. Washington St.
Alexandria, VA 22314-1552
Ph: (703)836-2272   Fax: (703)684-1924
E-mail: aapa@aapa.org
URL: http://www.aapa.org

Primary Exhibits: Pharmaceuticals, medical equipment and supplies, medical books, and medical software.

★9637★ **California Academy of Physician Assistants Convention**

California Academy of Physician Assistants
3100 W. Warner Ave., Ste. 3
Santa Ana, CA 92704-5331
Ph: (714)427-0321   Fax: (714)427-0324
E-mail: capa@capanet.org
URL: http://www.capanet.org

Semiannual. **Primary Exhibits:** Medical equipment, supplies, and services, including pharmaceuticals and employment recruitment services.

OTHER SOURCES

★9638★ American Academy of Physician Assistants (AAPA)

950 N Washington St.
Alexandria, VA 22314-1552
Ph: (703)836-2272   Fax: (703)684-1924
E-mail: aapa@aapa.org
URL: http://www.aapa.org

Description: Physician assistants and other interested parties. Seeks to promote quality, cost-effective, and accessible healthcare, and the professional and personal development of PAs. Provides services for members. **Activities:** Organizes annual National PA Day. Develops research and education programs; compiles statistics.

★9639★ American Almanac of Jobs and Salaries

HarperCollins
10 E. 53rd St.
New York, NY 10022
Ph: (212)207-7000   Fr: 800-242-7737
URL: http://www.harpercollins.com/

John W. Wright. Revised edition, 2000. $20.00 (paper). 672 pages. This is a comprehensive guide to the wages of hundreds of occupations in a wide variety of industries and organizations.

★9640★ American Association of Pathologists' Assistants (AAPA)

Rosewood Office Plz.
1711 W County Rd. B, Ste. 300 N
Roseville, MN 55113-4036
Ph: (651)697-9264   Fr: 800-532-AAPA
E-mail: msok@assocmgmt.org
URL: http://www.pathologistsassistants.org

Members: Pathologists' assistants and individuals qualified by academic and practical training to provide service in anatomic pathology under the direction of a qualified pathologist who is responsible for the performance of the assistant. **Purpose:** Promotes the mutual association of trained pathologists' assistants and informs the public and the medical profession concerning the goals of this profession. **Activities:** Compiles statistics on salaries, geographic distribution, and duties of pathologists' assistants. Sponsors a continuing medical education program; offers a job hotline for members only.

★9641★ Association of Physician Assistants in Cardiovascular Surgery (APACVS)

PO Box 4834
Englewood, CO 80155
Ph: (303)221-5651   Fax: (303)771-2550
Fr: 877-221-5651
E-mail: admin@apacvs.org
URL: http://www.apacvs.org

Description: Represents physician assistants who work with cardiovascular surgeons. Assists in defining the role of physician assistants in the field of cardiovascular surgery through educational forums.

★9642★ Commission on Accreditation of Allied Health Education Programs (CAAHEP)

1361 Park St.
Clearwater, FL 33756
Ph: (727)210-2350   Fax: (727)210-2354
E-mail: megivern@caahep.org
URL: http://www.caahep.org

Description: Serves as a nationally recognized accrediting agency for allied health programs in 18 occupational areas.

★9643★ EMTs, Nurses, Therapists, and Assistants

Cambridge Educational
PO Box 2053
Princeton, NJ 08543-2053
Ph: 800-257-5126   Fax: (609)671-0266
Fr: 800-468-4227
E-mail: custserv@films.com
URL: http://www.cambridgeeducational.com

VHS and DVD. $79.95. 2000. 18 minutes. Part of the series "Exploring Health Occupations."

★9644★ Exploring Health Occupations

Cambridge Educational
PO Box 2053
Princeton, NJ 08543-2053
Ph: 800-257-5126   Fax: (609)671-0266
Fr: 800-468-4227
E-mail: custserv@films.com
URL: http://www.cambridgeeducational.com

VHS and DVD. $159.90. 1999. Two-part series provides a detailed view of the field of medical technicians and technologists, EMTs, nurses, therapists, and assistants.

★9645★ Health Service Occupations

Delphi Productions
3159 6th St.
Boulder, CO 80304
Ph: (303)443-2100   Fax: (303)443-4022
Fr: 888-443-2400
E-mail: support@delphivideo.com
URL: http://www.delphivideo.com

$95.00. 50 minutes. Part of the Careers for the 21st Century Video Library.

★9646★ Joint Council of Allergy, Asthma and Immunology (JCAAI)

50 N Brockway, Ste. 3-3
Palatine, IL 60067
Ph: (847)934-1918   Fax: (847)934-1820
E-mail: info@jcaai.org
URL: http://www.jcaai.org

Description: Physicians specializing in allergy or clinical immunology. Members must belong to the American Academy of Allergy and Immunology or the American College of Allergy and Immunology. Serves as political

and socioeconomic arm for these sponsoring organizations.

★9647★ Medicine & Related Occupations

Delphi Productions
3159 6th St.
Boulder, CO 80304
Ph: (303)443-2100   Fax: (303)443-4022
Fr: 888-443-2400
E-mail: support@delphivideo.com
URL: http://www.delphivideo.com

$95.00. 45 minutes. Part of the Careers for the 21st Century Video Library.

★9648★ National Commission on Certification of Physician Assistants (NCCPA)

12000 Findley Rd., Ste. 200
Duluth, GA 30097
Ph: (678)417-8100   Fax: (678)417-8135
E-mail: nccpa@nccpa.net
URL: http://www.nccpa.net

Description: Certifies physician assistants at the entry level and for continued competence; has certified 22,750 physician assistants.

★9649★ National Rural Health Association (NRHA)

Administrative Office
521 E 63rd St.
Kansas City, MO 64110-3329
Ph: (816)756-3140   Fax: (816)756-3144
E-mail: mail@nrharural.org
URL: http://www.nrharural.org

Description: Administrators, physicians, nurses, physician assistants, health planners, academicians, and others interested or involved in rural health care. Creates a better understanding of health care problems unique to rural areas; utilizes a collective approach in finding positive solutions; articulates and represents the health care needs of rural America; supplies current information to rural health care providers; serves as a liaison between rural health care programs throughout the country. Offers continuing education credits for medical, dental, nursing, and management courses.

★9650★ Visiting Nurse Associations of America (VNAA)

Administration Office
99 Summer St., Ste. 1700
Boston, MA 02110
Ph: (617)737-3200   Fax: (617)737-1144
Fr: 800-426-2547
E-mail: vnaa@vnaa.org
URL: http://www.vnaa.org

Members: Home health care agencies. **Purpose:** Develops competitive strength among community-based nonprofit visiting nurse organizations; works to strengthen business resources and economic programs through contracting, marketing, governmental affairs and publications.

Physicians

★9651★ AACAP News

American Academy of Child and
  Adolescent Psychiatry (AACAP)
3615 Wisconsin Ave., NW
Washington, DC 20016-3007
Ph: (202)966-7300   Fax: (202)966-2891
E-mail: clinical@aacap.org
URL: http://www.aacap.org/

Description: Bimonthly. Publishes news of the Academy, child and adolescent psychiatrists, and AACAP members. Focuses on the practice of child and adolescent psychiatry. Recurring features include letters to the editor, legislative updates, news of research, statistics, announcements of open positions, and columns titled Ethics, Clinical Vignettes, Forensic Corner, and Clinical Marketing.

★9652★ AARC Times

Daedalus Enterprises Inc.
11030 Ables Ln.
PO Box 29686
Dallas, TX 75229
Ph: (972)243-2272   Fax: (972)484-2720
URL: http://aarc.org

Monthly. $85.00/year for individuals, 1-year subscription. Professional magazine for respiratory therapists and other cardiopulmonary specialists.

★9653★ Academic Emergency Medicine

Mosby Inc.
11830 Westline Industrial Dr.
St. Louis, MO 63146
Ph: (314)872-8370   Fax: (314)432-1380
Fr: 800-325-4177
URL: http://www.elsevier.com/wps/find/journaldescription.cws_home

Monthly. $259.00/year for institutions; $161.00/year for individuals; $77.00/year for students; $245.00/year for institutions; $151.00/year for individuals; $83.00/year for students. Journal publishing material relevant to the practice, education, and investi-

gation of emergency medicine; reaches a wide audience of emergency care practitioners and educators.

★9654★ ACP Observer

American College of Physicians
190 N Independence Mall W
Philadelphia, PA 19106-1572
Ph: (215)351-2600   Fr: 800-523-1546
URL: http://www.acponline.org/journals/news/obstoc.htm

Monthly. Free to members. Official membership tabloid of the American College of Physicians.

★9655★ American Family Physician

American Academy of Family Physicians
11400 Tomahawk Creek Pkwy.
PO Box 11210
Leawood, KS 66211-2672
Ph: (913)906-6000   Fax: (913)906-6010
Fr: 800-274-2237
E-mail: afpedit@aafp.org
URL: http://www.aafp.org/afp

Semimonthly. $120.00/year for individuals, U.S.; $200.00/year for out of country, individuals; $160.00/year for Canada, individuals; $160.00/year for institutions, U.S.; $200.00/year for institutions, Canada; $240.00/year for institutions, foreign countries; $68.00/year for students, medical; $108.00/year for students, medical; $148.00/year for students, medical; $11.00 for single issue, six copies. Peer reviewed clinical journal for family physicians and others in primary care. Review articles detail the latest diagnostic and therapeutic techniques in the medical field. Department features in each issue include 'Tips from other Journals,' CME credit opportunities and course calendar.

★9656★ American Heart Journal

Mosby
1600 John F. Kennedy Blvd., Ste. 1800
Philadelphia, PA 19103-2899
Ph: (215)239-3276   Fax: (215)239-3286
URL: http://www3.us.elsevierhealth.com/ahj/

Monthly. $258.00/year   for   individuals;

$320.00/year for institutions; $258.00/year for other countries, Includes air speed delivery; $509.00/year for institutions, other countries, Includes air speed delivery. Medical journal serving practicing cardiologists, university-affiliated clinicians, and physicians keeping abreast of developments in the diagnosis and management of cardiovascular disease.

★9657★ The American Journal of Cardiology

Excerpta Medica Inc.
685 US-202
Bridgewater, NJ 08807
Ph: (908)547-2100   Fax: (908)547-2200
URL: http://www.ajconline.org/

Semimonthly. $414.00/year for institutions, domestic; $132.00/year for individuals, domestic; $73.00/year for students, domestic; $625.00/year for institutions, international; $337.00/year for individuals, international; $77.00/year for students, international. Journal for heart specialists.

★9658★ American Journal of Clinical Nutrition

The American Society for Clinical
  Nutrition
9650 Rockville Pke.
L-2407A
Bethesda, MD 20814-3998
Ph: (301)634-7038   Fax: (301)634-7351
E-mail: dbier@nutrition.org
URL: http://www.ajcn.org

Annual. $470.00/year for institutions, print and online U.S.; $455.00/year for institutions, online U.S.; $200.00/year for individuals, print and online U.S.; $175.00/year for individuals, online U.S.; $85.00/year for students, print and online U.S.; $60.00/year for students, online U.S.; $495.00/year for Canada and Mexico, print and online; $455.00/year for Canada and Mexico, online only; $520.00/year for elsewhere, print and online; $455.00/year for elsewhere, online only. Journal of basic and clinical studies relevant to human nutrition.

★9659★ American Journal of Emergency Medicine

Mosby Inc.
11830 Westline Industrial Dr.
St. Louis, MO 63146
Ph: (314)872-8370   Fax: (314)432-1380
Fr: 800-325-4177
URL: http://www.elsevier.com/wps/find/journaldescription.cws_home

Bimonthly. $275.00/year for individuals; $419.00/year for institutions; $129.00/year for students; $397.00/year for individuals, international; $546.00/year for institutions, international; $198.00/year for students, international. Journal reporting on emergency medicine.

★9660★ American Journal of Epidemiology

Oxford University Press
2001 Evans Rd.
Cary, NC 27513
Ph: (919)677-0977   Fax: (919)677-1714
Fr: 800-852-7323
URL: http://aje.oupjournals.org

Semimonthly. $473.00/year for institutions, print & online; $709.00/year for institutions, print & online; $709.00/year for institutions, print & online; $449.00/year for individuals, online; $674.00/year for individuals, online; $674.00/year for individuals, online; $449.00/year for institutions, print; $674.00/year for institutions, print; $674.00/year for institutions, print. Science research and medical journal.

★9661★ American Journal of Medical Genetics

John Wiley & Sons Inc.
111 River St.
Hoboken, NJ 07030-5774
Ph: (201)748-6000   Fax: (201)748-6088
Fr: 800-825-7550
URL: http://as.wiley.com/WileyCDA/WileyTitle/productCd-AJMG.html

$635.00/year for individuals; $635.00/year for Canada and Mexico, in Canada, add 7% GST; $827.00/year for other countries; $11,610.00/year for institutions, print; $12,042.00/year for institutions, Canada and Mexico, print, in Canada add 7% GST; $12,294.00/year for institutions, other countries, print; $12,771.00/year for institutions, print and online, U.S.; $13,203.00/year for institutions, Canada and Mexico, print and online; $13,455.00/year for institutions, other countries, rest of world, print and online. Medical research journal.

★9662★ American Journal of Medicine

Excerpta Medica Inc.
685 US-202
Bridgewater, NJ 08807
Ph: (908)547-2100   Fax: (908)547-2200
URL: http://www.amjmed.com/

Monthly. $336.00/year for individuals, international; $131.00/year for U.S. and Canada; $81.00/year for students, international; $76.00/year for students, in U.S. Medical journal.

★9663★ American Journal of Obstetrics and Gynecology

Mosby Inc.
11830 Westline Industrial Dr.
St. Louis, MO 63146
Ph: (314)872-8370   Fax: (314)432-1380
Fr: 800-325-4177
E-mail: usjcs@elsevier.com
URL: http://www2.us.elsevierhealth.com

Monthly. $256.00/year for individuals; $588.00/year for institutions; $130.00/year for students; $318.00/year for individuals, Canada; $652.00/year for institutions, other countries; $159.00/year for students, Mexico. Journal for specialists in obstetrics and gynecology and for general practitioners. Official Journal of the American Gynecological and Obstetrical Society, American Board of Obstetrics and Gynecology, Society of Gynecologic Surgeons, and Society of Maternal-Fetal Medicine.

★9664★ The American Journal of Orthopedics

Quadrant Healthcom
7 Century Dr., Ste. 302
Parsippany, NJ 07054-4609
Ph: (973)206-3434
URL: http://www.quadranthealth.com

Monthly. $128.00/year for individuals; $184.00/year for institutions; $165.00/year for Canada and Mexico; $185.00/year for other countries; $266.00/year for individuals. Medical journal.

★9665★ The American Journal of Pathology

The American Journal of Pathology
9650 Rockville Pke.
Bethesda, MD 20814-3993
Ph: (301)634-7130   Fax: (301)634-7990
E-mail: asip@asip.org
URL: http://ajp.amjpathol.org

Monthly. $195.00/year for members, U.S. $270.00/year for members, Canada & Mexico; $290.00/year for members, elsewhere; $275.00/year for individuals, U.S. $375.00/year for individuals, Canada & Mexico; $375.00/year for individuals, elsewhere; $605.00/year for institutions, U.S. $685.00/year for institutions, Canada & Mexico; $710.00/year for institutions, elsewhere. Journal publishing original experimental and clinical studies in diagnostic and experimental pathology.

★9666★ American Journal of Psychiatry

American Psychiatric Publishing Inc.
1000 Wilson Blvd., Ste. 1825
Arlington, VA 22209-3901
Ph: (703)907-7322   Fax: (703)907-1091
Fr: 800-368-5777
E-mail: ajp@psych.org
URL: http://store.appi.org/main.aspx?pageid=journal/journal&id=AJ

Monthly. $205.00/year for nonmembers, print + online; $205.00/year for members, print + online, international; $308.00/year for nonmembers, print + online, international;

$370.00/year for nonmembers, 2 years, print + online; $370.00/year for members, 2 years, print + online, international; $554.00/year for nonmembers, 2 years, print + online, international. Psychiatry journal.

★9667★ The American Journal of Sports Medicine

The American Orthopaedic Society for Sports Medicine
6300 North River Rd., Ste. 500
Rosemont, IL 60018
Ph: (847)292-4900   Fax: (847)292-4905
URL: http://ajs.sagepub.com/

$721.00/year for institutions, print & e-access; $169.00/year for individuals, print & e-access. Medical journal.

★9668★ American Journal of Surgery

Excerpta Medica Inc.
685 US-202
Bridgewater, NJ 08807
Ph: (908)547-2100   Fax: (908)547-2200
URL: http://www.elsevier.com/wps/find/journaldescription.cws_home

Monthly. $562.00/year for institutions, outside U.S.; $373.00/year for individuals, outside U.S.; $82.00/year for students; $205.00/year for individuals; $334.00/year for institutions. Surgical journal.

★9669★ The American Journal of Surgical Pathology (AJSP)

Lippincott Williams & Wilkins
351 W Camden St.
Baltimore, MD 21201
Ph: (410)528-4000   Fax: (410)528-4305
Fr: 800-399-3110
URL: http://www.ajsp.com/

Monthly. $472.00/year for individuals; $1,017.00/year for institutions; $229.00/year for individuals, in-training; $613.00/year for individuals, other countries; $1,101.00/year for institutions, other countries; $245.00/year for other countries, in-training. Medical journal covering issues concerning diagnostic problems.

★9670★ Anesthesia & Analgesia

Lippincott Williams & Wilkins
530 Walnut St.
Philadelphia, PA 19106-3621
Ph: (215)521-8300   Fax: (215)521-8902
Fr: 800-638-3030
E-mail: editor@anesthesia-analgesia.org
URL: http://www.anesthesia-analgesia.org/

Monthly. $482.00/year for individuals, U.S.; $706.00/year for institutions, U.S.; $234.00/year for U.S., In-training; $614.00/year for institutions, other countries; $839.00/year for other countries; $371.00/year for other countries, In-training. Medical journal.

★9671★ Anesthesia & Analgesia

Society for Ambulatory Anesthesia
520 N. Northwest Hwy.
Park Ridge, IL 60068-2573
Ph: (847)825-5586   Fax: (847)825-5658

E-mail: samba@asahq.org
URL: http://www.sambahq.org/

Description: Quarterly. Reports on the educational and scientific work of the Society, which represents anesthesiologists who specialize in ambulatory anesthesia care in the U.S. Recurring features include editorials, letters to the editor, news of members, and a calendar of events.

★9672★ *Anesthesiology*
Lippincott Williams & Wilkins
530 Walnut St.
Philadelphia, PA 19106-3621
Ph: (215)521-8300   Fax: (215)521-8902
Fr: 800-638-3030
URL: http://www.anesthesiology.org/

Monthly. $408.00/year for individuals, U.S.; $753.00/year for institutions, U.S.; $575.00/year for other countries; $880.00/year for institutions, other countries; $207.00/year for U.S., in-training; $248.00/year for other countries, in-training. Medical journal publishing original manuscripts and brief abstracts from current literature on anesthesiology.

★9673★ *Annals of Behavioral Medicine*
Society of Behavioral Medicine
10 Industrial Ave.
Mahwah, NJ 07430
Ph: (201)258-2238   Fax: (201)760-3735
Fr: 800-926-6579

Quarterly. Journal describing the interactions of behavior and health.

★9674★ *Annals of Emergency Medicine*
Mosby Inc.
11830 Westline Industrial Dr.
St. Louis, MO 63146
Ph: (314)872-8370   Fax: (314)432-1380
Fr: 800-325-4177
URL: http://www.us.elsevierhealth.com/product.jsp?isbn=01960644

Monthly. Medical journal for emergency physicians.

★9675★ *Annals of Medicine*
Taylor & Francis Group Journals
325 Chestnut St., Ste. 800
Philadelphia, PA 19106
Ph: (215)625-8900   Fax: (215)625-8914
Fr: 800-354-1420
URL: http://www.ingentaconnect.com

$418.00/year for institutions, print and online; $397.00/year for institutions, online only; $155.00/year for individuals. Journal covering health science and medical education.

★9676★ *Annals of Neurology*
John Wiley & Sons Inc.
111 River St.
Hoboken, NJ 07030-5774
Ph: (201)748-6000   Fax: (201)748-6088
Fr: 800-825-7550

URL: http://as.wiley.com/WileyCDA/Wiley-Title/productCd-ANA.html

Monthly. $240.00/year for U.S. $240.00/year for Canada and Mexico; $312.00/year for other countries; $635.00/year for U.S., print only rates; $779.00/year for Canada and Mexico, print only rates; $863.00/year for institutions, other countries, print only rates; $699.00/year for U.S., combined print with online access rates; $843.00/year for Canada and Mexico, combined print with online access rates; $927.00/year for other countries, combined print with online access rates. Articles of scientific and clinical merit for neurologists.

★9677★ *Annals of Plastic Surgery*
Lippincott Williams & Wilkins
530 Walnut St.
Philadelphia, PA 19106-3621
Ph: (215)521-8300   Fax: (215)521-8902
Fr: 800-638-3030
URL: http://www.lww.com/product/?0148-7043

Monthly. $435.00/year for individuals, U.S.; $719.00/year for institutions, U.S.; $223.00/year for U.S., in-training; $562.00/year for individuals, international; $838.00/year for institutions, international; $239.00/year for other countries, in-training. Medical journal for the plastic surgeon.

★9678★ *Annals of Surgery*
Lippincott Williams & Wilkins
530 Walnut St.
Philadelphia, PA 19106-3621
Ph: (215)521-8300   Fax: (215)521-8902
Fr: 800-638-3030
E-mail: jumulliga@lww.com
URL: http://www.annalsofsurgery.com/

Monthly. $249.00/year for individuals; $646.00/year for institutions; $99.00/year for other countries, international; $392.00/year for individuals; $814.00/year for institutions; $99.00/year for other countries. Medical journal publishing original manuscripts promoting the advancement of surgical knowledge and practice.

★9679★ *Applied Radiology*
Anderson Publishing Ltd.
180 Glenside Ave.
Scotch Plains, NJ 07076
Ph: (908)301-1995
URL: http://www.appliedradiology.com

Monthly. $95.00/year for individuals; $165.00 for two years; $110.00/year for other countries, surface mail; $185.00 for other countries, two years (surface mail); $180.00/year for other countries, air mail; $185.00 for other countries, two years (air mail). Magazine for radiologists, chief radiologic technologists, radiology department administrators, and key managers in HMOs. Presents articles written by radiologic professionals on all aspects of general diagnostic radiology, the diagnostic radiologic subspecialties, radiation therapy, and the socioeconomics of imaging.

★9680★ *Archives of Dermatology*
American Medical Association
515 N State St.
Chicago, IL 60610
Fr: 800-621-8335
URL: http://archderm.ama-assn.org

Monthly. $245.00/year for individuals, print and online; $485.00/year for institutions, print and online; $30.00 for single issue. Educational/clinical journal for dermatologists.

★9681★ *Archives of General Psychiatry*
American Medical Association
515 N State St.
Chicago, IL 60610
Fr: 800-621-8335
E-mail: archgenpsychiatry@jama-archives.org
URL: http://archpsyc.ama-assn.org/

Monthly. $465.00/year for institutions, print and online; $135.00/year for members, print and online; $199.00/year for nonmembers, print and online. Educational/clinical journal for psychiatrists.

★9682★ *Archives of Neurology*
American Medical Association
515 N State St.
Chicago, IL 60610
Fr: 800-621-8335
E-mail: archneurol@mednet.swmed.edu
URL: http://archneur.ama-assn.org

Monthly. $245.00/year for individuals, print and online; $480.00/year for institutions, print and online; $30.00 for single issue. Educational/clinical journal for neurologists.

★9683★ *Archives of Ophthalmology*
American Medical Association
515 N State St.
Chicago, IL 60610
Fr: 800-621-8335
URL: http://archopht.ama-assn.org/

Monthly. $215.00/year for individuals. Educational/clinical journal for ophthalmologists.

★9684★ *Archives of Otolaryngology-Head & Neck Surgery*
American Medical Association
515 N State St.
Chicago, IL 60610
Fr: 800-621-8335
URL: http://archotol.ama-assn.org/

Monthly. $220.00/year for individuals. Educational/clinical journal for otolaryngologists.

★9685★ *Archives of Pathology & Laboratory Medicine*
American Medical Association
515 N State St.
Chicago, IL 60610
Fr: 800-621-8335
URL: http://arpa.allenpress.com

Monthly. $210.00/year for U.S. and Canada,

1 year; $315.00/year for other countries. Educational/clinical journal for pathologists. Published in cooperation with the College of American Pathologists.

★9686★ Archives of Surgery

American Medical Association
515 N State St.
Chicago, IL 60610
Fr: 800-621-8335
E-mail: archsurg@jama-archives.org
URL: http://archsurg.ama-assn.org/

Monthly. $190.00/year for individuals, print and online; $435.00/year for institutions, print and online. Educational/clinical journal for general surgeons and surgical specialists.

★9687★ Chinese American Medical Society Newsletter

Chinese American Medical Society
281 Edgewood Ave.
Teaneck, NJ 07666
Ph: (201)833-1506   Fax: (201)833-8252
E-mail: hw5@columbia.edu
URL: http://www.camsociety.org

Description: 3-4 issues/year. Publishes Society news. Recurring features include recent activities of the Society, coming scientific meetings, excerpts of presentations at the scientific meeting, new members, job listings and a calendar of events.

★9688★ Clinical Cardiology

Clinical Cardiology Publishing Company Inc.
PO Box 832
Mahwah, NJ 07430-0832
Ph: (201)818-1010   Fax: (201)818-0086
Fr: 800-443-0263
E-mail: clinicalcardiology@fams.org

Monthly. $120.00/year for individuals; $150.00/year for institutions, no online access; $166.50/year for individuals, foreign; $400.00/year for institutions, foreign; institutional with online access; $446.50/year for institutions, other countries, foreign; $196.50/year for institutions, no online access. Peer-reviewed indexed medical journal.

★9689★ Clinical Medicine & Research

Marshfield Clinic
1000 North Oak Ave.
Marshfield, WI 54449
Ph: (715)387-5511   Fr: 800-782-8581
URL: http://www.clinmedres.org/

Monthly. Journal that publishes scientific medical research that is relevant to a broad audience of medical researchers and healthcare professionals.

★9690★ Clinical Pediatrics

Sage Publications Inc.
2455 Teller Rd.
Thousand Oaks, CA 91320
Ph: (805)499-0721   Fax: (805)499-8096

URL: http://www.westminsterpublications.com

$660.00/year for institutions, print and e-access; $594.00/year for institutions, online; $647.00/year for institutions, print; $437.00/year for U.S., hospital, print and e-access; $256.00/year for individuals, print and e-access; $80.00/year for institutions, single print; $37.00/year for individuals, single print. Professional journal for pediatric practitioners.

★9691★ Clinical Psychiatry News

International Medical News Group
60-B Columbia Rd.
Morristown, NJ 07960
Ph: (973)290-8200   Fax: (973)290-8250
URL: http://journals.elsevierhealth.com/periodicals/cpnews

Monthly. $90.00/year for individuals; $144.00/year for other countries, surface mail. Medical and psychiatry tabloid.

★9692★ CME Supplement to Emergency Medicine Clinics of North America

Elsevier Science Inc.
360 Park Ave. S
New York, NY 10010
Ph: (212)989-5800   Fax: (212)633-3990
URL: http://www.elsevier.com

Quarterly. $190.00/year for individuals. Journal covering emergency medicine clinics.

★9693★ Contemporary OB/GYN

Advanstar Communications Inc.
641 Lexington Ave., 8th Fl.
New York, NY 10022
Ph: (212)951-6600   Fax: (212)951-6793
E-mail: cog@advanstar.com
URL: http://www.contemporaryobgyn.net/obgyn

Monthly. $109.20/year for individuals, U.S.; $139.65/year for individuals, Canada and foreign; $10.50/year for individuals, single copy U.S.; $15.75/year for individuals, single copy Canada and foreign. Magazine covering clinical, investigative, and socioeconomic aspects of obstetrics and gynecology for specialists.

★9694★ Contemporary Pediatrics

Advanstar Communications Inc.
641 Lexington Ave., 8th Fl.
New York, NY 10022
Ph: (212)951-6600   Fax: (212)951-6793
URL: http://www.contemporarypediatrics.com/contpeds/

Monthly. $89.00/year for institutions, inside U.S.; $150.00/year for institutions, for two years; $105.00/year for institutions, outside U.S.; $189.00/year for institutions, two years; $11.00/year for institutions, single copies inside U.S.; $16.00/year for institutions, single copies outside U.S.; $6.5/year for institutions, for additional postage and handling. Journal to help pediatricians diagnose, treat,

and prevent illness in infants, children, adolescents, and young adults.

★9695★ Contemporary Urology

Advanstar Communications Inc.
641 Lexington Ave., 8th Fl.
New York, NY 10022
Ph: (212)951-6600   Fax: (212)951-6793
URL: http://www.contemporaryurology.com/conturo

Monthly. Clinical magazine for urologists.

★9696★ Critical Care Medicine

Society of Critical Care Medicine
701 Lee St., Ste. 200
Des Plaines, IL 60016
Ph: (847)827-6869   Fax: (847)827-6886
URL: http://www.ccmjournal.com/

Monthly. $342.00/year for individuals, U.S.; $549.00/year for institutions, U.S.; $440.00/year for individuals, foreign; $649.00/year for institutions, international; $319.00/year for institutions, in-training. Interdisciplinary journal for ICU and CCU specialists.

★9697★ Current Surgery

Lippincott Williams & Wilkins
530 Walnut St.
Philadelphia, PA 19106-3621
Ph: (215)521-8300   Fax: (215)521-8902
Fr: 800-638-3030
URL: http://www.us.elsevierhealth.com/product.jsp?isbn=01497944

Bimonthly. $283.00/year for individuals; $707.00/year for institutions. Professional journal covering continuing education for surgical residents and general surgeons.

★9698★ Diagnostic Imaging

CMP Media L.L.C.
600 Community Dr.
Manhasset, NY 11030
Ph: (516)562-5000   Fax: (516)562-7830
URL: http://www.diagnosticimaging.com/

Monthly. News and analysis on clinical and economic developments in medical imaging.

★9699★ Dialysis & Transplantation

Creative Age Publications Inc.
7628 Densmore Ave.
Van Nuys, CA 91406-2042
Ph: (818)782-7328   Fax: (818)782-7450
Fr: 800-442-5667
URL: http://www.eneph.com

Monthly. $22.00/year for individuals, 12 issues; $26.00/year for out of country; $43.00/year for Canada and Mexico, by mail; $82.00/year for other countries. Multi-disciplinary, peer-reviewed journal on clinical applications in dialysis, transplantation and nephrology for renal-care teams.

★9700★ Discovery Medicine

Discovery Medicine
2245 Chapel Valley Ln.
Timonium, MD 21093
Ph: (410)560-9007   Fax: (410)560-9000
URL: http://www.discoverymedicine.com

Bimonthly. $39.95/year for individuals; $49.95/year for individuals, digital edition and online access; $69.95 for two years, online access; $84.95 for two years, digital edition and online access; $99.95/year for individuals, 3 years, online access; $119.95/year for individuals, 3 years, digital and online access; $299.00/year for individuals, medical report (PMR); $99.00/year for individuals, medical report update. Online journal that publishes articles on diseases, biology, new diagnostics, and treatments for medical professionals.

★9701★ Diseases of the Colon and Rectum

Lippincott Williams & Wilkins
530 Walnut St.
Philadelphia, PA 19106-3621
Ph: (215)521-8300   Fax: (215)521-8902
Fr: 800-638-3030
E-mail: oldenburg.patricia@mayo.edu

Monthly. Medical journal.

★9702★ The DO

American Osteopathic Association
142 East Ontario St.
Chicago, IL 60611
Ph: (312)202-8000   Fax: (312)202-8200
Fr: 800-621-1773
URL: http://www.osteopathic.org

Monthly. Osteopathic medical magazine.

★9703★ Ear, Nose & Throat Journal

Vendome Group, LLC
3800 Lakeside Ave., Ste. 201
Cleveland, OH 44114-3857
Ph: (216)391-9100   Fax: (216)391-9200
E-mail: entjournal@phillyent.com
URL: http://www.entjournal.com

Monthly. $50.00/year for individuals, 12 month special; $70.00/year for individuals, 12 month; $120.00/year for individuals, 24 month. Journal on otorhinolaryngology, head and neck surgery, and allergies.

★9704★ Education & Treatment of Children

West Virginia University Press
44 Stansbury Hall
PO Box 6295
Morgantown, WV 26506
Ph: (304)293-8400   Fax: (304)293-6585
Fr: (866)988-7737
URL: http://www.educationandtreatmentofchildren.net

Quarterly. $85.00/year for institutions; $45.00/year for individuals; $100.00/year for institutions, elsewhere; $60.00/year for individuals, elsewhere. Periodical featuring information concerning the development of services for children and youth. Includes reports written for educators and other child care and mental health providers focused on teaching, training, and treatment effectiveness.

★9705★ Emergency Medical Services

Cygnus Business Media
1233 Janesville Ave.
Fort Atkinson, WI 53538
Fr: 800-547-7377
URL: http://www.emsmagazine.com

Monthly. Magazine covering emergency care, rescue and transportation.

★9706★ Epigenetics

Landes Bioscience
1002 West Ave., 2nd Fl.
Austin, TX 78701
Ph: (512)637-6050   Fax: (512)637-6079
Fr: 800-736-9948
URL: http://www.landesbioscience.com/index.php

Journal devoted to practicing physicians, residents and students.

★9707★ Family Practice Management

American Academy of Family Physicians
11400 Tomahawk Creek Pkwy.
PO Box 11210
Leawood, KS 66211-2672
Ph: (913)906-6000   Fax: (913)906-6010
Fr: 800-274-2237
E-mail: fpmedit@aafp.org
URL: http://www.aafp.org/fpm

Monthly. $12.00/year for institutions, a copy for six or fewer copies; $8.00/year for institutions, Canada, a copy for seven or more copies; $79.00/year for institutions; $89.00/year for U.S. $101.00/year for Canada; $60.00/year for other countries; $70.00/year for individuals, physicians and other; $87.00/year for U.S., physicians and other; $47.00/year for Canada, Physicians and other; $63.00/year for other countries, Physicians and other. Magazine covering socio-economic and management topics concerning family physicians.

★9708★ Family Practice News

International Medical News Group
60-B Columbia Rd.
Morristown, NJ 07960
Ph: (973)290-8200   Fax: (973)290-8250
E-mail: fpnews@imng.com
URL: http://www.efamilypracticenews.com

$115.00/year for U.S. $230.00/year for other countries, International. Family physician medical tabloid.

★9709★ The Federal Physician

Federal Physicians Association
12427 Hedges Run Dr., Ste. 104
Lake Ridge, VA 22192
Fax: 800-528-3492   Fr: 800-403-3374
E-mail: info@fedphy.com
URL: http://www.fedphy.org/

Description: Bimonthly. Covers issues affecting physicians in the federal government. Recurring features include news of research, reports of meetings, and job listings.

★9710★ Fertility and Sterility

The American Society for Reproductive Medicine
1209 Montgomery Hwy.
Birmingham, AL 35216-2809
Ph: (205)978-5000   Fax: (205)978-5005
URL: http://www.asrm.org

Monthly. Medical journal covering all aspects of reproductive medicine.

★9711★ Forensic Science, Medicine and Pathology

Humana Press Inc.
999 Riverview Dr., Ste. 208
Totowa, NJ 07512
Ph: (973)256-1699   Fax: (973)256-8341
URL: http://www.humanapress.com/index.php?option=com_journalshome

Journal focusing on forensic science, medicine, and pathology.

★9712★ Genes and Nutrition

New Century Health Publishers LLC
PO Box 50702
New Orleans, LA 70150-0702
Fax: (504)305-3762
URL: http://www.newcenturyhealthpublishers.com/genes_and_nutritio

Quarterly. $428.00/year for institutions; $228.00/year for individuals. International, interdisciplinary peer reviewed scientific journal for critical evaluation of research on the relationship between genetics & nutrition with the goal of improving human health.

★9713★ Head & Neck Surgery

John Wiley & Sons Inc.
111 River St.
Hoboken, NJ 07030-5774
Ph: (201)748-6000   Fax: (201)748-6088
Fr: 800-825-7550
URL: http://as.wiley.com/WileyCDA/WileyTitle/productCd-HED.html

Monthly. $260.00/year for individuals, print with online access; $260.00/year for Canada and Mexico, print with online access; $332.00/year for other countries, print with online access; $1,415.00/year for institutions, print only rates; $1,559.00/year for Canada and Mexico, print only rates; $1,643.00/year for other countries, print only rates; $1,557.00/year for institutions, combined print with online access rates; $1,701.00/year for Canada and Mexico, combined print with online access rates; $1,785.00/year for other countries, combined print with online access rates. International, multidisciplinary publication of original contributions concerning diagnosis and surgical management of diseases of the head and neck. Publishes articles of interest to several medical and surgical specialists including general surgeons, neurosurgeons, otolaryngologists, and plastic surgeons.

★9714★ Heart and Lung

Mosby
1600 John F. Kennedy Blvd., Ste. 1800
Philadelphia, PA 19103-2899
Ph: (215)239-3276   Fax: (215)239-3286
URL: http://www.elsevier.com/wps/find/journaleditorialboard.cws_h

Bimonthly. $111.00/year for individuals; $321.00/year for institutions; $34.00/year for students; $99.00/year for other countries; $50.00/year for students, other countries; $289.00/year for institutions, other countries. Journal offering articles prepared by nurse and physician members of the critical care team, recognizing the nurse's role in the care and management of major organ-system conditions in critically ill patients.

★9715★ Hematology

American Society of Hematology
1900 M St. NW, Ste. 200
Washington, DC 20036
Ph: (202)776-0544   Fax: (202)776-0545
URL: http://asheducation-book.hematologylibrary.org

Semiweekly. $60.00/year for members; $90.00/year for nonmembers. Journal providing continuing medical education for physicians.

★9716★ Hospitals & Health Networks

Health Forum L.L.C.
1 N Franklin, 29th Fl.
Chicago, IL 60606
Ph: (312)893-6800   Fax: (312)422-4506
Fr: 800-821-2039
URL: http://www.hhnmag.com

Weekly. Publication covering the health care industry.

★9717★ The IHS Primary Care Provider

Indian Health Service (HQ)
The Reyes Bldg.
801 Thompson Ave., Ste. 400
Rockville, MD 20852-1627
URL: http://www.ihs.gov/PublicInfo/Publications/HealthProvider/Pr

Monthly. Journal for health care professionals, physicians, nurses, pharmacists, dentists, and dietitians.

★9718★ Infectious Disease News

SLACK Inc.
6900 Grove Rd.
Thorofare, NJ 08086-9447
Ph: (856)848-1000   Fax: (856)853-5991
E-mail: idn@slackinc.com
URL: http://infectiousdiseasenews.com

Monthly. $269.00/year for individuals; $457.00 for two years; $605.00/year for individuals, three years; $429.00/year for institutions; $729.00 for two years; $965.00/year for institutions, three years; $135.00/year for individuals; $36.00/year for individuals. Newspaper for infectious disease specialists.

★9719★ Infectious Diseases in Children

SLACK Inc.
6900 Grove Rd.
Thorofare, NJ 08086-9447
Ph: (856)848-1000   Fax: (856)853-5991
E-mail: idc@slackinc.com
URL: http://www.idinchildren.com

Monthly. $269.00/year for individuals; $429.00/year for institutions; $457.00/year for individuals, two years; $729.00/year for institutions, two years; $605.00/year for individuals, three years; $965.00/year for institutions, three years; $36.00 for single issue, resident. Newspapers for physician.

★9720★ Injury

Mosby Inc.
11830 Westline Industrial Dr.
St. Louis, MO 63146
Ph: (314)872-8370   Fax: (314)432-1380
Fr: 800-325-4177
URL: http://www.elsevier.com/wps/find/journaldescription.cws_home

Monthly. $1,106.00/year for institutions, all countries except Europe, Japan and Iran; $169.00/year for individuals, all countries except Europe, Japan and Iran. Journal publishing articles and research related to the treatment of injuries such as trauma systems and management; surgical procedures; epidemiological studies; surgery (of all tissues); resuscitation; biomechanics; rehabilitation; anaesthesia; radiology and wound management.

★9721★ The Journal of Allergy and Clinical Immunology

Mosby Inc.
11830 Westline Industrial Dr.
St. Louis, MO 63146
Ph: (314)872-8370   Fax: (314)432-1380
Fr: 800-325-4177
URL: http://www.jacionline.org

Monthly. $663.00/year for institutions; $342.00/year for individuals; $134.00/year for students, U.S.; $585.00/year for institutions, United States; $267.00/year for individuals, United States; $171.00/year for students, other countries. Journal for clinical allergists and immunologists, as well as dermatologists, internists, general practitioners, pediatricians, and otolaryngologists (ENT physicians) concerned with clinical manifestations of allergies in their practice.

★9722★ Journal of the American Academy of Child and Adolescent Psychiatry

Lippincott Williams & Wilkins
530 Walnut St.
Philadelphia, PA 19106-3621
Ph: (215)521-8300   Fax: (215)521-8902
Fr: 800-638-3030
URL: http://www.jaacap.com/

Monthly. $195.00/year for individuals, U.S.; $341.00/year for institutions, U.S.; $252.00/year for individuals, international; $402.00/year for institutions, international. Child psychiatry journal.

★9723★ Journal of the American Academy of Dermatology

Mosby Inc.
11830 Westline Industrial Dr.
St. Louis, MO 63146
Ph: (314)872-8370   Fax: (314)432-1380
Fr: 800-325-4177
E-mail: elspcs@elsevier.com
URL: http://www.elsevier.com

Monthly. $543.00/year for institutions; $601.00/year for institutions, international (includes air speed delivery). Journal for dermatologists and for family practitioners, pediatricians, and internists who are concerned with clinical manifestations of skin disease in their practice.

★9724★ Journal of the American Osteopathic Association

American Osteopathic Association
142 East Ontario St.
Chicago, IL 60611
Ph: (312)202-8000   Fax: (312)202-8200
Fr: 800-621-1773
URL: http://www.osteopathic.org

Monthly. Osteopathic clinical journal.

★9725★ Journal of the American Society of Echocardiography

Mosby
1600 John F. Kennedy Blvd., Ste. 1800
Philadelphia, PA 19103-2899
Ph: (215)239-3276   Fax: (215)239-3286
URL: http://www.elsevier.com/wps/find/journalbibliographicinfo.cw

Monthly. $260.00/year for other countries, print & online; $390.00/year for institutions, other countries, print & online; $243.00/year for individuals, print & online; $402.00/year for institutions, print & online; $127.00/year for students, other countries; $116.00/year for students. Official journal of the American Society of Echocardiography serving as a source of information on the technical basis and clinical application of echocardiography. Peer-reviewed publication featuring research, reviews, and case studies.

★9726★ Journal of the American Society of Podiatric Medical Assistants

American Society of Podiatric Medical Assistants
2124 S Austin Blvd.
Cicero, IL 60804
Ph: (708)863-6303   Fr: 888-882-7762
URL: http://www.aspma.org

Quarterly. Subscription included in membership. Professional journal covering issues in podiatry.

★9727★ The Journal of Arthroplasty

Elsevier
1600 John F. Kennedy Blvd., Ste. 1800
Philadelphia, PA 19103-2899
Ph: (215)239-3900   Fax: (215)238-7883
E-mail: elspcs@elsevier.com
URL: http://www.us.elsevierhealth.com/

product.jsp?isbn=08835403

$777.00/year for institutions, outside U.S.; $172.00/year for students; $638.00/year for institutions; $390.00/year for individuals; $200.00/year for students, outside U.S.; $512.00/year for individuals, outside U.S. Medical journal for orthopaedic surgeons. Covering clinical and basic science research on arthroplasty including surgical techniques, prosthetic design, biomechanics, biomaterials, and metallurgy.

★9728★ *Journal of Clinical Psychiatry*

Physicians Postgraduate Press Inc.
PO Box 752870
Memphis, TN 38175
Ph: (901)751-3800   Fax: (901)751-3444
E-mail: mwaters@psychiatrist.com
URL: http://www.psychiatrist.com

Monthly. Journal containing original papers about practical and clinical psychiatry.

★9729★ *Journal of Health Law*

American Health Lawyers Association
1025 Connecticut Ave., NW, Ste. 600
Washington, DC 20036-5405
Ph: (202)833-1100   Fax: (202)833-1105
URL: http://www.healthlawyers.org

Quarterly. Professional journal covering healthcare issues and cases and their impact on the health care arena.

★9730★ *Journal of Hospital Medicine*

John Wiley & Sons Inc.
111 River St.
Hoboken, NJ 07030-5774
Ph: (201)748-6000   Fax: (201)748-6088
Fr: 800-825-7550
URL: http://www.wiley.com/WileyCDA/WileyTitle/productCd-JHM.html

Bimonthly. $110.00/year for individuals, print only; Online version available with subscription. Journal on hospital medicine.

★9731★ *Journal of Intensive Care Medicine*

Sage Publications Inc.
2455 Teller Rd.
Thousand Oaks, CA 91320
Ph: (805)499-0721   Fax: (805)499-8096
E-mail: advertising@sagepub.com
URL: http://www.sagepub.com/journal.aspx?pid=340

Bimonthly. $676.00/year for institutions, print & e-access; $744.00/year for institutions, (current volume print & all online content); $608.00/year for institutions, e-access; $676.00/year for e-access plus backfile (all online content); $671.84/year for institutions, back file purchase, e-access content through 1999; $662.00/year for institutions, print only; $272.00/year for individuals, print only; $121.00 for institutions, single print issue; $59.00 for individuals, single print issue. Medical journal for specialists working in intensive care units.

★9732★ *Journal of the National Medical Association*

National Medical Association
1012 10th St. NW
Washington, DC 20001
Ph: (202)347-1895   Fax: (202)898-2510
URL: http://www.nmanet.org

Monthly. Journal on specialized clinical research related to the health problems of African-Americans and other minorities. Recognizes significant contributions by black physicians and others involved with minority health issues and health disparities.

★9733★ *Journal of Occupational and Environmental Medicine*

Lippincott Williams & Wilkins
530 Walnut St.
Philadelphia, PA 19106-3621
Ph: (215)521-8300   Fax: (215)521-8902
Fr: 800-638-3030
URL: http://www.lww.com/product/?1076-2752

Monthly. $319.00/year for individuals, U.S.; $432.00/year for institutions, U.S.; $435.00/year for individuals, other countries; $531.00/year for institutions, other countries. Occupational and environmental medicine journal.

★9734★ *Journal of Pediatric Hematology/Oncology*

Lippincott Williams & Wilkins
351 W Camden St.
Baltimore, MD 21201
Ph: (410)528-4000   Fax: (410)528-4305
Fr: 800-399-3110
URL: http://www.lww.com/product/0,0,1077-4114,00.html

Monthly. $407.00/year for individuals; $694.00/year for institutions; $152.00/year for individuals, in-training; $483.00/year for institutions; $798.00/year for institutions, other countries; $160.00/year for other countries, in-training. Journal containing reports on major advances in the diagnosis and treatment of cancer and blood diseases in children.

★9735★ *The Journal of Pediatrics*

Mosby Inc.
11830 Westline Industrial Dr.
St. Louis, MO 63146
Ph: (314)872-8370   Fax: (314)432-1380
Fr: 800-325-4177
URL: http://www.us.elsevierhealth.com/product.jsp?isbn=00223476

Monthly. $623.00/year for institutions; $249.00/year for individuals; $99.00/year for students; $573.00/year for institutions, within U.S.; $200.00/year for individuals, within U.S. Journal for physicians who diagnose and treat disorders in infants and children.

★9736★ *Journal of Trauma*

Lippincott Williams & Wilkins
530 Walnut St.
Philadelphia, PA 19106-3621
Ph: (215)521-8300   Fax: (215)521-8902
Fr: 800-638-3030
URL: http://www.jtrauma.com

Monthly. $362.00/year for individuals, U.S.; $489.00/year for institutions, U.S.; $210.00/year for other countries, in-training; $455.00/year for individuals, international; $582.00/year for institutions, other countries, international; $303.00/year for individuals, in-training, international. Surgery journal.

★9737★ *Journal of Urology*

Elsevier Science
PO Box 945
New York, NY 10159-0945
Ph: (212)989-5800   Fax: (212)633-3680
Fr: 888-615-4500
E-mail: publications@auanet.org
URL: http://www.jurology.com/

Monthly. $647.00/year for individuals; $866.00/year for individuals, other countries; $715.00/year for institutions; $933.00/year for institutions, other countries; $275.00/year for U.S., in-training; $515.00/year for other countries, in-training. Medical journal.

★9738★ *Journal of Vascular Surgery*

Mosby
1600 John F. Kennedy Blvd., Ste. 1800
Philadelphia, PA 19103-2899
Ph: (215)239-3276   Fax: (215)239-3286
E-mail: elspcs@elsevier.com
URL: http://us.elsevierhealth.com/product.jsp?isbn=07415214#descr

Monthly. $233.00/year for individuals; $460.00/year for institutions; $279.00/year for individuals, Includes air speed delivery; $509.00/year for institutions, Includes air speed delivery; $153.00/year for institutions, other countries, US Members of European Society of Vascular Surgery; $184.00/year for out of country, Members of European Society of Vascular Surgery; Add U.S. State tax & Canadian services tax, as applicable. Journal providing a forum for the advances in knowledge of the peripheral vascular system. Publishes peer-reviewed original articles on all aspects of disease and injury to the arterial and venous systems.

★9739★ *Laboratory Medicine*

American Society for Clinical Pathology
33 West Monroe, Ste. 1600
Chicago, IL 60603
Ph: (312)541-4999   Fax: (312)541-4998
Fr: 800-267-2727
E-mail: labmed@ascp.org
URL: http://www.labmedicine.com/

Monthly. $105.00/year for individuals, print and online; $105.00/year for other countries, print and online, individual; $140.00/year for other countries, print and online, individual expedited; $116.00/year for institutions, other countries, print and online, individual expedited; $20.00 for single issue, print and online; $15.00 for single issue, print and online, rest of world; $130.00/year for institutions, print and online; $130.00/year for institutions, other countries, print and online; $165.00/year for institutions, other countries, print and online, expedited. Professional journal covering medical technology and pathology.

★9740★ The Lancet (North American Edition)

Lippincott Williams & Wilkins
530 Walnut St.
Philadelphia, PA 19106-3621
Ph: (215)521-8300   Fax: (215)521-8902
Fr: 800-638-3030
URL: http://www.us.elsevierhealth.com/product.jsp?isbn=01406736

Weekly. Medical journal. Contents identical to British edition.

★9741★ Medical Economics

Advanstar Communications Inc.
641 Lexington Ave., 8th Fl.
New York, NY 10022
Ph: (212)951-6600   Fax: (212)951-6793
URL: http://www.memag.com/memag/

Semimonthly. Magazine covering physicians practice management, professional relations, and financial affairs.

★9742★ Medical Risks

Taylor & Francis Group Journals
325 Chestnut St., Ste. 800
Philadelphia, PA 19106
Ph: (215)625-8900   Fax: (215)625-8914
Fr: 800-354-1420
URL: http://www.tandf.co.uk

Monthly. Journal covering articles on medical risks.

★9743★ Medical Society of Milwaukee County-Membership Newsletter(MSMC)

Medical Society of Milwaukee County
1126 S. 70th St., Ste. N101A
Milwaukee, WI 53214-3104
Ph: (414)475-4750   Fax: (262)242-1862
E-mail: office@medicalsocietymilwaukee.org
URL: http://www.medicalsocietymilwaukee.org/

Description: Monthly. Serves as an informational newsletter for physicians. Contains IOCU medical business notes and practice announcements. Recurring features include letters to the editor, a calendar of events, reports of meetings, news of educational opportunities, job listings, and columns titled President's Letter.

★9744★ Medical Staff Development Professional

American Academy of Medical Management
Crossville Commons
560 W Crossville Rd., Ste. 103
Roswell, GA 30075
Ph: (770)649-7150   Fax: (770)649-7552

Periodic. Professional journal covering medical education.

★9745★ Military Medicine

AMSUS - The Society of the Federal Health Agencies
9320 Old Georgetown Rd.
Bethesda, MD 20814
Ph: (301)897-8800   Fax: (301)503-5446
Fr: 800-761-9320
URL: http://www.amsus.org/journal/

Monthly. $132.00/year for individuals; $177.00/year for other countries; $20.00 for single issue; $27.00 for single issue, other countries. Journal for professional personnel affiliated with the Federal medical services.

★9746★ Minnesota Medicine

Minnesota Medical Association
1300 Godward St. NE, Ste. 2500
Minneapolis, MN 55413
Ph: (612)378-1875   Fax: (612)378-3875
Fr: 800-342-5662
URL: http://www.minnesotamedicine.com/

Monthly. $45.00/year for individuals; $81.00 for two years; $80.00/year for other countries; $144.00/year for other countries, two years. Magazine on medical, socioeconomic, public health, medical-legal, and biomedical ethics issues of interest to physicians.

★9747★ Neonatal Intensive Care

Goldstein & Associates
1150 Yale St., Ste. 12
Santa Monica, CA 90403
Ph: (310)828-1309   Fax: (310)829-1169

Bimonthly. Intensive care, neonatal; perinatology; periodicals.

★9748★ Neuroscience Quarterly

Society for Neuroscience
1121 14th St., Ste. 1010
Washington, DC 20005
Ph: (202)962-4000   Fax: (202)962-4941
E-mail: info@sfn.org
URL: http://www.sfn.org/NL/current

Description: Bimonthly. Covers developments in neuroscience, with attention to research findings and funding, education, and interdisciplinary programs. Carries summaries or text of talks, papers, and of the prepared testimony of the Society's representatives before congressional committees. Recurring features include announcements of meetings and symposia, reports of foreign neuroscience societies, and Society news.

★9749★ The New England Journal of Medicine

The New England Journal of Medicine
860 Winter St.
Waltham, MA 02451-1413
Ph: (781)893-3800   Fr: 800-843-6356
URL: http://content.nejm.org/

Weekly. $99.00/year for individuals, online only; $149.00/year for individuals, print & online. Journal for the medical profession.

★9750★ Ob Gyn News

International Medical News Group
60-B Columbia Rd.
Morristown, NJ 07960
Ph: (973)290-8200   Fax: (973)290-8250
E-mail: obnews@imng.com
URL: http://www.eobgynnews.com

Semimonthly. $115.00/year for individuals; $230.00/year for other countries, surface mail. Obstetrics and gynecology tabloid distributed to obstetricians and gynecologists.

★9751★ Ocular Surgery News

SLACK Inc.
6900 Grove Rd.
Thorofare, NJ 08086-9447
Ph: (856)848-1000   Fax: (856)853-5991
URL: http://www.osnsupersite.com

Semimonthly. $399.00/year for individuals; $519.00/year for institutions; $199.00/year for individuals, resident; $48.00 for single issue. Medical newspaper for ophthalmologists. Covers scientific meetings and events, with emphasis on cataract/IOL, glaucoma treatment, refractive therapy, general ophthalmic topics, and legislative/ regulatory developments, and industry news.

★9752★ Oncology

S. Karger Publishers Inc.
26 W Avon Rd.
PO Box 529
Farmington, CT 06085
Ph: (860)675-7834   Fax: (203)675-7302
Fr: 800-828-5479
URL: http://content.karger.com/ProdukteDB/produkte.asp?Aktion=Jou

$1,974.00/year for institutions, print; $1,410.00/year for institutions, print; $1,974.00/year for institutions, print and online; plus postage and handling; $60.00/year for institutions, postage and handling; $43.20/year for institutions, postage and handling; $90.00/year for institutions, postage and handling, overseas; $82.40/year for institutions, postage and handling, overseas. Medical journal presenting experimental and clinical findings on cancer.

★9753★ Ophthalmic Surgery Lasers and Imaging

SLACK Inc.
6900 Grove Rd.
Thorofare, NJ 08086-9447
Ph: (856)848-1000   Fax: (856)853-5991
E-mail: osli@slackinc.com
URL: http://www.osli.com

Bimonthly. $139.00/year for individuals; $319.00/year for institutions; $236.00 for individuals, two years; $542.00 for institutions, two years; $312.00 for individuals, three years; $717.00 for institutions, three years. Journal publishing articles on ophthalmic surgery, lasers, research, and clinical approaches.

★9754★ **Optometric Management**

Lippincott Williams & Wilkins VisionCare Group
1300 Virginia Dr., Ste. 400
Fort Washington, PA 19034
Ph: (215)643-8000
E-mail: om@boucher1.com
URL: http://www.optometric.com

Monthly. Medical professional journal.

★9755★ **Orthopedics Today**

SLACK Inc.
6900 Grove Rd.
Thorofare, NJ 08086-9447
Ph: (856)848-1000   Fax: (856)853-5991
URL: http://www.orthosupersite.com/about.asp?pid=ot

Monthly. $269.00/year for individuals; $457.00 for individuals, two years; $605.00 for individuals, 3 years; $429.00/year for institutions; $729.00 for institutions, two years; $965.00 for institutions, 3 years; $135.00/year for individuals, resident; $36.00 for single issue. Newspaper covering orthopedic meetings, courses, and symposia.

★9756★ **Pacifica Review**

Taylor & Francis Group Journals
325 Chestnut St., Ste. 800
Philadelphia, PA 19106
Ph: (215)625-8900   Fax: (215)625-8914
Fr: 800-354-1420
URL: http://www.tandf.co.uk/

$462.00/year for individuals; $279.00/year for individuals; $487.00/year for individuals; $294.00/year for individuals; $123.00/year for individuals; $86.00/year for individuals. Journal promoting physical therapy and integration.

★9757★ **Patient Care**

Advanstar Communications Inc.
641 Lexington Ave., 8th Fl.
New York, NY 10022
Ph: (212)951-6600   Fax: (212)951-6793
URL: http://www.patientcareonline.com/patcare

Monthly. $57.00/year for individuals; $72.00/year for Canada and Mexico, individuals; $72.00/year for other countries, individuals. Medical journal publishing today's best clinical practices.

★9758★ **Pediatric Annals**

SLACK Inc.
6900 Grove Rd.
Thorofare, NJ 08086-9447
Ph: (856)848-1000   Fax: (856)853-5991
URL: http://www.slackinc.com/subscribe/pedann.asp

Monthly. $209.00/year for individuals; $359.00/year for institutions; $355.00 for individuals, two years; $610.00 for institutions, two years; $470.00 for individuals, three years; $807.00 for institutions, three years; $110.00/year for individuals, resident; $32.00 for individuals, single copy; $53.00/year for individuals, outside the U.S. Scholarly journal.

★9759★ **Pediatric News**

International Medical News Group
60-B Columbia Rd.
Morristown, NJ 07960
Ph: (973)290-8200   Fax: (973)290-8250
URL: http://www.epediatricnews.com

Monthly. $90.00/year for individuals, print. Tabloid covering pediatric medicine and distributed to pediatricians.

★9760★ **Pediatrics**

American Academy of Pediatrics
141 North West Point Blvd.
Elk Grove Village, IL 60007-1098
Ph: (847)434-4000   Fax: (847)434-8000
Fr: 800-433-9016
E-mail: journals@aap.org

Monthly. Medical journal reporting on pediatrics.

★9761★ **Psychiatric Annals**

SLACK Inc.
6900 Grove Rd.
Thorofare, NJ 08086-9447
Ph: (856)848-1000   Fax: (856)853-5991
E-mail: psyann@slackinc.com
URL: http://www.psychiatricannalsonline.com

Monthly. $219.00/year for individuals; $438.00 for individuals, two years; $657.00 for individuals, three years; $373.00/year for institutions; $746.00 for institutions, two years; $1119.00 for institutions, three years; $109.00/year for individuals, resident; $48.00 for single issue. Journal analyzing concepts and practices in every area of psychiatry.

★9762★ **Psychiatric News**

American Psychiatric Publishing Inc.
1000 Wilson Blvd., Ste. 1825
Arlington, VA 22209-3901
Ph: (703)907-7322   Fax: (703)907-1091
Fr: 800-368-5777
URL: http://pn.psychiatryonline.org/

Semimonthly. $93.00/year for individuals, U.S.; $126.00/year for members, international member; $140.00/year for nonmembers, international; $19.00 for single issue, U.S.; $31.00/year for single issue, international.

Professional magazine of the American Psychiatric Assn.

★9763★ **Psychiatric Services**

Association of Partners for Public Lands
2401 Blueridge Ave., Ste. 303
Wheaton, MD 20902
Ph: (301)946-9475   Fax: (301)946-9478

Monthly. Interdisciplinary mental health journal covering clinical, legal, and public policy issues.

★9764★ **Psychiatric Times**

CMP Media L.L.C.
600 Harrison St., 6th Fl.
San Francisco, CA 94107
Ph: (415)947-6000   Fax: (415)947-6055
URL: http://www.psychiatrictimes.com/

Monthly. $55.00/year for individuals; $90.00 individuals, for two years; $120.00/year for libraries, institutions; $120.00/year for other countries. Newspaper (tabloid) on psychiatric disorders and issues.

★9765★ **Resident & Staff Physician**

Pharmacy Times
103 College Rd. E
Princeton, NJ 08540-6612
Ph: (609)524-9560   Fax: (609)524-9699
URL: http://www.residentandstaff.com

Monthly. $92.00/year for individuals; $155.00 for two years; $165.00/year for institutions; $285.00/year for institutions, two years; $55.00/year for students; $95.00/year for students, two years; $150.00/year for Canada; $270.00/year for Canada, two years. Medical journal.

★9766★ **RETINA**

Lippincott Williams & Wilkins
530 Walnut St.
Philadelphia, PA 19106-3621
Ph: (215)521-8300   Fax: (215)521-8902
Fr: 800-638-3030
E-mail: brucker@retinajournal.com
URL: http://www.retinajournal.com

Monthly. $299.00/year for individuals; $653.00/year for institutions; $153.00/year for U.S., in-training; $400.00/year for other countries; $697.00/year for institutions, other countries; $153.00/year for other countries, in-training. Journal publishing clinically oriented articles for the general ophthalmologist and vitreoretinal specialist.

★9767★ **Seminars in Oncology**

Elsevier
1600 John F. Kennedy Blvd., Ste. 1800
Philadelphia, PA 19103-2899
Ph: (215)239-3900   Fax: (215)238-7883
E-mail: elspcs@elsevier.com
URL: http://www.elsevier.com

$228.00/year for individuals, U.S.; $114.00/year for students, U.S.; $311.00/year for individuals, Canada; $156.00/year for students, Canada; $311.00/year for individuals, Mexico; $156.00/year for students, Mexico;

$311.00/year for individuals, international; $156.00/year for students, international; $510.00/year for institutions, international; $424.00/year for institutions, U.S. Journal reviewing current diagnostic and treatment techniques used in oncology patient care.

★9768★ Skin & Allergy News

International Medical News Group
60-B Columbia Rd.
Morristown, NJ 07960
Ph: (973)290-8200   Fax: (973)290-8250
E-mail: sknews@imng.com
URL: http://www.eskinandallergynews.com/

Monthly. Dermatology/allergy tabloid.

★9769★ Southern Medical Journal

Southern Medical Association
35 Lakeshore Dr.
Birmingham, AL 35209
Ph: (205)945-1840   Fax: (205)945-1830
Fr: 800-423-4992
URL: http://www.sma.org/smj/index.cfm

Monthly. $35.00/year for individuals, resident and fellow SMA members; $169.00/year for nonmembers, individual; $331.00/year for nonmembers, institutions; $205.00/year for nonmembers, international; $371.00/year for nonmembers, institutions, international. Multispecialty medical journal.

★9770★ Stethoscope

National Association of Residents and Interns
Hillsboro Executive Ctr. N.
350 Fairway Dr., Ste. 200
Deerfield Beach, FL 33441-1834
Ph: (954)571-1877   Fax: (954)571-8582
Fr: 800-221-2168
E-mail: membership@assnservices.com
URL: http://www.nari-assn.com/

Description: Semiannual. Provides current information on the financial and practice management aspects of medical and dental practices. Focuses on the economic, tax, investment, and career concerns of the young doctor. Recurring features include Association news and news of research.

★9771★ Surgical Rounds

Pharmacy Times
103 College Rd. E
Princeton, NJ 08540-6612
Ph: (609)524-9560   Fax: (609)524-9699
URL: http://www.surgicalroundsonline.com/

Monthly. Journal featuring clinical articles of interest to office-based and hospital-based surgeons, including residents, full-time staff, and surgical faculty.

★9772★ USA Body Psychotherapy Journal

United States Association for Body Psychotherapy
7831 Woodmont Ave.
Bethesda, MD 20814
URL: http://www.usabp.org/displaycommon.cfm?an=4

Semiannual. Academic journal that seeks to support, promote and stimulate the exchange of ideas, scholarship and research within the field of body psychotherapy as well as an interdisciplinary exchange with related fields of clinical practice and inquiry.

★9773★ Year Book of Critical Care Medicine

Elsevier Science Inc.
360 Park Ave. S
New York, NY 10010
Ph: (212)989-5800   Fax: (212)633-3990
URL: http://www.elsevier.com

$180.00/year for institutions, U.S. $191.00/year for institutions, other countries; $121.00/year for individuals, U.S. $134.00/year for individuals, other countries; $59.00/year for students, U.S. $71.00/year for students, other countries. Journal focused on treatment of severe sepsis and septic shock, echocardiography in the evaluation of hemodynamically unstable patients & mechanical ventilation of acute respiratory distress syndrome.

PLACEMENT AND JOB REFERRAL SERVICES

★9774★ American Academy of Neurology (AAN)

1080 Montreal Ave.
St. Paul, MN 55116
Ph: (651)695-2717   Fax: (651)695-2791
Fr: 800-879-1960
E-mail: memberservices@aan.com
URL: http://www.aan.com

Description: Professional society of medical doctors specializing in brain and nervous system diseases. Maintains placement service. Sponsors research and educational programs. Compiles statistics. Publishes scientific journal.

★9775★ American Association of Certified Orthoptists (AACO)

Vanderbilt University
104 MAB TN Lions EYE Center
Nashville, TN 37212
Ph: (615)936-2250
E-mail: ron.biernacki@vanderbilt.edu
URL: http://www.orthoptics.org

Members: Orthoptists certified by the American Orthoptic Council, after completing a minimum of 24 months' special training, to treat defects in binocular function. **Activities:** Assists in postgraduate instruction courses; conducts programs and courses at international, national, and regional meetings; helps individual orthoptists with special or unusual problem cases; trains new orthoptists. Operates a placement listing.

★9776★ American Association for Geriatric Psychiatry (AAGP)

7910 Woodmont Ave., Ste. 1050
Bethesda, MD 20814-3069
Ph: (301)654-7850   Fax: (301)654-4137
E-mail: main@aagponline.org
URL: http://www.aagpgpa.org

Description: Psychiatrists interested in promoting better mental health care for the elderly. Maintains placement service and speakers' bureau.

★9777★ American College of Chest Physicians (ACCP)

3300 Dundee Rd.
Northbrook, IL 60062
Ph: (847)498-1400   Fax: (847)498-5460
Fr: 800-343-ACCP
E-mail: accp@chestnet.org
URL: http://www.chestnet.org

Description: Serves as a professional society of physicians and surgeons specializing in diseases of the chest (heart and lungs). Promotes undergraduate and postgraduate medical education and research in the field. Sponsors forums. Maintains placement service; conducts educational programs.

★9778★ American College Health Association (ACHA)

PO Box 28937
Baltimore, MD 21240-8937
Ph: (410)859-1500   Fax: (410)859-1510
E-mail: contact@acha.org
URL: http://www.acha.org

Purpose: Provides an organization in which institutions of higher education and interested individuals may work together to promote health in its broadest aspects for students and all other members of the college community. **Activities:** Offers continuing education programs for health professionals. Maintains placement listings for physicians and other personnel seeking positions in college health. Compiles statistics. Conducts seminars and training programs.

★9779★ American College of Occupational and Environmental Medicine (ACOEM)

25 NW Point Blvd., Ste. 700
Elk Grove Village, IL 60007-1030
Ph: (847)818-1800   Fax: (847)818-9266
E-mail: acoeminfo@acoem.org
URL: http://www.acoem.org

Description: Represents physicians specializing in occupational and environmental medicine. Promotes maintenance and improvement of the health of workers; works to increase awareness of occupational medicine as a medical specialty. Sponsors educational programs; maintains placement service.

★9780★ American College of Osteopathic Internists (ACOI)

3 Bethesda Metro Ctr., Ste. 508
Bethesda, MD 20814
Ph: (301)656-8877   Fax: (301)656-7133
Fr: 800-327-5183
E-mail: bjd@acoi.org
URL: http://www.acoi.org

Description: Osteopathic doctors who limit their practice to internal medicine and various subspecialties and who intend, through postdoctoral education, to qualify as certified specialists in the field. Aims to provide educational programs and to improve educational standards in the field of osteopathic internal medicine. Sponsors competitions. Compiles statistics; offers placement service.

★9781★ American College of Osteopathic Surgeons (ACOS)

123 N Henry St.
Alexandria, VA 22314-2903
Ph: (703)684-0416   Fax: (703)684-3280
Fr: 800-888-1312
E-mail: info@facos.org
URL: http://www.facos.org

Members: Professional society of osteopathic physicians specializing in surgery and surgical specialties. **Purpose:** Maintains placement service; conducts seminars in continuing surgical education.

★9782★ American College of Physician Executives (ACPE)

4890 W Kennedy Blvd., Ste. 200
Tampa, FL 33609
Ph: (813)287-2000   Fax: (813)287-8993
Fr: 800-562-8088
E-mail: acpe@acpe.org
URL: http://www.acpe.org

Description: Physicians whose primary professional responsibility is in management. Provides for continuing education and certification of the physician executive and the advancement and recognition of the physician executive and the profession. Offers specialized career planning, counseling, recruitment and placement services, and research and information data on physician executives.

★9783★ American Gastroenterological Association (AGA)

4930 Del Ray Ave.
Bethesda, MD 20814
Ph: (301)654-2055   Fax: (301)654-5920
E-mail: member@gastro.org
URL: http://www.gastro.org

Description: Physicians of internal medicine certified in gastroenterology; radiologists, pathologists, surgeons, and physiologists with special interest and competency in gastroenterology. Studies normal and abnormal conditions of the digestive organs and problems connected with their metabolism; conducts scientific research; offers placement services.

★9784★ American Health Quality Association (AHQA)

1155 21st St. NW
Washington, DC 20036
Ph: (202)331-5790   Fax: (202)331-9334
E-mail: info@ahqa.org
URL: http://www.ahqa.org

Description: Institutions and individuals. Develops communication programs for physicians, institutions, and others interested in peer review organizations (PROs). Provides a national forum for the interchange of ideas, techniques, and information relating to medical quality assessment. Conducts courses and on-site educational programs to increase physicians' involvement and leadership in PROs, improve practice patterns through review, understand and use PRO data to improve service delivery, pre-admission review, profile analysis, retrospective review, and organizational development. Sponsors placement service; maintains a speakers' bureau and a library.

★9785★ American Medical Association (AMA)

515 N State St.
Chicago, IL 60610
Ph: (312)464-5000   Fax: (312)464-4184
Fr: 800-621-8335
E-mail: msc@ama-assn.org
URL: http://www.ama-assn.org

Description: Represents county medical societies and physicians. Disseminates scientific information to members and the public. Informs members on significant medical and health legislation on state and national levels and represents the profession before Congress and governmental agencies. Cooperates in setting standards for medical schools, hospitals, residency programs, and continuing medical education courses. Offers physician placement service and counseling on practice management problems. Operates library that lends material and provides specific medical information to physicians. Maintains Ad-hoc committees for such topics as health care planning and principles of medical ethics.

★9786★ American Public Health Association (APHA)

800 I St. NW
Washington, DC 20001
Ph: (202)777-2742   Fax: (202)777-2534
E-mail: comments@apha.org
URL: http://www.apha.org

Members: Professional organization of physicians, nurses, educators, academicians, environmentalists, epidemiologists, new professionals, social workers, health administrators, optometrists, podiatrists, pharmacists, dentists, nutritionists, health planners, other community and mental health specialists, and interested consumers. **Purpose:** Seeks to protect and promote personal, mental, and environmental health. **Activities:** Services include: promulgation of standards; establishment of uniform practices and procedures; development of the etiology of communicable diseases; research in public health; exploration of medical care programs

and their relationships to public health. Sponsors job placement service.

★9787★ American Society of Anesthesiologists (ASA)

520 N Northwest Hwy.
Park Ridge, IL 60068-2573
Ph: (847)825-5586   Fax: (847)825-1692
E-mail: mail@asahq.org
URL: http://www.asahq.org

Members: Professional society of physicians specializing or interested in anesthesiology. **Purpose:** Seeks "to develop and further the specialty of anesthesiology for the general elevation of the standards of medical practice". Encourages education, research, and scientific progress in anesthesiology. **Activities:** Conducts refresher courses and other postgraduate educational activities. Maintains placement service.

★9788★ American Society of Colon and Rectal Surgeons (ASCRS)

85 W Algonquin Rd., Ste. 550
Arlington Heights, IL 60005
Ph: (847)290-9184   Fax: (847)290-9203
E-mail: ascrs@fascrs.org
URL: http://www.fascrs.org

Description: Professional society of surgeons specializing in the diagnosis and treatment of diseases of the colon, rectum, and anus. Offers placement service; conducts research programs.

★9789★ American Society of Extra-Corporeal Technology (AmSECT)

2209 Dickens Rd.
Richmond, VA 23230-2005
Ph: (804)565-6363   Fax: (804)282-0090
E-mail: stewart@amsect.org
URL: http://www.amsect.org

Description: Perfusionists, technologists, doctors, nurses, and others actively employed and using the applied skills relating to the practice of extracorporeal technology (involving heart-lung machines); student members. Disseminates information necessary to the proper practice of the technology. Conducts programs in continuing education and professional-public liaison and hands-on workshops. Maintains placement service.

★9790★ American Society for Histocompatibility and Immunogenetics (ASHI)

15000 Commerce Pkwy., Ste. C
Mount Laurel, NJ 08054
Ph: (856)638-0428   Fax: (856)439-0525
E-mail: info@ashi-hla.org
URL: http://www.ashi-hla.org

Members: Scientists, physicians, and technologists involved in research and clinical activities related to histocompatibility testing (a state of mutual tolerance that allows some tissues to be grafted effectively to others). **Activities:** Conducts proficiency testing and educational programs. Maintains liaison with regulatory agencies; offers placement services and laboratory accreditation. Has cosponsored development of histocompatibility specialist and laboratory certification program.

★9791★ **American Society of Nephrology (ASN)**

1725 I St. NW, Ste. 510
Washington, DC 20006
Ph: (202)659-0599   Fax: (202)659-0709
E-mail: email@asn-online.org
URL: http://www.asn-online.org

Members: Nephrologists united for the exchange of scientific information. **Purpose:** Seeks to contribute to the education of members and to improve the quality of patient care. **Activities:** Conducts educational courses. Maintains placement service.

★9792★ **Association for Academic Surgery (AAS)**

11300 W Olympic Blvd., Ste. 600
Los Angeles, CA 90064
Ph: (310)437-1606   Fax: (310)437-0585
E-mail: aaron@aasurg.org
URL: http://www.aasurg.org

Description: Active and senior surgeons with backgrounds in all surgical specialties in academic surgical centers at chief resident level or above. Encourages young surgeons to pursue careers in academic surgery; supports them in establishing themselves as investigators and educators by providing a forum in which senior surgical residents and junior faculty members may present papers on subjects of clinical or laboratory investigations; promotes interchange of ideas between senior surgical residents, junior faculty, and established academic surgeons; facilitates communication among academic surgeons in all surgical fields. Maintains placement service.

★9793★ **Association for the Advancement of Medical Instrumentation (AAMI)**

1110 N Glebe Rd., Ste. 220
Arlington, VA 22201-4795
Ph: (703)525-4890   Fax: (703)276-0793
Fr: 800-332-2264
E-mail: membership@aami.org
URL: http://www.aami.org

Description: Clinical engineers, biomedical equipment technicians, physicians, hospital administrators, consultants, engineers, manufacturers of medical devices, nurses, researchers and others interested in medical instrumentation. Works to improve the quality of medical care through the application, development, and management of technology. Maintains placement service. Offers certification programs for biomedical equipment technicians and clinical engineers. Produces numerous standards and recommended practices on medical devices and procedures. Offers educational programs.

★9794★ **Association for Research in Vision and Ophthalmology (ARVO)**

12300 Twinbrook Pkwy., Ste. 250
Rockville, MD 20852-1606
Ph: (240)221-2900   Fax: (240)221-0370
E-mail: arvo@arvo.org
URL: http://www.arvo.org

Members: Professional society of researchers in vision and ophthalmology. **Purpose:** Encourages ophthalmic research in the field of blinding eye disease. **Activities:** Operates placement service. Maintains 13 scientific sections.

★9795★ **Chinese American Medical Society (CAMS)**

281 Edgewood Ave.
Teaneck, NJ 07666
Ph: (201)833-1506   Fax: (201)833-8252
E-mail: hw5@columbia.edu
URL: http://www.camsociety.org

Members: Physicians of Chinese origin residing in the U.S. and Canada. **Purpose:** Seeks to advance medical knowledge, scientific research, and interchange of information among members and to promote the health status of Chinese Americans. **Activities:** Conducts educational meetings; supports research. Maintains placement service. Sponsors limited charitable program.

★9796★ **Clinical Ligand Assay Society (CLAS)**

3139 S Wayne Rd.
Wayne, MI 48184
Ph: (734)722-6290   Fax: (734)722-7006
E-mail: clas@clas.org
URL: http://www.clas.org

Description: Seeks to establish and promote high standards in the science and application of ligand assay technology by encouraging research, education practitioners, and fostering communication and cooperation among individuals in laboratories in medicine, academia, and industry. Sponsors job placement service.

★9797★ **College of American Pathologists (CAP)**

325 Waukegan Rd.
Northfield, IL 60093-2750
Ph: (847)832-7000   Fax: (847)832-8000
Fr: 800-323-4040
URL: http://www.cap.org

Description: Physicians practicing the specialty of pathology (diagnosis, treatment, observation, and understanding of the progress of disease or medical condition) obtained by morphologic, microscopic, chemical, microbiologic, serologic, or any other type of laboratory examination made on the patient. Fosters improvement of education, research, and medical laboratory service to physicians, hospitals, and the public. Provides job placement information for members. Conducts laboratory accreditation program and laboratory proficiency testing surveys. Maintains spokespersons network; provides free health information to the pub-

lic; compiles statistics; sponsors educational programs.

★9798★ **Congress of Neurological Surgeons (CNS)**

10 N Martingale Rd., Ste. 190
Schaumburg, IL 60173
Ph: (847)240-2500   Fax: (847)240-0804
Fr: 877-517-1267
E-mail: info@1cns.org
URL: http://www.neurosurgeon.org

Description: Professional society of neurological surgeons in the United States and 55 other countries who meet annually to express their views on various aspects of the principles and practice of neurological surgery; to exchange technical information and experience; to join study of the developments in scientific fields allied to neurological surgery. Promotes interest of neurological surgeons in their practice; provides placement service; honors a living leader in the field of neurological surgery annually.

★9799★ **Endocrine Society**

8401 Connecticut Ave., Ste. 900
Chevy Chase, MD 20815-5817
Ph: (301)941-0200   Fax: (301)941-0259
Fr: 888-363-6274
E-mail: societyservices@endo-society.org
URL: http://www.endo-society.org

Purpose: Promotes excellence in research, education, and clinical practice in endocrinology and related disciplines. **Activities:** Maintains placement service.

★9800★ **Islamic Medical Association of North America (IMANA)**

101 W 22nd St., Ste. 106
Lombard, IL 60148
Ph: (630)932-0000   Fax: (630)932-0005
E-mail: hq@imana.org
URL: http://www.imana.org

Members: Muslim physicians and allied health professionals. **Purpose:** Unites Muslim physicians and allied health professionals in the U.S. and Canada for the improvement of professional and social contact; provides assistance to Muslim communities worldwide. Charitable programs include: donation of books, journals, and educational and research materials to medical institutions; donation of medical supplies and equipment to charity medical institutions in Muslim countries. **Activities:** Maintains speakers' bureau to present Islamic viewpoints on medical topics; sponsors placement service; offers assistance in orientation.

★9801★ **National Association of Managed Care Physicians (NAMCP)**

4435 Waterfront Dr., Ste. 101
PO Box 4765
Glen Allen, VA 23058
Ph: (804)527-1905   Fax: (804)747-5316
Fr: 800-722-0376
E-mail: info@namcp.com
URL: http://www.namcp.com

Members: Licensed physicians and allied health professionals working in managed health care programs; medical residents and students interested in managed health care; corporations or agencies providing services or goods to the industry; interested others. **Purpose:** Enhances the ability of practicing physicians to proactively participate within the managed health care arena through research, communication, and education. Provides a forum for members to communicate their concerns about the changing health care environment, integrate into managed health care delivery systems, and assure continuous improvement in the quality of health care services provided. Develops practice criteria, quality assurance measures, and appropriate utilization management criteria. **Activities:** Offers educational programs; maintains speakers' bureau and placement services; conducts research programs; develops informational clearinghouse.

★9802★ Ruth Jackson Orthopaedic Society (RJOS)

6300 N River Rd., Ste. 727
Rosemont, IL 60018-4226
Ph: (847)698-1626   Fax: (847)823-4921
E-mail: rjos@aaos.org
URL: http://www.rjos.org

Members: Women orthopaedic surgeons, residents, fellows, and medical students. **Purpose:** Seeks to advance the science of orthopaedic surgery and to provide support for women orthopaedic surgeons. Named for practicing orthopaedic surgeon Dr. Ruth Jackson (1902-94), the first woman certified by the American Board of Orthopaedic Surgery and the first female member of the American Academy of Orthopaedic Surgeons. **Activities:** Conducts educational programs; operates placement service and speakers' bureau, holds biennial meeting, sponsors mentoring program, offers traveling fellowship and resident research award.

★9803★ Ukrainian Medical Association of North America (UMANA)

2247 W Chicago Ave.
Chicago, IL 60622
Fax: (773)278-6962   Fr: 888-RXU-MANA
E-mail: umana@umana.org
URL: http://www.umana.org

Description: Physicians, surgeons, dentists, and persons in related professions who are of Ukrainian descent. Provides assistance to members; sponsors lectures. Maintains placement service, museum, biographical and medical archives.

EMPLOYER DIRECTORIES AND NETWORKING LISTS

★9804★ AHA Guide to the Health Care Field

American Hospital Association
1 N Franklin
Chicago, IL 60606
Ph: (312)422-2050   Fax: (312)422-4700
Fr: 800-424-4301

Annual, August. Covers hospitals, networks, multi-health care systems, freestanding ambulatory surgery centers, psychiatric facilities, long-term care facilities, substance abuse programs, and other health-related organizations. Entries include: For hospitals–Facility name, address, phone, administrator's name, number of beds, facilities and services, number of employees, expenses, other statistics. For other organizations–Name, address, phone, fax, name and title of contact. Arrangement: Geographical. Indexes: Hospital name.

★9805★ American Association of Public Health Physicians-Membership Roster

American Association of Public Health Physicians
1300 W.Belmont Ave.
Chicago, IL 60657-3200
URL: http://www.aaphp.org/

Annual. Covers 200 physicians. Entries include: Name, address, professional affiliation. Arrangement: Available in alphabetical or geographical arrangement.

★9806★ American Group Psychotherapy Association-Membership Directory

American Group Psychotherapy Association Inc.
25 E 21st St., 6th Fl.
New York, NY 10010
Ph: (212)477-2677   Fax: (212)979-6627
Fr: 877-668-2472
URL: http://www.agpa.org

Covers 4,500 physicians, psychologists, clinical social workers, psychiatric nurses, and other mental health professionals interested in treatment of emotional problems by group methods. Entries include: Name, office or home address, highest degree held, office or home phone number. Arrangement: Alphabetical. Indexes: Geographical.

★9807★ American Holistic Medical Association-National Referral Directory

American Holistic Medical Association
12101 Menaul Blvd., NE, Ste. C
Albuquerque, MN 87112-2460
Ph: (505)292-7788   Fax: (505)293-7582
URL: http://www.holisticmedicine.org

Annual, Spring. $25.00 for individuals. Covers medical doctors, doctors of osteopathy, and health practitioners who are certified,

registered, or licensed by their state and are interested in or practice holistic medicine. Entries include: Name, address, specialty, description of practice. Arrangement: Geographical. Indexes: Geographical.

★9808★ American Osteopathic Association-Yearbook and Directory of Osteopathic Physicians

American Osteopathic Association
142 East Ontario St.
Chicago, IL 60611
Ph: (312)202-8000   Fax: (312)202-8200
Fr: 800-621-1773
URL: http://www.aoa-net.org

Annual; last print edition June 2000. Covers member and nonmember osteopathic physicians; includes associate members. Entries include: Name, office or home address, specialty, type of practice, age, date and institution granting degree and board certifications. Arrangement: Alphabetical. Indexes: Geographical; certifying board; field.

★9809★ Directory of Child Life Programs

Child Life Council Inc.
11820 Parklawn Dr., Ste. 240
Rockville, MD 20852-2529
Ph: (301)881-7090   Fax: (301)881-7092
URL: http://www.childlife.org/

Biennial; latest edition 14th, 2006. Covers over 400 child life programs. Entries include: Facility name, address, phone, name of child life department and director, reporting structure, staff statistics, educational requirements for employment, and internship or educational opportunities. Arrangement: Geographical. Indexes: Speciality areas, internship sessions, program size, fellowships.

★9810★ Directory of Hospital Personnel

Grey House Publishing
185 Millerton Rd.
PO Box 860
Millerton, NY 12546
Ph: (518)789-8700   Fax: (518)789-0556
Fr: 800-562-2139
URL: http://www.greyhouse.com/hospital_personnel.htm

Annual. $325.00 for print product; $545.00 for online database subscription; $650.00 for online database subscription and print product combined. Covers 200,000 executives at 7,000 U.S. hospitals. Entries include: Name of hospital, address, phone; number of beds; type and JCAHO status of hospital; names and titles of key department heads and staff; medical and nursing school affiliations; number of residents, interns, and nursing students. Arrangement: Geographical. Indexes: Hospital name, personnel, hospital size.

★9811★ Directory of Physicians in the United States

American Medical Association
515 N State St.
Chicago, IL 60610
Fr: 800-621-8335

URL: http://www.directoryofphysicians.org

Biennial, November of even years; latest edition 39th. $750.00 for individuals. Covers, in four volume set, more than 875,000 physicians in the United States, Puerto Rico, Virgin Islands, and certain Pacific Islands. Entries include: Name, address, year licensed in mailing address state, medical school, type of practice, primary and secondary specialties, board certifications, and Physician's Recognition award status. Both print and CD-ROM versions are available. Arrangement: Geographical by city; federal service separate section. Indexes: Alphabetical (constitutes Volume 1 of set); geographical.

★9812★ **Guide to Careers in the Health Professions**

The Princeton Review
2315 Broadway
New York, NY 10024
Ph: (212)874-8282   Fax: (212)874-0775
Fr: 800-733-3000
URL: http://www.princetonreview.com/

Published January, 2001. $24.95 for individuals. Presents advice and information for those searching for satisfying careers in the health professions. Publication includes: Directory of schools and academic programs. Entries include: Name, address, phone, tuition, program details, employment profiles.

★9813★ **Health & Wellness Resource Center**

Gale, Cengage Learning
27500 Drake Rd.
Farmington Hills, MI 48331-3535
Ph: (248)699-4253   Fax: (248)699-8065
Fr: 800-877-4253
URL: http://www.galegroup.com

Database includes: Located in the Health Organization Directory component-listings of agencies, schools and organizations; journals, newsletters, and publishers websites; hospitals, health care facilities, programs and special care. Data is derived from the Medical and Health Information Directory. Entries include: Contact information. Principal content of database is a medical encyclopedia, drug and herb locator, health assessment tools, medical dictionary, links to other sites, and health news. Indexes: Searchable by key term along with city and state.

★9814★ **Health & Wellness Resource Center-Alternative Health Module**

Gale, Cengage Learning
27500 Drake Rd.
Farmington Hills, MI 48331-3535
Ph: (248)699-4253   Fax: (248)699-8065
Fr: 800-877-4253
URL: http://www.galegroup.com

Database includes: Focus upon alternative medicine topics. This information is located in the Health Organization Directory component-listings of agencies, schools and organizations; journals, newsletters, and publishers websites; hospitals, health care facilities, programs and special care. Data is derived

from the Medical and Health Information Directory. Entries include: Contact information. Principal content of database consists of a medical encyclopedia, drug and herb locator, health assessment tools, medical dictionary, links to other sites, and health news and includes references to homeopathic treatments, yoga, massage therapy, etc.

★9815★ **HMO/PPO Directory**

Grey House Publishing
185 Millerton Rd.
PO Box 860
Millerton, NY 12546
Ph: (518)789-8700   Fax: (518)789-0556
Fr: 800-562-2139
URL: http://www.greyhouse.com/hmo_ppo.htm

Annual; latest edition November 2006. $325.00 for individuals, print product; $495.00 for individuals, online database subscription; $600.00 for individuals, print product and online database subscription,combined. Covers over 600 health maintenance organizations (HMOs) and more than 1,000 preferred provider organizations (PPOs). Entries include: Name of organization, address, phone, number of members, names of officers, employer references, geographical area served, parent company, average fees and co-payments, financial data, and cost control procedures. Arrangement: Geographical. Indexes: Organization name, personnel name, HMOs and PPOs by state, and number of members enrolled.

★9816★ **Hospital Blue Book**

Billian Publishing Inc./Transworld
  Publishing Inc.
2100 Powers Ferry Rd. SE
Atlanta, GA 30339
Ph: (770)955-5656   Fax: (770)952-0669
Fr: 800-533-8484
E-mail: blu-book@billian.com

2005. $300.00 for individuals. Covers more than 6,687 hospitals; some listings also appear in a separate southern edition of this publication. Entries include: Name of hospital, accreditation, mailing address, phone, fax, number of beds, type of facility (nonprofit, general, state, etc.); list of administrative personnel and chiefs of medical services, with specific titles. Arrangement: Geographical.

★9817★ **The JobBank Guide to Health Care Companies**

Adams Media Corp.
57 Littlefield St.
Avon, MA 02322
Ph: (508)427-7100   Fax: (508)427-6790
Fr: 800-872-5627
URL: http://www.amazon.com/Jobbank-Guide-Health-Care-Companies/dp

Biennial. Covers jobs nationwide in health care companies. Entries include: Firm or organization name, address, phone, name and title of contact; description of organization, headquarters location, typical titles for entry- and middle-level positions, education-

al backgrounds desired, fringe benefits fered, stock exchange listing, training grams, internships, parent company, nur of employees, revenues, e-mail and addresses, projected number of hires dexes: Alphabetical.

★9818★ **Journal of the American Medical Association-Physician Ser Opportunities Overseas Section**

American Medical Association
515 N State St.
Chicago, IL 60610
Fr: 800-621-8335
URL: http://jama.ama-assn.org/content/tract/289/1/34

Irregular; latest edition August 2002. P cation includes: List of more than 60 org zations that provide assignments overs for physicians from the United States. tries include: Organization name, addr phone, contact person, countries ser and medical specialties sought. Arrar ment: Alphabetical.

★9819★ **Medical and Health Information Directory**

Gale, Cengage Learning
27500 Drake Rd.
Farmington Hills, MI 48331-3535
Ph: (248)699-4253   Fax: (248)699-8
Fr: 800-877-4253
E-mail: businessproducts@gale.com
URL: http://www.gale.com

Annual; latest edition 20th, July 20 $375.00/volume. Covers in Volume 1, m than 26,500 medical and health orien associations, organizations, institutions, government agencies, including health m tenance organizations (HMOs), prefer provider organizations (PPOs), insura companies, pharmaceutical companies, search centers, and medical and al health schools. In Volume 2, over 12, medical book publishers; medical peri cals, directories, audiovisual producers services, medical libraries and informa centers, electronic resources, and health lated internet search engines. In Volume more than 35,500 clinics, treatment cente care programs, and counseling/diagno services for 34 subject areas. Entries clude: Institution, service, or firm nai address, phone, fax, email and URL; m include names of key personnel and, wl pertinent, descriptive annotations. Volum was formerly listed separately as Hea Services Directory. Arrangement: Classifi by organization activity, service, etc. dexes: Each volume has a complete alp betical name and keyword index.

★9820★ **Medical School Admission from High School**

The Graduate Group
PO Box 370351
West Hartford, CT 06137-0351
Ph: (860)233-2330   Fax: (860)233-23
URL: http://www.graduategroup.com/mec cal.htm

$30.00 for individuals. Reviews early-adm

sion medical programs and covers common issues, including application processes, grade point average, class rank and standardized tests. Publication includes: Program profiles and contacts for more than 75 schools.

★9821★ **The Official ABMS Directory of Board Certified Medical Specialists**

Marquis Who's Who L.L.C.
890 Mountain Ave., Ste. 300
New Providence, NJ 07974-1218
Ph: (908)673-1001   Fax: (908)673-1189
Fr: 800-473-7020
URL: http://www.marquiswhoswho.com/

Annual, October. $699.00 for individuals. Covers more than 565,000 board-certified specialists in 25 areas of medical practice from allergy to urology. Prior to 1997, all 25 areas were covered in separate publications. Entries include: Name, certifications, office address, phone, date and place of birth, education, career data, date certified, type of practice, professional memberships. Arrangement: Classified by specialty, then geographical. Indexes: Alphabetical within each speciality, and one alphabetical index of all physicians listed in the directory.

★9822★ **Physicians and Dentists Database**

Firstmark Inc.
25 Vintinner Rd.
PO Box 1270
Campton, NH 03223-1270
Ph: (603)726-4800   Fax: (603)726-4840
Fr: 800-729-2600
URL: http://www.firstmark.com

Updated continuously; printed on request. Database covers: Over 500,000 physicians and 160,000 dentists nationwide. Entries include: Individual name, address, phone, medical specialty, whether in single or group practice.

★9823★ **Principles and Practice of Clinical Research**

Academic Press
525 B St., Ste. 1900
San Diego, CA 92101-4495
Ph: (619)231-0926   Fax: (619)699-6422
Fr: 800-545-2522
URL: http://www.academicpress.com

Latest edition 2nd, April 2007. $99.95 for individuals. Publication includes: List of Web sites for further information about review processes and process changes for grants. Principal content of publication is a comprehensive review of clinical research including history, ethics, regulations, biostatistics, protocol development, and funding. Indexes: Alphabetical.

★9824★ **Student Resource Center-Health Module**

Gale, Cengage Learning
27500 Drake Rd.
Farmington Hills, MI 48331-3535
Ph: (248)699-4253   Fax: (248)699-8065
Fr: 800-877-4253

URL: http://www.galegroup.com

Database includes: Listing of individuals who have "made significant contributions to the world of health. " Entries include: Biographical data. Principal content of database is approximately 1,200 essays on all aspects of major health issues along with events, definitions, pamphlets and links to reviewed websites.

★9825★ **Transplantation Sourcebook**

Omnigraphics Inc.
615 Griswold St.
PO Box 31-1640
Detroit, MI 48226
Ph: (313)961-1340   Fax: (313)961-1383
Fr: 800-234-1340
URL: http://www.omnigraphics.com

Published 2002. $78.00 for individuals. Publication includes: List of transplant organizations, donor centers, and major transplant hospitals in the United States. Principal content of publication is a detailed discussion of the issues surrounding transplantation. Indexes: Alphabetical.

HANDBOOKS AND MANUALS

★9826★ **America's Top Medical, Education, and Human Service Jobs, Fifth Edition**

JIST Publishing
875 Montreal Way
St. Paul, MN 55102
Fax: 800-547-8329   Fr: 800-648-5478
E-mail: info@jist.com
URL: http://www.jist.com

Michael Farr. 2001. $9.95. 352 pages. Targeted reference organized into three sections that offer comprehensive job descriptions, job search advice, and current trends in jobs and industries.

★9827★ **Barron's Guide to Medical and Dental Schools**

Barron's Educational Series, Inc.
250 Wireless Blvd.
Hauppauge, NY 11788-3917
Ph: (631)434-3311   Fax: (631)434-3723
Fr: 800-645-3476
E-mail: fbrown@barronseduc.com
URL: http://barronseduc.com

Saul Wischnitzer and Edith Wischnitzer. Eleventh edition, 2000. $18.99. 625 pages. Updated with the latest facts and figures, this school directory and guidance manual presents profiles of all accredited medical, dental, and osteopathic schools in the United States and Canada.

★9828★ **Cardiac Nuclear Medicine**

McGraw-Hill Professional
PO Box 182604
Columbus, OH 43272
Fax: (614)759-3749   Fr: 877-883-5524

E-mail: customer.service@mcgraw-hill.com
URL: http://www.mcgraw-hill.com

Myron C. Gerson, editor. Third edition, 1996. $169.00. 830 pages.

★9829★ **Career Guide in Pathology**

A S C P Press
33 W. Monroe, Ste. 1600
Chicago, IL 60603
Ph: (312)541-4999   Fax: (312)541-4998
Fr: 800-267-2727
E-mail: info@ascp.org
URL: http://www.ascp.org

Ellis S. Benson, Barbara F. Atkinson, and Martin Flax. $20.00. 1999. 102 pages

★9830★ **Career Opportunities in Health Care (Career Opportunities)**

Facts On File Inc.
132 W. 31st St., 17th Fl.
New York, NY 10001-2006
Ph: (212)967-8800   Fax: 800-678-3633
Fr: 800-322-8755
E-mail: custserv@factsonfile.com
URL: http://www.factsonfile.com

Shelly Field. Arthur E. Weintraub. 2002. Reprint. $49.50. 243 pages. Part of the Career Opportunities Series.

★9831★ **Careers in Health Care**

The McGraw-Hill Companies
PO Box 182604
Columbus, OH 43272
Fax: (614)759-3749   Fr: 877-883-5524
E-mail: customer.service@mcgraw-hill.com
URL: http://www.mcgraw-hill.com

Barbara M. Swanson. Fifth edition, 2005. $15.95 (paper). 192 pages. Describes job duties, work settings, salaries, licensing and certification requirements, educational preparation, and future outlook. Gives ideas on how to secure a job.

★9832★ **Careers in Medicine**

The McGraw-Hill Companies
PO Box 182604
Columbus, OH 43272
Fax: (614)759-3749   Fr: 877-883-5524
E-mail: customer.service@mcgraw-hill.com
URL: http://www.mcgraw-hill.com

Terence J. Sacks. Third edition, 2006. $15.95 (paper). 192 pages. Examines the many paths open to M.D.s, D.O.s, and M.D./Ph.D.s, including clinical private or group practice, hospitals, public health organizations, the armed forces, emergency rooms, research institutions, medical schools, pharmaceutical companies and private industry, and research/advocacy groups like the World Health Organization. A special chapter on osteopathy and chiropractic explores this branch of medicine.

★9833★ Careers for Night Owls and Other Insomniacs

The McGraw-Hill Companies
PO Box 182604
Columbus, OH 43272
Fax: (614)759-3749   Fr: 877-883-5524
E-mail: customer.service@mcgraw-hill.com
URL: http://www.mcgraw-hill.com

Louise Miller. Second edition, 2002. $12.95 (paper). 160 pages.

★9834★ Evaluating and Negotiating Compensation Arrangements: Understanding the Process and Ensuring Your Future

American Medical Association
515 N. State St.
Chicago, IL 60610
Ph: (312)464-5000   Fax: (312)464-5226
Fr: 800-621-8335
URL: http://www.ama-assn.org/

American Medical Association Staff, authors. 1998. $45.00. 69 pages. Part of the Career Development Series. Concise text discussing benefits, compensation, and perquisites with a prospective employer.

★9835★ Expert Resumes for Health Care Careers

Jist Works
875 Montreal Way
St. Paul, MN 55102
Fr: 800-648-5478
E-mail: info@jist.com
URL: http://www.jist.com

Wendy S. Enelow and Louise M. Kursmark. December 2003. $16.95. 288 pages.

★9836★ Health Care Job Explosion! High Growth Health Care Careers and Job Locator

Bookhaven Press LLC
249 Field Club Cir.
McKees Rocks, PA 15136
Ph: (412)494-6926   Fax: (412)494-5749
Fr: 800-782-7424
E-mail: info@bookhavenpress.com
URL: http://www.bookhavenpress.com/

Dennis V. Damp. Third edition, 2006. 320 pages. $19.95.

★9837★ Health Careers Today

Elsevier
11830 Westline Industrial Dr.
St. Louis, MO 63146
Ph: (314)453-7010   Fax: (314)453-7095
Fr: 800-545-2522
E-mail: usbkinfo@elsevier.com
URL: http://www.elsevier.com

Gerdin, Judith. Fourth edition. 2007. $59.95. 496 pages. Covers more than 45 health careers. Discusses the roles and responsibilities of various occupations and provides a solid foundation in the skills needed for all health careers.

★9838★ How to Start a Private Practice

Yvonne Mart Fox
9454 Wilshire Blvd., Ste. 600
Beverly Hills, CA 90212
Ph: (323)934-9949   Fax: (323)935-7954
E-mail: yvonne@yvonnemartfox.com
URL: http://www.yvonnemartfox.com/home.html

Yvonne Mart Fox. 2000. $36.00 (paper). 149 pages.

★9839★ The Medical Job Interview

Blackwell Science, Incorporated
Commerce Pl.
350 Main St.
Malden, MA 02148-5018
Ph: (781)388-8200   Fax: (781)388-8210
Fr: 800-759-6102
URL: http://www.blackwellpublishing.com/

Colin Mumford. Second edition, 2005. $24.95 (paper). 76 pages.

★9840★ Opportunities in Health and Medical Careers

The McGraw-Hill Companies
PO Box 182604
Columbus, OH 43272
Fax: (614)759-3749   Fr: 877-883-5524
E-mail: customer.service@mcgraw-hill.com
URL: http://www.mcgraw-hill.com

I. Donald Snook, Jr. and Leo D'Orazio. 2004. $13.95 (paper). 157 pages. Covers the full range of medical and health occupations. Illustrated.

★9841★ Opportunities in Sports and Athletics Careers

The McGraw-Hill Companies
PO Box 182604
Columbus, OH 43272
Fax: (614)759-3749   Fr: 877-883-5524
E-mail: customer.service@mcgraw-hill.com
URL: http://www.mcgraw-hill.com

William Ray Heitzmann. 1993. 160 pages. $11.95 (paper). A guide to planning for and seeking opportunities in this growing field. Illustrated.

★9842★ Opportunities in Sports Medicine Careers

The McGraw-Hill Companies
PO Box 182604
Columbus, OH 43272
Fax: (614)759-3749   Fr: 877-883-5524
E-mail: customer.service@mcgraw-hill.com
URL: http://www.mcgraw-hill.com

William Ray Heitzmann. 1992. $11.95 (paper). 160 pages. Discusses a variety of opportunities in this field and how to pursue them. Contains bibliography and illustrations.

★9843★ Real People Working in Health Care

The McGraw-Hill Companies
PO Box 182604
Columbus, OH 43272
Fax: (614)759-3749   Fr: 877-883-5524
E-mail: customer.service@mcgraw-hill.com
URL: http://www.mcgraw-hill.com

Blythe Camenson, Jan Goldberg. 1996. $12.95 (paper). 144 pages. Interviews and profiles of working professionals capture a range of opportunities in this field.

★9844★ Resumes for Health and Medical Careers

The McGraw-Hill Companies
PO Box 182604
Columbus, OH 43272
Fax: (614)759-3749   Fr: 877-883-5524
E-mail: customer.service@mcgraw-hill.com
URL: http://www.mcgraw-hill.com

Third edition, 2003. $11.95 (paper). 160 pages.

★9845★ Resumes & Personal Statements for Health Professionals

Galen Press, Ltd.
PO Box 64400
Tucson, AZ 85728-4400
Ph: (520)577-8363   Fax: (520)529-6459
Fr: 800-442-5369
E-mail: sales@galenpress.com
URL: http://www.galenpress.com/

James W. Tysinger. Second edition, 1999. $18.95 (paper). 210 pages. Step-by-step, fool-proof instructions to guide any health professions student, graduate, or practitioner through the process of writing these documents.

★9846★ Your Career in Physical Medicine

W. B. Saunders Co.
6277 Sea Harbor Dr.
Orlando, FL 32887
Fr: 800-654-2452
URL: http://www.elsevier.com

Roberta C. Weiss. 1997. $54.95 (paper). 382 pages. Covers concepts, hands-on skills, and techniques for various health career opportunities in physical medicine.

EMPLOYMENT AGENCIES AND SEARCH FIRMS

★9847★ Alan Darling Consulting

374 Dover Rd., Ste. 18
South Newfane, VT 05351-7901
Ph: (802)348-6365   Fax: (802)348-7826
URL: http://www.alandarling.com

Executive search firm focused on the healthcare industry.

★9848★ The Bauman Group
350 Second St., Ste. 2
Los Altos, CA 94022
Ph: (650)941-0800   Fax: (650)941-1729
E-mail: info@thebaumangroup.com
URL: http://www.thebaumangroup.com

Executive search firm.

★9849★ BeechTree Partners LLC
875 N. Michigan Ave., Ste. 3100
Chicago, IL 60611
Ph: (312)794-7808
E-mail: brad@beechtreepartners.com
URL: http://www.beechtreepartners.com

Executive search firm.

★9850★ Breitner Clark & Hall Inc.
1017 Turnpike St., Ste. 22A
Canton, MA 02021
Ph: (781)828-6411   Fax: (781)828-6431
Fr: 800-331-7004
E-mail: info@breitner.com
URL: http://breitnerclarkandhall.com/site/about/default.asp

Executive search firm focused on the healthcare industry.

★9851★ Carson Kolb Healthcare Group Inc.
20301 Birch St., Ste. 101
Newport Beach, CA 92660-1754
Ph: (949)476-2988   Fax: (949)476-2155
Fr: 800-606-9439
E-mail: info@carsonkolb.com
URL: http://www.carsonkolb.com

Executive search firm focused on the healthcare industry.

★9852★ Cejka Search
4 CityPlace Dr., Ste. 300
St. Louis, MO 63141
Ph: (314)726-1603   Fax: (314)726-0026
Fr: 800-678-7858
E-mail: info@cejkasearch.com
URL: http://www.cejkasearch.com

Executive search firm for the healthcare industry. Branch in Norcross, GA.

★9853★ Drew Associates International
77 Park St.
Montclair, NJ 07042
Ph: (201)746-8877

Executive search firm focused on the healthcare industry.

★9854★ The Energists
10260 Westheimer Blvd., Ste. 300
Houston, TX 77042
Ph: (713)781-6881   Fax: (713)781-2998
E-mail: search@energists.com
URL: http://www.energists.com

Executive search firm.

★9855★ Foley Proctor Yoskowitz LLC
1 Cattano Ave.
Morristown, NJ 07960
Ph: (973)605-1000   Fax: (973)605-1020
Fr: 800-238-1123
E-mail: fpy@fpysearch.com
URL: http://www.fpysearch.com

Executive search firm for the healthcare industry. Second location in New York, NY.

★9856★ Forager
1516 Sudeenew Dr.
McHenry, IL 60051
Ph: (815)344-0006
E-mail: aaforager@comcast.net

Executive search firm. Branches in Alta Loma, CA; and Littleton, CO.

★9857★ Harper Associates
3100 NW Hwy., Ste. 240
Farmington Hills, MI 48334
Ph: (248)932-1170   Fax: (248)932-1214
E-mail: info@harperjobs.com
URL: http://www.harperjobs.com

Executive search firm and employment agency.

★9858★ Lee Calhoon & Company Inc.
1621 Birchrun Rd.
PO Box 201
Birchrunville, PA 19421
Ph: (610)469-9000   Fax: (610)469-0398
Fr: 800-469-0896
E-mail: info@leecalhoon.com
URL: http://www.leecalhoon.com

Executive search firm.

★9859★ MedSearch Staffing Services Inc.
7530 Lucerne Dr., Islander 2, Ste. 208
Plaza S 3
Middleburg Heights, OH 44130
Ph: (440)243-5300   Fax: (440)243-9117
E-mail: info@medicalreserves.com
URL: http://www.medicalreserves.com

Provides specialized recruitment of sales, marketing and management personnel. Also involved in top-level hospital management consulting and physician recruitment, interim/temporary staffing. Industries served: healthcare manufacturers and institutions.

★9860★ Merritt Hawkins & Associates
5001 Statesman Dr.
Irving, TX 75063
Ph: (469)524-1400   Fax: (469)524-1421
Fr: 800-876-0500
E-mail: info@mhagroup.com
URL: http://www.merritthawkins.com

Physician recruitment firm. Provides physician search and consulting services. Industries served: healthcare.

★9861★ O'Shea System of Employment Inc.
PO Box 2134
Aston, PA 19014
Ph: (610)364-3964   Fax: (610)364-3962
Fr: 800-220-5203
E-mail: fcomeau@osheasystem.com
URL: http://www.osheasystem.com

Offers personnel staff recruiting nationally in the following fields: Insurance, Health Care, Financial, Information Technology, Administration, Human resource, Manufacturing and Sales.

★9862★ Pate Resources Group Inc.
595 Orleans, Ste. 707
Beaumont, TX 77701
Ph: (409)833-4514   Fax: (409)833-4646
Fr: 800-669-4514
E-mail: opportunities@pateresourcesgroup.com
URL: http://www.pateresourcesgroup.com

Offers executive search and recruiting services to professionals who include physicians, healthcare administrators, engineers, accounting and financial disciplines, legal, outplacement, sales and marketing. Industries served: healthcare, petrochemicals, accounting, utility, legal, and municipalities.

★9863★ Phyllis Hawkins and Associates
7601 N. Central Ave., No. 5
Phoenix, AZ 85020
Ph: (602)263-0248   Fax: (602)678-1564
E-mail: phyllis@azlawsearch.com
URL: http://www.azlawsearch.com

Executive search firm focusing on attorney searches.

★9864★ Physician Executive Management Center
3403 W Fletcher Ave.
Tampa, FL 33618-2813
Ph: (813)963-1800   Fax: (813)264-2207
URL: http://www.physicianexecutive.com

Specialists in physician executive search for health care delivery organizations such as health systems, hospitals, group practice and managed care.

★9865★ Physicians Search, Inc.
5581 E. Stetson Ct.
Anaheim, CA 92807-4650
Ph: (714)685-1047   Fax: (714)685-1143
Fr: 800-748-6320
E-mail: info2@physicianssearch.com
URL: http://www.physicianssearch.com

Executive search firm. Affiliate office in Spokane, WA.

★9866★ P.J. Murphy & Associates Inc.
735 N Water St.
Milwaukee, WI 53202
Ph: (414)277-9777   Fax: (414)277-7626
E-mail: info@pjmurphy.com

URL: http://www.pjmurphy.com

Management consulting firm which specializes in retained executive search. Industries served: all industries, to include healthcare and physician recruiting.

★9867★ Professional Placement Associates, Inc.

287 Bowman Ave., Ste. 309
Purchase, NY 10577-2517
Ph: (914)251-1000   Fax: (914)251-1055
E-mail: careers@ppasearch.com
URL: http://www.ppasearch.com

Executive search firm specializing in the health and medical field.

★9868★ Shiloh Careers International, Inc.

7105 Peach Ct., Ste. 102
PO Box 831
Brentwood, TN 37024-0831
Ph: (615)373-3090   Fax: (615)373-3480
E-mail: maryann@shilohcareers.com
URL: http://www.shilohcareers.com

Employment agency serving the industry field.

★9869★ Team Placement Service, Inc.

1414 Prince St., Ste. 202
Alexandria, VA 22314
Ph: (703)820-8618   Fax: (703)820-3368
Fr: 800-495-6767
E-mail: 4jobs@teamplace.com
URL: http://www.teamplace.com

Full-service personnel consultants provide placement for healthcare staff, physician and dentist, private practice, and hospitals. Conduct interviews, tests, and reference checks to select the top 20% of applicants. Survey applicants' skill levels, provide backup information on each candidate, select compatible candidates for consideration, and insure the hiring process minimizes potential legal liability. Industries served: healthcare and government agencies providing medical, dental, biotech, laboratory, hospitals, and physician search.

★9870★ Weatherby Locums

6451 N Federal Hwy., Ste. 800
Fort Lauderdale, FL 33308
Ph: (954)343-3050   Fax: 800-463-2985
Fr: (866)906-1636
E-mail: jobs@weatherbylocums.com
URL: http://www.weatherbylocums.com

Executive search firm for physicians. Branch office in Fairfax, VA.

ONLINE JOB SOURCES AND SERVICES

★9871★ American Association of Anatomists Career Center

9650 Rockville Pike
Bethesda, MD 20814-3998
Ph: (301)634-7910   Fax: (301)634-7965
E-mail: exec@anatomy.org
URL: http://www.anatomy.org/resources/career_center.htm

Description: Job advertisers include academic sites in the U.S. and Canada. Job seekers may review these posted jobs through "Positions Offered" or post their own needs under "Positions Wanted." Offerings for Postdoctoral Positions also available. Contains Career Resources sections and links to online career resources.

★9872★ EmployMED: Healthcare Job Listings

URL: http://www.evalumed.com/employmed.cfm

Description: Lists practice opportunities throughout North America for all medical specialties. Contains job listings directory. Posting option is available for those who wish to advertise jobs. **Fee:** $25 per month per posting for minimum of two months.

★9873★ FCS - The 1st Choice in Psychiatric Recruitment

1711 Ashley Cir., Ste. 6
Bowling Green, KY 42104-5801
Fax: (270)782-1055   Fr: 800-783-9152
E-mail: admin@fcspsy.com
URL: http://www.fcspsy.com

Description: Physician search firm specializing in the recruitment of psychiatrists. After the applicant fills out an interest survey, a tailored search is run on the jobs database. Confidential and free.

★9874★ Health Care Job Store

395 South End Ave., Ste. 15-D
New York, NY 10280
Ph: (561)630-5201
E-mail: jobs@healthcarejobstore.com
URL: http://www.healthcarejobstore.com/

Description: Job sites include every job title in the healthcare industry, every healthcare industry and every geographic location in the U.S.

★9875★ Health Search USA

Fax: (602)650-0664   Fr: 800-899-2200
E-mail: info@healthsearchusa.com
URL: http://www.healthsearchusa.com

Description: A site for national physician recruitment. Offers job postings classified by region and salary comparison.

★9876★ MDJobsite.com

E-mail: contact@mdjobsite.com

URL: http://www.mdjobsite.com/

Description: Career search site for physicians. Physicians can search thousands of physician employment opportunities, register for email notifications of new jobs listed in their specialty and post a CV searchable by facilities and healthcare firms nationwide.

★9877★ MedExplorer

E-mail: medmaster@medexplorer.com
URL: http://www.medexplorer.com

Description: Employment postings make up one module of this general medical site. Other sections contain: Newsletter, Classifieds, and Discussion Forum.

★9878★ Medhunters.com

Fr: 800-664-0278
E-mail: info@medhunters.com
URL: http://www.medhunters.com

Description: Career search site for jobs in all health care specialties; educational resources; visa and licensing information for relocation; interesting articles; relocation tools; links to professional organizations and general resources.

★9879★ MedSource Consultants

300 Main St.
Stamford, CT 06901
Fax: (203)324-0555   Fr: 800-575-2880
E-mail: dpascale@medsourceconsultants.com
URL: http://www.medsourceconsultants.com

Description: Site houses a physician search and consulting company for psychiatrists. Consultants attempt to match job seekers to positions according to the individual's personal and professional needs. This page also aids institutions looking to recruit psychiatrists.

★9880★ Medzilla

URL: http://www.medzilla.com

Description: General medical website which matches employers and job hunters to their ideal employees and jobs through search capabilities. **Main files include:** Post Jobs, Search Resumes, Post Resumes, Search Jobs, Head Hunters, Articles, Salary Survey.

★9881★ Monster Healthcare

URL: http://healthcare.monster.com/

Description: Delivers nationwide access to healthcare recruiting. Employers can post job listings or ads. Job seekers can post and code resumes, and search over 150,000 healthcare job listings, healthcare career advice columns, career resources information, and member employer profiles and services.

TRADESHOWS

★9882★ American Academy of Pediatrics National Conference and Exhibition

American Academy of Pediatrics
141 Northwest Point Blvd., Elk Grove Village
PO Box 927
Elk Grove Village, IL 60007-1098
Ph: (847)228-5005   Fax: (847)434-8000
Fr: (847)434-4000
E-mail: commun@aap.org
URL: http://www.aap.org

Annual. **Primary Exhibits:** Prescription and over-the-counter drugs, infant formulas and baby foods, medical equipment, developmental toys, and publications.

★9883★ American Academy of Physical Medicine and Rehabilitation Annual Meeting

American Academy of Physical Medicine and Rehabilitation
330 N. Wabash Ave., Ste. 2500
Chicago, IL 60611-7617
Ph: (312)464-9700   Fax: (312)464-0227
E-mail: info@aapmr.org
URL: http://www.aapmr.org

Annual. **Primary Exhibits:** Pharmaceuticals, electrodiagnostic equipment, wheelchairs, and related equipment, supplies, and services.

★9884★ American College of Osteopathic Obstetricians and Gynecologists Annual Convention

American College of Osteopathic Obstetricians and Gynecologists
2615 Merrick St.
Fort Worth, TX 76107
Ph: (817)377-0421   Fax: (817)377-0439
Fr: 800-875-6360
E-mail: acoog@acoog.com
URL: http://www.acoog.com

Annual. **Primary Exhibits:** Pharmaceuticals and medical supplies pertaining to Ob/Gyn. Clothing, vitamins, personal toiletries (all relating to healthcare for women).

★9885★ American College of Sports Medicine Annual Meeting

American College of Sports Medicine
401 W. Michigan St.
PO Box 1440
Indianapolis, IN 46202-3233
Ph: (317)637-9200   Fax: (317)634-7817
Fr: 800-486-5643
E-mail: publicinfo@acsm.org
URL: http://www.acsm.org

Annual. **Primary Exhibits:** Exercise equipment, physiological monitoring equipment, ergometers, treadmills, scientific publications, sports medicine monitoring software, and pharmaceuticals. **Dates and Locations:** 2008 May 28-31; Indianapolis, IN; 2009 May 27-30; Seattle, WA.

★9886★ American College of Surgeons Annual Clinical Congress

American College of Surgeons
633 N. Saint Clair St.
Chicago, IL 60611-3211
Ph: (312)202-5000   Fax: (312)202-5001
Fr: 800-621-4111
E-mail: postmaster@facs.org
URL: http://www.facs.org

Annual. **Primary Exhibits:** Medical products, pritent care, practice management & educational services and products. **Dates and Locations:** 2008 Oct 12-16; San Francisco, CA.

★9887★ American Heart Association Scientific Sessions

American Heart Association
7272 Greenville Ave.
Dallas, TX 75231-4596
Ph: 800-242-8721
URL: http://www.americanheart.org

Annual. **Primary Exhibits:** Equipment, books, pharmaceuticals, exercise equipment, heart healthy food, and services relevant to cardiological research or physician practice.

★9888★ American Medical Women's Association Annual Meeting

American Medical Women's Association
211 N. Union St, Ste. 100
Alexandria, VA 22314
Ph: (703)838-0500   Fax: (703)549-3864
E-mail: info@amwa-doc.org
URL: http://www.amwa-doc.org/

Annual. **Primary Exhibits:** Medical equipment, supplies, pharmaceuticals, and services.

★9889★ American Pain Society Scientific Meeting

American Pain Society
4700 W. Lake Ave.
Glenview, IL 60025
Ph: (847)375-4715   Fax: 877-734-8758
Fr: 877-734-8758
E-mail: info@ampainsoc.org
URL: http://www.ampainsoc.org

Annual. **Primary Exhibits:** Pharmaceutical and medical instruments, medical equipment, products, supplies, services and alternative delivery systems (homecare, hospice). **Dates and Locations:** 2008 May 07-10; Tampa Bay, FL; Tampa Convention Center.

★9890★ American Society for Laser Medicine and Surgery Conference

American Society for Laser Medicine and Surgery
2404 Stewart Ave.
Wausau, WI 54401
Ph: (715)845-9283   Fax: (715)848-2493
E-mail: information@aslms.org
URL: http://www.aslms.org

Annual. **Primary Exhibits:** Laser medicine equipment, supplies, and services. **Dates and Locations:** 2008 Apr 02-06; Kissimmee, FL; Gaylord Palms Resort; 2009 Apr 01-05; Washington, DC; Gaylord National Resort.

★9891★ International College of Surgeons North American Federation Congress

International College of Surgeons - US
1516 N Lake Shore Dr.
Chicago, IL 60610-1694
Ph: (312)642-6502   Fax: (312)642-9516
Fr: 800-766-FICS
E-mail: info@imss.org
URL: http://www.icsglobal.org

Annual. **Primary Exhibits:** Medical equipment, including: pharmaceuticals, surgery books, surgical equipment, new hospital devices, and anatomy models.

★9892★ International Medical and Dental Hypnotherapy Association (IMDHA)

International Medical and Dental Hypnotherapy Association (IMDHA)
4110 Edgeland, Ste. 800
Royal Oak, MI 48073-2285
Ph: (248)549-5594   Fax: (248)549-5421
Fr: 800-257-5467
E-mail: aspencer@infinityinst.com
URL: http://www.infinityinst.com

Annual. **Primary Exhibits:** Hypnotherapy and Holistic Health.

★9893★ National Medical Association Annual Convention and Scientific Assembly

National Medical Association
1012 10th St. NW
Washington, DC 20001
Ph: (202)347-1895   Fax: (202)898-2510
URL: http://www.nmanet.org

Annual. **Primary Exhibits:** Medical equipment, supplies, and services.

OTHER SOURCES

★9894★ American Academy of Clinical Toxicology (AACT)

777 E Park Dr.
PO Box 8820
Harrisburg, PA 17105-8820
Ph: (717)558-7847   Fax: (717)558-7841
Fr: 888-633-5784
E-mail: swilson@pamedsoc.org
URL: http://www.clintox.org

Members: Physicians, veterinarians, pharmacists, nurses research scientists, and analytical chemists. **Purpose:** Objectives are to: unite medical scientists and facilitate the exchange of information; encourage the development of therapeutic methods and technology; **Activities:** Conducts professional training in poison information and emergency service personnel.

★9895★ American Academy of Craniofacial Pain (AACP)

1901 N Roselle Rd., Ste. 920
Schaumburg, IL 60195-3187
Ph: (847)885-1272   Fax: (847)885-8393
Fr: 800-322-8651
E-mail: central@aacfp.org
URL: http://www.aacfp.org

Members: Health Care Practitioners who treat head, facial, and neck pain. **Purpose:** Functions as a referral service for patients suffering from head, facial, and neck pain worldwide. Plans to establish computerized medical procedures and insurance database.

★9896★ American Academy of Dermatology (AAD)

PO Box 4014
Schaumburg, IL 60168-4014
Ph: (847)240-1280   Fax: (847)240-1859
Fr: (866)503-SKIN
E-mail: mrc@aad.org
URL: http://www.aad.org

Description: Serves as professional society of medical doctors specializing in skin diseases. Provides educational opportunities through meetings and publications. Provides support to members' practices. Promotes dermatologists as experts in treating skin, hair, and nail conditions. Maintains liaison with Congress, Federal agencies, State legislatures and State agencies.

★9897★ American Academy of Family Physicians (AAFP)

PO Box 11210
Shawnee Mission, KS 66207-1210
Ph: (913)906-6000   Fr: 800-274-2237
E-mail: fp@aafp.org
URL: http://www.aafp.org

Description: Serves as a professional society of family physicians who provide continuing comprehensive care to patients.

★9898★ American Academy of Medical Acupuncture (AAMA)

4929 Wilshire Blvd., Ste. 428
Los Angeles, CA 90010
Ph: (323)937-5514   Fax: (323)937-0959
E-mail: jdowden@prodigy.net
URL: http://www.medicalacupuncture.org

Members: Professional society of physicians and osteopaths who utilize acupuncture in their practices. **Purpose:** Provides ongoing training and information related to the Chinese practice of puncturing the body at specific points to cure disease or relieve pain. **Activities:** Offers educational and research programs.

★9899★ American Academy of Otolaryngology - Head and Neck Surgery (AAO-HNS)

1 Prince St.
Alexandria, VA 22314-3354
Ph: (703)836-4444   Fax: (703)299-1124
E-mail: webmaster@entnet.org

URL: http://www.entnet.org

Description: Professional society of medical doctors specializing in otolaryngology (diseases of the ear, nose, and throat) and head and neck surgery. Represents otolaryngology in governmental and socioeconomic areas and provides high-quality medical education for otolaryngologists. Coordinates Combined Otolaryngological Spring Meetings for ten national otolaryngological societies. Operates job information exchange service and museum.

★9900★ American Academy of Sports Physicians (AASP)

17445 Oak Creek Ct.
Encino, CA 91316
Ph: (818)501-8855   Fax: (818)501-8855
E-mail: aasp-@mindspring.com

Description: Clinical physicians engaged in the practice of sports medicine who have made contributions in research, academics, or related fields. Objectives are to educate and inform physicians whose practices comprise mainly sports medicine and to register and recognize physicians who have expertise in sports medicine. Sponsors seminars.

★9901★ American Association of Immunologists (AAI)

9650 Rockville Pike
Bethesda, MD 20814-3998
Ph: (301)634-7178   Fax: (301)634-7887
E-mail: infoaai@aai.org
URL: http://www.aai.org

Description: Represents scientists engaged in immunological research including aspects of virology, bacteriology, biochemistry, genetics, and related disciplines. Advances knowledge of immunology and related disciplines and facilitate the interchange of information among investigators in various fields. Promotes interaction between laboratory investigators and clinicians. Conducts training courses, symposia, workshop, and lectures. Compiles statistics.

★9902★ American Association of Neuropathologists (AANP)

University of Texas at San Antonio
College of Sciences
6900 N Loop 1604 W
San Antonio, TX 78249-0661
Ph: (216)368-3671   Fax: (216)368-8964
E-mail: aanp@case.edu
URL: http://www.neuropath.org

Description: Promotes neuropathology, especially the study of diverse aspects of diseases of the nervous system including changes at tissue, cellular, subcellular, and molecular levels with consideration of etiology and pathophysiology, genetics, epidemiology and clinical manifestations of such diseases.

★9903★ American Association of Oriental Medicine (AAOM)

PO Box 162340
Sacramento, CA 95816
Ph: (916)443-4770   Fax: (916)443-4766
Fr: (866)455-7999
E-mail: info@aaom.org
URL: http://www.aaom.org

Members: Professional acupuncturists and Oriental Medicine Practitioners. **Purpose:** Seeks to: elevate the standards of education and practice of acupuncture and oriental medicine; establish laws governing acupuncture; provide a forum to share information on acupuncture techniques; increase public awareness of acupuncture; support research in the field. **Activities:** Conducts educational programs; compiles statistics. Operates speakers' bureau.

★9904★ American Association of Physician Specialists (AAPS)

5550 W Executive Dr., Ste. 400
Tampa, FL 33609
Ph: (813)433-2277   Fax: (813)830-6599
E-mail: wcarbone@aapsus.org
URL: http://www.aapsga.org

Description: Represents twelve major specialties and twelve sub-specialties of medicine. Accepts qualified physicians into membership with either an allopathic (MD) or osteopathic (DO) degree. Serves as the official headquarters for 15 academies of medicine and boards of certification in the following specialties: anesthesiology, dermatology, disaster medicine, emergency medicine, family practice, internal medicine, geriatric medicine, neurology/psychiatry, obstetrics/gynecology, orthopedic surgery, plastic/reconstructive surgery, radiology, surgery.

★9905★ American College of Emergency Physicians (ACEP)

1125 Executive Cir.
Irving, TX 75038-2522
Ph: (972)550-0911   Fax: (972)580-2816
Fr: 800-798-1822
E-mail: execdirector@acep.org
URL: http://www.acep.org

Description: Supports quality emergency medical care and promotes the interests of emergency physicians. Represents more than 22,000 members and is the emergency medicine specialty society recognized by organized medicine.

★9906★ American College of Medical Quality (ACMQ)

4334 Montgomery Ave., Ste. B
Bethesda, MD 20814
Ph: (301)913-9149   Fax: (301)913-9142
Fr: 800-924-2149
E-mail: acmq@acmq.org
URL: http://www.acmq.org

Members: Physicians, affiliates, and institutions. **Purpose:** Seeks to educate and set standards of competence in the field of quality improvement and management. Offers a core curriculum in quality. Maintains Speaker's Bureau.

★9907★ American College of Radiology (ACR)

1891 Preston White Dr.
Reston, VA 20191
Ph: (703)648-8900   Fax: (703)264-2093
Fr: 800-227-5463
E-mail: info@acr.org
URL: http://www.acr.org

Description: Principal organization serving radiologists with programs that focus on the practice of radiology and the delivery of comprehensive radiological health services. These programs in medical sciences, education, and in practice management, serve the public interest and the interests of the medical community in which radiologists serve in both diagnostic and therapeutic roles. Seeks to "advance the science of radiology, improve radiologic service to the patient, study the economic aspects of the practice of radiology, and encourage improved and continuing education for radiologists and allied professional fields".

★9908★ American College of Sports Medicine (ACSM)

401 W Michigan St.
Indianapolis, IN 46202-3233
Ph: (317)637-9200   Fax: (317)634-7817
E-mail: publicinfo@acsm.org
URL: http://www.acsm.org

Purpose: Promotes and integrates scientific research, education, and practical applications of sports medicine and exercise science to maintain and enhance physical performance, fitness, health, and quality of life. **Activities:** Certifies fitness leaders, fitness instructors, exercise test technologists, exercise specialists, health/fitness program directors, and U.S. military fitness personnel. Grants Continuing Medical Education (CME) and Continuing Education Credits (CEC). Operates more than 50 committees.

★9909★ American Hospital Association (AHA)

1 N Franklin
Chicago, IL 60606-3421
Ph: (312)422-3000   Fax: (312)422-4796
URL: http://www.aha.org

Description: Represents health care provider organizations. Seeks to advance the health of individuals and communities. Leads, represents, and serves health care provider organizations that are accountable to the community and committed to health improvement.

★9910★ American Medical Group Association (AMGA)

1422 Duke St.
Alexandria, VA 22314-3403
Ph: (703)838-0033   Fax: (703)548-1890
E-mail: dfisher@amga.org
URL: http://www.amga.org

Description: Represents the interests of medical groups. Advocates for the medical groups and patients through innovation and information sharing, benchmarking, develop-

ing leadership, and improving patient care. Provides political advocacy, educational and networking programs and publications, benchmarking data services, and financial and operations assistance.

★9911★ American Mental Health Alliance (AMHA)

PO Box 4075
Portland, OR 97208-4075
Ph: (503)279-8160   Fr: 888-577-3386
E-mail: memberinfo@americanmentalhealth.com
URL: http://www.americanmentalhealth.com

Description: Represents mental health professionals licensed or certified for independen t practice. Creates a professional community that provides therapy of the highes t quality and ethical standards. Supports and markets competent, ethical mental health services that preserve privacy and confidentiality. Supports education, s upervision, and research opportunities for members. Opposes legislation and regu lations that invade patient privacy and confidentiality.

★9912★ American Mental Health Counselors Association (AMHCA)

801 N Fairfax St., Ste. 304
Alexandria, VA 22314
Ph: (703)548-6002   Fax: (703)548-4775
Fr: 800-326-2642
E-mail: mhamilton@amhca.org
URL: http://www.amhca.org

Description: Professional counselors employed in mental health services; students. Aims to: deliver quality mental health services to children, youth, adults, families, and organizations; improve the availability and quality of counseling services through licensure and certification, training standards, and consumer advocacy. Supports specialty and special interest networks. Fosters communication among members. A division of the American Counseling Association.

★9913★ American Osteopathic Association (AOA)

142 E Ontario St.
Chicago, IL 60611
Ph: (312)202-8000   Fax: (312)202-8200
Fr: 800-621-1773
E-mail: info@osteotech.org
URL: http://www.osteopathic.org

Description: Osteopathic physicians, surgeons, and graduates of approved colleges of osteopathic medicine. Associate members include teaching, research, administrative, and executive employees of approved colleges, hospitals, divisional societies, and affiliated organizations. Forms (with its affiliates) an officially recognized structure of the osteopathic profession. Promotes the public health to encourage scientific research, and to maintain and improve high standards of medical education in osteopathic colleges. Inspects and accredits colleges and hospitals; conducts a specialty certification program; sponsors a national examining board satisfactory to state licensing agencies;

maintains mandatory program of continuing medical education for members.

★9914★ American School Health Association (ASHA)

PO Box 708
Kent, OH 44240
Ph: (330)678-1601   Fax: (330)678-4526
E-mail: asha@ashaweb.org
URL: http://www.ashaweb.org

Description: School physicians, school nurses, counsellors, nutritionists, psychologists, social workers, administrators, school health coordinators, health educators, and physical educators working in schools, professional preparation programs, public health, and community-based organizations. Promotes coordinated school health programs that include health education, health services, a healthful school environment, physical education, nutrition services, and psycho-social health services offered in schools collaboratively with families and other members of the community. Offers professional reference materials and professional development opportunities. Conducts pilot programs that inform materials development, provides technical assistance to school professionals, advocates for school health.

★9915★ American Society of Psychopathology of Expression (ASPE)

74 Lawton St.
Brookline, MA 02446
Ph: (617)738-9821   Fax: (617)975-0411

Description: Psychiatrists, psychologists, art therapists, sociologists, art critics, artists, social workers, linguists, educators, criminologists, writers, and historians. At least two-thirds of the members must be physicians. Fosters collaboration among specialists in the United States who are interested in the problems of expression and in the artistic activities connected with psychiatric, sociological, and psychological research. Disseminates information about research and clinical applications in the field of psychopathology of expression. Sponsors consultations, seminars, and lectures on art therapy.

★9916★ American Society for Reproductive Medicine (ASRM)

1209 Montgomery Hwy.
Birmingham, AL 35216-2809
Ph: (205)978-5000   Fax: (205)978-5005
E-mail: asrm@asrm.org
URL: http://www.asrm.org

Description: Gynecologists, obstetricians, urologists, reproductive endocrinologists, veterinarians, research workers, and others interested in reproductive health in humans and animals. Seeks to extend knowledge of all aspects of fertility and problems of infertility and mammalian reproduction; provides a rostrum for the presentation of scientific studies dealing with these subjects. Offers patient resource information.

★9917★ American Urological Association (AUA)

1000 Corporate Blvd.
Linthicum, MD 21090
Ph: (410)689-3700   Fax: (410)689-3800
Fr: (866)746-4282
E-mail: aua@auanet.org
URL: http://www.auanet.org

Description: Serves as professional society of physicians specializing in urology. Provides education and formulation of health care policy for urologists.

★9918★ Association of Staff Physician Recruiters (ASPR)

1711 W County Rd. B, Ste. 300N
Roseville, MN 55113
Fax: (651)635-0307   Fr: 800-830-2777
E-mail: admin@aspr.org
URL: http://www.aspr.org

Description: Recruits physicians and other healthcare providers to staff hospitals, clinics and managed care organizations where the members are employed. Sponsors educational programs and meetings on various recruitment issues.

★9919★ Emergency Medicine Residents' Association (EMRA)

1125 Executive Cir.
Irving, TX 75038-2522
Ph: (972)550-0920   Fax: (972)580-2829
Fr: 800-798-1822
E-mail: emra@emra.org
URL: http://www.emra.org

Description: Physicians enrolled in emergency medicine residency training programs; medical students. Aims to provide a unified voice for emergency medicine residents and encourage high standards in training and education for emergency physicians. Encourages research to improve emergency medicine education; promotes community, state, and national representation for emergency medicine in organized and academic medicine.

★9920★ Exploring Health Occupations

Cambridge Educational
PO Box 2053
Princeton, NJ 08543-2053
Ph: 800-257-5126   Fax: (609)671-0266
Fr: 800-468-4227
E-mail: custserv@films.com
URL: http://www.cambridgeeducational.com

VHS and DVD. $159.90. 1999. Two-part series provides a detailed view of the field of medical technicians and technologists, EMTs, nurses, therapists, and assistants.

★9921★ Health Service Occupations

Delphi Productions
3159 6th St.
Boulder, CO 80304
Ph: (303)443-2100   Fax: (303)443-4022
Fr: 888-443-2400
E-mail: support@delphivideo.com
URL: http://www.delphivideo.com

$95.00. 50 minutes. Part of the Careers for the 21st Century Video Library.

★9922★ Holistic Dental Association (HDA)

PO Box 151444
San Diego, CA 92175
Ph: (619)923-3120   Fax: (619)615-2228
E-mail: info@holisticdental.org
URL: http://www.holisticdental.org

Description: Represents dentists, chiropractors, dental hygienists, physical therapists, and medical doctors. Aims to provide a holistic approach to better dental care for patients, and to expand techniques, medications, and philosophies that pertain to extractions, anesthetics, fillings, crowns, and orthodontics. Encourages the use of homeopathic medications, acupuncture, cranial osteopathy, nutritional techniques, and physical therapy in treating patients in addition to conventional treatments. Sponsors training and educational seminars.

★9923★ Institute on Psychiatric Services/American Psychiatric Association

1000 Wilson Blvd., Ste. 1825
Arlington, VA 22209-3901
Ph: (703)907-7300   Fax: (703)907-1085
Fr: 888-357-7924
E-mail: apa@psych.org
URL: http://www.psych.org

Description: Annual meeting sponsored by the American Psychiatric Association. Open to Physicians and all mental health professionals of all psychiatric and related health and educational facilities. Includes lectures by experts in the field and workshops and accredited courses on problems, programs, and trends. Offers on-site Job Bank, which lists opportunities for mental health professionals. Organized scientific exhibits.

★9924★ International Association of Hygienic Physicians (IAHP)

4620 Euclid Blvd.
Youngstown, OH 44512
Ph: (330)788-0526   Fax: (330)788-0093
E-mail: mhuberman@zoominternet.net
URL: http://www.iahp.net

Members: Doctors of medicine, osteopathy, chiropractic, and naturopathy who specialize in the supervision of therapeutic fasting as part of a natural hygiene regimen. **Purpose:** Promotes clinical advancement and ethical responsibility. Works for the health freedom of members. **Activities:** Provides certification for professionals and accreditation for schools and training programs; offers internship programs. Funds research.

★9925★ International Association of Pediatric Laboratory Medicine (IAPLM)

6728 Old McLean Village Dr.
McLean, VA 22101
E-mail: klausp.kohse@t-online.de
URL: http://www.uni-oldenburg.de/ec4/iaplm.htm

Description: Aims to enhance the science and practice of pediatric laboratory medicine. Encourages the development of scientific knowledge and use of improved methods, practices, and techniques applied to pediatric laboratory medicine. Seeks to advance the interests of pediatric clinical pathologists and scientists through continuing education. Fosters camaraderie and networking among international leaders in laboratory medicine.

★9926★ International Association of Transpersonal Therapists and Physicians (IATTP)

485 S Independence Blvd., Ste. 111
Virginia Beach, VA 23452
Ph: (757)216-8096   Fax: (757)216-8101
E-mail: iattpmembers@aol.com
URL: http://iattp.org

Description: Provides training and continuing education to professionals who work with clients across all aspects of their lives. Provides a forum for professionals to share their knowledge and expertise in the field of transpersonal healthcare.

★9927★ International Mobile Health Association (IMHA)

PO Box 7611
Huntington, WV 25777-7611
Ph: (228)238-9676
E-mail: lseim@chfund.org
URL: http://www.internationalmobilehealthassociation.or

Description: Promotes the development, enhancement, and implementation of global mobile health services. Aims to increase public access to vital healthcare services, especially among underserved populations. Provides educational support services and networking opportunities for mobile health specialists.

★9928★ International Society for Clinical Densitometry (ISCD)

342 N Main St.
West Hartford, CT 06117-2507
Ph: (860)586-7563   Fax: (860)586-7550
E-mail: iscd@iscd.org
URL: http://www.iscd.org

Description: Raises awareness and understanding of the clinical application of bone mass measurement technology. Seeks to adopt an industry and technology neutral approach towards advances in the field. Encourages improvements in patient care through appropriate utilization of densitometry. Fosters continuing professional education and certification for clinicians and technologists.

★9929★ International Society of Stress Analysts (ISSA)

9 Westchester Dr.
Kissimmee, FL 34744
Ph: (407)933-4839   Fax: (407)935-0911
E-mail: diogenesfl@aol.com

Members: Jurists, attorneys, physicians, private detectives, law enforcement personnel, security personnel, scholar/researchers, and individuals interested in stress analysis for lie detection/truth verification. **Purpose:** Purposes are to: promote the science of psychological stress evaluation and the efficient administration of justice; aid indigent persons, without cost, who may be wrongfully accused; develop and maintain high educational standards; observe and evaluate training programs for the purpose of accreditation and endorsement. **Activities:** Sponsors and certifies schools; offers workshops and research and educational programs; conducts forums. Offers expertise, consultation, and advice; invites inquiries.

★9930★ **Joint Council of Allergy, Asthma and Immunology (JCAAI)**

50 N Brockway, Ste. 3-3
Palatine, IL 60067
Ph: (847)934-1918   Fax: (847)934-1820
E-mail: info@jcaai.org
URL: http://www.jcaai.org

Description: Physicians specializing in allergy or clinical immunology. Members must belong to the American Academy of Allergy and Immunology or the American College of Allergy and Immunology. Serves as political and socioeconomic arm for these sponsoring organizations.

★9931★ **Medicine & Related Occupations**

Delphi Productions
3159 6th St.
Boulder, CO 80304
Ph: (303)443-2100   Fax: (303)443-4022
Fr: 888-443-2400
E-mail: support@delphivideo.com
URL: http://www.delphivideo.com

$95.00. 45 minutes. Part of the Careers for the 21st Century Video Library.

★9932★ **National Medical Association (NMA)**

1012 10th St. NW
Washington, DC 20001
Ph: (202)347-1895   Fax: (202)289-2662
URL: http://www.nmanet.org

Description: Serves as professional society of minority physicians.

★9933★ **National Physician's Association (NPA)**

PO Box 35215
Chicago, IL 60707-0215
Ph: (708)453-0080   Fax: (708)453-0083
E-mail: npa@rentamark.com

Members: Physicians. **Purpose:** Seeks to increase members' public visibility and professional influence. **Activities:** Provides trademark licensing and product and service endorsement services to support members' activities. Serves as a platform for doctors to find new patients and receive information about the latest healthcare "breakthroughs", and receive advice on healthcare matters.

★9934★ **National Rehabilitation Association (NRA)**

633 S Washington St.
Alexandria, VA 22314
Ph: (703)836-0850   Fax: (703)836-0848
E-mail: info@nationalrehab.org
URL: http://www.nationalrehab.org/website/index.html

Description: Provides opportunities through knowledge and diversity for professionals in the fields of rehabilitation of people with disabilities.

★9935★ **National Rural Health Association (NRHA)**

Administrative Office
521 E 63rd St.
Kansas City, MO 64110-3329
Ph: (816)756-3140   Fax: (816)756-3144
E-mail: mail@nrharural.org
URL: http://www.nrharural.org

Description: Administrators, physicians, nurses, physician assistants, health planners, academicians, and others interested or involved in rural health care. Creates a better understanding of health care problems unique to rural areas; utilizes a collective approach in finding positive solutions; articulates and represents the health care needs of rural America; supplies current information to rural health care providers; serves as a liaison between rural health care programs throughout the country. Offers continuing education credits for medical, dental, nursing, and management courses.

★9936★ **Neuro-Developmental Treatment Association (NDTA)**

1540 S Coast Hwy., Ste. 203
Laguna Beach, CA 92651
Fax: (949)376-3456   Fr: 800-869-9295
E-mail: info@ndta.org
URL: http://www.ndta.org

Members: Physical and occupational therapists, speech pathologists, special educators, physicians, parents, and others interested in neurodevelopmental treatment. (NDT is a form of therapy for individuals who suffer from central nervous system disorders resulting in abnormal movement. Treatment attempts to initiate or refine normal stages and processes in the development of movement.) **Purpose:** Informs members of new developments in the field and with ideas that will eventually improve fundamental independence. **Activities:** Locates articles related to NDT.

★9937★ **North American Sikh Medical and Dental Association (NASMDA)**

13801 Allied Rd.
Chester, VA 23836
Ph: (804)691-1906
E-mail: gurmitchilana@yahoo.com
URL: http://sikhdocs.org

Description: Promotes the interests of Sikh physicians and dentists in the United States, Canada and elsewhere. Supports Sikh physicians, dentists and other Sikh professionals pursuing their careers in those fields or any other fields. Assists Sikh medical and dental graduates to establish practices and help them obtain adequate post-graduate training. Seeks to improve the medical education and delivery of medical care in the parent homeland. Compiles a comprehensive directory of Sikh physicians and dentists residing in North America.

Physicists and Astronomers

SOURCES OF HELP-WANTED ADS

★9938★ AACG Newsletter

American Association for Crystal Growth
9 Red Hill Rd
Warren, NJ 07059
Ph: (908)575-0649   Fax: (908)575-0794
E-mail: aacg@att.net
URL: http://www.crystalgrowth.org/

Description: Three issues/year. Contains news and features on developments in crystal growth and characterization, international research, and historical retrospectives. Recurring features include news from local AACG chapters, employment notices, coverage of meetings and conferences, letters to the editor, a calendar of events, and columns titled Crystal Growth News, Historical Perspectives, and The President's Corner.

★9939★ Astronomy

Kalmbach Publishing Co.
PO Box 1612
21027 Crossroads Cir.
Waukesha, WI 53187-1612
Ph: (262)796-8776   Fax: (262)796-1615
Fr: 800-533-6644
URL: http://www.astronomy.com

Monthly. $42.95/year for Canada; $79.95/year for Canada, two years; $114.95/year for Canada, three years; $43.00/year for individuals; $80.00/year for individuals, two years; $115.00/year for individuals, three years; $58.00/year for out of country; $110.00/year for out of country, two years; $160.00/year for out of country, three years. Magazine for the "star gazing public."

★9940★ Astronomy Education Review

National Optical Astronomy Observatory
950 N Cherry Ave.
Tucson, AZ 85719
Ph: (520)318-8000
URL: http://aer.noao.edu/

Free, online. Scholarly journal publishing research and articles on astronomy.

★9941★ The Astrophysical Journal

University of Chicago Press, Journals Div.
PO Box 37005
Chicago, IL 60637
Ph: (773)753-3347   Fax: (773)753-0811
Fr: 877-705-1878
URL: http://www.journals.uchicago.edu/ApJ/front.html

$1,950.00/year for U.S.; $2,226.00/year for Canada; $2,090.00/year for Mexico; $2,280.00/year for other countries; $59.00 for single issue. Journal covering current events in astronomy and astrophysics.

★9942★ AWIS Magazine

Association for Women in Science
1200 New York Ave. NW, Ste. 650
Washington, DC 20005
Ph: (202)326-8940   Fax: (202)326-8960
Fr: (866)657-2947
E-mail: awis@awis.org
URL: http://www.awis.org/

Description: Bimonthly. Covers issues, legislation, and trends related to science education for girls, women, and minorities. Includes information on grants and fellowships, job openings, educational programs, events, and notices of publications available.

★9943★ The Electrochemical Society Interface

The Electrochemical Society Inc.
65 S Main St., Bldg. D
Pennington, NJ 08534-2839
Ph: (609)737-1902   Fax: (609)737-2743
E-mail: interface@electrochem.org
URL: http://www.electrochem.org/dl/interface/

Quarterly. $15.00/year for members; $68.00/year for nonmembers; $15.00 for single issue, members; $20.00 for single issue, nonmembers. Publication featuring news and articles of interest to members of the Electrochemical Society.

★9944★ International Archives of Bioscience

International Archives of Bioscience
PO Box 737254
Elmhurst, NY 11373-9997
URL: http://www.iabs.us/jdoc/aboutiabs.htm

Free, online only. Journal reporting multidisciplinary coverage and interaction between scientists in biology, informatics, mathematics, physics, engineering and other sciences.

★9945★ Journal of Vacuum Science and Technology A & B

American Institute of Physics
1 Physics Ellipse
College Park, MD 20740-3843
Ph: (301)209-3100
E-mail: jvst@mcnc.org
URL: http://www.virtualjournals.org/

Monthly. $1,700.00/year for individuals, print & online; $1,813.00/year for other countries, print & online (surface); $1,896.00/year for individuals, print & online (air). Journal containing research review articles in all areas of vacuum science.

★9946★ Laser Focus World

PennWell Corp.
98 Spit Brook Rd.
Nashua, NH 03062-5737
Ph: (603)891-0123
URL: http://lfw.pennnet.com

Monthly. $150.00/year for individuals; $200.00/year for individuals, Canada; $75.00/year for individuals, digital distribution; $250.00/year for other countries. Magazine covering advances and applications in optoelectronics and photonics.

★9947★ Lasers & Optronics

Reed Business Information
360 Park Ave. S
New York, NY 10010
Ph: (646)746-6400   Fax: (646)746-7431
URL: http://www.lasersoptrmag.com

Monthly. $55.00/year for individuals. Magazine serving the laser and optoelectronic market.

★9948★ Nature International Weekly Journal of Science

Nature Publishing Group
75 Varick St., 9th Fl.
New York, NY 10013-1917
Ph: (212)726-9200   Fax: (212)696-9006
Fr: 888-331-6288
E-mail: nature@natureny.com
URL: http://www.nature.com

Weekly. $145.00/year for individuals; $49.00/year for institutions. Magazine covering science and technology, including the fields of biology, biochemistry, genetics, medicine, earth sciences, physics, pharmacology, and behavioral sciences.

★9949★ Night Sky

Sky Publishing Corp.
49 Bay State Rd.
Cambridge, MA 02138-1200
Ph: (617)864-7360   Fax: (617)864-6117
Fr: 800-253-0245
URL: http://www.nightskymag.com

Bimonthly. $5.95/year for individuals. Magazine for amateur astronomers and stargazing enthusiasts.

★9950★ PE & RS Photogrammetric Engineering & Remote Sensing

The Imaging and Geospatial Information Society
5410 Grosvenor Ln., Ste. 210
Bethesda, MD 20814-2160
Ph: (301)493-0290   Fax: (301)493-0208
E-mail: asprs@asprs.org
URL: http://www.asprs.org/

Monthly. $250.00/year for individuals, U.S.D 15 discount per subscp. off the base rate; $120.00/year for individuals, active; $80.00/year for individuals, associate; $45.00/year for students, domestic. Journal covering photogrammetry, remote sensing, geographic information systems, cartography, and surveying, global positioning systems, digital photogrammetry.

★9951★ The Physics Teacher

American Association of Physics Teachers
1 Physics Ellipse
College Park, MD 20740-3845
Ph: (301)209-3300   Fax: (301)209-0845
E-mail: tpt@appstate.edu
URL: http://www.aapt.org/Publications/

$335.00/year for nonmembers, international; $105.00/year for members, regular. Scientific education magazine.

★9952★ Physics Today

American Institute of Physics
1 Physics Ellipse
College Park, MD 20740-3843
Ph: (301)209-3100
URL: http://www.aip.org

Monthly. $69.00/year for individuals; $59.00/year for members, in affiliated societies; $595.00/year for individuals, print + online backfile; $615.00/year for Canada and Mexi-co, print + online backfile; $625.00/year for other countries, print + online backfile; $395.00/year for institutions, print, domestic (U.S. and possessions); $415.00/year for Canada and Mexico, print, institution (surface delivery); $425.00/year for other countries, institution (air freight). Journal covering news of physics research and activities that affect physics.

★9953★ The Scientist

The Scientist Inc.
400 Market St., No. 1250
Philadelphia, PA 19106
Ph: (215)351-1660   Fax: (215)351-1146
URL: http://www.the-scientist.com

Bimonthly. $49.95/year for individuals, on-line; $74.95/year for individuals, online plus print edition; $124.95/year for out of country, online plus print edition (air freight); $29.95/year for individuals; $19.95 for individuals, 6 months; $14.95 for individuals, 1 month; $9.95 for individuals, 1 week; $4.95 for individuals, 1 week. News journal (tabloid) for life scientists featuring news, opinions, research, and professional section.

★9954★ Sky & Telescope

Sky Publishing Corp.
49 Bay State Rd.
Cambridge, MA 02138-1200
Ph: (617)864-7360   Fax: (617)864-6117
Fr: 800-253-0245
URL: http://www.skypub.com

Monthly. $37.95/year for individuals; $69.95 for individuals, 2 years; $49.95/year for Canada; $89.95 for Canada, 2 years; $61.95/year for other countries; $113.00 for other countries, 2 years. Magazine on astronomy and space science.

★9955★ The SPS Observer

Society of Physics Students
1 Physics Ellipse
College Park, MD 20740
Ph: (301)209-3007   Fax: (301)209-0839
E-mail: sps@aip.org
URL: http://www.spsnational.org/publications/

Description: Three issues/year and one issue per year online. Carries material of interest to undergraduate and graduate-level physics students, including articles on employment, available fellowships, meetings, and Society news.

PLACEMENT AND JOB REFERRAL SERVICES

★9956★ American Association of Physicists in Medicine (AAPM)

One Physics Ellipse
College Park, MD 20740
Ph: (301)209-3350   Fax: (301)209-0862
E-mail: 2007.aapm@aapm.org
URL: http://www.aapm.org

Members: Persons professionally engaged in application of physics to medicine and biology in medical research and educational institutions; Purpose: encourages interest and training in medical physics and related fields; promotes high professional standards; disseminates technical information. Activities: Maintains placement service. Conducts research programs. Member society of American Institute of Physics.

★9957★ American Institute of Physics (AIP)

1 Physics Ellipse
College Park, MD 20740
Ph: (301)209-3000   Fax: (301)209-3133
E-mail: brodsky@aip.org
URL: http://www.aip.org

Description: Consists of ten national societies in the fields of physics, astronomy and related disciplines with a total of 100,000 members, 17 affiliated societies, 47 corporate associates and 7,500 student members. Seeks to assist in the advancement and diffusion of the knowledge of physics and its application to human welfare. Publishes scientific journals devoted to physics and related sciences; provides secondary information services and online electronic journals; serves the public by making available to the press and other channels of public information reliable communications on physics and its progress; carries on extensive career services activities; maintains projects directed toward providing information about physics education to students, physics teachers and physics departments; encourages and assists in the documentation and study of the history of recent physics; cooperates with local, national and international organizations devoted to physics; and fosters the relations of the science of physics to other sciences and to the arts and industry. Provides placement service; compiles statistics; maintains biographical archives and Niels Bohr Library of History of Physics.

★9958★ Health Physics Society (HPS)

1313 Dolley Madison Blvd., Ste. 402
McLean, VA 22101
Ph: (703)790-1745   Fax: (703)790-2672
E-mail: hps@burkinc.com
URL: http://www.hps.org

Description: Persons engaged in some form of activity in the field of health physics (the profession devoted to radiation protection). Strives to improve public understanding of the problems and needs in radiation protection. Promotes health physics as a profession. Maintains Elda E. Anderson Memorial Fund to be used for teachers, researchers, and others. Provides placement service at annual meeting. Co-sponsors American Board of Health Physics for certification of health physicists.

★9959★ International Planetarium Society (IPS)

Imiloa Astronomy Center of Hawaii
600 Imiloa Pl.
Hilo, HI 96720
Ph: (808)969-9735   Fax: (808)969-9748
E-mail: slaatsch@imiloahawaii.org
URL: http://www.ips-planetarium.org

Description: Planetarium staff members; planetarium equipment suppliers; students in planetarium education and astronomy. Encourages exchange of ideas relating to planetariums and the profession. Operates placement service.

★9960★ Society for In Vitro Biology (SIVB)

514 Daniels St., Ste. 411
Raleigh, NC 27605
Ph: (919)420-7940   Fax: (919)420-7939
Fr: 888-588-1923
E-mail: sivb@sivb.org
URL: http://www.sivb.org

Description: Professional society of individuals using mammalian, invertebrate, plant cell tissue, and organ cultures as research tools in chemistry, physics, radiation, medicine, physiology, nutrition, and cytogenetics. Aims are to foster collection and dissemination of information concerning the maintenance and experimental use of tissue cells in vitro and to establish evaluation and development procedures. Operates placement service.

EMPLOYER DIRECTORIES AND NETWORKING LISTS

★9961★ American Men and Women of Science

Gale, Cengage Learning
27500 Drake Rd.
Farmington Hills, MI 48331-3535
Ph: (248)699-4253   Fax: (248)699-8065
Fr: 800-877-4253
URL: http://www.gale.com

Biennial, latest edition 23rd, October 2006; new edition expected 24th, January 2008. $1,075.00 for individuals. Covers over 129,700 U.S. and Canadian scientists active in the physical, biological, mathematical, computer science, and engineering fields; includes references to previous edition for deceased scientists and nonrespondents. Entries include: Name, address, education, personal and career data, memberships, honors and awards, research interest. Arrangement: Alphabetical. Indexes: Discipline (in separate volume).

★9962★ Directory of Physics, Astronomy, and Geophysics Staff

American Institute of Physics
1 Physics Ellipse
College Park, MD 20740-3843
Ph: (301)209-3100

URL: http://www.aip.org/pubs/books/dpags.html

Biennial; latest edition 2006. $82.00 for individuals. Covers 31,000 staff members at 2,300 colleges, universities, and laboratories throughout North America that employ physicists and astronomers; list of foreign organizations. Entries include: Name, address, phone, fax, e-mail address. Arrangement: Separate alphabetical sections for individuals, academic institutions, and laboratories. Indexes: Academic institution location, type of laboratory.

★9963★ Discovering Careers for Your Future: Science

Facts On File Inc.
132 W 31st St., 17th Fl.
New York, NY 10001
Ph: (212)967-8800   Fax: 800-678-3633
Fr: 800-322-8755
URL: http://www.factsonfile.com

Latest edition 2nd, 2004. $21.95 for individuals; $19.75 for libraries. Covers astronomers, biochemists, genetic scientists, marine biologists, pharmacologists, physicists, and zoologists; links career education to curriculum, helping children investigate the subjects they are interested in and the careers those subjects might lead to.

★9964★ Peterson's Job Opportunities in Engineering and Technology

Peterson's Guides
2000 Lenox Dr.
Box 67005
Lawrenceville, NJ 08648
Ph: (609)896-1800   Fax: (609)896-4531
Fr: 800-338-3282
E-mail: custsvc@petersons.com
URL: http://www.petersons.com

Compiled by the Peterson's staff. Fourth edition, 1996. $21.95 (paper). 379 pages. Profiles 2,000 high-tech companies looking primarily for technical personnel in such fields as biotechnology, telecommunications, software, computers and peripherals, defense, and aerospace. Contains job-search strategies and career options to help match education and expertise to the job market. Indexed geographically, by industry, and by hiring needs.

HANDBOOKS AND MANUALS

★9965★ The Best Resumes for Scientists and Engineers

John Wiley & Sons Inc.
1 Wiley Dr.
Somerset, NJ 08873
Ph: (732)469-4400   Fax: (732)302-2300
Fr: 800-225-5945
E-mail: custserv@wiley.com
URL: http://www.wiley.com/WileyCDA/

Adele Lewis and David J. Moore. Second edition, 1993. $37.50; $19.95 (paper). 224 pages. Presents an extensive collection of scientific and engineering resumes, highlighting the important differences between these and resumes written for other occupations.

★9966★ A Career in Theoretical Physics

World Scientific Publishing Co. Inc.
27 Warren St., Ste., 401-402
Hackensack, NJ 07601
Ph: (201)487-9655   Fax: (201)487-9656
Fr: 800-227-7562
URL: http://www.worldscientific.com/

Philip W. Anderson. Second edition. 2005. $98.00 (paper). 884 pages. Part of the Series in Twentieth Century Physics.

★9967★ Guide to Nontraditional Careers in Science

Taylor & Francis
325 Chestnut St., 8th Fl.
Philadelphia, PA 19106
Ph: (215)625-8900   Fax: (215)269-0363
Fr: 800-821-8312
URL: http://www.taylorandfrancis.com

Karen Young Kreeger. 1998. $45.95 (paper). Guidebook aids the reader in evaluating and finding career opportunities in non-academic research fields. 263 pages.

★9968★ Opportunities in Environmental Careers

The McGraw-Hill Companies
PO Box 182604
Columbus, OH 43272
Fax: (614)759-3749   Fr: 877-883-5524
E-mail: customer.service@mcgraw-hill.com
URL: http://www.mcgraw-hill.com

Odom Fanning. Revised, 2002. $12.95 (paper). 174 pages. Describes a broad range of opportunities in fields such as environmental health, recreation, physics, and hygiene, and provides job search advice. Part of the "Opportunities in ..." Series.

★9969★ Opportunities in High Tech Careers

The McGraw-Hill Companies
PO Box 182604
Columbus, OH 43272
Fax: (614)759-3749   Fr: 877-883-5524
E-mail: customer.service@mcgraw-hill.com
URL: http://www.mcgraw-hill.com

Gary Colter and Deborah Yanuck. 1999. $14.95; $11.95 (paper). 160 pages. Explores high technology careers. Describes job opportunities, how to make a career decision, how to prepare for high technology jobs, job hunting techniques, and future trends.

★9970★ Opportunities in Research and Development Careers

The McGraw-Hill Companies
PO Box 182604
Columbus, OH 43272
Fax: (614)759-3749   Fr: 877-883-5524

E-mail: customer.service@mcgraw-hill.com
URL: http://www.mcgraw-hill.com

Jan Goldberg. 1996. $11.95 (paper). 146 pages.

★9971★ *Resumes for Scientific and Technical Careers*

The McGraw-Hill Companies
PO Box 182604
Columbus, OH 43272
Fax: (614)759-3749   Fr: 877-883-5524
E-mail: customer.service@mcgraw-hill.com
URL: http://www.mcgraw-hill.com

Third edition, 2007. $12.95 (paper). 144 pages. Provides resume advice for individuals interested in working in scientific and technical careers. Includes sample resumes and cover letters.

★9972★ *To Boldly Go: A Practical Career Guide for Scientists*

Amer Global Pub
2000 Florida Ave., NW
Washington, DC 20009
Ph: (202)462-6900   Fax: (202)328-0566
Fr: 800-966-2481

Peter S. Fiske. 1996. $19.00 (paper). 188 pages.

EMPLOYMENT AGENCIES AND SEARCH FIRMS

★9973★ **Erspamer Associates**

4010 W. 65th St., Ste. 100
Edina, MN 55435
Ph: (952)925-3747   Fax: (952)925-4022
E-mail: hdhuntrel@aol.com

Executive search firm specializing in technical management.

★9974★ **International Staffing Consultants**

17310 Redhill Ave., No. 140
Irvine, CA 92614
Ph: (949)255-5857   Fax: (949)767-5959
E-mail: iscinc@iscworld.com
URL: http://www.iscworld.com

Employment agency. Provides placement on regular or temporary basis. Affiliate office in London.

TRADESHOWS

★9975★ **March Meeting of the American Physical Society**

American Physical Society
1 Physics Ellipse
College Park, MD 20740-3844
Ph: (301)209-3200   Fax: (301)209-0865

E-mail: exoffice@aps.org
URL: http://www.aps.org

Annual. **Primary Exhibits:** Physics equipment.

OTHER SOURCES

★9976★ *American Almanac of Jobs and Salaries*

HarperCollins
10 E. 53rd St.
New York, NY 10022
Ph: (212)207-7000   Fr: 800-242-7737
URL: http://www.harpercollins.com/

John W. Wright. Revised edition, 2000. $20.00 (paper). 672 pages. This is a comprehensive guide to the wages of hundreds of occupations in a wide variety of industries and organizations.

★9977★ **American Astronomical Society (AAS)**

2000 Florida Ave. NW, Ste. 400
Washington, DC 20009-1231
Ph: (202)328-2010   Fax: (202)234-2560
E-mail: aas@aas.org
URL: http://www.aas.org

Description: Represents astronomers, physicists, and scientists in related fields. Conducts Visiting Professor in Astronomy Program.

★9978★ **American Crystallographic Association (ACA)**

PO Box 96
Buffalo, NY 14207-0090
Ph: (716)898-8690   Fax: (716)898-8695
E-mail: aca@hwi.buffalo.edu
URL: http://aca.hwi.buffalo.edu

Members: Chemists, biochemists, physicists, mineralogists, and metallurgists interested in crystallography and in the application of X-ray, electron, and neutron diffraction. **Purpose:** Promotes the study of the arrangement of atoms in matter, its causes, its nature, and its consequences, and of the tools and methods used in such studies. **Activities:** Maintains employment clearinghouse for members and employers.

★9979★ **American Physical Society (APS)**

One Physics Ellipse
College Park, MD 20740-3844
Ph: (301)209-3200   Fax: (301)209-0865
E-mail: exoffice@aps.org
URL: http://www.aps.org

Description: Scientists worldwide, dedicated to the advancement and the diffusion of the knowledge of physics. Publishes some of the leading international physics journals, organizes major scientific meetings and provides strong outreach programs in physics

education and in international and public affairs.

★9980★ **ASPRS - The Imaging and Geospatial Information Society**

5410 Grosvenor Ln., Ste. 210
Bethesda, MD 20814-2160
Ph: (301)493-0290   Fax: (301)493-0208
E-mail: asprs@asprs.org
URL: http://www.asprs.org

Members: Firms, individuals, government employees and academicians engaged in photogrammetry, photointerpretation, remote sensing, and geographic information systems and their application to such fields as archaeology, geographic information systems, military reconnaissance, urban planning, engineering, traffic surveys, meteorological observations, medicine, geology, forestry, agriculture, construction and topographic mapping. Mission is to advance knowledge and improve understanding of these sciences and to promote responsible applications. **Activities:** Offers voluntary certification program open to persons associated with one or more functional area of photogrammetry, remote sensing and GIS. Surveys the profession of private firms in photogrammetry and remote sensing in the areas of products and services.

★9981★ **Association for International Practical Training (AIPT)**

10400 Little Patuxent Pkwy., Ste. 250
Columbia, MD 21044-3519
Ph: (410)997-2200   Fax: (410)992-3924
E-mail: aipt@aipt.org
URL: http://www.aipt.org

Description: Providers worldwide of on-the-job training programs for students and professionals seeking international career development and life-changing experiences. Arranges workplace exchanges in hundreds of professional fields, bringing employers and trainees together from around the world. Client list ranges from small farming communities to Fortune 500 companies.

★9982★ **Astronomical League**

9201 Ward Pkwy., Ste. 100
Kansas City, MO 64114
Ph: (816)333-7759
E-mail: aloffice@earthlink.net
URL: http://www.astroleague.org

Description: Members of 250 astronomical societies and other interested individuals. Promotes the science of astronomy; encourages and coordinates activities of amateur astronomical societies; fosters observational and computational work and craftsmanship in various fields of astronomy; correlates amateur activities with professional research. Sponsors educational programs.

★9983★ Minority Women In Science (MWIS)

Directorate for Education and Human
  Resources Programs
1200 New York Ave. NW
Washington, DC 20005
Ph: (202)326-7019   Fax: (202)371-9849
E-mail: ygeorge@aaas.org

Description: A national network group of the American association for the Advancement of Science (AAAS), Education and Human Resources Directorate. The objectives of this group are: to identify and share information on resources and programs that could help in mentoring young women and minorities interested in science and engineering careers, and to strengthen communication among women and minorities in science and education.

★9984★ Radiation Research Society (RRS)

PO Box 7050
Lawrence, KS 66044
Fax: (785)843-1274   Fr: 800-627-0326
E-mail: info@radres.org
URL: http://www.radres.org

Description: Professional society of biologists, physicists, chemists, and physicians contributing to knowledge of radiation and its effects. Promotes original research in the natural sciences relating to radiation; facilitates integration of different disciplines in the study of radiation effects.

★9985★ Scientific, Engineering, and Technical Services

Cambridge Educational
PO Box 2053
Princeton, NJ 08543-2053
Ph: 800-257-5126   Fax: (609)671-0266
Fr: 800-468-4227
E-mail: custserv@films.com
URL: http://www.cambridgeeducational.com

VHS and DVD. $89.95. 2002. 18 minutes. 2002. Part of the Career Cluster Series.

★9986★ Scientific Occupations

Delphi Productions
3159 6th St.
Boulder, CO 80304
Ph: (303)443-2100   Fax: (303)443-4022
Fr: 888-443-2400
E-mail: support@delphivideo.com
URL: http://www.delphivideo.com

$95.00. 60 minutes. Part of the Careers for the 21st Century Video Library.

Plumbers

SOURCES OF HELP-WANTED ADS

★9987★ Builder

Hanley-Wood L.L.C.
1 Thomas Cir., NW, Ste. 600
Washington, DC 20005
Ph: (202)452-0800   Fax: (202)785-1974
URL: http://www.hanleywood.com/default.aspx?page=b2bbd

$29.95/year for individuals, 13 issues; $54.95/year for Canada, 26 issues; $192.00/year for out of country, 13 issues. Magazine covering housing and construction industry.

★9988★ Constructor

Associated General Contractors of
    America
2300 Wilson Blvd., Ste. 400
Arlington, VA 22201
Ph: (703)548-3118   Fax: (703)548-3119
URL: http://www.agc.org

Monthly. Management magazine for the Construction Industry.

★9989★ Contractor Magazine

Penton Media Inc.
2700 South River Rd., Ste. 109
Des Plaines, IL 60018
Ph: (847)299-3101   Fax: (847)299-3018
URL: http://www.contractormag.com

Monthly. $90.00/year for other countries; $157.50 for two years, international. Free, to U.S. and Canadian residents. Industry news and management how-to magazine for heating, plumbing, piping, fire sprinkler, and other mechanical specialties contracting firms.

★9990★ MCAA Reporter

Mechanical Contractors Association of
    America Inc.
1385 Piccard Dr.
Rockville, MD 20850
Ph: (301)869-5800   Fax: (301)990-9690
Fr: 800-556-3653

URL: http://www.mcaa.org/reporter/

Description: Monthly, except in February and August. Covers labor issues and government affairs as they affect mechanical contractors in the plumbing, pipefitting, air conditioning, refrigeration, fire protection, and high-purity piping industries. Recurring features include reports on the activities of the Association and notices of pertinent seminars and meetings.

★9991★ PHC Profit Report

BNP Media
c/o Tim Fausch
2401 W Big Beaver Rd., Ste. 700
Troy, MI 48084-3333
Ph: (248)362-3700   Fax: (248)786-1383
E-mail: wrdwzrd@aol.com
URL: http://www.bnpmedia.com/

Description: Monthly. Provides information on marketing, financial management, employee relations, and news and commentary on the plumbing-heating-cooling industry.

★9992★ Plumbing Business Owner

Cahaba Media Group
PO Box 530067
Birmingham, AL 35253
Ph: (205)212-9402
URL: http://www.pbomag.com/

Monthly. Free. Business magazine for plumbers.

★9993★ Plumbing Engineer

TMB Publishing Inc.
1838 Techny Ct.
Northbrook, IL 60062
Ph: (847)564-1127   Fax: (847)564-1264
URL: http://www.tmbpublishing.com

Monthly. Trade journal for consulting engineering, mechanical engineering, architecture, and contracting professionals.

★9994★ Professional Builder

Reed Business Information
360 Park Ave. S
New York, NY 10010
Ph: (646)746-6400   Fax: (646)746-7431

E-mail: ncrum@reedbusiness.com
URL: http://www.housingzone.com/toc-archive-pbx

Monthly. Free. The integrated engineering magazine of the building construction industry.

★9995★ Southern PHC Magazine

Southern Trade Publications Inc.
Box 7344
Greensboro, NC 27417
Ph: (336)454-3516   Fax: (336)454-3649

Bimonthly. $10.00/year. Free to qualified subscribers; $10.00/year others. Trade magazine covering plumbing, heating, and air conditioning, targeted to contractors and wholesalers in 14 southern states.

★9996★ WIT

Vermont Works for Women
51 Park St.
Essex Junction, VT 05452
Ph: (802)878-0004   Fax: (802)878-0050
Fr: 800-639-1472
URL: http://www.nnetw.org/

Description: Three issues/year. Provides a network of support, information, and skill sharing for women in skilled trades professions.

PLACEMENT AND JOB REFERRAL SERVICES

★9997★ National Association of Home Builders (NAHB)

1201 15th St. NW
Washington, DC 20005
Ph: (202)266-8200   Fax: (202)266-8400
Fr: 800-368-5242
E-mail: info@nahb.com
URL: http://www.nahb.org

Description: Single and multifamily home builders, commercial builders, and others associated with the building industry. Lobbies on behalf of the housing industry and conducts public affairs activities to increase public understanding of housing and the economy. Collects and disseminates data on current developments in home building and home builders' plans through its Economics Department and nationwide Metropolitan Housing Forecast. Maintains NAHB Research Center, which functions as the research arm of the home building industry. Sponsors seminars and workshops on construction, mortgage credit, labor relations, cost reduction, land use, remodeling, and business management. Compiles statistics; offers charitable program, spokesman training, and placement service; maintains speakers' bureau, and Hall of Fame. Subsidiaries include the National Council of the Housing Industry. Maintains over 50 committees in many areas of construction; operates National Commercial Builders Council, National Council of the Multifamily Housing Industry, National Remodelers Council, and National Sales and Marketing Council.

EMPLOYER DIRECTORIES AND NETWORKING LISTS

★9998★ ABC Today-Associated Builders and Contractors National Membership Directory Issue

Associated Builders & Contractors Inc.
4250 N Fairfax Dr., 9th Fl.
Arlington, VA 22203-1607
Ph: (703)812-2000   Fax: (703)812-8203
URL: http://www.abc.org/
wmspage.cfm?parm1=2033

Annual, December. $150.00. Publication includes: List of approximately 19,000 member construction contractors and suppliers. Entries include: Company name, address, phone, name of principal executive, code to volume of business, business specialty. Arrangement: Classified by chapter, then by work specialty.

★9999★ Constructor-AGC Directory of Membership and Services Issue

AGC Information Inc.
2300 Wilson Blvd., Ste. 400
Arlington, VA 22201
Ph: (703)548-3118   Fax: (703)548-3119
Fr: 800-282-1423
URL: http://www.agc.org

Annual, August; latest edition 2004 edition. Publication includes: List of over 8,500 member firms and 24,000 national associate member firms engaged in building, highway, heavy, industrial, municipal utilities, and railroad construction (SIC 1541, 1542, 1611, 1622, 1623, 1629); listing of state and local chapter officers. Entries include: For firms–Company name, address, phone, fax, names of principal executives, and code indicating type of construction undertaken. For officers–Name, title, address. Arrangement: Geographical, alphabetical. Indexes: Company name.

★10000★ ENR-Top 400 Construction Contractors Issue

McGraw-Hill Inc.
1221 Ave. of the Americas
New York, NY 10020-1095
Ph: (212)512-2000   Fax: (212)512-3840
Fr: 877-833-5524
URL: http://construction.ecnext.com/coms2/
summary_0249-137077_ITM

Annual; 22nd, May 2006. $35.00 for individuals. Publication includes: List of 400 United States contractors receiving largest dollar volumes of contracts in preceding calendar year. Separate lists of 50 largest design/construction management firms; 50 largest program and construction managers; 25 building contractors; 25 heavy contractors. Entries include: Company name, headquarters location, total value of contracts received in preceding year, value of foreign contracts, countries in which operated, construction specialities. Arrangement: By total value of contracts received.

★10001★ Minnesota P-H-C Contractor-Membership Directory Issue

Minnesota Association of Plumbing-Heating-Cooling Contractors
6300 Shingle Creek Pky., No. 275
Brooklyn Center, MN 55430-2183
Ph: (763)569-0891   Fax: (763)569-0893
Fr: 800-646-6742

Annual, July. Publication includes: List of 450 member firms and associates. Entries include: Name of company, address, phone, fax, code indicating type of work, local association affiliation (chapter memberships and other), name and title of owner or officer. Arrangement: Alphabetical. Indexes: Alphabetical by business.

★10002★ Who's Who in the Plumbing-Heating-Cooling Contracting Business

National Association of Plumbing, Heating, Cooling Contractors
180 S Washington St.
PO Box 6808
Falls Church, VA 22046
Ph: (703)237-8100   Fax: (703)237-7442
Fr: 800-533-7694

Annual. $75.00. Covers about 4,000 professional plumbing/heating/cooling contractors and member firms. Entries include: Name, address, phone, fax, contact. Arrangement: Geographical. Indexes: Individual member.

HANDBOOKS AND MANUALS

★10003★ Opportunities in Building Construction Trades

The McGraw-Hill Companies
PO Box 182604
Columbus, OH 43272
Fax: (614)759-3749   Fr: 877-883-5524
E-mail: customer.service@mcgraw-hill.com
URL: http://www.mcgraw-hill.com

Michael Sumichrast. Second edition, 1998. $14.95; $11.95 (paper). 104 pages. From custom builder to rehabber, the many kinds of companies that employ craftspeople and contractors are explored. Includes job descriptions, requirements, and salaries for dozens of specialties within the construction industry. Contains a complete list of Bureau of Apprenticeship and Training state and area offices. Illustrated.

★10004★ Opportunities in Plumbing and Pipefitting Careers

The McGraw-Hill Companies
PO Box 182604
Columbus, OH 43272
Fax: (614)759-3749   Fr: 877-883-5524
E-mail: customer.service@mcgraw-hill.com
URL: http://www.mcgraw-hill.com

Patrick J. Galvin. Reprint edition, 1995. $14.95; $10.95 (paper). 160 pages. Provides information on getting into the trade, apprenticeship programs, and how to build a career in a variety of settings. Illustrated.

★10005★ Plumber's Licensing Study Guide

The McGraw-Hill Companies
PO Box 182604
Columbus, OH 43272
Fax: (614)759-3749   Fr: 877-883-5524
E-mail: customer.service@mcgraw-hill.com
URL: http://www.mcgraw-hill.com

R. Woodson. 2001. $39.95 (paper). 500 pages.

TRADESHOWS

★10006★ American Society of Plumbing Engineers Convention

American Society of Plumbing Engineers
8614 Catalpa Ave., Ste. 1007
Chicago, IL 60656-1116
Ph: (773)693-2773   Fax: (773)695-9007
E-mail: info@aspe.org
URL: http://www.aspe.org

Biennial. **Primary Exhibits:** Exhibits for the plumbing engineering industry. **Dates and Locations:** 2008 Oct 26-29; Long Beach, CA; Long Beach Convention Center.

★10007★ Massachusetts Association of Plumbing/Heating/Cooling Contractors Convention and Tradeshow

Massachusetts Association of Plumbing/Heating/Cooling Contractors
178 Forbes Rd., Ste. 218
Braintree, MA 02184-2610
Ph: (781)843-3800   Fax: (781)843-1178
Fr: 800-542-7422
E-mail: phcc.ma@verizon.net
URL: http://www.phccma.org

Annual. **Primary Exhibits:** Plumbing, heating and cooling equipment, supplies, and services.

★10008★ National Plumbing-Heating-Cooling Piping Producers Exposition

National Association of Plumbing, Heating and Cooling Contractors
180 S. Washington St.
PO Box 6808
Falls Church, VA 22040
Ph: (703)237-8100   Fax: (703)237-7442
Fr: 800-533-7694
E-mail: naphcc@naphcc.org
URL: http://www.phccweb.org

Annual. **Primary Exhibits:** Equipment, supplies, and services for plumbing, heating, and cooling.

★10009★ The Ohio Plumbing Heating Cooling Expo

Ohio Association of Plumbing-Heating-Cooling Contractors
18961 River's Edge Dr.
Chagrin Falls, OH 44023
Ph: (440)543-4011   Fax: (440)543-1699
E-mail: info@phccohio.org
URL: http://www.phccohio.org

Annual. **Primary Exhibits:** Products, tools, and services used by plumbing and heating contractors.

OTHER SOURCES

★10010★ American Society of Plumbing Engineers (ASPE)

8614 Catalpa Ave., Ste. 1007
Chicago, IL 60656-1116
Ph: (773)693-2773   Fax: (773)695-9007
E-mail: info@aspe.org
URL: http://www.aspe.org

Description: Represents engineers and designers involved in the design and specification of plumbing systems; manufacturers, governmental officials, and contractors related to the industry may become members on a limited basis. Seeks to resolve professional problems in plumbing engineering; advocates greater cooperation among members and plumbing officials, contractors, laborers, and the public. Code committees examine regulatory codes pertaining to the industry and submit proposed revisions to code writing authorities to simplify, standardize, and modernize all codes. Sponsors American Society of Plumbing Engineers Research Foundation; operates certification program.

★10011★ American Society of Sanitary Engineering (ASSE)

901 Canterbury, Ste. A
Westlake, OH 44145
Ph: (440)835-3040   Fax: (440)835-3488
E-mail: info@asse-plumbing.org
URL: http://www.asse-plumbing.org

Description: Plumbing officials, sanitary engineers, plumbers, plumbing contractors, building officials, architects, engineers, designing engineers, physicians, and others interested in health. Conducts research on plumbing and sanitation, and develops performance standards for components of the plumbing system. Sponsors disease research program and other studies of waterborne epidemics.

★10012★ Associated Builders and Contractors (ABC)

4250 N Fairfax Dr., 9th Fl.
Arlington, VA 22203-1607
Ph: (703)812-2000   Fax: (703)812-8200
E-mail: gotquestions@abc.org
URL: http://www.abc.org

Description: Construction contractors, subcontractors, suppliers, and associates. Aims to foster and perpetuate the principles of rewarding construction workers and management on the basis of merit. Sponsors management education programs and craft training; also sponsors apprenticeship and skill training programs. Disseminates technological and labor relations information.

★10013★ Associated General Contractors of America (AGC)

2300 Wilson Blvd., Ste. 400
Arlington, VA 22201
Ph: (703)548-3118   Fax: (703)548-3119
Fr: 800-242-1767
E-mail: info@agc.org
URL: http://www.agc.org

Description: General construction contractors; subcontractors; industry suppliers; service firms. Provides market services through its divisions. Conducts special conferences and seminars designed specifically for construction firms. Compiles statistics on job accidents reported by member firms. Maintains 65 committees, including joint cooperative committees with other associations and liaison committees with federal agencies.

★10014★ Associated Specialty Contractors (ASC)

3 Bethesda Metro Ctr., Ste. 1100
Bethesda, MD 20814
Ph: (703)548-3118
E-mail: dgw@necanet.org
URL: http://www.assoc-spec-con.org

Description: Works to promote efficient management and productivity. Coordinates the work of specialized branches of the industry in management information, research, public information, government relations and construction relations. Serves as a liaison among specialty trade associations in the areas of public relations, government relations, and with other organizations. Seeks to avoid unnecessary duplication of effort and expense or conflicting programs among affiliates. Identifies areas of interest and problems shared by members, and develops positions and approaches on such problems.

★10015★ Building Trades

Delphi Productions
3159 6th St.
Boulder, CO 80304
Ph: (303)443-2100   Fax: (303)443-4022
Fr: 888-443-2400
E-mail: support@delphivideo.com
URL: http://www.delphivideo.com

$95.00. 46 minutes. Part of the Careers for the 21st Century Video Library.

★10016★ COIN Career Guidance System

COIN Educational Products
3361 Executive Pky., Ste. 302
Toledo, OH 43606
Ph: (419)536-5353   Fax: (419)536-7056
Fr: 800-274-8515
URL: http://www.coinedu.com/

CD-ROM. Provides career information through seven cross-referenced files covering postsecondary schools, college majors, vocational programs, military service, apprenticeship programs, financial aid, and scholarships. Apprenticeship file describes national apprenticeship training programs, including information on how to apply, contact agencies, and program content. Military file describes more than 200 military occupations and training opportunities related to civilian employment.

★10017★ Mechanical Contractors Association of America (MCAA)

1385 Piccard Dr.
Rockville, MD 20850-4329
Ph: (301)869-5800   Fax: (301)990-9690
Fr: 800-556-3653
E-mail: membership@mcaa.org
URL: http://www.mcaa.org

Members: Contractors who furnish, install, and service piping systems and related equipment for heating, cooling, refrigeration, ventilating, and air conditioning systems. **Purpose:** Works to standardize materials and methods used in the industry. Conducts business overhead, labor wage, and statistical surveys. Maintains dialogue with key officials in building trade unions. Promotes apprenticeship training programs. Conducts seminars on contracts, labor estimating, job cost control, project management, marketing, collective bargaining, contractor insurance, and other management topics. Promotes methods to conserve energy in new and existing buildings. Sponsors Industrial Relations Council for the Plumbing and Pipe Fitting Industry.

★10018★ National Association of Women in Construction (NAWIC)

327 S Adams St.
Fort Worth, TX 76104
Ph: (817)877-5551   Fax: (817)877-0324
Fr: 800-552-3506
E-mail: nawic@nawic.org
URL: http://www.nawic.org

Description: Seeks to enhance the success of women in the construction industry.

★10019★ Plumbing-Heating-Cooling Contractors Association (PHCC)

PO Box 6808
Falls Church, VA 22046
Ph: (703)237-8100   Fax: (703)237-7442
Fr: 800-533-7694
E-mail: naphcc@naphcc.org
URL: http://www.phccweb.org

Members: Federation of state and local associations of plumbing, heating, and cooling contractors. **Purpose:** Seeks to advance sanitation, encourage sanitary laws, and generally improve the plumbing, heating, ventilating, and air conditioning industries. **Activities:** Conducts apprenticeship training programs, workshops, seminars, political action committee, educational and research programs.

★10020★ Women in Building Construction

Her Own Words
PO Box 5264
Madison, WI 53705-0264
Ph: (608)271-7083   Fax: (608)271-02
E-mail: herownword@aol.com
URL: http://www.herownwords.com/

Video. Jocelyn Riley. $95.00. 15 minute
Resource guide also available for $45.0

Podiatrists

SOURCES OF HELP-WANTED ADS

★10021★ APMA News

American Podiatric Medical Association
9312 Old Georgetown Rd.
Bethesda, MD 20814-1621
Ph: (301)581-9200   Fax: (301)530-2752
Fr: 800-275-2762
URL: http://www.apma.org

Monthly. $65.00/year for individuals, U.S.; $75.00/year for out of country. Non-scientific news for member podiatrists.

★10022★ Journal of the Academy of Ambulatory Foot Surgery

Academy of Ambulatory Foot and Ankle Surgery
1601 Walnut, Ste. 1005
Philadelphia, PA 19102
Ph: (215)569-3303   Fax: (215)569-3310
Fr: 800-433-4892
URL: http://www.academy-afs.org/

Periodic. Professional journal covering issues in podiatry.

★10023★ Journal of the American Podiatric Medical Association

American Podiatric Medical Association
9312 Old Georgetown Rd.
Bethesda, MD 20814-1621
Ph: (301)581-9200   Fax: (301)530-2752
Fr: 800-275-2762
URL: http://www.japmaonline.org

Bimonthly. $75.00/year for members, U.S. & other countries including Canada; $185.00/year for institutions, print + online; $165.00/year for institutions, online; $155.00/year for individuals, print + online; $140.00/year for individuals, online; $40.00 for single issue, institutional & individual; $220.00/year for institutions, print + online, other countries, Canada; $200.00/year for institutions, online, other countries including Canada; $185.00/year for individuals, print + online, other countries, including Canada; $165.00/year for individuals, online, other countries includ-

ing Canada. Professional journal for podiatrists.

★10024★ Journal of the American Society of Podiatric Medical Assistants

American Society of Podiatric Medical Assistants
2124 S Austin Blvd.
Cicero, IL 60804
Ph: (708)863-6303   Fr: 888-882-7762
URL: http://www.aspma.org

Quarterly. Subscription included in membership. Professional journal covering issues in podiatry.

★10025★ The New England Journal of Medicine

The New England Journal of Medicine
860 Winter St.
Waltham, MA 02451-1413
Ph: (781)893-3800   Fr: 800-843-6356
URL: http://content.nejm.org/

Weekly. $99.00/year for individuals, online only; $149.00/year for individuals, print & online. Journal for the medical profession.

★10026★ Podiatry Management Magazine

Kane Communications Inc.
10 E Athens Ave., Ste. 208
Ardmore, PA 19003
Ph: (610)645-6940   Fax: (610)645-6943
URL: http://www.podiatrym.com/

Monthly. Magazine serving as a medical and surgical management guide for podiatrists.

★10027★ Southern Medical Journal

Southern Medical Association
35 Lakeshore Dr.
Birmingham, AL 35209
Ph: (205)945-1840   Fax: (205)945-1830
Fr: 800-423-4992
URL: http://www.sma.org/smj/index.cfm

Monthly. $35.00/year for individuals, resident and fellow SMA members; $169.00/year for nonmembers, individual; $331.00/year for

nonmembers, institutions; $205.00/year for nonmembers, international; $371.00/year for nonmembers, institutions, international. Multispecialty medical journal.

PLACEMENT AND JOB REFERRAL SERVICES

★10028★ American Medical Association (AMA)

515 N State St.
Chicago, IL 60610
Ph: (312)464-5000   Fax: (312)464-4184
Fr: 800-621-8335
E-mail: msc@ama-assn.org
URL: http://www.ama-assn.org

Description: Represents county medical societies and physicians. Disseminates scientific information to members and the public. Informs members on significant medical and health legislation on state and national levels and represents the profession before Congress and governmental agencies. Cooperates in setting standards for medical schools, hospitals, residency programs, and continuing medical education courses. Offers physician placement service and counseling on practice management problems. Operates library that lends material and provides specific medical information to physicians. Maintains Ad-hoc committees for such topics as health care planning and principles of medical ethics.

★10029★ American Public Health Association (APHA)

800 I St. NW
Washington, DC 20001
Ph: (202)777-2742   Fax: (202)777-2534
E-mail: comments@apha.org
URL: http://www.apha.org

Members: Professional organization of physicians, nurses, educators, academicians, environmentalists, epidemiologists, new professionals, social workers, health administrators, optometrists, podiatrists, pharmacists, dentists, nutritionists, health planners, other community and mental health specialists, and interested consumers. **Purpose:** Seeks to protect and promote personal, mental, and environmental health. **Activities:** Services include: promulgation of standards; establishment of uniform practices and procedures; development of the etiology of communicable diseases; research in public health; exploration of medical care programs and their relationships to public health. Sponsors job placement service.

EMPLOYER DIRECTORIES AND NETWORKING LISTS

★10030★ AHA Guide to the Health Care Field

American Hospital Association
1 N Franklin
Chicago, IL 60606
Ph: (312)422-2050   Fax: (312)422-4700
Fr: 800-424-4301

Annual, August. Covers hospitals, networks, multi-health care systems, freestanding ambulatory surgery centers, psychiatric facilities, long-term care facilities, substance abuse programs, and other health-related organizations. Entries include: For hospitals–Facility name, address, phone, administrator's name, number of beds, facilities and services, number of employees, expenses, other statistics. For other organizations–Name, address, phone, fax, name and title of contact. Arrangement: Geographical. Indexes: Hospital name.

★10031★ Directory of Hospital Personnel

Grey House Publishing
185 Millerton Rd.
PO Box 860
Millerton, NY 12546
Ph: (518)789-8700   Fax: (518)789-0556
Fr: 800-562-2139
URL: http://www.greyhouse.com/hospital_personnel.htm

Annual. $325.00 for print product; $545.00 for online database subscription; $650.00 for online database subscription and print product combined. Covers 200,000 executives at 7,000 U.S. hospitals. Entries include: Name of hospital, address, phone; number of beds; type and JCAHO status of hospital; names and titles of key department heads and staff; medical and nursing school affiliations; number of residents, interns, and nursing students. Arrangement: Geographical. Indexes: Hospital name, personnel, hospital size.

★10032★ HMO/PPO Directory

Grey House Publishing
185 Millerton Rd.
PO Box 860
Millerton, NY 12546
Ph: (518)789-8700   Fax: (518)789-0556
Fr: 800-562-2139
URL: http://www.greyhouse.com/hmo_

ppo.htm

Annual; latest edition November 2006. $325.00 for individuals, print product; $495.00 for individuals, online database subscription; $600.00 for individuals, print product and online database subscription,combined. Covers over 600 health maintenance organizations (HMOs) and more than 1,000 preferred provider organizations (PPOs). Entries include: Name of organization, address, phone, number of members, names of officers, employer references, geographical area served, parent company, average fees and co-payments, financial data, and cost control procedures. Arrangement: Geographical. Indexes: Organization name, personnel name, HMOs and PPOs by state, and number of members enrolled.

★10033★ Hospital Blue Book

Billian Publishing Inc./Transworld Publishing Inc.
2100 Powers Ferry Rd. SE
Atlanta, GA 30339
Ph: (770)955-5656   Fax: (770)952-0669
Fr: 800-533-8484
E-mail: blu-book@billian.com

2005. $300.00 for individuals. Covers more than 6,687 hospitals; some listings also appear in a separate southern edition of this publication. Entries include: Name of hospital, accreditation, mailing address, phone, fax, number of beds, type of facility (nonprofit, general, state, etc.); list of administrative personnel and chiefs of medical services, with specific titles. Arrangement: Geographical.

★10034★ Journal of the American Medical Association-Physician Service Opportunities Overseas Section

American Medical Association
515 N State St.
Chicago, IL 60610
Fr: 800-621-8335
URL: http://jama.ama-assn.org/content/extract/289/1/34

Irregular; latest edition August 2002. Publication includes: List of more than 60 organizations that provide assignments overseas for physicians from the United States. Entries include: Organization name, address, phone, contact person, countries served, and medical specialties sought. Arrangement: Alphabetical.

★10035★ Medical and Health Information Directory

Gale, Cengage Learning
27500 Drake Rd.
Farmington Hills, MI 48331-3535
Ph: (248)699-4253   Fax: (248)699-8065
Fr: 800-877-4253
E-mail: businessproducts@gale.com
URL: http://www.gale.com

Annual; latest edition 20th, July 2007. $375.00/volume. Covers in Volume 1, more than 26,500 medical and health oriented associations, organizations, institutions, and government agencies, including health main-

tenance organizations (HMOs), preferred provider organizations (PPOs), insurance companies, pharmaceutical companies, research centers, and medical and allied health schools. In Volume 2, over 12,000 medical book publishers; medical periodicals, directories, audiovisual producers and services, medical libraries and information centers, electronic resources, and health-related internet search engines. In Volume 3, more than 35,500 clinics, treatment centers, care programs, and counseling/diagnostic services for 34 subject areas. Entries include: Institution, service, or firm name, address, phone, fax, email and URL; many include names of key personnel and, when pertinent, descriptive annotations. Volume 3 was formerly listed separately as Health Services Directory. Arrangement: Classified by organization activity, service, etc. Indexes: Each volume has a complete alphabetical name and keyword index.

HANDBOOKS AND MANUALS

★10036★ Expert Resumes for Health Care Careers

Jist Works
875 Montreal Way
St. Paul, MN 55102
Fr: 800-648-5478
E-mail: info@jist.com
URL: http://www.jist.com

Wendy S. Enelow and Louise M. Kursmark. December 2003. $16.95. 288 pages.

★10037★ Health Careers Today

Elsevier
11830 Westline Industrial Dr.
St. Louis, MO 63146
Ph: (314)453-7010   Fax: (314)453-7095
Fr: 800-545-2522
E-mail: usbkinfo@elsevier.com
URL: http://www.elsevier.com

Gerdin, Judith. Fourth edition. 2007. $59.95. 496 pages. Covers more than 45 health careers. Discusses the roles and responsibilities of various occupations and provides a solid foundation in the skills needed for all health careers.

★10038★ Opportunities in Health and Medical Careers

The McGraw-Hill Companies
PO Box 182604
Columbus, OH 43272
Fax: (614)759-3749   Fr: 877-883-5524
E-mail: customer.service@mcgraw-hill.com
URL: http://www.mcgraw-hill.com

I. Donald Snook, Jr. and Leo D'Orazio. 2004. $13.95 (paper). 157 pages. Covers the full range of medical and health occupations. Illustrated.

★10039★ **Opportunities in Paramedical Careers**

The McGraw-Hill Companies
PO Box 182604
Columbus, OH 43272
Fax: (614)759-3749   Fr: 877-883-5524
E-mail: customer.service@mcgraw-hill.com
URL: http://www.mcgraw-hill.com

Alex Kacen. 1999. 14.95 (hardcover). 160 pages. Discusses a variety of opportunities in this field and how to pursue them. Illustrated.

★10040★ **Opportunities in Sports Medicine Careers**

The McGraw-Hill Companies
PO Box 182604
Columbus, OH 43272
Fax: (614)759-3749   Fr: 877-883-5524
E-mail: customer.service@mcgraw-hill.com
URL: http://www.mcgraw-hill.com

William Ray Heitzmann. 1992. $11.95 (paper). 160 pages. Discusses a variety of opportunities in this field and how to pursue them. Contains bibliography and illustrations.

★10041★ **Resumes for Health and Medical Careers**

The McGraw-Hill Companies
PO Box 182604
Columbus, OH 43272
Fax: (614)759-3749   Fr: 877-883-5524
E-mail: customer.service@mcgraw-hill.com
URL: http://www.mcgraw-hill.com

Third edition, 2003. $11.95 (paper). 160 pages.

EMPLOYMENT AGENCIES AND SEARCH FIRMS

★10042★ **Harper Associates**

3100 NW Hwy., Ste. 240
Farmington Hills, MI 48334
Ph: (248)932-1170   Fax: (248)932-1214
E-mail: info@harperjobs.com
URL: http://www.harperjobs.com

Executive search firm and employment agency.

★10043★ **Phyllis Hawkins and Associates**

7601 N. Central Ave., No. 5
Phoenix, AZ 85020
Ph: (602)263-0248   Fax: (602)678-1564
E-mail: phyllis@azlawsearch.com
URL: http://www.azlawsearch.com

Executive search firm focusing on attorney searches.

★10044★ **Physicians Search, Inc.**

5581 E. Stetson Ct.
Anaheim, CA 92807-4650
Ph: (714)685-1047   Fax: (714)685-1143
Fr: 800-748-6320
E-mail: info2@physicianssearch.com
URL: http://www.physicianssearch.com

Executive search firm. Affiliate office in Spokane, WA.

★10045★ **Professional Placement Associates, Inc.**

287 Bowman Ave., Ste. 309
Purchase, NY 10577-2517
Ph: (914)251-1000   Fax: (914)251-1055
E-mail: careers@ppasearch.com
URL: http://www.ppasearch.com

Executive search firm specializing in the health and medical field.

★10046★ **Shiloh Careers International, Inc.**

7105 Peach Ct., Ste. 102
PO Box 831
Brentwood, TN 37024-0831
Ph: (615)373-3090   Fax: (615)373-3480
E-mail: maryann@shilohcareers.com
URL: http://www.shilohcareers.com

Employment agency serving the industry field.

★10047★ **Team Placement Service, Inc.**

1414 Prince St., Ste. 202
Alexandria, VA 22314
Ph: (703)820-8618   Fax: (703)820-3368
Fr: 800-495-6767
E-mail: 4jobs@teamplace.com
URL: http://www.teamplace.com

Full-service personnel consultants provide placement for healthcare staff, physician and dentist, private practice, and hospitals. Conduct interviews, tests, and reference checks to select the top 20% of applicants. Survey applicants' skill levels, provide backup information on each candidate, select compatible candidates for consideration, and insure the hiring process minimizes potential legal liability. Industries served: healthcare and government agencies providing medical, dental, biotech, laboratory, hospitals, and physician search.

★10048★ **Weatherby Locums**

6451 N Federal Hwy., Ste. 800
Fort Lauderdale, FL 33308
Ph: (954)343-3050   Fax: 800-463-2985
Fr: (866)906-1636
E-mail: jobs@weatherbylocums.com
URL: http://www.weatherbylocums.com

Executive search firm for physicians. Branch office in Fairfax, VA.

ONLINE JOB SOURCES AND SERVICES

★10049★ **MDJobsite.com**
E-mail: contact@mdjobsite.com
URL: http://www.mdjobsite.com/

Description: Career search site for physicians. Physicians can search thousands of physician employment opportunities, register for email notifications of new jobs listed in their specialty and post a CV searchable by facilities and healthcare firms nationwide.

★10050★ **Medhunters.com**
Fr: 800-664-0278
E-mail: info@medhunters.com
URL: http://www.medhunters.com

Description: Career search site for jobs in all health care specialties; educational resources; visa and licensing information for relocation; interesting articles; relocation tools; links to professional organizations and general resources.

★10051★ **ProHealthJobs**
Fr: 800-796-1738
E-mail: Info@prohealthedujobs.com
URL: http://www.prohealthjobs.com

Description: Career resources site for the medical and health care field. Lists professional opportunities, product information, continuing education and open positions.

TRADESHOWS

★10052★ **American College of Foot and Ankle Surgeons Annual Meeting and Scientific Seminar**

American College of Foot and Ankle Surgeons
8725 W. Higgins Rd., Ste. 555
Chicago, IL 60631-2724
Ph: (773)693-9300   Fax: (847)292-2022
Fr: 800-421-2237
E-mail: info@acfas.org
URL: http://www.acfas.org

Annual. **Primary Exhibits:** Surgical and podiatric products.

★10053★ **American Podiatric Medical Association Annual Meeting**

American Podiatric Medical Association
9312 Old Georgetown Rd.
Bethesda, MD 20814-1621
Ph: (301)571-9200   Fax: (301)530-2752
Fr: 800-FOOTCARE
E-mail: bshaub@apma.org
URL: http://www.apma.org

Annual. **Primary Exhibits:** Podiatric supplies and services.

OTHER SOURCES

★10054★ *American Almanac of Jobs and Salaries*

HarperCollins
10 E. 53rd St.
New York, NY 10022
Ph: (212)207-7000   Fr: 800-242-7737
URL: http://www.harpercollins.com/

John W. Wright. Revised edition, 2000. $20.00 (paper). 672 pages. This is a comprehensive guide to the wages of hundreds of occupations in a wide variety of industries and organizations.

★10055★ American Association of Hospital Podiatrists (AAHP)

8508 18th Ave.
Brooklyn, NY 11214
Ph: (718)259-1822   Fax: (718)259-4002
E-mail: info@hospitalpodiatrists.org
URL: http://www.hospitalpodiatrists.org

Description: A general specialty group of the American Podiatric Medical Association. Podiatrists (trained and certified persons dealing in the care and diseases of the foot) who are affiliated with hospitals. Seeks to: elevate the standards of podiatry practices in hospitals and health institutions; standardize hospital podiatry procedures, charting, recording forms, and methods; promote understanding among personnel in podiatry, medicine, and allied health professions; aid podiatrists in attaining institutional affiliations; assist in the educational and teaching programs of health institutions and hospitals; foster the development of podiatric internships and residencies in hospitals and institutions. Compiles statistics.

★10056★ American Board of Podiatric Orthopedics and Primary Podiatric Medicine (ABPOPPM)

3812 Sepulvada Blvd., Ste. 530
Torrance, CA 90505
Ph: (310)375-0700   Fax: (310)375-1386

E-mail: admin@abpoppm.org
URL: http://www.abpoppm.org

Description: Podiatrists who have taken a competency exam prepared by the board. Offers certifying examinations in podiatric orthopedics and primary podiatric medicine aims at improving public health by encouraging and elevating standards for practicing podiatrics.

★10057★ American Board of Podiatric Surgery (ABPS)

445 Fillmore St.
San Francisco, CA 94117-3404
Ph: (415)553-7800   Fax: (415)553-7801
E-mail: info@abps.org
URL: http://www.abps.org

Description: Podiatrists certified as diplomates. Protects and improves public health by advancing the science of foot surgery and by encouraging the study and evaluation of standards of foot surgery. Acts upon application for certification of legally licensed podiatrists to ascertain their competency in foot surgery. Grants certificates to candidates who have met all qualifications.

★10058★ American Hospital Association (AHA)

1 N Franklin
Chicago, IL 60606-3421
Ph: (312)422-3000   Fax: (312)422-4796
URL: http://www.aha.org

Description: Represents health care provider organizations. Seeks to advance the health of individuals and communities. Leads, represents, and serves health care provider organizations that are accountable to the community and committed to health improvement.

★10059★ American Podiatric Medical Association (APMA)

9312 Old Georgetown Rd.
Bethesda, MD 20814-1621
Ph: (301)571-9200   Fr: 800-FOOTCARE

E-mail: gbgastwirth@apma.org
URL: http://www.apma.org

Description: Serves as professional soci of doctors of podiatric medicine.

★10060★ Exploring Health Occupations

Cambridge Educational
PO Box 2053
Princeton, NJ 08543-2053
Ph: 800-257-5126   Fax: (609)671-02
Fr: 800-468-4227
E-mail: custserv@films.com
URL: http://www.cambridgeeducational.cc

VHS and DVD. $159.90. 1999. Two-p. series provides a detailed view of the field medical technicians and technologis EMTs, nurses, therapists, and assistants

★10061★ Health Service Occupations

Delphi Productions
3159 6th St.
Boulder, CO 80304
Ph: (303)443-2100   Fax: (303)443-40.
Fr: 888-443-2400
E-mail: support@delphivideo.com
URL: http://www.delphivideo.com

$95.00. 50 minutes. Part of the Careers the 21st Century Video Library.

★10062★ Medicine & Related Occupations

Delphi Productions
3159 6th St.
Boulder, CO 80304
Ph: (303)443-2100   Fax: (303)443-402
Fr: 888-443-2400
E-mail: support@delphivideo.com
URL: http://www.delphivideo.com

$95.00. 45 minutes. Part of the Careers f the 21st Century Video Library.

Political and Legislative Aides

SOURCES OF HELP-WANTED ADS

★10063★ American Experiment Quarterly

Center of the American Experiment
12 South 6th St.
Minneapolis, MN 55402
Ph: (612)338-3605   Fax: (612)338-3621
URL: http://www.americanexperiment.org/

Quarterly. Magazine covering political issues and politics.

★10064★ Contemporary Politics

Taylor & Francis Group Journals
325 Chestnut St., Ste. 800
Philadelphia, PA 19106
Ph: (215)625-8900   Fax: (215)625-8914
Fr: 800-354-1420
URL: http://www.tandf.co.uk/journals/titles/13569775.asp

Quarterly. $629.00/year for institutions, print and online; $597.00/year for institutions, online only; $119.00/year for individuals. Journal covering social, economic, developmental, environmental and gender issues.

★10065★ In These Times

Institute for Public Affairs Inc.
2040 North Milwaukee Ave.
Chicago, IL 60647
Ph: (773)772-0100   Fax: (773)772-4180
E-mail: itt@inthesetimes.com
URL: http://www.inthesetimes.com

Biweekly. $24.95/year for individuals, U.S. $49.90 for two years, U.S. $39.95/year for Canada; $59.95/year for other countries. National political newsmagazine.

★10066★ Leadership and Policy in Schools

Taylor & Francis Group Journals
325 Chestnut St., Ste. 800
Philadelphia, PA 19106
Ph: (215)625-8900   Fax: (215)625-8914
Fr: 800-354-1420

URL: http://www.tandf.co.uk/journals/titles/15700763.asp

Quarterly. $477.00/year for institutions, print and online; $453.00/year for institutions, online only; $227.00/year for individuals; $60.00/year for ICSEI members. Journal providing information about leadership and policy in primary and secondary education.

★10067★ Presidential Studies Quarterly

Wiley-Blackwell
350 Main St. Commerce Pl.
Malden, MA 02148
Ph: (781)388-8200   Fax: (781)388-8210
Fr: 800-759-6120
URL: http://www.blackwell-synergy.com

Quarterly. $355.00/year for institutions, print and premium online; $323.00/year for institutions, print and standard online; $307.00/year for institutions, premium online only; $266.00/year for institutions, other countries, print and premium online; $242.00/year for institutions, other countries, print and standard online; $230.00/year for institutions, other countries, premium online only. Publication covering political science and history.

★10068★ Theory and Research in Education

Sage Publications Inc.
2455 Teller Rd.
Thousand Oaks, CA 91320
Ph: (805)499-0721   Fax: (805)499-8096
URL: http://tre.sagepub.com/

$459.00/year for institutions, print and online; $413.00/year for institutions, online only; $450.00/year for institutions, print only; $77.00/year for individuals, print only. Interdisciplinary journal covering normative and theoretical issues concerning education including multi-faceted philosophical analysis of moral, social, political and epistemological problems and issues arising from educational practice.

PLACEMENT AND JOB REFERRAL SERVICES

★10069★ American Political Science Association (APSA)

1527 New Hampshire Ave. NW
Washington, DC 20036-1206
Ph: (202)483-2512   Fax: (202)483-2657
E-mail: apsa@apsanet.org
URL: http://www.apsanet.org

Description: College and university teachers of political science, public officials, research workers, and businessmen. Encourages the impartial study and promotes the development of the art and science of government. Develops research projects of public interest and educational programs for political scientists and journalists; seeks to improve the knowledge of and increase citizen participation in political and governmental affairs. Serves as clearinghouse for teaching and research positions in colleges, universities, and research bureaus in the U.S. and abroad and for positions open to political scientists in government and private business; conducts Congressional Fellowship Program. Conducts Committee on Professional Ethic, and Rights and Freedom. Offers placement service.

EMPLOYER DIRECTORIES AND NETWORKING LISTS

★10070★ Carroll's Federal Directory

Carroll Publishing
4701 Sangamore Rd., Ste. S-155
Bethesda, MD 20816
Ph: (301)263-9800   Fax: (301)263-9801
Fr: 800-336-4240
URL: http://www.carrollpub.com

Four times/year. $425.00 for single issue. Covers about 46,000 executive managers in federal government offices in Washington, D.C., including executive, congressional and judicial branches; members of Congress and Congressional committees and staff. Entries include: Agency names, titles, office address (including room numbers), e-mail addresses, and telephone and fax numbers. Also available as part of a "library edition" titled "Federal Directory Annual." Arrangement: By cabinet department or administrative agency. Indexes: Keyword, personal name (with phone) and e-mail addresses.

★10071★ **Congressional Directory**
Capitol Advantage
2751 Prosperity Ave., Ste. 600
Fairfax, VA 22031
Ph: (703)289-4670   Fax: (703)289-4678
Fr: 800-659-8708
URL: http://capitoladvantage.com/publishing/products.html

Annual. $17.95 for individuals. Covers 100 current senators and 440 House of Representative members. Entries include: Name, district office address, phone, fax; names and titles of key staff; committee and subcommittee assignments; biographical data, percentage of votes won, photo. Arrangement: Available in separate alphabetical, geographical, or condensed editions. Indexes: Name.

★10072★ **Congressional Yellow Book**
Leadership Directories Inc.
104 5th Ave.
New York, NY 10011
Ph: (212)627-4140   Fax: (212)645-0931
E-mail: congressional@leadershipdirectories.com
URL: http://www.leadershipdirectories.com/products/cyb.htm

Quarterly; latest edition 2007. $475.00 for individuals; $452.00 for individuals, standing order. Covers members of Congress and their principal aides, Congressional committees, leadership, and congressional support arms. Entries include: For members of Congress–Name, Washington office address, party affiliation, state or district represented, year began service, reelection year; names, titles, and legislative responsibilities of principal aides, member's committee assignments and other responsibilities; photograph, biographical data, fax, and map of district; state and district office addresses and phone; ZIP codes by congressional district. For committees–Committee name, office address, phone, members' names and parties, description of committee jurisdiction, fax, key staff for full and subcommittees. Arrangement: Alphabetical by member of Congress or committee name. Indexes: Name, subject, organization.

★10073★ **United States Government Manual**
Office of the Federal Register
c/o The National Archives and Records Administration
8601 Adelphi Rd.
College Park, MD 20740-6001
Ph: (301)837-0482   Fax: (301)837-0483
Fr: (866)272-6272
URL: http://www.gpoaccess.gov/gmanual/index.html

Annual, September; latest edition 2007-2008. $27.00 for individuals. Provides information on the agencies of the executive, judicial, and legislative branches of the Federal government. Contains a section on terminated or transferred agencies. Arrangement: Classified by department and agency. Indexes: Personal name, agency/subject.

★10074★ **Washington: A Comprehensive Directory of the Key Institutions and Leaders in the National Capital Area**
Columbia Books Inc.
8120 Woodmont Ave., Ste. 110
Bethesda, MD 20814
Ph: (202)464-1662   Fax: (202)464-1775
Fr: 888-265-0600
URL: http://www.columbiabooks.com

Annual, May. Covers over 5,000 federal and district government offices, businesses, associations, publications, radio and television stations, labor organizations, religious and cultural institutions, health care facilities and community organizations in the District of Columbia area. Entries include: Name, address, phone, names and titles of key personnel and board of directors. Arrangement: Classified by subject. Indexes: Individuals, organizations.

★10075★ **Washington Information Directory**
CQ Press
1255 22nd St. NW, Ste. 400
Washington, DC 20037
Ph: (202)729-1800   Fax: 800-380-3810
Fr: (866)427-7737
URL: http://www.cqpress.com

Annual; latest edition 2007. $128.00 for individuals. Covers 5,000 governmental agencies, congressional committees, and non-governmental associations considered competent sources of specialized information. Entries include: Name of agency, committee, or association; address, phone, fax, and Internet address; annotation concerning function or activities of the office; and name of contact. Arrangement: Classified by activity or competence (economics and business, housing and urban affairs, etc.). Indexes: Subject, agency/organization name, contact name.

HANDBOOKS AND MANUALS

★10076★ **The Book of US Government Jobs: Where They Are, What's Available and How to Get One**
Bookhaven Press LLC
249 Field Club Cir.
McKees Rocks, PA 15136
Ph: (412)494-6926   Fax: (412)494-5749
E-mail: info@bookhavenpress.com
URL: http://www.bookhavenpress.com

Dennis Damp. 9th edition. 2005. 278 pages.

★10077★ **Career Opportunities in Politics, Government, and Activism**
Checkmark Books
132 W. 31st St., 17th Fl.
New York, NY 10001-2006
Ph: (212)967-8800   Fax: (212)967-9196
Fr: 800-322-8755

Joan Axelrod-Contrada and John Kerry. May 2003. 274 pages.

★10078★ **Great Jobs for Political Science Majors**
The McGraw-Hill Companies
PO Box 182604
Columbus, OH 43272
Fax: (614)759-3749   Fr: 877-883-5524
E-mail: customer.service@mcgraw-hill.com
URL: http://www.mcgraw-hill.com

Mark Rowh. Second edition, 2003. $15.95 (paper). 240 pages. Includes index.

★10079★ **The Insider's Guide to Political Internships: What to Do Once You're in the Door**
Westview Press
2465 Central Ave.
Boulder, CO 80301
Ph: (720)406-7336
URL: http://www.perseusbooksgroup.com/westview/index.jsp

Grant Reeher, Mack Mariani. September 2002. 240 pages.

★10080★ **Washington Job Source**
Benjamin Scott Publishing
20 E. Colorado Blvd., No. 202
Pasadena, CA 91105
Ph: (626)449-1339   Fax: (626)449-1389
Fr: 800-448-4959

Mary McMahon. Fifth edition, 2002. 15.95. 482 pages.

ONLINE JOB SOURCES AND SERVICES

★10081★ **Political and Government Career Resources**
E-mail: info@dc.politixgroup.com
URL: http://www.politixgroup.com
Description: Job listings.

OTHER SOURCES

★10082★ **Congressional Black Caucus (CBC)**
2236 Rayburn Bldg.
Washington, DC 20515-3312
Ph: (202)226-9776   Fax: (202)225-1512
URL: http://

www.congressionalblackcaucus.net

Members: Black members of the U.S. House of Representatives. **Purpose:** Addresses the legislative concerns of black and other underrepresented citizens and to for-malize and strengthen the efforts of its members. Works to implement these objectives through personal contact with other House members, through the dissemination of information to individual black constituents, and by working closely with black elected officials in other levels of government. **Activities:** Establishes a yearly legislative agenda setting forth the issues which it supports: full employment, national health development, welfare reform, and international affairs.

Political Scientists

SOURCES OF HELP-WANTED ADS

★10083★ American Journal of Political Science

Wiley-Blackwell
350 Main St. Commerce Pl.
Malden, MA 02148
Ph: (781)388-8200   Fax: (781)388-8210
Fr: 800-759-6120
URL: http://www.ajps.org/

Quarterly. $388.00/year for institutions, print plus premium online; $353.00/year for institutions, print plus standard online; $335.00/year for institutions, premium online only; $301.00/year for institutions, other countries, print plus premium online; $274.00/year for institutions, other countries, print plus standard online; $260.00/year for institutions, other countries, premium online only. Journal focusing on all major areas of political science including American politics, public policy, international relations, comparative politics, political methodology, and political theory.

★10084★ BardPolitik

Bard College
PO Box 5000
Annandale on Hudson, NY 12504-5000
Ph: (845)758-6822
URL: http://bardcollege.com/about/publications/

Semiannual. Free. Magazine that covers debate and discussion on global political and international affairs.

★10085★ CNPS Newsletter

Caucus for a New Political Science
1527 New Hampshire Ave. NW
Washington, DC 20036
Ph: (202)483-2512   Fax: (202)483-2657
E-mail: bwright@fullerton.edu
URL: http://www.apsanet.org/~new/

Description: 3/yr. Contains association activities and news, and listings of members' publications.

★10086★ Federal Times

Army Times Publishing Co.
6883 Commercial Dr.
Springfield, VA 22159-0500
Ph: (703)750-7400   Fr: 800-368-5718
URL: http://www.armytimes.com/employment

Weekly (Mon.). Federal bureaucracy; technology in government.

★10087★ In These Times

Institute for Public Affairs Inc.
2040 North Milwaukee Ave.
Chicago, IL 60647
Ph: (773)772-0100   Fax: (773)772-4180
E-mail: itt@inthesetimes.com
URL: http://www.inthesetimes.com

Biweekly. $24.95/year for individuals, U.S. $49.90 for two years, U.S. $39.95/year for Canada; $59.95/year for other countries. National political newsmagazine.

★10088★ International Political Science Review

Sage Publications Inc.
2455 Teller Rd.
Thousand Oaks, CA 91320
Ph: (805)499-0721   Fax: (805)499-8096
URL: http://www.sagepub.com/journalsProdDesc.nav?prodId=Journal20

Quarterly. $571.00/year for institutions, print & e-access; $628.00/year for institutions, current volume print & all online content; $514.00/year for institutions, e-access; $571.00/year for institutions, backfile lease, e-access plus backfile; $830.11/year for institutions, backfile purchase, e-access (content through 1999); $560.00/year for institutions, print only; $104.00/year for individuals, print only; $123.00 for institutions, single print; $27.00 for individuals, single print. Journal for political scientists who are interested in studying political phenomena in the contemporary context of increasing international interdependence and global change; journal of the International Political Science Association (IPSA).

★10089★ Miller Center Report

Miller Center of Public Affairs
PO Box 400406
Charlottesville, VA 22904-4406
Ph: (434)924-7236   Fax: (434)982-2739
URL: http://www.millercenter.virginia.edu/

Description: Quarterly. Reports on the activities and programs of the Miller Center. Features information on the study of American governance and presidency. Recurring features include reports of meetings, and notices of publications available.

★10090★ Political Science Educator

American Political Science Association (APSA)
1527 New Hampshire Ave., NW
Washington, DC 20036-1206
Ph: (202)483-2512   Fax: (202)483-2657
E-mail: apsa@apsanet.org
URL: http://www.apsanet.org

Description: Quarterly. Provides information on The American Political Science Association. Includes news of meetings and conferences, and reviews of pertinent books.

★10091★ Presidential Studies Quarterly

Wiley-Blackwell
350 Main St. Commerce Pl.
Malden, MA 02148
Ph: (781)388-8200   Fax: (781)388-821
Fr: 800-759-6120
URL: http://www.blackwell-synergy.com

Quarterly. $355.00/year for institutions, print and premium online; $323.00/year for institutions, print and standard online; $307.00/year for institutions, premium online only; $266.00/year for institutions, other countries, print and premium online; $242.00/year for institutions, other countries, print and standard online; $230.00/year for institutions, other countries, premium online only. Publication covering political science and history.

★10092★ Quarterly Journal of Political Science

Now Publishers
PO Box 1024
Hanover, MA 02339
Ph: (781)871-0245
URL: http://www.qjps.com

Quarterly. $315.00/year for institutions, plus shipping cost; North America; $315.00/year for institutions, plus shipping cost; outside North America; $355.00/year for institutions, print and online; plus shipping costs; North America; $355.00/year for institutions, print and online; outside North America; $75.00/year for individuals, print and online; plus $16 shipping fee; $50.00/year for individuals, online only. Journal focusing on positive political science and contemporary political economy.

★10093★ State Politics & Policy Quarterly

University of Illinois Press
1325 S Oak St.
Champaign, IL 61820-6903
Ph: (217)333-0950   Fax: (217)244-8082
Fr: 800-537-5487
URL: http://www.press.uillinois.edu/journals/sppq.html

Quarterly. $42.00/year for individuals; $120.00/year for institutions; $82.00/year for individuals, out of country; $160.00/year for institutions, other countries; $48.00 for single issue, institutions; $12.00 for single issue, individuals. Official journal of the State Politics and Policy section of the American Political Science Association covering studies that develop general hypotheses of the political behavior and policymaking and test those hypotheses using methodological advantages of the states.

★10094★ White House Studies

Nova Science Publishers Inc.
400 Oser Ave., Ste. 1600
Hauppauge, NY 11788-3619
Ph: (631)231-7269   Fax: (631)231-8175
URL: http://www.novapublishers.com/catalog/product_info.php?cPat

Quarterly. $245.00/year for individuals. Publication covering political science and history.

PLACEMENT AND JOB REFERRAL SERVICES

★10095★ African Studies Association (ASA)

Douglass Campus
132 George St.
New Brunswick, NJ 08901-1400
Ph: (732)932-8173   Fax: (732)932-3394
E-mail: asaed@rci.rutgers.edu
URL: http://www.africanstudies.org

Members: Persons specializing in teaching, writing, or research on Africa including political cal scientists, historians, geographers, anthropologists, economists, librarians, linguists, and government officials; persons who are studying African subjects; institutional members are universities, libraries, government agencies, and others interested in receiving information about Africa. **Purpose:** Seeks to foster communication and to stimulate research among scholars on Africa. **Activities:** Sponsors placement service; conducts panels and discussion groups; presents exhibits and films.

★10096★ American Political Science Association (APSA)

1527 New Hampshire Ave. NW
Washington, DC 20036-1206
Ph: (202)483-2512   Fax: (202)483-2657
E-mail: apsa@apsanet.org
URL: http://www.apsanet.org

Description: College and university teachers of political science, public officials, research workers, and businessmen. Encourages the impartial study and promotes the development of the art and science of government. Develops research projects of public interest and educational programs for political scientists and journalists; seeks to improve the knowledge of and increase citizen participation in political and governmental affairs. Serves as clearinghouse for teaching and research positions in colleges, universities, and research bureaus in the U.S. and abroad and for positions open to political scientists in government and private business; conducts Congressional Fellowship Program. Conducts Committee on Professional Ethic, and Rights and Freedom. Offers placement service.

EMPLOYER DIRECTORIES AND NETWORKING LISTS

★10097★ American Political Science Association-Centennial Biographical Directory of Members

American Political Science Association
1527 New Hampshire Ave. NW
Washington, DC 20036-1206
Ph: (202)483-2512   Fax: (202)483-2657
URL: http://www.apsanet.org

Irregular; latest edition 2001. $95.00 for nonmembers, print product only; $50.00 for members, print product or CD-ROM; $65.00 for members, print product and CD-ROM, combined. Number of listings: 13,500. Entries include: Name, address, affiliation, highest degree, fields of interest, phone, e-mail, URL, honors, employment history, publications. Arrangement: Alphabetical. Indexes: Women members; African American members; Asian American members; Latino/a members; Native American members; fields of interest; geographical.

★10098★ Career Opportunities in Politics, Government, and Activism

Facts On File Inc.
132 W 31st St., 17th Fl.
New York, NY 10001
Ph: (212)967-8800   Fax: 800-678-3633
Fr: 800-322-8755
URL: http://www.factsonfile.com

Published 2003. $49.50 for individuals; $44.55 for libraries. Covers 70 jobs from government, human services, and international relations, such as mayor, governor, political consultant, urban/regional planner, press secretary, foreign service officer, community organizer, and human rights advocate.

★10099★ Carroll's Federal Directory

Carroll Publishing
4701 Sangamore Rd., Ste. S-155
Bethesda, MD 20816
Ph: (301)263-9800   Fax: (301)263-9801
Fr: 800-336-4240
URL: http://www.carrollpub.com

Four times/year. $425.00 for single issue. Covers about 46,000 executive managers in federal government offices in Washington, D.C., including executive, congressional and judicial branches; members of Congress and Congressional committees and staff. Entries include: Agency names, titles, office address (including room numbers), e-mail addresses, and telephone and fax numbers. Also available as part of a "library edition" titled "Federal Directory Annual." Arrangement: By cabinet department or administrative agency. Indexes: Keyword, personal name (with phone) and e-mail addresses.

★10100★ Encyclopedia of Governmental Advisory Organizations

Gale, Cengage Learning
27500 Drake Rd.
Farmington Hills, MI 48331-3535
Ph: (248)699-4253   Fax: (248)699-8065
Fr: 800-877-4253
E-mail: businessproducts@gale.com
URL: http://www.gale.com

Annual; latest edition 22nd, published May 2007. $850.00 for individuals. Covers more than 7,300 boards, panels, commissions, committees, presidential conferences, and other groups that advise the President, Congress, and departments and agencies of federal government; includes interagency committees and federally sponsored conferences. Also includes historically significant organizations. Entries include: Unit name, address, phone, URL and e-mail (if active), name of principal executive, legal basis for the unit, purpose, reports and publications, findings and recommendations, description of activities, members. Arrangement: Classified by general subject. Indexes: Alphabetical/keyword; personnel; publication; federal department/agency; presidential administration.

★10101★ Federal Yellow Book

Leadership Directories Inc.
104 5th Ave.
New York, NY 10011
Ph: (212)627-4140   Fax: (212)645-0931
E-mail: federal@leadershipdirectories.com
URL: http://www.leadershipdirectories.com/products/fyb.htm

Quarterly; latest edition 2007. $475.00 for individuals; $452.00 for individuals, standing order. Covers federal departments, including the Executive Office of the President, the Office of the Vice President, the Office of Management and Budget, the Cabinet, and the National Security Council, and over 40,000 key personnel and over 70 independent federal agencies. Entries include: For personnel–Name, address, phone, fax, e-mail, titles. For departments and agencies–Office, or branch name and address; names and titles of principal personnel, with their room numbers, direct-dial phone numbers, and e-mails. Arrangement: Classified by department or agency. Indexes: Subject, organization, individuals' names.

★10102★ Jewish Americans and Political Participation

ABC-CLIO
130 Cremona Dr.
PO Box 1911
Santa Barbara, CA 93117
Ph: (805)968-1911   Fax: (805)685-9685
Fr: 800-368-6868
URL: http://www.abc-clio.com

August 2002. Publication includes: List of American Jewish historical and political organizations. Entries include: Name, address, phone, and Web site address. Principal content of publication is a historical and current look at the participation of Jews in American politics. Indexes: Alphabetical.

★10103★ Personnel Service Newsletter

American Political Science Association
1527 New Hampshire Ave. NW
Washington, DC 20036-1206
Ph: (202)483-2512   Fax: (202)483-2657
E-mail: psn@apsanet.org
URL: http://www.apsanet.org

Monthly. Covers academic, governmental, and other positions currently open for political scientists, as well as opportunities for graduate research, study, travel, and scholarly exchange abroad. Entries include: For professional openings–Employer name, address, name of contact, description of position; some listings include phone. For fellowships–Name of sponsoring institution, contact name, address, phone, description of award, goals, requirements, deadline. Arrangement: Classified by type of position (administrative, academic, fellowship, late notice); academic positions are by subject area.

★10104★ United States Government Manual

Office of the Federal Register
c/o The National Archives and Records Administration
8601 Adelphi Rd.
College Park, MD 20740-6001
Ph: (301)837-0482   Fax: (301)837-0483
Fr: (866)272-6272
URL: http://www.gpoaccess.gov/gmanual/index.html

Annual, September; latest edition 2007-2008. $27.00 for individuals. Provides information on the agencies of the executive, judicial, and legislative branches of the Federal government. Contains a section on terminated or transferred agencies. Arrangement: Classified by department and agency. Indexes: Personal name, agency/subject.

★10105★ Washington: A Comprehensive Directory of the Key Institutions and Leaders in the National Capital Area

Columbia Books Inc.
8120 Woodmont Ave., Ste. 110
Bethesda, MD 20814
Ph: (202)464-1662   Fax: (202)464-1775
Fr: 888-265-0600
URL: http://www.columbiabooks.com

Annual, May. Covers over 5,000 federal and district government offices, businesses, associations, publications, radio and television stations, labor organizations, religious and cultural institutions, health care facilities and community organizations in the District of Columbia area. Entries include: Name, address, phone, names and titles of key personnel and board of directors. Arrangement: Classified by subject. Indexes: Individuals, organizations.

★10106★ Washington Information Directory

CQ Press
1255 22nd St. NW, Ste. 400
Washington, DC 20037
Ph: (202)729-1800   Fax: 800-380-3810
Fr: (866)427-7737
URL: http://www.cqpress.com

Annual; latest edition 2007. $128.00 for individuals. Covers 5,000 governmental agencies, congressional committees, and non-governmental associations considered competent sources of specialized information. Entries include: Name of agency, committee, or association; address, phone, fax, and Internet address; annotation concerning function or activities of the office; and name of contact. Arrangement: Classified by activity or competence (economics and business, housing and urban affairs, etc.). Indexes: Subject, agency/organization name, contact name.

HANDBOOKS AND MANUALS

★10107★ The Book of US Government Jobs: Where They Are, What's Available and How to Get One

Bookhaven Press LLC
249 Field Club Cir.
McKees Rocks, PA 15136
Ph: (412)494-6926   Fax: (412)494-5749
E-mail: info@bookhavenpress.com
URL: http://www.bookhavenpress.com

Dennis Damp. 9th edition. 2005. 278 pages.

★10108★ Career Opportunities in Politics, Government, and Activism

Checkmark Books
132 W. 31st St., 17th Fl.
New York, NY 10001-2006
Ph: (212)967-8800   Fax: (212)967-9196
Fr: 800-322-8755

Joan Axelrod-Contrada and John Kerry. May 2003. 274 pages.

★10109★ Careers in International Affairs

Georgetown University Press
3240 Prospect St., NW
Washington, DC 20007
Ph: (202)687-5889   Fax: (202)687-6340
Fr: 800-246-9606
E-mail: gupress@georgetown.edu
URL: http://www.press.georgetown.edu/

Maria Carland and Lisa Gihring (editors). Seventh edition, 2003. $24.95 (paper). 371 pages. Includes index and bibliography.

★10110★ Careers & the Study of Political Science: A Guide for Undergraduates

American Political Science Association
1527 New Hampshire Ave., NW
Washington, DC 20036-1206
Ph: (202)483-2512   Fax: (202)483-2657
E-mail: apsa@apsanet.org
URL: http://www.apsanet.org/

Sixth edition, 2001. $6.00 (paper). 35 pages.

★10111★ Great Jobs for Political Science Majors

The McGraw-Hill Companies
PO Box 182604
Columbus, OH 43272
Fax: (614)759-3749   Fr: 877-883-5524
E-mail: customer.service@mcgraw-hill.com
URL: http://www.mcgraw-hill.com

Mark Rowh. Second edition, 2003. $15.95 (paper). 240 pages. Includes index.

★10112★ The Insider's Guide to Political Internships: What to Do Once You're in the Door

Westview Press
2465 Central Ave.
Boulder, CO 80301
Ph: (720)406-7336

URL: http://www.perseusbooksgroup.com/westview/index.jsp

Grant Reeher, Mack Mariani. September 2002. 240 pages.

★10113★ Opportunities in Social Science Careers

The McGraw-Hill Companies
PO Box 182604
Columbus, OH 43272
Fax: (614)759-3749   Fr: 877-883-5524
E-mail: customer.service@mcgraw-hill.com
URL: http://www.mcgraw-hill.com

Rosanne J. Marek. 2004. $13.95. 160 Pages. VGM Opportunities Series.

TRADESHOWS

★10114★ American Political Science Association Meeting

American Political Science Association
1527 New Hampshire Ave., NW
Washington, DC 20036-1206
Ph: (202)483-2512   Fax: (202)483-2657
E-mail: apsa@apsanet.org
URL: http://www.apsanet.org

Annual. **Primary Exhibits:** Publications and computer software.

OTHER SOURCES

★10115★ Academy of Political Science (APS)

475 Riverside Dr., Ste. 1274
New York, NY 10115-1274
Ph: (212)870-2500   Fax: (212)870-2202
E-mail: aps@psqonline.org
URL: http://www.psqonline.org

Members: Individual members, libraries and institutions. **Purpose:** Promotes the cultivation of political science and its application to the solution of political, social, and economic problems.

★10116★ American Academy of Political and Social Science (AAPSS)

3814 Walnut St.
Philadelphia, PA 19104-6197
Ph: (215)746-6500   Fax: (215)573-3003
E-mail: phyllis.kaniss@sas.upenn.edu
URL: http://www.aapss.org

Members: Professionals and laymen concerned with the political and social sciences and related fields. **Purpose:** Promotes the progress of political and social science through publications and meetings. The academy does not take sides in controver-

sial issues, but seeks to gather and present reliable information to assist the public in forming an intelligent and accurate judgment.

★10117★ American Association of Political Consultants (AAPC)

600 Pennsylvania Ave. SE, Ste. 330
Washington, DC 20003
Ph: (202)544-9815   Fax: (202)544-9816
E-mail: info@theaapc.org
URL: http://www.theaapc.org

Description: Regular members are corporations and individuals who devote a major portion of their time to or earn a major portion of their livelihood from political counseling and related activities; associate members are persons who devote part of their time to or earn part of their living from political counseling, have an interest in the political process, are teachers of political science, or intend to become actively involved in political activities. Provides a vehicle for the exchange of information, resources, and ideas among persons involved in political activity. Arranges seminars and holds biennial updates on campaign techniques and professional advances.

★10118★ Congressional Black Caucus (CBC)

2236 Rayburn Bldg.
Washington, DC 20515-3312
Ph: (202)226-9776   Fax: (202)225-1512
URL: http://www.congressionalblackcaucus.net

Members: Black members of the U.S. House of Representatives. **Purpose:** Addresses the legislative concerns of black and other underrepresented citizens and to formalize and strengthen the efforts of its members. Works to implement these objectives through personal contact with other House members, through the dissemination of information to individual black constituents, and by working closely with black elected officials in other levels of government. **Activities:** Establishes a yearly legislative agenda setting forth the issues which it supports: full employment, national health development, welfare reform, and international affairs.

★10119★ International Studies Association (ISA)

University of Arizona
324 Social Sciences Bldg.
Tucson, AZ 85721
Ph: (520)621-7715   Fax: (520)621-5780
E-mail: isa@u.arizona.edu
URL: http://www.isanet.org

Members: Social scientists and other scholars from a wide variety of disciplines who are specialists in international affairs and cross-cultural studies; academicians; government officials; officials in international organizations; business executives; students. **Pur-

pose:** Promotes research, improved teaching, and the orderly growth of knowledge in the field of international studies; emphasizes a multidisciplinary approach to problems. **Activities:** Conducts conventions, workshops and discussion groups.

★10120★ Storming Washington: An Intern's Guide to National Government

American Political Science Association
1527 New Hampshire Ave., NW
Washington, DC 20036-1206
Ph: (202)483-2512   Fax: (202)483-2657
E-mail: apsa@apsanet.org
URL: http://www.apsanet.org/

Stephen E. Frantzich. Fourth edition, 2001. $6.00 (paper). 82 pages.

★10121★ U.S. Public Interest Research Group (USPIRG)

218 D St. SE
Washington, DC 20003-1900
Ph: (202)546-9707   Fax: (202)546-2461
E-mail: membershipservices@pirg.org
URL: http://www.uspirg.org

Description: Individuals who contribute time, effort, or funds toward public interest research and advocacy. Conducts research, monitors corporate and government actions, and lobbies for reforms on consumer, environmental, energy, and governmental issues. Current efforts include support for: laws to protect consumers from unsafe products and unfair banking practices; laws to reduce the use of toxic chemicals; strengthening clean air laws; efforts to reduce global warming and ozone depletion; energy conservation and use of safe, renewable energy sources. Sponsors internships for college students; provides opportunities for students to receive academic credit for activities such as legislative research, lobbying, and public education and organizing. Offers summer jobs.

★10122★ Women's Caucus for Political Science (WCPS)

SDSU Dept. of Political Science
5500 Campanile Dr.
San Diego, CA 92182
Ph: (803)777-7442
E-mail: rschreib@mail.sdsu.edu
URL: http://www.cas.sc.edu/poli/caucus/main.html

Members: Women professionally trained in political science. **Purpose:** Purposes are to: upgrade the status of women in the profession of political science; promote equal opportunities for women political scientists for graduate admission, financial assistance in such schools, and in employment, promotion, and tenure. **Activities:** Advances candidates for consideration for APSA offices and committees.

Postal Service Workers

SOURCES OF HELP-WANTED ADS

★10123★ The American Postal Worker
American Postal Workers Union, AFL-CIO
1300 L St. NW
Washington, DC 20005
Ph: (202)842-4200   Fax: (202)842-4297

Monthly. $3.00/year for individuals. AFL-CIO postal labor.

★10124★ Business Mailers Review
Business Mailers Review
PO Box 328
Boyds, MD 20841
Ph: (301)528-0011   Fax: (301)528-2497
URL: http://
www.businessmailersreview.com/

Description: Biweekly. Concerned with the monitoring of the U.S. Postal Service, private carriers, and suppliers. Offers volume mailers, traffic managers, parcel shippers, and operators of letter-shops news of current developments in the field of business mailings. Reports on new technologies and products, rate changes, metering alternatives, and relevant legislative activity. Recurring features include interviews and news of research.

★10125★ NAPS Letter
National Association of Postal Supervisors
1727 King St., Ste. 400
Alexandria, VA 22314-2753
Ph: (703)836-9660   Fax: (703)836-9665
URL: http://www.naps.org/

Description: Biweekly. Reports news of interest to postal supervisors on postal service policy, legislative actions, civil service benefits, and related subjects having an effect upon the postal service. Recurring features include a schedule of activities and columns titled Capitol Hill Notes and Resolutions Update.

★10126★ Postal Bulletin
U.S. Government Printing Office and
  Superintendent of Documents
PO Box 371954
Pittsburgh, PA 15250-7954
Ph: (202)512-1800   Fax: (202)512-2104
URL: http://www.usps.com/cpim/ftp/bulletin/
pb.htm

Bimonthly. $163.00/year for individuals, U.S.; $228.20/year for other countries; $13.00 for single issue, U.S.; $18.20/year for single issue, other countries. Bulletin reporting U.S. Postal Service news.

★10127★ Postal Record
National Association of Letter Carriers
100 Indiana Ave. NW
Washington, DC 20001-2144
Ph: (202)393-4695
URL: http://www.nalc.org/news/precord/in-dex.html

Monthly. Magazine for active and retired letter carriers.

★10128★ Postal World
United Communications Group
11300 Rockville Pike, Ste. 1100
Rockville, MD 20852-3030
Ph: (301)287-2700   Fax: (301)816-8945
Fr: 800-929-4824
E-mail: webmaster@ucg.com
URL: http://www.ucg.com/IndexForm.aspx

Description: Disseminates information to help readers run a more efficient mail operation. Discusses how to trim postage costs, speed delivery, improve mailroom productivity, and plan for rate increases. Recurring features include an annual salary survey and periodic special reports.

★10129★ Postmasters Advocate Express
National League of Postmasters of the
  United States
5904 Richmond Highway, Ste.500
Alexandria, VA 22303-1864
Ph: (703)329-4550   Fax: (703)329-0466
E-mail: information@postmasters.org
URL: http://www.postmasters.org

Description: 5-9 issues/year. Monitors the advocacy activities of the League, which sponsors the Postmasters Benefit Plan and represents postmasters and other federal employees before Congress and provides liaison to USPS. Covers pertinent legislative developments and postal issues. Recurring features include items on members and information on League officer training programs.

★10130★ Postmasters Gazette
National Association of Postmasters
8 Herbert St.
Alexandria, VA 22305-2628
Ph: (703)683-9027   Fax: (703)683-6820
URL: http://www.napus.org/mempubs/ga-zette.htm

Monthly. $18.00/year for nonmembers. Postal magazine.

PLACEMENT AND JOB REFERRAL SERVICES

★10131★ Mail Systems Management Association (MSMA)
PO Box 1145
North Riverside, IL 60546-1145
Ph: (708)853-0471   Fr: 800-714-6762
E-mail: fahyb@aol.com
URL: http://www.msmanational.org

Description: Mail management executives. Provides training, through the development of management skills, in reducing costs, improving services, and reducing employee turnover. Organizes meetings to discuss topics such as presort discounts, scheduling, and recruiting and training personnel. Conducts certification program, training programs for mail distribution clerks, and management programs for mail managers and supervisors. Maintains placement service. Conducts research; operates speakers' bureau and consulting service.

EMPLOYER DIRECTORIES AND NETWORKING LISTS

★10132★ National Five-Digit Zip Code and Post Offices Directory

United States Postal Service
6060 Primacy Pky., Ste. 201
Memphis, TN 38188-0001
Fax: (901)681-4409   Fr: 800-275-8777
URL: http://www.usps.com

Annual, January. Covers post offices, named stations, named branches, community post offices, and place names of former post offices frequently used as delivery addresses. Also includes Postal Service regional offices, bulk mail centers, etc. Zip codes are given for cities, for buildings having their own zip codes, and for streets and blocks within zip code areas. Entries include: For post offices–Post office name, county, state, and zip code. For Postal Service installations–Office name, mailing address, areas served. Arrangement: Post offices are listed alphabetically and by zip code. Cities that have more than one zip code are listed separately by state, then city, with buildings and other installations with their own zip codes listed first. Discontinued post offices and military installation zip code lists are also provided separately.

★10133★ Who's Who-The MFSA Buyer's Guide to Blue Ribbon Mailing Services

Mail & Fulfillment Service Association
1421 Prince St., Ste. 410
Alexandria, VA 22314-2806
Ph: (703)836-9200   Fax: (703)548-8204
Fr: 800-333-6272
URL: http://www.mfsanet.org

Annual, December. Covers 750 member firms that provide printing, addressing, inserting, sorting, and other mailing services, and mailing list brokers. Entries include: Firm name; MFSA representative name and title, address, phone, coded list of services, gross business volume for latest year. Arrangement: Geographical. Indexes: Company name; personal name; geographical; product/service.

HANDBOOKS AND MANUALS

★10134★ Post Office Jobs: How to Get a Job With the U.S. Postal Service

Bookhaven Press LLC
249 Field Club Cir.
McKees Rocks, PA 15136
Ph: (412)494-6926   Fax: (412)494-5749
E-mail: info@bookhavenpress.com
URL: http://www.bookhavenpress.com

Dennis V. Damp. Third edition. 2003. 256 pages. Includes tips on how to identify job openings, preparing for interviews, and a study guide for exams.

ONLINE JOB SOURCES AND SERVICES

★10135★ Mailman Stuff

E-mail: mailman@.rollanet.org
URL: http://www.mailmanstuff.com

Description: Shared resources for letter carriers.

★10136★ Postmasters Online

E-mail: rupzip@cs.com
URL: http://ourworld-top.cs.com/rupzip/home.htm

Description: Provides current news and links to other postal sites.

TRADESHOWS

★10137★ National Association of Postmasters of the United States Convention

National Association of Postmasters of the United States
8 Herbert St.
Alexandria, VA 22305-2600
Ph: (703)683-9027   Fax: (703)683-6820
E-mail: napusinfo@napus.org
URL: http://www.napus.org

Annual. **Primary Exhibits:** Office supplies and materials for the postal service. **Dates and Locations:** 2008 Aug 22-28; St. Louis, MO.

OTHER SOURCES

★10138★ American Postal Workers Union (APWU)

1300 L St. NW
Washington, DC 20005
Ph: (202)842-4200   Fax: (202)842-4297
E-mail: askthepresident@att.net
URL: http://www.apwu.org

Description: AFL-CIO. Works to advance the interest of members. Negotiates, interprets and enforces a national agreement with the U.S. Postal Service.

★10139★ Association of Mailing, Shipping, and Office Automation Specialists (AIMED)

949 Winding Brook Ln.
Walnut, CA 91789
Fax: (909)594-9743   Fr: 888-750-6245

E-mail: barbara@aimedweb.org
URL: http://www.aimedweb.org

Members: Independent dealers of mail-related products and services; manufacturers of mailing equipment. **Purpose:** Keeps members informed about industry changes and new products. **Activities:** Maintains speakers' bureau, hall of fame; conducts educational programs.

★10140★ Association for Postal Commerce (PostCom)

1901 N Ft. Myer Dr., Ste. 401
Arlington, VA 22209-1609
Ph: (703)524-0096   Fax: (703)524-1871
E-mail: info@postcom.org
URL: http://www.postcom.org

Members: Represents supporters and users of mail as an advertising, marketing, and fundraising medium. Seeks to protect interests of members with respect to postal rates and services before Congress, the U.S. Postal Service, and the Postal Rate Commission.

★10141★ National Association of Letter Carriers of the U.S.A. (NALC)

100 Indiana Ave. NW
Washington, DC 20001-2144
Ph: (202)393-4695   Fax: (202)737-1540
E-mail: nalcinf@nalc.org
URL: http://www.nalc.org

Description: AFL-CIO. Provides Collective Bargaining representation for city delivery letter carriers employed by the U.S. Postal Service. Maintains information center.

★10142★ National Association of Postal Supervisors (NAPS)

1727 King St., Ste. 400
Alexandria, VA 22314-2700
Ph: (703)836-9660   Fax: (703)836-9665
E-mail: napshq@naps.org
URL: http://www.naps.org

Description: Represents first-line supervisors who work both in facilities where postal employees process mail and where they deliver mail. Promotes and cooperates with USPS and other agencies of the federal government in a continuing effort to improve the service.

★10143★ National Association of Postmasters of the United States (NAPUS)

8 Herbert St.
Alexandria, VA 22305-2600
Ph: (703)683-9027   Fax: (703)683-6820
E-mail: napusinfo@napus.org
URL: http://www.napus.org

Purpose: Serves the professional interests of postmasters and promotes cooperation and interchange of ideas between members and officials of the U.S. Postal Service.

★10144★ National League of Postmasters of the United States (NLPM)

One Beltway Ctr.
5904 Richmond Hwy., Ste. 500
Alexandria, VA 22303-1864
Ph: (703)329-4550   Fax: (703)329-0466
E-mail: information@postmasters.org
URL: http://www.postmasters.org

Description: Independent. Sponsors the Postmasters Benefit Plan, an insurance program operated under the Federal Employees Health Benefit Program (FEHBP). Represents postmasters and other federal employees before Congress. Conducts annual league forum and national convention for league officer training.

★10145★ National Postal Forum (NPF)

3998 Fair Ridge Dr., Ste. 300
Fairfax, VA 22033
Ph: (703)218-5015   Fax: (703)218-5020
E-mail: info@npf.org
URL: http://www.npf.org

Members: Postal authorities and businesses making use of the postal service. **Purpose:** Seeks to ensure the most efficient use of postal services by businesses. **Activities:** Serves as a clearinghouse on products and services offered by the U.S. Postal Service; conducts educational and training programs for business mailers.

★10146★ National Postal Mail Handlers Union (NPMHU)

1101 Connecticut Ave. NW, Ste. 500
Washington, DC 20036-4325
Ph: (202)833-9095   Fax: (202)833-0008
E-mail: markgardner@npmhu.org
URL: http://www.npmhu.org

Description: AFL-CIO. Operates as a division of Laborers' International Union of North America. Aims to negotiate and enforce a National Agreement with the U.S. Postal Service, a contract that establishes wages, cost-of-living adjustments and other pay increases, working conditions, and fringe benefits for all workers within its jurisdiction.

★10147★ National Rural Letter Carriers' Association (NRLCA)

1630 Duke St., 4th Fl.
Alexandria, VA 22314-3426
Ph: (703)684-5545
URL: http://www.nrlca.org

Description: Works to improve the methods used by rural letter carriers, to benefit their conditions of labor with the United States Postal Service (USPS), and to promote a fraternal spirit among its members.

★10148★ National Star Route Mail Contractors Association (NSRMCA)

324 E Capitol St.
Washington, DC 20003-3897
Ph: (202)543-1661   Fax: (202)543-8863
E-mail: info@starroutecontractors.org
URL: http://www.starroutecontractors.org

Description: Highway mail contractors with the U.S. Postal Service transporting mail over the highway on authorized schedules.

★10149★ Parcel Shippers Association (PSA)

1211 Connecticut Ave. NW, Ste. 620
Washington, DC 20036-2701
Ph: (202)296-3690   Fax: (202)331-8318
E-mail: psa@parcelshippers.org
URL: http://www.parcelshippers.org

Members: Wholesalers, retailers, mail order houses, and other firms using parcel post service for distribution of products. **Purpose:** Promotes the efficient and economical distribution of small package shipments.

Preschool Teachers

SOURCES OF HELP-WANTED ADS

★10150★ AAEE Connections
American Association for Employment in
  Education
3040 Riverside Dr., Ste. 125
Columbus, OH 43221
Ph: (614)485-1111   Fax: (614)485-9609
E-mail: office@aaee.org
URL: http://www.aaee.org/

Description: Quarterly. Publishes news of
the Association, whose aim is "to enhance
and promote the concept of career planning
and placement as an integral part of the
educational process and to undertake activities designed to help schools, colleges, and
universities meet their educational staffing
needs." Also concerned with teacher education and the supply of/demand for teachers.
Recurring features include news of members, state and regional news, and announcements of upcoming conferences and
meetings.

★10151★ About Campus
John Wiley & Sons Inc.
111 River St.
Hoboken, NJ 07030-5774
Ph: (201)748-6000   Fax: (201)748-6088
Fr: 800-825-7550
URL: http://www3.interscience.wiley.com/
cgi-bin/jhome/86513696

Bimonthly. $60.00/year for individuals, for
print; $60.00/year for Canada and Mexico,
for print; $96.00/year for individuals, for print
(rest of world); $159.00/year for institutions,
for print; $219.00/year for institutions, Cana-
da and Mexico, for print; $270.00/year for
institutions, for print (rest of world); $175.00/
year for institutions, for print and online;
$235.00/year for institutions, Canada and
Mexico, for print and online; $286.00/year for
institutions, for print and online, (rest of
world); $111.00/year for individuals, print
only. Journal focused on the critical issues
faced by both student affairs and academic
affairs staff as they work on helping students
learn.

★10152★ American Academic
American Federation of Teachers
555 New Jersey Ave. NW
Washington, DC 20001
Ph: (202)879-4400
URL: http://www.aft.org/pubs-reports/ameri-
can_academic/index.htm

Higher education policy journal.

★10153★ Annals of Medicine
Taylor & Francis Group Journals
325 Chestnut St., Ste. 800
Philadelphia, PA 19106
Ph: (215)625-8900   Fax: (215)625-8914
Fr: 800-354-1420
URL: http://www.ingentaconnect.com

$418.00/year for institutions, print and on-
line; $397.00/year for institutions, online
only; $155.00/year for individuals. Journal
covering health science and medical education.

**★10154★ Assessment & Evaluation in
Higher Education**
Taylor & Francis Group Journals
325 Chestnut St., Ste. 800
Philadelphia, PA 19106
Ph: (215)625-8900   Fax: (215)625-8914
Fr: 800-354-1420
E-mail: aehe@bath.ac.uk
URL: http://www.tandf.co.uk/journals/titles/
02602938.asp

Bimonthly. $1,982.00/year for institutions,
print and online; $1,882.00/year for institu-
tions, online only; $466.00/year for individu-
als. Journal focusing on publishing papers
and reports on all aspects of assessment
and evaluation within higher education.

**★10155★ Brookings Papers on
Education Policy**
Brookings Institution Press
1775 Massachusetts Ave. NW
Washington, DC 20036-2188
Ph: (202)536-3600   Fax: (202)536-3623
Fr: 800-275-1447
URL: http://www.brookings.edu/press/jour-
nals.htm

$46.00/year for institutions; $35.00/year for

individuals. Journal dealing with all aspects
of American education.

★10156★ Communication Quarterly
MetaPress
PO Box 1943
Birmingham, AL 35201
Fr: 877-773-3833

Periodical focusing on research, criticism,
communication theory, and excellence in
teaching.

**★10157★ Community College Journal
of Research & Practice**
Taylor & Francis Group Journals
325 Chestnut St., Ste. 800
Philadelphia, PA 19106
Ph: (215)625-8900   Fax: (215)625-8914
Fr: 800-354-1420
URL: http://www.tandf.co.uk/journals/titles/
10668926.asphttp://www

Monthly. $778.00/year for institutions, print
and online; $739.00/year for institutions,
online only; $208.00/year for individuals.
Journal focusing on exchange of ideas,
research, and empirically tested educational
innovations.

**★10158★ E-Journal of Teaching and
Learning in Diverse Settings**
Southern University at Baton Rouge
PO Box 9942
Baton Rouge, LA 70813
Ph: (225)771-3184   Fax: (225)771-4400
URL: http://www.subr.edu/coeducation/ej-
ournal

Online academic journal that publishes research and scholarly articles in the field of
education and learning.

**★10159★ Education & Treatment of
Children**
West Virginia University Press
44 Stansbury Hall
PO Box 6295
Morgantown, WV 26506
Ph: (304)293-8400   Fax: (304)293-6585
Fr: (866)988-7737

URL: http://
www.educationandtreatmentofchildren.net

Quarterly. $85.00/year for institutions; $45.00/year for individuals; $100.00/year for institutions, elsewhere; $60.00/year for individuals, elsewhere. Periodical featuring information concerning the development of services for children and youth. Includes reports written for educators and other child care and mental health providers focused on teaching, training, and treatment effectiveness.

★10160★ Educational Policy

Sage Publications Inc.
2455 Teller Rd.
Thousand Oaks, CA 91320
Ph: (805)499-0721   Fax: (805)499-8096
URL: http://www.sagepub.com/journalsProdDesc.nav?prodId=Journal20

Annual. $749.00/year for institutions, combined (print & e-access); $824.00/year for institutions, backfile lease, combined plus backfile; $674.00/year for institutions, e-access; $749.00/year for institutions, backfile lease, e-access plus backfile; $687.48/year for institutions, backfile puchase, e-access (content through 1999); $734.00/year for institutions, print only; $159.00/year for individuals, print only; $135.00 for institutions, single print; $34.00 for individuals, single print. Journal for educators, policy makers, administrators, researchers, teachers, and graduate students.

★10161★ Educational Research and Evaluation

Taylor & Francis Group Journals
325 Chestnut St., Ste. 800
Philadelphia, PA 19106
Ph: (215)625-8900   Fax: (215)625-8914
Fr: 800-354-1420
URL: http://www.tandf.co.uk/journals/titles/13803611.asp

Bimonthly. $616.00/year for institutions, print and online; $585.00/year for institutions, online only; $239.00/year for individuals. Journal on theory and practice.

★10162★ Environmental Education Research

Taylor & Francis Group Journals
325 Chestnut St., Ste. 800
Philadelphia, PA 19106
Ph: (215)625-8900   Fax: (215)625-8914
Fr: 800-354-1420
URL: http://www.tandf.co.uk/journals/titles/13504622.asp

Journal covering all aspects of environmental education.

★10163★ Essays in Education

University of South Carolina
471 University Pky.
Aiken, SC 29801
Ph: (803)648-6851   Fax: (803)641-3461
Fr: 888-969-8722
URL: http://www.usca.edu/essays/

Monthly. Journal covering issues that impact and influence education.

★10164★ Hematology

American Society of Hematology
1900 M St. NW, Ste. 200
Washington, DC 20036
Ph: (202)776-0544   Fax: (202)776-0545
URL: http://asheducation-book.hematologylibrary.org

Semiweekly. $60.00/year for members; $90.00/year for nonmembers. Journal providing continuing medical education for physicians.

★10165★ The International Electronic Journal of Health Education

American Alliance for Health, Physical
Education, Recreation & Dance
1900 Association Dr.
Reston, VA 20191-1598
Ph: (703)476-3400   Fax: (703)476-9527
Fr: 800-213-7193
URL: http://www.aahperd.org/iejhe/template.cfm?template=about.htm

Annual. Free to health education professionals and students. Journal promoting health through education and other systematic strategies.

★10166★ International Journal of Early Years Education

Taylor & Francis Group Journals
325 Chestnut St., Ste. 800
Philadelphia, PA 19106
Ph: (215)625-8900   Fax: (215)625-8914
Fr: 800-354-1420
URL: http://www.tandf.co.uk/journals/titles/09669760.asp

$512.00/year for institutions, print and online; $486.00/year for institutions, online only; $184.00/year for individuals. Journal focusing on education world-wide.

★10167★ International Journal of Inclusive Education

Taylor & Francis Group Journals
325 Chestnut St., Ste. 800
Philadelphia, PA 19106
Ph: (215)625-8900   Fax: (215)625-8914
Fr: 800-354-1420
URL: http://www.tandf.co.uk/journals/titles/13603116.asp

Bimonthly. $320.00/year for individuals, print only; $616.00/year for institutions, online only; $649.00/year for individuals, print and online; $193.00/year for individuals, print only; $376.00/year for institutions, online only; $396.00/year for institutions, print and online. Journal providing information on the nature of schools, universities and technical colleges for the educators and educational policy-makers.

★10168★ International Journal of Leadership in Education

Taylor & Francis Group Journals
325 Chestnut St., Ste. 800
Philadelphia, PA 19106
Ph: (215)625-8900   Fax: (215)625-8914
Fr: 800-354-1420
E-mail: ijle@txstate.edu
URL: http://www.tandf.co.uk/journals/tf/13603124.html

Quarterly. $196.00/year for individuals; $536.00/year for institutions, print and online; $509.00/year for institutions, online only; Journal dealing with leadership in education.

★10169★ International Journal of Progressive Education

International Journal of Progressive
Education
c/o Mustafa Yunus Eryaman, Mng. Ed.
2108 S Orchard St., No. D
Urbana, IL 61801
URL: http://www.inased.org/ijpe.htm

$35.00/year for members; $45.00/year for individuals; $140.00/year for institutions, library; $35.00/year for students; $25.00/year for single issue, U.S. Peer reviewed online journal that aims to create an open and continuing dialogue about current educational issues and future conceptions of educational theory.

★10170★ International Journal of Research & Method in Education

Taylor & Francis Group Journals
325 Chestnut St., Ste. 800
Philadelphia, PA 19106
Ph: (215)625-8900   Fax: (215)625-8914
Fr: 800-354-1420
URL: http://www.tandf.co.uk/journals/titles/1743727x.asp

$1809.00/year for institutions, print and online; $1718.00/year for institutions, online only; $271.00/year for individuals. Professional journal to further international discourse in education with particular focus on method.

★10171★ International Journal of Whole Schooling

Whole Schooling Press
Wayne State University
217 Education
Detroit, MI 48202
URL: http://www.wholeschooling.net/Journal_of_Whole_Schooling/IJW

Free to qualified subscribers. International, refereed academic journal dedicated to exploring ways to improve learning and schooling for all children.

★10172★ Journal of Academic Leadership

Academic Leadership
600 Park St.
Rarick Hall 219
Hays, KS 67601-4099
Ph: (785)628-4547

URL: http://www.academicleadership.org/

Journal focusing on the leadership issues in the academic world.

★10173★ **Journal of Cases in Educational Leadership**

Sage Publications Inc.
2455 Teller Rd.
Thousand Oaks, CA 91320
Ph: (805)499-0721   Fax: (805)499-8096
URL: http://www.sagepub.com/journalsProdDesc.nav?prodId=Journal20

Quarterly. $319.00/year for institutions, e-access; $83.00/year for individuals, e-access. Journal covering cases appropriate for use in programs that prepare educational leaders.

★10174★ **Journal of Curriculum and Supervision**

Association for Supervision and
Curriculum Development
1703 N Beauregard St.
Alexandria, VA 22311-1714
Ph: (703)578-9600   Fax: (703)575-5400
Fr: 800-933-2723
URL: http://www.ascd.org/portal/site/ascd/menuitem.0545410c9839aa

Scholarly journal focusing on curriculum and supervision.

★10175★ **Journal of Direct Instruction**

Association for Direct Instruction
PO Box 10252
Eugene, OR 97440
Ph: (541)485-1293   Fax: (541)683-7543
Fr: 800-995-2464
URL: http://www.adihome.org/phpshop/articles/articles.php?type=JD

Quarterly. Subscription included in membership. Journal covering education.

★10176★ **Journal of Language, Identity, and Education**

Lawrence Erlbaum Associates Inc.
10 Industrial Ave.
Mahwah, NJ 07430
Ph: (201)258-2200   Fax: (201)236-0072
Fr: 800-926-6579
E-mail: journals@erlbaum.com
URL: http://www.erlbaum.com

Quarterly. $50.00/year for U.S. and Canada, individual, online and print; $80.00/year for elsewhere, individual, online and print; $360.00/year for U.S. and Canada, institution, online and print; $390.00/year for elsewhere, institution, online and print; $290.00/year for U.S. and Canada, institution, online only; $290.00/year for elsewhere, institution, online only; $325.00/year for U.S. and Canada, institution, print only; $355.00/year for elsewhere, institution, print only. Scholarly, interdisciplinary journal covering issues in language, identity and education worldwide for academics, educators and policy specialists in a variety of disciplines, and others.

★10177★ **Journal of Latinos and Education**

Lawrence Erlbaum Associates Inc.
10 Industrial Ave.
Mahwah, NJ 07430
Ph: (201)258-2200   Fax: (201)236-0072
Fr: 800-926-6579
URL: http://www.erlbaum.com/

Quarterly. $50.00/year for individuals, online and print - U.S./Canada; $80.00/year for individuals, online and print - all other countries; $360.00/year for institutions, online and print - U.S./Canada; $390.00/year for institutions, online and print - all other countries; $290.00/year for institutions, online only - U.S./Canada; $290.00/year for institutions, online only - all other countries; $325.00/year for institutions, print only - U.S./Canada; $355.00/year for institutions, print only - all other countries. Scholarly, multidisciplinary journal covering educational issues that impact Latinos for researchers, teaching professionals, academics, scholars, institutions, and others.

★10178★ **Journal of STEM Education**

Auburn University
9088 Haley Ctr.
Auburn, AL 36849
Ph: (334)844-4000   Fax: (334)844-9027
URL: http://www.auburn.edu/research/litee/jstem/index.php

Semiannual. Journal for educators in Science, Technology, Engineering, and Mathematics (STEM) education.

★10179★ **Journal of Teacher Education**

Boston College
140 Commonwealth Ave.
Chestnut Hill, MA 02467
URL: http://www.sagepub.com

$403.00/year for institutions, print & e-access; $423.00/year for institutions, volume print & all online; $363.00/year for institutions, e-access; $383.00/year for institutions, all online content; $1,512.00/year for institutions, backfile purchase, e-access; $395.00/year for institutions, print; $99.00/year for individuals, print; $87.00/year for institutions, single print; $26.00/year for individuals, single print. Magazine of interest to educators.

★10180★ **Leadership and Policy in Schools**

Taylor & Francis Group Journals
325 Chestnut St., Ste. 800
Philadelphia, PA 19106
Ph: (215)625-8900   Fax: (215)625-8914
Fr: 800-354-1420
URL: http://www.tandf.co.uk/journals/titles/15700763.asp

Quarterly. $477.00/year for institutions, print and online; $453.00/year for institutions, online only; $227.00/year for individuals; $60.00/year for ICSEI members. Journal providing information about leadership and policy in primary and secondary education.

★10181★ **NJEA Review**

New Jersey Education Association
180 West State St.
PO Box 1211
Trenton, NJ 08607-1211
Ph: (609)599-4561   Fax: (609)599-1201

Monthly. Educational journal for public school employees.

★10182★ **Oxford Review of Education**

Taylor & Francis Group Journals
325 Chestnut St., Ste. 800
Philadelphia, PA 19106
Ph: (215)625-8900   Fax: (215)625-8914
Fr: 800-354-1420
URL: http://www.tandf.co.uk/journals/titles/03054985.asp

$1,031.00/year for institutions, print and online; $979.00/year for institutions, online only; $396.00/year for individuals. Journal covering advance study of education.

★10183★ **Research Strategies**

Elsevier Science Inc.
360 Park Ave. S
New York, NY 10010
Ph: (212)989-5800   Fax: (212)633-3990
URL: http://www.elsevier.com

Journal covering library literature and the educational mission of the library.

★10184★ **School Effectiveness and School Improvement**

Taylor & Francis Group Journals
325 Chestnut St., Ste. 800
Philadelphia, PA 19106
Ph: (215)625-8900   Fax: (215)625-8914
Fr: 800-354-1420
URL: http://www.tandf.co.uk/journals/titles/09243453.asp

Quarterly. $305.00/year for institutions, print and online; $231.00/year for institutions, online only; $153.00/year for individuals, print only; $520.00/year for institutions, print and online; $494.00/year for institutions, online only; $255.00/year for individuals, print only. Journal focusing on educational progress of all students.

★10185★ **Teaching and Learning in Nursing**

Elsevier Science Inc.
360 Park Ave. S
New York, NY 10010
Ph: (212)989-5800   Fax: (212)633-3990
URL: http://www.elsevier.com

Quarterly. $119.00/year for institutions, U.S. $167.00/year for institutions, other countries; $75.00/year for individuals, U.S. $104.00/year for individuals, other countries. Journal devoted to associate degree nursing education and practice.

★10186★ Theory and Research in Education

Sage Publications Inc.
2455 Teller Rd.
Thousand Oaks, CA 91320
Ph: (805)499-0721   Fax: (805)499-8096
URL: http://tre.sagepub.com/

$459.00/year for institutions, print and on-line; $413.00/year for institutions, online only; $450.00/year for institutions, print only; $77.00/year for individuals, print only. Interdisciplinary journal covering normative and theoretical issues concerning education including multi-faceted philosophical analysis of moral, social, political and epistemological problems and issues arising from educational practice.

★10187★ Uratie

IDG Communications Inc.
5 Speen St., 3rd. Fl
Framingham, MA 01701
Ph: (508)875-5000   Fax: (508)988-7888
URL: http://www.idg.com

Magazine providing job offers for graduates, engineers and information technology professionals.

PLACEMENT AND JOB REFERRAL SERVICES

★10188★ American Montessori Society (AMS)

281 Park Ave. S
New York, NY 10010-6102
Ph: (212)358-1250   Fax: (212)358-1256
E-mail: info@amshq.org
URL: http://www.amshq.org

Description: School affiliates and teacher training affiliates; heads of schools, teachers, parents, non-Montessori educators, and other interested individuals dedicated to stimulating the use of the Montessori teaching approach and promoting better education for all children. Seeks to meet demands of growing interest in the Montessori approach to early learning. Assists in establishing schools; supplies information and limited services to member schools in other countries. Maintains school consultation and accreditation service; provides information service; assists research and gathers statistical data; offers placement service. Maintains Montessori and related materials exhibit.

★10189★ Association for Direct Instruction (ADI)

PO Box 10252
Eugene, OR 97440
Ph: (541)485-1293   Fax: (541)868-1397
Fr: 800-995-2464
E-mail: info@adihome.org
URL: http://www.adihome.org

Members: Public school regular and special education teachers and university instructors. **Purpose:** Encourages, promotes, and

engages in research aimed at improving educational methods. Promotes dissemination of developmental information and skills that facilitate the education of adults and children. **Activities:** Administers a preschool for developmentally delayed children. Offers educational training workshops for instructors. Maintains speaker's bureau and placement service.

EMPLOYER DIRECTORIES AND NETWORKING LISTS

★10190★ Career Ideas for Teens in Education and Training

Facts On File Inc.
132 W 31st St., 17th Fl.
New York, NY 10001
Ph: (212)967-8800   Fax: 800-678-3633
Fr: 800-322-8755
URL: http://www.factsonfile.com

Published 2005. $40.00 for individuals; $36.00 for libraries. Covers a multitude of career possibilities based on a teenager's specific interests and skills and links his/her talents to a wide variety of actual professions.

★10191★ Discovering Careers for Your Future: Teaching

Facts On File Inc.
132 W 31st St., 17th Fl.
New York, NY 10001
Ph: (212)967-8800   Fax: 800-678-3633
Fr: 800-322-8755
URL: http://www.factsonfile.com

Published 2002. $21.95 for individuals; $19.75 for libraries. Covers athletic and fitness trainers, career counselors, college professors, elementary school teachers, ESL teachers, music teachers, and pre-school teachers; links career education to curriculum, helping children investigate the subjects they are interested in and the careers those subjects might lead to.

★10192★ Independent School Guide for Washington DC and Surrounding Area

Lift Hill Press Inc.
c/o Washington Book Distributors
4930-A Eisenhower Ave.
Alexandria, VA 22304-4809
Ph: (703)212-9113   Fax: (703)212-9114
Fr: 800-699-9113
URL: http://www.washingtonbk.com

Biennial; latest edition 2004. Covers over 525 independent schools (including parochial schools) in the Washington, DC, area, including Maryland and Virginia. Entries include: School name, address, phone, name and title of contact, number of faculty, geographical area served, tuition, courses, admission procedures, summer programs, LD/ED programs, scholarships available. Ar-

rangement: Alphabetical. Indexes: Geographical.

HANDBOOKS AND MANUALS

★10193★ How to Get the Teaching Position You Want: Teacher Candidate Guide

Educational Enterprises
PO Box 1836
Spring Valley, CA 91979
Ph: (619)660-7720

Phyllis Murton. Second edition, revised, 1996. $19.95 (paper). 110 pages. This book provides a comprehensive guide for the teacher candidate's job search, as the format offers information that includes: interview questions most often asked in the teaching interview (grade-level and subject-matter specific); sample forms for applications, cover letters, and resumes that will impact principals and district personnel; strategies on preparing for the teaching interview; interview follow-up techniques; inside tips from a superintendent, a principal and a counselor.

★10194★ Inside Secrets of Finding a Teaching Job, Second Edition: The Most Effective Search Methods for Both New and Experienced Educators

JIST Publishing
875 Montreal Way
St. Paul, MN 55102
Fax: 800-547-8329   Fr: 800-648-5478
E-mail: info@jist.com
URL: http://www.jist.com

Jack Warner and Clyde Bryan. 2003. $12.95. 208 pages. Covers researching job opportunities; preparing resumes, cover letters, mission statements, teacher portfolios, and demonstration videos; preparing for interviews; and finding the inside track.

★10195★ Opportunities in Child Care Careers

The McGraw-Hill Companies
PO Box 182604
Columbus, OH 43272
Fax: (614)759-3749   Fr: 877-883-5524
E-mail: customer.service@mcgraw-hill.com
URL: http://www.mcgraw-hill.com

Renee Wittenberg. 2006. $13.95 (paper). 160 pages. Discusses various job opportunities and how to secure a position. Illustrated.

★10196★ Real People Working in Education

The McGraw-Hill Companies
PO Box 182604
Columbus, OH 43272
Fax: (614)759-3749   Fr: 877-883-5524
E-mail: customer.service@mcgraw-hill.com
URL: http://www.mcgraw-hill.com

Blythe Camenson, Jan Goldberg. 1997.

$17.95; $12.95 (paper). 160 pages/ Interviews and profiles of working professionals capture a range of opportunities in this field.

★10197★ *Skills for Preschool Teachers*
Prentice Hall PTR
1 Lake St.
Upper Saddle River, NJ 07458
Ph: (201)236-7000   Fax: 800-445-6991
Fr: 800-428-5331
URL: http://www.phptr.com/index.asp?rl=1

Janice J. Beaty. Eighth edition, 2007. $48.00 (paper). 416 pages. Focuses on training students to help young children become independent and self-directed in their learning.

EMPLOYMENT AGENCIES AND SEARCH FIRMS

★10198★ **Educational Placement Service**
6510-A S. Academy Blvd.
Colorado Springs, CO 80906
Ph: (719)579-9911   Fax: (719)579-5050
E-mail: accounting@educatorjobs.com
URL: http://www.educatorjobs.com

Employment agency. Focuses on teaching, administrative, and education-related openings.

TRADESHOWS

★10199★ **Association for Childhood Education International Annual International Conference & Exhibition**
Association for Childhood Education International
17904 Georgia Ave., Ste. 215
Olney, MD 20832
Ph: (301)570-2111   Fax: (301)570-2212
Fr: 800-423-3563
E-mail: headquarters@acei.org
URL: http://www.acei.org

Annual. **Primary Exhibits:** Commercial and educational exhibits of interest to teachers, teacher educators, college students, day care personnel and other care givers. **Dates and Locations:** 2008 Mar 26-29; Atlanta, GA; Westin Peachtree Plaza; 2009 Mar 18-21; Chicago, IL; Westin Michigan Avenue.

★10200★ **National Art Education Association Convention**
National Art Education Association
1916 Association Dr.
Reston, VA 20191-1590
Ph: (703)860-8000   Fax: (703)860-2960
E-mail: naea@dgs.dgsys.com
URL: http://www.naea-reston.org

Annual. **Primary Exhibits:** Art materials; art-related books and magazines; art career education information; arts and crafts supplies. **Dates and Locations:** 2008 Mar 26-30; New Orleans, LA.

★10201★ **National Association for the Education of Young Children Annual Conference**
National Association for the Education of Young Children
1509 16th St., NW
Washington, DC 20036
Ph: (202)232-8777   Fax: (202)328-1846
Fr: 800-424-2460
E-mail: naeyc@naeyc.org
URL: http://www.naeyc.org

Annual. **Primary Exhibits:** Educational materials and equipment designed for children ages birth through eight years old.

OTHER SOURCES

★10202★ **American Federation of Teachers (AFT)**
555 New Jersey Ave. NW
Washington, DC 20001
Ph: (202)879-4400   Fax: (202)879-4545
Fr: 800-238-1133
E-mail: online@aft.org
URL: http://www.aft.org

Description: Affiliated with the AFL-CIO. Works with teachers and other educational employees at the state and local level in organizing, collective bargaining, research, educational issues, and public relations. Conducts research in areas such as educational reform, teacher certification, and national assessments and standards. Represents members' concerns through legislative action; offers technical assistance. Serves professionals with concerns similar to those of teachers, including state employees, healthcare workers, and paraprofessionals.

★10203★ **Education and Training**
Cambridge Educational
PO Box 2053
Princeton, NJ 08543-2053
Ph: 800-257-5126   Fax: (609)671-0266
Fr: 800-468-4227
E-mail: custserv@films.com
URL: http://www.cambridgeeducational.com

VHS and DVD. $89.95. 2002. 18 minutes. Presents four distinct occupations in the field: elementary teachers, teacher's aides, administrators, and librarians. People working in these jobs discuss their responsibilities.

★10204★ **National Association for the Education of Young Children (NAEYC)**
1313 L St. NW, Ste. 500
Washington, DC 20005
Ph: (202)232-8777   Fax: (202)328-1846
Fr: 800-424-2460
E-mail: naeyc@naeyc.org
URL: http://www.naeyc.org

Description: Teachers and directors of preschool and primary schools, kindergartens, child care centers, and early other learning programs for young childhood; early childhood education and child development educators, trainers, and researchers and other professionals dedicated to young children's healthy development.

★10205★ *Overseas Employment Opportunities for Educators: Department of Defense Dependents Schools*
DIANE Publishing Co.
PO Box 617
Darby, PA 19023-0617
Ph: (610)461-6200   Fax: (610)461-6130
Fr: 800-782-3833
URL: http://www.dianepublishingcentral.com

Barry Leonard, editor. 2000. $15.00. 54 pages. An introduction to teachings positions in the Dept. of Defense Dependents Schools (DoDDS), a worldwide school system, operated by the DoD in 14 countries.

★10206★ **Teaching & Related Occupations**
Delphi Productions
3159 6th St.
Boulder, CO 80304
Ph: (303)443-2100   Fax: (303)443-4022
Fr: 888-443-2400
E-mail: support@delphivideo.com
URL: http://www.delphivideo.com

$95.00. 50 minutes. Part of the Careers for the 21st Century Video Library.

Printers and Bookbinders

SOURCES OF HELP-WANTED ADS

★10207★ *American Printer*
Penton Media Inc.
9800 Metcalf Ave.
Overland Park, KS 66212
Ph: (913)341-1300   Fax: (913)967-1898
E-mail: apeditor@prismb2b.com
URL: http://www.americanprinter.com/

Monthly. Magazine covering the printing and publishing market.

★10208★ *Economic Edge*
National Association for Printing
  Leadership
75 W. Century Rd.
Paramus, NJ 07652-1408
Ph: (201)634-9600   Fax: (201)986-2976
Fr: 800-642-6275
E-mail: perc@napl.org
URL: http://www.napl.org/

Description: Quarterly. Provides current economic data for the printing industry. Also covers sales growth projections, capital spending, and employment.

★10209★ *FLEXO*
Foundation of Flexographic Technical
  Association
900 Marconi Ave.
Ronkonkoma, NY 11779-7212
Ph: (631)737-6020   Fax: (631)737-6813
E-mail: flexo@flexography.org
URL: http://www.flexography.org/flexo/mediakit.cfm

Monthly. $55.00/year for U.S., Canada, and Mexico; $76.00/year for other countries; $30.00/year for individual special issues; $92.00 for U.S., Canada, and Mexico, two years; $125.00 for U.S., Canada, and Mexico, 3 years. Magazine covering the flexographic printing method.

★10210★ *Graphic Arts Monthly Magazine*
Reed Business Information
360 Park Ave. S
New York, NY 10010
Ph: (646)746-6400   Fax: (646)746-7431
URL: http://www.reedbusiness.com

Monthly. Free. Magazine featuring commercial printing and graphic arts, including digital technologies.

★10211★ *Guild of Book Workers Newsletter*
Guild of Book Workers Inc.
521 5th Ave.
New York, NY 10175-0038
Ph: (212)292-4444
E-mail: publicity@guildofbookworkers.allmail.net
URL: http://palimpsest.stanford.edu/byorg/gbw/news.shtml

Description: Bimonthly. Covers issues in book arts, binding, book conservation, calligraphy, and printing. Recurring features include letters to the editor, interviews, news of research, a calendar of events, reports of meetings, news of educational opportunities, job listings, book reviews, and notices of publications available.

★10212★ *High Volume Printing*
Innes Publishing Co.
28100 N Ashley Cir.
PO Box 7280
Libertyville, IL 60048
Ph: (847)816-7900   Fax: (847)247-8855
Fr: 800-247-3306
URL: http://www.innespub.com

Bimonthly. Magazine for printers, trade binderies, and color tradehouses with more than 20 employees.

★10213★ *In-Plant Printer*
Innes Publishing Co.
28100 N Ashley Cir.
PO Box 7280
Libertyville, IL 60048
Ph: (847)816-7900   Fax: (847)247-8855
Fr: 800-247-3306

URL: http://innespub.com

Bimonthly. Free. Magazine serving printing, graphics, typesetting facilities, educational, government, and non-profit organizations.

★10214★ *Instant and Small Commercial Printer*
Innes Publishing Co.
28100 N Ashley Cir.
PO Box 7280
Libertyville, IL 60048
Ph: (847)816-7900   Fax: (847)247-8855
Fr: 800-247-3306
URL: http://www.innespub.com

Monthly. Magazine serving the field of instant/quick printers, copy shops, small commercial printers, industry suppliers and others allied to the field, including typesetters and thermographers.

★10215★ *Printing Impressions*
North American Publishing Co.
1500 Spring Garden St., Ste. 1200
Philadelphia, PA 19130
Ph: (215)238-5482   Fax: (215)238-5412
Fr: 800-777-8074
URL: http://www.napco.com

Monthly. Free. Trade magazine.

★10216★ *Publish&Print*
IDG Communications Inc.
5 Speen St., 3rd. Fl
Framingham, MA 01701
Ph: (508)875-5000   Fax: (508)988-7888
URL: http://www.idg.com

Monthly. Magazine covering information on entire printing process from publishing to production, pre-press to postpress in one magazine.

★10217★ *Quick Printing*
Cygnus Business Media Inc.
3 Huntington Quadrangle, Ste. 301 N
Melville, NY 11747
Ph: (631)845-2700   Fax: (631)845-7109
Fr: 800-308-6397
URL: http://www.quickprinting.com

Monthly. For quick and small commercial printers.

PLACEMENT AND JOB REFERRAL SERVICES

★**10218**★ **Women in Production (WIP)**
276 Bowery
New York, NY 10012
Ph: (212)334-2108 Fax: (212)431-5786
E-mail: admin@p3-ny.org
URL: http://www.p3-ny.org

Description: Persons involved in all production phases of print and graphics, web and multimedia, including those working in magazine, book, and Web publishing, agency production, conventional and digital print manufacturing, print-related vending and buying, advertising production, catalogs, direct mail; seeks to improve job performance by sharing information with members and suppliers. Sponsors placement service.

EMPLOYER DIRECTORIES AND NETWORKING LISTS

★**10219**★ **International Literary Market Place**
Information Today Inc.
143 Old Marlton Pke.
Medford, NJ 08055-8750
Ph: (609)654-6266 Fax: (609)654-4309
Fr: 800-300-9868
URL: http://www.literarymarketplace.com

Annual; latest edition 2007. $249.00 for individuals. Covers over 10,799 publishers in over 180 countries outside the United States and Canada, and about 1,499 trade and professional organizations related to publishing abroad; includes major printers, binders, typesetters, book manufacturers, book dealers, libraries, literary agencies, translators, book clubs, reference books and journals, periodicals, prizes, and international reference section. Entries include: For publishers–Name, address, phone, fax, telex, names and titles of key personnel, branches, type of publications, subjects, ISBN prefix. Listings for others include similar information but less detail. Arrangement: Classified by business activities, then geographical. Indexes: Company name, subject, type of publication.

★**10220**★ **Literary Market Place**
Information Today Inc.
143 Old Marlton Pke.
Medford, NJ 08055-8750
Ph: (609)654-6266 Fax: (609)654-4309
Fr: 800-300-9868
URL: http://store.yahoo.com/infotoday/

Annual; latest edition 2007. $299.95 for

individuals. Covers over 14,500 firms or organizations offering services related to the publishing industry, including book publishers in the United States and Canada who issued three or more books during the preceding year, plus a small press section of publishers who publish less than three titles per year or those who are self-published. Also included: Book printers and binders; book clubs; book trade and literary associations; selected syndicates, newspapers, periodicals, and radio and television programs that use book reviews or book publishing news; translators and literary agents. Entries include: For publishers–Company name, address, phone, address for orders, principal executives, editorial directors, and managers, date founded, number of titles in previous year, number of backlist titles in print, types of books published, ISBN prefixes, representatives, imprints, and affiliations. For suppliers, etc.–Listings usually show firm name, address, phone, executives, services, etc. Arrangement: Classified by line of business. Indexes: Principal index is 35,000-item combined index of publishers, publications, and personnel; several sections have geographical and/or subject indexes; translators are indexed by source and target language.

★**10221**★ **Publishers Directory**
Gale, Cengage Learning
27500 Drake Rd.
Farmington Hills, MI 48331-3535
Ph: (248)699-4253 Fax: (248)699-8065
Fr: 800-877-4253
E-mail: businessproducts@gale.com
URL: http://www.galegroup.com

Annual; latest edition 30th, published November 2006. $540.00 for individuals. Covers over 20,000 new and established, commercial and nonprofit, private and alternative, corporate and association, government and institution publishing programs and their distributors; includes producers of books, classroom materials, prints, reports, and databases. Entries include: Firm name, address, phone, fax, company e-mail address, URL, year founded, ISBN prefix, Standard Address Number, whether firm participates in the Cataloging in Publication program of the Library of Congress, names of principal executives, personal e-mail addresses, number of titles in print, description of firm and its main subject interests, discount and returns policies, affiliated and parent companies, mergers and amalgamations, principal markets, imprints and divisions, alternate formats products are offered in; distributors also list firms for which they distribute, special services, terms to publishers and regional offices. Arrangement: Alphabetical; distributors listed separately. Indexes: Subject; geographical; publisher; imprints; and distributor.

★**10222**★ **Who's Who in SGIA**
Screenprinting and Graphic Imaging
  Association International
10015 Main St.
Fairfax, VA 22031
Ph: (703)385-1335 Fax: (703)273-0456
Fr: 888-385-3588

Annual, August. Covers about 3,800 screen

printers and graphic imaging companies, suppliers of screen printing equipment and graphic imaging materials, and investors in the Screen Printing Technical Foundation; international coverage. Entries include: Company name, address, phone, fax, e-mail, name of contact, products or services. Arrangement: Classified by type of business, then geographical. Indexes: Alphabetical by company, within state or country.

★**10223**★ **The Workbook**
Scott & Daughters Publishing Inc.
940 N Highland Ave.
Los Angeles, CA 90038
Ph: (213)856-0008 Fax: (323)856-4368
Fr: 800-547-2688
URL: http://www.workbook.com

Annual, February. Covers 49,000 advertising agencies, art directors, photographers, freelance illustrators and designers, artists' representatives, interactive designers, prepress services, and other graphic arts services in the U.S. Entries include: Company or individual name, address, phone, specialty. National in scope. Arrangement: Classified by product or service.

HANDBOOKS AND MANUALS

★**10224**★ **Degree of Mastery: A Journey Through Book Arts Apprenticeship**
Penguin
375 Hudson St.
New York, NY 10014
Ph: (212)366-2000 Fax: (212)366-2666
Fr: 800-847-5515
URL: http://us.penguingroup.com/

Annie Tremmel Wilcox. 2000. $27.95 (paper). 224 pages.

★**10225**★ **Opportunities in Printing Careers**
The McGraw-Hill Companies
PO Box 182604
Columbus, OH 43272
Fax: (614)759-3749 Fr: 877-883-5524
E-mail: customer.service@mcgraw-hill.com
URL: http://www.mcgraw-hill.com

Irvin Borowsky. 1998. $14.95; $11.95 (paper). 160 pages. Offers detailed information on the variety of pre-press, press, and post-press jobs available. Covers apprenticeships, unions, salaries, and how to get ahead. Illustrated.

EMPLOYMENT AGENCIES AND SEARCH FIRMS

★10226★ Burton & Grove Executive Search.

1320 Tower Rd.
Schaumburg, IL 60173
Ph: (847)919-8880
E-mail: support@burtonandgrove.com
URL: http://www.burtonandgrove.com

Executive search firm.

★10227★ Core Management Search LLC

5130 Saratoga Ln. N., Ste. 201
Minneapolis, MN 55442
Ph: (763)559-0977   Fax: (763)559-1664
E-mail: jlentner@coremanage.com
URL: http://www.coremanage.com

Executive search firm.

★10228★ Executive Resource Group Inc.

PO Box 10257
Portland, ME 04107
Ph: (207)767-1320   Fax: (207)799-8624
E-mail: sibyl@mediahunter.com
URL: http://www.mediahunter.com

Executive search firm focused on publishing, new media and broadcast industries.

★10229★ Gordon Wahls Executive Search Co.

450 Parkway Blvd., Ste. 104
PO Box 386
Broomall, PA 19008-0386
Fax: (610)359-8803   Fr: 800-523-7112
E-mail: search@gwahls.com

Offers executive search services for the printing, packaging, publishing and graphic arts industry.

★10230★ Graphic Arts Employment Service, Inc.

409 N Pacific Coast Hwy., Ste.455
Redondo Beach, CA 90277
Ph: (818)499-9722   Fax: (310)937-3760
Fr: 888-499-9722
E-mail: info@gaes.com
URL: http://www.gaes.com

Employment agency specializing in the publishing and packaging industries.

★10231★ Graphic Search Associates Inc.

1217 W. Chester Pike, Ste. 203
West Chester, PA 19382
Ph: (610)429-8077   Fax: (610)429-1355
Fr: 800-342-1777
E-mail: info@graphsrch.com
URL: http://www.graphsrch.com

Executive search firm for the graphic arts industry.

★10232★ LandaJob Advertising Staffing Specialists

8177 Wornall Rd.
Kansas City, MO 64114
Ph: (816)523-1881   Fax: (816)523-1876
Fr: 800-931-8806
E-mail: adstaff@landajobnow.com
URL: http://www.landajobnow.com

Personnel consultants and recruiters for advertising, marketing, and communications positions. Industries served: advertising, communications, marketing, graphic arts, printing and publishing.

★10233★ Printemps

18 Avery Pl.
Westport, CT 06880
Ph: (203)226-6869   Fax: (203)226-1594
E-mail: printemps7@aol.com

Specializes in providing temporary support for graphic design, document management and the electronic printing industry. Provides permanent placement for professionals and production personnel. Consults with printers and in-house printshops for greater production efficiency. Handles personnel management and policy programs as well. Industries served: printing, advertising, manufacturing, insurance, banking, and government agencies.

★10234★ Stewart and Associates

1717 Penn Ave.
Wilkinsburg, PA 15221
Ph: (412)244-0552   Fax: (717)299-4879

Executive search firm for the manufacturing industry.

★10235★ Zachary & Sanders Inc.

Linden Ln.
East Norwich, NY 11732
Ph: (516)922-5500   Fax: (516)922-2286
Fr: 800-540-7919
E-mail: zacharyserch@earthlink.net

Serves the printing, packaging, publishing, advertising, direct marketing industries.

ONLINE JOB SOURCES AND SERVICES

★10236★ PrintJobs.com

Newhouse Associates
PO Box 135
Bowmansville, NY 14026
Ph: (716)686-9251   Fax: (716)686-9258
E-mail: printjobs@roadrunner.com
URL: http://www.printjobs.com

Description: Aims to find suitable graphic arts jobs for qualified candidates. Over a hundred jobs are maintained and updated on the site. **Fee:** Must be paid by employers using the site; no registration charge for job hunters.

OTHER SOURCES

★10237★ Amalgamated Printers' Association (APA)

PO Box 18117
Fountain Hills, AZ 85269
E-mail: mikeatfh@cox.net
URL: http://www.apa-letterpress.com

Description: Active printers interested in furtherance of the art and craft of printing. Encourages excellence of printing content, design, and techniques among members. Sponsors competitions.

★10238★ American Institute of Graphic Arts (AIGA)

164 5th Ave.
New York, NY 10010
Ph: (212)807-1990   Fax: (212)807-1799
E-mail: comments@aiga.org
URL: http://www.aiga.org

Description: Graphic designers, art directors, illustrators and packaging designers. Sponsors exhibits and projects in the public interest. Sponsors traveling exhibitions. Operates gallery. Maintains library of design books and periodicals; offers slide archive.

★10239★ Behind the Scenes: Printing

Cambridge Educational
PO Box 2053
Princeton, NJ 08543-2053
Ph: 800-257-5126   Fax: (609)671-0266
Fr: 800-468-4227
E-mail: custserv@films.com
URL: http://www.cambridgeeducational.com

VHS and DVD. $69.95. 16 minutes. 2004. Part of the series "Behind the Scenes: Industrial Field Trips."

★10240★ Binding Industries Association International (BIA)

200 Deer Run Rd.
Sewickley, PA 15143
Ph: (412)259-1802   Fax: (412)259-1803
E-mail: lreynolds@piagatf.org
URL: http://www.gain.net

Members: Represents trade binders and loose-leaf manufacturers united to conduct seminars, hold conventions, and formulate and maintain standards.

★10241★ COIN Career Guidance System

COIN Educational Products
3361 Executive Pky., Ste. 302
Toledo, OH 43606
Ph: (419)536-5353   Fax: (419)536-7056
Fr: 800-274-8515
URL: http://www.coinedu.com/

CD-ROM. Provides career information through seven cross-referenced files covering postsecondary schools, college majors, vocational programs, military service, apprenticeship programs, financial aid, and scholarships. Apprenticeship file describes national apprenticeship training programs, including information on how to apply, contact agencies, and program content. Military file describes more than 200 military occupations and training opportunities related to civilian employment.

★10242★ **Employee Recognition Program**

200 Deer Run Rd.
Sewickley, PA 15143
Fax: (412)749-9890   Fr: 800-910-4283
E-mail: dhower@piagatf.org
URL: http://www.gain.net

Description: Serves as a division of Printing Industries of America. Supports pro-business labor law reform and modern industrial relations in plants. Conducts seminars for industrial relations directors and managers of local associations.

★10243★ **Graphic Arts Technical Foundation (GATF)**

200 Deer Run Rd.
Sewickley, PA 15143-2600
Fax: (412)741-2311   Fr: 800-910-GATF
E-mail: info@piagatf.org
URL: http://www.gain.net

Description: Scientific, research, technical, and educational organization serving the international graphic communications industries. Conducts research in all graphic processes and their commercial applications. Conducts seminars, workshops, and forums on graphic arts and environmental subjects. Conducts educational programs, including the publishing of graphic arts textbooks and learning modules, videotapes and CD-ROMs and broadcast video seminars. Conducts training and certification program in sheet-fed offset press operating, Web Offset press operating, Image Assembly, and desktop publishing. Produces test images and quality control devices for the industry. Performs technical services for the graphic arts indus-

try, including problem-solving, material evaluation, and plant audits.

★10244★ **National Association for Printing Leadership (NAPL)**

75 W Century Rd.
Paramus, NJ 07652-1408
Ph: (201)634-9600   Fax: (201)634-0324
Fr: 800-642-6275
E-mail: info@napl.org
URL: http://www.napl.org

Description: Represents commercial printers and suppliers to the commercial printing industry. Enables those in the industry to operate their businesses for maximum profitability. Offers following management products and services: sales and marketing, customer service, financial, human resources, operations, and economic. **Activities:** Maintains Management Institute, which conducts Executive Certification Program. Compiles extensive economic statistics.

★10245★ **Printing Brokerage/Buyers Association (PB/BA)**

PO Box 744
Palm Beach, FL 33480
Ph: (561)546-0116   Fax: (561)845-7130
Fr: 877-585-7141
E-mail: contactus@pbba.org
URL: http://www.pbba.org

Description: Printing buyers/brokers/distributors, printers, typographers, binders, envelope and book manufacturers, packagers, color separation houses, pre-press service organizations, and related companies in the graphic arts industry. Promotes understanding, cooperation, and interaction among members while obtaining the highest standard of professionalism in the graphic arts industry. Gathers information on current technology in the graphic communications industry. Sponsors seminars for members to learn how to work with buyers, brokers and printers; also conducts technical and man-

agement seminars. Maintains referral service; compiles statistics. Conducts charitable programs.

★10246★ **Printing Industries of America (PIA)**

200 Deer Run Rd.
Sewickley, PA 15143
Ph: (412)741-6860   Fax: (412)741-2311
Fr: 800-910-4283
E-mail: gain@piagatf.org
URL: http://www.gain.net

Description: Commercial printing firms (lithography, letterpress, gravure, platemakers, typographic houses); allied firms in the graphic arts. Provides extensive management services for member companies, including government relations, industry research and statistical information, technology information and assistance, and management education and publications. Compiles statistical and economic data, including annual ratio study that provides a benchmark for printers to compare profits as a basis for improving individual member company and industry profits. Provides reporting system on provisions, rates, and other matters relating to union contracts in effect throughout the industry. Sponsors annual Premier Print Awards Competition.

★10247★ **Typophiles**

30 E 23rd St., 8th Fl.
New York, NY 10010
E-mail: info@typophiles.org
URL: http://www.typophiles.org

Description: Represents designers, printers, book collectors, artists, calligraphers, private press owners, wood engravers, librarians and others interested in graphic arts. Promotes the love and appreciation of fine graphic design and printing. Conducts quarterly meeting-luncheons and maintains publications.

Private Detectives and Investigators

SOURCES OF HELP-WANTED ADS

★10248★ The Legal Investigator
National Association of Legal Investigators Inc.
235 N. Pine St.
Lansing, MI 48933
Ph: (517)702-9835   Fax: (517)372-1501
Fr: (866)520-6254
E-mail: info@NaliOnline.org
URL: http://www.nalionline.org/nalipublications.html

Description: Quarterly. Focuses on concerns of the legal investigator, especially on professionalization of the career through a certification program. Discusses issues and legal developments relating to the investigation of personal injury matters for the plaintiff and criminal defense.

PLACEMENT AND JOB REFERRAL SERVICES

★10249★ National Association of Investigative Specialists (NAIS)
PO Box 82148
Austin, TX 78708
Ph: (512)719-3595   Fax: (512)719-3594
E-mail: rthomas007@aol.com
URL: http://www.pimall.com/nais

Members: Private investigators, automobile repossessors, bounty hunters, and law enforcement officers. **Purpose:** Promotes professionalism and provides for information exchange among private investigators. Lobbies for investigative regulations. Offers training programs and issues certificates of completion. **Activities:** Sponsors charitable programs; compiles statistics; maintains speakers' bureau and placement service. Operates Investigators' Hall of Fame of Private Investigators. Offers seminars on cassette tape.

EMPLOYER DIRECTORIES AND NETWORKING LISTS

★10250★ Investigator's International All-In-One Directory
National Association of Investigative Specialists
PO Box 82148
Austin, TX 78708
Ph: (512)719-3595   Fax: (512)719-3594
URL: http://www.pimall.com/nais/dir.menu.html

Annual. Covers approximately 1,800 NAIS members; national, state, and foreign private investigative and related associations; online networks for private investigators; security associations; publications; information services; training programs and seminars; equipment sources; state investigative licensing agencies. Entries include: Company name or individual name, address, contact, investigative specialty, services provided, geographic area covered. Arrangement: Geographical.

★10251★ Legal Investigators Directory
FINDLAW
610 Opperman Dr.
Eagan, MN 55123
Ph: (651)687-7000   Fax: 800-392-6206
Fr: 800-344-5008
URL: http://marketcenter.findlaw.com/legal_investigators.html

Free. Database covers: Legal investigators (dealing with arson, asset, background checks, and surveillance) in the United States. Entries include: Name, address, phone, fax, e-mail, website, description of services, additional offices, area(s) of practice, states served. Arrangement: Classified by subject; alphabetical by state.

★10252★ Naked in Cyberspace
Information Today Inc.
143 Old Marlton Pke.
Medford, NJ 08055-8750
Ph: (609)654-6266   Fax: (609)654-4309
Fr: 800-300-9868

E-mail: custserv@infotoday.com
URL: http://www.infotoday.com

Latest edition 2002. $29.95 for individuals. Publication includes: Web sites for finding people via the Internet. Principal content of publication is information on how to investigate people, find genealogical information, find prospective customers, and access public records. Indexes: Alphabetical.

HANDBOOKS AND MANUALS

★10253★ Careers for Legal Eagles and Other Law-and-Order Types
The McGraw-Hill Companies
PO Box 182604
Columbus, OH 43272
Fax: (614)759-3749   Fr: 877-883-5524
E-mail: customer.service@mcgraw-hill.com
URL: http://www.mcgraw-hill.com

Blythe Camenson. Second edition, 2005. $13.95 (paper). 176 pages.

★10254★ Careers for Mystery Buffs and Other Snoops and Sleuths
The McGraw-Hill Companies
PO Box 182604
Columbus, OH 43272
Fax: (614)759-3749   Fr: 877-883-5524
E-mail: customer.service@mcgraw-hill.com
URL: http://www.mcgraw-hill.com

Blythe Camenson. Second edition, 2004. $12.95 (paper); $14.95 (cloth). 160 pages.

★10255★ Find Out Fast: The Instant Guide to Private Investigation
Thomas Investigative Publications, Inc.
PO Box 33244
Austin, TX 78764-3864
Ph: (512)719-3595   Fax: (512)719-3594

Kelly Riddle. 1997. $19.95 (paper). 120 pages.

★10256★ **Introduction to Private Investigation: Essential Knowledge and Procedures for the Private Investigator**

Charles C Thomas Publisher, Ltd.
2600 S. 1st St.
PO Box 19265
Springfield, IL 62794-9265
Ph: (217)789-8980   Fax: (217)789-9130
Fr: 800-258-8980
E-mail: books@ccthomas.com
URL: http://www.ccthomas.com

Joseph A. Travers. Second edition, 2005. $41.95. 270 pages.

★10257★ **An Introduction to Public and Private Investigations**

West Publishing Company
27500 Drake Rd.
Farmington Hills, MI 48331
Fr: 800-328-4880
URL: http://west.thomson.com/

John S. Dempsey. 1996. $93.95 (paper). 415 pages.

★10258★ **Primer on Success in the Private Investigative Profession**

Thomas Investigative Publications, Inc.
PO Box 33244
Austin, TX 78764-3864
Ph: (512)719-3595   Fax: (512)719-3594

Irv Baggett. 1996. $25.00 (paper). 65 pages. Subtitled, "A Business and Investigative Manual for Establishing a Successful Investigative Agency and Working the Most In-Demand Types of Cases." 65 pages.

★10259★ **Private Investigative Agency Start-Up Manual**

Thomas Investigative Publications, Inc.
PO Box 33244
Austin, TX 78764-3864
Ph: (512)719-3595   Fax: (512)719-3594

Jody Ball. 1997. $65.00 (paper). 247 pages.

★10260★ **Real People Working in Law**

The McGraw-Hill Companies
PO Box 182604
Columbus, OH 43272
Fax: (614)759-3749   Fr: 877-883-5524
E-mail: customer.service@mcgraw-hill.com
URL: http://www.mcgraw-hill.com

Blythe Camenson, Jan Goldberg. 1997. $12.95 (paper). 160 pages. Interviews and profiles of working professionals capture a range of opportunities in this field.

OTHER SOURCES

★10261★ **Council of International Investigators (CII)**

2150 N 107th St., Ste. 205
Seattle, WA 98133-9009
Ph: (206)361-8889   Fax: (206)367-8777
Fr: 888-759-8884
E-mail: office@cii2.org
URL: http://www.cii2.org

Description: Represents licensed and accredited professional private investigators and detectives in 28 countries. Conducts seminars on investigation, security work, criminology, and lie detection.

★10262★ **International Society of Stress Analysts (ISSA)**

9 Westchester Dr.
Kissimmee, FL 34744
Ph: (407)933-4839   Fax: (407)935-0911
E-mail: diogenesfl@aol.com

Members: Jurists, attorneys, physicians, private detectives, law enforcement personnel, security personnel, scholar/researchers, and individuals interested in stress analysis for lie detection/truth verification. **Purpose:** Purposes are to: promote the science of psychological stress evaluation and the efficient administration of justice; aid indigent persons, without cost, who may be wrongfully accused; develop and maintain high educational standards; observe and evaluate training programs for the purpose of accreditation and endorsement. **Activities:** Sponsors and certifies schools; offers workshops and research and educational programs; conducts forums. Offers expertise, consultation, and advice; invites inquiries.

★10263★ **National Association of Traffic Accident Reconstructionists and Investigators (NATARI)**

PO Box 2588
West Chester, PA 19382
Ph: (610)696-1919
E-mail: natari@natari.org
URL: http://www.natari.org

Description: Represents engineers, attorneys, police officers, private investigators, medical examiners, and other individuals involved in the analysis of motor vehicle traffic accidents. Gathers and disseminates information on techniques and equipment of potential use to members; reviews literature in the field. Participating Organization of the Accreditation Commission for Traffic Accident Reconstruction.

Professional Organizers

SOURCES OF HELP-WANTED ADS

★10264★ WorkingWorld.com
3600 Wilshire Blvd., Ste. 1526
Los Angeles, CA 90010
Ph: (213)385-4781   Fax: (213)385-3782
URL: http://www.workingworld.com

Monthly. Employment magazine that features a searchable jobs database and career-related articles, including information for professional organizers.

EMPLOYER DIRECTORIES AND NETWORKING LISTS

★10265★ National Association of Professional Organizers-Directory
National Association of Professional Organizers
4700 W Lake Ave.
Glenview, IL 60025
Ph: (847)375-4746
URL: http://www.napo.net

Annual. Covers over 500 member professionals involved with time management, information management, space planning, and productivity improvement in the workplace and in the home. Entries include: Name, company name, address, phone, description of services. Arrangement: Geographical; alphabetical; specialty.

HANDBOOKS AND MANUALS

★10266★ Becoming a Professional Organizer
1563 Solano Ave, Ste.306
Berkeley, CA 94707
URL: http://
www.becomingaprofessionalorganizer.com

$29.95 (kit). Offers a systematic guide that provides advice and practical guidance for starting a professional organizing business. Contains forms and business letters that will assist in starting the business.

★10267★ FabJob Guide to Become a Professional Organizer
FabJob.com
4616 25th Ave. NE, Ste. 224
Seattle, WA 98105
Ph: (403)949-4980
URL: http://www.fabjob.com

Grace Jasmine and Jennifer James. 2005. $34.95 (paper). 265 pages. Includes sections on residential organizing, office organizing, and how to start a professional organizing business.

★10268★ A Manual for Professional Organizers
Banter Books
520 Hudson St., Ste. 139
New York, NY 10014

Cyndi Seidler. 2004. $32.00 (paper). 148 pages. Covers an industry overview, the business of professional organizing, getting a professional organizing business started, establishing a business, running a business, organizing the client, and marketing and promoting a business.

★10269★ Newbie Pitfalls
Red Letter Day
Ph: (586)746-1428
URL: http://www.rldpo.com/ForOrganizers.htm

$29.95 (paper); $24.95 (PDF download). 50 pages. Includes lessons and tips from a veteran organizer to help those new to the profession avoid costly learning experiences.

★10270★ Secrets of a Professional Organizer and How to Become One
OverHall Consulting
PO Box 263
Port Republic, MD 20676
Ph: (410)586-9440   Fr: 800-687-3040
E-mail: janet@Soverhall.com
URL: http://www.overhall.com

Janet L. Hall. $49.95 (download). Includes information on establishing an organizing business, including business skills needed, how to set fees, writing contracts, and proven systems and techniques.

EMPLOYMENT AGENCIES AND SEARCH FIRMS

★10271★ America's Most Organized
441 Ski Lodge Rd.
McQueeney, TX 78123
Ph: (830)560-3248
E-mail: info@americasmostorganized.com
URL: http://americasmostorganized.com

Consults with individuals and businesses who seek professional organizing services and outsources services with a pool of freelance professional organizers and custom storage contractors.

ONLINE JOB SOURCES AND SERVICES

★10272★ BlueSuitMom.com
2335 E. Atlantic Blvd., Ste. 300
Pompano Beach, FL 33062
Ph: (954)943-2322   Fax: (954)943-2441
URL: http://www.bluesuitmom.com/career/

Description: An online database containing over 300,000 searchable job postings, including those in professional organizing. Offers career advice for the professional organizer.

★10273★ Clutterbug.net
URL: http://www.clutterbug.net/becomeap-rofessionalorganizer/
Description: Acts as an online clearing-house of information for those interested in becoming professional organizers. Also maintains a directory of professional organizers.

★10274★ OnlineOrganizing.com
PO Box 1942
Clinton, MD 20735
Ph: (301)659-2203
URL: http://www.onlineorganizing.com
Description: Serves as an online source for organizing advice, products, and other information related to professional organizing. Maintains an online listing of professional organizers.

★10275★ Organizing Network
PO Box 12312
Ogden, UT 84414-2312
Ph: (801)668-2410   Fax: (801)782-9832
E-mail: contact.info@organizingnetwork.com
URL: http://www.myorganizedlife.com
Description: Provides a searchable online list of professional organizers based on geographic location for those seeking professional organizing services.

★10276★ P-O News
Organizing Resources
PO Box 412
Plainville, CT 06062-0412
Ph: (860)747-8962
E-mail: Judith@OrganizingResources.com
URL: http://www.organizingresources.com
Description: A monthly, online newsletter, by subscription, that includes ideas, articles and pertinent information on the potentials and opportunities for the professional organizer.

★10277★ Professional Organizers Web Ring
PO Box 298
Mount Ephraim, NJ 08059
E-mail: ringmasters@organizerswebring.com

URL: http://www.organizerswebring.com
Description: Maintains a searchable member directory, as well as information on upcoming organizing events, seminars, workshops, and conferences. Provides an online collection of featured articles written by professional organizers and a section on frequently asked questions in the field of professional organizing.

★10278★ Red Letter Day
Ph: (586)746-1428
URL: http://www.rldpo.com
Description: Provides online advice for professional organizers and those looking to become professional organizers.

★10279★ Ryze Business Networking
Ph: (415)367-3795
E-mail: press@ryze.com
URL: http://po-network.ryze.com
Description: Provides an online classifieds section for the professional organizer, as well as networking services that allow organizers to share tips and advice.

OTHER SOURCES

★10280★ HG Training Academy
8209 Foothill Blvd. Ste. A-184
Sunland, CA 91040
Ph: (818)686-8888   Fax: (818)301-2525
E-mail: service@hgtrainingacademy.com
URL: http://www.hgtrainingacademy.com
Purpose: Provides online training for professional organizers. **Activities:** Offers courses in the basic principles of organization, as well as an apprenticeship program.

★10281★ National Association of Professional Organizers (NAPO)
4700 W Lake Ave.
Glenview, IL 60025
Ph: (847)375-4746   Fax: 877-734-8668
E-mail: hq@napo.net
URL: http://www.napo.net
Description: Professional organizers pro-

viding organization, time management, or productivity improvement services; persons in related fields such as organizational product sales and organizational development. Works to promote and educate the public about the profession and to offer support, education, and networking opportunities to members.

★10282★ Organizing Resources
PO Box 412
Plainville, CT 06062-0412
Ph: (860)747-8962
E-mail: Judith@OrganizingResources.com
URL: http://www.organizingresources.com
Purpose: Offers resources, tips, and techniques for the professional organizer. **Activities:** Provides learning modules, a mentoring program, and teleclasses for the professional organizer.

★10283★ The Professional Organizer
180 Worthington Dr., Ste. 1A
Marietta, GA 30068
Ph: (770)579-9866   Fax: (770)579-0314
E-mail: info@theprofessionalorganizer.com
URL: http://www.theprofessionalorganizer.com
Description: Provides advice, information, and products on organization. **Activities:** Administers Organizer U, a training, mentoring, and licensing program for professional organizers.

★10284★ Professional Organizers
609 Deep Valley Dr., Ste. 200
Rolling Hills Estates, CA 90274
Fr: 888-739-9965
E-mail: kathy@professionalorganizers.com
URL: http://www.professionalorganizers.com
Activities: Offers instructional seminars on becoming a professional organizer, as well as continuing education courses for those already in the profession.

Project Managers

SOURCES OF HELP-WANTED ADS

★10285★ Business Performance Management

Penton Media Inc.
249 W 17th St.
New York, NY 10011
Ph: (212)204-4200
URL: http://www.bpmmag.net/

Free to qualified subscribers. Magazine for business managers. Covers organizing, automating, and analyzing of business methodologies and processes.

★10286★ CXO

IDG Communications Inc.
5 Speen St., 3rd. Fl
Framingham, MA 01701
Ph: (508)875-5000   Fax: (508)988-7888
URL: http://www.idg.com

Monthly. Magazine providing technology information for chief officers and managers.

★10287★ D & O Advisor

American Lawyer Media L.P.
345 Pk. Ave. S
New York, NY 10010
Ph: (212)779-9200   Fax: (212)481-8110
Fr: 800-888-8300
URL: http://www.alm.com

Quarterly. Magazine that offers advice and perspective on corporate oversight responsibilities for directors and officers.

★10288★ E Journal of Organizational Learning and Leadership

WeLEAD Inc.
PO Box 202
Litchfield, OH 44253
Fr: 877-778-5494
URL: http://www.weleadinlearning.org/ejournal.htm

Continuous. Free. Online academic journal about organizational leadership.

★10289★ Event Management

Cognizant Communications Corp.
3 Hartsdale Rd.
Elmsford, NY 10523-3701
Ph: (914)592-7720   Fax: (914)592-8981
URL: http://www.cognizantcommunication.com/filecabinet/EventManag

Quarterly. $325.00/year for institutions, library; $360.00/year for institutions, rest of the world, library; $585.00/year for institutions, library, 2 years; $648.00/year for institutions, rest if the world, library, 2 years; $45.00/year professional; $52.00/year for other countries, professional. Journal covering research and analytic needs of a rapidly growing profession focused on events.

★10290★ Executive Legal Adviser

American Lawyer Media L.P.
345 Pk. Ave. S
New York, NY 10010
Ph: (212)779-9200   Fax: (212)481-8110
Fr: 800-888-8300
URL: http://www.executivelegaladviser.com

Bimonthly. Free to qualified subscribers. Magazine that offers legal advice for corporate executives.

★10291★ Forrester

Forrester Research Inc.
400 Technology Sq.
Cambridge, MA 02139
Ph: (617)613-6000   Fax: (617)613-5000
URL: http://www.forrester.com/mag

Free. Journal that aims to provide ideas and advice that are relevant to today's CEOs.

★10292★ International Journal of Business Research

Academy of International Business and Economics
PO Box 2536
Ceres, CA 95307
URL: http://www.aibe.org

Peer-reviewed journal publishing theoretical, conceptual, and applied research on topics related to research, practice and teaching in all areas of business, management, and marketing.

★10293★ Journal of Academic Leadership

Academic Leadership
600 Park St.
Rarick Hall 219
Hays, KS 67601-4099
Ph: (785)628-4547
URL: http://www.academicleadership.org/

Journal focusing on the leadership issues in the academic world.

★10294★ Journal of Business and Psychology

Springer-Verlag New York Inc.
233 Spring St.
New York, NY 10013
Ph: (212)460-1500   Fax: (212)460-1575
URL: http://www.springer.com/journal/10869/

Journal covering all aspects of psychology that apply to the business segment. Includes topics such as personnel selection and training, organizational assessment and development, risk management and loss control, marketing and consumer behavior research.

★10295★ Journal of International Business Strategy

Academy of International Business and Economics
PO Box 2536
Ceres, CA 95307
URL: http://www.AIBE.org

Peer-reviewed journal publishing theoretical, conceptual, and applied research on topics related to strategy in international business.

★10296★ Organization Management Journal

Eastern Academy of Management
c/o Craig Tunwall, VP
Empire State College
2805 State Hwy. 67
Johnstown, NY 12095
Ph: (518)762-4651   Fax: (518)736-1716

URL: http://www1.wnec.edu/omj

Free to qualified subscribers. Refereed, on-line journal focusing on organization management issues.

★10297★ **Project Management Journal**
Project Management Institute
4 Campus Blvd.
Newtown Square, PA 19073
Ph: (610)356-4600   Fax: (610)356-4647
URL: http://www.pmi.org/info/PIR_PMJournal.asp

Quarterly. Peer-reviewed professional journal devoted to theory and practice in the field of project management.

EMPLOYER DIRECTORIES AND NETWORKING LISTS

★10298★ **Harvard Business School Guide to Careers in Management Consulting**
Harvard Business School Publishing
60 Harvard Way
Boston, MA 02163
Ph: (617)783-7500   Fax: (617)783-7555
Fr: 800-988-0886
URL: http://www.hbsp.harvard.edu

$10.83 for individuals. Publication includes: Well-known consulting firms, a mailing list of recruiting contacts, and a selective bibliography of relevant books and directories compiled by the Harvard Business School.

★10299★ **Project Management Step-by-Step**
AMACOM
1601 Broadway
New York, NY 10019-7420
Ph: (212)586-8100   Fax: (518)891-0368
Fr: 800-262-9699
URL: http://www.amanet.org/

Latest edition 2002. $27.95 for individuals. Publication includes: List of resources for project management. Principal content of publication is information on the theory and practice of project management. Indexes: Alphabetical.

HANDBOOKS AND MANUALS

★10300★ **Essential People Skills for Project Managers**
Management Concepts, Inc.
8230 Leesburg Pke., Ste. 800
Vienna, VA 22182
Ph: (703)790-9595   Fax: (703)790-1371
Fr: 800-506-4450
URL: http://www.managementconcepts.com/

Steven Glannes and Ginger Levin. 2005. $29.00. People management skills for project managers are discussed.

★10301★ **PMP Project Management Professional Study Guide**
The McGraw-Hill Companies
PO Box 182604
Columbus, OH 43272
Fax: (614)759-3749   Fr: 877-883-5524
E-mail: customer.service@mcgraw-hill.com
URL: http://www.mcgraw-hill.com

Joseph Phillips. 2003. $59.99 (paper). 576 pages. Includes complete coverage of all objectives of the PMP examination, hundreds of practice questions, and hands-on exercises.

★10302★ **PMP: Project Management Professional Workbook**
Sybex
111 River St.
Hoboken, NJ 07030
Ph: (201)748-6000   Fax: (201)748-6088
Fr: 800-225-5945
E-mail: custserv@wiley.com
URL: http://www.sybex.com/WileyCDA/

Claudia Baca and Patti Jansen. 2003. $34.99 (paper). 320 pages. Offers hands-on experience in preparation for the PMP examination sponsored by the Project Management Institute.

★10303★ **Project Management: A Systems Approach to Planning, Scheduling, and Controlling**
John Wiley & Sons, Inc.
1 Wiley Dr.
Somerset, NJ 08873
Ph: (732)469-4400   Fax: (732)302-2300
Fr: 800-225-5945
E-mail: custserv@wiley.com
URL: http://www.wiley.com/WileyCDA/

Harold Kerzner. Ninth edition, 2005. $85.00. 1040 pages. Focuses on the critical aspects of project management and includes expanded problems and exercises.

★10304★ **Project Management Handbook**
John Wiley & Sons, Inc.
1 Wiley Dr.
Somerset, NJ 08873
Ph: (732)469-4400   Fax: (732)302-2300
Fr: 800-225-5945
E-mail: custserv@wiley.com
URL: http://www.wiley.com/WileyCDA/

Jeffrey K. Pinto. 1998. $89.00. 496 pages. A print-on-demand title that details project management's best practices. Experts in the field detail the essentials of project planning; describe team-building, motivation, and conflict management challenges; and delineate critical success factors.

★10305★ **Project Management Workbook and PMP/CAPM Exam Study Guide**
Sybex
111 River St.
Hoboken, NJ 07030
Ph: (201)748-6000   Fax: (201)748-6088
Fr: 800-225-5945
E-mail: custserv@wiley.com
URL: http://www.sybex.com/WileyCDA/

Harold Kerzner. Ninth Edition. 2006. $55.00. 416 pages. Provides problems and exercises to reinforce project management concepts. Prepares project managers for the Project Management Professional certification examination.

★10306★ **A Project Manager's Guide to Enterprise Project Management**
Sturgeon Publishing
PO Box 30291
Phoenix, AZ 85046-0291
Ph: (602)327-6969

Brent Knapp. 2006. $59.95. Detailed information for preparing for the PMP exam.

EMPLOYMENT AGENCIES AND SEARCH FIRMS

★10307★ **Acuity**
159 Samoset St.
Plymouth, MI 02360
Fax: (734)533-6606   Fr: (866)332-8489
URL: http://www.acuitybi.com

Provider of qualified project managers for various business needs.

★10308★ **EEG Recruiting**
16564 Garnet Ct.
Orland Park, IL 60467
Fr: 800-819-1841
E-mail: info@eegrecruiting.com
URL: http://www.eegrecruiting.com

Executive recruiting firm with a focus on project management.

★10309★ **Project Performance Corporation**
1760 Old Meadow Rd., 1st Fl.
McLean, VA 22102
Ph: (703)748-7000   Fax: (703)748-7001
E-mail: info@ppc.com
URL: http://www.ppc.com

Serves as a placement and recruiting firm for project management professionals.

★10310★ **Torch Group**
33595 Bainbridge Rd., Ste. 200
Cleveland, OH 44139
Ph: (440)519-1822   Fax: (440)519-1823
E-mail: info@torchgroup.com
URL: http://www.torchgroup.com

Professional employment services firm that supplies businesses with professional project managers.

★10311★ Woltcom, Inc.
650 San Benito St., Ste. 230
Hollister, CA 95023
Fax: (831)638-4944   Fr: 800-682-4949
E-mail: wci@woltcom.com
URL: http://www.woltcom.com

A national provider of contract and career staffing and management solutions for the telecommunications industry. Specializes in project management and telecommunications engineering.

ONLINE JOB SOURCES AND SERVICES

★10312★ CSC CareerSource
2100 E. Grand Ave.
El Segundo, CA 90245
Ph: (310)615-0311
URL: http://www.csc.com

Virtual recruiting site listing employment opportunities in the project management field.

★10313★ Dice
URL: http://seeker.dice.com

Description: Online job board that offers searchable databases, job alerts, and career resources to the project management professional.

★10314★ ProjectManager.com
E-mail: support@projectmanager.com
URL: http://www.projectmanager.com

Description: Allows job seekers to create an online resume, browse available jobs, and use a career alert tool linking them with potential employers. Also maintains a knowledge section containing employment information and resources for project managers.

★10315★ Projects@Work
E-mail: aaron@projectsatwork.com
URL: http://www.projectsatwork.com

Description: Online newsletter for project management professionals. Provides a forum for networking and examines trends in project management.

★10316★ StartWright
URL: http://www.startwright.com

Description: Provides a comprehensive list of links to various sites on project management, project management methodology, and the project management profession.

TRADESHOWS

★10317★ Project Management Institute Annual Seminars and Symposium
Project Management Institute
4 Campus Blvd.
Newtown Square, PA 19073-3299
Ph: (610)356-4600   Fax: (610)356-4647
E-mail: customercare@pmi.org
URL: http://www.pmi.org

Annual. **Primary Exhibits:** Project management related exhibits.

OTHER SOURCES

★10318★ 4PM
3547 S. Ivanhoe
Denver, CO 80237
Ph: (303)756-4247   Fr: 877-332-2599
URL: http://www.4pm.com

Activities: Provides project management training and certification courses for professional project managers.

★10319★ American Academy of Project Management
245 Glendale Dr., Ste. One
Metairie, LA 70001
E-mail:
info@projectmanagementcertification.org
URL: http://
projectmanagementcertification.org

Purpose: Acts as the global board of standards for project management professionals. **Activities:** Offers courses in conjunction with certification. Maintains a job board for certified project managers.

★10320★ American Association of Service Coordinators (AASC)
PO Box 1178
Powell, OH 43065-1178
Ph: (614)848-5958   Fax: (614)848-5954
E-mail: info@servicecoordinator.org
URL: http://www.servicecoordinator.org

Description: Advances the interests of the service coordinator profession. Increases awareness and understanding of service coordination and service-enriched housing. Provides guidance to members in the creation and maintenance of service-enhanced housing to families, the elderly and persons with disabilities. Strives to enhance the professionalism of its constituents through leadership, education, training, networking, and advocacy.

★10321★ American Society for the Advancement of Project Management (ASAPM)
6547 N Academy, No. 404
Colorado Springs, CO 80918
Ph: (931)647-7373   Fax: (719)487-0673
E-mail: info@asapm.org
URL: http://www.asapm.org

Description: Promotes the mainstreaming of project management as a profession and as a way to improve human welfare. Advances project management methods, standards, and practical application techniques. Seeks to improve understanding and practice of the profession.

★10322★ Association of Call Center Managers (ACCM)
2505 Living Rock Ave.
Las Vegas, NV 89106
Ph: (702)367-2288
E-mail: info@callcentermanagers.org

Description: Represents call center managers and leaders dedicated to advancing the profession of call center management. Provides networking, peer mentoring, research, education and other resources that elevate the role and value of a call center leader. Strives to raise awareness of the call center profession and to heighten awareness of the strategic and economic value of call/contact centers.

★10323★ International Association of Project and Program Management
426 Main St., No. 360
Spotswood, NJ 08884
Ph: (732)421-2306
E-mail: info@iappm.org
URL: http://www.iappm.org

Members: Professional project managers. **Purpose:** Enhances and adds value to members and the project community and assists them in managing projects and programs successfully. **Activities:** Conducts a certification program. Offers members a forum in which they can network with other project managers.

★10324★ Leading Edge Alliance (LEA)
621 Cedar St.
St. Charles, IL 60174
Ph: (630)513-9814   Fax: (630)524-9014
URL: http://www.leadingedgealliance.com

Description: Represents independently owned accounting and consulting firms. Provides business development, professional training and education, and peer-to-peer networking opportunities. Offers business advisory expertise and experience and conducts accounting, tax and consulting services.

★10325★ Location Managers Guild of America (LMGA)
8033 Sunset Blvd., Ste. 1017
West Hollywood, CA 90046
Ph: (310)967-2007
E-mail: boardofdirectors@locationmanagers.org
URL: http://www.locationmanagers.org

Description: Enhances recognition and respect for members within the entertainment and related industries. Strengthens their ability to develop meaningful and credible careers. Strives to serve the public and the production industries through philanthropic and educational programs. Identifies, improves, exchanges and encourages the mutual benefits of location filming among the entertainment industries and the communities.

★10326★ **Management Education Alliance (MEA)**

300 Cumnock Hall
Boston, MA 02163
Ph: (617)495-6494   Fax: (617)495-8736
URL: http://www.mgteducationalliance.org

Description: Seeks to help business schools that serve African-American and Hispanic-American students to provide the skills and knowledge that will lead to successful careers in management. Fosters the professional growth of faculty members, innovations in curriculum, and development of supporting institutional policies. Communicates and collaborates with business schools and US business corporations.

★10327★ **Project Management Institute (PMI)**

4 Campus Blvd.
Newtown Square, PA 19073-3299
Ph: (610)356-4600   Fax: (610)356-4647
E-mail: customercare@pmi.org
URL: http://www.pmi.org

Members: Corporations and individuals engaged in the practice of project management; project management students and educators. **Purpose:** Seeks to advance the study, teaching, and practice of project management. **Activities:** Establishes project management standards; conducts educational and professional certification courses; bestows Project Management Professional credential upon qualified individuals. Offers educational seminars and global congresses.

★10328★ **Schedule Associates International**

2604 Elmwood Ave., No. 328
Rochester, NY 14618-2213
Ph: (585)271-1450   Fax: (585)244-1249
Fr: 800-606-1450
E-mail: info@scheduleassociates.net
URL: http://www.scheduleassociates.net

Activities: Offers training courses and seminars for professional project managers and those asked to fill that roll. Courses can be applied towards CAPM or PMP project management certification.

Property and Real Estate Managers

SOURCES OF HELP-WANTED ADS

★10329★ Buildings

Stamats Communications Inc.
615 5th St. SE
PO Box 1888
Cedar Rapids, IA 52406-1888
Ph: (319)364-6167   Fax: (319)365-5421
Fr: 800-553-8878
URL: http://www.buildings.com

Monthly. The facilities construction and management magazine covering news, concepts and technologies related to commercial building ownership and facilities management.

★10330★ The Caretaker Gazette

Gary C. Dunn
3 Estancia Lane
Boerne, TX 78006
Ph: (830)755-2300
E-mail: caretaker@caretaker.org
URL: http://www.caretaker.org

Description: Bimonthly. Covers the property caretaking field. Recurring features include rent-free living opportunities, job listings, letters to the editor, interviews, and a column titled Caretaker Profile. Offers mailing labels.

★10331★ Clayton-Fillmore Report

Clayton-Fillmore Ltd.
PO Box 480894
Denver, CO 80248
Ph: (303)663-0606   Fax: (303)663-1616
URL: http://www.clayfil.com

Monthly. $195.00/year for individuals, 1 year. Periodical covering real estate and business.

★10332★ Commercial Property News

VNU Business Media USA
770 Broadway
New York, NY 10003
Ph: (646)654-4500
URL: http://

www.commercialpropertynews.com/cpn/index.jsp

Semimonthly. $10.00 for single issue. Twice-monthly magazine for senior level executives in the commercial real estate market, including brokers, developers, investors, lenders, property managers, owners, and corporate real estate executives.

★10333★ Journal of Property Management

Institute of Real Estate Management
430 North Michigan Ave.
Chicago, IL 60611
Ph: (312)329-6000   Fax: 800-338-4736
Fr: 800-837-0706
E-mail: jpmsub@irem.org
URL: http://www.irem.org/sechome.cfm?sec=JPM

Bimonthly. $65.74/year for Canada; $56.95/year for individuals; $105.00/year for individuals, 2 years; $122.70/year for Canada, 2 years; $153.72/year for individuals, 3 years. Magazine serving real estate managers.

★10334★ Journal of Real Estate Literature

American Real Estate Society
c/o Diane Quarles
Clemson University
Box 341323
Clemson, SC 29634-1323
Ph: (864)656-1373   Fax: (864)656-3748
URL: http://cbeweb-1.fullerton.edu/finance/jrel/

Semiannual. Professional journal covering real estate issues.

★10335★ Journal of Real Estate Portfolio Management

American Real Estate Society
c/o Diane Quarles
Clemson University
Box 341323
Clemson, SC 29634-1323
Ph: (864)656-1373   Fax: (864)656-3748
URL: http://cbeweb-1.fullerton.edu/finance/jrepm/

Quarterly. Journal for real estate professionals.

★10336★ Journal of Real Estate Research

American Real Estate Society
c/o Diane Quarles
Clemson University
Box 341323
Clemson, SC 29634-1323
Ph: (864)656-1373   Fax: (864)656-3748
URL: http://cbeweb-1.fullerton.edu/finance/journal/

Journal focusing on scholarly real estate research.

★10337★ Lives of Real Estate

REAL Trends Inc.
6898 S University Blvd., Ste. 200
Littleton, CO 80122
Ph: (303)741-1000   Fax: (303)741-1070
URL: http://www.loremagazine.com/

Bimonthly. Free to qualified subscribers. Magazine that profiles personnel in the residential real estate industry.

★10338★ New England Real Estate Journal

East Coast Publications
PO Box 55
Accord, MA 02018-0055
Ph: (781)878-4540   Fax: (781)871-1853
Fr: 800-654-4993
E-mail: nerej@rejournal.com
URL: http://www.rejournal.com/

Weekly (Fri.). $99.00/year for individuals; $159.00 for individuals, two years. Newspaper publishing commercial, industrial, and investment real estate news.

★10339★ Property Management Association-Bulletin

Property Management Association
7900 Wisconsin Ave., Ste. 305
Bethesda, MD 20814
Ph: (301)657-9200   Fax: (301)907-9326
URL: http://www.pma-dc.org/pubs.html

Description: Monthly. Reports market trends and other information related to property management. Contains information on the Association and tips for members. Recurring features include news of research, a calendar of events, reports of meetings, news of educational opportunities, job listings, book reviews, and notices of publications available.

★10340★ *Real Estate Issues*
The Counselors of Real Estate
430 N Michigan Ave.
Chicago, IL 60611-4089
Ph: (312)329-8427   Fax: (312)329-8881
URL: http://www.cre.org

$48.00/year for individuals, one year; $15.00 for single issue, per issue. Trade publication covering the real estate industry.

PLACEMENT AND JOB REFERRAL SERVICES

★10341★ **CoreNet Global**
260 Peachtree St., Ste. 1500
Atlanta, GA 30303-1237
Ph: (404)589-3200   Fax: (404)589-3201
Fr: 800-726-8111
E-mail: jclarke@corenetglobal.org
URL: http://www.corenetglobal.org

Description: Executives, attorneys, real estate department heads, architects, engineers, analysts, researchers, and anyone responsible for the management, administration, and operation of national and regional real estate departments of national and international corporations. Encourages professionalism within corporate real estate through education and communication; protects the interests of corporate realty in dealing with adversaries, public or private; maintains contact with other real estate organizations; publicizes the availability of fully qualified members to the job market. Conducts seminars, including concentrated workshops on the corporate real estate field. Compiles statistics; sponsors competitions; maintains biographical archives and placement service.

EMPLOYER DIRECTORIES AND NETWORKING LISTS

★10342★ *Executive Guide to Specialists in Industrial and Office Real Estate*
Society of Industrial and Office Realtors
1201 New York Ave. NW, Ste. 350
Washington, DC 20005-6126
Ph: (202)449-8200   Fax: (202)216-9325
URL: http://www.sior.com

Annual, July. Covers industrial and office

real estate practitioners: the society's 2,800 designees, affiliates, associates, and candidates. Updated annually, the guide lists SIOR designees and affiliates geographically. Associate members are listed alphabetically by company for easy reference to leading corporate users, developers, public utilities, universities, and more. Arrangement: Geographical. Indexes: Personal name.

★10343★ *National Association of Real Estate Companies-Membership Directory*
National Association of Real Estate Companies
216 W Jackson Blvd., Ste. 625
Chicago, IL 60606
Ph: (312)263-1755   Fax: (312)750-1203
E-mail: cindy@narec.org
URL: http://www.narec.org

Quarterly. Covers about 200 real estate development companies. Entries include: Company name, address, phone, name of contact.

HANDBOOKS AND MANUALS

★10344★ *Be A Successful Property Manager*
McGraw-Hill
PO Box 182604
Columbus, OH 43272
Fax: (614)759-3749   Fr: 877-833-5524
E-mail: customer.service@mcgraw-hill.com
URL: http://www.mcgraw-hill.com/edu/default.shtml

Roger Woodson. 2006. $29.95. Comprehensive guide offering information for managing rental properties.

★10345★ *Great Big Book for Landlords and Property Managers*
Entrepreneur Press
PO Box 432
Newburgh, NY 12551
Fax: (845)457-5029   Fr: 800-215-7814
E-mail: epresscs@etcdata.com
URL: http://www.entrepreneurpress.com/

Stuart Leland Rider. $29.95. 2006. Comprehensive guide for landlords that teaches how to find and retain quality tenants.

★10346★ *How About a Career in Real Estate?*
Real Estate Education Co
1070 Idylwood Dr. SW
Issaquah, WA 98027
Ph: (425)392-6914   Fax: (425)392-6414
Fr: 800-296-2599

Carla Cross. Second edition, 1993. $14.95 (paper). 177 pages.

★10347★ *The Landlord's Handbook: A Complete Guide to Managing Small Residential Properties*
Kaplan Business
1 Liberty Plaza, 24th Fl.
New York, NY 10006
Ph: (312)836-4400   Fax: (312)836-1021
Fr: 800-527-4836
URL: http://www.kaplanpublishing.com/

Daniel Goodwin and Richard Rusdorf. Third edition, 1997. $29.95 (paper). 218 pages.

★10348★ *Real Estate Blues: A Jump Start Guide to Your Real Estate Career*
PublishAmerica, Incorporated
PO Box 151
Frederick, MD 21705
Ph: (301)695-1707   Fax: (301)631-9073
URL: http://www.publishamerica.com

David H. Lawrence. May 2004. $19.95 (paper). 138 pages.

★10349★ *Real Estate Careers: Twenty-Five Growing Opportunities*
John Wiley & Sons Inc.
1 Wiley Dr.
Somerset, NJ 08873
Ph: (732)469-4400   Fax: (732)302-2300
Fr: 800-225-5945
E-mail: custserv@wiley.com
URL: http://www.wiley.com/WileyCDA/

Carolyn Janik and Ruth Rejnis. 1994. $24.95 (paper). 224 pages.

★10350★ *The Rental Property Manager's Tool Box: A Complete Guide Including Pre-Written Forms, Agreements, Letters, Legal Notices with Companion CD-ROM*
Atlantic Publishing Company
1210 SW 23rd Pl.
Ocala, FL 34474-7014
Fax: (352)622-1875   Fr: 800-814-1132
E-mail: sales@atlantic-pub.com
URL: http://www.atlantic-pub.com/

Jamaine Burrell. 2006. $29.95. 384 pages. Complete guide for managing rental property covering advertising, tenant screening, managing tenants, legal rights, discrimination, vacancies, lease clauses, crime prevention, drugs, gangs, security, liability, eviction, maintenance, recordkeeping, and taxes; includes companion CD-ROM.

EMPLOYMENT AGENCIES AND SEARCH FIRMS

★10351★ **The Alfus Group Inc.**
353 Lexington Ave., Fl. 8
New York, NY 10016
Ph: (212)599-1000   Fax: (212)599-1523
E-mail: mail@thealfusgroup.com
URL: http://www.thealfusgroup.com

Executive search firm. Specializes in the hospitality industry.

★10352★ Arlene Clapp Ltd.

4250 Park Glen Rd.
Minneapolis, MN 55416
Ph: (952)928-7474   Fax: (952)928-7475
E-mail: arlene@arleneclapp.com
URL: http://www.arleneclapp.com/

Executive search firm.

★10353★ The Barack Group Inc.

Grand Central Station
PO Box 4407
New York, NY 10163
Ph: (212)867-9700   Fax: (212)681-9555
URL: http://www.barackgroup.com

Executive search firm.

★10354★ Bennett Search & Consulting Company Inc.

285-1 W. Naomi Dr.
Naples, FL 34104
Ph: (239)352-0219   Fax: (239)353-7719
E-mail: robertbennett3@comcast.net
URL: http://www.bscinc.org

Executive search firm.

★10355★ Caruso & Associates Inc.

990 Stinson Way, Ste. 201
West Palm Beach, FL 33411
Ph: (561)683-2336
E-mail: info@carusoassociates.com
URL: http://www.carusoassociates.com

Executive search firm.

★10356★ ChaseAmerica Inc.

6231 PGA Blvd., Ste. 104
Palm Beach Gardens, FL 33418
Ph: (561)491-5000   Fax: (561)491-5001
E-mail: davidstefanjr@chaseamericainc
URL: http://www.chaseamericainc.com

Executive search firm.

★10357★ Contractor Marketing

346 Dayton St.
Dayton, OH 45387-1704
Ph: (937)767-2876   Fax: (937)767-7281
E-mail: larry@contractormarketing.com
URL: http://www.contractormarketing.com

Executive search firm.

★10358★ Crown Advisors Inc.

800 E. Northwest Hwy., Ste. 612
Palatine, IL 60074
Ph: (847)221-2213   Fax: (847)221-2219
Fr: (847)830-6998
E-mail: jdimare@crownsearch.com

Executive search firm.

★10359★ Cullen International Executive Search Inc.

50 North Crest Dr.
Newnan, GA 30265-1200
Ph: (678)230-5475   Fax: (678)423-1718
E-mail: info@cullenexecutivesearch.com

Executive search firm.

★10360★ Dean M. Coe Associates

32 Pine St.
Sandwich, MA 02563
Ph: (508)888-8029
E-mail: deancoeassociates@comcast.net

Executive search firm focused on real estate and non-profit industries.

★10361★ DLG Associates Inc.

1515 Mockingbird Ln., Ste. 560
Charlotte, NC 28209
Ph: (704)522-9993   Fax: (704)522-7730
E-mail: dguilford@dlgassociates.com
URL: http://www.dlgassociates.com

Executive search firm.

★10362★ Edward Dellon Associates Inc.

450 N. Brand Blvd., Ste. 600
Glendale, CA 91203
Ph: (310)286-0625   Fax: (818)291-6205
E-mail: Edward_dellon@yahoo.com
URL: http://edwarddellonassociatesinc.com

Executive search firm.

★10363★ Franchise Recruiters Ltd.

Lincolnshire Country Club
3500 Innsbruck
Crete, IL 60417
Ph: (708)757-5595   Fax: (708)758-8222
Fr: 800-334-6257
E-mail: franchise@att.net
URL: http://www.franchiserecruiter.com

Executive search firm. Second location in Toronto, Canada.

★10364★ Real Estate Executive Search, Inc.

306 SE 4th St.
Dania Beach, FL 33004
Ph: (954)927-6000   Fax: (954)927-6003
E-mail: reesearch954@aol.com
URL: http://reesearchinc.com

Executive search firm for the real estate and finance fields.

TRADESHOWS

★10365★ Building Owners and Managers Association International Annual Convention and The Office Building Show

Building Owners and Managers Association International
1201 New York Ave., NW, Ste. 300
Washington, DC 20005
Ph: (202)408-2662   Fax: (202)371-0181
E-mail: meetings@boma.org
URL: http://www.bomaconvention.org

Annual. **Primary Exhibits:** Products, supplies and equipment for the office building industry, including architectural and building hardware, asbestos abatement, building automation, carpeting, control systems, doors, elevators and elevator maintenance, electrical and lighting, environmental services, financial services, fire protection, flooring and floor machines, hazardous waste removal, interior design, landscaping, locks, paper products, parking, pest control, plumbing and fixtures, recycling, renovation and restoration, roofing, security, signage, water treatment, windows.

★10366★ World Congress of the World Federation of Building Service Contractors

World Federation of Building Service Contractors
10201 Lee Hwy., Ste. 225
Fairfax, VA 22030
Ph: (703)359-7090   Fax: (703)352-0493
E-mail: cdean@bscai.org
URL: http://www.wfbsc.org

Biennial. **Primary Exhibits:** Floor care and carpet care equipment, building service contracting equipment, supplies, and services. **Dates and Locations:** 2008 Dates and location not set.

OTHER SOURCES

★10367★ Administration and Management Occupations

Delphi Productions
3159 6th St.
Boulder, CO 80304
Ph: (303)443-2100   Fax: (303)443-4022
Fr: 888-443-2400
E-mail: support@delphivideo.com
URL: http://www.delphivideo.com

$95.00. 50 minutes. Part of the Careers for the 21st Century Video Library.

★10368★ Building Owners and Managers Association International (BOMA)

1201 New York Ave. NW, Ste. 300
Washington, DC 20005-3966
Ph: (202)408-2662   Fax: (202)326-6377

E-mail: info@boma.org
URL: http://www.boma.org

Description: Building owners, managers, developers, leasing professionals, facility managers, asset managers and the providers of goods and services. Represents all facets of the commercial real estate industry.

★10369★ **Institute of Real Estate Management (IREM)**
430 N Michigan Ave.
Chicago, IL 60611-3900
Ph: (312)329-6000   Fax: 800-338-4736
Fr: 800-837-0706
E-mail: custserv@irem.org
URL: http://www.irem.org

Description: Professional organization of real property and asset managers. Awards professional designation Certified Property Manager (CPM) to qualifying individuals, Accredited Management Organization (AMO) to qualifying management firms and also awards Accredited Residential Manager (ARM) accreditation to qualifying individuals who are primarily residential site managers. Monitors legislation affecting real estate management. Offers management courses and seminars; conducts research and educational programs, publishes books and reports; maintains formal code of ethics; compiles statistics; maintains employment Website for real estate management industry.

★10370★ **National Apartment Association (NAA)**
4300 Wilson Blvd., Ste. 400
Arlington, VA 22203-4168
Ph: (703)518-6141   Fax: (703)248-9440

E-mail: webmaster@naahq.com
URL: http://www.naahq.org

Members: Federation of 155 state and local associations of industry professionals engaged in all aspects of the multifamily housing industry, including owners, builders, investors, developers, managers, and allied service representatives. **Purpose:** Provides education and certification for property management executives, on-site property managers, maintenance personnel, property supervisors, and leasing agents. Offers a nationwide legislative network concerned with governmental decisions at the federal, state, and local levels.

★10371★ **National Association of Realtors (NAR)**
430 N Michigan Ave.
Chicago, IL 60611-4088
Fax: (312)329-5960   Fr: 800-874-6500
E-mail: infocentral@realtors.org
URL: http://www.realtor.org

Description: Federation of 54 state and territory associations and 1,860 local real estate boards whose members are real estate brokers and agents; terms are registered by the association in the U.S. Patent and Trademark Office and in the states. Promotes education, high professional standards, and modern techniques in specialized real estate work such as brokerage, appraisal, property management, land development, industrial real estate, farm brokerage, and counseling. Conducts research programs.

★10372★ **National Property Management Association (NPMA)**
28100 US Hwy. 19 N, Ste. 400
Clearwater, FL 33761
Ph: (727)736-3788   Fax: (727)736-6707
E-mail: hq@npma.org
URL: http://www.npma.org

Description: Aims to build leadership by educating, training and promoting standards of competency and ethical behavior in the asset management of personal property. Serves property professionals throughout the United States; members represent companies and organizations in both the public and private sectors, including scientific laboratories, universities, hospitals, public school systems, and local, state and federal government agencies.

★10373★ **Realtors Land Institute (RLI)**
430 N Michigan Ave.
Chicago, IL 60611
Fax: (312)329-8633   Fr: 800-441-5263
E-mail: rli@realtors.org
URL: http://www.rliland.com

Members: Real estate brokers and salespersons selling, managing, appraising, or developing all types of land. **Purpose:** Maintains educational programs for real estate brokers; promotes competence and accredits members. **Activities:** Sponsors courses for realtors and others seeking professional excellence on Land Brokerage, Agricultural Land Brokerage, Exchanging Properties, Estate Planning, Subdivision Development, and Financial Analysis of Land Investment.

Psychologists

news of research, and positions-available notices.

SOURCES OF HELP-WANTED ADS

★10374★ AAAP News

American Academy of Addiction Psychiatry
345 Blackstone Blvd., 2nd Fl. RCH
Providence, RI 02906
Ph: (401)524-3076   Fax: (401)272-0922
URL: http://www.aaap.org/pulications.htm

$45.00/year for individuals; $15.00 for individuals, per issue; $50.00/year for individuals, international; $20.00 for individuals, per issue, international. Professional journal covering addiction psychiatry.

★10375★ AACAP News

American Academy of Child and Adolescent Psychiatry (AACAP)
3615 Wisconsin Ave., NW
Washington, DC 20016-3007
Ph: (202)966-7300   Fax: (202)966-2891
E-mail: clinical@aacap.org
URL: http://www.aacap.org/

Description: Bimonthly. Publishes news of the Academy, child and adolescent psychiatrists, and AACAP members. Focuses on the practice of child and adolescent psychiatry. Recurring features include letters to the editor, legislative updates, news of research, statistics, announcements of open positions, and columns titled Ethics, Clinical Vignettes, Forensic Corner, and Clinical Marketing.

★10376★ The ABA Newsletter

Association for Behavior Analysis (ABA)
1219 South Park St.
Kalamazoo, MI 49001
Ph: (269)492-9310   Fax: (269)492-9316
E-mail: mail@abainternational.org
URL: http://www.abainternational.org

Description: Three issues/year. Covers Association activities, with reports of committees and special interest groups, and news from regional, state, and local associations for behavior analysis. Recurring features include convention details and overview,

★10377★ Academic Psychiatry

American Psychiatric Publishing Inc.
1000 Wilson Blvd., Ste. 1825
Arlington, VA 22209-3901
Ph: (703)907-7322   Fax: (703)907-1091
Fr: 800-368-5777
URL: http://ap.psychiatryonline.org/

$132.00/year for members, 1 year; $168.00/year for members, 1 year; $187.00/year for nonmembers, 1 year; $211.00/year for members, 1 year; $281.00/year for nonmembers, 1 year. Journal contributing to the efforts in furthering psychiatry as a profession and to knowledge pool of medicine.

★10378★ Alcoholism

Wiley-Blackwell
350 Main St. Commerce Pl.
Malden, MA 02148
Ph: (781)388-8200   Fax: (781)388-8210
Fr: 800-759-6120
E-mail: mnewcomb-acer@earthlink.net
URL: http://www.blackwellpublishing.com/journal.asp?ref=0145-6008

Monthly. Publishing original clinical and research studies on alcoholism and alcohol-induced organ damage.

★10379★ American Journal of Family Therapy

MetaPress
PO Box 1943
Birmingham, AL 35201
Fr: 877-773-3833

Quarterly. $248.00/year for individuals, one year. Periodical covering the techniques for treating families, theory on normal and dysfunctional family relationships, research on sexuality and intimacy, the effects of traditional and alternative family styles, and community approaches to family intervention. Also includes family measurement techniques, family behavioral medicine and health, family law issues in family therapy practice, and continuing education and training.

★10380★ American Journal of Geriatric Psychiatry

American Association for Geriatric Psychiatry
7910 Woodmont Ave., Ste. 1050
Bethesda, MD 20814-3004
Ph: (301)654-7850   Fax: (301)654-4137
URL: http://ajgponline.org

Monthly. $351.00/year for individuals; $965.00/year for institutions; $491.00/year for individuals, other countries; $849.00/year for institutions, other countries; $201.00/year for individuals, in-training; $253.00/year for individuals, other countries, in-training. Professional journal covering geriatric psychiatry.

★10381★ American Journal of Psychology

University of Illinois Press
1325 S Oak St.
Champaign, IL 61820-6903
Ph: (217)333-0950   Fax: (217)244-8082
Fr: 800-537-5487
URL: http://www.press.uillinois.edu/journals/ajp.html

Quarterly. $70.00/year for individuals; $126.00/year for individuals, two years; $178.00/year for individuals, three years; $190.00/year for institutions; $342.00/year for institutions, two years; $484.00/year for institutions, three years; $80.00/year for individuals, outside U.S.; $146.00/year for individuals, outside U.S., two years; $208.00/year for individuals, outside U.S., three years; $40.00 for single issue. Journal dealing with experimental psychology and basic principles of psychology.

★10382★ American Psychologist

American Psychological Association
750 1st St. NE
Washington, DC 20002-4242
Ph: (202)336-5540   Fax: (202)336-5549
Fr: 800-374-2721
URL: http://www.apa.org/journals/amp.html

$12.00/year for members, domestic; $249.00/year for nonmembers, domestic; $12.00/year for students, domestic; $649.00/year for institutions, domestic; $743.00/year for institutions, other countries, foreign, surface freight; $66.00/year for members, foreign, air freight; $66.00/year for students, foreign, air freight; $770.00/year for institutions, other countries, foreign, air freight; $295.00/year for nonmembers, foreign, surface freight; $322.00/year for nonmembers, foreign, air freight. Official journal of the association. Publishes empirical, theoretical, and professional articles.

★10383★ **Annals of Behavioral Medicine**
Society of Behavioral Medicine
10 Industrial Ave.
Mahwah, NJ 07430
Ph: (201)258-2238   Fax: (201)760-3735
Fr: 800-926-6579

Quarterly. Journal describing the interactions of behavior and health.

★10384★ **Annual Review of Psychology**
Annual Reviews Inc.
4139 El Camino Way
PO Box 10139
Palo Alto, CA 94303-0139
Ph: (650)493-4400   Fax: (650)424-0910
Fr: 800-523-8635

Annual. $75.00/year for individuals, print and online; $181.00/year for institutions, print only; $181.00/year for institutions, online only; $217.00/year for institutions, print and online. Publication covering psychology and mental health issues.

★10385★ **APS Observer**
Association for Psychological Science
1010 Vermont Ave. NW, 11th Fl.
Washington, DC 20005-4918
Ph: (202)783-2077   Fax: (202)783-2083
E-mail: apsobserver@aps.washington.dc.us
URL: http://www.psychologicalscience.org/

Description: Ten issues/year. Provides information on issues of interest to members. Offers a monthly employment listing for academic and scientific psychologists.

★10386★ **Archives of General Psychiatry**
American Medical Association
515 N State St.
Chicago, IL 60610
Fr: 800-621-8335
E-mail: archgenpsychiatry@jama-archives.org
URL: http://archpsyc.ama-assn.org/

Monthly. $465.00/year for institutions, print and online; $135.00/year for members, print and online; $199.00/year for nonmembers, print and online. Educational/clinical journal for psychiatrists.

★10387★ **Children & Society**
John Wiley & Sons Inc.
111 River St.
Hoboken, NJ 07030-5774
Ph: (201)748-6000   Fax: (201)748-6088
Fr: 800-825-7550

E-mail: children&society@ncb.org.uk
URL: http://www3.interscience.wiley.com/cgi-bin/jhome/4805

$655.00/year for institutions, print and online; $566.00/year for institutions, online only; $194.00/year for individuals, print and online. Journal focusing on children and services for children.

★10388★ **Clinical Psychiatry News**
International Medical News Group
60-B Columbia Rd.
Morristown, NJ 07960
Ph: (973)290-8200   Fax: (973)290-8250
URL: http://journals.elsevierhealth.com/periodicals/cpnews

Monthly. $90.00/year for individuals; $144.00/year for other countries, surface mail. Medical and psychiatry tabloid.

★10389★ **Contemporary Psychology**
American Psychological Association
750 1st St. NE
Washington, DC 20002-4242
Ph: (202)336-5540   Fax: (202)336-5549
Fr: 800-374-2721
URL: http://www.apa.org/journals/cnt.html

Bimonthly. $20.00 for single issue. Journal presenting critical reviews of books, films, tapes, and other media representing a cross section of psychological literature.

★10390★ **Counselling Psychology Quarterly**
Taylor & Francis Group Journals
325 Chestnut St., Ste. 800
Philadelphia, PA 19106
Ph: (215)625-8900   Fax: (215)625-8914
Fr: 800-354-1420
URL: http://www.tandf.co.uk/journals/titles/09515070.asp

Quarterly. $1,067.00/year for institutions, print and online; $1,013.00/year for institutions, online only; $303.00/year for individuals; $66.00/year for BPS and APA members. Journal covering practical counseling, clinical, occupational and medical psychology.

★10391★ **EAP Digest**
Performance Resource Press Inc.
1270 Rankin Dr., Ste. F
Troy, MI 48083
Ph: (248)588-7733   Fax: (248)588-6633
URL: http://www.prponline.net/Work/EAP/eap.htm

Quarterly. $36.00/year for individuals; $82.00 for two years, Canada, Hawaii, & Alaska; $99.00 for individuals for three years, Canada, Hawaii, & Alaska; $104.00 for other countries, three years; $87.00 for other countries, two years; $54.00/year for other countries; $49.00/year for individuals, Canada, Hawaii, & Alaska; $60.00 for two years. Magazine covering planning, development, and administration of employee assistance programs.

★10392★ **Ethical Human Psychology and Psychiatry**
Springer Publishing Co.
11 W 42nd St., 15th Fl.
New York, NY 10036
Ph: (212)431-4370   Fax: (212)941-7342
Fr: 877-687-7476
URL: http://www.springerpub.com/

$70.00/year for individuals; $105.00/year for individuals, print and online; $200.00/year for institutions; $300.00/year for institutions, print and online. Books on nursing, psychology, gerontology, geriatrics, social work, counseling, public health, rehabilitation and medical education.

★10393★ **GradPsych**
American Psychoanalytic Association
309 E 49th St.
New York, NY 10017
Ph: (212)752-0450   Fax: (212)593-0571
E-mail: gradpsych@apa.org
URL: http://www.gradpsych.apags.org

Quarterly. $18.00/year for members, domestic; $35.00/year for individuals, non-members; $70.00/year for institutions; $18.00/year for other countries, international affiliates; $18.00/year for individuals, high school teacher affiliates; $28.00/year for members, international surface; $50.00/year for individuals, international surface; $40.00/year for members, international air mail; $60.00/year for individuals, international air mail; $115.00/year for institutions, international air mail. Magazine that offers information about psychology careers, finance, and emerging trends in psychology practice, research, and education.

★10394★ **Intellectual and Developmental Disabilities**
American Association on Intellectual and Developmental Disabilities
444 N Capitol St. NW, Ste. 846
Washington, DC 20001-1512
Ph: (202)387-1968   Fax: (202)387-2193
Fr: 800-424-3688
URL: http://www.aamr.org

Bimonthly. $219.00/year for institutions, print + online; $252.00/year for institutions, other countries, print + online; $106.00/year for individuals, print + online; $139.00/year for individuals, print + online outside U.S.; $207.00/year for institutions, online only; $207.00/year for institutions, other countries, online only; $95.00/year for individuals, online only; $95.00/year for individuals, online only outside U.S. Magazine featuring articles on mental retardation for professionals and parents.

★10395★ **International Journal of Psychiatry in Clinical Practice**
Taylor & Francis Group Journals
325 Chestnut St., Ste. 800
Philadelphia, PA 19106
Ph: (215)625-8900   Fax: (215)625-8914
Fr: 800-354-1420
URL: http://www.tandf.co.uk/journals/titles/13651501.asp

Quarterly. Journal for health professionals with clinical, academic, and research interests in psychiatry.

★10396★ International Journal of Psychology

Psychology Press
270 Madison Ave.
New York, NY 10016
Ph: (212)216-7800   Fax: (212)563-2269
Fr: 800-634-7064
URL: http://www.tandf.co.uk/journals/titles/00207594.asp

$735.00/year for institutions, print and online; $698.00/year for institutions, online only; $171.00/year for individuals. Journal dealing with all aspects of development of international psychological science.

★10397★ Journal of the American Academy of Child and Adolescent Psychiatry

Lippincott Williams & Wilkins
530 Walnut St.
Philadelphia, PA 19106-3621
Ph: (215)521-8300   Fax: (215)521-8902
Fr: 800-638-3030
URL: http://www.jaacap.com/

Monthly. $195.00/year for individuals, U.S.; $341.00/year for institutions, U.S.; $252.00/year for individuals, international; $402.00/year for institutions, international. Child psychiatry journal.

★10398★ Journal of Business and Psychology

Springer-Verlag New York Inc.
233 Spring St.
New York, NY 10013
Ph: (212)460-1500   Fax: (212)460-1575
URL: http://www.springer.com/journal/10869/

Journal covering all aspects of psychology that apply to the business segment. Includes topics such as personnel selection and training, organizational assessment and development, risk management and loss control, marketing and consumer behavior research.

★10399★ Journal of Clinical Psychology

John Wiley & Sons Inc.
111 River St.
Hoboken, NJ 07030-5774
Ph: (201)748-6000   Fax: (201)748-6088
Fr: 800-825-7550
URL: http://www3.interscience.wiley.com/cgi-bin/jhome/31171

Monthly. $115.00/year for individuals, for print (U.S., Canada, and Mexico); $187.00/year for individuals, for print (rest of world); $725.00/year for institutions, print only; $809.00/year for institutions, other countries, print only; $798.00/year for institutions, combined print with online access rates; $882.00/year for Canada and Mexico, combined print with online access rates; $882.00/year for other countries, combined

print with online access rates. Journal for professionals in the field of psychology.

★10400★ Journal of Counseling Psychology

American Psychological Association
750 1st St. NE
Washington, DC 20002-4242
Ph: (202)336-5540   Fax: (202)336-5549
Fr: 800-374-2721
E-mail: journals@apa.org
URL: http://www.apa.org/journals/cou.html

Quarterly. $50.00/year for members, domestic; $66.00/year for members, foreign, surface freight; $78.00/year for members, foreign, air mail; $29.00/year for students, domestic; $45.00/year for students, foreign, surface freight; $57.00/year for students, foreign, air mail; $98.00/year for nonmembers, domestic; $119.00/year for nonmembers, foreign, surface freight; $129.00/year for nonmembers, foreign, air mail; $267.00/year for institutions, domestic. Journal presenting empirical studies about counseling processes and interventions, theoretical articles about counseling, and studies dealing with evaluation of counseling applications and programs.

★10401★ Journal of Family Psychotherapy

The Haworth Press Inc.
10 Alice St.
Binghamton, NY 13904
Ph: (607)722-5857   Fr: 800-429-6784
URL: http://www.haworthpress.com/store/product.asp?sid=3CXTKNPDX

Quarterly. Journal includes case studies, treatment reports, and strategies in clinical practice for psychotherapists.

★10402★ Journal of Positive Behavior Interventions

PRO-ED Inc.
8700 Shoal Creek Blvd.
PO Box 678370
Austin, TX 78757-6897
Ph: (512)451-3246   Fax: 800-397-7633
Fr: 800-897-3202
URL: http://www.proedinc.com

Quarterly. $48.00/year for individuals, North America,1 year; $78.00/year for individuals, North America,2 year; $128.00/year for institutions, North America, 1 year; $205.00/year for institutions, North America,2 year; $78.00/year for individuals, foreign subscriptions,1 year; $125.00/year for individuals, foreign subscriptions, 2 year; $161.00/year for institutions, foreign subscriptions,1 year; $258.00/year for institutions, foreign subscriptions, 2 year; $46.00/year for individuals, North America; $124.00/year for institutions, North America. Journal covering issues in mental health and psychology.

★10403★ The Journal of Psychology

Heldref Publications
1319 18th St., NW
Washington, DC 20036-1802
Ph: (202)296-6267   Fr: 800-365-9753

E-mail: jrl@heldref.org
URL: http://www.heldref.org/jp.php

Quarterly. $239.00/year for institutions, print or online; $207.00/year for individuals, online only; $217.00/year for individuals, print and online; $287.00/year for institutions, print and online. Psychology journal that publishes a variety of research and theoretical articles.

★10404★ Medical Economics

Advanstar Communications Inc.
641 Lexington Ave., 8th Fl.
New York, NY 10022
Ph: (212)951-6600   Fax: (212)951-6793
URL: http://www.memag.com/memag/

Semimonthly. Magazine covering physicians practice management, professional relations, and financial affairs.

★10405★ Monitor on Psychology

American Psychological Association
750 1st St. NE
Washington, DC 20002-4242
Ph: (202)336-5540   Fax: (202)336-5549
Fr: 800-374-2721
E-mail: journals@apa.org
URL: http://www.apa.org/monitor/

Monthly. $46.00/year for nonmembers; $86.00/year for individuals, foreign, surface freight; $113.00/year for individuals, foreign, air freight; $87.00/year for institutions, nonmember, foreign, surface freight; $168.00/year for institutions, foreign, air freight; $195.00/year for institutions, air freight; $3.00/year for single issue. Magazine of the APA. Reports on the science, profession, and social responsibility of psychology, including latest legislative developments affecting mental health, education, and research support.

★10406★ North American Society of Adlerian Psychology Newsletter (NASAP Newsletter)

North American Society of Adlerian Psychology
614 W. Chocolate Ave.
Hershey, PA 17033
Ph: (717)579-8795   Fax: (717)533-8616
E-mail: info@alfredadler.org
URL: http://www.alfredadler.org

Description: Bimonthly. Relates news and events of the North American Society of Adlerian Psychology and regional news of affiliated associations. Recurring features include lists of courses and workshops offered by affiliated associations, reviews of new publications in the field, professional employment opportunities, a calendar of events, and a column titled President's Message.

★10407★ Patient Education and Counseling

Mosby Inc.
11830 Westline Industrial Dr.
St. Louis, MO 63146
Ph: (314)872-8370   Fax: (314)432-1380
Fr: 800-325-4177
URL: http://www.elsevier.com/wps/find/journaldescription.cws_home

Monthly. $229.00/year for individuals; $2,169.00/year for institutions. Journal publishing articles on patient education and health promotion researchers, managers, physicians, nurses and other health care providers.

★10408★ Pediatrics

American Academy of Pediatrics
141 North West Point Blvd.
Elk Grove Village, IL 60007-1098
Ph: (847)434-4000   Fax: (847)434-8000
Fr: 800-433-9016
E-mail: journals@aap.org

Monthly. Medical journal reporting on pediatrics.

★10409★ Practice

Taylor & Francis Group Journals
325 Chestnut St., Ste. 800
Philadelphia, PA 19106
Ph: (215)625-8900   Fax: (215)625-8914
Fr: 800-354-1420
URL: http://www.tandf.co.uk/journals/titles/09503153.asp

$285.00/year for institutions, print and online; $270.00/year for institutions, online only; $98.00/year for individuals. Journal for a strong base in social work practice.

★10410★ Psychiatric Annals

SLACK Inc.
6900 Grove Rd.
Thorofare, NJ 08086-9447
Ph: (856)848-1000   Fax: (856)853-5991
E-mail: psyann@slackinc.com
URL: http://www.psychiatricannalsonline.com

Monthly. $219.00/year for individuals; $438.00 for individuals, two years; $657.00 for individuals, three years; $373.00/year for institutions; $746.00 for institutions, two years; $1119.00 for institutions, three years; $109.00/year for individuals, resident; $48.00 for single issue. Journal analyzing concepts and practices in every area of psychiatry.

★10411★ Psychiatric News

American Psychiatric Publishing Inc.
1000 Wilson Blvd., Ste. 1825
Arlington, VA 22209-3901
Ph: (703)907-7322   Fax: (703)907-1091
Fr: 800-368-5777
URL: http://pn.psychiatryonline.org/

Semimonthly. $93.00/year for individuals, U.S.; $126.00/year for members, international member; $140.00/year for nonmembers, international; $19.00 for single issue, U.S.;

$31.00/year for single issue, international. Professional magazine of the American Psychiatric Assn.

★10412★ Psychiatric Services

Association of Partners for Public Lands
2401 Blueridge Ave., Ste. 303
Wheaton, MD 20902
Ph: (301)946-9475   Fax: (301)946-9478

Monthly. Interdisciplinary mental health journal covering clinical, legal, and public policy issues.

★10413★ Psychiatric Times

CMP Media L.L.C.
600 Harrison St., 6th Fl.
San Francisco, CA 94107
Ph: (415)947-6000   Fax: (415)947-6055
URL: http://www.psychiatrictimes.com/

Monthly. $55.00/year for individuals; $90.00 individuals, for two years; $120.00/year for libraries, institutions; $120.00/year for other countries. Newspaper (tabloid) on psychiatric disorders and issues.

★10414★ Psychiatry

Elsevier Science Inc.
360 Park Ave. S
New York, NY 10010
Ph: (212)989-5800   Fax: (212)633-3990
URL: http://www.elsevier.com

$464.00/year for institutions in all countries except Europe, Japan and Iran. $243.00/year for individuals in all countries except Europe, Japan and Iran. $135.00/year for students in all countries except Europe, Japan and Iran. $87.00/year for nurses in all countries except Europe, Japan and Iran. Journal covering medical specialties dealing with diagnosis, treatment, and rehabilitation of mental illness.

★10415★ Psychological Bulletin

American Psychological Association
750 1st St. NE
Washington, DC 20002-4242
Ph: (202)336-5540   Fax: (202)336-5549
Fr: 800-374-2721
E-mail: journals@apa.org
URL: http://www.apa.org/journals/bul.html

Bimonthly. $93.00/year for members, domestic; $111.00/year for members, foreign, surface freight; $129.00/year for members, foreign, air mail; $59.00/year for students, domestic; $77.00/year for students, foreign, surface freight; $95.00/year for students, foreign, air mail; $198.00/year for nonmembers, domestic; $224.00/year for nonmembers, foreign, surface freight; $238.00/year for nonmembers, foreign, air mail; $555.00/year for institutions, domestic. Journal presenting comprehensive and integrative reviews and interpretations of critical substantive and methodological issues and practical problems from all the diverse areas of psychology.

★10416★ Psychological Services

American Psychological Association
750 1st St. NE
Washington, DC 20002-4242
Ph: (202)336-5540   Fax: (202)336-5549
Fr: 800-374-2721
URL: http://www.apa.org/journals/ser

Quarterly. $55.00/year for members, domestic; $71.00/year for members, international surface; $83.00/year for members, international airmail; $55.00/year for students, domestic; $71.00/year for students, international surface; $83.00/year for students, international airmail; $80.00/year for nonmembers, domestic; $101.00/year for nonmembers, international surface; $111.00/year for nonmembers, international airmail; $289.00/year for institutions, domestic. Journal of the Division of Psychologists in Public Service, publishing data-based articles on the broad range of psychological services.

★10417★ Psychology Journal

Psychological Publishing
PO Box 176
Natchitoches, LA 71458
URL: http://www.psychologicalpublishing.com/

$40.00/year for individuals; $75.00/year for institutions. Journal dedicated to all areas of the science and practice of counseling and clinical psychology.

★10418★ Review of General Psychology

American Psychological Association
750 1st St. NE
Washington, DC 20002-4242
Ph: (202)336-5540   Fax: (202)336-5549
Fr: 800-374-2721
URL: http://www.apa.org/journals/gpr.html

Quarterly. $55.00/year for members, domestic; $55.00/year for students, domestic; $80.00/year for nonmembers, domestic; $279.00/year for institutions, domestic; $71.00/year for members, surface mail; $71.00/year for students, surface mail; $101.00/year for nonmembers, surface mail; $317.00/year for institutions, surface mail; $83.00/year for members, airmail; $83.00/year for students, airmail. Journal including a wide variety of psychological research-related articles.

★10419★ Teaching Exceptional Children

Council for Exceptional Children
1110 N Glebe Rd., Ste. 300
Arlington, VA 22201-5704
Ph: (703)620-3660   Fax: (703)264-9494
Fr: 888-232-7733
E-mail: tec@bc.edu
URL: http://www.cec.sped.org

Bimonthly. $135.00/year for individuals; $250.00 for two years; $145.00 for two years, Canada; $270.00 for two years, Canada; $165.00/year for out of country, foreign-air printed matter; $310.00/year for out of country, two years, foreign-air printed matter; $25.00/year for institutions, single copy;

$170.00/year for institutions; $290.00 for two years, institutional. Journal exploring practical methods for teaching students who have exceptionalities and those who are gifted and talented.

★10420★ **USA Body Psychotherapy Journal**

United States Association for Body Psychotherapy
7831 Woodmont Ave.
Bethesda, MD 20814
URL: http://www.usabp.org/displaycommon.cfm?an=4

Semiannual. Academic journal that seeks to support, promote and stimulate the exchange of ideas, scholarship and research within the field of body psychotherapy as well as an interdisciplinary exchange with related fields of clinical practice and inquiry.

PLACEMENT AND JOB REFERRAL SERVICES

★10421★ **American Public Health Association (APHA)**

800 I St. NW
Washington, DC 20001
Ph: (202)777-2742   Fax: (202)777-2534
E-mail: comments@apha.org
URL: http://www.apha.org

Members: Professional organization of physicians, nurses, educators, academicians, environmentalists, epidemiologists, new professionals, social workers, health administrators, optometrists, podiatrists, pharmacists, dentists, nutritionists, health planners, other community and mental health specialists, and interested consumers. **Purpose:** Seeks to protect and promote personal, mental, and environmental health. **Activities:** Services include: promulgation of standards; establishment of uniform practices and procedures; development of the etiology of communicable diseases; research in public health; exploration of medical care programs and their relationships to public health. Sponsors job placement service.

★10422★ **American Society of Criminology (ASC)**

1314 Kinnear Rd., Ste. 212
Columbus, OH 43212-1156
Ph: (614)292-9207   Fax: (614)292-6767
E-mail: asc@osu.edu
URL: http://www.asc41.com

Description: Represents professional and academic criminologists, students of criminology in accredited universities, psychiatrists, psychologists, and sociologists. Develops criminology as a science and academic discipline. Aids in the construction of criminological curricula in accredited universities. Upgrades the practitioner in criminological fields (police, prisons, probation, parole, delinquency workers). Conducts research

programs and sponsors three student paper competitions. Provides placement service at annual convention.

★10423★ **Association for Behavior Analysis (ABA)**

1219 S Park St.
Kalamazoo, MI 49001-5607
Ph: (269)492-9310   Fax: (269)492-9316
E-mail: mail@abainternational.org
URL: http://www.abainternational.org

Description: Professionals, paraprofessionals, and students interested in the applied, experimental, and theoretical analysis of behavior. Promotes the development of behavior analysis as a profession and science. Provides a forum for the discussion of issues; disseminates information on behavior analysis. Conducts workshops and seminars in 16 specialty areas including: Behavioral Pharmacology and Toxicology; Developmental Disabilities; Organizational Behavior Analysis. Offers continuing education credits for psychologists. Maintains archives of the association's publications; offers placement service.

★10424★ **International Association of Counselors and Therapists (IACT)**

RR No. 2, Box 2468
Laceyville, PA 18623
Ph: (570)869-1021   Fax: (570)869-1249
Fr: 800-553-6886
E-mail: info@iact.org
URL: http://www.iact.org

Description: Mental health professionals, medical professionals, social workers, clergy, educators, hypnotherapists, counselors, and individuals interested in the helping professions. Promotes enhanced professional image and prestige for complementary therapy. Provides a forum for exchange of information and ideas among practitioners of traditional and nontraditional therapies and methodologies; fosters unity among "grassroots" practitioners and those with advanced academic credentials. Facilitates the development of new therapy programs. Conducts educational, research, and charitable programs. Awards credits for continuing education. Maintains speakers' bureau and library; operates referral and placement services; compiles statistics. Assists in the development of local chapters.

EMPLOYER DIRECTORIES AND NETWORKING LISTS

★10425★ **AHA Guide to the Health Care Field**

American Hospital Association
1 N Franklin
Chicago, IL 60606
Ph: (312)422-2050   Fax: (312)422-4700
Fr: 800-424-4301

Annual, August. Covers hospitals, networks,

multi-health care systems, freestanding ambulatory surgery centers, psychiatric facilities, long-term care facilities, substance abuse programs, and other health-related organizations. Entries include: For hospitals–Facility name, address, phone, administrator's name, number of beds, facilities and services, number of employees, expenses, other statistics. For other organizations–Name, address, phone, fax, name and title of contact. Arrangement: Geographical. Indexes: Hospital name.

★10426★ **American Association for Correctional Psychology-Directory**

American Association for Correctional Psychology
c/o Robert Smith, Ed.D.
Marshall University Graduate College
100 Angus E Peyton Dr.
South Charleston, WV 25303-1600
Ph: (304)746-1929   Fax: (304)746-1942

Continuously updated. Covers 400 mental health professionals engaged in correctional and rehabilitative work in prisons, reformatories, juvenile institutions, probation and parole agencies, and in other aspects of criminal justice. Entries include: Name, affiliation, address, phone. Arrangement: Alphabetical.

★10427★ **American Board of Forensic Psychology-Directory of Diplomates**

American Board of Forensic Psychology
638 Popular Ct.
Pittsburgh, PA 15238
Ph: (412)828-9685   Fax: (412)826-8279
URL: http://www.abfp.com

Biennial. Covers approximately 200 forensic psychologists. Entries include: Personal name, home and office addresses and phone numbers, biographical data, services. Arrangement: Alphabetical. Indexes: Geographical; specialty field.

★10428★ **American Board of Professional Psychology-Directory of Diplomates**

American Board of Professional Psychology
300 Drayton St., 3rd Fl.
Savannah, GA 31401
Ph: (912)234-5477   Fax: (912)234-5120
Fr: 800-255-7792
URL: http://www.abpp.org

Biennial, odd years. Covers 3,200 psychologists who have passed the board's examination. Entries include: Name, office address, highest degree held, date of certification, practice areas. Arrangement: Alphabetical. Indexes: Geographical; speciality.

★10429★ **American Group Psychotherapy Association-Membership Directory**

American Group Psychotherapy Association Inc.
25 E 21st St., 6th Fl.
New York, NY 10010
Ph: (212)477-2677   Fax: (212)979-6627
Fr: 877-668-2472

URL: http://www.agpa.org

Covers 4,500 physicians, psychologists, clinical social workers, psychiatric nurses, and other mental health professionals interested in treatment of emotional problems by group methods. Entries include: Name, office or home address, highest degree held, office or home phone number. Arrangement: Alphabetical. Indexes: Geographical.

★10430★ **American Psychological Association-APA Membership Register**
American Psychological Association
750 1st St. NE
Washington, DC 20002-4242
Ph: (202)336-5540   Fax: (202)336-5549
Fr: 800-374-2721
E-mail: regdir@apa.org
URL: http://www.apa.org/databases/mem_directory/homepage.html

Annual; latest edition 2007; level 2 access in process. Free. Covers over 83,000 members in the United States, Canada, and abroad; also includes membership rosters of American Board of Professional Psychology and American Board of Psychological Hypnosis. Entries include: Name, office or home address, phone, fax, degrees and universities where obtained, election date, membership and divisional affiliations. Arrangement: Alphabetical. Indexes: Association division.

★10431★ **American Society for Adolescent Psychiatry-Membership Directory**
American Society for Adolescent Psychiatry
PO Box 570218
Dallas, TX 75357-0218
Ph: (972)613-0985   Fax: (972)613-5532
URL: http://www.adolpsych.org

Covers 1,500 members. Entries include: Name, office address and phone, fax, home address and phone (when given). Arrangement: Alphabetical. Indexes: Geographical, chapter.

★10432★ **Christian Association for Psychological Studies International-Membership Directory**
Christian Association for Psychological Studies
PO Box 365
Batavia, IL 60510-0365
Ph: (630)639-9478   Fax: (630)454-3799

Annual, June. $12.00 for Canada; $12.00 for other countries. Covers 2,300 Christians involved in psychology, psychiatry, counseling, sociology, social work, ministry, and nursing. Entries include: Name, office address and phone number, highest degree held, area of occupational specialization, and career data. Arrangement: Geographical. Indexes: Alphabetical.

★10433★ **Directory of Child Life Programs**
Child Life Council Inc.
11820 Parklawn Dr., Ste. 240
Rockville, MD 20852-2529
Ph: (301)881-7090   Fax: (301)881-7092
URL: http://www.childlife.org/

Biennial; latest edition 14th, 2006. Covers over 400 child life programs. Entries include: Facility name, address, phone, name of child life department and director, reporting structure, staff statistics, educational requirements for employment, and internship or educational opportunities. Arrangement: Geographical. Indexes: Speciality areas, internship sessions, program size, fellowships.

★10434★ **Directory of Counseling Services**
International Association of Counseling Services
101 S Whiting St., Ste. 211
Alexandria, VA 22304-3416
Ph: (703)823-9840   Fax: (703)823-9843
URL: http://iacsinc.org/iacsmem.html

Annual, September. $50.00. Covers about 200 accredited services in the United States and Canada concerned with psychological, educational, and vocational counseling, including those at colleges and universities and public and private agencies. Entries include: Name, address, phone, hours of operation, director's name, service, clientele served. Arrangement: Geographical.

★10435★ **Directory of Hospital Personnel**
Grey House Publishing
185 Millerton Rd.
PO Box 860
Millerton, NY 12546
Ph: (518)789-8700   Fax: (518)789-0556
Fr: 800-562-2139
URL: http://www.greyhouse.com/hospital_personnel.htm

Annual. $325.00 for print product; $545.00 for online database subscription; $650.00 for online database subscription and print product combined. Covers 200,000 executives at 7,000 U.S. hospitals. Entries include: Name of hospital, address, phone; number of beds; type and JCAHO status of hospital; names and titles of key department heads and staff; medical and nursing school affiliations; number of residents, interns, and nursing students. Arrangement: Geographical. Indexes: Hospital name, personnel, hospital size.

★10436★ **Directory of Refugee Mental Health Professionals and Paraprofessionals**
Refugee Assistance Program–Mental Health Technical Assistance Center
University of Minnesota
Mayo MC 85
420 Delaware St. SE
Minneapolis, MN 55455

$99.95 for individuals. Covers professionals who specialize in refugee mental health. Entries include: Name, address, phone, geo-

graphical area served and area of specialty. Arrangement: Geographical.

★10437★ **Encyclopedia of Psychology**
Jacksonville State University
700 Pelham Rd.
Jacksonville, AL 36265-1602
Ph: (256)782-5402   Fax: (256)782-5406
Fr: 800-231-5291

Free. Database covers: Links to scientific aspects of psychology, including organizations related to the field.

★10438★ **The Encyclopedia of Suicide**
Facts On File Inc.
132 W 31st St., 17th Fl.
New York, NY 10001
Ph: (212)967-8800   Fax: 800-678-3633
Fr: 800-322-8755
URL: http://www.factsonfile.com

Latest edition 2nd, 2003. $75.00 for individuals; $67.50 for libraries. Publication includes: List of national organizations and suicide prevention/crisis intervention groups in the United States and Canada. Principal content of publication is detailed information about the problem and history of suicide. Indexes: Alphabetical.

★10439★ **Hospital Blue Book**
Billian Publishing Inc./Transworld Publishing Inc.
2100 Powers Ferry Rd. SE
Atlanta, GA 30339
Ph: (770)955-5656   Fax: (770)952-0669
Fr: 800-533-8484
E-mail: blu-book@billian.com

2005. $300.00 for individuals. Covers more than 6,687 hospitals; some listings also appear in a separate southern edition of this publication. Entries include: Name of hospital, accreditation, mailing address, phone, fax, number of beds, type of facility (nonprofit, general, state, etc.); list of administrative personnel and chiefs of medical services, with specific titles. Arrangement: Geographical.

★10440★ **International Council of Psychologists-Yearbook**
International Council of Psychologists
SW Texas State University
Dept. of Psychology
601 University Dr.
San Marcos, TX 78666
Ph: (512)245-2111
URL: http://www.icpweb.org/

Biennial; November of even years. Covers about 1,800 psychologists and related mental health professionals. Entries include: Name, office and home address, career data, languages spoken and written, highest degree, fields of interest. Arrangement: Alphabetical. Indexes: Geographical, major field of interest.

★10441★ Internship Programs in Professional Psychology, Including Post-Doctoral Training Programs

Association of Psychology Postdoctoral and Internship Centers
10 G St. NE, Ste. 440
Washington, DC 20002
Ph: (202)589-0600   Fax: (202)589-0603
URL: http://www.appic.org/directory/search_dol_internships.asp

Annual, September. $74.85 for nonmembers; reduced rates for persons associated with Association of Psychology Postdoctoral and Internship Centers. Covers institutions offering PhD internship programs in professional psychology. Entries include: Institution name, name and address of contact, description of program, theoretical orientation, number of interns, stipend, admission requirements. Arrangement: Geographical.

★10442★ Legal and Ethical Dictionary for Mental Health Professionals

University Press of America
4501 Forbes Blvd., Ste. 200
Lanham, MD 20706
Ph: (301)459-3366   Fax: (301)429-5748
Fr: 800-462-6420
URL: http://www.univpress.com/

$76.50 for print product, cloth-bound; $47.50 for print product, paperback. Publication includes: Lists of state licensure boards and Web sites for mental health organizations. Principal content of publication is a dictionary of legal and ethical responsibilities for mental health professionals.

★10443★ Magill's Encyclopedia of Social Science

Salem Press Inc.
2 University Plz., Ste. 121
Hackensack, NJ 07601
Ph: (201)968-9899   Fax: (201)968-1411
Fr: 800-221-1592
URL: http://www.salempress.com

Published January 2003. $404.00 for individuals. Publication includes: Lists of Web sites, organizations, and support groups in the field of psychology. Principal content of publication consists of entries on psychology including specific disorders, diagnosis, and therapies. Indexes: Alphabetical.

★10444★ Medical and Health Information Directory

Gale, Cengage Learning
27500 Drake Rd.
Farmington Hills, MI 48331-3535
Ph: (248)699-4253   Fax: (248)699-8065
Fr: 800-877-4253
E-mail: businessproducts@gale.com
URL: http://www.gale.com

Annual; latest edition 20th, July 2007. $375.00/volume. Covers in Volume 1, more than 26,500 medical and health oriented associations, organizations, institutions, and government agencies, including health maintenance organizations (HMOs), preferred provider organizations (PPOs), insurance companies, pharmaceutical companies, re-

search centers, and medical and allied health schools. In Volume 2, over 12,000 medical book publishers; medical periodicals, directories, audiovisual producers and services, medical libraries and information centers, electronic resources, and health-related internet search engines. In Volume 3, more than 35,500 clinics, treatment centers, care programs, and counseling/diagnostic services for 34 subject areas. Entries include: Institution, service, or firm name, address, phone, fax, email and URL; many include names of key personnel and, when pertinent, descriptive annotations. Volume 3 was formerly listed separately as Health Services Directory. Arrangement: Classified by organization activity, service, etc. Indexes: Each volume has a complete alphabetical name and keyword index.

★10445★ Mental Help Net

CenterSite L.L.C.
PO Box 20709
Columbus, OH 43220
Ph: (614)448-4055   Fax: (614)448-4055
URL: http://www.mentalhelp.net

Covers resources for finding mental help, including local therapists and self-help groups, as well as services such as upcoming conferences, professional education, and universities offering degrees in mental health fields.

★10446★ National Directory of Private Social Agencies

Croner Publications Inc.
10951 Sorrento Valley Rd., Ste. 1-D
San Diego, CA 92121-1613
Fax: 800-809-0334   Fr: 800-441-4033
URL: http://www.sdic.net/croner

$109.95 for individuals. Number of listings: Over 10,000. Entries include: Agency name, address, phone, name and title of contact, description of services. Arrangement: Geographical. Indexes: Service, agency type.

HANDBOOKS AND MANUALS

★10447★ Career Paths in Psychology: Where Your Degree Can Take You

American Psychological Association
750 1st St. NE
Washington, DC 20002-4242
Ph: (202)336-5500   Fax: (202)336-5620
Fr: 800-374-2721
URL: http://www.apa.org/

Robert J. Sternberg. 2006. $19.95 (paper). 376 pages.

★10448★ Careers for Mystery Buffs and Other Snoops and Sleuths

The McGraw-Hill Companies
PO Box 182604
Columbus, OH 43272
Fax: (614)759-3749   Fr: 877-883-5524

E-mail: customer.service@mcgraw-hill.com
URL: http://www.mcgraw-hill.com

Blythe Camenson. Second edition, 2004. $12.95 (paper); $14.95 (cloth). 160 pages.

★10449★ Careers in Social and Rehabilitation Services

The McGraw-Hill Companies
PO Box 182604
Columbus, OH 43272
Fax: (614)759-3749   Fr: 877-883-5524
E-mail: customer.service@mcgraw-hill.com
URL: http://www.mcgraw-hill.com

Geraldine O. Garner. 2001. $19.95; 14.95 (paper). 128 pages.

★10450★ Eighty Dots: Creating a Career in Psychology

Cengage Learning
PO Box 6904
Florence, KY 41022
Fax: 800-487-8488   Fr: 800-354-9706
URL: http://www.cengage.com

Thomas E. Heinzen. 2004. Novel about the experiences of five undergraduate psychology interns as they sort out their lives, each other, and their emerging careers.

★10451★ Employment in Community Psychology: The Diversity of Opportunity

Haworth Press, Inc.
10 Alice St.
Binghamton, NY 13904-1580
Ph: (607)722-5857   Fax: (607)722-6362
Fr: 800-429-6784
URL: http://www.haworthpress.com

Clifford R. O'Donnell and Joseph R. Ferrari. 2000. $30.00 (paper). 140 pages.

★10452★ Everything You Need to Get a Psychology Internship

Windmill Lane Press
1009 S. Bedford St.
Los Angeles, CA 90035-2101
Fax: (310)815-9865   Fr: 800-566-3659

Carl Levinger and Itzchack Schefres. 1996. $24.95 (paper). 144 pages.

★10453★ Great Jobs for Liberal Arts Majors

The McGraw-Hill Companies
PO Box 182604
Columbus, OH 43272
Fax: (614)759-3749   Fr: 877-883-5524
E-mail: customer.service@mcgraw-hill.com
URL: http://www.mcgraw-hill.com

Blythe Camenson. Second edition, 2001. $14.95 (paper). 256 pages.

★10454★ Independent Practice for the Mental Health Professional: Growing a Private Practice for the 21st Century

Routledge
270 Madison Ave.
New York, NY 10016
Ph: (212)216-7800   Fax: (212)563-2269
URL: http://www.routledge.com/

Ralph Earle and Dorothy Barnes. 1999. $33.95. 192 pages. Discusses pros and cons of going solo or joining a group, legal issues, marketing, physical arrangement of the office, collecting fees, and maintaining a practice in the age of managed care.

★10455★ Opportunities in Child Care Careers

The McGraw-Hill Companies
PO Box 182604
Columbus, OH 43272
Fax: (614)759-3749   Fr: 877-883-5524
E-mail: customer.service@mcgraw-hill.com
URL: http://www.mcgraw-hill.com

Renee Wittenberg. 2006. $13.95 (paper). 160 pages. Discusses various job opportunities and how to secure a position. Illustrated.

★10456★ Opportunities in Health and Medical Careers

The McGraw-Hill Companies
PO Box 182604
Columbus, OH 43272
Fax: (614)759-3749   Fr: 877-883-5524
E-mail: customer.service@mcgraw-hill.com
URL: http://www.mcgraw-hill.com

I. Donald Snook, Jr. and Leo D'Orazio. 2004. $13.95 (paper). 157 pages. Covers the full range of medical and health occupations. Illustrated.

★10457★ Opportunities in Mental Health Careers

The McGraw-Hill Companies
PO Box 182604
Columbus, OH 43272
Fax: (614)759-3749   Fr: 877-883-5524
E-mail: customer.service@mcgraw-hill.com
URL: http://www.mcgraw-hill.com

Philip A. Perry. 1996. $14.95; $11.95 (paper) 160 pages. Part of the "Opportunities in ..." Series.

★10458★ Opportunities in Research and Development Careers

The McGraw-Hill Companies
PO Box 182604
Columbus, OH 43272
Fax: (614)759-3749   Fr: 877-883-5524
E-mail: customer.service@mcgraw-hill.com
URL: http://www.mcgraw-hill.com

Jan Goldberg. 1996. $11.95 (paper). 146 pages.

★10459★ Opportunities in Social Science Careers

The McGraw-Hill Companies
PO Box 182604
Columbus, OH 43272
Fax: (614)759-3749   Fr: 877-883-5524
E-mail: customer.service@mcgraw-hill.com
URL: http://www.mcgraw-hill.com

Rosanne J. Marek. 2004. $13.95. 160 Pages. VGM Opportunities Series.

★10460★ Opportunities in Sports and Athletics Careers

The McGraw-Hill Companies
PO Box 182604
Columbus, OH 43272
Fax: (614)759-3749   Fr: 877-883-5524
E-mail: customer.service@mcgraw-hill.com
URL: http://www.mcgraw-hill.com

William Ray Heitzmann. 1993. 160 pages. $11.95 (paper). A guide to planning for and seeking opportunities in this growing field. Illustrated.

★10461★ Opportunities in Sports Medicine Careers

The McGraw-Hill Companies
PO Box 182604
Columbus, OH 43272
Fax: (614)759-3749   Fr: 877-883-5524
E-mail: customer.service@mcgraw-hill.com
URL: http://www.mcgraw-hill.com

William Ray Heitzmann. 1992. $11.95 (paper). 160 pages. Discusses a variety of opportunities in this field and how to pursue them. Contains bibliography and illustrations.

★10462★ Real People Working in Education

The McGraw-Hill Companies
PO Box 182604
Columbus, OH 43272
Fax: (614)759-3749   Fr: 877-883-5524
E-mail: customer.service@mcgraw-hill.com
URL: http://www.mcgraw-hill.com

Blythe Camenson, Jan Goldberg. 1997. $17.95; $12.95 (paper). 160 pages/ Interviews and profiles of working professionals capture a range of opportunities in this field.

★10463★ The Role of Work in People's Lives: Applied Career Counseling & Vocational Psychology

Wadsworth Publishing
PO Box 6904
Florence, KY 41022
Fax: 800-487-8488   Fr: 800-354-9706
URL: http://www.cengage.com

Nadine Peterson and Roberto Cortez Gonzalez. 2004. Second edition. $110.95. 624 pages.

ONLINE JOB SOURCES AND SERVICES

★10464★ Delta T Group
E-mail: pa@deltatg.com
URL: http://www.delta-tgroup.com

Description: Specialized contract temporary staffing source for healthcare professionals in the fields of social service, psychiatry, mental health, and substance abuse. Organizations may request services and staffing; job seekers may view services provided, submit a resume, or peruse jobs available.

★10465★ MedSource Consultants
300 Main St.
Stamford, CT 06901
Fax: (203)324-0555   Fr: 800-575-2880
E-mail: dpascale@medsourceconsultants.com
URL: http://www.medsourceconsultants.com

Description: Site houses a physician search and consulting company for psychiatrists. Consultants attempt to match job seekers to positions according to the individual's personal and professional needs. This page also aids institutions looking to recruit psychiatrists.

★10466★ RehabWorld
URL: http://www.rehabworld.com

Description: Site for rehabilitation professionals to learn about the profession and locate jobs. Includes user groups, salary surveys, and chat capabilities. **Main files include:** Physical Therapy, Occupational Therapy, Speech Therapy, Mental Health, Employer World, Student World, International World, Forum.

TRADESHOWS

★10467★ American Psychological Association Convention

American Psychological Association
750 1st St., NE
Washington, DC 20002-4242
Ph: (202)336-5500   Fr: 800-374-2721
E-mail: convention@apa.org
URL: http://www.apa.org

Annual. **Primary Exhibits:** Computers, publications, and related government services. **Dates and Locations:** 2008 Aug 14-17; Boston, MA.

★10468★ Southwestern Psychological Association Annual Meeting

Southwestern Psychological Association
Tarleton State University
PO Box T-0820
Dr. Bob Newby
Stephenville, TX 76401
Ph: (785)827-5541   Fax: (254)968-9947
E-mail: russinr@kwu.edu
URL: http://www.swpsych.org

Annual. **Primary Exhibits:** Publications, films, and health products.

OTHER SOURCES

★10469★ American Almanac of Jobs and Salaries

HarperCollins
10 E. 53rd St.
New York, NY 10022
Ph: (212)207-7000   Fr: 800-242-7737
URL: http://www.harpercollins.com/

John W. Wright. Revised edition, 2000. $20.00 (paper). 672 pages. This is a comprehensive guide to the wages of hundreds of occupations in a wide variety of industries and organizations.

★10470★ American Association of Mental Health Professionals in Corrections (AAMHPC)

PO Box 160208
Sacramento, CA 95816-0208
Fax: (916)649-1080
E-mail: corrmentalhealth@aol.com

Description: Psychiatrists, psychologists, social workers, nurses, and other mental health professionals; individuals working in correctional settings. Fosters the progress of behavioral sciences related to corrections. Goals are: to improve the treatment, rehabilitation, and care of the mentally ill, mentally retarded, and emotionally disturbed; to promote research and professional education in psychiatry and allied fields in corrections; to advance standards of correctional services and facilities; to foster cooperation between individuals concerned with the medical, psychological, social, and legal aspects of corrections; to share knowledge with other medical practitioners, scientists, and the public. Conducts scientific meetings to contribute to the advancement of the therapeutic community in all its institutional settings, including correctional institutions, hospitals, churches, schools, industry, and the family.

★10471★ American Association of Psychiatric Technicians (AAPT)

1220 S St., Ste. 100
Sacramento, CA 95811-7138
Ph: (916)443-1701   Fax: (916)329-9145
Fr: 800-391-7589
E-mail: loger@psychtechs.net
URL: http://www.psychtechs.org

Description: Administers the Nationally Certified Psychiatric Technician examination to non-licensed direct-care workers in the fields of mental illness, developmental disabilities and substance abuse.

★10472★ American Mental Health Alliance (AMHA)

PO Box 4075
Portland, OR 97208-4075
Ph: (503)279-8160   Fr: 888-577-3386
E-mail: memberinfo@americanmentalhealth.com
URL: http://www.americanmentalhealth.com

Description: Represents mental health professionals licensed or certified for independen t practice. Creates a professional community that provides therapy of the highes t quality and ethical standards. Supports and markets competent, ethical mental health services that preserve privacy and confidentiality. Supports education, s upervision, and research opportunities for members. Opposes legislation and regu lations that invade patient privacy and confidentiality.

★10473★ American Psychological Association (APA)

750 First St. NE
Washington, DC 20002-4242
Ph: (202)336-5500   Fax: (202)336-6069
Fr: 800-374-2721
E-mail: president@apa.org
URL: http://www.apa.org

Description: Scientific and professional society of psychologists; students participate as affiliates. Advances psychology as a science, a profession, and as a means of promoting health, education and the human welfare.

★10474★ American Society of Psychopathology of Expression (ASPE)

74 Lawton St.
Brookline, MA 02446
Ph: (617)738-9821   Fax: (617)975-0411

Description: Psychiatrists, psychologists, art therapists, sociologists, art critics, artists, social workers, linguists, educators, criminologists, writers, and historians. At least two-thirds of the members must be physicians. Fosters collaboration among specialists in the United States who are interested in the problems of expression and in the artistic activities connected with psychiatric, sociological, and psychological research. Disseminates information about research and clinical applications in the field of psychopathology of expression. Sponsors consultations, seminars, and lectures on art therapy.

★10475★ Association of Black Psychologists (ABPsi)

PO Box 55999
Washington, DC 20040-5999
Ph: (202)722-0808   Fax: (202)722-5941
E-mail: abpsi_office@abpsi.org
URL: http://www.abpsi.org

Members: Professional psychologists and others in associated disciplines. **Purpose:** Aims to: enhance the psychological well being of black people in America; define mental health in consonance with newly established psychological concepts and standards; develop policies for local, state and national decision-making that have impact on the mental health of the black community; support established black sister organizations and aid in the development of new, independent black institutions to enhance the psychological, educational, cultural and economic situation. **Activities:** Offers training and information on AIDS. Conducts seminars, workshops and research.

★10476★ Association of Psychology Postdoctoral and Internship Centers (APPIC)

10 G St. NE, Ste. 440
Washington, DC 20002
Ph: (202)589-0600   Fax: (202)589-0603
E-mail: appic@aol.com
URL: http://www.appic.org

Description: Veterans administration hospitals, medical centers, state hospitals, university counseling centers, and other facilities that provide internship and postdoctoral programs in professional psychology. Promotes activities that assist in the development of professional psychology training programs. Serves as a clearinghouse to provide Ph.D. candidates with internship placement assistance at member facilities. Conducts workshops and seminars on training procedures in clinical psychology at the PhD level.

★10477★ Counseling Association for Humanistic Education and Development (C-AHEAD)

PO Box 791006
Baltimore, MD 21279-1006
Ph: (703)823-9800   Fax: 800-473-2329
Fr: 800-347-6647
E-mail: lleech@gw.mp.sc.edu
URL: http://www.c-ahead.com

Description: A division of the American Counseling Association. Teachers, educational administrators, community agency workers, counselors, school social workers, and psychologists; others interested in the area of human development. Aims to assist individuals in improving their quality of life. Provides forum for the exchange of information about humanistically-oriented administrative and instructional practices. Supports humanistic practices and research on instructional and organizational methods for facilitating humanistic education; encourages cooperation among related professional groups.

★10478★ Employee Assistance Society of North America (EASNA)

2001 Jefferson Davis Hwy., Ste. 1004
Arlington, VA 22202-3617
Ph: (703)416-0060   Fax: (703)416-0014
E-mail: info@easna.org
URL: http://www.easna.org

Description: Individuals in the field of employee assistance, including psychiatrists, psychologists, and managers. Facilitates communication among members; provides resource information; serves as a network for employee assistance programs nationwide. Conducts research.

★10479★ International Association of Transpersonal Therapists and Physicians (IATTP)
485 S Independence Blvd., Ste. 111
Virginia Beach, VA 23452
Ph: (757)216-8096   Fax: (757)216-8101
E-mail: iattpmembers@aol.com
URL: http://iattp.org

Description: Provides training and continuing education to professionals who work with clients across all aspects of their lives. Provides a forum for professionals to share their knowledge and expertise in the field of transpersonal healthcare.

★10480★ Internship Selection in Professional Psychology: A Comprehensive Guide for Students, Faculty, and Training Directors
Charles C Thomas Publisher, Ltd.
2600 S 1st St.
PO Box 19265
Springfield, IL 62794-9265
Ph: (217)789-8980   Fax: (217)789-9130
Fr: 800-258-8980
E-mail: books@ccthomas.com
URL: http://www.ccthomas.com
Mary E. Oehlert, Scott Sumerall and Shane J. Lopez. 1998. $44.95. 153 pages.

★10481★ National Association of School Psychologists (NASP)
4340 E West Hwy., Ste. 402
Bethesda, MD 20814
Ph: (301)657-0270   Fax: (301)657-0275
Fr: (866)331-NASP
E-mail: membership@naspweb.org
URL: http://www.nasponline.org

Members: School psychologists. **Purpose:** Serves the mental health and educational needs of all children and youth. Encourages and provides opportunities for professional growth of individual members. Informs the public on the services and practice of school psychology, and advances the standards of the profession. **Activities:** Operates national school psychologist certification system. Sponsors children's services.

★10482★ Professional Specialty Occupations
Delphi Productions
3159 6th St.
Boulder, CO 80304
Ph: (303)443-2100   Fax: (303)443-4022
Fr: 888-443-2400
E-mail: support@delphivideo.com
URL: http://www.delphivideo.com
$95.00. 53 minutes. Part of the Careers for the 21st Century Video Library.

★10483★ Psychology Society (PS)
100 Beekman St.
New York, NY 10038-1810
Ph: (212)285-1872   Fax: (212)285-1872

Description: Professional membership is limited to psychologists who have a doctorate and are certified/licensed as such in the state where they practice. Associate membership is intended for teachers and researchers as well as persons who will attain professional status shortly. Seeks to further the use of psychology in therapy, family and social problems, behavior modification, and treatment of drug abusers and prisoners. Encourages the use of psychology in the solution of social and political conflicts. Operates an information bureau to answer inquiries of authors and media. Sponsors biennial overseas trip to enable members and their spouses to observe other programs and institutions. Collaborates with other associations. Evaluates programs in the use of psychology. Recommends legislation; appears in court cases where issues of mental health occur as expert and impartial witness.

Public Relations Specialists

SOURCES OF HELP-WANTED ADS

★10484★ Bulldog Reporter Business Media

Infocom Group
5900 Hollis St., Ste. L
Emeryville, CA 94608-2008
Ph: (510)596-9300   Fax: (510)596-9331
Fr: 800-959-1059
URL: http://www.infocomgroup.com

Description: Semimonthly. Covers U.S. news media for public relations professionals. Recurring features include interviews, media contact lists, and media personnel changes.

★10485★ Bulldog Reporter-Eastern Edition

Infocom Group
5900 Hollis St., Ste. L
Emeryville, CA 94608-2008
Ph: (510)596-9300   Fax: (510)596-9331
Fr: 800-959-1059
URL: http://www.infocomgroup.com

Description: Semimonthly. Features information on effective ways to place stories in newspapers, magazines, and radio and/or television programs. Recurring features include interviews, media contact listings, and media personnel changes.

★10486★ Cheap Relief

Star Lawrence
734 W El Alba Way
Chandler, AZ 85225
Ph: (480)855-0054
E-mail: jkellaw@aol.com
URL: http://www.sunoasis.com/webjean.html

Description: Monthly. Offers efficiency and money-saving advice in advertising, marketing, and public relations. Recurring features include news of research, news of educational opportunities, book reviews, and notices of publications available.

★10487★ Communication Briefings

Briefings Publishing Group
2807 N. Parham Rd, Ste. 200
Richmond, VA 23294
Ph: (570)567-1982   Fax: (804)217-8999
Fr: 800-791-8699
E-mail: customerservice@briefings.com
URL: http://www.briefings.com

Description: Monthly. Provides communication ideas and techniques for a wide variety of areas, including public relations, advertising, fund raising, speeches, media relations, human resources, and employee/manager relations. Carries interviews with top communicators, business leaders, university experts, and research specialists. Recurring features include news of research, book reviews, and abstracts of articles from national publications.

★10488★ Contacts: The Media Pipeline for PR People

Mercomm Inc.
500 Executive Blvd.
Ossining, NY 10562
Ph: (914)923-9400   Fax: (914)923-9484
E-mail: contacts@mercommawards.com
URL: http://www.mercommawards.com/contacts.htm

Description: Weekly. Contains media placement opportunities for publicists and public relations professionals.

★10489★ Editor & Publisher

Editor & Publisher Magazine
770 Broadway
New York, NY 10003-9595
Ph: (646)654-5500   Fax: (646)654-5370
Fr: 800-562-2706
URL: http://www.editorandpublisher.com/eandp/index.jsp

Weekly (Mon.). $99.00/year for individuals, print and online; $159.00/year for Canada, print and online; $320.00/year for other countries; $7.95/year for individuals, monthly. Magazine focusing on newspaper journalism, advertising, printing equipment, and interactive services.

★10490★ Healthcare Marketer's Executive Briefing

The E-Commerce Information Center
PO Box 456
Allenwood, NJ 08720
Ph: (732)292-1100   Fax: (732)292-1111
Fr: 800-516-4343
E-mail: info@healthresourcesonline.com.
URL: http://www.healthresourcesonline.com/management/12nl.htm

Description: Monthly. Designed to keep professionals abreast of the newest marketing and public relations techniques and strategies within the field of health care.

★10491★ Jack O'Dwyer's Newsletter

J.R. O'Dwyer Company Inc.
271 Madison Ave., No. 600
New York, NY 10016
Ph: (212)679-2471   Fax: (212)683-2750
Fr: (866)395-7710
URL: http://www.odwyerpr.com

Description: Weekly. Provides nationwide coverage of the public relations industry. Reports on executive and account changes, new public relations firms, and honors won in the field. Recurring features include a calendar of events, book reviews, lists of free pamphlets and other materials, new services available to public relations personnel, and media changes.

★10492★ Lifestyle Media-Relations Reporter

Infocom Group
5900 Hollis St., Ste. L
Emeryville, CA 94608-2008
Ph: (510)596-9300   Fax: (510)596-9331
Fr: 800-959-1059
URL: http://www.infocomgroup.com

Description: Semimonthly. Covers lifestyle/consumer media for public relations professionals. Recurring features include interviews.

★10493★ Magnet Marketing & Sales

Graham Communications
40 Oval Rd., Ste. 2
Quincy, MA 02170-3813
Ph: (617)328-0069   Fax: (617)471-1504
E-mail: info@grahamcomm.com
URL: http://www.grahamcomm.com/

Description: Quarterly. Contains information and advice on marketing, sales, and public relations.

★10494★ Marketer's Guidepost

Medical Group Management Association
104 Inverness Ter. E
Englewood, CO 80112-5306
Ph: (303)799-1111   Fax: (303)643-4439
Fr: 877-275-6462
E-mail: service@mgma.com
URL: http://www.mgma.com

Description: Bimonthly. Presents case studies and marketing techniques and offers advice for promotions and public relations campaigns. Recurring features include columns titled Quick tips, Guidepost-its, and What Would You Do?

★10495★ Media Relations Report

Lawrence Ragan Communications Inc.
111 E. Wacker Dr., Ste. 500
Chicago, IL 60601
Ph: (312)960-4100   Fax: (312)861-3592
Fr: 800-878-5331
E-mail: cservice@ragan.com
URL: http://www.ragan.com/ME2/Sites/Default.asp

Description: Semimonthly. Covers advertising and public relations media placement. Topics include placement opportunities, media news, pitching media campaigns, targeting ads, press releases, and others.

★10496★ O'Dwyers PR Marketplace

J.R. O'Dwyer Company Inc.
271 Madison Ave., No. 600
New York, NY 10016
Ph: (212)679-2471   Fax: (212)683-2750
Fr: (866)395-7710
URL: http://www.odwyerpr.com

Lists job opportunities and service available in Public Relations.

★10497★ Partyline Newsletter

Partyline Publishing Co.
35 Sutton Pl.
New York, NY 10022
Ph: (212)755-3487   Fax: (212)755-4859
E-mail: byarmon@ix.netcom.com
URL: http://www.partylinepublishing.com

Description: Weekly. Disseminates information about media placement opportunities for public relations professionals.

★10498★ PR Intelligence Report

Lawrence Ragan Communications Inc.
111 E. Wacker Dr., Ste. 500
Chicago, IL 60601
Ph: (312)960-4100   Fax: (312)861-3592
Fr: 800-878-5331
E-mail: cservice@ragan.com
URL: http://www.ragan.com

Description: Semimonthly. Internet newsletter providing news about the public relations industry, including tips for those in the industry.

★10499★ PR News

Access Intelligence L.L.C.
4 Choke Cherry Rd.
Rockville, MD 20850
Ph: (301)354-2000   Fax: (301)309-3847
Fr: 800-777-5006
E-mail: info@accessintel.com
URL: http://www.pbimedia.com/cgi/catalog/info?PRN

Description: Weekly. Carries public relations news and information of interest to high-level executives. Offers a two-page case study in each issue on an aspect of public relations within business, industry, and government. Recurring features include mention of awards and honors in the field, personnel and account changes, excerpts from major speeches, media insight chart, global PR and cyber PR.

★10500★ Public Relations Career Opportunities

Public Relations Career Opportunities
1220 L St. NW
Washington, DC 20005
Ph: (202)721-7656
E-mail: info@ceoupdate.com
URL: http://www.careeropps.com

Description: Semimonthly. Provides information about positions available in the fields of public affairs and public relations.

★10501★ The Ragan Report

Lawrence Ragan Communications Inc.
111 E. Wacker Dr., Ste 500
Chicago, IL 60601
Ph: (312)960-4100   Fax: (312)861-3592
Fr: 800-878-5331
E-mail: cservice@ragan.com
URL: http://www.ragan.com/ME2/Sites/Default.asp

Description: Weekly. Offers ideas and techniques for communications executives, especially the organizational press. Provides commentary; "how-to" advice on writing, photography, and design; plus examples of outstanding work in the field. Recurring features include editorials, news of research, letters to the editor, news of members, book reviews, a calendar of events, and columns titled The Typochondriac, Arnold on Typography, Douglis on Visuals, and The Do-It-Yourself Designer.

★10502★ Ragan's PR Intelligence Report

Lawrence Ragan Communications Inc.
111 E. Wacker Dr., Ste. 500
Chicago, IL 60601
Ph: (312)960-4100   Fax: (312)861-3592
Fr: 800-878-5331
E-mail: cservice@ragan.com
URL: http://www.ragan.com

Description: Monthly. Covers the public relations industry.

PLACEMENT AND JOB REFERRAL SERVICES

★10503★ Agricultural Relations Council (ARC)

62768 N Star Dr.
Montrose, CO 81401
Ph: (970)249-1465   Fax: (970)249-4385
E-mail: jmo@rmmc.biz
URL: http://www.agrelationscouncil.org

Description: Professional society of agricultural public relations executives employed by private business firms, associations, publications, and government agencies. Operates placement service.

★10504★ American Marketing Association (AMA)

311 S Wacker Dr., Ste. 5800
Chicago, IL 60606
Ph: (312)542-9000   Fax: (312)542-9001
Fr: 800-262-1150
E-mail: info@ama.org
URL: http://www.marketingpower.com

Description: Serves as a professional society of marketing and market research executives, sales and promotion managers, advertising specialists, academics, and others interested in marketing. **Activities:** Fosters research; sponsors seminars, conferences, and student marketing clubs; provides educational placement service and doctoral consortium.

★10505★ PROMAX

9000 W Sunset Blvd., Ste. 900
Los Angeles, CA 90069
Ph: (310)788-7600   Fax: (310)788-7616
E-mail: michael.d.benson@abc.com
URL: http://www.promax.tv

Members: Advertising, public relations, and promotion managers of cable, radio, and television stations, systems and networks; syndicators. **Purpose:** Seeks to: advance the role and increase the effectiveness of promotion and marketing within the industry, related industries, and educational communities. **Activities:** Conducts workshops and weekly fax service for members. Operates employment service. Maintains speakers' bureau, hall of fame, and resource center with print, audio, and visual materials.

EMPLOYER DIRECTORIES AND NETWORKING LISTS

★10506★ The ADWEEK Directory

ADWEEK Magazines
770 Broadway, 7th Fl.
New York, NY 10003-9595
Ph: (646)654-5105   Fax: (646)654-5350
Fr: 800-562-2706
URL: http://www.adweek.com

Annual. Covers over 6,400 U.S. advertising agencies, public relations firms, media buying services, direct marketing and related organizations. Entries include: Agency name, address, phone, fax/e-mail, URL; names and titles of key personnel; major accounts; parent company; headquarters location; major subsidiaries and other operating units; year founded; number of employees; fee income; billings; percentage of billings by medium. Individual listings for each agency branch. Arrangement: Alphabetical. Indexes: Geographical; parent company, subsidiary, branch; ethnic specialities; organization, name changes, agencies opened/closed.

★10507★ National School Public Relations Association-Directory

National School Public Relations Association
15948 Derwood Rd.
Rockville, MD 20855-2123
Ph: (301)519-0496   Fax: (301)519-0494
URL: http://www.nspra.org

Annual, January. Covers approximately 2,000 school system public relations directors, school administrators, principals, and others who are members of the National School Public Relations Association. Entries include: Name, affiliation, address, phone. Arrangement: Geographical.

★10508★ O'Dwyer's Directory of Corporate Communications

J.R. O'Dwyer Company Inc.
271 Madison Ave. No. 600
New York, NY 10016
Ph: (212)679-2471   Fax: (212)683-2750
Fr: (866)395-7710
URL: http://www.odwyerpr.com

Annual; latest edition 2005. $65.00 for individuals. Covers more than 18,000 PR professionals, including public relations departments of approximately 7,800 companies, associations, and government agencies. Entries include: Organization name, address, phone, sales, type of business; names and duties of principal public relations personnel at headquarters and other major offices, plus name and title of person to whom PR head reports; PR budget. Arrangement: Alphabetical. Indexes: Geographical, product.

★10509★ O'Dwyer's Directory of Public Relations Firms

J.R. O'Dwyer Company Inc.
271 Madison Ave., No. 600
New York, NY 10016
Ph: (212)679-2471   Fax: (212)683-2750
Fr: (866)395-7710
E-mail: sales@odwyerpr.com
URL: http://www.odwyerpr.com/

Annual; latest edition 2007 Edition. $175.00 for individuals. Covers over 1,900 public relations firms; international coverage. Entries include: Firm name, address, phone, principal executives, branch and overseas offices, billings, date founded, and 19,000+ clients, which are cross-indexed. Arrangement: Geographical by country. Indexes: Specialty (beauty and fashions, finance/investor, etc.); geographical; client.

★10510★ Public Relations Society of America, Chicago Chapter-Membership Directory

Public Relations Society of America, Chicago Chapter
1000 N Rand Rd., Ste. 214
Wauconda, IL 60084
Ph: (847)526-2010   Fax: (847)526-3993
URL: http://prsachicago.com/members.html

Annual, October. Covers about 550 individuals engaged in public relations and related occupations in Chicago. Entries include: Name, title, affiliation, address, phone, type of membership, year joined, employment history. Arrangement: Alphabetical. Indexes: Firm name.

★10511★ Public Relations Tactics-Member Services Directory-The Blue Book

Public Relations Society of America
33 Maiden Ln., 11th Fl.
New York, NY 10038-5150
Ph: (212)460-1400   Fax: (212)995-0757
Fr: 800-937-7772
E-mail: 74224.1456@compuserve.com
URL: http://www.prsa.org

Annual; latest edition 2007. Covers PRSA members–headquaters, staff contacts, and chapter, section, and district information. Entries include: Name, professional affiliation and title, address, phone, membership rank. Arrangement: Alphabetical. Indexes: Geographical, organizational.

★10512★ Reed's Worldwide Directory of Public Relations Organizations

Pigafetta Press
PO Box 39244
Washington, DC 20016
Ph: (202)244-2580   Fax: (202)244-2581
E-mail: 110104.1310@compuserve.com

Annual, October. $95.00. Covers approximately 225 professional public relations associations in 75 countries. Entries include: Association name, address, phone, publications, current officers, activities, and history of the organization. Arrangement: Geographical; separate section for international organizations.

★10513★ Sports Market Place

Sports Careers
2990 E Northern Ave., Ste. D107
Phoenix, AZ 85028
Ph: (602)485-5555   Fax: (602)485-5556

Annual, January. Covers manufacturers, organizations, professional sports teams, broadcasting networks, sports arenas, syndicators, publications, trade shows, marketing services, corporate sports sponsors, and other groups concerned with the business and promotional aspects of sports generally and with air sports, arm wrestling, auto sports, badminton, baseball, basketball, biathlon, bowling, boxing, curling, equestrian, exercise, fencing, field hockey, football, golf, gymnastics, ice hockey, lacrosse, martial arts, paddleball, paddle tennis, platform tennis, pentathlon, racquetball, rowing, rugby, running/jogging, skiing, soccer, softball, squash, swimming, table tennis, tennis, track and field, volleyball, water sports, weightlifting, and wrestling. Entries include: Name of company or organization, address, fax, e-mail, URL, name of key personnel with titles, and description of products or services. Arrangement: Classified by type of firm, sport, or activity. Indexes: Alphabetical; single sport; media; sport sponsors; agencies; manufacturers; brand name; facilities; executives; and geographical.

HANDBOOKS AND MANUALS

★10514★ Career Opportunities for Writers

Facts On File Inc.
132 W. 31st St., 17th Fl.
New York, NY 10001-2006
Ph: (212)967-8800   Fax: 800-678-3633
Fr: 800-322-8755
E-mail: custserv@factsonfile.com
URL: http://www.factsonfile.com

Rosemary Ellen Guiley and Janet Frick. 2nd edition, 1991. $49.50. 230 pages. Part of the Career Opportunities Series. Describes more than 100 jobs in eight major fields, offering such details as duties, salaries, perquisites, employment and advancement opportunities, organizations to join, and opportunities for women and minorities.

★10515★ Careers in Communications

The McGraw-Hill Companies
PO Box 182604
Columbus, OH 43272
Fax: (614)759-3749   Fr: 877-883-5524
E-mail: customer.service@mcgraw-hill.com
URL: http://www.mcgraw-hill.com

Shonan Noronha. Fourth edition, 2004. $15.95 (paper). 192 pages. Examines the fields of journalism, photography, radio, television, film, public relations, and advertising. Gives concrete details on job locations and how to secure a job. Suggests many resources for job hunting.

★10516★ Careers for Writers and Others Who Have a Way with Words

The McGraw-Hill Companies
PO Box 182604
Columbus, OH 43272
Fax: (614)759-3749   Fr: 877-883-5524
E-mail: customer.service@mcgraw-hill.com
URL: http://www.mcgraw-hill.com

Robert W. Bly. Second edition, 2003. $13.95 (paper). 208 pages.

★10517★ How to Get into Marketing and PR

Continuum International Publishing Group, Inc.
80 Maiden Ln., Ste. 704
New York, NY 10038
Ph: (212)953-5858   Fax: (212)953-5944
URL: http://www.continuumbooks.com/

Annie Gurton. June 2003. $129.99 (hardcover). 213 pages.

★10518★ Opportunities in Insurance Careers

The McGraw-Hill Companies
PO Box 182604
Columbus, OH 43272
Fax: (614)759-3749   Fr: 877-883-5524
E-mail: customer.service@mcgraw-hill.com
URL: http://www.mcgraw-hill.com

Robert M. Schrayer. Revised, 2007. $14.95 (paper). 160 pages. A guide to planning for and seeking opportunities in the field. Contains bibliography and illustrations.

★10519★ Opportunities in Journalism Careers

The McGraw-Hill Companies
PO Box 182604
Columbus, OH 43272
Fax: (614)759-3749   Fr: 877-883-5524
E-mail: customer.service@mcgraw-hill.com
URL: http://www.mcgraw-hill.com

Jim Patten and Donald L. Ferguson. 2001. $12.95 (paper). 160 pages. Outlines opportunities in every field of journalism, including newspaper reporting and editing, magazine and book publishing, corporate communications, advertising and public relations, freelance writing, and teaching. Covers how to prepare for and enter each field, outlining responsibilities, salaries, benefits, and job outlook for each specialty. Illustrated.

★10520★ Opportunities in Marketing Careers

The McGraw-Hill Companies
PO Box 182604
Columbus, OH 43272
Fax: (614)759-3749   Fr: 877-883-5524
E-mail: customer.service@mcgraw-hill.com
URL: http://www.mcgraw-hill.com

Margery Steinberg. 2005. $13.95; $11.95 (paper). 176. Gives guidance on identifying and pursuing job opportunities. Illustrated.

★10521★ Opportunities in Public Relations Careers

The McGraw-Hill Companies
PO Box 182604
Columbus, OH 43272
Fax: (614)759-3749   Fr: 877-883-5524
E-mail: customer.service@mcgraw-hill.com
URL: http://www.mcgraw-hill.com

Morris B. Rotman. 2001. $12.95 (paper). 160 pages. Tells the reader how to enter the field and how to build a career. Contains bibliography and illustrations.

★10522★ Opportunities in Sports and Athletics Careers

The McGraw-Hill Companies
PO Box 182604
Columbus, OH 43272
Fax: (614)759-3749   Fr: 877-883-5524
E-mail: customer.service@mcgraw-hill.com
URL: http://www.mcgraw-hill.com

William Ray Heitzmann. 1993. 160 pages. $11.95 (paper). A guide to planning for and seeking opportunities in this growing field. Illustrated.

★10523★ Opportunities in Writing Careers

The McGraw-Hill Companies
PO Box 182604
Columbus, OH 43272
Fax: (614)759-3749   Fr: 877-883-5524
E-mail: customer.service@mcgraw-hill.com
URL: http://www.mcgraw-hill.com

Elizabeth Foote-Smith. 2006. $13.95; $11.95 (paper). 160 pages. Discusses opportunities in the print media, broadcasting, advertising or publishing. Business writing, public relations, and technical writing are among the careers covered. Contains bibliography and illustrations.

★10524★ Real People Working in Communications

The McGraw-Hill Companies
PO Box 182604
Columbus, OH 43272
Fax: (614)759-3749   Fr: 877-883-5524
E-mail: customer.service@mcgraw-hill.com
URL: http://www.mcgraw-hill.com

Jan Goldberg. 1996. $17.95 (paper). 133 pages. Interviews and profiles of working professionals capture a range of opportunities in this field.

★10525★ Working in Public Relations: How to Gain the Skills and Opportunities for a Career in Public Relations

Trans-Atlantic Publications, Inc.
311 Bainbridge St.
Philadelphia, PA 19147
Ph: (215)925-5083   Fax: (215)925-1912
E-mail: bookinquiries@earthlink.net
URL: http://www.transatlanticpub.com/

Carole Chester. 1998. $21.95 (paper). 144 pages.

★10526★ Writing for Results: Keys to Success for the Public Relations Writer

Alta Villa Publishing, Incorporated
PO Box 17684
Indianapolis, IN 46217-0684
Ph: (317)885-1918
E-mail: editor@altavillapublishing.com
URL: http://altavillapublishing.com/

Ray Begovich. 2001. $12.00 (paper). 67 pages.

EMPLOYMENT AGENCIES AND SEARCH FIRMS

★10527★ Chaloner Associates

36 Milford St.
Boston, MA 02118
Ph: (617)451-5170   Fax: (617)451-8160
E-mail: info@chaloner.com
URL: http://www.chaloner.com

Executive search firm.

★10528★ The Esquire Staffing Group Ltd.

1 S. Wacker Dr., Ste. 1616
Chicago, IL 60606-4616
Ph: (312)795-4300   Fax: (312)795-4329
E-mail: d.williams@esquirestaffing.com
URL: http://www.esquirestaffing.com

Employment agency. Fills permanent as well as temporary openings.

★10529★ Howard-Sloan Professional Search Inc.

1140 Ave. of the Americas
New York, NY 10036
Ph: (212)704-0444   Fax: (212)869-7999
Fr: 800-221-1326
E-mail: info@howardsloan.com
URL: http://www.howardsloan.com

Executive search firm.

OTHER SOURCES

★10530★ ABA Marketing Network

1120 Connecticut Ave. NW
Washington, DC 20036
Fax: (202)828-4540   Fr: 800-BAN-KERS
E-mail: marketingnetwork@aba.com
URL: http://www.aba.com/MarketingNetwork/default.htm

Members: Marketing and public relations executives for commercial and savings banks, credit unions, and savings and loans associations, and related groups such as advertising agencies and research firms. **Purpose:** Provides marketing education, information, and services to the financial services industry. **Activities:** Conducts research; cosponsors summer sessions of fundamentals and advanced courses in marketing at the University of Colorado at Boulder; compiles statistics.

★10531★ *American Almanac of Jobs and Salaries*

HarperCollins
10 E. 53rd St.
New York, NY 10022
Ph: (212)207-7000   Fr: 800-242-7737
URL: http://www.harpercollins.com/

John W. Wright. Revised edition, 2000. $20.00 (paper). 672 pages. This is a comprehensive guide to the wages of hundreds of occupations in a wide variety of industries and organizations.

★10532★ Association for Women in Communications (AWC)

3337 Duke St.
Alexandria, VA 22314
Ph: (703)370-7436   Fax: (703)370-7437
E-mail: info@womcom.org

URL: http://www.womcom.org

Description: Professional association of journalism and communications.

★10533★ Media Alliance (MA)

1904 Franklin St., Ste. 500
Oakland, CA 94612
Ph: (510)832-9000   Fax: (510)238-8557
E-mail: information@media-alliance.org
URL: http://www.media-alliance.org

Description: Writers, photographers, editors, broadcast workers, public relations practitioners, videographers, filmmakers, commercial artists and other media workers and aspiring media workers. Supports free press and independent, alternative journalism that services progressive politics and social justice.

★10534★ National School Public Relations Association (NSPRA)

15948 Derwood Rd.
Rockville, MD 20855-2123
Ph: (301)519-0496   Fax: (301)519-0494

E-mail: nspra@nspra.org
URL: http://www.nspra.org

Description: Represents school system public relations directors, school administrators, and others interested in furthering public understanding of the public schools. Has adopted standards for public relations professionals and programs and an accreditation program.

★10535★ Public Relations Society of America (PRSA)

33 Maiden Ln., 11th Fl.
New York, NY 10038-5150
Ph: (212)460-1400   Fax: (212)995-0757
E-mail: exec@prsa.org
URL: http://www.prsa.org

Description: Professional society of public relations practitioners in business and industry, counseling firms, government, associations, hospitals, schools, and nonprofit organizations. Conducts professional development programs. Maintains a Professional Resource Center. Offers accreditation program.

Purchasing Agents and Managers

SOURCES OF HELP-WANTED ADS

★10536★ *Benchmarking Purchasing*
American Purchasing Society
8 E Galena Blvd., Ste. 203
Aurora, IL 60506
Ph: (630)859-0250   Fax: (630)859-0270
URL: http://www.american-purchasing.com
Annual. Professional journal covering issues in purchasing.

★10537★ *Electronic Business*
Reed Business Information
225 Wyman St.
Waltham, MA 02451-1216
URL: http://www.edn.com/index.asp?layout=businessCenter
Monthly. Magazine for purchasing managers and buyers of electronic components and materials used in end product manufacturing.

★10538★ *NAEB Bulletin*
National Association of Educational Procurement
5523 Research Pk. Dr.
Ste. 340
Baltimore, MD 21228
Ph: (443)543-5540   Fax: (443)543-5550
URL: http://www.naepnet.org/
Description: Monthly, except May and April. Features information on institutional purchasing and news of the Association. Recurring features include a calendar of events, reports of meetings, news of educational opportunities, job listings, book reviews, notices of publications available, and columns titled Professional Perspective, Market Index, and Roamin' With Yeoman.

★10539★ *Professional Purchasing*
American Purchasing Society
8 E Galena Blvd., Ste. 203
Aurora, IL 60506
Ph: (630)859-0250   Fax: (630)859-0270
E-mail: propurch@mgci.com
URL: http://www.american-purchasing.com/propurch.asp
Description: Monthly. Provides information on policies, procedures, methods, and prices of purchasing. Features price indexes. Recurring features include letters to the editor, news of research, reports of meetings, news of educational opportunities, job listings, book reviews, and notices of publications available.

★10540★ *Purchasing Magazine*
Reed Business Information
225 Wyman St.
Waltham, MA 02451-1216
URL: http://www.purchasing.com
Free. Magazine for buying professionals.

PLACEMENT AND JOB REFERRAL SERVICES

★10541★ **American Purchasing Society**
PO Box 256
Aurora, IL 60506
Ph: (630)859-0250   Fax: (630)859-0270
E-mail: support@american-purchasing.com
URL: http://www.american-purchasing.com
Description: Seeks to certify qualified purchasing personnel. Maintains speakers' bureau and placement service. Conducts research programs; compiles statistics including salary surveys. Provides consulting service for purchasing, materials management, and marketing. Conducts seminars and on-line courses.

EMPLOYER DIRECTORIES AND NETWORKING LISTS

★10542★ *Multi-Hospital Systems (MHSs) and Group Purchasing Organizations (GPOs) Report & Directory*
SMG Marketing Group Inc.
875 N Michigan Ave., Ste. 3100
Chicago, IL 60611
Ph: (312)642-3026   Fax: (312)642-9729
Fr: 800-678-3026
URL: http://www.smg.com
Annual. Covers over 750 multi-hospital systems and group purchasing organizations. Entries include: Company name, address, phone; hospital name, address, phone, type of hospital service, licensed number of beds, number of staffed beds, annual admission data, annual surgical information, status of hospital, activity in recent quarter, date and length of management contract with the hospital. Arrangement: Geographical. Indexes: Company name.

HANDBOOKS AND MANUALS

★10543★ *Opportunities in Hospital Administration Careers*
The McGraw-Hill Companies
PO Box 182604
Columbus, OH 43272
Fax: (614)759-3749   Fr: 877-883-5524
E-mail: customer.service@mcgraw-hill.com
URL: http://www.mcgraw-hill.com
I. Donald Snook. 2006. $13.95. 160 pages. Discusses opportunities for administrators in a variety of management settings: hospital, department, clinic, group practice, HMO, mental health, and extended care facilities.

★10544★ Opportunities in International Business Careers

The McGraw-Hill Companies
PO Box 182604
Columbus, OH 43272
Fax: (614)759-3749   Fr: 877-883-5524
E-mail: customer.service@mcgraw-hill.com
URL: http://www.mcgraw-hill.com

Jeffrey Arpan. 1994. $11.95 (paper). 147 pages. Describes what types of jobs exist in international business, where they are located, what challenges and rewards they bring, and how to prepare for and obtain jobs in international business.

EMPLOYMENT AGENCIES AND SEARCH FIRMS

★10545★ The Aspire Group

52 Second Ave, 1st Fl
Waltham, MA 02451-1129
Fax: (718)890-1810   Fr: 800-487-2967
URL: http://www.bmanet.com

Employment agency.

★10546★ Britt Associates Inc.

3533 Lake Shore Dr.
Joliet, IL 60431-8820
Ph: (815)436-8300   Fax: (815)436-9617
E-mail: brittassoc@aol.com

Employment agency.

★10547★ Colli Associates

414 Caboose Ln.
Valrico, FL 33594
Ph: (813)681-2145   Fax: (813)661-5217
E-mail: colli@gte.net

Employment agency. Executive search firm.

★10548★ The Esquire Staffing Group Ltd.

1 S. Wacker Dr., Ste. 1616
Chicago, IL 60606-4616
Ph: (312)795-4300   Fax: (312)795-4329
E-mail: d.williams@esquirestaffing.com
URL: http://www.esquirestaffing.com

Employment agency. Fills permanent as well as temporary openings.

★10549★ KForce

Fr: 888-663-3626
URL: http://www.kforce.com

Executive search firm. More than 30 locations throughout the United States.

★10550★ Rocky Mountain Recruiters, Inc.

1776 S. Jackson St., Ste. 412
Denver, CO 80210
Ph: (303)296-2000   Fax: (303)296-2223

E-mail: resumes@rmrecruiters.com
URL: http://www.rmrecruiters.com

Accounting, financial, and executive search firm.

TRADESHOWS

★10551★ Great Lakes Industrial Show

North American Exposition Co.
33 Rutherford Ave.
Boston, MA 02129
Ph: (617)242-6092   Fax: (617)242-1817
Fr: 800-225-1577
E-mail: naexpo@hotmail.com
URL: http://www.naexpo.com

Annual. **Primary Exhibits:** Industrial products, machine tools, hand tools, pneumatics, hydraulics, plant engineering, and maintenance, paper and packaging, plastics, rubber products, material handling equipment, and dies and stampings.

★10552★ The NAMSB Show

NSI
309 5th Ave., Ste. 307
New York, NY 10016
Ph: (212)685-4550   Fax: (212)685-4688
Fr: 800-936-2672

Semiannual. **Primary Exhibits:** Product lines include mens' and boy's clothing, sportswear, footwear, streetwear, unisex, and accessories.

★10553★ Supermarket Industry Convention and Educational Exposition

Food Marketing Institute
655 15th St., NW, Ste. 700
Washington, DC 20005
Ph: (202)452-8444   Fax: (202)429-4519
E-mail: fmi@fmi.org
URL: http://www.fmi.org

Annual. **Primary Exhibits:** Products, equipment, supplies, and services available to and through the supermarket industry, including grocery products, perishables, general merchandise, health and beauty aids, food service equipment, store design services, data processing equipment, advertising, and warehouse services.

OTHER SOURCES

★10554★ Administration and Management Occupations

Delphi Productions
3159 6th St.
Boulder, CO 80304
Ph: (303)443-2100   Fax: (303)443-4022
Fr: 888-443-2400
E-mail: support@delphivideo.com

URL: http://www.delphivideo.com
$95.00. 50 minutes. Part of the Careers for the 21st Century Video Library.

★10555★ American Almanac of Jobs and Salaries

HarperCollins
10 E. 53rd St.
New York, NY 10022
Ph: (212)207-7000   Fr: 800-242-7737
URL: http://www.harpercollins.com/

John W. Wright. Revised edition, 2000. $20.00 (paper). 672 pages. This is a comprehensive guide to the wages of hundreds of occupations in a wide variety of industries and organizations.

★10556★ Institute for Supply Management (ISM)

PO Box 22160
Tempe, AZ 85285-2160
Ph: (480)752-6276   Fax: (480)752-7890
Fr: 800-888-6276
E-mail: ashaw@ism.ws
URL: http://www.ism.ws

Members: Represents industrial, commercial, and utility firms; educational institutions and government agencies. **Purpose:** Disseminates information on procurement. Works to develop more efficient supply management methods. **Activities:** Conducts program for certification as a supply manager. Cosponsors executive purchasing management institutes at Michigan State University and Arizona State University. Provides in-company training. Maintains Speaker's Bureau and reference service.

★10557★ National Contract Management Association (NCMA)

21740 Beaumeade Cir., Ste. 125
Ashburn, VA 20147
Ph: (571)382-0082   Fax: (703)448-0939
Fr: 800-344-8096
E-mail: couture@ncmahq.org
URL: http://www.ncmahq.org

Description: Professional individuals concerned with administration, procurement, acquisition, negotiation and management of contracts and subcontracts. Works for the education, improvement and professional development of members and nonmembers through national and chapter programs, symposia and educational materials. Offers certification in Contract Management (CPCM, CFCM, and CCCM) designations as well as a credential program. Operates speakers' bureau.

★10558★ National Institute of Governmental Purchasing (NIGP)

151 Spring St.
Herndon, VA 20170-5223
Ph: (703)736-8900   Fax: (703)736-2818
Fr: 800-FOR-NIGP
E-mail: membershipinfo@nigp.org
URL: http://www.nigp.org

Description: Federal, state, provincial,

county, and local government buying agencies; hospital, school, prison, and public utility purchasing agencies in the U.S. and Canada. Also provides services to the International procurement community. Develops standards and specifications for governmental buying; promotes uniform purchasing laws and procedures; conducts specialized education and research programs. Administers certification program for the Universal Public Purchasing Certification Council (UPPCC) for Certified Professional Public Buyer (CPPB) and Certified Public Purchasing Officer (CPPO); offers audit consulting services and cost saving programs and tools

for governmental agencies, including product commodity code to online specifications library. Maintains speakers' bureau; compiles statistics, web based products and services.

★10559★ **National Management Association (NMA)**
2210 Arbor Blvd.
Dayton, OH 45439
Ph: (937)294-0421   Fax: (937)294-2374
E-mail: nma@nma1.org
URL: http://www.nma1.org

Description: Business and industrial management personnel; membership comes from supervisory level, with the remainder from middle management and above. Seeks to develop and recognize management as a profession and to promote the free enterprise system. Prepares chapter programs on basic management, management policy and practice, communications, human behavior, industrial relations, economics, political education, and liberal education. Maintains speakers' bureau and hall of fame. Maintains educational, charitable, and research programs. Sponsors charitable programs.

Rabbis and Jewish Religious Professionals

PLACEMENT AND JOB REFERRAL SERVICES

★10560★ Central Conference of American Rabbis (CCAR)
355 Lexington Ave.
New York, NY 10017
Ph: (212)972-3636 Fax: (212)692-0819
E-mail: info@ccarnet.org
URL: http://www.ccarnet.org
Description: National organization of Reform rabbis. Offers placement service; compiles statistics. Maintains 38 committees.

★10561★ Council for Jewish Education (CJE)
11 Olympia Ln.
Monsey, NY 10952
Ph: (845)368-8657 Fax: (845)369-6538
E-mail: mjscje@aol.com
Description: Teachers of Hebrew in universities; heads of Bureaus of Jewish Education and their administrative departments; faculty members of Jewish teacher training schools. Seeks to: further the cause of Jewish education in America; raise professional standards and practices; promote the welfare and growth of Jewish educational workers; improve and strengthen Jewish life. Conducts educational programs; cosponsors a Personnel Placement Committee with Jewish Education Service of North America.

★10562★ Jewish Community Centers Association of North America (JCCANA)
520 8th Ave.
New York, NY 10018
Ph: (212)532-4949 Fax: (212)481-4174
Fr: 877-452-2237
E-mail: info@jcca.org
URL: http://www.jcca.org
Description: Promotes the Jewish community center movement; aims to provide educational, cultural, social, Jewish identity building and recreational programs; fosters connections between North American Jews and Israel and world Jewry. Jewish military personnel and their dependents in the U.S. Armed Forces and Veterans Administration Hospitals through the JWB Jewish Chaplains Council. Operates research center; compiles statistics; maintains placement services for professional Jewish community center and YM and YWHA workers. Jewish military personnel and their dependents in the U.S. Armed Forces and Veterans Administration Hospitals through the JWB Jewish Chaplains Council. Operates research center; compiles statistics; maintains placement services for professional Jewish community center and YM andYWHA workers

★10563★ Jewish Educators Assembly (JEA)
PO Box 413
Cedarhurst, NY 11516
Ph: (516)569-2537 Fax: (516)295-9039
E-mail: jewisheducators@jewisheducators.org
URL: http://www.jewisheducators.org
Members: Educational and supervisory personnel serving Jewish educational institutions. **Purpose:** Seeks to: advance the development of Jewish education in the congregation on all levels in consonance with the philosophy of the Conservative Movement; cooperate with the United Synagogue of America Commission on Jewish Education as the policy-making body of the educational enterprise; join in cooperative effort with other Jewish educational institutions and organizations; establish and maintain professional standards for Jewish educators; serve as a forum for the exchange of ideas; promote the values of Jewish education as a basis for the creative continuity of the Jewish people. **Activities:** Maintains placement service and speaker's bureau.

★10564★ Jewish Reconstructionist Federation (JRF)
101 Greenwood Ave.
Jenkintown, PA 19046
Ph: (215)885-5601 Fax: (215)885-5603
E-mail: info@jrf.org
URL: http://www.jrf.org
Description: Federation of synagogues and fellowships committed to the philosophy and program of the Jewish Reconstructionist Movement. Maintains placement service and consulting services. Organize services to affiliates.

★10565★ National Association of Temple Administrators (NATA)
PO Box 936
Ridgefield, WA 98642
Ph: (360)887-0464 Fax: (866)767-3791
Fr: 800-966-NATA
E-mail: nataoffice@natanet.org
URL: http://natanet.org
Description: Full-time administrators of Jewish synagogues affiliated with the Union of American Hebrew Congregations. Conducts educational programs; has established code of standards and ethics. Offers congregational survey service and compiles synagogue research reports and salary reports. Conducts placement service and maintains speakers' bureau.

★10566★ National Association of Temple Educators (NATE)
633 Third Ave., 7th Fl.
New York, NY 10017-6778
Ph: (212)452-6510 Fax: (212)452-6512
E-mail: nateoff@aol.com
URL: http://nate.rj.org
Members: Directors of education in Reform Jewish religious schools, principals, heads of departments, supervisors, educational consultants, students, and authors. **Purpose:** Purposes are to: assist in the growth and development of Jewish religious education consistent with the aims of Reform Judaism; stimulate communal interest in Jewish religious education; represent and encourage the profession of temple educator. **Activities:** Conducts surveys on personnel practices, confirmation practices, religious school organization and administration, curricular practices, and other aspects of religious education. Sponsors institutes for principals and educational directors; maintains placement service.

★10567★ Rabbinical Alliance of America (RAA)

866 Eastern Pkwy., Apt. 3-E
Brooklyn, NY 11213
Ph: (718)493-5711   Fax: (718)493-5711

Description: Orthodox rabbis who serve in pulpits and as principals of Jewish day schools and Hebrew schools throughout the world. Supervises Hebrew Schools Program for Adult Studies. Provides placement service aid for indigent Torah scholars; contributes to Jewish charitable causes. Maintains the Rabbinical Court which handles orthodox Jewish divorces, court of arbitration, Dinei Torahs, and family and marriage counselling.

★10568★ Rabbinical Assembly (RA)

3080 Broadway
New York, NY 10027
Ph: (212)280-6000   Fax: (212)749-9166
E-mail: info@rabbinicalassembly.org
URL: http://www.rabbinicalassembly.org

Description: Seeks to be a creative force shaping the ideology, programs and practices of the Conservative movement; committed to building and strengthening the totality of Jewish life. Publishes learned textbooks, prayerbooks, and works of Jewish interest; administers the work of the Committee on Jewish Law and Standards for the Conservative Movement. Serves the professional and personal needs of members through publications, conferences, and benefit programs; coordinates the Joint Placement Commission of the Conservative movement.

★10569★ Solomon Schechter Day School Association (SSDSA)

155 5th Ave., 5th Fl.
New York, NY 10010-6802
Ph: (212)533-7800
E-mail: abramson@uscj.org
URL: http://www.ssdsa.org

Description: A division of the United Synagogue of Conservative Judaism Commission on Jewish Education. Jewish elementary day schools and high schools with a total of over 21,500 students. Named for Solomon Schecher (1850-1915), scholar of Talmud and rabbinical literature at Cambridge and founder of the United Synagogue of America and the Jewish Theological Seminary. Provides visitations and consultations regarding education, governance and administration; publication of advisories and position papers, biennial conferences for lay leaders, annual conferences of the principals council, Shibboley Schechter newsletter, listserves for presidents, School heads, Business managers, and development directors. Also provides dissemination of demographics and statistics, chartering and accreditation of schools, seminars and board training for lay leaders, Schechter website, SHAR"R, 7th and 8th grade trips to Israel, placement service, MaToK-TaNaKH curriculum development project for Solomon Schecter Day schools, residency fellowship program to prepare professional leadership (SREL) and a listing of consultants.

★10570★ Young Israel Council of Rabbis (YICR)

111 John St., Ste. 450
New York, NY 10038
Ph: (212)929-1525   Fax: (212)727-9526
Fr: 800-617-NCYI
E-mail: ncyi@youngisrael.org
URL: http://www.youngisrael.org

Description: Rabbis serving 200 Young Israel congregations in the U.S., Canada, and Israel. Encourages study and observance of Judaism and provides spiritual leadership to the Young Israel Movement. Adjudicates issues relating to the Young Israel Synagogues. Maintains speakers' bureau; conducts research and educational programs; provides placement service. Is concerned with welfare of rabbis.

HANDBOOKS AND MANUALS

★10571★ *Non-Profits and Education Job Finder*

Planning Communications
7215 Oak Ave.
River Forest, IL 60305-1935
Ph: (708)366-5200   Fax: (708)366-5280
Fr: 888-366-5200
E-mail: info@planningcommunications.com
URL: http://jobfindersonline.com

Daniel Lauber. 1997. $32.95; $16.95 (paper). 340 pages. Covers 1600 sources. Discusses how to use sources of non-profit sector job vacancies in a number of specialties and state-by-state, including job-matching services, job hotlines, specialty periodicals with job ads, salary surveys, and directories. Covers a variety of fields from education to religion. Includes chapters on resume and cover letter preparation and interviewing.

★10572★ *Opportunities in Religious Service Careers*

The McGraw-Hill Companies
PO Box 182604
Columbus, OH 43272
Fax: (614)759-3749   Fr: 877-883-5524
E-mail: customer.service@mcgraw-hill.com
URL: http://www.mcgraw-hill.com

John Oliver Nelson. 2003. $12.95; $11.95 (paper). 160 pages.

OTHER SOURCES

★10573★ Human Services Occupations

Delphi Productions
3159 6th St.
Boulder, CO 80304
Ph: (303)443-2100   Fax: (303)443-4022
Fr: 888-443-2400
E-mail: support@delphivideo.com
URL: http://www.delphivideo.com

$95.00. 50 minutes. Part of the Careers for the 21st Century Video Library.

★10574★ Jewish Education Service of North America (JESNA)

111 8th Ave., 11th Fl.
New York, NY 10011
Ph: (212)284-6950   Fax: (212)284-6951
E-mail: info@jesna.org
URL: http://www.jesna.org

Description: Widely recognized leader in the areas of research and program evaluation, organizational change and innovative program design and dissemination. Operates the Mandell J. Berman Jewish Heritage Center for Research and Evaluation. Supports the Covenant Foundation, a joint venture with the Crown Family, which makes awards and grants for creativity in Jewish education.

★10575★ National Council of Young Israel (NCYI)

111 John St., Ste. 450
New York, NY 10038
Ph: (212)929-1525   Fax: (212)727-9526
Fr: 800-617-NCYI
E-mail: ncyi@youngisrael.org
URL: http://www.youngisrael.org

Members: Families of traditional Jewish faith in the U.S., Canada, and Israel. **Purpose:** Seeks "to perpetuate traditional Judaism; instill a love for Americanism and the principles of democracy; bring Jewish youth back to the synagogue; educate the youth and adults in the heritage and culture of the Jewish people". Benevolent Association in the New York City area; conducts programs nationwide for adults and youths. **Activities:** Sponsors Institute for Jewish Studies, which provides specialized programs in Jewish education. The Institute maintains the Torah Tape Library of cassette tapes on Jewish philosophy, law, the Talmud, and related topics. Sponsors children's services, charitable program, and competitions. Maintains speakers' bureau; compiles statistics.

★10576★ Union of Sephardic Congregations (USC)

8 W 70th St.
New York, NY 10023
Ph: (212)873-0300   Fax: (212)724-6165
E-mail: office@shearithisrael.org

Description: Affiliated congregations practicing Sephardic (Spanish, Portuguese, or Middle Eastern) Judaism. Publishes and distributes Sephardic prayer books.

Radio and Television Announcers and Newscasters

SOURCES OF HELP-WANTED ADS

★10577★ AFTRA Magazine
American Federation of Television and
Radio Artists
260 Madison Ave.
New York, NY 10016-2401
Ph: (212)532-0800   Fax: (212)532-2242

$3.00/year for individuals, per year. Membership magazine covering issues in television and radio broadcasting.

★10578★ B-Stats
SNL Kagan
One Lower Ragsdale Dr. Bldg. One, Ste.
  130
Monterey, CA 93940
Ph: (831)624-1536   Fax: (831)625-3225
Fr: (866)296-3743
URL: http://www.snl.com/media_comm/

Description: Monthly. Discusses the sale of broadcast stations in the U.S., covering both AM and FM radio and television stations. Provides financial data on station transfers and contains five-year projections of revenues for all broadcast markets. Also available via e-mail and fax.

★10579★ Billboard Radio Monitor
VNU Business Media USA
770 Broadway
New York, NY 10003
Ph: (646)654-4500
URL: http://www.billboardradiomonitor.com/
radiomonitor/index.jsp

Weekly. $299.00 for individuals, per year; $6.99 for single issue. Magazine covering every format of music radio, regulatory developments, news radio, talk radio, and satellite radio.

★10580★ Broadcasting & Cable
Reed Business Information
360 Park Ave. S
New York, NY 10010
Ph: (646)746-6400   Fax: (646)746-7431

URL: http://www.reedbusiness.com

Weekly. $199.99/year for individuals. News magazine covering The Fifth Estate (radio, TV, cable, and satellite), and the regulatory commissions involved.

★10581★ Country Airplay Monitor
VNU Business Media USA
770 Broadway
New York, NY 10003
Ph: (646)654-4500

Weekly (Sun.). Trade publication covering the radio and music industry.

★10582★ Current
Heldref Publications
1319 18th St., NW
Washington, DC 20036-1802
Ph: (202)296-6267   Fr: 800-365-9753
URL: http://www.heldref.org/current.php

Monthly. $47.00/year for individuals, print only; $111.00/year for institutions, print only. Journal that reprints articles on education, politics, and other social issues.

★10583★ Daily Variety
Reed Business Information
5700 Wilshire Blvd., Ste. 120
Los Angeles, CA 90036
Ph: (323)857-6600   Fax: (323)857-0494
URL: http://www.reedbusiness.com/in-
dex.asp?layout=theListProfile&

Daily. Global entertainment newspaper (tabloid).

★10584★ Editor & Publisher
Editor & Publisher Magazine
770 Broadway
New York, NY 10003-9595
Ph: (646)654-5500   Fax: (646)654-5370
Fr: 800-562-2706
URL: http://www.editorandpublisher.com/
eandp/index.jsp

Weekly (Mon.). $99.00/year for individuals, print and online; $159.00/year for Canada, print and online; $320.00/year for other countries; $7.95/year for individuals, month-

ly. Magazine focusing on newspaper journalism, advertising, printing equipment, and interactive services.

★10585★ Feminist Media Studies
Taylor & Francis Group Journals
325 Chestnut St., Ste. 800
Philadelphia, PA 19106
Ph: (215)625-8900   Fax: (215)625-8914
Fr: 800-354-1420
URL: http://www.tandf.co.uk/journals/titles/
14680777.asp

Quarterly. $552.00/year for institutions, print and online; $106.00/year for individuals, print only; $524.00/year for institutions, online only. Journal covering media and communication studies.

★10586★ FMedia!
FM Atlas Publishing
PO Box 336
Esko, MN 55733-0336
Ph: (218)879-7676   Fr: 800-605-2219
URL: http://members.aol.com/fmatlas/
home.html

Description: Monthly. Lists information on the facilities and formats of FM radio, including new station grants and applications. Also provides official and unofficial news and comments, as well as FM Dxing and FM reception concerns. Recurring features include letters to the editor, news of research, job listings, and notices of publications available.

★10587★ The Hollywood Reporter
The Nielsen Co.
770 Broadway
New York, NY 10003
Ph: (646)654-5000   Fax: (646)654-5002
URL: http://www.hollywoodreporter.com/thr/
index.jsp

Daily (morn.). $3.00 for single issue; $6.00/year for U.S., weekly; $299.00/year for individuals, print; $175.00/year for U.S., weekly print; $299.00/year for U.S., print/online combination; $265.00/year for U.S., weekly print/online combination. Film, TV, and entertainment trade newspaper.

★10588★ Insiders Sportsletter

American Sportscasters Association Inc.
225 Broadway
New York, NY 10007
Ph: (212)227-8080   Fax: (212)571-0556
E-mail:
info@americansportscastersonline.com
URL: http://
www.americansportscastersonline.com

Description: Quarterly. Highlights Association programs promoting excellence and recognition in the field of sportscasting. Carries profiles of award winners and interviews with sportscasting professionals. Recurring features include news of research, employment opportunities, and a calendar of events.

★10589★ Journal of College Radio

Intercollegiate Broadcasting System Inc.
367 Windsor Hwy.
New Windsor, NY 12553
Ph: (845)565-0003   Fax: (845)565-7446
URL: http://www.ibsradio.org/

Description: Four issues/year. Provides informational and educational materials related to the establishment, operation, programming, and development of school and college radio stations. Recurring features include editorials, letters to the editor, news of members, book reviews, and a calendar of events.

★10590★ NAB RadioWeek

National Association of Broadcasters
1771 N St. NW
Washington, DC 20036
Ph: (202)429-5300   Fax: (202)429-4199
Fr: 800-368-5644
E-mail: nab@nab.org
URL: http://www.nab.org/

Description: Weekly. Covers radio broadcasting from legislative, regulatory, political, technical, management, and sales/marketing perspectives. Contains pertinent industry news, promotions of NAB conferences, product announcements, and coverage of awards competitions. Disseminated via broadcast fax only; not mailed. For NAB members only.

★10591★ NAB World

National Association of Broadcasters
1771 N St. NW
Washington, DC 20036
Ph: (202)429-5300   Fax: (202)429-4199
Fr: 800-368-5644
E-mail: nab@nab.org
URL: http://www.nab.org

Description: Monthly. Tracks the domestic and international broadcasting industry (radio and television) with emphasis on public policy, and engineering/technology issues. Features pertinent industry news and information on NAB conferences, products, and services.

★10592★ Public Broadcasting Report

Warren Communications News
2115 Ward Ct. NW
Washington, DC 20037
Ph: (202)872-9202   Fax: (202)318-8350
Fr: 800-771-9202
E-mail: info@warren-news.com
URL: http://www.warren-news.com

Description: Biweekly. Covers funding, programming, and regulations involving public television and radio. Monitors activities at National Public Radio (NPR), the Public Broadcasting System (PBS), the Federal Communications Commission (FCC), the National Telecommunications and Information Administration (NTIA), and the Corporation for Public Broadcasting (CPB).

★10593★ QST

American Radio Relay League Inc.
225 Main St.
Newington, CT 06111-1494
Ph: (860)594-0200   Fax: (860)594-0259
Fr: 888-277-5289
E-mail: qst@arrl.org
URL: http://www.arrl.org/qst/

Monthly. $34.00/year for individuals. Amateur radio magazine.

★10594★ Radio Journal

M Street Corp.
365 Union St.
Littleton, NH 03561
Ph: (603)444-5720   Fax: (603)444-2872
Fr: 800-242-9618
E-mail: info@theradiojournal.com
URL: http://www.theradiojournal.com

Description: Weekly. Reports on radio station regulatory applications, actions, and filings; construction permit activity; format changes; and other U.S. and Canadian radio news of interest to the broadcast industry. Covers all radio markets, large and small.

★10595★ Rock Airplay Monitor

VNU Business Media USA
770 Broadway
New York, NY 10003
Ph: (646)654-4500

Weekly. Trade publication covering the music and radio industries.

★10596★ Small Market Radio Newsletter

Jay Mitchell Associates
4 Ventana
Aliso Viejo, CA 92656-6062
Ph: (949)533-4912   Fax: (949)666-5045
Fr: 800-JAY-RADIO
E-mail: mitchell@jaymitchell.com
URL: http://www.smallmarketradio.com

Description: Weekly. Provides news and information for the radio industry and small market owners and managers. Recurring features include letters to the editor, interviews, news of research, a calendar of events, book reviews, and columns titled

FCC Actions, Editorials, and Promotions Page.

★10597★ SMPTE Journal

Society of Motion Picture and Television Engineers
3 Barker Ave.
White Plains, NY 10601
Ph: (914)761-1100
URL: http://www.smpte.org

Monthly. $130.00/year for individuals. Journal containing articles pertaining to new developments in motion picture and television technology; standards and recommended practices; general news of the industry.

★10598★ Sound Thinking

Jay Mitchell Associates
4 Ventana
Aliso Viejo, CA 92656-6062
Ph: (949)533-4912   Fax: (949)666-5045
Fr: 800-JAY-RADIO
E-mail: mitchell@jaymitchell.com
URL: http://www.smallmarketradio.com

Description: Weekly. Covers information about small market radio stations. Recurring features include letters to the editor, interviews, news of research, a calendar of events, book reviews, and columns titled Sound Bytes, Sales, and Promotions.

★10599★ Swap Shop

National Association of Broadcasters
1771 N St. NW
Washington, DC 20036
Ph: (202)429-5300   Fax: (202)429-4199
Fr: 800-368-5644
E-mail: nab@nab.org
URL: http://www.nab.org/nabstore

Description: Monthly. Provides money-making and money-saving ideas for the National Association of Broadcasters small market radio members.

★10600★ TelevisionWeek

Crain Communications Inc.
1155 Gratiot Ave.
PO Box 07924
Detroit, MI 48207-2997
Ph: (313)446-6000   Fax: (313)446-0347
Fr: 888-909-9111
URL: http://www.tvweek.com/

Weekly. $119.00/year for individuals; $171.00/year for Canada, including GST; $309.00/year for other countries, airmail. Newspaper covering management, programming, cable and trends in the television and the media industry.

★10601★ Weatherwise

Heldref Publications
1319 18th St., NW
Washington, DC 20036-1802
Ph: (202)296-6267   Fr: 800-365-9753
URL: http://www.heldref.org/ww.php

Bimonthly. $40.00/year for individuals, print only; $106.00/year for institutions, print only;

$44.00/year for individuals, print and online; $127.00/year for institutions, print and online. Popular weather magazine for students, teachers, and professionals.

PLACEMENT AND JOB REFERRAL SERVICES

★10602★ American Sportscasters Association (ASA)

225 Broadway, Ste. 2030
New York, NY 10007
Ph: (212)227-8080   Fax: (212)571-0556
E-mail: lschwa8918@aol.com
URL: http://www.americansportscastersonline.com

Members: Radio and television sportscasters. **Purpose:** Sponsors seminars, clinics, and symposia for aspiring announcers and sportscasters. **Activities:** Compiles statistics. Operates Speaker's Bureau, placement service, hall of fame, and biographical archives. Maintains American Sportscaster Hall of Fame Trust. Is currently implementing Hall of Fame Museum, Community Programs.

★10603★ Broadcast Foundation of College/University Students (BROADCAST)

89 Longview Rd.
Port Washington, NY 11050
Ph: (516)883-0159   Fax: (516)883-0159
E-mail: rstarleton@aol.com

Members: College students interested in broadcasting and professional broadcasters interested in encouraging practical broadcasting experience in colleges and universities. **Activities:** Conducts annual survey of all professional broadcasting stations for part-time and summer employment for college students. Sponsors job advisory and placement service.

★10604★ National Association of Broadcasters (NAB)

1771 N St. NW
Washington, DC 20036
Ph: (202)429-5300   Fax: (202)429-4199
E-mail: nab@nab.org
URL: http://www.nab.org

Description: Representatives of radio and television stations and networks; associate members include producers of equipment and programs. Seeks to ensure the viability, strength, and success of free, over-the-air broadcasters; serves as an information resource to the industry. Monitors and reports on events regarding radio and television broadcasting. Maintains Broadcasting Hall of Fame. Offers minority placement service and employment clearinghouse.

★10605★ National Association of Farm Broadcasting (NAFB)

PO Box 500
Platte City, MO 64079
Ph: (816)431-4032   Fax: (816)431-4087
E-mail: info@nafb.com
URL: http://www.nafb.com

Description: Radio and television farm directors actively engaged in broadcasting or telecasting farm news and information; associate members are persons with agricultural interests who are affiliated with advertising agencies, government agencies, farm organizations, and commercial firms. Works to improve quantity and quality of farm programming and serve as a clearinghouse for new ideas in farm broadcasting. Provides placement information.

★10606★ Radio-Television News Directors Association (RTNDA)

1600 K St. NW, Ste. 700
Washington, DC 20006-2806
Ph: (202)659-6510   Fax: (202)223-4007
Fr: 800-80-RTNDA
E-mail: rtnda@rtnda.org
URL: http://rtnda.org

Description: Comprises of heads of news departments for broadcast and cable stations and networks; associate members are journalists engaged in the preparation and presentation of broadcast news and teachers of electronic journalism; other members represent industry services, public relations departments of business firms, public relations firms, and networks. Works to improve standards of electronic journalism; defends rights of journalists to access news; promotes journalism training to meet specific needs of the industry. Operates placement service and speakers' bureau.

EMPLOYER DIRECTORIES AND NETWORKING LISTS

★10607★ ADWEEK Marketer's Guide to Media

ADWEEK Magazines
770 Broadway, 7th Fl.
New York, NY 10003-9595
Ph: (646)654-5105   Fax: (646)654-5350
Fr: 800-562-2706
URL: http://www.vnubusinessmedia.com

Annual, April. Covers television, radio, cable, magazines, newspapers, out-of-home, interactive, Hispanic, and promotion media. Entries include: Current rates, audience demographics, industry trends, market data for all areas of media. Arrangement: Classified by type of media.

★10608★ Bacon's Metro California Media

Cision US Inc.
332 S Michigan Ave., Ste. 900
Chicago, IL 60604
Ph: (312)922-2400   Fax: (312)922-9387
Fr: (866)639-5087
URL: http://www.bacons.com

Annual, November; latest edition 2005. $385.65 for individuals. Covers consumer media in the state of California, including newspapers, radio television and cable stations, magazines, and broadcast programs, ethnic media, news services and syndicates. Entries include: Name, address, phone, names of editors and creative staff, with titles or indication of assignments. Arrangement: Geographical, classified by type of outlet. Indexes: Alphabetical.

★10609★ Bacon's Radio/TV/Cable Directory, Volume 1

Cision US Inc.
332 S Michigan Ave., Ste. 900
Chicago, IL 60604
Ph: (312)922-2400   Fax: (312)922-9387
Fr: (866)639-5087
URL: http://www.bacons.com

Annual; latest edition 2007. $450.00 for individuals. Covers over 13,500 radio and television stations, including college radio and public television stations, and cable companies. Entries include: For radio and television stations–Call letters, address, phone, names and titles of key personnel, programs, times broadcast, name of contact, network affiliation, frequency or channel number, target audience data. For cable companies–Name, address, phone, description of activities. Arrangement: Geographical.

★10610★ BIA's Television Yearbook

BIA Financial Network Inc.
15120 Enterprise Ct.
Chantilly, VA 20151
Ph: (703)818-2425   Fax: (703)803-3299
Fr: 800-331-5086
E-mail: sales@bia.com
URL: http://www.bia.com

Annual, May. $150.00 for individuals. Covers U.S. Television markets and their inclusive stations, television equipment manufacturers, and related service providers and trade associations. Entries include: For stations–Call letters, address; name and phone number of general manager, owner, and other key personnel; technical attributes, rep. firm, network affiliation, last acquisition date and price and ratings for total day and prime time. For others–Company or organization name, address, phone, description. Arrangement: Classified by market. Indexes: Numerical by market rank; call letters.

★10611★ Bowker's News Media Directory

R.R. Bowker L.L.C.
630 Central Ave.
New Providence, NJ 07974
Ph: (908)286-1090   Fr: 888-269-5372

E-mail: wpn@bowker.com
URL: http://www.bowker.com

Annual; latest edition November 2006.
$635.00 for individuals, set; $385.00 for
individuals, per volume. Covers, in three
separate volumes, syndicates and over
8,500 daily and weekly newspapers; 1,750
newsletters; over 16,800 radio and television
stations; 5,500 magazines; 1,000 internal
publications. Entries include: Name of publication or station, address, phone, fax, e-mail
and URL, names of executives, editors,
writers, etc., as appropriate. Broadcasting
and magazine volumes include data on
kinds of material accepted. Technical and
mechanical requirements for publications
are given. Arrangement: Magazines are
classified by subject; newspapers and
broadcasting stations geographical. Indexes:
Newspaper department/editor by interest,
metro area, feature syndicate subject; magazine subject, publication title; television di-
rector/personnel by subject, radio personnel
and director by subject.

★10612★ **Broadcasting & Cable Yearbook**

R.R. Bowker L.L.C.
630 Central Ave.
New Providence, NJ 07974
Ph: (908)286-1090   Fr: 888-269-5372
URL: http://www.bowker.com

Annual; latest edition 2007, published October 2006. $235.00 for individuals. Covers
over 17,000 television and radio stations in
the United States, its territories, and Canada; cable MSOs and their individual systems; television and radio networks, broadcast and cable group owners, station representatives, satellite networks and services,
film companies, advertising agencies, government agencies, trade associations,
schools, and suppliers of professional and
technical services, including books, serials,
and videos; communications lawyers. Entries include: Company name, address,
phone, fax, names of executives. Station
listings include broadcast power, other operating details. Arrangement: Stations and
systems are geographical, others are alphabetical. Indexes: Alphabetical.

★10613★ **Career Opportunities in Radio**

Facts On File Inc.
132 W 31st St., 17th Fl.
New York, NY 10001
Ph: (212)967-8800   Fax: 800-678-3633
Fr: 800-322-8755
URL: http://www.factsonfile.com

Published 2004. $49.50 for individuals;
$44.55 for libraries. Covers more than 70
jobs, such as on-air personality/disc jockey,
business reporter, sportscaster, advertising
account representative, billing specialist,
publicist, studio engineer, program director,
website content producer, and more.

★10614★ **Careers in Focus: Broadcasting**

Facts On File Inc.
132 W 31st St., 17th Fl.
New York, NY 10001
Ph: (212)967-8800   Fax: 800-678-3633
Fr: 800-322-8755
URL: http://www.factsonfile.com

Latest edition 3rd, January 2007. $29.95 for
individuals; $26.95 for libraries. Covers an
overview of broadcasting, followed by a
selection of jobs profiled in detail, including
the nature of the job, earnings, prospects for
employment, what kind of training and skills
it requires, and sources for further information.

★10615★ **CPB Public Broadcasting Directory**

Corporation for Public Broadcasting
401 9th St. NW
Washington, DC 20004-2129
Ph: (202)879-9600   Fax: (202)879-9700
Fr: 800-272-2190
URL: http://www.cpb.org/stations/publicdi-
rectory/

Annual. Covers public television and radio
stations, national and regional public broadcasting organizations and networks, state
government agencies and commissions, and
other related organizations. Entries include:
For radio and television stations—Station call
letters, frequency or channel, address,
phone, licensee name, licensee type, date
on air, antenna height, area covered, names
and titles of key personnel. For organizations—Name, address, phone, name and title
of key personnel. Arrangement: National and
regional listings are alphabetical; state
groups and the public radio and television
stations are each geographical; other organizations and agencies are alphabetical. Indexes: Geographical, personnel, call letter,
licensee type (all in separate indexes for
radio and television).

★10616★ **Discovering Careers for Your Future: Radio & Television**

Facts On File Inc.
132 W 31st St., 17th Fl.
New York, NY 10001
Ph: (212)967-8800   Fax: 800-678-3633
Fr: 800-322-8755
URL: http://www.factsonfile.com

Published 2005. $21.95 for individuals;
$19.75 for libraries. Covers actors, audio
recording engineers, disc jockeys, radio and
television anchors, reporters, talent agents
and scouts, and weather forecasters; links
career education to curriculum, helping children investigate the subjects they are interested in and the careers those subjects
might lead to.

★10617★ **FM Atlas**

FM Atlas Publishing
PO Box 336
Esko, MN 55733-0336
Ph: (218)879-7676   Fr: 800-605-2219
URL: http://members.aol.com/fmatlas/

home.html

Irregular; latest edition 20th. $21.00 for indi-
viduals. Covers approximately 10,500 FM
stations located in North America. Entries
include: Call letters, location, musical format,
transmitting radius in kilometers, whether
stereo or monaural, FM subcarriers, etc.
Arrangement: Geographical, then by frequency.

★10618★ **Gebbie Press All-in-One Directory**

Gebbie Press Inc.
PO Box 1000
New Paltz, NY 12561
Ph: (845)255-7560   Fax: (845)256-1239
URL: http://www.gebbieinc.com/aio.htm

Annual; latest edition 37th, 2008. $170.00 for
individuals. Covers 1,577 daily newspapers,
6,200 weekly newspapers, 10,000 radio stations, 1,400 television stations, 268 general-
consumer magazines, 430 professional business publications, 3,100 trade magazines,
320 farm publications, list of the Black press
and radio, Hispanic press and radio, and a
list of news syndicates. Entries include: For
periodicals—Name, address, phone, fax, frequency, editor, circulation, readership. For
newspapers—Name, address, phone, fax,
circulation. For radio and television stations—Call letters, address, phone, format.
Arrangement: Classified by type of media.

★10619★ **International Television and Video Almanac**

Quigley Publishing Company Inc.
64 Wintergreen Ln.
Groton, MA 01450-4129
Ph: (860)228-0247   Fax: (860)228-0157
Fr: 800-231-8239
URL: http://hometown.aol.com/quigleypub/
mp.html

Annual, January; latest edition 2007.
$175.00 for individuals. Covers "Who's Who
in Motion Pictures and Television and Home
Video," television networks, major program
producers, major group station owners, cable television companies, distributors, firms
serving the television and home video industry, equipment manufacturers, casting agencies, literary agencies, advertising and publicity representatives, television stations, associations, list of feature films produced for
television, statistics, industry's year in review, award winners, satellite and wireless
cable providers, primetime programming,
video producers, distributors, wholesalers.
Entries include: Generally, company name,
address, phone; manufacturer and service
listings may include description of products
and services and name of contact; producing, distributing, and station listings include
additional details and contacts for cable and
broadcast networks. Arrangement: Classified by service or activity. Indexes: Full.

★10620★ M Street Radio Directory

M Street Corp.
365 Union St.
Littleton, NH 03561
Ph: (603)444-5720   Fax: (603)444-2872
Fr: 800-248-4242

Annual. $84.95 for individuals. Covers approximately 14,000 AM and FM radio stations in the U.S. and Canada. Entries include: Company name, address, phone, fax, personnel, geographical area served, format, audience ratings, markets served, technical and market information. Arrangement: Geographical. Indexes: Geographical, call letters, station frequency.

★10621★ The News Media

Lucent Books Inc.
10911 Technology Pl.
PO Box 9187
San Diego, CA 92127
Ph: (858)485-7424   Fax: 800-414-5043
Fr: 800-877-4253
URL: http://www.gale.com

Latest edition April 2002. Publication includes: List of organizations to contact for further information about careers in the news media. Principal content of publication is an examination of a variety of careers in the news media. Indexes: Alphabetical.

★10622★ North Carolina News Media Directory

News Media Directories
PO Box 316
Mount Dora, FL 32756-0316
Fax: (866)586-7020   Fr: 800-749-6399
URL: http://www.newsmediadirectories.info/

Annual; latest edition 2007. $65.00 for individuals. Covers about 730 newspapers, periodicals, radio and television broadcasting stations, and press services operating in North Carolina. Entries include: Publisher or company name, address, phone, names and titles of key personnel, publication title, call letters, hours of operation, and frequency. Arrangement: Classified by type of media. Indexes: Title; call letters; county.

★10623★ Pocket Media Guide

Media Distribution Services
307 W 36th St., Dept. P
New York, NY 10018-6496
Ph: (212)279-4800   Fax: (212)714-9092
Fr: 800-MDS-DATA
URL: http://www.mdsconnect.com/news_release/1_03.htm

Annual; latest edition 30th. Covers about 700 major market newspapers, radio and television stations and networks, foreign and national wire services, and trade and general interest publications in major United States cities and Canada. Entries include: Publication or call name, address, phone. Arrangement: Classified by line of business.

★10624★ The R & R Directory

Radio and Records Inc.
2049 Century Pk. E, 41St. Fl.
Los Angeles, CA 90067-4004
Ph: (310)553-4330   Fax: (310)203-9763
E-mail: moreinfo@rronline.com
URL: http://www.radioandrecords.com/RRDirectory/Directory_Main.as

Semiannual, spring and fall. $75.00. Covers more than 3,000 radio group owners, equipment manufacturers, jingle producers, TV production houses and spot producers, record companies, representative firms, research companies, consulting firms, media brokers, networks, program suppliers, trade associations, and other organizations involved in the radio and record industry. Entries include: Organization name, address, phone, fax, e-mail, name and title of contacts, branch offices or subsidiary names and locations. Arrangement: Alphabetical; classified by subject. Indexes: Company.

★10625★ Radio Advertising Source

SRDS
1700 Higgins Rd.
Des Plaines, IL 60018-5605
Ph: (847)375-5000   Fax: (847)375-5001
Fr: 800-851-7737
URL: http://www.srds.com

Quarterly. $614.00 for individuals. Covers over 10,500 AM and FM stations, networks, syndicators, group owners, and representative firms. Entries include: Call letters, name of owning company, address, phone; names of representatives and station personnel; demonstration detail, station format, signal strength, programming opportunities, special features. Arrangement: Geographical by state, then by Arbitron metro and non-metro areas.

★10626★ Radio Programming Profile

BF/Communication Services Inc.
66 Chestnut Ln.
Woodbury, NY 11797
Ph: (516)364-2593
URL: http://www.prplace.com/pr_pub.html

Three times yearly. Covers about 3,000 AM and FM radio stations in top 200 markets, with hour-by-hour format information (type of music, news, etc.) for each. Entries include: Station call letters, address, phone, names of executives, hour-by-hour format information. Arrangement: Alphabetical by market and call letters. Volume 1 has top 70 ranking markets; volume 2 has markets 71-200.

★10627★ RTNDA Communicator-Directory Issues

Radio-Television News Directors Association
1600 K St. NW, No. 700
Washington, DC 20006-2838
Ph: (202)659-6510   Fax: (202)223-4007
Fr: 800-80R-TNDA
URL: http://www.rtnda.org

Semiannual, January and July. Number of listings: 3,000; membership includes Canada and some foreign countries. Entries include: Member name, address, phone, and name of radio or television station, network, or other news organization with which affiliated. Arrangement: Same information given in alphabetical and geographical arrangements.

★10628★ Sports Market Place

Sports Careers
2990 E Northern Ave., Ste. D107
Phoenix, AZ 85028
Ph: (602)485-5555   Fax: (602)485-5556

Annual, January. Covers manufacturers, organizations, professional sports teams, broadcasting networks, sports arenas, syndicators, publications, trade shows, marketing services, corporate sports sponsors, and other groups concerned with the business and promotional aspects of sports generally and with air sports, arm wrestling, auto sports, badminton, baseball, basketball, biathlon, bowling, boxing, curling, equestrian, exercise, fencing, field hockey, football, golf, gymnastics, ice hockey, lacrosse, martial arts, paddleball, paddle tennis, platform tennis, pentathlon, racquetball, rowing, rugby, running/jogging, skiing, soccer, softball, squash, swimming, table tennis, tennis, track and field, volleyball, water sports, weightlifting, and wrestling. Entries include: Name of company or organization, address, fax, e-mail, URL, name of key personnel with titles, and description of products or services. Arrangement: Classified by type of firm, sport, or activity. Indexes: Alphabetical; single sport; media; sport sponsors; agencies; manufacturers; brand name; facilities; executives; and geographical.

★10629★ Television & Cable Factbook

Warren Communications News Inc.
2115 Ward Ct. NW
Washington, DC 20037
Ph: (202)872-9202   Fax: (202)318-8350
Fr: 800-771-9202
URL: http://www.warren-news.com/factbook.htm

Annual. $925.00 for individuals, print product; $995.00 for individuals, full online database. Covers commercial and noncommercial television stations and networks, including educational, low-power and instructional TV stations, as well as translators; United States cable television systems; cable and television group owners; program and service suppliers; and brokerage and financing companies. Entries include: For stations–Call letters, licensee name and address, studio address and phone; identification of owners, sales and legal representatives and chief station personnel; rates, technical data, map of service area, and Nielsen circulation data. For cable systems–Name, address, basic and pay subscribers, programming and fees, physical plant; names of personnel and ownership. Arrangement: Geographical by state, province, city, county, or country. Indexes: Call letters; product/service; name; general subject.

★10630★ TV and Cable Source

SRDS
1700 Higgins Rd.
Des Plaines, IL 60018-5605
Ph: (847)375-5000   Fax: (847)375-5001
Fr: 800-851-7737
URL: http://www.srds.com

Quarterly. $602.00 for single issue. Covers all domestic and international commercial television stations and networks; public television stations, cable networks, systems, interconnects, rep. firms, and group owners. Includes separate section showing production specifications of stations and systems. Entries include: Call letters, parent company, address, phone, representative, personnel, facilities, special features, programming. Production specifications section shows call letters or system name, address, and preferred specifications for ad copy. Arrangement: Classified by DMA ranking, then by call letters.

★10631★ What Can I Do Now

Facts On File Inc.
132 W 31st St., 17th Fl.
New York, NY 10001
Ph: (212)967-8800   Fax: 800-678-3633
Fr: 800-322-8755
URL: http://www.factsonfile.com

Latest edition 2nd, 2007. $29.95 for individuals; $26.95 for libraries. Covers radio producers and disc jockeys, radio and television anchors, reporters and correspondents, and television directors.

HANDBOOKS AND MANUALS

★10632★ 100 Best Careers in Entertainment

Arco Pub.
200 Old Tappan Rd.
Old Tappan, NJ 07675
Fr: 800-428-5331

Shelly Field. 1995. $15.00 (paper). 340 pages.

★10633★ Breaking into Television

Peterson's Guides
2000 Lenox Dr.
Box 67005
Lawrenceville, NJ 08648
Ph: (609)896-1800   Fax: (609)896-4531
Fr: 800-338-3282
E-mail: custsvc@petersons.com
URL: http://www.petersons.com

Dan Weaver. 1998. $14.95 (paper). 244 pages. Explains how to get a job in the television industry, with a list of internship opportunities.

★10634★ Career Opportunities in Radio

Checkmark Books
132 W. 31st St., 17th Fl.
New York, NY 10001-2006
Ph: (212)967-8800   Fax: (212)967-9196
Fr: 800-322-8755

Shelly Field Scherer. May 2004. $18.95 (paper). Illustrated. 288 pages.

★10635★ Careers in Communications

The McGraw-Hill Companies
PO Box 182604
Columbus, OH 43272
Fax: (614)759-3749   Fr: 877-883-5524
E-mail: customer.service@mcgraw-hill.com
URL: http://www.mcgraw-hill.com

Shonan Noronha. Fourth edition, 2004. $15.95 (paper). 192 pages. Examines the fields of journalism, photography, radio, television, film, public relations, and advertising. Gives concrete details on job locations and how to secure a job. Suggests many resources for job hunting.

★10636★ How to Launch Your Career in TV News

The McGraw-Hill Companies
PO Box 182604
Columbus, OH 43272
Fax: (614)759-3749   Fr: 877-883-5524
E-mail: customer.service@mcgraw-hill.com
URL: http://www.mcgraw-hill.com

Jeff Leshay. 1993. $14.95 (paper). 135 pages.

★10637★ Lights, Camera, Action!: Careers in Film, Television, & Video

BFI
601 N. Morton St.
Bloomington, IN 47404-3797
Ph: (812)855-4203   Fax: (812)855-7931
Fr: 800-842-6796

Josephine Langham. Second edition, 1997. $22.50 (paper). 287 pages.

★10638★ Making It in Broadcasting: An Insider's Guide to Career Opportunities

Macmillan Publishing Company
175 Fifth Ave.
New York, NY 10010
Ph: (646)307-5151   Fr: 800-428-5331
URL: http://www.macmillan.com/

Leonard Mogel. 1994. $15.00 (paper). 322 pages.

★10639★ The Media Jungle: A Survival Guide

Media Masters
872 Franklin Trace
Zionsville, IN 46077-1169
Ph: (317)733-9440   Fax: (317)873-4493

Carrie Van Dyke. 1996. $15.00. 87 pages.

★10640★ Opportunities in Broadcasting Careers

The McGraw-Hill Companies
PO Box 182604
Columbus, OH 43272
Fax: (614)759-3749   Fr: 877-883-5524
E-mail: customer.service@mcgraw-hill.com
URL: http://www.mcgraw-hill.com

Elmo I. Ellis. 2004. $14.95; $11.95 (paper). 176 pages. Discusses opportunities and job search techniques in broadcasting, television, and radio. Illustrated.

★10641★ Opportunities in Journalism Careers

The McGraw-Hill Companies
PO Box 182604
Columbus, OH 43272
Fax: (614)759-3749   Fr: 877-883-5524
E-mail: customer.service@mcgraw-hill.com
URL: http://www.mcgraw-hill.com

Jim Patten and Donald L. Ferguson. 2001. $12.95 (paper). 160 pages. Outlines opportunities in every field of journalism, including newspaper reporting and editing, magazine and book publishing, corporate communications, advertising and public relations, freelance writing, and teaching. Covers how to prepare for and enter each field, outlining responsibilities, salaries, benefits, and job outlook for each specialty. Illustrated.

★10642★ Opportunities in Sports and Athletics Careers

The McGraw-Hill Companies
PO Box 182604
Columbus, OH 43272
Fax: (614)759-3749   Fr: 877-883-5524
E-mail: customer.service@mcgraw-hill.com
URL: http://www.mcgraw-hill.com

William Ray Heitzmann. 1993. 160 pages. $11.95 (paper). A guide to planning for and seeking opportunities in this growing field. Illustrated.

★10643★ Opportunities in Television and Video Careers

The McGraw-Hill Companies
PO Box 182604
Columbus, OH 43272
Fax: (614)759-3749   Fr: 877-883-5524
E-mail: customer.service@mcgraw-hill.com
URL: http://www.mcgraw-hill.com

Shonan Noronha. Second edition, 2003. $12.95 (paper). 160 pages. Details the employment opportunities open in television, cable, corporate video, institutional and government media, including independent production, and discusses how to land a job. Illustrated.

★10644★ Opportunities in Writing Careers

The McGraw-Hill Companies
PO Box 182604
Columbus, OH 43272
Fax: (614)759-3749   Fr: 877-883-5524
E-mail: customer.service@mcgraw-hill.com

URL: http://www.mcgraw-hill.com

Elizabeth Foote-Smith. 2006. $13.95; $11.95 (paper). 160 pages. Discusses opportunities in the print media, broadcasting, advertising or publishing. Business writing, public relations, and technical writing are among the careers covered. Contains bibliography and illustrations.

★10645★ **Real People Working in Communications**

The McGraw-Hill Companies
PO Box 182604
Columbus, OH 43272
Fax: (614)759-3749   Fr: 877-883-5524
E-mail: customer.service@mcgraw-hill.com
URL: http://www.mcgraw-hill.com

Jan Goldberg. 1996. $17.95 (paper). 133 pages. Interviews and profiles of working professionals capture a range of opportunities in this field.

★10646★ **Real-Resumes for Media, Newspaper, Broadcasting and Public Affairs Jobs**

PREP Publishing
1110 1/2 Hay St., PMB 66
Fayetteville, NC 28305
Ph: (910)483-6611   Fax: (910)483-2439
Fr: 800-533-2814

Anne McKinney (Editor). October 2002. $16.95. 192 pages. Part of the Real-Resumes Series.

★10647★ **Resumes for Communications Careers**

The McGraw-Hill Companies
PO Box 182604
Columbus, OH 43272
Fax: (614)759-3749   Fr: 877-883-5524
E-mail: customer.service@mcgraw-hill.com
URL: http://www.mcgraw-hill.com

Third edition, 2003. $10.95 (paper). 160 pages.

★10648★ **What's up Dawg: How to Become a Superstar in the Music Business**

Hyperion Books
77 West 66th St., 11 Fl.
New York, NY 10023
Ph: (212)522-8700   Fr: 800-759-0190
URL: http://www.hyperionbooks.com

Randy Jackson. 2004. $19.95 (paper). 208 pages.

EMPLOYMENT AGENCIES AND SEARCH FIRMS

★10649★ **Adler Management Inc.**

66 Witherspoon St., Ste. 315
Princeton, NJ 08542
Ph: (609)443-3300   Fax: (609)443-4439

E-mail: jadler@amiconsulting.com
URL: http://www.amiconsulting.com

Executive search firm.

★10650★ **Joe Sullivan and Associates, Inc.**

9 Feather Hill
Southold, NY 11971-0612
Ph: (631)765-5050   Fax: (631)765-9047

Executive search firm. Recruits for the broadcasting, media, and entertainment industries.

ONLINE JOB SOURCES AND SERVICES

★10651★ **JournalismJobs.com**
Ph: (510)653-1521
E-mail: contact@journalismjobs.com
URL: http://www.journalismjobs.com

Description: Career-related site for journalists and other media professionals. Seekers can search for jobs, post a resume online, and manage the search online with the Job Seeker Folder feature. They also can receive free job announcements by e-mail.

TRADESHOWS

★10652★ **NAB Radio Show and World Media Expo**

National Association of Broadcasters
1771 N. St. NW
Washington, DC 20036
Ph: (202)429-5300   Fax: (202)429-4193
Fr: 800-342-2460
E-mail: nab@nab.org
URL: http://www.nab.org

Annual. **Primary Exhibits:** Radio and television broadcasting equipment, supplies, and services; supplies and services for production, post-production, computing, multimedia, telecommunications and corporate communications.

★10653★ **NATPE Annual Conference**

National Association Television Program Executives (NATPE)
5757 Wilshire Blvd.
Penthouse 10
Los Angeles, CA 90036-3681
Ph: (310)453-4440   Fax: (310)453-5258
Fr: 800-NATPE-GO
URL: http://www.natpe.com

Annual. **Primary Exhibits:** Equipment, supplies, and services for media content production, development, distribution, marketing, advertising, licensing and technology.

★10654★ **Radio-Television News Directors Association International Conference & Exhibition**

Radio-Television News Directors Association
1600 K St., NW, Ste. 700
Washington, DC 20006-2838
Ph: (202)659-6510   Fax: (202)223-4007
Fr: 800-807-8632
E-mail: rtnda@rtnda.org
URL: http://www.rtnda.org

Annual. **Primary Exhibits:** Equipment, supplies, and services for the radio and television news industries, including cameras, recorders, weather equipment, computers, and software.

OTHER SOURCES

★10655★ **American Almanac of Jobs and Salaries**

HarperCollins
10 E. 53rd St.
New York, NY 10022
Ph: (212)207-7000   Fr: 800-242-7737
URL: http://www.harpercollins.com/

John W. Wright. Revised edition, 2000. $20.00 (paper). 672 pages. This is a comprehensive guide to the wages of hundreds of occupations in a wide variety of industries and organizations.

★10656★ **Association for Women in Communications (AWC)**

3337 Duke St.
Alexandria, VA 22314
Ph: (703)370-7436   Fax: (703)370-7437
E-mail: info@womcom.org
URL: http://www.womcom.org

Description: Professional association of journalism and communications.

★10657★ **Broadcast Education Association (BEA)**

1771 N St. NW
Washington, DC 20036-2891
Ph: (202)429-3935   Fax: (202)775-2981
Fr: 888-380-7222
E-mail: beainfo@beaweb.org
URL: http://www.beaweb.org

Description: Universities and colleges; faculty and students; promotes improvement of curriculum and teaching methods, broadcasting research, television and radio production, and programming teaching on the college level.

★10658★ **Corporation for Public Broadcasting (CPB)**

401 9th St. NW
Washington, DC 20004-2129
Ph: (202)879-9600   Fax: (202)879-9700
Fr: 800-272-2190
E-mail: comments@cpb.org
URL: http://www.cpb.org

Description: Promotes and finances the growth and development of noncommercial radio and television. Makes grants to local public television and radio stations, program producers, and program distribution networks; studies emerging technologies; works to provide adequate long-range financing from the U.S. government and other sources for public broadcasting. Supports children's services; compiles statistics; sponsors training programs.

★10659★　Country Radio Broadcasters (CRB)

819 18th Ave. S
Nashville, TN 37203
Ph: (615)327-4487　　　Fax: (615)329-4492
E-mail: info@crb.org
URL: http://www.crb.org

Description: Seeks to advance and promote the study of the science of broadcasting through the mutual exchange of ideas by conducting seminars and workshops, as well as providing scholarships to broadcasting students.

★10660★　Media and the Arts Occupations

Delphi Productions
3159 6th St.
Boulder, CO 80304
Ph: (303)443-2100　　　Fax: (303)443-4022
Fr: 888-443-2400
E-mail: support@delphivideo.com
URL: http://www.delphivideo.com

$95.00. 50 minutes. Part of the Careers for the 21st Century Video Library.

★10661★　National Association of Black Owned Broadcasters (NABOB)

1155 Connecticut Ave. NW, Ste. 600
Washington, DC 20036
Ph: (202)463-8970　　　Fax: (202)429-0657
E-mail: nabob@nabob.org
URL: http://www.nabob.org

Description: Black broadcast station owners; black formatted stations not owned or controlled by blacks; organizations having an interest in the black consumer market or black broadcast industry; individuals interested in becoming owners; and communications schools, departments, and professional groups and associations. Represents the interests of existing and potential black radio and television stations. Works with the Office of Federal Procurement Policy to determine which government contracting major advertisers and advertising agencies are complying with government initiatives to increase

the amount of advertising dollars received by minority-owned firms. Conducts lobbying activities; provides legal representation for the protection of minority ownership policies. Sponsors annual Communications Awards Dinner each March. Conducts workshops; compiles statistics.

★10662★　National Religious Broadcasters (NRB)

9510 Technology Dr.
Manassas, VA 20110
Ph: (703)330-7000　　　Fax: (703)330-7100
E-mail: info@nrb.org
URL: http://www.nrb.org

Description: Christian communicators. Fosters electronic media access for the Gospel; promotes standards of excellence; integrity and accountability; and provides networking and fellowship opportunities for members.

★10663★　Women in Cable Telecommunications (WICT)

PO Box 791305
Baltimore, MD 21279-1305
Ph: (703)234-9810　　　Fax: (703)817-1595
E-mail: bfmosley@wict.org
URL: http://www.wict.org

Description: Empowers and educates women to achieve their professional goals by providing opportunities for leadership, networking and advocacy.

Radiologic Technologists

SOURCES OF HELP-WANTED ADS

★10664★ **ADVANCE for Imaging and Radiation Therapy Professionals**

Merion Publications Inc.
2900 Horizon Dr.
PO Box 61556
King of Prussia, PA 19406
Ph: (610)278-1400   Fr: 800-355-5627
URL: http://imaging-radiology-oncology-technologist.advanceweb.co

Biweekly. Professional medical magazine reaching radiology managers, technologists, and therapists.

★10665★ **Applied Radiation and Isotopes**

Mosby Inc.
11830 Westline Industrial Dr.
St. Louis, MO 63146
Ph: (314)872-8370   Fax: (314)432-1380
Fr: 800-325-4177
URL: http://www.elsevier.com/wps/find/journaldescription.cws_home

Monthly. $3,117.00/year for institutions (price for all countries except European countries, Japan and Iran). Journal for radiologists.

★10666★ **Applied Radiology**

Anderson Publishing Ltd.
180 Glenside Ave.
Scotch Plains, NJ 07076
Ph: (908)301-1995
URL: http://www.appliedradiology.com

Monthly. $95.00/year for individuals; $165.00 for two years; $110.00/year for other countries, surface mail; $185.00 for other countries, two years (surface mail); $180.00/year for other countries, air mail; $185.00 for other countries, two years (air mail). Magazine for radiologists, chief radiologic technologists, radiology department administrators, and key managers in HMOs. Presents articles written by radiologic professionals on all aspects of general diagnostic radiology, the diagnostic radiologic subspe-cialties, radiation therapy, and the socioeco-nomics of imaging.

★10667★ **ASTRO News**

American Society for Therapeutic Radiology and Oncology
8280 Willow Oaks Corporate Dr., Ste. 500
Fairfax, VA 22031
Ph: (703)502-1550   Fax: (703)502-7876
Fr: 800-962-7876
URL: http://www.astro.org/Publications/ASTROnews/index.asp

Quarterly. Subscription included in member-ship. Professional magazine covering radiol-ogy.

★10668★ **CME Supplement to Radiologic Clinics of North America**

Elsevier Science Inc.
360 Park Ave. S
New York, NY 10010
Ph: (212)989-5800   Fax: (212)633-3990
URL: http://www.elsevier.com

$431.00/year for institutions, U.S. $530.00/year for institutions, Canada; $290.00/year for individuals, U.S. $339.00/year for individ-uals, Canada; $142.00/year for students, U.S. 192.00/year for students, Canada. Jour-nal covering radiology, nuclear medicine and medical imaging.

★10669★ **Diagnostic Imaging**

CMP Media L.L.C.
600 Community Dr.
Manhasset, NY 11030
Ph: (516)562-5000   Fax: (516)562-7830
URL: http://www.diagnosticimaging.com/

Monthly. News and analysis on clinical and economic developments in medical imaging.

★10670★ **Investigative Radiology**

Lippincott Williams & Wilkins
530 Walnut St.
Philadelphia, PA 19106-3621
Ph: (215)521-8300   Fax: (215)521-8902
Fr: 800-638-3030
E-mail: runge@att.net
URL: http://www.investigativeradiology.com/

Monthly. $400.00/year for individuals, U.S.; $979.00/year for institutions, U.S.; $522.00/year for other countries; $1,147.00/year for institutions, other countries; $205.00/year for U.S., in-training; $221.00/year for other countries, in-training. Journal covering clini-cal and laboratory investigations in diagnos-tic imaging.

★10671★ **Journal of Clinical Ultrasound**

John Wiley & Sons Inc.
111 River St.
Hoboken, NJ 07030-5774
Ph: (201)748-6000   Fax: (201)748-6088
Fr: 800-825-7550
URL: http://as.wiley.com/WileyCDA/Wiley-Title/productCd-JCU.html

$295.00/year for individuals, print only rates; $295.00/year for Canada and Mexico, print only rates; $349.00/year for individuals, print only rates other; $1,265.00/year for institu-tions, print only rates; $1,373.00/year for institutions, Canada and Mexico, print only rates; $1,436.00/year for institutions, other countries, print only rates; $1,392.00/year for institutions, print with online access; $1,500.00/year for institutions, Canada and Mexico, print with online access; $1,563.00/year for institutions, other countries, print with online access. International journal de-voted to the clinical applications of ultra-sound in medicine. Features include scholar-ly, peer-reviewed articles on research proce-dures and techniques encompassing all phases of diagnostic ultrasound.

★10672★ **Journal of Computer-Assisted Tomography**

Lippincott Williams & Wilkins
351 W Camden St.
Baltimore, MD 21201
Ph: (410)528-4000   Fax: (410)528-4305
Fr: 800-399-3110
URL: http://www.jcat.org/

Bimonthly. $365.00/year for individuals; $1,037.00/year for institutions; $180.00/year for individuals, in-training; $453.00/year for individuals; $1,053.00/year for institutions;

$197.00/year for institutions, in-training. Radiology journal.

★10673★ **Magnetic Resonance Imaging Clinics**

Mosby Inc.
11830 Westline Industrial Dr.
St. Louis, MO 63146
Ph: (314)872-8370   Fax: (314)432-1380
Fr: 800-325-4177
URL: http://www.mri.theclinics.com

Quarterly. $345.00/year for individuals, international; $463.00/year for institutions, international; $167.00/year for students, international; $253.00/year for individuals; $376.00/year for institutions; $123.00/year for students. Journal publishing articles and research on the latest trends in magnetic resonance imagining clinics and patient management.

★10674★ **Magnetic Resonance in Medicine**

International Society for Magnetic Resonance in Medicine
2118 Milvia St., Ste. 201
Berkeley, CA 94704
Ph: (510)841-1899   Fax: (510)841-2340
URL: http://www.ismrm.org

Monthly. $850.00/year for individuals, U.S.; $850.00/year for individuals, Canada and Mexico; $892.00/year for individuals, rest of world; $1,795.00/year for institutions, U.S.; $1,795.00/year for institutions, Canada and Mexico; $1,867.00/year for institutions, rest of world; $1,975.00/year for U.S., combined print with online; $1,975.00/year for Canada and Mexico, combined print with online; $2,047.00/year for rest of world, combined print with online. Journal covering radiology worldwide.

★10675★ **Neuroimaging Clinics of North America**

Mosby Inc.
11830 Westline Industrial Dr.
St. Louis, MO 63146
Ph: (314)872-8370   Fax: (314)432-1380
Fr: 800-325-4177
URL: http://www.neuroimaging.theclinics.com

Quarterly. $454.00/year for institutions, international; $332.00/year for individuals, international; $166.00/year for students, international; $370.00/year for institutions, U.S.; $123.00/year for students, U.S.; $277.00/year for individuals, Canada; $166.00/year for students, Canada; $454.00/year for institutions, Canada. Journal publishing articles on newest advances in neuroimaging and patient treatment options.

★10676★ **RadioGraphics**

Radiological Society of North America
820 Jorie Blvd.
Oak Brook, IL 60523-2251
Ph: (630)571-2670   Fax: (630)571-7837
E-mail: rarnold@rsna.org
URL: http://www.rsna.org

Bimonthly. Scientific publication for radiologists.

★10677★ **Radiologic Clinics of North America**

Mountain Association for Community Economic Development
433 Chestnut St.
Berea, KY 40403
Ph: (859)986-2373   Fax: (859)986-1299
URL: http://www.radiologic.theclinics.com

Bimonthly. $259.00/year for individuals; $385.00/year for institutions; $127.00/year for students; $43.00 for individuals, single issue; $64.00 for institutions, single issue; $21.00 for students, single issue; $79.00 for single issue, non-subscribers; $352.00/year for individuals, international; $473.00/year for institutions, international; $171.00/year for students, international. Journal publishing articles written by leading experts, along with high-quality reproductions of radiographs, MR images, CT scans and sonograms.

★10678★ **Radiologic Technology**

American Society of Radiologic Technologists
15000 Central Ave. SE
Albuquerque, NM 87123-3909
Ph: (505)298-4500   Fax: (505)298-5063
Fr: 800-444-2778
E-mail: pubsdept@asrt.org
URL: http://www.asrt.org

Bimonthly. $60.00/year for individuals; $90.00/year for other countries; $108.00 for two years; $162.00 for two years, other countries. Medical imaging technology. Includes annual index.

★10679★ **Seminars in Roentgenology**

Mosby Inc.
11830 Westline Industrial Dr.
St. Louis, MO 63146
Ph: (314)872-8370   Fax: (314)432-1380
Fr: 800-325-4177
URL: http://www.seminarsinroentgenology.com/

Quarterly. $240.00/year for individuals, U.S.; $120.00/year for students, U.S.; $345.00/year for individuals, Canada; $173.00/year for students, Canada; $345.00/year for individuals, Mexico; $173.00/year for students, Mexico; $345.00/year for individuals, international; $173.00/year for students, international. Journal covering issues concerning the practicing radiologist and for the resident.

EMPLOYER DIRECTORIES AND NETWORKING LISTS

★10680★ **AHA Guide to the Health Care Field**

American Hospital Association
1 N Franklin
Chicago, IL 60606
Ph: (312)422-2050   Fax: (312)422-4700
Fr: 800-424-4301

Annual, August. Covers hospitals, networks, multi-health care systems, freestanding ambulatory surgery centers, psychiatric facilities, long-term care facilities, substance abuse programs, and other health-related organizations. Entries include: For hospitals–Facility name, address, phone, administrator's name, number of beds, facilities and services, number of employees, expenses, other statistics. For other organizations–Name, address, phone, fax, name and title of contact. Arrangement: Geographical. Indexes: Hospital name.

★10681★ **Directory of Hospital Personnel**

Grey House Publishing
185 Millerton Rd.
PO Box 860
Millerton, NY 12546
Ph: (518)789-8700   Fax: (518)789-0556
Fr: 800-562-2139
URL: http://www.greyhouse.com/hospital_personnel.htm

Annual. $325.00 for print product; $545.00 for online database subscription; $650.00 for online database subscription and print product combined. Covers 200,000 executives at 7,000 U.S. hospitals. Entries include: Name of hospital, address, phone; number of beds; type and JCAHO status of hospital; names and titles of key department heads and staff; medical and nursing school affiliations; number of residents, interns, and nursing students. Arrangement: Geographical. Indexes: Hospital name, personnel, hospital size.

★10682★ **Directory of Personnel Responsible for Radiological Health Programs**

Conference of Radiation Control Program Directors Inc.
205 Capital Ave.
Frankfort, KY 40601-2832
Ph: (502)227-4543   Fax: (502)227-7862
URL: http://www.crcpd.org

Annual, January. $50.00. Covers about 350 individuals who conduct radiological health program activities in federal, state, and local government agencies; members of the conferences. Entries include: For directors–Name and title, name of agency address, phone; office hours listed with state heading. For members–name, address, phone, affiliation, department, and title. Arrangement: Directors are by level of agency and geographical. Indexes: Personal name, agency, state.

★10683★ Hospital Blue Book

Billian Publishing Inc./Transworld
Publishing Inc.
2100 Powers Ferry Rd. SE
Atlanta, GA 30339
Ph: (770)955-5656   Fax: (770)952-0669
Fr: 800-533-8484
E-mail: blu-book@billian.com

2005. $300.00 for individuals. Covers more than 6,687 hospitals; some listings also appear in a separate southern edition of this publication. Entries include: Name of hospital, accreditation, mailing address, phone, fax, number of beds, type of facility (nonprofit, general, state, etc.); list of administrative personnel and chiefs of medical services, with specific titles. Arrangement: Geographical.

★10684★ Medical and Health Information Directory

Gale, Cengage Learning
27500 Drake Rd.
Farmington Hills, MI 48331-3535
Ph: (248)699-4253   Fax: (248)699-8065
Fr: 800-877-4253
E-mail: businessproducts@gale.com
URL: http://www.gale.com

Annual; latest edition 20th, July 2007. $375.00/volume. Covers in Volume 1, more than 26,500 medical and health oriented associations, organizations, institutions, and government agencies, including health maintenance organizations (HMOs), preferred provider organizations (PPOs), insurance companies, pharmaceutical companies, research centers, and medical and allied health schools. In Volume 2, over 12,000 medical book publishers; medical periodicals, directories, audiovisual producers and services, medical libraries and information centers, electronic resources, and health-related internet search engines. In Volume 3, more than 35,500 clinics, treatment centers, care programs, and counseling/diagnostic services for 34 subject areas. Entries include: Institution, service, or firm name, address, phone, fax, email and URL; many include names of key personnel and, when pertinent, descriptive annotations. Volume 3 was formerly listed separately as Health Services Directory. Arrangement: Classified by organization activity, service, etc. Indexes: Each volume has a complete alphabetical name and keyword index.

HANDBOOKS AND MANUALS

★10685★ Careers in Health Care

The McGraw-Hill Companies
PO Box 182604
Columbus, OH 43272
Fax: (614)759-3749   Fr: 877-883-5524
E-mail: customer.service@mcgraw-hill.com
URL: http://www.mcgraw-hill.com

Barbara M. Swanson. Fifth edition, 2005. $15.95 (paper). 192 pages. Describes job duties, work settings, salaries, licensing and certification requirements, educational preparation, and future outlook. Gives ideas on how to secure a job.

★10686★ Expert Resumes for Health Care Careers

Jist Works
875 Montreal Way
St. Paul, MN 55102
Fr: 800-648-5478
E-mail: info@jist.com
URL: http://www.jist.com

Wendy S. Enelow and Louise M. Kursmark. December 2003. $16.95. 288 pages.

★10687★ Health Careers Today

Elsevier
11830 Westline Industrial Dr.
St. Louis, MO 63146
Ph: (314)453-7010   Fax: (314)453-7095
Fr: 800-545-2522
E-mail: usbkinfo@elsevier.com
URL: http://www.elsevier.com

Gerdin, Judith. Fourth edition. 2007. $59.95. 496 pages. Covers more than 45 health careers. Discusses the roles and responsibilities of various occupations and provides a solid foundation in the skills needed for all health careers.

★10688★ Opportunities in Health and Medical Careers

The McGraw-Hill Companies
PO Box 182604
Columbus, OH 43272
Fax: (614)759-3749   Fr: 877-883-5524
E-mail: customer.service@mcgraw-hill.com
URL: http://www.mcgraw-hill.com

I. Donald Snook, Jr. and Leo D'Orazio. 2004. $13.95 (paper). 157 pages. Covers the full range of medical and health occupations. Illustrated.

★10689★ Opportunities in Medical Imaging Careers

The McGraw-Hill Companies
PO Box 182604
Columbus, OH 43272
Fax: (614)759-3749   Fr: 877-883-5524
E-mail: customer.service@mcgraw-hill.com
URL: http://www.mcgraw-hill.com

Clifford J. Sherry. 2006. $13.95. 160 pages.

★10690★ Opportunities in Medical Technology Careers

The McGraw-Hill Companies
PO Box 182604
Columbus, OH 43272
Fax: (614)759-3749   Fr: 877-883-5524
E-mail: customer.service@mcgraw-hill.com
URL: http://www.mcgraw-hill.com

Karen R. Karni. Revised, 1996. $14.95; $11.95 (paper). 148 pages. Details opportunities for various technical medical personnel and supplies up-to-date information on salary levels and employment outlook. Append-ices list associations and unions in each field. Illustrated.

EMPLOYMENT AGENCIES AND SEARCH FIRMS

★10691★ Cross Country TravCorps

6551 Park of Commerce Blvd.
Boca Raton, FL 33487-8247
Fax: (562)998-8533   Fr: 800-530-6125
URL: http://www.crosscountrytravcorps.com

Places traveling nurses in assignments nationwide.

★10692★ Harper Associates

3100 NW Hwy., Ste. 240
Farmington Hills, MI 48334
Ph: (248)932-1170   Fax: (248)932-1214
E-mail: info@harperjobs.com
URL: http://www.harperjobs.com

Executive search firm and employment agency.

★10693★ JPM International

26034 Acero
Mission Viejo, CA 92691
Ph: (949)699-4300   Fax: (949)699-4333
Fr: 800-685-7856
E-mail: trish@jpmintl.com
URL: http://www.jpmintl.com

Executive search firm and employment agency.

★10694★ Professional Placement Associates, Inc.

287 Bowman Ave., Ste. 309
Purchase, NY 10577-2517
Ph: (914)251-1000   Fax: (914)251-1055
E-mail: careers@ppasearch.com
URL: http://www.ppasearch.com

Executive search firm specializing in the health and medical field.

★10695★ Shiloh Careers International, Inc.

7105 Peach Ct., Ste. 102
PO Box 831
Brentwood, TN 37024-0831
Ph: (615)373-3090   Fax: (615)373-3480
E-mail: maryann@shilohcareers.com
URL: http://www.shilohcareers.com

Employment agency serving the industry field.

ONLINE JOB SOURCES AND SERVICES

★10696★ Medhunters.com
Fr: 800-664-0278
E-mail: info@medhunters.com
URL: http://www.medhunters.com

Description: Career search site for jobs in all health care specialties; educational resources; visa and licensing information for relocation; interesting articles; relocation tools; links to professional organizations and general resources.

★10697★ ProHealthJobs
Fr: 800-796-1738
E-mail: Info@prohealthedujobs.com
URL: http://www.prohealthjobs.com

Description: Career resources site for the medical and health care field. Lists professional opportunities, product information, continuing education and open positions.

★10698★ RadWorking.com
E-mail: info@atsradworking.com
URL: http://www.RadWorking.com

Description: Employment resource dedicated to the profession of radiology. Site is divided into various job-search sections based on job type or nature of support position.

TRADESHOWS

★10699★ Radiological Society of North America Scientific Assembly and Annual Meeting
Radiological Society of North America
820 Jorie Blvd.
Oak Brook, IL 60523-2251
Ph: (630)571-2670   Fax: (630)571-7837
Fr: 800-381-6600
E-mail: exhibits@rsna.org
URL: http://www.rsna.org

Annual. **Primary Exhibits:** Radiologic equipment, supplies, services, and publications. **Dates and Locations:** 2008 Nov 30 - Dec 05; Chicago, IL; McCormick Place ; 2009 Nov 29 - Dec 04; Chicago, IL; McCormick Place; 2010 Nov 28 - Dec 03; Chicago, IL; McCormick Place; 2011 Nov 27 - Dec 02; Chicago, IL; McCormick Place.

★10700★ SDMS Annual Conference
Society of Diagnostic Medical Sonographers
2745 Dallas Pkwy. Ste. 350
Plano, TX 75093-8730
Ph: (214)473-8057   Fax: (214)473-8563
Fr: 800-229-9506
E-mail: bclay@sdms.org
URL: http://www.sdms.org

Annual. **Primary Exhibits:** Exhibits related to the science of diagnostic medical sonography.

★10701★ Ultrasound/Women's Imaging
Brigham and Women's Hospital
Department of Radiology
75 Francis St.
Boston, MA 02115
Ph: (617)732-5500   Fax: (617)732-6458
E-mail: bwhteleservices@partners.org
URL: http://www.brighamandwomens.org

Primary Exhibits: Ultrasound scanners, gels, and related equipment; mammography equipment and supplies.

OTHER SOURCES

★10702★ American Institute of Ultrasound in Medicine (AIUM)
14750 Sweitzer Ln., Ste. 100
Laurel, MD 20707-5906
Ph: (301)498-4100   Fax: (301)498-4450
Fr: 800-638-5352
E-mail: admin@aium.org
URL: http://www.aium.org

Description: A multidisciplinary organization dedicated to advancing the art and science of ultrasound in medicine through its educational, scientific, literary and professional activities. Membership comprises professionals from many medical specialties, as well as basic scientists, engineers, manufacturers, nurses, physicists, radiologic technologists, sonographers and veterinarians involved with diagnostic medical ultrasound.

★10703★ American Registry of Diagnostic Medical Sonography (ARDMS)
51 Monroe St.
Plz. East One
Rockville, MD 20850-2400
Ph: (301)738-8401   Fax: (301)738-0312
Fr: 800-541-9754
E-mail: admin@ardms.org
URL: http://www.ardms.org

Members: Administers examinations in the field of diagnostic medical sonography and vascular technology throughout the U.S. and Canada and registers candidates passing those exams in the specialties of their expertise. **Activities:** Maintains central office for administering examination plans and schedules and assisting registered candidates and those interested in becoming registered.

★10704★ American Registry of Radiologic Technologists (ARRT)
1255 Northland Dr.
St. Paul, MN 55120-1155
Ph: (651)687-0048
URL: http://www.arrt.org

Description: Radiologic technologist certification board that administers examinations, issues certificates of registration to radiographers, nuclear medicine technologists, and radiation therapists, and investigates the qualifications of practicing radiologic technologists. Governed by trustees appointed from American College of Radiology and American Society of Radiologic Technologists.

★10705★ American Society of Radiologic Technologists (ASRT)
15000 Central Ave. SE
Albuquerque, NM 87123-3909
Ph: (505)298-4500   Fax: (505)298-5063
Fr: 800-444-2778
E-mail: customerinfo@asrt.org
URL: http://www.asrt.org

Description: Serves as professional society of diagnostic radiography, radiation therapy, ultrasound, and nuclear medicine technologists. Advances the science of radiologic technology; establishes and maintains high standards of education; evaluates the quality of patient care; improves the welfare and socioeconomics of radiologic technologists. Operates ASRT Education and Research Foundation, which provides educational materials to radiologic technologists.

★10706★ Exploring Health Occupations
Cambridge Educational
PO Box 2053
Princeton, NJ 08543-2053
Ph: 800-257-5126   Fax: (609)671-0266
Fr: 800-468-4227
E-mail: custserv@films.com
URL: http://www.cambridgeeducational.com

VHS and DVD. $159.90. 1999. Two-part series provides a detailed view of the field of medical technicians and technologists, EMTs, nurses, therapists, and assistants.

★10707★ Health Service Occupations
Delphi Productions
3159 6th St.
Boulder, CO 80304
Ph: (303)443-2100   Fax: (303)443-4022
Fr: 888-443-2400
E-mail: support@delphivideo.com
URL: http://www.delphivideo.com

$95.00. 50 minutes. Part of the Careers for the 21st Century Video Library.

★10708★ Health Technologists & Technicians
Delphi Productions
3159 6th St.
Boulder, CO 80304
Ph: (303)443-2100   Fax: (303)443-4022
Fr: 888-443-2400
E-mail: support@delphivideo.com
URL: http://www.delphivideo.com

$95.00. 50 minutes. Part of the Careers for the 21st Century Video Library.

★10709★ International Society for Clinical Densitometry (ISCD)
342 N Main St.
West Hartford, CT 06117-2507
Ph: (860)586-7563   Fax: (860)586-7550
E-mail: iscd@iscd.org
URL: http://www.iscd.org

Description: Raises awareness and understanding of the clinical application of bone mass measurement technology. Seeks to adopt an industry and technology neutral approach towards advances in the field. Encourages improvements in patient care through appropriate utilization of densitometry. Fosters continuing professional education and certification for clinicians and technologists.

★10710★ Medical Technicians and Technologists
Cambridge Educational
PO Box 2053
Princeton, NJ 08543-2053
Ph: 800-257-5126   Fax: (609)671-0266
Fr: 800-468-4227
E-mail: custserv@films.com
URL: http://www.cambridgeeducational.com

VHS and DVD. $79.95. 18 minutes. 2000. Part of the Exploring Health Occupations Series.

★10711★ Medicine & Related Occupations
Delphi Productions
3159 6th St.
Boulder, CO 80304
Ph: (303)443-2100   Fax: (303)443-4022
Fr: 888-443-2400
E-mail: support@delphivideo.com
URL: http://www.delphivideo.com

$95.00. 45 minutes. Part of the Careers for the 21st Century Video Library.

★10712★ Society of Diagnostic Medical Sonography (SDMS)
2745 N Dallas Pkwy., Ste. 350
Plano, TX 75093-8730
Ph: (214)473-8057   Fax: (214)473-8563
Fr: 800-229-9506
E-mail: dsanchez@sdms.org
URL: http://www.sdms.org

Description: Works to enhance the art and science of medicine by advancing medical sonography.

Real Estate Agents

SOURCES OF HELP-WANTED ADS

★10713★ Clayton-Fillmore Report

Clayton-Fillmore Ltd.
PO Box 480894
Denver, CO 80248
Ph: (303)663-0606   Fax: (303)663-1616
URL: http://www.clayfil.com

Monthly. $195.00/year for individuals, 1 year. Periodical covering real estate and business.

★10714★ Commercial Property News

VNU Business Media USA
770 Broadway
New York, NY 10003
Ph: (646)654-4500
URL: http://www.commercialpropertynews.com/cpn/index.jsp

Semimonthly. $10.00 for single issue. Twice-monthly magazine for senior level executives in the commercial real estate market, including brokers, developers, investors, lenders, property managers, owners, and corporate real estate executives.

★10715★ CONNECTIONS

Women's Council of Realtors
430 N. Michigan Ave.
Chicago, IL 60611
Ph: (312)329-8483   Fax: (312)329-3290
Fr: 800-245-8512
E-mail: wcr@wcr.org
URL: http://www.wcr.org/commq.htm

Description: Eight issues/year. Carries articles on personal and career growth topics relating to women in real estate. Includes council news.

★10716★ Florida Real Estate & Development Update

Mentor Communications
PO Box 290
Manhasset, NY 11030
Ph: (516)741-8887   Fax: (516)741-3131

URL: http://www.business-magazines.com

Description: Monthly. Covers financing of real estate projects. Includes legislative and regulatory updates and reports on national and state industry trends in all areas of real estate.

★10717★ Journal of Property Management

Institute of Real Estate Management
430 North Michigan Ave.
Chicago, IL 60611
Ph: (312)329-6000   Fax: 800-338-4736
Fr: 800-837-0706
E-mail: jpmsub@irem.org
URL: http://www.irem.org/sechome.cfm?sec=JPM

Bimonthly. $65.74/year for Canada; $56.95/year for individuals; $105.00/year for individuals, 2 years; $122.70/year for Canada, 2 years; $153.72/year for individuals, 3 years. Magazine serving real estate managers.

★10718★ Journal of Real Estate Literature

American Real Estate Society
c/o Diane Quarles
Clemson University
Box 341323
Clemson, SC 29634-1323
Ph: (864)656-1373   Fax: (864)656-3748
URL: http://cbeweb-1.fullerton.edu/finance/jrel/

Semiannual. Professional journal covering real estate issues.

★10719★ Journal of Real Estate Portfolio Management

American Real Estate Society
c/o Diane Quarles
Clemson University
Box 341323
Clemson, SC 29634-1323
Ph: (864)656-1373   Fax: (864)656-3748
URL: http://cbeweb-1.fullerton.edu/finance/jrepm/

Quarterly. Journal for real estate professionals.

★10720★ Journal of Real Estate Research

American Real Estate Society
c/o Diane Quarles
Clemson University
Box 341323
Clemson, SC 29634-1323
Ph: (864)656-1373   Fax: (864)656-3748
URL: http://cbeweb-1.fullerton.edu/finance/journal/

Journal focusing on scholarly real estate research.

★10721★ Lives of Real Estate

REAL Trends Inc.
6898 S University Blvd., Ste. 200
Littleton, CO 80122
Ph: (303)741-1000   Fax: (303)741-1070
URL: http://www.loremagazine.com/

Bimonthly. Free to qualified subscribers. Magazine that profiles personnel in the residential real estate industry.

★10722★ New England Real Estate Journal

East Coast Publications
PO Box 55
Accord, MA 02018-0055
Ph: (781)878-4540   Fax: (781)871-1853
Fr: 800-654-4993
E-mail: nerej@rejournal.com
URL: http://www.rejournal.com/

Weekly (Fri.). $99.00/year for individuals; $159.00 for individuals, two years. Newspaper publishing commercial, industrial, and investment real estate news.

★10723★ Real Estate Issues

The Counselors of Real Estate
430 N Michigan Ave.
Chicago, IL 60611-4089
Ph: (312)329-8427   Fax: (312)329-8881
URL: http://www.cre.org

$48.00/year for individuals, one year; $15.00 for single issue, per issue. Trade publication covering the real estate industry.

EMPLOYER DIRECTORIES AND NETWORKING LISTS

★10724★ **CRS Referral Directory**
Council of Residential Specialists
430 N Michigan Ave.
Chicago, IL 60611-4011
Ph: (312)321-4400   Fax: (312)329-8882
Fr: 800-462-8841
E-mail: crsdirectory@crs.com
URL: http://www.crs.com

Annual, November. Free. Covers 35,000 Certified Residential Specialists (CRS). Entries include: Member name, firm name, address, phone, fax, e-mail, web page address, voicemail, second business phone; designations held, areas of specialization, years of experience. Arrangement: Geographical. Indexes: Alphabetical.

★10725★ **Directory of Real Estate Development & Related Education Programs**
Urban Land Institute
1025 Thomas Jefferson NW, Ste. 500 W
Washington, DC 20007
Ph: (202)624-7000   Fax: (202)624-7140
Fr: 800-321-5011
URL: http://www.uli.org

Biennial; latest edition 10th, 2005. $19.95 for members; $24.95 for nonmembers. Covers over 60 real estate development education programs currently being offered at colleges and universities. Entries include: College or university name, address, list of faculty members, curriculum, tuition, length of program, degrees offered, financial aid information, job placement services, international programs, e-mail addresses. Indexes: Faculty; programs by degree type; programs by geographical area.

★10726★ **ERC Directory of Real Estate Appraisers and Brokers**
Employee Relocation Council
1717 Pennsylvania Ave. NW, Ste. 800
Washington, DC 20006
Ph: (202)857-0857   Fax: (202)659-8631
E-mail: membership@erc.org

Annual, March. Covers about 9,000 member brokers and appraisers worldwide, equipped to handle the relocation of employees. Entries include: For brokers–Firm name, address, phone, e-mail, number of offices, median price, code indicating services offered, list of corporations served, code indicating means of working with other brokers. For appraisers–Name, firm affiliation (if any), address, phone, e-mail, code indicating professional designations, names of corporations served. Arrangement: Appraisers and brokers are geographical.

★10727★ **National Association of Real Estate Companies-Membership Directory**
National Association of Real Estate Companies
216 W Jackson Blvd., Ste. 625
Chicago, IL 60606
Ph: (312)263-1755   Fax: (312)750-1203
E-mail: cindy@narec.org
URL: http://www.narec.org

Quarterly. Covers about 200 real estate development companies. Entries include: Company name, address, phone, name of contact.

★10728★ **National Referral Roster**
Stamats Communications Inc.
615 5th St. SE
PO Box 1888
Cedar Rapids, IA 52406-1888
Ph: (319)364-6167   Fax: (319)365-5421
Fr: 800-553-8878
E-mail: real-estate@roster.com
URL: http://www.roster.com

Annual; latest edition 2007. Covers 80,000 real estate firms nationwide. Entries include: Firm name, address, phone, fax, contact name, e-mail, and URL, included with their advertisers. Arrangement: Geographical.

★10729★ **Nelson Information's Directory of Institutional Real Estate**
Nelson Information
c/o Thomson Financial
195 Broadway
New York, NY 10007
Ph: (646)822-2000   Fax: (646)822-3000
Fr: 800-333-6357
URL: http://www.nelsoninformation.com

Annual, August. Covers 300 real estate investment managers, 1,700 plan sponsor investors in real estate, 1,400 real estate service firms and consultants, 1,000 insurance companies with real estate investments, 2,000 corporations with active real estate operations and 280 real estate investment trusts. Arrangement: Separate sections for real estate investment managers, plan sponsors, corporations, insurance companies, real estate service providers, and REITs. Indexes: Geographical; product/service.

★10730★ **U.S. Real Estate Register**
Barry Inc.
PO Box 551
Wilmington, MA 01887-0551
Ph: (978)658-0441   Fax: (978)657-8691
URL: http://www.usrealestateregister.com/

Annual; latest edition 37th. $95.00 for individuals. Covers real estate departments of large national companies, industrial economic/development organizations, utilities, real estate brokers, and railroads involved in commercial and industrial real estate development. Entries include: Company or organization name, address; many listings include name of contact. Arrangement: Companies are alphabetical; others are geographical.

★10731★ **Who's Who in Luxury Real Estate**
JBL Inc.
2110 W Ave.
Seattle, WA 98121
Ph: (206)695-4834   Fax: (206)695-4837
Fr: 800-488-4066
URL: http://www.luxuryrealestate.com

Annual, January. Covers approximately 500 international luxury real estate brokers. Entries include: Company name, address, phone, names and titles of key personnel, description, number of employees, geographical area served, number of offices, area price range, referral, logo. Arrangement: Geographical. Indexes: Geographical, trade name.

HANDBOOKS AND MANUALS

★10732★ **Agent's Guide to Real Estate: Power Your Career to Financial Success and Personal Happiness**
Realty Research Group
46879 Willowood Pl.
Potomac Falls, VA 20165
Ph: (571)434-9071

David Rathgeber. Third edition, 2001. 16.95. 138 pages.

★10733★ **The Everything Guide to Being a Real Estate Agent**
Adams Media Corporation
57 Littlefield St.
Avon, MA 02322
Ph: (508)427-7126   Fax: (508)427-6790
Fr: 800-872-5627
URL: http://www.adamsmedia.com/

Shahri Masters. 2006. $14.95.

★10734★ **How About a Career in Real Estate?**
Real Estate Education Co
1070 Idylwood Dr. SW
Issaquah, WA 98027
Ph: (425)392-6914   Fax: (425)392-6414
Fr: 800-296-2599

Carla Cross. Second edition, 1993. $14.95 (paper). 177 pages.

★10735★ **On Track to Success in 30 Days: Energize Your Real Estate Career To Become A Top Producer**
Dearborn Trade, A Kaplan Professional Co.
155 N. Wacker Dr.
Chicago, IL 60606-1719
Ph: (312)836-4400   Fax: (312)836-1021
Fr: 800-527-4836
URL: http://www.kaplanpublishing.com/

Carla Cross. 1996. $25.45 (paper). 160 pages.

★10736★ *Opportunities in Real Estate Careers*

The McGraw-Hill Companies
PO Box 182604
Columbus, OH 43272
Fax: (614)759-3749   Fr: 877-883-5524
E-mail: customer.service@mcgraw-hill.com
URL: http://www.mcgraw-hill.com

Mariwyn Evansand and Richard Mendenhal. Second edition, 2002. $12.95 (paper). 160 pages.

★10737★ *Real Estate Blues: A Jump Start Guide to Your Real Estate Career*

PublishAmerica, Incorporated
PO Box 151
Frederick, MD 21705
Ph: (301)695-1707   Fax: (301)631-9073
URL: http://www.publishamerica.com

David H. Lawrence. May 2004. $19.95 (paper). 138 pages.

★10738★ *Real Estate Brokerage: A Guide to Success*

Cengage Learning
PO Box 6904
Florence, KY 41022
Fax: 800-487-8488   Fr: 800-345-9706
URL: http://www.cengage.com/

Dan Hamilton. 2006. $50.95. Recruiting and retention strategies for running a successful real estate brokerage are covered. The book is designed to meet the requirements of a real estate brokerage course.

★10739★ *Real Estate Careers: Twenty-Five Growing Opportunities*

John Wiley & Sons Inc.
1 Wiley Dr.
Somerset, NJ 08873
Ph: (732)469-4400   Fax: (732)302-2300
Fr: 800-225-5945
E-mail: custserv@wiley.com
URL: http://www.wiley.com/WileyCDA/

Carolyn Janik and Ruth Rejnis. 1994. $24.95 (paper). 224 pages.

EMPLOYMENT AGENCIES AND SEARCH FIRMS

★10740★ **20-20 Foresight Executive Search Inc.**

One Lincoln Center, Fl. 15
Oakbrook Terrace, IL 60181
Ph: (708)246-2100
E-mail: bcavoto@202-4.com
URL: http://www.2020-4.com

Executive search firm. Affiliate offices in California and Washington DC.

★10741★ **Adams Partners**

205 W. Wacker Dr., Ste. 620
Chicago, IL 60606
Ph: (312)673-0389   Fax: (312)673-0390
URL: http://www.adamspartners.com

Executive search firm.

★10742★ **AET Advisors LLC**

4875 Olde Towne Pkwy., Ste. 150
Marietta, GA 30068
Ph: (770)578-6556
E-mail: aetadvisors@mindspring.com

Executive search and consultant firm. Focuses on the real estate industry.

★10743★ **American Human Resources Associates Ltd. (AHRA)**

PO Box 18269
Cleveland, OH 44118-0269
Ph: (440)995-7120   Fr: 877-342-5833
E-mail: inquiry@ahrasearch.com
URL: http://www.ahrasearch.com

Executive search firm. Focused on real estate, banking and credit & collection.

★10744★ **Crown Advisors Inc.**

800 E. Northwest Hwy., Ste. 612
Palatine, IL 60074
Ph: (847)221-2213   Fax: (847)221-2219
Fr: (847)830-6998
E-mail: jdimare@crownsearch.com

Executive search firm.

★10745★ **Liberty Screening Services**

2180 N Loop W, 3rd FL.
Houston, TX 77008-1374
Ph: (713)980-1751   Fax: (713)961-9889
Fr: 888-961-9990
E-mail: helpdesk@libertyscreening.com
URL: http://www.libertyscreening.com

Real estate specialists conducting retainer and contingency executive searches. Contract, temporary and permanent placement capability. Merger and acquisition expertise. National employment screening services and drug testing. Offers market research, policy manual and job description development, candidate search, contract negotiations, interview assistance, post-placement assistance and outplacement. Also offers career path guidance, creation of opportunities, resume critique, interview guidance, contract negotiation, relocation guidance and post placement assistance follow-up.

★10746★ **Real Estate Executive Search, Inc.**

306 SE 4th St.
Dania Beach, FL 33004
Ph: (954)927-6000   Fax: (954)927-6003
E-mail: reesearch954@aol.com
URL: http://reesearchinc.com

Executive search firm for the real estate and finance fields.

TRADESHOWS

★10747★ **American Real Estate Society Annual Meeting**

American Real Estate Society
5353 Parkside Dr.
Cleveland State University
College of Business
Department of Finance, UC513
Jupiter, FL 33458
Ph: (561)799-8664   Fax: (561)799-8535
E-mail: dcooper@fau.edu
URL: http://www.aresnet.org

Annual. **Primary Exhibits:** Exhibits relating to decision-making within real estate finance, real estate market analysis, investment, valuation, development, and other areas related to real estate in the private sector. Data providers, book publishers, etc.

★10748★ **NAIFA National Convention**

National Association of Independent Fee Appraisers
401 N. Michigan Ave.
Chicago, IL 60611
Ph: (312)321-6830   Fax: (312)673-6552
E-mail: info@naifa.com
URL: http://www.naifa.com

Annual. **Primary Exhibits:** Equipment, supplies, and services directed to appraisers for real estate groups, savings and loan associations, title insurance groups, and governmental agencies.

★10749★ **National Association of Realtors Trade Exposition**

National Association of Realtors
30700 Russell Ranch Rd.
Westlake Village, CA 91362
Ph: (805)557-2300   Fax: (805)557-2680
Fr: 800-628-6338
URL: http://www.realtor.com

Annual. **Primary Exhibits:** Real estate industry equipment, supplies, and services, including hardware and software, marketing programs, office products, mortgage and financial services, and insurance.

★10750★ **National Association of Review Appraisers and Mortgage Underwriters Convention - National Conference & Expo**

National Association of Review Appraisers and Mortgage Underwriters
1224 N Nokomis NE
Alexandria, MN 56308-5072
Ph: (320)763-6870   Fax: (320)763-9290
URL: http://iami.org/nara

Annual. **Primary Exhibits:** Real estate-related information and services.

★10751★ **ND/SD Realtors Convention**

South Dakota Association of Realtors
204 N. Euclid Ave.
Pierre, SD 57501
Ph: (605)224-0554   Fax: (605)224-8975

E-mail: sdar@sdrealtor.org
URL: http://www.sdrealtor.org

Annual. **Primary Exhibits:** Realty equipment, supplies, and services.

★10752★ New York State Association of Realtors Annual Conference and Trade Exposition

New York State Association of Realtors
130 Washington Ave.
Albany, NY 12210
Ph: (518)463-0300   Fax: (518)462-5474
Fr: 800-239-4432
E-mail: admin@nysar.com
URL: http://www.nysar.com

Annual. **Primary Exhibits:** Office equipment, publications, and real estate support services and technology.

★10753★ Realtor Annual Convention and Trade Expo

National Association of Realtors
30700 Russell Ranch Rd.
Westlake Village, CA 91362
Ph: (805)557-2300   Fax: (805)557-2680
Fr: 800-628-6338
URL: http://www.realtor.com

Annual. **Primary Exhibits:** Products and services related to the real estate business.

OTHER SOURCES

★10754★ American Real Estate and Urban Economics Association (AREUEA)

PO Box 9958
Richmond, VA 23228
Fax: 877-273-8323   Fr: (866)273-8321
E-mail: areuea@areuea.org
URL: http://www.areuea.org

Description: University faculty, individuals in real estate and related areas, and firms and organizations active in real estate and research. Promotes education and encourages research in real estate, urban land economics, and allied fields; improves communication in real estate and allied matters among college and university faculty who are teaching or conducting research in fields of interest to the association; facilitates the mutual association of academic and research persons in real estate, urban land economics, and allied fields.

★10755★ Counselors of Real Estate (CRE)

430 N Michigan Ave.
Chicago, IL 60611-4011
Ph: (312)329-8427   Fax: (312)329-8456
E-mail: info@cre.org
URL: http://www.cre.org

Description: Professional society of individuals with extensive experience in all phases of real estate who provide a counseling service. Members are entitled to use the Professional Designation CRE (Counselor of Real Estate). Conducts educational programs during three national meetings.

★10756★ Marketing & Sales Occupations

Delphi Productions
3159 6th St.
Boulder, CO 80304
Ph: (303)443-2100   Fax: (303)443-4022
Fr: 888-443-2400
E-mail: support@delphivideo.com
URL: http://www.delphivideo.com

$95.00. 50 minutes. Part of the Careers for the 21st Century Video Library.

★10757★ National Apartment Association (NAA)

4300 Wilson Blvd., Ste. 400
Arlington, VA 22203-4168
Ph: (703)518-6141   Fax: (703)248-9440
E-mail: webmaster@naahq.com
URL: http://www.naahq.org

Members: Federation of 155 state and local associations of industry professionals engaged in all aspects of the multifamily housing industry, including owners, builders, investors, developers, managers, and allied service representatives. **Purpose:** Provides education and certification for property management executives, on-site property managers, maintenance personnel, property supervisors, and leasing agents. Offers a nationwide legislative network concerned with governmental decisions at the federal, state, and local levels.

★10758★ National Association of Real Estate Brokers (NAREB)

225 S 42nd St., Ste. 303-A
Louisville, KY 40212
Ph: (502)774-8909   Fax: (502)774-5678
E-mail: chturner1@usa.net
URL: http://www.nareb.com

Description: Members of the real estate industry. Research, educational, and certification programs include: Real Estate Management Brokers Institute; National Society of Real Estate Appraisers; Real Estate Brokerage Institute; United Developers Council. Encourages unity among those who are engaged in real estate. Promotes and maintains high standards of conduct. Protects the public against unethical, improper, or fraudulent practices connected with the real estate business. Conducts research; compiles statistics on productivity, marketing, and development. Gives members license to use "Realtist" symbol. Sponsors educational seminars. Maintains Willis E. Carson Library.

★10759★ National Association of Real Estate Buyer Brokers (NAREBB)

2704 Wemberly Dr.
Belmont, CA 94002
Ph: (650)655-2500   Fax: (650)591-6807
E-mail: raymond@raymondstoklosa.com
URL: http://www.raymondstoklosa.com

Members: Real estate licensees. **Purpose:** Promotes buyer representation in real estate transactions. **Activities:** Informs consumers and professionals of the advantages and benefits of retaining a buyer's agent specialist when buying property. Conducts seminars and workshops to facilitate professionalism and enhance consumer awareness. Presents educational programs leading to a designation as a Certified Real Estate Buyer's Broker (CREBB). Manages free referral program for home buyers seeking representation.

★10760★ National Association of Realtors (NAR)

430 N Michigan Ave.
Chicago, IL 60611-4088
Fax: (312)329-5960   Fr: 800-874-6500
E-mail: infocentral@realtors.org
URL: http://www.realtor.org

Description: Federation of 54 state and territory associations and 1,860 local real estate boards whose members are real estate brokers and agents; terms are registered by the association in the U.S. Patent and Trademark Office and in the states. Promotes education, high professional standards, and modern techniques in specialized real estate work such as brokerage, appraisal, property management, land development, industrial real estate, farm brokerage, and counseling. Conducts research programs.

★10761★ Realtors Land Institute (RLI)

430 N Michigan Ave.
Chicago, IL 60611
Fax: (312)329-8633   Fr: 800-441-5263
E-mail: rli@realtors.org
URL: http://www.rliland.com

Members: Real estate brokers and salespersons selling, managing, appraising, or developing all types of land. **Purpose:** Maintains educational programs for real estate brokers; promotes competence and accredits members. **Activities:** Sponsors courses for realtors and others seeking professional excellence on Land Brokerage, Agricultural Land Brokerage, Exchanging Properties, Estate Planning, Subdivision Development, and Financial Analysis of Land Investment.

★10762★ Society of Industrial and Office Realtors (SIOR)

1201 New York Ave. NW, Ste. 350
Washington, DC 20005
Ph: (202)449-8200   Fax: (202)216-9325
E-mail: admin@sior.com
URL: http://www.sior.com

Members: Real estate brokers specializing in industrial and office properties; representatives of utilities, financial institutions, corporations, and industrial park developments. **Purpose:** Conducts studies on special problems of industrial development, development of sale-lease back techniques, surveys of plants or site locations, and availability. Conducts six educational courses and eight seminars annually. **Activities:** Sponsors

SIOR Educational Foundation. Compiles statistics.

★10763★ **Women's Council of Realtors (WCR)**
430 N Michigan Ave.
Chicago, IL 60611
Ph: (312)329-8481   Fax: (312)329-3290
Fr: 800-245-8512
E-mail: info@wcr.org
URL: http://www.wcr.org

Description: Women and men real estate brokers and salespeople. Provides opportunity for real estate professionals to participate at local, state, and national levels. Makes programs available for personal and career growth. Offers courses in leadership training, referral and relocation business. Members may earn the Leadership Training Graduate (LTG) designation.

Real Estate Appraisers

★10774★ **International Real Estate Institute (IREI)**
1224 N Nokomis NE
Alexandria, MN 56308-5072
Ph: (320)763-4648   Fax: (320)763-9290
E-mail: irei@iami.org
URL: http://www.iami.org/irei/home.cfm

Description: Professionals in 120 countries specializing in the development, finance, investment, and valuation of real estate. Conducts educational seminars and regional programs; operates speakers' bureau and placement service. Compiles statistics, consults United Nations on property issues.

★10775★ **National Association of Review Appraisers and Mortgage Underwriters (NARA/MU)**
1224 N Nokomis NE
Alexandria, MN 56308-5072
Ph: (320)763-6870   Fax: (320)763-9290
E-mail: nara@iami.org
URL: http://www.iami.org/nara

Description: Real estate professionals and mortgage underwriters who aid in determining value of property. Acts as umbrella group for real estate appraisers. Conducts educational seminars; maintains speakers' bureau; operates placement service.

EMPLOYER DIRECTORIES AND NETWORKING LISTS

★10776★ *Appraisal Institute-Directory of Designated Members*
Appraisal Institute
550 W Van Buren St., Ste. 1000
Chicago, IL 60607
Ph: (312)335-4100   Fax: (312)335-4400
E-mail: directory@appraisalinstitute.org
URL: http://www.appraisalinstitute.org/

Covers over 16,000 real estate appraisers of all types of real property in the United States and Canada who hold the MAI, SRPA, or SREA general appraisal, and/or SRA or RM residential appraisal membership designations of the Appraisal Institute; includes limited overseas listings. Entries include: Name of individual member, company name, address, phone, fax, and e-mail address. Arrangement: Geographical.

★10777★ *Directory of Professional Appraisers*
American Society of Appraisers
555 Herndon Pkwy., Ste. 125
Herndon, VA 20170
Ph: (703)478-2228   Fax: (703)742-8471
Fr: 800-272-8258
URL: http://www.appraisers.org

Annual, July. Covers approximately 3,000 appraisers of businesses, real property, personal property, machinery, equipment, gems and jewelry, and all other types of property; limited international coverage. Entries include: Personal and company name, ad-dress, phone, fax, e-mail, URL, specialty. Arrangement: Geographical.

★10778★ *ERC Directory of Real Estate Appraisers and Brokers*
Employee Relocation Council
1717 Pennsylvania Ave. NW, Ste. 800
Washington, DC 20006
Ph: (202)857-0857   Fax: (202)659-8631
E-mail: membership@erc.org

Annual, March. Covers about 9,000 member brokers and appraisers worldwide, equipped to handle the relocation of employees. Entries include: For brokers–Firm name, address, phone, e-mail, number of offices, median price, code indicating services offered, list of corporations served, code indicating means of working with other brokers. For appraisers–Name, firm affiliation (if any), address, phone, e-mail, code indicating professional designations, names of corporations served. Arrangement: Appraisers and brokers are geographical.

★10779★ *National Association of Independent Fee Appraisers-National Membership Directory*
National Association of Independent Fee Appraisers
401 N Michigan Ave., Ste. 2200
Chicago, IL 60611
Ph: (312)321-6830   Fax: (312)673-6652
URL: http://www.naifa.com

Annual, January. Covers 4,300 independent real estate appraisers. Entries include: Name, address, phone, level of membership. Arrangement: Geographical.

★10780★ *National Association of Master Appraisers-Membership Directory*
National Association of Master Appraisers
303 W Cypress St.
San Antonio, TX 78212
Ph: (512)271-0781   Fax: (512)225-8450
Fr: 800-229-6262
URL: http://www.masterappraisers.org/

Annual, January-March. Free. Covers approximately 2,400 real estate appraisers. Entries include: Personal name, address, phone, field of specialty. Arrangement: Geographical. Indexes: Name.

★10781★ *National Association of Real Estate Companies-Membership Directory*
National Association of Real Estate Companies
216 W Jackson Blvd., Ste. 625
Chicago, IL 60606
Ph: (312)263-1755   Fax: (312)750-1203
E-mail: cindy@narec.org
URL: http://www.narec.org

Quarterly. Covers about 200 real estate development companies. Entries include: Company name, address, phone, name of contact.

★10782★ *National Referral Roster*
Stamats Communications Inc.
615 5th St. SE
PO Box 1888
Cedar Rapids, IA 52406-1888
Ph: (319)364-6167   Fax: (319)365-5421
Fr: 800-553-8878
E-mail: real-estate@roster.com
URL: http://www.roster.com

Annual; latest edition 2007. Covers 80,000 real estate firms nationwide. Entries include: Firm name, address, phone, fax, contact name, e-mail, and URL, included with their advertisers. Arrangement: Geographical.

★10783★ *U.S. Real Estate Register*
Barry Inc.
PO Box 551
Wilmington, MA 01887-0551
Ph: (978)658-0441   Fax: (978)657-8691
URL: http://www.usrealestateregister.com/

Annual; latest edition 37th. $95.00 for individuals. Covers real estate departments of large national companies, industrial economic/development organizations, utilities, real estate brokers, and railroads involved in commercial and industrial real estate development. Entries include: Company or organization name, address; many listings include name of contact. Arrangement: Companies are alphabetical; others are geographical.

HANDBOOKS AND MANUALS

★10784★ *Best Websites for Financial Professionals, Business Appraisers, & Accountants*
John Wiley & Sons Inc.
111 River St.
Hoboken, NJ 07030-5774
Ph: (201)748-6000   Fax: (201)748-5774
E-mail: custserv@wiley.com
URL: http://www.wiley.com/WileyCDA/

Eva M. Lang and Jan Davis Tudor. Second edition, 2003. $49.95 (paper). 256 pages.

★10785★ *How About a Career in Real Estate?*
Real Estate Education Co
1070 Idylwood Dr. SW
Issaquah, WA 98027
Ph: (425)392-6914   Fax: (425)392-6414
Fr: 800-296-2599

Carla Cross. Second edition, 1993. $14.95 (paper). 177 pages.

★10786★ *Opportunities in Real Estate Careers*
The McGraw-Hill Companies
PO Box 182604
Columbus, OH 43272
Fax: (614)759-3749   Fr: 877-883-5524
E-mail: customer.service@mcgraw-hill.com
URL: http://www.mcgraw-hill.com

Mariwyn Evansand and Richard Mendenhal. Second edition, 2002. $12.95 (paper). 160 pages.

★10787★ Power Publicity for Personal Property Appraisers

Clifford Publishing
PO Box 43596
Upper Montclair, NJ 07043-0596
Ph: (973)857-4142

Paul Hartunian. 2006. $79.00. Profiles marketing ideas for personal property appraisers using press releases as a tool for publicity; includes a full year calendar with story ideas and headlines for each month.

★10788★ Power Publicity for Real Estate Appraisers

Clifford Publishing
PO Box 43596
Upper Montclair, NJ 07043-0596
Ph: (973)857-4142

Paul Hartunian. 2006. $79.00. Ideas for press releases for real estate appraisers seeking publicity are presented. A full year calendar with ideas for every month is included.

★10789★ Real Estate Careers: Twenty-Five Growing Opportunities

John Wiley & Sons Inc.
1 Wiley Dr.
Somerset, NJ 08873
Ph: (732)469-4400   Fax: (732)302-2300
Fr: 800-225-5945
E-mail: custserv@wiley.com
URL: http://www.wiley.com/WileyCDA/

Carolyn Janik and Ruth Rejnis. 1994. $24.95 (paper). 224 pages.

EMPLOYMENT AGENCIES AND SEARCH FIRMS

★10790★ Real Estate Executive Search, Inc.

306 SE 4th St.
Dania Beach, FL 33004
Ph: (954)927-6000   Fax: (954)927-6003
E-mail: reesearch954@aol.com
URL: http://reesearchinc.com

Executive search firm for the real estate and finance fields.

OTHER SOURCES

★10791★ American Real Estate and Urban Economics Association (AREUEA)

PO Box 9958
Richmond, VA 23228
Fax: 877-273-8323   Fr: (866)273-8321
E-mail: areuea@areuea.org
URL: http://www.areuea.org

Description: University faculty, individuals in real estate and related areas, and firms and organizations active in real estate and research. Promotes education and encourages research in real estate, urban land economics, and allied fields; improves communication in real estate and allied matters among college and university faculty who are teaching or conducting research in fields of interest to the association; facilitates the mutual association of academic and research persons in real estate, urban land economics, and allied fields.

★10792★ American Society of Agricultural Appraisers (ASAA)

PO Box 186
Twin Falls, ID 83303-0186
Ph: (208)733-2323   Fax: (208)733-2326
Fr: 800-488-7570
E-mail: ag@amagappraisers.com
URL: http://www.amagappraisers.com

Members: Appraisers of livestock, farm equipment, and other agricultural properties, supplies, and products. **Purpose:** Promotes adherence to high standards of ethics and practice in the field of agricultural appraising. **Activities:** Sponsors educational programs.

★10793★ Appraisal Institute (AI)

Headquarters Office
550 W Van Buren St., Ste. 1000
Chicago, IL 60607
Ph: (312)335-4100   Fax: (312)335-4400
E-mail: info@appraisalinstitute.org
URL: http://www.appraisalinstitute.org

Members: General appraisers who hold the MAI designation, and residential members who hold the SRA designation. **Purpose:** Enforces Code of Professional Ethics and Standards of Professional Appraisal Practice. Confers one general designation, the MAI, and one residential designation, the SRA. Provides training in valuation of residential and income properties, market analysis, and standards of professional appraisal practice. Sponsors courses in preparation for state certification and licensing; offers continuing education programs for designated members.

★10794★ Counselors of Real Estate (CRE)

430 N Michigan Ave.
Chicago, IL 60611-4011
Ph: (312)329-8427   Fax: (312)329-8456
E-mail: info@cre.org
URL: http://www.cre.org

Description: Professional society of individuals with extensive experience in all phases of real estate who provide a counseling service. Members are entitled to use the Professional Designation CRE (Counselor of Real Estate). Conducts educational programs during three national meetings.

★10795★ National Association of Master Appraisers (NAMA)

303 W Cypress St.
San Antonio, TX 78212
Fax: (210)225-8450   Fr: 800-229-6262
E-mail: maitca@bellsouth.net
URL: http://www.masterappraisers.org

Members: Appraisers, analysts, assessors, brokers, salespersons, and others involved in real estate appraisal. **Purpose:** Works to enhance competency in the appraisal industry through education. Provides basic and advanced courses and educational meetings in techniques, management practices, and marketing strategies. Offers certification. Areas of interest include: residential, commercial, and rural property; review appraisal; condemnation proceedings; tax assessing. Keeps members apprised of new legislation and legal changes in policy. **Activities:** Sponsors Lender Awareness Program to increase awareness among banks and savings association officers. Provides referral services and speakers' bureau.

★10796★ National Association of Real Estate Appraisers (NAREA)

1224 N Nokomis NE
Alexandria, MN 56308
Ph: (320)763-7626   Fax: (320)763-9290
E-mail: narea@iami.org
URL: http://www.iami.org/narea/home.cfm

Description: Real estate appraisers. Aims to make available the services of the most highly qualified real estate appraisers. Offers certification to members.

★10797★ National Association of Real Estate Brokers (NAREB)

225 S 42nd St., Ste. 303-A
Louisville, KY 40212
Ph: (502)774-8909   Fax: (502)774-5678
E-mail: chturner1@usa.net
URL: http://www.nareb.com

Description: Members of the real estate industry. Research, educational, and certification programs include: Real Estate Management Brokers Institute; National Society of Real Estate Appraisers; Real Estate Brokerage Institute; United Developers Council. Encourages unity among those who are engaged in real estate. Promotes and maintains high standards of conduct. Protects the public against unethical, improper, or fraudulent practices connected with the real estate business. Conducts research; compiles statistics on productivity, marketing, and development. Gives members license to use "Realtist" symbol. Sponsors educational seminars. Maintains Willis E. Carson Library.

★10798★ **National Association of Real Estate Buyer Brokers (NAREBB)**
2704 Wemberly Dr.
Belmont, CA 94002
Ph: (650)655-2500   Fax: (650)591-6807
E-mail: raymond@raymondstoklosa.com
URL: http://www.raymondstoklosa.com
Members: Real estate licensees. **Purpose:** Promotes buyer representation in real estate transactions. **Activities:** Informs consumers and professionals of the advantages and benefits of retaining a buyer's agent specialist when buying property. Conducts seminars and workshops to facilitate professionalism and enhance consumer awareness. Presents educational programs leading to a designation as a Certified Real Estate Buyer's Broker (CREBB). Manages free referral program for home buyers seeking representation.

★10799★ **National Association of Realtors (NAR)**
430 N Michigan Ave.
Chicago, IL 60611-4088
Fax: (312)329-5960   Fr: 800-874-6500
E-mail: infocentral@realtors.org
URL: http://www.realtor.org
Description: Federation of 54 state and territory associations and 1,860 local real estate boards whose members are real estate brokers and agents; terms are registered by the association in the U.S. Patent and Trademark Office and in the states. Promotes education, high professional standards, and modern techniques in specialized real estate work such as brokerage, appraisal, property management, land development, industrial real estate, farm brokerage, and counseling. Conducts research programs.

★10800★ **Realtors Land Institute (RLI)**
430 N Michigan Ave.
Chicago, IL 60611
Fax: (312)329-8633   Fr: 800-441-5263
E-mail: rli@realtors.org
URL: http://www.rliland.com
Members: Real estate brokers and salespersons selling, managing, appraising, or developing all types of land. **Purpose:** Maintains educational programs for real estate brokers; promotes competence and accredits members. **Activities:** Sponsors courses for realtors and others seeking professional excellence on Land Brokerage, Agricultural Land Brokerage, Exchanging Properties, Estate Planning, Subdivision Development, and Financial Analysis of Land Investment.

Recreation Workers

SOURCES OF HELP-WANTED ADS

★10801★ American City and County
Primedia Business
6151 Powers Ferry Rd., Ste. 200
Atlanta, GA 30339
Ph: (770)955-2500   Fax: (770)618-0204
URL: http://
www.americancityandcounty.com

Monthly. $67.00/year for individuals. Municipal and county administration magazine.

★10802★ Camping Magazine
American Camp Association
5000 State Rd., 67 N
Martinsville, IN 46151-7902
Ph: (765)342-8456   Fax: (765)342-2065
E-mail: magazine@aca-camps.org
URL: http://www.acacamps.org/campmag/

Bimonthly. $29.95/year for individuals, U.S. mainland; $56.00 for two years, U.S. mainland; $48.00/year for individuals, Alaska, Hawaii, Puerto Rico, Canada & Mexico; $92.00 for two years, Alaska, Hawaii, Puerto Rico, Canada & Mexico; $54.00/year for other countries; $104.00 for other countries, two years. Magazine on organized camp management.

★10803★ Earth Work
Student Conservation Association
689 River Rd.
PO Box 550
Charlestown, NH 03603
Ph: (603)543-1700   Fax: (603)543-1828
E-mail: earthwork@sca-inc.org
URL: http://www.thesca.org/

Description: Monthly. Contains listings of environmental positions, ranging from internships and administrative assistants for environmental groups to camp directors, state natural resource managers, and biologists.

★10804★ Job Line...and News from CPRS
California Park & Recreation Society Inc.
7971 Freeport Blvd.
Sacramento, CA 95832-9701
Ph: (916)665-2777   Fax: (916)665-9149
URL: http://www.cprs.org/publications-jobline.htm

Description: Monthly. Discusses parks and recreation news of interest.

★10805★ The Municipality
League of Wisconsin Municipalities
122 W Washington Ave., Ste. 300
Madison, WI 53703-2718
Ph: (608)267-2380   Fax: (608)267-0645
Fr: 800-991-5502
URL: http://www.lwm-info.org/index.asp?Type=B_BASIC&SEC=¢0702EE8F

Monthly. Magazine for officials of Wisconsin's local municipal governments.

★10806★ NRPA Job Bulletin
National Recreation and Park Association, Professional Services Div.
22377 Belmont Ridge Rd.
Ashburn, VA 20148
Ph: (703)858-0784   Fax: (703)858-0794
Fr: 800-626-6772
E-mail: info@nrpa.org
URL: http://www.nrpa.org

Description: Semimonthly. Provides listings of employment opportunities in the park, recreation, and leisure services field.

★10807★ Sailing World
Miller Sports Group L.L.C.
79 Madison Ave., 8th Fl.
New York, NY 10016-7802
Ph: (212)636-2700   Fax: (212)636-2730
Fr: 800-634-1953
E-mail: editor@sailingworld.com
URL: http://www.sailingworld.com/index.jsp

$14.97/year for individuals. Magazine on performance sailing.

★10808★ Ski Area Management
Beardsley Publishing Corp.
45 Main St. N
PO Box 644
Woodbury, CT 06798
Ph: (203)263-0888   Fax: (203)266-0452
URL: http://www.saminfo.com

Bimonthly. $48.00/year for individuals, one year; $66.00/year for two years; $81.00/year for individuals, three years offer good in U.S. only; $6.00/year for individuals, Canada add U.S. $22.00/year for other countries; $8.00/year for by mail, two years. Trade magazine covering ski area management.

★10809★ Strategies
American Alliance for Health, Physical Education, Recreation & Dance
1900 Association Dr.
Reston, VA 20191-1598
Ph: (703)476-3400   Fax: (703)476-9527
Fr: 800-213-7193
E-mail: strategies@aahperd.org
URL: http://www.aahperd.org/naspe/template.cfm?template=strategie

Bimonthly. $115.00/year for U.S. and Canada, institution; $45.00/year for nonmembers, U.S. and Canada, individual; $127.00/year for institutions, other countries; $57.00/year for nonmembers, foreign, individual. Journal providing practical, hands-on information to physical educators and coaches.

★10810★ Tourist Attractions & Parks Magazine
Kane Communications Inc.
10 E Athens Ave., Ste. 208
Ardmore, PA 19003
Ph: (610)645-6940   Fax: (610)645-6943
E-mail: tapmap@kanec.com
URL: http://www.tapmag.com

$49.00/year for individuals; $55.00 for two years; $55.00/year for individuals, foreign and Canada; $61.00 for two years, foreign and Canada. Magazine on the management of amusement parks, carnivals, arcades, museums, zoos, campgrounds, fun centers, arenas, miniature golf, and water sports.

★10811★ Western City

League of California Cities
1400 K St., Ste. 400
Sacramento, CA 95814
Ph: (916)658-8200   Fax: (916)658-8240
Fr: 800-262-1801
URL: http://www.westerncity.com

Monthly. $39.00/year for individuals; $63.00 for two years; $52.00/year for other counties; $26.50/year for students. Municipal interest magazine.

PLACEMENT AND JOB REFERRAL SERVICES

★10812★ American Alliance for Health, Physical Education, Recreation and Dance (AAHPERD)

1900 Association Dr.
Reston, VA 20191-1598
Ph: (703)476-3400   Fax: (703)476-9527
Fr: 800-213-7193
E-mail: info@aahperd.org
URL: http://www.aahperd.org

Members: Students and educators in physical education, dance, health, athletics, safety education, recreation, and outdoor education. **Purpose:** Works to improve its fields of education at all levels through such services as consultation, periodicals and special publications, leadership development, determination of standards, and research. Sponsors placement service.

★10813★ American Sail Training Association (ASTA)

PO Box 1459
Newport, RI 02840
Ph: (401)846-1775   Fax: (401)849-5400
E-mail: asta@sailtraining.org
URL: http://tallships.sailtraining.org

Members: Organizations operating sail training programs; corporations and educational institutions supporting sail training; private citizens with an interest in sailing and sail training. **Purpose:** Promotes sail training as an educational and character-building experience for youth of all ages. Seeks to bring together the sail training ships of the world in a spirit of friendship and international goodwill. **Activities:** Sponsors Tall Ships events including sail training rallies. Maintains billet bank/placement service; compiles statistics.

★10814★ Exercise Safety Association (ESA)

PO Box 547916
Orlando, FL 32854-7916
Ph: (407)246-5090
E-mail: askesa@aol.com
URL: http://www.exercisesafety.com

Description: Fitness instructors, personal trainers, health spas, YMCAs, community recreation departments, and hospital wellness programs. Purposes are: to improve the qualifications of exercise instructors; to train instructors to develop safe exercise programs that will help people avoid injury while exercising; to prepare instructors for national certification. Offers training in aerobics and exercise and on the physiological aspects of exercise. Conducts exercise safety and research programs. Sponsors charitable program; maintains speakers' bureau. Offers instructor placement services.

★10815★ Horsemanship Safety Association (HSA)

5304 Reeve Rd.
Mazomanie, WI 53560
Ph: (608)767-2593   Fax: (608)767-2590
E-mail: hoofbeat@midplains.net
URL: http://www.horsesafety.net

Description: Schools of horsemanship; equine programs at colleges and technical schools; riding instructors and students; medical personnel. To educate equestrians and instructors in safe horsemanship practices. Trains instructors in leadership techniques; conducts group and private lessons for children and adults; sponsors seminars and speaking engagements by certified clinicians. Conducts riding instructor clinics for adults. Certifies instructors at 4 levels: assistant riding instructor, horsemanship safety instructor, associate instructor, and clinic instructor. Certified instructors must renew certification every 3 years. Provides on-site consultation. Offers Expert Witness service. Compiles statistics; maintains speakers' bureau and placement service. Operates job placement services.

★10816★ Jackie Robinson Foundation (JRF)

One Hudson Sq.
75 Varick St., 2nd Fl.
New York, NY 10013-1947
Ph: (212)290-8600   Fax: (212)290-8081
E-mail: general@jackierobinson.org
URL: http://www.jackierobinson.org

Description: Seeks to develop the leadership and achievement potential of minority and urban youth. Founded by the friends and family of Jackie Robinson (1919-72), the first black athlete to play major league baseball. Trains minority and poor youths for sports management careers. Provides counseling, support, and placement services. Awards full college scholarships to promising minority students. Maintains collection of Jackie Robinson memorabilia; has produced a national touring exhibit of archival materials pertaining to Robinson.

★10817★ National Association of Underwater Instructors (NAUI)

PO Box 89789
Tampa, FL 33689-0413
Ph: (813)628-6284   Fax: (813)628-8253
Fr: 800-553-6284
E-mail: nauihq@nauiww.org
URL: http://www.nauiww.org

Members: Certified instructors of basic, advanced, and specialized courses in underwater diving. **Activities:** Offers instructor certification programs and training programs. Conducts seminars, workshops, and symposia. Sells diving education books. Sponsors competitions; maintains speakers' bureau and placement service; conducts charitable programs.

★10818★ Resort and Commercial Recreation Association (RCRA)

PO Box 1564
Dubuque, IA 52004
Fax: (563)690-3296
E-mail: bruce.boliver@sru.edu
URL: http://www.r-c-r-a.org

Members: Professionals, agencies, vendors, educators, and students involved in the resort and commercial recreation field. **Purpose:** Seeks to advance the resort and commercial recreation industries; increase the profitability of commercial recreation enterprises; foster communication among members; promote professionalism within the industry; provide opportunities for continuing education. **Activities:** Acts as a vehicle for networking; offers program exchange and job placement services. Holds specialized educational presentations; operates student chapters; encourages and facilitates internships. Provides car rental discount program.

★10819★ Society of Recreation Executives (SRE)

Box 520
Gonzalez, FL 32560-0520
Ph: (850)937-8354   Fr: 800-281-9186
E-mail: rltresoource@spydee.net

Description: Corporate executives in the recreation, leisure, and travel industry. To obtain individual and collective recognition for recreation executives. Works to: provide a perspective on needs, trends, and changes within the industry; provide opportunities for the exchange of ideas and expertise among members; inform, train, and instruct members in industry principles and practices. Supports favorable legislation. Sponsors continuing education and selfhelp programs. Operates placement service and speakers' bureau.

★10820★ YMCA International Camp Counselor Program (ICCP)

5 W 63rd St., 2nd Fl.
New York, NY 10023-9197
Ph: (212)727-8800   Fax: (212)727-8814
Fr: 888-477-9622
E-mail: ips@ymcanyc.org
URL: http://www.internationalymca.org/ICCP/home.html

Description: Serves as a work-travel program designed to introduce international university students and teachers and social workers aged 19-30 to life in America; the students spend 8 to 9 weeks counseling in children's camps across the country, followed by a period of independent or group travel. Sponsors ICCP-Abroad placement service for American university students aged 18-25 wishing to serve as camp counselors in Africa, Asia, Australia, Hungary, New Zealand, and South America.

EMPLOYER DIRECTORIES AND NETWORKING LISTS

★10821★ Directory of Public Garden Internships

American Association of Botanical
  Gardens and Arboreta
100 W 10th St., Ste. 614
Wilmington, DE 19801
Ph: (302)655-7100   Fax: (302)655-8100
E-mail: bvincent@aabga.org
URL: http://aabga.org

Annual, November; latest edition 2005. Covers 700 student internships and summer jobs at public gardens throughout North America. Entries include: Name of institution, address, name of contact, deadline for application, number of students hired, whether internships are available, employment period, hours, rate of pay, whether housing is available, other comments. Arrangement: Alphabetical. Indexes: By position, by state/province.

★10822★ Guide to ACA-Accredited Camps

American Camp Association
5000 State Rd., 67 N
Martinsville, IN 46151-7902
Ph: (765)342-8456   Fax: (765)342-2065
URL: http://bookstore.acacamps.org/

Annual, January; latest edition 2004. Covers Over 2,400 summer camps. Entries include: Name of camp, address, phone, fax, e-mail addresses, age and sex of children accepted, rates, season, capacity, facilities, programs, activities offered and camp philosophy. Arrangement: Geographical, then by day or resident camp. Indexes: Activity, special clientele, camp name, specific disabilities.

★10823★ Membership and Peer Network Directory

ESM Association
568 Spring Rd., Ste. D
Elmhurst, IL 60126-3896
Ph: (630)559-0020   Fax: (630)559-0025
URL: http://www.esmassn.org/members/login.asp

Annual, April. Covers over 4,500 personnel managers, recreation directors, suppliers, and certified administrators in employee recreation, fitness, and services. Entries include: Name, address, phone, fax and e-mail. Arrangement: Alphabetical.

★10824★ National Parks

U.S. National Park Service
Harpers Ferry Center
PO Box 50
Harpers Ferry, WV 25425-0050
Ph: (202)208-4747   Fax: (304)535-6144
URL: http://www.nps.gov/

Biennial, odd years. Covers over 379 areas administered by the National Park Service, including parks, shores, historic sites, 80 national trails, and wild and scenic rivers. Entries include: Name, location, address, acreage (federal, non-federal, and gross), federal facilities, brief description. Arrangement: Most areas are alphabetical by state; geographical and historical by state; wild and scenic rivers and national trails are alphabetical by state. Indexes: Alphabetical by state.

★10825★ Peterson's Summer Jobs for Students

Peterson's
Princeton Pke. Corporate Ctr., 2000
  Lenox Dr.
PO Box 67005
Lawrenceville, NJ 08648
Ph: (609)896-1800   Fax: (609)896-4531
Fr: 800-338-3282
URL: http://www.petersons.com/

Annual; latest edition 2002. $13.95 for individuals. Covers over 650 camps, resorts, amusement parks, hotels, businesses, national parks, conference and training centers, ranches, and restaurants offering about 45,000 temporary summer jobs; listings are paid. Entries include: Name and address, length of employment, pay rate, fringe benefits, duties, qualifications, application deadline and procedure. Arrangement: Geographical, then type of job. Indexes: Job title.

★10826★ Recreational Sports Directory

National Intramural-Recreational Sports
  Association
4185 SW Research Way
Corvallis, OR 97333-1067
Ph: (541)766-8211   Fax: (541)766-8284
URL: http://www.nirsa.org

Annual; latest edition 2008. $35.00 for members; $85.00 for nonmembers. Covers recreational sports programs in approximately 2,500 four-year colleges and universities, nearly 700 junior and community colleges, Canadian colleges and universities, and over 350 military installations. Entries include: Institution name and address; institution enrollment; name of president; names, phone numbers, fax numbers, Internet access, and job titles of recreational directors and staff; existing sports clubs; degrees offered in physical education and recreation; whether graduate assistantships or internships are available. A buyer's guide is included with supplier addresses and descriptions of products and services. Arrangement: Classified by institution type, then alphabetical. Indexes: Alphabetical; geographical; personal name; recreational sports program.

★10827★ Skiing USA

Fodor's Travel Publications Inc.
1745 Broadway
New York, NY 10019
Ph: (212)572-2313   Fax: (212)782-9054
Fr: 800-733-3000
URL: http://www.fodors.com

Biennial; latest edition 4th, published November 2002. Covers 30 top ski resorts in the U.S. Entries include: Resort name, address, phone; type of lifts, number of trails, snowmaking capabilities, length of season, hotels, restaurants, available transportation, other activities, and recommendations on the best trails for all levels. Arrangement: Geographical. Indexes: Resort name.

★10828★ White Book of Ski Areas

Inter-Ski Services Inc.
PO Box 3775, Georgetown Sta.
Washington, DC 20007
Ph: (202)342-0886   Fax: (202)338-1940
URL: http://www.inter-ski.com

Annual; latest edition 30th. Free. Covers about 500 lift-equipped ski areas and resorts. Entries include: Name of ski area, location, phone; snow condition phone numbers; ski statistics (elevation, lift capacity, etc.); season and rates; equipment and schooling available; lodging availability and phone, restaurants, apres-ski, and other recreational facilities in vicinity; shops; travel instructions. Special industry edition available with more comprehensive information for $395. Arrangement: Geographical within four regions–West, North Central, South, and Northeast. Indexes: Geographical.

★10829★ YMCA Resident Camp Directory

Camping Programs
101 N Wacker Dr.
Chicago, IL 60606
Ph: (312)419-8418   Fax: (312)977-4809
Fr: 800-872-9622
URL: http://www.ymca.net/find_ymca_camps/

Updated weekly. Database covers: over 235 resident camps and conference and retreat centers operated by local YMCA associations in the United States. Entries include: Association name, camp name, address and phone of winter office, camp location and summer address and phone, name of director, seasons of operation, capacity; whether coed or restricted to boys or girls, or available for family and adult camping; special programs offered. Arrangement: Classified by type of camp (resident, family, conference centers).

HANDBOOKS AND MANUALS

★10830★ **Athlete's Guide to Career Planning**
Human Kinetics Publishers
PO Box 5076
Champaign, IL 61825-5076
Ph: (217)351-5076   Fax: (217)351-1549
Fr: 800-747-4457
E-mail: info@hkusa.com
URL: http://www.humankinetics.com/

Delight Champagne, Judy Chartrand, Steven Danish, and Shane M. Murphy. 1997. $17.95 (paper). 240 pages.

★10831★ **Careers for Health Nuts and Others Who Like to Stay Fit**
The McGraw-Hill Companies
PO Box 182604
Columbus, OH 43272
Fax: (614)759-3749   Fr: 877-883-5524
E-mail: customer.service@mcgraw-hill.com
URL: http://www.mcgraw-hill.com

Blythe Camenson. Second edition, 2005. $13.95 (paper). 208 pages.

★10832★ **Careers in Travel, Tourism, and Hospitality**
The McGraw-Hill Companies
PO Box 182604
Columbus, OH 43272
Fax: (614)759-3749   Fr: 877-883-5524
E-mail: customer.service@mcgraw-hill.com
URL: http://www.mcgraw-hill.com

Marjorie Eberts, Linda Brothers, and Ann Gisler. Second edition, 2005. $15.95 (paper). 224 pages.

★10833★ **Great Careers for People Who Like Being Outdoors**
UXL
27500 Drake Rd.
Farmington Hills, MI 48331-3535
Ph: (248)699-GALE   Fax: 800-414-5043
Fr: 800-877-GALE
E-mail: galeord@cengage.com
URL: http://gale.cengage.com/uxl/

Helen Mason. Volume 6. 1993. $40.00. 48 pages. Part of Career Connections Series 1 Series.

★10834★ **Guiding Your Entry into the Hospitality, Recreation and Tourism Mega-Profession**
Prentice Hall PTR
1 Lake St.
Upper Saddle River, NJ 07458
Ph: (201)236-7000   Fax: 800-445-6991
Fr: 800-428-5331
URL: http://www.phptr.com/index.asp?rl=1

Jack B. Samuels and Reginald Foucar-Szocki. 1998. $60.80. 296 pages.

★10835★ **How to Get a Job with a Cruise Line**
Ticket to Adventure, Inc.
PO Box 41005
St. Petersburg, FL 33743-1005
Ph: (727)822-5029   Fax: (727)821-3409
Fr: 800-929-7447

Mary Fallon Miller. Fifth edition, 2001. $16.95 (paper). 352 pages. Explores jobs with cruise ships, describing duties, responsibilities, benefits, and training. Lists cruise ship lines and schools offering cruise line training. Offers job hunting advice.

★10836★ **It's More Than Just Making Them Sweat: A Career Training Guide for Personal Fitness Trainers**
Robert D. Reed Publishers
PO Box 1992
Bandon, OR 97411
Ph: (541)347-9882   Fax: (541)347-9883
E-mail: 4bobreed@msn.com
URL: http://www.rdrpublishers.com/home.html

Ed Thornton. 2001 (paper). $11.95. 120 pages.

★10837★ **Opportunities in Child Care Careers**
The McGraw-Hill Companies
PO Box 182604
Columbus, OH 43272
Fax: (614)759-3749   Fr: 877-883-5524
E-mail: customer.service@mcgraw-hill.com
URL: http://www.mcgraw-hill.com

Renee Wittenberg. 2006. $13.95 (paper). 160 pages. Discusses various job opportunities and how to secure a position. Illustrated.

★10838★ **Opportunities in Sports and Fitness Careers**
The McGraw-Hill Companies
PO Box 182604
Columbus, OH 43272
Fax: (614)759-3749   Fr: 877-883-5524
E-mail: customer.service@mcgraw-hill.com
URL: http://www.mcgraw-hill.com

William Ray Heitzmann. $12.95. 160 pages. 2003. E-book, netLibrary.

★10839★ **Opportunities in Travel Careers**
The McGraw-Hill Companies
PO Box 182604
Columbus, OH 43272
Fax: (614)759-3749   Fr: 877-883-5524
E-mail: customer.service@mcgraw-hill.com
URL: http://www.mcgraw-hill.com

Robert Scott Milne. Second edition, 2003. $14.95 (paper). 141 pages. Discusses what the jobs are and where to find them in airlines, shipping lines, and railroads. Discusses related opportunities in hotels, motels, resorts, travel agencies, public relation firms, and recreation departments. Illustrated.

TRADESHOWS

★10840★ **IDEA World Fitness and Personal Trainer Convention**
IDEA, Health & Fitness Association
10455 Pacific Center Ct.
San Diego, CA 92121-4339
Ph: (858)535-8979   Fax: (858)535-8234
Fr: 800-999-4332
E-mail: contact@ideafit.com
URL: http://www.ideafit.com

Annual. **Primary Exhibits:** Aerobic clothing and footwear, exercise products, equipment companies, related services.

★10841★ **North Carolina Recreation and Park Society Conference**
North Carolina Recreation and Park Society
883 Washington St.
Raleigh, NC 27605
Ph: (919)832-5868   Fax: (919)832-3323
E-mail: ncrps@bellsouth.net
URL: http://www.ncrps.org

Annual. **Primary Exhibits:** Parks and recreation equipment, supplies, and services.

OTHER SOURCES

★10842★ **American Association for Physical Activity and Recreation (AAPAR)**
1900 Association Dr.
Reston, VA 20191-1598
Ph: (703)476-3400   Fax: (703)476-9527
Fr: 800-213-7193
E-mail: aapar@aahperd.org
URL: http://www.aahperd.org/aapar

Description: Aims to promote and support education, physical activity, and recreation by developing quality programming and professional training; providing leadership opportunities; disseminating guidelines and standards; enhancing public understanding of the importance of leisure and recreation in maintaining a creative and healthy lifestyle. Goals and objectives are to serve as a forum for professionals, students and organizations to educate and exchange information and ideas on physical activity and recreation services; develop and promote professional standards for education, physical activity and recreation services; increase public awareness, understanding, appreciation, and support for lifelong education, physical activity and recreation services; encourage professional training for all with an interest in education, leisure and recreation services; advance, encourage, conduct and publish scientific knowledge and research in the field of education, physical activity, and recreation services.

★10843★ American Camp Association (ACA)

5000 State Rd. 67 N
Martinsville, IN 46151-7902
Ph: (765)342-8456   Fax: (765)342-2065
Fr: 800-428-CAMP
E-mail: psmith@acacamps.org
URL: http://www.acacamps.org

Description: Camp owners, directors, program directors, businesses, and students interested in resident and day camp programming for youth and adults. Conducts camp standards. Offers educational programs in areas of administration, staffing, child development, promotion, and programming.

★10844★ American Council on Exercise (ACE)

4851 Paramount Dr.
San Diego, CA 92123
Ph: (858)279-8227   Fax: (858)279-8064
Fr: 888-825-3636
E-mail: support@acefitness.org
URL: http://www.acefitness.org

Description: Promotes the benefits of physical activity and protects consumers against unsafe and ineffective fitness products and instruction. Sponsors university-based exercise science research and testing that targets fitness products and trends. Sets standards for fitness professionals.

★10845★ American Senior Fitness Association (SFA)

PO Box 2575
New Smyrna Beach, FL 32170
Ph: (386)423-6634   Fax: (386)427-0613
Fr: 800-243-1478
E-mail: sfa@ucnsb.net
URL: http://www.seniorfitness.net

Description: Promotes excellence in older adult fitness. Provides comprehensive training, recognized certification, professional resources and member support for fitness professionals who serve older adults. Offers senior fitness specialist courses for colleges and universities.

★10846★ Employee Services Management Association (ESM)

568 Spring Rd., Ste. D
Elmhurst, IL 60126-3896
Ph: (630)559-0020   Fax: (630)559-0025
E-mail: esmahq@esmassn.org
URL: http://www.esmassn.org

Description: Corporations and governmental agencies that sponsor recreation, fitness, and service programs for their employees;

associate members are manufacturers and suppliers in the employee recreation market and distributors of consumer products and services. Serves as an information resource network for members nationwide. Implements and maintains a diverse range of employee services; believes that employee services, as practical solutions to work/life issues, are essential to sound business management. Conducts programs that improves relations between employees and management, increases overall productivity, boosts morale, and reduces absenteeism and turnover. Covers the 10 Components of a Well-Rounded Employee Services Program such as employee stores, convenience services, recognition programs, recreation programs, travel services, and special events.

★10847★ Human Services Occupations

Delphi Productions
3159 6th St.
Boulder, CO 80304
Ph: (303)443-2100   Fax: (303)443-4022
Fr: 888-443-2400
E-mail: support@delphivideo.com
URL: http://www.delphivideo.com

$95.00. 50 minutes. Part of the Careers for the 21st Century Video Library.

★10848★ IDEA Health and Fitness Association

10455 Pacific Center Ct.
San Diego, CA 92121-3773
Ph: (858)535-8979   Fax: (858)535-8234
Fr: 800-999-IDEA
E-mail: contact@ideafit.com
URL: http://www.ideafit.com

Purpose: Provides continuing education for fitness professionals including; fitness instructors, personal trainers, program directors, and club/studio owners. **Activities:** Offers workshops for continuing education credits.

★10849★ International Council of Cruise Lines (ICCL)

2111 Wilson Blvd., 8th Fl.
Arlington, VA 22201
Ph: (703)522-8463   Fax: (703)522-3811
Fr: 800-595-9338
E-mail: info@cruising.org
URL: http://www.cruising.org

Description: Represents cruise ship operators. Aims to participate in the regulatory and policy development process and promote all measures that foster a safe, secure and healthy cruise ship environment. Advocates industry positions to key domestic and inter-

national regulatory organizations, policymakers and other industry partners.

★10850★ National Association for Girls and Women in Sport (NAGWS)

1900 Association Dr.
Reston, VA 20191-1598
Ph: (703)476-3400   Fax: (703)476-4566
Fr: 800-213-7193
E-mail: nagws@aahperd.org
URL: http://www.aahperd.org/nagws

Description: Represents teachers, coaches, athletic trainers, officials, athletic administrators, and students. Has 4 main structures: Advocacy Coaching Enhancement; Minority Representation; Professional Development Publications, and Student Representation. Supports and fosters the development of quality sports programs that will enrich the lives of all participants. Holds training sessions for leadership development. Conducts research programs.

★10851★ National Association of Recreation Resource Planners (NARRP)

PO Box 221
Marienville, PA 16239
Ph: (814)927-8212   Fax: (814)927-6659
E-mail: info@narrp.org
URL: http://www.narrp.org

Description: Individuals working in state and federal recreation and resource agencies and private organizations who are responsible for recreation planning. Seeks to increase the professional expertise of membership and to coordinate positions with respect to federal planning requirements and policy and funding issues.

★10852★ National Forest Recreation Association (NFRA)

PO Box 488
Woodlake, CA 93286
Ph: (559)564-2365   Fax: (559)564-2048
E-mail: info@nfra.org
URL: http://www.nfra.org

Description: Owners and operators of resorts, winter sports areas, marinas, campgrounds, stores, river trip outfitters, packer-outfitters, restaurants, and motels located on or adjacent to federal land. Participates in trade and public relations matters that is of interest to members, including legislation and relationships with U.S. agencies; state and local officials in matters of taxation, insurance, finance, health, and building requirements; and employment.

Recreational Therapists

PLACEMENT AND JOB REFERRAL SERVICES

★10853★ Special Recreation for disABLED International (SRDI)

701 Oaknoll Dr.
Iowa City, IA 52246-5168
Ph: (319)466-3192   Fax: (319)351-6772
E-mail: john-nesbitt@uiowa.edu
URL: http://www.globalvisionproject.org

Description: Seeks to serve and advocate special and therapeutic play and recreation for infants, children, youth, adults, and seniors throughout the world. Services include advisory and consultation, awards, employment information, professional education, public education, publishing, research, resource information and referral, technical assistance on programs and management methods, and an international library. Does international service work to: collect and disseminate international information on special recreation services for disabled persons, special recreation programs, and personnel training; conduct, provide, and support international exchange of technical, professional, and general information on special recreation for the disabled; cooperate with both governmental and voluntary organizations on national and international levels. Offers career guidance and placement service. Maintains speakers' bureau; compiles statistics.

EMPLOYER DIRECTORIES AND NETWORKING LISTS

★10854★ AHA Guide to the Health Care Field

American Hospital Association
1 N Franklin
Chicago, IL 60606
Ph: (312)422-2050   Fax: (312)422-4700
Fr: 800-424-4301

Annual, August. Covers hospitals, networks, multi-health care systems, freestanding am-
bulatory surgery centers, psychiatric facilities, long-term care facilities, substance abuse programs, and other health-related organizations. Entries include: For hospitals–Facility name, address, phone, administrator's name, number of beds, facilities and services, number of employees, expenses, other statistics. For other organizations–Name, address, phone, fax, name and title of contact. Arrangement: Geographical. Indexes: Hospital name.

★10855★ Directory of Hospital Personnel

Grey House Publishing
185 Millerton Rd.
PO Box 860
Millerton, NY 12546
Ph: (518)789-8700   Fax: (518)789-0556
Fr: 800-562-2139
URL: http://www.greyhouse.com/hospital_personnel.htm

Annual. $325.00 for print product; $545.00 for online database subscription; $650.00 for online database subscription and print product combined. Covers 200,000 executives at 7,000 U.S. hospitals. Entries include: Name of hospital, address, phone; number of beds; type and JCAHO status of hospital; names and titles of key department heads and staff; medical and nursing school affiliations; number of residents, interns, and nursing students. Arrangement: Geographical. Indexes: Hospital name, personnel, hospital size.

★10856★ Hospital Blue Book

Billian Publishing Inc./Transworld Publishing Inc.
2100 Powers Ferry Rd. SE
Atlanta, GA 30339
Ph: (770)955-5656   Fax: (770)952-0669
Fr: 800-533-8484
E-mail: blu-book@billian.com

2005. $300.00 for individuals. Covers more than 6,687 hospitals; some listings also appear in a separate southern edition of this publication. Entries include: Name of hospital, accreditation, mailing address, phone, fax, number of beds, type of facility (nonprofit, general, state, etc.); list of administrative personnel and chiefs of medical services,
with specific titles. Arrangement: Geographical.

★10857★ Medical and Health Information Directory

Gale, Cengage Learning
27500 Drake Rd.
Farmington Hills, MI 48331-3535
Ph: (248)699-4253   Fax: (248)699-8065
Fr: 800-877-4253
E-mail: businessproducts@gale.com
URL: http://www.gale.com

Annual; latest edition 20th, July 2007. $375.00/volume. Covers in Volume 1, more than 26,500 medical and health oriented associations, organizations, institutions, and government agencies, including health maintenance organizations (HMOs), preferred provider organizations (PPOs), insurance companies, pharmaceutical companies, research centers, and medical and allied health schools. In Volume 2, over 12,000 medical book publishers; medical periodicals, directories, audiovisual producers and services, medical libraries and information centers, electronic resources, and health-related internet search engines. In Volume 3, more than 35,500 clinics, treatment centers, care programs, and counseling/diagnostic services for 34 subject areas. Entries include: Institution, service, or firm name, address, phone, fax, email and URL; many include names of key personnel and, when pertinent, descriptive annotations. Volume 3 was formerly listed separately as Health Services Directory. Arrangement: Classified by organization activity, service, etc. Indexes: Each volume has a complete alphabetical name and keyword index.

HANDBOOKS AND MANUALS

★10858★ Careers in Health Care

The McGraw-Hill Companies
PO Box 182604
Columbus, OH 43272
Fax: (614)759-3749   Fr: 877-883-5524
E-mail: customer.service@mcgraw-hill.com

URL: http://www.mcgraw-hill.com

Barbara M. Swanson. Fifth edition, 2005. $15.95 (paper). 192 pages. Describes job duties, work settings, salaries, licensing and certification requirements, educational preparation, and future outlook. Gives ideas on how to secure a job.

★10859★ Careers in Social and Rehabilitation Services

The McGraw-Hill Companies
PO Box 182604
Columbus, OH 43272
Fax: (614)759-3749   Fr: 877-883-5524
E-mail: customer.service@mcgraw-hill.com
URL: http://www.mcgraw-hill.com

Geraldine O. Garner. 2001. $19.95; 14.95 (paper). 128 pages.

★10860★ Opportunities in Gerontology and Aging Services Careers

The McGraw-Hill Companies
PO Box 182604
Columbus, OH 43272
Fax: (614)759-3749   Fr: 877-883-5524
E-mail: customer.service@mcgraw-hill.com
URL: http://www.mcgraw-hill.com

Ellen Williams. Second edition, 2002. $12.95 (paper). 160 pages. Covers jobs in community, health and medical programs, financial, legal, residential, travel and tourism, and counseling, and how to go after them. Includes bibliography and illustrations.

★10861★ Opportunities in Health and Medical Careers

The McGraw-Hill Companies
PO Box 182604
Columbus, OH 43272
Fax: (614)759-3749   Fr: 877-883-5524
E-mail: customer.service@mcgraw-hill.com
URL: http://www.mcgraw-hill.com

I. Donald Snook, Jr. and Leo D'Orazio. 2004. $13.95 (paper). 157 pages. Covers the full range of medical and health occupations. Illustrated.

★10862★ Real People Working in the Helping Professions

The McGraw-Hill Companies
PO Box 182604
Columbus, OH 43272
Fax: (614)759-3749   Fr: 877-883-5524
E-mail: customer.service@mcgraw-hill.com
URL: http://www.mcgraw-hill.com

Blythe Camenson, Jan Goldberg. 1997. $12.95 (paper). 192 pages. Interviews and profiles of working professionals capture a range of opportunities in this field.

★10863★ Resumes for Health and Medical Careers

The McGraw-Hill Companies
PO Box 182604
Columbus, OH 43272
Fax: (614)759-3749   Fr: 877-883-5524
E-mail: customer.service@mcgraw-hill.com

URL: http://www.mcgraw-hill.com

Third edition, 2003. $11.95 (paper). 160 pages.

EMPLOYMENT AGENCIES AND SEARCH FIRMS

★10864★ Cross Country TravCorps

6551 Park of Commerce Blvd.
Boca Raton, FL 33487-8247
Fax: (562)998-8533   Fr: 800-530-6125
URL: http://www.crosscountrytravcorps.com

Places traveling nurses in assignments nationwide.

★10865★ Harper Associates

3100 NW Hwy., Ste. 240
Farmington Hills, MI 48334
Ph: (248)932-1170   Fax: (248)932-1214
E-mail: info@harperjobs.com
URL: http://www.harperjobs.com

Executive search firm and employment agency.

★10866★ Professional Placement Associates, Inc.

287 Bowman Ave., Ste. 309
Purchase, NY 10577-2517
Ph: (914)251-1000   Fax: (914)251-1055
E-mail: careers@ppasearch.com
URL: http://www.ppasearch.com

Executive search firm specializing in the health and medical field.

ONLINE JOB SOURCES AND SERVICES

★10867★ Medhunters.com

Fr: 800-664-0278
E-mail: info@medhunters.com
URL: http://www.medhunters.com

Description: Career search site for jobs in all health care specialties; educational resources; visa and licensing information for relocation; interesting articles; relocation tools; links to professional organizations and general resources.

★10868★ ProHealthJobs

Fr: 800-796-1738
E-mail: Info@prohealthedujobs.com
URL: http://www.prohealthjobs.com

Description: Career resources site for the medical and health care field. Lists professional opportunities, product information, continuing education and open positions.

OTHER SOURCES

★10869★ American Association for Physical Activity and Recreation (AAPAR)

1900 Association Dr.
Reston, VA 20191-1598
Ph: (703)476-3400   Fax: (703)476-9527
Fr: 800-213-7193
E-mail: aapar@aahperd.org
URL: http://www.aahperd.org/aapar

Description: Aims to promote and support education, physical activity, and recreation by developing quality programming and professional training; providing leadership opportunities; disseminating guidelines and standards; enhancing public understanding of the importance of leisure and recreation in maintaining a creative and healthy lifestyle. Goals and objectives are to serve as a forum for professionals, students and organizations to educate and exchange information and ideas on physical activity and recreation services; develop and promote professional standards for education, physical activity and recreation services; increase public awareness, understanding, appreciation, and support for lifelong education, physical activity and recreation services; encourage professional training for all with an interest in education, leisure and recreation services; advance, encourage, conduct and publish scientific knowledge and research in the field of education, physical activity, and recreation services.

★10870★ American Health Care Association (AHCA)

1201 L St. NW
Washington, DC 20005
Ph: (202)842-4444   Fax: (202)842-3860
E-mail: hr@ahca.org
URL: http://www.ahca.org

Description: Federation of state associations of long-term health care facilities. Promotes standards for professionals in long-term health care delivery and quality care for patients and residents in a safe environment. Focuses on issues of availability, quality, affordability, and fair payment. Operates as liaison with governmental agencies, Congress, and professional associations. Compiles statistics.

★10871★ American Kinesiotherapy Association (AKTA)

118 College Dr., No. 5142
Hattiesburg, MS 39406
Fr: 800-296-AKTA
E-mail: info@akta.org
URL: http://www.akta.org

Members: Professional society of kinesiotherapists, associate and student members with interest in therapeutic exercise and education. Kinesiotherapy is the application of scientifically-based exercise principles adapted to enhance the strength, endurance and mobility of individuals with functional limitations of those requiring extended physical reconditioning. Seeks to serve the interest of members and represent the profession to the public through the promotion of continuing competency and continuing educational opportunities.

★10872★ **American Therapeutic Recreation Association (ATRA)**

1414 Prince St., Ste. 204
Alexandria, VA 22314
Ph: (703)683-9420   Fax: (703)683-9431
E-mail: atra@atra-tr.org
URL: http://www.atra-tr.org/atra.htm

Members: Therapeutic recreation professionals and students; interested others. **Purpose:** Promotes the use of therapeutic recreation in hospitals, mental rehabilitation centers, physical rehabilitation centers, senior citizen treatment centers, and other public health facilities. **Activities:** Conducts discussions on certification, legislative and regulatory concerns that affect the industry. Sponsors seminars and workshops; conducts research.

★10873★ **Association on Higher Education and Disability (AHEAD)**

107 Commerce Center Dr., Ste. 204
Huntersville, NC 28078
Ph: (704)947-7779   Fax: (704)948-7779
E-mail: ahead@ahead.org
URL: http://www.ahead.org

Description: Individuals interested in promoting the equal rights and opportunities of disabled postsecondary students, staff, faculty, and graduates. Provides an exchange of communication for those professionally involved with disabled students; collects, evaluates, and disseminates information; encourages and supports legislation for the benefit of disabled students. Conducts surveys on issues pertinent to college students with disabilities; offers resource referral system and employment exchange for positions in disability student services. Conducts research programs; compiles statistics.

★10874★ **Child Life Council (CLC)**

11820 Parklawn Dr., Ste. 240
Rockville, MD 20852-2529
Ph: (301)881-7090   Fax: (301)881-7092
Fr: 800-CLC-4515
E-mail: clcstaff@childlife.org
URL: http://www.childlife.org

Members: Professional organization representing child life personnel, patient activities specialists, and students in the field. **Purpose:** Promotes psychological well-being

and optimum development of children, adolescents, and their families in health care settings. **Activities:** Works to minimize the stress and anxiety of illness and hospitalization. Addresses professional issues such as program standards, competencies, and core curriculum. Provides resources and conducts research and educational programs. Offers a Job Bank Service listing employment openings.

★10875★ **Exploring Health Occupations**

Cambridge Educational
PO Box 2053
Princeton, NJ 08543-2053
Ph: 800-257-5126   Fax: (609)671-0266
Fr: 800-468-4227
E-mail: custserv@films.com
URL: http://www.cambridgeeducational.com

VHS and DVD. $159.90. 1999. Two-part series provides a detailed view of the field of medical technicians and technologists, EMTs, nurses, therapists, and assistants.

★10876★ **Health Assessment & Treating Occupations**

Delphi Productions
3159 6th St.
Boulder, CO 80304
Ph: (303)443-2100   Fax: (303)443-4022
Fr: 888-443-2400
E-mail: support@delphivideo.com
URL: http://www.delphivideo.com

$95.00. 50 minutes. Part of the Careers for the 21st Century Video Library.

★10877★ **Health Service Occupations**

Delphi Productions
3159 6th St.
Boulder, CO 80304
Ph: (303)443-2100   Fax: (303)443-4022
Fr: 888-443-2400
E-mail: support@delphivideo.com
URL: http://www.delphivideo.com

$95.00. 50 minutes. Part of the Careers for the 21st Century Video Library.

★10878★ **Medicine & Related Occupations**

Delphi Productions
3159 6th St.
Boulder, CO 80304
Ph: (303)443-2100   Fax: (303)443-4022
Fr: 888-443-2400

E-mail: support@delphivideo.com
URL: http://www.delphivideo.com

$95.00. 45 minutes. Part of the Careers for the 21st Century Video Library.

★10879★ **National Council for Therapeutic Recreation Certification (NCTRC)**

7 Elmwood Dr.
New City, NY 10956
Ph: (845)639-1439   Fax: (845)639-1471
E-mail: nctrc@nctrc.org
URL: http://www.nctrc.org

Description: Objectives are to: establish standards for certification and recertification of individuals who work in the therapeutic recreation field; grant recognition to individuals who voluntarily apply and meet established standards; monitor adherence to standards by certified personnel.

★10880★ **National Rehabilitation Association (NRA)**

633 S Washington St.
Alexandria, VA 22314
Ph: (703)836-0850   Fax: (703)836-0848
E-mail: info@nationalrehab.org
URL: http://www.nationalrehab.org/website/index.html

Description: Provides opportunities through knowledge and diversity for professionals in the fields of rehabilitation of people with disabilities.

★10881★ **National Therapeutic Recreation Society (NTRS)**

22377 Belmont Ridge Rd.
Ashburn, VA 20148-4501
Ph: (703)858-0784   Fax: (703)858-0794
Fr: 800-626-6772
E-mail: ntrsnrpa@nrpa.org
URL: http://www.nrpa.org/content/default.aspx?documentId=530

Description: Serves as a branch of the National Recreation and Park Association. **Members:** Professionals, educators, and students involved in the provision of therapeutic recreation services for persons with disabilities in clinical and residential facilities and in the community. **Purpose:** Offers technical assistance services to agencies, institutions, and individuals.

Registered Nurses

SOURCES OF HELP-WANTED ADS

★10882★ AANA Journal

AANA Publishing Inc.
222 South Prospect Ave.
Park Ridge, IL 60068
Ph: (847)692-7050   Fax: (847)518-0938
URL: http://www.aana.com

Bimonthly. $45.00/year for individuals; $10.00 for single issue. Nursing and anesthesia journal.

★10883★ AAOHN Journal

SLACK Inc.
6900 Grove Rd.
Thorofare, NJ 08086-9447
Ph: (856)848-1000   Fax: (856)853-5991
E-mail: aaohn@slackinc.com
URL: http://www.aaohnjournal.com

Monthly. $99.00/year for individuals, U.S. Official journal of the American Association of Occupational Health Nurses.

★10884★ AAOHN News

American Association of Occupational Health Nurses Inc.
2920 Brandywine Rd., Ste. 100
Atlanta, GA 30341
Ph: (770)455-7757   Fax: (770)455-7271
URL: http://www.aaohn.org/member_services/newsletter/index.cfm

Description: Monthly. Covers Association events as well as trends and legislation affecting occupational and enivornmental health nursing. Recurring features include news of research, a calendar of events, reports of meetings, news of educational opportunities, job listings, notices of publications available, resources for career-building, briefs on governmental issues concerning occupational and environment health, and a President's column.

★10885★ ADVANCE for Nurse Practitioners

Merion Publications Inc.
2900 Horizon Dr.
PO Box 61556
King of Prussia, PA 19406
Ph: (610)278-1400   Fr: 800-355-5627
URL: http://nurse-practition-ers.advanceweb.com/main.aspx

Monthly. For practicing nurse practitioner students with senior status.

★10886★ Advances in Nursing Science (ANS)

Lippincott Williams & Wilkins
530 Walnut St.
Philadelphia, PA 19106-3621
Ph: (215)521-8300   Fax: (215)521-8902
Fr: 800-638-3030
URL: http://www.lww.com/product/?0161-9268

Quarterly. $97.91/year for individuals, U.S.; $272.96/year for institutions, U.S.; $52.94/year for U.S., in-training; $145.94/year for individuals, international; $320.94/year for institutions, international. Academic medical journal focusing on nursing research and education.

★10887★ American Family Physician

American Academy of Family Physicians
11400 Tomahawk Creek Pkwy.
PO Box 11210
Leawood, KS 66211-2672
Ph: (913)906-6000   Fax: (913)906-6010
Fr: 800-274-2237
E-mail: afpedit@aafp.org
URL: http://www.aafp.org/afp

Semimonthly. $120.00/year for individuals, U.S.; $200.00/year for out of country, individuals; $160.00/year for Canada, individuals; $160.00/year for institutions, U.S.; $200.00/year for institutions, Canada; $240.00/year for institutions, foreign countries; $68.00/year for students, medical; $108.00/year for students, medical; $148.00/year for students, medical; $11.00 for single issue, six copies. Peer reviewed clinical journal for family physicians and others in primary care. Review articles detail the latest diagnostic and therapeutic techniques in the medical field. Department features in each issue include 'Tips from other Journals,' CME credit opportunities and course calendar.

★10888★ American Journal of Medicine

Excerpta Medica Inc.
685 US-202
Bridgewater, NJ 08807
Ph: (908)547-2100   Fax: (908)547-2200
URL: http://www.amjmed.com/

Monthly. $336.00/year for individuals, international; $131.00/year for U.S. and Canada; $81.00/year for students, international; $76.00/year for students, in U.S. Medical journal.

★10889★ American Journal of Nursing

American Journal of Nursing
c/o Lippincott, Williams & Wilkins
530 Walnut St.
Philadelphia, PA 19106-3621
Ph: (215)521-8300   Fax: (215)521-8902
Fr: 800-627-0484
URL: http://www.nursingcenter.com

Monthly. $32.90/year for individuals; $159.00/year for institutions; $69.00/year for individuals, other countries; $199.00/year for institutions, other countries. Journal for staff nurses, nurse managers, and clinical nurse specialists. Focuses on patient care in hospitals, hospital ICUs and homes. Provides news coverage of health care from the nursing perspective.

★10890★ The American Nurse

American Nurses Association
8515 Georgia Ave., Ste. 400
Silver Spring, MD 20910
Ph: (301)628-5000   Fax: (301)628-5001
Fr: 800-274-4262
E-mail: adsales@ana.org
URL: http://nursingworld.org/tan/

Monthly. Newspaper (tabloid) for the nursing profession.

★10891★ AORN Journal

AORN Inc.
2170 S Parker Rd., Ste. 300
Denver, CO 80231
Ph: (303)755-6304   Fax: (303)750-3212
Fr: 800-755-2676
URL: http://www.aornjournal.org/authorinfo

Monthly. $113.00/year for individuals;
$151.00/year for individuals, Canada;
$151.00/year for other countries; $151.00/
year for individuals, Mexico. Journal for
perioperative nurses.

★10892★ Applied Nursing Research

Mountain Association for Community
  Economic Development
433 Chestnut St.
Berea, KY 40403
Ph: (859)986-2373   Fax: (859)986-1299
URL: http://www.elsevier.com/wps/find/jour-
naldescription.cws_home

Quarterly. $298.00/year for institutions, out-
side U.S; $88.00/year for individuals, inside
U.S.; $246.00/year for institutions, inside
U.S.; $125.00/year for individuals, outside
U.S. Nursing journal publishing peer-reviewed research findings for clinical applications.

★10893★ Cancer Nursing

Lippincott Williams & Wilkins
530 Walnut St.
Philadelphia, PA 19106-3621
Ph: (215)521-8300   Fax: (215)521-8902
Fr: 800-638-3030
E-mail: bguthy@lww.com
URL: http://www.cancernursingonline.com/

Bimonthly. $94.43/year for individuals;
$243.48/year for institutions; $49.48/year for
other countries, in-training; $167.46/year for
individuals; $284.46/year for institutions.
Medical journal covering problems arising in
the care and support of cancer patients.

**★10894★ Clinical Effectiveness in
  Nursing**

Mosby Inc.
11830 Westline Industrial Dr.
St. Louis, MO 63146
Ph: (314)872-8370   Fax: (314)432-1380
Fr: 800-325-4177
URL: http://www.us.elsevierhealth.com/
product.jsp?isbn=13619004

Quarterly. $70.00/year for individuals;
$316.00/year for institutions. Journal for
nurses demonstrating the impact of nursing
on patients and clients; addresses the effects of interventions on patients' well-being.

★10895★ Clinical Nurse Specialist

Lippincott Williams & Wilkins
530 Walnut St.
Philadelphia, PA 19106-3621
Ph: (215)521-8300   Fax: (215)521-8902
Fr: 800-638-3030
URL: http://www.cns-journal.com

Bimonthly. $97.91/year for individuals, U.S.;
$228.96/year for institutions, U.S.; $52.96/

year for other countries, U.S. in-training:;
$177.94/year for individuals, international;
$307.94/year for institutions, international in-
training. Nursing journal.

★10896★ Critical Care Medicine

Society of Critical Care Medicine
701 Lee St., Ste. 200
Des Plaines, IL 60016
Ph: (847)827-6869   Fax: (847)827-6886
URL: http://www.ccmjournal.com/

Monthly. $342.00/year for individuals, U.S.;
$549.00/year for institutions, U.S.; $440.00/
year for individuals, foreign; $649.00/year for
institutions, international; $319.00/year for
institutions, in-training. Interdisciplinary journal for ICU and CCU specialists.

★10897★ Critical Care Nurse

Critical Care Nurse
101 Columbia
Aliso Viejo, CA 92656
Ph: (949)448-7370   Fr: 800-899-2273
URL: http://ccn.aacnjournals.org

Bimonthly. Nursing journal.

★10898★ Dialysis & Transplantation

Creative Age Publications Inc.
7628 Densmore Ave.
Van Nuys, CA 91406-2042
Ph: (818)782-7328   Fax: (818)782-7450
Fr: 800-442-5667
URL: http://www.eneph.com

Monthly. $22.00/year for individuals, 12 is-
sues; $26.00/year for out of country; $43.00/
year for Canada and Mexico, by mail;
$82.00/year for other countries. Multi-disci-
plinary, peer-reviewed journal on clinical
applications in dialysis, transplantation and
nephrology for renal-care teams.

★10899★ Emergency Medical Services

Cygnus Business Media
1233 Janesville Ave.
Fort Atkinson, WI 53538
Fr: 800-547-7377
URL: http://www.emsmagazine.com

Monthly. Magazine covering emergency
care, rescue and transportation.

★10900★ EndoNurse

Virgo Publishing Inc.
PO Box 40079
Phoenix, AZ 85067-0079
Ph: (480)990-1101   Fax: (480)990-0819
URL: http://endonurse.com/

Bimonthly. $34.95/year in U.S.; $54.95/year
for Canada; $64.95/year for elsewhere. Mag-
azine covering endoscopic nursing.

★10901★ Fertility and Sterility

The American Society for Reproductive
  Medicine
1209 Montgomery Hwy.
Birmingham, AL 35216-2809
Ph: (205)978-5000   Fax: (205)978-5005

URL: http://www.asrm.org

Monthly. Medical journal covering all aspects
of reproductive medicine.

★10902★ Geriatric Nursing

Mosby Inc.
10801 Executive Center Dr., Ste. 509
Little Rock, AR 72211
Ph: (501)223-5165   Fax: (501)223-0519
URL: http://journals.elsevierhealth.com/peri-
odicals/ymgn

Bimonthly. $63.00/year for individuals;
$113.00/year for individuals, Canada;
$113.00/year for individuals, Mexico;
$113.00/year for individuals, international.
Magazine for nurses in geriatric and gerontologic nursing practice, the primary professional providers of care for the aging. Provides news on issues affecting elders and
clinical information on techniques and procedures.

★10903★ Health Progress

Catholic Health Association of the United
  States
4455 Woodson Rd.
St. Louis, MO 63134-3797
Ph: (314)427-2500
URL: http://www.chausa.org

Bimonthly. $50.00/year for members;
$61.00/year for others; $61.00/year for out of
country, foreign and Canada; $3.00/year for
nonmembers, special section reprints;
$10.00/year for nonmembers, single copy.
Magazine for administrative-level and other
managerial personnel in Catholic healthcare
and related organizations. Featured are articles on management concepts, legislative
and regulatory trends, and theological, sociological, ethical, legal, and technical issues.

★10904★ Heart and Lung

Mosby
1600 John F. Kennedy Blvd., Ste. 1800
Philadelphia, PA 19103-2899
Ph: (215)239-3276   Fax: (215)239-3286
URL: http://www.elsevier.com/wps/find/jour-
naleditorialboard.cws_h

Bimonthly. $111.00/year for individuals;
$321.00/year for institutions; $34.00/year for
students; $99.00/year for other countries;
$50.00/year for students, other countries;
$289.00/year for institutions, other countries.
Journal offering articles prepared by nurse
and physician members of the critical care
team, recognizing the nurse's role in the care
and management of major organ-system
conditions in critically ill patients.

★10905★ Home Healthcare Nurse

Lippincott Williams & Wilkins
530 Walnut St.
Philadelphia, PA 19106-3621
Ph: (215)521-8300   Fax: (215)521-8902
Fr: 800-638-3030
URL: http://
www.homehealthcarenurseonline.com/

Monthly. $56.43/year for individuals, U.S.; $202.95/year for institutions, U.S.; $126.46/year for individuals, other countries; $252.95/year for institutions, other countries; $43.48/year for U.S., in-training. Magazine for the practicing professional nurse working in the home health, community health, and public health areas.

★10906★ HomeCare Magazine

Miramar Communications Inc.
23805 Stuart Ranch Rd., Ste. 235
PO Box 8987
Malibu, CA 90265-8987
Ph: (310)317-4522   Fax: (310)317-9644
Fr: 800-543-4116
URL: http://www.homecaremag.com

Monthly. Free, in US; $135.00/year for Canada; $150.00/year for two years, Canada; $250.00/year for other countries; $250.00/year for two years, other countries. Magazine serving home medical equipment suppliers, including independent and chain centers specializing in home care, pharmacies or chain drug stores with home care products, and joint-ventured hospital home health care businesses. Contains industry news and new product launches and marketing strategies.

★10907★ Hospitals & Health Networks

Health Forum L.L.C.
1 N Franklin, 29th Fl.
Chicago, IL 60606
Ph: (312)893-6800   Fax: (312)422-4506
Fr: 800-821-2039
URL: http://www.hhnmag.com

Weekly. Publication covering the health care industry.

★10908★ The IHS Primary Care Provider

Indian Health Service (HQ)
The Reyes Bldg.
801 Thompson Ave., Ste. 400
Rockville, MD 20852-1627
URL: http://www.ihs.gov/PublicInfo/Publications/HealthProvider/Pr

Monthly. Journal for health care professionals, physicians, nurses, pharmacists, dentists, and dietitians.

★10909★ Imprint

National Student Nurses' Association Inc.
45 Main St., Ste. 606
Brooklyn, NY 11201
Ph: (718)210-0705   Fax: (718)210-7010
E-mail: nsna@nsna.org
URL: http://www.nsna.org/

Periodic. Magazine for nursing students, focusing on issues and trends in nursing.

★10910★ Intensive and Critical Care Nursing

Mosby Inc.
11830 Westline Industrial Dr.
St. Louis, MO 63146
Ph: (314)872-8370   Fax: (314)432-1380
Fr: 800-325-4177
URL: http://www.us.elsevierhealth.com/product.jsp?isbn=09643397&r

Bimonthly. $92.00/year for individuals, international; $422.00/year for institutions, international; $92.00/year for individuals; $422.00/year for institutions. Journal for nurses in intensive and critical care nursing.

★10911★ International Journal of Nursing Education Scholarship

Berkeley Electronic Press
2809 Telegraph Ave., Ste. 202
Berkeley, CA 94705
Ph: (510)665-1200   Fax: (510)665-1201
URL: http://www.bepress.com/ijnes

Semiannual. $525.00/year   corporate; $175.00/year academic. Journal that publishes original papers on nursing education issues and research.

★10912★ International Journal of Nursing Practice

Wiley-Blackwell
350 Main St. Commerce Pl.
Malden, MA 02148
Ph: (781)388-8200   Fax: (781)388-8210
Fr: 800-759-6120
URL: http://www.blackwellpublishing.com/journal.asp?ref=1322-7114

Bimonthly. $122.00/year for individuals, print and online; $759.00/year for institutions, print and premium online; $690.00/year for institutions, print and standard online; $656.00/year for institutions, premium online only; $469.00/year for institutions, other countries, print and premium online; $426.00/year for institutions, other countries, print and standard online; $405.00/year for institutions, other countries, premium online only; $311.00/year for institutions, print and premium online, Australia/New Zealand; $283.00/year for institutions, print and standard online, Australia/New Zealand; $269.00/year for institutions, premium online only, Australia/New Zealand. Journal publishing articles about advancing the international understanding and development of nursing, both as a profession and as an academic discipline.

★10913★ International Nursing Review

Wiley-Blackwell
350 Main St. Commerce Pl.
Malden, MA 02148
Ph: (781)388-8200   Fax: (781)388-8210
Fr: 800-759-6120
URL: http://www.blackwellpublishing.com/journal.asp?ref=0020-8132

Quarterly. $96.00/year for individuals, U.S. print and online; $77.00/year for individuals, print and online, Euro zone; $51.00/year for individuals, print and online, non Euro zone; $57.00/year for individuals, print and online,

rest of world; $277.00/year for institutions, print and premium online; $150.00/year for institutions, print and premium online, Euro zone; $150.00/year for institutions, print and premium online, non Euro zone; $165.00/year for institutions, print and premium online, rest of world; $239.00/year for institutions, premium online only; $129.00/year for institutions, premium online only, Euro zone. Journal focusing on current concerns and issues of modern day nursing and health care from an international perspective.

★10914★ Journal of Addictions Nursing

Taylor & Francis Group Journals
325 Chestnut St., Ste. 800
Philadelphia, PA 19106
Ph: (215)625-8900   Fax: (215)625-8914
Fr: 800-354-1420
URL: http://www.tandf.co.uk/journals/titles/10884602.asp

$443.00/year for institutions, print and online; $421.00/year for institutions, online only; $135.00/year for individuals. Journal for nursing addiction professionals.

★10915★ Journal of the Association of Nurses in AIDS Care

Mosby Inc.
11830 Westline Industrial Dr.
St. Louis, MO 63146
Ph: (314)872-8370   Fax: (314)432-1380
Fr: 800-325-4177
URL: http://www.elsevier.com/wps/find/journaldescription.cws_home

Bimonthly. $428.00/year for institutions; $119.00/year for individuals; $399.00/year for U.S. institutions; $90.00/year for U.S. individuals. Journal covering the spectrum of nursing issues in HIV/AIDS: education, treatment, prevention, research, practice, clinical issues, awareness, policies and program development.

★10916★ Journal of Clinical Nursing

Wiley-Blackwell
350 Main St. Commerce Pl.
Malden, MA 02148
Ph: (781)388-8200   Fax: (781)388-8210
Fr: 800-759-6120
E-mail: jcn@oxon.blackwellpublishing.com
URL: http://www.blackwellpublishing.com/journal.asp?ref=0962-1067

Monthly. $307.00/year for individuals, U.S. print and online; $167.00/year for students, U.S. print and online; $1,660.00/year for institutions, U.S. print and premium online; $1,509.00/year for institutions, U.S. print and standard online; $1,434.00/year for institutions, U.S. premium online only; $251.00/year for individuals, Europe print and online; $135.00/year for students, Europe print and online; $899.00/year for institutions, Europe print and premium online; $817.00/year for institutions, Europe print and standard online; $776.00/year for institutions, Europe premium online only. Journal focusing on all spheres of nursing and midwifery practice.

★10917★ The Journal of Continuing Education in Nursing

SLACK Inc.
6900 Grove Rd.
Thorofare, NJ 08086-9447
Ph: (856)848-1000   Fax: (856)853-5991
URL: http://www.slackinc.com/allied/jcen

Bimonthly. $99.00/year for individuals; $245.00/year for institutions; $168.00 for individuals, two years; $416.00 for institutions, two years; $32.00 for single issue. Journal for nurses involved in planning and implementing educational programs for the practitioner and others in patient care.

★10918★ Journal of Emergency Nursing

Mosby
1600 John F. Kennedy Blvd., Ste. 1800
Philadelphia, PA 19103-2899
Ph: (215)239-3276   Fax: (215)239-3286
URL: http://www.elsevier.com/wps/find/journaleditorialboard.cws_h

Bimonthly. $83.00/year for individuals; $299.00/year for institutions; $88.00/year for other countries, Includes air speed delivery; $256.00/year for institutions, other countries, Includes air speed delivery. Journal containing peer-reviewed articles on clinical aspects of emergency care by, and for, emergency nurses. Presents information about professional, political, administrative, and educational aspects of emergency nursing and nursing in general.

★10919★ Journal of Gerontological Nursing

SLACK Inc.
6900 Grove Rd.
Thorofare, NJ 08086-9447
Ph: (856)848-1000   Fax: (856)853-5991
E-mail: jgn@slackinc.com
URL: http://www.jognonline.com

Monthly. $84.00/year for individuals; $142.00 for individuals, two years; $189.00 for individuals, three years; $169.00/year for institutions; $287.00 for institutions, two years; $380.00 for institutions, three years; $21.00 for single issue. Gerontological nursing journal.

★10920★ Journal of Intensive Care Medicine

Sage Publications Inc.
2455 Teller Rd.
Thousand Oaks, CA 91320
Ph: (805)499-0721   Fax: (805)499-8096
E-mail: advertising@sagepub.com
URL: http://www.sagepub.com/journal.aspx?pid=340

Bimonthly. $676.00/year for institutions, print & e-access; $744.00/year for institutions, (current volume print & all online content); $608.00/year for institutions, e-access; $676.00/year for e-access plus backfile (all online content); $671.84/year for institutions, back file purchase, e-access content through 1999; $662.00/year for institutions, print only; $272.00/year for individuals, print only; $121.00 for institutions, single print issue;

$59.00 for individuals, single print issue. Medical journal for specialists working in intensive care units.

★10921★ Journal of the National Medical Association

National Medical Association
1012 10th St. NW
Washington, DC 20001
Ph: (202)347-1895   Fax: (202)898-2510
URL: http://www.nmanet.org

Monthly. Journal on specialized clinical research related to the health problems of African-Americans and other minorities. Recognizes significant contributions by black physicians and others involved with minority health issues and health disparities.

★10922★ Journal of Nursing Administration (JONA)

Lippincott Williams & Wilkins
530 Walnut St.
Philadelphia, PA 19106-3621
Ph: (215)521-8300   Fax: (215)521-8902
Fr: 800-638-3030
E-mail: jonaeditor@aol.com
URL: http://jonajournal.com/

Monthly. $108.91/year for individuals, U.S.; $345.79/year for institutions, U.S.; $202.94/year for other countries; $478.75/year for institutions, other countries. Journal covering developments and advances in nursing administration and management.

★10923★ Journal of Nursing Scholarship

Wiley-Blackwell
350 Main St. Commerce Pl.
Malden, MA 02148
Ph: (781)388-8200   Fax: (781)388-8210
Fr: 800-759-6120
URL: http://www.blackwellpublishing.com/journal.asp?ref=1527-6546

Quarterly. $51.00/year for individuals, print and online; $185.00/year for institutions, print and premium online; $168.00/year for institutions, print and standard online; $160.00/year for institutions, premium online only; $59.00/year for individuals, print and online; $135.00/year for institutions, other countries, print and premium online; $123.00/year for institutions, other countries, print and standard online; $117.00/year for institutions, other countries, premium online only; $39.00/year for individuals, print and online. Peer-reviewed journal covering nursing.

★10924★ Journal of Obstetric, Gynecologic and Neonatal Nursing (JOGNN)

Sage Publications Inc.
2455 Teller Rd.
Thousand Oaks, CA 91320
Ph: (805)499-0721   Fax: (805)499-8096
E-mail: advertising@sagepub.com
URL: http://www.sagepub.com/journal.aspx?pid=245

Bimonthly. $97.00/year for individuals, print

+ online; $762.00/year for institutions, print + premium online; $724.00/year for institutions, premium online only; $81.00/year for institutions, print + online; $424.00/year for institutions, print + premium online; $402.00/year for institutions, premium online only; $54.00/year for institutions, print + online; $402.00/year; $402.00/year for institutions, premium online only-All countries. Journal covering trends, policies, and research. Official publication of the Association of Women's Health, Obstetric, and Neonatal Nurses (AWHONN).

★10925★ Journal of Orthopaedic Nursing

Mosby Inc.
11830 Westline Industrial Dr.
St. Louis, MO 63146
Ph: (314)872-8370   Fax: (314)432-1380
Fr: 800-325-4177
URL: http://http://www.elsevier.com/wps/find/journaldescription.cws_home/623057/description#description

Quarterly. $84.00/year for individuals, U.S.; $326.00/year for institutions, U.S. Journal for orthopaedic nurses.

★10926★ Journal of Pediatric Health Care

Mosby
1600 John F. Kennedy Blvd., Ste. 1800
Philadelphia, PA 19103-2899
Ph: (215)239-3276   Fax: (215)239-3286
URL: http://www.elsevier.com/wps/find/journaldescription.cws_home

Bimonthly. $99.00/year for other countries; $210.00/year for institutions, other countries; $50.00/year for students, other countries, or resident; $83.00/year for individuals; $229.00/year for institutions; $40.00/year for students, resident in USA. Official publication of the National Association of Pediatric Nurse Practitioners. Provides current information on pediatric clinical topics as well as research studies, health policy, and legislative issues applicable to pediatric clinical practice.

★10927★ Journal of PeriAnesthesia Nursing

Mosby Inc.
11830 Westline Industrial Dr.
St. Louis, MO 63146
Ph: (314)872-8370   Fax: (314)432-1380
Fr: 800-325-4177
URL: http://www.elsevier.com/wps/find/journaldescription.cws_home

Bimonthly. $359.00/year for institutions; $249.00/year for individuals; $267.00/year for U.S. institutions; $119.00/year for U.S. individuals. Journal publishing original, peer-reviewed research for a primary audience that includes nurses in perianesthesia settings, including ambulatory surgery, preadmission testing, postanesthesia (Phases I, II, and III) care, and pain management. Journal providing forum for sharing professional knowledge and experience relating to management, ethics, legislation, research, and other aspects of perianesthesia nursing.

★10928★ Journal of Psychosocial Nursing and Mental Health Services

SLACK Inc.
6900 Grove Rd.
Thorofare, NJ 08086-9447
Ph: (856)848-1000   Fax: (856)853-5991
E-mail: jpn@slackinc.com
URL: http://www.psychnurse.org

Monthly. $85.00/year for individuals; $144.00 for individuals, two years; $191.00 for individuals, three years; $259.00/year for institutions; $440.00 for institutions, two years; $582.00 for institutions, three years. Journal presenting original, peer-reviewed articles on psychiatric/mental health nursing.

★10929★ Journal of Radiology Nursing

Mosby Inc.
11830 Westline Industrial Dr.
St. Louis, MO 63146
Ph: (314)872-8370   Fax: (314)432-1380
Fr: 800-325-4177
URL: http://www.radiologynursing.org

Quarterly. $72.00/year for individuals, U.S.; $122.00/year for institutions, U.S.; $103.00/year for individuals, International; $157.00/year for institutions, International. Journal publishing articles about patient care in the diagnostic and therapeutic imaging environments.

★10930★ Journal for Specialists in Pediatric Nursing

Wiley-Blackwell
350 Main St. Commerce Pl.
Malden, MA 02148
Ph: (781)388-8200   Fax: (781)388-8210
Fr: 800-759-6120
URL: http://www.blackwellpublishing.com/journal.asp?ref=1539-0136

Quarterly. $71.00/year for individuals, U.S. print and online; $158.00/year for institutions, U.S. print and premium online; $144.00/year for institutions, U.S. print and standard online; $137.00/year for institutions, U.S. premium online only; $74.00/year for individuals, Europe, print and online; $110.00/year for institutions, Europe, print and premium online; $100.00/year for institutions, Europe, print and standard online; $95.00/year for institutions, Europe, premium online only; $49.00/year for individuals, print and online; $110.00/year for institutions, other countries, print and premium online. Journal focusing on nurses who specialize in the care of children and families.

★10931★ LPN2008

Lippincott Williams & Wilkins
530 Walnut St.
Philadelphia, PA 19106-3621
Ph: (215)521-8300   Fax: (215)521-8902
Fr: 800-638-3030
URL: http://www.lww.com/product/?1553-0582

Bimonthly. $119.96/year for institutions; $27.86/year for individuals; $21.91/year for U.S., in-training; $67.96/year for individuals, other countries; $167.96/year for institutions,

other countries. Peer-reviewed journal that focuses on bedside care skills for practical nurses.

★10932★ McKnight's Long-Term Care News

McKnight's Long-Term Care News
1 Northfield Plz., Ste. 521
Northfield, IL 60093-1216
Ph: (847)784-8706   Fax: (847)784-9346
Fr: 800-558-1703
E-mail: ltcn-webmaster@mltcn.com
URL: http://www.mcknightsonline.com/home

Professional magazine.

★10933★ MCN, The American Journal of Maternal/Child Nursing

Lippincott Williams & Wilkins
530 Walnut St.
Philadelphia, PA 19106-3621
Ph: (215)521-8300   Fax: (215)521-8902
Fr: 800-638-3030
URL: http://www.mcnjournal.com/

Bimonthly. $53.91/year for individuals, U.S.; $131.95/year for institutions, U.S.; $121.94/year for other countries, individual; $161.95/year for institutions, other countries. Journal focusing on maternal/child nursing and health.

★10934★ Military Medicine

AMSUS - The Society of the Federal Health Agencies
9320 Old Georgetown Rd.
Bethesda, MD 20814
Ph: (301)897-8800   Fax: (301)503-5446
Fr: 800-761-9320
URL: http://www.amsus.org/journal/

Monthly. $132.00/year for individuals; $177.00/year for other countries; $20.00 for single issue; $27.00 for single issue, other countries. Journal for professional personnel affiliated with the Federal medical services.

★10935★ Minority Nurse Newsletter

Tucker Publications Inc.
PO Box 580
Lisle, IL 60532
Ph: (630)969-3809   Fax: (630)969-3895
E-mail: drsallie@gmail.com
URL: http://www.tuckerpub.com

Description: Quarterly. Provides health care information of interest to minority nursing faculty.

★10936★ Modern Healthcare

Crain Communications Inc.
360 N Michigan Ave.
Chicago, IL 60601
Ph: (312)649-5411   Fax: (312)280-3150
Fr: 888-909-9111
E-mail: subs@crain.com
URL: http://www.modernhealthcare.com

Weekly. $154.00/year for individuals; $244.00/year for Canada; $208.00/year for

other countries. Weekly business news magazine for healthcare management.

★10937★ Nephrology Nursing Journal

American Nephrology Nurses' Association
East Holly Ave.
PO Box 56
Pitman, NJ 08071-0056
Ph: (856)256-2320   Fax: (856)589-7463
URL: http://www.nephrologynursing.net/

Bimonthly. Nursing journal.

★10938★ The New England Journal of Medicine

The New England Journal of Medicine
860 Winter St.
Waltham, MA 02451-1413
Ph: (781)893-3800   Fr: 800-843-6356
URL: http://content.nejm.org/

Weekly. $99.00/year for individuals, online only; $149.00/year for individuals, print & online. Journal for the medical profession.

★10939★ Nurse Education in Practice

Mosby Inc.
11830 Westline Industrial Dr.
St. Louis, MO 63146
Ph: (314)872-8370   Fax: (314)432-1380
Fr: 800-325-4177
URL: http://www.us.elsevierhealth.com/product.jsp?isbn=14715953#a

Bimonthly. $77.00/year for individuals; $311.00/year for institutions. Journal enabling lecturers and practitioners to both share and disseminate evidence that demonstrates the actual practice of education as it is experienced in the realities of their respective work environments.

★10940★ Nurse Educator

Lippincott Williams & Wilkins
530 Walnut St.
Philadelphia, PA 19106-3621
Ph: (215)521-8300   Fax: (215)521-8902
Fr: 800-638-3030
E-mail: needitor@aol.com
URL: http://www.nurseeducatoronline.com/

Bimonthly. $103.91/year for individuals, U.S.; $292.96/year for institutions, U.S.; $189.94/year for individuals, international; $375.94/year for institutions, international. Journal for nursing educators.

★10941★ Nurse Leader

Mosby Inc.
11830 Westline Industrial Dr.
St. Louis, MO 63146
Ph: (314)872-8370   Fax: (314)432-1380
Fr: 800-325-4177
E-mail: roxane.spitzer@comcast.net
URL: http://www.nurseleader.com

Bimonthly. $64.00/year for individuals, domestic; $140.00/year for institutions, domestic; $219.00/year for institutions, international; $100.00/year for individuals, international. Journal publishing articles on the vision, skills, and tools needed by nurses currently aspiring to leadership positions.

★10942★ *The Nurse Practitioner*

Lippincott Williams & Wilkins
530 Walnut St.
Philadelphia, PA 19106-3621
Ph: (215)521-8300   Fax: (215)521-8902
Fr: 800-638-3030
E-mail: npedit@wolterskluwer.com
URL: http://www.tnpj.com

Monthly. $57.95/year for individuals; $209.00/year for institutions; $29.00/year for U.S., in-training; $120.98/year for other countries, individual; $258.98/year for institutions. Magazine presenting clinical information to nurses in advanced primary care practice. Also covers legal, business, economic, ethical, research, and pharmaceutical issues.

★10943★ *Nurse Practitioner Forum*

Elsevier
1600 John F. Kennedy Blvd., Ste. 1800
Philadelphia, PA 19103-2899
Ph: (215)239-3900   Fax: (215)238-7883
URL: http://202.117.24.24/html/xjtu/ckzl/ssci/ssci_n.htm

Quarterly. Journal for nurse practitioners.

★10944★ *Nursing Clinics of North America*

Mosby Inc.
11830 Westline Industrial Dr.
St. Louis, MO 63146
Ph: (314)872-8370   Fax: (314)432-1380
Fr: 800-325-4177
URL: http://www.elsevier.com/wps/find/bookdescription.cws_home/70

Quarterly. $55.00/year for individuals. Journal publishing articles by experts in the field; provides current, practical information geared to the active nurse.

★10945★ *Nursing Economics*

Jannetti Publications Inc.
East Holly Ave., Box 56
Pitman, NJ 08071-0056
Ph: (856)256-2300
E-mail: nejrnl@ajj.com
URL: http://www.ajj.com

Bimonthly. $65.00/year for individuals; $110.00 for individuals, 2 years; $80.00/year for institutions; $130.00 for institutions, 2 years; $89.00/year for individuals, other countries; $158.00 for individuals, other countries, 2 years; $104.00/year for institutions, other countries; $178.00 for institutions, other countries, 2 years. Business magazine for nursing administrators.

★10946★ *Nursing Education Perspectives*

National League for Nursing
61 Broadway, 33rd Fl.
New York, NY 10006-2701
Ph: (212)363-5555   Fax: (212)812-0391
Fr: 800-669-1656

URL: http://www.nln.org/nlnjournal/index.htm

Bimonthly. $40.00/year; $70.00/year for non-members; $90.00/year for Canada; $98.00/year for other countries, non-member; $137.00/year for individuals; $157.00/year for Canada; $165.00/year for other countries. Professional journal for nurses. Includes articles on health policy, social and economic issues affecting health care, and nursing education and practice.

★10947★ *Nursing Management*

Lippincott Williams & Wilkins
323 Norristown Rd., Ste. 200
Ambler, PA 19002-2758
Ph: (215)646-8700   Fax: (215)654-1328
URL: http://www.nursingmanagement.com/

Monthly. $46.95/year for individuals, U.S.; $199.00/year for institutions, U.S.; $103.00/year for individuals, international; $258.00/year for institutions, international. Magazine focusing on nursing management.

★10948★ *Nursing Outlook*

Mosby Inc.
10801 Executive Center Dr., Ste. 509
Little Rock, AR 72211
Ph: (501)223-5165   Fax: (501)223-0519
URL: http://journals.elsevierhealth.com/periodicals/ymno

Bimonthly. $65.00/year for individuals; $106.00/year for individuals, Canada; $106.00/year for individuals, other countries. Official journal of the American Academy of Nursing, reporting on trends and issues in nursing.

★10949★ *Nursing Science Quarterly*

Sage Publications Inc.
2455 Teller Rd.
Thousand Oaks, CA 91320
Ph: (805)499-0721   Fax: (805)499-8096
URL: http://www.sagepub.com

Quarterly. $443.00/year for institutions, combined (print & e-access); $465.00/year for institutions, combined plus backfile current volume print and all; $399.00/year for institutions, e-access; $421.00/year for institutions, e-access plus backfile (all online content); $399.00/year for institutions, e-access (content through 1999); $434.00/year for institutions, print only; $129.00/year for individuals, print only; $120.00 for institutions, single print; $42.00 for individuals, single print. Journal focusing on enhancement of nursing knowledge.

★10950★ *Ob Gyn News*

International Medical News Group
60-B Columbia Rd.
Morristown, NJ 07960
Ph: (973)290-8200   Fax: (973)290-8250
E-mail: obnews@imng.com
URL: http://www.eobgynnews.com

Semimonthly. $115.00/year for individuals; $230.00/year for other countries, surface

mail. Obstetrics and gynecology tabloid distributed to obstetricians and gynecologists.

★10951★ *Oncology*

S. Karger Publishers Inc.
26 W Avon Rd.
PO Box 529
Farmington, CT 06085
Ph: (860)675-7834   Fax: (203)675-7302
Fr: 800-828-5479
URL: http://content.karger.com/ProdukteDB/produkte.asp?Aktion=Jou

$1,974.00/year for institutions, print; $1,410.00/year for institutions, print; $1,974.00/year for institutions, print and online; plus postage and handling; $60.00/year for institutions, postage and handling; $43.20/year for institutions, postage and handling; $90.00/year for institutions, postage and handling, overseas; $82.40/year for institutions, postage and handling, overseas. Medical journal presenting experimental and clinical findings on cancer.

★10952★ *Orthopaedic Nursing*

National Association of Orthopaedic Nurses
401 North Michigan Ave., Ste. 2200
Chicago, IL 60611
Fax: (312)527-6658   Fr: 800-289-6266
URL: http://www.orthopaedicnursing.com

Bimonthly. Nursing magazine.

★10953★ *Pediatric Nursing*

Jannetti Publications Inc.
East Holly Ave., Box 56
Pitman, NJ 08071-0056
Ph: (856)256-2300
URL: http://www.pediatricnursing.net

Bimonthly. $42.00/year for individuals; $78.00 for individuals, two years; $65.00/year for institutions; $120.00 for institutions, two years; $66.00/year for individuals, foreign; $126.00 for individuals, foreign, two years; $89.00/year for institutions, foreign; $168.00 for institutions, foreign, two years; $15.00 for single issue, current issue; $15.00 for single issue, back future issue. Professional nursing magazine.

★10954★ *Provider*

American Health Care Association
1201 L St. NW
Washington, DC 20005
Ph: (202)842-4444   Fax: (202)842-3860
E-mail: sales@ahca.org
URL: http://www.providermagazine.com

Monthly. $48.00/year for U.S.; $61.00/year for Canada and Mexico; $85.00/year for other countries. Provider Magazine.

★10955★ *Rehabilitation Nursing*

Rehabilitation Nursing
4700 West Lake Ave.
Glenview, IL 60025
Ph: (847)375-4710   Fr: 800-229-7530
E-mail: info@rehabnurse.org

URL: http://www.rehabnurse.org/index.html

Bimonthly. $95.00/year for individuals; $125.00/year for institutions; $135.00/year for other countries; $18.00 for single issue; $125.00/year for Canada. Magazine focusing on rehabilitation nursing involving clinical practice, research, education, and administration.

★10956★ **Research in Nursing & Health**

John Wiley & Sons Inc.
111 River St.
Hoboken, NJ 07030-5774
Ph: (201)748-6000　　Fax: (201)748-6088
Fr: 800-825-7550
URL: http://as.wiley.com/WileyCDA/Wiley-Title/productCd-NUR.html

Bimonthly. $140.00/year for individuals, print only; $140.00/year for Canada and Mexico, in Canada, add 7% GST print only; $176.00/year for other countries, print only; $1,185.00/year for institutions, print only; $1,257.00/year for institutions, Canada and Mexico, print only in Canada, add 7% GST; $1,299.00/year for institutions, other countries, print only; $1,304.00/year for institutions, print and online U.S.; $1,376.00/year for institutions, Canada and Mexico, print and online, in Canada, add 7% GST; $1,418.00/year for institutions, other countries, print and online. Journal providing forum for research in the areas of nursing practice, education, and administration. Covers health issues relevant to nursing as well as investigations of the applications of research findings in clinical settings.

★10957★ **RN**

Advanstar Communications Inc.
641 Lexington Ave., 8th Fl.
New York, NY 10022
Ph: (212)951-6600　　Fax: (212)951-6793
E-mail: rnmagazine@advanstar.com
URL: http://www.rnweb.com/rnweb

Monthly. $25.00/year for individuals; $50.00/year for individuals, by surface mail. Clinical journal for registered nurses.

★10958★ **Seminars in Oncology**

Elsevier
1600 John F. Kennedy Blvd., Ste. 1800
Philadelphia, PA 19103-2899
Ph: (215)239-3900　　Fax: (215)238-7883
E-mail: elspcs@elsevier.com
URL: http://www.elsevier.com

$228.00/year for individuals, U.S.; $114.00/year for students, U.S.; $311.00/year for individuals, Canada; $156.00/year for students, Canada; $311.00/year for individuals, Mexico; $156.00/year for students, Mexico; $311.00/year for individuals, international; $156.00/year for students, international; $510.00/year for institutions, international; $424.00/year for institutions, U.S. Journal reviewing current diagnostic and treatment techniques used in oncology patient care.

★10959★ **Seminars in Oncology Nursing**

Mosby Inc.
11830 Westline Industrial Dr.
St. Louis, MO 63146
Ph: (314)872-8370　　Fax: (314)432-1380
Fr: 800-325-4177
URL: http://www.nursingoncology.com

Quarterly. $91.00/year for individuals; $227.00/year for institutions; $23.00 for individuals, single issue; $172.00/year for individuals, International; $298.00/year for institutions, International; $43.00 for individuals, single issue, international. Journal publishing material to disseminate knowledge in the complex field of cancer nursing.

★10960★ **Teaching and Learning in Nursing**

Elsevier Science Inc.
360 Park Ave. S
New York, NY 10010
Ph: (212)989-5800　　Fax: (212)633-3990
URL: http://www.elsevier.com

Quarterly. $119.00/year for institutions, U.S. $167.00/year for institutions, other countries; $75.00/year for individuals, U.S. $104.00/year for individuals, other countries. Journal devoted to associate degree nursing education and practice.

★10961★ **Worldviews on Evidence-Based Nursing**

Wiley-Blackwell
350 Main St. Commerce Pl.
Malden, MA 02148
Ph: (781)388-8200　　Fax: (781)388-8210
Fr: 800-759-6120
URL: http://www.blackwellpublishing.com/journals/WVN

Quarterly. $112.00/year for individuals, print and online; $116.00/year for individuals, online only; $49.00/year for members, print and online; $47.00/year for members, online only; $318.00/year for institutions, print and premium online; $289.00/year for institutions, print and standard online; $275.00/year for institutions, premium online only; $132.00/year for individuals, print and online; $126.00/year for individuals, online only; $53.00/year for members, print and online. Journal that offers research, policy and practice, education and management for nursing.

PLACEMENT AND JOB REFERRAL SERVICES

★10962★ **American Association of Occupational Health Nurses (AAOHN)**

2920 Brandywine Rd., Ste. 100
Atlanta, GA 30341
Ph: (770)455-7757　　Fax: (770)455-7271
E-mail: ann@aaohn.org
URL: http://www.aaohn.org

Description: Represents registered professional nurses employed by business and industrial firms; nurse educators, nurse editors, nurse writers, and others interested in occupational health nursing. Promotes and sets standards for the profession. Provides and approves continuing education; maintains governmental affairs program; offers placement service.

★10963★ **American College of Nurse-Midwives (ACNM)**

8403 Colesville Rd., Ste. 1550
Silver Spring, MD 20910
Ph: (240)485-1800　　Fax: (240)485-1818
E-mail: info@acnm.org
URL: http://www.midwife.org

Description: Seeks to develop and support the profession of certified nurse-midwives in order to promote the health and well-being of women and infants within their families and communities. Represents licensed health care practitioner educated in the two disciplines of nursing and midwifery. Provides gynecological services and care of mothers and babies throughout the maternity cycle. Cooperates with allied groups to enable nurse-midwives to concentrate their efforts in the improvement of services for mothers and newborn babies. Studies and evaluates activities of nurse-midwives in order to establish qualifications. Conducts research and continuing education workshops. Compiles statistics. Maintains speakers' bureau and archives; offers placement service.

★10964★ **American Organization of Nurse Executives (AONE)**

325 Seventh St. NW
Liberty Pl.
Washington, DC 20004
Ph: (202)626-2240　　Fax: (202)638-5499
E-mail: aone@aha.org
URL: http://www.aone.org

Description: Provides leadership, professional development, advocacy, and research to advance nursing practice and patient care, promote nursing leadership and excellence, and shape healthcare public policy. Supports and enhances the management, leadership, educational, and professional development of nursing leaders. Offers placement service through Career Development and Referral Center.

★10965★ **American Public Health Association (APHA)**

800 I St. NW
Washington, DC 20001
Ph: (202)777-2742　　Fax: (202)777-2534
E-mail: comments@apha.org
URL: http://www.apha.org

Members: Professional organization of physicians, nurses, educators, academicians, environmentalists, epidemiologists, new professionals, social workers, health administrators, optometrists, podiatrists, pharmacists, dentists, nutritionists, health planners, other community and mental health specialists, and interested consumers. **Purpose:** Seeks to protect and promote personal, mental, and environmental health. **Activities:** Services include: promulgation of standards; establishment of uniform practices and procedures; development of the etiology of communicable diseases; research in public health; exploration of medical care programs and their relationships to public health. Sponsors job placement service.

★10966★ **American Society of Extra-Corporeal Technology (AmSECT)**

2209 Dickens Rd.
Richmond, VA 23230-2005
Ph: (804)565-6363   Fax: (804)282-0090
E-mail: stewart@amsect.org
URL: http://www.amsect.org

Description: Perfusionists, technologists, doctors, nurses, and others actively employed and using the applied skills relating to the practice of extracorporeal technology (involving heart-lung machines); student members. Disseminates information necessary to the proper practice of the technology. Conducts programs in continuing education and professional-public liaison and hands-on workshops. Maintains placement service.

EMPLOYER DIRECTORIES AND NETWORKING LISTS

★10967★ **AHA Guide to the Health Care Field**

American Hospital Association
1 N Franklin
Chicago, IL 60606
Ph: (312)422-2050   Fax: (312)422-4700
Fr: 800-424-4301

Annual, August. Covers hospitals, networks, multi-health care systems, freestanding ambulatory surgery centers, psychiatric facilities, long-term care facilities, substance abuse programs, and other health-related organizations. Entries include: For hospitals—Facility name, address, phone, administrator's name, number of beds, facilities and services, number of employees, expenses, other statistics. For other organizations—Name, address, phone, fax, name and title of contact. Arrangement: Geographical. Indexes: Hospital name.

★10968★ **American Group Psychotherapy Association-Membership Directory**

American Group Psychotherapy
  Association Inc.
25 E 21st St., 6th Fl.
New York, NY 10010
Ph: (212)477-2677   Fax: (212)979-6627
Fr: 877-668-2472
URL: http://www.agpa.org

Covers 4,500 physicians, psychologists, clinical social workers, psychiatric nurses, and other mental health professionals interested in treatment of emotional problems by group methods. Entries include: Name, office or home address, highest degree held, office or home phone number. Arrangement: Alphabetical. Indexes: Geographical.

★10969★ **American Journal of Nursing-Career Guide**

American Journal of Nursing
c/o Lippincott, Williams & Wilkins
530 Walnut St.
Philadelphia, PA 19106-3621
Ph: (215)521-8300   Fax: (215)521-8902
Fr: 800-627-0484
URL: http://www.ajnonline.com

Annual, April. $34.90 for individuals; $234.95 for institutions; $26.95 for individuals, in-training; $87.00 for individuals, international; $299.00 for institutions, international. Publication includes: List of nursing organizations and agencies. Entries include: Name, address, names of officers or nursing representatives. Arrangement: Classified by type of organization.

★10970★ **Careers in Focus: Nursing**

Facts On File Inc.
132 W 31st St., 17th Fl.
New York, NY 10001
Ph: (212)967-8800   Fax: 800-678-3633
Fr: 800-322-8755
URL: http://www.factsonfile.com

Latest edition 3rd, 2006. $29.95 for individuals; $26.95 for libraries. Covers an overview of nursing, followed by a selection of jobs profiled in detail, including the nature of the job, earnings, prospects for employment, what kind of training and skills it requires, and sources for further information.

★10971★ **CriticalCare Choices**

Lippincott Williams & Wilkins
530 Walnut St.
Philadelphia, PA 19106-3621
Ph: (215)521-8300   Fax: (215)521-8902
Fr: 800-346-7844
URL: http://www.nursingcenter.com

Annual, May 2005. Free. Clinical and career directory for critical care nurses. Covers nonprofit and investor-owned hospitals and departments of the United States government that hire critical care nurses. Arrangement: Geographical. Indexes: Geographical.

★10972★ **Directory of Child Life Programs**

Child Life Council Inc.
11820 Parklawn Dr., Ste. 240
Rockville, MD 20852-2529
Ph: (301)881-7090   Fax: (301)881-7092
URL: http://www.childlife.org/

Biennial; latest edition 14th, 2006. Covers over 400 child life programs. Entries include: Facility name, address, phone, name of child life department and director, reporting structure, staff statistics, educational requirements for employment, and internship or educational opportunities. Arrangement: Geographical. Indexes: Speciality areas, internship sessions, program size, fellowships.

★10973★ **Directory of Hospital Personnel**

Grey House Publishing
185 Millerton Rd.
PO Box 860
Millerton, NY 12546
Ph: (518)789-8700   Fax: (518)789-0556
Fr: 800-562-2139
URL: http://www.greyhouse.com/hospital_personnel.htm

Annual. $325.00 for print product; $545.00 for online database subscription; $650.00 for online database subscription and print product combined. Covers 200,000 executives at 7,000 U.S. hospitals. Entries include: Name of hospital, address, phone; number of beds; type and JCAHO status of hospital; names and titles of key department heads and staff; medical and nursing school affiliations; number of residents, interns, and nursing students. Arrangement: Geographical. Indexes: Hospital name, personnel, hospital size.

★10974★ **Essentials of Internet Use in Nursing**

Springer Publishing Co.
11 W 42nd St., 15th Fl.
New York, NY 10036
Ph: (212)431-4370   Fax: (212)941-7342
Fr: 877-687-7476
URL: http://www.springerpub.com/prod.aspx?prod_id=15543

Latest edition August 2002. $32.95 for individuals. Publication includes: Appendix listing relevant Web sites. Principal content of publication is information on Internet usage for clinical nursing practice, for continuing nursing education, for medical research, and for nursing staff recruitment and development. Indexes: Topical.

★10975★ **Hitting the Road**

Lippincott Williams & Wilkins
530 Walnut St.
Philadelphia, PA 19106-3621
Ph: (215)521-8300   Fax: (215)521-8902
Fr: 800-638-3030
URL: http://www.lww.com

Published January 2003. $24.95 for individuals. Publication includes: List of 70 health care staffing agencies. Principal content of publication is discussion of and assistance in entering field of travel nursing.

★10976★ **Hospital Blue Book**

Billian Publishing Inc./Transworld
  Publishing Inc.
2100 Powers Ferry Rd. SE
Atlanta, GA 30339
Ph: (770)955-5656   Fax: (770)952-0669
Fr: 800-533-8484
E-mail: blu-book@billian.com

2005. $300.00 for individuals. Covers more than 6,687 hospitals; some listings also appear in a separate southern edition of this publication. Entries include: Name of hospital, accreditation, mailing address, phone, fax, number of beds, type of facility (nonprofit, general, state, etc.); list of administrative personnel and chiefs of medical services, with specific titles. Arrangement: Geographical.

★10977★ **How to Survive and Maybe Even Love Nursing School!**
F.A. Davis Co.
1915 Arch St.
Philadelphia, PA 19103
Ph: (215)568-2270   Fax: (215)568-5065
Fr: 800-523-4049

2nd edition 2004. $24.95 for individuals. Publication includes: List of resources for nursing students, such as Web sites and related organizations. Principal content of publication is information about succeeding in nursing school.

★10978★ **The JobBank Guide to Health Care Companies**
Adams Media Corp.
57 Littlefield St.
Avon, MA 02322
Ph: (508)427-7100   Fax: (508)427-6790
Fr: 800-872-5627
URL: http://www.amazon.com/Jobbank-Guide-Health-Care-Companies/dp

Biennial. Covers jobs nationwide in health care companies. Entries include: Firm or organization name, address, phone, name and title of contact; description of organization, headquarters location, typical titles for entry- and middle-level positions, educational backgrounds desired, fringe benefits offered, stock exchange listing, training programs, internships, parent company, number of employees, revenues, e-mail and web addresses, projected number of hires. Indexes: Alphabetical.

★10979★ **Medical and Health Information Directory**
Gale, Cengage Learning
27500 Drake Rd.
Farmington Hills, MI 48331-3535
Ph: (248)699-4253   Fax: (248)699-8065
Fr: 800-877-4253
E-mail: businessproducts@gale.com
URL: http://www.gale.com

Annual; latest edition 20th, July 2007. $375.00/volume. Covers in Volume 1, more than 26,500 medical and health oriented associations, organizations, institutions, and government agencies, including health maintenance organizations (HMOs), preferred provider organizations (PPOs), insurance companies, pharmaceutical companies, research centers, and medical and allied health schools. In Volume 2, over 12,000 medical book publishers; medical periodicals, directories, audiovisual producers and services, medical libraries and information centers, electronic resources, and health-related internet search engines. In Volume 3, more than 35,500 clinics, treatment centers, care programs, and counseling/diagnostic services for 34 subject areas. Entries include: Institution, service, or firm name, address, phone, fax, email and URL; many include names of key personnel and, when pertinent, descriptive annotations. Volume 3 was formerly listed separately as Health

Services Directory. Arrangement: Classified by organization activity, service, etc. Indexes: Each volume has a complete alphabetical name and keyword index.

★10980★ **Nursing Career Directory**
Lippincott Williams & Wilkins
530 Walnut St.
Philadelphia, PA 19106-3621
Ph: (215)521-8300   Fax: (215)521-8902
Fr: 800-346-7844
URL: http://www.springnet.com

Annual, January. Covers nonprofit and investor-owned hospitals and departments of the United States government that hire nurses. Does not report specific positions available. Entries include: Unit name, location, areas of nursing specialization, educational requirements for nurses, licensing, facilities, benefits, etc. Arrangement: Geographical. Indexes: Geographical.

★10981★ **The Nursing Job Search Handbook**
University of Pennsylvania Press
3905 Spruce St.
Philadelphia, PA 19104-4112
Ph: (215)898-6261   Fax: (215)898-0404
Fr: 800-445-9880
URL: http://www.upenn.edu/pennpress/book/13752.html

Latest edition 2002. $18.95 for individuals; $12.50 for individuals. Publication includes: Appendix listing state licensing boards and nursing organizations. Entries include: Name, address, phone. Principal content of publication is information on obtaining a job in the field of nursing. Indexes: Alphabetical.

★10982★ **Peterson's Guide to Nursing Programs**
Peterson's
Princeton Pke. Corporate Ctr., 2000 Lenox Dr.
PO Box 67005
Lawrenceville, NJ 08648
Ph: (609)896-1800   Fax: (609)896-4531
Fr: 800-338-3282
URL: http://www.petersons.com/

Annual; latest edition 12th, April 2006. $18.48 for individuals. Covers over 700 institutions offering approximately 2,000 accredited nursing programs in the U.S. and Canada. Entries include: Academic information, extracurricular issues, costs, financial aid.

★10983★ **Peterson's Job Opportunities for Health and Science Majors**
Peterson's
Princeton Pke. Corporate Ctr., 2000 Lenox Dr.
PO Box 67005
Lawrenceville, NJ 08648
Ph: (609)896-1800   Fax: (609)896-4531
Fr: 800-338-3282
URL: http://www.petersons.com

Irregular; latest edition 1999. Covers about 1,300 research, consulting, government, and

non-profit and profit service organizations that hire college and university graduates in science and health-related majors. Entries include: Organization name, address, phone, name and title of contact, type of organization, number of employees, Standard Industrial Classification (SIC) code; description of opportunities available including disciplines, level of education required, starting locations and salaries, level of experience accepted, benefits.

★10984★ **Saunders Student Nurse Planners**
W.B. Saunders Company
c/o Elsevier
30 Corporate Dr., 4th Fl.
Burlington, MA 01803
Ph: (781)313-4700   Fax: (781)313-4880
URL: http://www.elsevier.com/

Latest edition July, 2005. $10.99. Covers nursing orientation. Publication includes: telephone and address directory.

★10985★ **What Can I Do Now**
Facts On File Inc.
132 W 31st St., 17th Fl.
New York, NY 10001
Ph: (212)967-8800   Fax: 800-678-3633
Fr: 800-322-8755
URL: http://www.factsonfile.com

Latest edition 2nd, 2007. $22.95 for individuals; $20.65 for libraries. Covers licensed practical nurses, nurse anesthetists, nurse assistants, nurse midwives, nurse practitioners, registered nurses, and surgical nurses.

HANDBOOKS AND MANUALS

★10986★ **101 Careers in Nursing**
Springer-Verlag New York, Inc.
233 Spring St.
New York, NY 10013
Ph: (212)460-1501   Fax: (212)460-1595
URL: http://www.springer.com/

Jeanne M. Novotny, Doris T. Lippman, Nicole K. Sanders, Joyce J. Fitzpatrick. June 2006. $16.00 (paper). Illustrated. 222 pages.

★10987★ **Anatomy of a Job Search: A Nurse's Guide to Finding and Landing the Job You Want**
Lippincott Williams & Wilkins
530 Walnut St.
Philadelphia, PA 19106
Ph: (215)521-8300   Fax: (215)521-8902
Fr: 800-346-7844
URL: http://www.lww.com

Jeanna Bozell. 1999. $25.95 (paper). 146 pages.

★10988★ Building and Managing a Career in Nursing: Strategies for Advancing Your Career

Sigma Theta Tau International, Center for Nursing Press
550 W. North St.
Indianapolis, IN 46202
Ph: (317)634-8171   Fax: (317)634-8188
Fr: 888-634-7575

Terry W. Miller. May 2003. $25.00. Illustrated. 411 pages.

★10989★ Career Opportunities in Health Care (Career Opportunities)

Facts On File Inc.
132 W. 31st St., 17th Fl.
New York, NY 10001-2006
Ph: (212)967-8800   Fax: 800-678-3633
Fr: 800-322-8755
E-mail: custserv@factsonfile.com
URL: http://www.factsonfile.com

Shelly Field. Arthur E. Weintraub. 2002. Reprint. $49.50. 243 pages. Part of the Career Opportunities Series.

★10990★ Careers in Health Care

The McGraw-Hill Companies
PO Box 182604
Columbus, OH 43272
Fax: (614)759-3749   Fr: 877-883-5524
E-mail: customer.service@mcgraw-hill.com
URL: http://www.mcgraw-hill.com

Barbara M. Swanson. Fifth edition, 2005. $15.95 (paper). 192 pages. Describes job duties, work settings, salaries, licensing and certification requirements, educational preparation, and future outlook. Gives ideas on how to secure a job.

★10991★ Careers for Night Owls and Other Insomniacs

The McGraw-Hill Companies
PO Box 182604
Columbus, OH 43272
Fax: (614)759-3749   Fr: 877-883-5524
E-mail: customer.service@mcgraw-hill.com
URL: http://www.mcgraw-hill.com

Louise Miller. Second edition, 2002. $12.95 (paper). 160 pages.

★10992★ Careers in Nursing

The McGraw-Hill Companies
PO Box 182604
Columbus, OH 43272
Fax: (614)759-3749   Fr: 877-883-5524
E-mail: customer.service@mcgraw-hill.com
URL: http://www.mcgraw-hill.com

Terence J. Sacks. Second edition, 2003. $15.95 (paper). 192 pages.

★10993★ Developing Your Career in Nursing

Sage Publications, Inc.
2455 Teller Rd.
Thousand Oaks, CA 91320-2218
Ph: (805)499-0721   Fax: (805)499-0871

E-mail: info@sagepub.com
URL: http://www.sagepub.com/

Robert Newell, editor. 2003. $37.95. 184 pages.

★10994★ Expert Resumes for Health Care Careers

Jist Works
875 Montreal Way
St. Paul, MN 55102
Fr: 800-648-5478
E-mail: info@jist.com
URL: http://www.jist.com

Wendy S. Enelow and Louise M. Kursmark. December 2003. $16.95. 288 pages.

★10995★ Federal Jobs in Nursing and Health Sciences

Impact Publications
9104 Manassas Dr., Ste. N
Manassas Park, VA 20111-5211
Ph: (703)361-7300   Fax: (703)335-9486
Fr: 800-361-1055
E-mail: query@impactpublications.com
URL: http://www.impactpublications.com

Russ Smith. 1996. Part of "Federal Jobs in ..." Series. $14.95. 130 pages.

★10996★ Health Careers Today

Elsevier
11830 Westline Industrial Dr.
St. Louis, MO 63146
Ph: (314)453-7010   Fax: (314)453-7095
Fr: 800-545-2522
E-mail: usbkinfo@elsevier.com
URL: http://www.elsevier.com

Gerdin, Judith. Fourth edition. 2007. $59.95. 496 pages. Covers more than 45 health careers. Discusses the roles and responsibilities of various occupations and provides a solid foundation in the skills needed for all health careers.

★10997★ Mosby's Tour Guide to Nursing School: A Student's Road Survival Guide

Mosby
11830 Westline Industrial Dr.
St. Louis, MO 63146
Ph: (314)872-8370   Fax: 800-235-0256
Fr: 800-325-4177
URL: http://www.elsevier.com

Melodie Chenevert. Fifth edition, 2006. $27.95 (paper). 256 pages.

★10998★ The Nurses' Career Guide: Discovering New Horizons in Health Care

Sovereignty Press
1241 Johnson Ave., No. 353
San Luis Obispo, CA 93401
Ph: (805)543-6100   Fax: (805)543-1085
Fr: 888-201-2501

Zardoya E. Eagles and Marti Kock. 1999. $17.95 (paper). 118 pages. Helps the reader identify work skills and achievements, clarify

values and goals, explore career options, develop a personal action plan, prepare cover letters and resumes, and conduct informational and job interviews. Also addresses the dramatic changes that nurses currently face in the workplace. Includes a 65-page resource section which lists references, samples of resumes and letters, professional magazines, organizations, and online resources.

★10999★ Nursing (Career Portraits)

The McGraw-Hill Companies
PO Box 182604
Columbus, OH 43272
Fax: (614)759-3749   Fr: 877-883-5524
E-mail: customer.service@mcgraw-hill.com
URL: http://www.mcgraw-hill.com

Blythe Camenson. 1997. $13.95. 96 pages.

★11000★ The Nursing Experience: Trends, Challenges & Transitions

The McGraw-Hill Companies
PO Box 182604
Columbus, OH 43272
Fax: (614)759-3749   Fr: 877-883-5524
E-mail: customer.service@mcgraw-hill.com
URL: http://www.mcgraw-hill.com

Lucille A. Joel and L.Y. Kelly. Fifth edition, 2006. $44.95 (paper). 792 pages.

★11001★ Nursing Today: Transition and Trends

W. B. Saunders Co.
6277 Sea Harbor Dr.
Orlando, FL 32887
Fr: 800-654-2452
URL: http://www.elsevier.com

JoAnn Zerwekh and Jo C. Claborn, editors. Fifth edition, 2005. $47.95 (paper). 688 pages.

★11002★ Opportunities in Environmental Careers

The McGraw-Hill Companies
PO Box 182604
Columbus, OH 43272
Fax: (614)759-3749   Fr: 877-883-5524
E-mail: customer.service@mcgraw-hill.com
URL: http://www.mcgraw-hill.com

Odom Fanning. Revised, 2002. $12.95 (paper). 174 pages. Describes a broad range of opportunities in fields such as environmental health, recreation, physics, and hygiene, and provides job search advice. Part of the "Opportunities in ..." Series.

★11003★ Opportunities in Health and Medical Careers

The McGraw-Hill Companies
PO Box 182604
Columbus, OH 43272
Fax: (614)759-3749   Fr: 877-883-5524
E-mail: customer.service@mcgraw-hill.com
URL: http://www.mcgraw-hill.com

I. Donald Snook, Jr. and Leo D'Orazio. 2004. $13.95 (paper). 157 pages. Covers the full range of medical and health occupations. Illustrated.

★11004★ Opportunities in Mental Health Careers

The McGraw-Hill Companies
PO Box 182604
Columbus, OH 43272
Fax: (614)759-3749   Fr: 877-883-5524
E-mail: customer.service@mcgraw-hill.com
URL: http://www.mcgraw-hill.com

Philip A. Perry. 1996. $14.95; $11.95 (paper) 160 pages. Part of the "Opportunities in ..." Series.

★11005★ Opportunities in Nursing Careers

The McGraw-Hill Companies
PO Box 182604
Columbus, OH 43272
Fax: (614)759-3749   Fr: 877-883-5524
E-mail: customer.service@mcgraw-hill.com
URL: http://www.mcgraw-hill.com

Keville Frederickson and Judith A. Ryan. Second edition, 2003. $13.95 (paper). 160 pages. Discusses the employment outlook and job-seeking techniques for LVN's, LPN's, RN's, nurse practitioners, nurse anesthetists, and other nurse members of the medical team. Includes a complete list of state nurses associations, state nursing boards, and specialty nursing organizations. Contains bibliography and illustrations.

★11006★ Opportunities in Paramedical Careers

The McGraw-Hill Companies
PO Box 182604
Columbus, OH 43272
Fax: (614)759-3749   Fr: 877-883-5524
E-mail: customer.service@mcgraw-hill.com
URL: http://www.mcgraw-hill.com

Alex Kacen. 1999. 14.95 (hardcover). 160 pages. Discusses a variety of opportunities in this field and how to pursue them. Illustrated.

★11007★ Opportunities in Physician Assistant Careers

The McGraw-Hill Companies
PO Box 182604
Columbus, OH 43272
Fax: (614)759-3749   Fr: 877-883-5524
E-mail: customer.service@mcgraw-hill.com
URL: http://www.mcgraw-hill.com

Terence J. Sacks. 2005. $13.95 (paper). 151 pages.

★11008★ Opportunities in State and Local Government Careers

The McGraw-Hill Companies
PO Box 182604
Columbus, OH 43272
Fax: (614)759-3749   Fr: 877-883-5524
E-mail: customer.service@mcgraw-hill.com
URL: http://www.mcgraw-hill.com

Neale J. Baxter. Revised edition, 1992.

$14.95; $10.95 (paper). 148 pages. Points out the incentives and drawbacks of a government career. Describes hiring procedures and provides tips on filling out applications, taking physical and aptitude tests, handling interviews, and finding jobs. Describes the jobs in which 75% of all state and local government workers are employed. For each occupation, covers the nature of the work and the training required.

★11009★ Real People Working in Health Care

The McGraw-Hill Companies
PO Box 182604
Columbus, OH 43272
Fax: (614)759-3749   Fr: 877-883-5524
E-mail: customer.service@mcgraw-hill.com
URL: http://www.mcgraw-hill.com

Blythe Camenson, Jan Goldberg. 1996. $12.95 (paper). 144 pages. Interviews and profiles of working professionals capture a range of opportunities in this field.

★11010★ Real-Resumes for Nursing Jobs: Including Real Resumes Used to Change Careers and Resumes Used to Gain Federal Employment

PREP Publishing
1110 1/2 Hay St., PMB 66
Fayetteville, NC 28305
Ph: (910)483-6611   Fax: (910)483-2439
Fr: 800-533-2814

Anne McKinney. 2003. $16.95. 181 pages. Real-Resumes Series.

★11011★ Reinventing Your Nursing Career: A Handbook for Success in the Age of Managed Care

Aspen Publishers
1 Lake St.
Upper Saddle River, NJ 07458
Ph: (201)236-7000   Fax: 800-445-6991
Fr: 800-638-8437
URL: http://www.aspenpublishers.com/

Michael Newell and Mario Pinardo. 1998. $53.95 (paper). 253 pages. Helps nurses identify career goals and take practical steps to realize them using self-surveys, goal-setting methods, personal action plans, and networking techniques.

★11012★ Resumes for the Health Care Professional

John Wiley & Sons Inc.
1 Wiley Dr.
Somerset, NJ 08873
Ph: (732)469-4400   Fax: (732)302-2300
Fr: 800-225-5945
E-mail: custserv@wiley.com
URL: http://www.wiley.com/WileyCDA/

Kim Marino. Second edition, 2000. $21.50 (paper). 224 pages.

★11013★ Resumes for Health and Medical Careers

The McGraw-Hill Companies
PO Box 182604
Columbus, OH 43272
Fax: (614)759-3749   Fr: 877-883-5524
E-mail: customer.service@mcgraw-hill.com
URL: http://www.mcgraw-hill.com

Third edition, 2003. $11.95 (paper). 160 pages.

★11014★ Resumes for Nursing Careers

The McGraw-Hill Companies
PO Box 182604
Columbus, OH 43272
Fax: (614)759-3749   Fr: 877-883-5524
E-mail: customer.service@mcgraw-hill.com
URL: http://www.mcgraw-hill.com

2001. $11.95 (paper). 144 pages.

★11015★ Top 100 Health-Care Careers, Second Edition: Your Complete Guidebook to Training and Jobs in Allied Health, Nursing, Medicine, and More

JIST Publishing
875 Montreal Way
St. Paul, MN 55102
Fax: 800-547-8329   Fr: 800-648-5478
E-mail: info@jist.com
URL: http://www.jist.com

Dr. Saul Wischnitzer and Edith Wischnitzer. 2005. $24.95. 464 pages. Offers a self-assessmant for choosing the right career in the field, as well as guidance on common admissions tests, information on financial aid, and job search tips.

★11016★ Your Career in Nursing: Manage Your Future in the Changing World of Healthcare

Kaplan Publishing
1 Liberty Plaza, 24th Fl.
New York, NY 10006
Ph: (312)836-4400   Fax: (312)836-1021
Fr: 800-527-4836
URL: http://www.kaplanpublishing.com

Annette Vallano. November 2006. $16.00. Illustrated. 384 Pages. Vocational guide.

★11017★ Your First Year as a Nurse: Making the Transition from Total Novice to Successful Professional

Three Rivers Press
280 Park Ave. (11-3)
New York, NY 10017
Fax: (212)940-7381   Fr: 800-726-0600
URL: http://www.primapublishing.com/crown/trp.html

Donna Cardillo. 2001. $19.95 (paper). 267 pages.

EMPLOYMENT AGENCIES AND SEARCH FIRMS

★11018★ Cross Country TravCorps
6551 Park of Commerce Blvd.
Boca Raton, FL 33487-8247
Fax: (562)998-8533   Fr: 800-530-6125
URL: http://www.crosscountrytravcorps.com

Places traveling nurses in assignments nationwide.

★11019★ Educational Placement Service
6510-A S. Academy Blvd.
Colorado Springs, CO 80906
Ph: (719)579-9911   Fax: (719)579-5050
E-mail: accounting@educatorjobs.com
URL: http://www.educatorjobs.com

Employment agency. Focuses on teaching, administrative, and education-related openings.

★11020★ Harper Associates
3100 NW Hwy., Ste. 240
Farmington Hills, MI 48334
Ph: (248)932-1170   Fax: (248)932-1214
E-mail: info@harperjobs.com
URL: http://www.harperjobs.com

Executive search firm and employment agency.

★11021★ Medical Personnel Services, Inc.
1748 N St., NW
Washington, DC 20036
Ph: (202)466-2955   Fax: (202)452-1818
E-mail: jobs@medicalpersonnel.com
URL: http://www.medicalpersonnel.com

Employment agency specializing in permanent health/medical placements.

★11022★ Nursing Technomics
814 Sunset Hollow Rd.
West Chester, PA 19380-1848
Ph: (610)436-4551   Fax: (610)436-0255
E-mail: jimccrea@chesco.com

Administrative nursing consultants offer expertise in the design and implementation of customized software applications for departments of nursing, organizational design and implementation and executive nurse search. Also specializes in department staffing, scheduling and nurse recruitment. Serves private industries as well as government agencies.

★11023★ Professional Placement Associates, Inc.
287 Bowman Ave., Ste. 309
Purchase, NY 10577-2517
Ph: (914)251-1000   Fax: (914)251-1055
E-mail: careers@ppasearch.com
URL: http://www.ppasearch.com

Executive search firm specializing in the health and medical field.

★11024★ Team Placement Service, Inc.
1414 Prince St., Ste. 202
Alexandria, VA 22314
Ph: (703)820-8618   Fax: (703)820-3368
Fr: 800-495-6767
E-mail: 4jobs@teamplace.com
URL: http://www.teamplace.com

Full-service personnel consultants provide placement for healthcare staff, physician and dentist, private practice, and hospitals. Conduct interviews, tests, and reference checks to select the top 20% of applicants. Survey applicants' skill levels, provide backup information on each candidate, select compatible candidates for consideration, and insure the hiring process minimizes potential legal liability. Industries served: healthcare and government agencies providing medical, dental, biotech, laboratory, hospitals, and physician search.

ONLINE JOB SOURCES AND SERVICES

★11025★ GasWork.com: The Largest Internet Anesthesia Employment Resource
Ph: 800-828-2203
E-mail: support@gaswork.com
URL: http://www.gaswork.com

Description: The largest anesthesia employment resource. Lists positions for anesthesiologists, CRNA's, and more. Visitors may post or search jobs.

★11026★ Health Care Job Store
395 South End Ave., Ste. 15-D
New York, NY 10280
Ph: (561)630-5201
E-mail: jobs@healthcarejobstore.com
URL: http://www.healthcarejobstore.com/

Description: Job sites include every job title in the healthcare industry, every healthcare industry and every geographic location in the U.S.

★11027★ HealthCareerWeb
URL: http://www.healthcareerweb.com/

Description: Advertises jobs for healthcare professionals. **Main files include:** Jobs, Employers, Resumes, Jobwire. Relocation tools and career guidance resources available.

★11028★ MedExplorer
E-mail: medmaster@medexplorer.com
URL: http://www.medexplorer.com

Description: Employment postings make up one module of this general medical site.

Other sections contain: Newsletter, Classifieds, and Discussion Forum.

★11029★ Medhunters.com
Fr: 800-664-0278
E-mail: info@medhunters.com
URL: http://www.medhunters.com

Description: Career search site for jobs in all health care specialties; educational resources; visa and licensing information for relocation; interesting articles; relocation tools; links to professional organizations and general resources.

★11030★ Medzilla
URL: http://www.medzilla.com

Description: General medical website which matches employers and job hunters to their ideal employees and jobs through search capabilities. **Main files include:** Post Jobs, Search Resumes, Post Resumes, Search Jobs, Head Hunters, Articles, Salary Survey.

★11031★ Monster Healthcare
URL: http://healthcare.monster.com/

Description: Delivers nationwide access to healthcare recruiting. Employers can post job listings or ads. Job seekers can post and code resumes, and search over 150,000 healthcare job listings, healthcare career advice columns, career resources information, and member employer profiles and services.

★11032★ NursesRX.com
13620 Reese Blvd. E., Ste. 200
Huntersville, NC 28078
Fr: 800-733-9354
E-mail: info@nursesrx.com
URL: http://www.nursesrx.com

Description: Job board site for travel nursing. In addition to traditional travel nursing, Nurses RX provides staffing possibilities from temporary-to-permanent, traditional permanent placement, staffing/recruitment outsourcing, new graduate internship programs, and a full Canadian Placement Division.

TRADESHOWS

★11033★ American Association of Office Nurses Annual Meeting and Convention
American Association of Office Nurses
52 Park Ave. Ste. B4
Park Ridge, NJ 07656
Ph: (201)391-2600   Fax: (201)573-8543
Fr: 800-457-7504
E-mail: aaonmail@aaon.org
URL: http://www.aaon.org

Annual. **Primary Exhibits:** Exhibits of interest to nurses.

★11034★ American Nephrology Nurses Association Symposium

Anthony J. Jannetti, Inc.
E Holly Ave.
PO Box 56
Pitman, NJ 08071-0056
Ph: (856)256-2300   Fax: (856)589-7463
URL: http://www.ajj.com

Annual. **Primary Exhibits:** Equipment, supplies, pharmaceuticals, and services related to the field of nephrology.

★11035★ American Organization of Nurse Executives Annual Meeting and Exposition

Dallas Hyatt Regency
300 Reunion Blvd.
Dallas, TX 75207
Ph: (214)651-1234   Fax: (214)742-8126
URL: http://www.dallasregency.hyatt.com

Annual. **Primary Exhibits:** Patient-care equipment and supplies; computer hardware and software related to the administration of hospital nursing services; communications systems; intensive care units; medical supplies and equipment; recruiting and staffing services; and related equipment, supplies, and services. **Dates and Locations:** 2008 Apr 25-29; Seattle, WA.

★11036★ AORN World Conference on Surgical Patient Care

Association of Perioperative Registered Nurses (AORN)
2170 S. Parker Rd., Ste. 300
Denver, CO 80231-5711
Ph: (303)755-6304   Fax: (303)752-0299
Fr: 800-755-2676
E-mail: custserv@aorn.org
URL: http://www.aorn.org

Biennial. **Primary Exhibits:** Equipment, supplies, and services used in operating room suites and pre-surgical areas.

★11037★ Association of Perioperative Registered Nurses Annual Congress

Association of Perioperative Registered Nurses (AORN)
2170 S. Parker Rd., Ste. 300
Denver, CO 80231-5711
Ph: (303)755-6304   Fax: (303)752-0299
Fr: 800-755-2676
E-mail: custserv@aorn.org
URL: http://www.aorn.org

Annual. **Primary Exhibits:** Surgical equipment, supplies, and services; recruiting firms, computer software, endoscopes, online buying services.

★11038★ Conference on Classification of Nursing Diagnosis

North American Nursing Diagnosis Association
1211 Locust St.
Philadelphia, PA 19107
Ph: (215)545-8105   Fax: (215)545-8107
Fr: 800-647-9002
E-mail: info@nanda.org

URL: http://www.nanda.org
Biennial. **Primary Exhibits:** Exhibits relating to the development of a taxonomy of diagnostic terminology for use by professional nurses. Booth publishers, electronic media publishers.

★11039★ Conference of the National Association of Pediatric Nurse Associates and Practitioners

National Association of Pediatric Nurse Associates and Practitioners
20 Brace Rd., Ste. 200
Cherry Hill, NJ 08034-2634
Ph: (856)857-9700   Fax: (856)857-1600
Fr: 877-662-7627
E-mail: info@napnap.org
URL: http://www.napnap.org

Annual. **Primary Exhibits:** Equipment, supplies, and services for pediatric, school, and family nurse practitioners.

★11040★ Emergency Nurses Association Annual Meeting

Emergency Nurses Association
915 Lee St.
Des Plaines, IL 60016-6569
Ph: (847)460-4099   Fr: 800-900-9659
URL: http://www.ena.org

Annual. **Primary Exhibits:** Exhibits relating to emergency room care. **Dates and Locations:** 2008 Sep 24-27; Minneapolis, MN.

★11041★ House of Delegates Meeting

American Nurses Association
8515 Georgia Ave., Ste. 400
Silver Spring, MD 20910
Ph: (301)628-5000   Fax: (301)628-5001
Fr: 800-274-4262
E-mail: convention@ana.org
URL: http://www.ana.org

Annual. **Primary Exhibits:** Equipment, supplies, and services for nurses, including publications, uniforms and shoes, computers, laboratory services, medical equipment, and nutritional products.

★11042★ International Society of Psychiatric-Mental Health Nurses Annual Conference

International Society of Psychiatric - Mental Health Nurses
7600 Terrace Ave., Ste. 203
Middleton, WI 53562-3174
Ph: (608)836-3363   Fax: (608)831-5122
Fr: 800-826-2950
E-mail: info@ispn-psych.org
URL: http://www.ispn-psych.org

Annual. **Primary Exhibits:** Psychiatric nursing equipment, supplies, and services.

★11043★ National Association of Orthopedic Nurses Annual Congress

Smith, Bucklin and Associates, Inc. (Chicago)
401 N Michigan Ave.
Chicago, IL 60611-4267
Ph: (312)321-6610   Fax: (312)673-6670
Fr: 800-289-NAON
E-mail: info@smithbucklin.com
URL: http://www.smithbucklin.com

Annual. **Primary Exhibits:** Pharmaceuticals, medical equipment, medical instruments, and publications. **Dates and Locations:** 2008 May 17-21; San Jose, CA; McEnry Convention Center; 2009 May 16-20; Tampa, FL; Tampa Convention Center; 2010 May 15-19; Seattle, WA; Washington State Convention & Trade Center.

★11044★ National Student Nurses' Association Convention

National Student Nurse Association
45 Main St., Ste., 606
Brooklyn, NY 11201
Ph: (718)210-0705   Fax: (718)210-0710
E-mail: nsna@nsna.org
URL: http://www.nsna.org

Annual. **Primary Exhibits:** Equipment, supplies, and services for the student nurse.

★11045★ North Carolina Nurses Association Convention

North Carolina Nurses Association
103 Enterprise St.
PO Box 12025
Raleigh, NC 27607
Ph: (919)821-4250   Fax: (919)829-5807
Fr: 800-626-2153
E-mail: rns@ncnurses.org
URL: http://www.ncnurses.org

Annual. **Primary Exhibits:** Nursing equipment, supplies, and services, books.

★11046★ Oncology Nursing Society Meeting

Oncology Nursing Society
125 Enterprise Dr., RIDC Park W
Pittsburgh, PA 15275-1214
Ph: (412)859-6100   Fax: 877-369-5497
Fr: (866)257-4ONS
E-mail: customer.service@ons.org
URL: http://www.ons.org

Annual. **Primary Exhibits:** Oncology nursing equipment, supplies, and services.

OTHER SOURCES

★11047★ American Almanac of Jobs and Salaries

HarperCollins
10 E. 53rd St.
New York, NY 10022
Ph: (212)207-7000   Fr: 800-242-7737
URL: http://www.harpercollins.com/

John W. Wright. Revised edition, 2000. $20.00 (paper). 672 pages. This is a comprehensive guide to the wages of hundreds of occupations in a wide variety of industries and organizations.

★11048★ **American Assembly for Men in Nursing (AAMN)**
PO Box 130220
Birmingham, AL 35213
Ph: (205)802-7551   Fax: (205)802-7553
E-mail: aamn@aamn.org
URL: http://aamn.org

Members: Registered nurses. **Purpose:** Works to: help eliminate prejudice in nursing; interest men in the nursing profession; provide opportunities for the discussion of common problems; encourage education and promote further professional growth; advise and assist in areas of professional inequity; help develop sensitivities to various social needs; promote the principles and practices of positive health care. **Activities:** Acts as a clearinghouse for information on men in nursing. Conducts educational programs. Promotes education and research about men's health issues.

★11049★ **American Association of Nurse Attorneys (TAANA)**
PO Box 515
Columbus, OH 43216-0515
Fax: (614)221-2335   Fr: 877-538-2262
E-mail: taana@taana.org
URL: http://www.taana.org

Members: Nurse attorneys, nurses in law school, and attorneys in nursing school. **Purpose:** Aims to inform the public on matters of nursing, health care and law. Facilitates communication and information sharing between professional groups; establishes an employment network; assists new and potential nurse attorneys; develops the profession; promotes the image of nurse attorneys as experts and consultants in nursing and law. **Activities:** Maintains educational foundation.

★11050★ **American Health Care Association (AHCA)**
1201 L St. NW
Washington, DC 20005
Ph: (202)842-4444   Fax: (202)842-3860
E-mail: hr@ahca.org
URL: http://www.ahca.org

Description: Federation of state associations of long-term health care facilities. Promotes standards for professionals in long-term health care delivery and quality care for patients and residents in a safe environment. Focuses on issues of availability, quality, affordability, and fair payment. Operates as liaison with governmental agencies, Congress, and professional associations. Compiles statistics.

★11051★ **American Hospital Association (AHA)**
1 N Franklin
Chicago, IL 60606-3421
Ph: (312)422-3000   Fax: (312)422-4796
URL: http://www.aha.org

Description: Represents health care provider organizations. Seeks to advance the health of individuals and communities. Leads, represents, and serves health care provider organizations that are accountable to the community and committed to health improvement.

★11052★ **American Nurses Association (ANA)**
8515 Georgia Ave., Ste. 400
Silver Spring, MD 20910
Ph: (301)628-5000   Fax: (301)628-5001
Fr: 800-274-4262
E-mail: memberinfo@ana.org
URL: http://www.nursingworld.org

Description: Serves as membership association representing registered nurses. Advances the nursing profession by fostering high standards of nursing practice, promoting the rights of nurses in the workplace, projecting a positive and realistic view of nursing, and by lobbying the Congress and regulatory agencies on health care issues affecting nurses and the public.

★11053★ **American School Health Association (ASHA)**
PO Box 708
Kent, OH 44240
Ph: (330)678-1601   Fax: (330)678-4526
E-mail: asha@ashaweb.org
URL: http://www.ashaweb.org

Description: School physicians, school nurses, counsellors, nutritionists, psychologists, social workers, administrators, school health coordinators, health educators, and physical educators working in schools, professional preparation programs, public health, and community-based organizations. Promotes coordinated school health programs that include health education, health services, a healthful school environment, physical education, nutrition services, and psycho-social health services offered in schools collaboratively with families and other members of the community. Offers professional reference materials and professional development opportunities. Conducts pilot programs that inform materials development, provides technical assistance to school professionals, advocates for school health.

★11054★ **Association of Black Nursing Faculty (ABNF)**
PO Box 589
Lisle, IL 60532
Ph: (630)969-3809   Fax: (630)969-3895
E-mail: clay@tuckerpub.com

Members: Black nursing faculty teaching in nursing programs accredited by the National League for Nursing. **Purpose:** Works to promote health-related issues and educa-

tional concerns of interest to the black community and ABNF. **Activities:** Serves as a forum for communication and the exchange of information among members; develops strategies for expressing concerns to other individuals, institutions, and communities. Assists members in professional development; develops and sponsors continuing education activities; fosters networking and guidance in employment and recruitment activities. Promotes health-related issues of legislation, government programs, and community activities. Supports black consumer advocacy issues. Encourages research. Maintains speakers' bureau and hall of fame.

★11055★ **Association of Staff Physician Recruiters (ASPR)**
1711 W County Rd. B, Ste. 300N
Roseville, MN 55113
Fax: (651)635-0307   Fr: 800-830-2777
E-mail: admin@aspr.org
URL: http://www.aspr.org

Description: Recruits physicians and other healthcare providers to staff hospitals, clinics and managed care organizations where the members are employed. Sponsors educational programs and meetings on various recruitment issues.

★11056★ **EMTs, Nurses, Therapists, and Assistants**
Cambridge Educational
PO Box 2053
Princeton, NJ 08543-2053
Ph: 800-257-5126   Fax: (609)671-0266
Fr: 800-468-4227
E-mail: custserv@films.com
URL: http://www.cambridgeeducational.com

VHS and DVD. $79.95. 2000. 18 minutes. Part of the series "Exploring Health Occupations."

★11057★ **Exploring Health Occupations**
Cambridge Educational
PO Box 2053
Princeton, NJ 08543-2053
Ph: 800-257-5126   Fax: (609)671-0266
Fr: 800-468-4227
E-mail: custserv@films.com
URL: http://www.cambridgeeducational.com

VHS and DVD. $159.90. 1999. Two-part series provides a detailed view of the field of medical technicians and technologists, EMTs, nurses, therapists, and assistants.

★11058★ **Health Service Occupations**
Delphi Productions
3159 6th St.
Boulder, CO 80304
Ph: (303)443-2100   Fax: (303)443-4022
Fr: 888-443-2400
E-mail: support@delphivideo.com
URL: http://www.delphivideo.com

$95.00. 50 minutes. Part of the Careers for the 21st Century Video Library.

★11059★ Medicine & Related Occupations

Delphi Productions
3159 6th St.
Boulder, CO 80304
Ph: (303)443-2100   Fax: (303)443-4022
Fr: 888-443-2400
E-mail: support@delphivideo.com
URL: http://www.delphivideo.com

$95.00. 45 minutes. Part of the Careers for the 21st Century Video Library.

★11060★ National Association of Pediatric Nurse Practitioners (NAPNAP)

20 Brace Rd., Ste. 200
Cherry Hill, NJ 08034-2634
Ph: (856)857-9700   Fax: (856)857-1600
Fr: 877-662-7627
E-mail: info@napnap.org
URL: http://www.napnap.org

Members: Pediatric, school, and family nurse practitioners and interested persons. **Purpose:** Seeks to improve the quality of infant, child, and adolescent health care by making health care services accessible and providing a forum for continuing education of members. **Activities:** Facilitates and supports legislation designed to promote the role of pediatric nurse practitioners; promotes salary ranges commensurate with practitioners' responsibilities; facilitates exchange of information between prospective employers and job seekers in the field. Supports research programs; compiles statistics.

★11061★ National League for Nursing (NLN)

61 Broadway, 33rd Fl.
New York, NY 10006
Ph: (212)363-5555   Fax: (212)812-0393
Fr: 800-669-1656
E-mail: generalinfo@nln.org
URL: http://www.nln.org

Description: Champions the pursuit of quality nursing education. A professional association of nursing faculty, education agencies, health care agencies, allied/public agencies, and public members whose mission is to advance quality nursing education that prepares the nursing workforce to meet the needs of diverse populations in an ever-changing health care environment. Serves as the primary source of information about every type of nursing education program, from the LVN and LPN to the EdD and PhD. There are 20 affiliated constituent leagues that provide a local forum for members. The National League for Nursing Accrediting Commission is an independent corporate affiliate of the NLN, responsible for providing accreditation services to all levels of nursing education.

★11062★ National Rural Health Association (NRHA)

Administrative Office
521 E 63rd St.
Kansas City, MO 64110-3329
Ph: (816)756-3140   Fax: (816)756-3144
E-mail: mail@nrharural.org
URL: http://www.nrharural.org

Description: Administrators, physicians, nurses, physician assistants, health planners, academicians, and others interested or involved in rural health care. Creates a better understanding of health care problems unique to rural areas; utilizes a collective approach in finding positive solutions; articulates and represents the health care needs of rural America; supplies current information to rural health care providers; serves as a liaison between rural health care programs throughout the country. Offers continuing education credits for medical, dental, nursing, and management courses.

★11063★ National Student Nurses' Association (NSNA)

45 Main St., Ste. 606
Brooklyn, NY 11201
Ph: (718)210-0705   Fax: (718)210-0710
E-mail: nsna@nsna.org
URL: http://www.nsna.org

Members: Students enrolled in state-approved schools for the preparation of registered nurses. **Purpose:** Seeks to aid in the development of the individual nursing student and to urge students of nursing, as future leaders and health professionals, to be aware of and to contribute to improving the health care of all people. Encourages programs and activities in state groups concerning nursing, health, and the community. Provides assistance for state board review, as well as materials for preparation for state RN licensing examination. Cooperates with nursing organizations in recruitment of nurses and in professional, community, and civic programs. Sponsors Foundation of the National Student Nurses' Association in memory of Frances Tompkins.

★11064★ Nurses' House

Veronica M. Driscoll Center for Nursing
2113 Western Ave., Ste. 2
Guilderland, NY 12084-9559
Ph: (518)456-7858   Fax: (518)452-3760
E-mail: mail@nurseshouse.org
URL: http://www.nurseshouse.org

Members: Registered nurses and interested individuals united to assist registered nurses in financial and other crises. **Purpose:** Provides short-term financial aid for shelter, food, and utilities until nurses obtain entitlements or jobs. Offers counseling and referrals. Encourages homebound or retired nurses through a volunteer corps.

★11065★ The Patient Care Nursing Team

Cambridge Educational
PO Box 2053
Princeton, NJ 08543-2053
Ph: 800-257-5126   Fax: (609)671-0266
Fr: 800-468-4227
E-mail: custserv@films.com
URL: http://www.cambridgeeducational.com

VHS and DVD. $89.95. 2002. 15 minutes. Program describes the challenges that nurses face in a variety of work environments, including hospitals, clinics, schools, and homes, and outlines the education and licensing process that nurses must complete.

★11066★ Visiting Nurse Associations of America (VNAA)

Administration Office
99 Summer St., Ste. 1700
Boston, MA 02110
Ph: (617)737-3200   Fax: (617)737-1144
Fr: 800-426-2547
E-mail: vnaa@vnaa.org
URL: http://www.vnaa.org

Members: Home health care agencies. **Purpose:** Develops competitive strength among community-based nonprofit visiting nurse organizations; works to strengthen business resources and economic programs through contracting, marketing, governmental affairs and publications.

Reporters and Correspondents

★11067★ AeroSpaceNews.com

AeroSpaceNews.com
PO Box 1748
Ojai, CA 93024-1748
Ph: (805)985-2320
URL: http://www.aerospacenews.com/content/view/41/33/

Monthly. $19.95/year for individuals, private; $53.95/year for two years, individual, private; $79.95/year for individuals, trade; $143.95 for two years, individual. Journal reporting on the insights, impressions and images of tomorrow's technological wonders in the field of aerospace.

★11068★ Broadcasting & Cable

Reed Business Information
360 Park Ave. S
New York, NY 10010
Ph: (646)746-6400   Fax: (646)746-7431
URL: http://www.reedbusiness.com

Weekly. $199.99/year for individuals. News magazine covering The Fifth Estate (radio, TV, cable, and satellite), and the regulatory commissions involved.

★11069★ Columbia Journalism Review

Columbia Journalism Review
2950 Broadway, Journalism Bldg.
Columbia University
New York, NY 10027
Ph: (212)854-1881   Fax: (212)854-8580
Fr: 888-425-7782
E-mail: cjr@columbia.edu
URL: http://www.cjr.org/

Bimonthly. $19.95/year for U.S. $27.95 for single issue, Canadian & international orders. Magazine focusing on journalism.

★11070★ Current

Heldref Publications
1319 18th St., NW
Washington, DC 20036-1802
Ph: (202)296-6267   Fr: 800-365-9753

URL: http://www.heldref.org/current.php

Monthly. $47.00/year for individuals, print only; $111.00/year for institutions, print only. Journal that reprints articles on education, politics, and other social issues.

★11071★ Editor & Publisher

Editor & Publisher Magazine
770 Broadway
New York, NY 10003-9595
Ph: (646)654-5500   Fax: (646)654-5370
Fr: 800-562-2706
URL: http://www.editorandpublisher.com/eandp/index.jsp

Weekly (Mon.). $99.00/year for individuals, print and online; $159.00/year for Canada, print and online; $320.00/year for other countries; $7.95/year for individuals, monthly. Magazine focusing on newspaper journalism, advertising, printing equipment, and interactive services.

★11072★ Global Media Journal

Global Media Journal
c/o Yahya R. Kamalipour
Purdue University Calumet
Dept. of Communication & Creative Arts
2200 169th St.
Hammond, IN 46323-2094
Ph: (219)989-2880   Fax: (219)989-2008
URL: http://lass.calumet.purdue.edu/cca/gmj/gmj_about_us.htm

Semiannual. Free, e-mail. Electronic journal that seeks to address the interests of media and journalism scholars, researchers, teachers, students, and institutions engaged in international activities, particularly communication.

★11073★ The Hollywood Reporter

The Nielsen Co.
770 Broadway
New York, NY 10003
Ph: (646)654-5000   Fax: (646)654-5002
URL: http://www.hollywoodreporter.com/thr/index.jsp

Daily (morn.). $3.00 for single issue; $6.00/year for U.S., weekly; $299.00/year for individuals, print; $175.00/year for U.S., weekly

print; $299.00/year for U.S., print/online combination; $265.00/year for U.S., weekly print/online combination. Film, TV, and entertainment trade newspaper.

★11074★ In These Times

Institute for Public Affairs Inc.
2040 North Milwaukee Ave.
Chicago, IL 60647
Ph: (773)772-0100   Fax: (773)772-4180
E-mail: itt@inthesetimes.com
URL: http://www.inthesetimes.com

Biweekly. $24.95/year for individuals, U.S. $49.90 for two years, U.S. $39.95/year for Canada; $59.95/year for other countries. National political newsmagazine.

★11075★ Journalism Practice

Taylor & Francis Group Journals
325 Chestnut St., Ste. 800
Philadelphia, PA 19106
Ph: (215)625-8900   Fax: (215)625-8914
Fr: 800-354-1420
URL: http://www.tandf.co.uk/journals/titles/17512786.asp

$323.00/year for institutions, print and online; $306.00/year for institutions, online only; $77.00/year for individuals. Journal focusing on professional practice of journalism.

★11076★ Metro Magazine

Bobit Business Media
3520 Challenger St.
Torrance, CA 90503
Ph: (310)533-2400   Fax: (310)533-2500
E-mail: info@metro-magazine.com
URL: http://www.metro-magazine.com

Free. Magazine on public transportation.

★11077★ The New Republic

The New Republic L.L.C.
1331 H St. NW, Ste. 700
Washington, DC 20005
Ph: (202)508-4444   Fax: (202)628-9380
E-mail: tnrcustserv@cdsfulfillment.com
URL: http://www.tnr.com

Weekly. $39.97/year for individuals, print; $29.95/year for individuals, digital. Journal featuring current events comments and reviews.

★11078★ *Publishers Weekly*
Publishers Weekly
360 Park Ave. S.
New York, NY 10010
Ph: (646)746-6598
URL: http://www.publishersweekly.com

Weekly. $239.99/year for individuals; $299.99/year for Canada and Mexico; $399.99/year for other countries, air delivery. Magazine for publishers.

★11079★ *TelevisionWeek*
Crain Communications Inc.
1155 Gratiot Ave.
PO Box 07924
Detroit, MI 48207-2997
Ph: (313)446-6000   Fax: (313)446-0347
Fr: 888-909-9111
URL: http://www.tvweek.com/

Weekly. $119.00/year for individuals; $171.00/year for Canada, including GST; $309.00/year for other countries, airmail. Newspaper covering management, programming, cable and trends in the television and the media industry.

★11080★ *Writer's Digest*
F & W Publications Inc.
4700 E Galbraith Rd.
Cincinnati, OH 45236
Ph: (513)531-2690   Fax: (513)531-0798
Fr: 800-289-0963
URL: http://www.writersdigest.com

Monthly. $20.00/year for individuals; $30.00/year for Canada, including GST/HST; $30.00/year for other countries, surface delivery. Professional magazine for writers.

PLACEMENT AND JOB REFERRAL SERVICES

★11081★ **American Sportscasters Association (ASA)**
225 Broadway, Ste. 2030
New York, NY 10007
Ph: (212)227-8080   Fax: (212)571-0556
E-mail: lschwa8918@aol.com
URL: http://www.americansportscastersonline.com

Members: Radio and television sportscasters. **Purpose:** Sponsors seminars, clinics, and symposia for aspiring announcers and sportscasters. **Activities:** Compiles statistics. Operates Speaker's Bureau, placement service, hall of fame, and biographical archives. Maintains American Sportscaster Hall of Fame Trust. Is currently implementing Hall of Fame Museum, Community Programs.

★11082★ **Broadcast Foundation of College/University Students (BROADCAST)**
89 Longview Rd.
Port Washington, NY 11050
Ph: (516)883-0159   Fax: (516)883-0159
E-mail: rstarleton@aol.com

Members: College students interested in broadcasting and professional broadcasters interested in encouraging practical broadcasting experience in colleges and universities. **Activities:** Conducts annual survey of all professional broadcasting stations for part-time and summer employment for college students. Sponsors job advisory and placement service.

★11083★ **Education Writers Association (EWA)**
2122 P St. NW, Ste. 201
Washington, DC 20037
Ph: (202)452-9830   Fax: (202)452-9837
E-mail: ewa@ewa.org
URL: http://www.ewa.org

Members: Education writers and reporters of daily and weekly newspapers, national magazines of general circulation, and radio and television stations; associate members are school and college public relations personnel and others with a serious interest in education writing. **Purpose:** Improves the quality of education reporting and interpretation; encourages the development of education coverage by the press; to help attract top-notch writers and reporters to the education field. **Activities:** Sponsors regional and special workshops. Provides job referral/bank services.

★11084★ **National Association of Broadcasters (NAB)**
1771 N St. NW
Washington, DC 20036
Ph: (202)429-5300   Fax: (202)429-4199
E-mail: nab@nab.org
URL: http://www.nab.org

Description: Representatives of radio and television stations and networks; associate members include producers of equipment and programs. Seeks to ensure the viability, strength, and success of free, over-the-air broadcasters; serves as an information resource to the industry. Monitors and reports on events regarding radio and television broadcasting. Maintains Broadcasting Hall of Fame. Offers minority placement service and employment clearinghouse.

★11085★ **National Association of Hispanic Journalists (NAHJ)**
1000 National Press Bldg.
529 14th St. NW
Washington, DC 20045-2001
Ph: (202)662-7145   Fax: (202)662-7144
Fr: 888-346-NAHJ
E-mail: nahj@nahj.org
URL: http://www.nahj.org

Description: Aims to organize and support Hispanics involved in news gathering and dissemination. Encourages journalism and communications study and practice by Hispanics. Seeks recognition for Hispanic members of the profession regarding their skills and achievements. Promotes fair and accurate media treatment of Hispanics; opposes job discrimination and demeaning stereotypes. Works to increase educational and career opportunities and development for Hispanics in the field. Seeks to foster greater awareness of members' cultural identity, interests, and concerns. Provides a united voice for Hispanic journalists with the aim of achieving national visibility. Offers placement services to Hispanic students. Activities include: a census of Hispanic media professionals nationwide; writing contest for Hispanic students. Offers scholarships, seminars, and training workshops.

★11086★ **Radio-Television News Directors Association (RTNDA)**
1600 K St. NW, Ste. 700
Washington, DC 20006-2806
Ph: (202)659-6510   Fax: (202)223-4007
Fr: 800-80-RTNDA
E-mail: rtnda@rtnda.org
URL: http://rtnda.org

Description: Comprises of heads of news departments for broadcast and cable stations and networks; associate members are journalists engaged in the preparation and presentation of broadcast news and teachers of electronic journalism; other members represent industry services, public relations departments of business firms, public relations firms, and networks. Works to improve standards of electronic journalism; defends rights of journalists to access news; promotes journalism training to meet specific needs of the industry. Operates placement service and speakers' bureau.

EMPLOYER DIRECTORIES AND NETWORKING LISTS

★11087★ *ANR National Directory of Community Newspapers*
American Newspaper Representatives Inc.
2075 W Big Beaver Rd., Ste. 310
Troy, MI 48084
Ph: (248)643-7766   Fax: (248)643-9914
Fr: 800-550-7557
URL: http://www.anrinc.net/

Weekly (Mon.), May/June. Number of listings: 7,000. Entries include: Name of weekly newspaper, address, county, type of area, circulation, day published, name of publisher, and information on advertising rates and production specifications. Arrangement: Geographical.

★11088★ *Broadcasting & Cable Yearbook*
R.R. Bowker L.L.C.
630 Central Ave.
New Providence, NJ 07974
Ph: (908)286-1090   Fr: 888-269-5372

URL: http://www.bowker.com

Annual; latest edition 2007, published October 2006. $235.00 for individuals. Covers over 17,000 television and radio stations in the United States, its territories, and Canada; cable MSOs and their individual systems; television and radio networks, broadcast and cable group owners, station representatives, satellite networks and services, film companies, advertising agencies, government agencies, trade associations, schools, and suppliers of professional and technical services, including books, serials, and videos; communications lawyers. Entries include: Company name, address, phone, fax, names of executives. Station listings include broadcast power, other operating details. Arrangement: Stations and systems are geographical, others are alphabetical. Indexes: Alphabetical.

★11089★ **CPB Public Broadcasting Directory**

Corporation for Public Broadcasting
401 9th St. NW
Washington, DC 20004-2129
Ph: (202)879-9600   Fax: (202)879-9700
Fr: 800-272-2190
URL: http://www.cpb.org/stations/publicdirectory/

Annual. Covers public television and radio stations, national and regional public broadcasting organizations and networks, state government agencies and commissions, and other related organizations. Entries include: For radio and television stations–Station call letters, frequency or channel, address, phone, licensee name, licensee type, date on air, antenna height, area covered, names and titles of key personnel. For organizations–Name, address, phone, name and title of key personnel. Arrangement: National and regional listings are alphabetical; state groups and the public radio and television stations are each geographical; other organizations and agencies are alphabetical. Indexes: Geographical, personnel, call letter, licensee type (all in separate indexes for radio and television).

★11090★ **Directory of Small Magazine-Press Editors and Publishers**

Dustbooks
PO Box 100
Paradise, CA 95967
Ph: (530)877-6110   Fax: (530)877-0222
Fr: 800-477-6110
URL: http://www.dustbooks.com/

Annual; latest edition 37th, 2006-2007. $25.95 for individuals. Covers about 7,500 publishers and editors. Entries include: Individual name, title of press or magazine, address and phone number. Arrangement: Alphabetical.

★11091★ **Editor & Publisher International Year Book**

Editor & Publisher Magazine
770 Broadway
New York, NY 10003-9595
Ph: (646)654-5500   Fax: (646)654-5370
Fr: 800-562-2706
URL: http://www.editorandpublisher.com

Annual, 2005. Covers daily and Sunday newspapers in the United States and Canada; weekly newspapers; foreign daily newspapers; special service newspapers; newspaper syndicates; news services; journalism schools; foreign language and Black newspapers in the United States; news, picture, and press services; feature and news syndicates; comic and magazine services; advertising clubs; trade associations; clipping bureaus; house organs; journalism awards; also lists manufacturers of equipment and supplies. Entries include: For daily papers–Publication name, address, phone, fax, e-mail, web site URL, names of executives and departmental editors (business, financial, book, food, etc.), circulation and advertising data, production information including format of paper and equipment used. Similar but less detailed information for other publications. Arrangement: Publications and schools are geographical; most other lists are alphabetical.

★11092★ **Editorial Freelancers Association-Membership Directory**

Editorial Freelancers Association Inc.
71 W 23rd St., Ste. 1910
New York, NY 10010-4102
Ph: (212)929-5400   Fax: (212)929-5439
Fr: (866)929-5400
URL: http://66.241.221.102/EFADirectory/select.asp

Annual, spring. $25.00. Covers 1,100 member editorial freelancers. Entries include: Personal name, address, phone, services provided, specialties. Arrangement: Alphabetical. Indexes: Product/service; special interest; geographical; computer skills.

★11093★ **International Directory of Little Magazines and Small Presses**

Dustbooks
PO Box 100
Paradise, CA 95967
Ph: (530)877-6110   Fax: (530)877-0222
Fr: 800-477-6110
URL: http://www.dustbooks.com/lilmag.htm

Annual; latest edition 43rd, 2007-2008. $55.00 for individuals, cloth-bound; $37.95 for individuals, paperback. Covers over 4,000 small, independent magazines, presses, and papers. Entries include: Name, address, size, circulation, frequency, price, type of material used, number of issues or books published annually, and other pertinent data. Arrangement: Alphabetical. Indexes: Subject; regional.

★11094★ **International Television and Video Almanac**

Quigley Publishing Company Inc.
64 Wintergreen Ln.
Groton, MA 01450-4129
Ph: (860)228-0247   Fax: (860)228-0157
Fr: 800-231-8239
URL: http://hometown.aol.com/quigleypub/mp.html

Annual, January; latest edition 2007. $175.00 for individuals. Covers "Who's Who in Motion Pictures and Television and Home Video," television networks, major program producers, major group station owners, cable television companies, distributors, firms serving the television and home video industry, equipment manufacturers, casting agencies, literary agencies, advertising and publicity representatives, television stations, associations, list of feature films produced for television, statistics, industry's year in review, award winners, satellite and wireless cable providers, primetime programming, video producers, distributors, wholesalers. Entries include: Generally, company name, address, phone; manufacturer and service listings may include description of products and services and name of contact; producing, distributing, and station listings include additional details and contacts for cable and broadcast networks. Arrangement: Classified by service or activity. Indexes: Full.

★11095★ **National Directory of Magazines**

Oxbridge Communications Inc.
186 5th Ave.
New York, NY 10010
Ph: (212)741-0231   Fax: (212)633-2938
Fr: 800-955-0231
E-mail: custserv@oxbridge.com
URL: http://www.oxbridge.com/

Latest edition September 2007. $995.00 for individuals, print product; $1,195.00 for individuals, CD-ROM; $1,995.00 for individuals, print product and CD-ROM. Covers over 19,000 magazines; coverage includes Canada. Entries include: Title, publisher name, address, phone, fax number, names and titles of contact and key personnel, financial data, editorial and advertising information, circulation. Arrangement: Classified by subject. Indexes: Title; geographical; publisher.

★11096★ **The News Media**

Lucent Books Inc.
10911 Technology Pl.
PO Box 9187
San Diego, CA 92127
Ph: (858)485-7424   Fax: 800-414-5043
Fr: 800-877-4253
URL: http://www.gale.com

Latest edition April 2002. Publication includes: List of organizations to contact for further information about careers in the news media. Principal content of publication is an examination of a variety of careers in the news media. Indexes: Alphabetical.

★11097★ RTNDA Communicator-Directory Issues

Radio-Television News Directors
Association
1600 K St. NW, No. 700
Washington, DC 20006-2838
Ph: (202)659-6510   Fax: (202)223-4007
Fr: 800-80R-TNDA
URL: http://www.rtnda.org

Semiannual, January and July. Number of listings: 3,000; membership includes Canada and some foreign countries. Entries include: Member name, address, phone, and name of radio or television station, network, or other news organization with which affiliated. Arrangement: Same information given in alphabetical and geographical arrangements.

★11098★ Sports Market Place

Sports Careers
2990 E Northern Ave., Ste. D107
Phoenix, AZ 85028
Ph: (602)485-5555   Fax: (602)485-5556

Annual, January. Covers manufacturers, organizations, professional sports teams, broadcasting networks, sports arenas, syndicators, publications, trade shows, marketing services, corporate sports sponsors, and other groups concerned with the business and promotional aspects of sports generally and with air sports, arm wrestling, auto sports, badminton, baseball, basketball, biathlon, bowling, boxing, curling, equestrian, exercise, fencing, field hockey, football, golf, gymnastics, ice hockey, lacrosse, martial arts, paddleball, paddle tennis, platform tennis, pentathlon, racquetball, rowing, rugby, running/jogging, skiing, soccer, softball, squash, swimming, table tennis, tennis, track and field, volleyball, water sports, weightlifting, and wrestling. Entries include: Name of company or organization, address, fax, e-mail, URL, name of key personnel with titles, and description of products or services. Arrangement: Classified by type of firm, sport, or activity. Indexes: Alphabetical; single sport; media; sport sponsors; agencies; manufacturers; brand name; facilities; executives; and geographical.

★11099★ SRDS International Media Guide

SRDS
1700 Higgins Rd.
Des Plaines, IL 60018-5605
Ph: (847)375-5000   Fax: (847)375-5001
Fr: 800-851-7737
URL: http://www.srds.com

Annual. $395.00 for individuals. Covers approximately 2,500 newspapers and color newspaper magazines/supplements from 200 countries, including the United States. Entries include: Publication name; publisher name, address, phone, fax, e-mail, URL, names of editor, advertising manager, and representatives in the United States and worldwide; advertising rates in U.S. dollars and/or local currency, circulation, mechanical data, ad closing, readership description, etc. Arrangement: Geographical.

★11100★ Ulrich's Periodicals Directory

R.R. Bowker L.L.C.
630 Central Ave.
New Providence, NJ 07974
Ph: (908)286-1090   Fr: 888-269-5372
E-mail: ulrichs@bowker.com
URL: http://www.bowker.com

Annual; 45th edition, 2007. $875.00. Covers nearly 186,000 current periodicals and newspapers published worldwide. Entries include: In main list–Publication title; Dewey Decimal Classification number, Library of Congress Classification number (where applicable), CODEN designation (for sci-tech serials), British Library Document Supply Centre shelfmark number, country code, ISSN; subtitle, language(s) of text, year first published, frequency, subscription prices, sponsoring organization, publishing company name, address, phone, fax, e-mail and website addresses, editor and publisher names; regular features (reviews, advertising, abstracts, bibliographies, trade literature, etc.), indexes, circulation, format, brief description of content; availability of microforms and reprints; whether refereed; CD-ROM availability with vendor name; online availability with service name; services that index or abstract the periodical, with years covered; advertising rates and contact; rights and permissions contact name and phone; availability through document delivery. Arrangement: Main listing is classified by subject; U.S. general daily and weekly newspapers are listed in a separate volume; lists of cessations, online services, and CD-ROM vendors are alphabetical. Indexes: Cessations; subjects; title (including variant, former, and ceased titles); ISSN; periodicals available on CD-ROM; online periodical title; refereed serial; and international organization publication title.

HANDBOOKS AND MANUALS

★11101★ Career Opportunities for Writers

Facts On File Inc.
132 W. 31st St., 17th Fl.
New York, NY 10001-2006
Ph: (212)967-8800   Fax: 800-678-3633
Fr: 800-322-8755
E-mail: custserv@factsonfile.com
URL: http://www.factsonfile.com

Rosemary Ellen Guiley and Janet Frick. 2nd edition, 1991. $49.50. 230 pages. Part of the Career Opportunities Series. Describes more than 100 jobs in eight major fields, offering such details as duties, salaries, perquisites, employment and advancement opportunities, organizations to join, and opportunities for women and minorities.

★11102★ Careers in Communications

The McGraw-Hill Companies
PO Box 182604
Columbus, OH 43272
Fax: (614)759-3749   Fr: 877-883-5524
E-mail: customer.service@mcgraw-hill.com

URL: http://www.mcgraw-hill.com

Shonan Noronha. Fourth edition, 2004. $15.95 (paper). 192 pages. Examines the fields of journalism, photography, radio, television, film, public relations, and advertising. Gives concrete details on job locations and how to secure a job. Suggests many resources for job hunting.

★11103★ Careers in Journalism

The McGraw-Hill Companies
PO Box 182604
Columbus, OH 43272
Fax: (614)759-3749   Fr: 877-883-5524
E-mail: customer.service@mcgraw-hill.com
URL: http://www.mcgraw-hill.com

Jan Goldberg. Third edition, 2005. $15.95 (paper). 192 pages.

★11104★ Careers for Mystery Buffs and Other Snoops and Sleuths

The McGraw-Hill Companies
PO Box 182604
Columbus, OH 43272
Fax: (614)759-3749   Fr: 877-883-5524
E-mail: customer.service@mcgraw-hill.com
URL: http://www.mcgraw-hill.com

Blythe Camenson. Second edition, 2004. $12.95 (paper); $14.95 (cloth). 160 pages.

★11105★ Careers for Night Owls and Other Insomniacs

The McGraw-Hill Companies
PO Box 182604
Columbus, OH 43272
Fax: (614)759-3749   Fr: 877-883-5524
E-mail: customer.service@mcgraw-hill.com
URL: http://www.mcgraw-hill.com

Louise Miller. Second edition, 2002. $12.95 (paper). 160 pages.

★11106★ Careers for Writers and Others Who Have a Way with Words

The McGraw-Hill Companies
PO Box 182604
Columbus, OH 43272
Fax: (614)759-3749   Fr: 877-883-5524
E-mail: customer.service@mcgraw-hill.com
URL: http://www.mcgraw-hill.com

Robert W. Bly. Second edition, 2003. $13.95 (paper). 208 pages.

★11107★ Editorial Freelancing: A Practical Guide

Aletheia Publications, Inc.
46 Bell Hollow Rd.
Putnam Valley, NY 10579
Ph: (845)526-2873   Fax: (845)526-2905
E-mail: AlethPub@aol.com

Trumbull Rogers. 1995. 212 pages. $19.95 (paper). Contains everything the freelancer needs to know about building a basic reference library, choosing a computer and appropriate software, marketing editorial services, determining and negotiating rates, billing, and setting up a retirement plan.

★11108★ **Great Jobs for Communications Majors**

The McGraw-Hill Companies
PO Box 182604
Columbus, OH 43272
Fax: (614)759-3749   Fr: 877-883-5524
E-mail: customer.service@mcgraw-hill.com
URL: http://www.mcgraw-hill.com

Blythe Camenson. Second edition, 2001. $15.95 (paper). 256 pages.

★11109★ **Great Jobs for English Majors**

The McGraw-Hill Companies
PO Box 182604
Columbus, OH 43272
Fax: (614)759-3749   Fr: 877-883-5524
E-mail: customer.service@mcgraw-hill.com
URL: http://www.mcgraw-hill.com

Julie DeGalan. Third edition, 2006. $15.95 (paper). 192 pages.

★11110★ **Great Jobs for Liberal Arts Majors**

The McGraw-Hill Companies
PO Box 182604
Columbus, OH 43272
Fax: (614)759-3749   Fr: 877-883-5524
E-mail: customer.service@mcgraw-hill.com
URL: http://www.mcgraw-hill.com

Blythe Camenson. Second edition, 2001. $14.95 (paper). 256 pages.

★11111★ **Opportunities in Journalism Careers**

The McGraw-Hill Companies
PO Box 182604
Columbus, OH 43272
Fax: (614)759-3749   Fr: 877-883-5524
E-mail: customer.service@mcgraw-hill.com
URL: http://www.mcgraw-hill.com

Jim Patten and Donald L. Ferguson. 2001. $12.95 (paper). 160 pages. Outlines opportunities in every field of journalism, including newspaper reporting and editing, magazine and book publishing, corporate communications, advertising and public relations, freelance writing, and teaching. Covers how to prepare for and enter each field, outlining responsibilities, salaries, benefits, and job outlook for each specialty. Illustrated.

★11112★ **Opportunities in Sports and Athletics Careers**

The McGraw-Hill Companies
PO Box 182604
Columbus, OH 43272
Fax: (614)759-3749   Fr: 877-883-5524
E-mail: customer.service@mcgraw-hill.com
URL: http://www.mcgraw-hill.com

William Ray Heitzmann. 1993. 160 pages. $11.95 (paper). A guide to planning for and seeking opportunities in this growing field. Illustrated.

★11113★ **Opportunities in Technical Writing and Communications Careers**

The McGraw-Hill Companies
PO Box 182604
Columbus, OH 43272
Fax: (614)759-3749   Fr: 877-883-5524
E-mail: customer.service@mcgraw-hill.com
URL: http://www.mcgraw-hill.com

Jay Gould and Wayne Losano. Revised edition, 1994. $14.95; $11.95 (paper). 152 pages. Provides advice on acquiring a position in medical, engineering, pharmaceutical, and other technical fields. Illustrated.

★11114★ **Opportunities in Writing Careers**

The McGraw-Hill Companies
PO Box 182604
Columbus, OH 43272
Fax: (614)759-3749   Fr: 877-883-5524
E-mail: customer.service@mcgraw-hill.com
URL: http://www.mcgraw-hill.com

Elizabeth Foote-Smith. 2006. $13.95; $11.95 (paper). 160 pages. Discusses opportunities in the print media, broadcasting, advertising or publishing. Business writing, public relations, and technical writing are among the careers covered. Contains bibliography and illustrations.

★11115★ **Real People Working in Communications**

The McGraw-Hill Companies
PO Box 182604
Columbus, OH 43272
Fax: (614)759-3749   Fr: 877-883-5524
E-mail: customer.service@mcgraw-hill.com
URL: http://www.mcgraw-hill.com

Jan Goldberg. 1996. $17.95 (paper). 133 pages. Interviews and profiles of working professionals capture a range of opportunities in this field.

★11116★ **Real-Resumes for Media, Newspaper, Broadcasting and Public Affairs Jobs**

PREP Publishing
1110 1/2 Hay St., PMB 66
Fayetteville, NC 28305
Ph: (910)483-6611   Fax: (910)483-2439
Fr: 800-533-2814

Anne McKinney (Editor). October 2002. $16.95. 192 pages. Part of the Real-Resumes Series.

★11117★ **Resumes for Communications Careers**

The McGraw-Hill Companies
PO Box 182604
Columbus, OH 43272
Fax: (614)759-3749   Fr: 877-883-5524
E-mail: customer.service@mcgraw-hill.com
URL: http://www.mcgraw-hill.com

Third edition, 2003. $10.95 (paper). 160 pages.

EMPLOYMENT AGENCIES AND SEARCH FIRMS

★11118★ **Joe Sullivan and Associates, Inc.**

9 Feather Hill
Southold, NY 11971-0612
Ph: (631)765-5050   Fax: (631)765-9047

Executive search firm. Recruits for the broadcasting, media, and entertainment industries.

ONLINE JOB SOURCES AND SERVICES

★11119★ **JournalismJobs.com**
Ph: (510)653-1521
E-mail: contact@journalismjobs.com
URL: http://www.journalismjobs.com

Description: Career-related site for journalists and other media professionals. Seekers can search for jobs, post a resume online, and manage the search online with the Job Seeker Folder feature. They also can receive free job announcements by e-mail.

TRADESHOWS

★11120★ **Radio-Television News Directors Association International Conference & Exhibition**

Radio-Television News Directors Association
1600 K St., NW, Ste. 700
Washington, DC 20006-2838
Ph: (202)659-6510   Fax: (202)223-4007
Fr: 800-807-8632
E-mail: rtnda@rtnda.org
URL: http://www.rtnda.org

Annual. **Primary Exhibits:** Equipment, supplies, and services for the radio and television news industries, including cameras, recorders, weather equipment, computers, and software.

OTHER SOURCES

★11121★ **Asian American Journalists Association (AAJA)**

1182 Market St., Ste. 320
San Francisco, CA 94102
Ph: (415)346-2051   Fax: (415)346-6343
E-mail: national@aaja.org
URL: http://www.aaja.org

Description: Represents more than 2,000 members. Serves Asian Americans and Pacific Islanders by encouraging young people to consider journalism as a career, developing managers in the media industry, and promoting fair and accurate news coverage. Serves as an alliance partner in UNITY Journalists of Color, along with the Native American Journalists Association, National Association of Hispanic Journalists, and National Association of Black Journalists.

★11122★ **Association for Women in Communications (AWC)**

3337 Duke St.
Alexandria, VA 22314
Ph: (703)370-7436   Fax: (703)370-7437
E-mail: info@womcom.org
URL: http://www.womcom.org

Description: Professional association of journalism and communications.

★11123★ **Broadcast Education Association (BEA)**

1771 N St. NW
Washington, DC 20036-2891
Ph: (202)429-3935   Fax: (202)775-2981
Fr: 888-380-7222
E-mail: beainfo@beaweb.org
URL: http://www.beaweb.org

Description: Universities and colleges; faculty and students; promotes improvement of curriculum and teaching methods, broadcasting research, television and radio production, and programming teaching on the college level.

★11124★ **Dow Jones Newspaper Fund (DJNF)**

PO Box 300
Princeton, NJ 08543-0300
Ph: (609)452-2820   Fax: (609)520-5804
E-mail: newsfund@wsj.dowjones.com
URL: http://djnewspaperfund.dowjones.com

Description: Established by Dow Jones and Company, publisher of *The Wall Street Journal*, to encourage careers in journalism. Operates newspaper's editing, and Sports Copy Editing Internship Programs for all junior, senior, and graduate level college students interested in journalism. Also offers Business Reporting Intern Program for minority college sophomores and juniors to complete summer internships on daily newspapers as business reporters. Students re-

ceive monetary scholarships to return to school in the fall. Offers information on careers in journalism.

★11125★ **Editorial Freelancers Association (EFA)**

71 W 23rd St., 4th Fl.
New York, NY 10010-4181
Ph: (212)929-5400   Fax: (212)929-5439
Fr: (866)929-5400
E-mail: office@the-efa.org
URL: http://www.the-efa.org

Description: Represents persons who work full or part-time as freelance writers or editorial freelancers. Promotes professionalism and facilitates the exchange of information and support. Conducts professional training seminars; and offers job listings.

★11126★ *Interviewing Techniques for Newspapers*

Hyperion Books
77 West 66th St., 11 Fl.
New York, NY 10023
Ph: (212)522-8700   Fr: 800-759-0190
URL: http://www.hyperionbooks.com

Maurice Dunlevy. 1995. $20.00 (paper). 143 pages.

★11127★ **Media and the Arts Occupations**

Delphi Productions
3159 6th St.
Boulder, CO 80304
Ph: (303)443-2100   Fax: (303)443-4022
Fr: 888-443-2400
E-mail: support@delphivideo.com
URL: http://www.delphivideo.com

$95.00. 50 minutes. Part of the Careers for the 21st Century Video Library.

★11128★ **National Journalism Center (NJC)**

110 Elden St.
Herndon, VA 20170
Fax: (703)318-9122   Fr: 800-872-1776
E-mail: amooney@yaf.org
URL: http://njc.yaf.org

Description: Advances awareness and understanding of America's traditional values and free enterprise system through the publi-

cation and distribution of studies on major issues of public policy. Conducts educational programs for youth and trains college students in journalistic skills. Sponsors internship program that features research projects, writing assignments, and weekly seminars with professional journalists. Operates a job bank to match potential candidates with media-related jobs.

★11129★ **National Religious Broadcasters (NRB)**

9510 Technology Dr.
Manassas, VA 20110
Ph: (703)330-7000   Fax: (703)330-7100
E-mail: info@nrb.org
URL: http://www.nrb.org

Description: Christian communicators. Fosters electronic media access for the Gospel; promotes standards of excellence; integrity and accountability; and provides networking and fellowship opportunities for members.

★11130★ **Society of Professional Journalists (SPJ)**

3909 N Meridian St.
Indianapolis, IN 46208-4011
Ph: (317)927-8000   Fax: (317)920-4789
E-mail: tharper@spj.org
URL: http://www.spj.org

Members: Professional society - journalism. **Purpose:** Promotes a free and unfettered press; high professional standards and ethical behavior; journalism as a career. Conducts lobbying activities; maintains legal defense fund. Sponsors Pulliam/Kilgore Freedom of Information Internships in Washington, DC, and Indianapolis, IN. **Activities:** Holds forums on the free press.

★11131★ **Women in Cable Telecommunications (WICT)**

PO Box 791305
Baltimore, MD 21279-1305
Ph: (703)234-9810   Fax: (703)817-1595
E-mail: bfmosley@wict.org
URL: http://www.wict.org

Description: Empowers and educates women to achieve their professional goals by providing opportunities for leadership, networking and advocacy.

Respiratory Therapists

SOURCES OF HELP-WANTED ADS

★11132★ **AARC Times**
Daedalus Enterprises Inc.
11030 Ables Ln.
PO Box 29686
Dallas, TX 75229
Ph: (972)243-2272   Fax: (972)484-2720
URL: http://aarc.org

Monthly. $85.00/year for individuals, 1-year subscription. Professional magazine for respiratory therapists and other cardiopulmonary specialists.

★11133★ **ADVANCE for Respiratory Care Practitioners**
Merion Publications Inc.
2900 Horizon Dr.
PO Box 61556
King of Prussia, PA 19406
Ph: (610)278-1400   Fr: 800-355-5627
URL: http://www.advanceweb.com/publications.asp?pub=RC

Biweekly. Magazine for RRT's, CRTT's, and cardiopulmonary technologists across the country.

★11134★ **Annals of Medicine**
Taylor & Francis Group Journals
325 Chestnut St., Ste. 800
Philadelphia, PA 19106
Ph: (215)625-8900   Fax: (215)625-8914
Fr: 800-354-1420
URL: http://www.ingentaconnect.com

$418.00/year for institutions, print and online; $397.00/year for institutions, online only; $155.00/year for individuals. Journal covering health science and medical education.

★11135★ **Clinical Medicine & Research**
Marshfield Clinic
1000 North Oak Ave.
Marshfield, WI 54449
Ph: (715)387-5511   Fr: 800-782-8581

URL: http://www.clinmedres.org/

Monthly. Journal that publishes scientific medical research that is relevant to a broad audience of medical researchers and healthcare professionals.

★11136★ **CME Supplement to Emergency Medicine Clinics of North America**
Elsevier Science Inc.
360 Park Ave. S
New York, NY 10010
Ph: (212)989-5800   Fax: (212)633-3990
URL: http://www.elsevier.com

Quarterly. $190.00/year for individuals. Journal covering emergency medicine clinics.

★11137★ **Discovery Medicine**
Discovery Medicine
2245 Chapel Valley Ln.
Timonium, MD 21093
Ph: (410)560-9007   Fax: (410)560-9000
URL: http://www.discoverymedicine.com

Bimonthly. $39.95/year for individuals; $49.95/year for individuals, digital edition and online access; $69.95 for two years, online access; $84.95 for two years, digital edition and online access; $99.95/year for individuals, 3 years, online access; $119.95/year for individuals, 3 years, digital and online access; $299.00/year for individuals, medical report (PMR); $99.00/year for individuals, medical report update. Online journal that publishes articles on diseases, biology, new diagnostics, and treatments for medical professionals.

★11138★ **Education & Treatment of Children**
West Virginia University Press
44 Stansbury Hall
PO Box 6295
Morgantown, WV 26506
Ph: (304)293-8400   Fax: (304)293-6585
Fr: (866)988-7737
URL: http://
www.educationandtreatmentofchildren.net

Quarterly. $85.00/year for institutions; $45.00/year for individuals; $100.00/year for institutions, elsewhere; $60.00/year for individuals, elsewhere. Periodical featuring information concerning the development of services for children and youth. Includes reports written for educators and other child care and mental health providers focused on teaching, training, and treatment effectiveness.

★11139★ **Heart and Lung**
Mosby
1600 John F. Kennedy Blvd., Ste. 1800
Philadelphia, PA 19103-2899
Ph: (215)239-3276   Fax: (215)239-3286
URL: http://www.elsevier.com/wps/find/journaleditorialboard.cws_h

Bimonthly. $111.00/year for individuals; $321.00/year for institutions; $34.00/year for students; $99.00/year for other countries; $50.00/year for students, other countries; $289.00/year for institutions, other countries. Journal offering articles prepared by nurse and physician members of the critical care team, recognizing the nurse's role in the care and management of major organ-system conditions in critically ill patients.

★11140★ **Hospitals & Health Networks**
Health Forum L.L.C.
1 N Franklin, 29th Fl.
Chicago, IL 60606
Ph: (312)893-6800   Fax: (312)422-4506
Fr: 800-821-2039
URL: http://www.hhnmag.com

Weekly. Publication covering the health care industry.

★11141★ **The IHS Primary Care Provider**
Indian Health Service (HQ)
The Reyes Bldg.
801 Thompson Ave., Ste. 400
Rockville, MD 20852-1627
URL: http://www.ihs.gov/PublicInfo/Publications/HealthProvider/Pr

Monthly. Journal for health care professionals, physicians, nurses, pharmacists, dentists, and dietitians.

★11142★ Injury

Mosby Inc.
11830 Westline Industrial Dr.
St. Louis, MO 63146
Ph: (314)872-8370   Fax: (314)432-1380
Fr: 800-325-4177
URL: http://www.elsevier.com/wps/find/journaldescription.cws_home

Monthly. $1,106.00/year for institutions, all countries except Europe, Japan and Iran; $169.00/year for individuals, all countries except Europe, Japan and Iran. Journal publishing articles and research related to the treatment of injuries such as trauma systems and management; surgical procedures; epidemiological studies; surgery (of all tissues); resuscitation; biomechanics; rehabilitation; anaesthesia; radiology and wound management.

★11143★ Journal of the American Society of Podiatric Medical Assistants

American Society of Podiatric Medical Assistants
2124 S Austin Blvd.
Cicero, IL 60804
Ph: (708)863-6303   Fr: 888-882-7762
URL: http://www.aspma.org

Quarterly. Subscription included in membership. Professional journal covering issues in podiatry.

★11144★ Journal of Cardiopulmonary Rehabilitation (JCR)

Lippincott Williams & Wilkins
530 Walnut St.
Philadelphia, PA 19106-3621
Ph: (215)521-8300   Fax: (215)521-8902
Fr: 800-638-3030
E-mail: jcr@sba.com
URL: http://www.jcrjournal.com/

Bimonthly. $108.91/year for individuals, U.S.; $298.96/year for institutions, U.S.; $222.94/year for individuals, international; $375.94/year for institutions, international; $37.49/year for U.S., in-training. Medical journal.

★11145★ Journal of Health Law

American Health Lawyers Association
1025 Connecticut Ave., NW, Ste. 600
Washington, DC 20036-5405
Ph: (202)833-1100   Fax: (202)833-1105
URL: http://www.healthlawyers.org

Quarterly. Professional journal covering healthcare issues and cases and their impact on the health care arena.

★11146★ Journal of Hospital Medicine

John Wiley & Sons Inc.
111 River St.
Hoboken, NJ 07030-5774
Ph: (201)748-6000   Fax: (201)748-6088
Fr: 800-825-7550
URL: http://www.wiley.com/WileyCDA/WileyTitle/productCd-JHM.html

Bimonthly. $110.00/year for individuals, print only; Online version available with subscription. Journal on hospital medicine.

★11147★ Medical Risks

Taylor & Francis Group Journals
325 Chestnut St., Ste. 800
Philadelphia, PA 19106
Ph: (215)625-8900   Fax: (215)625-8914
Fr: 800-354-1420
URL: http://www.tandf.co.uk

Monthly. Journal covering articles on medical risks.

★11148★ Medical Staff Development Professional

American Academy of Medical Management
Crossville Commons
560 W Crossville Rd., Ste. 103
Roswell, GA 30075
Ph: (770)649-7150   Fax: (770)649-7552

Periodic. Professional journal covering medical education.

★11149★ Pacifica Review

Taylor & Francis Group Journals
325 Chestnut St., Ste. 800
Philadelphia, PA 19106
Ph: (215)625-8900   Fax: (215)625-8914
Fr: 800-354-1420
URL: http://www.tandf.co.uk/

$462.00/year for individuals; $279.00/year for individuals; $487.00/year for individuals; $294.00/year for individuals; $123.00/year for individuals; $86.00/year for individuals. Journal promoting physical therapy and integration.

★11150★ USA Body Psychotherapy Journal

United States Association for Body Psychotherapy
7831 Woodmont Ave.
Bethesda, MD 20814
URL: http://www.usabp.org/displaycommon.cfm?an=4

Semiannual. Academic journal that seeks to support, promote and stimulate the exchange of ideas, scholarship and research within the field of body psychotherapy as well as an interdisciplinary exchange with related fields of clinical practice and inquiry.

★11151★ Year Book of Critical Care Medicine

Elsevier Science Inc.
360 Park Ave. S
New York, NY 10010
Ph: (212)989-5800   Fax: (212)633-3990
URL: http://www.elsevier.com

$180.00/year for institutions, U.S. $191.00/year for institutions, other countries; $121.00/year for individuals, U.S. $134.00/year for individuals, other countries; $59.00/year for students, U.S. $71.00/year for students, other countries. Journal focused on treatment of severe sepsis and septic shock, echocardiography in the evaluation of hemodynamically unstable patients & mechanical ventilation of acute respiratory distress syndrome.

PLACEMENT AND JOB REFERRAL SERVICES

★11152★ American Public Health Association (APHA)

800 I St. NW
Washington, DC 20001
Ph: (202)777-2742   Fax: (202)777-2534
E-mail: comments@apha.org
URL: http://www.apha.org

Members: Professional organization of physicians, nurses, educators, academicians, environmentalists, epidemiologists, new professionals, social workers, health administrators, optometrists, podiatrists, pharmacists, dentists, nutritionists, health planners, other community and mental health specialists, and interested consumers. **Purpose:** Seeks to protect and promote personal, mental, and environmental health. **Activities:** Services include: promulgation of standards; establishment of uniform practices and procedures; development of the etiology of communicable diseases; research in public health; exploration of medical care programs and their relationships to public health. Sponsors job placement service.

EMPLOYER DIRECTORIES AND NETWORKING LISTS

★11153★ AHA Guide to the Health Care Field

American Hospital Association
1 N Franklin
Chicago, IL 60606
Ph: (312)422-2050   Fax: (312)422-4700
Fr: 800-424-4301

Annual, August. Covers hospitals, networks, multi-health care systems, freestanding ambulatory surgery centers, psychiatric facilities, long-term care facilities, substance abuse programs, and other health-related organizations. Entries include: For hospitals–Facility name, address, phone, administrator's name, number of beds, facilities and services, number of employees, expenses, other statistics. For other organizations–Name, address, phone, fax, name and title of contact. Arrangement: Geographical. Indexes: Hospital name.

★11154★ Directory of Hospital Personnel

Grey House Publishing
85 Millerton Rd.
PO Box 860
Millerton, NY 12546
Ph: (518)789-8700   Fax: (518)789-0556
Fr: 800-562-2139
URL: http://www.greyhouse.com/hospital_personnel.htm

Annual. $325.00 for print product; $545.00 for online database subscription; $650.00 for online database subscription and print product combined. Covers 200,000 executives at 7,000 U.S. hospitals. Entries include: Name of hospital, address, phone; number of beds; type and JCAHO status of hospital; names and titles of key department heads and staff; medical and nursing school affiliations; number of residents, interns, and nursing students. Arrangement: Geographical. Indexes: Hospital name, personnel, hospital size.

★11155★ Hospital Blue Book

Billian Publishing Inc./Transworld Publishing Inc.
2100 Powers Ferry Rd. SE
Atlanta, GA 30339
Ph: (770)955-5656   Fax: (770)952-0669
Fr: 800-533-8484
E-mail: blu-book@billian.com

2005. $300.00 for individuals. Covers more than 6,687 hospitals; some listings also appear in a separate southern edition of this publication. Entries include: Name of hospital, accreditation, mailing address, phone, fax, number of beds, type of facility (nonprofit, general, state, etc.); list of administrative personnel and chiefs of medical services, with specific titles. Arrangement: Geographical.

★11156★ Medical and Health Information Directory

Gale, Cengage Learning
27500 Drake Rd.
Farmington Hills, MI 48331-3535
Ph: (248)699-4253   Fax: (248)699-8065
Fr: 800-877-4253
E-mail: businessproducts@gale.com
URL: http://www.gale.com

Annual; latest edition 20th, July 2007. $375.00/volume. Covers in Volume 1, more than 26,500 medical and health oriented associations, organizations, institutions, and government agencies, including health maintenance organizations (HMOs), preferred provider organizations (PPOs), insurance companies, pharmaceutical companies, research centers, and medical and allied health schools. In Volume 2, over 12,000 medical book publishers; medical periodicals, directories, audiovisual producers and services, medical libraries and information centers, electronic resources, and health-related internet search engines. In Volume 3, more than 35,500 clinics, treatment centers, care programs, and counseling/diagnostic services for 34 subject areas. Entries include: Institution, service, or firm name, address, phone, fax, email and URL; many include names of key personnel and, when

pertinent, descriptive annotations. Volume 3 was formerly listed separately as Health Services Directory. Arrangement: Classified by organization activity, service, etc. Indexes: Each volume has a complete alphabetical name and keyword index.

HANDBOOKS AND MANUALS

★11157★ Careers in Health Care

The McGraw-Hill Companies
PO Box 182604
Columbus, OH 43272
Fax: (614)759-3749   Fr: 877-883-5524
E-mail: customer.service@mcgraw-hill.com
URL: http://www.mcgraw-hill.com

Barbara M. Swanson. Fifth edition, 2005. $15.95 (paper). 192 pages. Describes job duties, work settings, salaries, licensing and certification requirements, educational preparation, and future outlook. Gives ideas on how to secure a job.

★11158★ Expert Resumes for Health Care Careers

Jist Works
875 Montreal Way
St. Paul, MN 55102
Fr: 800-648-5478
E-mail: info@jist.com
URL: http://www.jist.com

Wendy S. Enelow and Louise M. Kursmark. December 2003. $16.95. 288 pages.

★11159★ Health Careers Today

Elsevier
11830 Westline Industrial Dr.
St. Louis, MO 63146
Ph: (314)453-7010   Fax: (314)453-7095
Fr: 800-545-2522
E-mail: usbkinfo@elsevier.com
URL: http://www.elsevier.com

Gerdin, Judith. Fourth edition. 2007. $59.95. 496 pages. Covers more than 45 health careers. Discusses the roles and responsibilities of various occupations and provides a solid foundation in the skills needed for all health careers.

★11160★ Opportunities in Health and Medical Careers

The McGraw-Hill Companies
PO Box 182604
Columbus, OH 43272
Fax: (614)759-3749   Fr: 877-883-5524
E-mail: customer.service@mcgraw-hill.com
URL: http://www.mcgraw-hill.com

I. Donald Snook, Jr. and Leo D'Orazio. 2004. $13.95 (paper). 157 pages. Covers the full range of medical and health occupations. Illustrated.

★11161★ Resumes for Health and Medical Careers

The McGraw-Hill Companies
PO Box 182604
Columbus, OH 43272
Fax: (614)759-3749   Fr: 877-883-5524
E-mail: customer.service@mcgraw-hill.com
URL: http://www.mcgraw-hill.com

Third edition, 2003. $11.95 (paper). 160 pages.

EMPLOYMENT AGENCIES AND SEARCH FIRMS

★11162★ Cross Country TravCorps

6551 Park of Commerce Blvd.
Boca Raton, FL 33487-8247
Fax: (562)998-8533   Fr: 800-530-6125
URL: http://www.crosscountrytravcorps.com

Places traveling nurses in assignments nationwide.

★11163★ JPM International

26034 Acero
Mission Viejo, CA 92691
Ph: (949)699-4300   Fax: (949)699-4333
Fr: 800-685-7856
E-mail: trish@jpmintl.com
URL: http://www.jpmintl.com

Executive search firm and employment agency.

★11164★ Professional Placement Associates, Inc.

287 Bowman Ave., Ste. 309
Purchase, NY 10577-2517
Ph: (914)251-1000   Fax: (914)251-1055
E-mail: careers@ppasearch.com
URL: http://www.ppasearch.com

Executive search firm specializing in the health and medical field.

ONLINE JOB SOURCES AND SERVICES

★11165★ Medhunters.com
Fr: 800-664-0278
E-mail: info@medhunters.com
URL: http://www.medhunters.com

Description: Career search site for jobs in all health care specialties; educational resources; visa and licensing information for relocation; interesting articles; relocation tools; links to professional organizations and general resources.

★11166★ ProHealthJobs
Fr: 800-796-1738

E-mail: Info@prohealthedujobs.com
URL: http://www.prohealthjobs.com

Description: Career resources site for the medical and health care field. Lists professional opportunities, product information, continuing education and open positions.

★11167★ **RehabJobs Online**
PO Box 480536
Los Angeles, CA 90048
Ph: (213)938-7718   Fax: (213)938-9609
Fr: 800-43-REHAB
E-mail: support@atsrehabjobs.com
URL: http://www.rehabjobs.com

Description: Resource center for the professional therapist. **Main files include:** Therapists Only, Therapy Forums, Nationwide Job Search (database), Therapy Job Outlook, Therapy Job Search Utilities, Therapy Links, Information for Employers and Recruiters.

OTHER SOURCES

★11168★ **American Association for Respiratory Care (AARC)**
9425 N MacArthur Blvd., Ste. 100
Irving, TX 75063-4706
Ph: (972)243-2272   Fax: (972)484-2720
E-mail: info@aarc.org
URL: http://www.aarc.org

Description: Allied health society of respiratory therapists and other respiratory caregivers employed by hospitals, skilled nursing facilities, home care companies, group practices, educational institutions, and municipal organizations. Encourages, develops, and provides educational programs for persons interested in the profession of respiratory care; and advances the science of respiratory care.

★11169★ **Committee on Accreditation for Respiratory Care (COARC)**
1248 Harwood Rd.
Bedford, TX 76021-4244
Ph: (817)283-2835   Fax: (817)354-8519
Fr: 800-874-5615
E-mail: bill@heasc.org
URL: http://www.coarc.com

Description: Physicians, respiratory therapists, and a public representative. Purposes are to develop standards and requirements for accredited educational programs of respiratory therapy for recommendation to the American Medical Association; to conduct evaluations of educational programs that have applied for accreditation of the AMA and to make recommendations to the AMA's Committee on Allied Health Education and Accreditation; to maintain a working liaison with other organizations interested in respiratory therapy education and evaluation.

★11170★ **Exploring Health Occupations**
Cambridge Educational
PO Box 2053
Princeton, NJ 08543-2053
Ph: 800-257-5126   Fax: (609)671-0266
Fr: 800-468-4227
E-mail: custserv@films.com
URL: http://www.cambridgeeducational.com

VHS and DVD. $159.90. 1999. Two-part series provides a detailed view of the field of medical technicians and technologists, EMTs, nurses, therapists, and assistants.

★11171★ **Health Assessment & Treating Occupations**
Delphi Productions
3159 6th St.
Boulder, CO 80304
Ph: (303)443-2100   Fax: (303)443-4022
Fr: 888-443-2400
E-mail: support@delphivideo.com
URL: http://www.delphivideo.com

$95.00. 50 minutes. Part of the Careers for the 21st Century Video Library.

★11172★ **Health Service Occupations**
Delphi Productions
3159 6th St.
Boulder, CO 80304
Ph: (303)443-2100   Fax: (303)443-4022
Fr: 888-443-2400
E-mail: support@delphivideo.com
URL: http://www.delphivideo.com

$95.00. 50 minutes. Part of the Careers for the 21st Century Video Library.

★11173★ **Medicine & Related Occupations**
Delphi Productions
3159 6th St.
Boulder, CO 80304
Ph: (303)443-2100   Fax: (303)443-4022
Fr: 888-443-2400
E-mail: support@delphivideo.com
URL: http://www.delphivideo.com

$95.00. 45 minutes. Part of the Careers for the 21st Century Video Library.

★11174★ **National Board for Respiratory Care (NBRC)**
18000 W 105th St.
Olathe, KS 66061-7543
Ph: (913)895-4900   Fax: (913)895-4650
E-mail: nbrc-info@nbrc.org
URL: http://www.nbrc.org

Description: Offers credentialing examinations for respiratory therapists, respiratory therapy technicians, pulmonary technologists, and perinatal/pediatric respiratory care specialists.

Restaurant and Food Service Managers

SOURCES OF HELP-WANTED ADS

★11175★ Airport Press
P.A.T.I. Inc.
PO Box 879, JFK Sta.
Jamaica, NY 11430-0879
Ph: (718)244-6788   Fax: (718)995-3432
Fr: 800-982-5832
E-mail: airprtpres@aol.com
URL: http://www.airportpress.us

Monthly. $48.00/year for individuals; $96.00/year for individuals, overseas. Newspaper for the airport industry.

★11176★ Beverage World
Beverage World
90 Broad St., Ste. 402
New York, NY 10004-3312
Ph: (646)708-7300   Fax: (646)708-7399
Fr: (866)890-8541
URL: http://www.beverageworld.com

Monthly. $99.00/year for individuals. Trade magazine for corporate, marketing, distribution, production, and purchasing top and middle management in the multi-product beverage industry.

★11177★ Chef
Talcott Communications Corp.
20 W Kinzie, Ste. 1200
Chicago, IL 60610
Ph: (312)849-2220   Fax: (312)849-2174
E-mail: chef@talcott.com
URL: http://www.chefmagazine.com

$32.00/year for individuals; $47.00 for two years; $64.00 for individuals, 3 years; $43.00/year for Canada; $96.00/year for other countries. Food information for chefs.

★11178★ Food Management
Penton Media Inc.
1300 E 9th St.
Cleveland, OH 44114
Ph: (216)696-7000   Fax: (216)696-1752
URL: http://www.food-management.com/

Monthly. Magazine for foodservice professionals in the onsite 'noncommercial' market.

★11179★ FoodService Director
Ideal Media LLC
303 E Wacker Dr., 21st Fl.
Chicago, IL 60601
Ph: (312)456-2822   Fax: (312)240-0742
URL: http://www.fsdmag.com

Monthly. $79.00/year for individuals; $99.00/year for Canada; $235.00/year for out of country. Tabloid newspaper of the noncommercial foodservice market.

★11180★ Foodservice East
The Newbury Street Group Inc.
165 New Boston St., No. 236
Woburn, MA 01801
Ph: (781)376-9080   Fax: (781)376-0010
Fr: 800-852-5212
E-mail: fdsvceast@.aol.com

Bimonthly. $30.00/year for individuals. Compact tabloid covering trends and analysis of the foodservice industry in the Northeast. A business-to-business publication featuring news, analysis and trends for the Northeast food service professional.

★11181★ Hotel F & B Executive
Hotel Forums LLC
5455 N Sheridan Rd., Ste. 2802
Chicago, IL 60640
Ph: (773)728-4995   Fax: (773)728-4996
URL: http://www.hfbexecutive.com/

Bimonthly. $49.00/year for individuals; $25.00/year for students; $76.00/year for institutions. Magazine that addresses the needs of the hospitality F&B markets, which include hotels, resorts, cruise lines and conference, and convention & meeting centers.

★11182★ Hotel & Motel Management
Questex Media Group
275 Grove St., 2-130
Newton, MA 02466
Ph: (617)219-8300   Fax: (617)219-8310
Fr: 888-552-4346

URL: http://www.hotelmotel.com
$53.50/year for individuals; $74.00/year for individuals, Canada and Mexico; $130.00/year for individuals, all other countries; $75.00/year for individuals, all other countries. Free to qualified subscribers. Magazine covering the global lodging industry.

★11183★ HOTELS
Reed Business Information
360 Park Ave. S
New York, NY 10010
Ph: (646)746-6400   Fax: (646)746-7431
URL: http://www.reedbusiness.com/

Monthly. Free. Magazine covering management and operations as well as foodservice and design in the hospitality industry.

★11184★ Journal of the American Dietetic Association
American Dietetic Association
120 S Riverside Plz., Ste. 2000
Chicago, IL 60606-6995
Fax: (312)899-4817   Fr: 800-877-1600
URL: http://www.eatright.org/cps/rde/xchg/ada/hs.xsl/home_7018_en

Monthly. Journal reporting original research on nutrition, diet therapy, education and administration.

★11185★ Midwest Food Network
Pinnacle Publishing Group
8205-F Estates Pky.
Plain City, OH 43064
Fax: (614)873-1650
URL: http://www.midwestfoodnetwork.com/

Bimonthly. $24.00/year. Free to qualified subscribers; $24.00/year for individuals, others. Food service trade magazine featuring new products and suppliers and other industry news including food news, restaurant association updates, news of chefs, restaurant concepts, earnings, and openings and closings.

★11186★ Nightclub & Bar Magazine

Oxford Publishing Inc.
307 West Jackson Ave.
Oxford, MS 38655-2154
Ph: (662)236-5510   Fax: (662)236-5541
Fr: 800-247-3881
URL: http://www.nightclub.com

Monthly. Free to qualified subscribers. Trade magazine covering management, lighting, sound, food, beverage, promotions, current trends, and other bar industry news.

★11187★ Restaurant Business

VNU Business Publications
770 Broadway
New York, NY 10003
Ph: (646)654-5000
URL: http://www.foodservicetoday.com

Monthly. $119.00/year for individuals; $212.00/year for Canada; $468.00/year for other countries, rest of the world. Trade magazine for restaurants and commercial food service.

★11188★ Restaurant Hospitality

Penton Media Inc.
1300 E 9th St.
Cleveland, OH 44114
Ph: (216)696-7000   Fax: (216)696-1752
URL: http://www.restaurant-hospitality.com/

Monthly. Free. Dedicated to the success of full service restaurants and edited for chefs and other commercial foodservice professionals. Includes new food and equipment products and trends, menu and recipe ideas, industry news, new technology, food safety, emerging new concepts, consumer attitudes and trends, labor and training, and profiles of successful operations.

★11189★ Restaurant Startup & Growth

Specialized Publications Company
5215 Crooked Rd.
Parkville, MO 64152
Ph: (816)741-5151   Fax: (816)741-6458
URL: http://www.restaurantowner.com/mag/

Monthly. $39.95/year for U.S. $48.95/year for Canada; $54.95/year for elsewhere; $69.95/year for U.S., 2 years; $87.95/year for Canada, 2 years; $99.95/year for elsewhere, 2 years; $89.95/year for U.S., 3 years; $116.95/year for Canada, 3 years; $134.95/year for elsewhere, 3 years. Magazine about starting and operating a restaurant business.

★11190★ Restaurants & Institutions

Reed Business Information
360 Park Ave. S
New York, NY 10010
Ph: (646)746-6400   Fax: (646)746-7431
URL: http://www.reedbusiness.com/

Semimonthly. Free. Magazine focusing on foodservice and lodging management.

★11191★ Southeast Food Service News

Southeast Publishing Company Inc.
5672 Peachtree Pky., Ste. E
Norcross, GA 30092
Ph: (770)499-9800   Fax: (770)499-9802

Monthly. $36.00/year for individuals, per year; $5.00 for individuals, per single copy; $59.00/year for individuals, per directory issue. Magazine (tabloid) serving the food industry.

★11192★ Special Events

Miramar Communications Inc.
23805 Stuart Ranch Rd., Ste. 235
PO Box 8987
Malibu, CA 90265-8987
Ph: (310)317-4522   Fax: (310)317-9644
Fr: 800-543-4116
E-mail: secs@pbsub.com
URL: http://www.specialevents.com

Monthly. $59.00/year. Free to qualified subscribers; $110.00/year for Canada; $106.00/year for other countries; $200.00 for Canada, two years; $200.00 for other countries, two years. Magazine for special event professionals.

★11193★ Sunbelt Foodservice

Shelby Publishing Company Inc.
517 Green St.
Gainesville, GA 30501
Ph: (770)534-8380   Fax: (770)535-0110
URL: http://www.shelbypublishing.com

Monthly. $36.00/year for individuals; $60.00 for two years. Trade newspaper (tabloid) covering the food industry; geared toward restaurant operators.

★11194★ Western Itasca Review & Deerpath Shopper

Lebhar-Friedman, Inc.
425 Park Ave., 6th Fl.
New York, NY 10022
Ph: (212)756-5000   Fax: (212)756-5215

Weekly (Mon.). $34.50/year for individuals. Local newspaper and shopper.

PLACEMENT AND JOB REFERRAL SERVICES

★11195★ Les Amis d'Escoffier Society of New York

787 Ridgewood Rd.
Millburn, NJ 07041
Ph: (212)414-5820   Fax: (973)379-3117
E-mail: kurt@escoffier-society.com
URL: http://www.escoffier-society.com

Members: An educational organization of professionals in the food and wine industries. **Activities:** Maintains museum, speakers' bureau, hall of fame, and placement service. Sponsors charitable programs.

★11196★ Society for Foodservice Management (SFM)

304 W Liberty St., Ste. 201
Louisville, KY 40202
Ph: (502)583-3783   Fax: (502)589-3602
E-mail: sfm@hqtrs.com
URL: http://www.sfm-online.org

Description: Operates or maintains food service and vending facilities in businesses and industrial plants, or supply food products, equipment, or other essential industry services. Serves the needs and interests of onsite employee food service executives and management. Provides an opportunity for the exchange of experiences and opinions through study, discussion, and publications develops greater efficiency and more economical methods of providing high-quality food and service at a reasonable cost assists members in solving specific operating and management problems; keeps pace with the rapidly changing conditions of the employee food service segment of the industry. Develops and encourages the practice of high standards and professional conduct among management and executive personnel; provides job placement and management personnel recruiting service; sends representative to the U.S. Air Force Hennessey Award Team, which selects the Air Force base having the most superior food service.

EMPLOYER DIRECTORIES AND NETWORKING LISTS

★11197★ Directory of Chain Restaurant Operators

Chain Store Guide
3922 Coconut Palm Dr.
Tampa, FL 33619
Fax: (813)627-6883   Fr: 800-778-9794
URL: http://www.csgis.com

Annual; latest edition 2004. $365.00 for individuals. Covers chain restaurant operators, chain hotel operators, nontraditional foodservice operators and food service management operators who operate two or more food service locations. Entries include: For chain restaurant operators–company name, address, phone and fax numbers; e-mail and web addresses; type of business; listing type; total annual sales; food service sales; system wide sales; percent of sales of alcohol; percent of sales from Internet; alcohol types served; total units; company owned units; units franchised to and from; trade names; co-branded names and numbers; food service management location types; trading areas; foreign trading areas; units by primary menu types and type of foodservice; self-distributing and catering services indicators; franchise affiliations names and locations; primary distributors names and locations; parent and subsidiary company names and locations; regional, divisional, and branch office locations; distribution centers locations; year founded; public company indicator; key personnel with titles. For chain hotel operators–includes number of restaurants in hotels. For food service management operators–includes number of food service management accounts and total number of locations served. Arrangement: Geographical. Indexes: Alphabetical; type of food service; menu type; franchisee; food service management; state; exclusions.

★11198★ **Directory of Hospital Personnel**

Grey House Publishing
185 Millerton Rd.
PO Box 860
Millerton, NY 12546
Ph: (518)789-8700   Fax: (518)789-0556
Fr: 800-562-2139
URL: http://www.greyhouse.com/hospital_personnel.htm

Annual. $325.00 for print product; $545.00 for online database subscription; $650.00 for online database subscription and print product combined. Covers 200,000 executives at 7,000 U.S. hospitals. Entries include: Name of hospital, address, phone; number of beds; type and JCAHO status of hospital; names and titles of key department heads and staff; medical and nursing school affiliations; number of residents, interns, and nursing students. Arrangement: Geographical. Indexes: Hospital name, personnel, hospital size.

HANDBOOKS AND MANUALS

★11199★ **Best Impressions in Hospitality: Your Professional Image for Excellence**

Cengage Learning
PO Box 6904
Florence, KY 41022
Fax: 800-487-8488   Fr: 800-354-9706
URL: http://www.cengage.com

Angie Michael. 1999. $63.95 (paper). 240 pages.

★11200★ **Career Opportunities in the Food and Beverage Industry**

Facts on File, Inc.
132 W. 31st St., 17th Fl.
New York, NY 10001-2006
Ph: (212)967-8800   Fax: 800-678-3633
Fr: 800-322-8755
E-mail: custserv@factsonfile.com
URL: http://www.factsonfile.com

Barbara Sims-Bell. Second edition, 2001. $18.95 (paper). 223 pages. Provides the job seeker with information about locating and landing 80 skilled and unskilled jobs in the industry. Includes detailed job descriptions for many specific positions and lists trade associations, recruiting organizations, and major agencies. Contains index and bibliography.

★11201★ **Career Opportunities in Travel and Tourism**

Facts On File Inc.
132 W. 31st St., 17th Fl.
New York, NY 10001-2006
Ph: (212)967-8800   Fax: 800-678-3633
Fr: 800-322-8755
E-mail: custserv@factsonfile.com
URL: http://www.factsonfile.com

John K. Hawks. 1996. $18.95 (paper). 224 pages. Includes detailed job descriptions, educational requirements, salary ranges, and advancement prospects for 70 different job opportunities in this fast-paced industry. Contains index and bibliography.

★11202★ **Careers for Gourmets and Others Who Relish Food**

The McGraw-Hill Companies
PO Box 182604
Columbus, OH 43272
Fax: (614)759-3749   Fr: 877-883-5524
E-mail: customer.service@mcgraw-hill.com
URL: http://www.mcgraw-hill.com

Mary Donovan. Second edition, 2002. $15.95; $12.95 (paper). 192 pages. Discusses such job prospects as foods columnist, cookbook writer, test kitchen worker, pastry chef, recipe developer, food festival organizer, restaurant manager, and food stylist.

★11203★ **Careers for Health Nuts and Others Who Like to Stay Fit**

The McGraw-Hill Companies
PO Box 182604
Columbus, OH 43272
Fax: (614)759-3749   Fr: 877-883-5524
E-mail: customer.service@mcgraw-hill.com
URL: http://www.mcgraw-hill.com

Blythe Camenson. Second edition, 2005. $13.95 (paper). 208 pages.

★11204★ **Careers for Night Owls and Other Insomniacs**

The McGraw-Hill Companies
PO Box 182604
Columbus, OH 43272
Fax: (614)759-3749   Fr: 877-883-5524
E-mail: customer.service@mcgraw-hill.com
URL: http://www.mcgraw-hill.com

Louise Miller. Second edition, 2002. $12.95 (paper). 160 pages.

★11205★ **Careers in Travel, Tourism, and Hospitality**

The McGraw-Hill Companies
PO Box 182604
Columbus, OH 43272
Fax: (614)759-3749   Fr: 877-883-5524
E-mail: customer.service@mcgraw-hill.com
URL: http://www.mcgraw-hill.com

Marjorie Eberts, Linda Brothers, and Ann Gisler. Second edition, 2005. $15.95 (paper). 224 pages.

★11206★ **Choosing a Career in the Restaurant Industry**

Rosen Publishing Group, Inc.
29 E. 21st St.
New York, NY 10010
Ph: (212)777-3017   Fax: 888-436-4643
Fr: 800-237-9932
URL: http://www.rosenpublishing.com/

Eileen Beal. Revised edition, 2000. $25.25. 64 pages. Explores various jobs in the restaurant industry. Describes job duties, salaries, educational preparation, and job hunting. Contains information about fast food, catering, and small businesses.

★11207★ **Culinary Arts Career Starter**

LearningExpress, LLC
55 Broadway, 8th Fl.
New York, NY 10006
Ph: (212)995-2566   Fax: (212)995-5512
Fr: 800-295-9556
E-mail: customerservice@learningexpressllc.com
URL: http://www.learningexpressllc.com

Mary Masi. 1999. $15.95 (paper). 208 pages.

★11208★ **How to Get a Job with a Cruise Line**

Ticket to Adventure, Inc.
PO Box 41005
St. Petersburg, FL 33743-1005
Ph: (727)822-5029   Fax: (727)821-3409
Fr: 800-929-7447

Mary Fallon Miller. Fifth edition, 2001. $16.95 (paper). 352 pages. Explores jobs with cruise ships, describing duties, responsibilities, benefits, and training. Lists cruise ship lines and schools offering cruise line training. Offers job hunting advice.

★11209★ **Opportunities in Culinary Careers**

The McGraw-Hill Companies
PO Box 182604
Columbus, OH 43272
Fax: (614)759-3749   Fr: 877-883-5524
E-mail: customer.service@mcgraw-hill.com
URL: http://www.mcgraw-hill.com

Mary Deirdre Donovan. 2003. $13.95; $11.95 (paper). 149 pages. Describes the educational preparation and training of chefs and cooks and explores a variety of food service jobs in restaurants, institutions, and research and development. Lists major culinary professional associations and schools. Offers guidance on landing a first job in cooking and related fields.

★11210★ **Opportunities in Hospital Administration Careers**

The McGraw-Hill Companies
PO Box 182604
Columbus, OH 43272
Fax: (614)759-3749   Fr: 877-883-5524
E-mail: customer.service@mcgraw-hill.com
URL: http://www.mcgraw-hill.com

I. Donald Snook. 2006. $13.95. 160 pages.

Discusses opportunities for administrators in a variety of management settings: hospital, department, clinic, group practice, HMO, mental health, and extended care facilities.

★11211★ Opportunities in Restaurant Careers

The McGraw-Hill Companies
PO Box 182604
Columbus, OH 43272
Fax: (614)759-3749   Fr: 877-883-5524
E-mail: customer.service@mcgraw-hill.com
URL: http://www.mcgraw-hill.com

Carol Caprione Chmelynski. 2004. $13.95 (paper). 150 pages. Covers opportunities in the food service industry and details salaries, benefits, training opportunities, and professional associations. Special emphasis is put on becoming a successful restaurant manager by working up through the ranks. Illustrated.

★11212★ The Professional Caterer's Handbook: How to Open and Operate a Financially Successful Catering Business

Atlantic Publishing Company
1210 SW 23rd Pl.
Ocala, FL 34474-7014
Fax: (352)622-1875   Fr: 800-814-1132
E-mail: sales@atlantic-pub.com
URL: http://www.atlantic-pub.com/

Douglas Robert Brown and Lora Arduser. 2005. $79.95. Comprehensive guide for planning, starting, and operating a catering business; includes companion CD-ROM. Covers marketing, management, budgeting, home-based catering, ways for restaurants to add catering services to existing businesses, forms, Web sites, and more.

EMPLOYMENT AGENCIES AND SEARCH FIRMS

★11213★ The Alfus Group Inc.

353 Lexington Ave., Fl. 8
New York, NY 10016
Ph: (212)599-1000   Fax: (212)599-1523
E-mail: mail@thealfusgroup.com
URL: http://www.thealfusgroup.com

Executive search firm. Specializes in the hospitality industry.

★11214★ Anderson & Associates

112 S. Tryon St., Ste. 700
Charlotte, NC 28284
Ph: (704)347-0090   Fax: (704)347-0064
E-mail: info@andersonexecsearch.com
URL: http://www.andersonexecsearch.com

Executive search firm. Branch in Cumming, Georgia.

★11215★ Bennett Search & Consulting Company Inc.

285-1 W. Naomi Dr.
Naples, FL 34104
Ph: (239)352-0219   Fax: (239)353-7719
E-mail: robertbennett3@comcast.net
URL: http://www.bscinc.org

Executive search firm.

★11216★ Cary & Associates

PO Box 2043
Winter Park, FL 32790-2043
Ph: (407)647-1145
E-mail: concary@caryassociates.com
URL: http://www.caryassociates.com

Executive search firm.

★11217★ The Cooper Executive Search Group Inc.

PO Box 375
Wales, WI 53183-0375
Ph: (262)968-9049   Fax: (262)968-9059
E-mail: cesgroup@aol.com

Executive search firm.

★11218★ CraigSearch

1130 E. Arapaho Rd., Ste. 180
Richardson, TX 75081
Ph: (972)644-3264   Fax: (972)644-3265
E-mail: search@craigsearch.com
URL: http://www.craigsearch.com

Executive search firm.

★11219★ Derba & Derba

7 Whispering Pines
Andover, MA 01810
Ph: (978)470-8270   Fax: (978)470-4592
E-mail: info@derbaandderba.com
URL: http://derbaandderba.com/

Executive search firm focused on the hospitality industry.

★11220★ Employment Advisors

815 Nicollet Mall
Minneapolis, MN 55402
Ph: (612)339-0521

Employment agency. Places candidates in variety of fields.

★11221★ Hospitality International

23 W 73rd St., Ste.100
New York, NY 10023
Ph: (212)769-8800   Fax: (212)769-2138
E-mail: jar@hospitalityinternational.com
URL: http://www.hospitalityinternational.com

Executive search firm. Branch office in New York, NY.

★11222★ J.D. Hersey and Associates

8 E. Poplar Ave.
Columbus, OH 43215
Ph: (614)228-4022   Fax: (614)228-4085
E-mail: requests@jdhersey.com
URL: http://www.jdhersey.com

Executive search firm for permanent and contingency placements.

★11223★ LW Foote Company

301 116th Ave. SE, Ste. 105
Bellevue, WA 98004
Ph: (425)451-1660   Fax: (425)451-1535
E-mail: email@lwfoote.com
URL: http://ww.lwfoote.com

Executive search firm.

★11224★ The Personnel Network, Inc.

1246 Lake Murray Blvd.
PO Box 1426
Irmo, SC 29063
Ph: (803)781-2087   Fax: (803)732-7986
E-mail: chuckirmo@aol.com

Executive search firm.

★11225★ Ritt-Ritt and Associates, Inc.

5105 Tollview Dr., Ste. 110
Rolling Meadows, IL 60008
Ph: (847)483-9330   Fax: (847)483-9331
E-mail: info@rittsearch.com

Food service and hospitality employment agency and executive search firm.

ONLINE JOB SOURCES AND SERVICES

★11226★ Bristol Associates, Inc.

5757 W. Century Blvd., Ste. 62B
Los Angeles, CA 90045
Ph: (310)670-0525   Fax: (310)670-4075
E-mail: lstern@bristolassoc.com
URL: http://www.bristolassoc.com

Description: Executive search firm specializing in direct marketing, hospitality and food industries. Applicants can post their resumes online for recruiters' viewing and search current job databank. Also contains job tools and resources.

★11227★ Food Industry Jobs.com

HRsmart, Inc.
2929 N. Central Expressway, Ste. 110
Richardson, TX 75080
E-mail: jobboards@hrsmart.com
URL: http://www.foodindustryjobs.com

Description: Job databank and resume submission service for food industry workers.

TRADESHOWS

★11228★ American School Food Service Association Annual National Conference

American School Food Service Association
700 S. Washington St., Ste. 300
Alexandria, VA 22314-4287
Ph: (703)739-3900 Fax: (703)739-3915
Fr: 800-877-8822
E-mail: servicecenter@asfsa.org
URL: http://www.asfsa.org

Annual. **Primary Exhibits:** Food service supplies and equipment, including educational services and computers.

★11229★ Annual Hotel, Motel, and Restaurant Supply Show of the Southeast

Leisure Time Unlimited, Inc.
708 Main St.
PO Box 332
Myrtle Beach, SC 29577
Ph: (843)448-9483 Fax: (843)626-1513
Fr: 800-261-5591
E-mail: dickensshow@sc.rr.com

Annual. **Primary Exhibits:** Carpeting, furniture, coffee makers, produce companies, wine and beer and food companies, and services to motels, hotels, and restaurants.

★11230★ Foodservice Expo

Kentucky Restaurant Association
133 N Evergreen Rd., Ste. 201
Louisville, KY 40243-1484
Ph: (502)896-0464 Fax: (502)896-0465
Fr: 800-896-0414
E-mail: info@kyra.org
URL: http://www.kyra.org

Annual. **Primary Exhibits:** Foodservice equipment, supplies, services, and products.

★11231★ International Hotel & Restaurant Expo

Diversified Business Communications
121 Free St.
PO Box 7437
Portland, ME 04112-7437
Ph: (207)842-5500 Fax: (207)842-5503
E-mail: custserv@divcom.com
URL: http://www.divbusiness.com

Primary Exhibits: Equipment, supplies, and services for the hotel and restaurant industries.

★11232★ International Restaurant & Foodservice Show of New York

Reed Exhibitions (North American Headquarters)
383 Main Ave.
Norwalk, CT 06851
Ph: (203)840-5337 Fax: (203)840-9570
E-mail: export@reedexpo.com
URL: http://www.reedexpo.com

Annual. **Primary Exhibits:** Equipment, supplies, and services for the food products, foodservice, restaurant, and institutional food service industries. **Dates and Locations:** 2008 Mar 09-11; New York, NY; Jacob K. Javits Convention Center.

★11233★ Louisiana Foodservice Expo

Louisiana Restaurant Association
2700 N. Arnoult Rd.
Metairie, LA 70002
Ph: (504)454-2277 Fax: (504)454-2663
Fr: 800-256-4572
E-mail: sandyr@lra.org

Annual. **Primary Exhibits:** Food service equipment, supplies, and services, food products.

★11234★ Midsouthwest Foodservice Convention and Exposition

Oklahoma Restaurant Association
3800 N. Portland
Oklahoma City, OK 73112
Ph: (405)942-8181 Fax: (405)942-0541
Fr: 800-375-8181
URL: http://www.okrestaurants.com

Annual. **Primary Exhibits:** Providers of foodservice and hospitality products, services and equipment.

★11235★ South Carolina Foodservice Expo

South Carolina Foodservice Expo
111 Shannon Dr.
Spartanburg, SC 29301
Ph: (864)574-9323 Fax: (864)574-0784
E-mail: scsfsa@aol.com

Annual. **Primary Exhibits:** Food and foodservice equipment, supplies, and services.

★11236★ Upper Midwest Hospitality, Restaurant, and Lodging Show - UP Show

Hospitality Minnesota - Minnesota's Restaurant, Hotel, and Resort Associations
305 E Roselawn Ave.
St. Paul, MN 55117-2031
Ph: (651)778-2400 Fax: (651)778-2424
E-mail: info@hospitalitymn.com
URL: http://www.hospitalitymn.com

Annual. **Primary Exhibits:** Food, beverages, hospitality business services, lodging supplies, and foodservice equipment.

OTHER SOURCES

★11237★ Administration and Management Occupations

Delphi Productions
3159 6th St.
Boulder, CO 80304
Ph: (303)443-2100 Fax: (303)443-4022
Fr: 888-443-2400

E-mail: support@delphivideo.com
URL: http://www.delphivideo.com

$95.00. 50 minutes. Part of the Careers for the 21st Century Video Library.

★11238★ Association of Correctional Food Service Affiliates (ACFSA)

406 Surrey Woods Dr.
St.Charles, IL 60174
Ph: (630)513-4736 Fax: (630)513-4653
E-mail: info@acfsa.org
URL: http://www.acfsa.org

Description: Food service professionals from federal, state and county correctional institutions and vendors that serve them. Works to advance skills and professionalism through education, information and networking.

★11239★ Association for International Practical Training (AIPT)

10400 Little Patuxent Pkwy., Ste. 250
Columbia, MD 21044-3519
Ph: (410)997-2200 Fax: (410)992-3924
E-mail: aipt@aipt.org
URL: http://www.aipt.org

Description: Providers worldwide of on-the-job training programs for students and professionals seeking international career development and life-changing experiences. Arranges workplace exchanges in hundreds of professional fields, bringing employers and trainees together from around the world. Client list ranges from small farming communities to Fortune 500 companies.

★11240★ Club Managers Association of America (CMAA)

1733 King St.
Alexandria, VA 22314
Ph: (703)739-9500 Fax: (703)739-0124
E-mail: cmaa@cmaa.org
URL: http://www.cmaa.org

Members: Professional managers and assistant managers of private golf, yacht, athletic, city, country, luncheon, university, and military clubs. **Purpose:** Encourages education and advancement of members and promotes efficient and successful club operations. **Activities:** Provides reprints of articles on club management. Supports courses in club management. Compiles statistics; maintains management referral service.

★11241★ International Council on Hotel, Restaurant, and Institutional Education (CHRIE)

2810 N Parham Rd., Ste. 230
Richmond, VA 23294
Ph: (804)346-4800 Fax: (804)346-5009
E-mail: kmccarty@chrie.org
URL: http://www.chrie.org

Description: Schools and colleges offering specialized education and training in hospitals, recreation, tourism and hotel, restaurant, and institutional administration; individuals, executives, and students. Provides networking opportunities and professional development.

★11242★ National Management Association (NMA)

2210 Arbor Blvd.
Dayton, OH 45439
Ph: (937)294-0421   Fax: (937)294-2374
E-mail: nma@nma1.org
URL: http://www.nma1.org

Description: Business and industrial management personnel; membership comes from supervisory level, with the remainder from middle management and above. Seeks to develop and recognize management as a profession and to promote the free enterprise system. Prepares chapter programs on basic management, management policy and practice, communications, human behavior, industrial relations, economics, political education, and liberal education. Maintains speakers' bureau and hall of fame. Maintains educational, charitable, and research programs. Sponsors charitable programs.

★11243★ National Restaurant Association (NRA)

1200 17th St. NW
Washington, DC 20036
Ph: (202)331-5900   Fax: (202)331-2429
Fr: 800-424-5156
E-mail: info@dineout.org
URL: http://www.restaurant.org

Description: Represents restaurants, cafeterias, clubs, contract foodservice management, drive-ins, caterers, institutional food services, and other members of the foodservice industry; also represents establishments belonging to non-affiliated state and local restaurant associations in governmental affairs. Supports foodservice education and research in several educational institutions. Is affiliated with the Educational Foundation of the National Restaurant Association to provide training and education for operators, food and equipment manufacturers, distributors, and educators. Has 300,000 member locations.

★11244★ National Restaurant Association Educational Foundation (NRAEF)

175 W Jackson Blvd., Ste. 1500
Chicago, IL 60604-2702
Ph: (312)715-1010   Fr: 800-765-2122
E-mail: info@nraef.org
URL: http://www.nraef.org

Description: Serves as an educational foundation supported by the National Restaurant Association and all segments of the foodservice industry including restaurateurs, foodservice companies, food and equipment manufacturers, distributors, and trade associations. Advances the professional standards of the industry through education and research. Offers video training programs, management courses, and careers information. Conducts research and maintains hall of fame.

Retail Sales Representatives

SOURCES OF HELP-WANTED ADS

★11245★ *Chain Store Age*
Lebhar-Friedman, Inc.
425 Park Ave., 6th Fl.
New York, NY 10022
Ph: (212)756-5000   Fax: (212)756-5215
URL: http://www.chainstoreage.com

Monthly. Magazine for management of retail chain headquarters. Reports on marketing, merchandising, strategic planning, physical supports, and shopping center developments, retail technology credit and communications.

★11246★ *The College Store*
The College Store
500 E Lorain St.
Oberlin, OH 44074
Fax: (440)775-4769   Fr: 800-622-7498
E-mail: thecollegestore@nacs.org
URL: http://www.nacs.org/

Bimonthly. Books and college supplies magazine.

★11247★ *Counterman*
Babcox
3550 Embassy Pky.
Akron, OH 44333
Ph: (330)670-1234   Fax: (330)670-0874
URL: http://www.aftermarketnews.com/default.aspx?type=wm&module=4

Monthly. Free to qualified subscribers. Magazine devoted to improving the effectiveness of professional automotive parts counter-sales personnel.

★11248★ *CRN*
CMP Media L.L.C.
600 Community Dr.
Manhasset, NY 11030
Ph: (516)562-5000   Fax: (516)562-7830
URL: http://www.crn.com

Weekly. Newspaper for value added resel-lers, retailers, and distributors in the computer market.

★11249★ *DNR*
Fairchild Publications Inc.
750 Third Ave.
New York, NY 10017
Ph: (212)630-4000
URL: http://www.dnrnews.com/

Daily (morn.). Daily newspaper reporting on men's and boys' clothing, retailing, and textiles.

★11250★ *Gifts & Decorative Accessories*
Reed Business Information
360 Park Ave. S
New York, NY 10010
Ph: (646)746-6400   Fax: (646)746-7431
URL: http://www.reedbusiness.com

Monthly. International magazine for retailers of gifts, greeting cards, decorative accessories, and stationery-related merchandise.

★11251★ *Home Channel News*
Lebhar-Friedman, Inc.
425 Park Ave., 6th Fl.
New York, NY 10022
Ph: (212)756-5000   Fax: (212)756-5215
URL: http://www.homechannelnews.com

$189.00/year for individuals. Business tabloid serving home center/building material retailers.

★11252★ *Modern Grocer*
GC Publishing Company Inc.
PO Box 2010
744 Main St., Rte. 6A
Dennis, MA 02638
Ph: (508)385-7700   Fax: (508)385-0089
URL: http://www.gccomm.net/mg.htm

Monthly. $50.00/year for individuals. Magazine for food retailers, wholesalers, distributors, brokers, manufacturers, and packers in the metro New York and New Jersey marketing area.

★11253★ *Money Making Opportunities*
Success Publishing International
11071 Ventura Blvd.
Studio City, CA 91604
Ph: (818)980-9166   Fax: (818)980-7829
URL: http://www.moneymakingopps.com/

Free. Magazine Source for small business opportunity seekers.

★11254★ *Music Inc.*
Maher Publications Inc.
102 N Haven Rd.
Elmhurst, IL 60126
Ph: (630)941-2030   Fax: (630)941-3210
Fr: 800-535-7496
URL: http://www.musicinc.com

$17.00/year for individuals. Magazine serving retailers of music and sound products.

★11255★ *National Jeweler*
The Nielsen Co.
770 Broadway
New York, NY 10003
Ph: (646)654-5000   Fax: (646)654-5002
URL: http://www.nationaljewelernetwork.com/njn/index.jsp

Semimonthly. $10.00 for single issue, cover; $89.00/year for U.S. $104.00/year for Canada; $330.00/year for other countries, airmail only. Jewelry industry magazine.

★11256★ *Photo Marketing*
Photo Marketing Association International
3000 Picture Pl.
Jackson, MI 49201
Ph: (517)788-8100   Fax: (517)788-8371
Fr: 800-762-9287
URL: http://www.photomarketing.com/

Monthly. $50.00/year for individuals; $55.00/year for Canada; $70.00/year for other countries; $5.00/year for single issue; $90.00 for two years; $100.00 for two years, Canada; $130.00 for two years, other countries. Trade magazine for photo/video dealers and photo finishers.

★11257★ Retailing Today

Lebhar-Friedman, Inc.
425 Park Ave., 6th Fl.
New York, NY 10022
Ph: (212)756-5000   Fax: (212)756-5215
URL: http://www.retailingtoday.com/

Semimonthly. Retailing business industry news and information.

★11258★ Sales & Marketing Management

The Nielsen Co.
770 Broadway
New York, NY 10003
Ph: (646)654-5000   Fax: (646)654-5002
URL: http://www.salesandmarketing.com

Monthly. $48.00/year for individuals. Business magazine.

★11259★ Sporting Goods Dealer

Bill Communications Inc.
1115 Northmeadow Pkwy.
Roswell, GA 30076
Ph: (770)569-1540   Fax: (770)569-5105
Fr: 800-241-9034
URL: http://www.sgdealer.com/sportinggoodsdealer/index.jsp

Bimonthly. Magazine that offers expert reporting on trends affecting team dealers and retailers who service schools, colleges, pro and local teams.

★11260★ Tire Business

Crain Communications Inc.
1725 Merriman Rd., Ste. 300
Akron, OH 44313-5283
Ph: (330)836-9180   Fax: (330)836-1005
URL: http://www.tirebusiness.com

Semimonthly. $79.00/year for individuals; $148.00 for two years; $107.00/year for individuals, Canada; $194.00 for two years, Canada; $119.00/year for other countries; $208.00 for two years, all other countries; $99.00/year for individuals, web only. Newspaper (tabloid) serving independent tire dealers, retreaders, tire wholesalers and others allied to the tire industry.

★11261★ Tire Review

Babcox
3550 Embassy Pky.
Akron, OH 44333
Ph: (330)670-1234   Fax: (330)670-0874
URL: http://www.tirereview.com/

Monthly. Free to qualified subscribers. Magazine containing news and business information about the tire, custom wheel, automotive service, and retreading industries.

★11262★ Visual Merchandising and Store Design

ST Media Group International Inc.
407 Gilbert Ave.
Cincinnati, OH 45202
Ph: (513)421-2050   Fax: (513)421-5144
Fr: 800-925-1110

E-mail: vmsd@stmediagroup.com
URL: http://www.stmediagroup.com/index.php3?d=pubs&p=vm

Monthly. $42.00/year for individuals, U.S.; $66.00/year for individuals, 2 years, U.S.; $62.00/year for individuals, Canada (surface); $100.00/year for individuals, 2 years, Canada (surface); $65.00/year for individuals, Mexico/Foreign (surface); $105.00/year for individuals, 2 years, Mexico/Foreign (surface); $100.00/year for individuals, Mexico, 1st Class; $175.00/year for individuals, 2 years, Mexico 1st Class; $115.00/year for individuals, Central/South America; $205.00/year for individuals, 2 years, Central/South America. The leading magazine of the retail design industry covering the latest trends in retail design, store planning, and merchandise presentation.

★11263★ Watch & Clock Review

Golden Bell Press
2403 Champa St.
Denver, CO 80205
Ph: (303)296-1600   Fax: (303)295-2159

Monthly. $19.50/year for individuals, 1 year; $35.00/year for individuals, 2 years. Magazine on watches and clocks.

EMPLOYER DIRECTORIES AND NETWORKING LISTS

★11264★ Careers in Focus: Retail

Facts On File Inc.
132 W 31st St., 17th Fl.
New York, NY 10001
Ph: (212)967-8800   Fax: 800-678-3633
Fr: 800-322-8755
URL: http://www.factsonfile.com

Latest edition 3rd, 2007. $29.95 for individuals; $26.95 for libraries. Covers an overview of retail, followed by a selection of jobs profiled in detail, including the nature of the job, earnings, prospects for employment, what kind of training and skills it requires, and sources for further information.

★11265★ Directory of Department Stores

Chain Store Guide
3922 Coconut Palm Dr.
Tampa, FL 33619
Fax: (813)627-6883   Fr: 800-778-9794
URL: http://www.csgis.com

Annual, 2005. $335.00 for individuals. Covers 214 department store companies, 1,500 shoe store companies, 200 jewelry store companies, 95 optical store companies, and 70 leather and luggage store companies in the United States and Canada, with annual sales of at least $250,000. Entries include: Company name; physical and mailing addresses; phone and fax numbers; company e-mail and web addresses; listing type; total sales; industry sales; total selling square footage; store prototype sizes; total units;

units by trade name; trading areas; projected openings and remodelings; self-distributing indicator; distribution center locations; resident buyers' name and location; leased departments area, name, and location; mail order catalog indicator; Internet order processing indicator; private label softlines, hardlines, and credit card indicators; furniture styles and price lines; average number of checkouts; year founded; public company indicator; parent company name and location; subsidiaries' names and locations; regional and divisional office locations; key personnel with titles; store locations, with address, phone number, and manager name (department stores only). Arrangement: Geographical. Indexes: Alphabetical; product lines; exclusions.

★11266★ Directory of Drug Store & HBC Chains

Chain Store Guide
3922 Coconut Palm Dr.
Tampa, FL 33619
Fax: (813)627-6883   Fr: 800-778-9794
URL: http://www.csgis.com

Annual, May. Covers more than 1,700 drug store chains operations of two or more units, including mass merchants and grocers with pharmacies; 215 wholesale drug companies in the United States and Canada. Entries include: For retailers–company name; phone and fax numbers; physical and mailing addresses; company e-mail and web addresses; listing type; number of stores; product lines; percentage of sales by product line; total sales; prescription drug sales; percentage of prescriptions filled with generic drugs; number of prescriptions filled daily; percentage of prescriptions filled with private third party, cash, and Medicaid; number of stores by type; mail order pharmacy indicator; managed care division indicator; projected openings and remodelings; store prototype sizes; total selling square footage; trading area; franchise group headquarters' name and location; distribution center and primary wholesaler names and locations; number of specialty departments; packaged liquor indicators; private label indicators; computerized pharmacy indicator; average number of checkouts; year founded; public company indicator; parent company name and location; regional and divisional office locations; headquarters personnel with titles. For wholesalers–company name, address, phone, and fax; e-mail and web addresses; listing type; product lines; percentage of sales by product line; total sales; percentage of sales by customer type; total stores served; number of member and non-member stores served; trading area; group store trading names; wholesaler type; distribution center locations; private label indicator; year founded; public company indicator; headquarters personnel with titles. Arrangement: Separate geographical sections for retailers and wholesalers. Indexes: Alphabetical, exclusions.

★11267★ STORES-Top 100 Retailers Issue

National Retail Federation
325 7th St. NW, Ste. 1100
Washington, DC 20004
Ph: (202)783-7971   Fax: (202)737-2849
Fr: 800-673-4692
URL: http://www.stores.org

Annual, July. $75.00. Publication includes: 100 U.S. retail companies having largest estimated sales during preceding year. Entries include: Name of store, city, number of stores included, and total sales. Arrangement: Ranked by sales.

HANDBOOKS AND MANUALS

★11268★ Great Jobs for Business Majors

The McGraw-Hill Companies
PO Box 182604
Columbus, OH 43272
Fax: (614)759-3749   Fr: 877-883-5524
E-mail: customer.service@mcgraw-hill.com
URL: http://www.mcgraw-hill.com

Stephen Lambert. Second edition, 2003. $15.95 (paper). 240 pages.

★11269★ Opportunities in Retailing Careers

The McGraw-Hill Companies
PO Box 182604
Columbus, OH 43272
Fax: (614)759-3749   Fr: 877-883-5524
E-mail: customer.service@mcgraw-hill.com
URL: http://www.mcgraw-hill.com

Roslyn Dolber. 2003. 160 pages. $13.95 (paper). Discusses a number of opportunities in retailing, from entry-level to retail management.

★11270★ Opportunities in Sales Careers

The McGraw-Hill Companies
PO Box 182604
Columbus, OH 43272
Fax: (614)759-3749   Fr: 877-883-5524
E-mail: customer.service@mcgraw-hill.com
URL: http://www.mcgraw-hill.com

James Brescoll and Ralph Dahm. 160 pages. 2001. $12.95 (paper). Details sales in retail, wholesale and industrial sales, sales of services and intangibles, and sales management. Illustrated.

★11271★ Real People Working in Sales and Marketing

The McGraw-Hill Companies
PO Box 182604
Columbus, OH 43272
Fax: (614)759-3749   Fr: 877-883-5524
E-mail: customer.service@mcgraw-hill.com
URL: http://www.mcgraw-hill.com

Blythe Camenson, Jan Goldberg. 1996.

$12.95 (paper). 144 pages. Interviews and profiles of working sales and marketing professionals capture a range of opportunities in this field.

EMPLOYMENT AGENCIES AND SEARCH FIRMS

★11272★ Allen Associates

4555 Lake Forest Dr., 6th Fl.
Cincinnati, OH 45242
Ph: (513)563-3040
E-mail: feedback@allensearch.com
URL: http://www.allensearch.com

Executive senior-level search firm.

★11273★ APA Search Inc.

1 Byram Brook Pl., Ste. 201
Armonk, NY 10504
Ph: (914)273-6000   Fax: (914)273-8025
E-mail: info@apasearch.com
URL: http://www.apasearch.com

Employment agency specializing in the automotive, retail, and hardware industries.

★11274★ Bender Executive Search

45 N. Station Plaza, Ste. 315
Great Neck, NY 11021
Ph: (516)773-3200   Fax: (516)482-5355
URL: http://www.marketingexecsearch.com

Executive search firm.

★11275★ Ecruiters.net

PO Box 1086
Chanhassen, MN 55317
Ph: (952)233-5750
E-mail: headhunter@ecruiters.net
URL: http://www.ecruiters.net

Executive search firm.

★11276★ Eggers Consulting Company Inc.

11272 Elm St., Eggers Plz.
Omaha, NE 68144
Ph: (402)333-3480   Fax: (402)333-9759
E-mail: admin@eggersconsulting.com
URL: http://www.eggersconsulting.com

Executive search consulting firm. Industries served: insurance, data processing, retail and banking.

★11277★ Employment Advisors

815 Nicollet Mall
Minneapolis, MN 55402
Ph: (612)339-0521

Employment agency. Places candidates in variety of fields.

★11278★ Fairfaxx Corp.

338 Commerce Dr.
Fairfield, CT 06825-0252
Ph: (203)337-3900   Fax: (203)337-3910
E-mail: jjt@fairfaxx.com
URL: http://www.fairfaxx.com

Offers specialization in apparel and retail industry positions.

★11279★ Gene Kaufman Associates Ltd.

450 Fashion Ave.
New York, NY 10123-0101
Ph: (212)643-0625   Fax: (212)643-8598

Personnel consultant specializing in recruiting on all levels for the apparel industry in the areas of design, sales, merchandising, production, operations and administration.

★11280★ J.D. Hersey and Associates

8 E. Poplar Ave.
Columbus, OH 43215
Ph: (614)228-4022   Fax: (614)228-4085
E-mail: requests@jdhersey.com
URL: http://www.jdhersey.com

Executive search firm for permanent and contingency placements.

★11281★ Joel H. Wilensky Associates, Inc.

PO Box 155
Sudbury, MA 01776-0155
Ph: (978)443-5176   Fax: (978)443-3009
E-mail: jhwassoc@joelhwilensky.com
URL: http://www.joelhwilensky.com

Executive search firm.

★11282★ John J. Sudlow and Co.

1044 Water St., Ste. 223
Port Townsend, WA 98368
Ph: (360)385-0703

Offers counsel emphasizing executive development and recruiting, particularly for manufacturing and retail oriented businesses.

★11283★ National Register Columbus, Inc.

550 Polaris Pkwy., Ste. 530
Westerville, OH 43082
Ph: (614)890-1200   Fax: (614)890-1259
E-mail: sales@nrcols.com
URL: http://www.nrcols.com

Employment agency. Offices in Akron and Toledo, OH.

★11284★ National Sales & Marketing Consultants Inc.

5650 Greenwood Plz. Blvd., Ste. 206
Englewood, CO 80111-2309
Ph: (303)771-4201   Fax: (303)740-8640
E-mail: nasmarc@aol.com

Locates, hires, and trains sales representatives, and coordinates on-going activities of manufacturer's representatives for clients in health-care, government, health and beauty aids, sporting goods, consumer products, hardware, and stationery/office supply industries. Assists clients in developing pricing, packaging, advertising, general sales, and promotional policies. Acts as national sales manager for multiple clients.

★11285★ The Personnel Network, Inc.
1246 Lake Murray Blvd.
PO Box 1426
Irmo, SC 29063
Ph: (803)781-2087   Fax: (803)732-7986
E-mail: chuckirmo@aol.com

Executive search firm.

★11286★ Retail Connection, Inc.
33 Newark Pompton Turnpike
Riverdale, NJ 07457
Ph: (973)569-9600   Fax: (973)569-9700
Fr: 800-770-4945
E-mail: email@retailconnectioninc.com
URL: http://www.retailconnectioninc.com

Executive search firm serving retail executives.

★11287★ Retail Recruiters
2189 Silas Deane Hwy.
Rocky Hill, CT 06067
Ph: (860)721-9550   Fax: (860)257-8813
E-mail: careers@retailrecruitersusa.com
URL: http://www.retailrecruitersusa.com

Employment agency. Affiliate offices in many locations across the country.

★11288★ Salespositions.com
450 7th Ave., Ste. 507A
New York, NY 10123
Ph: (609)407-4774
E-mail: salepositions@comcast.net
URL: http://www.salespositions.com

Employment agency.

ONLINE JOB SOURCES AND SERVICES

★11289★ Spherion
2050 Spectrum Blvd.
Fort Lauderdale, FL 33309
Ph: (954)308-7600
E-mail: help@spherion.com
URL: http://www.spherion.com

Description: Recruitment firm specializing in accounting and finance, sales and marketing, interim executives, technology, engineering, retail and human resources.

OTHER SOURCES

★11290★ Automotive Aftermarket Industry Association (AAIA)
7101 Wisconsin Ave., Ste. 1300
Bethesda, MD 20814-3415
Ph: (301)654-6664   Fax: (301)654-3299
E-mail: aaia@aftermarket.org
URL: http://www.aftermarket.org

Members: Automotive parts and accessories retailers, distributors, manufacturers, and manufacturers' representatives. **Activities:** Conducts research and compiles statistics. Conducts seminars and provides specialized education program.

★11291★ CBA
PO Box 62000
Colorado Springs, CO 80962-2000
Ph: (719)265-9895   Fax: (719)272-3510
Fr: 800-252-1950
E-mail: info@cbaonline.org
URL: http://www.cbaonline.org

Members: Serves as trade association for retail stores selling Christian books, Bibles, gifts, and Sunday school and church supplies. **Activities:** Compiles statistics; conducts specialized education programs.

★11292★ Computing Technology Industry Association (CompTIA)
1815 S Meyers Rd., Ste. 300
Oakbrook Terrace, IL 60181-5228
Ph: (630)678-8300   Fax: (630)678-8384
E-mail: information@comptia.org
URL: http://www.comptia.org

Description: Trade association of more than 19,000 companies and professional IT members in the rapidly converging computing and communications market. Has members in more than 89 countries and provides a unified voice for the industry in the areas of e-commerce standards, vendor-neutral certification, service metrics, public policy and workforce development. Serves as information clearinghouse and resource for the industry; sponsors educational programs.

★11293★ Marketing & Sales Occupations
Delphi Productions
3159 6th St.
Boulder, CO 80304
Ph: (303)443-2100   Fax: (303)443-4022
Fr: 888-443-2400
E-mail: support@delphivideo.com
URL: http://www.delphivideo.com

$95.00. 50 minutes. Part of the Careers for the 21st Century Video Library.

★11294★ National Association of College Stores (NACS)
500 E Lorain St.
Oberlin, OH 44074
Ph: (440)775-7777   Fax: (440)775-4769
Fr: 800-622-7498
E-mail: membership@nacs.org
URL: http://www.nacs.org

Members: Institutional, private, leased, and cooperative college stores (2,800) selling books, supplies, and other merchandise to college students, faculty, and staff; associate members include publishers and suppliers (1,200). **Purpose:** Seeks to effectively serve higher education by providing educational research, advocacy and other to college stores and their suppliers. **Activities:** Maintains NACSCORP, Inc., a wholly owned subsidiary corporation, which distributes trade and mass market books and educational software. Sponsors seminars. Conducts manager certification, specialized education, and research programs. Maintains College Stores Research and Educational Foundation which provides grants for educational programs and conducts research.

★11295★ National Retail Federation (NRF)
325 7th St. NW, Ste. 1100
Washington, DC 20004
Ph: (202)783-7971   Fax: (202)737-2849
Fr: 800-673-4692
E-mail: mullint@nrf.com
URL: http://www.nrf.com

Purpose: Represents state retail associations, several dozen national retail associations, as well as large and small corporate members representing the breadth and diversity of the retail industry's establishment and employees. **Activities:** Conducts informational and educational conferences related to all phases of retailing including financial planning and cash management, taxation, economic forecasting, expense planning, shortage control, credit, electronic data processing, telecommunications, merchandise management, buying, traffic, security, supply, materials handling, store planning and construction, personnel administration, recruitment and training, and advertising and display.

★11296★ Working with Children
Cambridge Educational
PO Box 2053
Princeton, NJ 08543-2053
Ph: 800-257-5126   Fax: (609)671-0266
Fr: 800-468-4227
E-mail: custserv@films.com
URL: http://www.cambridgeeducational.com

VHS and DVD. $89.95. 2000. 24 minutes. This program examines alternative positions offering the opportunity to work with children of different ages and the qualifications necessary for those jobs. A nanny, social worker, non-faculty school worker, and retail salesperson describe their job responsibilities and explain why they find their work so enjoyable.

Roofers

SOURCES OF HELP-WANTED ADS

★11297★ Builder

Hanley-Wood L.L.C.
1 Thomas Cir., NW, Ste. 600
Washington, DC 20005
Ph: (202)452-0800   Fax: (202)785-1974
URL: http://www.hanleywood.com/default.aspx?page=b2bbd

$29.95/year for individuals, 13 issues; $54.95/year for Canada, 26 issues; $192.00/year for out of country, 13 issues. Magazine covering housing and construction industry.

★11298★ Constructor

Associated General Contractors of
  America
2300 Wilson Blvd., Ste. 400
Arlington, VA 22201
Ph: (703)548-3118   Fax: (703)548-3119
URL: http://www.agc.org

Monthly. Management magazine for the Construction Industry.

★11299★ Professional Builder

Reed Business Information
360 Park Ave. S
New York, NY 10010
Ph: (646)746-6400   Fax: (646)746-7431
E-mail: ncrum@reedbusiness.com
URL: http://www.housingzone.com/toc-archive-pbx

Monthly. Free. The integrated engineering magazine of the building construction industry.

★11300★ Professional Roofing

National Roofing Contractors Association
10255 W Higgins Rd., Ste. 600
Rosemont, IL 60018-5607
Ph: (847)299-9070   Fax: (847)299-1183
Fr: 800-323-9545
URL: http://www.nrca.net

Monthly. Free. Roofing industry magazine.

★11301★ Roofing Contractor

BNP Media
2401 W Big Beaver Rd., Ste. 700
Troy, MI 48084-3333
Ph: (248)786-1642   Fax: (248)786-1388
URL: http://www.roofingcontractor.com/

Monthly. Trade publication covering roofing and the construction industry.

★11302★ WIT

Vermont Works for Women
51 Park St.
Essex Junction, VT 05452
Ph: (802)878-0004   Fax: (802)878-0050
Fr: 800-639-1472
URL: http://www.nnetw.org/

Description: Three issues/year. Provides a network of support, information, and skill sharing for women in skilled trades professions.

PLACEMENT AND JOB REFERRAL SERVICES

★11303★ National Association of Home Builders (NAHB)

1201 15th St. NW
Washington, DC 20005
Ph: (202)266-8200   Fax: (202)266-8400
Fr: 800-368-5242
E-mail: info@nahb.com
URL: http://www.nahb.org

Description: Single and multifamily home builders, commercial builders, and others associated with the building industry. Lobbies on behalf of the housing industry and conducts public affairs activities to increase public understanding of housing and the economy. Collects and disseminates data on current developments in home building and home builders' plans through its Economics Department and nationwide Metropolitan Housing Forecast. Maintains NAHB Research Center, which functions as the research arm of the home building industry. Sponsors seminars and workshops on construction, mortgage credit, labor relations, cost reduction, land use, remodeling, and business management. Compiles statistics; offers charitable program, spokesman training, and placement service; maintains speakers' bureau, and Hall of Fame. Subsidiaries include the National Council of the Housing Industry. Maintains over 50 committees in many areas of construction; operates National Commercial Builders Council, National Council of the Multifamily Housing Industry, National Remodelers Council, and National Sales and Marketing Council.

EMPLOYER DIRECTORIES AND NETWORKING LISTS

★11304★ ABC Today-Associated Builders and Contractors National Membership Directory Issue

Associated Builders & Contractors Inc.
4250 N Fairfax Dr., 9th Fl.
Arlington, VA 22203-1607
Ph: (703)812-2000   Fax: (703)812-8203
URL: http://www.abc.org/wmspage.cfm?parm1=2033

Annual, December. $150.00. Publication includes: List of approximately 19,000 member construction contractors and suppliers. Entries include: Company name, address, phone, name of principal executive, code to volume of business, business specialty. Arrangement: Classified by chapter, then by work specialty.

★11305★ Constructor-AGC Directory of Membership and Services Issue

AGC Information Inc.
2300 Wilson Blvd., Ste. 400
Arlington, VA 22201
Ph: (703)548-3118   Fax: (703)548-3119
Fr: 800-282-1423
URL: http://www.agc.org

Annual, August; latest edition 2004 edition. Publication includes: List of over 8,500 member firms and 24,000 national associate member firms engaged in building, highway, heavy, industrial, municipal utilities, and railroad construction (SIC 1541, 1542, 1611, 1622, 1623, 1629); listing of state and local chapter officers. Entries include: For firms–Company name, address, phone, fax, names of principal executives, and code indicating type of construction undertaken. For officers–Name, title, address. Arrangement: Geographical, alphabetical. Indexes: Company name.

★11306★ ENR-Top 400 Construction Contractors Issue

McGraw-Hill Inc.
1221 Ave. of the Americas
New York, NY 10020-1095
Ph: (212)512-2000   Fax: (212)512-3840
Fr: 877-833-5524
URL: http://construction.ecnext.com/coms2/summary_0249-137077_ITM

Annual; 22nd, May 2006. $35.00 for individuals. Publication includes: List of 400 United States contractors receiving largest dollar volumes of contracts in preceding calendar year. Separate lists of 50 largest design/construction management firms; 50 largest program and construction managers; 25 building contractors; 25 heavy contractors. Entries include: Company name, headquarters location, total value of contracts received in preceding year, value of foreign contracts, countries in which operated, construction specialities. Arrangement: By total value of contracts received.

★11307★ National Roofing Contractors Association-Membership Directory

National Roofing Contractors Association
10255 W Higgins Rd., Ste. 600
Rosemont, IL 60018-5613
Ph: (847)299-9070   Fax: (847)299-1183
URL: http://www.nrca.net

Annual, July. Covers 5,000 contractors applying all types of commercial and residential roofing; 600 associate member manufacturers, suppliers, and distributors; 300 foreign members; and 100 institutions and related industries. Entries include: Company name, address, phone, and names of voting representatives. Arrangement: Alphabetical. Indexes: Geographical; voting representative; alphabetical; member product guide.

HANDBOOKS AND MANUALS

★11308★ Opportunities in Building Construction Trades

The McGraw-Hill Companies
PO Box 182604
Columbus, OH 43272
Fax: (614)759-3749   Fr: 877-883-5524
E-mail: customer.service@mcgraw-hill.com
URL: http://www.mcgraw-hill.com

Michael Sumichrast. Second edition, 1998. $14.95; $11.95 (paper). 104 pages. From custom builder to rehabber, the many kinds of companies that employ craftspeople and

contractors are explored. Includes job descriptions, requirements, and salaries for dozens of specialties within the construction industry. Contains a complete list of Bureau of Apprenticeship and Training state and area offices. Illustrated.

ONLINE JOB SOURCES AND SERVICES

★11309★ National Roofing Contractors Association

10255 W. Higgins Rd., Ste. 600
Rosemont, IL 60018-5607
Ph: (847)299-9020   Fax: (847)299-1183
E-mail: llewis@nrca.net
URL: http://www.nrca.net

Description: Members have the opportunity to have their resume and business listed free of charge and are accessed by the zip codes they serve. NRCA provides a complimentary hyperlink to a member's Web site if an address is provided. Also, (800) USA-ROOF: NRCA's contractor referral network is accessed by more than 8,000 consumers each year who are searching for professional roofing contractors. **Fee:** Membership fees depend on annual sales volume and begin at $330.

TRADESHOWS

★11310★ Midwest Roofing Contractors Association Convention and Trade Show

Midwest Roofing Contractors Association
4840 Bob Billings Pkwy. Ste. 1000
Lawrence, KS 66049-3862
Ph: (785)843-4888   Fax: (785)843-7555
E-mail: mrca@mrca.org
URL: http://www.mrca.org

Annual. **Primary Exhibits:** Roofing products, materials, and related industries and services.

★11311★ National Roofing Contractors Association Annual Convention and Exhibit

National Roofing Contractors Association
O'Hare International Center
10255 W Higgins Rd., Ste. 600
Rosemont, IL 60018-5607
Ph: (847)299-9070   Fax: (847)299-1183
Fr: 800-323-9545
E-mail: nrca@nrca.net
URL: http://www.nrca.net

Annual. **Primary Exhibits:** Roofing, urethane foam, waterproofing materials, and computer programs. **Dates and Locations:** 2008 Feb 24-27; San Diego, CA.

★11312★ Southeast Roofing and Sheet Metal Spectacular Trade Exposition

Florida Roofing, Sheet Metal, and Air Conditioning Contractors Association FRSA
4111, Metric Dr., Ste. 6
Winter Park, FL 32792
Ph: (407)671-3772   Fax: (407)679-0010
E-mail: frsa@floridaroof.com
URL: http://www.floridaroof.com

Annual. **Primary Exhibits:** Roofing and sheet metal supplies, products and services.

OTHER SOURCES

★11313★ Associated Builders and Contractors (ABC)

4250 N Fairfax Dr., 9th Fl.
Arlington, VA 22203-1607
Ph: (703)812-2000   Fax: (703)812-8200
E-mail: gotquestions@abc.org
URL: http://www.abc.org

Description: Construction contractors, subcontractors, suppliers, and associates. Aims to foster and perpetuate the principles of rewarding construction workers and management on the basis of merit. Sponsors management education programs and craft training; also sponsors apprenticeship and skill training programs. Disseminates technological and labor relations information.

★11314★ Associated General Contractors of America (AGC)

2300 Wilson Blvd., Ste. 400
Arlington, VA 22201
Ph: (703)548-3118   Fax: (703)548-3119
Fr: 800-242-1767
E-mail: info@agc.org
URL: http://www.agc.org

Description: General construction contractors; subcontractors; industry suppliers; service firms. Provides market services through its divisions. Conducts special conferences and seminars designed specifically for construction firms. Compiles statistics on job accidents reported by member firms. Maintains 65 committees, including joint cooperative committees with other associations and liaison committees with federal agencies.

★11315★ Associated Specialty Contractors (ASC)

3 Bethesda Metro Ctr., Ste. 1100
Bethesda, MD 20814
Ph: (703)548-3118
E-mail: dgw@necanet.org
URL: http://www.assoc-spec-con.org

Description: Works to promote efficient management and productivity. Coordinates the work of specialized branches of the industry in management information, research, public information, government relations and construction relations. Serves as a liaison among specialty trade associations in the areas of public relations, government relations, and with other organizations. Seeks to avoid unnecessary duplication of effort and expense or conflicting programs among affiliates. Identifies areas of interest and problems shared by members, and develops positions and approaches on such problems.

★11316★ Building Trades

Delphi Productions
3159 6th St.
Boulder, CO 80304
Ph: (303)443-2100   Fax: (303)443-4022
Fr: 888-443-2400
E-mail: support@delphivideo.com
URL: http://www.delphivideo.com

$95.00. 46 minutes. Part of the Careers for the 21st Century Video Library.

★11317★ COIN Career Guidance System

COIN Educational Products
3361 Executive Pky., Ste. 302
Toledo, OH 43606
Ph: (419)536-5353   Fax: (419)536-7056
Fr: 800-274-8515

URL: http://www.coinedu.com/

CD-ROM. Provides career information through seven cross-referenced files covering postsecondary schools, college majors, vocational programs, military service, apprenticeship programs, financial aid, and scholarships. Apprenticeship file describes national apprenticeship training programs, including information on how to apply, contact agencies, and program content. Military file describes more than 200 military occupations and training opportunities related to civilian employment.

★11318★ National Association of Women in Construction (NAWIC)

327 S Adams St.
Fort Worth, TX 76104
Ph: (817)877-5551   Fax: (817)877-0324
Fr: 800-552-3506
E-mail: nawic@nawic.org
URL: http://www.nawic.org

Description: Seeks to enhance the success of women in the construction industry.

★11319★ Roofing Industry Educational Institute (RIEI)

10255 W Higgins Rd., Ste. 600
Rosemont, IL 60018-5607
Ph: (847)299-9070   Fax: (847)299-1183
E-mail: nrca@nrca.net
URL: http://www.nrca.net/rp/related/riei

Members: Participants are contractors, architects, specifiers, owners, consultants, and others involved in the roofing industry. **Activities:** Conducts seminars and educational programs covering all aspects of roofing, highlighting design, installation, and maintenance including topics such as thermal insulation, vapors and condensation, and fire and codes. Provides referral service and presents diplomas.

Sales Managers

★11320★ **Academy of Management Journal**

Academy of Management
PO Box 3020
Briarcliff Manor, NY 10510-8020
Ph: (914)923-2607   Fax: (914)923-2615
URL: http://www.aom.pace.edu/amr

Bimonthly. Professional journal covering management.

★11321★ **Academy of Management Learning & Education**

Academy of Management
PO Box 3020
Briarcliff Manor, NY 10510-8020
Ph: (914)923-2607   Fax: (914)923-2615
URL: http://journals.aomonline.org/amle

Quarterly. $80.00/year for individuals, print; $130.00/year for individuals, print & online; $165.00/year for libraries, print; $215.00/year for libraries, print and online; $100.00/year for individuals, other countries, print; $150.00/year for individuals, other countries, print & online; $185.00/year for other countries, print, corporate library; $235.00/year for other countries, print & online, corporate library. Journal covering management issues for professionals.

★11322★ **Business Performance Management**

Penton Media Inc.
249 W 17th St.
New York, NY 10011
Ph: (212)204-4200
URL: http://www.bpmmag.net/

Free to qualified subscribers. Magazine for business managers. Covers organizing, automating, and analyzing of business methodologies and processes.

★11323★ **Customer Service Advantage**

Progressive Business Publications
370 Technology Dr.
Malvern, PA 19355
Ph: (610)695-8600   Fax: (610)647-8089
Fr: 800-220-5000
E-mail: customer_service@pbp.com
URL: http://www.pbp.com

Description: Semimonthly. Presents practical methods for quantifying customer service benefits and motivating employees day in and day out. Recurring features include interviews, news of research, a calendar of events, news of educational opportunities, and a column titled Sharpen Your Judgment.

★11324★ **CXO**

IDG Communications Inc.
5 Speen St., 3rd. Fl
Framingham, MA 01701
Ph: (508)875-5000   Fax: (508)988-7888
URL: http://www.idg.com

Monthly. Magazine providing technology information for chief officers and managers.

★11325★ **D & O Advisor**

American Lawyer Media L.P.
345 Pk. Ave. S
New York, NY 10010
Ph: (212)779-9200   Fax: (212)481-8110
Fr: 800-888-8300
URL: http://www.alm.com

Quarterly. Magazine that offers advice and perspective on corporate oversight responsibilities for directors and officers.

★11326★ **E Journal of Organizational Learning and Leadership**

WeLEAD Inc.
PO Box 202
Litchfield, OH 44253
Fr: 877-778-5494
URL: http://www.weleadinlearning.org/ejournal.htm

Continuous. Free. Online academic journal about organizational leadership.

★11327★ **Event Management**

Cognizant Communications Corp.
3 Hartsdale Rd.
Elmsford, NY 10523-3701
Ph: (914)592-7720   Fax: (914)592-8981
URL: http://www.cognizantcommunication.com/filecabinet/EventManag

Quarterly. $325.00/year for institutions, library; $360.00/year for institutions, rest of the world, library; $585.00/year for institutions, library, 2 years; $648.00/year for institutions, rest if the world, library, 2 years; $45.00/year professional; $52.00/year for other countries, professional. Journal covering research and analytic needs of a rapidly growing profession focused on events.

★11328★ **Executive Legal Adviser**

American Lawyer Media L.P.
345 Pk. Ave. S
New York, NY 10010
Ph: (212)779-9200   Fax: (212)481-8110
Fr: 800-888-8300
URL: http://www.executivelegaladviser.com

Bimonthly. Free to qualified subscribers. Magazine that offers legal advice for corporate executives.

★11329★ **Fleet Maintenance**

Cygnus Business Media Inc.
3 Huntington Quadrangle, Ste. 301 N
Melville, NY 11747
Ph: (631)845-2700   Fax: (631)845-7109
Fr: 800-308-6397
URL: http://www.fleetmag.com

Bimonthly. Business tabloid magazine offering a chapterized curriculum of technical, regulatory and managerial information designed to help maintenance managers, directors and supervisors better perform their jobs and reduce their overall cost-per-mile.

★11330★ **Forrester**

Forrester Research Inc.
400 Technology Sq.
Cambridge, MA 02139
Ph: (617)613-6000   Fax: (617)613-5000
URL: http://www.forrester.com/mag

Free. Journal that aims to provide ideas and advice that are relevant to today's CEOs.

★11331★ International Journal of Business Research

Academy of International Business and Economics
PO Box 2536
Ceres, CA 95307
URL: http://www.aibe.org

Peer-reviewed journal publishing theoretical, conceptual, and applied research on topics related to research, practice and teaching in all areas of business, management, and marketing.

★11332★ Issues & Answers in Sales Management

Clement Communications Inc.
10 LaCrue Ave.
PO Box 36
PO Box 7000
Concordville, PA 19331
Ph: (610)459-4200   Fax: 800-459-1933
Fr: 888-358-5858
E-mail: customerservice@clement.com
URL: http://www.clement.com

Description: Biweekly. Provides sales managers and supervisors with techniques and strategies to improve customer service and profits. Includes topics such as the Internet, tradeshow tips, and cold-calling hints.

★11333★ Journal of Academic Leadership

Academic Leadership
600 Park St.
Rarick Hall 219
Hays, KS 67601-4099
Ph: (785)628-4547
URL: http://www.academicleadership.org/

Journal focusing on the leadership issues in the academic world.

★11334★ Journal of Business and Psychology

Springer-Verlag New York Inc.
233 Spring St.
New York, NY 10013
Ph: (212)460-1500   Fax: (212)460-1575
URL: http://www.springer.com/journal/10869/

Journal covering all aspects of psychology that apply to the business segment. Includes topics such as personnel selection and training, organizational assessment and development, risk management and loss control, marketing and consumer behavior research.

★11335★ Journal of International Business Strategy

Academy of International Business and Economics
PO Box 2536
Ceres, CA 95307
URL: http://www.AIBE.org

Peer-reviewed journal publishing theoretical, conceptual, and applied research on topics related to strategy in international business.

★11336★ Management Research

M.E. Sharpe Inc.
80 Business Pk. Dr.
Armonk, NY 10504
Ph: (914)273-1800   Fax: (914)273-2106
Fr: 800-541-6563
URL: http://www.mesharpe.com/mall/results1.asp?ACR=JMR

$72.00/year for individuals; $349.00/year for institutions; $84.00/year for other countries, individual; $391.00/year for institutions, other countries. International journal dedicated to advancing the understanding of management in private and public sector organizations through empirical investigation and theoretical analysis. Attempts to promote an international dialogue between researchers, improve the understanding of the nature of management in different settings, and achieve a reasonable transfer of research results to management practice in several contexts. Receptive to research across a broad range of management topics such as human resource management, organizational behavior, organizational theory, and strategic management. While not regional in nature, articles dealing with Iberoamerican issues are particularly welcomed.

★11337★ Master Salesmanship

Clement Communications Inc.
10 LaCrue Ave.
PO Box 36
PO Box 7000
Concordville, PA 19331
Ph: (610)459-4200   Fax: 800-459-1933
Fr: 888-358-5858
E-mail: editor@clement.com
URL: http://www.clement.com/

Description: Biweekly. Designed to help sales managers motivate, train, and inform their salespeople. Offers pointers on improving old sales skills and developing new ones. Recurring features include a motivation column, Q&A, and Selling Slants.

★11338★ Organization Management Journal

Eastern Academy of Management
c/o Craig Tunwall, VP
Empire State College
2805 State Hwy. 67
Johnstown, NY 12095
Ph: (518)762-4651   Fax: (518)736-1716
URL: http://www1.wnec.edu/omj

Free to qualified subscribers. Refereed, online journal focusing on organization management issues.

★11339★ Public Performance and Management Review

M.E. Sharpe Inc.
80 Business Pk. Dr.
Armonk, NY 10504
Ph: (914)273-1800   Fax: (914)273-2106
Fr: 800-541-6563

URL: http://www.mesharpe.com/mall/results1.asp?ACR=pmr

Quarterly. $85.00/year for individuals; $399.00/year for institutions; $101.00/year for other countries, individual; $431.00/year for institutions, other countries. Journal addressing a broad range of factors influencing the performance of public and nonprofit organizations and agencies. Aims to facilitate the development of innovative techniques and encourage a wider application of those already established; stimulate research and critical thinking about the relationship between public and private management theories; present integrated analyses of theories, concepts, strategies and techniques dealing with productivity, measurement and related questions of performance improvement; and provide a forum for practitioner-academic exchange. Continuing themes include managing for productivity, measuring and evaluating performance, improving budget strategies, managing human resources, building partnerships, and applying new technologies.

★11340★ Sales and Marketing Executive Report

The Dartnell Corp.
2272 Airport Rd. S.
Naples, FL 34112
Fr: 800-477-4030
E-mail: customerservice@dartnellcorp.com
URL: http://www.dartnellcorp.com/

Description: Biweekly. Discusses topics of interest to managers, including motivating and training sales personnel, executive self-improvement, and advertising and public relations strategies. Recurring features include news of research, letters to the editor, book reviews, a calendar of events, and columns titled Sales/Marketing Briefs and Special Report.

★11341★ Sales & Marketing Report

Lawrence Ragan Communications Inc.
111 E. Wacker Dr., Ste. 500
Chicago, IL 60601
Ph: (312)960-4100   Fax: (312)861-3592
Fr: 800-878-5331
E-mail: cservice@ragan.com
URL: http://www.ragan.com

Description: Monthly. Provides information about strategic sales coaching, building a high performance sales team, boosting morale and productivity, and managing time more effectively.

★11342★ The Selling Advantage

Progressive Business Publications
370 Technology Dr.
Malvern, PA 19355
Ph: (610)695-8600   Fax: (610)647-8089
Fr: 800-220-5000
E-mail: Customer_Service@pbp.com
URL: http://www.pbp.com

Description: Semimonthly. Explores new strategies and proven techniques to improve sales performance. Recurring features include book reviews and a column titled Tale of the Sale.

★11343★ Supply Chain Management Review

Reed Business Information
225 Wyman St.
Waltham, MA 02451-1216
URL: http://www.scmr.com

$199.00/year for U.S. and Canada; $241.00/year for other countries. Publication covering business and management.

★11344★ What's Working in Sales Management

Progressive Business Publications
370 Technology Dr.
Malvern, PA 19355
Ph: (610)695-8600   Fax: (610)647-8089
Fr: 800-220-5000
E-mail: Customer_Service@pbp.com
URL: http://www.pbp.com

Description: Semimonthly. Acts as a time-saving resource for busy sales managers. Recurring features include interviews, news of research, a calendar of events, and news of educational opportunities.

HANDBOOKS AND MANUALS

★11345★ Career Opportunities in the Retail and Wholesale Industry

Facts On File Inc.
132 W. 31st St., 17th Fl.
New York, NY 10001-2006
Ph: (212)967-8800   Fax: 800-678-3633
Fr: 800-322-8755
E-mail: custserv@factsonfile.com
URL: http://www.factsonfile.com

Field, Shelly and Groveman 2001. $18.95 (Trade paper). $49.50 (hardcover). 278 pages.

★11346★ How to Make Hot Cold Calls: Your Calling Card to Personal Success

Stoddart
4500 Witmer Industrial, E.
Niagara Falls, NY 14305-1386
Fax: 800-481-6207   Fr: 800-805-1083

Steven J. Schwartz. Revised, 2001. 145 pages.

★11347★ Opportunities in Retailing Careers

The McGraw-Hill Companies
PO Box 182604
Columbus, OH 43272
Fax: (614)759-3749   Fr: 877-883-5524
E-mail: customer.service@mcgraw-hill.com
URL: http://www.mcgraw-hill.com

Dolber, Roslyn. 2003. $13.95 (Trade paper). 160 pages.

★11348★ Opportunities in Sales Careers

The McGraw-Hill Companies
PO Box 182604
Columbus, OH 43272
Fax: (614)759-3749   Fr: 877-883-5524
E-mail: customer.service@mcgraw-hill.com
URL: http://www.mcgraw-hill.com

Dahm, Ralph M. and James Brescoll. 2001. $12.95 (Trade paper). $14.95 (Hardcover). 160 pages.

★11349★ Retailing Career Starter

LearningExpress, LLC
55 Broadway, 8th Fl.
New York, NY 10006
Ph: (212)995-2566   Fax: (212)995-5512
Fr: 800-295-9556
E-mail: customerser-vice@learningexpressllc.com
URL: http://www.learningexpressllc.com

Lipow, Valerie. 1998. $14.95 (Trade paper). 212 pages.

★11350★ Sales Careers: The Ultimate Guide to Getting a High-Paying Sales Job

Jist Works
875 Montreal Way
St. Paul, MN 55102
Fr: 800-648-5478
E-mail: info@jist.com
URL: http://www.jist.com

Edward R. Newill, Louise Kursmark. 2003. $12.95. 196 pages.

★11351★ Sales Management: A Career Path Approach

South-Western Pub
5191 Natorp Blvd.
Mason, OH 45040
Ph: (513)229-1000   Fr: 800-354-9706
URL: http://www.swlearning.com

Hughes, G. David, Daryl McKee, and Charles H. Singler. 1998. $98.95 (Cloth). 453 pages.

EMPLOYMENT AGENCIES AND SEARCH FIRMS

★11352★ AG Fishkin & Associates

PO Box 34413
Bethesda, MD 20827
Ph: (301)983-0303   Fax: (301)983-0415
E-mail: afishkin@comcast.net

Executive search firm.

★11353★ Aries Search Group

9925 Haynes Bridge Rd., Ste. 200-146
Alpharetta, GA 30022
Ph: (770)569-4708   Fax: (770)569-4709
E-mail: ariessearch@bellsouth.net

Executive search firm specializing in medical sales and marketing.

★11354★ The B & B Group

65 Sunset Hills Dr.
Edwardsville, IL 62025
Ph: (618)288-1372   Fax: (618)659-0302
E-mail: ron@bnbgrp.com
URL: http://www.bnbgrp.com

Executive search firm.

★11355★ Baldwin Gilman, LLC

4760 Red Bank Expressway
Cincinnati, OH 45227
Ph: (513)272-2400   Fax: (513)527-5929
Fr: 800-745-2373
E-mail: resumes@baldwingilman.com
URL: http://www.baldwin-assoc.com

Executive search firm.

★11356★ Barclay Consultants Inc.

201 Union Ln., Ste. F
Brielle, NJ 08730
Ph: (732)223-1131

Executive search firm.

★11357★ Barcus Associates

PO Box 1059
Van Alstyne, TX 75495
Ph: (903)482-1362   Fax: (903)482-1365
E-mail: moreinfo@barcusassociates.com
URL: http://www.barcusassociates.com

Executive search firm.

★11358★ Barrett & Co. Inc.

59 Stiles Rd., Ste. 105
Salem, NH 03079
Ph: (603)890-1111   Fax: (603)890-1118
E-mail: info@barrettcompany.com
URL: http://www.barrettcompany.com

Executive search firm.

★11359★ The Bentley Group Inc.

9090 Alexandra Cir.
Wellington, FL 33414
Ph: (561)734-3550   Fax: (561)734-3449
Fr: (866)734-3550
E-mail: Bennett@bentleygrp.com
URL: http://www.bentleygrp.com

Executive search firm.

★11360★ Bishop Partners

708 3rd Ave., Ste. 2200
New York, NY 10017
Ph: (212)986-3419   Fax: (212)986-3350
E-mail: info@bishoppartners.com
URL: http://www.bishoppartners.com

A retainer-based executive search firm specializing in media and communications. This includes cable, broadcasting, publishing, Internet and interactive media, entertainment. Consulting closely with clients, finds the right person to fill a specific need and/or solve a specific business issue in functional areas which include CEO and COO, sales, marketing, finance, human resources, programming and production, and e-commerce.

★11361★ **Bosch & Associates LLC**
PO Box 1030
Greens Farms, CT 06838
Ph: (203)255-8700   Fax: (203)259-4959
E-mail: human.resources@boschllc.com
URL: http://www.boschllc.com

Executive search firm.

★11362★ **Brownstone Sales & Marketing Group Inc.**
552 Broadway, Ste. 301
New York, NY 10012
Ph: (212)219-4022
E-mail: jn@b-stone.com
URL: http://www.b-stone.com

Executive search firm.

★11363★ **Bryant Bureau Sales Recruiters**
2435 Kimberly Rd., Ste. 110 N
Bettendorf, IA 52722-3505
Ph: (563)355-4411   Fax: (563)355-3635
Fr: 800-873-4411
E-mail: bbureau@netexpress.net
URL: http://www.bbureau.com

Executive search firm.

★11364★ **CAA Search**
5469 Sunbird Dr.
Loves Park, IL 61111
Ph: (815)654-8535   Fax: (815)654-0469
E-mail: christian@caasearch.com
URL: http://www.caasearch.com

Executive search firm.

★11365★ **Career Forum Inc.**
165 S Union Blvd., Ste.777
Lakewood, CO 80228
Ph: (303)279-9200   Fax: (303)279-9296
E-mail: jennprice@careerforum.com
URL: http://www.careerforum.com

Executive search firm.

★11366★ **CareerConnections USA Inc.**
12827 Westledge Lane
St. Louis, MO 63131
Ph: (314)909-8510   Fax: (314)909-8513
E-mail: deb@careerconnectionsusa.com
URL: http://www.careerconnectionsusa.com

Executive search firm.

★11367★ **Carter/MacKay**
777 Terrace Ave.
Hasbrouck Heights, NJ 07604
Ph: (201)288-5100   Fax: (201)288-2660
E-mail: info.nj@cartermackay.com

URL: http://www.cartermackay.com

Executive search firm.

★11368★ **Century Associates Inc.**
1420 Walnut St., Ste. 1402
Philadelphia, PA 19102
Ph: (215)732-4311   Fax: (215)735-1804
E-mail: dallen@centuryassociates.com
URL: http://www.centuryassociates.com

Executive search firm.

★11369★ **Clanton & Co.**
1 City Blvd. W, Ste. 820
Orange, CA 92868
Ph: (714)978-7100   Fax: (714)978-7103
E-mail: fssearch@aol.com

Executive search firm.

★11370★ **Clinton, Charles, Wise & Co.**
931 SR 434, Ste. 1201-319
Altamonte Springs, FL 32714
Ph: (407)682-6790   Fax: (407)682-1697
E-mail: sales@recruitersofccwc.com
URL: http://www.recruitersofccwc.com

Executive search firm.

★11371★ **Colton Bernard Inc.**
870 Market St., Ste. 822
San Francisco, CA 94102
Ph: (415)399-8700   Fax: (415)399-0750
E-mail: inquiry@coltonbernard.com
URL: http://www.coltonbernard.com

Executive search firm focused on textiles, apparel and retail industries.

★11372★ **Comprehensive Search Corp.**
201 W Padonia Rd., Ste. 101
Lutherville Timonium, MD 21093-2126
Ph: (410)252-8911   Fax: (410)252-7289
Fr: 800-535-8466

Provides recruitment services for sales, management, marketing and technical positions. Industries served: business, environmental, and engineering industries.

★11373★ **Corporate Dynamix**
6619 N Scottsdale Rd.
Scottsdale, AZ 85250
Ph: (480)607-0040   Fax: (480)607-0054
E-mail: david@cdynamix.com
URL: http://www.cdynamix.com

Executive search firm.

★11374★ **Corporate Resources, Inc.**
110 N. Potomac St.
Hagerstown, MD 21740
Ph: (301)797-3434   Fax: (301)797-3331
E-mail: jgocha1@aol.com

Executive search firm.

★11375★ **Criterion Search Group Inc.**
PO Box 466
Wayne, PA 19087
Ph: (610)581-0590   Fax: (610)581-0594
E-mail: hare@criterionsg.com
URL: http://www.criterionsg.com

Executive search firm.

★11376★ **Damon & Associates Inc.**
5716 Portsmouth Ln
Dallas, TX 75252
Ph: (972)671-6990
E-mail: damonoffice@sbcglobal.net

Executive search firm.

★11377★ **Dan Bolen & Associates LLC**
9741 N 90th Pl., Ste. 200
Scottsdale, AZ 85258-5045
Ph: (480)767-9000   Fax: (480)767-0100
E-mail: danbolen@mindspring.com
URL: http://www.danbolenassoc.com

Executive search firm.

★11378★ **David Blevins & Associates Inc.**
611 S. Palm Canyon Dr., Ste. 7140
Palm Springs, CA 92264
Ph: (707)495-3714
E-mail: DaveBlevins@daveblevins.com
URL: http://www.daveblevins.com/vineyards.swf

Executive search firm.

★11379★ **David Fockler & Associates Inc.**
25944 Paseo Estribo, Ste. 100
Monterey, CA 93940
Ph: (831)649-6666   Fax: (831)649-0600
E-mail: dave@fockler.com
URL: http://www.fockler.com

Executive search firm.

★11380★ **Despres & Associates Inc.**
515 S. Hough St.
Barrington, IL 60010
Ph: (847)382-0625   Fax: (847)382-1705
E-mail: rdespres@despres.net
URL: http://www.despres.net

Executive search firm.

★11381★ **Don Allan Associates Inc.**
PO Box 12988
La Jolla, CA 92039-2988
Ph: (858)587-4800   Fax: (858)777-3490
Fr: 800-291-6900
E-mail: resume@globalstaffing.com
URL: http://www.globalstaffing.com

Executive search firm.

★11382★ Don V. Poole and Associates, Inc
7700 S. Glencoe Way
Centennial, CO 80122
Ph: (303)721-6644   Fax: (303)721-7724
E-mail: dvpoole@attglobal.net
Executive search firm.

★11383★ The Donnelly Group Sales Recruiters Inc.
12536 Glenlea Dr.
St. Louis, MO 63043
Ph: (314)469-6400   Fax: (561)258-3187
E-mail: ddonnelly@primary.net
URL: http://www.donnellysearch.com/
Executive search firm.

★11384★ Dorothy W. Farnath & Associates Inc.
104B Centre Blvd.
Marlton, NJ 08053
Ph: (856)810-2200   Fax: (856)810-2140
E-mail: info@farnath.com
URL: http://www.farnath.com
Executive search firm.

★11385★ Ecruiters.net
PO Box 1086
Chanhassen, MN 55317
Ph: (952)233-5750
E-mail: headhunter@ecruiters.net
URL: http://www.ecruiters.net
Executive search firm.

★11386★ The Excel Group Inc.
18430 Brookhurst St., Ste. 202B
Fountain Valley, CA 92708
Ph: (714)593-5927   Fax: (714)593-6027
E-mail: frank@xlg.com
URL: http://www.xlg.com
Executive search firm.

★11387★ Execusearch
PO Box 3990
Plant City, FL 33564
Ph: (813)659-9665   Fax: (813)759-6303
E-mail: donna@execusearchusa.com
URL: http://www.execusearch.net
Executive search firm.

★11388★ Executive Sales Search Inc.
1815 Habersham Terrace
Cumming, GA 30041
Ph: (770)889-9665   Fax: (770)889-9350
E-mail: lindamende@earthlink.net
Executive search firm.

★11389★ Fast Switch Ltd.
37 W Bridge St., Ste. 200
Dublin, OH 43017
Ph: (614)336-1122   Fax: (614)336-3695
E-mail: webresumes@fastswitch.com

URL: http://www.fastswitch.com
Executive search firm.

★11390★ Fisher Todd Associates and Winston Advertising
122 E 42nd St., Ste. 320
New York, NY 10168
Ph: (212)557-5000   Fax: (212)682-1742
E-mail: fishertodd@winstonstaffing.com
URL: http://www.winstonresources.com
Executive search firm.

★11391★ Forsyte Associates Inc.
1749 Central St., Ste. 4
Stoughton, MA 02072
Ph: (781)344-8600   Fax: (781)344-1896
E-mail: exec-search@forsyte.com
URL: http://www.forsyte.com
Executive search firm.

★11392★ The Garrison Organization
5625 Mills Civic Pkwy, Ste. 101
West Des Moines, IA 50266-5324
Ph: (515)309-4440   Fax: (509)479-1213
Fr: (866)324-6068
E-mail: info@garrisonorg.com
URL: http://www.garrisonorg.com
Executive search firm.

★11393★ Georgia Sales Development Inc.
3700 Mansell Rd., Ste. 220
Alpharetta, GA 30022
Ph: (770)625-5075   Fax: (770)992-1601
E-mail: info@bridge2sales.com
URL: http://www.bridge2sales.com
Executive search firm.

★11394★ GlobalQuest Group
12 Greenway Plaza, Ste. 110
Houston, TX 77046
Ph: (713)964-4007   Fax: (713)964-4006
E-mail: rjhsearch@aol.com
Executive search firm.

★11395★ Gowdy Consultants
12059 Starcrest Dr.
San Antonio, TX 78247
Ph: (210)499-4444   Fax: (210)499-4676
E-mail: gowdycts@texas.net
URL: http://www.gowdyconsultants.com
Executive search firm.

★11396★ Harbeck Associates Inc.
2003 Claremont
Normal, IL 61761
Ph: (309)452-5773
E-mail: bill@harbeckassociates.com
URL: http://www.greatsalesjobs.com
Executive search firm.

★11397★ Hilleren & Associates
3800 American Blvd. W, Ste. 880
Minneapolis, MN 55431
Ph: (952)956-9090   Fax: (952)956-9009
E-mail: jerry@hilleren.com
URL: http://www.hilleren.com

Provides executive search services in sales, marketing and management in the medical and pharmaceutical manufacturing industry.

★11398★ The Howard-Sloan-Koller Group
300 E 42nd St.
New York, NY 10017
Ph: (212)661-5250   Fax: (212)557-9178
E-mail: hsk@hsksearch.com
URL: http://www.hsksearch.com
Executive search firm.

★11399★ International Search Consultants
1956 E Vinedo Lane
Tempe, AZ 85284
Ph: (480)839-8113   Fr: 888-866-7276
E-mail: AnnR@ISCJobs.com
URL: http://www.iscjobs.com/
Executive search firm.

★11400★ J H Dugan & Company
431 El Camino Real, Ste. 5302
Santa Clara, CA 95050
Ph: (408)920-7700   Fax: (408)920-7701
E-mail: info@jhdugan.com
URL: http://www.jhdugan.com
Executive search firm.

★11401★ Jivaro Group
5433 S Emporia Court
Greenwood Village, CO 80111
Ph: (303)740-0022   Fax: (303)843-9570
E-mail: sue@jivarogroup.com
URL: http://www.jivarogroup.com
Executive search firm.

★11402★ JS Robertson Retained Search
75 E. Santa Clara St., Ste. 1388
San Jose, CA 95113
Ph: (408)292-9292   Fax: (408)292-4555
E-mail: info@jsrobertson.com
URL: http://www.jsrobertson.com
Executive search firm.

★11403★ KDK Associates LLC
575 Waterford Dr.
Lake Zurich, IL 60047
Ph: (847)726-2902   Fax: (847)726-2903
E-mail: kdkassociates@aol.com
URL: http://www.kdkassociates.com
Executive search firm.

★11404★ Kensington International Inc.
1415 W 22nd St., Ste. 500
Oak Brook, IL 60523
Ph: (630)571-0123   Fax: (630)571-3139
E-mail: info@kionline.com
URL: http://www.kionline.com
Executive search firm.

★11405★ The Kirdonn Sales Pros
106 W. 11th St., Ste. 1520
Kansas City, MO 64105
Ph: (816)474-0700   Fax: (816)474-0702
E-mail: salespros@kirdonn.net
URL: http://www.kirdonn.com
Executive search firm.

★11406★ Kressenberg Associates
1112 E Copeland, Ste. 340
Arlington, TX 76011
Ph: (817)226-8990   Fax: (817)226-8999
Fr: 800-551-5361
E-mail: sammye@kressenberg.attbbs.com
URL: http://kressenbergassociates.com
Executive search firm with a specialty in veterinary medicine.

★11407★ A la Carte International Inc.
3330 Pacific Ave., Ste. 500
Virginia Beach, VA 23451-2997
Ph: (757)425-6111   Fax: (757)425-8507
Fr: 800-446-3037
E-mail: alacarte@wedofood.com
URL: http://www.wedofood.com
Executive search firm.

★11408★ Lawrence Glaser Associates Inc.
505 S. Lenola Rd., Ste. 202
Moorestown, NJ 08057
Ph: (856)778-9500   Fax: (856)778-4390
E-mail: larryg@lgasearch.com
URL: http://www.lgasearch.com
Executive search firm.

★11409★ Management Decision Systems Inc.
466 Kinderkamack Rd.
Oradell, NJ 07649
Ph: (201)986-1200   Fax: (201)986-1210
E-mail: amy@mdsisearch.com
URL: http://www.mdsisearch.com
Executive search firm.

★11410★ Marketing & Sales Resources Inc.
5455 N. Federal Hwy., Ste. 12
Boca Raton, FL 33487
Ph: (561)988-8557   Fax: (561)637-7555
E-mail: msresources@mindspring.com
Executive search firm.

★11411★ Medical Recruiters Inc.
7733 Forsyth Blvd., Ste. 670
St. Louis, MO 63105
Ph: (314)222-4200   Fax: (314)222-4211
E-mail: resumes@medrecinc.com
URL: http://medicalrecruitersincorporated.com/
Executive search firm.

★11412★ MH Executive Search Group
30617 US Hwy. 19 N, Ste. 502
Palm Harbor, FL 34684
Ph: (727)786-8877
E-mail: packagingjobs@mhgroup.com
URL: http://www.mhgroup.com
Executive search firm.

★11413★ Mid-American Placement Service Inc.
1941 S 42nd St., Ste. 520
Omaha, NE 68105-2945
Ph: (402)341-3338   Fax: (402)341-6266
Executive search firm.

★11414★ Morency Associates
301 Newbury St., Ste. 242
Danvers, MA 01923
Ph: (978)750-4460
E-mail: mmorency@aol.com
Executive search firm.

★11415★ MRI of the Baltimore Washington Corridor
7240 Parkway Dr., Ste. 150
Hanover, MD 21076
Ph: (410)712-0770   Fax: (410)712-0510
E-mail: mribwi@recruitergurus.com
URL: http://www.mrinetwork.com
Executive search firm.

★11416★ MRI Management Recruiters of Atlanta West
4260 Bankhead Hwy., Ste. A
Lithia Springs, GA 30122-1752
Ph: (770)948-5560   Fax: (770)948-5762
E-mail: steve@mraw.net
URL: http://www.mrinetwork.com/
Executive search firm.

★11417★ MRI Network Sales Consultants of St. Petersburg
275 104th Ave., Unit A
Treasure Island, FL 33706
Ph: (727)367-8787   Fax: (727)367-8532
E-mail: scstpete@netscape.net
URL: http://www.mrinetwork.com
Executive search firm.

★11418★ MRI Network Sales Consultants of Southampton
928 Jaymor Rd., Ste. A-200
Southampton, PA 18966
Ph: (215)364-7559   Fax: (215)364-7579
E-mail: infoscs@mriscs.com
URL: http://www.mriscs.com
Executive search firm.

★11419★ MRI Network The Lawler Group
1333 W. Towne Square Rd.
Mequon, WI 53092
Ph: (262)241-1600   Fax: (262)241-1640
E-mail: admin@lawlergroup.com
URL: http://www.lawlergroup.com
Executive search firm.

★11420★ MRI Sales Consultants of Morris County, NJ
364 Parsippany Rd.
Parsippany, NJ 07054-5109
Ph: (973)887-3838   Fax: (973)887-2304
E-mail: scmorris@marketing-sales.com
URL: http://www.marketing-sales.com
Executive search firm.

★11421★ MRI Sales Consultants of Rhode Island
2348 Post Rd., Ste. 101
Airport Professional Park
Warwick, RI 02886-2271
Ph: (401)737-3200   Fax: (401)737-4322
E-mail: BestSalesTalent@mrisales.net
URL: http://www.mrisales.net
Executive search firm.

★11422★ MRI Sales Consultants of Syracuse
212 Highbridge St., Ste. B
Fayetteville, NY 13066
Ph: (315)637-0619   Fax: (315)637-0621
E-mail: mri.sc@verizon.net
URL: http://www.mrinetwork.com
Executive search firm.

★11423★ MRI Search Consultants Intracoastal, Inc.
3000 NE 30th Place, Ste. 308
Fort Lauderdale, FL 33306
Ph: (954)772-5100   Fax: (954)772-0777
E-mail: resume@mri-sc-usa.com
URL: http://www.mri-sc-usa.com/
Executive search firm.

★11424★ MRINetwork Management Recruiters of Mercer
1717 Arch St., 36th Floor
Philadelphia, PA 19103
Fax: (215)751-1757   Fr: (866)836-9890
E-mail: info@mrmercer.com
URL: http://www.mrinetwork.com/
Executive search firm.

★11425★ National Sales & Marketing Consultants Inc.
5650 Greenwood Plz. Blvd., Ste. 206
Englewood, CO 80111-2309
Ph: (303)771-4201   Fax: (303)740-8640
E-mail: nasmarc@aol.com

Locates, hires, and trains sales representatives, and coordinates on-going activities of manufacturer's representatives for clients in health-care, government, health and beauty aids, sporting goods, consumer products, hardware, and stationery/office supply industries. Assists clients in developing pricing, packaging, advertising, general sales, and promotional policies. Acts as national sales manager for multiple clients.

★11426★ Navin Group
200 Cordwainer Dr., Ste. 100
Norwell, MA 02061
Ph: (781)871-6770   Fax: (781)878-8703
Fr: 888-837-1300
E-mail: search@navingroup.com
URL: http://www.navingroup.com

Executive search firm.

★11427★ Next Step Group, Inc
PO Box 25038
San Mateo, CA 94402
Ph: (650)577-8000   Fax: (650)577-9000
E-mail: info@4nextstep.com
URL: http://www.4nextstep.com

Executive search firm.

★11428★ Oliver & Rozner Associates
598 Madison Ave., Ste. 11
New York, NY 10022
Ph: (212)688-1850

Performs executive search for top tiers of management including presidents, general management, advertising account management, division management, group executive and vice presidential line positions in such areas as marketing, research, operations, sales, finance, human resources, and others; hard-to-find specialists including specific marketing/advertising executives, research and development expertise, computer/data processing knowledge, scientific, physicians-product efficacy and occupational medicine, and engineering. Industries served include pharmaceutical, healthcare, hospital, advertising, consumer products and packaged goods, housewares, direct selling, cosmetics/toiletries, industrial products, high technology products, forest products, engineering, construction, environment/resource recovery, graphic arts, chemical, and government agencies.

★11429★ Opus Productivity
23151 Moulton Pkwy.
Laguna Hills, CA 92653
Ph: (949)581-0962   Fax: (949)581-1497
URL: http://www.OpusProductivity.com

Executive search firm.

★11430★ Page Consulting LLC
Blue Heron Pines Golf Community
Egg Harbor City, NJ 08215
Ph: (609)965-3300   Fax: (609)965-3339
E-mail: abrown@turntothepage.com
URL: http://www.turntothepage.com/

Executive search firm.

★11431★ Pat Licata & Associates
200 Pinner Weald Way, Ste.101
Cary, NC 27513
Ph: (919)653-1180   Fax: (919)653-1199
E-mail: resumes@patlicata.com
URL: http://www.patlicata.com

Executive search firm for the pharmaceutical and medical industries.

★11432★ Paul J. Biestek Associates Inc.
800 E. NW Hwy., Ste. 700
PO Box 101
Palatine, IL 60074
Ph: (847)825-5131
E-mail: search@biestek-associates.com
URL: http://www.biestek-associates.com

Executive search firm.

★11433★ Price & Associates
1400 Midhurst Cir.
Virginia Beach, VA 23464
Ph: (757)306-4777   Fax: (757)306-8943
E-mail: vprice@earthlink.net

Executive search firm.

★11434★ Pro Search National Recruiting Services
216 W Pacific Ave., Ste. 104
Spokane, WA 99201
Ph: (509)363-1986   Fax: (509)363-1987
E-mail: pat@prosearchnational.com

Executive search firm.

★11435★ Professional Recruiters Inc.
705 1ST St., NE
Little Falls, MN 56345
Ph: (320)616-5849   Fr: 800-594-8414
E-mail: mail@professionalrecruiters.com
URL: http://www.professionalrecruiters.com

Executive search firm.

★11436★ The Professional Sales Search Company Inc.
12801 50th Ave. Ct. NW
Gig Harbor, WA 98332
Ph: (253)851-3528   Fax: (253)851-7505
E-mail: execadmin@psscinc.com
URL: http://www.psscinc.com

Executive search firm.

★11437★ Sales Consultants of Indianapolis
8200 Haverstick Rd., Ste. 240
Indianapolis, IN 46240-2472
Ph: (317)257-5411   Fax: (317)259-6886

Executive search firm.

★11438★ Sales Consultants of Laurel Park
17177 N Laurel Park Dr., Ste. 256
Livonia, MI 48152-2659
Ph: (734)542-9099

Executive search firm.

★11439★ Sales Consultants of Scottsdale
10245 E. Viaduct Linda
Scottsdale, AZ 85258
Ph: (480)424-7958
E-mail: scscottsdale@extremezone.com

Executive search firm.

★11440★ Sales Recruiters International Ltd.
2 Depot Plz., Ste. 303A
Bedford Hills, NY 10507
Ph: (914)631-0090   Fax: (914)244-3001
Fr: 800-836-0881
E-mail: info@salesrecruiters.net
URL: http://www.salesrecruiters.net

Offers management and consulting services including recruitment, selection, and retention of sales and marketing personnel, and teambuilding. Industries served: office products, telecommunications, data processing, financial, contract interiors, food service, hospitality, consumer products, and graphic arts.

★11441★ Sanford Rose Associates-Norcross
9810-B Medlock Bridge Rd., Ste. 201
Johns Creek, GA 30097
Ph: (770)232-9900   Fax: (770)232-1933
E-mail: norcrossresume@sanfordrose.com
URL: http://www.sanfordrose.com/norcross

Executive search firm.

★11442★ Satterfield & Associates Inc.
7875 Annesdale Dr.
Cincinnati, OH 45243
Ph: (513)561-3679
E-mail: info@satterfield3.com
URL: http://www.satterfield3.com

Executive search firm.

★11443★ Search North America Inc.
PO Box 3577
Sunriver, OR 97707-0577
Ph: (503)222-6461   Fax: (503)227-2804
E-mail: mylinda@searchna.com
URL: http://www.searchna.com

An executive search and recruiting firm whose focus is placing engineers, operations and maintenance managers, sales and marketing management, financial and general management executives (both domestic and international). Industries served: forest products, pulp and paper, waste to energy, environmental services, consulting and equipment suppliers for above related industries.

★11444★ Select Medical Solutions
16303 Autumn View Terrace
Ellisville, MO 63011
Ph: (636)405-0333   Fax: (636)458-4657
E-mail: info@smsrecruiters.com
URL: http://
www.selectmedicalsolutions.com

Executive search firm.

★11445★ SHS of Cherry Hill
496 N Kings Hwy., Ste. 125
Cherry Hill, NJ 08034
Ph: (856)779-9030   Fax: (856)779-0898
E-mail: shs@shsofcherryhill.com
URL: http://www.shsofcherryhill.com

Personnel recruiters operating in the disciplines of accounting, sales, insurance, engineering, and administration. Industries served: insurance, distribution, manufacturing, and service.

★11446★ Sondra Search
PO Box 101
Roswell, GA 30077-0101
Ph: (770)552-1910   Fax: (770)552-7340
E-mail: sondrasearch@earthlink.net

Executive search firm.

★11447★ SR & Associates
5001 Birch St.
Newport Beach, CA 92660
Ph: (949)756-3271
E-mail: sraross@srassociates.com
URL: http://www.srassociatesinc.com

Executive search firm.

★11448★ Strategic Associates Inc.
PO Box 203278
Austin, TX 78720-3278
Ph: (512)218-8222   Fax: (512)218-8102
E-mail: sai@strategicassociates.com
URL: http://www.strategicassociates.com

Executive search firm.

★11449★ Strategic Executive Search Solutions
14 Fernald Ave
PO Box 86
Corinna, ME 04928
Fax: 877-780-4777   Fr: 877-871-3800
E-mail: j.parker@strategicexecsearch.com
URL: http://www.parkerbusiness.com

Executive search firm.

★11450★ Todd Arro Inc.
3024 Delaware Ave.
PO Box 172
Buffalo, NY 14217
Ph: (716)871-0993   Fax: (716)871-1376

Recruiting and search consultants specializing in sales and marketing management in the industrial, commercial, consumer product, pharmaceutical and medical areas.

★11451★ Weterrings & Agnew Inc.
295 Woodcliff Dr., Ste. 101
Fairport, NY 14450
Ph: (585)641-2575   Fax: (585)641-2589
E-mail: info@weterrings.com
URL: http://www.weterrings.com

Executive search firm.

★11452★ Whitney Group
850 3rd Ave., 11th Fl
New York, NY 10022
Ph: (212)508-3500   Fax: (212)508-3589
E-mail: recruiter@whitneygroup.com
URL: http://www.whitneygroup.com

Executive search firm.

★11453★ William Halderson Associates Inc.
PO Box 20056
St. Simons Island, GA 31522
Ph: (912)638-8430
E-mail: bill@haldersonsearch.com
URL: http://www.haldersonsearch.com/

Executive search firm.

★11454★ The Wylie Group Ltd.
345 N Canal St., Ste. 1605
Chicago, IL 60606
Ph: (312)822-0333   Fax: (312)454-1375
E-mail: wrw@wyliegroup.net

Executive search firm.

ONLINE JOB SOURCES AND SERVICES

★11455★ Omni Search, Inc.
E-mail: omni@omnisearch.biz
URL: http://www.omnisearch.biz/opps.htm

Description: Job search engine for those in the sales and marketing positions in the pharmaceutical, medical and consumer industries.

★11456★ Spherion
2050 Spectrum Blvd.
Fort Lauderdale, FL 33309
Ph: (954)308-7600
E-mail: help@spherion.com
URL: http://www.spherion.com

Description: Recruitment firm specializing

in accounting and finance, sales and marketing, interim executives, technology, engineering, retail and human resources.

TRADESHOWS

★11457★ ERA Conference and Exposition
Electronic Retailing Association
2000 N. 14th St., Ste. 300
Arlington, VA 22201
Ph: (703)841-1751   Fax: (703)841-1860
Fr: 800-987-6462
E-mail: contact@retailing.org
URL: http://www.retailing.org

Annual. Primary Exhibits: Equipment, supplies, and services for the growth, development, and acceptance of electronic retailing worldwide.

OTHER SOURCES

★11458★ Administration and Management Occupations
Delphi Productions
3159 6th St.
Boulder, CO 80304
Ph: (303)443-2100   Fax: (303)443-4022
Fr: 888-443-2400
E-mail: support@delphivideo.com
URL: http://www.delphivideo.com

$95.00. 50 minutes. Part of the Careers for the 21st Century Video Library.

★11459★ American Management Association (AMA)
1601 Broadway
New York, NY 10019-7420
Ph: (212)586-8100   Fax: (212)903-8168
Fr: 800-262-9699
E-mail: membership@amanet.org
URL: http://www.amanet.org

Description: Provides educational forums worldwide where members and their colleagues learn superior, practical business skills and explore best practices of world-class organizations through interaction with each other and expert faculty practitioners. Purpose: Maintains a publishing program providing tools individuals use to extend learning beyond the classroom in a process of life-long professional growth and development through education.

★11460★ American Society of Association Executives (ASAE)
1575 I St. NW
Washington, DC 20005
Ph: (202)371-0940   Fax: (202)371-8315
Fr: 888-950-2723
E-mail: pr@asaenet.org

URL: http://www.asaecenter.org

Members: Professional society of paid executives of international, national, state, and local trade, professional, and philanthropic associations. **Purpose:** Seeks to educate association executives on effective management, including: the proper objectives, functions, and activities of associations; the basic principles of association management; the legal aspects of association activity; policies relating to association management; efficient methods, procedures, and techniques of association management; the responsibilities and professional standards of association executives. Maintains information resource center. **Activities:** Conducts resume, guidance, and consultation services; compiles statistics in the form of reports, surveys, and studies; carries out research and education. Maintains ASAE Services Corporation to provide special services and ASAE Foundation to do future-oriented research and make grant awards. Offers executive search services and insurance programs. Provides CEO center for chief staff executives. Conducts Certified Association Executive (CAE) program.

★11461★ **Marketing & Sales Occupations**

Delphi Productions
3159 6th St.
Boulder, CO 80304
Ph: (303)443-2100   Fax: (303)443-4022
Fr: 888-443-2400
E-mail: support@delphivideo.com
URL: http://www.delphivideo.com

$95.00. 50 minutes. Part of the Careers for the 21st Century Video Library.

★11462★ **National Management Association (NMA)**

2210 Arbor Blvd.
Dayton, OH 45439
Ph: (937)294-0421   Fax: (937)294-2374
E-mail: nma@nma1.org
URL: http://www.nma1.org

Description: Business and industrial management personnel; membership comes from supervisory level, with the remainder from middle management and above. Seeks to develop and recognize management as a profession and to promote the free enterprise system. Prepares chapter programs on basic management, management policy and practice, communications, human behavior, industrial relations, economics, political education, and liberal education. Maintains speakers' bureau and hall of fame. Maintains educational, charitable, and research programs. Sponsors charitable programs.

Science Technicians

SOURCES OF HELP-WANTED ADS

★11463★ American Biotechnology Laboratory

International Scientific Communications Inc.
30 Controls Dr.
PO Box 870
Shelton, CT 06484
Ph: (203)926-9300   Fax: (203)926-9310
URL: http://
www.americanbiotechnologylaboratory.com

Bimonthly. $160.00/year for individuals. Biotechnology magazine.

★11464★ Annual Review of Microbiology

Annual Reviews Inc.
4139 El Camino Way
PO Box 10139
Palo Alto, CA 94303-0139
Ph: (650)493-4400   Fax: (650)424-0910
Fr: 800-523-8635
URL: http://www.annualreviews.org/

Annual. $80.00/year for individuals, print & online; $80.00/year for out of country, print & online; $222.00/year for institutions, print & online; $222.00/year for institutions, other countries, print & online; $185.00/year for institutions, online; $185.00/year for institutions, other countries, online; $185.00/year for institutions, print; $185.00/year for institutions, other countries, print. Periodical covering microbiology and the biological sciences.

★11465★ AWIS Magazine
Association for Women in Science
1200 New York Ave., NW, Ste. 650
Washington, DC 20005
Ph: (202)326-8940   Fax: (202)326-8960
Fr: (866)657-2947
URL: http://www.awis.org/

Quarterly. $7.00 for nonmembers, price per issue; $5.00 for members, price per issue. Professional magazine covering the status of women in science.

★11466★ Chemical Equipment
Reed Business Information
360 Park Ave. S
New York, NY 10010
Ph: (646)746-6400   Fax: (646)746-7431
URL: http://
www.reedbusinessinteractive.com

Free, for qualified professionals; $72.90/year for individuals, cover price. Tabloid on the chemical process industry.

★11467★ Engineering in Life Sciences
John Wiley & Sons Inc.
111 River St.
Hoboken, NJ 07030-5774
Ph: (201)748-6000   Fax: (201)748-6088
Fr: 800-825-7550
URL: http://as.wiley.com/WileyCDA/Wiley-Title/productCd-2129.html

Bimonthly. $765.00/year for institutions, rest of Europe; $1,170.00/year for institutions, Switzerland and Liechtenstein; $1,005.00/year for institutions, rest of world; $842.00/year for institutions, print with online rest of Europe; $1,287.00/year for institutions, print with online Switzerland and Liechtenstein; $1,106.00/year for institutions, print with online rest of world. Journal focusing on the field of biotechnology and related topics including microbiology, genetics, biochemistry, and chemistry.

★11468★ Harvard Science Review
Harvard University Press
79 Garden St.
Cambridge, MA 02138
Ph: (401)531-2800   Fax: 800-406-9145
Fr: 800-405-1619
E-mail: hsr@hcs.harvard.edu
URL: http://www.harvardsciencereview.org

Semiannual. A science journal.

★11469★ InterJournal
New England Complex Systems Institute
24 Mt. Auburn St.
Cambridge, MA 02138
Ph: (617)547-4100   Fax: (617)661-7711
URL: http://www.interjournal.org/

Journal covering the fields of science and engineering.

★11470★ The Internet Journal of Forensic Science
Internet Scientific Publications L.L.C.
23 Rippling Creek Dr.
Sugar Land, TX 77479
Ph: (832)443-1193   Fax: (281)240-1532
URL: http://www.ispub.com/ostia/index.php?xmlFilePath=journals/ij

Free, online. Electronic journal for medical professionals focusing on the field of forensic science.

★11471★ Invertebrate Biology
Allen Press Inc.
810 E 10th St.
Lawrence, KS 66044
Ph: (785)843-1234   Fax: (785)843-1244
Fr: 800-627-0326
URL: http://www.amicros.org/

Quarterly. $38.00/year for members; $19.00/year for students. Scientific journal covering the biology of invertebrate animals and research in the fields of cell and molecular biology, ecology, physiology, systematics, genetics, biogeography and behavior.

★11472★ Nature Biotechnology
Nature Publishing Group
75 Varick St., 9th Fl.
New York, NY 10013-1917
Ph: (212)726-9200   Fax: (212)696-9006
Fr: 888-331-6288
E-mail: biotech@natureny.com
URL: http://www.nature.com/nbt/index.html

Monthly. Scientific research journal.

★11473★ Nature International Weekly Journal of Science
Nature Publishing Group
75 Varick St., 9th Fl.
New York, NY 10013-1917
Ph: (212)726-9200   Fax: (212)696-9006
Fr: 888-331-6288
E-mail: nature@natureny.com

URL: http://www.nature.com

Weekly. $145.00/year for individuals; $49.00/year for institutions. Magazine covering science and technology, including the fields of biology, biochemistry, genetics, medicine, earth sciences, physics, pharmacology, and behavioral sciences.

★11474★ *The Northeastern Naturalist*

Humboldt Field Research Institute
59 Eagle Hill Rd.
PO Box 9
Steuben, ME 04680-0009
Ph: (207)546-2821   Fax: (207)546-3042
URL: http://www.eaglehill.us/jngeninf.html

Quarterly. $40.00/year for individuals; $30.00/year for students; $60.00/year for institutions. Peer-reviewed interdisciplinary scientific journal covering field ecology, biology, behavior, biogeography, taxonomy, anatomy, physiology, geology and related fields in the northeastern United States.

★11475★ *Popular Science*

Time4 Media Inc.
2 Park Ave., 9th Fl.
New York, NY 10016-5614
Ph: (212)779-5000   Fax: (212)779-5588
URL: http://www.popsci.com/popsci

Monthly. $4.00/year; $20.00/year for individuals, 2 years, 24 issues; $30.00/year for individuals, 3 years, 36 issues; $28.00/year for Canada, 24 issues; $68.00/year for Canada, 36 issues. General interest science magazine.

★11476★ *Psychology Journal*

Psychological Publishing
PO Box 176
Natchitoches, LA 71458
URL: http://
www.psychologicalpublishing.com/

$40.00/year for individuals; $75.00/year for institutions. Journal dedicated to all areas of the science and practice of counseling and clinical psychology.

★11477★ *Science*

American Association for the
  Advancement of Science
1200 New York Ave. NW
Washington, DC 20005
Ph: (202)326-6400   Fax: (202)371-9227
URL: http://www.scienceonline.org

Weekly (Fri.). $142.00/year for members, professional; $119.00/year for individuals, NPA postdoctoral; $99.00/year for individuals, postdoctoral/resident; $75.00/year for students; $142.00/year for individuals, k-12 teacher; $310.00/year for individuals, patron; $110.00/year for individuals, emeritus. Magazine devoted to science, scientific research, and public policy.

★11478★ *The Scientist*

The Scientist Inc.
400 Market St., No. 1250
Philadelphia, PA 19106
Ph: (215)351-1660   Fax: (215)351-1146
URL: http://www.the-scientist.com

Bimonthly. $49.95/year for individuals, online; $74.95/year for individuals, online plus print edition; $124.95/year for out of country, online plus print edition (air freight); $29.95/year for individuals; $19.95 for individuals, 6 months; $14.95 for individuals, 1 month; $9.95 for individuals, 1 week; $4.95 for individuals, 1 week. News journal (tabloid) for life scientists featuring news, opinions, research, and professional section.

★11479★ *The Southeastern Naturalist*

Humboldt Field Research Institute
59 Eagle Hill Rd.
PO Box 9
Steuben, ME 04680-0009
Ph: (207)546-2821   Fax: (207)546-3042
E-mail: office@eaglehill.us
URL: http://www.eaglehill.us/jsgeninf.html

Quarterly. $45.00/year for individuals; $35.00/year for students; $75.00/year for institutions. Peer-reviewed interdisciplinary scientific journal covering field ecology, biology, behavior, biogeography, taxonomy, anatomy, physiology, geology and related fields in the southeastern United States.

★11480★ *Wetlands*

Society of Wetland Scientists
1313 Dolley Madison Blvd., Ste. 402
Mc Lean, VA 22101
Ph: (703)790-1745   Fax: (703)790-2672
URL: http://www.sws.org/wetlands/index.mgi

Quarterly. $100.00/year for individuals; $35.00/year for students; $500.00/year for institutions; $200.00/year for libraries. Scholarly journal covering all aspects of wetlands biology, ecology, hydrology, water chemistry, soil and sediment characteristics, management, and laws and regulations.

PLACEMENT AND JOB REFERRAL SERVICES

★11481★ *American Society of Agronomy (ASA)*

677 S Segoe Rd.
Madison, WI 53711
Ph: (608)273-8080   Fax: (608)273-2021
E-mail: headquarters@agronomy.org
URL: http://www.agronomy.org

Description: Professional society of agronomists, plant breeders, physiologists, soil scientists, chemists, educators, technicians, and others concerned with crop production and soil management, and conditions affecting them. Sponsors fellowship program and student essay and speech contests. Provides placement service.

★11482★ American Society for Histocompatibility and Immunogenetics (ASHI)

15000 Commerce Pkwy., Ste. C
Mount Laurel, NJ 08054
Ph: (856)638-0428   Fax: (856)439-0525
E-mail: info@ashi-hla.org
URL: http://www.ashi-hla.org

Members: Scientists, physicians, and technologists involved in research and clinical activities related to histocompatibility testing (a state of mutual tolerance that allows some tissues to be grafted effectively to others). **Activities:** Conducts proficiency testing and educational programs. Maintains liaison with regulatory agencies; offers placement services and laboratory accreditation. Has co-sponsored development of histocompatibility specialist and laboratory certification program.

EMPLOYER DIRECTORIES AND NETWORKING LISTS

★11483★ *Peterson's Job Opportunities in Engineering and Technology*

Peterson's Guides
2000 Lenox Dr.
Box 67005
Lawrenceville, NJ 08648
Ph: (609)896-1800   Fax: (609)896-4531
Fr: 800-338-3282
E-mail: custsvc@petersons.com
URL: http://www.petersons.com

Compiled by the Peterson's staff. Fourth edition, 1996. $21.95 (paper). 379 pages. Profiles 2,000 high-tech companies looking primarily for technical personnel in such fields as biotechnology, telecommunications, software, computers and peripherals, defense, and aerospace. Contains job-search strategies and career options to help match education and expertise to the job market. Indexed geographically, by industry, and by hiring needs.

HANDBOOKS AND MANUALS

★11484★ *The Best Resumes for Scientists and Engineers*

John Wiley & Sons Inc.
1 Wiley Dr.
Somerset, NJ 08873
Ph: (732)469-4400   Fax: (732)302-2300
Fr: 800-225-5945
E-mail: custserv@wiley.com
URL: http://www.wiley.com/WileyCDA/

Adele Lewis and David J. Moore. Second edition, 1993. $37.50; $19.95 (paper). 224 pages. Presents an extensive collection of scientific and engineering resumes, highlighting the important differences between these and resumes written for other occupations.

★11485★ Opportunities in Biological Science Careers

The McGraw-Hill Companies
PO Box 182604
Columbus, OH 43272
Fax: (614)759-3749   Fr: 877-883-5524
E-mail: customer.service@mcgraw-hill.com
URL: http://www.mcgraw-hill.com

Charles A. Winter. 2004. $13.95; $11.95 (paper). 160 pages. Identifies employers and outlines opportunities in plant and animal biology, biological specialties, biomedical sciences, applied biology, and other areas. Illustrated.

★11486★ Opportunities in High Tech Careers

The McGraw-Hill Companies
PO Box 182604
Columbus, OH 43272
Fax: (614)759-3749   Fr: 877-883-5524
E-mail: customer.service@mcgraw-hill.com
URL: http://www.mcgraw-hill.com

Gary Colter and Deborah Yanuck. 1999. $14.95; $11.95 (paper). 160 pages. Explores high technology careers. Describes job opportunities, how to make a career decision, how to prepare for high technology jobs, job hunting techniques, and future trends.

★11487★ Opportunities in Research and Development Careers

The McGraw-Hill Companies
PO Box 182604
Columbus, OH 43272
Fax: (614)759-3749   Fr: 877-883-5524
E-mail: customer.service@mcgraw-hill.com
URL: http://www.mcgraw-hill.com

Jan Goldberg. 1996. $11.95 (paper). 146 pages.

★11488★ Opportunities in Science Technician Careers

The McGraw-Hill Companies
PO Box 182604
Columbus, OH 43272
Fax: (614)759-3749   Fr: 877-883-5524
E-mail: customer.service@mcgraw-hill.com
URL: http://www.mcgraw-hill.com

JoAnn Chirico. 1996. 160 pages. $14.95; $11.95 (paper).

★11489★ Resumes for Science Careers

The McGraw-Hill Companies
PO Box 182604
Columbus, OH 43272
Fax: (614)759-3749   Fr: 877-883-5524
E-mail: customer.service@mcgraw-hill.com
URL: http://www.mcgraw-hill.com

1997. $11.95 (paper). 144 pages.

EMPLOYMENT AGENCIES AND SEARCH FIRMS

★11490★ Banner Personnel Service
125 S Wacker Dr., Ste. 1250
Chicago, IL 60606
Ph: (312)580-2500   Fax: (312)580-2515
URL: http://www.bannerpersonnel.com

Employment agency. Executive search firm. Branch offices in Oak Brook and Schaumburg, IL.

★11491★ Bruce Edwards & Associates Inc.
1502 W NC Highway 54, Ste. 610
Durham, NC 27707
Ph: (919)489-5368   Fax: (919)604-3157
E-mail: brucedwar@aol.com

Executive search firm.

★11492★ Eastbourne Associates Inc.
104 Sandy Hollow Rd.
Northport, NY 11768
Ph: (631)757-1217   Fax: (631)757-1417
E-mail: search@eastbourneassociates.com
URL: http://www.eastbourneassociates.com

Executive search firm.

★11493★ Franklin Allen Consultants Ltd.
1205 Franklin Ave., Ste. 350
Garden City, NY 11530-1629
Ph: (516)248-4511   Fax: (516)294-6646
E-mail: hroher@frankinallen.com

Executive search firm.

★11494★ Intech Summit Group, Inc.
3450 Bonita Rd., Ste. 203
Chula Vista, CA 91910
Ph: (619)862-2720   Fax: (619)862-2699
Fr: 800-750-8100
E-mail: isg@isgsearch.com
URL: http://www.isgsearch.com

Employment agency and executive recruiter with a branch in Carlsbad, CA.

TRADESHOWS

★11495★ American Association for the Advancement of Science Annual Meeting & Science Innovation Exposition
American Association for the Advancement of Science (AAAS)
1200 New York Ave. NW
Washington, DC 20005
Ph: (202)326-6450   Fax: (202)289-4021
URL: http://www.aaasmeetings.org

Annual. **Primary Exhibits:** Scientific supplies and services, including books and journals, educational and informational services, government agencies, and scientific associations. **Dates and Locations:** 2008 Feb 14-18; Boston, MA; 2009 Feb 12-16; Chicago, IL; 2010 Feb 18-22; San Diego, CA; 2011 Feb 17-21; Washington, DC.

OTHER SOURCES

★11496★ American Chemical Society (ACS)
1155 16th St. NW
Washington, DC 20036
Ph: (202)872-4600   Fax: (202)872-4615
Fr: 800-227-5558
E-mail: help@acs.org
URL: http://portal.chemistry.org/portal/acs/corg/memberapp

Members: Scientific and educational society of chemists and chemical engineers. **Activities:** Conducts: studies and surveys; special programs for disadvantaged persons; legislation monitoring, analysis, and reporting; courses for graduate chemists and chemical engineers; radio and television programming. Offers career guidance counseling; administers the Petroleum Research Fund and other grants and fellowship programs. Operates Employment Clearing Houses. Compiles statistics. Maintains Speaker's Bureau and 33 divisions.

★11497★ American Institute of Biological Sciences (AIBS)
1444 I St. NW, Ste. 200
Washington, DC 20005
Ph: (202)628-1500   Fax: (202)628-1509
Fr: 800-992-2427
E-mail: rogrady@aibs.org
URL: http://www.aibs.org

Members: Professional member organization and federation of biological associations, laboratories, and museums whose members have an interest in the life sciences. **Purpose:** Promotes unity and effectiveness of effort among persons engaged in biological research, education, and application of biological sciences, including agriculture, environment, and medicine. Seeks to further the relationships of biological sciences to other sciences and industries. Conducts roundtable series; provides names of prominent biologists who are willing to serve as speakers and curriculum consultants; provides advisory committees and other services to the Department of Energy, Environmental Protection Agency, National Science Foundation, Department of Defense, and National Aeronautics and Space Administration. Maintains educational consultant panel.

★11498★ Association for International Practical Training (AIPT)
10400 Little Patuxent Pkwy., Ste. 250
Columbia, MD 21044-3519
Ph: (410)997-2200   Fax: (410)992-3924

E-mail: aipt@aipt.org
URL: http://www.aipt.org

Description: Providers worldwide of on-the-job training programs for students and professionals seeking international career development and life-changing experiences. Arranges workplace exchanges in hundreds of professional fields, bringing employers and trainees together from around the world. Client list ranges from small farming communities to Fortune 500 companies.

★11499★ Minority Women In Science (MWIS)
Directorate for Education and Human
  Resources Programs
1200 New York Ave. NW
Washington, DC 20005
Ph: (202)326-7019   Fax: (202)371-9849
E-mail: ygeorge@aaas.org

Description: A national network group of the American association for the Advancement of Science (AAAS), Education and Human Resources Directorate. The objectives of this group are: to identify and share information on resources and programs that could help in mentoring young women and minorities interested in science and engineering careers, and to strengthen communication among women and minorities in science and education.

★11500★ Society for Range Management (SRM)
10030 W 27th Ave.
Wheat Ridge, CO 80215-6601
Ph: (303)986-3309   Fax: (303)986-3892
E-mail: info@rangelands.org
URL: http://www.rangelands.org

Description: Professional international society of scientists, technicians, ranchers, administrators, teachers, and students interested in the study, use, and management of rangeland resources for livestock, wildlife, watershed, and recreation.

Secondary School Teachers

SOURCES OF HELP-WANTED ADS

★11501★ AAEE Connections

American Association for Employment in Education
3040 Riverside Dr., Ste. 125
Columbus, OH 43221
Ph: (614)485-1111   Fax: (614)485-9609
E-mail: office@aaee.org
URL: http://www.aaee.org/

Description: Quarterly. Publishes news of the Association, whose aim is "to enhance and promote the concept of career planning and placement as an integral part of the educational process and to undertake activities designed to help schools, colleges, and universities meet their educational staffing needs." Also concerned with teacher education and the supply of/demand for teachers. Recurring features include news of members, state and regional news, and announcements of upcoming conferences and meetings.

★11502★ About Campus

John Wiley & Sons Inc.
111 River St.
Hoboken, NJ 07030-5774
Ph: (201)748-6000   Fax: (201)748-6088
Fr: 800-825-7550
URL: http://www3.interscience.wiley.com/cgi-bin/jhome/86513696

Bimonthly. $60.00/year for individuals, for print; $60.00/year for Canada and Mexico, for print; $96.00/year for individuals, for print (rest of world); $159.00/year for institutions, for print; $219.00/year for institutions, Canada and Mexico, for print; $270.00/year for institutions, for print (rest of world); $175.00/year for institutions, for print and online; $235.00/year for institutions, Canada and Mexico, for print and online; $286.00/year for institutions, for print and online, (rest of world); $111.00/year for individuals, print only. Journal focused on the critical issues faced by both student affairs and academic affairs staff as they work on helping students learn.

★11503★ American Academic

American Federation of Teachers
555 New Jersey Ave. NW
Washington, DC 20001
Ph: (202)879-4400
URL: http://www.aft.org/pubs-reports/american_academic/index.htm

Higher education policy journal.

★11504★ The American Biology Teacher

National Association of Biology Teachers
12030 Sunrise Valley Dr., Ste. 110
Reston, VA 20191-3409
Fax: (703)264-7778   Fr: 800-406-0775
E-mail: publication@nabt.org
URL: http://www.nabt.org

Monthly. Journal featuring articles on biology, science, and education for elementary, high school and college level biology teachers. Includes audio-visual, book, computer, and research reviews.

★11505★ Annals of Medicine

Taylor & Francis Group Journals
325 Chestnut St., Ste. 800
Philadelphia, PA 19106
Ph: (215)625-8900   Fax: (215)625-8914
Fr: 800-354-1420
URL: http://www.ingentaconnect.com

$418.00/year for institutions, print and online; $397.00/year for institutions, online only; $155.00/year for individuals. Journal covering health science and medical education.

★11506★ Assessment & Evaluation in Higher Education

Taylor & Francis Group Journals
325 Chestnut St., Ste. 800
Philadelphia, PA 19106
Ph: (215)625-8900   Fax: (215)625-8914
Fr: 800-354-1420
E-mail: aehe@bath.ac.uk
URL: http://www.tandf.co.uk/journals/titles/02602938.asp

Bimonthly. $1,982.00/year for institutions, print and online; $1,882.00/year for institutions, online only; $466.00/year for individuals. Journal focusing on publishing papers and reports on all aspects of assessment and evaluation within higher education.

★11507★ Brookings Papers on Education Policy

Brookings Institution Press
1775 Massashusetts Ave. NW
Washington, DC 20036-2188
Ph: (202)536-3600   Fax: (202)536-3623
Fr: 800-275-1447
URL: http://www.brookings.edu/press/journals.htm

$46.00/year for institutions; $35.00/year for individuals. Journal dealing with all aspects of American education.

★11508★ Communication Quarterly

MetaPress
PO Box 1943
Birmingham, AL 35201
Fr: 877-773-3833

Periodical focusing on research, criticism, communication theory, and excellence in teaching.

★11509★ Community College Journal of Research & Practice

Taylor & Francis Group Journals
325 Chestnut St., Ste. 800
Philadelphia, PA 19106
Ph: (215)625-8900   Fax: (215)625-8914
Fr: 800-354-1420
URL: http://www.tandf.co.uk/journals/titles/10668926.aspttp://www

Monthly. $778.00/year for institutions, print and online; $739.00/year for institutions, online only; $208.00/year for individuals. Journal focusing on exchange of ideas, research, and empirically tested educational innovations.

★11510★ The Council Chronicle

National Council of Teachers of English
1111 W Kenyon Rd.
Urbana, IL 61801-1096
Ph: (217)328-3870   Fax: (217)328-9645
Fr: 877-369-6283

URL: http://www.ncte.org/pubs/chron
Quarterly. Newspaper for teachers of English or language arts at all levels who are members of the National Council of Teachers of English.

★11511★ E-Journal of Teaching and Learning in Diverse Settings
Southern University at Baton Rouge
PO Box 9942
Baton Rouge, LA 70813
Ph: (225)771-3184   Fax: (225)771-4400
URL: http://www.subr.edu/coeducation/ejournal

Online academic journal that publishes research and scholarly articles in the field of education and learning.

★11512★ Education & Treatment of Children
West Virginia University Press
44 Stansbury Hall
PO Box 6295
Morgantown, WV 26506
Ph: (304)293-8400   Fax: (304)293-6585
Fr: (866)988-7737
URL: http://www.educationandtreatmentofchildren.net

Quarterly. $85.00/year for institutions; $45.00/year for individuals; $100.00/year for institutions, elsewhere; $60.00/year for individuals, elsewhere. Periodical featuring information concerning the development of services for children and youth. Includes reports written for educators and other child care and mental health providers focused on teaching, training, and treatment effectiveness.

★11513★ Education Week
Editorial Projects in Education Inc.
6935 Arlington Rd., Ste. 100
Bethesda, MD 20814-5233
Ph: (301)280-3100   Fax: (301)280-3200
Fr: 800-346-1834
E-mail: ew@epe.org
URL: http://www.edweek.org/ew

Weekly. $79.94/year for individuals, print plus online; $69.94/year for individuals, online; $135.94/year for Canada, online Monthly; $208.84/year for out of country. Professional newspaper for elementary and secondary school educators.

★11514★ Educational Policy
Sage Publications Inc.
2455 Teller Rd.
Thousand Oaks, CA 91320
Ph: (805)499-0721   Fax: (805)499-8096
URL: http://www.sagepub.com/journalsProdDesc.nav?prodId=Journal20

Annual. $749.00/year for institutions, combined (print & e-access); $824.00/year for institutions, backfile lease, combined plus backfile; $674.00/year for institutions, e-access; $749.00/year for institutions, backfile lease, e-access plus backfile; $687.48/year for institutions, backfile puchase, e-access

(content through 1999); $734.00/year for institutions, print only; $159.00/year for individuals, print only; $135.00 for institutions, single print; $34.00 for individuals, single print. Journal for educators, policy makers, administrators, researchers, teachers, and graduate students.

★11515★ Educational Research and Evaluation
Taylor & Francis Group Journals
325 Chestnut St., Ste. 800
Philadelphia, PA 19106
Ph: (215)625-8900   Fax: (215)625-8914
Fr: 800-354-1420
URL: http://www.tandf.co.uk/journals/titles/13803611.asp

Bimonthly. $616.00/year for institutions, print and online; $585.00/year for institutions, online only; $239.00/year for individuals. Journal on theory and practice.

★11516★ Educational Researcher
American Educational Research Association
1230 17th St. NW
Washington, DC 20036
Ph: (202)223-9485   Fax: (202)775-1824
URL: http://www.aera.net/publications/?id=317

Monthly. $48.00/year for individuals, plus foreign mailing charges; $150.00/year for institutions, plus foreign mailing charges. Educational research journal.

★11517★ Environmental Education Research
Taylor & Francis Group Journals
325 Chestnut St., Ste. 800
Philadelphia, PA 19106
Ph: (215)625-8900   Fax: (215)625-8914
Fr: 800-354-1420
URL: http://www.tandf.co.uk/journals/titles/13504622.asp

Journal covering all aspects of environmental education.

★11518★ Essays in Education
University of South Carolina
471 University Pky.
Aiken, SC 29801
Ph: (803)648-6851   Fax: (803)641-3461
Fr: 888-969-8722
URL: http://www.usca.edu/essays/

Monthly. Journal covering issues that impact and influence education.

★11519★ Hematology
American Society of Hematology
1900 M St. NW, Ste. 200
Washington, DC 20036
Ph: (202)776-0544   Fax: (202)776-0545
URL: http://asheducationbook.hematologylibrary.org

Semiweekly. $60.00/year for members; $90.00/year for nonmembers. Journal pro-

viding continuing medical education for physicians.

★11520★ The International Electronic Journal of Health Education
American Alliance for Health, Physical Education, Recreation & Dance
1900 Association Dr.
Reston, VA 20191-1598
Ph: (703)476-3400   Fax: (703)476-9527
Fr: 800-213-7193
URL: http://www.aahperd.org/iejhe/template.cfm?template=about.htm

Annual. Free to health education professionals and students. Journal promoting health through education and other systematic strategies.

★11521★ International Journal of Early Years Education
Taylor & Francis Group Journals
325 Chestnut St., Ste. 800
Philadelphia, PA 19106
Ph: (215)625-8900   Fax: (215)625-8914
Fr: 800-354-1420
URL: http://www.tandf.co.uk/journals/titles/09669760.asp

$512.00/year for institutions, print and online; $486.00/year for institutions, online only; $184.00/year for individuals. Journal focusing on education world-wide.

★11522★ International Journal of Inclusive Education
Taylor & Francis Group Journals
325 Chestnut St., Ste. 800
Philadelphia, PA 19106
Ph: (215)625-8900   Fax: (215)625-8914
Fr: 800-354-1420
URL: http://www.tandf.co.uk/journals/titles/13603116.asp

Bimonthly. $320.00/year for individuals, print only; $616.00/year for institutions, online only; $649.00/year for individuals, print and online; $193.00/year for individuals, print only; $376.00/year for institutions, online only; $396.00/year for institutions, print and online. Journal providing information on the nature of schools, universities and technical colleges for the educators and educational policy-makers.

★11523★ International Journal of Leadership in Education
Taylor & Francis Group Journals
325 Chestnut St., Ste. 800
Philadelphia, PA 19106
Ph: (215)625-8900   Fax: (215)625-8914
Fr: 800-354-1420
E-mail: ijle@txstate.edu
URL: http://www.tandf.co.uk/journals/tf/13603124.html

Quarterly. $196.00/year for individuals; $536.00/year for institutions, print and online; $509.00/year for institutions, online only; Journal dealing with leadership in education.

★11524★ International Journal of Progressive Education

International Journal of Progressive Education
c/o Mustafa Yunus Eryaman, Mng. Ed.
2108 S Orchard St., No. D
Urbana, IL 61801
URL: http://www.inased.org/ijpe.htm

$35.00/year for members; $45.00/year for individuals; $140.00/year for institutions, library; $35.00/year for students; $25.00/year for single issue, U.S. Peer reviewed online journal that aims to create an open and continuing dialogue about current educational issues and future conceptions of educational theory.

★11525★ International Journal of Research & Method in Education

Taylor & Francis Group Journals
325 Chestnut St., Ste. 800
Philadelphia, PA 19106
Ph: (215)625-8900   Fax: (215)625-8914
Fr: 800-354-1420
URL: http://www.tandf.co.uk/journals/titles/1743727x.asp

$1809.00/year for institutions, print and online; $1718.00/year for institutions, online only; $271.00/year for individuals. Professional journal to further international discourse in education with particular focus on method.

★11526★ International Journal of Whole Schooling

Whole Schooling Press
Wayne State University
217 Education
Detroit, MI 48202
URL: http://www.wholeschooling.net/Journal_of_Whole_Schooling/IJW

Free to qualified subscribers. International, refereed academic journal dedicated to exploring ways to improve learning and schooling for all children.

★11527★ Journal of Academic Leadership

Academic Leadership
600 Park St.
Rarick Hall 219
Hays, KS 67601-4099
Ph: (785)628-4547
URL: http://www.academicleadership.org/

Journal focusing on the leadership issues in the academic world.

★11528★ Journal of Cases in Educational Leadership

Sage Publications Inc.
2455 Teller Rd.
Thousand Oaks, CA 91320
Ph: (805)499-0721   Fax: (805)499-8096
URL: http://www.sagepub.com/journalsProdDesc.nav?prodId=Journal20

Quarterly. $319.00/year for institutions, e-access; $83.00/year for individuals, e-access. Journal covering cases appropriate for

use in programs that prepare educational leaders.

★11529★ Journal of Curriculum and Supervision

Association for Supervision and Curriculum Development
1703 N Beauregard St.
Alexandria, VA 22311-1714
Ph: (703)578-9600   Fax: (703)575-5400
Fr: 800-933-2723
URL: http://www.ascd.org/portal/site/ascd/menuitem.0545410c9839aa

Scholarly journal focusing on curriculum and supervision.

★11530★ Journal of Direct Instruction

Association for Direct Instruction
PO Box 10252
Eugene, OR 97440
Ph: (541)485-1293   Fax: (541)683-7543
Fr: 800-995-2464
URL: http://www.adihome.org/phpshop/articles/articles.php?type=JD

Quarterly. Subscription included in membership. Journal covering education.

★11531★ Journal of Language, Identity, and Education

Lawrence Erlbaum Associates Inc.
10 Industrial Ave.
Mahwah, NJ 07430
Ph: (201)258-2200   Fax: (201)236-0072
Fr: 800-926-6579
E-mail: journals@erlbaum.com
URL: http://www.erlbaum.com

Quarterly. $50.00/year for U.S. and Canada, individual, online and print; $80.00/year for elsewhere, individual, online and print; $360.00/year for U.S. and Canada, institution, online and print; $390.00/year for elsewhere, institution, online and print; $290.00/year for U.S. and Canada, institution, online only; $290.00/year for elsewhere, institution, online only; $325.00/year for U.S. and Canada, institution, print only; $355.00/year for elsewhere, institution, print only. Scholarly, interdisciplinary journal covering issues in language, identity and education worldwide for academics, educators and policy specialists in a variety of disciplines, and others.

★11532★ Journal of Latinos and Education

Lawrence Erlbaum Associates Inc.
10 Industrial Ave.
Mahwah, NJ 07430
Ph: (201)258-2200   Fax: (201)236-0072
Fr: 800-926-6579
URL: http://www.erlbaum.com/

Quarterly. $50.00/year for individuals, online and print - U.S./Canada; $80.00/year for individuals, online and print - all other countries; $360.00/year for institutions, online and print - U.S./Canada; $390.00/year for institutions, online and print - all other countries; $290.00/year for institutions, online only - U.S./Canada; $290.00/year for institutions, online only - all other countries; $325.00/

year for institutions, print only - U.S./Canada; $355.00/year for institutions, print only - all other countries. Scholarly, multidisciplinary journal covering educational issues that impact Latinos for researchers, teaching professionals, academics, scholars, institutions, and others.

★11533★ Journal of Learning Disabilities

PRO-ED Inc.
8700 Shoal Creek Blvd.
PO Box 678370
Austin, TX 78757-6897
Ph: (512)451-3246   Fax: 800-397-7633
Fr: 800-897-3202
URL: http://www.proedinc.com

Bimonthly. $60.00/year for individuals; $96.00 for individuals, 2 years; $161.00/year for institutions; $258.00 for institutions, 2 years; $96.00/year for individuals, international; $154.00 for individuals, 2 year international; $187.00/year for institutions, international; $300.00 for institutions, 2 year international. Special education journal.

★11534★ Journal of STEM Education

Auburn University
9088 Haley Ctr.
Auburn, AL 36849
Ph: (334)844-4000   Fax: (334)844-9027
URL: http://www.auburn.edu/research/litee/jstem/index.php

Semiannual. Journal for educators in Science, Technology, Engineering, and Mathematics (STEM) education.

★11535★ Journal of Teacher Education

Boston College
140 Commonwealth Ave.
Chestnut Hill, MA 02467
URL: http://www.sagepub.com

$403.00/year for institutions, print & e-access; $423.00/year for institutions, volume print & all online; $363.00/year for institutions, e-access; $383.00/year for institutions, all online content; $1,512.00/year for institutions, backfile purchase, e-access; $395.00/year for institutions, print; $99.00/year for individuals, print; $87.00/year for institutions, single print; $26.00/year for individuals, single print. Magazine of interest to educators.

★11536★ Leadership and Policy in Schools

Taylor & Francis Group Journals
325 Chestnut St., Ste. 800
Philadelphia, PA 19106
Ph: (215)625-8900   Fax: (215)625-8914
Fr: 800-354-1420
URL: http://www.tandf.co.uk/journals/titles/15700763.asp

Quarterly. $477.00/year for institutions, print and online; $453.00/year for institutions, online only; $227.00/year for individuals; $60.00/year for ICSEI members. Journal providing information about leadership and policy in primary and secondary education.

★11537★ Music Educators Journal
MENC: The National Association for
  Music Education
1806 Robert Fulton Dr.
Reston, VA 20191
Ph: (703)860-4000   Fax: (703)860-1531
Fr: 800-336-3768
URL: http://www.menc.org/publication/arti-
cles/journals.html

Journal covering all levels of music education. Published on alternate months with
Teaching Music.

★11538★ NJEA Review
New Jersey Education Association
180 West State St.
PO Box 1211
Trenton, NJ 08607-1211
Ph: (609)599-4561   Fax: (609)599-1201

Monthly. Educational journal for public
school employees.

★11539★ Oxford Review of Education
Taylor & Francis Group Journals
325 Chestnut St., Ste. 800
Philadelphia, PA 19106
Ph: (215)625-8900   Fax: (215)625-8914
Fr: 800-354-1420
URL: http://www.tandf.co.uk/journals/titles/
03054985.asp

$1,031.00/year for institutions, print and on-
line; $979.00/year for institutions, online
only; $396.00/year for individuals. Journal
covering advance study of education.

★11540★ The Physics Teacher
American Association of Physics
  Teachers
1 Physics Ellipse
College Park, MD 20740-3845
Ph: (301)209-3300   Fax: (301)209-0845
E-mail: tpt@appstate.edu
URL: http://www.aapt.org/Publications/

$335.00/year for nonmembers, international;
$105.00/year for members, regular. Scientif-
ic education magazine.

★11541★ Research Strategies
Elsevier Science Inc.
360 Park Ave. S
New York, NY 10010
Ph: (212)989-5800   Fax: (212)633-3990
URL: http://www.elsevier.com

Journal covering library literature and the
educational mission of the library.

**★11542★ Scholastic Coach & Athletic
Director**
Scholastic Library Publishing Inc.
90 Old Sherman Tpke.
PO Box 1795
Danbury, CT 06816
Ph: (203)797-3500   Fax: (203)797-3657
Fr: 800-621-1115
E-mail: magazines@scholastic.ca
URL: http://www.coachad.com/

$14.98/year for individuals, 10 issues;
$24.98/year for individuals, 20 issues;
$41.95/year for other countries, 10 issues.
Magazine on high school and college athletics.

★11543★ School and Community
Missouri State Teachers Association
407 South Sixth St.
PO Box 458
Columbia, MO 65205
Ph: (573)442-3127   Fax: (573)443-5079
Fr: 800-392-0532

Quarterly. Education magazine.

**★11544★ School Effectiveness and
School Improvement**
Taylor & Francis Group Journals
325 Chestnut St., Ste. 800
Philadelphia, PA 19106
Ph: (215)625-8900   Fax: (215)625-8914
Fr: 800-354-1420
URL: http://www.tandf.co.uk/journals/titles/
09243453.asp

Quarterly. $305.00/year for institutions, print
and online; $231.00/year for institutions,
online only; $153.00/year for individuals,
print only; $520.00/year for institutions, print
and online; $494.00/year for institutions,
online only; $255.00/year for individuals,
print only. Journal focusing on educational
progress of all students.

★11545★ The Science Teacher
National Science Teachers Association
1840 Wilson Blvd.
Arlington, VA 22201
Ph: (703)243-7100   Fax: (703)243-7177
URL: http://www.nsta.org/highschool/

Journal on science education.

★11546★ Strategies
American Alliance for Health, Physical
  Education, Recreation & Dance
1900 Association Dr.
Reston, VA 20191-1598
Ph: (703)476-3400   Fax: (703)476-9527
Fr: 800-213-7193
E-mail: strategies@aahperd.org
URL: http://www.aahperd.org/naspe/temp-
late.cfm?template=strategie

Bimonthly. $115.00/year for U.S. and Cana-
da, institution; $45.00/year for nonmembers,
U.S. and Canada, individual; $127.00/year
for institutions, other countries; $57.00/year
for nonmembers, foreign, individual. Journal
providing practical, hands-on information to
physical educators and coaches.

★11547★ Teacher Magazine
Editorial Projects in Education Inc.
6935 Arlington Rd., Ste. 100
Bethesda, MD 20814-5233
Ph: (301)280-3100   Fax: (301)280-3200
Fr: 800-346-1834
URL: http://www.edweek.org/ew/index.html

$10.00/year for individuals; $17.00/year for
individuals, two years. Professional magazine for elementary and secondary school
teachers.

**★11548★ Teaching Exceptional
Children**
Council for Exceptional Children
1110 N Glebe Rd., Ste. 300
Arlington, VA 22201-5704
Ph: (703)620-3660   Fax: (703)264-9494
Fr: 888-232-7733
E-mail: tec@bc.edu
URL: http://www.cec.sped.org

Bimonthly. $135.00/year for individuals;
$250.00 for two years; $145.00 for two
years, Canada; $270.00 for two years, Can-
ada; $165.00/year for out of country, foreign-
air printed matter; $310.00/year for out of
country, two years, foreign-air printed matter;
$25.00/year for institutions, single copy;
$170.00/year for institutions; $290.00 for two
years, institutional. Journal exploring practical methods for teaching students who have
exceptionalities and those who are gifted
and talented.

**★11549★ Teaching and Learning in
Nursing**
Elsevier Science Inc.
360 Park Ave. S
New York, NY 10010
Ph: (212)989-5800   Fax: (212)633-3990
URL: http://www.elsevier.com

Quarterly. $119.00/year for institutions, U.S.
$167.00/year for institutions, other countries;
$75.00/year for individuals, U.S. $104.00/
year for individuals, other countries. Journal
devoted to associate degree nursing education and practice.

★11550★ Tech Directions
Prakken Publications Inc.
832 Phoenix Dr.
PO Box 8623
Ann Arbor, MI 48108
Ph: (734)975-2800   Fax: (734)975-2787
Fr: 800-530-9673
E-mail: tdedit@techdirections.com
URL: http://www.techdirections.com

Monthly. $30.00/year for individuals, U.S.;
$20.00/year for students; $40.00/year for
elsewhere; $55.00 for two years, U.S.;
$75.00 for two years, elsewhere. Free to
qualified subscribers. Magazine covering issues, programs, and projects in industrial
education, technology education, trade and
industry, and vocational-technical career
education. Articles are geared toward teacher and administrator use and reference from
elementary school through postsecondary
levels.

★11551★ *The Technology Teacher*

International Technology Education Association
1914 Association Dr., Ste. 201
Reston, VA 20191-1539
Ph: (703)860-2100   Fax: (703)860-0353

$35.00/year for individuals, professional U.S., 2year; $70.00/year for individuals, professional U.S., 1year; $30.00/year for students, undergrad student- first time member, 1year; $35.00/year for students, full-time grad/renewing undergrad student, 1year; $55.00/year for students, bridge - one-time student to professional, 1year; $410.00/year for institutions, group membership, 2 year; $210.00/year for institutions, group membership, 1 year; $690.00/year for individuals, group membership, 2year; $350.00/year for individuals, group membership, 1year; $270.00/year for individuals, group membership, 2year. Magazine on technology education.

★11552★ *Theory and Research in Education*

Sage Publications Inc.
2455 Teller Rd.
Thousand Oaks, CA 91320
Ph: (805)499-0721   Fax: (805)499-8096
URL: http://tre.sagepub.com/

$459.00/year for institutions, print and online; $413.00/year for institutions, online only; $450.00/year for institutions, print only; $77.00/year for individuals, print only. Interdisciplinary journal covering normative and theoretical issues concerning education including multi-faceted philosophical analysis of moral, social, political and epistemological problems and issues arising from educational practice.

★11553★ *Uratie*

IDG Communications Inc.
5 Speen St., 3rd. Fl
Framingham, MA 01701
Ph: (508)875-5000   Fax: (508)988-7888
URL: http://www.idg.com

Magazine providing job offers for graduates, engineers and information technology professionals.

PLACEMENT AND JOB REFERRAL SERVICES

★11554★ American Alliance for Health, Physical Education, Recreation and Dance (AAHPERD)

1900 Association Dr.
Reston, VA 20191-1598
Ph: (703)476-3400   Fax: (703)476-9527
Fr: 800-213-7193
E-mail: info@aahperd.org
URL: http://www.aahperd.org

Members: Students and educators in physical education, dance, health, athletics, safety education, recreation, and outdoor educa-

tion. **Purpose:** Works to improve its fields of education at all levels through such services as consultation, periodicals and special publications, leadership development, determination of standards, and research. Sponsors placement service.

★11555★ American Association of Christian Schools (AACS)

National Office
602 Belvoir Ave.
East Ridge, TN 37412
Ph: (423)629-4280   Fax: (423)622-7461
E-mail: national@aacs.org
URL: http://www.aacs.org

Description: Maintains teacher/administrator certification program and placement service. Participates in school accreditation program. Sponsors National Academic Tournament. Maintains American Christian Honor Society. Compiles statistics; maintains speakers' bureau and placement service.

★11556★ American Association of Teachers of French (AATF)

Southern Illinois University
Mail Code 4510
Carbondale, IL 62901
Ph: (618)453-5731   Fax: (618)453-5733
E-mail: abrate@siu.edu
URL: http://www.frenchteachers.org

Members: Teachers of French in public and private elementary and secondary schools, colleges and universities. **Activities:** Sponsors National French Week each November to take French out of the classroom and into the schools and community. Conducts National French Contest in elementary and secondary schools and awards prizes at all levels. Maintains Materials Center with promotional and pedagogical materials; National French Honor Society (high school), Placement Bureau, summer scholarships.

★11557★ American Association of Teachers of Spanish and Portuguese (AATSP)

900 Ladd Rd.
Walled Lake, MI 48390
Ph: (248)960-2180   Fax: (248)960-9570
E-mail: corporate@aatsp.org
URL: http://www.aatsp.org

Description: Teachers of Spanish and Portuguese languages and literatures and others interested in Hispanic culture. Operates placement bureau and maintains pen pal registry. Sponsors honor society, Sociedad Honoraria Hispanica and National Spanish Examinations for secondary school students.

★11558★ American Classical League (ACL)

Miami University
422 Wells Mills Dr.
Oxford, OH 45056-1694
Ph: (513)529-7741   Fax: (513)529-7742
E-mail: info@aclclassics.org
URL: http://www.aclclassics.org

Members: Teachers of classical languages

in high schools and colleges. **Purpose:** Works to promote the teaching of Latin and other classical languages. Presents scholarship. **Activities:** Maintains placement service, teaching materials, and resource center at Miami University in Oxford, OH to sell teaching aids to Latin and Greek teachers.

★11559★ American Mathematical Society (AMS)

201 Charles St.
Providence, RI 02904-2213
Ph: (401)455-4000   Fax: (401)331-3842
Fr: 800-321-4AMS
E-mail: ams@ams.org
URL: http://www.ams.org

Description: Professional society of mathematicians and educators. Promotes the interests of mathematical scholarship and research. Holds institutes, seminars, short courses, and symposia to further mathematical research; awards prizes. Offers placement services; compiles statistics.

★11560★ Association for Direct Instruction (ADI)

PO Box 10252
Eugene, OR 97440
Ph: (541)485-1293   Fax: (541)868-1397
Fr: 800-995-2464
E-mail: info@adihome.org
URL: http://www.adihome.org

Members: Public school regular and special education teachers and university instructors. **Purpose:** Encourages, promotes, and engages in research aimed at improving educational methods. Promotes dissemination of developmental information and skills that facilitate the education of adults and children. **Activities:** Administers a preschool for developmentally delayed children. Offers educational training workshops for instructors. Maintains speaker's bureau and placement service.

★11561★ Christian Schools International (CSI)

3350 E Paris Ave. SE
Grand Rapids, MI 49512-2907
Ph: (616)957-1070   Fax: (616)957-5022
Fr: 800-635-8288
E-mail: info@csionline.org
URL: http://csionline.org

Description: Christian elementary and secondary schools enrolling 100,000 pupils and employing 7,800 teachers. Aims to: provide a medium for a united witness regarding the role of Christian schools in contemporary society; promote the establishment of Christian schools; help members function more effectively in areas of promotion, organization, administration, and curriculum; help establish standards and criteria to guide the operation of its members; foster high professional ideals and economic well-being among Christian school personnel; establish and maintain communication with member schools, colleges, churches, government agencies, and the public. Encourages study, research, and writing that embodies Christian theories of education; conducts salary studies, research, and surveys on operating costs; offers expert and confidential analysis of member school programs and operation. Sponsors meetings, workshops, and seminars; offers placement service. Administers the Christian School Pension and Trust Funds, Group Insurance Plans, and Life and Insurance Plans and Trust Funds.

★11562★ **International Association of Baptist Colleges and Universities (IABCU)**

8120 Sawyer Brown Rd., Ste. 108
Nashville, TN 37221-1410
Ph: (615)673-1896   Fax: (615)662-1396
E-mail: tim_fields@baptistschools.org
URL: http://www.baptistschools.org

Members: Southern Baptist senior colleges, universities, junior colleges, academies, and Bible schools. **Purpose:** Promotes Christian education through literature, faculty workshops, student recruitment, teacher placement, trustee orientation, statistical information, and other assistance to members.

★11563★ **International Educator's Institute (TIE)**

PO Box 513
Cummaquid, MA 02637
Ph: (508)790-1990   Fax: (508)790-1922
Fr: 877-375-6668
E-mail: tie@tieonline.com
URL: http://www.tieonline.com

Description: Facilitates the placement of teachers and administrators in American, British, and international schools. Seeks to create a network that provides for professional development opportunities and improved financial security of members. Offers advice and information on international school news, recent educational developments, job placement, and investment, consumer, and professional development opportunities. Makes available insurance and travel benefits. Operates International Schools Internship Program.

★11564★ **Jewish Educators Assembly (JEA)**

PO Box 413
Cedarhurst, NY 11516
Ph: (516)569-2537   Fax: (516)295-9039
E-mail: jewisheducators@jewisheducators.org
URL: http://www.jewisheducators.org

Members: Educational and supervisory personnel serving Jewish educational institutions. **Purpose:** Seeks to: advance the development of Jewish education in the congregation on all levels in consonance with the philosophy of the Conservative Movement; cooperate with the United Synagogue of America Commission on Jewish Education as the policy-making body of the educational enterprise; join in cooperative effort with other Jewish educational institutions and organizations; establish and maintain professional standards for Jewish educators; serve as a forum for the exchange of ideas; promote the values of Jewish education as a basis for the creative continuity of

the Jewish people. **Activities:** Maintains placement service and speaker's bureau.

★11565★ **National Alliance of Black School Educators (NABSE)**

310 Pennsylvania Ave.
Washington, DC 20003
Ph: (202)608-6310   Fax: (202)608-6319
Fr: 800-221-2654
E-mail: lavette@nabse.org
URL: http://www.nabse.org

Description: Black educators from all levels; others indirectly involved in the education of black youth. Promotes awareness, professional expertise, and commitment among black educators. Goals are to: eliminate and rectify the results of racism in education; work with state, local, and national leaders to raise the academic achievement level of all black students; increase members' involvement in legislative activities; facilitate the introduction of a curriculum that more completely embraces black America; improve the ability of black educators to promote problem resolution; create a meaningful and effective network of strength, talent, and professional support. Sponsors workshops, commission meetings, and special projects. Encourages research, especially as it relates to blacks, and the presentation of papers during national conferences. Plans to establish a National Black Educators Data Bank and offer placement service.

★11566★ **National Association for Sport and Physical Education (NASPE)**

1900 Association Dr.
Reston, VA 20191-1598
Ph: (703)476-3400   Fax: (703)476-8316
Fr: 800-213-7193
E-mail: naspe@aahperd.org
URL: http://www.naspeinfo.org

Description: Men and women professionally involved with physical activity and sports. Seeks to improve the total sport and physical activity experience in America. Conducts research and education programs in such areas as sport psychology, curriculum development, kinesiology, history, philosophy, sport sociology, and the biological and behavioral basis of human activity. Develops and distributes public information materials which explain the value of physical education programs. Supports councils involved in organizing and supporting elementary, secondary, and college physical education and sport programs; administers the National Council of Athletic Training in conjunction with the National Association for Girls and Women in Sport; serves the professional interests of coaches, trainers, and officials. Maintains hall of fame, placement service, and media resource center for public information and professional preparation. Member benefits include group insurance and discounts.

★11567★ **National Association of Teachers' Agencies (NATA)**

797 Kings Hwy.
Fairfield, CT 06825
Ph: (203)333-0611   Fax: (203)334-7224
E-mail: info@jobsforteachers.com

Description: Private employment agencies engaged primarily in the placement of teaching and administration personnel. Works to standardize records and promote a strong ethical sense in the placement field. Maintains speakers' bureau.

★11568★ **National Communication Association (NCA)**

1765 N St. NW
Washington, DC 20036
Ph: (202)464-4622   Fax: (202)464-4600
E-mail: rsmitter@natcom.org
URL: http://www.natcom.org

Members: Elementary, secondary, college, and university teachers, speech clinicians, media specialists, communication consultants, students, theater directors, and other interested persons; libraries and other institutions. **Purpose:** Works to promote study, criticism, research, teaching, and application of the artistic, humanistic, and scientific principles of communication, particularly speech communication. Sponsors the publication of scholarly volumes in speech. **Activities:** Conducts international debate tours in the U.S. and abroad. Maintains placement service.

★11569★ **U.S.-China Education Foundation (USCEF)**

4140 Oceanside Blvd., Ste. 159 - No. 112
Oceanside, CA 92056-6005
Ph: (760)644-0977
E-mail: uscef@sage-usa.net
URL: http://www.sage-usa.net/uscef.htm

Purpose: Aims to promote the learning of the Chinese languages (including Mandarin, Cantonese, and minority languages such as Mongolian) by Americans, and the learning of English by Chinese. **Activities:** Conducts short-term travel-study program to prepare Americans and Chinese for stays of four, six, or eight months or one to four years in China or the U.S., respectively. Operates teacher placement service and speakers' bureau. A project of The Society for the Development of Global Education (S.A.G.E. Inc.).

EMPLOYER DIRECTORIES AND NETWORKING LISTS

★11570★ *50 State Educational Directories*

Career Guidance Foundation
8090 Engineer Rd.
San Diego, CA 92111
Ph: (858)560-8051   Fax: (858)278-8960
Fr: 800-854-2670

URL: http://www.cgf.org

Annual. Microfiche. Collection consists of reproductions of the state educational directories published by the departments of education of individual 50 states. Directory contents vary, but the majority contain listings of elementary and secondary schools, colleges and universities, and state education officials. Amount of detail in each also varies. Entries include: Usually, institution name, address, and name of one executive.

★11571★ **Boarding Schools Directory**

Association of Boarding Schools
2141 Wisconsin Ave. NW, Ste. H
Washington, DC 20007
Ph: (202)965-8982   Fax: (202)965-8988
URL: http://www.schools.com/

Annual; latest edition 2007-2008. For U.S. and Canada. Covers boarding schools that are members of the Association of Boarding Schools. Entries include: School name, address, phone, e-mail and URL, grades for which boarding students are accepted, enrollment, brief description. Arrangement: Classified by type of school. Indexes: Geographical; program; alphabetical.

★11572★ **Career Ideas for Teens in Education and Training**

Facts On File Inc.
132 W 31st St., 17th Fl.
New York, NY 10001
Ph: (212)967-8800   Fax: 800-678-3633
Fr: 800-322-8755
URL: http://www.factsonfile.com

Published 2005. $40.00 for individuals; $36.00 for libraries. Covers a multitude of career possibilities based on a teenager's specific interests and skills and links his/her talents to a wide variety of actual professions.

★11573★ **Careers in Focus: Education**

Facts On File Inc.
132 W 31st St., 17th Fl.
New York, NY 10001
Ph: (212)967-8800   Fax: 800-678-3633
Fr: 800-322-8755
URL: http://www.factsonfile.com

Latest edition 2nd, 2003. $29.95 for individuals; $26.95 for libraries. Covers an overview of education, followed by a selection of jobs profiled in detail, including the nature of the job, earnings, prospects for employment, what kind of training and skills it requires, and sources for further information.

★11574★ **Christian Schools International-Directory**

Christian Schools International
3350 E Paris Ave. SE
Grand Rapids, MI 49512
Ph: (616)957-1070   Fax: (616)957-5022
Fr: 800-635-8288
URL: http://store.csionline.org

Annual; 2007-2008. $15.00 for members; $72.00 for nonmembers. Covers nearly 450

Reformed Christian elementary and secondary schools; related associations; societies without schools. Entries include: For schools–School name, address, phone; name, title, and address of officers; names of faculty members. Arrangement: Geographical.

★11575★ **Directory of Public Elementary and Secondary Education Agencies**

National Center for Education Statistics
1990 K St. NW
Washington, DC 20006
Ph: (202)502-7300
URL: http://nces.ed.gov/ccd/

Annual; latest edition 2002-2003. Covers about 17,000 local education agencies in the United States, the District of Columbia, and five territories that operate their own schools or pay tuition to other local education agencies. Also lists intermediate education agencies. Entries include: Agency name, address, phone, county, description of district, grade span, membership, special education students, metropolitan status, number of high school graduates, teachers, and schools. Also available from Superintendent of Documents, U.S. Government Printing Office. Arrangement: Geographical, then by type of agency.

★11576★ **Directory of Public School Systems in the U.S.**

American Association for Employment in Education
3040 Riverside Dr., Ste. 125
Columbus, OH 43221
Ph: (614)485-1111   Fax: (614)485-9609
URL: http://www.aaee.org/

Annual, winter; latest edition 2004-2005 edition. $10.00 for members (plus $2.00/copy for mailing); $20.00 for nonmembers (plus $2.00/copy for mailing). Covers about 14,500 public school systems in the United States and their administrative personnel. Entries include: System name, address, phone, website address, name and title of personnel administrator, levels taught and approximate student population. Arrangement: Geographical by state.

★11577★ **Educators Resource Directory**

Grey House Publishing
185 Millerton Rd.
PO Box 860
Millerton, NY 12546
Ph: (518)789-8700   Fax: (518)789-0556
Fr: 800-562-2139
E-mail: books@greyhouse.com
URL: http://www.greyhouse.com/education.htm

Annual; latest edition 2007/2008. $145.00 for individuals. Covers publishing opportunities, state by state information on enrollment, funding and grant resources, associations and conferences, and teaching jobs abroad all geared toward elementary and secondary school professionals. Also covers online databases, textbook publishers, school sup-

pliers, plus state and federal agencies. Entries include: Contact name, address, phone, fax, description, publications. A compilation of over 6,500 educational resources and over 130 tables and charts of education statistics and rankings. Arrangement: By subject categories. Indexes: Entry; geographical; publisher; web sites.

★11578★ **Employment Opportunities, USA**

Washington Research Associates
1090 Vermont Ave. NW, Ste. 800
Washington, DC 20005
Ph: (202)408-7025

Annual, quarterly updates. Publication includes: List of over 1,000 employment contacts in companies and agencies in banking, arts, telecommunications, education, and 14 other industries and professions, including federal government. Entries include: Company name, name of representative, address, description of products or services, hiring and recruiting practices, training programs, and year established. Principal content is industry overviews, career news, employment opportunity information on 14 different job markets, and comprehensive guidance to career resources on the Internet. Arrangement: Classified by industry. Indexes: Occupation.

★11579★ **Encyclopedia of Education**

Macmillan/McGraw-Hill
2 Penn Plz., 5th Fl.
New York, NY 10121-2298
Ph: (212)904-3834   Fax: (212)904-4878
URL: http://www.mheducation.com/home/index.shtml

Publication includes: List of assessment and achievement tests with contact information; list of state departments of education; list of Internet resources. Principal content of publication consists of a variety of topics within the field of education, including policy, curriculum, learning, assessment, legislation, history, and standards. Indexes: Alphabetical.

★11580★ **Ganley's Catholic Schools in America-Elementary/Secondary/College & University**

Fisher Publishing Co.
PO Box 15070
Scottsdale, AZ 85267-5070
Ph: (480)657-9422   Fax: (480)657-9422
Fr: 800-759-7615
URL: http://www.ganleyscatholicschools.com

Annual, summer; latest edition 34th, 2007 edition. $60.00 for individuals. Covers over 8,400 Catholic K-12 Schools. Arrangement: Geographical by state, then alphabetical by Diocese name.

★11581★ **Handbook of Private Schools**

Porter Sargent Publishers Inc.
11 Beacon St., Ste. 1400
Boston, MA 02108-3099
Ph: (617)523-1670   Fax: (617)523-1021
Fr: 800-342-7470

E-mail: orders@portersargent.com
URL: http://www.portersargent.com

Annual, latest edition 87th, 2006 edition. $99.00 for individuals. Covers more than 1,600 elementary and secondary boarding and day schools in the United States. Entries include: School name, address, phone, fax, e-mail, URL, type of school (boarding or day), sex and age range, names and titles of administrators, grades offered, academic orientation, curriculum, new admissions yearly, tests required for admission, enrollment and faculty, graduate record, number of alumni, tuition and scholarship figures, summer session, plant evaluation and endowment, date of establishment, calendar, association membership, description of school's offerings and history, test score averages, uniform requirements, and geographical and demographic data. Arrangement: Geographical. Indexes: Alphabetical by school name, cross indexed by state, region, grade range, sexes accepted, school features and enrollment.

★11582★ **Independent School Guide for Washington DC and Surrounding Area**

Lift Hill Press Inc.
c/o Washington Book Distributors
4930-A Eisenhower Ave.
Alexandria, VA 22304-4809
Ph: (703)212-9113   Fax: (703)212-9114
Fr: 800-699-9113
URL: http://www.washingtonbk.com

Biennial; latest edition 2004. Covers over 525 independent schools (including parochial schools) in the Washington, DC, area, including Maryland and Virginia. Entries include: School name, address, phone, name and title of contact, number of faculty, geographical area served, tuition, courses, admission procedures, summer programs, LD/ED programs, scholarships available. Arrangement: Alphabetical. Indexes: Geographical.

★11583★ **Independent Schools Association of the Southwest-Membership List**

Independent Schools Association of the Southwest
Energy Sq., Ste 406
505 North Big Spring St.
Midland, TX 79701
Ph: (432)684-9550   Fax: (432)684-9401
URL: http://www.isasw.org

Annual, August. Covers over 84 schools located in Arizona, Kansas, Louisiana, Mexico, New Mexico, Oklahoma, and Texas enrolling over 38,000 students. Entries include: School name, address, phone, chief administrative officer, structure, and enrollment. Arrangement: Geographical. Indexes: Alphabetical.

★11584★ **MDR's School Directories**

Market Data Retrieval
1 Forest Pkwy.
Shelton, CT 06484-0947
Ph: (203)926-4800   Fax: (203)926-1826
Fr: 800-333-8802
URL: http://www.schooldata.com

Annual, October. Covers over 90,000 public, 8,000 Catholic, and 15,000 other private schools (grades K-12) in the United States; over 15,000 school district offices, 76,000 school librarians, 27,000 media specialists, and 33,000 technology coordinators. Includes names of over 165,000 school district administrators and staff members in county and state education administration. Entries include: District name and address; telephone and fax number; number of schools; number of teachers in the district; district enrollment; special education students; limited-english proficient students; minority percentage by race; percentage of college bound students; expenditures per student for instructional materials; poverty level; title 1 dollars; site-based management; district open/close dates; construction indicator; technologies and quantities; district-level administrators, (new superintendents shaded); school name and address (new public shaded); telephone and fax number; principal (new principal shaded); librarian, media specialist and technology coordinator; grade span; special programs and school type; student enrollment; technologies and quantities (instructional computer brand, noting predominant brand); Multi-Media Computers; Internet connection or access; Tech Sophistication Index. Arrangement: Geographical. Indexes: District county; district personnel; principal; new public schools and key personnel; district and school telephone; district URLs.

★11585★ **National Directory for Employment in Education**

American Association for Employment in Education
3040 Riverside Dr., Ste. 125
Columbus, OH 43221
Ph: (614)485-1111   Fax: (614)485-9609
URL: http://www.aaee.org/

Annual, winter; latest edition 2005 edition. $20.00 for nonmembers; $10.00 for members. Covers about 600 placement offices maintained by teacher-training institutions and 300 school district personnel officers and/or superintendents responsible for hiring profesional staff. Entries include: Institution name, address, phone, contact name, email address, and website. Arrangement: Geographical. Indexes: Personal name; subject-field of teacher training; institutions that provide vacancy bulletins and placement services to non-enrolled students.

★11586★ **Opportunities Abroad for Educators**

Fulbright Teacher and Administrator Exchange Program
600 Maryland Ave. SW, Ste. 320
Washington, DC 20024-2520
Ph: (202)314-3527   Fax: (202)479-6806
Fr: 800-726-0479

URL: http://www.fulbrightexchanges.org

Annual. Covers opportunities available for elementary and secondary teachers, two-year college instructors, and school administrators to attend seminars or to teach abroad under the Mutual Educational and Cultural Exchange Act of 1961. Entries include: Countries of placement, dates, eligibility requirements, teaching assignments. Arrangement: Geographical.

★11587★ **Patterson's American Education**

Educational Directories Inc.
PO Box 68097
Schaumburg, IL 60168
Ph: (847)891-1250   Fax: (847)891-0945
Fr: 800-357-6183
URL: http://www.ediusa.com

Annual; latest edition October 2007. $94.00 for individuals. Covers over 11,400 school districts in the United States; more than 34,000 public, private, and Catholic high schools, middle schools, and junior high schools; Approximately 300 parochial superintendents; 400 state department of education personnel. Entries include: For school districts and schools–District and superintendent name, address, phone, fax; grade ranges, enrollment; school names, addresses, phone numbers, names of principals. For postsecondary schools–School name, address, phone number, URL, e-mail, names of administrator or director of admissions. For private and Catholic high schools–name, address, phone, fax, enrollment, grades offered, name of principal. Postsecondary institutions are also covered in 'Patterson's Schools Classified.' Arrangement: Geographical by state, then alphabetical by city.

★11588★ **Private Independent Schools**

Bunting and Lyon Inc.
238 N Main St.
Wallingford, CT 06492
Ph: (203)269-3333   Fax: (203)269-5697
URL: http://www.buntingandlyon.com

Annual; latest edition 60th, January 2007. $115.00 for individuals. Covers 1,200 English-speaking elementary and secondary private schools and summer programs in North America and abroad. Entries include: School name, address, phone, fax, e-mail, website, enrollment, tuition and other fees, financial aid information, administrator's name and educational background, director of admission, regional accreditation, description of programs, curriculum, activities, learning differences grid. Arrangement: Geographical. Indexes: school name; geographical.

★11589★ **QED's State School Guides**

Quality Education Data Inc.
1050 Seventeenth St, Ste. 1100
Denver, CO 80265
Ph: (303)209-9400   Fax: (303)209-9401
Fr: 800-525-5811
URL: http://www.qeddata.com/MarketKno/SchoolGuides/SchoolGuides.a

Annual, October. $1,345.00 for national print set; $3,565.00 for national online version; $4175.00 for print set and online version, combined. Covers over 100,000 public and private elementary and secondary schools in 16,000 school districts; in 52 volumes (national set). Entries include: School district name, address, phone, district enrollment, identification of site-based managed schools, number of teachers, number of schools, financial data, minority enrollment statistics, names and educational specializations of key personnel, list of member schools, including school name, address, phone, name of principal, name of librarian, grade levels taught, enrollment, services outsourced, number and brands of microcomputers used. Arrangement: Geographical - county within state. Indexes: School name, district name, geographical (county name), personal name.

★11590★ *Requirements for Certification of Teachers, Counselors, Librarians, Administrators for Elementary and Secondary Schools*
University of Chicago Press
Journals Division
1427 E 60th St.
Chicago, IL 60637-2954
Ph: (773)702-7600   Fax: (773)702-0694
Fr: 877-705-1878
Annual, June; latest edition 71st, 2006-07. $47.00. Publication includes: List of state and local departments of education. Entries include: Office name, address, phone. Principal content of publication consists of summaries of each state's teaching and administrative certification requirements. Arrangement: Geographical.

HANDBOOKS AND MANUALS

★11591★ *America's Top Medical, Education, and Human Service Jobs, Fifth Edition*
JIST Publishing
875 Montreal Way
St. Paul, MN 55102
Fax: 800-547-8329   Fr: 800-648-5478
E-mail: info@jist.com
URL: http://www.jist.com
Michael Farr. 2001. $9.95. 352 pages. Targeted reference organized into three sections that offer comprehensive job descriptions, job search advice, and current trends in jobs and industries.

★11592★ *Becoming a Secondary School Science Teacher*
Prentice Hall PTR
1 Lake St.
Upper Saddle River, NJ 07458
Ph: (201)236-7000   Fax: 800-445-6991
Fr: 800-428-5331
URL: http://www.phptr.com/index.asp?rl=1

Jazlin V. Ebenezer and Sharon M. Haggerty. 1999. $99.00 (paper). 512 pages.

★11593★ *Becoming a Teacher*
Pearson Allyn & Bacon
1 Lake St.
Upper Saddle River, NJ 07458
Ph: (201)236-7000   Fr: 800-922-0579
URL: http://www.pearsoned.com/higher-ed/
Gary Borich. 1995. $43.95 (paper). 152 pages. Part of The Falmer Press Teachers' Library Series No. 7.

★11594★ *Careers in Education*
The McGraw-Hill Companies
PO Box 182604
Columbus, OH 43272
Fax: (614)759-3749   Fr: 877-883-5524
E-mail: customer.service@mcgraw-hill.com
URL: http://www.mcgraw-hill.com
Roy A. Edelfelt, Alan Reiman. Fourth edition, 2003. $15.95. 192 pages E-book, netLibrary.

★11595★ *Careers in Horticulture and Botany*
The McGraw-Hill Companies
PO Box 182604
Columbus, OH 43272
Fax: (614)759-3749   Fr: 877-883-5524
E-mail: customer.service@mcgraw-hill.com
URL: http://www.mcgraw-hill.com
Jerry Garner. 2006. 15.95 (paper). 192 pages. Includes bibliographical references.

★11596★ *Careers in Journalism*
The McGraw-Hill Companies
PO Box 182604
Columbus, OH 43272
Fax: (614)759-3749   Fr: 877-883-5524
E-mail: customer.service@mcgraw-hill.com
URL: http://www.mcgraw-hill.com
Jan Goldberg. Third edition, 2005. $15.95 (paper). 192 pages.

★11597★ *Great Jobs for English Majors*
The McGraw-Hill Companies
PO Box 182604
Columbus, OH 43272
Fax: (614)759-3749   Fr: 877-883-5524
E-mail: customer.service@mcgraw-hill.com
URL: http://www.mcgraw-hill.com
Julie DeGalan. Third edition, 2006. $15.95 (paper). 192 pages.

★11598★ *Great Jobs for History Majors*
The McGraw-Hill Companies
PO Box 182604
Columbus, OH 43272
Fax: (614)759-3749   Fr: 877-883-5524
E-mail: customer.service@mcgraw-hill.com
URL: http://www.mcgraw-hill.com

Julie DeGalan and Stephen Lambert. 2001. $15.95 (paper). 256 pages.

★11599★ *Great Jobs for Liberal Arts Majors*
The McGraw-Hill Companies
PO Box 182604
Columbus, OH 43272
Fax: (614)759-3749   Fr: 877-883-5524
E-mail: customer.service@mcgraw-hill.com
URL: http://www.mcgraw-hill.com
Blythe Camenson. Second edition, 2001. $14.95 (paper). 256 pages.

★11600★ *Great Jobs for Music Majors*
The McGraw-Hill Companies
PO Box 182604
Columbus, OH 43272
Fax: (614)759-3749   Fr: 877-883-5524
E-mail: customer.service@mcgraw-hill.com
URL: http://www.mcgraw-hill.com
Jan Goldberg, Stephen Lambert, Julie De-Galan. Second edition, 2004. $15.95 (paper). 180 pages.

★11601★ *Great Jobs for Theater Majors*
The McGraw-Hill Companies
PO Box 182604
Columbus, OH 43272
Fax: (614)759-3749   Fr: 877-883-5524
E-mail: customer.service@mcgraw-hill.com
URL: http://www.mcgraw-hill.com
Jan Goldberg and Julie DeGalan. 2005. $15.95 (paper). 192 pages.

★11602★ *Handbook for Christian EFL Teachers: Christian Teacher-Preparation Programs, Overseas Teaching Opportunities, Instructional Materials and Resources*
Institute for Cross-Cultural Training, Billy Graham Center, Wheaton College; Berry Pub. Services
PO Box 794
Wheaton, IL 60189
Ph: (630)752-7158   Fax: (630)752-7155
Lonna J. Dickerson and Dianne F. Dow. 1997. $9.00 (paper). 96 pages. Part of the Monograph Series.

★11603★ *How to Get the Teaching Position You Want: Teacher Candidate Guide*
Educational Enterprises
PO Box 1836
Spring Valley, CA 91979
Ph: (619)660-7720
Phyllis Murton. Second edition, revised, 1996. $19.95 (paper). 110 pages. This book provides a comprehensive guide for the teacher candidate's job search, as the format offers information that includes: interview questions most often asked in the teaching interview (grade-level and subject-matter specific); sample forms for applica-

tions, cover letters, and resumes that will impact principals and district personnel; strategies on preparing for the teaching interview; interview follow-up techniques; inside tips from a superintendent, a principal and a counselor.

★11604★ The Inside Secrets of Finding a Teaching Job

Jist Works
875 Montreal Way
St. Paul, MN 55102
Fr: 800-648-5478
E-mail: info@jist.com
URL: http://www.jist.com

Jack Warner, Clyde Bryan, and Diane Warner. Third edition, 2006. $12.95. 196 pages. Tips from educators on finding an entry-level teaching position.

★11605★ Inside Secrets of Finding a Teaching Job, Second Edition: The Most Effective Search Methods for Both New and Experienced Educators

JIST Publishing
875 Montreal Way
St. Paul, MN 55102
Fax: 800-547-8329   Fr: 800-648-5478
E-mail: info@jist.com
URL: http://www.jist.com

Jack Warner and Clyde Bryan. 2003. $12.95. 208 pages. Covers researching job opportunities; preparing resumes, cover letters, mission statements, teacher portfolios, and demonstration videos; preparing for interviews; and finding the inside track.

★11606★ Non-Profits and Education Job Finder

Planning Communications
7215 Oak Ave.
River Forest, IL 60305-1935
Ph: (708)366-5200   Fax: (708)366-5280
Fr: 888-366-5200
E-mail: info@planningcommunications.com
URL: http://jobfindersonline.com

Daniel Lauber. 1997. $32.95; $16.95 (paper). 340 pages. Covers 1600 sources. Discusses how to use sources of non-profit sector job vacancies in a number of specialties and state-by-state, including job-matching services, job hotlines, specialty periodicals with job ads, salary surveys, and directories. Covers a variety of fields from education to religion. Includes chapters on resume and cover letter preparation and interviewing.

★11607★ Opportunities in Overseas Careers

The McGraw-Hill Companies
PO Box 182604
Columbus, OH 43272
Fax: (614)759-3749   Fr: 877-883-5524
E-mail: customer.service@mcgraw-hill.com
URL: http://www.mcgraw-hill.com

Blythe Camenson. 2004. $13.95 (paper). 173 pages.

★11608★ Opportunities in State and Local Government Careers

The McGraw-Hill Companies
PO Box 182604
Columbus, OH 43272
Fax: (614)759-3749   Fr: 877-883-5524
E-mail: customer.service@mcgraw-hill.com
URL: http://www.mcgraw-hill.com

Neale J. Baxter. Revised edition, 1992. $14.95; $10.95 (paper). 148 pages. Points out the incentives and drawbacks of a government career. Describes hiring procedures and provides tips on filling out applications, taking physical and aptitude tests, handling interviews, and finding jobs. Describes the jobs in which 75% of all state and local government workers are employed. For each occupation, covers the nature of the work and the training required.

★11609★ Opportunities in Teaching Careers

The McGraw-Hill Companies
PO Box 182604
Columbus, OH 43272
Fax: (614)759-3749   Fr: 877-883-5524
E-mail: customer.service@mcgraw-hill.com
URL: http://www.mcgraw-hill.com

Janet Fine. 2005. $13.95 (paper). 160 pages. Discusses licensing and accreditation programs, sources of placement information, job-seeking correspondence, selection procedures, and paths to advancement. Also covers professional associations, non-traditional teaching opportunities, and jobs abroad.

★11610★ Opportunities in Technical Education Careers

The McGraw-Hill Companies
PO Box 182604
Columbus, OH 43272
Fax: (614)759-3749   Fr: 877-883-5524
E-mail: customer.service@mcgraw-hill.com
URL: http://www.mcgraw-hill.com

Robert Connelly. 1998. 160 pages. $14.95; $11.95 (paper).

★11611★ Real People Working in Education

The McGraw-Hill Companies
PO Box 182604
Columbus, OH 43272
Fax: (614)759-3749   Fr: 877-883-5524
E-mail: customer.service@mcgraw-hill.com
URL: http://www.mcgraw-hill.com

Blythe Camenson, Jan Goldberg. 1997. $17.95; $12.95 (paper). 160 pages/ Interviews and profiles of working professionals capture a range of opportunities in this field.

EMPLOYMENT AGENCIES AND SEARCH FIRMS

★11612★ Educational Placement Service

6510-A S. Academy Blvd.
Colorado Springs, CO 80906
Ph: (719)579-9911   Fax: (719)579-5050
E-mail: accounting@educatorjobs.com
URL: http://www.educatorjobs.com

Employment agency. Focuses on teaching, administrative, and education-related openings.

TRADESHOWS

★11613★ American Council on the Teaching of Foreign Languages Convention

American Council on the Teaching of Foreign Languages
700 S. Washington St., Ste. 210
Alexandria, VA 22314
Ph: (703)894-2900   Fax: (703)894-2905
E-mail: headquarters@actfl.org
URL: http://www.actfl.org

Annual. **Primary Exhibits:** Textbooks, tapes, and supplementary material in foreign languages.

★11614★ Association for Childhood Education International Annual International Conference & Exhibition

Association for Childhood Education International
17904 Georgia Ave., Ste. 215
Olney, MD 20832
Ph: (301)570-2111   Fax: (301)570-2212
Fr: 800-423-3563
E-mail: headquarters@acei.org
URL: http://www.acei.org

Annual. **Primary Exhibits:** Commercial and educational exhibits of interest to teachers, teacher educators, college students, day care personnel and other care givers. **Dates and Locations:** 2008 Mar 26-29; Atlanta, GA; Westin Peachtree Plaza; 2009 Mar 18-21; Chicago, IL; Westin Michigan Avenue.

★11615★ NARST Annual Meeting

National Association for Research in Science Teaching
University of Missouri-Columbia
NARST Administrative Assistant
303 Townsend Hall
Columbia, MO 65211-2400
Ph: (573)884-1401   Fax: (573)884-2917
E-mail: narst-l@narst.org
URL: http://www.educ.sfu.ca/narstsite

Annual. **Primary Exhibits:** Science education, publications, equipment, supplies, and services.

★11616★ **National Art Education Association Convention**

National Art Education Association
1916 Association Dr.
Reston, VA 20191-1590
Ph: (703)860-8000   Fax: (703)860-2960
E-mail: naea@dgs.dgsys.com
URL: http://www.naea-reston.org

Annual. **Primary Exhibits:** Art materials; art-related books and magazines; art career education information; arts and crafts supplies. **Dates and Locations:** 2008 Mar 26-30; New Orleans, LA.

★11617★ **National Association for the Education of Young Children Annual Conference**

National Association for the Education of Young Children
1509 16th St., NW
Washington, DC 20036
Ph: (202)232-8777   Fax: (202)328-1846
Fr: 800-424-2460
E-mail: naeyc@naeyc.org
URL: http://www.naeyc.org

Annual. **Primary Exhibits:** Educational materials and equipment designed for children ages birth through eight years old.

★11618★ **National Council for Geographic Education Conference**

National Council for Geographic Education
206-A Martin Hall
Jacksonvill State University
Jacksonville, AL 36265-1602
Ph: (256)782-5293   Fax: (256)782-5336
E-mail: ncge@jsucc.jsu.edu
URL: http://www.ncge.org

Annual. **Primary Exhibits:** Geographic teaching aids and materials.

★11619★ **National Council for the Social Studies Conference**

National Council for the Social Studies
8555 16th St., Ste. 500
Silver Spring, MD 20910
Ph: (301)588-1800   Fax: (301)588-2049
E-mail: ncss@ncss.org
URL: http://www.ncss.org

Annual. **Primary Exhibits:** Educational materials, software, publications, and textbooks. **Dates and Locations:** 2008 Dates not set; Houston, TX; 2009 Dates not set; Atlanta, GA.

★11620★ **National Middle School Association Annual Conference & Exhibit**

National Middle School Association
4151 Executive Pkwy., No. 300
Westerville, OH 43081-3867
Ph: (614)895-4730   Fax: (614)895-4750
Fr: 800-528-6672
E-mail: info@NMSA.org
URL: http://www.nmsa.org

Annual. **Primary Exhibits:** Educational materials and services relating to middle level school (ages 10-15).

OTHER SOURCES

★11621★ **American Association for Health Education (AAHE)**

1900 Association Dr.
Reston, VA 20191-1599
Ph: (703)476-3437   Fax: (703)476-6638
Fr: 800-213-7193
E-mail: aahe@aahperd.org
URL: http://www.aahperd.org/aahe

Members: Professionals who have responsibility for health education in schools, colleges, communities, hospitals and clinics, and industries. **Purpose:** Aims to advance the health education through program activities and federal legislation; encourage close working relationships between all health education and health service organizations; achieve good health and well-being for all Americans automatically, without conscious thought and endeavor. Member of the American Alliance for Health, Physical Education, Recreation and Dance.

★11622★ **American Association of Teachers of German (AATG)**

112 Haddontowne Ct., No. 104
Cherry Hill, NJ 08034-3668
Ph: (856)795-5553   Fax: (856)795-9398
E-mail: headquarters@aatg.org
URL: http://www.aatg.org

Description: Represents teachers of German at all levels; individuals interested in German language and culture. Offers in-service teacher-training workshops, materials, student honor society, national German examination and stipends/scholarships.

★11623★ **American Federation of Teachers (AFT)**

555 New Jersey Ave. NW
Washington, DC 20001
Ph: (202)879-4400   Fax: (202)879-4545
Fr: 800-238-1133
E-mail: online@aft.org
URL: http://www.aft.org

Description: Affiliated with the AFL-CIO. Works with teachers and other educational employees at the state and local level in organizing, collective bargaining, research, educational issues, and public relations. Conducts research in areas such as educational reform, teacher certification, and national assessments and standards. Represents members' concerns through legislative action; offers technical assistance. Serves professionals with concerns similar to those of teachers, including state employees, healthcare workers, and paraprofessionals.

★11624★ **American Orff-Schulwerk Association (AOSA)**

PO Box 391089
Cleveland, OH 44139-8089
Ph: (440)543-5366   Fax: (440)543-2687
E-mail: info@aosa.org
URL: http://www.aosa.org

Description: Music and movement educators, music therapists, and church choir directors united to promote and encourage the philosophy of Carl Orff's (1895-1982, German composer) Schulwerk (Music for Children) in America. Distributes information on the activities and growth of Orff Schulwerk in America. Conducts research; offers information on teacher training. Operates clearinghouse.

★11625★ **Association of Christian Schools International (ACSI)**

PO Box 65130
Colorado Springs, CO 80962-5130
Ph: (719)528-6906   Fax: (719)531-0631
Fr: 800-367-0798
E-mail: info@acsi.org
URL: http://www.acsi.org

Description: Seeks to enable Christian educators and schools worldwide to effectively prepare students for life.

★11626★ **Council of American Instructors of the Deaf (CAID)**

PO Box 377
Bedford, TX 76095-0377
Ph: (817)354-8414
E-mail: caid@swbell.net
URL: http://www.caid.org

Members: Professional organization of teachers, administrators, and professionals in allied fields related to education of the deaf and hard-of-hearing. **Purpose:** Provides opportunities for a free interchange of views concerning methods and means of educating the deaf and hard-of-hearing. Promotes such education by the publication of reports, essays, and other information. Develops more effective methods of teaching deaf and hard-of-hearing children.

★11627★ **Education and Training**

Cambridge Educational
PO Box 2053
Princeton, NJ 08543-2053
Ph: 800-257-5126   Fax: (609)671-0266
Fr: 800-468-4227
E-mail: custserv@films.com
URL: http://www.cambridgeeducational.com

VHS and DVD. $89.95. 2002. 18 minutes. Presents four distinct occupations in the field: elementary teachers, teacher's aides, administrators, and librarians. People working in these jobs discuss their responsibilities.

★11628★ **Friends Council on Education (FCE)**

1507 Cherry St.
Philadelphia, PA 19102
Ph: (215)241-7245   Fax: (215)241-7299

E-mail: info@friendscouncil.org
URL: http://www.friendscouncil.org

Members: Representatives appointed by Friends Yearly Meetings; heads of Quaker secondary and elementary schools and colleges; members-at-large. **Purpose:** Acts as a clearinghouse for information on Quaker schools and colleges. **Activities:** Holds meetings and conferences on education and provides in-service training for teachers, administrators and trustees in Friends schools.

★11629★ International Reading Association (IRA)

PO Box 8139
Newark, DE 19714-8139
Ph: (302)731-1600   Fax: (302)731-1057
Fr: 800-336-7323
E-mail: pubinfo@reading.org
URL: http://www.reading.org

Description: Represents teachers, reading specialists, consultants, administrators, supervisors, researchers, psychologists, librarians, and parents interested in promoting literacy. Seeks to improve the quality of reading instruction and promote literacy worldwide. Disseminates information pertaining to research on reading, including information on adult literacy, early childhood and literacy development, international education, literature for children and adolescents, and teacher education and professional development. Maintains over 40 special interest groups and over 70 committees.

★11630★ International Technology Education Association - Council for Supervisors (ITEA-CS)

PO Box 144200
Salt Lake City, UT 84114-4200
Ph: (801)538-7598   Fax: (801)538-7868
E-mail: mrobinson@schools.utah.gov
URL: http://www.iteawww.net/CS

Description: Technology education supervisors from the U.S. Office of Education; local school department chairpersons; state departments of education, local school districts, territories, provinces, and foreign countries. Improves instruction and supervision of programs in technology education. Conducts research; compiles statistics. Sponsors competitions. Maintains speakers' bureau.

★11631★ Jewish Education Service of North America (JESNA)

111 8th Ave., 11th Fl.
New York, NY 10011
Ph: (212)284-6950   Fax: (212)284-6951
E-mail: info@jesna.org
URL: http://www.jesna.org

Description: Widely recognized leader in the areas of research and program evaluation, organizational change and innovative program design and dissemination. Operates the Mandell J. Berman Jewish Heritage Center for Research and Evaluation. Supports the Covenant Foundation, a joint venture with the Crown Family, which makes

awards and grants for creativity in Jewish education.

★11632★ NAFSA/Association of International Educators (NAFSA)

1307 New York Ave. NW, 8th Fl.
Washington, DC 20005-4701
Ph: (202)737-3699   Fax: (202)737-3657
E-mail: inbox@nafsa.org
URL: http://www.nafsa.org

Description: Individuals, organizations, and institutions dealing with international educational exchange, including foreign student advisers, overseas educational advisers, credentials and admissions officers, administrators and teachers of English as a second language, community support personnel, study-abroad administrators, and embassy cultural or educational personnel. Promotes self-regulation standards and responsibilities in international educational exchange; offers professional development opportunities primarily through publications, workshops, grants, and regional and national conferences. Advocates for increased awareness and support of international education and exchange on campuses, in government, and in communities. Offers services including: a job registry for employers and professionals involved with international education; a consultant referral service. Sponsors joint liaison activities with a variety of other educational and government organizations to conduct a census of foreign student enrollment in the U.S.; conducts workshops about specific subjects and countries.

★11633★ National Art Education Association (NAEA)

1916 Association Dr.
Reston, VA 20191-1502
Ph: (703)860-8000   Fax: (703)860-2960
E-mail: info@naea-reston.org
URL: http://www.naea-reston.org

Members: Teachers of art at elementary, middle, secondary, and college levels; colleges, libraries, museums, and other educational institutions. **Purpose:** Studies problems of teaching art; encourages research and experimentation. **Activities:** Serves as a clearinghouse for information on art education programs, materials, and methods of instruction. Sponsors special institutes. Cooperates with other national organizations for the furtherance of creative art experiences for youth.

★11634★ National Association of Blind Teachers (NABT)

1155 15th St. NW, Ste. 1004
Washington, DC 20005
Ph: (202)467-5081   Fax: (202)467-5085
Fr: 800-424-8666
E-mail: info@acb.org
URL: http://www.acb.org

Description: Public school teachers, college and university professors, and teachers in residential schools for the blind. Promotes employment and professional goals of blind persons entering the teaching profession or those established in their respective teach-

ing fields. Serves as a vehicle for the dissemination of information and the exchange of ideas addressing special problems of members. Compiles statistics.

★11635★ National Association of Catholic School Teachers (NACST)

1700 Sansom St., Ste. 903
Philadelphia, PA 19103
Ph: (215)568-4175   Fax: (215)568-8270
Fr: 800-99-NACST
E-mail: nacst.nacst@verizon.net
URL: http://www.nacst.com

Description: Catholic school teachers. Aims to unify, advise, and assist Catholic school teachers in matters of collective bargaining. Promotes the welfare and rights of Catholic schools and teachers; determines needs of Catholic schools and teachers. Monitors legislation, trends, and statistics concerning Catholic education; promotes legislation favorable to nonpublic schools and Catholic school teachers; offers legal advice and addresses issues such as unemployment compensation; assists teachers in organizing and negotiating contracts. Maintains speakers' bureau.

★11636★ National Association of Episcopal Schools (NAES)

815 2nd Ave., Ste. 819
New York, NY 10017-4594
Ph: (212)716-6134   Fax: (212)286-9366
Fr: 800-334-7626
E-mail: info@episcopalschools.org
URL: http://www.episcopalschools.org

Description: Represents episcopal day and boarding schools and preschools. Promotes the educational ministry of the Episcopal Church. Provides publications, consultation services and conference focusing on Episcopal identity of schools, worship, religious education, spirituality, leadership development and governance for heads/directors, administrators, chaplains and teachers of religion, trustees, rectors and other church and school leaders.

★11637★ National Association of Independent Schools (NAIS)

1620 L St. NW, Ste. 1100
Washington, DC 20036-5695
Ph: (202)973-9700   Fax: (202)973-9790
Fr: 800-793-6701
E-mail: info@nais.org
URL: http://www.nais.org

Description: Independent elementary and secondary school members; regional associations of independent schools and related associations. Provides curricular and administrative research and services. Conducts educational programs; compiles statistics.

★11638★ National Association for Research in Science Teaching (NARST)

12100 Sunset Hills Rd., Ste. 130
Reston, VA 20190-3221
Ph: (703)437-4377   Fax: (703)435-4390

E-mail: info@narst.org
URL: http://www.narst.org

Description: Science teachers, supervisors, and science educators specializing in research and teacher education. Promotes and coordinates science education research and interprets and reports the results.

★11639★ **National Association of State Directors of Special Education (NASDSE)**

1800 Diagonal Rd., Ste. 320
Alexandria, VA 22314
Ph: (703)519-3800   Fax: (703)519-3808
E-mail: nasdse@nasdse.org

Members: Professional society of state directors; consultants, supervisors, and administrators who have statewide responsibilities for administering special education programs. **Purpose:** Provides services to state agencies to facilitate their efforts to maximize educational outcomes for individuals with disabilities.

★11640★ **National Community Education Association (NCEA)**

3929 Old Lee Hwy., No. 91-A
Fairfax, VA 22030-2421
Ph: (703)359-8973   Fax: (703)359-0972
E-mail: ncea@ncea.com
URL: http://www.ncea.com

Description: Community school directors, principals, superintendents, professors, teachers, students, and laypeople. **Purpose:** Promotes and establishes community schools as an integral part of the educational plan of every community. Emphasizes community and parent involvement in the schools, lifelong learning, and enrichment of K-12 and adult education. Serves as a clearinghouse for the exchange of ideas and information, and the sharing of efforts. **Activities:** Offers leadership training.

★11641★ **National Council for Accreditation of Teacher Education (NCATE)**

2010 Massachusetts Ave. NW, Ste. 500
Washington, DC 20036
Ph: (202)466-7496   Fax: (202)296-6620
E-mail: ncate@ncate.org
URL: http://www.ncate.org

Members: Representatives from constituent colleges and universities, state departments of education, school boards, teacher, and other professional groups. **Purpose:** Voluntary accrediting body devoted exclusively to: evaluation and accreditation of institutions for preparation of elementary and secondary school teachers; preparation of school service personnel, including school principals, supervisors, superintendents, school psychologists, instructional technologists, and other specialists for school-oriented positions.

★11642★ **National Council for Geographic Education (NCGE)**

206A Martin Hall
Jacksonville State University
Jacksonville, AL 36265-1602
Ph: (256)782-5293   Fax: (256)782-5336
E-mail: ncge@ncge.org
URL: http://www.ncge.org

Description: Teachers of geography and social studies in elementary and secondary schools, colleges and universities; geographers in governmental agencies and private businesses. Encourages the training of teachers in geographic concepts, practices, teaching methods and techniques; works to develop effective geographic educational programs in schools and colleges and with adult groups; stimulates the production and use of accurate and understandable geographic teaching aids and materials.

★11643★ **National Council of Teachers of Mathematics (NCTM)**

1906 Association Dr.
Reston, VA 20191-1502
Ph: (703)620-9840   Fax: (703)476-2970
Fr: 800-235-7566
E-mail: inquiries@nctm.org
URL: http://www.nctm.org

Description: Aims to improve teaching and learning of mathematics.

★11644★ **Organization of American Historians (OAH)**

PO Box 5457
Bloomington, IN 47407-5457
Ph: (812)855-9852   Fax: (812)855-0696
E-mail: oah@oah.org
URL: http://www.oah.org

Description: Professional historians, including college faculty members, secondary school teachers, graduate students, and other individuals in related fields; institutional subscribers are college, university, high school and public libraries, and historical agencies. Promotes historical research and study. Sponsors 12 prize programs for historical writing; maintains speakers' bureau. Conducts educational programs.

★11645★ **Overseas Employment Opportunities for Educators: Department of Defense Dependents Schools**

DIANE Publishing Co.
PO Box 617
Darby, PA 19023-0617
Ph: (610)461-6200   Fax: (610)461-6130
Fr: 800-782-3833
URL: http://www.dianepublishingcentral.com

Barry Leonard, editor. 2000. $15.00. 54 pages. An introduction to teachings positions in the Dept. of Defense Dependents Schools (DoDDS), a worldwide school system, operated by the DoD in 14 countries.

★11646★ **Teaching & Related Occupations**

Delphi Productions
3159 6th St.
Boulder, CO 80304
Ph: (303)443-2100   Fax: (303)443-4022
Fr: 888-443-2400
E-mail: support@delphivideo.com
URL: http://www.delphivideo.com

$95.00. 50 minutes. Part of the Careers for the 21st Century Video Library.

Security Professionals and Investigators

SOURCES OF HELP-WANTED ADS

★11647★ ACJS Today
Academy of Criminal Justice Sciences (ACJS)
PO Box 960
Greenbelt, MD 20768-0960
Ph: (301)446-6300   Fax: (301)446-2819
Fr: 800-757-2257
URL: http://www.acjs.org/

Description: Four issues/year. Contains criminal justice information.

★11648★ National Locksmith
National Publishing Company Inc.
1533 Burgundy Pkwy.
Streamwood, IL 60107
Ph: (630)837-2044   Fax: (630)837-1210
E-mail: natlock@aol.com
URL: http://www.locksmithdownloads.com

Magazine focusing on physical security and locksmithing.

★11649★ Occupational Hazards
Penton Media Inc.
1300 E 9th St.
Cleveland, OH 44114
Ph: (216)696-7000   Fax: (216)696-1752
URL: http://www.occupationalhazards.com

Monthly. $72.00/year for individuals, Canada; $126.00 for two years, Canada; $50.00/year for individuals, Canada; $99.00/year for other countries; $162.00 for two years, international; $80.00/year for other countries, #. Monthly publication for safety professionals featuring information to meet OSHA and EPA compliance requirements, improve management of safety, industrial hygiene and environmental programs and find products and services to protect employees and property.

★11650★ Police & Security News
Days Communications
1208 Juniper St.
Quakertown, PA 18951-1520
Ph: (215)538-1240   Fax: (215)538-1208
E-mail: advertising@policeandsecuritynews.com
URL: http://www.policeandsecuritynews.com

Bimonthly. $18.00/year for by mail; $54.00/year for other countries, mail; $3.00 for single issue, mail. Tabloid for the law enforcement and private security industries. Includes articles on training, new products, and new technology.

★11651★ SafetyHealth
National Safety Council
1121 Spring Lake Dr.
Itasca, IL 60143-3201
Ph: (630)285-1121   Fax: (630)285-1315
Fr: 800-621-7615

Monthly. $56.00/year; $5.00 for single issue. Publication focusing on workplace safety and health issues.

★11652★ Security
BNP Media
2401 W Big Beaver Rd., Ste. 700
Troy, MI 48084
Ph: (248)362-3700   Fax: (248)362-0317
E-mail: security@cahners.com
URL: http://www.securitymagazine.com

Monthly. Free. Magazine presenting news and technology for loss prevention and asset protection.

★11653★ Security Sales & Integration
Bobit Business Media
3520 Challenger St.
Torrance, CA 90503
Ph: (310)533-2400   Fax: (310)533-2500
E-mail: secsales@bobit.com
URL: http://www.securitysales.com

Monthly. Free. Magazine covering the security industry.

PLACEMENT AND JOB REFERRAL SERVICES

★11654★ International Association for Healthcare Security and Safety (IAHSS)
PO Box 5038
Glendale Heights, IL 60139
Ph: (630)529-3913   Fax: (630)529-4139
Fr: 888-353-0990
E-mail: info@iahss.org
URL: http://www.iahss.org

Members: Administrative and supervisory personnel in the field of hospital security and safety. **Purpose:** Develops, promotes, and coordinates better security/safety programs in medical care facilities. **Activities:** Offers placement services; conducts specialized education programs.

★11655★ Nine Lives Associates (NLA)
Executive Protection Institute
PO Box 802
Berryville, VA 22611-0802
Ph: (540)554-2540   Fax: (540)554-2558
E-mail: info@personalprotection.com
URL: http://www.personalprotection.com

Description: Law enforcement, correctional, military, and security professionals who have been granted Personal Protection Specialist Certification through completion of the protective services program offered by the Executive Protection Institute; conducts research; EPI programs emphasize personal survival skills and techniques for the protection of others. Provides professional recognition for qualified individuals engaged in executive protection assignments. Maintains placement service. Operates speakers' bureau; compiles statistics.

EMPLOYER DIRECTORIES AND NETWORKING LISTS

★11656★ **Associated Locksmiths of America-Membership Directory**

Associated Locksmiths of America
3500 Easy St.
Dallas, TX 75247
Ph: (214)819-9733   Fax: (214)827-1810
Fr: 800-532-2562
URL: http://www.aloa.org/membersonly/

Annual, March. Publication includes: Roster of about 9,500 members of the association. Entries include: Name, address, phone. Arrangement: Alphabetical. Indexes: Geographical.

★11657★ **International Security Management Association-Membership Directory**

International Security Management Association
PO Box 623
Buffalo, IA 52728
Ph: (563)381-4008   Fax: (563)381-4283
Fr: 800-368-1894

Covers member senior security officers of multinational firms and chief executive officers of security consultation services.

HANDBOOKS AND MANUALS

★11658★ **Career Planning in Criminal Justice**

Anderson Publishing Co.
2035 Reading Rd.
Cincinnati, OH 45202-1576
Ph: (513)421-4142   Fax: (513)562-8116
Fr: 800-582-7295

Robert C. DeLucia and Thomas J. Doyle. Third edition, 1998. 225 pages. $21.95. Surveys a wide range of career and employment opportunities in law enforcement, the courts, corrections, forensic science, and private security. Contains career planning and job hunting advice.

★11659★ **Careers for Legal Eagles and Other Law-and-Order Types**

The McGraw-Hill Companies
PO Box 182604
Columbus, OH 43272
Fax: (614)759-3749   Fr: 877-883-5524
E-mail: customer.service@mcgraw-hill.com
URL: http://www.mcgraw-hill.com

Blythe Camenson. Second edition, 2005. $13.95 (paper). 176 pages.

★11660★ **Opportunities in Law Enforcement and Criminal Justice Careers**

The McGraw-Hill Companies
PO Box 182604
Columbus, OH 43272
Fax: (614)759-3749   Fr: 877-883-5524
E-mail: customer.service@mcgraw-hill.com
URL: http://www.mcgraw-hill.com

James Stinchcomb. Second edition, 2002. $13.95 (paper). 160 pages. Offers information on opportunities at the city, county, state, military, and federal levels. Contains bibliography and illustrations.

★11661★ **Real People Working in Law**

The McGraw-Hill Companies
PO Box 182604
Columbus, OH 43272
Fax: (614)759-3749   Fr: 877-883-5524
E-mail: customer.service@mcgraw-hill.com
URL: http://www.mcgraw-hill.com

Blythe Camenson, Jan Goldberg. 1997. $12.95 (paper). 160 pages. Interviews and profiles of working professionals capture a range of opportunities in this field.

EMPLOYMENT AGENCIES AND SEARCH FIRMS

★11662★ **Bill Young and Associates**

273 Oak Dale Lane
Stuarts Draft, VA 24477
Ph: (540)255-9909
E-mail: billyoung@ntelos.net
URL: http://www.billyoung.com

Employment agency. Executive recruiter.

★11663★ **Robert A. Borissoff, Security Consultant**

Nor-Cal Bldg., 2016 Oakdale Ave.
San Francisco, CA 94124
Ph: (415)221-0600   Fax: (415)668-7174
E-mail: rborissoff@aol.com

Safety and security specialist in the development, design, and installation of personnel security programs, guard services, surveillance services, and personnel testing. Industries served: legal, security and government agencies worldwide.

OTHER SOURCES

★11664★ **ASIS International**

1625 Prince St.
Alexandria, VA 22314-2818
Ph: (703)519-6200   Fax: (703)519-1501
E-mail: asis@asisonline.org
URL: http://www.asisonline.org

Purpose: Security professionals responsible for loss prevention, asset protection and security for businesses, government, or public organizations and institutions. Sponsors educational programs on security principles (basic through advanced levels) and current security issues. Administers professional certification programs (CPP, PCI, PSP). Offers networking opportunities to professionals; provides an online service for employment and resumes, publishes books, directories, and other resources.

★11665★ **Associated Locksmiths of America (ALOA)**

3500 Easy St.
Dallas, TX 75247
Ph: (214)819-9733   Fax: (214)819-9736
Fr: 800-532-2562
E-mail: charlie@aloa.org
URL: http://www.aloa.org

Members: Retail locksmiths; associate members are manufacturers and distributors of locks, keys, safes, and burglar alarms. **Purpose:** Aims to educate and provide current information to individuals in the physical security industry. **Activities:** Maintains information and referral services for members; offers insurance and bonding programs. Holds annual five-day technical training classes and 3-day technical exhibit. Maintains museum.

★11666★ **Federal Criminal Investigators Association (FCIA)**

PO Box 23400
Washington, DC 20026
Ph: (630)969-8537   Fax: 800-528-3492
Fr: 800-403-3374
E-mail: fcianat@aol.com
URL: http://www.fedcia.org

Description: Serves as professional fraternal organization dedicated to the advancement of federal law enforcement officers and the citizens they serve. Aims to ensure law enforcement professionals have the tools and support network to meet the challenges of future criminal investigations while becoming more community oriented. Intends to pursue mission by promoting professionalism, enhancing the image of federal officers, fostering cooperation among all law enforcement professionals, providing a fraternal environment for the advancement of the membership and community. Helps charitable programs and organizations.

★11667★ **Human Services Occupations**

Delphi Productions
3159 6th St.
Boulder, CO 80304
Ph: (303)443-2100   Fax: (303)443-4022
Fr: 888-443-2400
E-mail: support@delphivideo.com
URL: http://www.delphivideo.com

$95.00. 50 minutes. Part of the Careers for the 21st Century Video Library.

★11668★ **International Association of Campus Law Enforcement Administrators (IACLEA)**

342 N Main St., Ste. 301
West Hartford, CT 06117-2507
Ph: (860)586-7517   Fax: (860)586-7550
E-mail: info@iaclea.org
URL: http://www.iaclea.org

Description: Advances public safety for educational institutions by providing educational resources, advocacy, and professional development. Promotes professional ideals and standards in the administration of campus security/public safety/law enforcement. Works to make campus security/public safety/law enforcement an integral part of the educational community.

★11669★ **International Association of Professional Security Consultants (IAPSC)**

525 SW 5th St., Ste. A
Des Moines, IA 50309-4501
Ph: (515)282-8192   Fax: (515)282-9117
E-mail: iapsc@iapsc.org
URL: http://www.iapsc.org

Description: Security management, technical, training, and forensic consultants. Promotes understanding and cooperation among members and industries or individuals requiring such services. Seeks to enhance members' knowledge through seminars, training programs, and educational materials. Works to foster public awareness of the security consulting industry; serves as a clearinghouse for consultants' requirements. Maintains code of conduct, ethics, and professional standards. Offers consultant referral service; operates speakers' bureau.

★11670★ **International Security Management Association (ISMA)**

PO Box 623
Buffalo, IA 52728
Fax: (563)381-4283   Fr: 800-368-1894
E-mail: isma3@aol.com
URL: http://www.ismanet.com

Description: Senior security executives of multinational business firms and chief executive officers of full service security services companies. Aims to assist senior security executives in coordinating and exchanging information about security management and to establish high business and professional standards.

★11671★ **Math at Work: Women in Nontraditional Careers**

Her Own Words
PO Box 5264
Madison, WI 53705-0264
Ph: (608)271-7083   Fax: (608)271-0209
E-mail: herownword@aol.com
URL: http://www.herownwords.com/

Video. Jocelyn Riley. $95.00. 15 minutes. Resource guide also available for $45.00.

★11672★ **National Association of Legal Investigators (NALI)**

PO Box 8479
Portland, ME 04104
Fax: (207)893-1457   Fr: 888-244-5685
E-mail: info@nalionline.org
URL: http://www.nalionline.org

Description: Legal investigators, both independent and law firm staff, who specialize in investigation of personal injury matters for the plaintiff and criminal defense. Promotes professionalization of the legal investigator, accomplished by seminars and a professional certification program. Provides nationwide network of contact among members. Compiles statistics.

★11673★ **Professional Specialty Occupations**

Delphi Productions
3159 6th St.
Boulder, CO 80304
Ph: (303)443-2100   Fax: (303)443-4022
Fr: 888-443-2400
E-mail: support@delphivideo.com
URL: http://www.delphivideo.com

$95.00. 53 minutes. Part of the Careers for the 21st Century Video Library.

★11674★ **Society of Professional Investigators (SPI)**

PO Box 1128
Bellmore, NY 11710
Ph: (516)781-5100   Fax: (516)783-0000
E-mail: info@spionline.org
URL: http://www.spionline.org

Description: Persons with at least 5 years' investigative experience for an official federal, state, or local government agency or for a quasi-official agency formed for law enforcement or related activities. Seeks to advance knowledge of the science and technology of professional investigation, law enforcement, and police science; maintains high standards and ethics; promotes efficiency of investigators in the services they perform.

Services Sales Representatives

SOURCES OF HELP-WANTED ADS

★11675★ BtoB Magazine
Crain Communications Inc.
360 N Michigan Ave.
Chicago, IL 60601
Ph: (312)649-5411   Fax: (312)280-3150
Fr: 888-909-9111
URL: http://www.btobonline.com

Monthly. $59.00/year for individuals; $69.00/year for Canada; $89.00/year for other countries. Trade magazine on business-to-business marketing news, strategy, and tactics.

★11676★ CRM Buyer
NewsFactor Network
21700 Oxnard St., Ste. 2040
Woodland Hills, CA 91367
Ph: (818)713-2500
URL: http://www.crmbuyer.com/

Monthly. Magazine covering customer relationship management solutions.

★11677★ Money Making Opportunities
Success Publishing International
11071 Ventura Blvd.
Studio City, CA 91604
Ph: (818)980-9166   Fax: (818)980-7829
URL: http://www.moneymakingopps.com/

Free. Magazine Source for small business opportunity seekers.

★11678★ Sales & Marketing Management
The Nielsen Co.
770 Broadway
New York, NY 10003
Ph: (646)654-5000   Fax: (646)654-5002
URL: http://www.salesandmarketing.com

Monthly. $48.00/year for individuals. Business magazine.

★11679★ Service Revenue
Center for Services Marketing Inc.
300 Hess Ave., Bldg. II
Golden, CO 80401
Ph: (720)746-1900   Fax: (720)746-0599
URL: http://www.csmhub.com/

Semiannual. $129.00/year for individuals. Newsletter giving information on marketing and sales knowledge for the service industry.

HANDBOOKS AND MANUALS

★11680★ Career Opportunities in Travel and Tourism
Facts On File Inc.
132 W. 31st St., 17th Fl.
New York, NY 10001-2006
Ph: (212)967-8800   Fax: 800-678-3633
Fr: 800-322-8755
E-mail: custserv@factsonfile.com
URL: http://www.factsonfile.com

John K. Hawks. 1996. $18.95 (paper). 224 pages. Includes detailed job descriptions, educational requirements, salary ranges, and advancement prospects for 70 different job opportunities in this fast-paced industry. Contains index and bibliography.

★11681★ Careers for Talkative Types and Others with the Gift of Gab
The McGraw-Hill Companies
PO Box 182604
Columbus, OH 43272
Fax: (614)759-3749   Fr: 877-883-5524
E-mail: customer.service@mcgraw-hill.com
URL: http://www.mcgraw-hill.com

Marjorie Eberts and Margaret Gisler. Second edition, 2006. $13.95 (paper). 160 pages.

★11682★ The I Hate Selling Book: Business-Building Advice for Consultants, Attorneys, Accountants, Engineers, Architects, and Other Professionals
AMACOM
1601 Broadway, 12th Fl.
New York, NY 10019-7420
Ph: (212)586-8100   Fax: (212)903-8168
Fr: 800-262-9699
URL: http://www.amanet.org

Allan S. Boress. 2001. $29.95. 240 pages.

★11683★ Opportunities in Medical Sales Careers
The McGraw-Hill Companies
PO Box 182604
Columbus, OH 43272
Fax: (614)759-3749   Fr: 877-883-5524
E-mail: customer.service@mcgraw-hill.com
URL: http://www.mcgraw-hill.com

Chad Ellis. 1997. $14.95; $11.95 (paper). 160 pages. Includes index.

★11684★ Opportunities in Sales Careers
The McGraw-Hill Companies
PO Box 182604
Columbus, OH 43272
Fax: (614)759-3749   Fr: 877-883-5524
E-mail: customer.service@mcgraw-hill.com
URL: http://www.mcgraw-hill.com

James Brescoll and Ralph Dahm. 160 pages. 2001. $12.95 (paper). Details sales in retail, wholesale and industrial sales, sales of services and intangibles, and sales management. Illustrated.

★11685★ Resumes for Sales and Marketing Careers
The McGraw-Hill Companies
PO Box 182604
Columbus, OH 43272
Fax: (614)759-3749   Fr: 877-883-5524
E-mail: customer.service@mcgraw-hill.com
URL: http://www.mcgraw-hill.com

Chuck Cochran and Donna Peerce. 1998. $13.95. 336 pages. Sample resumes and cover letters from all levels of the sales and marketing field.

EMPLOYMENT AGENCIES AND SEARCH FIRMS

★11686★ Bender Executive Search
45 N. Station Plaza, Ste. 315
Great Neck, NY 11021
Ph: (516)773-3200   Fax: (516)482-5355
URL: http://www.marketingexecsearch.com

Executive search firm.

★11687★ The Culver Group, Inc.
600 City Parkway W., Ste. 320
Orange, CA 92868
Ph: (714)939-8900
URL: http://www.culvergroup.com

Employment agency specializing in sales positions.

★11688★ National Register Columbus, Inc.
550 Polaris Pkwy., Ste. 530
Westerville, OH 43082
Ph: (614)890-1200   Fax: (614)890-1259
E-mail: sales@nrcols.com
URL: http://www.nrcols.com

Employment agency. Offices in Akron and Toledo, OH.

★11689★ Sales Executives Inc.
33900 W. 8 Mile Rd., Ste. 171
Farmington Hills, MI 48335
Ph: (248)615-0100
E-mail: dale@salesexecutives.com
URL: http://www.salesexecutives.com

Employment agency. Executive search firm.

★11690★ Salespositions.com
450 7th Ave., Ste. 507A
New York, NY 10123
Ph: (609)407-4774
E-mail: salepositions@comcast.net
URL: http://www.salespositions.com

Employment agency.

OTHER SOURCES

★11691★ Marketing & Sales Occupations
Delphi Productions
3159 6th St.
Boulder, CO 80304
Ph: (303)443-2100   Fax: (303)443-4022
Fr: 888-443-2400
E-mail: support@delphivideo.com
URL: http://www.delphivideo.com

$95.00. 50 minutes. Part of the Careers for the 21st Century Video Library.

Social Workers

SOURCES OF HELP-WANTED ADS

★11692★ American City and County

Primedia Business
6151 Powers Ferry Rd., Ste. 200
Atlanta, GA 30339
Ph: (770)955-2500   Fax: (770)618-0204
URL: http://
www.americancityandcounty.com

Monthly. $67.00/year for individuals. Municipal and county administration magazine.

★11693★ Child and Adolescent Social Work Journal

Springer-Verlag New York Inc.
233 Spring St.
New York, NY 10013
Ph: (212)460-1500   Fax: (212)460-1575
URL: http://www.springer.com/sgw/cda/
frontpage/0,11855,5-0-70-355

Journal dealing with issues in clinical social work practice with children, adolescents, and their families.

★11694★ Children & Schools

National Association of Social Workers
750 1st St. NE, Ste. 700
Washington, DC 20002-4241
Ph: (202)408-8600
URL: http://www.naswpress.org/publications/journals/children/csin

Quarterly. $54.00/year for members; $89.00/year for nonmembers; $37.00/year for students; $125.00/year for institutions. Journal.

★11695★ Children & Society

John Wiley & Sons Inc.
111 River St.
Hoboken, NJ 07030-5774
Ph: (201)748-6000   Fax: (201)748-6088
Fr: 800-825-7550
E-mail: children&society@ncb.org.uk
URL: http://www3.interscience.wiley.com/
cgi-bin/jhome/4805

$655.00/year for institutions, print and on-line; $566.00/year for institutions, online only; $194.00/year for individuals, print and online. Journal focusing on children and services for children.

★11696★ EAP Digest

Performance Resource Press Inc.
1270 Rankin Dr., Ste. F
Troy, MI 48083
Ph: (248)588-7733   Fax: (248)588-6633
URL: http://www.prponline.net/Work/EAP/
eap.htm

Quarterly. $36.00/year for individuals; $82.00 for two years, Canada, Hawaii, & Alaska; $99.00 for individuals for three years, Canada, Hawaii, & Alaska; $104.00 for other countries, three years; $87.00 for other countries, two years; $54.00/year for other countries; $49.00/year for individuals, Canada, Hawaii, & Alaska; $60.00 for two years. Magazine covering planning, development, and administration of employee assistance programs.

★11697★ Intellectual and Developmental Disabilities

American Association on Intellectual and Developmental Disabilities
444 N Capitol St. NW, Ste. 846
Washington, DC 20001-1512
Ph: (202)387-1968   Fax: (202)387-2193
Fr: 800-424-3688
URL: http://www.aamr.org

Bimonthly. $219.00/year for institutions, print + online; $252.00/year for institutions, other countries, print + online; $106.00/year for individuals, print + online; $139.00/year for individuals, print + online outside U.S. $207.00/year for institutions, online only; $207.00/year for institutions, other countries, online only; $95.00/year for individuals, online only; $95.00/year for individuals, online only outside U.S. Magazine featuring articles on mental retardation for professionals and parents.

★11698★ International Sociology

Sage Publications Inc.
2455 Teller Rd.
Thousand Oaks, CA 91320
Ph: (805)499-0721   Fax: (805)499-8096
URL: http://www.sagepub.com/journalspro-
deditboards.nav?prodid=jou

Bimonthly. $662.00/year for institutions, print & e-access; $695.00/year for institutions, print & all online; $596.00/year for institutions, e-access; $629.00/year for institutions, e-access & all online; $659.00/year for institutions, e-access thru 1999; $649.00/year for institutions, print only; $88.00/year for individuals, print only; $119.00 for institutions, single print; $19.00 for individuals, single print. Journal publishing studies on social organization, societal change, and comparative sociology.

★11699★ Journal of Applied Sociology

Society for Applied Sociology
712 Pray-Harrold, EMU
Ypsilanti, MI 48197
Ph: (734)487-0012   Fax: (734)487-7010

Annual. Journal covering current research and policy in applied sociology.

★11700★ Journal of Family Social Work

The Haworth Press Inc.
10 Alice St.
Binghamton, NY 13904
Ph: (607)722-5857   Fr: 800-429-6784
URL: http://www.haworthpress.com/store/
product.asp?sid=9LJ67H8WF

Quarterly. $99.00/year for U.S., individual; $145.00/year for Canada, individual; $152.00/year for other countries, individual; $255.00/year for institutions, agency, library; $362.00/year for institutions, Canada, agency, library; $383.00/year for institutions, other countries, agency, library. Journal serves as a forum for family practitioners, scholars, and educators in the field of social work.

★11701★ The Lutheran

Augsburg Fortress, Publishers
100 S 5th St., Ste. 600
PO Box 1209
Minneapolis, MN 55402-1209
Ph: (612)330-3271   Fax: (612)330-3455
Fr: 800-328-4648
E-mail: lutheran@elca.org
URL: http://www.thelutheran.org

Monthly. $15.95/year for individuals; $1.50 for single issue; $29.95 for individuals for two years; $39.95/year for individuals, 3 years. Magazine of the Evangelical Lutheran Church in America.

★11702★ Modern Healthcare

Crain Communications Inc.
360 N Michigan Ave.
Chicago, IL 60601
Ph: (312)649-5411   Fax: (312)280-3150
Fr: 888-909-9111
E-mail: subs@crain.com
URL: http://www.modernhealthcare.com

Weekly. $154.00/year for individuals; $244.00/year for Canada; $208.00/year for other countries. Weekly business news magazine for healthcare management.

★11703★ NASW News

National Association of Social Workers
750 1st St. NE, Ste. 700
Washington, DC 20002-4241
Ph: (202)408-8600   Fax: (202)336-8312
E-mail: naswnews@naswdc.org
URL: http://www.socialworkers.org

Description: Ten issues/year. Recurring features include letters to the editor, job listings, notices of publications available, and columns titled From the President, From the Director, and Social Work in the Public Eye.

★11704★ The New Social Worker

White Hat Communications
PO Box 5390
Harrisburg, PA 17110-0390
Ph: (717)238-3787   Fax: (717)238-2090
URL: http://www.socialworker.com

Quarterly. $15.00/year for individuals. Publication offering career guidance for social work students.

★11705★ The NonProfit Times

NPT Publishing Group Inc.
120 Littleton Rd., Ste. 120
Parsippany, NJ 07054-1803
Ph: (973)394-1800   Fax: (973)394-2888
E-mail: ednchief@nptimes.com
URL: http://www.nptimes.com/

Biweekly. $69.00/year for individuals, subscribe at the one year rate; $49.00/year for individuals, digital only; $100.00/year for individuals, print & digital; $122.00 for two years, (48 issues); $101.00/year for Canada and Mexico; $137.00/year for other countries, international. Trade journal serving nonprofit organizations.

★11706★ The Pennsylvania Social Worker

National Association of Social Workers-Pennsylvania Chapter
2001 N. Front St., Ste. 321
Harrisburg, PA 17102
Ph: (717)232-4125   Fax: (717)232-4140
Fr: 800-272-6279
E-mail: exec@nasw-pa.org
URL: http://www.nasw-pa.org

Description: Bimonthly. Provides information on state, local, and national Association activities. Tracks legislative actions. Recurring features include interviews, a calendar of events, news of educational opportunities, job listings, book reviews, and columns titled President's Report and Division Report.

★11707★ Practice

Taylor & Francis Group Journals
325 Chestnut St., Ste. 800
Philadelphia, PA 19106
Ph: (215)625-8900   Fax: (215)625-8914
Fr: 800-354-1420
URL: http://www.tandf.co.uk/journals/titles/09503153.asp

$285.00/year for institutions, print and online; $270.00/year for institutions, online only; $98.00/year for individuals. Journal for a strong base in social work practice.

★11708★ Psychiatric Services

Association of Partners for Public Lands
2401 Blueridge Ave., Ste. 303
Wheaton, MD 20902
Ph: (301)946-9475   Fax: (301)946-9478

Monthly. Interdisciplinary mental health journal covering clinical, legal, and public policy issues.

★11709★ Social Work

National Association of Social Workers
750 1st St. NE, Ste. 700
Washington, DC 20002-4241
Ph: (202)408-8600
URL: http://www.naswpress.org

Quarterly. $37.00/year for students; $89.00/year for nonmembers; $129.00/year for institutions; subscription included in membership. Journal for social workers.

★11710★ Teaching Exceptional Children

Council for Exceptional Children
1110 N Glebe Rd., Ste. 300
Arlington, VA 22201-5704
Ph: (703)620-3660   Fax: (703)264-9494
Fr: 888-232-7733
E-mail: tec@bc.edu
URL: http://www.cec.sped.org

Bimonthly. $135.00/year for individuals; $250.00 for two years; $145.00 for two years, Canada; $270.00 for two years, Canada; $165.00/year for out of country, foreign-air printed matter; $310.00 for out of country, two years, foreign-air printed matter; $25.00/year for institutions, single copy; $170.00/year for institutions; $290.00 for two

years, institutional. Journal exploring practical methods for teaching students who have exceptionalities and those who are gifted and talented.

PLACEMENT AND JOB REFERRAL SERVICES

★11711★ Alliance for Children and Families (ACF)

11700 W Lake Park Dr.
Milwaukee, WI 53224-3099
Ph: (414)359-1040   Fax: (414)359-1074
E-mail: info@alliance1.org
URL: http://www.alliance1.org

Description: Membership organization of local agencies in more than 1,000 communities providing family counseling, family life education and family advocacy services, and other programs to help families with parent-child, marital, mental health, and other problems of family living. Assists member agencies in developing and providing effective family services. Works with the media, government, and corporations to promote strong family life. Compiles statistics; conducts research. Maintains extensive files of unpublished materials from member agencies. Offers career placement services.

★11712★ American Public Health Association (APHA)

800 I St. NW
Washington, DC 20001
Ph: (202)777-2742   Fax: (202)777-2534
E-mail: comments@apha.org
URL: http://www.apha.org

Members: Professional organization of physicians, nurses, educators, academicians, environmentalists, epidemiologists, new professionals, social workers, health administrators, optometrists, podiatrists, pharmacists, dentists, nutritionists, health planners, other community and mental health specialists, and interested consumers. **Purpose:** Seeks to protect and promote personal, mental, and environmental health. **Activities:** Services include: promulgation of standards; establishment of uniform practices and procedures; development of the etiology of communicable diseases; research in public health; exploration of medical care programs and their relationships to public health. Sponsors job placement service.

★11713★ International Association of Counselors and Therapists (IACT)

RR No. 2, Box 2468
Laceyville, PA 18623
Ph: (570)869-1021   Fax: (570)869-1249
Fr: 800-553-6886
E-mail: info@iact.org
URL: http://www.iact.org

Description: Mental health professionals, medical professionals, social workers, clergy, educators, hypnotherapists, counselors, and individuals interested in the helping professions. Promotes enhanced professional image and prestige for complementary therapy. Provides a forum for exchange of information and ideas among practitioners of traditional and nontraditional therapies and methodologies; fosters unity among "grassroots" practitioners and those with advanced academic credentials. Facilitates the development of new therapy programs. Conducts educational, research, and charitable programs. Awards credits for continuing education. Maintains speakers' bureau and library; operates referral and placement services; compiles statistics. Assists in the development of local chapters.

★11714★ National Staff Development and Training Association (NSDTA)

American Public Human Services
  Association
810 First St. NE, Ste. 500
Washington, DC 20002-4207
Ph: (202)682-0100   Fax: (202)289-6555
E-mail: dgross@aphsa.org
URL: http://nsdta.aphsa.org

Description: Social welfare workers engaged in staff development and training. Attempts to: support people in the field; influence welfare policy-making on the national level; form a network of contacts for members. Provides technical assistance. Maintains speakers' bureau; offers placement services.

EMPLOYER DIRECTORIES AND NETWORKING LISTS

★11715★ American Group Psychotherapy Association-Membership Directory

American Group Psychotherapy
  Association Inc.
25 E 21st St., 6th Fl.
New York, NY 10010
Ph: (212)477-2677   Fax: (212)979-6627
Fr: 877-668-2472
URL: http://www.agpa.org

Covers 4,500 physicians, psychologists, clinical social workers, psychiatric nurses, and other mental health professionals interested in treatment of emotional problems by group methods. Entries include: Name, office or home address, highest degree held, office or home phone number. Arrangement: Alphabetical. Indexes: Geographical.

★11716★ Christian Association for Psychological Studies International-Membership Directory

Christian Association for Psychological
  Studies
PO Box 365
Batavia, IL 60510-0365
Ph: (630)639-9478   Fax: (630)454-3799

Annual, June. $12.00 for Canada; $12.00 for other countries. Covers 2,300 Christians

involved in psychology, psychiatry, counseling, sociology, social work, ministry, and nursing. Entries include: Name, office address and phone number, highest degree held, area of occupational specialization, and career data. Arrangement: Geographical. Indexes: Alphabetical.

★11717★ Directory of Catholic Charities USA Directories

Catholic Charities USA
1731 King St.
Alexandria, VA 22314
Ph: (703)549-1390   Fax: (703)549-1656
URL: http://www.catholiccharitiesusa.org/

Annual. $25.00 for individuals. Covers nearly 1,200 Catholic community and social service agencies. Listings include diocesan agencies and state Catholic conferences. Entries include: Organization name, address, name and title of director, phone, fax. Arrangement: Geographical by state, then classified by diocese.

★11718★ Directory of Child Life Programs

Child Life Council Inc.
11820 Parklawn Dr., Ste. 240
Rockville, MD 20852-2529
Ph: (301)881-7090   Fax: (301)881-7092
URL: http://www.childlife.org/

Biennial; latest edition 14th, 2006. Covers over 400 child life programs. Entries include: Facility name, address, phone, name of child life department and director, reporting structure, staff statistics, educational requirements for employment, and internship or educational opportunities. Arrangement: Geographical. Indexes: Speciality areas, internship sessions, program size, fellowships.

★11719★ Mental Help Net

CenterSite L.L.C.
PO Box 20709
Columbus, OH 43220
Ph: (614)448-4055   Fax: (614)448-4055
URL: http://www.mentalhelp.net

Covers resources for finding mental help, including local therapists and self-help groups, as well as services such as upcoming conferences, professional education, and universities offering degrees in mental health fields.

★11720★ National Directory of Private Social Agencies

Croner Publications Inc.
10951 Sorrento Valley Rd., Ste. 1-D
San Diego, CA 92121-1613
Fax: 800-809-0334   Fr: 800-441-4033
URL: http://www.sdic.net/croner

$109.95 for individuals. Number of listings: Over 10,000. Entries include: Agency name, address, phone, name and title of contact, description of services. Arrangement: Geographical. Indexes: Service, agency type.

★11721★ Public Human Services Directory

American Public Human Services
  Association
810 1st St. NE, Ste. 500
Washington, DC 20002
Ph: (202)682-0100   Fax: (202)289-6555
E-mail: pubs@aphsa.org
URL: http://www.aphsa.org

Annual, September. $110.00 for members; $149.00 for nonmembers. Covers federal, state, territorial, county, and major municipal public human service agencies. Entries include: Agency name, address, phone, fax, e-mail address, web site address, names of key personnel, program area. Arrangement: Geographical.

★11722★ Social Workers Directory

infoUSA Inc.
5711 S 86th Cir.
PO Box 27347
Omaha, NE 68127-0347
Ph: (402)593-4593   Fax: (402)596-7688
Fr: 800-555-6124
URL: http://www.infousa.com

Annual. Number of listings: 4,859. Entries include: Name, address, phone (including area code), size of advertisement, year first in "Yellow Pages," name of owner or manager, number of employees. Compiled from telephone company "Yellow Pages," nationwide. Arrangement: Geographical.

HANDBOOKS AND MANUALS

★11723★ 100 Jobs in Social Change

John Wiley & Sons Inc.
1 Wiley Dr.
Somerset, NJ 08873
Ph: (732)469-4400   Fax: (732)302-2300
Fr: 800-225-5945
E-mail: custserv@wiley.com
URL: http://www.wiley.com/WileyCDA/

Harley Jebens. 1996. $14.95. 216 pages. Part of the One Hundred Jobs Series.

★11724★ Careers for Caring People and Other Sensitive Types

The McGraw-Hill Companies
PO Box 182604
Columbus, OH 43272
Fax: (614)759-3749   Fr: 877-883-5524
E-mail: customer.service@mcgraw-hill.com
URL: http://www.mcgraw-hill.com

Adrian Paradis. Second edition, 2003. $13.95 (paper). 208 pages.

★11725★ Careers for Good Samaritans and Other Humanitarian Types

The McGraw-Hill Companies
PO Box 182604
Columbus, OH 43272
Fax: (614)759-3749   Fr: 877-883-5524
E-mail: customer.service@mcgraw-hill.com

URL: http://www.mcgraw-hill.com

Marjorie Eberts and Margaret Gisler. Third edition, 2006. $13.95 (paper). 160 pages. Contains hundreds of ideas for turning good work into paid work. Inventories opportunities in service organizations like the Red Cross, Goodwill, and the Salvation Army; religious groups, VISTA, the Peace Corps, and UNICEF; and agencies at all levels of the government. Part of Careers for You series.

★11726★ **Careers in Health Care**

The McGraw-Hill Companies
PO Box 182604
Columbus, OH 43272
Fax: (614)759-3749   Fr: 877-883-5524
E-mail: customer.service@mcgraw-hill.com
URL: http://www.mcgraw-hill.com

Barbara M. Swanson. Fifth edition, 2005. $15.95 (paper). 192 pages. Describes job duties, work settings, salaries, licensing and certification requirements, educational preparation, and future outlook. Gives ideas on how to secure a job.

★11727★ **Careers in Social and Rehabilitation Services**

The McGraw-Hill Companies
PO Box 182604
Columbus, OH 43272
Fax: (614)759-3749   Fr: 877-883-5524
E-mail: customer.service@mcgraw-hill.com
URL: http://www.mcgraw-hill.com

Geraldine O. Garner. 2001. $19.95; 14.95 (paper). 128 pages.

★11728★ **Great Jobs for Liberal Arts Majors**

The McGraw-Hill Companies
PO Box 182604
Columbus, OH 43272
Fax: (614)759-3749   Fr: 877-883-5524
E-mail: customer.service@mcgraw-hill.com
URL: http://www.mcgraw-hill.com

Blythe Camenson. Second edition, 2001. $14.95 (paper). 256 pages.

★11729★ **Great Jobs for Sociology Majors**

The McGraw-Hill Companies
PO Box 182604
Columbus, OH 43272
Fax: (614)759-3749   Fr: 877-883-5524
E-mail: customer.service@mcgraw-hill.com
URL: http://www.mcgraw-hill.com

Stephen Lambert. Second edition, 2002. $15.95 (paper). 224 pages.

★11730★ **A Guide to Careers in Community Development**

Island Press
1718 Connecticut Ave. NW, Ste. 300
Washington, DC 20009
Ph: (202)232-7933   Fax: (202)234-1328
Fr: 800-621-2736
URL: http://www.islandpress.org/

Alice Shabecoff and Paul Brody. 2001. $35.00. 270 pages.

★11731★ **Non-Profits and Education Job Finder**

Planning Communications
7215 Oak Ave.
River Forest, IL 60305-1935
Ph: (708)366-5200   Fax: (708)366-5280
Fr: 888-366-5200
E-mail: info@planningcommunications.com
URL: http://jobfindersonline.com

Daniel Lauber. 1997. $32.95; $16.95 (paper). 340 pages. Covers 1600 sources. Discusses how to use sources of non-profit sector job vacancies in a number of specialties and state-by-state, including job-matching services, job hotlines, specialty periodicals with job ads, salary surveys, and directories. Covers a variety of fields from education to religion. Includes chapters on resume and cover letter preparation and interviewing.

★11732★ **Opportunities in Child Care Careers**

The McGraw-Hill Companies
PO Box 182604
Columbus, OH 43272
Fax: (614)759-3749   Fr: 877-883-5524
E-mail: customer.service@mcgraw-hill.com
URL: http://www.mcgraw-hill.com

Renee Wittenberg. 2006. $13.95 (paper). 160 pages. Discusses various job opportunities and how to secure a position. Illustrated.

★11733★ **Opportunities in Gerontology and Aging Services Careers**

The McGraw-Hill Companies
PO Box 182604
Columbus, OH 43272
Fax: (614)759-3749   Fr: 877-883-5524
E-mail: customer.service@mcgraw-hill.com
URL: http://www.mcgraw-hill.com

Ellen Williams. Second edition, 2002. $12.95 (paper). 160 pages. Covers jobs in community, health and medical programs, financial, legal, residential, travel and tourism, and counseling, and how to go after them. Includes bibliography and illustrations.

★11734★ **Opportunities in Health and Medical Careers**

The McGraw-Hill Companies
PO Box 182604
Columbus, OH 43272
Fax: (614)759-3749   Fr: 877-883-5524
E-mail: customer.service@mcgraw-hill.com
URL: http://www.mcgraw-hill.com

I. Donald Snook, Jr. and Leo D'Orazio. 2004. $13.95 (paper). 157 pages. Covers the full range of medical and health occupations. Illustrated.

★11735★ **Opportunities in Social Work Careers**

The McGraw-Hill Companies
PO Box 182604
Columbus, OH 43272
Fax: (614)759-3749   Fr: 877-883-5524
E-mail: customer.service@mcgraw-hill.com
URL: http://www.mcgraw-hill.com

Renee Wittenberg. Second edition, 2002. 160 pages. $12.95 (paper).

★11736★ **Opportunities in State and Local Government Careers**

The McGraw-Hill Companies
PO Box 182604
Columbus, OH 43272
Fax: (614)759-3749   Fr: 877-883-5524
E-mail: customer.service@mcgraw-hill.com
URL: http://www.mcgraw-hill.com

Neale J. Baxter. Revised edition, 1992. $14.95; $10.95 (paper). 148 pages. Points out the incentives and drawbacks of a government career. Describes hiring procedures and provides tips on filling out applications, taking physical and aptitude tests, handling interviews, and finding jobs. Describes the jobs in which 75% of all state and local government workers are employed. For each occupation, covers the nature of the work and the training required.

★11737★ **Passion and Policy: A Social Workers Career**

David Press
12127 Sperry Rd.
Chesterland, OH 44026-2230
Ph: (216)729-3252   Fax: (216)729-2003

Alvin L. Schorr. 1997. $29.95. 211 pages.

★11738★ **Resumes for Social Service Careers**

The McGraw-Hill Companies
PO Box 182604
Columbus, OH 43272
Fax: (614)759-3749   Fr: 877-883-5524
E-mail: customer.service@mcgraw-hill.com
URL: http://www.mcgraw-hill.com

2006. $11.95 (paper). 144 pages.

★11739★ **Social Work Career Development: A Handbook for Job Hunting and Career Planning**

National Association of Social Workers
750 1st St., NE, Ste. 700
Washington, DC 20002-4241
Ph: (202)408-8600   Fax: (202)336-8312
Fr: 800-638-8799

Carol Nesslein Doelling, editor. 2005. Second edition. $49.99 (paper). 251 pages.

ONLINE JOB SOURCES AND SERVICES

★11740★ **Delta T Group**
E-mail: pa@deltatg.com
URL: http://www.delta-tgroup.com
Description: Specialized contract temporary staffing source for healthcare professionals in the fields of social service, psychiatry, mental health, and substance abuse. Organizations may request services and staffing; job seekers may view services provided, submit a resume, or peruse jobs available.

★11741★ **RehabWorld**
URL: http://www.rehabworld.com
Description: Site for rehabilitation professionals to learn about the profession and locate jobs. Includes user groups, salary surveys, and chat capabilities. **Main files include:** Physical Therapy, Occupational Therapy, Speech Therapy, Mental Health, Employer World, Student World, International World, Forum.

★11742★ **Social Work and Social Services Jobs Online**
George Warren Brown School of Social Work Washington University
Campus Box 1196
1 Brookings Dr.
St. Louis, MO 63130-4899
Ph: (314)935-6600   Fax: (314)935-4859
Fr: 800-321-2426
E-mail: msw@wustl.edu
URL: http://gwbweb.wustl.edu/jobs/
Description: Specialized database of social work and social services jobs gives a large list of openings sorted by location (both within and outside the United States). Employers may submit job openings. Site also contains career resources and links to related internet job sites.

TRADESHOWS

★11743★ **National Association of Black Social Workers Convention**
National Black United Fund
40 Clinton St., 5th Fl.
Newark, NJ 07102
Ph: (973)643-5122   Fr: 800-223-0866
E-mail: nbuf@nbuf.org
URL: http://www.nbuf.org
Annual. **Primary Exhibits:** Items of interest to social workers and others concerned with community welfare projects and programs.

OTHER SOURCES

★11744★ *American Almanac of Jobs and Salaries*
HarperCollins
10 E. 53rd St.
New York, NY 10022
Ph: (212)207-7000   Fr: 800-242-7737
URL: http://www.harpercollins.com/
John W. Wright. Revised edition, 2000. $20.00 (paper). 672 pages. This is a comprehensive guide to the wages of hundreds of occupations in a wide variety of industries and organizations.

★11745★ **American Association of Mental Health Professionals in Corrections (AAMHPC)**
PO Box 160208
Sacramento, CA 95816-0208
Fax: (916)649-1080
E-mail: corrmentalhealth@aol.com
Description: Psychiatrists, psychologists, social workers, nurses, and other mental health professionals; individuals working in correctional settings. Fosters the progress of behavioral sciences related to corrections. Goals are: to improve the treatment, rehabilitation, and care of the mentally ill, mentally retarded, and emotionally disturbed; to promote research and professional education in psychiatry and allied fields in corrections; to advance standards of correctional services and facilities; to foster cooperation between individuals concerned with the medical, psychological, social, and legal aspects of corrections; to share knowledge with other medical practitioners, scientists, and the public. Conducts scientific meetings to contribute to the advancement of the therapeutic community in all its institutional settings, including correctional institutions, hospitals, churches, schools, industry, and the family.

★11746★ **American Association of Psychiatric Technicians (AAPT)**
1220 S St., Ste. 100
Sacramento, CA 95811-7138
Ph: (916)443-1701   Fax: (916)329-9145
Fr: 800-391-7589
E-mail: loger@psychtechs.net
URL: http://www.psychtechs.org
Description: Administers the Nationally Certified Psychiatric Technician examination to non-licensed direct-care workers in the fields of mental illness, developmental disabilities and substance abuse.

★11747★ **American Mental Health Alliance (AMHA)**
PO Box 4075
Portland, OR 97208-4075
Ph: (503)279-8160   Fr: 888-577-3386
E-mail: memberinfo@americanmentalhealth.com
URL: http://www.americanmentalhealth.com
Description: Represents mental health professionals licensed or certified for independen t practice. Creates a professional community that provides therapy of the highes t quality and ethical standards. Supports and markets competent, ethical mental health services that preserve privacy and confidentiality. Supports education, s upervision, and research opportunities for members. Opposes legislation and regu lations that invade patient privacy and confidentiality.

★11748★ **American Society of Psychopathology of Expression (ASPE)**
74 Lawton St.
Brookline, MA 02446
Ph: (617)738-9821   Fax: (617)975-0411
Description: Psychiatrists, psychologists, art therapists, sociologists, art critics, artists, social workers, linguists, educators, criminologists, writers, and historians. At least two-thirds of the members must be physicians. Fosters collaboration among specialists in the United States who are interested in the problems of expression and in the artistic activities connected with psychiatric, sociological, and psychological research. Disseminates information about research and clinical applications in the field of psychopathology of expression. Sponsors consultations, seminars, and lectures on art therapy.

★11749★ **Association on Higher Education and Disability (AHEAD)**
107 Commerce Center Dr., Ste. 204
Huntersville, NC 28078
Ph: (704)947-7779   Fax: (704)948-7779
E-mail: ahead@ahead.org
URL: http://www.ahead.org
Description: Individuals interested in promoting the equal rights and opportunities of disabled postsecondary students, staff, faculty, and graduates. Provides an exchange of communication for those professionally involved with disabled students; collects, evaluates, and disseminates information; encourages and supports legislation for the benefit of disabled students. Conducts surveys on issues pertinent to college students with disabilities; offers resource referral system and employment exchange for positions in disability student services. Conducts research programs; compiles statistics.

★11750★ **Child Welfare League of America (CWLA)**
2345 Crystal Dr., Ste. 250
Arlington, VA 22202
Ph: (703)412-2400   Fax: (703)412-2401
E-mail: register@cwla.org
URL: http://www.cwla.org
Purpose: Works to improve care and services for abused, dependent, or neglected children, youth, and their families. **Activities:** Provides training and consultation; conducts research; maintains information service and develops standards for child welfare practice.

★11751★ Counseling Association for Humanistic Education and Development (C-AHEAD)

PO Box 791006
Baltimore, MD 21279-1006
Ph: (703)823-9800   Fax: 800-473-2329
Fr: 800-347-6647
E-mail: lleech@gw.mp.sc.edu
URL: http://www.c-ahead.com

Description: A division of the American Counseling Association. Teachers, educational administrators, community agency workers, counselors, school social workers, and psychologists; others interested in the area of human development. Aims to assist individuals in improving their quality of life. Provides forum for the exchange of information about humanistically-oriented administrative and instructional practices. Supports humanistic practices and research on instructional and organizational methods for facilitating humanistic education; encourages cooperation among related professional groups.

★11752★ Employee Assistance Society of North America (EASNA)

2001 Jefferson Davis Hwy., Ste. 1004
Arlington, VA 22202-3617
Ph: (703)416-0060   Fax: (703)416-0014
E-mail: info@easna.org
URL: http://www.easna.org

Description: Individuals in the field of employee assistance, including psychiatrists, psychologists, and managers. Facilitates communication among members; provides resource information; serves as a network for employee assistance programs nationwide. Conducts research.

★11753★ Human Services Occupations

Delphi Productions
3159 6th St.
Boulder, CO 80304
Ph: (303)443-2100   Fax: (303)443-4022
Fr: 888-443-2400
E-mail: support@delphivideo.com
URL: http://www.delphivideo.com

$95.00. 50 minutes. Part of the Careers for the 21st Century Video Library.

★11754★ National Association of Social Workers (NASW)

750 First St. NE, Ste. 700
Washington, DC 20002-4241
Ph: (202)408-8600   Fax: (202)336-8313
Fr: 800-742-4089
E-mail: info@naswdc.org
URL: http://www.naswdc.org

Members: Regular members are persons who hold a minimum of a baccalaureate degree in social work. Associate members are persons engaged in social work who have a baccalaureate degree in another field. Student members are persons enrolled in accredited (by the Council on Social Work Education) graduate or undergraduate social work programs. **Purpose:** Works to create professional standards for social work practice; advocate sound public social policies through political and legislative action; provide a wide range of membership services, including continuing education opportunities and an extensive professional program. **Activities:** Operates National Center for Social Policy and Practice. Conducts research; compiles statistics.

★11755★ National Organization for Human Services (NOHS)

90 Madison St., Ste. 206
Denver, CO 80206
Ph: (303)320-5430   Fax: (303)322-1455
E-mail: info@nationalhumanservices.org
URL: http://www.nationalhumanservices.org

Description: Human service professionals, faculty, and students. Fosters excellence in teaching, research and curriculum planning in the human service area. Encourages and supports the development of local, state, and national human services organizations. Aids faculty and professional members in their career development. Provides a medium for cooperation and communication among members. Maintains registry of qualified consultants in human service education.

Conducts professional development workshop. Operates speakers' bureau.

★11756★ North American Association of Christians in Social Work (NACSW)

PO Box 121
Botsford, CT 06404-0121
Fax: (203)270-8780   Fr: 888-426-4712
E-mail: info@nacsw.org
URL: http://www.nacsw.org

Description: Professional social workers and related professionals, students, interested individuals. Supports the integration of Christian faith and professional social work practice in the lives of its members, the profession and the church, promoting love and justice in social service and social reform. Provides opportunities for Christian fellowship, education and service opportunities; articulates informed Christian voice on social welfare practice and policy to the social work profession; provides professional understanding and help for the social ministry of the church; and promotes social welfare services and policies in society that bring about greater justice and meet basic human needs.

★11757★ Working with Children

Cambridge Educational
PO Box 2053
Princeton, NJ 08543-2053
Ph: 800-257-5126   Fax: (609)671-0266
Fr: 800-468-4227
E-mail: custserv@films.com
URL: http://www.cambridgeeducational.com

VHS and DVD. $89.95. 2000. 24 minutes. This program examines alternative positions offering the opportunity to work with children of different ages and the qualifications necessary for those jobs. A nanny, social worker, non-faculty school worker, and retail salesperson describe their job responsibilities and explain why they find their work so enjoyable.

Sociologists

Sociologists

SOURCES OF HELP-WANTED ADS

★11758★ American Studies Association Newsletter

American Studies Association
1120 19th St. NW, Ste. 301
Washington, DC 20036
Ph: (202)467-4783   Fax: (202)467-4786
E-mail: asastaff@theasa.net
URL: http://www.theasa.net/

Description: Quarterly. Promotes the inter-disciplinary study of American culture. Presents news of research, publications, and conferences. Also includes information on grants, employment opportunities, and Association activities.

★11759★ Child and Adolescent Social Work Journal

Springer-Verlag New York Inc.
233 Spring St.
New York, NY 10013
Ph: (212)460-1500   Fax: (212)460-1575
URL: http://www.springer.com/sgw/cda/frontpage/0,11855,5-0-70-355

Journal dealing with issues in clinical social work practice with children, adolescents, and their families.

★11760★ Children & Society

John Wiley & Sons Inc.
111 River St.
Hoboken, NJ 07030-5774
Ph: (201)748-6000   Fax: (201)748-6088
Fr: 800-825-7550
E-mail: children&society@ncb.org.uk
URL: http://www3.interscience.wiley.com/cgi-bin/jhome/4805

$655.00/year for institutions, print and on-line; $566.00/year for institutions, online only; $194.00/year for individuals, print and online. Journal focusing on children and services for children.

★11761★ The Gerontologist

Gerontological Society of America
1030 15th St. NW, Ste. 250
Washington, DC 20005
Ph: (202)842-1275   Fax: (202)842-1150
E-mail: geron@geron.org
URL: http://gerontologist.gerontologyjournals.org

Bimonthly. $258.00/year for institutions, print + online, domestic; $288.00/year for institutions, print + online, foreign airmail only; $237.00/year for institutions, online only. Multidisciplinary peer-reviewed journal presenting new concepts, clinical ideas, and applied research in gerontology. Includes book and audiovisual reviews.

★11762★ Human Nature

Transaction Publishers
Rutgers - The State University of New Jersey
35 Berrue Cir.
Piscataway, NJ 08854-8042
Ph: (732)445-2280   Fax: (732)445-3138
URL: http://www.transactionpub.com

Quarterly. $85.00/year for individuals, online only; $85.00/year for individuals, print only; $95.00/year for individuals, print & online only; $320.00/year for institutions, online only; $320.00/year for institutions, print only; $338.00/year for institutions, print & online only. Interdisciplinary journal covering the biological, social and environmental factors behind human behavior.

★11763★ Innovations

National Council on the Aging
1901 L St. NW 4th Fl.
Washington, DC 20024
Ph: (202)479-1200   Fax: (202)479-0735
Fr: 800-373-4906
E-mail: scott.parkin@ncoa.org
URL: http://www.ncoa.org

Quarterly. Free, to members; $225.00/year for nonmembers, for organizations; $50.00/year for nonmembers. Magazine exploring significant developments in the field of aging.

★11764★ International Sociology

Sage Publications Inc.
2455 Teller Rd.
Thousand Oaks, CA 91320
Ph: (805)499-0721   Fax: (805)499-8096
URL: http://www.sagepub.com/journalsprodeditboards.nav?prodid=jou

Bimonthly. $662.00/year for institutions, print & e-access; $695.00/year for institutions, print & all online; $596.00/year for institutions, e-access; $629.00/year for institutions, e-access & all online; $659.00/year for institutions, e-access thru 1999; $649.00/year for institutions, print only; $88.00/year for individuals, print only; $119.00 for institutions, single print; $19.00 for individuals, single print. Journal publishing studies on social organization, societal change, and comparative sociology.

★11765★ Journal of Applied Sociology

Society for Applied Sociology
712 Pray-Harrold, EMU
Ypsilanti, MI 48197
Ph: (734)487-0012   Fax: (734)487-7010

Annual. Journal covering current research and policy in applied sociology.

★11766★ SINET-Social Indicators Network News

SINET
Department of Sociology
Box 90088
Durham, NC 27708-0088
Ph: (919)660-5615   Fax: (919)660-5623
E-mail: kland@soc.duke.edu
URL: http://www.soc.duke.edu/resources/sinet/

Description: Quarterly. Features information on social indicators, quality of life, social reports, related policy initiatives, and methodological developments covering Asia, the Pacific, Europe, and the Americas. Includes book reviews.

PLACEMENT AND JOB REFERRAL SERVICES

★11767★ American Society of Criminology (ASC)
1314 Kinnear Rd., Ste. 212
Columbus, OH 43212-1156
Ph: (614)292-9207   Fax: (614)292-6767
E-mail: asc@osu.edu
URL: http://www.asc41.com

Description: Represents professional and academic criminologists, students of criminology in accredited universities, psychiatrists, psychologists, and sociologists. Develops criminology as a science and academic discipline. Aids in the construction of criminological curricula in accredited universities. Upgrades the practitioner in criminological fields (police, prisons, probation, parole, delinquency workers). Conducts research programs and sponsors three student paper competitions. Provides placement service at annual convention.

EMPLOYER DIRECTORIES AND NETWORKING LISTS

★11768★ American Sociological Association-Directory of Members
American Sociological Association
1307 New York Ave. NW, Ste. 700
Washington, DC 20005
Ph: (202)383-9005   Fax: (202)638-0882
URL: http://www.asanet.org

Latest edition 2003. Covers 12,000 sociologists, worldwide. Entries include: Member name, preferred mailing address, educational background, and section memberships. Only the 1990 issue is biographical; others are cited as American Sociological Association-Directory of Members. Arrangement: Alphabetical. Indexes: Geographical.

★11769★ Christian Association for Psychological Studies International-Membership Directory
Christian Association for Psychological Studies
PO Box 365
Batavia, IL 60510-0365
Ph: (630)639-9478   Fax: (630)454-3799

Annual, June. $12.00 for Canada; $12.00 for other countries. Covers 2,300 Christians involved in psychology, psychiatry, counseling, sociology, social work, ministry, and nursing. Entries include: Name, office address and phone number, highest degree held, area of occupational specialization, and career data. Arrangement: Geographical. Indexes: Alphabetical.

HANDBOOKS AND MANUALS

★11770★ 100 Jobs in Social Change
John Wiley & Sons Inc.
1 Wiley Dr.
Somerset, NJ 08873
Ph: (732)469-4400   Fax: (732)302-2300
Fr: 800-225-5945
E-mail: custserv@wiley.com
URL: http://www.wiley.com/WileyCDA/

Harley Jebens. 1996. $14.95. 216 pages. Part of the One Hundred Jobs Series.

★11771★ Careers for Caring People and Other Sensitive Types
The McGraw-Hill Companies
PO Box 182604
Columbus, OH 43272
Fax: (614)759-3749   Fr: 877-883-5524
E-mail: customer.service@mcgraw-hill.com
URL: http://www.mcgraw-hill.com

Adrian Paradis. Second edition, 2003. $13.95 (paper). 208 pages.

★11772★ Careers in Health Care
The McGraw-Hill Companies
PO Box 182604
Columbus, OH 43272
Fax: (614)759-3749   Fr: 877-883-5524
E-mail: customer.service@mcgraw-hill.com
URL: http://www.mcgraw-hill.com

Barbara M. Swanson. Fifth edition, 2005. $15.95 (paper). 192 pages. Describes job duties, work settings, salaries, licensing and certification requirements, educational preparation, and future outlook. Gives ideas on how to secure a job.

★11773★ Careers for Mystery Buffs and Other Snoops and Sleuths
The McGraw-Hill Companies
PO Box 182604
Columbus, OH 43272
Fax: (614)759-3749   Fr: 877-883-5524
E-mail: customer.service@mcgraw-hill.com
URL: http://www.mcgraw-hill.com

Blythe Camenson. Second edition, 2004. $12.95 (paper); $14.95 (cloth). 160 pages.

★11774★ Careers in Sociology
Pearson Allyn & Bacon
1 Lake St.
Upper Saddle River, NJ 07458
Ph: (201)236-7000   Fr: 800-922-0579
URL: http://www.pearsoned.com/higher-ed/

W. Richard Stephens. Second edition, 2003. $11.40 (paper). 46 pages.

★11775★ Doing Fieldwork in Japan
University of Hawaii Press
2840 Kolowalu St.
Honolulu, HI 96822-1888
Ph: (808)956-8255   Fax: (808)988-6052
E-mail: uhpbooks@hawaii.edu

URL: http://www.uhpress.hawaii.edu

Theodore C. Bestor, Patricia G. Steinhoff, and Victoria Lyon Bestor. 2003. $28.00. Illustrated. 428 pages. Exploring social sciences in Japan.

★11776★ Embarking upon a Career with an Undergraduate Sociology Major
American Sociological Association
1307 New York Ave. NW, Ste. 700
Washington, DC 20005-4701
Ph: (202)383-9005   Fax: (202)638-0882
E-mail: apap@asanet.org
URL: http://www.asanet.org

Janet Mancini Billson and Bettina J. Huber. 1999. $10.00; $6.00 (paper). 65 pages. Aimed at the new college graduate with a sociology major. Reviews job search strategies.

★11777★ Great Jobs for Sociology Majors
The McGraw-Hill Companies
PO Box 182604
Columbus, OH 43272
Fax: (614)759-3749   Fr: 877-883-5524
E-mail: customer.service@mcgraw-hill.com
URL: http://www.mcgraw-hill.com

Stephen Lambert. Second edition, 2002. $15.95 (paper). 224 pages.

★11778★ A Guide to Careers in Physical Anthropology
Greenwood Publishing Group Inc.
80 Post Rd. W
Westport, CT 06881
Ph: (203)266-3571   Fax: (203)222-1502
Fr: 800-225-5800
URL: http://www.greenwood.com/

Alan S. Ryan. 2001. $109.95. 328 pages.

★11779★ Opportunities in Gerontology and Aging Services Careers
The McGraw-Hill Companies
PO Box 182604
Columbus, OH 43272
Fax: (614)759-3749   Fr: 877-883-5524
E-mail: customer.service@mcgraw-hill.com
URL: http://www.mcgraw-hill.com

Ellen Williams. Second edition, 2002. $12.95 (paper). 160 pages. Covers jobs in community, health and medical programs, financial, legal, residential, travel and tourism, and counseling, and how to go after them. Includes bibliography and illustrations.

★11780★ Opportunities in Research and Development Careers
The McGraw-Hill Companies
PO Box 182604
Columbus, OH 43272
Fax: (614)759-3749   Fr: 877-883-5524
E-mail: customer.service@mcgraw-hill.com
URL: http://www.mcgraw-hill.com

Jan Goldberg. 1996. $11.95 (paper). 146 pages.

★11781★ *Opportunities in Social Science Careers*

The McGraw-Hill Companies
PO Box 182604
Columbus, OH 43272
Fax: (614)759-3749   Fr: 877-883-5524
E-mail: customer.service@mcgraw-hill.com
URL: http://www.mcgraw-hill.com

Rosanne J. Marek. 2004. $13.95. 160 Pages. VGM Opportunities Series.

TRADESHOWS

★11782★ American Association for State and Local History Annual Meeting

American Association for State and Local History
1717 Church St.
Nashville, TN 37203-2991
Ph: (615)320-3203   Fax: (615)327-9013
E-mail: membership@AASLH.org
URL: http://www.aaslh.org

Annual. **Primary Exhibits:** Products and services directed toward the museum and history field, including: publications, fund-raising devices, software, exhibit design, historic preservation, historic research and technical information.

★11783★ American Sociological Association Annual Meeting

American Sociological Association
1307 New York Ave. NW, Ste. 700
Washington, DC 20005-4701
Ph: (202)383-9005   Fax: (202)638-0882
E-mail: executive.office@asanet.org
URL: http://www.asanet.org

Annual. **Primary Exhibits:** Scholarly book publishers, statistical software supplies, government agencies, and information/data centers.

★11784★ Eastern Sociological Society Annual Meeting

Exhibit Promotions Plus
11620 Vixens Path
Ellicott City, MD 21042-1539
Ph: (410)997-0763   Fax: (410)997-0764
E-mail: exhibit@epponline.com
URL: http://www.epponline.com

Annual. **Primary Exhibits:** Publishers with titles in fields of sociology, anthropology, and psychology. **Dates and Locations:** 2009 Mar 12-15; Balitmore, MD; Sheraton Inner Harbor.

OTHER SOURCES

★11785★ American Academy of Political and Social Science (AAPSS)

3814 Walnut St.
Philadelphia, PA 19104-6197
Ph: (215)746-6500   Fax: (215)573-3003
E-mail: phyllis.kaniss@sas.upenn.edu
URL: http://www.aapss.org

Members: Professionals and laymen concerned with the political and social sciences and related fields. **Purpose:** Promotes the progress of political and social science through publications and meetings. The academy does not take sides in controversial issues, but seeks to gather and present reliable information to assist the public in forming an intelligent and accurate judgment.

★11786★ American Society of Psychopathology of Expression (ASPE)

74 Lawton St.
Brookline, MA 02446
Ph: (617)738-9821   Fax: (617)975-0411

Description: Psychiatrists, psychologists, art therapists, sociologists, art critics, artists, social workers, linguists, educators, criminologists, writers, and historians. At least two-thirds of the members must be physicians. Fosters collaboration among specialists in the United States who are interested in the problems of expression and in the artistic activities connected with psychiatric, sociological, and psychological research. Disseminates information about research and clinical applications in the field of psychopathology of expression. Sponsors consultations, seminars, and lectures on art therapy.

★11787★ American Sociological Association (ASA)

1307 New York Ave. NW, Ste. 700
Washington, DC 20005
Ph: (202)383-9005   Fax: (202)638-0882
E-mail: executive.office@asanet.org
URL: http://www.asanet.org

Description: Sociologists, social scientists, and others interested in research, teaching, and application of sociology; graduate and undergraduate sociology students. Compiles statistics. Operates the ASA Teaching Resources Center, which develops a variety of materials useful in teaching sociology. Sponsors Minority Fellowship and Professional Development Programs and Teaching Project. Maintains 44 sections including: Aging; Criminology; Medical; Population.

★11788★ Institute for the Study of Man (ISM)

1133 13th St. NW, Ste. C-2
Washington, DC 20005
Ph: (202)371-2700   Fax: (202)371-1523
E-mail: iejournal@aol.com
URL: http://www.jies.org

Description: Aims to publish books and journals in areas related to anthropology, historical linguistics, and the human sciences.

★11789★ Population Association of America (PAA)

8630 Fenton St., Ste. 722
Silver Spring, MD 20910-3812
Ph: (301)565-6710   Fax: (301)565-7850
E-mail: info@popassoc.org
URL: http://www.popassoc.org

Description: Professional society of individuals interested in demography and its scientific aspects.

★11790★ Rural Sociological Society (RSS)

University of Missouri
104 Gentry Hall
Columbia, MO 65211-7040
Ph: (573)882-9065   Fax: (573)882-1473
E-mail: ruralsoc@missouri.edu
URL: http://www.ruralsociology.org

Description: Educators and others employed in the field of rural sociology. Promotes the development of rural sociology through research, teaching, and extension work.

★11791★ Sociological Practice Association (SPA)

Social Research Corp.
PO Box 15
Wyncote, PA 19095
Ph: (215)576-8221   Fax: (215)576-8346
E-mail: rkoppel@sas.upenn.edu
URL: http://www.socpractice.org

Purpose: Promotes the application of sociology to individual and social change and advances theory, research, and methods to this end; develops opportunities for the employment and use of clinically trained sociologists; provides a common ground for sociological practitioners, allied professionals, and interested scholars and students. Promotes training and educational opportunities to further sociological practice. **Activities:** Sponsors sessions and programs in clinical and applied sociology at national and regional meetings of other sociological associations. Has conducted a survey on skills, licenses, education, and experience of members. Conducts national certification program.

★11792★ Sociological Research Association (SRA)

1307 New York Ave. NW, Ste. 700
Washington, DC 20005
Ph: (202)383-9005   Fax: (202)638-0882
URL: http://www.asanet.org

Description: Persons, elected from membership of the American Sociological Association, "who have made significant contributions to sociological research, other than a doctoral dissertation, and who maintain an active interest in the advancement of sociological knowledge".

★11793★ Sociologists for Women in Society (SWS)
University of Akron
Chafee Social Science Center
Kingston, RI 02881
Ph: (401)874-9510   Fax: (401)874-2588
E-mail: sws@etal.uri.edu
URL: http://www.socwomen.org

Description: Members are mainly national and international professional social scientists, sociologists and students of sociology, though membership is open to anyone interested in the purposes of the organization. Maximizes the effectiveness of and professional opportunities for women in sociology. Explores the contributions which sociology can, does, and should make to the investigation of and improvement in the status of women in society. Acts as watchdog of the American Sociological Association to ensure that it does not ignore the special needs of women in the profession; has organized a job market service to bring potential jobs and applicants together; established a discrimination committee offering advice and organizational support for women who pursue cases charging sex discrimination; has aided women to establish social, professional, and intellectual contacts with each other. Supports minority scholarships, breast cancer research and academic mentoring activities.

Software Engineers

★11805★ CXO

IDG Communications Inc.
5 Speen St., 3rd. Fl
Framingham, MA 01701
Ph: (508)875-5000   Fax: (508)988-7888
URL: http://www.idg.com

Monthly. Magazine providing technology information for chief officers and managers.

★11806★ E-Business Advisor

e-Business Advisor
PO Box 429002
San Diego, CA 92142
Ph: (858)278-5600   Fax: (858)278-0300
Fr: 800-336-6060
URL: http://www.e-businessadvisor.com

Magazine for developing strategies, practices, and innovations for e-business applications.

★11807★ Eclipse Review

BZ Media LLC
7 High St., Ste. 407
Huntington, NY 11743
Ph: (631)421-4158   Fax: (631)421-4130
URL: http://www.eclipsesource.com/contact.htm

Magazine for IT professionals.

★11808★ Electronic Markets

Taylor & Francis Group Journals
325 Chestnut St., Ste. 800
Philadelphia, PA 19106
Ph: (215)625-8900   Fax: (215)625-8914
Fr: 800-354-1420
URL: http://www.tandf.co.uk/journals/titles/10196781.asp

$683.00/year for institutions, print and online; $648.00/year for institutions, online only; $189.00/year for individuals. Journal covering all system concepts of electronic commerce.

★11809★ ENA powered by Network World

IDG Communications Inc.
5 Speen St., 3rd. Fl
Framingham, MA 01701
Ph: (508)875-5000   Fax: (508)988-7888
URL: http://www.idg.com

Monthly. Journal covering information on networking.

★11810★ Foundations of Computational Mathematics

Springer-Verlag New York Inc.
233 Spring St.
New York, NY 10013
Ph: (212)460-1500   Fax: (212)460-1575

Academic journal that publishes articles related to the connections between mathematics and computation, including the interfaces between pure and applied mathematics, numerical analysis and computer science.

★11811★ Foundations and Trends in Networking

Now Publishers
PO Box 1024
Hanover, MA 02339
Ph: (781)871-0245
URL: http://www.nowpublishers.com/product.aspx?product=NET

$315.00/year online only; $355.00/year print and online; $315.00/year online only; $355.00/year print and online. Academic journal publishing new research in computer networking.

★11812★ Government Computer News

PostNewsweek Tech Media
10 G St. NE, Ste. 500
Washington, DC 20002-4228
Ph: (202)772-2500   Fax: (202)772-2511
Fr: (866)447-6864

Semimonthly. Magazine for professionals interested in government IT.

★11813★ Graduating Engineer & Computer Careers

Career Recruitment Media
211 W Wacker Dr., Ste. 900
Chicago, IL 60606
Ph: (312)525-3100
URL: http://www.graduatingengineer.com

Quarterly. $15.00/year for individuals. Magazine focusing on employment, education, and career development for entry-level engineers and computer scientists.

★11814★ High Technology Careers Magazine

HTC
4701 Patrick Henry Dr., No. 1901
Santa Clara, CA 95054-1847
Fax: (408)567-0242
URL: http://www.hightechcareers.com

Bimonthly. $29.00/year; $35.00/year for Canada; $85.00/year for out of country. Magazine (tabloid) containing employment opportunity information for the engineering and technical community.

★11815★ IEEE Computer Graphics and Applications

IEEE Computer Society
10662 Los Vaqueros Cir.
PO Box 3014
Los Alamitos, CA 90720-1314
Ph: (714)821-8380   Fax: (714)821-4010
Fr: 800-272-6657
URL: http://www.computer.org/cga/

Bimonthly. $20.00/year for members; $116.00/year for nonmembers. Magazine addressing the interests and needs of professional designers and users of computer graphics hardware, software, and systems.

★11816★ IEEE Security & Privacy Magazine

IEEE Computer Society
10662 Los Vaqueros Cir.
PO Box 3014
Los Alamitos, CA 90720-1314
Ph: (714)821-8380   Fax: (714)821-4010
Fr: 800-272-6657
URL: http://www.computer.org/portal/site/security/

Bimonthly. $24.00/year for members; $29.00/year for nonmembers; $28.00/year for members; $565.00/year for libraries, institution. Journal that aims to explore role and importance of networked infrastructure and developing lasting security solutions.

★11817★ IEEE Software

IEEE Computer Society
10662 Los Vaqueros Cir.
PO Box 3014
Los Alamitos, CA 90720-1314
Ph: (714)821-8380   Fax: (714)821-4010
Fr: 800-272-6657
E-mail: software@computer.org
URL: http://www.computer.org/software

Bimonthly. $77.00/year for nonmembers, individual; $46.00/year for members, plus online access to software articles; $76.00/year for members; $765.00/year for institutions, library. Magazine covering the computer software industry for the community of leading software practitioners.

★11818★ Information Security

TechTarget
117 Kendrick St., Ste. 800
Needham, MA 02494
Ph: (781)657-1000   Fax: (781)657-1100
URL: http://searchsecurity.techtarget.com/

Monthly. Free to qualified subscribers. Magazine covering information security topics.

★11819★ Intelligent Enterprise

CMP Media L.L.C.
600 Community Dr.
Manhasset, NY 11030
Ph: (516)562-5000   Fax: (516)562-7830
E-mail: tgibb@cmp.com
URL: http://www.intelligententerprise.com

Periodic. Free. Magazine serving business and IT professionals.

★11820★ International Journal of Computer Games Technology

Hindawi Publishing Corp.
410 Park Ave., 15th Fl.
287 PMB
New York, NY 10022
E-mail: ijcgt@hindawi.com
URL: http://www.hindawi.com/journals/ijcgt

$195.00/year for individuals. Journal covering research and development aspects of games technology.

★11821★ International Journal of Software Engineering and Knowledge Engineering

World Scientific Publishing
27 Warren St., Ste. 401-402
Hackensack, NJ 07601
Ph: (201)487-9655   Fax: (201)487-9656
Fr: 800-227-7562
URL: http://www.wspc.com

Bimonthly. $768.00/year for institutions, electronic + print; $677.00/year for institutions, electronic + print; $730.00/year for institutions, electronic only; $643.00/year for individuals, electronic only; $272.00/year for individuals, print only; $240.00/year for individuals, print only. Journal focusing on the interplay between software engineering and knowledge engineering.

★11822★ IT Focus

IDG Communications Inc.
5 Speen St., 3rd. Fl
Framingham, MA 01701
Ph: (508)875-5000   Fax: (508)988-7888
URL: http://www.idg.com

Online journal focusing mainly on information technology.

★11823★ IT Solutions Guide

SYS-CON Media
135 Chestnut Ridge Rd.
Montvale, NJ 07645
Ph: (201)802-3000   Fax: (201)782-9600
Fr: 888-303-5282
URL: http://itsolutions.sys-con.com/

Quarterly. $4.00/year for individuals, single pdf issue. Magazine for IT professionals.

★11824★ Journal of Active and Passive Electronic Devices

Old City Publishing
628 N 2nds St.
Philadelphia, PA 19123
Ph: (215)925-4390   Fax: (215)925-4371
URL: http://www.oldcitypublishing.com/ JAPED/JAPED.html

Quarterly. $412.00/year for institutions; $122.00/year for individuals. International journal devoted to the science and technology of all types of electronic components.

★11825★ Journal of Computer Science

Science Publications
Vails Gate Heights Dr.
PO Box 879
Vails Gate, NY 12584
URL: http://www.scipub.us/

Bimonthly. $3,500.00/year for individuals; $300.00/year for single issue. Scholarly journal covering many areas of computer science, including: concurrent, parallel and distributed processing; artificial intelligence; image and voice processing; quality software and metrics; computer-aided education; wireless communication; real time processing; evaluative computation; and data bases and information recovery and neural networks.

★11826★ Journal of Computer Systems, Networks, and Communications

Hindawi Publishing Corp.
410 Park Ave., 15th Fl.
287 PMB
New York, NY 10022
E-mail: jcsnc@hindawi.com
URL: http://www.hindawi.com/journals/ jcsnc/

$195.00/year for individuals. Journal covering important areas of information technology.

★11827★ Journal of Software Maintenance

John Wiley & Sons Inc.
111 River St.
Hoboken, NJ 07030-5774
Ph: (201)748-6000   Fax: (201)748-6088
Fr: 800-825-7550
URL: http://www3.interscience.wiley.com/ cgi-bin/jhome/5391

Bimonthly. $1,575.00/year for other countries, print; $2,100.00/year for institutions, other countries, print; $2,310.00/year for institutions, other countries, print and online combined. Journal devoted to maintaining the viability of software through swift software evolution cycles.

★11828★ Kompiuterija PC World

IDG Communications Inc.
5 Speen St., 3rd. Fl
Framingham, MA 01701
Ph: (508)875-5000   Fax: (508)988-7888
URL: http://www.idg.com

Monthly. Journal providing professionals, business people and users with up-to-date information on computers and the internet.

★11829★ Mikro PC

IDG Communications Inc.
5 Speen St., 3rd. Fl
Framingham, MA 01701
Ph: (508)875-5000   Fax: (508)988-7888
URL: http://www.idg.com

Monthly. Magazine focusing on information technology and digital lifestyle.

★11830★ Monitor

Capital PC User Group
19209 Mt. Airey Rd.
Brookeville, MD 20833
Ph: (301)560-6442   Fax: (301)760-3303
URL: http://monitor.cpcug.org/index.html

Quarterly. Magazine covering computer hardware and software reviews, special interest user group news, advertisers and author/subject index, and calendar of events.

★11831★ NetWorld

IDG Communications Inc.
5 Speen St., 3rd. Fl
Framingham, MA 01701
Ph: (508)875-5000   Fax: (508)988-7888

URL: http://www.idg.com

Monthly. Magazine focusing on networks, security, infrastructure management, wireless, mobile and VOIP technologies.

★11832★ PC WORLD

101 Communications
9121 Oakdale Ave., Ste. 101
Chatsworth, CA 91311
Ph: (818)734-1520   Fax: (818)734-1522
URL: http://www.pcworld.com

Quarterly. $20.00/year for individuals, 12 issues; $30.00/year for individuals, 24 issues. Technology or business magazine meeting the informational needs of tech-savvy managers, both at work and at home.

★11833★ Queue

Association for Computing Machinery
2 Penn Plz., Ste. 701
New York, NY 10121-0701
Ph: (212)869-7440   Fax: (212)944-1318
Fr: 800-342-6626
URL: http://www.acmqueue.org/

Monthly. Free, U.S./Canadian residents and all members. Online magazine aimed at the computer professional. Magazine editorial does not provide solutions for the "here-and-now," but instead helps decision-makers plan future projects by examining the challenges and problems they are most likely to face.

★11834★ Revenue

Montgomery Media International
300 Montgomery St., Ste. 1135
San Francisco, CA 94104
Ph: (415)397-2400   Fax: (415)397-2420
URL: http://www.revenuetoday.com/

$30.00/year for individuals. Magazine covering internet marketing strategies.

★11835★ SMB Data

IDG Communications Inc.
5 Speen St., 3rd. Fl
Framingham, MA 01701
Ph: (508)875-5000   Fax: (508)988-7888
URL: http://www.idg.com

Magazine focusing on information technology systems at small and medium-size businesses.

★11836★ SME World

IDG Communications Inc.
5 Speen St., 3rd. Fl
Framingham, MA 01701
Ph: (508)875-5000   Fax: (508)988-7888
URL: http://www.idg.com

Magazine covering articles on technology, technology investments, IT products and services.

★11837★ Software

John Wiley & Sons Inc.
111 River St.
Hoboken, NJ 07030-5774
Ph: (201)748-6000   Fax: (201)748-6088
Fr: 800-825-7550
URL: http://as.wiley.com/WileyCDA/Wiley-Title/productCd-SPE.html

$2,750.00/year for other countries, print; $3,665.00/year for institutions, other countries, print; $4,032.00/year for institutions, other countries, print and online combined. Journal for those who design, implement, or maintain computer software.

★11838★ Software Process

John Wiley & Sons Inc.
111 River St.
Hoboken, NJ 07030-5774
Ph: (201)748-6000   Fax: (201)748-6088
Fr: 800-825-7550
URL: http://as.wiley.com/WileyCDA/Wiley-Title/productCd-SPIP.html

Bimonthly. $170.00/year for individuals, print, U.K.; $295.00/year for other countries, print, rest of world; $649.00/year for institutions, other countries, print, rest of world. Journal for those involved in the software development process. Features experience reports, research papers, and critical discussion.

★11839★ SWE, Magazine of the Society of Women Engineers

Society of Women Engineers
230 East Ohio St., Ste. 400
Chicago, IL 60611-3265
Ph: (312)596-5223
E-mail: hq@swe.org
URL: http://www.swe.org

Quarterly. $30.00/year for nonmembers. Magazine for engineering students and for women and men working in the engineering and technology fields. Covers career guidance, continuing development and topical issues.

★11840★ TecCHANNEL Compact

IDG Communications Inc.
5 Speen St., 3rd. Fl
Framingham, MA 01701
Ph: (508)875-5000   Fax: (508)988-7888
URL: http://www.idg.com

Quarterly. Magazine covering issues of information technology.

★11841★ Tips & Trucs

IDG Communications Inc.
5 Speen St., 3rd. Fl
Framingham, MA 01701
Ph: (508)875-5000   Fax: (508)988-7888
URL: http://www.idg.com

Monthly. Magazine covering topics on computer hardware, software and the internet.

★11842★ Top 100

IDG Communications Inc.
5 Speen St., 3rd. Fl
Framingham, MA 01701
Ph: (508)875-5000   Fax: (508)988-7888
URL: http://www.idg.com

Annual. Magazine providing analyses, assessments and statistics on information technology industry.

★11843★ Ubiquity

Association for Computing Machinery
2 Penn Plz., Ste. 701
New York, NY 10121-0701
Ph: (212)869-7440   Fax: (212)944-1318
Fr: 800-342-6626
URL: http://www.acm.org/ubiquity/

Weekly. Free to members; $163.00/year for nonmembers, 12 issues. Web-based magazine of the Association for Computing Machinery dedicated to fostering critical analysis and in-depth commentary, including book reviews, on issues relating to the nature, constitution, structure, science, engineering, cognition, technology, practices and paradigms of the IT profession.

★11844★ WebLogic Pro

Fawcette Technical Publications
2600 S El Camino Real, Ste. 300
San Mateo, CA 94403-2332
Ph: (650)378-7100   Fax: (650)570-6307
Fr: 800-848-5523
URL: http://www.weblogicpro.com

Bimonthly. Free to qualified subscribers. Magazine that aims to provides IT solutions for developers, architects, and administrators.

★11845★ WITI FastTrack

CMP Media L.L.C.
600 Community Dr.
Manhasset, NY 11030
Ph: (516)562-5000   Fax: (516)562-7830
URL: http://www.witi.com/corporate/fasttrack.php

Semiannual. Semiannual publication featuring in-depth content on the issues facing today's women professionals in technology.

★11846★ The World Wide Web Journal of Biology

Epress, Inc.
130 Union Terrace Ln.
Plymouth, MN 55441
URL: http://www.epress.com/w3jbio/

Journal on Bio-informatics.

PLACEMENT AND JOB REFERRAL SERVICES

★11847★ American Indian Science and Engineering Society (AISES)

PO Box 9828
Albuquerque, NM 87119-9828
Ph: (505)765-1052   Fax: (505)765-5608
E-mail: info@aises.org
URL: http://www.aises.org

Description: Represents American Indian and non-Indian students and professionals in science, technology, and engineering fields; corporations representing energy, mining, aerospace, electronic, and computer fields. Seeks to motivate and encourage students to pursue undergraduate and graduate studies in science, engineering, and technology. Sponsors science fairs in grade schools, teacher training workshops, summer math/science sessions for 8th-12th graders, professional chapters, and student chapters in colleges. Offers scholarships. Adult members serve as role models, advisers, and mentors for students. Operates placement service.

★11848★ Engineering Society of Detroit (ESD)

2000 Town Ctr., Ste. 2610
Southfield, MI 48075
Ph: (248)353-0735   Fax: (248)353-0736
E-mail: esd@esd.org
URL: http://esd.org

Description: Engineers from all disciplines; scientists and technologists. Conducts technical programs and engineering refresher courses; sponsors conferences and expositions. Maintains speakers' bureau; offers placement services; although based in Detroit, MI, society membership is international.

★11849★ Society of Hispanic Professional Engineers (SHPE)

5400 E Olympic Blvd., Ste. 210
Los Angeles, CA 90022
Ph: (323)725-3970   Fax: (323)725-0316
E-mail: shpenational@shpe.org
URL: http://oneshpe.shpe.org/wps/portal/national

Description: Represents engineers, student engineers, and scientists. Aims to increase the number of Hispanic engineers by providing motivation and support to students. Sponsors competitions and educational programs. Maintains placement service and speakers' bureau; compiles statistics.

EMPLOYER DIRECTORIES AND NETWORKING LISTS

★11850★ American Men and Women of Science

Gale, Cengage Learning
27500 Drake Rd.
Farmington Hills, MI 48331-3535
Ph: (248)699-4253   Fax: (248)699-8065
Fr: 800-877-4253
URL: http://www.gale.com

Biennial, latest edition 23rd, October 2006; new edition expected 24th, January 2008. $1,075.00 for individuals. Covers over 129,700 U.S. and Canadian scientists active in the physical, biological, mathematical, computer science, and engineering fields; includes references to previous edition for deceased scientists and nonrespondents. Entries include: Name, address, education, personal and career data, memberships, honors and awards, research interest. Arrangement: Alphabetical. Indexes: Discipline (in separate volume).

★11851★ Computer Directory

Computer Directories Inc.
23815 Nichols Sawmill Rd.
Hockley, TX 77447
Ph: (281)356-7880   Fr: 800-234-4353
URL: http://www.compdirinc.com

Annual, fall. Covers approximately 130,000 computer installation companies; 19 separate volumes for Alaska/Hawaii, Connecticut/New Jersey, Dallas/Ft. Worth, Eastern Seaboard, Far Midwest, Houston, Illinois, Midatlantic, Midcentral, Mideast, Minnesota/Wisconsin, North Central, New England, New York Metro, Northwest, Ohio, Pennsylvania/West Virginia, Southeast, and Southwest Texas. Entries include: Company name, address, phone, fax, e-mail, name and title of contact, hardware used, software application, operating system, programming language, computer graphics, networking system. Arrangement: Geographical. Indexes: Alphabetical; industry; hardware.

★11852★ Directory of Contract Staffing Firms

C.E. Publications Inc.
PO Box 3006
Bothell, WA 98041-3006
Ph: (425)806-5200   Fax: (425)806-5585
URL: http://www.cjhunter.com/dcsf/overview.html

Covers nearly 1,300 contract firms actively engaged in the employment of engineering, IT/IS, and technical personnel for 'temporary' contract assignments throughout the world. Entries include: Company name, address, phone, name of contact, email, web address. Arrangement: Alphabetical. Indexes: Geographical.

★11853★ Discovering Careers for Your Future: Computers

Facts On File Inc.
132 W 31st St., 17th Fl.
New York, NY 10001
Ph: (212)967-8800   Fax: 800-678-3633
Fr: 800-322-8755
URL: http://www.factsonfile.com

Published 2001. $21.95 for individuals; $19.75 for libraries. Covers computer operators, programmers, database specialists, and software engineers; links career education to curriculum, helping children investigate the subjects they are interested in, and the careers those subjects might lead to.

★11854★ GIS Markets and Opportunities

Daratech Inc.
255 Bent St.
Cambridge, MA 02141-2001
Ph: (617)354-2339   Fax: (617)354-7822
URL: http://www.daratech.com

$5,950.00 for individuals. Covers over 310 geographic information system software vendors and products. Entries include: Company name, address, phone, names and titles of key personnel, number of employees, geographical area served, financial data, subsidiary and branch names and locations, description of software. Arrangement: Alphabetical. Indexes: Alphabetical by name and product.

★11855★ Indiana Society of Professional Engineers-Directory

Indiana Society of Professional Engineers
PO Box 20806
Indianapolis, IN 46220
Ph: (317)255-2267   Fax: (317)255-2530
URL: http://www.indspe.org

Annual, fall. Covers member registered engineers, land surveyors, engineering students, and engineers in training. Entries include: Member name, address, phone, type of membership, business information, specialty. Arrangement: Alphabetical by chapter area.

★11856★ Information Sources

Software & Information Industry Association
1090 Vermont Ave. NW, 6th Fl.
Washington, DC 20005-4095
Ph: (202)289-7442   Fax: (202)289-7097
Fr: 800-388-7478
URL: http://www.siia.net/

Continuous. Covers more than 800 companies involved in the creation, distribution, and use of information products, services, and technology. Entries are prepared by companies described. Entries include: Company name, address, phone, names of executives, international partners, regional offices, trade and brand names, and description of products and services. Arrangement: Alphabetical. Indexes: Product; personal name; trade name; geographical; corporate parents; international and niche markets.

★11857★ The Software Encyclopedia

R.R. Bowker L.L.C.
630 Central Ave.
New Providence, NJ 07974
Ph: (908)286-1090   Fr: 888-269-5372
URL: http://www.bowker.com/catalog/000103.htm

Annual; latest edition May 2007. $440.00 for individuals. Contains listings of over 44,600 software programs from 4,646 publishers and distributors. Arrangement: Two alphabetical sections for software, one by title, the other by system/application; also, one alphabetical section for publishers. Indexes: Title, system/application.

★11858★ Software Engineering Bibliography

Data & Analysis Center for Software
775 Daedalian Dr.
Rome, NY 13441-4909
Ph: (315)334-4905   Fax: (315)334-4964
Fr: 800-214-7921
URL: http://www.dacs.dtic.mil/

Annual. Database covers: Citations for over 100,000 technical reports, articles, theses, papers, and books concerned with software technology. Entries include: Title, author name, publisher name and address, number of pages, other bibliographic information, and abstract. Arrangement: By document accession number.

HANDBOOKS AND MANUALS

★11859★ Career Guide for the High-Tech Professional: Where the Jobs Are Now and How to Land Them

Career Press, Inc.
3 Tice Rd.
PO Box 687
Franklin Lakes, NJ 07417
Ph: (201)848-0310   Fax: (201)848-1727
Fr: 800-227-3371
URL: http://www.careerpress.com

David Perry. May 2004. $16.99 (paper). Illustrated. 216 pages.

★11860★ Career Insights: CEO's and CTO's from BEA, BMC, Peoplesoft and More on Achieving Personal and Professional Success

Aspatore Books, Incorporated
400 Commonwealth Ave., 2nd Fl.
Boston, MA 02115
Ph: (617)249-1960   Fax: (617)249-1970
Fr: (866)277-2863
URL: http://www.aspatore.com/

Aspatore Books. April 2004. $19.95 (paper). 120 pages.

★11861★ Career Opportunities in Computers and Cyberspace

Facts On File Inc.
132 W. 31st St., 17th Fl.
New York, NY 10001-2006
Ph: (212)967-8800   Fax: 800-678-3633
Fr: 800-322-8755
E-mail: custserv@factsonfile.com
URL: http://www.factsonfile.com

Harry Henderson. Second edition, 2004. $18.95 (paper). Part of the Career Opportunities Series. 256 pages.

★11862★ Careers for Computer Buffs and Other Technological Types

The McGraw-Hill Companies
PO Box 182604
Columbus, OH 43272
Fax: (614)759-3749   Fr: 877-883-5524
E-mail: customer.service@mcgraw-hill.com
URL: http://www.mcgraw-hill.com

Marjorie Eberts and Margaret Gisler. Third edition, 2006. $13.95 (paper). 160 pages. Suggested jobs in a wide range of settings, from the office to the outdoors.

★11863★ Careers in Computers

The McGraw-Hill Companies
PO Box 182604
Columbus, OH 43272
Fax: (614)759-3749   Fr: 877-883-5524
E-mail: customer.service@mcgraw-hill.com
URL: http://www.mcgraw-hill.com

Lila B. Stair and Leslie Stair. 2002. $19.95; $14.95 (paper). 192 pages. Describes trends affecting computer careers and explores a wide range of job opportunities from programming to consulting. Provides job qualifications, salary data, job market information, personal and educational requirements, career paths, and the place of the job in the organizational structure. Offers advice on education, certification, and job search.

★11864★ Careers in High Tech

The McGraw-Hill Companies
PO Box 182604
Columbus, OH 43272
Fax: (614)759-3749   Fr: 877-883-5524
E-mail: customer.service@mcgraw-hill.com
URL: http://www.mcgraw-hill.com

Nick Basta. Second edition, 1998. $17.95 (paper). 98 pages. Examines new career opportunities in such fields as biotechnology, computers, aerospace, telecommunications, and others.

★11865★ Careers Inside the World of Technology

Pearson Learning Group
135 S. Mt. Zion Rd.
PO Box 2500
Lebanon, IN 46052
Fax: 800-393-3156   Fr: 800-526-9907
URL: http://www.pearsonatschool.com

Jean W. Spencer. Revised edition, 2000. $13.50. 64 pages. Describes computer-related careers for reluctant readers.

★11866★ Careers for Number Crunchers and Other Quantitative Types

The McGraw-Hill Companies
PO Box 182604
Columbus, OH 43272
Fax: (614)759-3749   Fr: 877-883-5524
E-mail: customer.service@mcgraw-hill.com
URL: http://www.mcgraw-hill.com

Rebecca Burnett. Second edition, 2002. $22.95 (paper). 192 pages. Provides information to math-oriented job hunters on how to become statisticians, field researchers, computer programmers, stock analysts, investment managers, bankers, engineers, accountants, underwriters, economists, market analysts, mathematicians, systems analysts, and more.

★11867★ The Digital Frontier Job & Opportunity Finder

Moon Lake Media
PO Box 251466
Los Angeles, CA 90025
Ph: (310)535-2453

Don B. Altman. 1996. $19.95 (paper). 245 pages.

★11868★ Expert Resumes for Computer and Web Jobs

Jist Publishing
875 Montreal Way
St. Paul, MN 55102
Fr: 800-648-5478
E-mail: info@jist.com
URL: http://www.jist.com

Wendy Enelow and Louis Kursmark. Second edition, 2005. $16.95 (paper). 286 pages.

★11869★ Get Your IT Career in Gear!

The McGraw-Hill Companies
PO Box 182604
Columbus, OH 43272
Fax: (614)759-3749   Fr: 877-883-5524
E-mail: customer.service@mcgraw-hill.com
URL: http://www.mcgraw-hill.com

Leslie Goff. 2001. $24.99 (paper). 401 pages.

★11870★ Great Jobs for Computer Science Majors

The McGraw-Hill Companies
PO Box 182604
Columbus, OH 43272
Fax: (614)759-3749   Fr: 877-883-5524
E-mail: customer.service@mcgraw-hill.com
URL: http://www.mcgraw-hill.com

Jan Goldberg, Stephen Lambert, Julie De-Galan. Second edition, 2002. $14.95 (paper). 224 pages.

★11871★ Hidden Job Market

Peterson's Guides
2000 Lenox Dr.
Box 67005
Lawrenceville, NJ 08648
Ph: (609)896-1800   Fax: (609)896-4531
Fr: 800-338-3282
E-mail: custsvc@petersons.com
URL: http://www.petersons.com

Ninth edition, 1999. $18.95 (paper). 319 pages. Guide to 2,000 fast-growing companies that are hiring now. Focuses on high technology companies in such fields as environmental consulting, genetic engineering, home health care, telecommunications, alternative energy systems, and others. Part of Peterson's Hidden Job Market series.

★11872★ Job Seekers Guide to Silicon Valley Recruiters

John Wily and Sons, Inc.
605 Third Ave., 4th Fl.
New York, NY 10158-0012
Ph: (212)850-6276   Fax: (212)850-8641

Christopher W. Hunt, Scott A. Scanlon. First edition, 1998. $19.95 (paper). 371 pages. Includes a list of 2,400 recruiters specializing in high technology positions and explains how to work with them.

★11873★ The JobBank Guide to Computer and High-Tech Companies

Adams Media Corp.
57 Littlefield St.
Avon, MA 02322
Ph: (508)427-7100   Fax: (508)427-6790
Fr: 800-872-5627
URL: http://www.adamsmedia.com

Steven Graber, Marcie Dipietro, and Michelle Roy Kelly. Second edition, 1999. $17.95 (paper). 700 pages. Contains profiles of more than 4,500 high-tech employers.

★11874★ Opportunities in Engineering Careers

The McGraw-Hill Companies
PO Box 182604
Columbus, OH 43272
Fax: (614)759-3749   Fr: 877-883-5524
E-mail: customer.service@mcgraw-hill.com
URL: http://www.mcgraw-hill.com

Nicholas Basta. Revised second edition, 2002. $13.95; $11.95 (paper). 160 pages. Outlines typical job titles, salaries, career paths, and employment prospects.

★11875★ Opportunities in High Tech Careers

The McGraw-Hill Companies
PO Box 182604
Columbus, OH 43272
Fax: (614)759-3749   Fr: 877-883-5524
E-mail: customer.service@mcgraw-hill.com
URL: http://www.mcgraw-hill.com

Gary Colter and Deborah Yanuck. 1999. $14.95; $11.95 (paper). 160 pages. Explores high technology careers. Describes job opportunities, how to make a career decision,

how to prepare for high technology jobs, job hunting techniques, and future trends.

★11876★ *Peterson's Job Opportunities in Engineering and Technology*

Peterson's Guides
2000 Lenox Dr.
Box 67005
Lawrenceville, NJ 08648
Ph: (609)896-1800   Fax: (609)896-4531
Fr: 800-338-3282
E-mail: custsvc@petersons.com
URL: http://www.petersons.com

Compiled by the Peterson's staff. Fourth edition, 1996. $21.95 (paper). 379 pages. Profiles 2,000 high-tech companies looking primarily for technical personnel in such fields as biotechnology, telecommunications, software, computers and peripherals, defense, and aerospace. Contains job-search strategies and career options to help match education and expertise to the job market. Indexed geographically, by industry, and by hiring needs.

★11877★ *Preparing for an Outstanding Career in Computers: Questions and Answers for Professionals and Students*

Rafi Systems, Incorporated
750 N. Diamond Bar Blvd., Ste. 224
Diamond Bar, CA 91765
Ph: (909)593-8124   Fax: (909)629-1034
Fr: 800-584-6706
E-mail: rafisystems@rafisystems.com
URL: http://www.rafisystems.com/

Mohamed Rafiquzzaman. 2001. $19.95. 204 pages. Book contains over 300 questions and answers on various important aspects of computers. Topics include basic and state-of-the-art concepts from digital logic to the design of a complete microcomputer.

★11878★ *Resumes for Scientific and Technical Careers*

The McGraw-Hill Companies
PO Box 182604
Columbus, OH 43272
Fax: (614)759-3749   Fr: 877-883-5524
E-mail: customer.service@mcgraw-hill.com
URL: http://www.mcgraw-hill.com

Third edition, 2007. $12.95 (paper). 144 pages. Provides resume advice for individuals interested in working in scientific and technical careers. Includes sample resumes and cover letters.

★11879★ *Unlocking the Clubhouse: Women in Computing*

MIT Press
55 Hayward St.
Cambridge, MA 02142-1493
Ph: (617)253-5646   Fax: (617)258-6779
Fr: 800-405-1619
URL: http://mitpress.mit.edu/main/home/default.asp

Jane Margolis and Allan Fisher. 2003. $15.00. 182 pages.

★11880★ *The Unofficial Guide to Getting a Job at Microsoft*

The McGraw-Hill Companies
PO Box 182604
Columbus, OH 43272
Fax: (614)759-3749   Fr: 877-883-5524
E-mail: customer.service@mcgraw-hill.com
URL: http://www.mcgraw-hill.com

Rebecca Smith. 2000. $16.95 (paper). 192 pages.

★11881★ *Winning Resumes for Computer Personnel*

Barron's Educational Series, Inc.
250 Wireless Blvd.
Hauppauge, NY 11788-3917
Ph: (631)434-3311   Fax: (631)434-3723
Fr: 800-645-3476
E-mail: fbrown@barronseduc.com
URL: http://barronseduc.com

Anne Hart. Second edition, 1998. $14.95 (paper). 260 pages.

EMPLOYMENT AGENCIES AND SEARCH FIRMS

★11882★ **Amtec Engineering Corp.**

2749 Saturn St.
Brea, CA 92821
Ph: (714)993-1900   Fax: (714)993-2419
E-mail: info@amtechc.com
URL: http://www.amtec-eng.com

Employment agency.

★11883★ **The Arcus Group Inc.**

5001 LBJ Freeway, Ste. 875
Dallas, TX 75244
Ph: (214)294-0516   Fax: (214)871-1338
URL: http://www.arcusgroup.com

Executive search firm. Branch in Chicago.

★11884★ **Ashton Computer Professionals Inc.**

15 Chesterfield Pl., Unit C
North Vancouver, BC, Canada V6E 3V7
Ph: (604)904-0304   Fax: (604)904-0305
E-mail: acp@axionet.com
URL: http://www.acprecruit.com

Provides personnel recruitment and temporary contract services, specializing in advanced computer technology based fields, i.e., management information services, software engineering, product manufacturing, telecommunications, management personnel in all technology based disciplines. Serves private industries as well as government agencies.

★11885★ **Career Development Services**

150 State St.
Rochester, NY 14614
Ph: (585)244-0765   Fax: (585)244-7115
Fr: 800-736-6710
E-mail: info@careerdev.org
URL: http://www.careerdev.org

Employment agency.

★11886★ **Carol Maden Group**

2019 Cunningham Dr., Ste. 218
Hampton, VA 23666-3316
Ph: (757)827-9010   Fax: (757)827-9081
E-mail: cmaden@hroads.net

Personnel consultants offering placement service in computer technology and engineering; servicing manufacturing and private industries nationwide. Temporary placement servicing clerical and light industrial.

★11887★ **The Datafinders Group, Inc.**

25 E. Spring Valley Ave.
Maywood, NJ 07607
Ph: (201)845-7700   Fax: (201)845-7365
E-mail: info@datafinders.net
URL: http://www.datafinders.net

Executive search firm.

★11888★ **Erspamer Associates**

4010 W. 65th St., Ste. 100
Edina, MN 55435
Ph: (952)925-3747   Fax: (952)925-4022
E-mail: hdhuntrel@aol.com

Executive search firm specializing in technical management.

★11889★ **George Houchens Associates**

11356 Tall Shadows Ct.
Pinckney, MI 48169-8471
Ph: (734)649-9250   Fax: (734)665-4961
E-mail: houchens@techie.com
URL: http://www.houchens.com

Specializes in recruiting top quality executive, technical, and sales/marketing professionals for permanent positions in the computer, electronics, biomedical, and other high technology industries. Positions handled include: computer product engineering, (software and hardware), management information systems, office automation and related systems, computer networking and communications, Wireless/RF/Mobile, computer aided engineering, expert systems, quality assurance, CIM/CAM, industrial control, robotics, image processing, motion control, automated inspection, material handling, and other related specialties. served: Primarily Midwest.

★11890★ **Global Employment Solutions**

10375 Park Meadows Dr., Ste. 375
Littleton, CO 80124
Ph: (303)216-9500   Fax: (303)216-9533
E-mail: careers@global
URL: http://www.gesnetwork.com

Employment agency.

★11891★ Houser Martin Morris
110th Ave. NE, 110 Atrium Pl., Ste. 580
110 Atrium Pl.
Bellevue, WA 98004
Ph: (425)453-2700   Fax: (425)453-8726
E-mail: info@houser.com
URL: http://www.houser.com

Focus is in the areas of retained executive search, professional and technical recruiting. Areas of specialization include software engineering, sales and marketing, information technology, legal, human resources, accounting and finance, manufacturing, factory automation, and engineering.

★11892★ Huntington Personnel Consultants, Inc.
PO Box 1077
Huntington, NY 11743-0640
Ph: (516)549-8888

Executive search firm and employment agency.

★11893★ JES Search Firm Inc.
1021 Stovall Blvd., Ste. 600
950 E Paces Ferry Rd., Ste. 2245
Atlanta, GA 30319
Ph: (404)812-0622   Fax: (404)812-1910
E-mail: bde1@jessearch.com
URL: http://www.jessearch.com

Contract and permanent information technology search firm specializing in placing software developers as well as other information systems professionals.

★11894★ JPM International
26034 Acero
Mission Viejo, CA 92691
Ph: (949)699-4300   Fax: (949)699-4333
Fr: 800-685-7856
E-mail: trish@jpmintl.com
URL: http://www.jpmintl.com

Executive search firm and employment agency.

★11895★ Louis Rudzinsky Associates Inc.
394 Lowell St., Ste. 17
PO Box 640
Lexington, MA 02420
Ph: (781)862-6727   Fax: (781)862-6868
E-mail: lra@lra.com
URL: http://www.lra.com

Provides recruitment, placement, and executive search to industry (software, electronics, optics) covering positions in general management, manufacturing, engineering, and marketing. Personnel consulting activities include counsel to small and startup companies. Industries served: electronics, aerospace, optical, laser, computer, software, imaging, electro-optics, biotechnology, advanced materials, and solid-state/semiconductor.

★11896★ M.I.S. Consultants
55 Eglinton Ave. E, Ste. 701
Toronto, ON, Canada M4P 1G8
Ph: (416)489-4334   Fax: (416)489-0918
Fr: 800-311-2828
E-mail: info@misconsultants.ca
URL: http://www.misconsultants.ca

Specializes in contracting, consulting and recruitment in the information technology industry. Main focus is in the mainframe, mini and PC market, which includes database, case tool technology development, client/server, object oriented programming, RDB's, 4thGLs and software/technical support.

★11897★ Resources Objective Inc.
33 Broad St.
Boston, MA 02109-4216
Ph: (617)523-7788   Fax: (617)523-7939

Offers executive outplacement and executive search services particularly in the high-technology areas-software/hardware engineering, marketing/sales; quality engineering; manufacturing/engineering support, and communications.

★11898★ Technical Talent Locators Ltd.
5570 Sterrett Pl., Ste. 208
Columbia, MD 21044
Ph: (410)740-0091
E-mail: steve@ttlgroup.com
URL: http://www.ttlgroup.com

Permanent employment agency working within the following fields: software and database engineering; computer, communication, and telecommunication system engineering; and other computer-related disciplines.

★11899★ Wallach Associates Inc.
7811 Montrose Rd., Ste. 505
Potomac, MD 20854
Ph: (301)340-0300   Fax: (301)340-8008
Fr: 800-296-2084
E-mail: jobs@wallach.org
URL: http://www.wallach.org

Specialists in recruitment of professional personnel, primarily in information technology and electronic systems and engineering, energy research and development, management consulting, operations research, computers, defense systems, and programmers. Specializes in Internet and software engineer for intelligence community.

ONLINE JOB SOURCES AND SERVICES

★11900★ Computerwork.com
Fr: 800-691-8413
E-mail: contactus@computerwork.com
URL: http://www.computerwork.com/

Description: Job search and resume submission service for professionals in information technology.

★11901★ Computerworld Careers
URL: http://www.computerworld.com/careertopics/careers

Description: Offers career opportunities for IT (information technology) professionals. Job seekers may search the jobs database, register at the site, and read about job surveys and employment trends. Employers may post jobs.

★11902★ Computing Research Association Job Announcements
1100 17th St., NW
Washington, DC 20036-4632
Ph: (202)234-2111   Fax: (202)667-1066
URL: http://www.cra.org/main/cra.jobs.html

Description: Contains dated links to national college and university computer technology positions.

★11903★ Dice.com
4101 NW Urbandale Dr.
Urbandale, IA 50322
Fax: (515)280-1452   Fr: 877-386-3323
URL: http://www.dice.com

Description: Job search database for computer consultants and high-tech professionals, listing thousands of high tech permanent contract and consulting jobs for programmers, software engineers, systems administrators, web developers, and hardware engineers. Also free career advice e-mail newsletter and job posting e-alerts.

★11904★ Guru.com
5001 Baum Blvd., Ste. 760
Pittsburgh, PA 15213
Ph: (412)687-1316   Fax: (412)687-4466
URL: http://www.guru.com

Description: Job board specializing in contract jobs for creative and information technology professionals. Also provides online incorporation and educational opportunities for independent contractors along with articles and advice.

★11905★ Ittalent.com
E-mail: ewsmith@ITtalent.com
URL: http://www.ittalent.com

Description: Job search and resume submission service for professionals in information technology.

★11906★ Jobs for Programmers
E-mail: prgjobs@jfpresources.com
URL: http://www.prgjobs.com

Description: Job board site for computer programmers that allows them to browse through thousands of programming jobs, even search for special jobs with sign-on bonuses, relocation funding, and 4-day work weeks. Resume posting is free.

★11907★ Softwarejobs.com

E-mail: info@softwarejobs.com
URL: http://www.softwarejobs.com

Description: Job search website for software programmers. Registrants can post their resume and search available positions, review career resources, and activate e-mail job alerts. Registration is free.

★11908★ ZDNet Tech Jobs

URL: http://www.zdnet.com/

Description: Site houses a listing of national employment opportunities for professionals in high tech fields. Also contains resume building tips and relocation resources.

OTHER SOURCES

★11909★ American Association of Engineering Societies (AAES)

1620 I St. NW, Ste. 210
Washington, DC 20006
Ph: (202)296-2237   Fax: (202)296-1151
Fr: 888-400-2237
E-mail: dbateson@aaes.org
URL: http://www.aaes.org

Description: Coordinates the efforts of the member societies in the provision of reliable and objective information to the general public concerning issues which affect the engineering profession and the field of engineering as a whole; collects, analyzes, documents, and disseminates data which will inform the general public of the relationship between engineering and the national welfare; provides a forum for the engineering societies to exchange and discuss their views on matters of common interest; and represents the U.S. engineering community abroad through representation in WFEO and UPADI.

★11910★ Association for Women in Computing (AWC)

41 Sutter St., Ste. 1006
San Francisco, CA 94104
Ph: (415)905-4663   Fax: (415)358-4667
E-mail: info@awc-hq.org
URL: http://www.awc-hq.org

Members: Individuals interested in promoting the education, professional development, and advancement of women in computing.

★11911★ Computer Occupations

Delphi Productions
3159 6th St.
Boulder, CO 80304
Ph: (303)443-2100   Fax: (303)443-4022
Fr: 888-443-2400
E-mail: support@delphivideo.com
URL: http://www.delphivideo.com

$95.00. 50 minutes. Part of the Careers for the 21st Century Video Library.

★11912★ Information Technology Occupations

Delphi Productions
3159 6th St.
Boulder, CO 80304
Ph: (303)443-2100   Fax: (303)443-4022
Fr: 888-443-2400
E-mail: support@delphivideo.com
URL: http://www.delphivideo.com

$95.00. 52 minutes. Part of the Emerging Careers Video Library.

★11913★ Information Technology Services

Cambridge Educational
PO Box 2053
Princeton, NJ 08543-2053
Ph: 800-257-5126   Fax: (609)671-0266
Fr: 800-468-4227
E-mail: custserv@films.com
URL: http://www.cambridgeeducational.com

VHS and DVD. $89.95. 2002. 19 minutes. Part of the Career Cluster Series.

★11914★ Internet-Related Occupations

Delphi Productions
3159 6th St.
Boulder, CO 80304
Ph: (303)443-2100   Fax: (303)443-4022
Fr: 888-443-2400
E-mail: support@delphivideo.com
URL: http://www.delphivideo.com

$95.00. 47 minutes. Part of the Emerging Careers Video Library.

★11915★ National Action Council for Minorities in Engineering (NACME)

440 Hamilton Ave., Ste. 302
White Plains, NY 10601-1813
Ph: (914)539-4010   Fax: (914)539-4032
E-mail: webmaster@nacme.org
URL: http://www.nacme.org

Description: Leads the national effort to increase access to careers in engineering and other science-based disciplines. Conducts research and public policy analysis, develops and operates national demonstration programs at precollege and university levels, and disseminates information through publications, conferences and electronic media. Serves as a privately funded source of scholarships for minority students in engineering.

★11916★ National Society of Professional Engineers (NSPE)

1420 King St.
Alexandria, VA 22314-2794
Ph: (703)684-2800   Fax: (703)836-4875
Fr: 888-285-6773
E-mail: memserv@nspe.org
URL: http://www.nspe.org

Description: Represents professional engineers and engineers-in-training in all fields registered in accordance with the laws of states or territories of the U.S. or provinces of Canada; qualified graduate engineers, student members, and registered land surveyors. Is concerned with social, professional, ethical, and economic considerations of engineering as a profession; encompasses programs in public relations, employment practices, ethical considerations, education, and career guidance. Monitors legislative and regulatory actions of interest to the engineering profession.

★11917★ *Resumes for High Tech Careers*

The McGraw-Hill Companies
PO Box 182604
Columbus, OH 43272
Fax: (614)759-3749   Fr: 877-883-5524
E-mail: customer.service@mcgraw-hill.com
URL: http://www.mcgraw-hill.com

Third edition, 2003. $10.95 (paper). 160 pages. Demonstrates how to tailor a resume that catches a high tech employer's attention. Part of "Resumes for ..." series.

★11918★ Society of Women Engineers (SWE)

230 E Ohio St., Ste. 400
Chicago, IL 60611-3265
Ph: (312)596-5223   Fax: (312)596-5252
Fr: 877-SWE-INFO
E-mail: hq@swe.org
URL: http://www.swe.org

Description: Educational and service organization representing both students and professional women in engineering and technical fields.

★11919★ Special Interest Group on Accessible Computing (SIGACCESS)

IBM T.J. Watson Research Center
19 Skyline Dr.
Hawthorne, NY 10532
Ph: (914)784-6603   Fax: (914)784-7279
E-mail: chair_sigaccess@acm.org
URL: http://www.sigaccess.org

Description: Promotes the professional interests of computing personnel with physical disabilities and the application of computing and information technology in solving relevant disability problems. Works to educate the public to support careers for the disabled.

★11920★ Women in Engineering

Her Own Words
PO Box 5264
Madison, WI 53705-0264
Ph: (608)271-7083   Fax: (608)271-0209
E-mail: herownword@aol.com
URL: http://www.herownwords.com/

Video. Jocelyn Riley. $95.00. 15 minutes. Resource guide also available for $45.00.

Special Education Teachers

SOURCES OF HELP-WANTED ADS

★11921★ About Campus

John Wiley & Sons Inc.
111 River St.
Hoboken, NJ 07030-5774
Ph: (201)748-6000   Fax: (201)748-6088
Fr: 800-825-7550
URL: http://www3.interscience.wiley.com/cgi-bin/jhome/86513696

Bimonthly. $60.00/year for individuals, for print; $60.00/year for Canada and Mexico, for print; $96.00/year for individuals, for print (rest of world); $159.00/year for institutions, for print; $219.00/year for institutions, Canada and Mexico, for print; $270.00/year for institutions, for print (rest of world); $175.00/year for institutions, for print and online; $235.00/year for institutions, Canada and Mexico, for print and online; $286.00/year for institutions, for print and online, (rest of world); $111.00/year for individuals, print only. Journal focused on the critical issues faced by both student affairs and academic affairs staff as they work on helping students learn.

★11922★ American Academic

American Federation of Teachers
555 New Jersey Ave. NW
Washington, DC 20001
Ph: (202)879-4400
URL: http://www.aft.org/pubs-reports/american_academic/index.htm

Higher education policy journal.

★11923★ Annals of Medicine

Taylor & Francis Group Journals
325 Chestnut St., Ste. 800
Philadelphia, PA 19106
Ph: (215)625-8900   Fax: (215)625-8914
Fr: 800-354-1420
URL: http://www.ingentaconnect.com

$418.00/year for institutions, print and online; $397.00/year for institutions, online only; $155.00/year for individuals. Journal covering health science and medical education.

★11924★ Assessment & Evaluation in Higher Education

Taylor & Francis Group Journals
325 Chestnut St., Ste. 800
Philadelphia, PA 19106
Ph: (215)625-8900   Fax: (215)625-8914
Fr: 800-354-1420
E-mail: aehe@bath.ac.uk
URL: http://www.tandf.co.uk/journals/titles/02602938.asp

Bimonthly. $1,982.00/year for institutions, print and online; $1,882.00/year for institutions, online only; $466.00/year for individuals. Journal focusing on publishing papers and reports on all aspects of assessment and evaluation within higher education.

★11925★ Brookings Papers on Education Policy

Brookings Institution Press
1775 Massachusetts Ave. NW
Washington, DC 20036-2188
Ph: (202)536-3600   Fax: (202)536-3623
Fr: 800-275-1447
URL: http://www.brookings.edu/press/journals.htm

$46.00/year for institutions; $35.00/year for individuals. Journal dealing with all aspects of American education.

★11926★ Communication Quarterly

MetaPress
PO Box 1943
Birmingham, AL 35201
Fr: 877-773-3833

Periodical focusing on research, criticism, communication theory, and excellence in teaching.

★11927★ Community College Journal of Research & Practice

Taylor & Francis Group Journals
325 Chestnut St., Ste. 800
Philadelphia, PA 19106
Ph: (215)625-8900   Fax: (215)625-8914
Fr: 800-354-1420
URL: http://www.tandf.co.uk/journals/titles/10668926.aspttp://www

Monthly. $778.00/year for institutions, print and online; $739.00/year for institutions, online only; $208.00/year for individuals. Journal focusing on exchange of ideas, research, and empirically tested educational innovations.

★11928★ E-Journal of Teaching and Learning in Diverse Settings

Southern University at Baton Rouge
PO Box 9942
Baton Rouge, LA 70813
Ph: (225)771-3184   Fax: (225)771-4400
URL: http://www.subr.edu/coeducation/ejournal

Online academic journal that publishes research and scholarly articles in the field of education and learning.

★11929★ Education and Training in Developmental Disabilities

Council for Exceptional Children
1110 N Glebe Rd., Ste. 300
Arlington, VA 22201-5704
Ph: (703)620-3660   Fax: (703)264-9494
Fr: 888-232-7733
E-mail: etdd@asu.edu

Quarterly. $60.00/year for individuals; $20.00 for single issue; $95.00/year for institutions; $105.00/year for institutions, other countries. Journal covering theory and research in education of individuals with mental retardation and/or developmental disabilities.

★11930★ Education & Treatment of Children

West Virginia University Press
44 Stansbury Hall
PO Box 6295
Morgantown, WV 26506
Ph: (304)293-8400   Fax: (304)293-6585
Fr: (866)988-7737
URL: http://
www.educationandtreatmentofchildren.net

Quarterly. $85.00/year for institutions; $45.00/year for individuals; $100.00/year for institutions, elsewhere; $60.00/year for individuals, elsewhere. Periodical featuring information concerning the development of services for children and youth. Includes reports written for educators and other child care and mental health providers focused on teaching, training, and treatment effectiveness.

★11931★ Educational Policy

Sage Publications Inc.
2455 Teller Rd.
Thousand Oaks, CA 91320
Ph: (805)499-0721   Fax: (805)499-8096
URL: http://www.sagepub.com/journalsProdDesc.nav?prodId=Journal20

Annual. $749.00/year for institutions, combined (print & e-access); $824.00/year for institutions, backfile lease, combined plus backfile; $674.00/year for institutions, e-access; $749.00/year for institutions, backfile lease, e-access plus backfile; $687.48/year for institutions, backfile puchase, e-access (content through 1999); $734.00/year for institutions, print only; $159.00/year for individuals, print only; $135.00 for institutions, single print; $34.00 for individuals, single print. Journal for educators, policy makers, administrators, researchers, teachers, and graduate students.

★11932★ Educational Research and Evaluation

Taylor & Francis Group Journals
325 Chestnut St., Ste. 800
Philadelphia, PA 19106
Ph: (215)625-8900   Fax: (215)625-8914
Fr: 800-354-1420
URL: http://www.tandf.co.uk/journals/titles/13803611.asp

Bimonthly. $616.00/year for institutions, print and online; $585.00/year for institutions, online only; $239.00/year for individuals. Journal on theory and practice.

★11933★ Environmental Education Research

Taylor & Francis Group Journals
325 Chestnut St., Ste. 800
Philadelphia, PA 19106
Ph: (215)625-8900   Fax: (215)625-8914
Fr: 800-354-1420
URL: http://www.tandf.co.uk/journals/titles/13504622.asp

Journal covering all aspects of environmental education.

★11934★ Essays in Education

University of South Carolina
471 University Pky.
Aiken, SC 29801
Ph: (803)648-6851   Fax: (803)641-3461
Fr: 888-969-8722
URL: http://www.usca.edu/essays/

Monthly. Journal covering issues that impact and influence education.

★11935★ Hematology

American Society of Hematology
1900 M St. NW, Ste. 200
Washington, DC 20036
Ph: (202)776-0544   Fax: (202)776-0545
URL: http://asheducation-book.hematologylibrary.org

Semiweekly. $60.00/year for members; $90.00/year for nonmembers. Journal providing continuing medical education for physicians.

★11936★ The International Electronic Journal of Health Education

American Alliance for Health, Physical Education, Recreation & Dance
1900 Association Dr.
Reston, VA 20191-1598
Ph: (703)476-3400   Fax: (703)476-9527
Fr: 800-213-7193
URL: http://www.aahperd.org/iejhe/template.cfm?template=about.htm

Annual. Free to health education professionals and students. Journal promoting health through education and other systematic strategies.

★11937★ International Journal of Early Years Education

Taylor & Francis Group Journals
325 Chestnut St., Ste. 800
Philadelphia, PA 19106
Ph: (215)625-8900   Fax: (215)625-8914
Fr: 800-354-1420
URL: http://www.tandf.co.uk/journals/titles/09669760.asp

$512.00/year for institutions, print and online; $486.00/year for institutions, online only; $184.00/year for individuals. Journal focusing on education world-wide.

★11938★ International Journal of Inclusive Education

Taylor & Francis Group Journals
325 Chestnut St., Ste. 800
Philadelphia, PA 19106
Ph: (215)625-8900   Fax: (215)625-8914
Fr: 800-354-1420
URL: http://www.tandf.co.uk/journals/titles/13603116.asp

Bimonthly. $320.00/year for individuals, print only; $616.00/year for institutions, online only; $649.00/year for individuals, print and online; $193.00/year for individuals, print only; $376.00/year for institutions, online only; $396.00/year for institutions, print and online. Journal providing information on the nature of schools, universities and technical

colleges for the educators and educational policy-makers.

★11939★ International Journal of Leadership in Education

Taylor & Francis Group Journals
325 Chestnut St., Ste. 800
Philadelphia, PA 19106
Ph: (215)625-8900   Fax: (215)625-8914
Fr: 800-354-1420
E-mail: ijle@txstate.edu
URL: http://www.tandf.co.uk/journals/tf/13603124.html

Quarterly. $196.00/year for individuals; $536.00/year for institutions, print and online; $509.00/year for institutions, online only; Journal dealing with leadership in education.

★11940★ International Journal of Progressive Education

International Journal of Progressive Education
c/o Mustafa Yunus Eryaman, Mng. Ed.
2108 S Orchard St., No. D
Urbana, IL 61801
URL: http://www.inased.org/ijpe.htm

$35.00/year for members; $45.00/year for individuals; $140.00/year for institutions, library; $35.00/year for students; $25.00/year for single issue, U.S. Peer reviewed online journal that aims to create an open and continuing dialogue about current educational issues and future conceptions of educational theory.

★11941★ International Journal of Research & Method in Education

Taylor & Francis Group Journals
325 Chestnut St., Ste. 800
Philadelphia, PA 19106
Ph: (215)625-8900   Fax: (215)625-8914
Fr: 800-354-1420
URL: http://www.tandf.co.uk/journals/titles/1743727x.asp

$1809.00/year for institutions, print and online; $1718.00/year for institutions, online only; $271.00/year for individuals. Professional journal to further international discourse in education with particular focus on method.

★11942★ International Journal of Whole Schooling

Whole Schooling Press
Wayne State University
217 Education
Detroit, MI 48202
URL: http://www.wholeschooling.net/Journal_of_Whole_Schooling/IJW

Free to qualified subscribers. International, refereed academic journal dedicated to exploring ways to improve learning and schooling for all children.

★11943★ Journal of Academic Leadership

Academic Leadership
600 Park St.
Rarick Hall 219
Hays, KS 67601-4099
Ph: (785)628-4547
URL: http://www.academicleadership.org/

Journal focusing on the leadership issues in the academic world.

★11944★ Journal of Cases in Educational Leadership

Sage Publications Inc.
2455 Teller Rd.
Thousand Oaks, CA 91320
Ph: (805)499-0721   Fax: (805)499-8096
URL: http://www.sagepub.com/journalsProdDesc.nav?prodId=Journal20

Quarterly. $319.00/year for institutions, e-access; $83.00/year for individuals, e-access. Journal covering cases appropriate for use in programs that prepare educational leaders.

★11945★ Journal of Curriculum and Supervision

Association for Supervision and Curriculum Development
1703 N Beauregard St.
Alexandria, VA 22311-1714
Ph: (703)578-9600   Fax: (703)575-5400
Fr: 800-933-2723
URL: http://www.ascd.org/portal/site/ascd/menuitem.0545410c9839aa

Scholarly journal focusing on curriculum and supervision.

★11946★ Journal of Direct Instruction

Association for Direct Instruction
PO Box 10252
Eugene, OR 97440
Ph: (541)485-1293   Fax: (541)683-7543
Fr: 800-995-2464
URL: http://www.adihome.org/phpshop/articles/articles.php?type=JD

Quarterly. Subscription included in membership. Journal covering education.

★11947★ Journal of Language, Identity, and Education

Lawrence Erlbaum Associates Inc.
10 Industrial Ave.
Mahwah, NJ 07430
Ph: (201)258-2200   Fax: (201)236-0072
Fr: 800-926-6579
E-mail: journals@erlbaum.com
URL: http://www.erlbaum.com

Quarterly. $50.00/year for U.S. and Canada, individual, online and print; $80.00/year for elsewhere, individual, online and print; $360.00/year for U.S. and Canada, institution, online and print; $390.00/year for elsewhere, institution, online and print; $290.00/year for U.S. and Canada, institution, online only; $290.00/year for elsewhere, institution, online only; $325.00/year for U.S. and Canada, institution, print only; $355.00/year for elsewhere, institution, print only. Scholarly, interdisciplinary journal covering issues in language, identity and education worldwide for academics, educators and policy specialists in a variety of disciplines, and others.

★11948★ Journal of Latinos and Education

Lawrence Erlbaum Associates Inc.
10 Industrial Ave.
Mahwah, NJ 07430
Ph: (201)258-2200   Fax: (201)236-0072
Fr: 800-926-6579
URL: http://www.erlbaum.com/

Quarterly. $50.00/year for individuals, online and print - U.S./Canada; $80.00/year for individuals, online and print - all other countries; $360.00/year for institutions, online and print - U.S./Canada; $390.00/year for institutions, online and print - all other countries; $290.00/year for institutions, online only - U.S./Canada; $290.00/year for institutions, online only - all other countries; $325.00/year for institutions, print only - U.S./Canada; $355.00/year for institutions, print only - all other countries. Scholarly, multidisciplinary journal covering educational issues that impact Latinos for researchers, teaching professionals, academics, scholars, institutions, and others.

★11949★ The Journal of Special Education

PRO-ED Inc.
8700 Shoal Creek Blvd.
PO Box 678370
Austin, TX 78757-6897
Ph: (512)451-3246   Fax: 800-397-7633
Fr: 800-897-3202
URL: http://www.proedinc.com

Quarterly. $48.00/year for individuals, North America; $128.00/year for institutions, North America; $78.00/year for individuals, other countries; $161.00/year for other countries, others country. Journal presents research findings in the field of special education.

★11950★ Journal of Special Education Leadership

Council of Administrators of Special Education
Fort Valley State University
1005 State University Dr.
Fort Valley, GA 31030
Ph: (478)825-7667   Fax: (478)825-7811
Fr: 800-585-1753
URL: http://www.casecec.org/archives.htm

Semiannual. Subscription included in membership. Journal covering programs and developments affecting the special education field.

★11951★ Journal of STEM Education

Auburn University
9088 Haley Ctr.
Auburn, AL 36849
Ph: (334)844-4000   Fax: (334)844-9027
URL: http://www.auburn.edu/research/litee/jstem/index.php

Semiannual. Journal for educators in Science, Technology, Engineering, and Mathematics (STEM) education.

★11952★ Leadership and Policy in Schools

Taylor & Francis Group Journals
325 Chestnut St., Ste. 800
Philadelphia, PA 19106
Ph: (215)625-8900   Fax: (215)625-8914
Fr: 800-354-1420
URL: http://www.tandf.co.uk/journals/titles/15700763.asp

Quarterly. $477.00/year for institutions, print and online; $453.00/year for institutions, online only; $227.00/year for individuals; $60.00/year for ICSEI members. Journal providing information about leadership and policy in primary and secondary education.

★11953★ Oxford Review of Education

Taylor & Francis Group Journals
325 Chestnut St., Ste. 800
Philadelphia, PA 19106
Ph: (215)625-8900   Fax: (215)625-8914
Fr: 800-354-1420
URL: http://www.tandf.co.uk/journals/titles/03054985.asp

$1,031.00/year for institutions, print and online; $979.00/year for institutions, online only; $396.00/year for individuals. Journal covering advance study of education.

★11954★ Remedial and Special Education (RASE)

PRO-ED Inc.
8700 Shoal Creek Blvd.
PO Box 678370
Austin, TX 78757-6897
Ph: (512)451-3246   Fax: 800-397-7633
Fr: 800-897-3202
URL: http://www.proedinc.com

Bimonthly. $45.00/year for individuals, North America; $140.00/year for institutions, North America; $81.00/year for individuals, other countries; $165.00/year for institutions, other countries. Journal interprets research and makes recommendations for practice in the fields of remedial and special education.

★11955★ Research Strategies

Elsevier Science Inc.
360 Park Ave. S
New York, NY 10010
Ph: (212)989-5800   Fax: (212)633-3990
URL: http://www.elsevier.com

Journal covering library literature and the educational mission of the library.

★11956★ School Effectiveness and School Improvement

Taylor & Francis Group Journals
325 Chestnut St., Ste. 800
Philadelphia, PA 19106
Ph: (215)625-8900   Fax: (215)625-8914
Fr: 800-354-1420
URL: http://www.tandf.co.uk/journals/titles/

09243453.asp

Quarterly. $305.00/year for institutions, print and online; $231.00/year for institutions, online only; $153.00/year for individuals, print only; $520.00/year for institutions, print and online; $494.00/year for institutions, online only; $255.00/year for individuals, print only. Journal focusing on educational progress of all students.

★11957★ **Teacher Education and Special Education**

Allen Press Inc.
810 E 10th St.
Lawrence, KS 66044
Ph: (785)843-1234   Fax: (785)843-1244
Fr: 800-627-0326
URL: http://www.tese.org/

Quarterly. $50.00/year for individuals; $96.00/year for libraries, other institutions. Journal covering personnel preparation in special education.

★11958★ **Teaching and Learning in Nursing**

Elsevier Science Inc.
360 Park Ave. S
New York, NY 10010
Ph: (212)989-5800   Fax: (212)633-3990
URL: http://www.elsevier.com

Quarterly. $119.00/year for institutions, U.S. $167.00/year for institutions, other countries; $75.00/year for individuals, U.S. $104.00/year for individuals, other countries. Journal devoted to associate degree nursing education and practice.

★11959★ **Theory and Research in Education**

Sage Publications Inc.
2455 Teller Rd.
Thousand Oaks, CA 91320
Ph: (805)499-0721   Fax: (805)499-8096
URL: http://tre.sagepub.com/

$459.00/year for institutions, print and online; $413.00/year for institutions, online only; $450.00/year for institutions, print only; $77.00/year for individuals, print only. Interdisciplinary journal covering normative and theoretical issues concerning education including multi-faceted philosophical analysis of moral, social, political and epistemological problems and issues arising from educational practice.

★11960★ **Uratie**

IDG Communications Inc.
5 Speen St., 3rd. Fl
Framingham, MA 01701
Ph: (508)875-5000   Fax: (508)988-7888
URL: http://www.idg.com

Magazine providing job offers for graduates, engineers and information technology professionals.

EMPLOYER DIRECTORIES AND NETWORKING LISTS

★11961★ **Career Ideas for Teens in Education and Training**

Facts On File Inc.
132 W 31st St., 17th Fl.
New York, NY 10001
Ph: (212)967-8800   Fax: 800-678-3633
Fr: 800-322-8755
URL: http://www.factsonfile.com

Published 2005. $40.00 for individuals; $36.00 for libraries. Covers a multitude of career possibilities based on a teenager's specific interests and skills and links his/her talents to a wide variety of actual professions.

★11962★ **Directory of Programs for Preparing Individuals for Careers in Special Education**

National Clearinghouse for Professions in Special Education
1110 N Glebe Rd., Ste. 300
Arlington, VA 22201-4795
Ph: (703)620-3660   Fax: (703)264-9494
Fr: (866)915-5000
URL: http://www.special-ed-careers.org

Irregular; latest edition 1999. $75.00 for nonmembers. Covers approximately 850 institutions with programs in teacher preparation and administration in special education. Entries include: Institution name, program, contact name, address, coded description of program. Arrangement: Geographical.

★11963★ **Vocational Special Needs Teacher Education Directory**

National Association of Vocational Education Special Needs Personnel
101 Ostermayer University Dr.
4000 University Dr.
McKeesport, PA 15132-9065
Ph: (412)675-9065

Triennial. Covers National Association of Vocational Education Special Needs Personnel information, including special needs educators by state.

HANDBOOKS AND MANUALS

★11964★ **Becoming a Teacher**

Pearson Allyn & Bacon
1 Lake St.
Upper Saddle River, NJ 07458
Ph: (201)236-7000   Fr: 800-922-0579
URL: http://www.pearsoned.com/higher-ed/

Gary Borich. 1995. $43.95 (paper). 152 pages. Part of The Falmer Press Teachers' Library Series No. 7.

★11965★ **Building Blocks for Working with Exceptional Children & Youth: A Primer**

Houghton Mifflin Company
222 Berkeley St.
Boston, MA 02116
Ph: (617)351-5000
URL: http://www.hmco.com

Nancy Hunt and Kathleen Marshall. 1999. $14.75. 7 pages.

★11966★ **The Exceptional Teacher's Handbook: The First-Year Special Education Teacher's Guide for Success**

Corwin Press, Incorporated
2455 Teller Rd.
Thousand Oaks, CA 91320-2218
Ph: (805)499-9734   Fax: 800-499-5323
Fr: 800-417-2466
URL: http://www.corwinpress.com/

Carla F. Shelton and Alice B. Pollingue. Second edition, 2004. $74.95 (paper). 240 pages.

★11967★ **Great Jobs for Liberal Arts Majors**

The McGraw-Hill Companies
PO Box 182604
Columbus, OH 43272
Fax: (614)759-3749   Fr: 877-883-5524
E-mail: customer.service@mcgraw-hill.com
URL: http://www.mcgraw-hill.com

Blythe Camenson. Second edition, 2001. $14.95 (paper). 256 pages.

★11968★ **How to Get the Teaching Position You Want: Teacher Candidate Guide**

Educational Enterprises
PO Box 1836
Spring Valley, CA 91979
Ph: (619)660-7720

Phyllis Murton. Second edition, revised, 1996. $19.95 (paper). 110 pages. This book provides a comprehensive guide for the teacher candidate's job search, as the format offers information that includes: interview questions most often asked in the teaching interview (grade-level and subject-matter specific); sample forms for applications, cover letters, and resumes that will impact principals and district personnel; strategies on preparing for the teaching interview; interview follow-up techniques; inside tips from a superintendent, a principal and a counselor.

★11969★ **The Inside Secrets of Finding a Teaching Job**

Jist Works
875 Montreal Way
St. Paul, MN 55102
Fr: 800-648-5478
E-mail: info@jist.com
URL: http://www.jist.com

Jack Warner, Clyde Bryan, and Diane Warner. Third edition, 2006. $12.95. 196 pages.

Tips from educators on finding an entry-level teaching position.

★11970★ Opportunities in Special Education Careers

The McGraw-Hill Companies
PO Box 182604
Columbus, OH 43272
Fax: (614)759-3749   Fr: 877-883-5524
E-mail: customer.service@mcgraw-hill.com
URL: http://www.mcgraw-hill.com

Robert Connelly. 1995. 148 pages. $14.95; $11.95 (paper).

★11971★ Opportunities in Teaching Careers

The McGraw-Hill Companies
PO Box 182604
Columbus, OH 43272
Fax: (614)759-3749   Fr: 877-883-5524
E-mail: customer.service@mcgraw-hill.com
URL: http://www.mcgraw-hill.com

Janet Fine. 2005. $13.95 (paper). 160 pages. Discusses licensing and accreditation programs, sources of placement information, job-seeking correspondence, selection procedures, and paths to advancement. Also covers professional associations, nontraditional teaching opportunities, and jobs abroad.

★11972★ Real People Working in Education

The McGraw-Hill Companies
PO Box 182604
Columbus, OH 43272
Fax: (614)759-3749   Fr: 877-883-5524
E-mail: customer.service@mcgraw-hill.com
URL: http://www.mcgraw-hill.com

Blythe Camenson, Jan Goldberg. 1997. $17.95; $12.95 (paper). 160 pages/ Interviews and profiles of working professionals capture a range of opportunities in this field.

★11973★ Survival Guide for the First-Year Special Education Teacher

Council for Exceptional Children
1920 Association Dr.
Reston, VA 20191-1589
Ph: (703)264-9455   Fax: (703)620-2521
Fr: 888-232-7733
URL: http://www.cec.sped.org/

Mary Kemper Cohen, Maureen Gale and Joyce M. Meyer. Revised edition, 1994. $21.95 (paper). 47 pages.

EMPLOYMENT AGENCIES AND SEARCH FIRMS

★11974★ Educational Placement Service

6510-A S. Academy Blvd.
Colorado Springs, CO 80906
Ph: (719)579-9911   Fax: (719)579-5050
E-mail: accounting@educatorjobs.com
URL: http://www.educatorjobs.com

Employment agency. Focuses on teaching, administrative, and education-related openings.

TRADESHOWS

★11975★ Learning Disabilities Association of America

Learning Disabilities Association of America
4156 Library Rd.
Pittsburgh, PA 15234-1349
Ph: (412)341-1515   Fax: (412)344-0224
E-mail: info@LDAAmerica.org
URL: http://www.ldanatl.org

Annual. **Primary Exhibits:** Schools, universities, publishers and summer camps. **Dates and Locations:** 2008 Feb 27 - Mar 01; Chicago, IL.

★11976★ Lifelong Learning for Adults with Special Learning Needs

National Association for Adults with Special Learning Needs
c/o Correctional Education Association
8182 Lark Brown Rd., Ste. 202
Elkridge, MD 21075-6332
Fax: (614)939-4150   Fr: 888-562-2756
URL: http://www.naasln.org

Annual. **Primary Exhibits:** Equipment, supplies, and services for educating adults with special learning needs.

OTHER SOURCES

★11977★ American Council on Rural Special Education (ACRES)

Montana Center on Disabilities/MSU-Billings
1500 University Dr.
Billings, MT 59101
Ph: (406)657-2312   Fax: (406)657-2313
Fr: 888-866-3822
E-mail: inquiries@acres-sped.org
URL: http://www.acres-sped.org

Description: Represents rural special educators and administrators, parents of students with disabilities, and university and state department personnel. Works to enhance direct services to rural individuals and

agencies serving exceptional students and to increase educational opportunities for rural students with special needs; works to develop models for serving at-risk rural students, and a system for forecasting futures for rural special education and to plan creative service delivery alternatives. Provides professional development opportunities; disseminates information on the current needs of rural special education. Conducts task forces on specific rural problems and professional training.

★11978★ American Federation of Teachers (AFT)

555 New Jersey Ave. NW
Washington, DC 20001
Ph: (202)879-4400   Fax: (202)879-4545
Fr: 800-238-1133
E-mail: online@aft.org
URL: http://www.aft.org

Description: Affiliated with the AFL-CIO. Works with teachers and other educational employees at the state and local level in organizing, collective bargaining, research, educational issues, and public relations. Conducts research in areas such as educational reform, teacher certification, and national assessments and standards. Represents members' concerns through legislative action; offers technical assistance. Serves professionals with concerns similar to those of teachers, including state employees, healthcare workers, and paraprofessionals.

★11979★ AVKO Dyslexia Research Foundation (AVKOEFR)

3084 W Willard Rd., Ste. W
Clio, MI 48420-7801
Ph: (810)686-9283   Fax: (810)686-1101
Fr: (866)AVKO-612
E-mail: donmccabe@aol.com
URL: http://www.avko.org

Description: Teachers and individuals interested in helping others learn to read and spell and in developing reading training materials for individuals with dyslexia or other learning disabilities using a method involving audio, visual, kinesthetic, and oral (AVKO) techniques. Offers advice on the techniques of tutoring, classroom teaching, diagnosis, and remediation. Conducts research into the causes of reading, spelling, and writing disabilities. Publishes and disseminates information on research. Provides a reading and spelling center where children and adults with educational deficiencies can receive diagnostic attention and remediation. Sponsors adult community education courses to train adults in tutoring their spouses or children in reading and spelling skills. Maintains speakers' bureau; compiles statistics.

★11980★ Council of American Instructors of the Deaf (CAID)

PO Box 377
Bedford, TX 76095-0377
Ph: (817)354-8414
E-mail: caid@swbell.net
URL: http://www.caid.org

Members: Professional organization of teachers, administrators, and professionals in allied fields related to education of the deaf and hard-of-hearing. **Purpose:** Provides opportunities for a free interchange of views concerning methods and means of educating the deaf and hard-of-hearing. Promotes such education by the publication of reports, essays, and other information. Develops more effective methods of teaching deaf and hard-of-hearing children.

★11981★ **Council for Exceptional Children (CEC)**
1110 N Glebe Rd., Ste. 300
Arlington, VA 22201-5704
Ph: (703)620-3660   Fax: (703)264-9494
Fr: 888-232-7733
E-mail: service@cec.sped.org
URL: http://www.cec.sped.org

Members: Administrators, teachers, parents, and others who work with and on behalf of children with disabilities and/or gifts. **Purpose:** Seeks to improve the educational success for individuals with exceptionalities - children, youth, and young adults with disabilities and/or gifts. **Activities:** Advocates for appropriate government policies; provides information to the media. Operates the ERIC Clearinghouse on Disabilities and Gifted Education, and the National Clearinghouse for Professions in Special Education. Develops programs to help teachers, administrators, and related services professionals improve their practice.

★11982★ **Council for Learning Disabilities (CLD)**
11184 Antioch Rd.
Overland Park, KS 66210
Ph: (913)491-1011   Fax: (913)491-1012
E-mail: lnease@cldinternational.org
URL: http://www.cldinternational.org

Description: Professionals interested in the study of learning disabilities. Works to promote the education and general welfare of individuals having specific learning disabilities by: improving teacher preparation programs and local special education programs, and resolving important research issues. Sponsors educational sessions.

★11983★ **Education and Training**
Cambridge Educational
PO Box 2053
Princeton, NJ 08543-2053
Ph: 800-257-5126   Fax: (609)671-0266
Fr: 800-468-4227
E-mail: custserv@films.com
URL: http://www.cambridgeeducational.com

VHS and DVD. $89.95. 2002. 18 minutes. Presents four distinct occupations in the field: elementary teachers, teacher's aides, administrators, and librarians. People working in these jobs discuss their responsibilities.

★11984★ **Inter-American Conductive Education Association (IACEA)**
PO Box 3169
Toms River, NJ 08756-3169
Ph: (732)797-2566   Fax: (732)797-2599
Fr: 800-824-2232
E-mail: info@iacea.org
URL: http://www.iacea.org

Description: Promotes and disseminates the principles of conductive education using the services of parents, conductors, therapists, teachers, and other related health care professionals. Qualifies trained conductors as new professionals to obtain health care, Medicare, Medicaid, and private health insurance reimbursement. Trains and certifies conductive education practitioners working in the United States and Canada.

★11985★ **National Association of Special Education Teachers (NASET)**
1250 Connecticut Ave. NW, Ste. 200
Washington, DC 20036
Fr: 800-754-4421
E-mail: contactus@naset.org
URL: http://www.naset.org

Description: Provides support and assistance to professionals who teach children with special needs. Fosters exceptional teaching for exceptional children. Seeks to promote standards of excellence and innovation in special education research, practice, and policy.

★11986★ **National Association of State Directors of Special Education (NASDSE)**
1800 Diagonal Rd., Ste. 320
Alexandria, VA 22314
Ph: (703)519-3800   Fax: (703)519-3808
E-mail: nasdse@nasdse.org

Members: Professional society of state directors; consultants, supervisors, and administrators who have statewide responsibilities for administering special education programs. **Purpose:** Provides services to state agencies to facilitate their efforts to maximize educational outcomes for individuals with disabilities.

★11987★ **Teaching & Related Occupations**
Delphi Productions
3159 6th St.
Boulder, CO 80304
Ph: (303)443-2100   Fax: (303)443-4022
Fr: 888-443-2400
E-mail: support@delphivideo.com
URL: http://www.delphivideo.com

$95.00. 50 minutes. Part of the Careers for the 21st Century Video Library.

Speech-Language Pathologists and Audiologists

SOURCES OF HELP-WANTED ADS

★11988★ ADVANCE for Speech-Language Pathologists & Audiologists
Merion Publications Inc.
2900 Horizon Dr.
PO Box 61556
King of Prussia, PA 19406
Ph: (610)278-1400   Fr: 800-355-5627
URL: http://speech-language-pathology-audiology.advanceweb.com/

Weekly. Professional medical magazine for qualified speech-language pathologists and audiologists.

★11989★ American Annals of the Deaf
Conference of Educational Administrators
  Serving the Deaf
Gallaudet University Press
Denison House
Washington, DC 20002
Ph: (202)651-5488   Fax: (202)651-5489
URL: http://gupress.gallaudet.edu/annals/

Quarterly. $55.00/year   for   individuals;
$35.00 for single issue, foreign except Canada; $95.00/year for institutions; $50.00/year for members. Journal focusing on education of the deaf.

★11990★ American Journal of Speech Language Pathology
American Speech-Language-Hearing
  Association
10801 Rockville Pke.
Rockville, MD 20852
Ph: (301)897-5700   Fax: (240)333-4705
Fr: 800-498-2071
URL: http://www.asha.org

Quarterly. $30.00/year for members, print; $65.00/year for individuals, print plus online; $75.00/year for individuals, foreign; $157.00/year for institutions, print plus online; $209.00/year for institutions, foreign. Professional journal covering issues in speech, language, and hearing.

★11991★ Audiology Today
American Academy of Audiology
11730 Plaza America Dr., Ste. 300
Reston, VA 20190
Ph: (703)790-8466   Fax: (703)790-8631
Fr: 800-AAA-2336

Bimonthly. Professional magazine covering audiology.

★11992★ Topics in Language Disorders (TLD)
Aspen Publishers Inc.
76 Ninth Ave., 7th Fl.
New York, NY 10011
Ph: (212)771-0600   Fax: (212)771-0885
Fr: 800-638-8437
URL: http://www.lww.com/products/?0271-8294

Quarterly. $93.91/year   for   individuals;
$167.94/year for other countries, international; $272.96/year for institutions; $340.94/year for institutions, other countries. Journal intending to clarify the application of theory to practice in the treatment, rehabilitation, and education of individuals with language disorders.

★11993★ The Volta Review
Alexander Graham Bell Association for
  the Deaf
3417 Volta Pl. NW
Washington, DC 20007-2778
Ph: (202)337-5220   Fax: (202)337-8314
URL: http://www.agbell.org/DesktopDefault.aspx?p=The_Volta_Review

Quarterly. Scholarly journal relating to the field of deafness.

PLACEMENT AND JOB REFERRAL SERVICES

★11994★ National Communication Association (NCA)
1765 N St. NW
Washington, DC 20036
Ph: (202)464-4622   Fax: (202)464-4600
E-mail: rsmitter@natcom.org
URL: http://www.natcom.org

Members: Elementary, secondary, college, and university teachers, speech clinicians, media specialists, communication consultants, students, theater directors, and other interested persons; libraries and other institutions. **Purpose:** Works to promote study, criticism, research, teaching, and application of the artistic, humanistic, and scientific principles of communication, particularly speech communication. Sponsors the publication of scholarly volumes in speech. **Activities:** Conducts international debate tours in the U.S. and abroad. Maintains placement service.

EMPLOYER DIRECTORIES AND NETWORKING LISTS

★11995★ AHA Guide to the Health Care Field
American Hospital Association
1 N Franklin
Chicago, IL 60606
Ph: (312)422-2050   Fax: (312)422-4700
Fr: 800-424-4301

Annual, August. Covers hospitals, networks, multi-health care systems, freestanding ambulatory surgery centers, psychiatric facilities, long-term care facilities, substance abuse programs, and other health-related organizations. Entries include: For hospitals–Facility name, address, phone, administrator's name, number of beds, facilities and services, number of employees, expenses, other   statistics.   For   other   organizations–Name, address, phone, fax, name and title of contact. Arrangement: Geographical. Indexes: Hospital name.

★11996★ **Directory of Hospital Personnel**

Grey House Publishing
185 Millerton Rd.
PO Box 860
Millerton, NY 12546
Ph: (518)789-8700   Fax: (518)789-0556
Fr: 800-562-2139
URL: http://www.greyhouse.com/hospital_personnel.htm

Annual. $325.00 for print product; $545.00 for online database subscription; $650.00 for online database subscription and print product combined. Covers 200,000 executives at 7,000 U.S. hospitals. Entries include: Name of hospital, address, phone; number of beds; type and JCAHO status of hospital; names and titles of key department heads and staff; medical and nursing school affiliations; number of residents, interns, and nursing students. Arrangement: Geographical. Indexes: Hospital name, personnel, hospital size.

★11997★ **Hospital Blue Book**

Billian Publishing Inc./Transworld
  Publishing Inc.
2100 Powers Ferry Rd. SE
Atlanta, GA 30339
Ph: (770)955-5656   Fax: (770)952-0669
Fr: 800-533-8484
E-mail: blu-book@billian.com

2005. $300.00 for individuals. Covers more than 6,687 hospitals; some listings also appear in a separate southern edition of this publication. Entries include: Name of hospital, accreditation, mailing address, phone, fax, number of beds, type of facility (nonprofit, general, state, etc.); list of administrative personnel and chiefs of medical services, with specific titles. Arrangement: Geographical.

★11998★ **Medical and Health Information Directory**

Gale, Cengage Learning
27500 Drake Rd.
Farmington Hills, MI 48331-3535
Ph: (248)699-4253   Fax: (248)699-8065
Fr: 800-877-4253
E-mail: businessproducts@gale.com
URL: http://www.gale.com

Annual; latest edition 20th, July 2007. $375.00/volume. Covers in Volume 1, more than 26,500 medical and health oriented associations, organizations, institutions, and government agencies, including health maintenance organizations (HMOs), preferred provider organizations (PPOs), insurance companies, pharmaceutical companies, research centers, and medical and allied health schools. In Volume 2, over 12,000 medical book publishers; medical periodicals, directories, audiovisual producers and services, medical libraries and information centers, electronic resources, and health-related internet search engines. In Volume 3, more than 35,500 clinics, treatment centers, care programs, and counseling/diagnostic

services for 34 subject areas. Entries include: Institution, service, or firm name, address, phone, fax, email and URL; many include names of key personnel and, when pertinent, descriptive annotations. Volume 3 was formerly listed separately as Health Services Directory. Arrangement: Classified by organization activity, service, etc. Indexes: Each volume has a complete alphabetical name and keyword index.

HANDBOOKS AND MANUALS

★11999★ **Careers in Health Care**

The McGraw-Hill Companies
PO Box 182604
Columbus, OH 43272
Fax: (614)759-3749   Fr: 877-883-5524
E-mail: customer.service@mcgraw-hill.com
URL: http://www.mcgraw-hill.com

Barbara M. Swanson. Fifth edition, 2005. $15.95 (paper). 192 pages. Describes job duties, work settings, salaries, licensing and certification requirements, educational preparation, and future outlook. Gives ideas on how to secure a job.

★12000★ **Careers in Social and Rehabilitation Services**

The McGraw-Hill Companies
PO Box 182604
Columbus, OH 43272
Fax: (614)759-3749   Fr: 877-883-5524
E-mail: customer.service@mcgraw-hill.com
URL: http://www.mcgraw-hill.com

Geraldine O. Garner. 2001. $19.95; 14.95 (paper). 128 pages.

★12001★ **Clinical Practice Management for Speech-Language Pathologists**

Aspen Publishers Inc.
76 Ninth Ave., 7th Fl.
New York, NY 10011
Ph: (212)771-0786   Fax: (212)771-0796
Fr: 800-538-8437
URL: http://www.aspenpublishers.com

Becky Sutherland Cornett. 1999. $45.00. Discusses three attitudes central to clinical practice: scientific, therapeutic and, professional attitudes.

★12002★ **Funding Sources: A Guide for Future Audiologists, Speech-Language Pathologists, and Speech, Language, and Hearing Scientists**

American Speech-Language-Hearing
  Association
2200 Research Blvd.
Rockville, MD 20850
Ph: (301)897-5700   Fax: (301)296-8590
Fr: 888-498-6699
E-mail: productsales@asha.org
URL: http://www.asha.org/

Patricia A. Holliday. Second edition, 2000. $20.00 (paper). 132 pages.

★12003★ **Great Jobs for Communications Majors**

The McGraw-Hill Companies
PO Box 182604
Columbus, OH 43272
Fax: (614)759-3749   Fr: 877-883-5524
E-mail: customer.service@mcgraw-hill.com
URL: http://www.mcgraw-hill.com

Blythe Camenson. Second edition, 2001. $15.95 (paper). 256 pages.

★12004★ **Making a Difference for America's Children: Speech Language Pathologists in Public Schools**

Thinking Publications
PO Box 163
Eau Claire, WI 54702-0163
Ph: (715)832-2488   Fax: (715)832-9082
Fr: 800-225-4769

Barbara J. Moore-Brown and Judy K. Montgomery. 2005. $70.00.

★12005★ **On Your Own: A Resource Manual for Starting a Successful Private Practice as a Solo Practicioner in Speech-Language Pathology**

PRO-ED, Incorporated
8700 Shoal Creek Blvd.
Austin, TX 78757-6897
Ph: (512)451-3246   Fax: 800-397-7633
Fr: 800-897-3202
E-mail: info@proedinc.com
URL: http://www.proedinc.com

Ann M. Coleman. 2000. 61 pages.

★12006★ **Opportunities in Health and Medical Careers**

The McGraw-Hill Companies
PO Box 182604
Columbus, OH 43272
Fax: (614)759-3749   Fr: 877-883-5524
E-mail: customer.service@mcgraw-hill.com
URL: http://www.mcgraw-hill.com

I. Donald Snook, Jr. and Leo D'Orazio. 2004. $13.95 (paper). 157 pages. Covers the full range of medical and health occupations. Illustrated.

★12007★ **Resumes for Health and Medical Careers**

The McGraw-Hill Companies
PO Box 182604
Columbus, OH 43272
Fax: (614)759-3749   Fr: 877-883-5524
E-mail: customer.service@mcgraw-hill.com
URL: http://www.mcgraw-hill.com

Third edition, 2003. $11.95 (paper). 160 pages.

★12008★ Survival Guide for School-Based Speech-Language Pathologists

Singular Publishing Group, Incorporated
401 W. A St., Ste. 325
San Diego, CA 92101-7904
Ph: (619)238-6777   Fax: (619)238-6789
Fr: 800-521-8545

Ellen P. Dodge. 1999. $71.95 (paper). 464 pages.

EMPLOYMENT AGENCIES AND SEARCH FIRMS

★12009★ Educational Placement Service

6510-A S. Academy Blvd.
Colorado Springs, CO 80906
Ph: (719)579-9911   Fax: (719)579-5050
E-mail: accounting@educatorjobs.com
URL: http://www.educatorjobs.com

Employment agency. Focuses on teaching, administrative, and education-related openings.

ONLINE JOB SOURCES AND SERVICES

★12010★ Medhunters.com

Fr: 800-664-0278
E-mail: info@medhunters.com
URL: http://www.medhunters.com

Description: Career search site for jobs in all health care specialties; educational resources; visa and licensing information for relocation; interesting articles; relocation tools; links to professional organizations and general resources.

★12011★ ProHealthJobs

Fr: 800-796-1738
E-mail: Info@prohealthedujobs.com
URL: http://www.prohealthjobs.com

Description: Career resources site for the medical and health care field. Lists professional opportunities, product information, continuing education and open positions.

★12012★ RehabJobs Online

PO Box 480536
Los Angeles, CA 90048
Ph: (213)938-7718   Fax: (213)938-9609
Fr: 800-43-REHAB
E-mail: support@atsrehabjobs.com
URL: http://www.rehabjobs.com

Description: Resource center for the professional therapist. **Main files include:** Therapists Only, Therapy Forums, Nationwide Job Search (database), Therapy Job Outlook, Therapy Job Search Utilities, Ther-

apy Links, Information for Employers and Recruiters.

★12013★ RehabWorld

URL: http://www.rehabworld.com

Description: Site for rehabilitation professionals to learn about the profession and locate jobs. Includes user groups, salary surveys, and chat capabilities. **Main files include:** Physical Therapy, Occupational Therapy, Speech Therapy, Mental Health, Employer World, Student World, International World, Forum.

TRADESHOWS

★12014★ American Speech-Language-Hearing Association Annual Convention

American Speech-Language-Hearing Association
10801 Rockville Pke.
Rockville, MD 20852
Ph: (301)897-5700   Fax: (301)571-0457
Fr: 800-498-2071
E-mail: actioncenter@asha.org
URL: http://www.asha.org

Annual. **Primary Exhibits:** Scientific equipment, publications, and testing materials.

★12015★ National Student Speech Language Hearing Association Conference

National Student Speech Language Hearing Association
10801 Rockville Pike
Rockville, MD 20852
Ph: 800-498-2071   Fax: (301)571-0481
E-mail: nsslha@asha.org
URL: http://www.nsslha.org

Annual. **Primary Exhibits:** Exhibits relating to speech-language pathology, speech and hearing sciences, and audiology.

★12016★ North Carolina Speech, Hearing, and Language Association Convention

North Carolina Speech, Hearing, and Language Association
PO Box 28359
Raleigh, NC 27611-8359
Ph: (919)833-3984   Fax: (919)832-0445
E-mail: ncshla@juno.com
URL: http://www.ncshla.org

Annual. **Primary Exhibits:** Equipment, supplies, and services for speech and language pathology and/or audiology. **Dates and Locations:** 2008 Apr 02-05; Charlotte, NC; 2009 Apr 01-04; Dallas, TX.

★12017★ Summer Institute of the Academy of Rehabilitative Audiology

Academy of Rehabilitative Audiology
PO Box 26532
Minneapolis, MN 55426
Ph: (952)920-0484   Fax: (952)920-6098
E-mail: ara@incnet.com
URL: http://www.audrehab.org

Annual. **Primary Exhibits:** Exhibits relating to audiology, language, speech pathology, and the education of the deaf.

OTHER SOURCES

★12018★ American Almanac of Jobs and Salaries

HarperCollins
10 E. 53rd St.
New York, NY 10022
Ph: (212)207-7000   Fr: 800-242-7737
URL: http://www.harpercollins.com/

John W. Wright. Revised edition, 2000. $20.00 (paper). 672 pages. This is a comprehensive guide to the wages of hundreds of occupations in a wide variety of industries and organizations.

★12019★ American Auditory Society (AAS)

352 Sundial Ridge Cir.
Dammeron Valley, UT 84783-5196
Ph: (435)574-0062   Fax: (435)574-0063
E-mail: amaudsoc@aol.com
URL: http://www.amauditorysoc.org

Members: Audiologists, otolaryngologists, scientists, hearing aid industry professionals, and educators of hearing impaired people; individuals involved in industries serving hearing impaired people, including the amplification systems industry. **Purpose:** Works to increase knowledge and understanding of: the ear, hearing, and balance; disorders of the ear, hearing, and balance; prevention of these disorders; habilitation and rehabilitation of individuals with hearing and balance dysfunction.

★12020★ American Health Care Association (AHCA)

1201 L St. NW
Washington, DC 20005
Ph: (202)842-4444   Fax: (202)842-3860
E-mail: hr@ahca.org
URL: http://www.ahca.org

Description: Federation of state associations of long-term health care facilities. Promotes standards for professionals in long-term health care delivery and quality care for patients and residents in a safe environment. Focuses on issues of availability, quality, affordability, and fair payment. Operates as liaison with governmental agencies, Congress, and professional associations. Compiles statistics.

★12021★ Association on Higher Education and Disability (AHEAD)

107 Commerce Center Dr., Ste. 204
Huntersville, NC 28078
Ph: (704)947-7779   Fax: (704)948-7779
E-mail: ahead@ahead.org
URL: http://www.ahead.org

Description: Individuals interested in promoting the equal rights and opportunities of disabled postsecondary students, staff, faculty, and graduates. Provides an exchange of communication for those professionally involved with disabled students; collects, evaluates, and disseminates information; encourages and supports legislation for the benefit of disabled students. Conducts surveys on issues pertinent to college students with disabilities; offers resource referral system and employment exchange for positions in disability student services. Conducts research programs; compiles statistics.

★12022★ Council of American Instructors of the Deaf (CAID)

PO Box 377
Bedford, TX 76095-0377
Ph: (817)354-8414
E-mail: caid@swbell.net
URL: http://www.caid.org

Members: Professional organization of teachers, administrators, and professionals in allied fields related to education of the deaf and hard-of-hearing. **Purpose:** Provides opportunities for a free interchange of views concerning methods and means of educating the deaf and hard-of-hearing. Promotes such education by the publication of reports, essays, and other information. Develops more effective methods of teaching deaf and hard-of-hearing children.

★12023★ Exploring Health Occupations

Cambridge Educational
PO Box 2053
Princeton, NJ 08543-2053
Ph: 800-257-5126   Fax: (609)671-0266
Fr: 800-468-4227
E-mail: custserv@films.com
URL: http://www.cambridgeeducational.com

VHS and DVD. $159.90. 1999. Two-part series provides a detailed view of the field of medical technicians and technologists, EMTs, nurses, therapists, and assistants.

★12024★ Health Assessment & Treating Occupations

Delphi Productions
3159 6th St.
Boulder, CO 80304
Ph: (303)443-2100   Fax: (303)443-4022
Fr: 888-443-2400
E-mail: support@delphivideo.com
URL: http://www.delphivideo.com

$95.00. 50 minutes. Part of the Careers for the 21st Century Video Library.

★12025★ Health Service Occupations

Delphi Productions
3159 6th St.
Boulder, CO 80304
Ph: (303)443-2100   Fax: (303)443-4022
Fr: 888-443-2400
E-mail: support@delphivideo.com
URL: http://www.delphivideo.com

$95.00. 50 minutes. Part of the Careers for the 21st Century Video Library.

★12026★ International Association of Orofacial Myology (IAOM)

2000 NE 42nd Ave.
Portland, OR 97213-1305
Ph: (503)280-0614   Fax: (503)284-0041
E-mail: iaomec@msn.com
URL: http://www.iaom.com

Description: Supports the development of research in the area of orofacial myofunctional therapy. Develops communication with the insurance companies. Provides certification and continuing education to professionals and individuals in field of orofacial myology.

★12027★ Medicine & Related Occupations

Delphi Productions
3159 6th St.
Boulder, CO 80304
Ph: (303)443-2100   Fax: (303)443-4022
Fr: 888-443-2400
E-mail: support@delphivideo.com
URL: http://www.delphivideo.com

$95.00. 45 minutes. Part of the Careers for the 21st Century Video Library.

★12028★ Modern Language Association of America (MLA)

26 Broadway, 3rd Fl.
New York, NY 10004-1789
Ph: (646)576-5000   Fax: (646)458-0300
E-mail: execdirector@mla.org

URL: http://www.mla.org

Description: Provides opportunities for the members to share their scholarly findings and teaching experiences with colleagues and to discuss trends in the academy. Works to strengthen the study and teaching of language and literature.

★12029★ National Association of School Nurses for the Deaf (NASND)

CID
4560 Clayton Ave.
St. Louis, MO 63110
E-mail: drobarge@isd.k12.in.us
URL: http://www.nasnd.org

Description: Aims to enhance the quality of health education and services to deaf students. Fosters effective communication between school nurses and deaf students. Seeks to lessen workplace isolation by offering professional support and providing opportunities for its members to engage in networking activities.

★12030★ National Rehabilitation Association (NRA)

633 S Washington St.
Alexandria, VA 22314
Ph: (703)836-0850   Fax: (703)836-0848
E-mail: info@nationalrehab.org
URL: http://www.nationalrehab.org/website/index.html

Description: Provides opportunities through knowledge and diversity for professionals in the fields of rehabilitation of people with disabilities.

★12031★ Neuro-Developmental Treatment Association (NDTA)

1540 S Coast Hwy., Ste. 203
Laguna Beach, CA 92651
Fax: (949)376-3456   Fr: 800-869-9295
E-mail: info@ndta.org
URL: http://www.ndta.org

Members: Physical and occupational therapists, speech pathologists, special educators, physicians, parents, and others interested in neurodevelopmental treatment. (NDT is a form of therapy for individuals who suffer from central nervous system disorders resulting in abnormal movement. Treatment attempts to initiate or refine normal stages and processes in the development of movement.) **Purpose:** Informs members of new developments in the field and with ideas that will eventually improve fundamental independence. **Activities:** Locates articles related to NDT.

Sports Officials, Coaches, and Instructors

SOURCES OF HELP-WANTED ADS

★12032★ *The American Journal of Sports Medicine*

The American Orthopaedic Society for Sports Medicine
6300 North River Rd., Ste. 500
Rosemont, IL 60018
Ph: (847)292-4900   Fax: (847)292-4905
URL: http://ajs.sagepub.com/

$721.00/year for institutions, print & e-access; $169.00/year for individuals, print & e-access. Medical journal.

★12033★ *NAIA News*

National Association of Intercollegiate Athletics
1200 Grand Blvd
Kansas City, MO 64106
Ph: (816)595-8000   Fax: (816)595-8200
E-mail: naianews@naia.org
URL: http://www.naia.org

Description: Daily. Provides news and information on the Association, which strives to "develop intercollegiate athletic programs as an integral part of the total educational program of the college rather than as a separate commercial or promotional adjunct." Aims toward uniformity and equity in policies and practices. Recurring features include news of members and events, notices of awards, and job listings.

★12034★ *Sailing World*

Miller Sports Group L.L.C.
79 Madison Ave., 8th Fl.
New York, NY 10016-7802
Ph: (212)636-2700   Fax: (212)636-2730
Fr: 800-634-1953
E-mail: editor@sailingworld.com
URL: http://www.sailingworld.com/index.jsp

$14.97/year for individuals. Magazine on performance sailing.

★12035★ *Scholastic Coach & Athletic Director*

Scholastic Library Publishing Inc.
90 Old Sherman Tpke.
PO Box 1795
Danbury, CT 06816
Ph: (203)797-3500   Fax: (203)797-3657
Fr: 800-621-1115
E-mail: magazines@scholastic.ca
URL: http://www.coachad.com/

$14.98/year for individuals, 10 issues; $24.98/year for individuals, 20 issues; $41.95/year for other countries, 10 issues. Magazine on high school and college athletics.

PLACEMENT AND JOB REFERRAL SERVICES

★12036★ American Athletic Trainers Association and Certification Board (AATA)

146 E Duarte Rd.
Arcadia, CA 91006
Ph: (626)445-1978   Fax: (626)574-1999
E-mail: americansportsmedicine@hotmail.com

Purpose: Aims to qualify and certify active athletic trainers; establish minimum competence standards for individuals participating in the prevention and care of athletic injuries; to inform communities nationwide of the importance of having competent leadership in the area of athletic training. **Activities:** Conducts continuing education and charitable programs; maintains placement service.

★12037★ American Sail Training Association (ASTA)

PO Box 1459
Newport, RI 02840
Ph: (401)846-1775   Fax: (401)849-5400
E-mail: asta@sailtraining.org
URL: http://tallships.sailtraining.org

Members: Organizations operating sail training programs; corporations and educa-tional institutions supporting sail training; private citizens with an interest in sailing and sail training. **Purpose:** Promotes sail training as an educational and character-building experience for youth of all ages. Seeks to bring together the sail training ships of the world in a spirit of friendship and international goodwill. **Activities:** Sponsors Tall Ships events including sail training rallies. Maintains billet bank/placement service; compiles statistics.

★12038★ American Swimming Coaches Association (ASCA)

5101 NW 21st Ave., Ste. 200
Fort Lauderdale, FL 33309
Ph: (954)563-4930   Fax: (954)563-9813
Fr: 800-356-2722
E-mail: asca@swimmingcoach.org
URL: http://www.swimmingcoach.org

Members: Swimming coaches united for informational and educational purposes. **Activities:** Operates Swim America, a learn-to-swim program. Maintains placement service; conducts research programs; compiles statistics.

★12039★ Athletic Equipment Managers Association (AEMA)

460 Hunt Hill Rd.
Freeville, NY 13068
Ph: (607)539-6300   Fax: (607)539-6340
E-mail: dec13@cornell.edu
URL: http://www.aema1.com

Members: Athletic equipment managers and others who handle sports equipment for junior high and high schools, colleges, recreation centers, and professional sports; individuals involved in athletic management and coaching or the handling or purchasing of athletic, physical education, or recreational equipment. **Purpose:** Aims to improve the profession of equipment management and promote a better working relationship among those interested in problems of management. Works collectively to facilitate equipment improvement for greater safety among participants in all sports. **Activities:** Conducts workshops and clinics. Maintains job placement service.

★12040★ College Swimming Coaches Association of America (CSCAA)

10320 E Verbena Ln.
Scottsdale, AZ 85255
Ph: (480)628-5488   Fax: (480)699-4852
E-mail: swimphil@aol.com
URL: http://www.cscaa.org

Members: College and university swimming and diving coaches organized to promote college swimming. **Activities:** Disseminates information; maintains placement service and hall of fame.

★12041★ Exercise Safety Association (ESA)

PO Box 547916
Orlando, FL 32854-7916
Ph: (407)246-5090
E-mail: askesa@aol.com
URL: http://www.exercisesafety.com

Description: Fitness instructors, personal trainers, health spas, YMCAs, community recreation departments, and hospital wellness programs. Purposes are: to improve the qualifications of exercise instructors; to train instructors to develop safe exercise programs that will help people avoid injury while exercising; to prepare instructors for national certification. Offers training in aerobics and exercise and on the physiological aspects of exercise. Conducts exercise safety and research programs. Sponsors charitable program; maintains speakers' bureau. Offers instructor placement services.

★12042★ Jackie Robinson Foundation (JRF)

One Hudson Sq.
75 Varick St., 2nd Fl.
New York, NY 10013-1947
Ph: (212)290-8600   Fax: (212)290-8081
E-mail: general@jackierobinson.org
URL: http://www.jackierobinson.org

Description: Seeks to develop the leadership and achievement potential of minority and urban youth. Founded by the friends and family of Jackie Robinson (1919-72), the first black athlete to play major league baseball. Trains minority and poor youths for sports management careers. Provides counseling, support, and placement services. Awards full college scholarships to promising minority students. Maintains collection of Jackie Robinson memorabilia; has produced a national touring exhibit of archival materials pertaining to Robinson.

★12043★ National Association for Sport and Physical Education (NASPE)

1900 Association Dr.
Reston, VA 20191-1598
Ph: (703)476-3400   Fax: (703)476-8316
Fr: 800-213-7193
E-mail: naspe@aahperd.org
URL: http://www.naspeinfo.org

Description: Men and women professionally involved with physical activity and sports. Seeks to improve the total sport and physical activity experience in America. Conducts research and education programs in such areas as sport psychology, curriculum development, kinesiology, history, philosophy, sport sociology, and the biological and behavioral basis of human activity. Develops and distributes public information materials which explain the value of physical education programs. Supports councils involved in organizing and supporting elementary, secondary, and college physical education and sport programs; administers the National Council of Athletic Training in conjunction with the National Association for Girls and Women in Sport; serves the professional interests of coaches, trainers, and officials. Maintains hall of fame, placement service, and media resource center for public information and professional preparation. Member benefits include group insurance and discounts.

★12044★ National Association of Underwater Instructors (NAUI)

PO Box 89789
Tampa, FL 33689-0413
Ph: (813)628-6284   Fax: (813)628-8253
Fr: 800-553-6284
E-mail: nauihq@nauiww.org
URL: http://www.nauiww.org

Members: Certified instructors of basic, advanced, and specialized courses in underwater diving. **Activities:** Offers instructor certification programs and training programs. Conducts seminars, workshops, and symposia. Sells diving education books. Sponsors competitions; maintains speakers' bureau and placement service; conducts charitable programs.

★12045★ National Athletic Trainers' Association (NATA)

2952 Stemmons Fwy., No. 200
Dallas, TX 75247-6196
Ph: (214)637-6282   Fax: (214)637-2206
Fr: 800-879-6282
E-mail: mjalbohm@aol.com
URL: http://www.nata.org

Members: Athletic trainers from universities, colleges, and junior colleges; professional football, baseball, basketball, and ice hockey; high schools, preparatory schools, military establishments, sports medicine clinics, and business/industrial health programs. **Activities:** Maintains hall of fame and placement service. Conducts research programs; compiles statistics.

★12046★ National Christian College Athletic Association (NCCAA)

302 W Washington St.
Greenville, SC 29601-1919
Ph: (864)250-1199   Fax: (864)250-1141
E-mail: info@thenccaa.org
URL: http://www.thenccaa.org

Members: Christian colleges. **Purpose:** Provides national competition for the Christian college movement in baseball, basketball (men's and women's) cross-country (men's and women's), football, golf, soccer (men's and women's), tennis (men's and women's), men's volleyball, women's volleyball, track and field (men's and women's), and softball. **Activities:** Maintains placement service; compiles statistics.

★12047★ National Council of Secondary School Athletic Directors (NCSSAD)

1900 Association Dr.
Reston, VA 20191-1598
Ph: (703)476-3400   Fax: (703)476-8316
Fr: 800-213-7193
E-mail: naspe@aahperd.org
URL: http://www.aahperd.org/naspe

Description: A council of the National Association for Sport and Physical Education, which is a division of the American Alliance for Health, Physical Education, Recreation and Dance. Professional athletic directors in secondary schools. Purposes are to improve the educational aspects of interscholastic athletics; to provide for an exchange of ideas; to establish closer working relationships with related professional groups and promote greater unity; to establish and implement standards for the professional preparation of secondary school athletic directors. Provides in-service training programs. Maintains placement service and speakers' bureau.

★12048★ Professional Association of Diving Instructors (PADI)

30151 Tomas St.
Rancho Santa Margarita, CA 92688-2125
Ph: (949)858-7234   Fax: (949)267-1261
Fr: 800-729-7234
E-mail: webmaster@padi.com
URL: http://www.padi.com

Purpose: Educates and certifies underwater scuba instructors. Sanctions instructor training courses nationwide and in 175 foreign countries. Provides training course criteria, training aids, and national requirements for all aspects of diving instruction. Instructor training courses are held at geographically central locations. **Activities:** Sponsors PADI Travel Network and a retail dive store program. Offers courses in diving specialties; conducts educational programs. Offers placement service; compiles statistics.

★12049★ Professional Golfers' Association of America (PGA)

100 Ave. of the Champions
Palm Beach Gardens, FL 33418
Ph: (561)624-8400   Fax: (561)624-8430
E-mail: sales.pga@turner.com
URL: http://www.pga.com

Members: Recruits and trains men and women to manage a variety of golf businesses, including golf clubs, courses, and tournaments. **Activities:** Sponsors PGA Championship, PGA Seniors' Championship, Ryder Cup Matches, PGA Grand Slam of Golf, Club Professional Championship, PGA Foundation, and Senior Club Professional Championship; PGA Junior Championship; PGA Assistants Championship. Conducts Professional Golf Management; certifies college programs in golf management at

14 universities. Sponsors winter tournament program for club professionals including tournaments held in south Florida. Offers complementary employment services for PGA members and employers, owns and operates PGA Golf Club and PGA Learning Center.

★12050★ Professional Skaters Association (PSA)

3006 Allegro Park SW
Rochester, MN 55902
Ph: (507)281-5122   Fax: (507)281-5491
E-mail: office@skatepsa.com
URL: http://skatepsa.com

Members: Professional ice skaters engaged in the teaching, coaching and performing of ice skating. **Purpose:** Strives to form a cohesive body of all professional ice skaters for the benefit of the profession, to protect the interests of members' pupils, to advance all aspects of both ice figure skating and recreational skating, and to promote high ethical and professional standards in the field. **Activities:** Grades teachers on the basis of on-ice proficiency and oral examination. Operates placement service.

★12051★ Professional Tennis Registry (PTR)

PO Box 4739
Hilton Head Island, SC 29938
Ph: (843)785-7244   Fax: (843)686-2033
Fr: 800-421-6289
E-mail: ptr@ptrtennis.org
URL: http://www.ptrtennis.org

Purpose: Tests, certifies, and registers international tennis teaching professionals; Certification requires successful completion of a written and on-court examinations. **Activities:** Sponsors workshops, tennis clinics, and charitable program. Holds competitions; compiles statistics; maintains placement service.

★12052★ United States Association of Independent Gymnastic Clubs (USAIGC)

450 N End Ave., Ste. 20F
New York, NY 10282
Ph: (212)227-9792   Fax: (212)227-9793
Fr: 800-480-0201
E-mail: usaigcpsny2@aol.com
URL: http://www.usaigc.com

Members: Gymnastic clubs and independent gymnastic club businesses (725) offering professional class instruction and coaching; manufacturers (25) of gymnastic equipment, apparel, and supplies. **Purpose:** Aims to provide services, programs, and business advice to help gymnastic businesses to grow and prosper; locate organizations and individuals that will provide needed services for members' clientele; further coaching knowledge; advance the U.S. in gymnastic competitions throughout the world. **Activities:** Offers certification for coaches and developmental-training programs for gymnasts to prepare for international competitions. Provides placement service; conducts research

programs. Maintains Medical Advisory Board and hall of fame.

★12053★ United States Judo (USJ)

1 Olympic Plz., Ste. 505
Colorado Springs, CO 80909
Ph: (719)866-4730   Fax: (719)866-4733
E-mail: jose.h.rodriguez@usajudo.us
URL: http://www.usjudo.org

Description: Judo groups and athletes, referees, judges, and interested individuals. Serves as national governing body for amateur judo in the United States. Promotes the sport of judo and trains athletes for competition. Develops eligibility and safety standards; conducts training courses for referees, coaches, and athletes. Sanctions and sponsors national amateur judo competitions. Maintains placement service; compiles statistics.

★12054★ United States Professional Diving Coaches Association (USPDCA)

PO Box 268
Milford, OH 45150
E-mail: uspdca@cinci.rr.com
URL: http://www.uspdca.org

Description: Conducts educational programs; offers placement services.

★12055★ United States Professional Tennis Association (USPTA)

3535 Briarpark Dr., Ste. 1
Houston, TX 77042
Ph: (713)978-7782   Fax: (713)978-7780
Fr: 800-USPTA-4U
E-mail: uspta@uspta.org
URL: http://www.uspta.com

Members: Professional tennis instructors, tennis-teaching professionals and college coaches. **Purpose:** Seeks to improve tennis instruction in the United States; maintains placement bureau and library. Offers specialized education; sponsors competitions; administrates an adult tennis league and a nationwide program to introduce children ages 3-10 to tennis. Sponsors annual "Tennis Across America" program each spring.

★12056★ U.S. Ski Coaches Association (USSCA)

PO Box 100
Park City, UT 84060
Ph: (435)649-9090   Fax: (435)649-3613
E-mail: info@ussa.org
URL: http://www.usskiteam.com

Description: Alpine, Nordic, and Freestyle ski and snowboard coaches and instructors; persons interested in sports medicine. Promotes the highest standards of Alpine, Nordic, and Freestyle ski coaching. Provides educational and technical materials, supplies, and equipment necessary to the function of the ski coach. Offers courses, clinics, films, and placement service. Provides high standards of certification, recertification, accreditation, and coaching ethics; handles

problems of common concern to the ski coaching profession.

EMPLOYER DIRECTORIES AND NETWORKING LISTS

★12057★ *Blue Book of College Athletics for Senior, Junior & Community Colleges*

Athletic Publishing Company Inc.
PO Box 931
Montgomery, AL 36101
Ph: (334)263-4436   Fax: (334)263-4437
URL: http://www.athleticpubco.com

Annual; latest edition 76th, 2007-2008. $52.95 for individuals. Covers over 2,400 colleges and universities that have athletic programs, conferences, and related associations; coverage includes the U.S., Canada and Puerto Rico. Entries include: For colleges and universities–Name, address, phone, names and titles of governing officials, athletic department phone number, enrollment, school colors, team nickname, band nickname and size, band director's name, stadium name and size, other athletic facilities, conference membership; names and phone numbers of athletic directors, coaches, assistants, and trainers; previous year's team records. For conferences and associations–Name, headquarters address; names and titles of key personnel; name, address, phone commissioner; membership conference/associations championships for previous year. Arrangement: Classified by type of college, conference, or association, then alphabetical. Indexes: Senior colleges and universities in the U.S., colleges of Canada and Puerto Rico; senior conferences and associations, senior related associations and organizations; junior and community colleges; junior and community college conferences and associations.

★12058★ *Careers in Focus: Coaches & Fitness Professionals*

Facts On File Inc.
132 W 31st St., 17th Fl.
New York, NY 10001
Ph: (212)967-8800   Fax: 800-678-3633
Fr: 800-322-8755
URL: http://www.factsonfile.com

Published 2004. $29.95 for individuals; $26.95 for libraries. Covers an overview of coaches and fitness professionals, followed by a selection of jobs profiled in detail, including the nature of the job, earnings, prospects for employment, what kind of training and skills it requires, and sources for further information.

★12059★ *Careers in Focus: Sports*

Facts On File Inc.
132 W 31st St., 17th Fl.
New York, NY 10001
Ph: (212)967-8800   Fax: 800-678-3633
Fr: 800-322-8755

URL: http://www.factsonfile.com

Latest edition 3rd, 2003. $29.95 for individuals; $26.95 for libraries. Covers an overview of sports, followed by a selection of jobs profiled in detail, including the nature of the job, earnings, prospects for employment, what kind of training and skills it requires, and sources for further information.

★12060★ **Clell Wade Coaches Directory**

Clell Wade Coaches Directory Inc.
PO Box 177
Cassville, MO 65625
Ph: (417)847-2783   Fax: (417)847-5920
E-mail: info@coachesdirectory.com
URL: http://www.coachesdirectory.com

Annual, September 2007. Published in 50 state and/or regional editions as well as one Canadian province edition, this series covers high school and college athletic programs and their personnel. Entries include: For each school–Name and titles of athletic director, superintendent, principal, cheerleader sponsor, band director, and trainer; school name, address, phone; enrollment; conference memberships; school colors, nickname; interscholastic sports and names of coaches. College listings include name and seating capacity of the football stadium and basketball fieldhouse. Arrangement: Geographical.

★12061★ **Discovering Careers for Your Future: Sports**

Facts On File Inc.
132 W 31st St., 17th Fl.
New York, NY 10001
Ph: (212)967-8800   Fax: 800-678-3633
Fr: 800-322-8755
URL: http://www.factsonfile.com

Latest edition 2nd, 2005. $21.95 for individuals; $19.75 for libraries. Covers athletic trainers, fitness experts, lifeguards, sports broadcasters and announcers, sports physicians, sports scouts, and yoga and Pilates instructors; links career education to curriculum, helping children investigate the subjects they are interested in and the careers those subjects might lead to.

★12062★ **National Directory of College Athletics**

Collegiate Directories Inc.
PO Box 450640
Cleveland, OH 44145
Ph: (440)835-1172   Fax: (440)835-8835
Fr: 800-426-2232
URL: http://www.collegiatedirectories.com/shopping/index.asp

Annual; latest edition 2007-2008. $45.95 for individuals. Covers men's athletic departments of 2,100 senior and junior colleges in the United States and Canada. Entries include: School name, address, enrollment, colors, team nicknames, stadium and/or gym capacity; names of president, men's athletic director, athletic administrative staff, physical education director and coaches for each sport; athletic department phones, faxes,

etc.; association affiliations. Arrangement: Alphabetical. Indexes: Schools by program and division; alphabetical by advertisers and products.

★12063★ **National Directory of High School Coaches**

Athletic Publishing Company Inc.
PO Box 931
Montgomery, AL 36101
Ph: (334)263-4436   Fax: (334)263-4437
URL: http://www.athleticpubco.com/

Annual; latest edition 44, 2007-2008. $72.95 for individuals. Covers more than 240,000 high school coaches at over 19,500 high schools. Entries include: School name, address, phone, names of coaches, codes for sports coached, and ETS numbers. Arrangement: Geographical. Indexes: Advertiser; key to symbols; high schools by name, city and state.

★12064★ **Recreational Sports Directory**

National Intramural-Recreational Sports Association
4185 SW Research Way
Corvallis, OR 97333-1067
Ph: (541)766-8211   Fax: (541)766-8284
URL: http://www.nirsa.org

Annual; latest edition 2008. $35.00 for members; $85.00 for nonmembers. Covers recreational sports programs in approximately 2,500 four-year colleges and universities, nearly 700 junior and community colleges, Canadian colleges and universities, and over 350 military installations. Entries include: Institution name and address; institution enrollment; name of president; names, phone numbers, fax numbers, Internet access, and job titles of recreational directors and staff; existing sports clubs; degrees offered in physical education and recreation; whether graduate assistantships or internships are available. A buyer's guide is included with supplier addresses and descriptions of products and services. Arrangement: Classified by institution type, then alphabetical. Indexes: Alphabetical; geographical; personal name; recreational sports program.

★12065★ **Skiing USA**

Fodor's Travel Publications Inc.
1745 Broadway
New York, NY 10019
Ph: (212)572-2313   Fax: (212)782-9054
Fr: 800-733-3000
URL: http://www.fodors.com

Biennial; latest edition 4th, published November 2002. Covers 30 top ski resorts in the U.S. Entries include: Resort name, address, phone; type of lifts, number of trails, snowmaking capabilities, length of season, hotels, restaurants, available transportation, other activities, and recommendations on the best trails for all levels. Arrangement: Geographical. Indexes: Resort name.

★12066★ **Sports Market Place**

Sports Careers
2990 E Northern Ave., Ste. D107
Phoenix, AZ 85028
Ph: (602)485-5555   Fax: (602)485-5556

Annual, January. Covers manufacturers, organizations, professional sports teams, broadcasting networks, sports arenas, syndicators, publications, trade shows, marketing services, corporate sports sponsors, and other groups concerned with the business and promotional aspects of sports generally and with air sports, arm wrestling, auto sports, badminton, baseball, basketball, biathlon, bowling, boxing, curling, equestrian, exercise, fencing, field hockey, football, golf, gymnastics, ice hockey, lacrosse, martial arts, paddleball, paddle tennis, platform tennis, pentathlon, racquetball, rowing, rugby, running/jogging, skiing, soccer, softball, squash, swimming, table tennis, tennis, track and field, volleyball, water sports, weightlifting, and wrestling. Entries include: Name of company or organization, address, fax, e-mail, URL, name of key personnel with titles, and description of products or services. Arrangement: Classified by type of firm, sport, or activity. Indexes: Alphabetical; single sport; media; sport sponsors; agencies; manufacturers; brand name; facilities; executives; and geographical.

★12067★ **What Can I Do Now**

Facts On File Inc.
132 W 31st St., 17th Fl.
New York, NY 10001
Ph: (212)967-8800   Fax: 800-678-3633
Fr: 800-322-8755
URL: http://www.factsonfile.com

Latest edition 2nd, 2007. $29.95 for individuals; $26.95 for libraries. Covers professional athletes, sports broadcasters, coaches and trainers, sports physicians and surgeons, sports statisticians, umpires and referees.

★12068★ **White Book of Ski Areas**

Inter-Ski Services Inc.
PO Box 3775, Georgetown Sta.
Washington, DC 20007
Ph: (202)342-0886   Fax: (202)338-1940
URL: http://www.inter-ski.com

Annual; latest edition 30th. Free. Covers about 500 lift-equipped ski areas and resorts. Entries include: Name of ski area, location, phone; snow condition phone numbers; ski statistics (elevation, lift capacity, etc.); season and rates; equipment and schooling available; lodging availability and phone, restaurants, apres-ski, and other recreational facilities in vicinity; shops; travel instructions. Special industry edition available with more comprehensive information for $395. Arrangement: Geographical within four regions–West, North Central, South, and Northeast. Indexes: Geographical.

HANDBOOKS AND MANUALS

★12069★ Athlete's Guide to Career Planning

Human Kinetics Publishers
PO Box 5076
Champaign, IL 61825-5076
Ph: (217)351-5076   Fax: (217)351-1549
Fr: 800-747-4457
E-mail: info@hkusa.com
URL: http://www.humankinetics.com/

Delight Champagne, Judy Chartrand, Steven Danish, and Shane M. Murphy. 1997. $17.95 (paper). 240 pages.

★12070★ Career Game Plan for Student Athletes

Prentice Hall PTR
One Lake St.
Upper Saddle River, NJ 07458
Ph: (201)236-7000   Fr: 800-428-5331
URL: http://www.phptr.com/index.asp?rl=1

Jennifer Bohac. 1999. $41.00 (paper). 194 pages.

★12071★ Career Insights: Presidents/GMs from the NFL, MLB, NHL and MLS on Achieving Personal and Professional Success

Aspatore Books, Incorporated
400 Commonwealth Ave., 2nd Fl.
Boston, MA 02115
Ph: (617)249-1960   Fax: (617)249-1970
Fr: (866)277-2863
URL: http://www.aspatore.com/

Aspatore Books. April 2004. $19.95 (paper). 100 pages.

★12072★ Career Transitions in Sport: International Perspectives

Fitness Information Technology, Incorporated
PO Box 6116
Morgantown, WV 26506-6116
Ph: (304)293-6888   Fax: (304)293-6658
Fr: 800-477-4348
URL: http://www.fitinfotech.com/

Editors: David Lavallee, Paul Wylleman. 2000. $39.00. 305 pages.

★12073★ Chronicle of Sports Careers

Chronicle Guidance Publications Inc.
66 Aurora St.
Moravia, NY 13118-3576
Fax: (315)497-3359   Fr: 800-899-0454
URL: http://www.chronicleguidance.com/

Paul Downes, editor. 1994. $24.00.

★12074★ Developing a Lifelong Contract in the Sports Marketplace

Athletic Achievements
3036 Ontario Rd.
Little Canada, MN 55117
Ph: (612)484-8299   Fax: (612)484-8311
Fr: 800-680-8311

Greg J. Cylkowski. Fourth edition, 1999. $20.95. 400 pages. A guide to seeking opportunities in a variety of sports positions.

★12075★ Exploring Coaching: A Step-by-Step Guide to a Fulfilling and Rewarding Career

LearnMore Publishing
2245 Eagles Nest Dr.
Lafayette, CO 80026-9334
Ph: (303)464-0110
URL: http://www.willcraig.com/

Will Craig. Pdf format. April 2004. $9.95. 132 pages.

★12076★ Leading with the Heart: Coach K's Successful Strategies for Basketball, Business and Life

Hachette Book Group
237 Park Ave.
New York, NY 10017
Ph: (212)522-7200
URL: http://www.hachettebookgroupusa.com/

Mike Krzyzewski, Donald T. Phillips. 2001. $14.95 (paper). 336 pages.

★12077★ Opportunities in Sports and Athletics Careers

The McGraw-Hill Companies
PO Box 182604
Columbus, OH 43272
Fax: (614)759-3749   Fr: 877-883-5524
E-mail: customer.service@mcgraw-hill.com
URL: http://www.mcgraw-hill.com

William Ray Heitzmann. 1993. 160 pages. $11.95 (paper). A guide to planning for and seeking opportunities in this growing field. Illustrated.

★12078★ Opportunities in Sports Medicine Careers

The McGraw-Hill Companies
PO Box 182604
Columbus, OH 43272
Fax: (614)759-3749   Fr: 877-883-5524
E-mail: customer.service@mcgraw-hill.com
URL: http://www.mcgraw-hill.com

William Ray Heitzmann. 1992. $11.95 (paper). 160 pages. Discusses a variety of opportunities in this field and how to pursue them. Contains bibliography and illustrations.

★12079★ Real-Resumes for Sports Industry Jobs

PREP Publishing
1110 1/2 Hay St., PMB 66
Fayetteville, NC 28305
Ph: (910)483-6611   Fax: (910)483-2439
Fr: 800-533-2814

Anne McKinney (Editor). April 2004. $16.95 (paper). Illustrated. 192 pages. Real-Resumes Series.

ONLINE JOB SOURCES AND SERVICES

★12080★ Online Sports Career Center

Fr: 800-856-2638
E-mail: comments@atsonlinesports.com
URL: http://www.onlinesports.com/pages/careercenter.html

Description: Resource for sports-related career opportunities, as well as a resume bank for the perusal of potential employers within the sports and recreation industries. **Main files include:** Job Bank, Resume Bank, Newsletter, Work With Online Sports, Other Internet Resources.

OTHER SOURCES

★12081★ American Hockey Coaches Association (AHCA)

7 Concord St.
Gloucester, MA 01930
Ph: (781)245-4177   Fax: (781)245-2492
E-mail: jbertagna@hockeyeastonline.com
URL: http://www.ahcahockey.com

Description: Represents university, college, and secondary school ice hockey coaches. Conducts coaches' clinics throughout the U.S.

★12082★ Black Coaches Association (BCA)

Pan American Plz.
201 S Capitol Ave., Ste. 495
Indianapolis, IN 46225
Ph: (317)829-5600   Fax: (317)829-5601
Fr: 877-789-1222
E-mail: fkeith@bcasports.org
URL: http://bcasports.cstv.com

Description: Promotes equitable employment of ethnic minorities in all sports professions; the education, development and scholarship of members and ethnic minority student athletes. Promotes the creation of a positive environment in which issues such as stereotyping, lack of significant media coverage, and discrimination can be exposed, discussed, and resolved. Provides member services. Petitions the NCAA legislative bodies to design, enact, and enforce diligent guidelines and policies to improve professional mobility for minorities.

★12083★ **IDEA Health and Fitness Association**

10455 Pacific Center Ct.
San Diego, CA 92121-3773
Ph: (858)535-8979   Fax: (858)535-8234
Fr: 800-999-IDEA
E-mail: contact@ideafit.com
URL: http://www.ideafit.com

Purpose: Provides continuing education for fitness professionals including; fitness instructors, personal trainers, program directors, and club/studio owners. **Activities:** Offers workshops for continuing education credits.

★12084★ **National Association for Girls and Women in Sport (NAGWS)**

1900 Association Dr.
Reston, VA 20191-1598
Ph: (703)476-3400   Fax: (703)476-4566
Fr: 800-213-7193
E-mail: nagws@aahperd.org
URL: http://www.aahperd.org/nagws

Description: Represents teachers, coaches, athletic trainers, officials, athletic administrators, and students. Has 4 main structures: Advocacy Coaching Enhancement; Minority Representation; Professional Development Publications, and Student Representation. Supports and fosters the development of quality sports programs that will enrich the lives of all participants. Holds training sessions for leadership development. Conducts research programs.

★12085★ **National Association of Sports Officials (NASO)**

2017 Lathrop Ave.
Racine, WI 53405
Ph: (262)632-5448   Fax: (262)632-5460
Fr: 800-733-6100
E-mail: naso@naso.org
URL: http://www.naso.org

Description: Active sports officials, umpires, companies, and individuals interested in sports. Develops programs to assist in the education of sports officials; engages in programs to instruct fans, coaches, players, and the media on the role of sports officials. Conducts clinics and camps; sponsors public service ads.

★12086★ **National High School Athletic Coaches Association (NHSACA)**

PO Box 10065
Fargo, ND 58106
Ph: (701)293-2099   Fax: (701)293-8282
E-mail: office@hscoaches.org
URL: http://www.hscoaches.org

Description: High school coaches and athletic directors; athletic directors for school systems; executive secretaries of state high school coaches; state high school coaches associations. Aims to give greater national prestige and professional status to high school coaching and focuses on promoting cooperation among coaches, school administrators, the press, game officials, and the public. Promotes drug and alcohol abuse prevention through National Training Seminars in Drug Prevention in conjunction with the Drug Enforcement Administration, Washington, DC. Conducts Sports medicine/Medical Aspects of Sports seminars in conjunction with national sports and medical groups, and National College Credit Program for coaches and athletic directors.

★12087★ **National Strength and Conditioning Association (NSCA)**

1885 Bob Johnson Dr.
Colorado Springs, CO 80906
Ph: (719)632-6722   Fax: (719)632-6367
Fr: 800-815-6826
E-mail: nsca@nsca-lift.org
URL: http://www.nsca-lift.org

Description: Represents professionals in the sports science, athletic, and fitness industries. Promotes the total conditioning of athletes to a level of optimum performance, with the belief that a better conditioned athlete not only performs better but is less prone to injury. Gathers and disseminates information on strength and conditioning techniques and benefits. Conducts national, regional, state, and local clinics and work-shops. Operates professional certification program.

★12088★ **NFHS Coaches Association (NFCA)**

PO Box 690
Indianapolis, IN 46206
Ph: (317)972-6900   Fax: (317)822-5700
E-mail: tflannery@nfhs.org
URL: http://www.nfhs.org

Description: High school, middle school and youth athletic coaches. Promotes professional growth and image of interscholastic sports coaches; provides a forum for coaches to make suggestions on rules and procedures in high school sports in the U.S. Cooperates with state high school athletic associations and uses extensive committee structure to ensure grass roots involvement and input from the local, state, and national levels. Maintains hall of fame.

★12089★ **U.S. Lacrosse and The Lacrosse Museum and National Hall of Fame**

113 W University Pkwy.
Baltimore, MD 21210
Ph: (410)235-6882   Fax: (410)366-6735
E-mail: info@uslacrosse.org
URL: http://www.uslacrosse.org

Description: Serves as the national governing body of men's and women's lacrosse. Runs the Lacrosse Museum and National Hall of Fame.

★12090★ **Women in Nontraditional Careers: An Introduction**

Her Own Words
PO Box 5264
Madison, WI 53705
Ph: (608)271-7083   Fax: (608)271-0209
E-mail: herownword@aol.com
URL: http://www.herownwords.com/

Video. Jocelyn Riley. $95.00. 15 minutes. Resource guide also available for $45.00.

Statisticians

SOURCES OF HELP-WANTED ADS

★12091★ Journal of Financial and Quantitative Analysis

Journal of Financial & Quantitative Analysis
University of Washington
School of Business Administration
115 Lewis Hall
PO Box 353200
Seattle, WA 98195-3200
Ph: (206)543-4598   Fax: (206)616-1894
E-mail: jfqa@u.washington.edu

Quarterly. $70.00/year for individuals, U.S. and Canada; $80.00/year for other countries; $150.00/year for institutions; $160.00/year for institutions, other countries; $25.00/year for students; $30.00/year for students, other countries. Journal on research in finance.

★12092★ Journal of Mathematics and Statistics

Science Publications
Vails Gate Heights Dr.
PO Box 879
Vails Gate, NY 12584
URL: http://www.scipub.us/

Quarterly. $1,100.00/year for individuals; $300.00/year for single issue. Scholarly journal covering all areas of mathematics and statistics.

★12093★ Statistics

Taylor & Francis Group Journals
325 Chestnut St., Ste. 800
Philadelphia, PA 19106
Ph: (215)625-8900   Fax: (215)625-8914
Fr: 800-354-1420
URL: http://www.tandf.co.uk/journals/titles/02331888.asp

Bimonthly. $1,836.00/year for institutions, print and online; $1,744.00/year for institutions, online only; $328.00/year for individuals. Journal describing all aspects of statistical data analysis.

PLACEMENT AND JOB REFERRAL SERVICES

★12094★ International Society of Parametric Analysts (ISPA)

527 Maple Ave. E, Ste. 301
Vienna, VA 22180
Ph: (703)938-5090   Fax: (703)938-5091
E-mail: ispa@sceaonline.net
URL: http://www.ispa-cost.org

Members: Engineers, designers, statisticians, estimators, and managers in industry, the military, and government who develop and use computerized, parametric cost-estimating models. **Activities:** Conducts educational activities to promote usage of parametric modeling techniques for purposes of cost estimating, risk analysis, and technology forecasting. Sponsors placement service.

EMPLOYER DIRECTORIES AND NETWORKING LISTS

★12095★ American Men and Women of Science

Gale, Cengage Learning
27500 Drake Rd.
Farmington Hills, MI 48331-3535
Ph: (248)699-4253   Fax: (248)699-8065
Fr: 800-877-4253
URL: http://www.gale.com

Biennial, latest edition 23rd, October 2006; new edition expected 24th, January 2008. $1,075.00 for individuals. Covers over 129,700 U.S. and Canadian scientists active in the physical, biological, mathematical, computer science, and engineering fields; includes references to previous edition for deceased scientists and nonrespondents. Entries include: Name, address, education, personal and career data, memberships, honors and awards, research interest. Arrangement: Alphabetical. Indexes: Discipline (in separate volume).

HANDBOOKS AND MANUALS

★12096★ Careers for Number Crunchers and Other Quantitative Types

The McGraw-Hill Companies
PO Box 182604
Columbus, OH 43272
Fax: (614)759-3749   Fr: 877-883-5524
E-mail: customer.service@mcgraw-hill.com
URL: http://www.mcgraw-hill.com

Rebecca Burnett. Second edition, 2002. $22.95 (paper). 192 pages. Provides information to math-oriented job hunters on how to become statisticians, field researchers, computer programmers, stock analysts, investment managers, bankers, engineers, accountants, underwriters, economists, market analysts, mathematicians, systems analysts, and more.

★12097★ Opportunities in High Tech Careers

The McGraw-Hill Companies
PO Box 182604
Columbus, OH 43272
Fax: (614)759-3749   Fr: 877-883-5524
E-mail: customer.service@mcgraw-hill.com
URL: http://www.mcgraw-hill.com

Gary Colter and Deborah Yanuck. 1999. $14.95; $11.95 (paper). 160 pages. Explores high technology careers. Describes job opportunities, how to make a career decision, how to prepare for high technology jobs, job hunting techniques, and future trends.

★12098★ Opportunities in Research and Development Careers

The McGraw-Hill Companies
PO Box 182604
Columbus, OH 43272
Fax: (614)759-3749   Fr: 877-883-5524
E-mail: customer.service@mcgraw-hill.com
URL: http://www.mcgraw-hill.com

Jan Goldberg. 1996. $11.95 (paper). 146 pages.

★12099★ *Opportunities in Social Science Careers*

The McGraw-Hill Companies
PO Box 182604
Columbus, OH 43272
Fax: (614)759-3749   Fr: 877-883-5524
E-mail: customer.service@mcgraw-hill.com
URL: http://www.mcgraw-hill.com

Rosanne J. Marek. 2004. $13.95. 160 Pages. VGM Opportunities Series.

★12100★ *Opportunities in Sports and Athletics Careers*

The McGraw-Hill Companies
PO Box 182604
Columbus, OH 43272
Fax: (614)759-3749   Fr: 877-883-5524
E-mail: customer.service@mcgraw-hill.com
URL: http://www.mcgraw-hill.com

William Ray Heitzmann. 1993. 160 pages. $11.95 (paper). A guide to planning for and seeking opportunities in this growing field. Illustrated.

EMPLOYMENT AGENCIES AND SEARCH FIRMS

★12101★ **Analytic Recruiting, Inc.**

144 E. 44th St., 3rd Fl.
New York, NY 10017
Ph: (212)545-8511   Fax: (212)545-8520
E-mail: email@analyticrecruiting.com
URL: http://www.analyticrecruiting.com

Executive search firm.

★12102★ **Biomedical Search Consultants**

275 Wyman St.
Waltham, MA 02451
Ph: (978)952-6425   Fax: (781)890-1082
E-mail: kprovost@biomedicalsearchconsultants.com
URL: http://www.biomedicalsearchconsultants.com

Employment agency.

★12103★ **Placemart Personnel Service**

80 Haines St.
Lanoka Harbor, NJ 08734
Ph: (732)212-0144   Fax: (609)242-4347
Fr: 800-394-7522

E-mail: info@placemart.com
URL: http://www.placemart.com

Executive search firm focusing on the field of clinical research.

TRADESHOWS

★12104★ **Joint Statistical Meetings**

American Statistical Association
732 North Washington St.
Alexandria, VA 22314-1943
Ph: (703)684-1221   Fax: (703)684-2037
Fr: 888-231-3473
E-mail: asainfo@amstat.org
URL: http://www.amstat.org

Annual. **Primary Exhibits:** Publications, software, federal agencies, recruiters, consulting firms. **Dates and Locations:** 2008 Aug 03-07; Denver, CO; Denver Convention Center; 2009 Aug 02-06; Washington, DC; Washington Convention Center; 2010 Aug 01-05; Vancouver, BC, Canada; Vancouver Convention Center; 2011 Jul 31 - Aug 04; Miami Beach, FL; South Beach Convention Center.

OTHER SOURCES

★12105★ **American Statistical Association (ASA)**

732 N Washington St.
Alexandria, VA 22314-1943
Ph: (703)684-1221   Fax: (703)684-2037
Fr: 888-231-3473
E-mail: asainfo@amstat.org
URL: http://www.amstat.org

Members: Professional society of persons interested in the theory, methodology, and application of statistics to all fields of human endeavor.

★12106★ **Caucus for Women in Statistics (CWS)**

7732 Rydal Terr.
Rockville, MD 20855-2057
Ph: (301)827-0170   Fax: (301)827-6661
E-mail: anna.nevius@fda.hhs.gov
URL: http://caucusforwomeninstatistics.com

Description: Individuals, primarily statisticians, united to improve employment and professional opportunities for women in statistics. Conducts technical sessions concerning statistical studies related to women. Maintains biographical archives.

★12107★ **Institute of Mathematical Statistics (IMS)**

PO Box 22718
Beachwood, OH 44122
Ph: (216)295-2340   Fax: (216)295-5661
E-mail: ims@imstat.org
URL: http://www.imstat.org

Members: Professional society of mathematicians and others interested in mathematical statistics and probability theory. **Purpose:** Seeks to further research in mathematical statistics and probability.

★12108★ **Professional Specialty Occupations**

Delphi Productions
3159 6th St.
Boulder, CO 80304
Ph: (303)443-2100   Fax: (303)443-4022
Fr: 888-443-2400
E-mail: support@delphivideo.com
URL: http://www.delphivideo.com

$95.00. 53 minutes. Part of the Careers for the 21st Century Video Library.

★12109★ **Scientific, Engineering, and Technical Services**

Cambridge Educational
PO Box 2053
Princeton, NJ 08543-2053
Ph: 800-257-5126   Fax: (609)671-0266
Fr: 800-468-4227
E-mail: custserv@films.com
URL: http://www.cambridgeeducational.com

VHS and DVD. $89.95. 2002. 18 minutes. 2002. Part of the Career Cluster Series.

★12110★ **Scientific Occupations**

Delphi Productions
3159 6th St.
Boulder, CO 80304
Ph: (303)443-2100   Fax: (303)443-4022
Fr: 888-443-2400
E-mail: support@delphivideo.com
URL: http://www.delphivideo.com

$95.00. 60 minutes. Part of the Careers for the 21st Century Video Library.

Stenographers and Court Reporters

SOURCES OF HELP-WANTED ADS

★12111★ **Public Interest Employment Service Job Alert!**
Public Interest Clearinghouse
47 Kearny St., Ste. 705
San Francisco, CA 94108
Ph: (415)834-0100   Fax: (415)834-0202
E-mail: pies@pic.org
URL: http://www.pic.org

Description: Semimonthly. Lists job openings in legal aid offices and public interest law organizations. Also available via e-mail.

EMPLOYER DIRECTORIES AND NETWORKING LISTS

★12112★ **Law and Legal Information Directory**
Gale, Cengage Learning
27500 Drake Rd.
Farmington Hills, MI 48331-3535
Ph: (248)699-4253   Fax: (248)699-8065
Fr: 800-877-4253
E-mail: businessproducts@gale.com
URL: http://www.gale.com

Annual; latest edition 18th, published June 2007. $540.00 for individuals. Covers more than 19,000 national and international organizations, bar associations, federal and highest state courts, federal regulatory agencies, law schools, firms and organizations offering continuing legal education, paralegal education, sources of scholarships and grants, awards and prizes, special libraries, information systems and services, research centers, publishers of legal periodicals, books, and audiovisual materials, lawyer referral services, legal aid offices, public defender offices, legislature manuals and registers, small claims courts, corporation departments of state, state law enforcement agencies, state agencies, including disciplinary agencies, and state bar requirements. Entries include: All entries include institution or firm name, address, phone; many include names and titles of key personnel and, when pertinent, descriptive annotations. Contents based in part on information selected from several other Gale directories. Arrangement: Classified by type of organization, activity, service, etc. Indexes: Individual sections have special indexes as required.

HANDBOOKS AND MANUALS

★12113★ **Career Planning in Criminal Justice**
Anderson Publishing Co.
2035 Reading Rd.
Cincinnati, OH 45202-1576
Ph: (513)421-4142   Fax: (513)562-8116
Fr: 800-582-7295

Robert C. DeLucia and Thomas J. Doyle. Third edition, 1998. 225 pages. $21.95. Surveys a wide range of career and employment opportunities in law enforcement, the courts, corrections, forensic science, and private security. Contains career planning and job hunting advice.

★12114★ **The Court Reporter's Guide to Cyberspace**
CyberDawg Pub
4022 E. Stanford Dr.
Phoenix, AZ 85018
Ph: (602)808-7771   Fax: (602)808-7773

Richard A. Sherman and Gary Robson. 1996. $24.95. 356 pages.

★12115★ **Style and Sense For the Legal Profession: A Handbook for Court Reporters, Transcribers, Paralegals and Secretaries**
ETC Publications
1456 Rodeo Rd.
Palm Springs, CA 92262
Ph: (760)316-9695   Fax: (760)316-9681
Fr: (866)514-9969
URL: http://www.etcpublications.com/

Audrey Fatooh and Barbara R. Mauk. Revised, 1996. $22.95. 228 pages

EMPLOYMENT AGENCIES AND SEARCH FIRMS

★12116★ **Attorney Resources, Inc.**
750 North St. Paul, Ste. 540
Dallas, TX 75201
Ph: (214)922-8050   Fax: (214)871-3041
Fr: 800-324-4828
E-mail: dallas@attorneyresource.com
URL: http://www.attorneyresource.com

Employment agency. Offices in Austin, Dallas, Fort Worth, Houston and Tulsa, OK. Provides staffing assistance on regular or temporary basis.

★12117★ **Beverly Hills Bar Association Personnel Service**
300 S. Beverly Dr., Ste. 201
Beverly Hills, CA 90212-4805
Ph: (310)601-2422   Fax: (310)601-2423
URL: http://www.bhba.org

Employment agency.

★12118★ **Hallmark Services**
1511 Third Ave., Ste. 520
Seattle, WA 98101
Ph: (206)587-5360   Fax: (206)587-5319
E-mail: hallmark@hallmarkservices.com
URL: http://www.hallmarkservices.com/

Employment agency. Fills openings for permanent employment.

★12119★ **Legal Placement Services, Inc.**
6737 W. Washington St., Ste. 2390
West Allis, WI 53214
Ph: (414)276-6689   Fax: (414)276-1418
E-mail: info@legalplacementservices.com
URL: http://www.legalplacementservices.com

Employment agency. Periodically fills temporary placements, as well.

★12120★ **Pathfinders, Inc.**
229 Peachtree St. NE
International Tower, Ste. 1500
Atlanta, GA 30303
Ph: (404)688-5940 Fax: (404)688-9228
E-mail: resumes@pathfindersinc.com
URL: http://www.pathfindersinc.com

Permanent employment agency focusing on the secretarial field.

ONLINE JOB SOURCES AND SERVICES

★12121★ **Court Reporters Board of California**
2535 Capitol Oaks Dr., Ste. 230
Sacramento, CA 95833
Ph: (916)263-3660 Fax: (916)263-3664
URL: http://www.courtreportersboard.ca.gov

Description: Provides users of the Judicial System protection through disseminating information and through regulating and testing of the qualifications, performance, and ethical conduct of CSRs and entities regulated by the Board.

★12122★ **CourtReporterNet.com**
Fr: 800-960-1861
URL: http://www.courtreporternet.com

Description: Provides directory of court reporting firms worldwide.

★12123★ **JournalismJobs.com**
Ph: (510)653-1521
E-mail: contact@journalismjobs.com
URL: http://www.journalismjobs.com

Description: Career-related site for journalists and other media professionals. Seekers can search for jobs, post a resume online, and manage the search online with the Job Seeker Folder feature. They also can receive free job announcements by e-mail.

★12124★ **Law.com: Court Reporter Directory**
10 United Nations Plaza, 3rd Fl.
San Francisco, CA 94102
Fr: 800-903-9872
E-mail: courtreporter@corp.law.com
URL: http://courtreporter.law.com/index.cfm

Description: An online directory for those seeking services of court reporters.

OTHER SOURCES

★12125★ **California Court Reporters Association**
65 Enterprise
Aliso Viejo, CA 92656
Ph: (949)715-4682 Fax: (949)715-6931
E-mail: ccra@omgs.com
URL: http://www.cal-ccra.org

Description: Mission is to advance the profession of verbatim shorthand reporting by promoting professional reporting excellence through education, research, and the use of state-of-the-art technology; establishing and maintaining professional standards of practice; and advocating before legislative and regulatory bodies on issues which im-

pact the judicial system and others served by the court reporting profession of California.

★12126★ **Depo Depot: Certified Court Reporters and Videographers**
3535 Inland Empire Blvd.
Ontario, CA 91764-4908
Ph: (866)337-6337 Fax: 877-337-6329
URL: http://www.depodepot.com

Description: Provides professional court reporting services specializing in deposition reporting with realtime transcript deposition.

★12127★ **National Court Reporters**
500 S Ervay St., No. 120a
Dallas, TX 75201-6319
Fax: (866)819-2317 Fr: 888-800-9656
E-mail: NationalReport@aol.com
URL: http://www.nationalcourtreporters.com

Description: Provides comprehensive court reporting services throughout the United States, Canada and all countries overseas.

★12128★ **National Court Reporters Association (NCRA)**
8224 Old Courthouse Rd.
Vienna, VA 22182-3808
Ph: (703)556-6272 Fax: (703)556-6291
Fr: 800-272-6272
E-mail: msic@ncrahq.org
URL: http://www.ncraonline.org

Description: Represents Independent state, regional, and local associations. Verbatim court reporters who work as official reporters for courts and government agencies, as freelance reporters for independent contractors, and as captioners for television programming; retired reporters, teachers of court reporting, and school officials; student court reporters. Conducts research; compiles statistics; offers several certification programs; and publishes journal.

Stockbrokers and Securities Analysts

★12129★ Registered Rep.

Primedia Business
745 Fifth Ave.
New York, NY 10151
Ph: (212)745-0100   Fax: (212)745-0121
URL: http://www.registeredrep.com/

Monthly. Magazine providing comprehensive coverage of securities industry trends directly affecting the job performance and productivity of retail stockbrokers.

★12130★ Financial Women's Association of New York (FWA)

215 Park Ave. S, Ste. 1713
New York, NY 10003
Ph: (212)533-2141   Fax: (212)982-3008
E-mail: fwaoffice@fwa.org
URL: http://www.fwa.org

Members: Persons of professional status in the field of finance in the New York metropolitan area. **Purpose:** Works to promote and maintain high professional standards in the financial and business communities; provide an opportunity for members to enhance one another's professional contacts; achieve recognition of the contribution of women to the financial and business communities; encourage other women to seek professional positions within the financial and business communities. **Activities:** Activities include educational trips to foreign countries; college internship program including foreign student exchange; high school mentorship program; Washington and international briefings; placement service for members. Maintains speakers' bureau.

★12131★ New York Society of Security Analysts (NYSSA)

1177 Ave. of the Americas, 2nd Fl.
New York, NY 10036-2714
Ph: (212)541-4530   Fax: (212)541-4677
Fr: 800-248-0108
E-mail: staff@nyssa.org
URL: http://www.nyssa.org

Members: Security analysts and portfolio managers employed primarily in New York by brokerage houses, banks, insurance companies, mutual funds, and other financial institutions. **Activities:** Conducts educational forums on topics relating to the securities markets. Maintains placement service.

★12132★ Career Opportunities in Banking, Finance, and Insurance

Facts On File Inc.
132 W 31st St., 17th Fl.
New York, NY 10001
Ph: (212)967-8800   Fax: 800-678-3633
Fr: 800-322-8755
URL: http://www.factsonfile.com/

Latest edition 2nd, February 2007. $49.50 for individuals; $44.45 for libraries. Publication includes: Lists of colleges with programs supporting banking, finance, and industry; professional associations; professional certifications; regulatory agencies; and Internet resources for career planning. Principal content of publication consists of job descriptions for professions in the banking, finance, and insurance industries. Indexes: Alphabetical.

★12133★ National Association of Securities Dealers-Manual

CCH Inc.
4025 W Peterson Ave.
Chicago, IL 60646-6085
Fr: 888-224-7377
URL: http://www.onlinestore.cch.com

Monthly updates. $79.00. Publication includes: List of about 2,900 members of the National Association of Securities Dealers. Entries include: Company name, address. Principal contents of the manual are association by-laws and industry rules, arbitration code and code of procedure, and association's rules of fair practice. Arrangement: Alphabetical.

★12134★ Securities Industry Yearbook

Securities Industry and Financial Markets Association
120 Broadway, 35th Fl.
New York, NY 10271-0080
Ph: (212)608-1500   Fax: (212)968-0703
URL: http://www.sia.com

Annual, August; latest edition 2004-05. Covers over 600 member securities firms, with about 480 of them covered in detail. Entries include: For firms covered in detail–Company name, name of parent company, address, phone, capital position and rank, number of offices and type, number of employees, area of specialization, names and titles of key personnel, number of registered representatives, departments with name of department head, dollar volume of underwriting and syndication by type, other financial data. For other firms–Company name, address, name of delegated liaison to the association. Arrangement: Alphabetical. Indexes: National firms ranked by capital with capital and rank for prior year, number of offices and rank, number of employees and rank, and number of registered representatives and rank. Same data given in separate ranked list for regional firms.

★12135★ Standard & Poor's Security Dealers of North America

Standard & Poor's
55 Water St.
New York, NY 10041
Ph: (212)438-1000   Fax: (212)438-2000
Fr: 800-852-1641
URL: http://www2.standardandpoors.com

Semiannual, March and September; supplements available every six weeks. Covers over 12,000 security dealers; includes over 300 offices outside North America. Entries include: Company name, address, phone, main and branch offices, departments, names and titles of principal personnel, exchange memberships, teletype, wire systems, clearing facilities, employer identification number, and date established. Arrangement: Geographical.

HANDBOOKS AND MANUALS

★12136★ Careers in Banking and Finance

Rosen Publishing Group, Inc.
29 E. 21st St.
New York, NY 10010
Ph: (212)777-3017   Fax: 888-436-4643
Fr: 800-237-9932
URL: http://www.rosenpublishing.com/

Patricia Haddock. Revised edition, 2001. $31.95. 139 pages. Offers advice on job hunting. Describes jobs at all levels in banking and finance. Contains information about the types of financial organizations where the jobs are found, educational requirements, job duties, and salaries.

★12137★ Careers for Financial Mavens and Other Money Movers

The McGraw-Hill Companies
PO Box 182604
Columbus, OH 43272
Fax: (614)759-3749   Fr: 877-883-5524
E-mail: customer.service@mcgraw-hill.com
URL: http://www.mcgraw-hill.com

Marjorie Eberts and Margaret Gisler. Second edition, 2004. $13.95; $9.95 (paper). 153 pages.

★12138★ Careers for Number Crunchers and Other Quantitative Types

The McGraw-Hill Companies
PO Box 182604
Columbus, OH 43272
Fax: (614)759-3749   Fr: 877-883-5524
E-mail: customer.service@mcgraw-hill.com
URL: http://www.mcgraw-hill.com

Rebecca Burnett. Second edition, 2002. $22.95 (paper). 192 pages. Provides information to math-oriented job hunters on how to become statisticians, field researchers, computer programmers, stock analysts, investment managers, bankers, engineers, accountants, underwriters, economists, market analysts, mathematicians, systems analysts, and more.

★12139★ Job Seekers Guide to Wall Street Recruiters

John Wiley & Sons Inc.
1 Wiley Dr.
Somerset, NJ 08873
Ph: (732)469-4400   Fax: (732)302-2300
Fr: 800-225-5945
E-mail: custserv@wiley.com

URL: http://www.wiley.com/WileyCDA/
Christopher W. Hunt and Scott A. Scanlon. 1998. $26.95 (paper). 344 pages. Lists recruiters covering investment banking, investment management, and the securities industry.

★12140★ Opportunities in Financial Careers

The McGraw-Hill Companies
PO Box 182604
Columbus, OH 43272
Fax: (614)759-3749   Fr: 877-883-5524
E-mail: customer.service@mcgraw-hill.com
URL: http://www.mcgraw-hill.com

Michael Sumichrast. 2004. $13.95; $11.95 (paper). 160 pages. A guide to planning for and seeking opportunities in this challenging field.

★12141★ Vault Career Guide to Sales and Trading

Vault.com
150 W. 22nd St., 5th Fl.
New York, NY 10011
Ph: (212)366-4212   Fax: (212)366-6117
Fr: 888-562-8285
URL: http://www.vault.com

Gabriel Kim. April 2004. $29.95 (paper). 128 pages. Series of the Vault Career Library.

EMPLOYMENT AGENCIES AND SEARCH FIRMS

★12142★ Allen Personnel Agency Inc.

160 Broadway Lbby, Ste. 200
New York, NY 10038-4201
Ph: (212)571-1150   Fax: (212)766-1015
Fr: 800-486-1150

Personnel consultants specializing in business and finance recruitment, specifically insurance, banking, stock brokerage, law and accounting. Industries served: all.

★12143★ Baker Scott and Co.

1259 U.S. Highway 46, Ste. 1
Parsippany, NJ 07054
Ph: (973)263-3355   Fax: (973)263-9255
E-mail: exec.search@bakerscott.com
URL: http://www.bakerscott.com

Executive search firm.

★12144★ Essex Consulting Group Inc.

PO Box 550
Essex, MA 01929
Ph: (978)337-6633
E-mail: brad@essexsearch.com
URL: http://www.essexsearch.com/

Executive search firm.

★12145★ ExecuGroup Inc.

142 S. Main St.
PO Box 5040
Grenada, MS 38901
Ph: (662)226-9025   Fax: (662)226-9090
E-mail: tray@execugroup.com
URL: http://www.execugroup.com

Executive search firm. Second location in Bethlehem, PA.

★12146★ Fast Start Inc.

15 Pelican Pl.
Belleair, FL 33756-1512
Ph: (727)581-2224   Fax: (727)581-4743
E-mail: carolacfp@aol.com

Small consulting firm offering consulting, and broker/dealer referral services for the registered representative and the broker dealer. Offers assistance in areas of: practice management, broker/dealer selection, start-up interfacing, and career guidance. Start-up services include: starting an independent financial planning firm and feasibility studies on starting a broker/dealer and/or registered investment advisory firm. We match buyers and sellers of an RIA's Book of Business. We offer search services for mid-level and executive positions in financial services firms.

★12147★ Flagship Global Inc.

6308 Reserve Dr.
Boulder, CO 80303
Ph: (303)440-0280
E-mail: ac@flagshipboston.com
URL: http://www.flagshipglobal.com

Executive search firm focused on the financial industry.

★12148★ Fogec Consultants Inc.

PO Box 28806
Milwaukee, WI 53228
Ph: (414)427-0690   Fax: (414)427-0691
E-mail: tfogec@fogec.com
URL: http://www.fogec.com/fci/

Executive search firm focused on the financial industry.

★12149★ J.R. Scott and Associates

1 S Wacker Dr., Ste. 1616
Chicago, IL 60606-4616
Ph: (312)795-9999   Fax: (312)795-4329
E-mail: mark@esquirestaffing.com
URL: http://www.esquirestaffing.com

Executive search firm specializing in retail securities sales, investment banking, and equity and debt trading. A division of Esquire Personnel Services, Inc.

★12150★ Mark Elzweig Co. Ltd.

183 Madison Ave., Ste.1704
New York, NY 10016
Ph: (212)685-7070   Fax: (212)685-7761
E-mail: elzweig@elzweig.com
URL: http://www.elzweig.com

Executive search firm.

★12151★ People Management International
E-mail: info@peoplemanagement.org
URL: http://www.esearchgroup.com

Executive search firm with 2 dozens offices around the world.

★12152★ Straight and Company
1002 Brown Thrasher Pt.
St. Mary's, GA 31558
Ph: (912)882-3480   Fax: (912)882-3487
E-mail: gary.straight@straightco.com
URL: http://www.straightco.com

Financial services executive search firm.

ONLINE JOB SOURCES AND SERVICES

★12153★ Glocapsearch.com
156 W. 56th St., 4th Fl.
New York, NY 10019
Ph: (212)333-6400
E-mail: comments@glocap.com
URL: http://www.glocapsearch.com

Description: Recruitment firm for the private equity, venture capital and hedge fund marketplaces. After registering with website, seekers will be notified weekly of positions available that may interest them. Through returned e-mail, the firm will forward resumes and schedule preliminary interviews with prospective employers.

OTHER SOURCES

★12154★ CFA Institute
560 Ray C. Hunt Dr.
Charlottesville, VA 22903-2981
Ph: (434)951-5499   Fax: (434)951-5262
Fr: 800-247-8132
E-mail: info@cfainstitute.org
URL: http://www.cfainstitute.org

Description: Security and financial analyst association whose members are practicing investment analysts. Includes private, voluntary self-regulation program in which members are enrolled. Internationally renowned for its rigorous Chartered Financial Analyst curriculum and examination program, which has more than 86,000 candidates from 143 countries enrolled for exams. In addition, it is internationally recognized for its investment performance standards, which investment firms use to document and report investment results, as well as for its Code of Ethics and Standards of Professional Conduct.

★12155★ Financial Occupations
Delphi Productions
3159 6th St.
Boulder, CO 80304
Ph: (303)443-2100   Fax: (303)443-4022
Fr: 888-443-2400
E-mail: support@delphivideo.com
URL: http://www.delphivideo.com

$95.00. 50 minutes. Part of the Careers for the 21st Century Video Library.

★12156★ Securities Industry and Financial Markets Association (SIFMA)
120 Broadway, 35th Fl.
New York, NY 10271-0080
Ph: (212)608-1500   Fax: (212)968-0703
E-mail: rbrockhaus@sifma.org
URL: http://www.sifma.org

Description: Represents more than 650 member firms of all sizes, in all financial markets in the U.S. and around the world. Enhances the public's trust and confidence in the markets, delivering an efficient, enhanced member network of access and forward-looking services, as well as premiere educational resources for the professionals in the industry and the investors whom they serve. Maintains offices in New York City and Washington, DC.

Surgical Technicians

★12157★ *American Journal of Emergency Medicine*

Mosby Inc.
11830 Westline Industrial Dr.
St. Louis, MO 63146
Ph: (314)872-8370   Fax: (314)432-1380
Fr: 800-325-4177
URL: http://www.elsevier.com/wps/find/journaldescription.cws_home

Bimonthly. $275.00/year for individuals; $419.00/year for institutions; $129.00/year for students; $397.00/year for individuals, international; $546.00/year for institutions, international; $198.00/year for students, international. Journal reporting on emergency medicine.

★12158★ *American Journal of Surgery*

Excerpta Medica Inc.
685 US-202
Bridgewater, NJ 08807
Ph: (908)547-2100   Fax: (908)547-2200
URL: http://www.elsevier.com/wps/find/journaldescription.cws_home

Monthly. $562.00/year for institutions, outside U.S.; $373.00/year for individuals, outside U.S.; $82.00/year for students; $205.00/year for individuals; $334.00/year for institutions. Surgical journal.

★12159★ *Anesthesiology*

Lippincott Williams & Wilkins
530 Walnut St.
Philadelphia, PA 19106-3621
Ph: (215)521-8300   Fax: (215)521-8902
Fr: 800-638-3030
URL: http://www.anesthesiology.org/

Monthly. $408.00/year for individuals, U.S.; $753.00/year for institutions, U.S.; $575.00/year for other countries; $880.00/year for institutions, other countries; $207.00/year for U.S., in-training; $248.00/year for other countries, in-training. Medical journal publishing original manuscripts and brief abstracts from current literature on anesthesiology.

★12160★ *Annals of Medicine*

Taylor & Francis Group Journals
325 Chestnut St., Ste. 800
Philadelphia, PA 19106
Ph: (215)625-8900   Fax: (215)625-8914
Fr: 800-354-1420
URL: http://www.ingentaconnect.com

$418.00/year for institutions, print and online; $397.00/year for institutions, online only; $155.00/year for individuals. Journal covering health science and medical education.

★12161★ *Annals of Surgery*

Lippincott Williams & Wilkins
530 Walnut St.
Philadelphia, PA 19106-3621
Ph: (215)521-8300   Fax: (215)521-8902
Fr: 800-638-3030
E-mail: jumulliga@lww.com
URL: http://www.annalsofsurgery.com/

Monthly. $249.00/year for individuals; $646.00/year for institutions; $99.00/year for other countries, international; $392.00/year for individuals; $814.00/year for institutions; $99.00/year for other countries. Medical journal publishing original manuscripts promoting the advancement of surgical knowledge and practice.

★12162★ *Archives of Surgery*

American Medical Association
515 N State St.
Chicago, IL 60610
Fr: 800-621-8335
E-mail: archsurg@jama-archives.org
URL: http://archsurg.ama-assn.org/

Monthly. $190.00/year for individuals, print and online; $435.00/year for institutions, print and online. Educational/clinical journal for general surgeons and surgical specialists.

★12163★ *Clinical Medicine & Research*

Marshfield Clinic
1000 North Oak Ave.
Marshfield, WI 54449
Ph: (715)387-5511   Fr: 800-782-8581
URL: http://www.clinmedres.org/

Monthly. Journal that publishes scientific medical research that is relevant to a broad audience of medical researchers and healthcare professionals.

★12164★ *Clinical Nuclear Medicine*

Lippincott Williams & Wilkins
530 Walnut St.
Philadelphia, PA 19106-3621
Ph: (215)521-8300   Fax: (215)521-8902
Fr: 800-638-3030
E-mail: cnm@pond.com
URL: http://www.nuclearmed.com

Monthly. $329.00/year for individuals, U.S.; $613.00/year for institutions, U.S.; $436.00/year for other countries; $691.00/year for institutions, other countries; $186.00/year for other countries, in-training; $169.00/year for U.S., in-training. Journal publishing original manuscripts about scanning, imaging, and related subjects.

★12165★ *CME Supplement to Emergency Medicine Clinics of North America*

Elsevier Science Inc.
360 Park Ave. S
New York, NY 10010
Ph: (212)989-5800   Fax: (212)633-3990
URL: http://www.elsevier.com

Quarterly. $190.00/year for individuals. Journal covering emergency medicine clinics.

★12166★ *Current Surgery*

Lippincott Williams & Wilkins
530 Walnut St.
Philadelphia, PA 19106-3621
Ph: (215)521-8300   Fax: (215)521-8902
Fr: 800-638-3030
URL: http://www.us.elsevierhealth.com/product.jsp?isbn=01497944

Bimonthly. $283.00/year for individuals; $707.00/year for institutions. Professional journal covering continuing education for surgical residents and general surgeons.

★12167★ **Discovery Medicine**

Discovery Medicine
2245 Chapel Valley Ln.
Timonium, MD 21093
Ph: (410)560-9007   Fax: (410)560-9000
URL: http://www.discoverymedicine.com

Bimonthly. $39.95/year for individuals; $49.95/year for individuals, digital edition and online access; $69.95 for two years, online access; $84.95 for two years, digital edition and online access; $99.95/year for individuals, 3 years, online access; $119.95/year for individuals, 3 years, digital and online access; $299.00/year for individuals, medical report (PMR); $99.00/year for individuals, medical report update. Online journal that publishes articles on diseases, biology, new diagnostics, and treatments for medical professionals.

★12168★ **Education & Treatment of Children**

West Virginia University Press
44 Stansbury Hall
PO Box 6295
Morgantown, WV 26506
Ph: (304)293-8400   Fax: (304)293-6585
Fr: (866)988-7737
URL: http://
www.educationandtreatmentofchildren.net

Quarterly. $85.00/year for institutions; $45.00/year for individuals; $100.00/year for institutions, elsewhere; $60.00/year for individuals, elsewhere. Periodical featuring information concerning the development of services for children and youth. Includes reports written for educators and other child care and mental health providers focused on teaching, training, and treatment effectiveness.

★12169★ **Hospitals & Health Networks**

Health Forum L.L.C.
1 N Franklin, 29th Fl.
Chicago, IL 60606
Ph: (312)893-6800   Fax: (312)422-4506
Fr: 800-821-2039
URL: http://www.hhnmag.com

Weekly. Publication covering the health care industry.

★12170★ **The IHS Primary Care Provider**

Indian Health Service (HQ)
The Reyes Bldg.
801 Thompson Ave., Ste. 400
Rockville, MD 20852-1627
URL: http://www.ihs.gov/PublicInfo/Publications/HealthProvider/Pr

Monthly. Journal for health care professionals, physicians, nurses, pharmacists, dentists, and dietitians.

★12171★ **Injury**

Mosby Inc.
11830 Westline Industrial Dr.
St. Louis, MO 63146
Ph: (314)872-8370   Fax: (314)432-1380
Fr: 800-325-4177
URL: http://www.elsevier.com/wps/find/journaldescription.cws_home

Monthly. $1,106.00/year for institutions, all countries except Europe, Japan and Iran; $169.00/year for individuals, all countries except Europe, Japan and Iran. Journal publishing articles and research related to the treatment of injuries such as trauma systems and management; surgical procedures; epidemiological studies; surgery (of all tissues); resuscitation; biomechanics; rehabilitation; anaesthesia; radiology and wound management.

★12172★ **Journal of the American Society of Podiatric Medical Assistants**

American Society of Podiatric Medical Assistants
2124 S Austin Blvd.
Cicero, IL 60804
Ph: (708)863-6303   Fr: 888-882-7762
URL: http://www.aspma.org

Quarterly. Subscription included in membership. Professional journal covering issues in podiatry.

★12173★ **The Journal of Arthroplasty**

Elsevier
1600 John F. Kennedy Blvd., Ste. 1800
Philadelphia, PA 19103-2899
Ph: (215)239-3900   Fax: (215)238-7883
E-mail: elspcs@elsevier.com
URL: http://www.us.elsevierhealth.com/product.jsp?isbn=08835403

$777.00/year for institutions, outside U.S.; $172.00/year for students; $638.00/year for institutions; $390.00/year for individuals; $200.00/year for students, outside U.S.; $512.00/year for individuals, outside U.S. Medical journal for orthopaedic surgeons. Covering clinical and basic science research on arthroplasty including surgical techniques, prosthetic design, biomechanics, biomaterials, and metallurgy.

★12174★ **Journal of Health Law**

American Health Lawyers Association
1025 Connecticut Ave., NW, Ste. 600
Washington, DC 20036-5405
Ph: (202)833-1100   Fax: (202)833-1105
URL: http://www.healthlawyers.org

Quarterly. Professional journal covering healthcare issues and cases and their impact on the health care arena.

★12175★ **Journal of Hospital Medicine**

John Wiley & Sons Inc.
111 River St.
Hoboken, NJ 07030-5774
Ph: (201)748-6000   Fax: (201)748-6088
Fr: 800-825-7550

URL: http://www.wiley.com/WileyCDA/WileyTitle/productCd-JHM.html

Bimonthly. $110.00/year for individuals, print only; Online version available with subscription. Journal on hospital medicine.

★12176★ **Medical Risks**

Taylor & Francis Group Journals
325 Chestnut St., Ste. 800
Philadelphia, PA 19106
Ph: (215)625-8900   Fax: (215)625-8914
Fr: 800-354-1420
URL: http://www.tandf.co.uk

Monthly. Journal covering articles on medical risks.

★12177★ **Medical Staff Development Professional**

American Academy of Medical Management
Crossville Commons
560 W Crossville Rd., Ste. 103
Roswell, GA 30075
Ph: (770)649-7150   Fax: (770)649-7552

Periodic. Professional journal covering medical education.

★12178★ **Pacifica Review**

Taylor & Francis Group Journals
325 Chestnut St., Ste. 800
Philadelphia, PA 19106
Ph: (215)625-8900   Fax: (215)625-8914
Fr: 800-354-1420
URL: http://www.tandf.co.uk/

$462.00/year for individuals; $279.00/year for individuals; $487.00/year for individuals; $294.00/year for individuals; $123.00/year for individuals; $86.00/year for individuals. Journal promoting physical therapy and integration.

★12179★ **Surgical Rounds**

Pharmacy Times
103 College Rd. E
Princeton, NJ 08540-6612
Ph: (609)524-9560   Fax: (609)524-9699
URL: http://www.surgicalroundsonline.com/

Monthly. Journal featuring clinical articles of interest to office-based and hospital-based surgeons, including residents, full-time staff, and surgical faculty.

★12180★ **USA Body Psychotherapy Journal**

United States Association for Body Psychotherapy
7831 Woodmont Ave.
Bethesda, MD 20814
URL: http://www.usabp.org/displaycommon.cfm?an=4

Semiannual. Academic journal that seeks to support, promote and stimulate the exchange of ideas, scholarship and research within the field of body psychotherapy as well as an interdisciplinary exchange with related fields of clinical practice and inquiry.

★12181★ Year Book of Critical Care Medicine

Elsevier Science Inc.
360 Park Ave. S
New York, NY 10010
Ph: (212)989-5800   Fax: (212)633-3990
URL: http://www.elsevier.com

$180.00/year for institutions, U.S. $191.00/year for institutions, other countries; $121.00/year for individuals, U.S. $134.00/year for individuals, other countries; $59.00/year for individuals, other countries; $71.00/year for students, other countries. Journal focused on treatment of severe sepsis and septic shock, echocardiography in the evaluation of hemodynamically unstable patients & mechanical ventilation of acute respiratory distress syndrome.

EMPLOYER DIRECTORIES AND NETWORKING LISTS

★12182★ AHA Guide to the Health Care Field

American Hospital Association
1 N Franklin
Chicago, IL 60606
Ph: (312)422-2050   Fax: (312)422-4700
Fr: 800-424-4301

Annual, August. Covers hospitals, networks, multi-health care systems, freestanding ambulatory surgery centers, psychiatric facilities, long-term care facilities, substance abuse programs, and other health-related organizations. Entries include: For hospitals–Facility name, address, phone, administrator's name, number of beds, facilities and services, number of employees, expenses, other statistics. For other organizations–Name, address, phone, fax, name and title of contact. Arrangement: Geographical. Indexes: Hospital name.

★12183★ Directory of Hospital Personnel

Grey House Publishing
185 Millerton Rd.
PO Box 860
Millerton, NY 12546
Ph: (518)789-8700   Fax: (518)789-0556
Fr: 800-562-2139
URL: http://www.greyhouse.com/hospital_personnel.htm

Annual. $325.00 for print product; $545.00 for online database subscription; $650.00 for online database subscription and print product combined. Covers 200,000 executives at 7,000 U.S. hospitals. Entries include: Name of hospital, address, phone; number of beds; type and JCAHO status of hospital; names and titles of key department heads and staff; medical and nursing school affiliations; number of residents, interns, and nursing students. Arrangement: Geographical. Indexes: Hospital name, personnel, hospital size.

★12184★ Hospital Blue Book

Billian Publishing Inc./Transworld Publishing Inc.
2100 Powers Ferry Rd. SE
Atlanta, GA 30339
Ph: (770)955-5656   Fax: (770)952-0669
Fr: 800-533-8484
E-mail: blu-book@billian.com

2005. $300.00 for individuals. Covers more than 6,687 hospitals; some listings also appear in a separate southern edition of this publication. Entries include: Name of hospital, accreditation, mailing address, phone, fax, number of beds, type of facility (nonprofit, general, state, etc.); list of administrative personnel and chiefs of medical services, with specific titles. Arrangement: Geographical.

★12185★ Medical and Health Information Directory

Gale, Cengage Learning
27500 Drake Rd.
Farmington Hills, MI 48331-3535
Ph: (248)699-4253   Fax: (248)699-8065
Fr: 800-877-4253
E-mail: businessproducts@gale.com
URL: http://www.gale.com

Annual; latest edition 20th, July 2007. $375.00/volume. Covers in Volume 1, more than 26,500 medical and health oriented associations, organizations, institutions, and government agencies, including health maintenance organizations (HMOs), preferred provider organizations (PPOs), insurance companies, pharmaceutical companies, research centers, and medical and allied health schools. In Volume 2, over 12,000 medical book publishers; medical periodicals, directories, audiovisual producers and services, medical libraries and information centers, electronic resources, and health-related internet search engines. In Volume 3, more than 35,500 clinics, treatment centers, care programs, and counseling/diagnostic services for 34 subject areas. Entries include: Institution, service, or firm name, address, phone, fax, email and URL; many include names of key personnel and, when pertinent, descriptive annotations. Volume 3 was formerly listed separately as Health Services Directory. Arrangement: Classified by organization activity, service, etc. Indexes: Each volume has a complete alphabetical name and keyword index.

HANDBOOKS AND MANUALS

★12186★ Careers in Health Care

The McGraw-Hill Companies
PO Box 182604
Columbus, OH 43272
Fax: (614)759-3749   Fr: 877-883-5524
E-mail: customer.service@mcgraw-hill.com
URL: http://www.mcgraw-hill.com

Barbara M. Swanson. Fifth edition, 2005. $15.95 (paper). 192 pages. Describes job duties, work settings, salaries, licensing and certification requirements, educational preparation, and future outlook. Gives ideas on how to secure a job.

★12187★ Careers for Night Owls and Other Insomniacs

The McGraw-Hill Companies
PO Box 182604
Columbus, OH 43272
Fax: (614)759-3749   Fr: 877-883-5524
E-mail: customer.service@mcgraw-hill.com
URL: http://www.mcgraw-hill.com

Louise Miller. Second edition, 2002. $12.95 (paper). 160 pages.

★12188★ Expert Resumes for Health Care Careers

Jist Works
875 Montreal Way
St. Paul, MN 55102
Fr: 800-648-5478
E-mail: info@jist.com
URL: http://www.jist.com

Wendy S. Enelow and Louise M. Kursmark. December 2003. $16.95. 288 pages.

★12189★ Health Careers Today

Elsevier
11830 Westline Industrial Dr.
St. Louis, MO 63146
Ph: (314)453-7010   Fax: (314)453-7095
Fr: 800-545-2522
E-mail: usbkinfo@elsevier.com
URL: http://www.elsevier.com

Gerdin, Judith. Fourth edition. 2007. $59.95. 496 pages. Covers more than 45 health careers. Discusses the roles and responsibilities of various occupations and provides a solid foundation in the skills needed for all health careers.

★12190★ Opportunities in Health and Medical Careers

The McGraw-Hill Companies
PO Box 182604
Columbus, OH 43272
Fax: (614)759-3749   Fr: 877-883-5524
E-mail: customer.service@mcgraw-hill.com
URL: http://www.mcgraw-hill.com

I. Donald Snook, Jr. and Leo D'Orazio. 2004. $13.95 (paper). 157 pages. Covers the full range of medical and health occupations. Illustrated.

★12191★ Opportunities in Paramedical Careers

The McGraw-Hill Companies
PO Box 182604
Columbus, OH 43272
Fax: (614)759-3749   Fr: 877-883-5524
E-mail: customer.service@mcgraw-hill.com
URL: http://www.mcgraw-hill.com

Alex Kacen. 1999. 14.95 (hardcover). 160 pages. Discusses a variety of opportunities in this field and how to pursue them. Illustrated.

★12192★ *Resumes for Health and Medical Careers*

The McGraw-Hill Companies
PO Box 182604
Columbus, OH 43272
Fax: (614)759-3749   Fr: 877-883-5524
E-mail: customer.service@mcgraw-hill.com
URL: http://www.mcgraw-hill.com

Third edition, 2003. $11.95 (paper). 160 pages.

ONLINE JOB SOURCES AND SERVICES

★12193★ Medhunters.com

Fr: 800-664-0278
E-mail: info@medhunters.com
URL: http://www.medhunters.com

Description: Career search site for jobs in all health care specialties; educational resources; visa and licensing information for relocation; interesting articles; relocation tools; links to professional organizations and general resources.

★12194★ ProHealthJobs

Fr: 800-796-1738
E-mail: Info@prohealthedujobs.com
URL: http://www.prohealthjobs.com

Description: Career resources site for the medical and health care field. Lists professional opportunities, product information, continuing education and open positions.

OTHER SOURCES

★12195★ Association of Surgical Technologists (AST)

6 W Dry Creek Cir., Ste. 200
Littleton, CO 80120
Ph: (303)694-9130   Fax: (303)694-9169
Fr: 800-637-7433
E-mail: bteutsch@ast.org
URL: http://www.ast.org

Description: Individuals who have received specific education and training to deliver surgical patient care in the operating room. Membership categories are available for both certified and student surgical technologists. Emphasis is placed on encouraging members to participate actively in a continuing education program. Aims are: to study, discuss, and exchange knowledge, experience, and ideas in the field of surgical technology; to promote a high standard of surgical technology performance in the community for quality patient care; to stimulate interest in continuing education. Local groups sponsor workshops and institutes. Conducts research.

★12196★ Exploring Health Occupations

Cambridge Educational
PO Box 2053
Princeton, NJ 08543-2053
Ph: 800-257-5126   Fax: (609)671-0266
Fr: 800-468-4227
E-mail: custserv@films.com
URL: http://www.cambridgeeducational.com

VHS and DVD. $159.90. 1999. Two-part series provides a detailed view of the field of medical technicians and technologists, EMTs, nurses, therapists, and assistants.

★12197★ Health Service Occupations

Delphi Productions
3159 6th St.
Boulder, CO 80304
Ph: (303)443-2100   Fax: (303)443-4022
Fr: 888-443-2400

E-mail: support@delphivideo.com
URL: http://www.delphivideo.com

$95.00. 50 minutes. Part of the Careers for the 21st Century Video Library.

★12198★ Health Technologists & Technicians

Delphi Productions
3159 6th St.
Boulder, CO 80304
Ph: (303)443-2100   Fax: (303)443-4022
Fr: 888-443-2400
E-mail: support@delphivideo.com
URL: http://www.delphivideo.com

$95.00. 50 minutes. Part of the Careers for the 21st Century Video Library.

★12199★ Medical Technicians and Technologists

Cambridge Educational
PO Box 2053
Princeton, NJ 08543-2053
Ph: 800-257-5126   Fax: (609)671-0266
Fr: 800-468-4227
E-mail: custserv@films.com
URL: http://www.cambridgeeducational.com

VHS and DVD. $79.95. 18 minutes. 2000. Part of the Exploring Health Occupations Series.

★12200★ Medicine & Related Occupations

Delphi Productions
3159 6th St.
Boulder, CO 80304
Ph: (303)443-2100   Fax: (303)443-4022
Fr: 888-443-2400
E-mail: support@delphivideo.com
URL: http://www.delphivideo.com

$95.00. 45 minutes. Part of the Careers for the 21st Century Video Library.

Surveyors

SOURCES OF HELP-WANTED ADS

★12201★ American City and County
Primedia Business
6151 Powers Ferry Rd., Ste. 200
Atlanta, GA 30339
Ph: (770)955-2500   Fax: (770)618-0204
URL: http://
www.americancityandcounty.com

Monthly. $67.00/year for individuals. Municipal and county administration magazine.

★12202★ Architectural Record
McGraw-Hill Inc.
1221 Ave. of the Americas
New York, NY 10020-1095
Ph: (212)512-2000   Fax: (212)512-3840
Fr: 877-833-5524
URL: http://archrecord.construction.com

Monthly. $49.00/year for individuals. Magazine focusing on architecture.

★12203★ Builder
Hanley-Wood L.L.C.
1 Thomas Cir., NW, Ste. 600
Washington, DC 20005
Ph: (202)452-0800   Fax: (202)785-1974
URL: http://www.hanleywood.com/default.aspx?page=b2bbd

$29.95/year for individuals, 13 issues;
$54.95/year for Canada, 26 issues; $192.00/
year for out of country, 13 issues. Magazine
covering housing and construction industry.

★12204★ The Municipality
League of Wisconsin Municipalities
122 W Washington Ave., Ste. 300
Madison, WI 53703-2718
Ph: (608)267-2380   Fax: (608)267-0645
Fr: 800-991-5502
URL: http://www.lwm-info.org/index.asp?Type=B_BASIC&SEC=¢0702EE8F

Monthly. Magazine for officials of Wisconsin's local municipal governments.

★12205★ NAHRO Monitor
National Association of Housing and
  Redevelopment Officials
630 Eye St. NW
Washington, DC 20001
Ph: (202)289-3500   Fax: (202)289-8181
Fr: 877-866-2476
E-mail: nahro@nahro.org
URL: http://www.nahro.org/publications/
monitor.cfm

Description: Semimonthly. Disseminates
news on low-income housing and community
development issues. Intended for member
professionals and government officials.

**★12206★ PE & RS Photogrammetric
Engineering & Remote Sensing**
The Imaging and Geospatial Information
Society
5410 Grosvenor Ln., Ste. 210
Bethesda, MD 20814-2160
Ph: (301)493-0290   Fax: (301)493-0208
E-mail: asprs@asprs.org
URL: http://www.asprs.org/

Monthly. $250.00/year for individuals, U.S.D
15 discount per subscp. off the base rate;
$120.00/year for individuals, active; $80.00/
year for individuals, associate; $45.00/year
for students, domestic. Journal covering
photogrammetry, remote sensing, geographic information systems, cartography, and
surveying, global positioning systems, digital
photogrammetry.

★12207★ Western City
League of California Cities
1400 K St., Ste. 400
Sacramento, CA 95814
Ph: (916)658-8200   Fax: (916)658-8240
Fr: 800-262-1801
URL: http://www.westerncity.com

Monthly. $39.00/year for individuals; $63.00
for two years; $52.00/year for other countries; $26.50/year for students. Municipal
interest magazine.

PLACEMENT AND JOB REFERRAL SERVICES

**★12208★ National Association of
Home Builders (NAHB)**
1201 15th St. NW
Washington, DC 20005
Ph: (202)266-8200   Fax: (202)266-8400
Fr: 800-368-5242
E-mail: info@nahb.com
URL: http://www.nahb.org

Description: Single and multifamily home
builders, commercial builders, and others
associated with the building industry. Lobbies on behalf of the housing industry and
conducts public affairs activities to increase
public understanding of housing and the
economy. Collects and disseminates data on
current developments in home building and
home builders' plans through its Economics
Department and nationwide Metropolitan
Housing Forecast. Maintains NAHB Research Center, which functions as the research arm of the home building industry.
Sponsors seminars and workshops on construction, mortgage credit, labor relations,
cost reduction, land use, remodeling, and
business management. Compiles statistics;
offers charitable program, spokesman training, and placement service; maintains
speakers' bureau, and Hall of Fame. Subsidiaries include the National Council of the
Housing Industry. Maintains over 50 committees in many areas of construction; operates
National Commercial Builders Council, National Council of the Multifamily Housing
Industry, National Remodelers Council, and
National Sales and Marketing Council.

**★12209★ Professional Women in
Construction (PWC)**
315 E 56th St.
New York, NY 10022-3730
Ph: (212)486-7745   Fax: (212)486-0228
E-mail: pwcusa1@aol.com
URL: http://www.pwcusa.org

Description: Management-level women and
men in construction and allied industries;
owners, suppliers, architects, engineers,
field personnel, office personnel, and bond-

ing/surety personnel. Provides a forum for exchange of ideas and promotion of political and legislative action, education, and job opportunities for women in construction and related fields; forms liaisons with other trade and professional groups; develops research programs. Strives to reform abuses and to assure justice and equity within the construction industry. Sponsors mini-workshops. Maintains Action Line, which provides members with current information on pertinent legislation and on the association's activities and job referrals.

EMPLOYER DIRECTORIES AND NETWORKING LISTS

★12210★ ABC Today-Associated Builders and Contractors National Membership Directory Issue

Associated Builders & Contractors Inc.
4250 N Fairfax Dr., 9th Fl.
Arlington, VA 22203-1607
Ph: (703)812-2000   Fax: (703)812-8203
URL: http://www.abc.org/
wmspage.cfm?parm1=2033

Annual, December. $150.00. Publication includes: List of approximately 19,000 member construction contractors and suppliers. Entries include: Company name, address, phone, name of principal executive, code to volume of business, business specialty. Arrangement: Classified by chapter, then by work specialty.

★12211★ Constructor-AGC Directory of Membership and Services Issue

AGC Information Inc.
2300 Wilson Blvd., Ste. 400
Arlington, VA 22201
Ph: (703)548-3118   Fax: (703)548-3119
Fr: 800-282-1423
URL: http://www.agc.org

Annual, August; latest edition 2004 edition. Publication includes: List of over 8,500 member firms and 24,000 national associate member firms engaged in building, highway, heavy, industrial, municipal utilities, and railroad construction (SIC 1541, 1542, 1611, 1622, 1623, 1629); listing of state and local chapter officers. Entries include: For firms–Company name, address, phone, fax, names of principal executives, and code indicating type of construction undertaken. For officers–Name, title, address. Arrangement: Geographical, alphabetical. Indexes: Company name.

★12212★ Indiana Society of Professional Engineers-Directory

Indiana Society of Professional Engineers
PO Box 20806
Indianapolis, IN 46220
Ph: (317)255-2267   Fax: (317)255-2530
URL: http://www.indspe.org

Annual, fall. Covers member registered engi-

neers, land surveyors, engineering students, and engineers in training. Entries include: Member name, address, phone, type of membership, business information, specialty. Arrangement: Alphabetical by chapter area.

HANDBOOKS AND MANUALS

★12213★ Opportunities in Real Estate Careers

The McGraw-Hill Companies
PO Box 182604
Columbus, OH 43272
Fax: (614)759-3749   Fr: 877-883-5524
E-mail: customer.service@mcgraw-hill.com
URL: http://www.mcgraw-hill.com

Mariwyn Evansand and Richard Mendenhal. Second edition, 2002. $12.95 (paper). 160 pages.

TRADESHOWS

★12214★ California Land Surveyors Association Conference

California Land Surveyors Association
795 Farmers Ln., No. 11
PO Box 9098
Santa Rosa, CA 95405-9990
Ph: (707)578-6016   Fax: (707)578-4406
E-mail: clsa@californiasurveyors.org
URL: http://www.californiasurveyors.org

Annual. **Primary Exhibits:** Land surveying equipment, computers, vehicles, software, and two-way communication systems.

OTHER SOURCES

★12215★ American Congress on Surveying and Mapping (ACSM)

6 Montgomery Village Ave., Ste. 403
Gaithersburg, MD 20879
Ph: (240)632-9716   Fax: (240)632-1321
E-mail: curtis.sumner@acsm.net
URL: http://www.acsm.net

Members: Professionals, technicians, and students in the field of surveying and mapping including surveying of all disciplines, land and geographic information systems, cartography, geodesy, photogrammetry, engineering, geophysics, geography, and computer graphics; American Association for Geodetic Surveying, American Cartographic Association, and National Society of Professional Surveyors. **Purpose:** Objectives are to: advance the sciences of surveying and mapping; promote public understanding and use of surveying and mapping; speak on the national level as the collective voice of the

profession; provide publications to serve the surveying and mapping community. Member organizations encourage improvement of university and college curricula for surveying and mapping.

★12216★ ASPRS - The Imaging and Geospatial Information Society

5410 Grosvenor Ln., Ste. 210
Bethesda, MD 20814-2160
Ph: (301)493-0290   Fax: (301)493-0208
E-mail: asprs@asprs.org
URL: http://www.asprs.org

Members: Firms, individuals, government employees and academicians engaged in photogrammetry, photointerpretation, remote sensing, and geographic information systems and their application to such fields as archaeology, geographic information systems, military reconnaissance, urban planning, engineering, traffic surveys, meteorological observations, medicine, geology, forestry, agriculture, construction and topographic mapping. Mission is to advance knowledge and improve understanding of these sciences and to promote responsible applications. **Activities:** Offers voluntary certification program open to persons associated with one or more functional area of photogrammetry, remote sensing and GIS. Surveys the profession of private firms in photogrammetry and remote sensing in the areas of products and services.

★12217★ Associated Builders and Contractors (ABC)

4250 N Fairfax Dr., 9th Fl.
Arlington, VA 22203-1607
Ph: (703)812-2000   Fax: (703)812-8200
E-mail: gotquestions@abc.org
URL: http://www.abc.org

Description: Construction contractors, subcontractors, suppliers, and associates. Aims to foster and perpetuate the principles of rewarding construction workers and management on the basis of merit. Sponsors management education programs and craft training; also sponsors apprenticeship and skill training programs. Disseminates technological and labor relations information.

★12218★ Associated General Contractors of America (AGC)

2300 Wilson Blvd., Ste. 400
Arlington, VA 22201
Ph: (703)548-3118   Fax: (703)548-3119
Fr: 800-242-1767
E-mail: info@agc.org
URL: http://www.agc.org

Description: General construction contractors; subcontractors; industry suppliers; service firms. Provides market services through its divisions. Conducts special conferences and seminars designed specifically for construction firms. Compiles statistics on job accidents reported by member firms. Maintains 65 committees, including joint cooperative committees with other associations and liaison committees with federal agencies.

★12219★ National Association of Women in Construction (NAWIC)

327 S Adams St.
Fort Worth, TX 76104
Ph: (817)877-5551   Fax: (817)877-0324
Fr: 800-552-3506
E-mail: nawic@nawic.org
URL: http://www.nawic.org

Description: Seeks to enhance the success of women in the construction industry.

★12220★ National Center for Construction Education and Research (NCCER)

3600 NW 43rd St., Bldg. G
Gainesville, FL 32606
Ph: (352)334-0911   Fax: (352)334-0932
Fr: 888-622-3720
URL: http://www.nccer.org

Description: Education foundation committed to the development and publication of Contren(TM) Learning Series, the source of craft training, management education and safety resources for the construction industry.

★12221★ Technical & Related Occupations

Delphi Productions
3159 6th St.
Boulder, CO 80304
Ph: (303)443-2100   Fax: (303)443-4022
Fr: 888-443-2400
E-mail: support@delphivideo.com
URL: http://www.delphivideo.com

$95.00. 49 minutes. Part of the Careers for the 21st Century Video Library.

Talent Scouts and Agents

EMPLOYER DIRECTORIES AND NETWORKING LISTS

★12222★ Billboard's International Talent and Touring Guide
Billboard Books
770 Broadway
New York, NY 10003
Ph: (646)654-5000   Fax: (646)654-5487
Fr: 800-278-8477
URL: http://www.orderbillboard.com

Annual, published 2007. $139.00 for individuals. Covers over 12,900 artists, managers and agents from 76 countries worldwide, including the U.S. and Canada; tour facilities and services; venues; entertainers, booking agents, hotels, and others in the entertainment industry. Entries include: Company name, address, phone, fax, names and titles of key personnel. Arrangement: Classified by line of business; venues are then geographical. Indexes: Product/service.

★12223★ Hollywood Agents & Managers Directory
Hollywood Creative Directory
5055 Wilshire Blvd.
Los Angeles, CA 90036-4396
Ph: (323)525-2369   Fax: (323)525-2398
Fr: 800-815-0503
URL: http://www.hcdonline.com

$28.26. Covers 1,300 agencies and management companies, 4,500 agents and managers. Entries include: companies in Los Angeles, New York and across the nation.

★12224★ Model & Talent Directory
Peter Glenn Publications
235 SE 5th Ave., Ste. R
Delray Beach, FL 33483
Ph: (561)404-4275   Fax: (561)279-4672
Fr: 888-332-6700
URL: http://www.pgdirect.com

Annual; latest edition 25th, 2007. $29.95 for individuals. Covers over 2,200 listings of model and talent agencies worldwide. Arrangement: Geographical.

★12225★ New York City Model Agency Directory
Peter Glenn Publications
235 SE 5th Ave., Ste. R
Delray Beach, FL 33483
Ph: (561)404-4275   Fax: (561)279-4672
Fr: 888-332-6700
URL: http://www.pgdirect.com

Annual. $59.95 for individuals. Covers about 80 modeling agencies in New York City. Entries include: Company name, address, phone, fax, name and title of contact, type of modeling work handled, interview information, years of operation. Arrangement: Alphabetical. Indexes: Name.

HANDBOOKS AND MANUALS

★12226★ 100 Best Careers in Entertainment
Arco Pub.
200 Old Tappan Rd.
Old Tappan, NJ 07675
Fr: 800-428-5331

Shelly Field. 1995. $15.00 (paper). 340 pages.

★12227★ The Los Angeles Agent Book
Sweden Press
Box 1612
Studio City, CA 91614
Ph: (818)995-4250   Fax: (818)995-4399
URL: http://www.swedenpress.com/

K. Callan. Eighth edition, 2003. $19.95 (paper). 300 pages. Describes the actor-agent relationship, provides guidance for selecting the right agent, and gives a list of agents in Los Angeles with background information on each.

★12228★ The Media Jungle: A Survival Guide
Media Masters
872 Franklin Trace
Zionsville, IN 46077-1169
Ph: (317)733-9440   Fax: (317)873-4493

Carrie Van Dyke. 1996. $15.00. 87 pages.

★12229★ Opportunities in Entertainment Careers
The McGraw-Hill Companies
PO Box 182604
Columbus, OH 43272
Fax: (614)759-3749   Fr: 877-883-5524
E-mail: customer.service@mcgraw-hill.com
URL: http://www.mcgraw-hill.com

Jan Goldberg. 1999. $11.95 (paper). 148 pages.

EMPLOYMENT AGENCIES AND SEARCH FIRMS

★12230★ Executive Careers Ltd.
1801 Century Park E., Ste. 2400
Los Angeles, CA 90067
Ph: (310)552-3455   Fax: (310)578-7524
E-mail: eclresumes@att.net

Executive search firm.

★12231★ Joe Sullivan and Associates, Inc.
9 Feather Hill
Southold, NY 11971-0612
Ph: (631)765-5050   Fax: (631)765-9047

Executive search firm. Recruits for the broadcasting, media, and entertainment industries.

OTHER SOURCES

★12232★ **Agents: Tell It Like It Is!**
Joel Asher Studio
PO Box 4223
North Hollywood, CA 91617-4223
Ph: (818)785-1551
URL: http://www.joel-asher-studio.com

T. Michael. 1995. $29.95. This 50-minute videocassette introduces viewers to some veteran talent agents as well as to the nature of the job.

★12233★ **Association of Talent Agents (ATA)**
9255 Sunset Blvd., Ste. 930
Los Angeles, CA 90069
Ph: (310)274-0628   Fax: (310)274-5063
E-mail: shellie@agentassociation.com
URL: http://www.agentassociation.com

Members: Talent agencies that have clients in the Screen Actors Guild, American Federation of Television and Radio Artists, Directors Guild of America, Writers Guild of America, East, and Writers Guild of America, West. **Purpose:** Negotiates terms of franchise agreements with these guilds and maintains liaison with their representatives. Assists members with contract problems, interpretations, rulings, residual matters, and arbitrations. Employs legal counsel to prepare opinions upon request and to file briefs in arbitrations and labor commission hearings. Maintains liaison with labor commission representatives in San Francisco and Los Angeles, CA, and intervenes on behalf of individual members having special problems. **Activities:** Conducts seminars and symposia.

Tax Examiners and Revenue Agents

SOURCES OF HELP-WANTED ADS

★12234★ **Corporate Business Transactions Monthly**

CCH Inc.
4025 W Peterson Ave.
Chicago, IL 60646-6085
Fr: 888-224-7377

Monthly. Journal that publishes articles that contribute to professional practice in the area of corporate tax planning and related administration and compliance issues.

★12235★ **Journal of the American Taxation Association**

American Taxation Association
c/o American Accounting Association
5717 Bessie Dr.
Sarasota, FL 34233
Ph: (941)921-7747   Fax: (941)923-4093

Semiannual. Professional journal covering taxation.

★12236★ **Tax Adviser**

American Institute of Certified Public
  Accountants
1211 Ave. of the Americas
New York, NY 10036
Ph: (212)596-6200   Fax: (212)596-6213
URL: http://www.aicpa.org

Online magazine.

★12237★ **Taxes**

CCH Inc.
2700 Lake Cook Rd.
Riverwoods, IL 60015
Fr: 800-449-6439
URL: http://www.cch.com

Monthly. Publishes articles on legal, accounting, and economic aspects of federal and state taxes.

EMPLOYER DIRECTORIES AND NETWORKING LISTS

★12238★ **NAEA Annual Membership Directory**

National Association of Enrolled Agents
1120 Connecticut Ave. NW, Ste. 460
Washington, DC 20036-3922
Ph: (202)822-6232   Fax: (202)822-6270
Fr: 800-424-4339
URL: http://www.naea.org/

Annual. Covers individuals who have gained Enrolled Agent status and are thus qualified to represent all classes of taxpayers at any administrative level of the Internal Revenue Service.

HANDBOOKS AND MANUALS

★12239★ **Getting Started in Tax Consulting**

Wiley Publishing
1 Wiley Dr.
Somerset, NJ 08875-1272
Ph: (732)469-4400   Fax: (732)302-2300
Fr: 800-225-5945
E-mail: custserv@wiley.com
URL: http://www.wiley.com/WileyCDA/

Gary Carter. April 2001. $27.00. 304 pages. Discover how to break into the tax business, even with relatively limited education and training, and build a path to your new career with Carter's formula for success.

★12240★ **Revenue Agent**

National Learning Corporation
212 Michael Dr.
Syosset, NY 11791
Ph: (516)921-8888   Fax: (516)921-8743
Fr: 800-632-8888
URL: http://www.passbooks.com/

Rudman, Jack. 2002. $34.95 (Trade paper).

★12241★ **Tax Examiner**

National Learning Corporation
212 Michael Dr.
Syosset, NY 11791
Ph: (516)921-8888   Fax: (516)921-8743
Fr: 800-632-8888
URL: http://www.passbooks.com/

Rudman, Jack. 1994. $29.95 (Trade paper).

EMPLOYMENT AGENCIES AND SEARCH FIRMS

★12242★ **Boyce Cunnane Inc.**

PO Box 19064
Baltimore, MD 21284-9064
Ph: (410)583-5511   Fax: (410)583-5518
E-mail: bc@cunnane.com
URL: http://www.cunnane.com

Executive search firm.

★12243★ **The Directorship Search Group Inc.**

800 Boylston St., Ste. 402
Boston, MA 02199
Ph: (617)399-3090   Fax: (617)399-3092
E-mail: subs@directorship.com
URL: http://www.directorship.com

Executive search firm with a second office in New York.

★12244★ **ET Search Inc.**

1250 Prospect St., Ste. 101
La Jolla, CA 92037-3618
Ph: (858)459-3443   Fax: (858)459-4147
E-mail: ets@esearch.com
URL: http://www.etsearch.com

Executive search firm focused on the tax industry.

★12245★ Raymond Alexander Associates

97 Lackawanna Ave., Ste. 102
Totowa, NJ 07512
Ph: (973)256-1000   Fax: (973)256-5871
E-mail: raa@raymondalexander.com
URL: http://www.raymondalexander.com

Personnel consulting firm conducts executive search services in the specific areas of accounting, tax and finance. Industries served: manufacturing, financial services, and public accounting.

ONLINE JOB SOURCES AND SERVICES

★12246★ Association of Certified Fraud Examiners

716 W. Ave.
Austin, TX 78701-2727
Ph: (512)478-9000   Fax: (512)478-9297
Fr: 800-245-3321
E-mail: memberservices@acfe.com
URL: http://www.cfenet.com

Description: Website for membership organization contains Career Center with job databank, ability to post jobs and career resources and links. Must be a member of organization in order to access databank.

★12247★ Society of Financial Examiners

174 Grace Blvd.
Altamonte Springs, FL 32714
Ph: (407)682-4930   Fax: (407)682-3175
E-mail: pkeyes@sofe.org
URL: http://www.sofe.org

Description: Website for membership organization contains classified advertisements for financial examiner positions as well as links to resources about the profession and an opportunity to enroll in an annual career development seminar. Visitors do not have to be members of the association to view job postings.

OTHER SOURCES

★12248★ Accreditation Council for Accountancy and Taxation (ACAT)

1010 N Fairfax St.
Alexandria, VA 22314-1574
Fax: (703)549-2512   Fr: 888-289-7763
E-mail: info@acatcredentials.org
URL: http://www.acatcredentials.org

Description: Strives to raise professional standards and improve the practices of accountancy and taxation. Identifies persons with demonstrated knowledge of the principles and practices of accountancy and taxation. Ensures the continued professional growth of accredited individuals by setting stringent continuing education requirements. Fosters increased recognition for the profession in the public, private, and educational sectors.

★12249★ American Society of Tax Professionals (ASTP)

PO Box 1213
Lynnwood, WA 98046-1213
Ph: (425)774-1996   Fax: (425)672-0461
Fr: 877-674-1996
E-mail: carol.kraemer1@verizon.net

Members: Tax preparers, accountants, attorneys, bookkeepers, accounting services, and public accounting firms seeking to uphold high service standards in professional tax preparation. **Purpose:** Works to enhance the image of tax professionals and make tax practice more profitable; keep members abreast of tax law and service and delivery changes; promote networking among members for mutual assistance. **Activities:** Offers continuing education and training courses and public relations and marketing planning and preparation services. Supports Certified Tax Preparer Program.

★12250★ Council on State Taxation

122 C St. NW, Ste. 330
Washington, DC 20001-2109
Ph: (202)484-5222   Fax: (202)484-5229
E-mail: dlindholm@statetax.org
URL: http://www.statetax.org

Description: Seeks to preserve equitable local taxation practices.

★12251★ Financial Occupations

Delphi Productions
3159 6th St.
Boulder, CO 80304
Ph: (303)443-2100   Fax: (303)443-4022
Fr: 888-443-2400
E-mail: support@delphivideo.com
URL: http://www.delphivideo.com

$95.00. 50 minutes. Part of the Careers for the 21st Century Video Library.

★12252★ Institute for Professionals in Taxation

600 Northpark Town Center
1200 Abernathy Rd. NE, Ste. L-2
Atlanta, GA 30328-1040
Ph: (404)240-2300   Fax: (404)240-2315
E-mail: bcook@ipt.org
URL: http://www.ipt.org

Description: Offers networking and other job opportunities.

★12253★ National Association of Enrolled Agents

1120 Connecticut Ave. NW, Ste. 460
Washington, DC 20036-3953
Ph: (202)822-6232   Fax: (202)822-6270
E-mail: info@naeahq.org
URL: http://www.naea.org

Description: Professional society. Offers a career center.

★12254★ National Association of Tax Professionals (NATP)

PO Box 8002
Appleton, WI 54914-8002
Fax: 800-747-0001   Fr: 800-558-3402
E-mail: natp@natptax.com
URL: http://www.natptax.com

Description: Serves professionals who work in all areas of tax practice, including individual practitioners, enrolled agents, certified public accountants, accountants, attorneys and certified financial planners.

★12255★ National Society of Tax Professionals

10818 NE Coxley Dr., Ste. A
Vancouver, WA 98662
Ph: (360)695-8309   Fax: (360)695-7115
Fr: 800-367-8130
E-mail: taxes@nstp.org
URL: http://www.nstp.org

Description: Professional society.

Teacher Aides

★12265★ Education Week

Editorial Projects in Education Inc.
6935 Arlington Rd., Ste. 100
Bethesda, MD 20814-5233
Ph: (301)280-3100   Fax: (301)280-3200
Fr: 800-346-1834
E-mail: ew@epe.org
URL: http://www.edweek.org/ew

Weekly. $79.94/year for individuals, print plus online; $69.94/year for individuals, online; $135.94/year for Canada, online Monthly; $208.84/year for out of country. Professional newspaper for elementary and secondary school educators.

★12266★ Educational Policy

Sage Publications Inc.
2455 Teller Rd.
Thousand Oaks, CA 91320
Ph: (805)499-0721   Fax: (805)499-8096
URL: http://www.sagepub.com/journalsProdDesc.nav?prodId=Journal20

Annual. $749.00/year for institutions, combined (print & e-access); $824.00/year for institutions, backfile lease, combined plus backfile; $674.00/year for institutions, e-access; $749.00/year for institutions, backfile lease, e-access plus backfile; $687.48/year for institutions, backfile puchase, e-access (content through 1999); $734.00/year for institutions, print only; $159.00/year for individuals, print only; $135.00 for institutions, single print; $34.00 for individuals, single print. Journal for educators, policy makers, administrators, researchers, teachers, and graduate students.

★12267★ Educational Research and Evaluation

Taylor & Francis Group Journals
325 Chestnut St., Ste. 800
Philadelphia, PA 19106
Ph: (215)625-8900   Fax: (215)625-8914
Fr: 800-354-1420
URL: http://www.tandf.co.uk/journals/titles/13803611.asp

Bimonthly. $616.00/year for institutions, print and online; $585.00/year for institutions, online only; $239.00/year for individuals. Journal on theory and practice.

★12268★ Environmental Education Research

Taylor & Francis Group Journals
325 Chestnut St., Ste. 800
Philadelphia, PA 19106
Ph: (215)625-8900   Fax: (215)625-8914
Fr: 800-354-1420
URL: http://www.tandf.co.uk/journals/titles/13504622.asp

Journal covering all aspects of environmental education.

★12269★ Essays in Education

University of South Carolina
471 University Pky.
Aiken, SC 29801
Ph: (803)648-6851   Fax: (803)641-3461
Fr: 888-969-8722

URL: http://www.usca.edu/essays/

Monthly. Journal covering issues that impact and influence education.

★12270★ Hematology

American Society of Hematology
1900 M St. NW, Ste. 200
Washington, DC 20036
Ph: (202)776-0544   Fax: (202)776-0545
URL: http://asheducation-book.hematologylibrary.org

Semiweekly. $60.00/year for members; $90.00/year for nonmembers. Journal providing continuing medical education for physicians.

★12271★ The International Electronic Journal of Health Education

American Alliance for Health, Physical Education, Recreation & Dance
1900 Association Dr.
Reston, VA 20191-1598
Ph: (703)476-3400   Fax: (703)476-9527
Fr: 800-213-7193
URL: http://www.aahperd.org/iejhe/template.cfm?template=about.htm

Annual. Free to health education professionals and students. Journal promoting health through education and other systematic strategies.

★12272★ International Journal of Early Years Education

Taylor & Francis Group Journals
325 Chestnut St., Ste. 800
Philadelphia, PA 19106
Ph: (215)625-8900   Fax: (215)625-8914
Fr: 800-354-1420
URL: http://www.tandf.co.uk/journals/titles/09669760.asp

$512.00/year for institutions, print and online; $486.00/year for institutions, online only; $184.00/year for individuals. Journal focusing on education world-wide.

★12273★ International Journal of Inclusive Education

Taylor & Francis Group Journals
325 Chestnut St., Ste. 800
Philadelphia, PA 19106
Ph: (215)625-8900   Fax: (215)625-8914
Fr: 800-354-1420
URL: http://www.tandf.co.uk/journals/titles/13603116.asp

Bimonthly. $320.00/year for individuals, print only; $616.00/year for institutions, online only; $649.00/year for individuals, print and online; $193.00/year for individuals, print only; $376.00/year for institutions, online only; $396.00/year for institutions, print and online. Journal providing information on the nature of schools, universities and technical colleges for the educators and educational policy-makers.

★12274★ International Journal of Leadership in Education

Taylor & Francis Group Journals
325 Chestnut St., Ste. 800
Philadelphia, PA 19106
Ph: (215)625-8900   Fax: (215)625-8914
Fr: 800-354-1420
E-mail: ijle@txstate.edu
URL: http://www.tandf.co.uk/journals/tf/13603124.html

Quarterly. $196.00/year for individuals; $536.00/year for institutions, print and online; $509.00/year for institutions, online only; Journal dealing with leadership in education.

★12275★ International Journal of Progressive Education

International Journal of Progressive Education
c/o Mustafa Yunus Eryaman, Mng. Ed.
2108 S Orchard St., No. D
Urbana, IL 61801
URL: http://www.inased.org/ijpe.htm

$35.00/year for members; $45.00/year for individuals; $140.00/year for institutions, library; $35.00/year for students; $25.00/year for single issue, U.S. Peer reviewed online journal that aims to create an open and continuing dialogue about current educational issues and future conceptions of educational theory.

★12276★ International Journal of Research & Method in Education

Taylor & Francis Group Journals
325 Chestnut St., Ste. 800
Philadelphia, PA 19106
Ph: (215)625-8900   Fax: (215)625-8914
Fr: 800-354-1420
URL: http://www.tandf.co.uk/journals/titles/1743727x.asp

$1809.00/year for institutions, print and online; $1718.00/year for institutions, online only; $271.00/year for individuals. Professional journal to further international discourse in education with particular focus on method.

★12277★ International Journal of Whole Schooling

Whole Schooling Press
Wayne State University
217 Education
Detroit, MI 48202
URL: http://www.wholeschooling.net/Journal_of_Whole_Schooling/IJW

Free to qualified subscribers. International, refereed academic journal dedicated to exploring ways to improve learning and schooling for all children.

★12278★ Journal of Academic Leadership

Academic Leadership
600 Park St.
Rarick Hall 219
Hays, KS 67601-4099
Ph: (785)628-4547

URL: http://www.academicleadership.org/
Journal focusing on the leadership issues in the academic world.

★12279★ **Journal of Cases in Educational Leadership**

Sage Publications Inc.
2455 Teller Rd.
Thousand Oaks, CA 91320
Ph: (805)499-0721   Fax: (805)499-8096
URL: http://www.sagepub.com/journalsProdDesc.nav?prodId=Journal20

Quarterly. $319.00/year for institutions, e-access; $83.00/year for individuals, e-access. Journal covering cases appropriate for use in programs that prepare educational leaders.

★12280★ **Journal of Curriculum and Supervision**

Association for Supervision and Curriculum Development
1703 N Beauregard St.
Alexandria, VA 22311-1714
Ph: (703)578-9600   Fax: (703)575-5400
Fr: 800-933-2723
URL: http://www.ascd.org/portal/site/ascd/menuitem.0545410c9839aa

Scholarly journal focusing on curriculum and supervision.

★12281★ **Journal of Direct Instruction**

Association for Direct Instruction
PO Box 10252
Eugene, OR 97440
Ph: (541)485-1293   Fax: (541)683-7543
Fr: 800-995-2464
URL: http://www.adihome.org/phpshop/articles/articles.php?type=JD

Quarterly. Subscription included in membership. Journal covering education.

★12282★ **Journal of Language, Identity, and Education**

Lawrence Erlbaum Associates Inc.
10 Industrial Ave.
Mahwah, NJ 07430
Ph: (201)258-2200   Fax: (201)236-0072
Fr: 800-926-6579
E-mail: journals@erlbaum.com
URL: http://www.erlbaum.com

Quarterly. $50.00/year for U.S. and Canada, individual, online and print; $80.00/year for elsewhere, individual, online and print; $360.00/year for U.S. and Canada, institution, online and print; $390.00/year for elsewhere, institution, online and print; $290.00/year for U.S. and Canada, institution, online only; $290.00/year for elsewhere, institution, online only; $325.00/year for U.S. and Canada, institution, print only; $355.00/year for elsewhere, institution, print only. Scholarly, interdisciplinary journal covering issues in language, identity and education worldwide for academics, educators and policy specialists in a variety of disciplines, and others.

★12283★ **Journal of Latinos and Education**

Lawrence Erlbaum Associates Inc.
10 Industrial Ave.
Mahwah, NJ 07430
Ph: (201)258-2200   Fax: (201)236-0072
Fr: 800-926-6579
URL: http://www.erlbaum.com/

Quarterly. $50.00/year for individuals, online and print - U.S./Canada; $80.00/year for individuals, online and print - all other countries; $360.00/year for institutions, online and print - U.S./Canada; $390.00/year for institutions, online and print - all other countries; $290.00/year for institutions, online only - U.S./Canada; $290.00/year for institutions, online only - all other countries; $325.00/year for institutions, print only - U.S./Canada; $355.00/year for institutions, print only - all other countries. Scholarly, multidisciplinary journal covering educational issues that impact Latinos for researchers, teaching professionals, academics, scholars, institutions, and others.

★12284★ **Journal of Learning Disabilities**

PRO-ED Inc.
8700 Shoal Creek Blvd.
PO Box 678370
Austin, TX 78757-6897
Ph: (512)451-3246   Fax: 800-397-7633
Fr: 800-897-3202
URL: http://www.proedinc.com

Bimonthly. $60.00/year for individuals; $96.00 for individuals, 2 years; $161.00/year for institutions; $258.00 for institutions, 2 years; $96.00/year for individuals, international; $154.00 for individuals, 2 year international; $187.00/year for institutions, international; $300.00 for institutions, 2 year international. Special education journal.

★12285★ **Journal of STEM Education**

Auburn University
9088 Haley Ctr.
Auburn, AL 36849
Ph: (334)844-4000   Fax: (334)844-9027
URL: http://www.auburn.edu/research/litee/jstem/index.php

Semiannual. Journal for educators in Science, Technology, Engineering, and Mathematics (STEM) education.

★12286★ **Journal of Teacher Education**

Boston College
140 Commonwealth Ave.
Chestnut Hill, MA 02467
URL: http://www.sagepub.com

$403.00/year for institutions, print & e-access; $423.00/year for institutions, volume print & all online; $363.00/year for institutions, e-access; $383.00/year for institutions, all online content; $1,512.00/year for institutions, backfile purchase, e-access; $395.00/year for institutions, print; $99.00/year for individuals, print; $87.00/year for institutions, single print; $26.00/year for individuals, single print. Magazine of interest to educators.

★12287★ **Leadership and Policy in Schools**

Taylor & Francis Group Journals
325 Chestnut St., Ste. 800
Philadelphia, PA 19106
Ph: (215)625-8900   Fax: (215)625-8914
Fr: 800-354-1420
URL: http://www.tandf.co.uk/journals/titles/15700763.asp

Quarterly. $477.00/year for institutions, print and online; $453.00/year for institutions, online only; $227.00/year for individuals; $60.00/year for ICSEI members. Journal providing information about leadership and policy in primary and secondary education.

★12288★ **NJEA Review**

New Jersey Education Association
180 West State St.
PO Box 1211
Trenton, NJ 08607-1211
Ph: (609)599-4561   Fax: (609)599-1201

Monthly. Educational journal for public school employees.

★12289★ **Oxford Review of Education**

Taylor & Francis Group Journals
325 Chestnut St., Ste. 800
Philadelphia, PA 19106
Ph: (215)625-8900   Fax: (215)625-8914
Fr: 800-354-1420
URL: http://www.tandf.co.uk/journals/titles/03054985.asp

$1,031.00/year for institutions, print and online; $979.00/year for institutions, online only; $396.00/year for individuals. Journal covering advance study of education.

★12290★ **Research Strategies**

Elsevier Science Inc.
360 Park Ave. S
New York, NY 10010
Ph: (212)989-5800   Fax: (212)633-3990
URL: http://www.elsevier.com

Journal covering library literature and the educational mission of the library.

★12291★ **School Effectiveness and School Improvement**

Taylor & Francis Group Journals
325 Chestnut St., Ste. 800
Philadelphia, PA 19106
Ph: (215)625-8900   Fax: (215)625-8914
Fr: 800-354-1420
URL: http://www.tandf.co.uk/journals/titles/09243453.asp

Quarterly. $305.00/year for institutions, print and online; $231.00/year for institutions, online only; $153.00/year for individuals, print only; $520.00/year for institutions, print and online; $494.00/year for institutions, online only; $255.00/year for individuals, print only. Journal focusing on educational progress of all students.

★12292★ Strategies

American Alliance for Health, Physical Education, Recreation & Dance
1900 Association Dr.
Reston, VA 20191-1598
Ph: (703)476-3400   Fax: (703)476-9527
Fr: 800-213-7193
E-mail: strategies@aahperd.org
URL: http://www.aahperd.org/naspe/template.cfm?template=strategie

Bimonthly. $115.00/year for U.S. and Canada, institution; $45.00/year for nonmembers, U.S. and Canada, individual; $127.00/year for institutions, other countries; $57.00/year for nonmembers, foreign, individual. Journal providing practical, hands-on information to physical educators and coaches.

★12293★ Teaching Exceptional Children

Council for Exceptional Children
1110 N Glebe Rd., Ste. 300
Arlington, VA 22201-5704
Ph: (703)620-3660   Fax: (703)264-9494
Fr: 888-232-7733
E-mail: tec@bc.edu
URL: http://www.cec.sped.org

Bimonthly. $135.00/year for individuals; $250.00 for two years; $145.00 for two years, Canada; $270.00 for two years, Canada; $165.00/year for out of country, foreign-air printed matter; $310.00/year for out of country, two years, foreign-air printed matter; $25.00/year for institutions, single copy; $170.00/year for institutions; $290.00 for two years, institutional. Journal exploring practical methods for teaching students who have exceptionalities and those who are gifted and talented.

★12294★ Teaching/K-8

Teaching/K-8
40 Richards Ave.
Norwalk, CT 06854
Fr: 800-249-9363
E-mail: teachingk8@aol.com

$23.97/year for individuals; $4.50 for single issue; $12.00/year for institutions; $21.00 for institutions, two years; $30.00 for institutions, three years. Magazine for elementary teachers.

★12295★ Teaching and Learning in Nursing

Elsevier Science Inc.
360 Park Ave. S
New York, NY 10010
Ph: (212)989-5800   Fax: (212)633-3990
URL: http://www.elsevier.com

Quarterly. $119.00/year for institutions, U.S. $167.00/year for institutions, other countries; $75.00/year for individuals, U.S. $104.00/year for individuals, other countries. Journal devoted to associate degree nursing education and practice.

★12296★ Tech Directions

Prakken Publications Inc.
832 Phoenix Dr.
PO Box 8623
Ann Arbor, MI 48108
Ph: (734)975-2800   Fax: (734)975-2787
Fr: 800-530-9673
E-mail: tdedit@techdirections.com
URL: http://www.techdirections.com

Monthly. $30.00/year for individuals, U.S.; $20.00/year for students; $40.00/year for elsewhere; $55.00 for two years, U.S.; $75.00 for two years, elsewhere. Free to qualified subscribers. Magazine covering issues, programs, and projects in industrial education, technology education, trade and industry, and vocational-technical career education. Articles are geared toward teacher and administrator use and reference from elementary school through postsecondary levels.

★12297★ Theory and Research in Education

Sage Publications Inc.
2455 Teller Rd.
Thousand Oaks, CA 91320
Ph: (805)499-0721   Fax: (805)499-8096
URL: http://tre.sagepub.com/

$459.00/year for institutions, print and online; $413.00/year for institutions, online only; $450.00/year for institutions, print only; $77.00/year for individuals, print only. Interdisciplinary journal covering normative and theoretical issues concerning education including multi-faceted philosophical analysis of moral, social, political and epistemological problems and issues arising from educational practice.

★12298★ Uratie

IDG Communications Inc.
5 Speen St., 3rd. Fl
Framingham, MA 01701
Ph: (508)875-5000   Fax: (508)988-7888
URL: http://www.idg.com

Magazine providing job offers for graduates, engineers and information technology professionals.

PLACEMENT AND JOB REFERRAL SERVICES

★12299★ American Montessori Society (AMS)

281 Park Ave. S
New York, NY 10010-6102
Ph: (212)358-1250   Fax: (212)358-1256
E-mail: info@amshq.org
URL: http://www.amshq.org

Description: School affiliates and teacher training affiliates; heads of schools, teachers, parents, non-Montessori educators, and other interested individuals dedicated to stimulating the use of the Montessori teaching approach and promoting better education for all children. Seeks to meet demands of growing interest in the Montessori approach to early learning. Assists in establishing schools; supplies information and limited services to member schools in other countries. Maintains school consultation and accreditation service; provides information service; assists research and gathers statistical data; offers placement service. Maintains Montessori and related materials exhibit.

EMPLOYER DIRECTORIES AND NETWORKING LISTS

★12300★ 50 State Educational Directories

Career Guidance Foundation
8090 Engineer Rd.
San Diego, CA 92111
Ph: (858)560-8051   Fax: (858)278-8960
Fr: 800-854-2670
URL: http://www.cgf.org

Annual. Microfiche. Collection consists of reproductions of the state educational directories published by the departments of education of individual 50 states. Directory contents vary, but the majority contain listings of elementary and secondary schools, colleges and universities, and state education officials. Amount of detail in each also varies. Entries include: Usually, institution name, address, and name of one executive.

★12301★ Christian Schools International-Directory

Christian Schools International
3350 E Paris Ave. SE
Grand Rapids, MI 49512
Ph: (616)957-1070   Fax: (616)957-5022
Fr: 800-635-8288
URL: http://store.csionline.org

Annual; 2007-2008. $15.00 for members; $72.00 for nonmembers. Covers nearly 450 Reformed Christian elementary and secondary schools; related associations; societies without schools. Entries include: For schools–School name, address, phone; name, title, and address of officers; names of faculty members. Arrangement: Geographical.

★12302★ Directory of Public School Systems in the U.S.

American Association for Employment in Education
3040 Riverside Dr., Ste. 125
Columbus, OH 43221
Ph: (614)485-1111   Fax: (614)485-9609
URL: http://www.aaee.org/

Annual, winter; latest edition 2004-2005 edition. $10.00 for members (plus $2.00/copy for mailing); $20.00 for nonmembers (plus $2.00/copy for mailing). Covers about 14,500 public school systems in the United States and their administrative personnel. Entries include: System name, address, phone, website address, name and title of personnel administrator, levels taught and approximate student population. Arrangement: Geographical by state.

★12303★ Employment Opportunities, USA

Washington Research Associates
1090 Vermont Ave. NW, Ste. 800
Washington, DC 20005
Ph: (202)408-7025

Annual, quarterly updates. Publication includes: List of over 1,000 employment contacts in companies and agencies in banking, arts, telecommunications, education, and 14 other industries and professions, including federal government. Entries include: Company name, name of representative, address, description of products or services, hiring and recruiting practices, training programs, and year established. Principal content is industry overviews, career news, employment opportunity information on 14 different job markets, and comprehensive guidance to career resources on the Internet. Arrangement: Classified by industry. Indexes: Occupation.

★12304★ Ganley's Catholic Schools in America-Elementary/Secondary/College & University

Fisher Publishing Co.
PO Box 15070
Scottsdale, AZ 85267-5070
Ph: (480)657-9422   Fax: (480)657-9422
Fr: 800-759-7615
URL: http:// www.ganleyscatholicschools.com

Annual, summer; latest edition 34th, 2007 edition. $60.00 for individuals. Covers over 8,400 Catholic K-12 Schools. Arrangement: Geographical by state, then alphabetical by Diocese name.

★12305★ Handbook of Private Schools

Porter Sargent Publishers Inc.
11 Beacon St., Ste. 1400
Boston, MA 02108-3099
Ph: (617)523-1670   Fax: (617)523-1021
Fr: 800-342-7470
E-mail: orders@portersargent.com
URL: http://www.portersargent.com

Annual, latest edition 87th, 2006 edition. $99.00 for individuals. Covers more than 1,600 elementary and secondary boarding and day schools in the United States. Entries include: School name, address, phone, fax, e-mail, URL, type of school (boarding or day), sex and age range, names and titles of administrators, grades offered, academic orientation, curriculum, new admissions yearly, tests required for admission, enrollment and faculty, graduate record, number of alumni, tuition and scholarship figures, summer session, plant evaluation and endowment, date of establishment, calendar, association membership, description of school's offerings and history, test score averages, uniform requirements, and geographical and demographic data. Arrangement: Geographical. Indexes: Alphabetical by school name,

cross indexed by state, region, grade range, sexes accepted, school features and enrollment.

★12306★ Independent Schools Association of the Southwest-Membership List

Independent Schools Association of the Southwest
Energy Sq., Ste 406
505 North Big Spring St.
Midland, TX 79701
Ph: (432)684-9550   Fax: (432)684-9401
URL: http://www.isasw.org

Annual, August. Covers over 84 schools located in Arizona, Kansas, Louisiana, Mexico, New Mexico, Oklahoma, and Texas enrolling over 38,000 students. Entries include: School name, address, phone, chief administrative officer, structure, and enrollment. Arrangement: Geographical. Indexes: Alphabetical.

★12307★ MDR's School Directories

Market Data Retrieval
1 Forest Pkwy.
Shelton, CT 06484-0947
Ph: (203)926-4800   Fax: (203)926-1826
Fr: 800-333-8802
URL: http://www.schooldata.com

Annual, October. Covers over 90,000 public, 8,000 Catholic, and 15,000 other private schools (grades K-12) in the United States; over 15,000 school district offices, 76,000 school librarians, 27,000 media specialists, and 33,000 technology coordinators. Includes names of over 165,000 school district administrators and staff members in county and state education administration. Entries include: District name and address; telephone and fax number; number of schools; number of teachers in the district; district enrollment; special education students; limited-english proficient students; minority percentage by race; percentage of college bound students; expenditures per student for instructional materials; poverty level; title 1 dollars; site-based management; district open/close dates; construction indicator; technologies and quantities; district-level administrators, (new superintendents shaded); school name and address (new public shaded); telephone and fax number; principal (new principal shaded); librarian, media specialist and technology coordinator; grade span; special programs and school type; student enrollment; technologies and quantities (instructional computer brand, noting predominant brand); Multi-Media Computers; Internet connection or access; Tech Sophistication Index. Arrangement: Geographical. Indexes: District county; district personnel; principal; new public schools and key personnel; district and school telephone; district URLs.

★12308★ National Directory for Employment in Education

American Association for Employment in Education
3040 Riverside Dr., Ste. 125
Columbus, OH 43221
Ph: (614)485-1111   Fax: (614)485-9609
URL: http://www.aaee.org/

Annual, winter; latest edition 2005 edition. $20.00 for nonmembers; $10.00 for members. Covers about 600 placement offices maintained by teacher-training institutions and 300 school district personnel officers and/or superintendents responsible for hiring profesional staff. Entries include: Institution name, address, phone, contact name, email address, and website. Arrangement: Geographical. Indexes: Personal name; subject-field of teacher training; institutions that provide vacancy bulletins and placement services to non-enrolled students.

★12309★ Private Independent Schools

Bunting and Lyon Inc.
238 N Main St.
Wallingford, CT 06492
Ph: (203)269-3333   Fax: (203)269-5697
URL: http://www.buntingandlyon.com

Annual; latest edition 60th, January 2007. $115.00 for individuals. Covers 1,200 English-speaking elementary and secondary private schools and summer programs in North America and abroad. Entries include: School name, address, phone, fax, e-mail, website, enrollment, tuition and other fees, financial aid information, administrator's name and educational background, director of admission, regional accreditation, description of programs, curriculum, activities, learning differences grid. Arrangement: Geographical. Indexes: school name; geographical.

HANDBOOKS AND MANUALS

★12310★ Opportunities in Child Care Careers

The McGraw-Hill Companies
PO Box 182604
Columbus, OH 43272
Fax: (614)759-3749   Fr: 877-883-5524
E-mail: customer.service@mcgraw-hill.com
URL: http://www.mcgraw-hill.com

Renee Wittenberg. 2006. $13.95 (paper). 160 pages. Discusses various job opportunities and how to secure a position. Illustrated.

★12311★ Opportunities in Teaching Careers

The McGraw-Hill Companies
PO Box 182604
Columbus, OH 43272
Fax: (614)759-3749   Fr: 877-883-5524
E-mail: customer.service@mcgraw-hill.com
URL: http://www.mcgraw-hill.com

Janet Fine. 2005. $13.95 (paper). 160

pages. Discusses licensing and accreditation programs, sources of placement information, job-seeking correspondence, selection procedures, and paths to advancement. Also covers professional associations, nontraditional teaching opportunities, and jobs abroad.

EMPLOYMENT AGENCIES AND SEARCH FIRMS

★12312★ Educational Placement Service

6510-A S. Academy Blvd.
Colorado Springs, CO 80906
Ph: (719)579-9911   Fax: (719)579-5050
E-mail: accounting@educatorjobs.com
URL: http://www.educatorjobs.com

Employment agency. Focuses on teaching, administrative, and education-related openings.

OTHER SOURCES

★12313★ National Association of Independent Schools (NAIS)

1620 L St. NW, Ste. 1100
Washington, DC 20036-5695
Ph: (202)973-9700   Fax: (202)973-9790
Fr: 800-793-6701

E-mail: info@nais.org
URL: http://www.nais.org

Description: Independent elementary and secondary school members; regional associations of independent schools and related associations. Provides curricular and administrative research and services. Conducts educational programs; compiles statistics.

★12314★ National Community Education Association (NCEA)

3929 Old Lee Hwy., No. 91-A
Fairfax, VA 22030-2421
Ph: (703)359-8973   Fax: (703)359-0972
E-mail: ncea@ncea.com
URL: http://www.ncea.com

Description: Community school directors, principals, superintendents, professors, teachers, students, and laypeople. **Purpose:** Promotes and establishes community schools as an integral part of the educational plan of every community. Emphasizes community and parent involvement in the schools, lifelong learning, and enrichment of K-12 and adult education. Serves as a clearinghouse for the exchange of ideas and information, and the sharing of efforts. **Activities:** Offers leadership training.

★12315★ Overseas Employment Opportunities for Educators: Department of Defense Dependents Schools

DIANE Publishing Co.
PO Box 617
Darby, PA 19023-0617
Ph: (610)461-6200   Fax: (610)461-6130
Fr: 800-782-3833

URL: http://www.dianepublishingcentral.com

Barry Leonard, editor. 2000. $15.00. 54 pages. An introduction to teachings positions in the Dept. of Defense Dependents Schools (DoDDS), a worldwide school system, operated by the DoD in 14 countries.

★12316★ Working with Children

Cambridge Educational
PO Box 2053
Princeton, NJ 08543-2053
Ph: 800-257-5126   Fax: (609)671-0266
Fr: 800-468-4227
E-mail: custserv@films.com
URL: http://www.cambridgeeducational.com

VHS and DVD. $89.95. 2000. 24 minutes. This program examines alternative positions offering the opportunity to work with children of different ages and the qualifications necessary for those jobs. A nanny, social worker, non-faculty school worker, and retail salesperson describe their job responsibilities and explain why they find their work so enjoyable.

Telemarketing Representatives

SOURCES OF HELP-WANTED ADS

★12317★ Communications, IEEE Transactions

IEEE Electron Devices Society
445 Hoes Ln.
Piscataway, NJ 08855-1331
Ph: (732)981-0060   Fax: (732)981-1721
URL: http://ieeexplore.ieee.org

Journal relating to telecommunications.

★12318★ Customer Interaction Solutions

Technology Marketing Corp.
1 Technology Plz.
Norwalk, CT 06854
Ph: (203)852-6800   Fax: (203)853-2845
Fr: 800-243-6002
URL: http://www.tmcnet.com/call-center/

Monthly. Publication covering issues in the telecommunications industry.

★12319★ Journal of Municipal Telecommunications Policy

National Association of
Telecommunications Officers and
Advisors
1800 Diagonal Rd., Ste. 495
Alexandria, VA 22314
Ph: (703)519-8035   Fax: (703)519-8036
URL: http://www.natoa.org

Quarterly. $10.00/year for members; $15.00/year for nonmembers. Professional journal covering issues for the telecommunications industry.

★12320★ Mikro PC

IDG Communications Inc.
5 Speen St., 3rd. Fl
Framingham, MA 01701
Ph: (508)875-5000   Fax: (508)988-7888
URL: http://www.idg.com

Monthly. Magazine focusing on information technology and digital lifestyle.

★12321★ NetWorld

IDG Communications Inc.
5 Speen St., 3rd. Fl
Framingham, MA 01701
Ph: (508)875-5000   Fax: (508)988-7888
URL: http://www.idg.com

Monthly. Magazine focusing on networks, security, infrastructure management, wireless, mobile and VOIP technologies.

★12322★ SMB Data

IDG Communications Inc.
5 Speen St., 3rd. Fl
Framingham, MA 01701
Ph: (508)875-5000   Fax: (508)988-7888
URL: http://www.idg.com

Magazine focusing on information technology systems at small and medium-size businesses.

★12323★ SME World

IDG Communications Inc.
5 Speen St., 3rd. Fl
Framingham, MA 01701
Ph: (508)875-5000   Fax: (508)988-7888
URL: http://www.idg.com

Magazine covering articles on technology, technology investments, IT products and services.

PLACEMENT AND JOB REFERRAL SERVICES

★12324★ International Customer Service Association (ICSA)

401 N Michigan Ave.
Chicago, IL 60611
Ph: (312)321-6800   Fr: 800-360-4272
E-mail: icsa@smithbucklin.com
URL: http://www.icsa.com

Description: Customer service professionals in public and private sectors united to develop the theory and understanding of customer service and management. Goals are to: promote professional development; standardize terminology and phrases; provide career counseling and placement services; establish hiring guidelines, performance standards, and job descriptions. Provides a forum for shared problems and solutions. Compiles statistics.

EMPLOYER DIRECTORIES AND NETWORKING LISTS

★12325★ American Teleservices Association-Membership Directory and Resource Guide

American Teleservices Association
3815 River Crossing Pky., Ste. 20
Indianapolis, IN 46240
Ph: (317)816-9336
URL: http://www.ataconnect.org

Annual. $300.00 for nonmembers; free for members. Covers member companies in the teleservice industry; in-house call centers, services agencies, consultants and suppliers. Entries include: Company name, address, phone, name and title of contact, product or service provided, branch office location. Arrangement: Alphabetical, geographical, by business type. Indexes: Company; international/state member users of TM services, including agencies, consultants, and suppliers.

★12326★ Quirk's Marketing Research Review-Telephone Interviewing Facilities Directory Issue

Quirk Enterprises Inc.
4662 Slater Rd.
Eagan, MN 55122
Ph: (952)224-1919
URL: http://www.quirks.com

Annual, April. Publication includes: List of more than 800 telephone interviewing facilities that conduct marketing research projects. Entries include: Company name, address, phone, fax, description of interviewing stations. Arrangement: Geographical. Indexes: Geographical.

HANDBOOKS AND MANUALS

★12327★ Careers Inside the World of Sales

Pearson Learning Group
135 S. Mt. Zion Rd.
PO Box 2500
Lebanon, IN 46052
Fax: 800-393-3156   Fr: 800-526-9907
URL: http://www.pearsonatschool.com

Carlienne Frisch. Revised edition, 2000. $16.35. 64 pages. Describes different sales careers for reluctant readers.

★12328★ Careers in Marketing

The McGraw-Hill Companies
PO Box 182604
Columbus, OH 43272
Fax: (614)759-3749   Fr: 877-883-5524
E-mail: customer.service@mcgraw-hill.com
URL: http://www.mcgraw-hill.com

Lila B. Stair and Leslie Stair. Third edition, 2001. $13.95 (paper). 192 pages. Surveys career opportunities in marketing and related areas such as marketing research, product development, and sales promotion. Includes a description of the work, places of employment, employment outlook, trends, and salaries. Offers job hunting advice.

★12329★ The Complete Job-Finding Guide for Secretaries and Administrative Support Staff

AMACOM
1601 Broadway, 12th Fl.
New York, NY 10019-7420
Ph: (212)586-8100   Fax: (212)903-8168
Fr: 800-262-9699
URL: http://www.amanet.org

Paul Falcone. 1995. $16.95 (paper). 256 pages. Covers several secretarial and administrative staff support positions and includes tips on resume writing, interview preparation, and other aspects of the job search.

★12330★ How to Get Customers to Call, Buy and...Beg for More!

World Wide Publishing and Trading, LLC
5 Airport Rd.
Lakewood, NJ 08701
Ph: (732)364-1900   Fax: (732)364-3716
Fr: 800-545-4724

Kenneth J. Varga. 1997. $49.97. 323 pages.

★12331★ How to Make Hot Cold Calls: Your Calling Card to Personal Success

Stoddart
4500 Witmer Industrial, E.
Niagara Falls, NY 14305-1386
Fax: 800-481-6207   Fr: 800-805-1083

Steven J. Schwartz. Revised, 2001. 145 pages.

★12332★ Opportunities in Direct Marketing

The McGraw-Hill Companies
PO Box 182604
Columbus, OH 43272
Fax: (614)759-3749   Fr: 877-883-5524
E-mail: customer.service@mcgraw-hill.com
URL: http://www.mcgraw-hill.com

Anne Basye. 2008. $14.95; $11.95 (paper). 160 pages. Examines opportunities with direct marketers, catalog companies, direct marketing agencies, telemarketing firms, mailing list brokers, and database marketing companies. Describes how to prepare for a career in direct marketing and how to break into the field. Includes sources of short-term professional training.

★12333★ Opportunities in Sales Careers

The McGraw-Hill Companies
PO Box 182604
Columbus, OH 43272
Fax: (614)759-3749   Fr: 877-883-5524
E-mail: customer.service@mcgraw-hill.com
URL: http://www.mcgraw-hill.com

James Brescoll and Ralph Dahm. 160 pages. 2001. $12.95 (paper). Details sales in retail, wholesale and industrial sales, sales of services and intangibles, and sales management. Illustrated.

★12334★ Opportunities in Telecommunications Careers

The McGraw-Hill Companies
PO Box 182604
Columbus, OH 43272
Fax: (614)759-3749   Fr: 877-883-5524
E-mail: customer.service@mcgraw-hill.com
URL: http://www.mcgraw-hill.com

Jan Bone, Suzanne Nagle. 1995. $11.95 (paper).

★12335★ Opportunities in Telemarketing Careers

The McGraw-Hill Companies
PO Box 182604
Columbus, OH 43272
Fax: (614)759-3749   Fr: 877-883-5524
E-mail: customer.service@mcgraw-hill.com
URL: http://www.mcgraw-hill.com

Anne Basye. 1994. $14.95; $11.95 (paper). 160 pages. Discusses opportunities in inside sales, customer service, telesearch, multilingual marketing, and more.

★12336★ Real People Working in Sales and Marketing

The McGraw-Hill Companies
PO Box 182604
Columbus, OH 43272
Fax: (614)759-3749   Fr: 877-883-5524
E-mail: customer.service@mcgraw-hill.com
URL: http://www.mcgraw-hill.com

Blythe Camenson, Jan Goldberg. 1996. $12.95 (paper). 144 pages. Interviews and profiles of working sales and marketing professionals capture a range of opportunities in this field.

★12337★ Resumes for Sales and Marketing Careers

The McGraw-Hill Companies
PO Box 182604
Columbus, OH 43272
Fax: (614)759-3749   Fr: 877-883-5524
E-mail: customer.service@mcgraw-hill.com
URL: http://www.mcgraw-hill.com

Chuck Cochran and Donna Peerce. 1998. $13.95. 336 pages. Sample resumes and cover letters from all levels of the sales and marketing field.

EMPLOYMENT AGENCIES AND SEARCH FIRMS

★12338★ Career Development Services

150 State St.
Rochester, NY 14614
Ph: (585)244-0765   Fax: (585)244-7115
Fr: 800-736-6710
E-mail: info@careerdev.org
URL: http://www.careerdev.org

Employment agency.

★12339★ Churchill & Affiliates Inc.

1200 Bustleton Pike, Ste. 3
Feasterville, PA 19053
Ph: (215)364-8070   Fax: (215)322-4391
E-mail: hwasserman@churchillsearch.com
URL: http://www.churchillsearch.com

Executive search firm focusing on the telecommunications industry.

★12340★ The Culver Group, Inc.

600 City Parkway W., Ste. 320
Orange, CA 92868
Ph: (714)939-8900
URL: http://www.culvergroup.com

Employment agency specializing in sales positions.

★12341★ The Esquire Staffing Group Ltd.

1 S. Wacker Dr., Ste. 1616
Chicago, IL 60606-4616
Ph: (312)795-4300   Fax: (312)795-4329
E-mail: d.williams@esquirestaffing.com
URL: http://www.esquirestaffing.com

Employment agency. Fills permanent as well as temporary openings.

★12342★ Winters and Ross

442 Main St.
Fort Lee, NJ 07024
Ph: (201)947-8400   Fax: (201)947-1035
E-mail: wintersandross@aol.com
URL: http://www.wintersandross.com

Permanent employment agency serving a variety of industries.

ONLINE JOB SOURCES AND SERVICES

★12343★ Spherion
2050 Spectrum Blvd.
Fort Lauderdale, FL 33309
Ph: (954)308-7600
E-mail: help@spherion.com
URL: http://www.spherion.com

Description: Recruitment firm specializing in accounting and finance, sales and market-ing, interim executives, technology, engineering, retail and human resources.

OTHER SOURCES

★12344★ Association of Call Center Managers (ACCM)
2505 Living Rock Ave.
Las Vegas, NV 89106
Ph: (702)367-2288
E-mail: info@callcentermanagers.org

Description: Represents call center managers and leaders dedicated to advancing the profession of call center management. Provides networking, peer mentoring, research, education and other resources that elevate the role and value of a call center leader. Strives to raise awareness of the call center profession and to heighten awareness of the strategic and economic value of call/contact centers.

★12345★ Marketing & Sales Occupations
Delphi Productions
3159 6th St.
Boulder, CO 80304
Ph: (303)443-2100   Fax: (303)443-4022
Fr: 888-443-2400
E-mail: support@delphivideo.com
URL: http://www.delphivideo.com

$95.00. 50 minutes. Part of the Careers for the 21st Century Video Library.

Tissue Engineers

SOURCES OF HELP-WANTED ADS

★12346★ AIE Perspectives Newsmagazine

American Institute of Engineers
4630 Appian Way, Ste. 206
El Sobrante, CA 94803-1875
Ph: (510)758-6240   Fax: (510)758-6240

Monthly. Professional magazine covering engineering.

★12347★ Engineering Conferences International Symposium Series

Berkeley Electronic Press
2809 Telegraph Ave., Ste. 202
Berkeley, CA 94705
Ph: (510)665-1200   Fax: (510)665-1201
URL: http://services.bepress.com/eci/

Journal focusing on advance engineering science.

★12348★ Engineering Times

National Society of Professional
  Engineers
1420 King St.
Alexandria, VA 22314
Ph: (703)684-2800
URL: http://www.nspe.org

Monthly. Magazine (tabloid) covering professional, legislative, and techology issues for an engineering audience.

★12349★ ENR: Engineering News-Record

McGraw-Hill Inc.
1221 Ave. of the Americas
New York, NY 10020-1095
Ph: (212)512-2000   Fax: (212)512-3840
Fr: 877-833-5524
E-mail: enr_web_editors@mcgraw-hill.com
URL: http://www.mymags.com/moreinfo.php?itemID=20012

Weekly. $94.00/year for individuals, print. Magazine focusing on engineering and construction.

★12350★ High Technology Careers Magazine

HTC
4701 Patrick Henry Dr., No. 1901
Santa Clara, CA 95054-1847
Fax: (408)567-0242
URL: http://www.hightechcareers.com

Bimonthly. $29.00/year; $35.00/year for Canada; $85.00/year for out of country. Magazine (tabloid) containing employment opportunity information for the engineering and technical community.

★12351★ InterJournal

New England Complex Systems Institute
24 Mt. Auburn St.
Cambridge, MA 02138
Ph: (617)547-4100   Fax: (617)661-7711
URL: http://www.interjournal.org/

Journal covering the fields of science and engineering.

★12352★ International Archives of Bioscience

International Archives of Bioscience
PO Box 737254
Elmhurst, NY 11373-9997
URL: http://www.iabs.us/jdoc/aboutiabs.htm

Free, online only. Journal reporting multidisciplinary coverage and interaction between scientists in biology, informatics, mathematics, physics, engineering and other sciences.

★12353★ NSBE Magazine

NSBE Publications
205 Daingerfield Rd.
Alexandria, VA 22314
Ph: (703)549-2207   Fax: (703)683-5312
URL: http://www.nsbe.org/publications/premieradvertisers.php

Journal providing information on engineering careers, self-development, and cultural issues for recent graduates with technical majors.

★12354★ SWE, Magazine of the Society of Women Engineers

Society of Women Engineers
230 East Ohio St., Ste. 400
Chicago, IL 60611-3265
Ph: (312)596-5223
E-mail: hq@swe.org
URL: http://www.swe.org

Quarterly. $30.00/year for nonmembers. Magazine for engineering students and for women and men working in the engineering and technology fields. Covers career guidance, continuing development and topical issues.

★12355★ Tissue Engineering

Mary Ann Liebert Inc. Publishers
140 Huguenot St., 3rd Fl.
New Rochelle, NY 10801-5215
Ph: (914)740-2100   Fax: (914)740-2101
Fr: 800-654-3237
E-mail: info@liebertpub.com
URL: http://www.liebertpub.com

Monthly. Peer-reviewed journal that focuses on the engineering of new biologic tissues. The official journal of the Tissue Engineering and Regenerative Medicine International Society.

★12356★ Uratie

IDG Communications Inc.
5 Speen St., 3rd. Fl
Framingham, MA 01701
Ph: (508)875-5000   Fax: (508)988-7888
URL: http://www.idg.com

Magazine providing job offers for graduates, engineers and information technology professionals.

★12357★ WEPANEWS

Women in Engineering Programs &
  Advocates Network
1901 E. Asbury Ave., Ste. 220
Denver, CO 80208
Ph: (303)871-4643   Fax: (303)871-6833
E-mail: dmatt@wepan.org
URL: http://www.wepan.org

Description: 2/year. Seeks to provide greater access for women to careers in engineering. Includes news of graduate, undergraduate, freshmen, pre-college, and re-entry engineering programs for women. Recurring features include job listings, faculty, grant, and conference news, international engineering program news, action group news, notices of publications available, and a column titled Kudos.

PLACEMENT AND JOB REFERRAL SERVICES

★12358★ American Society for Cell Biology (ASCB)

8120 Woodmont Ave., Ste. 750
Bethesda, MD 20814-2762
Ph: (301)347-9300   Fax: (301)347-9310
E-mail: ascbinfo@ascb.org
URL: http://www.ascb.org

Description: Represents scientists with educational or research experience in cell biology or an allied field. Offers placement service.

★12359★ Engineering Society of Detroit (ESD)

2000 Town Ctr., Ste. 2610
Southfield, MI 48075
Ph: (248)353-0735   Fax: (248)353-0736
E-mail: esd@esd.org
URL: http://esd.org

Description: Engineers from all disciplines; scientists and technologists. Conducts technical programs and engineering refresher courses; sponsors conferences and expositions. Maintains speakers' bureau; offers placement services; although based in Detroit, MI, society membership is international.

★12360★ Society of Hispanic Professional Engineers (SHPE)

5400 E Olympic Blvd., Ste. 210
Los Angeles, CA 90022
Ph: (323)725-3970   Fax: (323)725-0316
E-mail: shpenational@shpe.org
URL: http://oneshpe.shpe.org/wps/portal/national

Description: Represents engineers, student engineers, and scientists. Aims to increase the number of Hispanic engineers by providing motivation and support to students. Sponsors competitions and educational programs. Maintains placement service and speakers' bureau; compiles statistics.

EMPLOYER DIRECTORIES AND NETWORKING LISTS

★12361★ Careers in Focus: Engineering

Facts On File Inc.
132 W 31st St., 17th Fl.
New York, NY 10001
Ph: (212)967-8800   Fax: 800-678-3633
Fr: 800-322-8755
URL: http://www.factsonfile.com

3rd edition, 2007. $29.95 for individuals; $26.95 for libraries. Publication includes: List of resources to consult for more information. Principal content of publication consists of job descriptions, advancement opportunities, educational requirements, employment outlook, salary information, and working conditions for careers in the field of engineering. Indexes: Alphabetical.

★12362★ Indiana Society of Professional Engineers-Directory

Indiana Society of Professional Engineers
PO Box 20806
Indianapolis, IN 46220
Ph: (317)255-2267   Fax: (317)255-2530
URL: http://www.indspe.org

Annual, fall. Covers member registered engineers, land surveyors, engineering students, and engineers in training. Entries include: Member name, address, phone, type of membership, business information, specialty. Arrangement: Alphabetical by chapter area.

HANDBOOKS AND MANUALS

★12363★ The Best Resumes for Scientists and Engineers

John Wiley & Sons Inc.
1 Wiley Dr.
Somerset, NJ 08873
Ph: (732)469-4400   Fax: (732)302-2300
Fr: 800-225-5945
E-mail: custserv@wiley.com
URL: http://www.wiley.com/WileyCDA/

Adele Lewis and David J. Moore. Second edition, 1993. $37.50; $19.95 (paper). 224 pages. Presents an extensive collection of scientific and engineering resumes, highlighting the important differences between these and resumes written for other occupations.

★12364★ Functional Tissue Engineering

Springer-Verlag New York, Inc.
233 Spring St.
New York, NY 10013
Ph: (212)460-1501   Fax: (212)460-1595
E-mail: custserv@springer-ny.com
URL: http://www.springer.com/

Farshid Guilak, David Butler, Steven Goldstein, and David Mooney. July 2004. $79.95. 426 pages.

★12365★ Great Jobs for Engineering Majors

The McGraw-Hill Companies
PO Box 182604
Columbus, OH 43272
Fax: (614)759-3749   Fr: 877-883-5524
E-mail: customer.service@mcgraw-hill.com
URL: http://www.mcgraw-hill.com

Geraldine O. Garner. Second edition, 2002. $14.95. 256 pages. Covers all the career options open to students majoring in engineering.

★12366★ Keys to Engineering Success

Prentice Hall PTR
One Lake St.
Upper Saddle River, NJ 07458
Ph: (201)236-7000   Fr: 800-428-5331
URL: http://www.phptr.com/index.asp?rl=1

Jill S. Tietjen, Kristy A. Schloss, Carol Carter, Joyce Bishop, and Sarah Lyman. 2000. $46.00 (paper). 288 pages.

★12367★ The New Engineer's Guide to Career Growth & Professional Awareness

Institute of Electrical & Electronics Engineers
445 Hoes Lane
Piscataway, NJ 08854
Ph: (732)981-0060   Fax: (732)981-9667
Fr: 800-678-4333
URL: http://www.ieee.org

Irving J. Gabelman, editor. 1996. $39.95 (paper). 275 pages.

★12368★ Orthopedic Tissue Engineering: Basic Science and Practice

Marcel Dekker Inc.
270 Madison Ave., 4th Fl.
New York, NY 10016
URL: http://www.dekker.com

Victor Goldbert and Arnold Caplan. January 2004. $249.95. 425 pages. Explores the basic science and clinical concepts impacting bone tissue engineering.

★12369★ Resumes for Engineering Careers

The McGraw-Hill Companies
PO Box 182604
Columbus, OH 43272
Fax: (614)759-3749   Fr: 877-883-5524
E-mail: customer.service@mcgraw-hill.com
URL: http://www.mcgraw-hill.com

Third edition, 2005. $11.95 (paper). 144 pages. Contains sample resumes and cover letters applicable to any engineering field.

★12370★ Tissue Engineering

CRC Press LLC
6000 Broken Sound Pkwy NW, Ste. 300
Boca Raton, FL 33487
Fax: 800-374-3401   Fr: 800-272-7737
URL: http://www.crcpress.com

Bernhard Pallson, Jeffrey A. Hubbell, Robert Pionsey and Joseph D. Bronzion. 2003. $99.95. 392 pages. Provides an overview of the major physiologic systems of current interest to biomedical engineers.

★12371★ Tissue Engineering: Engineering Principles for the Design of Replacement Organs and Tissues

Oxford University Press Inc.
198 Madison Ave.
New York, NY 10016
Ph: (212)726-6000   Fax: (919)677-1303
Fr: 800-445-9714
E-mail: custserv.us@oup.com
URL: http://www.oup.com/us/

W Mark Saltzman. $85.00. 544 pages.

★12372★ Tissue Engineering in Musculoskeletal Clinical Practice

American Academy of Orthopaedic Surgeons
6300 N. River Rd.
Rosemont, IL 60018
Ph: (847)823-7186   Fax: (847)823-8125
E-mail: orthoinfo@aaos.org
URL: http://www.aaos.org

Linda J. Sandell. 2004. 415 pages. $120.00.

★12373★ Tissue Engineering, Stem Cells, and Gene Therapies

Springer-Verlag New York, Inc.
233 Spring St.
New York, NY 10013
Ph: (212)460-1501   Fax: (212)460-1595
E-mail: custserv@springer-ny.com
URL: http://www.springer.com/

Y. Murat Elcin. July 2003. $199.00. 350 pages. Book includes manuscripts on tissue engineering, stem cells and gene therapies authored by world-renowned scientists of the field.

EMPLOYMENT AGENCIES AND SEARCH FIRMS

★12374★ Aureus Group

13609 California St.
Omaha, NE 68154
Ph: (402)891-6900   Fax: (402)891-1290
Fr: 888-239-5993
E-mail: info@aureusgroup.com
URL: http://www.aureusgroup.com

Provides human capital management services in a wide variety of industries. Executive search and recruiting consultants specializing in six areas: accounting and finance, data processing, aerospace, engineering, manufacturing and medical professionals. Industries served: hospitals, all mainframe computer shops and all areas of accounting.

TRADESHOWS

★12375★ American Society for Engineering Education Annual Conference and Exposition

American Society for Engineering Education
1818 N. St. NW, Ste. 600
Washington, DC 20036-2479
Ph: (202)331-3500   Fax: (202)265-8504
E-mail: conferences@asee.org
URL: http://www.asee.org

Annual. **Primary Exhibits:** Publications, engineering supplies and equipment, computers, software, and research companies all products and services related to engineering education.

OTHER SOURCES

★12376★ American Association of Engineering Societies (AAES)

1620 I St. NW, Ste. 210
Washington, DC 20006
Ph: (202)296-2237   Fax: (202)296-1151
Fr: 888-400-2237
E-mail: dbateson@aaes.org
URL: http://www.aaes.org

Description: Coordinates the efforts of the member societies in the provision of reliable and objective information to the general public concerning issues which affect the engineering profession and the field of engineering as a whole; collects, analyzes, documents, and disseminates data which will inform the general public of the relationship between engineering and the national welfare; provides a forum for the engineering societies to exchange and discuss their views on matters of common interest; and represents the U.S. engineering community abroad through representation in WFEO and UPADI.

★12377★ American Engineering Association (AEA)

4116 S Carrier Pkwy., Ste. 280-809
Grand Prairie, TX 75052
Ph: (201)664-6954
E-mail: info@aea.org
URL: http://www.aea.org

Description: Members consist of Engineers and engineering professionals. Purpose to advance the engineering profession and U.S. engineering capabilities. Issues of concern include age discrimination, immigration laws, displacement of U.S. Engineers by foreign workers, trade agreements, off shoring of U.S. Engineering and manufacturing jobs, loss of U.S. manufacturing and engineering capability, and recruitment of foreign students. Testifies before Congress. Holds local Chapter meetings.

★12378★ American Institute of Engineers (AIE)

4630 Appian Way, Ste. 206
El Sobrante, CA 94803-1875
Ph: (510)758-6240   Fax: (510)758-6240
E-mail: aie@members-aie.org
URL: http://www.members-aie.org

Description: Professional association for engineers, scientists, and mathematicians. Multi-disciplined, non-technical association who aims to improve the stature and image of engineers, scientists, and mathematicians. Provides endorsements, awards and opportunities for small business start-ups within the AIE Councils. Sponsors "LA Engineer", a comedy-drama television series; produces annual "Academy Hall of FAME (TV)".

★12379★ Biomedical Engineering Society

8401 Corporate Dr., Ste. 140
Landover, MD 20785-2224
Ph: (301)459-1999   Fr: (301)459-2444
E-mail: info@bmes.org
URL: http://www.bmes.org

Description: Provides resources including relevant publications and career links.

★12380★ Engineering Workforce Commission (EWC)

1620 I St. NW, Ste. 210
Washington, DC 20006
Ph: (202)296-2237   Fax: (202)296-1151
Fr: 888-400-2237
E-mail: dbateson@aaes.org
URL: http://www.ewc-online.org

Description: Represents commissioners appointed by member societies of the American Association of Engineering Societies to engage in studies and analyses of the supply, demand, use and remuneration of engineering and technical personnel. Provides representation to government groups dealing with professional manpower policy; consults with industry. Gathers and disseminates information on the engineering profession. Conducts surveys of engineering school enrollments, degrees, and salaries; monitors federal labor statistics.

★12381★ International Federation of Professional and Technical Engineers (IFPTE)

8630 Fenton St., Ste. 400
Silver Spring, MD 20910-3803
Ph: (301)565-9016   Fax: (301)565-0018
E-mail: gjunemann@ifpte.org
URL: http://www.ifpte.org

Description: Represents engineers, scientists, architects and technicians.

★12382★ National Action Council for Minorities in Engineering (NACME)

440 Hamilton Ave., Ste. 302
White Plains, NY 10601-1813
Ph: (914)539-4010   Fax: (914)539-4032
E-mail: webmaster@nacme.org
URL: http://www.nacme.org

Description: Leads the national effort to increase access to careers in engineering and other science-based disciplines. Conducts research and public policy analysis, develops and operates national demonstration programs at precollege and university levels, and disseminates information through publications, conferences and electronic media. Serves as a privately funded source of scholarships for minority students in engineering.

★12383★ National Society of Professional Engineers (NSPE)

1420 King St.
Alexandria, VA 22314-2794
Ph: (703)684-2800   Fax: (703)836-4875
Fr: 888-285-6773
E-mail: memserv@nspe.org
URL: http://www.nspe.org

Description: Represents professional engineers and engineers-in-training in all fields registered in accordance with the laws of states or territories of the U.S. or provinces of Canada; qualified graduate engineers, student members, and registered land surveyors. Is concerned with social, professional, ethical, and economic considerations of engineering as a profession; encompasses programs in public relations, employment practices, ethical considerations, education, and career guidance. Monitors legislative and regulatory actions of interest to the engineering profession.

★12384★ Society of Engineering Science (SES)

Pennsylvania State University
Dept. of Engineering Science and
Mechanics
212 EES Bldg.
University Park, PA 16802
E-mail: jtodd@psu.edu
URL: http://www.sesinc.org

Members: Individuals with at least a baccalaureate degree who are engaged in any aspect of engineering science or in other pursuits that contributes to the advancement of engineering science. **Purpose:** Fosters and promotes the interchange of ideas and information among the various fields of engineering science and among engineering science and the fields of theoretical and applied physics, chemistry, and mathematics. Is dedicated to the advancement of interdisciplinary research and to the establishment of a bridge between science and engineering.

★12385★ Society of Women Engineers (SWE)

230 E Ohio St., Ste. 400
Chicago, IL 60611-3265
Ph: (312)596-5223   Fax: (312)596-5252
Fr: 877-SWE-INFO
E-mail: hq@swe.org
URL: http://www.swe.org

Description: Educational and service organization representing both students and professional women in engineering and technical fields.

★12386★ The Tissue Engineering Society International

15 Arlen Rd., Apt. J
Baltimore, MD 21236
Ph: (410)931-7838   Fax: (410)931-7849
E-mail: swilburn@termis.org
URL: http://www.tesinternational.org

Description: Brings together the international community of persons engaged or interested in the field of tissue engineering and promotes education and research within the field of tissue engineering through regular meetings, publications and other forms of communication.

★12387★ United Engineering Foundation (UEF)

PO Box 70
Mount Vernon, VA 22121-0070
Ph: (973)244-2328   Fax: (973)882-5155
E-mail: engfnd@aol.com
URL: http://www.uefoundation.org

Description: Federation of 5 major national engineering societies: American Institute of Chemical Engineers; American Institute of Mining, Metallurgical and Petroleum Engineers; American Society of Civil Engineers; American Society of Mechanical Engineers; Institute of Electrical and Electronics Engineers. Supports research in engineering and advances the engineering arts and sciences through its conference program.

Tool Programmers, Numerical Control

Sources of Help-Wanted Ads

★12388★ American Machinist

Penton Media Inc.
1300 E 9th St.
Cleveland, OH 44114
Ph: (216)696-7000   Fax: (216)696-1752
URL: http://www.americanmachinist.com/

Monthly. $90.00/year for Canada, individual; $153.00 for Canada, 2 years, individual; $113.00/year for individuals; $176.00/year for out of country, 2 years, individual. Magazine serving the metalworking marketplace, consisting of plants in industries primarily engaged in manufacturing durable goods and other metal products.

★12389★ Tooling & Production

Nelson Publishing Inc.
2500 Tamiami Trl. N
Nokomis, FL 34275
Ph: (941)966-9521   Fax: (941)966-2590
URL: http://www.manufacturingcenter.com

Monthly. Magazine concerning metalworking.

Placement and Job Referral Services

★12390★ American Indian Science and Engineering Society (AISES)

PO Box 9828
Albuquerque, NM 87119-9828
Ph: (505)765-1052   Fax: (505)765-5608
E-mail: info@aises.org
URL: http://www.aises.org

Description: Represents American Indian and non-Indian students and professionals in science, technology, and engineering fields; corporations representing energy, mining, aerospace, electronic, and computer fields. Seeks to motivate and encourage students to pursue undergraduate and graduate stud-ies in science, engineering, and technology. Sponsors science fairs in grade schools, teacher training workshops, summer math/science sessions for 8th-12th graders, professional chapters, and student chapters in colleges. Offers scholarships. Adult members serve as role models, advisers, and mentors for students. Operates placement service.

★12391★ Composites Manufacturing Association of the Society of Manufacturing Engineers (CMA/SME)

PO Box 930
Dearborn, MI 48121-0930
Ph: (313)425-3000   Fax: (313)425-3400
Fr: 800-733-4763
E-mail: leadership@sme.org
URL: http://www.sme.org/cgi-bin/communities.pl?/communities/cma/cma-home.htm&&&SME&

Description: A division of the Society of Manufacturing Engineers. Composites manufacturing professionals and students in 21 countries. Addresses design, tooling, assembly, producibility, supportability, and future trends of composites materials and hardware; promotes advanced composites technology. Analyzes industry trends; evaluates composites usage. Conducts educational programs; facilitates exchange of information among members; operates placement service.

Handbooks and Manuals

★12392★ Careers in Computers

The McGraw-Hill Companies
PO Box 182604
Columbus, OH 43272
Fax: (614)759-3749   Fr: 877-883-5524
E-mail: customer.service@mcgraw-hill.com
URL: http://www.mcgraw-hill.com

Lila B. Stair and Leslie Stair. 2002. $19.95; $14.95 (paper). 192 pages. Describes trends affecting computer careers and explores a wide range of job opportunities from pro-gramming to consulting. Provides job qualifications, salary data, job market information, personal and educational requirements, career paths, and the place of the job in the organizational structure. Offers advice on education, certification, and job search.

★12393★ Careers for Number Crunchers and Other Quantitative Types

The McGraw-Hill Companies
PO Box 182604
Columbus, OH 43272
Fax: (614)759-3749   Fr: 877-883-5524
E-mail: customer.service@mcgraw-hill.com
URL: http://www.mcgraw-hill.com

Rebecca Burnett. Second edition, 2002. $22.95 (paper). 192 pages. Provides information to math-oriented job hunters on how to become statisticians, field researchers, computer programmers, stock analysts, investment managers, bankers, engineers, accountants, underwriters, economists, market analysts, mathematicians, systems analysts, and more.

Employment Agencies and Search Firms

★12394★ KForce

Fr: 888-663-3626
URL: http://www.kforce.com

Executive search firm. More than 30 locations throughout the United States.

★12395★ Mfg/Search, Inc.

431 E Colfax Ave., Ste.120
South Bend, IN 46617
Ph: (574)282-2547   Fr: 800-782-7976
E-mail: mfg@mfgsearch.com
URL: http://www.mfgsearch.com

Executive search firm. Offices in GA, IL, MI, NY.

TRADESHOWS

★12396★ METALFORM

Precision Metalforming Association
6363 Oak Tree Blvd.
Independence, OH 44131-2500
Ph: (216)901-8800   Fax: (216)901-9190
E-mail: pma@pma.org
URL: http://www.metalforming.com

Annual. **Primary Exhibits:** Presses and stamping equipment, tooling and fabricating machines, management aids, and related materials.

★12397★ Pacific Coast Industrial and Machine Tool Show

Cygnus Expositions
3167 Skyway Ct.
Fremont, CA 94538
Ph: (510)354-3131   Fax: (510)354-3159
Fr: 800-548-1407
E-mail: john.wright@cygnusexpos.com
URL: http://www.proshows.com

Annual. **Primary Exhibits:** Industrial equipment, machine tools, business services, hand tools, and related equipment, supplies, and services.

★12398★ Reno Industrial & Machine Tool Show

Cygnus Expositions
3167 Skyway Ct.
Fremont, CA 94538
Ph: (510)354-3131   Fax: (510)354-3159
Fr: 800-548-1407
E-mail: john.wright@cygnusexpos.com
URL: http://www.proshows.com

Annual. **Primary Exhibits:** Industrial and machine tool products.

★12399★ WESTEC - Advanced Productivity Exposition

Society of Manufacturing Engineers (SME)
Expositions Division
1 SME Dr.
PO Box 930
Dearborn, MI 48121
Ph: (313)271-1500   Fax: (313)425-3400
Fr: 800-733-3976
E-mail: service@sme.org
URL: http://www.sme.org

Annual. **Primary Exhibits:** Equipment, supplies, and services for the tool and manufacturing engineering industries.

OTHER SOURCES

★12400★ Math at Work: Women in Nontraditional Careers

Her Own Words
PO Box 5264
Madison, WI 53705-0264
Ph: (608)271-7083   Fax: (608)271-0209
E-mail: herownword@aol.com
URL: http://www.herownwords.com/

Video. Jocelyn Riley. $95.00. 15 minutes. Resource guide also available for $45.00.

★12401★ Precision Machined Products Association (PMPA)

6700 W Snowville Rd.
Brecksville, OH 44141
Ph: (440)526-0300   Fax: (440)526-5803
E-mail: webmaster@pmpa.org
URL: http://www.pmpa.org

Description: Addresses the information, training, and technical needs of manufacturers of component parts to customers' order, machined from rod, bar, or tube stock, of metal, fiber, plastic, or other material, using automatic or hand screw machines, automatic bar machines, and CNC machines.

★12402★ Special Interest Group on Accessible Computing (SIGACCESS)

IBM T.J. Watson Research Center
19 Skyline Dr.
Hawthorne, NY 10532
Ph: (914)784-6603   Fax: (914)784-7279
E-mail: chair_sigaccess@acm.org
URL: http://www.sigaccess.org

Description: Promotes the professional interests of computing personnel with physical disabilities and the application of computing and information technology in solving relevant disability problems. Works to educate the public to support careers for the disabled.

★12403★ Women in Machining

Her Own Words
PO Box 5264
Madison, WI 53705-0264
Ph: (608)271-7083   Fax: (608)271-0209
E-mail: herownword@aol.com
URL: http://www.herownwords.com/

Video. Jocelyn Riley. $95.00. 15 minutes. Resource guide also available for $45.00.

★12404★ Women in Nontraditional Careers: An Introduction

Her Own Words
PO Box 5264
Madison, WI 53705
Ph: (608)271-7083   Fax: (608)271-0209
E-mail: herownword@aol.com
URL: http://www.herownwords.com/

Video. Jocelyn Riley. $95.00. 15 minutes. Resource guide also available for $45.00.

Tour Guides and Operators

SOURCES OF HELP-WANTED ADS

★12405★ *Meeting News*

The Nielsen Co.
770 Broadway
New York, NY 10003
Ph: (646)654-5000   Fax: (646)654-5002
URL: http://www.meetingnews.com/

$89.00/year for individuals; $99.00/year for Canada; $205.00/year for other countries, by airmail. The newspaper for conventions, meetings, incentive travel and trade show professionals.

★12406★ *Tourism, Culture & Communication*

Cognizant Communications Corp.
3 Hartsdale Rd.
Elmsford, NY 10523-3701
Ph: (914)592-7720   Fax: (914)592-8981
URL: http://www.cognizantcommunication.com/filecabinet/Tourism_Cu

$250.00/year for institutions, library; $275.00/year for institutions, rest of the world, library; $40.00/year professional; $55.00/year for other countries, professional. Journal covering tourism, culture, and communication.

★12407★ *Travel Agent*

Questex Media Group Inc.
306 W Michigan St., Ste. 200
Duluth, MN 55802
Ph: (218)279-8800   Fax: (218)279-8810

Weekly. $250.00/year. Free to qualified subscribers; $250.00/year. Travel industry magazine.

★12408★ *Travel Trade*

Travel Trade
15 West 44th St.
New York, NY 10036
Ph: (212)730-6600   Fax: (212)730-7060

E-mail: travelcat@aol.com

Weekly. Travel industry magazine.

★12409★ *Travel Weekly*

Northstar Travel Media
100 Lighting Way, 2nd Fl.
Secaucus, NJ 07094
Ph: (201)902-2000   Fax: (201)902-2045
URL: http://www.northstartravelmedia.com

Weekly (Mon.). Free to qualified subscribers. Travel industry magazine.

★12410★ *TravelAge West*

Northstar Travel Media
100 Lighting Way, 2nd Fl.
Secaucus, NJ 07094
Ph: (201)902-2000   Fax: (201)902-2045
URL: http://www.northstartravelmedia.com

Biweekly. Magazine for retail travel agents in western U.S. and western Canada.

PLACEMENT AND JOB REFERRAL SERVICES

★12411★ **Connected International Meeting Professionals Association (CIMPA)**

9200 Bayard Pl.
Fairfax, VA 22032
Ph: (512)684-0889   Fax: (267)390-5193
E-mail: susan2@cimpa.org
URL: http://www.cimpa.org

Members: Meeting planners, incentive organizers, travel agents, tour operators, and seminar organizers in 42 countries. **Purpose:** Works to improve the skills of professional conference and convention planners. Serves as a clearinghouse of information on new travel destinations and planning technologies, techniques, and strategies. **Activities:** Facilitates exchange of information among Internet professionals. Produces a television program on travel and meetings. Conducts educational courses and awards Certified Internet Meeting Professional designation. Conducts research programs and placement service. Sponsors training courses on the Internet.

★12412★ **International Association of Tour Managers - North American Region (IATM North)**

24 Blevins Rd.
Kerhonkson, NY 12446-1302
Ph: (212)208-6800   Fax: (212)208-6800
E-mail: chairman@tourmanager.org
URL: http://www.tourmanager.org

Description: Works to maintain the highest possible standards of tour management; guarantee excellence of performance; educate the travel world on the role of the tour manager (also referred to as tour director, tour escort, or tour leader) in the successful completion of the tour itinerary and in bringing business to related industries. Represents members in influencing legislation and advising on travel policy. Trains tour managers to plan, research, and lead tours to specific domestic and foreign destinations; operates Advisory Board in Professional Tour Management; offers placement service; conducts Professional travel agents, travel wholesalers, airlines, hotel associations, shipping lines, tourist organizations, restaurants, shops, and entertainment organizations Tour Management International Certificate Program.

EMPLOYER DIRECTORIES AND NETWORKING LISTS

★12413★ *Specialty Travel Index*

Alpine Hansen, Publishers
PO Box 458
San Anselmo, CA 94979
Ph: (415)455-1643   Fax: (415)455-1648
Fr: 888-624-4030
E-mail: info@specialitytravel.com
URL: http://www.specialtytravel.com

Semiannual, January and August. Covers over 600 special interest tour operators, worldwide; all listings are paid. Entries include: Firm name, address, phone; description of tours offered, including nature of trip, destinations, sample cost and duration of trip. Arrangement: Alphabetical. Indexes: Special interest activity (with location of activity); geographical (and the special interest activities possible).

★12414★ **Survey of State Tourism Offices**

Travel Industry Association of America
1100 New York Ave. NW, Ste. 450
Washington, DC 20005-3934
Ph: (202)408-8422   Fax: (202)408-1255
URL: http://www.tia.org

Annual; latest edition 2007. $300.00 for members; $495.00 for nonmembers. Covers state and territorial government agencies responsible for travel and travel promotion in their states. Entries include: Agency name, address, phone, number of full- and part-time staff, number of professional staff directly involved in travel; name and title of state travel director, and length of service as director, length of service in agency, and whether employed under the Civil Service program; advertising director and agency and public relations director in separate sections. Extensive additional data is provided by a series of tables covering state activities in advertising, package tours, general promotion press and public relations, research, the establishment of welcome centers, and the department budget. Although addresses are not given, some listings do include name, title, and department of contact. Arrangement: By function (administration, advertising, etc.), then geographical.

HANDBOOKS AND MANUALS

★12415★ **Career Opportunities in Travel and Tourism**

Facts On File Inc.
132 W. 31st St., 17th Fl.
New York, NY 10001-2006
Ph: (212)967-8800   Fax: 800-678-3633
Fr: 800-322-8755
E-mail: custserv@factsonfile.com
URL: http://www.factsonfile.com

John K. Hawks. 1996. $18.95 (paper). 224 pages. Includes detailed job descriptions, educational requirements, salary ranges, and advancement prospects for 70 different job opportunities in this fast-paced industry. Contains index and bibliography.

★12416★ **Careers in Travel, Tourism, and Hospitality**

The McGraw-Hill Companies
PO Box 182604
Columbus, OH 43272
Fax: (614)759-3749   Fr: 877-883-5524
E-mail: customer.service@mcgraw-hill.com
URL: http://www.mcgraw-hill.com

Marjorie Eberts, Linda Brothers, and Ann

Gisler. Second edition, 2005. $15.95 (paper). 224 pages.

★12417★ **A Coach Full of Fun: A Handbook of Creative Solutions and Ideas for Tour Escorts**

Shoreline Creations, Ltd.
2465 112th Ave.
Holland, MI 49424
Ph: (616)393-2077   Fax: (616)393-0085
Fr: 800-767-3489

Jeane S. Klender, Amber Christman-Clark, and Amy Gustin. 1995. $19.95 (paper). 214 pages. Provides advice on how to be successful in the group tour industry. Contains information on tour procedures, preparation, and finances.

★12418★ **Conducting Tours**

Cengage Learning
PO Box 6904
Florence, KY 41022
Fax: 800-487-8488   Fr: 800-354-9706
URL: http://www.cengage.com

Marc Mancini. Third edition, 2000. $98.95. 272 pages.

★12419★ **Cruise Ship Jobs: The Insider's Guide to Finding and Getting Jobs on Cruise Ships Around the World**

Portofino Publications
PO Box 97-0252
Coconut Creek, FL 33097
Ph: (972)380-2161   Fax: (972)380-9521
Fr: 800-522-4693
URL: http://www.portofinopress.com/

Richard B Marin. 1998. $13.95 (paper). 143 pages.

★12420★ **Ecotourism Guidelines for Nature Tour Operator**

The International Ecotourism Society
1333 H St., NW, Ste. 300, East Tower
Washington, DC 20005
Ph: (202)347-9203   Fax: (202)789-7279
E-mail: info@ecotourism.org
URL: http://www.ecotourism.org/

Megan Epler-Wood. 1993. $8.00 (paper). 14 pages.

★12421★ **First Class: An Introduction to Travel and Tourism**

The McGraw-Hill Companies
PO Box 182604
Columbus, OH 43272
Fax: (614)759-3749   Fr: 877-883-5524
E-mail: customer.service@mcgraw-hill.com
URL: http://www.mcgraw-hill.com

Dennis L. Foster. 1995. $111.15. 385 pages.

★12422★ **Hospitality and Tourism Careers: A Blueprint for Success**

The McGraw-Hill Companies
PO Box 182604
Columbus, OH 43272
Fax: (614)759-3749   Fr: 877-883-5524
E-mail: customer.service@mcgraw-hill.com
URL: http://www.mcgraw-hill.com

Melissa Dallas and Carl Riegel. Second edition, 1997. $57.00 (paper). 252 pages.

★12423★ **How to Get a Job with a Cruise Line**

Ticket to Adventure, Inc.
PO Box 41005
St. Petersburg, FL 33743-1005
Ph: (727)822-5029   Fax: (727)821-3409
Fr: 800-929-7447

Mary Fallon Miller. Fifth edition, 2001. $16.95 (paper). 352 pages. Explores jobs with cruise ships, describing duties, responsibilities, benefits, and training. Lists cruise ship lines and schools offering cruise line training. Offers job hunting advice.

★12424★ **Opportunities in Travel Careers**

The McGraw-Hill Companies
PO Box 182604
Columbus, OH 43272
Fax: (614)759-3749   Fr: 877-883-5524
E-mail: customer.service@mcgraw-hill.com
URL: http://www.mcgraw-hill.com

Robert Scott Milne. Second edition, 2003. $14.95 (paper). 141 pages. Discusses what the jobs are and where to find them in airlines, shipping lines, and railroads. Discusses related opportunities in hotels, motels, resorts, travel agencies, public relation firms, and recreation departments. Illustrated.

★12425★ **Travel the World Free as an International Tour Director: How to Be an International Tour Director**

BookSurge Publishing
PO Box 21199
Charleston, SC 29413
Ph: (803)723-7400   Fax: (803)723-0751
Fr: 800-894-8687
URL: http://www.booksurge.com/

Gerald E. Mitchell. 2007. $26.99. 366 pages. Kit includes 250-page manual, 189-page site-inspection journal and resource start up kit with video.

TRADESHOWS

★12426★ **Luxury Travel Expo**

Advanstar Communications Inc.
One Park Ave.
New York, NY 10016
Ph: (212)951-6600   Fax: (212)951-6793
E-mail: info@advanstar.com
URL: http://www.advanstar.com

Semiannual. **Primary Exhibits:** Tours and tour packages sales agents.

★12427★ **WTM - World Travel Market**
Reed Exhibitions (North American
  Headquarters)
383 Main Ave.
Norwalk, CT 06851
Ph: (203)840-5337   Fax: (203)840-9570
E-mail: export@reedexpo.com
URL: http://www.reedexpo.com

Annual. **Primary Exhibits:** Goods and services related to tourism and travel.

OTHER SOURCES

★12428★ **United States Tour Operators
Association (USTOA)**
275 Madison Ave., Ste. 2014
New York, NY 10016-1101
Ph: (212)599-6599   Fax: (212)599-6744
E-mail: information@ustoa.com
URL: http://www.ustoa.com

Description: Represents wholesale tour operators, common carriers, associations, government agencies, suppliers, purveyors of travel services, trade press, communications media, and public relations and advertising representatives. Encourages and supports professional and financial integrity in tourism. Protects the legitimate interests of the consumer and the retail agent from financial loss from business conducted with members. Provides tour operators with an opportunity to formulate and express an independent industry voice on matters of common interest and self-regulation. Strives to facilitate and develop travel on a worldwide basis.

Traffic Technicians

SOURCES OF HELP-WANTED ADS

★12429★ Advanced Transportation Technology News
BCC Research
70 New Canaan Ave.
Norwalk, CT 06850
Ph: (203)750-9783   Fax: (203)229-0087
Fr: (866)285-7215
URL: http://www.bccresearch.com

Monthly. $2,850.00/year for individuals, hard copy mail delivery. Publication covering technology and related news for the transportation industry.

★12430★ Maine Trails
Maine Better Transportation Association
146 State St.
Augusta, ME 04330
Ph: (207)622-0526   Fax: (207)623-2928
URL: http://www.mbtaonline.org/publications.htm

Bimonthly. Magazine informing association members and the business community about Maine transportation issues.

★12431★ Traffic Safety
NSC Press
1121 Spring Lake Dr.
Itasca, IL 60143-3201
Ph: (630)285-1121   Fax: (630)285-1315
Fr: 800-621-7615
E-mail: info@nsc.org
URL: http://secure.nsc.org

Monthly. $24.00/year for members; $31.00/year for nonmembers; $20.00 for single issue; $13.00/year for members, quantity 10 - 24; $11.00/year for members, quantity 25 - 49; $9.00/year for members, quantity 50 - 74; $8.00/year for members, quantity 75 - 999; $15.00/year for nonmembers, quantity 5 - 9; $17.00/year for nonmembers, quantity 10 - 24; $14.00/year for nonmembers, quantity 25 - 49. Vehicle collision prevention magazine includes information on driver training, traffic and road engineering, and law enforcement.

EMPLOYER DIRECTORIES AND NETWORKING LISTS

★12432★ Careers in Focus: Transportation
Facts On File Inc.
132 W 31st St., 17th Fl.
New York, NY 10001
Ph: (212)967-8800   Fax: 800-678-3633
Fr: 800-322-8755
URL: http://www.factsonfile.com

Latest edition 3rd, 2007. $29.95 for individuals; $26.95 for libraries. Covers an overview of transportation, followed by a selection of jobs profiled in detail, including the nature of the job, earnings, prospects for employment, what kind of training and skills it requires, and sources for further information.

HANDBOOKS AND MANUALS

★12433★ Opportunities in Civil Engineering Careers
McGraw-Hill
PO Box 182604
Columbus, OH 43272
Fax: (614)759-3749   Fr: 877-883-5524
E-mail: customer.service@mcgraw-hill.com
URL: http://www.mcgraw-hill.com

Joseph Hagerty, Louis F. Cohn, Philip Pessy, and Tom Cosgrove. 1996. $11.95 (paper). 160 pages. Describes career opportunities in the different fields of civil engineering and tells how to prepare for and launch such a career.

ONLINE JOB SOURCES AND SERVICES

★12434★ Civil Engineering Jobs
URL: http://www.civilengineeringjobs.com

Description: Job postings for all civil engineering disciplines including positions in traffic/transportation.

TRADESHOWS

★12435★ ATSSA Annual Convention and Traffic Expo
American Traffic Safety Services Association
15 Riverside Pkwy., Ste. 100
Fredericksburg, VA 22406-1022
Ph: (540)368-1701   Fax: (540)368-1717
Fr: 800-272-8772
E-mail: meetings@atssa.com
URL: http://www.atssa.com

Annual. **Primary Exhibits:** Manufacturers or services oriented companies that provide traffic control, ITS, pavement marking, signing and various other roadway safety devices.

★12436★ International Municipal Signal Association
International Municipal Signal Association
165 E Union St.
PO Box 539
Newark, NY 14513-0539
Ph: (315)331-2182   Fax: (315)331-8205
Fr: 800-723-4672
E-mail: Info@IMSAsafety.org
URL: http://www.imsasafety.org

Annual. **Primary Exhibits:** Public Safety equipment, supplies, and services, including: traffic signals, street signs, alarms, roadway lighting, and communications equipment.

OTHER SOURCES

★12437★ American Association of State Highway and Transportation Officials

444 N. Capitol St. NW, Ste. 249
Washington, DC 20001
Ph: (202)624-5800   Fax: (202)624-5806
URL: http://www.transportation.org

Description: Strives to advocate transportation policies, provide technical services, and demonstrate the contributions of transportation and facilitate change.

★12438★ American Highway Users Alliance

1101 14th St. NW, Ste. 750
Washington, DC 20005
Ph: (202)857-1200   Fax: (202)857-1220
E-mail: info@highways.org
URL: http://www.highways.org

Description: Serves as the voice of the transportation community promoting safe highways and the enhanced freedom of mobility.

★12439★ American Planning Association (APA)

122 S Michigan Ave., Ste. 1600
Chicago, IL 60603-6107
Ph: (312)431-9100   Fax: (312)431-9985
E-mail: customerservice@planning.org
URL: http://www.planning.org

Description: Public and private planning agency officials, professional planners, planning educators, elected and appointed officials, and other persons involved in urban and rural development. Works to foster the best techniques and decisions for the planned development of communities and regions. Provides extensive professional services and publications to professionals and laypeople in planning and related fields; serves as a clearinghouse for information. Through Planning Advisory Service, a research and inquiry-answering service, provides, on an annual subscription basis, advice on specific inquiries and a series of research reports on planning, zoning, and environmental regulations. Supplies information on job openings and makes definitive studies on salaries and recruitment of professional planners. Conducts research; collaborates in joint projects with local, national, and international organizations.

★12440★ American Traffic Safety Services Association

15 Riverside Pkwy., Ste. 100
Fredericksburg, VA 22406-1022
Ph: (540)368-1701   Fax: (540)368-1717
Fr: 800-272-8772
URL: http://www.atssa.com

Description: Represents individuals and companies in the traffic control and roadway safety industry.

★12441★ Association for Commuter Transportation

1444 I St. NW, Ste. 700
Washington, DC 20005
Ph: (202)712-9021
E-mail: info@actweb.org
URL: http://tmi.cob.fsu.edu/act

Description: Professionals who specialize in commuter options and solutions.

★12442★ Association of Metropolitan Planning Organizations

1029 Vermont Ave., Ste. 710
Washington, DC 20005
Ph: (202)296-7051   Fax: (202)296-7054
URL: http://www.ampo.org/

Description: Offers a forum for transportation policy development, conferences and workshops, and research.

★12443★ Institute of Transportation Engineers

1099 14th St., Ste. 300 W
Washington, DC 20005
Ph: (202)289-0222   Fax: (202)289-7722
E-mail: ite_staff@ite.org
URL: http://www.ite.org

Description: Traffic engineers, transportation planners, and other related professionals.

★12444★ National Committee on Uniform Traffic Laws and Ordinances (NCUTLO)

107 S West St., No. 110
Alexandria, VA 22314-2824
Fax: (540)465-5383   Fr: 800-807-5290
E-mail: twogen2@yahoo.com
URL: http://www.ncutlo.org

Members: Federal, state, and local highway, police, motor vehicle, and other officials; legislators; educational institutions; manu-facturers of vehicles and equipment; insurance companies, motor clubs, and safety councils; other persons and organizations interested in uniform motor vehicle laws. **Activities:** Maintains small library on traffic law. Keeps the Uniform Vehicle Code, Collection of model laws.

★12445★ National Highway Traffic Safety Administration

1200 New Jersey Ave., SE, West Bldg.
Washington, DC 20590
Ph: (202)366-0388   Fax: (202)366-7237
Fr: 888-327-4236
URL: http://www.nhtsa.dot.gov

Description: Works to save lives, prevent injuries and reduce traffic-related health care.

★12446★ Roadway Safety Foundation

1101 14th St. NW, Ste. 750
Washington, DC 20005
Ph: (202)857-1200   Fax: (202)857-1220
URL: http://www.roadwaysafety.org

Description: Dedicated to reducing highway deaths and injuries by improving the physical characteristics of roadways.

★12447★ The Traffic Group, Inc.

9900 Franklin Square Dr., Ste. H
Baltimore, MD 21236
Ph: (410)931-6600   Fax: (410)931-6601
Fr: 800-583-8411
E-mail: lkielian@trafficgroup.com
URL: http://www.trafficgroup.com

Description: Consists of professionals in the Traffic Engineering and Transportation Planning fields.

★12448★ Transportation Research Board

500 5th St. NW
Washington, DC 20001
Ph: (202)334-2934   Fax: (202)334-2003
E-mail: kanafani@berkeley.edu
URL: http://www.trb.org

Description: Engineers, Scientists, and other transportation researchers and practitioners from the public and private sectors. Facilitates the sharing of information, promotes innovation and progress, and stimulates research.

Translators and Interpreters

SOURCES OF HELP-WANTED ADS

★12449★ LSA Bulletin

Linguistic Society of America
1325 18th St. NW, Ste. 211
Archibald A. Hill Ste.
Washington, DC 20036-6501
Ph: (202)835-1714   Fax: (202)835-1717
URL: http://www.lsadc.org

Description: Quarterly. Covers activities of the linguistic community. Recurring features include a grants calendar, conference and job announcements, a calendar of events, reports of meetings, and job listings.

PLACEMENT AND JOB REFERRAL SERVICES

★12450★ African Studies Association (ASA)

Douglass Campus
132 George St.
New Brunswick, NJ 08901-1400
Ph: (732)932-8173   Fax: (732)932-3394
E-mail: asaed@rci.rutgers.edu
URL: http://www.africanstudies.org

Members: Persons specializing in teaching, writing, or research on Africa including political scientists, historians, geographers, anthropologists, economists, librarians, linguists, and government officials; persons who are studying African subjects; institutional members are universities, libraries, government agencies, and others interested in receiving information about Africa. **Purpose:** Seeks to foster communication and to stimulate research among scholars on Africa. **Activities:** Sponsors placement service; conducts panels and discussion groups; presents exhibits and films.

EMPLOYER DIRECTORIES AND NETWORKING LISTS

★12451★ American Translators Association-Membership Directory

American Translators Association
225 Reinekers Ln., Ste. 590
Alexandria, VA 22314
Ph: (703)683-6100   Fax: (703)683-6122
URL: http://atanet.org/membership/membershipdirectory.php

Annual, summer. Includes more than 9,000 member translators, interpreters, and linguists in the United States and over 60 countries. Entries include: Name, address, phone, languages in which member has ATA certification. Arrangement: Alphabetical.

★12452★ ATA Directory of Translators and Interpreters

American Translators Association
225 Reinekers Ln., Ste. 590
Alexandria, VA 22314
Ph: (703)683-6100   Fax: (703)683-6122
URL: http://www.atanet.org

Covers over 5,800 member translators and interpreters. Entries include: Name, address, languages in which proficient, subject competencies, professional background. Arrangement: Alphabetical, area of specialization, language. Indexes: Language-subject competency (with state).

★12453★ International Literary Market Place

Information Today Inc.
143 Old Marlton Pke.
Medford, NJ 08055-8750
Ph: (609)654-6266   Fax: (609)654-4309
Fr: 800-300-9868
URL: http://www.literarymarketplace.com

Annual; latest edition 2007. $249.00 for individuals. Covers over 10,799 publishers in over 180 countries outside the United States and Canada, and about 1,499 trade and professional organizations related to publishing abroad; includes major printers, binders, typesetters, book manufacturers, book deal-ers, libraries, literary agencies, translators, book clubs, reference books and journals, periodicals, prizes, and international reference section. Entries include: For publishers–Name, address, phone, fax, telex, names and titles of key personnel, branches, type of publications, subjects, ISBN prefix. Listings for others include similar information but less detail. Arrangement: Classified by business activities, then geographical. Indexes: Company name, subject, type of publication.

★12454★ Literary Market Place

Information Today Inc.
143 Old Marlton Pke.
Medford, NJ 08055-8750
Ph: (609)654-6266   Fax: (609)654-4309
Fr: 800-300-9868
URL: http://store.yahoo.com/infotoday/

Annual; latest edition 2007. $299.95 for individuals. Covers over 14,500 firms or organizations offering services related to the publishing industry, including book publishers in the United States and Canada who issued three or more books during the preceding year, plus a small press section of publishers who publish less than three titles per year or those who are self-published. Also included: Book printers and binders; book clubs; book trade and literary associations; selected syndicates, newspapers, periodicals, and radio and television programs that use book reviews or book publishing news; translators and literary agents. Entries include: For publishers–Company name, address, phone, address for orders, principal executives, editorial directors, and managers, date founded, number of titles in previous year, number of backlist titles in print, types of books published, ISBN prefixes, representatives, imprints, and affiliations. For suppliers, etc.–Listings usually show firm name, address, phone, executives, services, etc. Arrangement: Classified by line of business. Indexes: Principal index is 35,000-item combined index of publishers, publications, and personnel; several sections have geographical and/or subject indexes; translators are indexed by source and target language.

HANDBOOKS AND MANUALS

★12455★ *Careers in International Affairs*
Georgetown University Press
3240 Prospect St., NW
Washington, DC 20007
Ph: (202)687-5889   Fax: (202)687-6340
Fr: 800-246-9606
E-mail: gupress@georgetown.edu
URL: http://www.press.georgetown.edu/

Maria Carland and Lisa Gihring (editors). Seventh edition, 2003. $24.95 (paper). 371 pages. Includes index and bibliography.

★12456★ *Great Jobs for Foreign Language Majors*
The McGraw-Hill Companies
PO Box 182604
Columbus, OH 43272
Fax: (614)759-3749   Fr: 877-883-5524
E-mail: customer.service@mcgraw-hill.com
URL: http://www.mcgraw-hill.com

Julie DeGalan and Stephen Lambert. Sec-
ond edition, 2000. $15.95 (paper). 192 pages. Part of "Great Jobs for ... Majors" series.

★12457★ *Opportunities in Foreign Language Careers*
The McGraw-Hill Companies
PO Box 182604
Columbus, OH 43272
Fax: (614)759-3749   Fr: 877-883-5524
E-mail: customer.service@mcgraw-hill.com
URL: http://www.mcgraw-hill.com

Wilga Rivers. 2004. $13.95 (paper). 196 pages. Explores a variety of foreign language careers and discusses how to pursue them. Contains bibliography and illustrations.

★12458★ *A Practical Guide for Translators*
Multilingual Matters Ltd.
325 Chestnut St.
Philadelphia, PA 19106
Ph: (215)625-8900   Fax: (215)625-2940
Fr: 800-634-7064
E-mail: info@multilingual-matters.com
URL: http://www.multilingual-matters.com

Geoffrey Samuelsson-Brown. Fourth edition, 2004. 220 pages. $29.95. Part of Topics in Translation series. Provides information on becoming a translator.

ONLINE JOB SOURCES AND SERVICES

★12459★ **TranslationDirectory.com**
E-mail: CEO@translationDirectory.com
URL: http://www.translationdirectory.com

Description: Offers a directory of a wide variety of resources: groups and mailing lists for translators, tools for language professionals, glossaries and dictionaries, translation organizations, payment collection agencies, translation blogs, freelance translators and translation agencies, language education companies and other related resources.

Travel Agents and Managers

★12460★ ARTAFAX

Association of Retail Travel Agents
73 White Bridge Road, Box 238
Nashville, TN 37205
Fax: (615)985-0600   Fr: 800-969-6069
URL: http://www.artaonline.com

Description: Daily. Reviews developments in the travel industry for retail travel agents. Covers topics such as ethics, tour operations, transportation services, educational opportunities, commissions, and political action in pertinent issues. Includes chapter and Association news.

★12461★ Business Travel News

VNU Business Media USA
770 Broadway
New York, NY 10003
Ph: (646)654-4500
URL: http://www.btnmag.com/businesstravelnews/index.jsp

Weekly. Tabloid newspaper covering business travel.

★12462★ ICTA Update

Travel Institute
148 Linden St., Ste. 305
PO Box 812059
Wellesley, MA 02482
Ph: (781)237-0280   Fax: (781)237-3860
Fr: 800-542-4282
E-mail: info@thetravelinstitute.com
URL: http://thetravelinstitute.com

Description: Four issues/year. Covers the educational activities of the Institute, which grants the Certified Travel Counselor (CTC) designation to travel industry personnel. Offers special news stories on topics relevant to the travel industry. Recurring features include news of members, management tips, and names of newly certified agents.

★12463★ Journal of Vacation Marketing

Sage Publications Inc.
2455 Teller Rd.
Thousand Oaks, CA 91320
Ph: (805)499-0721   Fax: (805)499-8096
URL: http://www.sagepub.com/journalsProdDesc.nav?prodId=Journal20

Quarterly. $621.00/year for institutions, print & e-access; $652.00/year for institutions, current volume print & all online content; $559.00/year for institutions, e-access; $590.00/year for institutions, all online content; $559.00/year for institutions; $609.00/year for institutions, print only; $189.00/year for individuals, print only; $168.00 for institutions, single print; $61.00 for individuals, single print. Journal focusing on the latest techniques, thinking and practice in the marketing of hotels, travel, tourism attractions, conventions and destinations.

★12464★ Meeting News

The Nielsen Co.
770 Broadway
New York, NY 10003
Ph: (646)654-5000   Fax: (646)654-5002
URL: http://www.meetingnews.com/

$89.00/year for individuals; $99.00/year for Canada; $205.00/year for other countries, by airmail. The newspaper for conventions, meetings, incentive travel and trade show professionals.

★12465★ TIA Newsline

Travel Industry Association of America
1100 New York Ave. NW, No. 450
Washington, DC 20005-3934
Ph: (202)408-8422   Fax: (202)408-1255
E-mail: jharris@tia.org
URL: http://www.tia.org/Pubs/enewsline.asp

Description: Semimonthly. Publishes news for the travel industry. Includes book reviews and notices of publications available, news of educational opportunities, and a calendar of events.

★12466★ Tourism, Culture & Communication

Cognizant Communications Corp.
3 Hartsdale Rd.
Elmsford, NY 10523-3701
Ph: (914)592-7720   Fax: (914)592-8981
URL: http://www.cognizantcommunication.com/filecabinet/Tourism_Cu

$250.00/year for institutions, library; $275.00/year for institutions, rest of the world, library; $40.00/year professional; $55.00/year for other countries, professional. Journal covering tourism, culture, and communication.

★12467★ Travel Agent

Questex Media Group Inc.
306 W Michigan St., Ste. 200
Duluth, MN 55802
Ph: (218)279-8800   Fax: (218)279-8810

Weekly. $250.00/year. Free to qualified subscribers; $250.00/year. Travel industry magazine.

★12468★ Travel Partners

Minnesota Office of Tourism
100 Metro Sq.
121, 7th Pl. E.
St. Paul, MN 55101
Ph: (651)296-5029   Fax: (651)296-7095
Fr: 800-657-3700
E-mail: explore@state.mn.us
URL: http://www.exploreminnesota.com

Description: Monthly. Reports news, research, advertising and marketing opportunities, meetings, workshops, and seminars for the travel industry. Recurring features include news of research, a calendar of events, reports of meetings, news of educational opportunities, and notices of publications available.

★12469★ Travel Trade

Travel Trade
15 West 44th St.
New York, NY 10036
Ph: (212)730-6600   Fax: (212)730-7060

E-mail: travelcat@aol.com

Weekly. Travel industry magazine.

★12470★ *Travel Weekly*

Northstar Travel Media
100 Lighting Way, 2nd Fl.
Secaucus, NJ 07094
Ph: (201)902-2000   Fax: (201)902-2045
URL: http://www.northstartravelmedia.com

Weekly (Mon.). Free to qualified subscribers. Travel industry magazine.

★12471★ *TravelAge West*

Northstar Travel Media
100 Lighting Way, 2nd Fl.
Secaucus, NJ 07094
Ph: (201)902-2000   Fax: (201)902-2045
URL: http://www.northstartravelmedia.com

Biweekly. Magazine for retail travel agents in western U.S. and western Canada.

PLACEMENT AND JOB REFERRAL SERVICES

★12472★ **Connected International Meeting Professionals Association (CIMPA)**

9200 Bayard Pl.
Fairfax, VA 22032
Ph: (512)684-0889   Fax: (267)390-5193
E-mail: susan2@cimpa.org
URL: http://www.cimpa.org

Members: Meeting planners, incentive organizers, travel agents, tour operators, and seminar organizers in 42 countries. **Purpose:** Works to improve the skills of professional conference and convention planners. Serves as a clearinghouse of information on new travel destinations and planning technologies, techniques, and strategies. **Activities:** Facilitates exchange of information among Internet professionals. Produces a television program on travel and meetings. Conducts educational courses and awards Certified Internet Meeting Professional designation. Conducts research programs and placement service. Sponsors training courses on the Internet.

★12473★ **International Association of Tour Managers - North American Region (IATM North)**

24 Blevins Rd.
Kerhonkson, NY 12446-1302
Ph: (212)208-6800   Fax: (212)208-6800
E-mail: chairman@tourmanager.org
URL: http://www.tourmanager.org

Description: Works to maintain the highest possible standards of tour management; guarantee excellence of performance; educate the travel world on the role of the tour manager (also referred to as tour director, tour escort, or tour leader) in the successful completion of the tour itinerary and in bring-

ing business to related industries. Represents members in influencing legislation and advising on travel policy. Trains tour managers to plan, research, and lead tours to specific domestic and foreign destinations; operates Advisory Board in Professional Tour Management; offers placement service; conducts Professional travel agents, travel wholesalers, airlines, hotel associations, shipping lines, tourist organizations, restaurants, shops, and entertainment organizations Tour Management International Certificate Program.

★12474★ **Society of Incentive and Travel Executives (SITE)**

401 N Michigan Ave.
Chicago, IL 60611
Ph: (312)321-5148   Fax: (312)527-6783
E-mail: brenda_anderson@site-intl.org
URL: http://www.site-intl.org

Description: Represents individuals responsible for the administration or sale of incentive programs including corporate users, incentive marketing companies, cruise lines, hotel chains, resort operators, airlines, and tourist boards. Unites individuals in the incentive industry and facilitates information exchange and problem solving on a personal and professional basis. Supports expansion of incentive programs through public relations, promotion, and speakers' bureau activities. Contributes to the continuing professional education of members through meetings, publications, and research services. Helps upgrade standards through educational services to nonmembers. Compiles statistics; provides placement service.

EMPLOYER DIRECTORIES AND NETWORKING LISTS

★12475★ *American Society of Travel Agents-Membership Directory*

American Society of Travel Agents
1101 King St., Ste. 200
Alexandria, VA 22314
Ph: (703)739-2782   Fax: (703)684-8319
URL: http://www.astanet.com

Annual, June. Covers about 13,500 travel agents representing over 25,600 members in 130 countries. Entries include: Company name, address, phone, fax, telex, name of principal executive and other officials, services. Arrangement: Classified by membership category, then geographical. Indexes: Personal name, company name.

★12476★ *Career Opportunities in the Travel Industry*

Facts On File Inc.
132 W 31st St., 17th Fl.
New York, NY 10001
Ph: (212)967-8800   Fax: 800-678-3633
Fr: 800-322-8755
URL: http://www.factsonfile.com

Published 2004. $49.50 for individuals; $44.55 for libraries. Covers more than 75 professional and hourly jobs available in both the private and public sectors, from travel agent to tour guide and hotel general manager to flight navigator.

★12477★ *Careers in Focus: Travel & Hospitality*

Facts On File Inc.
132 W 31st St., 17th Fl.
New York, NY 10001
Ph: (212)967-8800   Fax: 800-678-3633
Fr: 800-322-8755
URL: http://www.factsonfile.com

Latest edition 3rd, 2006. $29.95 for individuals; $26.95 for libraries. Covers an overview of travel and hospitality, followed by a selection of jobs profiled in detail, including the nature of the job, earnings, prospects for employment, what kind of training and skills it requires, and sources for further information.

★12478★ *National Business Travel Association-Membership Directory*

National Business Travel Association
110 N Royal St., 4th Fl.
Alexandria, VA 22314
Ph: (703)684-0836   Fax: (703)684-0263
URL: http://www.nbta.org/

Annual. Covers over 1,900 corporate travel managers and supplier members in the United States. Entries include: Individual name, corporate name, type of membership, office address, phone, fax, e-mail, URL address. Arrangement: Alphabetical by individual/company name. Indexes: Geographical; member type; advertiser; company category listing.

★12479★ *Specialty Travel Index*

Alpine Hansen, Publishers
PO Box 458
San Anselmo, CA 94979
Ph: (415)455-1643   Fax: (415)455-1648
Fr: 888-624-4030
E-mail: info@specialtytravel.com
URL: http://www.specialtytravel.com

Semiannual, January and August. Covers over 600 special interest tour operators, worldwide; all listings are paid. Entries include: Firm name, address, phone; description of tours offered, including nature of trip, destinations, sample cost and duration of trip. Arrangement: Alphabetical. Indexes: Special interest activity (with location of activity); geographical (and the special interest activities possible).

★12480★ *Survey of State Tourism Offices*

Travel Industry Association of America
1100 New York Ave. NW, Ste. 450
Washington, DC 20005-3934
Ph: (202)408-8422   Fax: (202)408-1255
URL: http://www.tia.org

Annual; latest edition 2007. $300.00 for

members; $495.00 for nonmembers. Covers state and territorial government agencies responsible for travel and travel promotion in their states. Entries include: Agency name, address, phone, number of full- and part-time staff, number of professional staff directly involved in travel; name and title of state travel director, and length of service as director, length of service in agency, and whether employed under the Civil Service program; advertising director and agency and public relations director in separate sections. Extensive additional data is provided by a series of tables covering state activities in advertising, package tours, general promotion press and public relations, research, the establishment of welcome centers, and the department budget. Although addresses are not given, some listings do include name, title, and department of contact. Arrangement: By function (administration, advertising, etc.), then geographical.

HANDBOOKS AND MANUALS

★12481★ Career Opportunities in Travel and Tourism

Facts On File Inc.
132 W. 31st St., 17th Fl.
New York, NY 10001-2006
Ph: (212)967-8800   Fax: 800-678-3633
Fr: 800-322-8755
E-mail: custserv@factsonfile.com
URL: http://www.factsonfile.com

John K. Hawks. 1996. $18.95 (paper). 224 pages. Includes detailed job descriptions, educational requirements, salary ranges, and advancement prospects for 70 different job opportunities in this fast-paced industry. Contains index and bibliography.

★12482★ Careers in Travel, Tourism, and Hospitality

The McGraw-Hill Companies
PO Box 182604
Columbus, OH 43272
Fax: (614)759-3749   Fr: 877-883-5524
E-mail: customer.service@mcgraw-hill.com
URL: http://www.mcgraw-hill.com

Marjorie Eberts, Linda Brothers, and Ann Gisler. Second edition, 2005. $15.95 (paper). 224 pages.

★12483★ A Coach Full of Fun: A Handbook of Creative Solutions and Ideas for Tour Escorts

Shoreline Creations, Ltd.
2465 112th Ave.
Holland, MI 49424
Ph: (616)393-2077   Fax: (616)393-0085
Fr: 800-767-3489

Jeane S. Klender, Amber Christman-Clark, and Amy Gustin. 1995. $19.95 (paper). 214 pages. Provides advice on how to be successful in the group tour industry. Contains information on tour procedures, preparation, and finances.

★12484★ First Class: An Introduction to Travel and Tourism

The McGraw-Hill Companies
PO Box 182604
Columbus, OH 43272
Fax: (614)759-3749   Fr: 877-883-5524
E-mail: customer.service@mcgraw-hill.com
URL: http://www.mcgraw-hill.com

Dennis L. Foster. 1995. $111.15. 385 pages.

★12485★ Home-Based Travel Agent: How to Cash in on the Exciting New World of Travel Marketing

Intrepid Traveler
15200 NBN Way
Blue Ridge Summit, PA 17214

Kelly Monaghan. Third edition, 1999. $29.95 (paper). 400 pages. Includes an extensive resource section, mini sales program and subject index.

★12486★ Hospitality and Tourism Careers: A Blueprint for Success

The McGraw-Hill Companies
PO Box 182604
Columbus, OH 43272
Fax: (614)759-3749   Fr: 877-883-5524
E-mail: customer.service@mcgraw-hill.com
URL: http://www.mcgraw-hill.com

Melissa Dallas and Carl Riegel. Second edition, 1997. $57.00 (paper). 252 pages.

★12487★ How to Get a Job with a Cruise Line

Ticket to Adventure, Inc.
PO Box 41005
St. Petersburg, FL 33743-1005
Ph: (727)822-5029   Fax: (727)821-3409
Fr: 800-929-7447

Mary Fallon Miller. Fifth edition, 2001. $16.95 (paper). 352 pages. Explores jobs with cruise ships, describing duties, responsibilities, benefits, and training. Lists cruise ship lines and schools offering cruise line training. Offers job hunting advice.

★12488★ Opportunities in Travel Careers

The McGraw-Hill Companies
PO Box 182604
Columbus, OH 43272
Fax: (614)759-3749   Fr: 877-883-5524
E-mail: customer.service@mcgraw-hill.com
URL: http://www.mcgraw-hill.com

Robert Scott Milne. Second edition, 2003. $14.95 (paper). 141 pages. Discusses what the jobs are and where to find them in airlines, shipping lines, and railroads. Discusses related opportunities in hotels, motels, resorts, travel agencies, public relation firms, and recreation departments. Illustrated.

★12489★ Travel Career Development

Institute of Certified Travel Agents
148 Linden St.
PO Box 56
Wellesley, MA 02482
Ph: (781)237-0280   Fax: (781)237-3860
E-mail: info@thetravelinstitute.com
URL: http://www.thetravelinstitute.com/

Patricia J. Gagnon and Bruno Ociepka. Revised edition, 1997. $46.95 (paper). 434 pages.

★12490★ Travel the World Free as an International Tour Director: How to Be an International Tour Director

BookSurge Publishing
PO Box 21199
Charleston, SC 29413
Ph: (803)723-7400   Fax: (803)723-0751
Fr: 800-894-8687
URL: http://www.booksurge.com/

Gerald E. Mitchell. 2007. $26.99. 366 pages. Kit includes 250-page manual, 189-page site-inspection journal and resource start up kit with video.

EMPLOYMENT AGENCIES AND SEARCH FIRMS

★12491★ ChaseAmerica Inc.

6231 PGA Blvd., Ste. 104
Palm Beach Gardens, FL 33418
Ph: (561)491-5000   Fax: (561)491-5001
E-mail: davidstefanjr@chaseamericainc.com
URL: http://www.chaseamericainc.com

Executive search firm.

★12492★ The Elliot Group LLC

505 White Plains Rd., Ste. 228
Tarrytown, NY 10591
Ph: (914)631-4904   Fax: (914)631-6481
URL: http://www.theelliotgroup.com

Executive search firm. Six locations throughout the United States.

★12493★ Travel People Personnel

1199 Park Ave., Ste. 3E
New York, NY 10128-1762
Ph: (212)348-6942   Fax: (617)542-0070
E-mail: sue@travelpeople.com
URL: http://www.travelpeople.com

Provides temporary and regular placement to travel related companies. Industries served: travel and hospitality.

TRADESHOWS

★12494★ WTM - World Travel Market

Reed Exhibitions (North American
  Headquarters)
383 Main Ave.
Norwalk, CT 06851
Ph: (203)840-5337   Fax: (203)840-9570
E-mail: export@reedexpo.com
URL: http://www.reedexpo.com

Annual. **Primary Exhibits:** Goods and services related to tourism and travel.

OTHER SOURCES

★12495★ Administration and Management Occupations

Delphi Productions
3159 6th St.
Boulder, CO 80304
Ph: (303)443-2100   Fax: (303)443-4022
Fr: 888-443-2400
E-mail: support@delphivideo.com
URL: http://www.delphivideo.com

$95.00. 50 minutes. Part of the Careers for the 21st Century Video Library.

★12496★ American Society of Travel Agents (ASTA)

1101 King St., Ste. 200
Alexandria, VA 22314
Ph: (703)739-2782   Fax: (703)684-8319
Fr: 800-440-2782

E-mail: askasta@astahq.com
URL: http://www.astanet.com

Members: Travel agents; allied members are representatives of carriers, hotels, resorts, sightseeing and car rental companies, official tourist organizations, and other travel interests. **Purpose:** Aims to: promote and encourage travel among people of all nations and the use of professional travel agents worldwide; serve as an information resource for the travel industry worldwide; promote and represent the views and interests of travel agents to all levels of government and industry; promote professional and ethical conduct in the travel agency industry worldwide; facilitate consumer protection and safety for the traveling public. **Activities:** Maintains biographical archives and travel hall of fame. Conducts research and education programs.

★12497★ Institute of Certified Travel Agents

148 Linden St., Ste. 305
Wellesley, MA 02482
Ph: (781)237-0280   Fax: (781)237-3860
Fr: 800-542-4282
E-mail: info@thetravelinstitute.com
URL: http://www.thetravelinstitute.com

Description: Individuals who have been accredited as Certified Travel Counselors (CTC) or Certified Travel Associates (CTA) must meet the institute's testing and experience requirements. Seeks to increase the level of competence in the travel industry. Provides continuing education, and examination and certification programs; conducts workshops and professional management seminars. Operates Travel Career Development Program to increase professional skills

and Destination Specialist Programs to enhance the geographical knowledge of sales agents. Organizes study groups of instruction with enrolled student bodies in most major cities.

★12498★ Marketing & Sales Occupations

Delphi Productions
3159 6th St.
Boulder, CO 80304
Ph: (303)443-2100   Fax: (303)443-4022
Fr: 888-443-2400
E-mail: support@delphivideo.com
URL: http://www.delphivideo.com

$95.00. 50 minutes. Part of the Careers for the 21st Century Video Library.

★12499★ U.S. Travel Data Center (USTDC)

1100 New York Ave. NW, Ste. 450
Washington, DC 20005-3934
Ph: (202)408-8422   Fax: (202)408-1255
E-mail: feedback@tia.org
URL: http://www.tia.org

Description: Conducts statistical, economic, and market research concerning travel; encourages standardized travel research terminology and techniques. Monitors trends in travel activity and the travel industry. Measures the economic impact of travel on geographic areas and the cost of travel in the U.S. Evaluates the effect of government programs on travel and the travel industry. Forecasts travel activity and expenditures.

Typesetters and Compositors

SOURCES OF HELP-WANTED ADS

★12500★ American Printer

Penton Media Inc.
9800 Metcalf Ave.
Overland Park, KS 66212
Ph: (913)341-1300   Fax: (913)967-1898
E-mail: apeditor@prismb2b.com
URL: http://www.americanprinter.com/

Monthly. Magazine covering the printing and publishing market.

★12501★ American Typecasting Fellowship Newsletter

American Typecasting Fellowship
102 Fourth St.
Terra Alta, WV 26764
Ph: (304)789-2455   Fax: (304)789-2300
Fr: 800-621-6612
E-mail: ppwvinfo@ppwv.com
URL: http://www.ppwv.com/

Description: Periodic. Devoted to conveying information on the preservation of equipment and technology related to metal typecasting. Covers type founding, type design, matrix making, and letterpress printing. Recurring features include letters to the editor and news of members.

★12502★ Graphic Arts Monthly Magazine

Reed Business Information
360 Park Ave. S
New York, NY 10010
Ph: (646)746-6400   Fax: (646)746-7431
URL: http://www.reedbusiness.com

Monthly. Free. Magazine featuring commercial printing and graphic arts, including digital technologies.

★12503★ In-Plant Printer

Innes Publishing Co.
28100 N Ashley Cir.
PO Box 7280
Libertyville, IL 60048
Ph: (847)816-7900   Fax: (847)247-8855
Fr: 800-247-3306
URL: http://innespub.com

Bimonthly. Free. Magazine serving printing, graphics, typesetting facilities, educational, government, and non-profit organizations.

★12504★ Letterspace

Type Directors Club
127 W. 25th St. 8th
New York, NY 10001
Ph: (212)633-8943   Fax: (212)633-8944
URL: http://www.tdc.org

Description: 2/year. Highlights interests of the Type Directors Club, an organization devoted to graphic arts and typography. Recurring features include book reviews, a calendar of events, news of educational opportunities, and news of members.

★12505★ Printing Impressions

North American Publishing Co.
1500 Spring Garden St., Ste. 1200
Philadelphia, PA 19130
Ph: (215)238-5482   Fax: (215)238-5412
Fr: 800-777-8074
URL: http://www.napco.com

Monthly. Free. Trade magazine.

★12506★ Publish&Print

IDG Communications Inc.
5 Speen St., 3rd. Fl
Framingham, MA 01701
Ph: (508)875-5000   Fax: (508)988-7888
URL: http://www.idg.com

Monthly. Magazine covering information on entire printing process from publishing to production, pre-press to postpress in one magazine.

PLACEMENT AND JOB REFERRAL SERVICES

★12507★ Women in Production (WIP)

276 Bowery
New York, NY 10012
Ph: (212)334-2108   Fax: (212)431-5786
E-mail: admin@p3-ny.org
URL: http://www.p3-ny.org

Description: Persons involved in all production phases of print and graphics, web and multimedia, including those working in magazine, book, and Web publishing, agency production, conventional and digital print manufacturing, print-related vending and buying, advertising production, catalogs, direct mail; seeks to improve job performance by sharing information with members and suppliers. Sponsors placement service.

EMPLOYER DIRECTORIES AND NETWORKING LISTS

★12508★ International Literary Market Place

Information Today Inc.
143 Old Marlton Pke.
Medford, NJ 08055-8750
Ph: (609)654-6266   Fax: (609)654-4309
Fr: 800-300-9868
URL: http://www.literarymarketplace.com

Annual; latest edition 2007. $249.00 for individuals. Covers over 10,799 publishers in over 180 countries outside the United States and Canada, and about 1,499 trade and professional organizations related to publishing abroad; includes major printers, binders, typesetters, book manufacturers, book dealers, libraries, literary agencies, translators, book clubs, reference books and journals, periodicals, prizes, and international reference section. Entries include: For publishers–Name, address, phone, fax, telex, names and titles of key personnel, branches, type of publications, subjects, ISBN prefix. Listings for others include similar information but less detail. Arrangement: Classified by business activities, then geographical. Indexes: Company name, subject, type of publication.

★12509★ *Literary Market Place*

Information Today Inc.
143 Old Marlton Pke.
Medford, NJ 08055-8750
Ph: (609)654-6266   Fax: (609)654-4309
Fr: 800-300-9868
URL: http://store.yahoo.com/infotoday/

Annual; latest edition 2007. $299.95 for individuals. Covers over 14,500 firms or organizations offering services related to the publishing industry, including book publishers in the United States and Canada who issued three or more books during the preceding year, plus a small press section of publishers who publish less than three titles per year or those who are self-published. Also included: Book printers and binders; book clubs; book trade and literary associations; selected syndicates, newspapers, periodicals, and radio and television programs that use book reviews or book publishing news; translators and literary agents. Entries include: For publishers–Company name, address, phone, address for orders, principal executives, editorial directors, and managers, date founded, number of titles in previous year, number of backlist titles in print, types of books published, ISBN prefixes, representatives, imprints, and affiliations. For suppliers, etc.–Listings usually show firm name, address, phone, executives, services, etc. Arrangement: Classified by line of business. Indexes: Principal index is 35,000-item combined index of publishers, publications, and personnel; several sections have geographical and/or subject indexes; translators are indexed by source and target language.

★12510★ *Publishers Directory*

Gale, Cengage Learning
27500 Drake Rd.
Farmington Hills, MI 48331-3535
Ph: (248)699-4253   Fax: (248)699-8065
Fr: 800-877-4253
E-mail: businessproducts@gale.com
URL: http://www.galegroup.com

Annual; latest edition 30th, published November 2006. $540.00 for individuals. Covers over 20,000 new and established, commercial and nonprofit, private and alternative, corporate and association, government and institution publishing programs and their distributors; includes producers of books, classroom materials, prints, reports, and databases. Entries include: Firm name, address, phone, fax, company e-mail address, URL, year founded, ISBN prefix, Standard Address Number, whether firm participates in the Cataloging in Publication program of the Library of Congress, names of principal executives, personal e-mail addresses, number of titles in print, description of firm and its main subject interests, discount and returns policies, affiliated and parent companies, mergers and amalgamations, principal markets, imprints and divisions, alternate formats products are offered in; distributors also list firms for which they distribute,

special services, terms to publishers and regional offices. Arrangement: Alphabetical; distributors listed separately. Indexes: Subject; geographical; publisher; imprints; and distributor.

★12511★ *The Workbook*

Scott & Daughters Publishing Inc.
940 N Highland Ave.
Los Angeles, CA 90038
Ph: (213)856-0008   Fax: (323)856-4368
Fr: 800-547-2688
URL: http://www.workbook.com

Annual, February. Covers 49,000 advertising agencies, art directors, photographers, freelance illustrators and designers, artists' representatives, interactive designers, prepress services, and other graphic arts services in the U.S. Entries include: Company or individual name, address, phone, specialty. National in scope. Arrangement: Classified by product or service.

HANDBOOKS AND MANUALS

★12512★ *Degree of Mastery: A Journey Through Book Arts Apprenticeship*

Penguin
375 Hudson St.
New York, NY 10014
Ph: (212)366-2000   Fax: (212)366-2666
Fr: 800-847-5515
URL: http://us.penguingroup.com/

Annie Tremmel Wilcox. 2000. $27.95 (paper). 224 pages.

★12513★ *Opportunities in Printing Careers*

The McGraw-Hill Companies
PO Box 182604
Columbus, OH 43272
Fax: (614)759-3749   Fr: 877-883-5524
E-mail: customer.service@mcgraw-hill.com
URL: http://www.mcgraw-hill.com

Irvin Borowsky. 1998. $14.95; $11.95 (paper). 160 pages. Offers detailed information on the variety of pre-press, press, and post-press jobs available. Covers apprenticeships, unions, salaries, and how to get ahead. Illustrated.

EMPLOYMENT AGENCIES AND SEARCH FIRMS

★12514★ **Gordon Wahls Executive Search Co.**

450 Parkway Blvd., Ste. 104
PO Box 386
Broomall, PA 19008-0386
Fax: (610)359-8803   Fr: 800-523-7112

E-mail: search@gwahls.com

Offers executive search services for the printing, packaging, publishing and graphic arts industry.

★12515★ **Graphic Arts Employment Service, Inc.**

409 N Pacific Coast Hwy., Ste.455
Redondo Beach, CA 90277
Ph: (818)499-9722   Fax: (310)937-3760
Fr: 888-499-9722
E-mail: info@gaes.com
URL: http://www.gaes.com

Employment agency specializing in the publishing and packaging industries.

★12516★ **Graphic Search Associates Inc.**

1217 W. Chester Pike, Ste. 203
West Chester, PA 19382
Ph: (610)429-8077   Fax: (610)429-1355
Fr: 800-342-1777
E-mail: info@graphsrch.com
URL: http://www.graphsrch.com

Executive search firm for the graphic arts industry.

★12517★ **Printemps**

18 Avery Pl.
Westport, CT 06880
Ph: (203)226-6869   Fax: (203)226-1594
E-mail: printemps7@aol.com

Specializes in providing temporary support for graphic design, document management and the electronic printing industry. Provides permanent placement for professionals and production personnel. Consults with printers and in-house printshops for greater production efficiency. Handles personnel management and policy programs as well. Industries served: printing, advertising, manufacturing, insurance, banking, and government agencies.

★12518★ **Stewart and Associates**

1717 Penn Ave.
Wilkinsburg, PA 15221
Ph: (412)244-0552   Fax: (717)299-4879

Executive search firm for the manufacturing industry.

★12519★ **Zachary & Sanders Inc.**

Linden Ln.
East Norwich, NY 11732
Ph: (516)922-5500   Fax: (516)922-2286
Fr: 800-540-7919
E-mail: zacharyserch@earthlink.net

Serves the printing, packaging, publishing, advertising, direct marketing industries.

OTHER SOURCES

★12520★ American Institute of Graphic Arts (AIGA)

164 5th Ave.
New York, NY 10010
Ph: (212)807-1990   Fax: (212)807-1799
E-mail: comments@aiga.org
URL: http://www.aiga.org

Description: Graphic designers, art directors, illustrators and packaging designers. Sponsors exhibits and projects in the public interest. Sponsors traveling exhibitions. Operates gallery. Maintains library of design books and periodicals; offers slide archives.

★12521★ Graphic Arts Technical Foundation (GATF)

200 Deer Run Rd.
Sewickley, PA 15143-2600
Fax: (412)741-2311   Fr: 800-910-GATF
E-mail: info@piagatf.org
URL: http://www.gain.net

Description: Scientific, research, technical, and educational organization serving the international graphic communications industries. Conducts research in all graphic processes and their commercial applications. Conducts seminars, workshops, and forums on graphic arts and environmental subjects. Conducts educational programs, including the publishing of graphic arts textbooks and learning modules, videotapes and CD-ROMs and broadcast video seminars. Conducts training and certification program in sheet-fed offset press operating, Web Offset press operating, Image Assembly, and desktop publishing. Produces test images and quality control devices for the industry. Performs technical services for the graphic arts industry, including problem-solving, material evaluation, and plant audits.

★12522★ National Association for Printing Leadership (NAPL)

75 W Century Rd.
Paramus, NJ 07652-1408
Ph: (201)634-9600   Fax: (201)634-0324
Fr: 800-642-6275

E-mail: info@napl.org
URL: http://www.napl.org

Description: Represents commercial printers and suppliers to the commercial printing industry. Enables those in the industry to operate their businesses for maximum profitability. Offers following management products and services: sales and marketing, customer service, financial, human resources, operations, and economic. **Activities:** Maintains Management Institute, which conducts Executive Certification Program. Compiles extensive economic statistics.

★12523★ Printing Brokerage/Buyers Association (PB/BA)

PO Box 744
Palm Beach, FL 33480
Ph: (561)546-0116   Fax: (561)845-7130
Fr: 877-585-7141
E-mail: contactus@pbba.org
URL: http://www.pbba.org

Description: Printing buyers/brokers/distributors, printers, typographers, binders, envelope and book manufacturers, packagers, color separation houses, pre-press service organizations, and related companies in the graphic arts industry. Promotes understanding, cooperation, and interaction among members while obtaining the highest standard of professionalism in the graphic arts industry. Gathers information on current technology in the graphic communications industry. Sponsors seminars for members to learn how to work with buyers, brokers and printers; also conducts technical and management seminars. Maintains referral service; compiles statistics. Conducts charitable programs.

★12524★ Printing Industries of America (PIA)

200 Deer Run Rd.
Sewickley, PA 15143
Ph: (412)741-6860   Fax: (412)741-2311
Fr: 800-910-4283
E-mail: gain@piagatf.org
URL: http://www.gain.net

Description: Commercial printing firms (lithography, letterpress, gravure, platemakers, typographic houses); allied firms in the

graphic arts. Provides extensive management services for member companies, including government relations, industry research and statistical information, technology information and assistance, and management education and publications. Compiles statistical and economic data, including annual ratio study that provides a benchmark for printers to compare profits as a basis for improving individual member company and industry profits. Provides reporting system on provisions, rates, and other matters relating to union contracts in effect throughout the industry. Sponsors annual Premier Print Awards Competition.

★12525★ Type Directors Club (TDC)

127 W 25th St., 8th Fl.
New York, NY 10001
Ph: (212)633-8943   Fax: (212)633-8944
E-mail: director@tdc.org
URL: http://www.tdc.org

Description: Serves as a professional society of typographic designers, type directors, and teachers of typography; sustaining members are individuals with interests in typographic education. Seeks to stimulate research and disseminate information. Provides speakers, classes and offers presentations on history and new developments in typography.

★12526★ Typophiles

30 E 23rd St., 8th Fl.
New York, NY 10010
E-mail: info@typophiles.org
URL: http://www.typophiles.org

Description: Represents designers, printers, book collectors, artists, calligraphers, private press owners, wood engravers, librarians and others interested in graphic arts. Promotes the love and appreciation of fine graphic design and printing. Conducts quarterly meeting-luncheons and maintains publications.

Typists, Word Processors, and Data Entry Keyers

SOURCES OF HELP-WANTED ADS

★12527★ OfficePRO

Stratton Publishing and Marketing Inc.
5285 Shawnee Rd., Ste. 510
Alexandria, VA 22312-2334
Ph: (703)914-9200   Fax: (703)914-6777

Magazine for administrative assistants, office managers, and secretaries featuring information on trends in business, technology, career development, and management.

PLACEMENT AND JOB REFERRAL SERVICES

★12528★ Network and Systems Professionals Association (NASPA)

7044 S 13th St.
Oak Creek, WI 53154
Ph: (414)908-4945   Fax: (414)768-8001
E-mail: helpdesk@netstream.net
URL: http://www.naspa.com

Description: Technicians and technical management personnel in 90 countries who work in corporate data processing. Works to enhance the level of technical education among members through publications, public domain software, electronic information sharing, job and career assistance, and scholarships and grants. Conducts charitable and educational programs; maintains speakers' bureau and placement service; compiles statistics.

HANDBOOKS AND MANUALS

★12529★ How to Prepare for the Civil Service Examinations for Stenographer, Typist, Clerk, and Office Manager

Barron's Educational Series, Inc.
250 Wireless Blvd.
Hauppauge, NY 11788-3917
Ph: (631)434-3311   Fax: (631)434-3723
Fr: 800-645-3476
E-mail: fbrown@barronseduc.com
URL: http://barronseduc.com

Jerry Bobrow. Fifth edition, 2005. $16.95 (paper). 342 pages.

★12530★ Opportunities in Data and Word Processing Careers

The McGraw-Hill Companies
PO Box 182604
Columbus, OH 43272
Fax: (614)759-3749   Fr: 877-883-5524
E-mail: customer.service@mcgraw-hill.com
URL: http://www.mcgraw-hill.com

Marianne Munday. Revised edition, 2001. $12.95; $11.95 (paper). 160 pages.

★12531★ Opportunities in High Tech Careers

The McGraw-Hill Companies
PO Box 182604
Columbus, OH 43272
Fax: (614)759-3749   Fr: 877-883-5524
E-mail: customer.service@mcgraw-hill.com
URL: http://www.mcgraw-hill.com

Gary Colter and Deborah Yanuck. 1999. $14.95; $11.95 (paper). 160 pages. Explores high technology careers. Describes job opportunities, how to make a career decision, how to prepare for high technology jobs, job hunting techniques, and future trends.

★12532★ Opportunities in Office Occupations

The McGraw-Hill Companies
PO Box 182604
Columbus, OH 43272
Fax: (614)759-3749   Fr: 877-883-5524
E-mail: customer.service@mcgraw-hill.com
URL: http://www.mcgraw-hill.com

Blanche Ettinger. 1995. $14.95; $11.95 (paper). 146 pages. Covers a variety of office positions and discusses trends for the next decade. Describes the job market, opportunities, job duties, educational preparation, the work environment, and earnings.

★12533★ Opportunities in Secretarial Careers

The McGraw-Hill Companies
PO Box 182604
Columbus, OH 43272
Fax: (614)759-3749   Fr: 877-883-5524
E-mail: customer.service@mcgraw-hill.com
URL: http://www.mcgraw-hill.com

Blanche Ettinger. 1999. 160 pages. $14.95; $11.95 (paper). Includes a chapter on finding a secretarial job with sample resumes and interview questions.

★12534★ Opportunities in State and Local Government Careers

The McGraw-Hill Companies
PO Box 182604
Columbus, OH 43272
Fax: (614)759-3749   Fr: 877-883-5524
E-mail: customer.service@mcgraw-hill.com
URL: http://www.mcgraw-hill.com

Neale J. Baxter. Revised edition, 1992. $14.95; $10.95 (paper). 148 pages. Points out the incentives and drawbacks of a government career. Describes hiring procedures and provides tips on filling out applications, taking physical and aptitude tests, handling interviews, and finding jobs. Describes the jobs in which 75% of all state and local government workers are employed. For each occupation, covers the nature of the work and the training required.

EMPLOYMENT AGENCIES AND SEARCH FIRMS

★12535★ Apple One Employment Services
990 Knox St.
Torrance, CA 90504
Ph: (310)516-1572   Fr: 800-564-5644
E-mail: cduque@appleonee.com
URL: http://www.appleone.com

Employment agency. Additional offices in Anaheim, Oakland, Cerritos, San Francisco, Manhattan Beach, and Glendale.

★12536★ The Aspire Group
52 Second Ave, 1st Fl
Waltham, MA 02451-1129
Fax: (718)890-1810   Fr: 800-487-2967
URL: http://www.bmanet.com

Employment agency.

★12537★ Beverly Hills Bar Association Personnel Service
300 S. Beverly Dr., Ste. 201
Beverly Hills, CA 90212-4805
Ph: (310)601-2422   Fax: (310)601-2423
URL: http://www.bhba.org

Employment agency.

★12538★ Davis-Smith, Inc.
27656 Franklin Rd.
Southfield, MI 48034
Ph: (248)354-4100   Fax: (248)354-6702
Fr: 800-541-4672
E-mail: info@davissmith.com
URL: http://www.davissmith.com

Healthcare staffing agency. Executive search firm.

★12539★ The Esquire Staffing Group Ltd.
1 S. Wacker Dr., Ste. 1616
Chicago, IL 60606-4616
Ph: (312)795-4300   Fax: (312)795-4329
E-mail: d.williams@esquirestaffing.com

URL: http://www.esquirestaffing.com

Employment agency. Fills permanent as well as temporary openings.

★12540★ Hallmark Services
1511 Third Ave., Ste. 520
Seattle, WA 98101
Ph: (206)587-5360   Fax: (206)587-5319
E-mail: hallmark@hallmarkservices.com
URL: http://www.hallmarkservices.com/

Employment agency. Fills openings for permanent employment.

★12541★ Pathfinders, Inc.
229 Peachtree St. NE
International Tower, Ste. 1500
Atlanta, GA 30303
Ph: (404)688-5940   Fax: (404)688-9228
E-mail: resumes@pathfindersinc.com
URL: http://www.pathfindersinc.com

Permanent employment agency focusing on the secretarial field.

OTHER SOURCES

★12542★ Association of Information Technology Professionals (AITP)
401 N Michigan Ave., Ste. 2400
Chicago, IL 60611-4267
Ph: (312)245-1070   Fax: (312)673-6659
Fr: 800-224-9371
E-mail: aitp_hq@aitp.org
URL: http://www.aitp.org

Members: Managerial personnel, staff, educators, and individuals interested in the management of information resources. Founder of the Certificate in Data Processing examination program, now administered by an intersociety organization. **Purpose:** Maintains Legislative Communications Network. Professional education programs include EDP-oriented business and management principles self-study courses and a series of videotaped management development seminars. Sponsors student organiza-

tions around the country interested in information technology and encourages members to serve as counselors for the Scout computer merit badge. Conducts research projects, including a business information systems curriculum for two- and four-year colleges.

★12543★ Black Data Processing Associates (BDPA)
6301 Ivy Ln., Ste. 700
Greenbelt, MD 20770
Ph: (301)220-2180   Fax: (301)220-2185
Fr: 800-727-BDPA
E-mail: president@bdpa.org
URL: http://www.bdpa.org

Description: Represents persons employed in the information processing industry, including electronic data processing, electronic word processing, and data communications; others interested in information processing. Seeks to accumulate and share information processing knowledge and business expertise in order to increase the career and business potential of minorities in the information processing field. Conducts professional seminars, workshops, tutoring services, and community introductions to data processing. Makes annual donation to the United Negro College Fund.

★12544★ Blind Information Technology Specialists (BITS)
1121 Morado Dr.
Cincinnati, OH 45238-4436
Ph: (513)921-3186
E-mail: rrrogers@nuvox.net
URL: http://www.acb.org/bits

Description: Represents visually impaired electronic data processing employees; those seeking employment; employers, instructors, manufacturers, and students in the electronic data processing field. Advocates high standards in training visually impaired students. Seeks to increase employment opportunities; encourages the exchange of work technique ideas and the development of new equipment. Works with agencies to increase the availability of braille and recorded materials. Supports a speakers' bureau.

Underwriters

SOURCES OF HELP-WANTED ADS

★12545★ Best's Review
A.M. Best Company, Inc.
Ambest Rd.
Oldwick, NJ 08858
Ph: (908)439-2200
E-mail: editor_br@ambest.com
URL: http://www.ambest.com/sales/news-overview.asp#br

Monthly. Magazine covering issues and trends for the management personnel of life/health insurers, the agents, and brokers who market their products.

★12546★ Business Insurance
Crain Communications Inc.
1155 Gratiot Ave.
Detroit, MI 48207-2997
Ph: (313)446-6000
URL: http://www.businessinsurance.com

Weekly. $97.00/year for individuals; $173.00 for two years; $200.00/year for individuals, daily online only; $130.00/year for Canada and Mexico; $234.00 for Canada and Mexico, two years; $230.00/year for individuals, includes expedited airmail other countries; $436.00 for two years, includes expedited airmail other countries. International newsweekly reporting on corporate risk and employee benefit management news.

★12547★ National Underwriter Property and Casualty/Risk and Benefits Management
National Underwriter Co.
5081 Olympic Blvd.
Erlanger, KY 41018
Ph: (859)692-2100   Fr: 800-543-0874
E-mail: nup&c@nuco.com
URL: http://www.nunews.com/pandc/subscribe/

Weekly. $94.00/year for individuals, 2nd class; $133.00/year for Canada, air mail; $178.00/year for U.S. and Canada, air mail; $211.00/year for other countries, air mail.

Newsweekly for agents, brokers, executives, and managers in risk and benefit insurance.

★12548★ The Standard
Standard Publishing Corp.
155 Federal St., 13th Fl.
Boston, MA 02110
Ph: (617)457-0600   Fax: (617)457-0608
E-mail: stnd@earthlink.net
URL: http://www.spcpub.com

Weekly (Fri.). $85.00/year for individuals, U.S. Trade newspaper covering insurance events, legislation, regulatory hearings, and court sessions for independent insurance agents in New England.

PLACEMENT AND JOB REFERRAL SERVICES

★12549★ National Association of Review Appraisers and Mortgage Underwriters (NARA/MU)
1224 N Nokomis NE
Alexandria, MN 56308-5072
Ph: (320)763-6870   Fax: (320)763-9290
E-mail: nara@iami.org
URL: http://www.iami.org/nara

Description: Real estate professionals and mortgage underwriters who aid in determining value of property. Acts as umbrella group for real estate appraisers. Conducts educational seminars; maintains speakers' bureau; operates placement service.

EMPLOYER DIRECTORIES AND NETWORKING LISTS

★12550★ Best's Insurance Reports
A.M. Best Co.
Ambest Rd.
Oldwick, NJ 08858
Ph: (908)439-2200   Fax: (908)439-2688
URL: http://www.ambest.com

Annual, latest edition 2007. $1,295.00 for individuals. Published in three editions–Life-health insurance, covering about 1,750 companies; property-casualty insurance, covering over 3,200 companies; and international, covering more than 1,200 insurers. Each edition lists state insurance commissioners and related companies and agencies (mutual funds, worker compensation funds, underwriting agencies, etc.). Entries include: For each company–Company name, address, phone; history; states in which licensed; names of officers and directors; financial data; financial analysis and Best's rating. Arrangement: Alphabetical.

★12551★ Business Insurance-Agent/Broker Profiles Issue
Business Insurance
360 N Michigan Ave.
Chicago, IL 60601-3806
Ph: (312)649-5319   Fax: (312)280-3174
Fr: 800-678-2724
URL: http://www.businessinsurance.com

Annual; latest edition 2007. Publication includes: List of top 10 insurance agents/brokers worldwide specializing in commercial insurance. Entries include: Firm name, address, phone, fax, branch office locations, year established, names of subsidiaries, gross revenues, premium volume, number of employees, principal officers, percent of revenue generated by commercial retail brokerage, acquisitions. Arrangement: Alphabetical by company. Indexes: Geographical.

★12552★ Insurance Phone Book and Directory

Douglas Publications L.L.C.
2807 N Parham Rd., Ste. 200
Richmond, VA 23294
Ph: (804)762-9600   Fax: (804)217-8999
Fr: 800-794-6086
URL: http://www.douglaspublications.com/

Annual; latest edition 2006-2007. $195.00 for print product; $249.00 for print product/CD, combined. Covers about 3,500 life, accident and health, worker's compensation, auto, fire and casualty, marine, surety, and other insurance companies; 2,100 executive contacts, from presidents and CEOs to claims and customer service managers. Entries include: Company name, address, phone, fax, toll-free number, type of insurance provided. Arrangement: Alphabetical.

★12553★ Kirshner's Insurance Directories

National Underwriter Co.
5081 Olympic Blvd.
Erlanger, KY 41018
Ph: (859)692-2100   Fr: 800-543-0874
URL: http://www.nationalunderwriter.com/kirschners/

Annual; latest edition 2007. Covers insurance agents and agencies in all 50 states and the District of Columbia. Published in separate editions for Southern California, Northern California, Pacific Northwest (AK, ID, HI, OR, WA, MT), Michigan, Illinois, New England states (CT, ME, MA, NH, RI, VT), Ohio, Rocky Mountain states (AZ, CO, NV, NM, UT, WY), South Central states (GA, AL, MS), Indiana, Texas, Kentucky/Tennessee, East Central states (VA, WV, NC, SC), South Central West states (AR, OK, LA), Wisconsin, Central states (KS, MO, NE), North Central states (IA, MN, ND, SD), Mid-Atlantic states (DE, MD, NJ, DC), Pennsylvania, Florida. Entries include: For companies–Name, address, key personnel (with addresses and phone numbers). Arrangement: Separate alphabetical sections for insurance companies, wholesalers, field agents, and agencies. Indexes: Type of insurance.

★12554★ Who's Who in Insurance

Underwriter Printing and Publishing Co.
50 E Palisade Ave.
Englewood, NJ 07631
Ph: (201)569-8808   Fr: 800-526-4700

Annual, February. Covers over 5,000 insurance officials, brokers, agents, and buyers. Entries include: Name, title, company name, address, home address, educational background, professional club and association memberships, personal and career data. Arrangement: Alphabetical.

HANDBOOKS AND MANUALS

★12555★ Careers for Number Crunchers and Other Quantitative Types

The McGraw-Hill Companies
PO Box 182604
Columbus, OH 43272
Fax: (614)759-3749   Fr: 877-883-5524
E-mail: customer.service@mcgraw-hill.com
URL: http://www.mcgraw-hill.com

Rebecca Burnett. Second edition, 2002. $22.95 (paper). 192 pages. Provides information to math-oriented job hunters on how to become statisticians, field researchers, computer programmers, stock analysts, investment managers, bankers, engineers, accountants, underwriters, economists, market analysts, mathematicians, systems analysts, and more.

★12556★ Opportunities in Insurance Careers

The McGraw-Hill Companies
PO Box 182604
Columbus, OH 43272
Fax: (614)759-3749   Fr: 877-883-5524
E-mail: customer.service@mcgraw-hill.com
URL: http://www.mcgraw-hill.com

Robert M. Schrayer. Revised, 2007. $14.95 (paper). 160 pages. A guide to planning for and seeking opportunities in the field. Contains bibliography and illustrations.

EMPLOYMENT AGENCIES AND SEARCH FIRMS

★12557★ Employment Advisors

815 Nicollet Mall
Minneapolis, MN 55402
Ph: (612)339-0521

Employment agency. Places candidates in variety of fields.

★12558★ Godfrey Personnel Inc.

300 W. Adams, Ste. 612
Chicago, IL 60606-5194
Ph: (312)236-4455   Fax: (312)580-6292
E-mail: jim@godfreypersonnel.com
URL: http://www.godfreypersonnel.com

Search firm specializing in insurance industry.

★12559★ International Insurance Personnel, Inc.

300 W. Wieuca Rd., Bldg. 2, Ste. 101
Atlanta, GA 30342
Ph: (404)255-9710   Fax: (404)255-9864
E-mail: info@intlinspersonnel.com
URL: http://yp.bellsouth.com/sites/intlin-spersonnel/index.html

Employment agency specializing in the area of insurance.

★12560★ Questor Consultants, Inc.

2515 N. Broad St.
Colmar, PA 18915
Ph: (215)997-9262   Fax: (215)997-9226
E-mail: sbevivino@questorconsultants.com
URL: http://www.questorconsultants.com

Executive search firm specializing in the insurance and legal fields.

ONLINE JOB SOURCES AND SERVICES

★12561★ UnderwritingJobs.com

Ph: (972)679-4542
E-mail: admin@underwritingjobs.com
URL: http://www.underwritingjobs.com

Description: Job search website for underwriters. Seekers may search databank by field of interest or geography, post their resume or visit career-related links.

TRADESHOWS

★12562★ CPCU Conferment Ceremony

American Institute for CPCU
720 Providence Rd.
PO Box 3016
Malvern, PA 19355-0716
Ph: (610)644-2100   Fax: (610)640-9576
Fr: 800-644-2101
E-mail: cserv@cpcuiia.org
URL: http://www.aicpcu.org

Annual. **Primary Exhibits:** Exhibits for insurance personnel and Chartered Property Casualty Underwriters (CPCUs). **Dates and Locations:** 2008 Sep 06-09; Philadelphia, PA ; 2009 Aug 29 - Sep 01; Denver, CO.

★12563★ Financial Services Forum

Society of Financial Service Professionals
270 S. Bryn Mawr Ave.
Bryn Mawr, PA 19010-2195
Ph: (610)526-2500   Fax: (610)527-1499
URL: http://www.financialpro.org

Annual. **Primary Exhibits:** Exhibitors who offer products and services for the leaders in the insurance and financial services industry.

★12564★ National Association of Insurance and Financial Advisors Annual Convention and Career Conference

National Association of Insurance and
Financial Advisors
2901 Telestar Ct.
Falls Church, VA 22042-1205
Ph: (703)770-8100   Fax: (703) 770-8229
Fr: 877-866-2432
E-mail: jedwards@naifa.org
URL: http://www.naifa.org

Annual. **Primary Exhibits:** Exhibits relating to life and health insurance, mutual funds, and financial services.

★12565★ National Association of Review Appraisers and Mortgage Underwriters Convention - National Conference & Expo

National Association of Review Appraisers
and Mortgage Underwriters
1224 N Nokomis NE
Alexandria, MN 56308-5072
Ph: (320)763-6870   Fax: (320)763-9290
URL: http://iami.org/nara

Annual. **Primary Exhibits:** Real estate-related information and services.

★12566★ Physician Insurers Association of America Annual Meeting

Physician Insurers Association of America
2275 Research Blvd., Ste. 250
Rockville, MD 20850
Ph: (301)947-9000   Fax: (301)947-9090
E-mail: wchao@thepiaa.org
URL: http://www.thepiaa.org

Annual. **Primary Exhibits:** Exhibits related to physician liability insurance.

★12567★ Public Agency Risk Managers Association Convention

Public Agency Risk Managers Association
PO Box 6810
San Jose, CA 95150
Ph: 888-907-2762   Fax: 888-412-5913
Fr: 888-90-PARMA
E-mail: brenda.reisinger@parma.com
URL: http://www.parma.com

Annual. **Primary Exhibits:** Risk management equipment, supplies, and services.

OTHER SOURCES

★12568★ *American Almanac of Jobs and Salaries*

HarperCollins
10 E. 53rd St.
New York, NY 10022
Ph: (212)207-7000   Fr: 800-242-7737
URL: http://www.harpercollins.com/

John W. Wright. Revised edition, 2000. $20.00 (paper). 672 pages. This is a com-prehensive guide to the wages of hundreds of occupations in a wide variety of industries and organizations.

★12569★ American Council of Life Insurers (ACLI)

101 Constitution Ave. NW
Washington, DC 20001-2133
Ph: (202)624-2000   Fax: (202)624-2319
Fr: 877-674-4659
E-mail: media@acli.com
URL: http://www.acli.com

Description: Represents the interests of legal reserve life insurance companies in legislative, regulatory and judicial matters at the federal, state and municipal levels of government and at the NAIC. Member companies hold majority of the life insurance in force in the United States.

★12570★ American Institute for CPCU (AICPCU)

720 Providence Rd., Ste. 100
PO Box 3016
Malvern, PA 19355-0716
Ph: (610)644-2100   Fax: (610)640-9576
Fr: 800-644-2101
E-mail: customersupport@cpcuiia.org
URL: http://www.aicpcu.org

Purpose: Determines qualifications for professional certification of insurance personnel; conducts examinations and awards designation of Chartered Property Casualty Underwriter (CPCU).

★12571★ CPCU Society

720 Providence Rd.
Malvern, PA 19355-3402
Ph: (610)251-2727   Fax: (610)251-2780
Fr: 800-932-2728
E-mail: membercenter@cpcusociety.org
URL: http://www.cpcusociety.org

Description: Serves as a professional society of individuals who have passed national examinations of the American Institute for Chartered Property Casualty Underwriters, have 3 years of work experience, have agreed to be bound by a code of ethics, and have been awarded CPCU designation. Promotes education, research, social responsibility, and professionalism in the field. Holds seminars, symposia, and workshops.

★12572★ Insurance Information Institute (III)

110 William St.
New York, NY 10038
Ph: (212)346-5500   Fr: 800-331-9146
E-mail: johns@iii.org
URL: http://www.iii.org

Description: Property and casualty insurance companies. Provides information and educational services to mass media, educational institutions, trade associations, businesses, government agencies, and the public.

★12573★ LOMA

2300 Windy Ridge Pkwy., Ste. 600
Atlanta, GA 30339-8443
Ph: (770)951-1770   Fax: (770)984-0441
Fr: 800-275-5662
E-mail: askloma@loma.org
URL: http://www.loma.org

Description: Life and health insurance companies and financial services in the U.S. and Canada; and overseas in 45 countries; affiliate members are firms that provide professional support to member companies. Provides research, information, training, and educational activities in areas of operations and systems, human resources, financial planning and employee development. Administers FLMI Insurance Education Program, which awards FLMI (Fellow, Life Management Institute) designation to those who complete the ten-examination program.

★12574★ National Association of Health Underwriters (NAHU)

2000 N 14th St., Ste. 450
Arlington, VA 22201
Ph: (703)276-0220   Fax: (703)841-7797
E-mail: info@nahu.org
URL: http://www.nahu.org

Description: Insurance agents and brokers engaged in the promotion, sale, and administration of disability income and health insurance. Sponsors advanced health insurance underwriting and research seminars. Testifies before federal and state committees on pending health insurance legislation. Sponsors Leading Producers Roundtable Awards for leading salesmen. Maintains a speakers' bureau and a political action committee.

★12575★ National Association of Insurance Women International (NAIW)

6528 E 101st St., Ste. D-1
PMB No. 750
Tulsa, OK 74133
Fax: (918)743-1968   Fr: 800-766-6249
E-mail: joinnaiw@naiw.org
URL: http://www.naiw.org

Members: Insurance industry professionals. **Purpose:** Promotes continuing education and networking for the professional advancement of its members. **Activities:** Offers education programs, meetings, services, and leadership opportunities. Provides a forum to learn about other disciplines in the insurance industry.

★12576★ Society of Financial Service Professionals (SFSP)

17 Campus Blvd., Ste. 201
Newtown Square, PA 19073-3230
Ph: (215)321-9662   Fax: (610)527-1499
Fr: 800-927-2427
E-mail: mpepe@financialpro.org
URL: http://www.financialpro.org

Description: Represents the interests of financial advisers. Fosters the development of professional responsibility. Assists clients to achieve personal and business-related financial goals. Offers educational programs, online professional resources and networking opportunities.

Urban and Regional Planners

year for out of country, 13 issues. Magazine covering housing and construction industry.

SOURCES OF HELP-WANTED ADS

★12577★ American City and County

Primedia Business
6151 Powers Ferry Rd., Ste. 200
Atlanta, GA 30339
Ph: (770)955-2500   Fax: (770)618-0204
URL: http://
www.americancityandcounty.com

Monthly. $67.00/year for individuals. Municipal and county administration magazine.

★12578★ Architectural Record

McGraw-Hill Inc.
1221 Ave. of the Americas
New York, NY 10020-1095
Ph: (212)512-2000   Fax: (212)512-3840
Fr: 877-833-5524
URL: http://archrecord.construction.com

Monthly. $49.00/year for individuals. Magazine focusing on architecture.

★12579★ Better Roads

James Informational Media Inc.
2720 S River Rd.
Des Plaines, IL 60018-5142
Ph: (847)391-9070   Fax: (847)391-9058
URL: http://www.betterroads.com

Monthly. Free to qualified subscribers; $95.00/year for other countries. Magazine serving federal, state, county, city, and township officials involved in road, street, bridge, and airport construction, maintenance and safety.

★12580★ Builder

Hanley-Wood L.L.C.
1 Thomas Cir., NW, Ste. 600
Washington, DC 20005
Ph: (202)452-0800   Fax: (202)785-1974
URL: http://www.hanleywood.com/default.aspx?page=b2bbd

$29.95/year for individuals, 13 issues; $54.95/year for Canada, 26 issues; $192.00/

★12581★ IDA

International Downtown Association
1250 H St., NW 10th Fl.
Washington, DC 20005
Ph: (202)393-6801   Fax: (202)393-6869
E-mail: question@ida-downtown.org
URL: http://www.ida-downtown.org

Description: Quarterly. Covers issues of downtown revitalization, management districts, planning, development, promotion, marketing, financing, and related legislation. Recurring features include news of organization and "member cities'" activities.

★12582★ ITE Journal

Institute of Transportation Engineers
1099 14th St. NW, Ste. 300 W
Washington, DC 20005-3438
Ph: (202)289-0222   Fax: (202)289-7722
URL: http://www.ite.org/itejournal/

Monthly. $65.00/year for individuals, U.S., Canada and Mexico; $85.00/year for out of country; $160.00 for three years for individuals, U.S., Canada and Mexico; $200.00 for three years for individuals, out of country. Technical magazine focusing on the plan, design, and operation of surface transportation systems.

★12583★ JobMart

American Planning Association
122 S. Michigan Ave., Ste. 1600
Chicago, IL 60603-6107
Ph: (312)431-9100   Fax: (312)431-9985
Fr: 800-273-2365
E-mail: CustomerService@planning.org
URL: http://www.planning.org

Description: Semimonthly. Reports on jobs in the planning field, covering urban and regional opportunities and related jobs in community development and transportation. Recurring features include educational opportunities and internships.

★12584★ Land Use Law Report

Business Publishers Inc.
PO Box 17592
Baltimore, MD 21297
Ph: (301)562-2450   Fax: (301)587-1081
Fr: 800-274-6737
E-mail: custserv@bpinews.com
URL: http://www.bpinews.com/

Description: Provides up-to-date information on court decisions, legislation, and regulations that impact today's most pressing land-use policy, planning, and legal issues. Readers receive in-depth coverage on zoning and planning policies, regulatory takings, undesirable land uses, environmental legislation, and much more. Also available via e-mail.

★12585★ MAPC News

Metropolitan Area Planning Council
60 Temple Pl.
Boston, MA 02111
Ph: (617)451-2270   Fax: (617)482-7185
E-mail: contactinfo@mapc.org
URL: http://www.mapc.org/whats_new/newsletter.html

Description: Monthly. Reports on regional planning news on issues concerning economic developers. Topics include housing, transportation, environment, and open space protection. Recurring features include a calendar of events, reports of meetings, and news of educational opportunities.

★12586★ Municipal Art Society Newsletter

Municipal Art Society
457 Madison Ave.
New York, NY 10022
Ph: (212)935-3960   Fax: (212)753-1816
E-mail: info@mas.org
URL: http://www.mas.org/GetInvolved/Urbanists.cfm#membership

Description: Six issues/year. Provides updates on advocacy efforts, exhibitions, and programming on urban issues. Recurring features include a calendar of events and tour schedule.

★12587★ The Municipality

League of Wisconsin Municipalities
122 W Washington Ave., Ste. 300
Madison, WI 53703-2718
Ph: (608)267-2380   Fax: (608)267-0645
Fr: 800-991-5502
URL: http://www.lwm-info.org/index.asp?Type=B_BASIC&SEC=¢0702EE8F

Monthly. Magazine for officials of Wisconsin's local municipal governments.

★12588★ NAHRO Monitor

National Association of Housing and
  Redevelopment Officials
630 Eye St. NW
Washington, DC 20001
Ph: (202)289-3500   Fax: (202)289-8181
Fr: 877-866-2476
E-mail: nahro@nahro.org
URL: http://www.nahro.org/publications/monitor.cfm

Description: Semimonthly. Disseminates news on low-income housing and community development issues. Intended for member professionals and government officials.

★12589★ New Urban News

New Urban Publications Inc.
PO Box 6515
Ithaca, NY 14851
Ph: (607)275-3087   Fax: (607)272-2685
URL: http://www.newurbannews.com/

Description: Eight issues/year. Devoted to new urbanism and news and analysis of new and additional development in urban planning. Recurring features include letters to the editor, interviews, news of research, calendar of events, book reviews, job listings, notices of publications available, and columns from guest contributors.

★12590★ PAS Memo

American Planning Association
122 S Michigan Ave., Ste. 1600
Chicago, IL 60603-6107
Ph: (312)431-9100   Fax: (312)431-9985
Fr: 800-273-2365
E-mail: CustomerService@planning.org
URL: http://www.planning.org/pasmemo/index.htm

Description: Monthly. Focuses on subjects related to urban planning, zoning, and renewal. Provides advice and commentary on topics such as economic development, land use planning, growth management, and suburbanization.

★12591★ PE & RS Photogrammetric Engineering & Remote Sensing

The Imaging and Geospatial Information
  Society
5410 Grosvenor Ln., Ste. 210
Bethesda, MD 20814-2160
Ph: (301)493-0290   Fax: (301)493-0208
E-mail: asprs@asprs.org
URL: http://www.asprs.org/

Monthly. $250.00/year for individuals, U.S.D 15 discount per subscp. off the base rate;

$120.00/year for individuals, active; $80.00/year for individuals, associate; $45.00/year for students, domestic. Journal covering photogrammetry, remote sensing, geographic information systems, cartography, and surveying, global positioning systems, digital photogrammetry.

★12592★ Planning & Zoning News

Planning & Zoning Center Inc.
715 N. Cedar St. 2
Lansing, MI 48906-5275
Ph: (517)886-0555   Fax: (517)886-0564
E-mail: pznsub@pzcenter.com
URL: http://www.pzcenter.com/pznews.cfm

Description: Monthly. Addresses state-specific current planning and zoning issues in Michigan. Recurring features include a calendar of events, job listings, and court case summaries.

★12593★ Progressive Planning

Planners Network
106 West Sibley Hall
Cornell University
Ithaca, NY 14853
Ph: (607)254-8890   Fax: (607)255-1971
E-mail: info@plannersnetwork.org
URL: http://www.plannersnetwork.org

Description: Quarterly. Covers news of the Planners Network. Recurring features include letters to the editor, a calendar of events, job listings, and notices of publications available.

★12594★ Roads & Bridges Magazine

Scranton Gillette Communications Inc.
3030 W Salt Creek Ln., Ste. 201
Arlington Heights, IL 60005-5025
Ph: (847)391-1000   Fax: (847)390-0408
URL: http://www.roadsbridges.com

Monthly. Free to qualified subscribers. Magazine containing information on highway, road, and bridge design, construction, and maintenance for government agencies, contractors, and consulting engineers.

★12595★ RPA Blueprint

Regional Plan Association
4 Irving Pl. 7th Fl.
New York, NY 10003
Ph: (212)253-2727   Fax: (212)253-5666
URL: http://www.rpa.org

Description: Quarterly. Focuses on regional planning, forums, and economic development.

★12596★ The Times

Council on Tall Buildings & Urban Habitat
Illinois Institute of Technology
S.R. Crown Hall
3360 S State St.
Chicago, IL 60616-3796
Ph: (312)567-3307   Fax: (610)694-0238
E-mail: awood@ctbuh.org
URL: http://www.ctbuh.org

Description: 3-4 issues/year. Concerned

with all aspects of the planning, design, construction, and operation of tall buildings. Examines the role of tall buildings in the urban environment and acts as a forum for exchange of information among engineering, architectural, and planning professionals. Recurring features include news of research, book reviews, notices of publications available, reports on the committees of the Council, a calendar of events, and a column titled On My Mind.

★12597★ The Urban Open Space Manager

Urban Wildlife Resources
5130 W. Running Brook Rd.
Columbia, MD 21044
Ph: (410)997-7161   Fax: (410)997-6849
URL: http://users.erols.com/urbanwildlife

Description: Quarterly. Contains substantive articles involving research, planning, design, education, and management relative to urban open spaces.

★12598★ Western City

League of California Cities
1400 K St., Ste. 400
Sacramento, CA 95814
Ph: (916)658-8200   Fax: (916)658-8240
Fr: 800-262-1801
URL: http://www.westerncity.com

Monthly. $39.00/year for individuals; $63.00 for two years; $52.00/year for other countries; $26.50/year for students. Municipal interest magazine.

★12599★ Zoning and Planning Law Report

Thomson West
610 Opperman Dr.
PO Box 64833
Eagan, MN 55123
Ph: (651)687-7000   Fr: 800-328-9352
URL: http://west.thomson.com/

Description: Monthly. Features articles on land use law, zoning by initiative and referendum, impact fees, affordable housing laws, wetlands regulations, First Amendment land use cases, due process and taking clause claims, and choice of forum in land use litigation. Recurring features include descriptions of recent cases and notices of upcoming conferences.

EMPLOYER DIRECTORIES AND NETWORKING LISTS

★12600★ ENR-Top 500 Design Firms Issue

McGraw-Hill Inc.
1221 Ave. of the Americas
New York, NY 10020-1095
Ph: (212)512-2000   Fax: (212)512-3840
Fr: 877-833-5524
URL: http://enr.construction.com/people/

sourcebooks/top500Design/
Annual, latest edition 2007. $50.00 for individuals. Publication includes: List of 500 leading architectural, engineering, and specialty design firms selected on basis of annual billings. Entries include: Company name, headquarters location, type of firm, current and prior year rank in billings, types of services, countries in which operated in preceding year. Arrangement: Ranked by billings.

HANDBOOKS AND MANUALS

★12601★ Opportunities in Environmental Careers

The McGraw-Hill Companies
PO Box 182604
Columbus, OH 43272
Fax: (614)759-3749   Fr: 877-883-5524
E-mail: customer.service@mcgraw-hill.com
URL: http://www.mcgraw-hill.com

Odom Fanning. Revised, 2002. $12.95 (paper). 174 pages. Describes a broad range of opportunities in fields such as environmental health, recreation, physics, and hygiene, and provides job search advice. Part of the "Opportunities in ..." Series.

★12602★ Opportunities in Social Science Careers

The McGraw-Hill Companies
PO Box 182604
Columbus, OH 43272
Fax: (614)759-3749   Fr: 877-883-5524
E-mail: customer.service@mcgraw-hill.com
URL: http://www.mcgraw-hill.com

Rosanne J. Marek. 2004. $13.95. 160 Pages. VGM Opportunities Series.

★12603★ Planners on Planning: Leading Planners Offer Real-Life Lessons on What Works, What Doesn't and Why

Jossey-Bass
989 Market St.
San Francisco, CA 94103
Ph: (415)433-1740   Fax: (415)433-0499
Fr: 800-255-5945
E-mail: custserv@wiley.com
URL: http://www.josseybass.com/WileyC-DA/

Bruce W. McClendon and Anthony J.Catanese. 1996. $43.00. 320 pages. Provides career advice from professionals in the planning industry.

★12604★ Resumes for Architecture and Related Careers

The McGraw-Hill Companies
PO Box 182604
Columbus, OH 43272
Fax: (614)759-3749   Fr: 877-883-5524
E-mail: customer.service@mcgraw-hill.com
URL: http://www.mcgraw-hill.com

VGM Career Horizons Editors. First edition. 2004. $10.95 (paper). 160 pages.

OTHER SOURCES

★12605★ American Institute of Certified Planners (AICP)

1776 Massachusetts Ave. NW
Washington, DC 20036-1904
Ph: (202)872-0611   Fax: (202)872-0643
Fr: 800-954-1669
E-mail: aicp@planning.org
URL: http://www.planning.org/aicp

Description: Serves as the professional institute of the American Planning Association education, practice, and examination established for the professional practice of public planning. **Activities:** Provides continuing education and a written professional examination. Maintains code of ethics; conducts research.

★12606★ American Planning Association (APA)

122 S Michigan Ave., Ste. 1600
Chicago, IL 60603-6107
Ph: (312)431-9100   Fax: (312)431-9985
E-mail: customerservice@planning.org
URL: http://www.planning.org

Description: Public and private planning agency officials, professional planners, planning educators, elected and appointed officials, and other persons involved in urban and rural development. Works to foster the best techniques and decisions for the planned development of communities and regions. Provides extensive professional services and publications to professionals and laypeople in planning and related fields; serves as a clearinghouse for information. Through Planning Advisory Service, a research and inquiry-answering service, provides, on an annual subscription basis, advice on specific inquiries and a series of research reports on planning, zoning, and environmental regulations. Supplies information on job openings and makes definitive studies on salaries and recruitment of professional planners. Conducts research; collaborates in joint projects with local, national, and international organizations.

★12607★ ASPRS - The Imaging and Geospatial Information Society

5410 Grosvenor Ln., Ste. 210
Bethesda, MD 20814-2160
Ph: (301)493-0290   Fax: (301)493-0208
E-mail: asprs@asprs.org
URL: http://www.asprs.org

Members: Firms, individuals, government employees and academicians engaged in photogrammetry, photointerpretation, remote sensing, and geographic information systems and their application to such fields as archaeology, geographic information systems, military reconnaissance, urban planning, engineering, traffic surveys, meteorological observations, medicine, geology, forestry, agriculture, construction and topographic mapping. Mission is to advance knowledge and improve understanding of these sciences and to promote responsible applications. **Activities:** Offers voluntary certification program open to persons associated with one or more functional area of photogrammetry, remote sensing and GIS. Surveys the profession of private firms in photogrammetry and remote sensing in the areas of products and services.

★12608★ Environmental Occupations: Professional

Delphi Productions
3159 6th St.
Boulder, CO 80304
Ph: (303)443-2100   Fax: (303)443-4022
Fr: 888-443-2400
E-mail: support@delphivideo.com
URL: http://www.delphivideo.com

$95.00. 49 minutes. Part of the Emerging Careers Video Library.

★12609★ National Urban Fellows (NUF)

102 W 38th St., Ste. 700
New York, NY 10018
Ph: (212)730-1700   Fax: (212)730-1823
E-mail: luisalvarez@nuf.org
URL: http://www.nuf.org

Description: Aims to meet the need for competent urban and rural administrators, particularly minority group members and women, by combining a nine-month, on-the-job assignment as special assistant to an experienced practitioner with several kinds of academic work.

★12610★ Professional Specialty Occupations

Delphi Productions
3159 6th St.
Boulder, CO 80304
Ph: (303)443-2100   Fax: (303)443-4022
Fr: 888-443-2400
E-mail: support@delphivideo.com
URL: http://www.delphivideo.com

$95.00. 53 minutes. Part of the Careers for the 21st Century Video Library.

Veterinarians

★12611★ **American Journal of Animal and Veterinary Sciences**

Science Publications
Vails Gate Heights Dr.
PO Box 879
Vails Gate, NY 12584
URL: http://scipub.org/scipub/index.php

Quarterly. $1,100.00/year for individuals; $300.00 for single issue. Scholarly journal covering animal husbandry and veterinary medicine.

★12612★ **American Journal of Veterinary Research**

American Veterinary Medical Association
1931 N Meacham Rd., Ste. 100
Schaumburg, IL 60173
Ph: (847)925-8070   Fax: (847)925-1329
Fr: 800-248-2862
URL: http://www.avma.org/journals/ajvr/ajvr_about.asp

Monthly. $205.00/year for individuals; $215.00/year for other countries; $25.00 for single issue; $30.00 for single issue, other countries. Veterinary research on nutrition and diseases of domestic, wild, and furbearing animals.

★12613★ **Animal Keepers' Forum**

American Association of Zoo Keepers Inc.
3601 SW 29th St., Ste. 133
Topeka, KS 66614-2054
E-mail: akfeditor@zk.kscoxmail.com
URL: http://aazk.org

Monthly. $10.00/year for members; $20.00/year for Canada, members. Professional journal of the American Association of Zoo Keepers, Inc.

★12614★ **The Chronicle of the Horse**

The Chronicle of the Horse Inc.
PO Box 46
108 De Plains
Middleburg, VA 20118
Ph: (540)687-6341   Fax: (540)687-3937
E-mail: staff@chronofhorse.com
URL: http://www.chronofhorse.com

Weekly. $59.00/year; $79.00/year, Canada and all other countries; $108.00 for two years; $148.00 for two years, Canada and all other countries. $2.95 for single issue. Magazine covering English riding and horse sports.

★12615★ **Clinical Techniques in Small Animal Practice**

Mosby Inc.
11830 Westline Industrial Dr.
St. Louis, MO 63146
Ph: (314)872-8370   Fax: (314)432-1380
Fr: 800-325-4177
URL: http://www.elsevier.com/wps/find/journaldescription.cws_home

Quarterly. $308.00/year for institutions; $192.00/year for individuals; $97.00/year for students; $266.00/year for U.S. institutions; $160.00/year for U.S. individuals; $82.00/year for U.S. students. Journal providing practitioners with a convenient, comprehensive resource to enhance their office practice of veterinary medicine.

★12616★ **CME Supplement to Veterinary Clinics of North America**

Elsevier Science Inc.
360 Park Ave. S
New York, NY 10010
Ph: (212)989-5800   Fax: (212)633-3990
URL: http://www.elsevier.com

$55.00/year for individuals. Journal covering veterinary medicine, surgical treatment of animals.

★12617★ **Dog World**

Fancy Publications - A Division of Bowtie, Inc.
PO Box 6050
Mission Viejo, CA 92690
Ph: (949)855-8822   Fax: (949)855-3045
E-mail: letters@dogworld.com
URL: http://www.dogworldmag.com/DogWorldMag

Monthly. $56.00/year for individuals, foreign surface delivery; $56.00/year for other countries, foreign air delivery. Magazine serving breeders, exhibitors, hobbyists and professionals in kennel operations, groomers, veterinarians, animal hospitals/clinics and pet suppliers.

★12618★ **DVM Newsmagazine**

Advanstar Communications
641 Lexington Ave.
8th Fl.
New York, NY 10022
Ph: (212)951-6600   Fax: (212)951-6793
Fr: 800-225-4569
E-mail: dvmnewsmagazine@advanstar.com
URL: http://www.advanstar.com

Monthly. Magazine for veterinarians in private practices in the U.S.

★12619★ **Equus**

Primedia Equine Network
656 Quince Orchard Rd., Ste. 600
Gaithersburg, MD 20878
Ph: (301)977-3900   Fax: (301)990-9015
E-mail: eqletters@primedia.com
URL: http://www.equisearch.com/equus

Monthly. $30.00 for two years; $20.00/year for individuals. Magazine featuring health, care, and understanding of horses.

★12620★ **The Internet Journal of Veterinary Medicine**

Internet Scientific Publications L.L.C.
23 Rippling Creek Dr.
Sugar Land, TX 77479
Ph: (832)443-1193   Fax: (281)240-1532
URL: http://www.ispub.com/ostia/index.php?xmlFilePath=journals/ij

Free, online. Electronic journal focusing on veterinary medicine.

★12621★ Journal of the American Veterinary Medical Association

American Veterinary Medical Association
1931 N Meacham Rd., Ste. 100
Schaumburg, IL 60173
Ph: (847)925-8070   Fax: (847)925-1329
Fr: 800-248-2862
URL: http://www.avma.org

Semimonthly. $165.00/year for nonmembers; $185.00/year for other countries; $15.00 for single issue; $20.00 for single issue, foreign. Trade journal for veterinary medical professionals.

★12622★ Journal of Animal Science

American Society of Animal Science
1111 N Dunlap Ave.
Savoy, IL 61874
Ph: (217)356-9050   Fax: (217)398-4119
URL: http://jas.fass.org/

Monthly. Professional journal covering animal science.

★12623★ Journal of Avian Medicine and Surgery

Allen Press Inc.
810 E 10th St.
Lawrence, KS 66044
Ph: (785)843-1234   Fax: (785)843-1244
Fr: 800-627-0326
URL: http://www.aav.org/publications.html

Quarterly. Medical journal for veterinarians treating birds, students and technicians with an interest in the field.

★12624★ Journal of Equine Veterinary Science

Mosby Inc.
11830 Westline Industrial Dr.
St. Louis, MO 63146
Ph: (314)872-8370   Fax: (314)432-1380
Fr: 800-325-4177
URL: http://www.elsevier.com/wps/find/journaldescription.cws_home

Monthly. $367.00/year for institutions; $250.00/year for individuals; $127.00/year for students; $297.00/year for U.S. institutions; $215.00/year for U.S. individuals; $67.00/year for U.S. students. Journal publishing articles for equine veterinarians and other equine health care specialists.

★12625★ Journal of Herpetological Medicine and Surgery

Association of Reptilian and Amphibian Veterinarians
c/o Wilbur B. Amand
PO Box 605
Chester Heights, PA 19017
Ph: (610)358-9530   Fax: (610)892-4813
URL: http://www.arav.org

Quarterly. $115.00/year for individuals, North America; $75.00/year for students; $130.00/year for other countries, international; $145.00/year for libraries. Journal covering issues for reptile and amphibian veterinarians.

★12626★ Journal of Veterinary Behavior

Elsevier Science Inc.
360 Park Ave. S
New York, NY 10010
Ph: (212)989-5800   Fax: (212)633-3990
URL: http://www.elsevier.com

Bimonthly. $208.00/year for institutions, U.S. and Canada; $230.00/year for institutions, other countries; $139.00/year for individuals, U.S. and Canada; $160.00/year for individuals, other countries; $70.00/year for students, U.S. $91.00/year for students, other countries. Journal focused on veterinary behavioral medicine.

★12627★ Lab Animal

Nature Publishing Group
75 Varick St., 9th Fl.
New York, NY 10013-1917
Ph: (212)726-9200   Fax: (212)696-9006
Fr: 888-331-6288
E-mail: editors@labanimal.com
URL: http://www.labanimal.com/laban/index.html

Monthly. $225.00/year for individuals; $1,260.00/year for institutions; $125.00/year for individuals; $780.00/year for institutions. Life science magazine.

★12628★ The Morgan Horse

American Morgan Horse Association
122 Bostwick Rd.
PO Box 960
Shelburne, VT 05482-0960
Ph: (802)985-4944   Fax: (802)985-8897

Monthly. $31.50/year for individuals, 2nd class; $70.00/year for individuals, 1st class; $53.50/year for Canada and Mexico; $61.50/year for other countries. Magazine for Morgan horse enthusiasts.

★12629★ New Methods

Ronald S. Lippert, A.H.T.
713 S Main St., C-1
Willits, CA 95490
Ph: (707)456-1262

Description: Monthly. Examines common problems and concerns in the field of animal health technology. Provides professionals with items on animal care and protection and medical breakthroughs. Recurring features include letters to the editor, interviews, notices of publications available, job listings, news of educational opportunities, and news of research.

★12630★ Newsletter-Animal Behavior Society

Animal Behavior Society
Animal Behavior Office
Indiana University
2611 E. 10th St., No. 170
Bloomington, IN 47408-2603
Ph: (812)856-5541   Fax: (812)856-5542
URL: http://www.animalbehavior.org/ABS/Newsletters/Directory/

Description: Quarterly. Informs members of the Society of activities, events, meetings, announcements and opportunities in the field of animal behavior. Recurring features include a news of educational opportunities, job listings, and notices of publications available.

★12631★ Preventive Veterinary Medicine

Mosby Inc.
11830 Westline Industrial Dr.
St. Louis, MO 63146
Ph: (314)872-8370   Fax: (314)432-1380
Fr: 800-325-4177
URL: http://www.elsevier.com/wps/find/journaldescription.cws_home

$2,142.00/year for institutions (price for all countries except European countries, Japan and Iran). Journal focusing on the epidemiology of domestic and wild animals, costs of epidemic and endemic diseases of animals, the latest methods in veterinary epidemiology, disease control or eradication by public veterinary services, relationships between veterinary medicine and animal production, and development of new techniques in diagnosing, recording, evaluating and controlling diseases in animal populations.

★12632★ Research in Veterinary Science

Mountain Association for Community Economic Development
433 Chestnut St.
Berea, KY 40403
Ph: (859)986-2373   Fax: (859)986-1299
URL: http://www.elsevier.com/wps/find/journaldescription.cws_home

Bimonthly. $321.00/year for individuals, for all countries except European countries, Japan and Iran; $515.00/year for institutions, for all countries except European countries, Japan and Iran. Journal publishing original articles, reviews and short communications of a high scientific and ethical standard in the veterinary sciences.

★12633★ Seminars in Avian and Exotic Pet Medicine

Mosby Inc.
11830 Westline Industrial Dr.
St. Louis, MO 63146
Ph: (314)872-8370   Fax: (314)432-1380
Fr: 800-325-4177
URL: http://www.us.elsevierhealth.com/product.jsp?isbn=1055937X&r

Quarterly. $116.00/year for individuals; $220.00/year for institutions; $54.00/year for individuals, resident; $180.00/year for individuals, international; $270.00/year for institutions, international; $90.00/year for individuals, international resident. Journal for veterinary practitioners.

★12634★ TRENDS Magazine

American Animal Hospital Association
12575 West Bayaud Ave.
Lakewood, CO 80228
Ph: (303)986-2800   Fax: (303)986-1700
Fr: 800-883-6301

URL: http://www.aahanet.org

Bimonthly. $60.00/year for U.S. and Canada; $70.00/year for other countries; $20.00 for single issue. Professional magazine covering the management of small animal veterinary practices.

★12635★ Veterinary Economics

Advanstar Communications
641 Lexington Ave.
8th Fl.
New York, NY 10022
Ph: (212)951-6600   Fax: (212)951-6793
Fr: 800-225-4569
URL: http://web.advanstar.com/advanstar/v42/index.cvn

Monthly. Free to qualified subscribers. Periodical publishing business and management information for veterinarians.

★12636★ Veterinary Medicine

Advanstar Communications
641 Lexington Ave.
8th Fl.
New York, NY 10022
Ph: (212)951-6600   Fax: (212)951-6793
Fr: 800-225-4569
URL: http://www.vetmedpub.com/vetmed

Monthly. Free to qualified subscribers. Periodical publishing peer-reviewed clinical articles for companion-animal practitioners.

★12637★ Veterinary Practice News

Bowtie Inc.
1500 Broadway, Ste. 2302
New York, NY 10036
Ph: (212)302-8080   Fax: (212)302-8289
URL: http://www.veterinarypracticenews.com/

Monthly. Magazine covering veterinary practice in the United States featuring developments and trends affecting companion animals and livestock.

★12638★ Veterinary Research Communications

Springer Publishing Co.
11 W 42nd St., 15th Fl.
New York, NY 10036
Ph: (212)431-4370   Fax: (212)941-7342
Fr: 877-687-7476
URL: http://www.springer.com

Journal focusing on the current developments in the entire field of veterinary science.

★12639★ Vetz Magazine

Vetz Magazine
608 Hampton Dr.
Venice, CA 90291
Ph: (310)452-3900   Fax: (310)452-3909
URL: http://www.vetzmagazine.com/

Quarterly. $27.80/year for individuals. Lifestyle magazine for veterinarians that address personal, financial, health, and business issues unique to those in veterinary practice.

★12640★ Western Horseman

Western Horseman
3850 N Nevada Ave.
PO Box 7980
Colorado Springs, CO 80933-7980
Ph: (719)633-5524   Fax: (719)473-0997
URL: http://www.westernhorseman.com/

Monthly. $22.00/year for individuals; $42.00/year for individuals, for international orders; $32.00/year for individuals, for U.S. orders. Magazine covering forms of horsemanship and all breeds of horses; emphasizing western stock horses and western lifestyle.

PLACEMENT AND JOB REFERRAL SERVICES

★12641★ American Veterinary Medical Association (AVMA)

1931 N Meacham Rd., Ste. 100
Schaumburg, IL 60173
Ph: (847)925-8070   Fax: (847)925-1329
Fr: 800-248-2862
E-mail: avmainfo@avma.org
URL: http://www.avma.org

Description: Professional society of veterinarians. Conducts educational and research programs. Provides placement service. Sponsors American Veterinary Medical Association Foundation (also known as AVMF Foundation) and Educational Commission for Foreign Veterinary Graduates. Compiles statistics. Accredits veterinary medical education programs and veterinary technician education programs.

EMPLOYER DIRECTORIES AND NETWORKING LISTS

★12642★ American College of Veterinary Pathologists-Membership Directory

American College of Veterinary
  Pathologists
7600 Terrace Ave., Ste. 203
Middleton, WI 53562
URL: http://www.acvp.org/

Annual, March. Covers 1,200 veterinary anatomic pathologists and veterinary clinical pathologists. Entries include: Name, office address, phone, e-mail. Arrangement: Alphabetical.

★12643★ American Society of Veterinary Ophthalmology-Directory

American Society of Veterinary
  Ophthalmology
1416 W Liberty
Stillwater, OK 74075
Ph: (405)377-4388   Fax: (405)744-6265
URL: http://www.asvo.org

Bimonthly, December. Covers 250 member veterinarians interested in animal ophthalmology. Entries include: Name, address, office and home phone numbers, and year of graduation. Arrangement: Geographical. Indexes: Alphabetical; chronological.

★12644★ American Veterinary Medical Association-Directory and Resource Manual

American Veterinary Medical Association
1931 N Meacham Rd., Ste. 100
Schaumburg, IL 60173
Ph: (847)925-8070   Fax: (847)925-1329
Fr: 800-248-2862
URL: http://www.avma.org

Annual, January. $150.00 for nonmembers, U.S. and territories; $175.00 for nonmembers, other countries. Covers AVMA members; code of ethics, AVMA bylaws. Entries include: Name, spouse's name, address, e-mail, phone numbers, codes for practice activity, type of employer, institution granting degree, and year received. Arrangement: Geographical and alphabetical. Indexes: Alphabetical.

★12645★ Association of Veterinary Practice Management Membership Directory

Association of Veterinary Practice
  Management
PO Box 121625
Clermont, FL 34712-1625
Ph: (352)243-2014   Fax: (352)243-2013
URL: http://www.avpmca.org/

Quarterly. Covers complete listing of members and their contact information based on expertise areas.

★12646★ Careers in Focus: Animal Care

Facts On File Inc.
132 W 31st St., 17th Fl.
New York, NY 10001
Ph: (212)967-8800   Fax: 800-678-3633
Fr: 800-322-8755
URL: http://www.factsonfile.com

Latest edition 3rd, 2006. $29.95 for individuals; $26.95 for libraries. Covers an overview of animal care, followed by a selection of jobs profiled in detail, including the nature of the job, earnings, prospects for employment, what kind of training and skills it requires, and sources for further information.

★12647★ Directory of Animal Care and Control Agencies

American Humane Association
63 Inverness Dr. E
Englewood, CO 80112-5117
Ph: (303)792-9900   Fax: (303)792-5333
Fr: 800-227-4645

Updated continuously; printed on request. Covers over 6,000 animal protection agencies; Canadian and some other foreign agencies are available; national and individual state editions are available. Entries include: Agency name, address, phone, contact. Arrangement: Geographical.

★12648★ **Discovering Careers for Your Future: Animals**

Facts On File Inc.
132 W 31st St., 17th Fl.
New York, NY 10001
Ph: (212)967-8800   Fax: 800-678-3633
Fr: 800-322-8755
URL: http://www.factsonfile.com

Latest edition 2nd, 2005. $21.95 for individuals; $19.75 for libraries. Covers animal shelter workers, aquarists, farmers, naturalists, veterinarians, wildlife photographers, and zoo and aquarium curators; links career education to curriculum, helping children investigate the subjects they are interested in and the careers those subjects might lead to.

★12649★ **Programs in Veterinary Technology**

American Veterinary Medical Association
1931 N Meacham Rd., Ste. 100
Schaumburg, IL 60173
Ph: (847)925-8070   Fax: (847)925-1329
Fr: 800-248-2862
URL: http://www.avma.org

Semiannual, June and December. Covers colleges and universities that offer accredited veterinary technology programs. Entries include: Institution name, address; department name, address, phone, name of departmental contact, degree offered, length of program, type of accreditation. Arrangement: Geographical.

HANDBOOKS AND MANUALS

★12650★ **101 Secrets of a High-Performance Veterinary Practice**

Veterinary Medicine Pub Co
8033 Flint St.
Lenexa, KS 66214
Ph: (913)492-4300   Fax: (913)492-4157
Fr: 800-255-6864

Bob Levoy. 1996. $19.95 (paper). 170 pages.

★12651★ **Career Choices for Veterinarians: Beyond Private Practice**

Smith Veterinary Services
PO Box 698
Peshastin, WA 98847
Ph: (509)548-2010
URL: http://smithvet.com/

Carin A. Smith. 1998. $27.95 (paper). 255 pages.

★12652★ **Careers with Dogs**

Barron's Educational Series, Inc.
250 Wireless Blvd.
Hauppauge, NY 11788-3917
Ph: (631)434-3311   Fax: (631)434-3723
Fr: 800-645-3476
E-mail: fbrown@barronseduc.com
URL: http://barronseduc.com

Audrey Pavia. 1998. $8.95 (paper). 137 pages. Covers various types of work available for animal lovers. Includes information on salaries, qualifications, and job-hunting.

★12653★ **Careers in Veterinary Medicine**

Rosen Publishing Group, Inc.
29 E. 21st St.
New York, NY 10010
Ph: (212)777-3017   Fax: 888-436-4643
Fr: 800-237-9932
URL: http://www.rosenpublishing.com/

Jane Caryl Duncan. Revised edition, 1994. $16.95; $9.95 (paper). Contains advice from a real veterinarian and a description of her work.

★12654★ **Expert Resumes for Health Care Careers**

Jist Works
875 Montreal Way
St. Paul, MN 55102
Fr: 800-648-5478
E-mail: info@jist.com
URL: http://www.jist.com

Wendy S. Enelow and Louise M. Kursmark. December 2003. $16.95. 288 pages.

★12655★ **Health Careers Today**

Elsevier
11830 Westline Industrial Dr.
St. Louis, MO 63146
Ph: (314)453-7010   Fax: (314)453-7095
Fr: 800-545-2522
E-mail: usbkinfo@elsevier.com
URL: http://www.elsevier.com

Gerdin, Judith. Fourth edition. 2007. $59.95. 496 pages. Covers more than 45 health careers. Discusses the roles and responsibilities of various occupations and provides a solid foundation in the skills needed for all health careers.

★12656★ **Large Animal Clinical Procedures for Veterinary Technicians**

Elsevier
1600 John F. Kennedy Blvd., Ste. 1800
Philadelphia, PA 19103
Ph: (215)239-3900   Fax: (215)239-3990
Fr: 800-523-4069
URL: http://us.elsevierhealth.com

Elizabeth A. Hanie. 2005. $48.95. Large animal medical and surgical techniques are described. The book is divided into four parts: equine, bovine, small ruminant (sheep and goats), and swine.

★12657★ **Marketing Your Veterinary Practice**

Mosby
11830 Westline Industrial Dr.
St. Louis, MO 63146
Ph: (314)872-8370   Fax: 800-235-0256
Fr: 800-325-4177
URL: http://www.elsevier.com

Shawn Messonnier. Volume 2. 1997. $43.95 (paper). 176 pages. Presents discussions on ways to market services offered by veterinary practices, in an effort to increase practice income.

★12658★ **Opportunities in Animal and Pet Care Careers**

The McGraw-Hill Companies
PO Box 182604
Columbus, OH 43272
Fax: (614)759-3749   Fr: 877-883-5524
E-mail: customer.service@mcgraw-hill.com
URL: http://www.mcgraw-hill.com

Mary Price Lee and Richard S. Lee. 2001. $13.95. 160 pages. Covers the field from small animal medicine to large animal medicine, and provides job-hunting advice. Illustrated.

★12659★ **Opportunities in Environmental Careers**

The McGraw-Hill Companies
PO Box 182604
Columbus, OH 43272
Fax: (614)759-3749   Fr: 877-883-5524
E-mail: customer.service@mcgraw-hill.com
URL: http://www.mcgraw-hill.com

Odom Fanning. Revised, 2002. $12.95 (paper). 174 pages. Describes a broad range of opportunities in fields such as environmental health, recreation, physics, and hygiene, and provides job search advice. Part of the "Opportunities in ..." Series.

★12660★ **Opportunities in Health and Medical Careers**

The McGraw-Hill Companies
PO Box 182604
Columbus, OH 43272
Fax: (614)759-3749   Fr: 877-883-5524
E-mail: customer.service@mcgraw-hill.com
URL: http://www.mcgraw-hill.com

I. Donald Snook, Jr. and Leo D'Orazio. 2004. $13.95 (paper). 157 pages. Covers the full range of medical and health occupations. Illustrated.

EMPLOYMENT AGENCIES AND SEARCH FIRMS

★12661★ **Management Search, Inc.**

3013 NW 59th St.
Oklahoma City, OK 73112
Ph: (405)842-3173   Fax: (405)842-8360
E-mail: dorwig@mgmtsearch.com

URL: http://www.mgmtsearch.com

Executive search firm specializing in the field of agri-business.

ONLINE JOB SOURCES AND SERVICES

★12662★ Medhunters.com
Fr: 800-664-0278
E-mail: info@medhunters.com
URL: http://www.medhunters.com

Description: Career search site for jobs in all health care specialties; educational resources; visa and licensing information for relocation; interesting articles; relocation tools; links to professional organizations and general resources.

★12663★ ProHealthJobs
Fr: 800-796-1738
E-mail: Info@prohealthedujobs.com
URL: http://www.prohealthjobs.com

Description: Career resources site for the medical and health care field. Lists professional opportunities, product information, continuing education and open positions.

★12664★ VeterinaryLife.com
URL: http://www.veterinarylife.com

Description: Posts classified ads for veterinarian and clinic jobs available worldwide.

TRADESHOWS

★12665★ ACVS Veterinary Symposium
American College of Veterinary Surgeons
4401 E.W. Hwy. Ste. 205
Bethesda, MD 20814-4523
Ph: (301)913-9550   Fax: (301)913-2034
E-mail: ACVS@acvs.org
URL: http://www.acvs.org

Annual. **Primary Exhibits:** Veterinary surgery equipment, supplies, and services.

★12666★ American Association of Bovine Practitioners Annual Conference
American Association of Bovine Practitioners
PO Box 3610
Auburn, AL 36831-3610
Ph: (334)821-0442   Fax: (334)821-9532
Fr: 800-269-2227
E-mail: aabphq@aabp.org
URL: http://www.aabp.org/

Annual. **Primary Exhibits:** Pharmaceutical & biological manufacturers, equipment companies, agricultural related companies, and computer programs and supplies. **Dates and**

Locations: 2008 Sep 25-27; Charlotte, NC; 2009 Sep 10-12; Omaha, NE.

★12667★ American College of Veterinary Ophthalmologists Conference
Grana Enterprises
24832 N. 91st Ave.
Peoria, AZ 85383-1243
Ph: (602)841-8793   Fax: (602)864-3734

Annual. **Primary Exhibits:** Veterinary ophthalmology equipment, supplies, and services.

★12668★ American College of Veterinary Pathologists Annual Meeting
American College of Veterinary Pathologists
7600 Terrace Ave., Ste. 203
Middleton, WI 53562-3174
Ph: (608)833-8725   Fax: (608)831-5122
E-mail: info@acvp.org
URL: http://www.acvp.org

Annual. **Primary Exhibits:** Veterinary pathology (origin, nature, and course of diseases in animals) equipment, supplies, and services.

★12669★ American Humane Association Annual Conference
American Humane Association
63 Inverness Dr., E.
Englewood, CO 80112-5117
Ph: (303)792-9900   Fax: (303)792-5333
URL: http://www.americanhumane.org

Annual. **Primary Exhibits:** Animal welfare equipment, including pet food, cages, trucks, ID programs, and health and veterinary products.

★12670★ American Society of Veterinary Ophthalmology Meeting
American Society of Veterinary Ophthalmology
1416 W Liberty Ave.
Stillwater, OK 74075
Ph: (405)377-4388
URL: http://www.asvo.org

Annual. **Primary Exhibits:** Veterinary ophthalmology equipment, supplies, and services.

★12671★ American Veterinary Medical Association Annual Convention
American Veterinary Medical Association
1931 N. Meacham Rd., Ste. 100
Schaumburg, IL 60173-4360
Ph: (847)925-8070   Fax: (847)925-1329
E-mail: avmainfo@avma.org
URL: http://www.avma.org

Annual. **Primary Exhibits:** Products, materials, equipment, data, and services for veterinary medicine. **Dates and Locations:** 2008 Jul 19-22; New Orleans, LA; 2009 Jul 11-14; Seattle, WA; 2010 Jul 31 - Aug 03; Atlanta, GA; 2011 Jul 16-19; St. Louis, MO; 2012

Aug 04-07; San Diego, CA; 2013 Jul 20-23; Chicago, IL.

★12672★ International Congress on Veterinary Acupuncture
International Veterinary Acupuncture Society (IVAS)
PO Box 271395
Fort Collins, CO 80527-1395
Ph: (970)266-0666   Fax: (970)266-0777
URL: http://www.ivas.org

Annual. **Primary Exhibits:** Veterinary acupuncture equipment, supplies, and services.

★12673★ International Wildlife Rehabilitation Council Conference
International Wildlife Rehabilitation Council
PO Box 8187
San Jose, CA 95155
Ph: (408)271-2685   Fax: (408)271-9285
E-mail: office@iwrc-online.org
URL: http://iwrc-online.org

Annual. **Primary Exhibits:** Equipment, supplies, and services for the rehabilitation of wildlife, including the handling and care of sick and injured wild animals. T-shirts, books, jewelry, artwork, etc.

★12674★ Joint Annual Meeting of the American Dairy Science Association and the American Society of Animal Science
Federation of Animal Science Societies
1111 N Dunlap Ave.
Savoy, IL 61874
Ph: (217)356-3182   Fax: (217)398-4119
E-mail: fass@assochq.org
URL: http://www.fass.org

Annual. **Primary Exhibits:** Exhibits related to the investigation, instruction, or extension in animal sciences and in the production, processing, and dissemination of livestock and livestock products.

★12675★ Southwest International Veterinary Symposium Expo
Texas Veterinary Medical Association
8104 Exchange Dr.
Austin, TX 78754
Ph: (512)452-4224   Fax: (512)452-6633
E-mail: info@tvma.org
URL: http://www.tvma.org

Annual. **Primary Exhibits:** Pharmaceuticals, publications, computer equipment, surgical and X-ray equipment, veterinary supplies, pet nutritional products, biologicals, and testing laboratories, pesticides, livestock equipment.

★12676★ Washington State Veterinary Medical Association Convention
Washington State Veterinary Medical Association
PO Box 962
Bellevue, WA 98009
Ph: (425)454-8381   Fax: (425)454-8382
E-mail: info@wsvma.org

URL: http://www.wsvma.org

Annual. **Primary Exhibits:** Veterinary drugs, medical supplies, and equipment.

★12677★ **Western Veterinary Conference**

Western Veterinary Conference
2425 E Oquendo Rd.
Las Vegas, NV 89120-2406
Ph: (702)739-6698   Fax: (702)739-6420
E-mail: info@westernveterinary.org
URL: http://www.wvc.org

Annual. **Primary Exhibits:** Veterinary equipment, supplies, and services, including drugs.

★12678★ **Wisconsin Veterinary Medical Association Annual Convention**

Wisconsin Veterinary Medical Association
301 N Broom St.
Madison, WI 53703
Ph: (608)257-3665   Fax: (608)257-8989
E-mail: wvma@wvma.org
URL: http://www.wvma.org

Annual. **Primary Exhibits:** Veterinary supplies, pharmaceuticals, pet food, business systems, and record-keeping equipment.

OTHER SOURCES

★12679★ **American Academy of Clinical Toxicology (AACT)**

777 E Park Dr.
PO Box 8820
Harrisburg, PA 17105-8820
Ph: (717)558-7847   Fax: (717)558-7841
Fr: 888-633-5784
E-mail: swilson@pamedsoc.org
URL: http://www.clintox.org

Members: Physicians, veterinarians, pharmacists, nurses research scientists, and analytical chemists. **Purpose:** Objectives are to: unite medical scientists and facilitate the exchange of information; encourage the development of therapeutic methods and technology; **Activities:** Conducts professional training in poison information and emergency service personnel.

★12680★ **American Association of Zoo Veterinarians (AAZV)**

581705 White Oak Rd.
Yulee, FL 32097
Ph: (904)225-3275   Fax: (904)225-3289
E-mail: rhilsenrothaazv@aol.com
URL: http://www.aazv.org

Description: Veterinarians actively engaged in the practice of zoo and wildlife medicine for at least four years; veterinarians who do not qualify for active membership; persons interested in diseases of wildlife; students of veterinary medicine in any accredited veterinary school. Purposes are to: advance programs for preventive medicine, husbandry, and scientific research dealing with captive and free-ranging wild animals; provide a forum for the presentation and discussion of problems related to the field; enhance and uphold the professional ethics of veterinary medicine.

★12681★ **Association for Women Veterinarians (AWV)**

K-State College of Veterinary Medicine
228 Coles Hall
Manhattan, KS 66506-5602
Ph: (785)532-1918   Fax: (785)532-4557
E-mail: bthomps@vet.ksu.edu
URL: http://www.vet.ksu.edu/AWV/index.htm

Description: Works to support veterinary medicine by providing leadership in women's issues.

★12682★ **Exploring Health Occupations**

Cambridge Educational
PO Box 2053
Princeton, NJ 08543-2053
Ph: 800-257-5126   Fax: (609)671-0266
Fr: 800-468-4227
E-mail: custserv@films.com
URL: http://www.cambridgeeducational.com

VHS and DVD. $159.90. 1999. Two-part series provides a detailed view of the field of medical technicians and technologists, EMTs, nurses, therapists, and assistants.

★12683★ **Health Service Occupations**

Delphi Productions
3159 6th St.
Boulder, CO 80304
Ph: (303)443-2100   Fax: (303)443-4022
Fr: 888-443-2400

E-mail: support@delphivideo.com
URL: http://www.delphivideo.com

$95.00. 50 minutes. Part of the Careers for the 21st Century Video Library.

★12684★ **International Veterinary Acupuncture Society**

PO Box 271395
Fort Collins, CO 80527-1395
Ph: (970)266-0666   Fax: (970)266-0777
E-mail: office@ivas.org
URL: http://www.ivas.org

Description: Veterinarians and veterinary students. Encourages knowledge and research of the philosophy, technique, and practice of veterinary acupuncture. Fosters high standards in the field; promotes scientific investigation. Accumulates resources for scientific research and education; collects data concerning clinical and research cases where animals have been treated with acupuncture; disseminates information to veterinary students, practitioners, other scientific groups, and the public. Offers 120-contact hour basic veterinary acupuncture course; administers certification examination; also offers advanced traditional Chinese herbal veterinary medicine.

★12685★ **Medicine & Related Occupations**

Delphi Productions
3159 6th St.
Boulder, CO 80304
Ph: (303)443-2100   Fax: (303)443-4022
Fr: 888-443-2400
E-mail: support@delphivideo.com
URL: http://www.delphivideo.com

$95.00. 45 minutes. Part of the Careers for the 21st Century Video Library.

★12686★ **National Association of Federal Veterinarians (NAFV)**

1101 Vermont Ave. NW, Ste. 170
Washington, DC 20005
Ph: (202)842-4360   Fax: (202)289-6334
E-mail: dboyle@nafv.org
URL: http://users.erols.com/nafv

Description: Professional society of veterinarians employed by the U.S. Government. Maintains speakers' bureau.

Video Game Designers

SOURCES OF HELP-WANTED ADS

★12687★ Game Informer Magazine
Sunrise Publications Inc.
724 North First St., 4th Fl.
Minneapolis, MN 55401
Ph: (612)486-6100   Fax: (612)486-6101
URL: http://www.gameinformer.com/default.htm

Monthly. $19.98/year for individuals; $24.98 for two years. Consumer magazine covering video and computer game information and reviews.

★12688★ Game Revolution
Game Revolution
732 Gilman St.
Berkeley, CA 94710
URL: http://www.gamerevolution.com/

Monthly. Consumer magazine covering gaming news, reviews, and information.

★12689★ GamePro Greece
IDG Communications Inc.
5 Speen St., 3rd. Fl
Framingham, MA 01701
Ph: (508)875-5000   Fax: (508)988-7888
URL: http://www.idg.com

Monthly. Magazine covering all major consoles, coin-operated systems and video game systems including Sony playstation, Nintendo and X-box.

★12690★ GameStar
IDG Communications Inc.
5 Speen St., 3rd. Fl
Framingham, MA 01701
Ph: (508)875-5000   Fax: (508)988-7888
URL: http://www.idg.com

Magazine covering news and events of computer games.

★12691★ GameStar China
IDG Communications Inc.
5 Speen St., 3rd. Fl
Framingham, MA 01701
Ph: (508)875-5000   Fax: (508)988-7888
URL: http://www.idg.com

Monthly. Magazine covering latest games, testing and evaluation of computer hardware, methodology of games, game players experience, and entertainment information.

★12692★ International Journal of Computer Games Technology
Hindawi Publishing Corp.
410 Park Ave., 15th Fl.
287 PMB
New York, NY 10022
E-mail: ijcgt@hindawi.com
URL: http://www.hindawi.com/journals/ijcgt/

$195.00/year for individuals. Journal covering research and development aspects of games technology.

★12693★ Next Generation
Imagine Media
4000 Shoreline Court, Ste. 400
South San Francisco, CA 94080
Ph: (650)872-1642
URL: http://www.next-gen.biz

Consumer magazine covering computers and games.

★12694★ PC Gamer
Imagine Media
4000 Shoreline Court, Ste. 400
South San Francisco, CA 94080
Ph: (650)872-1642
URL: http://www.futureus-inc.com/products/index.php?magazine=pc_g

Monthly. $19.95/year for individuals; $34.95/year for Canada, print & cd-rom; $49.95/year for other countries, print & cd-rom. Consumer magazine covering computer games.

EMPLOYER DIRECTORIES AND NETWORKING LISTS

★12695★ Casino Vendors Guide
Casino City Press
95 Wells Ave.
Newton, MA 02459
Ph: (617)332-2850   Fax: (617)964-2280
Fr: 800-490-1715
URL: http://www.casinocitypress.com

$49.95. Covers 10,000 industry suppliers, manufacturers, and distributors, 1,000 gaming products and services, 1,500 gaming properties around the world, gaming associations, analysts, attorneys, trade shows, and trade publications. Entries include: company name, address, branch office locations, phone and fax numbers, email and website addresses, executive contacts and company description.

★12696★ The Computer Game Company Directory
Infinite Monkey Systems Inc.
58 Burr Ave.
Middletown, CT 06457-3708
Ph: (860)704-8305   Fax: (860)704-8306

Listing of names and links to web sites of more than 130 companies that publish computer games or make tools for creating computer games.

★12697★ International Game Developers Association Membership Directory
19 Mantua Rd.
Mount Royal, NJ 08061
Ph: (856)423-2990   Fax: (856)423-3420
E-mail: contact@igda.org
URL: http://www.igda.org/community/members.php

Directory of the 15,021 members of the International Game Developers Association. Information consists of a listing of all members with a public member profile, including member country, job type, company type and more.

★12698★ Play Meter-Directory Issue

Play Meter Magazine
PO Box 337
Metairie, LA 70004-0337
Ph: (504)488-7003   Fax: (504)488-7083
Fr: 888-473-2376
E-mail: news@playmeter.com
URL: http://www.playmeter.com

Annual, January. Covers about 500 firms that manufacture and distribute coin-operated video and electronic games and other amusement machines; 300 firms that supply the industry; state and national trade associations; exporters and importers; foreign manufacturers and distributors. Entries include: Company name, address, phone, cable address, telex, names and titles of key personnel, product line. Arrangement: Alphabetical.

HANDBOOKS AND MANUALS

★12699★ Becoming a Digital Designer: A Guide to Careers in Web, Video, Broadcast, Game and Animation Design

Wiley Publishing
10475 Crosspoint Blvd.
Indianapolis, IN 46256
Ph: (317)572-3000
E-mail: info@wiley.com
URL: http://www.wiley.com

Steven Heller and David Womack. 2007. $35.00. 336 pages. Provides an ideal starting point for anyone considering a career in the video game design industry and includes information concerning the preparation of an effective portfolio and resources for finding a job within the field.

★12700★ Break Into the Game Industry: How to Get a Job Making Video Games

McGraw-Hill Osborne Media
2600 10th St.
Berkeley, CA 94710
Ph: (510)549-6600   Fax: (510)549-6603
URL: http://www.osborne.com

Ernest Adams. 2003. $24.99. 352 pages. Gives readers practical advice for landing a job in the video game design industry. Also provides hundreds of resources for job seekers.

★12701★ Business and Legal Primer for Game Development

Charles River Media
25 Thomson Pl.
Boston, MA 02210
Ph: (617)757-7900   Fax: (617)757-7969
Fr: 800-347-7707
E-mail: crminfo@cengage.com
URL: http://www.charlesriver.com

S. Gregory Boyd and Brian Green, editors. 2006. $49.95. 475 pages. Explores the major business and legal issues involved in game development and design. Also provides an excellent reference of information from issues as diverse as contract negotiation, employment law, taxation, licensing, and basic business operations.

★12702★ Career Opportunities in the Internet, Video Games, and Multimedia

Ferguson Publishing Company
132 W 31st St., 17th Fl.
New York, NY 10001
Fax: 800-678-3633   Fr: 800-322-8755
E-mail: custserv@factsonfile.com
URL: http://ferguson.infobasepublishing.com/

Allan Taylor, James Robert Parish and Dan Fiden. 2007. $49.50. 384 pages.

★12703★ Creating Casual Games for Profit and Fun

Course Technology PTR
25 Thomson Pl.
Boston, MA 02210
Ph: (617)757-7900   Fax: 800-487-8488
Fr: 800-648-7450
URL: http://www.courseptr.com

Allen Partridge. 2007. $39.99. 320 pages. Covers the video game industry's standards and expectations.

★12704★ Designing 3D Games that Sell!

Course Technology PTR
25 Thomson Pl.
Boston, MA 02210
Ph: (617)757-7900   Fax: 800-487-8488
Fr: 800-648-7450
URL: http://www.courseptr.com

Luke Ahearn. 2001. $44.96. 406 pages. Explains the video game industry and what publishers are looking for when hiring or producing a new game. Also details the game proposal and submission process.

★12705★ Designing a Digital Portfolio

Peachpit Press
1249 8th St.
Berkeley, CA 94710
Fr: 800-283-9444
E-mail: press@peachpit.com
URL: http://www.peachpit.com

Cynthia Baron. 2003. $26.40. 336 pages. Gives the reader inspiring examples of digital portfolios for those looking for a job as a digital artist, particularly video game designers. Also provides step-by-step instructions for creating a portfolio that will stand out in this competitive industry as well as important insights from the professionals who evaluate designer portfolios.

★12706★ Emergence in Games

Course Technology PTR
25 Thomson Pl.
Boston, MA 02210
Ph: (617)757-7900   Fax: 800-487-8488
Fr: 800-648-7450

URL: http://www.courseptr.com

Penny Sweetser. 2007. $49.99. 312 pages. Discusses the future direction of video game design and development and shows those looking for a job in the field how to use emergence to make video games more lifelike and interactive which will set them apart from the competition.

★12707★ FabJob Guide to Become a Video Game Designer

FabJob.com
4616 25th Ave. NE
No. 224
Seattle, WA 98105
Ph: (403)949-4980
URL: http://www.fabjob.com/video.html

Phil Marlof. $9.97. 180 pages. Provides information about how the video game industry works, the best ways to find out about and apply for jobs, how to ace the interview process, how to get a job through an agency, as well as a list of companies who are hiring, including their contact information.

★12708★ Fundamentals of Game Design

Prentice Hall PTR
1003 Gravenstein Hwy. N
Sebastopol, CA 95472
Ph: (707)827-4100   Fax: (707)829-5754
URL: http://safari.phptr.com/contactus

Ernest Adams and Andrew Rollings. 2006. $88.00. 600 pages. Focuses on designing for the commercial entertainment market and provides readers with resources in which to break into the video game industry or further develop their skills as a professional video game designer.

★12709★ The Game Asset Pipeline

Charles River Media
25 Thomson Pl.
Boston, MA 02210
Ph: (617)757-7900   Fax: (617)757-7969
Fr: 800-347-7707
E-mail: crminfo@cengage.com
URL: http://www.charlesriver.com

Ben Carter. 2004. $39.95. 302 pages. Overview of what it takes to get a video game into the marketplace.

★12710★ Game Creation and Careers: Insider Secrets from Industry Experts

Peachpit Press
1249 8th St.
Berkeley, CA 94710
Fr: 800-283-9444
E-mail: press@peachpit.com
URL: http://www.peachpit.com

Marc Saltzman. 2003. $49.99. 744 pages. Presents an overview of video game design and development and the industry as a whole. Includes resources for breaking into the video gaming industry and discusses the pros and cons of working with a franchise compared to working for oneself.

★12711★ Game Design: A Practical Approach

Course Technology PTR
25 Thomson Pl.
Boston, MA 02210
Ph: (617)757-7900   Fax: 800-487-8488
Fr: 800-648-7450
URL: http://www.courseptr.com

Paul Schuytema. 2006. $44.95. 375 pages. Provides a complete and practical examination of the craft of game design for new video game designers as well as practicing designers. Also includes invaluable insights and tips from the industry's top game designers about working in the field successfully.

★12712★ Game Design: From Blue Sky to Green Light

A K Peters, Ltd.
888 Worcester St., Ste. 230
Wellesley, MA 02482
Ph: (781)416-2888   Fax: (781)416-2889
E-mail: editorial@akpeters.com
URL: http://www.akpeters.com

Deborah Todd. 2007. $45.00. 308 pages. Covers the world of video game design and is an invaluable resource for those looking to start a career in the industry as well as for established professionals already working as video game designers.

★12713★ Game Design Perspectives

Course Technology PTR
25 Thomson Pl.
Boston, MA 02210
Ph: (617)757-7900   Fax: 800-487-8488
Fr: 800-648-7450
URL: http://www.courseptr.com

Francois Laramee. 2002. $35.96. 406 pages. Overview of how to write effective video game design documents and tips and techniques from a variety of designers provides aspiring video game designers with tools to succeed in the industry. Also gives information about the key aspects of managing a game development business which will help aspiring game designers develop real-world skills, making them a valuable addition to companies looking to hire.

★12714★ Game Design: Principles, Practice, and Techniques: The Ultimate Guide for the Aspiring Game Designer

Wiley Publishing
10475 Crosspoint Blvd.
Indianapolis, IN 46256
Ph: (317)572-3000
E-mail: info@wiley.com
URL: http://www.wiley.com

Jim Thompson, Barnaby Berbank-Green and Nic Cusworth. 2007. $50.00. 192 pages. Provides advice for those wanting to break into the video game design industry as well as a host of resources.

★12715★ Game Design, Second Edition

Course Technology PTR
25 Thomson Pl.
Boston, MA 02210
Ph: (617)757-7900   Fax: 800-487-8488
Fr: 800-648-7450
URL: http://www.courseptr.com

Bob Bates. Second edition, 2004. $39.99. 376 pages. Offers a behind-the-scenes look at how a video game gets designed and developed with interviews, document templates and the latest techniques and development models. Also includes various video game industry resources.

★12716★ Game Design: The Art and Business of Creating Games

Course Technology
25 Thomson Pl.
Boston, MA 02210
Fr: 800-648-7450
URL: http://www.course.com

Bob Bates. 2002. $21.89. 336 pages. Comprehensive guide provides insight on how to turn video game design into a career.

★12717★ Game Design Workshop: Designing, Prototyping, and Playtesting Games

CMP Media LLC
600 Community Dr.
Manhasset, NY 11030
Ph: (516)562-5000   Fax: (516)562-7830
E-mail: cmp@cmp.com
URL: http://www.cmp.com

Tracy Fullerton, Chris Swain and Steven Hoffman. 2004. $44.95. 480 pages. Gives those looking for a career as a video game designer an overview of elements that work as well as those that do not work when creating a video game. Also includes valuable resources.

★12718★ Game Development Essentials: Game Interface Design

Delmar, Cengage Learning
5 Maxwell Dr.
Clifton Park, NY 12065
Fax: 800-430-4445   Fr: 800-648-7450
E-mail: esales@cengage.com
URL: http://www.delmarlearning.com

Kevin Saunders and Jeannie Novak. 2006. $35.25. 296 pages. Gives advice from a host of professionals in the video game design industry about the topic of user interface design. Also includes resources for the aspiring video game designer.

★12719★ Game Development Essentials: Game Project Management

Delmar, Cengage Learning
5 Maxwell Dr.
Clifton Park, NY 12065
Fax: 800-430-4445   Fr: 800-648-7450
E-mail: esales@cengage.com
URL: http://www.delmarlearning.com

John Hight and Jeannie Novak. 2007. $52.95. 320 pages. Offers a comprehensive look at the video game project management process including: roles and responsibilities of team members, concept development, roles and responsibilities of team members, scheduling, marketing and budgeting.

★12720★ Game Interface Design

Course Technology PTR
25 Thomson Pl.
Boston, MA 02210
Ph: (617)757-7900   Fax: 800-487-8488
Fr: 800-648-7450
URL: http://www.courseptr.com

Brent Fox. 2004. $39.99. 232 pages. Outlines each step of the video game interface and defines goals in creating that interface. Also gives an overview of the video game industry with a look into developer and publisher relationships, budget constraints, scheduling, and the politics of the industry.

★12721★ The Game Localization Handbook

Course Technology PTR
25 Thomson Pl.
Boston, MA 02210
Ph: (617)757-7900   Fax: 800-487-8488
Fr: 800-648-7450
URL: http://www.courseptr.com

Heather Chandler. 2004. $44.95. 338 pages. Comprehensive guide to producing localized games for any platform discusses the importance for video game designers to start thinking in a global mindset. Manual provides an overview of each phase of the localization process including staffing needs, determining budgets, scheduling, working with third-party vendors and console submission process.

★12722★ Game Plan: The Insider's Guide to Breaking In and Succeeding in the Computer and Video Game Business

St. Martin's Griffin
175 5th Ave.
New York, NY 10010
Ph: (212)674-5151   Fax: (212)674-3179
Fr: 800-221-7945
URL: http://www.stmartins.com

Alan Gershenfeld, Mark Loparco and Cecilia Barajas. 2003. $9.39. 352 pages. Reveals how to break in, survive, and produce video games for successful video game companies.

★12723★ The Game Producer's Handbook

Course Technology PTR
25 Thomson Pl.
Boston, MA 02210
Ph: (617)757-7900   Fax: 800-487-8488
Fr: 800-648-7450
URL: http://www.courseptr.com

Dan Irish. 2005. $39.99. 352 pages. Provides an ideal reference guide for both students who want to acquire the knowledge to succeed in the video game design industry as well as veterans of the field.

★12724★ Game Production Handbook

Charles River Media
25 Thomson Pl.
Boston, MA 02210
Ph: (617)757-7900   Fax: (617)757-7969
Fr: 800-347-7707
E-mail: crminfo@cengage.com
URL: http://www.charlesriver.com

Heather Chandler. 2006. $44.95. 350 pages. Provides advice from video game industry professionals about succeeding in the industry and is an invaluable resource for those looking to begin a career as a video game designer as well as for professionals already working in the field.

★12725★ Game Programming Golden Rules

Charles River Media
25 Thomson Pl.
Boston, MA 02210
Ph: (617)757-7900   Fax: (617)757-7969
Fr: 800-347-7707
E-mail: crminfo@cengage.com
URL: http://www.charlesriver.com

Martin Brownlow. 2004. $11.34. 318 pages. Overview of the nine "Golden Rules" that help define a methodology for creating a modern video game in an attempt to empower the video game designer to take a more active role therefore bypassing the need for programmers involvement beyond the initial step of video game development.

★12726★ Game Testing All in One

Course Technology PTR
25 Thomson Pl.
Boston, MA 02210
Ph: (617)757-7900   Fax: 800-487-8488
Fr: 800-648-7450
URL: http://www.courseptr.com

Charles Schultz, Robert Bryant and Tim Langdell. 2005. $49.99. 416 pages. Describes how to apply software test engineer methodologies to the video game industry in order to test a new video game. Also includes tips for finding employment in the field.

★12727★ Get in the Game: Careers in the Game Industry

Peachpit Press
1249 8th St.
Berkeley, CA 94710
Fr: 800-283-9444
E-mail: press@peachpit.com
URL: http://www.peachpit.com

Marc Mencher. 2002. $29.99. 320 pages. Covers ways in which to find a job in the video game industry through research, meeting the right people, marketing oneself, accessing the unadvertised job market, creating the perfect demo, and also discusses ways to handle tough interview ques-

tions and gives tips for writing a remarkable resume.

★12728★ In the Mind of a Game

Course Technology PTR
25 Thomson Pl.
Boston, MA 02210
Ph: (617)757-7900   Fax: 800-487-8488
Fr: 800-648-7450
URL: http://www.courseptr.com

John Flynt, PhD. 2005. $39.99. 384 pages. Valuable resource for both professional video game designers and those looking to break into the field; covers video game development, use, marketing, financing, criticism and consumption of computer games as well as a personalized account of the author's direct experience developing a video game.

★12729★ Indie Game Development Survival Guide

Charles River Media
25 Thomson Pl.
Boston, MA 02210
Ph: (617)757-7900   Fax: (617)757-7969
Fr: 800-347-7707
E-mail: crminfo@cengage.com
URL: http://www.charlesriver.com

David Michael. 2003. $39.95. 384 pages. Provides an invaluable resource for those looking to break into the video game design industry.

★12730★ Introduction to Game Development

Course Technology PTR
25 Thomson Pl.
Boston, MA 02210
Ph: (617)757-7900   Fax: 800-487-8488
Fr: 800-648-7450
URL: http://www.courseptr.com

Steve Rabin. 2005. $62.95. 900 pages. Comprehensive guide based on the curriculum guidelines of the IGDA surveys all aspects of the theory and practice of video game development, design and production. Also includes resources

★12731★ Introduction to the Game Industry

Prentice Hall PTR
1003 Gravenstein Hwy. N
Sebastopol, CA 95472
Ph: (707)827-4100   Fax: (707)829-5754
URL: http://safari.phptr.com/contactus

Michael E. Moore and Jennifer Sward. 2006. $82.67. 500 pages. Provides an overview of how the video game industry works and describes how games are designed and built for those looking to break into the field.

★12732★ Mobile 3D Game Development: From Start to Market

Course Technology PTR
25 Thomson Pl.
Boston, MA 02210
Ph: (617)757-7900   Fax: 800-487-8488
Fr: 800-648-7450
URL: http://www.courseptr.com

Carlos Morales and David Nelson. 2007. $49.99. 496 pages. Provides an overview of the burgeoning mobile video game industry as well as instruction for developing commercial-quality 3D games for Java enabled mobile phones. Also includes resources for breaking into the 3D game market.

★12733★ The Official Guide to 3D GameStudio

Course Technology PTR
25 Thomson Pl.
Boston, MA 02210
Ph: (617)757-7900   Fax: 800-487-8488
Fr: 800-648-7450
URL: http://www.courseptr.com

Mike Duggan. 2007. $39.99. 480 pages. Provides information about video game design and gives readers tips regarding the game industry as a whole, including how video games are made, what job opportunities exist and how to break into the field.

★12734★ Paid to Play: An Insider's Guide to Video Game Careers

Prima Games
3000 Lava Ridge Ct., Ste. 100
Roseville, CA 95661
Fr: 800-733-3000
URL: http://www.primagames.com

Alice Rush, David Hodgson and Bryan Stratton. 2006. $19.95. 272 pages. Overview of the video game industry gives readers a career guide which outlines the differences in jobs available in the field and interviews over 100 professionals currently working in the industry.

★12735★ Patterns in Game Design

Course Technology PTR
25 Thomson Pl.
Boston, MA 02210
Ph: (617)757-7900   Fax: 800-487-8488
Fr: 800-648-7450
URL: http://www.courseptr.com

Staffan Bjork and Jussi Holopainen. 2004. $44.96. 423 pages. Resource provides professional and aspiring video game designers a practical collection of game design patterns that facilitate the design of a successful game and defines a common language video game designers can use to speak concisely about the essence of video games.

★12736★ Secrets of the Game Business

Charles River Media
25 Thomson Pl.
Boston, MA 02210
Ph: (617)757-7900   Fax: (617)757-7969
Fr: 800-347-7707

E-mail: crminfo@cengage.com
URL: http://www.charlesriver.com

Francois Dominic Laramee. 2005. $39.95. 410 pages. Provides an in-depth look into the video game industry for those seeking to begin a career in the field as well as those seeking to advance their careers.

★12737★ **Serious Games: Games That Educate, Train and Inform**
Course Technology PTR
25 Thomson Pl.
Boston, MA 02210
Ph: (617)757-7900   Fax: 800-487-8488
Fr: 800-648-7450
URL: http://www.courseptr.com

David Michael and Sandra Chen. 2005. $34.99. 352 pages. Provides information about the growing market of games used for education, training, healing and more. Also includes a detailed overview of all of the major markets for serious games and the goals of each of those markets as well as the types of games on which they focus and market-specific issues the video game designer must consider. Aims to show aspiring video game designers ways in which to successfully apply their skills to this growing area in order to stand out from the competition.

★12738★ **21st Century Game Design**
Charles River Media
25 Thomson Pl.
Boston, MA 02210
Ph: (617)757-7900   Fax: (617)757-7969
Fr: 800-347-7707
E-mail: crminfo@cengage.com
URL: http://www.charlesriver.com

Chris Bateman and Richard Boon. 2005. $39.95. 352 pages. Discusses the importance of the audience model when designing video games in an attempt to create better video game designers who will create interesting and innovative games for the public.

★12739★ **Ultimate 3D Game Engine Design and Architecture**
Course Technology PTR
25 Thomson Pl.
Boston, MA 02210
Ph: (617)757-7900   Fax: 800-487-8488
Fr: 800-648-7450
URL: http://www.courseptr.com

Allen Sherrod. 2006. $59.95. 556 pages. Aimed at video game designers and programmers aspiring to break into the field of video game development, this manual focuses on designing and creating a video game engine that can be used to create gaming application on the PC. Also includes resources for finding a job.

★12740★ **Ultimate Guide to Video Game Writing and Design**
Lone Eagle
770 Broadway
New York, NY 10003
E-mail: info@watsonguptill.com

URL: http://www.watsonguptill.com
Flint Dille and John Zuur Platten. 2008. $19.95. 272 pages. Provides an in-depth look into the video game industry for those looking to start a career in the field as well as those looking to advance their job position.

★12741★ **Video Game Design Revealed**
Course Technology PTR
25 Thomson Pl.
Boston, MA 02210
Ph: (617)757-7900   Fax: 800-487-8488
Fr: 800-648-7450
URL: http://www.courseptr.com

Guy Lecky-Thompson. 2007. $39.99. 336 pages. Provides an overview of the steps and processes involved in bringing a video game from concept to completion. Also includes tips and information on how to find and contact game studios and publishers.

★12742★ **The Virtual Handshake: Opening Doors and Closing Deals Online**
AMACOM
1601 Broadway
New York, NY 10019
Fax: (518)891-2372   Fr: 800-250-5308
URL: http://www.amanet.org/books/

David Teten and Scott Allen. 2005. $13.57 (paper). 272 pages. Covers such topics as finding a dream job in the video game design industry, how to meet more relevant senior employees, creating a powerful presence online, and building strong relationships within the industry.

EMPLOYMENT AGENCIES AND SEARCH FIRMS

★12743★ **GameRecruiter.com**
401 E Las Olas Blvd.
No. 130
Fort Lauderdale, FL 33301
Fax: (866)358-4219   Fr: (866)358-4263
E-mail: info@gamerecruiter.com
URL: http://www.gamerecruiter.com

Employment agency.

★12744★ **JobMonkey, Inc.**
PO Box 3956
Seattle, WA 98124
Fr: 800-230-1095
E-mail: adminstaff2@jobmonkey.com
URL: http://www.jobmonkey.com/videogamejobs/video_game_developer_jobs.html

Recruitment firm specializing in jobs in the technology fields, particularly video game designers.

★12745★ **Mary-Margaret.com, Inc.**
815-A Brazos St., No. 498
Austin, TX 78701
Ph: (512)388-4010   Fax: (206)888-6031
Fr: 877-662-3888
E-mail: jobs@mary-margaret.com
URL: http://www.mary-margaret.com/

Employment agency for the video gaming industry.

★12746★ **Showbizjobs.com, LLC**
3579 E Foothill Blvd.
Pasadena, CA 91107
Ph: (626)798-4533   Fax: (626)798-4533
URL: http://www.showbizjobs.com

Employment agency includes listings for jobs in the video gaming industry.

★12747★ **Studio Search, LLC**
7667 NE Park Ln.
Otis, OR 97369
Ph: (541)994-4441   Fax: (541)994-4473
E-mail: resumes@studio-search.com
URL: http://www.studio-search.com

Employment agency for the video gaming industry.

★12748★ **TSC Management Services Group**
112 Wool St.
Barrington, IL 60010
Ph: (847)381-0167
E-mail: grant@tscsearch.com
URL: http://www.tscsearch.com

Employment agency.

ONLINE JOB SOURCES AND SERVICES

★12749★ **Cold Milk**
19 Mantua Rd.
Mount Royal, NJ 08061
Ph: (856)423-2990   Fax: (856)423-3420
URL: http://www.coldmilk.org

Resource site run by video game professionals that includes industry job listings, tips for building a career as a video game designer, forums, articles, and new trends having an impact on video game developers.

★12750★ **Gamasutra**
CMP Media LLC
600 Harrison St., 6th Fl.
San Francisco, CA 94107
Ph: (415)947-6000   Fax: (415)947-6090
URL: http://www.gamasutra.com

Online resource provides up-to-date information about the video game industry as well as job listings, resumes, and featured companies.

★12751★ Game Discovery
107 SE Washington St., Ste. 520
Portland, OR 97214
Ph: (503)488-5763   Fr: 800-226-8887
E-mail: vegard@gamediscovery.com
URL: http://www.gamediscover.com

Online resource provides job listings for video game designers as well as news, reviews and tips on becoming a successful video game designer.

★12752★ GameDaily Biz
75 Rockefeller Plaza, 5th Fl.
New York, NY 10019
E-mail: libe.goad@corp.aol.com
URL: http://biz.gamedaily.com/

Online resource provides current news, interviews, featured companies and job listings for the video game industry.

★12753★ Gignews.com
2188 W Atlantic Blvd.
Delray Beach, FL 33445
Fax: 800-779-3369   Fr: 888-578-6882
E-mail: editor@gignews.com
URL: http://www.gignews.com

Online resource provides interviews, insider information, current news and job listings for those in the video game industry.

TRADESHOWS

★12754★ Austin Game Developers Conference
CMP Game Group
600 Community Dr.
Manhasset, NY 11030
Ph: (516)562-5000   Fax: (516)562-7830
URL: http://www.austingdc.net

Annual. Primary Exhibits: Three days of conference content, two days of exhibits, the Game Career Seminar, and industry-defining keynote speakers.

★12755★ E3 Media & Business Summit
Entertainment Software Association
575 7th St. NW
Ste. 300
Washington, DC 20004
Ph: (202)223-2400
E-mail: dhewitt@theesa.com

Annual. Primary Exhibits: Suite-based meetings for those in the video gaming industry, as well as video game demonstrations and panel discussions.

★12756★ Game Careers Seminar
CMP Game Group
600 Community Dr.
Manhasset, NY 11030
Ph: (516)562-5000   Fax: (516)562-7830
URL: http://www.cmpgame.com/events/ga-

mecareerseminar.html

Annual. Primary Exhibits: Several mini-conferences for those who are interested in getting a job in the video game industry includes networking opportunities, lessons in how to get a jumpstart in the field and keynote speakers willing to share their insights as professionals working in the industry.

★12757★ Game Developers Choice Awards
CMP Game Group
600 Community Dr.
Manhasset, NY 11030
Ph: (516)562-5000   Fax: (516)562-7830
URL: http://www.cmpgame.com/events/gdchoice.html

Annual. Primary Exhibits: Networking event seeks to recognize those in the video game design industry who are driving innovation providing a forum in which video game designers can share information thus moving the field forward.

★12758★ Game Developers Conference
CMP Game Group
600 Community Dr.
Manhasset, NY 11030
Ph: (516)562-5000
E-mail: jmoledina@cmp.com
URL: http://www.gdconf.com

Annual. Primary Exhibits: Keynote speakers highlight the most up-to-date topics facing game industry professionals.

★12759★ Game Developers Conference Mobile
CMP Game Group
600 Community Dr.
Manhasset, NY 11030
Ph: (516)562-5000   Fax: (516)562-7830
URL: http://www.cmpgame.com/events/gdcmobile.html

Annual. Primary Exhibits: Networking opportunity for the next generation of mobile video game designers includes keynote speakers and demonstrations.

★12760★ Game Developers Conference Prime
CMP Game Group
600 Community Dr.
Manhasset, NY 11030
Ph: (516)562-5000   Fax: (516)562-7830
URL: http://www.gdcprime.com

Annual. Primary Exhibits: Exclusive networking event for executives in the video game industry which seeks to identify solutions on how to improve the industry and drive innovations.

★12761★ Independent Games Festival
CMP Game Group
600 Community Dr.
Manhasset, NY 11030
Ph: (516)562-5000   Fax: (516)562-7830

URL: http://www.cmpgame.com/events/igf.html

Annual. Primary Exhibits: Networking opportunity for video game industry professionals that recognizes leaders within the field and serves as a forum in which to bring fresh new talent and groundbreaking material into the industry.

★12762★ The Interactive Achievement Awards
The Academy of Interactive Arts and Sciences
23622 Calabasas Rd., Ste. 220
Calabasas, CA 91302
Ph: (818)876-0826   Fax: (818)876-0850
E-mail: geri@interactive.org
URL: http://www.interactive.org

Annual. Primary Exhibits: Networking event aims to honor those video game developers and publishers who continue to move the industry forward with their talent and passion.

OTHER SOURCES

★12763★ CMP Game Group
600 Community Dr.
Manhasset, NY 11030
Ph: (516)562-5000   Fax: (516)562-7830
E-mail: cmp@cmp.com
URL: http://www.cmpgame.com

Provides a definitive source for reaching game industry professionals through a host of resources.

★12764★ Entertainment Software Association
575 7th St. NW
Ste. 300
Washington, DC 20004
E-mail: esa@theesa.com
URL: http://www.theesa.com

Dedicated to serving the needs of video game designers and developers through business and consumer research, government relations, an anti-piracy program, and a number of other resources provided to members.

★12765★ Game Career Guide
CMP Media LLC
600 Community Dr.
Manhasset, NY 11030
Ph: (516)562-5000   Fax: (516)562-7830
URL: http://www.cmpgame.com/print/careerguide.html

Annual. Important resource that gives students, recent graduates, and experienced professionals resources on ways to update their skillsets and take control of their careers.

★12766★ Game Developer Magazine

CMP Media LLC
600 Community Dr.
Manhasset, NY 11030
Ph: (516)562-5000   Fax: (516)562-7830
URL: http://www.cmpgame.com/print/gdmag.html

Monthly. Valuable reference for those looking to begin a career in the video game industry as well as professionals already in the field which includes strategies for creating innovative and successful video games as well as resources for getting a job.

★12767★ GameDaily Biz Newsletter

75 Rockefeller Plaza, 5th Fl.
New York, NY 10019
E-mail: libe.goad@corp.aol.com
URL: http://biz.gamedaily.com/

Daily. Newsletter provides both aspiring video game designers and professionals already working in the field resources and current news concerning the industry.

★12768★ Georgia Game Developers Association

5900 Sugarloaf Pkwy., Ste. 443
Lawrenceville, GA 30043
URL: http://www.ggda.org

Seeks to elevate the local video game industry by fostering relationships, providing vital resources to video game designers and other industry figures, representing concerns of the industry on issues appearing before Georgia lawmakers, and promoting aware-ness of the region's talented game developers to foster further economic growth and development within the region. Membership levels range in price.

★12769★ Georgia Interactive

Georgia Game Developers Association
5900 Sugarloaf Pkwy., Ste. 443
Lawrenceville, GA 30043
URL: http://www.ggda.org

Newsletter published by Georgia Game Developers Association provides pertinent information to professionals in the video game industry as well as to those who are looking for employment as video game designers.

★12770★ International Game Developers Association

19 Mantua Rd.
Mount Royal, NJ 08061
Ph: (856)423-2990   Fax: (856)423-3420
E-mail: contact@igda.org
URL: http://www.igda.org/

Seeks to advance the careers and enhance the lives of game developers through peer networking, promoting professional development, and advocating on issues affecting the developer community. Membership of 15,021 individuals includes programmers, designers, artists, producers and other development professions in the gaming industry.

★12771★ International Simulation and Gaming Association (ISAGA)

George Washington University
School of Business and Public Mgt.
Monroe Hall
Washington, DC 20052
Ph: (202)994-6918
E-mail: lobuts@gwu.edu
URL: http://www.isaga.info

Description: Individuals interested in any facet of simulation and gaming. Maintains resource lists; conducts specialized education; sponsors workshops, symposia, and research activities.

★12772★ North American Simulation and Gaming Association (NASAGA)

PO Box 78636
Indianapolis, IN 46278
Ph: (317)387-1424   Fax: (317)387-1921
Fr: 888-432-GAME
E-mail: info@nasaga.org
URL: http://www.nasaga.org

Description: Teachers, trainers, media specialists, faculty, and researchers in various disciplines. Seeks to promote training of specialists in the field of simulation and gaming; facilitate communication between these specialists, policymakers, students, and others; promote the development of better techniques in the field of simulation and gaming. Provides referrals to simulation-gaming consultants; maintains speakers' bureau and gaming archives. (Gaming is the application of experimental techniques to simulated conditions, especially for training or testing purposes.)

Vintners

★12773★ **Agricultural Technology Information Network**
2910 E Barstow Ave., MS 115
Fresno, CA 93740
Ph: (559)278-4872   Fax: (559)278-7753
E-mail: atimgr@atinet.org
URL: http://www.atinet.org

Listing of agricultural jobs for students and professionals, particularly those in the wine industry.

★12774★ **American Sommelier Association**
580 Broadway, Ste. 716
New York, NY 10012
Ph: (212)226-6805   Fax: (212)226-6407
E-mail: office@americansommelier.org
URL: http://www.americansommelier.com/

Provides certification courses and support to members as well as the American sommelier industry; also includes a list of job postings for professionals in the wine industry.

★12775★ **American Wine Society Journal**
American Wine Society
113 S Perry St.
Lawrenceville, GA 30045
Ph: (678)377-7070   Fax: (678)377-7005
E-mail: editor@mngolf.org
URL: http://www.americanwinesociety.com/

Quarterly. $4.00 for single issue; $57.00/year for individuals, individual or couple membership annual dues; $80.00/year for individuals, professional membership; $600.00/year for individuals, senior citizen 60 and over lifetime membership. Wine magazine.

★12776★ **Court of Master Sommeliers**
PO Box 6170
Napa, CA 94581
Ph: (707)255-5056

E-mail: klewis@mastersommeliers.org
URL: http://www.mastersommeliers.org

Educational program offers The Master Sommelier diploma, the highest distinction a professional can attain in fine wine and beverage service; also includes a list of job postings for professionals in the wine industry.

★12777★ **Department of Viticulture & Enology, University of California**
1 Shields Ave.
Davis, CA 95616
Ph: (530)752-0380   Fax: (530)752-0382
URL: http://wineserver.ucdavis.edu/

Website includes a listing of jobs in the grape growing and winemaking industries.

★12778★ **Grape Times**
Florida Grape Growers Association
111 Yelvington Rd., Ste. 1
East Palatka, FL 32131
Ph: (386)329-0318   Fax: (386)329-1262

Bimonthly. Magazine for wine enthusiasts and those working in wineyards and wineries.

★12779★ **New England Wine Gazette**
Recorder Publishing Company Inc.
17-19 Morristown Rd.
PO Box 687
Bernardsville, NJ 07924
Ph: (908)766-3900   Fax: (908)766-6365

Quarterly. $10.00/year for individuals. Newspaper covering wine and the wine industry in New England.

★12780★ **Restaurant Wine**
TasteTour Publications
306 Randolph St.
PO Box 222
Napa, CA 94559
Ph: (707)224-4777   Fax: (707)224-6740
E-mail: info@restaurantwine.com
URL: http://www.restarantwine.com/

Monthly. $109.00/per year for individuals. Magazine covers wine trends, winery pro-

files, tips for training wine staff, reviews, and other resources concerning the wine industry; also includes annual issues such as the Smart Business Issue and The USA Wine Market On-Premise Issue.

★12781★ **Richard Cartiere's Wine Market Report**
Richard Cartiere Publishing LLC
PO Box 641
Calistoga, CA 94515
Ph: (707)942-5044   Fax: (707)581-1770
E-mail: barbjen-nings@winemarketreport.com
URL: http://www.winemarketreport.com/

Biweekly. $345.00/year for individuals. Newsletter covers the United State's wine market and issues of interest to United States vintners abroad as well as additional information pertaining to winemakers.

★12782★ **Wine Business Insider**
Wine Communications Group
110 W Napa St.
Sonoma, CA 95476
Ph: (707)939-0822   Fax: (707)939-0833
E-mail: info@winebusiness.com
URL: http://www.winebusiness.com

Weekly. $295.00/year for individuals. Analyzes the week's top stories pertaining to the winemaking industry including key personnel changes, mergers and acquisitions, production and harvest reports, retail numbers and bulk wine and grape prices.

★12783★ **Wine Business Monthly**
Wine Communications Group
110 W Napa St.
Sonoma, CA 95476
Ph: (707)939-0822   Fax: (707)939-0833
E-mail: info@winebusiness.com
URL: http://www.winebusiness.com

Monthly. $39.00/year for individuals; $49.00/year for Canadian subscriptions; $89.00 for other countries. Magazine provides up-to-date information to growers, wineries, suppliers and distributors about the latest trends and developments in the global business of making wine; also covers the best practices and new products as they pertain to grape growing, winemaking, marketing, sales, finance and business administration.

★12784★ Wine Business Program, Sonoma State University

1801 E Catati Ave.
Rohnert Park, CA 94928
Ph: (707)664-2260
E-mail: winebiz@sonoma.edu
URL: http://www.sonoma.edu/winebiz/

Located within the university's School of Business & Economics, Sonoma State's Wine Business Program is the first and only in the United States to focus exclusively on the business aspects of the wine industry. Website includes listing of internships and industry employment.

★12785★ Wine East

L & H Photojournalism
620 N Pine St.
Lancaster, PA 17603
Ph: (717)393-0943
E-mail: editor@wineeast.com

Bimonthly. Trade magazine covering the wine industry east of the Rocky Mountains.

★12786★ Wine East-News of Grapes and Wine in Eastern North America

Wine East
620 N Pine St.
Lancaster, PA 17601
Ph: (717)393-0943　　Fax: (717)393-7398
E-mail: info@wineeast.com
URL: http://www.wineeast.com

$25.00/year for individuals; $35.00/year for Canada and Mexico; $40.00/year for international. Bi-monthly trade publication provides news and information concerning the Northeastern American wine industry.

★12787★ Wine Enthusiast Magazine

Wine Enthusiast Co.
103 Fairview Pk. Dr.
Elmsford, NY 10523
Ph: (914)345-8463
URL: http://www.winemag.com

$29.95/year for individuals; $49.95 for two years, individuals; $69.95 for three years, individuals; $49.95/year for Canada; $79.95/year for institutions, U.S. and international. Magazine reporting news on wines and spirits; includes profiles of industry leaders from around the world as well as a consumer wine report.

★12788★ Wine Spectator

M. Shanken Communications Inc.
387 Park Ave. S
New York, NY 10016
Ph: (212)684-4224
URL: http://www.winespectator.com

$50.00/year for individuals, online; $80.00 for two years, online; $80.00/year for Canada; $135.00 for two years, in Canada; $145.00/year for other countries, air mail;

$250.00/year for other countries, two years. Lifestyle Magazine for the wine consumer.

★12789★ Wine & Spirits Magazine

Wine & Spirits Magazine Inc.
2 W 32nd St., Ste. 601
New York, NY 10001
Ph: (212)695-4660
E-mail: winespir@aol.com
URL: http://www.wineandspiritsmagazine.com

Monthly. $26.00/year for individuals; $45.00 for two years; $36.00/year for Canada and Mexico; $55.00/year for Canada and Mexico, two years. Magazine containing consumer buying information on wine and spirits with in-depth articles on regions and trends in food and wine.

★12790★ WineJobs.com Daily Email Alert

Wine Communications Group
110 W Napa St.
Sonoma, CA 95476
Ph: (707)939-0822　　Fax: (707)939-0833
E-mail: info@winebusiness.com
URL: http://winebusiness.com/services/wj_emailalerts.cfm

Provides the latest job listings for all sectors of the winemaking industry including finance, winemaking and production, vineyards, sales and marketing, information systems, hospitality and retail, human resources and general administration.

★12791★ Wines & Vines

Hiaring Co.
1800 Lincoln Ave.
San Rafael, CA 94901-1298
Ph: (415)453-9700　　Fax: (415)453-2517
URL: http://www.winesandvines.com

Monthly. $32.50/year for individuals; $50.00/year for out of country. Periodical on wine industry.

PLACEMENT AND JOB REFERRAL SERVICES

★12792★ Automated Recruiter

WineAndHospitalityJobs.com
640 Michael Dr.
Sonoma, CA 95476
URL: http://www.wineandhospitalityjobs.com/

Free email newsletter which notifies subscribers with new wine and hospitality job positions that closely match the job skills and interests listed by the subscriber.

★12793★ WineAmerica

1212 New York Ave., Ste. 425
Washington, DC 20005
Ph: (202)783-2756

URL: http://www.wineamerica.org

Seeks to encourage the dynamic development and growth of American wineries and winegrowing through the advancement and advocacy of sound public policy; also provides membership services to assist wineries with a variety of business operations including job referral services.

EMPLOYER DIRECTORIES AND NETWORKING LISTS

★12794★ All American Wineries

PO Box 189
Pinnacle, NC 27043
E-mail: bobh007@cpvsvcs.com
URL: http://www.allamericanwineries.com/

Directory of wineries, vineyards, events and guides associated with the wine industry. Also includes information concerning wineries and the law, feedback about wineries featured in the directory and other resources.

★12795★ American Society for Enology and Viticulture-Membership Directory Issue

American Society for Enology and Viticulture
PO Box 1855
Davis, CA 95617-1855
Ph: (530)753-3142　　Fax: (530)753-3318
URL: http://www.asev.org

Approximately annual, latest edition 2000. for members. Publication includes: List of 2,500 member vineyard and winery owners, technicians, academicians interested in enology and viticulture, and agricultural advisors. Entries include: Name, membership classification, address. Arrangement: Alphabetical.

★12796★ The California Directory of Fine Wineries

Ten Speed Press
PO Box 7123
Berkeley, CA 94707
Ph: (510)559-1600　　Fax: (510)559-1629
E-mail: info@tenspeed.com
URL: http://www.tenspeed.com

Marty Olmstead, Tom Silberkleit and Robert Holmes. Third edition, 2006. $19.95. 142 pages. Directory includes Northern California wineries.

★12797★ The Complete Handbook of Winemaking

American Wine Society
113 S Perry St.
Lawrenceville, GA 30045
Ph: (678)377-7070　　Fax: (678)377-7005

Annual, September. $17.50 for individuals. Covers suppliers of juice, other products, equipment, and services for wine and beer making; publishers who have books, pamphlets, and textbooks on the process; colleges and universities offering courses in viticulture and enology. Entries include: For suppliers and publishers–Name, address, phone; product, service, or title of publication. For colleges and universities–Name, address, and phone.

★12798★ **East Coast Wineries**

Rutgers University Press
100 Joyce Kilmer Ave.
Piscataway, NJ 08854-8099
Ph: (732)445-7762 Fax: (732)445-7039
Fr: 800-446-9323
URL: http://rutgerspress.rutgers.edu/acatalog/__East_Coast_Wineri

Latest edition 2004. $21.95 for individuals. Covers nearly 300 wineries in the northeast coastal states of the United States (Connecticut, Delaware, Maine, Maryland, Massachusetts, New Hampshire, New Jersey, New York, Pennsylvania, Rhode Island, Vermont, Virginia, West Virginia). Entries include: Name, address, phone, brief history, list of wines offered with recommended buys, directions, and hours of operation. Also includes list of annual wine festivals and other special events.

★12799★ **LocalWineEvents.com**

2042 Gen. Alexander Dr.
Malvern, PA 19355
Ph: (610)647-4888
E-mail: info@localwineevents.com
URL: http://www.localwineevents.com

Online directory and events calendar for the wine industry.

★12800★ **The Oxford Companion to the Wines of North America**

Facts On File Inc.
132 W 31st St., 17th Fl.
New York, NY 10001
Ph: (212)967-8800 Fax: 800-678-3633
Fr: 800-322-8755
URL: http://www.lisaekus.com

Latest edition November 2000. Publication includes: Organizations and people associated with wineries in North America. Principal content of publication is encyclopedic information about wine. Indexes: Comprehensive index listing U.S. wine licensees, American Viticultural Areas, people, and techniques mentioned in the text.

★12801★ **Pennsylvania Wineries**

5067 Ritter Rd.
Mechanicsburg, PA 17055
Fax: (717)796-0412 Fr: 800-732-3669
E-mail: kweaver@stackpolebooks.com
URL: http://www.stackpolebooks.com/cgi-bin/stackpolebooks.storefront

Linda Jones McKee and Richard Carey. 2000. $19.95. 182 pages. Directory of wineries in Pennsylvania includes contact information, types of wine available, best-selling wines, hours and directions.

★12802★ **Pocket Encyclopedia of American Wine East of the Rockies**

Wine Appreciation Guild Ltd.
360 Swift Ave., Unit 30-40
South San Francisco, CA 94080
Ph: (650)866-3020 Fax: (650)866-3513
Fr: 800-231-9463
E-mail: shannon@wineappreciation.com
URL: http://www.wineappreciation.com

Biennial, even years. Covers more than 300 wineries in 24 states east of the continental divide. Entries include: Name of winery, address, phone, key personnel, wines produced, history. Arrangement: Alphabetical. Indexes: By state and by winery names.

★12803★ **Sonoma**

Chronicle Books L.L.C.
680 Second St.
San Francisco, CA 94107
Ph: (415)537-4200 Fax: (415)537-4460
Fr: 800-722-6657
URL: http://www.chroniclebooks.com

Published in February 2005. $19.95 for individuals. Covers 25 wineries throughout Sonoma county, California. Entries include: In-depth descriptions.

★12804★ **Uncork New York**

New York Wine and Grape Foundation
800 S Main St., Ste. 200
Canandaigua, NY 14424
Ph: (585)394-3620 Fax: (585)394-3649
E-mail: uncork@nywine.com
URL: http://www.newyorkwines.org

Annual, May. Covers over 120 wineries in New York state. Entries include: Winery name, address, phone. Arrangement: Geographical.

★12805★ **Vineyard & Winery Management-Directory Product Guide Issue**

Vineyard & Winery Management
PO Box 231
Watkins Glen, NY 14891-0231
Ph: (607)535-7133 Fax: (607)535-2998
Fr: 800-573-9192
URL: http://www.vwm-online.com

Annual, Latest edition 2007. $95.00 for individuals. Publication includes: List of about 1,000 grape growers and wine producers and processors in the U.S. and Canada; list of 950 suppliers of equipment, products, and services to the wine and grapegrowing industry; list of 27 wine competitions in the U.S. and Europe. Entries include: For growers and wine producers and processors–Name, address, phone, fax, names and titles of key personnel, description of products or services. For suppliers–Name, address, phone, fax, telex, name and title of contact, products and services. For competitions–Company name, address, phone, fax, names and titles of key personnel, geographical area served. Incorporates information from "Vineyard & Winery Management–Industry Directory Issue" and "Goldwyn's Directory of Wine Judgings,"

which have been discontinued. Arrangement: Geographical.

★12806★ **Virginia Wineries Festival and Tour Guide**

Virginia Department of Agriculture and Consumer Services
102 Governor St.
PO Box 1163
Richmond, VA 23219
Ph: (804)786-2373 Fax: (804)371-6079
URL: http://www.virginiawines.org

Annual, January 2003. Free. Covers 100 wineries in Virginia that are open for tours, passport to Virginia Wineries Program, festivals and events. Entries include: Winery name, address, phone, winery description, URL, directions, tour hours. Wine festivals, special events, dates, times, contact information. Arrangement: Regional. Indexes: Alphabetical.

★12807★ **Welcome to Tennessee Wine Country**

Market Development Div.
440 Hogan Rd.
PO Box 40627, Melrose Sta.
Nashville, TN 37220-9029
Ph: (615)837-5160 Fax: (615)837-5194
Fr: 800-342-8206
URL: http://www.tennesseewines.com

Latest edition March 1999. Free. Publication includes: List of approximately 17 wineries in Tennessee. Entries include: Company name, address, phone, location, hours of operation, products.

★12808★ **Wine Industry Index**

Vineyards & Winery Management, Inc.
3883 Airway Dr., Ste. 250
Santa Rosa, CA 95403
Ph: (707)577-7700 Fax: (707)577-7705
Fr: 800-535-5670
URL: http://www.vwm-online.com/

$95.00. Reference guide includes: wineries in the United States and Canada; vineyard and winery suppliers, products and services; North American Winery and Grower Associations; viticultural areas within the United States and Canada; wine competitions; regulatory office listings; wine industry universities, research centers and faculty and listings of trade shows, seminars and workshops.

★12809★ **Wine Industry Index CD**

Vineyards & Winery Management, Inc.
3883 Airway Dr., Ste. 250
Santa Rosa, CA 95403
Ph: (707)577-7700 Fax: (707)577-7705
Fr: 800-535-5670
URL: http://www.vwm-online.com/

CD. $595.00 (includes free Wine Industry Index book). Reference of wineries includes search categories by city, state, zip code, appellation, acres, grapes grown, gallons produced, varietals produced and more.

★12810★ The Wine Tours Project

PO Box 625
Troy, NY 12180
E-mail: sales@wine-tours.com
URL: http://www.wine-tours.com/wine-main.html

Covers more than 7,000 wine-related businesses. Entries include: business name, address, available Web and email address as well as phone and fax numbers.

★12811★ WineLinx.com

PO Box 5365
Scottsdale, AZ 85261
URL: http://alaquips.com/winelinx.htm

Online global directory covers wineries, vineyards, vintners, wine books and provides additional links related to wine and winemaking.

★12812★ Wines and Vines-Annual Directory/Buyer's Guide

Hiaring Co.
1800 Lincoln Ave.
San Rafael, CA 94901-1298
Ph: (415)453-9700   Fax: (415)453-2517
E-mail: geninfo@winesandvines.com

Annual, June. Publication includes: List of wineries and industry suppliers in the United States, Canada, and Mexico. Entries include: For wineries–Company name, address, phone, fax; names of principal executives; trade and brand names; types of wines made; date founded; storage, fermenting, and bottling capacity; area served; vineyard acreage; bonded premises types and number; top varietals, annual casegoods production. For suppliers–Company name, address, phone, products, representatives' names, maps of wine regions. Arrangement: Wineries are geographical; suppliers are alphabetical and classified by category. Indexes: Winery name, supplier product, brand name.

HANDBOOKS AND MANUALS

★12813★ The Business of Wine: Industry Insiders on the Production & Delivery of a Premium Product from Vine to Table

Aspatore Books
400 Commonwealth Ave., 2nd Fl.
Boston, MA 02215
Fax: (617)249-0219   Fr: (866)277-2867
E-mail:
west.customer.service@thomson.com
URL: http://www.aspatore.com

Thomas B. Selfridge, Paul Dolan, Brooks Firestone, Daniel Duckhorn and Patrick Duffeler. 2004. $27.95. 76 pages. Provides a comprehensive overview of the current shape and future state of the wine industry. Discusses wine trends and changes, successful marketing strategies, the role of retailers and distributors, building a reputa-

tion and other critical points wine industry professionals as well as potential workers need to understand.

★12814★ Introduction to Wine Laboratory Practices and Procedures

Springer Publishing Company
11 W 42nd St., 15th Fl.
New York, NY 10036
Fr: 877-687-7476
E-mail: contactus@springerpub.com
URL: http://www.springerpub.com/

Jean L. Jacobson. 2005. $69.95. 382 pages. Provides a step-by-step guide on performing routine and essential winemaking duties for small and large wineries, entry level chemists and enologists, students and professionals in the wine industry.

★12815★ Knowing and Making Wine

Wiley-Interscience
111 River St.
Hoboken, NJ 07030
Ph: (201)748-6000   Fax: (201)748-6088
URL: http://www3.interscience.wiley.com/cgi-bin/home?CRETRY=1&SRETRY=0

Emile Peynaud and Alan F. Spencer. 1984. $110.00. 416 pages. Provides a complete survey of winemaking techniques and wine appreciation for the student or professional who needs to solve the problems which arise in the winemaking industry.

★12816★ Principles and Practices of Winemaking

Springer Publishing Company
11 W 42nd St., 15th Fl.
New York, NY 10036
Fr: 877-687-7476
E-mail: contactus@springerpub.com
URL: http://www.springerpub.com/

Roger B. Boulton, Vernon L. Singleton, Linda F. Bisson and Ralph E. Kunkee. 1996. $147.00. 604 pages. Complete reference guide to winemaking for both students and professionals.

★12817★ The Science of Wine: From Vine to Glass

University of California Press
2120 Berkeley Way
Berkeley, CA 94704
Ph: (510)642-4247   Fax: (510)643-7127
E-mail: askucp@ucpress.edu
URL: http://www.ucpress.edu/

Jamie Goode. 2006. $34.95. 216 pages. Provides a comprehensive overview of current scientific and technological innovations that are now influencing how grapes are grown and how wine is made. Students, winemakers, wine professionals and those looking to get into the industry will find this a valuable reference book.

★12818★ Spinning the Bottle

Wine Appreciation Guild
360 Swift Ave., Unit 30-40
South San Francisco, CA 94080
Ph: (650)866-3020   Fr: 800-231-9463
E-mail: info@wineappreciation.com
URL: http://www.wineappreciation.com

Harvey Posert. 2004. $39.95. 224 pages. Collection of guidelines and case studies for promoting wine, wine companies and wine-related issues, is as relevant to the student of wine and marketing as it is to the seasoned executive or winery owner.

★12819★ Successful Wine Marketing

Springer Publishing Company
11 W 42nd St., 15th Fl.
New York, NY 10036
Fr: 877-687-7476
E-mail: contactus@springerpub.com
URL: http://www.springerpub.com/

James Lapsley and Kirby Moulton. 2001. $115.00. 307 pages. Covers the logistics, principles and strategies of wine marketing and sales. Provides resources, tips and information useful to students, small and large wineries, wine consultants and distributors and others looking to enter the field of winemaking.

★12820★ Wine Analysis & Production

Springer Publishing Company
11 W 42nd St., 15th Fl.
New York, NY 10036
Fr: 877-687-7476
E-mail: contactus@springerpub.com
URL: http://www.springerpub.com/

Bruce Zoecklein, Kenneth C. Fegelsang and Barry H. Gump. Second edition, 1995. $139.00. 621 pages. Provides practical information on wine analysis and production and is an essential resource for those looking for a job in the wine industry as well as laboratory personnel and winemakers already working in the business.

★12821★ Wine People

Vendome Press
1334 York Ave.
New York, NY 10021

Stephen Brook. 2001. $27.50. 189 pages. Provides information about individuals involved in all aspects of wine production.

★12822★ Winery Technology and Operations: A Handbook for Small Wineries

Wine Appreciation Guild
360 Swift Ave., Unit 30-40
South San Francisco, CA 94080
Ph: (650)866-3020   Fr: 800-231-9463
E-mail: info@wineappreciation.com
URL: http://www.wineappreciation.com

Yair Margalit. 1990. $29.95. 224 pages. Valuable reference for student winemakers, small commercial wineries, and for those looking for a job in the wine industry.

★12823★ Women of Wine

University of California Press
2120 Berkeley Way
Berkeley, CA 94704
Ph: (510)642-4247   Fax: (510)643-7127
E-mail: askucp@ucpress.edu
URL: http://www.ucpress.edu/

Ann B. Matasar. 2006. $24.95. 265 pages. Discusses the role of women in the wine industry and covers such issues of importance for women looking to work in the field such as mentorship, networking, education, corporate life and risk taking.

★12824★ The Wrath of Grapes: The Coming Wine Industry Shakeout and How to Take Advantage of It

Avon Books, Inc.
1350 Avenue of the Americas
New York, NY 10019
Ph: (212)207-7000
URL: http://www.harpercollins.com/imprints/index.aspx?imprintid=517994

Lewis Perdue. 1999. $13.50. 272 pages. Focuses on the business aspect of the wine industry; an invaluable resource for anyone already working in the wine industry and those looking for a job in the field of winemaking.

EMPLOYMENT AGENCIES AND SEARCH FIRMS

★12825★ Produce Careers Inc.

122 LePoint St., Ste. 202
Arroyo Grande, CA 93420
Ph: (805)481-3200   Fax: (805)481-3545
E-mail: support@producecareers.com
URL: http://www.producecareers.com

Employment agency and executive search firm.

ONLINE JOB SOURCES AND SERVICES

★12826★ Hospitality Link

866 SE 14th Terr., Ste. 128
Deerfield Beach, FL 33441
Ph: (954)579-1802   Fax: (954)421-1046
E-mail: sales@hospitalitylink.com
URL: http://www.hospitalitylink.com/

Online job site for the wine and hospitality industry.

★12827★ Juju Job Search Engine

151 1st Ave., No. 19
New York, NY 10003
Ph: (514)891-6283   Fax: (514)891-0679
E-mail: administrator@juju.com
URL: http://www.job-search-engine.com/

jobs?k=winemaking

Online listing of jobs, particularly those in the wine industry.

★12828★ Michigan Wines

Michigan Grape and Wine Industry
  Council
PO Box 30017
Lansing, MI 48909
Ph: (517)241-4468
E-mail: mda-michigan-wines@michigan.gov
URL: http://www.michiganwines.com

Online resource provides a directory of Michigan wineries, listings of meetings and events, articles, newsletters, and additional resources concerning the wine industry in Michigan.

★12829★ OregonWines.com

Canvas Dreams LLC
12725 SW Millikan Way, Ste. 300
Beaverton, OR 97005
URL: http://www.oregonwines.com

Online resource provides job postings, a directory of Oregon wineries, an events calendar, news concerning the wine industry and editorials.

★12830★ Professional Friends of Wine

642 W Harvard
Fresno, CA 93705
Ph: (559)225-4051
E-mail: jimlamar@winepros.org
URL: http://winepros.org

Online resource providing wine education, wine information and wine training as well as a directory of wineries and an events calendar.

★12831★ Squire Partners LLC: WineSquire.com

PO Box 70135
Bellevue, WA 98005
Ph: (425)641-7764   Fax: (425)653-5991
E-mail: scottmi@msn.com
URL: http://www.winesquire.com

Online resource provides job listings for the wine industry as well as directories, links, event listings and articles.

★12832★ Vault Inc.

150 W 22nd St., 5th Fl.
New York, NY 10011
Ph: (212)366-4212
URL: http://www.vault.com

Online resource provides job listings, particularly for the food and wine industry.

★12833★ Virginia Wines

Virginia Wine Marketing Office
1001 E Broad St., Ste. 140
Richmond, VA 23219
Ph: (804)344-8200   Fax: (804)344-8332
E-mail: info@virginiawine.org
URL: http://www.virginiawines.org/

Online guide dedicated to Virginia wines provides information and a directory of the region's wineries, an event calendar, current news concerning the region's winemakers, and other resources.

★12834★ Voice of the Vine

Washington State University
PO Box 646414
Pullman, WA 99164
Ph: (509)335-9502
E-mail: Hendrix@wsu.edu
URL: http://winegrapes.wsu.edu/

Biweekly. Free. Provides current news concerning Washington's wine industry as well as profiles of researchers, students and alumni working in the field.

★12835★ Wine Business Daily News

Wine Communications Group
110 W Napa St.
Sonoma, CA 95476
Ph: (707)939-0822   Fax: (707)939-0833
E-mail: info@winebusiness.com
URL: http://www.winebusiness.com/company/

Daily. Free. Emailed newsletter covers the top stories concerning the winemaking industry.

★12836★ Wine Business.com

Wine Communications Group
110 W Napa St.
Sonoma, CA 95476
Ph: (707)939-0822   Fax: (707)939-0833
E-mail: info@winebusiness.com
URL: http://www.winebusiness.com

Resource includes information about the business and technology of winemaking as well as classified ads and listings of jobs in the wine industry.

★12837★ Wine Events Calendar

PO Box 26280
San Jose, CA 95159
E-mail: events@wineevents-calendar.com
URL: http://www.wineevents-calendar.com

Online directory of regional wine events, classes, wine tastings, and other networking opportunities and resources also includes ratings, reviews and editorials concerning the wine industry.

★12838★ Wine and Spirits Jobs

PO Box 22
Mokena, IL 60448
Fr: (866)975-4473
E-mail: info@wineandspirits.com
URL: http://www.wineandspiritsjobs.com

Online resource lists jobs in the wine industry. Also encourages job seekers to post their resumes.

★12839★ WineAndHospitalityJobs.com

640 Michael Dr.
Sonoma, CA 95476
E-mail: margieotl@aol.com
URL: http://
www.wineandhospitalityjobs.com/

Online resource for both job seekers looking for work in the wine industry and employers from the wine industry in need of help. Website also includes articles, industry news, forums and other information concerning the industry and encourages job seekers to post their resumes.

★12840★ WineCountry.com

Freerun Technologies Inc.
570 Gateway Dr.
Napa, CA 94558
Ph: (707)265-1835   Fax: (707)265-1840
URL: http://www.winecountry.com

Online resource provides interviews and profiles of leading winemakers and wine professionals across the country as well as information about the business of wine; also includes message boards, an event calendar and a directory of wineries throughout the country.

★12841★ WineJobs.com

Wine Communications Group
110 W Napa St.
Sonoma, CA 95476
Ph: (707)939-0822   Fax: (707)939-0833
E-mail: info@winebusiness.com
URL: http://winebusiness.com/services

Online resource for the wine industry includes classified ads for used equipment, real estate, grapes and bulk wine, and is also the industry's leading online job site.

TRADESHOWS

★12842★ Boston Wine Expo

Resource Plus and Event Management
  International, Inc.
200 Seaport Blvd., Ste. 125
Boston, MA 02210
Ph: (617)385-5088   Fax: (617)385-5166
Fr: 800-544-1898
URL: http://www.resource-plus.com

Annual. **Primary Exhibits:** Wineries, fine foods, and wine-related products.

★12843★ Direct to Consumer Symposium

Coalition for Free Trade
PO Box 4277
Napa, CA 94558
URL: http://www.coalitionforfreetrade.org/symposium/

Annual. Primary Exhibits: Sessions about direct marketing and sales which include: consumer research findings about who is buying; starting a winning direct marketing program; food and wine marketing to increase sales; direct to consumer legislation and enforcement; lessons from those in the winery industry; telemarketing; tactics to increase mailing lists; shipping updates for various states; tips on building a successful wine club. Dates and Location: 2008 May 1-2; Napa, CA.

★12844★ Fifth Annual African American Wine Tasting Festival

Association of African American Vintners
1083 Vine St., No. 237
Healdsburg, CA 95448
Ph: (707)529-5955
E-mail: info@aaavintners.org
URL: http://www.aaavintners.org/news.html

Annual. Primary Exhibits: Networking opportunity aims to celebrate sommeliers, African American women in wine, winemakers and winery owners. Sessions include advice from California's leading African American vintners, growers and winemakers.

★12845★ From Bottle to Glass

The Ohio Wine Producers Association
33 Tegam Way
Geneva, OH 44041
Ph: (440)466-4417   Fax: (440)466-4427
E-mail: dwinchell@ohiowines.org
URL: http://www.ohiowines.org

Annual. Primary Exhibits: Sessions targeting winery tasting room staff wanting to improve sales, newbees looking to get into the wine business, decision makers planning the future of a winery's marketing program and winery owners.

★12846★ Managing the Winery Laboratory Seminar

Vineyards & Winery Management, Inc.
3883 Airway Dr., Ste. 250
Santa Rosa, CA 95403
Ph: (707)577-7700   Fax: (707)577-7705
Fr: 800-535-5670
URL: http://www.vwm-online.com/

Annual. Primary Exhibits: Networking and educational opportunity presents new technologies vital to running a successful lab as well as information pertaining to such issues as obtaining TTB certification or ISO accreditation.

★12847★ Tasting Room Profitability Conference & Trade Show

Vineyards & Winery Management, Inc.
3883 Airway Dr., Ste. 250
Santa Rosa, CA 95403
Ph: (707)577-7700   Fax: (707)577-7705
Fr: 800-535-5670
URL: http://www.vwm-online.com/

Annual. Primary Exhibits: Networking opportunity for wine industry and hospitality management professionals includes sessions by experts and an extensive array of merchandise.

★12848★ Telluride Wine Festival

Commission for Community Assistance,
  Arts & Special Events
113 W Columbia Ave.
Telluride, CO 81435
Ph: (970)728-3071
E-mail: info@telluridewinefestival.com
URL: http://www.telluridewinefestival.com

Annual. Primary Exhibits: Educational programs to increase awareness, interest and understanding of the new and developing aspects of wine and food production, preparation and consumption.

★12849★ Wine Club Summit

Vineyards & Winery Management, Inc.
3883 Airway Dr., Ste. 250
Santa Rosa, CA 95403
Ph: (707)577-7700   Fax: (707)577-7705
Fr: 800-535-5670
URL: http://www.vwm-online.com/

Annual. Primary Exhibits: Networking opportunity for wine industry professionals.

★12850★ Wineries Unlimited

Vineyards & Winery Management, Inc.
3883 Airway Dr., Ste. 250
Santa Rosa, CA 95403
Ph: (707)577-7700   Fax: (707)577-7705
Fr: 800-535-5670
URL: http://www.vwm-online.com/

Annual. Primary Exhibits: Networking opportunity includes expanded sessions on enology, viticulture, finance, management and marketing. Date and Location: 2008 March 4-7; King of Prussia, Pennsylvania.

OTHER SOURCES

★12851★ American Institute of Wine and Food

213-37 39th Ave.
PO Box 216
Bayside, NY 11361
Fax: (718)522-0204   Fr: 800-274-2493
E-mail: info@aiwf.org
URL: http://www.aiwf.org

National organization with 25 chapters in major cities across the United States which is made up of wine and food professionals and enthusiasts; seeks to provide a networking opportunity in which industry professionals are able to meet with enthusiasts so they will then know and understand their core consumers. Offers scholarships and additional resources.

★12852★ American Society for Enology and Viticulture (ASEV)

PO Box 1855
Davis, CA 95617-1855
Ph: (530)753-3142   Fax: (530)753-3318
E-mail: society@asev.org
URL: http://www.asev.org

Description: Persons concerned with the management and technical aspects of the wine and grape industry including owners, technicians, academic personnel, and farm advisors. Promotes technical advancement in enology and viticulture through integrated research by science and industry; provides a medium for the free exchange of technical information and information on problems of interest to the wine and grape industries.

★12853★ **American Vineyard Foundation (AVF)**

PO Box 5779
Napa, CA 94581
Ph: (707)252-6911   Fax: (707)252-7672
URL: http://www.avf.org

Description: Collects funds for research on grape growing and wine making.

★12854★ **American Wine Society (AWS)**

113 S Perry St.
Lawrenceville, GA 30045
Ph: (678)377-7070   Fax: (678)377-7005
E-mail: coskery@americanwinesociety.org
URL: http://www.americanwinesociety.org

Description: Amateur and professional winegrowers, winemakers, wine connoisseurs, wine merchants, and other interested persons. Seeks to further the knowledge, appreciation and enjoyment of wines produced on the American continent without bias toward European or other wines. Encourages legislation requiring honest labeling of both American and imported wines; fosters production of home wine-makers; seeks to further the use of American terms for American wines. Sponsors educational programs at national and local levels. Conducts wine tastings and trips to vineyards and wineries; arranges gourmet wine dinners; provides speakers on grape growing, wine-making, and wine appreciation.

★12855★ **Brotherhood of the Knights of the Vine (KOV)**

3343 Industrial Dr., Ste. 2
Santa Rosa, CA 95403
Ph: (707)579-3781   Fax: (707)579-3996
E-mail: info@kov.org
URL: http://www.kov.org

Description: Vintners, grape growers, wine wholesalers and retailers, professors of enology (the study of wine and wine-making), wine lovers with an interest in American grapes and wine. Seeks to promote wine as a healthy, hygienic beverage. Bestows titles of Supreme Knight, Master Knight, Knight or Gentle Lady, and Supreme Lady for services rendered to the cause of vines and wines of America. Sponsors Knights of the Vine Scholarship Fund at the University of California-Davis, Washington State University, Fresno State University, and Texas A&M University. National chapters conduct educational programs on wine.

★12856★ **California Association of Winegrape Growers (CAWG)**

601 University Ave., Ste. 135
Sacramento, CA 95825
Ph: (916)924-5370   Fax: (916)924-5374
Fr: 800-241-1800
E-mail: info@cawg.org
URL: http://www.cawg.org

Members: Corporations, associations, and individuals who grow grapes in California for wine and related products. **Purpose:** Serves as a unified voice to address issues aimed at improving the domestic and foreign market for California wines and wine grapes. **Activities:** Lobbies state and federal legislatures and regulatory agencies. Holds annual reception for the California Legislature and annual Wines of America Reception for Congress; co-sponsors the annual Unified Wine and Grape Symposium.

★12857★ **ENews Montior**

Benson Marketing Group LLC
2700 Napa Valley Corp. Dr., Ste. H
Napa, CA 94558
Ph: (707)254-9292   Fax: (707)254-0433
E-mail: info@bensonmarketing.com
URL: http://www.enewsmonitor.com

Email news clipping service about the wine industry delivers specific category subscriptions for the wine lover, retailer, restaurateur, wholesaler, winery, grape grower and media.

★12858★ **Finger Lakes Wine Growers Association (FLWGA)**

PO Box 222
Hammondsport, NY 14840
Ph: (607)569-6133   Fax: (607)569-6135
E-mail: mike@pleasantvalleywine.com

Description: Wineries in the New York State Finger Lakes wine-producing region. Promotes the wine industry.

★12859★ **Free the Grapes**

2700 Napa Valley Corporate Dr., Ste. H
Napa, CA 94558
Ph: (707)254-1107   Fax: (707)254-0433
E-mail: fedup@freethegrapes.org
URL: http://www.freethegrapes.org

Seeks to augment the three-tier system currently in place by many states which creates monopolies in wine distribution and prevents costumers from purchasing wine directly from the winemakers despite the consumer demand to buy wine products that are not always available by the wholesaler middlemen. These wholesalers aggressively support state-sanctioned legislation that further restrict consumer access and choice by reversing direct shipping provisions, introducing new felony legislation and placing arbitrary limitations on who can and cannot ship wine.

★12860★ **International Wine Guild**

12138 W Brittany Ave.
Littleton, CO 80127
Ph: (303)296-3966   Fax: (303)904-3245

E-mail: info@internationalwineguild.com
URL: http://www.internationalwineguild.com

Seeks to encourage study to develop professional and technical understanding and increased knowledge of wine throughout all areas of the food and wine service industry. Offers programs for certification as well as an advanced program path leading to a Guild Wine Master Educator.

★12861★ **Long Island Wine Council**

5120 Sound Ave.
Riverhead, NY 11901
Ph: (631)369-5887   Fax: (631)722-2221
E-mail: info@liwines.com
URL: http://www.liwines.com

Seeks to promote and develop the region's wine industry; offers educational programs for those looking to work in the field; sponsors wine events for networking and promotion.

★12862★ **Monterey County Vintners and Growers Association (MCVGA)**

PO Box 1793
Monterey, CA 93942-1793
Ph: (831)375-9400   Fax: (831)375-1116
E-mail: info@montereywines.org
URL: http://www.montereywines.org

Description: Represents grape growers and wine producers of Monterey County, CA. Seeks to develop awareness and promote the image of Monterey wines.

★12863★ **Napa Valley Grapegrowers (NVG)**

811 Jefferson St.
Napa, CA 94559
Ph: (707)944-8311   Fax: (707)224-7836
E-mail: info@napagrowers.org
URL: http://www.napagrowers.org

Description: Grape growers, wineries, businesses that work with growers, and others interested in the wine grape growing industry with particular emphasis on the Napa Valley. Provides marketing assistance to growers; promotes legislation at the local and state levels that will benefit growers. Has established a Napa Valley viticultural area designation, and is involved in the technical aspects of grape growing. Cosponsors marketing and promotional programs. Compiles statistical data on Napa Valley grapes and local markets.

★12864★ **Napa Valley Vintners Association (NVV)**

PO Box 141
St. Helena, CA 94574
Ph: (707)963-3388   Fax: (707)963-3488
Fr: 800-982-1371
E-mail: reception2@napavintners.com
URL: http://www.napavintners.com

Description: Promotes Napa Valley, CA, wines and wineries; disseminates information about Napa Valley wines to the public.

★12865★ Napa Valley Wine Library Association (NVWLA)

PO Box 328
St. Helena, CA 94574-0328
Ph: (707)963-5145
E-mail: info@napawinelibrary.org
URL: http://www.napawinelibrary.org

Description: Represents persons interested in wines, particularly those of the Napa Valley. Collects, preserves, and makes available books, publications, periodicals, and ephemera concerning Napa Valley wine. Conducts wine tasting courses.

★12866★ New York Wine/Grape Foundation (NYWGF)

800 S Main St., Ste. 200
Canandaigua, NY 14424
Ph: (585)394-3620   Fax: (585)394-3649
E-mail: info@newyorkwines.org
URL: http://www.newyorkwines.org

Description: Grape growers from New York State; wineries and juice processors, suppliers, financiers, insurance representatives, consultants to growers, restaurateurs, and consumers. Promotes the demand for and sale of grapes and grape products through advertising and promotional work; assist members by performing services relative to the production, harvesting, and marketing of wine grapes, and any related research; provide members with production and marketing information; promote mutual understanding and goodwill between growers and processors of grapes. Seeks to educate consumers on the variety and quality of grapes grown and grape products made in New York State. Sponsors Women for New York State Wines, consisting of women supporting the New York State wine industry; WNYSW promotes wine salesand holds wine tasting to teach people how to read wine labels and distinguish between wines made from various types of wine grapes

★12867★ Paso Robles Wine Country Alliance

530 10th St.
Paso Robles, CA 93446
Ph: (805)239-8463   Fax: (805)237-6439
Fr: 800-549-9463
E-mail: info@pasowine.com
URL: http://www.pasowine.com/

Seeks to enhance the status of Paso Robles as a world-class wine region by marketing and promoting the unique attributes of the region; offers educational resources that can help the membership to optimize business opportunities as well as their products; monitors local governments to protect member property rights, water rights and rights to farm. Website provides winery and vineyard profiles, event calendar, a wine directory and classified ads which offer job listings.

★12868★ Santa Cruz Mountains Winegrowers Association (SCMWA)

7605-A Old Dominion Ct.
Aptos, CA 95003
Ph: (831)685-8463   Fax: (831)688-6961

E-mail: info@scmwa.com
URL: http://www.scmwa.com

Description: Wineries in the Santa Cruz Mountains area. Facilitates exchange of information among members. Promotes wines of the Santa Cruz Mountains appellation. Holds grape growing and winemaking seminars. Publications: none.

★12869★ SF Sommelier Consulting

77 Sunview Dr.
San Francisco, CA 94131
Ph: (415)505-9382
E-mail: sfsommelier@sbcglobal.net
URL: http://www.sfsommelier.com

Provides educational programs and organizes wine events for the wine industry.

★12870★ Society of Wine Educators (SWE)

1212 New York Ave. NW, Ste. 425
Washington, DC 20005
Ph: (202)408-8777   Fax: (202)408-8677
E-mail: lairey@societyofwineeducators.org
URL: http://wine.gurus.com

Description: Represents individuals who teach or write about wine for the trade or academic communities; those associated with wineries, restaurants, or the wine retail, wholesale, or import industry; consumers with an interest in wine and wine education. Facilitates the flow of information among wine producers, marketers, retailers, and consumers.

★12871★ Sonoma County Grape Growers Association (SCGGA)

PO Box 1959
Sebastopol, CA 95473
Ph: (707)829-3963
E-mail: info@scgga.org
URL: http://www.scgga.org

Description: Growers of wine grapes for commercial sale to wineries. Promotes the wines of Sonoma County, CA; addresses agricultural issues that affect grape growers. Provides information on Sonoma County food and wine. Maintains speakers' bureau.

★12872★ Sonoma County Vintners (SCV)

420 Aviation Blvd., Ste. 106
Santa Rosa, CA 95403
Ph: (707)522-5840   Fax: (707)573-3942
Fr: 800-939-7666
E-mail: info@sonomawine.com
URL: http://www.sonomawine.com

Description: Wineries that produce and label at least one wine made in Sonoma County. Promotes the wines of Sonoma County. Conducts events designed to educate the public about wine, wine tasting, and wine-producing regions. Sponsors annual national wine tasting tour in March and April, and Canadian tour in October and November.

★12873★ Sonoma County Wine Library

Piper and Center Sts.
Healdsburg, CA 95448-3899
Ph: (707)433-3772   Fax: (707)433-7946
E-mail: bo@sonoma.lib.ca.us
URL: http://www.sonomalibrary.org/wine/

Four stated collections include: the science and technology of growing grapes and making wine; the history of wine worldwide; the history of wine in Sonoma County; the business and economics of the wine industry; also includes videos, 16mm films, photographs, and books about careers in the wine industry.

★12874★ Vinifera Wine Growers Association (VWGA)

PO Box 10045
Alexandria, VA 22310
Ph: (703)922-7049   Fax: (703)922-0617
E-mail: thewinexchange@aol.com

Description: Promotes public appreciation and understanding of wine and its production. Supports state and national wine educational forums and research. Provides technical, cultural, and historical wine information. Promotes wine enjoyment and responsible consumption as part of a healthy lifestyle. Supports quality production and sales of all grape wines. Lobbies on behalf of state and federal legislation favorable to the growth and economic viability of the U.S. wine industry. Strengthens cooperation with other wine organizations in addressing wine issues of common concern.

★12875★ Wine Appreciation Guild (WAG)

360 Swift Ave., Unit 30-40
South San Francisco, CA 94080
Ph: (650)866-3020   Fax: (650)866-3513
Fr: 800-231-9463
E-mail: info@wineappreciation.com
URL: http://www.wineappreciation.com

Description: Represents winery owners and distributors. Disseminates information on wine, with emphasis on American wines. Conducts wine evaluations and research programs on wine and health, cooking with wine, and consumer wine. Offers wine study courses and compiles statistics. Sponsors competitions.

★12876★ The Wine Institute

425 Market St., Ste. 1000
San Francisco, CA 94105
Ph: (415)512-0151   Fax: (415)442-0742
URL: http://www.wineinstitute.org

Advocacy and public policy association concerning California wineries brings together the resources of 1,000 wineries and affiliated businesses to support legislation and regulation, international market development, scientific research, media relations and educational programs that benefit the entire California wine industry.

★12877★ Wine Market Council
100 Lincoln Village Cir., No. 107
Larkspur, CA 94939
Ph: (415)925-1116
URL: http://www.winemarketcouncil.com/

Seeks to broaden and strengthen the consumer base of the United States wine market through its public relations plan, merchandising program, research studies, Internet programs and advertising campaigns; also includes consumer research and regional data as well as networking opportunities.

★12878★ Wine & Winemaking
World Fine Art
PO Box 5365
Scottsdale, AZ 85261
URL: http://alaquips.com/winelinx.htm

$9.00. Provides notes, quotes and anecdotes about the business of wine and winemaking.

★12879★ Winefiles.org
Sonoma County Library
3rd and E Sts.
Santa Rosa, CA 95404
Ph: (707)545-0831   Fax: (707)544-0854
E-mail: sclib@sonic.net
URL: http://www.winefiles.org

Online resource provides information about wine, winemaking and grape growing, including the business, technology and history associated with wine.

Visual Artists

SOURCES OF HELP-WANTED ADS

★12880★ Adweek

VNU Business Media USA
770 Broadway
New York, NY 10003
Ph: (646)654-4500
URL: http://www.adweek.com/aw/index.jsp

Weekly. $149.00/year for individuals, 12 months basic; $85.00 for individuals, 6 months basic; $135.00 for individuals, 6 months premium; $249.00/year for individuals, 12 months premium; $20.00/year for individuals, monthly online. Advertising news magazine.

★12881★ Afterimage

Visual Studies Workshop Press
31 Prince St.
Rochester, NY 14607
Ph: (585)442-8676
E-mail: afterimage@vsw.org
URL: http://www.vsw.org/afterimage/index.html

Bimonthly. $33.00/year for individuals; $61.00 for two years; $90.00/year for institutions, library. Publication providing independent critical commentary on issues in media arts, including scholarly research, in-depth reviews, investigative journalism, interviews, and the largest list of exhibitions, festivals, position announcements and calls for work of its kind.

★12882★ American Artist

VNU Business Media USA
770 Broadway
New York, NY 10003
Ph: (646)654-4500
URL: http://www.myamericanartist.com/

Monthly. $30.00/year for individuals; $53.00 for two years. Art and educational journal.

★12883★ Art in America

Brant Publications Inc.
575 Broadway
New York, NY 10012-3230
Ph: (212)941-2800   Fax: (212)941-2844
URL: http://www.artinamericamagazine.com

Monthly. $25.00/year for individuals; $85.00/year for individuals, Canada; $95.00/year for out of country, international; $45.00/year for two years; $60.00/year for individuals, 3 year; $170.00/year for two years, Canada; $190.00 for two years, international. Art magazine.

★12884★ Art Calendar

Art Calendar
1500 Park Center Dr.
Orlando, FL 32835
Ph: (407)563-7000   Fax: (407)563-7099
URL: http://www.artcalendar.com

Description: Monthly, except August. Lists art grants, shows, and commissions. Features articles on the psychology of creativity. Recurring features include interviews, a calendar of events, news of educational opportunities, job listings, book reviews, notices of publications available, and columns titled Marketing Strategies, Art Law, Perspective, and Federal Updates.

★12885★ Art and Living

Art and Living
8306 Wilshire Blvd., Ste. 2029
Beverly Hills, CA 90211
Ph: (310)313-3171   Fax: (310)313-2125

Bimonthly. $76.00/year for individuals, international; $36.00/year for U.S. and Canada; $30.00/year for elsewhere. Magazine covering art and art topics.

★12886★ Artary

National Conference of Artists
Gallery Row
409 7th St. NW
Washington, DC 20004
Ph: (202)393-3116

Semiannual. Magazine covering issues for artists.

★12887★ The Artist's Magazine

F & W Publications Inc.
4700 E Galbraith Rd.
Cincinnati, OH 45236
Ph: (513)531-2690   Fax: (513)531-0798
Fr: 800-289-0963
E-mail: tamedit@fwpubs.com
URL: http://www.artistsmagazine.com

Monthly. $20.00/year for individuals; $30.00/year for Canada, including GST/HST; $30.00/year for other countries, surface delivery; $59.00/year for other countries, airmail delivery. Magazine by artists for artists. Covers artwork, working methods, tools, and materials.

★12888★ ARTnews Magazine

Art News L.L.C.
48 W 38th St.
New York, NY 10018
Ph: (212)398-1690   Fax: (212)819-0394
Fr: 800-284-4625
URL: http://secure.artnews.com

Monthly. $59.95/year for individuals; $99.95/year for elsewhere. News magazine reporting on art, personalities, issues, trends, and events that shape the international art world.

★12889★ Dirty Goat

Host Publications, Inc.
451 Greenwich St., Ste. 7J
New York, NY 10013
Ph: (212)905-2365   Fax: (212)905-2369
URL: http://www.thedirtygoat.com/index.html

Semiannual. Journal covering poetry, prose, drama, literature and visual art.

★12890★ DM News

DM News
114 W 26th St., 4th Fl.
New York, NY 10001
Ph: (646)638-6000   Fax: (646)638-6159
E-mail: inquiry@dmnews.com
URL: http://www.dmnews.com/

Weekly. $49.00/year for U.S. $99.00/year for Canada and Mexico; $149.00/year for other countries. Tabloid newspaper for publishers, fund raisers, financial marketers, catalogers, package goods advertisers and their agencies, and other marketers who use direct mail, mail order advertising, catalogs, or other direct response media to sell their products or services.

★12891★ Editor & Publisher

Editor & Publisher Magazine
770 Broadway
New York, NY 10003-9595
Ph: (646)654-5500   Fax: (646)654-5370
Fr: 800-562-2706
URL: http://www.editorandpublisher.com/eandp/index.jsp

Weekly (Mon.). $99.00/year for individuals, print and online; $159.00/year for Canada, print and online; $320.00/year for other countries; $7.95/year for individuals, monthly. Magazine focusing on newspaper journalism, advertising, printing equipment, and interactive services.

★12892★ Film History

Indiana University Press
601 N Morton St.
Bloomington, IN 47404-3797
Ph: (812)855-6657   Fax: (812)855-8817
Fr: 800-842-6796
E-mail: filmhist@aol.com
URL: http://inscribe.iupress.org/loi/fil

Quarterly. $77.00/year for individuals, print and online, for U.S. $63.00/year for individuals, electronic only, for U.S. Journal tracing the history of the motion picture with reference to social, technological, and economic aspects, covering various aspects of motion pictures such as production, distribution, exhibition, and reception.

★12893★ GNSI Newsletter

Guild of Natural Science Illustrators Inc.
PO Box 652, Ben Franklin Sta.
Washington, DC 20044-0652
Ph: (301)309-1514   Fax: (301)309-1514
E-mail: gnsihome@his.com
URL: http://www.gnsi.org/join/publicat.html

Description: Ten issues/year. Serves as a forum for member professional scientific illustrators and technical artists. Provides information on supplies, techniques, methods, and materials for production of highly-rendered and accurate illustrations of natural science subjects. Also discusses business practices of interest to professional as well as aspiring illustrators. Recurring features include announcements of Guild activities, examples of members' work, book reviews and notices of publications available, and job listings.

★12894★ Graphic Arts Monthly Magazine

Reed Business Information
360 Park Ave. S
New York, NY 10010
Ph: (646)746-6400   Fax: (646)746-7431
URL: http://www.reedbusiness.com

Monthly. Free. Magazine featuring commercial printing and graphic arts, including digital technologies.

★12895★ HOW

F & W Publications Inc.
4700 E Galbraith Rd.
Cincinnati, OH 45236
Ph: (513)531-2690   Fax: (513)531-0798
Fr: 800-289-0963
URL: http://www.howdesign.com

Bimonthly. $29.96/year for U.S. $45.00/year for Canada; $52.00/year for other countries. Instructional trade magazine.

★12896★ Jobline News

Graphic Artists Guild
32 Broadway, ste.1114
New York, NY 10004
Ph: (212)791-3400   Fax: (212)791-0333
E-mail: jobline@gag.org
URL: http://www.gag.org/jobline/index.html

Description: Weekly. Lists jobs for freelance and staff artists in areas such as graphic design, illustration, and art education. Lists jobs from across the country; quantity and locales vary weekly.

★12897★ Me

Me Magazine
126 Winding Ridge Rd.
White Plains, NY 10603
Ph: (914)761-1860
URL: http://www.memagazinenyc.com

Quarterly. $25.00/year for individuals. Magazine devoted to people in creative professions. Provides biographical insight into the personal lives of people in the creative community.

★12898★ NSS News Bulletin

National Sculpture Society
237 Park Ave.
New York, NY 10017
Ph: (212)764-5643   Fax: (212)764-5651
E-mail: info@nationalsculpture.org
URL: http://www.nationalsculpture.org/nss/publications/bulletin.cfm

Description: Bimonthly. Covers sculpture competitions, awards, grants, exhibitions, and commissions. Reports members' works and activities. Recurring features include news of research, a calendar of events, reports of meetings, news of educational opportunities, job listings, notices of publications available, and Seeking and Offering.

★12899★ Producers Masterguide

Producers Masterguide
60 E 8th St., 34th Fl.
New York, NY 10003-6514
Ph: (212)777-4002   Fax: (212)777-4101
URL: http://www.producers.masterguide.com

Annual. $155.00/year for U.S. $165.00/year for Canada; $195.00/year for other countries. An international film and TV production directory and guide for the professional

motion picture, broadcast television, feature film, TV commercial, cable/satellite, digital and videotape industries in the U.S., Canada, the UK, the Caribbean Islands, Mexico, Australia, New Zealand, Europe, Israel, Morocco, the Far East, and South America.

★12900★ Publishers Weekly

Publishers Weekly
360 Park Ave. S.
New York, NY 10010
Ph: (646)746-6598
URL: http://www.publishersweekly.com

Weekly. $239.99/year for individuals; $299.99/year for Canada and Mexico; $399.99/year for other countries, air delivery. Magazine for publishers.

★12901★ The Salmagundian

Salmagundi Art Club
47 5th Ave.
New York, NY 10003
Ph: (212)255-7740
URL: http://www.salmagundi.org

Description: 2/year. Highlights activities of the Club, a fellowship and exhibition organization for painters, sculptors, writers, and artists. Profiles artists and their work. Recurring features include notes on members, coverage of Clubhouse activities.

★12902★ SignCraft

Signcraft Publishing Company Inc.
PO Box 60031
Fort Myers, FL 33906
Ph: (239)939-4644   Fax: (239)939-0607
Fr: 800-204-0204
E-mail: signcraft@signcraft.com
URL: http://www.signcraft.com

$39.00/year for individuals; $49.00/year for other countries. Trade magazine.

★12903★ Stained Glass Magazine

Stained Glass Association of America
10009 East 62nd St.
Raytown, MO 64133
Fr: 800-438-9581
E-mail: quarterly@sgaaonline.com

Quarterly. $36.00/year for individuals; $48.00/year for Canada and Mexico; $54.00/year for other countries. Magazine on architectural stained and decorative art glass.

★12904★ State of the Arts

Montana Arts Council
830 N. Warren St., 1st Fl.
PO Box 202201
Helena, MT 59601
Ph: (406)444-6430   Fax: (406)444-6548
E-mail: mac@mt.gov
URL: http://www.art.state.mt.us/soa/listing

Description: Bimonthly. Contains artists profiles; news of educational opportunities; updates of legislation and government support programs, especially the National Endowment for the Arts; news of conferences and Council activities; grant announcements; calls for exhibit entries; notices of publications available; a calendar of events; and job listings.

PLACEMENT AND JOB REFERRAL SERVICES

★12905★ Broadcast Designer's Association (BDA)

9000 W Sunset Blvd., Ste. 900
Los Angeles, CA 90069
Ph: (310)788-7600   Fax: (310)788-7616
E-mail: brett@ashyagency.com
URL: http://www.bda.tv

Members: Designers, artists, art directors, illustrators, photographers, animators, and other motion graphic professionals in the electronic media industry; educators and students; commercial and industrial companies that manufacture products related to design. **Purpose:** Seeks to promote understanding between designers, clients, and management; to stimulate innovative ideas and techniques; to encourage and provide a resource for young talents; and to provide a forum for discussion on industry issues and concerns. **Activities:** Maintains placement service; conducts surveys and compiles statistics.

★12906★ Health Science Communications Association (HeSCA)

39 Wedgewood Dr., Ste. A
Jewett City, CT 06351-2420
Ph: (860)376-5915   Fax: (860)376-6621
E-mail: hesca@hesca.org
URL: http://www.hesca.org

Description: Represents media managers, graphic artists, biomedical librarians, producers, faculty members of health science and veterinary medicine schools, health professional organizations, and industry representatives. Acts as a clearinghouse for information used by professionals engaged in health science communications. Coordinates Media Festivals Program that recognizes outstanding media productions in the health sciences. Offers placement service.

★12907★ Institute of American Indian Arts (IAIA)

83 Avan Nu Po Rd.
Santa Fe, NM 87508
Ph: (505)424-2300   Fax: (505)424-3900
Fr: 800-804-6423
E-mail: setzel@iaia.edu
URL: http://www.iaia.edu

Description: Federally chartered private institution. Offers learning opportunities in the arts and crafts to Native American youth (Indian, Eskimo, or Aleut). Emphasis is placed upon Indian traditions as the basis for creative expression in fine arts including painting, sculpture, museum studies, creative writing, printmaking, photography, communications, design, and dance, as well as

training in metal crafts, jewelry, ceramics, textiles, and various traditional crafts. Students are encouraged to identify with their heritage and to be aware of themselves as members of a race rich in architecture, the fine arts, music, pageantry, and the humanities. All programs are based on elements of the Native American cultural heritage that emphasizes differences between Native American and non-Native American cultures. Sponsors Indian arts-oriented junior college offering Associate of Fine Arts degrees in various fields as well as seminars, an exhibition program, and traveling exhibits. Maintains extensive library, museum, and biographical archives. Provides placement service.

EMPLOYER DIRECTORIES AND NETWORKING LISTS

★12908★ American Showcase Illustration

American Showcase Inc.
915 Broadway, 14th Fl.
New York, NY 10010
Ph: (212)673-6600   Fax: (212)673-9795
Fr: 800-894-7469

Annual. $29.90 for individuals. Covers illustrators and graphic designers. Entries include: Name, address, phone, sample of work. Arrangement: Geographical.

★12909★ Black Book Photography

Black Book Marketing Group
740 Broadway, Ste. 202
New York, NY 10003
Ph: (212)979-6700   Fax: (212)673-4321
Fr: 800-841-1246
URL: http://www.BlackBook.com

Annual; latest edition 2007. $88.00 for individuals. Publication includes: Over 19,000 art directors, creative directors, photographers and photographic services, design firms, advertising agencies, and other firms whose products or services are used in advertising. Entries include: Company name, address, phone. Principal content of publication consists of 4-color samples from the leading commercial photographers. Arrangement: Classified by product/service.

★12910★ Career Ideas for Teens in the Arts and Communications

Facts On File Inc.
132 W 31st St., 17th Fl.
New York, NY 10001
Ph: (212)967-8800   Fax: 800-678-3633
Fr: 800-322-8755
URL: http://www.factsonfile.com

Published 2005. $40.00 for individuals; $36.00 for libraries. Covers a multitude of career possibilities based on a teenager's specific interests and skills and links his/her talents to a wide variety of actual professions.

★12911★ Careers in Focus: Art

Facts On File Inc.
132 W 31st St., 17th Fl.
New York, NY 10001
Ph: (212)967-8800   Fax: 800-678-3633
Fr: 800-322-8755
URL: http://www.factsonfile.com

Published 2004. $29.95 for individuals; $26.95 for libraries. Covers an overview of art, followed by a selection of jobs profiled in detail, including the nature of the job, earnings, prospects for employment, what kind of training and skills it requires, and sources for further information.

★12912★ Discovering Careers for Your Future: Art

Facts On File Inc.
132 W 31st St., 17th Fl.
New York, NY 10001
Ph: (212)967-8800   Fax: 800-678-3633
Fr: 800-322-8755
URL: http://www.factsonfile.com

Published 2001. $21.95 for individuals; $19.75 for libraries. Covers artists, cartoonists, graphic designers, illustrators, and photographers; links career education to curriculum, helping children investigate the subjects they are interested in and the careers those subjects might lead to.

★12913★ Employment Opportunities, USA

Washington Research Associates
1090 Vermont Ave. NW, Ste. 800
Washington, DC 20005
Ph: (202)408-7025

Annual, quarterly updates. Publication includes: List of over 1,000 employment contacts in companies and agencies in banking, arts, telecommunications, education, and 14 other industries and professions, including federal government. Entries include: Company name, name of representative, address, description of products or services, hiring and recruiting practices, training programs, and year established. Principal content is industry overviews, career news, employment opportunity information on 14 different job markets, and comprehensive guidance to career resources on the Internet. Arrangement: Classified by industry. Indexes: Occupation.

★12914★ International Directory of Design

Penrose Press
1333 Gough, Ste. 8B
PO Box 470925
San Francisco, CA 94109
Ph: (415)567-4157   Fax: (415)567-4165
URL: http://penrose-press.com/idd/search_db.php

Covers fine art guides and periodicals. Entries include: Name, address, phone, fax and e-mail address. Arrangement: Alphabetical by country.

★12915★ National Directory of Arts Internships

National Network for Artist Placement
935 W Ave. 37
Los Angeles, CA 90065
Ph: (323)222-4035   Fax: (323)225-5711
Fr: 800-354-5348
URL: http://www.artistplacement.com

Biennial, odd years; latest edition 10th. $95.00 for individuals. Covers over 5,000 internship opportunities in dance, music, theater, art, design, film, and video & over 1,250 host organizations. Entries include: Name of sponsoring organization, address, name of contact; description of positions available, eligibility requirements, stipend or salary (if any), application procedures. Arrangement: Classified by discipline, then geographical.

★12916★ National Directory of Magazines

Oxbridge Communications Inc.
186 5th Ave.
New York, NY 10010
Ph: (212)741-0231   Fax: (212)633-2938
Fr: 800-955-0231
E-mail: custserv@oxbridge.com
URL: http://www.oxbridge.com/

Latest edition September 2007. $995.00 for individuals, print product; $1,195.00 for individuals, CD-ROM; $1,995.00 for individuals, print product and CD-ROM. Covers over 19,000 magazines; coverage includes Canada. Entries include: Title, publisher name, address, phone, fax number, names and titles of contact and key personnel, financial data, editorial and advertising information, circulation. Arrangement: Classified by subject. Indexes: Title; geographical; publisher.

★12917★ Printworld Directory of Contemporary Prints and Prices

Printworld International Inc.
PO Box 1957
West Chester, PA 19380
Ph: (610)431-6654   Fax: (610)431-6653
Fr: 800-788-9101
URL: http://www.printworlddirectory.com

Irregular; latest edition 2006, 11th edition. Publication includes: Biographical data on 5,000 international artists in contemporary printmaking; thousands of galleries that handle prints and hundreds of print publishers; and 600,000 print/price listings. Entries include: For artists–Name, address, personal and educational data, major exhibits, collections, publishers, printers, galleries, awards, teaching positions and documentation of prints. For galleries and publishers–Name, address. Arrangement: Alphabetical. Indexes: Artist name, printer/print workshop, publisher, gallery, art appraiser.

★12918★ RSVP

RSVP: The Directory of Illustration and Design
PO Box 050314
Brooklyn, NY 11205
Ph: (718)857-9267   Fax: (718)783-2376

URL: http://www.rsvpdirectory.com/

Annual, January/February; latest edition 2005. $20.00 for individuals. Covers about 250 illustrators and designers in the graphic arts industry. All listings are paid. Entries include: Name, address, phone, sample of work. Arrangement: Separate sections for illustrators and designers; each subdivided into color and black and white. Indexes: Specialty (with phone), geographical, alphabetical.

★12919★ Society of Illustrators-Annual of American Illustration

Society of Illustrators
128 E 63rd St.
New York, NY 10021-7303
Ph: (212)838-2560   Fax: (212)838-2561
URL: http://stage.societyillustrators.org/shop/annuals/index.cms

Annual, January. $45.00 for individuals. Covers 800 illustrators and art directors. Entries include: Personal or firm name, address, clients. Arrangement: Alphabetical.

★12920★ Top Careers for Art Graduates

Facts On File Inc.
132 W 31st St., 17th Fl.
New York, NY 10001
Ph: (212)967-8800   Fax: 800-678-3633
Fr: 800-322-8755
URL: http://www.factsonfile.com

Published 2004. $14.95 for individuals; $13.45 for libraries. Covers several of the best career opportunities for art graduates in a number of industries.

★12921★ The Workbook

Scott & Daughters Publishing Inc.
940 N Highland Ave.
Los Angeles, CA 90038
Ph: (213)856-0008   Fax: (323)856-4368
Fr: 800-547-2688
URL: http://www.workbook.com

Annual, February. Covers 49,000 advertising agencies, art directors, photographers, freelance illustrators and designers, artists' representatives, interactive designers, prepress services, and other graphic arts services in the U.S. Entries include: Company or individual name, address, phone, specialty. National in scope. Arrangement: Classified by product or service.

HANDBOOKS AND MANUALS

★12922★ 100 Best Careers for Writers and Artists

Macmillan Publishing Company
175 Fifth Ave.
New York, NY 10010
Ph: (646)307-5151   Fr: 800-428-5331
URL: http://www.macmillan.com/

Shelly Field. 1997. $15.95 (paper). 274 pages. Identifies job opportunities in communications and the arts.

★12923★ The Art Business Encyclopedia

Allworth Press
10 E. 23rd St., Ste. 510
New York, NY 10010
Ph: (212)777-8395   Fax: (212)777-8261
Fr: 800-491-2808
URL: http://www.allworth.com/

Leonard DuBoff. 1996. $29.95; $19.95 (paper). 255 pages.

★12924★ Art and Reality: the Standard Reference Guide and Business Plan for Actively Developing Your Career As an Artist

Seven Locks Press
3100 W. Warner Ave., Ste. 8
Santa Ana, CA 92704
Ph: (714)545-2526   Fax: (714)545-1572
Fr: 800-354-5348
E-mail: sevenlocks@aol.com
URL: http://www.sevenlockspublishing.com/

Robert J. Abbott. Second edition, 2001. $29.95 (paper). 256 pages.

★12925★ An Artist's Guide: Making It in New York City

Watson-Guptill Publications
770 Broadway
New York, NY 10003
Ph: (646)654-5400   Fax: (646)654-5487
Fr: 800-278-8477
E-mail: info@watsonguptill.com
URL: http://www.watsonguptill.com

Daniel Grant. 2001. $19.95 (paper). 224 pages. There are chapters to understanding the neighborhoods of New York, the vagaries of the real estate market, the realities of job hunting, the ins and outs of getting health insurance, and the perilous business of establishing contact with a reputable gallery.

★12926★ Becoming a Computer Graphics Designer Artist

John Wiley & Sons Inc.
111 River St.
Hoboken, NJ 07030-5774
Ph: (201)748-6000   Fax: (201)748-6088
E-mail: custserv@wiley.com
URL: http://www.wiley.com/WileyCDA/

Gardner. 2007. $29.95 (paper). 288 pages.

★12927★ Becoming a Successful Artist

North Light Books
4700 E Galbraith Rd.
Cincinnati, OH 45236
Ph: (513)531-2690   Fax: (513)531-4082
Fr: 800-289-0963

Lewis B. Lehrman. 1996. $24.99 (paper). 138 pages.

★12928★ Career Opportunities in Theater and the Performing Arts

Checkmark Books
132 W. 31st St., 17th Fl.
New York, NY 10001-2006
Ph: (212)967-8800   Fax: (212)967-9196
Fr: 800-322-8755

Shelly Field. Third edition, 2006. $18.95 (paper). 320 pages. Offers a complete range of information about job opportunities in the performing arts. Part of Career Opportunities Series.

★12929★ Career Solutions for Creative People: How to Balance Artistic Goals with Career Security

Allworth Press
10 E. 23rd St., Ste. 510
New York, NY 10010
Ph: (212)777-8395   Fax: (212)777-8261
Fr: 800-491-2808
URL: http://www.allworth.com/

Ronda Ormont. 2001. $19.95 (paper). 305 pages.

★12930★ Careers for Color Connoisseurs and Other Visual Types

The McGraw-Hill Companies
PO Box 182604
Columbus, OH 43272
Fax: (614)759-3749   Fr: 877-883-5524
E-mail: customer.service@mcgraw-hill.com
URL: http://www.mcgraw-hill.com

Jan Goldberg. Second edition, 2005. $13.95 (paper). 176 pages.

★12931★ Careers for Crafty People and Other Dexterous Types

The McGraw-Hill Companies
PO Box 182604
Columbus, OH 43272
Fax: (614)759-3749   Fr: 877-883-5524
E-mail: customer.service@mcgraw-hill.com
URL: http://www.mcgraw-hill.com

Mark Rowh. Third edition, 2006. $13.95; $9.95 (paper). 160 pages.

★12932★ Careers by Design: A Headhunter's Secrets for Success and Survival in Graphic Design

Allworth Press
10 E. 23rd St., Ste. 510
New York, NY 10010
Ph: (212)777-8395   Fax: (212)777-8261
Fr: 800-491-2808
URL: http://www.allworth.com/

Roz Goldfarb. Third edition, 2002. $18.95. 223 pages.

★12933★ Careers for Film Buffs and Other Hollywood Types

The McGraw-Hill Companies
PO Box 182604
Columbus, OH 43272
Fax: (614)759-3749   Fr: 877-883-5524
E-mail: customer.service@mcgraw-hill.com

URL: http://www.mcgraw-hill.com

Jaq Greenspon. Second edition, 2003. $13.95; $9.95 (paper). 208 pages. Describes job descriptions in production, camera, sound, special effects, grips, electrical, makeup, costumes, etc.

★12934★ Careers in Health Care

The McGraw-Hill Companies
PO Box 182604
Columbus, OH 43272
Fax: (614)759-3749   Fr: 877-883-5524
E-mail: customer.service@mcgraw-hill.com
URL: http://www.mcgraw-hill.com

Barbara M. Swanson. Fifth edition, 2005. $15.95 (paper). 192 pages. Describes job duties, work settings, salaries, licensing and certification requirements, educational preparation, and future outlook. Gives ideas on how to secure a job.

★12935★ Chronicle Artistic Occupations Guidebook

Chronicle Guidance Publications Inc.
66 Aurora St.
Moravia, NY 13118-3569
Fax: (315)497-3359   Fr: 800-899-0454
URL: http://www.chronicleguidance.com/

Paul Downes, editor. Revised, 1986. $81.80. 250 pages.

★12936★ The Fine Artist's Career Guide

Allworth Press
10 E. 23rd St.
New York, NY 10010
Ph: (212)777-8395   Fax: (646)654-5486
Fr: 800-323-9432
URL: http://www.allworth.com/

Daniel Grant. Second edition, 2004. $19.95 (paper). 320 pages. Covers the fine and applied arts.

★12937★ The Fine Artist's Guide to Marketing and Self-Promotion: Innovative Techniques to Build Your Career As an Artist

Watson-Guptill Publications
770 Broadway
New York, NY 10003
Ph: (646)654-5400   Fax: (646)654-5487
Fr: 800-278-8477
E-mail: info@watsonguptill.com
URL: http://www.watsonguptill.com

Julius Vitali. 2003. $19.95 (paper). 256 pages. Covers a variety of self-promotion techniques for artists, including preparing a resume.

★12938★ Get Noticed!: Self Promotion for Creative Professionals

North Light Books
4700 E Galbraith Rd.
Cincinnati, OH 45236
Ph: (513)531-2690   Fax: (513)531-4082
Fr: 800-289-0963

Sheree Clark, Kristin Lennert. 2000. $29.99 (paper). 143 pages.

★12939★ Graphic Designer's Ultimate Resource Directory

North Light Books
4700 E Galbraith Rd.
Cincinnati, OH 45236
Ph: (513)531-2690   Fax: (513)531-4082
Fr: 800-289-0963

Poppy Evans. 1999. $28.99 (paper). 192 pages.

★12940★ Great Jobs for Art Majors

The McGraw-Hill Companies
PO Box 182604
Columbus, OH 43272
Fax: (614)759-3749   Fr: 877-883-5524
E-mail: customer.service@mcgraw-hill.com
URL: http://www.mcgraw-hill.com

Blythe Camenson, Stephen Lambert, Julie DeGalan. Second edition, 2003. $15.95 (paper). 248 pages. Includes bibliographical references and index.

★12941★ How to Start and Succeed as an Artist

Allworth Press
10 E. 23rd St., Ste. 510
New York, NY 10010
Ph: (212)777-8395   Fax: (212)777-8261
Fr: 800-491-2808
URL: http://www.allworth.com/

Daniel Grant. 1996. $18.95 (paper). 231 pages. Covers a variety of self-promotion techniques for artists, including preparing a resume.

★12942★ How to Survive and Prosper as an Artist: Selling Yourself Without Selling Your Soul

Holt Paperbacks
175 Fifth Ave.
New York, NY 10010
Ph: (646)307-5095   Fax: (212)633-0748
Fr: 800-672-2054
URL: http://www.henryholt.com

Caroll Michels. 5 Revised edition, 2001. $18.00. 369 pages. Includes index and bibliographical references.

★12943★ The Lost Soul Companion: Comfort & Constructive Advice for Struggling Actors, Musicians, Artists, Writers & Other Free Spirits

Dell
1745 Broadway
New York, NY 10019
Ph: (212)782-9000   Fax: (212)572-6066
Fr: 800-733-3000

URL: http://www.randomhouse.com/bantamdell

Susan M. Brackney. 2001. $10.00. 176 pages.

★12944★ The Madness of Art: A Guide to Living and Working in Chicago

Chicago Review Press
814 N. Franklin St.
Chicago, IL 60610
Ph: (312)337-0747   Fax: (312)337-5985
Fr: 800-888-4741

Adam Langer. 1996. $12.95 (paper). 256 pages.

★12945★ New Media Careers for Artists and Designers

AuthorHouse
1663 Liberty Dr., Ste. 200
Bloomington, IN 47403
Ph: (812)961-1023   Fax: (812)339-8654
Fr: 888-519-5121
URL: http://www.authorhouse.com

Brenda S. Faison. February 2003. $13.95. 136 pages.

★12946★ Opportunities in Arts and Crafts Careers

The McGraw-Hill Companies
PO Box 182604
Columbus, OH 43272
Fax: (614)759-3749   Fr: 877-883-5524
E-mail: customer.service@mcgraw-hill.com
URL: http://www.mcgraw-hill.com

Elizabeth Gardner. 2005. $13.95 (paper). 211 pages.

★12947★ Opportunities in Commercial Art and Graphic Design Careers

The McGraw-Hill Companies
PO Box 182604
Columbus, OH 43272
Fax: (614)759-3749   Fr: 877-883-5524
E-mail: customer.service@mcgraw-hill.com
URL: http://www.mcgraw-hill.com

Barbara Gordon. 2003. $13.95; $11.95 (paper). 160 pages. Provides a survey of job opportunities in advertising and public relations, publishing, fashion, architecture, and newspapers, as well as in a variety of specialty markets. Illustrated.

★12948★ Opportunities in Drafting Careers

The McGraw-Hill Companies
PO Box 182604
Columbus, OH 43272
Fax: (614)759-3749   Fr: 877-883-5524
E-mail: customer.service@mcgraw-hill.com
URL: http://www.mcgraw-hill.com

Mark Rowh. 1994. $13.95; $11.95 (paper). 146 pages. Provides information on opportunities in mechanical, landscape, marine, and topographical drafting in civil service, archi-

tecture, electronics, and other fields. Contains index and illustrations.

★12949★ Opportunities in Magazine Publishing Careers

The McGraw-Hill Companies
PO Box 182604
Columbus, OH 43272
Fax: (614)759-3749   Fr: 877-883-5524
E-mail: customer.service@mcgraw-hill.com
URL: http://www.mcgraw-hill.com

S. William Pattis. 1994. $13.95; $14.95 (paper). 148 pages. Covers the scope of magazine publishing and addresses how to identify and pursue available positions. Illustrated.

★12950★ Opportunities in Printing Careers

The McGraw-Hill Companies
PO Box 182604
Columbus, OH 43272
Fax: (614)759-3749   Fr: 877-883-5524
E-mail: customer.service@mcgraw-hill.com
URL: http://www.mcgraw-hill.com

Irvin Borowsky. 1998. $14.95; $11.95 (paper). 160 pages. Offers detailed information on the variety of pre-press, press, and post-press jobs available. Covers apprenticeships, unions, salaries, and how to get ahead. Illustrated.

★12951★ Opportunities in Publishing Careers

The McGraw-Hill Companies
PO Box 182604
Columbus, OH 43272
Fax: (614)759-3749   Fr: 877-883-5524
E-mail: customer.service@mcgraw-hill.com
URL: http://www.mcgraw-hill.com

Robert A. Carter and S. William Pattis. 2000. $12.95 (paper). 160 pages. Covers all positions in book and magazine publishing, including new opportunities in multimedia publishing.

★12952★ Opportunities in Visual Arts Careers

The McGraw-Hill Companies
PO Box 182604
Columbus, OH 43272
Fax: (614)759-3749   Fr: 877-883-5524
E-mail: customer.service@mcgraw-hill.com
URL: http://www.mcgraw-hill.com

Mark Salmon and Bill Barrett. 2001. $12.95; $11.95 (paper). 160 pages. Points the way to a career in the visual arts, examining opportunities for designers, painters, sculptors, illustrators, animators, photographers, art therapists, educators, and others. Offers a view of the pros and cons of working for an art or design company or on your own.

★12953★ Taking the Leap: Building a Career as a Visual Artist

Chronicle Books LLC
680 Second St.
San Francisco, CA 94107
Ph: (415)537-4200   Fax: (415)537-4460
Fr: 800-722-6657
E-mail: frontdesk@chroniclebooks.com
URL: http://www.chroniclebooks.com

Cay Lang. 2006. $19.95. 256 pages.

EMPLOYMENT AGENCIES AND SEARCH FIRMS

★12954★ Claremont-Branan, Inc.

1298 Rockbridge Rd., Ste. B
Stone Mountain, GA 30087
Ph: (770)925-2915   Fax: (770)925-2601
Fr: 800-875-1292
E-mail: ohil@cbisearch.com
URL: http://cbisearch.com

Employment agency. Executive search firm.

★12955★ Graphic Arts Employment Service, Inc.

409 N Pacific Coast Hwy., Ste.455
Redondo Beach, CA 90277
Ph: (818)499-9722   Fax: (310)937-3760
Fr: 888-499-9722
E-mail: info@gaes.com
URL: http://www.gaes.com

Employment agency specializing in the publishing and packaging industries.

★12956★ Graphic Search Associates Inc.

1217 W. Chester Pike, Ste. 203
West Chester, PA 19382
Ph: (610)429-8077   Fax: (610)429-1355
Fr: 800-342-1777
E-mail: info@graphsrch.com
URL: http://www.graphsrch.com

Executive search firm for the graphic arts industry.

★12957★ Randolph Associates, Inc.

950 Massachusetts Ave., Ste. 105
Cambridge, MA 02139-3174
Ph: (617)441-8777   Fax: (617)441-8778
E-mail: jobs@greatjobs.com
URL: http://www.greatjobs.com

Employment agency. Provides regular or temporary placement of staff.

ONLINE JOB SOURCES AND SERVICES

★12958★ ArtJob Online
1743 Wazee St., Ste. 300
Denver, CO 80202
Ph: (303)629-1166   Fax: (303)629-9717
Fr: 888-JOBS-232
E-mail: artjob@westaf.org
URL: http://www.artjob.org

Description: Contains up-to-date national and international listings of arts employment and related opportunities in the arts: full- & part-time employment, internships, grants, public art projects, and residencies. User can search by region, art discipline, type of organization. **Fee:** Subscribers pay $25 for 3 months, $40 for six months and $75 for one year.

★12959★ Graphic Artists Guild
93 John St., Ste. 403
New York, NY 10038
Ph: (212)791-3400
E-mail: communications@gag.org
URL: http://www.gag.org

Description: JOBLine News section of Guild Resources page contains weekly e-mail newsletter of job listings. **Fee:** Must subscribe to e-mail newsletter non-member six-month rates start at $80. Visitors may download a free sample.

OTHER SOURCES

★12960★ Aid to Artisans (ATA)
331 Wethersfield Ave.
Hartford, CT 06114
Ph: (860)947-3344   Fax: (860)947-3350
E-mail: info@aidtoartisans.org
URL: http://www.aidtoartisans.org

Description: Offers practical assistance worldwide to artisans. Fosters artistic traditions and cultural vitality to improve livelihood and keep communities healthy, strong and growing. Works with its artisan partners to develop products with the appeal to compete successfully in new markets around the world and to improve their business skills so that the changes achieved are enduring.

★12961★ American Institute of Graphic Arts (AIGA)
164 5th Ave.
New York, NY 10010
Ph: (212)807-1990   Fax: (212)807-1799
E-mail: comments@aiga.org
URL: http://www.aiga.org

Description: Graphic designers, art directors, illustrators and packaging designers. Sponsors exhibits and projects in the public interest. Sponsors traveling exhibitions. Operates gallery. Maintains library of design books and periodicals; offers slide archives.

★12962★ American Society of Artists (ASA)
PO Box 1326
Palatine, IL 60078
Ph: (312)751-2500
E-mail: asoa@webtv.net
URL: http://www.americansocietyofartists.com

Description: Professional artists and craftspeople. Maintains art referral service and information exchange service. Sponsors art and craft festivals and a Lecture and Demonstration Service; the Special Arts Services Division aids disabled individuals to either practice or enjoy the visual arts. Presents demonstrations in visual arts to better acquaint the public with various processes in different media.

★12963★ American Society of Psychopathology of Expression (ASPE)
74 Lawton St.
Brookline, MA 02446
Ph: (617)738-9821   Fax: (617)975-0411

Description: Psychiatrists, psychologists, art therapists, sociologists, art critics, artists, social workers, linguists, educators, criminologists, writers, and historians. At least two-thirds of the members must be physicians. Fosters collaboration among specialists in the United States who are interested in the problems of expression and in the artistic activities connected with psychiatric, sociological, and psychological research. Disseminates information about research and clinical applications in the field of psychopathology of expression. Sponsors consultations, seminars, and lectures on art therapy.

★12964★ Art Directors Club (ADC)
106 W 29th St.
New York, NY 10001
Ph: (212)643-1440   Fax: (212)643-4266
E-mail: info@adcglobal.org
URL: http://www.adcglobal.org

Members: Art directors of advertising magazines and agencies, visual information specialists, and graphic designers; associate members are artists, cinematographers, photographers, copywriters, educators, journalists, and critics. **Purpose:** Promotes and stimulates interest in the practice of art direction. **Activities:** Sponsors Annual Exhibition of Advertising, Editorial and Television Art and Design; International Traveling Exhibition. Provides educational, professional, and entertainment programs; on-premise art exhibitions; portfolio review program. Conducts panels for students and faculty.

★12965★ Association of Medical Illustrators (AMI)
810 E 10th St.
Lawrence, KS 66044
Fax: (785)843-1274   Fr: (866)393-4264
E-mail: hq@ami.org
URL: http://www.ami.org

Description: Represents medical illustrators and individuals engaged in related pursuits.

Promotes the study and encourages the advancement of medical illustration and allied fields of visual education. Works to advance medical education and to promote understanding and cooperation with medical and related professions; accredits six postgraduate medical illustration programs. Offers continuing education program; provides professional certification; compiles statistics.

★12966★ Cartoonists Northwest (CNW)
PO Box 31122
Seattle, WA 98103
Ph: (425)226-7623   Fax: (425)227-0511
E-mail: cartoonistsnw@gmail.com
URL: http://www.cartoonists.net

Description: Cartoonists, writers, publishers, illustrators, agents, and others interested in cartooning. Members are accepted nationwide and internationally. Provides information on all aspects of the cartooning profession to amateur, aspiring, and practicing cartoonists. Promotes cartooning as an art form. Provides networking opportunities and referral services. Conducts educational programs.

★12967★ College Art Association (CAA)
275 7th Ave., 18th Fl.
New York, NY 10001
Ph: (212)691-1051   Fax: (212)627-2381
E-mail: nyoffice@collegeart.org
URL: http://www.collegeart.org

Description: Professional organization of artists, art historians and fine art educators, museum directors, and curators. Seeks to raise the standards of scholarship and of the teaching of art and art history throughout the country.

★12968★ Graphic Arts Technical Foundation (GATF)
200 Deer Run Rd.
Sewickley, PA 15143-2600
Fax: (412)741-2311   Fr: 800-910-GATF
E-mail: info@piagatf.org
URL: http://www.gain.net

Description: Scientific, research, technical, and educational organization serving the international graphic communications industries. Conducts research in all graphic processes and their commercial applications. Conducts seminars, workshops, and forums on graphic arts and environmental subjects. Conducts educational programs, including the publishing of graphic arts textbooks and learning modules, videotapes and CD-ROMs and broadcast video seminars. Conducts training and certification program in sheet-fed offset press operating, Web Offset press operating, Image Assembly, and desktop publishing. Produces test images and quality control devices for the industry. Performs technical services for the graphic arts industry, including problem-solving, material evaluation, and plant audits.

★12969★ Media and the Arts Occupations

Delphi Productions
3159 6th St.
Boulder, CO 80304
Ph: (303)443-2100   Fax: (303)443-4022
Fr: 888-443-2400
E-mail: support@delphivideo.com
URL: http://www.delphivideo.com

$95.00. 50 minutes. Part of the Careers for the 21st Century Video Library.

★12970★ National Polymer Clay Guild (NPCG)

PMB 345
1350 Beverly Rd., 115
McLean, VA 22101
E-mail: npcglibr@bellsouth.net
URL: http://www.npcg.org

Description: Seeks to educate the public about polymer clay and to study and promote interest in the use of polymer clay as an artistic medium. Promotes polymer clay work to galleries and museums as well as to the public. Develops opportunities for artists to show their work to the public and engage in public-service activities.

★12971★ Society of Illustrators (SI)

128 E 63rd St.
New York, NY 10021-7303
Ph: (212)838-2560   Fax: (212)838-2561
E-mail: info@societyillustrators.org
URL: http://www.societyillustrators.org

Description: Professional society of illustrators and art directors. Maintains Museum of American Illustration which sponsors continuous exhibits; holds annual exhibit (February-April) of best illustrations of the year; conducts benefit and sale in gallery in December. Participates in annual U.S. Air Force exhibits. Maintains hall of fame; traveling exhibition.

★12972★ Southeastern Theatre Conference (SETC)

PO Box 9868
Greensboro, NC 27429
Ph: (336)272-3645   Fax: (336)272-8810
E-mail: setc@setc.org
URL: http://www.setc.org

Description: Serves the needs of individuals and theatre organizations involved in professional, university/college, community, children/youth, and secondary school theatres. Brings together people interested in theatre and theatre artists and craftsmen from 10 southeastern states of the U.S., across the nation and internationally in order to promote high standards and to stimulate creativity in all phases of theatrical endeavor. Services include: job contact service for technical hiring and job listings, resume service, etc.; playwriting projects for new plays; scholarships for a variety of theatre interests; and annual auditions (spring and fall) for professional, dinner, repertory, summer indoor and outdoor theatres, cruise lines and entertainment venues.

★12973★ Women's Caucus for Art (WCA)

Canal St. Sta.
PO Box 1498
New York, NY 10013
Ph: (212)634-0007
E-mail: info@nationalwca.com
URL: http://www.nationalwca.org

Members: Professional women in visual art fields: artists, critics, art historians, museum and gallery professionals, arts administrators, educators and students, and collectors of art. **Purpose:** Aims to increase recognition for contemporary and historical achievements of women in art. Ensures equal opportunity for employment, art commissions, and research grants. Encourages professionalism and shared information among women in art. Stimulates and publicizes research and publications on women in the visual arts. **Activities:** Conducts workshops, periodic affirmative action research, and statistical surveys.

Website Designers

SOURCES OF HELP-WANTED ADS

★12974★ Computer Graphics World
PennWell Corp.
98 Spit Brook Rd.
Nashua, NH 03062-5737
Ph: (603)891-0123
URL: http://cgw.pennnet.com/home.cfm

Monthly. $55.00/year for individuals, U.S.; $75.00/year for Canada; $115.00/year for other countries; $90.00 for two years, U.S.; $104.00 for two years, Canada; $160.00 for two years, other countries; $27.00/year digital distribution; $10.00 for single issue. Publication reporting on the use of modeling, animation, and multimedia in the areas of science and engineering, art and entertainment, and presentation and training.

★12975★ E-Business Advisor
e-Business Advisor
PO Box 429002
San Diego, CA 92142
Ph: (858)278-5600   Fax: (858)278-0300
Fr: 800-336-6060
URL: http://www.e-businessadvisor.com

Magazine for developing strategies, practices, and innovations for e-business applications.

★12976★ IEEE Computer Graphics and Applications
IEEE Computer Society
10662 Los Vaqueros Cir.
PO Box 3014
Los Alamitos, CA 90720-1314
Ph: (714)821-8380   Fax: (714)821-4010
Fr: 800-272-6657
URL: http://www.computer.org/cga/

Bimonthly. $20.00/year for members; $116.00/year for nonmembers. Magazine addressing the interests and needs of professional designers and users of computer graphics hardware, software, and systems.

★12977★ PC WORLD
101 Communications
9121 Oakdale Ave., Ste. 101
Chatsworth, CA 91311
Ph: (818)734-1520   Fax: (818)734-1522
URL: http://www.pcworld.com

Quarterly. $20.00/year for individuals, 12 issues; $30.00/year for individuals, 24 issues. Technology or business magazine meeting the informational needs of tech-savvy managers, both at work and at home.

EMPLOYER DIRECTORIES AND NETWORKING LISTS

★12978★ Career Opportunities in Computers and Cyberspace
Facts On File Inc.
132 W 31st St., 17th Fl.
New York, NY 10001
Ph: (212)967-8800   Fax: 800-678-3633
Fr: 800-322-8755
URL: http://www.factsonfile.com

Published 2004. $49.50 for individuals; $44.55 for libraries. Covers nearly 200 professions, clustering them by skill, objectives, and work conditions. Entries include: Education, salaries, employment prospects.

★12979★ Careers in Focus: Internet
Facts On File Inc.
132 W 31st St., 17th Fl.
New York, NY 10001
Ph: (212)967-8800   Fax: 800-678-3633
Fr: 800-322-8755
URL: http://www.factsonfile.com

Latest edition 3rd, 2006. $29.95 for individuals; $26.95 for libraries. Covers an overview of the Internet, followed by a selection of jobs profiled in detail, including the nature of the job, earnings, prospects for employment, what kind of training and skills it requires, and sources for further information.

★12980★ Computer Directory
Computer Directories Inc.
23815 Nichols Sawmill Rd.
Hockley, TX 77447
Ph: (281)356-7880   Fr: 800-234-4353
URL: http://www.compdirinc.com

Annual, fall. Covers approximately 130,000 computer installation companies; 19 separate volumes for Alaska/Hawaii, Connecticut/New Jersey, Dallas/Ft. Worth, Eastern Seaboard, Far Midwest, Houston, Illinois, Midatlantic, Midcentral, Mideast, Minnesota/Wisconsin, North Central, New England, New York Metro, Northwest, Ohio, Pennsylvania/West Virginia, Southeast, and Southwest Texas. Entries include: Company name, address, phone, fax, e-mail, name and title of contact, hardware used, software application, operating system, programming language, computer graphics, networking system. Arrangement: Geographical. Indexes: Alphabetical; industry; hardware.

HANDBOOKS AND MANUALS

★12981★ Career Opportunities in Computers and Cyberspace
Facts On File Inc.
132 W. 31st St., 17th Fl.
New York, NY 10001-2006
Ph: (212)967-8800   Fax: 800-678-3633
Fr: 800-322-8755
E-mail: custserv@factsonfile.com
URL: http://www.factsonfile.com

Harry Henderson. Second edition, 2004. $18.95 (paper). Part of the Career Opportunities Series. 256 pages.

★12982★ Careers for Color Connoisseurs and Other Visual Types
The McGraw-Hill Companies
PO Box 182604
Columbus, OH 43272
Fax: (614)759-3749   Fr: 877-883-5524
E-mail: customer.service@mcgraw-hill.com
URL: http://www.mcgraw-hill.com

Jan Goldberg. Second edition, 2005. $13.95 (paper). 176 pages.

★12983★ Creating Online Media: A Guide to Research, Writing and Design on the Internet

The McGraw-Hill Companies
PO Box 182604
Columbus, OH 43272
Fax: (614)759-3749   Fr: 877-883-5524
E-mail: customer.service@mcgraw-hill.com
URL: http://www.mcgraw-hill.com

Carole Rich. 1998. $34.50. 366 pages.

★12984★ The Digital Frontier Job & Opportunity Finder

Moon Lake Media
PO Box 251466
Los Angeles, CA 90025
Ph: (310)535-2453

Don B. Altman. 1996. $19.95 (paper). 245 pages.

★12985★ Expert Resumes for Computer and Web Jobs

Jist Publishing
875 Montreal Way
St. Paul, MN 55102
Fr: 800-648-5478
E-mail: info@jist.com
URL: http://www.jist.com

Wendy Enelow and Louis Kursmark. Second edition, 2005. $16.95 (paper). 286 pages.

★12986★ Exploring Careers in Cyberspace

Rosen Publishing Group, Inc.
29 E. 21st St.
New York, NY 10010
Ph: (212)777-3017   Fax: 888-436-4643
Fr: 800-237-9932
URL: http://www.rosenpublishing.com/

Michael Fulton. 1998. $26.50. Over 114 pages. Provides information on preparation for cyberspace careers and available jobs.

★12987★ Get Your IT Career in Gear!

The McGraw-Hill Companies
PO Box 182604
Columbus, OH 43272
Fax: (614)759-3749   Fr: 877-883-5524
E-mail: customer.service@mcgraw-hill.com
URL: http://www.mcgraw-hill.com

Leslie Goff. 2001. $24.99 (paper). 401 pages.

★12988★ Job Seekers Guide to Silicon Valley Recruiters

John Wily and Sons, Inc.
605 Third Ave., 4th Fl.
New York, NY 10158-0012
Ph: (212)850-6276   Fax: (212)850-8641
Christopher W. Hunt, Scott A. Scanlon. First edition, 1998. $19.95 (paper). 371 pages.

Includes a list of 2,400 recruiters specializing in high technology positions and explains how to work with them.

★12989★ The JobBank Guide to Computer and High-Tech Companies

Adams Media Corp.
57 Littlefield St.
Avon, MA 02322
Ph: (508)427-7100   Fax: (508)427-6790
Fr: 800-872-5627
URL: http://www.adamsmedia.com

Steven Graber, Marcie Dipietro, and Michelle Roy Kelly. Second edition, 1999. $17.95 (paper). 700 pages. Contains profiles of more than 4,500 high-tech employers.

★12990★ Opportunities in High Tech Careers

The McGraw-Hill Companies
PO Box 182604
Columbus, OH 43272
Fax: (614)759-3749   Fr: 877-883-5524
E-mail: customer.service@mcgraw-hill.com
URL: http://www.mcgraw-hill.com

Gary Colter and Deborah Yanuck. 1999. $14.95; $11.95 (paper). 160 pages. Explores high technology careers. Describes job opportunities, how to make a career decision, how to prepare for high technology jobs, job hunting techniques, and future trends.

★12991★ Preparing for an Outstanding Career in Computers: Questions and Answers for Professionals and Students

Rafi Systems, Incorporated
750 N. Diamond Bar Blvd., Ste. 224
Diamond Bar, CA 91765
Ph: (909)593-8124   Fax: (909)629-1034
Fr: 800-584-6706
E-mail: rafisystems@rafisystems.com
URL: http://www.rafisystems.com/

Mohamed Rafiquzzaman. 2001. $19.95. 204 pages. Book contains over 300 questions and answers on various important aspects of computers. Topics include basic and state-of-the-art concepts from digital logic to the design of a complete microcomputer.

★12992★ Unlocking the Clubhouse: Women in Computing

MIT Press
55 Hayward St.
Cambridge, MA 02142-1493
Ph: (617)253-5646   Fax: (617)258-6779
Fr: 800-405-1619
URL: http://mitpress.mit.edu/main/home/default.asp

Jane Margolis and Allan Fisher. 2003. $15.00. 182 pages.

★12993★ The Unofficial Guide to Getting a Job at Microsoft

The McGraw-Hill Companies
PO Box 182604
Columbus, OH 43272
Fax: (614)759-3749   Fr: 877-883-5524

E-mail: customer.service@mcgraw-hill.com
URL: http://www.mcgraw-hill.com

Rebecca Smith. 2000. $16.95 (paper). 192 pages.

★12994★ Winning Resumes for Computer Personnel

Barron's Educational Series, Inc.
250 Wireless Blvd.
Hauppauge, NY 11788-3917
Ph: (631)434-3311   Fax: (631)434-3723
Fr: 800-645-3476
E-mail: fbrown@barronseduc.com
URL: http://barronseduc.com

Anne Hart. Second edition, 1998. $14.95 (paper). 260 pages.

EMPLOYMENT AGENCIES AND SEARCH FIRMS

★12995★ Capitol Search

215 E. Ridgewood Ave., Ste. 205
Ridgewood, NJ 07450
Ph: (201)444-6666

Employment agency.

★12996★ Graphic Arts Employment Service, Inc.

409 N Pacific Coast Hwy., Ste.455
Redondo Beach, CA 90277
Ph: (818)499-9722   Fax: (310)937-3760
Fr: 888-499-9722
E-mail: info@gaes.com
URL: http://www.gaes.com

Employment agency specializing in the publishing and packaging industries.

ONLINE JOB SOURCES AND SERVICES

★12997★ Aquent.com

711 Boylston St.
Boston, MA 02116
Ph: (617)535-5000   Fax: (617)535-5005
E-mail: questions@aquent.com
URL: http://www.aquent.com/FindWork/

Description: Aquent finds contract, project-based, and permanent work for a broad range of creative and information technology professionals. Applicants submit their applications, which are reviewed by an Aquent agent and, if qualifications match job opportunities, they will be called in for an interview and skills assessment. If skills and experience are appropriate, then will then be assigned an Aquent agent who will get to work finding contract or permanent jobs. Also offers free career resources.

★12998★ ComputerJobs.com
280 Interstate North Cir., SE, Ste. 300
Atlanta, GA 30339-2411
Ph: 800-850-0045
URL: http://www.computerjobs.com
Description: The site is an employment tool for technology professionals. Information on positions is updated hourly for seekers. Jobs may be searched by skill, or by location nationally or in a specific state or city job market. Contains thousands of job postings. National jobs may be posted for free. Also career resources for IT professionals.

★12999★ Computerwork.com
Fr: 800-691-8413
E-mail: contactus@computerwork.com
URL: http://www.computerwork.com/
Description: Job search and resume submission service for professionals in information technology.

★13000★ Computerworld Careers
URL: http://www.computerworld.com/careertopics/careers
Description: Offers career opportunities for IT (information technology) professionals. Job seekers may search the jobs database, register at the site, and read about job surveys and employment trends. Employers may post jobs.

★13001★ Computing Research Association Job Announcements
1100 17th St., NW
Washington, DC 20036-4632
Ph: (202)234-2111   Fax: (202)667-1066
URL: http://www.cra.org/main/cra.jobs.html
Description: Contains dated links to national college and university computer technology positions.

★13002★ Dice.com
4101 NW Urbandale Dr.
Urbandale, IA 50322
Fax: (515)280-1452   Fr: 877-386-3323
URL: http://www.dice.com
Description: Job search database for computer consultants and high-tech professionals, listing thousands of high tech permanent contract and consulting jobs for programmers, software engineers, systems administrators, web developers, and hardware engineers. Also free career advice e-mail newsletter and job posting e-alerts.

★13003★ Guru.com
5001 Baum Blvd., Ste. 760
Pittsburgh, PA 15213
Ph: (412)687-1316   Fax: (412)687-4466
URL: http://www.guru.com
Description: Job board specializing in contract jobs for creative and information technology professionals. Also provides online incorporation and educational opportunities for independent contractors along with articles and advice.

★13004★ Ittalent.com
E-mail: ewsmith@ITtalent.com
URL: http://www.ittalent.com
Description: Job search and resume submission service for professionals in information technology.

★13005★ ZDNet Tech Jobs
URL: http://www.zdnet.com/
Description: Site houses a listing of national employment opportunities for professionals in high tech fields. Also contains resume building tips and relocation resources.

OTHER SOURCES

★13006★ Computer Occupations
Delphi Productions
3159 6th St.
Boulder, CO 80304
Ph: (303)443-2100   Fax: (303)443-4022
Fr: 888-443-2400
E-mail: support@delphivideo.com
URL: http://www.delphivideo.com
$95.00. 50 minutes. Part of the Careers for the 21st Century Video Library.

★13007★ Internet Careers: College Not Required
Cambridge Educational
PO Box 2053
Princeton, NJ 08543-2053
Fax: (609)671-0266   Fr: 800-257-5126
E-mail: custserv@films.com
URL: http://www.cambridgeeducational.com
VHS and DVD. 1998. $79.95. 28 minutes. Covers careers and job opportunities related to developing, programming, and managing Internet sites.

★13008★ Internet-Related Occupations
Delphi Productions
3159 6th St.
Boulder, CO 80304
Ph: (303)443-2100   Fax: (303)443-4022
Fr: 888-443-2400
E-mail: support@delphivideo.com
URL: http://www.delphivideo.com
$95.00. 47 minutes. Part of the Emerging Careers Video Library.

Wedding Consultants

★13009★ Special Events

Miramar Communications Inc.
23805 Stuart Ranch Rd., Ste. 235
PO Box 8987
Malibu, CA 90265-8987
Ph: (310)317-4522   Fax: (310)317-9644
Fr: 800-543-4116
E-mail: secs@pbsub.com
URL: http://www.specialevents.com

Monthly. $59.00/year. Free to qualified subscribers; $110.00/year for Canada; $106.00/year for other countries; $200.00 for Canada, two years; $200.00 for other countries, two years. Magazine for special event professionals.

★13010★ Business of Wedding Photography

Watson-Guptill Publications
770 Broadway
New York, NY 10003
Ph: (646)654-5400   Fax: (646)654-5487
Fr: 800-278-8477
E-mail: info@watsonguptill.com
URL: http://www.watsonguptill.com

Ann Monteith. 1996. $35.00 (paper). 192 pages. Subtitled, "A Professional's Guide to Marketing and Managing a Successful Studio With Profiles of 30 Top Portrait Photographers."

★13011★ FabJob Guide to Become a Wedding Planner

FabJob.com
4616-25th Ave. NE
Seattle, WA 98105
Ph: (403)949-4980
URL: http://www.fabjob.com

2003. $39.95. 224 pages. Provides a step-by-step guide on how to plan a wedding. Includes advice for planning the wedding ceremony and reception, and how to chose reputable vendors (e.g. bridal shop, caterer, florist, limousine company, photographer, stationer, etc.)

★13012★ How to Start a Home-Based Event Planning Business

Globe Pequot Press
246 Goose Lane
Guilford, CT 06437
Ph: (203)458-4500   Fr: 800-820-2329
E-mail: info@globepequot.com
URL: http://www.globepequot.com

Jill Moran. 2004. $17.95. 197 pages. This insider's handbook reveals how to start a successful business planning a wide variety of events from home.

★13013★ Planning a Wedding to Remember

Wilshire Publications
12021 Wilshire Blvd., Ste. 208
Los Angeles, CA 90025

Beverly Clark. Fifth edition, 1999. $22.95 (paper). 248 pages.

★13014★ Start Your Own Wedding Consulting Business: Your Step-By-Step Guide to Success

Entrepreneur Press
PO Box 432
Newburgh, NY 12551-0432
Ph: 800-220-8186   Fax: (845)457-5029
E-mail: epresscs@etcdata.com
URL: http://www.entrepreneurpress.com

Eileen Figure Sandlin. 2003. $14.95. 152 pages. Provides information for someone who is starting their wedding consulting business.

★13015★ Coordinators' Corner

9947 Hull St. Rd., No. 289
Richmond, VA 23236
Ph: (804)814-1727
E-mail: nancy@coordinatorscorner.com
URL: http://www.coordinatorscorner.com

Description: Offers access to articles on managing a wedding consultant business. Provides information from the industry's top experts.

★13016★ American Society of Wedding Professionals (ASWP)

268 Griggs Ave.
Teaneck, NJ 07666
Ph: (973)472-1800   Fax: (973)574-7626
Fr: 800-526-0497
E-mail: lawrence@carroll.com
URL: http://www.sellthebride.com

Members: Professionals in the wedding industry. **Purpose:** Promotes the wedding professional and educates brides on the experience of working with a consultant. **Activities:** Provides trends, etiquette, marketing, consulting information, directory listing, referrals, networking, and co-op advertising. Offers local forums for information exchange among members. Compiles statistics and conducts educational programs and seminars.

★13017★ Association of Bridal Consultants (ABC)

56 Danbury Rd., Ste. 11
New Milford, CT 06776
Ph: (860)355-0464   Fax: (860)354-1404
E-mail: office@bridalassn.com
URL: http://www.bridalassn.com

Description: Represents independent bridal

and wedding consultants; persons employed by companies in wedding-related businesses and novices looking to get into the business. Strives to improve professionalism and recognition of bridal and wedding consultants. Offers professional development program, start-up manual and seminars. Provides advertising, publicity, referrals, and information services. Operates speakers' bureau; compiles statistics.

★13018★ Association of Certified Professional Wedding Consultants
7791 Prestwick Cir.
San Jose, CA 95135
Ph: (408)528-9000   Fax: (408)528-9333
E-mail: anola@acpwc.com
URL: http://www.acpwc.com

Description: Professional society. Offers personalized training courses.

★13019★ Association of Wedding Professionals
PO Box 743005
Dallas, TX 75374-3005
E-mail: info@awpdallas.com

URL: http://www.awpdallas.com
Description: Dedicated to helping its members grow through networking opportunities, education programs, and special event showcases.

★13020★ Association for Wedding Professionals International
6700 Freeport Blvd., Ste. 282
Sacramento, CA 95822
Ph: (916)392-5000   Fr: 800-242-4461
E-mail: richard@afwpi.com
URL: http://www.afwpi.com

Description: Acts as a central source of information and referrals.

★13021★ Bridal Association of America
531 H St.
Bakersfield, CA 93304
Ph: (661)633-1949   Fax: (661)633-9199
E-mail: kyle@bridalassociationofamerica.com
URL: http://www.bridalassociationofamerica.com

Description: Acts as a forum for wedding professionals.

★13022★ Wedding and Portrait Photographers International (WPPI)
1312 Lincoln Blvd.
PO Box 2003
Santa Monica, CA 90406-2003
Ph: (310)451-0090   Fax: (310)395-9058
URL: http://www.wppinow.com/index2.tml

Description: Represents wedding portrait and digital photographers and photographers employed at general photography studios. Promotes high artistic and technical standards in wedding photography. Serves as a forum for the exchange of technical knowledge and experience; makes available the expertise of top professionals in the field of photographic arts and technology, advertising, sales promotion, marketing, public relations, accounting, business management, tax, and profit planning. Members are offered the opportunity to purchase special products and services.

Wholesale and Retail Buyers

SOURCES OF HELP-WANTED ADS

★13023★ Aftermarket Business
Advanstar Communications
641 Lexington Ave.
8th Fl.
New York, NY 10022
Ph: (212)951-6600   Fax: (212)951-6793
Fr: 800-225-4569
URL: http://www.advanstar.com

Monthly. Free to qualified subscribers. Magazine (tabloid) for purchasing professionals in the retail automotive aftermarket.

★13024★ AudioVideo International
AudioVideo International
275 Madison Ave.
New York, NY 10016
Ph: (212)682-3755   Fax: (212)682-2730
E-mail: avi@dempa-us.com

Quarterly. $48.00/year for individuals, 1 year; $84.00/year for single issue, 2 years. Magazine for domestic retailers of consumer electronics products. Feature stories include trends and developments in audio, hi-fi, TV, video, car stereo, and home and personal electronics products.

★13025★ Benchmarking Purchasing
American Purchasing Society
8 E Galena Blvd., Ste. 203
Aurora, IL 60506
Ph: (630)859-0250   Fax: (630)859-0270
URL: http://www.american-purchasing.com

Annual. Professional journal covering issues in purchasing.

★13026★ Chain Store Age
Lebhar-Friedman, Inc.
425 Park Ave., 6th Fl.
New York, NY 10022
Ph: (212)756-5000   Fax: (212)756-5215
URL: http://www.chainstoreage.com

Monthly. Magazine for management of retail chain headquarters. Reports on marketing, merchandising, strategic planning, physical supports, and shopping center developments, retail technology credit and communications.

★13027★ DNR
Fairchild Publications Inc.
750 Third Ave.
New York, NY 10017
Ph: (212)630-4000
URL: http://www.dnrnews.com/

Daily (morn.). Daily newspaper reporting on men's and boys' clothing, retailing, and textiles.

★13028★ Electronic Business
Reed Business Information
225 Wyman St.
Waltham, MA 02451-1216
URL: http://www.edn.com/index.asp?layout=businessCenter

Monthly. Magazine for purchasing managers and buyers of electronic components and materials used in end product manufacturing.

★13029★ Electronics Supply and Manufacturing
CMP Media L.L.C.
600 Community Dr.
Manhasset, NY 11030
Ph: (516)562-5000   Fax: (516)562-7830
URL: http://www.cmp.com/products/pr_det_elecsupply.jhtml

Monthly. Reports business and technology trends of the electronics industry.

★13030★ Gifts & Decorative Accessories
Reed Business Information
360 Park Ave. S
New York, NY 10010
Ph: (646)746-6400   Fax: (646)746-7431
URL: http://www.reedbusiness.com

Monthly. International magazine for retailers of gifts, greeting cards, decorative accessories, and stationery-related merchandise.

★13031★ Home Channel News
Lebhar-Friedman, Inc.
425 Park Ave., 6th Fl.
New York, NY 10022
Ph: (212)756-5000   Fax: (212)756-5215
URL: http://www.homechannelnews.com

$189.00/year for individuals. Business tabloid serving home center/building material retailers.

★13032★ LDB Interior Textiles
E.W. Williams Publications Co.
2125 Center Ave., Ste. 305
Fort Lee, NJ 07024-5898
Ph: (201)592-7007   Fax: (201)592-7171
URL: http://www.ldbinteriortextiles.com

Monthly. $72.00/year for individuals; $125.00/year for Canada; $150.00/year for elsewhere; $100.00 for two years; $7.00/year for single issue; $12.00 for single issue, Canada; $18.00/year for single issue, elsewhere. Magazine for buyers of home fashions, including bed, bath and table linens, hard and soft window treatments, home fragrances, decorative pillows and home accessories, accent rugs, and decorative fabrics.

★13033★ Music Inc.
Maher Publications Inc.
102 N Haven Rd.
Elmhurst, IL 60126
Ph: (630)941-2030   Fax: (630)941-3210
Fr: 800-535-7496
URL: http://www.musicinc.com

$17.00/year for individuals. Magazine serving retailers of music and sound products.

★13034★ Music Trades
Music Trades Corp.
80 West St.
Englewood, NJ 07631
Ph: (201)871-1965   Fax: (201)871-0455
Fr: 800-423-6530
URL: http://www.musictrades.com/

Monthly. $23.00/year for individuals, foreign; $23.00 for two years, domestic; $16.00/year for individuals, domestic. Music trade magazine.

★13035★ National Jeweler

The Nielsen Co.
770 Broadway
New York, NY 10003
Ph: (646)654-5000   Fax: (646)654-5002
URL: http://www.nationaljewelernetwork.com/njn/index.jsp

Semimonthly. $10.00 for single issue, cover; $89.00/year for U.S. $104.00/year for Canada; $330.00/year for other countries, airmail only. Jewelry industry magazine.

★13036★ Purchasing Magazine

Reed Business Information
225 Wyman St.
Waltham, MA 02451-1216
URL: http://www.purchasing.com

Free. Magazine for buying professionals.

★13037★ Retailing Today

Lebhar-Friedman, Inc.
425 Park Ave., 6th Fl.
New York, NY 10022
Ph: (212)756-5000   Fax: (212)756-5215
URL: http://www.retailingtoday.com/

Semimonthly. Retailing business industry news and information.

★13038★ Southern PHC Magazine

Southern Trade Publications Inc.
Box 7344
Greensboro, NC 27417
Ph: (336)454-3516   Fax: (336)454-3649

Bimonthly. $10.00/year. Free to qualified subscribers; $10.00/year others. Trade magazine covering plumbing, heating, and air conditioning, targeted to contractors and wholesalers in 14 southern states.

★13039★ Sporting Goods Dealer

Bill Communications Inc.
1115 Northmeadow Pkwy.
Roswell, GA 30076
Ph: (770)569-1540   Fax: (770)569-5105
Fr: 800-241-9034
URL: http://www.sgdealer.com/sportinggoodsdealer/index.jsp

Bimonthly. Magazine that offers expert reporting on trends affecting team dealers and retailers who service schools, colleges, pro and local teams.

★13040★ Tire Business

Crain Communications Inc.
1725 Merriman Rd., Ste. 300
Akron, OH 44313-5283
Ph: (330)836-9180   Fax: (330)836-1005
URL: http://www.tirebusiness.com

Semimonthly. $79.00/year for individuals; $148.00 for two years; $107.00/year for individuals, Canada; $194.00 for two years, Canada; $119.00/year for other countries; $208.00 for two years, all other countries; $99.00/year for individuals, web only. Newspaper (tabloid) serving independent tire dealers, retreaders, tire wholesalers and others allied to the tire industry.

★13041★ Tire Review

Babcox
3550 Embassy Pky.
Akron, OH 44333
Ph: (330)670-1234   Fax: (330)670-0874
URL: http://www.tirereview.com/

Monthly. Free to qualified subscribers. Magazine containing news and business information about the tire, custom wheel, automotive service, and retreading industries.

★13042★ TWICE

Reed Business Information
360 Park Ave. S
New York, NY 10010
Ph: (646)746-6400   Fax: (646)746-7431
E-mail: mgrand@reedbusiness.com
URL: http://www.reedbusiness.com/

Biweekly. Free. Trade tabloid covering consumer electronics, appliance, and camera industries for retailers, manufacturers, and distributors.

EMPLOYER DIRECTORIES AND NETWORKING LISTS

★13043★ Directory of Department Stores

Chain Store Guide
3922 Coconut Palm Dr.
Tampa, FL 33619
Fax: (813)627-6883   Fr: 800-778-9794
URL: http://www.csgis.com

Annual, 2005. $335.00 for individuals. Covers 214 department store companies, 1,500 shoe store companies, 200 jewelry store companies, 95 optical store companies, and 70 leather and luggage store companies in the United States and Canada, with annual sales of at least $250,000. Entries include: Company name; physical and mailing addresses; phone and fax numbers; company e-mail and web addresses; listing type; total sales; industry sales; total selling square footage; store prototype sizes; total units; units by trade name; trading areas; projected openings and remodelings; self-distributing indicator; distribution center locations; resident buyers' name and location; leased departments area, name, and location; mail order catalog indicator; Internet order processing indicator; private label softlines, hardlines, and credit card indicators; furniture styles and price lines; average number of checkouts; year founded; public company indicator; parent company name and location; subsidiaries' names and locations; regional and divisional office locations; key personnel with titles; store locations, with address, phone number, and manager name (department stores only). Arrangement: Geographical. Indexes: Alphabetical; product lines; exclusions.

★13044★ Directory of Drug Store & HBC Chains

Chain Store Guide
3922 Coconut Palm Dr.
Tampa, FL 33619
Fax: (813)627-6883   Fr: 800-778-9794
URL: http://www.csgis.com

Annual, May. Covers more than 1,700 drug store chains operations of two or more units, including mass merchants and grocers with pharmacies; 215 wholesale drug companies in the United States and Canada. Entries include: For retailers–company name; phone and fax numbers; physical and mailing addresses; company e-mail and web addresses; listing type; number of stores; product lines; percentage of sales by product line; total sales; prescription drug sales; percentage of prescriptions filled with generic drugs; number of prescriptions filled daily; percentage of prescriptions filled with private third party, cash, and Medicaid; number of stores by type; mail order pharmacy indicator; managed care division indicator; projected openings and remodelings; store prototype sizes; total selling square footage; trading area; franchise group headquarters' name and location; distribution center and primary wholesaler names and locations; number of specialty departments; packaged liquor indicators; private label indicators; computerized pharmacy indicator; average number of checkouts; year founded; public company indicator; parent company name and location; regional and divisional office locations; headquarters personnel with titles. For wholesalers–company name, address, phone, and fax; e-mail and web addresses; listing type; product lines; percentage of sales by product line; total sales; percentage of sales by customer type; total stores served; number of member and non-member stores served; trading area; group store trading names; wholesaler type; distribution center locations; private label indicator; year founded; public company indicator; headquarters personnel with titles. Arrangement: Separate geographical sections for retailers and wholesalers. Indexes: Alphabetical, exclusions.

★13045★ STORES-Top 100 Retailers Issue

National Retail Federation
325 7th St. NW, Ste. 1100
Washington, DC 20004
Ph: (202)783-7971   Fax: (202)737-2849
Fr: 800-673-4692
URL: http://www.stores.org

Annual, July. $75.00. Publication includes: 100 U.S. retail companies having largest estimated sales during preceding year. Entries include: Name of store, city, number of stores included, and total sales. Arrangement: Ranked by sales.

★13046★ The Wholesaler-'The Wholesaling 100' Issue

TMB Publishing Inc.
1838 Techny Ct.
Northbrook, IL 60062
Ph: (847)564-1127   Fax: (847)564-1264

URL: http://www.plumbingengineer.com

Annual, July; $50.00 for individuals. Publication includes: Ranks 100 leading wholesalers of plumbing, heating, air conditioning, refrigeration equipment, and industrial pipe, valves and fittings. Entries include: Company name, address, phone, fax, names and titles of key personnel, number of employees, business breakdown (percentage). Arrangement: Ranked by sales.

HANDBOOKS AND MANUALS

★13047★ *Opportunities in Retailing Careers*

The McGraw-Hill Companies
PO Box 182604
Columbus, OH 43272
Fax: (614)759-3749   Fr: 877-883-5524
E-mail: customer.service@mcgraw-hill.com
URL: http://www.mcgraw-hill.com

Roslyn Dolber. 2003. 160 pages. $13.95 (paper). Discusses a number of opportunities in retailing, from entry-level to retail management.

★13048★ *Resumes for Sales and Marketing Careers*

The McGraw-Hill Companies
PO Box 182604
Columbus, OH 43272
Fax: (614)759-3749   Fr: 877-883-5524
E-mail: customer.service@mcgraw-hill.com
URL: http://www.mcgraw-hill.com

Chuck Cochran and Donna Peerce. 1998. $13.95. 336 pages. Sample resumes and cover letters from all levels of the sales and marketing field.

EMPLOYMENT AGENCIES AND SEARCH FIRMS

★13049★ The Aspire Group

52 Second Ave, 1st Fl
Waltham, MA 02451-1129
Fax: (718)890-1810   Fr: 800-487-2967
URL: http://www.bmanet.com

Employment agency.

★13050★ Britt Associates Inc.

3533 Lake Shore Dr.
Joliet, IL 60431-8820
Ph: (815)436-8300   Fax: (815)436-9617
E-mail: brittassoc@aol.com

Employment agency.

★13051★ Colli Associates

414 Caboose Ln.
Valrico, FL 33594
Ph: (813)681-2145   Fax: (813)661-5217
E-mail: colli@gte.net

Employment agency. Executive search firm.

TRADESHOWS

★13052★ Great Lakes Industrial Show

North American Exposition Co.
33 Rutherford Ave.
Boston, MA 02129
Ph: (617)242-6092   Fax: (617)242-1817
Fr: 800-225-1577
E-mail: naexpo@hotmail.com
URL: http://www.naexpo.com

Annual. **Primary Exhibits:** Industrial products, machine tools, hand tools, pneumatics, hydraulics, plant engineering, and maintenance, paper and packaging, plastics, rubber products, material handling equipment, and dies and stampings.

★13053★ The NAMSB Show

NSI
309 5th Ave., Ste. 307
New York, NY 10016
Ph: (212)685-4550   Fax: (212)685-4688
Fr: 800-936-2672

Semiannual. **Primary Exhibits:** Product lines include mens' and boy's clothing, sportswear, footwear, streetwear, unisex, and accessories.

★13054★ Supermarket Industry Convention and Educational Exposition

Food Marketing Institute
655 15th St., NW, Ste. 700
Washington, DC 20005
Ph: (202)452-8444   Fax: (202)429-4519
E-mail: fmi@fmi.org
URL: http://www.fmi.org

Annual. **Primary Exhibits:** Products, equipment, supplies, and services available to and through the supermarket industry, including grocery products, perishables, general merchandise, health and beauty aids, food service equipment, store design services, data processing equipment, advertising, and warehouse services.

OTHER SOURCES

★13055★ National Association of College Stores (NACS)

500 E Lorain St.
Oberlin, OH 44074
Ph: (440)775-7777   Fax: (440)775-4769
Fr: 800-622-7498
E-mail: membership@nacs.org
URL: http://www.nacs.org

Members: Institutional, private, leased, and cooperative college stores (2,800) selling books, supplies, and other merchandise to college students, faculty, and staff; associate members include publishers and suppliers (1,200). **Purpose:** Seeks to effectively serve higher education by providing educational research, advocacy and other to college stores and their suppliers. **Activities:** Maintains NACSCORP, Inc., a wholly owned subsidiary corporation, which distributes trade and mass market books and educational software. Sponsors seminars. Conducts manager certification, specialized education, and research programs. Maintains College Stores Research and Educational Foundation which provides grants for educational programs and conducts research.

★13056★ National Retail Federation (NRF)

325 7th St. NW, Ste. 1100
Washington, DC 20004
Ph: (202)783-7971   Fax: (202)737-2849
Fr: 800-673-4692
E-mail: mullint@nrf.com
URL: http://www.nrf.com

Purpose: Represents state retail associations, several dozen national retail associations, as well as large and small corporate members representing the breadth and diversity of the retail industry's establishment and employees. **Activities:** Conducts informational and educational conferences related to all phases of retailing including financial planning and cash management, taxation, economic forecasting, expense planning, shortage control, credit, electronic data processing, telecommunications, merchandise management, buying, traffic, security, supply, materials handling, store planning and construction, personnel administration, recruitment and training, and advertising and display.

Writers and Editors

SOURCES OF HELP-WANTED ADS

★13057★ **Adweek**
VNU Business Media USA
770 Broadway
New York, NY 10003
Ph: (646)654-4500
URL: http://www.adweek.com/aw/index.jsp

Weekly. $149.00/year for individuals, 12 months basic; $85.00 for individuals, 6 months basic; $135.00 for individuals, 6 months premium; $249.00/year for individuals, 12 months premium; $20.00/year for individuals, monthly online. Advertising news magazine.

★13058★ **American Markets Newsletter**
American Markets Newsletter
1974 46th Ave.
San Francisco, CA 94116
Ph: (415)753-6057   Fax: (415)753-6057
E-mail: sheila.oconnor@juno.com.

Description: Six issues/year. Contains market information for writers. Recurring features include letters to the editor, book reviews, job listings, notices of publications available, and columns titled American Markets, Overseas Markets, Writers Tips, Press Trips, and Market Guidelines of the Month.

★13059★ **Amherst Writers and Artists Newsletter**
Amherst Writers & Artists Press Inc.
190 University Dr., Ste. 1
PO Box 1076
Amherst, MA 01002
Ph: (413)253-3307   Fax: (413)256-1207
E-mail: info@amherstwriters.com
URL: http://www.amherstwriters.com/

Description: Semiannual, February and September. Newsletter of the Amherst Writers and Artists Press. Recurring features include a calendar of events, news of members, notices of publications available, and news of educational opportunities.

★13060★ **ASJA Members' Newsletter**
American Society of Journalists and
  Authors
1501 Broadway, Ste. 302
New York, NY 10036
Ph: (212)997-0947   Fax: (212)937-2315
URL: http://www.asja.org/

Description: Monthly. Includes confidential market information.

★13061★ **Authors Guild-Bulletin**
Authors Guild
31 E. 32nd St., 7th Fl.
New York, NY 10016
Ph: (212)563-5904   Fax: (212)564-5363
E-mail: staff@authorsguild.org
URL: http://www.authorsguild.org/

Description: Quarterly. Concerned with the business interests of professional authors, including copyright protection, contract problems, freedom of expression, taxation, and relevant legislation. Recurring features include listings of books by members, news of members and publishers, editorial job changes, job openings, surveys, symposia transcripts, and legal updates.

★13062★ **Authors' Newsletter**
Arizona Authors' Association
6145 W. Echo Lane
Glendale, AZ 85302
Ph: (623)847-9343
E-mail: info@azauthors.com
URL: http://www.azauthors.com/

Description: Bimonthly. Serves as a information and referral service of the Association.

★13063★ **AWP Job List**
Association of Writers & Writing Programs
Mailstop 1E3
George Mason Univ.
Fairfax, VA 22030-4444
Ph: (703)993-4301   Fax: (703)993-4302
E-mail: services@awpwriter.org
URL: http://www.awpwriter.org/careers/job-list.htm

Description: Monthly. Lists job opportunities

for writers, both in academia and in the business sector.

★13064★ **CAP Communications-Contacts**
CAP Communications
35-20 Broadway
Astoria, NY 11106
Ph: (718)721-0508   Fax: (718)274-3387
E-mail: contactspr@aol.com

Description: Weekly. Provides information on specific editorial needs of newspapers, magazines, wire feature services, and radio and television program directors. Carries media description, area of interest, and addresses and phone numbers of contact persons. Recurring features include a column titled Between the Lines.

★13065★ **Children's Book Insider**
Children's Book Insider
901 Columbia Rd.
Fort Collins, CO 80525
Ph: (970)495-0056   Fax: (970)493-1810
Fr: 800-807-1916
URL: http://www.write4kids.com

Description: Monthly. Discusses writing and selling books and stories for children. Recurring features include interviews, news of educational opportunities, job listings, and columns titled Writing Workshop, Market News, and Trends.

★13066★ **Columbia Journalism Review**
Columbia Journalism Review
2950 Broadway, Journalism Bldg.
Columbia University
New York, NY 10027
Ph: (212)854-1881   Fax: (212)854-8580
Fr: 888-425-7782
E-mail: cjr@columbia.edu
URL: http://www.cjr.org/

Bimonthly. $19.95/year for U.S. $27.95 for single issue, Canadian & international orders. Magazine focusing on journalism.

★13067★ **Creativity Connection**

University of Wisconsin
716 Langdon St.
Madison, WI 53706
Ph: (608)263-6960   Fax: (608)265-2475
E-mail: info@dcs.wisc.edu.
URL: http://www.dcs.wisc.edu/lsa/writing/creativity_connection.htm

Description: Quarterly. Features profiles and how-to articles for writers. Recurring features include letters to the editor, interviews, news of research, collection, book reviews, notices of publications available, and columns titled What Every Writer Should Know, Pub Tour, All Questions Considered, and Carson's Corner.

★13068★ **Daily Variety**

Reed Business Information
5700 Wilshire Blvd., Ste. 120
Los Angeles, CA 90036
Ph: (323)857-6600   Fax: (323)857-0494
URL: http://www.reedbusiness.com/index.asp?layout=theListProfile&

Daily. Global entertainment newspaper (tabloid).

★13069★ **Directory Marketplace**

Todd Publications
PO Box 500
Millwood, NY 10546
Ph: (914)373-4750   Fax: (914)373-4750
Fr: (866)896-0916
URL: http://www.toddpublications.com

Description: Quarterly. Serves as a means for directory and reference book publishers to advertise their publications. Listings for more than 300 directories and reference books for sale.

★13070★ **Dirty Goat**

Host Publications, Inc.
451 Greenwich St., Ste. 7J
New York, NY 10013
Ph: (212)905-2365   Fax: (212)905-2369
URL: http://www.thedirtygoat.com/index.html

Semiannual. Journal covering poetry, prose, drama, literature and visual art.

★13071★ **The Dramatists Guild Newsletter**

The Dramatists Guild of America Inc.
1501 Broadway, Ste. 701
New York, NY 10036
Ph: (212)398-9366   Fax: (212)944-0420
Fr: 800-289-9366
URL: http://www.dramatistsguild.com

Description: Bimonthly. Contains news of Guild activities, including seminars, regional playwriting news, playwriting contests, workshops and playreading units. Offers information on organizations which are looking for new plays. Features business advice columns and articles pertinent to professional theatre writing.

★13072★ **Editor & Publisher**

Editor & Publisher Magazine
770 Broadway
New York, NY 10003-9595
Ph: (646)654-5500   Fax: (646)654-5370
Fr: 800-562-2706
URL: http://www.editorandpublisher.com/eandp/index.jsp

Weekly (Mon.). $99.00/year for individuals, print and online; $159.00/year for Canada, print and online; $320.00/year for other countries; $7.95/year for individuals, monthly. Magazine focusing on newspaper journalism, advertising, printing equipment, and interactive services.

★13073★ **Fiction Writer's Guideline**

Fiction Writer's Connection
PO Box 72300
Albuquerque, NM 87195
Ph: (505)352-9490   Fax: (505)352-9495
Fr: 800-248-2758
E-mail: BCamenson@aol.com
URL: http://www.fictionwriters.com

Description: Bimonthly. Offers practical advice and support on writing and getting published. Recurring features include interviews, book reviews, and advice from agents and editors.

★13074★ **The Great Blue Beacon**

The Great Blue Beacon
1425 Patriot Dr.
Melbourne, FL 32940
Ph: (321)253-5869
URL: http://www.bluebeacongroup.com

Description: Quarterly. Newsletter for writers. Includes contest listings, publications of interested writers, writing-related cartoons, and writing-related articles. Recurring features include book reviews.

★13075★ **History News**

American Association for State & Local History
1717 Church St.
Nashville, TN 37203-2991
Ph: (615)320-3203   Fax: (615)327-9013
URL: http://www.aaslh.org/historynews.htm

Quarterly. Magazine for employees of historic sites, museums, and public history agencies. Coverage includes museum education programs and techniques for working with volunteers.

★13076★ **HOW**

F & W Publications Inc.
4700 E Galbraith Rd.
Cincinnati, OH 45236
Ph: (513)531-2690   Fax: (513)531-0798
Fr: 800-289-0963
URL: http://www.howdesign.com

Bimonthly. $29.96/year for U.S. $45.00/year for Canada; $52.00/year for other countries. Instructional trade magazine.

★13077★ **Independent Publisher Online**

Jenkins Group Inc.
1129 Woodmere Ave., Ste. B
Traverse City, MI 49684-2206
Ph: (231)933-0445   Fax: (231)933-0448
Fr: 800-706-4636
URL: http://www.independentpublisher.com/

Monthly. Free. Online magazine containing book reviews and articles about independent publishing.

★13078★ **Metro Magazine**

Bobit Business Media
3520 Challenger St.
Torrance, CA 90503
Ph: (310)533-2400   Fax: (310)533-2500
E-mail: info@metro-magazine.com
URL: http://www.metro-magazine.com

Free. Magazine on public transportation.

★13079★ **The New Republic**

The New Republic L.L.C.
1331 H St. NW, Ste. 700
Washington, DC 20005
Ph: (202)508-4444   Fax: (202)628-9380
E-mail: tnrcustserv@cdsfulfillment.com
URL: http://www.tnr.com

Weekly. $39.97/year for individuals, print; $29.95/year for individuals, digital. Journal featuring current events comments and reviews.

★13080★ **Novelists, Inc.**

Novelists, Inc.
PO Box 2037
Manhattan, KS 66505
E-mail: ninc@varney.com
URL: http://www.ninc.com/

Description: Monthly. Covers activities of Novelists, Inc. Reports on activities of Novelists, Inc, an association dedicated to serving the needs of multi-published writers of popular fiction. Offers advice and wisdom from other writers.

★13081★ **Ohio Writer**

Cleveland's Literary Center
2570 Superior Ave., Ste. 203
Cleveland, OH 44114
Ph: (216)694-0000
E-mail: judith@the-lit.org.
URL: http://www.pwlgc.com

Description: Six issues/year. Contains book reviews, announcements, calendars, interviews, and articles of interest to writers living in Ohio.

★13082★ **The Poetry Connection**

Poetry Connection
13455 SW 16 Ct., No. F-405
Pembroke Pines, FL 33027
Ph: (954)431-3016
URL: http://www.thepoetryconnection.com

Description: Monthly. Provides listings of poetry publishers and contests, greeting card opportunities, and performing arts publications/organizations. Offers Magic Circle (Poetry Distribution Network Service) and books on selling poetry, publicity, and self-publishing.

★13083★ Producers Masterguide

Producers Masterguide
60 E 8th St., 34th Fl.
New York, NY 10003-6514
Ph: (212)777-4002   Fax: (212)777-4101
URL: http://
www.producers.masterguide.com

Annual. $155.00/year for U.S. $165.00/year for Canada; $195.00/year for other countries. An international film and TV production directory and guide for the professional motion picture, broadcast television, feature film, TV commercial, cable/satellite, digital and videotape industries in the U.S., Canada, the UK, the Caribbean Islands, Mexico, Australia, New Zealand, Europe, Israel, Morocco, the Far East, and South America.

★13084★ Publishers Weekly

Publishers Weekly
360 Park Ave. S.
New York, NY 10010
Ph: (646)746-6598
URL: http://www.publishersweekly.com

Weekly. $239.99/year for individuals; $299.99/year for Canada and Mexico; $399.99/year for other countries, air delivery. Magazine for publishers.

★13085★ The Quarterly of the National Writing Project

National Writing Project
School of Education
University of California
2105 Bancroft Way No. 1042
Berkeley, CA 94720-1042
Ph: (510)642-0963   Fax: (510)642-4545
E-mail: nwp@nwp.org
URL: http://www.writingproject.org/cs/nwpp/
print/nwp_docs/322

Description: Four issues/year. Explores the teaching and learning of writing and the connections between research and practice. Recurring features include book reviews.

★13086★ Romance Writers Report

Romance Writers of America Inc.
16000 Stuebner Airline Rd., Ste. 140
Spring, TX 77379
Ph: (832)717-5200   Fax: (832)717-5201
E-mail: info@rwanational.org
URL: http://www.rwanational.org

Description: Bimonthly. Provides romance writers with information, assistance, knowledge, and support by publishing agents' special reports, author profiles, and how-to articles. Recurring features include editorials, news of members' activities, letters to the editor, interviews, reports of meetings, book reviews, and a calendar of events. Includes columns titled Market News, President's Column, Conferences and Contests, and Sparks 'N' Spice.

★13087★ The Salmagundian

Salmagundi Art Club
47 5th Ave.
New York, NY 10003
Ph: (212)255-7740
URL: http://www.salmagundi.org

Description: 2/year. Highlights activities of the Club, a fellowship and exhibition organization for painters, sculptors, writers, and artists. Profiles artists and their work. Recurring features include notes on members, coverage of Clubhouse activities.

★13088★ Scavenger's Newsletter

Janet Fox
833 Main St.
Osage City, KS 66523-1241
Ph: (785)528-3538
E-mail: jfoxtx@aol.com
URL: http://www.argentmoon.net/scavengers/index.htm

Description: Monthly. Provides information for fantasy, horror, science fiction and mystery writers and artists. Lists markets for these materials.

★13089★ Sojourners

Sojourners
2401 15th St. NW
Washington, DC 20009
Ph: (202)328-8842   Fax: (202)328-8757
Fr: 800-714-7474
URL: http://www.sojo.net/

Monthly. $39.95/year for individuals; $49.95/year for Canada; $59.95/year for other countries; $60.00/year for individuals, supporting; $110.00/year for individuals, partnership. Independent, ecumenical Christian magazine which analyzes faith, politics, and culture from a progressive, justice-oriented perspective.

★13090★ tech Comments

Society for Technical Communication, Southeastern Michigan Chapter
PO Box 1289
Ann Arbor, MI 48106
URL: http://www.stc-sm.org/

Description: Monthly. Keeps chapter members informed of events and shares information about the work of technical communicators. Recurring features include letters to the editor, a calendar of events, reports of meetings, news of educational opportunities, job listings, book reviews, notices of publications available, and messages from chapter president and regional director.

★13091★ Travel Writer

Society of American Travel Writers
7044 S. 13 St.
Oak Creek, WI 53154
Ph: (414)908-4949   Fax: (414)768-8001
E-mail: satw@satw.org
URL: http://www.satw.org/

Description: Ten issues/year. Advises and provides information for travel writers.

★13092★ A View from the Loft

A View from the Loft
Ste. 200, Open Book, 1011 Washington Ave. S.
Minneapolis, MN 55415
Ph: (612)215-2575   Fax: (612)215-2576
E-mail: loft@loft.org
URL: http://www.loft.org

Description: Bimonthly, except for July. Acts as a "forum for the exchange of information and opinions of writers." Presents articles on writing and publishing.

★13093★ The Writer Magazine

Kalmbach Publishing Co.
PO Box 1612
21027 Crossroads Cir.
Waukesha, WI 53187-1612
Ph: (262)796-8776   Fax: (262)796-1615
Fr: 800-533-6644
URL: http://www.writermag.com

Monthly. $32.00/year for individuals; $61.00 for individuals, two years; $88.00 for individuals, 3 years; $44.00/year for other countries; $82.00 for two years, outside USA; $119.00 for other countries, 3 years. Magazine for freelance writers. Publishing practical information and advice on how to write publishable material and where to sell it.

★13094★ Writers Ask

Glimmer Train Press Inc.
1211 NW Glisan St., Ste. 207
Portland, OR 97209
Ph: (503)221-0836   Fax: (503)221-0837
E-mail: info@glimmertrain.com
URL: http://www.glimmertrain.com/writersask.html

Description: Quarterly. Disseminates information of interest to writers.

★13095★ Writer's Digest

F & W Publications Inc.
4700 E Galbraith Rd.
Cincinnati, OH 45236
Ph: (513)531-2690   Fax: (513)531-0798
Fr: 800-289-0963
URL: http://www.writersdigest.com

Monthly. $20.00/year for individuals; $30.00/year for Canada, including GST/HST; $30.00/year for other countries, surface delivery. Professional magazine for writers.

★13096★ Writing That Works

Communications Concepts Inc.
7481 Huntsman Blvd., No. 720
Springfield, VA 22153-1648
Ph: (703)643-2200   Fax: (703)643-2329
URL: http://www.apexawards.com/selectedarticles.htm

Description: Monthly. Advises corporate, nonprofit, agency and independent communicators on business writing and publishing. Also covers writing techniques, style matters, publication management, and online publishing. Publisher also sponsors annual APEX Awards for Publication Excellence.

PLACEMENT AND JOB REFERRAL SERVICES

★13097★ Education Writers Association (EWA)

2122 P St. NW, Ste. 201
Washington, DC 20037
Ph: (202)452-9830　　Fax: (202)452-9837
E-mail: ewa@ewa.org
URL: http://www.ewa.org

Members: Education writers and reporters of daily and weekly newspapers, national magazines of general circulation, and radio and television stations; associate members are school and college public relations personnel and others with a serious interest in education writing. **Purpose:** Improves the quality of education reporting and interpretation; encourages the development of education coverage by the press; to help attract top-notch writers and reporters to the education field. **Activities:** Sponsors regional and special workshops. Provides job referral/bank services.

★13098★ Evangelical Press Association (EPA)

PO Box 28129
Crystal, MN 55428
Ph: (763)535-4793　　Fax: (763)535-4794
E-mail: director@epassoc.org
URL: http://www.epassoc.org

Members: Editors and publishers of Christian periodicals. **Activities:** Maintains placement service.

★13099★ Health Science Communications Association (HeSCA)

39 Wedgewood Dr., Ste. A
Jewett City, CT 06351-2420
Ph: (860)376-5915　　Fax: (860)376-6621
E-mail: hesca@hesca.org
URL: http://www.hesca.org

Description: Represents media managers, graphic artists, biomedical librarians, producers, faculty members of health science and veterinary medicine schools, health professional organizations, and industry representatives. Acts as a clearinghouse for information used by professionals engaged in health science communications. Coordinates Media Festivals Program that recognizes outstanding media productions in the health sciences. Offers placement service.

★13100★ National Association of Hispanic Journalists (NAHJ)

1000 National Press Bldg.
529 14th St. NW
Washington, DC 20045-2001
Ph: (202)662-7145　　Fax: (202)662-7144
Fr: 888-346-NAHJ
E-mail: nahj@nahj.org
URL: http://www.nahj.org

Description: Aims to organize and support Hispanics involved in news gathering and dissemination. Encourages journalism and communications study and practice by Hispanics. Seeks recognition for Hispanic members of the profession regarding their skills and achievements. Promotes fair and accurate media treatment of Hispanics; opposes job discrimination and demeaning stereotypes. Works to increase educational and career opportunities and development for Hispanics in the field. Seeks to foster greater awareness of members' cultural identity, interests, and concerns. Provides a united voice for Hispanic journalists with the aim of achieving national visibility. Offers placement services to Hispanic students. Activities include: a census of Hispanic media professionals nationwide; writing contest for Hispanic students. Offers scholarships, seminars, and training workshops.

EMPLOYER DIRECTORIES AND NETWORKING LISTS

★13101★ Agents Directory

Emmis Books
Old Firehouse, 1700 Madison Rd.
Cincinnati, OH 45206
Ph: (513)861-4045　　Fax: (513)861-4430
Fr: 800-913-9563
URL: http://www.emmisbooks.com

$13.59. Covers information about the type of work that agent accepts, recent sales, and contact information. Entries include: writer's organizations.

★13102★ American Society of Journalists and Authors-Directory

American Society of Journalists & Authors
1501 Broadway, Ste. 302
New York, NY 10036
Ph: (212)997-0947　　Fax: (212)937-2315
URL: http://www.asja.org

Annual, January. Covers 1,000 member freelance nonfiction writers. Entries include: Writer's name, home and office addresses and phone numbers, specialties, areas of expertise; name, address and phone number of agent; memberships; books; periodicals to which contributed; awards. Arrangement: Alphabetical. Indexes: Subject specialty; type of material written; geographical.

★13103★ ANR National Directory of Community Newspapers

American Newspaper Representatives Inc.
2075 W Big Beaver Rd., Ste. 310
Troy, MI 48084
Ph: (248)643-7766　　Fax: (248)643-9914
Fr: 800-550-7557
URL: http://www.anrinc.net/

Weekly (Mon.), May/June. Number of listings: 7,000. Entries include: Name of weekly newspaper, address, county, type of area, circulation, day published, name of publisher, and information on advertising rates and production specifications. Arrangement: Geographical.

★13104★ Association of American University Presses-Directory

Association of American University Presses
71 W 23rd St.
New York, NY 10010-4102
Ph: (212)989-1010　　Fax: (212)989-0275
URL: http://www.aaupnet.org

Annual; latest edition spring 2007. $21.00 for individuals. Covers 124 presses and affiliates worldwide. Entries include: Press name, address, phone, e-mail, URL; titles and names of complete editorial and managerial staffs; editorial program; mailing, warehouse, printing, and/or customer service addresses; other details. Arrangement: Classified by press affiliation, alphabetical by press name. Indexes: Personal name.

★13105★ Association of Professional Communication Consultants-Membership Directory

Association of Professional Communication Consultants
104 Trace Ridge Dr.
Clinton, MS 39056-6153
Ph: (601)924-2173　　Fax: (601)924-0522
E-mail: revadaniel@aol.com
URL: http://www.consultingsuccess.org/

Annual. Covers 200 members. Entries include: Company or individual name, address, phone, areas of consulting expertise, services. Arrangement: Geographical and alphabetical.

★13106★ Bowker's News Media Directory

R.R. Bowker L.L.C.
630 Central Ave.
New Providence, NJ 07974
Ph: (908)286-1090　　Fr: 888-269-5372
E-mail: wpn@bowker.com
URL: http://www.bowker.com

Annual; latest edition November 2006. $635.00 for individuals, set; $385.00 for individuals, per volume. Covers, in three separate volumes, syndicates and over 8,500 daily and weekly newspapers; 1,750 newsletters; over 16,800 radio and television stations; 5,500 magazines; 1,000 internal publications. Entries include: Name of publication or station, address, phone, fax, e-mail and URL, names of executives, editors, writers, etc., as appropriate. Broadcasting and magazine volumes include data on kinds of material accepted. Technical and mechanical requirements for publications are given. Arrangement: Magazines are classified by subject; newspapers and broadcasting stations geographical. Indexes: Newspaper department/editor by interest, metro area, feature syndicate subject; magazine subject, publication title; television director/personnel by subject, radio personnel and director by subject.

★13107★ Career Opportunities in the Publishing Industry

Facts On File Inc.
132 W 31st St., 17th Fl.
New York, NY 10001
Ph: (212)967-8800   Fax: 800-678-3633
Fr: 800-322-8755
URL: http://www.factsonfile.com

Published 2004. $49.50 for individuals; $44.55 for libraries. Covers more than 85 jobs, such as those in writing, editing, design, printing, selling, publicity, advertising, marketing, and distribution.

★13108★ Careers in Focus: Publishing

Facts On File Inc.
132 W 31st St., 17th Fl.
New York, NY 10001
Ph: (212)967-8800   Fax: 800-678-3633
Fr: 800-322-8755
URL: http://www.factsonfile.com

Latest edition 3rd, 2007. $29.95 for individuals; $26.95 for libraries. Covers an overview of publishing, followed by a selection of jobs profiled in detail, including the nature of the job, earnings, prospects for employment, what kind of training and skills it requires, and sources for further information.

★13109★ Careers in Focus: Writing

Facts On File Inc.
132 W 31st St., 17th Fl.
New York, NY 10001
Ph: (212)967-8800   Fax: 800-678-3633
Fr: 800-322-8755
URL: http://www.factsonfile.com

Latest edition 3rd, 2007. $29.95 for individuals; $26.95 for libraries. Covers an overview of writing, followed by a selection of jobs profiled in detail, including the nature of the job, earnings, prospects for employment, what kind of training and skills it requires, and sources for further information.

★13110★ Children's Writer's & Illustrator's Market

Writer's Digest Books
1507 Dana Ave.
PO Box 420235
Cincinnati, OH 45207
Fr: 800-221-5831
URL: http://www.writersdigest.com

Annual; latest edition 2007. $26.99 for individuals. Covers about 800 book and magazine publishers that publish works by authors and illustrators for young audiences; sponsors of writing and illustrating contests and awards; writers' organizations; and workshops. Entries include: For Publishers–Name, address, phone, name and title of contact, type of business, type and number of books published annually, average length of material bought, list of recently published material, reporting times, terms of payment to authors. Arrangement: Separate sections for book and magazine publishers. Indexes: Age level for books; general; magazine.

★13111★ Contemporary Theatre, Film, and Television

Gale, Cengage Learning
27500 Drake Rd.
Farmington Hills, MI 48331-3535
Ph: (248)699-4253   Fax: (248)699-8065
Fr: 800-877-4253
URL: http://www.gale.com

Bimonthly, volume 72; published December, 2006. $215.00 for individuals. Covers more than 15,000 leading and up-and-coming performers, directors, writers, producers, designers, managers, choreographers, technicians, composers, executives, and dancers in the United States, Canada, Great Britain and the rest of the world. Each volume includes updated biographies for people listed in previous volumes and in "Who's Who in the Theatre," which this series has superseded. Entries include: Name, agent and/or office addresses, personal and career data; stage, film, and television credits; writings, awards, other information. Arrangement: Alphabetical. Indexes: Cumulative name index also covers entries in "Who's Who in the Theatre" editions 1-17 and in "Who Was Who in the Theatre.".

★13112★ Directory of Poetry Publishers

Dustbooks
PO Box 100
Paradise, CA 95967
Ph: (530)877-6110   Fax: (530)877-0222
Fr: 800-477-6110
URL: http://www.dustbooks.com/dp.htm

Annual; latest edition 22nd, 2006-2007. $25.95 for individuals. Covers about 2,000 magazines, small presses, commercial presses, and university presses that accept poetry for publication. Entries include: Publisher name and address, number of submissions accepted, percentage of submissions published, deadlines, reporting time, list of recent contributors, rights purchased, and method of payment. Arrangement: Alphabetical. Indexes: Subject; geographical.

★13113★ Directory of Small Magazine-Press Editors and Publishers

Dustbooks
PO Box 100
Paradise, CA 95967
Ph: (530)877-6110   Fax: (530)877-0222
Fr: 800-477-6110
URL: http://www.dustbooks.com/

Annual; latest edition 37th, 2006-2007. $25.95 for individuals. Covers about 7,500 publishers and editors. Entries include: Individual name, title of press or magazine, address and phone number. Arrangement: Alphabetical.

★13114★ Discovering Careers for Your Future: English

Facts On File Inc.
132 W 31st St., 17th Fl.
New York, NY 10001
Ph: (212)967-8800   Fax: 800-678-3633
Fr: 800-322-8755

URL: http://www.factsonfile.com

Latest edition 2nd, 2005. $21.95 for individuals; $19.75 for libraries. Covers editors, education directors and museum teachers, interpreters and translators, literary agents, public relations specialists, screenwriters, teachers, and more; links career education to curriculum, helping children investigate the subjects they are interested in, and the careers those subjects might lead to.

★13115★ Discovering Careers for Your Future: Publishing

Facts On File Inc.
132 W 31st St., 17th Fl.
New York, NY 10001
Ph: (212)967-8800   Fax: 800-678-3633
Fr: 800-322-8755
URL: http://www.factsonfile.com

Published 2005. $21.95 for individuals; $19.75 for libraries. Covers book editors, columnists, desktop publishing specialists, literary agents, printing press workers, science and medical writers, and webmasters; links career education to curriculum, helping children investigate the subjects they are interested in and the careers those subjects might lead to.

★13116★ The Dramatists Guild Resource Directory

The Dramatists Guild of America Inc.
1501 Broadway, Ste. 701
New York, NY 10036-5505
Ph: (212)398-9366   Fax: (212)944-0420
URL: http://www.dramatistsguild.com

Annual, September. Publication includes: Lists of Broadway and off-Broadway producers; theater and producing organizations; agents; regional theaters; sources of grants, fellowships, residencies; conferences and festivals; playwriting contests; and sources of financial assistance. Entries include: For producers–Name, address, credits, types of plays accepted for consideration. For groups–Name, address, contact name, type of material accepted for consideration, future commitment, hiring criteria, response time. For agents–Name, address. For theaters–Theater name, address, contact name, submission procedure, types of plays accepted for consideration, maximum cast, limitations, equity contract, opportunities, response time. For grants, fellowships, residencies, financial assistance, conferences, and festivals–Name, address, contact name, description, eligibility and application requirements, deadline. For play contests–Name, address, prize, deadline, description. Arrangement: Contests are by deadline; others are classified.

★13117★ Editor & Publisher International Year Book

Editor & Publisher Magazine
770 Broadway
New York, NY 10003-9595
Ph: (646)654-5500   Fax: (646)654-5370
Fr: 800-562-2706
URL: http://www.editorandpublisher.com

Annual, 2005. Covers daily and Sunday newspapers in the United States and Canada; weekly newspapers; foreign daily newspapers; special service newspapers; newspaper syndicates; news services; journalism schools; foreign language and Black newspapers in the United States; news, picture, and press services; feature and news syndicates; comic and magazine services; advertising clubs; trade associations; clipping bureaus; house organs; journalism awards; also lists manufacturers of equipment and supplies. Entries include: For daily papers–Publication name, address, phone, fax, e-mail, web site URL, names of executives and departmental editors (business, financial, book, food, etc.), circulation and advertising data, production information including format of paper and equipment used. Similar but less detailed information for other publications. Arrangement: Publications and schools are geographical; most other lists are alphabetical.

★13118★ **Editorial Freelancers Association-Membership Directory**

Editorial Freelancers Association Inc.
71 W 23rd St., Ste. 1910
New York, NY 10010-4102
Ph: (212)929-5400   Fax: (212)929-5439
Fr: (866)929-5400
URL: http://66.241.221.102/EFADirectory/select.asp

Annual, spring. $25.00. Covers 1,100 member editorial freelancers. Entries include: Personal name, address, phone, services provided, specialties. Arrangement: Alphabetical. Indexes: Product/service; special interest; geographical; computer skills.

★13119★ **The Guide to Writers Conferences & Workshops**

ShawGuides Inc., Educational Publishers
PO Box 231295, Ansonia Sta.
New York, NY 10023
Ph: (212)799-6464   Fax: (212)724-9287
URL: http://writing.shawguides.com/

Continuously updated. Free. Covers listings for more than 1,500 conferences and workshops for writers in the U.S. and abroad, searchable by date, state or country, or by type. Entries include: Name of workshop or program, description of programs, fees, locations, contact name, address, phone, fax, e-mail, web site.

★13120★ **Hudson's Washington News Media Contacts Directory**

Howard Penn Hudson Associates Inc.
44 W Market St.
PO Box 311
Rhinebeck, NY 12572-0311
Ph: (845)876-2081   Fax: (845)876-2561
Fr: 800-572-3451
URL: http://www.hudsonsdirectory.com

Annual, 2006 edition. $289.00 for individuals, print or online subscription; $329.00 for individuals, print and online subscription, combined. Covers nearly 5,000 editors, freelance writers, and news correspondents,

plus 4,624 United States, Canadian, and foreign newspapers, radio/television networks and stations, magazines, and periodicals based or represented in Washington, D.C. Entries include: For publications and companies–Name, address, phone, and name of editor or key personnel. For individuals–Name, assignment. Arrangement: Classified by activity (e.g., correspondents), media type, etc.; newspapers and radio/television stations sections are arranged geographically; specialized periodicals section is arranged by subject. Indexes: Subject.

★13121★ **International Directory of Little Magazines and Small Presses**

Dustbooks
PO Box 100
Paradise, CA 95967
Ph: (530)877-6110   Fax: (530)877-0222
Fr: 800-477-6110
URL: http://www.dustbooks.com/lilmag.htm

Annual; latest edition 43rd, 2007-2008. $55.00 for individuals, cloth-bound; $37.95 for individuals, paperback. Covers over 4,000 small, independent magazines, presses, and papers. Entries include: Name, address, size, circulation, frequency, price, type of material used, number of issues or books published annually, and other pertinent data. Arrangement: Alphabetical. Indexes: Subject; regional.

★13122★ **International Literary Market Place**

Information Today Inc.
143 Old Marlton Pke.
Medford, NJ 08055-8750
Ph: (609)654-6266   Fax: (609)654-4309
Fr: 800-300-9868
URL: http://www.literarymarketplace.com

Annual; latest edition 2007. $249.00 for individuals. Covers over 10,799 publishers in over 180 countries outside the United States and Canada, and about 1,499 trade and professional organizations related to publishing abroad; includes major printers, binders, typesetters, book manufacturers, book dealers, libraries, literary agencies, translators, book clubs, reference books and journals, periodicals, prizes, and international reference section. Entries include: For publishers–Name, address, phone, fax, telex, names and titles of key personnel, branches, type of publications, subjects, ISBN prefix. Listings for others include similar information but less detail. Arrangement: Classified by business activities, then geographical. Indexes: Company name, subject, type of publication.

★13123★ **Literary Market Place**

Information Today Inc.
143 Old Marlton Pke.
Medford, NJ 08055-8750
Ph: (609)654-6266   Fax: (609)654-4309
Fr: 800-300-9868
URL: http://store.yahoo.com/infotoday/

Annual; latest edition 2007. $299.95 for individuals. Covers over 14,500 firms or organizations offering services related to the

publishing industry, including book publishers in the United States and Canada who issued three or more books during the preceding year, plus a small press section of publishers who publish less than three titles per year or those who are self-published. Also included: Book printers and binders; book clubs; book trade and literary associations; selected syndicates, newspapers, periodicals, and radio and television programs that use book reviews or book publishing news; translators and literary agents. Entries include: For publishers–Company name, address, phone, address for orders, principal executives, editorial directors, and managers, date founded, number of titles in previous year, number of backlist titles in print, types of books published, ISBN prefixes, representatives, imprints, and affiliations. For suppliers, etc.–Listings usually show firm name, address, phone, executives, services, etc. Arrangement: Classified by line of business. Indexes: Principal index is 35,000-item combined index of publishers, publications, and personnel; several sections have geographical and/or subject indexes; translators are indexed by source and target language.

★13124★ **Midwest Travel Writers Association-Membership Directory**

Midwest Travel Writers Association
PO Box 83542
Lincoln, NE 68501-3542
Ph: (402)438-2253   Fax: (866)365-4851
URL: http://www.mtwa.org

Annual, February. $50.00 for individuals, print product; $65.00 for individuals, print product and CD-ROM, combined. Covers over 100 travel writers, editors, and representatives of the travel and tourism industry, located in 13 midwestern states. Entries include: Name, spouse's name, address, phone; title, year membership began, publications, professional affiliations, writing specialties. Arrangement: Alphabetical. Indexes: Geographical.

★13125★ **National Directory of Arts Internships**

National Network for Artist Placement
935 W Ave. 37
Los Angeles, CA 90065
Ph: (323)222-4035   Fax: (323)225-5711
Fr: 800-354-5348
URL: http://www.artistplacement.com

Biennial, odd years; latest edition 10th. $95.00 for individuals. Covers over 5,000 internship opportunities in dance, music, theater, art, design, film, and video & over 1,250 host organizations. Entries include: Name of sponsoring organization, address, name of contact; description of positions available, eligibility requirements, stipend or salary (if any), application procedures. Arrangement: Classified by discipline, then geographical.

★13126★ **National Directory of Magazines**

Oxbridge Communications Inc.
186 5th Ave.
New York, NY 10010
Ph: (212)741-0231   Fax: (212)633-2938
Fr: 800-955-0231
E-mail: custserv@oxbridge.com
URL: http://www.oxbridge.com/

Latest edition September 2007. $995.00 for individuals, print product; $1,195.00 for individuals, CD-ROM; $1,995.00 for individuals, print product and CD-ROM. Covers over 19,000 magazines; coverage includes Canada. Entries include: Title, publisher name, address, phone, fax number, names and titles of contact and key personnel, financial data, editorial and advertising information, circulation. Arrangement: Classified by subject. Indexes: Title; geographical; publisher.

★13127★ **Novel & Short Story Writer's Market**

Writer's Digest Books
1507 Dana Ave.
PO Box 420235
Cincinnati, OH 45207
Fr: 800-221-5831
URL: http://www.writersdigest.com/

Annual; latest edition 2005. $26.99 for individuals. Publication includes: List of 2,000 literary magazines, general periodicals, small presses, book publishers, and authors' agents; contests awards; and writers' organizations. Entries include: For markets–Publication name (if a periodical), publisher name and address, phone, name of editor or other contact; description of periodical or type of work published; frequency and circulation for periodicals, number of titles published for others; needs, method of contact, terms, payment, advice, comments, or tips given by firm. For contests and awards–Name, sponsoring organization name and address, name and title of contact, frequency; purpose, requirements, other information. Arrangement: Contests and awards are alphabetical; markets are classified by type of publisher or type of periodical. Indexes: Market category.

★13128★ **Poet's Market**

Writer's Digest Books
1507 Dana Ave.
PO Box 420235
Cincinnati, OH 45207
Fr: 800-221-5831
E-mail: poetsmarket@fwpubs.com
URL: http://www.writersdigest.com

Annual. $26.99 for individuals. Covers 1,800 publishers, periodicals, and other markets accepting poetry for publication. Entries include: Name, address, phone, name and title of contact, types of poetry accepted, submission requirements. Arrangement: Alphabetical. Indexes: Subject; geographical; chapbook publishers.

★13129★ **Professional Freelance Writers Directory**

The National Writers Association
10940 South Parker Rd., No. 508
Parker, CO 80134
URL: http://www.nationalwriters.com/

Annual. Free. Database covers: about 200 professional members selected from the club's membership on the basis of significant articles or books, or production of plays or movies. Entries include: Name, address, phone (home and business numbers), special fields of writing competence, titles of books published by royalty firms, mention of contributions to specific magazines, journals, newspapers or anthologies, recent awards received, relevant activities and skills (photography, etc.). Arrangement: Alphabetical. Indexes: Alphabetical by author; by state; by subject.

★13130★ **Publishers Directory**

Gale, Cengage Learning
27500 Drake Rd.
Farmington Hills, MI 48331-3535
Ph: (248)699-4253   Fax: (248)699-8065
Fr: 800-877-4253
E-mail: businessproducts@gale.com
URL: http://www.galegroup.com

Annual; latest edition 30th, published November 2006. $540.00 for individuals. Covers over 20,000 new and established, commercial and nonprofit, private and alternative, corporate and association, government and institution publishing programs and their distributors; includes producers of books, classroom materials, prints, reports, and databases. Entries include: Firm name, address, phone, fax, company e-mail address, URL, year founded, ISBN prefix, Standard Address Number, whether firm participates in the Cataloging in Publication program of the Library of Congress, names of principal executives, personal e-mail addresses, number of titles in print, description of firm and its main subject interests, discount and returns policies, affiliated and parent companies, mergers and amalgamations, principal markets, imprints and divisions, alternate formats products are offered in; distributors also list firms for which they distribute, special services, terms to publishers and regional offices. Arrangement: Alphabetical; distributors listed separately. Indexes: Subject; geographical; publisher; imprints; and distributor.

★13131★ **Publishers, Distributors, and Wholesalers of the United States**

R.R. Bowker L.L.C.
630 Central Ave.
New Providence, NJ 07974
Ph: (908)286-1090   Fr: 888-269-5372
URL: http://www.bowker.com/

Annual; latest edition October 2006. $415.00 for individuals. Covers over 140,670 publishers, distributors, and wholesalers; includes associations, museums, software producers and manufacturers, and others not included in 'Books in Print.' Entries include: Publisher name, editorial and ordering addresses, e-mail, website, phone, Standard Address

Numbers (SANs), International Standard Book Number prefix. Arrangement: Alphabetical; distributors and wholesalers are listed separately. Indexes: ISBN prefix; abbreviation; type of business; imprint name; geographical; inactive and out of business company name; toll-free phone and fax; wholesaler and distributor.

★13132★ **Self-Employed Writers and Artists Network-Directory**

Self-Employed Writers and Artists
 Network Inc.
PO Box 440
Paramus, NJ 07653
Ph: (201)967-1313
URL: http://www.swan-net.com

Annual, spring. Covers over 135 freelance writers, graphic designers, illustrators, photographers, and other graphic arts professionals in northern New Jersey and New York city providing services in advertising, marketing, sales promotion, public relations, and telecommunications. Entries include: Name, address, phone, biographical data, description of services provided. Arrangement: Alphabetical. Indexes: Line of business.

★13133★ **Self-Publishing Manual**

Para Publishing
530 Ellwood Ridge
PO Box 8206-240
Santa Barbara, CA 93117-1047
Ph: (805)968-7277   Fax: (805)968-1379
Fr: 800-727-2782
URL: http://www.parapublishing.com

Biennial, odd years. $19.95 for individuals. Publication includes: Lists of wholesalers, reviewers, exporters, suppliers, direct mailing list sources, publishing organizations, and others of assistance in publishing. Entries include: Organization or company name, address, e-mail address and web address. Arrangement: Classified by ZIP code. Indexes: General subject.

★13134★ **Society of American Travel Writers-Membership Directory**

Society of American Travel Writers
7044 S 13 St.
Oak Creek, WI 53154
Ph: (919)861-5586   Fax: (919)787-4916
URL: http://www.satw.org/satw/index.asp?SId=27

Annual; latest edition 2007. $250.00 for individuals, print product or CD-ROM; $400.00 for individuals, print product and CD-ROM, combined. Covers about 1,200 newspaper and magazine travel editors, writers, columnists, photo journalists, and broadcasters in the United States and Canada. Also covers separately 400 executives in public relations who handle tourist attractions and travel industry accounts. Entries include: For regular members–Name, business address, phone, year joined; awards, publications, specialties, publications contributed to; spouse's name. For public relations executives–Name, address, phone, year joined, clients. Arrangement: Classified by type of membership. Indexes: Geographical; travel editor affiliation; freelance travel writers; public relations executive affiliation.

★13135★ *Space Coast Writers Guild-Membership Information/Directory*
Space Coast Writers' Guild
PO Box 262
Melbourne, FL 32902-0262
URL: http://www.scwg.org/

Annual. Free. Covers about 350 professional and aspiring writers in Florida. Entries include: Name, address, phone, area and form of specialty. Arrangement: Alphabetical. Indexes: By genre.

★13136★ *SRDS International Media Guide*
SRDS
1700 Higgins Rd.
Des Plaines, IL 60018-5605
Ph: (847)375-5000   Fax: (847)375-5001
Fr: 800-851-7737
URL: http://www.srds.com

Annual. $395.00 for individuals. Covers approximately 2,500 newspapers and color newspaper magazines/supplements from 200 countries, including the United States. Entries include: Publication name; publisher name, address, phone, fax, e-mail, URL, names of editor, advertising manager, and representatives in the United States and worldwide; advertising rates in U.S. dollars and/or local currency, circulation, mechanical data, ad closing, readership description, etc. Arrangement: Geographical.

★13137★ *Top Careers for Liberal Arts Graduates*
Facts On File Inc.
132 W 31st St., 17th Fl.
New York, NY 10001
Ph: (212)967-8800   Fax: 800-678-3633
Fr: 800-322-8755
URL: http://www.factsonfile.com

Published 2003. $14.95 for individuals; $13.45 for libraries. Covers what it takes to turn a major in liberal arts, such as one in history, English, or art history, into a top job.

★13138★ *Ulrich's Periodicals Directory*
R.R. Bowker L.L.C.
630 Central Ave.
New Providence, NJ 07974
Ph: (908)286-1090   Fr: 888-269-5372
E-mail: ulrichs@bowker.com
URL: http://www.bowker.com

Annual; 45th edition, 2007. $875.00. Covers nearly 186,000 current periodicals and newspapers published worldwide. Entries include: In main list–Publication title; Dewey Decimal Classification number, Library of Congress Classification number (where applicable), CODEN designation (for sci-tech serials), British Library Document Supply Centre shelfmark number, country code, ISSN; subtitle, language(s) of text, year first published, frequency, subscription prices, sponsoring organization, publishing compa-

ny name, address, phone, fax, e-mail and website addresses, editor and publisher names; regular features (reviews, advertising, abstracts, bibliographies, trade literature, etc.), indexes, circulation, format, brief description of content; availability of microforms and reprints; whether refereed; CD-ROM availability with vendor name; online availability with service name; services that index or abstract the periodical, with years covered; advertising rates and contact; rights and permissions contact name and phone; availability through document delivery. Arrangement: Main listing is classified by subject; U.S. general daily and weekly newspapers are listed in a separate volume; lists of cessations, online services, and CD-ROM vendors are alphabetical. Indexes: Cessations; subjects; title (including variant, former, and ceased titles); ISSN; periodicals available on CD-ROM; online periodical title; refereed serial; and international organization publication title.

★13139★ *Washington Independent Writers-Directory*
Washington Independent Writers
1001 Connecticut Ave. NW, Ste. 701
Washington, DC 20036
Ph: (202)775-5150   Fax: (202)775-5810
URL: http://www.washwriter.org/

Biennial. Covers about 2,500 member freelance writers in the Washington, D.C., area. Entries include: Name, address, home and office phone numbers, area of specialization; personal and career data usually included. Arrangement: Alphabetical. Indexes: Specialty.

★13140★ *Writer's Guide to Book Editors, Publishers, and Literary Agents*
Prima Publishing
3000 Lava Ridge Ct.
Roseville, CA 95661
Ph: (916)787-7000   Fax: (916)787-7003
Fr: 800-632-8676

Annual; latest edition 2002-2003. Covers more than 300 publishing houses and their editors. Entries include: Name of press, description, editors and their specialties. Appendixes list agents, model book proposal, and author-agency agreement. Indexes: Extensive.

★13141★ *The Writer's Handbook*
Kalmbach Publishing Co.
PO Box 1612
21027 Crossroads Cir.
Waukesha, WI 53187-1612
Ph: (262)796-8776   Fax: (262)796-1615
Fr: 800-533-6644

Annual; latest edition 2005. $29.95 for individuals. Publication includes: Compilation of 50-plus articles for publication, many by recognized authors and editors. Features list of 3,000-plus markets for the sale of manuscripts (fiction, nonfiction, poetry, drama, greeting card), plus lists of American literary agents, writers' organizations, literary contests, and writing conferences. Entries in-

clude: Markets-name of firm or publication, contact information, editorial preferences, payment rate. Agents–agency name, contact information, submission guidelines, commission rates. Organizations–name, contact information, description of purpose and activities. Contests–name, contact information, prize or award, deadline. Conferences–name, contact information, date/place, description of workshops/activities. Arrangement: Markets are classified by type: magazine (nonfiction and fiction/poetry) and book (general, juvenile, religious); other resources are alphabetical. Indexes: Alphabetical.

★13142★ *Writer's Market*
Writer's Digest Books
1507 Dana Ave.
PO Box 420235
Cincinnati, OH 45207
Fr: 800-221-5831
E-mail: writersmarker@fwpubs.com
URL: http://www.writersdigest.com/

Annual, September; latest edition 2006. $29.99 for individuals. Covers over 8,000 buyers of books, articles, short stories, plays, gags, verse, fillers, and other original written material. Includes book and periodical publishers, greeting card publishers, play producers and publishers, audiovisual material producers, syndicates, and contests and awards. Entries include: Name and address of buyer, phone, payment rates, editorial requirements, reporting time, how to break in. Arrangement: Classified by type of publication. Indexes: Subject; alphabetical.

★13143★ *WritersNet*
NetConcepts L.L.C.
2820 Walton Common West, Ste. 123
Madison, WI 53718
Ph: (608)285-6600   Fr: 888-207-1109
URL: http://www.writers.net

Database covers: Internet resources, books, and other materials for writers.

HANDBOOKS AND MANUALS

★13144★ *30-Minute Writer: How to Write & Sell Short Pieces*
Writers Digest Books
4700 E. Galbraith Rd.
Cincinnati, OH 45236
Ph: (513)531-2690   Fax: (513)531-4082
Fr: 800-289-0963
E-mail: writersdig@fwpubs.com
URL: http://www.writersdigest.com

Connie Emerson. 2000. $17.95 (paper). 260 pages.

★13145★ 30 Steps to Becoming a Writer & Getting Published

Writers Digest Books
4700 E. Galbraith Rd.
Cincinnati, OH 45236
Ph: (513)531-2690   Fax: (513)531-4082
Fr: 800-289-0963
E-mail: writersdig@fwpubs.com
URL: http://www.writersdigest.com

Scott Edelstein. 1993. $16.99. 176 pages.

★13146★ 100 Best Careers for Writers and Artists

Macmillan Publishing Company
175 Fifth Ave.
New York, NY 10010
Ph: (646)307-5151   Fr: 800-428-5331
URL: http://www.macmillan.com/

Shelly Field. 1997. $15.95 (paper). 274 pages. Identifies job opportunities in communications and the arts.

★13147★ Achieving Financial Independence As a Freelance Writer

Blue Heron Publishing
4205 SW Washington St., Ste. 303
Portland, OR 97204
Ph: (503)221-6841   Fax: (503)221-6843

Raymond Dreyfack. 2000. $16.95 (paper). 149 pages.

★13148★ Be a Successful Writer: New Expanded Common Sense Program for Anyone Who Wants to Write

Diamond Editions
3808 Georgia St., Apt. 212
San Diego, CA 92103-4673
Ph: (619)224-8907

Carolan Gladden. 1995. 123 pages.

★13149★ Career Opportunities for Writers

Facts On File Inc.
132 W. 31st St., 17th Fl.
New York, NY 10001-2006
Ph: (212)967-8800   Fax: 800-678-3633
Fr: 800-322-8755
E-mail: custserv@factsonfile.com
URL: http://www.factsonfile.com

Rosemary Ellen Guiley and Janet Frick. 2nd edition, 1991. $49.50. 230 pages. Part of the Career Opportunities Series. Describes more than 100 jobs in eight major fields, offering such details as duties, salaries, perquisites, employment and advancement opportunities, organizations to join, and opportunities for women and minorities.

★13150★ Careers in Communications

The McGraw-Hill Companies
PO Box 182604
Columbus, OH 43272
Fax: (614)759-3749   Fr: 877-883-5524
E-mail: customer.service@mcgraw-hill.com
URL: http://www.mcgraw-hill.com

Shonan Noronha. Fourth edition, 2004.

$15.95 (paper). 192 pages. Examines the fields of journalism, photography, radio, television, film, public relations, and advertising. Gives concrete details on job locations and how to secure a job. Suggests many resources for job hunting.

★13151★ Careers in Health Care

The McGraw-Hill Companies
PO Box 182604
Columbus, OH 43272
Fax: (614)759-3749   Fr: 877-883-5524
E-mail: customer.service@mcgraw-hill.com
URL: http://www.mcgraw-hill.com

Barbara M. Swanson. Fifth edition, 2005. $15.95 (paper). 192 pages. Describes job duties, work settings, salaries, licensing and certification requirements, educational preparation, and future outlook. Gives ideas on how to secure a job.

★13152★ Careers for Health Nuts and Others Who Like to Stay Fit

The McGraw-Hill Companies
PO Box 182604
Columbus, OH 43272
Fax: (614)759-3749   Fr: 877-883-5524
E-mail: customer.service@mcgraw-hill.com
URL: http://www.mcgraw-hill.com

Blythe Camenson. Second edition, 2005. $13.95 (paper). 208 pages.

★13153★ Careers in Journalism

The McGraw-Hill Companies
PO Box 182604
Columbus, OH 43272
Fax: (614)759-3749   Fr: 877-883-5524
E-mail: customer.service@mcgraw-hill.com
URL: http://www.mcgraw-hill.com

Jan Goldberg. Third edition, 2005. $15.95 (paper). 192 pages.

★13154★ Careers for Mystery Buffs and Other Snoops and Sleuths

The McGraw-Hill Companies
PO Box 182604
Columbus, OH 43272
Fax: (614)759-3749   Fr: 877-883-5524
E-mail: customer.service@mcgraw-hill.com
URL: http://www.mcgraw-hill.com

Blythe Camenson. Second edition, 2004. $12.95 (paper); $14.95 (cloth). 160 pages.

★13155★ Careers for Writers and Others Who Have a Way with Words

The McGraw-Hill Companies
PO Box 182604
Columbus, OH 43272
Fax: (614)759-3749   Fr: 877-883-5524
E-mail: customer.service@mcgraw-hill.com
URL: http://www.mcgraw-hill.com

Robert W. Bly. Second edition, 2003. $13.95 (paper). 208 pages.

★13156★ Editorial Freelancing: A Practical Guide

Aletheia Publications, Inc.
46 Bell Hollow Rd.
Putnam Valley, NY 10579
Ph: (845)526-2873   Fax: (845)526-2905
E-mail: AlethPub@aol.com

Trumbull Rogers. 1995. 212 pages. $19.95 (paper). Contains everything the freelancer needs to know about building a basic reference library, choosing a computer and appropriate software, marketing editorial services, determining and negotiating rates, billing, and setting up a retirement plan.

★13157★ Great Jobs for Communications Majors

The McGraw-Hill Companies
PO Box 182604
Columbus, OH 43272
Fax: (614)759-3749   Fr: 877-883-5524
E-mail: customer.service@mcgraw-hill.com
URL: http://www.mcgraw-hill.com

Blythe Camenson. Second edition, 2001. $15.95 (paper). 256 pages.

★13158★ Great Jobs for English Majors

The McGraw-Hill Companies
PO Box 182604
Columbus, OH 43272
Fax: (614)759-3749   Fr: 877-883-5524
E-mail: customer.service@mcgraw-hill.com
URL: http://www.mcgraw-hill.com

Julie DeGalan. Third edition, 2006. $15.95 (paper). 192 pages.

★13159★ Great Jobs for Liberal Arts Majors

The McGraw-Hill Companies
PO Box 182604
Columbus, OH 43272
Fax: (614)759-3749   Fr: 877-883-5524
E-mail: customer.service@mcgraw-hill.com
URL: http://www.mcgraw-hill.com

Blythe Camenson. Second edition, 2001. $14.95 (paper). 256 pages.

★13160★ How to Make a Living as a Travel Writer

Marlowe & Co.
841 Broadway, 4th Fl.
New York, NY 10003
Ph: (212)614-7880   Fax: (212)614-7887
Fr: 800-788-3123

Susan Farewell. Second edition, 1997. $10.95 (paper). 205 pages.

★13161★ How to Write and Sell Your Articles

Writer, Inc.
21027 Crossroads Cir.
Waukesha, WI 53187
Ph: (262)796-8776   Fax: (262)798-6592
Fr: 800-553-6644

Sylvia K. Burack, editor. 1997. $8.95 (paper). 112 pages.

★13162★ *How to Write What You Love and Make a Living at It*

Shaw Books
12265 Oracle Blvd., Ste. 200
Colorado Springs, CO 80921
Ph: (719)590-4999   Fax: (719)590-8977
Fr: 800-603-7051
URL: http://www.randomhouse.com/waterbrook/shaw/

Dennis E. Hensley. 2000. $12.99 (paper). 224 pages.

★13163★ *The Lost Soul Companion: Comfort & Constructive Advice for Struggling Actors, Musicians, Artists, Writers & Other Free Spirits*

Dell
1745 Broadway
New York, NY 10019
Ph: (212)782-9000   Fax: (212)572-6066
Fr: 800-733-3000
URL: http://www.randomhouse.com/bantamdell

Susan M. Brackney. 2001. $10.00. 176 pages.

★13164★ *Making Money Writing Newsletters*

National Book Network
4501 Forbes Blvd., Ste. 200
Lanham, MD 20706
Ph: (301)459-3366   Fax: (301)429-5746
Fr: 800-462-6420
E-mail: custserv@nbnbooks.com
URL: http://www.nbnbooks.com

Elaine Floyd. 1994. $29.95 (paper). 132 pages. How to start a newsletter writing and design service.

★13165★ *Opportunities in High Tech Careers*

The McGraw-Hill Companies
PO Box 182604
Columbus, OH 43272
Fax: (614)759-3749   Fr: 877-883-5524
E-mail: customer.service@mcgraw-hill.com
URL: http://www.mcgraw-hill.com

Gary Colter and Deborah Yanuck. 1999. $14.95; $11.95 (paper). 160 pages. Explores high technology careers. Describes job opportunities, how to make a career decision, how to prepare for high technology jobs, job hunting techniques, and future trends.

★13166★ *Opportunities in Journalism Careers*

The McGraw-Hill Companies
PO Box 182604
Columbus, OH 43272
Fax: (614)759-3749   Fr: 877-883-5524
E-mail: customer.service@mcgraw-hill.com
URL: http://www.mcgraw-hill.com

Jim Patten and Donald L. Ferguson. 2001. $12.95 (paper). 160 pages. Outlines opportunities in every field of journalism, including newspaper reporting and editing, magazine and book publishing, corporate communications, advertising and public relations, free-

lance writing, and teaching. Covers how to prepare for and enter each field, outlining responsibilities, salaries, benefits, and job outlook for each specialty. Illustrated.

★13167★ *Opportunities in Magazine Publishing Careers*

The McGraw-Hill Companies
PO Box 182604
Columbus, OH 43272
Fax: (614)759-3749   Fr: 877-883-5524
E-mail: customer.service@mcgraw-hill.com
URL: http://www.mcgraw-hill.com

S. William Pattis. 1994. $13.95; $14.95 (paper). 148 pages. Covers the scope of magazine publishing and addresses how to identify and pursue available positions. Illustrated.

★13168★ *Opportunities in Publishing Careers*

The McGraw-Hill Companies
PO Box 182604
Columbus, OH 43272
Fax: (614)759-3749   Fr: 877-883-5524
E-mail: customer.service@mcgraw-hill.com
URL: http://www.mcgraw-hill.com

Robert A. Carter and S. William Pattis. 2000. $12.95 (paper). 160 pages. Covers all positions in book and magazine publishing, including new opportunities in multimedia publishing.

★13169★ *Opportunities in Technical Writing and Communications Careers*

The McGraw-Hill Companies
PO Box 182604
Columbus, OH 43272
Fax: (614)759-3749   Fr: 877-883-5524
E-mail: customer.service@mcgraw-hill.com
URL: http://www.mcgraw-hill.com

Jay Gould and Wayne Losano. Revised edition, 1994. $14.95; $11.95 (paper). 152 pages. Provides advice on acquiring a position in medical, engineering, pharmaceutical, and other technical fields. Illustrated.

★13170★ *Opportunities in Writing Careers*

The McGraw-Hill Companies
PO Box 182604
Columbus, OH 43272
Fax: (614)759-3749   Fr: 877-883-5524
E-mail: customer.service@mcgraw-hill.com
URL: http://www.mcgraw-hill.com

Elizabeth Foote-Smith. 2006. $13.95; $11.95 (paper). 160 pages. Discusses opportunities in the print media, broadcasting, advertising or publishing. Business writing, public relations, and technical writing are among the careers covered. Contains bibliography and illustrations.

★13171★ *Power Freelancing: Home-Based Careers for Writers, Designers, & Consultants*

Mid-List Press
4324 12th Ave., S
Minneapolis, MN 55407-3218
Ph: (612)822-3733   Fax: (612)823-8387
Fr: 888-543-1138
E-mail: guide@midlist.org
URL: http://www.midlist.org/

George Sorenson. 1995. $14.95 (paper). 198 pages.

★13172★ *Real People Working in Communications*

The McGraw-Hill Companies
PO Box 182604
Columbus, OH 43272
Fax: (614)759-3749   Fr: 877-883-5524
E-mail: customer.service@mcgraw-hill.com
URL: http://www.mcgraw-hill.com

Jan Goldberg. 1996. $17.95 (paper). 133 pages. Interviews and profiles of working professionals capture a range of opportunities in this field.

★13173★ *Resumes for Advertising Careers*

The McGraw-Hill Companies
PO Box 182604
Columbus, OH 43272
Fax: (614)759-3749   Fr: 877-883-5524
E-mail: customer.service@mcgraw-hill.com
URL: http://www.mcgraw-hill.com

Third edition, 2003. $10.95 (paper). 160 pages. Aimed at job seekers trying to enter or advance in advertising. Provides sample resumes for copywriters, art directors, account managers, ad managers, and media people at all levels of experience. Furnishes sample cover letters.

★13174★ *Resumes for Communications Careers*

The McGraw-Hill Companies
PO Box 182604
Columbus, OH 43272
Fax: (614)759-3749   Fr: 877-883-5524
E-mail: customer.service@mcgraw-hill.com
URL: http://www.mcgraw-hill.com

Third edition, 2003. $10.95 (paper). 160 pages.

★13175★ *Stage Writers Handbook: A Complete Business Guide for Playwrights, Composers, Lyricists, and Librettists*

Theatre Communications Group
520 Eighth Ave., 24th Fl.
New York, NY 10018-4156
Ph: (212)609-5900   Fax: (212)609-5901
E-mail: custserv@tcg.org
URL: http://www.tcg.org/

Dana Singer. 1997. $22.95 (paper). 302 pages.

★13176★ Stein on Writing: A Master Editor of Some of the Most Successful Writers of Our Century Shares His Craft Techniques & Strategies

St. Martin's Press, LLC
175 5th Ave.
New York, NY 10010
Ph: (212)726-0200   Fax: (212)686-9491
Fr: 800-470-4767
URL: http://www.stmartins.com

Sol Stein. 2000. $15.95 (paper). 320 pages.

★13177★ Twenty Questions: Answers for the Inquiring Writer

Browder Springs Publishing
6238 Glennox Ln.
Dallas, TX 75214
Ph: (214)368-4360   Fax: (214)739-9149

Clay Reynolds. 1997. $12.95 (paper). 132 pages. Novelist Clay Reynolds provides "how to" advice on becoming a best-selling author.

★13178★ Write Your Way to Riches: How to Make a Fortune As a Technical Writer

J. G. Communications
200 Berkeley St.
Methuen, MA 01844
Ph: (978)682-4106

Joseph Gregg. 1998. $19.95. 114 pages.

★13179★ A Writer's Guide to Getting Published in Magazines

Aletheia Publications, Inc.
46 Bell Hollow Rd.
Putnam Valley, NY 10579
Ph: (914)526-2873   Fax: (914)526-2905
E-mail: AlethPub@aol.com

JJ Despain. 2000. $19.95 (paper). 183 pages.

★13180★ The Writer's Handbook

Writer, Inc.
21027 Crossroads Cir.
Waukesha, WI 53187
Ph: (262)796-8776   Fax: (262)798-6592
Fr: 800-553-6644

Elfrieda Abbe, editor. 2002. 29.95. 1,056 pages.

★13181★ Writing for Results: Keys to Success for the Public Relations Writer

Alta Villa Publishing, Incorporated
PO Box 17684
Indianapolis, IN 46217-0684
Ph: (317)885-1918
E-mail: editor@altavillapublishing.com
URL: http://altavillapublishing.com/

Ray Begovich. 2001. $12.00 (paper). 67 pages.

EMPLOYMENT AGENCIES AND SEARCH FIRMS

★13182★ Amtec Engineering Corp.

2749 Saturn St.
Brea, CA 92821
Ph: (714)993-1900   Fax: (714)993-2419
E-mail: info@amtechc.com
URL: http://www.amtec-eng.com

Employment agency.

★13183★ Ariel Associates

159-34 Riverside Dr. W., Apt. 5J
New York, NY 10032-1155
Ph: (212)923-1155
E-mail: info@arielassociates.com
URL: http://www.arielassociates.com

Executive search firm specializing in media, advertising and publishing.

★13184★ Bert Davis Publishing Placement Consultants

425 Madison Ave., Fl. 14
New York, NY 10017
Ph: (212)838-4000   Fax: (212)935-3291
E-mail: info@bertdavis.com
URL: http://www.bertdavis.com

Executive search firm.

★13185★ Brattle Temps

50 Congress St., Ste. 935
Boston, MA 02109-4008
Ph: (617)523-4600   Fax: (617)523-3939
E-mail: temps@brattletemps.com
URL: http://www.brattletemps.com

Personnel consulting firm specializes in providing temporary consultants. Skill areas available include: computer operators, secretaries, editors, librarians, graphic artists, and marketing professionals. Industries served: universities, publishing, engineering, manufacturing, and government agencies.

★13186★ Career Development Services

150 State St.
Rochester, NY 14614
Ph: (585)244-0765   Fax: (585)244-7115
Fr: 800-736-6710
E-mail: info@careerdev.org
URL: http://www.careerdev.org

Employment agency.

★13187★ Chaloner Associates

36 Milford St.
Boston, MA 02118
Ph: (617)451-5170   Fax: (617)451-8160
E-mail: info@chaloner.com
URL: http://www.chaloner.com

Executive search firm.

★13188★ The Esquire Staffing Group Ltd.

1 S. Wacker Dr., Ste. 1616
Chicago, IL 60606-4616
Ph: (312)795-4300   Fax: (312)795-4329
E-mail: d.williams@esquirestaffing.com
URL: http://www.esquirestaffing.com

Employment agency. Fills permanent as well as temporary openings.

★13189★ Howard-Sloan-Koller Group

300 E 42nd St.
New York, NY 10017
Ph: (212)661-5250   Fax: (212)557-9178
E-mail: hsk@hsksearch.com
URL: http://www.hsksearch.com

Provides professional search and recruitment services for the publishing, direct marketing, communications, and new media industries. Also consults with organizations regarding staffing, development, and growth strategies.

★13190★ Howard-Sloan Professional Search Inc.

1140 Ave. of the Americas
New York, NY 10036
Ph: (212)704-0444   Fax: (212)869-7999
Fr: 800-221-1326
E-mail: info@howardsloan.com
URL: http://www.howardsloan.com

Executive search firm.

★13191★ LandaJob Advertising Staffing Specialists

8177 Wornall Rd.
Kansas City, MO 64114
Ph: (816)523-1881   Fax: (816)523-1876
Fr: 800-931-8806
E-mail: adstaff@landajobnow.com
URL: http://www.landajobnow.com

Personnel consultants and recruiters for advertising, marketing, and communications positions. Industries served: advertising, communications, marketing, graphic arts, printing and publishing.

★13192★ Max Brown

3208 Q St. NW
Washington, DC 20007
Ph: (202)338-2727   Fax: (202)338-3131

Executive recruiter to the magazine and book publishing industries. Employment placements in all publishing disciplines, including operation and financial management, new product development, marketing, advertising sales, editorial, graphic design, production, manufacturing, circulation, distribution, corporate communications, promotion and administration. Secondary concentrations include management advising for publishers, providing the following services: marketing and product positioning for new and existing publications, market research and development, business planning and financial projections, publishing models, launch strategies and start-up operations and acquisitions and mergers counsel.

★13193★ Technical Talent Locators Ltd.

5570 Sterrett Pl., Ste. 208
Columbia, MD 21044
Ph: (410)740-0091
E-mail: steve@ttlgroup.com
URL: http://www.ttlgroup.com

Permanent employment agency working within the following fields: software and database engineering; computer, communication, and telecommunication system engineering; and other computer-related disciplines.

★13194★ Zachary & Sanders Inc.

Linden Ln.
East Norwich, NY 11732
Ph: (516)922-5500   Fax: (516)922-2286
Fr: 800-540-7919
E-mail: zacharyserch@earthlink.net

Serves the printing, packaging, publishing, advertising, direct marketing industries.

ONLINE JOB SOURCES AND SERVICES

★13195★ Guru.com

5001 Baum Blvd., Ste. 760
Pittsburgh, PA 15213
Ph: (412)687-1316   Fax: (412)687-4466
URL: http://www.guru.com

Description: Job board specializing in contract jobs for creative and information technology professionals. Also provides online incorporation and educational opportunities for independent contractors along with articles and advice.

★13196★ JournalismJobs.com

Ph: (510)653-1521
E-mail: contact@journalismjobs.com
URL: http://www.journalismjobs.com

Description: Career-related site for journalists and other media professionals. Seekers can search for jobs, post a resume online, and manage the search online with the Job Seeker Folder feature. They also can receive free job announcements by e-mail.

OTHER SOURCES

★13197★ American Almanac of Jobs and Salaries

HarperCollins
10 E. 53rd St.
New York, NY 10022
Ph: (212)207-7000   Fr: 800-242-7737
URL: http://www.harpercollins.com/

John W. Wright. Revised edition, 2000. $20.00 (paper). 672 pages. This is a com-prehensive guide to the wages of hundreds of occupations in a wide variety of industries and organizations.

★13198★ American Screenwriters Association (ASA)

269 S Beverly Dr., Ste. 2600
Beverly Hills, CA 90212-3807
Fax: (866)265-9091   Fr: (866)265-9091
E-mail: asa@goasa.com
URL: http://www.asascreenwriters.com

Description: Promotes the art and craft of screenwriting. Provides writers with practical resources and educational opportunities to enhance their skills. Assists writers who wish to sell their film and television scripts, or are currently working in film or television and are looking to advance their careers.

★13199★ American Society of Business Publication Editors (ASBPE)

214 N Hale St.
Wheaton, IL 60187
Ph: (630)510-4588   Fax: (630)510-4501
E-mail: info@asbpe.org
URL: http://www.asbpe.org

Description: Represents editors and writers working for business, trade, association, professional, technical print magazines and newsletters and Internet publications. Serves to enhance editorial standards and quality and raise the level of publication management skills of its members.

★13200★ American Society of Journalists and Authors (ASJA)

1501 Broadway, Ste. 302
New York, NY 10036
Ph: (212)997-0947   Fax: (212)937-2315
E-mail: execdir@asja.org
URL: http://www.asja.org

Description: Represents freelance writers of nonfiction magazine articles and books. Seeks to elevate the professional and economic position of nonfiction writers, provide a forum for discussion of common problems among writers and editors, and promote a code of ethics for writers and editors. Operates writer referral service for individuals, institutions, or companies seeking writers for special projects; sponsors Llewellyn Miller Fund to aid professional writers who no longer able to work due to age, disability, or extraordinary professional crisis.

★13201★ American Society of Magazine Editors (ASME)

810 7th Ave., 24th Fl.
New York, NY 10019
Ph: (212)872-3700   Fax: (212)906-0128
E-mail: asme@magazine.org
URL: http://www.magazine.org/Editorial

Purpose: Represents magazine editors. **Activities:** Sponsors annual editorial internship program for college juniors and the National Magazine Awards.

★13202★ American Society of Newspaper Editors (ASNE)

11690B Sunrise Valley Dr.
Reston, VA 20191-1409
Ph: (703)453-1122   Fax: (703)453-1133
E-mail: asne@asne.org
URL: http://www.asne.org

Description: Directs editors who determine editorial and news policies of daily newspapers and news gathering operations of daily newspapers.

★13203★ American Society of Psychopathology of Expression (ASPE)

74 Lawton St.
Brookline, MA 02446
Ph: (617)738-9821   Fax: (617)975-0411

Description: Psychiatrists, psychologists, art therapists, sociologists, art critics, artists, social workers, linguists, educators, criminologists, writers, and historians. At least two-thirds of the members must be physicians. Fosters collaboration among specialists in the United States who are interested in the problems of expression and in the artistic activities connected with psychiatric, sociological, and psychological research. Disseminates information about research and clinical applications in the field of psychopathology of expression. Sponsors consultations, seminars, and lectures on art therapy.

★13204★ Art Directors Club (ADC)

106 W 29th St.
New York, NY 10001
Ph: (212)643-1440   Fax: (212)643-4266
E-mail: info@adcglobal.org
URL: http://www.adcglobal.org

Members: Art directors of advertising magazines and agencies, visual information specialists, and graphic designers; associate members are artists, cinematographers, photographers, copywriters, educators, journalists, and critics. **Purpose:** Promotes and stimulates interest in the practice of art direction. **Activities:** Sponsors Annual Exhibition of Advertising, Editorial and Television Art and Design; International Traveling Exhibition. Provides educational, professional, and entertainment programs; on-premise art exhibitions; portfolio review program. Conducts panels for students and faculty.

★13205★ Asian American Journalists Association (AAJA)

1182 Market St., Ste. 320
San Francisco, CA 94102
Ph: (415)346-2051   Fax: (415)346-6343
E-mail: national@aaja.org
URL: http://www.aaja.org

Description: Represents more than 2,000 members. Serves Asian Americans and Pacific Islanders by encouraging young people to consider journalism as a career, developing managers in the media industry, and promoting fair and accurate news coverage. Serves as an alliance partner in UNITY Journalists of Color, along with the Native American Journalists Association, National

Association of Hispanic Journalists, and National Association of Black Journalists.

★13206★ Associated Press Managing Editors (APME)

19 Commerce Ct. W
Cranbury, NJ 08512-2416
Ph: (212)621-1838   Fax: (212)506-6102
E-mail: apme@ap.org
URL: http://www.apme.com

Description: Represents managing editors or executives on the news or editorial staff of The Associated Press newspapers. Aims to: advance the journalism profession; examine the news and other services of the Associated Press in order to provide member newspapers with services that best suit their needs; provide a means of cooperation between the management and the editorial representatives of the members of the Associated Press. Maintains committees dealing with newspapers and news services.

★13207★ Association for Business Communication (ABC)

PO Box 6143
Nacogdoches, TX 75962-0001
Ph: (936)468-6280   Fax: (936)468-6281
E-mail: abcjohnson@sfasu.edu
URL: http://
www.businesscommunication.org

Description: College teachers of business communication; management consultants in business communications; training directors and correspondence supervisors of business firms, direct mail copywriters, public relations writers, and others interested in communication for business.

★13208★ Association of Earth Science Editors (AESE)

554 Chess St.
Pittsburgh, PA 15205
E-mail: llindsay@sunbeltpub.com
URL: http://www.aese.org

Description: Editors, managing editors, and others in editorial management positions in the field of earth science publications; interested individuals. Seeks to provide efficient means for cooperation among earth science editors and to promote effective publishing of journals, reviews, monograph series, maps, abstract journals and services, indexes, micro cards, and other publications that disseminate information on the earth sciences.

★13209★ Association for Women in Communications (AWC)

3337 Duke St.
Alexandria, VA 22314
Ph: (703)370-7436   Fax: (703)370-7437
E-mail: info@womcom.org
URL: http://www.womcom.org

Description: Professional association of journalism and communications.

★13210★ Association of Writers and Writing Programs (AWP)

George Mason University
Mail Stop 1E3
Fairfax, VA 22030-4444
Ph: (703)993-4301   Fax: (703)993-4302
E-mail: awp@awpwriter.org
URL: http://www.awpwriter.org

Description: Writers; students and teachers in creative writing programs in university departments of English; editors, publishers, and freelance creative and professional writers. Fosters literary talent and achievement; advocates the craft of writing as primary to a liberal and humane education; provides publications and services to the makers and readers of contemporary literature. Operates career services and job listings; sponsors literary competitions.

★13211★ Authors Guild (AG)

31 E 32nd St., 7th Fl.
New York, NY 10016-7923
Ph: (212)563-5904   Fax: (212)564-5363
E-mail: staff@authorsguild.org
URL: http://www.authorsguild.org

Description: Professional book and magazine writers. Maintains legal staff to provide book and magazine contract reviews for members. Group health insurance available. Members of the guild are also members of the Authors League of America.

★13212★ Authors League of America (ALA)

31 E 32nd St., 7th Fl.
New York, NY 10016-7923
Ph: (212)563-5904   Fax: (212)564-5363
E-mail: staff@authorsguild.org
URL: http://www.authorsguild.org

Description: Serves as a professional organization of authors of books, magazine material, and plays.

★13213★ Catholic Press Association (CPA)

3555 Veterans Memorial Hwy., Unit O
Ronkonkoma, NY 11779
Ph: (631)471-4730   Fax: (631)471-4804
E-mail: cathjourn@catholicpress.org
URL: http://www.catholicpress.org

Description: Consists of Catholic writers and publishers of Catholic newspapers, magazines, newsletters and books. Maintains 25 committees, including Freedom of Information, Fair Publishing Practices Code, Catholic News Service Liaison.

★13214★ Construction Writers Association

PO Box 5586
Buffalo Grove, IL 60089-5586
Ph: (847)398-7756   Fax: (847)590-5241
E-mail: office@constructionwriters.org
URL: http://www.constructionwriters.org

Description: Writers and editors for media, public relations, and marketing in the construction field.

★13215★ Copywriter's Council of America (CCA)

CCA Bldg.
PO Box 102
Middle Island, NY 11953-0102
Ph: (631)924-8555   Fax: (631)924-3890
E-mail: cca4dmcopy@att.net
URL: http://lgroup.addr.com/freelance.htm

Description: Advertising copywriters, marketing and public relations consultants, copyeditors, proofreaders, and other individuals involved in print, radio, broadcast, video, and telecommunications. Provides freelance work; acts as agent for members; negotiates on members' behalf. Serves as a forum for professional and social contact between freelance communications professionals. Offers courses on copywriting, direct marketing, mail order, publishing screenplays, and how to get published. Conducts charitable programs. Maintains speakers' bureau, hall of fame, and word processing consultation service.

★13216★ Council for the Advancement of Science Writing (CASW)

PO Box 910
Hedgesville, WV 25427
Ph: (304)754-5077   Fax: (304)754-5076
E-mail: diane@nasw.org
URL: http://www.casw.org

Members: Operated by a council of 19 science writers, editors, television executives, scientists, and physicians. **Purpose:** Works to increase public understanding of science by upgrading the quality and quantity of science writing and improving the relationship between scientists and the press. **Activities:** Conducts seminars, workshops, and conferences; sponsors programs to train minority journalists in science and medical writing.

★13217★ Council of Science Editors (CSE)

12100 Sunset Hills Rd., Ste. 130
Reston, VA 20190
Ph: (703)437-4377   Fax: (703)435-4390
E-mail: cse@councilscienceeditors.org
URL: http://www.councilscienceeditors.org

Description: Active and former editors of primary and secondary journals in the life sciences and those in scientific publishing and editing. Through study and discussion groups, panels, and committees, considers all aspects of communication in the life sciences with emphasis on publication, especially in primary journals and retrieval in secondary media.

★13218★ Dow Jones Newspaper Fund (DJNF)

PO Box 300
Princeton, NJ 08543-0300
Ph: (609)452-2820   Fax: (609)520-5804
E-mail: newsfund@wsj.dowjones.com
URL: http://djnewspaperfund.dowjones.com

Description: Established by Dow Jones and Company, publisher of *The Wall Street Journal*, to encourage careers in journalism.

Operates newspaper's editing, and Sports Copy Editing Internship Programs for all junior, senior, and graduate level college students interested in journalism. Also offers Business Reporting Intern Program for minority college sophomores and juniors to complete summer internships on daily newspapers as business reporters. Students receive monetary scholarships to return to school in the fall. Offers information on careers in journalism.

★13219★ **Editorial Freelancers Association (EFA)**
71 W 23rd St., 4th Fl.
New York, NY 10010-4181
Ph: (212)929-5400   Fax: (212)929-5439
Fr: (866)929-5400
E-mail: office@the-efa.org
URL: http://www.the-efa.org

Description: Represents persons who work full or part-time as freelance writers or editorial freelancers. Promotes professionalism and facilitates the exchange of information and support. Conducts professional training seminars; and offers job listings.

★13220★ **Horror Writers Association (HWA)**
244 5th Ave., Ste. 2767
New York, NY 10001-7604
E-mail: hwa@horror.org
URL: http://www.horror.org

Members: Horror writers, including creators of comic strips, screenplays, and role-playing games, who have sold at least one work at professional rates are active members; horror writers who have sold something but not at professional rates are affiliate members. **Purpose:** Non-writing professionals are associate members. Seeks to assist aspiring and accomplished horror writers in advancing their art and careers. **Activities:** Facilitates networking among members; gathers and disseminates information on horror fiction markets; serves as liaison between members and writers' agents and publishers.

★13221★ **International Association of Media Tie-in Writers (IAMTW)**
PO Box 8212
Calabasas, CA 91372
E-mail: info@iamtw.org
URL: http://www.iamtw.org

Description: Enhances the professional and public image of tie-in writers. Works with the media to review tie-in novels and publicize their authors. Raises public awareness of media tie-in writers. Provides a forum for tie-in writers to share information and discuss issues related to the field of tie-in writing.

★13222★ **International Black Writers and Artists (IBWA)**
PO Box 43576
Los Angeles, CA 90043
Ph: (213)964-3721
E-mail: ibwa_la@yahoo.com

URL: http://members.tripod.com/~ibwa/home.htm

Description: Seeks to discover and support new black writers. Conducts research and monthly seminars in poetry, fiction, nonfiction, music, and jazz. Provides writing services and children's services. Maintains speakers' bureau. Offers referral service. Plans to establish hall of fame, biographical archives, and museum.

★13223★ **International Press Institute, American Committee (IPI)**
Missouri Scholarship of Journalism
132A Neff Annex
Columbia, MO 65211
Ph: (573)884-1599   Fax: (573)884-1699
E-mail: ipi@freemedia.at
URL: http://www.freemedia.at/cms/ipi

Description: Editors and editorial directors of newspapers, magazines, and news agencies and broadcasting system staff members who control or contribute to news policy in the press and broadcasting systems; educators, foreign correspondents, and others interested in journalism. Works to improve the flow of news and journalism practices. Seeks to protect freedom of the press and increase contacts and exchanges within the profession. Conducts research on news sources and presentation, foreign news reporting, and flow of news.

★13224★ **International Science Writers Association (ISWA)**
6666 N Mesa View Terr.
Tucson, AZ 85718
Ph: (520)529-6835
E-mail: cornelljc@earthlink.net
URL: http://www.internationalsciencewriters.org

Members: Science writers. **Purpose:** Seeks to insure a free press and maximize access to printed scientific information worldwide. **Activities:** Represents members' interests; conducts continuing professional development courses; gathers and disseminates information.

★13225★ **International Society of Weekly Newspaper Editors (ISWNE)**
Institute of International Studies
Missouri Southern State University
3950 E Newman Rd.
Joplin, MO 64801-1512
Ph: (417)625-9736   Fax: (417)659-4445
E-mail: stebbins-c@mssu.edu
URL: http://www.iswne.org

Description: Represents editors and writers of editorial comment in weekly newspapers. Promotes wise and independent editorial comments, news content and leadership in community newspapers throughout the world. Facilitates the exchange of ideas and viewpoints of community editors. Helps in the development of the community newspaper press as an instrument of mutual understanding and world peace and fosters freedom of the press in all nations.

★13226★ **International Thriller Writers (ITW)**
PO Box 311
Eureka, CA 95502
Fax: (707)442-9251
E-mail: info@thrillerwriters.org
URL: http://www.thrillerwriters.org

Description: Promotes suspense or thriller novels. Enhances the prestige and raises the profile of thriller writers. Provides opportunities for collegiality among authors and other industry professionals.

★13227★ **International Women's Writing Guild (IWWG)**
PO Box 810
Gracie Sta.
New York, NY 10028-0082
Ph: (212)737-7536   Fax: (212)737-9469
E-mail: dirhahn@iwwg.org
URL: http://www.iwwg.org

Members: Women writers in 24 countries interested in expressing themselves through the written word professionally and for personal growth regardless of portfolio. **Purpose:** Seeks to empower women personally and professionally through writing. **Activities:** Facilitates manuscript submissions to literary agents and independent presses. Participates in international network. Maintains dental and vision program at group rates.

★13228★ **Media Alliance (MA)**
1904 Franklin St., Ste. 500
Oakland, CA 94612
Ph: (510)832-9000   Fax: (510)238-8557
E-mail: information@media-alliance.org
URL: http://www.media-alliance.org

Description: Writers, photographers, editors, broadcast workers, public relations practitioners, videographers, filmmakers, commercial artists and other media workers and aspiring media workers. Supports free press and independent, alternative journalism that services progressive politics and social justice.

★13229★ **Mystery Writers of America (MWA)**
17 E 47th St., 6th Fl.
New York, NY 10017
Ph: (212)888-8171   Fax: (212)888-8107
E-mail: mwa@mysterywriters.org
URL: http://www.mysterywriters.org

Members: Professional writers in the mystery-crime field; publishers and agents are associate members.

★13230★ **National Association of Home and Workshop Writers (NAHWW)**
PO Box 12
Baker, NV 89311
Ph: (847)255-0210   Fr: (866)457-2582
E-mail: dstowe@arkansas.net
URL: http://www.nahww.org

Members: Writers and illustrators of materials on home maintenance and improvement projects, manual skills, woodworking, and do-it-yourself projects and techniques. **Purpose:** Aims to promote communication among colleagues by sharing information on publishers, marketing conditions, and mutual problems.

★13231★ National Association of Science Writers (NASW)

PO Box 890
Hedgesville, WV 25427
Ph: (304)754-5077   Fax: (304)754-5076
E-mail: director@nasw.org
URL: http://www.nasw.org

Members: Writers and editors engaged in the preparation and interpretation of science news for the public.

★13232★ National Association of Women Writers (NAWW)

24165 IH-10 W, Ste. 217-637
San Antonio, TX 78257
Fax: (866)821-5829   Fr: (866)821-5829
E-mail: naww@onebox.com
URL: http://www.naww.org

Description: Promotes appreciation of the work of women writers. Serves as a support and assistance network for women writers. Aims to create opportunities for its members to excel and become more prolific individuals in their own respective fields of writing.

★13233★ National Press Club (NPC)

National Press Bldg.
529 14th St. NW, 13th Fl.
Washington, DC 20045
Ph: (202)662-7500   Fax: (202)662-7512
E-mail: info@press.org
URL: http://www.press.org

Members: Reporters, writers, and news people employed by newspapers, wire services, magazines, radio and television stations, and other forms of news media; former news people and associates of news people are nonvoting members. **Activities:** Sponsors sports, travel, and cultural events, rap sessions with news figures and authors, and newsmaker breakfasts and luncheons. Offers monthly training.

★13234★ National Resume Writers' Association (NRWA)

PO Box 475
Tuckahoe, NY 10707
Ph: (631)930-6287   Fax: (631)980-4355
Fr: 877-843-6792
E-mail: adminmanager@nrwaweb.com
URL: http://www.nrwaweb.com

Description: Promotes high standards of excellence in resume writing through mentoring, education and support services. Represents the interests of writers, recruiters, counselors and other employment and career-related professionals.

★13235★ National Sportscasters and Sportswriters Association (NSSA)

PO Box 1545
Salisbury, NC 28145
Ph: (704)633-4275   Fax: (704)633-2027
E-mail: nssahalloffame@aol.com
URL: http://www.nssahalloffame.com

Description: Sportscasters and sportswriters. Pursues matters of common interest to members. Elects charter members to U.S. Olympic Hall of Fame.

★13236★ National Writers Association (NWA)

10940 S Parker Rd., No. 508
Parker, CO 80134
Ph: (303)841-0246   Fax: (303)841-2607
E-mail: anitaedits@aol.com
URL: http://www.nationalwriters.com

Members: Professional full- or part-time freelance writers who specialize in business writing. **Purpose:** Aims to serve as a marketplace whereby business editors can easily locate competent writing talent. **Activities:** Establishes communication among editors and writers.

★13237★ National Writers Union (NWU)

113 University Pl., 6th Fl.
New York, NY 10003
Ph: (212)254-0279   Fax: (212)254-0673
E-mail: nwu@nwu.org
URL: http://www.nwu.org

Members: Freelance writers; journalists, authors, poets, and technical and public relations writers who are not represented by any existing union. **Purpose:** Engages in collective bargaining and provides other services for members such as grievance handling and health insurance. Works to raise rates and improve treatment of freelance writers by magazine and book publishers. Holds conferences on legal, economic, trade, and craft issues affecting writers.

★13238★ New York Financial Writers' Association (NYFWA)

PO Box 338
Ridgewood, NJ 07451-0338
Ph: (201)612-0100   Fax: (201)612-9915
E-mail: info@nyfwa.org
URL: http://www.nyfwa.org

Members: Financial and business editors and reporters whose publications are located in metropolitan New York.

★13239★ Outdoor Writers Association of America (OWAA)

121 Hickory St., Ste. 1
Missoula, MT 59801
Ph: (406)728-7434   Fax: (406)728-7445
Fr: 800-692-2477
E-mail: owaa@montana.com
URL: http://www.owaa.org

Members: Professional organization of newspaper, magazine, radio, television and motion picture writers and photographers (both staff and free-lance) concerned with outdoor recreation and conservation. **Activities:** Conducts surveys for educational and industrial organizations; compiles market data for writer members and offers liaison aid in writer assignments.

★13240★ Romance Writers of America (RWA)

16000 Stuebner Airline Rd., Ste. 140
Spring, TX 77379
Ph: (832)717-5200   Fax: (832)717-5201
E-mail: info@rwanational.org
URL: http://www.rwanational.org

Members: Writers, editors, and publishers of romance novels. **Purpose:** Aims to support beginning, intermediate, and advanced romance writers; promotes recognition of the genre of romance writing as a serious literary form. **Activities:** Conducts workshops.

★13241★ Science Fiction and Fantasy Writers of America (SFWA)

PO Box 877
Chestertown, MD 21620
Fax: (410)778-3052
E-mail: execdir@sfwa.org
URL: http://www.sfwa.org

Description: Professional writers of science fiction stories, novels, radio plays, teleplays, or screenplays. Works to achieve the best working conditions possible for writers. Maintains legal fund and emergency medical fund to help members in time of need. Helps mediate between writers and publishers. Encourages public interest in science fiction literature through use of school and public library facilities; produces and disseminates science fiction literature of high quality. Conducts discussions, lectures, and seminars. Maintains speakers' bureau.

★13242★ Society of American Business Editors and Writers (SABEW)

385 McReynolds
Columbia, MO 65211-1200
Ph: (573)882-7862   Fax: (573)884-1372
E-mail: sabew@missouri.edu
URL: http://www.sabew.org

Members: Active business, economic, and financial news writers and editors for newspapers, magazines, and other publications; broadcasters of business news; teachers of business or journalism at colleges and universities. **Activities:** Plans periodic seminars on problems and techniques in business news coverage and occasional special meetings with business, financial, government and labor leaders, and other experts. Maintains the Resume Bank, a service that keeps resumes of members on file; editors looking for job candidates can request the resumes of candidates that meet their requirements.

★13243★ **Society of Professional Journalists (SPJ)**

3909 N Meridian St.
Indianapolis, IN 46208-4011
Ph: (317)927-8000   Fax: (317)920-4789
E-mail: tharper@spj.org
URL: http://www.spj.org

Members: Professional society - journalism. **Purpose:** Promotes a free and unfettered press; high professional standards and ethical behavior; journalism as a career. Conducts lobbying activities; maintains legal defense fund. Sponsors Pulliam/Kilgore Freedom of Information Internships in Washington, DC, and Indianapolis, IN. **Activities:** Holds forums on the free press.

★13244★ **Society for Technical Communication (STC)**

901 N Stuart St., Ste. 904
Arlington, VA 22203-1822
Ph: (703)522-4114   Fax: (703)522-2075
E-mail: stc@stc.org
URL: http://www.stc.org

Members: Writers, editors, educators, scientists, engineers, artists, publishers, and others professionally engaged in or interested in the field of technical communication; companies, corporations, organizations, and agencies interested in the aims of the society. **Purpose:** Seeks to advance the theory and practice of technical communication in all media. **Activities:** Sponsors high school writing contests.

★13245★ **Tall Grass Writers Guild (TWG)**

2036 N Winds Dr.
Dyer, IN 46311
Ph: (219)322-7270   Fr: 800-933-4680
E-mail: outriderpress@sbcglobal.net
URL: http://www.outriderpress.com

Members: Writers including individuals who write for publication or as a recreational pursuit. **Purpose:** Seeks to promote personal and literary development of members. **Activities:** Facilitates communication among members. Sponsors formal readings; makes available leadership training opportunities; conducts writing development courses.

★13246★ **Western Writers of America (WWA)**

1665 E Julio St.
Sandy, UT 84093
E-mail: wwa@unm.edu
URL: http://www.westernwriters.org

Description: Represents freelance writers of Western fiction and nonfiction, editors, literary agents, historians, romance writers, screenplay and scriptwriters, and journalists. Sponsors competitions; maintains speakers' bureau, hall of fame, and library.

★13247★ **Women in Scholarly Publishing (WISP)**

1070 Beacon St., Apt. 6D
Brookline, MA 02446-3951
E-mail: sworst@comcast.net

Description: Women involved in scholarly publishing and men who support the organization's goals. Promotes professional development and advancement, management skills, and opportunities for women in scholarly publishing. Concerns include career development, job-sharing information, and surveys of salaries and job opportunities for women, and practical workshops or other training opportunities. Provides a forum and network for communication among women in presses throughout the U.S. Sponsors educational workshops, programs, and seminars, in conjunction with the Association of American University Presses. Compiles statistics.

★13248★ **Women's National Book Association (WNBA)**

PO Box 237
New York, NY 10150
Ph: (212)208-4629   Fax: (212)208-4629
E-mail: publicity@bookbuzz.com
URL: http://www.wnba-books.org

Description: Women and men who work with and value books. Exists to promote reading and to support the role of women in the book community.

Broad Sources of Job-Hunting Information

REFERENCE WORKS

★13249★ 10 Insider Secrets to a Winning Job Search: Everything You Need to Get the Job You Want in 24 Hours or Less
Career Press
3 Tice Rd.
PO Box 687
Franklin Lakes, NJ 07417-1322
Ph: (201)848-0310   Fax: (201)848-1727
Fr: 800-227-3371

Todd Bermont. 2004. $14.99. 216 pages. Step-by-step guide to getting the job you want; shares secrets to finding a job in any economy.

★13250★ 50 Best Jobs for Your Personality
JIST Publishing
875 Montreal Way
St. Paul, MN 55102
Fax: 800-547-8329   Fr: 800-648-5478
E-mail: info@jist.com
URL: http://www.jist.com

Michael Farr and Laurence Shatkin, PhD. 2005. $16.95. 480 pages. Used to help job seekers match their personality to the right career.

★13251★ 101 Tips for Graduates
Facts On File Inc.
132 W 31st St., 17th Fl.
New York, NY 10001
Ph: (212)967-8800   Fax: 800-678-3633
Fr: 800-322-8755
URL: http://www.factsonfile.com

Published 2005. $34.95 for individuals; $31.45 for libraries. Covers the key principles a graduate needs to know about work skills, communication skills, leadership skills, social skills, self-discipline, and demonstrating a positive attitude.

★13252★ 200 Best Jobs for College Graduates, Third Edition
JIST Publishing
875 Montreal Way
St. Paul, MN 55102
Fax: 800-547-8329   Fr: 800-648-5478
E-mail: info@jist.com
URL: http://www.jist.com

Michael Farr. 2006. $16.95. 448 pages. 200 jobs with the best pay, fastest growth, and most openings for people with associate's, bachelor's, and higher degrees.

★13253★ 250 Best Jobs Through Apprenticeships
JIST Publishing
875 Montreal Way
St. Paul, MN 55102
Fax: 800-547-8329   Fr: 800-648-5478
E-mail: info@jist.com
URL: http://www.jist.com

Michael Farr and Laurence Shatkin, PhD. 2005. $24.95. 544 pages. Lists all 876 apprenticeships that are registered with the U.S. Department of Labor and explains how to become an apprentice, where the opportunities are, what the requirements are, and the pros and cons.

★13254★ 300 Best Jobs Without a Four-Year Degree, Second Edi
JIST Publishing
875 Montreal Way
St. Paul, MN 55102
Fax: 800-547-8329   Fr: 800-648-5478
E-mail: info@jist.com
URL: http://www.jist.com

Michael Farr. 2006. $16.95. 464 pages. 300 jobs with the best pay, fastest growth, and most openings with no four-year degree required.

★13255★ 303 Off-the-Wall Ways to Get a Job
Career Press, Inc.
3 Tice Rd.
Franklin Lakes, NJ 07417-1322
Ph: (201)848-0310   Fax: (201)848-1727
Fr: 800-227-3371

URL: http://www.careerpress.com
Brandon Toropov. 1995. $12.99 (paper). 311 pages. Provides a creative perspective on job hunting.

★13256★ 1000 Best Job Hunting Secrets
Sourcebooks, Inc.
1935 Brookdale Rd., Ste. 139
Naperville, IL 60563
Ph: (630)961-3900   Fax: (630)961-2168
Fr: 800-727-8866
URL: http://www.sourcebooks.com

Diane Stafford and Moritza Day. 2004. $10.36. 461 pages. Provides information on how to: customize the resume to suit the job; protect yourself and keep your job search confidential; write a cover letter that gets you noticed; secure a second interview; and guarantee a positive reference.

★13257★ 2007-2008 Guide to Employment Web Sites
Kennedy Information
1 Phoenix Mill Ln., 3rd Fl.
Peterborough, NH 03458
Ph: (603)924-1006   Fax: (603)924-4460
Fr: 800-531-0007
URL: http://www.kennedyinfo.com/hr/hrbookstore.html

Annual, Latest edition 2007. $39.95 for individuals. Covers more than 40,000 sites for locating high caliber job candidates. Entries include: Website address, duration of the site, visits per month, profile of frequent visitors, candidate visits, fees, number of records, resume acquisition, site features such as automatic notification of resume-job matches.

★13258★ Adams Electronic Job Search Almanac
Adams Media Corp.
57 Littlefield St.
Avon, MA 02322
Ph: (508)427-7100   Fax: (508)427-6790
Fr: 800-872-5627
URL: http://www.adamsmedia.com

Annual; latest edition 6th. Covers job listings

on the Internet; bulletin boards, Web networking, and online services for finding a job. Entries include: Firm or organization name, address, phone, name and title of contact; description of organization, headquarters location, typical titles for entry- and middle-level positions, educational backgrounds desired, fringe benefits offered, stock exchange listing, training programs, internships, parent company, number of employees, revenues, e-mail and web address, projected number of hires. Arrangement: Alphabetical.

★13259★ **Adams Jobs Almanac**
Adams Media Corp.
57 Littlefield St.
Avon, MA 02322
Ph: (508)427-7100   Fax: (508)427-6790
Fr: 800-872-5627
URL: http://adamsmedia.stores.yahoo.net/adjoal9thed.html

Annual; latest edition 9th. $19.95 for individuals. Covers job listings nationwide. Entries include: Firm or organization name, address, phone, name and title of contact; description of organization, headquarters location, typical titles for entry- and middle-level positions, educational backgrounds desired, fringe benefits offered, stock exchange listing, training programs, internships, parent company, number of employees, revenues, e-mail and web address, projected number of hires. Indexes: Alphabetical.

★13260★ **America's 101 Fastest Growing Jobs, Eighth Edition**
JIST Publishing
875 Montreal Way
St. Paul, MN 55102
Fax: 800-547-8329   Fr: 800-648-5478
E-mail: info@jist.com
URL: http://www.jist.com

Michael Farr. 2005. $15.95. 400 pages. More than 100 of the fastest growing jobs in America detailed in this reference; includes careers at every education and training level, and in a wide range of industries.

★13261★ **America's Career InfoNet**
U.S. Department of Labor
Frances Perkins Bldg.
200 Constitution Ave. NW
Washington, DC 20210
Ph: (886)487-2365   Fr: 877-889-5627
URL: http://www.acinet.org/acinet/

Covers links to and information about job banks, employment service providers, career education, and nationwide employer contacts.

★13262★ **America's Top 101 Jobs for College Graduates, Sixth Edition**
JIST Publishing
875 Montreal Way
St. Paul, MN 55102
Fax: 800-547-8329   Fr: 800-648-5478
E-mail: info@jist.com
URL: http://www.jist.com

Michael Farr. 2005. $15.95. 384 pages.

Current descriptions for more than 100 major jobs in alphabetical order within five degree levels: professional or doctoral, master's degree, bachelor's degree plus work experience, bachelor's degree, and jobs that may not require a bachelor's degree but are often held by college graduates.

★13263★ **America's Top 101 Jobs for People Without a Four-Year Degree, Seventh Edition**
JIST Publishing
875 Montreal Way
St. Paul, MN 55102
Fax: 800-547-8329   Fr: 800-648-5478
E-mail: info@jist.com
URL: http://www.jist.com

Michael Farr. 2005. $15.95. 368 pages. Current descriptions for more than 100 jobs that do not require a four-year degree.

★13264★ **America's Top 300 Jobs, Ninth Edition**
JIST Publishing
875 Montreal Way
St. Paul, MN 55102
Fax: 800-547-8329   Fr: 800-648-5478
E-mail: info@jist.com
URL: http://www.jist.com

U.S. Department of Labor. 2004. $18.95. 736 pages. Based on the latest edition of the Occupational Outlook Handbook, this reference includes information job seekers and students need to research careers, learn about pay, outlook, and education and skills needed to land a job.

★13265★ **Atlanta JobBank**
Adams Media Corp.
57 Littlefield St.
Avon, MA 02322
Ph: (508)427-7100   Fax: (508)427-6790
Fr: 800-872-5627
URL: http://www.adamsmedia.com

Latest edition 15th. $17.95 for individuals. Covers 3,900 employers in the state of Georgia, including Albany, Columbus, Macon, and Savannah. Entries include: Firm or organization name, address, local phone, toll-free phone, fax, description of organization, subsidiaries, other locations, recorded jobline, name and title of contact, typical titles for common positions, educational backgrounds desired, number of employees, benefits offered, training programs, internships, parent company, revenues, e-mail and URL address, projected number of hires. Arrangement: Classified by industry. Indexes: Alphabetical.

★13266★ **The Austin/San Antonio JobBank**
Adams Media Corp.
57 Littlefield St.
Avon, MA 02322
Ph: (508)427-7100   Fax: (508)427-6790
Fr: 800-872-5627
URL: http://www.adamsmedia.com

Biennial; latest edition 4th. $17.95 for individ-

uals. Covers More than 5,100 companies in metro Austin, metro San Antonio, and the surrounding area, including El Paso. Entries include: Firm or organization name, address, phone, name and title of contact; description of organization, headquarters location, typical titles for entry- and middle-level positions, educational backgrounds desired, fringe benefits offered, stock exchange listing, training programs, internships, parent company, number of employees, revenues, e-mail and web address, projected number of hires. Indexes: Alphabetical.

★13267★ **The Baby Boomer's Guide to a Successful Job Search**
AuthorHouse
1663 Liberty Dr., Ste. 200
Bloomington, IN 47403
Ph: (812)961-1023   Fax: (812)339-8654
Fr: 888-519-5121
URL: http://www.authorhouse.com

Don Theeuwes. April 2004. $13.95 (paper). 108 pages.

★13268★ **Best Career and Education Web Sites, Fourth Edition**
JIST Publishing
875 Montreal Way
St. Paul, MN 55102
Fax: 800-547-8329   Fr: 800-648-5478
E-mail: info@jist.com
URL: http://www.jist.com

Rachel Singer Gordon and Anne Wolfinger. 2004. $12.95. 208 pages. Provides URLs and objective reviews of the most helpful career and college-related sites on the Web; organized by category and target audience.

★13269★ **Best Entry-Level Jobs, 2006**
The Princeton Review
2315 Broadway
New York, NY 10024
Ph: (212)874-8282   Fax: (212)874-0775
URL: http://www.princetonreview.com

Princeton Review. 2005. $11. 320 pages. Reveals where the best first job opportunities in the country are and what you need to do to get them.

★13270★ **Best Jobs for the 21st Century, Fourth Edition**
JIST Publishing
875 Montreal Way
St. Paul, MN 55102
Fax: 800-547-8329   Fr: 800-648-5478
E-mail: info@jist.com
URL: http://www.jist.com

Michael Farr. 2006. $19.95. 688 pages. Reference book featuring "best jobs" list and detailed job descriptions organized according to interest area structure following the U.S. Department of Education career clusters.

★13271★ Career Exploration on the Internet

Facts On File Inc.
132 W 31st St., 17th Fl.
New York, NY 10001
Ph: (212)967-8800   Fax: 800-678-3633
Fr: 800-322-8755
URL: http://www.factsonfile.com

Published 2000. $24.95 for individuals; $22.45 for libraries. Covers descriptions and links to the most informative and useful career sites on the Internet.

★13272★ Career Exploration on the Internet Set

Facts On File Inc.
132 W 31st St., 17th Fl.
New York, NY 10001
Ph: (212)967-8800   Fax: 800-678-3633
Fr: 800-322-8755
URL: http://www.factsonfile.com

$49.90 for individuals; $42.40 for libraries. Covers descriptions and links to the most informative and useful career sites on the Internet.

★13273★ Career Guide to America's Top Industries, Sixth Edition

JIST Publishing
875 Montreal Way
St. Paul, MN 55102
Fax: 800-547-8329   Fr: 800-648-5478
E-mail: info@jist.com
URL: http://www.jist.com

U.S. Department of Labor. 2004. $13.95. 272 pages. Provides job seekers and career changers knowledge of businesses and industries to target their job search.

★13274★ Career Ideas for Teens Set

Facts On File Inc.
132 W 31st St., 17th Fl.
New York, NY 10001
Ph: (212)967-8800   Fax: 800-678-3633
Fr: 800-322-8755
URL: http://www.factsonfile.com

$320.00 for individuals; $272.00 for libraries. 8-volume set. Covers a multitude of career possibilities based on a teenager's specific interests and skills and links his/her talents to a wide variety of actual professions.

★13275★ Career Opportunities Set

Facts On File Inc.
132 W 31st St., 17th Fl.
New York, NY 10001
Ph: (212)967-8800   Fax: 800-678-3633
Fr: 800-322-8755
URL: http://www.factsonfile.com

$1,485.00 for individuals; $1,262.25 for libraries. 30-volume set. Covers in-depth profiles of approximately 60 to 100 jobs, providing thorough information on salary ranges, employment trends, necessary experience, advancement prospects, and helpful unions and associations.

★13276★ Career Skills Library: Communication Skills

Facts On File Inc.
132 W 31st St., 17th Fl.
New York, NY 10001
Ph: (212)967-8800   Fax: 800-678-3633
Fr: 800-322-8755
URL: http://www.factsonfile.com

Latest edition 2nd, 2004. $21.95 for individuals; $19.75 for libraries. Covers the importance of solid speaking, writing, listening, and conversational skills for thriving in the workplace, plus additional communication skills that are useful in specific situations, such as techniques for conducting structured and productive meetings.

★13277★ Career Skills Library: Leadership Skills

Facts On File Inc.
132 W 31st St., 17th Fl.
New York, NY 10001
Ph: (212)967-8800   Fax: 800-678-3633
Fr: 800-322-8755
URL: http://www.factsonfile.com

Latest edition 2nd, 2004. $21.95 for individuals; $19.75 for libraries. Covers the qualities of all successful leaders, such as courteousness, compassion, decisiveness, and willingness to give and receive criticism.

★13278★ Career Skills Library: Learning the Ropes

Facts On File Inc.
132 W 31st St., 17th Fl.
New York, NY 10001
Ph: (212)967-8800   Fax: 800-678-3633
Fr: 800-322-8755
URL: http://www.factsonfile.com

Latest edition 2nd, 2004. $21.95 for individuals; $19.75 for libraries. Covers what to expect from the first day on the job, how to successfully navigate the workplace environment, preparing for some of the realities of work life, including dress codes, organizational hierarchies, co-worker conflicts and resolutions, and some basic rights of every employee.

★13279★ Career Skills Library: Organization Skills

Facts On File Inc.
132 W 31st St., 17th Fl.
New York, NY 10001
Ph: (212)967-8800   Fax: 800-678-3633
Fr: 800-322-8755
URL: http://www.factsonfile.com

Latest edition 2nd, 2004. $21.95 for individuals; $19.75 for libraries. Covers time management, setting schedules, avoiding procrastination and time wasters, and organizing one's workplace.

★13280★ Career Skills Library: Problem Solving

Facts On File Inc.
132 W 31st St., 17th Fl.
New York, NY 10001
Ph: (212)967-8800   Fax: 800-678-3633
Fr: 800-322-8755
URL: http://www.factsonfile.com

Latest edition 2nd, 2004. $21.95 for individuals; $19.75 for libraries. Covers the difference between scientific and creative problem-solving techniques and outlines a five-step approach to dealing with dilemmas to apply to almost any situation.

★13281★ Career Skills Library: Research and Information Management

Facts On File Inc.
132 W 31st St., 17th Fl.
New York, NY 10001
Ph: (212)967-8800   Fax: 800-678-3633
Fr: 800-322-8755
URL: http://www.factsonfile.com

Latest edition 2nd, 2004. $21.95 for individuals; $19.75 for libraries. Covers different ways of approaching research and information management, such as using research methods, evaluating information for relevance, creating effective presentations, and managing information with spreadsheet and word processing software.

★13282★ Career Skills Library Set

Facts On File Inc.
132 W 31st St., 17th Fl.
New York, NY 10001
Ph: (212)967-8800   Fax: 800-678-3633
Fr: 800-322-8755
URL: http://www.factsonfile.com

$175.60 for individuals; $149.25 for libraries. 8-volume set. Covers the skills, traits, and attributes that are crucial to success in any field, including communication, problem solving, organization, and relating to others.

★13283★ Career Skills Library: Teamwork Skills

Facts On File Inc.
132 W 31st St., 17th Fl.
New York, NY 10001
Ph: (212)967-8800   Fax: 800-678-3633
Fr: 800-322-8755
URL: http://www.factsonfile.com

Latest edition 2nd, 2004. $21.95 for individuals; $19.75 for libraries. Covers the need for teams and how to achieve and encourage healthy team dynamics, including topics such as developing people skills, effectively setting goals and negotiating, appreciating diversity among team members, and resolving team conflicts.

★13284★ *Career Tips for 20 Something's: What You Should Know About Managing Your Career Before You're 30*

JIST Publishing
875 Montreal Way
St. Paul, MN 55102
Fax: 800-547-8329   Fr: 800-648-5478
E-mail: info@jist.com
URL: http://www.jist.com

Phillis Caves Rawley. 2004. $7.95. 212 pages. Book of common sense advice for career starters to prevent interview mistakes and dead-end career choices; includes starter guide for managing the first job, paycheck, budget, and future career successes.

★13285★ *Career Tips Workbook: What Career Will You See in Your Rear View Mirror Thirty Years from Now?*

JIST Publishing
875 Montreal Way
St. Paul, MN 55102
Fax: 800-547-8329   Fr: 800-648-5478
E-mail: info@jist.com
URL: http://www.jist.com

Phyllis Caves Rawley. 2004. $12.95. 72 pages. Assists people in learning what motivates them when looking for the best career fit.

★13286★ *Careers in Focus Series*

JIST Publishing
875 Montreal Way
St. Paul, MN 55102
Fax: 800-547-8329   Fr: 800-648-5478
E-mail: info@jist.com
URL: http://www.jist.com

1999-2005. $22.95. 176-192 pages. Each of the 45 books in this series is focused on a specific field.

★13287★ *CareerXRoads*

MMC GROUP
105 Decker Ct., Ste. 150
Irving, TX 75062
Ph: (972)893-0100   Fax: (972)893-0099
URL: http://www.careerxroads.com/about/

Latest edition 2002. Covers nearly 3,000 job and resume Web sites with reviews and descriptions of the top 500. Indexes: colleges; corporations: diversity; specialty/industry; location; listing services.

★13288★ *Change Your Job, Change Your Life: High Impact Strategies for Finding Great Jobs in the 21st Century*

Impact Publications
9104 Manassas Dr., Ste. N
Manassas Park, VA 20111-5211
Ph: (703)361-7300   Fax: (703)335-9486
Fr: 800-361-1055
E-mail: query@impactpublications.com
URL: http://www.impactpublications.com

Ronald Krannich. Seventh edition, 1999. $21.95 (paper). 317 pages. Details trends in the marketplace, how to identify opportuni-

ties, how to retrain for them, and how to land jobs. Includes a chapter on starting a business. Contains index, bibliography, and illustrations.

★13289★ *College Majors Handbook with Real Career Paths and Payoffs, Second Edition*

JIST Publishing
875 Montreal Way
St. Paul, MN 55102
Fax: 800-547-8329   Fr: 800-648-5478
E-mail: info@jist.com
URL: http://www.jist.com

Neeta P. Fogg, PhD; Paul E. Harrington, EdD; Thomas F. Harrington, PhD. 2004. $24.95. 656 pages. Gives job salary prospects for specific college majors, employment growth rates, and how many graduates go on to additional education, based on U.S. Census Bureau study.

★13290★ *Coming Alive from Nine to Five: The Career Search Handbook*

The McGraw-Hill Companies
PO Box 182604
Columbus, OH 43272
Fax: (614)759-3749   Fr: 877-883-5524
E-mail: customer.service@mcgraw-hill.com
URL: http://www.mcgraw-hill.com

Betty Neville Michelozzi. Seventh edition, 2003. $60.00. 360 pages. In addition to general job-hunting advice, provides special information for women, young adults, minorities, older workers, and persons with handicaps.

★13291★ *The Connecticut JobBank*

Adams Media Corp.
57 Littlefield St.
Avon, MA 02322
Ph: (508)427-7100   Fax: (508)427-6790
Fr: 800-872-5627
URL: http://adamsmedia.stores.yahoo.net/cojo3rded.html

Biennial; latest edition 3. $17.95 for individuals. Covers approximately 2,000 employers, career resources, industry associations, and employment services in Connecticut. Entries include: Company name, address, phone, fax, e-mail, and web address; names and titles of key personnel; number of employees; geographical area served; financial data; subsidiary names and addresses; description of services; Standard Industrial Classification (SIC) code. Indexes: Alphabetical.

★13292★ *Damn, I Need a Job. Again!*

Kanianthra Press
PO Box 23311
Seattle, WA 98102

Alex Dakotta. June 2005. $14.95. 266 pages.

★13293★ *Discovering Careers for Your Future Set*

Facts On File Inc.
132 W 31st St., 17th Fl.
New York, NY 10001
Ph: (212)967-8800   Fax: 800-678-3633
Fr: 800-322-8755
URL: http://www.factsonfile.com

$482.90 for individuals; $410.45 for libraries. 22-volume set. Covers 20 careers in each volume and offering a comprehensive look at everything from how to start preparing while still in school to what the future might hold in terms of job prospects and salaries.

★13294★ *Do What You Are: Discover the Perfect Career for You Through the Secrets of Personality Type*

JIST Publishing
875 Montreal Way
St. Paul, MN 55102
Fax: 800-547-8329   Fr: 800-648-5478
E-mail: info@jist.com
URL: http://www.jist.com

Paul D. Tieger and Barbara Barron-Tieger. 2001. $18.95. 416 pages. Helps readers discover their Myers-Briggs personality type and introduces the key ingredients work must have for it to be truly fulfilling.

★13295★ *The Don't Sweat Guide to Your Job Search: Finding a Career Your Really Love*

Hyperion Press
77 W. 66th St., 11th Fl.
New York, NY 10023-6298
Ph: (212)456-0100   Fax: (212)456-0108
Fr: 800-759-0190
URL: http://www.hyperionbooks.com/

$10.95 (paper). 208 pages. May 2004.

★13296★ *Effective Strategies for Career Success*

Jist Works
875 Montreal Way
St. Paul, MN 55102
Fr: 800-648-5478
E-mail: info@jist.com
URL: http://www.jist.com

$9.95 (paper). 380 pages.

★13297★ *Employment Opportunities, USA*

Washington Research Associates
1090 Vermont Ave. NW, Ste. 800
Washington, DC 20005
Ph: (202)408-7025

Annual, quarterly updates. Publication includes: List of over 1,000 employment contacts in companies and agencies in banking, arts, telecommunications, education, and 14 other industries and professions, including federal government. Entries include: Company name, name of representative, address, description of products or services, hiring and recruiting practices, training programs, and year established. Principal content is industry overviews, career news, employment opportunity information on 14 different job markets, and comprehensive guidance to career resources on the Internet. Arrangement: Classified by industry. Indexes: Occupation.

★13298★ **Encyclopedia of Careers and Vocational Guidance, Twelfth Edition**
JIST Publishing
875 Montreal Way
St. Paul, MN 55102
Fax: 800-547-8329   Fr: 800-648-5478
E-mail: info@jist.com
URL: http://www.jist.com

2002. $199.95. 3,216 pages. Four-volume comprehensive career reference.

★13299★ **Exploring Tech Careers, Third Edition**
JIST Publishing
875 Montreal Way
St. Paul, MN 55102
Fax: 800-547-8329   Fr: 800-648-5478
E-mail: info@jist.com
URL: http://www.jist.com

2001. $89.95. 1,056 pages. Answers questions students are likely to have about tech careers.

★13300★ **Ferguson Career Resource Guide Series-Directory Issue**
Ferguson Publishing Co.
200 W Jackson Blvd.
Chicago, IL 60606-6941
Fax: 800-306-9942   Fr: 800-306-9941
URL: http://www.fergpubco.com/

Published 2006. $625.00; $531.26. Covers descriptions and contact information for hundreds of organizations, schools, and associations.

★13301★ **Find and Get Your Dream Job**
Socrates Media LLC
736 N. Western Ave., Ste. 360
Lake Forest, IL 60045
Ph: (312)762-5600   Fax: (312)896-5850
Fr: 800-822-4566
URL: http://www.socrates.com

$9.95. Laminated. Step-by-step guide to determine what your dream job is, how to go after it, and how to land it.

★13302★ **Finding Your Perfect Work**
Penguin Putnam Inc.
375 Hudson St.
New York, NY 10014-3757
Ph: (212)366-2000   Fax: (212)366-2888
Fr: 800-631-8571
E-mail: ecommerce@us.penguingroup.com
URL: http://www.us.penguingroup.com

January 2003. $17.95. Covers Internet resources that help with career choices, including a list of Internet sites offering education grants and loans.

★13303★ **The First Job Hunt Survival Guide**
Drake Beam Morin Pub
750 Third Ave., 28th Fl.
New York, NY 10017
Ph: (212)692-7700   Fax: (212)297-0426
E-mail: inquiries@dbm.com
URL: http://www.dbm.com

Pat Morton and Marcia R. Fox, editors. 1995. $11.95 (paper). 176 pages. Helps new graduates navigate the entry-level job market.

★13304★ **Get A Job! Put Your Degree to Work**
Donna Kozik
2828 University Ave., Ste. 227
San Diego, CA 92104
Ph: (619)297-1749

Donna Kozik. 2004. $19.95. 128 pages.

★13305★ **Get That Job!: Job Openings**
The McGraw-Hill Companies
PO Box 182604
Columbus, OH 43272
Fax: (614)759-3749   Fr: 877-883-5524
E-mail: customer.service@mcgraw-hill.com
URL: http://www.mcgraw-hill.com

Susan Echaore-McDavid. 1997. $4.66 (paper). 32 pages. Part of an eight-book series that targets adult learners to improve communication and language skills to aid them in getting jobs.

★13306★ **Get That Job!: Work Experience**
The McGraw-Hill Companies
PO Box 182604
Columbus, OH 43272
Fax: (614)759-3749   Fr: 877-883-5524
E-mail: customer.service@mcgraw-hill.com
URL: http://www.mcgraw-hill.com

Susan Echaore-McDavid. 1997. $4.66 (paper). 32 pages. Part of an eight-book series that targets adult learners to improve communication.

★13307★ **Getting the Job You Really Want**
Jist Works
875 Montreal Way
St. Paul, MN 55102
Fr: 800-648-5478
E-mail: info@jist.com
URL: http://www.jist.com

J. Michael Farr. Fourth edition, 2001. $12.95 (paper). 232 pages. A step-by-step guide to career planning, job seeking, and job survival.

★13308★ **Getting, Keeping, and Growing in Your Job**
Jist Works
875 Montreal Way
St. Paul, MN 55102
Fr: 800-648-5478
E-mail: info@jist.com

URL: http://www.jist.com
William G. Corbin and Kim Corbin. 1997 $9.95. 128 pages. Covers job hunting topics such as writing resumes and cover letters interviews, and starting a new job.

★13309★ **Getting Your Foot in the Door When You Don't Have a Leg to Stand On**
The McGraw-Hill Companies
PO Box 182604
Columbus, OH 43272
Fax: (614)759-3749   Fr: 877-883-5524
E-mail: customer.service@mcgraw-hill.com
URL: http://www.mcgraw-hill.com

Rob Sullivan. 2001. $12.95 (paper). 192 pages.

★13310★ **Great Careers in 2 Years, Second Edition: The Associate Degree Option**
JIST Publishing
875 Montreal Way
St. Paul, MN 55102
Fax: 800-547-8329   Fr: 800-648-5478
E-mail: info@jist.com
URL: http://www.jist.com

Paul Phifer. 2003. $19.95. 368 pages. Profiles more than 100 promising and rewarding careers that require two-year degrees.

★13311★ **Great Jobs Series**
JIST Publishing
875 Montreal Way
St. Paul, MN 55102
Fax: 800-547-8329   Fr: 800-648-5478
E-mail: info@jist.com
URL: http://www.jist.com

$14.95 each. 24 title series, focusing on college majors with an overview of career fields with possible employers, job titles, related occupations, and professional associations.

★13312★ **Greater Philadelphia Chamber of Commerce Job Fair Job Seekers Guide**
Greater Philadelphia Chamber of Commerce
200 S Broad St., Ste. 700
Philadelphia, PA 19102
Ph: (215)545-1234   Fax: (215)790-3700

Covers more than 100 recruiting companies in Philadelphia. Entries include: Company profiles, contact information.

★13313★ **Guerilla Marketing: 400 Unconventional Tips, Tricks, and Tactics for Landing Your Dream Job**
John Wiley and Sons, Inc.
1 Wiley Dr.
Somerset, NJ 08875-1272
Ph: (732)469-4400   Fax: (732)302-2300
Fr: 800-225-5945
E-mail: custserv@wiley.com
URL: http://www.wiley.com/WileyCDA/

Jay Conrad Levinson and David Perry. 2005. $18.95. 288 pages. Provides steps to using a typically unconventional Guerilla approach covering all the basics of a winning campaign.

★13314★ **Guide to Apprenticeship Programs, Second Edition**

JIST Publishing
875 Montreal Way
St. Paul, MN 55102
Fax: 800-547-8329   Fr: 800-648-5478
E-mail: info@jist.com
URL: http://www.jist.com

1999. $89.95. 980 pages. 7,500 programs listed in 53 job categories with first-hand testimony of former apprentices.

★13315★ **Guide for the Pissed-off-Job-Seeker: Angry? Good! Use That Anger to Get Work!**

iUniverse, Inc.
2021 Pine Lake Rd. Ste. 100
Lincoln, NE 68512
Ph: (402)323-7800   Fax: (402)323-7824
Fr: 877-288-4677
URL: http://www.iuniverse.com/

Irv Zuckerman, David Abel. May 2004. $14.95 (paper). 132 pages.

★13316★ **Guide for the Unemployed Workbook**

Prosperity and Profits Unlimited
PO Box 416
Denver, CO 80201-0416
Ph: (303)575-5676   Fax: (970)292-2136

Frieda Carrol. 1997. $24.95 (ringbound). 60 pages.

★13317★ **The Harvard Business School Guide to Finding Your Next Job**

Harvard Business School Press
60 Harvard Way
Boston, MA 02163
Ph: (617)783-7500   Fax: (617)783-7555
Fr: 800-988-0886
URL: http://www.hbsp.harvard.edu

Robert S. Gardella. 2000. $19.95 (paper). 176 pages.

★13318★ **Have No Career Fear: A College Grad's Guide to Snagging a Job, Trekking the Career Path, and Reaching Job Nirvana**

Natavi Guides
19 Stuyvesant Oval, Ste. 8E
New York, NY 10009
Fax: (866)425-4218   Fr: (866)425-4218
E-mail: info@nataviguides.com
URL: http://www.nataviguides.com/

Ben Cohen-Leadholm, Rachel Skerritt, Ari Gerzon-Kessler. April 2004. $13.95 (paper). 206 pages.

★13319★ **Help Wanted: An Inexperienced Job Seekers Complete Guide to Career Success**

Waveland Press
4180 IL Route 83, Ste. 101
Long Grove, IL 60047
Ph: (847)634-0081   Fax: (847)634-9501
E-mail: info@waveland.com
URL: http://www.waveland.com/

Ann M. Gill and Stephen M. Lewis. 1996. $6.99 (paper). 212 pages.

★13320★ **How to Choose Your Next Employer**

Oakhill Press
461 Layside Dr., Ste. 102
Winchester, VA 22602-2123
Ph: (540)877-1689   Fax: (540)877-1360
Fr: 800-322-6657

Roger E. Herman. 2000. $15.95. 226 pages.

★13321★ **How to Find the Work You Love**

Penguin
375 Hudson St.
New York, NY 10014
Ph: (212)366-2000   Fax: (212)366-2666
Fr: 800-847-5515
URL: http://us.penguingroup.com/

Laurence G. Boldt. 2004. $12.00 (paper). 192 pages.

★13322★ **How to Get a Better Job in This Crazy World**

Signet Book
375 Hudson St.
New York, NY 10014-3657
Ph: (212)366-2000   Fax: (212)366-2666
Fr: 800-331-4624
URL: http://us.penguingroup.com/

Robert Half. 1994. $17.95. 256 pages.

★13323★ **How to Get Hired Today!**

The McGraw-Hill Companies
PO Box 182604
Columbus, OH 43272
Fax: (614)759-3749   Fr: 877-883-5524
E-mail: customer.service@mcgraw-hill.com
URL: http://www.mcgraw-hill.com

George E. Kent. 1994. $7.95 (paper). 128 pages. Directed at individuals who know the type of job they are looking for. Focuses the reader on activities that are likely to lead to a job and eliminates those that won't. Shows how to establish productive contacts and discover, evaluate, and pursue strong job leads.

★13324★ **How to Get a Job & Keep It**

Ferguson Publishing Co.
132 W. 31st St., 17th Fl.
New York, NY 10001
Fax: 800-678-3633   Fr: 800-322-8755
E-mail: custserv@factsonfile.com
URL: http://fergu-

son.infobasepublishing.com/
Susan Morem. 2007. $16.95. 320 pages.

★13325★ **How to Get the Job You Desire**

Dorrance Publishing Company, Inc.
701 Smithfield St., Ste. 301
Pittsburgh, PA 15222
Ph: (412)288-4543   Fax: (412)288-1786
Fr: 800-788-7654
URL: http://www.dorrancepublishing.com/

Peggy Redman. February 2004. $14.95 (paper). 42 pages.

★13326★ **How to Get That Job**

Pilot Books
127 Sterling Ave.
PO Box 2102
Greenport, NY 11944-0893
Ph: (516)477-1094   Fax: (516)477-0978
Fr: 800-797-4568
URL: http://www.pilotbooks.com

Ruby N. Gorter. 1997. $8.95. 94 pages. Provides information for first-time job seekers as well as those who want to change careers.

★13327★ **How to Get Your Dream Job in 60 Days: For College Graduates**

Althemus
PO Box 8634
Northridge, CA 91327
Fax: (818)831-1316

Kerry Gardette. February 2004. $12.95 (paper). Illustrated. 163 pages.

★13328★ **How to Market Your College Degree**

The McGraw-Hill Companies
PO Box 182604
Columbus, OH 43272
Fax: (614)759-3749   Fr: 877-883-5524
E-mail: customer.service@mcgraw-hill.com
URL: http://www.mcgraw-hill.com

Dorothy Rogers. 1993. $12.95 (paper). 149 pages. Provides a guide to self-marketing as a key component of an effective job search. Helps job seekers to develop a strategic marketing plan that targets niches with needs that match their skills, differentiate themselves from the competition by positioning themselves against other candidates, evaluate their potential worth from the employer's perspective, and manage their careers as they move up the career ladder or into another field.

★13329★ **How to Move from College into a Secure Job**

The McGraw-Hill Companies
PO Box 182604
Columbus, OH 43272
Fax: (614)759-3749   Fr: 877-883-5524
E-mail: customer.service@mcgraw-hill.com
URL: http://www.mcgraw-hill.com

Mary Dehner. 1993. $12.95 (paper). 205 pages.

★13330★ Hunt-Scanlon's Executive Recruiters of North America - Contingency Firms

Hunt-Scanlon Publishing
700 Fairfield Ave.
Stamford, CT 06902
Ph: (203)352-2920   Fax: (203)352-2930
Fr: 800-477-1199
URL: http://www.hunt-scanlon.com/

Annual. $235.00. Covers over 3,000 executive recruiters in a cross-section of contingency search firms in North America. Entries include: Individual and company name, phone number, and revenue statistics. Arrangement: Alphabetical. Indexes: Geographical; business sector.

★13331★ Hunt-Scanlon's Executive Recruiters of North America (Retained Firms Edition)

Hunt-Scanlon Publishing
700 Fairfield Ave.
Stamford, CT 06902
Ph: (203)352-2920   Fax: (203)352-2930
Fr: 800-477-1199
URL: http://www.hunt-scanlon.com/

Annual; latest edition 2005. $235.00. Covers Over 3,600 retained executive recruiters in the U.S., Canada, and Mexico. Entries include: Individual name, phone number, specialization, revenue, professional memberships, salary levels.

★13332★ Hunt-Scanlon's Select Guide to Human Resource Executives

Hunt-Scanlon Publishing
700 Fairfield Ave.
Stamford, CT 06902
Ph: (203)352-2920   Fax: (203)352-2930
Fr: 800-477-1199
URL: http://www.hunt-scanlon.com/shop/

Annual; latest edition 2005. $269.00. Covers over 23,000 human resource executives, personnel managers, and compensation, benefits, and training professionals in 10,000 companies in the U.S. Entries include: Company and individual name, title.

★13333★ The Indiana JobBank

Adams Media Corp.
57 Littlefield St.
Avon, MA 02322
Ph: (508)427-7100   Fax: (508)427-6790
Fr: 800-872-5627

Biennial. $72.24 for individuals. Covers 3,200 employers in Indiana, including Evansville, Fort Wayne, Gary, New Albany, and South Bend. Entries include: Firm or organization name, address, phone, name and title of contact; description of organization, headquarters location, typical titles for entry and middle-level positions, educational backgrounds desired, fringe benefits offered, stock exchange listing, training programs, internships, parent company, number of em-

ployees, revenues, e-mail and web address, projected number of hires. Indexes: Alphabetical.

★13334★ Insider's Guide to Finding a Job

JIST Publishing
875 Montreal Way
St. Paul, MN 55102
Fax: 800-547-8329   Fr: 800-648-5478
E-mail: info@jist.com
URL: http://www.jist.com

Wendy S. Enelow and Shelly Goldman. 2005. $12.95. First-hand advice from 66 top hiring managers, HR directors, and recruiters at the most sought-after companies in the U.S.

★13335★ The Job Hunter's Catalog

John Wiley & Sons Inc.
1 Wiley Dr.
Somerset, NJ 08873
Ph: (732)469-4400   Fax: (732)302-2300
Fr: 800-225-5945
E-mail: custserv@wiley.com
URL: http://www.wiley.com/WileyCDA/

Peggy Schmidt. First edition, 1996. $10.95 (paper). 192 pages.

★13336★ Job Hunting for Dummies

Running Press Book Publishers
2300 Chestnut St., Ste. 200
Philadelphia, PA 19103
Ph: (215)567-5080   Fax: (215)568-2919
Fr: 800-345-5359
E-mail: perseus.promos@perseusbooks.com
URL: http://www.perseusbooksgroup.com/runningpress/home.jsp

Robert Half, Max Massmer, Jr. 2001. $4.95. 128 pages. Presents strategies for determining what you want in a career and how to negotiate the best deal when you get a job offer.

★13337★ Job Hunting Made Easy

LearningExpress, LLC
55 Broadway, 8th Fl.
New York, NY 10006
Ph: (212)995-2566   Fax: (212)995-5512
Fr: 800-295-9556
E-mail: customerservice@learningexpressllc.com
URL: http://www.learningexpressllc.com

Carol Sonnenblick, Michaele Basciano, and Kim Crabbe. 1997. $13.95 (paper). 197 pages.

★13338★ Job Search 101

Jist Works
875 Montreal Way
St. Paul, MN 55102
Fr: 800-648-5478
E-mail: info@jist.com
URL: http://www.jist.com

Marcia Fox and Pat Morton. 1997. $12.95.

182 pages. An introductory guide to entry-level jobs.

★13339★ Job Search and Career Checklists: 101 Proven Time-Saving Checklists to Organize and Plan Your Career Search

JIST Publishing
875 Montreal Way
St. Paul, MN 55102
Fax: 800-547-8329   Fr: 800-648-5478
E-mail: info@jist.com
URL: http://www.jist.com

Arlene S. Hirsch. 2005. $14.95. 208 pages. Job search workbook including checklists and task lists for assessing needs, initiating job searches, improving current jobs and exploring career options.

★13340★ Job Search: Career Planning Guide

Wadsworth Publishing
PO Box 6904
Florence, KY 41022
Fax: 800-487-8488   Fr: 800-354-9706
URL: http://www.cengage.com

Robert D. Lock. Fifth edition, 2005. $58.95 (paper). 368 pages. Assists the reader in a productive job search. Part of Career Planning Guide series.

★13341★ Job Search Magic: Insider Secrets from America's Career and Life Coach

JIST Publishing
875 Montreal Way
St. Paul, MN 55102
Fax: 800-547-8329   Fr: 800-648-5478
E-mail: info@jist.com
URL: http://www.jist.com

Susan Britton Whitcomb. 2006. $18.95. 512 pages. Job search manual offers basic foundations of a complete resume, cover letters, and strategies for getting the interview and embarking on a career path.

★13342★ Job Seeker's Guide

Greater Dallas Chamber
700 N Pearl St., Ste. 1200
Dallas, TX 75201
Ph: (214)746-6600

Annual. $10.00 for nonmembers; $20.00 for members. Covers top 100 employers in the Dallas area, information on employment agencies, and labor market projections.

★13343★ Job Seeker's Online Goldmine: A Step-by-Step Guidebook to Government and No-Cost Web Tools

JIST Publishing
875 Montreal Way
St. Paul, MN 55102
Fax: 800-547-8329   Fr: 800-648-5478
E-mail: info@jist.com
URL: http://www.jist.com

Janet E. Wall, EdD. 2006. $13.95. 256

pages. Handbook pulls together, in a single source, a wealth of online options that are not widely publicized because they're funded by tax dollars or nonprofit organizations.

★13344★ Job Seeker's Workbook

JIST Publishing
875 Montreal Way
St. Paul, MN 55102
Fax: 800-547-8329   Fr: 800-648-5478
E-mail: info@jist.com
URL: http://www.jist.com

Editors at JIST. 2001. $6.95. 80 pages. For job seekers with lower reading level or limited English skills. Includes interactive worksheets, charts and checklists.

★13345★ JobSmarts 50 Top Careers

HarperCollins
10 E. 53rd St.
New York, NY 10022
Ph: (212)207-7000   Fax: (212)207-7633
Fr: 800-242-7737
URL: http://www.harpercollins.com/

Bradley G. Richardson. 1997. $16.00 (paper). 400 pages.

★13346★ Joyce Lain Kennedy's Career Book

The McGraw-Hill Companies
PO Box 182604
Columbus, OH 43272
Fax: (614)759-3749   Fr: 877-883-5524
E-mail: customer.service@mcgraw-hill.com
URL: http://www.mcgraw-hill.com

Joyce Lain Kennedy and Dr. Darryl Laramore. Third edition, 1997. $29.95; $17.95 (paper). 448 pages. Guides the reader through the entire career-planning and job-hunting process. Addresses how to find the kinds of jobs available and what to do once the job is secured. Provides a number of case histories to give examples.

★13347★ Knock 'Em Dead: The Ultimate Job Seeker's Handbook

Adams Media Corp.
4700 E. Galbraith Rd.
Cincinnati, OH 45236
Ph: (513)531-2690   Fax: (513)531-4082
Fr: 800-289-0963
URL: http://www.adamsmedia.com

Martin Yate. Revised edition, 2007. $14.95 (paper). Prepares the job seeker for the interview with advice on dress, manner, how to answer the toughest questions, and how to spot illegal questions. Discusses how to respond to questions of salary to maximize income. Features sections on executive search firms and drug testing. 352 pages.

★13348★ Last Minute Job Search Tips

Career Press, Inc.
PO Box 687
3 Tice Rd.
Franklin Lakes, NJ 07417
Ph: (201)848-0310   Fax: (201)848-1727
Fr: 800-227-3371

URL: http://www.CareerPress.com

Brandon Toropov. 1996. $7.99 (paper). 127 pages.

★13349★ Major Employers Directory

Greater Philadelphia Chamber of Commerce
200 S Broad St., Ste. 700
Philadelphia, PA 19102
Ph: (215)545-1234   Fax: (215)790-3700
URL: http://www.philachamber.com/

$25.00 for members; $35.00 for nonmembers. Covers over 500 top employers and pertinent information in each of the Greater Philadelphia area's 11 counties. Arrangement: Alphabetical.

★13350★ Making Good Career and Life Decisions: You Have to Know Who You Are to Get Where You're Going

JIST Publishing
875 Montreal Way
St. Paul, MN 55102
Fax: 800-547-8329   Fr: 800-648-5478
E-mail: info@jist.com
URL: http://www.jist.com

Staff of Northern Virginia Community College. 1997. $9.95. 160 pages. Designed for adults without college degrees to be led through the process of self-examination and taught how to make good decisions.

★13351★ Making a Life, Making a Living: Reclaiming Your Purpose and Passion in Business and in Life

Hachette Book Group
237 Park Ave.
New York, NY 10017
Ph: (212)522-7200
URL: http://www.hachettebookgroupusa.com/

Mark Albion. 2000. $28.00. 304 pages.

★13352★ Moving on in Your Career

Routledge
270 Madison Ave.
New York, NY 10016
Ph: (212)216-7800   Fax: (212)563-2269
URL: http://www.routledge.com/

Lynda Ali and Barbara Graham. 2000. $26.95.

★13353★ NACE Directory

National Association of Colleges and Employers
62 Highland Ave.
Bethlehem, PA 18017-9085
Ph: (610)868-1421   Fax: (610)868-0208
Fr: 800-544-5272
URL: http://www.naceweb.org

Annual. Covers names, addresses, phone numbers, interview schedules, and other key information about employers and career planning and placement offices.

★13354★ Nail It! Get a Job in 24 Hours Using 10 Insider Secrets

Entrepreneur Media Inc.
2445 McCabe Way, Ste. 400
Irvine, CA 92614-6244
Ph: (949)261-2325   Fax: (949)261-7729
Fr: 800-274-6229
URL: http://www.entrepreneur.com/

Todd Bermont. February 2004. $17.95 (paper). 208 pages.

★13355★ National JobBank

Adams Media Corp.
57 Littlefield St.
Avon, MA 02322
Ph: (508)427-7100   Fax: (508)427-6790
Fr: 800-872-5627
URL: http://www.adamsmedia.com

Annual; latest edition 19th. $475.00 for individuals. Covers over 20,000 employers nationwide. Entries include: Firm or organization name, address, local phone, toll-free phone, fax, contact name and title, description of organization, headquarters location, names of management, number of employees, other locations, subsidiaries, parent company, projected number of hires, training offered, internships, hours, recorded jobline, typical titles for common positions, educational backgrounds desired, stock exchange (if listed), fringe benefits offered. Several state and regional volumes are available and described separately. Arrangement: Geographical. Indexes: Geographical and classified by industry.

★13356★ The New Jersey JobBank

Adams Media Corp.
57 Littlefield St.
Avon, MA 02322
Ph: (508)427-7100   Fax: (508)427-6790
Fr: 800-872-5627
URL: http://adamsmedia.stores.yahoo.net/newjejobba3r.html

Biennial; latest edition 3. $17.95 for individuals. Covers approximately 4,000 employers, career resources, industry associations, and employment services in the Garden State. Entries include: Company name, address, phone, fax, email, and web address; names and titles of key personnel; number of employees; geographical area served; financial data; subsidiary names and addresses; description of services; standard industrial classification (SIC) code. Indexes: Alphabetical.

★13357★ New guide for Occupational Exploration, Fourth Edition

JIST Publishing
875 Montreal Way
St. Paul, MN 55102
Fax: 800-547-8329   Fr: 800-648-5478
E-mail: info@jist.com
URL: http://www.jist.com

Michael Farr, Laurence Shatkin PhD. 2006. Hardcover $49.95, softcover $39.95. Resource for matching interests to both job and learning options based on the 16 U.S. Department of Education clusters that connect learning to careers.

★13358★ No One is Unemployable: Creative Solutions for Overcoming Barriers to Employment

JIST Publishing
875 Montreal Way
St. Paul, MN 55102
Fax: 800-547-8329   Fr: 800-648-5478
E-mail: info@jist.com
URL: http://www.jist.com

Debra L. Angel and Elisabeth E. Harney. 1997. $29.95. 280 pages. Resource for welfare-to-work, ex-offender, and many other programs.

★13359★ No One Will Hire Me: Avoid 15 Mistakes and Win the Job

JIST Publishing
875 Montreal Way
St. Paul, MN 55102
Fax: 800-547-8329   Fr: 800-648-5478
E-mail: info@jist.com
URL: http://www.jist.com

Ron and Caryl Krannich, PhDs. 2002. $13.95. 184 pages. Identifies 15 major mistakes and offers analyses, self-tests, exercises, and resources to avoid the error.

★13360★ Occupational Outlook Handbook

U.S. Bureau of Labor Statistics
Postal Sq. Bldg., 2 Massachusetts Ave. NE
Washington, DC 20212-0001
Ph: (202)691-5200   Fax: (202)691-6325
Fr: 800-877-8339
E-mail: oohinfo@bls.gov
URL: http://www.bls.gov/oco/home.htm

Biennial, January of even years; latest edition 2006-07. $22.00 for individuals. Publication includes: Various occupational organizations that provide career information on hundreds of occupations. Entries include: For organizations–Organization name, address. Principal content of publication is profiles of various occupations, which include description of occupation, educational requirements, job outlook, and expected earnings. Arrangement: Organizations are classified by occupation.

★13361★ The Ohio JobBank

Adams Media Corp.
57 Littlefield St.
Avon, MA 02322
Ph: (508)427-7100   Fax: (508)427-6790
Fr: 800-872-5627
URL: http://www.adamsmedia.com

Biennial; latest edition 11th. $17.95 for individuals. Covers 4,800 employers and employment services in Ohio. Entries include: Firm or organization name, address, phone, name and title of contact; description of organization, headquarters location, typical titles for entry- and middle-level positions, educational backgrounds desired, fringe benefits offered, stock exchange listing, training programs, internships, parent company, number of employees, revenues, e-mail and web address, projected number of hires. Arrangement: Alphabetical.

★13362★ O*NET Dictionary of Occupational Titles, Third Edition

JIST Publishing
875 Montreal Way
St. Paul, MN 55102
Fax: 800-547-8329   Fr: 800-648-5478
E-mail: info@jist.com
URL: http://www.jist.com

Michael Farr. 2004. Hardcover $49.95, softcover $39.95. 720 pages. Reference book of job descriptions and other information from the U.S. Department of Labor's O-NET database put into print form.

★13363★ The Only Job Hunting Guide You'll Ever Need

Fireside
1230 Ave. of the Americas
New York, NY 10020
Ph: (212)698-7000   Fax: (212)698-7007
Fr: 800-897-7650

Kathryn and Ross Petras. 1995. $15.00 (paper). 400 pages. Covers the full range of the job search process for job hunters and career switchers.

★13364★ Outwitting the Job Market: Everything You Need to Locate and Land a Great Position

The Lyons Press
246 Goose Ln.
Guilford, CT 06437
Ph: (203)458-4500   Fax: (203)458-4604
Fr: 800-243-0495
URL: http://www.lyonspress.com/

Chandra Prasad. May 2004. $13.95 (paper). 256 pages. Part of the Outwitting Series.

★13365★ Over-40 Job Search Guide: 10 Strategies for Making Your Age an Advantage in Your Career

JIST Publishing
875 Montreal Way
St. Paul, MN 55102
Fax: 800-547-8329   Fr: 800-648-5478
E-mail: info@jist.com
URL: http://www.jist.com

Gail Geary, JD. 2005. $14.95. 256 pages. Helps over-40 job seekers learn to overcome negative stereotypes, conduct an "ageless" job search, and revitalize their career.

★13366★ Overnight Career Choice: Discover Your Ideal Job in Just a Few Hours

JIST Publishing
875 Montreal Way
St. Paul, MN 55102
Fax: 800-547-8329   Fr: 800-648-5478
E-mail: info@jist.com
URL: http://www.jist.com

Michael Farr. 2006. $8.95. 192 pages. Guide for job seekers to discover their ideal career quickly.

★13367★ The Pocket Book of Job Search Data and Tips, Second Edition

JIST Publishing
875 Montreal Way
St. Paul, MN 55102
Fax: 800-547-8329   Fr: 800-648-5478
E-mail: info@jist.com
URL: http://www.jist.com

Michael Farr. 2002. $1.95. 32 pages. Includes worksheets for personal information, job preferences, health information, school experience, other training, past employer contact information, work experience, and all other information required for employment applications.

★13368★ The Procrastinator's Guide to the Job Hunt

NAL
375 Hudson St.
New York, NY 10014-3657
Ph: (212)366-2000   Fax: (212)366-2666
Fr: 800-331-4624

Lorelei Lanum. June 2004. $14.00 (paper). 229 pages.

★13369★ Quick Guide to Career Training in Two Years or Less

JIST Publishing
875 Montreal Way
St. Paul, MN 55102
Fax: 800-547-8329   Fr: 800-648-5478
E-mail: info@jist.com
URL: http://www.jist.com

Laurence Shatkin, PhD. 2004. $16.95. 304 pages. Students use a set of self-assessments that examine interests, skills, favorite classes and work-related values to help them focus on training programs to investigate.

★13370★ Quick Guide to College Majors

JIST Publishing
875 Montreal Way
St. Paul, MN 55102
Fax: 800-547-8329   Fr: 800-648-5478
E-mail: info@jist.com
URL: http://www.jist.com

Laurence Shatkin, PhD. 2002. $16.95. 336 pages. Based on information from the O-NET database, this reference connects education to careers using self-assesment worksheets to help focus on college majors to investigate.

★13371★ The Quick Job Search, Third Edition

JIST Publishing
875 Montreal Way
St. Paul, MN 55102
Fax: 800-547-8329   Fr: 800-648-5478
E-mail: info@jist.com
URL: http://www.jist.com

Michael Farr. 2002. $2.95. 64 pages. Covers the basics on how to explore career options and conduct an effective job search; includes skills checklists, worksheets, and sample resumes.

★**13372**★ *Rea's Authoritative Guide to the Top 100 Careers to Year 2005*
Research and Education Association
61 Ethel Rd., W
Piscataway, NJ 08854
Ph: (732)819-8800   Fax: (732)819-8808
Fr: 800-822-0830
E-mail: info@rea.com
URL: http://www.rea.com/

Research and Education Association. 1997. $19.95 (paper). 368 pages.

★**13373**★ *Seven-Step Job Search, Second Edition: Cut Your Job Search Time in Half*
JIST Publishing
875 Montreal Way
St. Paul, MN 55102
Fax: 800-547-8329   Fr: 800-648-5478
E-mail: info@jist.com
URL: http://www.jist.com

Michael Farr. 2006. $8.95. 192 pages. Advice on finding a great job, from resumes to interviews.

★**13374**★ *Standard Occupational Classification Manual*
JIST Publishing
875 Montreal Way
St. Paul, MN 55102
Fax: 800-547-8329   Fr: 800-648-5478
E-mail: info@jist.com
URL: http://www.jist.com

2002. $29.95. 304 pages. Standardizes collection and reporting of occupational information among government agencies, businesses, and others who produce and need such data.

★**13375**★ *Stay in Control: How to Cope and Still Get the Job You Really Want*
Drake Beam Morin Pub
750 Third Ave., 28th Fl.
New York, NY 10017
Ph: (212)692-7700   Fax: (212)297-0426
E-mail: inquiries@dbm.com
URL: http://www.dbm.com

Carla-Krystin Andrade. $14.95. 1994. 212 pages. Focuses on stress management during the job search process.

★**13376**★ *Super Job Search: The Complete Manual for Job-Seekers and Career-Changers*
Jamenair Ltd.
PO Box 241957
Los Angeles, CA 90024-9757
Ph: (310)470-6688   Fax: (310)470-8106
Fr: 800-581-5953

Peter Studner. Third edition, 2003. $22.95 (paper). 352 pages. A step-by-step guidebook for getting a job, with sections on getting started, how to present accomplish-

ments, networking strategies, telemarketing tips, and negotiating tactics.

★**13377**★ *Taking Charge of Your Career Direction*
Wadsworth Publishing
PO Box 6904
Florence, KY 41022
Fax: 800-487-8488   Fr: 800-354-9706
URL: http://www.cengage.com

Robert D. Lock. Fifth edition, 2004. Three volumes. 504 pages. $69.95. Provides guidance for the job search process.

★**13378**★ *Tips for Finding the Right Job*
U.S. Government Printing Office
732 N. Capitol St. NW
Washington, DC 20401
Ph: (202)512-1800   Fax: (202)512-2104
Fr: (866)512-1800
E-mail: ContactCenter@gpo.gov
URL: http://www.gpoaccess.gov

United States. 029-014-002445. 1996. $2.50. 27 pages. General advice for job seekers. See website for current list of available publications.

★**13379**★ *The Top 10 Fears of Job Seekers*
Berkley Publishing Group
375 Hudson St.
New York, NY 10014
Ph: (212)366-2000   Fax: (212)366-2666
Fr: 800-847-5515
URL: http://us.penguingroup.com/static/html/aboutus/adult/berkley.html

Gary J. Grappo. 1996. 117 pages. $12.00 (paper). Shows effective ways to overcome common fears associated with job hunting.

★**13380**★ *Top Careers Set*
Facts On File Inc.
132 W 31st St., 17th Fl.
New York, NY 10001
Ph: (212)967-8800   Fax: 800-678-3633
Fr: 800-322-8755

6-volume set, each volume profiling approximately 35 jobs available to college graduates within a chosen major. Entries include: Duties and responsibilities, necessary qualifications or certification requirements, salary ranges, types of employers, job outlook.

★**13381**★ *The Two Best Ways to Find a Job*
Jist Works
875 Montreal Way
St. Paul, MN 55102
Fr: 800-648-5478
E-mail: info@jist.com
URL: http://www.jist.com

Michael J. Farr and Susan Christophersen. $7.95. 87 pages. Second edition, 1999. Presents techniques that emphasize non-traditional job search methods.

★**13382**★ *Ultimate Job Hunting Secrets: Essential Tips, Tricks, and Tactics for Today's Job Seeker*
AllCountyJobs.com LLC
674 Orchard St.
Trumbull, CT 06611
Fr: 800-399-6651
E-mail: info@allcountyjobs.com
URL: http://www.allcountyjobs.com

C.M. Russell. 2005. $20. 115 pages. Provides timely job hunting strategies ranging from breakthrough ideas, to clever ways of networking, to unique apply methods.

★**13383**★ *The Very Quick Job Search: Get a Better Job in Half the Time*
Jist Publishing
875 Montreal Way
St. Paul, MN 55102
Fr: 800-648-5478
E-mail: info@jist.com
URL: http://www.jist.com

J. Michael Farr. Third edition, 2003. $17.95. 512 pages.

★**13384**★ *The Virginia JobBank*
Adams Media Corp.
57 Littlefield St.
Avon, MA 02322
Ph: (508)427-7100   Fax: (508)427-6790
Fr: 800-872-5627
URL: http://www.adamsmedia.com

Biennial; latest edition 4th. $17.95 for individuals. Covers 3,700 employers in Virginia and West Virginia. Entries include: Firm or organization name, address, phone, name and title of contact; description of organization, headquarters location, typical titles for entry- and middle-level positions, educational backgrounds desired, fringe benefits offered, stock exchange listing, training programs, internships, parent company, number of employees, revenues, e-mail and web address, projected number of hires. Indexes: Alphabetical.

★**13385**★ *Weddle's Recruiter's and Job Seeker's Guide to Association Web Sites*
Paul & Co.
814 N Franklin St.
Chicago, IL 60610
Ph: (312)337-0747   Fax: (312)337-5985
Fr: 800-888-4741
URL: http://www.ipgbook.com/

$49.95. Covers 1,900 associations from around the world. Entries include: resume database, discussion forum, and association who offers a job board. Indexes: By career field, industry, and Geographical location.

★**13386**★ *What Can I Do Now*
Facts On File Inc.
132 W 31st St., 17th Fl.
New York, NY 10001
Ph: (212)967-8800   Fax: 800-678-3633
Fr: 800-322-8755

$22.95 for individuals; $20.65 for libraries. 5-

volume set to help students take a proactive, hands-on approach to career exploration and preparation. Covers accurate and important information on work environment, job outlook, education and training requirements, skill requirements, salary information, and advancement opportunities.

★13387★ What Color Is Your Parachute

Ten Speed Press
PO Box 7123
Berkeley, CA 94707
Ph: (510)559-1600   Fax: (510)559-1629
Fr: 800-841-2665
E-mail: order@tenspeed.com
URL: http://www.tenspeedpress.com

Richard N. Bolles. 2005. $27.95. Publication cancelled. 424 pages. Subtitled: "A Practical Manual for Job-Hunters and Career-Changers". One of the best-known works on job hunting, this book provides detailed and strategic advice on all aspects of the job search.

★13388★ What Employers Really Want: The Insider's Guide to Getting a Job

The McGraw-Hill Companies
PO Box 182604
Columbus, OH 43272
Fax: (614)759-3749   Fr: 877-883-5524
E-mail: customer.service@mcgraw-hill.com
URL: http://www.mcgraw-hill.com

Barbara S. Hawk. 1998. $14.95 (paper). 224 pages. Insider's guide to a successful and efficient job search giving you the candid and straightforward opinions of the managers and business leaders.

★13389★ You're Certifiable: The Alternative Career Guide to More than 700 Certificate Programs, Trade Schools and Job Opportunities

Fireside
1230 Ave. of the Americas
New York, NY 10020
Ph: (212)698-7000   Fax: (212)698-7007

Lee Naftali and Joel Naftali. 1999. $20.95 (paper). 384 pages.

NEWSPAPERS, MAGAZINES, AND JOURNALS

★13390★ AEC Professional News

AECWorkForce
IBM Plz.
330 North Wabash, Ste. 3201
Chicago, IL 60611
Ph: (312)628-5870   Fax: (312)628-5878
URL: http://www.aecworkforce.com

Free, e-mail. E-mail newsletter offering advice on job searches, resumes, and career development.

★13391★ Job Choices

National Association of Colleges and Employers
62 Highland Ave.
Bethlehem, PA 18017-9085
Ph: (610)868-1421   Fax: (610)868-0208
Fr: 800-544-5272
URL: http://www.jobweb.com/market/job-choices.htm

Magazine focusing on job-search and career planning.

★13392★ Journal of Job Placement

National Rehabilitation Association
633 S Washington St.
Alexandria, VA 22314
Ph: (703)836-0850   Fax: (703)836-0848
E-mail: info@natioanlrehab.org
URL: http://www.nationalrehab.org

Periodic. Employment journal.

★13393★ Kennedy's Career Strategist

Career Strategies
714 Sheridan Rd.
Wilmette, IL 60091
Ph: (847)251-1661   Fax: (847)251-5191
Fr: 800-728-1709
E-mail: MMKCareer@aol.com
URL: http://www.moatskennedy.com

Description: Ten issues/year. Offers advice on job hunting and discusses such topics as "how to win at office politics." Follows employment trends in various industries. Recurring features include interviewing techniques, salary strategies, and advice column.

★13394★ Occupational Outlook Quarterly

U.S. Government Printing Office and Superintendent of Documents
PO Box 371954
Pittsburgh, PA 15250-7954
Ph: (202)512-1800   Fax: (202)512-2104
URL: http://www.bls.gov/opub/ooq/o-oqhome.htm

Quarterly. $30.00 for two years, domestic; $15.00/year for individuals; $42.00 for two years, foreign; $6.00/year for single issue, domestic; $8.40 for single issue. Magazine providing occupational and employment information.

★13395★ Packaging Horizons Online

Women in Packaging, Inc.
4290 Bells Ferry Rd., Ste. 106-17
Kennesaw, GA 30144-1300
Ph: (678)594-6872
URL: http://www.womeninpackaging.org/

Weekly. E-zine comprising career guidance tips, advice, and industry know how.

★13396★ Professional Studies Review

St. John's University
8000 Utopia Pky.
Jamaica, NY 11439
URL: http://new.stjohns.edu/academics/undergraduate/professionals

Semiannual. $60.00/year for institutions; $35.00/year for individuals; $20.00 for single issue. Peer-reviewed journal devoted to the pedagogic needs and research interests of those working within career-oriented disciplines.

★13397★ Student Pharmacist

American Pharmaceutical Association
1100 15th St. NW, Ste. 400
Washington, DC 20037-2985
Ph: (202)628-4410   Fax: (202)783-2351
Fr: 800-237-2742
URL: http://www.aphanet.org//AM/Template.cfm?Section=Home

Bimonthly. Free to members of APhA-ASP. Magazine providing advice for pharmacy career planning.

★13398★ Today's Officer

Military Officers Association of America
201 N Washington St.
Alexandria, VA 22314
Ph: (703)549-2311   Fr: 800-234-6622
URL: http://www.todaysofficer.org

Quarterly. Subscription included in membership. Magazine that addresses issues important to new officers as well as officers transitioning to other careers.

★13399★ Uratie

IDG Communications Inc.
5 Speen St., 3rd. Fl
Framingham, MA 01701
Ph: (508)875-5000   Fax: (508)988-7888
URL: http://www.idg.com

Magazine providing job offers for graduates, engineers and information technology professionals.

AUDIO/VISUAL RESOURCES

★13400★ 10 Basics of Business Etiquette

Cambridge Educational
PO Box 2053
Princeton, NJ 08543-2053
Ph: 800-257-5126   Fax: (609)671-0266
Fr: 800-468-4227
E-mail: custserv@films.com
URL: http://www.cambridgeeducational.com

VHS and DVD. $69.95. 22 minutes. 1993. Prepares students for many different situations where a knowledge of professional etiquette will be essential. Includes inter-office etiquette, meeting protocol, introductions, dining etiquette, travel, and handling potentially awkward situations with grace.

★13401★ *The 50 Best Jobs for the 21st Century: Fastest-Growing Fields*

JIST Publishing
875 Montreal Way
St. Paul, MN 55102
Fax: 800-547-8329   Fr: 800-648-5478
E-mail: info@jist.com
URL: http://www.jist.com

2002. $149. 35 minutes. Jobs in this video include: physician's assistants, social workers, loan officers and counselors, medical records technicians, manicurists, amusement and recreation attendants, electrical engineers, special education teachers, human services workers, desktop publishing workers, personal and home care aides.

★13402★ *The 50 Best Jobs for the 21st Century: Good Pay, Most Openings, and Fastest Growth*

JIST Publishing
875 Montreal Way
St. Paul, MN 55102
Fax: 800-547-8329   Fr: 800-648-5478
E-mail: info@jist.com
URL: http://www.jist.com

2000. $149. 36 minutes. Jobs in this video include: systems analysts, computer engineers, securities and financial services sales workers, computer scientists, service managers, physical therapists, special education teachers, general managers and top executives.

★13403★ *The 50 Best Jobs for the 21st Century: Promising Careers With College Degrees*

JIST Publishing
875 Montreal Way
St. Paul, MN 55102
Fax: 800-547-8329   Fr: 800-648-5478
E-mail: info@jist.com
URL: http://www.jist.com

2001. $149. 42 minutes. Jobs in this video include: doctors, paralegals, designers, computer programmers, secondary school teachers, loan officers and counselors, electrical engineers, occupational therapists, writers and editors, and top executives.

★13404★ *The 50 Best Jobs for the 21st Century: Promising Careers Without College Degrees*

JIST Publishing
875 Montreal Way
St. Paul, MN 55102
Fax: 800-547-8329   Fr: 800-648-5478
E-mail: info@jist.com
URL: http://www.jist.com

2000. $149. 35 minutes. Jobs in this video include: musicians, vocational education instructors, clerical supervisors and managers, correction officers, insurance adjusters, examiners, and investigators, sales specialists, food service and lodging managers, cost estimators, police patrol officers, and flight attendants.

★13405★ *Accommodating*

Cambridge Educational
PO Box 2053
Princeton, NJ 08543-2053
Ph: 800-257-5126   Fax: (609)671-0266
Fr: 800-468-4227
E-mail: custserv@films.com
URL: http://www.cambridgeeducational.com

VHS and DVD. $69.95. 25 minutes. 1991. Part of the Video GOE series.

★13406★ *Artistic*

Cambridge Educational
PO Box 2053
Princeton, NJ 08543-2053
Ph: 800-257-5126   Fax: (609)671-0266
Fr: 800-468-4227
E-mail: custserv@films.com
URL: http://www.cambridgeeducational.com

VHS and DVD. $69.95. 46 minutes. 1991. Part of the Video GOE series.

★13407★ *Behind the Scenes: Industrial Field Trips*

Cambridge Educational
PO Box 2053
Princeton, NJ 08543-2053
Ph: 800-257-5126   Fax: (609)671-0266
Fr: 800-468-4227
E-mail: custserv@films.com
URL: http://www.cambridgeeducational.com

VHS and DVD. $209.85.

★13408★ *Business Detail*

Cambridge Educational
PO Box 2053
Princeton, NJ 08543-2053
Ph: 800-257-5126   Fax: (609)671-0266
Fr: 800-468-4227
E-mail: custserv@films.com
URL: http://www.cambridgeeducational.com

VHS and DVD. $69.95. 25 minutes. 1991. Part of the Video GOE series.

★13409★ *Career Clusters 2 Series*

JIST Publishing
875 Montreal Way
St. Paul, MN 55102
Fax: 800-547-8329   Fr: 800-648-5478
E-mail: info@jist.com
URL: http://www.jist.com

2004. $89.95 each. 18 minutes each. Men and women with experience in their fields talk about their jobs and the kinds of skills and training they needed to successfully acquire them.

★13410★ *Career Clusters 3 Series*

JIST Publishing
875 Montreal Way
St. Paul, MN 55102
Fax: 800-547-8329   Fr: 800-648-5478
E-mail: info@jist.com
URL: http://www.jist.com

2004. $89.95 each. 18 minutes each. Experienced workers talk about their jobs and the

kinds of skills and training needed to successfully acquire them.

★13411★ *Career Clusters Series*

JIST Publishing
875 Montreal Way
St. Paul, MN 55102
Fax: 800-547-8329   Fr: 800-648-5478
E-mail: info@jist.com
URL: http://www.jist.com

2002. $89.95 each. 18 minutes each. Men and women discuss background requirements and the rewards of their respective careers in this four-video series.

★13412★ *Career Evaluation*

Cambridge Educational
PO Box 2053
Princeton, NJ 08543-2053
Ph: 800-257-5126   Fax: (609)671-0266
Fr: 800-468-4227
E-mail: custserv@films.com
URL: http://www.cambridgeeducational.com

VHS and DVD. $79.95. 2007. 11 minutes. Program illustrates how to relate interests, skills, education, training, values, and lifestyle to specific occupations in the world of work.

★13413★ *Career Exploration and Planning: What Will I Do With My Life?*

JIST Publishing
875 Montreal Way
St. Paul, MN 55102
Fax: 800-547-8329   Fr: 800-648-5478
E-mail: info@jist.com
URL: http://www.jist.com

2003. $98. 25 minutes. Viewers learn ways to explore career fields and assess interests, skills and abilities; also suggests ways to match up with the right career.

★13414★ *Career Exploration: You're in the Driver's Seat*

Cambridge Educational
PO Box 2053
Princeton, NJ 08543-2053
Ph: 800-257-5126   Fax: (609)671-0266
Fr: 800-468-4227
E-mail: custserv@films.com
URL: http://www.cambridgeeducational.com

VHS and DVD. $179.90. Covers mapping your career plan and tracking your interests and abilities.

★13415★ *Careers in Science: From Archaeologist to Zoologist*

Cambridge Educational
PO Box 2053
Princeton, NJ 08543-2053
Ph: 800-257-5126   Fax: (609)671-0266
Fr: 800-468-4227
E-mail: custserv@films.com
URL: http://www.cambridgeeducational.com

VHS and DVD. $79.95. 20 minutes. 1997. Surveys the wide-ranging world of careers in science. Interviews with science professionals offer students a look at the diverse group of men and women working in science today.

★13416★ Careers Without College

Cambridge Educational
PO Box 2053
Princeton, NJ 08543-2053
Ph: 800-257-5126   Fax: (609)671-0266
Fr: 800-468-4227
E-mail: custserv@films.com
URL: http://www.cambridgeeducational.com

VHS and DVD. 1996. $79.95. 27 minutes. Covers career opportunities and other options for high school graduates.

★13417★ Choices Today for Career Satisfaction Tomorrow

Cambridge Educational
PO Box 2053
Princeton, NJ 08543-2053
Ph: 800-257-5126   Fax: (609)671-0266
Fr: 800-468-4227
E-mail: custserv@films.com
URL: http://www.cambridgeeducational.com

VHS and DVD. $209.85. 30 minutes. Includes student/teacher manual. Topics covered are preparing for an occupation, investigating the world of work, and self-awareness.

★13418★ The Complete Career Cluster

Cambridge Educational
PO Box 2053
Princeton, NJ 08543-2053
Ph: 800-257-5126   Fax: (609)671-0266
Fr: 800-468-4227
E-mail: custserv@films.com
URL: http://www.cambridgeeducational.com

VHS and DVD. $1,439.20. 2007. Covering 16 broad occupational categories, the Career Clusters system offers information on practically every job there is.

★13419★ The Complete Job Search System

Cambridge Educational
PO Box 2053
Princeton, NJ 08543-2053
Ph: 800-257-5126   Fax: (609)671-0266
Fr: 800-468-4227
E-mail: custserv@films.com
URL: http://www.cambridgeeducational.com

VHS and DVD. 2007. $399.75. Individual titles cover career planning, career evaluation, finding a job, interviewing for a job, and succeeding on the job.

★13420★ Dialing for Jobs, Revised Edition: Using the Phone in the Job Search

JIST Publishing
875 Montreal Way
St. Paul, MN 55102
Fax: 800-547-8329   Fr: 800-648-5478
E-mail: info@jist.com
URL: http://www.jist.com

2000. $129. 40 minutes. Practical techniques for effective telephone job searches.

★13421★ Directing Your Successful Job Search

Cambridge Educational
PO Box 2053
Princeton, NJ 08543-2053
Ph: 800-257-5126   Fax: (609)671-0266
Fr: 800-468-4227
E-mail: custserv@films.com
URL: http://www.cambridgeeducational.com

VHS and DVD. $69.95. 1988. 45 minutes. Describes the tools needed for a successful job search, networking, traditional sources of leads, and interviewing. Comes with an adapted version of the Cambridge Job Search Guide.

★13422★ Exceptional Employee: A Guide To Success On The Job

Cambridge Educational
PO Box 2053
Princeton, NJ 08543-2053
Ph: 800-257-5126   Fax: (609)671-0266
Fr: 800-468-4227
E-mail: custserv@films.com
URL: http://www.cambridgeeducational.com

VHS and DVD. $79.95. 1998. 24 minutes. Program emphasizes the traits and employee skills needed to take an active role in career success and advancement.

★13423★ Feedback on the Job: Accepting Criticism

Cambridge Educational
PO Box 2053
Princeton, NJ 08543-2053
Ph: 800-257-5126   Fax: (609)671-0266
Fr: 800-468-4227
E-mail: custserv@films.com
URL: http://www.cambridgeeducational.com

CD. $99.95. 1999. 22 minutes. Using live-action video, the CD-ROM program guides the user through a series of learning objectives and interactive testing.

★13424★ Finding a Job

Cambridge Educational
PO Box 2053
Princeton, NJ 08543-2053
Ph: 800-257-5126   Fax: (609)671-0266
Fr: 800-468-4227
E-mail: custserv@films.com
URL: http://www.cambridgeeducational.com

VHS and DVD. 2007. $79.95. 13 minutes. Covers conventional and unconventional job search methods.

★13425★ Finding a Job When Your Past Is Not So Hot

JIST Publishing
875 Montreal Way
St. Paul, MN 55102
Fax: 800-547-8329   Fr: 800-648-5478
E-mail: info@jist.com
URL: http://www.jist.com

1998. $125. 19 minutes. Presents tangible steps to overcome losing a job or dealing with a poor relationship with a former boss.

★13426★ From Pink Slip to Paycheck Series: The Road to Reemployment

JIST Publishing
875 Montreal Way
St. Paul, MN 55102
Fax: 800-547-8329   Fr: 800-648-5478
E-mail: info@jist.com
URL: http://www.jist.com

$199. 60 minutes. Five-video series produced especially for adult career changers, covering all essential job search topics: coping with job loss, planning the job search, networking, resumes, cover letters, and interviewing.

★13427★ Great Careers in Two Years or Less

JIST Publishing
875 Montreal Way
St. Paul, MN 55102
Fax: 800-547-8329   Fr: 800-648-5478
E-mail: info@jist.com
URL: http://www.jist.com

2005. $108. 29 minutes. This program provides information needed for a successful career in a field that takes less than two years.

★13428★ Great Jobs without a College Degree

JIST Publishing
875 Montreal Way
St. Paul, MN 55102
Fax: 800-547-8329   Fr: 800-648-5478
E-mail: info@jist.com
URL: http://www.jist.com

2000. $108. 30 minutes. Explores some of the hottest job categories and tells how job seekers can forge a challenging future without a degree.

★13429★ Humanitarian

Cambridge Educational
PO Box 2053
Princeton, NJ 08543-2053
Ph: 800-257-5126   Fax: (609)671-0266
Fr: 800-468-4227
E-mail: custserv@films.com
URL: http://www.cambridgeeducational.com

VHS and DVD. $69.95. 23 minutes. 1991. Part of the Video GOE series.

★13430★ Industrial

Cambridge Educational
PO Box 2053
Princeton, NJ 08543-2053
Ph: 800-257-5126   Fax: (609)671-0266
Fr: 800-468-4227
E-mail: custserv@films.com
URL: http://www.cambridgeeducational.com

VHS and DVD. $69.95. 21 minutes. 1991. Part of the Video GOE series.

★13431★ *Investigating the World of Work*

Cambridge Educational
PO Box 2053
Princeton, NJ 08543-2053
Ph: 800-257-5126   Fax: (609)671-0266
Fr: 800-468-4227
E-mail: custserv@films.com
URL: http://www.cambridgeeducational.com

VHS and DVD. $89.95. 26 minutes. 1988. Demonstrates techniques for relating knowledge of oneself to the world of work. Includes student/teacher manual.

★13432★ *The JIST Video Guide for Occupational Exploration: Real People, Real Jobs, Real Information*

JIST Publishing
875 Montreal Way
St. Paul, MN 55102
Fax: 800-547-8329   Fr: 800-648-5478
E-mail: info@jist.com
URL: http://www.jist.com

1997-1999. $29 each. 16 videos, 25-35 minutes each. TV-documentary style quality that supports career exploration for various age groups, emphasizing the connections betweeen education, work, and on-the-job success.

★13433★ *Job Survival Kit*

Cambridge Educational
PO Box 2053
Princeton, NJ 08543-2053
Ph: 800-257-5126   Fax: (609)671-0266
Fr: 800-468-4227
E-mail: custserv@films.com
URL: http://www.cambridgeeducational.com

VHS and DVD. $79.95. 30 minutes. 1994. Shows viewers how to strive to be as good at their job as they can, while making useful recommendations of how to keep a job diary, approach the annual review, and handle a disagreement in the office.

★13434★ *Mechanical I*

Cambridge Educational
PO Box 2053
Princeton, NJ 08543-2053
Ph: 800-257-5126   Fax: (609)671-0266
Fr: 800-468-4227
E-mail: custserv@films.com
URL: http://www.cambridgeeducational.com

VHS and DVD. $69.95. 45 minutes. 1991. Part of the Video GOE series.

★13435★ *Mechanical II*

Cambridge Educational
PO Box 2053
Princeton, NJ 08543-2053
Ph: 800-257-5126   Fax: (609)671-0266
Fr: 800-468-4227
E-mail: custserv@films.com
URL: http://www.cambridgeeducational.com

VHS and DVD. $69.95. 45 minutes. 1991. Part of the Video GOE series.

★13436★ *More Great Jobs Without a College Degree*

JIST Publishing
875 Montreal Way
St. Paul, MN 55102
Fax: 800-547-8329   Fr: 800-648-5478
E-mail: info@jist.com
URL: http://www.jist.com

2002. $108. 29 minutes. Continues the series on job opportunities for persons without a college degree.

★13437★ *The Networking Process*

Drake Beam Morin, Inc.
750 Third Ave., 28th Fl.
New York, NY 10017
Ph: (215)692-7700   Fax: (215)399-1391
Fr: 800-345-5627
E-mail: inquiries@dbm.com
URL: http://www.dbm.com

Video. $49.95. Presents networking techniques to find the job of your choice.

★13438★ *Occupational Preparation*

Cambridge Educational
PO Box 2053
Princeton, NJ 08543-2053
Ph: 800-257-5126   Fax: (609)671-0266
Fr: 800-468-4227
E-mail: custserv@films.com
URL: http://www.cambridgeeducational.com

VHS and DVD. $69.95. 30 minutes. 1988. Shows how to develop and implement an effective educational and training program. Includes student/teacher manual.

★13439★ *Physical Performing*

Cambridge Educational
PO Box 2053
Princeton, NJ 08543-2053
Ph: 800-257-5126   Fax: (609)671-0266
Fr: 800-468-4227
E-mail: custserv@films.com
URL: http://www.cambridgeeducational.com

VHS and DVD. $69.95. 31 minutes. 1991. Part of the Video GOE series.

★13440★ *Plants and Animals*

Cambridge Educational
PO Box 2053
Princeton, NJ 08543-2053
Ph: 800-257-5126   Fax: (609)671-0266
Fr: 800-468-4227
E-mail: custserv@films.com
URL: http://www.cambridgeeducational.com

VHS and DVD. $69.95. 24 minutes. 1991. Part of the Video GOE series.

★13441★ *Protective*

Cambridge Educational
PO Box 2053
Princeton, NJ 08543-2053
Ph: 800-257-5126   Fax: (609)671-0266
Fr: 800-468-4227
E-mail: custserv@films.com
URL: http://www.cambridgeeducational.com

VHS and DVD. $69.95. 24 minutes. 1991. Part of the Video GOE series.

★13442★ *Researching the Job Market*

Drake Beam Morin, Inc.
750 Third Ave., 28th Fl.
New York, NY 10017
Ph: (215)692-7700   Fax: (215)399-1391
Fr: 800-345-5627
E-mail: inquiries@dbm.com
URL: http://www.dbm.com

Video. $49.95. Follows three successful job seekers who use careful, planned research.

★13443★ *Scientific*

Cambridge Educational
PO Box 2053
Princeton, NJ 08543-2053
Ph: 800-257-5126   Fax: (609)671-0266
Fr: 800-468-4227
E-mail: custserv@films.com
URL: http://www.cambridgeeducational.com

VHS and DVD. $69.95. 46 minutes. 1990. Part of the Video GOE series.

★13444★ *Selling*

Cambridge Educational
PO Box 2053
Princeton, NJ 08543-2053
Ph: 800-257-5126   Fax: (609)671-0266
Fr: 800-468-4227
E-mail: custserv@films.com
URL: http://www.cambridgeeducational.com

VHS and DVD. $69.95. 22 minutes. 1991. Part of the Video GOE series.

★13445★ *Ten Ways to Get a Great Job: Back to the Basics*

Cambridge Educational
PO Box 2053
Princeton, NJ 08543-2053
Ph: 800-257-5126   Fax: (609)671-0266
Fr: 800-468-4227
E-mail: custserv@films.com
URL: http://www.cambridgeeducational.com

VHS and DVD. 1994. $79.95. 39 minutes. Reminds viewers of job search basics.

★13446★ *Think Small: Finding Big Jobs in Small Businesses*

JIST Publishing
875 Montreal Way
St. Paul, MN 55102
Fax: 800-547-8329   Fr: 800-648-5478
E-mail: info@jist.com
URL: http://www.jist.com

2002. $129. 25 minutes. Highlights the unique aspects of working in small business.

★13447★ The Tough New Labor Market, Revised Edition: And What It Takes to Succeed

JIST Publishing
875 Montreal Way
St. Paul, MN 55102
Fax: 800-547-8329   Fr: 800-648-5478
E-mail: info@jist.com
URL: http://www.jist.com

2000. $69. 29 minutes. Documentary news style format gives insight into labor market trends from labor market experts.

★13448★ Tough Times Job Strategies

JIST Publishing
875 Montreal Way
St. Paul, MN 55102
Fax: 800-547-8329   Fr: 800-648-5478
E-mail: info@jist.com
URL: http://www.jist.com

2003. $89.95. 24 minutes. This program presents strategies for finding and keeping a job in today's challenging economy.

★13449★ The Very Quick Job Search Video, Revised Edition

JIST Publishing
875 Montreal Way
St. Paul, MN 55102
Fax: 800-547-8329   Fr: 800-648-5478
E-mail: info@jist.com
URL: http://www.jist.com

Michael Farr. 1999. $99. 32 minutes. Video overview of results-oriented self-directed job search techniques.

★13450★ The Video Guide to JIST's Self-Directed Job Search Series: A Complete Job Search Course

JIST Publishing
875 Montreal Way
St. Paul, MN 55102
Fax: 800-547-8329   Fr: 800-648-5478
E-mail: info@jist.com
URL: http://www.jist.com

$199. 3 hours, 15 minutes. 10-video series provides outcome-oriented, self-directed, job search methods to cut job search time in half.

★13451★ The Video Guide to Occupational Exploration

Cambridge Educational
PO Box 2053
Princeton, NJ 08543-2053
Ph: 800-257-5126   Fax: (609)671-0266
Fr: 800-468-4227
E-mail: custserv@films.com
URL: http://www.cambridgeeducational.com

VHS and DVD. $979.30. 14 video programs covering each occupational cluster. Organized according to the 12 interest areas developed by the U.S. Department of Labor.

★13452★ Vocational Visions Career Series

Cambridge Educational
PO Box 2053
Princeton, NJ 08543-2053
Ph: 800-257-5126   Fax: (609)671-0266
Fr: 800-468-4227
E-mail: custserv@films.com
URL: http://www.cambridgeeducational.com

VHS and DVD. 10 videos. $399.50. 15 minutes each. Topics include auto mechanic, band director, florist, park ranger, potter, chef, insurance agent, physical therapist, letter carrier, and paralegal.

★13453★ The Winning Look

Cambridge Educational
PO Box 2053
Princeton, NJ 08543-2053
Ph: 800-257-5126   Fax: (609)671-0266
Fr: 800-468-4227
E-mail: custserv@films.com
URL: http://www.cambridgeeducational.com

VHS and DVD. $49.95. 11 minutes. 1991. Explains the importance of dressing appropriately in the business world–for job interviewing as well as for continued success on the job.

ONLINE AND DATABASE SERVICES

★13454★ 4Anything Network: 4Careers.com

URL: http://www.livve.com/promo/4anything/index.html

Description: Job hunters may search job ads placed by employers. Jobs are arranged in sub-categories. Also sections on personality assessments, salary research, and career counseling.

★13455★ CareerMag.com

URL: http://www.careermag.com

Description: Online magazine containing many columns, features and articles about job hunting. Also holds job listings for browsers. **Main files include:** Job Openings, Employers, Articles, Resume Bank, Career Forum, On Campus, Diversity, Be Your Own Boss, Job Fairs, Recruiter Directory, Consultant Directory, Products & Services, Relocation Resources, Career Links, Post Your Jobs. Has information section for self-employed and freelance workers.

★13456★ CareerOINK on the Web

JIST Publishing
875 Montreal Way
St. Paul, MN 55102
Fax: 800-547-8329   Fr: 800-648-5478
E-mail: info@jist.com
URL: http://www.jist.com

$300-$2,000 per year, depending on number

of users. A "one stop career center" web site; includes many new or improved features, all focused on careers, occupations, and self-directed job search.

★13457★ CareerPerfect.com

Ph: 800-716-0705
URL: http://www.careerperfect.com

Description: Provides links to career software and books; lists FAQ's on career planning, resumes, job searching, and interviewing; identifies online job databases; accepts resumes for posting.

★13458★ CollegeGrad.com

234 E. College Ave., Ste. 200
State College, PA 16801
Ph: (262)375-6700
URL: http://www.collegegrad.com

Description: Site contains the online version of the College Grad Job Hunter-an entry level job search book. **Main files include:** Preparation, Resumes and Cover Letters, Job Postings, Interviews and Negotiations, New Job. Employers may also search for candidates fitting positions.

★13459★ JobStar

E-mail: electrajobstar@earthlink.net
URL: http://jobstar.org/

Description: Job search guide based in California. Includes career guides and information on local, national and international career counseling centers, resumes, salaries, and hidden jobs.

★13460★ MonsterTRAK

11845 W. Olympic Blvd., Ste. 500
Los Angeles, CA 90064
Fr: 800-999-8725
URL: http://www.monstertrak.monster.com/

Description: College-targeted job hunting and recruiting site. Students and alumni may enter a user profile or resume to be reviewed by potential employers, or search job listings without doing so. Employers may enter full-time, part-time, temporary, and internship opportunities into the database to be reviewed by students and recent graduates, and may review resumes.

★13461★ NYU Stern School of Business

E-mail: ocd@stern.nyu.edu
URL: http://www.stern.nyu.edu

Description: Office of Career Development section of website provides career resources for business graduates, along with resume databases arranged by classes. Many resources restricted to Stern students and alumni.

★13462★ Quintessential Careers

E-mail: randall@quintcareers.com
URL: http://www.quintcareers.com

Description: Job search mega-site that links to several job board, provides information on every step of the job search process, and additional information on earning advanced degrees and certificates to increase one's value as a professional.

★13463★ **Recruiters Online Network**
E-mail: deb@recruitersonline.com
URL: http://www.recruitersonline.com/

Description: Site is used by over 8,000 recruiters, search firms, employment agencies, and employment professionals. Job seekers may read the Careers Online Magazine, post resumes, and search jobs. **Fee:** Free to job seekers; fee for recruiters.

★13464★ **The Riley Guide**
11218 Ashley Dr.
Rockville, MD 20852
Ph: (301)881-0122
E-mail: webmaster@rileyguide.com
URL: http://www.rileyguide.com

Description: Job search portal site. Also contains resources on writing and distributing resumes, targeting employers, interviewing, salary negotiations and more.

★13465★ **What Color Is Your Parachute? Job Hunters Bible**
URL: http://www.jobhuntersbible.com/

Description: Companion internet guide to the best selling job-hunting book, What Color is Your Parachute? Includes lists of helpful links to other resources on the internet. **Main files include:** Jobs, Resumes, Counseling, Contacts, Research, Dealing With Depression.

★13466★ **The World Wide Web Employment Office**
URL: http://www.employmentoffice.net/

Description: Portal to job and resume banks and board for employers and job hunters.

★13467★ **Yahoo! Careers**
700 1st. Ave
Sunnyvale, CA 94089
Fax: (408)349-3301   Fr: (408)349-3300
URL: http://careers.yahoo.com/

Description: Contains over 360,000 jobs for job seekers to search and post resumes for, as well as weekly features, relocation resources, a daily column, and links to resume banks and services and temp agencies. Special sections are devoted to industry research, company research, advice, high tech jobs, and first jobs and internships.

SOFTWARE

★13468★ **Career Finder Plus CD-ROM**
JIST Publishing
875 Montreal Way
St. Paul, MN 55102
Fax: 800-547-8329   Fr: 800-648-5478
E-mail: info@jist.com
URL: http://www.jist.com

1998. $99. Matches a person's interests to possible occupations and careers. Users answer just 18 questions and receive a list of 50 best-fitting jobs.

★13469★ **CareerExplorer CD-ROM, Version 3.0**
JIST Publishing
875 Montreal Way
St. Paul, MN 55102
Fax: 800-547-8329   Fr: 800-648-5478
E-mail: info@jist.com
URL: http://www.jist.com

2004. $295. Users can indicate their interests and get a list of the best 20 occupational matches in about 20 minutes.

★13470★ **Careers Without College Interactive CD-ROM**
JIST Publishing
875 Montreal Way
St. Paul, MN 55102
Fax: 800-547-8329   Fr: 800-648-5478
E-mail: info@jist.com
URL: http://www.jist.com

2002. $99.95. Tool for exploring career choices that do not require a four-year college degree.

★13471★ **Electronic Career Planner CD-ROM**
JIST Publishing
875 Montreal Way
St. Paul, MN 55102
Fax: 800-547-8329   Fr: 800-648-5478
E-mail: info@jist.com
URL: http://www.jist.com

2002. $295. Build a career portfolio with this software designed to organize and create all the tools needed to find, get, and keep a job.

★13472★ **Multimedia Job Search**
Cambridge Educational
PO Box 2053
Princeton, NJ 08543-2053
Ph: 800-257-5126   Fax: (609)671-0266
Fr: 800-468-4227
E-mail: custserv@films.com
URL: http://www.cambridgeeducational.com

CD-ROM. $99.95. 1997. Includes videos, narration, and on-screen text. Users learn about getting a competitive edge in today's job market, traditional and nontraditional job search tools, resumes and cover letters, and interviewing skills.

★13473★ **OOH: Career Center**
JIST Publishing
875 Montreal Way
St. Paul, MN 55102
Fax: 800-547-8329   Fr: 800-648-5478
E-mail: info@jist.com
URL: http://www.jist.com

2003. $349.95. Combines Occupational Outlook Handbook (OOH) career data with a variety of interactive tools designed to help users explore career options using today's technology.

OTHER SOURCES

★13474★ **Ady & Associates**
115 N Neil St., Ste. 216
Champaign, IL 61820-4083
Ph: (217)359-8080   Fax: (217)359-8082
URL: http://www.adyandassociates.com

Personnel consulting firm provides outplacement and career management services, employee and applicant assessment, and general human resource consulting. Additional expertise available in staffing and employment strategy, employee and organization development, plus effective employee communications programs. Industries served: All.

★13475★ **Al Gates & Associates**
2280A James White Blvd.
Sidney, BC, Canada V8L 1Z4
Ph: (250)656-5707   Fax: (250)654-0058
E-mail: info@cybercoaching.ca
URL: http://www.cybercoaching.ca

Specializes in executive coaching and career development. Helps organizations with ex human resource management, appraisals and human resource consulting.

★13476★ **Allied Search Inc.**
2030 Union St., Ste. 206
PO Box 472410
San Francisco, CA 94123
Ph: (415)921-2200   Fax: (415)921-3900
E-mail: consultants@alliedsearchinc.com
URL: http://www.alliedsearchinc.com

Eecutive search firm which will search, locate, recruit, and place the very best professionals and executives with client companies nationwide.

★13477★ **Amansco Inc.**
130 7th St., Ste. 430
Pittsburgh, PA 15222-3412
Ph: (412)281-5180

Executive search consultants active in all industries on worldwide basis.

★13478★ Career Connections

934 Dunlap St.
PO Box 9331
Santa Fe, NM 87501-2416
Ph: (505)983-9217   Fax: (505)983-8483
E-mail: barbaraconroy@earthlink.net

Provides individualized guidance in career planning, including job search strategies, assessment, goal-setting and networking strategies. Tailored networking techniques and strategies are employed to achieve specific aims. Ongoing support services include life/work coaching and consultations.

★13479★ Career Path

1240 Iroquois Ave., Ste. 100
Naperville, IL 60563
Ph: (630)369-3390
URL: http://www.career-path.info

Career planning consultants offering counseling in such areas as career development, career transition, and teambuilding.

★13480★ Clear Rock Inc.

Regus Business Ctr., 225 Franklin St., 26th Fl.
Boston, MA 02110
Ph: (617)217-2811   Fax: (617)217-2001
E-mail: info@clearrock.com
URL: http://www.clearrock.com

Focuses on executive and career development with an emphasis on coaching and outplacement. Approach focuses on individuals leadership, style, interpersonal relationships, career strategy, finances, stress, health and life balance.

★13481★ First Transitions Inc.

1211 W 22nd St., Ste. 1006
Oak Brook, IL 60523
Ph: (630)571-3311   Fax: (630)571-5714
Fr: 800-358-1112
E-mail: admin@firsttransitions.com
URL: http://www.firsttransitions.com

Provides corporate sponsored career transition services. Firm offers executive coaching, executive assessment and evaluation, organizational career development, 360 degree evaluations and leadership assessment.

★13482★ FREEdLANCE Group for Career & Workforce Innovation

1100 Washington Ave., Ste. 219
Carnegie, PA 15106
Ph: (412)429-7650   Fax: (412)429-7651
Fr: 877-937-6638
E-mail: info@freedlance.com
URL: http://www.freedlance.com

Specialized expertise in career and workforce development. Best practices and research-based innovations. Innovative stakeholder data accumulation, evaluation and analysis. Formal research methods/models and administration of testing, assessment and career case management systems; Grant writing; Contextual curriculum development and training, including career devel-

opment facilitator certification training; Independent pre and post-testing; Formal program evaluations; Technological interventions.

★13483★ Hill & Hill Consulting Inc.

12035 Cooperwood Ln.
Cincinnati, OH 45242
Ph: (513)984-8448   Fax: (513)856-5916

A career or life planning consulting firm specializing in helping persons to make successful career transitions and/or enhance their career. Clients include: associations, corporations, higher education and persons from diverse professions.

★13484★ Institute for Urban Family Health

16 E 16th St.
New York, NY 10003
Ph: (212)633-0800   Fax: (212)691-4610
E-mail: info@institute2000.org
URL: http://www.institute2000.org

Services in organization development, recruitment and retention, training and career development, diversity initiatives and performance management.

★13485★ J. Philip Associates Inc.

2120 Wilshire Blvd.
Santa Monica, CA 90403
Ph: (310)453-7700   Fax: (310)453-4660
Fr: 877-925-5446
E-mail: info@allignteam.com
URL: http://www.allignteam.com

Firm specializes in business solutions, search and recruitment services, executive search, hire recruitment campaigns, outsourcing or development of internal recruitment organizations and retention programs. Developer of ALLIGN business program tool.

★13486★ Job Search CD Series

JIST Publishing
875 Montreal Way
St. Paul, MN 55102
Fax: 800-547-8329   Fr: 800-648-5478
E-mail: info@jist.com
URL: http://www.jist.com

$98 each. Each CD is focused on a particular skill needed for a successful job search.

★13487★ The Murdock Group Holding Corp.

4084 S Commerce Dr.
Salt Lake City, UT 84107
Ph: (801)268-3232   Fax: (801)268-3289
Fr: 888-888-0892
E-mail: info@themurdockgroup.com

Specializes in providing full service career services and seminars for individuals and companies, including outplacements, 'The Hiring Series' and career expos.

★13488★ National Self-Help Clearinghouse (NSHC)

365 5th Ave., Ste. 3300
New York, NY 10016
Ph: (212)817-1822
E-mail: info@selfhelpweb.org
URL: http://www.selfhelpweb.org

Description: Clearinghouse on self-help groups; provides referral services. Conducts research and training activities. Maintains speakers' bureau. Conventions/Meetings: none.

★13489★ Norma Zuber and Associates

3585 Maple St., Ste. 237
Ventura, CA 93003-9504
Ph: (805)656-6220   Fax: (805)654-1523
E-mail: nzubercdlp@msn.com
URL: http://www.normazubercareers.com

Counselor/consultant offers formal assessment, evaluation and private counseling to individuals to discover their unique personal characteristics and potentials. This is done by combining self-understanding and an understanding of the world of work through personal assessment and occupational and educational exploration. Services provide an individualized career profile developed in order to help one make appropriate and satisfying career choices or changes at any age. Provides services to business and industry for staff development and team building. Serves clients located in central California.

★13490★ One Source Managed Solutions Inc.

1 Hollycrest Dr.
Brick, NJ 08723
Ph: (732)451-0035   Fax: (775)295-7475
E-mail: info@onesourcemanaged.com
URL: http://www.onesourcemanaged.com

A management consulting firm specializing in contract recruiting, executive search, contingency search.

★13491★ Reaction Search International Inc.

2682 Bishop Dr., Ste. 208
San Ramon, CA 94583
Ph: (925)275-0727   Fr: 800-832-8268
E-mail: info@reactionsearch.com
URL: http://www.reactionsearch.com

Executive recruiters specializing in search, assessment, selection processes and employer services. Provides custom-designed staffing searches and arrangements render us a preferred provider of executive search services.

★13492★ R.L. Stevens & Associates Inc.

800 South St., Ste. 295
Waltham, MA 02453
Ph: (781)647-4888   Fax: (781)647-2878
Fr: 800-721-9491
E-mail: jridge@rlstevens.com
URL: http://www.rlstevens.com

A career management firm that specializes in career marketing and outplacement.

★13493★ **RO-LAN Associates Inc.**
725 Sabattus St.
Lewiston, ME 04240
Ph: (207)784-1010   Fax: (207)782-3446
E-mail: rlapointe@aol.com

Professional placement specialists for permanent and temporary positions. Also offers executive search and recruiting expertise, outplacements, complete resume service,

new business consulting and job and career transition coaching.

★13494★ **Sociometrics Corp.**
170 State St., Ste. 260
Los Altos, CA 94022-2812
Ph: (650)949-3282   Fax: (650)949-3299
E-mail: socio@socio.com
URL: http://www.socio.com

Consulting firm offering program evaluation, needs assessment, personnel services and technical assistance and training. Company serves government and private industries worldwide.

★13495★ **T. Williams Consulting L.L.C.**
2570 Blvd. of the Generals, Ste. 110
Audubon, PA 19403
Ph: (610)635-0101   Fax: (610)635-0304
Fr: (866)892-1500
E-mail: info@twilliams.com
URL: http://www.twilliams.com

A management consulting firm specializing in human resources consulting and executive search and operational improvement services.

Career Transitions and Alternatives

REFERENCE WORKS

★13496★ America's Career InfoNet
U.S. Department of Labor
Frances Perkins Bldg.
200 Constitution Ave. NW
Washington, DC 20210
Ph: (886)487-2365   Fr: 877-889-5627
URL: http://www.acinet.org/acinet/

Covers links to and information about job banks, employment service providers, career education, and nationwide employer contacts.

★13497★ Career Bounce-Back!: The Professionals in Transition Guide to Recovery and Reemployment
AMACOM
1601 Broadway, 12th Fl.
New York, NY 10019-7420
Ph: (212)586-8100   Fax: (212)903-8168
Fr: 800-262-9699
URL: http://www.amanet.org

J. Damian Birkel and Stacey J. Miller. 1998. $14.95 (paper). 162 pages.

★13498★ Career Directions
The McGraw-Hill Companies
PO Box 182604
Columbus, OH 43272
Fax: (614)759-3749   Fr: 877-883-5524
E-mail: customer.service@mcgraw-hill.com
URL: http://www.mcgraw-hill.com

Donna J. Yena. Third edition, 1996. $41.33. 432 pages.

★13499★ Career Transition: A Guide for Federal Employees in a Time of Turmoil
FPMI Communications, Inc.
4901 Univ. St., Ste. 3
Huntsville, AL 35816
Ph: (256)539-1850   Fax: (256)539-0911

Robert Carey. 1996. $14.95 (paper). 105 pages.

★13500★ Career Transitions in Sport: International Perspectives
Fitness Information Technology, Incorporated
PO Box 6116
Morgantown, WV 26506-6116
Ph: (304)293-6888   Fax: (304)293-6658
Fr: 800-477-4348
URL: http://www.fitinfotech.com/

David Lavalle and Paul Wylleman. 2000. $39.00. 305 pages.

★13501★ Career Transitions in Turbulent Times: Exploring Work, Learning and Careers
Counseling and Psychological Services, Inc.
201 Ferguson Bldg., UNCG
Greensboro, NC 27402-6171
Ph: (336)334-4114   Fax: (336)334-4116
Fr: 800-414-9769

Rich Feller and Garry Walz, editors. 1996. $29.95 (paper). 458 pages.

★13502★ CareerXRoads
MMC GROUP
105 Decker Ct., Ste. 150
Irving, TX 75062
Ph: (972)893-0100   Fax: (972)893-0099
URL: http://www.careerxroads.com/about/

Latest edition 2002. Covers nearly 3,000 job and resume Web sites with reviews and descriptions of the top 500. Indexes: colleges; corporations: diversity; specialty/industry; location; listing services.

★13503★ Change Your Job, Change Your Life: High Impact Strategies for Finding Great Jobs in the 21st Century
Impact Publications
9104 Manassas Dr., Ste. N
Manassas Park, VA 20111-5211
Ph: (703)361-7300   Fax: (703)335-9486
Fr: 800-361-1055
E-mail: query@impactpublications.com
URL: http://www.impactpublications.com

Ronald Krannich. Seventh edition, 1999. $21.95 (paper). 317 pages. Details trends in the marketplace, how to identify opportunities, how to retrain for them, and how to land jobs. Includes a chapter on starting a business. Contains index, bibliography, and illustrations.

★13504★ College Majors and Careers
Facts On File Inc.
132 W 31st St., 17th Fl.
New York, NY 10001
Ph: (212)967-8800   Fax: 800-678-3633
Fr: 800-322-8755
E-mail: holli@inil.com
URL: http://www.fergpubco.com

Irregular; latest edition 5th, 2003. $16.95 for individuals. Publication includes: Lists of organizations and other sources of information on choosing a college field of concentration and a subsequent career path. Entries include: Organization name, address, phone. Principal content of publication is descriptions of 60 of the most popular major fields and discussions of their attributes.

★13505★ Dare to Change Your Job and Your Life
Jist Works
875 Montreal Way
St. Paul, MN 55102
Fr: 800-648-5478
E-mail: info@jist.com
URL: http://www.jist.com

Carole Kanchier. Second edition, 2000. $16.95. 325 pages. Based on a survey of more than 5,000 adults.

★13506★ Directory of Outplacement and Career Management Firms
Kennedy Information
1 Phoenix Mill Ln., 3rd Fl.
Peterborough, NH 03458
Ph: (603)924-1006   Fax: (603)924-4460
Fr: 800-531-0007
URL: http://www.kennedyinfo.com

Annual; latest edition 14th. $149.95 for individuals. Covers 407 consulting firms with special interest in career management and "outplacement" or "de-hiring" counseling executive employees being terminated because of poor performance, plant closings, etc., and assisting them in finding new jobs; firms that are compensated only by employers and those that also accept compensation from individuals are listed. Entries include: Firm name, address, phone, fax, e-mail, web address, description of philosophy and services, names and titles of principals, branches, area served, year established, revenue (within wide ranges), professional associations, minimum salary of positions handled, number of staff, percentage of business devoted to outplacement. Arrangement: Separate sections on basis of compensation arrangements, then alphabetical. Indexes: Industries, key principals, firm.

★13507★ **Do What You Love for the Rest of Your Life: A Practical Guide to Career Change and Personal Renewal**

Random House
1745 Broadway
New York, NY 10019
Ph: (212)782-9000   Fax: (212)572-6066
Fr: 800-733-3000
URL: http://www.randomhouse.com

Bob Griffiths. Reprint edition, December 2003. $13.95 (paper). 336 pages.

★13508★ **Effective Strategies for Career Success**

Jist Works
875 Montreal Way
St. Paul, MN 55102
Fr: 800-648-5478
E-mail: info@jist.com
URL: http://www.jist.com

$9.95 (paper). 380 pages.

★13509★ **Good News! You're Fired! A Comprehensive Guide for People in Career Transition**

Nebbadoon Press
PO Box 333
Etna, NH 03750
Ph: (603)643-0400   Fax: (603)643-0404
Fr: 800-500-9086

Elizabeth Tansey. 1998. $17.00. 137 pages.

★13510★ **How to Change Your Career**

The McGraw-Hill Companies
PO Box 182604
Columbus, OH 43272
Fax: (614)759-3749   Fr: 877-883-5524
E-mail: customer.service@mcgraw-hill.com
URL: http://www.mcgraw-hill.com

Kent Banning and Ardelle Friday. 1993. $9.95 (paper). 160 pages. Provides checklists, worksheets, and exercises to help career-changers identify and successfully enter new careers. Guides the reader in the production of a career-change resume.

★13511★ **How to Find the Work You Love**

Penguin
375 Hudson St.
New York, NY 10014
Ph: (212)366-2000   Fax: (212)366-2666
Fr: 800-847-5515
URL: http://us.penguingroup.com/

Laurence G. Boldt. 2004. $12.00 (paper). 192 pages.

★13512★ **How to Get That Job**

Pilot Books
127 Sterling Ave.
PO Box 2102
Greenport, NY 11944-0893
Ph: (516)477-1094   Fax: (516)477-0978
Fr: 800-797-4568
URL: http://www.pilotbooks.com

Ruby N. Gorter. 1997. $8.95. 94 pages. Provides information for first-time job seekers as well as those who want to change careers.

★13513★ **JobSmarts 50 Top Careers**

HarperCollins
10 E. 53rd St.
New York, NY 10022
Ph: (212)207-7000   Fax: (212)207-7633
Fr: 800-242-7737
URL: http://www.harpercollins.com/

Bradley G. Richardson. 1997. $16.00 (paper). 400 pages.

★13514★ **Occupational Outlook Handbook**

U.S. Bureau of Labor Statistics
Postal Sq. Bldg., 2 Massachusetts Ave. NE
Washington, DC 20212-0001
Ph: (202)691-5200   Fax: (202)691-6325
Fr: 800-877-8339
E-mail: oohinfo@bls.gov
URL: http://www.bls.gov/oco/home.htm

Biennial, January of even years; latest edition 2006-07. $22.00 for individuals. Publication includes: Various occupational organizations that provide career information on hundreds of occupations. Entries include: For organizations–Organization name, address. Principal content of publication is profiles of various occupations, which include description of occupation, educational requirements, job outlook, and expected earnings. Arrangement: Organizations are classified by occupation.

★13515★ **Outside the Ivory Tower: A Guide for Academics Considering Alternative Careers**

Harvard University, Office of Career Services
54 Dunster St.
Cambridge, MA 02138
Ph: (617)495-2595   Fax: (617)495-3584

Margaret Newhouse. 1993. $13.00 (paper). 163 pages.

★13516★ **Parting Company: How to Survive the Loss of a Job and Find Another Successfully**

Drake Beam Morin Pub
750 Third Ave., 28th Fl.
New York, NY 10017
Ph: (212)692-7700   Fax: (212)297-0426
E-mail: inquiries@dbm.com
URL: http://www.dbm.com

William J. Morin and James C. Cabrera. Third edition, 2000. $13.00 (paper). 388 pages. Covers the entire spectrum of termination issues.

★13517★ **Professional Careers Sourcebook**

Gale, Cengage Learning
27500 Drake Rd.
Farmington Hills, MI 48331-3535
Ph: (248)699-GALE   Fax: (248)699-8069
Fr: 800-877-GALE
E-mail: galeord@gale.com
URL: http://www.gale.com

Seventh edition, 2002. $174.63. 1,013 pages. Directs users to career information sources related to specific professions, such as civil engineering, psychology, law, public relations, dance and choreography, and more. Provides a listing of state professional and occupational licensing agencies and occupational rankings and statistics. Includes over 110 professional career profiles containing information on general career guides, career information and services provided by professional associations, standards and certification agencies, directories of educational programs and institutions, basic reference guides and handbooks related to the profession, professional and trade periodicals, and more. Indexes: Alphabetical.

★13518★ **Quick Prep Careers**

Ferguson Publishing Co.
200 W Jackson Blvd.
Chicago, IL 60606-6941
Fax: 800-306-9942   Fr: 800-306-9941

$18.95 for individuals. Publication includes: Lists of associations for further consultation for each of 75 jobs featured. Principal content of publication is detailed information on each job. Arrangement: By job. Indexes: Alphabetical.

★13519★ **Rea's Authoritative Guide to the Top 100 Careers to Year 2005**

Research and Education Association
61 Ethel Rd., W
Piscataway, NJ 08854
Ph: (732)819-8800   Fax: (732)819-8808
Fr: 800-822-0830
E-mail: info@rea.com
URL: http://www.rea.com/

Research and Education Association. 1997. $19.95 (paper). 368 pages.

★13520★ Starting Over: How to Change Careers or Start Your Own Business

Grand Central Publishing
237 Park Ave.
New York, NY 10017
Ph: (212)522-7200   Fax: 800-286-9471
Fr: 800-759-0190
URL: http://www.hachettebookgroupusa.com

Stephen M. Pollan and Mark Levine. 1997. $15.99 (paper). 256 pages.

★13521★ Taking Charge of Your Career Direction

Wadsworth Publishing
PO Box 6904
Florence, KY 41022
Fax: 800-487-8488   Fr: 800-354-9706
URL: http://www.cengage.com

Robert D. Lock. Fifth edition, 2004. Three volumes. 504 pages. $69.95. Provides guidance for the job search process.

★13522★ Ten Insider Secrets Career Transition Workshop: Your Complete Guide to Discovering the Ideal Job!

10 Step Publications
1151 N. State Pkwy., No. 253
Chicago, IL 60610
Ph: (312)493-0582   Fax: (312)873-3777

Todd Bermont. January 2004. $14.95. 108 pages.

★13523★ Vocational Careers Sourcebook

Gale, Cengage Learning
27500 Drake Rd.
Farmington Hills, MI 48331-3535
Ph: (248)699-GALE   Fax: (248)699-8069
Fr: 800-877-GALE
E-mail: galeord@gale.com
URL: http://www.gale.com

Sixth edition, 2006. $160.00. 700 pages. Directs users to career information sources related to specific occupations, such as insurance and real estate sales, corrections and police work, mechanics, armed forces options, agriculture and forestry, production work, and the trades. Contains information on general career guides, career information and services provided by trade associations, standards and certification agencies, directories of educational programs and institutions, basic reference guides and handbooks related to the occupation, trade periodicals, and more. Indexes: Alphabetical.

AUDIO/VISUAL RESOURCES

★13524★ E.M.P.O.Y.ability: Six Keys to Changing Your Career and Your Life

JIST Publishing
875 Montreal Way
St. Paul, MN 55102
Fax: 800-547-8329   Fr: 800-648-5478
E-mail: info@jist.com
URL: http://www.jist.com

2001. $69. 36 minutes. Motivational speaker Byron Ricks shares his EMPLOYability formula.

★13525★ Getting Fired, Getting Hired: Job Hunting From A to Z

Career Lab
10475 Park Meadows Dr. Ste. 600
Lone Tree, CO 80124-5437
Ph: (303)790-0505   Fax: (303)790-0606
Fr: 800-723-9675
E-mail: wsfrank@careerlab.com
URL: http://www.careerlab.com

Six-part video series.

★13526★ Rebounding from Job Loss

Cambridge Educational
PO Box 2053
Princeton, NJ 08543-2053
Ph: 800-257-5126   Fax: (609)671-0266
Fr: 800-468-4227
E-mail: custserv@films.com
URL: http://www.cambridgeeducational.com

VHS and DVD. $89.95. 2000. 16 minutes. Program helps viewers see how losing a job often parallels the trauma experienced after a death. In both cases, individuals must go through a grieving process that includes working through various stages. We also learn strategies for finding the positive opportunities in this dramatic change.

★13527★ Unemployment: Understanding The Grieving Process

Cambridge Educational
PO Box 2053
Princeton, NJ 08543-2053
Ph: 800-257-5126   Fax: (609)671-0266
Fr: 800-468-4227
E-mail: custserv@films.com
URL: http://www.cambridgeeducational.com

VHS and DVD. $89.95. 1999. 33 minutes. Includes section on taking action to find a new job.

ONLINE AND DATABASE SERVICES

★13528★ Career Leader
Fax: (617)738-9783
E-mail: help@careerleader.com
URL: http://www.careerdiscovery.com

Description: Online career assessment tool for job seekers, emphasis on business careers. **Fee:** Several levels of assessment available; starts at $95.

★13529★ CareerAdvantage.com

Bridges Transitions, Inc.
33637-B Hwy. 97 N.
Oroville, WA 98844
Ph: (250)869-4200   Fr: 800-281-1168
E-mail: resumes@bridges.com
URL: http://careeradvantage.com

Description: Career planning website with skills and interest aptitude assessments, daily feed of new career articles, exclusive library of career profiles and interviews with people in the field to help guide and direct professional development. **Fee:** Subscription to services $19.95.

★13530★ Keirsey Temperament Sorter and Temperament Web Site
E-mail: keirsey@orci.com
URL: http://www.keirsey.com

Description: Online personality questionnaire that identifies temperament and interest traits that may be applied towards career searches.

OTHER SOURCES

★13531★ Career Planning and Adult Development Network (CPADN)

PO Box 1484
Pacifica, CA 94044
Ph: (650)359-6911   Fax: (650)359-3089
E-mail: admin@careernetwork.org
URL: http://www.careernetwork.org

Description: Counselors, trainers, consultants, therapists, educators, personnel specialists, and graduate students who work in business, educational, religious, and governmental organizations, and focus on career planning and adult development issues. Seeks to: establish a link between professionals working with adults in a variety of settings; identify and exchange effective adult development methods and techniques; develop a clearer understanding of the directions and objectives of the career planning and the adult development movement. Keeps members informed of developments in career decision-making, career values clarification, preretirement counseling, dual-career families, job search techniques, and mid-life transitions. Cosponsors professional seminars; maintains biographical archives.

★13532★ New Ways to Work (NWW)
103 Morris St., Ste. A
Sebastopol, CA 95472
Ph: (707)824-4000   Fax: (707)824-4410
E-mail: newways@newwaystowork.org
URL: http://www.nww.org

Description: Helps communities build systems that connect schools, community organizations and businesses, and improve the services, educational programs and support the community provides for its youth. Engages and supports local communities in the invention and renewal of connected, comprehensive youth-serving systems.

Electronic Job Search Information

REFERENCE WORKS

★13533★ 110 Best Job Search Sites on the Internet
Linx Educational Publishing, Inc.
939 11th Ave. S.
Jacksonville Beach, FL 32250
Ph: (904)241-1861   Fax: 888-546-9338
Fr: 800-717-5469
E-mail: sales@linxedu.com
URL: http://www.linxedu.com/

Katherine K. Yonge. $12.95. 1998. 80 pages. Also includes tips on electronic resumes and other information.

★13534★ Adams Electronic Job Search Almanac
Adams Media Corp.
57 Littlefield St.
Avon, MA 02322
Ph: (508)427-7100   Fax: (508)427-6790
Fr: 800-872-5627
URL: http://www.adamsmedia.com

Annual; latest edition 6th. Covers job listings on the Internet; bulletin boards, Web networking, and online services for finding a job. Entries include: Firm or organization name, address, phone, name and title of contact; description of organization, headquarters location, typical titles for entry- and middle-level positions, educational backgrounds desired, fringe benefits offered, stock exchange listing, training programs, internships, parent company, number of employees, revenues, e-mail and web address, projected number of hires. Arrangement: Alphabetical.

★13535★ Be Your Own Headhunter
Crown Business
1540 Broadway
New York, NY 10036
Ph: (212)782-9000   Fax: (212)302-7985
Fr: 800-726-0600

P. Dickson and S. Tiersten. 1995. $16.00 (paper). 208 pages.

★13536★ Cyberspace Resume Kit
Jist Works
875 Montreal Way
St. Paul, MN 55102
Fr: 800-648-5478
E-mail: info@jist.com
URL: http://www.jist.com

Fred E. Jandt and Mary B. Nemnich. Second edition, 2000. $16.95. 332 pages. Teaches how to develop and post electronic resumes.

★13537★ Electronic Job Search Almanac
Adams Media Corp.
57 Littlefield St.
Avon, MA 02322
Ph: (508)427-7100   Fax: (508)427-6790
Fr: 800-872-5627

Edited by Adams Media Corp. staff. 1997. $10.95 (paper). 306 pages.

★13538★ Electronic Resumes and Online Networking: How to Use the Internet to Do a Better Job Search, Including a Complete, Up-to-Date Resource Guide
Career Press, Inc.
3 Tice Rd.
PO Box 687
Franklin Lakes, NJ 07417-1322
Ph: (201)848-0310   Fax: (201)848-1727
Fr: 800-227-3371
URL: http://www.careerpress.com

Rebecca Smith. Second edition, 2000. $15.99 (paper). Provides information on using the Internet as a resume networking tool. Covers locating employers, evaluating electronic resume options, and web pages. 224 pages.

★13539★ Electronic Resumes: The Complete Guide to Putting Your Resume On-Line
The McGraw-Hill Companies
PO Box 182604
Columbus, OH 43272
Fax: (614)759-3749   Fr: 877-883-5524
E-mail: customer.service@mcgraw-hill.com
URL: http://www.mcgraw-hill.com

Wayne M. Gonyea and James C. Gonyea. 1996. $19.95. 255 pages. Explains the basics of online, multimedia, video, and audio resumes in nontechnical language. Disk includes software that enables users to create their own electronic resume to upload via modem onto online resume databases.

★13540★ The Guide to Internet Job Searching
The McGraw-Hill Companies
PO Box 182604
Columbus, OH 43272
Fax: (614)759-3749   Fr: 877-883-5524
E-mail: customer.service@mcgraw-hill.com
URL: http://www.mcgraw-hill.com

Margaret Riley Dikel, Frances E. Roehm, Steve Oserman. $15.95. 2006. 288 pages. Helps readers develop an effective Internet job application, quickly locate major job listing sites in each career area, and use the computer to search for job opportunities.

★13541★ Guide to Internet Job Searching, 2004-2005 Edition
JIST Publishing
875 Montreal Way
St. Paul, MN 55102
Fax: 800-547-8329   Fr: 800-648-5478
E-mail: info@jist.com
URL: http://www.jist.com

Margaret Riley Dikel and Frances E. Roehm. 2000. $14.95. 288 pages. Describes how to find and use online bulletin boards, job listings, recruiter information, discussion groups, and resume posting services.

★13542★ Headhunters Revealed
Hunter Arts Publishing
PO Box 66578E
Los Angeles, CA 90066
Ph: (310)842-8864   Fax: (310)842-8868
Fr: 877-443-2348
URL: http://www.headhuntersrevealed.com/

Quarterly. $14.95 for individuals; $12.50 for out of country. Covers online career sites, career associations, and organizations.

★13543★ **Internet Resumes**
Impact Publications
9104 Manassas Dr., Ste. N
Manassas Park, VA 20111-5211
Ph: (703)361-7300   Fax: (703)335-9486
Fr: 800-361-1055
E-mail: query@impactpublications.com
URL: http://www.impactpublications.com

Peter D. Weddle. 1998. $14.95 (paper). 193 pages. Shows how to communicate qualifications to potential employers over the Internet.

★13544★ **Job Searching Online for Dummies**
For Dummies
1 Wiley Dr.
Somerset, NJ 08875-1272
Ph: (732)469-4400   Fax: (732)302-2300
Fr: 800-225-5945
E-mail: custserv@wiley.com
URL: http://www.dummies.com/WileyCDA/

Pam Dixon. Second edition, 2000. $24.99 (paper). 295 pages. Includes CD-ROM. Techniques for finding a job online through the Internet.

★13545★ **Plunkett's Employers' Internet Sites with Careers Information: The Only Complete Guide to Careers Websites Operated by Major Employers**
Plunkett Research, Ltd.
PO Box 541737
Houston, TX 77254-1737
Ph: (713)932-0000   Fax: (713)932-7080
E-mail: customersupport@plunkettresearch.com
URL: http://www.plunkettresearch.com

Jack W. Plunkett. Revised, 2004. $229.99 (includes CD-ROM). Provides profiles of Internet sites for major employers. Job hunters can use the profiles or indexes to locate the Internet job sites that best fit their needs. 681 pages.

★13546★ **Professional's Job Finder**
Planning Communications
7215 Oak Ave.
River Forest, IL 60305-1935
Ph: (708)366-5200   Fax: (708)366-5280
Fr: 888-366-5200
E-mail: projf@planningcommunications.com
URL: http://www.planningcommunications.com/jf/index.htm

$7.58 for individuals. Covers over 3,000 sources of jobs in the private sector of the United States, including job matching services, job hotlines, periodicals and directories, Internet job sites, salary surveys, databases, and electronic online job services. Includes coupons for over $200 in discounts and free job resources. Entries include: For job services–Name, sponsor or operator name, address, phone, length of registration period, cost, description (including number of job vacancies listed). For publications–Title, publisher name, address, phone, frequency of publication, price, description (including

number of job vacancies listed). Arrangement: Classified by occupational specialty; geographical by state. Indexes: Subject.

★13547★ **Using the Internet and the World Wide Web in Your Job Search**
Jist Works
875 Montreal Way
St. Paul, MN 55102
Fr: 800-648-5478
E-mail: info@jist.com
URL: http://www.jist.com

Fred Jandt and Mary Nemnich. Second edition, 1996. $16.95 (paper). 300 pages. Explains how to connect to the Internet, find job listings, research potential employers, use news groups to get leads, and adapt standard resumes to electronic formats.

AUDIO/VISUAL RESOURCES

★13548★ **Connect on the Net: Finding a Job on the Internet**
Cambridge Educational
PO Box 2053
Princeton, NJ 08543-2053
Ph: 800-257-5126   Fax: (609)671-0266
Fr: 800-468-4227
E-mail: custserv@films.com
URL: http://www.cambridgeeducational.com

VHS and DVD. $79.95. 24 minutes. 1995. Viewers learn how to use traditional and non-traditional job search strategies as they navigate job search directories and bulletin boards on the Internet.

★13549★ **How to Find a Job on the Inernet: Why Work Without a "Net"?**
JIST Publishing
875 Montreal Way
St. Paul, MN 55102
Fax: 800-547-8329   Fr: 800-648-5478
E-mail: info@jist.com
URL: http://www.jist.com

1999. $69. 40 minutes. Video answers common questions and misconceptions about internet job searching with step-by-step demonstrations, screen captures, and animation.

★13550★ **Log On for Success: Internet Job Searching**
JIST Publishing
875 Montreal Way
St. Paul, MN 55102
Fax: 800-547-8329   Fr: 800-648-5478
E-mail: info@jist.com
URL: http://www.jist.com

2004. $69.95. 18 minutes. Teaches job seekers how to search mega-job sites, industry specific sites, and individual company sites; also teaches the elements needed to prepare web-ready and e-mail compatible resumes and cover letters.

★13551★ **Networking on the WWW and Beyond**
Cambridge Educational
PO Box 2053
Princeton, NJ 08543-2053
Ph: 800-257-5126   Fax: (609)671-0266
Fr: 800-468-4227
E-mail: custserv@films.com
URL: http://www.cambridgeeducational.com

VHS and DVD. 1997. $79.95. 28 minutes. This three-part video includes an introduction to search engines, how to network and find jobs using Internet resources, and interviewing via the Internet.

★13552★ **Web Resumes**
Cambridge Educational
PO Box 2053
Princeton, NJ 08543-2053
Ph: 800-257-5126   Fax: (609)671-0266
Fr: 800-468-4227
E-mail: custserv@films.com
URL: http://www.cambridgeeducational.com

VHS and DVD. 1998. $69.95. 30 minutes. Topics covered include Web and electronic resumes, creative resumes, target resumes, and mid-life and reentry resumes.

ONLINE AND DATABASE SERVICES

★13553★ **4Anything Network: 4Careers.com**
URL: http://www.livve.com/promo/4anything/index.html

Description: Job hunters may search job ads placed by employers. Jobs are arranged in sub-categories. Also sections on personality assessments, salary research, and career counseling.

★13554★ **Academic Employment Network**
244 Fifth Ave., Ste. R266
New York, NY 10001
Ph: (917)331-8703
URL: http://www.academploy.com/

Description: Online position announcement service. Lists available positions in colleges, primary and secondary educational institutions for faculty, staff, and administrative professionals. **Fee:** Free searching and browsing features.

★13555★ **Academic360.com**
Internet Employment Linkage, Inc.
E-mail: webmaster@academic360.com
URL: http://www.academic360.com/

Description: Site is a collection of internet resources gathered for the academic job hunter. Contains links to over 1,400 colleges and universities that advertise job openings online. Positions listed are not limited to teaching positions.

★13556★ American Academy of Ophthalmology Professional Choices Career Center

American Academy of Ophthalmology
655 Beach St.
PO Box 7424
San Francisco, CA 94120-7424
Ph: (415)561-8500   Fax: (415)561-8533
E-mail: pchoices@atsaao.org
URL: http://www.aao.org/careers/

Description: A site providing regularly updated ophthalmology positions. Applicants for jobs contact the AAO with resume, cover letter, and listing reference number. Job hunters may post resumes for free. Employers may post 90-day job listings at the rate of $335 for members, $535 for nonmembers.

★13557★ American Academy of Physician Assistants Career Opportunities

950 N. Washington St.
Alexandria, VA 22314-1352
Ph: (703)836-2272   Fax: (703)684-1924
E-mail: aapa@aapa.org
URL: http://www.aapa.org

Description: Online newsletter of the AAPA. Job opportunities may be searched by state or type. Members may also post position wanted on AAPA website.

★13558★ American Accounting Association Placement Advertising

5717 Bessie Dr.
Sarasota, FL 34233-2399
Ph: (941)921-7747   Fax: (941)923-4093
E-mail: office@aahq.org
URL: http://aaahq.org/placements/default.cfm

Description: Visitors may apply for membership to the Association at this site. **Main files include:** Placement Postings, Placement Submission Information, Faculty Development, Marketplace, more.

★13559★ American Association of Anatomists Career Center

9650 Rockville Pike
Bethesda, MD 20814-3998
Ph: (301)634-7910   Fax: (301)634-7965
E-mail: exec@anatomy.org
URL: http://www.anatomy.org/resources/career_center.htm

Description: Job advertisers include academic sites in the U.S. and Canada. Job seekers may review these posted jobs through "Positions Offered" or post their own needs under "Positions Wanted." Offerings for Postdoctoral Positions also available. Contains Career Resources sections and links to online career resources.

★13560★ American Chemical Society

1155 16th St. NW
Washington, DC 20036
Ph: 800-227-5558   Fr: 888-667-7988
E-mail: service@acs.org
URL: http://www.cen-chemjobs.org

Description: Offers online interviewing between employers and potential employees, postings for positions available and situations wanted, and regularly updated career advice and information for American Chemical Society members only.

★13561★ American Institute of Aeronautics and Astronautics Career Planning and Placement Services

1801 Alexander Bell Dr., Ste. 500
Reston, VA 20191-4344
Ph: (703)264-7500   Fax: (703)264-7551
Fr: 800-639-2422
E-mail: custserv@aiaa.org
URL: http://www.aiaa.org

Description: Site for AIAA members to place recruitment advertisements, browse career opportunities listings, post resumes, and seek additional employment assistance. Non-members may become members though this site.

★13562★ American Institute of Biological Sciences Classifieds

1444 I St., Ste. 200
Washington, DC 20005
Ph: (202)628-1500   Fax: (202)628-1509
URL: http://www.aibs.org/classifieds/

Description: Section of the American Institute of Biological Sciences website used for posting available positions, research awards and fellowships, and other classified ads.

★13563★ American Library Association Education and Employment

50 E. Huron
Chicago, IL 60611
Fr: 800-545-2433
URL: http://www.ala.org

Description: Contains links to monthly job and career leads lists posted in American Libraries and College & Research Libraries NewsNet and other sources, as well as a Conference Placement Service and accreditation information.

★13564★ American Oil Chemists Society Career Opportunities

2710 S. Boulder
Urbana, IL 61802-6996
Ph: (217)359-2344   Fax: (217)351-8091
E-mail: general@aocs.org
URL: http://www.aocs.org/member/jobcent/

Description: Section of the AOCS homepage intended to aid members in finding jobs in the oil chemistry field. Job areas include analytical, health and nutrition, processing, surfactants and detergents, general fats and oils/chemistry, and others. Jobs may be posted and searched.

★13565★ American Society of Landscape Architects JobLink

American Society of Landscape Architects
636 Eye St. NW
Washington, DC 20001-3736
Ph: (202)898-2444   Fax: (202)898-1185
URL: http://www.asla.org/nonmembers/joblink.cfm

Description: A job-search site of the American Society of Landscape Architects. **Fee:** Resume postings cost $100 (nonmembers) or $10 (members) for a two-month listing. Job postings cost $560 (nonmembers) or $280 (members) for a one-month listing.

★13566★ American Society of Plant Biologists Job Bank

15501 Monona Dr.
Rockville, MD 20855-2768
Ph: (301)251-0560   Fax: (301)279-2996
E-mail: info@aspb.org
URL: http://www.aspb.org/jobbank/

Description: A service of the American Society of Plant Biologists, intended to aid its members in locating jobs and job resources. Site lists new jobs weekly in its job bank. **Fee:** A fee of $150 is charged for all academic/government/industry permanent positions and for all positions, regardless of rank, posted by private companies. Postdoctoral Positions; Research/Technical Positions (non-Ph.D.); and Assistantships, Fellowships, and Internships at universities and not-for-profit agencies are published for a fee of $25.

★13567★ AppleOne.com
Fr: 800-564-5644
URL: http://www.appleone.com

Description: Search site with job databank, resume posting and online e-newsletter subscriptions. Applicants can also interview with prospective employers online. Registration is free.

★13568★ ArtJob Online

1743 Wazee St., Ste. 300
Denver, CO 80202
Ph: (303)629-1166   Fax: (303)629-9717
Fr: 888-JOBS-232
E-mail: artjob@westaf.org
URL: http://www.artjob.org

Description: Contains up-to-date national and international listings of arts employment and related opportunities in the arts: full- & part-time employment, internships, grants, public art projects, and residencies. User can search by region, art discipline, type of organization. **Fee:** Subscribers pay $25 for 3 months, $40 for six months and $75 for one year.

★13569★ Best Jobs USA
E-mail: rci@atsbestjobsusa.com
URL: http://www.bestjobsusa.com

Description: Employment search engine and database offering employment ads from @IT1Employment Review Magazine@IT2. **Main files include:** Career Guide (job opportunities, resume posting, career fairs, company profiles); HR Solutions (trends, statistics, resume searching); News to Peruse (industry information and news).

★13570★ **Bio.com Career Center**
E-mail: careers@bio.com
URL: http://www.bio.com/jobs/index.jhtml
Description: Contains a job index searchable by employer name, discipline, or location. Suitable for job hunters tracking down specific medical, biological, biochemical, or pharmaceutical companies and positions. Also references at Career Guide and Career Forum sections.

★13571★ **Brass Ring**
343 Winter St.
Waltham, MA 02451
Ph: (781)530-5000   Fax: (781)530-5500
URL: http://www.brassring.com
Description: Site offers a database of over 15,000 job listings searchable by job title, technology, and location/company. Also provides a resume posting service, career article search, salary calculator, and Human Resource Center, as well as schedules for career fairs and expos.

★13572★ **California Society of Certified Public Accountants Classifieds**
1235 Radio Rd.
Redwood City, CA 94065-1217
Fr: 800-922-5272
E-mail: info@calcpa.org
URL: http://www.calcpa.org
Description: An accounting job search tool for CPAs in California. Details steps to become a CPA, provides job search posting opportunities for seekers and candidates' pages for employers looking to fill positions.

★13573★ **Career Mag**
URL: http://www.careermag.com
Description: Searchable database with resume bank. **Main files include:** Post Your Jobs; Post Internships; Relocation Assistance Center, Resume Writing Advice; Featured Employers.

★13574★ **Careerbuilder**
URL: http://www.careerbuilder.com
Description: Employment database featuring job listings from national and international newspapers. Employers may also post jobs. Listings are updated on a daily basis. Also contains sections on resumes, interviews, relocation services, and more. Also links to Resumezapper.com for rapid resume distribution. E-mail system for job lead alert.

★13575★ **CareerBuilder.com**
URL: http://www.careerbuilder.com
Description: Job-seekers may search job board through several different career headers, such as field of interest, location or keyword search, also may post resume to Career Builder database. Employers and recruiters may log on to post jobs and review resumes. Also contains resume and career resources, e-mail alerts.

★13576★ **Career.com**
E-mail: info@career.com
URL: http://www.career.com
Description: Users can perform job searches by company, location, discipline, and for new graduates. Other features include "Hot Jobs," CyberFair, and a resume save option.

★13577★ **CareerMag.com**
URL: http://www.careermag.com
Description: Online magazine containing many columns, features and articles about job hunting. Also holds job listings for browsers. **Main files include:** Job Openings, Employers, Articles, Resume Bank, Career Forum, On Campus, Diversity, Be Your Own Boss, Job Fairs, Recruiter Directory, Consultant Directory, Products & Services, Relocation Resources, Career Links, Post Your Jobs. Has information section for self-employed and freelance workers.

★13578★ **CareerOneStop**
Fr: 877-348-0502
E-mail: info@careeronestop.org
URL: http://www.careeronestop.org/
Description: Provides detailed job listings in all areas. Use the site's self-directed search feature to find a job opening in a particular field, browse by company name, or connect to one of the local job banks in each state. **Main files include:** Employers, Job Seekers, Job Market Info, Search Tips, Instructions, America's Talent Bank, and America's Career Infonet.

★13579★ **CareerPerfect.com**
Ph: 800-716-0705
URL: http://www.careerperfect.com
Description: Provides links to career software and books; lists FAQ's on career planning, resumes, job searching, and interviewing; identifies online job databases; accepts resumes for posting.

★13580★ **CareerShop.com**
12200 W. Colonial Dr., No. 201
Winter Garden, FL 34787
Ph: (407)877-5992   Fax: (407)877-5932
URL: http://www.careershop.com
Description: Database of resume profiles and employment opportunites. Job hunters can post resumes and perform job searches. Employers can search resumes and post job openings. AutoHire system offers the ability to enhance the recruiting section of an organization's current web site. It can also be used as a stand-alone site for organizations that have no current site.

★13581★ **Chronicle of Higher Education Career Network**
1255 Twenty-Third St., NW 7th Fl.
Washington, DC 20037
Fax: (202)452-1033
E-mail: help@chronicle.com
URL: http://www.chronicle.com/jobs/
Description: Provided by the Chronicle of Higher Education, a fully searchable online listing of jobs currently available at universities and colleges in the U.S. and abroad. Position listings include faculty, research, administrative and executive openings. Also provides an e-mail notification service for specific jobs, job market news, and links.

★13582★ **Classified Solutions Group, Inc.**
PO Box 1542
Radio City Station
New York, NY 10101-1542
Ph: (646)416-6665   Fax: (212)604-9361
E-mail: info@classifiedsolutionsgroup.com
URL: http://www.careerengine.com
Description: Job board where seekers may search for jobs, recruit a job search agent to assist them, and take advantage of relocation tools. Provides links to specific field information and diversity-concentrated sites.

★13583★ **CollegeGrad.com**
234 E. College Ave., Ste. 200
State College, PA 16801
Ph: (262)375-6700
URL: http://www.collegegrad.com
Description: Site contains the online version of the College Grad Job Hunter-an entry level job search book. **Main files include:** Preparation, Resumes and Cover Letters, Job Postings, Interviews and Negotiations, New Job. Employers may also search for candidates fitting positions.

★13584★ **ComputerJobs.com**
280 Interstate North Cir., SE, Ste. 300
Atlanta, GA 30339-2411
Ph: 800-850-0045
URL: http://www.computerjobs.com
Description: The site is an employment tool for technology professionals. Information on positions is updated hourly for seekers. Jobs may be searched by skill, or by location nationally or in a specific state or city job market. Contains thousands of job postings. National jobs may be posted for free. Also career resources for IT professionals.

★13585★ **Computerworld Careers**
URL: http://www.computerworld.com/careertopics/careers
Description: Offers career opportunities for IT (information technology) professionals. Job seekers may search the jobs database, register at the site, and read about job surveys and employment trends. Employers may post jobs.

★13586★ Computing Research Association Job Announcements

1100 17th St., NW
Washington, DC 20036-4632
Ph: (202)234-2111   Fax: (202)667-1066
URL: http://www.cra.org/main/cra.jobs.html

Description: Contains dated links to national college and university computer technology positions.

★13587★ Contract Job Hunter

C.E. Publications Inc.
PO Box 3006
Bothell, WA 98041-3006
Ph: (425)806-5200   Fax: (425)806-5585
E-mail: staff@cjhunter.com
URL: http://www.cjhunter.com/

Description: Contains information on immediate and anticipated contract job openings throughout the United States, Canada, and overseas. All jobs listed are temporary technical jobs that are usually higher paying than similar direct jobs. Jobs database is updated every hour. Hosts Subscribers' Lounge, advertisers section, a guest area, and links. Also directory of contract staffing firms.

★13588★ Delta T Group

E-mail: pa@deltatg.com
URL: http://www.delta-tgroup.com

Description: Specialized contract temporary staffing source for healthcare professionals in the fields of social service, psychiatry, mental health, and substance abuse. Organizations may request services and staffing; job seekers may view services provided, submit a resume, or peruse jobs available.

★13589★ Dice.com

4101 NW Urbandale Dr.
Urbandale, IA 50322
Fax: (515)280-1452   Fr: 877-386-3323
URL: http://www.dice.com

Description: Job search database for computer consultants and high-tech professionals. listing thousands of high tech permanent contract and consulting jobs for programmers, software engineers, systems administrators, web developers, and hardware engineers. Also free career advice e-mail newsletter and job posting e-alerts.

★13590★ The Digital Financier

URL: http://www.dfin.com

Description: Job postings from financial companies. Offers links to major job search websites. Has leads for further training and allows companies to post their own job links.

★13591★ EmployMED: Healthcare Job Listings

URL: http://www.evalumed.com/employmed.cfm

Description: Lists practice opportunities throughout North America for all medical specialties. Contains job listings directory. Posting option is available for those who wish to advertise jobs. **Fee:** $25 per month per posting for minimum of two months.

★13592★ Employment Guide.com

Trader Publishing Co.
Fr: 877-876-4039
URL: http://www.employmentguide.com/

Description: Users may search job listings, file their resume online, hunt for international jobs, search employers, and visit the specialized healthcare job database. Employers may list jobs and search resumes. Site also lists affiliated and associated job sites.

★13593★ Employment Resources for People with Disabilities

E-mail: familyvillage@waisman.wisc.edu
URL: http://www.familyvillage.wisc.edu/general/employmt.htm

Description: Site offering employment and career-related links to job seekers with disabilities.

★13594★ Employment911.com

175 Strafford Ave., Ste. 1
Wayne, PA 19087
E-mail: contact@employment911.com
URL: http://www.employment911.com

Description: Seekers can access free email, resume posting, job search organizer & personal web calendar. Also contains job meta-search engine, career resources, and links to online education. Registration is free.

★13595★ FASEB Career Resources

9650 Rockville Pike
Bethesda, MD 20814-3998
Ph: (301)634-7000   Fax: (301)634-7001
E-mail: careers@faseb.org.
URL: http://www.faseb.org/careers/

Description: A career opportunity site combined with a development service that attempts to pair applicants at all career levels with employers who hire biomedical scientists and technicians. Biomedical career development is highlighted through career resource tools. **Main files include:** Careers Online DataNet, Career Online Classified.

★13596★ FCS - The 1st Choice in Psychiatric Recruitment

1711 Ashley Cir., Ste. 6
Bowling Green, KY 42104-5801
Fax: (270)782-1055   Fr: 800-783-9152
E-mail: admin@fcspsy.com
URL: http://www.fcspsy.com

Description: Physician search firm specializing in the recruitment of psychiatrists. After the applicant fills out an interest survey, a tailored search is run on the jobs database. Confidential and free.

★13597★ FedWorld Federal Job Search

National Technical Information Service
5285 Port Royal Rd.
Springfield, VA 22161
Ph: (703)605-6000   Fr: 800-553-6847
E-mail: helpdesk@fedworld.gov
URL: http://www.fedworld.gov/

Description: Database containing employment information in the public sector. Listings include address, job title and information, contact information, geographic location, and data of availability, among others. **Main files include:** NTIS Federal Job Opportunities; Atlanta Regional Federal Jobs; Chicago Regional Federal Jobs; Dallas Regional Federal Jobs; Philadelphia Regional Federal Jobs; San Francisco Regional Federal Jobs; Washington DC Regional Federal Jobs; National Federal Jobs; S&S Federal Positions Available; Public Health Service Positions; Federal Jobs Listed by State; Atlantic Overseas; Pacific Overseas; Puerto Rico; Virgin Islands; Information on Downloading Files; Federal Jobs EMail Forum; Exit to Main Menu; and Enter Jobs File Library. **Fee:** Free.

★13598★ Financial Job Network

15030 Ventura Blvd., No. 378
Sherman Oaks, CA 91403
E-mail: info@fjn.com
URL: http://www.fjn.com

Description: Contains information on international and national employment opportunities for those in the financial job market. Job listings may be submitted, as well as resumes. **Main files include:** Testimonials, Calendar, Corporate Listings, FJN Clients, more. **Fee:** Free to candidates.

★13599★ First Steps in the Hunt: Daily News for Online Job Hunters

E-mail: suggestions@interbiznet.com
URL: http://www.interbiznet.com/hunt/index.html

Description: Database provides a wide variety of information on job hunting on the Internet, as well as links to other sources of information. Included are examples of online web page resumes and links to information about publishing them. Also includes current and archived articles, company job sites, and a listing of job hunting tools and products that may help in the job search. **Main files include:** Sponsors; Tools; Archives; Products; and Info.

★13600★ FlipDog.com

Monster.com
URL: http://www.flipdog.com

Description: A Monster.com web site. Job search site with job board, resume posting, automated job finders with e-mail alert, resume coaching and broadcasting, career resource center and semi-monthly newsletter. Registration is free.

★13601★ Freeality Online Career and Job Search
E-mail: freeality@juno.com
URL: http://www.freeality.com/jobst.htm
Description: Listing of career-related search engines, along with links to other career resources.

★13602★ FreeJobSearchEngines.com
URL: http://www.freejobsearchengines.com/
Description: Job board meta-search engine grouping jobs by geography. Seekers can search in the United States, the United Kingdom, Australia, Canada and Hong Kong.

★13603★ GasWork.com: The Largest Internet Anesthesia Employment Resource
Ph: 800-828-2203
E-mail: support@gaswork.com
URL: http://www.gaswork.com
Description: The largest anesthesia employment resource. Lists positions for anesthesiologists, CRNA's, and more. Visitors may post or search jobs.

★13604★ Genetics Society of America:Positions Open
E-mail: society@genetics-gsa.org
URL: http://www.genetics-gsa.org
Description: Listing of position announcements formerly published in Genetics. Members may e-mail job listings to the site to be posted.

★13605★ Graduate School of Library and Information Science Resources
University of Illinois at Urbana-Champaign
501 E. Daniel St.
MC 493
Champaign, IL 61820-6211
Ph: (217)333-3280   Fax: (217)244-3302
Fr: 800-982-0914
E-mail: gslis@uiuc.edu
URL: http://www.lis.uiuc.edu
Description: Database contains links to site posting library science related jobs available.

★13606★ GrantsNet
E-mail: grantsnet@aaas.org
URL: http://www.grantsnet.org/search/srch_specify.cfm
Description: Grant-locating site intended for scientists in training who may become vulnerable in an era of competitive funding. Includes a directory of over 600 programs with contact information within a searchable database.

★13607★ Great Insurance Jobs
Fr: 800-818-4898
URL: http://www.greatinsurancejobs.com
Description: Contains varied insurance positions. Job seekers may browse employee profiles, post resumes, and read descriptions

of hundreds of recently-posted insurance jobs.

★13608★ Guru.com
5001 Baum Blvd., Ste. 760
Pittsburgh, PA 15213
Ph: (412)687-1316   Fax: (412)687-4466
URL: http://www.guru.com
Description: Job board specializing in contract jobs for creative and information technology professionals. Also provides online incorporation and educational opportunities for independent contractors along with articles and advice.

★13609★ Health Care Job Store
395 South End Ave., Ste. 15-D
New York, NY 10280
Ph: (561)630-5201
E-mail: jobs@healthcarejobstore.com
URL: http://www.healthcarejobstore.com/
Description: Job sites include every job title in the healthcare industry, every healthcare industry and every geographic location in the U.S.

★13610★ Health Care Recruitment Online
Ph: 800-322-1463
E-mail: info@HealthcareRecruitment
URL: http://www.healthcareers-online.com/
Description: Helps seekers find healthcare positions through on-line postings with national staffing companies and hospital partners. **Main files include:** Featured Employers, Job Search, Immediate Openings, Relocating, Career Management, State boards, and more.

★13611★ Health Search USA
Fax: (602)650-0664   Fr: 800-899-2200
E-mail: info@healthsearchusa.com
URL: http://www.healthsearchusa.com
Description: A site for national physician recruitment. Offers job postings classified by region and salary comparison.

★13612★ HealthCareerWeb
URL: http://www.healthcareerweb.com/
Description: Advertises jobs for healthcare professionals. **Main files include:** Jobs, Employers, Resumes, Jobwire. Relocation tools and career guidance resources available.

★13613★ HelpWanted.com
E-mail: admin@helpwanted.com
URL: http://www.helpwanted.com
Description: Site providing job postings, resume service, and listing of employment agencies and recruiters. Caters to job seekers, employers, and agencies.

★13614★ Illinois Certified Public Accountant Society Career Services
550 W. Jackson, Ste. 900
Chicago, IL 60661-5716
Ph: (312)993-0407   Fax: (312)993-9954
URL: http://www.icpas.org/icpas/career-services/job-seekers.asp
Description: Offers job hunting aid to members of the Illinois CPA Society only. Opportunity for non-members to join online. **Main files include:** Overview of Services, Resume Match, Career Seminars, Career Resources, Free Job Listings, Per Diem Pool, and Career Bibliographies.

★13615★ Institute of Food Technologists - IFT Career Center
525 W. Van Buren, Ste. 1000
Chicago, IL 60607
Ph: (312)782-8424   Fr: (312)782-8348
E-mail: info@atsift.org
URL: http://www.ift.org
Description: Offers job information and resources for those considering the Food Science and Technology field. Employers may post for full- or part-time positions and have the option of receiving a resume file of current job seekers. IFT members may register for a six-month confidential service to have their credentials reviewed by food industry employers. Job seekers who list credentials will receive the monthly Jobs Available bulletin. **Main files include:** Employment and Salary Information, How to Find Your First Job in the Food Sciences, Resources for Non-US Job Seekers, and more.

★13616★ Internet Career Connection
Gonyea and Associates, Inc.
URL: http://www.iccweb.com/
Description: Online career and employment guidance agency. Site's services include: Help Wanted USA-job seekers can access one million help wanted ads; U.S. Government Employment Opportunities; Worldwide Resume/Talent Bank-job seekers can post resumes. Employers may view over 50,000 Resumes and career advice articles.

★13617★ Job.com
E-mail: jobseekersupport@job.com
URL: http://www.job.com
Description: Seekers can post resume free, search through job databank and use website "powertools" such as resume coaching and distribution, career direction report, personal salary report, online education and self-employment links, and more.

★13618★ JobFind.com
Ph: (617)426-3000
E-mail: jobfind@jobfind.com
URL: http://www.jobfind.com
Description: Job site that includes job search board, resume posting with HTML capabilities, "inbox" for e-mail job alerts, corporate profiles, job fair search and career resources.

★13619★ JobHunt: On-Line Job Meta-list
E-mail: info@job-hunt.org
URL: http://www.job-hunt.org/
Description: Database containing list of career search websites from various sources in the United States. **Main files include:** Categories: Academia; Classified Ads; Companies; General; Newsgroup Searches; Recruiting Agencies; Science, Engineering, and Medicine. Other Job Resources: Commercial Services; Other Meta-lists; Reference Material; Resume Banks; University Career Resource Centers. Also contains links to other job sites and free PDF file on choosing a career search site.

★13620★ JobListings.net
URL: http://www.joblistings.net
Description: Job search and resume posting site. Registration and posting is free.

★13621★ Jobs.com
E-mail: sales@wantedtech.com
URL: http://hoovers.wantedjobs.com
Description: Search engine for job postings.

★13622★ JobStar
E-mail: electrajobstar@earthlink.net
URL: http://jobstar.org/
Description: Job search guide based in California. Includes career guides and information on local, national and international career counseling centers, resumes, salaries, and hidden jobs.

★13623★ JobWeb
National Association of Colleges and Employers
62 Highland Ave.
Bethlehem, PA 18017-9085
Ph: (610)868-1421   Fax: (610)868-0208
Fr: 800-544-5272
URL: http://www.jobweb.com
Description: Site is maintained by the National Association of Colleges and Employers (NACE). Provides career-related information and job listings to college students and graduates.

★13624★ Law.com: Law Jobs
URL: http://www.lawjobs.com
Description: Visitors can post job openings for attorneys, legal support staff and temporary workers. Also resources for legal recruiters and temporary staffing agencies.

★13625★ Library and Information Technology Association Job Listing
E-mail: lita@ala.org
URL: http://www.lita.org
Description: Contains weekly postings of available library jobs. Searchable by region.

★13626★ Library Job Postings on the Internet
E-mail: sarah@libraryjobpostings.org
URL: http://www.libraryjobpostings.org
Description: Employers may post library position announcements. Also contains links to around 250 library employment sites and links to library-related e-mail lists. Positions are searchable by region and type of library.

★13627★ Mandy's International Film and TV Production Directory
E-mail: Directory@mandy.com
URL: http://www.mandy.com/1/filmtvjobs.cfm
Description: Employment site intended for film and tv professionals. Employers may post free Jobs Offered listings. Job seekers may post free Jobs Wanted ads.

★13628★ MBA Careers
3934 SW Corbett Ave.
Portland, OR 97239
Ph: (503)221-7779   Fax: (503)221-7780
E-mail: eric@careerexposure.com
URL: http://www.mbacareers.com
Description: Job site that provides resume posting, databank search and e-mail alert services to MBA and other advanced graduate degree holders.

★13629★ MedExplorer
E-mail: medmaster@medexplorer.com
URL: http://www.medexplorer.com
Description: Employment postings make up one module of this general medical site. Other sections contain: Newsletter, Classifieds, and Discussion Forum.

★13630★ MedSource Consultants
300 Main St.
Stamford, CT 06901
Fax: (203)324-0555   Fr: 800-575-2880
E-mail: dpascale@medsourceconsultants.com
URL: http://www.medsourceconsultants.com
Description: Site houses a physician search and consulting company for psychiatrists. Consultants attempt to match job seekers to positions according to the individual's personal and professional needs. This page also aids institutions looking to recruit psychiatrists.

★13631★ Medzilla
URL: http://www.medzilla.com
Description: General medical website which matches employers and job hunters to their ideal employees and jobs through search capabilities. **Main files include:** Post Jobs, Search Resumes, Post Resumes, Search Jobs, Head Hunters, Articles, Salary Survey.

★13632★ Monster
E-mail: webmaster@atsmonster.com
URL: http://www.monster.com
Description: An interactive, continually expanding database of current job openings, including an online career fair, career search help, employer profiles, and a resume posting service. Searching is available by industry, location, company, discipline and keyword. Users can search over 50,000 of position openings, advertise openings, or submit resumes. Employers pay a fee for posting position openings and company profiles. An online form allows for contact with the producers of the database. **Main files include:** Press Box, Career Center, Job Search Agent, Recruiters' Center. **Fee:** Free to job seekers; fees for job advertisers.

★13633★ Monster Healthcare
URL: http://healthcare.monster.com/
Description: Delivers nationwide access to healthcare recruiting. Employers can post job listings or ads. Job seekers can post and code resumes, and search over 150,000 healthcare job listings, healthcare career advice columns, career resources information, and member employer profiles and services.

★13634★ MonsterTRAK
11845 W. Olympic Blvd., Ste. 500
Los Angeles, CA 90064
Fr: 800-999-8725
URL: http://www.monstertrak.monster.com/
Description: College-targeted job hunting and recruiting site. Students and alumni may enter a user profile or resume to be reviewed by potential employers, or search job listings without doing so. Employers may enter full-time, part-time, temporary, and internship opportunities into the database to be reviewed by students and recent graduates, and may review resumes.

★13635★ National Insurance Recruiters Association
URL: http://www.insurancerecruiters.com
Description: Contains lists of recruiters (listed by department and line of business) and available insurance positions.

★13636★ NationJob Network
URL: http://www.nationjob.com/
Description: Online job database containing job listings and company profiles. **Main files include:** Specialty Pages; Custom Jobs Pages; Community Pages; Customer Success Stories.

★13637★ Net Temps
URL: http://www.net-temps.com/
Description: Site specializing in the Staffing industry serving direct placement and temporary (contract) professionals. Net-Temps provides a convenient and free method to post resumes, inquire about available positions and apply for jobs online. Recruiters

utilize Net-Temps to publicize available employment opportunities and search the Resume Bank to identify qualified job candidates.

★13638★ **NetJobs**
E-mail: info@atsnetjobs.com
URL: http://www.netjobs.com

Description: Source for Canadian job hunters and employers. Job seekers may post resumes online and search through job openings. Searches can be performed by job category, company name, or location, or on listings posted within the last ten days.

★13639★ **NowHiring.com**
PowerOne Media, Inc.
130 S. 1st St., 3rd Fl.
Ann Arbor, MI 48104
URL: http://www.nowhiring.com

Description: Job seekers can scan job opportunities either by employer or by type of work, and reply electronically to job listings. They can submit a resume and confidential profile to be placed in the database. The job seeker's identity is released to employers only with the listee's permission. Employers can list job postings for a 30-day period at the rate of $195 for one job, $495 for three jobs, $975 for ten jobs or $7,500 for an unlimited amount of job postings for one year.

★13640★ **NSBE Online**
URL: http://www.nsbe.org/careers/jobs.php

Description: A section of the website of the National Society of Black Engineers. **Main files include:** Job Search (includes full-time, co-ops, internships, and student jobs), Post a Job, Post a Resume. **Fee:** $250 to post a job for 60 days.

★13641★ **Online Sports Career Center**
Fr: 800-856-2638
E-mail: comments@atsonlinesports.com
URL: http://www.onlinesports.com/pages/careercenter.html

Description: Resource for sports-related career opportunities, as well as a resume bank for the perusal of potential employers within the sports and recreation industries. **Main files include:** Job Bank, Resume Bank, Newsletter, Work With Online Sports, Other Internet Resources.

★13642★ **The Paquin Group**
1134 Celebration Blvd.
Celebration, FL 34747
Ph: (407)566-1010
E-mail: info@thepaquingroup.com
URL: http://www.thepaquingroup.com

Description: Healthcare retail consulting firm.

★13643★ **Premier Careers, Inc.**
117 Main Ave. N.
Fayetteville, TN 37334
Ph: (931)438-7070
E-mail: info@atspremiercareers.com
URL: http://www.premiercareers.com

Description: Contains a database with information on candidates searching for jobs in the property and casualty insurance industry and with national sales organizations. Houses resumes and letters of reference. Candidate searches may be run by industry, geography, job title, years of experience, compensation, education, and/or accreditation. Also offers resume writing and interviewing tips to job hunters.

★13644★ **PrintJobs.com**
Newhouse Associates
PO Box 135
Bowmansville, NY 14026
Ph: (716)686-9251   Fax: (716)686-9258
E-mail: printjobs@roadrunner.com
URL: http://www.printjobs.com

Description: Aims to find suitable graphic arts jobs for qualified candidates. Over a hundred jobs are maintained and updated on the site. **Fee:** Must be paid by employers using the site; no registration charge for job hunters.

★13645★ **Quintessential Careers**
URL: http://www.quintcareers.com/business_jobs.html

Description: Site contains information on jobs in the business sector, primarily in accounting, finance, and consulting. Provides detailed information on job search aids and employer profiles, with job areas broken down into subject. Data on salaries, skill requirements, trends and other important factors are expanded from each subject-specific occupation listing. There are also many links to other job-seeking related sites and dozens of company sites on the Internet. **Main files include:** Careers in Finance; Careers in Accounting; Careers in Management; Other Career Sites; Recommended Books.

★13646★ **RadWorking.com**
E-mail: info@atsradworking.com
URL: http://www.RadWorking.com

Description: Employment resource dedicated to the profession of radiology. Site is divided into various job-search sections based on job type or nature of support position.

★13647★ **Recruiters Online Network**
E-mail: deb@recruitersonline.com
URL: http://www.recruitersonline.com/

Description: Site is used by over 8,000 recruiters, search firms, employment agencies, and employment professionals. Job seekers may read the Careers Online Magazine, post resumes, and search jobs. **Fee:** Free to job seekers; fee for recruiters.

★13648★ **RehabJobs Online**
PO Box 480536
Los Angeles, CA 90048
Ph: (213)938-7718   Fax: (213)938-9609
Fr: 800-43-REHAB
E-mail: support@atsrehabjobs.com
URL: http://www.rehabjobs.com

Description: Resource center for the professional therapist. **Main files include:** Therapists Only, Therapy Forums, Nationwide Job Search (database), Therapy Job Outlook, Therapy Job Search Utilities, Therapy Links, Information for Employers and Recruiters.

★13649★ **RehabWorld**
URL: http://www.rehabworld.com

Description: Site for rehabilitation professionals to learn about the profession and locate jobs. Includes user groups, salary surveys, and chat capabilities. **Main files include:** Physical Therapy, Occupational Therapy, Speech Therapy, Mental Health, Employer World, Student World, International World, Forum.

★13650★ **Resume-Net**
Myrtle Ave. S., Unit 2
Clearwater, FL 33756
Ph: (727)443-3233
E-mail: info@atsresume-net.com
URL: http://www.resumenet.com

Description: Online resume publishing service. Assists job seekers in creating online resumes. Resumes are searchable by location and profession.

★13651★ **Resume Safari**
URL: http://www.resumesafari.com/

Description: Site serves as a resume distribution service. Once submitted, a job hunter's resume will be distributed to over 1,500 locations on the web **Fee:** $60 or $80 depending on tier.

★13652★ **Saludos.com**
Ph: (323)726-2188   Fax: 800-730-3560
Fr: 800-748-6426
E-mail: info@atssaludos.com
URL: http://www.saludos.com

Description: Supported by Saludos Hispanos magazine, this site is devoted to promoting Hispanic careers and education. It is a prime resource for employers to gain access to the resumes of bilingual college graduates. Online job listings and a resume pool are offered, as well as a career center, links to Hispanic resources, career links, and access to Saludos Magazine.

★13653★ **The SciWeb Biotechnology Career Home Page**
E-mail: info@biocareer.com
URL: http://www.biocareer.com

Description: Career resource center resulting from the collaboration of the Biotechnology Industry Organization (BIO) and *SciWeb*. Aims to connect job seekers with recruiters in the biotechnology industry. **Main files include:** Post Resume, Search Resume, Post Job, Search Job, Career Resources. **Fee:** 150.00 for the first two months, $75.00 per additional monthly renewal. Academic PostDoctoral Listings are posted for free.

★13654★ **Social Work and Social Services Jobs Online**
George Warren Brown School of Social Work Washington University
Campus Box 1196
1 Brookings Dr.
St. Louis, MO 63130-4899
Ph: (314)935-6600　　Fax: (314)935-4859
Fr: 800-321-2426
E-mail: msw@wustl.edu
URL: http://gwbweb.wustl.edu/jobs/

Description: Specialized database of social work and social services jobs gives a large list of openings sorted by location (both within and outside the United States). Employers may submit job openings. Site also contains career resources and links to related internet job sites.

★13655★ **Society of Broadcast Engineers Job Line**
Ph: (317)846-9000　　Fax: (317)846-9120
E-mail: kjones@sbe.org
URL: http://www.sbe.org/jobline.html

Description: Job Line is one benefit of membership in the Society of Broadcast Engineers. Includes a resume service to distribute resumes to employers, job contact information, and descriptions of job openings. Also accessible via telephone.

★13656★ **Summer Jobs**
URL: http://www.summerjobs.com

Description: Database listing seasonal and part-time job opportunities. Job listings are organized by country, state, region, and city. Primary focus is on summer jobs for students and education professionals.

★13657★ **Telecommuting Jobs**
E-mail: contact@atstjobs.com
URL: http://www.tjobs.com

Description: Job hunters may enter a resume or post a job-wanted listing. Employers may search talent available and post job availabilities. Site also includes tools to connect telecommuters with employers and job news about telecommuting.

★13658★ **TMP/Hudson Global Resources**
URL: http://job.us.hudson.com

Description: Professional staffing firm website. Job seekers can search job databank and submit their resume to the firm for posting to employers.

★13659★ **Today's Military**
URL: http://www.todaysmilitary.com/app/tm/careers

Description: Site provides details on many enlisted and officer occupations and describes training, advancement, and educational services within each of the major services. Includes browsing capabilities to match positions with interests.

★13660★ **TopEchelon.com**
PO Box 21390
Canton, OH 44701-1390
Ph: (330)455-1433　　Fax: (330)455-8813
E-mail: info@topechelon.com
URL: http://www.topechelon.com

Description: Online placement recruiter network. Job seekers may search job board compiled by network member recruiters. They can also create an online profile for recruiters' reviews. They can also contact specific member recruiters in their field of business.

★13661★ **United Search Associates: Health Network USA**
PO Box 52
Hoopeston, IL 60942
E-mail: info@unitedsearch.com
URL: http://www.hnusa.com

Description: Visitors may explore healthcare positions, submit an electronic resume, or advertise with the site.

★13662★ **USAJOBS - United States Office of Personnel Management**
URL: http://www.usajobs.opm.gov

Description: Provides information about jobs that are available in the Federal government. The online search program allows users to search job announcements on the bulletin board by either series number or job title. Also has resume builder and e-mail alert services. **Fee:** Free.

★13663★ **Vault.com**
150 W. 22nd St.
New York, NY 10011
E-mail: feedback@staff.vault.com
URL: http://www.vault.com

Description: Job board website with searches emphasizing jobs in legal, business, consulting and finance fields of practice. Contains online profile posting, resume review, company research, salary calculators and relocation tools.

★13664★ **Wall Street Journal Executive Career Site**
URL: http://www.careerjournal.com

Description: Wall Street Journal CareerJournal.com contains numerous job-related resources, search engines and resume databases for job-seekers, employers and executive recruiters. Contains career columnists, salary negotiating instruments, discussion forums and e-mail alerting system. **Fee:** Must be subscribers to WSJ.com in order to fully utilize resources; year's subscription is $99.

★13665★ **WetFeet.com**
The Folger Bldg.
101 Howard St. Ste. 300
San Francisco, CA 94105
Ph: (415)284-7900　　Fr: (415)284-7910
E-mail: services@wetfeet.com
URL: http://www.wetfeet.com

Description: Job board website with free membership for job seekers. Contains job board, resume listing, self assessment guides, company and city research, discussion forums, e-guides and online bookstore, salary calculators and listings of internship opportunities.

★13666★ **What Color Is Your Parachute? Job Hunters Bible**
URL: http://www.jobhuntersbible.com/

Description: Companion internet guide to the best selling job-hunting book, What Color is Your Parachute? Includes lists of helpful links to other resources on the internet. **Main files include:** Jobs, Resumes, Counseling, Contacts, Research, Dealing With Depression.

★13667★ **Women at Work**
50 N. Hill Ave., Ste. 300
Pasadena, CA 91106
Ph: (626)796-6870　　Fax: (626)793-7396
E-mail: info@womenatwork.org
URL: http://www.womenatwork1.org/

Description: Site of nonprofit job and career resource center, serving the greater Los Angeles area.

★13668★ **Work from Home**
URL: http://www.jobs-telecommuting.com

Description: Contains a listing of over 700 companies currently looking for telecommuters. Employers may add or remove job listings. Also information on starting a home business available.

★13669★ **WorkTree.com**
E-mail: support@worktree.com
URL: http://www.worktree.com

Description: Job search engine portal, listing career-related search engines and websites by geography, field of practice, experience level, company and more. Also lists links to career resources such as resume coaching and interviewing tips. Resume broadcast service available. **Fee:** Membership available in several levels, depending on length of membership desired; three months' unlimited access is $47.

★13670★ **The World Wide Web Employment Office**
URL: http://www.employmentoffice.net/

Description: Portal to job and resume banks and board for employers and job hunters.

★13671★ **WSA Executive Job Search Center**
E-mail: info@execcoachkc.com
URL: http://www.wsacorp.com
Description: A site intended for $50K-$700K range executives. Offers resume preparation, critiques and distribution, and interview preparation.

★13672★ **Yahoo! Careers**
700 1st. Ave
Sunnyvale, CA 94089
Fax: (408)349-3301   Fr: (408)349-3300
URL: http://careers.yahoo.com/

Description: Contains over 360,000 jobs for job seekers to search and post resumes for, as well as weekly features, relocation resources, a daily column, and links to resume banks and services and temp agencies. Special sections are devoted to industry research, company research, advice, high tech jobs, and first jobs and internships.

★13673★ **Yahoo! Hotjobs**
45 W. 18th St., 6th FL.
New York, NY 10011
Ph: (646)351-3500
E-mail: support@hotjobs.com
URL: http://hotjobs.yahoo.com/

Description: Job board searchable by fields, company or geographic location. Seekers may also post resumes and receive e-mail alerts. Also resources for relocation, resumes and interview tips, salary negotiation and self-assessment.

★13674★ **ZDNet Tech Jobs**
URL: http://www.zdnet.com/

Description: Site houses a listing of national employment opportunities for professionals in high tech fields. Also contains resume building tips and relocation resources.

SOFTWARE

★13675★ **Multimedia Job Search**
Cambridge Educational
PO Box 2053
Princeton, NJ 08543-2053
Ph: 800-257-5126   Fax: (609)671-0266
Fr: 800-468-4227
E-mail: custserv@films.com
URL: http://www.cambridgeeducational.com

CD-ROM. $99.95. 1997. Includes videos, narration, and on-screen text. Users learn about getting a competitive edge in today's job market, traditional and nontraditional job search tools, resumes and cover letters, and interviewing skills.

Environmental Opportunities

REFERENCE WORKS

★13676★ 100 Jobs in the Environment
Macmillan Publishing Company
175 Fifth Ave.
New York, NY 10010
Ph: (646)307-5151   Fr: 800-428-5331
URL: http://www.macmillan.com/

Debra Quintana. 1997. $14.95 (paper). 218 pages. Each job profile includes prospects for finding work and describes a typical day.

★13677★ Association of Consulting Foresters-Membership Specialization Directory
Association of Consulting Foresters
312 Montgomery St., Ste. 208
Alexandria, VA 22314
Ph: (703)548-0990   Fax: (703)548-6395
URL: http://www.acf-foresters.org

Annual, August. Free. Covers nearly 500 member forestry consulting firms and professional foresters who earn the largest part of their income from consulting. Entries include: Name, address, phone, specialties, background, career data, staff (if a consulting firm), geographic area served, capabilities, including equipment available and foreign language proficiency. Arrangement: Alphabetical. Indexes: Name, office location, language, international capability.

★13678★ Careers in the Environment
The McGraw-Hill Companies
PO Box 182604
Columbus, OH 43272
Fax: (614)759-3749   Fr: 877-883-5524
E-mail: customer.service@mcgraw-hill.com
URL: http://www.mcgraw-hill.com

Michael Fasulo and Paul Walker. Second edition, 2000. $17.95; $13.95 (paper). 290 pages. Comprehensive information on the diverse career opportunities available in environmental services.

★13679★ Careers for Environmental Types and Others Who Respect the Earth
The McGraw-Hill Companies
PO Box 182604
Columbus, OH 43272
Fax: (614)759-3749   Fr: 877-883-5524
E-mail: customer.service@mcgraw-hill.com
URL: http://www.mcgraw-hill.com

Jane Kinney and Mike Fasulo. Second edition, 2001. $13.95; $10.74 (paper). 192 pages. Describes environmentally friendly positions with corporations, government, and environmental organizations.

★13680★ Careers for Health Nuts and Others Who Like to Stay Fit
The McGraw-Hill Companies
PO Box 182604
Columbus, OH 43272
Fax: (614)759-3749   Fr: 877-883-5524
E-mail: customer.service@mcgraw-hill.com
URL: http://www.mcgraw-hill.com

Blythe Camenson. Second edition, 2005. $13.95 (paper). 208 pages.

★13681★ The Complete Guide to Environmental Careers in the 21st Century
Island Press
1718 Connecticut Ave. NW, Ste. 300
Washington, DC 20009
Ph: (202)232-7933   Fax: (202)234-1328
Fr: 800-621-2736
URL: http://www.islandpress.org/

Environmental Careers Organization Staff. Third edition, 1998. (paper). 447 pages. $28.50

★13682★ Conservation Directory
National Wildlife Federation
11100 Wildlife Center Dr.
Reston, VA 20190-5362
Ph: (703)638-6000   Fax: (703)438-6061
Fr: 800-822-9919
E-mail: admin@nwf.org
URL: http://www.nwf.org/conservationdirectory/

Annual; latest edition March 2007. $80.00 for individuals. Covers over 4,000 organizations, agencies, colleges and universities with conservation programs and more than 18,000 officials concerned with environmental conservation, education, and natural resource use and management. Entries include: Agency name, address, branch or subsidiary office name and address, names and titles of key personnel, descriptions of program areas, size of membership (where appropriate), telephone, fax, e-mail and URL addresses. Arrangement: Classified by type of organization. Indexes: Personal name, keyword, geographic, organization.

★13683★ Exploring Careers in the National Parks
Rosen Publishing Group, Inc.
29 E. 21st St.
New York, NY 10010
Ph: (212)777-3017   Fax: 888-436-4643
Fr: 800-237-9932
URL: http://www.rosenpublishing.com/

Bob Gartner. Revised edition, 1999. $9.95. 192 pages. Describes working for the park service and how to get a job there.

★13684★ Green at Work
Island Press
1718 Connecticut Ave. NW, Ste. 300
Washington, DC 20009
Ph: (202)232-7933   Fax: (202)234-1328
Fr: 800-621-2736
URL: http://www.islandpress.org/

Susan Cohn, Horst Rechelbacher and Lynda Grose. 1995. $25.00 (paper). 452 pages. Identifies career options with an environmental focus and profiles more than 250 companies with environmental initiatives.

★13685★ Hidden Job Market
Peterson's Guides
2000 Lenox Dr.
Box 67005
Lawrenceville, NJ 08648
Ph: (609)896-1800   Fax: (609)896-4531
Fr: 800-338-3282
E-mail: custsvc@petersons.com
URL: http://www.petersons.com

Ninth edition, 1999. $18.95 (paper). 319 pages. Guide to 2,000 fast-growing companies that are hiring now. Focuses on high technology companies in such fields as environmental consulting, genetic engineering, home health care, telecommunications, alternative energy systems, and others. Part of Peterson's Hidden Job Market series.

★13686★ **National Parks**

U.S. National Park Service
Harpers Ferry Center
PO Box 50
Harpers Ferry, WV 25425-0050
Ph: (202)208-4747   Fax: (304)535-6144
URL: http://www.nps.gov/

Biennial, odd years. Covers over 379 areas administered by the National Park Service, including parks, shores, historic sites, 80 national trails, and wild and scenic rivers. Entries include: Name, location, address, acreage (federal, non-federal, and gross), federal facilities, brief description. Arrangement: Most areas are alphabetical by state; geographical and historical by state; wild and scenic rivers and national trails are alphabetical by state. Indexes: Alphabetical by state.

★13687★ **Nature (Career Portraits)**

The McGraw-Hill Companies
PO Box 182604
Columbus, OH 43272
Fax: (614)759-3749   Fr: 877-883-5524
E-mail: customer.service@mcgraw-hill.com
URL: http://www.mcgraw-hill.com

Marjorie Eberts. 1996. $13.95. 96 pages. Highlights a range of careers that focus on the environment, with descriptions of a typical day on the job and interactive exercises for readers.

★13688★ **The New Complete Guide to Environmental Careers**

Island Press
1718 Connecticut Ave. NW, Ste. 300
Washington, DC 20009
Ph: (202)232-7933   Fax: (202)234-1328
Fr: 800-621-2736
URL: http://www.islandpress.org/

John R. Cook, Kevin Doyle, and Bill Sharp. Second edition, 2001. $17.95 (paper). 364 pages. Covers job outlook, entry requirements, examples of actual jobs, and in-depth interviews with more than 100 professionals.

★13689★ **Opportunities in Environmental Careers**

The McGraw-Hill Companies
PO Box 182604
Columbus, OH 43272
Fax: (614)759-3749   Fr: 877-883-5524
E-mail: customer.service@mcgraw-hill.com
URL: http://www.mcgraw-hill.com

Odom Fanning. Revised, 2002. $12.95 (paper). 174 pages. Describes a broad range of opportunities in fields such as environmental health, recreation, physics, and hygiene, and provides job search advice. Part of the "Opportunities in ..." Series.

★13690★ **Opportunities in Forestry Careers**

The McGraw-Hill Companies
PO Box 182604
Columbus, OH 43272
Fax: (614)759-3749   Fr: 877-883-5524
E-mail: customer.service@mcgraw-hill.com
URL: http://www.mcgraw-hill.com

Christopher M. Wille. 2003. $11.95 (paper). 160 pages. Describes the forestry opportunities available in governmental agencies, commercial enterprises, education, and private conservation association, and how to pursue openings. Illustrated. Part of the "Opportunities in ..." Series.

★13691★ **Opportunities in Waste Management Careers**

The McGraw-Hill Companies
PO Box 182604
Columbus, OH 43272
Fax: (614)759-3749   Fr: 877-883-5524
E-mail: customer.service@mcgraw-hill.com
URL: http://www.mcgraw-hill.com

Mark Rowh. 1994. $14.95; $11.95 (paper). 145 pages. Outlines the diverse opportunities in waste management and examines the duties, working conditions, salaries, and future of a variety of positions. Profiles jobs and opportunities in solid waste and waste water management, environmental engineering, soil and wildlife conservation, and related career areas.

★13692★ **Resumes for Environmental Careers**

The McGraw-Hill Companies
PO Box 182604
Columbus, OH 43272
Fax: (614)759-3749   Fr: 877-883-5524
E-mail: customer.service@mcgraw-hill.com
URL: http://www.mcgraw-hill.com

Second edition, 2002. $10.95 (paper). 160 pages. Provides resume advice tailored to people pursuing careers focusing on the environment. Includes sample resumes and cover letters.

NEWSPAPERS, MAGAZINES, AND JOURNALS

★13693★ **Appalachian Trailway News**

Appalachian Trail Conservancy
799 Washington St.
PO Box 807
Harpers Ferry, WV 25425-0807
Ph: (304)535-6331   Fax: (304)535-2667
URL: http://www.appalachiantrail.org/site/c.jkLXJ8MQKtH/b.850199/

$15.00/year for individuals. Magazine on hiking, Appalachian Trail protection, and general conservation issues.

★13694★ **Applied Occupational & Environmental Hygiene**

Applied Industrial Hygiene Inc.
1330 Kemper Meadow Dr., Ste. 600
Cincinnati, OH 45240
Ph: (513)742-2020   Fax: (513)742-3355
URL: http://www.acgih.org

Monthly. $223.00/year for individuals, individual membership; $623.00/year for institutions, institution or organization. Peer-reviewed journal presenting applied solutions for the prevention of occupational and environmental disease and injury.

★13695★ **Earth Work**

Student Conservation Association
689 River Rd.
PO Box 550
Charlestown, NH 03603
Ph: (603)543-1700   Fax: (603)543-1828
E-mail: earthwork@sca-inc.org
URL: http://www.thesca.org/

Description: Monthly. Contains listings of environmental positions, ranging from internships and administrative assistants for environmental groups to camp directors, state natural resource managers, and biologists.

★13696★ **Job Line...and News from CPRS**

California Park & Recreation Society Inc.
7971 Freeport Blvd.
Sacramento, CA 95832-9701
Ph: (916)665-2777   Fax: (916)665-9149
URL: http://www.cprs.org/publications-job-line.htm

Description: Monthly. Discusses parks and recreation news of interest.

★13697★ **The Job Seeker**

The Job Seeker
403 Oakwood St.
Warrens, WI 54666
Ph: (608)378-4450   Fax: (267)295-2005
URL: http://www.thejobseeker.net

Description: Semimonthly. Specializes "in environmental and natural resource vacancies nationwide." Lists current vacancies from federal, state, local, private, and nonprofit employers. Also available via e-mail.

★13698★ **Journal of Forestry**

Society of American Foresters
5400 Grosvenor Ln.
Bethesda, MD 20814-2198
Ph: (301)897-8720   Fax: (301)897-3690
Fr: (866)897-8720
E-mail: journal@safnet.org
URL: http://www.safnet.org/periodicals/jof/

$85.00/year for nonmembers, U.S./Canada, print only; $185.00/year for institutions, U.S./Canada, print only; $70.00/year for nonmembers, online only; $116.00/year for institutions, online only; $94.00/year for nonmembers, U.S./Canada, print and online; $204.00/year for institutions, U.S./Canada, print and online; $115.00/year for nonmembers, foreign, print only; $215.00/year for institutions, foreign, print only; $127.00/year for nonmembers, foreign, print and online; $237.00/year for institutions, other countries, print and online. Journal of forestry serves to advance the profession by keeping professionals informed about significant developments and ideas in forest science, natural resource management, and forest policy.

★13699★ **Nature International Weekly Journal of Science**

Nature Publishing Group
75 Varick St., 9th Fl.
New York, NY 10013-1917
Ph: (212)726-9200   Fax: (212)696-9006
Fr: 888-331-6288
E-mail: nature@natureny.com
URL: http://www.nature.com

Weekly. $145.00/year for individuals; $49.00/year for institutions. Magazine covering science and technology, including the fields of biology, biochemistry, genetics, medicine, earth sciences, physics, pharmacology, and behavioral sciences.

★13700★ **NRPA Job Bulletin**

National Recreation and Park Association, Professional Services Div.
22377 Belmont Ridge Rd.
Ashburn, VA 20148
Ph: (703)858-0784   Fax: (703)858-0794
Fr: 800-626-6772
E-mail: info@nrpa.org
URL: http://www.nrpa.org

Description: Semimonthly. Provides listings of employment opportunities in the park, recreation, and leisure services field.

★13701★ **Recycling Today**

G.I.E. Media, MC
4020 Kinross Lakes Pkwy., Ste. 201
Richfield, OH 44286
Ph: (216)961-4130   Fax: (216)925-5038
Fr: 800-456-0707
URL: http://www.recyclingtoday.com

Monthly. Magazine covering recycling of secondary raw materials and solid-waste management.

★13702★ **Resource Recycling**

Resource Recycling
PO Box 42270
Portland, OR 97242-0270
Ph: (503)233-1305   Fax: (503)233-1356
E-mail: info@resource-recycling.com
URL: http://www.resource-recycling.com/rr.html

Monthly. $52.00/year for individuals. Journal reporting on all aspects of recycling and composting of solid waste, from collection and materials processing to markets and governmental policies.

★13703★ **Water Environment Research**

Water Environment Federation
601 Wythe St.
Alexandria, VA 22314-1994
Ph: (703)684-2452   Fax: (703)684-2492
Fr: 800-666-0206
E-mail: msc@wef.org
URL: http://www.wef.org

Bimonthly. $125.00/year for individuals, WEF Member, print plus online; $308.00/year for individuals, print plus online; $780.00/year for institutions, print plus online; $200.00/year for individuals, WEF Member, print plus online; $350.00/year for individuals, print plus online; $830.00/year for institutions, print plus online; $812.00/year for institutions, Domestic; $883.00/year for institutions, international. Technical journal covering municipal and industrial water pollution control, water quality, and hazardous wastes.

OTHER SOURCES

★13704★ **Air and Waste Management Association (A&WMA)**

1 Gateway Ctr., 3rd Fl.
420 Ft. Duquesne Blvd.
Pittsburgh, PA 15222-1435
Ph: (412)232-3444   Fax: (412)232-3450
Fr: 800-270-3444
E-mail: info@awma.org
URL: http://www.awma.org

Description: Serves as environmental, educational, and technical organization. **Purpose:** Seeks to provide a neutral forum for the exchange of technical information on a wide variety of environmental topics.

★13705★ **American Academy of Environmental Engineers (AAEE)**

130 Holiday Ct., Ste. 100
Annapolis, MD 21401
Ph: (410)266-3311   Fax: (410)266-7653
E-mail: info@aaee.net
URL: http://www.aaee.net

Members: Environmentally oriented registered professional engineers certified by examination as Diplomates of the Academy. **Purpose:** Seeks to improve the standards of environmental engineering. Certifies those with special knowledge of environmental engineering. Furnishes lists of those certified to the public. **Activities:** Maintains speakers' bureau. Recognizes areas of specialization: Air Pollution Control; General Environmental; Hazardous Waste Management; Industrial Hygiene; Radiation Protection; Solid Waste Management; Water Supply and Wastewater. Requires written and oral examinations for certification. Works with other professional organizations on environmentally oriented activities. Identifies potential employment candidates through Talent Search Service.

★13706★ **American Public Health Association (APHA)**

800 I St. NW
Washington, DC 20001
Ph: (202)777-2742   Fax: (202)777-2534
E-mail: comments@apha.org
URL: http://www.apha.org

Members: Professional organization of physicians, nurses, educators, academicians, environmentalists, epidemiologists, new professionals, social workers, health administrators, optometrists, podiatrists, pharmacists, dentists, nutritionists, health planners, other community and mental health specialists, and interested consumers. **Purpose:** Seeks to protect and promote personal, mental, and environmental health. **Activities:** Services include: promulgation of standards; establishment of uniform practices and procedures; development of the etiology of communicable diseases; research in public health; exploration of medical care programs and their relationships to public health. Sponsors job placement service.

★13707★ **Environmental Careers Organization (ECO)**

30 Winter St., 6th Fl.
Boston, MA 02108-4720
Ph: (617)426-4375   Fax: (617)423-0998
E-mail: kdoyle@eco.org
URL: http://www.eco.org

Description: Seeks to protect and enhance the environment through the development of professionals, the promotion of careers, and the inspiration of individual action. Offers paid internships, career development educational programs and related publications. Participants in programs are mostly upper-level undergraduate, graduate, and doctoral students, or recent graduates seeking professional experience relevant to careers in the environmental fields. Individual subject areas of placement service include biology, chemistry, community development, hazardous waste, natural resources, pollution, public/occupational health, transportation, and wildlife.

★13708★ **Environmental Technology Council (ETC)**

734 15th St. NW, Ste. 720
Washington, DC 20005-1013
Ph: (202)783-0870
E-mail: comments@etc.org
URL: http://www.etc.org

Description: Firms dedicated to the use of high technology treatment in the management of hazardous wastes and to the restricted use of land disposal facilities in the interests of protecting human health and the environment. Advocates minimization of hazardous wastes and the use of alternative technologies in their treatment, including chemical and biological treatments, fixation, neutralization, reclamation, recycling, and thermal treatments such as incineration. Encourages land disposal prohibitions. Promotes reductions in the volume of hazardous waste generated annually and expansion of EPA hazardous waste list. Advocates use of treatment technology as a more cost-effective approach to Superfund site cleanups. Works with state, national, and international officials and firms to assist in development of programs that utilize treatment and minimize land disposal. Provides technical and placement assistance to members; sponsors special studies, technical seminars, and workshops; participates in federal legislation, litigation, and regulatory development. Maintains library of materials on new technologies; operates speakers' bureau; compiles statistics and mailing list.

★13709★ **National Association of Conservation Districts (NACD)**

509 Capitol Ct. NE
Washington, DC 20002-4937
Ph: (202)547-6223   Fax: (202)547-6450
E-mail: krysta-harden@nacdnet.org
URL: http://www.nacdnet.org

Description: Soil and water conservation districts organized by the citizens of watersheds, counties, or communities under provisions of state laws. Directs and coordinates, through local self-government efforts, the conservation and development of soil, water, and related natural resources. Includes districts over 90% of the nation's privately owned land. Conducts educational programs and children's services.

★13710★ **National Environmental Health Association (NEHA)**

720 S Colorado Blvd., Ste. 1000-N
Denver, CO 80246-1926
Ph: (303)756-9090   Fax: (303)691-9490
E-mail: staff@neha.org
URL: http://www.neha.org

Description: Represents all professionals in environmental health and protection, including Registered Sanitarians, Registered Environmental Health Specialists, Registered Environmental Technicians, Certified Environmental Health Technicians, Registered Hazardous Substances Professionals and Registered Hazardous Substances Specialists. Advances the environmental health and protection profession for the purpose of providing a healthful environment for all. Provides educational materials, publications, credentials and meetings to members and non-member professionals who strive to improve the environment.

★13711★ **Student Conservation Association (SCA)**

PO Box 550
Charlestown, NH 03603-0550
Ph: (603)543-1700   Fax: (603)543-1828
E-mail: ask-us@thesca.org
URL: http://www.thesca.org

Description: Works to build the next generation of conservation leaders and inspire lifelong stewardship of the environment and communities by engaging young people in hands-on service to the land. Provides conservation service opportunities, outdoor education and leadership development for young people. Offers college and graduate students, as well as older adults expense-paid conservation internships, these positions includes wildlife research, wilderness patrols and interpretive opportunities and provide participants with valuable hands-on career experience. Places 15-19 year old high school students in four-week volunteer conservation crews in national parks forests and refuges across the country each summer to accomplish a range of trail building and habitat conservation projects. Offers year-round diversity conservation programs for young women and young persons of color in leading metropolitan areas of U.S.

★13712★ **United States Committee for the United Nations Environment Program (US UNEP)**

47914 252nd St.
Sioux Falls, SD 57198-0002
Ph: (605)594-6117   Fax: (605)594-6119
E-mail: singh@usgs.gov
URL: http://grid2.cr.usgs.gov

Description: Individuals interested in raising public awareness of the importance of a global environmental effort. Encourages activism in support of the United Nations Environment Program. Acts as a liaison between the UNEP and the public. Sponsors educational programs and children's services. Offers placement services to job seekers in international environmental work. Maintains speakers' bureau.

★13713★ **U.S. Public Interest Research Group (USPIRG)**

218 D St. SE
Washington, DC 20003-1900
Ph: (202)546-9707   Fax: (202)546-2461

E-mail: membershipservices@pirg.org
URL: http://www.uspirg.org

Description: Individuals who contribute time, effort, or funds toward public interest research and advocacy. Conducts research, monitors corporate and government actions, and lobbies for reforms on consumer, environmental, energy, and governmental issues. Current efforts include support for: laws to protect consumers from unsafe products and unfair banking practices; laws to reduce the use of toxic chemicals; strengthening clean air laws; efforts to reduce global warming and ozone depletion; energy conservation and use of safe, renewable energy sources. Sponsors internships for college students; provides opportunities for students to receive academic credit for activities such as legislative research, lobbying, and public education and organizing. Offers summer jobs.

★13714★ **Water Environment Federation (WEF)**

601 Wythe St.
Alexandria, VA 22314-1994
Ph: (703)684-2400   Fax: (703)684-2492
Fr: 800-666-0206
E-mail: csc@wef.org
URL: http://www.wef.org

Description: Technical societies representing chemists, biologists, ecologists, geologists, operators, educational and research personnel, industrial wastewater engineers, consultant engineers, municipal officials, equipment manufacturers, and university professors and students dedicated to the enhancement and preservation of water quality and resources. Seeks to advance fundamental and practical knowledge concerning the nature, collection, treatment, and disposal of domestic and industrial wastewaters, and the design, construction, operation, and management of facilities for these purposes. Disseminates technical information; and promotes good public relations and regulations that improve water quality and the status of individuals working in this field. Conducts educational and research programs.

Government Agencies

★13715★ Equal Employment Opportunity Commission

1801 L St. NW
Washington, DC 20507
Ph: (202)663-4900   Fr: 800-669-4000
E-mail: info@eeoc.gov
URL: http://www.eeoc.gov

The Equal Employment Opportunity Commission enforces laws which prohibit discrimination based on race, color, religion, sex, national origin, disability, or age in hiring, promoting, firing, setting wages, testing, training, apprenticeship, and all other terms and conditions of employment. The Commission conducts investigations of alleged discrimination; makes determinations based on gathered evidence; attempts conciliation when discrimination has taken place; files lawsuits; and conducts voluntary assistance programs for employers, unions, and community organizations. The Commission also has adjudicatory and oversight responsibility for all compliance and enforcement activities relating to equal employment opportunity among Federal employees and applicants, including discrimination against individuals with disabilities.

★13716★ Federal Labor Relations Authority

1400 K St., NW, 2nd Fl.
Washington, DC 20424-0001
Ph: (202)357-6029   Fax: (202)482-6724
URL: http://www.flra.gov

The Federal Labor Relations Authority oversees the Federal service labor-management relations program. It administers the law that protects the right of employees of the Federal Government to organize, bargain collectively, and participate through labor organizations of their own choosing in decisions affecting them. The Authority also ensures compliance with the statutory rights and obligations of Federal employees and the labor organizations that represent them in their dealings with Federal agencies.

★13717★ Federal Mediation and Conciliation Service

2100 K St. NW
Washington, DC 20427
Ph: (202)606-8100   Fax: (202)606-4251

E-mail: sblake@fmcs.gov
URL: http://www.fmcs.gov

The Federal Mediation and Conciliation Service assists labor and management in resolving disputes in collective bargaining contract negotiation through voluntary mediation and arbitration services; provides training to unions and management in cooperative processes to improve long-term relationships under the Labor Management Cooperation Act of 1978, including Federal sector partnership training authorized by Executive Order 12871; provides alternative dispute resolution services and training to Government agencies, including the facilitation of regulatory negotiations under the Administrative Dispute Resolution Act and the Negotiated Rule-making Act of 1996; and awards competitive grants to joint labor-management committees to encourage innovative approaches to cooperative efforts.

★13718★ Merit Systems Protection Board

1615 M St. NW, Fifth Fl.
Washington, DC 20419
Ph: (202)653-7200   Fax: (202)653-7130
Fr: 800-209-8960
E-mail: mspb@mspb.gov
URL: http://www.mspb.gov

The Merit Systems Protection Board protects the integrity of Federal merit systems and the rights of Federal employees working in the systems. In overseeing the personnel practices of the Federal Government, the Board conducts special studies of the merit systems, hears and decides charges of wrongdoing and employee appeals of adverse agency actions, and orders corrective and disciplinary actions when appropriate.

★13719★ National Labor Relations Board

1099 Fourteenth St. NW
Washington, DC 20570
Ph: (202)273-1000   Fr: (866)667-6572
URL: http://www.nlrb.gov

The National Labor Relations Board is vested with the power to prevent and remedy unfair labor practices committed by private sector employers and unions and to safe-

guard employees' rights to organize and determine whether to have unions as their bargaining representative.

★13720★ Occupational Safety and Health Review Commission

1120 Twentieth St. NW
Washington, DC 20036-3457
Ph: (202)606-5398   Fax: (202)606-5050
E-mail: lt_gpo@oshrc.gov
URL: http://www.oshrc.gov

The Occupational Safety and Health Review Commission works to ensure the timely and fair resolution of cases involving the alleged exposure of American workers to unsafe or unhealthy working conditions.

★13721★ Office of Personnel Management

1900 E St. NW
Washington, DC 20415
Ph: (202)606-1800
E-mail: General@opm.gov
URL: http://www.opm.gov

The Office of Personnel Management (OPM) administers a merit system to ensure compliance with personnel laws and regulations and assists agencies in recruiting, examining, and promoting people on the basis of their knowledge and skills, regardless of their race, religion, sex, political influence, or other non-merit factors. OPM's role is to provide guidance to agencies in operating human resources programs which effectively support their missions and to provide an array of personnel services to applicants and employees. OPM supports Government program managers in their human resources management responsibilities and provide benefits to employees, retired employees, and their survivors.

★13722★ U.S. Commission on Civil Rights

624 Ninth St. NW, Ste. 500
Washington, DC 20425
Ph: (202)376-7533
URL: http://www.usccr.gov

The Commission on Civil Rights collects and

studies information on discrimination or denials of equal protection of the laws because of race, color, religion, sex, age, disability, national origin, or in the administration of justice in such areas as voting rights, enforcement of Federal civil rights laws, and equal opportunity in education, employment, and housing.

★13723★ U.S. Department of Justice, Civil Rights Division

950 Pennsylvania Ave., NW
Washington, DC 20530
Ph: (202)514-4609   Fax: (202)514-0293
URL: http://www.usdoj.gov/crt

The Division is the primary institution within the Federal Government responsible for enforcing Federal statutes prohibiting discrimination on the basis of race, sex, disability, religion, and national origin.

★13724★ U.S. Department of Labor

200 Constitution Ave. NW
Washington, DC 20210
Ph: 877-889-5627   Fr: (866)487-2365
URL: http://www.dol.gov

Seeks to foster, promote, and develop the welfare of the wage earners of the United States, to improve their working conditions, and to advance their opportunities for profitable employment. In carrying out this mission, the Department administers a variety of Federal labor laws guaranteeing workers' rights to safe and healthful working conditions, a minimum hourly wage and overtime pay, freedom from employment discrimination, unemployment insurance, and workers' compensation. The Department also protects workers' pension rights; provides for job training programs; helps workers find jobs; works to strengthen free collective bargaining; and keeps track of changes in employment, prices, and other national economic measurements. As the Department seeks to assist all Americans who need and want to work, special efforts are made to meet the unique job market problems of older workers, youths, minority group members, women, the handicapped, and other groups.

★13725★ U.S. Department of Labor, Adult Services Administration

200 Constitution Ave. NW
Washington, DC 20210
Fr: 877-872-5625
URL: http://www.doleta.gov

The Adult Services Administration is responsible for planning and developing policies, legislative proposals, goals, strategies, budgets, and resource allocation for the operation of comprehensive services to adults in the work force investment system; designing, developing, and administering employment and training services for welfare recipients, Native Americans, migrant and seasonal farm workers, older workers, individuals with disabilities, and individuals dislocated due to mass layoffs and emergencies; and providing direction for the investigation of worker petitions and the preparation of

industry impact studies relating to trade adjustment assistance.

★13726★ U.S. Department of Labor, Bureau of International Labor Affairs

200 Constitution Ave. NW
Washington, DC 20210
Ph: (202)693-4770   Fax: (202)693-4780
Fr: 800-827-5335
URL: http://www.dol.gov/ilab

The Bureau of International Labor Affairs assists in formulating international economic, social, trade, and immigration policies affecting American workers, with a view to maximizing higher wage and higher value U.S. jobs derived from global economic integration; gathers and disseminates information on child labor practices worldwide; promotes respect for international labor standards to protect the economic and physical well-being of workers in the United States and around the world; gathers and disseminates information on foreign labor markets and programs so that U.S. employment policy formulation might benefit from international experiences; carries out overseas technical assistance projects; and conducts research on the labor market consequences of immigration proposals and legislation.

★13727★ U.S. Department of Labor, Bureau of Labor Statistics

2 Massachusetts Ave. NW, Rm. 4110
Washington, DC 20212-0001
Ph: (202)691-5200
URL: http://www.bls.gov

The Bureau of Labor Statistics (BLS) is the principal fact-finding agency of the Federal Government in the broad field of labor economics and statistics. The Bureau is an independent national statistical agency that collects, processes, analyzes, and disseminates essential statistical data to the American public, Congress, other Federal agencies, State and local governments, businesses, and labor.

★13728★ U.S. Department of Labor, Employee Benefits Security Administration

200 Constitution Ave. NW
Washington, DC 20210
Fr: (866)444-3272
URL: http://www.dol.gov/ebsa

The Employee Benefits Security Administration (EBSA) is responsible for promoting and protecting the pension, health, and other benefits of the over 150 million participants and beneficiaries in over 6 million private sector employee benefit plans. In administering its responsibilities, PWBA assists workers in understanding their rights and protecting their benefits; facilitates compliance by plan sponsors, plan officials, service providers, and other members of the regulated community; encourages the growth of employment-based benefits; and deters and corrects violations of the relevant statutes. ERISA is enforced through 15 PWBA field offices nationwide and the national office in Washington, DC.

★13729★ U.S. Department of Labor, Employment Standards Administration

200 Constitution Ave. NW
Washington, DC 20210
Fr: (866)487-2365
URL: http://www.dol.gov/esa

The Employment Standards Administration is responsible for managing and directing employment standards programs dealing with minimum wage and overtime standards; registration of farm labor contractors; determining prevailing wage rates to be paid on Government contracts and subcontracts; nondiscrimination and affirmative action for minorities, women, veterans, and handicapped Government contract and subcontract workers; workers' compensation programs for Federal and certain private employers and employees; safeguarding the financial integrity and internal democracy of labor unions; and administering statutory programs to certify employee protection provisions for various federally sponsored transportation programs.

★13730★ U.S. Department of Labor, Employment and Training Administration

200 Constitution Ave. NW
Washington, DC 20210
Fr: 877-872-5625
URL: http://www.doleta.gov

The Employment and Training Administration fulfills responsibilities assigned to the Secretary of Labor that relate to employment services, job training, and unemployment insurance. Component offices and services administer a Federal/State employment security system; fund and oversee programs to provide work experience and training for groups having difficulty entering or returning to the work force; formulate and promote apprenticeship standards and programs; and conduct continuing programs of research, development, and evaluation.

★13731★ U.S. Department of Labor, Mine Safety and Health Administration

1100 Wilson Boulevard, 21st Fl.
Arlington, VA 22209-3939
Ph: (202)693-9400   Fax: (202)693-9401
E-mail: mshahelpdesk@dol.gov
URL: http://www.msha.gov

The Mine Safety and Health Administration is responsible for safety and health in the Nation's mines. The Administration develops and promulgates mandatory safety and health standards, ensures compliance with such standards, assesses civil penalties for violations, and investigates accidents. It cooperates with and provides assistance to the States in the development of effective State mine safety and health programs; improves and expands training programs in cooperation with the States and the mining industry; and contributes to the improvement and expansion of mine safety and health research and development. All of these activities are aimed at preventing and reducing mine accidents and occupational diseases in the mining industry.

★13732★ U.S. Department of Labor, Occupational Safety and Health Administration

200 Constitution Ave. NW
Washington, DC 20210
Fr: 800-321-6742
URL: http://www.osha.gov

The Occupational Safety and Health Administration (OSHA) sets and enforces workplace safety and health standards and assists employers in complying with those standards.

★13733★ U.S. Department of Labor, Office of Apprenticeship

200 Constitution Ave. NW
Washington, DC 20210
Fr: 877-872-5625
URL: http://www.doleta.gov

The Administration is responsible for developing materials and conducting a program of public awareness to secure the adoption of training in skilled occupations and related training policies and practices used by employers, unions, and other organizations; developing policies and plans to enhance opportunities for minority and female participation in skilled training; and coordinating the effective use of Federal, labor, and employer resources to create a clear training-to-employment corridor for customers of the work force development system.

★13734★ U.S. Department of Labor, Office of Federal Contract Compliance Programs

200 Constitution Ave. NW
Washington, DC 20210
Fr: (866)487-2365
URL: http://www.dol.gov/esa/ofccp

The Office of Federal Contract Compliance Programs (OFCCP) ensures that companies that do business with the Government promote affirmative action and equal employment opportunity on behalf of minorities, women, the disabled, and Vietnam veterans.

★13735★ U.S. Department of Labor, Office of Labor-Management Standards

200 Constitution Ave. NW
Washington, DC 20210
Fr: (866)487-2365
URL: http://www.dol.gov/esa/olms

The Office of Labor-Management Standards conducts criminal and civil investigations to safeguard the financial integrity of unions and to ensure union democracy, and conducts investigative audits of labor unions to uncover and remedy criminal and civil violations of the Labor-Management Reporting and Disclosure Act and related statutes.

★13736★ U.S. Department of Labor, Office of Small Business Programs

200 Constitution Ave. NW
Washington, DC 20210
Ph: 877-889-5627   Fr: (866)487-2365
URL: http://www.dol.gov/osbp

The Office of Small Business Programs administers the Department's efforts to ensure procurement opportunities for small businesses, disadvantaged businesses, women-owned businesses, HUBZone businesses, and businesses owned by service-disabled veterans.

★13737★ U.S. Department of Labor, Office of Workers' Compensation Programs

200 Constitution Ave. NW, Rm. S-3524
Washington, DC 20210
Fr: (866)487-2365
URL: http://www.dol.gov/esa/owcp

The Office of Workers' Compensation Programs is responsible for programs providing workers' compensation for Federal employees; benefits to employees in private enterprise while engaged in maritime employment on navigable waters in the United States; benefits to coal miners who are totally disabled due to pneumoconiosis, a respiratory disease contracted after prolonged inhalation of coal mine dust, and to their survivors when the miner's death is due to pneumoconiosis; and to energy employees who contract occupational illnesses.

★13738★ U.S. Department of Labor, Veterans' Employment and Training Service

200 Constitution Ave. NW
Washington, DC 20210
Fr: (866)487-2365
URL: http://www.dol.gov/vets

The Veterans' Employment and Training Service (VETS) is responsible for administering veterans' employment and training programs and activities to ensure that legislative and regulatory mandates are accomplished.

★13739★ U.S. Department of Labor, Wage and Hour Division

200 Constitution Ave. NW, Rm. S-3502
Washington, DC 20210
Fr: (866)487-2365
E-mail: OFCCP-Public@dol.gov.
URL: http://www.dol.gov/esa/whd

The Wage and Hour Division is responsible for planning, directing, and administering programs dealing with a variety of Federal labor legislation. These programs are designed to protect low-wage incomes; safeguard the health and welfare of workers by

discouraging excessively long hours of work; safeguard the health and well-being of minors; prevent curtailment of employment and earnings for students, trainees, and handicapped workers; minimize losses of income and job rights caused by indebtedness; and direct a program of farm labor contractor registration designed to protect the health, safety, and welfare of migrant and seasonal agricultural workers.

★13740★ U.S. Department of Labor, Women's Bureau

200 Constitution Ave. NW
Washington, DC 20210
Ph: 877-889-5627   Fr: 800-827-5335
URL: http://www.dol.gov/wb

The Women's Bureau is responsible for formulating standards and policies that promote the welfare of wage earning women, improve their working conditions, increase their efficiency, and advance their opportunities for profitable employment.

★13741★ U.S. Department of Labor, Workforce Security Administration

200 Constitution Ave. NW
Washington, DC 20210
Fr: 877-872-5625
URL: http://www.doleta.gov

The Administration is responsible for interpreting Federal legislative requirements for State unemployment compensation and employment service programs and one-stop systems; guiding and assisting States in adopting laws, regulations, and policies that conform with and support Federal law; developing, negotiating, and monitoring reimbursable agreements with States to administer the Targeted Jobs Tax Credit Program; providing policy guidance for the Immigration and Nationality Act concerning aliens seeking admission into the United States in order to work; and overseeing the development and implementation of the Nation's labor market information system.

★13742★ U.S. Department of Labor, Youth Services Administration

200 Constitution Ave. NW
Washington, DC 20210
Ph: (202)693-3030   Fr: 877-872-5625
URL: http://www.doleta.gov

The Administration is responsible for planning, developing, and recommending objectives, policies, and strategies for operations of a comprehensive youth employment and training system; and providing policy guidance and program performance oversight for Job Corps youth employment and training services and youth services grant programs authorized under the Workforce Investment Act and the school-to-work system.

Government Employment Opportunities

REFERENCE WORKS

★13743★ *9 Steps to a Great Federal Job*
LearningExpress, LLC
55 Broadway, 8th Fl.
New York, NY 10006
Ph: (212)995-2566   Fax: (212)995-5512
Fr: 800-295-9556
E-mail: customerservice@learningexpressllc.com
URL: http://www.learningexpressllc.com

Lee Wherry Brainerd, C. Roebuck Reed. February 2004. $19.95. Illustrated. 176 pages.

★13744★ *The Book of U.S. Government Jobs*
Bookhaven Press L.L.C.
249 Field Club Cir.
McKees Rocks, PA 15136
Ph: (412)494-6926

Annual. $13.95 for individuals. Publication includes: Lists of Washington, D.C., departments and agencies, Web sites, and job centers nationwide. Indexes: Alphabetical.

★13745★ *Career Ideas for Teens in Government and Public Service*
Facts On File Inc.
132 W 31st St., 17th Fl.
New York, NY 10001
Ph: (212)967-8800   Fax: 800-678-3633
Fr: 800-322-8755
URL: http://www.factsonfile.com

Published 2005. $40.00 for individuals; $36.00 for libraries. Covers a multitude of career possibilities based on a teenager's specific interests and skills and links his/her talents to a wide variety of actual professions.

★13746★ *Career Transition: A Guide for Federal Employees in a Time of Turmoil*
FPMI Communications, Inc.
4901 Univ. St., Ste. 3
Huntsville, AL 35816
Ph: (256)539-1850   Fax: (256)539-0911

Robert Carey. 1996. $14.95 (paper). 105 pages.

★13747★ *Careers in Horticulture and Botany*
The McGraw-Hill Companies
PO Box 182604
Columbus, OH 43272
Fax: (614)759-3749   Fr: 877-883-5524
E-mail: customer.service@mcgraw-hill.com
URL: http://www.mcgraw-hill.com

Jerry Garner. 2006. 15.95 (paper). 192 pages. Includes bibliographical references.

★13748★ *Careers Inside the World of the Government*
Rosen Publishing Group, Inc.
29 E. 21st St.
New York, NY 10010
Ph: (212)777-3017   Fax: 888-436-4643
Fr: 800-237-9932
URL: http://www.rosenpublishing.com/

Sue Hurwitz. Revised edition, 1999. $29.25. 64 pages.

★13749★ *Careers in Law*
The McGraw-Hill Companies
PO Box 182604
Columbus, OH 43272
Fax: (614)759-3749   Fr: 877-883-5524
E-mail: customer.service@mcgraw-hill.com
URL: http://www.mcgraw-hill.com

Gary Munneke. Third edition, 2003. $15.95 (paper). 192 pages. Overview of opportunities available to lawyers in private practice, corporate law, in federal, state, and local governments, and in teaching. Provides information on the typical law school curriculum plus opportunities in internships and clerkships.

★13750★ *Carroll's Federal Directory*
Carroll Publishing
4701 Sangamore Rd., Ste. S-155
Bethesda, MD 20816
Ph: (301)263-9800   Fax: (301)263-9801
Fr: 800-336-4240
URL: http://www.carrollpub.com

Four times/year. $425.00 for single issue. Covers about 46,000 executive managers in federal government offices in Washington, D.C., including executive, congressional and judicial branches; members of Congress and Congressional committees and staff. Entries include: Agency names, titles, office address (including room numbers), e-mail addresses, and telephone and fax numbers. Also available as part of a "library edition" titled "Federal Directory Annual." Arrangement: By cabinet department or administrative agency. Indexes: Keyword, personal name (with phone) and e-mail addresses.

★13751★ *Carroll's State Directory*
Carroll Publishing
4701 Sangamore Rd., Ste. S-155
Bethesda, MD 20816
Ph: (301)263-9800   Fax: (301)263-9801
Fr: 800-336-4240
URL: http://www.carrollpub.com/state-print.asp

3x/yr. $385.00 for individuals. Covers about 73,000 state government officials in all branches of government; officers, committees and members of state legislatures; managers of boards and authorities. Entries include: Name, address, phone, fax, title. Arrangement: Geographical; separate sections for state offices and legislatures. Indexes: Personal name (with phone and e-mail address), organizational, keyword.

★13752★ *Congressional Directory*
Capitol Advantage
2751 Prosperity Ave., Ste. 600
Fairfax, VA 22031
Ph: (703)289-4670   Fax: (703)289-4678
Fr: 800-659-8708
URL: http://capitoladvantage.com/publishing/products.html

Annual. $17.95 for individuals. Covers 100 current senators and 440 House of Representative members. Entries include: Name, district office address, phone, fax; names and titles of key staff; committee and subcommittee assignments; biographical data, percentage of votes won, photo. Arrangement: Available in separate alphabetical, geographical, or condensed editions. Indexes: Name.

★13753★ **Discovering Careers for Your Future: Government**

Facts On File Inc.
132 W 31st St., 17th Fl.
New York, NY 10001
Ph: (212)967-8800   Fax: 800-678-3633
Fr: 800-322-8755
URL: http://www.factsonfile.com

Published 2002. $21.95 for individuals; $19.75 for libraries. Covers ambassadors, city managers, customs officials, foreign service workers, lobbyists, police officers, secret service special agents, and spies; links career education to curriculum, helping children investigate the subjects they are interested in and the careers those subjects might lead to.

★13754★ **Employment Guide for the Military, Intelligence and Special Operations Communities**

The Graduate Group
PO Box 370351
West Hartford, CT 06137-0351
Ph: (860)233-2330   Fax: (860)233-2330
Fr: 800-484-7280
E-mail: graduategroup@hotmail.com
URL: http://www.graduategroup.com

Mark W. Merritt. 1997. $27.50

★13755★ **Employment Opportunities, USA**

Washington Research Associates
1090 Vermont Ave. NW, Ste. 800
Washington, DC 20005
Ph: (202)408-7025

Annual, quarterly updates. Publication includes: List of over 1,000 employment contacts in companies and agencies in banking, arts, telecommunications, education, and 14 other industries and professions, including federal government. Entries include: Company name, name of representative, address, description of products or services, hiring and recruiting practices, training programs, and year established. Principal content is industry overviews, career news, employment opportunity information on 14 different job markets, and comprehensive guidance to career resources on the Internet. Arrangement: Classified by industry. Indexes: Occupation.

★13756★ **Encyclopedia of Governmental Advisory Organizations**

Gale, Cengage Learning
27500 Drake Rd.
Farmington Hills, MI 48331-3535
Ph: (248)699-4253   Fax: (248)699-8065
Fr: 800-877-4253

E-mail: businessproducts@gale.com
URL: http://www.gale.com

Annual; latest edition 22nd, published May 2007. $850.00 for individuals. Covers more than 7,300 boards, panels, commissions, committees, presidential conferences, and other groups that advise the President, Congress, and departments and agencies of federal government; includes interagency committees and federally sponsored conferences. Also includes historically significant organizations. Entries include: Unit name, address, phone, URL and e-mail (if active), name of principal executive, legal basis for the unit, purpose, reports and publications, findings and recommendations, description of activities, members. Arrangement: Classified by general subject. Indexes: Alphabetical/keyword; personnel; publication; federal department/agency; presidential administration.

★13757★ **FBI Careers, Second Edition**

JIST Publishing
875 Montreal Way
St. Paul, MN 55102
Fax: 800-547-8329   Fr: 800-648-5478
E-mail: info@jist.com
URL: http://www.jist.com

Thomas H. Ackerman. 2006. $19.95. 352 pages. Guide to handling the FBI's rigorous selection process; reveals what it takes to succeed in landing a job. Useful for special agents as well as professional support personnel.

★13758★ **Federal Career Opportunities**

Federal Research Service Inc.
PO Box 1708
Annandale, VA 22003
Ph: (703)914-JOBS   Fax: (703)914-0628
Fr: 800-822-5027
URL: http://www.fedjobs.com/index.html

Biweekly. Covers more than 3,000 current federal job vacancies in the United States and overseas; includes permanent, part-time, and temporary positions. Entries include: Position title, location, series and grade, job requirements, special forms, announcement number, closing date, application address. Arrangement: Classified by occupation.

★13759★ **Federal Jobs for College Graduates**

Macmillan Publishing Company
175 Fifth Ave.
New York, NY 10010
Ph: (646)307-5151   Fr: 800-428-5331
URL: http://www.macmillan.com/

Robert Goldenkoff. 1991. $15.95 (paper). 392 pages. Identifies job opportunities in numerous government agencies.

★13760★ **Federal Jobs Digest**

Federal Jobs Digest
326 Main St.
Emmaus, PA 18049
Ph: (610)965-5825

URL: http://www.jobsfed.com

25x/yr. Covers over 10,000 specific job openings in the federal government in each issue. Vacancies from over 300 federal agencies are covered. Entries include: Position name, title, General Schedule (GS) grade, and Wage Grade (WG), closing date for applications, announcement number, application address, phone, and name of contact. Arrangement: By federal department or agency, then geographical.

★13761★ **Federal Law Enforcement Careers, Second Edition: Profiles of 250 High-Powered Positions and Tactics for Getting Hired**

JIST Publishing
875 Montreal Way
St. Paul, MN 55102
Fax: 800-547-8329   Fr: 800-648-5478
E-mail: info@jist.com
URL: http://www.jist.com

Thomas H. Ackerman. 2005. $19.95. 368 pages. Provides information about federal law enforcement jobs with detailed profiles of 250 careers with more than 130 agencies, plus qualification requirements and training program descriptions.

★13762★ **Federal Staff Directory**

CQ Press
1255 22nd St. NW, Ste. 400
Washington, DC 20037
Ph: (202)729-1800   Fax: 800-380-3810
Fr: (866)427-7737
URL: http://www.staffdirectories.com/

Latest edition 52, April 2007. $450.00 for individuals. Covers approximately 45,000 persons in federal government offices and independent agencies, with biographies of 2,600 key executives; includes officials at policy level in agencies of the Office of the President, Cabinet-level departments, independent and regulatory agencies, military commands, federal information centers, and libraries, and United States attorneys, marshals, and ambassadors. Entries include: Name, title, location (indicating building, address, and/or room), phone, fax, e-mail address, website, symbols indicating whether position is a presidential appointment and whether senate approval is required. Arrangement: Classified by department/agency. Indexes: Office locator page; extensive subject/keyword; individual name.

★13763★ **Federal Yellow Book**

Leadership Directories Inc.
104 5th Ave.
New York, NY 10011
Ph: (212)627-4140   Fax: (212)645-0931
E-mail: federal@leadershipdirectories.com
URL: http://www.leadershipdirectories.com/products/fyb.htm

Quarterly; latest edition 2007. $475.00 for individuals; $452.00 for individuals, standing order. Covers federal departments, including the Executive Office of the President, the Office of the Vice President, the Office of Management and Budget, the Cabinet, and the National Security Council, and over 40,000 key personnel and over 70 independent federal agencies. Entries include: For personnel–Name, address, phone, fax, e-mail, titles. For departments and agencies–Office, or branch name and address; names and titles of principal personnel, with their room numbers, direct-dial phone numbers, and e-mails. Arrangement: Classified by department or agency. Indexes: Subject, organization, individuals' names.

★13764★ *Government Job Finder*
Planning Communications
7215 Oak Ave.
River Forest, IL 60305-1935
Ph: (708)366-5200   Fax: (708)366-5280
Fr: 888-366-5200
E-mail: info@planningcommunications.com
URL: http://jobfindersonline.com

Daniel Lauber. Fourth edition, 2006. 300 pages. $18.95. Covers 1800 sources. Discusses how to use sources of local, state, and federal government job vacancies in a number of specialties and state-by-state, including job-matching services, job hotlines, specialty periodicals with job ads, salary surveys, and directories. Explains how local, state, and federal hiring systems work. Includes chapters on resume and cover letter preparation and interviewing.

★13765★ *Guide to America's Federal Jobs, Third Edition*
JIST Publishing
875 Montreal Way
St. Paul, MN 55102
Fax: 800-547-8329   Fr: 800-648-5478
E-mail: info@jist.com
URL: http://www.jist.com

Bruce Maxwell. 2005. $18.95. 448 pages. Provides summaries of all federal agencies plus guidance on creating federal resumes; applying online; interviewing for federal jobs; and special programs for students, veterans, and people with disabilities.

★13766★ *Insider's Guide to Finding a Job in Washington*
CQ Press
1255 22nd St. NW, Ste. 400
Washington, DC 20037
Ph: (202)729-1800   Fax: 800-380-3810
Fr: (866)427-7737
URL: http://www.cqpress.com

Latest edition November, 1999. $24.95 for individuals. Publication includes: Contact details for organizations; Web sites for government job hunting. Principal content of publication consists of jobs and careers available in public policy in Washington, including internship positions, congressional jobs, jobs within federal agencies or departments, interest group positions, trade association or labor union jobs, or media jobs. Indexes: Bibliography, subject, contact.

★13767★ *Internships in Federal Government: A Guide for Faculty Coordinators and Instructors.*
Iowa State University Press
2121 S. State Ave.
Ames, IA 50014-8300
Ph: (515)292-0140   Fax: (515)292-3348
Fr: 800-862-6657
URL: http://www.iastate.edu/

James P. Alexander. Seventh edition, 1995. $27.50. 207 pages

★13768★ *Internships in State Government*
The Graduate Group
PO Box 370351
West Hartford, CT 06137-0351
Ph: (860)233-2330   Fax: (860)233-2330
Fr: 800-484-7280
E-mail: graduategroup@hotmail.com
URL: http://www.graduategroup.com

Sixth edition, 1996. $27.50.

★13769★ *Opportunities in Federal Government Careers*
The McGraw-Hill Companies
PO Box 182604
Columbus, OH 43272
Fax: (614)759-3749   Fr: 877-883-5524
E-mail: customer.service@mcgraw-hill.com
URL: http://www.mcgraw-hill.com

Neale Baxter. Second edition, 1994. $14.95; $10.95 (paper). 150 pages. Describes the spectrum of government employment, including professional, administrative, scientific, blue-collar, clerical, and technical opportunities, and how to land a job. Illustrated. Part of the "Opportunities in ..." Series.

★13770★ *Opportunities in Government Careers*
The McGraw-Hill Companies
PO Box 182604
Columbus, OH 43272
Fax: (614)759-3749   Fr: 877-883-5524
E-mail: customer.service@mcgraw-hill.com
URL: http://www.mcgraw-hill.com

Neale J. Baxter. 2003. $12.95. 160 pages. VGM Opportunities Series.

★13771★ *Opportunities in Overseas Careers*
The McGraw-Hill Companies
PO Box 182604
Columbus, OH 43272
Fax: (614)759-3749   Fr: 877-883-5524
E-mail: customer.service@mcgraw-hill.com
URL: http://www.mcgraw-hill.com

Blythe Camenson. 2004. $13.95 (paper). 173 pages.

★13772★ *Opportunities in State and Local Government Careers*
The McGraw-Hill Companies
PO Box 182604
Columbus, OH 43272
Fax: (614)759-3749   Fr: 877-883-5524

E-mail: customer.service@mcgraw-hill.com
URL: http://www.mcgraw-hill.com

Neale J. Baxter. Revised edition, 1992. $14.95; $10.95 (paper). 148 pages. Points out the incentives and drawbacks of a government career. Describes hiring procedures and provides tips on filling out applications, taking physical and aptitude tests, handling interviews, and finding jobs. Describes the jobs in which 75% of all state and local government workers are employed. For each occupation, covers the nature of the work and the training required.

★13773★ *The Paralegal's Guide to U.S. Government Jobs: How to Land a Job in 140 Law-Related Career Fields*
Federal Reports, Inc.
1010 Vermont Ave. NW, Ste. 408
Washington, DC 20005
Ph: (202)393-3311

Richard L. Hermann, Jeanette J. Sobajian and Linda P. Sutherland. Seventh edition, 1996. $19.95. 140 pages. Explains U.S. Government procedures and describes 140 law-related federal careers for which paralegals may qualify. Includes a directory of several hundred Federal Agency personnel offices that hire the most paralegal and law-related talents.

★13774★ *Real Resumes and Other Resumes for Federal Government Jobs: Including Samples of Real Resumes Used to Apply for Federal Government Jobs*
PREP Publishing
1110 1/2 Hay St., PMB 66
Fayetteville, NC 28305
Ph: (910)483-6611   Fax: (910)483-2439
Fr: 800-533-2814

Anne McKinney (Editor). March 2003. $24.95. Illustrated. 195 pages. Government Job Series.

★13775★ *State Yellow Book*
Leadership Directories Inc.
104 5th Ave.
New York, NY 10011
Ph: (212)627-4140   Fax: (212)645-0931
E-mail: state@leadershipdirectories.com
URL: http://www.leadershipdirectories.com/products/syb.htm

Quarterly; latest edition 2007. $475.00 for individuals; $452.00 for individuals, standing order. Covers contact information for elected and appointed officials in the executive branches, as well as state legislators and their committees with direct-dial telephone numbers, fax numbers, individual addresses, and e-mail addresses. Arrangement: Alphabetical. Indexes: Subject; personnel.

★13776★ Storming Washington: An Intern's Guide to National Government

American Political Science Association
1527 New Hampshire Ave., NW
Washington, DC 20036-1206
Ph: (202)483-2512   Fax: (202)483-2657
E-mail: apsa@apsanet.org
URL: http://www.apsanet.org/

Stephen E. Frantzich. Fourth edition, 2001. $6.00 (paper). 82 pages.

★13777★ The Student's Federal Career Guide

JIST Publishing
875 Montreal Way
St. Paul, MN 55102
Fax: 800-547-8329   Fr: 800-648-5478
E-mail: info@jist.com
URL: http://www.jist.com

Kathryn Kramer and Emily K. Troutman. 2005. $21.95. 244 pages. Comprehensive guide to federal government jobs for young adults.

★13778★ Ten Steps to a Federal Job: Navigating the Federal Job System

JIST Publishing
875 Montreal Way
St. Paul, MN 55102
Fax: 800-547-8329   Fr: 800-648-5478
E-mail: info@jist.com
URL: http://www.jist.com

Kathryn Kraemer Troutman. 2003. $38.95. 256 pages. Provides information for developing resumes and cover letters that will get noticed in the federal system, as well as guidance to landing a federal job.

★13779★ United States Government Manual

Office of the Federal Register
c/o The National Archives and Records
 Administration
8601 Adelphi Rd.
College Park, MD 20740-6001
Ph: (301)837-0482   Fax: (301)837-0483
Fr: (866)272-6272
URL: http://www.gpoaccess.gov/gmanual/index.html

Annual, September; latest edition 2007-2008. $27.00 for individuals. Provides information on the agencies of the executive, judicial, and legislative branches of the Federal government. Contains a section on terminated or transferred agencies. Arrangement: Classified by department and agency. Indexes: Personal name, agency/subject.

★13780★ Vault Guide to Capitol Hill Careers: An Inside Look Inside the Beltway

Vault.com
150 W. 22nd St., 5th Fl.
New York, NY 10011
Ph: (212)366-4212   Fax: (212)366-6117
Fr: 888-562-8285
URL: http://www.vault.com

William McCarthy. December 2003. $29.95 (paper). 128 pages. Part of the Vault Career Library.

★13781★ Vault Guide to the Top Government and Non-Profit Legal Employers

Vault.com
150 W. 22nd St., 5th Fl.
New York, NY 10011
Ph: (212)366-4212   Fax: (212)366-6117
Fr: 888-562-8285
URL: http://www.vault.com

Marcy Lerner. October 2003. $29.95 (paper). 176 pages. Part of the Vault Career Library Series.

★13782★ Washington Information Directory

CQ Press
1255 22nd St. NW, Ste. 400
Washington, DC 20037
Ph: (202)729-1800   Fax: 800-380-3810
Fr: (866)427-7737
URL: http://www.cqpress.com

Annual; latest edition 2007. $128.00 for individuals. Covers 5,000 governmental agencies, congressional committees, and non-governmental associations considered competent sources of specialized information. Entries include: Name of agency, committee, or association; address, phone, fax, and Internet address; annotation concerning function or activities of the office; and name of contact. Arrangement: Classified by activity or competence (economics and business, housing and urban affairs, etc.). Indexes: Subject, agency/organization name, contact name.

★13783★ Washington Job Source

Benjamin Scott Publishing
20 E. Colorado Blvd., No. 202
Pasadena, CA 91105
Ph: (626)449-1339   Fax: (626)449-1389
Fr: 800-448-4959

Mary McMahon. Fifth edition, 2002. 15.95. 482 pages.

★13784★ Who's Who in Local Government Management

International City/County Management
 Association
777 N. Capitol St., NE, Ste. 500
Washington, DC 20002-4201
Ph: (202)289-4262   Fax: (202)962-3500
URL: http://www.icma.org

Annual, September. Covers 8,000 appointed administrators of cities, counties, and councils of governments. Entries include: Name, position, office address, educational history, career data, offices held in ICMA. Arrangement: Alphabetical by individual name.

NEWSPAPERS, MAGAZINES, AND JOURNALS

★13785★ Federal Acquisition Report

Management Concepts Inc.
8230 Leesburg Pke., Ste. 800
Vienna, VA 22182
Ph: (703)790-9595   Fax: (703)790-1371
Fr: 800-506-4450
E-mail: publications@managementconcepts.com
URL: http://www.managementconcepts.com

Description: Monthly. Focuses on developments in federal contracting, legislation, changes in rules and regulations, and recent decisions by the board of contract appeals and by the courts. Features job listings and guest essays.

★13786★ Federal Times

Army Times Publishing Co.
6883 Commercial Dr.
Springfield, VA 22159-0500
Ph: (703)750-7400   Fr: 800-368-5718
URL: http://www.armytimes.com/employment

Weekly (Mon.). Federal bureaucracy; technology in government.

★13787★ FEW's News and Views

Federally Employed Women Inc.
1666 K St. NW, Ste. 440
Washington, DC 20006
Ph: (202)898-0994
E-mail: editor@few.org
URL: http://www.few.org/publications.asp

Description: Bimonthly. Concerned with women's issues, particularly those involving women in the federal government. Reports on administration actions affecting the status of women and analyzes significant legislation. Recurring features include letters to the editor, news of members, a calendar of events, book reviews, and notices of career development and training opportunities.

★13788★ Government Finance Officers Association Newsletter

Government Finance Officers Association
203 N. LaSalle St., Ste. 2700
Chicago, IL 60601-1210
Ph: (312)977-9700   Fax: (312)977-4806
URL: http://www.gfoa.org/

Description: Semimonthly. Provides updates on current events, innovations, and federal legislation affecting public finance management for state and local government finance officers. Covers cash management, budgeting, accounting, auditing, and financial reporting, public employee retirement administration, and related issues. Recurring features include news of research, news of members, a calendar of events, and columns titled Career Notes and Employment Opportunities. Subscription includes the bimonthly magazine Government Finance Review.

★13789★ The Municipality

League of Wisconsin Municipalities
122 W Washington Ave., Ste. 300
Madison, WI 53703-2718
Ph: (608)267-2380   Fax: (608)267-0645
Fr: 800-991-5502
URL: http://www.lwm-info.org/in-dex.asp?Type=B_BASIC&SEC=¢0702EE8F

Monthly. Magazine for officials of Wisconsin's local municipal governments.

★13790★ Postal Record

National Association of Letter Carriers
100 Indiana Ave. NW
Washington, DC 20001-2144
Ph: (202)393-4695
URL: http://www.nalc.org/news/precord/in-dex.html

Monthly. Magazine for active and retired letter carriers.

ONLINE AND DATABASE SERVICES

★13791★ ExecSearches.com

E-mail: info@execsearches.com
URL: http://www.execsearches.com

Description: Job site specializing in matching seekers with non-profit, public sector, academic and "socially conscious" positions. Contains job board, resume databank, e-mail alert system and reference articles. Employers may also post jobs and check resume references.

SOFTWARE

★13792★ Focus Learning Corp.

173 Cross St., Ste. 200
San Luis Obispo, CA 93401
Ph: (805)543-4895   Fax: (805)543-4897
Fr: 800-458-5116
E-mail: info@focuslearning.com
URL: http://www.focuslearning.com

Provides professional services to corporations for the development and implementation of training programs. Assists clients with needs assessment related to training and professional development, goals definition, and development of training materials. Industries served include: government, utility, aerospace, business, and computer.

★13793★ Quick and Easy Federal Jobs Kit

Datatech Software, Inc.
4800 Linglestown Rd., No. 201
Harrisburg, PA 17112
Ph: (717)652-4334   Fax: (717)652-3222
Fr: 800-556-7526
E-mail: tech@quickandeasy.com

URL: http://www.quickandeasy.com

$49.95 (personal version), $129.95 (office pack), $499.95 (professional version). Requires Windows 95. Designed to ensure that federal job applicants include all of the required information on the necessary forms.

OTHER SOURCES

★13794★ African Studies Association (ASA)

Douglass Campus
132 George St.
New Brunswick, NJ 08901-1400
Ph: (732)932-8173   Fax: (732)932-3394
E-mail: asaed@rci.rutgers.edu
URL: http://www.africanstudies.org

Members: Persons specializing in teaching, writing, or research on Africa including political scientists, historians, geographers, anthropologists, economists, librarians, linguists, and government officials; persons who are studying African subjects; institutional members are universities, libraries, government agencies, and others interested in receiving information about Africa. **Purpose:** Seeks to foster communication and to stimulate research among scholars on Africa. **Activities:** Sponsors placement service; conducts panels and discussion groups; presents exhibits and films.

★13795★ Celia D. Crossley & Associates Ltd.

3011 Bethel Rd., Ste. 201
Columbus, OH 43220
Ph: (614)538-2808   Fax: (614)442-8886
E-mail: crosworks@aol.com
URL: http://www.crosworks.com

Firm specializes in career planning and development, executive and organizational career coaching, assessment, key employee selection and team integration. Also offers career transition services, including in-placement, outplacement, and career coaching. Serves government, nonprofit, health-care, higher education and service industries.

★13796★ Civil Service Employees Association (CSEA)

PO Box 7125
Capitol Sta.
Albany, NY 12224-0125
Ph: (518)257-1000   Fax: (518)462-3639
Fr: 800-342-4146
E-mail: donohue@cseainc.org
URL: http://www.csealocal1000.org

Description: AFL-CIO. Represents state and local government employees from all public employee classifications. Negotiates work contracts; represents members in grievances; provides legal assistance for on-the-job problems; provides advice and assistance on federal, state, and local laws affecting public employees. Conducts research,

training and education programs. Compiles statistics.

★13797★ Federally Employed Women (FEW)

1666 K St. NW, Ste. 440
Washington, DC 20006
Ph: (202)898-0994
E-mail: few@few.org
URL: http://www.few.org

Members: Represents men and women employed by the federal government. **Purpose:** Seeks to end sexual discrimination in government service; to increase job opportunities for women in government service and to further the potential of all women in the government; to improve the merit system in government employment; to assist present and potential government employees who are discriminated against because of sex; to work with other organizations and individuals concerned with equal employment opportunity in the government. **Activities:** Provides speakers and sponsors seminars to publicize the Federal Women's Program; furnishes members with information on pending legislation designed to end discrimination against working women; informs and provides members opportunities for training to improve their job potential; issues fact sheets interpreting civil service rules and regulations and other legislative issues; provides annual training conference for over 3,000 women and men.

★13798★ National Alliance of Postal and Federal Employees (NAPFE)

1628 11th St. NW
Washington, DC 20001
Ph: (202)939-6325   Fax: (202)939-6389
E-mail: headquarters@napfe.org
URL: http://www.napfe.com

Description: Independent. Works to eliminate employment discrimination.

★13799★ National Association of Civil Service Employees (NACSE)

6829 Park Ridge Blvd.
San Diego, CA 92120
Ph: (619)466-3150

Description: Federal, state, county, and city civil service employees; association employees and counselors. Assists nonprofit charitable, educational, and scientific organizations in promoting social welfare. Conducts service and product consumer research and educational programs and symposia; sponsors competitions; maintains placement service.

★13800★ National Association of Government Communicators (NAGC)

201 Park Washington Ct.
Falls Church, VA 22046-4527
Ph: (703)538-1787   Fax: (703)241-5603
E-mail: info@nagconline.org
URL: http://www.nagc.com

Members: Government employees, retired persons, non-government affiliates, and students. **Purpose:** Seeks to advance communications as an essential professional resource at every level of national, state, and local government by: disseminating information; encouraging professional development, public awareness, and exchange of ideas and experience; improving internal communications. **Activities:** Maintains placement service.

★13801★ National Association of Government Employees (NAGE)
159 Burgin Pkwy.
Quincy, MA 02169
Ph: (617)376-0220   Fax: (617)376-0285
URL: http://www.nage.org

Members: Union of civilian federal government employees with locals and members in military agencies, Internal Revenue Service, Post Office, Veterans Administration, General Services Administration, Federal Aviation Administration, and other federal agencies, as well as state and local agencies. **Activities:** Activities include direct legal assistance, information service, legislative lobbying and representation, trained leadership in contract negotiations, employment protection, and insurance. Offers seminars; sponsors competitions.

★13802★ National Association of Hispanic Federal Executives (NAHFE)
PO Box 23270
Washington, DC 20026-3270
Ph: (202)315-3942   Fax: (202)478-0806
E-mail: president@nahfe.org
URL: http://www.nahfe.org

Members: Hispanic and other federal employees ranked GS-12 and above; individuals in the private sector whose positions are equivalent to rank GS-12. **Purpose:** Promotes the federal government as a model employer by encouraging qualified individuals to apply for federal government positions. **Activities:** Offers increased productivity training to federal employees. Maintains speakers' bureau and placement service. Offers educational programs; compiles statistics; conducts research.

Help-Wanted Ads

REFERENCE WORKS

★13803★ Affirmative Action Register

Affirmative Action Register
8356 Olive Blvd.
St. Louis, MO 63132
Ph: (314)991-1335   Fax: (314)997-1788
Fr: 800-537-0655
URL: http://www.aar-eeo.com

Monthly. Covers, in each issue, about 300 positions at a professional level (most requiring advanced study) available to women, minorities, veterans, and the handicapped; listings are advertisements placed by employers with affirmative action programs. Entries include: Company or organization name, address, contact name; description of position including title, requirements, duties, application procedure, salary, etc. Arrangement: Classified by profession.

★13804★ EEO Bi-monthly

Career Recruitment Media
211 W Wacker Dr., Ste. 900
Chicago, IL 60606
Ph: (312)525-3100

Bimonthly. Covers about 100 employers nationwide who anticipate having technical, professional or management employment opportunities in the coming six months; five regional editions for Pacific, Western, Midwestern, Southern, and Eastern states. Listings are paid. Entries include: Company name, address, phone, name of contact, date established, number of employees, description of the company and its products, and general description of openings expected. Arrangement: Alphabetical and geographical.

★13805★ Federal Career Opportunities

Federal Research Service Inc.
PO Box 1708
Annandale, VA 22003
Ph: (703)914-JOBS   Fax: (703)914-0628
Fr: 800-822-5027
URL: http://www.fedjobs.com/index.html

Biweekly. Covers more than 3,000 current federal job vacancies in the United States and overseas; includes permanent, part-time, and temporary positions. Entries include: Position title, location, series and grade, job requirements, special forms, announcement number, closing date, application address. Arrangement: Classified by occupation.

★13806★ Federal Jobs Digest

Federal Jobs Digest
326 Main St.
Emmaus, PA 18049
Ph: (610)965-5825
URL: http://www.jobsfed.com

25x/yr. Covers over 10,000 specific job openings in the federal government in each issue. Vacancies from over 300 federal agencies are covered. Entries include: Position name, title, General Schedule (GS) grade, and Wage Grade (WG), closing date for applications, announcement number, application address, phone, and name of contact. Arrangement: By federal department or agency, then geographical.

★13807★ Help Wanted: Job and Career Information Resources

American Library Association
50 E. Huron St.
Chicago, IL 60611
Fr: 800-545-2433
URL: http://www.ala.org/

Gary W. White. 2003. $25. 74 pages. Provides job and career information resources.

★13808★ How to Get Interviews from Classified Job Ads

Random House Inc.
1745 Broadway
New York, NY 10019
Ph: (212)782-9000   Fax: (212)572-6066
Fr: 800-733-3000
URL: http://www.randomhouse.com

Kenton Elderkin. Details how classifieds can be used for job leads, to find out more about hiring practices, and to provide networking opportunities.

★13809★ International Employment Hotline

International Employment Hotline
PO Box 6729
Charlottesville, VA 22906-6729
Ph: (434)985-6444   Fax: (434)985-6828
E-mail: ieo@mindspring.com
URL: http://www.internationaljobs.org/monthly.html

Monthly. $69.00 for individuals, one year; $21.00 for individuals, three months; $39.00 for individuals, six months; $129.00 for individuals, two years. Covers temporary and career job openings overseas and advice for international job hunters. Entries include: Company name, address, job title, description of job, requirements, geographic location of job. Arrangement: Geographical.

NEWSPAPERS, MAGAZINES, AND JOURNALS

★13810★ Employment & the Economy: Northern Region

New Jersey Department of Labor and Workforce Development
1 John Fitch Plaza
PO Box 110
Trenton, NJ 08625-0110
Ph: (609)292-7376   Fax: (609)633-8888
URL: http://lwd.dol.state.nj.us/

Description: Quarterly. Covers economic trends and developments in 11 northern New Jersey counties, including employment conditions and construction project updates. Recurring features include list of job opportunities.

★13811★ Employment & the Economy: Southern Region

New Jersey Department of Labor and Workforce Development
1 John Fitch Plaza
PO Box 110
Trenton, NJ 08625-0110
Ph: (609)292-7376   Fax: (609)633-8888
URL: http://www.wnjpin.state.nj.us

Description: Quarterly. Covers economic developments in six counties in southern New Jersey, including employment conditions and construction project updates. Recurring features include a list of job opportunities.

★13812★ *Federal Jobs Digest*

Breakthrough Publications Inc.
326 Main St.
Emmaus, PA 18049
Ph: (610)965-5825
E-mail: peter@jobsfed.com
URL: http://www.jobsfed.com

Nationwide federal employment newspaper.

★13813★ *Item-Interference Technology Engineers Master*

Robar Industries Inc.
3 Union Hill Rd.
West Conshohocken, PA 19428-2788
Fax: (610)834-7337
E-mail: item@rbitem.com
URL: http://www.interferencetechnology.com/rebrand_redirect.asp

Design magazine about measurement and control of electromagnetic interference.

★13814★ *The NonProfit Times*

NPT Publishing Group Inc.
120 Littleton Rd., Ste. 120
Parsippany, NJ 07054-1803
Ph: (973)394-1800   Fax: (973)394-2888
E-mail: ednchief@nptimes.com
URL: http://www.nptimes.com/

Biweekly. $69.00/year for individuals, subscribe at the one year rate; $49.00/year for individuals, digital only; $100.00/year for individuals, print & digital; $122.00 for two years, (48 issues); $101.00/year for Canada and Mexico; $137.00/year for other countries, international. Trade journal serving nonprofit organizations.

ONLINE AND DATABASE SERVICES

★13815★ **Beyond.com**

1060 First Ave., Ste. 100
King of Prussia, PA 19406
Ph: (610)878-2800
URL: http://careers.beyond.com

Description: Website providing free tools to job seekers including job database, career test, magazines, career evaluation, job alerts, personal portfolio, and career videos.

★13816★ **bigemployment.com**

URL: http://www.bigemployment.com

Description: Website for employers and job-seekers to locate candidates, companies and employers who match their needs.

★13817★ **Biz Classifieds**

5720 Green Cir. Dr., Ste. 100
Minnetonka, MN 55343
Ph: (952)401-0677   Fax: (952)401-0669
E-mail: support@bizclassifiedsplace.com
URL: http://www.bizclassifiedsplace.com

Description: Business resource providing an interactive internet community with tools, education, information and resources necessary to compete in the global entreprenurial arena.

★13818★ **HelpWanted.com**

E-mail: editor@helpwanted.com
URL: http://www.helpwanted.com

Description: Job postings.

★13819★ **Simply Hired, Inc.**

2513 Charleston Rd., Ste. 200
Mountain View, CA 94043
URL: http://www.simplyhired.com

Description: A vertical search engine company providing an online database of jobs.

Identifying Prospective Employers

REFERENCE WORKS

★13820★ America's Corporate Families

Dun & Bradstreet Information Services
899 Eaton Ave.
Bethlehem, PA 18025
Ph: (610)882-7000   Fax: (610)882-7269
Fr: 800-526-0651

Sharon Exner, Kathleen Mumbower, Traci Hilbert, and John Stinner. 2003. Volume I lists all American divisions and subsidiaries; Volume II lists all international divisions and subsidiaries. $495.00.

★13821★ The Career Guide-Dun's Employment Opportunities Directory

Dun & Bradstreet Corp.
103 JFK Pkwy.
Short Hills, NJ 07078
Ph: (973)921-5500   Fax: (973)921-6056
Fr: 800-234-3867
URL: http://dnb.com/us/

Annual. Covers more than 5,000 leading employers throughout the U.S. that provide career opportunities in sales, marketing, management, engineering, life and physical sciences, computer science, mathematics, statistics planning, accounting and finance, liberal arts fields, and other technical and professional areas; based on data supplied on questionnaires and through personal interviews. Also covers personnel consultants; includes some public sector employers (governments, schools, etc.) usually not found in similar lists. Entries include: Company name, location of headquarters and other offices or plants; entries may also include name, title, address, and phone of employment contact; disciplines or occupational groups hired; brief overview of company, discussion of types of positions that may be available, training and career development programs, benefits offered, internship and work-study programs. Arrangement: Employers are alphabetical; geographically by industry; employer branch offices geographically; disciplines hired geographically; employers offering work-study or internship programs and personnel consultants. Indexes: Geographical; SIC code.

★13822★ Corporate Affiliations Library

LexisNexis Group
PO Box 933
Dayton, OH 45401-0933
Ph: (937)865-6800   Fax: (518)487-3584
Fr: 800-543-6862
URL: http://www.corporateaffiliations.com

Annual; latest edition 2004. An 8-volume set listing public and private companies worldwide. Comprises the following: Master Index (volumes 1 and 2); U.S. Public Companies (volume 3 & 4), listing 6,200 parent companies and 52,000 subsidiaries, affiliates, and divisions worldwide; U.S. Private Companies (volume 5), listing 20,000 privately held companies and 24,000 U.S. and international subsidiaries; and International Public and Private Companies (volume 7 & 8), listing 4,800 parent companies and 69,000 subsidiaries worldwide. Entries include: Parent company name, address, phone, fax, telex, e-mail addresses, names and titles of key personnel, financial data, fiscal period, type and line of business, SIC codes; names and locations of subsidiaries, divisions, and affiliates, outside service firms (accountants, legal counsel, etc.). Arrangement: Alphabetical within each volume. Indexes: Each volume includes company name index; separate Master Index volume lists all company names in the set in alphabetic sequence in five indexes including private, public, international, alphabetical, geographical, brand name, SIC, and corporate responsibilities information.

★13823★ The Corporate Directory of U.S. Public Companies

Gale, Cengage Learning
27500 Drake Rd.
Farmington Hills, MI 48331-3535
Ph: (248)699-GALE   Fax: (248)699-8069
Fr: 800-877-GALE
E-mail: galeord@gale.com
URL: http://www.gale.com

2007. Annual. $360.00. 2600 pages. Provides information on more than 9,500 publicly-traded firms having at least $5,000,000 in assets. Entries include: General background, including name, address and phone, number of employees; stock data; description of areas of business; major subsidiaries; officers; directors; owners; and financial data. Indexes: Officers and directors, owners, subsidiary/parent, geographic, SIC, stock exchange, company rankings, and newly registered corporations.

★13824★ D & B Million Dollar Directory

Dun & Bradstreet Corp.
103 JFK Pkwy.
Short Hills, NJ 07078
Ph: (973)921-5500   Fax: (973)921-6056
Fr: 800-234-3867
URL: http://www.dnbmdd.com

Annual. Covers 1,600,000 public and private businesses with either a net worth of $500,000 or more, 250 or more employees at that location, or $25,000,000 or more in sales volume; includes industrial corporations, utilities, transportation companies, bank and trust companies, stock brokers, mutual and stock insurance companies, wholesalers, retailers, and domestic subsidiaries of foreign corporations. Entries include: Company name, address, phone, state of incorporation; annual sales; number of employees, company ticker symbol on stock exchange, Standard Industrial Classification (SIC) number, line of business; principal bank, accounting firm; parent company name, current ownership date, division names and functions, directors or trustees; names, titles, functions of principal executives; number of employees; import/export designation. Arrangement: Alphabetical, cross referenced geographically and by industry classification. Indexes: Geographical (with address and SIC); product by SIC (with address).

★13825★ Directory of Career Training and Development Programs

Ready Reference Press
PO Box 5249
Santa Monica, CA 90405
Ph: (310)475-4895   Fr: 800-424-5627

Alvin Renetzky. $47.50. 286 pages. Provides details on hundreds of professional career training programs offered by some of America's top corporations. Each company profile contains type of training, length of training, and qualifications.

★13826★ Employment Opportunities, USA

Washington Research Associates
1090 Vermont Ave. NW, Ste. 800
Washington, DC 20005
Ph: (202)408-7025

Annual, quarterly updates. Publication includes: List of over 1,000 employment contacts in companies and agencies in banking, arts, telecommunications, education, and 14 other industries and professions, including federal government. Entries include: Company name, name of representative, address, description of products or services, hiring and recruiting practices, training programs, and year established. Principal content is industry overviews, career news, employment opportunity information on 14 different job markets, and comprehensive guidance to career resources on the Internet. Arrangement: Classified by industry. Indexes: Occupation.

★13827★ Finding a Job Just Got a Lot Easier!

Village WordSmith
251 Hilltop Dr., No. 106
Redding, CA 96003
Ph: (530)242-1107
URL: http://villagewordsmith.com/

2001. $24.95. 128 pages. Made for individuals who have been recently fired or quit and now need a job; individuals scheduled for an interview but don't have a current resume; individuals entering or returning to the workforce but don't know how; individuals over 40, 50, 60 and considering a career change. Also provides assistance with focusing on appropriate jobs, composing your resume, targeting prospective employees, or preparing for the job interview.

★13828★ Forbes-Up-and-Comers 200

Forbes Magazine
90 5th Ave.
New York, NY 10011
Ph: (212)366-8900   Fr: 800-295-0893
URL: http://www.forbes.com

Weekly. Publication includes: List of 200 small companies judged to be high quality and fast-growing on the basis of 5-year return on equity and other qualitative measurements. Also includes a list of the 100 best small companies outside the U.S. Note: Issue does not carry address or CEO information for the foreign companies. Entries include: Company name, shareholdings data on chief executive officer; financial data. Arrangement: Alphabetical. Indexes: Ranking.

★13829★ Headquarters USA

Omnigraphics Inc.
615 Griswold St.
PO Box 31-1640
Detroit, MI 48226
Ph: (313)961-1340   Fax: (313)961-1383
Fr: 800-234-1340
URL: http://www.omnigraphics.com

Annual; latest edition 29th. $195.00 for indi-

viduals. Covers approximately 123,000 U.S. businesses, federal, state, and local government offices, banks, colleges and universities, associations, labor unions, political organizations, newspapers, magazines, TV and radio stations, foundations, postal and shipping services, hospitals, office equipment suppliers, airlines, hotels and motels, top cities, accountants, law firms, computer firms, foreign corporations, overseas trade contacts, and other professional services. Also covers internet access providers; internet mailing lists, publications, and sources; freenets. Personal names now included. Entries include: Company, organization, agency, or firm name, address, phone, fax, website addresses as available, toll-free phone. Arrangement: Arranged alphabetically by name (white pages) and in a classified subject arrangement (yellow pages). Indexes: Classified headings.

★13830★ Hidden Job Market

Peterson's Guides
2000 Lenox Dr.
Box 67005
Lawrenceville, NJ 08648
Ph: (609)896-1800   Fax: (609)896-4531
Fr: 800-338-3282
E-mail: custsvc@petersons.com
URL: http://www.petersons.com

Ninth edition, 1999. $18.95 (paper). 319 pages. Guide to 2,000 fast-growing companies that are hiring now. Focuses on high technology companies in such fields as environmental consulting, genetic engineering, home health care, telecommunications, alternative energy systems, and others. Part of Peterson's Hidden Job Market series.

★13831★ International Directory of Company Histories

St. James Press
PO Box 9187
Farmington Hills, MI 48331-9187
Ph: (248)699-4253   Fax: (248)699-8035
Fr: 800-877-4253
URL: http://www.gale.com

Latest edition Vol. 82, published 2006. $230.00 for individuals. Covers 55 volumes, over 5,700 leading companies world-wide. Entries include: Company name, address, phone, names of subsidiaries, dates of founding, sales data, SICs or NAICS, products or services, company history, key dates, principal subsidaries, principal competitors, sources for further reading. Arrangement: Alphabetical. Indexes: Company; industry; geographical.

★13832★ Manufacturing and Distribution USA

Gale, Cengage Learning
27500 Drake Rd.
Farmington Hills, MI 48331-3535
Ph: (248)699-4253   Fax: (248)699-8065
Fr: 800-877-4253
E-mail: ecdi@statrom.com
URL: http://www.gale.com

Biennial; latest edition 4th, published August 2006. $435.00 for individuals. Publication

includes: Lists of up to 75 leading companies for each manufacturing industry (Standard Industrial Classification, or SIC, code range 2011 to 3999), selected on the basis of annual sales. Entries include: Company name, address, phone, name of chief executive, type of company, annual sales, number of employees. Principal content of publication consists of statistical profiles of 458 manufacturing industries and over 21,000 public and private companies. Each industry division includes tables, graphs, and maps that provide general statistics on number of firms and employees, compensation, and production; change in these statistics since 1982 (through 1998 where available); materials consumed statistics; outputs; product share breakdowns by subsector; occupations of employees in the industry; and industry data by state. Arrangement: Classified by industry, then ranked by annual sales. Indexes: Company name, product, occupation, SIC.

★13833★ National Directory of Minority-Owned Business Firms

Business Research Services Inc.
7720 Wisconsin Ave., Ste. 213
Bethesda, MD 20814
Ph: (301)229-5561   Fax: (301)229-6133
Fr: 800-845-8420
URL: http://www.sba8a.com

Annual; latest edition 13th. $295.00 for individuals. Covers over 30,000 minority-owned businesses. Entries include: Company name, address, phone, name and title of contact, minority group, certification status, date founded, number of employees, description of products or services, sales volume, government contracting experience, references. Arrangement: Standard Industrial Classification (SIC) code, geographical. Indexes: Alphabetical by company name; SIC.

★13834★ National Directory of Nonprofit Organizations

The Taft Group
27500 Drake Rd.
Farmington Hills, MI 48331-3535
Ph: (248)699-4253   Fax: 800-414-5043
Fr: 800-877-4253
E-mail: businessproducts@gale.com
URL: http://www.gale.com

Annual; latest edition 21, December 2007. $750.00 for individuals. Covers over 265,000 nonprofit organizations; volume 1 covers organizations with annual incomes of over $100,000; volume 2 covers organizations with incomes between $25,000 and $99,999. Entries include: Organization name, address, phone, annual income, IRS filing status, employer identification number, tax deductible status, activity description. Arrangement: Alphabetical. Indexes: Area of activity, geographical.

★13835★ National Directory of Woman-Owned Business Firms

Business Research Services Inc.
7720 Wisconsin Ave., Ste. 213
Bethesda, MD 20814
Ph: (301)229-5561   Fax: (301)229-6133
Fr: 800-845-8420
URL: http://www.sba8a.com

Annual. $295.00 for individuals. Covers 28,000 woman-owned businesses. Entries include: Company name, address, phone, name and title of contact, minority group, certification status, date founded, number of employees, description of products or services, sales volume, government contracting experience, references. Arrangement: Standard Industrial Classification (SIC) code, geographical. Indexes: Alphabetical by company.

★13836★ Peterson's Job Opportunities for Business Majors

Peterson's
Princeton Pke. Corporate Ctr., 2000
  Lenox Dr.
PO Box 67005
Lawrenceville, NJ 08648
Ph: (609)896-1800   Fax: (609)896-4531
Fr: 800-338-3282
URL: http://www.petersons.com/

Irregular; latest edition 16th, 2000. Covers the 2,000 largest U.S. employers hiring in several fields, including financial services, management consulting, consumer products, and media/entertainment. Entries include: Organization name, address, phone, name and title of contact, number of employees, type of organization. Arrangement: Alphabetical. Indexes: Type of organization.

★13837★ Peterson's Job Opportunities in Engineering and Technology

Peterson's Guides
2000 Lenox Dr.
Box 67005
Lawrenceville, NJ 08648
Ph: (609)896-1800   Fax: (609)896-4531
Fr: 800-338-3282
E-mail: custsvc@petersons.com
URL: http://www.petersons.com

Compiled by the Peterson's staff. Fourth edition, 1996. $21.95 (paper). 379 pages. Profiles 2,000 high-tech companies looking primarily for technical personnel in such fields as biotechnology, telecommunications, software, computers and peripherals, defense, and aerospace. Contains job-search strategies and career options to help match education and expertise to the job market. Indexed geographically, by industry, and by hiring needs.

★13838★ Plunkett's Employers' Internet Sites with Careers Information: The Only Complete Guide to Careers Websites Operated by Major Employers

Plunkett Research, Ltd.
PO Box 541737
Houston, TX 77254-1737
Ph: (713)932-0000   Fax: (713)932-7080
E-mail: customersupport@plunkettresearch.com
URL: http://www.plunkettresearch.com

Jack W. Plunkett. Revised, 2004. $229.99 (includes CD-ROM). Provides profiles of Internet sites for major employers. Job hunters can use the profiles or indexes to locate the Internet job sites that best fit their needs. 681 pages.

★13839★ Standard & Poor's Register of Corporations, Directors and Executives

Standard & Poor's
55 Water St.
New York, NY 10041
Ph: (212)438-1000   Fax: (212)438-2000
Fr: 800-852-1641
URL: http://www2.standardandpoors.com/

Annual, January; supplements in April, July, and October. Covers over 55,000 public and privately held corporations in the United States, including names and titles of over 400,000 officials (Volume 1); 70,000 biographies of directors and executives (Volume 2). Entries include: For companies–Name, address, phone, names of principal executives and accountants; primary bank, primary law firm, number of employees, estimated

annual sales, outside directors, Standard Industrial Classification (SIC) code, product or service provided. For directors and executives–Name, home and principal business addresses, date and place of birth, fraternal organization memberships, business affiliations. Arrangement: Alphabetical. Indexes: Volume 3 indexes companies geographically, by Standard Industrial Classification (SIC) code, and by corporate family groups.

★13840★ Thomas Register of American Manufacturers

Thomas Publishing Co.
5 Penn Plz.
New York, NY 10001
Ph: (212)695-0500   Fax: (212)290-7362
URL: http://www.thomasregister.com

Annual, January. More than 168,000 manufacturing firms are listed in this 34 volume set. Volumes 1-23 list the firms under 68,000 product headings. Thomas Register is enhanced with over 8,000 manufacturers' catalogs and is available in print, CD-ROM, DVD or online. Logistics Guide is a reference manual for freight and shipping sourcing. Arrangement: Volumes 1-23, classified by product or service; Volumes 24-26 alphabetical by company; Volumes 27-34 company catalogs alphabetical by company. Indexes: Product/service, brand/trade name.

AUDIO/VISUAL RESOURCES

★13841★ Effective Use of the Telephone in Your Job Search

Cambridge Educational
PO Box 2053
Princeton, NJ 08543-2053
Ph: 800-257-5126   Fax: (609)671-0266
Fr: 800-468-4227
E-mail: custserv@films.com
URL: http://www.cambridgeeducational.com

VHS and DVD. 1998. $98.95. 22 minutes. Covers using the telephone to identify potential employers and set up interviews.

International Job Opportunities

REFERENCE WORKS

★13842★ 2007-2008 Guide to Employment Web Sites

Kennedy Information
1 Phoenix Mill Ln., 3rd Fl.
Peterborough, NH 03458
Ph: (603)924-1006   Fax: (603)924-4460
Fr: 800-531-0007
URL: http://www.kennedyinfo.com/hr/hrbookstore.html

Annual, Latest edition 2007. $39.95 for individuals. Covers more than 40,000 sites for locating high caliber job candidates. Entries include: Website address, duration of the site, visits per month, profile of frequent visitors, candidate visits, fees, number of records, resume acquisition, site features such as automatic notification of resume-job matches.

★13843★ Alternative Travel Directory

Transitions Abroad Publishing
PO Box 745
Bennington, VT 05201
Ph: (802)442-4827   Fax: (802)442-4827
URL: http://www.transitionsabroad.com/publications/atd/index.shtm

Annual, January; latest edition 7th edition. $19.95 for individuals. Covers over 2,000 sources of information on international employment, education, and specialty travel opportunities. Entries include: Source name, address, phone, description, cost dates. Arrangement: Classified by subject and country. Indexes: Geographical.

★13844★ Careers in International Affairs

Georgetown University Press
3240 Prospect St., NW
Washington, DC 20007
Ph: (202)687-5889   Fax: (202)687-6340
Fr: 800-246-9606
E-mail: gupress@georgetown.edu
URL: http://www.press.georgetown.edu/

Maria Carland and Lisa Gihring (editors).

Seventh edition, 2003. $24.95 (paper). 371 pages. Includes index and bibliography.

★13845★ Careers in International Business

The McGraw-Hill Companies
PO Box 182604
Columbus, OH 43272
Fax: (614)759-3749   Fr: 877-883-5524
E-mail: customer.service@mcgraw-hill.com
URL: http://www.mcgraw-hill.com

Ed Halloran. Second edition, 2003. $14.95 (paper). 192 pages.

★13846★ Craighead's International Business, Travel, and Relocation Guide to 81 Countries

Gale, Cengage Learning
27500 Drake Rd.
Farmington Hills, MI 48331-3535
Ph: (248)699-GALE   Fax: (248)699-8069
Fr: 800-877-GALE
E-mail: galeord@gale.com
URL: http://www.gale.com

First edition, 2002. $695.00. 5366 pages. Arranged geographically into regions of Asia, Africa, Europe, the Mideast, and the Americas. Profiles include information on maps, statistics, travel restrictions, currency, transportation, and health. A separate section covers details of international travel such as instructions for passports and visas and information on transportation and shopping. An international relocation chapter covers financial planning, legal matters, insurance, education, housing, and other family concerns.

★13847★ Directory of American Firms Operating in Foreign Countries

Uniworld Business Publications Inc.
6 Seward Ave.
Beverly, MA 01915
Ph: (978)927-0219
URL: http://www.uniworldbp.com

Biennial; latest edition 19th; published January 2007. $435.00 for individuals. Covers about 4,000 American corporations with 63,000 subsidiaries or affiliates outside the United States. Entries include: Company name, address, phone; names and titles of key personnel; number of employees, annual sales, NAICS code, web address, locations and types of facilities in foreign countries, number of employees, product/service. Separate country editions also available. Arrangement: Alphabetical. Indexes: Foreign operation by country.

★13848★ Directory of International Internships

Dean's Office of International Studies and Programs
Michigan State University
209 International Ctr.
East Lansing, MI 48824-1035
Ph: (517)355-2350   Fax: (517)353-7254
URL: http://www.isp.msu.edu/students/internships/intlguide/

Irregular; latest edition 5th. $30.00 for students; $37.00 for other individuals. Covers international internships sponsored by academic institutions, private sector, and the federal government. Entries include: Institution name, address, phone, names and titles of key personnel, subject areas in which internships are available, number available, location, duration, financial data, academic credit available, evaluation procedures, application deadline, requirements of participation. Arrangement: Classified by type of sponsor, then alphabetical. Indexes: Sponsor; subject; geographical.

★13849★ Directory of Websites for International Jobs

Impact Publications
9104 Manassas Dr., Ste. N
Manassas Park, VA 20111-5211
Ph: (703)361-7300   Fax: (703)335-9486
Fr: 800-361-1055
URL: http://www.impactpublications.com/

2002 edition. $19.95. Covers 1,400 websites.

★13850★ Federal Career Opportunities

Federal Research Service Inc.
PO Box 1708
Annandale, VA 22003
Ph: (703)914-JOBS   Fax: (703)914-0628
Fr: 800-822-5027
URL: http://www.fedjobs.com/index.html

Biweekly. Covers more than 3,000 current federal job vacancies in the United States and overseas; includes permanent, part-time, and temporary positions. Entries include: Position title, location, series and grade, job requirements, special forms, announcement number, closing date, application address. Arrangement: Classified by occupation.

★13851★ Finding Work Overseas: How and Where to Contact International Recruitment Agencies, Consultants and Employers

Trans-Atlantic Publications, Inc.
311 Bainbridge St.
Philadelphia, PA 19147
Ph: (215)925-5083   Fax: (215)925-1912
E-mail: jeffgolds@comcast.net
URL: http://www.transatlanticpub.com/

Matthew Cunningham. 1996. 205 pages. Part of the Living and Working Abroad Series.

★13852★ Great Jobs for Foreign Language Majors

The McGraw-Hill Companies
PO Box 182604
Columbus, OH 43272
Fax: (614)759-3749   Fr: 877-883-5524
E-mail: customer.service@mcgraw-hill.com
URL: http://www.mcgraw-hill.com

Julie DeGalan and Stephen Lambert. Second edition, 2000. $15.95 (paper). 192 pages. Part of "Great Jobs for ... Majors" series.

★13853★ How to Get a Job in Europe

Planning Communications
7215 Oak Ave.
River Forest, IL 60305-1935
Ph: (708)366-5200   Fax: (708)366-5280
Fr: 888-366-5200
E-mail: info@planningcommunications.com
URL: http://jobfindersonline.com

Robert Sanborn and Cheryl Matherly. Fifth edition, 2003. 496 pages. $22.95. Directory of employers, associations, job referral services, and other sources of employment information. Part of Insider's Guide series.

★13854★ International Employment Hotline

International Employment Hotline
PO Box 6729
Charlottesville, VA 22906-6729
Ph: (434)985-6444   Fax: (434)985-6828
E-mail: ieo@mindspring.com
URL: http://www.internationaljobs.org/monthly.html

Monthly. $69.00 for individuals, one year; $21.00 for individuals, three months; $39.00 for individuals, six months; $129.00 for individuals, two years. Covers temporary and career job openings overseas and advice for international job hunters. Entries include: Company name, address, job title, description of job, requirements, geographic location of job. Arrangement: Geographical.

★13855★ International Jobs Directory

Impact Publications
9104 Manassas Dr., Ste. N
Manassas Park, VA 20111-5211
Ph: (703)361-7300   Fax: (703)335-9486
Fr: 800-361-1055
E-mail: query@impactpublications.com
URL: http://www.impactpublications.com

Ronald L. Krannich and Caryl R. Krannich. 1998. $19.95 (paper).323 pages.

★13856★ Korea Calling: The Essential Handbook for Teaching English and Living in South Korea

Woodpecker Press
41 N. Palmer Dr.
Port Townsend, WA 98368-9427
Ph: (360)379-0297

Jay Freeborne and Allegra Specht. 1996. $14.95 (paper). 174 pages.

★13857★ Major Companies of the Far East and Australasia

Gale, Cengage Learning
27500 Drake Rd.
Farmington Hills, MI 48331-3535
Ph: (248)699-GALE   Fax: (248)699-8069
Fr: 800-877-GALE
E-mail: galeord@gale.com
URL: http://www.gale.com

Twentieth edition, 2003. Four volumes. $1,625.00/set. Listings are organized by country.

★13858★ Opportunities Abroad for Educators

Fulbright Teacher and Administrator Exchange Program
600 Maryland Ave. SW, Ste. 320
Washington, DC 20024-2520
Ph: (202)314-3527   Fax: (202)479-6806
Fr: 800-726-0479
URL: http://www.fulbrightexchanges.org

Annual. Covers opportunities available for elementary and secondary teachers, two-year college instructors, and school administrators to attend seminars or to teach abroad under the Mutual Educational and Cultural Exchange Act of 1961. Entries include: Countries of placement, dates, eligibility requirements, teaching assignments. Arrangement: Geographical.

★13859★ Opportunities in International Business Careers

The McGraw-Hill Companies
PO Box 182604
Columbus, OH 43272
Fax: (614)759-3749   Fr: 877-883-5524

E-mail: customer.service@mcgraw-hill.com
URL: http://www.mcgraw-hill.com

Jeffrey Arpan. 1994. $11.95 (paper). 147 pages. Describes what types of jobs exist in international business, where they are located, what challenges and rewards they bring, and how to prepare for and obtain jobs in international business.

★13860★ Opportunities in Overseas Careers

The McGraw-Hill Companies
PO Box 182604
Columbus, OH 43272
Fax: (614)759-3749   Fr: 877-883-5524
E-mail: customer.service@mcgraw-hill.com
URL: http://www.mcgraw-hill.com

Blythe Camenson. 2004. $13.95 (paper). 173 pages.

★13861★ Overseas Employment Opportunities for Educators: Department of Defense Dependents Schools

DIANE Publishing Co.
PO Box 617
Darby, PA 19023-0617
Ph: (610)461-6200   Fax: (610)461-6130
Fr: 800-782-3833
URL: http://www.dianepublishingcentral.com

Barry Leonard, editor. 2000. $15.00. 54 pages. An introduction to teachings positions in the Dept. of Defense Dependents Schools (DoDDS), a worldwide school system, operated by the DoD in 14 countries.

★13862★ Overseas Exotic Jobs-$100 to $1000 Daily: For Unskilled, Skilled, Professionals

Zinks International Career Guidance
PO Box 587
Marshall, MI 49068-0587

Richard M. Zink. Eighth edition, 1995. $14.95 (paper). 64 pages.

★13863★ Part Time Prospects: International Comparison of Part Time Work in Europe, North America and the Pacific Rim

Taylor & Francis
325 Chestnut St., 8th Fl.
Philadelphia, PA 19106
Ph: (215)625-8900   Fax: (215)269-0363
Fr: 800-821-8312
URL: http://www.taylorandfrancis.com

Jacqueline O'Reilly and Colette Fagan. 2007. $48.95 (paper). 308 pages. Presents for the first time a systematically comparative analysis of the common and divergent patterns in the use of part-time work in Europe, America and the Pacific Rim.

★13864★ Peterson's Job Opportunities for Business Majors

Peterson's
Princeton Pke. Corporate Ctr., 2000 Lenox Dr.
PO Box 67005
Lawrenceville, NJ 08648
Ph: (609)896-1800   Fax: (609)896-4531
Fr: 800-338-3282
URL: http://www.petersons.com/

Irregular; latest edition 16th, 2000. Covers the 2,000 largest U.S. employers hiring in several fields, including financial services, management consulting, consumer products, and media/entertainment. Entries include: Organization name, address, phone, name and title of contact, number of employees, type of organization. Arrangement: Alphabetical. Indexes: Type of organization.

★13865★ Peterson's Job Opportunities in Engineering and Technology

Peterson's Guides
2000 Lenox Dr.
Box 67005
Lawrenceville, NJ 08648
Ph: (609)896-1800   Fax: (609)896-4531
Fr: 800-338-3282
E-mail: custsvc@petersons.com
URL: http://www.petersons.com

Compiled by the Peterson's staff. Fourth edition, 1996. $21.95 (paper). 379 pages. Profiles 2,000 high-tech companies looking primarily for technical personnel in such fields as biotechnology, telecommunications, software, computers and peripherals, defense, and aerospace. Contains job-search strategies and career options to help match education and expertise to the job market. Indexed geographically, by industry, and by hiring needs.

★13866★ Resumes for Overseas & Stateside Jobs

Zinks International Career Guidance
PO Box 587
Marshall, MI 49068-0587

Richard M. Zink. 1994. $14.95 (paper). 80 pages.

★13867★ Summer Jobs Britain

Peterson's Guides
2000 Lenox Dr.
Box 67005
Lawrenceville, NJ 08648
Ph: (609)896-1800   Fax: (609)896-4531
Fr: 800-338-3282
E-mail: custsvc@petersons.com
URL: http://www.petersons.com

David Woodworth and Guy Hobbs (editors). First edition, 2007. $19.95 (paper). 320 pages. Part of Summer Jobs Britain series.

★13868★ Vacation Work's Overseas Summer Jobs

Peterson's
Princeton Pke. Corporate Ctr., 2000 Lenox Dr.
PO Box 67005
Lawrenceville, NJ 08648
Ph: (609)896-1800   Fax: (609)896-4531
Fr: 800-338-3282
URL: http://www.petersons.com/

Annual. Covers over 30,000 summer jobs worldwide. Entries include: Complete job data, length of employment, number of openings, pay, job description, qualifications needed, application/contact information.

★13869★ Weddle's Recruiter's and Job Seeker's Guide to Association Web Sites

Paul & Co.
814 N Franklin St.
Chicago, IL 60610
Ph: (312)337-0747   Fax: (312)337-5985
Fr: 800-888-4741
URL: http://www.ipgbook.com/

$49.95. Covers 1,900 associations from around the world. Entries include: resume database, discussion forum, and association who offers a job board. Indexes: By career field, industry, and Geographical location.

NEWSPAPERS, MAGAZINES, AND JOURNALS

★13870★ Center for European Studies Newsletter

Center for European Studies
FedEx Global Education Center
Univ. of North Carolina
Campus Box 3449
Chapel Hill, NC 27599
Ph: (919)962-6765
E-mail: europe@unc.edu
URL: http://www.unc.edu/depts/europe/

Description: Bimonthly. Announces events, visiting scholars, fellowships, scholarships, and grants at the Center. Recurring features include a calendar of events, news of educational opportunities, notes from the director, and job listings.

★13871★ International Living

Agora Inc.
PO Box 1936
Baltimore, MD 21203
Ph: (410)783-8499   Fax: (410)837-1999
Fr: 800-433-1528
E-mail: csteam@agorapublishinggroup.com
URL: http://www.agora-inc.com

Description: Monthly. Features articles about international travel, lifestyles, investments, retirement, employment, and real estate. Includes monthly currency reports. Recurring features include news briefs, letters to the editor, book reviews, and a calendar of events.

★13872★ International Studies Newsletter

International Studies Association
Social Sciences, No. 324
University of Arizona
Tucson, AZ 85721
Ph: (520)621-7715   Fax: (520)621-5780
E-mail: isa@u.arizona.edu
URL: http://www.isanet.org/

Description: Eight issues/year. Promotes the Association's interest in a multidisciplinary approach to international affairs and cross-cultural studies. Acts as a forum for discussion among scholars, students, and the general public. Recurring features include Association news; information on publications by members; notices of employment opportunities; calls for papers; and announcements of meetings, conferences, lectures, awards, grants, and fellowships.

★13873★ NewsNet, the Newsletter of the AAASS

American Association for the Advancement of Slavic Studies (AAASS)
8 Story St.
Cambridge, MA 02138
Ph: (617)495-0677   Fax: (617)495-0680
E-mail: aaass@fas.harvard.edu
URL: http://www.fas.harvard.edu/~aaass/

Description: Bimonthly. Reports on Association activities and on Slavic study research in institutions throughout the world. Alerts readers to research grants, internships, and fellowship opportunities as well as to employment opportunities in universities across the country. Announces awards, upcoming conferences, courses, new scholarly publications, and annual research.

ONLINE AND DATABASE SERVICES

★13874★ FreeJobSearchEngines.com
URL: http://www.freejobsearchengines.com/
Description: Job board meta-search engine grouping jobs by geography. Seekers can search in the United States, the United Kingdom, Australia, Canada and Hong Kong.

OTHER SOURCES

★13875★ Association for International Practical Training (AIPT)

10400 Little Patuxent Pkwy., Ste. 250
Columbia, MD 21044-3519
Ph: (410)997-2200   Fax: (410)992-3924
E-mail: aipt@aipt.org
URL: http://www.aipt.org

Description: Providers worldwide of on-the-job training programs for students and professionals seeking international career development and life-changing experiences. Arranges workplace exchanges in hundreds of professional fields, bringing employers and trainees together from around the world. Client list ranges from small farming communities to Fortune 500 companies.

★13876★ Chinese Christian Mission (CCM)

PO Box 750759
Petaluma, CA 94975-0759
Ph: (707)762-1314   Fax: (707)762-1713
E-mail: ccm@ccmusa.org
URL: http://www.ccmusa.org

Purpose: Serves as an evangelical faith mission dedicated to reaching Chinese people around the world with the gospel of Jesus Christ. Broadcasts radio programs to foster Christianity in China. **Activities:** Operates placement service providing ministers with churches. Sponsors short-term mission trips to Latin America and East Asia.

★13877★ International Educator's Institute (TIE)

PO Box 513
Cummaquid, MA 02637
Ph: (508)790-1990   Fax: (508)790-1922
Fr: 877-375-6668
E-mail: tie@tieonline.com
URL: http://www.tieonline.com

Description: Facilitates the placement of teachers and administrators in American, British, and international schools. Seeks to create a network that provides for professional development opportunities and improved financial security of members. Offers advice and information on international school news, recent educational developments, job placement, and investment, consumer, and professional development opportunities. Makes available insurance and travel benefits. Operates International Schools Internship Program.

★13878★ NAFSA/Association of International Educators (NAFSA)

1307 New York Ave. NW, 8th Fl.
Washington, DC 20005-4701
Ph: (202)737-3699   Fax: (202)737-3657
E-mail: inbox@nafsa.org
URL: http://www.nafsa.org

Description: Individuals, organizations, and institutions dealing with international educational exchange, including foreign student advisers, overseas educational advisers, credentials and admissions officers, administrators and teachers of English as a second language, community support personnel, study-abroad administrators, and embassy cultural or educational personnel. Promotes self-regulation standards and responsibilities in international educational exchange; offers professional development opportunities primarily through publications, workshops, grants, and regional and national conferences. Advocates for increased awareness and support of international education and exchange on campuses, in government, and in communities. Offers services including: a job registry for employers and professionals involved with international education; a consultant referral service. Sponsors joint liaison activities with a variety of other educational and government organizations to conduct a census of foreign student enrollment in the U.S.; conducts workshops about specific subjects and countries.

★13879★ U.S.-China Education Foundation (USCEF)

4140 Oceanside Blvd., Ste. 159 - No. 112
Oceanside, CA 92056-6005
Ph: (760)644-0977
E-mail: uscef@sage-usa.net
URL: http://www.sage-usa.net/uscef.htm

Purpose: Aims to promote the learning of the Chinese languages (including Mandarin, Cantonese, and minority languages such as Mongolian) by Americans, and the learning of English by Chinese. **Activities:** Conducts short-term travel-study program to prepare

Americans and Chinese for stays of four, six, or eight months or one to four years in China or the U.S., respectively. Operates teacher placement service and speakers' bureau. A project of The Society for the Development of Global Education (S.A.G.E. Inc.).

★13880★ United States Committee for the United Nations Environment Program (US UNEP)

47914 252nd St.
Sioux Falls, SD 57198-0002
Ph: (605)594-6117   Fax: (605)594-6119
E-mail: singh@usgs.gov
URL: http://grid2.cr.usgs.gov

Description: Individuals interested in raising public awareness of the importance of a global environmental effort. Encourages activism in support of the United Nations Environment Program. Acts as a liaison between the UNEP and the public. Sponsors educational programs and children's services. Offers placement services to job seekers in international environmental work. Maintains speakers' bureau.

★13881★ YMCA International Camp Counselor Program (ICCP)

5 W 63rd St., 2nd Fl.
New York, NY 10023-9197
Ph: (212)727-8800   Fax: (212)727-8814
Fr: 888-477-9622
E-mail: ips@ymcanyc.org
URL: http://www.internationalymca.org/ICCP/home.html

Description: Serves as a work-travel program designed to introduce international university students and teachers and social workers aged 19-30 to life in America; the students spend 8 to 9 weeks counseling in children's camps across the country, followed by a period of independent or group travel. Sponsors ICCP-Abroad placement service for American university students aged 18-25 wishing to serve as camp counselors in Africa, Asia, Australia, Hungary, New Zealand, and South America.

Interviewing Skills

REFERENCE WORKS

★13882★ 50 Winning Answers to Interview Questions

Drake Beam Morin Pub
750 Third Ave., 28th Fl.
New York, NY 10017
Ph: (212)692-7700   Fax: (212)297-0426
E-mail: inquiries@dbm.com
URL: http://www.dbm.com

Charles F. Albrecht, Jr., editor. 1995. $10.95 (paper). 160 pages. Provides question-by-question guidance.

★13883★ The 90 Minute Interview Prep Book

Peterson's Guides
2000 Lenox Dr.
Box 67005
Lawrenceville, NJ 08648
Ph: (609)896-1800   Fax: (609)896-4531
Fr: 800-338-3282
E-mail: custsvc@petersons.com
URL: http://www.petersons.com

Peggy Schmidt. 1996. $15.95 (paper). 155 pages. Includes diskette. Provides step-by-step instructions for conducting practice interviews. Software allows users to evaluate the practice interviews.

★13884★ 101 Great Answers to the Toughest Interview Questions

Cengage Learning
PO Box 6904
Florence, KY 41022
Fax: 800-487-8488   Fr: 800-354-9706
URL: http://www.cengage.com

Ronald Fry. Fifth edition, 2006. $12.95 (paper). 224 pages. Identifies some of the toughest interview questions and provides proven responses.

★13885★ A Better Job Interview: Questions and Techniques

Rampant Techpress
PO Box 511
Kittrell, NC 27544
Ph: (252)431-0050   Fax: (252)433-9311
Fr: (866)729-8145
URL: http://www.rampant-books.com/

Damen Choy. May 2004. $17.95 (paper). 150 pages.

★13886★ Dynamite Networking for Dynamite Jobs: 101 Interpersonal Telephone and Electronic Techniques for Getting Job Leads, Interviews, and Offers

Impact Publications
9104 Manassas Dr., Ste. N
Manassas Park, VA 20111-5211
Ph: (703)361-7300   Fax: (703)335-9486
Fr: 800-361-1055
E-mail: query@impactpublications.com
URL: http://www.impactpublications.com

Caryl R. Krannich and Ronald L. Kannich. 1996. $15.95 (paper). 188 pages.

★13887★ Effective Interviewing for Paralegals

Anderson Publishing Co.
2035 Reading Rd.
Cincinnati, OH 45202-1576
Ph: (513)421-4142   Fax: (513)562-8116
Fr: 800-582-7295

Fred E. Jandt. Second edition, 1994. $28.95. 300 pages.

★13888★ Essential Interviewing: A Programmed Approach to Effective Communication

Wadsworth Publishing
PO Box 6904
Florence, KY 41022
Fax: 800-487-8488   Fr: 800-354-9706
URL: http://www.cengage.com

Allen Ivey, Margaret T. Hearn, Max R. Uhlemann and David R. Evans. $79.95. Sixth edition, 2007. 320 pages.

★13889★ A Funny Thing Happened at the Interview: Wit, Wisdom, and War Stories from the Job Hunt

Edin Books, Inc.
102 Sunrise Dr.
Gillette, NJ 07933
Ph: (908)647-3346   Fax: (908)580-1008
Fr: 800-334-6477
E-mail: edinbooks@patmedia.net.
URL: http://www.edinbooks.com/

Gregory F. Farrell, Linda Sue Nathanson, and Chris McDonough. 1996. $12.95 (paper). 272 pages. Humorous, true job interview stories.

★13890★ Get That Interview: The Indispensable Guide for College Grads

Barron's Educational Series, Inc.
250 Wireless Blvd.
Hauppauge, NY 11788-3917
Ph: (631)434-3311   Fax: (631)434-3723
Fr: 800-645-3476
E-mail: fbrown@barronseduc.com
URL: http://barronseduc.com

R. Theodore Moock, Jr. 1996. $8.95 (paper). 145 pages. Offers strategies, tactics, and advice for the recent college graduate.

★13891★ Get That Job!: Interviews

The McGraw-Hill Companies
PO Box 182604
Columbus, OH 43272
Fax: (614)759-3749   Fr: 877-883-5524
E-mail: customer.service@mcgraw-hill.com
URL: http://www.mcgraw-hill.com

Susan Echaore-McDavid. 1997. $7.40 (paper). 32 pages.

★13892★ Government Job Finder

Planning Communications
7215 Oak Ave.
River Forest, IL 60305-1935
Ph: (708)366-5200   Fax: (708)366-5280
Fr: 888-366-5200
E-mail: info@planningcommunications.com
URL: http://jobfindersonline.com

Daniel Lauber. Fourth edition, 2006. 300 pages. $18.95. Covers 1800 sources. Discusses how to use sources of local, state, and federal government job vacancies in a number of specialties and state-by-state, including job-matching services, job hotlines, specialty periodicals with job ads, salary surveys, and directories. Explains how local, state, and federal hiring systems work. Includes chapters on resume and cover letter preparation and interviewing.

★13893★ **How to Have a Winning Job Interview**

The McGraw-Hill Companies
PO Box 182604
Columbus, OH 43272
Fax: (614)759-3749   Fr: 877-883-5524
E-mail: customer.service@mcgraw-hill.com
URL: http://www.mcgraw-hill.com

Deborah Perlmutter Bloch. Third edition, 1998. $14.95 (paper). 150 pages. Guides the reader through the steps of making the best impression on a future employer, including getting the appointment for the interview and planning an approach, what to emphasize, and what to minimize.

★13894★ **How to Turn an Interview into a Job**

Simon & Schuster Inc
1230 Ave. of the Americas
New York, NY 10020
Ph: (212)698-7000   Fax: (212)698-7007
Fr: 800-897-7650
URL: http://www.simonsays.com/

Jeffrey G. Allen. Rev edition, April 2004. $11.95 (paper). 128 pages. Presents proven advice on the A to Zs of successful interviewing.

★13895★ **Information Interviewing: How to Tap Your Hidden Job Market**

Ferguson Publishing Co.
132 W. 31st St.
New York, NY 10001
Fax: 800-678-3633   Fr: 800-322-8755
E-mail: custserv@factsonfile.com
URL: http://ferguson.infobasepublishing.com/

Martha Stoodley. Second edition, 1996. 170 pages. Details the why, how, and where of information interviewing and provides suggestions for incorporating this technique into an effective job search.

★13896★ **Interview Strategies That Will Get You the Job You Want**

F & W Publications, Inc.
4700 E Galbraith Rd.
Cincinnati, OH 45236
Ph: (513)531-2690   Fax: (513)531-4082
Fr: 800-289-0963
URL: http://www.fwpublications.com/

Andrea G. Kay. 1996. $12.99 (paper). 132 pages.

★13897★ **Interview for Success: A Practical Guide to Increasing Job Interviews, Offers, and Salaries**

Impact Publications
9104 Manassas Dr., Ste. N
Manassas Park, VA 20111-5211
Ph: (703)361-7300   Fax: (703)335-9486
Fr: 800-361-1055
E-mail: query@impactpublications.com
URL: http://www.impactpublications.com

Caryl Rae Krannich and Ronald L. Krannich. Eighth edition, 2002. $15.95 (paper). 209 pages. Subtitled: "A Practical Guide to Increasing Job Interviews, Offers and Salaries". Offers hundreds of tips for more successful job interviews.

★13898★ **Interviewing & Helping Skills for Health Professionals**

Wadsworth Publishing
PO Box 6904
Florence, KY 41022
Fax: 800-487-8488   Fr: 800-354-9706
URL: http://www.cengage.com

L. Sherilyn Cormier. Second edition, 1999. $37.50 (paper). 334 pages.

★13899★ **Interviewing Principles and Practices**

The McGraw-Hill Companies
PO Box 182604
Columbus, OH 43272
Fax: (614)759-3749   Fr: 877-883-5524
E-mail: customer.service@mcgraw-hill.com
URL: http://www.mcgraw-hill.com

Charles J. Stewart and William B. Cash. Eighth edition, 2007. $71.25 (paper). 456 pages.

★13900★ **Interviewing Techniques for Newspapers**

Hyperion Books
77 West 66th St., 11 Fl.
New York, NY 10023
Ph: (212)522-8700   Fr: 800-759-0190
URL: http://www.hyperionbooks.com

Maurice Dunlevy. 1995. $20.00 (paper). 143 pages.

★13901★ **Job Interview Tips for People with Not-So-Hot Backgrounds: How to Put Red Flags Behind You**

Impact Publications
9104 Manassas Dr., Ste. N
Manassas Park, VA 20111-5211
Ph: (703)361-7300   Fax: (703)335-9486
Fr: 800-361-1055
E-mail: query@impactpublications.com
URL: http://www.impactpublications.com

Ron Krannich. March 2004. $14.95 (paper). 160 pages.

★13902★ **Job Interviewing for College Students**

The McGraw-Hill Companies
PO Box 182604
Columbus, OH 43272
Fax: (614)759-3749   Fr: 877-883-5524
E-mail: customer.service@mcgraw-hill.com
URL: http://www.mcgraw-hill.com

John D. Singleton. 1995. $11.95 (paper). 112 pages.

★13903★ **Job Interviews for Dummies**

For Dummies
1 Wiley Dr.
Somerset, NJ 08875-1272
Ph: (732)469-4400   Fax: (732)302-2300
Fr: 800-225-5945
URL: http://www.dummies.com/WileyCDA/

Joyce L. Kennedy. Third edition, 2008. $16.99 (paper). 336 pages. Covers basic steps of interviewing from preparation to salary negotiation. Part of For Dummies series.

★13904★ **Job Interviews Made Easy**

The McGraw-Hill Companies
PO Box 182604
Columbus, OH 43272
Fax: (614)759-3749   Fr: 877-883-5524
E-mail: customer.service@mcgraw-hill.com
URL: http://www.mcgraw-hill.com

Jan Bailey Mattia. 1997. $7.44 (paper). 96 pages.

★13905★ **Job Interviews That Mean Business**

Random House
1745 Broadway
New York, NY 10019
Ph: (212)782-9000   Fax: (212)572-6066
Fr: 800-733-3000
URL: http://www.randomhouse.com

David R. Eyler. Third edition, 1999. $12.95 (paper). 272 pages.

★13906★ **Key Words to Nail Your Job Interview: What to Say to Win Your Dream Job**

Impact Publications
9104 Manassas Dr., Ste. N
Manassas Park, VA 20111-5211
Ph: (703)361-7300   Fax: (703)335-9486
Fr: 800-361-1055
E-mail: query@impactpublications.com
URL: http://www.impactpublications.com

Wendy S. Enelow. March 2004. $17.95 (paper). 222 pages.

★13907★ **Knock 'Em Dead: The Ultimate Job Seeker's Handbook**

Adams Media Corp.
4700 E. Galbraith Rd.
Cincinnati, OH 45236
Ph: (513)531-2690   Fax: (513)531-4082
Fr: 800-289-0963
URL: http://www.adamsmedia.com

Martin Yate. Revised edition, 2007. $14.95 (paper). Prepares the job seeker for the interview with advice on dress, manner, how to answer the toughest questions, and how to spot illegal questions. Discusses how to respond to questions of salary to maximize income. Features sections on executive search firms and drug testing. 352 pages.

★13908★ Last Minute Interview Tips

Cengage Learning
PO Box 6904
Florence, KY 41022
Fax: 800-487-8488   Fr: 800-354-9706
URL: http://www.cengage.com

Brandon Toropov. 1996. $12.95 (paper). 128 pages.

★13909★ The Medical Job Interview

Blackwell Science, Incorporated
Commerce Pl.
350 Main St.
Malden, MA 02148-5018
Ph: (781)388-8200   Fax: (781)388-8210
Fr: 800-759-6102
URL: http://www.blackwellpublishing.com/

Colin Mumford. Second edition, 2005. $24.95 (paper). 76 pages.

★13910★ More Successful Less Stressful Interviewing for Women: A Guide to Improving Your Interviewing Skills While Reducing Stress

StellWest Publishing Co., Inc.
PO Box 190
River Edge, NJ 07661
Ph: (201)692-8306   Fax: (201)692-0302

Jessica Woods. 1995. $9.95 (paper). 105 pages. Specialty publication geared toward women which teaches interviewing and personal skills to gain the edge over competitors.

★13911★ The New Job Interview

P P I Publishing
PO Box 292239
Kettering, OH 45429
Ph: (937)294-5057   Fax: (937)294-9442
Fr: 800-773-6825

Dinah Tallent. 1995. $6.95 (paper). 149 pages.

★13912★ The Perfect Interview: How to Get the Job You Really Want

Cengage Learning
PO Box 6904
Florence, KY 41022
Fax: 800-487-8488   Fr: 800-354-9706
URL: http://www.cengage.com

John D. Drake. Fifth edition, 2005. $17.95 (paper). 224 pages. Contains skill-building exercises and tips on preparing for the interview, framing good questions, and following through.

★13913★ Power Interviews: Job-Winning Tactics from Fortune 500 Recruiters

John Wiley and Sons, Inc.
1 Wiley Dr.
Somerset, NJ 08875-1272
Ph: (732)469-4400   Fax: (732)302-2300
Fr: 800-225-5945
E-mail: custserv@wiley.com
URL: http://www.wiley.com/WileyCDA/

Neil Yeager and Lee Hough. Revised, 1998. $15.95 (paper). 238 pages.

★13914★ The Quick Interview & Salary Negotiation Book: Dramatically Improve Your Interviewing Skills & Pay in a Matter of Hours

Jist Works
875 Montreal Way
St. Paul, MN 55102
Fr: 800-648-5478
E-mail: info@jist.com
URL: http://www.jist.com

Michael J. Farr. 1995. $14.95 (paper). 400 pages. Tells how to research before an interview, how to understanding traditional and nontraditional interview approaches used by employers, and how to take charge of the negotiation process.

★13915★ Resumes, Cover-Letters & Interviewing: Setting the Stage for Success

Wadsworth Publishing
PO Box 6904
Florence, KY 41022
Fax: 800-487-8488   Fr: 800-354-9706
URL: http://www.cengage.com

Clifford W. Eischen and Lynn A. Eischen. 1999. $25.95 (paper). 128 pages. Professional resume using today's business technologies including the Internet and E-mail. Specifically targeted to help individuals with a two-year degree showcase their skills and experiences to get the job they want. Scanable resumes, Internet-based resumes, and etiquette for sending resumes via fax or E-mail are addressed to prepare readers to apply for jobs using today's business technologies. Dedicated chapter on the interview process coaches readers on proper interview attire, preparing for interview questions, introductions, and how to follow up after an interview. Exercises on listing qualifications, producing a first draft, gathering references, and drafting a follow-up letter, all help readers build a finished resume step by step.

★13916★ Tips for Finding the Right Job

U.S. Government Printing Office
732 N. Capitol St. NW
Washington, DC 20401
Ph: (202)512-1800   Fax: (202)512-2104
Fr: (866)512-1800
E-mail: ContactCenter@gpo.gov
URL: http://www.gpoaccess.gov

United States. 029-014-002445. 1996. $2.50. 27 pages. General advice for job

seekers. See website for current list of available publications.

★13917★ Top Answers to Job Interview Questions: Which Questions the Applicant Should Ask

Rampant TechPress
PO Box 511
Kittrell, NC 27544
Ph: (252)431-0050   Fax: (252)433-9311
Fr: (866)729-8145
URL: http://www.rampant-books.com/

Donald Burleson, Robert Strickland. April 2004. $16.95 (paper).

★13918★ Your First Interview

The Career Press, Inc.
3 Tice Rd.
PO Box 687
Franklin Lakes, NJ 07417-1322
Ph: (201)848-0310   Fax: (201)848-1727
Fr: 800-227-3371
URL: http://www.careerpress.com

Ronald Fry. Fourth edition, 2001. $14.95 (paper). 154 pages. Takes the reader from making the initial contact with a prospective employer to negotiating salary.

AUDIO/VISUAL RESOURCES

★13919★ Access Unlimited: The Job Search Series for People with Disabilities

Cambridge Educational
PO Box 2053
Princeton, NJ 08543-2053
Ph: 800-257-5126   Fax: (609)671-0266
Fr: 800-468-4227
E-mail: custserv@films.com
URL: http://www.cambridgeeducational.com

VHS and DVD. 1998. $269.85. Three 30-minute videos cover job search tactics, resumes and applications, and job interviewing.

★13920★ Common Mistakes People Make in Interviews

Cambridge Educational
PO Box 2053
Princeton, NJ 08543-2053
Ph: 800-257-5126   Fax: (609)671-0266
Fr: 800-468-4227
E-mail: custserv@films.com
URL: http://www.cambridgeeducational.com

VFHS and DVD. 2003. $79.95. 27 minutes. Helps job seekers anticipate what interviewers are looking for.

★13921★ **The Complete Job Search System**

Cambridge Educational
PO Box 2053
Princeton, NJ 08543-2053
Ph: 800-257-5126   Fax: (609)671-0266
Fr: 800-468-4227
E-mail: custserv@films.com
URL: http://www.cambridgeeducational.com

VHS and DVD. 2007. $399.75. Individual titles cover career planning, career evaluation, finding a job, interviewing for a job, and succeeding on the job.

★13922★ **Developing Your Interviewing Skills for the Executive**

Drake Beam Morin, Inc.
750 Third Ave., 28th Fl.
New York, NY 10017
Ph: (215)692-7700   Fax: (215)399-1391
Fr: 800-345-5627
E-mail: inquiries@dbm.com
URL: http://www.dbm.com

Video. $49.95.

★13923★ **Effective Use of the Telephone in Your Job Search**

Cambridge Educational
PO Box 2053
Princeton, NJ 08543-2053
Ph: 800-257-5126   Fax: (609)671-0266
Fr: 800-468-4227
E-mail: custserv@films.com
URL: http://www.cambridgeeducational.com

VHS and DVD. 1998. $98.95. 22 minutes. Covers using the telephone to identify potential employers and set up interviews.

★13924★ **Exceptional Interviewing Tips: A View from the Inside**

Cambridge Educational
PO Box 2053
Princeton, NJ 08543-2053
Ph: 800-257-5126   Fax: (609)671-0266
Fr: 800-468-4227
E-mail: custserv@films.com
URL: http://www.cambridgeeducational.com

VHS and DVD. 1996. $79.95. 28 minutes. Includes workbook. Representative from successful businesses cover what to do before, during, and after a job interview.

★13925★ **Extraordinary Answers to Common Interview Questions**

Cambridge Educational
PO Box 2053
Princeton, NJ 08543-2053
Ph: 800-257-5126   Fax: (609)671-0266
Fr: 800-468-4227
E-mail: custserv@films.com
URL: http://www.cambridgeeducational.com

VHS and DVD. 1995. $79.95. 22 minutes. Follows a quiz format, with advice from career experts.

★13926★ **First Impressions: The Key to Turning Job Interviews into Job Offers**

JIST Publishing
875 Montreal Way
St. Paul, MN 55102
Fax: 800-547-8329   Fr: 800-648-5478
E-mail: info@jist.com
URL: http://www.jist.com

Video. 2001. $199.00. 22 minutes. A humorous, informative look at making a good first impression on a potential employer. Also available in Spanish.

★13927★ **From Parole to Payroll**

Cambridge Educational
PO Box 2053
Princeton, NJ 08543-2053
Ph: 800-257-5126   Fax: (609)671-0266
Fr: 800-468-4227
E-mail: custserv@films.com
URL: http://www.cambridgeeducational.com

VHS and DVD. 2008. $269.85. Contains solid, real-world content designed to help job seekers find satisfying work, and features informative interviews, helpful tips, and colorful graphics.

★13928★ **Interviewing for a Job**

Cambridge Educational
PO Box 2053
Princeton, NJ 08543-2053
Ph: 800-257-5126   Fax: (609)671-0266
Fr: 800-468-4227
E-mail: custserv@films.com
URL: http://www.cambridgeeducational.com

VHS and DVD. 2007. $79.95. 12 minutes. Covers preparing for an interview, dressing for an interview, using body language to good advantage, articulating skills and abilities, answering difficult questions, and handling salary and benefits issues.

★13929★ **The Job Interview**

Cambridge Educational
PO Box 2053
Princeton, NJ 08543-2053
Ph: 800-257-5126   Fax: (609)671-0266
Fr: 800-468-4227
E-mail: custserv@films.com
URL: http://www.cambridgeeducational.com

VHS and DVD. $59.95. 1995. 15 minutes. Part of the From Parole to Payroll Series.

★13930★ **Job Interviewing for People with Disabilities**

Cambridge Educational
PO Box 2053
Princeton, NJ 08543-2053
Ph: 800-257-5126   Fax: (609)671-0266
Fr: 800-468-4227
E-mail: custserv@films.com
URL: http://www.cambridgeeducational.com

VHS and DVD. $89.95. 23 minutes. 1998. Part of the series "Access Unlimited: The Job Search Series for People with Disabilities."

★13931★ **Networking on the WWW and Beyond**

Cambridge Educational
PO Box 2053
Princeton, NJ 08543-2053
Ph: 800-257-5126   Fax: (609)671-0266
Fr: 800-468-4227
E-mail: custserv@films.com
URL: http://www.cambridgeeducational.com

VHS and DVD. 1997. $79.95. 28 minutes. This three-part video includes an introduction to search engines, how to network and find jobs using Internet resources, and interviewing via the Internet.

★13932★ **Power Interviewing Skills: Both Sides of the Desk**

Cambridge Educational
PO Box 2053
Princeton, NJ 08543-2053
Ph: 800-257-5126   Fax: (609)671-0266
Fr: 800-468-4227
E-mail: custserv@films.com
URL: http://www.cambridgeeducational.com

VHS and DVD. 1998. $159.90. Two volume series: Strategies for the Interviewer and Strategies for the Interviewee look at the interview process from both sides.

★13933★ **Strategies For The Interviewee**

Cambridge Educational
PO Box 2053
Princeton, NJ 08543-2053
Ph: 800-257-5126   Fax: (609)671-0266
Fr: 800-468-4227
E-mail: custserv@films.com
URL: http://www.cambridgeeducational.com

VHS and DVD. $79.95. 1998. 27 minutes. Part of the Series "Power Interviewing Skills Both Sides of the Desk."

★13934★ **Your First Resume and Interview**

Cambridge Educational
PO Box 2053
Princeton, NJ 08543-2053
Ph: 800-257-5126   Fax: (609)671-0266
Fr: 800-468-4227
E-mail: custserv@films.com
URL: http://www.cambridgeeducational.com

VHS and DVD. 1999. $89.95. 17 minutes. Learn why employers like resumes and what kinds of information should be included. See the different styles of resumes and why one style might be preferable to another. The interviewing process will also be covered, including an overview of what the employer hopes to learn.

SOFTWARE

★13935★ Adams Job Interview Almanac

Adams Media Corp.
4700 E. Galbraith Rd.
Cincinnati, OH 45236
E-mail: techsupport@adamsmedia.com
URL: http://www.adamsmedia.com

2006. Second Edition. $17.95. 832 pages. Features over 1,800 job interview questions and successful responses.

★13936★ Interview Skills of the Future: Interview Challenges for Minorities, Women, and People with Disabilities

Program Development Associates
PO Box 2038
Syracuse, NY 13220-2038
Ph: (315)452-0643   Fax: (315)452-0710
Fr: 800-543-2119
E-mail: info@disabilitytraining.com
URL: http://www.pdassoc.com

$199.00. CD-ROM. Teaches a tactful and positive response to challenging interview questions for those having a hard time breaking through the traditional hiring barriers.

★13937★ Multimedia Job Search

Cambridge Educational
PO Box 2053
Princeton, NJ 08543-2053
Ph: 800-257-5126   Fax: (609)671-0266
Fr: 800-468-4227
E-mail: custserv@films.com
URL: http://www.cambridgeeducational.com

CD-ROM. $99.95. 1997. Includes videos, narration, and on-screen text. Users learn about getting a competitive edge in today's job market, traditional and nontraditional job search tools, resumes and cover letters, and interviewing skills.

Legal Information

REFERENCE WORKS

★13938★ Age Discrimination in the American Workplace: Old at a Young Age

Rutgers University Press
100 Joyce Kilmer Ave.
Piscataway, NJ 08854-8099
Ph: (732)445-7762   Fax: 800-272-6817
Fr: 800-848-6224
E-mail: customerservice@longleafservices.org
URL: http://rutgerspress.rutgers.edu

Gregory, Raymond F. 2001. $29.95 (Trade cloth). 238 pages. Study of a variety of discriminatory practices confronting older workers in the current American workplaces, and the approaches these workers use to fight back.

★13939★ Eastman on Defending Your Employee Rights: Preventing and Stopping Discriminatory and Wrongful Terminations

Northern Star Publishing
181 Springbrook Tr.
Sparta, NJ 07871
Ph: (973)729-9508   Fax: (973)729-9508

Eastman, J. D. 1997. $49.95 (Trade paper). 140 pages.

★13940★ The Employee Rights Handbook: The Essential Guide for People on the Job

Hachette Book Group
237 Park Ave.
New York, NY 10017
Ph: (212)522-7200
URL: http://www.hachettebookgroupusa.com/

Sack, Steven Mitchell. Rev edition, 2000. $14.95 (Trade paper). 480 pages. Covers every aspect of life on the job from getting hired to leaving with all the benefits and pay an employee deserves.

★13941★ Employee Rights in the Workplace

Oceana Publications, Inc.
198 Madison Ave.
New York, NY 10016
Fax: (919)677-1303   Fr: (866)445-8685
E-mail: custserv.us@oup.com
URL: http://www.oceanalaw.com/

Jasper, Margaret C. Second edition, 2004. $31.50 (Cloth). 120 pages.

★13942★ Federal Employees Legal Survival Guide: How to Protect and Enforce Your Job Rights

National Employee Rights Institute
2031 Florida Ave., NW, Ste. 500
414 Walnut St.
Washington, DC 20009
Ph: (202)243-7660   Fax: (202)282-8801
URL: http://www.workplacefairness.org/

1999. 520 pages. $39.95.

★13943★ Fired, Downsized, or Laid Off: Negotiating Secrets from the No. 1 Severance Attorney

Owl Books
1050 31st St. NW
Washington, DC 20007
Ph: (202)965-3500   Fr: 800-424-2725
E-mail: help@atlahq.com
URL: http://www.atla.org

Sklover, Alan L. 2005. $5.95 (Trade paper). 352 pages.

★13944★ Getting Fired: What to Do If You're Fired, Downsized, Laid off, Restructured, Discharged, Terminated or Forced to Resign

Grand Central Publishing
237 Park Ave.
New York, NY 10017
Ph: (212)522-7200   Fax: 800-286-9471
Fr: 800-759-0190
URL: http://www.hachettebookgroupusa.com

Sack, Steven Mitchell. 2001. $24.00 (Trade cloth). 496 pages.

★13945★ Job Discrimination II: How to Fight, How to Win

R & R Writers Agents, Inc.
364 Mauro Rd.
Englewood Cliffs, NJ 07632
Ph: (201)567-8986   Fax: (201)567-8987
Fr: 888-567-6785

Bernbach, Jeffrey M. 1998. $15.00 (Trade paper). 192 pages.

★13946★ Job Rights and Survival Strategies: A Handbook for Terminated Employees

Jist Publishing
875 Montreal Way
St. Paul, MN 55102
Fr: 800-648-5478
E-mail: info@jist.com
URL: http://www.jist.com

Tobias, Paul H. and Susan Sauter. 1997. $19.95 (Trade paper). 160 pages.

★13947★ The Law of the Workplace: Rights of Employers & Employees

BNA Books
PO Box 7814
Edison, NJ 08818-7814
Fax: (732)346-1624   Fr: 800-960-1220
E-mail: books@bna.com.
URL: http://www.bnabooks.com/

Hunt, James W. and Patricia K. Strongin. 1997. $45.00 (Trade paper). 318 pages.

★13948★ Meeting the Needs of Employees with Disabilities

Resources for Rehabilitation
22 Bonad Rd.
Winchester, MA 01890
Ph: (781)368-9094   Fax: (781)368-9096
URL: http://www.rfr.org

Biennial, odd years; latest edition 4th, 2004. $46.95 for individuals. Publication includes: Descriptions of organizations and products that assist those involved in the employment of people with disabilities. Entries include: Organization name, address, phone, requirements for membership, admission, or eligibility, description, prices of product. Principal content of publication consists of information and advice for employers and counselors who recruit and retain employees with disabilities, including coverage of government programs and laws, supported employment, environmental adaptations, mobility impairments, vision impairments, and communication impairments (hearing and speech). Chapters on assistive technology, environmental modification, transition from school to work, and older workers. Arrangement: Alphabetical.

★13949★ Personnel Law

Prentice Hall PTR
One Lake St.
Upper Saddle River, NJ 07458
Ph: (201)236-7000   Fr: 800-428-5331
URL: http://www.phptr.com/index.asp?rl=1

Sovereign, Kenneth L. 1998. $94.80 (Trade paper). 362 pages.

★13950★ Regulation, Litigation and Dispute Resolution under the Americans with Disabilities Act: A Practitioner's Guide to Implementation

American Bar Association
321 N. Clark St.
Chicago, IL 60610
Ph: (312)988-5561   Fax: (312)988-6030
Fr: 800-285-2221
URL: http://www.abanet.org/

John Parry, 1996. $35.00 (Trade paper). 185 pages.

★13951★ Sexual Identity on the Job: Issues and Services

Haworth Press, Inc.
10 Alice St.
Binghamton, NY 13904-1580
Ph: (607)722-5857   Fax: (607)722-6362
Fr: 800-429-6784
URL: http://www.haworthpress.com

Ellis, Alan L. and Ellen D. Riggle (Editors). 1996. $72.00 (trade cloth). $15.95 (paperback). 108 pages.

★13952★ State Individual Employment Rights Laws: Labor Relations, Employee Leave, Employee Rights & Protections

CCH, Inc.
2700 Lake Cook Rd.
Riverwoods, IL 60015
Ph: (847)267-7000   Fr: 800-248-3248
URL: http://www.cch.com/

2001. $125.00 (Trade paper). 1753 pages.

★13953★ Workplace Accommodations under the ADA

Thompson Publishing Group, Inc.
PO Box 26185
Tampa, FL 33623
Fax: 800-759-7179   Fr: 800-677-3789
URL: http://www.thompson.com

Magill, Barbara Gamble, Allen Smith and

Anne Woodworth. 1999. $99.00 (Trade paper). 118 pages.

★13954★ Workplace Law Advisor: From Harassment and Discrimination Policies to Hiring & Firing Guidelines - What Every Manager and Employee Needs to Know

Basic Books
387 Park Ave. S., 12th Fl.
New York, NY 10016
Ph: (212)340-8100   Fax: (212)207-7703
URL: http://www.perseusbooksgroup.com/basic/

Covey, Anne. 2000. $17.00 (Paper). 257 pages.

★13955★ Your Rights in the Workplace

Nolo.com
950 Parker St.
Berkeley, CA 94710
Ph: (510)549-1976   Fax: 800-645-0895
Fr: 800-728-3555
URL: http://www.nolo.com

Repa, Barbara K. Eighth edition, 2007. $29.99 (Trade paper). 544 pages. Covers everything from hiring and getting paid through privacy and firing.

NEWSPAPERS, MAGAZINES, AND JOURNALS

★13956★ Alabama Employment Law Letter

M. Lee Smith Publishers L.L.C.
PO Box 5094
Brentwood, TN 37024-5094
Ph: (615)373-7517   Fax: 800-785-9212
Fr: 800-274-6774
E-mail: custserv@mleesmith.com
URL: http://www.hrhero.com/alemp.shtml

Description: Monthly. Covers laws regulating employment activities in Alabama.

★13957★ American Academy of Psychiatry and the Law Newsletter

American Academy of Psychiatry and the Law
1 Regency Dr.
PO Box 30
Bloomfield, CT 06002
Ph: (860)242-5450   Fax: (860)286-0787
Fr: 800-331-1389
E-mail: execoff@aapl.org
URL: http://www.aapl.org/newsltr.htm

Description: Three issues/year. Discusses psychiatry as it relates to the law. Recurring features include recent legal cases, legislative updates, letters to the editor, notices of publications available, news of educational opportunities, job listings, a calendar of events, and columns.

★13958★ Bank Employment Law Report

A.S. Pratt & Sons
1725 K St., NW, Ste. 700
Washington, DC 20006
Ph: (703)528-0145   Fax: (703)528-1736
Fr: 800-524-2003
URL: http://www.aspratt.com

Description: Monthly. Presents legal matters for financial institutions' human resources officers.

★13959★ BNA's Corporate Counsel Weekly

Bureau of National Affairs Inc.
1801 S. Bell St.
Arlington, VA 22202
Fax: 800-253-0332   Fr: 800-372-1033
E-mail: customercare@bna.com
URL: http://www.bna.com/products/ens/oshr.htm

Description: Weekly. Covers law that affects business, including corporate law, securities law, antitrust law, and employment law. Carries brief reports of court cases, looks at government regulation of trade and the environment, and focuses each week on a topic of current importance. Includes texts of regulatory material and practitioner analysis.

★13960★ California Employer Advisor

Employer Resource Institute Inc.
1819 Polk St. No. 290
San Francisco, CA 94109
Fax: 888-321-5066   Fr: 800-695-7178
URL: http://www.employeradvice.com

Description: Monthly. The award-winning guide to California employment law and employee relations.

★13961★ California Employment Law Letter

M. Lee Smith Publishers L.L.C.
PO Box 5094
Brentwood, TN 37024-5094
Ph: (615)373-7517   Fax: 800-785-9212
Fr: 800-274-6774
E-mail: custserv@mleesmith.com
URL: http://www.hrhero.com/caemp.shtml

Description: Monthly. Provides coverage of court cases and other situations involving employment laws in California.

★13962★ California Labor and Employment ALERT Newsletter

Castle Publications Ltd.
PO Box 580
Van Nuys, CA 91408
Ph: (818)708-3208   Fax: (818)708-9287
E-mail: info@castlepublications.com
URL: http://www.castlepublications.com/alert.htm

Description: Bimonthly. Reports on current developments in California and federal laws concerning personnel and employment issues. Recurring features include notices of publications available.

★13963★ California Labor and Employment Law Quarterly

State Bar of California
180 Howard St.
San Francisco, CA 94105
Ph: (415)538-2000   Fax: (415)538-2368
URL: http://www.calbar.ca.gov

Description: Quarterly. Contains information and news on California's labor and employment laws and regulations.

★13964★ Colorado Employment Law Letter

M. Lee Smith Publishers L.L.C.
PO Box 5094
Brentwood, TN 37024-5094
Ph: (615)373-7517   Fax: 800-785-9212
Fr: 800-274-6774
E-mail: custserv@mleesmith.com
URL: http://www.hrhero.com/coemp.shtml

Description: Monthly. Addresses litigation and court decisions affecting employment issues.

★13965★ Commercial Laws of the World

Thomson RIA
395 Hudson St.
New York, NY 10014
Ph: (212)367-6300   Fr: 800-950-1216
URL: http://ria.thomson.com/

Description: Biweekly. Provides loose-leaf supplements covering commercial laws for countries across the world. Includes amendments to laws of over 100 countries translated into English. Covers commercial registers, employment of foreigners, branches of foreign companies, registration of foreigners, cost of registration, cost of business, commercial acts, brokers, limited partnerships, joint ventures, distribution of profits, legal reserves, treatment of foreigners, foreign judgments, balance sheets, nature and kinds of companies, forms of company contracts, foreign corporations, partnerships, dissolution, mergers, prescription period, capital stock, insurance companies, formation expenses, stockholders resident abroad, dividends, and inventories.

★13966★ Compensation

Bureau of National Affairs Inc.
1801 S. Bell St.
Arlington, VA 22202
Fr: 800-372-1033
E-mail: customercare@bna.com
URL: http://www.bna.com

Description: Weekly. Offers legal clarification and practical advice on employers' pay and benefit policies. Discusses such topics as health care cost containment, payroll laws and taxes, workers compensation laws, pension law (ERISA), job evaluation, benefit plans, compensation administration, incentive systems, and independent contractors. Compensation is part of the BNA Policy and Practice Series, and can be purchased separately or in any combination with other binder sets entitled Fair Employment Prac-

tices, Labor Relations, Personnel Management, or Wages and Hours.

★13967★ Connecticut Employment Law Letter

M. Lee Smith Publishers L.L.C.
PO Box 5094
Brentwood, TN 37024-5094
Ph: (615)373-7517   Fax: 800-785-9212
Fr: 800-274-6774
E-mail: custserv@mleesmith.com
URL: http://www.hrhero.com/ctemp.shtml

Description: Monthly. Addresses legislation and court decisions affecting employment issues.

★13968★ Disability Issues

Information Center for Individuals With Disabilities
PO Box 750119
Arlington Heights, MA 02475-0119
Fax: (781)860-0673
E-mail: contact@disability.net
URL: http://disability.net

Description: Quarterly. Addresses persons with disabilities, their relatives and friends, and service providers through articles on education, employment, transportation, housing, legislation, equipment, and entertainment. Recurring features include a calendar of events and columns titled Resources, Sports Scoop, Book Shelf, Support Column, On Screen, To Your Health, and Disability and the law.

★13969★ Employee Advocate

National Employment Lawyers Association
44 Montgomery St., Ste. 2080
San Francisco, CA 94104
Ph: (415)296-7629   Fax: (415)677-9445
URL: http://www.nela.org/

Description: Quarterly. Contains NELA activities, latest developments in employment law, best practice tips, briefs, and articles of interest to NELA members.

★13970★ Employment Law Counselor

Thomson West
610 Opperman Dr.
PO Box 64833
Eagan, MN 55123
Ph: (651)687-7000   Fr: 800-328-9352
URL: http://west.thomson.com/

Description: Monthly. Describes developments in all areas of employee relations law. Discusses such topics as Title VII, age discrimination, the Americans with Disabilities Act, reasonable accommodation, OSHA, wrongful discharge, employment contracts, drug testing, smoking in the workplace, employee benefit laws, arbitration, privacy in the workplace, and immigration laws. Recurring features include forms, checklists, policy statements, a calendar of events, case summaries, summaries of pending legislation, and the Executive Legal Summaries.

★13971★ Employment Litigation Reporter

Thomson West
610 Opperman Dr.
PO Box 64833
Eagan, MN 55123
Ph: (651)687-7000   Fr: 800-328-9352
URL: http://west.thomson.com/

Description: Biweekly. Reports on job termination lawsuits alleging tort and contract claims against employers. Follows pretrial, trial, and appellate proceedings and reprints complete texts of important case documents.

★13972★ Fair Employment Practices Summary of Latest Developments

Bureau of National Affairs Inc.
1801 S. Bell St.
Arlington, VA 22202
Fax: 800-253-0332   Fr: 800-372-1033
E-mail: customercare@bna.com
URL: http://www.bna.com/products/ens/oshr.htm

Description: Biweekly. Highlights developments in employment opportunity and affirmative action, and affirmative action programs. Reports on federal and state court decisions, Equal Employment Opportunity Commission (EEOC) rulings and Office of Federal Contract Compliance Programs (OFCCP) decisions, new laws, regulations, and agency directives. Also provides information on special programs for minorities, the handicapped, women, and older workers.

★13973★ Florida Employment Law Letter

M. Lee Smith Publishers L.L.C.
PO Box 5094
Brentwood, TN 37024-5094
Ph: (615)373-7517   Fax: 800-785-9212
Fr: 800-274-6774
E-mail: custserv@mleesmith.com
URL: http://www.hrhero.com/flemp.shtml

Description: Monthly. Addresses legal issues in employment and labor relations.

★13974★ Georgia Employment Law Letter

M. Lee Smith Publishers L.L.C.
PO Box 5094
Brentwood, TN 37024-5094
Ph: (615)373-7517   Fax: 800-785-9212
Fr: 800-274-6774
E-mail: custserv@mleesmith.com
URL: http://www.hrhero.com/gaemp.shtml

Description: Monthly. Covers court cases involving employment issues. Outlines employers' legal rights and responsibilities.

★13975★ HR Fact Finder

Jamestown Area Labor-Management Committee Inc.
Rm. 340, 1093 E. 2nd St.
PO Box 819
Jamestown, NY 14702-0819
Ph: (716)665-3654   Fax: (716)665-8060
Fr: 800-542-7869

URL: http://www.jalmc.org/Newsletters/Sales/HR_Fact_Finder/

Description: Monthly. Summarizes articles from various publications on such topics as company benefits, health, the Family Leave Act, Americans with Disabilities Act, hiring practices, employment law, workers compensation, budgets, and sexual harassment.

★13976★ HR Manager's Legal Reporter

Business & Legal Reports Inc.
141 Mill Rock Rd. E.
Old Saybrook, CT 06475
Ph: (860)510-0100   Fr: 800-727-5257
E-mail: service@blr.com
URL: http://www.blr.com/product.cfm/product/31510400

Description: Monthly. Provides information, news, and how-to articles on employment law. Recurring features include columns titled Washington Watch, You Be the Judge, From the States, and In Brief.

★13977★ Human Resources Practice Ideas

Thomson RIA
395 Hudson St.
New York, NY 10014
Ph: (212)367-6300   Fr: 800-950-1216
URL: http://ria.thomson.com/

Description: Monthly. Provides information about employment laws and regulations.

★13978★ Illinois Employment Law Letter

M. Lee Smith Publishers L.L.C.
PO Box 5094
Brentwood, TN 37024-5094
Ph: (615)373-7517   Fax: 800-785-9212
Fr: 800-274-6774
E-mail: custserv@mleesmith.com
URL: http://www.hrhero.com/ilemp.shtml

Description: Monthly. Addresses Illinois legislation and court decisions affecting employment issues.

★13979★ Indiana Employment Law Letter

M. Lee Smith Publishers L.L.C.
PO Box 5094
Brentwood, TN 37024-5094
Ph: (615)373-7517   Fax: 800-785-9212
Fr: 800-274-6774
E-mail: custserv@mleesmith.com
URL: http://www.hrhero.com/inemp.shtml

Description: Monthly. Contains legal information pertinent to employers in Indiana.

★13980★ Kentucky Employment Law Letter

M. Lee Smith Publishers L.L.C.
PO Box 5094
Brentwood, TN 37024-5094
Ph: (615)373-7517   Fax: 800-785-9212
Fr: 800-274-6774
E-mail: custserv@mleesmith.com
URL: http://www.hrhero.com/kyemp.shtml

Description: Monthly. Addresses the legal rights of employees and obligations of employers as dictated by Kentucky law. Contains case summaries.

★13981★ Labor and Employment Law

Section of Labor and Employment Law
321 N. Clark St
Chicago, IL 60610
Ph: (312)988-5000   Fr: 800-285-2221
URL: http://www.abanet.org/labor/

Description: Quarterly. Covers all developments, from recent decisions and new regulations to emerging trends and important people in the profession. Recurring features include a calendar of events, reports of meetings, news of educational opportunities, and notices of publications available.

★13982★ Labor & Employment Law Section Newsletter

New York State Bar Association
1 Elk St.
Albany, NY 12207
Ph: (518)463-3200   Fax: (518)487-5517
Fr: 800-582-2452
URL: http://www.nysba.org/

Description: Four issues/year. Provides topical information about labor and employment law. Recurring features include chair's comments, article from the editor, cartoon, biographical updates, and columns titled Ethics Matters and Legislative Update.

★13983★ Labor Relations Bulletin

Aspen Publishers Inc.
76 Ninth Ave., 7th Fl.
New York, NY 10011
Ph: (212)771-0600   Fax: (212)771-0885
Fr: 800-234-1660
URL: http://www.aspenpublishers.com/

Description: Quarterly. Provides information and insight to management and labor officials to help them avoid or resolve conflicts. Recurring features include reports on current developments in labor law and relations, discipline and grievance cases based on actual arbitration, a question and answer column on labor and employment relations, and a column titled Reflections of an Arbitrator, offering the insight and experience of prominent national arbitrators.

★13984★ Louisiana Employment Law Letter

M. Lee Smith Publishers L.L.C.
PO Box 5094
Brentwood, TN 37024-5094
Ph: (615)373-7517   Fax: 800-785-9212
Fr: 800-274-6774
E-mail: custserv@mleesmith.com
URL: http://www.hrhero.com/laemp.shtml

Description: Monthly. Addresses legislation and court decisions affecting employment issues.

★13985★ Managing Today's Federal Employees

LRP Publications
PO Box 24668
West Palm Beach, FL 33416-4668
Fax: (561)622-2423   Fr: 800-341-7874
E-mail: custserve@lrp.com
URL: http://www.lrp.com/

Description: Monthly. Provides information about federal employment law concerning government employees.

★13986★ Maryland Employment Law Letter

M. Lee Smith Publishers L.L.C.
PO Box 5094
Brentwood, TN 37024-5094
Ph: (615)373-7517   Fax: 800-785-9212
Fr: 800-274-6774
E-mail: custserv@mleesmith.com
URL: http://www.hrhero.com/mdemp.shtml

Description: Monthly. Covers Maryland laws and court cases involving employment-related issues.

★13987★ Massachusetts Employment Law Letter

M. Lee Smith Publishers L.L.C.
PO Box 5094
Brentwood, TN 37024-5094
Ph: (615)373-7517   Fax: 800-785-9212
Fr: 800-274-6774
E-mail: custserv@mleesmith.com
URL: http://www.hrhero.com/maemp.shtml

Description: Monthly. Addresses legal issues of interest to employers and employees in Massachusetts.

★13988★ Michigan Employment Law Letter

M. Lee Smith Publishers L.L.C.
PO Box 5094
Brentwood, TN 37024-5094
Ph: (615)373-7517   Fax: 800-785-9212
Fr: 800-274-6774
E-mail: custserv@mleesmith.com
URL: http://www.hrhero.com/miemp.shtml

Description: Monthly. Addresses employers' legal responsibilities and employee rights as dictated by Michigan law.

★13989★ Minnesota Employment Law Letter

M. Lee Smith Publishers L.L.C.
PO Box 5094
Brentwood, TN 37024-5094
Ph: (615)373-7517   Fax: 800-785-9212
Fr: 800-274-6774
E-mail: custserv@mleesmith.com
URL: http://www.hrhero.com/mnemp.shtml

Description: Monthly. Contains analysis of issues regarding employment law in Minnesota.

★13990★ **Missouri Employment Law Letter**

M. Lee Smith Publishers L.L.C.
PO Box 5094
Brentwood, TN 37024-5094
Ph: (615)373-7517   Fax: 800-785-9212
Fr: 800-274-6774
E-mail: custserv@mleesmith.com
URL: http://www.hrhero.com/moemp.shtml

Description: Monthly. Presents issues in Missouri employment law.

★13991★ **National Partnership News**

National Partnership for Women & Families
1875 Connecticut Ave. NW, Ste. 650
Washington, DC 20009
Ph: (202)986-2600   Fax: (202)986-2539
E-mail: info@nationalpartnership.org
URL: http://www.nationalpartnership.org

Description: Four issues/year. Monitors developments in employment discrimination, reproductive health, family leave policies, quality health care issues, and areas of sex discrimination law that affect women's status. Contains updates on the organization's services and activities and discussions of women's rights issues.

★13992★ **New Jersey Employment Law Letter**

M. Lee Smith Publishers L.L.C.
PO Box 5094
Brentwood, TN 37024-5094
Ph: (615)373-7517   Fax: 800-785-9212
Fr: 800-274-6774
E-mail: custserv@mleesmith.com
URL: http://www.hrhero.com/njemp.shtml

Description: Monthly. Addresses legislation and court decisions affecting employment issues.

★13993★ **New Jersey Labor and Employment Law Quarterly**

New Jersey State Bar Association
New Jersey Law Center
1 Constitution Sq.
New Brunswick, NJ 08901-1520
Ph: (732)249-5000   Fax: (732)249-2815
URL: http://www.njsba.com/

Description: Quarterly. Deals with labor and employment legal matters and legislation in New Jersey, including grievances, mediation, and arbitration. Recurring features include Section news and columns titled Editor's Corner and Director's Corner.

★13994★ **North Carolina Employment Law Letter**

M. Lee Smith Publishers L.L.C.
PO Box 5094
Brentwood, TN 37024-5094
Ph: (615)373-7517   Fax: 800-785-9212
Fr: 800-274-6774
E-mail: custserv@mleesmith.com
URL: http://www.hrhero.com/ncemp.shtml

Description: Monthly. Contains information

on court cases and legislation affecting employment law in North Carolina.

★13995★ **Ohio Employment Law Letter**

M. Lee Smith Publishers L.L.C.
PO Box 5094
Brentwood, TN 37024-5094
Ph: (615)373-7517   Fax: 800-785-9212
Fr: 800-274-6774
E-mail: custserv@mleesmith.com
URL: http://www.hrhero.com/ohemp.shtml

Description: Monthly. Addresses legal issues of interest to Ohio employers.

★13996★ **Oklahoma Employment Law Letter**

M. Lee Smith Publishers L.L.C.
PO Box 5094
Brentwood, TN 37024-5094
Ph: (615)373-7517   Fax: 800-785-9212
Fr: 800-274-6774
E-mail: custserv@mleesmith.com
URL: http://www.hrhero.com/okemp.shtml

Description: Monthly. Addresses legislation and court decisions affecting employment issues.

★13997★ **Payroll Administration Guide**

Bureau of National Affairs Inc.
1801 S. Bell St.
Arlington, VA 22202
Fr: 800-372-1033
URL: http://www.bna.com/products/hr/pylw.htm

Description: Biweekly. Concerned with federal and state employment tax, and wage-hour and wage-payment laws.

★13998★ **Payroll Legal Alert**

Alexander Hamilton Institute Inc.
70 Hilltop Rd.
Ramsey, NJ 07446-1119
Ph: (201)825-3377   Fax: (201)825-8696
Fr: 800-879-2441
E-mail: payla@ahipubs.com
URL: http://www.ahipubs.com

Description: Monthly. Covers aspects of payroll operations, including key tax and benefits laws, regulations, rulings, and cases. Includes new trends in tax law, ideas on benefits, wage and hour traps, and unemployment issues.

★13999★ **Pennsylvania Employment Law Letter**

M. Lee Smith Publishers L.L.C.
PO Box 5094
Brentwood, TN 37024-5094
Ph: (615)373-7517   Fax: 800-785-9212
Fr: 800-274-6774
E-mail: custserv@mleesmith.com
URL: http://www.hrhero.com/paemp.shtml

Description: Monthly. Details court cases and laws affecting employer/employee rights and responsibilities in Pennsylvania.

★14000★ **Personnel Legal Alert**

Alexander Hamilton Institute Inc.
70 Hilltop Rd.
Ramsey, NJ 07446-1119
Ph: (201)825-3377   Fax: (201)825-8696
Fr: 800-879-2441
E-mail: pla@ahipubs.com
URL: http://www.ahipubs.com

Description: Semimonthly. Provides information about employment law. Topics include court opinions and government regulations.

★14001★ **Personnel Management**

Bureau of National Affairs Inc.
1801 S. Bell St.
Arlington, VA 22202
Fax: 800-253-0332   Fr: 800-372-1033
E-mail: customercare@bna.com
URL: http://www.bna.com/products/ens/oshr.htm

Description: Weekly. Provides legal clarification and practical advice on employers' pay and benefit policies, including detailed discussions of pertinent federal and state laws. Discusses such topics as health care compensation laws, pension law (ERISA), job evaluation, benefit plans, compensation administration, incentive systems, and independent contractors. Part of the BNA Policy and Practice Series; can be purchased alone or in any combination with other binder sets titled Compensation, Fair Employment Practices, Wages and Hours, and Labor Relations.

★14002★ **South Carolina Employment Law Letter**

M. Lee Smith Publishers L.L.C.
PO Box 5094
Brentwood, TN 37024-5094
Ph: (615)373-7517   Fax: 800-785-9212
Fr: 800-274-6774
E-mail: custserv@mleesmith.com
URL: http://www.hrhero.com/scemp.shtml

Description: Monthly. Addresses legislation and court decisions affecting employment issues.

★14003★ **State Labor Laws**

Bureau of National Affairs Inc.
1801 S. Bell St.
Arlington, VA 22202
Fax: 800-253-0332   Fr: 800-372-1033
E-mail: customercare@bna.com
URL: http://www.bna.com/products/ens/oshr.htm

Description: Biweekly. Provides full texts, digests, and charts of state labor laws, covering their scope, jurisdiction, administration, and enforcement. Also discusses how state labor law relates to federal laws affecting labor relations and employment regulation and provides directories of state agencies that administer and enforce these laws.

★14004★ Supervisors Legal Update
Progressive Business Publications
370 Technology Dr.
Malvern, PA 19355
Ph: (610)695-8600   Fax: (610)647-8089
Fr: 800-220-5000
E-mail: Customer_Service@pbp.com.
URL: http://www.pbp.com/slu.html
Description: Semimonthly. Supplies brief updates on employment law for supervisors. Review a column titled Sharpen Your Judgment.

★14005★ Tennessee Employment Law Update
M. Lee Smith Publishers L.L.C.
PO Box 5094
Brentwood, TN 37024-5094
Ph: (615)373-7517   Fax: 800-785-9212
Fr: 800-274-6774
E-mail: custserv@mleesmith.com
URL: http://www.hrhero.com/tnemp.shtml
Description: Annual. Profiles legal issues of interest to employers in Tennessee.

★14006★ Texas Employment Law Letter
M. Lee Smith Publishers L.L.C.
PO Box 5094
Brentwood, TN 37024-5094
Ph: (615)373-7517   Fax: 800-785-9212
Fr: 800-274-6774
E-mail: custserv@mleesmith.com
URL: http://www.hrhero.com/txemp.shtml
Description: Monthly. Covers laws and legislation affecting Texas employers.

★14007★ Unemployment Insurance Reports with Social Security
CCH Inc.
4025 W Peterson Ave.
Chicago, IL 60646-6085
Ph: (847)267-7000   Fax: (773)866-3895
Fr: 888-224-7377
URL: http://www.cch.com
Description: Weekly. Issues of CCH's Unemployment Insurance Reports with Social Security provide timely information on social security and federal/state unemployment insurance taxes, coverage, and benefits. Pertinent federal and state laws are reported promptly and reflected in place in the explanatory guides, as are regulations, judicial and administrative decisions, rulings, releases, and forms. Explanatory guides include examples showing how rules apply and offer practical information regarding the tax management, coverage, and benefit aspects of the social security and unemployment insurance systems. Each issue starts off with an informative Report Letter summarizing recent developments in these areas.

★14008★ Virginia Employment Law Letter
M. Lee Smith Publishers L.L.C.
PO Box 5094
Brentwood, TN 37024-5094
Ph: (615)373-7517   Fax: 800-785-9212
Fr: 800-274-6774
E-mail: custserv@mleesmith.com
URL: http://www.hrhero.com/vaemp.shtml
Description: Monthly. Examines legal issues pertinent to employers in Virginia.

★14009★ What's Working in Human Resources
Progressive Business Publications
370 Technology Dr.
Malvern, PA 19355
Ph: (610)695-8600   Fax: (610)647-8089
Fr: 800-220-5000
E-mail: Service@pbp.com
URL: http://www.pbp.com
Description: Semimonthly. Reports on the latest trends in Human Resources, including the latest employment law rulings. Recurring features include interviews, news of research, a calendar of events, news of educational opportunities, and a column titlted Sharpen Your Judgment.

★14010★ You & the Law
National Institute of Business Management
PO Box 906
Williamsport, PA 17703-9933
Fax: (570)567-0166   Fr: 800-433-0622
E-mail: customer@nibm.net
URL: http://www.nibm.net/newsletter.asp?pub=YATL
Description: Monthly. Covers the employment law area. Provides information for managers and business owners interested in the relationship between the law and their business.

Looking to Relocate

REFERENCE WORKS

★14011★ Atlanta JobBank

Adams Media Corp.
57 Littlefield St.
Avon, MA 02322
Ph: (508)427-7100   Fax: (508)427-6790
Fr: 800-872-5627
URL: http://www.adamsmedia.com

Latest edition 15th. $17.95 for individuals. Covers 3,900 employers in the state of Georgia, including Albany, Columbus, Macon, and Savannah. Entries include: Firm or organization name, address, local phone, toll-free phone, fax, description of organization, subsidiaries, other locations, recorded jobline, name and title of contact, typical titles for common positions, educational backgrounds desired, number of employees, benefits offered, training programs, internships, parent company, revenues, e-mail and URL address, projected number of hires. Arrangement: Classified by industry. Indexes: Alphabetical.

★14012★ The Austin/San Antonio JobBank

Adams Media Corp.
57 Littlefield St.
Avon, MA 02322
Ph: (508)427-7100   Fax: (508)427-6790
Fr: 800-872-5627
URL: http://www.adamsmedia.com

Biennial; latest edition 4th. $17.95 for individuals. Covers More than 5,100 companies in metro Austin, metro San Antonio, and the surrounding area, including El Paso. Entries include: Firm or organization name, address, phone, name and title of contact; description of organization, headquarters location, typical titles for entry- and middle-level positions, educational backgrounds desired, fringe benefits offered, stock exchange listing, training programs, internships, parent company, number of employees, revenues, e-mail and web address, projected number of hires. Indexes: Alphabetical.

★14013★ Baltimore Job Source: The Only Source You Need to Land the Job of Your Choice in Baltimore.

Benjamin Scott Publishing
20 E. Colorado Blvd., No. 202
Pasadena, CA 91105
Ph: (626)449-1339   Fax: (626)449-1389
Fr: 800-448-4959

Mary McMahon, Ruth E. Thaler-Carter and Betty Glascoe. 2005. $15.95. 312 pages. Over 5000 job contacts in the Baltimore/Annapolis Metro Areas, including small and large companies, Fortune 500 corporations, non-profits, government agencies, and internships.

★14014★ Boston JobBank

Adams Media Corp.
57 Littlefield St.
Avon, MA 02322
Ph: (508)427-7100   Fax: (508)427-6790
Fr: 800-872-5627
URL: http://www.adamsmedia.com

Annual; latest edition 20th. $17.95 for individuals. Covers over 7,000 employers in Massachusetts. Entries include: Firm or organization name, address, local phone, toll-free phone, fax, e-mail, URL, recorded jobline, hours, names of management, name and title of contact, titles of common positions, entry-level positions, fringe benefits offered, stock exchange listing, description of organization, subsidiaries, location of headquarters, educational background desired, projected number of hires, training programs, internships, parent company, number of employees, revenues, other U.S. Locations, international locations. Arrangement: Classified by industry. Indexes: Alphabetical.

★14015★ California Job Journal

California Job Journal
2033 Howe Ave., Ste. 100
Sacramento, CA 95825
Ph: (916)925-0800   Fax: (916)925-0101
Fr: 800-655-5627
E-mail: cjj@jobjournal.com
URL: http://www.jobjournal.com

Weekly. Free. Covers employment issues and job openings in California from entry-level to executive positions. Entries include: Company name, address, phone, type of business, name and title of contact; comprehensive description of position and required skills/background, salary and/or benefits offered. Arrangement: Classified by field of employment.

★14016★ Carolina JobBank

Adams Media Corp.
57 Littlefield St.
Avon, MA 02322
Ph: (508)427-7100   Fax: (508)427-6790
Fr: 800-872-5627
URL: http://www.adamsmedia.com

Latest edition 7th. $17.95 for individuals. Covers 4,600 employers in North Carolina and South Carolina. Entries include: Firm or organization name, address, local phone, toll-free phone, fax, e-mail, URL, recorded jobline, description of organization, subsidiaries, other locations, hours, names of management, name and title of contact, location of headquarters, typical titles for common positions, educational backgrounds desired, projected number of hires, company benefits, stock exchange listing, training programs and internships, parent company, number of employees, revenues. Arrangement: Classified by industry. Indexes: Alphabetical.

★14017★ Central Florida Career Guide

Edge Publishing
555 Republic Dr., Ste. 200
Plano, TX 75074
Ph: (972)424-1953   Fax: (214)774-2441

Annual. Covers employment needs of over 400 firms in the Orlando metropolitan area. Entries include: Company name, address, phone, name and title of contact, number of employees, products or services provided, staffing needs. Arrangement: Classified by line of business.

★14018★ Chicago JobBank

Adams Media Corp.
57 Littlefield St.
Avon, MA 02322
Ph: (508)427-7100   Fax: (508)427-6790
Fr: 800-872-5627
URL: http://www.adamsmedia.com

Annual; latest edition 19th. $17.95 for individuals. Covers about 5,500 major employers in northern and central Illinois including Aurora, Peoria, Rockford, and Springfield. Entries include: Firm or organization name, address, local phone, toll-free phone, fax, e-mail, URL, description of organization, hours, recorded jobline, subsidiaries, names of management, name and title of contact, headquarters locations, typical titles for entry-level and middle-level positions, educational backgrounds desired, company benefits, stock exchange listing, training programs, internships, parent company, number of employees, revenues, other U.S. locations, international locations. Arrangement: Classified by industry. Indexes: Alphabetical.

★14019★ The Connecticut JobBank

Adams Media Corp.
57 Littlefield St.
Avon, MA 02322
Ph: (508)427-7100   Fax: (508)427-6790
Fr: 800-872-5627
URL: http://adamsmedia.stores.yahoo.net/cojo3rded.html

Biennial; latest edition 3. $17.95 for individuals. Covers approximately 2,000 employers, career resources, industry associations, and employment services in Connecticut. Entries include: Company name, address, phone, fax, e-mail, and web address; names and titles of key personnel; number of employees; geographical area served; financial data; subsidiary names and addresses; description of services; Standard Industrial Classification (SIC) code. Indexes: Alphabetical.

★14020★ Craighead's International Business, Travel, and Relocation Guide to 81 Countries

Gale, Cengage Learning
27500 Drake Rd.
Farmington Hills, MI 48331-3535
Ph: (248)699-GALE   Fax: (248)699-8069
Fr: 800-877-GALE
E-mail: galeord@gale.com
URL: http://www.gale.com

First edition, 2002. $695.00. 5366 pages. Arranged geographically into regions of Asia, Africa, Europe, the Mideast, and the Americas. Profiles include information on maps, statistics, travel restrictions, currency, transportation, and health. A separate section covers details of international travel such as instructions for passports and visas and information on transportation and shopping. An international relocation chapter covers financial planning, legal matters, insurance, education, housing, and other family concerns.

★14021★ Dallas/Ft. Worth JobBank

Adams Media Corp.
57 Littlefield St.
Avon, MA 02322
Ph: (508)427-7100   Fax: (508)427-6790
Fr: 800-872-5627
URL: http://www.adamsmedia.com

Annual; latest edition 14th. $17.95 for individuals. Covers 4,000 employers in the Dallas/Ft. Worth, Texas, area including Abilene, Amarillo, Arlington, Garland, Irving, Lubbock, and Plano. Entries include: Firm or organization name, address, local phone, toll-free phone, fax, e-mail, URL, recorded jobline, hours, description of organization, subsidiaries, names of management, name and title of contact, location of headquarters, typical titles for common positions, educational backgrounds desired, company benefits, stock exchange listing, training programs, internships, parent company, number of employees, revenues, projected number of hires. Arrangement: Classified by industry. Indexes: Alphabetical.

★14022★ Denver JobBank

Adams Media Corp.
57 Littlefield St.
Avon, MA 02322
Ph: (508)427-7100   Fax: (508)427-6790
Fr: 800-872-5627
URL: http://www.adamsmedia.com

Latest edition 14th. $17.95 for individuals. Covers 3,500 employers in Denver and the rest of Colorado including Aurora, Boulder, Colorado Springs, and Lakewood. Entries include: Firm or organization name, address, local phone, toll-free phone, fax, e-mail, URL, description of organization, subsidiaries, other locations, hours, recorded jobline, names of management, name and title of contact, headquarters location, projected number of hires; listings may also include typical titles for common positions, educational backgrounds desired, company benefits, stock exchange listing, training programs, internships, parent company, number of employees, revenues. Arrangement: Classified by industry. Indexes: Alphabetical.

★14023★ Detroit JobBank

Adams Media Corp.
57 Littlefield St.
Avon, MA 02322
Ph: (508)427-7100   Fax: (508)427-6790
Fr: 800-872-5627

Annual. Covers 4,200 employers throughout Michigan including Dearborn, Flint, Grand Rapids, and Lansing. Entries include: Firm or organization name, address, local phone, toll-free phone, fax, e-mail, URL, recorded jobline, description of organization, other locations, subsidiaries, names of management, name and title of contact, location of headquarters, typical titles for common positions, educational backgrounds desired, projected number of hires, company benefits, stock exchange listing, training programs, internships, parent company, number of employees, revenues. Arrangement: Classified by industry. Indexes: Alphabetical.

★14024★ Florida JobBank

Adams Media Corp.
57 Littlefield St.
Avon, MA 02322
Ph: (508)427-7100   Fax: (508)427-6790
Fr: 800-872-5627
URL: http://www.adamsmedia.com/

Latest edition 16th. $17.95 for individuals. Covers 5,500 employers in Florida including Fort Lauderdale, Jacksonville, Miami, Orlando, Tampa. Entries include: Firm or organization name, address, local phone, toll-free phone, fax, e-mail addresses, web addresses, description of organization, subsidiaries, hours, recorded jobline, name and title of contact, headquarters location, typical titles for common positions, educational backgrounds desired, number of projected hires, company benefits, stock exchange listing, training programs, internships, parent company, number of employees, revenues, other U.S. Locations, international locations. Arrangement: Classified by industry. Indexes: Alphabetical.

★14025★ Greater Philadelphia JobBank

Adams Media Corp.
57 Littlefield St.
Avon, MA 02322
Ph: (508)427-7100   Fax: (508)427-6790
Fr: 800-872-5627
URL: http://www.adamsmedia.com

Annual; latest edition 14th. $16.95 for individuals. Covers 5,200 employers in metropolitan Philadelphia, the eastern half of Pennsylvania, southern New Jersey, and Delaware. Entries include: Firm or organization name, address, phone, description of organization, name and title of contact, typical titles for entry-level and middle-level positions, educational backgrounds desired, company benefits, stock exchange listing, training programs, internships, parent company, number of employees, revenues, web address, e-mail address, corporate headquarters, and projected number of hires for this location in the next year. Arrangement: Classified by industry. Indexes: Alphabetical.

★14026★ Houston JobBank

Adams Media Corp.
57 Littlefield St.
Avon, MA 02322
Ph: (508)427-7100   Fax: (508)427-6790
Fr: 800-872-5627
URL: http://www.adamsmedia.com

Annual; latest edition 12th. $17.95 for individuals. Covers over 3,500 employers in Houston, Texas, and the surrounding areas including Bayton, Beaumont, Galveston, and Pasadena. Entries include: Firm or organization name, address, local phone, toll-free phone, fax, recorded jobline, e-mail, URL, hours, name and title of contact, description of organization, headquarters location, subsidiaries, operations at the facility, names of management, typical titles for common positions, educational backgrounds desired, number of projected hires, fringe benefits offered, stock exchange listing, training programs, internships, parent company, number of employees, revenues, other U.S. Locations, international locations. Arrangement: Classified by industry. Indexes: Alphabetical.

★14027★ **How to Get a Job in Atlanta**

Surrey Books, Inc.
230 E. Ohio St., Ste. 120
Chicago, IL 60611
Ph: (312)751-7330   Fax: (312)751-7334
Fr: 800-326-4430
URL: http://www.agatepublishing.com/

Robert Sanborn, A. Tariq Shakoor and Rosita Jackson. Fourth edition, 1997. $16.95 (paper). 349 pages. Directory of employers, associations, job referral services, and other sources of employment information. Part of How to get a Job series.

★14028★ **How to Get a Job in Dallas and Fort Worth**

Surrey Books, Inc.
230 E. Ohio St., Ste. 120
Chicago, IL 60611
Ph: (312)751-7330   Fax: (312)751-7334
Fr: 800-326-4430
URL: http://www.agatepublishing.com/

Robert Sanborn and Richard Citrin. Sixth edition, 1998. $17.95 (paper). 354 pages. Directory of employers, associations, job referral services, and other sources of employment information.

★14029★ **How to Get a Job in Denver and Central Colorado**

Surrey Books, Inc.
230 E. Ohio St., Ste. 120
Chicago, IL 60611
Ph: (312)751-7330   Fax: (312)751-7334
Fr: 800-326-4430
URL: http://www.agatepublishing.com/

Robert Sanborn and Christopher Ott. 1999. $18.95 (paper). 363 pages. Directory of employers, associations, job referral services, and other sources of employment information. Part of How to get a Job series.

★14030★ **How to Get a Job in Europe**

Planning Communications
7215 Oak Ave.
River Forest, IL 60305-1935
Ph: (708)366-5200   Fax: (708)366-5280
Fr: 888-366-5200
E-mail: info@planningcommunications.com
URL: http://jobfindersonline.com

Robert Sanborn and Cheryl Matherly. Fifth edition, 2003. 496 pages. $22.95. Directory of employers, associations, job referral services, and other sources of employment information. Part of Insider's Guide series.

★14031★ **How to Get a Job in New York City and the Metropolitan Area**

Surrey Books, Inc.
230 E. Ohio St.. Ste. 120
Chicago, IL 60611
Ph: (312)751-7330   Fax: (312)751-7334
Fr: 800-326-4430
URL: http://www.agatepublishing.com/

Robert Sanborn and Eva Lederman. Sixth edition, 1998. $17.95 (paper). 388 pages. Directory of employers, associations, job referral services, and other sources of employment information. Part of Insider's Guide series.

★14032★ **How to Get a Job in the San Francisco Bay Area**

Surrey Books, Inc.
230 E. Ohio St., Ste. 120
Chicago, IL 60611
Ph: (312)751-7330   Fax: (312)751-7334
Fr: 800-326-4430
URL: http://www.agatepublishing.com/

Robert Sanborn and Will Flowers. Fifth edition, 1998. $17.95 (paper). 378 pages. Directory of employers, associations, job referral services, and other sources of employment information. Part of Insider's Guide series.

★14033★ **How to Get a Job in Southern California**

Surrey Books, Inc.
230 E. Ohio St., Ste. 120
Chicago, IL 60611
Ph: (312)751-7330   Fax: (312)751-7334
Fr: 800-326-4430
URL: http://www.agatepublishing.com/

Robert Sanborn and Naomi Sandweiss. Seventh edition, 1999. $18.95 (paper). 330 pages. Directory of employers, associations, job referral services, and other sources of employment information. Part of How to get a Job series.

★14034★ **The Indiana JobBank**

Adams Media Corp.
57 Littlefield St.
Avon, MA 02322
Ph: (508)427-7100   Fax: (508)427-6790
Fr: 800-872-5627

Biennial. $72.24 for individuals. Covers 3,200 employers in Indiana, including Evansville, Fort Wayne, Gary, New Albany, and South Bend. Entries include: Firm or organization name, address, phone, name and title of contact; description of organization, headquarters location, typical titles for entry and middle-level positions, educational backgrounds desired, fringe benefits offered, stock exchange listing, training programs, internships, parent company, number of employees, revenues, e-mail and web address, projected number of hires. Indexes: Alphabetical.

★14035★ **Los Angeles JobBank**

Adams Media Corp.
57 Littlefield St.
Avon, MA 02322
Ph: (508)427-7100   Fax: (508)427-6790
Fr: 800-872-5627
URL: http://www.adamsmedia.com

Annual; latest edition 17th. $16.95 for individuals. Covers over 7,900 southern California employers including Orange, Riverside,

San Bernadino, San Diego, Santa Barbara and Ventura counties. Entries include: Firm or organization name, address, local phone, toll-free phone, fax, e-mail, URL, recorded jobline, hours, subsidiaries, other locations, names of management, name and title of contact, description of organization, number of employees, headquarters location, typical titles for common positions, educational backgrounds desired, fringe benefits offered, stock exchange listing, training programs, internships, parent company, number of employees, revenues, and number of projected hires. Arrangement: Classified by industry. Indexes: Alphabetical.

★14036★ **Metro Washington DC JobBank**

Adams Media Corp.
57 Littlefield St.
Avon, MA 02322
Ph: (508)427-7100   Fax: (508)427-6790
Fr: 800-872-5627
URL: http://www.adamsmedia.com

Latest edition 15th. $17.95 for individuals. Covers 6,900 employers in Washington, D.C., greater Baltimore, and northern Virginia. Entries include: Firm or organization name, address, local phone, toll-free phone, fax, recorded jobline, name and title of contact, description of organization, subsidiaries, other locations, names of management, hours, titles for common positions, educational backgrounds desired, company benefits, stock exchange listing, location of headquarters, training programs, internships, parent company, number of employees, revenues, email and URL address, projected number of hires. Arrangement: Classified by industry. Indexes: Alphabetical.

★14037★ **Metropolitan New York JobBank**

Adams Media Corp.
57 Littlefield St.
Avon, MA 02322
Ph: (508)427-7100   Fax: (508)427-6790
Fr: 800-872-5627
URL: http://www.adamsmedia.com

Latest edition 19th. $17.95 for individuals. Covers over 7,900 New York City, Northern New Jersey, Southwestern Connecticut, Long Island, and Westchester employers. Entries include: Firm or organization name, address, local phone, toll-free phone, fax, e-mail, URL, recorded jobline, hours, name and title of contact, description of organization, subsidiaries, other locations, names of management, headquarters location, typical titles for common positions, educational backgrounds desired, fringe benefits offered, stock exchange listing, training programs, internships, parent company, number of employees, revenues, projected number of hires. Arrangement: Classified by industry. Indexes: Alphabetical.

★14038★ Missouri JobBank

Adams Media Corp.
57 Littlefield St.
Avon, MA 02322
Ph: (508)427-7100　　Fax: (508)427-6790
Fr: 800-872-5627

Covers 3,700 employers in the Kansas City area and the rest of Missouri, as well as southern Illinois. Entries include: Firm or organization name, address, local phone, toll-free phone, fax, e-mail, URL, recorded jobline, hours, description of organization, name and title of contact, location of headquarters, typical titles for entry-level and middle-level positions, educational backgrounds desired, projected number of hires, company benefits, stock exchange listing, training programs, internships, parent company, projected hiring, number of employees, revenues. Arrangement: Classified by industry. Indexes: Alphabetical.

★14039★ Multinational Firms & International Relocation

Edward Elgar Publishing, Inc.
136 West St., Ste. 202
Northampton, MA 01060
Ph: (413)584-5551　　Fax: (413)584-9933

Peter J. Buckley and Jean Louis Mucchielli, editors. 1997. $140.00. 255 pages.

★14040★ National JobBank

Adams Media Corp.
57 Littlefield St.
Avon, MA 02322
Ph: (508)427-7100　　Fax: (508)427-6790
Fr: 800-872-5627
URL: http://www.adamsmedia.com

Annual; latest edition 19th. $475.00 for individuals. Covers over 20,000 employers nationwide. Entries include: Firm or organization name, address, local phone, toll-free phone, fax, contact name and title, description of organization, headquarters location, names of management, number of employees, other locations, subsidiaries, parent company, projected number of hires, training offered, internships, hours, recorded jobline, typical titles for common positions, educational backgrounds desired, stock exchange (if listed), fringe benefits offered. Several state and regional volumes are available and described separately. Arrangement: Geographical. Indexes: Geographical and classified by industry.

★14041★ Nevada in Your Future: The Complete Relocation Guide for Job-Seekers, Retirees and Snowbirds

DiscoverGuides
PO Box 231954
Las Vegas, NV 89123
Ph: (702)558-8242　　Fax: (702)558-4355

Don W. Martin and Betty W. Martin. Second edition, 2003. $17.95. 296 pages.

★14042★ The New Jersey JobBank

Adams Media Corp.
57 Littlefield St.
Avon, MA 02322
Ph: (508)427-7100　　Fax: (508)427-6790
Fr: 800-872-5627
URL: http://adamsmedia.stores.yahoo.net/newjejobba3r.html

Biennial; latest edition 3. $17.95 for individuals. Covers approximately 4,000 employers, career resources, industry associations, and employment services in the Garden State. Entries include: Company name, address, phone, fax, email, and web address; names and titles of key personnel; number of employees; geographical area served; financial data; subsidiary names and addresses; description of services; standard industrial classification (SIC) code. Indexes: Alphabetical.

★14043★ The Ohio JobBank

Adams Media Corp.
57 Littlefield St.
Avon, MA 02322
Ph: (508)427-7100　　Fax: (508)427-6790
Fr: 800-872-5627
URL: http://www.adamsmedia.com

Biennial; latest edition 11th. $17.95 for individuals. Covers 4,800 employers and employment services in Ohio. Entries include: Firm or organization name, address, phone, name and title of contact; description of organization, headquarters location, typical titles for entry- and middle-level positions, educational backgrounds desired, fringe benefits offered, stock exchange listing, training programs, internships, parent company, number of employees, revenues, e-mail and web address, projected number of hires. Arrangement: Alphabetical.

★14044★ Phoenix JobBank

Adams Media Corp.
57 Littlefield St.
Avon, MA 02322
Ph: (508)427-7100　　Fax: (508)427-6790
Fr: 800-872-5627
URL: http://www.adamsmedia.com

Latest edition 9th. $17.95 for individuals. Covers 2,100 employers in the Arizona area including Tucson, Phoenix, Flagstaff, and Yuma. Entries include: Firm or organization name, address, local phone, toll-free phone, fax, e-mail, URL, recorded jobline, description of organization, hours, names of management, name and title of contact, location of headquarters, typical titles for common positions, educational backgrounds desired, projected number of hires, company benefits, stock exchange listing, training programs, internships, parent company, number of employees, revenues. Arrangement: Classified by industry. Indexes: Alphabetical.

★14045★ San Francisco Bay Area JobBank

Adams Media Corp.
57 Littlefield St.
Avon, MA 02322
Ph: (508)427-7100　　Fax: (508)427-6790
Fr: 800-872-5627

URL: http://www.adamsmedia.com

Latest edition 17th. $17.95 for individuals. Covers about 5,600 employers in the San Francisco Bay area and the Northern half of California including Oakland, Sacramento, San Jose, and Silicon Valley. Entries include: Firm or organization name, address, local phone, toll-free phone, fax, e-mail, URL, recorded jobline, hours, description of organization, subsidiaries, other locations, number of employees, name and title of contact, headquarters location, typical titles for common positions, educational backgrounds desired, company benefits, stock exchange listing, training programs, internships, parent company, number of employees, revenues, and number of projected hires. Arrangement: Classified by industry. Indexes: Alphabetical.

★14046★ Seattle JobBank

Adams Media Corp.
57 Littlefield St.
Avon, MA 02322
Ph: (508)427-7100　　Fax: (508)427-6790
Fr: 800-872-5627
URL: http://www.adamsmedia.com

Latest edition 13th. $17.95 for individuals. Covers about 4,800 employers in Washington state, including Spokane, Tacoma, and Bellevue. Entries include: Firm or organization name, address, local phone, toll-free phone, fax, e-mail, URL, description of organization, subsidiaries, name and title of contact, headquarters location, recorded jobline, typical titles for common positions, educational backgrounds desired, projected number of hires, company benefits, stock exchange listing, training programs, internships, parent company, number of employees, revenues. Arrangement: Classified by industry. Indexes: Alphabetical.

★14047★ Tennessee JobBank

Adams Media Corp.
57 Littlefield St.
Avon, MA 02322
Ph: (508)427-7100　　Fax: (508)427-6790
Fr: 800-872-5627

Biennial. Covers 2,700 employers in Tennessee, including Chattanooga, Knoxville, Memphis, and Nashville. Entries include: Firm or organization name, address, local phone, toll-free phone, fax, e-mail, URL, recorded jobline, description of organization, subsidiaries, hours, names of management, name and title of contact, location of headquarters, typical titles for common positions, educational backgrounds desired, projected number of hires, company benefits, stock exchange listing, training programs, internships, parent company, number of employees, revenues. Arrangement: Classified by industry. Indexes: Alphabetical.

★14048★ The Virginia JobBank

Adams Media Corp.
57 Littlefield St.
Avon, MA 02322
Ph: (508)427-7100　　Fax: (508)427-6790
Fr: 800-872-5627

URL: http://www.adamsmedia.com

Biennial; latest edition 4th. $17.95 for individuals. Covers 3,700 employers in Virginia and West Virginia. Entries include: Firm or organization name, address, phone, name and title of contact; description of organization, headquarters location, typical titles for entry- and middle-level positions, educational backgrounds desired, fringe benefits offered, stock exchange listing, training programs, internships, parent company, number of employees, revenues, e-mail and web address, projected number of hires. Indexes: Alphabetical.

NEWSPAPERS, MAGAZINES, AND JOURNALS

★14049★ Arizona Business Gazette

Phoenix Newspapers Inc.
200 East Van Buren St.
Phoenix, AZ 85004-2238
Ph: (602)444-8000   Fax: (602)444-7363
URL: http://www.abgnews.com

Weekly (Thurs.). $30.00/year for individuals, 52 weeks; $60.00 for two years, 104 weeks; $20.00 for institutions, 26 weeks. Business and legal newspaper.

★14050★ Arkansas Business

Arkansas Business Publishing Group
122 East Second St.
PO Box 3686
Little Rock, AR 72203
Ph: (501)372-1443   Fax: (501)375-7933
URL: http://www.arkansasbusiness.com

Weekly. $55.00/year for individuals, in state; $85.00/year for other countries, international; $85.00/year for individuals, out of state; $136.00 for two years, in state; $189.00 for two years, out of state; $5.00/year for individuals, 6 months, in state; $15.00/year for individuals, premium. Business magazine on the Arkansas business community, covering people and recent news events statewide.

★14051★ Atlanta Business Chronicle

American City Business Journals Inc.
120 W Morehead St., Ste. 200
Charlotte, NC 28202
Ph: (704)973-1000   Fax: (704)973-1001
E-mail: bizchron@mindspring.com
URL: http://atlanta.bizjournals.com/atlanta

Weekly. $96.00/year for individuals, 56 issues; $173.00/year for individuals, 108 issues; $221.00/year for individuals, 160 issues. Local business newspaper.

★14052★ Austin Business Journal

Austin Business Journal Inc.
111 Congress Ave., Ste. 750
Austin, TX 78701
Ph: (512)494-2500   Fax: (512)494-2525

Weekly. Newspaper (tabloid) serving business and industry in Central Texas.

★14053★ Baltimore Business Journal

American City Business Journals Inc.
120 W Morehead St., Ste. 200
Charlotte, NC 28202
Ph: (704)973-1000   Fax: (704)973-1001
URL: http://baltimore.bizjournals.com/baltimore

Weekly. $93.00/year for individuals, 56 issues; $153.00/year for individuals, 108 issues; $183.00/year for individuals, 160 issues. Newspaper reporting Baltimore business news.

★14054★ Boston Business Journal

American City Business Journals Inc.
120 W Morehead St., Ste. 200
Charlotte, NC 28202
Ph: (704)973-1000   Fax: (704)973-1001
E-mail: boston@bizjournals.com
URL: http://www.bizjournals.com/boston/

Weekly. $115.00/year for individuals; $179.00 for two years, 108 issues; $226.00 for individuals, 160 issues. Business newspaper specializing in local and regional business for upper management and CEO's of large and mid-sized businesses.

★14055★ Business First of Buffalo

American City Business Journals Inc.
120 W Morehead St., Ste. 200
Charlotte, NC 28202
Ph: (704)973-1000   Fax: (704)973-1001
URL: http://buffalo.bizjournals.com/buffalo

Weekly. $94.00/year for individuals; $158.00 for individuals, two years, 108 issues; $204.00 for individuals, 160 issues. Business Newspaper.

★14056★ The Business Journal of Charlotte

American City Business Journals Inc.
120 W Morehead St., Ste. 200
Charlotte, NC 28202
Ph: (704)973-1000   Fax: (704)973-1001
E-mail: charlotte@bizjournals.com
URL: http://www.bizjournals.com/charlotte

Weekly. $88.00/year for individuals, 56 issues; $147.00/year for individuals, 108 issues; $197.00/year for individuals, 160 issues. Newspaper for the business community of Charlotte and the surrounding thirteen-county area.

★14057★ Business Times

Choice Media L.L.C.
PO Box 580
New Haven, CT 06513-0580
Ph: (203)782-1420   Fax: (203)782-3793
E-mail: cbtimes@ctbusinesstimes.com
URL: http://www.ctbusinesstimes.com

Monthly. $36.00/year for individuals, per year. Business journal (tabloid).

★14058★ Capital District Business Review

American City Business Journals Inc.
120 W Morehead St., Ste. 200
Charlotte, NC 28202
Ph: (704)973-1000   Fax: (704)973-1001
URL: http://www.bizjournals.com

Business tabloid providing local business news for Capital Region area.

★14059★ Crain's Chicago Business

Crain Communications Inc.
360 N Michigan Ave.
Chicago, IL 60601
Ph: (312)649-5411   Fax: (312)280-3150
Fr: 888-909-9111
URL: http://www.chicagobusiness.com

Weekly. $94.95/year for individuals, in the Midwest; $109.00/year for individuals, outside the Midwest; $148.00/year for other countries. Newspaper covering news stories about various aspects of business and labor activity in the Chicago market.

★14060★ Crain's Cleveland Business

Crain Communications Inc.
700 W St. Clair, Ste. 310
Cleveland, OH 44113-1256
Ph: (216)522-1383
URL: http://www.crainscleveland.com/apps/pbcs.dll/frontpage

Weekly. $52.00/year for individuals, print; $102.00/year for individuals, outside Ohio. Metropolitan business newspaper serving seven counties.

★14061★ Crain's Detroit Business

Crain Communications Inc.
1155 Gratiot Ave.
PO Box 07924
Detroit, MI 48207-2997
Ph: (313)446-6000   Fax: (313)446-0347
Fr: 888-909-9111
URL: http://www.crainsdetroit.com

Weekly (Mon.). $59.00/year for individuals, Michigan; $79.00/year for out of state; $127.00/year for other countries. Local business tabloid covering Wayne, Macomb, Oakland, Livingston, and Washtenaw counties.

★14062★ Crain's New York Business

Crain Communications Inc.
1155 Gratiot Ave.
Detroit, MI 48207-2997
Ph: (313)446-6000
URL: http://www.crainsny.com

Weekly. $90.00/year for individuals, print/digital combo; $125.00/year for individuals, print; $110.00/year for individuals, Canada and international; $35.00/year for individuals, digital edition with premium access. Regional business tabloid.

★14063★ Daily Journal of Commerce

New Orleans Publishing Group Inc.
111 Veterans Blvd., Ste. 1440
Metairie, LA 70005
Ph: (504)834-9292   Fax: (504)832-3550
URL: http://www.djc-gp.com

Daily. $495.00/year for individuals, online. Trade newspaper covering construction news in Louisiana and Mississippi.

★14064★ Des Moines Business Record

Business Publications Corp.
The Depot at Fourth
100 4th St.
Des Moines, IA 50309
Ph: (515)288-3336   Fax: (515)288-0309
URL: http://www.businessrecord.com

Weekly. $50.00/year for individuals, introductory; $65.00/year for individuals; $70.00/year for individuals, limited time offer - work and play package; $80.00/year for individuals, two years. Newspaper covering local business news.

★14065★ Florida Trend

Trend Magazines Inc.
490 First Ave., S
St. Petersburg, FL 33701
Ph: (727)821-5800
E-mail: custrelations@floridatrend.com
URL: http://www.floridatrend.com

Monthly. Business.

★14066★ Houston Business Journal

American City Business Journals Inc.
120 W Morehead St., Ste. 200
Charlotte, NC 28202
Ph: (704)973-1000   Fax: (704)973-1001
E-mail: houston@bizjournals.com
URL: http://www.bizjournals.com/houston

Weekly. $92.00/year for individuals; $130.00 for individuals, 2 years; $156.00/year for individuals, 3 year. Magazine for metropolitan Houston business community.

★14067★ Long Island

Long Island Association Inc.
300 Broadhollow Rd., Ste. 110W
Melville, NY 11747-4840
Ph: (631)493-3000   Fax: (631)499-2194
Fr: 800-564-6542
E-mail: info@longislandassociation.org
URL: http://www.longislandassociation.org/li_magazine.cfm

Monthly. $49.95/year for individuals, special member, for a limited time; $69.95/year for nonmembers. Long Island Association magazine.

★14068★ Long Island Business News

Long Island Business News
2150 Smithtown Ave., Ste. 7
Ronkonkoma, NY 11779
Ph: (631)913-4261   Fax: (631)737-1890
URL: http://www.libn.com

Weekly (Fri.). $104.00/year for individuals;

$166.00/year for two years; $224.00/year for individuals, three years. Business tabloid serving Long Island.

★14069★ The Los Angeles Business Journal

The Los Angeles Business Journal
5700 Wilshire, No. 170
Los Angeles, CA 90036
Ph: (213)549-5225   Fax: (213)549-5255
URL: http://www.labusinessjournal.com

Weekly (Mon.). $99.95/year for individuals; $179.95 for two years. Newspaper (tabloid) covering local business news, business trends, executive profiles, and information for the Los Angeles area executive.

★14070★ Miami Today

Today Enterprises Inc.
710 Brickell Ave.
Miami, FL 33131
Ph: (305)358-2663
E-mail: whatisok@aol.com
URL: http://www.miamitodaynews.com

Weekly (Thurs.). $2.00 for single issue; $80.00/year USA. Newspaper (tabloid) covering business and community information targeted to the upper management levels.

★14071★ Nashville Business Journal

Nashville Business Journal
344 4th Ave. N
Nashville, TN 37219
Ph: (615)248-2222   Fax: (615)248-6246
E-mail: nashville@bizjournals.com
URL: http://nashville.bizjournals.com/nashville/

Weekly. $87.00/year for individuals; $145.00 for two years. Regional business newspaper.

★14072★ Northeast Pennsylvania Business Journal

The Scranton Times
149 Penn Ave.
Scranton, PA 18505-3311
Ph: (570)348-9100   Fr: 800-228-4637
URL: http://www.npbj.com

Monthly. Business publication serving 19 counties.

★14073★ Orlando Business Journal

American City Business Journals Inc.
120 W Morehead St., Ste. 200
Charlotte, NC 28202
Ph: (704)973-1000   Fax: (704)973-1001
E-mail: orlando@bizjournals.com
URL: http://www.bizjournals.com/orlando/

Weekly. $86.00 for individuals, 56 issues; $129.00 for individuals, 108 issues; $172.00 for individuals, 160 issues. Newspaper (tabloid) covering local business news, trends, and ideas of interest to industry, trade, agribusiness, finance, and commerce.

★14074★ Pacific Business News

American City Business Journals Inc.
120 W Morehead St., Ste. 200
Charlotte, NC 28202
Ph: (704)973-1000   Fax: (704)973-1001
URL: http://pacific.bizjournals.com/pacific/

Weekly. $83.95/year for individuals, 56 issues; $169.95/year for individuals, 160 issues. Business tabloid.

★14075★ Philadelphia Business Journal

Philadelphia Business Journal
400 Market St., Ste. 1200
Philadelphia, PA 19106
Ph: (215)238-1450
URL: http://www.philadelphia.bizjournals.com

Weekly. Regional and general business newspaper.

★14076★ Pittsburgh Business Times

American City Business Journals Inc.
120 W Morehead St., Ste. 200
Charlotte, NC 28202
Ph: (704)973-1000   Fax: (704)973-1001
E-mail: pittsburgh@bizjournals.com
URL: http://pittsburgh.bizjournals.com/pittsburgh

Weekly. $104.00/year for individuals; $170.00 for two years. Metropolitan business newspaper.

★14077★ Providence Business News

Providence Business News
220 West Exchange St., Ste. 200
Providence, RI 02903-1004
Ph: (401)273-2201   Fax: (401)274-0670
E-mail: circulation@pbn.com
URL: http://www.pbn.com

Weekly. $89.00/year for individuals, Per year; $134.00/year for two years. Newspaper (tabloid) covering business news in Southeastern New England. Regular editorial focus sections include banking/finance, computers, boating, industry, real estate and health care.

★14078★ Puget Sound Business Journal (Seattle)

American City Business Journals Inc.
120 W Morehead St., Ste. 200
Charlotte, NC 28202
Ph: (704)973-1000   Fax: (704)973-1001
E-mail: seattle@bizjournals.com
URL: http://seattle.bizjournals.com/seattle/

Weekly. $88.00/year for individuals; $165.00/year for individuals, 108 issues; $176.00/year for individuals, 160 issues. Regional business newspaper (tabloid).

★14079★ St. Louis Business Journal

American City Business Journals Inc.
120 W Morehead St., Ste. 200
Charlotte, NC 28202
Ph: (704)973-1000   Fax: (704)973-1001

URL: http://stlouis.bizjournals.com/stlouis/

Weekly. $86.00/year for individuals; $146.00 for individuals, 108 issues; $194.00 for individuals, 160 issues. Business newspaper.

★14080★ St. Louis Countian
Legal Communications Corp.
612 North 2nd St., 4th Fl.
St. Louis, MO 63102
Ph: (314)421-1880   Fax: (314)436-2718
Business and legal newspaper.

★14081★ San Antonio Business Journal
American City Business Journals Inc.
120 W Morehead St., Ste. 200
Charlotte, NC 28202
Ph: (704)973-1000   Fax: (704)973-1001
E-mail: sanantonio@bizjournals.com
URL: http://sanantonio.bizjournals.com/sanantonio/

Weekly. $88.00/year for individuals; $176.00/year for individuals, 3 years. Newspaper featuring news and information about the San Antonio and south Texas business community.

★14082★ San Diego Business Journal
San Diego Business Journal
4909 Murphy Canyon Rd., Ste. 200
San Diego, CA 92123
Ph: (858)277-6359
URL: http://www.sdbj.com

Weekly (Mon.). Metropolitan business newspaper specializing in investigative and enterprise reporting on San Diego County businesses and related issues.

★14083★ San Diego Daily Transcript
San Diego Daily Transcript
2131 3rd Ave.
San Diego, CA 92101
Ph: (619)232-4381   Fax: (619)236-8126
E-mail: webmaster@sddt.com
URL: http://www.sddt.com

Daily (morn.). $200.00/year for individuals, print + online; $337.50 for two years, print + online. Local business newspaper.

★14084★ San Francisco Business Times
American City Business Journals Inc.
120 W Morehead St., Ste. 200
Charlotte, NC 28202
Ph: (704)973-1000   Fax: (704)973-1001
E-mail: sanfrancisco@bizjournals.com
URL: http://sanfrancisco.bizjournals.com/sanfrancisco

Weekly. $93.00/year for individuals; $158.00 for individuals, for two years; $188.00/year for individuals, for three years. Local business newspaper (tabloid) serving the San Francisco Bay Area.

★14085★ Vermont Business Magazine
Elk Publishing Inc.
531 Main St.
Colchester, VT 05446-7222
Fax: (802)879-2015   Fr: 800-499-0447
E-mail: info@vermontbiz.com
URL: http://www.vermontbiz.com/

Monthly. $28.00/year for individuals, 15 issues, regular subscription; $55.00/year; $55.00/year for individuals, 15 issues, business subscription. Regional business magazine.

★14086★ Washington Business Journal
American City Business Journals Inc.
120 W Morehead St., Ste. 200
Charlotte, NC 28202
Ph: (704)973-1000   Fax: (704)973-1001
E-mail: washington@bizjournals.com
URL: http://washington.bizjournals.com/washington

Weekly. $98.00/year for individuals, 56 issues; $158.00/year for individuals, 108 issues; $198.00/year for individuals, 160 issues. Metropolitan business newspaper (tabloid).

ONLINE AND DATABASE SERVICES

★14087★ BostonSearch.com
E-mail: webmaster@bostonsearch.com
URL: http://www.bostonsearch.com/

Description: Job search site for those interested in relocating to or remaining in the Boston, MA area. Visitors may post resume, search job databank and activate e-mail alert service.

★14088★ Corporate Search Consultants, Inc.
509 W. Colonial Dr.
Orlando, FL 32804
Ph: (407)578-3888   Fax: (407)578-5153
Fr: 800-800-7231
E-mail: webmanager@corpsearch.com
URL: http://jobs.corpsearch.com

Description: Job search consultants. Job board and resume posting for jobs in the healthcare and medical community.

★14089★ JobBus.com
E-mail: webmaster@jobbus.com
URL: http://www.jobbus.com

Description: Job search engine portal for those looking to remain in or relocate to Canada. Contains career resources and articles.

★14090★ PensacolaJobs.com
Ph: (850)475-9945
E-mail: contact@pensacolajobs.com

URL: http://www.pensacolajobs.com/

Description: Job search and resume posting database for those interested in remaining in or relocating to the Pensacola, Florida area.

OTHER SOURCES

★14091★ Aberdeen Area Chamber of Commerce
516 S. Main St.
PO Box 1179
Aberdeen, SD 57401
Ph: (605)225-2860   Fax: (605)225-2437
Fr: 800-874-9038
E-mail: info@aberdeen-chamber.com
URL: http://www.aberdeen-chamber.com

Promotes business and community development in the Aberdeen and Brown County, SD area.

★14092★ Abilene Chamber of Commerce
174 Cypress St., Ste. 200
Abilene, TX 79601
Ph: (325)677-7241   Fax: (325)677-0622
E-mail: info@abilenechamber.com
URL: http://www.abilenechamber.com

Promotes business and community development in Abilene, TX.

★14093★ Affiliated Chambers of Greater Springfield
1441 Main St., Ste. 136
Springfield, MA 01103-1449
Ph: (413)787-1555   Fax: (413)731-8530
E-mail: denver@myonlinechamber.com
URL: http://www.myonlinechamber.com

Promotes business and community development in the Springfield, MA area.

★14094★ Aiken Chamber of Commerce
121 Richland Ave. E
PO Box 892
Aiken, SC 29802
Ph: (803)641-1111   Fax: (803)641-4174
E-mail: chamber@aikenchamber.net
URL: http://www.aikenchamber.net

Promotes business and community development in Aiken, SC.

★14095★ Alaska State Chamber of Commerce
217 2nd St., Ste. 201
Juneau, AK 99801
Ph: (907)586-2323   Fax: (907)463-5515
E-mail: info@alaskachamber.com
URL: http://www.alaskachamber.com

Promotes business and community development in Alaska.

★14096★ Alexandria Chamber of Commerce (ACC)

801 N Fairfax St., Ste. 402
Alexandria, VA 22314
Ph: (703)549-1000   Fax: (703)739-3805
E-mail: info@alexchamber.com
URL: http://www.alexchamber.com

Promotes business and community development in Alexandria, VA.

★14097★ Amarillo Chamber of Commerce

1000 S Polk St.
Amarillo, TX 79105-9480
Ph: (806)373-7800   Fax: (806)373-3909
E-mail: chamber@amarillo-chamber.org
URL: http://www.amarillo-chamber.org

Promotes business and community development in Amarillo, TX. Sponsors local festival.

★14098★ Anaheim Chamber of Commerce

201 E Center St.
Anaheim, CA 92805
Ph: (714)758-0222   Fax: (714)758-0468
E-mail: info@anaheimchamber.org
URL: http://www.anaheimchamber.org

Works to promote and support healthy diverse and broad-based economic growth in Anaheim.

★14099★ Anchorage Chamber of Commerce (ACC)

1016 W 6th Ave., Ste. 303
Anchorage, AK 99501-2309
Ph: (907)272-2401   Fax: (907)272-4117
E-mail: info@anchoragechamber.org
URL: http://www.anchoragechamber.org

Promotes business and community development in Anchorage, AK.

★14100★ Ann Arbor Area Chamber of Commerce (AAACC)

425 S Main St., Ste. 103
Ann Arbor, MI 48104-2303
Ph: (734)665-4433   Fax: (734)665-4191
E-mail: info@annarborchamber.org

Promotes business and community development in the Ann Arbor, MI area.

★14101★ Arizona Chamber of Commerce

1850 N. Central Ave., Ste. 1010
Phoenix, AZ 85004
Ph: (602)248-9172   Fax: (602)265-1262
Fr: 800-498-6973
E-mail: info@azchamber.com
URL: http://www.azchamber.com

Promotes business and community development in Arizona.

★14102★ Arkansas State Chamber of Commerce

1200 W. Capitol Ave.
PO Box 3645
Little Rock, AR 72203-3645
Ph: (501)372-2222   Fax: (501)372-2722
E-mail: pharvel@arkansasstatechamber.com
URL: http://ascc.weknowarkansas.org/

Promotes business and community development in Arkansas.

★14103★ Arlington Chamber of Commerce (ACC)

505 E Border St.
Arlington, TX 76010
Ph: (817)275-2613   Fax: (817)261-7589
E-mail: wjurey@arlingtontx.com
URL: http://www.arlingtontx.com

Promotes business and community development in the Arlington, TX area. Seeks to create job opportunities and diversify the city's economic base. Represents business leadership on policy issues affecting city's economic growth.

★14104★ Arvada Chamber of Commerce

7305 Grandview Ave.
Arvada, CO 80002-9960
Ph: (303)424-0313   Fax: (303)424-5370
E-mail: director@arvadachamber.org
URL: http://www.arvadachamber.org

Promotes business and community development in the Arvada and Westminster, CO area. Facilitates communication and cooperation among area business people.

★14105★ Association of Commerce And Industry of New Mexico

2201 Buena Vista Dr., SE, Ste. 410
Albuquerque, NM 87106
Ph: (505)842-0644   Fax: (505)842-0734
URL: http://www.acinm.org/

Promotes business and community development in the state of New Mexico.

★14106★ Association of Washington Business

1414 Cherry St., SE
PO Box 658
Olympia, WA 98501
Ph: (360)943-1600   Fax: (360)943-5811
E-mail: members@awb.org
URL: http://www.awb.org

Promotes business and community development in the state of Washington.

★14107★ Athens Area Chamber of Commerce (AACC)

246 W Hancock Ave.
Athens, GA 30601
Ph: (706)549-6800   Fax: (706)549-5636
E-mail: info@athenschamber.net
URL: http://www.athenschamber.net

Promotes business and community development in the Athens, GA area.

★14108★ Augusta Metro Chamber of Commerce

PO Box 1837
Augusta, GA 30903
Ph: (706)821-1300   Fax: (706)821-1330
Fr: 888-639-8188
E-mail: smacgregor@augustagausa.com
URL: http://www.augustagausa.com

Promotes business and community development in the Augusta, GA area.

★14109★ Aurora Chamber of Commerce

562 Sable Blvd., Ste. 200
Aurora, CO 80011-0809
Ph: (303)344-1500   Fax: (303)344-1564
E-mail: info@aurorachamber.org
URL: http://www.aurorachamber.org

Strives to maintain a strong business climate and a thriving community. Provide business networking and services in Aurora, CO area.

★14110★ Baltimore - Washington Corridor Chamber of Commerce (BWCC)

312 Marshall Ave., Ste. 104
Laurel, MD 20707-4824
Ph: (410)792-9714   Fax: (301)725-0776
E-mail: bwcc@baltwashchamber.org
URL: http://www.baltwashchamber.org

Promotes business and community development along the Baltimore, MD/Washington, D.C. corridor. Sponsors periodic seminars, business mixers and signature events. Manages a regional bus system, Connect-A-Ride, Howard Transit and others. Provides scholarships and hosts an annual symposium for middle and high school math teachers.

★14111★ Beaumont Chamber of Commerce

726 Beaumont Ave.
PO Box 637
Beaumont, CA 92223
Ph: (951)845-9541   Fax: (951)769-9080
E-mail: info@beaumontcachamber.com
URL: http://www.beaumontcachamber.com

Works to help small business grow and succeed. Creates and maintains a climate for business growth and strong quality of life, serves as business advocate in city and provides credibility for business through association.

★14112★ Bellevue Chamber of Commerce

302 Bellevue Sq.
Bellevue, WA 98004
Ph: (425)454-2464   Fax: (425)462-4660
E-mail: staffteam@bellevuechamber.org
URL: http://www.bellevuechamber.org

Promotes business and community development in Bellevue, WA.

★14113★ Birmingham Regional Chamber of Commerce (BACC)

505 20th St. N
Birmingham, AL 35203
Ph: (205)324-2100   Fax: (205)324-2314
E-mail: jcoleman@birminghamchamber.com
URL: http://www.birminghamchamber.com

Promotes business and community development in the Birmingham, AL region. Provides liaison with local agencies.

★14114★ Bismarck - Mandan Chamber of Commerce

1640 Burnt Boat Dr.
PO Box 1675
Bismarck, ND 58502-1675
Ph: (701)223-5660   Fax: (701)255-6125
E-mail: info@bismarckmandan.com
URL: http://www.bismarckmandan.com

Promotes business and community development in the Bismarck, ND Area.

★14115★ Boise Metro Chamber of Commerce

250 S 5th St., Ste. 800
PO Box 2368
Boise, ID 83701
Ph: (208)472-5200   Fax: (208)472-5201
E-mail: info@boisechamber.org
URL: http://www.boisechamber.org

Promotes business and community development in the Boise, ID area.

★14116★ Bridgeport Regional Business Council (BRBC)

10 Middle St., 14th Fl.
Bridgeport, CT 06604
Ph: (203)335-3800   Fax: (203)366-0105
E-mail: info@brbc.org
URL: http://www.brbc.org

Promotes business and community development in Bridgeport region.

★14117★ Brownsville Chamber of Commerce

1600 University Blvd.
Brownsville, TX 78520
Ph: (956)542-4341   Fax: (956)504-3348
E-mail: info@brownsvillechamber.com
URL: http://www.brownsvillechamber.com

Promotes business and community development in Brownsville, TX.

★14118★ Buffalo Niagara Partnership

665 Main St., Ste. 200
Buffalo, NY 14203
Ph: (716)852-7100   Fax: (716)852-2761
Fr: 800-241-0474
E-mail: info@thepartnership.org
URL: http://www.thepartnership.org

Promotes business and community development in West Seneca, NY. Holds seminars.

★14119★ Burbank Chamber of Commerce

200 W. Magnolia Blvd.
Burbank, CA 91502-1724
Ph: (818)846-3111   Fax: (818)846-0109
E-mail: info@burbankchamber.org
URL: http://www.burbankchamber.org

Promotes business and community development in Burbank, CA.

★14120★ Business Council of Alabama

PO Box 76
2 N. Jackson St.
Montgomery, AL 36101
Ph: (334)834-6000   Fax: (334)262-7371
Fr: 800-665-9647
URL: http://www.bcatoday.org

Promotes business and community development in the state of Alabama.

★14121★ Business Council of New York State, Inc.

The Schuler Bldg.
152 Washington Ave.
Albany, NY 12210-2289
Ph: (518)465-7511   Fax: (518)465-4389
Fr: 800-358-1202
URL: http://www.bcnys.org/

Promotes business and community development in the state of New York.

★14122★ California Chamber of Commerce

1215 K St., Ste. 1400
PO Box 1736
Sacramento, CA 95814
Ph: (916)444-6670   Fax: (916)325-1272
E-mail: information@calchamber.com
URL: http://www.calchamber.com

Acts as legislative advocate for all California business interests. Offers educational seminars.

★14123★ Cambridge Chamber of Commerce

859 Massachusetts Ave.
Cambridge, MA 02139
Ph: (617)876-4100   Fax: (617)354-9874
E-mail: ccinfo@cambridgechamber.org
URL: http://www.cambridgechamber.org

Promotes business and community development in Cambridge, MA.

★14124★ Cedar Rapids Area Chamber of Commerce (CRACC)

424 1st Ave. NE
Cedar Rapids, IA 52401-1196
Ph: (319)398-5317   Fax: (319)398-5228
E-mail: chamber@cedarrapids.org
URL: http://www.cedarrapids.org

Promotes business and community development in the Cedar Rapids, IA area.

★14125★ Chamber of Commerce of Cape Coral

2051 Cape Coral Pkwy. East
PO Box 100747
Cape Coral, FL 33904
Ph: (239)549-6900   Fax: (239)549-9609
Fr: 800-226-9609
E-mail: info@capecoralchamber.com
URL: http://www.capecoralchamber.com

Promotes business and community development in Cape Coral, FL.

★14126★ Chamber of Commerce of Huntsville/Madison County (CCHMC)

PO Box 408
Huntsville, AL 35804-0408
Ph: (256)535-2000   Fax: (256)535-2015
E-mail: hcc@hsvchamber.org
URL: http://www.huntsvillealabamausa.com

Promotes business and community development in Madison County, AL.

★14127★ ChamberWest

1241 W. Village Main Dr. , Ste. B
West Valley City, UT 84119
Ph: (801)977-8755   Fax: (801)977-8329
E-mail: chamber@chamberwest.com
URL: http://www.chamberwest.com

The Chamber of Commerce for West Valley City, Taylorsville and Kearns, UT.

★14128★ Chandler Chamber of Commerce

25 S. Arizona Place, No. 201
Chandler, AZ 85225
Ph: (480)963-4571   Fax: (480)963-0188
Fr: 800-963-4571
E-mail: becky@chandlerchamber.com
URL: http://www.chandlerchamber.com

Promotes business and community development in Chandler, AZ.

★14129★ Chattanooga Area Chamber of Commerce

811 Broad St.
Chattanooga, TN 37402
Ph: (423)756-2121   Fax: (423)267-7242
E-mail: frontdesk@chattanooga-chamber.com
URL: http://www.chattanoogachamber.com

Promotes regional business growth that creates prosperity and enhances quality of life.

★14130★ Chicagoland Chamber of Commerce (CCoC)

Aon Center
200 E Randolph St., Ste. 2200
Chicago, IL 60601
Ph: (312)494-6700   Fax: (312)861-0660
E-mail: staff@chicagolandchamber.org
URL: http://www.chicagolandchamber.org

Promotes business and community development in Chicago, IL. Conducts drug-free workplace program.

★14131★ Chula Vista Chamber of Commerce

233 4th Ave.
Chula Vista, CA 91910
Ph: (619)420-6603
E-mail: lisa@chulavistachamber.org
URL: http://www.chulavistachamber.org

Promotes business and community development in Chula Vista, CA.

★14132★ Cincinnati USA Regional Chamber (GCCC)

441 Vine St., Ste. 300
Cincinnati, OH 45202-2812
Ph: (513)579-3100   Fax: (513)579-3101
E-mail: info@cincinnatichamber.com
URL: http://www.cincinnatichamber.com

Promotes business and community development in the Cincinnati, OH area.

★14133★ Clarksville Area Chamber of Commerce

25 Jefferson St., Ste. 300
PO Box 883
Clarksville, TN 37041
Ph: (931)647-2331   Fr: 800-530-2487
E-mail: cmcedc@clarksville.tn.us
URL: http://www.clarksville.tn.us

Promotes business and community development in the Clarksville, TN area.

★14134★ Clearwater Regional Chamber of Commerce

1130 Cleveland St.
PO Box 2457
Clearwater, FL 33757-2457
Ph: (727)461-0011   Fax: (727)449-2889
E-mail: info@clearwaterflorida.org
URL: http://www.clearwaterflorida.org

Promotes business and community development in the Clearwater, FL area. Provides networking opportunities and small business assistance.

★14135★ Colorado Association of Commerce and Industry

1600 Broadway, Ste. 1000
Denver, CO 80202-4935
Ph: (303)831-7411   Fax: (303)860-1439
E-mail: info@COchamber.com
URL: http://www.cochamber.com/

Promotes business and community development in the state of Colorado.

★14136★ Connecticut Business and Industry Association

350 Church St.
Hartford, CT 06103-1126
Ph: (860)244-1900   Fax: (860)278-8562
E-mail: bellj@cbia.com
URL: http://www.cbia.com

Promotes business and community development in the state of Connecticut.

★14137★ Corona Chamber of Commerce

904 E. 6th St.
Corona, CA 92879
Ph: (951)737-3350   Fax: (951)737-3531
E-mail: info@coronachamber.org
URL: http://www.coronachamber.org

Promotes business and community development in Corona, CA.

★14138★ Costa Mesa Chamber of Commerce

1700 Adams Ave., Ste. 101
Costa Mesa, CA 92626
Ph: (714)885-9090   Fax: (714)885-9094
E-mail: info@costamesachamber.com
URL: http://www.costamesachamber.com

Promotes business and community development in Costa Mesa, CA.

★14139★ Daly City - Colma Chamber of Commerce

355 Gellert Blvd., No. 138
Daly City, CA 94015
Ph: (650)755-3900   Fax: (650)755-5160
E-mail: agonzalez@dalycity-colmachamber.org
URL: http://www.dalycity-colmachamber.org

Promotes business and community development in the Daly City/Colma, CA area.

★14140★ Dayton Area Chamber of Commerce

PO Box 2408
Dayton, NV 89403
Ph: (775)246-7909   Fax: (775)246-5838
E-mail: info@daytonnvchamber.org
URL: http://www.daytonnvchamber.org

Promotes community and business growth in Dayton, Nevada.

★14141★ Delaware State Chamber of Commerce

1201 N. Orange St., Ste. 200
PO Box 671
Wilmington, DE 19899-0671
Ph: (302)655-7221   Fax: (302)654-0691
Fr: 800-292-9507
E-mail: dscc@dscc.com
URL: http://www.dscc.com

Promotes business and community development in Delaware.

★14142★ Denver Metro Chamber of Commerce

1445 Market St.
Denver, CO 80202
Ph: (303)534-8500   Fax: (303)534-2145
E-mail: info@denverchamber.org
URL: http://www.denverchamber.org

Works to promote the development of civic leadership in the business community and fosters opportunities for increased cooperation among the private, public, and nonprofit sectors in Denver, CO area.

★14143★ District of Columbia Chamber of Commerce (DCCC)

1213 K St., NW
Washington, DC 20005
Ph: (202)347-7201   Fax: (202)638-6762
E-mail: dedwards@dcchamber.org
URL: http://www.dcchamber.org

Promotes business and community development in Washington, DC.

★14144★ El Monte-South El Monte Chamber of Commerce

10505 Valley Blvd., Ste. 312
PO Box 5866
El Monte, CA 91734-1866
Ph: (626)443-0180
E-mail: chamber@ksb8.com
URL: http://www.emsem.com

Promotes business and community development in the El Monte, CA area.

★14145★ Erie Area Chamber of Commerce

208 E. Bayfront Pkwy., Ste. 100
Erie, PA 16507
Ph: (814)454-7191   Fax: (814)459-0241
E-mail: erie-chamber@erie.net
URL: http://www.eriechamber.com

Promotes business and community development in Erie County, PA.

★14146★ Escondido Chamber of Commerce

720 N. Broadway
Escondido, CA 92025
Ph: (760)745-2125
E-mail: info@escondidochamber.org
URL: http://www.escondidochamber.org

Promotes business and community development in Escondido, CA.

★14147★ Eugene Area Chamber of Commerce

1401 Willamette St.
PO Box 1107
Eugene, OR 97401
Ph: (541)484-1314   Fax: (541)484-4942
E-mail: admin@eugenechamber.com
URL: http://www.eugenechamber.com

Promotes a healthy local economy within the Eugene community by influencing business success, public policy and community development.

★14148★ Fayetteville Chamber of Commerce

201 Hay St.
PO Box 9
Fayetteville, NC 28302
Ph: (910)483-8133   Fax: (910)483-0263

E-mail: receptionist@ccbusinesscouncil.org
URL: http://www.fayettevillencchamber.org

Promotes business and community development in the Fayetteville, NC area.

★14149★ **Florida Chamber of Commerce**
136 S. Bronough St.
PO Box 11309
Tallahassee, FL 32302-3309
Ph: (850)521-1200   Fax: (850)521-1219
E-mail: info@flchamber.com
URL: http://www.flchamber.com

Promotes business and community development in the state of Florida.

★14150★ **Fontana Chamber of Commerce**
8491 Sierra Ave.
Fontana, CA 92335-3860
Ph: (909)822-4433   Fax: (909)822-6238
E-mail: info@fontanachamber.com
URL: http://www.fontanaacc.org

Promotes business and community development in the Fontana, CA area.

★14151★ **Fort Collins Area Chamber of Commerce**
225 S Meldrum St.
Fort Collins, CO 80521
Ph: (970)482-3746   Fax: (970)482-3774
E-mail: general@fcchamber.org
URL: http://www.fortcollinschamber.com

Promotes business and community development in the Ft. Collins, CO area.

★14152★ **Fort Worth Chamber of Commerce**
777 Taylor St., Ste. 900
Fort Worth, TX 76102-4997
Ph: (817)336-2491   Fax: (817)877-4034
E-mail: dbecker@fortworthchamber.com
URL: http://www.fortworthchamber.com

Promotes business and community development in Ft. Worth, TX.

★14153★ **Fremont Chamber of Commerce**
39488 Stevenson Pl., Ste. 100
Fremont, CA 94539
Ph: (510)795-2244
E-mail: fmtcc@fremontbusiness.com
URL: http://www.fremontbusiness.com

Promotes business and community development in Fremont, CA. Conducts business education and assistance programs.

★14154★ **Fullerton Chamber of Commerce**
444 N. Harbor Blvd., Ste. 200
Fullerton, CA 92832
Ph: (714)871-3100   Fax: (714)871-2871
E-mail: info@fullertonchamber.com
URL: http://www.fullertonchamber.com

Promotes business and community development in Fullerton, CA.

★14155★ **Garden Grove Chamber of Commerce**
12866 Main St., Ste. 102
Garden Grove, CA 92840-5298
Ph: (714)638-7950   Fax: (714)636-6672
Fr: 800-959-5560
E-mail: connie.margolin@gardengrovechamber.org
URL: http://gardengrovechamber.org

Promotes business and community development in Garden Grove, CA.

★14156★ **Garland Chamber of Commerce**
914 S. Garland Ave.
Garland, TX 75040
Ph: (972)272-7551   Fax: (972)276-9261
E-mail: information@garlandchamber.com
URL: http://www.garlandchamber.com

Promotes business and community development in Garland, TX.

★14157★ **Gary Chamber of Commerce**
839 Broadway, Ste. S103
Gary, IN 46402
Ph: (219)885-7407   Fax: (219)885-7408
E-mail: info@garychamber.com
URL: http://www.garychamber.com

Promotes business and community development in the Gary, IN area.

★14158★ **Genesee Regional Chamber of Commerce**
519 S Saginaw St., Ste. 200
Flint, MI 48502-1802
Ph: (810)600-1404   Fax: (810)600-1461
E-mail: info@thegrcc.org
URL: http://flintchamber.org

Business and professional organizations that promote business and community development in the Flint, MI area.

★14159★ **Georgia Chamber of Commerce**
233 Peachtree St. NE, Ste. 2000
Atlanta, GA 30303-1564
Ph: (404)233-2264   Fax: (404)223-2290
Fr: 800-241-2286
URL: http://www.gachamber.com

Promotes business and community development in the state of Georgia.

★14160★ **Gilbert Chamber of Commerce**
119 N. Gilbert Rd., Ste. 101
PO Box 527
Gilbert, AZ 85299-0527
Ph: (480)892-0056   Fax: (480)892-1980
E-mail: info@gilbertchamber.com
URL: http://www.gilbertaz.com

Promotes business and community development in Gilbert, AZ.

★14161★ **Glendale (AZ) Chamber of Commerce**
7105 N. 59th Ave.
PO Box 249
Glendale, AZ 85311
Ph: (623)937-4754   Fax: (623)937-3333
Fr: 800-437-8669
E-mail: info@glendaleazchamber.org
URL: http://www.glendaleazchamber.org

Promotes business and community development in Glendale, AZ.

★14162★ **Glendale (CA) Chamber of Commerce**
200 S. Louise St.
Glendale, CA 91205
Ph: (818)240-7870   Fax: (818)240-2872
E-mail: info@glendalechamber.com
URL: http://www.glendalechamber.com

Promotes business and community development in Glendale, CA.

★14163★ **Grand Prairie Chamber of Commerce**
900 Conover Dr.
Grand Prairie, TX 75051
Ph: (972)264-1558   Fax: (972)264-3419
E-mail: info@grandprairiechamber.org
URL: http://www.grandprairiechamber.org

Promotes business and community development in Grand Prairie, TX.

★14164★ **Grand Rapids Area Chamber of Commerce (GRACC)**
111 Pearl St. NW
Grand Rapids, MI 49503-2831
Ph: (616)771-0300   Fax: (616)771-0318
E-mail: info@grandrapids.org
URL: http://grandrapids.org

Creates opportunities for business success in the Grand Rapids, MI area.

★14165★ **Greater Akron Chamber of Commerce**
1 Cascade Plz., 17th Fl.
Akron, OH 44308-1192
Ph: (330)376-5550   Fax: (330)379-3164
Fr: 800-621-8001
E-mail: info@greaterakronchamber.org
URL: http://www.greaterakronchamber.org

Serves business organizations to improve the economic and social status of Greater Akron.

★14166★ **Greater Aurora Chamber of Commerce (GACC)**
43 W Galena Blvd.
Aurora, IL 60506
Ph: (630)897-9214   Fax: (630)897-7002
E-mail: jhenning@aurora-il.org
URL: http://www.aurorachamber.com

Promotes business and community development in the Aurora, IL area.

★14167★ Greater Austin Chamber of Commerce

PO Box 212
Austin, NV 89310-0212
Ph: (775)964-2200   Fax: (775)964-2447
E-mail: austinnvchamber@yahoo.com
URL: http://www.austinnevada.com

Promotes business and community development in the Austin, NV area. Promote tourism through Nevada area.

★14168★ Greater Bakersfield Chamber of Commerce

1725 Eye St.
PO Box 1947
Bakersfield, CA 93301
Ph: (661)327-4421   Fax: (661)327-8751
E-mail: info@bakersfieldchamber.org
URL: http://www.bakersfieldchamber.org

Bankers and beauticians, communications consultants and caterers. Provides leadership to promote a healthy environment for business through networking, advocacy, learning and community service.

★14169★ Greater Bethesda-Chevy Chase Chamber of Commerce

7910 Woodmont Ave., Ste. 1204
Bethesda, MD 20814
Ph: (301)652-4900   Fax: (301)657-1973
E-mail: info@bccchamber.org
URL: http://www.bccchamber.org

Promotes business and community development in the Bethesda and Chevy Chase communities within Maryland.

★14170★ Greater Bloomington Chamber of Commerce

400 W. 7th St., Ste. 102
PO Box 1302
Bloomington, IN 47402
Ph: (812)336-6381   Fax: (812)336-0651
E-mail: info@chamberbloomington.org
URL: http://www.chamberbloomington.org/

Promotes business and community development in the Bloomington, IN area.

★14171★ Greater Boston Chamber of Commerce

75 State St., 2nd Fl.
Boston, MA 02109
Ph: (617)227-4500   Fax: (617)227-7505
E-mail: info@bostonchamber.com
URL: http://www.bostonchamber.com

Promotes business and community development in Boston, MA area.

★14172★ Greater Colorado Springs Chamber of Commerce (GCSCC)

2 N Cascade Ave., Ste. 110
Colorado Springs, CO 80903
Ph: (719)635-1551   Fax: (719)635-1571

E-mail: info@cscc.org
URL: http://www.coloradospringschamber.org

Promotes business and community development in Colorado Springs, CO.

★14173★ Greater Columbia Chamber of Commerce (GCCVB)

930 Richland St.
Columbia, SC 29201
Ph: (803)733-1110   Fax: (803)733-1149
E-mail: info@columbiachamber.com
URL: http://www.columbiachamber.com

Promotes convention business and tourism in Columbia, SC.

★14174★ Greater Columbus Area Chamber of Commerce

37 N High St.
Columbus, OH 43215
Ph: (614)221-1321   Fax: (614)221-1408
E-mail: membership@columbus.org
URL: http://www.columbus.org

Promotes business and community development in Columbus, OH area.

★14175★ Greater Columbus Chamber of Commerce

1200 6th Ave.
Columbus, GA 31902
Ph: (706)327-1566   Fax: (706)327-7512
Fr: 800-360-8552
E-mail: mgaymon@columbusgachamber.com
URL: http://www.columbusgachamber.com

Promotes business and community development in Columbus, GA.

★14176★ Greater Concord Chamber of Commerce

2280 Diamond Blvd., Ste. 200
Concord, CA 94520-5750
Ph: (925)685-1181   Fax: (925)685-5623
E-mail: info@concordchamber.com
URL: http://www.concordchamber.com

Promotes business and community development in Concord, CA.

★14177★ Greater Dallas Chamber of Commerce

700 N Pearl St., Ste. 1200
Dallas, TX 75201
Ph: (214)746-6600   Fax: (214)746-6799
E-mail: information@dallaschamber.org
URL: http://www.dallaschamber.org

Works to unite and engage the Dallas region's business community. Provides dynamic business and civic leadership to develop and sustain a prosperous economy and a vibrant community.

★14178★ Greater Des Moines Partnership

700 Locust St., Ste. 100
Des Moines, IA 50309
Ph: (515)286-4950   Fax: (515)286-4974
Fr: 800-451-2625
E-mail: info@desmoinesmetro.com
URL: http://www.desmoinesmetro.com

Promotes business and community development in the greater Des Moines, IA area.

★14179★ Greater Durham Chamber of Commerce (DCC)

PO Box 3829
Durham, NC 27702-3829
Ph: (919)682-2133   Fax: (919)688-8351
E-mail: info@durhamchamber.org
URL: http://www.durhamchamber.org

Promotes business and community development in the Durham, NC area.

★14180★ Greater El Paso Chamber of Commerce (GEPCC)

10 Civic Center Plz.
El Paso, TX 79901
Ph: (915)534-0500   Fax: (915)534-0510
E-mail: gepccreceptionist@elpaso.org
URL: http://www.elpaso.org

Promotes business and community development in El Paso, TX.

★14181★ Greater Elizabeth Chamber of Commerce

456 N. Broad St., 2nd Fl.
Elizabeth, NJ 07208
Ph: (908)355-7600   Fax: (908)436-2054
E-mail: gecc@juno.com
URL: http://www.elizabethchamber.com

Promotes business and community development in Elizabeth, NJ.

★14182★ Greater Fairbanks Chamber of Commerce

100 Cushman St., Ste. 102
Fairbanks, AK 99701
Ph: (907)452-1105   Fax: (907)456-6968
E-mail: info@fairbankschamber.org
URL: http://www.fairbankschamber.org

Promotes business and community development in the Greater Fairbanks, AK area.

★14183★ Greater Fort Lauderdale Chamber of Commerce

512 NE 3rd Ave.
Fort Lauderdale, FL 33301
Ph: (954)462-6000
E-mail: info@ftlchamber.com
URL: http://www.ftlchamber.com

Promotes business, tourism, and community development in the Greater Ft. Lauderdale, FL area.

★14184★ Greater Fort Wayne Chamber of Commerce (GFWCC)

826 Ewing St.
Fort Wayne, IN 46802
Ph: (260)424-1435   Fax: (260)426-7232
E-mail: ppl@fwchamber.org
URL: http://www.fwchamber.org

Promotes business and community development in the Ft. Wayne, IN area.

★14185★ Greater Fresno Area Chamber of Commerce

2331 Fresno St.
Fresno, CA 93721
Ph: (559)495-4800   Fax: (559)495-4811
E-mail: info@fresnochamber.com
URL: http://www.fresnochamber.com

Promotes business and community development in the Fresno County, CA area. Serves as a voice of business on local and state level.

★14186★ Greater Hollywood Chamber of Commerce

330 N. Federal Hwy.
Hollywood, FL 33020
Ph: (954)923-4000   Fax: (954)923-8737
Fr: 800-231-5562
E-mail: tourism@hollywoodchamber.org
URL: http://www.hollywoodchamber.org

Promotes business and community development in the Hollywood, FL area.

★14187★ Greater Hot Springs Chamber of Commerce

659 Ouachita
PO Box 6090
Hot Springs, AR 71901
Ph: (501)321-1700   Fax: (501)321-3551
E-mail: info@hotspringschamber.com
URL: http://www.hotspringschamber.com

Promotes business and community development in the Hot Springs, AR area.

★14188★ Greater Houston Partnership

1200 Smith, Ste. 700
Houston, TX 77002-4400
Ph: (713)844-3600   Fax: (713)844-0200
E-mail: ghp@houston.org
URL: http://www.houston.org

Works to promote the business community in Houston. Seeks to establish economic prosperity in the region.

★14189★ Greater Irving - Las Colinas Chamber of Commerce

5221 N. O'Connor Blvd., Ste. 100
Irving, TX 75062
Ph: (214)217-8484   Fax: (214)384-2513
E-mail: chamber@irvingchamber.com
URL: http://www.irvingchamber.com

Promotes business and community development in Irving, TX.

★14190★ Greater Kansas City Chamber of Commerce

2600 Commerce Tower
911 Main St., Ste. 2600
Kansas City, MO 64105
Ph: (816)221-2424   Fax: (816)221-7440
E-mail: waltz@kcchamber.com
URL: http://www.kcchamber.com

Promotes business and community development in the Greater Kansas City, MO area.

★14191★ Greater Lafayette (IN) Chamber of Commerce

337 Columbia St.
PO Box 348
Lafayette, IN 47902-0348
Ph: (765)742-4041   Fax: (765)742-6276
E-mail: information@lafayettechamber.com
URL: http://www.lafayettechamber.com

Promotes business and community development in the Lafayette, IN area.

★14192★ Greater Lafayette (LA) Chamber of Commerce

804 E. Saint Mary Blvd.
PO Box 51307
Lafayette, LA 70503
Ph: (337)233-2705   Fax: (337)234-8671
E-mail: rob@lafchamber.org
URL: http://www.lafchamber.org

Promotes business and community development in the Lafayette, LA area.

★14193★ Greater Las Cruces Chamber of Commerce

760 W. Picacho Ave.
PO Drawer 519
Las Cruces, NM 88005
Ph: (575)524-1968   Fax: (575)527-5546
E-mail: jberryats@lascruces.org
URL: http://www.lascruces.org

Promotes business and community development in Las Cruces, NM.

★14194★ Greater Lehigh County Chamber of Commerce (LCCC)

840 Hamilton St., Ste. 205
Allentown, PA 18101
Ph: (610)841-5860   Fax: (610)437-4907
E-mail: info@lehighvalleychamber.org
URL: http://www.lehighvalleychamber.org

Seeks to improve the economy and quality of life in the Lehigh Valley, PA area.

★14195★ Greater Louisville Inc. - The Metro Chamber of Commerce (GLI)

614 W Main St., Ste. 6000
Louisville, KY 40202
Ph: (502)625-0000   Fax: (502)625-0010
E-mail: sfarnsworth@greaterlouisville.com
URL: http://www.greaterlouisville.com

Promotes business and community development in Louisville, KY.

★14196★ Greater Lowell Chamber of Commerce

131 Merrimack St.
Lowell, MA 01852
Ph: (978)459-8154   Fax: (978)452-4145
E-mail: info@greaterlowellchamber.org
URL: http://www.glcc.biz

Promotes business and community development in the Lowell, MA area.

★14197★ Greater Madison Chamber of Commerce (GMCC)

PO Box 71
615 E Washington Ave., 2nd Fl.
Madison, WI 53701-0071
Ph: (608)256-8348   Fax: (608)256-0333
E-mail: info@greatermadisonchamber.com
URL: http://
www.greatermadisonchamber.com

Promotes business and community development in Dane County, WI.

★14198★ Greater Manchester Chamber of Commerce

889 Elm St.
Manchester, NH 03101
Ph: (603)666-6600   Fax: (603)626-0910
E-mail: info@manchester-chamber.org
URL: http://www.manchester-chamber.org

Promotes business and community development in Manchester and northern Hillsborough County, NH.

★14199★ Greater Miami Chamber of Commerce (GMCC)

1601 Biscayne Blvd.
Ballroom Level
Miami, FL 33132-1260
Ph: (305)350-7700   Fax: (305)374-6902
E-mail: info@miamichamber.com
URL: http://www.greatermiami.com

Promotes business and community development in the Miami, FL area.

★14200★ Greater New Haven Chamber of Commerce (GNHCC)

900 Chapel St., 10th Fl.
New Haven, CT 06510
Ph: (203)787-6735   Fax: (203)782-4329
E-mail: info@gnhcc.com
URL: http://www.newhavenchamber.com

Provides leadership in marshalling the physical, economic, and human resources of the South Central Connecticut region.

★14201★ Greater North Dakota Chamber of Commerce

2000 Schafer St.
PO Box 2639
Bismarck, ND 58502-2639
Ph: (701)222-0929   Fax: (701)222-1611
Fr: 800-382-1405
E-mail: ndchamber@ndchamber.com
URL: http://www.ndchamber.com/

Promotes business and community development in the state of North Dakota.

★14202★ Greater Oklahoma City Chamber of Commerce

123 Park Ave.
Oklahoma City, OK 73102
Ph: (405)297-8900   Fax: (405)297-8916
E-mail: info@okcchamber.com
URL: http://www.okcchamber.com

Promotes business and community development in Oklahoma City, OK.

★14203★ Greater Omaha Chamber of Commerce

1301 Harney St.
Omaha, NE 68102
Ph: (402)346-5000   Fax: (402)346-7050
E-mail: info@omahachamber.org
URL: http://www.omahachamber.org

Promotes business and community development in the Omaha, NE area.

★14204★ Greater Paterson Chamber of Commerce

100 Hamilton Plaza, Ste. 1201
Paterson, NJ 07505
Ph: (973)881-7300   Fax: (973)881-8233
E-mail: gpcc@greaterpatersoncc.org
URL: http://www.greaterpatersoncc.org

Promotes business and community development in the Paterson, NJ area.

★14205★ Greater Philadelphia Chamber of Commerce

200 S Broad St., Ste. 700
Philadelphia, PA 19102
Ph: (215)545-1234   Fax: (215)790-3600
E-mail: memberrelations@philachamber.com
URL: http://www.gpcc.com

Seeks to facilitate and promote quality and excellence in business, governmental, and educational organizations in the Delaware Valley area of Delaware, New Jersey, and Pennsylvania. Offers custom designed and project team training and consultant referral. Provides print and video resources. Sponsors 20 seminars per year and PACE Network.

★14206★ Greater Phoenix Chamber of Commerce

201 N Central Ave., 27th Fl.
Phoenix, AZ 85004
Ph: (602)254-5521   Fax: (602)495-8913
E-mail: info@phoenixchamber.com
URL: http://www.phoenixchamber.com

Supports the growth and development of business and the quality of life in the Phoenix, AZ area. Champions the voice of business in government and keeps businesses informed, connected, and prosperous.

★14207★ Greater Pittsburgh Chamber of Commerce

Regional Enterprise Tower
425 6th Ave., Ste. 1100
Pittsburgh, PA 15219-1811
Ph: (412)392-1000   Fax: (412)281-1896
Fr: 877-392-1300
E-mail: info@alleghenyconference.org
URL: http://www.pittsburghchamber.com

Promotes business and community development in Greater Pittsburgh, PA.

★14208★ Greater Portland Chamber of Commerce

60 Pearl St.
Portland, ME 04101
Ph: (207)772-2811   Fax: (207)772-1179
E-mail: chamber@portlandregion.com
URL: http://www.portlandregion.com

Promotes business and community development in the Portland, ME area.

★14209★ Greater Portsmouth Chamber of Commerce

500 Market St.
PO Box 239
Portsmouth, NH 03802-0239
Ph: (603)436-3988   Fax: (603)436-5118
E-mail: info@portsmouthchamber.org
URL: http://www.portsmouthchamber.org

Promotes business and community development in the Portsmouth, New Hampshire area and southwestern Maine.

★14210★ Greater Providence Chamber of Commerce

30 Exchange Terr.
Providence, RI 02903
Ph: (401)521-5000   Fax: (401)751-2434
E-mail: chamber@provchamber.com
URL: http://www.providencechamber.com

Strives to develop a positive and productive business climate for the community through economic development, political action and civic endeavor. Helps member to grow and prosper in Rhode Island. Promotes program of a civic, social and cultural nature. Provides leadership, ideas, energy and finances to help address major community challenges.

★14211★ Greater Pueblo Chamber of Commerce

302 N. Santa Fe Ave.
PO Box 697
Pueblo, CO 81003
Ph: (719)542-1704
E-mail: info@pueblochamber.org
URL: http://www.pueblochamber.org

Promotes business and community development in Pueblo County, CO.

★14212★ Greater Raleigh Chamber of Commerce (GRCC)

800 S Salisbury St.
Raleigh, NC 27601
Ph: (919)664-7000   Fax: (919)664-7099

E-mail: hschmitt@the-chamber.org
URL: http://www.raleighchamber.org

Promotes business and community development in Raleigh and Wake County, NC.

★14213★ Greater Richmond Chamber of Commerce (GRCC)

201 E Franklin St.
PO Box 12280
Richmond, VA 23219
Ph: (804)648-1234   Fax: (804)783-9366
E-mail: chamber@grcc.com
URL: http://www.grcc.com

Seeks to improve the economy and quality of life of Greater Richmond region through its programs and initiatives.

★14214★ Greater Riverside Chamber of Commerce (GRCC)

3985 University Ave.
Riverside, CA 92501
Ph: (951)683-7100   Fax: (951)683-2670
E-mail: croth@riverside-chamber.com
URL: http://www.riverside-chamber.com

Promotes business and community development in the Riverside, CA area.

★14215★ Greater San Antonio Chamber of Commerce (GSACC)

602 E Commerce St.
San Antonio, TX 78295
Ph: (210)229-2100   Fax: (210)229-1600
E-mail: skolitz@sachamber.org
URL: http://www.sachamber.org

Promotes business and community development in the San Antonio, TX area. Represents the business community in legislative affairs and provides service programs.

★14216★ Greater Sarasota Chamber of Commerce

1945 Fruitville Rd.
Sarasota, FL 34236
Ph: (941)955-8187   Fax: (941)366-5621
E-mail: info@sarasotachamber.org
URL: http://www.sarasotachamber.org

Promotes business and community development in Sarasota County, FL.

★14217★ Greater Scranton Chamber of Commerce

222 Mulberry St.
PO Box 431
Scranton, PA 18501-0431
Ph: (570)342-7711   Fax: (570)347-6262
E-mail: jstetz@scrantonchamber.com
URL: http://www.scrantonchamber.com

Promotes business and community development in the greater Scranton, PA area.

★14218★ Greater Seattle Chamber of Commerce

1301 5th Ave., Ste. 2500
Seattle, WA 98101-2611
Ph: (206)389-7200   Fax: (206)389-7288

E-mail: info@seattlechamber.com
URL: http://www.seattlechamber.com

Promotes business and community development in Seattle, WA area.

★14219★ Greater Shreveport Chamber of Commerce (GSCC)

400 Edwards St.
Shreveport, LA 71101
Ph: (318)677-2500   Fax: (318)677-2541
Fr: 800-448-5432
E-mail: info@shreveportchamber.org
URL: http://www.shreveportchamber.org

Promotes business and community development in Shreveport/Bossier City, LA area.
Convention/Meeting: none.

★14220★ Greater Southwest Houston Chamber of Commerce

6900 S. Rice Ave.
PO Box 788
Bellaire, TX 77401
Ph: (713)666-1521   Fax: (713)666-1523
Fr: (866)517-8114
E-mail: swcinfo@gswhcc.org
URL: http://
www.southwesthoustonchamber.com

Promotes business and community development in Bellaire and Greater Southwest Houston, TX.

★14221★ Greater Springfield Chamber of Commerce

3 S. Old State Capitol Plaza
Springfield, IL 62701
Ph: (217)525-1173   Fax: (217)525-8768
E-mail: info@gscc.org
URL: http://www.gscc.org

Promotes business and community development in the Springfield, IL area.

★14222★ Greater Stockton Chamber of Commerce

445 W. Weber Ave., No. 220
Stockton, CA 95203
Ph: (209)547-2770   Fax: (209)466-5271
E-mail: schamber@stocktonchamber.org
URL: http://www.stocktonchamber.org

Promotes business and community development in the Stockton, CA area.

★14223★ Greater Syracuse Chamber of Commerce

572 S Salina St.
Syracuse, NY 13202-3320
Ph: (315)470-1800   Fax: (315)471-8545
E-mail: info@syracusechamber.com
URL: http://www.syracusechamber.com

Promotes business and community development in Syracuse, NY area.

★14224★ Greater Tampa Chamber of Commerce (GTCC)

PO Box 420
Tampa, FL 33601
Ph: (813)228-7777   Fax: (813)223-7899
Fr: 800-298-2672
E-mail: info@tampachamber.com
URL: http://www.tampachamber.com

Seeks to advance the general business conditions of the Tampa area.

★14225★ Greater Topeka Chamber of Commerce (GTCC)

120 SE 6th St., Ste. 110
Topeka, KS 66603-3515
Ph: (785)234-2644   Fax: (785)234-8656
E-mail: dkinsinger@topekachamber.org
URL: http://www.topekachamber.org

Promotes business and community development in the Topeka, KS area.

★14226★ Greater Vancouver Chamber of Commerce

1101 Broadway, Ste. 100
Vancouver, WA 98660
Ph: (360)694-2588   Fax: (360)693-8279
E-mail: yourchamber@vancouverusa.com
URL: http://www.vancouverusa.com

Promotes business and community development in the Vancouver and Clark County, WA areas.

★14227★ Greater Waco Chamber of Commerce

900 Washington Ave.
PO Box 1220
Waco, TX 76703-1220
Ph: (254)752-6551
E-mail: info@wacochamber.com
URL: http://www.wacochamber.com

Promotes business and community development in the Waco, TX area.

★14228★ Greater Winston-Salem Chamber of Commerce

601 W 4th St.
PO Box 1408
Winston-Salem, NC 27102
Ph: (336)728-9200   Fax: (336)721-2209
E-mail: anderson@winstonsalem.com
URL: http://www.winstonsalem.com

Promotes business and community development in Winston-Salem, NC area.

★14229★ Green Bay Area Chamber of Commerce (GBACC)

400 S Washington St.
PO Box 1660
Green Bay, WI 54305-1660
Ph: (920)437-8704   Fax: (920)437-1024
E-mail: @titletown.org
URL: http://www.titletown.org

Promotes business and community development in the Green Bay, WI area.

★14230★ Greensboro Area Chamber of Commerce

342 N Elm St.
PO Box 3246
Greensboro, NC 27402
Ph: (336)275-8675   Fax: (336)275-9299
E-mail: msamet@greensboro.org
URL: http://www.greensborochamber.com

Promotes business and community development in Greensboro, NC.

★14231★ Hampton Roads Chamber of Commerce

PO Box 327
Norfolk, VA 23501-0327
Ph: (757)622-2312   Fax: (757)622-5563
E-mail: jhornbeck@hrccva.com
URL: http://
www.hamptonroadschamber.com

Promotes business and community development in the Chesapeake, VA area.

★14232★ Hawaii Island Chamber of Commerce

106 Kamehameha Ave.
Hilo, HI 96720
Ph: (808)935-7178   Fax: (808)961-4435
E-mail: hicc@interpac.net
URL: http://www.gohilo.com

Promotes business and community development in the Hawaiian Islands.

★14233★ Hayward Chamber of Commerce

22561 Main St.
Hayward, CA 94541
Ph: (510)537-2424
E-mail: harryOrner@harryOrner.com
URL: http://www.haywardbusiness.com

Promotes business and community development in Hayward, CA.

★14234★ Henderson Chamber of Commerce

861 Coronado Center Dr., Ste 240
Henderson, NV 89052
Ph: (702)688-5500   Fax: (702)897-2720
E-mail: info@hendersonchamber.com
URL: http://www.hendersonchamber.com

Promotes business and community development in Henderson, NV.

★14235★ Hialeah Chamber of Commerce and Industry

1840 W. 49th St., Ste. 700
Hialeah, FL 33012
Ph: (305)828-9898
E-mail: info@hialeahchamber.com
URL: http://www.hialeahchamber.com

Seeks to promote and develop the economy through trade missions and government relations.

★14236★ Hudson County Chamber of Commerce

660 Newark Ave., Ste. 220
Jersey City, NJ 07306
Ph: (201)386-0699   Fax: (201)386-8480
E-mail: info@hudsonchamber.org
URL: http://www.hudsonchamber.org

Promotes business and community development in Hudson County, NJ.

★14237★ Huntington Beach Chamber of Commerce

19891 Beach Blvd., Ste. 140
Huntington Beach, CA 92648
Ph: (714)536-8888   Fax: (714)960-7654
E-mail: lmartin@hbcoc.com
URL: http://www.hbchamber.org

Strives to promote a favorable business climate to support and develop the city.

★14238★ Idaho Association of Commerce and Industry

PO Box 389
225 N. 9th St., Ste. 230
Boise, ID 83701-0389
Ph: (208)343-1849   Fax: (208)338-5623
E-mail: iaci@iaci.org
URL: http://www.iaci.org

Promotes business and community development in the state of Idaho.

★14239★ Illinois State Chamber of Commerce

311 S. Wacker Dr., Ste. 1500
Chicago, IL 60606
Ph: (312)983-7100   Fax: (312)983-7101
E-mail: info@ilchamber.org
URL: http://www.ilchamber.org

Promotes business and community development in Illinois.

★14240★ Independence Chamber of Commerce

210 W. Truman Rd.
PO Box 1077
Independence, MO 64051
Ph: (816)252-4745   Fax: (816)252-4917
E-mail: info@independencechamber.org
URL: http://www.independencechamber.com

Promotes business and community development in Independence, MO.

★14241★ Indiana Chamber of Commerce

115 W. Washington St., Ste. 850S
Indianapolis, IN 46204
Ph: (317)264-3110   Fax: (317)264-6855
E-mail: kbrinegar@indianachamber.com
URL: http://www.indianachamber.com

Businesses and other organizations. Promotes free enterprise and the preservation and advancement of the business climate. Monitors legislative activity. Holds seminars and workshops.

★14242★ Inglewood - Airport Area Chamber of Commerce

330 E. Queen St.
Inglewood, CA 90301
Ph: (310)677-1121   Fax: (310)677-1001
E-mail: inglewoodchamber@.sbcglobal.net
URL: http://www.inglewoodchamber.com

Promotes business and community development in Inglewood, CA.

★14243★ Irvine Chamber of Commerce

2485 McCabe Way, Ste. 150
Irvine, CA 92614
Ph: (949)660-9112
E-mail: icc@irvinechamber.com
URL: http://www.irvinechamber.com

Promotes business and community development in Irvine, CA.

★14244★ Jacksonville Regional Chamber of Commerce

3 Independent Dr.
Jacksonville, FL 32202
Ph: (904)366-6600
E-mail: info@jacksonvillechamber.org
URL: http://www.myjaxchamber.com

Promotes business and community development in Jacksonville, FL. Conducts seminars and other programs.

★14245★ Joliet Region Chamber of Commerce and Industry

63 N. Chicago St.
PO Box 752
Joliet, IL 60434-0752
Ph: (815)727-5371
E-mail: info@jolietchamber.com
URL: http://www.jolietchamber.com

Promotes business and community development in the Joliet, IL area.

★14246★ Kansas Chamber of Commerce and Industry

835 SW Topeka Blvd.
Topeka, KS 66612-1671
Ph: (785)357-6321   Fax: (785)357-4732
E-mail: info@kansaschamber.org
URL: http://www.kansaschamber.org

Promotes business and community development in Kansas.

★14247★ Kansas City, Kansas Area Chamber of Commerce

727 Minnesota Ave.
PO Box 171337
Kansas City, KS 66117
Ph: (913)371-3070   Fax: (913)371-3732
E-mail: chamber@kckchamber.com
URL: http://www.kckchamber.com

Promotes business and community development in the Kansas City, KS area.

★14248★ Kentucky Chamber of Commerce

464 Chenault Rd.
Frankfort, KY 40601
Ph: (502)695-4700   Fax: (502)695-6824
E-mail: kcc@kychamber.com
URL: http://www.kychamber.com

Promotes business and community development in Kentucky.

★14249★ Knoxville Area Chamber Partnership

17 Market Sq., No. 201
Knoxville, TN 37902
Ph: (865)637-4550   Fax: (865)523-2071
E-mail: partnership@kacp.com
URL: http://www.knoxvillechamber.com

Provides business and community development in Knoxville, TN area.

★14250★ Lake Champlain Region Chamber of Commerce (LCRCC)

60 Main St., Ste. 100
Burlington, VT 05401-8418
Ph: (802)863-3489   Fax: (802)863-1538
Fr: 877-686-5253
E-mail: vermont@vermont.org
URL: http://www.vermont.org

Promotes business and community development in Chittenden County, VT. Advocates for issues favorable to business.

★14251★ Lancaster Chamber of Commerce and Industry

100 S. Queen St.
PO Box 1558
Lancaster, PA 17603
Ph: (717)397-3531
E-mail: info@lcci.com
URL: http://www.lancaster-chamber.com

Promotes business and community development in Lancaster, PA.

★14252★ Lansing Regional Chamber of Commerce

112 E. Allegan St., Ste. 700
PO Box 14030
Lansing, MI 48901
Ph: (517)487-6340   Fax: (517)484-6910
E-mail: thansen@lansingchamber.org
URL: http://www.lansingchamber.org

Promotes business and community development in the Lansing, MI area.

★14253★ The Laredo Chamber of Commerce

2310 San Bernardo Ave.
PO Box 790
Laredo, TX 78042
Ph: (956)722-9895   Fax: (956)791-4503
Fr: 800-292-2122
E-mail: chamber@laredochamber.com
URL: http://www.laredochamber.com

Promotes business and community development in Laredo, TX.

★14254★ Las Vegas Chamber of Commerce (LVCC)

3720 Howard Hughes Pkwy.
Las Vegas, NV 89109-0937
Ph: (702)735-1616   Fax: (702)735-2011
E-mail: info@lvchamber.com
URL: http://www.lvchamber.com

Promotes business and community development in Las Vegas, NV.

★14255★ Lincoln Chamber of Commerce

1135 M St., Ste. 200
PO Box 83006
Lincoln, NE 68501-3006
Ph: (402)436-2350   Fax: (402)436-2360
E-mail: info@lcoc.com
URL: http://www.lcoc.com

Promotes business and community development in Lincoln, NE.

★14256★ Little Rock Regional Chamber of Commerce

One Chamber Plz.
Little Rock, AR 72201-1618
Ph: (501)374-2001   Fax: (501)374-6018
E-mail: chamber@littlerockchamber.com
URL: http://www.littlerockchamber.com

Promotes business and community development in the Little Rock, AR area.

★14257★ Livonia Chamber of Commerce

33233 Five Mile Rd.
Livonia, MI 48154
Ph: (734)427-2122   Fax: (734)427-6055
E-mail: chamber@livonia.org
URL: http://www.livonia.org

Business association that promotes economic and community development in the city of Livonia, MI.

★14258★ Long Beach Area Chamber of Commerce (LBACC)

1 World Trade Ctr., Ste. 206
Long Beach, CA 90831-0206
Ph: (562)436-1251   Fax: (562)436-7099
E-mail: info@lbchamber.com
URL: http://www.lbchamber.com

Promotes business and community development in the Long Beach, CA area.

★14259★ Los Angeles Area Chamber of Commerce

350 S Bixel St.
Los Angeles, CA 90017
Ph: (213)580-7500   Fax: (213)580-7511
E-mail: info@lachamber.org
URL: http://www.lachamber.org

Promotes business and community development in the Los Angeles, CA area.

★14260★ Louisiana Association of Business and Industry

3113 Valley Creek Dr.
PO Box 80258
Baton Rouge, LA 70898-0258
Ph: (225)928-5388   Fax: (225)929-6054
E-mail: jouanar@.labi.org
URL: http://www.labi.org

Promotes business and community development in the state of Louisiana.

★14261★ Lubbock Chamber of Commerce

1301 Broadway, Ste. 101
Lubbock, TX 79401
Ph: (806)761-7000   Fax: (806)761-7013
E-mail: info@lubbockbiz.org
URL: http://www.lubbockchamber.com

Promotes business and community development in Lubbock, TX area.

★14262★ Macomb County Chamber of Commerce

28 First St., Ste. B
Mount Clemens, MI 48043
Ph: (586)493-7600   Fax: (586)493-7602
URL: http://www.macombcountychamber.com

Promotes business and community development in Macomb County, MI.

★14263★ Maine State Chamber of Commerce

7 University Dr.
Augusta, ME 04330
Ph: (207)623-4568   Fax: (207)622-7723
Fr: 800-821-2230
E-mail: rstoddard@mainechamber.org
URL: http://www.mainechamber.org

Promotes business and community development in Maine.

★14264★ Maryland Chamber of Commerce

60 West St., Ste. 100
Annapolis, MD 21401
Ph: (410)269-0642   Fax: (410)269-5247
E-mail: mcc@mdchamber.org
URL: http://www.mdchamber.org

Promotes business and community development in the state of Maryland.

★14265★ Massachusetts Chamber of Commerce

34 Market St.
Everett, MA 02149
Ph: (617)389-4900   Fax: (617)387-0051
URL: http://www.massonline.com

Promotes business and community development in the state of Massachusetts.

★14266★ McAllen Chamber of Commerce

1200 Ash Ave.
PO Box 790
McAllen, TX 78501
Ph: (956)682-2871   Fax: (956)687-2917
Fr: 877-622-5536
E-mail: steve@mcallenchamber.com
URL: http://www.mcallenchamber.com

Promotes business and community development in McAllen, TX.

★14267★ Memphis Regional Chamber of Commerce

22 N Front St., Ste. 200
PO Box 224
Memphis, TN 38101-0224
Ph: (901)543-3500   Fax: (901)543-3510
E-mail: info@memphischamber.com
URL: http://www.memphischamber.com

Works to establish the Memphis region as a dynamic, growing, energetic metropolitan region strongly connected to the global marketplace.

★14268★ Mesa Chamber of Commerce (MCC)

120 N Center St.
Mesa, AZ 85201
Ph: (480)969-1307   Fax: (480)827-0727
E-mail: info@mesachamber.org
URL: http://www.mesachamber.org

Promotes business, tourism, and community development in Mesa, AZ. Encourages civic involvement in tourism, community betterment, and winter visitor marketing. Conducts annual Business Showcase.

★14269★ Mesquite Chamber of Commerce and CVB

617 N. Ebrite
Mesquite, TX 75149
Ph: (972)285-0211   Fax: (972)285-3535
Fr: 800-541-2355
E-mail: info@mesquitechamber.com
URL: http://www.mesquitechamber.com

Promotes business and community development in the Mesquite, TX area.

★14270★ Metro Atlanta Chamber of Commerce (MACOC)

235 Andrew Young Intl. Blvd. NW
Atlanta, GA 30303-2718
Ph: (404)880-9000   Fax: (404)586-8464
E-mail: samwilliams@macoc.com
URL: http://www.metroatlantachamber.com

Aims to improve the quality of life and promote economic growth in Atlanta.

★14271★ Metro Evansville Chamber of Commerce

100 NW 2nd St., Ste. 100
Evansville, IN 47708-2101
Ph: (812)425-8147   Fax: (812)421-5883
E-mail: info@evansvillechamber.com
URL: http://www.evansvillechamber.com

Promotes business and community development in the Evansville, IN area.

★14272★ Metrocrest Chamber of Commerce

1204 Metrocrest Dr.
Carrollton, TX 75006
Ph: (972)416-6600   Fax: (972)416-7874
E-mail: ed@metrocrestchamber.com
URL: http://metrocrestchamber.com

Promotes business and community development in Carrollton, TX.

★14273★ Metropolitan Milwaukee Association of Commerce (MMAC)

756 N Milwaukee St., Ste. 400
Milwaukee, WI 53202
Ph: (414)287-4100   Fax: (414)271-7753
E-mail: info@mmac.org
URL: http://www.mmac.org

Works to serve as advocate for metro Milwaukee companies to encourage business development, capital investment and job creation.

★14274★ Michigan Chamber of Commerce

600 S. Walnut St.
Lansing, MI 48933
Ph: (517)371-2100   Fax: (517)371-7224
Fr: 800-748-0266
E-mail: info@michamber.com
URL: http://www.michamber.com

Promotes business and community development in the state of Michigan.

★14275★ Minneapolis Regional Chamber of Commerce

81 S 9th St., Ste. 200
Minneapolis, MN 55402-3223
Ph: (612)370-9100   Fax: (612)370-9195
E-mail: info@minneapolischamber.org
URL: http://www.minneapolischamber.org

Promotes business and community development in the Minneapolis, MN area.

★14276★ Miramar-Pembroke Pines Regional Chamber of Commerce

10100 Pines Blvd., 4th Fl.
Pembroke Pines, FL 33026-3900
Ph: (954)432-9808   Fax: (954)432-9193
E-mail: membership@miramarpembrokepines.org
URL: http://www.miramarpembrokepines.org/

Promotes business and community development in Miramar and Pembroke Pines, FL.

★14277★ Mississippi Economic Council

PO Box 23276
248 E. Capitol St., Ste. 940
Jackson, MS 39225-3276
Ph: (601)969-0022   Fax: (601)353-0247
Fr: 800-748-7626

URL: http://www.msmec.com

Promotes business and community development in the state of Mississippi.

★14278★ Missoula Area Chamber of Commerce and Convention and Visitors' Bureau

825 E. Front
PO Box 7577
Missoula, MT 59802-7577
Ph: (406)543-6623   Fax: (406)543-6625
E-mail: info@missoulachamber.com
URL: http://www.missoulachamber.com

Promotes business and community development in the Missoula, MT area.

★14279★ Missouri Chamber of Commerce

428 E. Capitol Ave.
PO Box 149
Jefferson City, MO 65102
Ph: (573)634-3511   Fax: (573)634-8855
E-mail: kbuschmann@mochamber.com
URL: http://www.Mochamber.org

Promotes business and community development in the state of Missouri.

★14280★ Mobile Area Chamber of Commerce (MACC)

451 Government St.
PO Box 2187
Mobile, AL 36652-2187
Ph: (251)433-6951   Fax: (251)432-1143
Fr: 800-422-6952
E-mail: info@mobilechamber.com
URL: http://www.mobilechamber.com

Promotes business and community development in the Mobile, AL area. Serves as a progressive advocate for business needs to promote the Mobile Alabama area's economic well-being.

★14281★ Modesto Chamber of Commerce

1114 J St.
PO Box 844
Modesto, CA 95353-0844
Ph: (209)577-5757   Fax: (209)577-2673
E-mail: info@modchamber.org
URL: http://www.modchamber.org

Promotes business and community development in Modesto, CA.

★14282★ Montana Chamber of Commerce

2030 11th Ave., Ste. 21
PO Box 1730
Helena, MT 59624-1730
Ph: (406)442-2405   Fax: (406)442-2409
E-mail: dee@montanachamber.com
URL: http://www.montanachamber.com

Promotes business and community development in the state of Montana.

★14283★ Montgomery Area Chamber of Commerce (MACOC)

41 Commerce St.
PO Box 79
Montgomery, AL 36101
Ph: (334)834-5200   Fax: (334)265-4745
E-mail: macoc@montgomerychamber.com
URL: http://www.montgomerychamber.com

Promotes business and community development in the Montgomery, AL area.

★14284★ Morgantown Area Chamber of Commerce

1009 University Ave.
PO Box 658
Morgantown, WV 26507-0658
Ph: (304)292-3311   Fr: 800-618-2525
E-mail: info@morgantownchamber.org
URL: http://www.mgnchamber.org

Promotes business and community development in the Morgantown, WV area.

★14285★ Naperville Area Chamber of Commerce

55 S. Main St., Ste. 351
Naperville, IL 60540
Ph: (630)355-4141   Fax: (630)355-8335
E-mail: chamber@naperville.net
URL: http://www.naperville.net

Promotes business and community development in the Naperville, IL area.

★14286★ Nashville Area Chamber of Commerce

211 Commerce St., Ste. 100
Nashville, TN 37201-1806
Ph: (615)743-3000   Fax: (615)256-3074
E-mail: info@nashvillechamber.com
URL: http://www.nashvillechamber.com

Provides leadership that fosters growth and prosperity by ensuring the Nashville/Music City region is the best place to operate and grow a business, as well as the most desirable place to live, work, play and visit.

★14287★ Nebraska Chamber of Commerce and Industry

PO Box 95128
1320 Lincoln Mall
Lincoln, NE 68509-5128
Ph: (402)474-4422   Fax: (402)474-5681
E-mail: nechamber@nechamber.com
URL: http://www.nechamber.com

Promotes business and community development in Nebraska.

★14288★ New Hampshire State Chamber of Commerce

122 N. Main St.
Concord, NH 03301
Ph: (603)224-5388   Fax: (603)224-2872
Fr: 800-709-2810
URL: http://www.nhbia.org

Promotes business and community development in the state of New Hampshire.

★14289★ New Jersey Chamber of Commerce

216 W. State St.
Trenton, NJ 08608
Ph: (609)989-7888   Fax: (609)989-9696
URL: http://www.njchamber.com

Promotes business and community development in the state of New Jersey.

★14290★ Newport County Chamber of Commerce (NCCC)

45 Valley Rd.
Middletown, RI 02842-6377
Ph: (401)847-1600   Fax: (401)849-5848
E-mail: info@newportchamber.com
URL: http://www.newportchamber.com

Promotes business and community development in Newport County, RI.

★14291★ North Carolina Chamber

701 Corporate Center Dr., Ste. 400
PO Box 2508
Raleigh, NC 27607
Ph: (919)836-1400   Fax: (919)836-1425
E-mail: info@nccbi.org
URL: http://www.nccbi.org

Promotes business and community development in the state of North Carolina.

★14292★ North Las Vegas Chamber of Commerce

3345 W. Craig Rd., Ste B
North Las Vegas, NV 89032
Ph: (702)642-9595   Fax: (702)642-0439
E-mail: contact@nlvchamber.com
URL: http://
www.northlasvegaschamber.com

Promotes business and community development in North Las Vegas, NV and neighboring communities.

★14293★ Norwalk Chamber of Commerce

12040 Foster Rd.
Norwalk, CA 90650
Ph: (562)864-7785   Fax: (562)864-8539
E-mail: Info@norwalkchamber.com
URL: http://www.norwalkchamber.com

Promotes business and community development in Norwalk, CA.

★14294★ Oakland Metropolitan Chamber of Commerce

475 14th St.
Oakland, CA 94612-1903
Ph: (510)874-4800   Fax: (510)839-8817
E-mail: jharaburda@oaklandchamber.com
URL: http://www.oaklandchamber.com

Promotes business and community development in Oakland, CA.

★14295★ Oceanside Chamber of Commerce

928 N. Coast Hwy.
Oceanside, CA 92054
Ph: (760)722-1534   Fax: (760)722-8336
Fr: 800-350-7873
E-mail: info@oceansidechamber.com
URL: http://www.oceansidechamber.com

Promotes business and community development in Oceanside, CA.

★14296★ Ohio Chamber of Commerce

230 E. Town St.
PO Box 15159
Columbus, OH 43215-0159
Ph: (614)228-4201   Fax: (614)228-6403
Fr: 800-622-1893
E-mail: occ@ohiochamber.com
URL: http://www.ohiochamber.com

Businesses organized to foster economic and industrial growth in Ohio. Serves as liaison between government and business. Keeps members informed of employment conditions, economic developments, and pertinent regulations. Conducts lobbying activities.

★14297★ Orlando Regional Chamber of Commerce

PO Box 1234
75 S Ivanhoe Blvd.
Orlando, FL 32802-1234
Ph: (407)425-1234   Fax: (407)835-2500
E-mail: info@orlando.org
URL: http://www.orlando.org

Promotes business and community development in Orange, Osceola, and Seminole, FL. Provides governmental activities, small business and international trade programs.

★14298★ Overland Park Chamber of Commerce

9001 W. 110th, Ste. 150
Overland Park, KS 66210
Ph: (913)491-3600   Fax: (913)491-0393
E-mail: opcc@opks.org
URL: http://www.opks.org

Promotes business and community development in Overland Park and Johnson County, KS.

★14299★ Oxnard Chamber of Commerce

400 E. Esplanade Dr., Ste. 302
Oxnard, CA 93036
Ph: (805)983-6118   Fax: (805)604-7331
E-mail: ross@oxnardchamber.org
URL: http://www.oxnardchamber.org

Promotes business and community development in Oxnard, CA area.

★14300★ Palmdale Chamber of Commerce

817 E. Ave. Q9
Palmdale, CA 93550
Ph: (661)273-3232   Fax: (661)273-8508
E-mail: bbarnard@palmdalechamber.org
URL: http://www.palmdalechamber.org

Promotes business and community development in Palmdale, CA.

★14301★ Pasadena Chamber of Commerce

4334 Fairmont Pkwy.
Pasadena, TX 77504-3306
Ph: (281)487-7871   Fax: (281)487-5530
E-mail: info@pasadenachamber.org
URL: http://www.pasadenachamber.org

Promotes business and community development in Pasadena, TX.

★14302★ Pasadena Chamber of Commerce and Civic Association

865 E. Del Mar Blvd.
Pasadena, CA 91101
Ph: (626)795-3355
E-mail: info@pasadena-chamber.org
URL: http://www.pasadena-chamber.org

Promotes business and community development in Pasadena, CA.

★14303★ Pennsylvania Chamber of Business and Industry

417 Walnut St.
Harrisburg, PA 17101
Ph: (717)255-3252   Fax: (717)255-3298
Fr: 800-225-7224
E-mail: info@pachamber.org
URL: http://www.pachamber.org

Promotes business and community development in Pennsylvania.

★14304★ Peoria Area Chamber of Commerce

124 SW Adams St., Ste. 300
Peoria, IL 61602-1388
Ph: (309)676-0755   Fax: (309)676-7534
E-mail: chamber@chamber.h-p.org
URL: http://www.peoriachamber.org

Promotes business and community development in the Peoria, IL area.

★14305★ Peoria Chamber of Commerce

8765 W. Kelton Lane, Bldg C-1
Peoria, AZ 85380
Ph: (623)979-3601   Fax: (623)486-4729
Fr: 800-580-2645
E-mail: info@peoriachamber.com
URL: http://www.peoriachamber.com

Promotes business and community development in the Peoria, AZ area.

★14306★ Plano Chamber of Commerce

1200 E. 15th St.
Plano, TX 75074
Ph: (972)424-7547   Fax: (972)422-5182
E-mail: info@planocc.org
URL: http://www.planocc.org

Promotes business and community development in Plano, TX.

★14307★ Portland Business Alliance

200 SW Market, Ste. 1770
Portland, OR 97201
Ph: (503)224-8684   Fax: (503)323-9186
E-mail: info@portlandalliance.com
URL: http://www.portlandalliance.com

Works to ensure economic prosperity in the Portland region by providing strong leadership, partnership and programs that encourage business growth and vitality.

★14308★ Provo-Orem Chamber of Commerce (POACC)

51 S University Ave., Ste. 215
Provo, UT 84601
Ph: (801)851-2555   Fax: (801)851-2557
E-mail: info@thechamber.org
URL: http://www.thechamber.org

Promotes business and community development in Provo and Orem, UT. Conducts networking activities.

★14309★ Rancho Cucamonga Chamber of Commerce

7945 Vineyard Ave., Ste. D-5
Rancho Cucamonga, CA 91730-2314
Ph: (909)987-1012
E-mail: info@ranchochamber.org
URL: http://www.ranchochamber.org

Promotes business and community development in Rancho Cucamonga, CA.

★14310★ Regional Business Partnership (RBP)

744 Broad St., 26th Fl.
Newark, NJ 07102-3802
Ph: (973)522-0099   Fax: (973)824-6587
E-mail: info@newarkrbp.org
URL: http://www.rbp.org

Works to promote the economic growth and development of the Newark, NJ region.

★14311★ Reno-Sparks Chamber of Commerce

1 E 1st St., Ste. No. 1600
PO Box 3499
Reno, NV 89501
Ph: (775)337-3030   Fax: (775)337-3038
E-mail: info@renosparkschamber.org
URL: http://www.renosparkschamber.org

Promotes business and community development in the northern NV area. Sponsors community events. Conducts business seminars and events.

★14312★ Ricklin-Echikson Associates Inc.

374 Millburn Ave.
Millburn, NJ 07041
Ph: (973)376-2020   Fax: (973)376-2072
Fr: 800-544-2317
E-mail: jcowan@reacareers.com

URL: http://www.r-e-a.com

Assists spouses of relocating or newly recruited employees nationwide in the transfer or establishment of a new career, as well as entry into the employment market. Each spouse relocation career assistance program is customized with continuous, on-going counseling until the spouse is properly situated. Individual and group programs available as well as outplacement services to clients worldwide.

★14313★ Rochester Area Chamber of Commerce (RACC)

220 S Broadway, Ste. 100
Rochester, MN 55904-6517
Ph: (507)288-1122   Fax: (507)282-8960
E-mail: chamber@rochestermnchamber.com
URL: http://www.rochestermnchamber.com

Promotes business and community development in the Rochester/Olmsted County, MN area.

★14314★ Rockford Area Chamber of Commerce

308 W. State St., Ste. 190
PO Box 1747
Rockford, IL 61110
Ph: (815)987-8100   Fax: (815)987-8122
E-mail: info@rockfordchamber.com
URL: http://www.rockfordchamber.com

Promotes business and community development in the Rockford, IL area.

★14315★ Sacramento Metro Chamber of Commerce

917 7th St.
Sacramento, CA 95814
Ph: (916)552-6800   Fax: (916)443-2672
E-mail: chamber@metrochamber.org
URL: http://www.metrochamber.org

Promotes business and community development in the Sacramento, CA area.

★14316★ St. Paul Area Chamber of Commerce

PO Box 153
619 Howard Ave.
St. Paul, NE 68873
Ph: (308)754-5558
E-mail: stpaulcham@cornhusker.net

Promotes business and community development in St. Paul, NE. Hosts the Museum of Nebraska Major League Baseball.

★14317★ St. Petersburg Area Chamber of Commerce

PO Box 1371
100 2nd Ave. N, Ste. 150
St. Petersburg, FL 33701
Ph: (727)821-4069   Fax: (727)895-6326
E-mail: mbaker@stpete.com
URL: http://www.stpete.com

Promotes business and community development in the St. Petersburg, FL area.

★14318★ Salem Area Chamber of Commerce

200 S Main St.
Salem, MO 65560
Ph: (573)729-6900   Fax: (573)729-6741
E-mail: chamber@salemmo.com
URL: http://www.salemmo.com

Promotes business, community development, and tourism in Salem, MO.

★14319★ Salinas Valley Chamber of Commerce

119 E. Alisal St.
PO Box 1170
Salinas, CA 93902
Ph: (831)424-7611   Fax: (831)424-8639
E-mail: info@salinaschamber.com
URL: http://www.salinaschamber.com

Promotes business and community development in the Salinas, CA area.

★14320★ Salt Lake Chamber (SLACC)

175 E 400 S, Ste. 600
Salt Lake City, UT 84111-2329
Ph: (801)364-3631   Fax: (801)328-5098
E-mail: info@saltlakechamber.org
URL: http://www.saltlakechamber.org

Promotes business and community development in the Salt Lake City, UT area.

★14321★ San Diego Regional Chamber of Commerce

402 W Broadway, Ste. 1000
San Diego, CA 92101-3585
Ph: (619)544-1300
E-mail: webinfo@sdchamber.org
URL: http://www.sdchamber.org

Promotes business and community development in the Greater San Diego, CA area.

★14322★ San Francisco Chamber of Commerce

235 Montgomery St., 12th Fl.
San Francisco, CA 94104
Ph: (415)392-4520   Fax: (415)392-0485
E-mail: sfalk@sfchamber.com
URL: http://www.sfchamber.com

Promotes business and community development in San Francisco, CA.

★14323★ San Jose - Silicon Valley Chamber of Commerce

310 S 1st St.
San Jose, CA 95113
Ph: (408)291-5250   Fax: (408)286-5019
E-mail: info@sjchamber.com
URL: http://www.sjchamber.com

Promotes economic development and the improvement of quality of life in the Silicon Valley area of CA by being the leading voice for business through delivering innovative products and services, engaging in aggressive government advocacy, and producing premier networking opportunities.

★14324★ Santa Ana Chamber of Commerce

202 N. Broadway, 2nd Fl.
Santa Ana, CA 92706
Ph: (714)541-5353   Fax: (714)541-2238
URL: http://www.santaanachamber.com

Promotes business and community development in the Santa Ana, CA area.

★14325★ Santa Clara Chamber of Commerce and Convention and Visitors Bureau

1850 Warburton Ave., Ste. 101
PO Box 387
Santa Clara, CA 95050
Ph: (408)244-8244   Fax: (408)244-7830
Fr: 800-272-6822
URL: http://www.santaclara.org

Promotes business, community development, tourism and the convention trade in Santa Clara, CA.

★14326★ Santa Clarita Valley Chamber of Commerce

28460 Ave. Stanford, Ste. 100
Santa Clarita, CA 91355
Ph: (661)702-6977   Fax: (661)702-6980
E-mail: info@scvchamber.com
URL: http://www.scvchamber.com

Promotes business and community development in the Santa Clarita Valley, CA area. Sponsors business expo.

★14327★ Santa Rosa Chamber of Commerce

637 1st St.
Santa Rosa, CA 95404
Ph: (707)545-1414
E-mail: chamber@santarosachamber.com
URL: http://www.santarosachamber.com

Promotes business and community development in Santa Rosa, CA.

★14328★ Savannah Area Chamber of Commerce (SACC)

PO Box 1628
101 E Bay St.
Savannah, GA 31402-1628
Ph: (912)644-6400   Fax: (912)644-6499
E-mail: ebrowne@savcvb.com
URL: http://www.savannahchamber.com

Promotes business and community development in the Savannah, GA area.

★14329★ Scottsdale Area Chamber

4725 N. Scottsdale Rd., No. 210
Scottsdale, AZ 85251-4498
Ph: (480)355-2700   Fax: (480)355-2710
E-mail: info@scottsdalechamber.com
URL: http://www.scottsdalechamber.com

Promotes business and community development in the Scottsdale, AZ area.

★14330★ Simi Valley Chamber of Commerce

40 W. Cochran St., No. 100
Simi Valley, CA 93065
Ph: (805)526-3900   Fax: (805)526-6234
E-mail: info@sjchamber.org
URL: http://simivalleychamber.org

Promotes business and community development in Simi Valley, CA.

★14331★ Sioux Falls Area Chamber of Commerce (SFACC)

200 N Phillips Ave., Ste. 102
PO Box 1425
Sioux Falls, SD 57104
Ph: (605)336-1620   Fax: (605)336-6499
E-mail: sfacc@siouxfalls.com
URL: http://www.siouxfallschamber.com

Promotes business and community development in the Sioux Falls, SD area. Supports industry and agriculture. Maintains convention bureau.

★14332★ South Carolina Chamber of Commerce

1201 Main St., Ste. 1700
Columbia, SC 29201
Ph: (803)799-4601   Fax: (803)779-6043
Fr: 800-799-4601
E-mail: chamber@sccc.net
URL: http://www.scchamber.net

Promotes business and community development in South Carolina.

★14333★ South Dakota Chamber of Commerce and Industry

180 N. Euclid Ave.
PO Box 190
Pierre, SD 57501
Ph: (605)224-6161   Fax: (605)224-7198
Fr: 800-742-8112
E-mail: contactus@sdchamber.biz
URL: http://www.sdchamber.biz/

Promotes business and community development in the state of South Dakota.

★14334★ Spokane Regional Chamber of Commerce (SRCC)

801 W Riverside, Ste. 100
Spokane, WA 99201
Ph: (509)624-1393   Fax: (509)747-0077
E-mail: info@chamber.spokane.net
URL: http://www.spokanechamber.org

Promotes business and community development in the Spokane, WA area.

★14335★ Springfield Area Chamber of Commerce

202 S. John Q. Hammons Pkwy.
PO Box 1687
Springfield, MO 65806
Ph: (417)862-5567   Fax: (417)862-1611
E-mail: info@springfieldchamber.com
URL: http://www.springfieldchamber.com

Promotes business and community development in the Springfield, MO area.

★14336★ Stamford Chamber of Commerce

733 Summer St.
Stamford, CT 06901-1019
Ph: (203)359-4761   Fax: (203)363-5069
E-mail: jcondlin@stamfordchamber.com
URL: http://www.stamfordchamber.com

Aims to advance the civic and economic vitality of Stamford, Connecticut.

★14337★ State Chamber - Oklahoma's Association of Business and Industry

330 NE 10th St.
Oklahoma City, OK 73104-3220
Ph: (405)235-3669
E-mail: info@okstatechamber.com
URL: http://www.okstatechamber.com

Promotes business and community development in Oklahoma.

★14338★ Sterling Heights Area Chamber of Commerce

12900 Hall Rd., Ste. 190
Sterling Heights, MI 48313
Ph: (586)731-5400   Fax: (586)731-3521
E-mail: ladams@suscc.com
URL: http://www.suscc.com

Promotes business and community development in the Sterling Heights, Utica, Shelby Township, MI area.

★14339★ Sunnyvale Chamber of Commerce

260 S. Sunnyvale Ave., Ste. 4
Sunnyvale, CA 94086
Ph: (408)736-4971   Fax: (408)736-1919
E-mail: sblackman@svcoc.org
URL: http://www.svcoc.org

Promotes business and community development in Sunnyvale, CA.

★14340★ Tacoma-Pierce County Chamber of Commerce (TPCC)

950 Pacific Ave., Ste. 300
PO Box 1933
Tacoma, WA 98401-1933
Ph: (253)627-2175   Fax: (253)597-7305
E-mail: lindsay.bull@tacomachamber.org
URL: http://www.tacomachamber.org

Promotes business and community development in Pierce County, WA.

★14341★ Tempe Chamber of Commerce

909 E. Apache Blvd.
PO Box 28500
Tempe, AZ 85285-8500
Ph: (480)967-7891
E-mail: info@tempechamber.org
URL: http://www.tempechamber.org

Promotes business and community development in Tempe, AZ.

★14342★ Tennessee Chamber of Commerce and Industry

611 Commerce St., Ste. 3030
Nashville, TN 37203-3742
Ph: (615)256-5141   Fax: (615)256-6726
E-mail: info@tnchamber.org
URL: http://www.tnchamber.org

Promotes business and community development in the state of Tennessee.

★14343★ Texas Association of Business and Chamber of Commerce

1209 Nueces St.
Austin, TX 78701-1209
Ph: (512)477-6721   Fax: (512)477-0836
E-mail: info@txbiz.org
URL: http://www.txbiz.org

Promotes business and community development in the state of Texas.

★14344★ Thousand Oaks - Westlake Village Chamber of Commerce

600 Hampshire Rd., Ste. 200
Westlake Village, CA 91361
Ph: (805)370-0035   Fax: (805)370-1083
E-mail: info@towlvchamber.org
URL: http://www.towlvchamber.org

Promotes business and community development in Thousand Oaks and Westlake Village, CA. Offers networking opportunities.

★14345★ Toledo Area Chamber of Commerce (TACC)

Enterprise Ste. 200
300 Madison Ave.
Toledo, OH 43604-1575
Ph: (419)243-8191   Fax: (419)241-8302
E-mail: joinus@toledochamber.com
URL: http://www.toledochamber.com

Businesses. Promotes business and community development in the Toledo, OH area. Offers cost-saving benefits and networking opportunities to members.

★14346★ Torrance Area Chamber of Commerce Foundation

3400 Torrance Blvd, Ste. 100
Torrance, CA 90503
Ph: (310)540-5858   Fax: (310)540-7662
E-mail: barbara@torrancechamber.com
URL: http://www.torrancechamber.com

Promotes business and community development in the Torrance, CA area.

★14347★ Tucson Metropolitan Chamber of Commerce (TMCC)

PO Box 991
Tucson, AZ 85701
Ph: (520)792-2250   Fax: (520)882-5704
E-mail: info@tucsonchamber.org
URL: http://www.tucsonchamber.org

Promotes business and community development in the Tucson, AZ area.

★14348★ Utah State Chamber of Commerce

Heber M. Wells Bldg.
160 E. 300 S.
Salt Lake City, UT 84106
Ph: (801)621-8300   Fax: (801)932-7609
URL: http://www.commerce.state.ut.us/

Promotes business and community development in the state of Utah.

★14349★ Vallejo Chamber of Commerce

2 Florida St.
Vallejo, CA 94590
Ph: (707)644-5551   Fax: (707)644-5590
URL: http://www.vallejochamber.com

Promotes business and community development in Vallejo, CA.

★14350★ Ventura Chamber of Commerce

801 S. Victoria Ave., Ste. 200
Ventura, CA 93003
Ph: (805)676-7500   Fax: (805)650-1414
E-mail: info@ventura-chamber.org
URL: http://www.ventura-chamber.org

Promotes business and community development in the Ventura, CA area.

★14351★ Vermont Chamber of Commerce

PO Box 37
Montpelier, VT 05601
Ph: (802)223-3443   Fax: (802)223-4257
E-mail: info@vtchamber.com
URL: http://www.vtchamber.com

Promotes business and community development in the state of Vermont. Conducts educational programs. Lobbies state government.

★14352★ Virginia Chamber of Commerce

9 S. 5th St.
Richmond, VA 23219
Ph: (804)644-1607   Fax: (804)783-6112
URL: http://www.vachamber.com

Promotes business and community development in Virginia.

★14353★ Virginia Peninsula Chamber of Commerce

21 Enterprise Pkwy., Ste. 100
Hampton, VA 23666
Ph: (757)262-2000   Fax: (757)262-2009
Fr: 800-556-1822
E-mail: vpcc@vpcc.org
URL: http://www.vpcc.org

Promotes the economic and business interests of the Virginia Peninsula.

★14354★ West Chamber of Commerce Serving Jefferson County

1667 Cole Blvd., Bldg. 19, Ste. 400
Lakewood, CO 80401
Ph: (303)233-5555   Fax: (303)237-7633
E-mail: info@westchamber.org
URL: http://www.westchamber.org

Promotes business and community development in Lakewood and Jefferson County, CO.

★14355★ West Covina Chamber of Commerce

811 S. Sunset Ave.
West Covina, CA 91790-3599
Ph: (626)338-8496   Fax: (626)960-0511
Fr: 888-763-3232
E-mail: sdunn@westcovinachamber.com
URL: http://www.westcovinachamber.com

Promotes business and community development in West Covina, CA.

★14356★ West Virginia Chamber of Commerce

1624 Kanawha Blvd. E
Charleston, WV 25311
Ph: (304)342-1115
E-mail: forjobs@wvchamber.com
URL: http://www.wvchamber.com

Promotes business and community development in West Virginia. Sponsors seminars.

★14357★ Wichita Area Chamber of Commerce (WACC)

350 W Douglas Ave.
Wichita, KS 67202-2970
Ph: (316)265-7771   Fax: (316)265-7502
E-mail: info@wichitachamber.org
URL: http://www.wichitakansas.org

Promotes business and community development in the Wichita, KS area.

★14358★ Wichita Falls Board of Commerce and Industry

900 8th St., No. 218
PO Box 1860
Wichita Falls, TX 76307
Ph: (940)723-2741   Fax: (940)723-8773
E-mail: wfbci@wf.net
URL: http://www.wichitafallscommerce.com

Promotes business and community development in Wichita Falls, TX.

★14359★ Wisconsin Manufacturers and Commerce

501 E. Washington Ave.
PO Box 352
Madison, WI 53703-2944
Ph: (608)258-3400   Fax: (608)258-3413
URL: http://www.wmc.org

Promotes business and community development in the state of Wisconsin.

★14360★ **Yonkers Chamber of Commerce**
55 Main St., 2nd Fl.

Yonkers, NY 10701
Ph: (914)963-0332   Fax: (914)963-0455
E-mail: info@yonkerschamber.com

URL: http://www.yonkerschamber.com
Promotes business and community development in Yonkers, NY.

Negotiating Compensation Packages

URL: http://www.dbm.com

Video. $49.95. Shows an actual job offer negotiation session.

ONLINE AND DATABASE SERVICES

★14371★ JobStar Central
URL: http://www.jobstar.org
Description: Offers salary negotiation strategies and links to other resources.

★14372★ Salary.com
195 West St.
Waltham, MA 02451
Fr: (866)725-2791
URL: http://www.salary.com

Description: Offers salary reports based upon occupation. Also provides self-tests, learning and career links.

★14373★ SalaryExpert.com
9817 NE 54th St., Ste. 100
Vancouver, WA 98662
Fax: 877-799-3428   Fr: 877-799-3427
E-mail: techsupport@salaryexpert.com

URL: http://www.salaryexpert.com
Description: Salary reports.

★14374★ WageWeb.com
11820 Durrington Dr.
Richmond, VA 23236
Ph: (804)363-1792   Fax: (804)294-3721
E-mail: custserv@.wageweb.com
URL: http://www.wageweb.com

Description: Provides salaries according to industry. Also offers consulting services.

Networking

REFERENCE WORKS

★14375★ Dynamite Networking for Dynamite Jobs: 101 Interpersonal Telephone and Electronic Techniques for Getting Job Leads, Interviews, and Offers

Impact Publications
9104 Manassas Dr., Ste. N
Manassas Park, VA 20111-5211
Ph: (703)361-7300   Fax: (703)335-9486
Fr: 800-361-1055
E-mail: query@impactpublications.com
URL: http://www.impactpublications.com

Caryl R. Krannich and Ronald L. Kannich. 1996. $15.95 (paper). 188 pages.

★14376★ Electronic Resumes and Online Networking: How to Use the Internet to Do a Better Job Search

Career Press, Inc.
3 Tice Rd.
PO Box 687
Franklin Lakes, NJ 07417
Ph: (201)848-0310   Fr: 800-227-3371
URL: http://www.careerpress.com

Rebecca Smith. 224 pages. Second Edition. Explains how to use the Internet as a marketing tool for getting noticed in an increasingly online job market.

★14377★ Networking and Interviewing for Jobs

JIST Publishing
875 Montreal Way
St. Paul, MN 55102
Fax: 800-547-8329   Fr: 800-648-5478
E-mail: info@jist.com
URL: http://www.jist.com

$6.95. Techniques geared toward ex-offenders for finding the hidden job market, using the Yellow Pages and cold calling to get interviews and preparing for the inevitable question about prison time.

★14378★ Networking for Job Search and Career Success

JIST Publishing
8902 Otis Ave.
Indianapolis, IN 46216
Fr: 800-648-5478
E-mail: info@jist.com
URL: http://www.jist.com

Michelle Tullier. 2004. $16.95. 372 pages. Debunks the myths and misconceptions about networking while demonstrating how to cultivate and maintain rewarding professional relationships.

★14379★ Networking for Job Search and Career Success, Second Edition

JIST Publishing
875 Montreal Way
St. Paul, MN 55102
Fax: 800-547-8329   Fr: 800-648-5478
E-mail: info@jist.com
URL: http://www.jist.com

L. Michelle Tullier, PhD. 2004. $16.95. 384 pages. Shows how building relationships can lead to finding hidden jobs, choosing a career, advancing a current career, or starting a business.

★14380★ The Networking Survival Guide: Get the Success You Want by Tapping into People You Know

McGraw-Hill Trade
PO Box 182604
Columbus, OH 43272
Ph: 877-833-5524   Fax: (614)759-3749
E-mail: customer.service@mcgraw-hill.com
URL: http://www.mcgraw-hill.com

Diane Darling. 2003. Walks readers through the process of networking, including setting goals, identifying and developing potential contacts, and following up on leads and turning them into opportunities.

★14381★ Networking Works!: The WetFeet Insider Guide to Networking

WetFeet, Inc.
101 Howard St., Ste. 300
San Francisco, CA 94105
Ph: (415)284-7900   Fax: (415)284-7910

URL: http://www.wetfeet.com

2004. $19.95. 122 pages. Shows how to network effectively by tapping into an existing network, reading about alternative means of networking, and using alternative means of networking.

★14382★ Power Networking: Using the Contacts You Don't Even Know You Have to Succeed in the Job You Want

McGraw-Hill Trade
PO Box 182604
Columbus, OH 43272
Ph: 877-833-5524   Fax: (614)759-3749
E-mail: customer.service@mcgraw-hill.com
URL: http://www.mcgraw-hill.com

Marc Kramer. 1997.

★14383★ Practical Networking: How to Give and Get Help with Jobs

AuthorHouse
1663 Liberty Dr., Ste. 200
Bloomington, IN 47403
Fax: (812)339-8654   Fr: 888-519-5121
URL: http://www.authorhouse.com

Edward L. Flippen. October 2003. $22.95. 108 pages. Provides creative networking ideas for establishing contacts.

★14384★ Success Runs in Our Race: The Complete Guide to Effective Networking in the Black Community

HarperTrade
10 E. 53rd St.
New York, NY 10022
Ph: (212)207-7000   Fax: (212)207-7633
Fr: 800-242-7737
URL: http://www.harpercollins.com/

$13.95. 1996. 352 pages. Demonstrates how to network for information, for influence, and for resources.

★14385★ *Table Talk: The Savvy Girl's Alternative to Networking*
AuthorHouse
1663 Liberty Dr., Ste. 200
Bloomington, IN 47403
Fr: 888-519-5121
E-mail: 1stbooks@1stbooks.com
URL: http://www.authorhouse.com

Diane K. Danielson. April 2003. $17.50. 196 pages.

AUDIO/VISUAL RESOURCES

★14386★ *Job Search Strategies*
The Learning Seed
641 W. Lake St., Ste. 301
Chicago, IL 60661
Fax: 800-998-0854   Fr: 800-634-4941
E-mail: info@learningseed.com
URL: http://www.learningseed.com

Video. $89.00. 23 minutes. Learn how to network with companies without going through the personnel department.

ONLINE AND DATABASE SERVICES

★14387★ **Monster Networking**
URL: http://network.monster.com
An online community of professionals that provide jobseekers with the opportunity to learn about various companies, industries, and fields through personal contact.

OTHER SOURCES

★14388★ **Business Network International**
9903 Santa Monica Blvd., Ste. 812
Beverly Hills, CA 90212
Ph: (818)667-8967   Fax: (323)395-0987
Fr: 800-825-8286
URL: http://bni4success.com

Description: Offers a structured system of giving and receiving business by providing an environment in which individuals can develop personal relationships with other business professionals.

★14389★ **Small Business Network**
3 Woodthorne Ct.
Owings Mills, MD 21117
Ph: (410)581-1373
URL: http://www.usahomebusiness.com

Description: Maintains Business and Consumer Market-Sharing Network.

Non-Profit Opportunities

REFERENCE WORKS

★14390★ Alternatives to the Peace Corps

Food First Books
398 60th St.
Oakland, CA 94618
Ph: (510)654-4400   Fax: (510)654-4551
URL: http://www.foodfirst.org

Annual; latest edition 11th. $11.95 for individuals. Covers more than 100 foreign service organizations (excluding the Peace Corps) that offer long- or short-term volunteer service or travel opportunities in developing countries and U.S.-based volunteer opportunities. Entries include: Program name, address, phone, e-mail, website, description of program, including geographical areas served and admission requirements. Arrangement: Classified by type of program. Indexes: Organization.

★14391★ Careers for Good Samaritans and Other Humanitarian Types

The McGraw-Hill Companies
PO Box 182604
Columbus, OH 43272
Fax: (614)759-3749   Fr: 877-883-5524
E-mail: customer.service@mcgraw-hill.com
URL: http://www.mcgraw-hill.com

Marjorie Eberts and Margaret Gisler. Third edition, 2006. $13.95 (paper). 160 pages. Contains hundreds of ideas for turning good work into paid work. Inventories opportunities in service organizations like the Red Cross, Goodwill, and the Salvation Army; religious groups, VISTA, the Peace Corps, and UNICEF; and agencies at all levels of the government. Part of Careers for You series.

★14392★ Directory of Catholic Charities USA Directories

Catholic Charities USA
1731 King St.
Alexandria, VA 22314
Ph: (703)549-1390   Fax: (703)549-1656
URL: http://www.catholiccharitiesusa.org/

Annual. $25.00 for individuals. Covers nearly 1,200 Catholic community and social service agencies. Listings include diocesan agencies and state Catholic conferences. Entries include: Organization name, address, name and title of director, phone, fax. Arrangement: Geographical by state, then classified by diocese.

★14393★ Federal Support for Nonprofits

Cengage Learning
PO Box 6904
Florence, KY 41022
Fax: 800-487-8488   Fr: 800-354-9706
URL: http://www.cengage.com

Cynthia R. Spomer. 1995. $150.00. 986 pages.

★14394★ Great Jobs for Business Majors

The McGraw-Hill Companies
PO Box 182604
Columbus, OH 43272
Fax: (614)759-3749   Fr: 877-883-5524
E-mail: customer.service@mcgraw-hill.com
URL: http://www.mcgraw-hill.com

Stephen Lambert. Second edition, 2003. $15.95 (paper). 240 pages.

★14395★ How to Form Your Own Profit or Non-Profit Corporation Without a Lawyer

Do-It-Yourself Legal Publishers
60 Park Pl., Ste. 1013
Newark, NJ 07102
Ph: (973)639-0400   Fax: (973)639-1801

Benji O. Anosike. 1999. $25.95.

★14396★ How to Successfully Start a Grassroots Non-Profit Organization

Achievement U.S.A. Corporation
PO Box 9328
Washington, DC 20005
Ph: (202)319-9057   Fr: 800-891-3296

Darryl Webster. 2001. $20.00 The author provides a unique grassroots perspective on the pros and cons of getting started in the non-profit world. This book was written to save its reader's money, time and energy looking for information to help them start a non-profit organization. Some of the subjects covered in the book are: incorporating, obtaining tax exemption, garnering community support, marketing, proposal writing for grants, fundraising, getting publicity, giving interviews, and also comments on the significance and impact that grass-roots' citizens are having in the non-profit sector.

★14397★ A Legal Guide to Starting and Managing a Nonprofit Organization

John Wiley and Sons, Inc.
1 Wiley Dr.
Somerset, NJ 08875-1272
Ph: (732)469-4400   Fax: (732)302-2300
Fr: 800-225-5945
E-mail: custserv@wiley.com
URL: http://www.wiley.com/WileyCDA/

Bruce R. Hopkins. Fourth edition, 2004. $39.95 (paper). 360 pages.

★14398★ National Directory of Nonprofit Organizations

The Taft Group
27500 Drake Rd.
Farmington Hills, MI 48331-3535
Ph: (248)699-4253   Fax: 800-414-5043
Fr: 800-877-4253
E-mail: businessproducts@gale.com
URL: http://www.gale.com

Annual; latest edition 21, December 2007. $750.00 for individuals. Covers over 265,000 nonprofit organizations; volume 1 covers organizations with annual incomes of over $100,000; volume 2 covers organizations with incomes between $25,000 and $99,999. Entries include: Organization name, address, phone, annual income, IRS filing status, employer identification number, tax deductible status, activity description. Arrangement: Alphabetical. Indexes: Area of activity, geographical.

★14399★ National Directory of Private Social Agencies

Croner Publications Inc.
10951 Sorrento Valley Rd., Ste. 1-D
San Diego, CA 92121-1613
Fax: 800-809-0334   Fr: 800-441-4033
URL: http://www.sdic.net/croner

$109.95 for individuals. Number of listings: Over 10,000. Entries include: Agency name, address, phone, name and title of contact, description of services. Arrangement: Geographical. Indexes: Service, agency type.

★14400★ Non-Profits and Education Job Finder

Planning Communications
7215 Oak Ave.
River Forest, IL 60305-1935
Ph: (708)366-5200   Fax: (708)366-5280
Fr: 888-366-5200
E-mail: info@planningcommunications.com
URL: http://jobfindersonline.com

Daniel Lauber. 1997. $32.95; $16.95 (paper). 340 pages. Covers 1600 sources. Discusses how to use sources of non-profit sector job vacancies in a number of specialties and state-by-state, including job-matching services, job hotlines, specialty periodicals with job ads, salary surveys, and directories. Covers a variety of fields from education to religion. Includes chapters on resume and cover letter preparation and interviewing.

★14401★ Opportunities in Nonprofit Organizations

The McGraw-Hill Companies
PO Box 182604
Columbus, OH 43272
Fax: (614)759-3749   Fr: 877-883-5524
E-mail: customer.service@mcgraw-hill.com
URL: http://www.mcgraw-hill.com

Adrian Paradis. 1994. $14.95; $11.95 (paper). 151 pages. Covers a range of career opportunities with nonprofit organizations.

★14402★ Public Human Services Directory

American Public Human Services
  Association
810 1st St. NE, Ste. 500
Washington, DC 20002
Ph: (202)682-0100   Fax: (202)289-6555
E-mail: pubs@aphsa.org
URL: http://www.aphsa.org

Annual, September. $110.00 for members; $149.00 for nonmembers. Covers federal, state, territorial, county, and major municipal public human service agencies. Entries include: Agency name, address, phone, fax, e-mail address, web site address, names of key personnel, program area. Arrangement: Geographical.

★14403★ Real Resumes for Jobs in Non-Profit Organizations

PREP Publishing
1110 1/2 Hay St., PMB 66
Fayetteville, NC 28305
Ph: (910)483-6611   Fax: (910)483-2439
Fr: 800-533-2814

Anne McKinney (Editor). April 2004. $16.95 (paper). Illustrated. 192 pages. Real-Resumes Series.

★14404★ Search: Winning Strategies to Get Your Next Job in the Nonprofit World

Piemonte Press
PO Box 639
Glen Echo, MD 20812
Ph: (301)320-0680   Fax: (301)320-9471

Larry Slesinger. March 2004. $16.95. Illustrated. 104 pages.

★14405★ Vault Guide to the Top Government and Non-Profit Legal Employers

Vault.com
150 W. 22nd St., 5th Fl.
New York, NY 10011
Ph: (212)366-4212   Fax: (212)366-6117
Fr: 888-562-8285
URL: http://www.vault.com

Marcy Lerner. October 2003. $29.95 (paper). 176 pages. Part of the Vault Career Library Series.

NEWSPAPERS, MAGAZINES, AND JOURNALS

★14406★ The Chronicle of Philanthropy

The Chronicle of Philanthropy
1255 23rd St. NW, Ste. 700
Washington, DC 20037
Ph: (202)466-1200
E-mail: editor@philanthropy.com
URL: http://philanthropy.com

$72.00/year for individuals; $125.00 for two years; $72.00/year for individuals, online access only; $99.75/year for Canada; $72.00/year for Canada, online access only; $135.00/year for other countries; $72.00/year for other countries, online access only. Magazine covering fundraising, philanthropy, and non-profit organizations. Includes information on tax rulings, new grants, and statistics, reports on grant makers, and profiles of foundations.

★14407★ The NonProfit Times

NPT Publishing Group Inc.
120 Littleton Rd., Ste. 120
Parsippany, NJ 07054-1803
Ph: (973)394-1800   Fax: (973)394-2888
E-mail: ednchief@nptimes.com
URL: http://www.nptimes.com/

Biweekly. $69.00/year for individuals, subscribe at the one year rate; $49.00/year for individuals, digital only; $100.00/year for individuals, print & digital; $122.00 for two years, (48 issues); $101.00/year for Canada and Mexico; $137.00/year for other countries, international. Trade journal serving nonprofit organizations.

★14408★ Public Interest Employment Service Job Alert!

Public Interest Clearinghouse
47 Kearny St., Ste. 705
San Francisco, CA 94108
Ph: (415)834-0100   Fax: (415)834-0202
E-mail: pies@pic.org
URL: http://www.pic.org

Description: Semimonthly. Lists job openings in legal aid offices and public interest law organizations. Also available via e-mail.

AUDIO/VISUAL RESOURCES

★14409★ Humanitarian

Cambridge Educational
PO Box 2053
Princeton, NJ 08543-2053
Ph: 800-257-5126   Fax: (609)671-0266
Fr: 800-468-4227
E-mail: custserv@films.com
URL: http://www.cambridgeeducational.com

VHS and DVD. $69.95. 23 minutes. 1991. Part of the Video GOE series.

ONLINE AND DATABASE SERVICES

★14410★ American Society of Association Executives

E-mail: career@asaenet.org
URL: http://www.asaecenter.org/YourCareer/

Description: Membership site for executives of non-profit associations. "Career Headquarters" section contains resources both for searching for employees and new positions. Executives can also search resumes and review a list of executive recruiters, plus read information on a number of employment-related issues. You do not have to be a member to view job boards.

★14411★ ExecSearches.com

E-mail: info@execsearches.com
URL: http://www.execsearches.com

Description: Job site specializing in matching seekers with non-profit, public sector, academic and "socially conscious" positions. Contains job board, resume databank, e-mail alert system and reference articles.

Employers may also post jobs and check resume references.

★14412★ OpportunityKnocks.org

50 Hurt Plaza, Ste. 845
Atlanta, GA 30303
Ph: (678)916-3070
E-mail: support@opportunityknocks.org
URL: http://www.opportunitynocks.org

Description: Job board website for those interested in careers in non-profit organizations. Visitors may search job bank, receive listserv, and subscribe to free updates e-newsletter. Also contains career resources.

OTHER SOURCES

★14413★ Brigham Hill Consultancy

2909 Cole Ave., Ste. 220
Dallas, TX 75204
Ph: (214)871-8700   Fax: (214)871-6004
E-mail: brigham@brighamhill.com
URL: http://www.brighamhill.com

Firm provides retained executive search and related management consulting services to not-for-profit organizations.

★14414★ Campaign Service Consultants

7 Andrew Cir.
Hampstead, NH 03841-0370
Ph: (603)329-4534   Fax: (603)329-4534
E-mail: cscunningham@mediaone.net
URL: http://home.comcast.net/~cscunningham

Firm provides managerial and fund-raising counsel to nonprofit organizations. Services include feasibility studies, development audits, constituency analysis, campaign management, board and staff development, special event planning and management, interim staffing needs, computerization guidance and assessment, and ongoing counsel and support.

★14415★ Capability Co.

2818 Anderson Dr.
Raleigh, NC 27608
Ph: (919)791-3700   Fax: (919)882-9401
E-mail: rebecca@capabilitycompany.com
URL: http://www.capabilitycompany.com

Executive search for nonprofits. Company

helps nonprofit organizations find the best executive directors, development officers and chief financial officers.

★14416★ Celia D. Crossley & Associates Ltd.

3011 Bethel Rd., Ste. 201
Columbus, OH 43220
Ph: (614)538-2808   Fax: (614)442-8886
E-mail: crosworks@aol.com
URL: http://www.crosworks.com

Firm specializes in career planning and development, executive and organizational career coaching, assessment, key employee selection and team integration. Also offers career transition services, including in-placement, outplacement, and career coaching. Serves government, nonprofit, health-care, higher education and service industries.

★14417★ Institutional Advantage L.L.C.

340 Lothrop Rd.
Grosse Pointe Farms, MI 48236
Ph: (313)886-6349   Fax: (313)557-1331
E-mail: kts@ia-llc.com
URL: http://www.ia-llc.com

Retained executive search for higher education and not-for-profit clients.

★14418★ Intercristo

19303 Fremont Ave. N
MS No. 20
Seattle, WA 98133
Fax: (206)546-7375
E-mail: careerhelp@intercristo.com
URL: http://intercristo.searchease.com

Members: Division of CRISTA Ministries.
Purpose: Provides job exploration and job information service with computerized referrals on current openings with Christian organizations. Has career counseling, which is available through The Birkman Method Assessment Tool.

★14419★ McCormack & Farrow Co.

949 S Coast Dr., Ste. 620
Costa Mesa, CA 92626
Ph: (714)549-7222   Fax: (714)549-7227
E-mail: resumes@mfsearch.com
URL: http://www.mfsearch.com

General practice retained search in most industries. Special emphasis on high-technology, start-up and emerging companies, manufacturing, healthcare, financial services, nonprofit and privately owned businesses.

★14420★ Synergy Search Partners Inc.

11921 Freedom Dr., Ste. 550
Reston, VA 20190
Ph: (703)481-9936   Fax: (703)481-9938
E-mail: resume@synergysearchpartners.com
URL: http://www.synergysearchpartners.com

Executive Search firm provides recruitment services to a diverse client base. Firm provides consultative advice throughout the search and recruitment process. With a global network of senior-level candidates and human capital resources, firm has the reach and expertise to assist clients in finding talent with the right skill-sets, experiences, cultural compatibility, business astuteness, and leadership savvy.

★14421★ Third Sector Search Associates

1155 University St., Ste. 1414
Montreal, QC, Canada H3B 3A7
Ph: (514)906-1333   Fax: (514)878-2473
Fr: (866)273-8796
E-mail: info@thirdsectorsearch.com
URL: http://www.thirdsectorsearch.com

An executive search firm dedicated to not-for-profit organizations.

★14422★ U.S. Public Interest Research Group (USPIRG)

218 D St. SE
Washington, DC 20003-1900
Ph: (202)546-9707   Fax: (202)546-2461
E-mail: membershipservices@pirg.org
URL: http://www.uspirg.org

Description: Individuals who contribute time, effort, or funds toward public interest research and advocacy. Conducts research, monitors corporate and government actions, and lobbies for reforms on consumer, environmental, energy, and governmental issues. Current efforts include support for: laws to protect consumers from unsafe products and unfair banking practices; laws to reduce the use of toxic chemicals; strengthening clean air laws; efforts to reduce global warming and ozone depletion; energy conservation and use of safe, renewable energy sources. Sponsors internships for college students; provides opportunities for students to receive academic credit for activities such as legislative research, lobbying, and public education and organizing. Offers summer jobs.

Opportunities for Disabled Workers

REFERENCE WORKS

★14423★ Adult Agencies: Linkages for Adolescents in Transition

PRO-ED, Incorporated
8700 Shoal Creek Blvd.
Austin, TX 78757-6897
Ph: (512)451-3246   Fax: 800-397-7633
Fr: 800-897-3202
E-mail: info@proedinc.com
URL: http://www.proedinc.com

Gary Cozzens. 1999. $19.90. 111 pages.

★14424★ Affirmative Action Register

Affirmative Action Register
8356 Olive Blvd.
St. Louis, MO 63132
Ph: (314)991-1335   Fax: (314)997-1788
Fr: 800-537-0655
URL: http://www.aar-eeo.com

Monthly. Covers, in each issue, about 300 positions at a professional level (most requiring advanced study) available to women, minorities, veterans, and the handicapped; listings are advertisements placed by employers with affirmative action programs. Entries include: Company or organization name, address, contact name; description of position including title, requirements, duties, application procedure, salary, etc. Arrangement: Classified by profession.

★14425★ Career Planning and Employment Strategies for Postsecondary Students with Disabilities

National Clearinghouse on Postsecondary Education for Individuals with Disabilities
2121 K St. NW, Ste. 220
Washington, DC 20052
Ph: (202)973-0904   Fax: (202)973-0908
Fr: 800-544-3284
URL: http://www.heath.gwu.edu

Annual. Free. Covers about 30 educational institutions and organizations offering career placement programs for handicapped postsecondary students. Entries include: Institution name, address, phone, name and title of contact, program name, description of program. Arrangement: Classified by type of program.

★14426★ Coming Alive from Nine to Five: The Career Search Handbook

The McGraw-Hill Companies
PO Box 182604
Columbus, OH 43272
Fax: (614)759-3749   Fr: 877-883-5524
E-mail: customer.service@mcgraw-hill.com
URL: http://www.mcgraw-hill.com

Betty Neville Michelozzi. Seventh edition, 2003. $60.00. 360 pages. In addition to general job-hunting advice, provides special information for women, young adults, minorities, older workers, and persons with handicaps.

★14427★ Demystifying Job Development: Field-Based Approaches to Job Development for People with Disabilities

Training Resource Network, Incorporated
PO Box 439
St. Augustine, FL 32085-0439
Ph: (904)823-9800   Fax: (904)823-3554
Fr: (866)823-9800
URL: http://www.trninc.com/

David Hoff, Cecilia Gandolfo, Marty Gold, and Melanie Jordan. 2000. $29.95 (paper). 105 pages.

★14428★ Directory of Information Resources for the Handicapped

Ready Reference Press
PO Box 5249
Santa Monica, CA 90405
Ph: (310)475-4895   Fr: 800-424-5627

$47.50. 236 pages. Three separate volumes provide a guide to information resources and services for the handicapped, covering the fields of employment, vocational rehabilitation, and education and training, among others. Discusses how to locate specialized career placement services.

★14429★ Disabilities/Different Abilities: A New Perspective for Job Hunters

JIST Publishing
875 Montreal Way
St. Paul, MN 55102
Fax: 800-547-8329   Fr: 800-648-5478
E-mail: info@jist.com
URL: http://www.jist.com

Paula Reuben Vieillet. 2002. $18.95. 84 pages. A workbook for job hunters with disabilities.

★14430★ Job Search Handbook for People with Disabilities, Second Edition

JIST Publishing
875 Montreal Way
St. Paul, MN 55102
Fax: 800-547-8329   Fr: 800-648-5478
E-mail: info@jist.com
URL: http://www.jist.com

Daniel J. Ryan, PhD. 2004. $17.95. 288 pages. Career planning guide identifies strengths, gives job search tips, and provides options for career exploration from the perspective of people who have physical or mental disabilities.

★14431★ No More Job Interviews!: Self-Employment Strategies for People with Disabilities

Training Resource Network, Incorporated
PO Box 439
St. Augustine, FL 32085-0439
Ph: (904)823-9800   Fax: (904)823-3554
Fr: (866)823-9800
URL: http://www.trninc.com/

Alice Weiss. 2000. $29.95 (paper). 183 pages.

★14432★ Shoot for the Moon

Saunderstown Press
PO Box 307
Saunderstown, RI 02874-0307
Ph: (401)295-8810

Allen A. Johnson. Second edition, 1996. $12.95 (paper). 37 pages. Designed for people starting or reentering employment, with special emphasis on handicapped and minorities.

★14433★ So You're On Disability...& You Think You Might Want to Get Back into Action

Daniel Thomas McAneny
1417 Bexley Dr.
Wilmington, NC 28412-2001

Daniel T. McAneny. 2005. $12.99 (paper). 164 pages. This book includes over 40 stories of people who have successfully gotten jobs or started businesses after long term disability.

NEWSPAPERS, MAGAZINES, AND JOURNALS

★14434★ ADARA Update

ADARA
PO Box 480
Myersville, MD 21773
Ph: (410)495-8440　Fax: (410)495-8442
E-mail: ADARAorgn@aol.com
URL: http://www.adara.org/pages/publications.shtml

Description: Quarterly. Surveys news events, resources, legislation, and developments in services related to the deaf. Recurring features include notices of employment opportunities, news of the national Association and its local chapters, information on new publications, announcements of awards granted, and a calendar of events.

★14435★ Fair Employment Practices Summary of Latest Developments

Bureau of National Affairs Inc.
1801 S. Bell St.
Arlington, VA 22202
Fr: 800-372-1033
E-mail: customercare@bna.com
URL: http://www.bna.com/

Description: Biweekly. Highlights developments in employment opportunity and affirmative actions, and affirmative action programs. Reports on federal and state court decisions, Equal Employment Opportunity Commission (EEOC) rulings and Office of Federal Contract Compliance Programs (OFCCP) decisions, new laws, regulations, and agency directives. Also provides information on special programs for minorities, the handicapped, women, and older workers.

★14436★ Opportunity

National Industries for the Blind
1310 Braddock Place
Alexandria, VA 22314-1691
Ph: (703)310-0500　Fr: 800-433-2304
URL: http://www.nib.org

Description: Quarterly. Publishes news and feature articles on agencies for individuals

who are blind, and describes industries, agencies, and projects that employ blind workers. Recurring features include legislative updates, conference news, and news of programs and events of various associations employing blind individuals.

★14437★ Paraplegia News

PVA Publications
2111 E. Highland Ave., Ste. 180
Phoenix, AZ 85016-4702
Ph: (602)224-0500　Fax: (602)224-0507
Fr: 888-888-2201
URL: http://www.pvamagazines.com/pnnews/services/contact.php

Description: Monthly. Presents articles and briefs on wheelchair living, education, employment, housing, transportation, travel, spinal cord injury, research, legislation, new products, and sports and recreation for the wheelchair user.

★14438★ SIGCAPH Newsletter

Special Interest Group on Programming Languages
Department of Computer Science
151 Engineer's Way
Charlottesville, VA 22904
Ph: (212)869-7440　Fax: (212)944-1318
Fr: 800-342-6626

Description: Quarterly. Supports the Group's concern to promote professional interests of computing personnel with the physically handicapped; promotes the "application of computing and information technology toward solutions of disability problems and to perform a public education function in support of computing careers for suitably trained blind, deaf, or motor impaired persons."

★14439★ Tapping New Talent for Business Success

Rehabilitation Research and Training Center on Workplace Supports
1314 W. Main St.
PO Box 842011
Richmond, VA 23284-2011
Ph: (804)828-2494　Fax: (804)828-2193
E-mail: tcblanke@saturn.vcu.edu
URL: http://www.worksupport.com

Description: Irregular. Reports on diversity and disabilities in the workplace. Publishes original research, new resources, and human interest features.

★14440★ Vendorscope

Randolph-Sheppard Vendors of America
1808 Faith Pl., Ste. B
Terrytown, LA 70056-4104
Ph: (504)368-7785　Fax: (504)368-7739
Fr: 800-467-5299
E-mail: rsva@juno.com
URL: http://www.acb.org/rsva/fall2002.html

Description: Quarterly. Reports on issues pertinent to the Business Enterprise Program for Blind Vendors. Recurring features include letters to the editor, interviews, news of research, a calendar of events, reports of

meetings, news of educational opportunities, job listings, book reviews, notices of publications available, news of conventions and legislative action, and a column titled Mini-Mumbles from "Mean Dean." Also available on audiocassette.

AUDIO/VISUAL RESOURCES

★14441★ Access Unlimited: The Job Search Series for People with Disabilities

Cambridge Educational
PO Box 2053
Princeton, NJ 08543-2053
Ph: 800-257-5126　Fax: (609)671-0266
Fr: 800-468-4227
E-mail: custserv@films.com
URL: http://www.cambridgeeducational.com

VHS and DVD. 1998. $269.85. Three 30-minute videos cover job search tactics, resumes and applications, and job interviewing.

★14442★ Everybody's Working Video

Attainment Co., Inc.
PO Box 930160
Verona, WI 53593
Ph: (608)845-7880　Fax: 800-942-3865
Fr: 800-327-4269
E-mail: info@attainmentcompany.com
URL: http://www.attainmentcompany.com/

1997. $59.00 This 22-minute videocassette features success stories of five employees with disabilities.

★14443★ Everyone Can Work Video

Attainment Co., Inc.
PO Box 930160
Verona, WI 53593
Ph: (608)845-7880　Fax: 800-942-3865
Fr: 800-327-4269
E-mail: info@attainmentcompany.com
URL: http://www.attainmentcompany.com/

Paul Wehman and Pamela Sherron. 1996. $79.00. This 55-minute videocassette provides information on employment for persons with disabilities. Covers advantages of supported employment, including job coaches. Includes interviews with employers.

★14444★ Job Interviewing for People with Disabilities

Cambridge Educational
PO Box 2053
Princeton, NJ 08543-2053
Ph: 800-257-5126　Fax: (609)671-0266
Fr: 800-468-4227
E-mail: custserv@films.com
URL: http://www.cambridgeeducational.com

VHS and DVD. $89.95. 23 minutes. 1998. Part of the series "Access Unlimited: The Job Search Series for People with Disabilities."

★14445★ Job Search Tactics for People with Disabilities

Cambridge Educational
PO Box 2053
Princeton, NJ 08543-2053
Ph: 800-257-5126   Fax: (609)671-0266
Fr: 800-468-4227
E-mail: custserv@films.com
URL: http://www.cambridgeeducational.com

VHS and DVD. $89.95. 23 minutes. 1998. Part of the series "Access Unlimited: The Job Search Series for People with Disabilities."

★14446★ Resumes and Applications for People with Disabilities

Cambridge Educational
PO Box 2053
Princeton, NJ 08543-2053
Ph: 800-257-5126   Fax: (609)671-0266
Fr: 800-468-4227
E-mail: custserv@films.com
URL: http://www.cambridgeeducational.com

VHS and DVD. $89.95. 1998. 25 minutes. Part of the series "Access Unlimited: The Job Search Series for People with Disabilities."

SOFTWARE

★14447★ Interview Skills of the Future: Interview Challenges for Minorities, Women, and People with Disabilities

Program Development Associates
PO Box 2038
Syracuse, NY 13220-2038
Ph: (315)452-0643   Fax: (315)452-0710
Fr: 800-543-2119
E-mail: info@disabilitytraining.com
URL: http://www.pdassoc.com

$199.00. CD-ROM. Teaches a tactful and positive response to challenging interview questions for those having a hard time breaking through the traditional hiring barriers.

OTHER SOURCES

★14448★ Abilities!

201 I.U. Willets Rd.
Albertson, NY 11507-1599
Ph: (516)465-1400   Fax: (516)465-1591
E-mail: ecortez@ncds.org
URL: http://www.ncds.org

Description: Serves as a center providing educational, vocational, rehabilitation, and research opportunities for persons with disabilities. Work is conducted through the following: Abilities Health and Rehabilitation Services, a New York state licensed diagnostic and treatment center which offers comprehensive outpatient programs in physical therapy, occupational therapy, speech therapy, and psychological services; Career and Employment Institute, which evaluates, trains, and counsels more than 600 adults with disabilities each year, with the goal of productive competitive employment; Henry Viscardi School, which conducts early childhood, elementary, and secondary programs, as well as adult and continuing education programs; Research and Training Institute, which conducts research on the education, employment, and career development of persons with disabilities, and holds seminars and workshops for rehabilitation services professionals. Maintains library and speakers' bureau; compiles statistics; offers placement service; conducts research and educational programs.

★14449★ AFL-CIO Working for America Institute

815 16th St. NW
Washington, DC 20006
Ph: (202)508-3717   Fax: (202)508-3719
E-mail: info@workingforamerica.org
URL: http://www.workingforamerica.org

Purpose: Serves as the employment and training arm of the AFL-CIO. Works to assure full labor participation in employment and training programs funded under the Job Training Partnership Act. Assists in developing JTPA programs for dislocated and economically disadvantaged workers; provides technical services in support of labor-operated programs. **Activities:** Offers job search and placement services for disabled persons and early intervention and return-to-work services for recently disabled union members. Sponsors demonstration program to develop effective ways of improving workers' skills through structured workplace training; also offers workplace literacy study. Works with affected labor groups to help workers displaced by plant closings. Provides education and training to labor members of JTPA planning councils, labor leaders, and employment and training professionals.

★14450★ Goodwill Industries International (GII)

15810 Indianola Dr.
Rockville, MD 20855
Ph: (301)530-6500   Fr: 800-741-0186
E-mail: contactus@goodwill.org
URL: http://www.goodwill.org

Description: Federation of Goodwill Industries organizations across North America and the world concerned primarily with providing employment, training, evaluation, counseling, placement, job training, and other vocational rehabilitation services and opportunities for individual growth for people with disabilities and other special needs. Collects donated goods and sell them in Goodwill retail stores as a means of providing employment and generating income. Conducts seminars and training programs; compiles statistics.

★14451★ Helen Keller National Center for Deaf-Blind Youths and Adults (HKNC)

141 Middle Neck Rd.
Sands Point, NY 11050-1218
Ph: (516)944-8900   Fax: (516)944-7302
E-mail: hkncinfo@hknc.org
URL: http://www.hknc.org

Description: Provides diagnostic evaluations, comprehensive vocational and personal adjustment training, job preparation and placement for adults who are deaf-blind from every state and territory. Includes field services such as: information, referral, advocacy, and technical assistance to professionals, consumers, and families. Sponsors annual National Helen Keller Deaf-Blind Awareness Week.

★14452★ Inspiration Ministries (IM)

PO Box 948
Corner State Rd. 67 and County F
Walworth, WI 53184
Ph: (262)275-6131   Fax: (262)275-3355
E-mail: info@inspirationministries.org
URL: http://www.inspirationministries.org

Members: Seeks to provide fully accessible, permanent residence with attendant care in room and board facility for physically disabled adults. Conducts summer camping program for disabled persons and retreat opportunities for groups.

★14453★ Job Accommodation Network (JAN)

PO Box 6080
Morgantown, WV 26506-6080
Ph: (304)293-7186   Fax: (304)293-5407
Fr: 800-526-7234
E-mail: jan@jan.wvu.edu
URL: http://www.jan.wvu.edu

Description: A service of U.S. Department of Labor's Office of Disability Employment Policy. **Purpose:** An international toll-free consulting service that provides information about job accommodation and the employability of people with disabilities. Calls are answered by consultants who understand the limitations associated with disabilities and who have instant access to the most comprehensive and up-to-date information about accommodation methods, devices, and strategies.

★14454★ Just One Break (JOB)

570 Seventh Ave.
New York, NY 10018
Ph: (212)785-7300   Fax: (212)785-4513
E-mail: jobs@justonebreak.com
URL: http://www.justonebreak.com

Description: Serves as an employment service for people with disabilities, to help them find jobs and lead to productive lives. Finds competitive employment for people with disabilities by bringing together leading employers and qualified JOB applicants. Concentrates efforts in New York, and is working to include New Jersey and Connecticut, but advises companies nationwide. Offers placement services, employment counseling, skills evaluation, college recruitment, resume writing assistance service referrals, and computer access. Provides JOB's Student Internship Program (SIP), a hands-on work experience for college students with disabilities and works in collaboration with college disability and career service offices. Provides on-site disability awareness training to support initiatives related to interviewing, hiring, and retaining employees with disabilities.

★14455★ National Association of the Deaf (NAD)
8630 Fenton St., Ste. 820
Silver Spring, MD 20910-3819
Ph: (301)587-1788   Fax: (301)587-1791
E-mail: nadinfo@nad.org
URL: http://www.nad.org

Description: Safeguards accessibility and civil rights of America's deaf population in areas of education, employment, healthcare, and telecommunications.

★14456★ National Business and Disability Council (NBDC)
201 I.U. Willets Rd.
Albertson, NY 11507
Ph: (516)465-1516   Fax: (516)465-3730
E-mail: lbroder@abilitiesonline.org
URL: http://www.nbdc.com

Description: Acts as a resource for employers seeking to integrate people with disabilities into the workplace and companies seeking to reach them in the consumer market.

★14457★ NTID's Center on Employment (NCE)
Lyndon Baines Johnson Bldg.
Rochester Institute of Technology
52 Lomb Memorial Dr.
Rochester, NY 14623-5604
Ph: (585)475-6219   Fax: (585)475-7570
E-mail: ntidcoe@rit.edu
URL: http://www.ntid.rit.edu/nce

Members: Operated by the National Techni-cal Institute for the Deaf. **Purpose:** Promotes successful employment of Rochester Institute of Technology's deaf students and graduates. Offers resources and training for employers.

★14458★ Special Interest Group on Accessible Computing (SIGACCESS)
IBM T.J. Watson Research Center
19 Skyline Dr.
Hawthorne, NY 10532
Ph: (914)784-6603   Fax: (914)784-7279
E-mail: chair_sigaccess@acm.org
URL: http://www.sigaccess.org

Description: Promotes the professional interests of computing personnel with physical disabilities and the application of computing and information technology in solving relevant disability problems. Works to educate the public to support careers for the disabled.

Opportunities for Ex-Offenders

REFERENCE WORKS

★14459★ The Ex-Offender's Job Search Companion
Cambridge Career Products
PO Box 2153
Charleston, WV 25328-2153
Ph: (304)744-9323   Fax: (304)744-9351
Fr: 800-468-4227
URL: http://www.cambridgeol.com
1997. $11.95. 72 pages. This workbook covers all of the situations, problems, and obstacles the job hunter will encounter.

★14460★ I Need a Job!: The Ex-Offender's Job Search Manual
ConquestHouse, Inc.
Po Box 73873
Washington, DC 20056-3873
Ph: (202)723-2014   Fax: (202)291-1759
Louis Jones. May 2005. $15.00. 88 pages.

★14461★ Prisoners' Assistance Directory
National Prison Project
733 15th St. NW, Ste. 620
Washington, DC 20005
Ph: (202)393-4930   Fax: (202)393-4931
URL: http://www.aclu.org
Irregular; latest edition January 2007. $30.00 for individuals. Covers organizations in the U.S. offering assistance to prisoners and their families, including legal, ex-offender, and family support services. Entries include: Organization name, address, phone, fax, URL, name and title of contact, geographical area served, subsidiary and branch names and locations, description of services. Arrangement: Geographical by state. Indexes: Geographical.

AUDIO/VISUAL RESOURCES

★14462★ After Prison: How the Ex-Convict Can Find a Place to Live, Get Work, and Stay Straight
JIST Publishing
875 Montreal Way
St. Paul, MN 55102
Fax: 800-547-8329   Fr: 800-648-5478
E-mail: info@jist.com
URL: http://www.jist.com
1999. $129. 25 minutes. Focuses on the critical factors while in transition: food, shelter, and employment.

★14463★ Finding a Job
Cambridge Educational
PO Box 2053
Princeton, NJ 08543-2053
Ph: 800-257-5126   Fax: (609)671-0266
Fr: 800-468-4227
E-mail: custserv@films.com
URL: http://www.cambridgeeducational.com
VHS and DVD. 2008. $89.95. 23 minutes. Covers conventional and unconventional job search methods, and which are more likely to work for ex-offenders.

★14464★ From Parole to Payroll
Cambridge Educational
PO Box 2053
Princeton, NJ 08543-2053
Ph: 800-257-5126   Fax: (609)671-0266
Fr: 800-468-4227
E-mail: custserv@films.com
URL: http://www.cambridgeeducational.com
VHS and DVD. 2008. $269.85. Contains solid, real-world content designed to help job seekers find satisfying work, and features informative interviews, helpful tips, and colorful graphics.

★14465★ The Job Interview
Cambridge Educational
PO Box 2053
Princeton, NJ 08543-2053
Ph: 800-257-5126   Fax: (609)671-0266
Fr: 800-468-4227
E-mail: custserv@films.com
URL: http://www.cambridgeeducational.com
VHS and DVD. $59.95. 1995. 15 minutes. Part of the From Parole to Payroll Series.

★14466★ Life after Prison: Success on the Outside
Cambridge Educational
PO Box 2053
Princeton, NJ 08543-2053
Ph: 800-257-5126   Fax: (609)671-0266
Fr: 800-468-4227
E-mail: custserv@films.com
URL: http://www.cambridgeeducational.com
Video and DVD. 1999. $98.95. 40 minutes. Contains interviews and covers where to look for employment.

★14467★ Resumes and Job Applications
Cambridge Educational
PO Box 2053
Princeton, NJ 08543-2053
Ph: 800-257-5126   Fax: (609)671-0266
Fr: 800-468-4227
E-mail: custserv@films.com
URL: http://www.cambridgeeducational.com
$89.95. 2008. 20 minutes. Part of the "From Parole to Payroll" Series.

OTHER SOURCES

★14468★ Court Services and Offender Supervision Agency
633 Indiana Ave., NW
Washington, DC 20004-2902
Ph: (202)220-5300
E-mail: webmaster@csosa.gov
URL: http://www.csosa.gov

Description: Provides services for individuals on parole and probation.

★14469★ **Delancey Street Foundation**

600 Embarcadero
San Francisco, CA 94107
Ph: (415)957-9800
URL: http://
www.delanceystreetfoundation.org

Description: Provides a structured educational and living environment for ex-felons. Teaches life skills.

★14470★ **Fortune Society (FS)**

53 W 23rd St., 8th Fl.
New York, NY 10010
Ph: (212)691-7554   Fax: (212)255-4948
E-mail: kkidder@fortunesociety.org
URL: http://www.fortunesociety.org

Description: Ex-offenders and others interested in penal reform. Addresses the needs of ex-offenders and high-risk youth. Promotes greater public awareness of the prison system and of the problems confronting inmates before, after, and during incarceration. Works on a personal basis with men and women recently released from prison; helps ex-offenders find jobs. Offers educational services including literacy training and G.E.D. preparation. Sends teams of ex-offenders to talk to school, church, and civic groups and on radio and television to relate

first-hand experiences of prison life and to create a greater understanding of the causes of crime in the United States. Conducts Alternatives to Incarceration programs; offers AIDS and general counseling services. Acts as referral agency for half-way houses and drug and alcohol addiction programs.

★14471★ **Osborne Association**

809 Westchester Ave.
Bronx, NY 10455
Ph: (718)707-2600   Fax: (718)707-3102
URL: http://www.osborneny.org

Description: Provides assessment, testing, career and educational counseling for ex-offenders.

★14472★ **Sentencing Project**

514 Tenth St. NW, Ste. 1000
Washington, DC 20004
Ph: (202)628-0871   Fax: (202)628-1091
E-mail: staff@sentencingproject.org
URL: http://www.sentencingproject.org

Description: Training and technical assistance.

★14473★ **Wildcat Service Corporation (WSC)**

17 Battery Pl.
New York, NY 10004
Ph: (212)209-6000

E-mail: rmandor@wildcatatwork.org

Description: Provides transitional employment and training for chronically unemployed persons (former substance abusers, ex-offenders, welfare mothers, out-of-school youth, and illiterate and delinquent youth). Systematically prepares and grooms employees to accept the full responsibility of full-time work within a 12-month time period. Placement rate of terminees is about 70% in a variety of industries. Operates clerical school in basic and advanced office practices; conducts specialized "life skills" educational program. Compiles statistics; maintains placement service. Operates three high schools.

★14474★ **Women's Prison Association (WPA)**

110 2nd Ave.
New York, NY 10003
Ph: (646)336-6100   Fax: (212)677-1981
E-mail: ajacobs@wpaonline.org
URL: http://www.wpaonline.org

Purpose: Service agency that aids women involved in the criminal justice system and their families. Promotes alternatives to incarceration; sponsors transitional programs for women being released from prison; assists homeless ex-offenders seeking to reunite with their children who are in kinship or foster-care.

Opportunities for Gay and Lesbian Workers

REFERENCE WORKS

★14475★ The 100 Best Companies for Gay Men and Lesbians

Pocket Books
1230 Ave. of the Americas
New York, NY 10020
Ph: (212)698-7000   Fr: 800-223-2348

Ed Mickens. 1994. $12.00 (paper). 288 pages. Provides profiles of 100 "gay-friendly" companies and their policies and benefits. Also includes a discussion of gay and lesbian workplace issues and opportunities.

★14476★ Career and Life Planning With Gay, Lesbian, and Bisexual Persons

American Counseling Association
5999 Stevenson Ave.
Alexandria, VA 22304-3300
Ph: (703)823-9800   Fax: 800-473-2329
Fr: 800-347-6647
URL: http://www.counseling.org/

Susan Owre Gelberg and Joseph T. Chojnacki. 1996. $35.95. 199 pages. Addresses the issues of overt and covert discrimination in the workplace. Designed by combining career theory and application within a counseling framework specific to the needs of gay, lesbian, and bisexual persons.

★14477★ Community Yellow Pages

G & L Community Yellow Pages
5657 Wilshire Blvd., Ste. 500
Los Angeles, CA 90036-3736
Ph: (323)930-3220   Fax: (323)857-0503
Fr: 800-745-5669

Annual, January. Covers approximately 2,500 gay and lesbian-owned businesses; professionals and organizations serving the gay and lesbian community in the Los Angeles, Ventura, Inland Empire, and Long Beach/Orange County areas. Entries include: Company, organization, or individual name, address, phone and display advertising. Arrangement: Classified by type of service or profession.

★14478★ Corporate Closet: The Professional Lives of Gay Men in America

The Free Press
1230 Ave. of the Americas
New York, NY 10020
Ph: (212)698-7000   Fr: 800-223-2348

James D. Woods and Jay H. Lucas. 1994. $14.95. Addresses the risks and benefits of coming out on the job in the United States. 341 pages.

★14479★ Gay Issues in the Workplace

St. Martin's Press, LLC
175 5th Ave.
New York, NY 10010
Ph: (212)726-0200   Fax: (212)686-9491
Fr: 800-470-4767
URL: http://www.stmartins.com

Brian McNaught. 1994. $12.95. 180 pages. Deals with homophobia in the workplace, the importance of dealing with gay issues within corporations, and techniques for encouraging understanding between all employees. The book includes a sample workshop outline and a list of resources for companies and individuals. Part of Stonewall Inn Edition series.

★14480★ Gayellow Pages: A Classified Directory of Gay Services and Businesses in USA and Canada

Gayellow Pages
Village Sta.
PO Box 533
New York, NY 10014-0544
Ph: (646)213-0263   Fax: (646)292-5170
URL: http://gayellowpages.com/

Annual; latest edition February 2005. Covers gay- or lesbian-oriented business enterprises, organizations, resources, churches, bars, restaurants, and publications; many AIDS/HIV resources. Includes a separate listing of national organizations. Entries include: Name, address, phone, business hours, and an annotation describing programs, products, or services. Also available in regional editions. Arrangement: Geographical; national listings are classified by subject category.

★14481★ Outing Yourself: How to Come Out to Your Family, Your Friends, & Your Coworkers

Random House
1745 Broadway
New York, NY 10019
Ph: (212)782-9000   Fax: (212)572-6066
Fr: 800-733-3000
URL: http://www.randomhouse.com

Michelangelo Signorile. 1997. $13.00. 208 pages.

★14482★ Personal Financial Planning for Gays and Lesbians

Irwin Professional Pub
PO Box 545
Blacklick, OH 43004-0545
Fax: (614)755-5645   Fr: 800-722-4726

Peter M. Berkery, Jr. 1996. $24.95. Addresses challenges of financial planning and achieving financial goals. 400 pages.

★14483★ Sexual Orientation in the Workplace: Gay Men, Lesbians, Bisexuals, & Heterosexuals Working Together

Sage Publications, Inc.
2455 Teller Rd.
Thousand Oaks, CA 91320-2218
Ph: (805)499-9774   Fax: (805)499-0871
Fr: 800-818-7243
URL: http://www.sagepub.com/

Amy J. Zuckerman and George F. Simons. 1995. $52.95 (paper). 125 pages.

★14484★ Straight Jobs, Gay Lives

Fireside
1230 Ave. of the Americas
New York, NY 10020
Ph: (212)698-7000   Fax: (212)698-7007
Fr: 800-897-7650

Annette Friskopp and Sharon Silverstein. 1996. $23.95. 528 pages. Provides an in-depth look at the careers and lives of a wide array of gay professionals. Also provides over 200 contact listings.

NEWSPAPERS, MAGAZINES, AND JOURNALS

★14485★ The Advocate

Liberation Publications Inc.
6922 Hollywood Blvd., 10th Fl.
Los Angeles, CA 90028
Ph: (323)871-1225   Fax: (323)467-0173
E-mail: newsroom@advocate.com
URL: http://www.advocate.com

Biweekly. $39.97/year for individuals; $69.97/year for Canada; $69.97/year for out of country; $70.00 for two years. National gay and lesbian news and lifestyle magazine.

★14486★ Fair Employment Practices Summary of Latest Developments

Bureau of National Affairs Inc.
1801 S. Bell St.
Arlington, VA 22202
Fr: 800-372-1033
E-mail: customercare@bna.com
URL: http://www.bna.com/

Description: Biweekly. Highlights developments in employment opportunity and affirmative actions, and affirmative action programs. Reports on federal and state court decisions, Equal Employment Opportunity Commission (EEOC) rulings and Office of Federal Contract Compliance Programs (OFCCP) decisions, new laws, regulations, and agency directives. Also provides information on special programs for minorities, the handicapped, women, and older workers.

★14487★ Out & About

PlanetOut Corp.
PO Box 500
San Francisco, CA 94104-0500
Ph: (415)834-6500   Fax: (415)834-6502
Fr: 800-929-2268
E-mail: billing@planetout.com
URL: http://www.outandabout.com

Description: Ten issues/year. Provides "travel information free from bias for experienced lesbian and gay travelers and their travel agents." Explores U.S. and international destinations and experiences that are gay or gay-friendly. Recurring features include letters to the editor, calendar of events, book reviews, notices of publications available, and columns titled Out at the Inn, Three Ways to Save, Ask the Experts, Editor's Letter, and Traveler's Diary.

ONLINE AND DATABASE SERVICES

★14488★ Chicago Area Gay and Lesbian Chamber of Commerce

3656 N. Halsted
Chicago, IL 60613
Ph: (773)303-0167
E-mail: info@glchamber.org
URL: http://www.glchamber.org/

Description: Site offering business, consumer and travel information to gays and lesbians in the Chicago area. Also includes classified ads for jobhunting members.

★14489★ Queer Net Online Policy Group

E-mail: majordomo@queernet.org
URL: http://groups.queernet.org/

General e-mail news and discussion list dealing with gay, lesbian, bisexual, and transgender issues within the workplace.

OTHER SOURCES

★14490★ Association for Gay, Lesbian, and Bisexual Issues in Counseling (AGLBIC)

640 Glen Iris Dr., No. 510
Georgia State University
Atlanta, GA 30308
Ph: (404)651-3409   Fax: (404)651-1109
E-mail: bdew@gsu.edu
URL: http://www.aglbic.org

Members: Counselors, personnel and guidance workers concerned with lesbian and gay issues. **Purpose:** Seeks to eliminate discrimination against and stereotyping of gay and lesbian individuals, particularly gay counselors. Works to educate heterosexual counselors on how to overcome homophobia and to best help homosexual clients. **Activities:** Provides a referral network and support for gay counselors and administrators; encourages objective research on gay issues. Organizational affiliate of the American Counseling Association.

★14491★ Gay and Lesbian Medical Association (GLMA)

459 Fulton St., Ste. 107
San Francisco, CA 94102
Ph: (415)255-4547   Fax: (415)255-4784
E-mail: info@glma.org
URL: http://www.glma.org

Members: Healthcare professionals. **Purpose:** Seeks elimination of discrimination on the basis of gender identity and sexual orientation in the health profession; promotes unprejudiced medical care for LGBT patients through advocacy and education. Maintains a referral and support program for HIV infected health care workers. Sponsors annual continuing medical education (CME, CEU) symposium on LGBT issues. Offers support to lesbian, gay, bisexual, and transgendered health care workers; encourages research into the health needs of gays and lesbians. Maintains liaison with medical schools and other organizations concerning needs of gay patients and professionals; fosters communication and cooperation among members and other groups and individuals supportive of gay and lesbian physicians. Sponsors Lesbian Health Fund for researching lesbian health needs.

★14492★ Lesbian, Bisexual, Gay and Transgendered United Employees at AT&T (LEAGUE)

One AT&T Way, Rm. 4B214J
Bedminster, NJ 07921-2694
Ph: (703)691-5734
E-mail: league@att.com
URL: http://www.league-att.org

Description: Individuals employed at or retired from AT&T or any of its subsidiaries. Fosters the value of mutual respect and appreciation of cultural differences among employees. Offers educational programs and support groups to address issues that affect lesbian, gay, and bisexual employees, and their friends and families. Acts as an information clearinghouse on homosexuality, bisexuality, and lesbian and gay issues. Provides referral services to support groups and community and service organizations.

★14493★ Lesbian, Gay, Bisexual, and Transgender People in Medicine (LGBTPM)

1902 Association Dr.
Reston, VA 20191
Ph: (703)620-6600   Fax: (703)620-5873
Fr: 800-767-2266
E-mail: bhurley@usc.edu
URL: http://www.amsa.org/advocacy/lgbtpm

Description: Advocacy Group of the American Medical Student Association. Physicians and physicians in training; others interested in gay/lesbian issues. Purposes are to improve the quality of health care for gay patients; to improve working conditions and professional status of gay health professionals and students. Administers educational workshops for health professionals; designs training materials; conducts research on the health problems of gay people and surveys on admissions, hiring, and promotion policies of medical schools and hospitals; provides referrals; sponsors support groups for gay professionals to meet, socialize, and organize; presses for legislative and political action to end discrimination against gay people. Maintains speakers' bureau.

★14494★ Lesbian Resource Center (LRC)

227 S Orcas St.
Seattle, WA 98108
Ph: (206)322-3953   Fax: (206)322-0586
E-mail: lrc@lrc.net
URL: http://www.lrc.net

Description: Provides classes, groups, workshops, and information on housing, employment, and lesbian community groups and events. Represents the lesbian community in areas of political and social concern.

★14495★ **National Association of Social Workers National Committee on Lesbian, Gay and Bisexual Issues (NASW)**

750 First St. NE, Ste. 700
Washington, DC 20002-4241
Ph: (202)408-8600   Fr: 800-742-4089
E-mail: membership@naswdc.org
URL: http://www.socialworkers.org/governance/cmtes/nclgbi.asp

Description: A committee of the National Association of Social Workers. Seeks to ensure equal employment opportunities for lesbian, gay and bisexual individuals. Informs the NASW about: domestic, racial, and antigay violence; civil rights; family and primary associations. Encourages the NASW to support legislation, regulations, policies, judicial review, political action, and other activities that seek to establish and protect equal rights for all persons without regard to affectional and/or sexual orientation. Advises government bodies and political candidates regarding the needs and

concerns of social workers and lesbian and gay people; reviews proposed legislation.

★14496★ **National Center for Lesbian Rights (NCLR)**

870 Market St., Ste. 370
San Francisco, CA 94102
Ph: (415)392-6257   Fax: (415)392-8442
E-mail: info@nclrights.org
URL: http://www.nclrights.org

Description: A legal resource center specializing in sexual orientation discrimination cases, particularly those involving lesbians. Activities include: legal counseling and representation, community education, and technical assistance. Provides legal services to lesbian, gay and transgender youths, adults and elders on issues of custody and foster parenting, visitation rights second parent adoption.

★14497★ **National Gay and Lesbian Task Force (NGLTF)**

1325 Massachusetts Ave. NW, Ste. 600
Washington, DC 20005
Ph: (202)393-5177   Fax: (202)393-2241
E-mail: thetaskforce@thetaskforce.org
URL: http://www.ngltf.org

Description: Works to end violence and discrimination against gay, lesbian, bisexual, and transgendered people at the state, local, and federal level. Does grassroots organizing, training, and legislative advocacy. Monitors and tracks legislation in 50 states. Houses GLBT think tank producing research and analysis on GLBT issues. Maintains speakers' bureau.

★14498★ **National Organization of Gay and Lesbian Scientists and Technical Professionals (NOGLSTP)**

PO Box 91803
Pasadena, CA 91109
Ph: (626)791-7689   Fax: (626)791-7689
E-mail: office@noglstp.org
URL: http://www.noglstp.org

Members: Gay and lesbian individuals employed or interested in high-technology or scientific fields; interested organizations. **Purpose:** Works to: educate the public, especially the gay and scientific communities; improve members' employment and professional environment; provide role models through mentoring and recognition awards; interact with professional organizations; foster intercity contacts among members.

Opportunities for Independent Contractors and Freelance Workers

REFERENCE WORKS

★14499★ 101 Best Freelance Careers

Macmillan Publishing Company
175 Fifth Ave.
New York, NY 10010
Ph: (646)307-5151   Fr: 800-428-5331
URL: http://www.macmillan.com/

Kelly Reno. 1999. $14.95. 209 pages. Presents a guide with 101 options for freelance careers, ranging from the tried and true to cutting edge to the unusual.

★14500★ Achieving Financial Independence As a Freelance Writer

Blue Heron Publishing
4205 SW Washington St., Ste. 303
Portland, OR 97204
Ph: (503)221-6841   Fax: (503)221-6843

Raymond Dreyfack. 2000. $16.95 (paper). 149 pages.

★14501★ Editorial Freelancing: A Practical Guide

Aletheia Publications, Inc.
46 Bell Hollow Rd.
Putnam Valley, NY 10579
Ph: (845)526-2873   Fax: (845)526-2905
E-mail: AlethPub@aol.com

Trumbull Rogers. 1995. $19.95 (paper). 212 pages. Presents what a freelancer needs to know about building a basic reference library, choosing a computer and appropriate software, marketing editorial services, determining and negotiating rates, billing, and setting up a retirement plan. Offers guidelines for establishing and equipping the home office, finding and keeping clients, and maintaining business records.

★14502★ Freelance Teaching and Tutoring: How to Earn Good Money by Teaching Others What You Know

How to Books Ltd.
311 Bainbridge St.
Philadelphia, PA 19147
Ph: (215)925-5083   Fax: (215)925-1912

John T. Wilson. 1997. 120 pages. Part of the Jobs and Careers Series.

★14503★ In Concert: The Freelance Musician's Keys to Financial Success

Thimbleberry Press
1506 E. Fox. Ln.
Milwaukee, WI 53217-2853
Ph: (414)241-9711

Gail Nelson and Pamela Foard. 1994. $16.95 (paper). 91 pages.

★14504★ The Joy of Working from Home: Making a Life While Making a Living

Berrett-Koehler Publishers
235 Montgomery St., Ste. 650
San Francisco, CA 94104
Ph: (415)288-0260   Fax: (415)362-2512
Fr: 800-929-2929
E-mail: bkpub@bkpub.com
URL: http://www.bkconnection.com/

Jeff Berner. 1994. $12.95 (paper). 63 pages.

★14505★ Marketing for the Home-based Business

The McGraw-Hill Companies
PO Box 182604
Columbus, OH 43272
Fax: (614)759-3749   Fr: 877-883-5524
E-mail: customer.service@mcgraw-hill.com
URL: http://www.mcgraw-hill.com

Jeffrey P. Davidson. Second edition, 1999. $10.95 (paper). 204 pages. Addresses how to market the home-based business after you've started it.

★14506★ On Your Own: A Guide to Working Happily, Productively & Successfully at Home

Prentice Hall PTR
1 Lake St.
Upper Saddle River, NJ 07458
Ph: (201)236-7000   Fr: 800-428-5331
URL: http://www.phptr.com/index.asp?rl=1

Lionel L. Fisher. 1994. $10.95 (paper). 224 pages.

★14507★ The Perfect Business: How to Make a Million from Home with No Payroll, No Employee Headaches, No Debt, and No Sleepless Nights

Sound Ideas
1230 Ave. of the Americas
New York, NY 10020
Ph: (212)698-7000   Fax: (212)698-7007
Fr: 800-223-2336

Michael LeBoeuf. 1997. $14.95 (paper).224 pages

★14508★ Photos That Sell: The Art of Successful Freelance Photography

Watson-Guptill Publications
770 Broadway
New York, NY 10003
Ph: (646)654-5400   Fax: (646)654-5487
Fr: 800-278-8477
E-mail: info@watsonguptill.com
URL: http://www.watsonguptill.com

Lee Frost. 2004. $27.95 (paper). 192 pages.

★14509★ Rocky Mountain Publishing Professionals Guild-Directory

Rocky Mountain Publishing Professionals Guild
PO Box 17721
Boulder, CO 80308-7721
Ph: (303)282-9294
URL: http://www.rmppg.org

Annual. Included in membership. Covers approximately 60 freelancers serving the publishing industry nationwide. Entries include: Name, address, phone, fax, description of services offered, list of representative clients, year founded. Arrangement: Alphabetical. Indexes: Service.

★14510★ Self-Employed Writers and Artists Network-Directory

Self-Employed Writers and Artists
Network Inc.
PO Box 440
Paramus, NJ 07653
Ph: (201)967-1313
URL: http://www.swan-net.com

Annual, spring. Covers over 135 freelance writers, graphic designers, illustrators, photographers, and other graphic arts professionals in northern New Jersey and New York city providing services in advertising, marketing, sales promotion, public relations, and telecommunications. Entries include: Name, address, phone, biographical data, description of services provided. Arrangement: Alphabetical. Indexes: Line of business.

★14511★ Self-Publishing Manual

Para Publishing
530 Ellwood Ridge
PO Box 8206-240
Santa Barbara, CA 93117-1047
Ph: (805)968-7277   Fax: (805)968-1379
Fr: 800-727-2782
URL: http://www.parapublishing.com

Biennial, odd years. $19.95 for individuals. Publication includes: Lists of wholesalers, reviewers, exporters, suppliers, direct mailing list sources, publishing organizations, and others of assistance in publishing. Entries include: Organization or company name, address, e-mail address and web address. Arrangement: Classified by ZIP code. Indexes: General subject.

★14512★ Streetwise Guide to Freelance Design and Illustration

Writers Digest Books
4700 E. Galbraith Rd.
Cincinnati, OH 45236
Ph: (513)531-2690   Fax: (513)531-4082
Fr: 800-289-0963
E-mail: writersdig@fwpubs.com
URL: http://www.writersdigest.com

Theo S. Williams. 1998. $24.99 (paper). 144 pages.

★14513★ Working Solo Sourcebook: Essential Resources for Independent Entrepreneurs

John Wiley & Sons Inc.
1 Wiley Dr.
Somerset, NJ 08873
Ph: (732)469-4400   Fax: (732)302-2300
Fr: 800-225-5945
E-mail: custserv@wiley.com
URL: http://www.wiley.com/WileyCDA/

Terri Lonier. Second edition, 1998. $24.95 (paper). 315 pages.

★14514★ WritersNet

NetConcepts L.L.C.
2820 Walton Common West, Ste. 123
Madison, WI 53718
Ph: (608)285-6600   Fr: 888-207-1109

URL: http://www.writers.net
Database covers: Internet resources, books, and other materials for writers.

ONLINE AND DATABASE SERVICES

★14515★ FreeAgent

E-mail: support@workplacehomebiz.com
URL: http://www.freeagent.com

Description: Information site provides free job board for freelance and independent contractors. Site also contains resources for hosted e-presence, tax services, and business opportunities.

★14516★ FreelanceWorkExchange.com

45 Main St., Ste. 309, No. 178
Brooklyn, NY 11201
Ph: (718)249-4822
E-mail: support@freelanceworkexchange.com
URL: http://www.freelanceworkexchange.com

Description: Project and contract search board for the freelance worker. E-mail newsletters and freelancing e-books available. **Fee:** Must register as a member; pricing based on length of membership; one month is $19.95. Trial seven-day membership available.

★14517★ Guru.com

5001 Baum Blvd., Ste. 760
Pittsburgh, PA 15213
Ph: (412)687-1316   Fax: (412)687-4466
URL: http://www.guru.com

Description: Job board specializing in contract jobs for creative and information technology professionals. Also provides online incorporation and educational opportunities for independent contractors along with articles and advice.

★14518★ Work from Home

URL: http://www.jobs-telecommuting.com

Description: Contains a listing of over 700 companies currently looking for telecommuters. Employers may add or remove job listings. Also information on starting a home business available.

OTHER SOURCES

★14519★ American Society of Journalists and Authors (ASJA)

1501 Broadway, Ste. 302
New York, NY 10036
Ph: (212)997-0947   Fax: (212)937-2315

E-mail: execdir@asja.org
URL: http://www.asja.org

Description: Represents freelance writers of nonfiction magazine articles and books. Seeks to elevate the professional and economic position of nonfiction writers, provide a forum for discussion of common problems among writers and editors, and promote a code of ethics for writers and editors. Operates writer referral service for individuals, institutions, or companies seeking writers for special projects; sponsors Llewellyn Miller Fund to aid professional writers who no longer able to work due to age, disability, or extraordinary professional crisis.

★14520★ American Society of Media Photographers (ASMP)

150 N 2nd St.
Philadelphia, PA 19106
Ph: (215)451-2767   Fax: (215)451-0880
E-mail: mopsik@asmp.org
URL: http://www.asmp.org

Members: Professional society of freelance photographers. **Purpose:** Works to evolve trade practices for photographers in communications fields. Provides business information to photographers and their potential clients; promotes ethics and rights of members. **Activities:** Holds educational programs and seminars. Compiles statistics.

★14521★ Association of Food Journalists (AFJ)

7 Avienda Vista Grande, Ste. B7 467
Santa Fe, NM 87508-9199
E-mail: caroldemasters@yahoo.com
URL: http://www.afjonline.com

Description: Represents individuals employed as food journalists by newspapers, magazines, internet services, and broadcasters; freelance food journalists. Aims to encourage communication and professional development among food journalists and to increase members' knowledge of food and food-related issues. Promotes professional ethical standards.

★14522★ Copywriter's Council of America (CCA)

CCA Bldg.
PO Box 102
Middle Island, NY 11953-0102
Ph: (631)924-8555   Fax: (631)924-3890
E-mail: cca4dmcopy@att.net
URL: http://lgroup.addr.com/freelance.htm

Description: Advertising copywriters, marketing and public relations consultants, copyeditors, proofreaders, and other individuals involved in print, radio, broadcast, video, and telecommunications. Provides freelance work; acts as agent for members; negotiates on members' behalf. Serves as a forum for professional and social contact between freelance communications professionals. Offers courses on copywriting, direct marketing, mail order, publishing screenplays, and how to get published. Conducts charitable programs. Maintains speakers' bureau, hall of fame, and word processing consultation service.

★14523★ Dance Critics Association (DCA)

PO Box 1882
Old Chelsea Sta.
New York, NY 10011
E-mail: dancecritics@hotmail.com
URL: http://www.dancecritics.org

Description: Critics who review dance as a major professional responsibility either on a regular basis or as a freelance reviewer, in print and/or broadcast media; teachers, historians, publicists, and other individuals interested in dance writing. Encourages excellence in dance criticism through education, research, and the exchange of ideas. Conducts clinics on practical topics of interest to critics.

★14524★ National Court Reporters Association (NCRA)

8224 Old Courthouse Rd.
Vienna, VA 22182-3808
Ph: (703)556-6272   Fax: (703)556-6291
Fr: 800-272-6272
E-mail: msic@ncrahq.org
URL: http://www.ncraonline.org

Description: Represents Independent state, regional, and local associations. Verbatim court reporters who work as official reporters for courts and government agencies, as freelance reporters for independent contractors, and as captioners for television programming; retired reporters, teachers of court reporting, and school officials; student court reporters. Conducts research; compiles statistics; offers several certification programs; and publishes journal.

★14525★ National Writers Association (NWA)

10940 S Parker Rd., No. 508
Parker, CO 80134
Ph: (303)841-0246   Fax: (303)841-2607
E-mail: anitaedits@aol.com
URL: http://www.nationalwriters.com

Members: Professional full- or part-time freelance writers who specialize in business writing. **Purpose:** Aims to serve as a marketplace whereby business editors can easily locate competent writing talent. **Activities:** Establishes communication among editors and writers.

★14526★ National Writers Union (NWU)

113 University Pl., 6th Fl.
New York, NY 10003
Ph: (212)254-0279   Fax: (212)254-0673
E-mail: nwu@nwu.org
URL: http://www.nwu.org

Members: Freelance writers; journalists, authors, poets, and technical and public relations writers who are not represented by any existing union. **Purpose:** Engages in collective bargaining and provides other services for members such as grievance handling and health insurance. Works to raise rates and improve treatment of freelance writers by magazine and book publishers. Holds conferences on legal, economic, trade, and craft issues affecting writers.

Opportunities for Liberal Arts Graduates

REFERENCE WORKS

★14527★ The Career Guide-Dun's Employment Opportunities Directory
Dun & Bradstreet Corp.
103 JFK Pkwy.
Short Hills, NJ 07078
Ph: (973)921-5500   Fax: (973)921-6056
Fr: 800-234-3867
URL: http://dnb.com/us/
Annual. Covers more than 5,000 leading employers throughout the U.S. that provide career opportunities in sales, marketing, management, engineering, life and physical sciences, computer science, mathematics, statistics planning, accounting and finance, liberal arts fields, and other technical and professional areas; based on data supplied on questionnaires and through personal interviews. Also covers personnel consultants; includes some public sector employers (governments, schools, etc.) usually not found in similar lists. Entries include: Company name, location of headquarters and other offices or plants; entries may also include name, title, address, and phone of employment contact; disciplines or occupational groups hired; brief overview of company, discussion of types of positions that may be available, training and career development programs, benefits offered, internship and work-study programs. Arrangement: Employers are alphabetical; geographically by industry; employer branch offices geographically; disciplines hired geographically; employers offering work-study or internship programs and personnel consultants. Indexes: Geographical; SIC code.

★14528★ Career Planning & Development for College Students & Recent Graduates
The McGraw-Hill Companies
PO Box 182604
Columbus, OH 43272
Fax: (614)759-3749   Fr: 877-883-5524
E-mail: customer.service@mcgraw-hill.com
URL: http://www.mcgraw-hill.com
John E. Steele and Marilyn S. Morgan. 1995. $29.95; $17.95 (paper). 430 pages.

★14529★ College Grad Job Hunter: Insider Techniques and Tactics for Finding a Top-Paying Entry Level Job
Adams Media Corp.
57 Littlefield St.
Avon, MA 02322
Ph: (508)427-7100   Fax: (508)427-6790
Fr: 800-872-5627
URL: http://www.adamsmedia.com
Brian D. Krueger. Fifth edition, 2003. $14.95 (paper). 352 pages.

★14530★ Great Jobs for English Majors
The McGraw-Hill Companies
PO Box 182604
Columbus, OH 43272
Fax: (614)759-3749   Fr: 877-883-5524
E-mail: customer.service@mcgraw-hill.com
URL: http://www.mcgraw-hill.com
Julie DeGalan. Third edition, 2006. $15.95 (paper). 192 pages.

★14531★ Great Jobs for Foreign Language Majors
The McGraw-Hill Companies
PO Box 182604
Columbus, OH 43272
Fax: (614)759-3749   Fr: 877-883-5524
E-mail: customer.service@mcgraw-hill.com
URL: http://www.mcgraw-hill.com
Julie DeGalan and Stephen Lambert. Second edition, 2000. $15.95 (paper). 192 pages. Part of "Great Jobs for ... Majors" series.

★14532★ Great Jobs for History Majors
The McGraw-Hill Companies
PO Box 182604
Columbus, OH 43272
Fax: (614)759-3749   Fr: 877-883-5524
E-mail: customer.service@mcgraw-hill.com
URL: http://www.mcgraw-hill.com
Julie DeGalan and Stephen Lambert. 2001. $15.95 (paper). 256 pages.

★14533★ Great Jobs for Liberal Arts Majors
The McGraw-Hill Companies
PO Box 182604
Columbus, OH 43272
Fax: (614)759-3749   Fr: 877-883-5524
E-mail: customer.service@mcgraw-hill.com
URL: http://www.mcgraw-hill.com
Blythe Camenson. Second edition, 2001. $14.95 (paper). 256 pages.

★14534★ The Liberal Arts Advantage
HarperCollins
10 E. 53rd St.
New York, NY 10022
Ph: (212)207-7000   Fr: 800-242-7737
URL: http://www.harpercollins.com/
Gregory Giangrande. 1998. $12.00 (paper). 184 pages. How to find the right company, create the perfect resume, land a hard to-get interview, make the most of that all-important meeting, and more.

★14535★ Opening Doors: A Job Search Guide for Graduates
The Graduate Group
PO Box 370351
West Hartford, CT 06137-0351
Ph: (860)233-2330   Fax: (860)233-2330
Fr: 800-484-7280
E-mail: graduategroup@hotmail.com
URL: http://www.graduategroup.com
Janet G. Revelt. 1996. $27.50 (paper).

★14536★ Path: A Career Workbook for Liberal Arts Students
Sulzburger & Graham Publishing, Ltd.
793 Arbuckle Ave.
Woodmere, NY 11598-2723
Ph: (212)947-0100   Fax: (212)947-0360
Fr: 800-366-7086
Howard E. Figler and Gordon Brooks. Third edition, 1993. $13.50. 128 pages.

★14537★ Peterson's Job Opportunities for Business Majors

Peterson's
Princeton Pke. Corporate Ctr., 2000
  Lenox Dr.
PO Box 67005
Lawrenceville, NJ 08648
Ph: (609)896-1800   Fax: (609)896-4531
Fr: 800-338-3282
URL: http://www.petersons.com/

Irregular; latest edition 16th, 2000. Covers the 2,000 largest U.S. employers hiring in several fields, including financial services, management consulting, consumer products, and media/entertainment. Entries include: Organization name, address, phone, name and title of contact, number of employees, type of organization. Arrangement: Alphabetical. Indexes: Type of organization.

★14538★ Real Life Guide to Starting Your Career: How to Get the Right Job Right Now!

TIPS Technical Publishing, Inc.
108 E. Main St., Ste. 4
Carrboro, NC 27510-2374
Ph: (919)933-2629   Fax: (919)832-9717

Margot C. Lester. 1998. $16.95 (paper). 193 pages. Part of the "Real Life Guides Series."

ONLINE AND DATABASE SERVICES

★14539★ College Job Board.com
766 Turnpike St.
Canton, MA 02021
Ph: (781)821-0045

E-mail: contactus@myjobboard.com
URL: http://www.collegejobboard.com

Description: Job search site specializing in the career search of recent college, vocational and grad school graduates. Free resume posting, job board search, job tracking, scholarship and loan search and career resources.

★14540★ True Careers: Campus
12061 Bluemont Way
Reston, VA 20190
Fr: 800-441-4062
URL: http://www.truecareerscampus.com/

Description: Recent college graduates can post their resume and search for jobs. Also contains interviewing tips and career resources, and career expert advice posting.

Opportunities for Military Personnel and Veterans

REFERENCE WORKS

★14541★ Affirmative Action Register

Affirmative Action Register
8356 Olive Blvd.
St. Louis, MO 63132
Ph: (314)991-1335   Fax: (314)997-1788
Fr: 800-537-0655
URL: http://www.aar-eeo.com

Monthly. Covers, in each issue, about 300 positions at a professional level (most requiring advanced study) available to women, minorities, veterans, and the handicapped; listings are advertisements placed by employers with affirmative action programs. Entries include: Company or organization name, address, contact name; description of position including title, requirements, duties, application procedure, salary, etc. Arrangement: Classified by profession.

★14542★ America's Top Military Careers: The Official Guide to Occupations in the Armed Forces

Jist Publishing
875 Montreal Way
St. Paul, MN 55102
Fr: 800-648-5478
E-mail: info@jist.com
URL: http://www.jist.com

JIST Publishing staff. Fourth edition, 2003. $24.95 (paper). 384 pages.

★14543★ Career Opportunities in the Armed Forces

Facts On File Inc.
132 W 31st St., 17th Fl.
New York, NY 10001
Ph: (212)967-8800   Fax: 800-678-3633
Fr: 800-322-8755
URL: http://www.factsonfile.com

Latest edition 2nd, 2007. $49.50 for individuals; $44.55 for libraries. Covers 80 jobs from all branches of the service with emphasis not only on the career opportunities available in the military, but how military experience can be applied to a career in the civilian world; among the jobs profiled are communications manager, special operations officer, aerospace engineer, physicist, physician/surgeon, social worker, firefighter, and air traffic controller.

★14544★ Career Progression Guide for Soldiers

Stackpole Books
5067 Ritter Rd.
Mechanicsburg, PA 17055
Ph: (717)796-0411   Fax: (717)796-0412
Fr: 800-732-3669
URL: http://www.stackpolebooks.com

Audie G. Lewis. Second revised edition, 2003. $14.95 (paper). 160 pages.

★14545★ The Civilian Career Guide

Grant's Guide, Inc.
PO Box 613
Lake Placid, NY 12946
Ph: (518)523-3498   Fax: (518)523-2974
Fr: 800-922-1923

James L. Grant, editor. 1993. $9.95 (paper). 220 pages.

★14546★ Employment Guide for the Military, Intelligence and Special Operations Communities

The Graduate Group
PO Box 370351
West Hartford, CT 06137-0351
Ph: (860)233-2330   Fax: (860)233-2330
Fr: 800-484-7280
E-mail: graduategroup@hotmail.com
URL: http://www.graduategroup.com

Mark W. Merritt. 1997. $27.50

★14547★ Financial Aid for Veterans, Military Personnel, and Their Dependents

Reference Service Press
5000 Windplay Dr., Ste. 4
El Dorado Hills, CA 95762-9600
Ph: (916)939-9620   Fax: (916)939-9626
URL: http://www.rspfunding.com

Biennial, January of even years; latest edition 2004-2006 edition. $40.00 for individuals. Covers organizations that offer approximately 1,100 scholarships, fellowships, loans, grants, awards, and internships to veterans, military personnel, and their families. Entries include: Organization name, address, phone, financial data, requirements for eligibility, duration, special features and limitations, deadline, number of awards. Arrangement: Classified by type of program and target audience. Indexes: Organization name, program, residency, tenability, subject, and deadline date.

★14548★ Future Career Management Systems for U.S. Military Officers

Rand Corp.
PO Box 2138
Santa Monica, CA 90407-2138
Ph: (310)393-0411   Fax: (310)393-4818
URL: http://www.rand.org/

Harry A.Thie and Roger A. Brown. 1994. $15.00 (paper). 372 pages.

★14549★ A Guide to Civilian Jobs for Enlisted Naval Personnel

Barron's Educational Series, Inc.
250 Wireless Blvd.
Hauppauge, NY 11788-3917
Ph: (631)434-3311   Fax: (631)434-3723
Fr: 800-645-3476
E-mail: fbrown@barronseduc.com
URL: http://barronseduc.com

Rodney Voelker. 1996. $14.95 (paper). 392 pages.

★14550★ IMCEA-Membership Directory

International Military Community Executives Association
1530 Dunwoody Village Pky., Ste. 203
Atlanta, GA 30338
Ph: (770)396-2101   Fax: (770)396-2198
URL: http://www.imcea.com/

Annual, May. Covers about 1,000 Navy, Army, Air Force, Marine Corps, and Coast Guard personnel who manage military clubs and golf and bowling centers; supplier members are also listed. Entries include: For military club and Morale, Welfare and Recreation (MWR) personnel–Name, office address and phone. For suppliers–Company name, address, product or service. Arrangement: Personnel are alphabetical; suppliers are classified by product, then alphabetical. Indexes: Geographical, product.

★14551★ In or Out of the Military: How to Make Your Own Best Decision

Pepper Press
1254 W. Pioneer Way, Ste. A266
Oak Harbor, WA 98277-3288
D.F. Reardon. 1993. $14.95 (paper). 108 pages.

★14552★ Job Search: Marketing Your Military Experience

Stackpole Books
5067 Ritter Rd.
Mechanicsburg, PA 17055
Ph: (717)796-0411   Fax: (717)796-0412
Fr: 800-732-3669
URL: http://www.stackpolebooks.com

David G. Henderson. Fourth edition, 2004. $16.95 (paper). 240 pages.

★14553★ Millitary-to-Civilian Career Transition Guide: The Essential Job Search Handbook for Service Members

JIST Publishing
875 Montreal Way
St. Paul, MN 55102
Fax: 800-547-8329   Fr: 800-648-5478
E-mail: info@jist.com
URL: http://www.jist.com

Janet I. Farley. 2005. $15.95. 208 pages. Provides a framework for career transition for service members leaving any branch of the military; includes step-by-step directions, checklists, worksheets, and sample resumes.

★14554★ Opportunities in Aerospace Careers

The McGraw-Hill Companies
PO Box 182604
Columbus, OH 43272
Fax: (614)759-3749   Fr: 877-883-5524
E-mail: customer.service@mcgraw-hill.com
URL: http://www.mcgraw-hill.com

Wallace R. Maples. Third edition, 2002 $13.95 (paper). 160 pages. Surveys jobs with the airlines, airports, the government, the military, in manufacturing, and in research and development. Includes information on job opportunities with NASA in the U.S. space program.

★14555★ Opportunities in Law Enforcement and Criminal Justice Careers

The McGraw-Hill Companies
PO Box 182604
Columbus, OH 43272
Fax: (614)759-3749   Fr: 877-883-5524
E-mail: customer.service@mcgraw-hill.com

URL: http://www.mcgraw-hill.com

James Stinchcomb. Second edition, 2002. $13.95 (paper). 160 pages. Offers information on opportunities at the city, county, state, military, and federal levels. Contains bibliography and illustrations.

★14556★ Opportunities in Military Careers

The McGraw-Hill Companies
PO Box 182604
Columbus, OH 43272
Fax: (614)759-3749   Fr: 877-883-5524
E-mail: customer.service@mcgraw-hill.com
URL: http://www.mcgraw-hill.com

Adrian A. Paradis. 2005. $14.95; $13.95 (paper). 159 pages. Illustrates what it's like to work in a variety of job situations unique to the armed forces. Opportunities for civilian employment are also included. Illustrated.

★14557★ Punching Out: Launching a Post-Military Career

St. Martin's Press, LLC
175 5th Ave.
New York, NY 10010
Ph: (212)726-0200   Fax: (212)686-9491
Fr: 800-470-4767
URL: http://www.stmartins.com

Fred Mastin. 1994. $22.00. 196 pages.

★14558★ Yes, There Is Life after Aerospace: Career Transition from Military Defense Aerospace to Commercial Civilian Life

A B P Associates
116 W. Santa Fe Ave.
Placentia, CA 92870-5632
Ph: (909)982-7595

Marie H. Reichelt. 1994. $14.95 (paper). 126 pages.

NEWSPAPERS, MAGAZINES, AND JOURNALS

★14559★ Air Force Times

Army Times Publishing Co.
6883 Commercial Dr.
Springfield, VA 22159-0500
Ph: (703)750-7400   Fr: 800-368-5718
URL: http://www.airforcetimes.com

Weekly (Mon.). $55.00/year for individuals, 52 issues. Independent newspaper serving Air Force personnel worldwide.

★14560★ Armed Forces Journal International

Defense News Media Group
6883 Commercial Dr.
Springfield, VA 22159
Ph: (703)642-7330   Fax: (703)642-7386
Fr: 800-252-5825

URL: http://www.armedforcesjournal.com/

Periodic. Free, qualified individuals. Magazine concerning the armed services, national security, and defense.

★14561★ Army Aviation Magazine

Army Aviation Publications Inc.
755 Main St. Ste. 4D
Monroe, CT 06468-2830
E-mail: magazine@quad-a.org
URL: http://www.quad-a.org/magazine.htm

Monthly. $30.00/year for individuals; $3.00/year for single issue. Army aviation magazine.

★14562★ Checkpoint

Veterans of Foreign Wars of the United States
VFW National Headquarters
406 W. 34th St.
Kansas City, MO 64111
Ph: (816)756-3390   Fax: (816)968-1177
E-mail: RCherry@vfw.org
URL: http://www.vfw.org

Description: Six issues/year. Concerned with the organization's work of promoting patriotism. Covers national news of the VFW's community service activities, holiday observances, patriotic promotion campaigns, youth activities, safety, etc. Recurring features include editorials, legislation updates, veterans services, employment opportunities, and national security/foreign affairs.

★14563★ G.I. Jobs

Victory Media Inc.
PO Box 26
Sewickley, PA 15143
Ph: (412)269-1663   Fax: (412)291-2772
URL: http://www.gijobs.net/

Monthly. $19.95/year. Magazine for military personnel transitioning to civilian employment or seeking civilian education.

★14564★ Military Medicine

AMSUS - The Society of the Federal Health Agencies
9320 Old Georgetown Rd.
Bethesda, MD 20814
Ph: (301)897-8800   Fax: (301)503-5446
Fr: 800-761-9320
URL: http://www.amsus.org/journal/

Monthly. $132.00/year for individuals; $177.00/year for other countries; $20.00 for single issue; $27.00 for single issue, other countries. Journal for professional personnel affiliated with the Federal medical services.

★14565★ National Military Family Association Public Relations & Marketing

National Military Family Association Inc.
2500 N. Van Dorn St., Ste. 102
Alexandria, VA 22302-1601
Ph: (703)931-6632   Fax: (703)931-4600
Fr: 800-260-0218
E-mail: families@nmfa.org

URL: http://www.nmfa.org

Description: Monthly. Reports on current and proposed legislation affecting military families, quality of military life, and problems facing military families. Covers topics such as health care, relocation and housing, spouse employment, education, and retirement and survivor benefits. Recurring features include Association news and legislative updates.

★14566★ *Navy Times*

Army Times Publishing Co.
6883 Commercial Dr.
Springfield, VA 22159-0500
Ph: (703)750-7400   Fr: 800-368-5718
URL: http://www.navytimes.com/

Weekly (Mon.). Independent newspaper serving Navy, Marine, and Coast Guard personnel.

★14567★ *The Officer*

The Reserve Officers Association
1 Constitution Ave. NE
Washington, DC 20002
Ph: (202)479-2200   Fax: (202)547-1641
Fr: 800-809-9448
URL: http://www.roa.org/site/PageServer?pagename=publications

$12.00/year for individuals; $1.15 for single issue. Magazine for active and reserve officers of all uniformed services.

ONLINE AND DATABASE SERVICES

★14568★ Today's Military

URL: http://www.todaysmilitary.com/app/tm/careers

Description: Site provides details on many enlisted and officer occupations and describes training, advancement, and educational services within each of the major services. Includes browsing capabilities to match positions with interests.

SOFTWARE

★14569★ COIN Career Guidance System

COIN Educational Products
3361 Executive Pky., Ste. 302
Toledo, OH 43606
Ph: (419)536-5353   Fax: (419)536-7056
Fr: 800-274-8515
URL: http://www.coinedu.com/

CD-ROM. Provides career information through seven cross-referenced files covering postsecondary schools, college majors, vocational programs, military service, ap-

prenticeship programs, financial aid, and scholarships. Apprenticeship file describes national apprenticeship training programs, including information on how to apply, contact agencies, and program content. Military file describes more than 200 military occupations and training opportunities related to civilian employment.

OTHER SOURCES

★14570★ Air Force Association (AFA)

1501 Lee Hwy.
Arlington, VA 22209-1198
Ph: (703)247-5800   Fax: (703)247-5853
Fr: 800-727-3337
E-mail: polcom@afa.org
URL: http://www.afa.org

Description: Promotes public understanding of aerospace power and the pivotal role it plays in the security of the nation.

★14571★ American Military Retirees Association (AMRA)

5436 Peru St., Ste. 1
Plattsburgh, NY 12901
Ph: (518)563-9479   Fax: (518)324-5204
Fr: 800-424-2969
E-mail: info@amra1973.org
URL: http://www.amra1973.org

Description: Persons honorably retired for length of service or disability from all branches and grades of the armed forces and their widows or widowers; persons still on active duty. Aims to: maintain "COLA" Program; authorization for all military retirees regardless of age; maintain adequate care at military/VA medical facilities. Works to support or oppose Legislation in the best interests of members and to protect the earned privileges and benefits of military retirees. Testifies before Congress on Legislation affecting members. Sponsors Letter-writing campaigns. Offers supplemental health insurance program. Member of National Military and Veterans Alliance.

★14572★ Army Aviation Association of America (AAAA)

755 Main St., Ste. 4D
Monroe, CT 06468-2830
Ph: (203)268-2450   Fax: (203)268-5870
E-mail: aaaa@quad-a.org
URL: http://www.quad-a.org

Description: Commissioned officers, warrant officers, and enlisted personnel serving in U.S. Army aviation assignments in the active U.S. Army, Army National Guard, and Army Reserve; Department of Army civilian personnel and industry representatives affiliated with army aviation. Fosters fellowship among military and civilian persons connected with army aviation, past or present; seeks to advance status, overall esprit, and general knowledge of professionals engaged in army aviation. Activities include locator and placement services, technical assis-

tance, and biographical archives. Sponsors speakers' bureau; maintains hall of fame.

★14573★ Army and Navy Union, U.S.A. (ANU)

2178 Harmon Ave.
Niles, OH 44446
Ph: (330)673-9373   Fax: (330)673-8371
E-mail: anu@armynavy.net
URL: http://www.armynavy.net

Description: Servicemen and veterans of the armed forces during peace or war. Participates in veterans service work of all types. Provides children's services. Maintains nine county councils and 11 departments.

★14574★ Association of Graduates of the United States Air Force Academy (AOG)

3116 Academy Dr.
USAF Academy, CO 80840-4475
Ph: (719)472-0300   Fax: (719)333-4194
E-mail: aog@usafa.org
URL: http://www.usafa.org

Description: Graduates and friends of the U.S. Air Force Academy. Promotes interest in and dedication to the mission, ideals, objectives, activities, and history of the Academy; encourages young people to attend the Academy; encourages and supports fundraising for the Academy; fosters camaraderie among Academy graduates and U.S. armed forces officer corps; professional development of the armed forces officer corps. Sponsors annual class reunions/homecomings. Offers scholarships to graduates of the academy and their dependents; provides placement service. Operates charitable program, including humanitarian support for next-of-kin of academy graduates. Compiles statistics.

★14575★ Association of the United States Army (AUSA)

2425 Wilson Blvd.
Arlington, VA 22201
Ph: (703)841-4300   Fax: (703)525-9039
Fr: 800-336-4570
E-mail: ausa-info@ausa.org
URL: http://www.ausa.org

Members: Professional society of: active, retired, and reserve military personnel; West Point and Army ROTC cadets; civilians interested in national defense. **Purpose:** Seeks to advance the security of the United States and consolidate the efforts of all who support the United States Army as an indispensable instrument of national security. **Activities:** Conducts industrial symposia for manufacturers of Army weapons and equipment, and those in the Department of the Army who plan, develop, test, and use weapons and equipment. Symposia subjects have included guided missiles, army aviation, electronics and communication, telemedicine, vehicles, and armor. Sponsors monthly PBS TV series America's Army.

★14576★ Blinded Veterans Association (BVA)

477 H St. NW
Washington, DC 20001-2694
Ph: (202)371-8880   Fax: (202)371-8258
Fr: 800-669-7079
E-mail: bva@bva.org
URL: http://www.bva.org

Description: Veterans who lost their sight as a result of military service in the armed forces of the U.S.; associate members are veterans whose loss of sight was not connected with military service. Assists blinded veterans in attaining benefits and employment and with reestablishing themselves as adjusted, active, and productive citizens in their communities. Offers placement service; supports research programs; compiles statistics. Constructs initiatives designed to improve blind rehabilitation programs for veterans.

★14577★ Federal Employees Veterans Association (FEVA)

PO Box 183
Merion Station, PA 19066

Members: Federal government employees who have veterans' preference in federal employment under the G. I. Bill. **Purpose:** Works to maintain and increase veterans' preference in federal employment and prevent "the discrimination against the veteran that was rampant in federal agencies in the post-World War II era."

★14578★ Marine Corps Association (MCA)

715 Broadway St.
Quantico, VA 22134
Ph: (703)640-6161   Fax: (703)640-0823
Fr: 800-336-0291
E-mail: mca@mca-marine.org
URL: http://www.mca-marines.org

Description: Represents active duty, reserve, retired, Fleet Reserve, honorably discharged Marines, and members of other services who have served with Marine Corps units. Disseminates information about the military arts and sciences to members; assists members' professional advancement; fosters the spirit and works to preserve the traditions of the United States Marine Corps. Maintains discount book service and group insurance plan for members. Association founded by members of the Second Provisional Marine Brigade at Guantanamo Bay, Cuba.

★14579★ Marine Corps Reserve Association (MCRA)

2020 General Booth Blvd., Ste. 200
Virginia Beach, VA 23454
Ph: (757)301-2032   Fax: (757)301-6884
Fr: 800-927-6270
E-mail: kathleen@usmcra.org
URL: http://www.mcrassn.org

Description: Marines who have served on active duty in peace or war. Seeks to: advance the professional skills of marines; represent and assist individual members;

promote the interests of the U.S. Marine Corps in order to advance the welfare and preserve the security of the United States. Maintains speakers' bureau and placement service.

★14580★ Military Officers Association of America (MOAA)

201 N Washington St.
Alexandria, VA 22314-2520
Ph: (703)549-2311   Fax: (703)838-8173
Fr: 800-234-6622
E-mail: msc@moaa.org
URL: http://www.moaa.org

Members: Active duty, retired, National Guard, Reserve, former commissioned officers, warrant officers of the following uniformed services and their surviving spouse: Army, Marine Corps, Navy, Air Force, Coast Guard, Public Health Service, NOAA. **Purpose:** Supports strong national defense and represents and assists members, their dependents and survivors with active duty and retirement issues and benefits. **Activities:** Sponsors educational assistance program, survivor assistance, and travel, insurance, and career transition services.

★14581★ National Association for Uniformed Services (NAUS)

5535 Hempstead Way
Springfield, VA 22151-4094
Ph: (703)750-1342   Fax: (703)354-4380
E-mail: info@naus.org
URL: http://www.naus.org

Members: Members of the uniformed military services, active, retired or reserve, veteran, enlisted and officers, and their spouses or widows. **Purpose:** Develops and supports legislation that upholds the security of the U.S., sustains the morale of the uniformed services, and provides fair and equitable consideration for all service people. Protects and improves compensation, entitlements, and benefits. **Activities:** Provides discount rates on travel, insurance, auto rentals, charge cards, prescription medicine, and legal services.

★14582★ National Naval Officers Association (NNOA)

PO Box 10871
Alexandria, VA 22310-0871
Ph: (703)997-1068
E-mail: webmaster@nnoa.org
URL: http://www.nnoa.org

Members: Active, reserve, and retired Navy, Marine, and Coast Guard officers and students in college and military sea service programs. **Purpose:** Promotes and assists recruitment, retention, and career development of minority officers in the naval service. **Activities:** Conducts specialized education; maintains counseling, referral, and mentorship. Makes available non-ROTC grants-in-aid. Sponsors competitions; operates charitable program.

★14583★ National Veterans Outreach Program (NVOP)

5038 W 127th St.
Alsip, IL 60803
Ph: (708)371-9800   Fax: (708)371-1150

Description: A program sponsored by the American G.I. Forum of United States funded by local, state, and national government contracts. **Purpose:** Provides services to the economically disadvantaged, recently separated veterans (within the last 48 months), and Vietnam era veterans. **Activities:** Counsels veterans in making a smooth transition to the civilian community and mobilizes and coordinates all available resources serving veterans. Provides family counseling to Vietnam veterans who served in or near Vietnam between 1961-1972. Works with the private sector and local, state, and national employment services in order to place the economically disadvantaged and veterans in meaningful jobs. Offers V.A. benefit counseling and outreach follow-up and referral, including field counseling, home contacts, public service announcements, and street leaflet distribution.

★14584★ Non Commissioned Officers Association of the United States of America (NCOA)

10635 IH 35 N
San Antonio, TX 78233
Ph: (210)653-6161   Fax: (210)637-3337
Fr: 800-662-2620
E-mail: natdir@ncoausa.org
URL: http://www.ncoausa.org

Description: Noncommissioned and petty officers of the United States military serving in grades E1 through E9 from all five branches of the U.S. Armed Forces; includes active duty and retired personnel, members of the Reserve and National Guard components, and personnel who held the rank of NCO/PO at the time of separation from active duty under honorable conditions. Formed for patriotic, fraternal, social, and benevolent purposes. Offers veterans job assistance, legislative representation, and grants. Conducts charitable programs.

★14585★ Vietnam Veterans Against the War (VVAW)

PO Box 408594
Chicago, IL 60640
Ph: (773)276-4189
E-mail: vvaw@vvaw.org
URL: http://www.vvaw.org

Description: Works for: improvement of VA conditions and job opportunities; elimination of the possibility of future military conflicts such as Vietnam; no draft or registration; testing and treatment of Agent Orange poisoning. Offers traumatic stress disorder counseling and discharge upgrading; provides Agent Orange self-help information.

★14586★ Vietnam Veterans of America (VVA)
8605 Cameron St., No. 400
Silver Spring, MD 20910
Ph: (301)585-4000   Fax: (301)585-0519
Fr: 800-NAM-VETS
E-mail: communications@vva.org

URL: http://www.vva.org

Members: Acts as congressionally chartered, nationwide veterans service organization formed specifically for Vietnam veterans. **Purpose:** Aims to work for the employment, education benefits, improved psychological assistance, and health care of Vietnam veterans. **Activities:** Provides referral services and research and public information programs to help veterans in developing a positive identification with their Vietnam service and with fellow veterans. Offers annual training for veterans service representatives.

Opportunities for Minorities

REFERENCE WORKS

★14587★ Affirmative Action Register

Affirmative Action Register
8356 Olive Blvd.
St. Louis, MO 63132
Ph: (314)991-1335   Fax: (314)997-1788
Fr: 800-537-0655
URL: http://www.aar-eeo.com

Monthly. Covers, in each issue, about 300 positions at a professional level (most requiring advanced study) available to women, minorities, veterans, and the handicapped; listings are advertisements placed by employers with affirmative action programs. Entries include: Company or organization name, address, contact name; description of position including title, requirements, duties, application procedure, salary, etc. Arrangement: Classified by profession.

★14588★ American Indian National Business Directory

National Center for American Indian
  Enterprise Development
953 E Juanita Ave.
Mesa, AZ 85204
Ph: (480)545-1298   Fax: (480)545-4208
Fr: 800-462-2433
URL: http://www.ncaied.org/

Annual, May. Covers firms offering professional, commercial, and industrial products and services. Entries include: Firm name, address, phone, name and title of owner or chief executive, product or service, year established, work locations, license type/specialty, bonding capacity/sales. Arrangement: Classified by line of business.

★14589★ Best Careers for Bilingual Latinos

The McGraw-Hill Companies
PO Box 182604
Columbus, OH 43272
Fax: (614)759-3749   Fr: 877-883-5524
E-mail: customer.service@mcgraw-hill.com
URL: http://www.mcgraw-hill.com

Graciela Kenig. 1998. $14.95 (paper). 256 pages.

★14590★ Black Enterprise-Top Black Businesses Issue

Earl Graves Publishing Co.
130 5th Ave., 10th Fl.
New York, NY 10011-4399
Ph: (212)242-8000   Fr: 800-727-7777
E-mail: customerservice@blackenterprise.com
URL: http://www.blackenterprise.com

Annual, June. Publication includes: Lists of 100 Black-owned industrial/service companies with sales of $18 million or above; 25 banks with total assets of $3.6 billion or more; 10 insurance companies with total assets of about $689 million or more; 100 auto dealers with sales of $17 million or above; 20 advertising agencies with total billings of $795 million or more; 15 investment banks with issues totalling $123 billion. Entries include: Company name, city and state, name of chief executive, year founded, number of employees, financial data. Arrangement: In categories, with rankings by financial size.

★14591★ Career Counseling for African Americans

Lawrence Erlbaum Associates, Inc.
10 Industrial Ave.
Mahwah, NJ 07430-2262
Ph: (201)258-2200   Fax: (201)236-0072
Fr: 800-926-6579
URL: http://www.leaonline.com

Bruce W. Walsh, Michael T. Brown, and Connie M. Ward, Editors. 2000. $55.00; $24.50 (paperback).

★14592★ Career Guide and Directory for Immigrant Professionals

Scarecrow Press Inc.
4501 Forbes Blvd., Ste. 200
Lanham, MD 20706
Ph: (301)459-3366   Fax: (301)429-5748
Fr: 800-462-6420
URL: http://www.scarecrowpress.com

Latest edition October 2003. $27.95 for individuals. Covers federal, state, local, and private career resources in the District of Columbia, Maryland, and northern Virginia. Also included is information on all aspects of advancing in the American workplace.

★14593★ Career Opportunities for Minority College Graduates

Paoli Publishing Inc.
1708 E Lancaster Ave., Ste. 287
Paoli, PA 19301
E-mail: collegeindex@aol.com

Annual; latest edition 12th, March 2002. Free. Covers over 900 companies, organizations and schools representing 24 occupational fields and five continuing educational alternatives. Entries include: Name, address, personnel contact name or department; phone and fax number listed in many entries. Arrangement: Classified by occupation, then geographical.

★14594★ Coming Alive from Nine to Five: The Career Search Handbook

The McGraw-Hill Companies
PO Box 182604
Columbus, OH 43272
Fax: (614)759-3749   Fr: 877-883-5524
E-mail: customer.service@mcgraw-hill.com
URL: http://www.mcgraw-hill.com

Betty Neville Michelozzi. Seventh edition, 2003. $60.00. 360 pages. In addition to general job-hunting advice, provides special information for women, young adults, minorities, older workers, and persons with handicaps.

★14595★ Council of Asian American Business Associations of California-Directory

Council of Asian American Business
  Associations of California
1167 Mission St.
San Francisco, CA 94103
Ph: (415)928-5910   Fax: (415)921-0182
URL: http://www.caaba.org/

Annual, April. $50.00 for individuals. Covers over 2,000 Asian-American professional, commercial, and industrial firms; 10-plus trade associations. Entries include: Company name, address, phone, name of contact, product or service provided, number of employees, whether minority certified, market area, licenses; some listings include clients. Arrangement: Classified by Standard Industrial Classification (SIC) code; alphabetical. Indexes: Company name, association name, SIC number.

★14596★ **Directory of Indian Owned Businesses**

All Indian Pueblo Council Inc.
2301 Yale SE, Ste. C-B
Albuquerque, NM 87106
Ph: (505)766-9200   Fax: (505)766-8840

Annual. Covers about 200 firms offering professional, commercial, and industrial products and services in New Mexico. Entries include: Firm name, address, phone, name and title of owner or chief executive, product or service. Arrangement: Classified by Standard Industrial Classification (SIC) code. Indexes: Product/service.

★14597★ **Ferguson Career Resource Guide for Women and Minorities**

Impact Publications
9104 Manassas Dr., Ste. N
Manassas Park, VA 20111-5211
Ph: (703)361-7300   Fax: (703)335-9486
Fr: 800-361-1055
URL: http://www.impactpublications.com/

$125.00. Covers information on hundreds of organizations, colleges, foundations, and publications devoted to the careers and educational advancement of women minorities.

★14598★ **Finding a Job in the United States**

The McGraw-Hill Companies
PO Box 182604
Columbus, OH 43272
Fax: (614)759-3749   Fr: 877-883-5524
E-mail: customer.service@mcgraw-hill.com
URL: http://www.mcgraw-hill.com

John E. Friedenberg and Curtis H. Bradley. Third edition, 1994. $7.15 (paper). 120 pages. Written for those whose native language is not English. Contains job information based on the successful experience of job seekers, plus advice from the U.S. Department of Labor. Includes information about American job customs and laws related to immigration, as well as a systematic plan for job hunting.

★14599★ **Migrant Education**

ABC-CLIO
130 Cremona Dr.
PO Box 1911
Santa Barbara, CA 93117
Ph: (805)968-1911   Fax: (805)685-9685
Fr: 800-368-6868
URL: http://www.abc-clio.com

November 2001. $27.50 for individuals. Publication includes: List of additional resources for further information about migrant educa-

tion. Principal content of publication is discussion of issues facing educators who work with migrant families. Indexes: Alphabetical.

★14600★ **Minority Business Information Center**

National Minority Supplier Development Council Inc.
1040 Ave. of the Americas, 2nd Fl.
New York, NY 10018
Ph: (212)944-2430   Fax: (212)719-9611
URL: http://www.nmsdcus.org/infocenter/facts.html

Current. Updated as needed. Database covers: Approximately 350 companies that are certified by the NMSDC as minority owned. Database includes: Company name, address, phone, parent company name, Standard Industrial Classification (SIC) code/North American Industry Classification System (NAICS), description of products and services, year founded, ownership structure, number of employees; name, title, ethnicity, and sex of owners; major customers, annual sales, geographical area served, most recent certification date and accrediting council.

★14601★ **The Minority Executive's Handbook**

HarperCollins
10 E. 53rd St.
New York, NY 10022
Ph: (212)207-7000   Fax: (212)207-7633
Fr: 800-242-7737
URL: http://www.harpercollins.com/

Randolph W. Cameron. Revised edition, 1997. $12.95 (paper). 282 pages.

★14602★ **Multicultural and Diversity Education**

ABC-CLIO
130 Cremona Dr.
PO Box 1911
Santa Barbara, CA 93117
Ph: (805)968-1911   Fax: (805)685-9685
Fr: 800-368-6868
URL: http://www.abc-clio.com

Published September 2002. Publication includes: List of associations and organizations for further information about multicultural and diversity education. Principal content of publication is discussion of the trends, challenges, approaches, and future of diversity education. Indexes: Alphabetical.

★14603★ **National Directory of Minority-Owned Business Firms**

Business Research Services Inc.
7720 Wisconsin Ave., Ste. 213
Bethesda, MD 20814
Ph: (301)229-5561   Fax: (301)229-6133
Fr: 800-845-8420
URL: http://www.sba8a.com

Annual; latest edition 13th. $295.00 for individuals. Covers over 30,000 minority-owned businesses. Entries include: Company name, address, phone, name and title of contact, minority group, certification status,

date founded, number of employees, description of products or services, sales volume, government contracting experience, references. Arrangement: Standard Industrial Classification (SIC) code, geographical. Indexes: Alphabetical by company name; SIC.

★14604★ **National Minority and Women-Owned Business Directory**

Diversity Information Resources Inc.
2105 Central Ave. NE
Minneapolis, MN 55418
Ph: (612)781-6819   Fax: (612)781-0109
URL: http://www.diversityinforesources.com

Annual; latest edition 38th, published 2007. $129.00 for individuals. Covers over 9,000 minority-owned companies capable of supplying their goods and services on national or regional levels. Entries include: Company name, address, phone, fax, e-mail, Web site, number of employees, year established, products or services, certification status, minority identification, annual sales, NAICS code. Arrangement: Classified by product or service, then geographical and alphabetical. Indexes: Alphabetical; commodity; keyword.

★14605★ **Native American Education**

ABC-CLIO
130 Cremona Dr.
PO Box 1911
Santa Barbara, CA 93117
Ph: (805)968-1911   Fax: (805)685-9685
Fr: 800-368-6868
URL: http://www.abc-clio.com

July 2002. $27.50 for individuals. Publication includes: Principal content of publication is a discussion of issues facing educators of Native Americans. Indexes: Alphabetical.

★14606★ **SER-Jobs for Progress-Network Directory**

SER - Jobs for Progress National
1925 W John Carpenter Fwy., Ste. 5D
Irving, TX 75063-3224
Ph: (972)541-0616   Fax: (972)650-1860
Fr: 800-427-2306

Annual. Covers information about SER (Service, Employment, and Redevelopment), which aims to provide employment training and opportunities for Spanish-speaking and disadvantaged Americans. Includes main offices of local SER corporations, affiliates, and satellites.

★14607★ **SER Network Directory**

SER-Jobs for Progress National Inc.
5215 N O'Conner Blvd., Ste. 2550
Irving, TX 75039
Ph: (972)506-7815   Fax: (972)506-7832

Annual, April. Covers approximately 130 affiliated agencies in 90 U.S. cities of SER ("Service, Employment, Redevelopment")-Jobs for Progress National, Inc., an organization of Hispanics that provides employment training and services to disadvantaged youth and adults, especially Hispanics. Entries include: Organization name, address, phone, name of president, services provided, satellite offices, if any. Arrangement: Geographical.

★14608★ Shoot for the Moon

Saunderstown Press
PO Box 307
Saunderstown, RI 02874-0307
Ph: (401)295-8810

Allen A. Johnson. Second edition, 1996. $12.95 (paper). 37 pages. Designed for people starting or reentering employment, with special emphasis on handicapped and minorities.

NEWSPAPERS, MAGAZINES, AND JOURNALS

★14609★ African-American Career World

Equal Opportunity Publications Inc.
445 Broad Hollow Rd., Ste. 425
Melville, NY 11747
Ph: (631)421-9421   Fax: (631)421-0359
URL: http://www.eop.com/aacw.html

Semiannual. $18.00/year for individuals; $34.00 for two years; $49.00 for three years. Magazine that aims to be a recruitment link between students and professionals who are African American and the major corporations that seek to hire them.

★14610★ CAA Voice

Chinese for Affirmative Action
17 Walter U. Lum Pl.
San Francisco, CA 94108
Ph: (415)274-6750   Fax: (415)397-8770
E-mail: info@caasf.org
URL: http://www.caasf.org

Description: Quarterly. Reports on legislation and court rulings which affect the civil rights of Chinese Americans. Publicizes recent acts of discrimination against Chinese Americans and examines media stereotypes of Asians. Supports affirmative action programs and informs readers of career counseling services, and employment and apprenticeship opportunities. Promotes bilingual education and services; announces events of the organization.

★14611★ Chinese American Medical Society Newsletter

Chinese American Medical Society
281 Edgewood Ave.
Teaneck, NJ 07666
Ph: (201)833-1506   Fax: (201)833-8252
E-mail: hw5@columbia.edu
URL: http://www.camsociety.org

Description: 3-4 issues/year. Publishes Society news. Recurring features include recent activities of the Society, coming scientific meetings, excerpts of presentations at the scientific meeting, new members, job listings and a calendar of events.

★14612★ Fair Employment Practices Summary of Latest Developments

Bureau of National Affairs Inc.
1801 S. Bell St.
Arlington, VA 22202
Fr: 800-372-1033
E-mail: customercare@bna.com
URL: http://www.bna.com/

Description: Biweekly. Highlights developments in employment opportunity and affirmative actions, and affirmative action programs. Reports on federal and state court decisions, Equal Employment Opportunity Commission (EEOC) rulings and Office of Federal Contract Compliance Programs (OFCCP) decisions, new laws, regulations, and agency directives. Also provides information on special programs for minorities, the handicapped, women, and older workers.

★14613★ Hispanic Career World

Equal Opportunity Publications Inc.
445 Broad Hollow Rd., Ste. 425
Melville, NY 11747
Ph: (631)421-9421   Fax: (631)421-0359
URL: http://www.eop.com/hcw.html

Semiannual. $18.00/year for individuals; $34.00 for individuals, two years; $49.00/year for individuals, three years. Magazine that aims to be a recruitment link between students and professionals who are Hispanic and the major corporations that seek to hire them.

★14614★ Hispanic Link Weekly Report

Hispanic Link News Service
1420 N. St. NW
Washington, DC 20005
Ph: (202)234-0280   Fax: (202)234-4090
E-mail: zapoteco@aol.com
URL: http://www.hispaniclink.org/weeklyreport/index.htm

Description: Weekly. Covers Hispanic issues nationwide, including politics, employment, education, arts and entertainment, and relevant events. Recurring features include interviews, news of research, a calendar of events, reports of meetings, news of educational opportunities, and job listings.

★14615★ Hispanic Times Magazine

Hispanic Times Magazine
PO Box 579
Winchester, CA 92596
Ph: (909)926-2119

Quarterly. $30.00/year for individuals; $3.50 for single issue. Magazine focusing on business and careers (English and Spanish).

★14616★ Indian Heritage Council Quarterly

Indian Heritage Council Publishing
PO Box 732
McCall, ID 83638
Ph: (208)315-0916

Description: Quarterly. Covers issues of interest to Native Americans. Recurring features include letters to the editor, interviews, news of research, a calendar of events, reports of meetings, news of educational opportunities, job listings, book reviews, and notices of publications available.

★14617★ Item-Interference Technology Engineers Master

Robar Industries Inc.
3 Union Hill Rd.
West Conshohocken, PA 19428-2788
Fax: (610)834-7337
E-mail: item@rbitem.com
URL: http://www.interferencetechnology.com/rebrand_redirect.asp

Design magazine about measurement and control of electromagnetic interference.

★14618★ National Association of Black Accountants-News Plus

National Association of Black Accountants Inc.
7249-A Hanover Pkwy.
Greenbelt, MD 20770
Ph: (301)474-6222   Fax: (301)474-3114
Fr: 888-571-2939
E-mail: customerservice@nabainc.org
URL: http://www.nabainc.org/

Description: Quarterly. Addresses concerns of black business professionals, especially in the accounting profession. Reports on accounting education issues, developments affecting the profession, and the Association's activities on the behalf of minorities in the accounting profession. Recurring features include member profiles, job listings, reports of meetings, news of research, and a calendar of events.

★14619★ Saludos Hispanos

Saludos Hispanos
73-121 Fred Waring Dr., Ste. 100
Palm Desert, CA 92260
Ph: (760)776-1206   Fax: (760)776-1214
Fr: 800-371-4456
URL: http://www.saludos.com/

Bimonthly. Magazine showcasing successful Hispanic Americans and promoting higher education (English and Spanish).

ONLINE AND DATABASE SERVICES

★14620★ Latpro
3050 Universal Blvd., Ste. 120
Weston, FL 33331
Ph: (954)727-3844   Fax: (954)727-3845
E-mail: support@latpro.com
URL: http://www.latpro.com

Description: Job site dedicated to finding jobs for Spanish, Portuguese and bilingual workers. Seekers may post resumes, search the job databank and receive job alerts via e-mail. Contains e-mail newsletters, recruiter lists, relocation tools and salary calculators and ESL education opportunities, among other resources. Also available in Spanish and Portuguese.

★14621★ MBA Careers
3934 SW Corbett Ave.
Portland, OR 97239
Ph: (503)221-7779   Fax: (503)221-7780
E-mail: eric@careerexposure.com
URL: http://www.mbacareers.com

Description: Job site that provides resume posting, databank search and e-mail alert services to MBA and other advanced graduate degree holders.

★14622★ NSBE Online
URL: http://www.nsbe.org/careers/jobs.php

Description: A section of the website of the National Society of Black Engineers. **Main files include:** Job Search (includes full-time, co-ops, internships, and student jobs), Post a Job, Post a Resume. **Fee:** $250 to post a job for 60 days.

SOFTWARE

★14623★ Interview Skills of the Future: Interview Challenges for Minorities, Women, and People with Disabilities
Program Development Associates
PO Box 2038
Syracuse, NY 13220-2038
Ph: (315)452-0643   Fax: (315)452-0710
Fr: 800-543-2119
E-mail: info@disabilitytraining.com
URL: http://www.pdassoc.com

$199.00. CD-ROM. Teaches a tactful and positive response to challenging interview questions for those having a hard time breaking through the traditional hiring barriers.

OTHER SOURCES

★14624★ American Indian Science and Engineering Society (AISES)
PO Box 9828
Albuquerque, NM 87119-9828
Ph: (505)765-1052   Fax: (505)765-5608
E-mail: info@aises.org
URL: http://www.aises.org

Description: Represents American Indian and non-Indian students and professionals in science, technology, and engineering fields; corporations representing energy, mining, aerospace, electronic, and computer fields. Seeks to motivate and encourage students to pursue undergraduate and graduate studies in science, engineering, and technology. Sponsors science fairs in grade schools, teacher training workshops, summer math/science sessions for 8th-12th graders, professional chapters, and student chapters in colleges. Offers scholarships. Adult members serve as role models, advisers, and mentors for students. Operates placement service.

★14625★ Asian American Architects and Engineers (AAAE)
The Albert Group
114 Sansome St., Ste. 710
San Francisco, CA 94104
Ph: (415)957-8788
E-mail: leschau@kennedyjenks.com
URL: http://www.aaaenc.org

Members: Minorities. **Purpose:** Provides contracts and job opportunities for minorities in the architectural and engineering fields. **Activities:** Serves as a network for the promotion in professional fields.

★14626★ Chinese for Affirmative Action (CAA)
17 Walter U. Lum Pl.
San Francisco, CA 94108
Ph: (415)274-6750   Fax: (415)397-8770
E-mail: info@caasf.org
URL: http://www.caasf.org

Description: Works towards equal rights and justice for Asian Americans, women and other people of color. Conducts policy advocacy in the areas of education, employment, hate crimes and affirmative action. Provides direct services for people interested in non-traditional blue collar work where women and people of color have been historically underrepresented.

★14627★ Gatti & Associates
266 Main St.
Medfield, MA 02052
Ph: (508)359-4153   Fax: (508)359-5902
E-mail: info@gattihr.com
URL: http://www.gattihr.com

Executive search firm specializing exclusively in the search and placement of Human Resources professionals.

★14628★ Juan Menefee & Associates
503 S Oak Park Ave., Ste. 206
Oak Park, IL 60304
Ph: (708)848-7722   Fax: (708)848-6008
E-mail: jmenefee@jmarecruiter.com
URL: http://www.jmarecruiter.com

Diversity Search Firm. Firm places executives in the sales, marketing, finance, engineering, medical, high tech and insurance industries.

★14629★ Ludot Personnel Services Inc.
6056 N Sheldon Rd.
Canton, MI 48187-2861
Ph: (248)353-9720   Fax: (248)459-2012

Professional placement and executive search in regard to professionals from entry level through senior managers. Also maintains a specialized division for recruitment of females and minorities. Conducts human resources management studies and recommendations in regard to personnel and organization planning, wage and salary, and recruitment within small to medium-size businesses. Industries served: automotive and allied suppliers, chemical and petrochemical, defense/electronics, consumer products, heavy manufacturing, research and development, and legal, as well as government agencies.

★14630★ National Association for the Advancement of Colored People (NAACP)
4805 Mt. Hope Dr.
Baltimore, MD 21215
Ph: (410)580-5777   Fax: (410)358-3818
Fr: 877-NAACP-98
E-mail: info@naacp.org
URL: http://www.naacp.org

Description: Persons "of all races and religions" who believe in the objectives and methods of the NAACP. Works to achieve equal rights through the democratic process and eliminate racial prejudice by removing racial discrimination in housing, employment, voting, schools, the courts, transportation, recreation, prisons, and business enterprises. Offers referral services, tutorials, job referrals, and day care. Sponsors seminars; maintains law library. Sponsors the NAACP National Housing Corporation to assist in the development of low and moderate income housing for families. Compiles statistics.

★14631★ National Association of Hispanic Journalists (NAHJ)
1000 National Press Bldg.
529 14th St. NW
Washington, DC 20045-2001
Ph: (202)662-7145   Fax: (202)662-7144
Fr: 888-346-NAHJ
E-mail: nahj@nahj.org
URL: http://www.nahj.org

Description: Aims to organize and support Hispanics involved in news gathering and dissemination. Encourages journalism and communications study and practice by Hispanics. Seeks recognition for Hispanic members of the profession regarding their skills and achievements. Promotes fair and accurate media treatment of Hispanics; opposes job discrimination and demeaning stereotypes. Works to increase educational and career opportunities and development for Hispanics in the field. Seeks to foster greater awareness of members' cultural identity, interests, and concerns. Provides a united voice for Hispanic journalists with the aim of achieving national visibility. Offers placement services to Hispanic students. Activities include: a census of Hispanic media professionals nationwide; writing contest for Hispanic students. Offers scholarships, seminars, and training workshops.

★14632★ **National Black MBA Association (NBMBAA)**

180 N Michigan Ave., Ste. 1400
Chicago, IL 60601
Ph: (312)236-2622   Fax: (312)236-0390
E-mail: mail@nbmbaa.org
URL: http://www.nbmbaa.org

Description: Business professionals, lawyers, accountants, and engineers concerned with the role of blacks who hold advanced management degrees. Works to create economic and intellectual wealth for the black community. Encourages blacks to pursue continuing business education; assists students preparing to enter the business world. Provides programs for minority youths, students, and professionals, and entrepreneurs including workshops, panel discussions, and Destination MBA seminar. Sponsors job fairs. Works with graduate schools. Operates job placement service.

★14633★ **National Coalition of 100 Black Women (NCBW)**

1925 Adam C. Powell Jr. Blvd., Ste. 1L
New York, NY 10026
Ph: (212)222-5660   Fax: (212)222-5675
E-mail: nc100bw@aol.com
URL: http://www.ncbw.org

Description: Represents African-American women actively involved with issues such as economic development, health, employment, education, voting, housing, criminal justice, the status of black families, and the arts. Seeks to provide networking and career opportunities for African-American women in the process of establishing links between the organization and the corporate and political arenas. Encourages leadership develop-

ment; sponsors role-model and mentor programs to provide guidance to teenage mothers and young women in high school or who have graduated from college and are striving for career advancement.

★14634★ **National Puerto Rican Forum (NPRF)**

1910 Webster Ave.
Bronx, NY 10457
Ph: (718)466-3992   Fax: (718)466-5262
Fr: 800-662-1220
E-mail: elopez@nprf.org
URL: http://www.nprf.org

Description: Concerned with the overall improvement of Puerto Rican and Hispanic communities throughout the U.S. Seeks to identify the obstacles preventing the advancement of the Puerto Rican and Hispanic communities and to develop strategies to remove them. Designs and implements programs in areas of job counseling, training and placement, and English language skills, to deal effectively with the problems of Puerto Ricans and other Hispanics. Sponsors Career Services and Job Placement Program at the national level. Also provides specialized programs in New York, such as: Employment Placement Initiative, Access and Family Services in the schools, and job counseling.

★14635★ **National Society of Hispanic MBAs (NSHMBA)**

1303 Walnut Hill Ln., Ste. 100
Irving, TX 75038
Ph: (214)596-9338   Fax: (214)596-9325
Fr: 877-467-4622
E-mail: lhassler@nshmba.org
URL: http://www.nshmba.org

Description: Hispanic MBA professional business network dedicated to economic and philanthropic advancement.

★14636★ **Organization of Chinese American Women (OCAW)**

4641 Montgomery Ave., Ste. 208
Bethesda, MD 20814
Ph: (301)907-3898   Fax: (301)907-3899
E-mail: info@ocawwomen.org
URL: http://www.ocawwomen.org

Description: Advances the cause of Chinese American women in the U.S. and fosters public awareness of their special

needs and concerns. Seeks to integrate Chinese American women into the mainstream of women's activities and programs. Addresses issues such as equal employment opportunities at both the professional and nonprofessional levels; overcoming stereotypes; racial and sexual discrimination and restrictive traditional beliefs; assistance to poverty-stricken recent immigrants; access to leadership and policymaking positions. Serves as networking for Chinese American women. Sponsors annual opera and Mother's Day and Award Banquet. Establishes scholarships for middle school girls in rural China.

★14637★ **SER - Jobs for Progress National**

5215 N O'Connor Blvd., Ste. 2550
Irving, TX 75039
Ph: (972)506-7815   Fax: (972)506-7832
E-mail: info@ser-national.org
URL: http://www.ser-national.org

Description: Aims to provide employment training and opportunities for Spanish-speaking and disadvantaged Americans. Seeks to increase business and economic opportunities for minority communities and ensure optimum participation by the Hispanic community in public policy forums. Gives funds to SER performance contracts that are funded by the federal government. (The acronym SER stands for service, employment, and redevelopment.) Organizes its own training and management program and is responsible for recruitment and selection of job trainees, counseling, pre-job orientation and vocational preparation, basic education, employer relations, and follow-up services to trainees after training and job placement.

★14638★ **Wealth in Diversity Consulting Group Inc.**

544 Black Mountain
Cambridge, VT 05444
Ph: (802)644-5140   Fax: (802)644-2140
E-mail: info@wealthindiversity.com
URL: http://www.wealthindiversity.com

Group specializes in diversity initiatives, leadership and management development, organizational culture, team building, coaching, assessments, recruitment, conflict resolution, career development and health care educational development.

Opportunities for Older Workers

REFERENCE WORKS

★14639★ *Affirmative Action Register*
Affirmative Action Register
8356 Olive Blvd.
St. Louis, MO 63132
Ph: (314)991-1335   Fax: (314)997-1788
Fr: 800-537-0655
URL: http://www.aar-eeo.com

Monthly. Covers, in each issue, about 300 positions at a professional level (most requiring advanced study) available to women, minorities, veterans, and the handicapped; listings are advertisements placed by employers with affirmative action programs. Entries include: Company or organization name, address, contact name; description of position including title, requirements, duties, application procedure, salary, etc. Arrangement: Classified by profession.

★14640★ *Coming Alive from Nine to Five: The Career Search Handbook*
The McGraw-Hill Companies
PO Box 182604
Columbus, OH 43272
Fax: (614)759-3749   Fr: 877-883-5524
E-mail: customer.service@mcgraw-hill.com
URL: http://www.mcgraw-hill.com

Betty Neville Michelozzi. Seventh edition, 2003. $60.00. 360 pages. In addition to general job-hunting advice, provides special information for women, young adults, minorities, older workers, and persons with handicaps.

★14641★ *How to Find a New Career upon Retirement*
The McGraw-Hill Companies
PO Box 182604
Columbus, OH 43272
Fax: (614)759-3749   Fr: 877-883-5524
E-mail: customer.service@mcgraw-hill.com
URL: http://www.mcgraw-hill.com

Duane Brown. 1994. $9.95 (paper). 235 pages.

★14642★ *Jobs for People Over 50: 101 Companies That Hire Senior Workers*
Brattle Communications
24 Computer Dr., W.
Albany, NY 12205

Arthur Kuman, Jr. and Richard D. Salmon. 1994. 112 pages.

★14643★ *New Work Opportunities for Older Americans*
iUniverse, Inc.
2021 Pine Lake Rd. Ste. 100
Lincoln, NE 68512
Ph: (402)323-7800   Fax: (402)323-7824
Fr: 877-288-4677
URL: http://www.iuniverse.com/

Robert S. Menchin. 2000. $18.95 (paper). 356 pages.

★14644★ *Part-Time Employment for the Low-Income Elderly: Experiences from the Field*
Routledge
270 Madison Ave.
New York, NY 10016
Ph: (212)216-7800   Fax: (212)563-2269
URL: http://www.routledge.com/

Leslie B. Alexander. 1997. $95.00. Part of Issues in Aging series. 182 pages.

★14645★ *Resumes for Re-Entering the Job Market*
The McGraw-Hill Companies
PO Box 182604
Columbus, OH 43272
Fax: (614)759-3749   Fr: 877-883-5524
E-mail: customer.service@mcgraw-hill.com
URL: http://www.mcgraw-hill.com

Second edition, 2002. $10.95 (paper). 160 pages. Part of VGM Professional Resumes series.

★14646★ *Unretirement: A Career Guide for the Retired...the Soon-to-Be Retired...the Never Want-to-Be-Retired*
AMACOM
1601 Broadway, 12th Fl.
New York, NY 10019-7420
Ph: (212)586-8100   Fax: (212)903-8168
Fr: 800-262-9699
URL: http://www.amanet.org

Catherine D. Fyock and Anne M. Dorton. 1994. $17.95 (paper). 184 pages.

NEWSPAPERS, MAGAZINES, AND JOURNALS

★14647★ *Fair Employment Practices Summary of Latest Developments*
Bureau of National Affairs Inc.
1801 S. Bell St.
Arlington, VA 22202
Fr: 800-372-1033
E-mail: customercare@bna.com
URL: http://www.bna.com/

Description: Biweekly. Highlights developments in employment opportunity and affirmative actions, and affirmative action programs. Reports on federal and state court decisions, Equal Employment Opportunity Commission (EEOC) rulings and Office of Federal Contract Compliance Programs (OFCCP) decisions, new laws, regulations, and agency directives. Also provides information on special programs for minorities, the handicapped, women, and older workers.

ONLINE AND DATABASE SERVICES

★14648★ *Jobs In Dallas.com*
Ph: (214)522-9944   Fr: 888-900-3775
E-mail: in@localjobnetwork.com
URL: http://www.jobsindallas.com

Description: Job postings for the Dallas, TX area.

★14649★ Senior Job Bank
PO Box 508
Marlborough, MA 01752
URL: http://www.seniorjobbank.com
Description: Job postings for seniors.

★14650★ Seniors 4 Hire
c/o The Forward Group
7071 Warner Ave., F466
Huntington Beach, CA 92647
Ph: (714)848-0996   Fax: (714)848-5445
E-mail: info@seniors4hire.org
URL: http://www.seniors4hire.org

Description: Online career center for people 50 and over.

OTHER SOURCES

★14651★ Experience Works
2200 Clarendon Blvd., Ste. 1000
Arlington, VA 22201
Ph: (703)522-7272   Fax: (703)522-0141
Fr: (866)EXP-WRKS
E-mail: info@experienceworks.org
URL: http://www.experienceworks.org

Description: Provides training and employment services for mature workers. Reaches more than 125,000 mature individuals.

★14652★ National Council on the Aging
10501 Montgomery Blvd. NE, Ste. 210
Albuquerque, NM 87111
Ph: (505)292-2001   Fax: (505)292-1922

E-mail: info@ncoa.org
URL: http://www.nicoa.org

Description: Offers MaturityWorks-a partnership that places mature workers with jobs.

★14653★ Senior Employment Resources
4201 John Marr Dr., Ste. 236
Annandale, VA 22003-3204
Ph: (703)750-1936   Fax: (703)750-0269
E-mail: office@seniorjobs.org
URL: http://www.seniorjobs.org

Description: Job placement service that matches companies and job seekers age 50 and above.

Opportunities for Teenagers

REFERENCE WORKS

★14654★ Cents-Able Summer Self-Employment: An Entrepreneurial Guide for High School & College Students

Tamarax Press
PO Box 450
2A Taylor Way
Washington Crossing, PA 18977
Ph: (215)493-2136   Fax: (215)493-2057

E.K. Shepard. 1994. $12.95 (paper). 220 pages.

★14655★ Coming Alive from Nine to Five: The Career Search Handbook

The McGraw-Hill Companies
PO Box 182604
Columbus, OH 43272
Fax: (614)759-3749   Fr: 877-883-5524
E-mail: customer.service@mcgraw-hill.com
URL: http://www.mcgraw-hill.com

Betty Neville Michelozzi. Seventh edition, 2003. $60.00. 360 pages. In addition to general job-hunting advice, provides special information for women, young adults, minorities, older workers, and persons with handicaps.

★14656★ How to Get a Job If You're a Teenager

Upstart Books
PO Box 800
Fort Atkinson, WI 53538-0800
Ph: (920)563-9571   Fax: 800-835-2329
Fr: 800-448-4887
E-mail: service@highsmith.com
URL: http://www.highsmith.com

Cindy Pervola and Debby Hobgood. Second edition, revised 2000. $24.95 (paper). 68 pages. Covers the different steps in getting a job.

★14657★ Opportunities in Summer Camp Careers

The McGraw-Hill Companies
PO Box 182604
Columbus, OH 43272
Fax: (614)759-3749   Fr: 877-883-5524
E-mail: customer.service@mcgraw-hill.com
URL: http://www.mcgraw-hill.com

Blythe Camenson. 1998. $11.95 (paper). 160 pages. Part of "Opportunities in ..." Series.

★14658★ Peterson's Guide to College for Careers in Computing

Peterson's
Princeton Pke. Corporate Ctr., 2000 Lenox Dr.
PO Box 67005
Lawrenceville, NJ 08648
Ph: (609)896-1800   Fax: (609)896-4531
Fr: 800-338-3282

Publication includes: College-level programs in computing. Principal content of publication is career information on what it's like to work in the field, skills required, job outlook, career paths, education needed, and where to get more information.

★14659★ Peterson's International Directory of Summer Opportunities for Kids & Teenagers

Peterson's Guides
2000 Lenox Dr.
Box 67005
Lawrenceville, NJ 08648
Ph: (609)896-1800   Fax: (609)896-4531
Fr: 800-338-3282
E-mail: custsvc@petersons.com
URL: http://www.petersons.com

Fifth edition, 1998. $29.95 (paper). 110 pages.

★14660★ Peterson's Summer Jobs for Students

Peterson's
Princeton Pke. Corporate Ctr., 2000 Lenox Dr.
PO Box 67005
Lawrenceville, NJ 08648
Ph: (609)896-1800   Fax: (609)896-4531
Fr: 800-338-3282
URL: http://www.petersons.com/

Annual; latest edition 2002. $13.95 for individuals. Covers over 650 camps, resorts, amusement parks, hotels, businesses, national parks, conference and training centers, ranches, and restaurants offering about 45,000 temporary summer jobs; listings are paid. Entries include: Name and address, length of employment, pay rate, fringe benefits, duties, qualifications, application deadline and procedure. Arrangement: Geographical, then type of job. Indexes: Job title.

★14661★ Peterson's Summer Opportunities for Kids and Teenagers

Peterson's Guides
2000 Lenox Dr.
Box 67005
Lawrenceville, NJ 08648
Ph: (609)896-1800   Fax: (609)896-4531
Fr: 800-338-3282
E-mail: custsvc@petersons.com
URL: http://www.petersons.com

Peterson's. Twenty-second edition, 2004. $29.95 (paper). 1608 pages. In addition to information about 1,400 summer activities and programs, covers job opportunities for high school and college students. Part of Summer Opportunities for Kids and Teenagers series.

★14662★ Resumes for High School Graduates

The McGraw-Hill Companies
PO Box 182604
Columbus, OH 43272
Fax: (614)759-3749   Fr: 877-883-5524
E-mail: customer.service@mcgraw-hill.com
URL: http://www.mcgraw-hill.com

Third edition, 2005. $11.95. 144 pages. Designed for the person with little or no full-time work experience. Shows how to emphasize part-work experience and highlight educational, extra-curricular and volunteer experience. Provides sample resumes and cover letters.

★14663★ **Teen Guide to Getting Started in the Arts**

Greenwood Publishing Group Inc.
80 Post Rd. W
Westport, CT 06881
Ph: (203)266-3571   Fax: (203)222-1502
Fr: 800-225-5800
URL: http://www.greenwood.com/

Carol L. Ritzenthaler. 2001. $43.95. 176 pages.

★14664★ **A Teen's Guide to Finding a Job**

AuthorHouse
1663 Liberty Dr., Ste. 200
Bloomington, IN 47403
Ph: (812)961-1023   Fax: (812)339-8654
Fr: 888-519-5121
URL: http://www.authorhouse.com

Naomi Vernon. 2003. $15.50 (paper). 172 pages.

★14665★ **Your First Interview**

The Career Press, Inc.
3 Tice Rd.
PO Box 687
Franklin Lakes, NJ 07417-1322
Ph: (201)848-0310   Fax: (201)848-1727
Fr: 800-227-3371
URL: http://www.careerpress.com

Ronald Fry. Fourth edition, 2001. $14.95 (paper). 154 pages. Takes the reader from making the initial contact with a prospective employer to negotiating salary.

AUDIO/VISUAL RESOURCES

★14666★ **Teens for Hire**

Cambridge Educational
PO Box 2053
Princeton, NJ 08543-2053
Ph: 800-257-5126   Fax: (609)671-0266
Fr: 800-468-4227
E-mail: custserv@films.com
URL: http://www.cambridgeeducational.com

VHS and DVD. $89.95. 1999. 135 minutes. By following teens on the job and examining the responsibilities each job holds, viewers gain invaluable insight into what awaits them in the workplace.

OTHER SOURCES

★14667★ **National Youth Employment Coalition (NYEC)**

1836 Jefferson Pl. NW
Washington, DC 20036
Ph: (202)659-1064   Fax: (202)659-0399
E-mail: nyec@nyec.org
URL: http://www.nyec.org

Members: A network of over 180 community-based organizations, research organizations, public interest groups, policy analysis organizations, and others dedicated to promoting improved policies and practices related to youth employment/development, to help youth succeed in becoming lifelong learners, productive workers and self-sufficient citizens.

★14668★ **Operation Enterprise (OE)**

1601 Broadway
New York, NY 10019-7420
Ph: (212)903-8038   Fax: (212)903-8509
Fr: 800-797-7483
E-mail: govops@openterprise.com
URL: http://www.openterprise.com

Description: Gives high school and college

students an opportunity to learn about management by working with executives and managers. Learning techniques used include small group discussions, panel forums, a business simulation, and role playing. Sponsors Career Skills program, to encourage development of job skills. Candidates are sponsored in a variety of ways by companies, civic organizations, or individuals.

★14669★ **Vocational Foundation, Inc. (VFI)**

52 Broadway, 6th Fl.
New York, NY 10004
Ph: (212)823-1001   Fax: (718)230-8784
E-mail: erodriguez@vfinyc.org
URL: http://www.vfinyc.org

Description: Serves as a free voluntary vocational training, guidance, and job placement service for economically and educationally disadvantaged young people (ages 16-21) who are referred by other accredited public and voluntary agencies in New York City. **Purpose:** Seeks to aid high school dropouts and young people with correctional and drug abuse histories. Conducts GED prop and testing.

★14670★ **WAVE**

525 School St. SW, Ste. 500
Washington, DC 20024-2795
Ph: (202)484-0103   Fax: (202)484-7595
Fr: 800-274-2005
E-mail: info@waveinc.org
URL: http://www.waveinc.org

Description: Helps disadvantaged 16-21 year old high school dropouts and students at risk of dropping out to find unsubsidized jobs and careers. Provides classes for students to prepare for their high school equivalency diplomas and to learn basic living skills, such as how to find an apartment, how to dress for a job interview, and how to balance a checkbook. Holds seminars and competitions that foster motivation and leadership and conducts national employment and training seminars for enrollees, and annual staff training institutes.

Opportunities for Temporary Workers

REFERENCE WORKS

★14671★ *America's Career InfoNet*

U.S. Department of Labor
Frances Perkins Bldg.
200 Constitution Ave. NW
Washington, DC 20210
Ph: (886)487-2365   Fr: 877-889-5627
URL: http://www.acinet.org/acinet/

Covers links to and information about job banks, employment service providers, career education, and nationwide employer contacts.

★14672★ *CareerXRoads*

MMC GROUP
105 Decker Ct., Ste. 150
Irving, TX 75062
Ph: (972)893-0100   Fax: (972)893-0099
URL: http://www.careerxroads.com/about/

Latest edition 2002. Covers nearly 3,000 job and resume Web sites with reviews and descriptions of the top 500. Indexes: colleges; corporations: diversity; specialty/industry; location; listing services.

★14673★ *Directory of Outplacement and Career Management Firms*

Kennedy Information
1 Phoenix Mill Ln., 3rd Fl.
Peterborough, NH 03458
Ph: (603)924-1006   Fax: (603)924-4460
Fr: 800-531-0007
URL: http://www.kennedyinfo.com

Annual; latest edition 14th. $149.95 for individuals. Covers 407 consulting firms with special interest in career management and "outplacement" or "de-hiring" counseling executive employees being terminated because of poor performance, plant closings, etc., and assisting them in finding new jobs; firms that are compensated only by employers and those that also accept compensation from individuals are listed. Entries include: Firm name, address, phone, fax, e-mail, web address, description of philosophy and services, names and titles of principals, branches, area served, year established, revenue (within wide ranges), professional associations, minimum salary of positions handled, number of staff, percentage of business devoted to outplacement. Arrangement: Separate sections on basis of compensation arrangements, then alphabetical. Indexes: Industries, key principals, firm.

★14674★ *Half a Job: Bad and Good Part-Time Jobs in Changing Labor Market*

Temple University Press
University Services Bldg., Rm 306
1601 N. Broad St.
Philadelphia, PA 19122-6099
Ph: (215)204-8787   Fax: 800-621-8471
Fr: 800-621-2736
URL: http://www.temple.edu/tempress/

Chris Tilly. 1996. $26.95 (paper). 228 pages.

★14675★ *Harvard Business School Guide to Careers in Management Consulting*

Harvard Business School Publishing
60 Harvard Way
Boston, MA 02163
Ph: (617)783-7500   Fax: (617)783-7555
Fr: 800-988-0886
URL: http://www.hbsp.harvard.edu

$10.83 for individuals. Publication includes: Well-known consulting firms, a mailing list of recruiting contacts, and a selective bibliography of relevant books and directories compiled by the Harvard Business School.

★14676★ *Job Choices for Business & Liberal Arts Students*

National Association of Colleges and
  Employers
62 Highland Ave.
Bethlehem, PA 18017-9085
Ph: (610)868-1421   Fax: (610)868-0208
Fr: 800-544-5272
URL: http://www.naceweb.org

Annual. $16.95 for individuals. Covers information about prospective employers, as well as career advice.

★14677★ *NSEA News*

National Student Employment Association
c/o Joan Adams
PO Box 23606
Eugene, OR 97402
Ph: (541)484-6935   Fax: (541)484-6935
URL: http://nseastudemp.org

Quarterly. Covers information regarding the National Student Employment Association. Discusses such issues as job development, summer employment, and student financial aid. Includes book reviews.

★14678★ *Peterson's Summer Jobs for Students*

Peterson's
Princeton Pke. Corporate Ctr., 2000
  Lenox Dr.
PO Box 67005
Lawrenceville, NJ 08648
Ph: (609)896-1800   Fax: (609)896-4531
Fr: 800-338-3282
URL: http://www.petersons.com/

Annual; latest edition 2002. $13.95 for individuals. Covers over 650 camps, resorts, amusement parks, hotels, businesses, national parks, conference and training centers, ranches, and restaurants offering about 45,000 temporary summer jobs; listings are paid. Entries include: Name and address, length of employment, pay rate, fringe benefits, duties, qualifications, application deadline and procedure. Arrangement: Geographical, then type of job. Indexes: Job title.

★14679★ *Quick Prep Careers*

Ferguson Publishing Co.
200 W Jackson Blvd.
Chicago, IL 60606-6941
Fax: 800-306-9942   Fr: 800-306-9941

$18.95 for individuals. Publication includes: Lists of associations for further consultation for each of 75 jobs featured. Principal content of publication is detailed information on each job. Arrangement: By job. Indexes: Alphabetical.

★14680★ Temp: How to Survive and Thrive in the World of Temporary Employment

Shambhala Publications, Incorporated
Horticultural Hall, 300 Massachusetts Ave.
Boston, MA 02115
Ph: (617)424-0030   Fax: (617)236-1563
Fr: 888-424-2329
E-mail: custserv@shambhala.com
URL: http://www.shambhala.com/

Deborahann Smith. 1994. $15.95 (paper). 144 pages. Explains working with agencies, self-marketing, short- and long-term assignments, and more.

★14681★ The Temp Worker's Guide to Self-Fulfillment: How to Slack Off, Achieve Your Dreams, and Get Paid for It!

Loompanics Unlimited
PO Box 1197
Port Townsend, WA 98368
Ph: (360)385-5087   Fax: (360)385-7785
Fr: 800-380-2230
E-mail: service@loompanics.com
URL: http://www.loompanics.com

Dennis Fiery. 1997. $12.95 (paper). 156 pages.

★14682★ VGM's Guide to Temporary Employment

The McGraw-Hill Companies
PO Box 182604
Columbus, OH 43272
Fax: (614)759-3749   Fr: 877-883-5524
E-mail: customer.service@mcgraw-hill.com
URL: http://www.mcgraw-hill.com

Lewis Baratz. 1995. $11.95 (paper). 192 pages.

OTHER SOURCES

★14683★ AAA Personnel Associates

14 Hayestown Ave.
Danbury, CT 06811-4882
Ph: (203)744-1820   Fax: (203)744-1878

Personnel consultancy offers recruitment and placement of permanent and temporary help (Western Temporary Services division). Firm maintains a professional placement division, EDP search division, secretarial/clerical permanent division, temporary division, and tech-search jobbers division. Industries served: manufacturing, corporate, service, financial institutions, and government agencies.

★14684★ Ambassador Personnel Services Inc.

1541 Fording Island Rd., Ste. 4
PO Box 22448
Hilton Head Island, SC 29925
Ph: (843)837-9066   Fax: (843)837-6477
E-mail:
k.wilson@ambassadorpersonnel.com
URL: http://www.teamambassador.com

Full service employment agency that includes local temporary and permanent placements, medical home health provider and regional and national hospitality placement. Industries served: locally: administrative and clerical, home health; regionally: food and beverage and hospitality.

★14685★ American Staffing Association (ASA)

277 S Washington St., Ste. 200
Alexandria, VA 22314-3675
Ph: (703)253-2020   Fax: (703)253-2053
E-mail: asa@americanstaffing.net
URL: http://www.americanstaffing.net

Description: Promotes and represents the staffing industry through legal and legislative advocacy, public relations, education, and the establishment of high standards of ethical conduct.

★14686★ National Association of Part-Time and Temporary Employees (NAPTE)

5800 Barton, Ste. 201
PO Box 3805
Shawnee, KS 66203
Ph: (913)962-7740
E-mail: napte-champion@worldnet.att.net
URL: http://www.members.tripod.com/~napte

Purpose: Promotes the economic and social interests of persons working on a part-time, contingent, or temporary basis through research, advocacy, and member services. Offers short-term portable health insurance.

★14687★ RO-LAN Associates Inc.

725 Sabattus St.
Lewiston, ME 04240
Ph: (207)784-1010   Fax: (207)782-3446
E-mail: rlapointe@aol.com

Professional placement specialists for permanent and temporary positions. Also offers executive search and recruiting expertise, outplacements, complete resume service, new business consulting and job and career transition coaching.

★14688★ Spear-Izzo Associates L.L.C.

651 Holiday Dr., Ste. 300
Pittsburgh, PA 15220
Ph: (412)928-3290   Fax: (724)940-1959
E-mail: info@siasearch.com
URL: http://www.siasearch.com

An executive search management company. Provides permanent, temporary, and contract placements, for the consulting industry.

Opportunities for Women

REFERENCE WORKS

★14689★ 101 Best Extra-Income Opportunities for Women

Prima Lifestyles
401 Franklin Ave.
Garden City, NY 11530
Ph: (516)873-4561   Fax: (516)873-4714

Jennifer Basye Sandom. 1997. 192 pages.

★14690★ Affirmative Action Register

Affirmative Action Register
8356 Olive Blvd.
St. Louis, MO 63132
Ph: (314)991-1335   Fax: (314)997-1788
Fr: 800-537-0655
URL: http://www.aar-eeo.com

Monthly. Covers, in each issue, about 300 positions at a professional level (most requiring advanced study) available to women, minorities, veterans, and the handicapped; listings are advertisements placed by employers with affirmative action programs. Entries include: Company or organization name, address, contact name; description of position including title, requirements, duties, application procedure, salary, etc. Arrangement: Classified by profession.

★14691★ Coming Alive from Nine to Five: The Career Search Handbook

The McGraw-Hill Companies
PO Box 182604
Columbus, OH 43272
Fax: (614)759-3749   Fr: 877-883-5524
E-mail: customer.service@mcgraw-hill.com
URL: http://www.mcgraw-hill.com

Betty Neville Michelozzi. Seventh edition, 2003. $60.00. 360 pages. In addition to general job-hunting advice, provides special information for women, young adults, minorities, older workers, and persons with handicaps.

★14692★ Directory of Career Resources for Women

Ready Reference Press
PO Box 5249
Santa Monica, CA 90405
Ph: (310)475-4895   Fr: 800-424-5627

Alvin Renetzky, Daniel J. Jacobson, and Hynda Rudd. $89.50. 1979. 287 pages. Offers details on hundreds of programs and services, including job referral services, talent banks, re-entry programs, special training programs, career counseling, resume preparation, workshops, and others. Entries include organization name, general information, resources offered, special features, hours, fees (if any), and address. Subject and geographic indexes.

★14693★ Every Woman's Essential Job Hunting & Resume Book

Adams Media Corp.
57 Littlefield St.
Avon, MA 02322
Ph: (508)427-7100   Fax: (508)427-6790
Fr: 800-872-5627
URL: http://www.adamsmedia.com

Laura Morin. 1994. $11.95 (paper). 221 pages.

★14694★ Ferguson Career Resource Guide for Women and Minorities

Impact Publications
9104 Manassas Dr., Ste. N
Manassas Park, VA 20111-5211
Ph: (703)361-7300   Fax: (703)335-9486
Fr: 800-361-1055
URL: http://www.impactpublications.com/

$125.00. Covers information on hundreds of organizations, colleges, foundations, and publications devoted to the careers and educational advancement of women minorities.

★14695★ Finding the Work You Love: A Woman's Career Guide

Resource Publications, Inc.
160 E. Virginia St., No. 290
San Jose, CA 95112-5876
Ph: (408)286-8505   Fax: (408)287-8748
Fr: 888-273-7782

URL: http://www.rpinet.com/

Astrid Berg. 1994. $15.95 (paper). 203 pages.

★14696★ National Directory of Woman-Owned Business Firms

Business Research Services Inc.
7720 Wisconsin Ave., Ste. 213
Bethesda, MD 20814
Ph: (301)229-5561   Fax: (301)229-6133
Fr: 800-845-8420
URL: http://www.sba8a.com

Annual. $295.00 for individuals. Covers 28,000 woman-owned businesses. Entries include: Company name, address, phone, name and title of contact, minority group, certification status, date founded, number of employees, description of products or services, sales volume, government contracting experience, references. Arrangement: Standard Industrial Classification (SIC) code, geographical. Indexes: Alphabetical by company.

★14697★ Pathways to Career Success for Women: A Resource Guide to Colleges, Financial Aid, and Work

JIST Publishing
875 Montreal Way
St. Paul, MN 55102
Fax: 800-547-8329   Fr: 800-648-5478
E-mail: info@jist.com
URL: http://www.jist.com

2000. $29.95. 320 pages. Details hundreds of organizations, colleges, foundations, and publications devoted to the advancement of women.

★14698★ Professional by Choice: Milady's Career Development Guide

Milady Pub Corp
5 Maxwell Dr.
Clifton Park, NY 12065
Fax: (859)647-5963   Fr: 800-998-7498
E-mail: milady@delmar.com
URL: http://www.milady.com

Victoria Harper. 1994. $20.95 (paper). 143 pages. Part of Salon Ovations series.

★14699★ Resumes for Women

Arco Pub.
200 Old Tappan Rd.
Old Tappan, NJ 07675
Fr: 800-428-5331

Eva Shaw. 1995. $10.00 (paper). 158 pages.

★14700★ The Self-Employed Woman's Guide to Launching a Home-Based Business

Three Rivers Press
280 Park Ave. (11-3)
New York, NY 10017
Fax: (212)940-7381   Fr: 800-726-0600
URL: http://www.primapublishing.com/crown/trp.html

Priscilla Huff. 2002. $14.95 (paper). 368 pages.

★14701★ The Smart Woman's Guide to Career Success

The Career Press, Inc.
3 Tice Rd.
PO Box 687
Franklin Lakes, NJ 07417-1322
Ph: (201)848-0310   Fax: (201)848-1727
Fr: 800-227-3371
URL: http://www.careerpress.com

Janet Hauter. 1996. $21.95. 158 pages. Part of the "Smart Woman's Guides Series."

★14702★ The Smart Woman's Guide to Interviewing and Salary Negotiations

Cengage Learning
PO Box 6904
Florence, KY 41022
Fax: 800-487-8488   Fr: 800-354-9706
URL: http://www.cengage.com

Julie A. King. 1997. $15.95 (paper). 221 pages. Part of the "Smart Woman's Guide Series."

★14703★ The Smart Woman's Guide to Resumes and Job Hunting

The Career Press, Inc.
3 Tice Rd.
PO Box 687
Franklin Lakes, NJ 07417-1322
Ph: (201)848-0310   Fax: (201)848-1727
Fr: 800-227-3371
URL: http://www.careerpress.com

Julie Adair King and Betsy Sheldon. 1995. $11.99. 214 pages. Addresses job-search challenges unique to women in the '90s. Discusses breaking through the glass ceiling and other gender barriers, commanding a fair salary, networking to hidden job opportunities, using "power language", translating volunteer experiences into powerful accomplishments, and offers other guidance. Takes the reader through a resume-creating process.

★14704★ Unlocking the Clubhouse: Women in Computing

MIT Press
55 Hayward St.
Cambridge, MA 02142-1493
Ph: (617)253-5646   Fax: (617)258-6779
Fr: 800-405-1619
URL: http://mitpress.mit.edu/main/home/default.asp

Jane Margolis and Allan Fisher. 2003. $15.00. 182 pages.

★14705★ Wisconsin Women's Resources

Wisconsin Women's Council
101 E Wilson, 8th Fl.
Madison, WI 53702
Ph: (608)266-2219   Fax: (608)267-0626
URL: http://womenscouncil.wi.gov/section.asp?linkid=41&locid=2

Latest edition 2005-2006. Covers agencies, organizations, services, and other programs of interest to and concerned with women, including career planning, displaced homemaker services, legal aid, women's studies programs, child care services, etc. Entries include: Organization name, address, phone, e-mail, URL, purpose. Arrangement: Classified by area of concern.

★14706★ Women's Business Resource Guide

McGraw-Hill Professional Publishing (New York, New York)
2 Penn Plz.
New York, NY 10121-0101
Ph: (212)904-2000   Fax: (212)904-4760
URL: http://books.mcgraw-hill.com/

Biennial; latest edition 1st. $18.95 for individuals. Covers Over 600 training, technical assistance, and counseling programs, information sources, government agencies, membership organizations, and other associations of interest to women in business. Entries include: Resource name, address, phone, geographical area served, description. Arrangement: Classified by topic. Indexes: Product/service, organization name, subject.

★14707★ Work of Her Own: A Woman's Guide to Success off the Career Track

Tarcher
375 Hudson St.
New York, NY 10014-3657
Ph: (212)366-2000   Fax: (212)366-2666
Fr: 800-331-4624
URL: http://us.penguingroup.com/

Susan W. Albert. 1994. $12.95 (paper). 272pages. Reprint.

NEWSPAPERS, MAGAZINES, AND JOURNALS

★14708★ BusinessWoman Magazine

Business and Professional Women/USA
1900 M St. NW, Ste. 310
Washington, DC 20036
Ph: (202)293-1100   Fax: (202)861-0298
E-mail: businesswoman@bpwusa.org
URL: http://www.bpwusa.org/

Magazine for working women that promotes workplace equity issues.

★14709★ Center for Research on Women-Standpoint

Center for Research on Women
The University of Memphis
337 Clement Hall
Memphis, TN 38152-3550
Ph: (901)678-2770   Fax: (901)678-3652
E-mail: crow@memphis.edu
URL: http://cas.memphis.edu/isc/crow/

Description: 2/year. Features news on issues of concern to women, including careers, education, ethnic minority affairs, sexual harrassment, violence, and economics. Includes information on Center activities and conferences, and Race, Class, and Gender Scholarship.

★14710★ Fair Employment Practices Summary of Latest Developments

Bureau of National Affairs Inc.
1801 S. Bell St.
Arlington, VA 22202
Fr: 800-372-1033
E-mail: customercare@bna.com
URL: http://www.bna.com/

Description: Biweekly. Highlights developments in employment opportunity and affirmative actions, and affirmative action programs. Reports on federal and state court decisions, Equal Employment Opportunity Commission (EEOC) rulings and Office of Federal Contract Compliance Programs (OFCCP) decisions, new laws, regulations, and agency directives. Also provides information on special programs for minorities, the handicapped, women, and older workers.

★14711★ FEW's News and Views

Federally Employed Women Inc.
1666 K St. NW, Ste. 440
Washington, DC 20006
Ph: (202)898-0994
E-mail: editor@few.org
URL: http://www.few.org/publications.asp

Description: Bimonthly. Concerned with women's issues, particularly those involving women in the federal government. Reports on administration actions affecting the status of women and analyzes significant legislation. Recurring features include letters to the editor, news of members, a calendar of events, book reviews, and notices of career development and training opportunities.

★14712★ *Making Bread*

Making Bread Magazine
1528 Walnut St., Ste. 1925
Philadelphia, PA 19102
Ph: (215)670-2471
URL: http://
www.makingbreadmagazine.com/NEW-
Home.htm

Irregular. $20.00/year for individuals. Online magazine for professional and entrepreneurial women.

★14713★ *Math/Science Network-Broadcast*

Math/Science Network
Mills College
5000 Macarthur Blvd.
Oakland, CA 94613
Ph: (510)430-2222   Fax: (510)430-2090
E-mail: msneyh@mills.edu
URL: http://
www.expandingyourhorizons.org/

Description: Quarterly. Carries news of the Network, which is interested in promoting the continuing development in mathematics and science of all people, with special emphasis on the needs of women. Recurring features include information on career education conferences, teacher education programs which encourage girls and women to pursue scientific careers, and news of resources available.

★14714★ *The NAWIC Image*

National Association of Women in
  Construction
327 S. Adams St.
Fort Worth, TX 76104
Ph: (817)877-5551   Fax: (817)877-0324
Fr: 800-552-3506
E-mail: nawic@nawic.org
URL: http://www.nawic.org

Description: Six issues/year. Fosters career advancement for women in construction. Features women business owners, training for construction trades and educational programs. Recurring features include columns titled "Issues and Trends," "Road to Success," "Chapter Highlights," "Members on the Move," and "Q&A."

★14715★ *Southern Association for Women Historians Newsletter*

Southern Association for Women
  Historians
c/o Dr. Melissa Walker
Dept. of History and Politics
310 Auditorium Bldg.
East Lansing, MI 48824
Ph: (517)432-5134   Fax: (517)355-8363
E-mail: h-sawh@h-net.msu.edu
URL: http://www.h-net.org/~sawh/newsletters/index.htm

Description: Three issues/year. Informs members of the Association's activities aimed at advancing the professional development of women historians and historians of women. Carries minutes of the annual meeting, announcements of awards and prizes available for work published in a variety of areas, and calls for papers at various conferences. Recurring features include notices of publications available, job listings, and member updates.

★14716★ *WEPANEWS*

Women in Engineering Programs &
  Advocates Network
1901 E. Asbury Ave., Ste. 220
Denver, CO 80208
Ph: (303)871-4643   Fax: (303)871-6833
E-mail: dmatt@wepan.org
URL: http://www.wepan.org

Description: 2/year. Seeks to provide greater access for women to careers in engineering. Includes news of graduate, undergraduate, freshmen, pre-college, and re-entry engineering programs for women. Recurring features include job listings, faculty, grant, and conference news, international engineering program news, action group news, notices of publications available, and a column titled Kudos.

★14717★ *WIT*

Vermont Works for Women
51 Park St.
Essex Junction, VT 05452
Ph: (802)878-0004   Fax: (802)878-0050
Fr: 800-639-1472
URL: http://www.nnetw.org/

Description: Three issues/year. Provides a network of support, information, and skill sharing for women in skilled trades professions.

★14718★ *Women in Business*

The ABWA Company Inc.
9100 Ward Pkwy.
PO Box 8728
Kansas City, MO 64114-0728
Ph: (816)361-6621   Fax: (816)361-4991
Fr: 800-228-0007
E-mail: abwa@abwa.org

Bimonthly. $20.00/year for individuals; $24.00/year for other countries. Women's business magazine.

★14719★ *Women Work!*

Women Work!-The National Network for
  Women's Employment
1625 K St., NW, Ste. 300
Washington, DC 20006
Ph: (202)467-6346   Fax: (202)467-5366
Fr: 800-235-2732
E-mail: info@womenwork.org
URL: http://www.womenwork.org/

Description: Quarterly. Provides information on some of the issues women in transition face in their lives. Recurring features include legislative information and columns titled Career Ladder, which provides career tips; Occupation Profile, which highlights a high-wage growth occupation; Money Issues, which provides financial tips; Health Watch, which focuses on women's health issues; and President's Message.

AUDIO/VISUAL RESOURCES

★14720★ **Math at Work: Women in Nontraditional Careers**

Her Own Words
PO Box 5264
Madison, WI 53705-0264
Ph: (608)271-7083   Fax: (608)271-0209
E-mail: herownword@aol.com
URL: http://www.herownwords.com/

Video. Jocelyn Riley. $95.00. 15 minutes. Resource guide also available for $45.00.

★14721★ **Women in Building Construction**

Her Own Words
PO Box 5264
Madison, WI 53705-0264
Ph: (608)271-7083   Fax: (608)271-0209
E-mail: herownword@aol.com
URL: http://www.herownwords.com/

Video. Jocelyn Riley. $95.00. 15 minutes. Resource guide also available for $45.00.

★14722★ **Women in Dentistry**

Her Own Words
PO Box 5264
Madison, WI 53705-0264
Ph: (608)271-7083   Fax: (608)271-0209
E-mail: herownword@aol.com
URL: http://www.herownwords.com/

Video. Jocelyn Riley. $95.00. 15 minutes. Resource guide also available for $45.00.

★14723★ **Women in Engineering**

Her Own Words
PO Box 5264
Madison, WI 53705-0264
Ph: (608)271-7083   Fax: (608)271-0209
E-mail: herownword@aol.com
URL: http://www.herownwords.com/

Video. Jocelyn Riley. $95.00. 15 minutes. Resource guide also available for $45.00.

★14724★ **Women in Firefighting**

Her Own Words
PO Box 5264
Madison, WI 53705-0264
Ph: (608)271-7083   Fax: (608)271-0209
E-mail: herownword@aol.com
URL: http://www.herownwords.com/

Video. Jocelyn Riley. $95.00. 15 minutes. Resource guide also available for $45.00.

★14725★ **Women in Highway Construction**

Her Own Words
PO Box 5264
Madison, WI 53705-0264
Ph: (608)271-7083   Fax: (608)271-0209
E-mail: herownword@aol.com
URL: http://www.herownwords.com/

Video. Jocelyn Riley. $95.00. 15 minutes. Resource guide also available for $45.00.

★14726★ Women in Machining

Her Own Words
PO Box 5264
Madison, WI 53705-0264
Ph: (608)271-7083   Fax: (608)271-0209
E-mail: herownword@aol.com
URL: http://www.herownwords.com/

Video. Jocelyn Riley. $95.00. 15 minutes. Resource guide also available for $45.00.

★14727★ Women in Nontraditional Careers: An Introduction

Her Own Words
PO Box 5264
Madison, WI 53705
Ph: (608)271-7083   Fax: (608)271-0209
E-mail: herownword@aol.com
URL: http://www.herownwords.com/

Video. Jocelyn Riley. $95.00. 15 minutes. Resource guide also available for $45.00.

★14728★ Women in Policing

Her Own Words
PO Box 5264
Madison, WI 53705
Ph: (608)271-7083   Fax: (608)271-0209
E-mail: herownword@aol.com
URL: http://www.herownwords.com/

Video. Jocelyn Riley. $95.00. 15 minutes. Resource guide also available for $45.00.

★14729★ *Work Talk: Women in Nontraditional Careers in Their Own Words*

Her Own Words
PO Box 5264
Madison, WI 53705
Ph: (608)271-7083   Fax: (608)271-0209
E-mail: herownword@aol.com
URL: http://www.herownwords.com/

Video. Jocelyn Riley. $95.00. 15 minutes. Resource guide also available for $45.00.

ONLINE AND DATABASE SERVICES

★14730★ MBA Careers

3934 SW Corbett Ave.
Portland, OR 97239
Ph: (503)221-7779   Fax: (503)221-7780
E-mail: eric@careerexposure.com
URL: http://www.mbacareers.com

Description: Job site that provides resume posting, databank search and e-mail alert services to MBA and other advanced graduate degree holders.

★14731★ Women at Work

50 N. Hill Ave., Ste. 300
Pasadena, CA 91106
Ph: (626)796-6870   Fax: (626)793-7396
E-mail: info@womenatwork.org

URL: http://www.womenatwork1.org/

Description: Site of nonprofit job and career resource center, serving the greater Los Angeles area.

SOFTWARE

★14732★ Interview Skills of the Future: Interview Challenges for Minorities, Women, and People with Disabilities

Program Development Associates
PO Box 2038
Syracuse, NY 13220-2038
Ph: (315)452-0643   Fax: (315)452-0710
Fr: 800-543-2119
E-mail: info@disabilitytraining.com
URL: http://www.pdassoc.com

$199.00. CD-ROM. Teaches a tactful and positive response to challenging interview questions for those having a hard time breaking through the traditional hiring barriers.

OTHER SOURCES

★14733★ 9 to 5, National Association of Working Women

207 E Buffalo St., No. 211
Milwaukee, WI 53202
Ph: (414)274-0925   Fax: (414)272-2870
Fr: 800-522-0925
E-mail: 9to5@9to5.org
URL: http://www.9to5.org

Description: Represents women office workers. Seeks to build a national network of local office worker chapters that strives to gain better pay, proper use of office automation, opportunities for advancement, elimination of sex and race discrimination, and improved working conditions for women office workers. Works to introduce legislation or regulations at state level to protect video display terminal operators. Produces studies and research in areas such as reproductive hazards of Video Display Terminals (VDTs), automation's effect on clerical employment, family and medical leaves, and stress. Conducts annual summer school for working women. Maintains speakers' bureau.

★14734★ 9 to 5 Working Women Education Fund (WWEF)

207 E Buffalo St., No. 211
Milwaukee, WI 53202
Ph: (414)274-0925   Fax: (414)272-2870
Fr: 800-522-0925
E-mail: 9to5@9to5.org
URL: http://www.9to5.org

Purpose: Conducts research on the concerns of women workers. Includes topics such as: work/family, anti-discrimination, welfare/workfare, contingent work. **Activi-**

ties: Conducts public presentations and seminars upon request; provides speakers and trainers on sexual harassment. Compiles statistics of women in the workforce.

★14735★ Association for Women Geoscientists (AWG)

PO Box 30645
Lincoln, NE 68503-0645
Ph: (402)489-8122
E-mail: office@awg.org
URL: http://www.awg.org

Members: Represents men and women geologists, geophysicists, petroleum engineers, geological engineers, hydrogeologists, paleontologists, geochemists, and other geoscientists. **Purpose:** Aims to encourage the participation of women in the geosciences. Exchanges educational, technical, and professional information. Enhances the professional growth and advancement of women in the geosciences. Provides information through web site on opportunities and careers available to women in the geosciences. **Activities:** Sponsors educational booths and programs at geological society conventions. Operates charitable program. Maintains speaker's bureau, and Association for Women Geoscientists Foundation (educational arm).

★14736★ Business and Professional Women's Foundation (BPWF)

1900 M St. NW, Ste. 310
Washington, DC 20036
Ph: (202)293-1100   Fax: (202)861-0298
E-mail: foundation@bpwusa.org
URL: http://www.bpwfoundation.org

Purpose: Dedicated to improving the economic status of working women through their integration into all occupations. **Activities:** Conducts and supports research on women and work, with special emphasis on economic issues. Maintains Marguerite Rawalt Resource Center of 20,000 items on economic issues involving women and work and provides public reference and referral service.

★14737★ Catalyst

120 Wall St., 5th Fl.
New York, NY 10005-3904
Ph: (212)514-7600   Fax: (212)514-8470
E-mail: info@catalyst.org
URL: http://www.catalystwomen.org

Description: Works to advance women in Business and the professions. Serves as a source of information on women in business for past four decades. Helps companies and women maximize their potential. Holds current statistics, print media, and research materials on issues related to women in business.

★14738★ Center for Economic Options (CEO)

910 Quarrier St., Ste. 206
Charleston, WV 25301
Ph: (304)345-1298   Fax: (304)342-0641
E-mail: info@economicoptions.org

URL: http://www.centerforeconomicoptions.org

Description: Seeks to improve the economic position and quality of life for women, especially low-income and minority women. Works to provide access to job training and employment options to women. Supports self-employed women and small business owners by offering training and technical assistance and information. Advocates women's legal right to employment, training, education, and credit. Seeks to inform the public on economic issues related to women; while activities are conducted on local and state levels, group cooperates with national and international organizations on issues relating to employment and economic justice for women. Maintains speakers' bureau and library. Compiles statistics; conducts research.

★14739★ **Federally Employed Women (FEW)**

1666 K St. NW, Ste. 440
Washington, DC 20006
Ph: (202)898-0994
E-mail: few@few.org
URL: http://www.few.org

Members: Represents men and women employed by the federal government. **Purpose:** Seeks to end sexual discrimination in government service; to increase job opportunities for women in government service and to further the potential of all women in the government; to improve the merit system in government employment; to assist present and potential government employees who are discriminated against because of sex; to work with other organizations and individuals concerned with equal employment opportunity in the government. **Activities:** Provides speakers and sponsors seminars to publicize the Federal Women's Program; furnishes members with information on pending legislation designed to end discrimination against working women; informs and provides members opportunities for training to improve their job potential; issues fact sheets interpreting civil service rules and regulations and other legislative issues; provides annual training conference for over 3,000 women and men.

★14740★ **The International Alliance for Women (TIAW)**

8405 Greensboro Dr., Ste. 800
McLean, VA 22102-5120
Ph: (703)506-3284   Fax: (905)305-1548
Fr: (866)533-8429
E-mail: info@tiaw.org
URL: http://www.tiaw.org

Members: Local networks comprising 50,000 professional and executive women in 12 countries; individual businesswomen without a network affiliation are alliance associates. **Purpose:** Promotes recognition of the achievements of women in business. Encourages placement of women in senior executive positions. Maintains high standards of professional competence among members. Facilitates communication on an international scale among professional women's networks and their members. Represents members' interests before policymaking business and government. **Activities:** Sponsors programs that support equal opportunity and enhance members' business and professional skills. Operates appointments and directors service. Maintains speakers' bureau.

★14741★ **Ludot Personnel Services Inc.**

6056 N Sheldon Rd.
Canton, MI 48187-2861
Ph: (248)353-9720   Fax: (248)459-2012

Professional placement and executive search in regard to professionals from entry level through senior managers. Also maintains a specialized division for recruitment of females and minorities. Conducts human resources management studies and recommendations in regard to personnel and organization planning, wage and salary, and recruitment within smallto medium-size businesses. Industries served: automotive and allied suppliers, chemical and petrochemical, defense/electronics, consumer products, heavy manufacturing, research and development, and legal, as well as government agencies.

★14742★ **National Coalition of 100 Black Women (NCBW)**

1925 Adam C. Powell Jr. Blvd., Ste. 1L
New York, NY 10026
Ph: (212)222-5660   Fax: (212)222-5675
E-mail: nc100bw@aol.com
URL: http://www.ncbw.org

Description: Represents African-American women actively involved with issues such as economic development, health, employment, education, voting, housing, criminal justice, the status of black families, and the arts. Seeks to provide networking and career opportunities for African-American women in the process of establishing links between the organization and the corporate and political arenas. Encourages leadership development; sponsors role-model and mentor programs to provide guidance to teenage mothers and young women in high school or who have graduated from college and are striving for career advancement.

★14743★ **Organization of Chinese American Women (OCAW)**

4641 Montgomery Ave., Ste. 208
Bethesda, MD 20814
Ph: (301)907-3898   Fax: (301)907-3899
E-mail: info@ocawwomen.org
URL: http://www.ocawwomen.org

Description: Advances the cause of Chinese American women in the U.S. and fosters public awareness of their special needs and concerns. Seeks to integrate Chinese American women into the mainstream of women's activities and programs. Addresses issues such as equal employment opportunities at both the professional and nonprofessional levels; overcoming stereotypes; racial and sexual discrimination and restrictive traditional beliefs; assistance to poverty-stricken recent immigrants; access to leadership and policymaking positions. Serves as networking for Chinese American women. Sponsors annual opera and Mother's Day and Award Banquet. Establishes scholarships for middle school girls in rural China.

★14744★ **Wealth in Diversity Consulting Group Inc.**

544 Black Mountain
Cambridge, VT 05444
Ph: (802)644-5140   Fax: (802)644-2140
E-mail: info@wealthindiversity.com
URL: http://www.wealthindiversity.com

Group specializes in diversity initiatives, leadership and management development, organizational culture, team building, coaching, assessments, recruitment, conflict resolution, career development and health care educational development.

★14745★ **Wider Opportunities for Women (WOW)**

1001 Connecticut Ave. NW, Ste. 930
Washington, DC 20036
Ph: (202)464-1596   Fax: (202)464-1660
E-mail: info@wowonline.org
URL: http://www.wowonline.org

Description: Expands employment opportunities for women through information, employment training, technical assistance, and advocacy. Works to overcome barriers to women's employment and economic equity, including occupational segregation, sex stereotyped education and training, discrimination in employment practices and wages. Sponsors Women's Work Force Network, a national network of 500 women's employment programs and advocates. Monitors current policies to increase the priority given to employment needs of women; provides information to congressional staffs to clarify the impact of various legislative proposals on women; issues public policy alerts and informational materials when relevant federal policy is being proposed or undergoing revision; conducts investigative projects to assess how legislative programs are implemented and their impact on women. Offers technical assistance to education institutions, government agencies, and private industry on programs to increase women's participation in non-traditional employment and training. Maintains National Commission on Working Women and Industry Advisory Councils.

★14746★ **Women Employed Institute (WEI)**

111 N Wabash, Ste. 1300
Chicago, IL 60602
Ph: (312)782-3902   Fax: (312)782-5249
E-mail: info@womenemployed.org
URL: http://www.womenemployed.org

Description: Serves as a research and education division of Women Employed devoted to promoting economic equity for women. Analyzes government programs and employer policies; develops recommendations for public and corporate policy to promote equal opportunity. Sponsors advocacy programs to increase women's accessibility to vocational education and training for higher paying and nontraditional jobs. Develops model employment awareness/readiness programs for disadvantaged women. Conducts research projects; compiles statistics on women's economic status.

★14747★ Women in Management (WIM)
PO Box 1032
Dundee, IL 60118-7032
Ph: (708)386-0496   Fax: (847)683-3751
Fr: 877-946-6285
E-mail: nationalwim@wimonline.org
URL: http://www.wimonline.org

Description: Supports network of women in professional and management positions that facilitate the exchange of experience and ideas. Promotes self-growth in management; provides speakers who are successful in management; sponsors workshops and special interest groups to discuss problems and share job experiences.

★14748★ Women Work! The National Network for Women's Employment
1625 K St. NW, Ste. 300
Washington, DC 20006
Ph: (202)467-6346   Fax: (202)467-5366
Fr: 800-235-2732

E-mail: info@womenwork.org
URL: http://www.womenwork.org

Description: Works to "advocate for the economic security of women and families through policies, programs and partnerships". Represents displaced homemakers and single parents, women's training services, persons from related organizations, and supporters. Fosters development of programs and services for women preparing for the workforce. Acts as a clearinghouse to provide communications, technical assistance, public information, data collection, legislative monitoring, funding information, and other services. Compiles statistics. Provides referrals, information on research in progress, and publication distribution.

Outplacement

REFERENCE WORKS

★14749★ The Changing Outplacement Process: New Methods and Opportunities for Transition Management
Greenwood Publishing Group Inc.
88 Post Rd. W
Westport, CT 06881
Ph: (203)266-3571   Fax: (203)222-1502
Fr: 800-225-5800
URL: http://www.greenwood.com
1994. John Meyer and Carolyn Shadle. $109.95. 312 pages.

★14750★ Complete Guide to Outplacement Counseling
Lawrence Erlbaum
10 Industrial Ave.
Mahwah, NJ 07430
Ph: (201)258-2200   Fax: (201)236-0072
Fr: 800-926-6579
URL: http://www.leaonline.com
Alan Pickman. 168 pages. 1994. $49.95.

★14751★ Directory of Outplacement and Career Management Firms
Kennedy Information
1 Phoenix Mill Ln., 3rd Fl.
Peterborough, NH 03458
Ph: (603)924-1006   Fax: (603)924-4460
Fr: 800-531-0007
URL: http://www.kennedyinfo.com
Annual; latest edition 14th. $149.95 for individuals. Covers 407 consulting firms with special interest in career management and "outplacement" or "de-hiring" counseling executive employees being terminated because of poor performance, plant closings, etc., and assisting them in finding new jobs; firms that are compensated only by employers and those that also accept compensation from individuals are listed. Entries include: Firm name, address, phone, fax, e-mail, web address, description of philosophy and services, names and titles of principals, branches, area served, year established, revenue (within wide ranges), professional associations, minimum salary of positions handled, number of staff, percentage of business devoted to outplacement. Arrangement: Separate sections on basis of compensation arrangements, then alphabetical. Indexes: Industries, key principals, firm.

★14752★ Your Outplacement Handbook: Redesigning Your Career
CRC
6000 Broken Sounds Pkwy. NW, Ste. 300
Boca Raton, FL 33487
Ph: (561)994-0555   Fax: 800-374-3401
Fr: 800-272-7737
E-mail: orders@crcpress.com
URL: http://www.crcpress.com
Fern Lebo. 1996. $44.95. 240 pages.

NEWSPAPERS, MAGAZINES, AND JOURNALS

★14753★ Self-Employed America
National Association for the Self-Employed
DFW Airport
PO Box 612067
Dallas, TX 75261-2067
Fax: 800-551-4446   Fr: 800-232-6273
URL: http://nase.org/
Bimonthly. Magazine deseminating information on topics of interest to small-business owners, such as marketing, management, and pertinent legislative developments. Also presents success stories concerning Association members and describes Association activities.

AUDIO/VISUAL RESOURCES

★14754★ Getting Fired, Getting Hired: Job Hunting From A to Z
Career Lab
10475 Park Meadows Dr. Ste. 600
Lone Tree, CO 80124-5437
Ph: (303)790-0505   Fax: (303)790-0606
Fr: 800-723-9675
E-mail: wsfrank@careerlab.com
URL: http://www.careerlab.com
Six-part video series.

ONLINE AND DATABASE SERVICES

★14755★ HR-Guide.com
E-mail: webmaster@hr-guide.com
URL: http://www.hr-guide.com
Description: Online guide to ouplacement services.

★14756★ Transition Solutions: Executive Center for Transition
300 Crown Colony
Quincy, MA 02169
Ph: (617)471-5895   Fax: (617)471-7296
E-mail: jpoirier@transitionsolutions.com
URL: http://www.transitionsolutions.com
Description: Provides tailored transition support for senior executives with compensation of six figures or more.

OTHER SOURCES

★14757★ Association of Career Management Consulting Firms International (AOCFI)
204 E St. NE
Washington, DC 20002
Ph: (202)547-6344   Fax: (202)547-6348
E-mail: acf@acfinternational.org
URL: http://www.aocfi.org

Members: Represents firms providing displaced employees, who are sponsored by their organization, with counsel and assistance in job searching and the techniques and practices of choosing a career. **Purpose:** Develops, improves and encourages the art and science of outplacement consulting and the professional standards of competence, objectivity, and integrity in the service of clients. Cooperates with other industrial, technical, educational, professional, and governmental bodies in areas of mutual interest and concern.

★14758★ Career Concepts Inc.
140 W. Germantown Pike
Plymouth Meeting, PA 19462
Ph: (610)941-4455   Fax: (610)941-0267
URL: http://www.cciconsulting.com

Description: Privately held career consulting and human performance firm.

★14759★ CareerSoar
PO Box 905
Wappingers Falls, NY 12590
Ph: (845)790-5229   Fax: (845)790-5105
E-mail: info@CareerSoar.com
URL: http://www.careersoar.com

Description: Provides consulting services solutions.

★14760★ Five O'Clock Club
300 E. 40th St., Ste. 6L
New York, NY 10016
Fr: 800-538-6645
URL: http://www.fiveoclockclub.com

Description: Career Counseling network.

★14761★ The Miles/LeHane Group Inc.
205 N. King St.
Leesburg, VA 20176
Ph: (703)777-3370   Fax: (703)777-4861
E-mail: feedback@mileslehane.com
URL: http://www.mileslehane.com

Description: Provides transition support consultants to facilitate transition report process.

★14762★ National Career Development Association (NCDA)
305 N Beech Cir.
Broken Arrow, OK 74012
Ph: (918)663-7060   Fax: (918)663-7058
Fr: (866)367-6232
E-mail: dpenn@ncda.org
URL: http://www.ncda.org

Description: Represents professionals and others interested in career development or counseling in various work environments. Supports counselors, education and training personnel, and allied professionals working in schools, colleges, business/industry, community and government agencies, and in private practice. Provides publications, support for state and local activities, human equity programs, and continuing education and training for these professionals. Provides networking opportunities for career professionals in business, education, and government.

★14763★ National Self-Help Clearinghouse (NSHC)
365 5th Ave., Ste. 3300
New York, NY 10016
Ph: (212)817-1822
E-mail: info@selfhelpweb.org
URL: http://www.selfhelpweb.org

Description: Clearinghouse on self-help groups; provides referral services. Conducts research and training activities. Maintains speakers' bureau. Conventions/Meetings: none.

Self Employment

REFERENCE WORKS

★14764★ Being Self-Employed

Allyear Tax Guides
20484 Glen Brae Dr.
Saratoga, CA 95070
Ph: (408)867-2626   Fax: (408)867-6466

Holmes F. Crouch. Second edition, 1998. Part of the Series 100 Tax Guides: Individuals and Families. $19.95. 224 pages.

★14765★ The Bootstrapper's Bible: How to Start and Build a Business with a Great Idea And (Almost) No Money

Upstart Pub Co
155 N. Wacker Dr.
Chicago, IL 60606-1719
Ph: (312)836-4400   Fax: (312)836-1021
Fr: 800-621-9621

Seth Godin. 2001. $2.86 (paper). 280 pages.

★14766★ Careers in Focus: Entrepreneurs

Facts On File Inc.
132 W 31st St., 17th Fl.
New York, NY 10001
Ph: (212)967-8800   Fax: 800-678-3633
Fr: 800-322-8755
URL: http://www.factsonfile.com

Latest edition 2nd, 2004. $29.95 for individuals; $26.95 for libraries. Covers an overview of entrepreneurship, followed by a selection of jobs profiled in detail, including the nature of the job, earnings, prospects for employment, what kind of training and skills it requires, and sources for further information.

★14767★ Careers for Self-Starters and Other Entrepreneurial Types

The McGraw-Hill Companies
PO Box 182604
Columbus, OH 43272
Fax: (614)759-3749   Fr: 877-883-5524
E-mail: customer.service@mcgraw-hill.com
URL: http://www.mcgraw-hill.com

Blythe Camenson. Second edition, 2004. $13.95 (paper). 129 pages.

★14768★ Change Your Job, Change Your Life: High Impact Strategies for Finding Great Jobs in the 21st Century

Impact Publications
9104 Manassas Dr., Ste. N
Manassas Park, VA 20111-5211
Ph: (703)361-7300   Fax: (703)335-9486
Fr: 800-361-1055
E-mail: query@impactpublications.com
URL: http://www.impactpublications.com

Ronald Krannich. Seventh edition, 1999. $21.95 (paper). 317 pages. Details trends in the marketplace, how to identify opportunities, how to retrain for them, and how to land jobs. Includes a chapter on starting a business. Contains index, bibliography, and illustrations.

★14769★ A Consumer Guide to Buying a Franchise

Franchise Rule Information Hotline
6th and Pennsylvania Ave. NW
Washington, DC 20580
Ph: (202)326-2222
URL: http://www.ftc.gov

2005. 21 pages. Describes owning and selecting a franchise.

★14770★ The Directory of Home-Based Business Resources

Pilot Books
127 Sterling Ave.
PO Box 2102
Greenport, NY 11944-0893
Ph: (516)477-1094   Fax: (516)477-1094
Fr: 800-797-4568
URL: http://www.pilotbooks.com

$7.95. 35 pages. 1997. Provides information on starting and running a homebased business and lists sources of additional information.

★14771★ Entrepreneur's Be Your Own Boss

Entrepreneur Media Inc.
2445 McCabe Way, Ste. 400
Irvine, CA 92614
Ph: (949)261-2325   Fax: (949)261-0234
Fr: 800-274-6229
URL: http://www.entrepreneur.com

Three times/year (February, May, September). Covers over 1,100 franchise and business opportunities; coverage includes Canada. Febuary issue: low-investment franchises; May issue: directory of home-based franchises and business opportunities; September issue: completed directory of franchise and business opportunities. Entries include: Company name, address, phone, description of opportunity, geographical areas available, costs. Arrangement: Classified by line of business.

★14772★ Fired Up: The Proven Principles of Successful Entrepreneurs

Penguin
375 Hudson St.
New York, NY 10014
Ph: (212)366-2000   Fax: (212)366-2666
Fr: 800-847-5515
URL: http://us.penguingroup.com/

Michael Gill and Sheila Paterson. 1999. $8.95 (paper). 272 pages.

★14773★ Free Help from Uncle Sam to Start Your Own Business or Expand the One You Have

Puma Publishing Co.
1670 Coral Dr.
Santa Maria, CA 93454
Ph: (805)925-3216   Fax: (805)925-2656
Fr: 800-255-5730

William M. Alarid. Fifth edition, 2000. $15.95 (paper). 234 pages.

★14774★ Guide to Self-Employment

John Wiley & Sons Inc.
1 Wiley Dr.
Somerset, NJ 08873
Ph: (732)469-4400   Fax: (732)302-2300
Fr: 800-225-5945

E-mail: custserv@wiley.com
URL: http://www.wiley.com/WileyCDA/

National Business Employment Weekly staff. 1996. $12.95 (paper). 256 pages.

★14775★ How to Run Your Own Home Business

McGraw-Hill Companies
PO Box 182604
Columbus, OH 43272
Fax: (614)759-3749   Fr: 877-883-5524
E-mail: customer.service@mcgraw-hill.com
URL: http://www.mcgraw-hill.com

Coralee Smith Kern and Tammara Hoffman Wolfgram. Revised edition, 2001. $10.95 (paper). 128 pages. Helps the reader determine if he/she is suited to working at home, choose a product or service, set up a comfortable, efficient working environment, and keep abreast of zoning and tax laws.

★14776★ How to Write What You Love and Make a Living at It

Shaw Books
12265 Oracle Blvd., Ste. 200
Colorado Springs, CO 80921
Ph: (719)590-4999   Fax: (719)590-8977
Fr: 800-603-7051
URL: http://www.randomhouse.com/waterbrook/shaw/

Dennis E. Hensley. 2000. $12.99 (paper). 224 pages.

★14777★ The Ideal Entrepreneurial Business for You

John Wiley and Sons, Inc.
1 Wiley Dr.
Somerset, NJ 08875-1272
Ph: (732)469-4400   Fax: (732)302-2300
Fr: 800-225-5945
E-mail: custserv@wiley.com
URL: http://www.wiley.com/WileyCDA/

Glenn Desmond and Monica Faulkner. 1995. $55.00; $12.95 (paper). 261 pages.

★14778★ Independent Practice for the Mental Health Professional: Growing a Private Practice for the 21st Century

Routledge
270 Madison Ave.
New York, NY 10016
Ph: (212)216-7800   Fax: (212)563-2269
URL: http://www.routledge.com/

Ralph Earle and Dorothy Barnes. 1999. $33.95. 192 pages. Discusses pros and cons of going solo or joining a group, legal issues, marketing, physical arrangement of the office, collecting fees, and maintaining a practice in the age of managed care.

★14779★ Kiss off Corporate America: A Young Professional's Guide to Independence

Andrews McMeel Publishing
100 Front St.
Riverside, NJ 08075
Fax: 800-943-9831   Fr: 800-943-9839
URL: http://www.andrewsmcmeel.com/

Lisa Kivirist. 1998. $12.95 (paper). 198 pages.

★14780★ Lifescripts For the Self Employed

John Wiley & Sons Inc.
1 Wiley Dr.
Somerset, NJ 08873
Ph: (732)469-4400   Fax: (732)302-2300
Fr: 800-225-5945
E-mail: custserv@wiley.com
URL: http://www.wiley.com/WileyCDA/

Stephen M. Pollan and Mark Levine. 1999. $14.95. Part of Lifescripts series. 176 pages.

★14781★ Making Money Writing Newsletters

National Book Network
4501 Forbes Blvd., Ste. 200
Lanham, MD 20706
Ph: (301)459-3366   Fax: (301)429-5746
Fr: 800-462-6420
E-mail: custserv@nbnbooks.com
URL: http://www.nbnbooks.com

Elaine Floyd. 1994. $29.95 (paper). 132 pages. How to start a newsletter writing and design service.

★14782★ Marketing for the Home-based Business

The McGraw-Hill Companies
PO Box 182604
Columbus, OH 43272
Fax: (614)759-3749   Fr: 877-883-5524
E-mail: customer.service@mcgraw-hill.com
URL: http://www.mcgraw-hill.com

Jeffrey P. Davidson. Second edition, 1999. $10.95 (paper). 204 pages. Addresses how to market the home-based business after you've started it.

★14783★ Mind Your Own Business!

Jist Works
875 Montreal Way
St. Paul, MN 55102
Fr: 800-648-5478
E-mail: info@jist.com
URL: http://www.jist.com

LaVerne L. Ludden and Bonnie R. Maitlen. 1999. $9.95. 213 pages. Explains how to get started as an entrepreneur.

★14784★ Modern Moonlighting: How to Earn Thousands Extra without Leaving Your Day Job

The McGraw-Hill Companies
PO Box 182604
Columbus, OH 43272
Fax: (614)759-3749   Fr: 877-883-5524

E-mail: customer.service@mcgraw-hill.com
URL: http://www.mcgraw-hill.com

Roger Woodson. 1997. $14.95 (paper). 288 pages. Explores part-time self-employment business opportunities.

★14785★ Money Smart Secrets for the Self-Employed

Random House
1745 Broadway
New York, NY 10019
Ph: (212)782-9000   Fax: (212)572-6066
Fr: 800-733-3000
URL: http://www.randomhouse.com

Linda Stern. 1997. $20.00 (paper). 336 pages.

★14786★ No More Job Interviews!: Self-Employment Strategies for People with Disabilities

Training Resource Network, Incorporated
PO Box 439
St. Augustine, FL 32085-0439
Ph: (904)823-9800   Fax: (904)823-3554
Fr: (866)823-9800
URL: http://www.trninc.com/

Alice Weiss. 2000. $29.95 (paper). 183 pages.

★14787★ On Your Own: A Guide to Working Happily, Productively & Successfully at Home

Prentice Hall PTR
1 Lake St.
Upper Saddle River, NJ 07458
Ph: (201)236-7000   Fr: 800-428-5331
URL: http://www.phptr.com/index.asp?rl=1

Lionel L. Fisher. 1994. $10.95 (paper). 224 pages.

★14788★ Opportunities in Franchising Careers

The McGraw-Hill Companies
PO Box 182604
Columbus, OH 43272
Fax: (614)759-3749   Fr: 877-883-5524
E-mail: customer.service@mcgraw-hill.com
URL: http://www.mcgraw-hill.com

Kent B. Banning and Brook Carey. Revised, 1995. $14.95; $11.95 (paper). 143 pages.

★14789★ The Perfect Business: How to Make a Million from Home with No Payroll, No Employee Headaches, No Debt, and No Sleepless Nights

Sound Ideas
1230 Ave. of the Americas
New York, NY 10020
Ph: (212)698-7000   Fax: (212)698-7007
Fr: 800-223-2336

Michael LeBoeuf. 1997. $14.95 (paper). 224 pages

★14790★ **Secrets of Self-Employment: Surviving and Thriving on the Ups and Downs at Being Your Own Boss**

Tarcher
375 Hudson St.
New York, NY 10014-3657
Ph: (212)366-2000   Fax: (212)366-2666
Fr: 800-331-4624
URL: http://us.penguingroup.com/

Paul Edwards and Sarah Edwards. 1996. $15.95 (paper). 400 pages. Part of the Working from Home Series.

★14791★ **The Self-Employed Woman's Guide to Launching a Home-Based Business**

Three Rivers Press
280 Park Ave. (11-3)
New York, NY 10017
Fax: (212)940-7381   Fr: 800-726-0600
URL: http://www.primapublishing.com/crown/trp.html

Priscilla Huff. 2002. $14.95 (paper). 368 pages.

★14792★ **Self-Employment: From Dream to Reality!**

Jist Publishing
875 Montreal Way
St. Paul, MN 55102
Fr: 800-648-5478
E-mail: info@jist.com
URL: http://www.jist.com

Linda D. Gilkeson and Theresia Paauwe. Second Wrkbk edition, 2003. $16.95. 160 pages. An interactive workbook for starting a small business.

★14793★ **The Self-Employment Survival Manual: How to Start and Operate a One-Person Business Successfully**

A. William Benitez Ltd.
PO Box 150266
Austin, TX 78715-0266
Ph: (512)447-4744   Fax: (512)292-1778
Fr: 800-887-4017
E-mail: bill.benitez@yahoo.com
URL: http://abenitez-ebooksandmore.com/

A. William Benitez. 1993. $18.95 (paper). 102 pages. The book helps individuals to discover the work they are best suited for and then teaches them how to get started and organized, get and keep customers, how to price work, handle complaints and all other aspects of small business operation.

★14794★ **Small Business Sourcebook**

Gale, Cengage Learning
27500 Drake Rd.
Farmington Hills, MI 48331-3535
Ph: (248)699-4253   Fax: (248)699-8065
Fr: 800-877-4253
E-mail: businessproducts@gale.com
URL: http://www.gale.com

Annual; latest edition 22nd; Published April 2007. $499.00 for individuals. Contains profiles for 341 specific types of small businesses. Each profile contains sources of related start-up information, associations, educational programs, reference works, sources of supplies, statistical sources, trade periodicals, videos, trade shows and conventions, consultants, franchises, databases, business systems and software, libraries, research centers, and Internet databases. Publication also lists 99 general small business topics of interest to entrepreneurs and sources of small business information and assistance. Entries include: Organization, individual, event, or publication name, address, contact numbers; description of contents, activities, services, publications, or programs; and other details relevant to the type of source, such as show dates and location, investment preferences and limitations, etc. Arrangement: Volume 1 contains small business profiles A-Z; volume 2 contains general small business topics, state listings, federal government assistance. Indexes: Alphabetical.

★14795★ **Small Time Operator: How to Start Your Own Small Business, Keep Your Books, Pay Your Taxes, and Stay out of Trouble!**

Bell Springs Publishing
PO Box 1240
106 State St.
Willits, CA 95490
Ph: (707)459-6372   Fax: (707)459-8614
Fr: 800-515-8050
E-mail: publisher@bellsprings.com.
URL: http://www.bellsprings.com/

Bernard Kamoroff. Eighth edition, 2004. $17.95 (paper). 208 pages.

★14796★ **Solo Success**

Random House
1745 Broadway
New York, NY 10019
Ph: (212)782-9000   Fax: (212)572-6066
Fr: 800-733-3000
URL: http://www.randomhouse.com

David Perlstein. 1999. $1.99 (paper).

★14797★ **Start Small, Finish Big: 15 Key Lessons to Start-and Run-Your Own Successful Business**

Hachette Book Group
237 Park Ave.
New York, NY 10017
Ph: (212)522-7200
URL: http://www.hachettebookgroupusa.com/

Fred DeLuca and John P. Hayes. 2001. $14.95. 368 pages.

★14798★ **Start Up Financing: An Entrepreneur's Guide to Financing a New or Growing Business**

The Career Press, Inc.
3 Tice Rd.
PO Box 687
Franklin Lakes, NJ 07417-1322
Ph: (201)848-0310   Fax: (201)848-1727
Fr: 800-227-3371
URL: http://www.careerpress.com

William J. Stolze. 1997. $16.99. 239 pages. Written for the reader about to embark on a new venture or who has started a business within the past few years. Addresses key problems crucial to the small business owner, such as adequacy of funding and how to write a business plan.

★14799★ **Starting Over: How to Change Careers or Start Your Own Business**

Grand Central Publishing
237 Park Ave.
New York, NY 10017
Ph: (212)522-7200   Fax: 800-286-9471
Fr: 800-759-0190
URL: http://www.hachettebookgroupusa.com

Stephen M. Pollan and Mark Levine. 1997. $15.99 (paper). 256 pages.

★14800★ **Supplier Diversity Information Resource Guide**

Diversity Information Resources Inc.
2105 Central Ave. NE
Minneapolis, MN 55418
Ph: (612)781-6819   Fax: (612)781-0109
URL: http://www.diversityinforesources.com

Annual; latest edition 15th, 2007. $70.00 for individuals. Covers business opportunity fairs, seminars, and workshops; National Supplier Development Council regional offices; Small Business Administration and Minority Business Development Administration offices; minority and women-owned business directories; and other resources for minority and women-owned businesses.

★14801★ **Why Aren't You Your Own Boss?**

JIST Publishing
875 Montreal Way
St. Paul, MN 55102
Fax: 800-547-8329   Fr: 800-648-5478
E-mail: info@jist.com
URL: http://www.jist.com

Paul and Sarah Edwards, Peter Economy. 2003. $15.95. 320 pages. Guide to self-employment that identifies typical barriers and offers research-based strategies, case histories, and success stories.

★14802★ **Working Solo Sourcebook: Essential Resources for Independent Entrepreneurs**

John Wiley & Sons Inc.
1 Wiley Dr.
Somerset, NJ 08873
Ph: (732)469-4400   Fax: (732)302-2300
Fr: 800-225-5945
E-mail: custserv@wiley.com
URL: http://www.wiley.com/WileyCDA/

Terri Lonier. Second edition, 1998. $24.95 (paper). 315 pages.

NEWSPAPERS, MAGAZINES, AND JOURNALS

★14803★ *Entrepreneur Magazine*

Entrepreneur Media Inc.
2445 McCabe Way, Ste. 400
Irvine, CA 92614
Ph: (949)261-2325   Fax: (949)261-0234
Fr: 800-274-6229
E-mail: entmag@entrepreneur.com
URL: http://www.entrepreneur.com

Monthly. $11.97/year for individuals, special online rate. Magazine covering small business management and operation.

★14804★ *Franchising World*

International Franchise Association
1501 K St. NW, Ste. 350
Washington, DC 20005
Ph: (202)628-8000   Fax: (202)628-0812
Fr: 800-543-1038
URL: http://www.franchise.org/

Monthly. $50.00/year for individuals. Trade magazine covering topics of interest to franchise company executives and the business world.

★14805★ *innkeeping*

Professional Association of Innkeepers International
207 White Horse Pike
Haddon Heights, NJ 08035
Ph: (856)310-1102   Fax: (856)310-1105
Fr: 800-468-7244

E-mail: membership@paii.org
URL: http://www.paii.org/

Description: Monthly. Addresses topics of interest to innkeepers who own and operate bed and breakfast operations. Recurring features include letters to the editor, news of research, news of educational opportunities, and notices of publications available.

★14806★ *Self-Employed America*

National Association for the Self-Employed
DFW Airport
PO Box 612067
Dallas, TX 75261-2067
Fax: 800-551-4446   Fr: 800-232-6673
URL: http://nase.org/

Bimonthly. Magazine deseminating information on topics of interest to small-business owners, such as marketing, management, and pertinent legislative developments. Also presents success stories concerning Association members and describes Association activities.

ONLINE AND DATABASE SERVICES

★14807★ National Homeworkers Alliance

1925 Pine Ave., Ste. 9035
Niagara Falls, NY 14301
Ph: (905)521-0703   Fax: (905)521-9799

E-mail: support@homeworkers.org
URL: http://www.homeworkers.org

Description: Job databank and resource site for the self-employed. Contains links, online courses, resume submission and more. FEE Membership plans start at $14.88 for one month. $9.99 registration fee.

OTHER SOURCES

★14808★ National Association for the Self-Employed (NASE)

PO Box 612067
DFW Airport
Dallas, TX 75261-2067
Fax: 800-551-4446   Fr: 800-232-6673
E-mail: mpetron@nase.org
URL: http://www.nase.org

Members: Self-employed and small independent businesspersons. **Purpose:** Acts as an advocate at the state and federal levels for self-employed people. Provides discounts on products and services important to self-employed and small business owners.

Using Recruiters and Employment Agencies

REFERENCE WORKS

★14809★ Adams Executive Recruiters Almanac

Adams Media Corp.
57 Littlefield St.
Avon, MA 02322
Ph: (508)427-7100   Fax: (508)427-6790
Fr: 800-872-5627

Covers executive recruiters in the United States. Entries include: Firm or organization name, address, phone, name and title of contact; description of organization, headquarters location, typical titles for entry- and middle-level positions, educational backgrounds desired, fringe benefits offered, stock exchange listing, training programs, internships, parent company, number of employees, revenues, e-mail and web address, projected number of hires. Indexes: Alphabetical and by specialization.

★14810★ The Directory of Executive Recruiters

Kennedy Information Inc.
1 Phoenix Mill Lane, 3rd Fl.
Peterborough, NH 03458
Ph: (603)924-1006   Fax: (603)924-4460
Fr: 800-531-0007
E-mail: bookstore@kennedyinfo.com
URL: http://www.kennedyinfo.com/

2006. $59.95 (paper). 2,100 pages. Lists and describes more than 5,600 firms in North America and indexes these by function, industry, and geographic area. Names key principals of recruiting firms. Includes narrative section on executive search and how it affects job candidates. Also available: Corporate Edition, expanded for use by corporate staffs, $299.00 (paper).

★14811★ Executive Search Firms and Employment Agencies in Seattle: Job-Search Resources for the Executive, Manager and Professional

Barrett Street Productions
PO Box 99642
Seattle, WA 98199
Ph: (206)284-8202   Fax: (206)352-0944

Linda Carlson. 1998. $21.95 (paper). 192 pages.

★14812★ Executive Search Research Directory

Recruiting & Search Report
PO Box 9433
Panama City Beach, FL 32417
Ph: (850)235-3733   Fax: (850)233-9695
Fr: 800-634-4548
URL: http://www.rsronline.com

Latest edition 10th. $15.00 for individuals. Covers 389 freelance executive search researchers that specialize in candidate locating, screening, and development for executive recruiters and corporate (in-house) recruiters; publishers of directories, books, periodicals, and other resources related to recruitment research. Entries include: For researchers–Name, address, phone, rates, year established, first year listed, a description of services and specialties, hourly rates. Arrangement: Researchers are geographical by zip code. Indexes: Geographical; means of industry or functional concentration; unusual expertise; specialty.

★14813★ Finding Work Overseas: How and Where to Contact International Recruitment Agencies, Consultants and Employers

Trans-Atlantic Publications, Inc.
311 Bainbridge St.
Philadelphia, PA 19147
Ph: (215)925-5083   Fax: (215)925-1912
E-mail: jeffgolds@comcast.net
URL: http://www.transatlanticpub.com/

Matthew Cunningham. 1996. 205 pages. Part of the Living and Working Abroad Series.

★14814★ Headhunters Revealed

Hunter Arts Publishing
PO Box 66578E
Los Angeles, CA 90066
Ph: (310)842-8864   Fax: (310)842-8868
Fr: 877-443-2348
URL: http://www.headhuntersrevealed.com/

Quarterly. $14.95 for individuals; $12.50 for out of country. Covers online career sites, career associations, and organizations.

★14815★ Hunt-Scanlon's Executive Recruiters of North America - Contingency Firms

Hunt-Scanlon Publishing
700 Fairfield Ave.
Stamford, CT 06902
Ph: (203)352-2920   Fax: (203)352-2930
Fr: 800-477-1199
URL: http://www.hunt-scanlon.com/

Annual. $235.00. Covers over 3,000 executive recruiters in a cross-section of contingency search firms in North America. Entries include: Individual and company name, phone number, and revenue statistics. Arrangement: Alphabetical. Indexes: Geographical; business sector.

★14816★ Hunt-Scanlon's Executive Recruiters of North America (Retained Firms Edition)

Hunt-Scanlon Publishing
700 Fairfield Ave.
Stamford, CT 06902
Ph: (203)352-2920   Fax: (203)352-2930
Fr: 800-477-1199
URL: http://www.hunt-scanlon.com/

Annual; latest edition 2005. $235.00. Covers Over 3,600 retained executive recruiters in the U.S., Canada, and Mexico. Entries include: Individual name, phone number, specialization, revenue, professional memberships, salary levels.

★14817★ Job Seeker's Guide

Greater Dallas Chamber
700 N Pearl St., Ste. 1200
Dallas, TX 75201
Ph: (214)746-6600

Annual. $10.00 for nonmembers; $20.00 for members. Covers top 100 employers in the Dallas area, information on employment agencies, and labor market projections.

★14818★ Job Seekers Guide to Executive Recruiters

John Wiley & Sons Inc.
1 Wiley Dr.
Somerset, NJ 08873
Ph: (732)469-4400   Fax: (732)302-2300
Fr: 800-225-5945
E-mail: custserv@wiley.com
URL: http://www.wiley.com/WileyCDA/

Christopher W. Hunt and Scott A. Scanlon. 1997. $34.95 (paper). 516 pages. Provides listings for executive search consultants, as well as advice on interviewing and resume preparation.

★14819★ Job Seekers Guide to Silicon Valley Recruiters

John Wily and Sons, Inc.
605 Third Ave., 4th Fl.
New York, NY 10158-0012
Ph: (212)850-6276   Fax: (212)850-8641

Christopher W. Hunt, Scott A. Scanlon. First edition, 1998. $19.95 (paper). 371 pages. Includes a list of 2,400 recruiters specializing in high technology positions and explains how to work with them.

★14820★ Job Seekers Guide to Wall Street Recruiters

John Wiley & Sons Inc.
1 Wiley Dr.
Somerset, NJ 08873
Ph: (732)469-4400   Fax: (732)302-2300
Fr: 800-225-5945
E-mail: custserv@wiley.com
URL: http://www.wiley.com/WileyCDA/

Christopher W. Hunt and Scott A. Scanlon. 1998. $26.95 (paper). 344 pages. Lists recruiters covering investment banking, investment management, and the securities industry.

★14821★ Knock 'Em Dead: The Ultimate Job Seeker's Handbook

Adams Media Corp.
4700 E. Galbraith Rd.
Cincinnati, OH 45236
Ph: (513)531-2690   Fax: (513)531-4082
Fr: 800-289-0963
URL: http://www.adamsmedia.com

Martin Yate. Revised edition, 2007. $14.95 (paper). Prepares the job seeker for the interview with advice on dress, manner, how to answer the toughest questions, and how to spot illegal questions. Discusses how to respond to questions of salary to maximize income. Features sections on executive search firms and drug testing. 352 pages.

★14822★ National Directory of Personnel Service Firms

National Association of Personnel Services
The Village At Banner Elk, Ste. 108
PO Box 2128
Banner Elk, NC 28604
Ph: (828)898-4929   Fax: (828)898-8098
URL: http://www.recruitinglife.com

Annual, spring. Covers over 1,100 member private (for-profit) personnel service firms and temporary service firms. Entries include: Firm name, address, phone, fax, contact, area of specialization. Arrangement: Same information given geographically by employment specialty.

★14823★ Navigating Your Career: 21 of America's Leading Headhunters Tell You How It's Done

John Wiley and Sons, Inc.
1 Wiley Dr.
Somerset, NJ 08875-1272
Ph: (732)469-4400   Fax: (732)302-2300
Fr: 800-225-5945
E-mail: custserv@wiley.com
URL: http://www.wiley.com/WileyCDA/

Christopher W. Hunt and Scott A. Scanlon. 1998. $21.50 (paper). 256 pages. Provides job-hunting advice from executive recruiters.

★14824★ O'Dwyer's New York Public Relations Directory

J.R. O'Dwyer Company Inc.
271 Madison Ave., Ste. 600
New York, NY 10016
Ph: (212)679-2471   Fax: (212)683-2750
Fr: (866)395-7710

Annual. $50.00 for individuals. Covers approximately 600 public relations firms, 840 corporations, 225 trade associations, and 500 public relations service firms; over 50 executive recruiters and employment agencies. Entries include: Contact information.

★14825★ The Recruiter's Research Blue Book

Kennedy Information Inc.
1 Pheonix Mill Ln., 3rd Fl.
Peterborough, NH 03458
Ph: (603)924-1006   Fax: (603)924-4460
Fr: 800-531-0007

$179.00 for individuals. Publication includes: An annotated bibliography of print and electronic resources in 220 categories. Principal content of publication is a guide book to the executive search process for professional recruiters and human resources departments.

ONLINE AND DATABASE SERVICES

★14826★ Association of Executive Search Consultants

E-mail: aesc@aesc.org
URL: http://www.aesc.org

Description: Partnership with BlueSteps.com allows member search consultants to add their names to a directory of firms, which may then be referred to senior executives who contact the organization to help fill executive vacancies within their own organizations.

★14827★ Corporate Search Consultants, Inc.

509 W. Colonial Dr.
Orlando, FL 32804
Ph: (407)578-3888   Fax: (407)578-5153
Fr: 800-800-7231
E-mail: webmanager@corpsearch.com
URL: http://jobs.corpsearch.com

Description: Job search consultants. Job board and resume posting for jobs in the healthcare and medical community.

★14828★ FutureStep

1900 Ave. of the Stars, Ste. 2600
Los Angeles, CA 90067
Ph: (310)552-1834
E-mail: info@futurestep.com
URL: http://www.futurestep.com

Description: An executive search service for management professionals brought to you by Korn/Ferry International, the world's largest executive search firm. Seekers can register for free, and search for jobs posted. Also contains assessment information, career resources, and useful links.

★14829★ Glocapsearch.com

156 W. 56th St., 4th Fl.
New York, NY 10019
Ph: (212)333-6400
E-mail: comments@glocap.com
URL: http://www.glocapsearch.com

Description: Recruitment firm for the private equity, venture capital and hedge fund marketplaces. After registering with website, seekers will be notified weekly of positions available that may interest them. Through returned e-mail, the firm will forward resumes and schedule preliminary interviews with prospective employers.

★14830★ MRINetwork.com

URL: http://www.mrinetwork.com/

Description: Management-level job seekers can review job board and/or contact an executive recruiter seeking for prospective candidates. Site also contains resume building and career transitioning resources.

★14831★ **Spherion**
2050 Spectrum Blvd.
Fort Lauderdale, FL 33309
Ph: (954)308-7600
E-mail: help@spherion.com
URL: http://www.spherion.com
Description: Recruitment firm specializing in accounting and finance, sales and marketing, interim executives, technology, engineering, retail and human resources.

SOFTWARE

★14832★ **Executive Search System**
Custom Databanks, Inc.
60 Sutton Pl. S, Ste. 14BN
New York, NY 10022-4168
Fr: 800-445-3557
E-mail: email@customdatabanks.com
URL: http://www.customdatabanks.com
$300.00 (latest update). Databases contain 25,700+ search firms. Can download and merge data directly into your cover letters.

Working at Home

REFERENCE WORKS

★14833★ *Complete Work-at-Home Companion: Everything You Need to Know to Prosper as a Home-Based Entrepreneur or Employee*
Prima Publishing
3000 Lava Ridge Ct.
Roseville, CA 95661
Ph: (916)787-7000   Fax: (916)787-7001
Herman R. Holtz. Second edition, 1994. $14.95 (paper). 368 pages.

★14834★ *The Directory of Home-Based Business Resources*
Pilot Books
127 Sterling Ave.
PO Box 2102
Greenport, NY 11944-0893
Ph: (516)477-1094   Fax: (516)477-1094
Fr: 800-797-4568
URL: http://www.pilotbooks.com
$7.95. 35 pages. 1997. Provides information on starting and running a homebased business and lists sources of additional information.

★14835★ *The Home Team: How Couples Can Make a Life and a Living by Working at Home*
Panda Publishing
PO Box 5900
Navarre, FL 32566
Ph: (850)936-4050   Fax: (850)939-4953
Shirley Siluk Gregory. 1999. $14.95 (paper). 256 pages.

★14836★ *Homemade Money*
M. Evans & Company Inc.
4501 Forbes Blvd., Ste. 200
Lanham, MD 20706
Ph: (301)459-3366   Fax: (301)429-5743
Fr: 800-462-6420
URL: http://www.mevans.com
Published in two volumes. Publication includes: A special 76-page, updated "A-Z Crash Course" on business basics and a directory of 300 listings. Entries include: Supplier name, address, description of information, price, order information. Principal content of the book is editorial matter on beginning and developing a home-based business. Arrangement: Classified by subject. Indexes: Alphabetical.

★14837★ *How to Run Your Own Home Business*
McGraw-Hill Companies
PO Box 182604
Columbus, OH 43272
Fax: (614)759-3749   Fr: 877-883-5524
E-mail: customer.service@mcgraw-hill.com
URL: http://www.mcgraw-hill.com
Coralee Smith Kern and Tammara Hoffman Wolfgram. Revised edition, 2001. $10.95 (paper). 128 pages. Helps the reader determine if he/she is suited to working at home, choose a product or service, set up a comfortable, efficient working environment, and keep abreast of zoning and tax laws.

★14838★ *The Ideal Entrepreneurial Business for You*
John Wiley and Sons, Inc.
1 Wiley Dr.
Somerset, NJ 08875-1272
Ph: (732)469-4400   Fax: (732)302-2300
Fr: 800-225-5945
E-mail: custserv@wiley.com
URL: http://www.wiley.com/WileyCDA/
Glenn Desmond and Monica Faulkner. 1995. $55.00; $12.95 (paper). 261 pages.

★14839★ *The Joy of Working from Home: Making a Life While Making a Living*
Berrett-Koehler Publishers
235 Montgomery St., Ste. 650
San Francisco, CA 94104
Ph: (415)288-0260   Fax: (415)362-2512
Fr: 800-929-2929
E-mail: bkpub@bkpub.com
URL: http://www.bkconnection.com/
Jeff Berner. 1994. $12.95 (paper). 63 pages.

★14840★ *Making Money with Your Computer at Home*
Midwest Book Review
278 Orchard Dr.
Oregon, WI 53575
Ph: (608)835-7937
E-mail: mwbookrevw@aol.com
URL: http://www.midwestbookreview.com
Paul Edwards and Sarah Edwards. 2005. $5.95 (paper). 368 pages. Profiles 75 different home-based computer businesses.

★14841★ *Marketing for the Home-based Business*
The McGraw-Hill Companies
PO Box 182604
Columbus, OH 43272
Fax: (614)759-3749   Fr: 877-883-5524
E-mail: customer.service@mcgraw-hill.com
URL: http://www.mcgraw-hill.com
Jeffrey P. Davidson. Second edition, 1999. $10.95 (paper). 204 pages. Addresses how to market the home-based business after you've started it.

★14842★ *Mompreneurs: A Mother's Step-by-Step Guide to Work-at-Home Success*
Perigee Trade
375 Hudson St.
New York, NY 10014
Ph: (212)366-2000   Fax: (212)366-2385
Fr: 800-631-8571
Ellen H. Parlapiano and Patricia Cobe. Reprint edition, 2002. $14.95 (paper). 320 pages.

★14843★ *Moneymaking Moms: How Work at Home Can Work for You*
Citadel Press
850 Third Ave.
New York, NY 10022
Fr: 800-221-2647
URL: http://www.kensingtonbooks.com/
Caroline Hull and Tanya Wallace. 1998. $12.00 (paper). 242 pages.

★14844★ On Your Own: A Guide to Working Happily, Productively & Successfully at Home

Prentice Hall PTR
1 Lake St.
Upper Saddle River, NJ 07458
Ph: (201)236-7000   Fr: 800-428-5331
URL: http://www.phptr.com/index.asp?rl=1

Lionel L. Fisher. 1994. $10.95 (paper). 224 pages.

★14845★ The Perfect Business: How to Make a Million from Home with No Payroll, No Employee Headaches, No Debt, and No Sleepless Nights

Sound Ideas
1230 Ave. of the Americas
New York, NY 10020
Ph: (212)698-7000   Fax: (212)698-7007
Fr: 800-223-2336

Michael LeBoeuf. 1997. $14.95 (paper).224 pages

★14846★ The Road to Self-Employment: A Practical Guide to Microbusiness Development

Women's Business Training Center
PO Box 126305
San Diego, CA 92101
Ph: (619)239-9282   Fax: (619)238-5205

Gerri P. Norington. 1997. $24.95. 163 pages. Part of The Rose Program Series. Deals with personal growth as a tool for business success and lets the reader know what to expect from and how to prepare for microbusiness development.

★14847★ The Selling-From-Home Sourcebook

Betterway Publications
4700 E Galbraith Rd.
Cincinnati, OH 45236
Ph: (513)531-2690   Fax: (513)531-4082
Fr: 800-289-0963

Kathryn Caputo. 1996. $17.99 (paper). 262 pages.

★14848★ Starting a Home Based Business (Full or Part-Time)

Citadel Press
850 Third Ave.
New York, NY 10022
Fr: 800-221-2647
URL: http://www.kensingtonbooks.com/

Irene Korn and Bill Zanker. 1993. $8.95 (paper). 122 pages.

★14849★ Work-at-Home Sourcebook

Live Oak Publications
6003 N 51st St. No. 105
PO Box 2193
Boulder, CO 80306

Latest edition 2002. $12.97 for individuals. Covers over 1,000 companies and home business franchises that employ home workers. Entries include: Company name, ad-

dress, contact person, description of job position, pay scale, requirements, equipment, and training provided. Arrangement: Classified by occupational category. Indexes: Alphabetical; geographical.

★14850★ Work at Home Wisdom: A Collection of Quips, Tips, and Inspirations to Balance Work, Family, and Home.

Upstart Pub Co.
155 N. Wacker Dr.
Chicago, IL 60606-1719
Ph: (312)836-4400   Fax: (312)836-1021
Fr: 800-621-9621

David H. Bangs and Andi Axman. 1998. $9.95 (paper). 189 pages. Offers advice on how to work smarter from home, including balancing the demands of home, work, and family.

★14851★ Working from Home: Everything You Need to Know About Living and Working Under the Same Roof

Tarcher
375 Hudson St.
New York, NY 10014-3657
Ph: (212)366-2000   Fax: (212)366-2666
Fr: 800-331-4624
URL: http://us.penguingroup.com/

Paul Edwards and Sarah Edwards Fifth edition, 1999. $19.95. 436 pages.

★14852★ Working at Home While the Kids Are There Too

Career Press, Inc.
3 Tice Rd.
PO Box 687
Franklin Lakes, NJ 07417-1322
Ph: (201)848-0310   Fax: (201)848-1727
Fr: 800-227-3371
URL: http://www.careerpress.com

Loriann H. Oberlin. 1997. $12.99 (paper). 191 pages.

★14853★ Working and Living Spaces: Working at Home

Loft and HBI
770 Broadway
New York, NY 10003
Ph: (646)654-5400   Fax: (646)654-5486
Fr: 800-323-9432

Aurora Cuito (editor). 2000. $35.00 (paper). 176 pages. Book examines the many imaginative ways architects and interior designers have combined working and living spaces in a variety of settings, shown in numerous photographs, detailed plans, and sketches.

★14854★ Working Smarter from Home: Your Day, Your Way

Crisp Publications, Inc.
1200 Hamilton Ct.
Menlo Park, CA 94025
Ph: (650)323-6100   Fax: (650)323-5800
Fr: 800-442-7477

Nancy Struck. 1995. $13.95 (paper). 111 pages. Part of Fifty-Minute series.

NEWSPAPERS, MAGAZINES, AND JOURNALS

★14855★ The Home Business Report

The Kerner Group Inc.
121 Bulifants Blvd., Ste. A
Williamsburg, VA 23188-5709
Ph: (757)229-6269   Fax: (757)229-8027
URL: http://www.kernergroup.com

Description: Monthly. Provides information on how to operate a home-based business or work from home. Features real life success stories, "how-to" articles on marketing, and strategies to keep focused on goals. Recurring features include letters to the editor, interviews, news of research, job listings, book reviews, and notices of publications available.

★14856★ Our Place

Home-Based Working Moms
PO Box 1628
Spring, TX 77383-1628
Ph: (512)266-0900
URL: http://www.hbwm.com

Description: Biweekly. Advocates home employment and home businesses to allow parents more time with their children. Offers ideas, marketing tips, member profiles to promote successful employment at home. Recurring features include interviews, job listings, and book reviews.

ONLINE AND DATABASE SERVICES

★14857★ FreelanceWorkExchange.com

45 Main St., Ste. 309, No. 178
Brooklyn, NY 11201
Ph: (718)249-4822
E-mail: support@freelanceworkexchange.com
URL: http://www.freelanceworkexchange.com

Description: Project and contract search board for the freelance worker. E-mail newsletters and freelancing e-books available. **Fee:** Must register as a member; pricing based on length of membership; one month is $19.95. Trial seven-day membership available.

★14858★ Independent Homeworkers Alliance

1925 Pine Ave., Ste. 9035
Niagara Falls, NY 14301
Ph: (905)521-0703   Fax: (905)521-9799
E-mail: support@homeworkers.org
URL: http://www.homeworkers.org

Description: Job databank and resource site for the self-employed. Contains links, online courses, resume submission and more. FEE Membership plans start at $14.88 for one month. $9.99 registration fee.

★14859★ Telecommuting Jobs

E-mail: contact@atstjobs.com
URL: http://www.tjobs.com

Description: Job hunters may enter a resume or post a job-wanted listing. Employers may search talent available and post job availabilities. Site also includes tools to connect telecommuters with employers and job news about telecommuting.

★14860★ Work from Home

URL: http://www.jobs-telecommuting.com

Description: Contains a listing of over 700 companies currently looking for telecommuters. Employers may add or remove job listings. Also information on starting a home business available.

Working Part-Time, Summer Employment, and Internships

REFERENCE WORKS

★14861★ *Administration of Justice: An Internship Guide to the Quest for Justice*
Kendall Hunt Publishing Company
4050 Westmark Dr.
PO Box 1840
Dubuque, IA 52002
Ph: (319)589-1000   Fax: (319)589-1046
Fr: 800-228-0810
URL: http://www.kendallhunt.com/

Carol L. Fine. 2001. $55.95 (paper). 370 pages.

★14862★ *Baltimore Job Source: The Only Source You Need to Land the Job of Your Choice in Baltimore.*
Benjamin Scott Publishing
20 E. Colorado Blvd., No. 202
Pasadena, CA 91105
Ph: (626)449-1339   Fax: (626)449-1389
Fr: 800-448-4959

Mary McMahon, Ruth E. Thaler-Carter and Betty Glascoe. 2005. $15.95. 312 pages. Over 5000 job contacts in the Baltimore/Annapolis Metro Areas, including small and large companies, Fortune 500 corporations, non-profits, government agencies, and internships.

★14863★ *The Best 109 Internships*
The Princeton Review
2315 Broadway
New York, NY 10024
Ph: (212)874-8282   Fax: (212)874-0775
Fr: 800-733-3000
URL: http://www.princetonreview.com/

Latest edition January 2003. $21.00 for individuals. Covers more than 20,000 internship opportunities. Entries include: Summary of the internship program and contact information.

★14864★ *Cents-Able Summer Self-Employment: An Entrepreneurial Guide for High School & College Students*
Tamarax Press
PO Box 450
2A Taylor Way
Washington Crossing, PA 18977
Ph: (215)493-2136   Fax: (215)493-2057

E.K. Shepard. 1994. $12.95 (paper). 220 pages.

★14865★ *Creating a Flexible Workplace: How to Select & Manage Alternative Work Options*
AMACOM
1601 Broadway, 12th Fl.
New York, NY 10019
Ph: (212)586-8100   Fax: (212)903-8168
Fr: 800-262-9699
URL: http://www.amanet.org

Barney Olmsted and Suzanne Smith. Second edition, 1994. $59.95. 402 pages.

★14866★ *Directory of Child Life Programs*
Child Life Council Inc.
11820 Parklawn Dr., Ste. 240
Rockville, MD 20852-2529
Ph: (301)881-7090   Fax: (301)881-7092
URL: http://www.childlife.org/

Biennial; latest edition 14th, 2006. Covers over 400 child life programs. Entries include: Facility name, address, phone, name of child life department and director, reporting structure, staff statistics, educational requirements for employment, and internship or educational opportunities. Arrangement: Geographical. Indexes: Speciality areas, internship sessions, program size, fellowships.

★14867★ *Directory of International Internships*
Dean's Office of International Studies and Programs
Michigan State University
209 International Ctr.
East Lansing, MI 48824-1035
Ph: (517)355-2350   Fax: (517)353-7254

URL: http://www.isp.msu.edu/students/internships/intlguide/

Irregular; latest edition 5th. $30.00 for students; $37.00 for other individuals. Covers international internships sponsored by academic institutions, private sector, and the federal government. Entries include: Institution name, address, phone, names and titles of key personnel, subject areas in which internships are available, number available, location, duration, financial data, academic credit available, evaluation procedures, application deadline, requirements of participation. Arrangement: Classified by type of sponsor, then alphabetical. Indexes: Sponsor; subject; geographical.

★14868★ *Directory of Public Garden Internships*
American Association of Botanical Gardens and Arboreta
100 W 10th St., Ste. 614
Wilmington, DE 19801
Ph: (302)655-7100   Fax: (302)655-8100
E-mail: bvincent@aabga.org
URL: http://aabga.org

Annual, November; latest edition 2005. Covers 700 student internships and summer jobs at public gardens throughout North America. Entries include: Name of institution, address, name of contact, deadline for application, number of students hired, whether internships are available, employment period, hours, rate of pay, whether housing is available, other comments. Arrangement: Alphabetical. Indexes: By position, by state/province.

★14869★ *Everything You Need to Get a Psychology Internship*
Windmill Lane Press
1009 S. Bedford St.
Los Angeles, CA 90035-2101
Fax: (310)815-9865   Fr: 800-566-3659

Carl Levinger and Itzchack Schefres. 1996. $24.95 (paper). 144 pages.

★14870★ Grants, Fellowships, and Prizes of Interest to Historians

American Historical Association
400 A St. SE
Washington, DC 20003-3889
Ph: (202)544-2422   Fax: (202)544-8307
E-mail: grantguide@theaha.org
URL: http://www.historians.org

Annual; latest edition 2006. For American Historical Association members. Covers over 450 sources of funding (scholarships, fellowships, internships, awards, and book and essay prizes) in the United States and abroad for graduate students, postdoctoral researchers, and institutions in the humanities. Entries include: Name of source, institution name or contact, address, phone, eligibility and proposal requirements, award or stipend amount, location requirements for research, application deadlines. Arrangement: Alphabetical in three categories: support for individual research and teaching; grants for groups and organizations for research and education; and book, article, essay, and manuscript prizes.

★14871★ A Guide to a Successful Legal Internship

Anderson Publishing Co.
2035 Reading Rd.
Cincinnati, OH 45202-1576
Ph: (513)421-4142   Fax: (513)562-8116
Fr: 800-582-7295

Hedi Nasheri and Peter C. Kratcoski. 1996. $22.95 (paper). 171 pages.

★14872★ Half a Job: Bad and Good Part-Time Jobs in Changing Labor Market

Temple University Press
University Services Bldg., Rm 306
1601 N. Broad St.
Philadelphia, PA 19122-6099
Ph: (215)204-8787   Fax: 800-621-8471
Fr: 800-621-2736
URL: http://www.temple.edu/tempress/

Chris Tilly. 1996. $26.95. 228 pages.

★14873★ The Imaginative Soul's Guide to Foreign Internships: A Roadmap to Envision, Create and Arrange Your Own Experience

Ivy House
PO Box 391262
Cambridge, MA 02139
Ph: (617)489-0599

Laura Hitchcock. 1993. $16.95 (paper). 125 pages.

★14874★ Internship Bible

Princeton Review
2315 Broadway
New York, NY 10024
Ph: (212)874-8282   Fax: (212)874-0775
URL: http://www.princetonreview.com

Mark Oldman and Samer Hamadeh. 2005. 672 pages.

★14875★ The Internship, Practicum and Field Placement Handbook: A Guide for the Helping Professions

Prentice Hall PTR
1 Lake St.
Upper Saddle River, NJ 07458
Ph: (201)236-7000   Fr: 800-428-5331
URL: http://www.phptr.com/index.asp?rl=1

Brian N. Baird. Fourth edition, 2004. $77.40. 212 pages.

★14876★ Internship Selection in Professional Psychology: A Comprehensive Guide for Students, Faculty, and Training Directors

Charles C Thomas Publisher, Ltd.
2600 S 1st St.
PO Box 19265
Springfield, IL 62794-9265
Ph: (217)789-8980   Fax: (217)789-9130
Fr: 800-258-8980
E-mail: books@ccthomas.com
URL: http://www.ccthomas.com

Mary E. Oehlert, Scott Sumerall and Shane J. Lopez. 1998. $44.95. 153 pages.

★14877★ Internships in Communications

Iowa State University Press
2121 S. State Ave.
Ames, IA 50014-8300
Ph: (515)292-0140   Fax: (515)292-3348
Fr: 800-862-6657
URL: http://www.iastate.edu/

James P. Alexander. 1995. $22.99 (paper). 207 pages.

★14878★ Internships in Federal Government: A Guide for Faculty Coordinators and Instructors.

Iowa State University Press
2121 S. State Ave.
Ames, IA 50014-8300
Ph: (515)292-0140   Fax: (515)292-3348
Fr: 800-862-6657
URL: http://www.iastate.edu/

James P. Alexander. Seventh edition, 1995. $27.50. 207 pages

★14879★ Internships Leading to Careers

The Graduate Group
PO Box 370351
West Hartford, CT 06137-0351
Ph: (860)233-2330   Fax: (860)233-2330
Fr: 800-484-7280
E-mail: graduategroup@hotmail.com
URL: http://www.graduategroup.com

Sixth edition, 2001. $25.00.

★14880★ Internships in Recreation and Leisure Services: A Practical Guide for Students

Venture Publishing, Inc.
1999 Cato Ave.
State College, PA 16801
Ph: (814)234-4561   Fax: (814)234-1651

E-mail: vpublish@venturepublish.com
URL: http://www.venturepublish.com/

Edward E. Seagle, Ralph W. Smith and Lola M. Dalton. Third Spiral edition, 2002. $28.95 (paper). 190 pages.

★14881★ Internships in State Government

The Graduate Group
PO Box 370351
West Hartford, CT 06137-0351
Ph: (860)233-2330   Fax: (860)233-2330
Fr: 800-484-7280
E-mail: graduategroup@hotmail.com
URL: http://www.graduategroup.com

Sixth edition, 1996. $27.50.

★14882★ Internships: The Hotlist for Job Hunters

Arco Pub.
10475 Crosspoint Blvd.
Indianapolis, IN 46256
Fax: (317)572-4000   Fr: 800-667-1115

Sara D. Gilbert. Second edition, 1997. $19.95 (paper). 418 pages. Part of Arco Internships series.

★14883★ Internships: The Largest Source of Internships Available

Peterson's Guides
2000 Lenox Dr.
Box 67005
Lawrenceville, NJ 08648
Ph: (609)896-1800   Fax: (609)896-4531
Fr: 800-338-3282
E-mail: custsvc@petersons.com
URL: http://www.petersons.com

Twenty first Rev edition, 2000. $24.95 (paper). 721 pages. Lists 35,000 paid and unpaid internships. Part of Peterson's Guides series.

★14884★ The JobBank Guide to Health Care Companies

Adams Media Corp.
57 Littlefield St.
Avon, MA 02322
Ph: (508)427-7100   Fax: (508)427-6790
Fr: 800-872-5627
URL: http://www.amazon.com/Jobbank-Guide-Health-Care-Companies/dp

Biennial. Covers jobs nationwide in health care companies. Entries include: Firm or organization name, address, phone, name and title of contact; description of organization, headquarters location, typical titles for entry- and middle-level positions, educational backgrounds desired, fringe benefits offered, stock exchange listing, training programs, internships, parent company, number of employees, revenues, e-mail and web addresses, projected number of hires. Indexes: Alphabetical.

★14885★ Jobs in Paradise

HarperCollins
10 E. 53rd St.
New York, NY 10022
Ph: (212)207-7000   Fax: (212)207-7145
Fr: 800-242-7737
URL: http://www.harpercollins.com/

Jeffrey Maltzman. Revised, 1993. $16.00 (paper). 448 pages.

★14886★ Modern Moonlighting: How to Earn Thousands Extra without Leaving Your Day Job

The McGraw-Hill Companies
PO Box 182604
Columbus, OH 43272
Fax: (614)759-3749   Fr: 877-883-5524
E-mail: customer.service@mcgraw-hill.com
URL: http://www.mcgraw-hill.com

Roger Woodson. 1997. $14.95 (paper). 288 pages. Explores part-time self-employment business opportunities.

★14887★ National Directory of Arts Internships

National Network for Artist Placement
935 W Ave. 37
Los Angeles, CA 90065
Ph: (323)222-4035   Fax: (323)225-5711
Fr: 800-354-5348
URL: http://www.artistplacement.com

Biennial, odd years; latest edition 10th. $95.00 for individuals. Covers over 5,000 internship opportunities in dance, music, theater, art, design, film, and video & over 1,250 host organizations. Entries include: Name of sponsoring organization, address, name of contact; description of positions available, eligibility requirements, stipend or salary (if any), application procedures. Arrangement: Classified by discipline, then geographical.

★14888★ New Internships

The Graduate Group
PO Box 370351
West Hartford, CT 06137-0351
Ph: (860)233-2330   Fax: (860)233-2330
Fr: 800-484-7280
E-mail: graduategroup@hotmail.com
URL: http://www.graduategroup.com

Robert Wigman, editor. 1997. $27.50.

★14889★ Opportunities in Part-Time and Summer Jobs

The McGraw-Hill Companies
PO Box 182604
Columbus, OH 43272
Fax: (614)759-3749   Fr: 877-883-5524
E-mail: customer.service@mcgraw-hill.com
URL: http://www.mcgraw-hill.com

Adrian A. Paradis. 1998. $14.95 (paper). 160 pages.

★14890★ Opportunities in Summer Camp Careers

The McGraw-Hill Companies
PO Box 182604
Columbus, OH 43272
Fax: (614)759-3749   Fr: 877-883-5524
E-mail: customer.service@mcgraw-hill.com
URL: http://www.mcgraw-hill.com

Blythe Camenson. 1998. $11.95 (paper). 160 pages. Part of "Opportunities in ..." Series.

★14891★ Paralegal Internships: Finding, Managing & Transitioning Your Career

Cengage Learning
PO Box 6904
Florence, KY 41022
Fax: 800-487-8488   Fr: 800-354-9706
URL: http://www.cengage.com

Ruth-Ellen Post. 1998. $51.95 (paper). 288 pages. Part of the Paralegal Series. Text covers all stages of the internship experience, including identifying learning objectives, finding the "right office," managing "office politics," self-monitoring and documentation an finally how to use the internship to land a permanent job.

★14892★ Part-Time Employment: A Bridge or a Trap?

Avebury
101 Cherry St.
Ste. 420
Burlington, VT 05401-4405
Ph: (802)865-7641   Fax: (802)865-7847
URL: http://www.ashgate.com

May Tam. 1997. 259 pages.

★14893★ Part-Time Employment for the Low-Income Elderly: Experiences from the Field

Routledge
270 Madison Ave.
New York, NY 10016
Ph: (212)216-7800   Fax: (212)563-2269
URL: http://www.routledge.com/

Leslie B. Alexander. 1997. $95.00. Part of Issues in Aging series. 182 pages.

★14894★ Part Time Prospects: International Comparison of Part Time Work in Europe, North America and the Pacific Rim

Taylor & Francis
325 Chestnut St., 8th Fl.
Philadelphia, PA 19106
Ph: (215)625-8900   Fax: (215)269-0363
Fr: 800-821-8312
URL: http://www.taylorandfrancis.com

Jacqueline O'Reilly and Colette Fagan. 2007. $48.95 (paper). 308 pages. Presents for the first time a systematically comparative analysis of the common and divergent patterns in the use of part-time work in Europe, America and the Pacific Rim.

★14895★ Peterson's Internships

Peterson's
Princeton Pke. Corporate Ctr., 2000 Lenox Dr.
PO Box 67005
Lawrenceville, NJ 08648
Ph: (609)896-1800   Fax: (609)896-4531
Fr: 800-338-3282
URL: http://www.petersons.com

Annual; latest edition 25th, 2005. Covers 50,000 career-oriented internship positions with over 2,000 organizations in the U.S., with focuses ranging from business to theater, communications to science. Entries include: Company name, address, phone, name and title of contact, types of internships available, number of internships offered, salary where applicable, qualifications, how to apply. Arrangement: Classified by career field. Indexes: Geographical.

★14896★ Peterson's Job Opportunities for Business Majors

Peterson's
Princeton Pke. Corporate Ctr., 2000 Lenox Dr.
PO Box 67005
Lawrenceville, NJ 08648
Ph: (609)896-1800   Fax: (609)896-4531
Fr: 800-338-3282
URL: http://www.petersons.com/

Irregular; latest edition 16th, 2000. Covers the 2,000 largest U.S. employers hiring in several fields, including financial services, management consulting, consumer products, and media/entertainment. Entries include: Organization name, address, phone, name and title of contact, number of employees, type of organization. Arrangement: Alphabetical. Indexes: Type of organization.

★14897★ Peterson's Job Opportunities in Engineering and Technology

Peterson's Guides
2000 Lenox Dr.
Box 67005
Lawrenceville, NJ 08648
Ph: (609)896-1800   Fax: (609)896-4531
Fr: 800-338-3282
E-mail: custsvc@petersons.com
URL: http://www.petersons.com

Compiled by the Peterson's staff. Fourth edition, 1996. $21.95 (paper). 379 pages. Profiles 2,000 high-tech companies looking primarily for technical personnel in such fields as biotechnology, telecommunications, software, computers and peripherals, defense, and aerospace. Contains job-search strategies and career options to help match education and expertise to the job market. Indexed geographically, by industry, and by hiring needs.

★14898★ Peterson's Summer Jobs for Students

Peterson's
Princeton Pke. Corporate Ctr., 2000 Lenox Dr.
PO Box 67005
Lawrenceville, NJ 08648
Ph: (609)896-1800   Fax: (609)896-4531
Fr: 800-338-3282
URL: http://www.petersons.com/

Annual; latest edition 2002. $13.95 for individuals. Covers over 650 camps, resorts, amusement parks, hotels, businesses, national parks, conference and training centers, ranches, and restaurants offering about 45,000 temporary summer jobs; listings are paid. Entries include: Name and address, length of employment, pay rate, fringe benefits, duties, qualifications, application deadline and procedure. Arrangement: Geographical, then type of job. Indexes: Job title.

★14899★ Peterson's Summer Opportunities for Kids and Teenagers

Peterson's Guides
2000 Lenox Dr.
Box 67005
Lawrenceville, NJ 08648
Ph: (609)896-1800   Fax: (609)896-4531
Fr: 800-338-3282
E-mail: custsvc@petersons.com
URL: http://www.petersons.com

Peterson's. Twenty-second edition, 2004. $29.95 (paper). 1608 pages. In addition to information about 1,400 summer activities and programs, covers job opportunities for high school and college students. Part of Summer Opportunities for Kids and Teenagers series.

★14900★ Storming Washington: An Intern's Guide to National Government

American Political Science Association
1527 New Hampshire Ave., NW
Washington, DC 20036-1206
Ph: (202)483-2512   Fax: (202)483-2657
E-mail: apsa@apsanet.org
URL: http://www.apsanet.org/

Stephen E. Frantzich. Fourth edition, 2001. $6.00 (paper). 82 pages.

★14901★ Summer Jobs Britain

Peterson's Guides
2000 Lenox Dr.
Box 67005
Lawrenceville, NJ 08648
Ph: (609)896-1800   Fax: (609)896-4531
Fr: 800-338-3282
E-mail: custsvc@petersons.com
URL: http://www.petersons.com

David Woodworth and Guy Hobbs (editors). First edition, 2007. $19.95 (paper). 320 pages. Part of Summer Jobs Britain series.

★14902★ Summer Theater Directory

American Theatre Works Inc.
2349 W. Rd.
PO Box 159
Dorset, VT 05251
Ph: (802)867-9333   Fax: (802)867-2297
URL: http://www.theatredirectories.com

Annual, December. $29.50 for individuals. Covers summer theater companies, theme parks and cruise lines that offer employment opportunities in acting, design, production, and management; summer theater training programs. Entries include: Company name, address, phone, name and title of contact; type of company, activities and size of house; whether union affiliated, whether nonprofit or commercial; year established; hiring procedure and number of positions hired annually/seasonally; description of stage; internships; description of company's artistic goals and audience. Arrangement: Geographical. Indexes: Company name.

★14903★ Survival Jobs: 118 Ways to Make Money While Pursuing Your Dreams

Windtree Pub
1540 Broadway
New York, NY 10036
Ph: (212)354-6500   Fax: (212)782-8338
Fr: 800-223-6834

Deborah Jacobson. 1998. $19.00 (paper). 256 pages.

★14904★ Vacation Work's Overseas Summer Jobs

Peterson's
Princeton Pke. Corporate Ctr., 2000 Lenox Dr.
PO Box 67005
Lawrenceville, NJ 08648
Ph: (609)896-1800   Fax: (609)896-4531
Fr: 800-338-3282
URL: http://www.petersons.com/

Annual. Covers over 30,000 summer jobs worldwide. Entries include: Complete job data, length of employment, number of openings, pay, job description, qualifications needed, application/contact information.

★14905★ Washington Job Source

Benjamin Scott Publishing
20 E. Colorado Blvd., No. 202
Pasadena, CA 91105
Ph: (626)449-1339   Fax: (626)449-1389
Fr: 800-448-4959

Mary McMahon. Fifth edition, 2002. 15.95. 482 pages.

NEWSPAPERS, MAGAZINES, AND JOURNALS

★14906★ Earth Work

Student Conservation Association
689 River Rd.
PO Box 550
Charlestown, NH 03603
Ph: (603)543-1700   Fax: (603)543-1828
E-mail: earthwork@sca-inc.org
URL: http://www.thesca.org/

Description: Monthly. Contains listings of environmental positions, ranging from internships and administrative assistants for environmental groups to camp directors, state natural resource managers, and biologists.

★14907★ Job Line...and News from CPRS

California Park & Recreation Society Inc.
7971 Freeport Blvd.
Sacramento, CA 95832-9701
Ph: (916)665-2777   Fax: (916)665-9149
URL: http://www.cprs.org/publications-job-line.htm

Description: Monthly. Discusses parks and recreation news of interest.

★14908★ NRPA Job Bulletin

National Recreation and Park Association, Professional Services Div.
22377 Belmont Ridge Rd.
Ashburn, VA 20148
Ph: (703)858-0784   Fax: (703)858-0794
Fr: 800-626-6772
E-mail: info@nrpa.org
URL: http://www.nrpa.org

Description: Semimonthly. Provides listings of employment opportunities in the park, recreation, and leisure services field.

ONLINE AND DATABASE SERVICES

★14909★ College Job Board.com

766 Turnpike St.
Canton, MA 02021
Ph: (781)821-0045
E-mail: contactus@myjobboard.com
URL: http://www.collegejobboard.com

Description: Job search site specializing in the career search of recent college, vocational and grad school graduates. Free resume posting, job board search, job tracking, scholarship and loan search and career resources.

★14910★ WetFeet.com

The Folger Bldg.
101 Howard St. Ste. 300
San Francisco, CA 94105
Ph: (415)284-7900   Fr: (415)284-7910

E-mail: services@wetfeet.com
URL: http://www.wetfeet.com

Description: Job board website with free membership for job seekers. Contains job board, resume listing, self assessment guides, company and city research, discussion forums, e-guides and online bookstore, salary calculators and listings of internship opportunities.

OTHER SOURCES

★14911★ **Association of Psychology Postdoctoral and Internship Centers (APPIC)**

10 G St. NE, Ste. 440
Washington, DC 20002
Ph: (202)589-0600   Fax: (202)589-0603
E-mail: appic@aol.com
URL: http://www.appic.org

Description: Veterans administration hospitals, medical centers, state hospitals, university counseling centers, and other facilities that provide internship and postdoctoral programs in professional psychology. Promotes activities that assist in the development of professional psychology training programs. Serves as a clearinghouse to provide Ph.D. candidates with internship placement assistance at member facilities. Conducts workshops and seminars on training procedures in clinical psychology at the PhD level.

★14912★ **INROADS**

10 S Broadway, Ste. 300
St. Louis, MO 63102
Ph: (314)241-7488   Fax: (314)241-9325
E-mail: info@inroads.org
URL: http://www.INROADS.org

Description: Provides internships for ethnically diverse students which lead to full-time career opportunities for the interns. Aims to develop and place talented Black, Hispanic/Latino, and Native American Indian high school and college students in business and industry and to prepare them for corporate and community leadership. Recruits, trains, and matches over 5000 individuals with paid internships for over 500 business corporations per year. Offers professional training seminars on time management, business presentation skills, team building, and decision making. Provides personal and professional guidance to pre-college and college interns. Operates in the U.S.; Mexico City; and Toronto and Saskatchewan, Canada.

★14913★ **National Association of Part-Time and Temporary Employees (NAPTE)**

5800 Barton, Ste. 201
PO Box 3805
Shawnee, KS 66203
Ph: (913)962-7740
E-mail: napte-champion@worldnet.att.net
URL: http://www.members.tripod.com/~napte

Purpose: Promotes the economic and social interests of persons working on a part-time, contingent, or temporary basis through research, advocacy, and member services. Offers short-term portable health insurance.

★14914★ **New Ways to Work (NWW)**

103 Morris St., Ste. A
Sebastopol, CA 95472
Ph: (707)824-4000   Fax: (707)824-4410
E-mail: newways@newwaystowork.org
URL: http://www.nww.org

Description: Helps communities build systems that connect schools, community organizations and businesses, and improve the services, educational programs and support the community provides for its youth. Engages and supports local communities in the invention and renewal of connected, comprehensive youth-serving systems.

★14915★ **U.S. Public Interest Research Group (USPIRG)**

218 D St. SE
Washington, DC 20003-1900
Ph: (202)546-9707   Fax: (202)546-2461
E-mail: membershipservices@pirg.org
URL: http://www.uspirg.org

Description: Individuals who contribute time, effort, or funds toward public interest research and advocacy. Conducts research, monitors corporate and government actions, and lobbies for reforms on consumer, environmental, energy, and governmental issues. Current efforts include support for: laws to protect consumers from unsafe products and unfair banking practices; laws to reduce the use of toxic chemicals; strengthening clean air laws; efforts to reduce global warming and ozone depletion; energy conservation and use of safe, renewable energy sources. Sponsors internships for college students; provides opportunities for students to receive academic credit for activities such as legislative research, lobbying, and public education and organizing. Offers summer jobs.

Writing Resumes and Other Job-Search Correspondence

REFERENCE WORKS

★14916★ 101 Best Resumes: Endorsed by the Professional Association of Resume Writers

The McGraw-Hill Companies
PO Box 182604
Columbus, OH 43272
Fax: (614)759-3749   Fr: 877-883-5524
E-mail: customer.service@mcgraw-hill.com
URL: http://www.mcgraw-hill.com

Jay A. Block and Michael Betrus. 2001. $12.95 (paper). 241 pages.

★14917★ 101 Great Resumes

Cengage Learning
PO Box 6904
Florence, KY 41022
Fax: 800-487-8488   Fr: 800-354-9706
URL: http://www.cengage.com

Ron Fry. Second edition, 2002. $12.95 (paper). 216 pages. Sample resumes cover 39 common situations and 62 career fields.

★14918★ 175 High-Impact Resumes

John Wiley and Sons, Inc.
1 Wiley Dr.
Somerset, NJ 08875-1272
Ph: (732)469-4400   Fax: (732)302-2300
Fr: 800-225-5945
E-mail: custserv@wiley.com
URL: http://www.wiley.com/WileyCDA/

Richard Beatty. Third edition, 2002. $14.95 (paper). Includes information on preparing electronic resumes for posting on the Internet. 304 pages.

★14919★ 200 Letters for Job Hunters

Ten Speed Press
PO Box 7123
Berkeley, CA 94707
Ph: (510)559-1600   Fax: (510)559-1629
Fr: 800-841-2665
E-mail: order@tenspeed.com
URL: http://www.tenspeedpress.com

William S. Frank. Revised edition, 1993.

$21.95 (paper). 344 pages. Provides over 250 letters to cover a variety of situations.

★14920★ 201 Dynamite Job Search Letters

Impact Publications
9104 Manassas Dr., Ste. N
Manassas Park, VA 20111-5211
Ph: (703)361-7300   Fax: (703)335-9486
Fr: 800-361-1055
E-mail: query@impactpublications.com
URL: http://www.impactpublications.com

Ron Krannich. Fifth edition, 2005. $19.95. 271 pages. Shows how to write nine different types of letters.

★14921★ Best Resumes for $75,000 Plus Executive Jobs

John Wiley and Sons, Inc.
1 Wiley Dr.
Somerset, NJ 08875-1272
Ph: (732)469-4400   Fax: (732)302-2300
Fr: 800-225-5945
E-mail: custserv@wiley.com
URL: http://www.wiley.com/WileyCDA/

William E. Montag. Second edition, 1998. The revised edition covers launching a job search campaign, interviewing, job selection criteria, and a guide to the Internet aimed at executives. $16.95. 304 pages.

★14922★ The Best Resumes for Scientists and Engineers

John Wiley & Sons Inc.
1 Wiley Dr.
Somerset, NJ 08873
Ph: (732)469-4400   Fax: (732)302-2300
Fr: 800-225-5945
E-mail: custserv@wiley.com
URL: http://www.wiley.com/WileyCDA/

Adele Lewis and David J. Moore. Second edition, 1993. $37.50; $19.95 (paper). 224 pages. Presents an extensive collection of scientific and engineering resumes, highlighting the important differences between these and resumes written for other occupations.

★14923★ Better Resumes in 3 Easy Steps

Cengage Learning
PO Box 6904
Florence, KY 41022
Fax: 800-487-8488   Fr: 800-354-9706
URL: http://www.cengage.com

Wright Field. 1999. Covers how to write an effective resume and cover letter. $33.95 (paper). 77 pages.

★14924★ Better Resumes for Executives and Professionals

Barron's Educational Series, Inc.
250 Wireless Blvd.
PO Box 8040
Hauppauge, NY 11788-3917
Ph: (631)434-3311   Fax: (631)434-3723
Fr: 800-645-3476
E-mail: fbrown@barronseduc.com
URL: http://barronseduc.com

Robert F. Wilson and Adele Lewis. Fourth edition, 2000. $16.95 (paper). 280 pages. Explains how to write resumes and cover letters for executives and professionals in most fields.

★14925★ Blue Collar Resumes

Cengage Learning
PO Box 6904
Florence, KY 41022
Fax: 800-487-8488   Fr: 800-354-9706
URL: http://www.cengage.com

Steve Provanzano. 1999. $14.95 (paper). 224 pages. Includes hundreds of examples.

★14926★ The Business Writer's Companion

St. Martin's Press, LLC
175 5th Ave.
New York, NY 10010
Ph: (212)726-0200   Fax: (212)686-9491
Fr: 800-470-4767
URL: http://www.stmartins.com

Gerald J, Charles T. Brusaw, Walter E. Oliu, and Roger Munger. Alred. Fourth edition, 2006. $19.50 (paper). 452 pages.

★14927★ The Complete Resume Guide

Arco Pub.
10475 Crosspoint Blvd.
Indianapolis, IN 46256
Ph: (317)572-2000   Fr: 800-428-5331

Marian Faux. Fifth edition, 1995. $8.95 (paper). 188 pages.

★14928★ Cover Letters for Dummies

For Dummies
1 Wiley Dr.
Somerset, NJ 08875-1272
Ph: (732)469-4400   Fax: (732)302-2300
Fr: 800-225-5945
E-mail: custserv@wiley.com
URL: http://www.dummies.com/WileyCDA/

Joyce Lane Kennedy. Second edition, 2000. $16.99, $14.99 (paper). 283 pages. Includes dozens of examples.

★14929★ Cover Letters Made Easy

The McGraw-Hill Companies
PO Box 182604
Columbus, OH 43272
Fax: (614)759-3749   Fr: 877-883-5524
E-mail: customer.service@mcgraw-hill.com
URL: http://www.mcgraw-hill.com

Jan B. Mattia and Patty Marley. 1996. $6.95 (paper). Part of Made Easy series. 96 pages.

★14930★ Cover Letters That Knock 'em Dead

Adams Media Corp.
57 Littlefield St.
Avon, MA 02322
Ph: (508)427-7100   Fax: (508)427-6790
Fr: 800-872-5627
URL: http://www.adamsmedia.com

Martin Yate. Seventh edition, 2006. $12.95 (paper). 302 pages. Discusses the fundamentals of writing a superior cover letter; how to match the letter style with the resume it accompanies; which format is right for which applicant; what always goes in, what always stays out, and why. Includes a number of samples. Part of Cover Letters That Knock 'em Dead series.

★14931★ Creating Your High School Portfolio

Jist Works
875 Montreal Way
St. Paul, MN 55102
Fr: 800-648-5478
E-mail: info@jist.com
URL: http://www.jist.com

2003. $8.95. 160 pages. This workbook shows students how to collect and store essential documents needed to apply for first jobs or college.

★14932★ Creating Your High School Resume

Jist Works
875 Montreal Way
St. Paul, MN 55102
Fr: 800-648-5478

E-mail: info@jist.com
URL: http://www.jist.com

Kathryn Kraemer Troutman. 2003. $8.95. 154 pages. This workbook provides a step-by-step guide to preparing an effective resume for a career or college.

★14933★ CV's and Job Applications

Oxford University Press, Inc.
198 Madison Ave.
New York, NY 10016-4314
Ph: (212)726-6000   Fax: (919)677-1303
Fr: 800-445-9714
E-mail: custserv.us@oup.com
URL: http://www.oup.com/us/

Judith Leigh. John Seely. 2004. $16.51 Paper. Illustrated. 144 pages.

★14934★ Cyberspace Resume Kit

Jist Works
875 Montreal Way
St. Paul, MN 55102
Fr: 800-648-5478
E-mail: info@jist.com
URL: http://www.jist.com

Fred E. Jandt and Mary B. Nemnich. Second edition, 2000. $16.95. 332 pages. Teaches how to develop and post electronic resumes.

★14935★ The Damn Good Resume Guide

Ten Speed Press
PO Box 7123
Berkeley, CA 94707
Ph: (510)559-1600   Fax: (510)559-1629
Fr: 800-841-2665
E-mail: order@tenspeed.com
URL: http://www.tenspeedpress.com

Yana Parker. Fourth edition, 2004. $11.95 (paper). 80 pages. Concentrates on producing an effective resume, with examples of functional and chronological resumes.

★14936★ Designing the Perfect Resume

Barron's Educational Series, Inc.
250 Wireless Blvd.
Hauppauge, NY 11788-3917
Ph: (631)434-3311   Fax: (631)434-3723
Fr: 800-645-3476
E-mail: fbrown@barronseduc.com
URL: http://barronseduc.com

Pat Criscito. Third edition, 2005. $16.99 (paper). 300 pages. Focuses on resume appearance. Includes hundreds of sample resumes created using WordPerfect software.

★14937★ Dynamic Cover Letters

Ten Speed Press
PO Box 7123
Berkeley, CA 94707
Ph: (510)559-1600   Fax: (510)559-1629
Fr: 800-841-2665
E-mail: order@tenspeed.com
URL: http://www.tenspeedpress.com

Katherine Hansen and Randall S. Hansen. Revised edition, 2001. $14.95 (paper). 144 pages. Helps sell the employer with a cover letter that will get a resume read, get an interview, and get the job.

★14938★ The Edge Resume and Job Search Strategy

Jist Works
875 Montreal Way
St. Paul, MN 55102
Fr: 800-648-5478
E-mail: info@jist.com
URL: http://www.jist.com

Third edition, 2000. $24.95. 176 pages. A unique collection of fancy resumes in full color and unusual shapes.

★14939★ Effective Resume Writing: A Guide to Successful Employment

Neal Publications, Inc.
127 W. Indiana
PO Box 451
Perrysburg, OH 43551
Ph: (419)874-4787

James E. Neal Jr. Second edition, 1996. $7.95 (paper). 104 pages.

★14940★ Electronic Resumes and Online Networking: How to Use the Internet to Do a Better Job Search, Including a Complete, Up-to-Date Resource Guide

Career Press, Inc.
3 Tice Rd.
PO Box 687
Franklin Lakes, NJ 07417-1322
Ph: (201)848-0310   Fax: (201)848-1727
Fr: 800-227-3371
URL: http://www.careerpress.com

Rebecca Smith. Second edition, 2000. $15.99 (paper). Provides information on using the Internet as a resume networking tool. Covers locating employers, evaluating electronic resume options, and web pages. 224 pages.

★14941★ Electronic Resumes: The Complete Guide to Putting Your Resume On-Line

The McGraw-Hill Companies
PO Box 182604
Columbus, OH 43272
Fax: (614)759-3749   Fr: 877-883-5524
E-mail: customer.service@mcgraw-hill.com
URL: http://www.mcgraw-hill.com

Wayne M. Gonyea and James C. Gonyea. 1996. $19.95. 255 pages. Explains the basics of online, multimedia, video, and audio resumes in nontechnical language. Disk includes software that enables users to create their own electronic resume to upload via modem onto online resume databases.

★14942★ Every Woman's Essential Job Hunting & Resume Book

Adams Media Corp.
57 Littlefield St.
Avon, MA 02322
Ph: (508)427-7100   Fax: (508)427-6790
Fr: 800-872-5627
URL: http://www.adamsmedia.com

Laura Morin. 1994. $11.95 (paper). 221 pages.

★14943★ Expert Resumes for Computer and Web Jobs

Jist Publishing
875 Montreal Way
St. Paul, MN 55102
Fr: 800-648-5478
E-mail: info@jist.com
URL: http://www.jist.com

Wendy Enelow and Louis Kursmark. Second edition, 2005. $16.95 (paper). 286 pages.

★14944★ The Five-Minute Interview

John Wiley and Sons, Inc.
1 Wiley Dr.
Somerset, NJ 08875-1272
Ph: (732)469-4400   Fax: (732)302-2300
Fr: 800-225-5945
E-mail: custserv@wiley.com
URL: http://www.wiley.com/WileyCDA/

Richard H. Beatty. Third edition, 2002. $21.50 (paper). 266 pages.

★14945★ Gallery of Best Resumes

Jist Works
875 Montreal Way
St. Paul, MN 55102
Fr: 800-648-5478
E-mail: info@jist.com
URL: http://www.jist.com

David F. Noble. Third edition, 2004. $18.95. 432 pages. Includes a wide range of styles, formats, designs, occupations, and situations.

★14946★ Get That Job!: Job Applications

The McGraw-Hill Companies
PO Box 182604
Columbus, OH 43272
Fax: (614)759-3749   Fr: 877-883-5524
E-mail: customer.service@mcgraw-hill.com
URL: http://www.mcgraw-hill.com

Susan Echaore-McDavid and Winifred H. Roderman. 1998. $7.00. 32 pages.

★14947★ Government Job Finder

Planning Communications
7215 Oak Ave.
River Forest, IL 60305-1935
Ph: (708)366-5200   Fax: (708)366-5280
Fr: 888-366-5200
E-mail: info@planningcommunications.com
URL: http://jobfindersonline.com

Daniel Lauber. Fourth edition, 2006. 300 pages. $18.95. Covers 1800 sources. Dis-

cusses how to use sources of local, state, and federal government job vacancies in a number of specialties and state-by-state, including job-matching services, job hotlines, specialty periodicals with job ads, salary surveys, and directories. Explains how local, state, and federal hiring systems work. Includes chapters on resume and cover letter preparation and interviewing.

★14948★ High Impact Resumes and Letters: How to Communicate Your Qualifications to Employers

Impact Publications
9104 Manassas Dr., Ste. N
Manassas Park, VA 20111-5211
Ph: (703)361-7300   Fax: (703)335-9486
Fr: 800-361-1055
E-mail: query@impactpublications.com
URL: http://www.impactpublications.com

Ronald L. Krannich and William J. Banis. Seventh edition, 1997. $19.95 (paper). 289 pages.

★14949★ How to Prepare Your Curriculum Vitae

The McGraw-Hill Companies
PO Box 182604
Columbus, OH 43272
Fax: (614)759-3749   Fr: 877-883-5524
E-mail: customer.service@mcgraw-hill.com
URL: http://www.mcgraw-hill.com

Acy L. Jackson. Third edition, 2003. $12.95 (paper). 136 pages. Dozens of examples from academics in all disciplines and at all career levels illustrate the principles of writing an effective C.V. Worksheets guide the reader through a step-by-step process that begins with describing, in draft form, all pertinent experiences, and then helps shape, organize, and edit experiences and credentials into a professional curriculum vitae. Includes sample cover letters tailored to academic institutions.

★14950★ How to Write Better Resumes

Barron's Educational Series, Inc.
250 Wireless Blvd.
Hauppauge, NY 11788-3917
Ph: (631)434-3311   Fax: (631)434-3723
Fr: 800-645-3476
E-mail: fbrown@barronseduc.com
URL: http://barronseduc.com

Gary J. Grappo and Adele Lewis. Fifth edition, 1998. $11.95 (paper). 282 pages.

★14951★ How to Write an Effective Resume

The Saunderstown Press
PO Box 307
Saunderstown, RI 02874-0307
Ph: (401)295-8810
URL: http://www.amanet.org

Allen A. Johnson. Twenty-first edition, 1996. $7.95 17 pages.

★14952★ How to Write a Winning Resume

The McGraw-Hill Companies
PO Box 182604
Columbus, OH 43272
Fax: (614)759-3749   Fr: 877-883-5524
E-mail: customer.service@mcgraw-hill.com
URL: http://www.mcgraw-hill.com

Deborah Perlmutter Bloch. Fourth edition, 1998. $14.95 (paper). 128 pages. Explains what a resume does, the various kinds that exist, and occasions where it should be used. Contains advice on what and what not to include in a resume, how to respond to the want ads, and an appendix of job descriptions.

★14953★ Internet Resumes

Impact Publications
9104 Manassas Dr., Ste. N
Manassas Park, VA 20111-5211
Ph: (703)361-7300   Fax: (703)335-9486
Fr: 800-361-1055
E-mail: query@impactpublications.com
URL: http://www.impactpublications.com

Peter D. Weddle. 1998. $14.95 (paper). 193 pages. Shows how to communicate qualifications to potential employers over the Internet.

★14954★ Last Minute Cover Letters

Cengage Learning
PO Box 6904
Florence, KY 41022
Fax: 800-487-8488   Fr: 800-354-9706
URL: http://www.cengage.com

Brandon Toropov. 1998. $12.95 (paper). 160 pages. Provides templates for cover letters.

★14955★ Non-Profits and Education Job Finder

Planning Communications
7215 Oak Ave.
River Forest, IL 60305-1935
Ph: (708)366-5200   Fax: (708)366-5280
Fr: 888-366-5200
E-mail: info@planningcommunications.com
URL: http://jobfindersonline.com

Daniel Lauber. 1997. $32.95; $16.95 (paper). 340 pages. Covers 1600 sources. Discusses how to use sources of non-profit sector job vacancies in a number of specialties and state-by-state, including job-matching services, job hotlines, specialty periodicals with job ads, salary surveys, and directories. Covers a variety of fields from education to religion. Includes chapters on resume and cover letter preparation and interviewing.

★14956★ The Perfect Cover Letter

John Wiley & Sons Inc.
1 Wiley Dr.
Somerset, NJ 08873
Ph: (732)469-4400   Fax: (732)302-2300
Fr: 800-225-5945
E-mail: custserv@wiley.com
URL: http://www.wiley.com/WileyCDA/

Richard H. Beatty. Third edition, 2003. $19.95 (paper). 224 pages. Provides examples and analysis of a range of letters, including executive search, advertising response, networking, personal introduction, and general broadcast targeted pieces. Also contains tips on what information to include or omit, as well as proper letter design.

★14957★ **The Perfect Resume: Today's Ultimate Job Search Tool**
Broadway Books
1745 Broadway
New York, NY 10019
Ph: (212)782-9000   Fax: (212)572-6066
Fr: 800-733-3000
URL: http://www.randomhouse.com/broadway/

Tom Jackson. June 2004. $12.95 (paper). 240 pages.

★14958★ **Power Resumes**
John Wiley & Sons Inc.
1 Wiley Dr.
Somerset, NJ 08873
Ph: (732)469-4400   Fax: (732)302-2300
Fr: 800-225-5945
E-mail: custserv@wiley.com
URL: http://www.wiley.com/WileyCDA/

Ron Tepper. Third edition, 1998. $14.95 (paper). Covers the key parts and techniques that make for a successful resume. 272 pages.

★14959★ **Professional Resumes for Executives, Managers and Other Administrators: A New Gallery of Best Resumes**
Jist Works
875 Montreal Way
St. Paul, MN 55102
Fr: 800-648-5478
E-mail: info@jist.com
URL: http://www.jist.com

David F. Noble. 1998. $19.95. 606 pages.

★14960★ **The Quick Resume and Cover Letter Book**
Jist Works
875 Montreal Way
St. Paul, MN 55102
Fr: 800-648-5478
E-mail: info@jist.com
URL: http://www.jist.com

Third edition, 2005. $14.95. 416 pages. Explains how to write and use a resume in one day.

★14961★ **Real Life Resumes That Work!**
Drake Beam Morin Pub
750 Third Ave., 28th Fl.
New York, NY 10017
Ph: (212)692-7700   Fax: (212)297-0426
E-mail: inquiries@dbm.com
URL: http://www.dbm.com

Bob Stirling and Pat Morton, editors. 1994. 197 pages. $11.00 (paper). Includes a wide range of sample resumes as well as networking, ad response, and follow-up letters.

★14962★ **The Resume Catalog: 200 Damn Good Examples**
Ten Speed Press
PO Box 7123
Berkeley, CA 94707
Ph: (510)559-1600   Fax: (510)559-1629
Fr: 800-841-2665
E-mail: order@tenspeed.com
URL: http://www.tenspeedpress.com

Yana Parker. 2002. $19.95 (paper). 314 pages. Contains a range and variety of 200 sample resumes. Indexed and cross-referenced for ease of use.

★14963★ **Resume and Cover Letter Writing Guide**
Voc-Offers
PO Box 700252
San Jose, CA 95170-0252
Ph: (408)255-6579

Carey E. Harbin. Second edition, 1998. $5.95 (paper). 36 pages.

★14964★ **The Resume Handbook**
Adams Media Corp.
57 Littlefield St.
Avon, MA 02322
Ph: (508)427-7100   Fax: (508)427-6790
Fr: 800-872-5627
URL: http://www.adamsmedia.com

Arthur D. Rosenberg and David V. Hizer. Fourth edition, 2003. $9.95 (paper). 144 pages. Includes specific examples of excellent resumes and cover letters and examples of how weaker resumes and cover letters can be improved. Presents resumes for many types of job hunters, including recent college graduates, seasoned professionals, and women re-entering the job market. Chapters on cover letters and 'personal sales' letters and design and layout of resumes are also included.

★14965★ **The Resume Kit**
John Wiley & Sons Inc.
1 Wiley Dr.
Somerset, NJ 08873
Ph: (732)469-4400   Fax: (732)302-2300
Fr: 800-225-5945
E-mail: custserv@wiley.com
URL: http://www.wiley.com/WileyCDA/

Richard H. Beatty. Fifth edition, 2003. $16.95 (paper). 356 pages. Details effective resume preparation. Discusses both chronological and functional resumes. Includes sample resumes and cover letters.

★14966★ **Resume Magic: Trade Secrets of a Professional Resume Writer**
Jist Works
875 Montreal Way
St. Paul, MN 55102
Fr: 800-648-5478
E-mail: info@jist.com
URL: http://www.jist.com

Susan Britton Whitcomb. Third edition, 2006. $18.95. 585 pages. Covers every element of resume writing, with nearly 100 "before and after" examples.

★14967★ **The Resume Makeover: The Resume Writing Guide That Includes Personalized Feedback**
John Wiley & Sons Inc.
1 Wiley Dr.
Somerset, NJ 08873
Ph: (732)469-4400   Fax: (732)302-2300
Fr: 800-225-5945
E-mail: custserv@wiley.com
URL: http://www.wiley.com/WileyCDA/

Jeffrey G. Allen. 2001. $14.95 (paper). 276 pages.

★14968★ **Resume Power: Selling Yourself on Paper**
Mount Vernon Press
1750 112th St. NE, C-224
Bellevue, WA 98004
Ph: (425)454-6982   Fax: (425)455-4729

Tom Washington. Seventh edition, 2003. $14.95 (paper). 295 pages.

★14969★ **Resume Winners from the Pros: 177 of the Best from the Professional Association of Resume Writer**
Impact Publications
9104 Manassas Dr., Ste. N
Manassas Park, VA 20111-5211
Ph: (703)361-7300   Fax: (703)335-9486
Fr: 800-361-1055
E-mail: query@impactpublications.com
URL: http://www.impactpublications.com

Wendy S. Enelow. 1998. $17.95 (paper). 395 pages.

★14970★ **The Resume Writer's Handbook**
HarperCollins
10 E. 53rd St.
New York, NY 10022
Ph: (212)207-7000   Fax: (212)207-7145
Fr: 800-242-7737
URL: http://www.harpercollins.com/

Michael Holley Smith. 1994. $4.99 (paper). A writing guide aimed at people at all job levels. Provides examples and advice on common problems. 240 pages.

★14971★ Resume Writing Made Easy

Prentice Hall PTR
1 Lake St.
Upper Saddle River, NJ 07458
Ph: (201)236-7000   Fr: 800-428-5331
URL: http://www.phptr.com/index.asp?rl=1

Lola Brown. Eighth edition, 2006. $22.00. 192 pages.

★14972★ Resumes for Advertising Careers

The McGraw-Hill Companies
PO Box 182604
Columbus, OH 43272
Fax: (614)759-3749   Fr: 877-883-5524
E-mail: customer.service@mcgraw-hill.com
URL: http://www.mcgraw-hill.com

Third edition, 2003. $10.95 (paper). 160 pages. Aimed at job seekers trying to enter or advance in advertising. Provides sample resumes for copywriters, art directors, account managers, ad managers, and media people at all levels of experience. Furnishes sample cover letters.

★14973★ Resumes for Banking and Financial Careers

The McGraw-Hill Companies
PO Box 182604
Columbus, OH 43272
Fax: (614)759-3749   Fr: 877-883-5524
E-mail: customer.service@mcgraw-hill.com
URL: http://www.mcgraw-hill.com

Second edition, 2001. $11.95 (paper). 160 pages.

★14974★ Resumes for Business Management Careers

The McGraw-Hill Companies
PO Box 182604
Columbus, OH 43272
Fax: (614)759-3749   Fr: 877-883-5524
E-mail: customer.service@mcgraw-hill.com
URL: http://www.mcgraw-hill.com

Third edition, 2006. $11.95 (paper). 144 pages. Resume guide for supervisors and line and staff managers. Provides advice on compiling a business management resume; includes a number of sample resumes and cover letters. Part of VGM Professional Resumes series.

★14975★ Resumes for College Students and Recent Graduates

The McGraw-Hill Companies
PO Box 182604
Columbus, OH 43272
Fax: (614)759-3749   Fr: 877-883-5524
E-mail: customer.service@mcgraw-hill.com
URL: http://www.mcgraw-hill.com

Third edition, 2004. $11.95 (paper). 153 pages. Shows how to write a resume that capitalizes on pertinent work experience, academic background, and volunteer and extracurricular activities. Includes sample resumes and cover letters.

★14976★ Resumes for Communications Careers

The McGraw-Hill Companies
PO Box 182604
Columbus, OH 43272
Fax: (614)759-3749   Fr: 877-883-5524
E-mail: customer.service@mcgraw-hill.com
URL: http://www.mcgraw-hill.com

Third edition, 2003. $10.95 (paper). 160 pages.

★14977★ Resumes, Cover-Letters & Interviewing: Setting the Stage for Success

Wadsworth Publishing
PO Box 6904
Florence, KY 41022
Fax: 800-487-8488   Fr: 800-354-9706
URL: http://www.cengage.com

Clifford W. Eischen and Lynn A. Eischen. 1999. $25.95 (paper). 128 pages. Professional resume using today's business technologies including the Internet and E-mail. Specifically targeted to help individuals with a two-year degree showcase their skills and experiences to get the job they want. Scanable resumes, Internet-based resumes, and etiquette for sending resumes via fax or E-mail are addressed to prepare readers to apply for jobs using today's business technologies. Dedicated chapter on the interview process coaches readers on proper interview attire, preparing for interview questions, introductions, and how to follow up after an interview. Exercises on listing qualifications, producing a first draft, gathering references, and drafting a follow-up letter, all help readers build a finished resume step by step.

★14978★ Resumes for Engineering Careers

The McGraw-Hill Companies
PO Box 182604
Columbus, OH 43272
Fax: (614)759-3749   Fr: 877-883-5524
E-mail: customer.service@mcgraw-hill.com
URL: http://www.mcgraw-hill.com

Third edition, 2005. $11.95 (paper). 144 pages. Contains sample resumes and cover letters applicable to any engineering field.

★14979★ Resumes for Environmental Careers

The McGraw-Hill Companies
PO Box 182604
Columbus, OH 43272
Fax: (614)759-3749   Fr: 877-883-5524
E-mail: customer.service@mcgraw-hill.com
URL: http://www.mcgraw-hill.com

Second edition, 2002. $10.95 (paper). 160 pages. Provides resume advice tailored to people pursuing careers focusing on the environment. Includes sample resumes and cover letters.

★14980★ Resumes Etc.

Prototype Career Press
1086 Seventh St., W.
St. Paul, MN 55102-3829
Fax: (612)224-5526   Fr: 800-368-3197

Amy Lindgren. $2.95. 112 pages. 1995. Covers resumes, cover letters, follow-up letters, and applications.

★14981★ Resumes for the First-Time Job Hunter

The McGraw-Hill Companies
PO Box 182604
Columbus, OH 43272
Fax: (614)759-3749   Fr: 877-883-5524
E-mail: customer.service@mcgraw-hill.com
URL: http://www.mcgraw-hill.com

Third edition, 2005. $11.95 (paper). 144 pages.

★14982★ Resumes that Get Jobs

Book Marketing Works
50 Lovely St.
Avon, CT 06001
Fax: (203)729-5335   Fr: 800-562-4357
E-mail: brianjud@bookmarketing.com
URL: http://www.bookmarketingworks.com

Brian Jud. $1.45. 20 pages. 1995. Provides tips on resume writing.

★14983★ Resumes for Government Careers

The McGraw-Hill Companies
PO Box 182604
Columbus, OH 43272
Fax: (614)759-3749   Fr: 877-883-5524
E-mail: customer.service@mcgraw-hill.com
URL: http://www.mcgraw-hill.com

1996. $9.95 (paper). 151 pages.

★14984★ Resumes for Health and Medical Careers

The McGraw-Hill Companies
PO Box 182604
Columbus, OH 43272
Fax: (614)759-3749   Fr: 877-883-5524
E-mail: customer.service@mcgraw-hill.com
URL: http://www.mcgraw-hill.com

Third edition, 2003. $11.95 (paper). 160 pages.

★14985★ Resumes for High School Graduates

The McGraw-Hill Companies
PO Box 182604
Columbus, OH 43272
Fax: (614)759-3749   Fr: 877-883-5524
E-mail: customer.service@mcgraw-hill.com
URL: http://www.mcgraw-hill.com

Third edition, 2005. $11.95. 144 pages. Designed for the person with little or no full-time work experience. Shows how to emphasize part-work experience and highlight educational, extra-curricular and volunteer experience. Provides sample resumes and cover letters.

★14986★ *Resumes for High Tech Careers*

The McGraw-Hill Companies
PO Box 182604
Columbus, OH 43272
Fax: (614)759-3749   Fr: 877-883-5524
E-mail: customer.service@mcgraw-hill.com
URL: http://www.mcgraw-hill.com

Third edition, 2003. $10.95 (paper). 160 pages. Demonstrates how to tailor a resume that catches a high tech employer's attention. Part of "Resumes for ..." series.

★14987★ *Resumes for Higher Paying Positions: A Complete Guide to Resume Writing for a More Rewarding Career*

Best Seller Publications, Inc.
12146 Island View Cir.
Germantown, MD 20874
Ph: (301)869-0072   Fax: (301)972-4456

Cory Schulman. 1997. $17.95 (paper). 187 pages.

★14988★ *Resumes for Law Careers*

The McGraw-Hill Companies
PO Box 182604
Columbus, OH 43272
Fax: (614)759-3749   Fr: 877-883-5524
E-mail: customer.service@mcgraw-hill.com
URL: http://www.mcgraw-hill.com

Third edition, 2007. $12.95 (paper). 144 pages.

★14989★ *Resumes for Nursing Careers*

The McGraw-Hill Companies
PO Box 182604
Columbus, OH 43272
Fax: (614)759-3749   Fr: 877-883-5524
E-mail: customer.service@mcgraw-hill.com
URL: http://www.mcgraw-hill.com

2001. $11.95 (paper). 144 pages.

★14990★ *Resumes for Overseas & Stateside Jobs*

Zinks International Career Guidance
PO Box 587
Marshall, MI 49068-0587

Richard M. Zink. 1994. $14.95 (paper). 80 pages.

★14991★ *Resumes for Performing Arts Careers*

The McGraw-Hill Companies
PO Box 182604
Columbus, OH 43272
Fax: (614)759-3749   Fr: 877-883-5524
E-mail: customer.service@mcgraw-hill.com
URL: http://www.mcgraw-hill.com

2004. $10.95 (paper). 160 pages.

★14992★ *Resumes & Personal Statements for Health Professionals*

Galen Press, Ltd.
PO Box 64400
Tucson, AZ 85728-4400
Ph: (520)577-8363   Fax: (520)529-6459
Fr: 800-442-5369
E-mail: sales@galenpress.com
URL: http://www.galenpress.com/

James W. Tysinger. Second edition, 1999. $18.95 (paper). 210 pages. Step-by-step, fool-proof instructions to guide any health professions student, graduate, or practitioner through the process of writing these documents.

★14993★ *Resumes for Re-Entering the Job Market*

The McGraw-Hill Companies
PO Box 182604
Columbus, OH 43272
Fax: (614)759-3749   Fr: 877-883-5524
E-mail: customer.service@mcgraw-hill.com
URL: http://www.mcgraw-hill.com

Second edition, 2002. $10.95 (paper). 160 pages. Part of VGM Professional Resumes series.

★14994★ *Resumes for Sales and Marketing Careers*

The McGraw-Hill Companies
PO Box 182604
Columbus, OH 43272
Fax: (614)759-3749   Fr: 877-883-5524
E-mail: customer.service@mcgraw-hill.com
URL: http://www.mcgraw-hill.com

Chuck Cochran and Donna Peerce. 1998. $13.95. 336 pages. Sample resumes and cover letters from all levels of the sales and marketing field.

★14995★ *Resumes for Science Careers*

The McGraw-Hill Companies
PO Box 182604
Columbus, OH 43272
Fax: (614)759-3749   Fr: 877-883-5524
E-mail: customer.service@mcgraw-hill.com
URL: http://www.mcgraw-hill.com

1997. $11.95 (paper). 144 pages.

★14996★ *Resumes for Scientific and Technical Careers*

The McGraw-Hill Companies
PO Box 182604
Columbus, OH 43272
Fax: (614)759-3749   Fr: 877-883-5524
E-mail: customer.service@mcgraw-hill.com
URL: http://www.mcgraw-hill.com

Third edition, 2007. $12.95 (paper). 144 pages. Provides resume advice for individuals interested on working in scientific and technical careers. Includes sample resumes and cover letters.

★14997★ *Resumes for Social Service Careers*

The McGraw-Hill Companies
PO Box 182604
Columbus, OH 43272
Fax: (614)759-3749   Fr: 877-883-5524
E-mail: customer.service@mcgraw-hill.com
URL: http://www.mcgraw-hill.com

2006. $11.95 (paper). 144 pages.

★14998★ *Resumes That Knock 'Em Dead*

Adams Media Corp.
57 Littlefield St.
Avon, MA 02322
Ph: (508)427-7100   Fax: (508)427-6790
Fr: 800-872-5627
URL: http://www.adamsmedia.com

Martin Yate. Seventh edition, 2006. $12.95 (paper). 309 pages. Presents resumes that were successfully used by individuals to obtain jobs. Resumes target the most commonly-sought positions on all levels.

★14999★ *Resumes for Women*

Arco Pub.
200 Old Tappan Rd.
Old Tappan, NJ 07675
Fr: 800-428-5331

Eva Shaw. 1995. $10.00 (paper). 158 pages.

★15000★ *The Smart Woman's Guide to Resumes and Job Hunting*

The Career Press, Inc.
3 Tice Rd.
PO Box 687
Franklin Lakes, NJ 07417-1322
Ph: (201)848-0310   Fax: (201)848-1727
Fr: 800-227-3371
URL: http://www.careerpress.com

Julie Adair King and Betsy Sheldon. 1995. $11.99. 214 pages. Addresses job-search challenges unique to women in the '90s. Discusses breaking through the glass ceiling and other gender barriers, commanding a fair salary, networking to hidden job opportunities, using "power language", translating volunteer experiences into powerful accomplishments, and offers other guidance. Takes the reader through a resume-creating process.

★15001★ *Sure-Hire Resumes*

AMACOM
1601 Broadway, 12th Fl.
New York, NY 10019
Ph: (212)586-8100   Fax: (212)903-8168
Fr: 800-262-9699
URL: http://www.amanet.org

Robbie M. Kaplan. Second edition, 1998. $14.95 (paper). 148 pages. Includes 'ideal' cover letters written by personnel directors. Presents 25 actual resumes (indexed by occupation) and includes discussions of useful resume-writing software and word processing.

★15002★ Winning Cover Letters

John Wiley & Sons Inc.
1 Wiley Dr.
Somerset, NJ 08873
Ph: (732)469-4400   Fax: (732)302-2300
Fr: 800-225-5945
E-mail: custserv@wiley.com
URL: http://www.wiley.com/WileyCDA/

Robin Ryan. 2002. $14.95 (paper). Covers the techniques needed to draft an effective cover letter. 192 pages. Part of Career Coach series.

★15003★ Winning Resumes

John Wiley & Sons Inc.
1 Wiley Dr.
Somerset, NJ 08873
Ph: (732)469-4400   Fax: (732)302-2300
Fr: 800-225-5945
E-mail: custserv@wiley.com
URL: http://www.wiley.com/WileyCDA/

Robin Ryan. Second edition. 2002. $14.95 (paper). 288 pages.

★15004★ Write a Winning Resume

The McGraw-Hill Companies
PO Box 182604
Columbus, OH 43272
Fax: (614)759-3749   Fr: 877-883-5524
E-mail: customer.service@mcgraw-hill.com
URL: http://www.mcgraw-hill.com

Deborah P. Bloch. 1997. $12.95 (paper). 146 pages. Part of Here's How series.

★15005★ Writing Resumes That Work: A How-to-Do-It Manual for Librarians

Neal-Schuman Publishers, Inc.
100 William St., Ste. 2004
New York, NY 10038
Ph: (212)925-8650   Fax: (212)219-8916
E-mail: info@neal-schuman.com
URL: http://www.neal-schuman.com/

Robert R. Newlen. 2006. $55.00 (paper). 206 pages. Provides ideas for alternate library careers in this new edition of a 1980 publication. Most of the 62 contributors have information science, academic, and other adult-focused backgrounds; four come from the fields of children's and elementary school media services and one from the YA ranks.

★15006★ Your First Resume

The Career Press Inc.
3 Tice Rd.
PO Box 687
Franklin Lakes, NJ 07417-1322
Ph: (201)848-0310   Fax: (201)848-1727
Fr: 800-227-3371
URL: http://www.careerpress.com

Ronald W. Fry. Fifth edition, 2001. $14.99 (paper). 190 pages. Subtitled: "The Comprehensive Guide for College Students or Anyone Preparing to Enter or Reenter the Job Market."

★15007★ Your Resume: Key to a Better Job

Arco Pub.
200 Old Tappan Rd.
Old Tappan, NJ 07675
Fr: 800-428-5331

Leonard Corwen. Sixth edition, 1996. $10.95 (paper). 176 pages. Provides guidelines for resume writing; explains what employers look for in a resume, including contents and style. Includes model resumes for high-demand careers such as computer programmers, health administrators, and high-tech professionals. Notes basic job-getting information and strategies.

AUDIO/VISUAL RESOURCES

★15008★ Access Unlimited: The Job Search Series for People with Disabilities

Cambridge Educational
PO Box 2053
Princeton, NJ 08543-2053
Ph: 800-257-5126   Fax: (609)671-0266
Fr: 800-468-4227
E-mail: custserv@films.com
URL: http://www.cambridgeeducational.com

VHS and DVD. 1998. $269.85. Three 30-minute videos cover job search tactics, resumes and applications, and job interviewing.

★15009★ Defining and Developing Your Portfolio

Cambridge Educational
PO Box 2053
Princeton, NJ 08543-2053
Ph: 800-257-5126   Fax: (609)671-0266
Fr: 800-468-4227
E-mail: custserv@films.com
URL: http://www.cambridgeeducational.com

VHS and DVD. $79.95. 2000. 17 minutes. Program focuses on the steps involved in compiling a career portfolio, from gathering the individual components to tailoring them for use with different job categories. Work samples and other elements, such as a statement of confidentiality, a mission statement, a set of goals, a resume, and letters of reference, are highlighted.

★15010★ Effective Resumes: Reading Between The Lines

Cambridge Educational
PO Box 2053
Princeton, NJ 08543-2053
Ph: 800-257-5126   Fax: (609)671-0266
Fr: 800-468-4227
E-mail: custserv@films.com
URL: http://www.cambridgeeducational.com

VHS and DVD. $79.95. 60 minutes. 1991. Students learn the difference an effective resume makes in a successful job search and tips for giving theirs the vital edge over competitors. Employers discuss what turns them on and off.

★15011★ From Parole to Payroll

Cambridge Educational
PO Box 2053
Princeton, NJ 08543-2053
Ph: 800-257-5126   Fax: (609)671-0266
Fr: 800-468-4227
E-mail: custserv@films.com
URL: http://www.cambridgeeducational.com

VHS and DVD. 2008. $269.85. Contains solid, real-world content designed to help job seekers find satisfying work, and features informative interviews, helpful tips, and colorful graphics.

★15012★ The Ideal Resume

Cambridge Educational
PO Box 2053
Princeton, NJ 08543-2053
Ph: 800-257-5126   Fax: (609)671-0266
Fr: 800-468-4227
E-mail: custserv@films.com
URL: http://www.cambridgeeducational.com

VHS and DVD. 1997. $79.95. 21 minutes. Appropriate for both adults and youth.

★15013★ The Portfolio Resume Series

Cambridge Educational
PO Box 2053
Princeton, NJ 08543-2053
Ph: 800-257-5126   Fax: (609)671-0266
Fr: 800-468-4227
E-mail: custserv@films.com
URL: http://www.cambridgeeducational.com

VHS and DVD. $159.90. 2000. Topics include defining and developing your portfolio and using and maintaining your portfolio.

★15014★ Resumes and Applications for People with Disabilities

Cambridge Educational
PO Box 2053
Princeton, NJ 08543-2053
Ph: 800-257-5126   Fax: (609)671-0266
Fr: 800-468-4227
E-mail: custserv@films.com
URL: http://www.cambridgeeducational.com

VHS and DVD. $89.95. 1998. 25 minutes. Part of the series "Access Unlimited: The Job Search Series for People with Disabilities."

★15015★ Resumes and Job Applications

Cambridge Educational
PO Box 2053
Princeton, NJ 08543-2053
Ph: 800-257-5126   Fax: (609)671-0266
Fr: 800-468-4227
E-mail: custserv@films.com
URL: http://www.cambridgeeducational.com

$89.95. 2008. 20 minutes. Part of the "From Parole to Payroll" Series.

★15016★ *Ten Commandments of Resumes*

Cambridge Educational
PO Box 2053
Princeton, NJ 08543-2053
Ph: 800-257-5126   Fax: (609)671-0266
Fr: 800-468-4227
E-mail: custserv@films.com
URL: http://www.cambridgeeducational.com

VHS and DVD. 1997. $79.95. 35 minutes. This contains ten important tips for writing an excellent resume, providing the knowledge needed to stand out in a crowd of job seekers.

★15017★ *Using and Maintaining Your Portfolio*

Cambridge Educational
PO Box 2053
Princeton, NJ 08543-2053
Ph: 800-257-5126   Fax: (609)671-0266
Fr: 800-468-4227
E-mail: custserv@films.com
URL: http://www.cambridgeeducational.com

VHS and DVD. $79.95. 2000. 21 minutes. Part of the Portfolio Resume Series.

★15018★ *Web Resumes*

Cambridge Educational
PO Box 2053
Princeton, NJ 08543-2053
Ph: 800-257-5126   Fax: (609)671-0266
Fr: 800-468-4227
E-mail: custserv@films.com
URL: http://www.cambridgeeducational.com

VHS and DVD. 1998. $69.95. 30 minutes. Topics covered include Web and electronic resumes, creative resumes, target resumes, and mid-life and reentry resumes.

★15019★ *Your First Resume and Interview*

Cambridge Educational
PO Box 2053
Princeton, NJ 08543-2053
Ph: 800-257-5126   Fax: (609)671-0266
Fr: 800-468-4227
E-mail: custserv@films.com
URL: http://www.cambridgeeducational.com

VHS and DVD. 1999. $89.95. 17 minutes. Learn why employers like resumes and what kinds of information should be included. See the different styles of resumes and why one style might be preferable to another. The interviewing process will also be covered, including an overview of what the employer hopes to learn.

ONLINE AND DATABASE SERVICES

★15020★ **CareerXpress.com**

Interweb Connections, Inc.
Dept. 732
PO Box 34069
Seattle, WA 98124
E-mail: info@Careerxpress.com
URL: http://www.careerxpress.com

Description: Resume writing and distribution service. **Fee:** Pricing depending on desired range of search; begins at $69.

★15021★ **Resume Safari**

URL: http://www.resumesafari.com/

Description: Site serves as a resume distribution service. Once submitted, a job hunter's resume will be distributed to over 1,500 locations on the web **Fee:** $60 or $80 depending on tier.

★15022★ **SeeMeResumes.com**

6767 W. Tropicana Ave.
Las Vegas, NV 89103
Ph: (702)248-1032
URL: http://www.seemeresumes.com

Description: Resume coaching and distribution service. Confidential e-mail inboxes available. **Fee:** Pricing based on desired intensity and range of search; starts at $39.

SOFTWARE

★15023★ **Adams Cover Letter Almanac**

Adams Media Corp.
4700 E. Galbraith Rd.
Cincinnati, OH 45236
E-mail: techsupport@adamsmedia.com
URL: http://www.adamsmedia.com

2006. Second Edition. $17.95 736 pages. Contains more than 600 sample cover letters.

★15024★ **Adams Resume Almanac**

Adams Media Corp.
4700 E. Galbraith Rd.
Cincinnati, OH 45236
E-mail: techsupport@adamsmedia.com

URL: http://www.adamsmedia.com

Second Edition $17.95. 768 pages. Contains more than 600 sample resumes.

★15025★ **Multimedia Job Search**

Cambridge Educational
PO Box 2053
Princeton, NJ 08543-2053
Ph: 800-257-5126   Fax: (609)671-0266
Fr: 800-468-4227
E-mail: custserv@films.com
URL: http://www.cambridgeeducational.com

CD-ROM. $99.95. 1997. Includes videos, narration, and on-screen text. Users learn about getting a competitive edge in today's job market, traditional and nontraditional job search tools, resumes and cover letters, and interviewing skills.

★15026★ **ResumePro**

Cambridge Educational
PO Box 931
Monmouth Junction, NJ 08852-0931
Fax: (732)536-4429   Fr: 800-967-3846
E-mail: mw@gilbertresumes.com
URL: http://www.resumepro.com/

CD-ROM. 1998. $69.95. Requires Widows 95 or higher. Teaches resume formats and includes a word processor.

★15027★ **Resumes Quick & Easy**

Individual Software, Inc.
4255 Hopyard Rd., Ste. 2
Pleasanton, CA 94588
Ph: (925)734-6767   Fax: (925)734-8337
Fr: 800-822-3522
E-mail: orders@individualsoftware.com
URL: http://www.individualsoftware.com

CD-ROM. $19.95. Helps create resumes, write cover letters, find your salary range, manage contacts, and fax or email your resume.

★15028★ **WinWay Resume Deluxe**

PO Box 1097
Folsom, CA 95763-1097
URL: http://www.winway.com

Version 11. Windows. $39.95. Includes more than 13,000 resume examples and job descriptions.

Index to Information Sources

This Index is an alphabetical listing of all entries contained in both Parts One and Two. Index references are to **entry numbers** rather than to page numbers. Publication and film titles are rendered in italics.

American College of Medical
Genetics **5590**
American College of Medical Quality **5961**,
9906
American College of Nurse-Midwives **10963**
American College of Occupational and
Environmental Medicine **9779**
American College of Osteopathic
Internists **9780**
American College of Osteopathic
Obstetricians and Gynecologists Annual
Convention **9884**
American College of Osteopathic
Surgeons **9781**
American College Personnel
Association **3163**, **4100**
American College of Physician
Executives **9782**
American College of Prosthodontists **3472**,
3535, **3588**, **3713**
American College of Radiology **9907**
American College of Sports Medicine **4968**,
9908
American College of Sports Medicine Annual
Meeting **9885**
American College of Surgeons Annual
Clinical Congress **9886**
American College of Trial Lawyers **6956**
American College of Veterinary
Ophthalmologists Conference **12667**
American College of Veterinary Pathologists
Annual Meeting **12668**
American College of Veterinary Pathologists-
Membership Directory **12642**
American Congress on Surveying and
Mapping **12215**
American Conservatory Theater
Foundation **165**
American Correctional Association **3074**
American Correctional Health Services
Association **5870**
American Council on Alcoholism **819**
American Council on Exercise **4969**, **10844**
American Council of Life Insurers **288**,
6448, **12569**
American Council on Rural Special
Education **11977**
American Council on the Teaching of
Foreign Languages Convention **11613**
American Counseling Association **3215**
American Counseling Association World
Conference **815**, **3209**, **7942**
American Credit Union Mortgage
Association **3352**
American Crystallographic
Association **1891**, **9978**
American Culinary Federation **1166**, **1693**
American Dance Guild **3391**
American Dental Assistants
Association **3473**
American Dental Association **3474**, **3536**,
3589, **3714**
American Dental Association Annual Session
& Technical Exhibition **3467**, **3526**, **3682**
American Dental Education
Association **3475**, **3537**, **3590**, **3715**
American Dental Hygienists'
Association **3538**
American Dental Hygienists' Association
Access **3426**, **3487**, **3549**, **3615**, **5812**,
6064
American Dental Hygienists' Association
Convention **3527**
American Dental Society of Anesthesiology
Scientific Meeting **3683**
American Design Drafting Association **3797**,
3989
American Dietetic Association **3898**
American Dietetic Association Annual
Meeting and Exhibition **3894**
American Disc Jockey Association **3936**
American Economic Association **4036**
American Education Finance
Association **4101**

American Electrology Association Annual
Convention **3103**, **7552**
American Electronics Association-Member
Directory **4254**, **4320**
American Engineering Association **517**,
576, **2031**, **4575**, **4673**, **5163**, **6312**, **8305**,
8528, **12377**
American Executive Management
Inc. **4826**, **5307**, **7786**
American Experiment Quarterly **10063**
American Family Physician **7273**, **9580**,
9655, **10887**
American Family Therapy Academy **3216**
American Federation of Musicians of the
United States and Canada **8469**
American Federation of Police and
Concerned Citizens **6793**
American Federation of School
Administrators **4169**
American Federation of Teachers **417**,
6650, **10202**, **11623**, **11978**
American Feed Industry Association Feed
Industries Show **623**
American Financial Services
Association **1195**, **3353**, **4919**
American Floral Industry Association **5010**
American Foreign Law Association **6957**
American Forests **5120**
American Gaming Association **5226**
American Gastroenterological
Association **9783**
American Genetic Association **5591**
American Geographical Society **5620**
American Geological Institute **5662**
American Geophysical Union **5639**, **7966**
American Group Practice **5893**
American Group Psychotherapy Association-
Membership Directory **3172**, **9806**,
10429, **10968**, **11715**
American Guild of Musical Artists **8470**
American Guild of Organists **8471**
American Hardware Manufacturers
Association-Rep/Factory Contact Service
Directory **7606**
American Harp Society National
Conference **8454**
American Health Care Association **5962**,
6134, **7412**, **8718**, **8788**, **9522**, **10870**,
11050, **12020**
American Health Care Association Annual
Convention and Exposition **5955**
American Health Information Management
Association **8148**
American Health Lawyers Association **6958**
American Health Quality Association **9784**
American Heart Association Scientific
Sessions **9887**
American Heart Journal **4213**, **9656**
American Highway Users Alliance **12438**
American Historical Association **6052**
American Historical Association Annual
Meeting **6044**
American Hockey Coaches
Association **12081**
American Holistic Medical Association-
National Referral Directory **9807**
American Hospital Association **5963**, **7413**,
8719, **9328**, **9909**, **10058**, **11051**
American Hospital Association-Ambulatory
Outreach **4414**
American Hotel and Lodging
Association **6197**
American Hotel and Motel Association
Annual Conference and Leadership
Forum **6184**
American Human Resources Associates Ltd.
(AHRA) **1189**, **4827**, **10743**
American Humane Association Annual
Conference **862**, **12669**
American Humanics **6208**
American Hydrogen Association **5164**
American Immigration Lawyers
Association **6959**
American Incite **5308**

American Indian National Business
Directory **14588**
American Indian Rock Art **927**
American Indian Science and Engineering
Society **451**, **1352**, **1730**, **1991**, **2564**,
2835, **4313**, **4546**, **4613**, **6266**, **8017**,
8184, **8276**, **8498**, **9208**, **11847**, **12390**,
14624
American Industrial Hygiene Association-
Directory **6394**
American Industrial Hygiene Association
Journal **6383**
American Institute of Aeronautics and
Astronautics **452**
American Institute of Aeronautics and
Astronautics Career Planning and
Placement Services **504**, **13561**
American Institute of Architects **1014**
American Institute of Architects-
AIArchitect **955**
American Institute of Architects National
Convention **1011**
American Institute of Baking **1167**
American Institute of Biological
Sciences **634**, **1310**, **11497**
American Institute of Biological Sciences
Annual Meeting **1301**
American Institute of Biological Sciences
Classifieds **1295**, **13562**
American Institute of Certified
Planners **12605**
American Institute of Certified Public
Accountants **117**
American Institute of Chemical
Engineers **1798**
American Institute of Chemical Engineers
Journal **1701**, **1813**
American Institute of Chemists **1799**, **1892**
American Institute of Chemists-Professional
Directory **1736**, **1851**
American Institute for Conservation of
Historic and Artistic Works **1071**, **6053**
American Institute of Constructors Annual
Forum **3023**
American Institute of Constructors
Newsletter **2955**
American Institute for CPCU **6449**, **12570**
American Institute of Engineers **5165**,
12378
American Institute of Floral Designers **5011**
American Institute of Graphic Arts **5757**,
10238, **12520**, **12961**
American Institute of Physics **9957**
American Institute of Professional
Geologists **5663**
American Institute of Ultrasound in
Medicine **10702**
American Institute of Wine and
Food **12851**
American Intellectual Property Law
Association **6960**
American Jail Association Training
Conference & Jail Expo **3073**
American Journal of Agricultural and
Biological Science **1205**
American Journal of Alternative
Agriculture **585**
American Journal of Animal and Veterinary
Sciences **12611**
American Journal of Archaeology **928**
The American Journal of Cardiology **4214**,
9657
American Journal of Clinical Nutrition **3849**,
9658
The American Journal of Drug and Alcohol
Abuse **785**
American Journal of Emergency
Medicine **4415**, **8073**, **9581**, **9659**, **12157**
American Journal of Epidemiology **4683**,
9660
American Journal of Family Therapy **7917**,
10379
American Journal of Geriatric
Psychiatry **8584**, **10380**

National Association of Pastoral
  Musicians **8368, 8478**
National Association of Pastoral Musicians
  National Convention **8464**
National Association of Pediatric Nurse
  Practitioners **7421, 11060**
National Association of Personnel
  Services **4518**
National Association of Photoshop
  Professionals **3846**
National Association of Postal
  Supervisors **10142**
National Association of Postmasters of the
  United States **10143**
National Association of Postmasters of the
  United States Convention **10137**
National Association for Practical Nurse
  Education and Service **7422**
National Association for the Practice of
  Anthropology **916**
National Association for Printing
  Leadership **10244, 12522**
National Association of Professional Geriatric
  Care Managers **6138**
National Association of Professional
  Insurance Agents **6460**
National Association of Professional
  Organizers **10281**
*National Association of Professional
  Organizers-Directory* **10265**
National Association of Professional
  Organizers (NAPO) **9099**
National Association of Professional Pet
  Sitters **9100**
National Association of Public Auto
  Auctions **1113**
National Association of Public Insurance
  Adjusters **2067**
National Association of Real Estate
  Appraisers **10796**
National Association of Real Estate
  Brokers **10758, 10797**
National Association of Real Estate Buyer
  Brokers **10759, 10798**
*National Association of Real Estate
  Companies-Membership Directory* **10343,
  10727, 10781**
National Association of Realtors **10371,
  10760, 10799**
National Association of Realtors Trade
  Exposition **10749**
National Association of Recreation Resource
  Planners **10851**
National Association of Rehabilitation
  Providers and Agencies **9576**
National Association for Research in
  Science Teaching **6666, 11638**
National Association of Review Appraisers
  and Mortgage Underwriters **10775, 12549**
National Association of Review Appraisers
  and Mortgage Underwriters Convention -
  National Conference & Expo **10750,
  12565**
National Association of School Nurses for
  the Deaf **12029**
National Association of School
  Psychologists **10481**
National Association of Science
  Writers **13231**
National Association of Secondary School
  Principals **4183**
National Association of Secondary School
  Principals Annual Convention **4160**
*National Association of Securities Dealers-
  Manual* **12133**
National Association for the Self-
  Employed **14808**
National Association of Social
  Workers **11754**
National Association of Social Workers
  National Committee on Lesbian, Gay and
  Bisexual Issues **14495**
National Association of Special Education
  Teachers **11985**

National Association for Sport and Physical
  Education **2203, 6603, 11566, 12043**
National Association of Sports
  Officials **12085**
National Association of State Directors of
  Special Education **3230, 4184, 6667,
  11639, 11986**
National Association of State
  Telecommunications Directors
  Conference **1534**
National Association of Student
  Anthropologists **917**
National Association of Student Personnel
  Administrators **4185**
National Association of Substance Abuse
  Trainers and Educators **829**
National Association of Tax
  Professionals **138, 12254**
National Association of Tax Professionals
  Conference **108**
National Association of Teachers'
  Agencies **2204, 4112, 6604, 11567**
National Association of Teachers of
  Singing **8479**
National Association of Temple
  Administrators **10565**
National Association of Temple
  Educators **4113, 10566**
National Association of Traffic Accident
  Reconstructionists and
  Investigators **2037, 6804, 6987, 10263**
National Association of Underwater
  Instructors **10817, 12044**
National Association for Uniformed
  Services **14581**
National Association of Women in
  Construction **1481, 1603, 2949, 3138,
  4409, 6008, 10018, 11318, 12219**
National Association of Women
  Lawyers **6988**
National Association of Women
  Writers **13232**
National Athletic Trainers' Association **4962,
  12045**
National Auction List **1107**
National Auctioneers Association **1114**
*National Auto Auction Association-
  Membership Directory* **1104**
National Automotive Radiator Service
  Association Annual Trade Show and
  Convention **1140**
National Bankers Association **3322, 4786,
  7434**
*National Bankers Association-Roster of
  Minority Banking Institutions* **3329, 4793,
  7438**
National Bar Association **6989**
National Bar Association Annual Convention
  & Exhibits **6944**
National Beauty Culturists' League **3113**
National Beauty Show -
  HAIRWORLD **3108, 7555**
National Black Coalition of Federal Aviation
  Employees **713, 778**
National Black Law Students
  Association **6990**
National Black MBA Association **5261,
  14632**
National Board for Certification in Dental
  Laboratory Technology **3602**
National Board for Certification in
  Occupational Therapy **8798, 8834**
National Board for Certified Counselors and
  Affiliates **5601**
National Board for Respiratory Care **11174**
National Border Patrol Council **1427**
National Business Aviation Association
  Annual Meeting & Convention **775**
National Business and Disability
  Council **14456**
*National Business Travel Association-
  Membership Directory* **12478**
National Cable and Telecommunications
  Association **1544**

National Career Development
  Association **3231, 14762**
The National Casting Guide **228**
National Center for Construction Education
  and Research **1018, 2950, 3139, 12220**
National Center for Database
  Marketing **7870**
National Center for Lesbian Rights **14496**
National Certification Commission for
  Acupuncture and Oriental Medicine **321**
National Christian College Athletic
  Association **12046**
National Coalition of 100 Black
  Women **14633, 14742**
National Coalition of Black Meeting
  Planners **4723**
National Coalition of Creative Arts Therapies
  Associations **1095**
National Coalition for Health Professional
  Education in Genetics **5602**
National Coalition for History **6057**
National Commission on Certification of
  Physician Assistants **9648**
National Commission on Orthotic and
  Prosthetic Education **8992**
National Committee on Uniform Traffic Laws
  and Ordinances **12444**
National Communication Association **2205,
  6605, 11568, 11994**
National Community Education
  Association **424, 4186, 6668, 11640,
  12314**
National Conference for Catechetical
  Leadership **8333**
National Contact Lens Examiners **3967**
National Contract Management
  Association **10557**
National Cosmetology Association **3114,
  7556**
National Council for Accreditation of Teacher
  Education **3232, 4187, 6669, 11641**
National Council for Adoption **387**
National Council for Adoption
  Conference **376**
National Council on the Aging **14652**
National Council of Architectural Registration
  Boards **1019**
National Council on Economic
  Education **4041**
National Council on Family Relations **7949**
National Council For Adoption-Memo **366**
National Council for Geographic
  Education **2298, 5624, 6670, 11642**
National Council for Geographic Education
  Conference **11618**
National Council News **7933**
National Council on Public History **6058**
National Council on Rehabilitation
  Education **3169**
National Council of Secondary School
  Athletic Directors **4114, 12047**
National Council for the Social Studies
  Conference **11619**
National Council of Teachers of
  Mathematics **425, 2299, 6671, 7989,
  11643**
National Council for Therapeutic Recreation
  Certification **10879**
National Council of Young Israel **10575**
National Counsel of Black Lawyers **6851**
National Court Reporters **12127**
National Court Reporters
  Association **12128, 14524**
National Credentialing Agency for Laboratory
  Personnel **2120**
National Criminal Justice Association **6991**
The National Culinary Review **1614, 1661**
National Dance Association **3394**
National Dental Assistants Association **3484**
National Dental Association **3724**
National Dental Association Annual
  Convention **3528, 3695**
National Dental Hygienists'
  Association **3546**